NELSON'S
New Illustrated
Bible Commentary

NELSON'S

New Illustrated

Bible Commentary

NELSON'S
New Illustrated
Bible Commentary

Earl D. Radmacher, Th.D.
General Editor

Ronald B. Allen, Th.D.
Old Testament Editor

H. Wayne House, Th.D., J.D.
New Testament Editor

THOMAS NELSON PUBLISHERS
Nashville

Unless otherwise indicated, Scripture quotations are from the New King James Version of the Bible, © 1979, 1980, 1982, 1990, Thomas Nelson, Inc., Publishers.

Bible maps are from the Nelson Study Bible, copyright © 1997 by Thomas Nelson, Inc. and the Word In Life Study Bible, copyright © 1996 by Thomas Nelson, Inc.

Book design and composition by Mark McGarry, Texas Type & Book Works, Dallas, Texas
Set in Meridien

Library of Congress Cataloging-in-Publication Data
 Nelson's new illustrated Bible commentary / Earl D. Radmacher, general editor;
  Ronald B. Allen, Old Testament editor; H. Wayne House, New Testament editor.
   p. cm.
  ISBN 0-7852-1438-0
  1. Bible—Commentaries. I. Radmacher, Earl D.
 II. Allen, Ronald Barclay. III. House, H. Wayne.
 BS491.2.N43   1999
 220.7—dc21

99-11281
CIP

Printed in the United States of America

2 3 4 5 6 7—04 03 02 01 00 99

Contents

■

APPENDIXES

A Different Kind of Commentary

E VERYONE WHO READS THE BIBLE AT ALL WANTS to know more about it and understand it better. A variety of helps have been developed to that end, although most of them are focused on specific categories of information—atlases for map study, dictionaries or lexicons for words studies, or individual books dealing with specific books of the Bible.

For a general yet thorough study of the whole Bible, the best resource is a commentary. Commentaries come in all sorts of shapes and sizes, from one volume to sixty! Unfortunately they also come with some negative baggage, at least for ordinary Bible students. Do a word association on "commentary" with most people and you will hear words like "long," "dry," "boring"—perhaps even "confusing." Many commentaries are written and designed for scholars and specialists, and by and large they do a good job of meeting the needs of those people. If you are not in that elite group, however, commentaries may leave you feeling intimidated.

Nelson's New Illustrated Bible Commentary breaks the commentary mold. From conception to final production, it has been planned and developed for people who are not typical commentary users—ordinary Bible readers and students, Sunday school teachers, and Bible study leaders. This book does have scholarship too—more than forty evangelical scholars have contributed to its contents. But it offers much more. It is brief yet complete, with verse-by-verse annotations on the whole Bible in less than 2,000 pages. It is at the same time clear and relevant, speaking to issues people face in their daily lives today. Perhaps most conspicuously it is attractive and appealing, with one or more interesting features on almost every two-page spread.

Watch for these in-text features as you move through this commentary.

 —word studies to help you grasp what the original writers of the Greek and Hebrew words actually meant

 —brief pieces of background information that you might otherwise have missed

 —longer pieces of background or historical information, helping you discover the how and why of biblical incidents

 —articles that emphasize life-application principles, so you can more readily put the Word to work in *your* life

 —articles describing cultural factors that have some bearing on a biblical incident and thus shedding new light on the world of the Bible

 —charts and tables, so you can recognize the relationship between people and events more quickly and easily

 —personality profiles to help you see Bible characters as fully rounded individuals

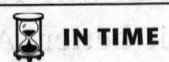 —timelines to go with every Bible book, allowing you to place the books within their historical setting

All of these are listed by page number in the pages following this article.

In addition, each Bible book commentary opens with a helpful introduction and an outline. Maps and photographs are scattered appropriately throughout the volume. Major feature articles offer an overview of the Old and New Testaments as well as a look at key biblical themes and doctrines. An article between the testaments helps you bridge that 400-year period. Other features in the Appendix help you

gain a better grasp of how biblical archaeology illuminates the Bible and how church history shows the Bible's message in action. Closing the book is a General Bibliography, offering you carefully selected resources to extend and deepen your studies more.

Not only do we believe that *Nelson's New Illustrated Bible Commentary* is unique in the marketplace—we believe that you will find it uniquely helpful in your life as a Christian who wants God's Word to shine into your world.

List of In-text Features

●

IN DEPTH

(Longer pieces of background/historical information)

IN FOCUS

(Word studies)

IN LIFE

(Articles that emphasize life-application principles)

IN PERSON

(Personality profiles)

INSIGHT

(Brief pieces of background information)

IN TIME

(Timelines)

List of Maps

List of Illustrations

———————————————◼———————————————

Contributors

■

Ronald B. Allen, Th.D.

Ray Bakke, D.Min., Th.D.

Calvin Beisner, M.A.

Barry J. Beitzel, Ph.D.

Darrell Lane Bock, Ph.D.

James Borland, Th.D.

Dick Chewning, Ph.D.

Robert B. Chisholm Jr., Th.D.

Michael G. Cocoris, D.D.

Ronald Dennis Cole, Th.D.

Joseph Edward Coleson, Ph.D.

W. Robert Cook, Th.D.

Sue Cotten

Barry C. Davis, Ph.D.

Darryl DelHoussaye, D.Min.

Gary Wayne Derickson, Ph.D.

Joseph C. Dillow, Th.D.

Duane Arthur Dunham, Th.D.

David J. Eckman, Ph.D.

Stanley A. Ellisen, Th.D.

Arthur L. Farstad, Th.D. (deceased)

Dietrich Gruen, M.Div.

Pete Hammond, M.Div.

William Hendricks, M.A., M.S.

H. Wayne House, Th.D., J.D.

David M. Howard Jr., Ph.D.

Thomas Ice, Ph.D.

S. Lewis Johnson Jr., Th.D.

Sharon Johnson, D.B.A.

Walter C. Kaiser Jr., Ph.D.

Deborah Jane Kappas, Th.M.

J. Carl Laney, Th.D.

Donald H. Launstein, Th.D.

Asa Boyd Luter Jr., Ph.D.

Walter Creighton Marlowe, Ph.D.

Eugene H. Merrill, Ph.D.

Bruce M. Metzger, Ph.D.

Thomas Kem Oberholtzer, Th.D.

Gregory W. Parsons, Th.D.

Dorothy Kelley Patterson, D. Min, Th. D.

Richard D. Patterson, Ph.D.

Susan Perlman

Earl D. Radmacher, Th.D.

Neil Rendall, B.Div.

Moishe Rosen

Ray C. Stedman, D.D. (deceased)

Clinton Stockwell, Ph.D., Th.D.

Stanley D. Toussaint, Th.D.

Willem VanGemeren, Ph.D.

Bruce K. Waltke, Ph.D., Th.D.

John F. Walvoord, Th.D., D.D., Litt.D.

Abbreviations

—————————————————————— ■ ——————————————————————

BIBLE BOOK ABBREVIATIONS

Old Testament

Gen.	Genesis
Ex.	Exodus
Lev.	Leviticus
Num.	Numbers
Deut.	Deuteronomy
Josh.	Joshua
Judg.	Judges
Ruth	Ruth
1 Sam.	1 Samuel
2 Sam.	2 Samuel
1 Kin.	1 Kings
2 Kin.	2 Kings
1 Chr.	1 Chronicles
2 Chr.	2 Chronicles
Ezra	Ezra
Neh.	Nehemiah
Esth.	Esther
Job	Job
Ps.(Pss.)	Psalm(s)
Prov.	Proverbs
Eccl.	Ecclesiastes
Song	Song of Solomon
Is.	Isaiah
Jer.	Jeremiah
Lam.	Lamentations
Ezek.	Ezekiel
Dan.	Daniel
Hos.	Hosea
Joel	Joel
Amos	Amos

Obad.	Obadiah
Jon.	Jonah
Mic.	Micah
Nah.	Nahum
Hab.	Habakkuk
Zeph.	Zephaniah
Hag.	Haggai
Zech.	Zechariah
Mal.	Malachi

New Testament

Matt.	Matthew
Mark	Mark
Luke	Luke
John	John
Acts	Acts
Rom.	Romans
1 Cor.	1 Corinthians
2 Cor.	2 Corinthians
Gal.	Galatians
Eph.	Ephesians
Phil.	Philippians
Col.	Colossians
1 Thess.	1 Thessalonians
2 Thess.	2 Thessalonians
1 Tim.	1 Timothy
2 Tim.	2 Timothy
Titus	Titus
Philem.	Philemon
Heb.	Hebrews
James	James
1 Pet.	1 Peter
2 Pet.	2 Peter

1 John	1 John
2 John	2 John
3 John	3 John
Jude	Jude
Rev.	Revelation

OTHER ABBREVIATIONS

A.D.	*Anno Domini*, in the year of our Lord
B.C.	Before Christ
c. *circa*,	about
cf.	*confer*, compare
chap.	chapter
chaps.	chapters
ed.	edited, edition, editor
eds.	editors
e.g.	*exempli gratia*, for example
Gk.	Greek
Heb.	Hebrew
Ibid.	*ibidem*, in the same place
i.e.	*id est*, that is
lit.	literal, literally
NT	New Testament
OT	Old Testament
p., pp.	page(s)
trans.	translation, translator, translated
vol(s)	volume(s)
v., vv.	verse(s)

FEATURE
ARTICLES

———————————————■———————————————

The Old Testament at a Glance

The Classification of the Hebrew Bible

*E*NGLISH READERS ARE FAMILIAR WITH THE CLASSIfications and order of the Old Testament in the English Bible. The divisions are the Law of Moses, the Historical Books, the Poetical Books, and lastly the Prophets. The Jews of today and in the days of Christ, however, had a different structure and order. The major divisions were the Law, the Prophets, and the Psalms or Writings (Luke 24:27, 44).

The Law

The Law contains the books of Moses, which present the beginnings of the world and of the covenant people Israel. God is presented as the Creator of the material universe, then more specifically as the Creator of the people that bear His name. Moses received the family histories (Gen. 2:4; 5:1; 10:1) that had been passed down from the various faithful of mankind through the father of Israel, Abraham. Moses probably used these to write the Genesis account, plus the oral tradition which surely would have come through the children of God in bondage in Egypt concerning their heritage and the acts of their leaders. The majority of the remainder of the Pentateuch (the five books) would have been concurrent with Moses' own life and experience.

The Prophets

The Hebrew Scriptures list the Prophets as Joshua, Judges, Samuel, and Kings ("the Former Prophets"), and Isaiah, Jeremiah, Ezekiel, and the twelve Minor Prophets ("the Latter Prophets"). The inclusion of so many books in this category comes about because the Hebrews correctly understood prophecy to be *forth*telling

from God as well as *fore*telling. Moreover, the term "prophets" stands over an entire portion of sacred text even if every part of the section might not be predictive in nature. The books of Samuel and Kings, for example, are called Prophets even though their content is largely historical. The Prophets set forth the words of God to the covenant people regarding His promises to them and their duty to obey His law given through Moses. In addition, the stories tell of men like Elijah and Elisha, as well as the rising star of Israel, David, whom Peter tells us was a prophet (Acts 2:30).

The Writings

The Writings were sometimes broadly called "the Psalms," and consist of Psalms, Proverbs, Job, Song of Solomon, Ruth, Lamentations, Ecclesiastes, Esther, Daniel, Ezra, Nehemiah, and Chronicles. (Song of Solomon through Esther are termed "The Five Scrolls.") These portions of the Hebrew Bible contain the devotional and wisdom literature of Israel, as well as some historical and prophetic material. Nonpoetic books that are relatively late chronologically find their place among the Writings in the Hebrew canon.

Divisions and Books of the Old Testament

Type of Literature	Book	Theme
LAW* (the foundation of the Hebrew faith)	Genesis (1–11)	God Begins His Earthly Work
	Genesis (12—50)	God the Sovereign Establishes His Plan
		God the Savior Redeems His People
	Exodus	God the Holy Provides True Worship
	Leviticus	God Chastens His People in Love
	Numbers	God the King Loves His People
	Deuteronomy	
HISTORY (the record of Israel's spiritual growth and decline)	Joshua	God Fulfills His Promise for the Land
	Judges	God Tests His People
	Ruth	God Portrays His Redemption
	1 Samuel	God Chooses His King
	2 Samuel	
	1 Kings	God Rules the Nation
	2 Kings	
	1 Chronicles	God Preserves His Royal Seed
	2 Chronicles	
	Ezra	God Restores His People
	Nehemiah	God Rebuilds His City
	Esther	God Protects His People
POETRY (a presentation of the worship of the Lord and individual faith)	Job	God Tries His Servant
	Psalms	God Enjoys True Worship
	Proverbs	God Teaches True Wisdom
	Ecclesiastes	God Unveils Our Finitude
	Song of Solomon	God Extols Human Love
PROPHETS (the Lord's revelation of His blessings, judgments, and promises)	Isaiah	God Manifests His Great Salvation
	Jeremiah	God Reveals His Heart
	Lamentations	God Weeps
	Ezekiel	God Envisions Hope
	Daniel	God Preserves His Servants
	Hosea	God Loves the Sinner
	Joel	God Announces His Day
	Amos	God Displays His Displeasure
	Obadiah	God Judges His Enemies
	Jonah	God Loves the World
	Micah	God Is Incomparable
	Nahum	God Avenges His People
	Habakkuk	God Enlists the Nations
	Zephaniah	God Shelters His People
	Haggai	God Restores His Worship
	Zechariah	God Remembers
	Malachi	God Sends His Messenger

*The Hebrew canon has the categories of Law, Prophets, and Writings, and different ordering of books.

Author	Date
Moses (with Deuteronomy 34 probably written by Joshua)	1445—1440 B.C.**
Joshua	1405–1390 B.C.
Anonymous	1043–1004 B.C.
Unknown	Uncertain
Samuel	1050–750 B.C.
Anonymous	1050–750 B.C.
Unknown, but possibly Jeremiah	590–570 B.C.
Possibly Ezra	430–425 B.C.
Ezra	457–444 B.C.
Nehemiah	457–444 B.C.
Unknown	464–435 B.C.
Unknown	Uncertain
David, Asaph, sons of Korah, Solomon, Moses	1410-c. 430 B.C.
Solomon, Agur, Lemuel	
Solomon	950–700 B.C.
Solomon	935 B.C.
	965 B.C.
Isaiah	740–680 B.C.
Jeremiah	626–586 B.C.
Jeremiah	586–584 B.C.
Ezekiel	593–571 B.C.
Daniel	605–530 B.C.
Hosea	750–720 B.C.
Joel	830 or 600 B.C.
Amos	760 B.C.
Obadiah	586 B.C.
Jonah	750 B.C.
Micah	730 B.C.
Nahum	620 B.C.
Habakkuk	612 B.C.
Zephaniah	607 B.C.
Haggai	520 B.C.
Zechariah	515 B.C.
Malachi	430 B.C.

**All dates are approximate

Old Testament Time Line

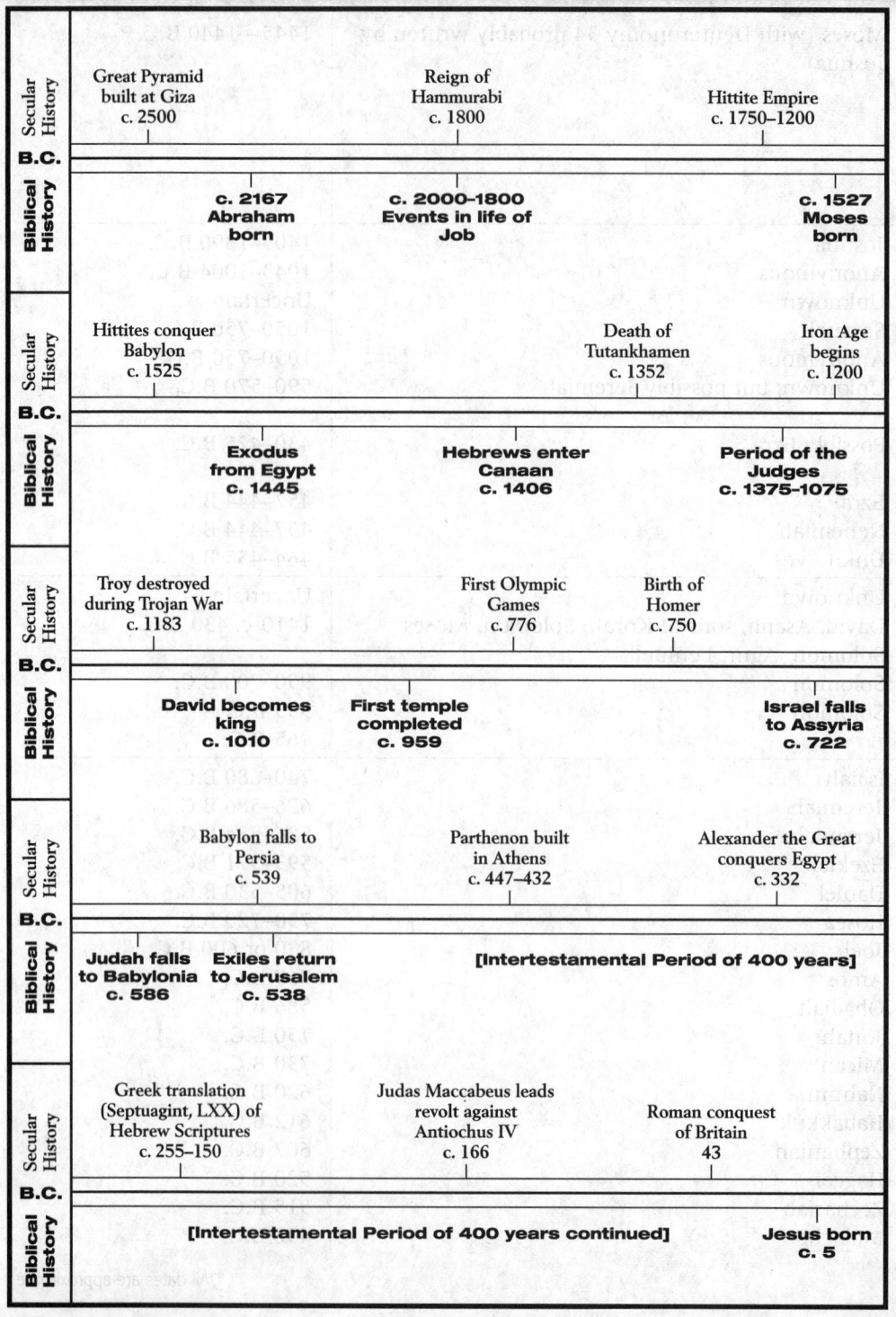

Secular History B.C.	Great Pyramid built at Giza c. 2500	Reign of Hammurabi c. 1800	Hittite Empire c. 1750–1200
Biblical History	c. 2167 Abraham born	c. 2000–1800 Events in life of Job	c. 1527 Moses born
Secular History B.C.	Hittites conquer Babylon c. 1525	Death of Tutankhamen c. 1352	Iron Age begins c. 1200
Biblical History	Exodus from Egypt c. 1445	Hebrews enter Canaan c. 1406	Period of the Judges c. 1375–1075
Secular History B.C.	Troy destroyed during Trojan War c. 1183	First Olympic Games c. 776	Birth of Homer c. 750
Biblical History	David becomes king c. 1010	First temple completed c. 959	Israel falls to Assyria c. 722
Secular History B.C.	Babylon falls to Persia c. 539	Parthenon built in Athens c. 447–432	Alexander the Great conquers Egypt c. 332
Biblical History	Judah falls to Babylonia c. 586 — Exiles return to Jerusalem c. 538	[Intertestamental Period of 400 years]	
Secular History B.C.	Greek translation (Septuagint, LXX) of Hebrew Scriptures c. 255–150	Judas Maccabeus leads revolt against Antiochus IV c. 166	Roman conquest of Britain 43
Biblical History	[Intertestamental Period of 400 years continued]		Jesus born c. 5

The New Testament at a Glance

L IKE THE OLD TESTAMENT, THE NEW TESTAMENT has several noticeable divisions. They are Gospels, History, Letters, and Apocalypse (Revelation).

What Exactly Is a Gospel?

The Gospels present a kind of literature that is very different from other ancient and modern writings. They are not biographies of Christ, seeking to develop a full-orbed understanding of Jesus' life, His friendships, His family, or His mental and psychological dimensions. They are also not histories of heroic deeds or collections of His famous sayings, though some of these kinds of materials are found in the Gospel accounts.

The four Gospels appear to be a new genre for which other categories are inadequate. These accounts of the life, works, and words of Jesus are preaching material regarding the redemptive work of God in Jesus Christ. They are the good news from God that is manifested in the life, ministry, death, burial, resurrection, and ascension of Christ.

The Growth of Christianity Through the Eyes of Luke

The Book of Acts is part two of Luke's book. He presents to Theophilus the results of his investigation of the life and work of Jesus in his Gospel, and then in Acts he continues to recount the work of the apostles of Christ through the power of the Holy Spirit sent from Him. Acts sets forth the growth of Christianity in six stages: 1:1—6:7; 6:8—9:31; 9:32—12:24; 12:25—16:5; 16:6—19:20; 19:21—28:31.

The Nature of New Testament Letters

The letters written by the apostles and their companions are different from the letters most people would write today. Writing tools and materials were not plentiful, so the authors sought to conserve space when writing. Moreover, the greetings and benedictions in the New Testament letters are unlike the sort of correspondence we would see now, but they are similar to the introductions and conclusions found in other first-century letters. The New Testament authors composed their letters in order to solve problems in the church or to communicate the gospel of Jesus Christ to those who needed to hear about it.

The Revelation of Jesus Christ

The Book of Revelation is unique among the New Testament books, reflecting a genre of literature familiar to the Jews, called apocalyptic. It sets forth in vivid and emotional terms the triumph of Christ over His enemies, in agreement with the prophetic teachings about the conquering Messiah and the discourses of Jesus in Matt. 24 and Mark 13 concerning His second coming.

Divisions and Books of the New Testament

Type of Literature	Book	Theme
GOSPELS (the good news of Jesus the Messiah)	Matthew Mark Luke John	God Announces His King God Presents His Servant God Becomes True Man Jesus Is God
HISTORY (history of the spread of Christianity to the west)	Acts	God Creates His Church
LETTERS (personal letters and letters to Christian churches)	Romans 1 Corinthians 2 Corinthians Galatians Ephesians Philippians Colossians 1 Thessalonians 2 Thessalonians 1 Timothy 2 Timothy Titus Philemon Hebrews James 1 Peter 2 Peter 1 John 2 John 3 John Jude	God Defends His Righteousness God Corrects His Church God Defends His Minister God Defines His Gospel God Unveils His Mystery God Gives Joy Through Solving God Exalts Christ as Lord God Encourages His Church God Enlightens His Church God Exhorts His Minister God Rewards His Servants God Commends Sound Teaching God Values Human Dignity God Certifies Christ's Supremacy God Extols Faith That Works God Compensates Endurance God Keeps His Promises God Clarifies True Love God Warns Against Loss God Encourages Doing Good God Commissions the Fight
APOCALYPSE (victory of Christ and the church over sin and the world)	Revelation	God Completes His Plan and Creates All Things New

Author	Date
Matthew the tax collector	50s or 60s
John Mark the cousin of Barnabas	60s
Luke the physician and companion of Paul	Early 60s
John the beloved disciple	Late 80s or early 90s
Luke the physician and companion of Paul	Early 60s
Paul the apostle	Spring 57
Paul the apostle	Spring 56
Paul the apostle	Fall 56
Paul the apostle	48
Paul the apostle	60
Paul the apostle	61
Paul the apostle	60
Paul the apostle	51
Paul the apostle	51
Paul the apostle	Fall 62
Paul the apostle	Fall 67
Paul the apostle	64
Paul the apostle	60
Unknown	64
James the brother of the Lord	Mid 40s
Peter the apostle	64
Peter the apostle	65
John the beloved disciple	90
John the beloved disciple	90
John the beloved disciple	90
Jude the brother of the Lord	Early 60s
John the beloved disciple	96

New Testament Time Line

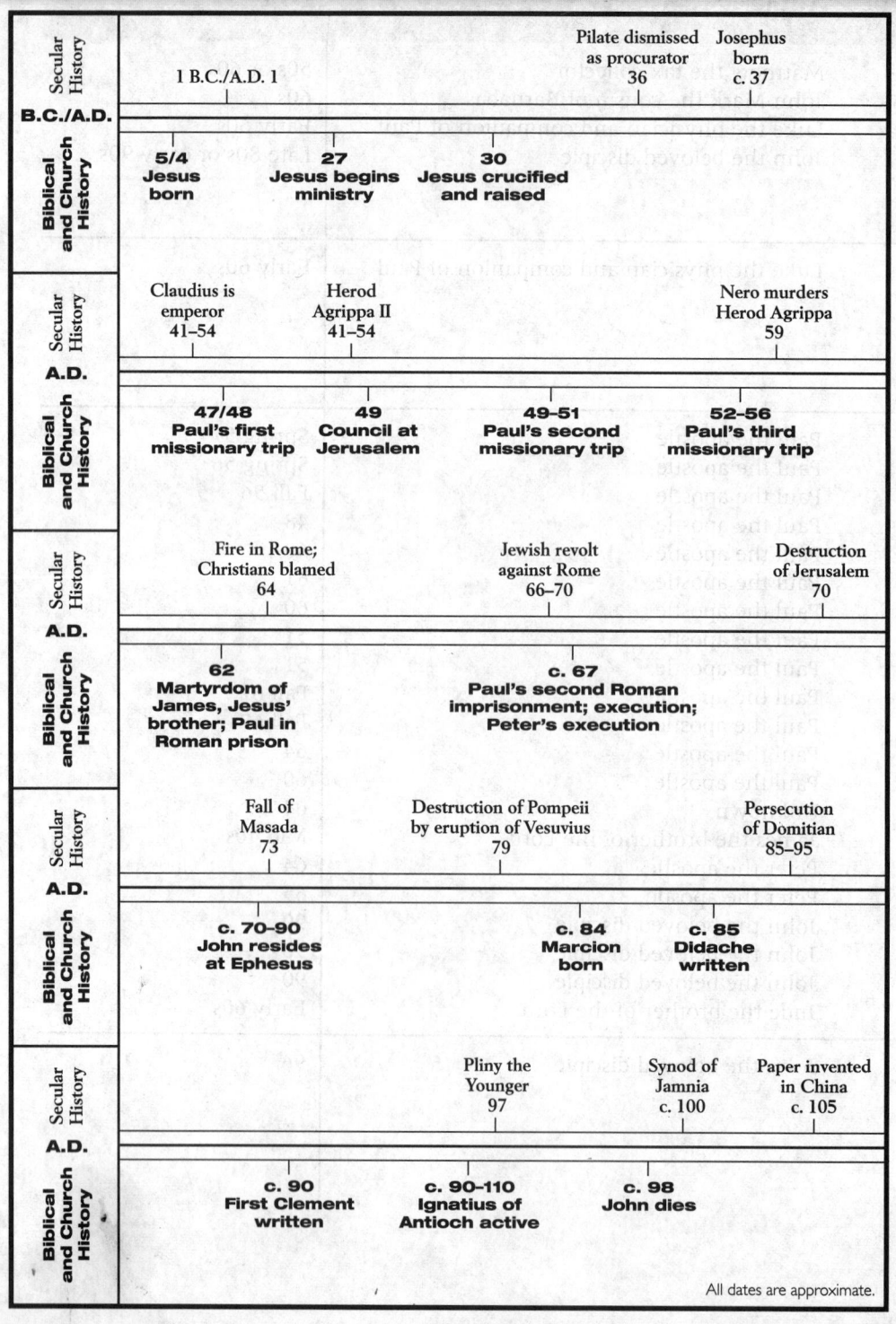

Secular History	1 B.C./A.D. 1			Pilate dismissed as procurator 36 / Josephus born c. 37

B.C./A.D.

Biblical and Church History	**5/4** Jesus born	**27** Jesus begins ministry	**30** Jesus crucified and raised	

Secular History	Claudius is emperor 41–54	Herod Agrippa II 41–54		Nero murders Herod Agrippa 59

A.D.

Biblical and Church History	**47/48** Paul's first missionary trip	**49** Council at Jerusalem	**49–51** Paul's second missionary trip	**52–56** Paul's third missionary trip

Secular History	Fire in Rome; Christians blamed 64		Jewish revolt against Rome 66–70	Destruction of Jerusalem 70

A.D.

Biblical and Church History	**62** Martyrdom of James, Jesus' brother; Paul in Roman prison		**c. 67** Paul's second Roman imprisonment; execution; Peter's execution	

Secular History	Fall of Masada 73	Destruction of Pompeii by eruption of Vesuvius 79		Persecution of Domitian 85–95

A.D.

Biblical and Church History	**c. 70–90** John resides at Ephesus		**c. 84** Marcion born	**c. 85** Didache written

Secular History		Pliny the Younger 97	Synod of Jamnia c. 100	Paper invented in China c. 105

A.D.

Biblical and Church History	**c. 90** First Clement written	**c. 90–110** Ignatius of Antioch active	**c. 98** John dies	

All dates are approximate.

Themes of the Bible

*A*S WE READ THE BIBLE, WE NOTICE THAT THROUGH-out God's word certain important themes are repeatedly mentioned or implied. Several of these basic scriptural topics are described below.

Faithfulness

God reveals Himself in the Bible as One who can be fully trusted. He exhibits complete integrity in all He says and promises; consequently His people are to have complete confidence in His promises concerning them (Num. 23:19; Is. 55:11). Studying the faithfulness of God will bring about spiritual stability and confidence in a believer's daily walk.

Love

In the Old Testament the verb "to love" (Heb. *ahab*) and its related words cover the full range of meanings the English word "love" has, including love for God (Ex. 20:6; Ps. 40:16) and the love God has for His people (Deut. 7:13; Hos. 3:1). The Old Testament also uses the Hebrew word *chesed* specifically for the covenant love the Lord has for His people, referring to His steadfastness or loyalty.

In the New Testament the primary Greek verbs expressing the concept of love are *agapao*, loving as an act of will, and *phileo*, loving as a response to a person or object. In the synoptic Gospels, one notes that the primary use of the word "love" is with regard to the great commandment (Matt. 22:34–40; Mark 12:28–34; Luke 10:26–28). Love is a possibility only because the believer has responded in faith to

God's saving act in the death and resurrection of Christ (Rom. 5:8; Gal. 2:20).

Justice

Justice is founded in the being of God and is an extension of His holiness. God is shown to be a sure defender of the poor and the oppressed (Ps. 10:17, 18; Jer. 9:23, 24). The Psalms base justice on God's role as the sovereign creator of the universe (Ps. 99:1–4), so the idea extends beyond the nation of Israel (Ps. 9:7–9; Dan. 4:27). In view of God's concern for the poor and the weak, a corresponding quality is expected from God's people (Deut. 10:18, 19). When they properly carry out justice, they are agents of the divine will (Is. 59:15, 16; 2 Cor. 9:8–10). God's demand for justice is so central that other responses to Him are empty or diminished if they exist without it (Amos 5:21–24; Mic. 6:6–8; Matt. 23:23). Paul (primarily in Romans) uses the language of justice to describe God's work of salvation as he expounds the righteousness of God.

Judgment

In the Old Testament God appears frequently in the role of "Judge of all the earth" (Gen. 18:25), or more generally the "God of justice" (Mal. 2:17). Judgment implies not only an unbiased weighing of good and evil, but also vigorous

(cont'd on p. xl)

Major Bible Themes

Category	Primary Definition
FAITHFULNESS	Faithfulness describes the dependability, loyalty, and stability of God, particularly in relation to His people. God's faithfulness in keeping His word is a consistent theme in the Bible. Faithfulness is also something that God's people are to demonstrate in their relationship with Him.
LOVE	Love is both an attribute of God and an essential part of His nature. Lovingkindness is another term used throughout the Old Testament to refer to the loyal esteem and favor God has toward His covenant people. In the New Testament the two main terms used for love refer to the positive regard God has for His Son and His people, and to the affection of brothers and friends toward each other.
JUSTICE	When the Bible refers to the justice of God it means that God is honorable in His treatment of people. All of His decisions are righteous and true. God requires that His people also deal justly in all the situations of life (Mic. 6:8). God's actions in the Bible give us the pattern by which we can make right decisions.
JUDGMENT	God is the Judge of all the universe. He judges according to His standard of Law as revealed in the Bible. Judgment can refer either to the process of determining guilt or innocence or to the punishment given out to those who fall under God's wrath.
MERCY	Mercy is seen in God's compassion toward the suffering and in His willingness to restore those whose own sins have separated them from Him. God sovereignly determines to extend mercy by withholding punishment from sinners and restoring them to fellowship with Himself. God also exhibits His mercy through acts of His providence, such as healing and rescue from danger. God expects us to show mercy to others as well.
TRUTH	The biblical concept regarding truth is not conformity to an external standard but faithfulness or reliability. Concerning God, of course, faithfulness or reliability is not measured by any external standard; the standard is God Himself.
HOLINESS	God is holy, separate from His creation by His very nature. To be holy literally means to be cut off or separate, and denotes apartness, the separation of a person or thing from the common or profane to a divine use.
MISSIONS	God uses His people to proclaim His Word to those outside His covenant. By this proclamation those He has elected unto salvation come to faith in Him. Israel was to proclaim His goodness and today the church is commanded to go into all the world and proclaim the good news of salvation in Christ.

Major Old Testament Verses	Major New Testament Verses
Faithfulness part of God's character (Is. 49:7); great (Lam. 3:23); established (Ps. 89:2); incomparable (Ps. 89:8); unfailing (Ps. 89:33); infinite (Ps. 36:5); everlasting (Ps. 119:90).	Faithfulness part of God's character (1 Cor. 1:9; 1 Thess. 5:24); unfailing (2 Tim. 2:13); in fulfilling His promises (Heb. 10:23); in forgiving sins (1 John 1:9); to His saints (2 Thess. 3:3); to be depended on (1 Pet. 4:19); a characteristic of saints (Eph. 1:1; Col. 1:2; 1 Tim. 1:12; Rev. 17:14).
God's love described as and seen in being: sovereign (Deut. 7:8; 10:15); assuring (Zeph. 3:17); unfailing (Is. 49:15, 16); everlasting (Jer. 31:3); irrespective of merit (Deut. 7:7; Job 7:17); by election (Mal. 1:2, 3); by redemption (Is. 43:3, 4; 63:9); by forgiving sin (Is. 38:17); by drawing us to Himself (Hos. 11:4); by temporal blessings (Deut. 7:13).	God's love a part of His character (2 Cor. 13:11; 1 John 4:8); Christ, the special object of (John 15:9; 17:26); Christ abides in (John 15:10); God's love manifested toward: perishing sinners (John 3:16; Titus 3:4); His saints (John 16:27; 17:23; 2 Thess. 2:16); shed abroad in the heart by the Holy Spirit (Rom. 5:5); saints know and believe (1 John 4:16); saints should abide in (Jude 21).
Justice a part of God's character (Deut. 32:4; Is. 45:21); concerning His justice God is plenteous (Job 37:23); incorruptible (Deut. 10:17; 2 Chr. 19:7); impartial (Jer. 32:19); unfailing (Zeph. 3:5); undeviating (Job 8:3).	God's justice without respect of persons (Rom. 2:11; Col. 3:25; 1 Pet. 1:17); exhibited in: forgiving sins (1 John 1:9); redemption (Rom. 3:26).
Judgment comes from God (Deut. 32:39; Job 12:23; Amos 3:6; Mic. 6:9); God judges by: blotting out one's name (Deut. 29:20); abandonment (Hos. 4:17); cursing men's blessings (Mal. 2:2); pestilence (Deut. 28:21, 22; Amos 4:10).	All judgment is in the hands of Jesus Christ (John 5:22); He has this authority because He is the Son of Man (John 5:27). Believers are not to stand in the place of Christ as Judge because we all will stand before Christ's judgment seat (Rom. 14:10).
God's mercy described as great (Is. 54:7); sure (Is. 55:3); tender (Ps. 25:6); new every morning (Lam. 3:22, 23); seen especially in forgiveness (Ps. 51:1); believers are to cast themselves on God's mercy (2 Sam. 24:14).	God's mercy seen in Christ's mission (Luke 1:72, 78); salvation (1 Cor. 7:25; Titus 3:5); regeneration (1 Pet. 1:3); practiced as a gift (Rom. 12:8); shown in God's providences (Phil. 2:27); obtained through prayer (Heb. 4:16); believers are enjoined to "put on mercy" (Col. 3:12).
God is a God of truth (Deut. 32:4; Ps. 31:5); His Word is truth (Ps. 119:160; Dan. 10:21); He regards truthful people with favor (Jer. 5:3); the judgments of God are according to His truth (Ps. 96:13).	Jesus Christ is the Truth (John 7:18; 14:6); He was full of truth (John 1:14); He spoke truth (John 8:45); the Holy Spirit is the Spirit of Truth (John 14:17) who guides us into all truth (John 16:13).
The character of God is the standard (Lev. 19:2); is incomparable (Ex. 15:11; 1 Sam. 2:2); commanded (Lev. 11:45; 19:2; 20:7); necessary to worship of God (Ps. 24:3, 4); we are to avoid everything inconsistent with it (Lev. 21:6).	We are to bear fruit unto holiness (Rom. 6:22); we are chastened by God so we may partake of His holiness (Heb. 12:10); called by God to a holy life (1 Thess. 4:7).
The king of Assyria allowed a Jewish priest to teach the way of God (2 Kin. 17:27, 28); Israel was commanded to proclaim the day of His salvation to all the earth (1 Chr. 16:23, 24); the prophet Jonah was commanded to proclaim God's message to Nineveh (Jon. 3:1, 2).	The Gospel of the Kingdom shall be preached in all the world and then the end shall come (Matt. 24:14); the church is commanded to teach the truth of Christ to all the world (Matt. 28:19); people come to faith by hearing the Word preached (Rom. 10:14).

action against evil. It is because of this understanding that the people of God are summoned to exercise judgment in turn (Is. 1:17; Zech. 8:16). It is a strongly personal notion, closely linked to God's characteristics of mercy, lovingkindness, righteousness, and truth.

The New Testament continues to stress judgment as part of God's nature and essential activity (Rom. 1:18; Heb. 12:23; 1 Pet. 1:17; 2:23; Rev. 16:5). His judgments are not confined to the future but are already at work in the present age (John 8:50; Rom. 1:18, 22, 24, 26, 28; Rev. 18:8). Judgment is associated even now with Christ, who exercises the Father's judgments.

Mercy

Just as strong as the emphasis on judgment is the Bible's recognition of God's mercy. By His grace God extends help and forgiveness to sinners who deserve only condemnation, as well as practical help to those who are suffering under life's burdens. God shows compassion toward those who have broken His law (Dan. 9:9; 1 Tim. 1:13, 16), although such mercy is selectively bestowed upon the undeserving (Rom. 9:14–18). God's mercy extends beyond withheld punishment (Eph. 2:4–6) to include the blessings of salvation.

Jesus showed mercy toward the afflicted when he healed them, as in the case of blind men (Matt. 9:27–31; 20:29–34) and lepers (Luke 17:11–19). Jesus was modeling the behavior He expects from His followers: because God is merciful, He expects us to be merciful as well (Matt. 5:7; James 1:27).

Truth

The Hebrew idea of truth is generally associated with constancy, permanence, faithfulness, and reliability. God above all is true, that is, real and reliable (Is. 65:16; Jer. 10:10); His people are to seek God's truth (Ps. 25:5; 51:6; 86:11) and judge truly. The lack of truth is lamented (Is. 59:14, 15; Zech. 8:16).

For the Hebrews, truth was basically moral and relational, not simply intellectual. For the Greeks, the emphasis of truth was intellectual rather than a matter of trust or reliance. The New Testament usage draws on both understandings. The word is found mainly in Paul's writings and in John's Gospel and letters. John builds on the understanding that God is true or real (John 3:33; 7:28). Christ reveals God and thus reveals truth (John 8:26, 40; 18:37). Christ is full of grace and truth (John 1:14, 17), He is "the truth" (John 14:6; read John 1:9; 15:1), and He sends the Spirit of truth (John 15:26).

Paul teaches that truth is to be obeyed (Rom. 2:8; Gal. 5:7), that it proves reliable (2 Cor. 7:14; 11:10), and that its opposite is malice and evil (1 Cor. 5:8). The Greek idea of truth as correct knowledge appears most clearly in Paul's pastoral letters. One is to know the truth (1 Tim. 4:3; 2 Tim. 2:25) and avoid false beliefs (2 Tim. 2:18; 4:4).

Holiness

In Hebrew, to be holy primarily means to be separate from the ordinary or profane. God is holy, and people, things, and actions may be holy by association with God. Psalms and Isaiah frequently refer to God as the Holy One (Ps. 78:41; 89:18; Is. 1:4; 5:19; 30:15). Places where God appeared and was customarily worshiped were also holy (Gen. 28:11–22; Ex. 3:5). The temple in Jerusalem was the most holy place in Israel because God's presence dwelled there (1 Kin. 8:10, 11); consequently, persons and things relating to the temple were holy (Lev. 22; 27). Israel itself was a holy nation (Ex. 19:4; Lev. 19:2; Deut. 7:6) because the Lord set it apart for His purposes.

The New Testament reaffirms the ideas of holiness found in Judaism. God, the temple, and the law are all holy. The physical temple is deemphasized because Gentile Christians had moved away from the practice of Judaism and because the temple was destroyed in A.D. 70, but the temple occurs as a metaphor for Christian holiness (1 Cor. 3:17; 6:19). God is addressed as "Holy Father" by Jesus (John 17:11), praised in heaven by the threefold "holy" of Isaiah (Is. 6:3; Rev. 4:6–10), and addressed by the petition of the Lord's Prayer, "Hallowed be Your name" (Matt. 6:9; Luke 11:2).

Missions

God has always used His people to proclaim His mighty deeds and saving grace. The nation of Israel was to declare the goodness of God to the Gentiles so that they might enter into covenant with God. The Book of Isaiah is filled with declarations regarding the salvation of the Gentiles (Is. 11:10; 42:6; 49:6; 60:11).

It was not until the advent of the church that the good news of God's salvation in Christ was being proclaimed widely in the world. Jesus commands His people to go into all the world and preach the gospel (Mark 16:15). It is through "the foolishness of the message preached" (1 Cor. 1:21) that people are drawn to faith in Jesus Christ. Salvation is of God, but He uses His people as the means by which He saves sinners.

Doctrine in Scripture

Classifications of Theology

*T*HEOLOGY IS SIMPLY ORGANIZED THINKING ABOUT God. Different ways of organizing those thoughts has resulted in different types of theology, each with its own merit. Christian theology presupposes the existence of God (theology proper) and His revelation of Himself in the Bible (bibliology). These presuppositions are not without firm intellectual foundation; in fact, they comprise two large categories of doctrine

in their own right. Theology proper and bibliology form the starting point and foundation for true Christian theology. The more the doctrines are studied, the more certain the foundation becomes; but they are necessary presuppositions if the student of the Scriptures is to start correctly. As the adage goes, "Well begun is half done."

Doctrine is the summation or description of the truth found in the Bible. Theology is the process of arriving at that doctrine. The major ways to approach the study of theology are biblical theology, historical theology, systematic theology, and practical theology.

Biblical theology concerns the unfolding of truth in specific books and passages of Scripture. It recognizes the progressive revelation of God (defined below) and therefore does not necessarily aim to present the whole of a biblical doctrine, but to establish that portion of doctrine taught in the Scripture under consideration. The different books of the Bible were occasioned by specific circumstances and needs. Therefore, often the intent of the author was not to develop a doctrine fully, but rather to teach the truth necessary to accomplish a purpose that the occasion required.

Historical theology deals with the theological perspectives set forth by Christians through the centuries. This approach looks at the teaching as it has developed over time. Studying the way that the Scriptures have been understood helps the modern seeker of truth to clarify his or her own thought concerning many important doctrines.

Systematic theology is the organized presentation of the various doctrines, with full consideration of both biblical theology and historical theology. Doctrines are developed and articulated as a part or subset of the total structure of systematic theology. This does not mean that tradition has equal weight with the Bible in development of doctrine. Rather, it humbly respects the fact that other thinkers through the ages have wrestled with the same biblical truths, aided by the illumination of the same Holy Spirit. The conclusions and thoughts of the people of God through the centuries can contribute to the present understanding of the Scriptures.

Practical theology emphasizes the correlation of theology to life's needs. It shows the connections between doctrine and application, paying

(cont'd on p. xliv)

Classifications of Doctrine in Scripture

Classification	Meaning	Key Books
BIBLIOLOGY	The doctrine of the Bible, regarding the nature of revelation, inspiration, inerrancy, and illumination	Deuteronomy, Psalms, Matthew, 1 & 2 Timothy, 2 Peter
THEOLOGY PROPER	The doctrine of God based on His revelation of Himself to man	Genesis, Job, Isaiah, John, Romans
CHRISTOLOGY	The doctrine of Jesus Christ	Isaiah, Micah, John, Philippians, Colossians, Hebrews
PNEUMATOLOGY	The doctrine of the Holy Spirit	Genesis, John, Acts, Romans, 1 Corinthians
ANGELOLOGY	The doctrine of fallen and unfallen angels	Genesis, Job, Daniel, Zechariah, Matthew, Acts, 1 Corinthians, 2 Corinthians, Hebrews, Revelation
ANTHROPOLOGY	The doctrine of man, or humanity	Genesis, Psalms, 2 Corinthians
HAMARTIOLOGY	The doctrine of sin	Genesis, Job, Psalms, Romans
SOTERIOLOGY	The doctrine of salvation	Genesis, Psalms, Isaiah, John, Romans, Hebrews
ECCLESIOLOGY	The doctrine of the church	Acts, 1 Corinthians, Ephesians
ESCHATOLOGY	The doctrine of last things	Genesis, Major and Minor Prophets, Matthew, 1 and 2 Thessalonians, 2 Peter, Revelation

Old Testament Passages	New Testament Passages
Deut. 6:4–9; 1 Kin. 16:1; Ps. 19; 111:7, 8; 119; Is. 40:8; Jer. 1:9; 13:1	Matt. 5:18; Luke 11:51; John 10:34–36; 1 Tim. 5:18 (with Deut. 25:4 and Luke 10:7); 2 Tim. 3:15, 16; 2 Pet. 1:4, 20; 3:15, 16
Gen. 1:1; Ex. 3:14; Deut. 6:4; 1 Kin. 8:27; Job 42:1–6; Ps. 139:7–12; Is. 57:15; 65:1; 66:1; Jer. 32:17, 27	John 4:24; 5:26; 17:3; Rom. 1; 9:18; 11:22, 33–36; 1 Cor. 1:20; 1 Tim. 1:17; James 1:17
Gen. 3:15; Ps. 2:7; Is. 7:14; 9:6; 53; 61:1, 2; Mic. 5:2; Zech. 9:9	John 1:1–18; 14:7–11; Phil. 2:6–8; Col. 1:15–19; 2:9; Heb. 1:1–8; 2:18; Rev. 1:13–18
Gen. 1:2; 6:3; Judg. 14:19; 1 Sam. 16:13; Ps. 139:7; Is. 40:13, 14; Ezek. 2:2; Mic. 3:8; Zech. 12:10	Luke 1:35; John 14–16; Acts 2:1–4; 13:2, 4; Rom. 8; 1 Cor. 6:19; 12—14; 2 Cor. 13:14; Gal. 5:22, 23; Eph. 1:13; 4:30; 5:18
Gen. 16; 18; 19; 24:7, 40; Job 1:6; 38:7; Ps. 103:20; 148:2, 5; Is. 6:1–3; Dan. 9:20–27; Zech. 1:9, 13, 14; 3:1, 2; 4:1	Matt. 13:41, 49; 28:2–5; Acts 1:10; 5:19; 12:7; 1 Cor. 13:1; 2 Cor. 11:14; Heb. 1:6, 7; 2:2, 5; Rev. 1:1; 5:2; 7:2; 8:5; 22:16
Gen. 1:27; 2:20–23; 3:19; 9:6; Ps. 8:4, 5; 139:14; Is. 43:7; Eccl. 7:29	2 Cor. 4:16; 5:1, 6–8; Eph. 5:29; Heb. 9:27
Gen. 2:17; 3:14–24; Job 14:4; 15:14; Ps. 51:4, 5; Is. 53:6; Hab. 1:13	Rom. 1:21, 28; 3:23; 6:20; 7:20; 2 Cor. 4:4; Eph. 4:18; Titus 1:15; Rev. 20:11–15
Gen. 3:15; 22:12–14; Ex. 12:1–13; Lev. 1:1–9; Ps. 51; Is. 53:3–12	John 1:29; 3:3–8; Rom. 5:12–21; 8:1–4; Eph. 2:5, 8; Titus 2:11; Heb. 1:3; 2:10–18; 5:9; 9:28; Rev. 1:5, 6; 5:9, 10; 12:11
Not revealed as such in the Old Testament (Eph. 3:4–6)	Matt. 16:18; 18:15–20; Rom. 16:5; 1 Cor. 16:19; Eph. 1:22, 23; 5:23–32; Phil. 2; Col. 4:15; 1 Tim. 3; Titus 1:5–9
Gen. 12:2; 13:14, 15; 15:7; 2 Sam. 7:12–16; Ezek. 20:34–38; Dan. 12:13	Matt. 24:4–51; 1 Thess. 4:13–18; 5:1–3; 2 Thess. 2:1–12; 1 Pet. 4:7; 2 Pet. 3:3–13; Jude 6–7; Rev. 1:7–8; 4:1–11; 20:4–15; 21:1–8

attention to the ways in which theology pertains to issues concerning ethics and society, the interaction of people, and the mission of the church.

The Major Categories of Doctrine:

Bibliology	The doctrine of the Bible
Theology Proper	The doctrine of God
Christology	The doctrine of Jesus Christ
Pneumatology	The doctrine of the Holy Spirit
Angelology	The doctrine of angels (including Satan and demons)
Anthropology	The doctrine of man
Hamartiology	The doctrine of sin
Soteriology	The doctrine of salvation
Ecclesiology	The doctrine of the church
Eschatology	The doctrine of last things

The Development of Doctrine in the Bible

To understand the development of doctrine, it is necessary to understand two concepts: progressive revelation, and how the church developed its theology.

Progressive revelation means that God worked over time, with different persons and through different means, to reveal Himself and His truth in the Bible. A clear indication of this in Scripture is found in Heb. 1:1–3 as well as 1 Pet. 1:10–12. Because of this, we often weigh the later portions of Scripture more heavily regarding doctrine, for they provide the fuller explanation of many teachings. However, later biblical writers sometimes presuppose certain well-developed knowledge on the part of their readers and so do not state the assumed knowledge. In such cases, earlier portions of Scripture may give us a fuller understanding of certain aspects of doctrine.

Theological development in the church has been necessary because of the occasional and nonsystematic nature of the New Testament writings. The Bible contains enough truth for the establishment of clear, coherent doctrine, but it rarely presents that truth in a systematic teaching. Therefore, the people in the church have necessarily and appropriately contributed thought and organization as the truths of the Bible have been expressed and extended within their own historical and intellectual setting.

The Practical Importance of Doctrine

Biblical teaching, or doctrine, is not intended by God to stop with the enlightenment of the intellect. Enlightenment is a necessary first step, but truth is intended to impact the thinking, habits, and behaviors of its recipients.

Examples of this are abundant in Scripture (for example, Rom. 12:1; 2 Pet. 3:11). It is the intended pattern of Scripture that understanding of truth should motivate application of truth. Always learning but never acknowledging the truth (2 Tim. 3:7) is a description of the process of Christian thought short-circuiting at the mind and not getting to practical outworking. The writer of Hebrews tells us in Heb. 5:11–14 that Christian maturity comes through practicing biblical truth, not just by possessing the knowledge. James writes that we are to be "doers of the word and not hearers only" (James 1:22).

It is a theological and practical error, however, to reverse the order and take an application of truth and build a doctrine from it. As an example, the application of self-denial for one person should not become a prescription of lifestyle for another. Romans 14 illustrates clarity in conviction and charity in extension of that conviction to others. Dogmatic practices without foundational truth become a system of religion without power.

The Trinity in the Bible

Historical Development of the Doctrine of the Trinity

HE TERM *TRINITY* IS NOT FOUND IN THE BIBLE but is a theological word which expresses the clear teaching of Holy Scripture, especially the New Testament. The first theologian of the church to use the term was Theophilus who spoke of God as *trias*. The great Latin church father Tertullian first developed the concept of *trinitas*, one God in three persons. Though the fathers of the church in the second and third centuries spoke of the three persons of the Godhead while recognizing that there is but one God, the councils of Nicea (A.D. 325) and Constantinople (A.D. 381) gave the fullest expression to the Biblical doctrine.

The Bible Explicitly Teaches That There Is Only One God

The Teaching of the Old Testament

Belief in one God in the ancient Mediterranean world was unique to the nation of Israel. The faith of Israel is given in the famous Shema: "Hear, O Israel: The Lord our God, the Lord is one" (Deut. 6:4). Repeatedly the teaching of the Law and the pronouncements of God's prophets confirm this absolute truth.

The Teaching of the New Testament

The church continued the teaching of the Hebrew Scriptures, as well as the teaching of the Lord Jesus Christ, that there is only one God (1 Cor. 8:6; Eph. 4:6; 1 Tim. 2:5). This it did in contrast to the rampant polytheism that permeated the Greco-Roman world with its multitude of gods, including worship of the emperor as a god during the latter half of the first century. As the apostles and later the church began to articulate this monotheism against pagan religion, it was necessary to explain how this belief in one God was consistent with the concurrent belief that the Father, Son, and Holy Spirit are each God and yet still only one God.

Scripture Teaches That Three Persons Are One God

Glimpses of the Trinity in the Old Testament

Use of the Word Elohim with Singular Verbs   The usual word for God in the Hebrew is *Elohim*. This noun is in the plural, whereas in several places the term for God is a singular, such as *El* or *Eloah*. In spite of the plural term for God, the true Jewish faith was strongly monotheistic. When *Elohim* is used regarding the God of Israel, it is used with singular verbs, indicating that the God

(cont'd on p. xlviii)

Biblical Teaching About the Trinity

Teaching	Old Testament
THE BIBLE TEACHES THAT THERE IS ONLY ONE GOD.	The creed of Israel, the Shema (Deut. 6:4), emphasizes the uniqueness of God: "Hear, O Israel: The LORD our God, the LORD is one" (Ex. 20:2, 3; 3:13–15).
THE BIBLE SPEAKS OF GOD AS THREE DISTINCT PERSONS.	God the Father is distinguished from the Son in Ps. 2:7 (Ps. 68:18; Is. 9:6; 61:1–3; Heb. 1:1–13), and the Holy Spirit is set forth as distinct from them both. The Father is seen to be God in Is. 63:16, the Son in Is. 9:6, and the Spirit in Gen. 1:1, 2 (Ex. 31:3; Judg. 15:14; Is. 11:2).
THE BIBLE TEACHES THAT THREE DISTINCT PERSONS HAVE THE ATTRIBUTES OF GOD.	The Father possesses the divine attributes (Ps. 90:2; Jer. 17:10; 23:24). The Son has the attributes of deity (Is. 9:6, 7; Dan 7:13, 14). The Holy Spirit possesses the divine attributes (Gen. 1:2; Ps. 139:7; Neh. 9:20).
THE BIBLE TEACHES THAT THREE DISTINCT PERSONS PERFORM THE WORKS OF GOD.	The Father is presented in the Old Testament as the Creator (Ps. 102:25), and the other members of the Godhead are as well. Genesis 2:7 uses the plural to identify more than one person to the being of God. If we understand Jesus, the Logos, as the Wisdom of God by which He made the world, then the Son is intimated in the Old Testament as Creator too. The Spirit of God is the creative force brooding over the waters in Gen. 1:2 (compare Job 26:13).

New Testament

The early apostles of the Lord believed in only one God (1 Cor. 8:4–6; 1 Tim. 1:17; 2:5, 6; James 2:19).

The New Testament sets forth in clear terms that the Father of the Lord Jesus Christ is God (John 1:18; 1 Cor. 8:6; Phil. 2:11; 1 Pet. 1:2). No one disputes this truth. The New Testament authors at numerous places present Jesus Christ as God Himself, yet distinct from God the Father (John 1:1, 18; 8:58; Rom. 9:5; Titus 2:13; 2 Pet. 1:1). Moreover, the Holy Spirit is called God by Peter (Acts 5:4), yet He is introduced at the baptism of Jesus as different from Jesus, and as distinct from the Father and Son in the apostolic benedictions.

The Father possesses divine characteristics (John 7:28; Rom. 2:4; 1 Pet. 1:5; Rev. 15:4). The Son is presented as having the nature of God (Matt. 18:20; John 1:2; 2 Cor. 12:9; Rev. 3:7), and the Spirit of God is presented similarly (Acts 1:8; Rom. 15:19; 1 Cor. 2:11; 1 John 5:6).

Whereas the Father and Spirit are more clearly identified in the Old Testament, the New Testament strongly presents Jesus as the creator God (John 1:1–3; Col. 1:16).

of Israel is a single being. The plural allows for a plurality of expression for God, as later revealed in the New Testament, but Hebrew grammar may also simply be using a plural of plenitude.

Use of Plural Personal Pronouns On three occasions the Old Testament uses plural personal pronouns when speaking of God. The first occurrence refers to the creation of humanity: "Let Us make man in Our image" (Gen. 1:26). The second pertains to God deciding to confuse human languages at the tower of Babel: "Let Us go down" (Gen. 11:6–9). The last reference is to the call to mission: "Who will go for Us?" (Is. 6:1–8).

The Angel of the Lord Several times in the Hebrew Scriptures, reference is made to "the Angel of the LORD" (Yahweh). It is evident from the contexts that these references do not speak simply of a created messenger of God but of God Himself. In certain contexts the Angel of the LORD is identified as God Himself (Gen. 16:7–13; 18:1–22), but in others He is distinguished from God (Gen. 19:1–28, especially v. 24; Zech. 1:12, 13; Mal. 3:1). Such appearances most likely are of the preincarnate Christ, who is the revelation of the Father (John 1:18; Heb. 1:1–3). After the incarnation such appearances of the Angel of the LORD end, for now the revelation of God is present as a human in the person of Jesus Christ (compare Ex.14:19 with Ex. 23:20; 1 Cor. 10:4).

The Explicit Teaching of the New Testament

The Teaching of Jesus Christ on His Relationship to the Father and the Holy Spirit Jesus is the Son of the Father. Jesus calls Himself the Son of God, and He also calls God His Father in a way that implies a profoundly unique association. Moreover, Jesus claims a relationship with God the Father as a partner from all eternity. At other times Jesus makes statements and does deeds that cause others to recognize His claim to equality with God. The specific charge of blasphemy made against Christ was His admission to being the Son of God (Luke 22:70). These texts identify the person Jesus, preexistent to the world, as being God and yet distinct from God the Father.

Like Jesus the Son, the Holy Spirit is also a divine Person. Before Christ left the earth to be with the Father, He promised a Comforter similar to but distinct from Himself. He and the Father come to the believer through this Person, the Holy Spirit.

In a sense, each Christian is identified with the Triune God. Jesus in His prayer for believers in John 17 indicated that God would dwell with believers in Christ, "I in them and You in Me" (John 17:23).

The Teaching of the Apostles on the Trinity God is called the Father of the Lord Jesus Christ as well as of Christians (Eph. 1:2; Phil. 1:2; 2 John 3). The apostle John specifically calls Jesus God (John 1:1, 18; 8:58). In several places Paul identifies Jesus as God (Rom. 9:5; Phil. 2:6; Titus 2:13), as does Peter (2 Pet. 1:1). The Holy Spirit is declared to be God by Peter (Acts 5:4) and is listed alongside the Father and the Son (Matt. 28:19; 2 Cor. 13:14).

The Doctrine of Salvation

■

The Meaning of Salvation in the Bible

*G*ENERALLY IN THE OLD TESTAMENT, THE TERM *salvation* concerns physical deliverance or preservation. The major Hebrew verb for salvation, *yasha*, carries the sense of help, deliver, or save, and is used about 205 times in the Bible. It occurs in contexts of removing a burden or danger (Ex. 2:17) and can be used of removing someone from the danger of defeat (Josh. 10:6). At other times the term refers to being liberated or set free

(Judg. 12:2). Used in civil law, *yasha* pertains to the obligation of one who hears the cry of someone who needs to be saved from mistreatment (Deut. 22:27; 28:29; 2 Sam. 14:4). The Hebrew word appears in many prayer petitions in reference to war and judicial issues (Pss. 3:7; 20:9; 72:4; 86:2). The noun speaks of preservation from threatened, impending, and perhaps deserved danger and suffering (Gen. 49:18; 1 Sam. 14:45; Is. 12:3).

New Testament

The New Testament concept of salvation includes most of the elements of the Old Testament concept and adds spiritual dimensions. The Greek term *soteria* has both national and personal aspects. National deliverance is discussed in Luke 1:69. There is personal deliverance from the sea (Acts 27:34) and prison (Phil. 1:19), and spiritual and eternal deliverance through repentance and faith in Jesus Christ (Acts 4:12; Rom. 10:10). The New Testament uses *soteria* and the related verb *sozo* with regard to God's power to deliver from the bondage of sin (Phil. 2:12); the future deliverance of believers at the coming of Christ (Rom. 13:11; 1 Thess. 5:8, 9); and the deliverance of the nation of Israel at the second advent of Christ (Luke 1:71; 2 Thess. 2:10; Rev. 12:10).

Jesus the Savior

The designation of Jesus told to His mother by the angel Gabriel was that of Savior, namely, "you shall call His name Jesus, for He will save His people from their sins" (Matt. 1:21). That He carried that sense of mission throughout His life is clear from His statements in Mark 10:45: "For even the Son of Man did not come to be served, but to serve, and to give His life a ransom for many"; and in John 12:27: "Now My soul is troubled, and what shall I say? 'Father, save Me from this hour'? But for this purpose I came to this hour." The role of Jesus Christ as Savior of the world is further exhibited by His willingness to go to the Cross when He could have called the forces of heaven to rescue Him (Matt. 26:53, 54). Rather, He freely gave Himself on the Cross,

(cont'd on p. lii)

Salvation in the Bible

Category	Kind/Type	When
PHYSICAL	From Sickness	Present
	From Death	Past
	From Danger	Present
	From God's wrath	Future
SPIRITUAL	From Sin	Past
		Present
		Future
	From False Doctrine	Latter times

What	How	Passages
From sickness that is possibly through sin	Prayer of faith by church elders	James 5:14, 15
David, from physical death	Guidance into truth	Ps. 56:13
From attack by the enemies of God's people	God's deliverance of His people's enemies into their hands	Josh. 10:6–8; Hos. 13:10
Coming of Christ for the church	Rapture of the church	1 Thess. 1:10
Penalty	Justification	Rom. 3:21—4:12; Gal. 3:11–14
Power	Sanctification	Rom. 6:22; 2 Thess. 2:13; 2 Tim. 2:21
Presence	Glorification	Rom. 8:17, 18, 30; 1 Thess. 4:13–18
Avoidance of departure from the faith	Give special attention to sound doctrine	1 Tim. 4:13–16

as depicted in all four Gospels. Ironically, the ones standing by the Cross spoke true words: "He saved others; Himself He cannot save" (Mark 15:31).

Terms Used in Reference to Spiritual Salvation

Election is that aspect of the eternal purpose of God whereby He certainly and eternally determines who will believe and be saved (Matt. 22:14; Acts 13:48; Eph. 1:4; 2 Thess. 2:13). Yet no one is excused from believing by this doctrine. God "desires all men to be saved and to come to the knowledge of the truth" (1 Tim. 2:4). Acts 2:21 states that "whoever calls on the name of the Lord shall be saved." Whoever does not accept God's free offer of salvation has no one but himself to blame.

Predestination differs from election in that predestination relates specifically to the intent of God to conform those whom He has chosen to the image of Christ (Rom. 8:29, 30).

Calling is used in two senses. The first is the general call of the gospel addressed to all humans (Matt. 22:14; John 3:16–18; 16:7–11). The second call is the application of the word of the gospel to the ones God has chosen, and results in regeneration (John 6:44; Rom. 8:28, 30; 1 Cor. 1:23, 24).

Law is the means by which God *governed* His covenant people in the Old Testament, whereas He *established* His covenant by grace (Gen. 17:7). The New Testament demonstrates that the role of the law is not to justify, but to show us what sin is. It was only a schoolmaster to bring us to Christ (Gal. 2:16; 3:24)

Regeneration refers to the spiritual change brought about in a person by the Holy Spirit, namely a new life. This change is from spiritual death to spiritual life. It is a change in one's very nature, to one in communion with God. The New Testament explicitly presents the doctrine (2 Cor. 5:17; Eph. 2:1; 1 John 4:7), whereas the Old Testament implies it. Moses spoke of Israelites who would have "circumcised hearts" (Deut. 30:6). Isaiah also described changes that resemble the New Testament depiction of the new birth (Is. 57:15).

Justification is first presented in the Bible with regard to Abraham. The Scripture says that Abraham believed God's promises to him and this faith was accounted to him as righteousness (Gen. 15:6; Rom. 3:23—4:12; Gal. 3:6). If personal fulfillment of the law were necessary to justification before God, no one would have been saved. Believers in God are justified by faith in Christ, who is God's sacrifice. This satisfies God's righteous demands; all those who trust in Christ are counted righteous (Rom. 4:5; 5:1).

Sanctification is the work of God in developing the new life and bringing it to perfection before God. It is being separated from the sinful life and being set apart for a sacred purpose. Though Christians are sanctified fully in Christ, they are gradually becoming experientially what they already are positionally (Rom. 6:11; 12:1; 1 Cor. 1:2).

Glorification is the completion of the work of God in the believer. In justification, God placed us in a righteous position before Himself. In sanctification, God is working in the Christian to bring him to the image of Jesus Christ. Glorification is when God presents the believer perfect without sin in heaven (Rom. 8:30).

How We Got Our Bible

―■―

How the Word of God Came to Be Written

THE AUTHORS OF HEBREW SCRIPTURES ARE NOT AS identifiable as those of the New Testament. The books arose in the midst of the law given by Moses and the prophets sent by God to the children of Israel. The first five books (the Law) were written by Moses almost entirely. The remainder of the Old Testament is composed of the prophets and writings in the Hebrew canon, whereas the English Bible includes the following categories: historical books, poetic books, and prophetic books. These books include such authors as Samuel, David, Joshua, Solomon, and major prophets such as Isaiah, Jeremiah, and a number of lesser-known figures who wrote smaller books called the minor prophets. Each of these authors presents his words as being the Word of God.

New Testament

The New Testament was written by apostles of Jesus Christ and companions of the apostles. Letters were written to individuals, churches, or larger groups of persons either to confirm the truth of Christianity, engender belief in Christ, correct problems in the local churches, or argue against error. The Book of Revelation also seeks to present God's plans for the end of the age.

How the Inspired Writings Were Passed Down

Old Testament

The Old Testament was written between 1440 B.C. and approximately 400 B.C. The Law of Moses was maintained in the Hebrew community by the priests of the temple. Later books continued to be deposited with these leaders until the destruction of the temple and then found their way into the teaching community begun by Ezra and continued in the synagogues. Trained scribes copied biblical texts by hand until the modern printing press came into use. The copies of the Masoretes of the ninth century A.D. are very close to the recently discovered Dead Sea Scrolls, which originated a thousand years earlier.

New Testament

The New Testament books were copied by local Christian communities and passed from one to the other for decades before an entire collection was made. Since the early letters were written on papyrus, they wore out rapidly and required regular copying. In the early fourth century A.D., fifty copies of the entire Old and New Testament Greek Scriptures were made at the order of the first Christian emperor, Constantine. It is likely that the Vaticanus and Sinaiticus codexes, two of the longest early manuscripts to survive, originated from this order.

(cont'd on p. lvi)

History of the New King James Version

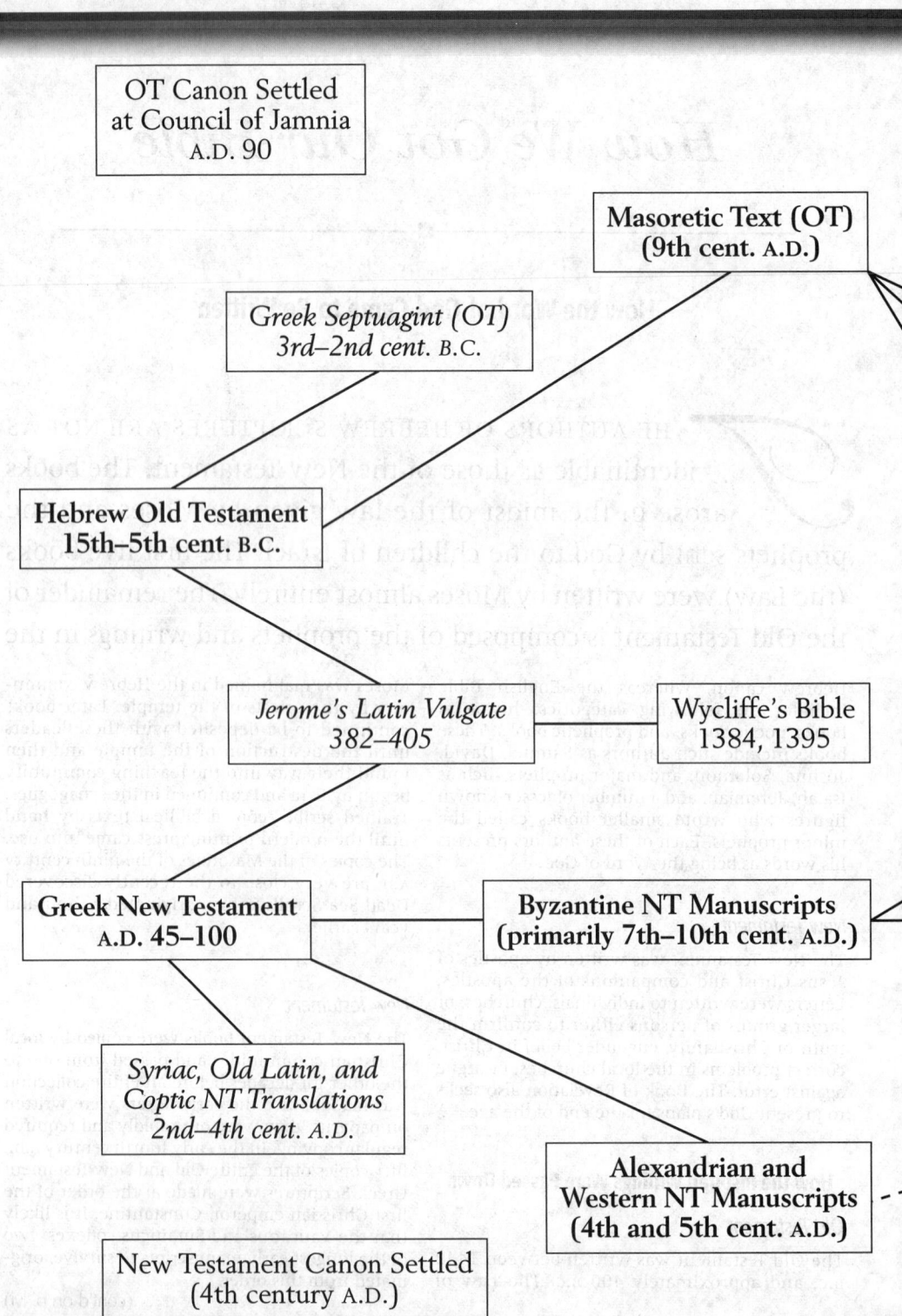

OT Canon Settled at Council of Jamnia A.D. 90

Masoretic Text (OT) (9th cent. A.D.)

Greek Septuagint (OT) 3rd–2nd cent. B.C.

Hebrew Old Testament 15th–5th cent. B.C.

Jerome's Latin Vulgate 382–405

Wycliffe's Bible 1384, 1395

Greek New Testament A.D. 45–100

Byzantine NT Manuscripts (primarily 7th–10th cent. A.D.)

Syriac, Old Latin, and Coptic NT Translations 2nd–4th cent. A.D.

Alexandrian and Western NT Manuscripts (4th and 5th cent. A.D.)

New Testament Canon Settled (4th century A.D.)

For further explanation and
details see the Preface to
the New King James
Version, p. viii.

Coverdale's Bible 1535
Matthew's Bible 1537
Great Bible 1539
Geneva Bible 1557, 1560
Bishop's Bible 1568

Tyndale's Bible
N.T. 1525
Part of O.T.
1530–31

King James Version 1611
(revisions 1613, 1616,
1629, 1638, 1762, 1769)

New King James
Version 1982

Erasmus' Greek NT Text 1516
Stephanus' Greek NT Text 1550

- - - - = NT footnotes
bold = original languages
italic = non-English translations

What is the Canon of Scripture?

The word *canon* is a word used to identify the writings of the prophets, the apostles, and their companions, which are inspired by God and authoritative for truth pertaining to doctrine and life. It means "rule" or "standard." A book is not inspired because it is declared to be canonical but is canonical because it is considered inspired. Therefore, the church discovered the canonicity of the Old and New Testament books; it did not determine or cause their canonicity.

How the Canon Was Decided

The books accepted by the Jewish community originated over a period of approximately one thousand years. The first question regarding a writing's acceptance was whether the book was written by a prophet of God. Generally the book would have statements of "thus says the Lord," or "the word of the Lord came." Second, miraculous signs or accuracy of fulfillment served as confirmation of a prophet's message. Third, the book had to be internally consistent with the revelation of God found in the teachings of other canonical books, especially what God gave through Moses.

The first question for the church to answer about a book's inclusion in the canon accepted by Christians was whether it came through the apostles of the Lord or through persons under the guidance of an apostle, such as Luke. Second, the book had to come with the power of God and be effective for changing lives. Third, it must have been generally accepted by the people of God. This latter test refers first to the ones who received the book and next to the transmission in the church. Determination of the New Testament canon took place over a period of years, reaching its final form at the Synod of Carthage in 397.

The Manuscripts of the Bible

Old Testament

Fragments of the Hebrew Scriptures number in the tens of thousands, the majority dating between the third century B.C. and the fourteenth century A.D. The greatest attestation to the Hebrew Old Testament is the manuscripts found in the Dead Sea Scrolls, which mostly date from the third century B.C. to the first century A.D.

New Testament

Manuscript evidence for the New Testament is abundant. There are more than five thousand existing copies, many with New Testament books entirely or largely intact. Also there are several older translations of the New Testament into languages like Syriac, Coptic, and Latin that survive in thousands of manuscripts. No work of antiquity even approaches the New Testament for authenticity.

THE
OLD TESTAMENT

The First Book of Moses Called

Genesis

∎

THE WORDS, "IN THE BEGINNING, GOD CREATED the heavens and the earth," have evoked considerable debate; but without apology, that is how Genesis begins. In the words of one of the historic creeds: "I believe in God the Father almighty, Maker of heaven and earth." These words are only the beginning of this book of beginnings—a prologue to a prologue. Genesis gives more than an account of creation. It also describes other beginnings—humanity's Fall into sin and the start of God's elaborate rescue mission for all peoples. It tells what happened *first* in many important respects (creation, sin, judgment, languages, races, marriage). But at the center of Genesis lies God's sovereign call to Abram and Sarai, a couple of idol worshipers in the Middle East.

The book has two parts. The first part (chs. 1—11) serves as a prologue to the second part (chs. 12—50), which is the book's main event: God's sovereign work in Abraham's family to accomplish His good will for all nations. The prologue (chs. 1—11) provides keys that unlock the rest of the book and the rest of the Bible as well.

Four key concepts presented in Genesis 1—11 are crucial for comprehending the rest of the Bible. First, the God who entered the lives of Abram and Sarai is the same God who created the entire universe. He is the only true and living God: Yahweh, the Creator and the Savior of the world. Second, all people have rebelled against God, their benevolent Creator, and His good will for them. Humanity has inherited a state of sinfulness from Adam and Eve's rebellion in the

garden of Eden. Third, God judges and will judge the actions of all people. By sending the Flood, God made it clear to Noah and to everyone that human wickedness is entirely unacceptable. God cannot let evil reign free in His creation. Fourth, sin continues to plague all of humanity even after the Flood. Although the Flood did not wash away sin, God, as the second half of Genesis (chs. 12—50) reveals, has a plan to save humanity from its own evil deeds.

The first part of Genesis provides the setting for the story of Abram and Sarai (chs. 12—50). Their world is populated by a broad spectrum of "people groups," each with its own language, customs, values, and beliefs, and all have adopted their own imaginary gods.

Genesis' main story—God's plan to bless all nations through Abraham's descendants—starts in chapter 12. It begins with God's call to Abram and Sarai (Abraham and Sarah) to become the parents of a new people, a new nation. This new nation would become God's tool for blessing all peoples. Even though Abram and Sarai were merely an elderly couple with the means to travel, God chose to begin His plan of redemption for the entire world with them. The Genesis description of their experiences demonstrates the *irruption* (breaking in from without) of God's blessing into their lives.

Central to God's blessing was His covenant with Abraham—the *Abrahamic covenant* (Gen. 12:1–3; 15:1–21). God, the awesome Creator of the entire universe, freely chose to make everlasting promises to Abraham and his descendants. These promises in the Abrahamic covenant were the foundation for all of God's subsequent promises and covenants in the Bible. Genesis is not merely a beginning; it provides the foundation for the rest of the biblical narrative.

The Book of Genesis was written and compiled by Moses in the Wilderness of Sinai. Biblical and extrabiblical evidence points to this fact. Jesus clearly assumes Mosaic authorship of Genesis in the statement, "Moses therefore gave you circumcision" (Acts 15:1). Since the reason for circumcision is mentioned only in Genesis 17, Jesus had to be referring to Moses' compilation of the story. Second, both Jewish and Christian tradition unanimously agree with this biblical testimony: Moses compiled and wrote the Pentateuch, the first five books of the Bible, in the Wilderness of Sinai. This would place his authorship of Genesis around the fifteenth century B.C.

Many scholars since the nineteenth century have denied Moses' authorship of Genesis. Some of these scholars have suggested that the Pentateuch, including Genesis, was compiled at a later date, perhaps in the sixth century B.C. According to this analysis, anonymous editors used at least four documents to piece together the Pentateuch. These four documents were identified by tracing the divine names, such as *Elohim* and *Yahweh,* through the Pentateuch, and by tracing certain variations in phraseology and word choice. The four documents are called the J document, which uses *Yahweh* for God; the E document, which uses *Elohim* for God; the P, or Priestly, document; and the D, or Deuteronomic, document. More recently, this dissection of the Pentateuch has been challenged and no real consensus has emerged from the ensuing scholarly debate.

By appreciating the unified structure of Genesis, Moses' guiding hand in the compilation and authorship of Genesis can be discerned. Certainly, Moses used other literary sources to piece together his narrative. Sometimes these sources are identified, such as in Genesis 5:1. Moses presumably edited these older documents to make them understandable to his readers, the second Israelite generation after the Exodus. And later prophets updated the language for the ensuing generations of Israelite readers.

But after all the analysis, it is clear that Moses wrote and compiled Genesis to encourage the early Israelites while they were preparing to enter the land of Canaan, the Promised Land. The content of Genesis would have been especially significant to them. It explains why their ancestors went to Egypt in the first place, why their nation was destined for another Promised Land, and why God had revealed Himself so dramatically to them in the wilderness.

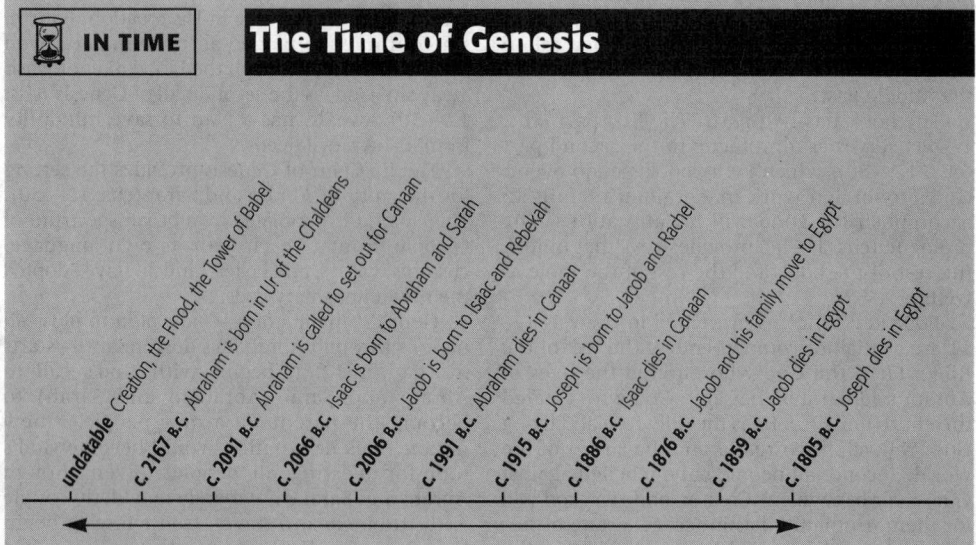

IN TIME — **The Time of Genesis**

- undatable — Creation, the Flood, the Tower of Babel
- c. 2167 B.C. — Abraham is born in Ur of the Chaldeans
- c. 2091 B.C. — Abraham is called to set out for Canaan
- c. 2066 B.C. — Isaac is born to Abraham and Sarah
- c. 2006 B.C. — Jacob is born to Isaac and Rebekah
- c. 1991 B.C. — Abraham dies in Canaan
- c. 1915 B.C. — Joseph is born to Jacob and Rachel
- c. 1886 B.C. — Isaac dies in Canaan
- c. 1876 B.C. — Jacob and his family move to Egypt
- c. 1859 B.C. — Jacob dies in Egypt
- c. 1805 B.C. — Joseph dies in Egypt

Outline

 **IN DEPTH** | **Twin Themes in the Bible**

Two major themes run like railroad tracks through the Bible, from the original creation of the heavens and the earth (Gen. 1:1) to the creation of a new heaven and earth (Rev. 21:1). One track is *creation,* the other is *redemption* (closely related to *salvation*). It's important to keep both in mind when reading and interpreting Scripture.

The creation track reminds us that . . .

- God in Christ has made everything there is. He is Creator and Lord (Gen. 1:31; Col. 1:16, 17).
- God has created and called people to oversee the earth as His managers (Gen. 1:27, 30; Ps. 8:6). People have been given a mandate to care for the earth—to preserve, protect, and use it wisely.
- Everyday work matters to God. We are His coworkers, called to accomplish meaningful tasks for which He will hold us accountable (Gen. 2:8, 15; Eccl. 9:10; 12:13, 14).
- What happens here and now, in this present, physical world, matters to God (John 5:17; Eph. 2:10).

The redemption track reminds us that . . .

- God has committed Himself to reclaiming this fallen world and rescuing sinful people through His Son, Jesus Christ (Gen. 3:15; Rom. 8:19–22).
- God desires that no one be lost, but that every person come to repentance and faith in Jesus (2 Pet. 3:9). As believers, we have a mandate to spread the gospel to the ends of the earth (Mark 16:15; Acts 1:8).
- Salvation affects everything about us, our relationships, our character, and our conduct (Col. 3:17).
- What happens here and now affects us spiritually and has eternal consequences (Matt. 25:31–46).

To ignore either of these two tracks is to get derailed from a balanced understanding of God's work in the world as revealed in the Bible.

Commentary

1:1 In the beginning is a thesis statement, which can be paraphrased, "Here is the story of God's creation of the heavens and the earth." John 1:1 speaks of a time that predates Gen. 1:1, but no information is given here on what happened before this time. It is possible that the rise, rebellion, and judgment of Satan transpired before these events. In ch. 3 Satan has already fallen (he tempts Eve in the guise of the serpent), and Gen. 6:1–4 speaks of angels who are already fallen. Furthermore, God's angels already have been created (3:24). In ch. 1 the focus is on the creation of the material world—the heavens and the earth. **God:** This standard Hebrew term for deity, *Elohim,* is in the form called the plural of majesty or the plural of intensity. In contrast to the ordinary plural (gods), this plural means "the fullness of deity" or "God—very full." Even though the word for God is plural, the verb for **created** is singular. It means "to fashion anew." This often used word in the Bible always has God as its subject. Here,

it means that God renewed what was in a chaotic state. God changed chaos into cosmos, disorder into order, emptiness into fullness. **The heavens and the earth** mean "all of creation" or "the cosmos."

1:2 The two words **without form** and **void** express one concept—chaos. The earth had been reduced to this state (Jer. 4:23); it was not the way God had first created it (Is. 45:18). **Darkness** is a potent biblical symbol of evil and wrong (Job 3:5; Ps. 143:3; Is. 8:22; John 3:19). The **deep** is a term for the secret places of the waters (7:11). This term sounds enough like the name of the Babylonian goddess Tiamat to remind the ancient reader of the Babylonian story of creation, to which the biblical story stands in dramatic contrast. All these images together portray chaos, disaster, and devastation. From this portrait of utter ruin, God brought an orderly creation. **The Spirit of God was hovering** like a mother stork might hover over her nest—a portent of life to come from the dark, murky depths of the chaos below (the Spirit is described as a dove in Matt. 3:16).

✠ IN CONTEXT | The Creator Is Not Sun or Moon

In Gen. 1:16, the words "sun" and "moon" were not omitted by accident, for the writer was aware that two prominent gods in the Near East were the sun and the moon.

In Egypt, the sun was associated with the gods Amon-Re, Re, and Aton. The Egyptians believed that Re created the world, and that one of Re's "eyes" was the moon god Tefnut. Another Egyptian god, Ptah, was also considered Creator, and its two eyes were the sun and the moon.

In Mesopotamia, the sun god Shamash was worshiped as the benefactor of the oppressed. Canaanite worshipers knew the sun as Shemesh. The appearance of this god's name in place names (1 Sam. 6:12) hints at its importance to that polytheistic people, whose moon god was of secondary importance.

The author of Gen. 1:14-19 makes the case that the Creator of the world is on a different plane than the sun or the moon. They are only "greater" or "lesser" lights, creations of God, and therefore not to be worshiped.

1:3 Let there be light: These words express a principal theme of the Bible: God bringing light into the darkness (Is. 9:1, 2). Here, God produced physical light. The NT records God sending His Son to be the light of the world (John 8:12). In the end, there will no longer be any darkness at all (Rev. 21:23). God **said** it, and it was done: **there was light.** His command caused reality.

1:4 Having examined the light, God declared it to be **good**—a powerful term of God's blessing.

1:5 Day . . . Night: The naming of these elements of creation is a mark of God's sovereignty. In the thinking of the peoples of the ancient Near East, naming something was a mark of power or lordship. For them, names were not merely labels, but descriptions with some force to them. Since the sun was not yet created (vv. 14–19), the **first day** (literally, a day, one) is ambiguous. Some say that the "seven days" is a literary frame on which the story of creation is draped. Others argue for a strict pattern of seven twenty-four-hour days.

1:6 In biblical usage, **firmament** means "heavens." Literally, it means "something stretched out, like hammered metal."

1:7, 8 divided the waters: The notion of upper and lower waters is somewhat mysterious. The language may simply refer to waters gathered in a liquid state and to moisture in the atmosphere. The division of the waters is another of God's acts in bringing order out of disorder.

1:9 The gathering of the waters and the separation of the **dry land** are further actions of God in establishing control over the chaos described in v. 2. Each act of separation and distinction brings order out of disorder, form out of formlessness, cosmos out of chaos. Each act also

demonstrates the Lord's power and wisdom (Prov. 8:22–31).

1:10 The naming of the **earth** in this verse suggests that the term was used in anticipation in v. 2.

1:11–13 The broad words **grass, tree,** and **fruit tree** encompass all plants, shrubs, and trees. The reference to **seed** and **kind** speaks of the fact that the plant kingdom will continue to reproduce. God not only created plant life but also set in motion the processes that make plant life reproduce.

1:14, 15 The creation of the sun, moon, and stars is described in general terms in these verses; vv. 16–18 spell out the details. **Lights** (Heb. *me'orot*) **in the firmament** are luminaries (objects that shine). They produce the division between the day and night. **signs and seasons:** Some have mistakenly viewed these words as a biblical basis for astrology. The signs in this case relate to phases of the moon and the relative positions of stars that mark the passage of time from the vantage point of earth. The two words form a pair that may be translated *seasonal signs.*

1:16 As in vv. 14, 15, the term for **lights** can mean "luminaries." The word can either designate the sun, which emits light, or the moon, which reflects light. **He made the stars also:** This is a remarkable statement. In the ancient Near East, other religions worshiped, deified, and mystified the stars. Israel's neighbors revered the stars and looked to them for guidance. In contrast, the biblical creation story gives the stars only the barest mention, as though the writer shrugged and said, "And, oh, yes. He also made the stars." Such a statement showed great contempt for ancient Babylonian astrology (Pss. 29; 93).

1:17–19 God set them: Interestingly, the

sun and moon are not named here, though they are clearly intended. The principal issue throughout these verses is that God alone is in control.

1:20, 21 The verb for **created** (Heb. *bara'*) is the same one used in 1:1 (also in v. 27 for the creation of man). **According to its kind** suggests that these things have the capability to reproduce themselves (v. 12). God not only made the living creatures but also gave them the power to propagate and to proliferate, to fill the air and the seas in great numbers and in wonderful variety.

1:22, 23 **God blessed them:** The first use of this important phrasing in the Bible (1:28; 2:3; 12:2, 3), and it is used of fish and birds!

1:24 The expression **living creature** contains the word sometimes used for the soul, but the word can also mean "life," "being," "living thing," or "person," depending on the context. The same phrase is used for man in 2:7. **cattle and creeping thing and beast of the earth:** Three sweeping categories, like those of vv. 11 and 20, make the point that God created all living things.

1:25 **God saw that it was good:** This is the sixth time this phrasing is used (1:4, 10, 12, 18, 21). Everything that God had made so far was good.

1:26–28 This is the high point of the text, that toward which the passage drives from the beginning. In the viewpoint of Scripture, there is nothing grander in all of God's creation than mankind, whom He has made in His image to reflect His glory.

1:26 **Let Us make** is emphatic, emphasizing the majesty of the speaker. Furthermore, the use of a plural for God allows for the later revelation of the Trinity (Gen. 11:7; Matt. 28:19). "Us" cannot refer to the angels that are present with God because man is made in the image of God alone, not also in that of the angels. **in Our image:** What is the image of God in man? The traditional view is that God's image is certain moral, ethical, and intellectual abilities. A more recent view, based on Hebrew grammar and the knowledge of the ancient Near East, interprets the phrase as meaning, "Let us make man *as* our image" (the Hebrew preposition in this phrase can be translated *as*). In ancient times an emperor might command statues of himself to be placed in remote parts of his empire. These symbols would declare that these areas were under his power and reign. So God placed humankind as living symbols of Himself on earth to represent His reign. This interpretation fits well with the command that follows: to reign over all that God has made. **according to Our likeness:** This phrase draws attention to the preceding figure of speech.

Since God is Spirit (John 4:24), there can be no "image" or "likeness" of Him in the normal sense of these words. Indeed, image-making was later strongly prohibited because of the clear ties that it has with idolatry (Ex. 20:4–6). We may not make images of God, for He has already done so! *We are His images; it is we who are*

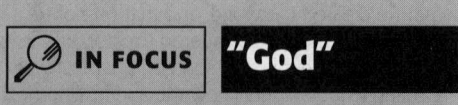

(Heb. pl. *elohim*) (Gen. 1:1, 26; Deut. 7:9; Is. 45:18) Strong's #430: The standard Hebrew term for God. This word is related to similar words for deity found throughout almost all Semitic languages. The basic meaning is probably "Mighty" or "the Almighty." In Hebrew this word often occurs in a form called "the plural of majesty" or "the plural of intensity." In contrast to a normal plural (that is, "gods," such as the false gods of 1 Kin. 19:2), the Hebrew uses this plural to mean "The Fullness of Deity" or "God— Very God!" Many Christians point to the plural form of this word as revealing the plural nature of God. God is one, but He is also three distinct persons: the Father, the Son, and the Holy Spirit.

in His likeness. This is the reason God values people so much: we are made to reflect His majesty on earth. **have dominion:** Rule as God's regent. That is, people are to rule as God would—wisely and prudently—over all that God has made (fish, birds, cattle, and so on).

1:27 **So God created man:** This is the third time the verb for *create* is used in Gen. 1 (vv. 1, 21). Here it is used three times. The language of vv. 26, 28 is elevated prose; this verse is pure poetry. The twelve words of the original Hebrew are arranged in three lines that have their own poetic repetition and cadence. The term for "man" (Heb. *'adam*) is likely associated with the term for "red earth" (Heb. *'adamâ*). Here the word is generic, including **male and female.** These words are sexual. Some have thought that Adam's and Eve's "discovery" of human sexuality was the forbidden fruit of ch. 3. However, these words indicate that human sexuality was a part of the original creation (5:2). Although the misuse of human sexuality is soundly condemned in Scripture (Lev. 18), its proper use is celebrated (Gen. 2:24, 25; Song). Verses 26–28 include the woman no less than the man in the story of creation.

1:28 **God blessed them:** God's smile, the

warmth of His pleasure (1:22; 2:3; 9:1; 12:2, 3). God delighted in what He had made (Prov. 8:30, 31). The word translated **subdue** (Heb. *kabash*) means "bring into bondage." This harsh term is used elsewhere of military conquest (Zech. 9:15) and of God subduing our iniquities (Mic. 7:19). As a king sets off to war to conquer a territory, so humans are told by the Great King to subdue the earth and rule it. Why this need to subjugate the earth? There are at least four possibilities: (1) sin would ruin the earth, and people would have to expend great effort to live there (3:17–19). (2) Satan would defy the will of God and make all good efforts difficult. (3) The earth left to itself would not remain good. Instead, God planned that people would need to manage and control it. (4) The beauty of the

vegetarians because God gave them **every herb** and **every tree.**

1:50 to every beast: The implication is that animal life may have been herbivores at the beginning. This is speculative, however. The text may speak in an abbreviated way of the ultimate nature of the food chain, that vegetation is at the base of that chain by divine design.

1:31 This is the seventh use of the term **good** in the creation story (1:4, 10, 12, 18, 21, 25). It is only one of several key terms that are used in multiples of seven in this text.

2:1 While mention is made of the heavens, the focus in the first chapter has been on the earth. Although the earth is not the physical center of the universe, it is the center of God's great creative work.

In this painting by Michelangelo in the Sistine Chapel in Rome, God is portrayed as the Creator. After six days of work, God was pleased with His creation (Gen. 1:31).

earth was only in the garden that God planted (2:8); the rest of the earth would be hostile. Whatever the case, subdue does not mean "destroy" or "ruin." It means to "act as managers who have the authority to run everything as God planned." This command applies equally to male and female.

1:29 Many suggest that Adam and Eve were

2:2 God did not rest because of fatigue but because of His accomplishment. God is never weary (Is. 40:28, 29). The verb translated as **rested** (Heb. *shabat)* is related to the word for Sabbath (Heb. *shabbat*), which means "rest." Many assume that the basic meaning of the Sabbath is worship, but this is not the case (Ex. 20:9–11; Deut. 5:12–14). By God's blessed inactivity on this seventh day, He showed that He was satisfied with the work He had done.

2:3 God blessed the birds and fish (1:22), humans (1:28), and now **the seventh day** (Saturday). He **sanctified** it; He made it holy. Thus, from the beginning of time, God placed special value on a certain day of the week.

2:4 The term translated as **history** is found in ten significant passages in Genesis (5:1; 6:9; 10:1; 11:10, 27; 25:12, 19; 36:1, 9; 37:2). The term may be translated *family histories* and is a major marker of the different sections of the Book of Genesis. **In the day** means "when." **The LORD God** is a significant new term for God. The word translated as *God* is the same word as in 1:1. The word translated as *LORD* is the proper name for God, Yahweh, or Jehovah (Ex. 3:14, 15). The God of ch. 1 and the LORD God of ch. 2 are the same.

2:5 The order of events in the second creation story is somewhat different from the first account (1:1—2:3). Conditions were radically different from those we now know and understand. The phrase **not caused it to rain** anticipates the story of the Flood (chs. 6—9). Here was an element of creation that was still in process. **man to till the ground:** The Hebrew term for man sounds similar to the term for ground (1:26; 2:7).

2:6 The precise meaning of the term translated as **mist** is unknown. Obviously it refers to some manner of irrigation before the Lord brought the cycles of rain into being.

2:7 Formed is the term for a potter's shaping of pots. Since man is made from the **dust of the ground,** that is where he returns when he dies (3:19). Although God created light with a mere word (1:3), He created man by fashioning a body out of mud and clay, transforming the clay into something new, and then breathing life into it. This **breath** may be the narrator's way of describing the infusion of the

---

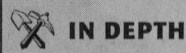 **IN DEPTH**   **A Day of Rest**

When God "rested on the seventh day from all His work which He had done" (Gen. 2:2), He was modeling for humanity His intention for a weekly day of rest. Clearly He did this for the sake of Adam and Eve (and for us), because God Himself does not tire or need to rest as people do. In what sense, then, did He rest from His labors, and in what sense should we rest from ours?

The term *Sabbath* has the root meaning of "cessation." On the seventh day God ceased His work of creating the world (Ex. 20:8–11). However, He did not cease His work of sustaining and maintaining the world (Ps. 145:15, 16; Col. 1:17). This distinction helps to clarify the significance of the Sabbath, a day that God set aside (or sanctified) and blessed. His clear intention was that people would emulate Him by pausing from their labors—the exercise of their dominion over the creation (Gen. 1:28–31)—for one day out of seven.

Was this day of rest given merely as a day off? No, for one of the most important purposes of the Sabbath today is to provide a day for believers to worship and focus on God, as individuals and communities (Is. 58:13, 14). This, of course, does not mean that we are free to ignore God on the other six days; every day belongs to Him (compare Rom. 14:5–13). But by designating one day as a special opportunity to come before the Lord, we demonstrate our dependence on Him as Creator and our obedience to Him as Lord.

This means that the Sabbath—or in NT times, the Lord's Day—was not intended simply as a "day off" to catch up on chores or pursue leisure activities. Not that these are wrong, but the point of the day is to "stir up love and good works, not forsaking the assembling of ourselves together, as is the manner of some, but exhorting one another" (Heb. 10:24, 25).

There is an obvious tension here regarding how we should treat the Lord's Day as a Christian Sabbath. In deciding the issue, it is worth remembering that Jesus pointed out that God established a day of rest for the sake of people, not the other way around (Mark 2:27). Sabbath observance is not to become a legalistic obligation. In fact, conditions occasionally require work on the Sabbath: an ox can get stuck in a ditch and must be gotten out (Luke 14:5). Likewise, human beings have basic needs even on Sundays (John 5:8, 9).

When God rested on the seventh day and set it aside, He did not intend to turn Sabbath-keeping into a strangling rule. The Sabbath was meant to provide true freedom, freedom from turning work into tyranny and freedom to enjoy fellowship with God, our neighbors, and our loved ones.

human spirit, with its moral, intellectual, relational, and spiritual capacities. God showed tender care and intimate concern in the way He shaped man. **living being:** This is the same term that was used of animal life in 1:24. In this phrase we see how humans and animal life are similar, but the breath of life makes humans distinct from all other creatures.

2:8 The term **Eden** is not explained except that it is **eastward.** The exact location is unknown. The planting of a garden is a touch of God's meticulous, personal care. This picture of a caring and loving God complements the picture of the strong and transcendent Creator in ch. 1.

2:9 As created, man was able to enjoy **pleasant** sights, something that would later become corrupted by sin and give rise to lust (1 John 2:16). Eden was an extraordinarily appointed garden, with choice specimens of the finest trees and plants. Two trees of very special importance were also there, **the tree of life** and **the tree of the knowledge of good and evil** (2:17; 3:24).

2:10–14 This river and its four tributaries would not have survived the great Flood (chs. 6—9). The provision of this grand river is a powerful demonstration of God's great care for His

---

🔍 **IN FOCUS**   **"Heavens"**

(Heb. *shamayim*) (Gen. 1:1, 8, 9; 2:1; Ps. 2:4) Strong's #8064: The Hebrew word for *heavens* may refer to either the physical heavens, the sky or atmosphere of earth (2:1, 4, 19), or to the dwelling place of God (Ps. 14:2), the spiritual heaven. The expression is probably derived from a word meaning "to be high, lofty." To describe God as living in the heavens is to describe His exalted position over all people. The physical heavens testify to God's glorious position and also to His creative genius (Ps. 19:1, 6).

---

garden. The names Pishon (v. 11), Gihon (v. 13), Hiddekel (v. 14), and Euphrates (v. 14) relate to later rivers that were known to the first readers of the text. These later rivers likely would only approximate the location of the original rivers. Here, the Christian reader thinks of the river found in the future vision of the New Jerusalem, where there is also a new tree of life (Rev. 22:1, 2).

2:15 The **garden** was perfectly prepared. It

was man's home and he had **to tend and keep it.** Even the biblical paradise required work (1:26–28)!

2:16 In His great grace, God gave permission before He gave restriction. The permission was broad, **of every tree,** while the restriction was narrow (v. 17). Man could do almost anything he wanted. It appears that man limited his diet to vegetation at first; only after the Flood is there mention of God's gift of meat as well (9:3).

2:17 the tree of the knowledge of good and evil: The phrase suggests "full knowledge" by tying together two contrasting words (as in 1:1, "heavens and earth"). We know little about this tree. Presumably, God wanted man to learn wisdom, but wisdom tied to his relationship with his Creator. **shall surely die:** These emphatic words are made of two forms of the verb meaning "to die." The point is not that the guilty person would drop dead right then but that it would certainly happen some time; there is no escape (Heb. 9:27).

2:18 It is not good: This is the first time a negative assessment appears in Genesis. God did not want Adam to be lonely, so He fashioned a **helper comparable to him.** This phrase indicates that this helper (or partner) would be truly fitting and fully adequate—just right. Some have thought that the term is demeaning, but it simply means "one who helps," and in fact is used to describe God when He comes to our aid (Pss. 33:20; 115:9, 10, 11). It does not refer to someone who is secondary or inferior.

2:19 The same verb for **formed** used here for God's creation of animals is also used for His creation of man in v. 7. Again, the verb suggests a potter at work casting his pots. But now, the pots are a lion and a raccoon, a raven and a stork. It appears that God created each animal (or group of animals) for the man too serve, study, and classify, **to see what he would call them.** In giving each animal its **name,** Adam demonstrated his right as God's regent (1:26–28). He was lord over all created order. Furthermore, Adam's names "stuck." That is, he demonstrated perfect insight in the names he used for the animals. They were more than titles; they were terms that described the animals accurately.

2:20 In his close study of the living things that God paraded before him, Adam did not find **a helper comparable to him.** He needed a companion just like him (v. 18), not a servant or an aide but another life like himself, having intelligence, personality, ethical and moral sensitivity, and spirituality. Yet the only living things that Adam found were some fascinating animals!

2:21 This is the first surgery, and God was the Surgeon. In His kindness, God used an

---

IN DEPTH — God as Creator

od created the heavens and the earth" (Gen. 1:1). These words form one of the Bible's principal assertions about the material world: that God created it all.

The first two chapters of Genesis present two complementary accounts of creation (Ps. 104 and Prov. 8 present two additional accounts). Chapter 1 pictures God in sublime terms, grand and awesome. The Hebrew term used for deity in this section (*Elohim*) speaks of God's majesty, sovereignty, and awesome power. With a mere word, God spoke the entire universe into existence. When He finished, He called every part of His creation "very good" (1:31).

Chapter 2, on the other hand, presents a more personal picture of creation. It focuses on the creation of man and woman, the only beings in creation who reflect the very image of God. In this section, God's personal name (*Yahweh,* or LORD) is used rather than His title, "God." This is because God personally shaped Adam from the dust of the earth, breathing life into him, and forming Eve from Adam's flesh and bone. Moreover, the section depicts God placing Adam and Eve in a beautiful garden and interacting with them.

Of course, these two chapters are not written in terms of modern science. But neither are they written in what would have passed for science in ancient times. If the Bible had been written in the "scientific" language of its day, it would be little more than a relic today. Had it been written in the scientific language of the Middle Ages, it would have been a mystery to its first readers and nonsense to us. Had it been written in the scientific language of our own day, it would have been unintelligible to prior generations and, to be sure, a relic in future years.

These first chapters of Genesis reveal God's identity as Creator in language that makes sense to every sort of audience. The chapters spoke first to a people on the move, at the dawn of Hebrew history. Over the ages, they have spoken to ancient and medieval peoples. And today, they speak to people from all backgrounds. The modern person sometimes wonders why the language is not more precise. Yet these chapters do not aim at precision; their aim is clarity concerning one certain truth: *God created the heavens and the earth.*

---

unusually **deep sleep** as an anesthetic. Later, the Lord would bring a "deep sleep" (perhaps meaning a "trance") upon Abram when He was about to establish His covenant with him. Abram, in his "sleep," was still aware of what was going on; the memory would be lasting. Adam's response (v. 23) suggests that he, too, had an awareness of what was happening during his supernatural slumber. God's use of a **rib** was fitting. He might have started over with dust and clay. But by using a part of Adam himself, the identification of Adam with his partner would be ensured. As Luther observed, God might have taken a bone from a toe and thus signified that Adam was to rule over her; or He might have taken a bone from his head to indicate her rule over him. But by taking a bone from his side, God implied equality and mutual respect.

2:22 The verb **made** means "to build." The expansion of one small part into a complete body makes sense in today's understanding of molecular structure and DNA.

2:23 This is now means "At last!" **bone of my bones:** Adam's wording is poetic and exalted; seeing Eve was a shocking and exhila-rating experience because the match was perfect. Here was a mirror of himself, someone just like him, and yet different! **She shall be called Woman:** In giving the woman her name, Adam was functioning as he had in naming the animals (v. 19). Yet the name that he gave her matched his own. She was woman, and he was man; they were perfectly suited for each other.

2:24 In marriage, a man is to **leave** his family, join his wife, and unite with her. Though this process establishes a new home distinct from the parents' home, it does not sever all ties with the extended family (the clan). In the biblical period, extended families were quite close and interdependent. The words **be joined** speak of both a physical embrace and more general aspects of marital bonding. In marriage, man and woman are a "we," not just a "me and you." **One flesh** suggests both a physical, sexual bonding and a lifelong relationship. There are still two persons, but together they are as one (Eph. 5:31). The term speaks of a unity with diversity (Heb. *'ehad*) rather than absolute unity (as Heb. *yahîd*). This term (Heb *'ehad*) is the same term used in the famed *Shema`,* the creed of Israel, where it is commonly translated, "the LORD is one (Deut. 6:4; compare Eph. 5:31). In the NT, Jesus refers to this text (Gen. 2:24) as the foundation of the biblical view of marriage (Matt. 19:5; 1 Cor. 6:16).

2:25 Because the man and the woman knew only good, they **were not ashamed** even though **they were both naked.** They were comfortable in their physical bodies, in their sexuality, in their relationship, and in their work—with no wrongdoing. The wording of vv. 24, 25 suggests the couple experienced sexual relations in the garden as a part of their God-intended experience. At 4:1 we first read of procreation, not necessarily the couple's first sexual experience together.

3:1–5 Though not equated with Satan in the OT, the **serpent** is clearly identified as such in the NT (Rev. 12:9). Here, then, is Satan's first deception of the human mind and will.

3:1 With no introduction, **the serpent** appeared in Paradise. This is the first clue in Scripture of creation outside the one Adam and Eve experienced. The serpent symbolizes something both fascinating and loathsome. Yet neither Adam nor Eve saw the danger embodied in the serpent. The Hebrew word for **cunning** sounds like the Hebrew word for naked in 2:25. Adam and Eve were naked in innocence; the serpent was crafty and sneaky. In Eve's innocence and naïveté, she showed no surprise on hearing a strange voice from the snake. **Has God indeed said:** Note that the serpent did not use the divine name Yahweh.

3:2 We may eat: Eve repeated the positive words of God (2:16).

3:3 There was one tree Eve knew to be off limits. This tree was in the middle of the garden. **nor shall you touch it:** Some interpreters suggest that the woman was already sinning by adding to the word of God, for these words were not part of God's instructions in 2:17. Yet the first sin was not lying; it was eating the fruit that God had forbidden. Her words reflected the original command well enough and indeed they would have ensured that the command would be kept. In fact, in 20:6 and 26:11 the word expresses the taking of a person sexually to be one's own. Thus, it may be translated, "You may not eat it; that is, consume it," which would be a common Hebrew way of saying the same thing twice for clarification or emphasis.

3:4 For the first time (here), Satan lied: **You will not surely die.** Lying was Satan's craft right from the beginning (John 8:44). The serpent boldly denied the truth of what God had said. In essence, the serpent called God a liar.

3:5 By arguing that God had an ulterior motive, the serpent appealed to Eve's sense of fair play. **you will be like God:** God's fullness of knowledge was only one of the superiorities that set Him apart from the woman. But the serpent combined all of God's superiority over the woman into this one audacious appeal to her pride.

3:6 Notice the parallel to 2:9; this tree was like the other trees. It was **good for food.** These words imply that this was the first time Eve considered disobeying God's command. After all, there was nothing in the tree that was poisonous or harmful, and it was **desirable.** The issue was one of obedience and disobedience to the word of God. **She took** and **ate:** Once she disobeyed God, all the world changed. (Note, however, that Rom. 5:12 speaks of the sin of Adam rather than the sin of Eve.) Because she did not die, she **gave** it **to her husband. And he ate:** Adam sinned with his eyes wide open. He did not even ask a question. He knew as well as she that the fruit was forbidden. Adam and Eve had now broken faith with the Lord, and the world was forever changed.

3:6 This verse records the tragic story of the fall of mankind in four clearly defined steps. First, sin begins with the sight of sin (Gen. 9:22; Job 31:1): **the woman saw.** The sight of sin itself is not sin, but that is where the pathway that leads to sin embarks. Her second step was desire in that direction. Sight alone is no crime, but to desire that which we have innocently seen, if it cannot be ours, is sin (Deut. 5:21; Matt. 5:28; James 1:13, 14; 1 John 2:15–17). Eve's third step on the pathway to sin went beyond coveting to indulging. **She took** what was not rightfully hers according to the prohibition of God. Desiring the forbidden fruit was covert sin; taking and eating it was overt and active sin. The final step was the involvement of another in the sin: **she gave to her husband.** There is no such thing as private sin; every sin affects someone else. Eve's sin affected Adam; and consequently, Adam's sin affected the entire race. The whole human race sinned in Adam, for "through one man sin entered the world" (Rom. 5:12). Sin always involves others and thus becomes compounded. Other striking examples of these same steps on the pathway to sin can be found in the lives of Achan (Josh. 7:21) and David (2 Sam. 11:1–5, 15, 24).

3:7 The serpent was right; they knew good and evil (v. 5). This is the awful truth about a skilled liar: the deception comes mixed with truth. Their eyes **were opened.** They discovered that **they were naked.** All of a sudden with no one around but the two of them, they were ashamed (2:25). Their lovely naïveté was now replaced by evil thoughts, and they covered themselves with **fig leaves.**

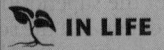 **IN LIFE** **Sin Is a Choice**

What is it in human nature—a nature which God created—that makes it temptable, vulnerable to sin? Adam and Eve were created apart from sin, and without the need to sin, yet some characteristic in their makeup allowed sin to enter their lives (Gen. 3:6, 7). What was that characteristic?

Scripture offers two answers. For Eve, the choice to believe a lie was the doorway through which sin entered her life (Gen. 3:13; 2 Cor. 11:3; 1 Tim. 2:14). For Adam, it was the choice to ignore God's voice of authority (Gen. 3:17). These two choices—self-deception and self-will—are two sides of the same coin. Both remain as complicating realities in our own lives today, allowing sin to continue to take root and bear its deadly fruit in us, until Christ enters our lives and breaks the bonds of sin, empowering us to resist it.

Temptation is sin's call to our basic needs and desires to be satisfied in self-serving or perverted ways. It is also a call to practice self-deception, finding ways to justify doing as we please even though we know in our heart of hearts that it is wrong.

For this reason, Scripture frequently speaks of blindness as a willful act in which we choose to practice rebellion and self-deception. But when Christ enters our lives, He regenerates our hearts and sets us free to choose what is true and righteous (1 Cor. 6:9–11; James 1:26, 27; 1 John 3:7–9).

3:8 The scene is pathetic and sad. Here comes the Lord for an evening walk and a cozy chat. But Adam and Eve, who have "become wise," cower in the trees to avoid being seen by the Creator of the universe. What had been a perfect, shameless fellowship has turned into dreadful fear of God. This was not fear in the sense of true piety, as with Abraham, Moses, David, and Solomon, but the raw terror of being discovered in the wrong.

3:9 God in His mercy did not destroy both of them immediately. He even called out to them and interacted with them (vv. 10–12). God's mercy reaches further than we usually believe, or else we would all be destroyed.

3:10 I was afraid: They had not become like God but were now estranged from God.

3:11 The Lord carried the interrogation to its sad ending by posing one question after another.

3:12 A guilty man's first line of defense is blame. Adam blamed **the woman,** and then he blamed God for having given her to him (for David's contrasting response to Nathan, read 2 Sam. 12:13).

3:13 the serpent deceived me and I ate: A simple statement of fact.

3:14 to the serpent: The Lord turned first to the serpent and brought His judgment upon him. God did not excuse the woman because she was deceived, but He did bring the harsher judgment on the one who deceived her. The language in these verses is poetry, something that adds solemnity to them. The word translated as **cursed** here is used only of the curse on the serpent and on the ground (v. 17). The

woman and the man faced harsh new realities, but they were not cursed (God had already blessed them; 1:28). The text suggests that the serpent became a creature that slithers on the ground and appears to eat dust. This implies that before this the serpent had some other bodily form.

3:14 The effects of the Fall reached well beyond the man and woman to the animal kingdom, which began to suffer along with man through the Edenic Curse (Jer. 12:4; Rom. 8:20).

3:15 enmity between you and the woman: This is not just about snakes; it is about the enemy of our souls, Satan. **your seed and her Seed:** The language is ambiguous but still contains the promise of a child. The term *seed* is exceedingly important. It may be translated *offspring* (15:3) or *descendants* (15:5, 13, 18). The term may refer to an individual (Gal. 3:16) or a group of people. This means, among other things, that Eve would live, at least for a while. The Seed of the woman is the Promised One, the coming Messiah of Israel. *Seed* continues to be used throughout the Bible as a messianic term (Num. 24:7; Is. 6:13). The meaning of the phrase **your seed** as it applies to the serpent is uncertain (John 8:37–47). The reference is ultimately to Satan. **your head:** This is sometimes called the "first gospel" because these words, as indirect as they are, promise the Coming One whom we know to be the Lord Jesus, the Messiah. The Lord was showing mercy even as He judged (4:15). **Bruise His heel** speaks of a serious injury, but it is contrasted with the bruising of the **head**—the defeat—of the ser-

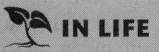 **IN LIFE** | **Is Work a Curse?**

What was the curse that God put on creation (Gen. 3:17–19)? One of the most stubborn myths in Western culture is that God imposed work as a curse to punish Adam and Eve's sin. As a result, some people view work as evil. Scripture does not support that idea:

- *God Himself is a worker.* The fact that God works shows that work is not evil, since by definition God cannot do evil. On the contrary, work is an ongoing activity of God (John 5:17).
- *God created people in His image to be His coworkers.* He gives them ability and authority to manage His creation.
- *God established work before the Fall.* Genesis 1 and 2 record how God created the world. The account tells how He placed the first humans in a garden "to tend and keep it" (Gen. 2:15). This work assignment was given before sin entered the world and before God pronounced the curse (Gen. 3). Obviously, then, work cannot be a result of the Fall since people were working before the Fall.
- *God commends work even after the Fall.* If work were evil in and of itself, God would never encourage people to engage in it. But He does. For example, He told Noah and his family the same thing He told Adam and Eve, to have dominion over the earth (Gen. 9:1–7). In the NT, Christians are commanded to work (Col. 3:23; 1 Thess. 4:11).
- *Work itself was not cursed in the Fall.* A careful reading of Gen. 3:17–19 shows that God cursed the ground, not work, as a result of Adam's sin: "Cursed is the ground for your sake; In toil you shall eat of it."

Notice three ways that the curse affected work: (1) Work had been a joy, but now it would be "toil." People would feel burdened by it and even come to hate it. (2) "Thorns and thistles" would hamper people's efforts to exercise dominion. In other words, the earth would not be as cooperative as it had been. (3) People would have to "sweat" to accomplish their tasks. Work would require enormous effort and energy.

Most people know how burdensome work can be. Workplace stresses and pressures, occupational hazards, the daily grind, office politics, crushing boredom, endless routine, disappointments, setbacks, catastrophes, frustration, cutthroat competition, fraud, deception, injustice—there is no end of evils connected with work. But work itself is not evil. Far from calling it a curse, the Bible calls work and its fruit a gift from God (Eccl. 3:13; 5:18, 19).

pent's seed. When Jesus went to the Cross, He was bruised in His heel. That is, He suffered a terrible but temporary injury (John 12:31; Col. 2:15). In His resurrection, He defeated His enemy. From that moment on, Satan has lived on borrowed time. He is already defeated; only the announcement of victory needs to be given (Rom. 16:20).

3:16 **your sorrow and your conception:** These two words mean "your sorrowful conception" (1:2; 4:12; 9:2; Ps. 9:2). That is, the woman's joy in conceiving and bearing children will be saddened by the pain of it. The word **desire** (Heb. *teshûqâ*) can also mean "an attempt to usurp or control" as in 4:7. We can paraphrase the last two lines of this verse this way: "You will now have a tendency to dominate your husband, and he will have the tendency to act as a tyrant over you." The battle of the sexes has begun. Each strives for control and neither lives in the best interest of the other (Phil. 2:3,

4). The antidote is in the restoration of mutual respect and dignity through Jesus Christ (Eph. 5:21–33).

3:17–19 Adam got his share of blame, even though he tried to escape it (v. 12). **Cursed is the ground:** Though the curse was not directed at the man, it is trouble for him. Now his life will be marked by **toil, thorns and thistles, sweat,** and finally death. These words imply that before the Fall the ground was not filled with noxious weeds and work would have been more pleasant (2:15). **to dust you shall return:** Death will now come to humankind, whereas there had been the possibility of living forever (Rom. 5:12–14). The word of God was sure: God had stated that they would certainly die (2:17). Now they were served notice concerning the process of aging and decay that was already at work (5:5; 6:3). Although some have termed the words of this section as God's Covenant with Adam, the Hebrew term "covenant" (*berît*) is lacking and the content appears to be less than that of a covenant.

3:20 The name **Eve** (Heb. *hawwâ*) is related to the verb meaning "to live." Eve is our common mother, just as Adam is our common father. This is Adam's second name for her. The first was *woman*, the feminine complement to his own masculinity (2:23).

3:21 This is the first place that the Bible mentions killing animals for human use. The shedding of the blood of these animals was a shadow, in a way, of the shedding of the blood of innumerable animals in the sacrificial system that would be enacted under Moses. And all the sacrifices under Torah would one day point to the greatest sacrifice of them all, the death of Savior Jesus as the propitiation of our sins.

3:22 become like one of us: By means of their rebellious act, the man and woman now shared something with God. But they were also at enmity with Him because of their sin. Adam and Eve's knowledge of good and evil had made them not wise but foolish. The fruit of the **tree of life** stopped aging. To eat of this tree was **to live forever.** One day this tree will be planted anew and its fruit will be for the healing of the nations (Rev. 22:2).

3:23 The man had been formed by God outside the **garden** (2:5–8, 15) and had been given the task of tending and keeping it. Now he was removed from the garden and sent to till the soil **from which he was taken** (2:5; 3:17–19).

3:24 Even though Eve sinned first, this section (vv. 22–24) focuses on the **man,** Adam. This is the first reference to holy angels or the **cherubim** in Genesis. The creation of the angels (including those who rebelled against God; 6:1–4) preceded the creation activities described in chs. 1 and 2. A cherub (plural, cherubim) is an angel who takes on a particular form (Ex. 25:18–22; compare Ezek. 1:5–28). Cherubim, like all angels, are spirit beings, but they can take on physical bodies. Adam and Eve were barred by **a flaming sword** from the garden that God had planted for their enjoyment. There was no way back in. The fact that the **tree of life** remained, even though guarded by angels and a sword, was a ray of hope. Is it not possible that because He had it guarded and did not uproot it, that one day its fruit may be eaten again? Indeed, one day we will see it again (Rev 22:2). Adam and Eve were no longer welcome in God's presence, but they had the hope that one day Paradise would be regained.

4:1 The verb **knew** (Heb. *yada*) is a splendid euphemism for sexual intercourse. It describes an intimate relationship that includes ardor, passion, mutuality, and oneness. This was an act of procreation, but most likely not the first sexual union between Adam and Eve. The name **Cain** is related to a word meaning "craftsman" or "metalworker," but it also sounds like the Hebrew word translated **I have acquired.** At times in Genesis the meaning for a name is taken directly from it (for example, Ishmael in 16:11); at other times the meaning is based on a pun—a word that sounds similar to the name itself.

4:2 We have no explanation of the name **Abel** as we have with Cain (v. 1). Perhaps after Abel was murdered (v. 8), the parents looked back with sadness on the brevity of his life and called him Abel (meaning "vapor") because his life was over so quickly. Keeping **sheep** and tilling the **ground** were equally valid occupations. They reflected merely different interests of the two brothers, not their character. The story of Cain and Abel begins a motif in Genesis of competing sons (like Esau and Jacob; 25:26).

4:3 Genesis does not explain how the practice of sacrificial worship began. The first readers of the book understood it well because they had been instructed in full by God through Moses (Lev.). Some people assume that Cain's sacrifice of **fruit** was deficient because it did not involve shedding blood, which God required for forgiveness of sins (Heb. 9:22). But nothing in ch. 4 indicates that Cain and Abel came to God for forgiveness: their sacrifices were acts of worship. In the later sacrificial system of Israel, God blessed the presentation of grain offerings alongside the sacrifices of animals (Lev. 6:14–23). A farmer presented a portion of his produce just as a herdsman presented a sample of his flock. Cain's sacrifice was deficient because Cain did not "do well" (v. 7), not because the sacrifice was the "fruit of the ground."

4:4 Abel's sacrifice was the best that he had to offer, **the firstborn** and **their fat.** There are no similar descriptive words for Cain's sacrifice. That is, Cain brought a token gift of his produce to the Lord, but Abel brought the very best. God **respected** or looked with favor first upon the person, *then* on his sacrifice (Ps. 40:6–8). Abel's offering was "more excellent" than Cain's because of Abel's faith in the Lord (Heb. 11:4).

4:5 Something deficient in Cain's attitude was reflected in his offering. Instead of repenting of his wrongdoing, Cain became angry and, we discover, filled with jealousy (v. 8).

4:6, 7 The gracious words of the Lord were that Cain could get it right! He did not have to go on being angry and morose, he could **do well.** Sin was lying at the **door,** about to pounce on him as a lion.

4:8 The murder was stunning in its lack of precedent, its suddenness, and its finality. Jesus spoke of this ghastly event as historical fact (Matt. 23:35).

4:9 your brother: The words emphasize the horror of the murder; it was in the family. Indeed, all muder is "in the family," for we are all related in Adam.

4:10 That **blood** of Abel **cries** out until the blood of One more innocent than Abel is shed as well (Heb. 12:24). In the manner of his death, Abel depicts the Savior Jesus.

4:11, 12 Cain was the third to be **cursed** of God; first was the serpent (3:14) and then the ground (3:17).

4:13 My punishment: Usually rendered "iniquity" (Ex. 20:5), here the term speaks of the result of iniquity.

4:14 Sadly, Cain expressed his distress only at the punishment he received, not at his crime. Nor was there any note of repentance concerning his dreadful action. **anyone who finds me:** Most have assumed that the others whom Cain feared were sisters and brothers already born but not mentioned or those yet to be born. This idea is based on the wording of 5:4, "and he {Adam} had sons and daughters." Some have proposed that God created others outside the Garden of Eden, but the Scriptures give no indication of this. It makes sense to conclude that Cain was afraid of his siblings.

4:15 It is remarkable to observe the mercy of the Lord in Cain's life. Though Cain had murdered his brother, the Lord did not slay Cain. And though the Lord brought a curse on Cain, He still protected him, by a **mark**, from being slain by others. In His wrath, God remembers mercy.

4:16 The land of Nod is a wordplay on the term for vagabond (vv. 12, 14). The point is more theological than geographical; to be apart from the presence of the Lord is to be a vagabond in a "vagabond-land."

4:17 Cain most likely acquired a **wife** from among his other siblings (v. 14). The name **Enoch** means "Dedicated One," the same name as the godly descendant of Seth who "walked with God" (5:21–24). The fact that Cain built a **city** named after his son speaks of a dramatic, rapid increase in population.

4:18 In quick succession, six generations from Cain to Lamech are mentioned. The verse indicates a rapidly expanding population, for the listing of each of these sons includes corresponding wives.

4:19–21 Here, the story of **Lamech**'s most celebrated descendants is given. Lamech represents skill and strength as well as arrogance and vengeance. This Lamech is not the same as

INSIGHT | The City of Enoch

The city of Enoch is the first city mentioned in the Bible. Its location is unknown. It was founded by Cain (Gen. 4:17), a fugitive in the land of Nod ("wandering"), who named the city after his son, Enoch ("dedicated" or "initiated"). The city was probably small, perhaps even a settlement of several families, but nonetheless called a "city" (Hebrew, *ir*), implying an enclosed space with permanent dwellings, in contrast to the tents of nomadic shepherds. Possibly it was the birthplace of civilization, specialized occupations, and the arts (4:20–22).

Lamech, the son of Methuselah (5:28–31). **two wives:** This notable act suggests a deliberate attempt by Lamech to subvert the original pattern of God of one man and one woman (2:24; read the words of Jesus on the subject in Matt. 19:4–6). **Adah . . . Zillah:** Only rarely in these accounts are the names of women mentioned.

4:20, 21 Jabal is celebrated for the guild of tent dwellers associated with his name. **Jubal** is celebrated for the guild of musicians associated with his name.

4:22 Some suggest that **iron** was not known during the time of **Tubal-Cain,** and this verse means that later metal workers who did work with iron could look back to Tubal-Cain as the "father" of metallurgy in general. **Naamah:** Even more rare than the names of mothers in

INSIGHT | Bronze and Iron

True bronze (Gen. 4:22) is an alloy of copper and tin. Iron (v. 22) is an element that in its pure state is soft. Its usefulness for making tools and weapons did not appear until it could be reliably combined with carbon to make steel. It was still rare in the time of Pharaoh Tutankhamen (1336–1327 B.C.). One dagger was discovered in his tomb.

these accounts (v. 19) are the names of daughters and sisters.

4:23, 24 What follows is a boastful taunt song that captures the violent spirit of **Lamech.** The words of Lamech are poetic, making the passage memorable and powerful (12:1). **I have killed a man:** In this boast, Lamech indicates that he has followed in the worst pattern of his ancestor Cain. In his wicked braggadocio, he taunted God by his words **seventy-sevenfold.** Whereas the Lord would bring vengeance on the slayer of Cain "sevenfold" (v. 15), Lamech boasted that by himself he would greatly magnify the vengeance on anyone who attacked him. This is another example (although in wickedness) of the inflation of numbers for effect (Num. 1:46).

4:25 and Adam knew his wife again: These words recall the opening words of the section (4:1) and bring the section to its conclusion. After the long, sad digression about Cain and his descendants, we return to Adam and Eve and their new progeny. With the death of Abel (v. 8) and the expulsion of Cain (vv. 11, 12), Adam and Eve had no son to carry on their line for good and for the promise of the Messiah. Hence the importance of the birth of **Seth.** His name is related to a Hebrew verb meaning "to place" or "to set," for he was **appointed** to take the *place* of the murdered son in the plan of God.

4:26 The birth of **Enosh** meant that the line of Seth would continue; the promise of the Lord (3:15) would not be forgotten. **began to call on the name of the LORD**: These words can

hardly mean that only now did people begin to pray to God. Rather, the verb *call* means "to make proclamation." That is, this is the beginning of preaching, of witnessing, and testifying *in* the name of the Lord (12:8).

5:1–32 This chapter abbreviates the family history that connects Adam to Noah. We do not know how much time the chapter represents. Its purpose is *connection* rather than chronology.

5:1 The word **genealogy** (or "family histories") is found in ten significant passages in Genesis (2:4, note). The term is a major building block of Genesis. **In the day** means "when." **likeness of God:** What God made humankind to be (1:26–28) continues after the Fall (ch. 3; compare also 9:6, after the Flood).

5:2 The original creation of humanity is in two complementary genders, **male and female,** as 1:26–28 clearly states (1:27).

5:3 one hundred and thirty years: The long lives of the people of the early chapters of Genesis have led to considerable speculation. One suggestion is that these ages were possible because of tremendously different climate and environmental conditions before the Flood (chs. 6—9). A second suggestion is that these ages are ways of expressing the relative importance of the figures; that is, that these are hyperbolic figures that use exaggeration to indicate significance in the ancient world. **likeness . . . image:** These are the same terms, but in reverse order, that are used of humankind in God's creation in 1:26.

5:4 sons and daughters: There may have

✠ IN CONTEXT   **The Purpose of Genealogies**

enealogies appear at a number of places in the Bible. Some readers may be tempted to skip over these lists as if they were inconsequential, but that would be a mistake. The genealogies of Scripture serve several important purposes. For example, some of them trace the ancestry of important people in the narrative (Gen. 5:1). Others show the links between the people and nations of the world (Gen. 10:1). Others reveal God's sovereign plan at work down through generations (Ruth 4:18–22).

Generally speaking, there are two kinds of genealogies, linear and segmented. A linear genealogy traces the history of a people to a particular goal, person, or office. For example, the extended genealogy of 1 Chr. 1—9 highlights the royal line of David, among other things. By contrast, a segmented genealogy shows how various social groups are related. For example, Gen. 25:1–4 gives the names of Abraham's sons through his wife Keturah, believed to be the ancestors of some of the Arabian tribes.

The genealogies of the Bible help to show that faith in God is not just a subjective experience but an objective, historical reality based in fact. Belief can be rooted in history, which is moving toward a goal. On the other hand, genealogies help to remind us that genuine faith involves human beings who are linked together by blood. History is handed down from parents to children, generation after generation, until it reaches its dramatic conclusion in God's good time.

been a very large number of children born from our first parents. We may presume intermarriage among them, of course. The problems associated with incest, addressed in Lev. 18, would not have occurred when the genetic pool was pure and unpolluted.

5:5 When God made Adam and Eve, the expectation was that they would live forever. There is a profound sadness in Adam's death, for it reminds us of Adam's mortality, and our own. **and he died:** This refrain is given at the conclusion of each of the ten names in this chapter except one (Enoch; v. 24). The judgment of God on fallen man was fulfilled in the death of Adam and each of his successors (3:19; 6:3). Death entered the world through this one man, and through him passed to all people (Rom. 5:12; 1 Cor. 15:22).

5:6-20 The pattern of the genealogies is as follows: (1) name "A" lived "x" years; (2) name "A" begot name "B"; (3) name "A" then lived "y" years; (4) name "A" lived "z" ("x"+ "y") years in all; (5) and he died. See also the pattern in the line of Shem (11:10–26). These lists are incomplete (compare Matt. 1:1–17); they serve merely to indicate major figures over an extended period of time. As in many such genealogical listings, which were originally oral, these were designed to be recited by memory to mark certain key figures through time for purposes of *connection,* for tying two great periods or names together. In this case, the point is to tie the line of continuity between Adam and Noah through the line of Seth. Thus, when the text says that name "A" begot name "B" at a certain age, the name given for "B" may not be the immediate child but a remote descendant. This conforms to biblical patterns elsewhere and to patterns in the ancient Near East and in many tribal societies even in our own day.

5:21-24 The most fascinating name in this listing is that of **Enoch** (not the son of Cain of the same name, 4:17). The phrase, **Enoch walked with God** (vv. 22, 24), expresses a life of fellowship with and obedience to the Lord (as was true of Noah, 6:8). It also recalls the experience of Adam and Eve, who had lived in even closer proximity to the Lord before the Fall (3:8). **he was not:** This phrase does not mean that Enoch ceased to exist but that he was taken into God's presence, **for God took him.** Only Enoch and Elijah (2 Kin. 2:11) ever had this experience. Enoch's remarkable experience was both a testimony of his deep faith in God (Heb. 11:5, 6) and a strong reminder at the beginning of biblical history that there is life in God's presence after death for the people of God. What Enoch experienced in a remarkable, dramatic fashion is what each person who "walks with God" will experience—everlasting life with the Savior.

5:25-27 Methuselah is said to have lived longer than any other figure mentioned in Genesis, 969 years.

5:28-31 The most important thing **Lamech** is remembered for is his descendant Noah. The

IN FOCUS **"Walked"**

(Heb. *halak*) (Gen. 5:24; 6:9; Deut. 13:4; Ps. 128:1; Mic. 6:8) Strong's #1980: The basic meaning of the Hebrew verb translated here as *walk* is "to go" or "to travel." The word is used often in the OT to signify merely a simple act of motion (Gen. 13:17; 2 Sam. 11:2). In 6:9 and other passages, the word possesses connotations of a habitual manner of life or a constant relationship with God. Thus the word describes Noah, Enoch, and other people of faith as living in a close relationship with their God and in obedience to His commands. Throughout Scripture, believers are called to *walk* with God daily, abiding in Him completely (Gal. 5:16; 1 John 2:6).

name **Noah** is the only one that is commented upon by the narrator in this chapter. It is a form of the word meaning "to rest" and is associated with **comfort.** Noah's name refers to a reversal of the curse.

5:32 These sons of Noah, **Shem, Ham, and Japheth,** figure in the ensuing story of the Flood (chs. 6–9).

6:1-4 This is one of the most debated OT passages. Three principal interpretations are: (1) The **sons of God** represent the godly line of Seth, and the **daughters of men** represent the ungodly line of Cain; their intermarriage led to apostasy, compromise, and sin. (2) The sons of God are powerful kings who practiced an enforced polygamy by taking wives of **all whom they chose,** leading to other wicked practices. (3) The sons of God are fallen angels who cohabited with human women (the daughters of men), producing offspring that were tyrants. Whichever view one settles on, it is important to see that this paragraph is a prologue to the story of the Flood. It accounts for the general description of wickedness mentioned in v. 5. The most likely interpretation is that the sons of God were fallen angels. This is the view of Jewish scholars and best explains the text. There are two principal objections to the fallen angel view. (1) Angels do not marry (Matt. 22:30), so the whole notion is impossible.

(2) This idea is so abhorrent to biblical thought that it breaks all analogy. Yet it is possible that these were angels who left "their proper domain" (Jude 6) and whose sin led to a special divine judgment (2 Pet. 2:4). It may be that in this isolated case, fallen angels did assume human form and marry human women; this was such a monumental breach of God's order that it provoked God's judgment on the world through the Flood.

6:1 The term **daughters** clearly means female children of human parents. The daughters were simply women.

6:2 The sons of God refer to a different group from either the **men** or their **daughters.** The phrase occurs elsewhere in the Bible and clearly means "angels." Job 1:6 presents Satan and his angels coming into the presence of the Lord for an audience with His Majesty. Satan's angels are there called "the sons of God," with the suggestion that these angelic beings were once holy ones who served the Lord, but were now allied with the evil one. Genesis assumes the existence of the good angels of the Lord (3:24), and of Satan and his angels. It also assumes that the latter are already fallen and under God's judgment (1:2). In 3:1, the serpent (Satan) was already at work as the father of lies (John 8:44). Here it appears that some of Satan's angels, spirit beings, took on human form (3:24) and, out of a perverted lust, seduced women. In response, God reserved these angels for special judgment (Jude 6; 2 Pet. 2:4) and cleansed the earth itself (with the Flood).

6:3 My Spirit: This is the second reference to the Holy Spirit in Genesis. The first is in anticipation of order and wonder (1:2); this second is in anticipation of destruction. Scholars are not sure what the Hebrew term **strive** means; it is found only here. **Flesh** speaks of the mortality of humankind (3:19; 5:5). **his days:** Some interpret this phrase as suggesting that the human life span will be reduced to 120 years. However, the reduction of the human life span to modern levels does not occur until well into the stories of the Patriarchs. More likely, this phrase means that God will extend a "grace period" of 120 years before expending His wrath (in the Flood).

6:4 The Hebrew word for **giants** means "fallen ones" (from the Heb. verb *napal,* meaning "to fall"). Many ancient cultures have legends of titans and demigods. This verse appears to be explaining this common memory of humankind.

6:5, 6 was sorry: This language is what theologians call anthropopathic (1:31); that is, the Lord is described as having human emotions (Num. 23:19). In these words we sense the passion of the Lord. He had desired so much from humanity and was overwhelmingly disappointed.

6:7 I will destroy: Humanity's ruin extends to all living things that God had made on the earth.

6:8 But Noah: In this contrast lies the hope of all of subsequent human history. Were there not a man and a family who by God's grace stood out from the wickedness of their day, there would have been a new beginning on the part of God that would have omitted all of us!

6:8 Grace in Hebrew comes from a root meaning "to bend or stoop"; thus, the condescending or unmerited favor of a superior person to an inferior one is implied. This is its first occurrence in Scripture and it is often used redemptively (Jer. 31:2; Zech. 12:10). Mankind, the beasts of the field, and the fowl of the air would be destroyed. But God would call out a remnant unto Himself.

6:9–13 Noah was a just man, and like Enoch, **walked with God.** "Just" relates to Noah's relationship with God; he was in a right relationship with God. He was also **perfect,** which conveys the idea of maturity or completeness. The phrase **in his generations** explains that Noah lived this way among his contemporaries, who were so wicked that God was going to destroy the world.

6:10 These **three sons,** first mentioned in 5:32, will form the family tree of the nations following the Flood.

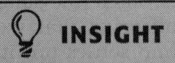 **INSIGHT** | **The Flood Through Other Eyes**

Divine destruction of the world by means of a flood is known in cultures around the world. Most of these stories appear to have had their origin in the biblical account (Gen. 6:5–9:29). The ancient Near East, however, has numerous myths of the great flood, which are separate retellings of the same event producing numerous versions. Mesopotamian flood stories are first found written in the Sumerian language in the earliest known literature (third millennium B.C.). Two of the most famous are the Gilgamesh Epic and the story of Atrahasis.

6:11 The verb translated **corrupt** has the idea of being ruined, spoiled, or destroyed. Sinful people were bringing ruin to the world that belonged to the living God (Ps. 24:1).

6:12 all flesh: The language is similar to that of Ps. 14:2, 3.

6:13 God's message to Noah was graphic and severe. But the faithful reader of the Bible is also impressed with God's grace. The Creator of the universe, who owes man nothing, took one man into His confidence. **end of all flesh:** It would appear that the God's "grace period" of 120 years (v. 3) was now complete.

6:14 The word **ark** (Heb. *tebâ*) means "a box." An Egyptian word from which this term may be drawn means "chest" or "coffin"; the same term is used of the box in which the baby Moses was placed in the Nile (Ex. 2:3). We usually picture a boat or a ship with bow and stern. But a ship is designed to move through the water as a conveyance; the ark was built merely to float on the water. The Hebrew word for **gopherwood** is merely transliterated because that type of wood is not known today. Noah made **rooms** in the ark and used **pitch** to seal the ark against leaks. It is not certain what this sealing agent was. What a comical thing this must have been! We do not know where Noah lived in the pre-Flood earth, but there is nothing that indicates he was near an ocean. Yet he was building the largest floating box that had ever been seen.

6:15 The **cubit** is about 18 inches. Hence, the ark was about 450 feet long, 75 feet wide, and 45 feet high.

6:16 The **window** was an "opening." The need for circulation of air, yet protection from the torrents of water, demanded a good deal of engineering and crafting. This opening could be covered (8:6).

6:17 I Myself: The Hebrew text places significant emphasis on the personal role of God in the ensuing storm.

6:18–21 In strongest contrast to God's punishment in the preceding verse, God in His mercy established His **covenant** with Noah. This is the first time the word covenant is used in the Bible; some believe the concept of covenant is found in 3:15, but the word doesn't occur until here. The details of this covenant were given after the Flood (9:9). Here, in the midst of judgment, the Lord stooped down to meet the needs of His servant (Pss. 40:1; 113:6) and to enter into a binding oath with him. In order to perpetuate the human family, God promised to preserve Noah's family and **two of every sort** of animal.

6:22 Noah's complete obedience is similar to Abram's (Gen. 12:4; 22:3). God has told Noah to build an ark, but Noah has never seen an ark.

Nevertheless, in total faith and trust in his God with whom he walks **Noah did according to all that God commanded him.** Little wonder is it recorded that, "By faith Noah, being divinely warned of things not yet seen, moved with godly fear, prepared an ark for the saving of his household, by which he condemned the world and became heir of the righteousness which is according to faith" (Heb 11:7).

7:1 The initiative is **the Lord's** (8:15), just as in the call of Abram (12:1).

7:2, 3 The command to take **seven each of every clean animal** is a new detail (6:19). The additional clean animals could be used for food and for sacrifice once the waters subsided (8:20–22).

7:4 The number **forty** is a significant number, representing a special fullness of time (v. 12; Num. 32:13; 1 Kin. 19:8; Matt. 4:2).

7:5 Again, **Noah** obeyed the Lord fully.

7:6 six hundred years old: This is the second notice of the age of Noah; he was 500 years old when he became a father (5:32).

7:7–9 The time had now come for the family and the animals to enter **the ark.** The events of these few verses summarize an immense labor; yet the gathering of the animals must have been largely the work of the Lord and their management the work of Noah and his sons.

7:10 The number **seven** follows the pattern of symbolic numbers begun in 2:3 (4:24).

7:11, 12 seventeenth day: The detail is remarkable; but then, so was the day! **fountains of the great deep . . . windows of heaven:** The waters of the ocean were raised, and the waters of the heavens fell, both converging in a super-inundation of **rain** for the forty days (v. 4).

7:13–15 The animals seem to have been drawn to the ark and **to Noah** by the compelling force of the Lord.

7:16 shut him in: The Lord who had drawn them now closed the door on them. That shut door was a symbol of closure, safety, and God's deliverance.

7:17, 18 Four times in this passage the phrase **the waters prevailed** is used (vv. 18–20, 24). The verb means "to be strong" or "to be mighty." From this word, numerous words are derived for strength, might, and powerful people.

7:19, 20 the high hills under the whole heaven were covered: The question of hyperbolic language is naturally raised here; yet these words do suggest a flood that covers the whole of the earth.

7:21, 22 Without exception, death extended to every creature—**all flesh**—whose home was on the land.

7:23, 24 man: People died—old people and

young; beautiful and brave along with the grisly and gray. **Only Noah** and those with him escaped the terrible, universal death of the wicked. Jesus affirmed the historicity of the "days of Noah" when he compared them to the end days (Matt. 24:37, 38; Luke 17:26, 27). Peter similarly used the story of Noah and the Flood as a pattern for the final judgment (1 Pet. 3:20; 2 Pet. 2:5; 3:5, 6).

8:1, 2 God, in His great mercy, **remembered** Noah. God faithfully loved the people with whom He had covenanted.

8:3 hundred and fifty days: Note the symmetry of time. It took the same amount of time for the waters to recede as it took for them to rage over the earth (7:24).

8:4, 5 tops of the mountains: The surging of the waters had been so great that the mountains had been submerged (7:19, 20).

8:6 Again, observe the symmetry of the numbers in this account. The rains had come for forty days (7:12); now the ark was subsiding for **forty days.**

8:7 The flight of the **raven** was observed from the ark; this hardy bird kept flying until it was able to locate land.

8:8, 9 The more gentle bird, the **dove,** sought land; finding none this bird returned to the ark.

8:10, 11 The **olive leaf** is a potent symbol of peace and restoration.

8:12 which did not return: This proved to Noah that the earth had once again become an inhabitable environment.

8:13, 14 After over a full year, the waters had returned to their place (7:11). As in the beginning (1:9–13), God had again brought the waters of the earth into their place, and He had **dried** the earth. The Flood began in Noah's year 600, month 2, day 17 (7:11) and ended in Noah's year 601, month 2, day 27 (8:14).

8:15 The fact that **God spoke to Noah** is another mark of God's great grace to Noah and of how much He valued him (7:1; for God's words to Abram, read 12:1).

8:16–19 As God called Noah and his family to enter the ark (7:1), so now with all danger past He graciously invited them to **go out of the ark.**

8:20 an altar: This is the first mention of sacrificial worship since the days of Cain and Abel (4:3–5); yet we may assume that the prin-

---

☑ IN COMPARISON — A New Beginning

By saving Noah and his family, God gave humanity a second chance, a fresh start. Note the similarities between the Creation story and Noah's story.

	The First Beginning: Adam and Eve	The Second Beginning: Noah and His Family
God's Action	God created Adam and Eve from the dust (2:7).	God saved Noah and his family from destruction (7:23).
God's Provision	God planted the Garden and gave Adam and Eve plants to eat (1:29–31; 2:8).	God saved animal species along with Noah and gave Noah and his family animals for food (6:17–22).
God's Blessing	Be fruitful and multiply; have dominion over all living things (1:28).	Be fruitful and multiply; all living things will be filled with fear and dread of you (9:1, 2).
God's Covenant		Never again will God destroy the earth with a flood; He will always provide the annual seasons (8:21, 22; 9:11).
God's Prohibition	Do not eat of the tree of the knowledge of good and evil (2:16).	Do not shed the blood of any person (9:5, 6).
God's Warning	Those who eat of it will die (2:17).	Of those who shed blood God will demand a reckoning (9:5).
God's Evaluation	It is very good (1:31).	Humanity's heart is evil (8:21).

ciple of sacrificial worship was perpetuated through the line of faithful people (ch. 5). In joyful and magnificent devotion to the Lord, Noah sacrificed animals and birds from all the clean animals and birds he had preserved on the ark (7:2).

8:21 a soothing aroma: By these words we understand that the sacrifices were acceptable and pleasing to God (4:3; Lev. 1:9). The Lord received Noah's offering as an act of devotion to Him (Num. 15:3). **I will never again curse the ground:** The awful devastation of the earth and its fullness that the Flood caused will never be repeated. It is also possible that this is a reference back to 3:17. This is the good news. The bad news is that God knew that the conditions of humankind had not changed. **the imagination of man's heart is evil from his youth:** This is the same charge against man with which the Flood story began (6:5). Nonetheless, the promise of God is that overwhelming judgment will not be repeated—not until the final judgment (2 Pet. 2:5).

8:22 while the earth remains: The words of this verse are in a poem of powerful effect (12:1–3). These words might easily have become a song of faith, the response of the people of God to the promise He made (v. 21). Later in Israel's history, the prophets recalled God's great promise to Noah (Is. 54:9, 10).

9:1 The blessing of God on the family of Noah provided a new beginning for humankind.

The word **blessed** expresses the idea of God's smile, the warmth of His pleasure (1:22, 28; 2:3; 12:2, 3). In a way, the promises that God had given to the first people were now restated for Noah, a "new Adam" (1:26–28). Among other things, the new populating of the earth by Noah's family means that human society began again with a shared understanding of earliest human history, including the creation and Flood stories. **Be fruitful and multiply** was God's command in the beginning (1:28).

9:2 the fear of you and the dread of you: The two phrases express the same idea. The language of God's blessing here is far stronger than the language of the first (1:28, 29); now the animals and birds will have an innate fear of humans, and they are placed under human control.

9:3–5 you: Three new realities mark the post-Flood world: (1) meat may be eaten along with plants; (2) blood is not to be eaten with meat; and (3) the taking of a person's life is now punishable by death.

9:3 From this verse it may be argued that up to this point men and women ate only vegetation (2:16).

9:4 blood: This restriction gets more attention in Leviticus (Lev. 17:11, 12). Blood represents the animal's life. It may be used in sacrifice, for all life belongs to the Lord.

9:5 lifeblood: More sacred than the life of an animal is the life of a person. Animals may be

---

 **IN DEPTH**   ## The Noahic Covenant

The rainbow that appears after a summer thunderstorm symbolizes God's mercy, His compassion on all. Moreover, it is a sign of God's covenant, His binding agreement with all humanity to never destroy the earth with a flood.

God initiated this covenant under the worst circumstances: "The earth was filled with violence" (Gen. 6:11, 13). Even though humanity's decline into evil greatly troubled God, He favored one man, Noah, and determined to save him and his family from the coming judgment and establish His covenant with them.

Although Noah was surrounded by violence and all kinds of evil, he walked with God (6:9) by seeking to obey Him. Noah's simple obedience is recorded five times in this story (6:22; 7:5, 9, 16; 8:17, 18). God called this obedient man to build an ark. With this large boat, God saved Noah from the cleansing waters of the Flood. With the past evils and sins washed away from the earth, Noah and his family could start anew (read 1 Pet. 3:21 for Peter's analogy comparing baptism with the Flood).

God not only gave them a fresh start but also an unconditional promise, or covenant, not to destroy the earth with a flood no matter how evil Noah's descendants became. Indeed, He promised that until the end of the earth there would be the seasons of planting and harvest and day and night. God unilaterally promised to uphold the rhythms of the earth in order to sustain human life, even though humans had rebelled against Him, their Creator.

Today all of us—Noah's children—should remember God's mercy to us when we see the beauty of the rainbow.

slain for food, but no wanton slaying of humans is allowed.

9:6, 7 These verses are poetry for impact and memorability. The **image of God** (1:26, 27; 5:1) is still in man (or is man); sin did not destroy it. God values humans more highly than animal life because only humankind possesses God's image.

9:8–10 This is the second occurrence of this enormously important concept, the **covenant,** in Genesis (6:18). God promised that He would establish His covenant with Noah and here He accomplished this great work (Gen. 15:18; contrast 3:15). This covenant extends to animals of every sort (v. 10).

9:11 There will **never again** be another Flood like that described in chs. 6—8.

9:12–15 The **rainbow** is a memorial to God's promise never to flood the earth again and a constant reminder of His oath. Later, Abram (Abraham) would ask the Lord for a sign of the covenant promise He had made to him.

9:16, 17 I will look on it is a precious note. For not only do people stop to look at a rainbow, but God will look on it also.

9:18, 19 The sons of Noah have been mentioned earlier (5:32; 6:10; 7:13); their mention here assures us of their survival through the Flood and sets the stage for what happens next. **the father of Canaan:** This identification was particularly important to the first readers of Genesis, the people of Israel, who were about to enter the land of Canaan (Deut. 1:1). But this

INSIGHT

Ancient Vineyards

To be fruitful, vineyards require considerable care. When the grapes are crushed for their juice, organisms found on the outside of the peel reach the juice. The organisms multiply and cause the juice to ferment and become wine (Gen. 9:20, 21). If it ferments too long, it becomes vinegar. Ancient farmers had to balance these different factors.

notice also prepares the reader for the shameful story that is about to be recalled (vv. 20–23).

9:20, 21 The **vineyard** was a standard feature in the agricultural setting of ancient Israel. Here it is noted because of Noah's drunkenness (v. 21).

9:22 It is not clear whether seeing his father's **nakedness** was Ham's chief offense.

The following verses (especially v. 23) imply that Ham made fun of his father, and that this news reached Noah after he awoke.

9:23, 24 Shem and Japheth took great pains to honor their father, not wanting even to glance at his nakedness.

9:25 The three sons had been blessed with their father (v. 1). Thus Noah **cursed** Ham indirectly by cursing his son **Canaan** (10:6). Some once believed that this verse justified the slavery of African peoples (who, it was alleged, were descended from Canaan), but those people misinterpreted the verse. Canaan was under the curse of his father. As the Hebrews stood on the banks of the Jordan River about to enter the land of Canaan (Deut. 1:1), they would have been encouraged by this verse because it promised victory over the Canaanites.

9:26, 27 Shem is given precedence over his brothers, while **Japeth** is also blessed. Eber and Abram were descended from Shem (11:10–30) so Shem's blessing is ultimately a blessing on Israel. Again, the poetic cast of these words (vv. 25–27) adds power and memorability to them (Gen. 12:1–3). Just as Noah blessed (and cursed) his sons before his death, so Jacob was later to bless his sons before his death (ch. 49).

9:28, 29 Noah's death was the end of an era. Only he and his family spanned two worlds, that of the earth before and after the Flood. His long life (950 years) gave him opportunity to transmit to his many descendants the dramatic story that he had lived out with his family. Peoples in places and cultures the world over have memories and stories of a great Flood in antiquity. The details differ, but the stories remain.

10:1—11:32 From these chapters, we learn that the peoples of the earth are all descended from the family of Noah, but there remain a few mysteries. For one thing, the mention of names moves from individuals to peoples to cities. Second, the point of view is from a later date, when the people of Israel had as their geographical center the land of Canaan. While the words imply universal humanity, they omit a global perspective. Finally, the chapters give no clear sense of time: they span many thousands of years.

10:1 Genealogy (or "family histories"; Heb. *tôledôt*) is found in ten significant passages in Genesis (2:4, note). The names of the **sons of Noah** were first given in 5:32 (6:10; 7:13 9:18).

10:2–4 The listing of **the sons of Japheth** is more brief than the others. Among the persons and peoples mentioned is **Javan** (vv. 2, 4), an ancient name for the Greek people. It may be that many of Japheth's descendants migrated to Europe.

10:5 The migrations of the peoples to different **lands** would have come after the events of 11:1–9 (the Tower of Babel).

10:6 Ham's family included more than just his son Canaan (9:25). **Cush, Mizraim, Put, and Canaan** are Ham's four sons. Cush is the

suggests great arrogance. Like Lamech the descendant of Cain (4:19–24), his infamy was proverbial. His territory was in the lands of the east, the fabled ancient cities of Mesopotamia; these include **Babel, Erech, Accad, and**

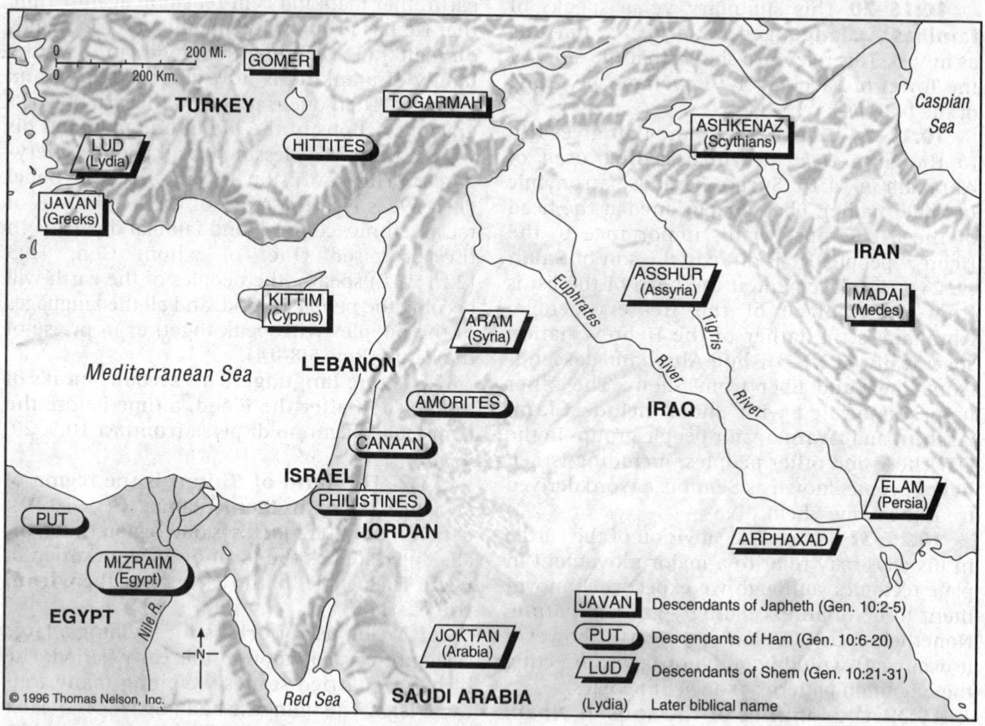

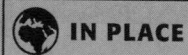

The Nations of Genesis 10

Map labels: GOMER, TOGARMAH, ASHKENAZ (Scythians), Caspian Sea, TURKEY, LUD (Lydia), HITTITES, JAVAN (Greeks), KITTIM (Cyprus), ARAM (Syria), ASSHUR (Assyria), IRAN, MADAI (Medes), Euphrates, Mediterranean Sea, LEBANON, AMORITES, IRAQ, Tigris, River, River, CANAAN, ISRAEL, PHILISTINES, ELAM (Persia), JORDAN, PUT, ARPHAXAD, MIZRAIM (Egypt), EGYPT, Nile R., JOKTAN (Arabia), Red Sea, SAUDI ARABIA, 200 Mi., 200 Km., © 1996 Thomas Nelson, Inc.

Legend: JAVAN Descendants of Japheth (Gen. 10:2–5); PUT Descendants of Ham (Gen. 10:6–20); LUD Descendants of Shem (Gen. 10:21–31); (Lydia) Later biblical name

ancient name for Ethiopia; Mizraim is a name for Egypt. The sons of Cush are given in vv. 7–12, the sons of Mizraim in vv. 13, 14, and the sons of Canaan in verses 15–19. This section does not list the sons of Put.

10:7–11 The sons of Cush include the infamous **Nimrod** (vv. 9–12). The description of him as **a mighty hunter before the Lord**

Calneh (v. 10). The term Accad (or Akkad) supplies the name of the language of ancient Babylon and Assyria, Akkadian. The prophet Micah would later use the name Nimrod to describe the region of Assyria, which would come under God's judgment (Mic. 5:5, 6).

10:12–15 The names associated with Canaan (9:22) are peoples who settled in the

---

🌍 IN PLACE　The First Major City

Erech is the biblical form of Uruk, a Sumerian city on the Euphrates river in ancient Mesopotamia. Although Erech is cited only in Gen. 10:10 and Ezra 4:9, its historical importance far exceeds its scant biblical mention. It played a major role in the development of urbanization and was one of the world's great religious centers.

The first evidence of public architecture, cylinder seals, and the origins of writing come from Erech, and building projects included the earliest known ziggurat. Late in the fourth century B.C., the population of Uruk began to expand its culture and controlled the major trade routes and the surrounding regions economically.

region of greater Canaan. Some of these names were still associated with the land at the time of Abraham. The sites of **Sodom** and its allied cities were later destroyed in the firestorm of Gen. 19.

10:16–20 This summary verse speaks of **families . . . languages . . . lands . . . nations** as in v. 5. This reference shows that the story of the Tower of Babel (11:1–9) overlaps the listing of the nations in ch. 10.

10:21–24 Eber is the name that gives rise to the term *Hebrew,* which is first used of Abraham in 14:13. Such a name is patronymic (a father name). Eber is mentioned at the head of the list because of his importance to the Hebrew people. He is directly the son of **Salah** (v. 24). His placement at the head of the list is from the vantage of the Hebrew people. Abraham is the father of the Hebrew nation specifically (12:1–3); but Abraham descends from Eber, and Eber from Shem. The other names associated with Shem include **Elam, Asshur,** and **Aram,** major people groups in the OT. These and other peoples, including Israel, have become known as Semitic, a word derived from the name Shem.

10:25–31 Peleg: The "division of the earth" in his days may refer to a major movement in plate tectonics, although we expect such movement to be of an exceedingly gradual nature. Nonetheless, the division of the earth (however it occurred) would be a major factor affecting the migration patterns of ancient peoples.

10:32 the families of the sons of Noah: Although not every ancient people group is listed in this "Table of the Nations," its clear teaching is that all the varied peoples of the earth, no matter of what land or language, are descended from Noah. The divisions among them are merely the results of the later incidents.

11:1–9 With the famous story of the confu-

sion of languages at the Tower of Babel, the prologue to the Bible draws to a close. It is necessary for the reader who comes to Gen. 12 to know that Yahweh, who speaks to Abram (Abraham) in Gen. 12, is the Creator of the earth, that mankind is in rebellion against Him, that He has brought judgments of varied kinds on mankind, including the Flood, and that the family of mankind is now greatly diverse and complex. Then one is prepared to learn of God's gracious actions in the life of one man and his wife to bring His blessing on all peoples everywhere. The confusion of languages at Babel (11:1–9) is also the story of the beginnings of racial, ethnic, cultural, and familial diversity. In the promised One, of whom Gen. 12:3 (22:15–18) speaks, the peoples of the earth will become the people of God, and all the languages of the peoples will speak together in praise of the Lamb (Rev. 5:8–14).

11:1 one language: This account speaks of a time soon after the Flood, a time before the family had begun to disperse (contrast 10:5, 20, 31, 32).

11:2 The land of Shinar is the region of ancient Babylon in Mesopotamia (Gen. 10:10), part of modern Iraq. This is one region traditionally suggested as the location of the Garden of Eden. The peoples of the earth came there **from the east.**

11:3 The use of **bricks** for building a large structure was common in this early period. Use of huge quarried stones weighing many tons came later. The immense building blocks of later times were dressed so well that they could be fitted together without **mortar.**

11:4 to the heavens: This hyperbole may have reflected the memory of these people regarding the mountains to the east, where they once lived and worshiped their gods "in the heights." They had migrated to the plain. They wanted to become famous as the Nephilim

---

✠ IN CONTEXT   Brickmaking

Bricks (Gen. 11:3) made of clay or a claylike mixture of mud and straw were one of the primary materials used for construction in the ancient world

There were probably two methods for making bricks. The easiest was to pack clay into a mold and let the block dry in the sun. The Hebrews probably used this method in Egypt (Ex. 5:7) and later in the Promised Land (2 Sam. 12:31; Jer. 43:9).

The Babylonians, whose ancestors probably constructed the tower of Babel (Gen. 11:4), used a more advanced technology of firing their bricks in kilns to make them harder and more durable. They also made them larger, up to a foot square, and flatter in order to support more weight than an ordinary brick.

(giants) were before the Flood. Motivated by pride and arrogance, they wanted to **make a name** for themselves. **lest we be scattered:** They feared that they might be dispersed—by implication, by the Lord—and not achieve the greatness they sought.

11:5 the LORD came down to see: A figurative way of speaking that indicates the omniscience (the all-embracing knowledge) of the Lord (Gen. 18:21).

11:6 nothing that they propose: The potential is that humankind will become as willfully sinful as they were before the Flood. God will not allow this to happen.

11:7 Us in this passage is similar to the language of 1:26–28. The plural pronoun emphasizes the majesty of the speaker. Variation in **language,** culture, values, and clans all started at this point. Were it not for human arrogance, this division would not have been necessary. One day peoples of all languages and cultures will unite to celebrate the grace of God's risen Son, lifting their voices together in praise of the Lamb (Rev. 5:8–14).

11:8 the LORD scattered them: There are three great judgments on sinful humanity in the first section of Genesis (chs. 1—11). The first is the expulsion from Eden (ch. 3); the second is the Flood (chs. 6—9), and the third is the scattering of the people from Babel (Luke 1:51).

11:9 There is a pun in the name **Babel** that no Hebrew reader would miss. The verb meaning "to confuse" (Heb. *balal*) sounds similar to the name of the city (Heb. *babel*). The principal city of ancient paganism (Babylon) is merely a site of confusion because **there the LORD** confused the language. Babel (and Babylon) serves as a name and symbol in the Bible for activities directed against God by the nations of the earth (Rev. 17).

11:10 Genealogy (or family histories) is found in ten significant passages in the Book of Genesis (2:4, note). The Jewish nation came from **Shem.** Hence, the accounts that follow make much of him and his family.

11:10–25 The pattern in this **genealogy** is similar to that in ch. 5; but here only the first three elements are given: (1) name "A" lived "x" years; (2) name "A" begot name "B"; (3) name "A" then lived "y" years. As does ch. 5, the list leaves out some names, focusing on major figures in the line from Noah to Abraham. "B" may be a remote descendant rather than the immediate child of "A" (5:20). Thus the genealogy shows that Abraham was a descendant of Noah through Shem, just as Noah was a descendant of Adam through Seth. Note also that while the people listed in ch. 11 lived very long lives, they did not live nearly as long as those mentioned in ch. 5. In fact, the people lived progressively *shorter* lives, from the 600 years of Shem (vv. 10, 11) to the 148 years of Nahor (vv. 24, 25). Note also the absence of a total for the time from Shem to Abram (vv. 26–30); it must have been at least several thousand years, but we do not know exactly how long. Excavations from Ebla in north Syria include texts from around 2500 B.C., and the ancient texts from Sumer, the first literate culture in the ancient Near East, date from around 3500 B.C. These ancient texts speak of a great flood many generations before their own time. The approximate date for the birth of Abraham is 2150 B.C.

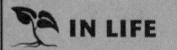 **IN LIFE** | **From Babel to Pentecost: Scattering and Gathering**

The confusion of languages at Babel was an explosive moment in history. It introduced geographic and linguistic barriers that survive to this day. However, in breaking up the unified community at Babel, God was working out His purposes. He knew that the people were united around a sinful desire to thwart His will, not to honor it (Gen. 11:6). Therefore, He miraculously disrupted their communication as an act of grace. He was preventing humanity from committing itself en masse to rebellion and eventual self-destruction.

Many centuries later, the same God who scattered the peoples at Babel began to gather them together again. At Pentecost, His Spirit began to create a new community unified around Jesus Christ (Acts 2:1–13). The Lord even breached linguistic barriers on that day—a miracle to match the miracle of creating different languages at Babel.

Since the beginning of history, God has been at work to save people from sin. He still uses the principles of scattering and gathering to do that. Only now, after Pentecost, the people that He "scatters" are equipped with the message of His grace and the power of His Spirit. He is helping them overcome every barrier that stands in the way of people knowing Him.

11:26 Terah: At long last we come to the family of Terah and the births of **Abram, Nahor, and Haran.** Years later, Abram would be renamed Abraham (17:5), and would become the father of Isaac (21:1–5). He was the progenitor of the Hebrew people from which the Promised Deliverer, Jesus, comes.

11:27 The term **genealogy** (or family histories) is found in ten significant passages in Genesis (2:4, note). **Abram, Nahor, and Haran:** These three sons of Terah would be expected to carry on his name (11:31). **Haran begot Lot:** Lot is a nephew of Abram; he figures prominently in the upcoming account (12:4, 5; 13:1–13).

11:28 The untimely death of **Haran** leaves his son Lot to carry on his name and to establish his destiny. For generations, scholars have believed **Ur of the Chaldeans** to be the famous Ur located near the ancient delta in the Persian Gulf where the Tigris and Euphrates Rivers flow together. More recently, some scholars have noted the tablets at Ebla that speak of an Ur in the region of north Syria and suggest that this is the city of Haran's death.

11:29 Sarai means "Princess," implying a person of noble birth. Sarah (as she is later called; 17:15) has the same meaning. The name **Milcah** is related to the verb that would be translated "to reign" and means "Queen." **daughter of Haran:** Evidently, Nahor married his niece. We learn later that Sarai was Abram's half sister. Milcah, who later gave birth to Bethuel, became the mother of Rebekah, the bride of Isaac (24:14). Although Rebekah's father and brother speak of faith in Yahweh, Josh. 24:2 reveals that the family had been idol worshipers in earlier times.

11:30 The sad fact that **Sarai was barren** marred her life and yet led to an opportunity for God to accomplish a miracle on her behalf (Gen. 21:1–5).

11:31, 32 Abram's epic move to Canaan begins in ch. 12 with Abram receiving a command from the Lord to leave his land to go to a new land. Did the journey begin with **Terah** or with Abram? It appears that Terah, for his own reasons, decided to move from Ur to Canaan. He began the journey with several members of his family. However, they went to Haran, where **Terah died.** This was the first step of the journey of Abram and Sarai to the land of promise. We should not charge Abram (Abraham) with sin, as is sometimes done, for moving to Haran, "when God wanted him to go to Canaan." Abram (Abraham) is presented as the great hero of the faith in 12:1–9, not as a person of only partial obedience to the Lord. The Lord was at work in the family's move from Ur to Haran. He becomes even more active and directive in the move from Haran to Canaan (12:1–4). And Abram (Abraham) becomes the father of the faithful (Rom. 4:16).

12:1–15:21 This section of the Bible begins with God's call of Abram and Sarai (later named Abraham and Sarah) to become the parents of a new people through whom God would reach all the families of the earth.

12:1 The name Yahweh, translated as LORD, is not explained until Ex. 3:14, 15. But the readers of Genesis needed to know that the one who spoke to Abram is the same Yahweh who later would form the nation of Israel and who had created all things (Gen. 2:4). To a world that believed in many gods, the name of the true and living God was significant. The account begins with the revelation of the word of the Lord, the irrupting grace of Yahweh, with He who sovereignly breaks into the lives of needy people from without. Gen. 1:3 records God speaking the words, "let there be light." Genesis 12:1 shows Yahweh speaking to Abram in words of great grace (7:1; 8:15, the words of Yahweh to Noah).

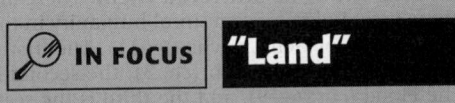 **IN FOCUS** "Land"

(Heb. *'erets*) (Gen. 1:1, 10; 4:16; 12:1; 13:10; Deut. 34:2; Ps. 98:3) Strong's #776: The common OT word *land* possesses several nuances of meaning, including: earth in contrast to the heavens (1:1); land in contrast to the sea (1:10); ground as a plot of real estate or a geographical location (4:16); the land of a sovereign nation (13:10, 12); or even the people who live upon the earth (Pss. 98:3; 100:1). In essence, all land belongs to God as its Creator (Ps. 24:1). Thus when God promised the Israelites the "land" of Canaan, it was His to give. Because the land of Canaan was an important element in God's covenant with the Israelites (12:1), it became one of their identifying characteristics—the "people of the land" (Gen. 13:15; 15:7).

John 1:1 speaks of the incarnation of the Word. In all the Bible the message is the same; it is Yahweh, the Lord, who reaches out to people, who reveals Himself, who extends His great grace. **had said:** God had spoken the promise to Abram in Ur (11:31). Now that Abram's father had died and been buried in Haran, Abram recalled Yahweh's words and acted upon them. **Abram** means "Exalted Father." Later it will be changed to Abraham, meaning "Father of

Many." **Get out:** Verses 1–3 are poetry, aiding memorability and a sense of solemnity and gravity (14:19, 20; 16:11, 12; 25:23). **country . . . family . . . father's house:** Here are three levels of ever-increasing demands on the life of Abram and Sarai. The country was the region of his dwelling, the family was his clan, and his father's house was where he had responsibility and leadership. Upon the death of Terah, Abram would have become the leader of the family group. God's commands to Abram were intensely demanding because they caused him to leave his place, his clan, and his family in a world where such actions were simply not done. Only the poverty-stricken or the defeated would wander; only the landless and the fugitive would move about and leave their ancestral homes. But the Lord's words to Abram commanded that he was to leave everything and go to a place that God would not even define until Abram got there: **a land that I will show you.**

12:2, 3 There are seven elements in God's promise to Abram in these two verses. The number seven suggests fullness and completeness, as in Gen. 2:2, 3. This celebrated passage is a prologue to the set of passages that together form the *Abrahamic covenant* (15:1–21, note), the irrevocable promise of God. (1) God commanded Abram to leave his home and family, promising to create **a great nation** through him—the people of God (18:18). This people would be the Hebrew nation. God set them apart to be His agents to reach other nations. This first element and the seventh element are the most significant in the set. (2) God promised to **bless** Abram. The blessing of God is His smile, the warmth of His pleasure (1:22, 28; 2:3; 9:1). The Lord's promise of His personal blessing to Abram and Sarai included the benefits of a long and healthy life (15:15; especially 24:1), plus wealth and importance (13:2). (3) That one's **name** would live on long after one's lifetime was a supreme honor (6:4). Those who brought

shame on themselves would be forgotten (11:4). The name Abraham, by which we remember Abram (17:5), is one of the most honored of all names in history. (4) **be a blessing:** The phrase is a command. That is, Abram was under divine orders to be a blessing to others. This he did whenever he told about the living God before other nations and peoples (v. 8). (5) **those who bless:** Elements five and six are closely related; together they form a poetic couplet. (6) **him who curses:** Whereas God would bless the peoples (plural) who blessed Abram or his descendants, His curse came upon the individual (singular) who cursed Abram or his descendants. (7) The final and most significant of the Lord's promises to Abram and his descendants was that **all the families of the earth** would be blessed through them, the Jewish people who are descended from Abram.

12:4 With the magnificent promise of the Lord as his sole motivation, **Abram departed.** He obeyed (Gen. 17:23; 22:3). In his obedience, Abram behaved as Noah had, demonstrating genuine righteousness (6:22; 7:5). **Lot went with him:** Some have imagined that Abram disobeyed God by taking Lot with him. However, the verse suggests that Lot made the decision. **seventy-five years old:** The Bible rarely indicates a person's age when events occur, but it does so several times for Abram. As we will see, this testifies to God's mighty works in Abram's life at his advanced age.

12:5 This is the first mention in the Bible of **Canaan,** the geographical stage for God's acts of salvation. Canaan was populated with peoples involved in gross idolatry (15:16). God promised this land to Abram and Sarai.

12:6 passed through: This verb resembles the name Hebrew (Gen. 14:13). Here the Hebrew Abram was "passing through" the land, crossing over to his destination. **Shechem:** This ancient site was in the center of the land; later under Joshua's leadership the people would

---

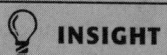 **INSIGHT**   ## The Patriarchs

Genesis 12—50 tells the accounts of Israel's "patriarchs." The events of the first three patriarchs Abraham, Isaac, and Jacob (chs. 12—38) take place primarily in Canaan, although Abraham originated in Mesopotamia (Ur and Haran). The life of the patriarch Joseph (chs. 33—50) is set primarily in Egypt.

"Patriarch" refers to the founder or ruler of a tribe, family, or clan. The Israelites traced their ancestry to one man, "the patriarch Abraham" (Heb. 7:4; compare Is. 51:2), and they laid claim to Canaan based on God's covenant with the first three patriarchs to "possess the land" (Deut. 1:8). The phrase "the patriarchs" eventually referred to Jacob's twelve sons (Acts 7:8, 9). Exact dates for the period in which they lived cannot be established.

commemorate the Lord's covenant there (Josh. 24:1). **tree of Moreh:** A terebinth or ancient oak tree would serve as a lasting marker for future generations to observe (13:18; 18:1; 23:17). The term *Moreh* means "The Teacher." It is related to the term *Torah*, which means "Instruction." Here Abraham began symbolically taking possession of the land that would one day be the territory of the Great Teacher and His instruction. The land was already occupied by **the Canaanites** (13:7), but by God's promise it would belong to Abraham's descendants.

12:7 the LORD appeared: This was the first time God appeared (theophany, or divine appearance) to Abram in the land of Canaan, but certainly not the last (13:14–17). **To your descendants:** The land of Canaan was a gift to the descendants of Abram. God owned the land (Ps. 24:1); it was His to do with as He pleased. The people of Canaan had lost their right to occupy the land due to their awful depravity (15:16). Thus God declared that **this land** would become the land of Israel (15:18–21; 17:6–8). This verse forms a part of the Abrahamic covenant (15:1–21, note), and Abraham quoted it many years later to his servant (24:7).

12:8 Later, in the time of Jacob, the site of **Bethel** would play an important role (Gen. 28:10–22). **Ai** means "Ruin." The name suggests that the site was a ruin of an ancient city. Abram responded to God's appearance by building **an altar** and worshiping the Lord. **called on the name of the LORD:** Not a private prayer, but a public proclamation. Abram was evangelizing—telling others about the Lord. God had commanded him to be a blessing to the nations (12:2) and he was doing it. The meaning "to proclaim" or "to preach" for this Hebrew verb is found also in 4:26; 21:33; 26:25.

12:9 South: This Hebrew word is often transliterated as the *Negev* (13:1; 24:62). The population of Canaan, along with their flocks and herds, kept Abram from finding a location for his own herds and flocks. He kept wandering further south, into the Negev, until he had room for them.

12:10 Sometime after Abram's arrival in Canaan, **famine** forced him to leave. Famine can arise either from forces of nature or from war and its disruption of farming (26:1; Ruth 1:1). **to Egypt:** The Scripture does not say whether Abram wanted to go.

12:11 beautiful countenance: Only rarely does the Bible refer to a person's appearance (other examples are Joseph at 39:6 and David at 1 Sam. 16:12). The comment on Sarai's beauty compares to ones on Rebekah (Gen. 24:16) and Rachel (29:17). Sarai's physical beauty was remarkable given her advanced age—she was ten years younger than Abram, or about sixty-five (12:4; 17:17).

12:12 The point is that Abram and his entourage would not be able to slip into Egypt secretly. They were many, with plenty of possessions, herds, and flocks. The Egyptians would **see** them, and Abram knew that Sarai's beauty would be noticed too.

12:13, 14 my sister: Sarai *was* Abram's half sister, the daughter of his father but not of his mother (20:12).

12:15 commended her: A form of praise (much like that in Ps. 113:1). **to Pharaoh's house:** Abram's ploy backfired!

12:16 treated Abram well: Abram was enriched by Pharaoh's actions, but at the possible loss of his wife. Some critical scholars used to think that **camels** were not domesticated nearly so early as this; they viewed the term camels as an error. It is now known that camels had been domesticated, although rarely. They represented great wealth; to have a camel in this period was like having an expensive limousine.

12:17 the LORD plagued Pharaoh: The first example of the cursing and blessing element of God's promise (12:2, 3).

12:18–20 In his indignation, Pharaoh dismissed the couple. The Lord protected Abram and Sarai for their role in salvation history.

13:1, 2 Abram and Sarai returned from Egypt **to the South** or to the Negev (12:9; 24:62), a region where they could live with their considerable wealth in **livestock, silver, and gold.** From there they journeyed back to **Bethel,** the site where God had appeared to him. Again Abram **called on the name of the LORD** (12:8).

13:3–7 Lot shared in his uncle Abram's prosperity to some degree. The crowding of range lands led to disputes and **strife** between their herdsmen. **The Canaanites and the Perizzites:** As in 12:6, the point of this phrase is that the land was already populated; Abram and Lot did not come into a region that was empty. They had to compete for available land for their rapidly growing herds and flocks.

13:8, 9 we are brethren: Abram acted with kindness, not wanting to fight his nephew's family and herdsmen. Abram gave Lot his choice. In doing this, Abram not only showed a lack of self-interest, but also confidence in God's continuing provision for him.

13:10–12 Lot was greedier than Abram; he wanted the well-watered region in **the plain of Jordan,** near the Dead Sea. **Sodom and Gomorrah:** In light of the fate of these infamous cities (chs. 18; 19); the first readers would be amazed to learn of the abundant water the region had once enjoyed. **like the garden of the LORD:** This exuberant comparison recalls the conditions of Eden (2:10). In an arid region, abundance of water would evoke images of Paradise. The "little" town of **Zoar** later figured in Lot's life (19:22).

13:13 Lot's choice of the more favorable land led him into territory that was populated by the worst of the Canaanites, the infamous evil people of **Sodom** (chs. 18; 19). The rest of the peoples of Canaan were given 400 years before their idolatry and wickedness demanded judgment (15:16).

13:14–17 This section forms part of the set of texts that set the stage for the Abrahamic covenant (15:1–21, note). This section builds on 12:1–3, 7, the passage in which God first gave His great promise to Abram.

13:14 The LORD reaffirmed the promise to Abram after his lack of faith in Egypt (12:10–20) and his **separation from Lot.**

is a symbolic act of taking possession. Abraham himself would not take possession of the land (Heb. 11:13–16); his descendants would (12:7; 15:17–21).

13:18 Hebron became one of the principal centers for Abram's stay in the land (23:2). Abram was still living in a tent, not in the cities. Abram continued to build **altars** to worship the living God (12:7, 8; 13:4).

14:1, 2 Most scholars no longer think it is likely that **Amraphel king of Shinar** was the famous Hammurabi of Babylon.

14:3 The Valley of Siddim is most likely submerged under the waters of the Dead Sea.

14:4 they served: That is, the kings from Mesopotamia forced the kings of the cities in the Valley of Siddim to pay tribute.

14:5–9 The punitive raid of the foreign alliance took at least a year to organize. The raid

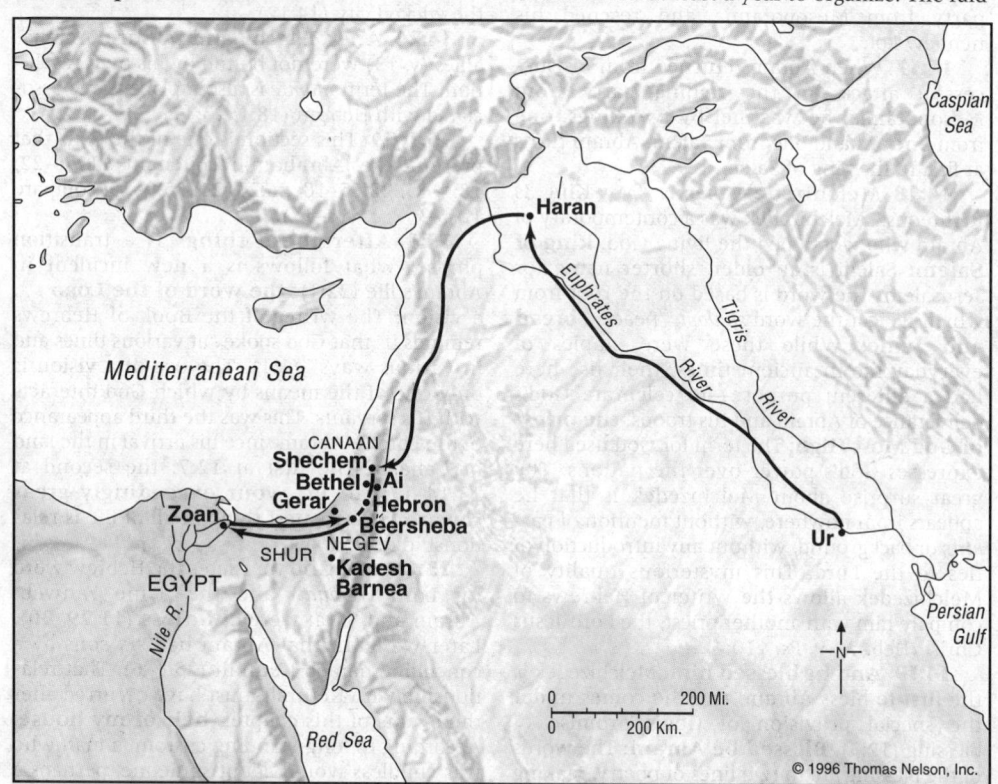

The Journeys of Abraham

13:15–17 all the land: None of the land was outside the promise. **Your descendants** translates the Hebrew word for seed (*zera'*). At times this term refers to many descendants and at other times to a unique individual, the Coming One (Gen. 22:18; Gal. 3:16). **as the dust of the earth:** A hyperbole or overstatement (15:5; 22:17). Abram's **walk in the land**

must have been formidable, given the list of cities they **attacked** as they made their way to the encounter with the rebellious kings.

14:10 asphalt pits: The Hebrew term for pits is written twice ("pits pits"), meaning that bitumen pits were everywhere.

14:11, 12 all the goods . . . Lot: Lot was not only captured, but he was also now living in the city of Sodom, an "exceedingly wicked and sinful" city (13:11–13). This sets the stage for the events of chs. 18; 19.

14:13 Here is this first use of the word **Hebrew** in the Bible. It comes from the name Eber, first mentioned in the table of the nations in ch. 10. The word (Heb. *'ibri*) is related to a verb meaning "cross over" or "pass through" (Heb. *'abar*), perhaps reminding us that Abram "passed through" or "crossed over" from another place in order to obey the Lord's command. Abram had moved to Hebron at the terebinth trees of **Mamre** (13:18, 24).

14:14, 15 The fact that Abram could field 318 fighting men from among his own **servants** is an indication of the great wealth and honor that the Lord had given him (12:2, 3).

14:16 Abram's raid was a complete success. He regained **all the goods** stolen by the raiding party from Mesopotamia and rescued his nephew Lot.

14:17 When Abram returned from his successful attack on the raiding party from Mesopotamia, he was met by two kings, one from **Sodom** and one from Salem. Abram turns at first to the king of Salem.

14:18 **Melchizedek** means "My King Is Righteous." Melchizedek was a contemporary of Abram who worshiped the living God. **king of Salem:** Salem is an older, shorter name for Jerusalem. The word is based on the root from which we get the word *shalom,* "peace." **bread and wine:** While these were staples of everyday life in ancient times, their use here had a different purpose—to celebrate God's deliverance of Abram and his troops. **the priest of God Most High:** The term for God used here expresses God's power over the nations. The great surprise about Melchizedek is that he appears from nowhere, without mention of parents or background, without any introduction of ties to the Lord. This mysterious quality of Melchizedek allows the writer of Hebrews to compare him with another priest, the Lord Jesus Christ (Heb. 5—9; Ps. 110:4).

14:19 **And he blessed him:** Melchizedek is the first to bless Abram; thus he comes under the special provision of God's promise of blessing (12:3). **Blessed be Abram:** The words of the blessing are in two lines of poetry, making them more memorable as well as adding a sense of power and effectiveness. The phrase **God Most High** is used in both lines of the blessing for special emphasis. **Possessor** may also mean "Creator" (Prov. 8:22).

14:20 **blessed be God Most High:** When we bless God, we acknowledge Him as the source of all our blessings (Ps. 103:1, 2). Melchizedek declared the true nature of Abram's victory—God **delivered** him. Here is

the first mention of the **tithe** in the Bible (Deut. 14:22). Abram's gift indicates that he considered Melchizedek a true priest of the living God; in giving this gift Abram seems to have ignored the king of **Sodom** (v. 17) until he had worshiped with the king of Salem. Now he hears the demands of this king, who asked for his people but not for his goods.

14:21 Abram seems to have ignored the **king of Sodom** (v. 17) until he had worshiped with the king of Salem. Now he hears the demands of this king, who asked for his people but not for his goods.

14:22 Abram **raised** his **hand** as a symbol of a strong oath. In other passages it is a sign of defiance. Abram identified Yahweh, translated here as **the Lord**, with the **God Most High.** This is a clear statement that he and Melchizedek both worshiped the true, living God.

14:23 **I will take nothing . . . strap:** In these words, Abram strongly rebuked Sodom and its king (13:12, 13). Abram stood in strong contrast to his nephew Lot who had moved into the wicked city (14:12).

14:24 **Aner, Eshcol, and Mamre:** Abram's allies (v. 13) were not bound by his own resolution. The term *Mamre* is also a place name associated with Hebron (18:1; 23:17).

15:1–21 This section is one of the texts that present the Abrahamic covenant (17:1–22; 18:1–15; 22:15–18; 26:23, 24; 35:9–15; compare 12:1–3, 7; 13:14–17).

15:1 **After these things** is a transition phrase; what follows is a new incident in Abram's life (22:1). **the word of the Lord . . . a vision:** The writer of the Book of Hebrews reminds us that God spoke "at various times and in various ways" (1:1). The use of a vision is only one of the means by which God interacts with His servants. This was the third appearance of the Lord to Abram since his arrival in the land of Canaan (the first at 12:7; the second at 13:14–17; ch. 17). **your exceedingly great reward:** The greatest thing in all of life is relationship to God.

15:2 **Lord God** translates the Hebrew word for Lord (*Adonai*) and the name Yahweh. Abram and Sarai were **childless** (11:29, 30). Later we learn that Abram had six sons by a concubine named Keturah (25:1–6). That relationship with Keturah must have occurred after the events of this chapter. **heir of my house:** According to long-standing custom, a man who was childless would adopt someone, perhaps a slave, to be his principal heir. If the man later had a child, then the natural child would replace the adopted son as the principal heir. Similar laws were part of the legal codes of the Near East, including the famed Code of Hammurabi of Babylon. We read of **Eliezer of Damascus** only here, but he had the honor of being Abram's heir because Abram and Sarai had no child of their own. Some have wondered if Eliezer is also the unnamed servant of

Abraham who went on the quest for a wife for Isaac (Gen. 22:5; 24:2).

15:3 Offspring represents a word that is also translated *seed* and *descendants* (3:15; 15:5, 13, 18).

15:4 from your own body: Eliezer was not a physical son of Abram; God promised that

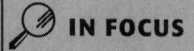

"Believe"

(Heb. *'aman*) (Gen. 15:6; Ex. 4:31; 2 Chr. 20:20; Ps. 116:10) Strong's #539: The Hebrew word translated *believe* is from a root meaning "establish" or "confirm." The English word *amen,* which is used to express approval, comes from the same root (Neh. 5:13; Ps. 41:13). Belief is one of the most important ideas in all the Bible, because a person must *believe* God in order to be saved from sin. For this very reason, the NT makes much of the fact that Abraham *believed* God (Heb. 11:8–12). Whenever the Scriptures, OT or NT, state that a person "believed in the Lord," it signals that the person has made a decision to treat God's word as certain and has made a commitment to do what God wants (15:6; John 1:12).

Abram himself would father a child, even in his advanced age.

15:5 Only God can count **the stars** (Ps. 147:4; Is. 40:26). The saying means that the descendants of Abram would be innumerable (Gen. 22:17; compare 13:16). **Your descendants** translates the Hebrew word for *seed*. This word is used to refer to the coming Messiah (Num. 24:7; Is. 6:13).

15:6 When God made a promise, Abram **believed in the Lord**. "Believed" is from the Hebrew root *'aman,* meaning "to be established," "to be confirmed." When God commanded Abram, he obeyed (12:4; 22:3). Nothing so marks the lives of Abram and Sarai as their *belief in God* (Heb. 11:8–19). It is this belief, faith in the only living God, that saves the sinner from sin (John 12:11). **He accounted it to him for righteousness:** Some have thought that in OT times people were saved by their good deeds rather than by faith, but this idea is mistaken. Abram was not saved because of righteous living or obedience, but by believing in God and so being declared righteous by Him. The only valid work is the work of faith (John 6:28, 29).

15:7 I am the Lord, who brought you

out: This is the self-authenticating declaration of the Lord. His grace enables a person to believe. **Ur:** See 11:28, 31.

15:8 how shall I know: The text suggests that Abram was asking the Lord for a commemorative sign of His promise, not that he was troubled by unbelief.

15:9, 10 Abram had only to prepare the sacrifice and **bring** it to God; the Lord would enact the sign (v. 17). This emphasizes the unilateral, unconditional nature of the covenant.

15:11 Abram had come not to feed the **vultures,** but to see a great sign from the Lord. For the rest of the day he kept the vultures away from the animals while waiting for God's sign.

15:12 Abram fell into the same sort of **deep sleep** that God placed on Adam (2:21). Abram was still aware of events around him. His trancelike state allowed him to remember these events for the rest of his life. **horror . . . darkness:** These two words give great emphasis to the meaning: "an overwhelmingly dark horror." This kind of reaction to the indescribable holiness of the Lord (Ps. 113:4–6; Is. 6:3; 40:25) is natural; Abram was about to experience the presence of the Almighty. This was a moment of profound dread and holy awe.

15:13 Know certainly is the same construction as "you shall surely die" at Gen. 2:17. **Your descendants** translates the Hebrew word for seed (vv. 3, 5, 18). **Strangers** are those who dwell temporarily in a foreign place. Abram was a *stranger* in the land of Canaan; his descendants would become strangers in another land (Egypt). **four hundred years:** No doubt this would impress Abram, but consider how it would impress the first readers of the book. They were the generation who came to fulfill God's promise! (Ex. 12:40–42.)

15:14 I will judge: God fulfilled this prophecy in the ten plagues (Ex. 7–11). The Israelites of the Exodus acquired **great possessions** when they plundered the Egyptians (Ex. 12:31–36).

15:15 to your fathers: A way of speaking about death; the phrase may include the promise of life after death as well (Gen. 25:8; 35:29; 49:33; 1 Sam. 12:23).

15:16 in the fourth generation: This expression reflects the longer life spans of people in Abram's day (compare 400 years in v. 13). **iniquity of the Amorites:** In a sense, the Lord was granting a stay of execution for the peoples of Canaan (12:5). He would allow their sin to reach a critical level—the word "iniquity" (Heb. *'awôn*) also speaks of "guilt." The command of God to take the land from the Canaanite peoples (Deut. 20) would come only when their iniquity was **complete.**

15:17 The deep sleep came on Abram when

the **sun** was setting (v. 12). Now in heavy darkness, he saw supernatural light. **a smoking oven and a burning torch:** These symbols represented the glory of the Lord to Abram. Smoke and fire, with clouds and darkness, often precede God's acts of judgment (Ex. 19:16–20; Ps. 97:2–6; Is. 6:1–5; Joel 2:2, 3; Zeph. 1:14–16). This oven and torch imagery may indicate the impending judgment on Canaan, the promise that God's word to Abram will be kept. **between those pieces:** This last element has profound implications. In solemn agreements between equals (parity treaties), both parties would pass between the bloody pieces of slain animals and birds. The symbol would be evident to all: "May I become like this if I do not keep my part of the deal." But Abram was not to walk this grisly pathway. Only God made that journey in the symbols of smoke and fire. The fulfillment of the promise of God to Abram, the Abrahamic covenant, is as sure as is the ongoing life of the Lord (22:15–18)!

15:18 The **same day** that Abram believed in the Lord (v. 6) and God counted it to him for righteousness, God made a covenant with him. Belief in God remains the model for us today (Rom. 4:22–25). **covenant:** The first time this very significant word is used of God's promise to Abraham. In this case the agreement is between a superior and an inferior. Compare 21:27, where the word is used in a parity treaty between Abraham and Abimelech. See Gen. 26:28 for a parity treaty between Isaac and Abimelech. **Descendants** translates the Hebrew word for seed, which may refer to a populace or to an individual. The Jews who would descend from Abram would fulfill this promise as the seed (collectively); so also the Christ who is the Seed (singular) would ultimately fulfill this promise (Gal. 3:16). One day, both the Savior and His people will fulfill this promise to the uttermost (Mic. 5:2–5). **This land** is the key term for this section. As already noted, God's promise to Abraham included his descendants

and the Promised One, the Seed of Gen. 3:15 (Is. 6:13). But the promise also included the land of Canaan (which was to become the land of Israel). We first see this in 12:7. This section greatly emphasizes it, and in later texts it is renewed repeatedly (17:6–8). God removed the people of Israel from the land of Canaan several times, but He never revoked His everlasting promise (17:8). The promise will be fulfilled in its fullness when Jesus Christ returns (Is. 9:1–7). **The river of Egypt** may be the Nile, or it may be what is called today the Wadi el'Arish, a smaller watercourse at the natural boundary of Egypt and the land of Israel. **the River Euphrates:** The northern arm of the Euphrates in Syria.

15:19–21 the Kenites . . . Jebusites: This list of nations served two purposes. (1) It defined the borders of the land. (2) It impressed: no fewer than ten nations would be supplanted by the nation of Israel. The Israelites who heard these words must have been greatly encouraged.

15:20 Most **Hittites** lived in Asia Minor (modern Turkey), but there were some Hittites in Canaan (ch. 23). **the Rephaim:** A people of unusually tall stature; they are called giants in 2 Sam. 21:15–22 (Num. 13:33; Deut. 2:11; 3:11, 13).

15:21 The term **Canaanite** could be used broadly to include all the people groups in Canaan (12:6), or more narrowly, as here, to indicate a particular people group (10:15–20).

16:1 had borne him no children: One of the principal themes in Genesis is the quest for children, especially sons. This appears in 4:1 with the birth of Cain. In Abram and Sarai's lives the theme gets a lot of attention (11:29, 30; 12:1–3; 15:1–4; also chs. 17; 18; 21). In the OT world, infertility caused great distress (25:21). At that time, the woman was always blamed. When a woman was not able to conceive a child, her husband might divorce her. Sarai's desperate ploy to have a child through **Hagar**

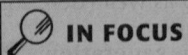 **IN FOCUS** | **"Accounted"**

(Heb. *chashab*) (Gen. 15:6; Ex. 26:1; Is. 33:8) Strong's #2803: This complex verb has two distinct ranges of meaning. The first is associated with calculations of some sort: "count" (Lev. 25:27; Prov. 17:28), "esteem" (Is. 53:3), "impute" (2 Sam. 19:19), "reckon" (Lev. 27:18, 23). The second includes the element of planning. Thus the word has the meaning of "think" (1 Sam. 1:13), "devise" (Esth. 8:3), "artistic design" (Ex. 26:1; 35:35), or "regard" (Is. 33:8). As used in 15:6, the word has commercial connotations. Abram's faith was "accounted" to him for righteousness; that is, computed or tallied as a credit or deposit in Abram's favor. Paul also appeals to this credit and debit language of the accounting ledger in his explanation of justification by faith (Rom 4:3).

was fully in accord with the practices of those days.

16:2 Sarai knew that conception was from the Lord (4:1); her words, **the LORD has** restrained me, expressed her grief. Earlier her husband had complained to the Lord that he was childless (15:2). **go in to my maid:** In the culture of the ancient Near East this would have been expected. Abram's peers would not have regarded it as immoral. **obtain children by her:** Hagar would become a surrogate mother for Sarai. At the time of birth, the mother would undress herself and stay near the birth mother. As the child was born it might be placed on the wife's body, a ritual indicating that it was born on behalf of the woman who was unable to have children herself.

16:3 Sarai and Abram enlisted Hagar's aid only after **ten years** of waiting for God's promise to be fulfilled. At this point, Abram would have been eighty-five years old and Sarai seventy-five (12:4; 17:17).

16:4 despised: Sarai paid an emotional price for doing what the culture accepted. Using a surrogate mother may have been expedient and acceptable to the culture, but the hatred and belittling by the arrogant young servant woman was excruciating for Sarai. Now that she saw the pride of her servant, Sarai was humiliated.

16:5 The LORD judge: This is as close as we come to the use of cursing among God's people in the Bible; such words arose out of Sarai's utter desperation.

16:6 Sarai's frustration led her to treat Hagar **harshly.** Neither she nor Abram behaved well during this stressful time. The Bible often shows its best characters at their worst moments.

16:7 the Angel of the LORD: This wonderful phrase is used to speak of God as He relates Himself directly to His people. Angel means "messenger." **by a spring of water in the wilderness:** The detail is appropriate for Hagar's experience. There she was, alive with a child within her, and yet she had no place to go and no future. Hagar was like that spring in the wilderness.

16:8, 9 and He said: On several occasions this passage states that the Angel of the Lord spoke directly to Hagar (vv. 9, 10, 11). **where … where:** The Lord asks these questions not from a lack of knowledge but to give Hagar an opportunity to express herself.

16:10 God's promise to Hagar to **multiply** her descendants is similar to the one given to Abram and Sarai (15:5; 17:20; 22:15–18). **Descendants** translates the Hebrew word for seed (for its use elsewhere, see 3:15; 15:3, 5, 13, 18). The promise is meant to encourage Hagar, and later God renews the promise (17:20).

16:11 The name **Ishmael** uses the divine name *El* and means "God hears."

16:12 This is something of a mixed blessing as is Isaac's to Esau (27:39, 40). **Wild man** suggests that Ishmael and his descendants would be unsettled, ever on the move. **His hand … against** suggests that his descendants would often be at war. Still this people would endure. They would **dwell in the presence of all his brethren.** This has indeed been the case, for Ishmael's descendants are the Arab peoples who populate most of the Middle East today. Very few of the peoples of the OT world have survived to our own day. For example, all ten nations of 15:19–21 have ceased to exist. But two peoples survive: Israel, the Jewish people, descended from Isaac; and the Arabs, descended from Ishmael (17:19–22).

16:13–16 Though Hagar was Egyptian, she had evidently come to faith in **the LORD** of

---

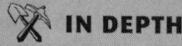 **IN DEPTH**   **The Abrahamic Covenant**

God burst into the lives of an older, childless couple, Abram and Sarai, with words of strong determination: "I will make you a great nation; I will bless you" (Gen. 12:2). This gracious promise was unconditional. God would multiply Abram's descendants and give them the land of Canaan (13:14–17). He formalized His promise to Abram as a formal agreement between a superior king and an inferior servant (15:1–21). Finally, He swore by Himself that He would do it (22:15–18). His word was irrevocable.

Yet within His unconditional promises, God made demands. He commanded Abram and Sarai to leave their home and their extended family to go to a new land (12:1). He commanded them to be a blessing to others (12:2), to walk before Him and be blameless (17:1), and to circumcise the males in their household as a sign of the covenant (17:10). Although God's promises were unconditional, Abram's temporal participation in God's blessing was conditioned on his faithfulness and his obedience to God's commands. Abram withstood the test—he believed and obeyed (15:6; 22:1–18).

Abram and Sarai. As a recipient of God's blessing, she gave Him a commemorative name, **You-Are-the-God-Who-Sees.** Her words, **have I also seen him,** suggest amazement at God's grace and humility in His presence. After the death of Abraham, his son Isaac lived at **Beer Lahai Roi** (25:11).

17:1–22 This text is a part of the complex of passages that form the Abrahamic covenant (see list at 15:1–21), the irrevocable promise of God.

17:1 ninety-nine years old: From Abram's perspective, God waited a long time to fulfill his promise. Abram was seventy-five years old when he came to the land of Canaan (12:4). At eighty-six he became the father of Ishmael (16:16). Then thirteen more years passed without a son being born to Sarai (12:1–3; 15:3, 5, 13, 18). For the fourth time, **the LORD** appeared to Abram after he came to the land of Canaan (the first is in 12:7; the second in 13:14–17; the third in ch. 15; the next in ch. 18). **I am Almighty God:** God used the name Shaddai for Himself for the first time (28:3; Ex. 3:14, 15; 6:2, 3). This word is similar to a word for mountain, to which God's strength and endurance can be compared. **walk before me:** As Enoch had walked with God (5:21–24), so now Abram was commanded to walk *before* God. He was to conduct his life as an open display of faithfulness to the Lord. **Be blameless** means to have integrity.

17:2, 3 This is the second time the word **covenant** is used of God's relationship with Abram (15:18). Before God instituted His covenant with Abram, He had already spoken to him with wonderful words of His great promise (12:1–3, 7; 13:14–17). The verb translated **will make** is not really a future tense in Hebrew. The covenant had already been established; here God is restating it to Abram (v. 4). The verb may be understood to mean, "{Again} I make." The words **multiply you exceedingly** are a different formation than is usual (16:10), giving the statement a highly emphatic sense.

17:4 a father of many nations: Abram's principal descendants are the Israelites, who are the centerpiece of biblical history and are the line from which the Savior Jesus comes. But Abram is also the father of other nations. He is the father of Ishmael and the Arab peoples (ch. 16), as well as a number of other people groups descended from Keturah, a concubine (25:1–6).

17:5, 6 Abram . . . Abraham: This name change is significant. Abram means "Exalted Father." Abraham means "Father of Many"—a direct reflection of his new role. The new name is unequivocally a name of relationship with the living God, to whom Abram had turned from idols (1 Thess. 1:9).

17:7 The Abrahamic **covenant** (12:1–3) is the foundation upon which all later divine covenants with God's people are based. **Everlasting** means the covenant would last through all time. **to be God to you:** With these remarkable words, God pledged His ongoing relationship with the people of Abraham (2 Sam. 7: 14; Is. 52:11; Ezek. 37:26, 27; 2 Cor. 6:14—7:1). This was later celebrated in the creed of Israel, the great *Shema* (Deut. 6:4; Ps. 100:3). **Descendants** is from the Hebrew word for seed; it may mean an individual person as well as a people (3:15; 15:3, 5, 13, 18).

17:8, 9 The promise clearly included the Israelite people *and* **the land** (Canaan). The two are linked in the language of the covenant in ch. 15. Even though God removed Israel more than once from the land; He promised them ultimate possession of Canaan. It is **an everlasting possession.** The same word used of God's covenant (v. 7) is used of the land.

17:10, 11 Circumcision means "cutting around," a minor operation that removes the foreskin from the male organ.

17:12, 13 An **eight**-day-old boy and his immune system would be strong enough for the operation, but he would be too young to remember the pain. **or bought with money:** The regulation extended to slaves and foreigners in the community of Israel. Thus circumcision was the distinctive sign of all men in the household.

17:14 There is something of a pun in the expression **cut off.** Any man who did not accept circumcision would be cut off from the community. Some have thought that this section of Scripture concerns only the external act of circumcision, but we know God's concern to be greater (Deut. 10:12–20). Circumcision—an outward sign—stood for a thorough commitment to God—an inward reality. Hence the apostle Paul demands that the heart be circumcised to God (Rom. 2:25–29).

17:15 Sarai . . . Sarah: Both names mean "Princess." Like the name change from Abram to Abraham (vv. 4, 5), the new name accompanied a new relationship with God.

17:16 bless her: The Lord's blessing was for Sarah as well as Abraham (12:1–3). A summary of the language used for Abraham in vv. 6–8 is used of her in these verses. The writer to the Hebrews also celebrated Sarah's faithfulness to the Lord (Heb. 11:11).

17:17 Fell on his face recalls the words of v. 3. Abraham's laugh is unexpected and shocking but completely understandable! For twenty-four years Abraham had heard, and believed, the same promise: one day he would become the father of a son who would found the nation of promise. He had tried to force the birth of a legitimate heir (chs. 15; 16), but God had assured him that the true heir would not be an adopted slave (15:4) nor the child of a surrogate mother (16:11, 12). But now, after nearly a quarter of a century and at the age of ninety-nine (17:1), Abraham had reached his limit. Even if Sarah were to conceive now, she would be ninety when the baby was born and he would be one hundred! At this point it seemed as though the whole thing might be a joke. And so at last he **laughed.**

17:18 Abraham's plea shows his love for his son **Ishmael** and his desire that in some tangible way the covenant promise of God would finally come to pass.

17:19 Isaac means "Laughter" (21:1–6).

17:20 God had **blessed** Ishmael before he was born (16:11, 12) and here He renewed and amplified the blessing. As the Hebrew people would have twelve tribes, so Ishmael's people would also have **twelve** families (25:12–18).

17:21 Isaac whom Sarah shall bear: The promise was plain. The father and mother were named, the child was named, and the time was named.

17:22 God went up: We sometimes read of the Lord coming down from heaven; here we read of Him returning there. Such language is expressive of God's holiness, transcendence, and wonder (Ps. 113:4–6).

17:23–27 Abraham took Ishmael: Again we see Abraham completely obey the command

of the Lord (12:4; 22:3). On the very day he received the command from God, he did just as the Lord commanded. All the males in his household from little boys to aged men were treated alike.

18:1–15 God reaffirmed His covenant with Abraham, reconfirming His promise to Sarah. This section is also a part of the complex of texts that make up the Abrahamic covenant (15:1–21, note).

18:1 This is the fifth time **the LORD** appeared to Abraham since he had come into the land of Canaan. (1) The first was the appearance at the altar Abram built in Shechem when he first entered the land (12:7). (2) The second was after Lot had separated from Abram when they came back to Canaan from Egypt (13:14–17). (3) The third followed Abram's heroic rescue of Lot from the league of invading kings and the subsequent encounter with Melchizedek (15:1–21). (4) The fourth came thirteen years after the birth of Ishmael, when the Lord renewed His covenant with Abraham and instituted the rite of circumcision (17:1–22). **Mamre** was one of Abram's allies in his battle against the invading kings from Mesopotamia (14:13). The place name Mamre was probably associated with a personal name. This region came to be known as Hebron (13:18; 23:17). **in the heat of the day:** The southern desert or the Negev (12:9) can become very hot in the summer, reaching above

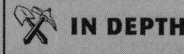 **IN DEPTH** | **Circumcision**

The rite of circumcision (Gen. 17:10) became a powerful, enduring symbol of God's covenant relationship with Abraham and his offspring.

Technically speaking, circumcision refers to the surgical removal of a male's foreskin. The procedure was widely practiced in the ancient world, including the Egyptian and Canaanite cultures. But they performed the rite at the beginning of puberty as an initiation into manhood. By contrast, the Hebrews circumcised infant boys as a sign of their responsibility to serve God as His special, holy people in the midst of a pagan world.

God instructed Abraham to circumcise every male child in his household, including servants (17:11) as a visible, physical sign of the covenant between the Lord and His people. Any male not circumcised was to be "cut off from his people" and regarded as a covenant breaker (17:14). The custom was performed on the eighth day after birth (17:12), at which time a name was given to the son (Luke 1:59; 2:21). In the early history of the Hebrews, the rite was performed by the father but eventually was carried out by a specialist.

The Hebrew people came to take great pride in circumcision. In fact, it became a badge of their spiritual and national superiority. This attitude fostered a spirit of exclusivism instead of compassion to reach out to other nations as God intended. Gentiles came to be regarded as the "uncircumcision," a term of disrespect implying that non-Jewish peoples were outside the circle of God's love.

Eventually the terms "circumcised" and "uncircumcised" became charged with emotion, as is plain from the discord the issue brought about centuries later in the early church (Gal. 2:12).

110° F. People usually did hard, physical work early in the morning or late in the afternoon.

18:2–3 Verse 1 states that it was the Lord who appeared to Abraham; v. 2 speaks of **three men;** v. 13 suggests that one of these men was the Lord. Who were the other two? Probably attending angels; each of the three visitors looked like men, but one was even greater than angels (19:1). The writer of Hebrews used this account to encourage hospitality to strangers, "for by so doing some have unwittingly entertained angels" (Heb. 13:2). Abraham's words **My Lord** suggests that he suspected the identity of the visitors, but perhaps he was not sure until later of the full significance of the event.

18:4–6 Abraham hurried: His rapidity of motion is remarkable for a man his age, and for "the heat of the day" (v. 1)

18:7 Tender and good point to "an exceptionally fine calf." In biblical times, one could not carve out a steak and then put the rest in the freezer! When a calf was slaughtered for a meal, it was for a feast (Luke 15:23) and had to be consumed in its entirety or the meat would quickly go bad (Prov. 9:1–4). Abraham and Sarah are pictured here as preparing a wonderful feast for their divine guest(s).

18:8 butter and milk and the calf: Because of a misunderstanding of a passage in Torah, later Jewish people determined that it was sinful to eat milk products with meat products. Strangely, this became one of the most deeply imbedded ideas in traditional post-biblical Judaism. But it is based on an erroneous interpretation of the Bible. The texts in question prohibit boiling a young goat in its mother's milk (Ex. 23:19; 34:26; Deut. 14:21). The passage actually prohibits an odious practice the Canaanites did to appease their gods. It appears that they would boil a goat doe's first kid alive in its mother's milk with the hope that the goat doe would have many kids in subsequent years. These texts had nothing to do with dietary laws; they regulated the religious practices of sacrifice. The feast that Abraham and Sarah served to their mysterious guests clearly includes both milk and meat products being served together. No prohibition of mixing the two is implied here, or in any other biblical passage.

18:9 Where is Sarah: Although the focus of God's promise in ch. 17 was on Abraham, the focus here is on Sarah.

18:10 Sarah your wife shall have: The wording was important because the couple had tried in the past to achieve the fulfillment of God's promise (chs. 15; 16).

 **IN COMPARISON** | **Barrenness**

Sarah laughed at the thought of bearing children at such an advanced age (Gen. 18:11, 12). But she may have laughed more out of pain than surprise, for in the ancient world to be barren, as she was, was considered a curse (Gen. 16:2; 20:17, 18; Luke 1:25). It was even considered grounds for divorce.

Several women in Scripture illustrate the predicament of the childless woman. Yet it's interesting that each of those named eventually gave birth to a child.

Sarah (Gen. 16:1, 2; 18:11, 12; 21:6, 7)	Used her maid Hagar as a surrogate childbearer, but then rejected both Hagar and the child, Ishmael; eventually gave birth to Isaac, changing laughter of pain to laughter of joy.
Rebekah (Gen. 25:21)	Conceived after her husband Isaac prayed to the Lord on her behalf; gave birth to twins, Esau and Jacob
Rachel (Gen. 29:31—30:24)	Driven by despair, used her maid Bilhah to compete with the other wife of her husband Jacob, her older sister Leah; eventually gave birth to Joseph and later Benjamin, whose birth caused her death.
Manoah's wife (Judg. 13)	Told by God that she would conceive a son who would be a Nazirite; gave birth to Samson, a judge of Israel.
Hannah (1 Sam. 1)	Desperately prayed for a son, whom she vowed to dedicate to the Lord; gave birth to Samuel, a judge of Israel.
Elizabeth (Luke 1:5–25, 57–66)	Conceived after her husband Zacharias was promised a son who would be the forerunner to the Messiah; gave birth to John the Baptist.

18:11 had passed the age of child-bearing: The text uses three phrases to describe the advanced age of Abraham and Sarah, with a special focus on the fact that Sarah had ceased to menstruate.

18:12 therefore Sarah laughed: She acted like Abraham had on an earlier occasion (17:17). She knew the facts of life, but she would soon be greatly surprised by the One who determined them.

18:13 the LORD said: Here the text makes it plain that the Lord Himself was one of the three guests. **Why did Sarah laugh:** This is one of the most wonderfully human passages in the Bible. The woman of faith, like her husband, had believed for years in God's promise. But now she found her faith stretched to the limit. God knew she had laughed.

18:14 Is anything too hard for the LORD: That is, there is no wonder that God cannot do. The verb for "too hard" (Heb. *pale'*) is a term of "wonder-working." One of the names for the Coming One is "Wonder-Working (Heb. *pele'*, a noun) Counselor" (Is. 9:6). **At the appointed time:** This section makes much of the fact that God chose the timing (Gen. 17:21; Eccl. 3:9–11). **time of life:** A reference to the length of pregnancy.

18:15 Afraid of being found out, Sarah **denied** that she had laughed. In His mercy God did not punish her, as He had not punished Abraham who also laughed. (17:17). But neither did He allow her embarrassed denial to stand. She *had* laughed. Sarah would laugh again, but that time it would be in joy rather than disbelief (21:1–7).

18:16 In 19:1 two of these **men** are called angels. **looked toward Sodom:** This verse begins the account of God's judgment on the sinful cities of Sodom and Gomorrah. **and Abraham went with them:** Abraham's hospitality enabled him to talk further with the living God.

18:17, 18 the LORD said: When this phrase is compared with 18:1, 2, 13, 16; 19:1, we come to the conclusion that two of the guests of Abraham and Sarah were angels and the third was none other than the living God! **Shall I hide:** The language of God in this section lets us "hear his thoughts," as if He were a man reflecting on the fact that Abraham had a vested interest in the city of Sodom because Lot lived there (14:12; 19:1).

18:19 for I have known him: The language here speaks of the intimate relationship, which motivates the Lord to accomplish His purpose in Abraham (22:12). **to do righteousness and justice:** One idea in two words—"genuine righteousness" (Mic. 3:1; 4:8).

18:20 The outcry against Sodom and Gomorrah suggests a moral center in the universe; the outrageous sins of these cities are an affront to the righteousness of God (19:4–8).

18:21 I will go down now: This picturesque way of speaking of the omniscience of the Lord (His all-embracing knowledge) heightens the sense of wonder (11:5). There is nothing that God does not know, although we may say that He "comes down" to see "what is going on" in His earth (Ps. 113:4–6).

18:22 stood before the LORD: An intercessor, pleading for the salvation of others.

18:23 The exchange between Abraham and God serves as a dramatic *theodicy,* a justification of the Lord's ways. Abraham's great concern, of course, was for his nephew Lot and his family (14:12; 19:1).

18:24 fifty righteous: That Abraham

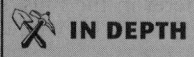 **IN DEPTH** ## Sodom and Gomorrah

- Two of the five "cities of the plain" (Gen. 13:12) at the southern base of the Dead Sea in a fertile area that was said to be like Eden (13:10).
- Sodom means "place of lime," Gomorrah means "submersion."
- Notorious in the Bible and elsewhere for wickedness and rebellion against God (for example, 2 Pet. 2:6)
- Area chosen by Lot, Abraham's nephew, as the place to graze his flocks and pitch his tent (Gen. 13:11).
- Judged by God for a variety of sins, including failure to care for the poor and needy despite incredible wealth (Ezek. 16:49), and for sexual immorality (Jude 7).
- Destroyed by brimstone and fire that rained from the sky (Gen. 19:24, 25). The region is still barren, even though it was once "well watered everywhere" (13:10).
- Site of frequent earthquakes and other geological events. Nearby repositories of salt, asphalt, and sulphur are abundant.

begins with a fairly low number may indicate that the overwhelming majority of the city of Sodom were wicked.

18:25 far be it from You: There is in Jewish tradition a boldness of expression to the Lord based on a strong sense of faith in Him and a confidence in Him that ultimately He is good (Ps. 100:5). When the famous question **Shall not the Judge of all the earth do right** is turned into an assertion it becomes the bedrock of faith in the justice of God (1 John 1:9). The Judge of all the earth will do right!

18:26 That the Lord would **spare the city** for the sake of fifty righteous men (later for the sake of ten, v. 32) is a mark of His extraordinary grace.

18:27–33 Abraham was determined to go on bargaining, but he knew that he was arguing with God. So he went one step at a time, pleading the case for the **righteous** in smaller and smaller numbers: from **forty-five** down to **ten.** Perhaps Abraham thought there were at least ten righteous persons in the city; but alas, there were not (as the report of ch. 19 shows).

19:1 **Lot's** fortunes had gone very well. The **gate** of a city was the place where the town elders met (Ruth 4:1). Lot had become so enmeshed in the life of the city that he had become a ruling elder. **bowed himself:** A term commonly used for the worship of God (22:5; 24:26); here it describes Lot's act of reverence to special guests (compare 18:2). The angels appeared as men (18:2), and Lot greeted them as such.

19:2 My lords is a greeting of respect for special visitors. **your servant's house:** Lot's generous offer of hospitality may have been motivated out of kindness toward them as well as his sense of the dangers his city might hold for them.

19:3 Feast here indicates much drinking as well as eating.

19:4 The men of Sodom were aggressive homosexuals, bent on raping innocent travelers. Under the circumstances, Lot showed great courage by inviting his guests to stay at his house under his protection.

19:5 The Hebrew verb for **know** is ordinarily used of normal sexual relations between a male and female (4:1). Here it is used to describe the perversion of homosexual sex between men (Rom. 1:18–32, especially vv. 26, 27). The term sodomite comes from this passage.

19:6–8 Lot's plight was severe; he had invited guests into his home for protection and was now in danger of seeing them abused by an unruly mob. Lot's desperation led him to risk the lives of his own **two daughters** to protect the lives of strangers from the mob. We can see

why an outcry from the city had gone up to the Lord (18:20, 21).

19:9, 10 Stand back: The crazed crowd was now about to attack Lot, whom they resented as an outsider even though he had risen to a position of prominence in the city.

19:11 Those who were morally blind were now stricken with physical **blindness** by the angelic guests (read about a similar angelic blight in 2 Kin. 6:18). Only the confusion and panic of these wicked men spared Lot and his family from vicious assault.

19:12 The angelic guests had completed their search and were now about to bring down the judgment of God on the city. In mercy, they offered an escape to Lot's immediate family. There simply were not sufficient righteous persons in the city for it to be spared (v. 13; 18:24–33).

19:13–15 Arise can mean "make haste."

19:16 Lot **lingered.** He had mixed feelings about the destruction that was to come. Lot and his family needed to be propelled from their home by physical force. The verb for **took hold** means "to seize." **the Lord** being merciful: This is the whole point of the story. God could have destroyed the city of Sodom with no word to Lot or Abraham (18:17). But because of God's mercy here (Heb. *hemlâ,* from the verb *hamal,* "to spare," "to have compassion"), His angels grabbed Lot and his family and brought them forcefully to safety.

19:17–19 There is something pathetic about Lot's words **and I die.** All "hell" was breaking loose and he was worried about a possible wild animal in the mountains! Lot was quite unstable. The only reason he was being spared was because of God's love for his uncle Abraham (vv. 27, 28).

19:20, 21 this city: Despite the gravity of the situation, Lot was still bargaining. He could not see himself as a wanderer in the hills, so even a little city was preferable to a life with no home at all.

19:22 Zoar: "Insignificant in Size."

19:23–26 Sun had risen: Throughout the account, special attention is given to time. The rain of **brimstone and fire** may be explained in a couple of ways. It is possible that God used a volcanic eruption or some similar kind of natural disaster. Then, the miracle would be in the Lord's timing and in the narrow escape of Lot and his family. See Ex. 14 for a similar possibility. It is also possible that the destruction of these cities was an act of judgment outside the normal range of natural occurrences.

19:26 The command was clear, not to look back or linger (v. 17). Lot's wife disobeyed and looked back. By implication, she was reluctant to leave. **pillar of salt:** Her destruction was sudden. Nothing was left of her but a mineral heap. Jesus referred to her in His teaching on the sudden destruction that will come in the last days. "Remember Lot's wife," Jesus warned (Luke 17:32).

19:27, 28 On the very **morning** that the cities were destroyed, Abraham looked on from a distance and saw the destruction. When he saw the **smoke,** he must have known the truth: there were not even ten righteous in the city (18:32).

19:29 Part of the reason for God's grace to Lot was that **God remembered Abraham.** Lot could barely tolerate the wickedness in the city (2 Pet. 2:7, 8), but only he felt that way. If it were not for Abraham, Lot would have died with the other inhabitants.

19:30, 31 Lot had begged the angels to give him a safe haven in the little city of **Zoar** (vv. 18–22), a request they granted. But following the devastation of the cities of the plain, Lot did not even feel safe in this city. So he lived in a **cave.**

19:32 Lot's daughters now conspired together to make their father drunk so that he would have sexual relations with them. **the**

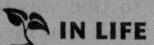 **IN LIFE** | # The Legacy of Sodom and Gomorrah

Throughout Scripture and in countless extrabiblical works, Sodom and Gomorrah and the other cities of the plain (Gen. 13:12) stand as a symbol of divine judgment for collective wickedness. What was once a well-watered, fertile region is today barren, full of tar pits, mounds of asphalt, and marsh. These ill-fated cities remind us that wickedness will not go unpunished. They also show that God not only judges sinful individuals, such as Lot's wife (19:26), but also entire cities and their surroundings.

However, the story is not all bad news. After the tragic end of Sodom and Gomorrah, "God remembered Abraham" (19:29). When we remember the patriarch's righteous example, several lessons of the story become clear:

- *Prayer makes a difference.* Abraham shows us that it is legitimate to pray for cities, as he did (18:22–33). We may not always be able to go to a city, but we can still pray for it. Abraham prayed more for a place than for individual people. He prayed persistently for an entire city, believing that nothing was too hard for the Lord (18:14). Moreover, he prayed for justice in the city, as well as for its peace and salvation. His example challenges us to ask: Are we praying for cities today? If so, what are we asking God to do? Save the city, or judge it?
- *People count.* Ten believing persons living in Sodom could have saved it (18:32). In other words, the presence of righteous persons acting as salt and light can preserve places where evil runs rampant. Even though Sodom was filled with wickedness, God would have saved it if He had found even a handful of righteous people. He spared Zoar, for the sake of one righteous man—Lot (19:16–22; 2 Pet. 2:6, 7). As God's people, are we living righteously in the places to which He has called us?
- *God is sovereign.* God's decision to destroy four cities of the plain but to preserve the fifth, Zoar, shows that He is ultimately in control. Let there be no mistake: God does not want to destroy cities or their systems and people (2 Pet. 3:9); but He can, and will. He decides when, where, and how judgment will fall. On the other hand, God can rescue people from evil places when and if He wishes. We might ask: Do we trust and respect the sovereignty of God? Do we live with a perspective that He is ultimately in control? Do we act as though we are accountable to Him?
- *Pride goes before a fall.* Sodom was destroyed not only because of sexual sin (Gen. 19:1–17; Jude 7), but because it had pride and a surplus of wealth, yet failed to care for its poor and needy (Ezek. 16:48–50). Its example challenges us: What are we doing with the resources God has put under our control?
- *Fleeing from the city does not avoid sin; it only spreads it around.* The behavior of Lot and his daughters after fleeing from Sodom shows that sin is not confined to the city; they exported Sodom-like immorality to the hinterlands (Gen. 19:19–22, 30–36). Are we running from the city in order to "escape" its problems and evils? Is it possible that God wants us to stay and live as His representatives of righteousness?

INSIGHT | **The Fear of the Lord**

Interestingly, the OT has no word for "religion." But the phrases "the fear of the Lord" and "the fear of God" come close to expressing what we today mean by religion. The phrases take into account a lifestyle in which people take seriously an all-wise, all-powerful, and all-righteous God who holds them responsible for their behavior.

lineage of our father: We can hardly approve of their action, yet their desperation was real. Their husbands had died and they were not likely to remarry. Their mother was also dead and they judged their father unlikely to remarry and have more children. Should they die child-less, there would be no one to carry on their family name. For the peoples of biblical cultures, this was an overwhelming loss (ch. 38).

19:33–35 and he did not know: The nar-rator inserts this phrase twice (v. 35) to protect Lot. This was not deliberate incest on his part; the daughters alone were responsible for what happened.

19:36–38 The shameful act of incest led to the births of two sons who would later greatly trouble Israel, **Moab** and **Ben-Ammi.**

20:1 Abraham's deception about Sarah in the city of **Gerar** was later to be repeated by his son Isaac (ch. 26). This is an example of a son taking after his father. The present story is also a replay of Abraham's earlier mistakes in Egypt (12:10–20).

20:2 Sarah was the half **sister** of Abraham (v. 12). **Abimelech . . . took her:** This action put Sarah in the king's harem, but not in his bed. Because of her advanced age, it is probable that Sarah was more desirable to Abimelech for her wealth than for her physical appearance.

20:3 Presumably, Abimelech was a pagan king. Yet God warned him of the wrong that he was about to commit. This is another instance of the protective care that the Lord gives His people (Gen. 31:24; compare Num. 22:12, 20). **a man's wife:** The Hebrew words speak of Sarah and Abraham on a level of equality and dignity. Both are spoken of as lords or nobles, literally "a noble wife of a noble man."

20:4, 5 Lord, will You slay a righteous nation also: Abimelech had not even touched Sarah; he did not want to die for a sin he had not committed. He argued that his actions so far were innocent. They were based on what Abraham and Sarah had told him.

20:6 This passage emphasizes the **dream** state Abimelech was in. The Lord's response to him was one of grace; God had kept the king from touching Sarah.

20:7 This is the first use of the term **prophet** in the Bible. The term indicates more a relationship to God than an ability to speak for Him. Abraham's relationship to God was the basis for God's command that Sarah be restored to her husband.

20:8–10 The gravity of the situation must have touched the king so strongly that his fear quickly spread to his family and servants. Abim-elech's questions of Abraham are especially touching: **What have you done to us?** is fol-lowed by the reverse **How have I offended you?** This last question uses the verb meaning "to sin" (Heb. *hata'*), a word that fits more strongly with the noun to follow in **a great sin** (the Hebrew noun is from the same root as the verb). His last question of Abraham might be paraphrased, "What were you thinking?"

20:11–13 Abraham gave two reasons for his actions. The first was based on his assumption that he was in hostile territory. That is, with **no fear of God,** there would be no justice among the people. A king set on doing whatever he wanted might seize Sarah as a first step toward subjugating Abraham and taking over his prop-erty. Second, Sarah was **truly my sister.** The marriages of the family of Terah were very close. In this patrician society, the marriages of close relatives was regarded as a sign of rank. Abraham and Sarah apparently agreed that she would invoke the plea that she was his sister wherever they might happen to be (v. 13). Later, the Law would prohibit the marriage of people so closely related.

20:14–16 Abimelech made a significant payment to Abraham in silver in order to com-pensate **Sarah**'s hardship. His words **your brother** may have been sarcastic. The Hebrew verb translated as **rebuked** can merely mean "vindicated." This verb is used in legal termi-nology to describe the settlement of a dispute.

20:17 So Abraham prayed to God: How-ever the situation began, it ended in mercy with Abraham acting as a priest for Abimelech before the true and living God. In this way, the people of Gerar learned about the Lord, as had hap-pened in Egypt years earlier (12:10–20).

20:18 the LORD had closed up all the

41 **Genesis 21:10**

wombs: Three things are indicated by these words. First, the stay of Abraham and Sarah had been prolonged in Gerar before Sarah's identity became known. Some months would have had to pass before the people realized that they were no longer conceiving at normal rates. This means that Sarah had lived in the harem of the king for several months. Second, the Lord reached out to these people in a way they would find difficult to resist; the wish to procreate was relentless in the ancient world, as these accounts consistently emphasize. Third, God graciously protected Sarah—and Abraham. The chapter ends with irony. Because of God's desire to protect Sarah, He had closed the wombs of the women of Abimelech's house. Soon the Lord would open Sarah's womb to give her a child, long after she was too old to conceive naturally (21:1, 2).

21:1 And the Lord visited Sarah: The Bible stresses that the Lord causes conception; that children are a gift of the Lord (Ps. 127:3). The verb *visit* is an extraordinary choice here, because it means that the Lord entered directly into the affairs of His people. This was what He did for Sarah **as He had said . . . as He had spoken:** These two phrases speak of the exact fulfillment of His promise to Abraham (17:21) and Sarah (18:14).

21:2 It appears that **Sarah conceived** while she and Abraham were living in Gerar (20:1; 21:22). The contrast is wonderful: God had closed the wombs of the family of Abimelech (20:18), and now He opened Sarah's womb. **bore Abraham a son:** A great fact that the Bible elsewhere celebrates (25:19; Heb. 11:11). **in his old age:** The writer of Hebrews says Abraham was "as good as dead" (Heb. 11:12). What a miracle this was! To both Abraham (17:21) and Sarah (18:14), God had emphasized the concept of His **set time.**

21:3 Isaac means "He (God) Is Laughing (Now)." At one time Abraham had laughed at the improbability of having a son in his old age (17:17); Sarah had laughed too (18:12). But now, with the birth of the child, laughter took on its happier meaning. Sarah got the joke (vv. 5, 6)!

21:4 circumcised his son: Abraham's pattern of obedience to the Lord continued unchanged (12:4; 17:23; 22:3). The sign of the covenant was most important for the son of promise (17:9–14).

21:5 one hundred years old: (Compare 12:4; 16:16; 17:1.) Amusingly, Abraham was precisely the age that caused him to laugh aloud (17:17).

21:6 Among the many name jokes in the Bible, few are as wonderful as this one; the words for **laugh** in this verse are related to the name Isaac (v. 3).

21:7 nurse children: Wondrously, this woman of ninety (17:17) now had breasts filled with milk and her arms full with a child! In the theology of the Bible, Isaac's birth suggests the promise of an even greater miracle, the miracle-Son, Jesus.

21:8 weaned: In biblical times children were nursed through the toddler period. The life of Isaac was to be marked by celebration, **a feast.** As glad parents, Abraham and Sarah rejoiced in each major step of his life. This makes the story of Isaac's near death (ch. 22) all the more suspenseful.

21:9 The Hebrew verb for **scoffing** is related to the name for Isaac (21:3, 5). Here is a bad turn on a wonderful joke. Young Ishmael, now perhaps seventeen, was mocking the joy of Sarah and Abraham in their young son.

21:10 Sarah's greatest moment came at the birth of her child; this moment was one of her worst. It is understandable, of course, that she would find Ishmael's derision hurtful even as she had Hagar's (16:5). But even in that culture it was reprehensible to send Ishmael away. When a surrogate wife had borne a son to one's husband, that mother and child could not be dismissed even if the first wife subsequently gave birth to a son. This partly explains Abraham's reluctance to do what Sarah demanded (v. 11). What is more, he still loved **his son** Ishmael (16:15; 17:18).

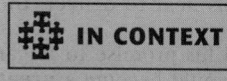 **IN CONTEXT** | **Gaining a Son from a Slave**

Ancient marriage contracts obligated wives to provide a son. Contracts dating from the mid-second millennium B.C. have been discovered in the city of Nuzi specifying that if a wife bore no male children she had the obligation to provide a child via a female servant. A child thus born would be considered the child of the wife, which meant that a barren wife had fulfilled her marriage obligation. Hence Sarai's words, "Perhaps I shall obtain a child by her" (Gen. 16:2).

Abram's reluctance to send Hagar and Ishmael away (21:9–11) reflects another aspect of the Nuzi tablets. Servants who provided such children were not supposed to be sent away but treated favorably. Thus it took the voice of God (21:12) to convince Abram to listen to Sarai's desire.

21:11, 12 but God said: This is the sixth time Abraham received a direct word from the Lord since coming to the land of Canaan. **listen to her voice:** Abraham needed to hear God give him permission to send Hagar and Ishmael from his home. **In Isaac** alone would the principal covenant be fulfilled. Ishmael had his own promise (v. 13; compare 16:10–12), but nothing God promised to Ishmael would replace His promise to Isaac.

21:13, 14 This scene must have been exceedingly difficult for Abraham. He had no idea that another **morning** in his life would be even worse (22:3). **Bread and a skin of water** are meager provisions. The skin refers to a water bag made of animal skin. **sent her away:** Years before, Hagar had had to leave the same household while pregnant with Ishmael (16:6). **wilderness of Beersheba** (v. 31): Later there would be a city built in this place; in this early period it was merely a region for herding sheep and goats. Isaac was later to rediscover water in this region (26:33).

21:15 water . . . used up: It would not take long for the two refugees to use up their meager provisions.

21:16 let me not see: Despite her sometimes mean spirit against Sarah, Hagar loved her son. The thought that she was about to lose her son to the desert heat was unbearable for her.

21:17 God heard: What wonderful words these are! There is no pain of His people that He does not see or hear about (Is. 40:27, 28; Heb. 2:10, 18; 4:15). God was near to deliver; the child would not die.

21:18 God renewed his promise to Hagar and Ishmael; Ishmael would become a **great nation** (16:10–12).

21:19 Hagar was so overcome with grief that she was unaware of the provision of water right before her. God showed **a well of water.** How fitting that the promise of God would again be beside a provision of water (Gen. 16:7, 14). Often in the pages of the OT, a spring or well of water is a symbol of spiritual salvation as well as physical deliverance (Is. 12:3; Jer. 2:13).

21:20 God's promise was realized in Ishmael's life. He became **an archer;** that is, he learned to hunt.

21:21 wife: Hagar made sure that Ishmael married an Egyptian, one of her own people, much as Abraham's servant searched for a wife for Isaac from among his parents' people (24:4).

21:22 Abimelech: It appears from this verse that Abraham and Sarah were still living in the region of Gerar (20:15). **Phichol:** This commander of the army is also mentioned in the later encounter with Isaac (26:26), unless the name is a hereditary term, as perhaps was that of Abimelech (26:8). **God is with you:**

With these words, Abimelech and Phichol introduced their desire to form a treaty with Abraham.

21:23, 24 swear to me by God: This kind of oath was a complete, binding obligation (22:16). God would be witness to the act and a witness against anyone who might break it. **kindness:** This exceedingly important term (Heb. *hesed*) sometimes translated "loyal love" is often used in the Psalms to describe God's character (Ps. 100:5). Here we see its proper context in a binding relationship. The term basically describes covenant loyalty (24:12).

21:25, 26 It turned out that there was a dispute between the two concerning a **well.** For those who tended sheep and goats, water rights and wells mattered a great deal. **Abimelech** agreed to settle the issue promptly.

21:27 This is the first use of the word **covenant** for a parity treaty (15:18). A parity treaty is a binding agreement between two equals, similar to today's business contract. At 26:28 there is a parity treaty between Abimelech and Isaac, and at 31:43–55 there is a covenant between Jacob and Laban.

21:28–31 Abraham made the occasion all the more memorable by his presentation of **seven ewe lambs** to Abimelech. The Hebrew number seven is similar in sound to the verb meaning "to swear" (v. 24). Thus **Beersheba** would be the well where they swore and the well of the seven ewe lambs. In the next generation the ritual would be repeated with a similar meaning given to the site (26:33).

21:32, 33 The hope was that the **tamarisk tree** would long mark the spot of this major treaty. **called on the name:** As in 12:8, Abraham did more than just pray to the Lord; he made proclamation in the Lord's name, telling everyone about **the Lord,** the Everlasting God, the Master of eternity. Not only does He live forever, but He meets the needs of His people for all eternity.

21:34 Although Abraham had been promised the whole of the land for his posterity (Gen. 12:7; 15:18–21), in his own life he lived under agreements with others in their **land** (Heb. 11:13–16). The name Palestine comes from the word for Philistine.

22:1–19 Without question, this narrative is one of the most shocking and memorable in the whole Bible. And yet in its outcome it is one of the finest texts describing the loyalty of the Lord to His covenant and to His servant Abraham. It also reveals remarkable faith on the part of Abraham, Sarah, and Isaac and points to the future sacrifice of God's only Son, Jesus.

22:1 after these things: A new story is about to begin (15:1). The term **God** includes the definite article ("the God"; Gen. 6:2; 27:28;

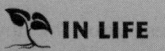 **IN LIFE** | ## Kill My Own Son?

It seems incredible that God would tell Abraham to "take . . . your son, your only son Isaac, whom you love," and offer him up as a sacrifice (Gen. 22:2). What sort of God would ask such a thing? What sort of God would test a man's faith with such a weighty request?

It was a severe test of Abraham's faith. Perhaps most of us would have failed the test. We might even have rejected God as cruel and bloodthirsty. But Abraham believed God. Though the sacrifice of Isaac seemed to go against God's promise of an heir, Abraham believed that God would still fulfill His Word, even if it required Him to raise Isaac from the dead (Rom. 4:17).

The request was also a harsh lesson that all of life comes from and belongs to God (Gen. 2:7; Job 27:3; 33:4). In essence, life is merely on loan to us, both as parents and children. God can ask for its return at any time. So in that respect, the request to slay Isaac was similar to the difficult period that Abram and Sarai endured as they waited for the birth of this very son (Gen. 18:1–15; 21:1–7). Their lives and the lives of any children they might have were in the hands of God.

Let there be no mistake: God abhors human sacrifice, as many OT passages make clear (Lev. 18:21; 20:2; Deut. 12:31; Ps. 106:35–38; Ezek. 20:30, 31). So when Abraham was about to slay His son, God stopped him short of the actual sacrifice and provided an alternative in Isaac's place. It proved to Abraham that his faith was well-placed: God is the God of mercy.

He is also the God of wisdom. He sometimes makes what to us may seem like strange requests. But if like Abraham we will believe and obey, He will reward our faith with His goodness and righteousness.

31:11; 46:3; 48:15). This is a way of indicating that the "Genuine Deity" or the "True God" is making these demands, not a false god or a demon. Note that the same use of the definite article occurs in 41:32 twice. This is the seventh time that God revealed Himself to Abraham since Abraham came to the land of Canaan. God **tested Abraham** in order to give Abraham an opportunity to show his true character. The verb does not suggest entrapment to harm or to destroy Abraham and his faith, but to refine him, to allow him to display his inner character. The words "do not lead us into temptation" in Matt. 6:13 suggest thee same idea.

22:2 only son: Abraham had one son by Hagar (ch. 16), and as we learn later he had six sons by Keturah (ch. 25). But only Isaac was *uniquely born* (the same idea is in the description of Jesus as the "only begotten," John 1:18). Indeed, the Greek term for "only begotten" is used to describe Isaac in Heb. 11:17. The point is not that Abraham had no other children, but that this was the unique child in whom all the promises of God resided. But that wasn't the only reason God's command would test Abraham's faith; this was Isaac, the son who had brought God's "laughter" to Abraham and Sarah (21:12). **Moriah:** "Where the Lord Provides" or "Where the Lord Appears." **burnt offering:** Abraham was not simply to strike his son and wound him, and then nurse him back to health. He was commanded to go through the steps of offering a sacrifice that burned an

animal or person entirely. The toll of this command on Abraham and Sarah must have been enormous. What a poignant picture of what our God did to His unique Son for us!

22:3, 4 Nothing is said of Abraham's thoughts, or the thoughts of the boy's mother. All we read is the account of the father's complete obedience to God (12:4; 17:23; compare the complete obedience of Noah in 6:22; 7:5). Difficult, heavy tasks were usually done in the early **morning** because of the heat of the midday in this part of the world (18:1).

22:5 If the **young men** (servants) had accompanied Abraham and his son to the sacrificial site, they might have tried to restrain him from his awful deed. He told them to **stay** with the donkey, he and his son were on their way to **worship** the Lord. **we will come back:** In the Hebrew text, these words are even more arresting than in a translation. The three verbs all show a strong determination on the part of the speaker (12:2): "We are determined to go, we are determined to worship, we are determined to return." There are three possibilities for Abraham's speech: (1) he was lying to the servants to buy time; (2) he was suffering from delusion, and no longer speaking rationally; or (3) he believed that he *and the boy* would return. He had heard, many times, God's promise to create a nation through Isaac (12:1–3, 7; 13:14–17; 15:1–21; 17:1–22; 18:1–15). He still believed it. He had concluded that even if he had to destroy his son, God would bring him back from death (Heb. 11:17–19). Only in this way could Abraham have gone ahead with the task before him.

22:6 As Christ on His way to Golgotha to be crucified, the son of Abraham also bore an instrument of death on his back. The **fire** would be live coals in a clay pot of some kind. A special **knife** was used in sacrificial worship.

22:7 My father . . . where is the lamb: Isaac still did not know what Abraham planned to do.

22:8 for Himself: The wording is stronger in this order: "God Himself will provide." **went together:** These words appear again in v. 19.

22:9, 10 the place: The site of Moriah is significant (vv. 2–4, 14). **bound Isaac:** Jewish scholars call this text "the binding of Isaac." At this point, Isaac knew that he was the sacrificial victim. Surely he could have run away from his aged father! Yet, like the Savior on an even darker day (John 10:17, 18), he was willing to do his father's will (Mark 14:36).

22:11, 12 the Angel of the LORD: An appearance of God (16:7; compare 24:7; 48:16). At the last moment, God spoke to **Abraham** from heaven; twice He called out his name. **Do not lay your hand:** The words used demanded an instant response. Abraham was just about to strike his son, then God stopped his hand (15:1). **now I know:** Certainly God knew ahead of time how this event would end. But in these words, God stood beside his servant Abraham, experiencing each moment with him and applauding his complete trust (18:19). The term for **fear** means to hold God in awe; this is the central idea of piety in the Bible (Ex. 20:20; Prov. 1:7).

22:13 With his attention solely on the awful task at hand, Abraham had not seen the **ram** until he looked for it. In an amazing manner, his earlier words of God's provision came to pass (v. 8).

22:14 The wonderful name **The-LORD-Will-Provide** is developed from the faith statement of Abraham to Isaac in v. 8. Compare the name of faith that Hagar gave to the Lord, "The-God-Who-Sees" (16:13). As God provided a ram instead of Abraham's son, so one day He would provide His own Son! Moriah is where Jerusalem and later the temple were built. And it was at Jerusalem that the Savior would die.

22:15–18 This is one of the texts that contain the Abrahamic covenant (see list at 15:1–21)—God's unbreakable promise to create a nation through Isaac.

22:16 By Myself I have sworn ("sworn," Heb. *shaba'*) means "By Myself I swear" or "I bring Myself under complete obligation." When a man took an oath, it was considered unchangeable (25:33). When God took an oath,

His eternity guaranteed the fulfillment of His word.

22:17 blessing I will bless you: The doubling of these verbs and the ones that follow (**multiplying I will multiply**) is a Hebrew idiom that powerfully emphasizes the certainty of the action. **as the stars . . . as the sand:** This use of hyperbole or exaggeration on God's part (Gen. 15:5; 13:16) must have overwhelmed Abraham. In ancient walled cities, the structure protecting the **gate** was the most important; to control the gate was to control the city. Later, the blessing of her family on Rebekah would contain the same prayer for her (24:60).

22:18 At times the term **seed** refers to a large number of descendants (13:16); at other times it refers to one unique descendant, the Coming One (as here and in Gal. 3:16). Here it is a grand play on words: The seed was Isaac; and by extension the Jewish nation; and the Seed was also Jesus.

22:19 As he had said (v. 5), Abraham **returned** with his son, and they all **went together** (v. 8) back to **Beersheba**.

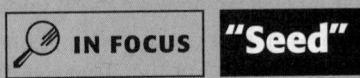

IN FOCUS "Seed"

(Heb. *zera'*) (Gen. 3:15; 13:15; 15:3; 22:18; 28:13; Ps. 89:4) Strong's #2233: The Hebrew word translated *seed* can literally mean a seed sown in the ground (1:11, 12) or figuratively one's offspring or descendants (13:15). The word can refer to a large group of people, such as the descendants of Abraham or the nation of Israel, or to an individual. In some parts of Genesis it refers specifically to the coming Messiah, as in God's promise that the woman's "Seed" would defeat the serpent (3:15; Num. 24:7; Is. 6:13; Gal. 3:16). As such, the term takes on great importance in the Bible: It is through Abraham's *seed*, both collectively in Israel and singularly in Christ, that God would reach out to save all people (15:3).

22:20–24 Milcah: The family of Nahor had first been noted at 11:29. It is touching to observe that there was correspondence between the families; but this genealogical notice also leads to the birth of **Rebekah**, who would figure significantly in the story to follow. This little piece is one of the family histories that help tie the Bible together.

23:1 Sarah 's 127 years allowed her to see her son Isaac reach adulthood.

23:2 Kirjath Arba means the "Village of Arba" or the "Village of Four" (Josh. 14:15). Abraham had lived for a while near **Hebron** at the location of some ancient terebinth trees (13:18; 18:1; 23:17). At this point the name **Canaan** would be particularly bitter to Abraham. None of the land was his. He had negotiated for water rights and herding privileges (21:22–34), but the land was not his; it still belonged to the Canaanites (12:6).

23:3 The Hittites had their principal center in Anatolia (modern Turkey). But there were some enclaves of Hittites (**sons of Heth**) in Canaan (15:20), and the region of Hebron was apparently one of them. It was with Hittites that Abraham negotiated to buy a burial spot for his beloved wife, Sarah.

23:4, 5 I am a foreigner and a visitor: Abraham was a "resident alien" in the land. His words were self-deprecating, to help him establish a bargaining position.

Abraham's posture followed the customs of the time (v. 12). Abraham was not willing to bury Sarah in a borrowed tomb; he wanted to have a place that would belong to his family long after his death. His words **meet with Ephron** indicated that he wanted to purchase some property, **the cave of Machpelah.** Ephron the Hittite responded to Abraham's request by generously offering to give him what he sought, plus the nearby field as well.

23:12, 13 I will give you money: He was not interested in the field, and he offered again to buy the cave. (Perhaps he believed a gift so easily given might as easily be withdrawn at a later time.) In any case, by money Abraham did not mean coins as we might think today. Coins were not invented until at least 650 B.C. Abraham was offering a generous weight of silver.

23:14, 15 The dialogue of the chapter is wonderful; it presents a step-by-step description

Photo by Howard Vos

Modern Hebron, successor to the ancient city of the same name where Abraham bought a burial cave for Sarah and his descendants (Gen. 23:19).

23:6 The sons of Heth (Hittites) responded with complimentary words. The adjective **mighty** is the term for deity (*elohim* as in 1:1). As an act of kindness, the Hittites let Abraham use one of their places for the **burial** of his dead family members.

23:7–11 Abraham stood up and bowed:

of the bargaining process. Ephron gave the purchase price, then seemed to dismiss it (**What is that between you and me?**).

23:16 Abraham weighed out the silver: He could have received the property without cost, but since he paid the agreed upon amount there could be no question at a later date.

23:17 Abraham had to purchase not only the **field** and the **cave,** but also the **trees.** This meant that he was responsible for the maintenance of these trees as well. All was done in the formal, legal manner of the time. The record is fascinating to read, but also noteworthy for this: the only land Abraham ever really possessed was a burial spot for his wife.

23:18–20 Abraham buried Sarah. Years later, Abraham would be buried in the same cave (25:10).

24:1–67 The passage tells how an unnamed servant of Abraham found a suitable wife for Isaac. The account is marked by a lingering style, with the loving details and repetition so treasured by the storytellers in Hebrew tradition. Above all it records the kind providence of the Lord toward His people.

24:1 The LORD had blessed Abraham in all things is a fulfillment of Gen. 12:2, 3, the original promise.

24:2 Some have thought **the oldest servant** to be Eliezer of 15:2 because of his high position over all that Abraham had.

24:3 swear by the LORD: Such an oath indicated how exceedingly important the matter was to Abraham. **from the daughters of the Canaanites:** This was not an issue of racism, as is sometimes thought—it was theological. The Canaanite peoples worshiped the false gods Baal and Asherah (15:16; compare Deut. 7:3).

24:4–7 The LORD God: The terms used of God in this chapter are extraordinarily rich, describing the strong faith not only of Abraham but also of his servant. Abraham repeated a major theme of God's covenant to him. His **descendants** would inherit the land (see list at 15:1–21). **His angel:** This phrase is grammatically equivalent to the expression "the Angel of the Lord." It is a way of referring to God's presence (Gen. 16:7; 22:11; 48:16).

24:8–10 The possession of **camels** in this ancient period was regarded as a mark of extraordinary wealth. **Mesopotamia** means "Aram of the Two Rivers." The location is northern Syria beyond the Euphrates (compare the location of Balaam's homeland, Num. 22:5; 23:7). The **city of Nahor** is known as Haran (11:31).

24:11 Traditionally, women drew water in the early morning or in the **evening** to avoid doing this heavy task during the heat of day.

24:12–14 O LORD God of my master Abraham: This language does not mean that the servant himself did not believe in the living God; rather, it was *because* of his faith that he prayed in this manner. The Lord had made His covenant with Abraham. The servant was making his appeal on the basis of God's covenant loyalty to Abraham, as is seen in his appeal to God's **kindness** (his covenant loyalty,

21:23). In the Psalms, this is the principal word used to describe God's "loyal love" (Ps. 100:5).

24:15 Rebekah's name may mean "Ensnaring Beauty." She was of the family circle of Abraham (22:20–23).

24:16–18 Such commentary on a woman's **beautiful** appearance is rare in the Bible (see the description of Sarai in 12:11; Rachel in 29:17; Joseph in 39:6; compare 1 Sam. 16:12). Her chastity is noted: **a virgin; no man had known her.** The word translated *virgin* is not a precise term; hence the clarification, "no man had known her."

24:19 I will draw water for your camels: This gesture went far beyond her social duties. This was precisely the proof that the servant had requested from the Lord.

24:20–22 The young woman must have been wondering what was happening to her

INSIGHT   **The Value of Gold**

Gold can be found in nature as a metal, either pure or mixed with silver or copper. It is easily worked and does not corrode. It has been used as a measure of value from early times and is a perennial symbol of wealth and rank (Gen. 24:22).

because expensive gifts, such as a **golden nose ring** and **two** (gold) **bracelets,** would not ordinarily be given to a stranger.

24:23 Whose daughter are you: In biblical times, a young woman's identity was closely tied to her father's (Ruth 2:5), and a married woman's to her husband's. After stating her family ties (v. 24; 22:20–23), Rebekah responded that there was plenty of room for him to lodge with them (v. 25).

24:24–26 Abraham's servant was overwhelmed by God's grace, so he **worshiped the LORD.** He prostrated himself to the ground (the meaning of worshiped; 19:1; 22:5). No wonder Abraham had so greatly trusted him (vv. 1–9).

24:27 Blessed be the LORD: In these and the following words, Abraham's servant gave God true, public praise, as is later to be found in the Book of Psalms (Ps. 105:1, 2). **Mercy** and **truth** together mean something like "the Lord's utterly unswerving loyalty." **being on the way, the Lord led me:** What an outstanding pairing of concepts! God did not lead someone who was being lazy but who was already actively pursuing the will of God.

24:28, 29 We tend to remember **Laban** from his subsequent dealings with Jacob (chs. 29—31). Here he appears to be a gentle servant of God, recognizing Abraham's servant with gracious hospitality (v. 31).

24:30–49 I will not eat shows the servant's enthusiasm. The Lord had done a marvel, and the servant wished to delay eating until he had told his great story to Rebekah's family. The servant's story continues with a dramatic flair, noting details of timing and activity.

24:50, 51 It is surprising that **Bethuel** the father was not more active in these proceedings (vv. 29–31). Perhaps he was aged or infirm; in any event, Laban, Rebekah's brother, seems to be the one making decisions. **The thing comes from the LORD**: In these words and in Laban's first responses to the servant of Abraham, v. 31, it appears that the family of Bethuel and Laban also worshiped the living God (11:27—12:4; Josh. 24:2). **Here is Rebekah:** Brother and father recognized the work of God and they responded graciously and immediately.

24:52 Before doing anything else, Abraham's servant **worshiped the LORD** by prostrating himself before God and by giving public acknowledgment of His provision (v. 26).

24:53–57 In the manner of the East and with the abundance that belonged to Abraham, the servant gave lovely and costly gifts of **jewelry,** first to Rebekah and then to her family. Again, the father is not mentioned.

24:58 Until now nothing had been said about Rebekah's desires, but her words **I will go** showed her willingness.

24:59 It was no easier for this family to send away their beloved daughter and sister **Rebekah** than it would be for us. This was an act of courage and faith in the Lord for all concerned.

24:60 they blessed Rebekah: In the customs of the ancient Near East, the family gave a formal blessing on her wedded life (Ruth 4:11, 12). These words are not mere sentiment nor are they a magical charm, but a prayer for God's blessing on her life. **The mother of thousands of ten thousands:** The two poetic lines echo

the promise of God to Abraham and Sarah (17:15, 16). The term translated *ten thousands* means "myriads," "uncountable." It may be a play on the name Rebekah because in Hebrew the words sound similar. As in God's promise to Abraham (22:17), the possession of the **gates** of one's enemies meant power over them.

24:61–63 Rebekah and her maids must have made quite an entourage as they took off that day from Haran. Meanwhile, **Isaac** was also on the move (v. 62). **Beer Lahai Roi** was named in the story of Hagar's first expulsion from Abraham and Sarah's household (16:13, 14).

24:62 The South is the Negev (12:9; 13:1).

24:63, 64 The precise meaning of the term translated **to meditate** is in dispute; perhaps it means "to walk about in thought."

24:65 In the manner of the East, wearing **a veil** would have been appropriate behavior for a young, unmarried woman who was about to come into the company of a man.

24:66 From the earlier recital to Laban (vv. 32–49), we can imagine the enthusiasm of the **servant** speaking to Isaac.

24:67 Isaac brought Rebekah to his mother's **tent,** a public act. **his wife, and he loved her:** Only rarely in the Bible do we read of romantic love (the Book of Ruth). But the Song of Songs rhapsodizes on it. Isaac's sense of grief at the death of his mother was now replaced by joy in the newness of married love. The story is lovely as it stands, a dramatic portrayal of God's kind providence toward His people.

25:1 The Hebrew phrase **again took** can be interpreted as "had taken." **Keturah:** She was not Abraham's second official wife. Instead she was a concubine (v. 6; 1 Chr. 1:32). As an unofficial wife, Keturah was probably with Abraham for life. Her sons had a status similar to that of Ishmael, Abraham's son by Hagar (ch. 16), but without Ishmael's particular blessing (16:10–16).

25:2 Midian was the father of the Midianites, some of whom later bought Joseph from his brothers (Gen. 36:35; 37:28, 36).

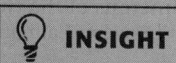 **INSIGHT** | **Burials in Caves**

Caves were not usually used as burial sites but as places of refuge (Gen. 19:30; Josh. 10:16; 1 Sam. 22:1; 24:1–3; 1 Kin. 19:13), or storage areas. In some periods, cadavers were buried in floors of houses, but mostly tombs were carved in the soft limestone rock of the Palestinian hills or dug into the dirt. Burial sites were used by families for generations. Abraham's purchase of the cave of Machpelah began a burial tradition continued by his descendants (Gen. 25:9, 10; 49:29–33; 50:13).

25:3–5 As the legal firstborn, **Isaac** received the grand share of his father's fortune; beyond that, he received the blessing of God (v. 11; 26:2–5).

25:6 The **concubines** were Hagar and Keturah. To protect Isaac's inheritance after his death, Abraham gave appropriate gifts to his lesser sons and sent them away.

25:7 God gave Abraham a long **life** as He had promised (12:2; 15:15).

25:8 gathered to his people: A burial. The phrase also indicates that there is an afterlife (15:15; 35:29; 49:33).

25:9 Abraham purchased **the cave of Machpelah** for the burial of his wife, **Sarah** (ch. 23).

25:10, 11 God blessed Isaac because He had already established "an everlasting covenant" with him (Gen. 17:19; Heb. 11:17). Later, God renewed the covenant with Isaac (26:2–5). **Beer Lahai Roi** means "The Well of the One Who Lives and Who Sees Me." At this well, an Angel of the Lord had appeared to Hagar (16:7–14).

25:12–18 genealogy of Ishmael: This passage distinguishes Ishmael's line, the line of the lesser promise (16:10–15), from Isaac's line (starting at v. 19), the line of the greater promise (for other genealogies in Genesis read note at 2:4).

25:16 God fulfilled his promise to Abraham (17:20). The descendants of Ishmael had **twelve princes** to govern them, just as the Israelites were divided into twelve tribes (ch. 49).

25:17 Ishmael . . . died: This notation of the death, following a long life, is a mark of significance to the narrator. The principal story will focus on Isaac, but Ishmael is not to be forgotten.

25:18 they dwelt: The descendants of Ishmael lived in a large area, including the Arabian peninsula and the desert land between Canaan and Mesopotamia.

25:19 genealogy of Isaac: There are ten significant genealogies in Genesis (2:4, note).

25:20 The story of the marriage of **Rebekah** and Isaac is recorded in ch. 24.

25:21 The Hebrew verb for **pleaded** ('*atar*; used infrequently in the Bible) indicates that Isaac prayed passionately for his wife. For examples of passionate prayer, see Ex. 8:30; 2 Sam. 21:14; 24:25. Isaac waited twenty years for God to grant his prayer (vv. 20, 26). **barren:** Rebekah experienced a period of infertility just like Sarah, Rachel, and Leah (16:1; 29:31; 30:9). After a period of barrenness, the **Lord** specifically gave each child in the line of promise. In the OT world, the inability of a woman to conceive a child was regarded as a problem with the

woman. In these ancient times, there was no understanding of sperm vitality and mobility, of course. Consequently, a barren woman might be both an object of pity and genuinely miserable herself (1 Sam. 1:6). In the Code of Hammurabi, barrenness was a legitimate reason for divorce. A woman divorced for this reason would not likely be remarried; her lot in life was truly pitiable. The recurring motif of barrenness in the family of God's promise may serve as a generation-by-generation reminder that the children finally born to these women were born because of the intervention of the Lord; thus, **the Lord** granted his plea. In this way, the children would not be regarded as simply the natural order of things, for each child in the line of promise was a distinct grace-gift from the Lord.

25:22 struggled: Rebekah's pregnancy was difficult. It seemed as though the two children were competing in her womb. **inquire:** In the context of sacrificial worship, Rebekah prayed to the Lord.

25:23 The **Lord** spoke directly to Rebekah (16:8–11). **two nations:** A theme of two sons recurs in Genesis: the sons of Eve (ch. 4), the sons of Tamar and Judah (38:27–30), and the sons of Joseph (ch. 48). In the ancient Near East, the firstborn would have preeminence. But this time God chose to bless the **younger** (compare 1 Sam. 16).

25:24 The birth of **twins** was regarded as a special blessing.

25:25 The name **Esau** sounds like the Hebrew word that means "hairy."

25:26 The younger brother grasped for his older brother's **heel** from birth. The Hebrew word that means "heel" sounds similar to the name **Jacob.** The name may mean either "He Who Grasps at the Heel (of Another)" or "He (the Lord) Is at His Heels (Is His Protector)." Later, Esau would taunt Jacob with the negative connotations of his name (27:36). Eventually God gave Jacob a new name, Israel (32:28).

25:27–34 A study of the patriarchal narratives indicates that there were two outstanding features associated with birthright, leadership of the clan and the guardianship of the promise.

25:27 hunter . . . mild man: The contrasting temperaments and interests of the two sons is similar to the contrast between Cain and Abel (4:2).

25:28 Isaac loved Esau: The following story illustrates the folly of parental favoritism.

25:29, 30 The ruddy color of his complexion (v. 25) was tied to his strong desire for the red food and later to the red land he inherited (36:8). Now Esau was known as "Red," that is, **Edom.**

25:31, 32 Esau, as the firstborn, had a **birthright** to a double portion of the family

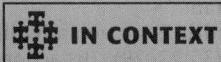 **IN CONTEXT**   **Birthrights**

When Jacob asked Esau to sell him his birthright (Gen. 25:31), he was looking to obtain a position that had both legal and spiritual benefits.

In Bible times, the firstborn son enjoyed a favored position, which was his by right of birth (hence birthright). He was privileged to inherit a double portion of his father's assets (Deut. 21:17) and could expect to receive a special blessing before the father died. After his father's death, a firstborn son became the head of the family, carrying on the family name and even acting as the family priest.

The inheritance rights of the firstborn were protected by law; a father could not give his benefits to a younger son (Deut. 21:15–17). However, the firstborn himself could lose, forfeit, or sell his birthright. Jacob's son Reuben lost his favored position because he committed incest with his father's concubine (Gen. 35:22; 1 Chr. 5:1, 2). Likewise, Esau sold his birthright for a stew of lentils (Gen. 25:29–34), or "one morsel of food" (Heb. 12:16).

In doing so, Esau committed a grave sin. It was bad enough to squander his inheritance for a single meal. Far worse, he was throwing away the blessing of God, who he knew had promised to make him a great nation of Abraham (22:15–18).

In this way, Esau serves as an example to believers today to hold onto what God has promised. Nothing is more important.

estate. Moreover he inherited from Isaac the privilege of an everlasting covenant with God (Gen. 12:1–3).

25:33 swear to me: The formal oath, even though unwitnessed, would have been regarded as binding by both parties.

25:34 The Hebrew verb for **despised** implies utter contempt (Num. 15:31; 2 Sam. 12:9; Mal. 1:6). Esau scorned God's promises given to the heirs of Isaac. Later, Esau greatly regretted his cavalier actions (Gen. 27:38).

26:1 An earlier famine occurred during the **days of Abraham** and led to Abraham going to Egypt (12:10–20). Abraham later had a similar misadventure in Gerar (ch. 20), a story that amazingly was repeated in some ways in the life of his son in the present narrative. The **Philistines** came to the coastland of Canaan following their defeat by the Egyptians around 1200 B.C. The Egyptians called them the "Sea Peoples." The Philistines were apparently Greek peoples who migrated eastward (1 Sam. 4:1; 2 Sam. 5:17).

26:2 The LORD appeared to Isaac for the first time on record. Interestingly, God had already spoken to Rebekah (25:22, 23). Even though Egypt's conditions may have been hospitable, the Lord prohibited Isaac from going **to Egypt** as his father had during the earlier famine (12:10).

26:3 bless you: The Lord fulfilled His promise to Abraham concerning Isaac (17:19). He established His everlasting covenant with Isaac just as He had with Abraham.

26:4, 5 God promised to make Isaac's

descendants innumerable **as the stars** because of His covenant with Abraham (22:17). God promised to bless the entire world, **all the nations,** through Abraham's descendants (12:3; 22:18; 28:14).

26:6 Gerar was better for farming than the arid regions of the Negev.

26:7 Rebekah was a close relative (22:20–23) but not Isaac's **sister.** Isaac was even more deceitful than his father Abraham was (20:2, 12).

26:8 In this early period, **window** does not describe a pane of glass but an opening in the wall for ventilation, or an opening in the lattice work at the top of the building. **showing endearment:** This Hebrew wordplay for "sexual caress" and the name "Isaac" could be rendered: "He Who Laughs was laughing with Rebekah his wife."

26:9, 10 how could you: A sense of moral outrage from the Philistine king. Ironically, Abimelech became the protector of Isaac and his wife.

26:11–13 God's special work for Abraham was extended to the son. The **Lord blessed** him so much that he became **very prosperous** and the envy of his neighbors.

26:14, 15 Abraham had made a covenant with Abimelech concerning the rights to **wells** (21:22–34). But enmity had led to acts of sabotage against these old wells.

26:16, 17 Although Isaac moved from **Gerar,** he did not leave the area.

26:18, 19 On the basis of Isaac's rights to the water in the area, his men **dug** new wells, giving these wells the same names as the old ones.

26:20 Esek comes from a verb meaning "to contend" and is used only here in the Bible.

26:21 Sitnah means "hostility" and is related to the Hebrew term for Satan.

26:22, 23 Isaac moved out of Gerar as the famine ended and water became more available. He returned **to Beersheba,** the land of his youth (22:19).

26:24 God of your father Abraham: God was faithful. He promised to the son what He had already promised to the father. This passage repeats the Abrahamic covenant (read references at 15:1–21).

26:25 Isaac followed the practice of his father (12:8). He made **an altar** and **called on the name of the LORD:** At this altar Isaac not only prayed to the Lord but also affirmed the reality of the living God in this special land (12:8; 21:33).

26:26 Abimelech came to end the animosity between his people and Isaac's family because he recognized God's blessing on Isaac (vv. 28, 29). **Ahuzzath . . . and Phichol,** associates of Abimelech, would witness the agreement.

26:27, 28 the LORD is with you: This was God's design. He wanted to bless Abraham's family because Abraham and his family followed Him. Then, God's extraordinary blessing on His people would attract others to Himself (12:2, 3). The **covenant** formally bound both parties. The covenant here was as between two equals (for similar covenants, see Abraham and Abimelech in 21:2–34; Laban and Jacob in 31:43–55). The covenant between God and Abraham was of a different type, a covenant between a king and a servant (15:18).

26:29, 30 ate and drank: This ceremonial meal expressed the new relationship and memorialized the alliance (27:3, 4; 31:46, 54).

26:31 peace: The Hebrew term *shalom* suggests that things were "as they ought to be" between the two contracting parties.

26:32 This was either a brand new **well** or a redigging of Abraham's well at that location (21:30, 31). The discovery of **water** was regarded as a blessing from God on their actions.

26:33 Shebah: The name is a wordplay on the Hebrew words that mean "swear" (v. 31) and "seven." The name **Beersheba** may mean either "Well of the Oath" or "Well of the Seven."

26:34, 35 Esau married Hittite women, who believed in many different gods. His parents wanted him to marry a woman who worshiped the living God (27:46; 28:8; 36:1–8). The name **Judith** is related to the word that means "praise," similar to the name "Judah." She is not mentioned among the wives of Esau in ch. 36.

Perhaps, the marriage did not last. The name **Basemath** means "Fragrant."

27:1–3 Isaac was old: Isaac actually did not die for many years (35:27–29). His actions were precautionary. **his eyes:** Isaac's failed vision allowed Jacob and his mother to trick him (vv. 11–29). For other blessings affected by Isaac's vision see Gen. 48:8–22. Ordinarily, a father would give the primary blessing to the firstborn, in this case **Esau** (25:29–34). Yet God worked contrary to cultural expectations and Isaac's favoritism (37:4). God had already blessed the younger (25:23).

27:4 Isaac wanted to memorialize his blessing on Esau with a ceremonial meal of **savory food** (27:30). **my soul:** This phrase is simply a substitute for the personal pronoun, "I." **bless you:** The father may have been unaware of the "deal" between the two sons where Esau sold his birthright to his brother (25:29–34). But Esau's words to his father (27:36) suggest that this was known to Isaac. Thus Isaac wished to overcome the loss of his son's birthright by the power of the words of great blessing. As it happened, Jacob would get both.

27:5 The mother had her favorite son as well, and the lack of understanding and agreement between the parents is an example of what today we might call a "dysfunctional family."

INSIGHT   **Becoming Head of the Family**

Primogeniture is the social custom of giving the firstborn son the natural right to succeed his father as supreme head of the family (Gen. 27:32). Like the right of a prince to become king, it is not based on merit or talent but only on being the firstborn son. The Bible recounts several struggles between firstborn and younger sons.

27:6, 7 her son: Rebekah, of course, was mother of both sons, but the phrasing here indicates her her special relationship with Jacob.

27:8–10 obey my voice: Rebekah wanted to circumvent the blessing that her husband planned to give to Esau. Here Rebekah appears to be calculating and devious. Yet God had told her that her younger son would have precedence over the older (25:23).

27:11, 12 Jacob wanted to know how he could pass as his brother. Esau had been **hairy** from birth (25:25). **deceiver:** Jacob feared that he would be discovered, not that he was doing wrong.

27:13–20 I am Esau: Jacob lied, then his lies led him to blasphemy. The attribution of his "good fortune" to **the Lord** indicates how far Jacob would go to achieve his aims.

27:21–27 come near: Isaac had to **feel** Jacob (vv. 21, 22), hear him (v. 22), question him (v. 24), **kiss** and **smell** him (v. 26, 27) before he finally believed Jacob's repeated lies. Each one of Jacob's lies needed another lie.

27:27–29 Ironically, Isaac began his blessing by describing the rustic **smell** of his son's clothing. **peoples serve you:** Isaac predicted that Jacob's descendants would obtain supremacy over other peoples. Jesus, as the King of kings and a descendant of Jacob, ultimately fulfilled this prediction (1 Tim. 6:14–16). **master:** This Hebrew word (*gebîr;* also used in v. 37) is related to a word meaning "hero" (Heb. *gibbôr;* Josh. 1:2; Is. 9:6) and describes one who is valiant and powerful. **mother's sons:** Isaac intended that Jacob would bow to Esau. Yet because of Jacob's deception, Isaac blessed Jacob instead. **Cursed . . . blessed:** Unwittingly, Isaac blessed Jacob with the words originally spoken by the Lord to Abram (12:3). Jacob became the heir to the everlasting covenant between Abraham's descendants and the Lord.

27:30–32 Who are you: Surely Isaac recognized his older son's voice.

27:33 In this word of despair, **Who,** Isaac realizes he had been duped by his own son. **he shall be blessed:** In this ancient culture, words could not be easily withdrawn as they often are today. Isaac's words of blessing had power; indeed, they were backed by the power of the Lord (vv. 27–29). They could not be withdrawn.

27:34 He cried: Esau's anguish was unbearable. **Bless me:** Surely Isaac had reserved some blessing for Esau.

27:35 Jacob had stolen the blessing Isaac had intended for Esau. **deceit:** Later, Jacob would be deceived by his uncle Laban (29:25).

27:36–38 rightly named: One meaning of the name Jacob is "He Who Grasps at the Heel (of Another)." Jacob lived up to the meaning of his name by trying to steal Esau's right as the firstborn. Actually, the **blessing** was one of the birthrights of the firstborn son. Esau, as the firstborn, probably hoped to overcome the loss of his **birthright** (25:29–34) with Isaac's powerful blessing. As it turned out, Jacob achieved both through underhanded means. The blessing was irrevocable (v. 37). **Have you only one blessing:** Esau repeated his pleas (v.

34). This repetition suggests a prolonged period of grieving.

27:39 Behold: The blessing for Esau was much weaker than the blessing for Jacob (for the "reserve blessing" for Ishmael, see 16:11, 12).

27:40 The blessing affirmed that Esau's descendants would **serve** his **brother.** Yet eventually they would free themselves from domination.

27:41 The feelings of Esau are now fully understandable; he **hated Jacob.** And they are shocking, for his plan was nothing less than to murder his brother, which recalls the fratricide of Gen. 4.

27:42–45 Apparently Esau revealed his evil decision to someone. Again, **Rebekah** intervened to help her favorite son. **Laban** was Rebekah's brother and **Haran** was her homeland (ch. 24). Earlier, Laban had welcomed Abraham's servant (24:29). The expression **a few days** is ironic, considering the great length, twenty years, of Jacob's subsequent sojourn (31:38, 41). **bereaved:** Rebekah would lose both her sons if Esau killed Jacob—the one to death and the other, like Cain, to exile. Sadly, she died before Jacob returned (31:18; 35:27–29).

27:46 daughters of Heth: Rebekah spoke to Isaac about Jacob's future wife because they had already regretted Esau's marrying Hittite women (26:34, 35). Furthermore, Isaac had found Rebekah in Haran.

28:1 Isaac agreed with Rebekah that intermarriage with the pagan women of **Canaan** was dangerous. These women would bring their own false gods into the household.

28:2 Padan Aram is a region of Haran in northern Aram (Syria) near the Euphrates River.

28:3 God Almighty: This Hebrew phrase, *El Shaddai,* is used by or in the hearing of Abraham, Isaac, and Jacob (35:11). God later identified Himself to Moses with this same name (Ex. 6:3).

28:4 Isaac formally passed on to his son Jacob the **blessing** that God had first given to his father Abraham (12:1–3). **descendants:** The Hebrew term *seed* may refer to a single individual (3:15) or to a number of people. This same term is used in prophecy to designate the coming Messiah, Jesus Christ (Num. 24:7; Is. 6:13).

28:6–9 Esau attempted to find favor in Isaac's eyes by doing what Isaac wished. By marrying **Mahalath the daughter of Ishmael,** Esau believed he had met the standard Isaac had given Jacob (v. 1). Sadly, Esau could not regain his lost blessing. Mahalath is the same woman as Basemath, the daughter of Ishmael, in 36:2. Her name probably means "Dance."

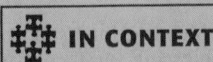 **IN CONTEXT** **The Mari Tablet Towns**

It is not known exactly when the patriarchs lived. Estimates for dating Abraham, Isaac, and Jacob rage from 2100 to 1800 B.C. These dates would locate the patriarchal period before, or simultaneous with, the Mari tablets, which have been placed between 1813 and 1760 B.C.

Mari was a powerful city, halfway between Babylon and the Mediterranean Sea on the banks of the Euphrates. It became rich through trading, and though it is not mentioned in the Bible it is well-known today because of the large archive of official documents discovered there. More than 20,000 clay tablets were dug up at the excavation site.

The Mari tablets frequently mention the cities Nahor and Haran. Abraham (Gen. 11:31) and Jacob (27:43; 28:10) lived in Haran, and Abraham's servant traveled to Nahor (24:10). Much of what is written in the Mari tablets may reflect aspects of culture known by the patriarchs.

28:10, 11 The uses of the word **stone** to describe the pillow is problematic. Perhaps the stone was near rather than under his head.

28:12 dreamed: The manner of revelation in the patriarchal stories varies. This is the first where a revelation of the Lord came via a dream.

28:13 I am the LORD: God identified Himself as the God whom both Abraham and Isaac believed. Later, He becomes known as the God of Jacob (Ex. 3:15). Isaac, in his blessing, predicted Jacob would inherit this **land** (vv. 3, 4). Now God promised it!

28:14 The Lord ratified Isaac's blessing on Jacob's **descendants** (vv. 3, 4). **all the families:** Every time the covenant was renewed, God repeated His promise to show mercy to all people through Abraham's descendants (12:3;

22:18; 26:4). **Seed** refers to Jacob's sons; Jacob's descendants, the nation of Israel; and the Promised One (as in 3:15; Is. 6:13).

28:15 I am with you: Right when Jacob was running away from the consequences of his lies, God mercifully chose to reaffirm His promises. Jacob was in no position to earn God's favor. Yet God promised to be with him. God's choice of Jacob was not based on merit but grace. This is always true. God also saw in Jacob a man who would grow in faithfulness and in character strength. One day he would no longer be "Jacob,"—"He who supplants" (28:36)—but "Israel,"—"God persists!" (32:28).

28:16 I did not know: God takes the initiative in seeking and confronting us.

28:17 Afraid indicates a fear of God similar to terror. **Afraid** and **awesome** are related and

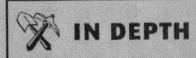 **IN DEPTH** **Bethel**

- A city of Palestine twelve miles north of Jerusalem.
- Originally called Luz ("light"), renamed Bethel ("house of God," Gen. 28:19) by Jacob; later derided by the prophets (Jer. 48:13), especially Hosea, who called it Beth Aven ("house of idols or harlotry," Hos. 4:15; 5:8; 10:5).
- Near the site of Abraham's altar to God's covenant (Gen. 12:8; 13:3).
- Place where Jacob erected a pillar to mark his dream of angels ascending and descending a ladder (28:10–22).
- Home of the ark of the covenant in the period of the judges (Judg. 20:26, 27).
- Place where King Jeroboam of Judah established a rival, idolatrous sanctuary to the temple at Jerusalem by setting up a golden calf (1 Kin. 12:28–33; 13:1–32; 2 Kin. 10:29).
- Purged by King Josiah, the reformer who destroyed pagan shrines and idols (2 Kin. 23:15).
- Resettled after the Babylonian exile (Ezra 2:28; Neh. 7:32).
- Unmentioned in the New Testament.
- Site today of the village of Beitin.
- Not to be confused with Bethel in the territory of Simeon (1 Sam. 30:27), which may be the same as Bethul (Josh. 19:4) or Bethuel (1 Chr. 4:30).

indicate a fear of God similar to wonder and worship (22:12; Ex. 20:20; Prov. 1:7). In Jacob's case, these twin emotions were mixed together. **house of God . . . gate of heaven:** God and heaven had come down to the very place where Jacob was sleeping!

28:18 stone . . . as a pillar: To commemorate the great event, Jacob set a stone on end and **poured oil on top** to consecrate it to God. Later he would refer to the Lord as "The Stone of Israel" (49:24). For Moses' use of oil to consecrate the tabernacle see Lev. 8:10–12.

28:19 Bethel means "House of God." God had also appeared to Abraham near Bethel (12:7, 8).

28:20 vow: Although Jacob made a conditional promise to be faithful to God, he based it on God's promises to him (v. 15).

28:21, 22 Jacob promised to give **a tenth** of his possessions to God. It is not known what prompted this percentage. His grandfather Abraham had given the same proportion to Melchizedek, the priest of God Most High (14:20). Later, the Mosaic law required giving a tenth to God (Deut. 14:22).

29:1 The **people of the East** were not Canaanites.

29:2–4 Shepherds would naturally gather at a **well.** As in the case of Abraham's servant (24:10, 11), Jacob met Rachel at a well, perhaps even at the same well. Because God allowed a number of significant events to occur at wells, they become a symbol of God's blessing and care (16:14; 21:19, 30; 26:32; Is. 12:3; John 4:1–26).

29:5 The term **son** is being used in a loose sense. **Nahor** was actually the grandfather of **Laban** (22:20–23). Laban's father was Bethuel (24:15, 50).

29:6–8 is he well: The expression involves the familiar term *shalom* in an idiom that was common in biblical speech. **Rachel** is a term of endearment, meaning "Ewe Lamb." As the daughter of his mother's brother, Rachel was a cousin of Jacob.

29:9, 10 still speaking: Rachel's arrival at that moment is a mirror of Rebekah's action to Abraham's servant so long ago (24:15–20). Again, God's timing is perfect (for Boaz and Ruth read Ruth 2:3).

29:11 kissed Rachel: Doubtless Jacob had heard the story of his mother's encounter with the servant of Abraham many times. He knew their meeting was from God.

29:12–15 your wages: The story takes a new turn. Laban turns out to be a "sharp dealer," a good match for Jacob "the supplanter."

29:16 Leah was Rachel's older sister. Her name may be a term of endearment meaning "Wild Cow."

29:17 Delicate here may mean a special loveliness in her eyes or a weakness. **beautiful of form:** Rachel's description is similar to the descriptions of Sarai (12:11) and of Rebekah (24:16).

29:18, 19 loved Rachel: A rare biblical example of "love at first sight" (for his father's similar response to Rebekah read Gen. 24:67).

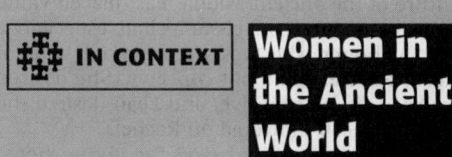

Women in the Ancient World

The record of Leah and Rachel stands out among the writings and stories that survive from ancient times. As near as we can tell, many cultures in the ancient world viewed women as little more than property. Furthermore, the men who recorded the literature of those times tended to overlook the presence and significance of their female counterparts. By contrast, the Bible not only includes women but also tells about their leadership, contributions, and feelings, and not just their sins and failures. Overall, Scripture provides an honest account of women as well as men in a fallen world.

The long **seven years** of service provides a stunning demonstration of the value Jacob placed on Rachel.

29:20, 21 seemed only a few days: A rare statement in the Bible on romantic love.

29:22 The Hebrew term **feast** indicates that there was drinking.

29:23 A public feast in recognition of the union made the marriage between Jacob and Leah official, even though Leah was the wrong woman.

29:24, 25 behold, it was Leah: The revelation of the morning light must have been nearly unbelievable to Jacob and a great hurt to Leah. We may also assume it was distressing for Rachel. Laban's "dirty trick" not only showed contempt for Jacob but also demonstrated little care for his daughters' feelings. The events also show how powerless women were in these circumstances in the ancient world. The Hebrew name **deceived** means "to act treacherously with" or "to betray" (1 Sam. 19:17). Jacob the deceiver had been deceived by Laban (27:35).

29:26 must not be done: The cultural necessity of Laban's actions is doubtful.

29:27 Laban deceived Jacob in order to get **another seven years'** work from him (for more of Laban's sharp deals read Gen. 31:7, 41). Jacob loved Rachel so much that he was willing to work another seven years (v. 28).

29:28, 29 As did Zilpah (v. 24), **Bilhah** later served as a surrogate mother when Rachel was barren (30:3–8).

29:30, 31 **Unloved** (v. 33) actually means "hated." The Lord graciously enabled Leah to conceive a child because she was unloved. The culture of the ancient Middle East placed value on a woman who could bear a child, especially a son. Although she was the beloved wife of Jacob, **Rachel** could not conceive. She desired Leah's ability to conceive, and Leah desired the love that Jacob showered on Rachel.

29:32 Leah praised God for giving her a son. Perhaps Leah joyfully shouted "Behold a Son!" at **Reuben**'s birth, which is what "Reuben" means. Leah's faith in Yahweh is attested in her acknowledgment that He had indeed seen her trouble and had reached out to meet her need. We are reminded of the story of Hannah (1 Sam. 1) and the great illustration of Yahweh's loyal love in Ps. 113:9. But there is more to the story than the isolated instance of child-bearing. From the birth of the first son of Eve our mother (4:1), OT accounts describe parents' quests for sons. Leah and Rachel fit this pattern, as do Sarah and Rebekah before them. Ultimately this quest leads to the birth of the Savior to Blessed Mary (Matt. 1:18–25), the fulfillment of the original promise of God to Eve that she would produce a Seed who would be the One to triumph over our great enemy (Gen. 3:15).

29:33 The name **Simeon** celebrates the fact that the Lord hears. He had heard Leah's prayers and He knew about her tragic relationship with Jacob.

29:34 Later, God chose the tribe of Levi to become priests and caretakers of the tabernacle. Then, the name **Levi** implied "Attached to the Lord."

29:35 **Judah,** the last of the first four sons of Leah and Jacob, was given a name related to (or sounding much like) a principal word for "praise of God" in the Bible (yadâ). This verb is translated "give thanks," but more properly means "to give public acknowledgment" (Ps. 118:1). Leah (in this verse) and Jacob (49:8) tie this name to the praise of Yahweh. Each of these four names then was an expression of the anticipation of Leah finally achieving loving acceptance by her husband. But it seems that in each case, Leah was to be denied her greater joy. We may also observe in the giving of these names that the narrator is not a modern philologist giving precise meanings to these words in their historical, linguistic development. Some of these names sound like the words to which they are related (Zebulun, at 30:20). Others are based on multilayered puns (Joseph, at 30:24). And some of the names mean precisely what they are said to mean.

30:1 The Hebrew verb for **envied** describes a strong inner feeling of rage (37:11), and may be translated "to act in zeal" (Num. 25:11; 1 Kin. 19:10; Zech. 8:2). Rachel's envy mirrored Sarai's envy of Hagar (ch. 16). **or else I die:** bitter feelings of jealousy and rage.

30:2 **Jacob's anger was aroused:** We sometimes speak of someone being "livid with rage." In the midst of the bitterness in the family, which was growing with accusations and countercharges, the Hebrew idiom for anger is fascinating. Literally, it may be translated, "the nose of Jacob burned." The flushed face of the heavily bearded Semitic adult male would be most noticeable in the reddened nose—the origin of this expression. In the common Hebrew saying "the Lord is longsuffering" (compare Ex. 34:6), the Hebrew idiom means "long of nose," meaning that it is exceedingly difficult to cause Him to get angry. Unlike us, the Lord has a very long fuse (Ps. 103:8; Mic. 7:18). Jacob's rage against his hurting wife showed

✠ IN CONTEXT **Concubines**

Leah and Rachel, the wives of Jacob, used their maids to compete with each other for their husband's favor by having them bear his children (Gen. 30:3–13). Thus the maids, Zilpah and Bilhah, became secondary wives or "concubines" to Jacob.

The practice of "marrying" concubines, a form of polygamy, was known throughout the ancient Middle East. A concubine was usually a female slave with whom the leading male of the family was free to have sexual relations. She was not considered an equal to his "full" wife (or wives), but she could not be sold if the man lost interest in her. However, rights varied from culture to culture.

One of the main justifications for keeping a concubine was to give birth to children, particularly a son and therefore an heir.

itself in a shifting of blame. Basically he said, "Don't blame me; blame God!"

30:3–5 Rachel's desperation led her to bring her maid **Bilhah** to Jacob as a surrogate wife (for Sarah doing the same thing with Hagar read ch. 16). This was accepted practice in the ancient Middle East to protect an infertile wife. A woman could be divorced if she failed to conceive.

30:6 Dan: In giving a name related to the Hebrew word that means "judge," Rachel thanked the Lord for hearing and answering her pleas.

30:7, 8 With the name **Naphtali,** which seems to mean "my wrestling," Rachel expressed the vehemence of her struggle with her sister.

30:9–13 Leah was **happy** because of her numerous sons, so she named her son **Asher.**

30:14 Mandrakes are a special type of herb that the peoples of the ancient Middle East regarded as an aid to conception. Their aroma was associated with lovemaking (Song 7:13). Reuben's discovery of the mandrakes led to another squabble between Leah and Rachel. In the end, Leah **hired** Jacob for a night with her.

30:15–18 The meaning of **Issachar** is in some dispute. It is treated as if meant "to hire out." Thus Issachar is "the Hired One," the one conceived because of the deal made between Leah and Rachel. Yet Leah again gives praise to the Lord, who had brought about the miracle.

30:19, 20 The verb "has endowed" in the Hebrew sounds something like **Zebulun.** The name is from the verb meaning "to be exalted." Thus Zebulun is "the Exalted One."

30:21 The name **Dinah** is related to the word that means "judgment."

30:22 Finally, God enabled Rachel to have a child. The three verbs, **remembered, listened,** and **opened,** emphasize that conception is a gift from God.

30:23 my reproach: In Rachel's culture a married woman without children was scorned.

30:24 By giving Rachel a son, God had removed her shame and brought joy to her life. The name she gave to him, **Joseph,** is a wordplay in Hebrew on two similar sounding verbs that end up meaning, "He (Yahweh) Adds {Even as He Removes}."

30:25 With the birth of Joseph by his beloved wife, Jacob was ready to go to his **own place.** Jacob had always wanted to return to Canaan (27:43, 44). Indeed, God had promised to bring him back to his homeland (28:4, 15).

30:26 Since Genesis speaks only of Laban's daughters during Jacob's visit, Laban probably did not have a son at the time (29:16). Therefore he adopted Jacob as his son and principal heir. The Code of Hammurabi attests that this was a common practice in the ancient Middle East. As the principal heir, Jacob and his family were regarded as a part of Laban's household (v. 43). But in the intervening years, Laban had fathered sons who would threaten Jacob's status in the family (31:1). Hence, he asked Laban to **let** him **go.**

30:27 God had promised to bless others through Abraham's descendants (12:2, 3). Now, God **blessed** Laban through Jacob, and later He would bless an Egyptian household through Joseph (39:5).

30:28 name your wages: These words must have sounded hollow to Jacob, given his earlier experience in striking a deal with Laban (29:15–30; 31:7).

30:29, 30 the LORD has blessed you: Both Laban (v. 27) and Jacob recognize the work of God in the increase of the livestock.

30:31, 32 Presumably, the **speckled and spotted sheep** would be the smaller part of the flock. The deal was to Laban's advantage.

30:33 my righteousness: Jacob asserted his trustworthiness.

30:34 according to your word: The deal was struck.

30:35, 36 three days' journey: A distance of about sixty miles separated Jacob's and Laban's herds so the animals would not mix. Jacob still tended **Laban's flocks.**

30:37–40 rods of green poplar: Jacob placed sticks of various colors in the watering troughs to symbolize his belief that God would bless him with more speckled and spotted lambs (v. 27; compare 31:5, 9, 10). Indeed, God blessed Jacob as He had promised (28:13–15). Jacob added all the speckled and spotted animals to his own herd.

30:41–43 With the symbolic multicolored rods, Jacob asked God to bless him with speckled and spotted animals from the **stronger livestock** in Laban's herd. Indeed, God promised to do just that in a dream (31:10), and Jacob became wealthy (v. 43).

31:1 These sons probably were born to **Laban** after Jacob had arrived in Haran (30:26). Concerned about their welfare, the sons accused Jacob of being a thief.

31:2 The countenance of Laban: Jacob realized that he had lost favor with his father-in-law, Laban.

31:3–6 God repeated the promises He gave Jacob at Bethel. He promised to be with Jacob as he returned to his homeland. This promise, **I will be with you,** is in fact related to the very name of God, Yahweh (Ex. 3:12, 14). Verses 11–13 describe more of this revelation.

31:7 Deceived may also mean "to trifle with" (compare 29:29).

31:8 speckled . . . streaked: Apparently,

〰 IN PERSON | **Helping God Out**

As his experience with Laban shows, Jacob had a tendency to try to "help God out" in solving thorny problems.

Laban must have been a difficult father-in-law at best. He constantly found new ways to cheat his son-in-law, whether it involved a "bait-and-switch" bride (Gen. 29:14–30) or manipulation in the family business (30:25–36). At times Jacob responded as a principled man. But at other times he resorted to treating Laban in kind, using his own style of deception and scheming.

Eventually God told Jacob to return to his homeland with the promise, "I will be with you" (31:3). But instead of trusting God and making a clean break with Laban, Jacob began complaining to his wives (31:4–16), with the result that the family stole away, taking some of Laban's property with them (31:17–21). Pursued and caught by Laban, Jacob grew angry and attempted to justify himself (31:36–42).

Much of this could have been avoided if Jacob had simply trusted and acted upon God's promise to be with him. Instead, he further complicated his troubled family by causing Laban's daughters to turn on their father in deceit and treachery.

Laban kept on switching the deal as he watched the births of a variety of colored animals. But with every new deal, God always increased Jacob's herd.

31:9–11 The Angel of God may be translated *The Angel of Genuine Deity.* God revealed Himself in Jacob's **dream** (Gen. 28:13–17; 32:22–30). **Jacob:** Here, God used the positive meaning of the name Jacob "He (the Lord) Supplants." For the negative sense see Gen. 25:26; 27:36. In the past, Jacob ("He Who Supplants") had achieved what he wanted by deceit and trickery. Now he had achieved great wealth because of God's blessing. The Lord is the Great Supplanter! Although Jacob's name was later changed to Israel (32:28), the name Jacob continued to be a term indicating God's work in Jacob's life (46:2; Ps. 114:7).

31:12, 13 The Lord identified Himself as the same God who had revealed Himself to Jacob at **Bethel** (28:10–19).

31:14 Rachel and Leah agreed that it was proper to leave their father's home, despite the cultural ties that ordinarily would have kept them there (30:26).The births of sons to their father may have displaced their **inheritance.**

31:15 Both daughters resented the way their father had **sold** them (29:15). Furthermore, they argued that whatever God had taken from their father belonged to them anyway.

31:16–19 household idols: Laban's family was either polytheistic—believing in many gods—or henotheistic—believing in Yahweh as one god above all other gods (for Joshua's recollection of the polytheism of Abraham's relatives read Josh. 24:1–3). In this culture, possession of the household idols was the right of the principal heir. Rachel probably did not steal the idols

in order to worship them, but to retain the rights of the principal heir for Jacob. Ultimately, the Lord's blessing on Jacob was more important for him than any rights derived from being Laban's principal heir.

31:20, 21 When a **river** is not named, it is often the Euphrates in these contexts. Jacob was about to repeat the journey made by his grandfather and grandmother years earlier. Like Abram and Sarai (12:1–4), he was going to Canaan.

31:22–25 But God: What great words! Man does what he can, but God is still in control. As is said, "Man proposes, but God disposes." Man plans, but God intervenes and delivers. The descriptive phrase **Laban the Syrian** is arresting. The term "Syrian" (better, "Aramian") reminds us that while Laban was of the extended family of Jacob, he was not part of the covenant community. **in a dream:** From time to time, God warned others not to harm His people (for Abimelech's dreams read 20:3, 6; for God's encounter with Balaam read Num. 22:12, 20).

31:26 The sudden departure, Laban charges, was similar to a raiding party that took **captives.**

31:27 This was all bluff and they both knew it.

31:28 Done foolishly carries a threat with it, again showing the strange admixture of his words.

31:29 God of your father: Only God's warning in v. 24 stilled Laban's rage.

31:30 The principal charge is the theft of the **gods.** Laban needed these household gods in his possession to secure his sons' heritage.

31:31, 32 Jacob explained that he left in secret because of a genuine fear that he would

Jacob's Travels in the Land of Canaan

not be permitted to leave with his family. Furthermore, he declared his household innocent of the alleged theft and cursed the thief of the idols with death.

31:33 Laban, certain that Jacob had stolen the idols, began his search in **Jacob's tent.** Last, he entered **Rachel's tent.** The fact that each wife had her own tent indicates that Jacob was rich.

31:34, 35 Rachel hid the idols in her saddle bags and sat on them while she made her excuses. Laban did not ask Rachel to move because of a male taboo respecting a woman who was experiencing her monthly period.

31:36 Jacob, in his anger, recited the woes of working for Laban. **Trespass** (Heb. *pesha'*) means to "overstep a boundary." **Sin** (Heb. *hatta't*) means "to miss a target" (as an archer might do). These words are used more often of actions against God than man, of course.

31:37 they may judge: Jacob had some leverage. Laban had been humiliated before his own men. His resolve to stop Jacob necessarily had to weaken.

31:38 Jacob had served fourteen years for his two wives (29:15–30). After that, he worked another six years for his flocks (v. 41). **not miscarried:** Here, Jacob affirmed his superior skills in managing the herds and God's blessing.

31:39–41 Jacob never charged Laban for any **loss** so that he could never charge Jacob for mismanagement. Furthermore, Jacob described the seasonal extremes that he suffered.

31:42 The Fear of Isaac: This name for God means that Isaac feared God with a reverential awe (Ps. 119:120). **rebuked you last night:** Perhaps Jacob knew that God had appeared to Laban.

31:43 Laban considered Jacob's **children** part of his extended family because he had adopted Jacob as a son and principal heir.

31:44 Covenant in this situation refers to a parity covenant, an agreement between equals. The word **witness** refers to a lasting reminder of a significant agreement or to a testimony that can be used in a court.

31:45, 46 Jacob, for a second time, set up a **stone** as a memorial. On the way to Haran at Bethel, he had already set up a pillar to mark the place where God spoke to him (28:18). Later he would erect another pillar at Bethel (35:14). In addition to the stone pillar, they also made a stone **heap** (v. 51). A ceremonial meal memorialized the agreement (26:30). At this meal, Jacob and Laban **ate** some of the animals that had been sacrificed while making the covenant.

31:47, 48 Jegar Sahadutha, Laban's term, is in Aramaic, and **Galeed,** Jacob's term, is in Hebrew. This is remarkable. Laban's term constitutes the only Aramaic words in the Book of

Genesis. Further, even though this is a serious situation, we wonder if there may be some humor in the fact that they have two names and symbols (a pillar, v. 45, and a **heap**). Were the two men able to agree on anything?

31:49 Mizpah means "Outlook Point" and is related to the Hebrew word that means "to watch." God above had His eyes on both men to make them keep their covenant!

31:50 It is not easy to make up one's mind about Laban! Here he seems to show regard for his daughters' welfare; a moment ago he might have had to face the possibility of executing one of them. **God is witness** is the point of the text. They could not watch one another, but God would watch them both.

31:51, 52 The **heap** and the **pillar** (vv. 45–48) were a double **witness** between the two men. Neither was to cross these symbols in order to **harm** the other.

31:53 The wording in Laban's oath suggests that Abraham, Nahor, and their father, Terah, all worshiped the same God, **the God of Abraham.** Possibly, the family believed in the Lord as the one God above many other gods— henotheism (for an indication of Terah's polytheism compare Josh. 24:1–3).

31:54, 55 Jacob offered a sacrifice: This is the only time Genesis records Jacob engaging in sacrificial worship (compare 12:7, 8; 22:13). **ate bread:** As in other cases, the act of eating together further solemnized the agreement (26:30).

32:1 the angels of God: In a magnificent display of His care for him, God allowed Jacob to see that he was not traveling alone (2 Kin. 6:17).

32:2 Jacob discovered that God's armies were encamped around his family's camp. **Mahanaim** means "a double camp."

32:3–5 Jacob sent **messengers** to Esau with a report of his life over the last twenty

---

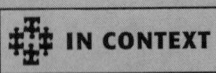 **IN CONTEXT** **Household Gods**

One of the most curious patriarchal accounts is the theft of Laban's household gods by his daughter Rachel (Gen. 31:19). The story is peculiar because of Laban's insistence on finding these gods (31:33–35), and that they are not mentioned either before or after this incident. After all, they were probably made of clay, like the hundreds of other household gods that have been excavated, and had little intrinsic value.

The account also presents other puzzles, such as both men's claim of ownership of the wives, children, and flocks (31:43). Solving these puzzles is helped by evidence from the second millennium B.C. Nuzi tablets, which say that these household gods were at times used as evidence of family leadership. This may explain that Rachel stole the gods to give her husband the position of tribal leader. It may also explain why Laban was so insistent to have these gods back.

years and with a request for **favor,** that is, grace.

32:6 Jacob viewed his brother's coming as a threat to his family, particularly when he learned that **four hundred men** were with him.

32:7 Here, the Hebrew term for **afraid** (*yare'*) refers to fright or terror (31:42). Jacob divided his family into two groups in order to save one from the rage of his brother.

32:8–11 Jacob prayed to God that he might be delivered from Esau's rage. The Hebrew term for **father** indicates either the immediate father or a more remote male ancestor. By mentioning both **Isaac** and Abraham, Jacob appealed to the God who had spoken to his fathers. Jacob reminded **the LORD** of His promises to him. Then Jacob confessed his humility before God's mercy in the words **I am not worthy.** Next, Jacob asked God to **deliver** him. He did not pray in generalities. Instead, he named his concern: Esau! Finally, he concluded with another appeal to God's promises. Christians today can likewise base their prayers on God's proven character and His promises in the Bible.

32:12–21 a present for Esau: Jacob had prayed in faith; now he acted in faith. He gave Esau an overabundance of gifts. By giving the gifts at three different times, Jacob hoped to appease Esau gradually.

32:22–24 Jacob had been struggling all his life; even at the moment of his birth he was struggling with Esau (25:26). Later he struggled with Laban (ch. 31). Yet right before meeting Esau, Jacob had the struggle of his life! He who had once grasped his brother's heel now clung

to the bodily form of the living God. Some believe that the **Man** who **wrestled** Jacob was the preincarnate Jesus Christ. Others believe the Man was the Angel of God (Gen. 21:17; 31:11). In any case, Jacob wrestled with a manifestation of God (vv. 28–30), and because of God's mercy he survived.

32:25, 26 He did not prevail against him: The Man could not turn Jacob away from the struggle—even though He could have easily defeated Jacob. This Hebrew verb translated **touched** (*naga'*) refers here to God's special touch, as when God touches the earth (Amos 9:5) or the human heart (1 Sam. 10:26). Here, God's touch caused pain (Josh. 9:19; 2 Sam. 14:10). Yet Jacob would not give up. He would not release the Man until he received a blessing.

32:27, 28 God had burst into Jacob's life, had given him the sure promises that were given to Abraham (28:13–15), and now—following a nightlong struggle with him—He gave him a new name. The name **Israel** can mean "Prince with God," or perhaps it carries the idea of struggling or persisting, as the wordplay in this passage implies.

32:29 Jacob asks for the Man's **name** because Jacob had given his name. The Man does not answer. But Jacob might have developed his own name for the Man who had wrestled with him: "The Mighty God of Jacob" (49:24). God would one day reveal His name more fully to Moses (Ex. 3:14, 15).

32:30, 31 Jacob's experience with God physically changed him; he **limped.** The experience also had a spiritual impact on his life.

IN LIFE | **When You Least Expect It**

Sometimes good happens to us when we least expect it. Sometimes we receive far more good than we deserve.

When Jacob learned that Esau was approaching (Gen. 32:6), he was terrified. Here was his older twin brother—the brother that he and his mother had cheated out of his rightful portion of the family inheritance (27:1–29)—coming toward him with 400 men. Jacob assumed the worst. He cried out to God for mercy and deliverance (32:9–12) and sent his own extended family and his possessions to his brother's "welcoming committee" (32:13–23).

Yet to Jacob's surprise, Esau ran to him, embraced him, kissed him, and wept (33:4). This kind of grace was completely unexpected. It proved disarming to Jacob, and he could only respond by pressing his gifts on Esau, perhaps as a small remuneration for the lost inheritance (33:8–11).

Like Jacob, we, too, were extended grace and forgiveness when we least expected it, or deserved it. In providing salvation through Christ, God offers unmerited favor to people who actually deserve judgment (Rom. 3:23–25; 5:15–17; James 4:1–6).

Jacob insisted on paying back his brother, and Esau finally accepted. But we can never pay back God for what He has done for us. However, we can respond to His gift of love by showing that same kind of love to others, especially as God teaches us how (1 John 3:11–17).

32:32 to this day: As always in Genesis, this phrase means the day of the first readers of the book. The Jewish rule against eating this muscle continues into modern times within Judaism.

33:1 For all Jacob knew, **Esau was coming** with 400 men to destroy his family.

33:2 maidservants and their children in front: Jacob aligned his family in a pattern that would protect them. He placed his favorite wife, Rachel, in the rear.

33:3 That Jacob **bowed himself** was an act of humility and a sign of contrition.

33:4–9 Instead of taking his revenge, **Esau** welcomed Jacob with joy. The event turned into a grand family reunion (for Joseph's family reunion read 45:15).

33:10 your face as . . . face of God: Jacob presented his gifts to his brother as if they were gifts to God. In this manner, he reenacted Abraham's gifts to Melchizedek (14:20) and indeed, he fulfilled his vow to the Lord (28:22).

33:11 take my blessing: Before, Jacob had done all he could to take Esau's blessing (25:29–34; 27:1–45). Now a wiser man, Jacob wanted to bless his brother with what God had given him. He wanted to restore the broken relationship with his brother.

33:12–16 Following their reconciliation, the two brothers discussed the best manner for the completion of their journey. Jacob seems not to wish to be under obligation to Esau, so he resists each act of kindness from Esau. There is also no covenant made between the two brothers. Perhaps this means that while the brothers were no longer hostile to one another they would still never become "pals."

33:17 Jacob stopped his journey and built temporary shelters east of the Jordan, perhaps at Deir `Alla, one mile north of the Jabbok River.

33:18 Jacob retraced his grandparents' route into Canaan through **Shechem** (12:6). Jacob did not live in the city, because it was devoted to pagan gods. Instead, he lived outside the city in a **tent.**

33:19 As his grandfather had purchased land for a burial place for Sarah (ch. 23), so Jacob bought a **parcel of land.** Even though God promised the entire land to Abraham's family (12:7), they had to buy it one little piece at a time.

33:20 Jacob, now named Israel, built an **altar** for the worship of the Lord, just as his grandfather had (12:7). The name he gave the altar reflected his mature faith in "God, the God of Israel." The God of Jacob's fathers was now Jacob's personal God, for He had fulfilled His promises and protected him (28:13–15).

34:1 Apparently **Dinah** was Leah's only daughter (30:21). It was natural for her to seek the companionship of other women.

34:2 Shechem noticed Dinah and forced her to have intercourse. The term **violated** translates the same word used for Amnon's rape of Tamar (2 Sam. 13:12, 14). Despite what he did, Shechem **loved** Dinah. The expression **spoke kindly** literally means, "spoke to her heart."

34:3, 4 Shechem's appeal to his father suggests that marriages were commonly arranged by parents.

34:5 When Jacob heard, he must have been enraged. The verb translated **defiled** here means "to make unclean."

34:6–10 Hamor presents what appears to be a reasonable position. The problem, of course, was that in these intermarriages there would be a loss of particularity, a loss of the sense of the promise, and a loss of the true worship of God. These concerns would have been lost on Hamor.

34:11, 12 Shechem is appealing in his naive expression of love.

34:13 spoke deceitfully: The proposal of the brothers was disingenuous (Heb. *mirmâ*, the same word used by Esau to describe the actions of Jacob in Gen. 27:35).

34:14–17 uncircumcised: Here, Jacob's sons took the symbol of their holy faith (17:9–14) and used it as a weapon against their foes.

34:18 Shechem proved his love for Dinah by his willingness to undergo circumcision as an adult.

34:19 Delighted is also the verb used in Hebrew with God as the subject in His delight in His people (Ps. 147:10, 11).

34:20–29 Most likely, Jacob's other **sons** joined Simeon and Levi in plundering the city. Jacob's sons let righteous anger over sin turn into unrighteous, unforgiving vengeance (Eph. 4:26).

34:30, 31 Jacob rebuked his sons for their terrible behavior (done in the name of the Lord). Instead of making the family a blessing to other nations (12:3), they were making the family **obnoxious** to its neighbors. The Hebrew word means "to stink." Jacob's family had become an embarrassing odor to their neighbors, something that at best needed to be ignored and at worst to be scorned. Sadly, Jacob's sons did not repent. Instead, they protested their father's rebuke.

35:1 God, for a fifth time, visited Jacob (Gen. 28:10–16; 31:3, 11–13; 32:1, 22–30; also Gen. 35:9–15). After the debacle at Shechem (ch. 34), God told Jacob to continue **to Bethel,** the place where God had first appeared to him (28:10–19). Again, Jacob retraced his grandfather Abraham's route (12:8). This is the first time in the Bible that God commanded **an altar** to be made for Him. Abraham constructed an altar, but no divine command was recorded (12:7, 8).

35:2 Jacob's command included the household idols that Rachel had stolen (31:22–35) as well as any idols among his servants. These **foreign gods** were gods of other people, not of Jacob. Indeed, the only true and living God is Jacob's God. **purify yourselves, and change your garments:** Jacob's household prepared for an encounter with the living and holy God. They cleaned themselves. Later, the Israelites would clean themselves in similar ways at the foot of Mount Sinai (Ex. 19) and at other times and places.

35:3 I will make an altar: Jacob declared his intention to obey God's command (v. 1). **who answered me . . . has been with me:** Jacob recalled God's constant protection (ch. 32) and His fulfillment of His promises (28:13–15) as a reason to obey and worship God.

35:4 As suggested by the nearby phrase **foreign gods,** these **earrings** probably represented some form of idolatry. In two other passages, earrings are mentioned in connection with idolatry (Judg. 8:22–28; Hos. 2:13). In many other passages, earrings are simply items of jewelry (Ex. 32:2, 3; 35:22; Prov. 25:12). The **terebinth tree** is a long-living deciduous tree, such as an oak. The tree has red berries and leaves shaped like feathers. Because the tree lived a long time, ancient people often used the terebinth tree to commemorate important events or to mark places of worship (Hos. 4:13).

35:5 God protected Jacob's family as they traveled. The Hebrew term for **terror** is related to the verb meaning "to be shattered" or "to be dismayed" (for examples of the use of this verb for divine judgment read Is. 7:8; 30:31).

35:6 Luz . . . Bethel: The change of name is explained at 28:19 (Josh. 18:13; Judg. 1:23).

35:7 El Bethel: Naming **an altar** added to the solemnity of the worship conducted there (22:14).

35:8 Deborah was a nurse of Rebekah (24:59). The Hebrew verb translated as **died** means "had died." Deborah had already died, but at this point the family commemorated her death and buried her at Bethel.

35:9 God renewed His everlasting covenant with Jacob. This is the eighth passage dealing with the Abrahamic covenant (15:1–21, note).

35:10 God validated Jacob's change of **name** and reaffirmed His promises to him. Now Jacob would be called Israel (32:28). Note that Genesis uses the names Jacob and Israel interchangeably (vv. 14, 20–22; 46:2).

35:11, 12 This is the third use of the name *El Shaddai,* **God Almighty** (17:1; 28:3; compare Ex. 6:3). God used His great name to attest His strong relationship with Jacob. **Be fruitful** is the language of the covenant and is used of Jacob here to demonstrate that it was he and not Esau who was the true heir of the promises (27:26–29;

28:3, 4). **Nation** and **land** are two words used by God in the promises to Abram (12:2, 7) and reconfirmed in the formal covenant (15:18–21).

35:13 God went up: The living God had made His will known and now returned to His

> **INSIGHT**   **Pillars of Stone**

Pillars of stone are the oldest kind of monument (Gen. 35:14). There are more than *3000* stone pillars at Carnac, France, dating from before 2000 B.C. When no writing accompanies a pillar, it is usually impossible to determine its meaning. The pyramids and obelisks of Egypt are in effect elaborations of the pillar.

abode. This is one of the rare expressions in the Bible of God ascending (Acts 1:9).

35:14 This is the second **pillar** Jacob set up to commemorate God's revelation at Bethel (28:18). Later, Jacob referred to God as "The Stone of Israel" (49:24). **drink offering:** Jacob consecrated the pillar by pouring wine and **oil** over it.

35:15, 16 Ephrath is an alternative name for the region around Bethlehem (v. 19; 48:7; compare Ruth 1:3; Mic. 5:2). The King of Glory would one day be born near the birthplace of Benjamin (Matt. 2:1).

35:17, 18 fear: Rachel's sorrow and fear that her second son might be stillborn became a symbol for all mothers who fear for their child's life (Jer. 31:15; Matt. 2:18). Jacob's name for his new son **Benjamin** indicates his youngest son's special place in the family: at Jacob's right hand. Benjamin would commemorate his beloved wife.

35:18 The phrase **as her soul was departing** does not indicate that the soul was considered a separate entity from the body with an existence of its own, but only that the life was departing.

35:19 Rachel was the only one of the principal characters in Abraham's family of promise who was not **buried** at the cave of Machpelah (Gen. 23:19, 20).

35:20 Jacob had set up pillars to mark the Lord's great works in his life (28:18; 35:14) and to commemorate his agreement with Laban (31:45). Here he erected a **pillar** to mark his sorrow.

35:21 Eder means "flock." This flock tower is mentioned only here and perhaps in Mic. 4:8.

35:22–26 Reuben, Jacob's firstborn son, may have been asserting his right to be the principal heir. Maybe he felt slighted by Jacob's implication that the youngest son, Benjamin, was the son of his right hand. By sleeping with his father's concubine, he was asserting that he would succeed his father. Ironically, this very action caused him to lose the blessing he desired (49:3, 4).

35:27, 28 After more than twenty years of absence, **Jacob** finally visited **his father.** Sadly, his mother Rebekah was probably dead since she is not mentioned. **Mamre** is identified as Hebron, where Isaac passed his youth with his father Abraham (Gen. 13:18).

35:29 The expression **gathered to his people** may also suggest a belief in the afterlife (15:15; 25:8; 49:33; 2 Sam. 12:23). Isaac's formerly feuding sons, **Esau and Jacob,** joined together to bury Isaac with his father and mother in the cave at Machpelah (49:31). Leah and Jacob would be buried there also (49:29–33; 50:12, 13).

36:1 The Hebrew term for **genealogy** means "family history" (2:4, note). At birth, **Esau** was notably ruddy in color (25:25) and he was called **Edom,** meaning "Red" (v. 8).

36:2, 3 Because Esau took **his wives from the daughters of Canaan,** his family would be no different from other families of Canaan. Rebekah and Isaac worried about Esau's **wives** (26:34, 35; 28:6–9). Would they tempt Esau's family to abandon the Lord, the holy and living God? **Adah** means "Ornament." Her father's name **Elon** means "Terebinth." **Aholibamah** means "My Tent Is a High Place." **Anah** may mean "Sing!" and **Basemath** means "Fragrant."

It appears that the names of Esau's wives are confused in Genesis. The names of his wives earlier in Genesis are: Judith the daughter of Beeri the Hittite (26:34), Basemath the daughter of Elon the Hittite (26:34), and Mahalath the daughter of Ishmael, sister of Nebajoth (28:9). In 36:2, 3 his wives are named as Adah the daughter of Elon the Hittite, Aholibamah (or better, Ohilibamah) daughter of Anah, the daughter of Zibeon the Hivite, and Basemath the daughter of Ishmael, sister of Nebajoth. The confusion in these names may have occurred because of scribal errors through the centuries. The versions show attempts to correct the name spellings to show some consistency. It is also possible that two of these wives of Esau had double names and that four, not three, women are in view. The confusion of names may be solved in the following manner:

(1) Judith the daughter of Beeri (26:34) may not have survived, or may not have lasted as a wife to Esau. She is not included in the listing of wives in ch. 36.

(2) Basemath the daughter of Elon the Hittite (26:34) is the same as Adah the daughter of Elon the Hittite (36:2); apparently she bore both names. Thus she is distinct from Basemath the daughter of Ishmael (number 4, below).

(3) Aholibamah (better, Oholibamah) the daughter of Anah the daughter of Zibeon the Hivite is mentioned only in ch. 36.

(4) Mahalath the daughter of Ishmael the sister of Nebajoth (28:9) is the same person as Basemath the daughter of Ishmael the sister of Nebajoth (36:2); apparently she bore both names.

In this way, the confusion of names is more apparent than real. Even in our own day we find that certain names seem to have a "run" in families, not only among their children but also

---

✣ IN CONTEXT   The Horites of Mount Seir

At one time, Seir and Edom may have been two separate geographical regions. Seir was mountainous and Edom was part of the Transjordanian plateau. Eventually Seir became part of the Edomite state and the names Seir and Edom were used interchangeably.

Two diferent peoples, the Horites and the Edomites, lived in the area known as Seir and Edom. The Horite genealogy in Gen. 36:20–30 is distinct from the Edomite genealogy in 36:9–19. The Horites appear to have been more pastoral, different from the agricultural Edomites. In the Bible the Horites are described as inhabiting the mountains of Seir until they were displaced by the Edomites (Gen. 14:6; Deut. 2:12).

When, in the nineteenth century, scholars discovered a people called the Hurrians, they assumed a connection with the biblical Horites. But the Hurrians were a political and cultural force in north Syria and in the Tigris area; their whereabouts in the northern regions does not correspond with the Horite association with Mount Seir. Thus the Horites should not be confused with the Edomites or the Hurrians. All that can be determined about them now is that they were very early inhabitants of Seir.

among their children's spouses and in-laws. Thus we may say "Big David" and "Little David," or "Lisa A" and "Lisa B."

36:4–8 Genesis describes the growth of Esau's family and possessions. He moved to **Mount Seir.** Eventually, the region would be named after Esau—Edom, the "Red" land (v. 43). Esau's separation from Jacob was similar to the separation of Lot from Abraham (13:6–13).

36:6–8 This separation had occurred probably between Jacob's purchase of Esau's birthright (25:29–34) and the stealing of Esau's blessing (27:18–29), before Jacob was sent to Haran (28:5). When Jacob returned to Canaan, Esau was already living in **Mount Seir** (32:3), southeast of the Dead Sea.

36:9–19 These verses parallel and expand on the genealogical list of Esau's family in vv. 1–8. Verses 15–19 expand further on this same list. More care is given to the genealogy of Jacob. When the material is pulled together, we have the following family line: The sons of Esau (born before leaving Canaan): Eliphaz, whose mother is Adah (36:4); Reuel, whose mother is Basemath (36:4); and Jeush, Jaalam, and Korah, whose mother is Aholibamah (36:5). The sons of Eliphaz (son of Esau and Adah): Teman, Omar, Zepho, Gatam, Kenaz (36:11), and Amalek, whose mother is Timna (36:12). The sons of Reuel (son of Esau and Basemath): Nahath, Zerah, Shammah, and Mizzah (36:13). No sons are named for Esau's sons by Aholibamah (36:14).

36:12 Timna's son, **Amalek,** founded a people that later would trouble the Israelites (Num. 14:39–45).

36:20–30 The people of **Seir,** the Horites, had close interrelationships with Esau's family. These family histories are repeated in 1 Chr. 1:38–42.

36:31–39 This list follows the list of the chiefs of **Edom** (vv. 15–19). The eight names in this list are unrelated to each other. This indicates that they were chosen for reasons other than royal descent.

36:40–43 These chiefs probably followed the kings listed in vv. 31–39. They bear some of the names of their forebears (vv. 1–14). **Esau was the father of the Edomites:** Although Esau is not the heir of God's everlasting covenant with the family of Abraham, God still blessed his family. They too became a nation.

Modern readers may understandably ask why a chapter like this is placed in the Bible. Why all this detail of names and chiefs? But readers in some parts of the world even today would find this material fascinating if not valuable. In many cultures, a great prize is placed on the accurate recital of the names of one's forebears. Such must also have been the case among many of the peoples of biblical periods. These listings may evince

several values: (1) A sense of connection that the descendant of Esau would have had in this recital of names; such a person would think highly of the fact that he or she had such an illustrious family line. (2) A sense of history that these names produce; any reader may look at this list and gain a sense, even in a cursory way, that the ancients had a strong desire for historical ties. (3) A sense of pride and worth in the memory of these details. In every culture there are those who are able (or who claim to be able) to trace back their ancestry through many centuries. (4) A sense of promise in that Esau was also given a promise from his father and from the Lord; that promise was kept (27:39, 40).

37:1–50:26 This last major section of Genesis is widely regarded as one of the finest works of narrative literature from the ancient world. Few characters in the OT are presented with as much clarity as is Joseph, and few story lines in the OT are given with as much detail and interest. Perhaps only the stories of Moses and of David surpass the account of Joseph. The story has a classic "U" shaped design, moving from a pastoral scene of familial prosperity, through an extended period of adversity and disintegration of the family unit, to a climax of restoration and reuniting of the family unit that result in a greater position of prosperity than when the story began.

37:1 in the land: When he left Laban, Jacob at first settled near Shechem (33:18–20). Then at the Lord's bidding he went to Bethel (35:1–15), where the divine covenant was renewed. Jacob traveled south again to Ephrath (later Bethlehem, 35:16–20), where Rachel died while giving birth to Benjamin. Finally, Jacob went to Hebron (Kirjath Arba), where he buried his father (35:27–29). Chapter 37 continues Jacob's story at Hebron (v. 14). The word for **stranger** (Heb. *gûr*) can also mean "sojourner" or "alien." The Lord had promised that this land would become a permanent possession of Abraham's family (12:7). To the third generation that promise was still not realized. Jacob and his family were still aliens in the land.

37:2 history of Jacob: This is the tenth time this Hebrew phrasing is used in Genesis (2:4, note). **Joseph** was the first son of Jacob's favorite wife, Rachel (30:22–24). **seventeen years old:** This is one of the few places the Bible gives the age of a person at a certain event (12:4). Usually, it records only the length of a person's whole life. **Bilhah** is the maid of Rachel, who gave birth to Dan and Naphtali (30:4–8); **Zilpah** is the maid of Leah, who gave birth to Gad and Asher (30:9–11). **a bad report:** Since Joseph in general demonstrated his integrity (ch. 39), he was probably not slandering his brothers but accurately reporting

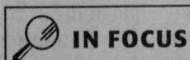 **IN FOCUS** | **"Dream"**

(Heb. *chalom*) (Gen. 37:5; 40:5; 41:7; Joel 2:28) Strong's #2472: The word simply means "to dream." The ancients understood a dream or a vision as "watching during sleep," suggesting a special state of consciousness. Often dreams were recognized as revelations from the gods, or from the Lord God Himself in the case of the Hebrews. Many times these dreams and visions were encoded in symbolic language that needed interpretation. Those who could interpret dreams possessed power in the ancient world (41:37–40; Dan. 2:46–48). Joseph both received and interpreted such messages but was able to interpret the figures and symbols of dream-events only as God enabled him (40:8; 41:16).

some negligence on their part. Whatever his intentions, his brothers naturally would have resented him.

37:3 The name **Israel** was given to Jacob following his wrestling with the Lord (32:22–32). It is used interchangeably with Jacob (35:21, 22; 43:6). **son of his old age:** Jacob's favoritism for his son Joseph may be explained as well by the special love he had for the boy's mother (29:30). **a tunic of many colors:** This is a traditional

translation. The Hebrew phrase (*ketonet passîm*) may simply mean a garment with long sleeves. The robe was distinctive in color or design and was probably costly.

37:4 they hated him: Unwittingly, Jacob's discriminatory actions made Joseph unpopular in the family.

37:5 In his youthful enthusiasm, Joseph told his family about his **dream.** Although the dream was prophetic, it alienated his brothers **even more.**

37:6 please hear: Joseph may be accused of willful action here, but more likely he was just not aware of how his words would be received. His exuberance led him to an unfortunate display of superiority over his older brothers.

37:7 my sheaf arose: Joseph's dream pictured the prominence that he would eventually have in the family. In the culture of his day, the firstborn was the prominent one (35:23). Joseph's dream not only insulted his older brothers, it also violated custom.

37:8 shall you indeed reign: The brothers understood immediately the meaning of Joseph's dream. Of course what they and he could not have known was that this dream would be fulfilled literally.

37:9 Joseph could have been more sensitive to his family's response to his **dreams.** His second dream was even more alarming. According to this dream, even the sun and moon, presumably his father and mother (though his mother was already deceased;

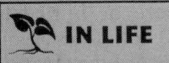 **IN LIFE** | **Sin Is Passed On Through Generations**

People often assume that their "private" sins hurt no one but themselves. For instance, how could the sin of envy affect anyone else? Isn't coveting strictly a matter between them and the Lord?

But sins of character have a way of touching everyone with whom we have contact, especially those we love the most, our family. That is what happened in three generations of Isaac's family. His wife, Rebekah, was determined to gain Isaac's blessing for her favorite son, Jacob, even if it meant deceiving her husband (Gen. 25:28; 27:5–29). Thus she helped her son Jacob grow up to be a deceiver (27:35, 36).

Years later, Jacob's second wife, Rachel, became frustrated as her sister and rival, Leah, bore four sons for Jacob. Rachel's anguish developed into such strong envy that it created tension and anger in her husband, even though he loved Rachel dearly (29:34–30:2).

A bitter harvest of Rebekah and Jacob's deception and Rachel's envy was reaped in the third generation when Joseph's brothers began to envy him (37:11). They sold him into slavery and then deceived their father about it (37:23–35). Where had they learned to treat their sibling with jealousy and their father with such cruel deception? Clearly, they were following in their elders' footsteps!

Sin can pass from generation to generation, not just by what is said, but by what is lived. Attitudes are not so much taught as caught.

35:16–20), would bow to Joseph. The eleven stars were his brothers.

37:10, 11 Now, even **his father** was insulted by Joseph's behavior. The son could have talked about his dreams with more tact. **kept the matter:** Although he was insulted, Jacob pondered (compare Luke 2:19) Joseph's dreams for they were clearly from God.

37:12 The brothers journeyed north from Hebron (35:27–29), presumably in order to find better pastures for their flocks. **Shechem** plays a continuing role in the Genesis narrative.

suggest that when God is working out all the details, even this does not guarantee that a journey will be what we desire. **Dothan** is about ten miles north of Shechem, near Mount Gilboa.

37:18 saw him a far off: His distinctive tunic allowed the brothers to recognize Joseph at a distance (vv. 3, 23, 31). **to kill him:** His brothers' hatred and envy led them to discuss murder (vv. 4, 5, 8, 11).

37:19, 20 this dreamer: The Hebrew phrase expresses contempt and literally means "master of dreams." The brothers feared that

Photo by Howard Vos

The mound of Dothan (center), the Old Testament city where Joseph's brothers threw him into a pit and later sold him to slave traders (Gen. 37:17–28).

Abram had built his first altar to God there (12:6; 33:18).

37:13 I will send you: The story of young Joseph being sent by his father to join his brothers is somewhat similar to that of David being sent by his father to join his brothers (1 Sam. 17:17–19).

37:14–16 well: The Hebrew word here, *shalom,* means "well, whole, sound" and is often translated by the word "peace." **bring back word:** Because Joseph had earlier brought back a bad report, he would not be welcomed by his brothers.

37:17 I heard them say: This unnamed (v. 15) individual was able to help Joseph, which we regard as providential provision: just the right person at just the right place and time to aid Joseph. Nevertheless, as it turns out, Joseph's journey soon ends in disaster, from which we

Joseph's **dreams** may actually come true. By killing him, they could prevent this.

37:21 Reuben, as the firstborn son and principal heir, had the most to lose if Joseph's dreams came true (35:23). Yet Reuben intervened to spare Joseph's life. This was something of a contrast with his earlier wicked actions (35:22).

37:22 shed no blood: Reuben attempted to save Joseph's life by getting his brothers to leave Joseph in a pit. Without water in the pit, Joseph could only survive a few days. Reuben planned to rescue him in time. Reuben may have been motivated by a love for his **father** and a desire to ease the strained relationship with him that had resulted from his abuse of Bilhah (35:22; compare 49:4). Once Reuben convinced his brothers not to kill Joseph, he left (v. 29).

37:23 The action of the brothers toward the

tunic shows how hateful to them this distinctive garment was, for they did not want him to have this garment even in death.

37:24 That **the pit** (v. 20) **was empty** of **water** meant that the brothers were leaving Joseph to die. A person can live for a considerable period of time without food but only a several days without water.

INSIGHT   **The Slave Traders**

It is ironic that Joseph was sold to a band of Midianites (Gen. 37:28), because the Midianites were distant relatives of Joseph and his brothers through Abraham's concubine Keturah (25:1, 2). The Midianites lived as nomads in the desert region southeast of Canaan, along the northern coast of the Red Sea. They were often linked with the Ishmaelites (37:27, 28; Judg. 7:25; 8:24), with whom they apparently shared the slave trade to Egypt.

37:25 The crassness of the brothers toward Joseph is further seen in the words **to eat a meal.** Presumably even Cain did not sit down and eat a meal after killing Abel (4:1–9). The **Ishmaelites** were wandering traders. The name (it refers to the descendants of Ishmael, the son of Abraham; 16:11–16; 17:18–27; 25:12–18; 28:9; 36:3) is loosely equivalent to the name Midianite (v. 28). **Gilead** is a mountainous region in the Transjordan (31:21), famed for aromatic spices (Jer. 8:22; 46:11). Only the rich

owned the few **camels** that were domesticated at this time.

37:26 What profit: The brothers not only considered killing Joseph, but started discussing how they could make the crime profitable.

37:27, 28 Midian was a son of Abraham by his concubine Keturah (25:2, 4; 36:35). The name **Midianites** is used interchangeably with the name Ishmaelites (v. 25), most likely indicating an alliance between the two peoples. Both terms refer to wandering Arab traders. **Twenty shekels of silver** may have been the going rate for a slave at the time. On the other hand, the Midianites may have paid a little less because they knew something was amiss (the standard price for a slave in later Israelite law was thirty shekels; Ex. 21:32). According to 42:21, Joseph begged his brothers not to sell him. The brothers considered Joseph as good as dead; he would never return from Egyptian slavery. The account would later be memorialized in song (Ps. 105:17), and the despicable act finds its parallel in the price paid to Judas for betraying the Savior (Matt. 27:3–10; compare Zech. 11:12).

37:29 Reuben returned, failed to find Joseph, and **tore his clothes** to express his grief. Tearing one's clothes was a common expression of profound dismay. Reuben's grief was genuine feeling for his younger brother mixed with the fear that he, the oldest brother, would be blamed.

37:30–35 Bringing the blood-covered **tunic** to their **father** was an attempt at legal deceit. This garment of Joseph's would constitute proof of his death (compare Ex. 22:13). Jacob then would be expected to confirm Joseph's death publicly, absolving the brothers of any further liability.

37:31, 32 The brothers used **Joseph's tunic,** the symbol of his favored position, as a

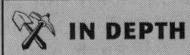

IN DEPTH   **The Actions of Judah**

Even though the actions of Judah were evil throughout most of the events recorded in Gen. 38, he was nonetheless by these events brought into contact with the peoples of the land. While they influenced him for evil throughout much of the story, at the end he had an effect on them for good. That is, God used Judah's sojourn among the Canaanites to bring a remnant of that people into contact with His family of faith.

In time, the people of Israel learned to celebrate the fact that among their mothers was a Canaanite woman of bold daring (Ruth 4:12, 18–22). Indeed, the Bible does not let us forget this. It comes to a head in the genealogy of Jesus the Messiah (Matt. 1:3). He who came to be the Savior not only of the Jewish people but also of the nations was descended not only from Jewish people but also from the nations whom He came to save. In these and many ways God displays His heart for the nations to know Him.

the identification of David as the guilty person by Nathan (2 Sam. 12:7).

38:26 She has been more righteous: Judah, one of the heirs of the everlasting covenant with the living God, was put to shame by a Canaanite woman. To his credit, Judah confessed his sins.

38:27 The birth of **twins** was a special blessing from the Lord. This section continues a biblical theme of competing sons (chs. 4; 25—28).

38:28 his hand: There could be no mistakes in identifying the firstborn. The midwife used a scarlet thread to make sure everyone knew which baby had been born first.

38:29 breach: The other baby burst forth after his brother's hand had been withdrawn. Despite the brother's hand, Perez was the firstborn. He became the one who is in the lineage of David, and ultimately Jesus (Ruth 4:18; Matt. 1:3).

38:30 Both Perez and **Zerah** established families in the house of Judah (1 Chr. 2:3–8); even Shelah established a family (Num. 26:19–22). Tamar became a member of the family of promise, even though she was a Canaanite (Ruth 4:12). Matthew mentions Tamar—a woman—in the lineage of the Messiah. She had become a heroine of the faith, despite her origins and the nature of her actions (Matt. 1:3).

39:1 Joseph had been taken down to Egypt: This verse repeats the sense of 37:36 and resumes the Joseph story that was interrupted by the story of Judah and Tamar (ch. 38). The first readers of Genesis were the second generation that had come out of Egypt under Moses. This narrative explained to them why their parents were Egyptian slaves. **Potiphar:** Joseph's brothers probably expected that he would be sold as a common laborer in a heavy construction project. Such heavy phys-

ical labor under harsh conditions could make a young man's life short. Yet because of God's mercy, Joseph was sold to a rich and important royal official. See the note at 37:28 for the interchange of the words **Ishmaelites** and Midianites.

39:2 The LORD was with Joseph: This key phrase of this section is repeated (vv. 21, 23). This phrase indicates that God cared for, protected, and blessed Joseph. Joseph occupied a very high station for a slave. He lived and worked in his master's **house** as **a successful man;** that is, as someone whose work was productive, who could be trusted, and who succeeded in his tasks.

39:3 Potiphar recognized that Joseph was successful because **the Lord was with him.** Perhaps Joseph had had some effect on his master's spiritual condition.

39:4 found favor: Joseph exemplified the faithful steward and illustrated the principle that one who is faithful in a little will be given charge over much (Matt. 25:21; 1 Cor. 4:2).

39:5 the LORD blessed the Egyptian's house: God commanded Abraham and his descendants to be a blessing to everyone (Gen. 12:2, 3). Here Joseph, thrust into a foreign country by the anger of his brothers, brought God's blessing to an Egyptian official's home. What is more, the Egyptian knew that the blessing was from God.

39:6 all that he had: Potiphar's trust in Joseph was so complete that Potiphar had no care except for his menu (v. 23). **handsome:** Seldom does the Bible mention a character's physical traits. This description is similar to the description of David (1 Sam. 16:12; for Sarai, see Gen. 12:11; for Rebekah, see 24:16; for Rachel, see 29:17).

39:7 Potiphar's **wife** began to flirt with Joseph. Perhaps she was bored. On the other

 **IN PERSON** **Potiphar's House and Joseph's Temptation**

Joseph's activities in Potiphar's house meant that day by day (Gen. 38:10) he was passing through the chamber that would be used for sleeping at night. The house would have had a front entrance, living or sleeping quarters, and storeroom at the back. Since his master's wife continued to lounge on her bed, presumably in ever-increasingly alluring attire and manner, the pressure on young Joseph must have been nearly unbearable.

From a human point of view, he might have decided that things were not going to get much better for him as a slave in a foreign land. As a young man with raging hormones, and as an insightful man with a realistic appraisal of his prospects, he might have yielded to her cries, even though the pleasures would be short lived. But he did not yield. Compare the seduction scene in Prov. 7 for someone, a fool, who did.

hand, the Hebrew term *sarîs* translated "officer" in v. 1 ordinarily means "eunuch." If Potiphar was literally a eunuch, this might help to explain his wife's actions.

39:8 But he refused: Joseph exemplified the highest standard of personal behavior. The recurring phrase, "the LORD was with him" (vv. 2, 21, 23) helps to explain Joseph's goodness. The empowering presence of God in his life helped Joseph to resist temptation.

39:9, 10 sin against God: Here Joseph not only stood up for his ethical beliefs, but he also told a woman who probably believed in many gods about the righteousness of the only true God!

39:11 none of the men: This time, the master's wife caught Joseph alone.

39:12, 13 The clothing of a slave in the hot climate of Egypt probably did not consist of much. She grabbed Joseph. In the ensuing struggle, she wound up holding **his garment.** Joseph fled.

39:14–18 he has brought: She insulted her husband in front of other slaves. The term **Hebrew** is used only four times in Genesis (14:13; 39:17; 41:12). Here it is a racial slur. **to mock:** The verb suggests racial hatred. The Hamitic Egyptians scorned the Semitic peoples of Canaan (43:32). The Egyptian slaves must have envied Joseph's success. Potiphar's wife must have found ready ears among these men to believe her lies. She had not **cried out,** of course. But the charge of rape was as serious then as it is in our day. The attempted rape of a master's wife by a foreign slave would have been an exceptional outrage.

39:19 The **anger** of Potiphar is understandable and expected.

39:20 Because Potiphar, **Joseph's master,** was a royal officer (39:1), his slave Joseph would be a legal member of his household and therefore put in a special **prison.**

39:20 into the prison: Surprisingly, Potiphar did not have Joseph put to death or simply killed outright. Is it possible that Joseph had so impressed Potiphar during the considerable time

he had been in his service that Potiphar found himself not fully believing the story his wife told him? Is it possible that Potiphar determined to throw Joseph into the royal prison, over which he had command (39:1; 40:3; 41:9–11) in order to spare Joseph's life? In any case, Joseph wound up in prison for something he had steadfastly refused to do.

39:21 The **LORD** continued to be **with Joseph,** even in prison (Ps. 139:7–12). **Mercy** can be translated "loyal love" (Ps. 13:5). Here in an Egyptian prison, Joseph experienced God's loyal love. God faithfully kept His promises by staying with His people—even in rough circumstances (for God's promises to be with Abraham's descendants see 12:1–3; 50:24). **The keeper of the prison** was the warden who was under the "captain of the guard" (40:3), namely, Potiphar (39:1).

39:22 The warden would have known, as Potiphar had (39:3), that the animating factor in Joseph's life was the presence of Yahweh. Thus Joseph spread the knowledge of the true God even to a prison (as Paul and other apostles were later to do).

39:23 the LORD made it prosper: Because of God's blessing, everything Joseph did prospered (Ps. 1:1–3).

40:1, 2 The butler and the baker of the king were important offices in the royal court. **Offended** stands for the word ordinarily translated as "sinned." Its principal meaning is "to miss the mark." The nature of their offenses is not explained.

40:3 The reference to **the house** implies that there were two holding areas for prisoners in this situation. One was the prison proper, the other was a type of house arrest associated with, but not in, the prison itself.

40:4 As a trustee of the prison, Joseph also **served** the high officials who were under house arrest awaiting the disposition of the charges against them.

40:5 Each . . . dream had **its own interpretation;** these were not ordinary dreams. They contained symbols that demanded explanation.

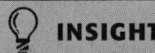 **INSIGHT**   **God's Mercy to Joseph**

The mercy (Heb. *chesed*) that God showed to Joseph (Gen. 39:21) involved His faithful loyalty to Abraham, Isaac, and Jacob. God made promises to these patriarchs (12:1–3; 15:13, 14; 28:3, 4, 13–15), and in order to fulfill His commitments, He preserved Joseph through his prison ordeal. God often demonstrated His mercy by delivering His people from their troubles. For example, He delivered Lot from Sodom before destroying the city in judgment (19:19), and He showed mercy to the Israelites by leading them out of Egypt (Ex. 15:13).

40:6 Joseph came to see the butler and baker because it was part of his duties as the prison trustee.

40:7, 8 Joseph's statement that **interpretations belong to God** was a bold testimony. But Joseph not only announced his faith, he then quickly acted upon it. Joseph had received such dreams as a younger man and had understood their meaning (37:5–11).

40:9–12 Joseph's words to the butler, **lift up your head,** form a grisly pun in the passage. Here they speak of the restoration of the butler to his former honor; in v. 19 they speak of death.

40:13, 14 Joseph asked the butler to **remember me** so that his case might be reviewed and he might be delivered from a false imprisonment. **Kindness** represents a word that also means "loyal love." Joseph spoke of a binding obligation that his interpretation of the dream had placed upon the butler.

40:15 Joseph had two good reasons for seeking his release: being sold by his brothers into slavery and being framed by Potiphar's wife. In both cases he was an innocent victim. Presumably the butler would recognize the unfairness of Joseph's condition, since he himself had been unfairly charged and badly treated as well.

40:16, 17 Perhaps **the chief baker's** sense of guilt had held him back, but now he sensed that the time was right to announce his own dream. Both of these men respected Joseph's interpretations as true. Like the butler's, the baker's dream used the number three.

40:18 The interpretation of the baker's dream was bad news indeed: In three days the baker would be executed.

40:19 The pun in **lift off your head** is more evident in the Hebrew text (v. 13). More literally, the words read, "Pharaoh will lift your head . . . from you." That is, the line begins exactly as in v. 13, but with a deadly zinger at the end! It is not simply baked goods **the birds** will eat (v. 17), but the flesh of the baker. That is, he will not be allowed even a proper burial; he will instead be hanged and then his body will be left for the vultures. Clearly there was no point for Joseph to ask to be remembered by the baker (vv. 14, 15).

40:20–22 Only here do we learn that **the third day** was Pharaoh's birthday. The play on words of vv. 13, 19 comes to its culmination here in **he lifted the head.** Pharaoh brought both of the prisoners from their house arrest for all the other servants to see. The one he restored (v. 21), and the other he hanged (v. 22). It could be that there had been a threat against Pharaoh's life that involved the poisoning of food. Presumably the investigation led to two possible culprits, the butler who would serve Pharaoh his wine and the baker who would prepare bread for Pharaoh. The guilty party was executed; the other was given back his prestigious position. Pharaoh did this in the presence of **all of Pharaoh's servants** in order to both warn and encourage the servant household. Pharaoh would reward those who served him well, but would destroy any who meant him harm.

40:23 The butler **did not remember** his promise made to Joseph. The euphoria of his release and restoration took his mind away from his distressing days under arrest. Soon the sheer business of his life precluded any action on behalf of Joseph. So Joseph stayed in prison. And God was still with him.

41:1–57 This chapter describes the turning point in Joseph's life. He rose from a dungeon to the Egyptian throne room. God engineered the circumstances so that through Joseph, He could meet the needs of a nation during the coming famine and reunite Jacob's family.

41:1–8 This providential series of dream-pairs is now concluded. The dreams in 40:5 proved the means for involving Joseph in the dreams here, and it was these dreams that served to fulfill the first pair (37:5–9).

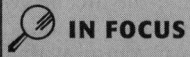 **IN FOCUS** | **"Pharaoh"**

(Heb. *Par 'oh*) (Gen. 41:1; Ex. 1:11) Strong's #6547: The name Pharaoh comes from the Egyptian word *pr-'o,* which means "the great house." Originally the word *Pharaoh* was not a designation for the king of Egypt but a reference to his palace. The ancient Egyptians believed that Pharaoh was the living representation of the god Horus in Egyptian religion, identified with the cult of the sun god and symbolized by the falcon. The plagues against the Egyptians prior to the Israelite exodus from Egypt were cosmic in nature, a kind of spiritual warfare between the living God and the false gods of Egypt (Ex. 12:12; 15:11). The tenth plague, resulting in the death of the firstborn among the Egyptians (including Pharaoh's), was divine judgment upon Pharaoh's claim to deity (Ex. 12:29, 30; 18:11, 12).

✠ IN CONTEXT   Egypt's Seven Lean Years

The record of Egypt's seven lean years (Gen. 41:27) appears to have an antecedent in Egyptian literature. A text called *The Tradition of the Seven Lean Years in Egypt* is attributed to pharaoh Djoser of the Third Dynasty of Egypt's Old Kingdom (c. 2650 B.C.). The text of this Egyptian story as it now exists came from scribes during the reign of Ptolemy V (204–180 B.C.). While this text is much later than the Genesis account, it is possible that it was copied from an earlier text.

The text recounts a letter that Djoser wrote to his overseer in Elephantine in southern Egypt, lamenting that the "Nile has not come up in my time for a space of seven years." Consequently grain was scarce, fruits had dried up, and "every man robbed his companion." Imhotep, the renowned vizier, or chief minister, to Djoser then tells him about the god Khnum, who resides at the birthplace of the Nile, namely Elephantine. Pharaoh Djoser then has a dream in which the god tells him that the Nile will soon "pour forth for you."

41:1 As in the case of his servants (40:5), **Pharaoh** had an unusual **dream** to which he attached great significance. **The river** is the Nile, the life stream of Egypt.

41:2 In ancient Semitic thought, the number **seven** had special significance. This significance probably had its roots in the seven days of creation (ch. 1).

41:3, 4 ugly and gaunt: The second group of seven cows contrasts strongly with the first. **ate up:** The bucolic scene quickly turns into a nightmare as the scrawny cows devour the healthy ones.

41:5–7 The **second** dream was very much like the first, only this time it presented heads of grain rather than cows. The numeral **seven** again was prominent.

41:8 magicians: The Hebrew term is related to the word for stylus, a writing instrument. Thus, the magicians were associated in some manner with writing and knowledge, no doubt of the occult. Yet here, as on a later occasion (Ex. 8:18, 19), the power of the magicians was shown to be limited. The **wise men** (Heb. *hakam*; also used for the "wise" man of Israel in Prov. 1:5) were a class of scholars associated with the courts of the ancient Middle East. They were either functionaries of pagan religions as here, or merely observers and interpreters of life. **No one who could interpret** is a scene similar to Dan. 2:1–13.

41:9 faults: The Hebrew word is usually translated "sins" (*hata'îm*). At long last the butler remembered his experience with the young Hebrew prisoner who interpreted his dream (40:9–15).

41:10–12 captain of the guard: In vv. 10, 12, this phrase refers to Potiphar (39:1, 19, 20).

41:13, 14 out of the dungeon: Joseph was manager of the prison (39:22, 23). Egyptian men not only **shaved** their face, but their entire body. They generally wore wigs. Egyptian officials scorned the "hairy" Canaanites, including the Hebrews (43:32). While in the service of Potiphar, Joseph probably adopted the manner and dress of the Egyptians. But in prison, Joseph could not keep up his appearance.

41:15 you can understand a dream: Pharaoh was desperate. He wanted a correct interpretation of his dream.

41:16 There is a strong emphasis on the word **God.** Joseph praised the power of the living God in the pagan court of Pharaoh. He would not take credit for his ability to interpret dreams or use his innocence to plead for his freedom. His **answer of peace** (Heb. *shalôm*) suggests that Joseph already knew the dream contained some good news for the Pharaoh.

41:17–24 in my dream: Pharaoh repeated the information he had given earlier to his own magicians and wise men (41:1–8; compare vv. 1–4). One new detail is recorded here (v. 21): the seven ugly cows do not look better after eating the good cows (v. 30).

41:25 Led by the Spirit of God, Joseph revealed that the **dreams** have the same meaning (22:15). **God has shown Pharaoh:** Again Joseph testified to the living God in a pagan court (39:3). God sent the dreams; God enabled Joseph to understand them; and ultimately God controlled and will control all things.

41:26–28 God has shown Pharaoh: The repetition of this phrase (v. 25) is for emphasis (v. 32). God put Joseph in Egypt during this critical time so that He could bless Egypt through a Hebrew. Then the true and living God's blessing would become known throughout the ancient world, for God had promised to bless all nations through the people of Israel (12:2).

41:29, 30 the plenty will be forgotten: The famine would be so severe that everyone would forget the years of plenty.

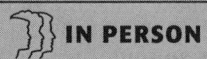 **IN PERSON** | **Joseph—A Model for Marketplace Christians**

People who work in today's marketplace may wonder at times how their faith applies in a tough business environment. If so, it helps to study the life of Joseph. He and Daniel (Dan. 1:6) are two of the best models in Scripture for how to honor God in a "secular" workplace.

Consider Joseph's circumstances. He was cut off from his family. He was part of a culture that worshiped pagan gods, and apparently he alone there worshiped the true God. Thus he had no support system for his beliefs or values and no one to turn to for godly counsel as he made far-reaching decisions. His boss, Pharaoh, was considered a god by the Egyptians. Likewise Joseph's wife was an Egyptian and his father-in-law a priest of the sun-god.

How did Joseph maintain his faith in such an environment? Consider several ways:

- (1) *He maintained his integrity.* Joseph steadfastly resisted the sexual advances of Potiphar's wife (Gen. 39:7–10). He realized that moral compromise would have been an offense not only against his master, but even worse, against God. He remained committed to what he knew was right, despite the consequences.
- (2) *He kept doing his best even when the situation was the worst.* Unjustly thrown into prison, Joseph easily could have become bitter at God. He could have given up with the attitude, "What's the use?" Instead, he kept doing what God had designed Him to do—exercising authority, even in prison (39:22, 23).
- (3) *He carried out the task he was given.* Promoted to Pharaoh's right hand, Joseph was faithful in the responsibility. He wisely planned for the coming famine and managed the Egyptian economy in a way that saved many lives (41:46–49, 53–57). He recognized that the work itself was what God wanted him to do.
- (4) *He used his power and influence compassionately.* Second-in-command under Pharaoh, Joseph could have used his position as an opportunity to pay back his enemies, such as his brothers, the slave traders, and Potiphar's wife. Instead, the record shows just the opposite: he used his power to bring reconciliation (45:3–15; 50:20).

God used Joseph's faithfulness to preserve the children of Jacob (Israel) in order to fulfill His promise to Abraham (45:5–8). In the same way, God intends to use believers today in positions great and small to accomplish His purposes. Therefore it is crucial that we honor God through our work. Like Joseph, we need to be people of whom there can be no doubt—we are those "in whom is the Spirit of God" (41:38).

41:31, 32 God, and God: Joseph emphasized his reference to the true God as he witnessed to the reality of the only true God. He made it clear that he was speaking about the one God, not the numerous false gods that filled the Egyptian court, or even Pharaoh himself who was believed to be a god (22:1; 42:18).

41:33 a discerning and wise man: An exceedingly wise man.

41:34 One-fifth may seem large. However, the large amount would allow for spoilage, for extra grain for trade, and for extra grain to plant after the seven years of famine.

41:35 Pharaoh would view this large tax as an expansion of his own **authority.**

41:36–38 in whom is the Spirit of God: At least Pharaoh acknowledged that Joseph was

extraordinarily wise. Or more likely, he testified to the reality of God's power in Joseph's life.

41:39, 40 You shall be over my house: Since Joseph was so wise, naturally he was the first choice for administering the collection of grain. **in regard to the throne:** Joseph was given enormous power. Only Pharaoh was above him.

41:41 over all the land of Egypt: The Book of Genesis begins with the story of the fall of our first parents from paradise. It concludes with the story of the rise of a Hebrew slave from a dungeon to a seat beside the throne of the king. In Joseph's elevation there is a symbol of hope for all who believe in his God. One day all such believers will be lifted from the murky dungeons and dank habitats of their present experiences to positions of wonder and glory (Ps. 113:7–9).

41:42 With the **signet ring,** Joseph's orders would have the same authority as the word of Pharaoh (Esth. 3:10; 8:2). The ring had the signature of the Pharaoh in Egyptian hieroglyphics (38:18). Joseph would use the ring to mark clay or wax to authenticate royal documents and laws. Now wearing fine **garments** and a **gold chain,** Joseph must have felt a world removed from that of the prison dungeon.

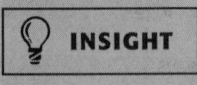

INSIGHT

Stone Storehouses

The Egyptians maintained large stone storehouses, primarily for grain (Gen. 41:48). This protected them from famine and helped stabilize prices. The granaries were often associated with the temples. The ruler was regarded as divine, and the department devoted to grain growing and distribution was one of the most important in the fundamentally religious government of Egypt.

41:43 Bow the knee: The Egyptian people bowed as a sign of respect and homage to Joseph's position, not as a sign of worship.

41:44 The hyperbole **hand or foot** here suggests the enormous power that Pharaoh accorded Joseph.

41:45 Zaphnath-Paaneah: Pharaoh honors Joseph by giving him an Egyptian name that probably means "The God Speaks and Lives." While in some contexts, this would refer to an Egyptian god, in this case it refers to the true God of Joseph. Wherever Joseph went in Egypt, his name would point to the reality of his God. **Asenath:** An Egyptian name meaning "Belonging to (the Goddess) Neith." **Poti-Pherah** means "He Whom Ra (the sun god) Gave." **On** is a city in northern Egypt that was noted for its worship of Ra. But Joseph and Asenath's sons were worshipers of the Lord, not Ra. Although Joseph married a pagan priest's daughter, he trained his sons to worship the living God. Probably Asenath also became a worshiper of the Lord.

41:46 thirty years old: Thirteen years had passed since Joseph was sold by his brothers (37:2).

41:47 seven plentiful years: Just as God had revealed, the years of plenty came.

41:48, 49 The task was enormous for there was **much grain.** Joseph had to be a wise administrator. The skills he learned in Potiphar's

household and in the royal prison must have been helpful during this busy time. But in the end, God made Joseph succeed (v. 52; 39:23).

41:50–53 Asenath's **two sons** carry on the two-son motif in Genesis (Ishmael and Isaac, chs. 16; 21; Esau and Jacob, 25:19–28; Perez and Zerah, 38:27–30).

41:54, 55 the seven years of famine: As Joseph had warned (41:30), bad years followed the seven years of plenty. Pharaoh allowed Joseph to handle the crisis. He trusted completely Joseph's leadership.

41:56, 57 Joseph enriched the treasury of Pharaoh by selling grain to the Egyptians. **all countries:** The whole known world came to Egypt to buy grain. Just as Joseph had testified to Egypt concerning the reality of the true God, so now he was able to testify to all nations.

42:1 Jacob said to his sons: By this time, Judah had returned to Jacob (ch. 38).

42:2–4 Benjamin: Jacob still played favorites (37:3). However, there is no mention of jealousy among the other brothers as there had been before (37:8).

42:5, 6 bowed before him: God fulfilled the dreams He gave to Joseph at the age of seventeen (37:5–11).

42:7, 8 acted as a stranger: These men standing before Joseph had sold him as a slave twenty years before; yet they were his brothers! Now suddenly here they were, bowing before him, just as he had dreamed! Joseph's life was now thoroughly Egyptian. In fact, he had named his first son "Forgetfulness," as a sign of his estrangement from the painful memories of his family (41:51). What went through Joseph's mind as he recognized his brothers? No doubt shock, confusion, and anger. Joseph may have **spoke roughly** in order to control his emotions.

42:9–12 Joseph **remembered the dreams** and released his pent-up feelings. He accused his brothers of something he knew they did not do. In this way, Joseph set out to learn whether his brothers had changed for the better. Would they betray each other when under pressure?

42:13 the youngest: At the mention of his younger brother, Benjamin, Joseph must have had great difficulty hiding his feelings. **and one is no more:** These words must have been unbearable to Joseph. Although his brothers supposed he was dead, he was right before their eyes!

42:14, 15 Twice, Joseph accused them of being **spies.** The brothers must have been overcome with fear. They were standing before a man who had absolute, autocratic power. At his word they could be executed.

42:16, 17 Joseph demanded that Benjamin, his full **brother,** be brought to him. At the time, Benjamin was with Jacob (v. 4).

42:18–20 Here, Joseph gave his brothers a clue about who he was. In effect, Joseph told them, "**I fear** the one **God**" (41:32). For all of his more than twenty years in Egypt, Joseph had not lost his belief in the true God.

42:21 truly guilty: The brothers realized that they were being punished for what they had done to Joseph so many years ago. **when he pleaded with us:** The first account (37:18–28) does not include this detail.

42:22 Only **Reuben** had tried to save Joseph on that awful day (37:22). His plan to rescue Joseph was thwarted when the brothers decided to sell him to the Midianite traders instead of abandoning him in a pit to die. **his blood:** According to Reuben, the brothers would be punished for killing Joseph.

42:23 Joseph had been speaking in Egyptian and an **interpreter** was translating to the brothers. The brothers did not suspect that this Egyptian official **understood** what they said in their own language.

42:24 wept: At last Joseph's emotions went beyond his control. **he took Simeon:** Since Reuben, the firstborn son, had been Joseph's principal defender years ago, Joseph took Simeon, the next son, hostage (35:23–26).

42:25–27 fill their sacks: Joseph's actions here are both gracious and unsettling. The returned money would enable the brothers to come another time for another purchase. On the other hand, they might be accused of stealing it. **money:** This word refers to a certain weight of silver. Coinage had not yet been invented.

42:28 The discovery of some of their **money** frightened the brothers (but see v. 35). They accused God for their troubles.

42:29–34 The brothers truthfully reported to their father **Jacob** all that had transpired.

42:35 The discovery of the **money** in the sack of one of the brothers (vv. 27, 28) could have been explained as a mistake. But now they learned that each man's money was in his sack!

42:36 You have bereaved me: Jacob's grief increased. One son was dead; another was in prison; and now a third was threatened by an Egyptian official.

42:37 Kill my two sons: Reuben took the lead. He tried to comfort his father, just as he had tried to stop his brothers from hurting Joseph (37:22). The rash vow Reuben makes concerning his own sons is an attempt to show how determined he was. Nonetheless, such vows sometimes brought disaster in biblical times (read the story of Jephthah's daughter, Judg. 11:29–40). Better to follow Jesus' instruction for "Yes" and "No" in Matt. 5:33–37.

42:38 My son shall not go: Jacob was resolute. He had lost enough sons; he didn't want to risk Benjamin, his favorite. **with sorrow:** He assured his sons that risking the loss of Benjamin in addition to having already lost Joseph would lead him into depression and cause his premature death.

43:1–6 deal so wrongfully: Jacob blamed his sons for telling the Egyptian there was still another brother. His sons replied that they had simply answered the questions they were asked (v. 7).

43:7, 8 Send the lad with me: Judah promised that he would keep Benjamin safe. Judah had changed tremendously (contrast 38:1). Instead of leaving the family, he protected his brother and was concerned about his father's welfare.

43:9 The verb for **be surety** is related to the noun "pledge" in Gen. 38:17, 18. **Blame** is from the Hebrew verb often translated as *sin* (40:1; 41:9).

43:10, 11 Because of the famine, the **fruits** that they took may have been dried and the **nuts** may have been from earlier harvests. The principle staple they needed was grain.

43:12–14 This is the fourth time in Genesis that **God** is called *El Shaddai* (Gen. 17:1; 28:3; 35:11). **If I am bereaved:** Jacob finally realized there was no other option. **Mercy,** here, is a word that speaks in an unusual manner of the warmth of God's love for His people. The word is the plural of a word related to the womb; it may describe the maternal affection of God for His people. This is the OT basis for the Paul's words "the mercies of God" in Rom. 12:1. Old Jacob did not yet know that God in His great maternal affection for him had already made a

 INSIGHT | **The Importance of Age**

Joseph seated his brothers in order of their ages (Gen. 43:33). Rights of inheritance were almost inflexibly linked to the order of birth. In society as a whole, age was regarded as a title to respect. Contempt for one's parents or elders was a serious offense, in certain cases calling for extreme punishment (Ex. 21:17; Lev. 19:32).

full reunion of the family possible, including the son presumed to be dead.

43:15–18 The brothers must have been surprised. The last time, they were treated as spies and criminals (42:9–14). Now Joseph invited them into his house to **dine** with him.

43:19–23 The steward responded in an unexpected manner. He did not accuse them of anything; instead, he invited them into the house with a blessing of **peace. Your God and the God of your father:** Surprisingly, the steward expressed his own faith in the God of Joseph and Jacob. **I had your money:** Of course, this is not the whole truth.

43:24 They **washed their feet** because they wore open sandals on dusty trails.

43:25, 26 For the second time (42:6) the brothers of Joseph **bowed** down to him, just as his revelatory dreams had predicted (37:5–11).

43:27–29 Benjamin had not been a part of the earlier conspiracy against Joseph. The relationship between Joseph and his younger brother must have been particularly close, since Joseph was overwhelmed when he saw Benjamin (v. 30).

43:30–32 place by himself: Joseph maintained his disguise, so he followed the Egyptian custom of eating at a table separate from the Hebrews. **abomination:** This word can indicate the strongest revulsion, something that might cause physical illness (46:34). The Egyptians might have been repulsed by bodily hair.

43:33, 34 according to his birthright: The brothers might have been surprised and unsettled that they had been seated according to their ages.

44:1–5 Joseph continued to test the character of his brothers by commanding his servants to place his brothers' **money** in their sacks and a **silver cup** in Benjamin's sack.

44:6–12 In response to the servant's accusations, Joseph's brothers insisted on their innocence and promised to give up whoever had Joseph's silver cup. After searching all the brothers' sacks, the servant found the cup with Benjamin.

44:13 In genuine despair for Benjamin's predicament, the brothers **tore their clothes.** They could not let Benjamin die! Ironically a few years earlier, the same brothers had been debating whether to kill Joseph. Instead of tearing their own clothes in grief, they had torn Joseph's robe in order to cover up what they had done.

44:14 Although Reuben was the oldest, **Judah** took the leadership role in this section (46:28).

44:15 Here, **divination** is the practice of consulting the will of the gods by observing the liquid in a special cup. Allegedly Benjamin had

stolen not only a silver cup from an Egyptian ruler, but a significant one. His action could have had grave consequences. The words **such a man as I** do not clearly mean that Joseph practices divination, only that he might be expected to.

44:16 The contrition of **Judah** was complete. He offered no excuse; what had happened was the will of **God.** He presented himself and all his brothers as slaves to Joseph.

44:17 Joseph demanded that the youngest son, the presumably guilty one, become his slave. Joseph's parting words, **go up in peace to your father,** were a test. Would the brothers leave Benjamin as a slave in Egypt as they had left Joseph? For the brothers, Joseph's words must have been especially bitter. There would be no peace in their father's household if Benjamin became an Egyptian slave.

44:18–29 Then Judah came near: The process that Joseph was imposing on his brothers was having a special effect on Judah. How remarkably he has changed from that period of his indifference to the rest of the family of promise (ch. 38).

44:30–34 Judah explained to Joseph the deep despair his father would experience if he lost Benjamin. Then he offered himself as a slave in Benjamin's place. Instead of showing indifference to his family as he had in the past (ch. 38), Judah offered his own life to save Benjamin's.

45:1 could not restrain himself: Joseph's emotions were now stretched to their limits. His feelings were as tight bands about to break. All control is gone.

45:2 Joseph **wept** so loudly that his voice was heard throughout the whole palace (46:29)!

45:3 I am Joseph: Joseph must have said this in Hebrew and not in Egyptian (42:23). Still, the brothers could not believe their ears. They had sold Joseph as a slave. He would certainly be dead. Could it be true? The Egyptian lord who held their lives in his hands was their brother!

45:4 Joseph realized that his physical appearance, his Egyptian manner, his high position, and his total power over them all conspired to make his words unbelievable. He told them to **come** closer so that they could recognize his face and voice. Joseph identified himself as the brother whom they had **sold.** Fear overcame Joseph's brothers again. Would Joseph take revenge?

45:5–7 Joseph used kindness to calm his brothers' fears. **God sent me before you to preserve life:** God had worked through the brothers' evil actions and hateful attitudes to preserve not only Jacob's family but also the

IN PERSON | Joseph's Story

The remarkable story of Joseph's rise to power in Egypt is not just another rags-to-riches story. Fundamentally, the story is about how the Lord created a nation out of a troubled family.

Jacob's family was plagued by jealousy. Rachel envied Leah, and Leah envied Rachel (Gen. 30:1). Leah's sons inherited this pattern of jealousy. They envied Joseph so much that they sold him as a slave (37:28). It may even be that Reuben abused Bilhah because of jealousy toward Benjamin (35:18–22). Also, the family was separating. After Joseph was sold into slavery, Judah left the family, associated with the Canaanites, and married a Canaanite woman (38:1–3). Simeon followed Judah's lead by also taking a Canaanite wife (46:10). With these jealousies and divisions, Jacob's family, the family of God's eternal promises (12:1–3), was becoming more and more like the pagan Canaanite community around them.

But the Lord did not let the troubles of this family thwart His good purposes. He had promised to shape a great nation from it, a nation that would spread His blessings to the whole earth (12:1–3). Jacob's family was divided, but God worked the events so that the family was reunited. Through a remarkable series of circumstances, God elevated Joseph from the positions of slave and prisoner to administrator of Egypt, Pharaoh's right-hand man. God transformed the evil plans of Joseph's brothers into something good (37:19–28; 50:20). As the administrator of the Egyptians' plan to survive the coming famine, Joseph could save the lives of many people in the ancient world. With his new name, Zaphnath-Paaneah ("God Speaks and Lives"), and his remarkable story, Joseph could witness to these people about the power and goodness of the living God (41:45).

But God's good plan did not end there. God used the physical hardship of famine to reunite Israel's family. When Joseph's brothers saw him, not only did they express sorrow for their former evil actions (42:21; 45:5), but they demonstrated a new loyalty to their other half brother, Benjamin. Judah, who had left the family before (38:1), begged for Benjamin's life, even at the cost of his own freedom (44:18–34). The reunion of the family and the pressures of famine prompted Jacob to move closer to Egypt, to the land of Goshen. God used the evil attitudes of the Egyptians—their hatred of shepherds—to isolate the family there (43:32; 46:34). In this isolation, God could develop a nation dedicated to worshiping and obeying Him. In all the exceptional events of Joseph's story, God remained faithful to His promises to Abraham (12:1–3). He created a great nation out of Jacob's family through a maze of human jealousy, family divisions, and racial hatred (50:20).

lives of many in the ancient world. Yahweh had worked through their actions to bring about His greater work. This pattern may be found throughout Scripture and history. It comes to its grand climax in the death and resurrection of the Lord Jesus Christ, which is the great point made by Peter in his pivotal sermon on the Pentecost Sunday, when the Church was created by God. While unbelieving Jewish officials and wicked Roman soldiers had conspired together to put Jesus to death, this was all done "by the determined purpose and foreknowledge of God" (Acts 2:23). In the same manner, the barbarous actions of Joseph's brothers prepared the scenario for the great saving work of the living God (50:20).

45:8 Joseph repeated that **God** had accomplished His good purpose through the evil actions of his brothers. **a father to Pharaoh:** Joseph was an adviser to Pharaoh much as a father might be an adviser to his son.

45:9, 10 Joseph told his brothers that they must live in Egypt during the famine. This was God's plan, for He had told Abram that his descendant would live in a foreign land (15:13–16).

45:11 I will provide for you: With his family close by, Joseph could make sure his family had enough during the famine.

45:12, 13 my mouth: Joseph still had to convince his brothers that he was really their brother.

45:14 Benjamin was Joseph's only full brother. Finally they were reunited.

45:15–20 It is another mark of the very high esteem with which Joseph was held by Pharaoh that the report of his reunion with his brothers was greeted with pleasure by Pharaoh and his officials. Pharaoh went beyond any expected act of hospitality to Joseph.

45:18, 19 Because Joseph was preserving the nation from destruction, Pharaoh was providing the **best** for Joseph.

45:20, 21 Joseph sent his brothers back to

his father with the Pharaoh's blessing and many gifts.

45:22 Benjamin, the brother who was at the greatest risk (ch. 44) now received the greatest blessing.

45:23–28 When the brothers told their father the great news concerning Joseph, Jacob was stunned. But he revived, saw the gifts, and believed his sons. **before I die:** These words are triumphant. Jacob could see his favorite son, whom he had believed to be dead.

46:1 Jacob's **journey** to Egypt began a 400-year sojourn away from the Promised Land of Canaan. Jacob entered Egypt with his twelve sons, including Joseph; 400 years later Jacob's descendants would leave Egypt as a small nation. Jacob went to the site that was so important to both his grandfather Abram (21:22–34) and his father Isaac (26:26–33). At **Beersheba,** Jacob (or Israel) had left his family to go to Haran (28:10). **offered sacrifices:** Jacob worshiped God at Beersheba. He consecrated his family to the Lord before he left the Promised Land.

46:2 God appeared to **Israel** for the seventh time (35:1, 9). The fact that the names **Israel** and **Jacob** are used interchangeably indicates that the earlier negative connotations of the name Jacob have faded (31:11; 32:28; 35:10). Instead of meaning that Jacob "Supplants," the name Jacob now means that God "Supplants."

46:3 God, the God of your father: The self-identification of the Lord is a bit different here than at earlier times. The Lord is saying, "I am the true deity." By adding the words, "(even) the God of your father," the Lord identifies Himself as the God in whom Isaac had believed, even the One who had brought great blessing to Isaac. God had forbidden Isaac at a previous time to go **to Egypt** (26:2), and Isaac's father Abram had had an unpleasant experience in Egypt (12:10–20). Despite Joseph's gifts and words, Jacob feared what would happen in Egypt. Jacob's family numbered seventy (v. 27). Out of this family, God would bring **a great nation** (Ex. 1:1–7). Again, God renewed His promises to Jacob (35:11).

46:3 Do not fear was the same assurance given to Abraham and Isaac (Gen. 15:1; 26:24).

46:4 go down with you: God promised to be with His people, even in a foreign land. **Joseph will put:** Jacob's life was nearing its end. But God promised Jacob that his beloved Joseph, who he had thought was dead, would be with him at his deathbed.

46:5–7 It is the style of Hebrew prose to announce an important event and then to describe it as having happened. This adds solemnity and dignity to the text. The entire family and all their possessions were now in Egypt.

46:8–27 these were the names: The listing of the family of Jacob is not only a remarkable historical document, but also a source of pride. From this family would come the whole nation of Israel, God's people who would enter the Promised Land according to His promise (15:13–21). The order of the sons of Jacob is given according to their birth mothers (as in 35:23–26; their birth order is given in 29:31–30:24; 35:16–22).

46:8–15 First are the sons of Leah: Reuben, Simeon, Levi, Judah, Issachar, and Zebulun, along with their sons.

46:8 Reuben: The identifying phrase, **Jacob's firstborn,** which should have been a mark of great pride, became a mark of sadness. Reuben lost the right of the firstborn because of his sin with Bilhah (35:22; 49:3, 4).

46:9, 10 Shaul, the son of a Canaanite woman: This phrase indicates that marrying a Canaanite was unusual in Jacob's family. Only Simeon and Judah married Canaanite women (Joseph's wife is Egyptian).

46:11 The sons of **Levi, Gershon, Kohath, and Merari** became the founders of the Levitical families (Ex. 6:16–19). The sons of Kohath in particular became the founders of the priestly family, from which Aaron and Moses descended (Ex. 6:20–25).

46:12–14 The story of **Judah**'s family, including the untimely deaths of **Er and Onan,** is found in ch. 38. **Shelah** was the only surviving son of Judah by his Canaanite wife, Shua. The other two sons, **Perez** and **Zerah,** were born to Tamar, his daughter-in-law.

46:15 Dinah's sad story is reported in ch. 34.

46:16–26 The total is **sixty-six,** and when Jacob, Joseph, and Joseph's two sons are added, the grand total is **seventy.** The number did not include the wives of Jacob's sons. Ancient Israelites regarded the number seventy as a token of God's special blessing on them.

46:27, 28 Jacob treated **Judah** as the leader among the brothers (44:18). Normally the firstborn, Reuben, would have been expected to lead (46:8).

46:29 Joseph, the great leader of Egypt, went to meet his family in **Goshen,** where they would settle.

46:30 Now let me die: Jacob's reunion with his son Joseph was the crowning event of his long life. Jacob lived for seventeen more years (47:28).

46:31–34 These verses show Joseph's leadership ability. He accomplished his goals by maintaining a genuinely deferential attitude to those in authority, by skill in making suggestions, and by a knowledge of the customs of the people. The Egyptians scorned **shepherds** (43:32). **Abomination** is a term referring to the strongest revulsion and distaste. God used the racial and ethnic prejudice of the Egyptians as a way of preserving the ethnic and spiritual identity of His own people. Jacob's family was already intermarrying with Canaanites (ch. 38) and was in danger of losing its identity as the people of God.

46:34 This verse is an inappropriate place for the chapter to end; this section extends to 47:12. There are several places in the Genesis where the chapter divisions are not at the best place in the narrative (2:1, 4; 27:46; 29:31; 30:25). It would seem that the better place for the end of ch. 46 would be at 47:12, with ch. 47 beginning with what is presently 47:13.

47:1–6 Joseph's plan worked. Pharaoh let Jacob's family live in Goshen (46:31) because the Egyptians detested **shepherds** (46:31–34).

47:6 **Goshen** is an area in the Nile delta that is well watered and ideally suited for the shepherding family of Jacob.

47:7–10 The presentation of Joseph's father **before Pharaoh** must have been a grand occasion. But surprisingly, **Jacob blessed Pharaoh** (vv. 7, 10). Pharaoh as the host might have thought of pronouncing a blessing on Jacob because of his great admiration for Joseph. But instead the visitor blessed the host in the name of the living God! Literally Jacob obeyed God's command to Abram's descendants to "be a blessing" (Gen. 12:2).

47:8–10 **how old:** Pharaoh's question suggests that the long ages of the patriarchal family were truly exceptional, even for this period. Jacob responded in humility and honesty. Jacob had experienced sadness or **evil.** Years of rivalry with his brother, Esau, and struggle with Laban had marked the early part of his life. For long years he grieved the supposed death of his son Joseph. His 130 years were fewer than the 175 years of Abraham (25:7) and the 180 years of Isaac (35:28). But his life was not over. He would live to the age of 147 and would die in Egypt (47:28).

47:11 With Pharaoh's blessing, Joseph arranged the perfect place for his family members to live.

47:12 **provided . . . bread:** As the one in charge of the distribution of food during the famine, Joseph made sure that his family was well supplied.

47:13 **Now there was no bread:** The famine was severe even in Egypt.

47:14 The **money** was quantities of silver. Because the stored foods belonged to the Egyptian state, the state's power and wealth

---

🐾 IN PERSON   Seizing an Opportunity

Sometimes God puts an opportunity in our way that could advance our career and bring prosperity. That's what happened to Jacob and his sons when they migrated to Egypt. Of course, they were hardly looking for a career move; mainly they wanted to escape the famine in Canaan, and they ended up relocating largely at the request of Joseph. But once they arrived, circumstances created a unique opportunity.

Joseph was faced with a bit of a problem: how to introduce his long-lost family to Pharaoh. Pharaoh had an extremely high regard for Joseph. But what would be his reaction when he learned that Jacob and his sons were shepherds and ranchers? Those occupations were an "abomination" to the Egyptians (Gen. 46:34), fit only for slaves. One can gain some idea of how detestable they were by noting that when the brothers came on their second journey to Egypt, bringing Benjamin with them, they were forced to eat by themselves, away from the Egyptians (43:32). Apparently Hebrews and shepherds were synonymous in the Egyptian mind.

Joseph turned this potential embarrassment into an opportunity. He instructed his brothers to boldly claim their skills rather than downplay their occupation. He knew that Pharaoh probably would never change his opinion of shepherds, but most likely the ruler at least would allow the family to live by themselves in the Goshen district.

That's exactly how the plan worked out (47:1–6). In addition, Pharaoh's respect for Joseph led to a request that the brothers have oversight over Pharaoh's own livestock. He still detested shepherds, but when it came to the care of his own animals, apparently he preferred to employ the kin of someone he trusted.

The assignment matched the skills and experience of the brothers. Like many immigrants around the world today, they were willing and able to do work that people in host cultures find unacceptable. As a result, they prospered in the land (47:27; compare Ex. 1:7).

grew immensely. The Egyptians gave up their silver, their cattle, and their property in the process of buying food to keep themselves alive. **Canaan** also continued to suffer from the famine.

47:15–19 When they ran out of **money** (silver), the people brought their **livestock** (v. 17) to purchase grain. When they no longer had livestock they sold their **land.** In this way the collective wealth of Canaan and Egypt went into Pharaoh's treasury.

47:20 Pharaoh's ownership of **the land** would eventually lead to gross abuses of power. For the abuse of the Israelites, see the Book of Exodus.

47:21 The movements of peoples from their farms **into the cities** was a significant event in the social and political affairs of ancient Egypt.

47:22 That Joseph gave preferential treatment to **the priests** of the pagan religions of that nation may be the most troubling issue for us in his administration of Egypt. Doubtless this was due to some extent to the powerful lobby that the priests would have had in the palace. Nonetheless, this seems to be a strange concession to idolatrous worship by Joseph, the man of God. The fact that the priests were under a system of rations from the throne may simply have tied Joseph's hands with regard to reform measures he might have wished to make.

47:23–26 With the land now in the possession of the state, Joseph imposed a system of

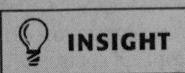

INSIGHT: Egyptian Bureaucracy

The Egyptian state supervised a bureaucracy capable of building pyramids and temples that required thousands of workers and decades of effort. Meticulous records were kept regarding commodities and the disbursements of food and drink to workers (Gen. 47:24). Standard-sized loaves of bread were common.

taxation on the people. The state supplied the seed for planting, but one-fifth of the proceeds became the property of Pharaoh. This became standard practice in Egypt (v. 26). The people responded with gratitude (v. 25) because Joseph had saved their lives.

47:27 Jacob's family did not have to sell their **possessions** in order to acquire food. Since Joseph controlled all the supplies, he gave his family what they needed.

47:28 seventeen years: Even though Jacob had been willing to die when he rejoined his son Joseph (45:28; 46:30), God gave him a good number of years to enjoy his family.

47:29–31 Jacob wanted to do a few more things before his death. First, He wanted Joseph to promise to bury him in Canaan. Second, he wanted to bless each of Joseph's sons (chs. 48; 49).

47:29–31 your hand under my thigh: The action suggests a most solemn and binding promise (for the same sign between Abraham and his servant read Gen. 24:2). **deal kindly and truly with me:** The expression means "demonstrate to me the utmost covenant loyalty." In other words be faithful, just as God has been faithful to His promises. **do not bury me in Egypt:** Jacob asked to be buried in Canaan. He demonstrated his vigorous faith in God's promises by asking to be buried in the land promised to his descendants.

48:1, 2 Joseph knew the end of Jacob's life was approaching (47:29), but the news came that he was **sick.** This chapter continues a theme in Genesis of **two** competing **sons.** For Cain and Abel see ch. 4; for Jacob and Esau see chs. 25–28; for Perez and Zerah see 38:27–30. Often the younger supplants the older. God works in ways different from the ordinary and expected course of events.

48:3, 4 God Almighty: This is the fifth time the name *El Shaddai* is found in Genesis (17:1; 28:3; 35:11; 43:14; 49:25). **Luz** is the older name for Bethel. Jacob recalled God's appearances to him (28:10–15, 19; 35:6–13) and God's promises to his family.

48:5–7 The **two sons** of Joseph were Manasseh and Ephraim (41:50–52). Jacob reversed their birth order. He also said that they were as much his sons as were **Reuben and Simeon,** his first and second sons (29:32, 33). Because of the outrageous acts of Reuben (35:22) and Simeon (34:25), both of them had fallen from favor. Levi was also implicated in the outrage of Simeon (34:25). Therefore the rights and privileges of the firstborn son were passed down to two other sons, Judah (49:8–12) and Joseph (49:22–26). Reuben as the firstborn could have received a double portion of the father's inheritance. But Jacob gave the double share to Joseph (v. 22). Joseph's two sons are then counted with their uncles as founders of the tribes of Israel.

48:7 Rachel died beside me: The aged Jacob remembered the great love of his life, Rachel, who died giving birth to Benjamin.

48:8–11 I had not thought to see: Jacob recalled again his grief at the thought of Joseph's death and his joy at being able to see him again in this life (46:29). Now he could see Joseph's sons as well!

INSIGHT | Jacob's Blessing

The last great event in the life of old Jacob was the prophetic blessing he gave to each of his twelve sons. The destiny of the nation was principally in their lives, for good or for ill. In Gen. 49 we read the Spirit-empowered blessings that Jacob gave to each son. The poetic casting of these words made them memorable, incisive, and powerful. These were oracles from God, much as any prophecy from Isaiah or Jeremiah.

48:12–14 Joseph presented his sons to his father in an act of humility and respect. He placed his sons so that his father's right hand would rest on the head of the older son and the left hand on the younger. But Jacob deliberately reversed his hands, putting Ephraim first.

48:15 In his blessing, Jacob reaffirmed his great faith in the living God. Despite the self-serving acts of his youth, Jacob's faith had matured. Jacob used the definite article with the word **God** to emphasize "the Genuine Deity" (as in Gen. 6:2; 22:1; 27:28; 31:11; 46:3). He identified God as the One whom Abraham and Isaac served.

48:16 The Angel is an abbreviated way of referring to the Angel of the Lord (16:7; 22:11; 24:7). **my name:** Jacob wanted Joseph's two sons to inherit the blessing God gave to Abraham, Isaac, and himself.

48:17 Joseph realized that his father's right hand was on the head of the younger boy, and he attempted to rearrange his father's hands. But despite his dimmed eyesight, Jacob knew completely what he was doing. Once again in Genesis, God overturned the expected order of things. The older would serve the younger, just as Jacob himself had been elevated over his older brother so long ago (27:1—28:9).

48:18–20 as Ephraim and as Manasseh: Jacob recited the names of Joseph's sons with the youngest first. From then on, Joseph's two sons were known in that order.

48:21 Jacob promised Joseph that he would return to the land of Canaan. The promise was fulfilled after Joseph's death (50:24–26).

48:22 one portion above: By blessing the two sons of Joseph on the same level as his own sons, Jacob gave to Joseph the double share. **from the hand of the Amorite:** This promise would be fulfilled when the Israelites returned to Canaan to possess the land God had given them (15:12–21).

49:1 in the last days: The expression may be translated "in the glorious future." Jacob described the future for his descendants.

49:2 Listen to these words are a formal introduction to what follows.

49:3, 4 Jacob began with warm words of praise to **Reuben,** his **firstborn** son (for his birth see 29:31, 32). But he ended with a rebuke of Reuben's presumptuous actions with Bilhah (35:22). By going to his **father's bed,** Reuben was attempting to solidify his claims as the firstborn son. In fact, he doomed his cause.

49:5–7 Simeon and Levi are linked because of the fierce and cruel revenge they took against Shechem and his people (ch. 34). Even though Shechem had raped their sister, their vengeance was excessive and an outrage against the sacred rite of circumcision. Because of what they did, Jacob described them as **instruments of cruelty.** Their anger was fierce and cruel, not righteous or zealous for God's honor (vv. 6, 7). Because of their actions, they would be scattered in Israel. Later, Simeon's allotment was scattered within the larger sphere of the tribe of Judah (Josh. 19:1–9), and Levi's allotment was scattered in cities throughout the land (Josh. 21).

49:8 Judah . . . shall praise: This verse is a wordplay on the meaning of Judah's name, "Let God Be Praised" (for the birth of Judah read 29:35). Jacob's praise for Judah was surpassed only by his praise for Joseph (vv. 22–26; ch. 48). Judah rose to the leadership of the twelve sons as Jacob passed over Reuben, Simeon, and Levi. Judah's selfless actions to save his brother Benjamin were exemplary (44:18–34), especially after the sorry episodes described in ch. 38.

49:9 The **lion** is an ancient royal symbol. It appears in Balaam's oracle (Num. 23; 24).

49:10 The **scepter** is an ornate staff or rod that is a symbol of royal authority. A **lawgiver** is the one who issues statutes. With these words, Jacob predicted that a royal line would rise from Judah's descendants. **Shiloh** is an obscure word, probably meaning the one "To Whom It Belongs." That is, until the One to whom all royal authority belongs comes, the tribe of Judah will always have a lawgiver in its ranks (Is. 9:1–6). Shiloh, like Seed (3:15), is a name for the coming Messiah.

49:11, 12 The imagery in this verse describes the warfare that the Messiah will wage to estab-

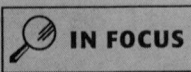

IN FOCUS — "Almighty"

(Heb. *shadday*) (Gen. 17:1; 28:3; 35:11; 43:14; 48:3; 49:25; Job 37:23) Strong's #7706: This divine name in Hebrew is *'El Shadday*. *'El* means God, and *Shadday* is probably related to the Akkadian word for mountain, or to a Hebrew verb meaning "mighty." God is "mountainlike." He is powerful, majestic, awe-inspiring, and enduring. Just like a mountain, He provides a shelter from the elements and from evil (Ps. 91:1, 2). Therefore, *'El Shadday* can mean "Majestic Deity" or "the God Who Provides My Refuge."

lish His reign (Pss. 2; 110; Rev. 19:11–21). **Wine** recalls the color of **blood.** The colors of his **eyes** and **teeth** speak of vitality and victory. The language of this passage expresses the mystery and wonder surrounding this Coming One, Shiloh.

49:13 Zebulun is given precedence over his brother Issachar (vv. 14, 15; for Zebulun's birth read 30:19, 20). His blessing will be the northern coastlands bordering Phoenicia (compare Josh. 18:10–16).

49:14 Jacob's words to **Issachar** portend a heavy enslavement following a time of plenty (Is. 9:1) For the birth of Issachar read 30:14–18. For Issachar's allotment, compare Josh. 19:17–23.

49:15, 16 Dan shall judge: Dan's name is related to the word meaning "judge" (for his birth read 30:1–6).

49:17, 18 a viper by the path: This possibly means that some of Dan's descendants would abandon their faith in the Lord. Yet the godly can still expect **salvation** from the Lord.

49:19 Gad, a troop shall tramp upon him: Although the tribe of Gad will endure hardship, ultimate victory is promised (for Gad's birth read 30:9–11).

49:20 The brief words to **Asher** were happy and hopeful (for Asher's birth read 30:12, 13).

49:21 Naphtali: Again, the brief words promised hope and joy. For Naphtali's birth to Rachel's maid Bilhah read 30:7, 8.

49:22 Joseph: Only the promises given to Judah (vv. 8–12) can rival the praise Jacob gave to Joseph. For Joseph's birth to Rachel read 30:22–24; for the exaltation of Joseph's family read ch. 48.

49:23 The imagery of **archers** who **shot at him** represents Joseph's personal experience at the hands of his brothers and then the Egyptians (chs. 37; 39; 40).

49:24 Jacob described Joseph's eventual triumph. Not only did Joseph have great strength of character represented by the strong **bow,** he was protected by **the Mighty God of Jacob.** This is the first of five titles that Jacob used to describe God as he blessed Joseph (vv. 24, 25). The word translated as **Mighty** is found also at Ps. 132:2, 5; Is. 1:24; 49:26; 60:16. In all of these places it serves as a name for God. Perhaps this is Jacob's special name for God drawn from his experience with the divine wrestler (32:22–30). Using this special term for God in his blessing shows what great affection he had for his son Joseph. Second, Jacob called the Lord the great **Shepherd.** This term also would have great significance for a family of shepherds. God shepherds and cares for their family just as they shepherded their own flocks so often. God is the one Good Shepherd, who truly cares for the flock (Ps. 23; John 10). Even the Egyptian Pharaoh, who despised shepherds (46:28—47:6), appeared in statues with a shepherd's crook to represent his benevolent care for the nation. Third, Jacob praised God as **the Stone of Israel.** On the occasions when God spoke to him, Jacob (or Israel) erected stone pillars to commemorate the event (28:18). God had become for him the "Stone of Israel," the Rock that typifies stability and trustworthiness.

49:25 The fourth term Jacob used for God in the blessing of Joseph is **the God of your father.** Earlier, Jacob had described the Lord as the God of Abraham and Isaac (48:15). Here he expressed his faith in the God who had blessed him. Finally, Jacob called God **the Almighty.** This is the sixth and final time *El Shaddai* is used in Genesis. This name of God is found in association with Abraham (17:1), Isaac (28:3), Jacob (28:3; 35:11; 43:14; 48:3), and Joseph (here). In Exodus, God identified Himself to Moses with this name (Ex. 6:3). In this way, with five titles for God, Jacob prayed manifold **blessings** on Joseph.

49:26 Jacob's blessing on Joseph concluded with the most enthusiastic words. **Separate** (Heb. *nazîr*) is the word also used for the Nazirites (Num. 6:1–21). Both Joseph and later Nazirites were separated from others in order to serve God's holy purposes.

49:27 Benjamin: The image of a **wolf** is ominous (Judg. 20:21–25). For Benjamin's birth and the death of his mother Rachel read 35:16–20.

49:28 the twelve tribes of Israel: Jacob's blessings are prophecies about the destiny of each tribe. Some of the blessings are obscure. But the blessings on Judah (vv. 8–12) and Joseph (vv. 22–26) are clear prophecies from God about their destinies (compare Moses' blessing of the tribes of Israel, Deut. 33).

⚒ IN DEPTH Many People

Who were the "many people to be saved alive" encompassed by Joseph's statement (Gen. 50:20)? Certainly they included Jacob's family, said to be at least seventy persons (46:27; Ex. 1:5). Joseph's position in Egypt enabled him to save this group from starvation (Gen. 45:5–8). Yet many more people than just Joseph's family benefited from his presence in Egypt. God used Joseph to rescue Pharaoh and the Egyptians from the famine (41:53–55). In fact, as a result of Joseph's wise planning and management, people from all countries in that part of the world were able to find food in Egypt (41:56, 57).

But God's goodness through Joseph did not stop there. Because the Israelites were preserved in Egypt, they eventually became a great nation (Ex. 1:7), in fulfillment of God's promise to Abraham (Gen. 12:2; 15:5). In turn, it was through the Israelites that God brought Jesus into the world, and through Him made salvation available to every person and nation (Gen. 12:3; John 3:17; Rom. 3:21–26, 29).

Given this perspective, we can see that the "many people" far exceeded even those that Joseph probably had in mind. In fact, Christians today are among the "many" who have benefited from the good purposes carried out by Joseph. This suggests that the OT is not only about God's dealings with the Israelites, but about God's plan to reach the entire world through the Israelites.

God's purpose has always been to "save alive" as many people as possible by bringing them into right relationship with Him.

49:29 bury me with my fathers: Jacob challenged his sons not to bury him in Egypt. Certainly Jacob knew that many thousands of his descendants would be buried in Egypt during the 400 years of their prophesied sojourn (15:13–16). But God had promised him that he would return to the Promised Land (46:4) His son Joseph had sworn a solemn oath to bury him in Canaan (47:29–31). Now at the moment of death, Jacob wanted more assurance that this oath would be kept.

49:30–33 Jacob identified the place as **the cave . . . Machpelah,** where Jacob's father, mother, grandfather, and grandmother were buried. Abraham had purchased this land as a burial place for Sarah (ch. 23). **gathered to his people:** This phrase refers to death (Gen. 15:15; 25:8; 35:29), but it also may refer to immortality (2 Sam. 12:23).

50:1 wept: Joseph expressed his strong, genuine love for his father (45:1–3; 46:29).

50:2 embalm: Joseph directed that his father be embalmed (Heb. *hanat,* related to "spices") so that he could be buried in Canaan. One day Joseph would also be embalmed (v. 26).

50:2, 3 Embalming a body originated in Egypt. Vital organs were removed and placed in jars to be buried with the mummy. Body cavities were filled with salt, soda, spices, and gums to effect drying and preservation. The limbs and the body were tightly wrapped with several layers of linen cloth. A person's status during life determined the elaborateness of the mummy case.

50:4–9 Joseph made his request to leave Egypt to bury his father's remains in Canaan. The expression **to the household of Pharaoh** indicates that even Joseph did not always have immediate access to the Pharaoh's presence.

50:10, 11 At **Atad** in the Transjordan, the delegation mourned another seven days. This is the entrance to the Promised Land. The Canaanites were so impressed with the party of mourners that they named the place for them.

50:12–15 Joseph's brothers had a new fear. What if Joseph's kindness to them were something Joseph showed merely to please his father? With Jacob dead, would Joseph take revenge?

50:16, 17 The message may have been truthful or it might have been an invention of the brothers reacting to their fear. **trespass . . . sin:** The evil the brothers had done to Joseph (for Jacob's use of the same words to Laban see 31:36). **Joseph wept:** Joseph accepted the confession in the message as a sincere confession from his brothers.

50:18–21 you meant evil: Joseph spoke clearly about how he viewed the events of his life (45:4–8). **God meant it for good:** God transformed the evil of a group of men into an exceedingly great work. Joseph not only saved the lives of numerous people in the ancient world, he also testified to the power and goodness of the living God. God works His good plan even through the evil plans of evil people. Even the worst events can be used in the hand of kindly Providence for His good. The most impressive example of this is the death of Jesus.

Their evil brought God's best, the gospel of Jesus Christ. The experience of Joseph at the hands of his then-evil brothers was a miniature demonstration of God's saving actions in Jesus, the Coming One. Here the typology of Joseph is most strongly a pointer to the experience of the

INSIGHT

Preserving the Dead Body

Egyptian ideas about death and the afterlife emphasized preserving the dead body from decay (Gen. 50:26). Since Egyptian climate is very dry, the Egyptians were able to preserve bodies by drying them completely. They accomplished this by burying the bodies in natron, a naturally found combination of baking soda and sodium carbonate.

Savior. So with these kind words he comforted them, dispersing their fear.

50:22 one hundred and ten years: God blessed Joseph with a long life. This age may be compared to the 175 years of Abraham (25:7), 180 years of Isaac (35:28), and 147 years of Jacob (47:28).

50:23 children of Machir: The listing of

the children of Ephraim before the children of Manasseh is a step in the fulfillment of Jacob's blessing. The younger son of Joseph was elevated over his older brother (48:8–22).

50:24 God will surely visit you: On his deathbed, Joseph expressed continuing faith in the promises of God. He reassured his relatives that God would continue to work in the family. In His time (15:12–16), God would keep His promise to give Canaan to Abraham's descendants (12:7; 26:3; 35:12; 46:4). **to Abraham, to Isaac, and to Jacob:** This phrase is the standard way of referring to God's covenant to Abraham's family (48:15; 49:25; Ex. 2:24; 3:16). The recital of the three names reaffirms the certainty of the promise and God's commitment to fulfill it.

50:25 an oath: Joseph had buried his father Jacob in Canaan (50:7–14). Now he had the Israelites swear that they would take his bones to the Promised Land when the entire nation of Israel returned to Canaan. In this oath Joseph expressed his complete belief that God would keep His promise to give the land of Canaan to the Israelites (Heb. 11:22). Hundreds of years later, Moses would keep the Israelites' oath by taking Joseph's bones with the people into the wilderness (Ex. 13:19). Finally, Joshua would bury the bones of Joseph at Shechem after the conquest of Canaan (Josh. 24:32).

50:26 Joseph was **embalmed,** like Jacob (vv. 1–3) and like all members of the Egyptian ruling class.

The Second Book of Moses Called

Exodus

▪

THE BOOK OF EXODUS DESCRIBES THE CENTRAL historical event for the Israelites: their salvation from slavery in Egypt. In addition to being the Creator of the entire universe and the One who had covenanted with Abraham's family, God emerges in Exodus as the Savior of the Israelites. He saved them from Egyptian slavery and in the process molded them into a nation, as He promised Abram in

Gen. 12:1–3. Similar to a child, Israel was "born" as a nation in the Exodus, grew and developed in the wilderness, and reached adulthood in the Promised Land. The Book of Exodus records the origin of this nation and can be considered the foundational charter for Israel.

Moses, the main character in this book, participated in an epic drama that featured unforgettable confrontations with a stubborn pharaoh, a last-minute escape, and a joyful celebration. Throughout this entire drama, God demonstrated His power and holiness through miraculous signs and wonders. Finally, through Moses at Mount Sinai, God taught His people how to become a kingdom of priests and a holy nation dedicated to serving and worshiping Him (19:6).

Exodus has two principal sections. The first section, written as a story of epic prose (chs. 1—18), portrays God as the Savior and Provider of His people. God first saved the infant Moses from a watery death and then provided him with the best education in the ancient world, Pharaoh's court. In this royal court and later in the Midianite wilderness, God shaped Moses into an instrument for saving His people, the

Israelites, from slavery. Then at the chosen time, God sent Moses and Aaron to confront Pharaoh, the Israelites' oppressor.

The miraculous signs and plagues displayed in this dramatic encounter demonstrated God's power over the supposed gods of Egypt, especially Pharaoh, who claimed he was an incarnate deity. Since Pharaoh had attempted to destroy God's firstborn son (the people of Israel; Ex. 4:22, 23), the Lord, in the tenth plague, destroyed the Egyptians' firstborn sons. But the Lord passed over, or saved, the firstborn sons of the Israelites because they were His people and had obeyed His instructions concerning the Passover feast (ch. 12). With this tenth plague, the Lord saved His people from slavery. At the Red Sea, God saved them again, this time from the power of the Egyptian army (12:31–42; 13:17—15:21). The enslaved people were free! God was their Savior!

Not only did God save these slaves, He provided for them. When the Israelites left Egypt, God prompted the Egyptians to give them all kinds of goods (12:36). Then in the wilderness He turned bitter waters sweet (15:22–27), gave manna (food) from heaven (ch. 16), and brought water from a rock (17:1–7). Yet even with these miraculous provisions, the Israelites murmured and complained. They had barely finished singing the praises of the Lord (15:1–21) when they begin to murmur against His goodness (15:24). When would they trust in God their Provider?

The second section of the Book of Exodus is a series of detailed laws and instructions (chs. 19—40). But these laws are no ordinary laws. They reveal the very character of God. They reveal God as a Lawgiver and as the Holy One. This section records God's benevolent laws given in the context of a treaty with the Israelites. The Hebrew word translated *law* always has a positive meaning—"instruction." The Law is like an outstretched finger, pointing out the direction a person should take in life. In the Ten Commandments (20:1–17), God mercifully pointed out His way to His people, the way to life. But benevolent instruction was only part of God's plan for the Israelites. His larger plan was to establish a relationship with them based on a formal treaty (ch. 20).

Exodus concludes with instructions about the tabernacle—its construction, furnishing, and services. Many of these instructions point to the person and work of the Lord Jesus Christ. These instructions and the Israelite's encounter with God at Mount Sinai taught them that God is perfect and holy. He can be approached only in the way He prescribes.

At the close of Exodus, we read how the Israelites completed the construction of the tabernacle (39:33) and that the glory of the Lord came to fill it (40:34). God had saved His people,

provided for them, made a treaty with them, and taught them how to live. Finally He lived with them (Ex. 25:8; 29:45). All was ready, it seemed, for the journey to the Land of Promise.

Traditionally, Jewish and Christian scholars have agreed that Moses compiled and wrote Exodus, along with the other books of the Pentateuch (Genesis through Deuteronomy). With the exception of the historical summary in the first chapter and the genealogical section in the sixth chapter, Moses participated in or observed all the events described in the book. Furthermore, unlike Genesis, Exodus mentions Moses' writing (17:14; 24:4; 34:27). Moses' training in Pharaoh's court (2:10; Acts 7:22) would have prepared him wonderfully for the task of the writing. However, Moses may not have written every word in Exodus. For example, the genealogical section in 6:14–27 appears to be a later scribal addition to the book. Yet, it is still reasonable to identify Moses as the architect and principal author of Exodus.

Some have observed that it would be unlikely for an author to use the third person ("he" or "Moses") rather than the first person ("I") in a narrative in which the author was so intimately involved. Yet in ancient cultures, the use of the third person for the narrator was customary.

Moses probably wrote his memoirs—which became the Pentateuch—while he was wandering in the wilderness with the Israelites. He wrote the early portions of Exodus, we suspect, with the full assurance that he would be a participant in Israel's blessing in the Land of Promise. Only much later (Num. 20:1–13) did Moses lose his opportunity to enter the land.

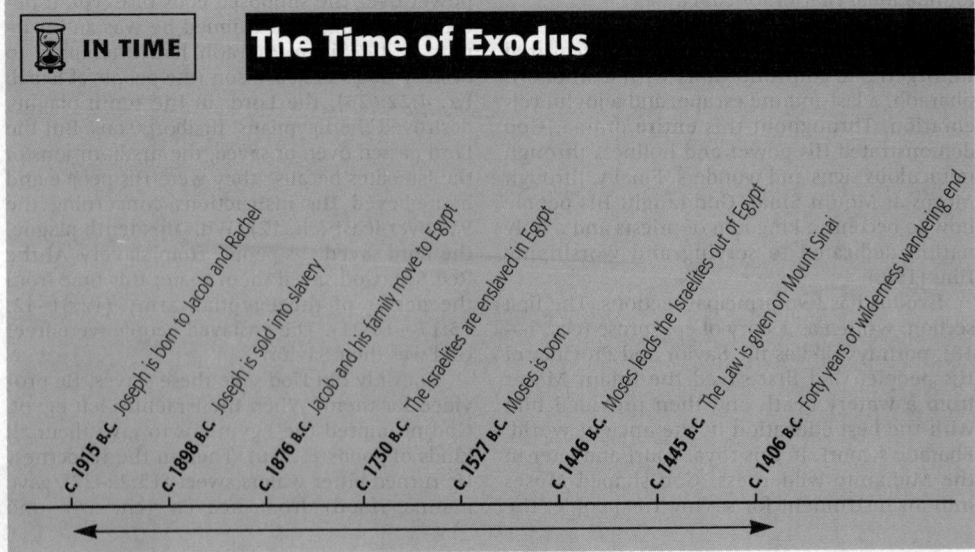

IN TIME — **The Time of Exodus**

c. 1915 B.C. Joseph is born to Jacob and Rachel

c. 1898 B.C. Joseph is sold into slavery

c. 1876 B.C. Jacob and his family move to Egypt

c. 1730 B.C. The Israelites are enslaved in Egypt

c. 1527 B.C. Moses is born

c. 1446 B.C. Moses leads the Israelites out of Egypt

c. 1445 B.C. The Law is given on Mount Sinai

c. 1406 B.C. Forty years of wilderness wandering end

Outline

I. Preparation of Israel for deliverance 1:1–12:36
   A. Preparation of Moses for Israel's deliverance 1:1–4:31
      1. The suffering of the Israelites in Egypt 1:1–22
      2. The birth and early years of Moses 2:1–22
      3. God's first revelation to Moses 2:23–3:22
      4. Moses' initial reluctance 4:1–31
   B. Moses' confrontation with Pharaoh 5:1–7:7
      1. Moses' first encounter with Pharaoh 5:1–19
      2. The aftermath of the first encounter 5:20–6:13
      3. Parenthesis: The family history of Moses, Aaron, and Miriam 6:14–27
      4. Aaron's appointment to speak for Moses 6:28–7:7
   C. God's empowerment of Moses to confront Pharaoh 7:8–12:36
      1. Moses' second encounter with Pharaoh 7:8–13
      2. The first plague: blood red waters of Egypt 7:14–25
      3. The second plague: frogs 8:1–15
      4. The third plague: lice 8:16–19
      5. The fourth plague: flies 8:20–32
      6. The fifth plague: disease among the livestock 9:1–7
      7. The sixth plague: boils 9:8–12
      8. The seventh plague: hail 9:13–35
      9. The eighth plague: locusts 10:1–20
      10. The ninth plague: darkness 10:21–29
      11. The tenth plague announced: death of the firstborn of Egypt 11:1–10
      12. The Passover instituted 12:1–28
      13. The tenth plague enacted 12:29, 30
      14. The beginning of the Exodus 12:31–36
II. Israel's journey to Mount Sinai 12:37–18:27
   A. The initial stages of the journey 12:37–51
   B. Foundational institutions for Israel and an unexpected direction 13:1–22
   C. The Great Event: the crossing of the Red Sea 14:1–15:21
      1. The crisis at the Red Sea 14:1–14
      2. The deliverance at the Red Sea 14:15–31
      3. The praise of God for His great deliverance 15:1–21
   D. The journey from the Red Sea to Mount Sinai 15:22–18:27
      1. Bitter waters at Marah and an oasis at Elim 15:22–27
      2. Provision of miraculous food 16:1–36
      3. Water from a rock at Rephidim 17:1–7
      4. Victory over the Amalekites 17:8–16
      5. Jethro's meeting with Moses 18:1–27
III. The Lord's revelation at His holy mountain, Mount Sinai 19:1–40:38
   A. The Ten Commandments at Mount Sinai 19:1–20:21
   B. Various laws for the people of God 20:22–23:33
   C. The establishment of the Lord's covenant with His people 24:1–18
   D. The design for the tabernacle of the Lord 25:1–31:18
   E. Israel's sin of worshiping a golden calf 32:1–35
   F. The renewal of the covenant between the Lord and His people 33:1–34:35
   G. The construction of the tabernacle and the indwelling of God's glory 35:1–40:38

Commentary

1:1–22 The suffering of the people of Israel in the land of Egypt. Exodus picks up where Genesis ended, but with a significant difference. The family of Jacob is still in Egypt after four hundred years, but they are now reduced to servility, despite the evident blessing of the Lord in their lives.

1:1 Israel is also called Jacob. His twelve sons became the founders of the twelve tribes of the nation Israel.

1:2–4 The sons are listed according to their mothers and their ages. **Reuben, Simeon, Levi, Judah, Issachar** and **Zebulun** are all sons of Leah. **Benjamin** is the son of Rachel. **Dan** and **Naphtali** are sons of Bilhah, the maid of Rachel. **Gad** and **Asher** are sons of Zilpah, the maid of Leah (for each son's birth, read Gen. 29:31–35; 35:16–20, 23–26).

1:5, 6 seventy persons: See Gen. 46:1–27. **Joseph** was not included among the seventy (for Joseph's death, read Gen. 50).

1:7 The extraordinary growth of the family of promise in Egypt is a great miracle and evidence of God's blessing. God **multiplied** a small family of twelve sons and one daughter into a nation that would conquer Canaan. This verse piles one descriptive phrase upon another to emphasize the incredible growth of Israel's family and God's hand in this miracle.

1:8–10 The **new king** did not remember Joseph—his privileged position in the older pharaoh's administration, his administrative

IN PLACE — The Land of Goshen

The "land" (Ex. 1:7) which the Hebrews inhabited during their years in Egypt was the land of Goshen (meaning "mound of earth," Gen. 47:27). This district is believed to have been in the northeastern territory of the Nile delta, but it was probably not irrigated by the Nile or its canals. For that reason, Goshen was more suited to grazing animals than to farming, and thus it was given to Jacob and his family during Joseph's days in power, because they owned many flocks (46:28–34).

By the time of Exodus, however, Joseph was long forgotten and the Israelites had become slaves to the Egyptians (Ex. 1:8–11). During this period, the Goshen district may have functioned as a Hebrew ghetto, housing the workers while they built the storage cities of Pithom and Raamses, both located in Goshen. However, Goshen later served as a place of protection as God kept His people from the plagues that He visited on Egypt.

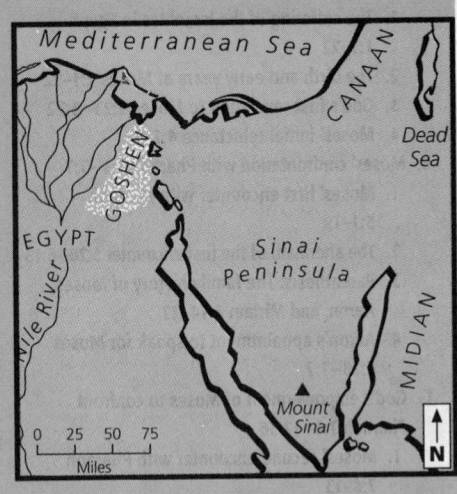

skill that saved the Egyptians from starvation, and his enrichment of the pharaoh's treasury. This new pharaoh probably did not reign immediately after the death of the pharaoh of Joseph's day. More likely, this pharaoh was one of the Hyksos kings who descended from foreign invaders. Ethnically they were a minority in Egypt. These kings may have perceived the growing numbers of Hebrews as a challenge to themselves and to their control over Egypt. **Deal shrewdly** is a form of the verb meaning "to be wise" (Heb. *hakam*, in the Hithpael formation) and is used here in a negative, conspiratorial sense. In other places, it is used of godly, pious wisdom (as in the Book of Proverbs).

1:9, 10 more and mightier than we: This declares that Israel was more numerous and powerful than policies for Egyptian security could tolerate. Egypt feared the consequences of a war in which Israel might side with the invaders.

1:11 By God's mercy, the Israelites were left to themselves for most of the four hundred years they were in Egypt. They increased dramatically during this period. But the time finally came when Pharaoh put **taskmasters,** (Heb. *sarê*) meaning "chiefs of slave gangs," over them. **Pithom and Raamses:** These store cities are mentioned according to the names by which they were known in later times. The Pharaoh Ramses (whose name presumably relates to the name of one of these cities) was not yet in power.

1:12 God **multiplied** His people in times of distress. The fear of the Egyptians toward the people of Israel was based on misjudgment and hatred. The term **dread** means "to feel a sickening dread" (Num. 21:4).

1:13, 14 The harsher the Egyptians made the lives of the Hebrews, the more they flourished. **made their lives bitter:** Later God commanded the Israelites to eat something bitter with the Passover meal so that they might remember the bitterness of their time in Egypt (ch. 12). **rigor:** This term (Heb. *perek*) means "harshness" or "severity." With every task the Egyptians gave to the Hebrews, they made things increasingly difficult for them. They hoped to break the Israelites' spirit with abusive slavery.

1:15 This chapter summarizes nearly four centuries of history. The **king of Egypt** mentioned here is probably not the Hyksos king alluded to in vv. 8–14. This king, perhaps Thutmose I (c. 1539–1514 B.C.), ruled Egypt when Moses was born (2:1–10). **Hebrew midwives:** Probably Hebrews themselves, or perhaps Egyptians who were given Hebrew names of honor. Most likely, these two women headed a guild of midwives. One thing is certain: they knew the living God (vv. 17, 21). Their names, **Shiphrah** ("Beautiful One") and **Puah** ("Splendid One"), are preserved in this account because they were godly women with a courageous faith. At the same time, the names of the pharaohs—the "important" people of the day—are omitted.

1:16 The custom was to support the mother on a **birthstool** during delivery. Pharaoh ordered the midwives to kill the baby boys because he feared the increasing numbers of Hebrew **sons** as a military threat.

1:17, 18 The Hebrew term for **fear** here (*yare'*) is the word regularly used for piety, obedience, and the true worship of God (Gen. 22:12; Ex. 20:20). This is not the term for the sickening "dread" (v. 12) used to describe Egyptian responses to the Hebrew's increase. The midwives would not obey the evil commands of a human ruler, even when their own lives were at risk, because they wanted to please the God of heaven.

1:19 These evasive words are wonderful wit and not likely to have fooled anyone.

1:20, 21 God blessed the midwives because they **feared God.** The phrase of v. 17 is repeated for emphasis. **He provided households for them:** Ordinarily households were established for men. God established the families of these two midwives (Gen. 18:19) because they were faithful to Him.

1:22 Because he could not count on the midwives, Pharaoh commanded the Egyptians to kill the Hebrew male babies by drowning them in **the river**—the Nile.

2:1 Both of Moses' parents were from **the house of Levi.** Later, God chose this family to be the priestly family for Israel.

2:2–4 bore a son: As v. 4 shows, this is not their first child. The older sister was Miriam; Aaron was three years older than this son (Ex. 7:7). **He was beautiful:** The Hebrew word is the common term meaning "good" (Heb. *tôb*), a natural and expected observation of a loving mother seeing her new baby the first time. The mother hid her baby from the authorities, who wanted to kill him. But after **three months,** she found it impossible (1:22). Just as the ark of Noah had been the means by which a family was saved from a watery death (Gen. 7:1), so this **ark** in which she placed her baby would be the means of saving him. She hoped that someone would find the ark and adopt the boy. She sent his **sister,** Miriam, to see what would happen.

2:5 This **daughter of Pharaoh** was probably one of many daughters. Even though the Egyptians were accustomed **to bathe** frequently, bathing in the Nile was a ritual dipping in the waters the Egyptians believed to be sacred.

2:6 The baby was **one of the Hebrews' children.** A Hebrew baby would have been circumcised on the eighth day. Although circumcision was practiced in Egypt, it was not done to infants. Upon unwrapping the infant's clothing, the women would have seen his "special mark."

2:7 The daughter of Pharaoh was not prepared to care for the baby. Since it was a Hebrew child, who would be better than a Hebrew woman to **nurse** it?

2:8 the maiden: The Hebrew term means a young woman of marriageable age; this is the word translated *virgin* in Is. 7:14. Miriam would have been in her mid-to-late teens.

2:9 Not only did God, through Pharaoh's daughter, protect the child from the river death that Pharaoh had commanded (1:22), but through Pharaoh's treasury He provided **wages** to the mother for caring for her own son!

2:10 After what was likely a prolonged period of nursing the child, the mother brought **her son** to Pharaoh's daughter, who then adopted the boy. The name **Moses** is probably related to the Egyptian word *ms* meaning "born," which is commonly found in Egyptian names. For example, "Thutmose" means "the god Thut is born." Pharaoh's daughter explains the meaning of the name: **"Because I drew him out of water."** In Hebrew, "Moses" means "He Who Draws Out" (Heb. *mosheh*). In this

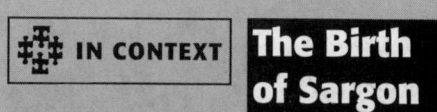

IN CONTEXT | The Birth of Sargon

The account of Moses' birth (Ex. 2:1–10) resembles a familiar theme in ancient Near Eastern folklore: the exposure and rescue of an infant son and his ascent to a position of royalty. One of the most famous of these legends is the birth of Sargon of Accad, a ruler in central Mesopotamia around 2350 B.C.

According to the story, found in eighth century B.C. records, Sargon was born to a high priestess and an unknown father. His birth was kept secret and his mother set him in a basket among the bulrushes, where he was found by a person drawing water. As Sargon grew, he is said to have been granted the love of Ishtar, goddess of love and war, whose love is regarded as a token of Sargon's title to the throne.

manner, Moses' name can refer the reader to the living God, who is the true Deliverer, and also to Moses, who would deliver the Israelites from the Red Sea (chs. 14, 15). The one who was drawn out of water would be the means of drawing the Israelite nation out of water. Yet he was one whose enemies wanted to drown him in the Nile (1:22).

2:11 The years of Moses' experience in the pharaoh's court are not detailed. Yet Stephen, the NT martyr, reports a long-held and surely accurate tradition: "Moses was learned in all the wisdom of the Egyptians and was mighty in words and deeds" (Acts 7:22). The training of Moses was the best education in the world at that time. He would have learned three languages: Egyptian, Akkadian, and Hebrew. When Moses came into the presence of a later pharaoh to demand the freedom of the Israelites (chs. 7—14), he was no stranger to the royal family. **his brethren:** At about the age of forty, Moses was confronted with a great personal crisis. He saw the mistreatment of his own people by his adopted people. He realized that while he had been living a life of disciplined luxury, his people were being abused.

2:12–14 Despite his privilege and position, Moses realized that there was no legal procedure for him to stop the abuses of the Egyptian

29:4–12; 30:37–43), a well played a significant role in the story of Moses.

2:16 Like Melchizedek, the priest-king of Salem or Jerusalem (Gen. 14:18–20), **the priest of Midian** appears to be a foreigner who had come to worship the true and living God. His **daughters** came to the well since, in the ancient world, typically the women **drew water** (Gen. 24).

2:17 The shepherds had probably acted churlishly toward these women before. Unmarried women with no brothers had little protection in the ancient East. **Moses stood up** and came to the aid of the women. Once again, Moses demonstrated his sensitivity to injustice (vv. 11–13). That Moses **helped them** was a magnanimous action and must have been astonishing to the seven women (compare Jacob helping Rachel; Gen. 29:9, 10). The word translated "helped" is the principal OT verb for salvation (Heb. *yasha`*). Its basic meaning, seen

Arab bedouin tents in the land of Midian, where Moses fled after killing an Egyptian (Ex. 2:11–15).

taskmasters. Moved by a sense of injustice, he rashly **killed** the taskmaster.

2:15 Pharaoh **sought to kill** Moses because he had committed a capital crime. **The land of Midian** is the region of the Sinai Peninsula and Arabian deserts where the seminomadic Midianites lived (for the Abrahamic origin of the Midianites, read Gen. 25:1, 2). **by a well:** As in the stories of the fathers and mothers of Israel in Genesis (Gen. 16:7–13; 21:22–34; 24:10–14;

nicely here, is "to make room for." These churlish shepherds had come crowding in on the well, driving the women away, but Moses "made room for" the women, acting as their "savior."

2:18, 19 Reuel is also called Jethro (4:18). His daughters reported to him that they had been delivered by **an Egyptian.** The dress, appearance, and language of Moses would have given this impression.

2:20 Reuel's invitation to **eat bread** was about more than a casual bite to eat. He was recruiting Moses to marry one of his seven daughters.

2:21 Moses was content: For a fugitive from the powerful hand of the Egyptian pharaoh, the offer of a home, protection, and a new life would be appealing. Moses had come as an alien. He had nothing to offer but himself, and thus he would have become part of Reuel's household in the deal (Ex. 4:18). **Zipporah** means "Bird."

2:22 Gershom means "A Stranger There." Moses was doubly removed from his land. He and his people, the Israelites, were strangers in Egypt (Gen. 15:13). Now he was cast off from them and was estranged in yet another waiting place. For all he knew, he would be a stranger for the rest of his days.

2:22–3:22 Here is the first revelation of Yahweh to His servant Moses. This revelation of the divine Person and Name is given in four sections: (1) the setting in the need of the people (2:23–25); (2) the encounter at the burning bush (3:1–12); the revelation of the divine Name (3:13–15); (4) the commission that Yahweh gave to Moses (3:16–22).

2:23–25 the king of Egypt died: The death of Pharaoh (likely Thutmose III, who died about 1447 B.C.) meant that Moses could return to Egypt. At the death of a pharaoh, Egyptian authorities dropped all pending charges, even in capital cases (4:19). The plight of the Israelite people had reached fever pitch during the time of Moses' absence. Four different Hebrew words—translated **groaned, cried out, cry,** and **groaning**—are used to describe the Israelites' complaint (6:5). Corresponding to the four terms for the people's distress, four wonderful verbs are used to describe the Lord's response to His people: **heard, remembered, looked,** and **acknowledged.** Indeed, these four verbs are an introduction to the meaning of His Name, Yahweh. We may speak of them as present tense realities, for they are the ways in which God responds to His people. He hears, He remembers, He sees, and He knows. Each of these words separately, and all of them collectively, express not just an awareness of Israel's trouble but also a participation in their distress, as well as the assurance that He will deliver them from it (Ex. 6:5).

3:1 God now had another "flock" for Moses to tend, the people of Israel. Much as Jacob had become part of Laban's family when he married Leah and Rachel (Gen. 29), Moses, for forty years (a generation in most circles), had been a part of the family of **Jethro,** whose name means "His [that is, the Lord's] Abundance." This word (Heb. *hotenô*) is related to

the Arabic term meaning "the one who circumcises," which helps us to understand the difficult text in Ex. 4:24–26. **Horeb,** another name for Mount Sinai, means "Desolate Place." Yet because of God's appearance on the moun-

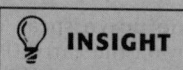

INSIGHT   Midian

Within the official boundaries of the Egyptian empire, in Palestine and the arid Sinai Peninsula, lived a diverse group called the Midianites. They appeared around the thirteenth century B.C. and were known as traders (Gen. 37:36) and metalworkers. Less clearly known is their religion, but some evidence indicates that they worshiped in tent shrines in the desert. The tabernacle that Moses was commanded to build (Ex. 26) may be related to Midianite practices. Moses' father-in-law was, after all, a priest of Midian (Ex. 2:16, 18).

tain (here and in chs. 19; 20), this desolate place would become holy, **the mountain of God** (4:27). Usually this site is identified as Jebel el-Musa, a mountain in the southern Sinai Peninsula.

3:2 the Angel of the LORD: An appearance of God. This is the first occurrence in Exodus of this frequently used phrase (14:19; 23:20, 23; 32:34; 33:2; compare Gen. 22:11, 15). The **flame of fire** was an extraordinary sight, particularly since the bush **was not consumed.**

3:3–5 The ground had become **holy;** it was set apart by the divine presence. For Moses' vivid memory of this experience with God at the end of his life, read Deut. 33:16.

3:4, 5 The dramatic encounter of Moses with the living God is an unforgettable moment in biblical history. God's call to him with the repetition of his name evokes memories of God's call to Abraham as he was about to sacrifice his son (Gen. 22:11); similarly, Moses' response was similar to Abraham's (Gen. 22:1, 11).

3:6 God identified Himself as **the God of your father**—the God worshiped by Abraham, Isaac, and Jacob (v. 15). In announcing these names, the Lord was assuring Moses that His covenant with the fathers of Israel was still in effect. **Moses hid:** Moses had once hidden a body out of fear (2:12, 14); now he hides his face from the presence of Yahweh. Toward the end of his great life, Moses would reflect on this experience. As he pronounced his blessing on the tribe of Joseph, he included the words, ". . . and the favor Him who dwelt in the bush" (Deut. 33:16).

3:7 Three of the four verbs of relationship from 2:24, 25 are repeated: **seen, heard, know.** The first is in the emphatic state. This verse ties the introduction into the chapter's story line.

3:8–10 The words **come down** speak of God's gracious intervention on the earth (Ps. 40:1). Not only was God intimately aware of the

3:11–4:17 Moses' objections to serving are ultimately questions about God. (1) Will He be with me? (3:11, 12). (2) What is He like? (3:13–25). (3) Does He have enough power? (4:1–9). (4) Can He accommodate Himself to me? (4:10–17). God answers these underlying questions.

3:12 God promised to **be with** Moses. Not only had God "come down" to deliver (v. 8), but now He promised to be present. This prefigures the Incarnation: Jesus would come down to

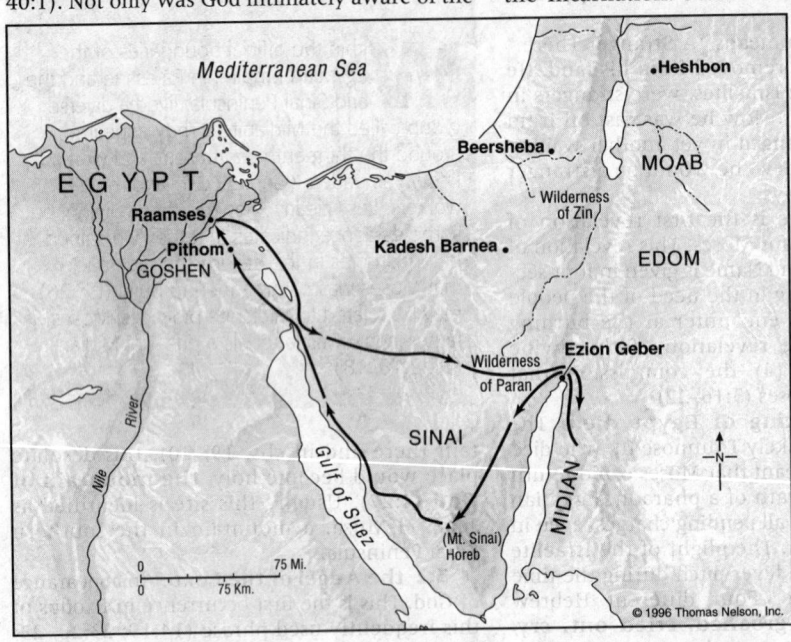

Moses' Flight and Return to Egypt

After killing an Egyptian, Moses fled through the Sinai and settled in Midian, where he married Zipporah. God spoke to Moses at the burning bush at Horeb, after which Moses returned to Egypt to assist the Israelites.

troubles of His people, but now He would act on their behalf. The **good and large land** of Canaan was God's great pledge to His people (Gen. 12:7; 15:12–21; Ex. 6:8). **flowing with milk and honey:** The land of Canaan would sustain God's people well, with some sections given to agriculture and others for herds and flocks. Under God's blessing, milk and honey would seem to flow. The listing of the peoples reminds the reader of three things. (1) The land was not just a figure of speech; it was a real place with real people living in its borders. (2) As to the inhabitants, their time was nearly up; their cup of iniquity was now full and God's judgment was about to fall on them (Gen. 15:16). (3) While the land was God's gift, it was not vacant property; the land would have to be seized from the inhabitants. This could be done with the power of God.

deliver us from our sins and be with us. God gave Moses **a sign,** a final proof that this experience was a divine manifestation and not a dream. Here the sign is a reminder, memorial, or symbol (Ex. 8:23; 12:13). But the word can also mean a miracle of God, a wonder that demonstrates His power and presence (7:3).

3:13 His mind reeling with questions and wonder, Moses asked for the Name of God. His request was for a mark of authority. He had been absent from Egypt for forty years, and even his early years were spent aloof from his own people. He must have wondered how he would be believed. Thus, Moses asked for a sign of authority, a Name to use to ensure that the message would be received.

3:14 I AM WHO I AM: The One who spoke to Moses declared Himself to be the Eternal One—uncaused and independent. Only

INSIGHT | Deliverance from Oppression

God is a God of justice. Therefore He notices when people are oppressed and abused, such as by governments, employers, and others in power. As the ultimate Judge, He can be counted on to right the world's wrongs, if not in this life then in the life to come. Exodus is the story of what God did when He heard His chosen people, Israel, crying out for justice and deliverance (Ex. 3:7–10). The theme of deliverance is developed through hundreds of biblical passages about the poor and oppressed. Many of those passages remind us that such people ought to receive justice and reform, not just mercy or relief.

the Creator of all things can call Himself the **I AM** in the absolute sense; all other creatures are in debt to Him for their existence. But in addition, God the Creator declares His relationship with the people of Israel. The future tense of the Hebrew verb related to God's name is used in v. 12: The I Am *will be* with His people. Thus God declares His covenantal relationship with Israel with His name. Many refer to the "I Am" as the covenantal name of God.

3:15 the LORD: This represents the Hebrew name Yahweh. The Hebrew word meaning "I Am" used in v. 14 is very similar. Translations into English often use LORD in small capitals to represent God's name Yahweh. Here, God does not merely declare His absolute existence, He also declares His relationship to His people. It is not simply that He exists, or even that He will ever exist, but that He declares that He is *for* His people. This is His name of grace, of relatedness, of covenant, and of condescending wonder. He is not a "new" deity but the same who made an eternal covenant with the fathers—**Abraham, Isaac,** and **Jacob**—and was worshiped by them (v. 6). But He has a Name. It is Yahweh. The last part of the verse is a couplet: this is My Name forever, and this is My memorial to all generations. As in other significant OT passages (Gen. 22:11–18), repetition and restatement are used for emphasis. Here they indicate the paramount importance of the divine Name.

3:16, 17 The instructions were now given to Moses so that he would hear again his part in the divine scheme of things (vv. 8–10).

3:18 you shall say to him: Moses is instructed in precisely what to say to Pharaoh. He is not required to come up with his own line of argumentation; only to serve as God's spokesman.

3:18 Three day's journey seems to be an example of an Eastern manner of expression, an argument from the lesser to the greater. That is, the first request was for a few days' distance from Egypt for the purpose of the worship of the living God. Since this request would not be hon-

ored (v. 19), it is certain that the demand to be set free altogether would not be honored either. The fact that Israelites had **to go** somewhere else to **sacrifice to the LORD** may have been an implied slur on the land of Egypt. The wickedness of the Egyptians polluted the land and made it unsuitable for worshiping their God. The Israelites needed neutral soil to worship God in purity (7:16).

3:19 The Hebrew words **But I am sure** are quite strong. They may be translated: "But as for Me, I know that the king of Egypt will not give you permission to go." The question many ask of this verse is important: Does this verse speak of the knowledge of God in the sense that "He knew how things would work out"? Or, does this verse present the foreknowledge of God in the sense that "He determined how things would work out"? See note at 4:21 for an answer and for a development of this theme. The **mighty hand** is the Lord's hand. God was the One who forced Pharaoh to free the Israelites (v. 20; 6:1).

3:20 The Lord's extended **hand** of mercy to the Israelites and of rage against the Egyptians is a constant theme in Exodus (for God's outstretched arm, read 6:6; for God's right hand, read 15:6, 12). **My wonders** are the ten plagues of chs. 7—12. The word "wonders" in Hebrew (*niphla'ot*) refers to things only God can do, things designed to inspire reverence in His worshipers and fear in His enemies.

3:21, 22 God would so humiliate their leader Pharaoh that the common people of Egypt would become favorably disposed toward Israel. The Israelites, who had been slaves in Egypt, would not leave **empty-handed.** They would **plunder the Egyptians** by merely asking for precious goods (for the fulfillment of this prophecy, read 11:2; 12:35, 36). Later, the Israelites gave these very same precious goods to God as offerings for the tabernacle (ch. 35). Thus God enriched a slave populace so that they in turn were able to give their riches back to Him with thanksgiving.

4:1 But suppose: Daunted by the enormity of the task, Moses in a very human way began to think of the problems he might face.

4:2–5 God turned Moses' **rod**—probably a long wooden pole with the familiar shepherd's crook at one end—into a snake to demonstrate the reality of His power and presence during Moses' coming mission.

4:6, 7 Again God demonstrated His power to Moses by making **his hand** leprous and then healing it. Leprosy in the Bible included a wide variety of skin diseases.

4:8, 9 The third sign would be the transformation of the water from the Nile into **blood.** In fact, this occurred in the first plague (7:14–25).

4:10–12 In great patience, God reminded Moses that it was He who had made Moses' **mouth,** even as it is He who has fashioned each individual according to His wisdom. Then He promised to instruct Moses as to precisely what to **say.**

4:13, 14 At this point, Moses saw a flash of God's **anger** (read his words in Ps. 90:11). Although Moses did not know it, God was already arranging some assistance for Moses. He was sending **Aaron** to him (for their meeting, read v. 27).

4:15, 16 words in his mouth: As Moses was a prophet of God, so Aaron was to be a prophet of Moses (7:1). The prophet had one job: to represent accurately the message of the one who sent him or her. Moses would be **as God** to Aaron because he would tell him what to say, just as God would tell Moses what to say.

4:17, 18 Moses needed to gain permission from his father-in-law, **Jethro,** to leave (for a similar predicament involving Jacob, read Gen. 31). Moses had become an official part of Jethro's family (2:16–22; 3:1). Jethro's blessing **Go in peace** was covenantal in nature.

4:19 The words **Now the LORD said** are likely not a new revelation but a reference to the revelations of Yahweh to Moses (chs. 3 and 4). The verb may be translated "had said" (Ex. 6:28; 12:1).

4:20 Moses took **his sons.** Gershom, Moses' firstborn, is mentioned in 2:22. The name of the second son is not given until Ex. 18:4, after Israel's deliverance. This is Eliezer, whose name means "My God Is Help." Moses also took **the rod of God,** that is, the rod that God had used to demonstrate His power (vv. 2–5, 17).

4:21 In the following passage, **Pharaoh,** most likely Amenhotep II (c. 1447–1421 B.C.), is not simply the king of Egypt, but a symbol for all who resist God, for all of God's enemies. **I will harden his heart:** Some interpret these words as meaning that God would confirm what Pharaoh had stubbornly determined to do. In the first five plagues, the hardening is attributed to Pharaoh (7:13, 22; 8:15, 19, 32; 9:7). Then for the sixth plague, God hardened a heart that Pharaoh had already hardened (9:12). Others insist that God had determined Pharaoh's negative response to Moses long before Pharaoh could harden his heart. These interpreters point to this verse and to 9:16, in which God says that He raised up Pharaoh for the purpose of demonstrating His power.

4:22, 23 The nation Israel is God's **son** and naturally God is its Father. In the course of time, others—all those who would believe in God's Son—would become God's children (John 1:12). (The Lord also has a daughter; the "daughter of Zion" is a beloved expression for Jerusalem; Ps. 87). But the nation Israel is His **firstborn.** Eventually God would claim all of the Israelites' firstborn as His own because He saved them from the tenth plague—the destruction of the firstborn sons of all the Egyptians (Num. 3:12, 13).

4:24 The **encampment** might have been a primitive inn on Moses' route back to Egypt. **the Lord met him and sought to kill him:** The precise meaning of this passage is unclear. Clearly someone in Moses' family was not circumcised, despite what God had commanded. Most likely, Moses had kept one of his sons uncircumcised in order to please his Midianite family. (The Midianites practiced circumcision

---

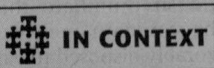 **IN CONTEXT**   ## A Heavy Mouth

Among his objections against going to Pharaoh, Moses considered himself "slow of speech and slow of tongue" (Ex. 4:10). His difficulties in speech are not unprecedented in ancient Near Eastern literature.

Enmerker, the Sumerian king of Uruk and third successor to the famous Gilgamesh, is the main character in *Enmerkar and the Lord of Aratta,* an epic written in Sumerian near the end of the third millennium B.C. In a brief passage, a messenger is unable to comprehend a message given to him by Enmerkar. Like Moses, Enmerkar was "slow of speech," expressed in this epic as "heavy of mouth."

on a groom right before his marriage instead of circumcising male infants.) Moses' neglect was a crime deserving of death, especially for the future leader of God's people. For this reason God **met** or "seized" Moses (for another use of this same Hebrew verb, read v. 27).

4:25, 26 At this time, circumcision was practiced with **sharp stone** knives rather than bronze because of associations with ancient traditions that may even have predated Israelite circumcision (Gen. 17). Many of Israel's neighboring peoples practiced circumcision, but none except Israel circumcised infants. **husband of blood:** Zipporah may have been angry that she could not follow the Midianite custom and leave her son uncircumcised.

4:26 The Lord who had met or "seized" Moses (v. 24), now **let him go.**

4:27, 28 The meeting of these two brothers after forty years must have been a very emotional moment. The Hebrew verb translated **met** encompasses the idea of a forceful, direct encounter, a bear hug (this same Hebrew verb is used in v. 24). How fitting that the two would meet **on the mountain of God** (3:1). Later at this mountain they would both minister together.

4:29–31 When they arrived in Egypt, they gathered the **elders** together. Aaron acted as Moses' prophet (vv. 14–16). It is not clear whether it was Aaron or Moses who did the **signs.** But the people's response was appropriate. They **believed** and **worshiped** the God who had sent these signs and messengers. God **had visited** them! Here God's visitation is for deliverance (Ruth 1:6). In other places the verb (Heb. *paqad*) refers to a visitation in wrath (Is. 10:12).

5:1 God emboldened Moses and Aaron to approach the powerful tyrant of Egypt with strong, daring words in the name of their God: **"Let My people go."** These word come repeatedly beginning with 7:16 (8:1, 20, 21; 9:1, 13; 10:3, 4). Yet the Lord told them what to expect (3:19; 4:21–23). It was God's plan that Pharaoh would not agree to their demand.

5:2 Who is the LORD: Later these arrogant words would haunt Pharaoh (12:31, 32). Indeed, he would ascribe greatness to God and shamefulness to himself and his people (9:27). Meanwhile, Pharaoh believed himself to be a god. He certainly felt no need to cave in to the demands of some other, unknown god. Sadly for him, he had never encountered the true and living God, hence his response, **nor will I let Israel go,** just as God had predicted (Ex. 3:19; 4:21–23). Note that Pharaoh had not yet hardened his heart (something not stated until 7:13). In the next encounter (ch. 7), Pharaoh would harden his heart resolutely.

5:2 Moses' first encounter reveals Pharaoh's central problem: **I do not know the LORD.**

5:3 The boldness of Moses and Aaron's first words (v. 1) is replaced with panic. The Israelites had to obey their God.

5:4–9 To punish Moses and Aaron for insolence, Pharaoh imposed severe measures on the Hebrew workers, who needed **straw** to strengthen the sun-dried bricks they were making. With no reduction in their daily quota, the people would have to gather the straw during their off-hours. Until now the Egyptians had provided it for them. Pharaoh invented a suitable excuse: The Hebrews had too much free time.

5:10–19 The **officers** (Heb. *shoterim,* meaning "subordinate officials"), the Hebrew leaders of the work gangs, understandably complained about the new work rules. Pharaoh repeated his excuse that the people were **idle** (v. 8) and ordered them to continue. The Hebrew crew chiefs were in a more precarious position than ever.

5:20, 21 The Hebrew crew chiefs turned their anger on Moses and Aaron. Indeed their words, **Let the LORD** look on you and judge, are a harsh curse. They felt that Moses and Aaron's words to Pharaoh were futile and only made him hate them more. The word translated **abhorrent** means "to cause to stink."

5:22–6:1 Greatly shaken at the outcome of his first encounter with Pharaoh, Moses offers a prayer of complaint.

5:22 Lord, why: While incongruous, these words are often linked in the experience of God's people. After people come to faith in the Lord, they often expect that their lives will be marked only by God's blessing. When troubles come, they almost inevitably wish to cry aloud, "O Lord, why?" Clearly, there is incongruity in these words. If He indeed is "Lord," then His ways are not to be questioned. The Hebrew crew chiefs' harsh charge against Moses greatly troubled him. His complaint to God, **Why is it You have sent me?** alludes to his initial reluctance to be the Lord's agent of deliverance (4:10–17).

5:23 speak in Your name: It seems that Moses expected Pharaoh to cave in as soon as he heard the use of the Lord's name Yahweh (3:14, 15; 5:1). Yet God had warned Moses that Pharaoh would do the opposite (3:19; 4:21). Moses had forgotten this clear revelation.

6:1 The Lord's response to Moses, **Now you shall see,** was designed to encourage him. Nothing had happened yet because God had not yet begun to act. **strong hand:** The reference seems to be to Pharaoh, although consistently the "strong hand" of Exodus is the Lord's (3:19; 20; 6:6; 15:6, 12). Thus the sense of the verse is, "Because of My strong hand Pharaoh will let them go, and because of My strong hand Pharaoh will drive them out of his land."

6:2–9 Yahweh's purpose in the Exodus. In the Lord's plan, Moses' futile and disheartening experience in his first encounter with Pharaoh (5:1-9) led to this most significant statement of the purpose that God intended in the Exodus.

INSIGHT

Dangers of Idolatry

God's promise to give the land of Canaan to Abraham's descendants (Ex. 6:4) meant dispossessing the Canaanites, a group of tribes descended from Noah's grandson Canaan (Gen. 10:15–20). They had been neighbors of Abraham and still lived in the land at the time of the Exodus. In the intervening years, however, their idolatries and immoral behavior had increased to the point where God was ready to judge them.

This section is so important that some biblical theologians believe this passage to be the heart of the Pentateuch. Here the living God explains His purpose for His people Israel.

6:2 By explaining His purpose for Israel, God encouraged Moses after his disheartening experience with Pharaoh (5:1-9). This passage builds strongly on the revelation of God to Moses at the burning bush (2:23—3:22). The words **I am the LORD** begin and conclude this section (vv. 2, 8). LORD stands for God's name, "Yahweh."

6:3 The patriarchs had known **God Almighty.** It is not that they had never heard the name Yahweh, but they had not **known** God in an intimate way. The patriarchs knew a great deal about God and had experienced His goodness in many ways. But they had not had the revelation that was granted to Moses and the people of his day.

6:4 My covenant: The Abrahamic covenant celebrated in Genesis (Gen. 12:1–3, 7; 15:12–21; 17; 22:15–18). **pilgrimage:** The fathers and mothers of Israel had wandered about in the land of Canaan without ever owning more than grazing rights, well treaties, and a burial ground for Sarah (Gen. 23; Heb. 11:8–10). They were **strangers** in Egypt, resident aliens, without citizenship in their own country.

6:5 groaning: This verse recalls the Israelites' cry in Ex. 2:23–25. With this wonderful introduction of Himself, the Lord was now ready to state His plan for Israel (vv. 6–8).

6:6–8 These verses express four aspects of God's plan for Israel. (1) He would deliver them from Egypt. This was more than freedom from slavery; it was a picture of their national salvation, for in the process the nation was redeemed from their sin (Ex. 14:31). (2) He would make them His people, a fellowship of believers. (3) He would be their God, a description of a one-on-one relationship. (4) He would bring them to Canaan, the Promised Land.

6:9 Despite God's powerful words to Moses, the people were still unwilling to believe. Their cruel suffering overwhelmed them. But they would eventually believe! They needed to experience the reality of the living God (14:31).

6:10, 11 The Lord renewed His command to Moses (4:22, 23). Pharaoh's arrogant rejection was not the end of the story, just the beginning.

6:12 Moses complained that his own people would not listen to him. How then would **Pharaoh?** Moses was still convinced that his **uncircumcised lips** (he was a poor speaker) would ruin everything (4:10).

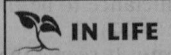

IN LIFE

Positive Authority

Authority can be used in ways that bring liberty to people, not just limitation.

Authority is sometimes thought of as nothing more than telling others what they cannot do and keeping people in line. But in God's instruction to Moses (Ex. 6:13), we are reminded that authority can bring freedom when applied wisely under the Lord's direction.

For example, a judge can use authority to release an innocent person from jail. A high school principal can use authority to obtain resources for teachers to teach effectively. A manager can use authority to reward a worker's performance and encourage creativity and excellence. So authority can be affirming and supportive rather than controlling and punitive.

Paul exercised a great deal of authority in the early church. But he recognized that his power was given to build others up not to tear them down (1 Cor. 13:10).

6:13 The Lord's response was to repeat the initial **command.** This was not something to be negotiated, but something to be done. Following the parenthesis of vv. 14–27, the story continues in v. 28. There we learn that there was more to the interaction between Moses and the Lord than these verses suggest.

6:14–27 The family history of Moses, Aaron, and Miriam briefly interrupts the narrative. But this was not just a matter of public record, it was something to celebrate! All of Israel's priests would eventually come from this line.

6:14–16 Reuben was the firstborn of Jacob by his wife Leah (Gen. 29:32; 35:23; 49:3, 4). His sons are also listed in Gen. 46:9 and in Num. 26:5–11. **Simeon** was the second son of Jacob by his wife Leah (Gen. 29:33; 35:23; 49:5–7). His sons are also listed in Gen. 46:10 and in Num. 26:12–14. **Jemuel** in some lists is spelled "Nemuel" (Num. 26:12). **Shaul the son of a Canaanite woman:** This factor is also noted in Gen. 4:10. It is an ominous notation suggesting the problem of assimilation with the Canaanite peoples had God not brought the nation Israel to Egypt where such a practice could not continue (notes at Gen. 38). **Levi** was the third son of Jacob by his wife Leah (Gen. 29:34; 35:23; 49:5–7). His sons are also listed in Gen. 46:11 and in Num. 26:57–62 (1 Chron. 6:1–30). Based on Ex. 6:17–27, it is clear that the purpose of this section is to describe the family history of Moses, Aaron, and Miriam and not to describe the families of each of the tribes. The mention of the families of Reuben and Simeon here seems to be simply a "courtesy" based on their precedence among the sons of Jacob. Despite his sinfulness in association with his brother Simeon in avenging the rape of their sister Dinah (Gen. 34; 49:5–7), Levi lived a very long life, 137 years.

6:17–19 The three sons of Levi each fathered several families (1 Chron. 6:1–30) that would have significant roles to play in the worship of God. All true priests and Levites would come from their numbers.

6:20 The verses above have led to the mention of **Amram**, the patriarch in the family of Levi from whom Moses and his siblings were descended. According to the lists in similar genealogies (Num. 26:57–59; 1 Chron. 6:1–3), Amram the son of Kohath was a grandson of Levi. **Jochebed,** his wife, was also his aunt, the daughter of Levi. Later, the Law would prohibit marriages among such close relatives (Lev. 18), but the early families of Israel must have had many such "close" marriages. **she bore him:** The biblical use of language allows a remote ancestor to be regarded as one's "parent." A paraphrase would read, "She bore to her husband the family that resulted in the later birth of

Moses." The actual names of Moses' mother, father, and his siblings are lost to us. By the time of Moses, many generations had passed from that of Amram, the grandson of Levi, and from Jochebed the daughter of Levi; indeed, the family of the descendants of Amram numbered in the thousands (Num. 3:27, 28). It is somewhat surprising for the modern reader to see language used in this manner. For the ancient Semite, it was sometimes more important to preserve the name of famous ancestors than even the names of persons closer in time, including the names of one's parents. The genealogy of Moses and his siblings was certifiable from the family of Levi. This was the important issue, for Aaron would become the father of the priests of the nation. See also the comments in the genealogies in Gen. 5 and 10, for similar "missing generations." The order of the sons is given here: **Aaron** was three years older than **Moses** (7:7). Miriam is not mentioned in this verse; most genealogies in Israel listed only sons. But the readers of Torah will not forget her; nor should we (Mic. 6:4). She, along with her celebrated brothers, were Yahweh's gifts to Israel.

6:21–23 Izhar, the second son of Kohath (v. 18) and **Uzziel,** the third son of Kohath, also founded significant families. Among the names mentioned is **Korah,** the priest who would later lead a rebellion against Moses (Num. 16). Korah's sons (v. 24) would survive his judgment (Num. 26:11) and would become a famous musical family whose songs became part of temple singing for generations (read the superscriptions to Pss. 84, 85, 87). **Elisheba:** The name of Aaron's wife (her Heb. name means "God is an Oath," that is, "It is by God One Swears") became "Elizabeth" in the Greek NT (Luke 1:5). Her father **Amminadab** (Heb., "My Kinsman [the Lord] Is Noble") was from a well-known family in the tribe of Judah (Num. 1:7; 2:3; 7:12, 17; 10:14) that later figured in the line of David, and thus of the Messiah (Ruth 4:19, 20; 1 Chron. 2:10). The sons **Nadab** and **Abihu** became proverbial in Israel of priests who used their office for evil purposes (Lev. 10:1–7; Num. 3:2–4). **Eleazar and Ithamar** were faithful priests.

6:24 sons of Korah: See v. 21.

6:25 Phineas: This son of Eleazar was the hero of God during one of the darkest moments of Israel's spiritual journey (Num. 25).

6:26, 27 the same Aaron and Moses: The wording of this whole section (vv. 14–27) seems to come from a period quite a bit removed from the time of Moses and Aaron. This is an example of a section that may have been added to the Book of Exodus at a later period. As mentioned in Introduction, it is not

✠ IN CONTEXT Moses as God

The Lord's statement to Moses that "I have made you as God to Pharaoh" (Ex. 7:1) may seem puzzling to a modern reader. But it helps to realize that the Egyptian pharaohs were considered gods, and that their words were seen as divine pronouncements. Thus they held absolute sway over the people.

Moses had been raised in a pharaoh's court (2:8–10), so he was well aware that Pharaoh would pay little attention to the statements of an ordinary human. Thus the Lord's message was a reassuring promise to Moses. God would persuade the ruler that in Moses he was dealing with someone who deserved a hearing.

necessary to argue that Moses wrote all the sections that the book contains. It is necessary, however, to believe that the entirety of the book, and all its parts, are authentic, authoritative, and inspired. Later scribes might have felt it very necessary to give the family history of Moses as a parenthesis in the story line so that readers would be well-aware of the connections Moses and Aaron had with the people of Israel. The repetition of the phrase with inversion of names not only identifies these men but also celebrates their memory.

6:28–30 These verses repeat the material of 6:10–13. **The Lord spoke** may be translated, "The Lord had spoken" (Ex. 4:19; 12:1). It is possible that the inclusion of the parenthetical genealogical material (6:14–27) necessitated a review. On the words **uncircumcised lips** see 6:12. Also, the chapter division at 7:1 is poorly placed; the new chapter should come at 7:8.

7:1, 2 These verses repeat the issues of 4:10–17. Repetition with variation is a part of Hebrew prose style to show emphasis. **you as God:** As Moses was the prophet of the Lord, so Aaron became Moses' **prophet.** Aaron would speak for Moses, for a prophet was the "mouth" of the one who sent him (or her).

7:3, 4 I will harden Pharaoh's heart: It was in God's plan that Pharaoh would be inflexibly stubborn (note at 4:21), thus setting the scene for God to deliver His people by powerful **signs and . . . wonders.** The word *sign* (Heb. 'ôt; Ex. 4:8, 9; 8:23) may be used to describe a reminder, a memorial, or a symbol, as in 3:12 (12:13), but here it speaks of a pledge or attestation of God's presence. The term *wonder* (Heb. *mophet*) similarly describes a special display of God's power. These two words paired together mean "irrefutable works." God would demonstrate His power and authenticate His agents, Moses and Aaron, with such works. The doubling of the personal pronoun, **My . . . My,** makes this assertion of God's irruption even more forceful.

7:5 God also planned from the beginning that **the Egyptians** would **know** that He and He alone was the living God. In the first nine plagues, God used forces of creation in a supernatural way to bring judgment on the Egyptians. In the tenth plague, the destruction of the firstborn of Egypt, God would **stretch out His hand** and bring judgment Himself (Ex. 12:12, 13, 29, 30).

7:6 did so . . . so they did: The obedience of Moses and Aaron is a recurring theme in the Pentateuch (Ex. 12:28; Num. 8:20–22). But even these men of God did not always obey Him.

7:7 eighty . . . eighty-three: In a sense, these men had already lived a lifetime (Ps. 90:10) before their principal life work had begun! Moses was to lead the nation of Israel for another forty years before he died (Deut. 29:5; 31:2; 34:5). Aaron died in the same year as his younger brother, at the age of 123 (Num. 20:22–29; 33:38, 39).

7:8–12:36 The Lord empowers His servant Moses against Pharaoh to enact His great plan of redemption. This section is the heart of the drama of redemption, containing the stories of the ten plagues, the institution of the Passover, the deliverance from Egypt, and the beginning of the journey into the Wilderness. It is one of the most dramatic OT narratives; it is epic prose at its best from the ancient world.

7:8 Then the Lord spoke to Moses and Aaron: This is the first time Moses and Aaron are referred to as receiving a message from God together.

7:9, 10 In the first confrontation with Pharaoh there was no talk of miracles (5:1–9). This time they would perform a **miracle,** a special display of God's power. Aaron's **rod** would figure prominently in several plagues (7:20; 8:5, 16; 9:23; 10:13, 22; 14:16; 17:5, 9). The sign that God had done before Moses, turning his rod into **a serpent** (4:1–5), was now repeated before Pharaoh and his courtiers.

⚒ IN DEPTH	**Magic and Magicians in Egypt**

Throughout the ancient Near East, magicians were important members of royal courts. Magic was a means by which power could be transferred from the gods to humans. Magicians were generally well-educated and literate persons who had studied the incantations and actions that were needed to cause the gods or demons to honor human requests. Their official services were needed to understand the will of the gods, or to bring down curses on treaty-breakers, or to create catastrophes for enemies.

Egypt's magical traditions are the best known of all the ancient traditions. This is partly because other civilizations were impressed by Egyptian traditions, but mostly because a wealth of their magical texts remain, to give the world great understanding of their incantations, amulets, secret signs, geometric shapes, acrostic patterns, and names of famous persons.

In Exodus, Moses is presented as directing the plagues in the same manner as the Egyptians understood their magic to work. Except that through the miracles, Moses conveyed the power of his God. When the Egyptian magicians turned rods into snakes, water into blood, or called frogs out of the Nile, they believed it was the power of their gods working through them.

Pharaoh's magicians were largely unimpressed with Moses and his God as long as they were able to do the same tricks through their magical arts. But when they could not produce gnats, the Egyptians expressed admiration for Moses with the words, "This is the finger of God" (Ex. 8:19), which quotes an actual Egyptian magical phrase. In this way they acknowledged that Moses' God was greater than their gods.

7:11 Pharaoh was not about to be outdone. **Wise men** (Heb. *hakamîn*) refers to his counselors, men of learning and insight. **Sorcerers** refers to those who practiced divination. They were prominent in the courts of ancient kings (Deut. 18:10; Dan. 2:2; Mal. 3:5). The **magicians** (Heb. *hartumîn*, a word related to one that means "engraver," "writer") of Egypt were believed to possess occult knowledge (Gen. 41:8, 24; Ex. 8:7, 18, 19; 9:11; Dan. 1:20; 2:2). The power of these persons may have been in trickery and slight-of-hand illusions, or demonic power. The word **enchantments** (Heb. *lahatîm*, a noun from the verb *lût*, meaning "to enwrap closely") speaks of "secret things" or "mysteries" (7:22); to paraphrase, "their bag of tricks." But in their encounter with Moses and Aaron, these men were no match for the power of God (8:19; 9:11)! Later, the royal courts of Israel had wise men (1 Kin. 4:34; Prov. 25:1), but the black arts of sorcery, divination, and astrology were forbidden (Deut. 18:9–14).

7:12 his rod . . . serpents: The text does not say whether this was a genuine transformation or a trick of Pharaoh's evil sorcerers. It is possible that they knew what the first sign would be and had drugged or stunned serpents in some manner so that they might appear to be rods. In any event, their serpents were no match for Aaron's serpent; his swallowed theirs!

7:13 Many times **Pharaoh's heart grew hard,** meaning he became insensitive and dull

to the demonstration of God's power (vv. 14, 22, 23; 8:15, 19, 32; 9:7, 12, 34, 35; 10:1, 20, 27; 11:10; 14:4, 5, 8). This was **as the LORD** had said—as God had planned from the beginning (3:19; 4:21; 7:3, 4). Pharaoh was willful (5:1–9). But he was captive to the dulling work of God's Spirit (Is. 6:10, concerning the people of Judah).

7:14 On other occasions (Ex. 4:21; 7:13, 22; 8:19) the term **hard** translates a form of the verb (Heb. *hazaq*) meaning "to strengthen," with the idea of being "perverse." Here the verb (Heb. *ka bed*) has the idea of being "heavy," "dulled," "insensitive," "peevish." See note at 4:21.

7:15 Some of the plagues were announced **to Pharaoh** beforehand; others came without warning. Those that were announced were the first (7:14–18), second (8:1–4), fourth (8:20–23), fifth (9:1–5), seventh (9:13–19), eighth (10:1–6), and tenth (11:4–8). Those not announced were the third (8:16, 17), sixth (9:8–10), and ninth (10:21–23). Note the pattern: two are announced, then a third comes without warning. This pattern occurs three times, culminating in the last, worst plague. **to the water . . . the river's bank:** Pharaoh went to the waters of the Nile not to bathe, but to be empowered. Pharaoh's bath in the Nile was a sacred Egyptian rite connected to Pharaoh's claim of divinity. **rod:** This rod is called the rod of God (Ex. 4:20) and the rod of Aaron (7:9).

7:16 The LORD God of the Hebrews: A similar identification of the Lord was used in the initial, disastrous encounter of Moses before Pharaoh (Ex. 5:1, 3). This time, Pharaoh would see a display of God's power, not just hear God's name (Ex. 2:23—3:15; 6:2–8; 9:1). The verb **serve** (Heb. *'ābad*, "to serve,") conveys the idea of sacred worship (Ex. 8:20; 9:1, 13). There is an implied criticism of Egypt as unfit for such worship because of its idolatry (3:18; 8:26, 27).

7:17, 18 The waters of the Nile may have chemically changed to **blood.** However, elements of the account suggest another possibility: (1) The first nine plagues form a set. Each of these is a natural event that occurs in a miraculous way, in quantity or timing. The change of the waters into blood would not be a natural event. (2) The plagues grow in severity with each successive one, coming to a climax with the tenth. A change of the water to actual blood would be out of step with this pattern. (3) The Hebrew word translated *blood* can refer to a red color, as in Joel 2:31. An appropriate miracle of natural timing might be that God caused torrential rains to flood and pollute the sources of the Nile to create this plague at the time it was needed. Red soil and algae would make the waters of the Nile red, unfit for drinking and deficient in oxygen for the fish.

7:19 The waters of Egypt came from the Nile and its annual flooding. The plague affected the entire water system of the nation, even the wooden and stone reservoirs that held additional supplies of drinking water.

7:20, 21 Moses and Aaron obeyed God's command and invoked the plague with **the rod** (4:1–8, 20; 7:9; 8:5, 16; 9:23; 10:13, 22; 14:16; 17:5, 9). Later believers in Israel would cele-brate this great event in a song (Pss. 78:44; 105:29, 30).

7:22 magicians . . . with their enchantments: Perhaps the tricksters of Pharaoh were able secretly to color containers of water in an attempt to duplicate the sign of the Lord in the Nile River (7:11). Their attempts were feeble by comparison. Even with this demonstration of God's power, the heart of Pharaoh **grew hard . . . as the LORD had said** (3:19; 4:21; 7:3, 13, 14).

7:23–25 Pharaoh showed his utter disdain for the revelation of God's power over the Nile when he **turned and went into his house.** He also seemed oblivious to the suffering of his people.

8:1, 2 Frogs, which in moderate numbers were regarded as signs of life, renewal, and happiness, would now become pests.

8:3–5 The **rod** of Aaron (7:19) was not a magician's wand; it was a powerful symbol of God's power in the hand of His servant (4:1–8, 20; 7:9, 20; 8:16; 9:23; 10:13, 22; 14:16; 17:5, 9). It is not clear in this passage, but it is likely, based on the words in 8:22; 9:4, 26; 10:23; 11:7, that the Hebrews were spared the effects of this plague **on the land of Egypt.** Only the polluting of the Nile (7:14–25) would have affected the Hebrew people directly.

8:6, 7 the magicians . . . with their enchantments: We do not know how or in what quantity the magicians (7:11) produced frogs; but doing so hardly helped the situation!

8:8 Note that Pharaoh did not turn to his magicians to relieve the land of the frogs; he **called for Moses and Aaron** to **entreat the**

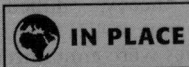 **IN PLACE**   **The Nile**

As the saying goes, "Egypt is a gift of the Nile." Therefore it is not surprising that with the first plague on the Egyptians, their river of life became a river of blood (Ex. 7:20).

Apart from the Nile, Egypt would be nothing but desert. The Nile not only brings irrigation for the country's crops but also the soil in which those crops grow. It is a rich source of fish, and in ancient times it was the main means of transportation, a source of papyrus for writing material, and even a calendar to mark the seasons.

The most striking feature of the Nile is its annual flood stage. During the spring and early summer, heavy rains and melting snow in the south, where the Nile's headwaters begin, create a dramatic rise in the river's level downstream. The Egyptians kept careful track of this flood stage using water-level gauges or Nilometers. By trapping the floodwaters through a system of channels, dikes, and irrigation works, farmers along the river's banks were able to sustain their crops in an area where rainfall was unknown except in late winter.

The Lord turned the Nile to blood to impress upon Pharaoh that he was dealing with a far more powerful God than any he had yet encountered (compare Ex. 5:2).

LORD (translated "intercede" in v. 9) on his behalf.

8:9 Accept the honor: Moses rises to Pharaoh's challenge and even invites him to set the time for Moses' prayer for relief from the frogs. In this way, Pharaoh would not be able to

world in which gods seemed to be more plentiful than trees in a forest, the living God, Yahweh, was not to be compared to a one of them. He, and He alone, is distinct from all that is in His creation (Ps. 113:4–6). The question, "Who is like Yahweh?" has no answer (Mic. 7:18).

Photo by Howard Vos

The Nile River near Luxor, Egypt. God turned the waters of this river into blood to punish the Egyptians for not freeing His people (Ex. 7:14–25).

say that it was just a coincidence that the frogs began to abate at a certain time.

8:10, 11 The Bible, especially the prophetic books, asserts again and again that **there is no one like the LORD our God**. Here the living God was being contrasted to the false gods of Egypt (Ex. 9:14; 15:11; Is. 40:25). That God alone is incomparable (Ex. 9:14; 15:11; Is. 40:25) is one of the major teachings of the OT prophets. In a

8:12 cried out to the LORD: The Hebrew verb translated *cry* places emphasis on the need at hand and suggests God's willingness to stoop down to answer that need (Ex. 22:27; Ps. 40:1). This same sort of prayer provoked the Lord to rescue His people (Ex. 2:23; 14:10, 15; 15:25; 17:4; 22:23, 27).

8:13, 14 There were so many dead frogs **the land stank.** The miraculous nature of this

---

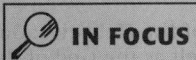 **IN FOCUS**   **"Entreat"**

(Heb. *'atar*) (Ex. 8:8, 9, 29, 30; 9:28; 10:17, 18) Strong's #6279: This Hebrew word translated *entreat* (8:8) or *intercede* (8:9) is one of the biblical words for prayer. The word depicts a person earnestly beseeching God and basically means "to ask" (Gen. 25:21; Is. 19:22). Spreading out one's hands before the Lord in the OT was a common gesture associated with prayer (Ex. 9:29). This gesture expressed the petitioner's receptiveness to God and his or her need. Empty-handed, with nothing to offer but oneself, petitioners were asking God to fill their hands with His blessings. For this reason, God warned worshipers to petition Him with hands that were not soiled by unclean and halfhearted offerings (Mal. 1:9).

plague lay in the timing and magnitude of the invasion. God did not create new frogs from nothing; He caused frogs to come up in unnaturally large numbers at exactly the right time, and then to die at exactly the right time (vv. 30, 31; 9:33; 10:18, 19).

8:15 Pharaoh's behavior exhibits a pattern. During the time of stress, Pharaoh was willing to promise anything. But as soon as the stress ended, he **hardened his heart** and became unwilling to do what he had promised (3:19; 4:21; 5:2; 7:3, 13, 14).

8:16, 17 The plague of **lice** was the first not to be announced to Pharaoh beforehand. **all the land of Egypt:** It is not clear in this passage, but it is likely, based on the wording in 8:22; 9:4, 26; 10:23; 11:7, that the Hebrews were spared the effects of this plague. **All the dust of the land became lice** is hyperbole indicating unprecedented trouble with tiny insects in countless numbers.

8:18 The magicians . . . with their enchantments (7:11) failed this time. Perhaps

---

✠ IN CONTEXT — An Ecological Disaster

The infestation of frogs (Ex. 8:1–15) and the other nine plagues created an ecological nightmare in Egypt. The Nile and its related waterways, the air over the land, the flora and fauna of the region, and many other natural systems were degraded by the region's ecological disasters.

But let there be no mistake. The responsibility for these natural disasters was Pharaoh's not God's. Although, as the Creator, God knew how to upset the intricate and delicate balance of Egypt's environment. The plagues were awesome and undeniable demonstrations of His power, and the fact that the Israelites were spared showed that God was in control of nature's forces.

---

the lack of announcement meant they had no time to prepare.

8:19 It is remarkable that Pharaoh's magicians attributed the plague to **the finger of God.** But what choice did they have? Their own competence was on the line. Still their words had no impact on Pharaoh (3:19; 4:21; 5:2; 7:3, 13, 14).

8:20–22 The pressure on Pharaoh intensified with this plague. For the first time (read 9:4, 26; 10:23; 11:7), God vowed to **set apart the land of Goshen** for the protection of His people. Swarms of flies would be everywhere except near the Hebrews. By this means God would make Himself known among all in Egypt. In some ways this exclusion is the most remarkable aspect of the plagues, especially in the last one (Ex. 11:7; 12).

8:23 Make a difference, here, is "to set a ransom," but that meaning is not clear in this context. The translation "distinction" from the Septuagint (the LXX) may be the superior reading here (this follows the meaning of the key verb in 8:22).

8:24 There is no mention of the rod of Moses in this instance (compare 7:20). Perhaps the rod was lifted by Moses or Aaron, but the emphasis here is on the action of **the LORD.** As the Lord had warned, the flies brought havoc. **Corrupted** can be used of moral corruption (Gen. 6:12) as well as in physical ruin, as here.

8:25 The response of Pharaoh was one of only partial submission; **in the land** refers to staying within the confines of Egypt.

8:26 By using the strong terminology **the abomination of the Egyptians** (Deut. 17:1; 18:12; 22:5), Moses employed the ethnic and cultural sensibilities of the Egyptians to free the Israelites (Gen. 43:32; 46:34). The sacrificial animals of Israel would include sheep, something the Egyptians regarded as detestable. The Egyptians' anger against the Hebrews might lead them to stone the Hebrews to death.

8:27 Three days journey: See 3:18.

8:28 Pharaoh capitulates, but with strings attached.

8:29 Moses promised to pray for relief from the plague of **flies,** but he also warned Pharaoh to keep his promise (7:22; 8:15, 19).

8:30–32 As soon as the Lord removed the swarms of flies, Pharaoh reverted to his earlier stubbornness against Moses, Israel, and God— and **hardened his heart** (3:19; 4:21; 5:2; 7:3, 13, 14).

9:1, 2 the LORD God of the Hebrews: God forcefully identified Himself as the God of the Hebrews just as He said He would (3:18). The first time Moses spoke to Pharaoh in God's name, he was rebuffed (5:1–9). On subsequent occasions, God demonstrated to Pharaoh the power of His name (6:2–8; 7:16).

9:3 A very severe pestilence on the livestock of Egypt would destroy much of the economy of Egypt as well as its military preparedness.

9:4 make a difference: The same verb is used in 8:22 (11:7). Among the Hebrews, nothing would die. The miracles of the Lord in the first nine plagues lay in their timing, their intensity, and as here, whom they affected. As the Egyptians' animals would fall all about them, the animals of the Hebrews would continue to flourish.

9:5 Just as it had been announced, the plague began at **a set time.** The timing was a significant part of these plagues as was the subsequent relief (9:18).

9:6, 7 As with the fourth plague (8:24), **the LORD did this thing.** There is no mention of the rod of Moses (7:20). Even though **Pharaoh sent** his agents and confirmed that the animals of the Hebrews had been spared this calamity, **the heart of Pharaoh became hard** (3:19; 4:21; 5:2; 7:3, 13, 14).

9:8 to Moses and Aaron: This is the second plague to arrive with no warning (7:15). **ashes:** Moses' use of a symbolic act **in the sight of Pharaoh** indicated that the outbreak of disease was not a coincidence. This disease was from the Lord.

9:9, 10 It is not clear from the text whether the Hebrews were spared the plague of **boils** as they were spared the others, but it seems reasonable to think so (8:22; 9:4, 26; 10:23; 11:7). As in the case of the fourth (8:24) and fifth (9:6) plagues, there is no mention of the rod of Moses in connection with the plague of boils (7:20).

9:11 The reference to the hapless **magicians** (7:11) is almost humorous. Not only were they powerless, but they also suffered from the plague.

9:12 hardened the heart of Pharaoh: See Ex. 3:19; 4:21; 5:2; 7:3, 13, 14.

9:13, 14 The words **to your very heart** suggest a growing intensity in the plagues (chs. 11; 12). **none like Me:** God is beyond comparison (8:10). He is distinct from all the supposed gods of Egypt, who were now under His direct attack.

9:15 if I had: The Lord points out that He could have destroyed the stubborn Pharaoh right at the beginning.

9:16 for this . . . I have raised you up: God used Pharaoh's stubbornness (Ex. 4:21): (1) to demonstrate His **power;** and (2) to make

known His **name** (10:2; Rom. 9:17, 18). Pharaoh was not only an evil ruler in a powerful state; he was an evil man, ungodly, unrighteous, and anti-God. Pharaoh set himself up as a god who maintained the stability of his kingdom. The Lord's judgment on him was an appropriate response to this fraud.

9:17 The term **you exalt yourself** has the idea of self-aggrandizement. In this, Pharaoh is behaving in a manner similar to that of the Prince of Tyre (Ezek. 28:1–10) and Satan, whom the Prince of Tyre emulated (Ezek. 28:11–19).

9:18 tomorrow: One theme in the plagues is the certainty of their timing (7:20; 9:5).

9:19–21 The fact that God was judging Pharaoh does not mean He was unmerciful. The Lord could have destroyed Pharaoh and his people in a moment (v. 15), but He did not. He could have brought each plague without warning, but in most cases He served notice (7:16). In anticipation of this plague, He warned the Egyptians to **gather** their **livestock** so they might be spared the hailstorm. Even some members of Pharaoh's court now took the **word of the LORD** seriously.

9:22–25 The wording of this paragraph is detailed, repetitious, and altogether frightening. We hear from time to time of terrible hailstorms with hail as large as baseballs. The wording of this text suggests that no hailstorm had ever been as terrible as this. The **rod** used here is the same one that was first described in 4:1–8 (4:20; 7:9; 8:5, 16; 10:13, 22; 14:16; 17:5, 9). The reference to **fire** probably means lightning (Lev. 10:2; 1 Kin. 18:38; Ps. 78:48).

9:26 The exclusion of **the land of Goshen** from the Lord's plagues was part of the miracle (8:22; 11:7).

9:27, 28 Pharaoh's response was more yielding than ever in the aftermath of this terrible blow. For such a proud man to say **I have sinned** was a stunning admission, as was his confession, **the LORD is righteous.** What a change from his initial arrogance (5:2)! But sadly, these words of contrition would not hold. Pharaoh would repeat them later (10:16, 17), only to take them back in the end.

9:29 I will spread out my hands: This is a

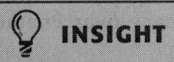 **INSIGHT**   **Flax**

Flax (Ex. 9:31) was grown mainly for its fibers, from which linen was made. Spelt is a food grain similar to wheat and can be grown is a less fertile soil. Wheat and barley have been grown in Egypt since 5000 B.C., and in Palestine since about 8000 B.C. All Egyptian agriculture depends on the Nile for water.

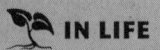 **IN LIFE** | **The Biting Edge of Sarcasm**

othing takes the heart out of a person quite like biting sarcasm from an authority figure. It can be hard enough just to get up the courage to approach a powerful leader, but if that figure responds with derision, even the bravest can lose hope.

Pharaoh used sarcasm with Moses and Aaron when they came to warn of the plague of locusts (Ex. 10:10). There is no clear indication that they were disheartened by the ruler's taunts. But given Moses' fears before returning to Egypt, perhaps he and his brother were not exactly rejoicing as they went out from Pharaoh's presence.

There are at least three ways to handle biting sarcasm, especially when it is directed against one's faith:

(1) Know who God is and why He has sent you. If people do not have much confidence in God to begin with, it won't take much to knock their faith out of them. Likewise, if they do not know God's purpose, it will be easy for a sarcastic comment to make them forget why they are doing what they are doing.

(2) Know yourself—your strengths and your weaknesses. What is the worst that someone could say to you, or about you? To what sort of comments would you be most sensitive and vulnerable?

(3) Know your enemy. What does your opponent stand to gain by turning you aside, or to lose if you prevail? Most importantly, do you know who your real enemy is?

However Moses and Aaron were affected by Pharaoh's words here, they nevertheless did not let it take the heart of what God had called them to do.

---

gesture of prayer (Ps. 134:2) tied here to a request (v. 28; 8:8). Pharaoh finally admitted that **the earth is the LORD's** (Ps. 24:1).

9:30 you will not yet fear: Moses sees through Pharaoh's veneer; his repentance is not sincere.

9:31, 32 As in Canaan (Ruth 1:22; 2:23), **barley** was the first of the crops to be harvested in the late spring; **wheat** would be harvested in the summer. From this verse the timing of the yearlong series of plagues can be estimated (7:19).

9:33–35 It took a miracle to stop the plague as well as to start it (8:10–14, 30, 31; 10:18, 19). Sadly, Pharaoh's remorse (v. 27) was short-lived; **he hardened his heart** (v. 34; 3:19; 4:21; 5:2; 7:3, 13, 14).

10:1 The coming plague of locusts would be preceded by a warning, so God commanded Moses to **go in to Pharaoh** (7:15). **I have hardened his heart:** Three verbs are used in Exodus to describe God's hardening of Pharaoh's heart. Usually the verb meaning "to make hard" is used (4:21). In 7:3, the Hebrew verb meaning "to make stiff" is used. Here the Hebrew verb that means "to make heavy" or "to make insensitive" is used.

10:2 your son and your son's son: The story of God's deliverance of Israel from Egypt was to be told by one generation to the next. **the mighty things I have done:** This whole

phrase translates an unusual Hebrew verb that literally means "to make sport of" or "to toy with." The Lord was saying, "I have just been playing games with Pharaoh." The word **signs** refers to God's power, His revelation of Himself (v. 1; 7:9; 9:16).

10:3 refuse to humble yourself: Pharaoh's pride was his undoing. He believed himself to be a god, and paraded himself as one. God resists the proud but gives grace to the humble (Pss. 18:27; 147:6; Is. 57:15–21; 1 Pet. 5:5).

10:4 As in each of the first nine plagues, the Lord used a part of His own creation, **locusts**—well known as a recurring cause of destruction—to bring unparalleled devastation to Egypt.

10:5–7 The term **snare** (Heb. *môqesh*) can be used to describe a trap for birds (Amos 3:5). Here it speaks of Moses as a symbol of destruction for the Egyptians. **Egypt is destroyed:** This admission by Pharaoh's counselors fulfilled God's prediction that the Egyptians would acknowledge God's supremacy over Pharaoh (7:5; 8:19; 9:20; 12:33).

10:8, 9 Pharaoh's questions implied that he was not serious about releasing the Israelites. For example, **Who are the ones that are going?** was a preposterous question. From the beginning, Moses had demanded the release of the entire population of Hebrews, and he stated this again.

10:10, 11 Pharaoh grudgingly gave permission for the **men** to leave. Keeping wives, families, flocks, and possessions under his control would assure that the men would return.

10:12–15 Since Pharaoh was still obstinate, the Lord brought on the **locusts** and **they covered the face of the whole earth.** This is a hyperbolic way of expressing that this was an unprecedented disaster in **all the land of Egypt.** It is not clear in this passage, but it is likely (based on the words in 8:22; 9:4, 26; 10:23; 11:7) that the Hebrews were spared the effects of this plague.

10:16–18 Pharaoh confessed **I have sinned,** and Moses **entreated the LORD** on his behalf because Pharaoh could not stop the plague himself, nor could his magicians. The text is careful to attribute the relief to God and not to Moses. God was winning.

10:19 a very strong wind: As in the case of the frogs (8:10–14) and the hail (9:33), Pharaoh saw God's power over the forces of nature. Truly the earth was the Lord's (9:29; Ps. 24:1).

10:20 But the LORD hardened Pharaoh's heart: See 3:19; 4:21; 5:2; 7:3, 13, 14.

10:21–23 The ninth plague, **thick darkness,** came upon Egypt without warning. This plague, which could be **felt,** struck at the very heart of Egyptian religion, the deification of the sun as personified by the great gods Re, Amun, Aten, and Horus (the winged Sun disc). Re was to the Egyptians what Yahweh was to the Israelites. He was the ultimate supreme being who sustained all life. The "thick darkness" blotted out his supposed power in the land of Egypt.

10:22–26 A comparison with other passages (vv. 12, 13) suggests that when **Moses stretched out his hand** he was holding the rod of God (4:1–8, 20; 7:9, 20; 8:5, 16; 9:23; 14:16; 17:5, 9), an indication to Pharaoh that he was opposing the living God. The Hebrew expression **thick darkness** comes from a pair of words. The first is the common word for darkness. The second is used less often and describes deep gloom (Job 3:6, 10:21, 22; Ps. 91:6; Is. 29:18). This calamity would have affected the Egyptians the most. They worshiped many gods, but none so much as the sun. Even a normal solar eclipse would have had an impact, but an enshrouding darkness that lasted **for three days** was a frontal attack on their gods (12:12), on their Pharaoh and his supposed control of nature, and on all Pharaoh's counselors who were as helpless as he was. **see . . . nor rise:** The people must have been terrified.

10:27 But the LORD hardened Pharaoh's heart: See 3:19; 4:21; 5:2; 7:3, 13, 14.

10:28, 29 There can be no mistaking the intent of Pharaoh's threat, **you shall die,** or of Moses' reply, **I will never see your face again.** It is likely that Moses spoke the words of 11:4–8 as a part of this same conversation, interrupted only by the prophecy that begins in 11:1. This would explain Moses' "great anger" toward Pharaoh (Ex. 11:8).

11:1, 2 one more plague: At this point, the series of plagues had come to its climax. **lets you go . . . drive you out:** Pharaoh would be glad to be rid of the Israelites. **ask from his neighbor:** God had announced this from the beginning (3:21, 22; read 12:35, 36 for the result).

INSIGHT   **Silver and Gold**

Long before coins were introduced in about 625 B.C., silver and gold were used as a way of storing value. Ancient Egyptian bracelets and other items of gold jewelry were sometimes thick and heavy. A necklace buried with Psusennes I in about 991 B.C. (recovered in 1940) weighs more than forty-two pounds.

11:3 Another remarkable component of the Exodus was the Egyptians' **favor** (Heb. *hen,* also translated "grace") toward the Hebrews and admiration for their leader. After all that had happened, we might expect the opposite. But the positive feelings for Moses were shared, amazingly enough, even by **Pharaoh's servants.** This, too, is a part of the wit and irony of this great victory (15:3) the Lord had won over His enemy Pharaoh, who represents evil, sin, ungodliness, and even Satan.

11:4 Then Moses said: The text here is a bit ambiguous, and one might ask, "To whom was Moses speaking?" Verse 8 says that Moses left the presence of Pharaoh in great anger. It is likely that the words of 11:4–8 were spoken to Pharaoh on the occasion of Moses' last interview with him (10:27–29, and notes). The report of this part of that interview is delayed until ch. 11 in order to set it apart and make it even more memorable. This interpretation means that the last plague (the tenth) was one of those that was announced to Pharaoh as a solemn warning beforehand (7:15, note). **About midnight I will go out:** The Lord was the power behind all ten plagues. But in none of the earlier ones did He become personally involved as He did here. When it came to the death of the firstborn, He came to do that in person. The analogy to the Gospel is inescapable. When God planned the salvation of mankind, it was not something He left to an agent, to a messenger, to an angel. It was work He came to do Himself. It demanded the Incarnation; God became man. Thus in the deliverance of Israel from Egypt, this saving work was not delegated to another. God says in effect, "In salvation work, it is I Myself, and no other."

11:5 firstborn of Pharaoh . . . of the female servant: The use of these social opposites indicates totality (another use of social opposites is in 12:29). None of the Egyptians would escape this plague.

11:6 Prediction of the **great cry** to come (12:30) only intensified the tragedy. Pharaoh had been warned of this (4:22, 23).

11:7 In some of the other nine plagues, the text specifically says that God protected His people from the effects (Ex. 8:22; 9:4, 26; 10:23). Here, too, it states emphatically that **none of the children of Israel** would suffer in this last, most ghastly plague. God served notice that He did recognize **a difference between the Egyptians and Israel** (8:22; 9:4). The institution of the Passover (ch. 12) accentuated this great distinction. The Lord in His mercy protected His people even as He executed judgment on those who opposed Him.

11:8 Moses repeated God's prophecy: Pharaoh's **servants** would honor Moses and beg him for mercy. This was certainly an affront to Pharaoh, along with the fact that Moses left **in great anger** (most likely soon after the words of 10:28, 29).

11:9, 10 As in each of the other plagues, it was part of God's plan that Pharaoh would **not heed** God's commands or warnings. Only in the face of Pharaoh's stubbornness might the power of God be displayed.

12:1 Now the LORD spoke: It is likely that

this revelation of Yahweh had already occurred before the events of chs. 10; 11. The verb may be rendered "had spoken" (Ex. 4:19; 6:28). Although we often read words of divine revelation in Exodus, it is important to understand that such words convey a tremendous sense of God's condescending grace. What a wonder it is that God would speak to a man! It is also imperative to understand by these words that Moses (and at times Aaron), because of divine revelation, was not instituting Israel's traditions and rituals by his own clever mind. Thus, whenever we speak of "the Law of Moses," it is the Law of Yahweh conveyed through His agent, Moses, the man of God.

12:2 This month, called Abib in 13:4, corresponds to April-May and is also called Nisan. **first month:** As the Christian world dated time with respect to the birth of Christ, so Hebrew people began to mark time relative to the month of their departure from Egypt. In later Judaism an alternate dating system developed, with the new year celebrated in the fall (September–October).

12:3 Each family took a lamb on the **tenth of the month** but waited until the fourteenth day to kill it (v. 6), perhaps allowing time to notice any problems that might make the animal unfit for this holy sacrifice. The word for **lamb** can refer to either a young sheep or a young goat (v. 5). The Passover feast involved the whole family, the **household.**

12:4 Any household **too small** to eat a lamb in one meal was to join with another. No one was to be excluded.

12:5 Sacrifice was not a way to get rid of unwanted animals. Only the best lambs **without blemish** were suitable. **a male of the first year:** God meant the Passover lamb sacrificed for the Israelites to be a type (a picture or model) of the coming death of the Savior, Jesus

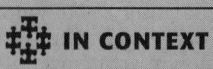 **IN CONTEXT**   ## Origins of the Passover Meal

Certain elements of the Passover ritual can be traced to ancient ceremonies that celebrated the new agricultural year. These elements include a sacrifice to be eaten by the community, or eating a new crop, or bitter herbs, or unleavened bread. They might also include rituals of thanksgiving for not dying during the period between harvests, or for a new start. Through Moses, God revealed a new meaning for the Israelite meal.

To this day Passover is celebrated by Jewish families, prepared and eaten according to the regulations of Ex. 12. As the meal is eaten, the Passover story is told, not only as something that happened long ago but as happening now. It is now that God brings every person who partakes of the meal to freedom and salvation. The feast establishes identity: we are God's people, because God did these things for us. Anticipating the coming of God's Messiah, Jewish tradition added a place at the table for Elijah, should the prophet come "this year" to proclaim the Messiah's advent.

Christ (1 Cor. 5:7). **sheep . . . goats:** We usually speak of the Passover lamb, but it could be a young goat as well.

12:6, 7 Each family took a lamb on the tenth of the month but waited until the **four-teenth day** to kill it (v. 3). The **blood** of the Passover lamb on the **doorposts and . . . lintel** was the Lord's provision for salvation from physical death, just as the blood of Christ is the Lord's provision for our salvation from spiritual death.

12:8 Verses 15–20 expand on the instructions for **unleavened bread.** See 1 Cor. 5:8 for Paul's comparison of sincerity and truth with unleavened bread. **Bitter herbs** reminded the people of the unpleasantness of slavery. The famous rabbi Gamaliel, the teacher of the great rabbinic student Saul (Acts 22:3), who became the Apostle Paul (Acts 13:9), is remembered in the Passover Haggadah (liturgy) for his words, "Whoever eats the Passover rightly must eat the lamb along with unleavened bread and bitter herbs." Paul himself was later to draw an analogy from unleavened bread to purity in keeping the feast of the Lord's Table (1 Cor. 5:8).

12:9 roasted in fire: The manner of cooking is emphasized as is the idea of the totality of the lamb. In this way, none of its bones would be broken in preparation (Num. 9:12).

12:10 none remain: This was not an ordinary meal with expected leftovers; it was a sacred feast.

12:11 The people were to dress for travel, in readiness to march at the Lord's bidding. Ordinarily they would not wear **sandals** (or shoes) in the house. One's **staff** would be propped near the door, but not on this night. They were to **eat in haste,** ready to leave. **It is the Lord's Passover:** (See v. 13 for the meaning of "Passover"). The commands for this night were not for the people's comfort. They readied the people for God's quick and miraculous deliverance. By the time of Jesus, the Jews ate this meal in a very leisurely manner, reclining on cushions around a three-winged table, the Roman *triclinium* (John 13:23). The first Passover meal was eaten in haste, but subsequent Passover meals could be less hurried, because the deliverance from Egypt had already been accomplished.

12:12 Pass through (v. 23) refers to linear motion, as in crossing over a stream (Gen. 31:21), crossing a border (Num. 20:17), or going across a territory (Num. 21:23). Abram used this word to describe his journey to Canaan (Gen. 12:6). This word is related to the name Hebrew (Ex. 1:15, 16; 2:6), perhaps meaning, "one who has come from the other side." Here it is used ominously of the antici-

pated journey of the Lord to destroy the **first-born in the land of Egypt** as threatened at the beginning (4:21–23) and told to Pharaoh's face (11:4–8). **I will pass through . . . I will strike . . . I will execute . . . I am the Lord:** The repetition of the pronoun *I* emphasizes that God did this, not an angel or some other agent.

12:13 The term **sign** can mean a reminder, memorial, or symbol, as it does here (3:12), or a miracle that points to the power of God (7:3). The verb translated **pass over** (Heb, *pasah;* v. 12), from which the Hebrew name for Passover comes (v. 11), means "to spare" or "skip" (vv. 23, 27). It is used only in these three verses and in Is. 31:5. This judgment was carried out personally by the living God. **I see . . . I will pass over you . . . I strike the land:** As in v. 12, *I* is repeated for emphasis (read the report in v. 29).

12:14 Henceforth the day would be **a memorial** (similar to the word describing God's name in 3:15). **feast to the Lord:** Some of the religious duties are somber and require fasting. The Passover, however, was a feast of celebration. (The name of the prophet Haggai was based on the Hebrew word for feast.) The same term translated **everlasting** here was also used to describe God's name (3:15). The word means "in perpetuity," for time without end (Ps. 90:2).

12:15, 16 seven days: The Passover was tied directly to the Feast of Unleavened Bread, so named in v. 17 (Ex. 23:15; Lev. 23:4–8). **Shall be cut off** means "shall be executed" (Gen. 17:14). The term **convocation** means "gathering." On the days of holy convocation the only work permitted was the preparation of food.

12:17–24 As vv. 17–20 repeat and expand on the ideas of vv. 15, 16, so vv. 21–24 take up the main ideas of the Passover (vv. 1–14) and expand on them.

12:25–28 To ensure against forgetting this festival, these verses include instructions on how one generation should teach the next concerning its importance. **to the land:** The hope for entry into the Promised Land was an essential part of the salvation story. **when your children say:** These words are implemented in a significant part of the Passover Haggadah (liturgy): Questions are provided for children to ask, and the answers are prepared as well. **He struck:** The language of this verse is consistent with that of vv. 12, 13. The Lord Himself passed over the homes of the faithful in Israel, and the Lord Himself struck the homes of the Egyptians (v. 29). **bowed their heads and worshiped:** This is the second time that such words are used of the Israelites in the Exodus. **so they did:** The Israelites not only worshiped God, but they believed His words and obeyed Him.

12:29 Moses, at the very beginning of his commission, was told about the death of the Egyptians' **firstborn** (4:22, 23). Furthermore, he announced it directly to Pharaoh (11:4–8). God regarded the nation of Israel as His firstborn. In exchange for the attacks on His firstborn son, the Lord attacked the firstborn son of Pharaoh (vv. 12, 13, 23, 27). **the firstborn of Pharaoh ... to the firstborn of the captive:** This use of opposites indicates totality—everyone in Egypt. **and also livestock:** Though not nearly as awful as the death of firstborn children, the death of the livestock was a blow to the Egyptians economically. These deaths were also attacks on their gods (v. 12).

12:30 The **great cry in Egypt** gives us only a glimpse of how Pharaoh's people paid for his choices. **Not a house** escaped. Wherever there was a family there was a death.

12:31 called for Moses and Aaron: Based on the words of Moses reported in 10:29, it is likely that this message was delivered by an intermediary. Pharaoh was grief-stricken at the death of his firstborn son.

12:32 your flocks and your herds: At last Pharaoh capitulated (10:9, 26). His words **and bless me also** show a softening of his heart. The death of his son, and the deaths of firstborn

sons everywhere, must have shattered him to the core of his being.

12:33 The Egyptians urged the people to leave because they feared they might all die if the Israelites did not leave soon. A Psalm written later celebrated this miraculous deliverance from slavery: "Egypt was glad when they departed, / For the fear of them had fallen upon them" (Ps. 105:38).

12:34 The dough before it was leavened explains the "unleavened bread" of vv. 15–20. The Israelites did not have enough time to let the leaven (yeast) work in their dough. They left Egypt with unleavened dough. From that day on, unleavened bread would remind them of the haste of that night of flight from slavery.

12:35 asked from the Egyptians: This was God's plan from the beginning (Ex. 3:21, 22; 11:2, 3). The slaves were now being paid for their years of servitude. Pharaoh was no longer respected by his people. The ones who suffered through all ten plagues respected the nation of the God who had humiliated Pharaoh.

12:36 plundered the Egyptians: Newly freed slaves do not usually make their escape with their masters pushing the family silver into their hands. But this is what happened when Israel left Egypt.

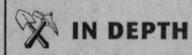 **IN DEPTH** | **The Destroyer**

The term "the destroyer" in Ex. 12:23 (a Heb. participle from *shahat*, in the Hiphil theme) seems to suggest that the agent of destruction is someone other than the Lord (but compare Ex. 12:12, 13).

Who then, or what, is "the destroyer?" If striking the firstborn of Egypt is done by none other than the Lord (vv. 12, 13), yet if the Lord is the one who may restrain "the destroyer" (v. 23), three possible solutions present themselves. (1) As with critical scholars, one might conclude that different "sources" were used in compiling this chapter, or that the texts are simply in disagreement with one another. For those who believe in the coherence of inspired Scriptures, this is not an adequate solution. (2) The use of the term "the destroyer" may be viewed as a way of speaking of God, but from a distance; it may be that this work of divine judgment was so distasteful that a substitute term needed to be used. The idea would still be that the destroying would be done by God. This is a possible notion, similar to an explanation given for the use of the phrase, "the Angel of the LORD" (Ex. 23:20). (3) The term "the destroyer" does refer to an agent of the Lord. Nevertheless, to remain consistent with the teaching of vv. 12, 13, that agent can be none other than the Lord Himself.

It seems that only with the NT revelation may this conundrum be solved. The "Destroyer" (the term should be spelled with a capital letter) appears to be another reference to the pre-incarnate Jesus! (This is also, we believe, the better solution to the meaning of the term "the Angel of Yahweh"; 23:20.) Certainly many will cringe at the notion of Jesus being described with this dark title; but they cringe as well at the picture of the Savior in Rev. 19:11–21. (Perhaps the same image is intended in the account of the Angel of the Lord with a drawn sword in His hand standing over the infamous Balaam; Num. 22:31.) Scriptural categories should not be established by "cringe-quotients"! There are many and varied portraits of the Savior-King in Scripture. Here is a neglected one, "the Destroyer!"

12:37 The familiar phrase **the children of Israel** refers to the heirs of God's promises to Abraham, Isaac, and Jacob. The Lord gave the name Israel to Jacob (Gen. 32:22–32). The reference to **Rameses** most likely relates to the store city Ramses mentioned in Ex. 1:11, perhaps Tell el-Daba in the Eastern Delta region. **Succoth** is possibly Tell el-Maskhuta further to the east. The number **six hundred thousand men** indicates a total population of some three million people. The actual numbering of the people did not take place until later (Num. 1). Thus, this verse should not be regarded as an independent witness to the number of fighting men in Israel at the time of the Exodus from Egypt, since it is derived from the later census (Num. 1:46).

12:38 The **mixed multitude** included Egyptians and perhaps other ethnic groups who had their own reasons for leaving. Some of these people later caused trouble when things did not go smoothly or as anticipated (Num. 11:4). The movement of this vast population was further complicated by their **flocks and herds,** which they needed to provide milk, meat, and hides, as well as sacrifices to the Lord.

12:39 The people baked **unleavened cakes** (bread without leaven) in obedience to God's command (vv. 1–20). **and could not wait:** The symbolism in this has to do with the haste of their departure, not (as some have supposed) something evil in leaven itself. If leaven were intrinsically evil, Israel would have been forbidden to eat leavened bread at any time.

12:40, 41 four hundred and thirty years: If the Exodus took place around 1446 B.C., Jacob's arrival in Egypt would have been around 1876 B.C.

12:42 The departure of Israel from Egypt was to be **a night of solemn observance.** The Passover has been carefully observed by Jews since that time. In a sense, Christians also celebrate the Passover when they celebrate the Lord's Supper, Jesus' last supper with his disciples that took place at the time of the Passover. When at the Lord's Supper Christians recall Jesus' saving acts for them, they can also thank God for His saving acts for the Israelites at the time of the Exodus.

12:43–51 The regulations concerning Passover may have been given at another time, but are included here because of the description of the first Passover earlier in the chapter.

12:43 no foreigner: The holy feast was designed for those who had come to faith in the living God. To invite others to share in the meal would cause people to lose their understanding of its sacred nature. However, this exclusion was certainly not designed to keep foreigners away from God (read the next verses).

12:44, 45 A **servant** who had faith in God and was circumcised could partake of the holy feast (Gen. 17:12). But persons who did not share in Israel's faith were excluded (v. 45).

12:46 in one house: The first Passover was celebrated in each home (vv. 1–13), for each house was marked by the blood of the Passover lamb. **nor . . . break one of its bones:** Not breaking the bones of the lamb foreshadowed Jesus' death: None of the Savior's bones were broken even though He suffered a horrible death (Ps. 34:20; John 19:33, 36).

12:47 All the congregation of Israel: This limited participation by outsiders and demanded participation from all of those who were part of the community.

12:48 The term **stranger** (Heb. *ger*) is different from "foreigner" (Heb. *nekar*) in v. 43. Both may speak of foreigners, but the term in v. 43 sometimes has negative overtones as well (for example, the word used for "foreign gods" in Gen. 35:2, 3; Josh. 24:20, 23). It would not be a light decision for a male sojourner to come to the Passover meal, for he would have to be **circumcised!** This rite would demand faith in the Lord and a determination to share in the responsibilities and promises of Israel. **he shall be as a native of the land:** These words anticipate Israel's residence in Canaan. But they also anticipate the idea of the new birth. In God's reckoning, a person of foreign birth who shares in Israel's faith has become as one who is native-born (Heb. *'ezrah;* Lev. 17:15; 18:26; 19:34; 24:16, 22). That is, the foreign-born believer becomes "Zion-born" (Ps. 87 develops this more fully). Here are biblical roots for the NT teaching of a person of faith being "born again" or "born from above" (John 3:3–21).

12:49, 50 One law is the Hebrew term *tôrâ,* basically meaning "teaching."

12:51 Armies refers to the hosts of multitudes of Israel, not necessarily to enlisted fighting men.

13:1–22 Before the dramatic story of the crossing of the Red Sea there is a record of foundational institutions that the Lord gave to Israel. These are: (1) the consecration of the firstborn (vv. 1, 2); (2) the Feast of Unleavened Bread (vv. 3–10); and (3) the law concerning the firstborn (vv. 11–16). This is followed by the Lord's command to the Israelites to travel in an unexpected direction (vv. 17–22).

13:1 The LORD spoke to Moses often, but Moses' close relationship with God was special (33:11; Num. 12:8).

13:2 The term translated **consecrate** means "to make holy." **it is Mine:** The explanation of the rite of consecration of the firstborn males to the Lord is developed further in vv. 11–16.

13:3 Remember this day: See 12:41, 42, 51.

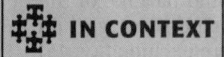

Eastern Literary Style

The nearly verbatim repetition of the Feast of Unleavened Bread exhortation in Ex. 12:14–20 and 13:3–10 represents a literary style used occasionally in the OT.

In presenting the laws of Israel, Hebrew style is "episodic." One finds here a little, there a little. In a more "Western book," the materials on a particular theme are often gathered to one place with repetitions being deleted. In the very "Eastern book" that the Bible is, there is a different literary and aesthetic style.

Further, even though the materials of Exodus were written (Ex. 24:4), most people would not have access to the written scrolls. Thus for purposes of common understanding, the text was frequently read aloud, and it is a feature of oral literature to be repetitive, which helps to fix the ideas in the minds of the hearers.

13:4 in the month Abib: This verse defines the month of 12:2.

13:5–7 into the land of: There are several lists of the nations of the land of Canaan, but the lists have variations. The most complete list is in Gen. 15:18–21, where ten nations are mentioned. In the lists in Exodus, three, five, or six nations are mentioned, and not always in the same order (3:8, 17; 23:23, 28; 33:2; 34:11). Here, the Perizzites are not mentioned. These variations suggest that the point is not a complete catalog so much as a reminder that the land of Canaan was inhabited and that the inhabitants would have to be removed by force if Israel were to realize her divine destiny.

13:8 Even later generations of Israelites who had not been part of the Exodus were to say, "This is what **the LORD did for me.**" They all shared in God's deliverance because of its lasting effects and God's promise of its permanence.

13:9–11 Sign: A similar commandment is found in Deut. 6:8. Jews would fasten a small box containing passages of Scripture to their hand and forehead during prayer to serve as a memorial. With or without such a physical sign, the symbol represented an internal reality: God's instructions were to become a rule for one's life.

13:12 Set apart helps explain the meaning of *consecrate* in v. 2. The idea is "to treat as distinct," "to mark out as special." The term **males** qualifies the term **every firstborn.**

13:13, 14 A firstborn male **donkey** was redeemed with a lamb; a donkey was not allowed as a sacrifice to the Lord. Similarly, the Israelites were to **redeem** their firstborn sons; they were never to slay them in human sacrifice. In this way the people were dramatically reminded of the extent to which the Lord had gone to free them from slavery. He had spared their firstborn even as He slew the firstborn of Egypt, human and animal, to buy their freedom. Later the Lord claimed the Levites for Himself in exchange for the firstborn sons of the people (Num. 3:40–51).

13:15 sacrifice . . . all males: This was a heavy reminder of the costly sacrifice of their redemption. **redeem:** The strategy was later changed by the Lord by taking the Levites to Himself in exchange for the firstborn sons (Num. 3:40–51).

The Road Through Philistia

There were three ancient routes between Asia and Egypt. One ran from Elath near Ezion Geber (1 Kin. 9:26) across the Sinai Peninsula to an area of the Suez around the city of On (Heliopolis). Another stretched from near Beersheba in the Negev to the area of the Suez. A third route, and most used, especially by Egyptian armies, was the "way of the land of the Philistines" (Ex. 13:17).

In Egypt, this roadway was called the "way of Horus," after Egypt's earliest state god. A coastal route that left Egypt from the northeast, it ran along the northern reaches of the Sinai Peninsula and along the coast of Canaan. Since the land closest to the Mediterranean Sea was marshy, the route did not lie within sight of the Sea but lay inland a few miles.

The biblical name "way of the land of the Philistines" alludes to the coastal area where the Philistines lived and through which the way of Horus passed. In later times, when the Philistines were not a distinguished people, the route was simple called "the way of the sea" (Is. 9:1).

13:16 A sign was a reminder, memorial, or symbol (v. 9; compare Deut. 6:8).

13:17 If the people of Israel had traveled directly to Canaan, it would have been in a northerly direction along the coastal plain. Later this plain would be known as **the land of the Philistines.** There were some Philistine people in Canaan from an early period, but their main invasion and settlement of the land did not come before the mid-twelfth century B.C. The use of this name is similar to the use of later names for the store cities Israel had worked on in Egypt (Ex. 1:11). **change their minds:** The Egyptians had heavily fortified this coastal route ʿor their own defensive purposes. The people might have been forced into battle with the Egyptians before they were prepared.

13:18 the way of the wilderness: The fact of the journey of Israel from Egypt is not in dispute. The route is another matter. The text is clear that the people did not go directly toward Canaan. Hence many alternative routes have been proposed to explain the direction they did

13:19 the bones of Joseph: The story of the last wish of Joseph and his death is found in Gen. 50:22–26. How wonderful that more than four hundred years later this dying wish, which required great faith in the living God, was accomplished!

13:20 We do not know the location of **Succoth, Etham,** and certain other early encampments of Israel (for Succoth, read 12:37.)

13:21, 22 God's presence with His people was made dramatically apparent in **a pillar of cloud** and **a pillar of fire** (Ex. 14:19, 20, 24; 40:38; Num. 9:21). God stayed with His people throughout the Exodus experience. By these and other wonderful signs He made Himself unforgettable! Because God is Spirit (John 4:24), it is a mark of His gracious character that He made His presence seen and felt among His people. If the people focused on the fact of His presence, they would not need to fear.

14:1–15:21 The crossing of the Red Sea (or Sea of Reeds), the climactic part of the Exodus from Egypt, is given both in a prose account

Photo by Howard Vos

A rocky shore along the Red Sea, at a point north of where the Israelites crossed during the Exodus from Egypt (Ex. 14).

take. The traditional route has the people moving in a southerly direction along the western shore of the Sinai Peninsula until they reached Mount Sinai in the far south-central region of the peninsula. The rendering **the Red Sea** comes from the Septuagint, the Greek translation of the OT completed about 150 B.C.; the Hebrew phrase means "Sea of Reeds." This phrase may refer to the ancient northern extension of the Red Sea. Many believe it was one of the marshy lakes in the region.

(ch. 14) and in poetry, a psalm of praise to God (ch. 15).

14:2 The locations of **Pi Hahiroth, Migdol,** and **Baal Zephon** are not known today. Pi Hahiroth may be a translation of an Egyptian name, perhaps "Dwelling of Hathor" or something similar. Migdol means "Tower" and might refer to some topographical feature. Baal Zephon means "Baal of the North," a name suggesting that Canaanite religious ideas had extended to this region. God told the Israelites to camp **by the sea** so that later He could deliver them miraculously.

14:3 The Egyptians would note Israel's route of escape, note the change in direction (v. 2), and conclude that **they** were **bewildered.** This was a ruse, of course, orchestrated by God Himself.

14:4, 5 then I will harden Pharaoh's heart: See Ex. 3:19; 4:21; 5:2; 7:3, 13, 14; 14:8. One more blow against Pharaoh was determined. The meaning of the verb **gain honor** is significant. When Moses and Aaron had first approached Pharaoh (5:1–9), he had treated the men and their God with contempt. With Pharaoh's final defeat, the name **the LORD** (that is, Yahweh) and its association with the people of Israel would be known and honored abroad.

14:6, 7 he made ready his chariot: At Pharaoh's command, the commander of the chariots pursued the Israelites. **Six hundred choice chariots** was a most formidable force. Chariots in the wars of the ancient world provided a decisive advantage over foot soldiers.

14:8 the LORD hardened the heart of Pharaoh: As He promised in 14:4.

14:9–11 We cannot fault the people for being **very afraid;** fear itself is not a sin. However, the sarcastic remark to Moses (and hence to the Lord) that there were **no graves in Egypt** showed a lack of faith. This is just the first of a series of complaints that they leveled against Moses. With each one their grumbling grew into open hostility (Ex. 16:2, 3; 17:2, 3).

14:12 The statement **let us alone** refers to Israel's response to Moses and Aaron after their first, disastrous approach to Pharaoh (5:21).

14:13 Stand still is a great statement of faith from Moses.

14:13, 14 Despite their harsh words, Moses did not lash out against the complaining people. Instead he sought to encourage them with a promise that they would see **the salvation of the LORD.** The Hebrew word for salvation, *yeshû'â,* comes from a term that has to do with "room" or "space." The people were under great pressure, squeezed between the waters before them and the armies of Pharaoh behind them. Salvation would relieve the pressure in a most dramatic way. This salvation was to come from God for He was pleased to provide it (v. 30; 15:2).

14:15 The people were to **go forward**—not to go back, not to give up.

14:16–18 Moses' **rod** is the same celebrated rod of God (Ex. 4:20) that Moses and Aaron had used in bringing forth many of the plagues against the Egyptians (4:1–8; 7:9, 20; 8:5, 16; 9:23; 10:13, 22; 17:5, 9). **stretch out your hand:** The power of God was going to be demonstrated in a most formidable manner. The

Israelites, like the Canaanites, thought of **the sea** as an uncontrollable enemy. The parting of the Red Sea was an unforgettable demonstration that every force in all creation was completely under God's control (Ps. 93).

14:19 Here, the **Angel of God** and the **pillar of cloud** cooperated to protect and lead the Israelites (Ex. 23:20, 23; 33:9–11). The name Angel of God is an alternative expression for the Angel of the LORD. The pillar is later strongly associated with the Lord Himself (Ex. 33:9–11).

14:20 The pillar became two different realities, a curse to the pursuing Egyptians and a blessing to the entrapped Israelites. **all that night:** At night, God confused the Egyptians and let the Israelites pass through the sea.

14:21 Moses stretched . . . and the LORD caused: God commanded Moses to stretch out the rod of God (v. 16). This was not a magical wand. The power was from God Himself; it was not in the stick. One of the forces the Lord used to part the waters was a **strong east wind.** We may picture an exceedingly strong wind with a narrow focus, driving a wedge between the two walls of water that were formed.

14:22 The effects of the wind on the waters was so strong that the ground of the watercourse had become dry. It was an act of faith on Israel's part to cross over on this **dry ground.** They might have refused to go and would then not have been delivered from the Egyptian army.

14:23 Egyptians pursued: The startled and confused Egyptians pursued the Israelites even into the Red Sea.

14:24 The Lord waited until the time was just right. Then He caused confusion to fall among the Egyptians **in the morning watch,** while it was still dark.

14:25–27 Without their **wheels,** the chariots were more liability than threat. **the LORD** fights for them: This was the confession the Lord demanded; word spread widely. The Lord fought for the Israelites (vv. 4, 17, 18).

14:28, 29 Of all the Egyptian men, horses, and equipment that entered the dry bed of the sea, **not so much as one** survived. The defeat was total. No doubt some Egyptian warriors had not actually entered the water and had survived. It was they who would spread the word about the Lord, the Warrior of Israel.

14:30 Saved, here, is a wonderful picture of deliverance expressed in the Hebrew meaning of the verb "to save," *yasha'.* They had been given "room to breathe."

14:31 The great work literally means "the great hand." That is, God did it; Moses was just the visible executor (15:6). This great, climactic verse speaks of the genuine faith of the people of

---

⚒ IN DEPTH | Miracles—Not an Everyday Occurrence

The parting of the Red Sea (Ex. 14:21) is one of the most well-known biblical examples of miracles, which are supernatural interventions by God into the natural order in a way that accomplishes His purposes and brings glory to His name.

One might suppose that every act of God is a miracle, and from the human perspective that may be so. Nevertheless, God usually seems to allow nature to operate according to the principles or laws with which He originally created it. Thus, for example, the normal course for the Red Sea would be for its waters to obey the laws of gravity and remain unparted.

But the Bible reveals certain times when God sovereignly overrules natural laws and causes matter to operate in ways that go beyond the ordinary. These are miracles, also called "signs," "wonders," or "mighty acts." At the Red Sea, God caused the waters to temporarily "disobey" the normal principles of gravity and thus the children of Israel were able to cross on dry ground.

Israel at the end of their experience of God's saving works and at the beginning of their journey of faith. When we read **so the people feared the LORD** and the words that follow, we are meant to understand that the community had come to saving faith and so were a reborn people. They **believed the LORD** (the same wording used of Abraham's saving faith in Gen. 15:6; read Paul's comments in Rom. 4). It was also significant that the people believed **His servant Moses.** At the beginning of this miraculous ordeal, they had not believed him at all (Ex. 6:9). The people were transformed spiritually even as they were delivered physically. It is no wonder that they broke out in song (ch. 15).

15:1–19 This section contains the first psalm (or song) of any length in the Bible. It is a song of deliverance. Other poetic sections in Genesis (Gen. 1:27; 3:14–16, 17–19; 4:23, 24) are too brief to be called psalms. Moses composed this psalm, and its grammar, structure, and vocabulary testify to its ancient origin (read Deut. 32 and Ps. 90 for two other psalms by Moses).

15:1 Moses and the children of Israel sang in worship together, as a community of believers, not just as a nation. And they sang **to the LORD**; the living God was their main audience. The term **triumphed gloriously** is an emphatic construction, expressing exuberant joy over God's great victory (Ex. 18:8). **Horse and rider** can also be rendered "horse and chariot." The Hebrew verb for **thrown** is a rare and pictorial expression. It describes God as reaching down and tossing members of the Egyptian army into the water one by one.

15:2 Because **my strength and my song** is such an unusual pairing of words, some have thought that the word translated *song* must mean "power," "fortress," or something similar. However, the idea as it is expressed is wonderful: God is my *strong song.* That is, a person of

faith may regard the living, omnipotent God as the reason for singing! **my salvation:** The word *save* and its related nouns have to do with room or space (14:13). With the terrifying sea before them and the pursuing Egyptians behind them, they were trapped. Yet God surprised them with His deliverance! The words of the first half of this verse are quoted in Ps. 118:14; Is. 12:2. **I will praise Him:** There are numerous words for praise in the Bible. But the Hebrew verb here (*nawâ*) is unique; it means "to bring God beauty." By the sacrifices of one's lips (Heb. 13:15), people of all ages can bring beauty to the One who created all that is beautiful. **my father's God:** The Israelites worshiped the same God that Abraham, their father, had worshiped, believed, and obeyed. Today, Christians are part of Abraham's line because they also believe, obey, and worship the same God (Gal. 3:6, 7). Many faithful believers have preceded us.

15:3–5 To call God **a man of war** is most appropriate in this context. The battle has been won, and the praise belongs to the Victor. **the LORD is His name:** It is difficult to exaggerate the importance of God's name Yahweh in the Bible (Ex. 3:14, 15). Other supposed gods had secret names that only guilds of priests knew. By knowing a god's secret name, a priest supposedly had special access to that god. But the living God has made His name known to all, and salvation is found in His name alone.

15:6 The Exodus narrative has emphasized the extended, powerful **right hand** of God throughout (vv. 12, 16). This was a way of describing God's active and powerful presence among His people. God did not deliver Israel "from afar"; He "came down" to act among them (3:8).

15:7, 8 Moses used more figures of speech to convey the great feeling of the moment. The powerful wind that made the waters pile up on either side of the people (14:21) is described in poetry as a **blast of Your nostrils.**

15:9–12 The arrogance of the pursuing armies trying to fight the living God is described in v. 9. **Who is like You:** Many times, the Bible uses this language of incomparability to describe the true God. In a world in which there were many supposed gods, the Lord was unique. He alone is God. He is not just better than other gods; there *are* no other gods. No person, god, or thing can be compared to the one true God (Ps. 96:4, 5; Is. 40:25, 26; Mic. 7:18). **Fearful** means that God inspired wonder, worship, and obedience from the Israelites.

15:13 mercy: Best rendered as "loyal love," God's faithful love for His people (Ps. 13:5). **Redeemed** is from a word that has to do with protecting family rights. God had protected His family, the Israelites. **Holy habitation** refers to the land of Israel in general, the land that God was giving to His people for their enjoyment (v. 17).

15:14, 15 The news of Israel's deliverance from Egypt spread abroad (Josh. 2:9). God's powerful deliverance was not to be kept a secret. The nations of the world were to be put on alert: God fought for Israel, and Israel was on the march! These words should have encouraged the Israelites to have courage. Instead, the subsequent story illustrates the cowardice of the Israelites. They struggled to trust in their powerful God (Num. 13, 14).

15:16 fear and dread: A pairing of two words to express one emphatic thought, "overwhelming dread." The expression **Your arm** is interchangeable with *right hand* (vv. 6, 12). The verb for **purchased** ("to acquire," "to possess") can also mean "to create" (Gen. 14:19).

15:17 bring them in: The verse speaks of the hope for the near future, the conquest of the land of Canaan (soon to be the land of Israel), as

well as the hope for the more distant future, the building of the temple.

15:18 the LORD shall reign forever and ever: Ultimately the salvation of Israel from Egypt points to the coming reign of the living God on earth over His redeemed people.

15:19, 20 Miriam, Moses' sister, is mentioned here by name for the first time. Most likely she is the one intended in the story of Moses' birth in ch. 2. She is called a **prophetess.** Although there is no record of women serving as priests in ancient Israel, women did serve as prophetesses (Deborah, Judg. 4:4; the wife of Isaiah, Is. 8:3; Huldah, 2 Kin. 22:14). As a prophetess (Mic. 6:4), Miriam spoke authoritatively from God. However neither she nor her brother **Aaron** was ever Moses' equal in intimacy with God (Num. 12). This passage also describes the Israelites' first worship service following their deliverance from the Red Sea. Women led this worship **with timbrels and with dances,** something later celebrated in the Psalms (Ps. 68:25).

15:21 The word **answered** may be translated "sang." The words of v. 21 are the first words of the psalm (v. 1). The point seems to be: Moses was the author of the psalm (v. 1); Miriam led in the singing, or perhaps in antiphonal response. The celebration included music, instruments, dance, and great praise of the living God.

15:22 Hagar had been found by the Angel of the Lord by a spring on the way to **Shur** (Gen. 16:7; 20:1; 25:18). The lack of **water** in this area would prove a constant test of Israel's faith in the God who had so miraculously rescued them (ch. 17).

15:23, 24 The verb **complained** is not so harsh as the verb in 17:2, but it expresses dissatisfaction. It is sometimes rendered "to murmur" (Ex. 16:2, 7; Num. 14:2; 16:11; 17:5). The people's recent deliverance from the Egyptian

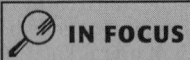 **IN FOCUS**   **"Redeemed"**

(Heb. *ga'al*) (Ex. 15:13; Ruth 4:4; Is. 43:14) Strong's #1350: The basic meaning of the Hebrew verb translated *redeem* is "to protect family rights" or "to deliver." The word refers to the responsibility of a close relative to buy back family land that had been sold because of debt (Lev. 25:25). The same Hebrew word is used to describe Boaz's kindness to Ruth. Boaz not only bought back the family's land but also saved Ruth from poverty (Ruth 4:3–10). Boaz's kindness and willingness to save Ruth is a picture of the kindness of God. The Israelites had become the "family of God" (Ex. 4:22; 13:2). God had freely taken on the responsibility to buy them back, to pay the price to free them from slavery. The Lord was Israel's Redeemer as Isaiah proclaimed (Is. 43:14), but He was also the personal Redeemer of both Job and David (Job 19:25; Ps. 19:14). We too have a Redeemer, Jesus, who was willing to pay the price—His death on the cross—to free us from our sins (Gal. 4:5; Titus 2:14).

armies makes this complaint seem fickle and a true test of God's mercy. We are often like the Israelites, turning from praise to complaint far too easily.

15:25 The use of the **tree** made the miracle of cleansing easier to perceive.

15:26 none of the diseases: As God had transformed the bitterness of the waters of

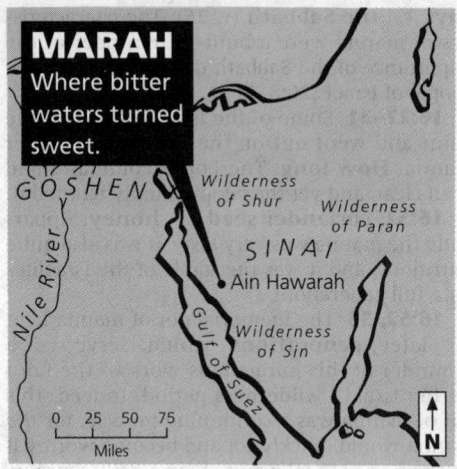

MARAH
Where bitter waters turned sweet.

Marah, so He promised to preserve His people from illness (Ex. 23:25). The descriptive phrase **I am the Lord who heals you** testifies to the mercy and power of God. It is still true: all healing comes from the Lord.

15:27 Elim means "Place of Trees." The **wells** and **palms** of Elim were a welcome relief from the barrenness of the wasteland. Many times the Bible compares wells and springs to salvation and palm trees to blessing (Ps. 1). **Elim** is probably Wadi Gharandal, near the traditional (southerly) site of Mount Sinai.

16:1 The location of the wasteland called **the Wilderness of Sin** is uncertain; its position between **Elim** and **Sinai** depends on the location of Mount Sinai. (The name Sin has nothing to do with the English word *sin*.) The term **second month** means one month from the time of their departure from Egypt (compare 12:2, 18, 40).

16:2 the whole congregation: This phrase indicates a general dissent, not that there were no exceptions. **Complained** here is the same word used in Ex. 15:24 and 16:16:7. The point here is their impatience.

16:3 died by the hand of the Lord: How could the Israelites voice this outrageous complaint? All that God had done for Israel by His great right hand was in mercy and deliverance. This complaint centered on food (for a similar complaint concerning water, read 15:22–16).

After God's great deliverance of the Israelites from the Egyptians and his provision of water, couldn't they see that providing sufficient food for them would be a small thing for their great God?

16:4 The Lord's response to the people's complaint was a promise of **bread from heaven** (manna, v. 15). God Himself would

Marah

Marah was a pool or well of water located in the Wilderness of Shur (Ex. 15:23–25; Num. 33:8, 9). Its name means "bitter," indicating that its water was undrinkable. The well was the first stop for the Israelites after crossing the Red Sea and the site where God satisfied the Israelites' thirst by miraculously turning bitter waters to sweet. This was a test of the people's faith, after which the Lord made a covenant with them (Ex. 15:25, 26). Marah today is identified with modern Ain Hawarah on the Sinai Peninsula.

supply their food. But the Israelites' reception of this wonderful blessing from God was already tarnished by their attitude. What could have been a joyful discovery became a bittersweet one. **A certain quota** meant a daily amount (v. 5). The verb translated **test** (with God as subject) does not mean "to tempt one to fail," but "to prove what one really is" (Ex. 15:25; 20:20).

16:5 The gathering of **twice as much** on the sixth day would allow for the Sabbath rest (v. 25).

16:6, 7 you shall know: The people would experience God's power in a new way (v. 12). **see the glory:** They would have a renewed sense of God's presence and further evidence of God's mercy.

16:8, 9 Come near: The idea is relative; they were not to come too close (19:21).

16:10, 11 Because God is Spirit (John 4:24), He has varied the ways in which He has shown Himself. **The glory of the Lord** is one of the grand *theophanies* (appearances of God) recorded in Exodus. God first appeared to Moses in the burning bush (ch. 3). We do not know exactly what the people saw **in the cloud,** but the sight certainly made them aware of God's majestic and somewhat ominous presence (Ps. 97:2–5).

16:12 God promised ample provision for His people in **meat** and **bread. And you shall know:** God supplied the heavenly food so that the Israelites would know beyond a doubt that

God was with them and was providing for them.

16:13 God provided meat through a natural event, the migration of **quails** through the region. It still was God's benevolent provision; the quails came at just the right time and in large numbers. On a later occasion, the gift of quails would come with judgment (Num. 11:31–35).

16:14, 15 a small round substance: There have been many attempts to explain manna as a naturally occurring substance that still might be found in the desert. Some have identified it as insect or plant secretions. The wording of these verses belies every one of these approaches. The description of the manna in these two verses (v. 31) is necessary precisely because it was *not* a naturally occurring substance (read the description in Num. 11:1–15.) The Israelites' question **What is it?** named the mystery bread: manna (v. 31). **This is the bread:** The manna could be made into bread. **the LORD has given:** The bread was a specific gift from God.

16:16 There would be sufficient manna for **each person.** Thus, no one was to take more than he or she needed. The Hebrew measure **one omer** is used only in this chapter in the Bible. It was about two quarts; v. 36 explains that it was one tenth of an ephah.

16:17–19 The Israelites' daily dependence on manna was an act of faith, hence the instruction **let no one leave any.** No one needed to gather more than one day's worth because there would be more manna on the next day. To do otherwise would only show doubt in God's provision.

16:20 The Hebrew word translated **stank** is a form of the Hebrew word *ba'ash* used by the crew chiefs to describe how the Hebrew people fared when Moses and Aaron first approached Pharaoh: "you have made us abhorrent (stink) in the sight of Pharaoh" (Ex. 5:21). **Moses became angry:** Concerning one of many occasions on which the people would not follow the Lord's directions!

16:21 it melted: The ungathered manna would disappear during the day.

16:22–26 Perhaps the most amazing feature

of the manna concerned the Sabbath. On the sixth day of the week, the people were to gather a two-day supply for each person. On any other day, manna that was kept from the day before would spoil and fill with worms. But on the Sabbath, the manna from the previous day would be as fresh as when first gathered. This is the most convincing argument that this "bread" was not a naturally occurring substance. **six days . . . the Sabbath** (v. 26): The characteristics of manna were a built-in reminder of the importance of the Sabbath day in the life of the people of Israel (20:8–11).

16:27–31 Some of the Israelites missed the point and went out on the Sabbath to gather manna. **How long:** The Lord's command had been clear, and yet the people simply ignored it.

16:31 coriander seed . . . honey: Apparently the manna was very tasty. It was also quite nutritious, and it was the staple of the Israelites for a full generation!

16:32, 33 The memorial pot of manna kept for later **generations** would serve as a reminder of this miraculous work of the Lord during Israel's wilderness period. Indeed, this pot of manna was a continuing miracle, for the manna would quickly rot and become wormy if a person tried to take more than a daily share (v. 20). Yet apparently the pot of manna **before the LORD** was kept for centuries without turning bad!

16:34–36 forty years: The completion of the story is anticipated before the intervening steps are recorded.

17:1 Rephidim may be located at Wadi Refayid in southwest Sinai (v. 8; 19:2; Num. 33:14, 15). **no water:** The need for water for the people and for their flocks must have been an immense problem, regardless of how we interpret the large number of 12:37.

17:2 There would have been no sin in asking for water. But the Israelites **contended** (Heb. *rîb*) with Moses. This verb is often used in the prophets to describe a judicial dispute (Mic. 6:2). Here it means a grumpy complaining. Moses judged this to be a challenge to God's faithful mercy and evidence of unbelief in His provision. This was not the first time that the

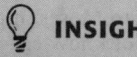 **INSIGHT** | **The Weekly Rhythm**

The seven-day week, with its rhythm of six days of work and one day of rest (Ex. 16:30), is revealed in Gen. 1 and Ex. 20. The early Assyrians and the Egyptians divided time into ten-day periods, while the Sumerians used a seven-day period. The recognized number of planets was seven, but this was not necessarily the reason for the length of the week.

people had railed against Moses (14:11, 12; 16:2, 3); sadly, it would not be the last.

17:3 Why . . . to kill us: Their genuine concern for water led the people to accuse Moses of having an outrageous motivation. Ultimately their attacks pointed at God.

17:4 cried out to the LORD: Whereas the words of the people were couched in malicious accusations, the words of Moses were given in a cry for help. God does not condemn one who screams to Him for help (Ex. 2:23, 24; the same verb, Heb. *sa`aq*, is found often in the Psalms of Lament; Ps. 142:1).

17:5 The participation of **some of the elders** shows that not all the people were

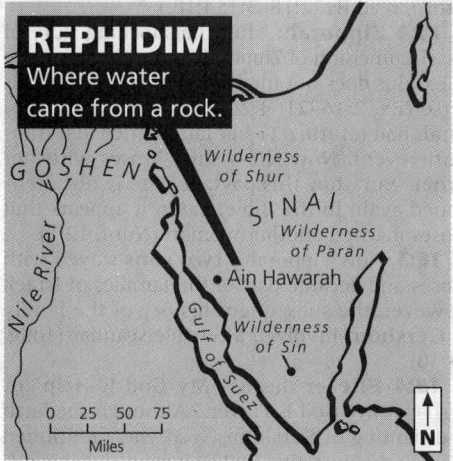

REPHIDIM
Where water came from a rock.

GOSHEN
Wilderness of Shur
SINAI
Wilderness of Paran
• Ain Hawarah
Wilderness of Sin
Nile River
Gulf of Suez

0 25 50 75
Miles

N

Rephidim

Rephidim was an Israelite encampment in the Wilderness of Sin (not to be confused with the English word "sin") at the foot of Mount Horeb. Its name meant "refreshments," even though there was no water there for the people to drink. However, God miraculously provided water by having Moses strike a rock. It was renamed Massah ("tested" or "tempted") and Meribah ("rebellion," "strife," or "contention") because of the Israelites' unbelief (Ex. 17:7). Rephidim was also the site of an attack by the Amalekites (17:8–16). During the battle, Moses lifted up his rod to assure victory. Aaron and Hur supported his arms throughout the day. Moses erected an altar there to commemorate the victory.

making the strong, malicious accusations that are described in vv. 2, 3. Moses' **rod** here is the same rod of God (v. 9; 4:20) that Moses and Aaron had used during the plagues of Egypt (Ex. 7:9, 20; 8:5, 16; 9:23; 10:13, 22) and with which Moses had signaled the parting of the waters (14:16).

17:6 The enveloping presence of God came down **on the rock** in a unique way. Later Paul said, "that Rock was Christ!" (1 Cor. 10:4; compare Deut. 32:30, 31, 37). Once before, Moses had been commanded to hold his rod over a body of water, and it became dry (Ex.14:21); here he was to **strike** a **rock** in a dry desert so that water would come from it. The striking of the rock pictured the coming death of the Savior. Water to satisfy the people's thirst came from the rock that was struck. One day, living water to satisfy spiritual thirst would come from the death of Jesus, our Rock. **Moses did so:** The text does not say so, but the implication seems to be that the water came rushing out and the people had plenty to drink and to water their flocks. Indeed, it is likely that the water from the rock became a steady source.

17:7 Massah . . . Meribah: Had the people not behaved so horribly, God would have provided the water in a context of blessing, and the names for the place would have been positive. Sadly, the names referred to the temptation and contention that occurred there (read Num. 20:13, 24 for the use of these names again). From our point of view, we wonder how the question **Is the LORD among us?** could even be asked! The people had seen God's power in the plagues, the Exodus, the crossing of the Red Sea, and the provision of manna. Every day they saw the pillar of His presence. Yet had we been part of this crowd, we would likely have been as impatient and questioning as they were.

17:8 The people of **Amalek** were descendants of Esau, the Edomites (Gen. 36:1, 12). Their attack on Israel was unprovoked. The Israelites—and the Lord—regarded this attack as particularly heinous (vv. 14–16).

17:9 This is the first mention of **Joshua,** the man who would later succeed Moses. He had chosen Joshua to be his close aide (Ex. 24:13; 32:17; 33:11). **the rod of God:** The second time this wonderful phrase is used (4:20) and the last mention of the rod in Exodus (Num. 20:8, 9).

17:10 Joshua led the battle; this field training would serve him well later in Canaan. God had trained Moses for his work; He was now training Joshua to succeed him. **Hur:** The first mention of this close associate of Moses and Aaron (24:14). He should not be confused with the grandfather of Bezalel (Ex. 31:2; 35:30; 38:22).

17:11 Moses **held up his hand** (holding the rod of God, v. 9) not as form of magic, but as a visible sign that Israel's victory was in God's hands.

17:12 Moses was not a young man, and even a youth would grow weary sooner or later, so his aides **supported his hands.** Only in this way would Israel prevail; only in the power of God would they win their battle.

17:13 Joshua defeated: The armies of Israel would fight, as all armies might fight, with normal combat techniques. But the victory was assured because of God's power on His people's behalf.

17:14 Write this: Some people allege that the first five books of the OT, the Pentateuch, were not actually written down until centuries after Moses' death. Others concede that Moses may have written certain small sections, such as the one to which this verse seems to refer (Ex. 24:4). Yet it is reasonable to assert that Moses wrote some passages of the first five books at the clear command of God, as this verse indicates, and then the rest later to record the full story of God's dealing with the Israelites during his lifetime (Ex. 34:27, 28). The word **memorial** (Heb. *zikkarôn*) is used of the Passover in Ex. 12:14. **The book** (Heb. *sepher*) refers to a scroll; bound books were not developed until many centuries after the time of Moses. **recount it:** The public announcement of an oracle of the Lord gave the sense that it was that much more certain. **Joshua**'s later role as Moses' successor would make him an important witness to this oracle of the Lord. **utterly blot out:** Moses reiterated God's command to the second generation (Deut. 25:19). Saul's failure to complete this terrible work led to his own rejection by God (1 Sam. 15). Finally, King David completed the judgment of the Lord on the Amalekites (2 Sam. 1:1).

17:15 Moses built and named an **altar,** just as Abraham and Isaac had (Gen. 8:20; 12:7; 26:25; 33:20; 35:1). Naming an altar gave it special significance by marking out a characteristic of God that was associated with worship there; the name memorialized the idea. **The-Lord-Is-My-Banner** (Heb. *Yahweh nissî; nissî* may mean "pole" or "standard") is the name of the altar, not a name for God. This phrase is not a sweet sentiment; the standing pole at the altar was an inexorable battle call for the extermination of the Amalekites.

17:16 The Hebrew word translated as **the Lord has sworn** is somewhat obscure, but appears to mean "Surely there is a hand on the throne of the Lord." In this phraseology, the Creator of the universe is pictured as seated on His throne while raising His hand in a solemn oath. It is a fearful thing for the wicked to fall into the hands of the just and righteous Judge of the universe.

18:1 God wanted the salvation of **Israel out of Egypt** to be **heard** throughout the world (Ex.15:14, 15). Word of God's deliverance of the Israelites had reached the remote dwelling place of **Jethro, the priest of Midian** (for more on Jethro, read Ex. 2:18; 3:1; 4:18.)

18:2 Zipporah: After the shocking story of the circumcision of Zipporah's son, the narrative of Exodus does not mention her again until this verse (Ex. 2:16–21; 4:24–26). Most likely, Zipporah had returned to her father after that traumatic event. Now she visited Moses with her father. But after this passage, she is not mentioned again in the Bible. Later, it appears that Moses married another woman (Num. 12:1).

18:3 Now Zipporah's **two sons** stayed with Moses and became part of the families of Israel. However, the subsequent history of the family of **Gershom** involved a terrible scandal (Judg. 18:30).

18:4 Eliezer means "My God Is Help" or perhaps "My God Is Power." Although the birth and naming of Gershom (v. 3) was mentioned early in the narrative (2:22), it is only at this relatively late point in the second son's life—after the Exodus—that his name is mentioned. Furthermore, his name is tied directly to the Exodus: **and delivered me from the sword of Pharaoh.** Since naming a boy child was done at the time of circumcision, the delay to report the name of this son, and its association with the completion of the Exodus, lends more evidence to the meaning we have given to the tan-

 **IN FOCUS**   **"Delivered"**

(Heb. *natsal*) (Ex. 3:8; Judg. 6:9; 1 Sam. 10:18). Strong's #5337: This verb may mean either "to strip, to plunder" or "to snatch away, to deliver." The word is often used to describe God's work in delivering (3:8), or rescuing (6:6), the Israelites from slavery. Sometimes it signifies deliverance of God's people from sin and guilt (Ps. 51:14). But in Ex. 18:8, the word is a statement of God's supremacy over the Egyptian pantheon of deities. The Lord was so powerful that He could "snatch" the entire nation of Israel from Pharaoh's grasp (18:10). This was only the beginning, for God repeatedly delivered the Israelites from their enemies (Josh. 11: 6; Judg. 3:9). The Lord was their Deliverer, and the psalmists proclaimed this fact with joy (Pss. 18:12; 144:2).

gled story in Ex. 4:24–26. Since the second son had not been circumcised on the eighth day of his life, Moses, the father, was in danger of losing his own life for this breach of covenant. The events of the circumcision of the son were such that the happy time of naming was not experienced. Zipporah seems to have returned with her father, Jethro, taking her two sons with her. Now, when Moses saw his second son again, he bestowed on him the name that represented God's saving work.

18:5, 6 The language in these verses suggests formality. Moses had been adopted into the family of **Jethro** when he had been a man adrift; his marriage brought certain lasting oblig-

ations. He had asked Jethro's permission to return to his own people in obedience to God's call (4:18). The heavy-handed repetition of the term **father-in-law** in this passage (vv. 1, 2, 5, 6, 7, 8, 12, 14, 15, 17, 24, 27) suggests that this is more than a courtesy title. Jethro had true authority over Moses.

18:7 bowed down, and kissed him: The ancient Middle Eastern acts of bowing and kissing were not acts of worship, but signs of respect and reminders of obligations between two people. It is strange that the narrative does not mention Moses' meeting with his wife. **Well-being** is a translation of the familiar Hebrew word *shalom,* meaning "peace."

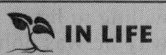 **IN LIFE**   ## Practical Principles of Leadership

L eadership has become a popular topic today, and for good reason. Effectiveness in any endeavor is largely a function of good leadership.

The Bible offers many principles and models to help leaders serve their people more effectively. Of course, Scripture was not written as a management manual, and one has to be careful about misinterpreting and misapplying the biblical text. Nevertheless, a number of passages are directly related to leadership issues. Moses' conversation with Jethro (Ex. 18:13–23) is one of the most significant. Several principles flow out of this exchange:

- (1) *Moses, himself a man of authority, respected the authority of Jethro (18:7, 24).* It would have been easy and perhaps even natural for Moses to become defensive and protect his own political "turf" when Jethro offered advice. But instead, Moses showed him respect, listened, and responded to the counsel of his father-in-law.
- (2) *Authority has a way of becoming intoxicating (18:14, 15).* Moses apparently knew little about delegation of responsibility. That may explain why he was overburdened. But when Jethro asked Moses why he sat "alone" advising everyone, Moses replied, "The people come to me to inquire of God." Could it be that the statement reflects the intoxicating allure of being in charge? Fortunately, Moses seemed eager to give up some of his centralized control.
- (3) *Authority should be invested in others prudently (18:21).* Jethro did not suggest that Moses merely fill a handful of leadership positions, the way so many do, with relatives and cronies. Rather, he described job qualifications based on proven character. In doing so, Jethro gave a reminder that delegation is a privilege, not a right. A leader ought to consider the quality and ability of prospective appointees.
- (4) *Authority is a resource to be invested in others (18:22–23).* By delegating authority to subordinates, Moses would unleash incredible energy that would take the people much further as a community than if he retained centralized control. People often think of authority as a position to be preserved. In fact, authority is a resource to be used up in empowering others to act more effectively.
- (5) *Effective leadership increases the health and longevity of an organization and its people (18:22, 23).* Moses probably prolonged his own life and ensured the progress of the nation by appointing effective judges. No organization can long survive if only a handful of its workers are involved in the task. By giving each member a stake in the outcome, leaders can bring far more eyes, ears, brains, and hands to bear on complex decisions.

Additional principles of leadership can be gleaned from the life of Nehemiah. And it ought to emphasized here that biblical kinds of leadership start with humility (Luke 22:24–27; John 13:2–17).

18:9, 10 When Jethro **rejoiced** (*hadad*, a rare verb in Hebrew), he did more than express personal happiness. His joy came from his acknowledgment of the true and living God. The priest who may have known something about the true God now gave praise to God in the words and manner of a true believer.

18:11 Jethro's words **now I know that the LORD is greater** imply that he had once regarded the Lord as one among many gods or perhaps as the principal among them. Here he declares full faith in God as the supreme Deity. **behaved proudly:** This verb (Heb. *zîd*, "to boil up," "to act presumptuously") is found elsewhere in Exodus only at 21:14; read Neh. 9: 10, 16, 29 for significant usage.

18:12 The **burnt offering** was totally consumed. However the **other sacrifices** were fellowship offerings. The priests of the Lord and the priest of Midian ate their part of the sacrifices together in common faith in the one true God. The scene is reminiscent of the one in which Abram celebrated the Lord together with Melchizedek (Gen. 14:18–20).

18:13 Judge here means "to render decisions."

18:14, 15 The lively interchange between Moses and Jethro shows a very human side of Moses. He was driven by a desire to do everything perfectly, but his activities were far too time-consuming for one man to bear alone. Jethro observed this (vv. 17, 18).

18:16 The verb **make known** (Heb. *yarâ*, in the Hiphil theme, "to teach," "to direct") is a form of the word from which the noun *Torah* ("law," Heb. *tôrâ*) is derived. This fascinating verse suggests that God's laws were general when they were first given, then applied on a case-by-case basis. Doubtless, many of the specific laws in the Book of Exodus are the result of this process, the application of general principles to specific cases (21:1).

18:17–24 It is sometimes said that believers may only take suggestions from other people of faith. Many people, however, who do not have faith in the living God have experience and understanding of important issues. The wise believer is able to learn truth no matter what the source.

18:18, 19 Jethro gave his **counsel** in the context of his new faith in God, but it was rooted in experience and wisdom he had gained throughout his life.

18:20–22 Moses would teach the broad areas of God's instruction, and others would deal with more mundane cases. Major matters would still be brought to Moses. Jethro listed only five qualifications for the men who would aid Moses. His list has some similarities to the qualifications for church offices in the NT (1

Tim. 3:1–13). (1) They were to be **able men** having strength, efficiency, and wealth (Gen. 47:6; Ruth 3:11; Prov. 12:4; 31:10). (2) They were to **fear God,** showing piety, reverence, godly humility, and ready obedience (Gen. 22:12). (3) They were to be **men of truth,** conforming to God's character (Ex. 34:6). (4) They were to be haters of (turners from) **covetousness,** so they could not be bribed. (5) They were to be ranked, with **rulers** over them. In other words, each man was to be accountable to someone else.

18:23 and God so commands: Any arrangement must be in keeping with God's will if it is to be blessed by Him. **in peace:** That is, this would be for the general welfare of all concerned (v. 7).

18:24–27 heeded: We see Moses' character in this interaction. He was willing to listen to others and to improve the way he was doing things. This was also a mark of his leadership ability and his lack of self-absorbing pride (Num. 12). The report that Jethro **went his way** was not a moral judgment, merely a statement about his travels. By going back to his land, Jethro was able to extend the knowledge of the true God at a time when the Israelites mostly kept to themselves. Jethro the priest of Midian had become Jethro the minister of the Lord.

19:1, 2 The arrival of the community of Israel at Mount Sinai was a momentous event that would shape their subsequent history. The narrator (Moses) was tremendously impressed with the Lord's timing (Ex. 12:41, 51). Likely, **the same day** means exactly two months after the Exodus, the fourteenth day of **the third month** (12:2, 18; 13:4; 16:1). When the Lord first confronted Moses, it was **before the mountain.** At that time, the Lord had promised that the Israelites would worship God at this place (3:12). This promise of God was about to be fulfilled.

19:3 Moses went up to God because God had made His presence known on the mountain, and Moses was the only one who had access to the Lord (Ex. 33:9–11; Num. 12). Moses was the intermediary between the Lord and the people.

19:4 The poetic expression **on eagles' wings** is a lovely way of describing the people's deliverance from Egypt. The Lord had whisked the Israelites away from slavery and brought them to Himself. This type of language not only describes Israel's salvation from slavery, but it can also describe our salvation from sin.

19:5–8 For the first time in Exodus, the term **covenant** (Heb. *berît*) is used to refer to the Lord's solemn arrangement with the Israelites at Mount Sinai, sometimes called the Mosaic Covenant (Ex. 24:1–8; 31:12–18; 34:27,

28). In previous passages in Exodus, this term has been used of the Abrahamic Covenant (Ex. 2:24; 6:3–5). This same word is also used for binding treaties between Israel and other nations (Ex. 23:32; 34:12, 15).

19:9 God was able to reveal only so much of His splendor to a people who were unprepared for a full revelation. Hence, He appeared to them **in the thick cloud.** One scholar calls this "His elusive Presence," in the sense that the holiness of God makes demands on His character when it comes to revealing His wonder to people.

19:10, 11 The people were instructed as to how they might prepare for the visitation of the living God. They were to **consecrate** them-

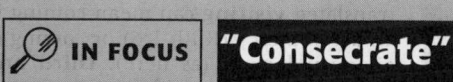

IN FOCUS "Consecrate"

(Heb. *qadash*) (Ex. 13:2; 19:10; 29:44) Strong's #6942: This Hebrew verb means "to make holy," "to declare distinct," or "to set apart." The word describes dedicating an object or person to God. By delivering the Israelites from slavery in Egypt, God made the nation of Israel distinct. Through His mighty acts of deliverance, God demonstrated that the Israelites were His people, and He was their God (6:7). By having the people wash themselves at Mount Sinai, the Lord made it clear that they as a people were being set apart for Him (19:10). Just like the Israelites, Christians also have been delivered, from slavery to sin. This deliverance has set us apart: we have been dedicated to our Savior and His purposes. We have been called to be His holy people (1 Pet. 1:15, 16; 2:9).

selves, that is, go through purifying rites to be ceremonially prepared for the meeting.

19:12 God commanded Moses to **set bounds** for the people. None could come near the mountain; they were all to keep their distance. When Moses first approached God at the burning bush, he was commanded to remove his sandals (Ex. 3:5). The people were not even to get that close.

19:13 not live: The threat of death demonstrated the seriousness of what was about to happen. What must it have been like, we wonder, to anticipate with terror and wonder a close encounter with the living God? The **trumpet** was a ram's horn (as in Josh. 6:4; the word in v. 16 is different).

19:14, 15 Sexual relations were also forbidden during the three days, for they would make the people ritually unclean.

19:16, 17 The epiphany of the Lord was a spectacular event of **thunderings and lightnings and a thick cloud.** The Canaanite god Baal was associated with these elements in the mythology of the day. His adherents believed him to be a god of storm, so clouds, thunder, and lightning would often be associated with him. But Israel learned that their God alone was the living God. He alone surrounded Himself in thick clouds, sent forth thunder and lightning, illuminated the earth, and filled the heavens with His wonders. Amazingly, one of the heavenly visitors played the **trumpet** rather than someone in the camp of Israel (compare Is. 27:13; 1 Cor. 15:52; 1 Thess. 4:16). None of the Israelites had ever heard such a blast. No wonder they **trembled** (Ex. 20:18, 19).

19:18 Even though we know God is everywhere, language such as **the LORD descended** gives us a greater appreciation of His merciful grace. The omnipotent Creator came down to meet the Israelites. His presence evoked an overwhelming sense of awe. The **smoke** was an enveloping cover for God's glory, even as the associated **fire** reminded the Israelites of that great glory.

19:19–25 The **blast of the trumpet** (v. 16) was not simply a distraction. It was a part of the physical assault on the senses—a sound and sight overload. Despite the ever grander display of God's glory, Moses drew closer to God even as the people were shrinking back from Him.

20:1–17 This passage conforms to the pattern of ancient Middle Eastern treaties between a king and his vassals or servants. The Great King presented to His servants, the Israelites, the duties and obligations of the covenant He made with them.

20:1 And God spoke: The following words of God are known as the Law of Moses. However, Moses was merely a reluctant prophet, a mouthpiece for God's words. This law is really the Law of God.

20:2 I am the LORD your God: First, the Great King identified Himself by speaking His name (Ex. 3:14, 15). **who brought you out:** Then, God reminded the Israelites of His gracious actions on their behalf (chs. 12—15). In ancient treaties, a king would describe the history of relations between his kingdom and the one being contracted. In this treaty between the Lord and the Israelites, God described His gracious deliverance of Israelites from cruel slavery.

20:3 no other gods: God was not to be viewed by Israel as one God among many nor as the best of the gods. He was and is the only living God. He and He alone was to be worshiped, obeyed, and adored by the Israelites. Critical scholarship has long argued that the concept of monotheism was an achievement of Israel, such as art was the achievement of the Greeks and order was the achievement of the Romans. These critical scholars believe that it was not until the time of Amos (eighth century B.C.) that true monotheism (the belief in one

Mount Sinai

The meeting between God and Moses on Mount Sinai (Ex. 19:20) has had a profound impact on the world. Its effects are still being felt to this day. But the exact location of Mount Sinai is unknown. As far as we know, the site never became a religious shrine attracting the devout on pilgrimages.

Mount Sinai is the same as Mount Horeb (Ex. 3:1), where God spoke to Moses in a burning bush and commissioned him to lead Israel out of Egypt (3:2–10). Horeb may refer to a mountain range or ridge, with Sinai indicating a particular summit on the ridge. Usually the Bible uses the name Sinai to indicate the actual place where Israel met God (Ex. 19:11), and it uses the name Horeb in reflecting on the events that happened there (Deut. 1:6).

A few peaks in the Sinai Peninsula have been suggested as the biblical Mount Sinai: Jebel Musa (named after Moses; 7,519 feet), which has a broad plain at its base that could have held the Hebrew encampment; Jebel Serbal (6,759 feet); and Jebel Katerina (8,551 feet).

God) was achieved. But the witness of the Bible is very different than this critical approach. The biblical story has the belief in one God as the true faith from the beginning of Israel's history as a nation. The first commandment is witness to this. And this was not something that Israel

achieved; Israel was the recipient of the revelation of God.

20:4 not make . . . a carved image: Peoples in the ancient world produced many kinds of idols, images, and other substitutes for God. Israel was forbidden to do this from the beginning. They could not make anything that would detract from the exclusive worship of the living God. However, the prohibition of fashioning images was not an injunction against every kind of art.

20:5 The phrase **bow down . . . nor serve** form a pair of Hebrew words that describe one idea: any form of worship to another god. God is **a jealous God** (Heb. *'el ganna'*); that is, He has a *zeal* for the truth that He alone is God, and He is *jealous* of any rivals. The Hebrew verb translated **visiting** can mean coming in an act of mercy (Ruth 1:6) or coming in divine judgment (as here). **third and fourth:** Idolatry would bring judgment that would affect the idolaters' descendants.

20:6 The Lord's **mercy** (Heb. *hesed*, "loyal love") would extend even more to the descendants of righteous people. The contrasting of the phrases "third and fourth" (v. 5) with **thousands** demonstrates that God's mercy is greater than His wrath. The lingering effects of righteousness will last far longer than the lingering effects of wickedness. The pairing of the words **love** and **keep** is found also in Jesus' teaching (John 14:15).

20:7 The third commandment concerns the sanctity of God's name (Ex. 3:14, 15). The revelation of God's name, Yahweh, entailed some risk. If it was broadcast among the people there was more likelihood that people would not hold it in reverence. Use of God's name **in vain** (Heb. *shaw'*) involved: (1) trivializing His name by regarding it as insignificant; (2) trying to use it to advance evil purposes by coaxing God to violate His character and purposes (one of the ways priests of false religions often used the names of their false gods); and even (3) using it in worship thoughtlessly.

20:8–11 The fourth commandment, **remember the Sabbath day,** was the special sign of the covenant with Israel at Mount Sinai (Ex. 31:12–18). With this command, God set Israel apart from its neighbors. Other peoples had their own various patterns of work and rest, but Israel was to set aside one day in seven for rest. The word Sabbath means "Rest." The day was kept **holy** by ceasing all labor on that day. The Sabbath was specifi-

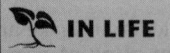

IN LIFE | Keep It Holy

What was God's will for the Sabbath (or "day of cessation," as the term literally means)? The fourth commandment is straightforward: "keep it holy" (Ex. 20:8). But what does it mean to keep the Sabbath "holy"?

The prologue to the Ten Commandments (20:2) provides a clue. All ten laws rest on the close relationship that God has to His people:

- He is their sovereign Lord.
- He is their Almighty God.
- He is their Deliverer.
- He is their Savior.
- They are His children.

If God's people keep in mind their relationship to the Lord and value it in their hearts, they will exhibit the kind of behaviors outlined in the Ten Commandments. For example, they will set aside one day of the week, the "day of cessation," in order to consciously emulate what their Lord did on the seventh day of creation.

God "rested" or ceased from His creative labors on that seventh day. He did not stop sustaining, maintaining, and redeeming the world, but He did cease from creating, shaping, and forming it. And that is what He asks His people to do, to set the day apart for Him, in order to do whatever He loves and desires, everything except the routine labors that are normally carried out on the other six days of the week.

Christians today have a degree of latitude in how they fulfill God's intentions for the Sabbath (Rom. 14:5–13). But the spirit of "keeping the Sabbath holy" still means to honor God, to focus on the needs of others rather than ourselves, and to pursue fellowship, unity, and concern for other believers.

---

cally **the seventh day,** Saturday. It was patterned after the seventh day of rest for God following the six days of creation. During the Sabbath, the Israelites worshiped God and recalled His deliverance of them from slavery (Deut. 5:15). The observance of the Sabbath included even foreign guests.

20:12 Before the discovery of ancient treaty patterns and their relation to the Ten Commandments, many people assumed that the two tablets of the Law (Ex. 34:1) were divided on the basis of laws relating to God and those relating to other people. In this approach, the fifth command, in this verse, would begin the second tablet. Following our understanding of ancient treaties, however, it is probable that each of the tablets contained all ten commandments. In the ancient world, one copy of a treaty would be placed in the principal temple of each contracting party. Here both copies were kept together before God and the people in the Most Holy Place. **Honor your father and your mother:** The term *honor* means "to treat with significance." It is the opposite of **in vain** (v. 7). Care of one's elderly parents was a basic element of social responsibility and godly piety in Israel. Here it is tied directly to how a person would fare in **the land.** People who were faithless to God in disregarding their parents would not last long in the new Promised Land.

20:13 The sixth to ninth commandments were designed to build a cohesive society in ancient Israel. Each was based on the value that God placed on people (their lives, their relationships, their property, and their reputation). Each of these commands was reaffirmed in the NT. The sixth commandment, **you shall not murder,** did not forbid all taking of life, for the Law itself included provisions for capital punishment (21:15–17, 23) as well as warfare (17:8–16). The deliberate murder of another person (outside the legitimate provisions of capital punishment or war) flagrantly violated the sanctity of life. This included murder committed by officers of the state (read the story of Naboth, 1 Kin. 21). The first murder recorded in the Bible was the killing of Abel by Cain (Gen. 4:8–14). Indeed, the death of Jesus, based on false charges and an illegal trial, was the most horrible murder of all time!

20:14 The seventh commandment concerned **adultery.** God regarded the sanctity of marriage as a sacred trust similar to the sanctity of life (v. 13). The marriage relationship was a symbol of faithfulness.

20:15 The eighth commandment protected the sanctity of property by prohibiting theft.

20:16 The ninth commandment prohibited bearing **false witness.** First, this command protected the reputation of people from libel by others. Second, this command established the ancient Israelite system of justice on a firm foundation. In ancient Israelite law, the judging of a person's guilt or innocence was based on testimony by faithful witnesses (Deut. 17:6). False witnesses would undermine justice.

20:17 Covet (Heb. *hamad*) means "to have a strong desire for." Coveting was not merely an appreciation of something from a distance, but an uncontrolled, inordinate, selfish desire. This tenth command governed an internal matter: the sin of coveting occurred in the mind. This demonstrated that God intended the Israelites not only to avoid the actions named in the previous commands, but also to turn away from the evil thoughts that led to those actions.

20:18–20 The response of Moses in this verse forms one of the most significant concepts in the first five books of the Bible. Note the interchange between the words **do not fear** and **His fear.** Moses told the people to stop being afraid; God was not going to hurt them. Yet they were very much afraid of the Lord (19:16; 20:18, 19). God did not want His people to live in terror of Him, as though He were an irrational, uncontrolled, violent force ready to be unleashed on innocent people without provocation. Rather, God wanted His people to respect the obvious hazards of wanton sin. Appropriate fear of God in this sense would make them circumspect, reverent, obedient, and worshipful, so that they might **not sin.**

20:21 God remained in **thick darkness**—a symbol of His elusive presence (Ps. 97:2). Only Moses could come near.

20:22–24 Israel was forbidden to make any altar more elaborate than **an altar of earth.** These individual altars would be used only until the selection of the central place for the worship of God (later in Jerusalem, Deut. 12). See Ex. 24:4 for an example of an altar built by Moses at Mount Sinai and 1 Kin. 18:31, 32 for an altar built by Elijah on Mount Carmel. **Where I record My name** can mean "where I cause My name to be remembered."

20:25, 26 your nakedness: The worship of the gods of Canaan involved sexually perverse acts. Nothing obscene or unseemly was permitted in the pure worship of the living God.

21:1 The word translated **the judgments** here (Heb. *mishpatîm*) is one of several Hebrew words that describe the Law (the Torah). This word describes God's response to a specific action, something like an umpire's call. Laws that appear in this section are responses to specific cases among the Israelites. Often the people would present critical or difficult disputes to Moses (ch. 18). When Moses had to render a decision on an issue that he was not sure about, he would ask the Lord. The decisions that he gave became known as *case law* or *casuistic law.* Such laws differed from the Ten Commandments (20:1–17), known as *apodictic law.* The Ten Commandments were general laws not based on specific cases. It is believed by some that among the nations of the ancient world, only Israel had both casuistic and apodictic law. The purpose of these judgments seems to be to place limits on people's behavior.

21:2 if you buy a Hebrew servant: Indebtedness or other crises might force a person

---

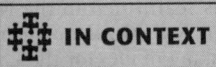 **IN CONTEXT** ## Of Slaves and Servants

Slavery (Ex. 21:2) has existed throughout a great many cultures throughout history. Just as the Hebrews had been slaves in Egypt, it was "normal" for them to have servants and slaves in the Promised Land.

The laws concerning slavery did not condone it, but they did limit its worst aspects. And there were some peculiarities. For instance, the Law commanded that a man who had become a slave to pay his debts should be freed in the seventh year of his service (Ex. 21:2). However, no such law was given for setting free female debt slaves. Why? One reason might be that a female slave often became a concubine of her master's (Gen. 30:9), and therefore unlikely to find a man willing to marry her should the case arise. Without marriage, she would have had difficulty surviving on her own, for the culture of that day was not conducive to anyone, male or female, living as a single person. Thus the Law may have assumed that a female slave would remain permanently in her master's household.

Centuries later, Christians in the early church wrestled with the problems created by the conflict between their faith and the institution of slavery. To see how one believing master had to deal with the implications of a slave becoming a brother in Christ, see Philemon.

to be sold into slavery. But what was to be done if that slave were a member of the Hebrew community? Moses ruled that the period of enslavement was not to exceed six years, and **in the seventh he shall go free.** Perpetual slavery of Hebrew men and women was prohibited.

21:2–5 Other rulings followed. (1) A slave who was married at the time of his enslavement would keep his wife. (2) If the marriage took place during the period of slavery, the wife and children belonged to the master.

21:6 If the slave being freed did not wish to leave his family behind, he was allowed to make a commitment of lifelong servitude. The slave would be taken before **judges,** where he would be given the opportunity to declare his intentions. **pierce his ear:** A sign of voluntary, lifelong servitude. This passage is not the explanation of the "opening of the ears" in Ps. 40:6, as is commonly supposed; that pictorial phrase is about the "coring of the ears" as the instrument of hearing, rather than a reference to voluntary slavery.

21:7–11 Women also endured the hardship of slavery. In ancient times, a family might be reduced to such a desperate state that it **sells a daughter** into bondage. The law in this section served to protect the purchased bride. If she were not acceptable to her new master, she would **let her be redeemed,** that is, her freedom might be purchased by another. In no case was she to be sold to a **foreign people.** If she were purchased as a bride for a man's son, she was to be treated as one would treat a daughter. If the man took another wife later, he was to continue to treat the purchased bride with respect. **Her food, her clothing, and her marriage rights** would continue. A husband who refused these necessities was to let the woman **go free.**

21:12 This verse lays out the basic circumstances for capital punishment. In ancient Israel, as in our own day, cases often had mitigating circumstances that might weigh against a death penalty. Complicating the matter was the common practice of family retribution. A family who had suffered death or injury believed they had just cause to exact a penalty from the offender. These laws were meant to place limits on the penalties that might be carried out.

21:13 A person who accidentally murdered another could escape punishment by fleeing to a city of refuge (Num. 35:9–34). **God delivered him:** A phrase indicating that the death was accidental.

21:14, 15 acts with premeditation: The Hebrew word *zîd* here means "to boil up" or "to act with presumption." See 18:11 for the only other use of this verb in Exodus. Deliberate acts of murder, including the particularly heinous act of killing one's parents, were punishable by death.

21:16 Kidnapping was a capital offense.

21:17 curses: Breaking the fifth commandment (20:12) in this harsh manner was also a capital offense.

21:18, 19 This ruling allowed the victim of a fight to be compensated for lost time and treatment of injury. Like other such laws, it is likely that a particular case resulted in this judgment.

21:20, 21 These provisions guarded somewhat against the abuse of slaves. They did not endorse the practice of slavery.

21:22–23 Defenders of abortion have sometimes cited this verse to support the idea that life in the womb is something less than a person. No matter how it is translated, this verse contains nothing that would support the modern practice of abortion on demand. **She gives birth prematurely** is one possible translation of the

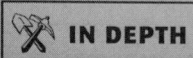 **IN DEPTH** | **Suing for Damages**

The Law was given to an agricultural society. Thus we find codes concerning goring oxen and open pits (Ex. 21:28–36). Nevertheless, the principles of care for human life and safety and for awarding restitution for personal injury carry over into any society and work environment.

For instance, God took a strong interest in preventive health care (Lev. 13:1–59), and that involved safety in the workplace and community. When an injury occurred, the injured party was due restitution in an amount and to a degree appropriate to the case. And the Law provided penalties for injuring another human being to an extent that would approximate the loss suffered by the injured party (Ex. 21:23–24; Lev. 24:17–22).

Further, nothing in Scripture suggests that injured persons should profit from their losses. Nor do we find anything about damages for pain, suffering, fear, psychological stress, or similar emotional conditions. We would do well today to consider carefully the OT prescriptions for settling property and injury cases. They show us the spirit with which we should seek restitution.

Hebrew. If this is a correct rendering, the subsequent "harm" would be harm to the baby (or perhaps to the mother and to the baby). More probably the Hebrew means that the woman suffers a miscarriage. **If no harm follows:** If the woman did not die from the blow, then the offender would be fined for the loss of her child. If, however, she were to die, then the penalty was **life for life.**

21:23–25 Here we encounter the best-known statement of *lex talionis* ("law of retaliation"). Many ancient cultures allowed punishments greatly out of proportion to the offense. In Israel, a judgment corresponded to the nature of the injury. The idea is *no more than* **eye for eye, tooth for tooth,** and so on.

21:26, 27 In this instance, the verb **strike** (Heb. *nagaph*) means to cause injury (in 12:23, 29, it includes the idea of causing fatality). A master who inflicted harm on his slaves could be compelled to set them free.

21:28–32 The judgments concerning the **ox** have a modern ring to them. An ox that caused human death was to be destroyed, but the owner suffered no further punishment. If, however, the ox had a history of injuring others and subsequently killed a free person, the owner could be put to death as well. In other cases, a heavy fine might be imposed but the owner's life spared. A shekel was about two-fifths of an ounce. **Thirty shekels of silver** was likely a sizable sum at that time. In those times, a slave did not have the same rights as the free person; thus the Law sought to place limits on the master in terms of abusive behavior.

21:33, 34 An unattended **pit** that caused the death of an animal would require restitution to the animal's owner because animals were the livelihood of their owners.

21:35, 36 The legislation in these verses has given rise to the expression: "it depends on whose ox was gored." In each of these instances,

we believe particular cases were presented for judgment. The loss of one's ox presented a serious financial drain.

22:1–4 Just as stealing a horse in the days of the American frontier was sometimes punished by hanging (because of the great loss suffered by the person affected by that theft), so the stealing of **an ox or a sheep** carried heavy penalties. The restitution was usually greater than the value of the stolen animal. **the sun has risen on him:** To strike the thief after the act would be considered inappropriate use of force (*lex talionis*, 21:23–25). The thief who could not offer restitution was to **be sold** into slavery.

22:5–13 Restitution also played a role when animals were allowed to forage in another's field (v. 5), when unattended fires raged out of control (v. 6), and when goods left in another's care would disappear under suspicious circumstances (vv. 7, 8). As in the earlier laws, we surmise that each of these provisions was the result of specific instances of grievance being brought to Moses for judgment from the Lord.

22:10–13 In some cases of suspected mismanagement, an **oath of the LORD** would be an acceptable testimony of innocence. In other cases, restitution was demanded, unless it might be proven that the loss was due to circumstances beyond one's reasonable control.

22:14, 15 Borrowing had its consequences, as in our day, but the owner's presence was also a factor to be considered.

22:16, 17 The violation of a young woman was regarded as a serious affront. The payment of the **bride price** also meant that the one who had enticed her had to marry her (with the father's permission). The steep fine was meant to discourage young men from reckless behavior.

22:18–21 The Bible does not record any executions of sorcerers or sorceresses, but it does recount the deadly consequences of false worship (ch. 32; Num. 25).

✠ IN CONTEXT   **The Code of Hammurabi**

Babylon's King Hammurabi (1792–1750 B.C.) is best know for his law code, the Code of Hammurabi, which contains 282 laws and has numerous parallels with Scripture. Few of the laws, however, were ever cited in Babylonian court cases, and the Code ignores many subjects. Hammurabi did not create these laws; they appear to be a collection from diverse traditions.

The format of the Code shows some similarities with that of laws in Exodus, Leviticus, and Deuteronomy. For instance, both the Code of Hammurabi and the Covenant Code found in Ex. 20:22–23:33 carry a series of laws structured in an "if . . . then" format. This format, or style, is often called case law, since it describes particular cases or situations.

Similarities between these two Codes are further evidence that there was a widespread legal tradition in the second millennium B.C.

22:22–24 Particular concern is expressed for the welfare of the **widow** and orphans, for they were powerless people. Yet those who might be their potential abusers needed to know that they were not entirely powerless, for God was on their side. **they cry . . . to me:** See note at 8:12. **My wrath:** One does not wish to place himself in "the line of fire" of the wrath of God. His own destruction would lead his family to be helpless as well. The issue of the treatment of widows and orphans forms a significant theme in public and private morality in biblical thought.

22:25–27 God also had a special concern for **the poor** in Israel. They were not to be subject to the abusive practices of moneylenders nor have goods they needed for survival taken as collateral. **When he cries to me:** At the conclusion of this verse, the Lord declares why it is right and fitting for one in distress to call out to Him. He says **I am gracious,** an anticipation of the great revelation of His compassionate character to Moses in Ex. 34:6, 7.

22:28 revile God nor curse a ruler: Since God is the ultimate sovereign, to curse a lesser ruler might encourage disrespect for God's authority.

22:29, 30 Promptness was commanded both in offering the firstfruits of the field and in the presentation of one's sons to the Lord. The sons were to be redeemed (Ex. 13:11–16) **on the eighth day.** This verse reminded the Israelites that all they had was a gift from the Lord.

22:31 holy: Israel was to be set apart from other nations (19:5, 6). **Meat torn by beasts** was not to be eaten, presumably because the blood had not been drained from it.

23:1 false report: Malicious talk is everywhere condemned in Scripture (James 3:1–12).

23:2 not follow a crowd: What modern words these are, and how appropriate for today.

23:3 partiality to a poor man: God's support of the poor (22:25–27) did not overrule His justice. Here God anticipated that some would use poverty as an excuse for greedy, even criminal, activity.

23:4, 5 The **enemy** in this context would be another member of the Hebrew community.

23:6–8 no bribe: true justice cannot be bought.

23:9–12 In addition to the weekly Sabbath (20:8–11; 31:12–18), Israel was also to practice a Sabbath year after arriving in the land (Lev. 25:1–7). **Let it rest and lie fallow:** Letting the land rest allowed the poor to glean any produce that might grow during the fallow year. It also gave the land time to rejuvenate for greater productivity in subsequent years. Of course, the **vineyard** and **olive grove** would continue to produce, but the owners were not to harvest the fruit. The year of rest was also an act of faith, for the Israelites would have to trust God to meet their needs.

23:13–19 Here is instruction concerning three annual feasts. The people of God were given a number of instructions concerning what life would be like when they entered the Promised Land. Among the most important was the requirement to appear before Him three times each year. This requirement corresponds to the similar demand for vassals to appear each year before their suzerain in the international treaties of the period.

23:16 The Feast of Harvest is also called the Feast of Weeks (34:22). **The Feast of Ingathering** is also called the Feast of Tabernacles or Sukkoth (Ex. 34:22; Lev. 23).

23:17 Lord God: Here two names for God, Adonai, translated as *Lord,* and Yahweh, trans-

IN FOCUS **"Lord God"**

(Heb. *'adonay YHWH*) (Ex. 23:17; Gen. 24:7) Strong's #113; 3068: This rare description of God links the title *'adonay,* meaning "Lord" or "Master," with God's personal name Yahweh. The title Lord speaks of God's unlimited power and authority, just as a master had unlimited power over a slave. On the other hand, God's personal name Yahweh invokes His merciful and righteous character. Yahweh is spelled with four consonants in Hebrew. The Jews do not pronounce this sacred name and instead read *'adonay* wherever the name occurs in the Scriptures. Its precise meaning and pronunciation is unknown. Most probably the name Yahweh is derived from the Hebrew verb for "to be," and means "I AM WHO I AM" (Ex. 3:14).

lated as *God,* are used together. This expression emphasizes God's sovereignty.

23:18, 19 You shall not boil a young goat in its mother's milk is a command (Ex. 34:26; Deut. 14:21) that forbade the Israelites to imitate the cruel sacrifices of their pagan neighbors.

23:20–23 behold, I send: The Hebrew construction here may be rendered: "I am about to send," presenting a sense of excitement about the impending action. **an Angel:** In v. 23, this being is described as "My Angel," an equivalent to the expression "the Angel of the Lord." The Hebrew word translated "angel" (*ma'lak*) can mean a supernatural angel or a human messenger (the prophet Malachi's name means "My Messenger"). Compare Ex. 3:2; 14:19; 32:34; 33:2. **To keep you . . . to bring you:** The Angel led and protected the Israelites just as the pillar of cloud did (Ex. 13:21, 22; 14:19, 20, 24; 16:10; 19:9, 16; 24:15–18; 33:9–11; 34:5; 40:34–38). **My name is in Him:** This is perhaps the strongest identification of the Angel with God. **His voice . . . I speak:** The interplay of these words also identifies the Angel with God.

23:24 The Canaanite gods, including Baal and his consorts, Anat and Asherah, were to be utterly destroyed. The **sacred pillars,** symbols of the overt sexuality of the Canaanite cult, were also to be destroyed.

23:25 Serve here means to worship as well as to obey (3:12). **Bread and water,** the necessities of life, would be in the care of Yahweh, not the supposed fertility gods of the Canaanite cults. The people of Israel were to have no reason to look to false gods (v. 24); the true God would meet their needs.

23:26 miscarriage . . . be barren: God's promises to make the Israelites fertile reminded the Israelites that there was no need to turn to the fertility cult that was so pervasive in Canaan.

23:27 This is one of several words in the Hebrew Bible for **fear,** "terror" (Heb. *'êmâ*), but it is not one of the more common words. See its use in Gen. 15:12, as one of the words describing Abram's experience with the covenant-making Yahweh. This word can be used in a general sense, as when paired to another word for fear, as in Ex. 15:16. But it is possible that more is meant here (v. 28, notes). It is almost as though the term is personified here. We propose that the stronger reading for *fear* in this context would be *My wrath*.

23:28 Hornets: The Hebrew is in the singular, "the hornet," although the word may be translated in the plural, as here. **Send:** This is the third use of the verb meaning "to send" in this passage (vv. 20, 27) with Yahweh as the subject. The scheme seems to be as follows:

(1) "Behold I am about to send [My] Angel before you . . ." (v. 20).
(2) "My Wrath I will send before you . . ." (v. 27).
(3) "And I will send the Hornet before you . . ." (v. 28).

It is possible that the first in the scheme, the Angel, is a direct reference to the pre-incarnate Savior (v. 20), but that the second and third terms are simply more general and abstract ideas. The structure of the passage, however, leads one to explore the idea that both *Wrath* and *Hornet* are words that also express ways in which *the Angel* will operate on behalf of the people of God. That is, He who is comfort and protection to the people of Israel (*My Angel*), is also an expression of the wrath of God (*My Fear*) against the wickedness of the peoples of the land of Canaan, whose iniquities are now complete (compare Gen. 15:16) and who are now about to feel His sting (*the Hornet*). It was the promise of Yahweh that it would be He who would judge these wicked people (Gen. 15:14). Is it not possible that the *Wrath* in v. 27 is a personification of God's righteous indignation against the wicked? If so, is it also possible that this is a hitherto unrecognized prophetic picture of the Christ? We know that one day the Savior will come as the avenging Judge (Rev. 19:11–21; compare Pss. 2; 110). Here, as the Wrath of God, He is presented as about to bring judgment on the peoples of Canaan.

Similarly, it is possible that He is also *the Hornet*. Since there is no record of God using any insects whatsoever in the conquest of the land of Canaan, as He had used insects and other natural phenomena in the plagues against Egypt (chs. 7—10), we conclude that the term *the Hornet* may be used here as a metaphor of God's power (Deut. 7:20; Josh. 24:12). Moreover, it is possible that both this word and *Wrath* in v. 27 are used in a similar manner to *My Angel* in v. 20 to speak of a preincarnation appearance of the living Savior Jesus. As a hornet has a frightful sting, so the Lord Himself would fight on behalf of His people, bringing a terrifying sting to the enemies of Israel.

This proposed use of the terms *Wrath* and *Hornet* as descriptive words for the work of Christ before His incarnation is similar to the suggestion in Ex. 12:23, that *the Destroyer* is also a term describing the Savior in acts of divine judgment.

23:29–31 not drive . . . in one year: This is the first description of God's plan for the gradual conquest of Canaan. **your bounds:** These boundaries concur with the original promise given to Abraham (Gen. 15:18–21). In biblical times these boundaries were never quite achieved.

23:32, 33 The word **covenant** here describes a binding agreement that recognizes the rights of each party. Israel was forbidden to make such treaties lest they be corrupted by the perverse customs of their neighbors. **their gods:** Principally, Baal and other fertility gods.

24:1, 2 Come up to the Lord speaks of God's grace and His holiness. God could be approached only on His terms. That any were invited to come near was because of His marvelous grace. **Aaron** and his sons **Nadab and Abihu** were allowed to join Moses, along with **seventy of the elders.** The later demise of

Nadab and Abihu (Lev. 10:1, 2) was tragic, given their esteemed privilege before the Lord. The number seventy is applied for the first time to the number of elders Moses had appointed following his discussion with Jethro (Ex. 18:24–27; 24:9; Num. 11:16, 24, 25). **Worship from afar** was the command given to all except Moses. Here, *worship* meant literally "to bow down to the earth."

24:3 words . . . judgments: This is one of the places where we discover one of the ways that the word of the Lord came to Moses (Ex. 13:1).

24:4 Moses wrote: Some scholars of the Pentateuch believe that Israel's leaders invented or exaggerated the life of Moses to heroic proportions to unify the nation, and that the laws and stories found in Exodus were not written until centuries after his death. Yet Scripture attests that Moses wrote down everything that he had heard from the Lord (Ex. 17:14; 34:27, 28; Num. 33:2). The **pillars** here should not be confused with the sacred pillars of the Canaanite gods (23:24). **Twelve tribes:** The whole nation was to be represented in worship.

24:5 Young men offered the sacrifices because the priesthood had not yet been instituted.

24:5 Burnt offerings were incinerated in their entirety on the altar (Lev. 1). **Peace offerings** were the prelude to a great, celebratory meal before the Lord (Lev. 3).

24:6 The sprinkling of **blood** on the altar must have been an awe-inspiring ceremony.

The blood of the OT sacrifice anticipated, of course, the death of the Lord Jesus Christ. The sacrifice of bulls and goats was an imperfect system that would be superseded by Christ's work (Ex. 12:7; Rom. 3:23–26; Heb. 10:4, 10).

24:7 The Book of the Covenant was likely the instructions and judgments of 20:22—23:33 that had been recorded by Moses (vv. 3, 4). Although the book (more precisely, the scroll) existed in written form, it was **read** to the people. Written documents were not widely available, and literacy was restricted to a few. Thus the Law was communicated orally. **We will do:** For the second time (v. 3), the people made a solemn oath of obedience to the Lord.

24:8 The sprinkling of **blood** on the people brought them into a covenant with the Lord. As their houses had been "under the blood" at the time of the Passover in Egypt (ch. 12), now the people themselves were under **the blood of the covenant** of the Lord. This resembles our own relationship to God, made possible by the blood of the Lamb of God (1 Pet. 1:2).

24:9–11 The people mentioned in v. 1 **saw the God of Israel.** The mention of **His feet** and **His hand** indicates that they saw a manifestation of God in some human form. Perhaps this was an appearance of Jesus before His Incarnation (23:20). The lack of details reminds us that any attempt to describe the glory of God is always inadequate. **Nobles** are the elders of vv. 1, 9. This passage could imply that the Lord did indeed **lay His hand** on Moses (vv. 12–18). **So they saw God:** The repetition of this indescrib-

---

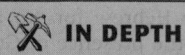 **IN DEPTH** | **The Book of the Covenant**

The Book of the Covenant includes various judgments for the people of God (for the term "judgment," read Ex. 21:1). Again we have a misplaced chapter division; the new chapter should have begun at 20:22.

These three chapters (21—23) include varied judgments and instructions on the following topics: (1) instruction concerning the altar of the Lord (20:22–26); (2) judgments concerning servants and slaves (21:1–11); (3) judgments concerning violent actions (21:12–27); (4) judgments concerning animals (21:28–36); (5) judgments concerning property (22:1–15); (6) a variety of judgments concerning personal behavior (22:16–31); (7) judgments concerning even-handed justice (23:1–9); (8) a judgment concerning Sabbaths (23:10–13). After these judgments are two appended instructions: (9) instructions concerning three annual feasts (23:14–19) and (10) the promise of Yahweh's Angel and the conquest of the land (23:20–33).

Sometimes this section is called "The Book of the Covenant" (Ex. 24:7, 8). It is often alleged that this section is the most ancient law code in the Bible. When critical scholars state this assertion, they base their notion on the ideas that the laws in the Bible grew very gradually and did not come to their fullness until nearly a thousand years after the time of Moses. It would be better to describe this section as a collection of miscellaneous judgments that Moses arranged for the people early in their experience at Mount Sinai. With the passing of time in Moses' life, he would have added other sections to the Book of Exodus, some of which supplemented these early sections.

able reality is for emphasis. **And they ate and drank:** The festive covenant meal, likely including meat from the peace offerings as well as bread and wine, was a grand celebration of the presence of the living God. It was also a prophetic glimpse of the supper of the Lord Jesus and His disciples, in which He transformed the ancient symbols of deliverance from Egypt (bread and wine) into the new symbols of His impending death and resurrection (Matt. 26:17–30).

24:12 Come up to me: Only Moses could draw near to God at that time. Today, we are all called to draw near to God through Jesus (Heb. 4:14–16). Here also is the first mention of the **tablets of stone** on which the Lord had **written** His **law and commandments.** These are sometimes pictured with the first four commandments (concerning one's relationship to God) written on one tablet and the last six (concerning one's responsibility before others) written on the other tablet. It is more likely, however, that all ten commandments appeared on each tablet. Middle Eastern treaties were typically written in duplicate. One copy was placed in the temple of the god of each of the contracting parties. Therefore the gods of both peoples witnessed the agreement. But in this case, both copies were placed before the only living God. **Teach** here is the source for the noun translated "law" (Heb. *tôrâ*).

24:13, 14 Assistant here (Heb. *misharet*) is ordinarily rendered "minister." **Joshua** was first mentioned during Israel's battle with Amalek (Ex. 17:9–14; 32:17; 33:11). **for us:** The plural wording of these verses suggests that Joshua accompanied Moses at least partway up Mount Sinai. Perhaps Joshua aided Moses during the strenuous ascent up the mountain but was not allowed to come into the presence of the Lord with Moses (vv. 15, 18). Joshua was not with the people during this time, but he was able to hear their boisterous, debased worship of the golden calf and report that startling news to Moses. **Hur:** See 17:10.

24:15, 16 Moses then witnessed the appearance of the Lord in the midst of a **cloud** (19:9). **The glory of the LORD** is closely associated with the cloud, as in Ex. 33:9. It is possible that the **seventh day** of waiting was also the seventh day of the week, the Sabbath. "Glory" (Heb. *kabôd*) refers to weight, significance, and importance (Ex. 16:7, 10; 33:18, 22; 40:34, 35).

24:17, 18 The sight of the glory of the **LORD** again is not described for us. All that the people could see was something like **a consuming fire.** Moses had seen such a fire in the burning bush (Ex. 3:2). The significance of the **forty days and forty nights** is not specified in Scripture. However, based on the response of the people (32:1), it was considered to be a very long period of time.

25:1, 2 bring me . . . willingly: God does not need the gifts of His people, but He receives their gifts as a part of their true worship of Him. Yet in this passage God asks His people for specific, voluntary gifts. This is because He wanted gifts that were given freely and gladly, not under compulsion. Also, he specified the gifts so that Moses could accomplish the plan that God was about to present to him.

25:3–7 Bronze was commonly used in this period. Widespread use of iron was still centuries away. The list contains items and materials of significant value. The people gave these valuables to the Lord to express their desire to worship Him in spirit and in truth.

25:8 Sanctuary means "holy place" (Heb. *migdash*). As the ground had become holy because of the presence of God in the burning bush (Ex. 3:5) so the sanctuary would be holy (*migdash* is related to the Hebrew for "to be holy," *qadash*) because of the presence of God that overshadowed the structure and dwelled in its symbols. God, whose true dwelling place is beyond the heavens, desired a structure that would represent His holy presence among His people. Thus, the sanctuary is a remarkable condescension of God's grace. He whose true dwelling place is in the heavenlies desired a structure

IN CONTEXT The Acacia Tree

The wood of the acacia tree, from which the ark and the tabernacle were constructed (Ex. 25:10; 36:20), was orange-brown in color, hard grained, and insect repellent. Many species of acacia grew in the desert of the Sinai Peninsula, as well as in southern Canaan and Egypt. The large, thorny tree had rough, gnarled bark and bore long, locust-like pods with seeds inside. It produced round, fragrant clusters of yellow blossoms. A site northeast of the Dead Sea where Israel camped prior to entering Canaan was apparently so thick with acacia trees that it was named Acacia Grove (Josh. 2:1).

to serve as the symbolic center for His presence among His people. **That I may dwell** is related to the Hebrew verb from which we derive the word *Shekinah,* which designates the radiance, glory, and presence of God dwelling among His people.

25:9 The pattern suggests that there is a heavenly reality that the earthly tabernacle was designed to resemble (v. 40; 26:30; 27:8; Acts 7:44; Heb. 8:5).

25:10 The most important religious symbol associated with the tabernacle was the holy **ark** or box. In contrast to the idolatry of Israel's neighbors, the shrine of the living God had no likeness or idol of any sort (Ex. 20:2–6). The highly decorated, beautifully fashioned ark kept the charter of the nation's relationship with God—the two stone tablets of the Ten Commandments—along with other symbols of God's mercy to them. **Acacia** wood was durable and resistant to disease and insects, making it the most suitable material for constructing the ark. The **cubit** was a measurement taken from the length of a man's arm from elbow to extended middle finger. The measurement could vary, but the commonly accepted estimate for the cubit is eighteen inches. Therefore, the ark was about four feet long and two and one quarter feet wide and high.

25:11–15 The **gold** would have made the box resplendent and costly. In addition to the gold used to **overlay** the ark, within and without, a decorative **molding of gold** adorned the box. The **rings of gold** allowed the ark to be carried on poles. It was not to be picked up by hand or carted about (2 Sam. 6).

25:16 The Testimony was the two tablets of the Ten Commandments.

25:17 The mercy seat is a familiar English translation of a Hebrew noun (*kapporet*) derived from the verb meaning "atone for," "to cover over," or "to make propitiation." The noun means "the place of propitiation." The mercy seat was the lid for the ark as well as the base on which the cherubim were to be placed. In the old covenant, the mercy seat was a place of propitiation for sin, resulting in peace with God. For ancient Israelites, the mercy seat had a meaning similar to that of the Cross for Christians.

25:18–20 two cherubim: The only likenesses permitted in the holy worship of the Lord were these beautiful artistic representations of mysterious, angelic beings. The cherub (Heb. *kerub*) was likely a composite creature with the body of a lion, a human-like face, and the wings of a great bird. Other ancient cultures had similar devices. Embroidered patterns of cherubim were also woven into the tapestry of the curtains of the tabernacle (26:1). The cherubim's **wings** stretched out and faced inward, shading the mercy seat. Their **faces** gazed on the mercy seat itself.

25:21, 22 The Lord promised Moses that He would **meet** with him at the mercy seat. The verb carries a specific meaning, "to meet at an appointed place." The Lord would also meet with Moses at the tent of meeting (Ex. 29:42, 43; 30:36). Some have thought that the mercy seat and the cherubim were something of a throne for the Lord, with the extended wings of the cherubs forming an exquisite seat for Him, or perhaps a footstool (1 Chr. 28:2).

25:23 The **table** was used to display twelve loaves of bread in the presence of the Lord. It was approximately three feet long, eighteen inches wide, and twenty-seven inches high.

IN LIFE   Beauty in Worship

All of the design elements for the sanctuary and its contents (Ex. 25) suggest God's great love of beauty, of design, of loveliness. We have sometimes imagined that God enjoys plainness. This is hardly the case. God's love for beautiful things, for craftsmanship, for design and art, is displayed throughout His creation, and it is mirrored in the wonderfully designed elements of furnishings He commanded Israel to fashion for His holy worship.

The church has often struggled with the issue of beauty in places of worship. Some have argued that since Christians are God's temple today, places of worship should be austere, stark, plain. Others have argued that large expenditures on our places of worship are self-serving in view of the great and continuing needs of so many of the peoples of the world.

But in the biblical descriptions of both the tabernacle and the later temple, other Christians have found models of beauty, craftsmanship, and artistry that bring joy both to man and God. As one woman lavished exquisite ointment over the Savior's feet as a gift of her love for Him (Luke 7:37–50), many Christians believe that lovely spiritual symbols of divine worship in the places where the church gathers are legitimate expressions of love for God.

25:24, 25 Like the ark, the table was to be overlaid with **gold** and was to have a decorative **molding of gold** (v. 11). The **frame** was a decorative element that kept objects on the table from being disturbed.

25:26–28 The table was to have **rings** and **poles** so that it could be transported properly. The poles protected the holy object from being touched by human hands.

25:29 pure gold: All of the implements for making bread were also to be costly and won-

---

✠ IN CONTEXT

The Ark of the Covenant

The ark (Ex. 25:10–22), commonly known as the ark of the covenant, was the most sacred of all the furniture in the tabernacle. A chest that measured approximately 45 inches long, 27 inches wide, and 27 inches deep, it held three priceless items: a copy of the stone tablets on which the Ten Commandments were written (25:16, 21), a golden pot of manna from the wilderness journey (16:32–34), and Aaron's rod that budded (Num. 17:1–11).

During the latter years of the period of the judges, the Israelites suffered a major spiritual, political, and military defeat when they foolishly carried the ark into battle, where it was captured by the enemy (1 Sam. 5:1).

---

derfully designed to physically represent their holiness. They were "set apart" to God.

25:30 The **showbread** itself is described more fully in Lev. 24:5–9. Twelve loaves representing the twelve tribes were placed in two rows with six loaves in each row. It was called showbread (Heb. *lehem panîm*, literally, "bread of the face") because it was placed symbolically before the "face" of God.

25:31 Perhaps the loveliest ornament in the tabernacle was the menorah, the golden **lampstand.** Lamps in biblical times were ordinarily oven-baked clay bowls that contained olive oil. A pinched edge or groove held the wick. These seven lamps, fashioned with much greater care and precision, were to be placed on a magnificent lampstand. Chapter 37 describes how the artisans made the lampstand (37:17–24). **of one piece:** All of the elements of the lampstand were to be hammered out of one solid piece of

gold, requiring skill, knowledge of metalworking, and great artistry.

25:32 One of the seven lamps was to be placed in the center, flanked by three **branches** on either side. This became the basic design for the menorah of later Judaism. The symbolism of the number seven goes back to the creation account of Gen. 1 and represents completion.

25:33–36 The **bowls, branches,** and **knobs** were highly decorative. The lamp illuminated the interior of the holy place, but it also was a work of art in its own right, showing God's pleasure in artistry.

25:37 light in front: The wicks would all be on the same side of the lampstand so that the light would be shed principally in one direction. The lights would burn even when no priest was present.

25:38 The implements used in servicing the lamps were also to be made **of gold.**

25:39 A talent weighed about seventy-five pounds. It is very difficult to estimate the monetary value of the lampstand, since there were no coins or currency at this time. We can assume it was enormously valuable and exquisitely beautiful.

25:40 the pattern: Moses was not only told how to make the implements, he actually "saw" in some manner on Sinai a heavenly pattern for them (v. 9; 26:30; 27:8; Acts 7:44; Heb. 8:5).

26:1 The English word **tabernacle** comes from the Latin *tabernaculum,* meaning "tent." The Hebrew word (*mishkan*) means literally "dwelling place." Sometimes it refers only to the tent. In other places, it means the tent with the surrounding courtyard. The same Hebrew word is used for the later shrine in Shiloh (Ps. 78:60) and for the worship shrines in Jerusalem before and after the temple was built (Pss. 26:8; 46:4; 74:7). In Exodus, the description of the tabernacle begins with the inside, according to "God's view," so to speak, and moves to the outside. Thus the **ten curtains** are described first. These ten curtains were divided into two sets. The inner curtains were made of delicate fabric with brilliant colors and exquisite design. All of this was hidden from public view.

26:1 These **curtains** formed the ceiling of the tabernacle.

26:2, 3 Each curtain was about forty-two feet long and six feet wide. The curtains were grouped in ten sections so they could be moved more easily.

26:4–6 Every detail of the curtains was specified, including directions for making the **loops** and **clasps.** With these the curtains were linked together to form the tent.

26:7 curtains of goat's hair: The coarse fabric of the outer curtains protected the delicate fabrics within from the elements. Goat's hair was a rich, black fabric highly prized in the ancient world. **Eleven curtains:** The outer curtains had to be larger than the inner curtains to assure complete coverage (vv. 1, 2). The extra outer curtain was used over the front of the tent (v. 9).

26:8 The approximate dimensions for each outer **curtain** was forty-five feet by six feet. This would allow an overage of one cubit on each side (vv. 12, 13).

26:9–25 There have been two principal views concerning the meaning of this section. One view pictures the frame as a solid wood structure that would be used to support the considerable weight of the four fabrics suspended above the wooden structure. But a solid wood building would have obscured completely the fabrics, particularly the inner fabric of fine linen, that seemed designed to be particularly fashioned for the "pleasure of the Lord." Thus the second view seems preferable. The frame was more of a lattice-work structure, through which the fabric of the inner covering would be clearly visible.

26:16–19 The boards were designed to be put together and taken apart easily, as befits a portable tent. As in the case of the design for the fabric, precise directions were given for making of the **boards,** their **tenons** (or tabs), and their **sockets.** Each **board** was about fifteen feet long and two and a half feet wide. **Twenty boards** were on the north side, twenty on the south, and six on the west. Corner posts stabilized the structure. The **sockets of silver** were costly and beautiful but functional. They were made from silver that was donated as redemption money by males over the age of twenty (Ex. 38:25–28).

26:20–30 The **bars** (or crossbars) were placed at right angles to the upright **boards** (vv. 15–25) to stabilize the lattice-work structure. **Five bars . . . the middle bar:** On each

of the three paneled sides of the tabernacle (north, south, and west), five bars were added to make the frame strong and rigid. The considerable weight of the fabrics and the prospect of inclement weather necessitated additional supports.

26:29 The fine acacia wood used to form the **boards** and **bars** also was overlaid with **gold.** This step added considerable weight to the structure, yet increased its beauty and intrinsic worth.

26:30 according to its pattern: Again, Moses was reminded of the pattern he had seen (25:9, 40; 27:8; Acts 7:44; Heb. 8:5).

26:31–35 The **veil** separated the holy place from the Most Holy Place. (See the record of the completion of this veil in Ex. 36:35, 36.) Only the ark would stay in the Most Holy Place.

26:31–33 Perhaps the most beautiful and intricate of all the fabrics in the tabernacle, the **veil** (Heb. *paroket,* compare v. 36) was to hang from **pillars** by **clasps,** dividing the chamber into two separate rooms. The larger room would be called **the holy place** and the smaller room **the Most Holy** Place. The Hebrew expression can also be translated "the Holiest Place" or "the Holy of Holies" (compare Heb. 9:2, 3 for "the Holiest of All").

26:34, 35 The **ark** with its **mercy seat** was the only object that would stay in the **Most Holy** Place. The **lampstand** and the **table** were to be in the holy place. Each object was purposely placed to reflect the pattern, order, and design given to Moses (v. 30).

26:36, 37 The same Hebrew word (*masak*) is used to describe the **screen** at the gate of the court (27:16; 35:17; 38:18; 39:40; 40:8, 33). At times, this word is used for the curtain separating the Holy Place from the Most Holy Place (35:12; 39:34; 40:21; compare the term "veil" in 26:31). This screen was made of multicolored threads and fine artistry, and it was held in place by **five pillars,** overlaid with **gold,** and fitted

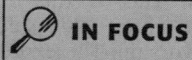 **IN FOCUS**   **"Altar"**

(Heb. *mizbeach*) (Ex. 27:1; 30:1). Strong's #4196: This word depicts a "place of slaughtering" and is derived from the verb meaning "to slaughter for sacrifice" (Ex. 20:24; Deut. 16:2). Altars were the site of sacrificial worship (Gen. 8:20) and were made of earth (Ex. 20:24), stones (Josh 8:31; Judg 13:19), or even bronze (Ex. 38:1–7). The ritual slaughtering of animals to the Lord was central to Hebrew worship at the temple (Lev. 1:5). But throughout Scripture, the Lord warned that righteousness, justice, and a humble heart submitted to Himself were more important than bringing sacrificial gifts to the altar (Ps. 51:17; Prov. 21:3; Matt. 5:23, 24). The sacrifices on the altar in the temple were a sign that God had forgiven the Israelites' sins. That sign pointed to the ultimate sacrifice: the sacrifice of His Son on the Cross for the sins of humanity (Heb. 9:11–15; 13:10–13).

with **sockets.** It would not be a flimsy fabric that the wind might blow open. Entrance into the inner Tabernacle was highly restricted by this heavy, ornamental barrier. The Christian is reminded here of the wonder of access to the living God because of Christ's completed work (Heb. 4:16).

27:1 The **altar** was about seven and a half feet square, with a height of four and a half feet. The **cubit** was approximately eighteen inches.

27:2 The **horns** were projections on each corner of the square altar. They could have been used to secure the sacrificial animal to the altar. They were also sprinkled with blood from the sacrifices (29:12).

27:3–7 Various implements were made of **bronze,** including the **grate,** which was to be suspended above the altar. The grate would allow the ashes to drop below.

27:8 A hollow altar would allow the ashes to fall down through its center. It is possible that the altar was partially filled with dirt to protect it from the intense heat of the sacrificial fires.

27:9–18 The courtyard of the tabernacle separated the ceremonies of worship from common areas. It was arranged to keep people and stray animals from wandering into the tabernacle. Entering the tent could only be a deliberate act. The construction of the court is described in 38:9–20.

27:16 The **gate** itself was made of a **screen** (26:36) thirty feet long. It was to be beautiful, like the screen inside the tabernacle.

27:17–19 utensils: These numerous tools and utensils were used only for the tabernacle. "Common" tools could not be used for holy tasks. The **pegs** made of bronze **were** used for ropes to hold the supporting pillars of the courtyard. Everything was designed for portability.

27:20 The fuel for the lamps, **pure oil of pressed olives** (Lev. 24:1–4), burned with little smoke. The purity of the oil was indicative of the standard God demanded for all sacrifices offered to Him.

27:21 shall tend it: The lamp was never to go out. This command was a perpetual **statute** throughout the period of the Aaronic priesthood. The priests were also to burn the sweet incense on the altar of incense (30:7, 8).

28:1 Aaron and Aaron's sons: Aaron is first mentioned when he is reunited with his **brother** Moses after Moses' forty-year exile in Midian (Ex. 4:14, 27–31). Their family history and early experience is given in Ex. 6:14—7:7. **from among the children of Israel:** This is a significant phrase concerning the nature of a true priesthood. If the priest is to be a true representative of the people, he must come from the people (Heb. 5:1). In order for the Lord Jesus to serve properly as our High Priest, it was

necessary first for Him to become a part of the people whom He would represent. Thus, the Incarnation was a necessity not only for His human life, His death, and His resurrection, but also for His priestly ministry in the heavenlies for His people (Book of Hebrews). **minister to me as priest:** The ministry of the priests was for the sake of the people, but its principal focus was toward the Lord. As the holy angels are

IN CONTEXT — **The Priests' Holy Garments**

The priests' garments (Ex. 28:2–4) represented their function as mediators between God and the people. Over his regular priestly garments, the high priest wore an ephod, a two-piece apron or vest that was ornamented. He also wore a breastplate of judgment to which were attached twelve precious stones engraved with the names of the twelve tribes of Israel (28:15–30). In the pocket of the breastplate, directly over the high priest's heart, were the Urim and Thummim (Ex. 28:30), a means by which God communicated His will to the people.

God's attending spirits, so the holy priests are His attending priests.

28:2 The **holy garments** were made holy by their consecration to God's service, as the materials of the tabernacle had been. **For glory and for beauty:** It is likely that the magnificent clothing of the priests represented the concept of imputed righteousness before the Lord (Zech. 3:1–5).

28:3 gifted artisans: This is the first description of the craftsmen who would fashion the items for tabernacle worship. The expression literally means those "who are wise at heart" (in 35:25, the same expression is used of skillful women who did the weaving). These people possessed divinely given skills of craftsmanship. **the spirit of wisdom:** God added to this skill a special endowment of the Spirit to aid their work. The study of the "gifts of the Spirit" (Rom. 12:3–8; 1 Cor. 12:1–11) can begin with this record of the spiritually guided artisans.

28:4 The **garments** of the priest are specified: **ephod** (vv. 5–14), **breastplate** (vv. 15–30), **robe** (vv. 31–35), **tunic** (v. 39), turban (vv. 36–38), **sash** (v. 39). Other garments were prepared for Aaron's **sons** (vv. 40–43).

28:5–14 The **ephod** (it is a transliteration of the Heb word *'ephod*) has been described variously as a cape or a vest made of fine linen with brilliant colors. Its two main sections covered the chest and back, with seams at the shoulders and a band at the waist. The shoulders were emblazoned with beautiful memorial stones.

28:5, 6 There are varied ideas concerning possible symbolic meanings for these varied colors. It is difficult, however, to discover *in the text of Scripture* the alleged symbolic values. It appears that a better approach is simply that the brilliant use of colors resulted in an exceedingly beautiful garment. For as the text says, it was **artistcally worked.**

28:7–12 The two **onyx stones,** engraved with the names of the tribes of Israel, were set in **gold.** They symbolized the intercessory work of the priest. He was to represent the people before the Lord. The names of the tribes were literally written on his shoulders, so that the priest would **bear their names before the LORD** on his two shoulders as a memorial.

28:13, 14 The use of **gold** enhanced the beauty and value of the garment. Everything about the garments of the priest was to speak of the wonder of his approach to the living God. Imagine what our garments may be like in heaven, when we shall behold Him!

28:15 The **breastplate** was a small pouch that hung from the neck of the priest. It was decorated with twelve stones, one for each of the tribes of Israel. Within the pouch were the Urim and Thummim (v. 30). The **breastplate of judgment** was used by the priest in seeking judgment; that is, a decision from the Lord on an issue presented for divine discernment. The breastplate was made of the same fabric as the ephod, to which it would be securely tied.

28:16 a square: It measured nine inches on each side. The **span** was determined as the length from the tip of the thumb to the tip of the small finger on an outstretched hand.

28:17–28 Four rows of precious and semiprecious **stones** were fastened to the breastplate. These twelve stones bore the names of the **twelve tribes.** This was another symbol of the priest's representation of the people before the Lord. Not all of the stones can be identified precisely today.

28:29 Over his heart was a touching phrase that reminded the priest of his solemn responsibility. He represented the nation before the living God. Any lesser devotion merited divine judgment (see the sad fate of Aaron's sons, Nadab and Abihu, at Lev. 10:1, 2).

⚒ IN DEPTH | # Guidance Through Urim and Thummin

The Urim and Thummim (meaning "lights and perfections," Ex. 28:30) were intended as a means of divine guidance for Israel. They involved gems or stones that were either attached to or carried inside the breastplate worn by the high priest when he consulted with God. For this reason, the breastplate is often called the breastplate of judgment or decision.

However, while we know that this decision-making system existed, no one knows for sure how it worked. The Urim and Thummim are mentioned only three other times in the Pentateuch (Lev. 8:8; Num. 27:21; Deut. 33:8), once during the early monarchy (1 Sam. 28:6), and twice after the Babylonian exile (Ezra 2:63; Neh. 7:65). Otherwise, there is no indication that the nation used them to make decisions.

Thus there is a great deal of speculation about how the Urim and Thummim delivered a verdict. Some believe that the gemstones were cast like dice. Others believe that the stones were engraved with symbols that signified yes or no, true or false.

The Jewish historian Josephus (A.D. 37–100?) believed that the Urim and Thummim had to do with the flashing of the precious stones in the breastplate. Other writers held that the letters in the names of the twelve tribes of Israel engraved on the stones stood out or flashed in succession to spell out God's reply. Another theory is that by staring at the glow of the stones, the high priest would go into a trance during which God would speak to him.

These theories are pure guesswork. However, it is easy to see that in the days before much of the Scriptures were written or collected, there was a need for some kind of divine guidance. Today, of course, we have God's complete written revelation, and therefore have no need of devices such as the Urim and Thummim.

28:30 The **breastplate** held the mysterious stones called **the Urim and the Thummim.** These transliterated Hebrew words mean "Lights" and "Perfections" (both superlative plurals). Together their names may mean "perfect knowledge" or a similar idea. It is not known how Aaron and his successors used these stones (if indeed they were stones). We do know that God instructed his priests in many ways. It is possible that these stones were meant to assure the priest that God would reveal His true judgment to him. Hence, the expression "to consult with the Urim and the Thummim" might mean presenting a matter before the Lord with Urim and Thummim in the breastplate, a sign that the priest confidently expected the Lord to resolve the issue (compare Lev. 8:8; Num. 27:21; Deut. 33:8; 1 Sam. 28:6; Ezra 2:63; Neh. 7:65).

28:31, 32 The **robe** was a long, flowing garment made of **blue.** It may have been a seamless garment. An opening for the **head** is mentioned, but not for the arms. There must have been slits for the arms.

28:33–35 The **pomegranates** on the hem were decorative. The **bells** would tinkle as the priest moved about within the sacred places. This sound would assure those outside that the priest was interceding on their behalf.

28:36–38 The **turban** of the high priest was made of white linen on which was secured a gold **plate** engraved with the words **HOLINESS TO THE LORD**. The plate rested on the **forehead** of the priest. The meaning of the phrase **bear the iniquity** seems to indicate that the **holy gifts** of the people would be acceptable only when presented through mediations of a holy priest. These words anticipate the work of the Savior, who bore our iniquities in His own body (1 Pet. 2:24).

28:39 The record of the completion of these items is given in 39:27–29.

28:40, 41 put them on . . . anoint . . . **consecrate . . . sanctify:** The rites of consecrating the priests for their holy work are detailed more fully in ch. 29, in 40:13–15, and in Lev. 8–10.

28:42 This command to wear **trousers** protected the modesty of the priests. Given the sexually preoccupied worship of Israel's neighbors, this provision was decidedly countercultural.

28:43 that they do not incur iniquity and die: It is difficult for us to grasp the gravity of the priests' responsibility as they ministered before the living God. They had to serve God with a pure heart, to represent the people without guile, and to worship without deviating from the commands of God. To fail would invite judgment, even death. Sadly,

priests did die because they failed to show respect for the holiness of God (Lev. 10:1, 2; 1 Sam. 4:17; 2 Sam. 6:7).

29:1–46 This section is devoted to instructions for the consecration of Aaron and his sons to the priesthood. It is not enough that the priests be correctly dressed.

29:1 The Hebrew word translated **hallow** describes actions that would mark the priests as distinct, holy, or set aside for God's purposes—as people who would approach Him in His service. The instruction to present animals **without blemish** reminds us that sacrifice was not an occasion to rid oneself of sick or defective livestock. Offering the best animals was an act of faith that expressed thanksgiving and confidence in God's provision. Blameless too was the death of the Savior Jesus, who was without fault in every particular.

29:2 unleavened **bread:** As it was at Passover (12:8), the use of leaven was prohibited in this rite also. Leaven was allowed for everyday baking.

29:3, 4 wash them: The bathing of the priests symbolized the necessity of cleanness before the Lord. Bathing was a rare luxury in the desert of Sinai.

29:5–7 The directions for mixing **the anointing oil** are given in 30:22–33. To **pour it on his head** was a lavish gesture, later celebrated by a psalmist (Ps. 133:2). **And anoint him:** As the priests of old were anointed for holy service, so would the Messiah (meaning "Anointed One") be anointed for His great service of sacrifice to the living God.

29:8, 9 The **sons** were to be dressed after their father was. The verb translated **consecrate** literally means "to fill one's hand." The idea seems to be that of "empowerment." A king was handed a rod as the symbol of his political power; so the hand of the priest was filled with spiritual power.

29:10, 11 The slaying of the **bull** would happen only after the priests had **put their hands** on its **head.** This gesture showed that the animal had been designated as their substitute. To **kill the bull,** the priests cut an artery in the bull's neck to cause a quick death.

29:12 blood: The application of the blood to **the horns of the altar** may have been to make the display of blood more prominent (12:7). The operation was not a tidy one. The sacrifice of a large animal, in the open air with a hot sun overhead and flies buzzing around, was a formidable task. The rest of the blood was poured **at the base of the altar.**

29:13, 14 sin offering: The burning of the **fat** and the **kidneys** on the altar would have produced an acrid odor. Yet because sin was consumed, these sacrifices are described at times as "sweet-smelling" to the Lord (v. 18). The rest of the animal was burned **outside the camp,** for it was unsuitable before the Lord (for more on the sin offering, read Lev. 4).

29:15–18 Burnt offering is a translation of a Hebrew term that can be rendered "that which goes up (in smoke)." Aaron and his sons needed to offer sacrifices for themselves as much as for their fellow Israelites (Heb. 5:1–4). However, no sacrifices were needed for the Savior, Jesus; He alone came as the sinless priest. **Sweet aroma** is an ironic use of language, for the odors of burning flesh, skin, hair, entrails would be an acrid smell. But because of the benefit that these odors bring to man (the forgiveness of sins), the Lord viewed them as a sweet aroma (notes at Num. 7).

29:19–28 One of the most obscure rites in the Book of Exodus is the use of **the ram of consecration.** The Hebrew expression can mean "the ram of the filling"; that is, the ram that results in the filling of the hands of the priests with their divine service (v. 9). Much of this section remains somewhat mysterious to us, but we can sense the priests carefully preparing for the worship of the Holy God with this sacrifice.

29:19 the other ram: That is, the second of the two rams mentioned in v. 1 (compare the first ram, vv. 15–18).

29:20, 21 The **blood** that was daubed on the priests signified that they were entirely "under the blood" that atoned for sin (12:7). It is possible that the anointing of the **ear** represented the hearing of the Word of God, that the anointing of the **thumb** represented the accomplishment of the will of God, and that the anointing of the **toe** represented the journey of the walk with God. Not only were the persons of the priests to be sprinkled with blood and anointed with **oil,** but so were their **garments.** In this way, the beautiful clothing of the priests would be made holy or **hallowed.** The substitution of the death of the animal pointed forward to the death of Christ (Heb. 10:1–14).

29:22–24 A **wave offering** was to be made of the **fat** of the **ram** and the **unleavened bread** (described first in v. 2). The elements would be held high and then waved back and forth before the altar. The offering made clear that everything was owed to God, but some was received back as God's gift. For more on the wave offering, read Lev. 7:30; 10:14.

29:25 After this symbolic act (vv. 22–24), the fat and the unleavened breads were burned as a **burnt offering** (v. 18). This is also called **an offering made by fire.**

29:26 The **breast of the ram** was **waved** as a symbol of giving and receiving, and was then kept by the priests as their portion to eat as a gift from the Lord.

29:27 Wave offering and **heave offering** are general terms that cover different kinds of sacrifices. The terms are used, as here, for parts of the peace offering (Lev. 7:29–34). But they are also used for a special grain offering (Num. 15:19–21) and for the tithe (Num. 18:24–29).

29:27, 28 The word translated **heave offering** (Heb. *terûmâ*) means "something held up (before the Lord)." Another meaning is "contribution."

29:29–34 The priests were to eat the meat of **the ram of the consecration** (vv. 19–28) in a meal of celebration, along with the **bread** (vv. 2, 23) that had not been burned. **An outsider** was not to eat this food, nor were any leftovers permitted. Anything not eaten as a part of the sacred feast had to be burned.

29:35–39 The rites of consecration (v. 9) lasted **seven days.** The repetition of these actions, day after day, dramatically emphasized the need for holiness and faithfulness in worship.

29:40, 41 One tenth of an ephah was about two quarts; **one fourth of a hin** was about one quart. The same offering was presented at twilight. This offering may actually have had a more **sweet aroma** than the burnt

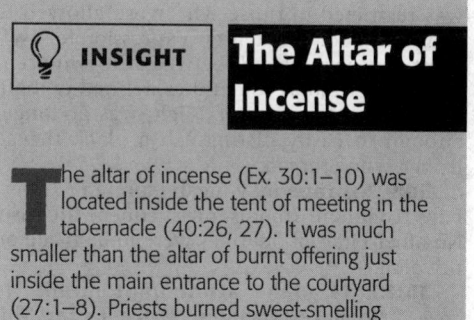

INSIGHT

The Altar of Incense

The altar of incense (Ex. 30:1–10) was located inside the tent of meeting in the tabernacle (40:26, 27). It was much smaller than the altar of burnt offering just inside the main entrance to the courtyard (27:1–8). Priests burned sweet-smelling incense on this altar every day.

offering of v. 18 because of the addition of the **wine** and **oil.**

29:42, 43 The purpose of the **tabernacle** and its **offering** are reiterated. It was here that the Lord would **meet** with His people, **speak** with them, and display His **glory.**

29:44 consecrate: The same idea, to set apart for God's service, is expressed in v. 9 with the Hebrew idiom "to fill the hand."

29:45 The words **they shall know** take us back to Yahweh's intention in His redemptive work and glorious covenant with Israel (6:1–8).

29:46 I am the Lord their God: Using His

personal name, God declared to the Israelites that He was *their* God. He had redeemed them and delivered them in order that they might become His people and He in turn *their* God (Ex. 15:2).

30:1, 2 This smaller **altar** was a stand used for burning the sweet-smelling incense. As with the ark of the covenant (25:10), the table of the showbread (25:23), and the altar of burnt offering (27:1), this altar was made of **acacia wood** (25:10). It was eighteen inches square and three feet high.

30:3 Like the larger altar, the smaller was overlaid with **gold.** The **horns** were a decorative copy of those on the altar of burnt offering (27:2).

30:4, 5 Rings and **poles** were used to carry the altar, signaling again the great respect that was demanded in the transportation of these holy furnishings.

30:6 The altar was situated within the holy place near the **veil** that divided it from the Most Holy Place. The mention of the **ark of the Testimony** reminds us of the most significant furnishing in the tabernacle.

30:7, 8 Aaron was directed to burn **sweet incense** each morning and at twilight, along with his tending of the **lamps** (27:20, 21).Why, we might ask, was the high priest charged with carrying out such a simple act? Burning incense actually was a privilege, for it was restricted to those who were allowed to approach God. The Hebrew expression for **twilight** may be rendered "between the two evenings." Later rabbis sometimes defined twilight as the point when natural light was no longer enough to easily distinguish a black thread from a white thread.

30:9 Strange may mean "foreign" or perhaps "common" (that is, unsanctified) **incense.** No other kinds of offerings were to be made on this altar.

30:10, 11 Make atonement means "to cover," "to make expiation." **Once a year:** This

Day of Atonement was later specified in Lev. 16. The "atoning" of objects such as this was a ritual cleansing to make these objects **holy** before the Lord. Since man was sinful, the things he came in contact with were associated with his sinfulness. Once a year, everything in the tabernacle that man touched had to be ceremonially cleansed. The phrase translated **it is most holy** is literally "holy of holies," the same Hebrew construction used in 26:34. Here the phrase describes not the Most Holy Place, but the supreme holiness of the articles of worship before the Lord (v. 29).

30:12, 13 This text is not clear if a command is being given or a concession. That is, it is not clear whether they were to take a **census** and then were to do as follows, or whether they might take a census and would have to do as follows. The term **ransom** (Heb. *kopher*) is related to the words for atonement and propitiation (v. 10; 29:36, 37). The idea is to pay a price for one's life. The Israelites had to acknowledge that their lives were from God and governed by Him by giving Him an offering of money. A **half-shekel** was about one-fifth of an ounce (Ex. 21:32; 38:26).

30:14–17 Every male was to provide a half-shekel ransom. The sum was not based on the worth or wealth of the person. The collection supported the Levites who cared for the tabernacle.

30:18 laver of bronze . . . its base: The shape of the laver is not specified, but it clearly had two parts, the laver itself and its base. Women provided the bronze mirrors that became the building materials for the laver (Ex. 38:8).

30:19–21 wash their hands and their feet: The constant need for cleansing the priests' hands is understandable. But the feet of the priests would also be readily soiled because they wore sandals. The continual washing was symbolic of the need to be cleansed from sin regularly. **Lest they die** emphasizes the seri-

---

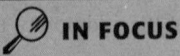 **IN FOCUS**   **"Washing"**

(Heb. *rachats*) (Ex. 2:5; 30:18; Prov. 30:12). Strong's #7364: In the Bible, washing or bathing has important cultural and religious associations. The ancient custom of washing a guest's feet was an act of hospitality that lasted into NT period (Gen. 18:4; John 13:5). Ritual washing was an important step in the purification of the priests for service in the tabernacle (40:12). Washing with water symbolized spiritual cleansing, the preparation necessary for entering God's presence (Pss. 26:6; 73:13). The OT prophets continued to use this imagery of washing and applied it symbolically to the act of repentance (Is. 1:16; Ezek. 16:4). In the NT, Paul describes redemption in Christ as "the washing of regeneration" (Titus 3:5).

ousness of maintaining the priests' holiness before God (28:43).

30:22–25 The priests used the holy oil in rites of anointing (29:7). This costly and treasured mixture must have had an unforgettable, wonderful aroma. The **holy anointing oil** was declared holy because it was set aside for use only in religious rites specified by the law (vv. 32, 33). The **perfumer,** like his counterparts who worked with wood, fabric, and metal, was a highly skilled craftsman (v. 35).

30:26–29 Everything connected with divine worship had to be anointed with the special oils. In this way, the creations of the workmen became holy, set aside for special use in the worship of God.

30:30 Anointing initiated the **priests** into the privilege of God's service.

30:31–33 The oil was reserved exclusively for the consecration of the tabernacle and all its furnishings. Any other use would result in divine judgment. **Cut off** means put to death (Gen. 17:14).

30:34–38 As in the case of the anointing oil (vv. 22–25), the directions for making the incense are precise. The resulting mixture was a lavish, expensive, precious commodity.

30:36 before the testimony: A portion of the fragrant incense was to be taken into the Most Holy Place as a holy symbol for the people before the Lord.

30:37, 38 No **incense** was to be made for personal use nor was it to be used for any other purpose than that which God commanded. **It shall be to you holy for the Lord** was a succinct reminder of the importance of reserving holy things for worshiping God.

31:1–11 The importance of the tabernacle and its furnishings was such that the Lord sovereignly prepared gifted artisans to do the work of construction under the detailed instructions of Moses. Everything was to be done in accordance with the plan that the Lord had shown to Moses on the mountain (26:30).

31:2 called by name: The Lord now designated specifically the man who would be the principal artisan for the tabernacle. The name **Bezalel** (Heb. *besal'el*) means "in the shadow of God." **Hur,** the grandfather of Bezalel, should not be confused with the more famous associate of Aaron and Moses (17:10; 24:14).

31:3–5 filled him with the Spirit of God: This wonderful phrase is indicative of the work of the Holy Spirit during OT times. We are familiar with the "filling of the Spirit" that came upon the disciples at Pentecost (Acts 2) and brought into being the new community of faith, the church. But we often neglect the work of the Spirit among the Israelites. Passages such as this one help us to see the continuity of God's

work among His people through the ages. In this case, the Spirit empowered uniquely gifted people to design and build a tabernacle befitting a holy and magnificent God. The piling up of the words **wisdom, understanding, knowledge,**

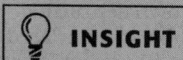

INSIGHT | **Spices**

Spices (Ex. 30:34) were important to trade and commerce. They were imported from Arabia and from as far away as India, which could be reached from Egypt by sea. Most spices came from plant products, such as gums and resins. Onycha (v. 34) was taken from a mollusk that lives in the Red Sea. Its exotic origins added to its perceived value.

and **all workmanship** is similar to the sevenfold Spirit endowment of the coming King (Is. 11:2). It is done here to impress readers with the tremendous importance of the sheer *artistry* of the tabernacle, which demanded such gifted persons empowered uniquely by the Holy Spirit for their work (35:30, 31).

31:6 The name **Aholiab,** given to the principal assistant to Bezalel, means "Tent of the Father" (Heb. *'oholi'ab*). It describes one who lives closely with God, the Father of His people (35:34; 36:1, 2; 38:23). The **wisdom in the hearts** was "the spirit of wisdom" spoken of in 28:3, or "the Spirit of God, in wisdom" of 31:3. Such wisdom was a divine gift that allowed these craftsmen to complete their holy work.

31:7–11 The bill of particulars is given concerning all the products that the two gifted men and their many associates were to produce. The wonderful thing to contemplate is that they were to do this work not only the basis of their own native talent (a gift from the Lord), but also by the indwelling presence of God's Spirit at work in them. Thus, the Spirit of God (v. 3) has concerns not only for the lives of people before the Lord, but also for the objects of holy worship of the living God. Craftsmen and craftswomen (35:25) were empowered by the Holy Spirit to produce the works commanded them by God.

31:12–18 This is one of the significant sections in Exodus that focuses on the meaning of Yahweh's covenant with Israel at Mount Sinai (19:5, 6; 24:1–8; 34:27, 28). The principal contribution of this section is on the role of the Sabbath as the special sign of the covenant.

31:13, 14 My Sabbaths reminds us that keeping the Sabbath is the Lord's idea, not a human invention. Such days of rest must be kept in righteousness before Him (Is. 1:10–15). **a sign:** a reminder, memorial, or symbol. The Sabbath distinguished Israel from its pagan neighbors, an idea reinforced by the last phrase, **the LORD who sanctifies you. put to death:** The Sabbath was not for casual recreation, but for worshiping God. Those who observed the Sabbath carelessly invited their own destruction.

31:15–17 Here the **Sabbath** is declared to be **a sign** between the Lord and Israel forever. The idea of Sabbath can be found in the pattern of **six days** of creation, followed by a seventh day of rest.

31:18 an end of speaking: This dramatic verse reminds the reader that the entire section beginning at 25:1 is a report of the divine encounter Moses experienced on the mountain (24:18; 25:1). When he returned to the people, he wrote down what he had seen and heard. The Spirit of God directed him to recall the amazing complex of details, ideas, and concepts of holy worship. The **two tablets of Testimony,** similar to ancient treaties, bore the Ten Commandments on each tablet. Both tablets were kept together before God in His holy tabernacle. The **stone** emphasized the permanence of the Word of God. **The finger of God** is a bold anthropomorphism (a quality of God expressed as a human characteristic) that underscores the divine origin of the Law. Scholars of religion have long spoken of Israel's religious ideas as its unique contribution to civilization, much as the Greeks developed philosophy and the Romans displayed a genius for organization and empire-building. Yet such a comparison misses the point of Scripture. The Bible speaks not of the genius of Israel, but of the *finger of God*. The Ten Commandments were not the product of man, but the revelation of the Lord.

32:1–35 The story of the Israelites' worship of the gold calf reveals both the unfaithfulness of the Israelites and God's great mercy. Even though the people had broken their promise to obey Him in such a short time, God forgives their sin and begins again with them.

32:1 This infamous story begins on a very human level. **The people saw that Moses delayed coming down from the mountain:** The extended absence of Moses (24:18) and the terrifying setting into which he had disappeared (24:9–17) led the people to think that he might never return. The people were the redeemed of Israel (ch. 12; 14:31), but in their discouragement they wandered to other gods. It is most shocking to discover the role that **Aaron** played in this debacle. It appears as though he also had given up hope for his brother's return. Moses was gone for forty days, yet we may conclude that the people ran out of patience before then. The preparation of the idol would have taken some time. **make us gods that shall go before us:** The people were asking not for the true God, but for other gods. **This Moses** is spoken of in scathing, sarcastic, and demeaning tones. What are we to make of this? Is it possible that the entire community had turned against Moses? Or is it possible that doubters and unbelievers in their midst took advantage of the situation to spread evil? We may also consider the possibility of spiritual warfare—that unseen and unrecognized forces worked to encourage evil among God's people. Stephen alluded to this event when he said that the fathers "turned back to Egypt" (Acts 7:39, 40).

32:2, 3 The golden earrings were part of the treasure from Egypt that should have been used for building the tabernacle (35:20–29).

32:4 A molded calf was an ominous worship symbol. Not only were the cow and the bull worshiped in Egypt, but the bull was a familiar embodiment of Baal seen in Canaan. **This is your god** can be rendered "these are your gods," suggesting that the worship of the Lord had been blended with the symbols of Baal and other fertility gods. Aaron thus had led the people in breaking the first three command-

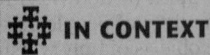 **IN CONTEXT**   **"Divine" Calves, Cows, and Bulls**

The stories of Aaron molding the golden calf (Ex. 32:1–4) and Jeroboam building golden calves for his new temples at Bethel and Dan (1 Kin. 12:28–31) are similar. For instance, both men broke God's commands soon after God had given the commands.

But why make calves? Cattle were common images for deities in that period. In Egypt, the popular goddess Hathor was represented as having various features of a cow, such as its horns and ears. Male deities in other cultures, such as Syria-Palestine and Babylon, were often depicted as having some cow features, usually horns. And Canaanite deities such as El and Baal are associated with bulls in the Ugaritic texts.

If the golden calf represents a Canaanite god, such worship was a blatant rejection of Israel's God.

ments: they had bowed to another god beside the Lord; they had made a graven image; and they used the Lord's name in false worship (v. 5). God had said repeatedly that it was He and only He who had brought the Israelites out of Egypt (Ex. 20:1, 2; 29:45, 46), an event they had all witnessed.

32:5 a feast to the Lord: Apostasy blinds us to the fact that we have rejected God.

32:6 The worship expressed here involved sacrifices combined with possibly sexual acts of profane worship. The words **and rose up to play** suggest the latter idea. See 34:12–16 for an elaboration of such Canaanite practices that Israel was forbidden to follow.

32:7, 8 The Lord alerted Moses to the fact of Israel's sin. **Have corrupted themselves:** The Hebrew (*shahat*) means "to pervert," "to ruin." It is used also to describe the ruin of humankind that provoked the Flood (Gen. 6:12).

32:9 a stiff-necked people: This is the first occasion of this doleful phrase, which describes the stubbornness of the people who refused to follow the ways of God (Ex. 33:3, 5; 34:9; Deut. 9:6, 13; 10:16).

32:10 The words of God then turned very ominous. He threatened to destroy the nation entirely and begin anew with Moses (Num. 14:11, 12). This declaration prompted Moses to intercede on behalf of the people for God's mercy (vv. 11–13).

32:11–13 Moses used three principal arguments in this great prayer to assuage the anger of the Lord. (1) The deliverance of Israel from Egypt was the work of the Lord. How could He abandon them now? (2) The Egyptians would hear of this judgment and would believe that they had triumphed after all. How could He destroy them now? (3) The covenant had been established long before by divine oath. How could He revoke this promise now? We see clearly Moses' own humility, his compassion for the Israelites, and his zeal for God's glory and honor.

32:14 so the Lord relented: Here is a wonderful example of the interaction of faithful intercessory prayer and the purpose of the Lord. God intended to spare Israel. But He drew Moses into the process by causing him to pray for the right outcome. He uses our prayer combined with His own determination to make His will come to pass.

32:15, 16 The two tablets of the Testimony are the tablets of the Ten Commandments (31:18).

32:17 It appears that **Joshua** had accompanied Moses on at least a part of the journey to Mount Sinai (24:13, 14). While Moses was alone with God, Joshua seems to have remained nearby. From his base, he was the first to hear the raucous worship of the golden calf and report that startling news to Moses.

32:18 Moses' response to the words of Joshua comes in a three-colon poem that is highly styled with twelve words (in Hebrew, perhaps reflective of the twelve tribes of Israel). In this poem, **noise** (twice) is also translated **sound,** and **shout** is also translated **cry** and sounds very much like the word translated **singing.** Moses knew that the **sound of singing** could only mean trouble. Since he had not left instructions on the worship of the Lord, the people must have been up to mischief with the worship of another god. How interesting, however, that the term singing was associated in Moses' mind with worship.

32:19, 20 In great rage, Moses destroyed the **tablets.** This gesture, highly symbolic, suggested that the law had been "broken" by the actions of the people. Then Moses destroyed the **calf,** finally making the people drink its residue mixed with water.

32:21–24 Moses then turned on Aaron, demanding to know how such wickedness had happened. Aaron's feeble response reminds us of Adam's weak reply to God in Gen. 3:12. Aaron passed the blame onto the people rather than admit his own complicity in this terrible sin.

32:25 Despite the return of Moses, some of

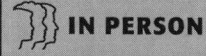 **IN PERSON** **Watch Moses Grow**

I t's amazing that God offered to make a great nation of Moses and his descendants (Ex. 32:10). Failures and mistakes had plagued his life to that point. In fact, they would plague him again before his life was over. Perhaps God was merely testing His servant to find out what sort of man he really was.

Christians who have struggled with personal growth and spiritual development can take heart from a study of the life of Moses. He did not start out as a giant of the faith. Nor did he end his career in a blaze of glory. Nevertheless, God honored this man's lifelong quest for godliness. His life record shows a path like the ones to which all believers are called (Eph. 4:15; Col. 1:10; 2 Pet. 3:18).

the people were unrestrained, perhaps still conducting themselves in the unseemly behavior of worshipers of Baal (Num. 25).

32:26 whoever is on the Lord's side: The first to respond to Moses were men from the tribe of Levi, an act that drew them more fully into the Lord's service.

32:27, 28 Moses sent the Levites to **kill** the people engaged in evil (most likely sexual degen-

---

INSIGHT   Pleading for Forgiveness

The incident with the golden calf brought the Israelites very close to being instantly consumed by the Lord's wrath. Only Moses' earnest intervention averted judgment (Ex. 32:31–35). This is one of numerous examples in Scripture of how important it is for sins to be brought before the Lord in order to seek His mercy and forgiveness.

---

eracy, Num. 25). It was painful for a Levite to slay **his brother . . . his companion . . . his neighbor.** But the wicked, even if they were relatives, had to be destroyed lest the whole camp perish under God's judgment.

32:29 consecrate yourselves: The people needed to turn completely back to the living God in the hope that He would receive them in **blessing** again.

32:30, 31 The terrible sin of the people needed to be removed. Moses hoped to **make atonement** for the people.

32:32, 33 Blot me out of your book: This is the most touching moment in Moses' leadership of the Israelites. Like Paul many centuries later, he could almost wish himself to be cursed, if by being so he could secure the salvation of his people (Rom. 9:3). Moses' offer could not be accepted. But his selfless gesture also resembles the self-sacrifice of Jesus, which God accepted as the atonement for the sins of every generation of humanity (Mark 10:45). **My book** is the Book of Life (Ps. 87:6; Rev. 3:5).

32:34 God promises that His **Angel** (23:20–23) will still lead the people, but coupled with that promise is a solemn threat of **punishment.** The expression **in the day** may refer to the Day of the Lord, proclaimed by later prophets (Joel 2, Zeph. 1).

32:35 It is not clear whether the Lord plagued **the people** after Moses' prayer or if this passage refers to the judgment God had already sent upon the people (vv. 26–28). It is

possible that this refers both to the punishment of the Lord for this particular sin and to later plagues (punishments) that would befall the Israelites in the wilderness as they continued to disobey the Lord.

33:1–34:35 Following their debacle as described in ch. 32, God in great mercy renewed His commitment to His covenant with them. The principal issue in the Hebrew Bible is not the display of the wrath of God, as is so often supposed. It is His mercy that shines through the darkness of His people's disobedience, and it is His grace that overcomes the despair caused by the doubts of His people.

33:1 depart . . . go up: The time had come for the march into Canaan. **Which I swore:** For God's covenant with Abraham and Isaac, read Gen. 12:7; 15:13–21; 22:15–18.

33:2 And drive out is language similar to that used of the hornet(s) in Ex. 23:28.

33:3, 4 God announced that He would **not go up** among his people because they were **stiff-necked.** Thus the hope of reaching the Promised Land was darkened by God's withdrawal from their presence. **This bad news,** the command to move on without the presence of the Lord, was hardly a message that they wanted to hear.

33:5, 6 I could come suggested that the threat of judgment was still very real (32:35). The **ornaments** were associated with the idolatrous worship of the golden calf (32:2, 3). Their removal was a mark of genuine repentance and renewal.

33:7 his tent . . . the tabernacle of meeting: Moses moved his own tent **outside the camp** to symbolize the Lord's departure from His people. Moses called his tent **the tabernacle of meeting,** for here he met with the living God. The people **who sought the Lord,** that is, who needed a divine decision, would consult Moses at his tent far from the center of the camp.

33:8 all the people rose . . . stood: In contrast to their earlier wickedness, the people now responded reverently to the living God. Only Moses could approach God, but those who were nearby could respond from a distance in awe and worship.

33:9 This **pillar of cloud** is the same one that guided the Israelites out of Egypt (13:21, 22; 24:15, 16). **Descended, stood** and **talked** are verbs that indicate personality within the pillar.

33:10 saw . . . worshiped: The people could not approach the Lord as Moses did. Moses saw and spoke with the Lord as one would to a friend. From a distance, the people saw the pillar and recognized the presence of God, and they worshiped by bowing low to the

---

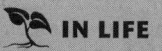 IN LIFE | ## The Glory of the Lord

G od allowed Moses to experience something of His glory (Ex. 33:12–23). The Hebrew term most often translated "glory" (*kabod*) means "weight, importance, or significance" and does not connote something light and ephemeral as does the English "glory." The word is sometimes applied to persons, indicating their excellence, or to things, describing their perfect functioning.

In Scripture, however, glory is most often used to indicate God's presence and power (Deut. 5:24). Sometimes it occurs as a synonym of the Hebrew word *qodesh,* indicating holiness. Sometimes it is associated with fire, as when He revealed Himself on Sinai (Ex. 24:16, 17), or with cloud or smoke, as when the tabernacle was dedicated (Ex. 40:34) or when Isaiah had his vision (Is. 6:3, 4).

In these cases, the awful reality of God is being emphasized. Compared to this, humanity is but a wisp of smoke or a blade of grass. It is in this context that God's determination to share His glory with us becomes the more astounding. In place of our frailty, He offers us His reality (John 1:14, 32, 34; Rom. 9:23; 2 Cor. 4:17).

---

ground. The text is careful to say that the people stayed off at some distance. Only Moses could come near the pillar, God's Presence.

33:11 the LORD: The identification of the pillar with the Lord is now unmistakable. **His servant Joshua:** Here we glimpse again (17:9; 24:13; 32:17) the bold man of God who would become Moses' successor. The word translated "servant" here does not mean slave, but rather a minister, one who does spiritual service.

33:12–33 Moses prays for an even closer experience with Yahweh. This section is in two units. (1) Moses demands the assurance of Yahweh's Presence with His people and with him personally (vv. 12–17). (2) Moses requests an unusually close encounter with the living God as a mark of His special relationship with His servant (vv. 18–23).

33:12 The message the Lord had given to Moses and the people, recorded at the beginning of the chapter (vv. 1–3), troubled Moses. Thus, he pressed the Lord to grant His presence in the adventure of faith that the people were to undertake. **Whom you will send with me** was Moses' indirect way of seeking assurance that the Lord Himself would accompany the people.

33:13 The words **Your way** refer in this context to the divine Presence among His people. **Your people** was Moses' reminder of God's promise that He would make the Israelites His people (6:1–8).

33:14–16 My Presence means literally in Hebrew "My Face." This extraordinary promise of God's Presence with His people was ultimately fulfilled in Jesus, God made man. **Rest** refers to the land of Canaan, when the conquest would be over and the land could be enjoyed by the Israelites. Moses even dared to say that the **Presence** of the Lord in the midst

of His people was the only acceptable condition for further advance. Only the Lord's Presence would demonstrate to surrounding nations that Israel's deliverance was really the work of the true and merciful God.

33:17 God's **grace** was accompanied by his intimate knowledge of and care for Moses, represented in the expression **I know you by name.**

33:18 The word **glory** conveys the idea of weight, significance, and importance (16:7, 10; 24:16, 17; 40:34, 35). Here, astoundingly, Moses requested an even greater sense of God's Presence than up to then had been experienced by any person.

33:19 Amazingly, the Lord responded positively. **My goodness** speaks of the sense of the wonder of God, of His divine attributes, of His essential worth and majesty. **Proclaim the name of the LORD:** The name of God is the expression of His person, who He is. **be gracious . . . have compassion:** The Lord's sovereignty is paramount in His dealings with people. God can do anything He wants. Yet, in His mercy, He responded to Moses' plea. What a great gift this is: The Creator of the universe tenderly granting the audacious request of His servant (Ps. 40:1).

33:20 cannot see my face: We cannot begin to describe what Moses experienced in this dramatic encounter. God is Spirit (John 4:24). Any experience of the living God requires Him to enter our finite sphere of space and time. Whatever Moses experienced was only a glimpse of what is still to be experienced! Human language is simply too limited to express the mysteries these verses describe. "My face" was earlier translated "My Presence" (v. 14).

33:21 The **place** is generally assumed to be a cleft in the rock of Mount Sinai. How fitting that Moses would experience the Lord who is his Rock (Deut. 32:4) while standing **on the rock.**

33:22, 23 The use of words such as **hand, back,** and **face** is anthropomorphic, a way of describing God, who is Spirit, in terms familiar to humankind. The point of these verses is clear enough. Moses would see something wonderful, but not so much as would take his life. This great revelation is described in 34:5–9.

34:1 The command to **cut two tablets of stone** is one of the great demonstrations of God's mercy. Despite the failure of the people at the very time that the Lord was instructing Moses on how they should worship, He was willing to begin again with them. Once more He would instruct them concerning His righteous ways.

34:2 The mercy of Yahweh is seen in His acquiescence to Moses' request for an even closer experience with the living God than he had ever had.

34:3, 4 As in the preparation of the people in ch. 19, the warning that **no man shall come up with you** was meant to protect the careless or the curious who would die if they trespassed on holy ground.

34:5 Like ch. 19, these verses describe an epiphany, the appearance of the Lord in His grand descent to encounter humans. As at other times (33:9–11) the people saw the **cloud,** which Moses knew as the visible symbol of the living God before him. The living God **proclaimed** His name to Moses by expressing His character, His awesome wonder, and His mercy.

34:6 The Hebrew verb translated **passed** (ʿabar, "to cross over") is the same verb that describes Abram's journey through the land of Canaan (Gen. 12:6). The name Hebrew is probably derived from this verb. Here the word speaks of the "movement" of the Lord before Moses. As the Lord moved by Moses, He proclaimed the meaning of His name Yahweh (Ex.

3:14, 15), revealing His gracious character in an unforgettable manner. Indeed, this verse is the foundation for understanding the character of the Lord. The words **merciful** and **gracious** convey the idea of "overwhelmingly gracious."
long-suffering: The idea of the Hebrew idiom is that God is very slow to anger. In our idiom, we would say He has "a very long fuse." The Hebrew word for **goodness** means "loyal love"; the word for **truth** means "faithfulness," "truth," and "constancy." When the Gospel of John introduces Jesus as the Word, there is celebration of the fact that He is "full of grace and truth" (John 1:14, 17). In this way John echoes the words of this passage. To see Jesus is to see the Father! (John 1:18).

34:7, 8 thousands . . . the third and the fourth: This phrase resembles the words of 20:5, 6, but the order is changed for emphasis here. The point is that God is more willing to show his **mercy** than His wrath. Yet His wrath is also real (32:34, 35; Ps. 90:11).

34:9 Go among us indicates that Moses was still praying for a reversal of God's judgment announced in 33:1–3. The Lord responded to these pleasing words by restoring the covenant (vv. 10–28).

34:10, 11 I make a covenant: This verse introduces the renewal of covenant; the message is completed in vv. 27, 28. Concurrent with the announcement of the covenant is the promise that the people will experience **an awesome thing** (Heb. nôraʾ, from yareʾ, a verb meaning "to fear"), namely the conquest of Canaan. The enormity of Israel's refusal to obey God's command and conquer the land (Num. 13; 14) is to be seen in the light of this extraordinary promise (Deut. 4:32–40).

34:12 covenant: Israel was forbidden to make treaties with nearby peoples. Instead, they were to destroy those nations, lest they be ruined by their perverted ideas and false religious affections. The next verses (vv. 13–26)

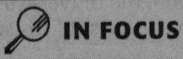 **IN FOCUS**   **"Goodness"**

(Heb. chesed) (Ex. 15:13; 20:6; 34:6) Strong's #2617: When God revealed Himself to Moses on Mount Sinai, He described Himself as overflowing with *goodness*. This is one of the most significant words that describes God's character (Ps. 13:5). It is often translated as *mercy* (Ex. 20:6; Ps. 6:4) and sometimes as *lovingkindness* (Ps. 17:7). The basic meaning of the word is "loyal love" or "steadfast love." It refers to God's loyalty and faithfulness to His covenant. This love is very similar to marital love, a love that is obligatory because of the marriage contract, but still intimate and voluntary. Hosea's actions toward his unfaithful wife are a striking picture of God's "faithful love" for the people of Israel (Hos. 1:1–3, 2:19; 3:1–5). In the NT, this characteristic of God is described as His grace (Gk. *charis*; John 1:17).

repeat some of the salient features of the Lord's covenant with Israel. We read these words with sadness in retrospect. They are the very commands Israel abandoned so quickly.

34:13 Pillars (Ex. 23:24) and **wooden images** were sexually centered images; the latter were representations of Asherah, the fertility goddess of the Canaanites. (Asherah was known to the Greeks as Astarte.)

34:14 No other gods is a reiteration of the basic stipulation of the Ten Words (Ex. 20:3).

34:15 Unfortunately, the phrase **to play the harlot** was probably not just a figure of speech. Unfaithfulness to the Lord was often

INSIGHT — Forbidden Religious Objects

Altars, sacred pillars, and wooden images continually appear in the Bible as a group of banned religious objects (Ex. 34:13). All three were common in religions of Syria-Palestine, which included Canaan. Thus to allow these to remain would have breached the commands not to worship other gods (Ex. 20:30). Incorporating indigenous religious practices into the worship of God posed a continual danger. Only when devoted to God and restricted to certain locations were altars acceptable for Israel.

manifested in sexual rites with temple prostitutes (male and female), an act of supposed union with Baal, Asherah, and other pagan deities. **To eat of his sacrifice** alludes to the love feast that preceded the orgy, reminiscent of the episode with the golden calf (32:5, 6, 19, 25).

34:16 take of his daughters for your sons: God's prohibition against intermarriage was not a matter of prejudice. The influence of immoral religious practices was subtle, pervasive, and unrelenting. Intermarriage would be the quickest route to compromise with false religion and immoral behavior.

34:17 Israel had, in fact, already paid the price for fashioning **molded gods.**

34:18 The Feast of Unleavened Bread recalls the commands of Ex. 12:15–20; 23:15.

34:19, 20 The law of the **firstborn** is also found in Ex. 13:2; 22:29, 30.

34:21 The law of the Sabbath is repeated from Ex. 20:8–11; 31:12–18.

34:22–24 The commands of the three annual **feasts** are repeated from Ex. 23:14–17. Faithful participation in these feasts was linked to God's promise in v. 24 to preserve the people in the land.

34:25–27 In the Hebrew text, the grammar used in the command to **Write these words** has a strong personal directive (see notes at 17:14; 24:4). It might be paraphrased: "Write—that is *you* do it!" This is the **covenant** of Yahweh with Israel at Mount Sinai (sometimes called the Mosaic Covenant; see notes at 19:5, 6; 24:1–8; 31:12–18; 34:10). The writing of Moses here is a remarkable attestation of biblical truth.

34:28 The period of **forty days and forty nights** matched Moses' earlier pilgrimage to Sinai (24:18). **bread . . . water:** A person can survive without food for weeks. But no one can go without water for more than three or four days. If Moses drank no water for forty days, then we must view his continued existence as a miracle of the Lord. Is it possible that he was removed into a heavenly sphere for this long period of time? We simply do not know. We are confident that God was able to sustain His servant in any way He pleased! The Lord then **wrote . . . the Ten Commandments,** equated once again with the words of the covenant. The Writer was the Lord Himself (Ex. 31:18; 32:15, 16; 34:1, 4).

34:29–35 skin of his face shone: One of the Bible's most wonderful descriptions is that of Moses' shining face. His proximity to the Presence of God transformed his very appearance (2 Cor. 3:7–18).

34:30 The people were **afraid to come near.** With all they had seen and heard, they had reason to be cautious.

34:31, 32 Moses sought to allay their fear and to teach them the **commandments** the Lord had sent him to proclaim.

34:33–35 The **veil** Moses wore concealed the glow of his face. This supernatural glow was enhanced on each subsequent encounter with the Lord. Paul taught that Moses wore the veil because the glow faded, a sign of imperfect glory (2 Cor. 3:7, 13).

35:1–40:38 These chapters have little new material. They are highly repetitive of instructions concerning building the tabernacle, fashioning its furnishings, and fabricating the priests' garments for their holy service before the Lord. There is a sense of celebration in this recital. The importance of the tabernacle and all connected with it is made even stronger with these repeated instructions.

35:1–3 The principal teaching concerning the **Sabbath** is the fourth commandment (20:8–11), and this teaching is expanded in

31:12–18. Here is another repetition of the command for emphasis (34:21). To **kindle . . . fire** was considered a breach of the command. To some Jews today, turning on a light switch on the Sabbath is the equivalent of kindling a fire.

35:4–9 This section is based on the instructions of 25:1–8. Here we observe Moses doing as God commanded him when he was on the mountain of the Lord.

35:10–19 gifted artisans: The call now went out for artisans who would create the tabernacle furnishings and the garments for the priests, the details of which appeared in chs. 25—31.

35:20–29 The offerings for the tabernacle are perhaps the most impressive offering ever taken from God's people for any endeavor! The key was the stirring of the **heart** and the willingness of the **spirit** of those who gave. **Both men and women** gave. Even in this patriarchal time, women participated actively in God's work. All people came with gifts that were sumptuous, varied, and abundant. At last they had to be told to stop giving (36:2–7)!

35:25–30 women . . . gifted artisans: Here the artisans, usually referred to in the masculine (28:3), are distinctly identified as women.

35:31–33 filled him with the Spirit of God: See the parallel passage at 31:3. Compare the comments at 28:3. The special endowment of the Spirit of God in this artisan and in those who worked with him attested to the importance the Lord attached to the aesthetic beauty of the tabernacle. The preparations for building the tabernacle and later the temple foreshadowed the incarnation of the Savior. For it was both in the tabernacle and temple and in the Incarnation that "heaven came down," that God drew near to His people in saving wonder and divine fellowship.

35:34, 35 The ability to teach is similar to the gift of teaching mentioned by Paul (Rom. 12:7). The same Spirit was at work among His people in the OT period as in the NT.

36:1–7 What a problem! Has there ever been another time in history when God's people had to be **restrained** for giving **too much**? The pattern of the "cheerful giver" (2 Cor. 9:7) could have no better basis than here.

36:8 gifted artisans: This is a wonderful comment carried through from 35:30—36:4 (28:3; 31:6; 35:10, 25). The demands of God's design (ch. 26) called for careful, detailed, and artistic work. The skillful work was of high quality.

36:9–19 Here we read about the fashioning of the outer **curtains** (v. 14). See 26:7–14 for God's command concerning their design.

36:20–30 A discussion of the tabernacle frame. See 26:15–25 for its design.

36:31–34 The construction of the crossbars for the outer structure of the tabernacle. See 26:26–30 for the earlier instructions for their design.

36:35, 36 The description of the **veil** that divided the holy place and the Most Holy Place. See 26:31–35 for God's command concerning its design.

36:37, 38 The description of the screen for the **door** of the tabernacle. See 26:36, 37 for its design.

37:1–9 This section describes how **Bezalel** (31:2) constructed the holy ark, including the mercy seat and the cherubs, following the pattern that the Lord gave to Moses on the mountain (25:10–22). This text follows the earlier passage in every particular concerning its actual

---

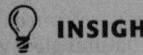 **INSIGHT** | ## God's Spirit in the Workplace

God's Holy Spirit was actively involved with the workers as they built the tabernacle (Ex. 35:31–36:1). The Spirit was the source of the many skills and abilities required for the design and construction of the tabernacle—metalwork, jewelry making, carpentry, engraving, weaving, and other related talents. Notice some of the characteristics of these Spirit-led workers:

- They were men and women (Ex. 35:20–22, 25).
- Their hearts were "willing" or "stirred" (35:5, 21, 22, 26), meaning that they were motivated to accomplish the task.
- They were skilled or "gifted" by God to carry out their various assignments (35:10, 25, 34, 35; 36:1, 2).
- They were generous with their skills, as well as their possessions, in order to get the job done (35:5, 22, 29; 36:3–7), which suggests that they were hard and loyal workers.
- The finished product shows that excellence was a hallmark of their work.

construction. The only detail not repeated here is the instruction to put the Testimony in the ark and the mercy seat on top (25:21). This is found again in 40:20.

37:10–16 The construction of the table for the showbread. This section corresponds in every detail to the instructions given to Moses by the Lord in 25:23–30. The only aspect not repeated here from the earlier text is the instruction to place the showbread on the table (40:4, 22, 23).

37:17–29 The creation of the golden **lampstand.** Again, this section corresponds in every detail to the instructions given to Moses in 25:31–40. The earlier text contains instruction for lighting the lamps, which Moses did when everything was completed (40:4, 25).

38:1–7 The construction of the altar of burnt offering. The corresponding instructions are found in 27:1–19. The details from the preceding section are presented again to demonstrate that all was done as the Lord had commanded. Throughout these sections, the pronoun **he** (v. 1) refers to Bezalel (37:1; compare 35:30–34), who was working according to the commands that the Lord had given Moses. Bezalel was the overseer. He would have had many artisans working under his leadership (36:8).

38:8 The crafting of the bronze **laver.** For the corresponding instructions, read 30:17–21.

38:9–23 The building of the **court** of the tabernacle. For the corresponding instructions, read 27:9–19.

38:24 The weight of **all the gold** used in the work may have been about a ton. The **talent** weighed about seventy pounds and equaled 3,000 **shekels.**

38:25 all the silver: The quantity of silver was simply enormous, about 7,000 pounds.

38:26 A **bekah** (half-shekel) of silver, required of each man over the age of twenty, came from 603,550 people, which corresponds with other estimates of the Exodus community (Num. 1). The number may be literal, but some contend that it is far too large for the time and the events of the Exodus.

38:27, 28 Enormous amounts of **silver** appeared in the most mundane elements of the

INSIGHT — The Use of Gold

Gold is the most malleable and ductile of metals. It can be hammered into very thin sheets (Ex. 39:3), thinner than a piece of paper. It can therefore be easily worked into different shapes, and it does not corrode. These characteristics help account for its value.

tabernacle and its furnishings. Although the tabernacle was a tent, it was not a makeshift dwelling. It was a glorious shrine that symbolized the presence of the living God in the midst of His people.

38:29–31 The weight of the **bronze** was about 5,000 pounds.

39:1 This verse is a summary statement that confirms the completion of the priests' garments first described in 28:1–4.

39:2–7 This section details the crafting of Aaron's **ephod,** according to the explicit instructions given to Moses in 28:5–14.

39:8–21 Here we read about the **breastplate,** made according to the directions spelled out in 28:15–30. The only detail not repeated is the placement of the Urim and the Thummim within the breastplate (28:30). This is reported in Lev. 8:8.

39:22–26 The fashioning of the **robe** is

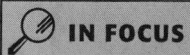

IN FOCUS — "Tabernacle"

(Heb. *mishkan*) (Ex. 25:9; 26:1; 40:2). Strong's #4908: The word *tabernacle* signifies "a dwelling place" and is related to the verb meaning "to dwell," "to settle down," and "to live among" (Ex. 29:45; Gen. 14:13). In Exodus, the tabernacle is a temporary place to live—a tent (Song 1:8). God's tent, the tabernacle, functioned as an object lesson in God's holiness and a symbol of His divine presence among His people (Ex. 33:7–11). It was a sign that God wanted to live among His people and establish an intimate relationship with them (Ex. 5:8, 9). The ultimate outworking of that desire was that Jesus Christ, who was Himself God, became a man. As the Son of God, Jesus lived among us, walked with us, and revealed God the Father to us (John 1:14–18). This is why His name is Immanuel, meaning "God with us" (Matt. 1:23).

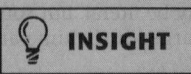

Excellence Starts at the Top

Moses set an excellent example for his workforce by doing his own job "according to all that the Lord had commanded him" (Ex. 40:16). That kind of precision set the pace for everyone else and reaped invaluable rewards. The management team and the workers under them all carried out their tasks as the Lord wanted (Ex. 35:30–35; 36:1; 39:1–43).

described, following the divine commands given to Moses in 28:31–35.

39:27–29 The fashioning of the **tunics,** the **turban,** and the **sash** follow the commands given in 28:39. **short trousers:** These were provided for the priests for modesty as they ascended the steps (see the command in 28:42).

39:30, 31 The fashioning of the **plate** that was attached to the **turban** of the high priest

vades these verses. One can sense the pride of accomplishment coupled with the reverence for all of these holy objects.

39:42 according to all that LORD had commanded: The constant stress throughout these chapters is for Israel to construct the tabernacle and all of its furnishings in compliance with divine command. These projects would only have significance in their holy worship of God if they were done just as He had commanded.

39:43 The words **Moses looked** suggest that Moses conducted a final inspection. He was satisfied that everything was finished according to the pattern he had seen on the mountain. Then **Moses blessed them,** a magnanimous gesture of approval for the work accomplished.

40:1, 2 This **first month** was the month Abib, also called Nisan (Ex. 12:2; 13:4). The tabernacle was completed nine months after the arrival of the people at Mount Sinai (Ex. 19:1) and two weeks before the second celebration of the Passover (v.17).

40:3–8 Moses now directed the placement of furnishings in the tabernacle, including the **ark,** the **table** of showbread, the **altar for the incense,** the **altar of the burnt offering,** the **laver,** and the **court** along with appropriate **screens.** The lamps were to be **lit** and **water**

A model of the tabernacle, constructed in the wilderness at God's command. After its completion, it was filled with God's glory and covered by a cloud, signifying God's presence (Ex. 40:34, 35).

followed precisely the commands that the Lord had given to Moses (28:36–38).

39:32–43 These verses list **all the work** that God had commanded through Moses. It was now completed. A mood of celebration per-

was to be placed in the laver. See ch. 25 for a list of the furnishings.

40:9–11 Following the placement of the furnishings, the Lord instructed Moses to **anoint** everything in the tabernacle so that it would be **holy** (separated to the Lord). For the anointing, Moses would have used the special olive oil that was mixed with spices (30:22–33). **The altar shall be most holy,** in Hebrew, is a superlative (*qodesh qodashîm*) literally meaning "holy of holies."

40:12–15 The Lord's next command to Moses was to prepare the priests for their holy service. These verses recall the extensive commands in ch. 29. **wash them:** The priests had to be clean before they were dressed in their **holy garments** (see the description at 28:1–4). Moses, acting as God's representative, was then to **anoint** them as he had anointed the furnishings. The family of Aaron was to have **an everlasting priesthood.** The same declaration also appears in ch. 29 (28:1).

40:16–19 Moses scrupulously obeyed every detail of God's commands (Ex. 7:10). Since Israel's welfare depended on the obedience of its leaders, Moses' faithfulness allowed untold blessings to follow God's wandering people. **as the LORD commanded Moses:** The repetition of this phrase emphasizes that Moses precisely obeyed God.

40:20, 21 The **Testimony** is the stone tablets of the Ten Commandments (25:16). **The mercy seat on top of the ark:** See the description in 25:17–22.

40:22, 23 the table . . . the bread: See the description in 25:23–30.

40:24, 25 the lampstand . . . lamps: See the description in 25:31–40; 27:20, 21.

40:26, 27 the gold altar: See the description in 30:1–10. **incense:** See the description in 30:34–38.

40:28 the screen: See the description in 26:36, 37.

40:29 the altar of burnt offering: See the description in 27:1–8.

40:30–32 the laver (v. 30): See the description in 30:17–21.

40:33 the court: See the description in 27:9–19.

40:34 cloud . . . glory: When everything the Lord had commanded had been completed, He came near in an epiphany, a dramatic descent that manifested His glory among His people (19:20; 34:5). When the Lord came near in the event described at 19:20, the people were terrified. But in His coming near the tabernacle described here, the people were overjoyed. This was not a descent in judgment, but in mercy. The **glory of the LORD** filling the tabernacle demonstrated His Presence with the Israelites, His significance to them, and His awe-inspiring wonder. The words of John 1:1–18 are appropriate to recall here. In the Incarnation, the glory of God was manifest not in a tent, but in His Son.

40:35 Although Moses had been intimately involved in preparing the tabernacle, its completion meant that the glory of the Lord was present and that even Moses could not enter it. **The cloud rested** speaks of God living among His people (John 1:14). Throughout this section we encounter two attributes of God. One is His great grace and tender mercy. The King of glory was in the midst of His people! The second is His indescribable holiness. The Lord filled the tent and no one could draw near!

40:36, 37 the cloud: The glory of the Lord, which now was among His people also directed the Israelites' movement (Ex. 13:21, 22; Num. 9:15–23). The appearance of His glory is sometimes called the Shekinah or the Shekinah glory, from the Hebrew for "to dwell."

40:38 the cloud of the Lord: How wonderful that the Book of Exodus concludes with this image of the gracious God, hovering protectively over His people. Christians today emphasize the indwelling presence of the Holy Spirit in their lives (Acts 2). But God was also present with His people before Jesus came. A faithful Israelite follower of God could see the tabernacle and realize that God was there in His splendor and power. And with Him the people advanced to Canaan, the land He had promised to them.

The Third Book of Moses Called

Leviticus

—————————————◆—————————————

*G*OD'S CONCERN FOR HIS PEOPLE AND HIS DESIRE for fellowship with them becomes more and more clear to anyone who reads carefully through the Book of Leviticus. Every detailed regulation recorded in Leviticus is a revelation *from* God *through* Moses *for* His people. With these laws, God personally instructed the Israelites how to live before Him. Christian readers sometimes get lost in all the regulations

governing various types of sacrifices, what was clean or unclean, who was eligible to be a priest, and so on. However, when these details are placed within the context of God's desire to have fellowship with the Israelites and live with them, the seemingly "dead" Law takes on a new life.

The name of the book is derived from the name of the tribe of Levi, the tribe that supplied the priests for Israel. Leviticus addresses many of the activities of the priests. It gives extensive instructions for the sacrificial system that atoned for both ceremonial and moral impurity. Yet Leviticus is not merely a manual for priests. It was intended for the entire Israelite community, with at least two purposes: (1) that people would know and value their privileges and responsibilities before God; and (2) that priests could not gain oppressive power over the people with any monopoly on the knowledge of how to approach God.

The purpose of Leviticus was to show the Israelites how they could live in ritual and moral purity. When they maintained their purity, God could live among them and they could approach Him in worship. Many of the required sacrifices

described in Leviticus were for the atonement of sins. On the other hand, the voluntary sacrifices brought the people to fellowship and feast with God, their family, and others.

The instructions in Leviticus were not given to the Israelites in order to help them achieve their own salvation. Salvation can never be earned. It is always a gift of God's grace appropriated by faith. These instructions were given to a redeemed nation so that its members would know how to maintain their fellowship with God.

The distinctions between clean and unclean and the various laws for holy living promoted the Israelites' own welfare and marked them out as a people separated to God. Israel's witness to God's holiness and their visible well-being as a result of holy living before Him would vividly demonstrate to their neighbors God's power and His care for His people. The directive found first in Leviticus 11:44 and many times afterward clearly expresses this purpose for the laws: "You shall be holy, for I am holy." Holiness must be maintained before God, and holiness can only be attained through a proper atonement. Rightly seen, these concepts, sacrifices, and regulations picture in many ways the person and work of our Savior, the Lord Jesus Christ.

Modern Christians can learn much from Leviticus. The holiness of God, the necessity of holy living, the great cost of atonement and forgiveness, the privilege and responsibility of presenting only our best to God, the generosity of God that enables His people to be generous—these are only some of the lessons. Leviticus reveals the holiness of God and His love for His people in ways found nowhere else in the Bible. Ultimately, Leviticus calls God's people of all ages to the great adventure of patterning life after God's holy purposes.

Jewish and Christian tradition has regarded Moses as the author of Leviticus. After delivering Israel out of Egypt, God revealed His covenant to Moses at Mount Sinai. When God entered into a covenant with the Israelites, He transformed them from a band of refugee slaves into a nation. Leviticus records a large part of that covenant. If Moses or a scribe acting as his secretary wrote down the revelation as God gave it, Leviticus was composed shortly after 1440 B.C. or shortly after 1290 B.C., depending on the date assigned to the Exodus.

Critical biblical scholarship of the late nineteenth century challenged the traditional dating and authorship of Leviticus. According to that scholarship, which is still influential today, Leviticus was written much later, during the post-exilic period. This would be a date after 530 B.C. During the past century, however, our understanding of the history, languages, cultures, and religions of the ancient Middle East including Israel has advanced greatly. Many of the premises on which the late dating of Leviticus was based have been shown to be unreliable.

Although Leviticus does not itself claim to be written by Moses, twenty of the twenty-seven chapters begin, "And the LORD spoke to Moses," or a variation of that statement. The phrase occurs fourteen other places in the book as well. The intent is that this is the word of God given through Moses at Mount Sinai. As with the rest of the Pentateuch, later editorial activity may have occurred. The material could have been arranged by someone other than Moses, though Moses certainly was as capable of its arrangement as anyone. The important point is that Leviticus is what it says it is, a series of revelations from God about how God's people may approach Him through sacrifice and honor Him in holy living.

Outline

I. The system of sacrifices (1:1–7:38)
  A. The burnt offering (1:1–17)
  B. The grain offering (2:1–16)
  C. The peace offering (3:1–17)
  D. The sin offering (4:1–5:13)
  E. The trespass or reparation offering (5:14–6:7)
  F. Instructions about offerings (6:8–7:38)
II. Ordination of priests (8:1–10:20)
  A. Ordination of Aaron as high priest and his sons as priests (8:1–36)
  B. First sacrifices of the newly ordained priests (9:1–24)

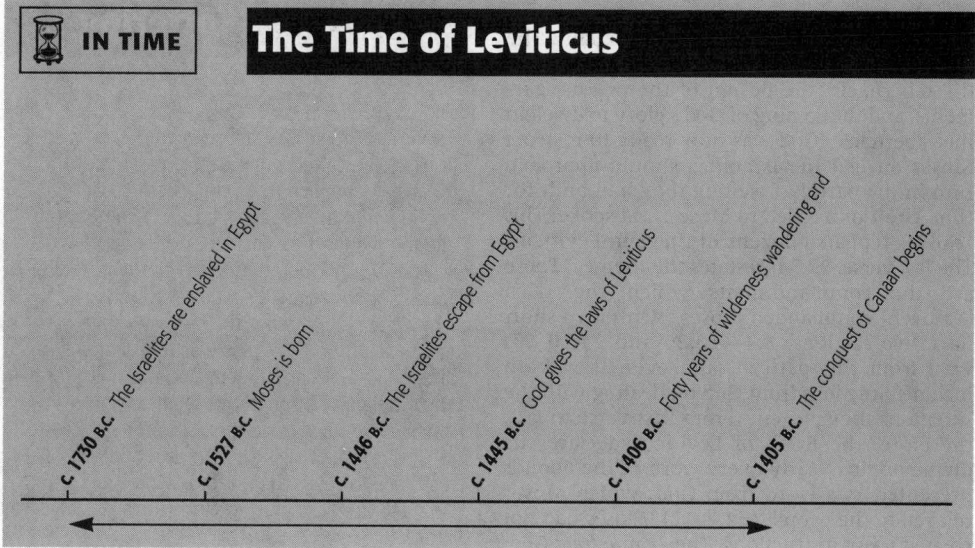

IN TIME — The Time of Leviticus

c. 1730 B.C. The Israelites are enslaved in Egypt
c. 1527 B.C. Moses is born
c. 1446 B.C. The Israelites escape from Egypt
c. 1445 B.C. God gives the laws of Leviticus
c. 1406 B.C. Forty years of wilderness wandering end
c. 1405 B.C. The conquest of Canaan begins

Commentary

1:1 Now connects Leviticus with Exodus. The last sections of Exodus describe the building of the tabernacle, the design of the priests' garments, and the coming of God's glory to dwell in the tabernacle. God was now ready to instruct Moses on *how* the Israelites should approach Him in the earthly dwelling they had built for Him. **the LORD** called to Moses, and spoke: This "call" is repeated dozens of times in Leviticus. The last verse, 27:34, restates the theme, "These are the commandments which the LORD {Yahweh} commanded Moses." Only two short narrative sections, 8:4—10:20 and 24:10–23, vary from this pattern, and even they both include directions from God on dealing with the situations they present. From first verse to last, therefore, the Book of Leviticus declares its divine origin. Nearly every word of the book is presented as a word from God, which Moses relayed to the people (Ex. 4:12). Moses had not created these instructions. They came *from* God,

through Moses, God's prophet (Deut. 34:10). **The tabernacle of meeting** was the center of Israel's public worship until Solomon's temple was built in Jerusalem centuries later. The tabernacle's plan is revealed in Ex. 25—30 and its construction is described in Ex. 36—39.

1:2 The children of Israel means "the people of Israel." Now that God had entered into covenant with them, Israel was a people and no longer just a band of refugees (Ex. 6:2–8). Most of the occasions when God spoke to Moses (1:1), He directed Moses to deliver the instructions to all the people. Even when the word was just for Aaron, or just for the priests, it was delivered publicly. This was an important safeguard against the priests gaining control over the people by a monopoly of knowledge on the rituals of worship. An informed laity could check the priests, making sure they were performing the rituals correctly and were not enriching themselves unethically through improper appropriation of the sacrifices. An informed laity could not be intimidated through threats of excommunication or of God's wrath if they did not do as the priests said. History abundantly illustrates the abuses of priestly classes holding a monopoly of esoteric religious and ritualistic knowledge and using that knowledge to oppress and exploit people. Priestly duties and privileges in other cultures in the ancient Near East were closely guarded secrets, passed along hereditary lines within elite guilds. It was by their secret crafts that the priests of these other peoples could maintain their power. Israel was distinct from all these nations, as is her God dis-

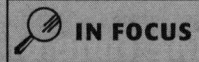

IN FOCUS "offering"

(Heb. *qorban*) (Lev. 1:2; 2:1; Ezek. 20:28) Strong's #7133: This Hebrew word is derived from the verb "to bring near," and it literally means "that which one brings near to God." The fact that the Israelites had such an opportunity to present their gifts to God reveals His mercy. Even though they were sinful and rebellious, God instituted a sacrificial system in which they could reconcile themselves to Him. Jesus' death on the Cross was the ultimate offering, the offering that ended the need for any others. For through the sacrifice of His sinless life, we have once for all been reconciled to God (Heb. 10:10–18). An appropriate response to Jesus' death for us is to offer our lives as living sacrifices to God (Rom. 12:1).

tinct from all their gods. **any one:** This is a general term (Heb. *'dm;* compare *adam*, "man") and specifically includes women. The term can refer to those who are not descendants of Abraham. Any person may come to faith in God and worship with God's people (Num. 15:14, 16, 29).

1:3 The **burnt sacrifice** (Heb. *'ola*, meaning "rising up") was the only sacrifice that was entirely consumed on the altar. It foreshadows the total sacrifice of Christ on the Cross. It also symbolizes that the worshiper must hold nothing in reserve when coming to God; everything is consumed in the relationship between God and the sincere worshiper. **male without blemish:** The use of males for sacrifice did not threaten the Israelites' flocks and herds, which required no more than one male to every five females to continue breeding. Still, a male without blemish was of great value to the worshiper. It would have been prime breeding stock and was a potential source of wool and meat, or of money if sold. To offer it on the altar was a real sacrifice. The principle still holds: God's people are to offer their best as a symbol that they are offering all that is theirs. A person should offer **of his own free will.** True sacrifice to the Lord is to be done with an attitude of joy—no half-hearted obedience. **door of the**

tabernacle: A person's sins had to be atoned for before he or she could come before God. **before the LORD**: God was present everywhere, but His presence was felt in an unusual manner at the site of His holy worship.

1:4 Each worshiper brought his or her own offering and then placed his or her own **hand** on the animal's **head.** No one could send another person to offer sacrifices for his or her own sins. By the same token, no one today can send someone else to accept the atonement that Jesus Christ purchased with His sacrifice on Calvary. This key idea (from the Heb. verb *kaphar*, "to wipe clean," "to ransom") has the meaning here, "to expiate." The life of the sacrificial animal, substituted for the life of the offender, expiated the offender's sin, thus averting God's wrath.

1:5–9 This section details the procedures when the sacrifice was a bull. Both the worshiper and the priests had several tasks. The worshiper killed the sacrifice; the priests collected the blood and sprinkled it on the altar. The worshiper skinned and cut up the sacrifice; the priests laid the wood and the cleaner parts of the sacrifice upon the altar. The worshiper washed the entrails and the legs; the priests burned the entire sacrifice. True worship is

---

🌱 IN LIFE   **Taking Sin Seriously**

The ancient Israelites took sin far more seriously that many people today do. Consider the impact of carrying out the instructions given for burnt-offering sacrifices (Lev. 1:3–5):

- *The psychological impact.* If you were a Hebrew at the time of Moses, you had to do the killing of your animal sacrifice. You had to place your hand on the animal's head as you slit its throat and felt its life drain away, all the while knowing that the animal was symbolically dying in your place.
- *The financial impact.* The required sacrifice for the burnt offering was a bull, which was to be among the best of your herd. No doubt you had other animals for food and trade. Still, no rancher likes to lose even one animal, particularly a prize bull. So the sacrifice involved a financial burden, a tangible reminder of the penalty of sin. Even those who could not afford bulls had to make sacrifices in line with their means (Lev. 1:10, 14; 5:7, 8).
- *The social impact.* As you slaughtered your animal, you were accompanied by other worshipers slaughtering their animals. As you listened to the death cries of cattle, sheep, and birds, you realized that every person around you—your relatives, your neighbors, even your leaders—were sinners who needed God's forgiveness.
- *The spiritual impact.* Overall, the sacrificial system reminded you that sin stood between you and God, and that the penalty for sin was death. You were also reminded of God's mercy, in that He accepted the death of an animal instead of your own death.

In short, regular animal sacrifices made it difficult to regard sin lightly. We do well to remember the ultimate substitutionary sacrifice that the animals' deaths represented, one far more precious, the very body and blood of Jesus Christ.

active; the worshiper cannot be a passive observer. One of the terms for "worship" in the Hebrew Bible is drawn from the verb meaning "to serve" (Heb. *'abad*). This is appropriate because a great deal of the procedures of biblical worship were actions of strong exertion and involvement.

1:5–8 the priests, Aaron's sons: Aaron was Moses' older brother and the one whom God had designated to be high priest of Israel (Ex. 28:1). Aaron's sons were Nadab, Abihu, Eleazar, and Ithamar. They and their descendants would be priests in the tabernacle. For details concerning Nadab and Abihu's untimely end, read ch. 10. **sprinkle the blood:** The blood, the bearer of life, was the most important part of the sacrifice. The lifeblood of the sacrificial animal on the altar substituted for the life of the guilty worshiper.

1:9 sweet aroma to the Lord: Never, in this image or elsewhere, does Scripture represent God as eating the offerings brought to Him, as the pagan gods were thought to do. When sacrifice was done in faith and with a free will (v. 3), it was accepted by the Lord as desirable or "sweet." The same is true of the death of His Son. Because the death of Jesus provided our salvation, Isaiah said, "It pleased the Lord to bruise Him" (Is. 53:10).

1:10–13 The procedure for the burnt offering was the same when the animal was a sheep or a goat (Ex. 12:5).

1:14–17 While the richest Israelites offered bulls, most of the people offered sheep or goats. The poorest were allowed to bring **turtledoves or young pigeons.** All sacrifices required the active participation of the worshiper. The Israelite who brought a pair of birds was required to help prepare them for the altar. The different offerings were accepted by God without prejudice or favoritism. Economic standing is not a measure of acceptability before God (James 2:1–9).

2:1–16 This chapter outlines the procedures for the grain offering and what could and could not be included. The offerings from livestock emphasized the aspect of substitution in Israel's

sacrificial worship, the life of the animal for the life of the worshiper. The grain offering emphasized Israel's dependence upon God for daily existence; bread was, then as now, the "staff of life." To present an offering from the most important daily food was to thank God for providing that food; it also was to declare one's trust that He would continue to provide it.

2:1 Anyone (Heb. *nephesh*, often translated "soul") is an inclusive term emphasizing that male or female, native Israelite or convert, could come to God with an offering (1:2). **Fine flour** was from the best grain and was free from impurities. This flour was fit for the king's table (1 Kin. 4:22; Ezek. 16:13) and was served to honored guests (Gen. 18:6). As with animal sacrifices, the offering was to be from the best the worshiper had. Olive **oil,** an important product of the Promised Land, was a primary part of the diet and a prominent symbol of blessing and prosperity, not just in Israel but around the Mediterranean. **Frankincense** was a costly incense from South Arabia and East Africa. Both its fragrance and value enhanced the grain offering. As an imported luxury, frankincense had to be bought with money. By including frankincense in this offering, every aspect of an Israelite's wealth was made a part of what he or she offered to God.

2:2 The handful of the offering burned on the altar included **all the frankincense.** This helped to make the offering **a sweet aroma to the Lord.**

2:3 Aaron's and his sons': A significant portion of the priests' daily food came from this part of the grain offering. **most holy:** Only the consecrated priests were allowed to eat the offerings, and only within the tabernacle (6:16). What is holy must be used in a holy place, by holy people, in a holy manner.

2:4–7 These verses list three types of *cooked* grain offerings: (1) bread **baked in the oven;** (2) cakes **baked** or fried **in a pan**—that is, on a flat plate or griddle; and (3) cakes **baked in a covered pan.** All were made of **fine flour mixed with oil.** Since most of these offerings were eaten by the priests, frankincense was left

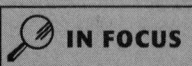 **IN FOCUS**   **"memorial portion"**

(Heb. *'azkarah*) (Lev. 2:2, 9, 16; Num. 5:26) Strong's #234: A memorial portion of a grain offering was a small portion burnt on the altar in place of the whole amount. The rest was a gift to the priest, to support him in his ministry. The word for *memorial portion* is related to the Hebrew verb *zakar*, which means "to remember." It signifies the worshiper's remembering of God's gracious character and generosity, especially God's remembering and blessing of the worshiper.

out of them. Frankincense would have permeated a cake if baked into it.

2:8–10 The priests' presentation of these cooked grain offerings on the **altar** was essentially the same as for the uncooked grain offerings.

2:9 The term **memorial portion** (Heb. *'azkaratah,* from the verb *zakar,* "to remember") occurs three times in the descriptions of the cereal offerings (2:2, 9, 16). It may well signify both the worshiper's remembering of God's gracious character and gracious acts toward the worshiper and God's remembering and blessing of the worshiper, for which he or she prayed in the act of offering.

2:10, 11 Prohibiting **leaven** in grain offerings that were burned on the altar might have been based on the same principle that prohibited eating the blood of animals. As blood is the life force of animals, leaven represents the life force of the vegetable kingdom. It is also possible that leaven and honey were both prohibited because they cause fermentation, which represents corruption.

2:12 A separate offering of the **firstfruits** of the harvest is described later (23:9–21).

2:13 The salt of the covenant of your God was to be used in every grain offering. (Salt as a symbol of covenant was also known among the Greeks and the Arabs.) Every such offering was a reminder of the covenant God had made with Israel at Sinai and of the worshiper's obligation and privilege to remain faithful to God and God's covenant. Jesus may have had covenant faithfulness in mind when He told His followers, "You are the salt of the earth" (Matt. 5:13).

2:14–16 This **grain offering** was prepared and presented at the altar in the same way as those already described. As they had to be prepared from fine flour, so this one had to be prepared from the first of the year's grain harvest. The principle was reaffirmed: only the best of a person's resources is good enough to offer to God.

3:1–7 When sin had been atoned with the burnt offering, it was appropriate to bring the **peace offering.** After this sacrifice, the meat was returned to the worshiper and his family to be eaten as a festive meal. Birds were not among the species listed for the peace offering because they would not supply sufficient meat for such a meal. Also, that special provision for the poor was unnecessary, since this was a voluntary offering. The procedures for offering the sacrifice were the same, whether it was from the cattle, the sheep, or the goats. However, the chapter reviews the procedures for each separately, so it is essentially three repetitions of the same instructions, with minor variations.

3:1 peace offering: The Hebrew word for *peace* (*shalôm*) means "wholeness, completeness, soundness, health." When a person has this, in all its dimensions, that person is at peace. The peace offerings were times of feasting, drinking, talking, singing, and enjoying salvation as a great gift from God (7:11–21). Paul describes Jesus Christ as our perfect peace offering (Col. 1:20). Unlike the burnt sacrifice, the peace offering could be either **male or female.** Like the burnt sacrifice, it had to be **without blemish** because it was offered **before the LORD.**

3:2 As with the burnt sacrifice, the presenter was an active participant in the peace offering (vv. 8, 13). He brought the animal, laid **his hand** on its **head,** and killed it. Then the priests sprinkled **the blood all around on the altar.** The blood, representing life, was the first sacrifice to God.

3:3, 4 The fat, the **two kidneys,** and the fatty lobe attached to the **liver** (vv. 9, 10, 14, 15) specifically belonged to God. The fat was the most prized portion of the meat. The kidneys were viewed as the seat of the emotions. The liver was the essential organ for telling the future in the pagan cultures surrounding Israel (Ezek. 21:21); such fortune-telling was strictly forbidden in Israel (Deut. 18:10). These portions, burned on the altar, were given to God as the best of the sacrificial animal. In addition, the offering of the fatty lobe attached to the liver demonstrated reliance on God for the future rather than on pagan gods. Burning the liver, or even a portion of it, meant that it could not be used for fortune-telling.

3:5, 6 Upon the burnt sacrifice indicates that the peace offering normally followed the burnt offering, which was entirely consumed on the altar. Being reconciled to God through the burnt offering, the worshiper was in a position to fellowship with God and with his or her family by sharing in the feast of the peace offering. Repentance and reconciliation must come before genuine fellowship.

3:7 before the LORD: Not a redundancy, but a reminder of the Lamb of God and that all offerings are offered before God (1:3).

3:8, 9 the whole fat tail: The tail of the Palestinian broad-tailed sheep is almost entirely fat and can weigh more than 16 pounds. This explains its special mention in the regulations for offering the fat of the sheep.

3:10, 11 The mention of **food** does not mean that God desired, needed, or ate the sacrifice, as the pagan gods were thought to do.

3:12–15 In the regulations for offering a **goat,** the animal's sex is not mentioned as it is in the regulations for cattle and sheep. Otherwise, the regulations for the sacrifice of a goat are the same as those for the sacrifice of a sheep.

3:16 **All the fat is the LORD's** is a reminder that our gifts to God must be from the best that we have.

3:17 **perpetual . . . dwellings:** Some regulations in the Law of Moses could be observed only in the land that God was giving the Israelites. However, this prohibition of eating fat or blood applied wherever an Israelite might live. There were no exceptions. These sacrificial regulations consistently emphasize the theme of *only the best for God.* As it was in ancient Israel, so it is today. Only our best is good enough to give to God. The prohibition of **blood** is explained in 17:11–14. It is worth noting that this prohibition was laid on Noah as well (Gen. 9:4). The prohibition here in 3:17 was for the Hebrew people as a part of God's plan in making them distinct from the nations.

4:1–5:13 These are the offerings for purification from unintentional sin. Not only the purification of the sinner is in view here but also the purity of the tabernacle because of pollution from people's sin. The sin, or purification, offering was prescribed according to the position of the person(s) committing the offense. The sin of the high priest, or of the entire congregation, polluted more deeply, requiring a more serious remedy. A ruler of the people, likewise, incurred more serious pollution than an ordinary citizen, so the remedy was more radical. The same principle holds today; the more prominent and influential the sinner, the more widely harmful the sin.

4:1, 2 **sins unintentionally:** Sin that occurred without the sinner realizing it still offended the holiness of God and polluted His earthly dwelling place, just as clothing may be soiled without the wearer knowing it. To be used again, both the clothing and the tabernacle required cleansing.

4:3 **anointed priest:** Since the high priest represented the people before God, his sin

brought **guilt on the people.** Until the sin was atoned for, the priest could not come before God, and the people's most important intermediary with God was set aside. **A young bull** was the most expensive sacrifice required for the purification offering, reflecting the importance of the high priest's office.

4:4, 5 The steps in offering different animals were similar, with small but important variations (vv. 14, 15, 22–24, 27–29, 33). Whether it was the **bull** for the **anointed priest** or the **whole congregation,** the male **kid** for the **ruler,** or the female **kid** or **lamb** for the **common** person, the worshiper brought the animal, laid a hand on its head, and killed it. These actions emphasized that the offering was to atone for the worshiper's sin. The most elaborate ritual was the blood ritual for the anointed priest. He himself did this, for there was no one higher to represent him before God. Since only the High Priest was allowed to enter the Most Holy Place, his was the only individual sin to pollute it.

4:6 **Seven** symbolizes completeness in the Bible, based on the seven days of creation in Gen. 1; 2. The **veil** was a heavy linen curtain that separated the Most Holy Place from the rest of the tabernacle (Ex. 26:31). Sprinkling the **blood** before, or on, the **veil** purified the Most Holy Place.

4:7 **The altar of sweet incense** was in the Holy Place (Ex. 30:1–6). Incense, not an animal sacrifice, was burned on this altar. Still, this part of the tabernacle also needed purification— through the application of blood—from the pollution of the priest's sin.

4:8–10 The instructions concerning the **fat** were the same as for the fat of the peace offering.

4:11, 12 Burning **the whole bull** ensured that the priest did not profit in any way from his own sin or from the atonement for his sin. Car-

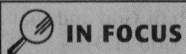 **IN FOCUS** | **"blood"**

(Heb. *dam*) (Lev. 3:2; 4:5; Ex. 12:13; Is. 1:11). Strong's #1818: This word is related to the Hebrew word *'adom,* which means "red" (Gen. 25:30) and refers to the blood of animals (Ex. 23:18) or human beings (Gen. 4:10). In the Scriptures, blood may be a synonym for death (Judg. 9:24) or even murder (Jer. 19:4). The word *blood* may also represent a person's guilt, as in the phrase "his blood shall be upon him"—that is, he is responsible for his own guilt (20:9). The OT equates *life* with *blood* (Gen. 9:4; Deut. 12:23), which vividly illustrates the sanctity of human life (Gen. 9:6). According to the NT, "without shedding of blood there is no remission" of sin (Heb. 9:22). Thus the emphasis on blood in the OT sacrifices pointed to the blood Christ would shed on our behalf (Rom. 5:9; 1 Cor. 11:25, 26).

rying it **outside the camp** was another way of symbolizing the seriousness of the pollution of the tabernacle caused by the high priest's sin. The part of the bull not burned on the altar could not be used for any other purpose. It needed to be disposed of entirely.

4:12 Even the **ashes** from the altar symbolized the atonement necessary for sin. Therefore, the ground **outside the camp** where they were **poured out** was considered **clean.**

4:13 whole congregation: All the people of Israel. **hidden:** A sin committed without anyone being aware of it, or without the one responsible knowing that it was sin.

4:14–21 Because the sin was the responsibility of the whole congregation, including the priests and the High Priest himself, the pollution of the sin reached into the innermost part of the tabernacle, as it did with the sin of the High Priest. Thus the ritual was the same, including the sprinkling of the blood of the sacrifice **in front of the veil,** and the placing of blood upon **the horns of the altar.**

4:15 The elders represented the whole **congregation** as they laid their **hands on the head of the bull.**

4:16–22 ruler: Literally, "one lifted up" (Heb. *nasi'*), a leader or chief of the people. The leader of the whole nation (judge or king) or a group (such as the chiefs and representatives of all the tribes) could be called by this name.

4:23, 24 A kid of the goats was designated for a ruler of the people. Since he was a civil and not a religious leader, his sin polluted the sanctuary less seriously than did the sin of the high priest or the sin of the whole congregation.

4:25 The altar of burnt offering stood in the outer court of the tabernacle. The pollution of a ruler's sin did not penetrate to the holy place or to the Most Holy Place (where the ark of the covenant stood), as did the pollution due to the sin of the high priest or the congregation.

4:26 The priest was not guilty of sin in this case, so he was entitled to the meat from the sacrificial animal brought by the ruler.

4:27–35 common people: Literally, "the people of the land," those who held no religious, civil, or military office.

5:1 utterance of an oath: Anyone with information regarding the oath was obligated to come forward and give testimony. Regardless of whether the person's information was firsthand or secondhand, if he did not testify, he became guilty and had to bring a purification offering. It was not *having* the information, but *withholding* it that made the person guilty.

5:2 unclean: The difference between clean and unclean animals is carefully spelled out in ch. 11. **beast:** Larger wild animals. **livestock:** Domesticated animals. **creeping things:**

Smaller wild animals, including reptiles, small mammals, and insects. **unaware of it:** Either by not noticing that he had touched the carcass or by forgetting before bringing the purification offering.

5:3 human uncleanness: Primarily the body fluids that caused a person to become unclean (ch. 15). Contact with a corpse would also be included, as would contact with another

INSIGHT Ritual Uncleanness

The uncleanness treated in Leviticus is ritual uncleanness. Being unclean in this sense means to be excluded from normal participation in religious acts. For instance, a person could become unclean due to touching a corpse (Lev. 5:2), but this is not an immoral or a sinful act. The offerings were the means for removing such uncleanness.

person's waste. The ancient Israelites knew nothing about microbiology. But God, who knows everything, gave the Israelites certain laws that prevented disease and made them distinct from their neighbors.

5:4 thoughtlessly: Rashly, in the grip of strong emotion or without thinking the matter through. **to do evil or to do good:** A rash vow is rash, whether the intention is good or evil. In any case, the guilt brought on by a rash vow needed to be atoned for. **unaware of it:** Certainly a person would know when he was making a vow, but he might not realize its full implications. He could also forget a vow to do good and fail to fulfill it. **when he realizes it:** At that point, the person's guilt had to be atoned for by the purification offering. The rash vow of Jephthah should be considered in this light (Judg. 11). Jephthah should have considered the sin of his vow and confessed his folly, rather than to proceed with further evil by keeping a vow that never should have been made. It is not a light thing to fail to perform a vow that has been made to the living God. But neither is it a wise thing to act upon a vow when that vow itself was sinful from its inception.

5:5 in any of these matters: Any of the situations described in vv. 1–4. This was a reminder that these sins were to be taken seriously; they required atonement. **confess:** The rituals of sacrifice were not automatic in their effect. The worshiper had to recognize, acknowledge, and repent of the sin.

5:6 trespass offering: This offering is not the same as the trespass offering prescribed in the next section. This section still deals with purification offerings for inadvertent guilt.

5:7 If he is not able: If he cannot afford it. **two turtledoves:** Part of the purification offering was burned on the altar and part was not burned. To accomplish this when offering birds, the worshiper brought two.

5:8–10 The first bird for the sin offering was sacrificed for its blood. The second was burned, like the fat and vital organs of the larger animals.

5:11–13 The purification offering was for inadvertent sin. Since every person sins inadvertently, whether by commission or by omission, provision was made for those who could not even afford to bring two birds.

5:11 one-tenth of an ephah: Approximately two quarts. **Oil** and **frankincense** were not added as they were to the grain offering. This was a purification offering; it had to be pure flour.

5:12, 13 Part of the offering was burned **on the altar,** as was part of the animal sacrifices. The rest belonged to the priests, as did the remainder of the animal sacrifices (except the burnt offerings) brought by ordinary citizens.

5:14–6:7 This section deals with the trespass, or reparation, offering for a breach of faith against God. This could be with regard to the sanctuary, to its holy things, to one of the commandments, or to another person. In the Hebrew text this section is a part of ch. 5.

5:15 commits a trespass: This phrase refers both to the objective responsibility of a sinner for his or her actions and the subjective feeling of guilt experienced by the offender. The

offering righted the wrong of the offense and cleared the conscience of the sinner. **the holy things of the Lord:** Anything separated from common use and dedicated to the sacred use of the Lord—the tabernacle, its furnishings and utensils, the sacrificial food reserved for the priests, the tithes, and any other gifts given to the sanctuary. **the shekel of the sanctuary:** Slightly heavier than the shekel used in ordinary transactions in the marketplace. The common shekel was about eleven and a half grams, or four-tenths of an ounce; the sanctuary shekel was about twelve and a half grams.

5:16 make restitution: A guiding principle of biblical law and ethics is that when a person has caused harm to another, whether to God or to another human being, the one offending is responsible to make good the loss. **add one-fifth to it:** As a fine, in addition to the ram and the full **restitution.** The restitution and fine were paid first, as evidence of the offender's genuine repentance. Then the priest sacrificed the ram as atonement.

5:17 he does not know: Ignorance did not make an offense harmless. The offender was still **guilty** and bore responsibility for his **iniquity.** He might also be troubled in his conscience, though he might never learn the exact nature of his offense. People often experienced dread that they had committed unwitting offense against God, His sanctuary, or His holy things.

5:18 In such a situation, the offering of a ram (without restitution or fine, since the value of what had been taken or harmed could not be determined) brought atonement for the unknown offense. **His ignorance in which he erred and did not know it:** This was not a sin of rebellion, but one for which the offender

IN LIFE **Making Restitution**

Some modern law-makers, educators, and others concerned with human behavior often make proposals based on the idea that people are basically good. In Leviticus, God held a more realistic view. For example, He knew that there would be cases of dishonesty among His people. So instead of excusing the offenses as the result of bad upbringing and proposing more education as a preventative, He instituted a system of sacrifices for the sin of the offender and restitution to the offended party (Lev. 6:1–7). It's easy to see why such laws were needed. Israel was a refugee nation traveling through a desert. Every day the people faced limited resources, so they may have found it easy to rationalize theft and deception. Temptations were many, and sooner or later people succumbed.

To address this problem, God called sin *sin* and devised a guide for forgiveness and restitution. If someone deceived another in a transaction, the perpetrator was required to sacrifice a ram and to repay the loss with 20 percent interest. The guiding law behind restitution was that of loving one's neighbor as oneself (Lev. 19:18). Centuries later, Christ reaffirmed this as the guiding principle for moral and social issues (Matt. 5:43, 44; 19:19).

earnestly desired to atone, though he did not know what it was.

5:19 he has certainly trespassed against the LORD: This could also be phrased as "He has certainly made reparation to the Lord." The emphasis on the worshiper's ignorance of his sin and his uneasy conscience was matched here by the statement that his offering had been accepted. He was forgiven, and his conscience could rest. Isaiah (53:10) used this verb (Heb. *'asham*) to assure the believer that the Coming One would make reparation for all sin, even the sin the offender does not know of and cannot discover. Thus the Hebrew wording of this verse is nearly the opposite of the common translation. A guilty conscience need not torment the believer today; reparation has been made.

6:1–7 This section deals with the trespass/reparation offering as it applies to harm caused to other people.

6:2, 3 a trespass against the LORD: The offenses listed were against people. However, they also wronged God because the offender used God's name in vain in the oath he used to swear his innocence in court. **lying to his neighbor:** Saying the property was lost, stolen, or destroyed, when he had kept it for himself. **delivered to him for safekeeping:** In the absence of banks, people would leave valuables with trusted neighbors or business associates when they went on a long journey. **a pledge:** A security deposit or collateral on a loan. **any one of these things:** In all these cases, a person betrayed his neighbor's trust, taking or keeping property illegally and then lying about it under oath. Since in court it was one person's sworn word against another's, the wronged person had little recourse.

6:4 is guilty: Objectively, he had done wrong. Subjectively, he became conscience-stricken. Since his oath in court had placed him beyond the reach of punishment, only the offender's guilty conscience could bring him to

justice. **shall restore:** Restitution was necessary before anything else when someone had wronged another by taking what was rightfully his. Zacchaeus recognized the principle of restitution when he encountered Jesus (Luke 19:8).

6:5, 6 As with sin concerning the holy things (5:16), restitution and a **one-fifth** fine were evidence of genuine repentance. Then the offender could bring the ram for the trespass offering and be forgiven for the sin against God of swearing falsely in God's name. Jesus preserved this order for the person who remembered at the altar that he had offended his brother (Matt. 5:23, 24).

6:7–9 Aaron and his sons, the priests, were responsible for the correct preparation and presentation of all offerings. **shall be kept burning:** The fire on the altar was never to go out. This was accomplished at night with a burnt offering that was not extinguished. It could have been stoked with wood through the night to keep it burning. After being renewed in the morning (v. 12), the fire was kept going throughout the day for the succession of burnt or whole offerings from various individuals (ch. 1), for the grain offerings burned on the altar (ch. 2), and for the fat of the peace offerings (ch. 3), the sin offerings (4:1—5:13), and the trespass offerings (5:14—6:7).

6:10 linen garment . . . linen trousers: The sacred clothing of the priests, worn only in the tabernacle (16:4; Ex. 28:40–43). The trousers were a linen undergarment that prevented immodest exposure as the priest ascended and descended the altar ramp. This modesty communicated to the Israelites that human sexuality could not influence God. That idea was a central feature of Baal worship, which continually tempted the Israelites. The priests of Baal would use obscene gestures and actions in the pagan worship of their depraved god.

6:11 The linen **garments** were worn only

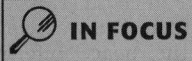 **IN FOCUS**   **"priest"**

(Heb. *kohen*) (Lev. 1:5; 6:6; 27:21; 2 Chr. 35:2) Strong's #3548: Priesthood was not unique to the Israelites. From the Egyptians to the Philistines, all the ancient Middle Eastern nations had a class of priests. At Mount Sinai, God consecrated Aaron and his descendants as priests (Ex. 28:1). They were to be representatives of the people before God, offering sacrifices and prayers on their behalf. Furthermore, they instructed the people about their religious duties and the character of God (Deut. 33:8–10). The NT describes Jesus Christ as our High Priest (Heb. 5:10). Through His death on the Cross, the formal priesthood was abolished (Heb. 10:11, 12). In its stead, all believers become priests—not to offer sacrifices but to pray, worship God, and witness to others about Jesus (Heb. 13:15, 16; 1 Pet. 2:5, 9; Rev. 1:5, 6).

within the tabernacle. They were not worn when carrying the ashes **outside the camp.**

6:12, 13 the fire . . . shall not be put out: Five times in this paragraph the priests are instructed to keep the fire burning. There are at least three reasons for this: (1) The original fire on the altar came from God (9:24). (2) Perpetual fire symbolized the perpetual worship of God. (3) Perpetual fire symbolized the continual need for atonement and reconciliation with God, which was the purpose of the offerings. If the ashes were cleaned off the altar every morning, the fire would have been at its lowest at that point. It was renewed with **wood.** Then the morning **burnt offering** was sacrificed, followed by other offerings through the day.

6:14–18 all the males . . . Aaron: This included all the priests, as well as descendants of Aaron who were disqualified from the priesthood for some reason (21:16–23). **statute forever:** "For all the age," or for as long as sacrifices are offered. **must be holy:** Only those who had been made holy or had been consecrated to God could touch or use the reserved sacrificial portions.

6:19–23 Because this was the daily grain offering of the high priest it was not included in the instructions for the sacrifices of the congregation.

6:20, 21 beginning . . . anointed: The high priest personally was to offer this sacrifice twice daily for as long as he was in office. **one-tenth of an ephah:** About two quarts. **half of it . . . at night:** The idea of a morning and an evening appointment with God is ancient. It is a precious privilege, open to every believer through the high priestly work of Christ. **at night:** More precisely, "in the evening"—at the time of the evening sacrifice.

6:22 The priest . . . in his place: Aaron's successors as high priest, beginning with his son Eleazar (Num. 20:25–28). **statute forever:** This grain offering and the burnt offering were sacrificed daily—with some interruptions, most notably during the Exile—until the destruction of the temple in A.D. 70. Even in the periods of Judah's worst apostasy, the evidence suggests that the daily offerings continued, though often for incorrect or inadequate reasons (Is. 1:10–17; Jer. 7:8–15; Mic. 6:6–8).

6:23 it shall not be eaten: The priests could eat most of the grain offerings brought by the people (2:3, 10). The principle here was that no one should profit from an offering which he himself had given.

6:24–30 Instructions for the priests about the sin, or purification, offering (4:1—5:13).

6:27 The blood of the sin offering was for the atonement of the one bringing the offering;

as such, the blood was holy, intended for a specific, holy purpose. The blood could be washed from a **garment** only **in a holy place.**

6:28, 29 It here refers to the flesh of the sin offering. The breaking of the **earthen vessel,** a clay cooking pot, is a striking contrast to the scouring of the **bronze pot.** No reason is given for the different treatment. However, the answer may be that a clay vessel is permeable and the residue of cooking could never be removed completely from it, even by a thorough scrubbing. The ancients knew nothing about microbiology; but God knows all things! Broth would not permeate a bronze pot and could be removed completely from it. That which is holy must not be profaned. Sacrificing

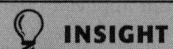

INSIGHT | Pottery

Pottery was a common product in ancient times. The objects made of clay were baked to make them hard and permanent. Quality was determined by the type of clay, the heat, and the evenness of firing. The firing process required experience and skill. Still, the whole process was cheap enough that even in ancient times some pottery vessels were intended to be disposed (Lev. 6:28).

the clay vessel, as it were, prevented profaning even the smallest part of the flesh of the sin offering, which was most holy (vv. 25, 29).

6:30 The blood of the sin offering for the priest and of that for the entire congregation was **brought into the tabernacle of meeting** (4:5–7, 16–18). Because no one should profit from an offering given to atone for his own sin, the priests were forbidden to eat the flesh of these offerings.

7:1, 2 In the place: At the door of the tabernacle of meeting before the Lord (1:3).

7:3, 4 The burning of the **fat** was commanded as it was for the peace offering (3:9–11). The fat was considered the best part of the meat. As such, it was not to be eaten by the worshiper or the priest. Instead, it was offered to God. Our best is still the measure of what we should offer to God.

7:5–7 the priest who makes atonement: That is, the individual officiating priest. Since many individual Israelites would have brought both trespass and sin offerings, the priests would take turns officiating for them and would receive equal proportions of the sacrifices.

7:8 The skin was the only part of the burnt

offering that was not burned (1:6). The officiating priest received it as part of his wages.

7:9 Each Israelite's baked **grain offering** belonged to the individual priest **who offered it,** as did the flesh of an animal offered as a sin or a trespass offering (v. 7).

7:10 By contrast, an offering of unbaked grain belonged to **all the sons of Aaron, to one as much as the other.** No priest was to be deprived of his rightful share in the sacrifices brought by the congregation. The priests were consecrated to the service of God, and their welfare and that of their families depended on the provisions from the sacrifices. The principle remains valid: No one called to serve the people of God as a vocation may be deprived of a fair living.

7:11–21 Instructions for the priests concerning the peace offering (commanded in Lev. 3). Three kinds of peace offering were possible: (1) thanksgiving, a confession of human dependence on God's grace and mercy, and a praise of the living God (v. 12); (2) marking the fulfillment of a vow (v. 16); (3) and voluntary, or free-will, offering (v. 16). A peace offering could be a male or female animal from the cattle, the sheep, or the goats.

7:12, 13 The sacrifice of **thanksgiving** (Heb. *tôdâ*, "a public acknowledgement {in praise}") was a public proclamation of who God is and what He does. The word is familiar from the Book of Psalms. A thanksgiving offering required three kinds of **unleavened cakes** and **leavened bread.**

7:14 The **heave offering** was a "present" or contribution to the officiating priest as his portion of the thanksgiving offering (Ex. 29:26–28; Lev. 7:29–34). The offering was waved before the Lord as an acknowledgment that He is the giver of all gifts.

7:15 the same day it is offered: The festive worshiper bringing his peace offering for a family feast at the tabernacle demonstrated trust in God for the next day's provision. He did not worry about saving food for the next day. When feasting and rejoicing in the presence of God, generosity is entirely appropriate.

7:16, 17 the next day . . . may be eaten: The **vow** and the **voluntary** peace offering were slightly less solemn than the thanksgiving (or confession) peace offering. Therefore, any leftovers from them could be eaten on the second day without jeopardizing the purity of the tabernacle.

7:18 it shall not be . . . imputed: The sacrifice would lose all its benefit to the worshiper. This was so even if the one eating the meat was not the one who had brought the offering. **It shall be an abomination** may be rephrased, "It shall be rotten or spoiled." This would be true

first in the physical sense: Unrefrigerated two-day-old meat would spoil. But it also would be rotten in the sense of an unclean thing that contaminated the holy precincts.

7:19 touches any unclean thing: An unclean object pollutes a clean object. A similar principle applies to sterile objects in medicine. Touching a sterile object with a dirty object makes the sterile object unsterile.

7:20, 21 unclean: Chapters 11—15 and 22 detail various kinds of uncleanness in persons and things. **shall be cut off:** The person will be removed from membership in the covenant community. This meant either execution, banishment, or denial of citizenship privileges (worship, inheritance, and so on; Gen. 17:14). This concern for approaching God's presence in a state of ritual purity is reflected in Paul's instructions about the reverence and self-examination the Christian should use in approaching the Lord's Supper (1 Cor. 11:27–29).

7:22, 23 The **fat** was considered the best portion of the sacrificial animal; as such, it belonged to God.

7:24 used in any other way: That is, for softening leather, for fuel, or in any other way but eating it.

7:25–29 The portions of the peace **offering** that belonged to the Lord included the fat, which was burned on the altar (v. 31), and the breast and thigh, which were the priests' portions (vv. 30–34).

7:30 His own hands: A worshiper could not delegate his worship, thanksgiving, or praise. Worship by proxy was impossible. **The breast** was one of the finer portions of the meat that was allowed to be eaten. The breast of the sacrificial animal was brought to the priest as a **wave offering** or an elevated offering—raised by the worshiper in the presence of God and the priest—symbolizing that the entire sacrifice was dedicated to God.

7:31 The **breast** (the elevated offering) was **Aaron's and his sons';** it belonged to all the priests.

7:32, 33 heave offering: The **right** (front) **thigh** of the sacrificial animal belonged to the priest who performed the sacrifice. Thus the officiating priest received his individual portion the thigh (heave offering), and all the priests received a further portion the breast (wave offering).

7:34–36 So no one would begrudge the priests a share in the meat of the sacrificial animals, God reminded Israel that these portions really belonged to Him: **I have taken.** By this means, God provided for the livelihood of the priests and their families. Those who spend their lives in God's service deserve the support of God's people.

7:37, 38 A summary listing of the offerings of chs. 1—7, with the reminder that these sacrifices were prescribed by God Himself on Mount Sinai. What God **commanded** He made possible, by giving careful instruction (**the law of the . . . offering**) regarding the proper way to bring the offerings before Him. God does not leave His people to wonder how they may approach Him and please Him. All these offerings foreshadow, in one way or another, the perfect sacrifice of Christ upon Calvary.

8:1–10:20 The first of two narrative sections in Leviticus. This one describes the inauguration of Israel's priesthood. The ordination of Aaron and his sons (ch. 8) was followed by Aaron's first offering of sacrifices (ch. 9). Chapter 10 concerns the deaths of Nadab and Abihu and the aftermath.

8:1, 2 Aaron had presided over Israel's idolatry with the golden calf. Now God gave him a second chance by allowing him to be ordained as God's own high priest. His ministry would affect all Israelites by atoning for their sins and bringing them into fellowship with God. **the garments:** The high priestly clothing that Aaron wore, prescribed by God to Moses in Ex. 28:1–39. **anointing oil:** Made from myrrh, cinnamon, cane, cassia, and olive oil (Ex. 30:23–25).

8:3 the congregation: The ordination of the priests was so important that all the people needed to witness it.

8:4, 5 This is what the LORD commanded, or similar words, is noted nine times in this chapter (vv. 4, 5, 9, 13, 17, 21, 29, 34, 36). It was important that God's instructions for worship be carried out meticulously. Sloppy, careless, or thoughtless worship did not honor God.

8:6 Moses brought Aaron: As the prophet of God and the leader of God's people (Deut. 18:15–18; 34:1–12), Moses was the only person qualified to ordain Aaron and his sons as Israel's priests. Until Moses ordained them, they were not priests and could not lead Israel's worship. Moses' prophetic ministry took precedence over

Aaron's priestly ministry. **washed them with water:** This symbolized moral purity.

8:7 The **ephod** was the magnificent outer garment of the high priest, made of gold thread; violet, purple, and scarlet woolen thread; and fine linen thread (Ex. 28:5, 6).

8:8 the Urim and the Thummim: Sacred lots used to determine the will of God. What they looked like and how they were used is not known. Apparently, the high priest phrased questions so the answers would be "yes" or "no," depending on how the lots came up.

8:9 The golden plate was also known as **the holy crown** of the high priest. On it was engraved HOLINESS TO THE LORD (Ex. 28:36).

8:10–12 The anointing of the tabernacle and all its furnishings, and of Aaron as High Priest, removed them *from* common use and **consecrated** them—set them apart, sanctified them *to* and made them fit *for* the service of God. The anointing of Aaron began the consecration of people for special service in and for the community of God which continues in the church to the present day.

8:11 Since **the altar** was the central furnishing of the tabernacle for the atonement for sin, sprinkling it **seven times** represented the complete consecration of the tabernacle and all its furnishings and utensils to God's service.

8:12 anointed: The high priests of Israel, beginning here with Aaron, were anointed, as were the kings of Israel (1 Sam. 10:1; 16:13) and at least some of the prophets (1 Kin. 19:16). Jesus combines in His person the offices of High Priest, King, and Prophet, so He is *the* Anointed One, which is the meaning of the names Messiah and Christ.

8:13 While **Aaron's sons** were set apart or ordained as priests, they were not anointed. Only the high priest was anointed.

8:14–29 These verses describe Moses' offering of three sacrifices for Aaron and his sons. The first was the sin, or purification, offering (vv. 14–17), the second was the burnt offering (vv. 18–21), and the third (vv. 22–29) followed basi-

---

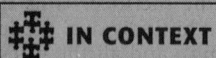 **IN CONTEXT** ## What Does It Take to Serve God?

Prospective priests had to be trained in the elaborate rituals detailed in the Law. But the text makes it plain that neither special ability nor the good fortune to be born into the tribe of Levi fully qualified a man to serve as a priest to the Lord. A man was fit for service only after his sins had been forgiven. For example, Moses prepared Aaron and his sons (Lev. 8:2, 3) by assembling them in front of the tabernacle and initiating their ministry with sacrifices to atone for their sins (8:14–36). Various qualifications might be mentioned for service in ministry today. But chief among them is still the requirement of being cleansed from sin (2 Tim. 2:1, 20).

cally the ritual of the peace offering. Because these were the very first sacrifices, some rituals were observed relating to the consecration of the altar and of Aaron and his sons which were not part of the "ordinary" sacrifices prescribed in Lev. 1—7. Because these sacrifices were part of the

Photo: Amsterdam Bible Museum

A model of Aaron in the distinctive dress of the high priest, including the ephod, breastplate, and turban (Lev. 8:6–9).

consecration service of the Aaronic priesthood (Aaron and his sons were not yet priests), Moses performed the priestly duties.

8:15–21 Moses' actions here were slightly different from the normal sin offering prescribed in ch. 4. The purpose is clear from the statement that he **purified the altar . . . and consecrated it.** The priests, the altar, and everything associated with the sacrificial system had to be pure and consecrated to God. Otherwise the sacrifices would not atone for the sins of Israel.

8:22–29 The manner of sacrificing the second ram with the unleavened bread most nearly resembled the peace offering (3:1–5) and

the grain offering (2:4–6). But there were significant differences because this was **the ram of consecration** for Aaron and his sons as priests.

8:23, 24 The reason for applying the blood of the sacrifice to Aaron's **ear, thumb,** and **big toe** is unclear. They were his extremities, top to bottom, possibly to represent the total covering of his sins by the sacrificial blood. Blood offering had also been applied to the horns of the altar (v. 15), signaling the close connection between the altar and the priests who ministered before it.

8:25, 26 The right thigh normally was the individual officiating priest's portion of the peace offering (7:32). In this case, it was a consecration offering for all the priests, so it was burned on the altar.

8:27–29 God received the **right thigh** burned upon the altar; Moses received the **breast.** Since both these portions normally went to the priests 7:31, 32, this arrangement may symbolize God and Moses together acting as priests to consecrate Aaron and his sons to Israel's priesthood, in keeping with the idea that one must be consecrated (made holy) by one who is already consecrated (holy).

8:29 Moses' part: Moses, acting as priest in this first sacrifice, received the breast, which from that time on would go to Aaron and his sons.

8:30–32 Moses' act of consecration here, though it used anointing oil together with blood from the altar, was different from his anointing of Aaron alone in v. 12.

8:33, 34 seven days: Becoming intercessors between God and the people was an extremely important step for Aaron and his sons—and for Israel. This period of confinement to the tabernacle emphasized the significance of the event. **consecrate you:** Literally, "fill your hand." In the physical sense, this referred to the fact that the priests' hands often would be filled with sacrifices as they served God in the tabernacle. In a greater sense, their consecration meant that their hands always would be filled with God's service to the exclusion of everything else.

8:35 That you may not die was a reminder that it is dangerous to approach God carelessly, without reverence, ignoring His instructions. Two of Aaron's sons failed to heed this warning and died (ch. 10).

8:36 For now, all those involved obeyed all the LORD had commanded. Their ordination was complete; their priesthood was valid. God would accept their service and their intercession for the people.

9:1 the eighth day: After the seven days of Aaron and his sons' consecration (8:33–36) were completed.

9:2 A young bull was the prescribed **sin offering** for the high priest (4:3). Before he could offer the sacrifices of others, his own sin needed atonement. The bull of the sin offering and the **ram** of the **burnt offering** (1:4, 10) accomplished this.

9:3 you shall speak: To this point Moses had given all the directions. Now that Aaron had been anointed high priest, it was fitting that he begin to instruct Israel on how to bring sacrifices. **A kid of the goats** was prescribed as the **sin offering** for individuals, a male goat for leaders (4:22, 23), and a female for ordinary citizens (4:27, 28).

9:4 All four of the regular public offerings—the burnt offering, the sin offering, the **peace** offering, and the **grain offering**—were performed on this first day of Israel's sacrificial worship in the tabernacle. The first two were specifically to atone for sin; the second two were for a feast of fellowship with God. Only the trespass, or reparation, offering was missing because it was a private offering (5:14—6:7). **the LORD** will appear to you: The purpose of all worship is to fellowship with God. The sacrifices were not an end in themselves; they allowed the worshiper to meet with God without being destroyed. The Israelites looked forward; we look back to Christ's atonement, by which we are ushered into God's presence.

9:5, 6 So they brought . . . and . . . drew near: The immediate and total obedience of the people is emphasized, in contrast with the complaining and rebellion that marked their response to Moses and to God (Ex. 32; Num. 14).

9:7 Before Aaron could **make atonement** for the people, he had to make atonement for himself.

9:8–21 Aaron offers the first sacrifices. The biblical narrators often took great pains to relate how people carried out the instructions. What to the modern reader seems like needless repetition of detail was to the ancients a satisfying

reassurance that what had been commanded had been completed faithfully.

9:8 The high priest had to kill **the calf of the sin offering** himself, since the sacrifice was for him. In Aaron's first attempt at being a priest for Israel, he had made a golden calf for the people to worship (Ex. 32). His first sacrifice as God's anointed high priest was a calf for his own sin offering. Aaron undoubtedly recognized the irony and praised God for His mercy. God had given Aaron a second chance. Truly, God is the God of the second chance for any who will respond to Him in faith!

9:9–11 Aaron did not sprinkle the **blood** before the veil (4:6). Also, the **altar** here is the altar of burnt offering, not the altar of incense (4:7). This variation from the normal pattern of the sin offering for the high priest was probably due to the fact that Aaron had not yet committed any sin that polluted the inner sanctuary. Therefore, its cleansing was not necessary. For regulations concerning the fat, flesh, and hide, read 4:8–12.

9:12–14 Because there was no variation from the general procedure for the **burnt offering,** the record of Aaron's performing this sacrifice is less detailed than the regulations for it (1:10–13). Aaron killed the ram himself (9:2), since it was a burnt offering for him and not for all the people.

9:15–17 The goat as the **sin offering** looked forward to the Day of Atonement (16:5, 9), rather than back to the normal sin offering for all the people, which required a bull (4:14).

9:18–21 The **peace offerings** for the people concluded the four offerings. Aaron had sacrificed a bull, a calf, and a ram for himself; and a kid, a calf, a lamb, a bull, a ram, and a grain offering for the people. On Aaron's first day as high priest, he offered all but one of the various sacrifices. The fact that God sent fire to consume these offerings signaled His future acceptance of all the sacrifices He had commanded the Israelites to bring—if they would

---

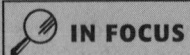 **IN FOCUS** | **"make atonement"**

(Heb. *kaphar*) (Lev. 1:4; 9:7; 14:18; 2 Sam. 21:3) Strong's #3722: In its various uses this word can mean "to cover," "to appease," or "to ransom." It can refer to monetary transaction, but in the Scriptures it more commonly speaks of payment for sin. All of the various offerings in the Jewish sacrificial system are described as effecting *atonement*. The key idea is that these offerings gained the favor of God, and God removed the worshiper's guilt. The sacrifice was presented as a substitute for the life of the offender. The sacrifice of an animal atoned for the offender's sin and turned aside God's wrath. Like the lambs offered to atone for the sins of the Israelites, Jesus' life was offered as a substitute for ours. His death turned away God's wrath and atoned for our sin (Rom. 3:25).

bring them with a repentant and trusting spirit, as He had instructed.

9:22 Aaron . . . blessed them: The ultimate function of the priests was to bless the people. When God gave the priestly blessing, He said that the priests would put His name on the children of Israel, and He would bless them (Num. 6:27). The purpose of the priests' sacrifices was to cleanse the priests so they could bless the people (Deut. 10:8). The purpose of the people's sacrifices was to cleanse the people so they could receive God's blessing, and in turn be a blessing to all other peoples (Gen. 12:3; 22:18). **came down:** The altar of burnt offering was five by five by three cubits (about seven and a half feet square and four and a half feet high). The priest climbed a ramp to offer on it.

9:23 the tabernacle of meeting: Moses, Aaron, and Aaron's sons were in the courtyard in front of the altar of burnt offering. Moses and Aaron went into the tent itself where the altar of incense, the table of showbread, and the golden lampstand (the menorah) stood. **blessed the people:** This was the second time that day that the people had been blessed. The fact that Moses and Aaron could bless the people after they met with God signaled that God was pleased with the inaugural sacrifices Aaron had offered on behalf of himself and the people. **glory of the Lord** appeared: as God had promised through Moses (vv. 4, 6).

9:24 fire came out: The sacrifices were consumed, not by fire ignited by Aaron, but by fire **from before the Lord**. This is the first of only five times that the OT records fire from God

as a sign that a sacrifice was accepted (Judg. 6:21; 1 Kin. 18:38; 1 Chr. 21:26; 2 Chr. 7:1). Since the fire on this altar was never to go out, all Israel's sacrifices from this time forward would be consumed by fire that originated from God. In the NT, the fire from God symbolized the coming of the Holy Spirit upon the believers in the Upper Room on the Day of Pentecost (Acts 2:3). That fire signaled, as had the ancient one, God's acceptance of the worship and dedication of His people, and His commitment to dwell among them. **they shouted:** The Hebrew verb (*ranan*) usually connotes a ringing cry of joy and exultation, not fearfulness and terror. The people understood that God's fire upon the altar meant God's presence in their midst. God's acceptance of their sacrifices meant His acceptance of them, and they could receive His dwelling with them with joy rather than fear. So it is today. Guilt makes people fearful of God's presence. God's forgiveness through Christ's perfect sacrifice upon Calvary allows people to dwell in God's presence without guilty fear. **fell on their faces:** This response to the glory of God's presence was called fear by previous generations. Today we call it reverence. The pattern of the Israelites' sacrifice established a valid pattern for approaching God today. Sin must be confessed, repented, and atoned for. When God accepted the sacrifice, He accepted the one who offered it into His presence.

10:1 Nadab and Abihu were Aaron's eldest sons. With Aaron and seventy elders of Israel, they had accompanied Moses partway up Mount Sinai and had seen God (Ex. 24:1, 9–11).

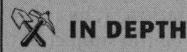 **IN DEPTH** | **Purified by Fire**

As Israel began offering sacrifices according to God's instructions, His presence was revealed through a fire that consumed the first burnt offering (Lev. 9:24). Not surprisingly, the people fell down in worship. They had instant respect for the fire of the presence of the One they served. Elsewhere in Scripture fire signifes things that must be respected, beginning with God:

- Moses described Him as "a consuming fire, a jealous God" (Deut. 4:24).
- God's deliverance of David was described in images of fire (Ps. 18:8–14).
- He appeared to Ezekiel in a cloud of fire (Ezek. 1:4).
- Malachi said that the Lord would act like a refiner's fire in the day of His coming (Mal. 3:2).
- John the Baptist said that Jesus would baptize people with the Holy Spirit and fire (Matt. 3:11; Acts 2:3, 4).
- The Lord's final evaluation of believers is described in terms of a smelter's fire (1 Cor. 3:13–15).
- John the apostle saw a vision of Jesus in which His eyes were like flames of fire (Rev. 1:14).

Peter reminds us that our trials and tribulations are "testings by fire" that help to purify our faith and make it genuine, like pure gold (1 Pet. 1:6, 7; 4:12, 13).

They had participated with their father in the inaugural sacrifices recorded in ch. 9. They had obeyed, and God had accepted all that had been done on that day. **profane fire:** Nadab and Abihu violated God's holiness in some way the author does not spell out. **Profane** is literally "strange." Two ideas may be combined here. Leviticus 16:12 directs that, at least for the Day of Atonement, incense had to be burned with coals from the altar of burnt offering. If this was true for other times as well, "strange" may mean that the two priests took their fire not from the altar but from another, illicit, source. S e c o n d , "strange" often refers to foreigners, including their pagan, "strange," gods. Aaron (Nadab's and Abihu's father) had fashioned a strange god, the golden calf (Ex. 32:4). Possibly they were now attempting to follow in his footsteps and incorporate the worship of a pagan god here, just as Israel was beginning its worship of Yahweh according to the forms He had given them. **Which He had not commanded them** is in striking contrast with the careful obedience to God's commands recorded in chs. 8 and 9. Whatever the details, their act was clearly disobedient, and they knew it.

10:2 Fire went out from the Lord in punishment. Two verses earlier (9:24), fire had come from the Lord in acceptance of Israel and its worship. What is a blessing when it comes as a result of faithfulness can be deadly when provoked by disobedience. **devoured them:** killed them. Their cousins picked them up in their priestly tunics and carried them outside the camp for burial (v. 5). **they died:** Their deaths were a result of their own rebellious action. God is a jealous God, unwilling to allow His people to be unfaithful to Him.

10:3 those who come near Me: In this context, God referred to the priests, Aaron and his sons. Those who are closest to God—those who minister before Him and teach the people—have a greater responsibility to be careful about God's holiness. James stresses this principle in his letter (James 3:1). **I must be glorified** is still a good principle by which to measure our worship. Anything that does not glorify God is not truly worship and should not be allowed in our worship gatherings. **Aaron held his peace:** Though he certainly was grieving the sudden loss of his sons, Aaron recognized that their action was rebellion against God. If it had not been dealt with promptly, it would have spread and disrupted Israel's holy worship. Aaron's grief may have been intensified by the memory of his own rebellion against God in making the golden calf (Ex. 32), an act his sons certainly had witnessed.

10:4 carry: Though priests were forbidden to come into contact with the dead, a brother's corpse normally was an exception to this rule (21:1–4). However, Moses called Aaron's cousins to carry the bodies of Nadab and Abihu **out of the camp** because their rebellion had been the cause of their deaths, and because their father and brothers had only just begun their priestly duties. **your brethren:** The Hebrew word for *brother* can include cousins, as it does here.

10:5 as Moses had said: The pattern of obedience interrupted by Nadab and Abihu's sin was reestablished.

10:6, 7 Aaron and his surviving sons were forbidden to mourn the deaths because they needed to remain in a state of ritual purity; also, so they would not appear to condone the sin of Nadab and Abihu. If they were to die as well, Israel would have no priests to intercede with God. But Israel as a whole was allowed to mourn the two.

10:6 uncover your heads nor tear your clothes: These were conventional signs of mourning (Ezek. 24:16, 17).

10:7, 8 the Lord spoke to Aaron: This is the only place in Leviticus where God speaks to Aaron alone.

10:9–11 Whether intoxication contributed to their sin, the author does not say. But it certainly would in future cases, if the priests allowed themselves to drink while on duty, and would bring upon them the same punishment Nadab and Abihu had suffered. Ministering before the altar and teaching the Israelites **all the statutes** required clear thinking and memory. Alcohol must not be allowed to impair the priests' functioning as priests.

10:10 Holy and unholy had been the subject of the preceding instructions about sacrifices and their first implementation (chs. 1—9). **Unclean and clean** would be the subject of the following instructions about animals, diseases, bodily discharges, and so on (chs. 11—15).

10:11–13 you may teach . . . the statutes: In the OT era, the priests were primarily responsible for teaching the people of Israel the Law of God. Parents, in turn, were to teach their children (Deut. 6:6–9, 20–25). **a holy place:** within the tabernacle. For instructions about the **grain offering,** read 2:10.

10:12–15 Moses took care to see that God's instructions (about the priests' portions of the sacrifices) were carried out in spite of the tragedy that just had occurred. When a new order is inaugurated, the first time of doing something has great symbolic significance. The sacrifices had been offered; Moses wanted to be sure the priests had eaten their allotted portions this first time.

10:14 a clean place: a place that had not been defiled by (or had been ritually cleansed

IN PERSON | Learning from Aaron's Weaknesses

Aaron had reason to do some serious thinking. He realized that the misbehavior of his sons raised serious questions about his fitness for ministry (Lev. 10:19). Thus Aaron provides an instructive lesson in the painful fact that good people have weaknesses, shortcomings, and a sinful, dark side.

Aaron was not a worthless individual. He was a good speaker, which was one reason why God called him to assist his brother, Moses, in leading Israel out of Egypt (Ex. 4:14). He and his descendants were also appointed by God to be the priests over Israel's worship (28:1–4). But the biblical account shows that Aaron struggled with some things that led to serious problems on several occasions:

- Even though he was aware of God's jealous love and holiness, he gave in to the people at Sinai and led them into idolatry (Ex. 32:1–4). Later, he avoided taking responsibility for his appalling lapse of leadership (32:21–25).
- He joined his sister, Miriam, in speaking against Moses because of Moses' possibly interracial marriage to an Ethiopian woman. God judged them harshly, so that Aaron pleaded for forgiveness (Num. 12:1–16).
- Though the text does not explicitly comment on Aaron as a parent, the back-to-back incidents involving all four of his sons raise serious questions about his effectiveness as a family leader (Lev. 10:1–3, 16–20).

No one can completely avoid failure and sin. Fortunately, God does not make us His children on the basis of our own ability not to commit sin, but on Christ's ability to deal with it. When the "greats" in the Bible fell short of God's holiness they could find forgiveness and restoration through repentance. Aaron is a good example.

---

from) the kinds of uncleanness described in chs. 11—15. This place was not specifically near the tabernacle, where some of the priests' portions had to be eaten, but presumably in the priests' dwellings or any other clean place within the camp (before they reached the Promised Land) or within the land (after they reached it). **your daughters:** The right of the women in the priests' families to share in their portions of the offerings is described more fully in 22:10–13. For instructions on the **wave** and **heave offerings,** read 7:32, 33.

10:15 Moses reassured his brother that God would allow him to remain as high priest, in spite of the sin and death of two of his sons.

10:16 careful inquiry: Moses was responsible to see that Nadab and Abihu's sin did not cause further punishment to fall on Israel. **burned up:** The flesh of the sin offering, if it was not for the priest or the whole congregation, was not to be burned completely. Only its fat should have been burned (4:26, 31, 35). This sin offering was not for Aaron and his sons, even though it was for all the people, since Aaron was to offer a separate sin offering for himself (and presumably for his sons, too). Moses **was angry.** Much had gone wrong already. The worship rituals had been carried

out improperly. What more might God do because of this further breach?

10:17, 18 The priests were to eat the flesh (except for the fat) of any sin offering whose **blood was not brought inside the holy place**—that is, of any sin offering that was not intended to atone for them (4:5–7, 16–18). Eleazar and Ithamar had not done this, but had burned up all the goat of the sin offering.

10:19 Aaron said: Moses had spoken to Eleazar and Ithamar, perhaps out of respect for his older brother, since Aaron should have eaten the meat of the sin offering also. But Aaron replied, taking responsibility for his family, as was proper in Israel's patriarchal society. **such things:** Aaron was referring to the deaths of his two eldest sons. **would it have been accepted:** Aaron did not eat the sacrificial meat because he was afraid of what more God might do. He was not being rebellious, as his dead sons had been in burning the incense. Aaron was arguing that in circumstances such as the one he faced that day, God would prefer the priest to err on the side of caution rather than presumption. Aaron's reply to Moses illustrates that the interpretation of the Law was not static.

10:20 Moses . . . was content: Rebellion arises from a heart that is not right toward God.

Moses recognized that Aaron's failure was not rebellion, that his argument had merit, and that Aaron could be forgiven. The first great crisis in establishing Israel's worship of God had passed.

11:1-47 Animals permissible for food (clean); animals not permissible for food (unclean). Various explanations of this division are proposed but most fail to explain it fully. One popular explanation is hygienic. Unclean animals were forbidden as food because they carried diseases (pork, trichinosis; hares and hyrax, tularemia), or because, as carrion eaters, they were more likely to transmit diseases to humans. True, but these are modern medical discoveries. If hygiene and health were the reason for forbidding them as food, it would have been as easy for God to reveal that pork needed thorough cooking, which prevents human infection with trichinosis. More importantly, some unclean animals do not necessarily transmit diseases and some clean animals do. Protection of health was an important result of declaring some of these animals unclean, but it cannot have been the main reason for doing so. Another explanation is that some animals were used in the pagan sacrifices of Israel's neighbors. But this would have required that the sheep and above all the bull—very prominent in Egyptian and Canaanite religion—be declared unclean, and they were not.

Some say clean and unclean were arbitrary distinctions that God used to test Israel's faithfulness and obedience. But Israel had plenty of other opportunities to demonstrate faith and obedience, just as the modern believer does. Some see the clean animals as representing righteous people of faith and the unclean as representing wicked, faithless persons. Such an allegorical approach has no controls; it is limited only by one's imagination, and for that reason ought not to be taken seriously.

A better explanation is that the clean animals were clean because their characteristics associated them with life and order in the culture of ancient Israel. The unclean animals were associated, by Israel's culture, with death and disorder because of their habits or their habitat. Ritual purity (cleanness), holiness, life, and order thus were associated concepts; ritual impurity (uncleanness), common or profane usage, death and disorder were associated concepts. This approach gives unity to the entire section on the distinction between the clean and the unclean (chs. 11—15).

11:1 the LORD spoke: Now that Aaron was high priest, he was responsible for teaching and administering the Law. So God spoke to Moses and Aaron together when He gave these further instructions (10:10, 11).

11:2 on the earth: As distinct from the sea and the air. A similar grouping of animal life is found in the creation account (Gen. 1:20–31).

11:3 chewing the cud: That is, the ruminants, like cows, sheep, goats, deer, and antelope. The ruminants eat only plants, mainly grasses and grains. No meat-eating animal chews the cud. The animals allowed for food are not mentioned by name (as they are in Deut. 14:4, 5). Cattle, sheep, and goats provided most of the meat for the ancient Israelites. They ate meat much less often than we do, usually only on special occasions such as the sacrificial feasts or to honor guests in the home.

11:4–7 Several species are specifically mentioned as unclean because they possessed one of the features of clean animals, but not both. One feature without the other was not enough to make an animal clean. While it might seem that this would be clear, God was gracious, providing examples and even rationales, so no one needed to be anxious about whether he was breaking the law. The believer today, seeking to avoid overt sin, will find God equally gracious.

11:4 The camel was eaten by some of Israel's neighbors, who considered it a delicacy. But the camel would not have been an important source of meat for Israel even if it had been permitted, for it never was as numerous in Israel or as important to Israel's economy as it was to their neighbors. The camel does have a split hoof, but its sole or pad is so thick that its imprint is like a single pad.

11:5 The rock hyrax lives in colonies among the rocks (Prov. 30:26). Though it is sometimes called a rock badger, it is not a badger. The rock hyrax is about the same size as a rabbit. Hyraxes appear to chew constantly while sitting outside their dens sunning themselves.

11:6 The hare is not a ruminant, although it does appear to chew constantly. It does not have a hoof.

11:7 The swine is the best known of the unclean animals and continues to be avoided by both Jews and Muslims. The swine was most commonly eaten by Israel's neighbors in both the OT and NT periods. All the reasons for labeling an animal as unclean fit the swine. (1) Inadequately cooked pork could transmit disease to humans. (2) Pigs were sacrificed to pagan deities. (3) Because pork tasted good, refusing it would be a suitable test of faithfulness and obedience.

11:8 In the case of these **unclean** animals, eating their meat or touching their dead carcasses caused an Israelite to be unclean or ritually impure. However, touching a live animal did not make a person unclean, and an Israelite could raise and use a donkey or camel as a beast of burden without becoming unclean.

11:9 A water creature had to possess both **fins and scales** in order to be eaten. Only true fish—and not all of them—fit this description. Oysters, clams, crabs, lobsters, and eels were unclean. **Whether in the seas or in the rivers** applied this command to both saltwater and freshwater species.

11:10–12 The phrasing is careful, deliberate, and repetitive to remove any possibility of finding any exception anywhere. **Abomination** is a stronger word than *unclean*. It implies not just avoidance, but active, fierce repulsion. Fins and scales are "appropriate" for water creatures. Fish that have them are clean. Water creatures that appear to mix categories—suggesting disorder—are not merely unclean; they are an abomination. There are good health reasons for being cautious in eating some of these creatures, but this was not the main reason for classifying them as unclean.

11:13–19 This listing differs from the previous two in that it did not establish criteria for judging which creatures were clean. Rather, it listed the birds that were an abomination; we may assume other birds were clean and edible. These birds were forbidden because they are birds of prey or carrion eaters. Also, many of them inhabit desert areas or ruins. The association with death and disorder made them unclean, as it did carnivorous mammals. Many names in this list are uncertain, for one of two reasons. Some refer not to a single species but to several similar species, such as eagles and vultures, or hawks, or members of the crow family. Others cannot be identified now with certainty, and many conflicting suggestions have been made. The effect of this lack of precision in naming would have been to consider all related species as being forbidden. That was the intent of the list, so no birds of prey or carrion eaters would be eaten in Israel. **After its kind** repeated four times, also suggests that several of these names each designated several similar species, perhaps not even recognized as different in an age before scientific classification became an important human endeavor.

11:19 The hoopoe is a migratory bird. It spends its winters in tropical Africa and its summers in Israel and farther north. **The bat** of course is not a bird. But in the prescientific age it was grouped with birds because it has wings and flies.

> *God was gracious, providing examples and even rationales, so no one needed to be anxious about whether he was breaking the Law. The believer today, seeking to avoid overt sin, will find God equally gracious.*

11:20 Creep on all fours is an idiom for crawling on the ground, as insects do on their six legs. Many insects move about in filth and eat refuse. Their association with death, impurity, and disorder made them unclean.

11:21 Insects with **jointed legs . . . with which to leap** were permitted to be eaten. The joints are the enlarged third legs of locusts and grasshoppers that enable them to leap. Locusts and grasshoppers do not live in filth or eat dung. They eat only plants.

11:22, 23 Only the first name, **the locust,** is certain. The rest may be different kinds of locusts or grasshoppers. The second and third names, **the destroying locust, the cricket,** occur only here in the OT. **After its kind** suggests the possibility of several species, as in 11:14–19.

11:24 These refers to just the flying insects of the previous paragraph or possibly to all the unclean animals discussed so far. Merely to touch an unclean carcass caused a person to be **unclean until evening,** when the new day began for the Israelites.

11:25 If a person **carried** or picked up a **carcass,** or part of a carcass, that person's uncleanness was greater. Therefore, the remedy had to be more thorough.

11:26 The word **carcass** is not in the Hebrew text, but clearly that is what is meant here. A live unclean animal, such as a donkey or camel, could not make a person unclean simply by touching it. Otherwise, many people would have been unclean all the time.

11:27, 28 Whatever goes on its paws is **unclean** because it does not have a cloven hoof. As with the previous group, to touch a **carcass** was to be **unclean** and to carry a carcass was to be even more unclean, requiring a more thorough cleansing.

11:29, 30 Another group of animals is introduced here. Many of these animals could to be found in or around human dwellings. Since these animals were unclean, it was important to know how to deal with them and with objects and utensils they touched. These are small creatures **that creep on the earth.** This refers not only to their great numbers, but also to their quickness of movement. The group includes small rodents in general, such as mice, voles, shrews, and hamsters, as well as some kinds of lizard.

11:31 when they are dead: Literally, "in their death" or "in their dying." The Israelite farmer was more likely to kill a small rodent in the course of the day than any other creature named in this chapter. It was important to remember as they killed these pests that they themselves would be **unclean until evening** if they touched them.

11:32–38 These are regulations for household items touched by the carcass of a small unclean animal falling on or in them. Again, good hygiene is an important result of these regulations, but their underlying purpose was to avoid those things associated with death and disorder. A carcass, unless it was a clean animal killed for food in the proper way, always defiled anyone or anything touching it.

11:32 Expensive vessels of wood, fabric, leather, or fiber were to **be put in water.** Whether they were only to be washed, or soaked **until evening,** is unclear. But at evening, the start of the new Jewish day, they would **be clean.**

11:33 Any earthen vessel . . . you shall break: Pottery was plentiful, cheap, and easily replaced. Vessels made of pottery were also used for food preparation and eating. Again, hygiene was an important result of avoiding the unclean.

11:34 The contents of any vessel made **unclean** in this way became unclean also.

11:35 These ovens were made of clay and so had to be **broken** also.

11:36 A spring or a cistern could hardly be emptied. Only the person removing the **carcass** became unclean, probably until evening.

11:37, 38 Dry **planting seed** did not become unclean.

11:39, 40 if any animal . . . dies: This refers to animals that died of natural causes, and not those killed for food. The **carcass** caused the person who touched it to be **unclean** because its blood had not been drained. Eating from or carrying the carcass involved more than merely touching it and required a greater remedy— washing one's clothes as well as waiting until evening. Eating meat without draining its blood apparently was not as serious an offense as eating and drinking blood by itself (7:26, 27). Carrying the carcass would have been unavoidable in many situations—removing the animal for burial, for example. Uncleanness often was not a moral issue, at least in the way a person became unclean.

11:41–43 Crawls on its belly and **has many feet** are new descriptions. They were not mentioned in the previous ban on eating **creeping things.**

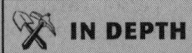 **IN DEPTH**   ## Not Like Others

People tend to put a lot of effort into being like those around them. But God challenges His people not to be like everybody else.

In the OT, God instructed Israel not to pattern itself after the nations around it. Instead, He called the Israelites to consecrate themselves (set themselves apart from others) and be holy, for He, the Lord their God, was holy (Lev. 11:44, 45).

One of the main ways that Israel was to be different was in its worship. Worship in the surrounding cultures included many rituals that Israel was not to follow. These forbidden practices were based on values that were not holy or rooted in a high view of God, people, or creation. Among them were:

- Divination or magic.
- Frenzied, chaotic dances.
- Self-mutilation.
- Ritual prostitution.
- Sensuality and orgiastic fertility rites.
- Human sacrifices.
- Sacrifices for the dead.

By contrast, Israel's worship was measured against God's holiness and defined the nation as God's people. There was no need to compete with other nations, cultures, or religions. The closing song at the end of Leviticus, Israel's manual for ritual and worship, says: "I will walk among you and be your God, and you shall be My people" (Lev. 26:12). This promise became a watchword for Israel (Hos. 1:9, 10; 2:23; Jer. 31:33; Ezek. 36:28). Later, the church also came to define itself as belonging to God first and foremost, with a responsibility for holy worship and living (1 Pet. 1:13–16; 2:9, 10).

11:44 I am the LORD your God: The word for LORD is *Yahweh*, the name by which God had revealed Himself to Moses (Ex. 3:14, 15; 6:2, 3). **Consecrate yourselves** means "make yourselves holy." **You shall be holy; for I am holy:** This is the foundation of the so-called Holiness Code of chs. 17—26. To be holy means to "be separate." God is holy as the transcendent Creator, above and apart from nature. To be separate *to* God is much more important than to be separate *from* other things. As God's people are separated *to* Him, we become more and more conformed to His image, to be the persons God intended us to be when He created the first man and the first woman in His image (Gen. 1:26, 27). Holiness in God's people involves grace, righteousness, integrity, peace, and mercy, because these are characteristics of the God who has redeemed us and whom we serve.

11:45 For emphasis, God reaffirmed His identity. Then He added an astounding commitment to Israel. His purpose in bringing them **up out of the land of Egypt** was **to be** their **God.** Because of God's holy nature, they too had to **be holy.**

11:46, 47 This statement summarizes the content and purpose of the chapter by listing again the four broad groupings of animals. **To distinguish** reminds the reader that these were instructions for the people as well as the priests. The priests were responsible for teaching the Israelites.

12:1, 2 The child did not cause the mother to be **unclean.** God had ordained and blessed childbirth from the beginning, even before the sin in the Garden (Gen. 1:28). Rather, it was the blood and other fluids in childbirth that made the mother ritually unclean for a period of time, just as other bodily fluids caused people to be unclean (ch. 15). This uncleanness was not necessarily a moral judgment on the mother. **Seven days** of uncleanness for a male child was the same length of time as the uncleanness for the woman's menstrual period or **customary impurity** (15:19–24).

12:3 Recent medical science has concluded that **the eighth day** is the best time for circumcision. Before the eighth day, blood does not clot as well, and after it, sensitivity to pain becomes greater. Circumcision was also practiced by groups such as the Ammonites, Moabites, and Edomites. However, in Israel it was the outward symbol of God's covenant with Abraham (Gen. 17:9–14). The fact that the symbol involved the male reproductive organ was a reminder that God had promised Abraham many descendants.

12:4 The eighth day also marked the end of the mother's uncleanness with regard to everyday objects and activities; she no longer would make them unclean by touching them.

But her personal uncleanness would continue for another **thirty-three days.** This corresponds with the medical characteristics of childbirth. After seven days, most discharges have ceased, but slight signs may continue for as long as six weeks. The phrase **blood of her purification** reminds us of this. Blood is the carrier of life in the body and the agent of purification from sin, both in the OT sacrificial system and Christ's sacrifice. At the same time, blood may become a source of pollution and death if it is taken lightly or not handled appropriately.

12:5 The birth of **a female child** doubled the period of ritual impurity. No reason is given.

12:6 The sacrifices required were the same **for a son or a daughter,** showing that God places equal value upon both sexes and that He intends His people to do the same. The **burnt offering** (ch. 1) and the **sin offering** (ch. 4) were two of the five regular offerings Israel had been instructed to bring before God. Following the birth of a child, these sacrifices were a woman's responsibility, though her husband normally would accompany her (Luke 2:22–24). The fact that the mother was to offer the sacrifices for herself reminds us that women were to be active participants in Israel's worship. **A young pigeon or a turtledove** was the least expensive offering. The poor could bring these birds when they could not afford a lamb (5:7).

12:7 The repetition here of the phrase **a male or a female** reemphasizes the equal worth of a girl and a boy.

12:8 If she is not able to bring a lamb is, literally, "If she cannot find in her hand enough for a lamb." Buying an animal for sacrifice was perhaps as common as raising one. Two points emphasized by this provision are: (1) the poor are not *excluded* from participation in the worship life of the community by reason of their poverty, and (2) the poor are not *excused* from participation by reason of their poverty. Mary, following the birth of Jesus and the days of her purification, went to the temple in Jerusalem in accordance with this regulation (Luke 2:22–24). Her offering was a pair of birds. Joseph and Mary obviously were poor; the Magi had not yet visited them with their expensive gifts for the newborn King.

13:1, 2 The Hebrew word for **a man** (*'adam*) means a "human being"—anyone. **A swelling, a scab, or a bright spot** would often be a minor ailment that healed within a few days and caused no further concern. If a condition persisted, and became **like a leprous sore**, it required further attention. Any given sore might or might not be leprous; that was for **the priest** to determine by examination.

The Hebrew word *tsara'at* (translated "leprous" here) denotes many serious skin and scalp diseases; rabbinic discussions noted as many as seventy-two. Whether classic leprosy (Hansen's disease) is included is a matter of vigorous debate; none of its typical symptoms is covered in the prescribed diagnoses of this chapter. While Hansen's disease may be included, it is not the primary focus of the chapter. **he shall be brought:** The most serious result of the priest's examination was to be declared unclean and banished from the camp. The natural tendency would be to put off seeing the priest about a condition. However, ritual uncleanness was a serious matter for all the people. It was important to diagnose skin problems immediately so that the whole camp did not become unclean. If the afflicted person did not come on his own initiative, his family and clan leaders were responsible for bringing him.

13:3–44 Seven cases of diseases involving the skin, the scalp, and the hair are in view. Basic cases are given with their diagnoses, followed by variations with their diagnoses. Several general principles emerge. (1) Often a second (even a third) examination after seven, and fourteen, days was required to make the diagnosis. (2) If the malady had not spread or deepened in the skin, or if discoloration had faded, the person was **clean.** (3) If the malady had spread, deepened, or become more raw or discolored, it was **leprosy** (13:2), and the person was **unclean.** (4) Between examinations, the patient could be **isolated,** or quarantined, for the protection of the community, in case the diagnosis should be "unlcean."

13:3 The priest shall examine: The priest made the diagnosis. However, nothing is said about how to treat the ailments. The subject of the passage is not medical treatment but ritual impurity, and making sure that the community of Israel, and particularly the tabernacle, would not become unclean.

13:4–6 he shall wash his clothes: Personal hygiene was an important factor in identifying and preventing the spread of infectious diseases, even those that did not cause a person to be unclean.

13:7–11 shall not isolate him: Isolation, or quarantine, was for the purpose of protecting the community until a diagnosis was reached. In this case, the patient was already diagnosed as **unclean,** which meant he had to live outside the camp (v. 46).

13:12–15 Raw flesh, here, is ulcerated, literally, "living," flesh. Flesh normally is hidden by the skin. If the skin is so damaged or eaten away by the disease that it can be seen, that disease is serious and dangerous and the person is **unclean.**

13:16–44 Some of these diseases were healed, either spontaneously or with treatment. After another examination, **the priest** would then **pronounce** the patient **clean.**

13:45, 46 his clothes . . . his mustache: These actions were signs of mourning because the afflictions were symbolic of death and decay. The afflicted person might as well have been dead as far as contact with the community or opportunity to worship in the sanctuary was

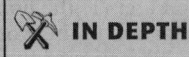 **IN DEPTH** **Leprosy**

Leprosy (Lev. 13:12) was one of the most feared diseases in the ancient world. Lepers suffered from a slowly progressing, ordinarily incurable skin disease that was believed to be highly contagious. As a result, anyone who appeared to have leprosy, even if the symptoms were caused by some other condition, was banished from the community.

True leprosy is caused by a bacterium that spreads across the skin, creating sores, scabs, and white shining spots. The most serious problem, however, is a loss of sensation. Without the ability to feel, lepers injure their tissue, leading to further infection, deformity, muscle loss, and eventual paralysis. Fortunately, modern medicine has all but eliminated the disease.

The Law was quite detailed in its instructions regarding recognition and quarantine of leprous persons. Priests became the central figures for diagnosis, care of patients, and taking sanitary precautions to protect the rest of the community. The Law required that a leper be isolated from the rest of society (Lev. 13:45, 46). Infected persons were required to wear mourning clothes, leave their hair in disorder, keep their beards covered, and cry 'Unclean! Unclean!' so that others could avoid them. Any contact would defile the person who touched a leper.

Sometimes lepers were miraculously cured, as in the case of Moses (Ex. 4:7), his sister Miriam (Num. 12:10), and Naaman (2 Kin. 5:1, 10), and Jesus healed lepers as a sign to vindicate His ministry. On one occasion He healed ten of them but only one returned to thank Him (Luke 17:11–15).

concerned. **'Unclean! Unclean!':** The afflicted person had to warn people away. Others would become unclean by coming into contact with him. **All the days:** Not every disease was incurable. Some people recovered and upon examination by the priest were allowed back into society and worship in the sanctuary. **He shall dwell alone . . . outside the camp:** This ensured that the rest of the community and the sanctuary did not become ritually impure. The community was also protected from the unchecked spread of the disease. The serious skin diseases became a metaphor for sin. Like them, sin is dangerous and ultimately fatal, often difficult to diagnose, and incurable without God's intervention. Sin isolates its victims from God and His worship, and from the community of faith.

13:47–59 These are regulations about impurities in fabric and leather. They are grouped with human skin diseases and identified by the same Hebrew term (*tsara'at*; 13:2) because they also are impurities on the surface and tend to spread, decay, and destroy the garment, just as the skin diseases do the persons afflicted with them.

13:47 Leprous plague would include any mold, mildew, or other fungus growths on clothing.

13:48 Warp and woof is a difficult phrase, probably meaning the entirety of the garment through and through, though not necessarily throughout its length and breadth.

13:49–58 The procedures for diagnosing a problem with a garment were similar to those for diagnosing human skin ailments. A seven-day period of quarantine and a second examination were required. Infected garments had to be burned. If the **plague** had not spread, a garment could be salvaged.

13:56–59 The fact that a **garment** was considered worth saving even after a piece had been torn out of it indicates how valuable cloth was in the ancient world. Cloth was the product of many hours of hard work and was not lightly thrown away.

14:1–32 This passage details the ritual for cleansing a healed leper.

14:2 He shall be brought to the priest: The priest was responsible for diagnosing the uncleanness, so it was necessary for him to administer the sacrifices and other rituals that marked and celebrated the return of the person to the community of Israel.

14:3 The priest shall go out of the camp: Even if the person was healed, he still was unclean and could not come into the camp until the proper rituals had been carried out (v. 8). This does not contradict the instructions to bring the person to the priest; the priest came outside

the camp and the person was brought to him there. **if the leprosy is healed:** These rites were not for healing. They were to confirm and celebrate the healing that already had occurred, to cleanse the recovered patient, and to readmit him or her into the community and its worship.

14:4 Cedar wood was used perhaps because of its durability and resistance to decay, symbolizing the patient's recovery from the decay that had threatened his life. **Scarlet** was probably a scarlet thread or cord. Scarlet symbolized blood, the agent in the sacrificial system that brought victory over sin and death. **Hyssop** was an aromatic herb used for food flavoring, fragrance, and medicine.

14:5 Running water is literally, "living water." This is water from a spring or stream, as opposed to water from a cistern, vessel, or pool. Stagnant water symbolized potential death; living water symbolized life. The blood of the bird ran into the water in the **earthen vessel.**

14:6, 7 It is likely that the sprigs of **hyssop** were tied to the **cedar wood** with the **scarlet** thread. With that in one hand and the **living bird** in the other hand, the priest would **dip** them all in the **blood** and water mixture in the pottery bowl and then shake them over the head of the one **to be cleansed.** This procedure was performed **seven times.** The dead bird represented the death the patient had escaped; the sprinkling began the process of ritual cleansing that allowed the person to reenter the community and its worship. After being dipped in the blood of the dead bird, **the living bird** was let **loose in the open field.** It symbolically took away from the camp and the tabernacle the uncleanness of the person who was returning to the camp.

14:8, 9 Two washings of clothes and body and two head shavings, seven days apart, completed the ritual cleansing. These certainly served a hygienic purpose, removing residual scales and flakes that might have passed on contagious diseases to others. Shaving was a drastic procedure for ancient Israel (2 Sam. 10:4, 5). New growing hair would have reassured everyone that the person truly was healed.

14:10–12 The eighth day was the day of circumcision for a newborn male. The symbolism of starting again, almost of being born again into the community of faith, was continued. **three-tenths of an ephah:** About nine pounds. **one log of oil:** About two-thirds of a pint.

14:13 in the place . . . holy place: These offerings were brought to the door of the tabernacle (1:3; 4:4, 14). The place where the lamb was killed is referred to as the *holy place.* Therefore, it must have been inside the door, in the court of the tabernacle, rather than outside.

⚒ **IN DEPTH** | **Rituals Against Fungus**

Israel's laws included regulations for dealing with a "leprous plague in the house" (Lev. 14: 33–53). The Hebrew word translated "leprous plague" pertains to various infestations. When used to describe the deterioration of garments (Lev. 13:47) and houses, it probably refers to decay caused by fungus, mildew, mold, or dry rot.

Any house in Israel that was discolored with mildew caused by fungus-producing organisms was quarantined (14:36–38). The structure had to be cleansed physically and ritually, with effected areas of stone being scraped, or replaced and re-mortared (14:40–42). If efforts were successful, the priest pronounced the house clean and performed a purification ritual (14:48–53).

This Mosaic cleansing ritual can be compared with two Mesopotamian texts. One is a quotation from a Babylonian omen series, which prescribes a ritual to the gods Ea and Ishum. Another ritual is mentioned in a letter to Esarhaddon, the king of Assyria (680–669 B.C.).

The omen reads: "If there is a fungus in a man's house, on the outer north wall, the owner of the house will die and his house will be scattered." To avert evil, the owner is instructed to gather the fungus (in a particular manner) and burn it with a torch, placing mud and gypsum around it. The person must then recite an incantation to Ea (the god of wisdom) and sacrifice a sheep to the god Ishum. Holy water is then sprinkled on the person while another incantation is recited.

The letter to Esarhaddon confirms the existence of a prayer and a ritual for two types of fungus that had appeared on the inner courtyard of the temple of Nabu. The author of the letter states that a technician, meaning a priest, will perform the appropriate ritual several times the next morning.

14:14–18 These rites are similar to Moses' actions in consecrating Aaron and his sons as priests (8:23). They encompassed the entire body, symbolizing a reversal in the person's status before God, from unclean and outside the community to a full member of the community once again.

14:19, 20 With these three offerings and the trespass offering (v. 12), the formerly unclean person had brought all the mandatory sacrifices that it was impossible to bring during the time of uncleanness.

14:21–32 God's legislation for Israel showed special concern for the **poor**. In these sacrifices, the poor Israelite still had to bring a lamb for the **trespass offering**. But for the **sin offering** and the **burnt offering**, he was allowed to bring **turtledoves** or **pigeons**. In addition, the **grain offering** was reduced from three-tenths to **one-tenth of an ephah of fine flour**. The ritual for restoring a poor person to the community was essentially the same as it was for other Israelites.

14:33–53 Regulations about mildew and mold in houses. Like humans and clothing, the house had to be inspected by the priest. If the symptoms were present, the house was quarantined for a week, as garments and humans were. As with garments, an attempt was made to save the house by replacing only the infected portion. If the mildew or mold reappeared, the house was torn down. Israelite houses typically were built of mud brick on a stone foundation.

The walls were plastered with a lime plaster. Mildew and other growths on the plaster, or coming through from the inside, were possible though probably not common. When they occurred and spread aggressively, they would have been a serious problem.

14:34–44 The land of Canaan, which I give you refers to the land God had promised Abraham He would give to his descendants (Gen. 15:18–21; Deut. 6:10, 11; 8:7–9). **Leprous plague** is the same Hebrew term used in 13:2 to indicate serious skin diseases that could come upon humans. All of these were harmful growths, whether on human skin, clothing, or the wall of a house.

14:45, 46 If every effort to save the house failed, it was destroyed and removed so the rest of the houses of the town would not become infected with the problem.

14:47 Lies down probably means to sleep overnight in the house.

14:48–53 The rite for cleansing a house of its uncleanness was the same as for cleansing a person.

14:54–57 This statement concludes the section 13:1—14:57. Again, the common characteristic of these problems, whether on persons, garments, or the walls of houses, was that they were harmful surface growths. Their uncleanness required action. If it could not be removed, the thing that carried the uncleanness had to be removed from among God's people. Uncleanness today still requires action. But God has provided an infinitely stronger remedy for human uncleanness—the blood of Christ, which cleanses initially and then continues to cleanse the believer moment by moment.

15:1, 2 any man: Regulations about female discharges begin in v. 19. **Discharge** refers to any abnormal flow. **Body,** literally, "flesh," is used here as a euphemism for the sexual organ.

15:3 A Hebrew verb for **runs** is used only here; a noun denotes a thick slimy substance. **His body is stopped up** may better be translated, "His body has stopped its discharge." If the urinary tract were completely blocked, uncleanness would not be the concern, but life and death; the subject would die in about a day. This verse seems to mean that even if the abnormal discharge stopped temporarily, the man still was regarded as unclean. A remission of seven days was required for him to consider himself cleansed from his discharge (v. 13).

15:4–12 A man with a discharge was unclean, as was anyone who came into contact with him, his spit, or any object that he touched. The other person made unclean was required to wash his clothes and himself and would be unclean **until evening.** Whether Israel understood the hygienic principles or not, this practice of cleanliness promoted better health by reducing the transmission of disease. Its primary purpose remained, however, to teach Israel that God is holy and requires a holy people for His own. Disease and uncleanness tend toward disorder, decay, and death, the opposite of the holiness, wholeness, and health that God ultimately intends His people to enjoy in every dimension of their lives.

15:12 The vessel of earth . . . of wood: Here the purpose was to prevent the spread of the disease through food and food utensils.

15:13 Seven days was enough time to be sure the discharge really had ceased.

15:14, 15 Two turtledoves or two young pigeons was the smallest, least expensive sacrifice allowed. The degree of uncleanness caused by genital discharges was less than that caused by skin diseases. These sacrifices would have atoned for any sins he had committed while he was unclean and barred from the tabernacle.

15:16, 17 This passage concerns emissions of semen apart from sexual intercourse, which is the subject of v. 18.

15:18 Both the male and the female are involved in sexual intercourse. Both had to wash afterward, and both were ritually **unclean** until evening. Gen. 1 and 2 portray sexual intercourse as God's plan from the beginning. Therefore, this uncleanness and requirement of washing does not mean that sexual intercourse is sinful. Here, too, hygiene is a limited consideration; washing promoted cleanliness and health. But the greater concern of this regulation was with ritual purity; sexual intercourse prevented access to the tabernacle until evening. Obviously, then, sexual intercourse was forbidden within the precincts of the tabernacle. By contrast, the Canaanites used sexual rites within their temples to remind Baal, the storm god, to "impregnate" the earth by bringing on the winter rainy season and thus ensure the fertility of field, flock, and family. God's removal of sex from the sanctuary through this regulation was intended to prevent Israel confusing Baal worship with the worship of Yahweh.

15:19–24 This passage provides regulations concerning a woman's menstrual period. Her ritual uncleanness lasted seven days. As was the case with a man's discharge, any person or object she touched became **unclean.**

15:24 This regulation did not forbid intercourse during menstruation; read, however, 18:19; 20:18. The man became ritually unclean for seven days, the same length of time as for the woman. No sacrifice was required; menstruation was not regarded as sinful.

15:25–27 If a woman had a flow of blood at any time other than her normal monthly period, or if her period lasted longer than usual, her uncleanness continued the whole time and passed to all she touched. Such was the case with the woman who touched Jesus secretly (Luke 8:43–48).

15:28–30 At the end of her abnormal discharge, a woman's obligation was the same as a man's. This is another indication of her standing before God, of her right and duty to offer sacrifice on her own behalf in the tabernacle. She was to bring the smallest allowable sacrifice for the atonement of sins she may have committed during the period of her uncleanness, when she was barred from the tabernacle.

15:31–33 Hygiene and health were important byproducts, but the *focus* of these regulations concerning **uncleanness** was on keeping God's **tabernacle** undefiled so that Israel would have a place to come for the atonement of sin and the privilege of meeting with God.

16:1–34 This chapter about the Day of Atonement stands at the center of Leviticus at the center of the Pentateuch. The Day of Atonement marked the most important, most comprehensive drawing near of all Israel to God in the entire year. The rabbis called it "the day," or "the great day." An entire tractate of the *Mishnah* is devoted to it, and it remains the most sacred day of the Jewish faith. Luke called it "the Fast" (Acts 27:9). Much of its symbolism relates to Christ's atoning death.

16:1 The two sons of Aaron died because of how they **offered profane fire,** literally, "drew near," **before the LORD**. If Aaron was to draw near to the Lord and be Israel's intermediary, he had to know how to do it properly to avoid the fate his sons had suffered. This reference continues the narrative of ch. 10. Chapters 11—15 intervene not for chronological but for theological reasons. The physical uncleannesses of individuals, barring their access to the tabernacle until they were cleansed, stood as metaphors, object lessons, for the moral uncleannesses of all the people that needed expiation on the Day of Atonement.

16:2, 3 God's command **not to come at just any time** refers to the arrogant attitude with which Aaron's sons had approached to offer unauthorized sacrifice (10:1). **the Holy Place inside the veil:** The Most Holy Place, the inner sanctuary of the tabernacle, was separated from the larger room (the holy place) by a veil of fine blue, purple, and scarlet linen (Ex. 26:31). **lest he die:** Carelessly approaching the presence of God was dangerous.

16:4, 5 Holy garments are not the elaborate robe and accessories described in Ex. 28, but the simple linen garments the priests wore when on duty at the altar. On this day, the high priest went in simplicity and humility; he offered atonement for himself first, then for his family, and finally for all of Israel.

16:6, 7 After atoning **for himself,** the high priest could offer the sacrifice to atone for the people. The author of Hebrews places great emphasis on this point in discussing the superior priesthood of Jesus (Heb. 7:26–28; 9:11–28; 10:19–22).

16:8–10 For the scapegoat is literally, "for Azazel." The meaning of the term is vigorously debated. Some take it to be an abstract noun, meaning "for complete removal." Others see it as a place name, or the name of a wilderness demon. If the third position is correct, it is important to stress that this goat was not a sacrifice to a demon. Sending the goat to the wilderness demon then would signify sending the people's sins far away from them and back to their demonic source, where they never again could harm them.

16:11–14 Only on this day each year did the High Priest enter the Holy of Holies. He carried a container of bull's blood (his own sin offering) together with the censer of burning coals and two handfuls **of sweet incense.** It is not clear whether he placed the incense in the censer before or after entering the Holy of Holies. But it was the aroma of the burning incense that protected him (compare Num. 16:46–50).

16:12 beaten fine: That is, of the highest quality.

16:13, 14 on the east side: That is, at Yahweh's feet, since Yahweh was represented as sitting **on the mercy seat,** facing eastward.

16:15–19 Aaron offered **the goat . . . for the people.** The further actions involved in this sacrifice made it clear that the sins of the people had a defiling effect on the tabernacle. If not removed, the sins would have caused the ministry to be ineffective in atoning for the people.

16:17 Though on other days, other priests officiated **in the tabernacle of meeting,** on this day only the High Priest himself was to be within the entire sacred precinct, including both the Holy Place and the Holy of Holies.

16:18, 19 The altar is either the altar of incense within the Holy Place or the altar of sacrifice in the outer court of the tabernacle; both had horns. Since no other furniture is mentioned, it may be that the atonement for the Holy of Holies covered all the furnishings inside the tabernacle and that the atonement for the altar of sacrifice covered all the furnishings in the tabernacle's outer court.

16:20 Aaron performed these actions out of the sight of the people.

16:21 Sending the goat into the wilderness was a public ceremony. Everyone could see Aaron symbolically place the sins of the people on the goat's head. **Iniquities . . . transgressions . . . sins** cover all of the ways in which

---

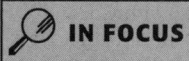 **IN FOCUS** | **"transgression"**

(Heb. *pesha'*) (Lev. 16:16, 21; Ps. 32:1, 5). Strong's #6588: This Hebrew word is derived from the verb *pasha',* which can mean "to revolt" (2 Kin. 8:20), "to offend" (Prov. 18:19), or "to transgress" in the sense of crossing a boundary (Jer. 3:13). It refers to violations of God's Law as revealed to Moses; in other words, someone crossing the limits that God had established. Although rebelling against God was a grave mistake, the Lord made provision for Israel's "transgressions" in the Day of Atonement (Lev. 16:15–19). The priest could make atonement for Israel's sin, and the nation could be reconciled to God. Like ancient Israel, we are in rebellion against God. In fact, it was "our transgressions" that wounded Jesus (Is. 53:5, 8; 1 Pet. 2:24).

people could offend God. All of these offenses were placed on the head of the goat, which took them away from the camp, away from the people, and away from God. A **suitable man** was a man who was ready and waiting to perform this task.

16:22 shall bear on itself all their iniquities: This is the origin of the common expression "scapegoat." This goat was not guilty of the sins he bore, but he bore them anyway, allowing the guilty to escape the consequences of their sins. In Jesus' bearing the sins of the human race, and in His death outside the city (outside the camp), He fulfilled this annual ritual of the Day of Atonement. Not only was Jesus the perfect High Priest; He was the perfect Sacrifice.

16:23–28 With the tabernacle cleansed of the accumulated guilt of the people, Aaron could sacrifice the **burnt offering** for himself and the one for the people in the normal manner, as prescribed in Lev. 1.

16:25, 26 Aaron burned **the fat of the sin offering** as instructed in 4:8–10.

16:27, 28 The bull and goat of the two sin offerings were burned according to the instructions in 4:11, 12.

16:29–34 A summary of the rites of the Day of Atonement. Three times the phrase **a statute forever** occurs (vv. 29, 31, 34). This was to be the most important day of the year for Israel, and it was not to cease until the One came who would fulfill permanently all its provisions. The Hebrew word translated "forever" may mean "to the end of the age." The death of Christ, a permanently effectual sacrifice—by contrast with those of the Day of Atonement, that had to be repeated every year—brought to a close one age and ushered in the beginning of another. Even now, however, it would not be inappropriate to observe this as a day of remembrance for Christ's atonement. Some Jewish believers do observe the day in this way.

16:29, 30 In the seventh month: The Day of Atonement fell between mid-September and mid-October. **afflict your souls:** Examine yourselves, repent of wrong actions and attitudes, and seek God's forgiveness. The mere actions of the sacrifices, without genuine repentance, were useless.

16:31 **A sabbath of solemn rest** was more sacred and more strictly observed than the normal weekly Sabbath.

16:32, 33 In his father's place emphasizes that this day was to be observed throughout Israel's generations.

16:34 And he did as the Lord commanded Moses indicates that Aaron, as high priest, carried out everything God had commanded for this all-important day.

17:1–26:46 This section, mostly of laws for

ethical and moral living, is often called the Holiness Code. After the first half of the book, dealing with sacrifices, ritual purity, and the Day of Atonement (how to become and remain clean and forgiven), this section gives instruction on how a clean and forgiven people, a holy people, are to live.

17:1–7 From the way this regulation begins, some have understood it to mean that every slaughtered animal had to be brought to the tabernacle, whether it was killed as a sacrifice or only for the private use of its owner. But its language, and the reasons given, indicate that this regulation covers only animals intended for, or used for, sacrifice. These were to be brought to the door of the tabernacle in accordance with the earlier sacrificial regulations. This was intended to prevent two abuses: (1) killing an animal for the private use, saying liturgical words over it, and imagining one had offered a legitimate sacrifice to Yahweh, and (2) offering a sacrifice to a demon of the field or other pagan deity.

17:3 Whatever man: There were to be no exceptions. **Kills** probably indicates a sacrifice, for only the sacrificial animals the **ox, lamb,** and **goat** are listed. Animals with defects that did not threaten human health were slaughtered for their meat, but were not acceptable for sacrifice.

17:4 The guilt of bloodshed usually refers to killing a human being. However, the blood of the sacrifice was the only means of atonement for sin; to desecrate this provision from God was not a light offense.

17:5 Which they offer means "which they might offer." Sacrifice in an open field was prohibited.

17:6, 7 Demons were pagan deities in the form of goats, like satyrs, who were thought to inhabit the wilderness. Israel probably came in contact with satyr worship when they settled in Goshen (Gen. 47:1–6). **They have played the harlot** indicates (1) Israel's worship of other gods and (2) God's attitude to this worship. Adultery was a serious sin; forsaking one's faith in God was an even more serious sin. Apostasy hurts Him deeply. **A statute forever** is another clue that this regulation was not about slaughtering animals for meat, but about animals offered in sacrifice. When Israel's worship was centralized in Jerusalem, some families lived more than a hundred miles from the temple. It would have been impossible for them to travel to Jerusalem each time they killed an animal for meat. However, they could travel to Jerusalem every time they offered a sacrifice.

17:8, 9 This regulation specifically extends the command to **strangers who dwell among you.**

17:10 Eating **blood** was forbidden in the

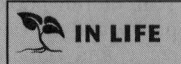 **IN LIFE**

A Place to Be Forgiven

For the Hebrews, there was only one place to worship God by offering sacrifices—at the tabernacle (Lev. 17:8, 9). This is not to say that one could not worship God elsewhere. But to make atonement for sin, one had to come to the altar, where a priest offered up a sacrifice according to the highly detailed instructions in the Law. Believers today are fortunate. Our high priest, Jesus, offered a sacrifice for our sins once and for all when He died on the Cross (Heb. 10:11–14). As a result, we can receive forgiveness for sins anytime, anyplace. We are not required to go to a specific location for this purpose or to perform a certain ritual. We need only draw near to God through Christ with a "true heart" and confess our sins (Heb. 10:19–22).

strongest possible terms. **Any blood** means blood in any form, including blood not drained from the animal when it was slaughtered.

17:11, 12 This verse explains the basis of blood atonement. The **life** of animals and of humans **is in the blood.** If a creature loses its blood, it loses its life. **I have given** emphasizes that blood has no *intrinsic* power to atone for sin. God appointed blood to have this power because it represents the life of the creature. A life may receive atonement only by the sacrifice of a life. The author of Hebrews emphasized the temporary nature of animal blood sacrifices. They required constant renewal. However, Jesus' one-time sacrifice of Himself is effective eternally (Heb. 9:12–14, 25–28).

17:13, 14 Wild animals and most birds were not eligible for sacrifice even if they were clean.

Their blood poured out and covered with dust, however, acknowledged God's claim on all blood as the sustainer of the creature's life and the medium to effect atonement. Blood was not to be handled carelessly but reverently.

17:13 That may be eaten refers to animals that are clean according to the regulations in ch. 11. **Cover it with dust** is a token of burial.

17:14, 15 The reason for uncleanness in this context was contact with a carcass in which there was still blood that had not been drained. The Law forbade eating any animal that had died a natural death (Deut. 14:21). In such cases, a person became ritually **unclean** until evening, the mildest degree of uncleanness.

17:16 guilt: The mild degree of ritual uncleanness became a serious sin if the required cleansing was not done.

18:1, 2 The Lord here translates the divine name Yahweh, the name by which God revealed Himself to Moses in Ex. 6:2, 3. In using this name, God was basing His claim to the Israelites' devotion on His willingness to reveal Himself to them, to redeem them, and to be their God.

18:3 Israel had lived in **Egypt** for generations and had been dominated by the Egyptians. **Canaan** is the land God was going to give Israel. The Israelites would be tempted to imitate the Canaanites physically, culturally, and religiously.

18:4, 5 ordinances . . . statutes: These are decrees, laws, and acts of a permanent nature. **Judgments** (Heb. *mishpatim*) refers to judicial decisions involving situations that might not be addressed in the statutes. Through the ordinances and the judgments of God, Israel would know how to live. **he shall live by them:** God gave the law as a means of life on all levels— physical, moral, spiritual, and relational. However, as Paul observed, when the law was violated, it became a cause of death (Rom. 7:10–12). At that point, a greater remedy than the law was needed. This remedy is in Christ.

18:6–18 Israel's laws against incest were

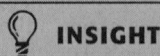 **INSIGHT**

Saved by Grace Or Effort?

God promised that whoever kept His statutes and judgments "shall live by them" (Lev. 18:5; compare Gal. 3:10–12), but the question remains exactly what is meant by the term "live." The context makes it doubtful that He was speaking of eternal salvation. More likely, He was indicating a quality of life that those who honor His ways will tend to experience. God wanted His people to live in purity, as distinct from the Egyptians, whose ordinances and customs He regarded as "abominable" (Lev. 18:3, 30). As for eternal life, Scripture is clear that salvation does not depend on human effort. It is always a gift of God's grace (Rom. 10:12, 13; Eph. 2:8, 9).

more complete and more advanced than any others in the ancient world. Genetic consequences of inbreeding and harmony in domestic relations are practical reasons for observing these taboos. But these are not the reasons emphasized in this list of forbidden unions. The incentive to obey lay in the positive urge to be faithful to Yahweh and to avoid the entrapments of the pagan practices of Israel's neighbors.

18:6 Anyone who is near of kin covers cases such as incest between father and daughter and between brother and full sister, even though they are absent from the following list. All the cases that appear in the list are based on blood relationship or marriage. To **uncover** someone's **nakedness** is to have sexual intercourse with that person.

18:7 The nakedness of your father does not imply a homosexual act. Rather, it emphasizes that to commit incest with the wife of one's father is symbolically to uncover the father's nakedness also, because the two are one flesh through marriage.

18:8 Father's wife may refer to a father's marriage partner after the death or divorce of one's mother, or it may refer to a wife or concubine who is not one's mother.

18:9, 10 Your sister refers to a half sister, since she is defined either as **the daughter of your father** or **the daughter of your mother. Elsewhere** refers to cases in which a father maintained multiple households of wives or concubines. It may also refer to illegitimate half sisters.

18:11, 12 Here, **begotten by your father** is a legal and not a biological term to indicate adoption. Legally she would be a full sister.

18:13–17 a woman and her daughter: This might involve a widow who lived with her daughter and son-in-law. **Nor shall you take** is a different verb; usually it means "to marry" in a context like this. Perhaps to marry a woman's granddaughter after having sexual union with her was not technically incest but close enough to be labeled **wickedness** and to be unacceptable.

18:18 as a rival to her sister: An example of the problems this situation can cause is the family life of Jacob, who married the sisters Leah and Rachel. Jacob, of course, did not violate this restriction, since it had not yet been given.

18:19 Her customary impurity refers to a woman's menstrual period. Sexual intercourse during this time was forbidden because the woman was ritually impure, and intercourse would make the man ritually impure as well.

18:20 Adultery is forbidden in Ex. 20:14; its penalty is given in Lev. 20:10.

18:21 Any of your descendants is liter-

ally, "of your seed." This usage ties this prohibition to the rest of the section on misuse of one's seed. Little is known about the Canaanite deity **Molech,** whose worshipers sacrificed their children to him as a whole burnt offering. Late in the Monarchy period this was done at a location called Tophet in the Hinnom Valley on the west side of Jerusalem (Jer. 7:31). Of course this practice was abhorrent to Yahweh. Ezekiel 16, which portrays Judah as His faithless wife, depicts these children sacrificed to Molech as God's own sons and daughters, slain by their own mother (vv. 20, 21).

18:22 Homosexuality here is labeled an **abomination,** something detestable to God both ritually and morally. Ritually, it was detestable partly because it was practiced in Canaanite religion, which God had commanded Israel not to follow.

18:23 Bestiality is labeled **perversion,** something out of the natural order. It, too, was a feature of some of the religions of Israel's neighbors.

18:24–30 The land had become so **defiled** by the perverted practices of the Canaanites that it was vomiting them out. For that reason, the land would be available to Israel to settle. The Israelites, however, needed to be careful to live as God's holy people in the land or it would vomit them out as well.

19:1–37 These laws about holy living in the community of faith seem quite diverse and unorganized. But they reflect three principle themes: (1) faithfulness and love to Yahweh; (2) faithfulness and love in personal relationships; (3) faithfulness defined as justice in business and legal affairs. Together they represent most areas of daily living; all of life is to be lived holy unto God. We should notice also that these laws relate back to the Ten Commandments (Ex. 20:3–17). Many do so quite directly, some less so, but all find their foundation there.

19:1–3 Revere means to respect and to obey. Under normal circumstances, young children are to obey their parents. Adult children are to respect their parents and concern themselves with their parents' welfare. **keep My Sabbaths:** The weekly Sabbath was an acknowledgment that not everything depended on the Israelites' efforts. It was an acknowledgment of God's lordship and His grace. It was valuable for worship, for rest and healing, for building relationships with family, and for regaining or strengthening an eternal perspective (Mark 2:23—3:5).

19:4, 5 The **peace offering** was a **free will** offering. Just like the Israelites, when we have peace, or wholeness, in God through the peace offering of Christ (Col. 1:19, 20), we can offer freely everything we are, everything we have, and everything we do.

19:6–10 Providing for **the poor and the stranger** (the alien who could not own land) was a priority in ancient Israelite society. Reserving the **gleanings** of a harvest for the poor is a very effective way of providing food for them. **I am the LORD** your God: The generosity of God's people was rooted in God's generosity toward the Israelites.

19:11–13 wages . . . until morning: A day laborer needed his pay daily to provide food for himself and his family. To withhold it for one's own gain or convenience created a hardship for him and was forbidden (Deut. 24:14, 15; James 5:4).

19:14 Taking advantage of those with physical limitations is forbidden, whether for profit, for spite, for ridicule, or as a practical joke. Not only is it wrong, it is dangerous, for God himself is their Champion.

19:15 In court, neither **the poor,** nor **the mighty,** nor even a person's **neighbor** were to be given any special treatment.

19:16 A **talebearer** is not just a gossip, but a slanderer, actively seeking to destroy another's reputation. **take a stand . . . neighbor:** Probably several kinds of cases could be included. In the context of the court in this paragraph, probably false swearing causing the death of the defendant, or failing to give testimony that would exonerate the accused, are most prominently in view.

19:17 hate your brother in your heart: Jesus addressed this principle in the Sermon on the Mount (Matt. 5:21–24). **rebuke your neighbor:** The way to avoid letting hatred build up was to confront the person. Ideally this would involve resolving the issue face to face. However, it also could involve taking the issue to court to settle it legally rather than taking it into one's own hands or allowing it to fester in one's heart.

19:18 Vengeance belongs to God (Deut. 32:35), partly because human vengeance often is carried out too zealously. God's vengeance is entirely just. **Bear any grudge** means actively keeping a grudge alive with an eye toward vengeance. **You shall love your neighbor as yourself:** Jesus identified this as one of only two commandments that, if kept, would fulfill all of the Law (Matt. 22:37–40).

19:19 Holiness means purity, in three important areas: (1) animal husbandry, (2) agriculture, and (3) domestic life. This principle also reflects reverence for creation as God made it.

19:20 The concubine, a woman of low social standing and few rights, may not have had the freedom to cry out when approached sexually. Therefore, she remained guiltless. Because the woman was a slave, the man escaped death but remained guilty before God. Atonement was necessary for him to receive forgiveness. **There shall be scourging** may be rephrased as "damages must be paid." The woman's owner probably received the compen-

---

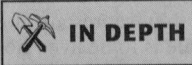 **IN DEPTH | What a Difference God Makes!**

The commands of God always flow out of His character. The numerous commands in Lev. 19 are related to holiness because "I the LORD your God am holy" (Lev. 19:2). Here are several standards that a holy God enacted on His people:

- Respect for parents (19:3).
- Keeping the Sabbath (19:3, 30).
- Forsaking idolatry (19:4).
- Concern for the poor (19:10).
- Honesty and integrity in business (19:11, 12, 35, 36).
- Protection of the physically challenged (19:14).
- Justice and truth in speech (19:16).
- Loving one's neighbor as oneself (19:18).
- Five years without harvesting a fruit tree for food (19:25).
- Dignified mourning (19:28).
- Forsaking magic and witchcraft (19:31).
- Respect for the elderly (19:32).
- Loving treatment of aliens (the "stranger," 19:34).
- Keeping the whole Law (19:37).

Notice the single reason given for all of the preceding statutes: "I am the LORD your God!"

sation, since the passage emphasizes that no money had yet been paid for her.

19:21-25 The most common reason suggested for this regulation is that young trees need to preserve their strength for themselves rather than putting it into fruit. In that case, the owner probably would have clipped off the blossoms in the first three years. The harvest of the fourth year was a kind of firstfruits (2:14). From the fifth year, the harvest belonged to the owner—after the firstfruits of each year's harvest had been given to God. **that it may yield to you its increase:** Faithfulness in observing this regulation was rewarded by increase in the production of fruit from the fifth year on.

19:26 Divination and **soothsaying** reveal a lack of trust in God to bring the best possible future. God, and not some demon or impersonal force, is all-powerful and directs the future.

19:27 Beards were standard among Israelite men. Shaving one's hair or beard often was a sign of mourning.

19:28 The human body was designed by God, who intended it to be whole and beautiful. Disfiguring the body dishonored God, in whose image the person was created. Cutting one's flesh **for the dead** and tattooing (or perhaps painting) one's body had religious significance among Israel's pagan neighbors. In Israel, such practices were signs of rebellion against God.

19:29 Fathers exercised total control over their daughters in Israel's patriarchal society. For a man in debt, facing the loss of his land, hiring out his daughter as a prostitute might have seemed like an attractive alternative. However, sexual relations are sacred. Forcing a daughter to violate that sanctity defiled her against her will.

19:30 An important, if familiar reminder. Repetition indicates its great importance.

19:31 Mediums and familiar spirits are different from what is mentioned in v. 26. Both of these may involve consulting the spirits of the dead. All contact with these or other spirits was strictly forbidden in Israel. It demonstrated lack of faith in and rebellion against God.

19:32 To **rise** when an elder entered one's presence was another way of showing reverence for God and submission to Him..

19:33, 34 Generous treatment of a **stranger,** or a resident alien, in the land was based on God's generous treatment of the Israelites when they were **strangers in the land of Egypt.** What God had done for them they were to pass along to others. This is still a good principle for God's people to follow. In v. 18, the Israelites were instructed, "Love your neighbor as yourself." Verse 34 expands that standard to include strangers. Jesus gave the

definitive illustration of this principle in His story of the Good Samaritan (Luke 10:30–36).

19:35-37 Injustice in judgment is injustice in legal transactions (vv. 11, 12, 15–18). **Injustice . . . in measurement** is one kind of

(Heb. *miqdash*) (Lev. 19:30; Ex. 15:17; 25:8) Strong's #4720: This noun means "holy place," a place separated and dedicated to God. It was the place where God had chosen to meet the Israelites. There priests would atone for the people's sin; in turn, the people would offer their worship and praise. Because it was God's dwelling place, the priests were prohibited from defiling it by entering while they were ceremonially unclean (21:12). But most important, the Israelites had to respect the sanctuary by approaching it with a contrite heart and a determination to praise their Creator. Just as Moses had to respect the ground where God made His presence known (Ex. 3:5), so now the Israelites had to respect the place where God had chosen to meet them.

injustice in business transactions. **ephah:** About five gallons. **hin:** A little less than a gallon. Once again, the fact that God had brought the Israelites **out of the land of Egypt** is cited as reason to believe He would provide for all of their needs. God had treated the Israelites generously. They could afford to treat each other fairly in their business dealings.

20:1-27 Specific penalties for specific transgressions. Every offence dealt with in Lev. 20 had been touched on before, mostly in chs. 18 and 19. The laws of those two chapters are mostly apodictic; that is, they are absolute commands or prohibitions setting forth laws in the form of timeless principles. The laws of ch. 20 are mostly casuistic; that is, they present laws in the form of specific cases with specific penalties attached. In most of the cases presented in this chapter, the penalty was death; these are serious offences. In three cases, the manner of execution was prescribed, the first and the last (vv. 2, 27) by stoning, the other (v. 14) by fire. The offences dealt with were pagan worship practices and illicit sexual relationships, which were often found in Canaanite religious practices.

20:2-5 strangers: All of the people dwelling in the land, whether citizens or not, were required to abstain from religious practices that defiled God's **sanctuary** and profaned His **holy name. I will . . . cut him off:** Execution by stoning seems to have been the way God set His face against the offender. However, if those responsible did not carry out the sentence on a guilty person, God executed judgment Himself. **prostitute themselves:** God "wed" Israel to Himself at Sinai. The Israelites' betrayal of that sacred bond by going after other gods was often portrayed as prostitution.

20:6–8 Who sanctifies you means "who sets you apart (to Myself)." There is an aspect of the worshiper's being set apart to God for which the worshiper was responsible, and an aspect God took upon Himself. The worshiper accepted God's gifts and agreed to forsake all other allegiances. God gave the Law to show the worshiper how to live set apart *to* God and *from* all other allegiances.

20:9 One **who curses his father or his mother** was very far from honoring them (Lev. 19:3; Ex. 20:12). **His blood shall be upon him** signifies that capital punishment was deserved. This statement also reassured the executioners that they were not guilty of shedding the offenders' blood. This was important, since there was no professional justice system at this time in ancient Israel. Nearly all functions of the law were performed by private citizens.

20:10–16 The penalties for these illicit sexual unions are grouped in this chapter with worship of other gods partly because Canaanite worship involved numerous sexual aberrations, such as in the practice of sympathetic magic, which attempted to influence the gods to bless the land with fertility.

All these sexual offences carried the death penalty, explicitly pronounced. Death for sexual misconduct sounds harsh to the modern ear, especially to many who believe there is no such thing as sexual misconduct. These offences, however, were not *merely* sexual in nature; in many cases, they also represented rebellion against God and participation in the sexual worship of Canaan's fertility deities, primarily Baal

and his sister-consort. And in most cases they also involve disruption of one or more families, a grave offence in and of itself.

20:10, 11 The adulterer and the adulteress both entered freely into the affair. Both were punished.

20:12 Perversion literally means "mixing, confusion"—in this case, of the natural order.

20:13, 14 Marries (literally, *takes*) probably means to have as a common-law wife. **burned . . . he and they:** Perhaps this was done after the stoning to prevent burial, which was very important to the ancients. Not to be buried was thought to make a peaceful afterlife impossible.

20:15–17 In these two cases the death penalty is prescribed by the less direct phrase **shall be cut off.**

20:18 her sickness: That is, her menstrual flow (15:19–24; 18:19). **exposed . . . her blood:** In menstruation, the mysterious powers of blood and sex are drawn together. Casual disregard shows disrespect for God as the Creator as well as for the human role in procreation.

20:19, 20 They shall die childless may not seem to be a severe penalty, but it was greatly dreaded in the ancient world, where continuation of the family line was extremely important. If this situation were an extramarital affair, as implied by the verb **lies with,** the childlessness would affect two families. The man would have no heirs, and the woman would lose her status as a faithful wife.

20:21 takes: If a man died childless before his father's death and the division of the family property, his brother was to marry the widow. Their firstborn would be considered the dead brother's heir. Otherwise it was forbidden for a surviving brother to marry his dead brother's widow. It might seem that he was trying to gain the dead man's estate for himself. **They shall be childless:** The Hebrew implies that if the man already had heirs, none would survive him, and that this marriage would not produce others.

20:22, 23 I am casting out: God took full

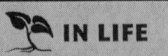 **IN LIFE**   ## A Definitive Standard

Believe anything you want." "You've got your truth, I've got mine." The frightening thing about such modern viewpoints is that those who believe them become the definers of truth and reality. They leave no room for objective truth or absolutes. Yet if there are no absolutes determined by a Source above ourselves then we are all gods, or else no truth exists, and we have nothing to bind us together or define how we should treat each other. God did not leave His people Israel in such a philosophical morass. He clearly spelled out moral and spiritual absolutes and warned His people to seek ultimate truth from Him, not from other sources (Lev. 20:6–8).

responsibility for His judgment on the wickedness of the people of Canaan, for which He would use Israel as His instrument.

20:24–26 Flowing with milk and honey conveys the agricultural potential of the land. Abundant wildflowers were the source of the honey and point to the excellent grazing for flocks and herds that would provide the milk. **Has separated you** emphasizes that the people of Israel were distinct from the people of Canaan whom they would displace. Israel's God was different from the gods of Canaan. Israel

INSIGHT
Mediums and Spiritists

The medium or spiritist pretends to find out things, especially about the future, through contact with the dead or other kinds of spirits from the realm of the dead (Lev. 20:27). This common sort of magic appears with many variations and methods, in both ancient and modern times. The Bible subjects these practices to ridicule and forbids them.

needed to operate on a different, higher standard of morality to demonstrate that to the world.

20:27 This verse is not out of place; it is necessary to complete the chiastic arrangement of the chapter, a frequent and important literary stylistic device in the Hebrew Bible.

21:1–24 Here are regulations for the priests about mourning, marriage, and fitness for the priesthood.

21:1 defile himself: Contact with a dead body made a person unclean. Since the priests ministered before the altar of the Lord, the occasions on which they were allowed to be unclean were restricted. While they were unclean they could not perform their priestly duties. This was in marked contrast to much of the ancient world, where the dead often were regarded as holy and even worshiped. In the revelation of God to Israel, it was clear that death was *the* great defilement, the greatest perversion of God's purpose for the human race. Death could not be holy; the dead only could be rescued from the uncleanness of death through resurrection, a topic on which Israel received little revelation this early in her history.

21:2, 3 The only exceptions for the priest were his closest relatives. For them he could attend mourning rites. The wife is probably included in the term **relatives who are**

nearest to him. The **virgin sister** still belonged to the priest's father's family. A married sister belonged to her husband's family; the priest could not attend mourning rites for her.

21:4, 5 These were pagan mourning customs. All Israel was forbidden to observe them (19:27, 28). Naturally, that prohibition began with the priests.

21:6 The bread belonged to God because it was sacrificed on His altar. There is no suggestion that God needed or ate this food, only that it belonged to Him. The priests received portions of it as one part of God's provision for them and their families (6:14—7:36).

21:7 A priest could marry a widow, but other women who had been with a man in any sexual relationship were forbidden to him. A priest's marriage symbolized his special, holy relationship to God.

21:8, 9 Prostitution, the ultimate promiscuity, was the opposite of holiness, the ultimate faithfulness. The priest's daughter was to reflect her father's holiness to God, especially in an age when everything one did reflected on one's family.

21:10–12 The high priest was not allowed to become ritually unclean, even at the death of his father or mother. Nor could he display any signs of mourning. His duties in the sanctuary could not be interrupted. For his exalted position before God, the high priest sometimes paid a high personal price.

21:13–15 The standard for the high priest's wife was higher than for the wife of an ordinary priest. The high priest could marry only a **virgin. Of his own people** could mean either another priest's daughter or an Israelite woman. **His posterity** had to be pure. By marrying a woman without sexual experience, the High Priest would ensure that his son truly was his. Alternatively, this verse could mean that the High Priest was not to defile his seed by lying with any woman other than his wife. Perhaps these two possible meanings are not mutually exclusive.

21:16–23 Prohibition of priestly service by those with physical imperfections. In the service of the sanctuary, physical wholeness was intended to model ritual and moral wholeness and perfection. Animals brought for sacrifice had to be without blemish; so, too, the priests who offered them upon the altar. This did not mean a priest with a physical deformity was immoral, only that he could not be the object lesson and model the priest was intended to be. Therefore, he could not serve as a priest.

21:18–20 Most of these physical conditions were permanent; a person afflicted by them could never serve as a priest. But some, like a broken limb or a skin condition, would heal with time. The priest suffering from them was barred from serving as a priest only so long as he was afflicted.

21:20, 21 Neither **eczema** nor **scab** is included in the list of things that made an ordinary Israelite unclean (13:1–46). As with mourning rites and marriage partners, the priests were held to a higher standard than the people because the priests had a more public role in modeling holiness to God. This was not because God had a double standard of moral behavior, one for the "religious" and one for the "non-religious." Rather, the priests had a more public role in the physical, outward modeling of holiness to God, which is both inward and outward, affecting and transforming all aspects of life.

21:22 He may eat: Physical defect did not imply a moral defect. The person afflicted still had access to the food of the altar by which the priests lived. He was not denied his provision, nor was he forced to leave the sanctuary.

21:23 My sanctuaries probably refers to the two divisions of the tabernacle: (1) the holy place, where the altar of incense stood; and (2) the Most Holy Place, where the ark of the covenant rested. This implies that the person with a physical defect had access to the outer court around the tabernacle as long as he did not come too close to the **altar** of burnt offering, which stood in the outer court.

21:24 These instructions were not given secretly to the priests, but publicly. Each Israelite was to know what God expected of him or her, and what God expected of the priests.

22:1, 2 separate . . . holy things: When the priests were ritually impure, they were not to come near the offerings the Israelites had brought to the tabernacle for dedication to God. **profane My holy name by what they dedicate:** If a ritually unclean priest officiated at a sacrifice, the value of sacrifice would be nullified.

22:3 All . . . your generations made the restriction as broad as possible in any one generation, and as broad as possible through all time. **Cut off from My presence** does not mean executed or banished from the community, but permanently denied the privilege of ministering as a priest.

22:4 leper: Regulations concerning leprosy are given in Lev. 13:1–46; 14:1–32. Regulations about **discharge** are found in 15:1–18.

22:5, 6 creeping thing . . . until evening: Clean and unclean animals are listed in ch. 11.

22:7 it is his food: The sacrifices brought by the Israelites were a major part of the daily provisions for the priests.

22:8, 9 Ordinary Israelites could eat this meat (17:15, 16). The priests were held to a higher standard.

22:10 Three groups of persons were denied access to the meat of the offerings: (1) the **outsider** (literally, *any stranger*), whether a foreigner or an Israelite not of Aaron's family line; (2) the **one who dwells** as a guest **with the priest;** and (3) **a hired servant,** who was not a member of the priest's household but worked in it on a daily basis.

22:11 Slaves, whether bought or born in the household, were allowed to eat of the priest's share of the consecrated food. They were part of his household.

22:12 A priest's daughter became a member of her husband's family when she married. If her husband was not a priest, she lost her right to eat consecrated food.

22:13 no outsider shall eat it: A repetition of the first injunction, marking the close of these prohibitions and strengthening the emphasis on this one.

22:14–17 Restitution plus one-fifth was the penalty here for an ineligible person who ate of the **holy offering.** In 5:14–16, the penalty was the sacrifice of a ram and restitution plus one-fifth. Both contexts are concerned with one who had eaten consecrated food without knowing it. The higher penalty (5:14–16) may have been for an Israelite, who never was eligible to eat such food; the lower penalty (22:14–16) was for a priest who usually could eat it, but on the occasion in question he should not have eaten because of ritual uncleanness.

22:18 strangers: Resident aliens in Israel were permitted to worship God with the Israelites. If a resident alien accepted the Israelites' God as his God, he was accepted at God's sanctuary under the same conditions as any Israelite was.

22:19–21 without blemish . . . no defect in it: This standard was addressed later by the prophet Malachi when some in his day were bringing defective animals to sacrifice on God's altar (Mal. 1:7–14). We are not to offer God less than our best.

22:22, 23 The prohibitions on sacrificial animals with bodily defects parallel many of the prohibitions on priests with bodily defects serving before the altar of God (21:17–23).

22:23 An exception was made for a **freewill offering,** since it was not required and was not made in fulfillment of **a vow.**

22:24, 25 cut: Castrated animals were not acceptable for sacrifice. **from a foreigner's hand:** Israel's sacrificial animals were to be raised by Israelites who worshiped God, not by foreigners who worshiped a multitude of pagan gods. This also removed the temptation for an Israelite to buy an inferior animal from a foreigner in an attempt to save money and avoid sacrificing an animal from his own flock or herd.

22:26, 27 The eighth day parallels the time of circumcision for the human male baby. This regulation probably was chiefly kindhearted. The mother, though an animal, was not to be deprived of her newborn in the first

INSIGHT

Give God Your Best

When it came to sacrifices, offerings, and the payment of vows, God required that the Israelites bring their best animals and goods to Him. Nothing with a defect was allowed (Lev. 22:20–23). This was because God is a holy, perfect God. He was worthy of the best that His people had to offer. In the end, all that they had belonged to Him anyway (compare Deut. 8:18; 1 Chr. 29:14, 15).

days after its birth, when both her maternal instincts and her milk supply were at their highest.

22:28–30 This also may have had a humanitarian aim, to avoid taking the life of a mother and her offspring on the same day. Economic care also may be reflected here; a man with a small flock who offered two animals on the same day was being perhaps foolish and wasteful, besides zealous. We do God no favors if we give all our substance to His worship place and then depend on charity for our own existence from that time on.

22:31–33 All of these elements had been expressed before, but not all together. God's person, His name, His present action in sanctifying His people, and His past action in rescuing them from slavery in Egypt all were given as the basis of Israel's worship.

23:1–44 The holy convocations of Israel. These are called "appointed times" and "sacred assemblies," and most called for special sacrifices above the regular sacrifices. These assemblies all had religious significance, of course. Some were agricultural harvest festivals, having as their focus the successive stages of the harvest season; they were times of thanksgiving for God's bounty to the nation. Others became associated with historical events of the nation. The celebrations, then, had a two-fold character, of thanks for God's goodness in giving food and for His mighty acts in history on behalf of His people. Together, the sacred assemblies encompassed the agricultural and the religious aspects of the life of the nation, memorialized its history and

marking the beginnings of both its religious and its civil calendars. All this emphasized that God and one's faith in God cannot be compartmentalized and set aside from the affairs of daily life. Different in character as they were, these sacred assemblies served a common purpose of bringing the nation together to reflect on and rejoice in God's goodness.

Each speech giving instructions for a sacred assembly includes: (1) the name or definition of the occasion; (2) most importantly, the time of its celebration; (3) some general indication, usually short and seldom with details, of how it was to be observed.

23:1 the LORD spoke to Moses: The instructions about each convocation are marked off in this chapter by the normal introduction for a speech in Leviticus. The instructions for each could be read separately, while still reminding the people that each had been ordained by God.

23:2 Speak to the children of Israel: These instructions were for all of the people, and not just for the priests. **The feasts of the LORD** literally means "appointed times of the Lord." This phrase emphasizes that these were specifically appointed holy days. Here *of* means both "ordained by" and "consecrated to" or "honoring" the Lord. **Holy convocations** were sacred assemblies of all the people called together at the appointed times by the priests. The Feast of Unleavened Bread and the Feast of Tabernacles lasted seven and eight days, respectively. The first and the last day of each were holy meetings. The days between were part of the holiday, though there were no special meetings on them.

23:3, 4 Six days shall work be done: Perhaps as important to human well-being as the day of rest are the six days of work. Work was given to the human race in the Garden. Work is one of the ways humans bear the image of God. Work itself is not a curse on the race. Instead, it remains, even after the Fall, God's good gift. The regular **seventh day** of rest and other holidays from work are ordained for our refreshment and the chance to commune more closely with God and His people. **A Sabbath of solemn rest** may be restated as "a Sabbath that is all a Sabbath should be"—a day of rest and of solemn, joyful worship. **In all your dwellings** emphasized the universal nature of the Sabbath. It was not to be observed only in the sanctuary; it was to be celebrated in every household.

23:5 fourteenth day of the first month: This would fall between mid-March and mid-April. The **Passover** celebrated Israel's exodus from Egypt (Ex. 12:1–28).

23:6–9 The Feast of Unleavened Bread immediately followed Passover, beginning the **fifteenth day** of Nisan. Later in Israel's history, this and other festivals involved pilgrimages to the central sanctuary, first in Shiloh and later in Jerusalem. This feast marked the beginning of the barley harvest, the first important grain harvest of the year. In practice, the Passover and the Feast of Unleavened Bread were observed together as an eight-day festival. In the instructions of Ex. 12:1–28 they are treated as one. **Unleavened** means without yeast. **Customary work** was work that could be left a day or two without problems. Essential or emergency tasks could be done. For example, animals could be milked. **an offering:** Instructions for this offering are given in Num. 28:16–25.

23:10 a sheaf of the firstfruits: This bundle of the first harvested barley belonged to God as a special offering, acknowledging God's provision of the harvest. Paul called Christ "the firstfruits of those who have fallen asleep"—the first of the dead to be resurrected (1 Cor. 15:20).

23:11, 12 To **wave the sheaf** was to elevate the offering before God. This **Sabbath** was either the first or the last day of the Feast of Unleavened Bread, or the seventh-day Sabbath during the week of the Feast, or the seventh-day Sabbath following the Feast. If one of the latter two, **the day after the Sabbath** would have been the first day of the week. The symbolism of Christ, the firstfruits of the Resurrection, rising on the first day of the week, the day of firstfruits, makes the last two alternatives attractive. But there is strong evidence also that this Sabbath was the first day of the Feast.

23:13 Two-tenths of an ephah was twice the grain offering for the regular morning and evening burnt offerings (Ex. 29:40). Exodus 29:38–42 specifies a **drink offering** to accompany the regular morning and evening offerings. **Wine** was the third major agricultural product of the land, along with grain and oil.

23:14 An Israelite could not eat the grain of a new harvest until he had brought the offering of the firstfruits to the sanctuary. **Parched grain** was a favorite food of those working in the harvest. Newly harvested heads of grain were roasted in a fire and eaten when cool (Ruth 2:14).

23:15–21 The Feast of Weeks (Pentecost). Though not named here, it is called the Feast of Weeks in Ex. 34:22. It received its name from its timing **seven sabbaths** (seven weeks) after the **wave offering** of the firstfruits during the Feast of Unleavened Bread, the week of Passover. The Christian celebration of Pentecost is fixed fifty days after Easter, the Passover on which Jesus became the Paschal Lamb.

23:17 Firstfruits refers to the firstfruits of wheat. The Feast of Weeks comes near the end of the wheat harvest in Palestine. Either the grain for baking these firstfruit loaves was set aside at the beginning of the harvest or the first grain used from the new harvest qualified as its firstfruits.

23:18–21 for the priest: Grain and meat from the sacrificial offerings were a large part of God's provision for the priests and their families (Lev. 7:1–14, 31–36).

23:22 The Israelites were to be generous when they reaped a plentiful harvest because God gave the harvest to them (19:9, 10). Grapes are not mentioned here because the Feast of Weeks came well before the grape harvest.

23:23–25 The Feast of Trumpets was the first of the fall festivals, marking the New Year according to the civil calendar (the religious year began in the spring).

23:24 The seventh month . . . first day falls in mid-September. **a memorial:** Israel remembered God's goodness, which was expressed in the covenant, and asked God to continue to remember that covenant. **Blowing of trumpets** marked solemn, joyful, and urgent occasions in ancient Israel.

23:25 an offering made by fire: The animals and amounts of grain for this offering are listed in Num. 29:2–5.

23:26–32 A fuller prescription for The Day of Atonement is given in Lev. 16.

23:27 Day of Atonement: The day was not given this name in ch. 16. Literally, it is the "Day of Atonements"; that is, the day above all days, when complete atonement was made for all Israel.

23:28 do no work: On the Day of Atonement, the most important work of all was done by the high priest in the Most Holy Place. To do any lesser work would have been sacrilegious.

23:29, 30 I will destroy: God Himself would see to it that the transgressor of this most holy day would be called to account.

23:31, 32 This is the third time in this passage that the Israelites were commanded to **afflict** their **souls,** indicating the importance of this duty for this day. **from evening to evening:** This is the only place in the regulations of Leviticus where the beginning time of a day of observance is noted.

23:33–36 The Feast of Tabernacles was the fall harvest festival to thank God for the success of the fruit crops, of which the most important were the grape and the olive. It also had a historical foundation, to remind Israel about their temporary dwellings in the Wilderness for the forty years. Thus, it also was a thanks to God for preserving Israel during that time and for bringing them safely into the land they would occupy when they began to observe this festival week.

23:36 A sacred assembly indicates the last day of a joyous eight-day celebration.

23:37, 38 Besides . . . which you give was a gentle warning not to bring an offering for a special festival day and then attempt to use it again for one of the regular offerings commanded in chs. 1—7. God is generous beyond measure with His people. God's people should be generous with their offerings to Him.

23:39, 40 the fruit of beautiful trees: In celebrating the Feast of Tabernacles today, people use the citron, a fruit like the lemon, but

A temporary booth, or shelter, near Jerusalem, set up to celebrate the Feast of Tabernacles, also known as the Feast of Booths (Lev. 23:33–43).

larger. **Leafy trees** is thought to be the myrtle.

23:41, 42 The implication is that the **booths** were made of the tree branches.

23:43 Dwelling in booths for seven days would remind the Israelites of God's goodness in preserving them through the hardships in the wilderness. The Feast of Tabernacles was both a celebration of harvest and a thanksgiving for God's protection of His people.

23:44 A final notice that Moses had obeyed; the people had heard the instructions God had for them.

24:1–4 Pure oil was needed for the lampstand because it stood within the tabernacle. **pressed olives:** Oil for the sacred lampstand was extracted by pounding olives in a mortar by hand, a process that produced the finest, lightest olive oil. **The veil of the Testimony** separated the holy place from the Most Holy Place. **Aaron:** Aaron and his sons (Ex. 27:21). **From evening until morning** indicates tending the lamps twice a day, not tending them throughout the night.

24:5–9 twelve cakes: One for each of the tribes of Israel. The **frankincense on each row** was not poured on the loaves because the priests had to eat them. When the loaves were replaced, the frankincense was burned as **a memorial, an offering made by fire to the LORD**. Every Sabbath, new loaves replaced the ones that had been there for a week. **eat it in a holy place:** See Lev. 7:1–14, 31–36 for regulations concerning the priests' food. Jesus referred to the light of the menorah and the showbread when He called Himself the "light of the world" (John 8:12) and "the bread of life" (John 6:35). The showbread eaten by the priests foreshadowed the bread of the Lord's Supper eaten by Christians. David, even though he was not a priest, ate the showbread when he fled from Saul (1 Sam. 21:1–6). In a conversation with His opponents, Jesus approved of David's action (Luke 6:1–5). The Law could be set aside to meet genuine human needs.

24:10–12 Blaspheming **the name of the LORD** was forbidden (Ex. 22:28). The question in this case was whether Israel's law applied to those who were not full-blooded Israelites. Note the care in recording that the offender's father was an Egyptian, as well as his mother's name, her father's name, and their tribe.

24:13, 14 The offender was taken **outside the camp** as a sign that he had been cut off from the people of Israel, and so that his death would not defile the camp. **Lay their hands on his head** was a witness that they had heard the words of blasphemy and a sign that his sin was his own responsibility.

24:15 His God can refer to either the Creator or any pagan deities the person worshiped. Anyone who cursed the Creator bore the responsibility for the **sin** and was executed. If an Israelite worshiped a pagan deity, he was liable for the death penalty on those grounds. Foreigners were allowed to worship Israel's God, but if they did not, they were not to worship their own gods while living among the people of Israel (Lev. 17:8, 9). For such a person to curse his own god in Israel's presence was of no concern to Israel. In that case, he **shall bear his sin** meant, "If his god desires to punish him, let him." Of course, faithful Israelites would have understood that other gods do not exist, and could not punish anyone who curses them.

24:16 To blaspheme **the name of the LORD** was a different matter. God had rescued the Israelites from Egypt and bound them to

Himself in covenant at Sinai. To blaspheme His name was rebellion. Rebellion, even against human governments, carried the death penalty. **Stranger as well as him who is born in the land** literally means "like stranger, like native." The laws of Israel applied to resident aliens as well as to citizens.

24:17–22 The verb suggests murder not accidental homicide in the case of killing a human. Yet in the case of killing an animal, the penalty of restitution to its owner for its value anticipates and denies the claim that an animal's life requires a human life in punishment. By arrangement and by repetition, this passage strongly teaches that animals are not equal to human beings.

24:19, 20 eye for eye: This law is also found in Ex. 21:23–25. Its purpose was not to *require* the injured party to inflict *equal* bodily harm on the one who had injured him, but to *forbid* him from inflicting *greater* bodily harm.

24:21, 22 One reason for these seemingly unrelated laws at this place in Leviticus was to anticipate the question of whether other laws would also apply to non-Israelites. The answer was yes, they would apply to the **stranger.**

24:23 If this closure to the narrative passage were missing, the readers would feel the incompleteness.

25:1 Mount Sinai was where God gave the covenant. Thus the following was part of the covenant and should be observed in order to keep faith with God.

25:2 The land which I give you is a reminder that the land belongs to God. The Israelites lived in it by His grace and under His direction. All of the laws of the Sabbath year and of the Jubilee were based on this premise. If Israel would follow God's direction while occupying the land, He would bless them abundantly. To that end, these instructions were aimed at restoring the social order that had become unbalanced as time passed. Unchecked, the rich would continue to get richer, and the poor would never have a chance to escape their poverty. **A sabbath to the LORD** is the same phrase used for the weekly Sabbath (23:3). The

people rested weekly from their work; the land was to rest every seventh year from its work. The principle of the land needing rest has been rediscovered in recent years and is practiced in various ways by farmers of many nations. The prophets denounced Israel for many violations of this principle. The Chronicler interpreted Jeremiah to mean that one reason for the seventy-year Babylonian exile was that the land could enjoy all the sabbatical years it had missed because Judah had ignored them (2 Chr. 36:21). In the list of curses for disobedience in Lev. 26:34, 35, this is exactly what God threatened.

25:3–7 shall not reap: Reaping and gathering for storage and selling were not permitted in the Sabbath year. However, harvesting for daily needs was permitted. Since the purpose of these laws was to promote social equality in Israel, anyone, regardless of social standing, was permitted to use anything that grew, wherever it grew. Even the wild **beasts** of the field are mentioned here, to emphasize that God would provide for every creature. Of course, Israel's main provision during this time was the bumper crop produced the year before the Sabbath year (vv. 21, 22).

25:8–17 The institution of the Year of Jubilee. After seven cycles of sabbatical years came the fiftieth year, the year of Jubilee. The seventh month was the beginning of the civil year. Its tenth day, the Day of Atonement, was an annual day of liberty from sin and guilt. Appropriately, in the fiftieth year it was to be the day to **proclaim liberty throughout all the land to all its inhabitants,** a day of liberty from debt and bond-service and the end of separation from one's ancestral land. In keeping with the concept of God's ownership of the land, no Israelite was to sell the land allotted to him as his inheritance. If an Israelite fell on hard times, he might be forced, in effect, to lease his land, probably his creditor, but only until the Jubilee year, when all debts were to be forgiven. The "sale" (long-term lease) of land was negotiated according to the number of years left until the next Jubilee. More years meant a greater price; fewer years, a smaller price. This precept

 **INSIGHT** | **The Year of Jubilee**

Israel's Jubilee year (Lev. 25:9) occurred every fiftieth year. It was like a Sabbath year (25:3–7) except that it had the additional purpose of returning property and lands to their owners and servants to their families (25:10). This meant that twice each century, the economy of Israel was somewhat leveled, though by no means redistributed. The point was that no family's lands should be permanently lost to creditors and no one's freedom permanently lost to servitude.

was intended to allow every Israelite family to begin again about once a generation, regardless of what had happened in the past. Thus, a few bad crop years in a row did not wipe out the family forever. Not even the laziness or moral lapses of the father could impoverish his descendants for more than one generation. Unfortunately, this wise provision, designed to give hope to individuals and social stability to the nation, was seldom, if ever, observed.

25:9, 10 To **proclaim liberty** meant specifically that all debts were canceled, all Israelites who had had to sell themselves into slavery were freed, and all land reverted to its original owner. The same phrase occurs in Is. 61:1, the passage Jesus read in the synagogue in Nazareth at the beginning of His earthly ministry. Jesus' mission on this earth was to proclaim liberty to all who have lost their inheritance and become servants of the Evil One.

25:11, 12 The fiftieth or **Jubilee** year was itself a Sabbath year (vv. 2–7). Observing the Jubilee year would have meant two years of rest in a row for the land.

25:13–17 To refrain from oppressing a fellow citizen is one way of showing **fear,** or reverence and respect, for God.

25:18, 19 If those who live in God's land follow His instructions, they will **dwell there in safety,** free from want and external threats.

25:18–22 Rather than waiting for the obvious question of provision for the year when harvest was forbidden, God raised and answered the question himself.

25:21, 22 I will command My blessing on you: If the Israelites would obey God's command to let the land rest, they could be sure that the land would provide for their needs. Parts of **three years** were involved. In the seventh year, no planting or harvesting for storage would be allowed. Some of the crops of the eighth year would not be harvested and ready for use until the ninth year had begun.

25:23, 24 The principle governing all of these laws was that the land did not belong to Israel; it belonged to God. **you are strangers and sojourners with Me:** God emphasized that the Israelites would live in a land that was not their own. Likewise, the Christian believer lives on this earth as a stranger and a sojourner, looking for a city "whose builder and maker is God" (Heb. 11:10).

25:25–28 Each family's land was the source of their food and income. For a family to be dispossessed meant, in most cases, becoming someone else's servants and dependents. Most people would have worked hard to avoid that, but illness, crop failure, or other misfortune could force a man into debt to the point that his only option was to sell (lease) his land. In that

case, three options of increasing hardship came into play. (1) **A redeeming relative** could redeem (buy) the land of the man in difficulty (v. 25). From the proceeds he could pay off his creditors. The land stayed in the extended family, the poor family stayed on their land, and eventually the redeemer was repaid. The redeemer was the nearest male relative; if he could not fulfill this obligation, it passed down the kinship line until someone could. This is the scenario of Ruth 4, when Boaz acted as redeemer and bought Naomi's field. (2) A man might have no relative to redeem his land but be able in time to save enough to buy it back himself. The purchase price would be prorated according to the number of years left until the next Jubilee year, and the appropriate amount would be returned to the purchaser (vv. 26, 27). (3) A man might have to wait until the Jubilee year to return to the land of his inheritance (v. 28). But even in that most extreme situation, there was hope that the family would be able to return to their inheritance debt-free and make a fresh start. The law of redemption and the law of the Jubilee year are vivid symbols of what Jesus Christ did on the Cross for every person. What our first father and mother lost in the Garden, we could not by any means retrieve. Jesus Christ, our elder Brother, redeemed it for us. We have been evicted from our inheritance, but in the year of Jubilee we will be allowed to return. This is part of the already-but-not-yet tension of the kingdom of God. It has broken through already here on this earth, but its complete realization is not yet. For that we hope, just as the ancient Israelite family waited and hoped for the year of Jubilee.

25:29, 30 A walled city indicates one of the larger cities of the land. These provided more economic diversity than unwalled villages. A person's survival did not depend on owning a city house. Therefore, the time limit to redeem these houses was one year. They were bought and sold without regard to the Jubilee year.

25:31 An unwalled village in ancient Israel was tiny by today's standards. Many had only a handful of families. The basic economic activity was farming the land within a walking radius of the village. For people living in these villages, losing the family home would be nearly as great a disaster as the loss of their farmland. Therefore, village **houses** were included in the laws of redemption and Jubilee.

25:32–34 The Levites' **houses,** too, were protected under the basic law of redemption and Jubilee (vv. 25–28) because their homes were their only substantial assets.

25:35–38 Charging interest on a loan to a poor Israelite—**your brother**—would only hinder his financial progress. This law probably did not prohibit interest on commercial loans, which was another level of economic activity, one that did not threaten anyone's survival. Some might have been tempted to refuse to lend money to a poor fellow citizen, preferring to lend to non-Israelites in order to collect interest. This explains the command **then you shall help him, like a stranger or a sojourner.** Mercy and generosity were to be stronger motivations than financial gain. That remains a valid principle today.

25:37 Perhaps seed for planting, as well as **food** for eating, is meant here.

25:38 The motivation to be generous to the poor should have come from a person's gratitude to God for His generosity in bringing Israel out of **Egypt,** giving them **the land of Canaan,** and making a covenant **to be** their **God.** Serving a generous God, God's people can afford to be generous, too.

25:39–55 The treatment and redemption of bondservants. For more than one hundred years the world has been virtually free of that slavery defined as the ownership of one human being by another; any mention of slavery naturally raises serious questions. These Levitical laws deal not with true slavery but with the case of any Israelite indebted so deeply he could not clear his debt with money. He would pay his creditor instead with labor. Several principles are set forth here. (1) An Israelite was not to be reckoned or treated as a permanent possession; he and his children could not be inherited. (2) He was not to be put to the humiliating or severe treatment of a slave (severe treatment of a slave is discouraged elsewhere). (3) A kinsman could redeem him, or he could redeem himself if that became possible. (4) If not redeemed before it, he was to go out in the year of Jubilee. (5) These rules applied whether he was bonded to a fellow Israelite, to a resident alien, or to a temporary resident. These rules have the same foundation as redemption and Jubilee for the land. All Israel belonged to God; if they were God's servants, they could not become the possession of another human, whether fellow Israelite or alien. Reverence for God was a further basis for the humane treatment of any person coming under one's authority.

25:44–47 Foreign **slaves** could be bought, sold, and inherited like other property. This does not mean God approves of slavery. He made laws to ameliorate the practices of that time.

25:48–55 Though this order of kinship in redeeming is not mandatory, it was the natural progression from close relative to more distant relative. A brother, if he could, would be the one to **redeem.** If no brother could or if the man had no brother, an uncle would be next, and then a cousin.

26:1–46 Blessings for obedience and curses for disobedience are two important elements of the ancient Near Eastern covenant treaty form, after which God's covenant with Israel at Sinai was modeled. The blessings are set forth in a list, followed by a list of threatened disasters that would follow Israel's disobedience and rebellion. The list of curses typically was longer; this list follows that pattern.

26:1 A sacred pillar was a stone or wooden column erected to represent a pagan god or goddess. It was not a likeness, but a symbol. Together, the four terms used in this verse cover all the possibilities for pagan images. **I am the LORD** your God confronts the Israelites with a choice of allegiances. Would they love the living God or idols?

26:2–13 This section uses an *if-then* format. Verse 3 is the *if* section, the conditions under which God's blessings would be poured out on the land and the people.

26:4, 5 The blessings were in three areas of Israel's life. First, God promised the resources for abundant supplies of food, including rain whenever it would be needed. **threshing . . . sowing:** The grain harvest was finished by early- to mid-June. The grape harvest began about two months later. Having two months to thresh the grain indicated a large harvest. Sowing could not occur until after the first rains

INSIGHT | **Establish Ground Rules**

God clearly defined rewards for obedience (Lev. 26:3–13) and punishments for disobedience (26:39). And He also promised to remember His people when they repented (26:40–45). In doing so, God modeled two important principles for the effective use of authority. (1) Leaders need to establish and clearly communicate what they expect others to do and to refrain from doing. (2) Leaders need to clarify the consequences for fulfilling or not fulfilling those expectations.

softened the ground enough to plow, usually from mid-October on. A two-month grape harvest also would be a bumper crop. **Dwell in your land safely** hints at the next area of God's blessing on Israel.

26:6–10 Second, God promised security or **peace** in the land. Neither animal nor human adversaries would be successful against Israel. The bears and lions, which were dangerous to humans, would be neutralized. Any human enemy daring to attack Israel would be routed easily, even at odds of a hundred to one.

26:10 clear out the old: Israel would not finish eating the old harvest before the new one was brought in.

26:11–13 Third, God promised His presence in Israel's midst. He would **set** His **tabernacle among** them. Furthermore, He would actively **walk among** them, looking out for their welfare, helping and protecting them. **I will be your God, and you shall be My people** is the covenant by which God bound Himself to Israel and Israel to Him. Later prophets often reminded Israel of this when they called the nation back to faithfulness to God.

26:14–39 These are curses upon Israel for unfaithfulness to God and God's covenant. They contain many points of contact with the blessings, reversing specific blessings into correspondingly opposite curses. For instance, if Israel remained faithful, one hundred Israelites would rout 10,000 of their enemy in battle (v. 8), but if they rebelled against God, they would flee at the sound of a rattling leaf (v. 36). These curses are divided into five sections.

26:14, 15 As with the blessings, the curses are presented in an *if-then* format. These two verses are the *if* section, the conditions under which God would bring disaster on His people in an effort to turn their hearts back to Him. **Commandments . . . statutes . . . judgments . . . covenant** cover all of the legislation God had given at Sinai and the agreement Israel had entered into with God there.

26:16, 17 Terror, various diseases, and famine caused by military defeat would be God's first attempts to call Israel back to Himself.

26:18–20 This second series of curses would be fulfilled if the first failed to get Israel's attention. This was characterized as **seven times more** punishment. **your heavens like iron and your earth like bronze:** Rainfall was essential to the agriculture of ancient Israel. The summer heat baked the land. If the early rains of winter did not fall and soften the soil, the primitive plows of ancient agriculture could not break it up for planting. Of course, without rainfall, planting was futile anyway; the seeds would not grow.

26:21, 22 If drought did not bring the Israelites to their senses, God would visit them with **seven times more plagues**—this time **wild beasts.** When the human population was far below today's levels, a sharp increase in the number of large predators would have been a serious threat to the people and their domestic animals.

26:23–26 If Israel did not repent after the wild beasts, God would multiply their punishment another **seven times** with war, resulting in epidemics and famine. **when you are gathered:** When enemies invaded a land in the ancient world, the people living in unwalled villages fled to the walled cities for refuge, causing great overcrowding. If a city then was besieged for a long time, unsanitary conditions led to **pestilence,** epidemics of deadly communicable diseases. Another result of a long siege was famine. The flour ration allotted to **ten women** would be so small that they would bake it all together **in one oven.** The bread itself would be weighed to ensure equal distribution.

26:27–39 If siege did not cause Israel to repent, the warfare would continue **seven times** greater, as punishment from God. Cannibalism, the complete desolation of the land, and exile to foreign lands—the end of the nation—would be the final result.

26:29 Further disobedience would result in cannibalism. This occurred centuries later during a siege of Samaria, and later still during the Babylonian siege of Jerusalem (2 Kin. 6:28, 29; Lam. 2:20; 4:10).

26:30–32 High places and **incense altars** were dedicated to the worship of pagan gods. To defile them with human **carcasses** would make them permanently unfit for worship. There is mocking irony in this threat of human carcasses being tossed upon the carcasses (the **lifeless forms**) of pagan deities.

26:33–35 scatter: This threat was fulfilled in the Babylonian exile of 587–536 B.C.

26:36, 37 those of you who are left: Survivors would not enjoy relief or peace of mind after escaping the disasters. They would still be timid, even when no one pursued them.

26:38, 39 Having been exiled to foreign lands, the people were not to think they were beyond God's punitive reach. They would **waste away,** perhaps wishing they had not escaped the quick death that had overtaken so many others.

26:40–45 This is a promise not to abandon Israel forever. God's purpose in all these disasters would not be to destroy Israel but to bring them to repentance and restore them to their land.

26:41, 42 God's **covenant** with the patriarchs took precedence over the covenant at Sinai (Gal. 3:15–18). Even when Israel violated the Sinai covenant, God honored the patriarchal covenant.

26:43–45 Ultimately, God's character is grace, mercy, love, and redemption. On that basis, God would **remember the covenant.** He would not **utterly destroy them.** God remembers and redeems because God is God.

⚒ IN DEPTH | God Bends but Does Not Break

Israel repeatedly broke God's commandments. For example, within a generation or two of entering the Promised Land, the people were worshiping idols (Judg. 2:10–13). Throughout their history, they failed to keep the Sabbatical and Jubilee years (Jer. 34:12–16). And they repeatedly dishonored the Lord's sanctuary and its implements (1 Sam. 4:3, 11; 13:7–13). These were direct violations of the covenant (Lev. 26:1, 2). And Israel broke almost every other law as well.

In every case, God responded with firm correction, just as He had warned (26:14–39; compare Judg. 2:14, 15; Jer. 34:17–22; 1 Sam. 7:2; 13:14). Finally He allowed foreigners to take His people into exile (2 Chr. 36:17–21). Nevertheless, God's relationship with his recalcitrant and rebellious people always included a place for forgiveness if they repented:

- He would remember His covenant with Israel's ancestors, Jacob and Abraham (Lev. 26:42, 45).
- He would remember the Promised Land (26:42).
- He would not cast His people away completely, or "abhor" them (26:44).
- He would not utterly destroy them or break His covenant with them (26:44).
- He would remain their God (26:44, 45).

God shows that a leader must practice loyalty toward disobedient followers even when correcting them. Following His example, leaders can exercise discipline in a way that helps people rather than destroys them; they can "bend" under the pressure of disobedience but not break.

26:46 This summary statement confirms the authority of Leviticus because its source is **the Lord**.

27:1–34 On vows and their redemption. People make vows to God for many reasons. Most vows are promises to give something to God, either a possession or a service. In any given situation, there may or may not be a valid reason why a vow should not (or cannot) be kept as it was spoken; then the redemption of the thing vowed becomes possible, and perhaps necessary. This chapter may seem strangely placed. Since it deals with redemption, and, like all of Leviticus, is concerned with the holy living of a redeemed people, it was regarded by the ancient author as a fitting conclusion to the book. A vow is a spoken word. James said that whoever can control his tongue can control his entire body (James 3:2). Careful consideration of vows and their proper disposition helps one keep the holy living of the redeemed constantly in view.

27:1–8 While people could dedicate themselves or their children (1 Sam. 1:11, 22) to God, only the Levites were allowed to serve God as priests. Therefore, those vowed in service to God had to be redeemed. The chief factor in determining value was relative physical strength. A man brought a higher price than a woman because he could do heavier work. Age also was a factor. By redeeming at a certain price the person dedicated to the sanctuary, the Israelite gave the value of the gift he had vowed.

27:8 A person might dedicate himself as

God's possession and go redeem the vow—since he could not personally serve in the sanctuary—only to have the priest discover he was **too poor to pay** that value. At this time, fifty shekels (v. 3) might have represented about four years' earnings. In that case, the priest set a redemption value **according to the ability** to pay.

27:9, 10 Rash vows and afterthoughts about vows were discouraged. If one vowed or brought a clean animal for sacrifice, then regretted the decision, the animal could not be exchanged.

27:11–13 Unclean animals could not be sacrificed. Therefore, the priest set a value on any such animal brought as a gift so that the sanctuary would receive the monetary value of the gift.

27:14, 15 The priest also set the value of a house given to fulfill a vow. Obviously, the priests had to be knowledgeable in many kinds of commercial enterprises. A house in a walled city could be dedicated to God if it was not part of the inheritance that was to stay in the family perpetually (25:29, 30).

27:16–25 A field could be dedicated to the Lord. If it was part of a family's inheritance, it could be redeemed before the Jubilee. The price for a parcel requiring a **homer of barley seed** to sow it was **fifty shekels.** A **homer** was a donkey-load. Over the full 49-year inter-Jubilee period, the price to redeem the parcel was about a shekel a year, the cost of its seed each year. A person was encouraged to redeem the land as

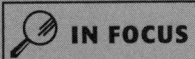

IN FOCUS "jubilee"

(Heb. *yobel*) (Lev. 25:10; 27:17; Ex. 19:13). Strong's #3104: This word literally means "ram" or "ram's horn" (Josh. 6:5), and in one instance it is rendered "trumpet" (Ex. 19:13). The term is associated with the Year of Jubilee in Leviticus (25:10) and in Numbers (36:4). The fiftieth year was a "jubilee" year for the Hebrews, marked by the blowing of a trumpet (Lev. 25:9). During this year, the Israelites experienced freedom and liberty: slaves were freed; debts were canceled; the land was left fallow; family property was redeemed (25:10–17). The fact that Jesus quoted Is. 48:8, 9 seems to indicate that Jesus equated his earthly ministry with the principles of the Year of Jubilee (Luke 4:18, 19).

soon as he could so that his family would not be deprived of its support. The priests and Levites would not have had time to work land dedicated to the sanctuary; apparently the person dedicating it continued to work it, perhaps paying the homer of barley each year toward its redemption, though the text does not mention such an arrangement. To dedicate land to the sanctuary, then sell (lease) it to a another person until the following Jubilee, probably represented an attempt to realize a profit from that which had been dedicated. It resulted in forfeiture of the right to redeem the land in the year of Jubilee.

27:22–25 A dedicated field not part of the family inheritance but bought from another was redeemable before the Jubilee under the same terms as a field belonging to the family inheritance. However, if it was not redeemed, it reverted to the original owner in the Year of Jubilee.

27:26, 27 Animal firstborns could not be dedicated to God, since they belonged to Him already (Ex. 13:2). One could not pay a vow with a firstborn animal, expecting to gain double credit with God from a single sacrifice. Clean animals could not be redeemed; they would have been sacrificed. Unclean animals could not be sacrificed, and they could be redeemed with money.

27:28, 29 Devoting a possession was a stronger act than dedication. Nothing devoted could be redeemed. Persons devoted (**under the ban**) were to **be put to death.** No private citizen would have had the power to put himself or anyone else under the ban.

27:30, 31 For a person living a distance from the sanctuary, it may have been easier to redeem the tithes of his crops than to bring the crops to the sanctuary.

27:32, 33 Sheep and goats were counted and inspected when they passed **under the rod,** which the shepherd placed across the entrance to the fold. Each year, the newborn animals were counted this way. Every tenth animal was part of the tithe that belonged to God. The owner was not allowed to adjust this procedure so that the animal for the tithe was small, weak, or sickly, nor could he substitute a poor animal for a better one.

27:34 Though it was given to an ancient people of another culture and is not binding on the modern believer in most of its details, the Book of Leviticus still has much to teach the follower of Christ. Holy living still should be our goal because we have been redeemed through the blood of Christ, which is infinitely more precious than the blood of any sacrificial animal.

The Fourth Book of Moses Called

Numbers

—•—

THE BOOK OF NUMBERS DESCRIBES THE EVENTS right before the Israelites entered the Promised Land. Similar to the tension-filled days before a great battle or election day, these events reveal the Israelites' restlessness and impatience, but also the anticipation of what God would do. The Israelites made grave mistakes during this crucial period, and God disciplined them. But through His discipline and instruction God trained the Israelites not only to worship Him but also to trust in Him for the ultimate victory.

The long lists of numbers and names in Numbers discourage many readers. However, these must be viewed as the ancient Israelites viewed them. The lists were the final roll call before the battle. They prompted praise to God for His faithfulness to the Israelites. He had protected them and multiplied their numbers even in the middle of a barren wilderness.

Numbers has two basic sections. Each of them begins with a census. The first census (chs. 1—4) numbered the men of war of the first generation of those who had left Egypt. This census and the triumphal march into the Promised Land quickly turned into disaster. The first generation of Israelites did not trust God and did not thank Him for His provision. Instead, they doubted God, accused Him, and rebelled against His gracious instructions. This demanded discipline: the first generation would not inherit the land because they had been faithless.

But while the Lord would not let them enter the land, He still had not abandoned His people. He allowed these rebellious people to live out their lives in the wilderness. Further, He graciously continued to instruct them in His ways and how they could prepare their sons and daughters to enter the land. The faithless first generation had not altered God's purposes or discouraged God from fulfilling His promises. One day, the Israelites would obey God and would conquer the Promised Land.

After forty years of wandering in the wilderness, the second census (ch. 26) numbered the men of war of the second generation. Finally, they were prepared to do what their parents had failed to do. But underlying the narrative of chs. 26—36 is the nagging question: "Will the second generation be successful, or will they repeat the errors of their fathers?" The book ends with a positive expectation. The second generation would succeed; the people of God would inherit the promise of the land of Canaan—at last!

The Book of Numbers is the fourth of the first five books of the Old Testament, the Pentateuch. The English name "Numbers" comes from the title that the translators of the Septuagint (a Greek translation of the Old Testament completed around 150 B.C.) gave the book, a name that refers to the two prominent census lists contained within.

Until the nineteenth century, Jewish and Christian scholars had unanimously agreed that Moses wrote the entire Pentateuch. Educated by the Egyptians, he certainly had the credentials to compose the five books, and he was a primary character in Exodus through Deuteronomy.

However, many nineteenth- and twentieth-century scholars have doubted that the historical Moses composed the first five books of the Old Testament. Instead, they have suggested that these books, including Genesis, were compiled at a later date. According to this analysis, anonymous editors used at least four documents to piece together the Pentateuch. These four documents were identified by tracing the divine names, such as Elohim and Yahweh, through the Pentateuch, and by tracing certain variations in subject matter, phrasing, and word choice. The four documents are the called J document, which uses the name Yahweh for God; the E document, which uses the name Elohim for God; the P or Priestly document; and the D or Deuteronomic document. More recently, this dissection of the Pentateuch has been challenged, and no real consensus has emerged from the ensuing scholarly debate.

On the other hand, most evangelical writers have insisted on Moses' authorship and compilation of the Pentateuch. Given the long sojourn of the Israelites in the wilderness, Moses would certainly have had the time to compile the materials and write most of the books. However, he may have overseen some additions to the books, and certain later editors under the leading of the Spirit may have added other materials. For example, the remarkable story of Balaam (chs. 22—24) may have been written by someone other than Moses, for Moses was neither a participant in nor an observer of these events.

At the same time, there are many positive indications in Numbers that Moses did write the principal narrative. For example, Numbers 33:2 speaks specifically of Moses writing the itinerary. Also, 3:40 certainly implies that Moses wrote down the number and names of Israel's firstborn. Moreover, the constant refrain "then the LORD spoke to Moses," found at the beginning of nearly every major section of the book, testifies not only to its divine origin but also to Moses' significant role in communicating these divine instructions to the Israelites.

Outline

I. The first generation in the wilderness (1:1–25:18)
A. The triumphal march (1:1–10:36)
  1. The setting apart of the people in preparation for the march (1:1–10:10)
    a. The census of the first generation (1:1–4:49)
    b. Rituals for purity (5:1–10:10)
  2. The beginning of the march (10:11–36)
B. The rebellion and judgment of the people (11:1–25:18)
  1. The cycle of rebellion and atonement for the people (11:1–20:29)
  2. A climax of rebellion and hope (21:1–25:18)

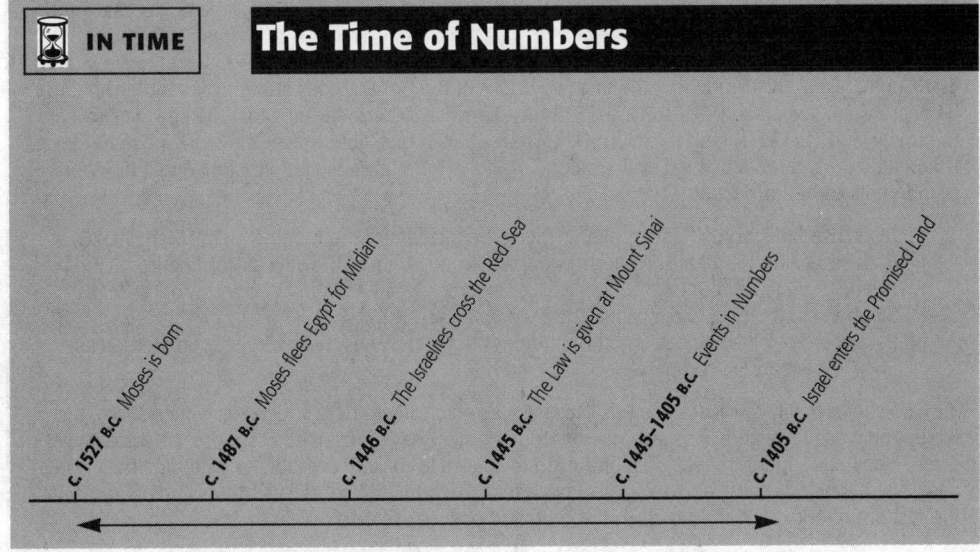

⌛ IN TIME   **The Time of Numbers**

c. 1527 B.C. Moses is born

c. 1487 B.C. Moses flees Egypt for Midian

c. 1446 B.C. The Israelites cross the Red Sea

c. 1445 B.C. The Law is given at Mount Sinai

c. 1445–1405 B.C. Events in Numbers

c. 1405 B.C. Israel enters the Promised Land

II. **The second generation's march to the Promised Land (26:1–36:13)**
   A. The census of the second generation (26:1–65)
   B. The inheritance of women in the land (27:1–11)
   C. The successor to Moses (27:12–23)
   D. Offerings, festivals, and vows for the new generation (28:1–30:16)
   E. The war against the Midianites (31:1–54)
   F. The settlement of the Transjordan tribes (32:1–42)
   G. Words of warning and encouragement (33:1–56)
   H. An anticipation of the Promised Land (34:1–36:13)

Commentary

1:1 The phrase **now the LORD spoke to Moses** sets the tone for the book. God's act of revelation to His servant Moses is mentioned over 150 times (in more than twenty different ways) in Numbers. **Wilderness of Sinai:** The geographical setting of Numbers is the wilderness. This setting serves as a powerful spiritual metaphor: Not only did the Israelites live in the wilderness, but they as a nation were spiritually traveling through a wasteland. God had already delivered them from slavery, but He hadn't yet brought them to the Promised Land. They had to endure physical hardships and other experiences that tested their faith (Num. 21:4–9). The place of revelation was **the tabernacle of meeting,** also called "the tabernacle of the Testimony" (1:50, 53). The time reference, **on the first day of the second month, in the second year,** is dated from the pivotal event in Israel's history, the deliverance of the people from slavery in Egypt. The Exodus was to the OT Israelites what the death and resurrection of Jesus is to Christians. The Exodus constituted the birth of the nation Israel. The second month corresponds roughly to April, a time that would be known later in Canaan as the month of the general harvest between Firstfruits and Pentecost. The census of Numbers is, in a sense, "God's harvest" of His people. The events of Numbers cover a period of thirty-eight years, most likely in the second half of the fifteenth century B.C.

1:2, 3 The stated purpose of this **census** was to be a military roster. It was not a census for social, political, or taxation purposes. Instead, the census would help Israel to prepare its

IN LIFE   God Has Spoken—to You!

Imagine hearing God's voice! Moses did (Num. 1:1). Scripture gives little indication of what that experience was like, but it does say that the Lord spoke to Moses "face to face, as a man speaks to his friend" (Ex. 33:11). For those who wish that God would speak to them directly, He has: through the Bible.

The Bible claims to be from God. Though its words were written down by people, they are words that God has spoken. Throughout the first five books of the Bible, Moses states again and again that he is presenting what God said to him (Ex. 24:4). Likewise, Moses declares that the Law was revealed to him by God (Ex. 25:1, Lev. 1:1; Num. 1:1; Deut. 1:6). In fact, the phrase "the Lord spoke to Moses" is repeated thirty-three times in Leviticus alone. And the NT affirms Moses' insistence that his commandments came from God:

- Jesus used the words "God spoke" in citing the incident of the burning bush (Mark 12:26).
- Both Jesus and the Pharisees acknowledged the authority of the Law as coming from God (Matt. 19:4–7; John 9:29).
- Stephen cited Moses' writings as God's words (Acts 7:6).
- Peter indicated that Moses and the other prophets "spoke as they were moved by the Holy Spirit" (2 Pet. 1:21; compare Heb. 1:1).

God spoke clearly to Moses. He has likewise spoken clearly to us, through His written Word, the Bible. Countless Jews and Christians down through history have preserved His message since it was given. Many have spent their careers and even their lives to make it available to us today. The Bible has been banned, burned, and, to some, supposedly "debunked," yet still its truth stands. It remains the test of orthodoxy for all who claim to be of God or speak of God's ways.

armies for the war of conquest against the peoples of Canaan. Therefore, those who were numbered were able-bodied males over the age of **twenty.** Just as He promised Abraham long ago (Gen. 15:16–21), God was preparing the Israelites to occupy Canaan. God was in the process of giving the Promised Land to them! Furthermore, the census demonstrated to the Israelites God's faithfulness in fulfilling another promise to Abraham, the multiplication of his descendants (Gen. 12:2; 15:5; 17:4–6; 22:17). Read ch. 26 for the second census.

1:4 A man from every tribe would aid Moses and Aaron in the immense task of numbering the nation. The participation of one person from each tribe would ensure that the numbering was done fairly and that each tribe was represented accurately.

1:5–15 the names: This listing has a certain poignancy to it. It was to have been a list of heroic persons, for they would have been the tribal leaders immortalized in the story of conquest. Because of the actions of unbelief of the nation at Kadesh (chs. 13 and 14), these men and all numbered with them perished in the wilderness. Many of these names are formed with compounds of terms for God. We call such names "theophoric," speaking of faith in the presence and provision of God in the lives of His people: **Elizur** (My God is a Rock) son of **Shedeur** (Shaddai is a Flame), chief of **Reuben** (v. 5); **Shelumiel** (My Peace is God) son of **Zurishaddai** (My Rock is Shaddai), chief of **Simeon** (v. 6); **Nahshon** (Serpentine—significance not known) son of **Amminadab** (My Kinsman [God] is Noble), chief of Judah (v. 7); **Nethaneel** (God has given) son of **Zuar** (Little one), chief of **Issachar** (v. 8); **Eliab** (My God is Father) son of **Helon** (perhaps "Rampart-like"), chief of **Zebulun** (v. 9); **Elishama** (My God has heard) son of **Ammihud** (My Kinsman [God] is Majesty), chief of **Ephraim** (v. 10); **Gamaliel** (Reward of God) son of **Pedahzur** (The Rock [God] has ransomed), chief of **Manasseh** (v. 10); **Abidan** (My Father [God] is Judge) son of **Gideoni** ([God is] My hewer), chief of **Benjamin** (v. 11); **Ahiezer** (My Brother [God] is Help) son of **Ammishaddai** (My Kinsman [God] is Shaddai), chief of **Dan** (v. 12); **Pagiel** (Encountered by God) son of **Ocran** (Troubled), chief of **Asher** (v. 13); **Eliasaph** (God has Added) son of **Deuel** (Know God!), chief of **Gad** (v. 14); **Ahira** (My Brother [God] is Calamity—perhaps a statement of warning to enemies) son of **Enan** (Seeing), chief of **Naphtali** (v. 15).

1:16–18 leaders: The leaders (Heb. *nasi'*) were "lifted up" or "selected" for their positions of leadership.

1:19 As the LORD commanded: The tone in

chs. 1–10 is one of compliance on the part of Moses and the people to the revealed will of God. When God commanded, Moses and his agents responded.

1:20–43 Now the children of Reuben: Each of the twelve mini-paragraphs in vv. 20–43 follows the same pattern, giving the name of the tribe, the particulars of the family houses, the stipulation that the ones numbered were able-bodied males over the age of twenty, the name of the tribe again, and then the number in that tribe. The only variation is in vv. 32–35, where it is explained that Ephraim and Manasseh are sons of Joseph (as in v. 10). This notice reminds the reader that Joseph received a double share among the tribes of Israel. His two sons had equal shares with their uncles in Israel's posterity. See vv. 47–50 regarding the tribe of Levi. This entire section has an aura of celebration about it. The details may appear repetitive and tedious to us, but they would stir the passions of the respective tribal units: "This is our family! Here are our numbers among the thousands of Israel."

1:44–46 These are the ones who were numbered: The total number of able-bodied men (who were at least twenty years old) was 603,550. The likely number of women, children, and older or infirm men not counted in this census would indicate a total population between of two and five million.

1:47, 48 The Levites were not to be included among the "lay" tribes. The tribe of Levi was sacred. It belonged to the Lord alone. (Chapter 3 records the families, numbers, and duties of the Levites.) In order to maintain the twelve separate tribes even though the Levites were not counted as a tribe, the tribe of Joseph was given two portions, one to each of Joseph's sons, Ephraim and Manasseh (1:10, 32–35). In this way, the tribe of Joseph received a double share (Gen. 49:22–26).

1:49, 50 The tabernacle of the Testimony is called "the tabernacle of meeting" in v. 1 and "the tabernacle" in v. 51. The term *tabernacle* by itself points to the temporary and portable nature of the tent; it was a movable shrine, specially designed for the worship of God by a people on the march. *Testimony* suggests the covenantal significance of the tent. Within that tent were the symbols of the presence of God among His people, His signs of a continuing relationship with the Israelites.

1:51–53 The outsider refers not to a person of foreign birth but to a non-Levite (Ex. 12:43). The punishment of death is reiterated in 3:10, 38; 18:7 and was imposed in 16:31–33 (1 Sam. 6:19). God's presence was both a blessing and a curse in the camp, a blessing for those who had a proper sense of awe and respect of the nearness of the Deity and a curse for those who had no respect for the Divine Presence.

1:54 So they did sets the tone of obedience for the first part of Numbers. The later rebellion (ch. 11) surprises the reader after phrases such as this.

2:1, 2 The chapter begins, as do most of the chapters in Numbers, with the notice of revelation from God to Moses. **by his own standard:** This chapter is one of consummate design and order; it speaks of the joy of knowing one's place in relation to the living and holy God. Late Jewish tradition suggests that each tribe had its own standard corresponding in color to the twelve stones in the high priest's breastplate (Ex. 28:15–21). In addition, each triad of tribes had its own **emblem.** The designs, or motifs, of these emblems are not known to us today. Late Jewish tradition suggests that the standard of the triad led by Judah had the figure of a lion, of Reuben the figure of a man, of Ephraim the figure of an ox, and of Dan the figure of an eagle (see the four living creatures described in Ezek. 1:10; compare Rev. 4:7). These traditions are difficult to substantiate historically. Further, whereas we today think of the beauty and order of God's work in creation (Gen. 1; Prov. 8:22–31; Ps. 104) and of His work in the coming new heavens and new earth (Rev. 21; 22), Num. 2 presents the notion of the beauty and order of God's work in the formation of His people Israel, a concept akin to the beauty of the church as the body of Christ (Eph. 2:19-22). God Himself placed each tribe in a specific place around His **tabernacle.** A person's identity was not only derived from his or her tribe, but also from his or her place in relation to the tabernacle. This is an OT portrait of God's dwelling among His people. The beauty and order of this chapter points ultimately to the beauty of being in the presence of the risen King. **some distance** (Heb. *minneged,* "some way off," "from a distance"): None dared draw too close to the tabernacle, so that God's holiness might be maintained (Is. 6:1–5). In contrast, a person may come *very* close to Jesus. This is not because Jesus as God is any less holy, but because He has come so very near to us in order to save us.

2:3–9 The three tribes **on the east side** had pride of place. The ancient people of Israel were not seafaring; in effect they turned their backs to the sea, so the word for *back* could mean "west" or "the sea." The west was the place of the setting sun. On the other hand, the east faced the rising sun, a picture of promise and power (Ps. 19:4–6). In the line of march, **Judah,** with its allied tribes **Issachar** and **Zebulun,** set out first. The names of the worthies of each tribe and the numbers of the men of war are the same as in ch. 1.

2:10–16 Positioned **on the south side** were the tribe of **Reuben** and its allied tribes **Simeon** and **Gad.** The subtotal of the men of war in these three tribes was 151,450. They set out second, after the tribes allied with Judah.

2:14–16 There is a well-known textual difficulty in v. 14 respecting the name **Reuel.** The Hebrew text in our standard edition actually reads "Reuel" in this place but "Deuel" in 1:14. The Hebrew letters *d* and *r* were easily confused by scribes because of their similarity in form in certain stages of the formation of the written alphabet symbols. (A similar problem is found in Gen. 10:4, where the name "Dodanim" is "Rodanim" in the Samaritan Pentateuch and in 1 Chr. 1:7.) Many other Hebrew manuscripts, along with the versions, read Deuel in Num. 2:14, which we suspect is the superior reading. Incidentally, most of the textual critical problems of the Book of Numbers are similar to this spelling issue of an ancient name (but read 21:14, 15). Wholesale textual corruption that would make the numbers of chs. 1 and 2 entirely suspect is simply not evident.

2:17 Levites in the middle: Only the consecrated people were allowed to move with the **tabernacle of meeting.** In the line of march, the tabernacle was in the central position—a symbol of not only Israel's protection of the holy objects, but also of the presence of God among His people.

2:18–24 Positioned **on the west side** were the tribe of **Ephraim** and its allied tribes **Manasseh** and **Benjamin.** The subtotal of the men of war in these three tribes was 108,100. In the line of march, they were the third group to move out from their encampments.

2:25–31 The tribe of **Dan** and its allied tribes **Asher** and **Naphtali** were positioned **on the north side.** The subtotal of the men of war in these three tribes was 157,600. In the line of march, they were the last group to move out of the camp.

2:32–34 These verses summarize this stately chapter. The four sets of triads yielded the same total as the sum of the twelve individual units: 603,550 (1:46). There is a studied consistency in the use of these numbers. Chapter 2 presents an almost idealized picture of the tribes of Israel as they are prepared for their triumphal march toward the land of promise. The greater sorrow of their subsequent rebellion is a warning to us all.

3:1 the records of Aaron: The focus of ch. 3 is on the priests and the families of the tribes of Levi.

3:2–4 the sons of Aaron: When we read **Nadab, the firstborn,** it must be with a sense of parental grief. Aaron's expected heir would prove to be such a disappointment. With his brother **Abihu,** Nadab offered **profane fire** before God, an offense that cost them their lives (Lev. 10:1, 2). Two of Aaron's other sons were still living. **Eleazar** and **Ithamar** continued to minister as priests before God. However, the supervision of their father was even more necessary, given the errors of their older, deceased brothers. The words of 2:2, "some distance," become more poignant in the context of the punishment of Nadab and Abihu. If priests who were given permission to draw near the holiest places were subject to violent judgment because of an improper approach, what would be the fate of the intrusive layperson?

3:5–10 Twice the narrator distinguished **the tribe of Levi** from the "lay" tribes (1:47–50; 2:33). Here the Levites were given their sphere of work in the care of the tabernacle. The Levites, however, were not the priests; only **Aaron and his sons** could be priests. The Levites, who assisted in the care of the holy things, drew near to the Divine Presence. Yet the priests, who ministered in the tabernacle, drew even nearer. But only the high priest, on whose ministry the hope of the community was based, entered the Most Holy Place where the Divine Presence resided. God is holy. Only the high priest, separated from the community for this holy purpose, could approach God in order to intercede for the people before Him. In contrast, Christians can approach the Divine Presence on an even footing with one another. Jesus' death has covered our sins and made us holy in God's sight.

3:11–13 I Myself points to God's direct involvement in redemption. When God redeemed and saved His people, it was by His own person (Ex. 12:29; 13:3, 17, 21; 14:19, 30, 31). Similarly, when God selected the Levites to be a special tribe in the ministry of His presence, it was His personal work, not something He delegated to a created being. Likewise, God would later select Jesus to be a perfect High Priest for all those who would believe in Him (Ps. 110:4; Heb. 6:20—8:6). **The firstborn are Mine:** When God passed over the homes of the Hebrew families who had obeyed His commands in the Passover (Ex. 12:29–51), He declared the surviving firstborn Hebrew children—and also the firstborn of animals—to be His own (Ex. 13:1, 2). Now the firstborn children needed to be redeemed. An exchange was made. God took the entire tribe of Levi as His special possession, instead of the firstborn child of each family (3:40–51). **I am the LORD**

> *None dared draw too close to the tabernacle, so that God's holiness might be maintained.*

emphasizes the authority of the speaker and the importance of His words.

3:14–20 the children of Levi: The three families of the Levites were **Gershon, Kohath, and Merari.** The Levites were distinguished from the other, non-priestly, tribes in several ways. (1) They were numbered separately from those numbered for war. (2) They were appointed as ministers in the worship of God rather than as soldiers in His army. (3) They were given certain restrictions for the conduct of their life. (4) They represented the gift of the firstborn of each family to the Lord (3:40–51). (5) They would live in cities amidst the various tribes instead of living together in a single region (35:1–8).

3:21–37 In the listing of the tribes' placement around the central sanctuary, there is a movement from the most favored tribe, Judah, to the lesser tribes (2:3–31). In the listing of the placement of the Levitical families, there is a different movement, from west to east. The Levitical families that were assigned the most important tasks were the families of Kohath in the south. The families of Gershon and Merari were assigned subsidiary tasks. The priests in the east were in leadership positions. The order was: **Gershon** to the west; **Kohath** to the south; **Merari** to the north; Moses, Aaron, and Aaron's sons to the east.

3:22–26 The family of **Gershon** cared for and handled the elements of the **tabernacle.** Males over the age of one month in this family numbered 7,500. **screen:** There were three curtains, coverings, or screens for the tabernacle: one at the gate of the court (4:26), a second at the entrance of the tent (v. 31; 4:25), and a third separating the Most Holy Place within the tent (4:5).

3:27–32 The work of the family of **Kohath** concerned the sacred implements and furnishings within the tabernacle. Aaron's son **Eleazar** supervised their work as the **chief over the leaders,** likely because the holy furnishings could only be carried in certain prescribed ways. The **Amramites** were the family of Moses, Aaron, and Miriam (Ex. 6:20). Males over the age of one month in Kohath's family numbered 8,600.

3:33–37 The work of the family of **Merari** concerned the structural elements of the tabernacle along with its utensils. In this family, males over the age of one month numbered 6,200.

3:38, 39 The placement of Moses, Aaron,

and Aaron's sons **on the east** indicated a most-favored status. Their responsibility was to guard against improper approach to God's holy tabernacle. The total of the families of the Levites is given as 22,000.

3:40–42 Number all the firstborn: The firstborn of the families of the Exodus belonged to the Lord because He saved them. The firstborn of the Israelites' animals were to be offered as a sacrifice to the Lord. But the firstborn sons of the Israelites were *not* to be killed (as were the firstborn sons of the Egyptians; Ex. 13). The Israelites' firstborn sons were redeemed by the dedication of the Levites to the Lord's service. Now, in the wilderness in the second year of their deliverance, the actual exchange of the Levites for the firstborn was made. The phrase **instead of** strongly emphasizes the substitution of the Levites for the firstborn. This ancient substitution reminds us of the substitution of Jesus for sinners. We all deserved death because of our sins; but He died on the Cross in our place.

3:43–48 The number of the firstborn, 22,273, seems small for a population of two million. Some argue that this figure suggests that the strength of the Israelites was 250,000 people. Others suggest that the number reflects the number of Israelite firstborn at the time of the first Passover. The payment of **five shekels** was as much a lesson to the Israelites on the importance of the individual as it was an act of substitution for those involved. Each individual's redemption had to be covered. The payment of the shekels **to Aaron and his sons** was appropriate. Just as the Levites were given to the Lord in order to assist Aaron in his duties at the holy tabernacle, the redemption money was also given to Aaron to further this same holy work.

3:49–51 The weight of the collected **money** (1,365 shekels) indicates the impressive nature of the transaction . The number is five times 273, since there was one Levite for each firstborn and five shekels for each firstborn beyond the number of Levites. In this way, each of the firstborn was accounted for in God's plan of redemption.

4:1, 2 The Book of Numbers moves in an orderly, planned manner, following the pattern of Hebrew thought, which moves from the general to the specific, from the whole to the parts. The numbering of the tribes in ch. 1 is followed by the order of the camps in ch. 2. The general explanation of the duties of the priests and the Levitical families, and the issue of the redemption of the firstborn are the subjects of ch. 3. Now ch. 4 deals more specifically with the functions of the Levitical families. The fact that **Kohath** took precedence over Gershon, who was probably his older brother (see the order in 3:17), was one of the recurring marks of God's sovereignty in elevating younger brothers over their seniors (see Cain and Abel, Ishmael and Isaac, Esau and Jacob, Joseph among his brothers, David among his brothers, and so on). This **census** was distinct from the one in ch. 3. This census numbered those between the ages of thirty and fifty, those who were specifically able to work in the service of the Lord in the holy things of worship.

4:3 According to 8:24, the Levites were to be twenty-five years old, which seems to contradict the **thirty years** here. The work of the Levites and that of the priests whom they served was complex and demanding. It is possible that the extra five years of 8:24 includes a period of apprenticeship to prepare these servants of the Lord for the tasks that lay before them.

4:4 The care and preservation of the **most holy things** were given to the Kohathites (3:29–31). The details are spelled out in vv. 4–20. The Kohathites were not to touch the holy items nor even look casually on them, lest they die. **Holy** means "separate," "removed," or "distinct." **Holy things** are items and utensils that have been taken out of common use and given over to the service of the Lord. At the same time, describing God as holy draws attention to His transcendence, the fact that He is altogether separate from His creation, not bound to it, and never to be confused with it.

4:5–20 The section presents a complex picture of service, in which order and structure are important elements, in which colors, textures, and layers are aesthetic aspects, in which care for detail is planned, in which a hierarchy of person and responsibility is well in place, and in which seriousness of purpose is inescapable. Overall, we are impressed with the sheer volume of material things that were parts of ancient Israel's worship services. This is not "primitive" but highly sophisticated, not simple but highly demanding. These duties must have been unusually fatiguing for the participants. How we are drawn to the image of the High Priest, who is finally able to sit down because His work finally is done (Heb. 8:1).

4:6 The various materials used in the tabernacle and its furnishings may have had symbolic meanings to the ancients which have not been preserved for us. We do get a sense that the materials were costly and dear.

4:7–13 Colors—including **blue, scarlet,** and **purple**—played a significant role in Israel's worship.

4:14, 15 The means of transporting the holy things of the tabernacle was to **carry them** by poles on foot. The sad story of Uzzah, who attempted to steady the ark as it was being carried on a cart (2 Sam. 6:6, 7), is a vivid reminder of the seriousness of obeying God's commands.

4:16–20 duty of Eleazar: The priest had functions that were reserved only for him. Any other approach to God would result in death. This was both a gracious gift and a warning. On one hand, God mercifully granted that a priest could serve Him and approach Him. On the other hand, if the priest were faithless, no person could substitute for him. The Israelites had to approach God in the way He prescribed.

4:21–28 In wording that is similar to the description of the Kohathites' responsibilities (vv. 4–15), the men of **Gershon** were given their responsibilities in more detail than the instructions found in 3:21–26. The men of Gershon were responsible for the **curtains** and for numerous parts of the tabernacle worship system. These men were allowed to touch the holy things they dealt with, but they could not be casual in their work. **Ithamar,** the other surviving son of Aaron, was made their chief.

4:29–33 The tasks of **Merari** first mentioned in 3:33–37 are reiterated here. The men of Merari cared for tabernacle posts and pegs, boards and sockets, and so on. There was no unimportant work in the care and maintenance of the tabernacle. Each individual son of Merari was given **by name** the items he had to carry. **Ithamar** was given the responsibility to oversee the work of Merari as well as the work of Gershon.

4:34–49 According to the commandment of the Lord: According to Hebrew prose style, a summary of Moses' compliance with God's commands is given. The numbers for each of the Levitical families can be viewed two ways. It is possible that since these numbers are smaller than those of ch. 1, they are rounded off to the nearest ten. A core of Levites of about 8,500 would seem quite suitable for a population of 250,000 persons. It is also possible that these numbers (as perhaps in the case of the numbers of the tribal census in ch. 1) have been inflated by a factor of ten, in which the total number would be 858, and the Levites considerably busier!

5:1–10:10 The principal issue in this section is the development of purity within the camp and preparations for the triumphal entry of the Israelites into the land of Canaan. At 10:11 they begin the long-anticipated march.

This ancient substitution reminds us of the substitution of Jesus for sinners. We all deserved death because of our sins; but He died on the Cross in our place.

5:1–4 defile: Ritual purity was an outward sign of an inward reality. God's principal concern was the purity of the heart of an individual (Deut. 10:12–20) and not just skin problems (Lev. 15:2, 25). The observable signs of disease and decay were opportunities to implement rules of purity within the camp. With these rules, the Israelites could maintain a camp free from disease and learn about the importance of purity, moral as well as physical. Contact with a dead body was included because of the clearly visible process of decomposition (6:6). However, the central issue in these restrictions was not disease; it was the fact of God's presence in the camp. God was holy, and hence the people had to maintain their purity and holiness. Jesus seems to have reached out particularly to those who were excluded by this section. He healed and brought back into the community those with skin diseases (Matt. 8:1–4; Luke 5:12–16; 17:11–19) and one who had a bleeding condition (Luke 8:43–48). He even touched the dead (Luke 8:54). In each of these cases, there was the danger of Jesus Himself becoming "unclean"; but by His healing touch the unclean were made clean, a fulfillment of His prophetic ministry (Is. 61:1, 2).

5:5–10 This section moves from the physical signs of uncleanness (vv. 1–4) to those that are no less severe but harder to detect. To keep the camp pure and holy, no one could mistreat another.

5:7–10 restitution: As in Lev. 6:1–7, it was not sufficient merely to confess a wrongdoing. One had to repay in full and add a penalty of one-fifth of the value to the one wronged (Lev. 22:14; 27:11–13, 31). Such rules emphasize the seriousness with which God held the people of the camp responsible to one another. If the one who was defrauded was no longer alive and had no relative surviving either, then the debt had to be paid to the priest. **Relative** is a translation of the Hebrew word *gô'el* (Ruth 3:3), which often depicts the protector of family rights. If the one who is defrauded is no longer alive and has no *gô'el* surviving either, then the debt must be made to the priest.

5:11–31 Infidelity is a third class of actions that brought defilement to the camp. Two considerations factor in the focus of this text on the woman. (1) A wife was regarded as a possession of her husband. Therefore, her infidelity was an offense against her husband (the Hebrew word "husband" is *ba'al,* "master"). (2) Paternity is harder to establish than maternity. Hence, there was a somewhat greater burden on the woman to be faithful to her husband so that reliable family lines would be maintained. This text can be read as an exceptionally harsh judgment on an unfaithful wife. But there is a sense in which this law ameliorated the harsh realities for a woman in this time period. A woman could be divorced in the ancient world on the mere suspicion of unfaithfulness. Without the limitation of laws such as this, a woman might even have been murdered by a jealous husband just on the suspicion of unfaithfulness. Here at least there was an opportunity for the woman to prove her innocence before an enraged husband.

5:12–15 Determining impurity in marital relations (when not detected "in the act") was more difficult than noting skin disorders, but the issue was similar. God was in the camp (v. 3). Therefore, the issue had to be resolved by **the priest** in the presence of God.

5:16–18 Bitter water that brings a curse was not a "magic potion," nor was there some hidden ingredient in the water. The addition of dust from the floor of the tabernacle to a vessel of holy water and the scrapings from the bill of indictment (v. 23) were signs of a spiritual reality. Holy water and dust from the holy place symbolized that God was the One who determined the innocence or guilt of the woman who had come before the priest.

5:19–21 Your thigh rot and your belly swell symbolically speaks of a miscarriage (of an illicit child) if the woman was pregnant, and an inability to conceive subsequently (v. 28). In the biblical world, a woman who was unable to bear children was regarded as being under a curse; in this case it would have been true.

5:22 Amen is the woman's strong agreement to the terms of the ritual. If she were innocent, this ritual was the means of her protection. If she were guilty, she would be bringing judgment upon herself.

5:23–31 her guilt: The gravity of the ritual

demonstrates that marital infidelity was regarded as a serious matter in Israel. However, the burden was largely on the woman, probably due to the possible conception of an illegitimate child. Yet the very provision of this law was a means of limiting unjust accusations made against a faithful wife.

6:1–8 Not to be confused with Nazarene (one from Nazareth; Matt. 2:23), the **Nazirite** (Heb. *pala',* meaning "difficult") was one who made a special vow to the Lord for a time of unusual devotion to God. Ordinarily this public vow was for a limited time (v. 13). There were three prohibitions: (1) total abstinence from everything associated with wine; (2) no trimming of the hair; and (3) no contact with a dead body. In all of this, the Nazirite was to regard himself or herself as **holy to the LORD**. After the vow was complete, the Nazirite would return to normal daily life (v. 20).

6:3, 4 wine and similar drink: The Hebrew term translated "drink" (*shekar*) is now understood to be "beer" (Prov. 31:6). Wine is made from fermented fruit, usually grapes; beer is produced from fermented grains. The Nazirite, for the period of the vow, renounced this part of ordinary life as a mark of his or her special devotion to God. The modern reader should resist associating unsavory ideas with wine and beer in this passage. Verse 20 demonstrates the drinking of wine was an expected part of life in biblical times (note on 28:7), and vv. 5–8 describe normal, everyday events as well, the cutting of one's hair and attending to the body of a deceased relative. Further, the sacrifices at the end of the period of the vow included the drink offerings, the pouring of wine on the altar in worship to the Lord (v. 15). The mandated abstinence of drinking wine and beer was a part of the voluntary action of taking a special vow to the Lord, not a judgment on the nature of wine itself.

6:5, 6 no razor: The male Nazirite over a period of time would have had unusually long hair, a sign of his special vow of devotion to the Lord (Judg. 16:17). It is more difficult to under-

---

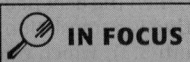 **IN FOCUS**   **"anointed"**

(Heb. *mashach*) (Num. 7:1; Ex. 30:26) Strong's #4886: This verb means to wet or daub a person with olive oil. This ritual designated a person or object as set apart for God's special purposes. Kings, priests, and prophets were anointed at the beginning of their service (Lev. 8:12, 16:32, 2 Sam. 2:4, 5:3; 1 Kin. 19:15, 16). During the Exodus, many holy things were anointed, including the tabernacle itself. In 7:1, the olive oil is an exquisite and expensive blend of oil and spices. This special oil symbolized the significance of the consecration of the tabernacle and its furnishings to God.

stand how this provision might have applied to a female Nazirite, who—presumably—would have been expected to have longer hair than her male counterpart. Perhaps in the case of a female Nazirite, as well as not cutting her hair she would not take ordinary care of it—a visible sign of her special vow of devotion to the Lord.

6:7 The extent of the prohibition concerning contact with a dead body is profoundly moving when it extends to the unexpected death of a **father, mother, brother, or sister.** In such a case, the Nazirite could not even fulfill the normal obligations that would be expected of a grieving relative. Such was the nature of the Nazirite vow of **separation to God.**

6:8, 9 So important was the concept of separation from contact with a dead body that the law included a provision for unexpected contact with the body of a person who **dies very suddenly** in one's proximity. In this case, the hair of the Nazirite was to be shaved, certain offerings presented, and the provisions of the vow continued, with allowance for the time inadvertently lost.

6:10–13 days of his separation are fulfilled: A vow as serious as the Nazirite's needed to have not only a process for initiation, but a solemn ritual for its culmination. The focus is on the hair, a visible symbol of the temporary vow. Therefore, in addition to presenting the required sacrifices (vv. 14–17), the man or woman who completed a Nazirite vow had to shave his or her head and burn the hair along with the peace offering (v. 18).

6:14–21 law of the Nazirite: The summary in this verse not only adds detail but also serves to solemnize the nature of the Nazirite vow. There is no indication in the NT that Jesus took the vow of a Nazirite. Yet it is likely that John the Baptist, who presumably did practice abstinence, was a Nazirite from birth.

6:22, 23 you shall bless: This famous Aaronic benediction is a blessing on all of the people. This blessing follows the section describing the special blessing that would result in the life of the man or woman who took on the Nazirite vow. God's blessing on the people was not gained by outstanding acts of devotion on their part. Rather, God freely blessed His people as a mark of His outstanding grace and mercy.

6:24 The word **bless** is the operative term in this passage. It is a general word indicating God's desire to bring good and significance to His people, to make their lives worthwhile and their relationship to Him remarkable. As God reached out to Abram and Sarai with His blessing (Gen. 12:1–3), so now He reaches out to the whole nation. There are those who seem to think that God's intent in the "Old" Testa-

ment was to make the lives of His people difficult, and that only in the NT does God reach out to people in grace. Such misconceptions fly in the face of texts such as this.

6:25 The idea of the phrase **make His face shine** is that of pleasure in the presence of God, of an intimate experience that is not unlike that experienced by Moses when he talked with God on Mount Sinai (Ex. 34:29–35). The people as a whole would have some sense of the God's glorious presence in their lives.

6:26 The idea of the phrase **lift up His countenance** is that of sensing God's smile. When a person was given an audience in an ancient Middle Eastern court, the monarch might not even look in that person's direction. The monarch might look at the claimant, but with an expression of wrath. How pleasant it was, however, when the monarch looked with pleasure on the one who had come before his throne. How wondrous when that smiling monarch is the King of kings and Lord of lords, and when He grants His peace!

6:27 Perhaps the most impressive element of the passage is this conclusion. God intended to place His **name** on the people. They would bear the benediction of His name as a spiritual brand, a mark of identification that they were a people peculiarly related to God Himself.

7:1 when Moses had finished: This phrasing places the events of this chapter before the taking of the census in chs. 1—4. The tabernacle was completed on the first day of the first month of the second year (Ex. 40:2). The census began on the first day of the second month of that year (1:1). Moses **anointed** and **consecrated** the tabernacle, its furnishings, the altar, and its utensils.

7:2–9 Covered carts would have been especially appropriate for the transportation of the elements of the tabernacle. The carts were distributed according to their use: two to the sons of Gershon for the transportation of the curtains (4:24–28) and four to the sons of Merari for the transportation of the heavier frames and support elements (4:29–33). None of the carts went to the Kohathites, for they had to carry the most holy things on poles on their shoulders (4:1–20).

7:10 Each of the leaders of the twelve tribes brought a special gift from his tribe to the Lord **for the altar.**

7:11–83 The paragraph for each tribe is almost exactly the same as for the other tribes, with the exception of the day of the presentation, the name of the leader, and the name of the tribe. The passage was designed to be read aloud in a slow and stately manner. As each tribal leader and his tribe was mentioned, members of that tribe would take special pleasure.

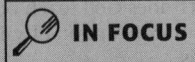 **IN FOCUS** | **"sacrifice"**

(Heb. *zebach*) (Num. 7:17; Ex. 10:25; Zeph. 1:7) Strong's #2077: The Hebrew word comes from a verb meaning "to slaughter for an offering." In accordance with the Law of Moses, a priest would offer sacrifices on behalf of a worshiper by burning them on the altar (Ex. 20:24). Sacrifices could either be grain offerings (the firstfruits of the harvest) or animal sacrifices. Which animals could be sacrificed at the tabernacle (and later the temple) was clearly stipulated by the Law; they had to be the best one had, with "no defect" (Lev. 22:21). Animal sacrifices under the Law served one primary function: to cover or atone for sin (Heb. 9:22). The sin of an individual was symbolically transferred to the animal to be sacrificed, thereby providing a substitutionary atonement. The sacrifices had to be repeated each year because they only partially dealt with sin (Heb. 10:4). Ultimately, all sacrifices in the OT point forward to and are types of the final, all-sufficient sacrifice made by Christ (Is. 53; 1 Cor. 5:7; Heb. 9:10).

Each would sense, "These were our gifts. This was our moment to give to the Lord." Chapter 7 presents a scene of pageantry, pomp, ceremony, and ritual.

7:84–88 This was the dedication offering: The totals of the twelve gifts are enumerated, demonstrating again the sense of order and control in the Book of Numbers.

7:89 More stunning than the gifts and their totals is this last verse of the chapter. When all was done, Moses **heard the voice** of God speaking from the innermost sanctuary. This was a mark of God's approval. The Israelites' gifts had been received with pleasure.

8:1–4 The seven lamps must have been exquisite, the finest work possible by artisans of the day. But the placement of these oil lamps was as important as their craftsmanship.

8:5–19 This section concerns the cleansing of the **Levites** in order to make them fit for their special service of the Lord in His holy worship. The Levites belonged to the Lord in exchange for the firstborn of Israel whom He spared during the tenth plague in Egypt (3:40, 41; 8:16–19).

8:7–9 To **shave** the entire **body** of the Levites was, in a sense, a physical symbol of a return to innocence. This act of devotion initiated the Levites into the service of the Lord. In addition to shaving their bodies, the Levites were also sprinkled with the water of purification and their clothing was washed.

8:10–12 lay their hands on: This ancient symbol of dedication (1) specified with a physical gesture the ones being dedicated, (2) expressed identification with the ones on whom the hands were placed, and (3) called for a divine sanction of this public and physical act. Aaron then presented the Levites to the Lord, perhaps with his hands swaying back and forth as though they were being waved before the Lord. Then those on whom hands had been placed reached out their own hands to the sacrificial bulls as a mark of identification.

8:13–16 The Hebrew words for **wholly given to Me** are an emphatic doubling: "given, given." The story of the Exodus—in this case, the Passover—was always just under the surface of OT theology, for this saving event shaped the nation of Israel.

8:17–19 no plague: With their service in the tabernacle, the Levites functioned as a protective hedge between the people and the symbols of the Divine Presence. Here God's mercy complements His holiness. His holiness would not bear an improper approach. But in His mercy, He provided a protective hedge in the Levites. They both warned others not to draw too close and instructed them on how to approach the living God appropriately.

8:20–26 This concluding paragraph serves to summarize the material of the chapter as well as to report on the actions of the priests and the people in obedience to the word of the Lord. Throughout the first ten chapters there is a regular pattern: (1) an announcement of the coming of the word of the Lord, (2) the details of that word, and (3) a report of compliance. With this pattern, we are conditioned to expect that obedience will regularly follow God's commands as the people make their way in triumphal procession to the Promised Land.

8:24–26 From twenty-five years old seems to disagree with the lower limit of thirty years given in 4:3. The difference is not easily resolved, but there is the possibility that the five years in dispute may have served as some sort of apprenticeship. Later in Israel's history, David reduced the lower age for the Levites to twenty (1 Chr. 23:24, 27).

9:1 The first month of the second year indicates that the material of this chapter precedes the command to take a census in 1:1. With the tabernacle completed, the camp ritu-

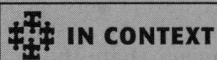 **IN CONTEXT** | **The Congregation**

The "congregation" which Moses was to call by blowing the silver trumpets (Num. 10:2, 3) included the entire population of Israel as God's chosen people. Often this group was referred to as the "assembly" (Heb., *edah* or *qahal*), especially when it gathered at an appointed time (for example, on the Sabbath or a feast day) and place (such as at the "tabernacle of meeting," Num. 10:3) for religious purposes.

Centuries later, when the synagogue was developed (Mark 1:21), the group that gathered there was referred to as the "assembly." The Greeks also described gatherings of their citizens as "assemblies" (*ekklesia*). When the OT was translated into Greek, the Hebrew word for "assembly" was often rendered *ekklesia*, a term that early Christians adopted. Eventually *ekklesia* was translated into English as "church."

ally purified, the religious functionaries cleansed and in place, the hovering symbols of God being experienced in the camp, and the Passover celebrated anew; all was ready for the triumphal march of God's citizen army to the Promised Land.

9:2–5 When the first **Passover** was celebrated in Egypt, the command was given to commemorate it throughout Israel's generations (Ex. 12:14). It was time now at the base of Mount Sinai to celebrate the Passover anew before the people began their march to Canaan.

9:6–10 Because of their defilement from touching the body of a dead person (5:2), there were some who **could not keep the Passover** at its appointed time. These people came willingly to ask Moses what they might do. God's intent was that the Passover would be celebrated by all of His people. Reasons of ritual impurity should not prevent a person from enjoying the night. Neither should one think that the celebration was unnecessary. Thus the ritually impure would celebrate the Passover a month later.

9:11 The specification of **bitter herbs** indicates that those who celebrated the Passover a month later would celebrate the exact details of it. They were not to rush through the ceremony, but were to take part in it fully, eating the lamb, the unleavened bread, and the bitter herbs.

9:12 nor break one of its bones: The Passover was not an ordinary meal. The food commemorated the great saving event of God in Israel's history. The meal was to be eaten with extraordinary attention to the lamb itself. It is fitting to remember that when the Savior was crucified as our "Passover Lamb," none of His bones was broken (John 19:36)—a fulfillment of the typology of this verse (Ex. 12:46; Ps. 34:20).

9:13 ceases to keep the Passover: Some people would simply refuse to celebrate the Passover, not for legitimate reasons, but because of ingratitude and insolence. Such persons would be **cut off from among** the people and would bear the responsibility for their sins.

9:14 Those who lived with the Hebrew people could be included in the celebration of Passover, but they first had to be circumcised (Ex. 12:48). This was a rite that applied to the citizen as well as to the alien. As **a stranger** heard the story of God's gracious, powerful actions in the salvation of His people, that person would naturally question the Israelites on how he or she could participate in Israel's blessing.

9:15–23 The cloud (Ex. 13:21) was a dramatic symbol of the active presence of God with His people, hovering over them in protection, moving ahead of them for direction, coming near at night as **fire** for comfort in the darkness. The rest of this paragraph serves as a summary of the activities of the cloud and the fire throughout Israel's experience in the wilderness.

9:23 at the command of the LORD: The cloud and the fire were manifestations of God's will. When the cloud rose, the people were to set out. When the cloud settled, the people were to encamp. There was nothing predictable in the movement or settling of the cloud; all was dependent on God's sovereignty. The people saw the glory and the will of God in the cloud's actions.

10:1, 2 The two silver trumpets were different from the curved ram's horn trumpets (Lev. 25:9; Ps. 81:3). Made of hammered silver, these instruments were straight with a flaring bell, like the post horns of medieval Europe. Since they did not have valves, they were played like a bugle. The pattern was as follows: The cloud would begin to move, the trumpets would sound, and the people would begin to break camp and move out within their ordered ranks. When the ark, the symbol of the Divine Presence, was moved, Moses recited the words of the song of triumph (v. 35).

10:3, 4 but if they blow only one: The number of trumpets that sounded and the notes they played were signals for various groups within the encampments as well as for the people as a whole.

10:5–8 begin their journey: Even when the trumpets sounded, there was never to be a pell-mell rush of the people. The tone throughout this section is one of discipline and order. God is a God of order, and this would be reflected in the conduct of the Israelites' camp (1 Cor. 14:40; Eph. 4).

10:9 The trumpets were not signals for the movement of the camp in the wilderness; later they functioned as signals for the army in Canaan. The sounding of the trumpets would be a part of Israel's **war** against the inhabitants of the **land.** In addition to functioning as signals at certain occasions, trumpet-blowing also became a symbol of calling on the Lord and a reminder that God was at work among the Israelites. In all symbols such as this, there is the danger of degenerating into magic, of substituting the symbol for the reality it represents. But the biblical world is filled with similar symbols of divine sanction. The abuse of symbols by some people is not an argument against their proper use, any more than the abuse of prayer (Is. 1:15) is a mandate for all prayer to cease.

10:10 day of your gladness: The trumpets were also played in the context of worship, particularly on days of feasting and the celebrations of the beginning of the month. **I am the Lord** your God indicates that the preceding was a divine revelation of the will of God. Furthermore, these words serve as a benediction on the people at the beginning of their march.

10:11 At long last, the time had come for the people to set out on the triumphal journey for which God had been preparing them. When **the cloud was taken up** by the Lord Himself, the Israelites packed up their camp and left. The cloud was a symbol of God's presence, His protection, and His guidance. The people could fearlessly march into the unknown.

10:12, 13 This verse is a summary statement of the initial march. **The Wilderness of Paran** was not actually reached until 12:16. The Wilderness of Paran is in the northeastern Sinai peninsula, south of the Negev, the desert area below Judah. Paran was a good staging area for the conquest of the land, away from the more fortified cities toward Egypt in the west.

10:14–28 This section, like so many others in Numbers, conveys a sense of pageantry, drama, and ordered design. The section was designed to be read aloud as a narrative of God's faithfulness to all of His people and of their proper response to His guidance. The repetition of the names from each tribe (chs. 1; 7) must have been an eloquent statement at the time.

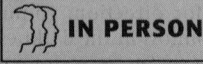

A Combination of Divine and Human Guidance

IN PERSON

The way that Moses led Israel through the wilderness serves as an instructive model for Christians seeking guidance in today's complex world. On the one hand, Moses invited a relative, Hobab, to act as a guide (Num. 10:29–31). On the other, he continued to follow the fiery cloud of the Lord's presence (10:34; 9:15–23). Moses used a combination of human and divine guidance to lead Israel to the Promised Land.

The fiery cloud, the tablets of stone, the Law, and other direct communications from God were the primary means of guidance, to be sure. But for many if not most day-to-day decisions, human judgment and wisdom—such as Hobab's knowledge of the wilderness—were required. The appearance of Hobab at this point is interesting. Earlier, Moses' father-in-law had counseled him to appoint judges to assist him in leading the people (Ex. 18:17–23). Now Moses appealed strongly to Hobab to "be our eyes" (Num. 10:31). So in both cases Moses realized the value of human resources.

Actually, the text doesn't say whether Hobab gave in to Moses' insistent appeals. It may be that Hobab returned to his own land and people as he had intended (10:30). Yet even if he left, the combination of human and divine leadership remained, as Moses, Aaron, Miriam, and the leaders appointed earlier continued to make decisions. This takes nothing away from God's leadership. Rather it demonstrates that God uses a variety of ways to lead His people. As we seek guidance today, we need to pay attention to divine revelation—particularly to the Bible, God's written Word—but we also need to recruit, listen to, and follow those whom God has gifted with insight and leadership.

One would expect these names to be memorialized as the leaders of the first generation who led their tribes into Canaan. Because of the events that follow (chs. 11–14), however, these names take on a certain sadness. These people did not achieve their destiny in the land. Rather, they were buried in the desert.

10:29–32 Reuel (perhaps to be identified with Jethro) is mentioned in Ex. 2:18–21 as the priest of Midian who befriended Moses and gave his daughter Zipporah to him as his wife. Moses invited **Hobab the son of Reuel** to join Israel on their triumphal journey. At first Hobab declined. But at Moses' insistence, Hobab continued with the Israelites (Judg. 1:16), serving as the **eyes** of the people in the wilderness. In this example of OT evangelism, Hobab joined in the destiny of Israel just as Ruth the Moabitess would later (Ruth 2). Joining Israel was not just a change of location; it involved a radical transformation of one's life and purpose so that it was centered around the living God.

10:33, 34 So they departed: These summary words are all of grace, all of mercy. As we read them, we fully expect that the journey will proceed with similar guidance and compliance until the victory is fully won.

10:35, 36 Rise up, O LORD and **Return, O LORD** are words of a triumphant song. These are not magical incantations, but poetic affirmations of God's presence among His people and prayers that His presence would have its effect in the lives and destiny of the people. The expression **many thousands** means the same as "untold thousands" or "teeming millions."

11:1–3 Now when the people complained: After the Israelites had traveled just three days following their deliverance from Egypt, they murmured against the Lord because of a lack of water (Ex. 15:22–24). Here again, after a journey of only three days, they murmured against the Lord for unspecified reasons.

This was not the "good-natured complaining" of people doing a difficult task. Murmuring demonstrated unfaithfulness and was an act of rebellion that demanded God's judgment. The **fire of the LORD** seems to have come both as a warning and as a purifying agent, since it hit only the outskirts of the camps. In the midst of wrath, the Lord remained merciful. He had long-standing patience with a people who continuously rebelled.

11:4 The mixed multitude indicates the presence of others who had escaped from slavery or poverty in Egypt, but were not Israelites (Ex. 12:38). These people were an encouragement to the continual murmuring that characterized the Israelites in the wilderness. It was understandable that those who did not share Israel's faith in God would make every discomfort an excuse to agitate rebellion against Him and His appointed leadership in Moses.

11:5, 6 The tone of the words **this manna** is one of contempt (an attitude that would peak years later; 21:5). The foods of Egypt were plentiful and varied, even for slaves and the poor. The provision of manna was regarded by the Israelites as monotonous, something that caused the inner being to be dried up.

11:7–9 The clear implication of these verses is that the provision of **manna** was something that later generations would not know about or understand without an explanation. Its daily appearance, with a double measure on the day before the Sabbath and none at all on the Sabbath, is clearly miraculous. One pot of manna was kept in the ark of the covenant for generations (Ex. 16:33). God provided manna throughout the forty-year experience in the wilderness. Then it ceased to appear as mysteriously as it had begun (Ex. 16:35). Jesus described Himself as the bread of life, better than the manna in the wilderness (John 6:48–58).

11:10, 11 In this instance, the fact that

 **IN FOCUS** | **"elders"**

(Heb. *zaqen*) (Num. 11:24; Ex. 24:1; Josh. 24:1) Strong's #2205: The word *elder* means "aged" or "old" (Gen. 18:12, 13). In the OT, the word *elder* refers to either an aged, decrepit person (Gen. 44:20; Job 42:17) or to a mature person who had authority within the Israelite community (Ex. 3:16; Josh. 8:33). Elders could serve as judges (Ex. 18:12), advisors (Ezek. 7:26), and ruling officials (Deut. 19:12; Ruth 4:2). Their duties were carried out at the city gate (Lam. 5:14), and their position was one of great honor (Prov. 31:23; Is. 9:15). At certain times in Israel's history, elders played a significant part in selecting Israel's king (1 Sam. 30:26; 2 Sam. 17:4) and establishing the correct worship of God (1 Kin. 8:1). In addition to age (Hebrew tradition states that an elder had to be a man at least fifty years of age), an elder had demonstrate his maturity by fearing God, being truthful, and not coveting (Ex. 18:21).

Moses also was displeased caused him to pray for help in dealing with the complaints of the people and their many needs (vv. 12–15). On another occasion, Moses' displeasure would lead to his own sin and would cost him the opportunity to enter the land of Canaan (20:1–13).

11:12–15 Did I conceive all these people? God was the "mother" of the Israelites; Moses was their "wet nurse." The people were like whining children who cannot be satisfied. In a flourish of rhetoric, Moses asked the Lord to kill him (1 Kin. 19:4) rather than force him to continue in this sorry situation.

11:16, 17 Moses' provocation led to the appointment of **seventy men** to assist him in the administration of the camp. These men would have been in addition to the leaders of each tribe. Presumably they formed a body of administrative assistants for Moses to reduce the burden he felt in attempting to meet the needs of the vast population by himself. These elders were Spirit- empowered (v. 25).

11:18–20 you shall eat meat: The complaint of the people had so angered the Lord that He determined to cause them to have an overabundance of meat. The Israelites had rejected the manna, describing it as something that dried their being (v. 6). God was going to give them so much meat that it would become sickening to them, causing them to realize what a great gift manna really was. The issue here was not really meat and manna, but whether the people would serve God as their God. To reject the provision was, in essence, to reject the Provider.

11:21–24 The idea of such plentiful meat in the wilderness was something even Moses balked at, wondering how even God could provide food for a company so large. God's response to Moses, **has the LORD's arm been shortened?** is a challenge to all people of faith. There is simply no limiting the power of God. Jesus' feedings of the multitudes are NT examples of God's continuing ability to provide food for thousands (Matt. 14:13–21; 15:32–39).

11:25 The Spirit rested upon them (Acts 2) is a divine empowerment of the seventy elders who would aid Moses in the administration of the camp. The prophesying they did on that occasion was a mark of the divine presence, much like the extraordinary speaking in other languages by the Spirit-empowered disciples of the risen Christ (Acts 2:6–12). We may describe this OT event as a "sign gift," marking the men

as specially empowered by God's Spirit. We note as well in this verse the association of Yahweh with the cloud of His presence (10:11).

11:25–30 For reasons that were not recorded, **Eldad and Medad** did not join the other elders at the tabernacle of meeting (v. 16). Nonetheless, the Spirit of God came upon them and empowered them in their own camp. When the word came to Moses that these men were prophesying even though they were not where they were supposed to be, Joshua was afraid

A quail trapped in a net. This bird is probably similar to those provided miraculously to sustain the Israelites in the wilderness (Num. 11:31, 32).

that their possible influence in the community would detract from the authority of Moses. Here Joshua showed his loyalty to Moses by deferring to Moses' leadership and authority. Moses responded by wishing that all of God's people were Spirit-empowered. (This is the first time Joshua is mentioned.)

11:31–33 True to His promise (vv. 18–20), the Lord provided meat in the form of **quail from the sea.** He sent a strong wind that brought vast numbers of quail fluttering about three feet off the ground. The people fell into a frenzy, killing the birds and gathering them all through the night and on into the next day.

11:34 Kibroth Hattaavah ("Graves of Craving") was a vast graveyard of needlessly craving, ungrateful people.

11:35 Hazeroth ("Enclosures") allowed the people a respite from the journey and its judgments.

12:1 The order of the names **Miriam and Aaron** suggests that Miriam was the instigator of the attack against Moses. Note also that the principal punishment falls on Miriam (v. 10). Pointing at the **Ethiopian woman** whom Moses married seems to have been merely a pretext for attacking Moses. Miriam and Aaron might have had a disagreement with Zipporah, Moses' wife (Ex. 2:21), or they might have been referring to a second wife who Moses married without their approval. In any event, the real issue dividing Miriam and Aaron from their brother was the special relationship Moses had with God.

12:2 only through Moses: The prophetess Miriam (Ex. 15:20) had very high status in the camp. Certainly Aaron, through whom God also spoke and who ministered before God as the high priest (2:1; 3:1; 4:1), was also in a most privileged position. Nonetheless, neither Miriam nor Aaron had the same proximity to God that Moses had. This must have galled Miriam and her brother. The verse ends ominously with the words **And the LORD** heard it. God was going to act on what He had heard.

12:3 Some people argue that a **very humble** man would hardly write about his unparalleled humility. Others contend that a humble man who was writing through God's inspiration might speak of his own humility. Still others have suggested that the verse comes from a later period and is a comment inserted to place the challenge against Moses in perspective. Another possibility is that the Hebrew word *'anaw,* translated as *humble,* may mean "miserable" in this context. The events described in ch. 11 may have taken an enormous toll on Moses. This verse may be a description of Moses' utter sense of brokenness as he experienced his brother and sister's betrayal.

12:4, 5 Then the LORD came down: Suddenly God spoke to Moses, Aaron, and Miriam, and then descended dramatically in the midst of the cloud. This theophany (appearance of God) was ominous. The language of this verse is more directly physical than usual. God came down, stood, and then called Aaron and Miriam forward.

12:6–8 The framework of this section is poetry, making the pronouncement of the Lord more vivid and memorable. The language conveys that God was in control. He spoke to whomever He wished and in the manner of His choosing. God is Spirit (John 4:24). Language about His "face" is a concession to our way of thinking of a person. Hence, **face to face** speaks of the most intimate relationship that God had with Moses.

12:9, 10 The singling out of **Miriam** suggests that she was the instigator in this challenge

to Moses (v. 1). **Leprous** refers to a serious skin disorder that made her unclean (5:1–4).

12:11 Aaron's words of confession—**we have done foolishly**—on behalf of his sister and himself are touching, and a sure sign of his deference to the leadership of his brother.

12:12–14 Moses' appeal to God on behalf of his sister was met with stern words from God that speak of a public humiliation. We are not told what might provoke a father to **spit** in the **face** of his daughter, but it would have had to be something quite shameful. The incident at hand was not trivial, but God's grace was abundant.

12:15 The delay in moving the camp for the seven days of Miriam's isolation indicates the high regard that Moses and the people held for Miriam. It is sad that, as in the case of Eve, the thing that Miriam is most noted for is her sin. Nevertheless, biblical writers continued to hold her in high esteem (Mic. 6:4).

12:16 The Wilderness of Paran had been the destination of the people since they set out from Mount Sinai (10:12). Sadly, the character

IN FOCUS "cloud"

(Heb. *'anan*) (Num. 11:25; 12:5; Ex. 24:16; Deut. 31:15) Strong's #6051: The OT word for *cloud* is derived from a verb that means "to cover" or "to intervene as an obstacle" (Gen. 9:14). In the OT, clouds often accompanied appearances of God (Ex. 16:10; 1 Kin. 8:10, 11). In fact, God demonstrated His presence and guided the Israelites through the Sinai desert with a cloud (Num. 9:15–23). Sometimes the OT describes God as the One who "rides" on the clouds (Pss. 68:4; 104:3; Is. 19:1). In ancient Palestine, this was often a description of Baal's power over the wind and rain. But with these words, the prophets and psalmists proclaimed that only God was truly in control of the elements. Other OT passages use clouds as symbols of the divine judgments associated with the day of the Lord (Joel 2:2; Zeph. 1:15).

of the people had changed en route. The people had murmured and rebelled against God and Moses, God's anointed.

13:1–3 According to Deut. 1:21–23, the sending of **men to spy** was the idea of the people. They might have urged Moses to send spies to the land to discover the best approach for conquest. Moses was then instructed by the Lord to proceed with the plan. The staging position in the Wilderness of Paran (12:16), southeast of the land of Canaan, was ideal for a northward sweep of the spies and then of the armies of Israel.

13:4–15 The list of **names** of the men from each of the twelve tribes was not a mere duplicate of earlier lists (ch. 1). Presumably, these men were regarded not only as leaders in their tribal units, but also as men who were physically and spiritually capable of great exploits.

13:16 Changing **Hoshea**'s name to **Joshua** probably indicated great esteem on Moses' part. As God often changed the names of people who had a special relationship with Him, so Moses changed the name of the one who would eventually become his spiritual heir. This was an act

than a year in the wilderness since the time of the Exodus, the mere sight of fresh fruit from the land would be sign enough that God's word was about to be fulfilled. That they brought back grapes is so appropriate, as "eshkol" is the Jewish symbol of joy and is used frequently to decorate the place of joyous events. It is no coincidence that the Israeli tourist bureau of today has as its symbol the two men carrying a great cluster of grapes.

13:21–25 Although the spies went all the way north to the region of Syria—**near the entrance of Hamath**—few details are recorded of their journey. Emphasis is given to **Hebron,** where **descendants of Anak** were found (v. 28), and to **the Valley of Eshcol,** where an enormous cluster of grapes was discovered.

13:26 The report of the spies came as a

The Valley of Eshcol, where the twelve spies sent out by Moses picked a huge cluster of grapes (Num. 13:17, 23).

of ritual adoption. Hoshea means "Salvation"; Joshua means "the Lord Saves." Joshua and Jesus are two forms of the same name.

13:17–20 Moses' commands to the spies were broad but definite. They were to spy out the land, determine what they could about the people and their cities, and observe the produce and forests. Then they were to bring back **some of the fruit of the land,** because it was the season of the first grape harvest. After more

grievous surprise. The spies went to the people at **Kadesh** in the **Wilderness of Paran.** The name Kadesh is associated with the Hebrew word that means "holy." Had the story turned out differently, this name would have been associated with positive memories. It would have been here that they would have sanctified themselves for their campaign of conquest of the land.

13:27 The phrase **flows with milk and**

honey is a slogan of redemption, a slogan expressing God's goodness in His promise of the land of Canaan (Num. 14:8; 16:13, 14; Ex. 3:8, 17; 13:5; 33:3; Lev. 20:24; Deut. 6:3; 11:9; 26:9, 15; 27:3; 31:20). *Milk* probably refers to goats' milk; *honey* refers to bees, which were especially associated with the propagation of fruitful pastures and fields in Canaan. The phrase evoked visions of pleasure and plenty for the Israelites. Canaan was a good land, and enjoyment of the land would follow faithfulness to God.

13:28 The spies quickly focused on the troubles of the land—the strength of its inhabitants, the fortification of its cities, and the immense size of **the descendants of Anak** in Hebron (v. 22). Apparently, this was a family whose hereditary stature was legendary in the ancient Middle East (v. 33).

13:29 The spies listed **the Amalekites** and the other peoples to support their claim that the land was not empty, that people had settled throughout its borders (Gen. 15:18–21). God did not promise Israel virgin territory, but a place that was inhabited by those whom God wished to displace because of their iniquity.

13:30 Only **Caleb** spoke out against the flow of negative reports. He urged immediate attack based on his confidence in the armies of Israel, and, we may presume, on his underlying faith in God, who would fight for His people (10:35, 36).

13:31–33 The other spies were steadfast in their **bad report,** which included their exaggerations. They described the land as evil and its inhabitants as giants. Their contentious description was ultimately an attack on God, the giver

of the land. Such scandalous language could not be tolerated (14:36, 37).

14:1 Following the scandalous report of the spies, **the people wept that night.** They wept not because of the sinful attitude of the spies, but because of their own loss of dream, their own sense that they had made a mistake in leaving Egypt.

14:2–4 Following the night of weeping, the people conspired together in despair. They **complained against Moses and Aaron.** They speculated that they would have been better off dying in Egypt or in the desert. They plotted to select a leader to take them back to Egypt. But they did a worse thing by slandering God, in saying that He would bring them to a place where they would die along with their **wives and children.**

14:5–10 The response of Moses, Aaron, Joshua, and Caleb contrasted remarkably with the foolish terror of the people. They also wept, but for the sins of the people against the Lord and His mercy. The two faithful spies, Caleb and Joshua, gave a good report of the land in the context of robust faith in God. They knew that the living and faithful God would give it to His people. They repeated the slogan of redemption concerning the land: **a land which flows with milk and honey** (13:27). They reasoned, **if the Lord** delights in us, then He will bring us into this land. These words of encouragement were followed by words of strong warning. To speak as the people had done was an act of rebellion and cowardice. The people were not trusting God. **They are our bread** was a boastful manner of

---

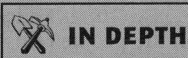 **IN DEPTH**   **Kadesh**

- A site in northeastern Sinai that probably included a well or spring and a settlement; located between the Wilderness of Zin and the Wilderness of Paran, seventy miles southwest of Hebron and fifty miles from Beersheba.
- Also referred to as Kadesh Barnea (Num. 32:8; Deut. 1:2).
- Known as En Mishpat ("spring of judgment") in Abraham's day, when warring kings marched through (Gen. 14:7).
- Base camp from which Moses sent out twelve spies to spy out Canaan (Num. 13:3, 26) and the scene of the people's refusal to go up and possess the land.
- Scene of Korah's rebellion against Moses (16:1–3).
- Burial site of Moses' sister and co-leader, Miriam (20:1).
- The site at which Moses dishonored God by striking a rock to produce water, rather than speaking to it as the Lord commanded; thus the waters were called Meribah Kadesh ("quarreling" or "strife" at Kadesh, Deut. 32:51; compare Num. 20:1–13; 27:14).
- Marker for the southern border with Edom (Num. 34:3, 4), whose king refused the Israelites direct access to the Promised Land (20:14–21).

speaking of the victory envisioned by the good spies, approximating the exaggerated language of the rebellious spies (13:33). The words **their protection has departed from them** speaks of God's forbearance; for 400 years He had endured the wickedness of the people of Canaan. Now the cup of iniquity was full (Gen. 15:16).

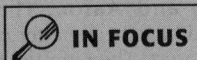

IN FOCUS   "rebel"

(Heb. *marad*) (Num. 14:9; Josh. 22:18, 19; Dan. 9:5) Strong's #4775: The word translated *rebel* means to "revolt" or "flagrantly disobey a recognized authority." God regards rebellion as a serious matter. He does not take it lightly when His people, whom He loves, reject His words. The OT compares rebellion with the terrible sins of witchcraft and sorcery (1 Sam. 15:23). Israel, who had seen the Lord deliver them from bondage in Egypt, often rebelled despite God's frequent warnings against doing so (Deut. 1:26, 43; 9:23, 24). The one who rebels against God departs from His precepts and refuses to heed His warnings (Dan. 9:5, 6). Scripture gives many examples of rebellion that illustrate its consequences—divine chastisement (Is. 1:20). These should serve as warnings to the believer (1 Cor. 10:1–12).

14:10 The bold words of the good spies elicited two responses: rejection by the congregation, who attempted to stone them, and the sudden appearance of the glory of God to save the lives of His faithful servants.

14:11, 12 Not unlike the leaders of Israel in Jesus' day, the people rejected God's miraculous **signs.** God's preliminary judgment was to utterly reject the nation. They clearly had rejected Him, dismissing the signs that He had done among them. In response, God again offered to use Moses to begin a new people.

14:13–19 As Gen. 22 records the divine testing of Abraham, this chapter records the divine testing of Moses. Moses might have accepted the Lord's offer and stood aside while the Lord swept the desert clean of this rebellious people. Instead, Moses protested that this drastic act of judgment would taint the reputation of God among the nations. Moses argued that **the Egyptians** would **hear it,** and that the great victory of God over their gods would be dismissed by their reinterpretation of events, if God were not able to bring His people into their new home. Then Moses quoted the Lord concerning His great mercy (v. 18 cites Ex. 34:6, 7) and begged Him to pardon the iniquity of the people.

14:20–25 Moses' dramatic recitation led to God's pardon of the rebels. The passion of God was seen in the exclamation of the words **as I live, all the earth shall be filled with the glory of the Lord.** This is an oath of deity that one day there will be the fullness of His glory throughout the earth, repeated by the Seraphim in Isaiah 6. The Christian thinks of the portraits of Jesus as the manifested glory of God (John 1:14) and in the coming age when His glory will illumine the earth (Rev. 21:23). God scolded the people who had ignored the many evidences of His glory in their midst, and who had put Him to the test **now these ten times.** It is possible that the expression "ten times" is a rounded number that speaks of the people's complete rejection of the Lord. This is another example of the ways numbers are used in the Book of Numbers. It is also possible (with some caution) to enumerate ten instances of rejection: (1) at the Red Sea where it seemed that Pharaoh's army would destroy them (Ex. 14:10–12); (2) at Marah where they found bitter water (Ex. 15:22–24); (3) in the Desert of Sin as they hungered (Ex. 19:1–3); (4) in the Desert of Sin as they paid no attention to Moses concerning storing manna until morning (Ex. 16:19, 20); (5) in the Desert of Sin as they disregarded Moses concerning gathering manna on the seventh day (Ex. 16:27–30); (6) at Rephadim as they complained for water (Ex. 17:1–4); (7) at Mount Sinai as Aaron led the people to make a golden calf (Ex. 32:1–35); (8) at Taberah where the people raged against the Lord (Num 11:1–3); (9) at Kibroth Hattaavah in the grumbling provoked by the rabble for quail (Num 11:4–34); (10) at Kadesh in the Desert of Paran when the people refused to receive the good report of Joshua and Caleb and wished themselves dead (Num 14:1–3). God's judgment was that the people who rejected Him would not see the land. Everyone was included except Caleb, whom God called **My servant,** and Joshua (v. 38). God then warned the people to bypass the region of the Amalekites. This was no longer a time for war, but for retreating into the wilderness.

14:26–38 This section forms what seems to be God's second response to the prayer of Moses (vv. 13–19). This second response contains some new elements. First, the **little ones** would be the only survivors of the wilderness wanderings. All over the age of twenty would die in the wilderness over the period of the next **forty years.** The forty days of the spies' journey would correspond to forty years of aimless wandering in the wilderness. For forty days the people had the opportunity to move with purpose; now for forty years there would be no purpose in their wandering. Finally, a distinction was made between the cowardly spies and the two faithful ones. Only Joshua and Caleb lived. The evil spies died immediately by a plague from the Lord. In the preservation of Joshua and Caleb from the fate of the others, we sense again the justice of the Lord. In His wrath He remembered to be merciful.

14:39–45 An abortive attempt at an invasion of the land by a still-rebellious people concludes this sad narrative. The people shouted their acknowledgment that they had sinned, but they had not taken to heart the seriousness of God's judgment on them. Heedless of Moses' warning that **the Lord** was **not among** them, the people went into battle. The result was disastrous. They go apart from the symbols of the divine presence and, indeed, apart from the presence of Yahweh. The Amalekites and the Canaanites route the disobedient armies of Israel, driving them deep into the wilderness. This is a classic example of way too little, very much too late. Only a disheartening, disastrous defeat could convince the armies that all was lost for themselves. The name **Hormah** means "Utter Destruction." At this point, the focus of Numbers shifts to the younger generation, who would enter the land.

15:1, 2 The words **when you have come into the land** may seem inappropriate following the events of chs. 13; 14. Yet God had not rejected the Israelites entirely. Their children would enter the land that their parents had rejected. Chapter 15, which concentrates on offerings and sacrifices, not only instructs the people about the worship of God, it is also is a sign of God's continuing promise: the people would eventually enter the land.

15:3–16 This section presents instructions on special offerings (the Hebrew word is *lepalle'*, "to make a special offering," from the verb *pale'*, "to be special," "extraordinary," "wondrous"; it is a verb used of the person and work of the Lord himself). These offerings were to be presented to the Lord by the people when they entered Canaan. There is a sense in which this chapter is a supplement to the teaching on sacrifices in Lev. 1—7.

15:4 a grain offering: The use of grain was as important in the sacrificial system of ancient Israel as was the offering of animals. **Fine flour** (Heb. *solet*) was luxurious, rather than ordinary. The mixing of certain proportions of fine flour with olive oil indicated that only the very best could be used in the celebratory worship of God.

15:5–12 a drink offering: Wine was used in drink offerings (vv. 7, 10) as an accompaniment to the burnt offerings of the goat, lamb, ram, and bull. In the pouring out of this wine on the altar, the worshiper poured out something of great value. As was the case with most of the other offerings, this represented the self-deprivation of the worshipers before God.

15:13–16 The words **all who are native-born** seem to point to a time after the wilderness experience, when the Israelites had already entered the land. As in the celebration of the Passover, the presentation of these offerings was to be done in the same way, whether the worshiper was born in the land or **a stranger.**

15:17–21 The **heave offering** is also known as the wave offering. Right at the beginning of the harvest, the harvester had to acknowledge that his produce was a gift from God. By holding up the very first produce from a harvest or of the first cake made from the first grain of the season, the worshiper thanked God as the giver of all good gifts.

15:22–29 If you sin unintentionally: Some sacrifices were offered on behalf of the nation as a whole, for there was always the possibility of an unintentional or unknown sin in the life of the people. Such sins may have been committed by the people as a whole (vv. 24–26) or by an individual (vv. 27, 28).

15:30, 31 The Hebrew phrase translated **presumptuously** means "with a high hand," with open disdain for the will and work of God. This is a sin that is done, as it were, while looking God in the eye and shaking one's fist at Him.

15:32–36 It is quite possible that **gathering sticks on the Sabbath day** is a specific example of the kind of thing mentioned in vv. 30, 31. One who flagrantly went out gathering sticks on the Sabbath was clearly in breach of the command to honor the Sabbath day (Ex. 20:8–11). This individual was caught and then brought to Moses for judgment.

15:37–41 The wearing of **tassels** (Heb. *sisit*) on the corners of garments was a beautiful sign of great significance. The tassels were memory devices to keep the wearer focused on the commandments of God. **To which your own heart and your own eyes are inclined** speaks vividly of the believer's old sin nature. The tendency to sin is always present, as the psalmist observes (Ps. 119:11). **Harlotry** of the **heart** is unfaithfulness to God. Each of us needs to have reminders to keep us thinking rightly about God and ourselves.

15:41 I am the Lord your God: God identified Himself as the One who gave these commands. He declared that He had a relationship with the Israelites. He was their God, and He had saved them from slavery. The Israelites had every reason to obey His directives, for He was their Lord *and* their Savior.

16:1 Yet another rebellion against Moses was led by **Korah,** a Kohathite (1 Chr. 6:22, 23). Korah and his allies challenged Aaron and Moses in much the same way that Miriam and Aaron had challenged Moses earlier (ch. 12). Korah and his allies were not satisfied with the role God had given them in the service of the tabernacle, so they decided to press for the priesthood (v. 10). This rebellion, then, was against Aaron as well as Moses (v. 11).

16:2, 3 Korah and the 250 leaders argued that the entire nation was **holy** to the Lord (Ex. 6:7) and that Moses and Aaron had presumptuously taken leadership positions. The root of their complaint was that God had not elevated them sufficiently.

16:4–8 Moses' response was complex. First, he submitted to the will of God, as seen in his action of falling **on his face.** Then he issued a challenge based on an expectation of an overt display of the will of God. He instructed each of the dissenters to take a **censer,** a metal holder for incense used in worship, and place incense on it as a sign of approach to God. Then each would await God's decision. Finally Moses tossed their own words back to them. Earlier they had said to him and to Aaron that they had gone too far (v. 3, "You take too much upon yourselves"); now Moses says that *they* have gone too far (v. 7, "You take too much upon yourselves"). The words are precisely the same in the Hebrew text.

16:9–11 The men who were seeking a higher position were in fact being contemptuous of the place to which God had appointed

them. Moses' response was condescending and scathing: **Is it a small thing to you?** The dissenters should have realized how gracious God had been in giving them the life work He had provided. They were not unlike people who complain about the gifts God has given them.

16:12–17 Dathan and Abiram, two allies of Korah, were so arrogant that they would not even come to stand before Moses. They attacked Moses, claiming he acted like a prince. These two approached absurdity when they charged Moses with leading them away from the land that flows **with milk and honey.** Possibly they were blaming Moses for the fact that the people had to turn away from the land after the rebellion at Kadesh (chs. 13; 14). In addition, they charged Moses with brutality: **Will you put out the eyes of these men?** Nothing in the story of the Exodus leads us to think that Moses might have done such a thing.

16:18, 19 The next day, each man lit incense in his censer. Korah brought the people near because he wanted witnesses to the events. **Then the glory of the LORD** appeared is a somber reminder of the words of 12:5, a similar setting of impending judgment.

16:20–22 The announcement of judgment begins with God's warning to Moses and Aaron that they should back away so that He might destroy the entire congregation. The very leaders who were under assault intervened for the people, asking God to spare them even if He had to judge the guilty. The expression **the God of the spirits of all flesh** suggests the comprehensive rule of God. He is sovereign over all.

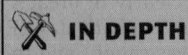 **IN DEPTH** | # Why Earthquakes?

Did God use an earthquake to judge Korah and his family (Num. 16:31, 32)? The text does not say, but the phenomena described resemble those of an earthquake. Certainly the geology of Palestine predisposed it to earthquake activity. In fact, to this day, between 200 and 300 tremors a day are recorded in Israel, most of them minor.

Modern geological studies have shown why. The Jordan River valley and the Dead Sea lie on top of a major north-south fault line which is actually part of a massive trans-continental system known as the Afro-Arabian Rift Valley. The two parallel faults that make up this rift probably indicate the overlap of two of the earth's underlying tectonic plates. Numerous secondary faults fan out east and west from the Palestinian portion of this fault.

As a result of these features, the Middle East has experienced numerous earthquakes down through the centuries, some of which have been catastrophic. A few are mentioned in the Bible:

• In the days of Saul during a campaign against the Philistines (1 Sam. 14:15)
• On Mount Horeb where Elijah hid (1 Kin. 19:11)
• In the days of King Uzziah (Amos 1:1; Zech. 14:5)
• At the crucifixion of Jesus (Matt. 27:51)
• In Philippi when Paul and Silas were in jail (Acts 16:26)

16:23–27 God demanded that the people back away from the tents of the rebels, and the people withdrew. Korah, Dathan, and Abiram were isolated at their tents with their families. It appears that Korah had left the 250 other rebels and was now standing beside Dathan and Abiram in wicked solidarity.

16:28–30 Moses called for a sign from God because he did not want anyone to think that what was about to happen was merely coincidence. Indeed, he asks for **a new thing** from God. This word describes the call for a new phenomenon (Heb. *beri'a*, a word related to the verb *bara'*, "to create," as in Gen. 1:1), something unmistakably the work of God.

16:31–35 In answer to Moses' prayer, God's judgment was sudden, dramatic, and memorable. He caused the earth to swallow the rebels alive. The words **the earth opened its mouth and swallowed them up** suggest a sudden action, like that of a sinkhole that opens with great speed. The families of Dathan and Abiram died with those two men. But the family of Korah was spared (26:11). In fact, Korah's descendants contributed a considerable number of psalms for temple worship (Ps. 42); yet another example of God displaying His mercy even as He justly punished rebels. The judgment was so sudden and severe that the people rushed back in fear, thinking that they might suffer the same fate. The 250 would-be priests were destroyed by fire **from the LORD**.

16:36–40 the censers . . . are holy: An amazing thing about this chapter is the Lord's concern that the censers be reused. Since these elements had been presented to Him, they were holy, despite the wickedness of those who presented them to God. The censers were gathered and hammered together for a covering for the altar. Henceforth, anyone who saw the altar would see its covering. This would be a warning not to wander too near for any reason. Only the true priests of the line of Aaron had that privilege.

16:41–45 Israel complained: Unbelievably, the people attacked Moses and Aaron as being the ones who caused the deaths of the popular leaders, **the people of the LORD**. In calling them this, the people asserted that they recognized Korah and the rest as spiritual leaders. Their affection for Korah and his associates had caused them to miss the greater reality, the leadership roles God had given to Moses and Aaron and God's judgment on those rebellious men. Again, there was a sudden appearance of the **glory of the LORD**—a symbol of further judgment. Again the Lord threatened to destroy the congregation, and again Moses and Aaron fell on their faces, interceding for the people's wickedness.

16:46–50 Moses' command to Aaron to **take a censer** is a fitting end to this chapter. Aaron and his sons were the divinely appointed priests. Only they could minister at the altar of God. Aaron rushed to the sacred tasks to make **atonement** for the sinning congregation because a **plague** had fallen on them. The picture of this aged priest running to save the people who had spoken against him is quite remarkable. The words of v. 48 are quite dramatic. Aaron stood between the living and the dead to stop the plague—a symbol of the Savior, who takes a similar stand in the gap between life and death.

17:1–5 The rebellion of Korah and its aftermath (ch. 16) left a level of uncertainty among the people concerning the divine appointment of Aaron and his sons as the true priests of God. The point of Aaron's rod budding was to eliminate the continuing complaint of the people against Moses and Aaron by another divine sign. One rod was presented from each tribe with the name of the tribal leader inscribed on it. Then the **twelve rods** were placed in the Most Holy Place. God would signal His choice of priestly leadership by causing the rod of one tribe and its leader to **blossom**—life from a dead stick.

17:6, 7 The text focuses on **the rod of Aaron** among the twelve. Aaron was near the end of his life. He and his wife, Elisheba, had four sons. Two, Nadab and Abihu, had died because of their own improper approach to God (3:2–4). Two, Eleazar and Ithamar, lived. On the impending death of Aaron, there had to be no question as to which family was divinely ordered to continue in the priestly office.

17:8, 9 When the rods were examined the next day, not only had the rod of Aaron sprouted, it had even **yielded ripe almonds.** This was a complete vindication of Aaron as the true priest of God. Each of the other rods was still a dead stick. But the rod of Aaron had sent forth such a sprout of life that the entire process of almond production had occurred in a single evening—all from a dead stick! Moses made each of the other tribal representatives take his own rod back, a physical symbol of agreement to the divine will.

17:10, 11 as a sign: Just as the stone tablets of the Law (Ex. 25:16) and a pot of manna were placed in the ark as signs of the enduring testimony of God's mercy to His people (Ex. 16:34), so now the rod of Aaron that budded and produced ripe almonds was placed there as well. Since the ark was in the Most Holy Place, only God would ordinarily look at this rod. Hence, Aaron's rod was a sign to God of His mercy. He had chosen the Levites to minister before Him. There would be one other besides God who

---

⚜ IN CONTEXT **Third-Party Assistance**

When a relationship has broken down, what can be done? It helps if a third party can be found to mediate a settlement, and that was a function of the priests in ancient Israel. By favoring Aaron's rod over those of others, God made it clear who should stand between Him and the people (Num. 17:10, 11).

God's relationship with Israel repeatedly broke down as a result of the violated commandments and rebellious complaints of the Israelites. Sometimes the offenses were so substantial that God immediately punished the offenders (Num. 14:40–45; 15:32–36; 16:31–35). Yet even when His character was violated and the people deserved judgment, God listened to Moses and Aaron as they intervened on the people's behalf (16:22, 46–48).

After Korah was taken away, the situation continued to deteriorate (16:41). Apparently the people had already forgotten whom God had placed in charge and whom He had made priests. So the Lord devised a plan to again make it clear that one group—the sons of Aaron—were to serve as intermediaries or priests between Him and the rebellious nation (17:1–11).

The Lord Jesus Christ is the intermediary between God and sinful people. All who depend on Christ's atoning work on their behalf have direct access to God (Heb. 10:19–25). Christ has become our High Priest (Heb. 8:1–6; 9:11–15), a permanent third-party Advocate who is fully worthy to intercede for our sin and rebellion (1 John 2:1).

---

would see these sacred items, the high priest of God's own choosing.

17:12, 13 Surely we die: Finally, the people realized that God had revealed His will through His miraculous actions among them. None of them except the one whom God had designated could approach God in His Holy Place. Any person who approached without heeding God's clear instructions could only expect death. The fact that God allowed anyone to approach Him demonstrated His mercy. Indeed, He not only allowed the high priest to approach, but He instructed him how he could atone for the sins of the people. Today, the same merciful God provides a more perfect way to find His forgiveness—through Jesus' death. With Jesus acting as our High Priest, we can boldly approach the Holy One and not fear death (Heb. 4:14–16).

18:1 Chapters 18 and 19 deal with the duties of priests and Levites, matters that flow quite naturally from the vindication of the true priesthood in ch. 17 and the crisis concerning the priesthood in ch. 16. The expression **bear the iniquity** speaks of the formidable work that was demanded of the priests of God. The word *iniquity* (Heb. 'awon) relates to the whole sphere of sin, guilt, and responsibility for an offense. If the people had no advocate before the Lord, they would die in their offenses. The priests stood as the intermediaries between God and man. Ultimately, all such priestly work points forward to the work of Jesus, our High Priest.

18:2–4 The Levites were the servants of the priests, but were limited in what they were able

to do. This was what had bothered Korah (ch. 16); he was a Levite who wanted to function as a priest.

18:5–7 Only the priests were allowed to attend to the duties of the sanctuary and the altar. The **outsider** was not a foreigner but a non-authorized Israelite. When one who was not authorized approached the holy places, that person was inviting punishment. Always in these contexts there is the sense of the priest standing between the dead and the living, between grace and mercy, between sin and forgiveness, the Christian reader thinks of the Savior.

18:8–20 The priests earned their livelihood in their work of the ministry of God (Lev. 6:14—7:36). Offerings that were not burned on the altars, although made to the Lord, became the food for the priests. **I am your portion:** The priests had no inheritance in the land itself. They lived off the produce of the land as God provided for them through the gifts of His people. Hence, the priests had a special relationship with God. He was their inheritance. Like the priests, believers today have no promise of an inheritance in this world. Nevertheless, believers are promised an inheritance in the future kingdom (Rom. 8:17).

18:21–24 all the tithes in Israel: The Levites also were the beneficiaries of the Lord's service. Like the priests, the Levites would not inherit land inheritances, but would be provided for in a manner suitable for their service to God.

18:25–32 The Levites who lived from the tithes of the people were themselves under obligation to make offerings to the Lord, **a tenth of the tithe.** Those who lived from the tithes were to give tithes so that they also might thank God for what He had given them. In all their work, the Levites were to remember the sense of the holy. Though they served God in mercy, they might be subject to His wrath if they behaved in a careless manner.

19:1, 2 The phrasing **this is the ordinance of the law** is somewhat awkward and unexpected. It is likely that we have a textual problem in the word "law" in this verse. The issue in this section is the sacrifice of the red heifer. The preferred Hebrew reading of the opening words of v. 2 is: "This is the ordinance of the heifer" (reading *hapara* for *hatora,* a copyist error). The **red heifer** was to be sacrificed in a special ritual outside the camp. Everything about this sacrifice was unusual. Ordinarily, the sacrificial animal was male; this one was female. The mention of the color of the animal is also unusual; in no other animal sacrifice was the color of the animal specified.

19:3 The naming of **Eleazar the priest** was a logical sequel to the test of the true priestly family in ch. 17. Before his father Aaron died, Eleazar had to start functioning in a prominent position before the congregation to ensure a smooth transition to his leadership. Ordinarily animals were sacrificed on or near the altar; in this case the animal was slaughtered **outside the camp.**

19:4–8 The total burning of the animal was also unusual, particularly since this animal was burned away from the altar. Symbolic items associated with cleansing—**cedar wood and hyssop and scarlet** (Lev. 14:4)—were then added to the fire. All were burned to ashes. The ritual made both the priest and those who helped him unclean.

19:9, 10 The **ashes of the heifer** were used in sacrificial rituals. The ashes were added to water, and the resultant mixture was used in certain rites of purification. **for purifying from sin:** What might be regarded as magical in a pagan context is here a visible symbol of God's inner work of purifying a person or object from sin.

19:11–13 The ashes and water had particular meaning for a person who had touched a **dead body.** Again, the sprinkling of **the water of purification** was more than a physical cleansing; it signified a submission to spiritual cleansing as well. It may be that contact with a dead body came under such strong sanction in ancient Israel due to that which death represented, the end result of sin. Death entered the world through sin (Rom. 5:12); death then is a grim reminder of the effects of sin. To touch a dead body was to make one in some spiritual

manner "unclean" for participation in the ritual of the worship of God.

19:14–19 Various instances of death and uncleanness are listed in these verses. This passage may have been a response to practical questions posed by the people. For example, if a man died in a tent, the people would certainly want to know what was required of them and how far the uncleanness extended. And what would happen if a person touched the body of a dead man in the field or in a grave?

19:20–22 One who did not **purify himself** rejected God's grace and consequently incurred His wrath. The issues were so serious that the one who applied the waters of purification to another became unclean also. These rituals were not given to make the lives of the people difficult. They were given to graciously instruct the people about the nature of true holiness.

20:1 The expression **the first month** lacks the notice of a year. Most likely, this was the fortieth year, the end of the sojourn in the wilderness. This chapter begins with the report of the Miriam's death, concludes with the report of Aaron's death (vv. 22–29), and records the major failure of Moses (vv. 1–13) and the resistance of Edom to the movement of the nation (vv. 14–21). It is a most dismal record. There is a sense that the deaths of Miriam and Aaron, as recorded in this chapter, are acts of mercy. The Lord has allowed them to live as long as possible before the first generation is utterly replaced by the second.

20:2–7 The words **no water** convey a sense of déjà vu. Having no water was the subject of the first crisis that the Israelites had in their journey out of Egypt (Ex. 17). Here, in the fortieth year since the Exodus, the same problem arose, provoking the same ingratitude and anger from the people.

20:8, 9 Moses was to take his rod, but was only to **speak to the rock.** A generation earlier, God's words were equally specific. At that time, Moses was told to take his rod and "strike the rock" (Ex. 17:6). On the first occasion, Moses did exactly what God had commanded; on the second occasion, he did not. Some have imagined what these differences in commands might mean. Since the text does not interpret them, here or elsewhere, it seems better just to observe the language and then to watch Moses' behavior. God is jealous for His word. We are not to change it but obey it explicitly (Rev. 22:18, 19).

20:10 The words of Moses are shocking: **Hear now, you rebels!** These words are understandable to be sure. But they are the words of one who had crossed the line, whose patience had been tried to the breaking point.

20:11 In his rage, Moses did not speak to

the rock as God had commanded. Instead he raised his rod and **struck the rock twice.** When he disobeyed, Moses violated all that he had stood for over the last forty years! God was not displaying anger, but Moses fell into deliberate, unrighteous anger. And in his anger, Moses lost his own stake in the Promised Land. What a huge loss for just a moment of disobedience! In the scheme of things, Moses did more than strike against the rock. He struck out against God. In some mysterious way, that rock was a symbol of the divine presence; the water

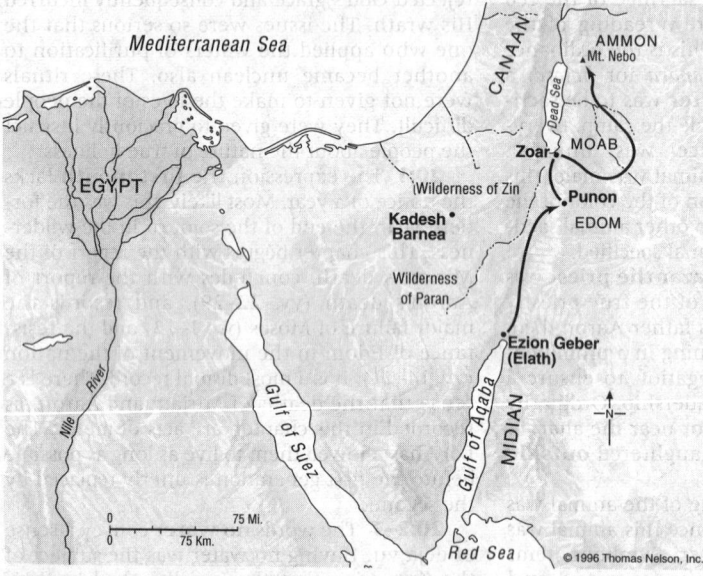

From the Wilderness to Canaan

The attempt forty years earlier to move from Kadesh Barnea north into Canaan had been rebuffed. This time Moses wanted to go east through Edom and north through Moab toward Canaan. However, the Hebrews were refused passage through both territories despite kinship with the peoples. Instead, Moses went south to Elath, then north and east, bypassing Edom and Moab. North of the Arnon River, they defeated the Amorites and were poised to cross the Jordan from the east to enter Canaan.

that gushed out so abundantly was a marker of His grace. The rock was miracle. It was Christ (1 Cor. 10:4).

20:12 God's judgment comes in expected severity, given the nature of Moses' offense. Moses is charged with the double sin of not believing in God and not hallowing Him before the people. **Hallow** means to "treat as holy." God saw Moses' action as a lack of respect and awe for His holiness. God's instructions were not honored. Moses, who for so long had been concerned with the reputation of God (14:13–19), slighted the Lord by not following His clear instructions in the presence of the con-

gregation. Aaron also was indicted and sentenced by the Lord. For both brothers, the sentence was to join the death march of the older generation. Neither of them would enter Canaan.

20:13 Meribah, or "Contention," is the name given to the place of Moses' sin. This is the same name that was given forty years earlier to the location of the first water crisis (Ex. 17:7).

20:14–21 Moses used diplomacy in his appeal to **the king of Edom,** testifying to the saving work of the Lord in delivering the people of Israel from Egypt. He also made what appears to be a most reasonable request: **let us pass through your country.** When Edom refused passage, Moses countered with an even more gentle request and reassured the Edomites that the Israelites had not come to conquer. This request was refused with a show of force.

20:22–29 Mount **Hor** is possibly Jebel Madurah, a mountain about fifteen miles northeast of Kadesh, on the northwest border of Edom. The mountain is on the direct route from Kadesh to Moab. It was here that the sad news came that Aaron was going to die. **Eleazar** received the duties of Aaron's priesthood. Soon the body of Moses would be left on another mountain, and Joshua would join Eleazar as a spiritual leader of the new generation. The **thirty days** of mourning for Aaron indicates the high esteem in which he was held by his brother and the people.

21:1–3 The first of Israel's military victories against the Canaanites came as the result of an attack by **the king of Arad.** Arad is located in the Negev, some twenty miles south of Hebron. However, it is likely that here the word "Arad" refers to a region even more south, as there is no sign of a city on the site of Arad from this period. It is not unusual for names of biblical places to "float" from one place to another over the centuries. The text emphasizes that the attackers were Canaanites and that the attack

---

N

☶ INSIGHT | Transfer of Authority

The transfer of authority is always a delicate task. Changing leaders can be a time of great stress for an organization, as old alliances and political forces vie with new ones to determine who will shape the future.

Aaron's death (Num. 20:22–29) was a major event in Israel. He was not only high priest for the nation but also the nation's first high priest. Furthermore, he had been Moses' primary spokesman (Ex. 4:16; 7:1) and was also Moses' brother. Aaron's successor, Eleazar, was his third son. Nadab and Abihu, Aaron's two older sons, had been consumed in the Lord's anger after offering "profane fire" before the Lord (Lev. 10:1–3). Thus Eleazar was, in a sense, the "third choice" for the position of high priest.

Despite these and other factors, the transition from Aaron to Eleazar went smoothly. Perhaps it was because God Himself oversaw the transfer of power. Scripture tells of several other transitions, not all of which went as smoothly.

---

was unprovoked. Israel made a vow of *herem*, devotion to the ban, should Yahweh give them victory. The people of Arad were distinct from peoples such as Edom and Moab. They were under the interdict of Yahweh. The Israelites fought valiantly and God fought for them. The Israelites triumphed over the army of Arad and destroyed its cities. This victory was the beginning of Israel's triumphant march into the Promised Land. But, as expected, even this turnabout will not be without troubles. The name **Hormah** is built on the word *herem*, something completely destroyed. It is possible that the name "Hormah" in 14:45 is based on this passage. That is, the region of Israel's earlier defeat only receives its proper name in this context. For the convenience of the reader, this name was inserted in the earlier story.

21:4, 5 The long journey **around the land of Edom** was necessary because the king of Edom refused to grant Moses' request for passage through his territory (20:14–21). After the first flush of victory (21:1–3), this circuitous route was particularly unpleasant to the people of Israel. Once again, they started complaining against Moses and God. The people again (11:6) protested God's provision of manna, calling it **this worthless bread.** As the psalmist later observed: "How often they provoked Him in the wilderness, And grieved Him in the desert!" (Ps. 78:40). In their contempt of the "bread of heaven" (Ps. 78:23, 24), the people were actually spurning God, who had given them this miraculous food.

21:6 God's discipline came upon the people in the form of **fiery serpents.** Snakes with poisonous venom for which there was no antidote caused raging fevers and agonizing deaths.

21:7–9 The pain of the venomous bites drove the people to repent, and they begged

Moses to intervene on their behalf. God instructed Moses to make an image of one of the serpents and to **set it on a pole.** Anyone who had been bitten and looked at the image **lived.** The raising of such a contemptible symbol on a pole ordinarily would have caused the people to shrink away in revulsion. But in this case the Israelites had to look at the serpent's image in order to live. Jesus pointed to this stunning image in His dialogue with Nicodemus (John 3:14, 15) as an analogy to His own execution. To the Jews, crucifixion was a sign of a curse. Therefore, just as the Israelites had to look on the repugnant, uplifted image of a serpent to be saved, we today have to look at the uplifted image of Jesus on a cross in order to be saved from our sins. So it is that this shameful account of Israel's rebellion becomes an incident that Jesus uses to explain the significance of His death. Hence we have the converging of a double symbol, a double type of the Savior. (1) The bread is a picture of Jesus the blessed; as bread of heaven, He is the proper nourisher of His people. (2) The snake is a picture of Jesus the cursed, who became sin for us as He hung on that awful tree.

21:10–13 The Israelites went around the region of Edom and entered the territory of Moab, which was just east of Jericho. It became the new staging area for the conquest of the land.

21:14, 15 The Book of the Wars of the **Lord** refers to an early collection of songs and writings known today only from this citation. The fact that Numbers draws upon other early Hebrew writings shows that the ancient Hebrew peoples had other literature in addition to Scripture. The song is difficult to translate today. The words **Waheb in Suphah,** if place names, are unknown.

21:16–20 Beer means "Well." At last the people had come to a place where they could dig a well and find adequate water. God had graciously provided for them and had given them a taste of the Promised Land that they would soon occupy. The song of vv. 17, 18 may be called "The Song of the Well." **Mattanah, Nahaliel, Bamoth,** and the tableland of **Pisgah** are not known to us today; they were merely stopping places of the nation along the route to the land of promise.

21:21–26 The defeat of **Sihon king of the Amorites** began with his rejection of a request for safe passage, not unlike a similar rejection from the king of Edom (20:14–21). In the case of Edom, Israel was not permitted by God to engage in a war of conquest. The territory of Edom was protected by the Lord in an ancient covenant (Gen. 36; Deut. 2:4, 5). No such protection was given to the Amorites, however;

Israel would live in the cities of her vanquished foes (Deut. 2:26–37).

21:27–32 The song of victory in these verses may also have come from "the Book of the Wars of the LORD" (v. 14). In any event, this chapter is notable in its use of lyrics from ancient songs of victory. Here again, this is a taunt song that celebrates the victory of Israel over a formidable force. **Those who speak in proverbs** refers not to wisdom sayings as in the Book of Proverbs but to taunt songs, as seen elsewhere in this chapter. The song begins with a recital of the earlier victory of the Amorites over the people of Moab and their god **Chemosh.** After defeating Sihon and the Amorites, Israel became a formidable threat to Moab (22:3). Verses 31, 32 refer to further encroachments of Israel in the land of the Amorites.

21:33–35 The defeat of **Og king of Bashan** immediately followed the defeat of the

Photo by Ben Chapman

Heshbon, capital city of Sihon, king of the Amorites, was captured by the Israelites during the wilderness wandering years (Num. 21:27–32).

they were among the peoples whom Israel was commissioned to destroy (Ex. 33:2; 34:11). Sihon not only rejected the request of Israel, but gathered for war against Israel at **Jahaz.** Israel completely defeated Sihon. This was the first of her victories east of the Jordan River. Israel conquered all of the cities that had belonged to the Amorites. This was part of the plan of God:

Amorites. The people of Israel had gained the control of all the land east of the Jordan River and north of the Arnon River. These early victories were part of the holy war of God and were celebrated by Israel as a part of her worship tradition (Deut. 3:1–11; Pss. 135:8–12; 136:17–22). God righteously and faithfully fulfilled His promise to Abraham (Gen. 15:7–21) that one day the sins of the Amorites would be judged and the people of promise would inherit their land.

22:1 the plains of Moab: With these words we come to the end of the travels of Israel described in the Book of Numbers. Not until the Book of Joshua does the story line of travel and conquest resume. **On the side of the Jordan across from Jericho** refers to the area they had conquered so far, territory that would be settled by two and a half tribes (ch. 32). However, the heart of the land was west of the Jordan River. The first city there that the Israelites would need to conquer was the oldest walled city in the world, ancient Jericho.

22:2-4 Remarkably, chs. 22—24 take the reader away from the camp of Israel and into hostile territory. These chapters focus on **Balak,** the king of Moab, and **Balaam,** whom Balak hired to destroy Israel by spiritual means. Moab was not yet facing Israel's threatening armies. But Balak knew that his enemy Sihon of Heshbon had been defeated by Israel (21:21–32), and he had reason to fear that he and his kingdom would be next. God had forbidden Israel to attack Moab (Deut. 2:1–9), but Balak either did not know this or did not believe it. He and the people of Moab were **exceedingly afraid** and **sick with dread.** Balak believed that he could not fight Israel on the field of battle and win. So he decided to fight them on another level, that of spiritual warfare. **The elders of Midian** with whom Balak consulted were the leaders of a mobile people with whom Balak may have had a mutual agreement of protection.

22:5 Balak sought out a pagan prophet who might engage Israel in spiritual warfare by causing her "gods," as they thought, to cease protecting them. Only then would Balak and Moab be safe from this formidable foe. The Moabites believed that blessings and cursings from the gods could be manipulated by skilled agents, who presumed to be able to traffic with the gods. At the time, the most famous of these agents was **Balaam** of Mesopotamia. In 1967, a discovery was made in Jordan of an eighth-century B.C. inscription of prophecies of Balaam. This discovery in what was ancient Moab is stunning evidence of the renown of this prophet even hundreds of years after his death. Yet the Balaam of Scripture is thoroughly reprehensible. In Scripture he becomes a paradigm of evil, a nearly satanic figure (Num. 31:8, 16; Deut. 23:4, 5; Josh. 13:22; 24:9, 10; Neh. 13:2; Mic. 6:5; 2 Pet. 2:15; Jude 11; Rev. 2:14). Balaam was a *baru* prophet, one who specialized in animal divination. He would inspect the liver of a ritually slain animal to ascertain from its shape and markings the will of the gods. Such prophets also observed the movements of animals and birds in order to ascertain certain signs from the gods. It was thought that such prophets could in some mysterious manner influence the gods by various rites. If Balaam could influence the "god" of Israel (as Balak supposed), then he might reverse their blessing, bring them under a curse, and destroy them. Yet this pagan prophet became an unwilling agent of some of the most sublime prophecies of the glorious future of Israel (chs. 23, 24). Balaam himself remained an enemy of Israel and sought to destroy them. He died in the camp of the people of Midian (ch. 31), enemies of Israel in their holy war.

22:6-8 The strong reputation of Balaam, who was believed to be able to influence the gods, is indicated in the phrasing **he whom you bless is blessed, and he whom you curse is cursed.** Behind all of this, of course, is the reality of God's irrevocable blessing on Israel and His standing curse on all who attempted to curse them (Gen. 12:2, 3). From the vantage of biblical theology, the story of Balaam is a test of the Abrahamic Covenant (Gen. 12:1–3; 15). Since Israel's experience in the wilderness was so dissolute, with repeated murmurings and rebellions, extending from the mixed rabble to her finest leaders, one might well wonder: is Israel still under Yahweh's blessing? Behind the story of paganism and magic, therefore, is a theological issue of the deepest significance for the future of God's people. In v. 8, Balaam speaks of **the Lord** as though he were intimate with Him. Because he was an internationally known soothsayer, it's likely that he had heard enough about Israel from emissaries of Moab and Midian to have learned the name of the God of Israel. Indeed, the story of God's deliverance of Israel from Egypt would have been widely known throughout the Middle East (Deut. 2:25).

22:9-14 The first encounter of the servants of Moab and Midian with Balaam ended in failure. God mercifully instructed Balaam, in what may have been a night vision, that he was not to go with the men to curse Israel, because they were **blessed.** Since Israel was under the blessing of God, any attempt to curse that nation would have been an attack on the word of God that would have brought the one who cursed Israel under God's curse (Gen. 12:3).

22:15-21 The second encounter of the emissaries of Moab and Midian with Balaam seemed to reverse things. The emissaries came with more noble persons and with grander gifts, bribes, and promises. Again, Balaam spoke of God in a familiar manner: **the word of the Lord** my God. This was not a confession of faith in God. Rather, it was a sly manipulation on the part of Balaam, a bold and false claim to be a medium of Israel's "god" just as he was the agent for many other gods. The duplicity of Balaam is seen in the way that God came to him the second time, reversing the clear orders He had given before (v. 12). Had Balaam been a true prophet, the words of God in v. 12 would have been definitive. But motivated by greed (2 Pet. 2:15; Jude 11), Balaam went to get a "new" word from God.

22:22–30 God's anger was aroused against Balaam, apparently because Balaam intended to do what Balak had hired him to do, to curse Israel. God could not have been angry at his going, for He had given Balaam permission (v. 20). But He had also given Balaam orders to speak "only the word which I speak to you" (v. 20). Apparently, Balaam planned to say whatever brought the highest amount of money. The Angel of the Lord refers to the presence of God (Gen. 22:11, 15). God was an adversary to Balaam. The donkey saw the Angel of the Lord: Balaam was supposed to have been able to communicate with the gods through animals. However, in this situation, the "seer" was blind to the presence of the true God. It was the animal who was the seer, perceiving the true will of God in the angel that blocked the path. In this context we read the stunning words the Lord opened the mouth of the donkey. While this sentence has been the subject of considerable ridicule, it hardly presents a significant challenge to a person of biblical faith. Anyone who has an adequate view of God can hardly balk at the concept of God's ability to give an animal a momentary ability to mimic human speech. After all, what is this compared to the Incarnation? The only issue in respect to miracles in the Bible is their import. That is, what would it mean were God to do such a thing? As C. S. Lewis has argued, every miracle in the Bible should be compared to the Grand Miracle of God becoming man. If we may believe that God became man, died, and was resurrected from the dead, what is hard to accept about the possibility of a man once hearing a sentence or two from a dumb animal? But if the Incarnation is not true, if Christ is not risen from the dead, then the speaking of all the animals of God's creation will do nothing to assuage our grief. But neither should we make more of this miracle than the Bible does. The donkey does not preach. The donkey does not give the word of God. *Balaam* will do that. All the donkey says is what an abused animal might say, were God to give it the opportunity: What have I done to you? The more amusing thing is that Balaam answers without surprise. And all the while there is the foreboding presence of the Angel of Yahweh (could this be

Christ?) with sword drawn to eviscerate the pagan rogue.

22:31–35 Then the Lord opened Balaam's eyes: The spiritually blind seer finally saw the majesty of the One whom the donkey saw all along. Now the pagan prophet was brought to his knees. His sin was the sin of willfulness: he had wanted to curse those whom God had blessed. In the strongest manner, the Angel of the Lord instructed Balaam to speak only what God spoke to him.

22:36–40 Balaam's statement, the word that God puts in my mouth, that I must speak, must have been puzzling to Balak (23:11, 25; 24:10, 25). The sacrifices of v. 40 were not to God, of course. These were pagan sacrifices to idols. That which Balak sent to Balaam included the livers, which Balaam used in divination (24:1).

22:41 The high places of Baal were selected not only because of the view they afforded. They were places of pagan worship.

23:1–6 The use of seven altars and the offering of a bull and a ram on each one was a part of Balaam's pagan ritual. Afterward, God in His mercy gave Balaam a true message to speak. The expression the Lord put a word in Balaam's mouth is the same type of language used of true prophets (Jer. 1:9). God used this pagan to bless His people.

23:7–10 The first oracle of Balaam set the pace for the rest. There were seven oracles in all. Each is introduced with the words he took up his oracle and said (23:7, 18; 24:3, 15, 20, 21, 23). The word translated *oracle* is the word usually translated *proverb*. In this case, it means "prophetic speeches." In the first oracle, Balaam described the purpose for which he was called, to curse Israel. However, he was unable to curse Israel because God would not allow it. From the worship site of pagan idolatry (22:41), he viewed Israel from a distance and saw that they were a people distinct from all other nations. Who can count the dust of Jacob suggests his attempt at ascertaining their number by divination. The numbers were vast, and he had no handle on them. my end: This is a reference to Balaam's destiny. He would not share Israel's glorious life in heaven.

23:11, 12 The response of Balak was one of stunned horror. He had brought Balaam to curse Israel, but Balaam had blessed them bountifully!

23:13–17 Balak foolishly thought that going to another place would influence God to allow a curse to be placed on His people. Then the Lord met Balaam: The language implies that Balaam was still attempting to be the channel for a curse. Perhaps he was looking for a stronger force that would override the power of

God that had made him bless Israel. But it was not to be. Again Balaam's words came from the only living God.

23:18–24 The second oracle was addressed to Balak, an unwilling listener. Balaam confessed a wondrous truth about the God of Israel: He is unable to change; He cannot lie. Because God had blessed Israel, Balaam was powerless to change this to a curse. God had seen many examples of evil in His people during the wilderness years. Nevertheless, there simply was no means of sorcery or divination that Balaam could use to destroy their blessing. We who live in Christ can be encouraged by these words today. God cannot lie, nor can He renege on His promise of life for His people (Rom. 8:31–39).

23:25–30 Neither curse them at all, nor bless them at all! Balak nearly said, "I will pay you just to be quiet!" But again he thought all that was needed was a better location.

24:1, 2 it pleased the LORD to bless Israel: God was determined to bless His own people. The words **the Spirit of God came upon him** refer to the empowerment that gave Balaam his message and its direction. Dramatically, God controlled Balaam and spoke clearly through a person who was His enemy.

24:3–9 The third **oracle** is marked by a lengthy introduction that speaks of the powerful things that had taken place within Balaam. The heart of the third oracle is a blessing on the tribes of Israel as they were about to enter the land of Canaan. Their **tents** were beautiful in their placement, but soon they would fill the land in great prosperity. Their king would be prodigious, for God would empower them to destroy all enemies. Israel is pictured as a **lion,** not to be trifled with. Finally in v. 9, Balaam quoted Gen. 12:3. Those who bless Israel will be blessed. Those who curse Israel will be cursed.

24:10–14 In the aftermath of the third oracle, Balak wanted to dismiss Balaam entirely. But Balaam was not to be stopped.

24:15–19 The fourth oracle has the longest introduction, which builds on the introduction to the third oracle (vv. 3, 4). **I see Him, but not now . . . A Star shall come out of Jacob:** This poetic language clearly refers to the Messiah. The pagan Balaam had a vision of the coming of the Hebrew Messiah, the Lord Jesus Christ! He was visible from afar. He was like a Star, radiant and beautiful. He was like a **Scepter,** majestic and powerful. And He is the victor over His enemies, including Moab—the nation that hired Balaam to curse Israel! All nations who resisted Israel and God's work would come under the curse they unwittingly embraced. Among them was **Edom,** who rejected the request of Moses for safe passage (20:14–21). The One **out of**

Jacob, the Messiah, will be victor over all His foes (Pss. 2; 110; Rev. 19:11–21).

24:20 The fifth oracle is brief, coming without a pause. It is a curse on **Amalek,** the first people to fight with Israel in their wilderness experience, and the first to bring defeat

IN FOCUS "scepter"

(Heb. *shebet*) (Num. 24:17; Gen. 49:28; Lev. 27:32) Strong's #7626: The word can vary in meaning depending upon its context. Potential meanings include "tribe" (Gen. 49:28), "staff" (1 Chr. 11:23), and "rod" (Ps. 23:4). Because a king would often hold a scepter, it became a symbol of a king, especially the kingship of the Messiah: He would rule God's people (24:17; Gen. 49:10; 1 Cor. 15:24–28). Yet when this Hebrew word is translated *staff,* it symbolizes the concern and care of a shepherd for his sheep, the kind of care the Lord has for His people (Mic. 7:14). When the word is translated *rod* it symbolizes judgment (Ps 2:9).

upon themselves (Ex. 17:8–16). A requital was coming.

24:21, 22 The Kenites were a Midianite tribe (Num. 10:29; Judg. 1:16). This oracle makes a wordplay between the word *Kenite* and the similar Hebrew word for *nest.* **Asshur** is Assyria here.

24:23–25 In this last oracle the identification of the nations is difficult, but the general sense is clear enough: One nation would rise against another, only to face its own doom. The Hebrew word translated **Cyprus** was used later in reference to Rome (Dan. 11:30).

25:1, 2 Acacia Grove (Heb. *shittim*) is another name for the staging area of Israel in the Transjordan across from Jericho. With these words, the focus of Numbers returns to the camp of Israel. At the end of their long wilderness wanderings, the Israelites had their first encounter with the false religion of Canaan. The phrase **the women of Moab** is the connecting link between this chapter and chs. 22—24. What the men of Moab could not do, the women were able to accomplish. They trapped the Israelite men in sexual immorality and false worship. For this God punished them. In 31:16, we learn that the principal instigator of this sorry affair was none other than Balaam.

25:3 Baal of Peor: Balaam had taken his stance at this high place for pagan worship

(23:28) in preparation for his last set of oracles. It is grimly fitting that the near destruction of the people of Israel should be associated with the debased sexual and idolatrous practices of this site.

25:4, 5 God's **anger** flashed yet again toward His errant people. But this was not just another time of trouble, this was the most serious challenge yet. The people had been seduced into joining the worship of Baal. And it was Baal worship that they had been sent to Canaan to eliminate!

25:6–9 The most egregious sort of pagan worship and debased sexual expression comes in these verses, although the language here is somewhat reserved. It may be that the narrator was not willing to be as candid as he might have been because the incident was so distasteful. This is much the same as the reserved expression in Gen. 6:1–4. Zimri (v. 14), a Hebrew man, became involved with a Midianite woman named Cozbi (v. 15), who may have been a priestess of Baal. Although the nature of the offense isn't made clear in the text, it could be that their sinful actions were performed **at the door of the tabernacle,** in full view of **the congregation. Phinehas the son of Eleazar,** zealous for God's honor, killed both Zimri and Cozbi with a javelin, thus ending the plague that resulted from this offense.

25:10–15 zealous with My zeal: God's response is one of praise for Phinehas. The Hebrew word translated *zealous* can also be translated *jealous*. Phinehas did not want the Israelite camp to be defiled with immorality connected to Baal worship. God honored Phinehas for his zeal with what He called **My covenant of peace.**

25:16–18 Harass the Midianites: God commanded Moses to institute a holy war against Midian in retaliation for the unholy and immoral war waged against Israel by that nation. The war was engaged in shortly, but this is not reported until ch. 31. The repetition of the names and the place of the debacle in v. 18 serves to memorialize the event.

26:1 after the plague: These words are a turning point in Numbers. The plague was the end of the first generation. Under God's grace, their sons and daughters were ready to begin anew. They would inherit the Promised Land.

26:2–4 The words **take a census** remind us of the beginning of the Book of Numbers (1:2). This is a new beginning and a new census. The numbers compare favorably with the numbers of the first generation. Despite all the people who had died in the wilderness, the total population was not markedly different. Again, this was a sign of God's blessing on the Israelites.

26:5–50 The children of Reuben: This chapter focuses specifically on the tribal units, with considerable attention paid to the family groupings and the notable persons. It is fitting that this census is considerably more complete than the one in ch. 1. These were the people who would actually enter and inherit the Promised Land.

26:51 who were numbered: The totals of the twelve tribes are very similar in the two census listings. Reuben decreased from 46,500 to 43,730; Simeon decreased from 59,300 to 22,200; Gad decreased from 45,650 to 40,500; Judah increased from 74,600 to 76,500; Issachar increased from 54,400 to 64,300; Zebulun increased from 57,400 to 60,500; Manasseh increased from 32,200 to 52,700; Ephraim decreased from 40,500 to 32,500; Benjamin increased from 35,400 to 45,600; Dan increased from 62,700 to 64,400; Asher increased from 41,500 to 53,400; Naphtali decreased from 53,400 to 45,400. The total decreased slightly, from 603,550 to 601,730.

26:52–56 The land of Canaan was the **inheritance** of the people from the Lord. It was His gift to them, prompted by His love. Two principles were to be used in dividing the land: large tribes were to get large portions, but the determinations were to be made by lot.

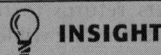 **INSIGHT**   **A Second Census**

Just as Israel's wilderness wanderings began with a census (Num. 1:2–19), so they ended with one (26:2). As before, the census counted only men of military age and probably functioned much like a draft. This second registration was required because some forty years had elapsed since the previous census. During that period, an entire generation of males had died, those who had been twenty years of age and older at the incident at Kadesh Barnea. The only survivors, aside from Moses, were Joshua and Caleb (14:29, 30; 26:64, 65). This was the second census recorded in Numbers, but actually the third for Israel that we know about. Scripture tells about seven major censuses.

26:57–62 The numbering of the **Levites** follows that of the other tribes, just as in the first census. In this case more names and families are given, for this was the list that would be used once the people were in the land. The total number of Levite males had increased to 23,000, which was quite close to the earlier total of 22,000 (3:39).

26:63–65 not a man of those: The persons numbered in the second census did not include any who were numbered in the first census. Of the survivors, only Caleb and Joshua had been over the age of twenty at the time of the debacle at Kadesh (chs. 13; 14).

27:1–5 Five sisters—**the daughters of Zelophehad**—approached Moses and Eleazar to make a claim for their inheritance in the land. Their father had died in the wilderness, as had his entire generation. Since he had no sons, there was no inheritance for him. On the basis of their father's memory, the daughters asked Moses for **a possession among our father's brothers.** In doing this, they were cutting across the social mores of the day. In ancient Israel, women did not inherit land. Yet because their case made sense, Moses took the issue to the Lord. This situation gives us some insight as to how law worked in Israel. Decisions were made on the basis of need and request. If a decision was difficult, the leaders would go the Lord for direction.

27:6–11 speak what is right: God's decision was that the daughters of Zelophehad had presented a just cause. They would inherit land in the name of their father. The case would become a precedent for other families in which there were no sons, only daughters. If there were no daughters, the inheritance would go to the nearest surviving relative. This was a significant departure from the custom of the day. See ch. 36 for complications that arose from this issue.

27:12–14 The time for the beginning of the conquest was near, which meant that the end of Moses' life was also near. Although God would not allow Moses to enter the land, He would, by His grace, allow Moses to **see the land** from afar.

27:15–17 set a man over the congregation: Moses' concern was for the well-being of the community, not for himself. Who would lead Israel after his death?

27:18–23 It appears that there were two candidates to succeed Moses: Caleb and Joshua, the two spies who had honored the Lord when the entire nation would not (ch. 14). God's choice was **Joshua.** One of the qualifications for the job was the presence of the Holy Spirit, a mark not unlike the qualification for spiritual leadership in the NT (Acts 6:3). The Lord

instructed Moses to present Joshua to the congregation so that there would not be a power struggle after his death. Further, Moses began to delegate work to Joshua so that the transition would begin while Moses was still alive. Moses **laid his hands** on Joshua, a symbol of the transfer of power. He invested Joshua with the authority to lead Israel (Acts 13:1–3).

28:1–6 My offerings made by fire: Numbers frequently inserts various materials into the flow of the narrative. Among such materials are the sections on sacrifice in chs. 28 and 29. The

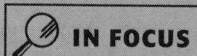

IN FOCUS — "sabbath"

(Heb. *shabbath*) (Num. 28:9; Ex. 20:8; Lev. 19:3; 23:3; Deut. 5:12; Jer. 17:22) Strong's #7676: The word derives from the verb meaning "to cease" or "to rest" (Gen. 2:3; Ex. 31:17). The Sabbath is the seventh day in the Hebrew calendar, or Saturday (Ex. 16:26; 20:10). God established this day as a time to rest because He had created all things in six days and had rested on the seventh day (Ex. 20:11). The Sabbath not only mirrored His own actions at creation, but it also was designed as a day to remember God, specifically His covenant with Israel (Ex. 31:12–18). In addition to this special day, the principle of a Sabbath rest was also applied to the land every seventh year (Lev. 25:1–7).

following chapters focus on the nature of the offerings God required on a seasonal and festival basis.

28:7, 8 In this case, the **drink offering** was beer; usually it was wine. Beer is made from fermented grains; wine is made from fruit, usually grapes. Both were used in the worship of God, to be poured on the altar in required measure.

28:9, 10 The offerings **on the Sabbath day** were in addition to the offerings made every day.

28:11–15 The offerings **at the beginnings of your months** were in addition to daily and weekly offerings.

28:16–25 The celebration of **Passover** (9:1–14) included special sacrifices at the altar. On the first and seventh day of the period, no work was done. The entire period was marked by the eating of unleavened bread.

28:26–31 The **Feast of Weeks** occurred fifty days after Passover and the Feast of Unleavened Bread.

29:1–6 The celebration of the Feast of

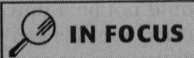

🔍 IN FOCUS   "vow"

(Heb. *neder*) (Num. 6:2, 5; 21:2; 30:2; 1 Sam. 1:11; Nah. 1:15) Strong's #5088: A *vow* to God is a voluntary commitment to do something that pleases Him or to abstain from certain practices to demonstrate devotion to Him. A vivid example is the OT Nazirite vow (6:1–21). Scripture admonishes the believer against making rash vows, since they are made before God, the righteous and holy Judge (Eccl. 5:4). The reason for the warning is that a vow made to Him is binding and must be fulfilled. The Hebrew word can also refer to a thank offering (Deut. 12:6), as the psalmists often speak of paying their vows as an act of praise to God (Pss. 66:13; 116:14).

Trumpets involved blowing ram's horns (contrast the silver trumpets in 10:2). Later, this festival became identified with the new year festival.

29:7–11 The Day of Atonement, or Yom Kippur, was regarded as the most holy day of all. Lev. 16 describes this as a day of fasting rather than feasting, of solemnity rather than rejoicing.

29:12–38 The celebration of the Feast of Tabernacles, or Succoth, was complex. There was an order to be followed over a period of eight days, and the eighth day had its own distinct ceremony. As in ch. 7, the mini-paragraphs for the days of the festival make use of deliberate repetition in order to evoke the pageantry and solemn ritual of these occasions.

29:39, 40 These verses conclude the summary of sacrifices of chs. 28 and 29. The sacrifices and offerings listed in these two chapters are the bare minimum the people had to present to the Lord throughout the year.

30:1, 2 The key issue is clear: one who makes a vow **shall not break his word.** Vows that are made to the Lord must be carried out (Deut. 23:21–23; Eccl. 5:1–7).

30:3–5 if a woman makes a vow to the LORD: In Israelite culture, an unmarried young woman was under the protection of her father. If she entered into a vow, that vow might have brought her father into an obligation he did not want to fulfill or could not fulfill. For that reason, the father could overrule the vow. If he did not, **then all her vows** would **stand,** including any complications that they might bring.

30:6–8 The preexisting **vows** of a newly married woman could have brought her husband under some obligation. Therefore, the husband had the opportunity to overrule vows his wife may have made before she came under his protection. In such a case, God would release the woman from her vow. If the husband heard the vow but did not overrule it, then the vow with all its possible complications would stand. A comparison with vv. 10–15 suggests that this woman is newly married.

30:9 The **vow of a widow or a divorced woman** would stand, because it did not complicate the obligations of either father or husband.

30:10–15 In the case of a woman who entered into a vow to the Lord after marriage, the husband could overrule the vow. His silence would allow it to remain in force. Many of these situations may have been decided in much the same manner as the case of the daughters of Zelophehad (ch. 27); that is, on the basis of particular cases that were brought before God for a decision.

30:16 This summary statement speaks of God's authority and the decisions He gave to Moses respecting the complications of vows

🔍 IN FOCUS   "vengeance"

(Heb. *naqam*) (Num. 31:2; 1 Sam. 24:12; Is. 1:24) Strong's #5358: The Hebrew verb translated *take vengeance* can have a negative or a positive connotation. On the one hand, the Israelites were forbidden to take revenge because such actions were ultimately self-serving (Lev. 19:18). On the other hand, the Scriptures speak of a righteous vengeance that involves the pursuit of justice, virtue, and the defense of God's majesty. God declared that only He can seek this type of vengeance: "Vengeance is Mine" (Deut. 32:35). But He often uses people, as in 31:2, to carry out His revenge.

where women were involved in the culture of ancient Israel.

31:1, 2 Chapter 31 refers back to ch. 25, the debacle of Israel's sin at Baal Peor and the role that the Midianites played in orchestrating the event.

31:3–6 The preparations for battle included setting apart **a thousand from each tribe,** a way of ensuring the sense of participation of the whole people in the war. **Phinehas,** the heroic figure who stemmed a plague with his bold action (25:7, 8), was commander in the field. As a priest, he led the armies of Israel with **holy articles and the signal trumpets.** This was not an ordinary conflict; it was a holy war, done in the name and power of God.

31:7–11 Victory was assured, given the blessing of God on the armies of Israel. The Israelites killed **all the males** and the **kings,** and took the **women** and **their little ones** as captives.

31:12–24 When the victors made their way back to the encampments of Israel, they found not praise but anger. **Have you kept all the**

be killed as well. Only the young girls who were still virgins were to be kept alive, for only they were provably innocent of the sexual sins of their mothers. Since this was a holy war, the soldiers and their possessions needed to go through extraordinary purification rites. This purification demanded both cleansing fire and water.

31:25–47 The balance of the chapter details the division of the plunder. The numbers are huge, suggesting a great victory. The division among those who had gone to war and those who had not set a standard for future battles. The portion that was to be regarded as the Lord's also became a standard.

31:48–54 While the record of the destruction of the people of Midian is distressing, the report from the officers of Israel that **not a man of us is missing** is awe-inspiring. None of

---

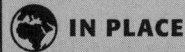 **IN PLACE** ## The Journeys of Israel

No one knows the exact route that Israel took from Egypt to Canaan (Num. 33:1). However, it was not a direct journey.

After the people left Egypt, they traveled south to Mount Sinai, where they received the Law. Then they eventually made their way north to Kadesh (Num. 13:26), from which they sent spies to survey the Promised Land. There they lost faith in the Lord's promises and as a result spent the next forty years "wandering" through the wilderness while an entire generation died off (14:34, 35). The term "wandering" is a misnomer, for the multitude was led by God Himself, who gave His people a cloud to follow by day and a fiery cloud by night (Ex. 13:21, 22).

The next major leg in the journey was the attempt to pass through Edom (Num. 20:14–21). Because the king of Edom refused access to the King's Highway, Israel was forced to take a route around Edom in order to travel north for the Transjordan valley east of Canaan. It was from this area that they eventually began the conquest of the land.

The list in Num. 33 includes many of the sites that the Israelites visited. However, not many have been positively identified by modern-day archaeologists.

Map labels:
The Great Sea · Spies sent north to Canaan. · CANAAN · Dead Sea · MOAB · Raamses · GOSHEN · Wilderness of Shur · EDOM · 40 years "wandering" through the wilderness; exact route unknown. · Wilderness of Paran · Ezion Geber · SINAI · Israelites travel around Edom toward Moab. · General locale of Mount Sinai. · Rephidim · 0 25 50 75 Miles · N

---

women alive: The key to Moses' anger is the sinfulness of the women. **These women** had caused Israel to sin, as they had been counseled by **Balaam.** Balaam had been slain, along with the kings and notables of the people (v. 8). Now the women and their male children needed to

their soldiers, not one, was lost in the battle. In praise and gratitude to God, the officers made a special offering, which Moses brought into the tabernacle as a memorial. The size of the officers' gift was extraordinary: a total of over 400 pounds of gold.

32:1–5 The tribes of **Reuben** and **Gad** wanted the land east of the Jordan which Israel had taken from Sihon and Og (ch. 21). The flocks and herds of Reuben and Gad were large, and the people of these tribes believed that the conquered area east of the Jordan would be good for them. Therefore, they came to Moses to request this land as their tribal inheritance.

32:6–15 And Moses said: Moses' initial response was one of outrage and dismay. It appears that he was concerned that these tribes were going to shirk their duty to help the other tribes conquer the territory west of the Jordan. Moses was afraid they were going to drop out of the battle before it was fully joined. The encounter with these men gave Moses an opportunity to rehearse the story of God's redemption of Israel and Israel's subsequent history and to use that story as a warning for these people.

32:16–19 The men of Reuben and Gad attempted to reassure Moses that they were not opting out of the battle at all. They simply wanted to build some provision for their wives and families while they were gone, and then they would join Israel's army until the entire Promised Land was secured. **We will not return:** Their promise of faithfulness to the Israelite army is couched in strong words. They would return to their wives only when every tribe had received its inheritance.

32:20–27 Moses and the men of Reuben and Gad negotiated. Plans were made for the fighting men of these tribes to join the armies of Israel for the period of the conquest. But first they wanted time to prepare for their families, flocks, and herds. Their confident promise of faithfulness to the battle, even when separated so far from their families, is couched in strong words (32:18). For the Jewish people to live in the land, it was considered a *mitzvah*, a holy act.

32:28–32 Finally the deal is struck between Moses and the leaders of Reuben and Gad. If the people would do as they had promised, if they would fight alongside the others until the conquest was complete, they could certainly live in the land they chose—the land east of the Jordan. If not, they would lose all choice in the land at all.

32:33–42 It is not until the end of the narrative that we learn that one-half of the tribe of Manasseh had joined Reuben and Gad in their proposal. Moses agreed to their plan and led them in the distribution of the land east of the Jordan. The villages and cities are listed, praising God for victory over them. Naming them shows how God had led His people to the Promised Land and enabled them to build cities and villages.

33:1 These are the journeys: Chapter 33 records the journey of the people of Israel from Rameses in Egypt (v. 3) to the plains of Moab (v. 49). The chapter is marked by significant difficulties. Most of the places cited are not known today. This is because for the most part they were not cities but merely encampments in the wilderness of the Sinai.

33:2 Moses wrote down: These remarkable words indicate that Moses himself wrote down the following passage. Curiously, on the basis of prior decisions against the writing activity of Moses, some critical scholars dismiss this phrase as not even worthy of consideration. The critical stance respecting Mosaic authorship of the Pentateuch is so deeply entrenched that even when the text says he did write, that is denied! That so many of the places mentioned in this chapter are not known to us or are even found elsewhere in the Bible are marks of the antiquity of the chapter, and, we may aver, its authenticity. Whereas Christians tend to describe Moses' profession as being that of a shepherd, Jewish people tend to regard his profession as either a teacher or a scribe.

33:3–5 Rameses is usually identified with Tanis (Gen. 47:11; Ex. 1:11). There is a certain structural symmetry to the listing of these place names in this chapter. In essence, this list of place names is a song of praise to God's faithfulness. With every step and with every encampment, God led them triumphantly to the Promised Land. Significantly, there are forty places mentioned between Rameses and the plains of Moab. Some of the sites recorded here (including many of the ones in vv. 5–18) are mentioned elsewhere in Exodus and Numbers; some are recorded only here (including most of those listed in vv. 19–29). In addition, some of the places mentioned in Exodus and Numbers are not recorded here (including Taberah, in 11:3).

33:6–37 Succoth, Etham, and **Pi Hahiroth** were west of the Sea of Reeds. The rest of the sites were in the Sinai Desert.

33:38–49 Mount Hor: With the mention of this place, a quick memorial is given of **Aaron,** the high priest. **fortieth year:** The journey from Rameses to Mt. Hor completed the forty-year cycle. Aaron died on the last year of the Israelites' wanderings in the desert.

33:50–56 On the staging area for the invasion of the Promised Land, God gave Moses instructions for the people about the conquest of Canaan. Israel was to exterminate the Canaanites and take full possession of their land. For over 400 years, from the time of God's covenant with Abram in Gen. 15:17–21, God had warned that a time would come when He would punish the sinfulness of the Canaanites. The Canaanites, by their continual wicked acts, had no right to live in the land of Canaan. God, whose land it really was, transferred the right of possession to Israel. Therefore, the words come as a legal transfer: **for I have given you the land to possess.** It was to be divided by lot, with the larger tracts going to the larger tribes, as already described in 26:52–56.

33:55, 56 if you do not drive out the inhabitants of the land: God's commands to Israel to eradicate the Canaanites from the land were ultimately expressions of His mercy to Israel. If the idolatrous Canaanites were allowed to live among God's people, they would have been a constant source of trouble for the Israelites, like an irritant in the eye or a thorn in the side. Indeed, if the Canaanites were allowed to remain, Israel would become like them. The result would necessitate the expulsion of Israel from the land. Sadly, the experience of Israel in the land led to this very result. This chapter serves as the emotional and logical conclusion of Numbers. The recital of places and the commission for conquest provide the reader a sense of closure for this phase of Israel's life, as well as an anticipation of the future. The last three chapters serve as appendices.

34:1–12 the land of Canaan to its boundaries: Chapter 34 serves as a detailed display of the grandeur of the land that God was about to give to His people (33:53). The information in this chapter is based on an intimate knowledge of the contours of the land, something that one might not expect Moses to have had. The information, however, may have been part of that gathered by the spies (ch. 13), and Caleb and Joshua might have assisted Moses in this list.

34:13–15 To the nine tribes and to the half-tribe is a reminder that Reuben, Gad, and the half-tribe of Manasseh would have their settlements east of the Jordan (32:33). The land of Canaan proper would be inhabited by the remaining nine tribes and the other half-tribe of Manasseh.

34:16–29 The listing of **the names of the men** serves several purposes: (1) to give authenticity to the record; (2) to memorialize these individuals in the history of Israel; (3) to serve as a legal arrangement so that the transfer of the land to the tribes would be done in order.

34:29 There is a sense in the words **these are the ones** that the second generation was now the fully accredited substitute for the rebellious first generation.

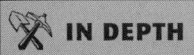 **IN DEPTH**   # Cities of Refuge

In the ancient Middle East, custom dictated that the taking of a life, even by accident, had to be avenged by a member of the victim's family. In response to this ancient practice, God ordered six Levitical cities to be stationed in the land as cities of refuge. A person guilty of unintentional manslaughter could escape blood revenge by fleeing to one of these cities (Josh. 20). No matter where a person lived, there would be a city of refuge within a reasonable distance, because they were strategically spread all over the land—three to the east of the Jordan and three to the west. The Hebrew term translated *refuge* or *asylum* designates a place of escape from the *avenger,* who was the protector of the family's rights, the one who made things right. (The Hebrew word for *avenger* is the same word used for Boaz, translated *relative* in Ruth 2:1.)

Seeking refuge was not a private act, however. Certain regulations governed whether it was applicable to a specific situation, and judgments would be made about each case (Num. 35:22–25). The provisions for seeking refuge in one of the designated cities were spelled out in some detail. (1) The slaying had to have been accidental and not premeditated (Num. 35:16–21). (2) The person had to flee immediately to the city of refuge. The person was safe from the avenger only when he or she was within the city. (3) The person was not safe from vengeance if he or she decided to leave the city. Basically, the unintentional murderer was a virtual prisoner within the city's walls (Num. 35:26–28). (4) The statute of limitations was based on the death of the high priest. When the high priest died, the avenger could no longer pursue the offender. The latter was free to return home (Num. 35:25, 28). (5) The law of asylum pertained to the alien as well as the citizen (Num. 35:15). (6) The manslayer could not pay a ransom instead of fleeing to or staying in a city of refuge. Otherwise a poor person would have been at a great disadvantage (Num. 53:31).

With all these specific regulations, God demonstrated His gracious concern for the innocent. He provided a place for an innocent person to find mercy and safety from the harsh ancient practice of avenging for family deaths.

35:1–8 give the Levites cities: The Levites were separated from the rest of the population for the holy service of God (1:47–53). They were not to have an allotment of land along with the other tribes (18:24). Nonetheless, the Levites needed places to live and to manage their herds and flocks. The decision of the Lord was that they would be distributed throughout the land in forty-eight cities. In this way, the Levites were distributed among the people as a symbol of the holy service of God (Josh. 20; 21).

35:9–29 Six Levitical cities were to be stationed strategically in the land—three in Transjordan and three in Canaan proper—as cities of refuge, or asylum cities, where a person guilty of unintentional manslaughter might escape blood revenge. Joshua 20 describes the sites that were eventually chosen.

Refuge, or "asylum" (Heb *ha-miqlat*), speaks of a place of escape from the "avenger" (Heb., *gô'el*) for the one who has committed manslaughter. The avenger is the protector of the family rights; the same word is used of the "kinsman redeemer" in Ruth 2:1 (Lev. 25:48). The avenger is more the "rectifier," the one who makes things right. Again, this is an institution that is highly culturalized, much like the making of vows by a woman in ch. 30.

35:30–34 Whoever kills a person: The people were not to confuse accidental manslaughter with premeditated murder. One who had committed homicide was not permitted to flee to a city of refuge. His crime was to be punished by death.

36:1–4 Chapter 36 presents the interest of the relatives of **Zelophehad,** who were worried about possible complications of the decision to allow Zelophehad's daughters to inherit their father's possession in the land (ch. 27). If the daughters were to marry outside their tribe and family, then the tribal allowances would be hopelessly confused and perhaps even lost.

36:5–13 they may marry only within the family: Moses decided that the family's concern was legitimate. He did not overrule the earlier decision to allow the women to inherit the portion that would have gone to their father, but he regulated their marriage choices to maintain the integrity of the tribal allotments. In this account, we see the way case law worked in ancient Israel. Specific instances that were not covered clearly in the general legislation would be brought to Moses for disposition. He would seek the word of the Lord on that specific issue and then would pronounce the decision.

The Fifth Book of Moses Called

Deuteronomy

*W*ITH THE NATION OF ISRAEL POISED AT THE entrance of Canaan, Moses seized one last opportunity to prepare the people for their new life in the land of their inheritance. Since Moses would not be entering the land with the people, he wanted to make sure that the nation did not forget its covenant with God. Moses' careful review of the laws of God is recorded in the Book of Deuteronomy.

The speeches in this book are set against the historical background of all the events of Israel's history until the time they were spoken, including the Exodus from Egypt, the revelation of God at Mount Sinai, the rebellious responses of Israel to the Lord's goodness, and God's constant protection of them. Yet there are a few pivotal events that the book particularly addresses.

The idolatry at Baal Peor was one of those significant moments (Num. 25). It was there that Israel first experienced the attraction of Baal worship, which would plague its existence for centuries. The people whom Moses addressed in Deuteronomy were those who had survived the plague that the Lord brought in punishment for the sins of the people (Deut. 4:3). In light of this experience, Moses pleaded with this new generation to be faithful to God's laws. He frequently used the word *today* in order to emphasize that this new generation could start anew (1:10, 39; 4:4, 40; 5:1, 3; 6:6; 7:11); they did not have to focus on their rebellious past.

Moses concluded his exhortations with a description of the covenant renewal ceremony that would take place between Mount Ebal and Mount Gerizim. He instructed the Levites to recite on the barren mountaintop of Ebal the curses for those who rejected God's Law. On the lush slopes of Gerizim, the rich blessings for those who obeyed God's Law would be recited. With these instructions, Moses anticipated the renewal of the covenant on the other side of the Jordan River. There, the people would gather for the grand moment when they would renew the covenant once again, but this time as inhabitants of the Promised Land (11:29, 30; 27:1–8, 12, 13; Josh. 8:30–35). After describing this future covenantal renewal, Moses himself challenged the people to renew their commitment to God (30:11–20).

Finally, the expectation of Moses' imminent death explains why he gave the book as a testimony to God's Law. The Lord had commanded him to leave the words of the Law as a testimony to Israel. In response, Moses wrote the words down, gave them to the priests for safekeeping, and commanded the priests to read the word of God every seven years. In this way, Moses not only prepared the new generation for the coming conquest of the land, but also insured that every generation after that would hear God's laws (31:9–13).

Moses' emphasis on the covenant throughout Deuteronomy is remarkable. He testified to its importance by repeatedly calling the new generation of Israelites to follow its provisions (30:11–20).

In fact, Deuteronomy as a whole reflects the pattern of an ancient Middle Eastern treaty between a lord and a servant. The typical pattern of such a treaty with its approximate corresponding sections in Deuteronomy is as follows:

(1) A preamble or introduction (1:1–5)
(2) A review of the past relationship between the parties (1:6—4:49)
(3) Basic stipulations that ensured fidelity to the treaty (5:1—26:19)
(4) Sanctions in the form of blessings and curses (27:1—30:20)
(5) Witnesses to the treaty (32:1)
(6) A provision for the storage and reading of the treaty (31:1—34:12)

While these similarities exist, the Book of Deuteronomy does not slavishly follow the typical treaty structure, but we can conclude that it was written with a basic treaty pattern in mind. Moses impressed on his readers the importance of the covenant not only with his repeated exhortations but also with the structure of the book itself. With Moses' warnings and their renewed commitment to God's covenant, the people were finally ready to enter the Promised Land.

The English title of the fifth book of the Pentateuch is derived from the Septuagint, the ancient Greek translation of the Old Testament, which interprets the words in 17:18, "a copy of this law," as "the second law." The name "Deuteronomy" means "the second law." The name is somewhat of a misnomer because Deuteronomy does not contain a second law. However, it does explain God's Law revealed at Mount Sinai to a second generation of Israelites.

Throughout the centuries, Jews and Christians have believed that Moses wrote Deuteronomy. But during the last 200 years, some have challenged this position. They have argued that the theology of the book is too advanced for the primitive Israelites at this early stage in their history. But others have maintained that Moses compiled Deuteronomy and wrote most of it. They argue that Mosaic authorship is supported by the book's consistent covenantal theology, its claims of Mosaic authorship, and the witness of NT writers.

Deuteronomy is basically the last will of Moses. In this will, he challenged Israel to remain faithful to the covenant, reminded them of their past history, and pointed to their future of blessings or cursings in the land of Canaan, depending upon their belief and behavior. Moses' speeches (31:24), the recitation of the Song of Moses (31:30—32:43), and Moses' blessing on the tribes (33:1–29) largely constitute the Book of Deuteronomy. To this, another author was led by the Spirit of God to add the account of the death of Moses and the tribute to his legacy (34:1–12). Some have argued that Moses himself might have written the account of his death and succession, having foreseen them by divine inspiration. This is certainly possible, but it is not a necessary conclusion for those who hold to Mosaic authorship of the Pentateuch as a whole.

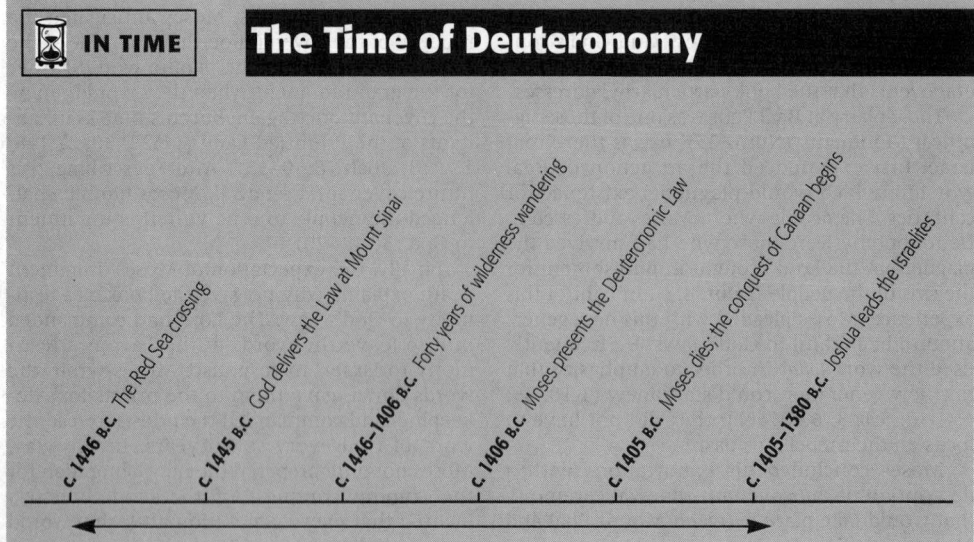

IN TIME

The Time of Deuteronomy

c. 1446 B.C. The Red Sea crossing

c. 1445 B.C. God delivers the Law at Mount Sinai

c. 1446–1406 B.C. Forty years of wilderness wandering

c. 1406 B.C. Moses presents the Deuteronomic Law

c. 1405 B.C. Moses dies; the conquest of Canaan begins

c. 1405–1380 B.C. Joshua leads the Israelites

Outline

I. **Prologue (1:1–5)**

II. **A review of Israel's history (1:6–4:43)**
   A. God's promises and the need for leadership (1:6–18)
   B. Israel's rebellion at Kadesh Barnea (1:19–46)
   C. Israel's journey into Transjordan (2:1–25)
   D. Israel's victory over Sihon and Og (2:26–3:11)
   E. The division of the conquered territory in Transjordan (3:12–22)
   F. Joshua's selection to lead Israel into the land (3:23–29)
   G. An invitation to live as a wise people (4:1–43)

III. **The Law, the promises, and the covenant community (4:44–11:32)**
   A. Historical prologue (4:44–49)
   B. The Lord's covenant (5:1–5)
   C. The Ten Commandments (5:6–22)
   D. Moses, the mediator of the covenant (5:23–31)
   E. A challenge to love God (5:32–6:25)
   F. Instructions concerning the conquest of the land (7:1–26)
   G. God, the only source of blessing (8:1–20)
   H. Israel's history and future (9:1–10:11)
   I. A challenge to seek God (10:12–11:32)

IV. **The development of the covenant fellowship (12:1–26:19)**
   A. The worship of God (12:1–16:17)
   B. The administration of justice and the purity of worship (16:18–17:13)
   C. The leadership of the people and the revelation of God (17:14–18:22)
   D. The administration of justice and the rules of war (19:1–21:14)
   E. The individual and the community (21:15–25:19)
   F. The anticipation of life in Canaan (26:1–15)
   G. The final exhortation of Moses (26:16–19)

V. **The covenant renewal (27:1–30:20)**
   A. The renewal of the covenant in Canaan under Joshua (27:1–26)
   B. Moses' address to Israel (28:1–29:1)
   C. Review and application (29:2–29)
   D. A choice of life or death, blessing or curse (30:1–20)

VI. **The last acts of Moses (31:1–33:29)**
   A. The transition of authority to Joshua (31:1–8)
   B. The reading of the law by the priests (31:9–13)
   C. God's appearance to Moses and Joshua (31:14–23)
   D. The placement of the law by the ark of the covenant (31:24–29)
   E. The Song of Moses (31:30–32:47)
   F. Moses' blessing on the tribes (32:48–33:29)

VII. **The epilogue: Moses' death, Joshua's succession, and Moses' legacy (34:1–12)**

Commentary

1:1–5 These preliminary verses connect Deuteronomy with Numbers (Num. 36:13) and give the setting.

1:1 words which Moses spoke: Most of Deuteronomy consists of Moses' explanation of God's Law and His exhortation to follow it. The reference to Moses and to **all Israel** is repeated in the final verse (34:12). **This side of the Jordan** is literally, "across the Jordan." This is the land east of the Jordan, or across it from the perspective of the land of Canaan (3:8, 20, 25; 4:41; 11:30). The **plain** is probably the region north of Moab.

1:2 eleven days: A journey that might have taken Israel less than two weeks to complete lasted forty years because of unbelief and disobedience (Num. 13; 14). **Horeb** is a name for Mount Sinai (4:10, 15; Ex. 3:1), where the Lord revealed His glory, gave His law, and made a covenant with Israel. **Kadesh Barnea,** an oasis in the Negev, fifty miles southwest of Beersheba, figured prominently in the story of the wilderness wandering (Num. 13; 14).

1:3 fortieth year: In early Israel, dates were given with reference to the Exodus from Egypt. Hence, this is forty years after the Exodus. It had taken Israel about a year to arrive at Kadesh Barnea from Mt. Horeb and another year to reach the place where Moses was addressing them in this passage. The thirty-eight years between had been spent wandering in the desert, God's punishment for their disobedience. **The eleventh month** would correspond to January-February. **Moses spoke . . . commandments:** The Law (Torah) of God was mediated through His servant Moses.

1:4 These victories under Moses' leadership (2:26–37; 21:21–35) opened up the conquest of the land from the east. They were a foretaste of the victories God would give the Israelites under Joshua's leadership. The Israelites celebrated these initial victories as having great significance in the history of redemption (2:26–36; 3:1–11; 4:46–49; Josh. 2:10; 9:10; 12:2–6; 13:10–12; Pss. 135:11; 136:19, 20).

1:5 The Hebrew word translated **law** (*tôrâ*) basically means "instruction." It is God's gracious teaching to the Israelites on the right way for them to live (6:1–3; Ps. 19). Deuteronomy is the exposition and application of the Law of God revealed at Mount Sinai.

1:6—4:43 This is a review of Israel's history. The section is reminiscent of the historical pro-

Abraham, Isaac, and Jacob long ago (Gen. 15:18–21; 26:2–4; 35:10–12). The verb "to swear" (Heb. *shaba'* in the Niphal formation) is similar in sound to the numeral "seven" (Heb. *sheba'*). The basic meaning of the verb may

The snow-capped Lebanon Mountains formed the northwestern boundary of the land promised by the Lord to Abraham and his descendants (Deut. 1:5–8).

logue so common in ancient Near Eastern treaties. Its focus is in God's promises to the patriarchs, God's ability to fulfill His promises, and Israel's stubborn resistance in not trusting Him.

1:6–18 God's promises and the need for leadership. God promised Abraham that His people would be living in the land and receive the blessing from the Lord (Gen. 15:13–21). This was now about to happen (vv. 6–8). But as Israel had increased in numbers, so had the need for a vital leadership (vv. 9–18).

1:6 The LORD our God is an emphatic reference to the divine revelation at Mount Sinai. Moses reminded Israel that God had revealed His glory, made His covenant with them, and assured them of His presence.

1:7, 8 Turn . . . and go refers to the departure for the Promised Land. The extent of God's gift was enormous, even as the people were numerous. Moses emphasized God's faithfulness to His promises. The Promised Land extended from the Negev, **the South** (Gen. 12:9) to **the River Euphrates** (Gen. 15:18–21). **swore to your fathers:** God had promised this land to

mean to bind oneself fully; that is, seven times. What a wonder that the sovereign Lord would "bind Himself" to meet the needs of His people (Heb. 6:13–18). Contrast another oath by Yahweh in 1:35.

1:9 I alone: Moses felt inadequate to take care of all aspects of leadership himself because the people were so numerous (Ex. 18:13–26).

1:10, 11 multiplied . . . stars of heaven Moses' rhetoric celebrates God's faithfulness in fulfilling His word to Abraham (Gen. 15:5; 22:17). **your God . . . the LORD** God of your fathers: God is the God of the patriarchs, but also the God of their descendants. This language indicates that the patriarchs still live; it is not that He *was* their God, but that He *is* their God! **bless you:** Moses prayed that God's promises would be even more dramatically fulfilled. **a thousand times:** The Lord had greatly blessed Israel in numbers (Ex. 1:1–7); His blessing in their past was to be a measure of His blessing in their future.

1:12, 13 wise . . . knowledgeable: The qualities of the leaders reflect attributes of God. Wisdom refers to the ability to bring harmony

---

🔍 **IN FOCUS** | **"swore"**

(Heb. *shaba'*) (Deut. 1:8; Gen. 24:7; Ex. 13:5; 1 Sam. 20:3; Ps. 95:11) Strong's #7650: In Hebrew, the verb translated *swore* is related to the word used for the number seven. In effect, the verb means "to bind oneself fully,"—that is, "seven times." In ancient times, oaths were considered sacred. People who made oaths to God or to others were accepting the greatest accountability. They were promising to be faithful to their word no matter what the personal cost. The OT describes God as taking an oath (Gen. 24:7; Ex. 13:5). He was not forced to do this; He did not have to swear in order to insure His own compliance with His word. Instead, He made an oath so that His people would be assured that His promises were completely trustworthy.

---

even when great differences exist. Understanding refers to the ability to penetrate the realities of life from God's perspective and to deal fairly with all parties in a dispute. Knowledge is the broad experience gained by living life, by watching people, and by making correct choices based on God's word.

1:14–16 Agreement with the counsel of the Lord is truly a **good** thing! **heads:** A number of men were charged with the administrative, judicial, and military tasks of creating unity among the people. Some of them were also called **judges.**

1:17, 18 not show partiality: God demanded absolute fairness regardless of age or social status. **all the things:** God's instruction was comprehensive. It covered all aspects of life.

1:19 Great and terrible wilderness describes the Israelites' journey by using two words for one idea, that of "a truly horrible wilderness."

1:20 The Amorites were one of the groups Israel encountered in their approach to the Promised Land. The term is often a general designation for the Canaanites, particularly those who lived in mountainous regions (Num. 13:29).

1:21 do not fear or be discouraged: Even though the future seemed uncertain, Moses exhorted the Israelites to have faith that God would take care of their needs (1:29; 3:22; 20:1, 3; 31:6, 8).

1:22, 23 every one of you: The initiative for sending the spies out came from the people, but it was something the Lord agreed to as well (Num. 13:2).

1:24, 25 The Valley of Eshcol was a region near Hebron (Num. 13:23); it is remembered for the huge clusters of grapes the spies found there.

1:26 you would not go up, but rebelled: The present generation was not directly involved in this rebellion, but as the descendants of the rebellious generation they shared in

the guilt of the disobedience of their forebears (Ps. 78:5–8). On the other hand, they were also the inheritors of God's promises to those who had gone before.

1:27 hates us . . . to destroy us: The rebels refused to acknowledge God's clear expressions of saving love to them. They did not trust the God who had saved them from slavery and provided for their needs on numerous occasions. Instead, they charged Him with hating them.

1:28 The Anakim were an ancient people known for their great size (Num. 13:28).

1:29, 30 goes before you . . . fight for you: The Lord would fight for His people and give them victory. **in Egypt:** Moses especially seems to have had the victory over the Egyptians at the Red Sea in mind (Ex. 14:1–15:19).

1:31 carried: God cared for His people and loved them as an adoring parent cares for a child (Ex. 19:4). **his son:** The Israelites were God's children by covenant (Is. 63:16; 64:8, 9). This image was well known in the OT period, but only rarely was God actually called "Father."

1:32 you did not believe: The people did not walk by faith, despite all that God had done in their lives. The language indicates that God could hardly believe the ingratitude and lack of obedience on the part of those to whom He had demonstrated such lavish love.

1:33 to search out: The Lord had always explored the next step for the Israelites, since He was leading them Himself. **The cloud** over the Most Holy Place symbolized God's presence. Whenever the cloud moved, Israel had followed the Lord (Num. 10:33–36).

1:34, 35 one . . . of this evil generation: Because of their rebellion, God excluded adults age twenty and older at that time from the blessing of the land (Num. 14:29).

1:36 Caleb was faithful (Num. 13:30—14:28). God permitted him to enter the land and receive the area of Hebron as his family estate (Josh. 15:13). **He wholly followed the Lord** by not wavering in his faith.

1:37 also angry with me: Even Moses, the leader of the people, was the object of God's wrath. He could not enter the land because he disobeyed God by striking the rock at Meribah (Num. 20:10–13).

1:38 God allowed **Joshua** to lead the Israelites into the land because of his trust in God (Num. 13:30–14:28). Before his death, Moses exhorted Joshua, encouraged him, and transferred to him the authority to lead the people into the Promised Land (3:28; 31:1–29; 34:9).

1:39 your little ones and your children: The most outrageous of Israel's complaints against God was that He had wanted their children to die (Num. 14:31). But the Lord demonstrated His love and faithfulness to His people by protecting those younger than twenty so that they could inherit the land. **you say will be victims:** This phrase reminds the people of the false accusations of the previous generation. **no knowledge of good and evil:** At that time, children less than a few years old were considered to be not yet fully responsible (Is. 7:15). By extending the age limit to twenty, the Lord again showed His compassion (Num. 14:18).

1:40 The Way of the Red Sea probably means the way toward Elath by the Red Sea (the Gulf of Aqaba).

1:41 In their statement, **we have sinned,** the Israelites showed regret but not true repentance. **we will go up and fight:** Their confidence was in themselves. They still would not follow God's commands.

1:42, 43 I am not among you: The Lord would not protect them. Therefore, victory was out of the question. **presumptuously:** The people were arrogant. They did not submit to the Lord.

1:44–46 As bees do is an expression that signifies alarming pursuit by a swarm of menacing enemies (Ex. 23:28; Ps. 118:12; Is. 7:18). **Hormah,** a name meaning "Destruction," probably refers to a site south of the Amorite hill country by Kadesh Barnea that came to be called subsequently by that name. **wept:** The tears were of regret, not repentance.

2:1–25 Israel's journey into Transjordan. The precise itinerary is difficult to reconstruct, and several proposals have been made. According to some critics, the biblical accounts record different migrations and project the facts into one account, the details of which make it difficult to reconstruct what really happened. Conservatives are in no agreement. Some hold that the Israelites returned from Kadesh to Elath by the Red Sea by a direct route and from there they took the Way of the Wilderness of Edom, around Edom and Moab. Others posit a journey through the Wilderness of Zin to Punon in the 'Arabah, from where Israel turned either north-ward to cross through Edom or descended further south to Ezion Geber before turning northward.

2:1–3 the Lord spoke to me: We see regularly in Genesis through Deuteronomy that Moses reported God's very words to him.

2:4 The descendants of Esau are the Edomites (Gen. 36:1–8).

2:5 I have given . . . to Esau: God had extended His blessing to the Edomites by giving them land, just as He was about to give Israel the Promised Land. All lands are His to give and to take (Ex. 19:5; Ps. 50:12).

2:6, 7 The Israelites could not take **food** or **water** by force, beg for it, or steal it. God demanded that they pay the expenses of their journey through Edom. The term **money** indicates not coinage but silver that was weighed out.

2:8 Away from Elath and Ezion Geber refers to turning away from the way of the Red Sea, on which these cities were located. **The Wilderness of Moab** was the area east of Moab (Num. 33:44).

2:9–11 The Moabites were related to the Israelites through **Lot** (Gen. 19:37). **Ar** is a synonym for the region of Moab. The Lord had given land to both Edom and Moab. However, His principal gift of land was to Israel. (God had also made provision for the people of Ammon, v. 19.)

2:12, 13 The Valley of the Zered was east of the Dead Sea at the border between Edom and Moab.

2:14 men of war: The generation that had rebelled at **Kadesh** were of age to make war but rarely fought. Instead they made war against the Lord by their bitter words.

2:15–19 When God saved His people, it was by His **hand** (Ex. 15:6). Sadly, it was by His hand that He brought judgment on them as well. The term *hand* suggests God's personal involvement in both acts of deliverance and chastening. **until they were consumed:** The Lord is a consuming fire (Heb. 12:29), by whom the generation perished (Jude 5).

2:20 The **Zamzummin** were a people who lived in the Ammonite territory, possibly the Zuzim (Gen. 14:5).

2:21–23 The **Avim** lived in villages between the Jordan and the Mediterranean coast. **Gaza** was a Philistine city on the Mediterranean coast. The **Caphtorim** were a group of the tribes that came by sea to the coasts of Canaan and Egypt. **Caphtor** is possibly the same as Crete (Gen. 10:14).

2:24 The River Arnon was the traditional border between Moab and Ammon. **Heshbon** refers both to the city and the territory ruled by Sihon.

2:25 The mighty acts of God through Israel would fill the nations with **dread and fear** (Ex. 15:14–16; Josh. 2:9). The deliverance of Israel from Egypt and God's subsequent acts of protection were known abroad. The fear of the nations would soften them for the time of conquest. But the dissemination of knowledge about God's works would glorify Him (4:6).

2:26–29 The Wilderness of Kedemoth was a desert within the territory of Sihon, located on its eastern border, east of the Dead Sea. **words of peace:** Israel made an offer of peaceful passage (vv. 27–29).

2:30 Sihon was responsible for his refusal to permit Israel to pass through his land. **God hardened his spirit and made his heart obstinate:** God is sovereign over human hearts (Ex. 3:19, 21, for God's hardening of the Pharaoh's heart). This is a great mystery, as we can never understand the inner working of human responsibility and of divine sovereignty. In and through it all God was working out His plan of redemption.

> *This is a great mystery, as we can never understand the inner working of human responsibility and of divine sovereignty.*

2:31, 32 Jahaz was located north of Kedemoth (Is. 15:4).

2:33 our God delivered . . . we defeated him: God gave Israel the victory, but the Israelites still had to fight courageously.

2:34, 35 By the law of the ban, every living thing, human and animal, was to be **utterly destroyed**—that is, put to death (7:1, 2; 20:17). Exceptions could be made, but only when permitted by the Lord. In this case, the Israelites took livestock and property as spoil. The ban included fighting men and civilians, males and females, adults and children. God used the people of Israel to punish the Canaanites for their continual wickedness through the generations. Further, the destruction of the Canaanites was designed to protect Israel from following the Canaanites' evil practices. Israel's failure to destroy all of the Canaanites in the subsequent conquests led finally to their own undoing.

2:36, 37 Aroer was a city on the northern bank of the River Arnon at the border between Sihon's territory and the Moabite kingdom. **Gilead** was the northern boundary of Sihon's kingdom. **Jabbok** was the river Jacob crossed on his way back to Canaan (Gen. 32:22).

3:1–3 Bashan was the region east of the Sea of Galilee. **Og:** The territory of Og may have extended south of the River Yarmuk into Gilead. The account of the victory over Og is similar to that of Sihon (2:26–37), but significantly shorter.

3:4–7 The **Argob** was an unidentified region in Bashan. **All these cities:** The Hebrew text is ambiguous here. Some understand that not all of the sixty cities were fortresses; others, also being called "cities" in the Hebrew text, were "rural towns." Others interpret "sixty" to refer to the fortified cities, exclusive of rural towns. **utterly destroyed:** See note at 2:34. The reasons for the ban (Heb. *herem*) may never be fully known by us.

3:8 The territory of Sihon and Og extended **from the River Arnon to Mount Hermon** (2:24–3:7). Mount Hermon is the mountain range in the north between Canaan and Lebanon.

3:9–13 The **Sidonians** were the Phoenicians. **Salach** was a city located at the eastern border of Bashan. **Bedstead** could also be translated "sarcophagus," that is, stone coffin. **Rabbah** was on the site of the capital of modern Jordan, Amman. **Nine cubits** is about thirteen feet, and **four cubits** is about six feet, according to the **standard cubit** (about eighteen inches).

3:14 Jair had captured these settlements (Num. 32:41). The **Geshurites** lived east of the Sea of Galilee and south of Mount Hermon. The **Maachathites** were descended from Abraham's brother Nahor (Gen. 22:24) and lived north of the Geshurites.

3:15–17 The northernmost section of **Gilead** was given to **Machir** (Num. 32:39), son of Manasseh (Gen. 50:23). The southern section was given to Reuben and Gad. **Chinnereth** is another name for the Sea of Galilee.

3:18, 19 The Lord . . . has given: The text regularly emphasizes that the land was God's gift (1:39). **men of valor:** Women, children, and animals were not to be put in danger during the conquest. The battle would be fought by armed men under the command of God (Ex. 15:3).

3:20, 21 Joshua, as one of the original spies (Num. 13; 14), had a great advantage. Along with Caleb, he had **seen** the land, had spied it out, and would be able to use his knowledge to prepare his military strategy. Joshua also had witnessed the victories the Lord had given east of the Jordan. Those experiences encouraged him when he led the Israelites across the river.

3:22 your God Himself fights: The Lord is the Divine Warrior who delivers and fights for His faithful people (Ex. 15:3).

3:23 Moses **pleaded** (Heb. *hanan*, "to implore favor") with God. But God refused to answer Moses' prayer, not because Moses lacked faith, but because Moses had disobeyed God and had not treated Him as holy (Num. 20:12).

3:24 O Lord God: The Hebrew has the word for "Lord" or "Master" followed by the personal name of God, Yahweh. This phrase indicates the depth of Moses' relationship with the Lord (9:26). **what god is there . . . mighty deeds:** Moses began his prayer with praise for God's holiness and power (Ex. 15:11). God is incomparable; there was none like Him (Is. 40:25, 26).

3:25 let me cross over: The verb is charged with energy expressing Moses' deep emotion. Moses did not ask that Joshua be removed as leader of the nation. He merely requested to **see** the land that God had promised. **The good land** is a lovely expression for the land that God had promised His people (4:21). It is not that the soil, land, topography, setting, or geography were magical; rather, this land was God's good gift to His people. One day it will be the "holy land," when the King of Righteousness reigns there!

3:26–28 angry: The Lord responded with great irritation and agitation. There is a play on words between the verb used in Moses' request, "let me cross over" (v. 25) and the verb translated "was angry" (v. 26). But verbs are spelled with the same letters (*'abar*), but whereas the former is a common enough translation the latter is from an uncommon root meaning "to infuriate oneself," (compare Ps. 78:21, 59, 62). **Enough:** God ordered Moses not to ask Him about it again. But God showed His mercy to Moses by showing him the land from a distance (34:1–3). Moses was not to wallow in self-pity, but was to **encourage** Joshua as his replacement in leading the Israelites.

3:29 Beth Peor was a pagan site dedicated to Baal of Peor (Num. 25:3, 5) and was the scene of Israel's first disastrous encounter with the sexually-centered worship of Baal (4:3).

4:1 The exhortation to **listen** includes an encouragement to obey (5:1; 6:3, 4; 9:1; 20:3; 27:9). **you may live:** In contrast, Moses could not enter the land (v. 22). But for the people, God's gift of His law was designed for their good. By obeying the Law, the people could experience a fruitful life (6:1–3).

4:2 not add . . . nor take from it: The Israelites had to learn to live by God's word without trying to justify their disobedience or explaining away God's clear commands (Rev. 22:18, 19).

4:3, 4 Baal Peor: See 3:29. Twenty-four thousand were executed there by plague (Num.

25:9). That name reminded the Israelites of the terror of God's judgment.

4:5–8 Those who live by God's revelation will direct others to the Lord, the giver of every good gift.

4:5 Moses was the mediator of God's word, not its originator (compare 2 Pet. 1:20, 21). **my God commanded me:** Throughout Deuteronomy, Moses always deferred to the Lord as the source of his message.

4:6–8 in the sight of the peoples: By living in obedience to God, Israel would become a countercultural force by its manner of life, government, and society (Rom. 12:2). God's blessings on Israel would cause the nations to seek to learn about Him. Since God was so **near** and had promised to respond to their prayers, the Israelites could approach the Lord with all kinds of requests. **statutes . . . judgments:** Living so close to God meant that the Israelites were especially obligated to live for Him, in the way revealed in His covenant with them.

4:9–14 At **Horeb** Yahweh had impressed His awesome glory upon Israel, made a covenant with them, and given them the moral law through Moses.

4:9 Moses warned against the sin of presumption. **your eyes have seen:** The people had witnessed God's redemption, His revelation,

💡 **INSIGHT**   **Leaving a Legacy**

Some of the Israelites who listened to Moses as he addressed Israel in the plain of Moab had stood as children and teenagers at Mount Sinai four decades earlier. Now they had a responsibility to teach both their children and grandchildren what they had seen, heard, and experienced on that occasion and in the years afterward (Deut. 4:9, 10). That way the faith would be passed down through the generations. So, too, parents and grandparents today are to instruct young people in the ways of the Lord.

and the giving of His gracious covenant. Now, they had to adhere to the covenantal regulations and **teach** their **children** the story of God's saving acts and His promises to Israel. **Heart** refers to the center of one's being, the source of direction for one's thoughts, actions, and speech (Matt. 12:34; 15:18, 19).

4:10 My words are the Ten Commandments (v. 13).

4:11 The appearance of God is often described as accompanied by **darkness** and **fire** (Ex. 19:18). The fire speaks of His holiness, majesty, and transcendence, but also of His judgment against evil (v. 24). The darkness speaks of His unapproachable nature, of our sin, and of the possibility of impending judgment. One scholar says that this language presents "the elusive presence" of Yahweh. That God is perceived at all is a mark of His great condescending grace. That He is perceived remotely is a reminder of the gulf that exists between the Divine One and His fallen creatures.

4:12 heard . . . but saw no form: The Lord revealed His glory to the Israelites, but they saw no visual image other than darkness and fire. They did hear God's voice, however (v. 15). This verse reminds us that God is Spirit (John 4:24).

4:13 Obedience to God's commandments was an expression of loyalty to and love for the Lord who had initiated a **covenant** with Israel. **The Ten Commandments** were given in the form of **two tablets of stone** (Ex. 31:18), each containing a full and complete copy of the commandments. The older view, popularized in art, is that part of the commands were on one tablet (perhaps those relating to one's duty to God, and the other commands (one's duty to others) were written on the second.

4:14 teach: Moses mediated God's revelation to the people. As their teacher, he applied the Law (Ex. 20:19).

4:15–24 Faith in the Lord excludes idolatry of any kind (compare 12:1–4). The revelation at Mt. Horeb was attended by stunning phenomena. Since God did not reveal any images or representations of Himself, He rejected any form of worship in which the divine is represented by anything that is created. He alone will be worshiped, not His works.

4:15, 16 There was no way of describing or of giving shape with any image to the experience of God's presence at Sinai (Ex. 20:18). Since Israel had not seen the **form** of God, they could not represent Him in any way. **likeness of male or female:** Although people were created in the likeness of God, no image created in human likeness could represent God (Gen. 1:26, 27).

4:17–19 likeness of any animal: Animals were created by God (Gen. 1:20–25). They cannot serve as a medium for spiritual awareness or as a representation for God. **sun . . . host of heaven:** Furthermore, heavenly bodies were created by God. They could not serve as representation of the Creator (Gen. 1:14–19; Ps. 19:1).

4:20 This verse forms a "slogan of redemption." **taken you and brought you:** God chose Israel to be His people and to have a covenant

with Him. **Iron furnace** refers to the period of affliction in Egypt (Is. 48:10; Jer. 11:4). **inheritance:** The people redeemed by the Lord belonged to Him and had a glorious future with Him.

4:21, 22 I must die: How hard these words must have been to Moses! He had to encourage the people to enter the same land which he himself would not enter.

4:23, 24 God is a **consuming fire.** He is free to destroy disobedient and rebellious people. Israel had witnessed His righteous anger during the wilderness journey as well as in Canaan (Heb. 12:29). **Jealous** (Heb. *ganna*) may also be translated as "zealous." God is zealous for His holiness. Both in His wrath and in His love, the Lord remains holy. The emphasis here on God's wrath should be balanced with the emphasis on His mercy (4:31).

4:25–31 God will severely judge idolaters but will have compassion on those who seek Him. Moses anticipates the future when a generation departs from the Lord. They will be judged and exiled from the country. Yet even in exile they must return to the Lord, for He is gracious and compassionate. This teaching is the basis of the prophetic proclamation of the remnant and of the apostolic teaching on God's grace for unregenerate Israel (Rom. 9—11).

4:25 Children and grandchildren is a reference to a future rebellion, when a generation would disobey the Lord.

4:26 Heaven and earth signifies all creation. **witness against you:** Creation would act as God's witness against a rebellious and obstinate people (Deut. 30:19; Is. 1:2). **utterly perish . . . be utterly destroyed:** The curses of the covenant would overtake the Israelites (Ps. 1:6). The Lord would discipline them and exile them from the land.

4:27 Scatter you among the peoples is a prophetic warning of the exiles that would take place in 722 and 586 B.C.

4:28, 29 Moses warned against the folly of idolatry. **Neither see . . . nor smell** declares the impotence of idols (Ps. 115:6; Is. 40:19, 20; 41:7, 22–24). These "gods" were not merely lesser gods. They did not exist at all; they were dead. Hence turning from the living God to false, nonexistent "gods" was in effect moving from life to death (1 Thess. 1:9, 10). But seeking the living God and Him alone brought life. There are times when one still hears people say that only in the NT does one come to inner reality; that in the "Old" Testament everything was external and merely symbolic. Words such as **seek Him with all your heart and with all your soul,** here, dispel that notion.

4:30 All these things refers to the curses of the covenant. **The latter days** simply means

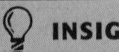 **INSIGHT**   ## There Is No Other God

The declaration that the Lord is uniquely God, that "there is none other besides Him" (Deut. 4:35), was a remarkable statement given the land that the Hebrews had just left, and the lands through which they had just traveled, and the land they were about to inhabit. The Egyptians, Moabites, Edomites, and Canaanites worshiped numerous gods, and in that context Israel's monotheism was unique (Deut. 32:39). Monotheism also addresses the popular view today that "all religions are basically the same" and that Christianity has no right to make claims of exclusivity.

"in the future." But the prophets developed this phrase into a more technical designation for a new era characterized by God's blessings, the age of Messiah. **turn to the LORD**: God would bless the nation when they returned to Him.

4:31 merciful God: The future of God's people depends on God's love. The emphasis on God's mercy (Heb. *rahûm*, related to the Hebrew for "womb," and so suggesting here "maternal affection" and "deep compassion") is a necessary balance to the emphasis that Moses placed on God's refining wrath (v. 24). **not forsake . . . nor forget**: The Lord was free to scatter His people. But after His discipline, He would re-gather them and show them His favor. God was and is faithful to His promises. **The covenant of your fathers** is God's solemn commitment to fulfill the promises He made to the patriarchs (Gen. 17:6–8; 22:16, 17; Ex. 3:15–17).

4:32–40 The revelation of Yahweh is a unique expression of His commitment to His covenant. Moses speaks with remarkable eloquence again on the uniqueness of God's revelation. Yahweh is incomparable (3:24; Is. 40:25, 26). This is unique because paganism cannot lay claim on revelation, and unique because God has demonstrated His love for Israel in redeeming them from Egypt, and unique because Israel lived to witness the revelation from heaven.

4:32–34 The Creator of all the earth is the same God who spoke to the Israelites at Mount Sinai. **By trials . . . and by great terrors,** the Creator had demonstrated His power in Egypt and had used it to save the Israelites.

4:35 there is none other besides Him: Moses emphasizes the theme that the living God is the only one there is (4:39; 5:7; 6:4; 32:39).

4:36 God's revelation to the Israelites was intended to graciously **instruct,** guide, and discipline the Israelites in the way of righteousness (compare 2 Tim. 3:16, 17).

4:37 He loved . . . He chose: Moses brings together the greatness of God in relation to Israel's election. These words also define the NT concept of "foreknowledge" (Rom. 8:29). God's

love for the fathers continues. The verb can be translated in the present tense: "He loves your fathers."

4:38 nations greater and mightier: The Scriptures have two different ways of regarding the size of the nation of Israel at the time of the Exodus. God is praised for the miraculous growth of Israel's family during their sojourn in Egypt (Ex. 1:7, 9, 10). On the other hand, the nation of Israel is described as small in number compared to the other nations around her. Hence, God deserves the glory for Israel's victories.

4:39 God in heaven . . . there is no other: Since no other God was Creator, Lord of history, Teacher, and the Lover of His people, Israel had to respond to God alone. This is a major theme of Deuteronomy and of the prophets. The incomparability of Yahweh is also the heart of the basic creed of Israel, the "Shema" (6:4).

4:40 keep . . . that it may go well with you: How wonderful that the basic meaning in the Torah was that God would bring good into the lives of His people by means of His Law. **your children**: Parents are responsible for the well-being of their children. None has such a treasure to give to their children as does the believer in the living God. The promise of blessing **in the land** was conditional; it required obedience (5:29; 6:24; 14:23; 19:9; 28:29, 33).

4:41–43 The regulations concerning the cities to which a person guilty of manslaughter could flee are further developed in 19:1–13. The narrative concerning the division of the land (3:12–20) resumes with the appointment of the **three cities** of refuge in the Transjordan (Num. 35:9–28; Josh. 20). **Ramoth** was located between the Yarmuk and the Jabbok in Gilead. The locations of **Bezer** and **Golan** are uncertain.

4:44–11:32 The central revelation of Yahweh: the Law, the promises, and the covenant community. Moses expounds the nature of the moral law of God and its related statutes and ordinances.

🔍 IN FOCUS | "statutes"

(Heb. *choq*) (Deut. 5:1; Ex. 18:16) Strong's #2706: The word conveys a variety of meanings in the OT, including: a "portion" or "ration" of food (Gen. 47:22); the "boundary" or "limit" of the sea (Prov. 8:29); and an "allotment" of the sacrifices for the priests (Lev. 10:13). This term is derived from a verb that means "to decree," or "to inscribe" (Prov. 8:15; Is. 10:1; 49:16). The term often refers to commands, civil enactments, legal prescriptions, and ritual laws decreed by someone in authority, whether by humans (Mic. 6:16) or by God Himself (Deut. 6:1). The Law of Moses includes commandments (*miswah*), judgments (*mispat*), and statutes (*hoq*) (Deut. 4:1–2). Israel was charged to obey God's statutes, and they pledged to do so (Deut 26:16–17). Accordingly, God's judgment was meted out against the Israelites when they disobeyed them (Amos 2:4; Ezek. 11:12; Mal. 3:7).

4:44–49 An historical prologue. These verses form a transition between the review of Israel's history (1:6—4:43) and the revelation of God: the Law, the promises, and the covenant community (5:1—11:32). Again we have an example of a misplaced chapter division. These verses should have begun ch. 5.

4:44 The law refers to the commandments detailed in chs. 5—26. *Law* basically means "instruction." God points out the path of righteousness for His covenant people.

4:45 These are . . . the judgments: This Law is the same as that given to the previous generation at Mount Sinai. Deuteronomy is a second delivery of the Law to those who would occupy the land.

4:46–49 in the land of Sihon . . . of Og: Israel had recently acquired this land east of the Jordan and was now preparing to cross the river and enter Canaan.

5:1–5 The Lord's covenant. The good news is that God has been faithful to the covenant, in that the present generation, whom Moses was addressing, are heirs of the covenant. The fact that God speaks to His people is a mark of His grace. The provision of His Torah is one of the great demonstrations of His mercy. It is a misreading of the Torah to regard it as a manifestation of God's anger. There was a time when some teachers of Scripture represented the giving of the Law as a punishment by God because His people had rejected His grace. The Law of God *is* a manifestation of His grace in this period of Hebrew history.

5:2 a covenant with us in Horeb: The Mosaic covenant is a divine administration of grace and promise by which the Lord consecrated Israel to Himself under the sanctions (curse and blessing) of His revealed will. It was from the Lord, and therefore not properly "the Law of Moses." It was the Law (Torah) of Yahweh, mediated through Moses.

5:3, 4 Did not make this covenant with our fathers, but with us emphasizes the privileged position of the present generation as they were preparing to enter Canaan. **Face to face** indicates intimacy. Moses stressed the special relationship the people had with the living God.

5:5 I stood between the Lord and you reflects Moses' role as mediator of the covenant (Ex. 20:18–21).

5:6–22 The Ten Commandments (4:13) encapsulate God's will for His people, teaching them how to love Him and how to love their neighbor as themselves. These Ten Words (as they are known in Hebrew) form a concentrated summary of the basic elements of the Torah. They have come to us in two versions, one given at Mt. Sinai (Ex. 20:3–17) and one coming shortly before Moses' death (5:6–21). The differences must be explained in terms of the new era, as Israel is about to enter the land. Jesus confirmed the validity of the moral law (Matt. 5:17, 18; Mark 12:31). The authority of the Law in the new covenant administration lies in Jesus' teaching, interpretation, and application of the Law.

5:6 I am the Lord your God: In the pattern of the Hittite treaties, these words speak of the identification of the covenant party of the first part. Instead of a grandiose listing of titles and descriptions, the basic elements are stated in just a few words. He is the living God who has acted in great grace to His people. He has the right as their redeemer to speak to them with His Ten Words.

5:7 no other gods: Many ancient Middle Eastern cultures absorbed other gods into their own belief systems, modifying and using these new gods for their own purposes. But the Israelites were unique: They served only one God, who would not allow any rivals.

5:8–10 Even when an **image** functioned as a symbol for deity, it led worshipers away from the true worship of the living God. **visiting the iniquity:** God would discipline the sinner. **to**

the third and fourth generations: Even as God would bless generation upon generation for their true worship of Him, He would also punish generation upon generation for faithlessness to Him. **Mercy to thousands** refers to thousands of generations in contrast to the three and four generations that would be punished. The comparison between four and thousands is a proportional measurement of God's mercy. His grace is far more expansive than His wrath.

5:11 Take . . . in vain refers to the abuse, misuse, blasphemy, cursing, or manipulation of the Lord's name. No wonder the ancient Israelites developed the practice of not pronouncing the sacred name aloud. Yet God delights in those who love and respect His name.

IN LIFE

The Blessing of the Sabbath

The commandment to keep the Sabbath holy (Deut. 5:12) did not mean that the other days of the week and their activities were unholy. The Sabbath was to remind Israel that human beings were dependent on God, and that they have strong tendencies to exalt themselves and their accomplishments, to turn them into gods even—to borrow an OT expression. In today's terms, we might say that our pursuits become addictions. The Sabbath enforced a day of rest and worship in the weekly cycle to keep their focus on the Lord rather than on themselves and their accomplishments. Sunday, as the Lord's Day, can help Christians set boundaries on who and what we worship and make the god of our lives.

5:12–15 These verses contain the positive command to regard the Sabbath as **holy**—separated for God's purposes. **as . . . commanded you:** The Lord did so at Mount Sinai (Ex. 20:8–11). **the Sabbath of the LORD:** The primary significance of the Sabbath was that it belonged to the Lord. **you shall do no work . . . rest:** On this Lord's day, the Israelites were to rest from work and celebrate God's good gifts. **remember that you were a slave:** The Israelites were to remember Israel's past oppression and celebrate their current freedom. Christians differ as to how this commandment relates to believers in Jesus Christ. The Sabbath was Saturday, the seventh day of the week. Christians

generally worship God on Sunday, the first day of the week, because it was on a Sunday that the Lord rose from the dead. Even so, Christians follow the principle of this command. They dedicate time to the Lord by resting, by praising Him for His blessings, and by remembering His saving acts written in the Bible.

5:16 Honor your father and your mother: Respect for parents would build strong families. Strong, godly families, in turn, would teach children the ways of God, and the covenant community dedicated to serving and worshiping God would remain intact. The benefits of respecting one's parents would be **long** life and success.

5:17 Premeditated **murder** was the concern of this law. For commands concerning other forms of homicide (chs. 19—21). The basis of respect for life lay in God's act of creating humans in His image (Gen. 9:6).

5:18 Adultery was a betrayal not only of a commitment, but of a relationship. Anyone who treated marriage lightly would also treat his or her relationship with God lightly.

5:19 not steal: Stealing could take many forms: illegitimate removal of property, kidnaping, manipulation of a person and his property to one's advantage, and so on.

5:20 not bear false witness: This included any testimony that falsely incriminated someone or negatively affected someone's reputation, such as gossip and slander.

5:21 You shall not covet: The only command that specifically prohibited an attitude. Desiring what someone else possessed was self-interestedness. This attitude was the opposite of a concern for the other person's welfare. The Law can be summed up in the last and first commandments: a person must truly love God and truly be concerned for his or her neighbor (Mark 12:28–31).

5:22 He wrote them on two tablets: The two tablets were two complete copies of the Law. Usually, two copies were made of ancient Near Eastern treaties. One was retained by each of the two contracting parties as a witness to the agreement. But with the Ten Commandments, both copies were placed before God. Not only did the Lord covenant with the Israelites, He also witnessed the agreement.

5:23–31 Because of their rebellious and sinful nature, the Israelites feared God's holy presence and were unprepared to face Him. Subsequently, they asked Moses to serve as their spokesman before the Lord, and God approved their request. Moses became the mediator of the covenant between God and His people. He not only communicated God's ways to the people, but he begged God to show His mercy to them.

5:24 His glory and His greatness: The

awe-inspiring revelation of God's presence. What glory this is!

5:25, 26 why should we die . . . living God: The Israelites' fear was necessary. The people needed to realize that the living God was powerful, great, and demanded perfection, so that they as sinners would recognize their need for His mercy.

5:27, 28 we will hear and do it: God's awe-inspiring revelation of Himself prompted the people to express their willingness to comply with the Lord's commands. However, their steadfastness to their promise would be tested.

5:29–31 The people were impressed with what they saw and heard, but their **heart** was unchanged.

5:32–6:25 A challenge to love Yahweh. Moses persuades the people to love Yahweh as the source of all goodness, in the present and in the future. God is good and faithful, but He expects His people to be responsible. Since the future also depends on the faithfulness of each generation, the family unit is vital. The godly family is God's appointed institution in which instruction in godliness takes place.

5:32, 33 in all the ways . . . God has commanded you: Out of all the nations, God had chosen Israel to be instructed in His law. But the real test of the distinctiveness of these people was their response to God's revelation. **and that it may be well with you, and that you may prolong your days:** These promises, attached to the fifth commandment, were applicable to all of the commandments.

6:1–9 The fear of God begins with an expression of love for God. Indeed, love for God and fear of God are inter-related responses to the wonders of His being.

6:1 The commandment refers to the instruction to love the Lord (v. 5). **commanded to teach you:** Moses was God's instrument in giving His Law to Israel (5:22, 23). It was not really "the Law of Moses" but the Law of God.

6:2 The **fear** of the Lord includes awe for His greatness and holiness, love for Him, and submission to His will. Initially, the fear of God may involve fright. Yet it leads to a sense of wonder, a commitment to worship, and delight in knowing God. **you . . . and your grandson:** Since God promised to bless generation after generation (Gen. 17:7, 8), He expected His people to follow His ways from generation to generation as well. **all the days of your life:** The Lord presented Israel with blessedness in the land as a covenantal benefit (4:40; 5:29; 6:24; 14:23; 18:5; 30:15), conditioned on loyalty (4:26). It was the point of God's gift of His Law to bring fullness of life under His grace (4:1). Disobedience would lead to forfeiture of the

land and of the covenant privileges (4:26; 30:15–19; Pss. 1:6; 112:10). Thus, God taught them that He alone is life and that the abandonment of God is the rejection of life in favor of death (30:20; John 3:16–20).

6:3 that it may be well with you: God instructed His people so they might live good lives full of meaning and peace. They would live in His glorious presence. **A land flowing with milk and honey** indicates a fruitful and blessed land (11:9; 26:9, 15; 27:3; 31:20). The land promised to the Israelites was better than the land of Egypt to which they had wanted to return (Num. 16:12–14).

6:4 This verse is the celebrated Shema, the basic confession of faith in Judaism (Matt. 22:37, 38; Mark 12:29, 30; Luke 10:27). **Hear:** The Hebrew word is *shema'*. The verse starts with a command for the people to respond properly to God. They must listen and obey. **The Lord our God** indicates the people's relationship with the living God. He had come into the lives of His people; it was not that they had ascended to Him. He had saved them from slavery in Egypt, guided them through the wilderness, and given them His instructions. Further, He was about to give them His land. **The Lord is one** means "the Lord alone." There is only one God.

6:5, 6 Moses repeatedly exhorted the Israelites to respond to God's love with devotion. In this context, the word translated as **love** may mean "to make one's choice in." God commanded His people to choose Him with all their being, and in the process to deny all other supposed deities.

6:7 talk of them when you sit . . . and when you rise up: God's revelation should be so central to a godly family that they should naturally talk about Him while they perform other activities.

6:8, 9 a sign . . . frontlets: In later years the Jews interpreted these instructions in a physical way. They instructed men to wear phylacteries, boxes containing passages of Scripture, when they prayed (Matt. 23:5). In any case the idea is that God's laws should be close to the mind and hands of His people at all times (compare Ex. 13:9, 16; Prov. 3:3; 6:21). **write them on the doorposts:** Jewish custom is to attach a small vessel called a *mezuzah* to the doorpost. In it is placed a small scroll containing the text of Deut. 6:4–9; 11:13–21 and God's name Shaddai.

6:10–25 The blessings of God point to Giver of every good gift. The fear of the Lord expresses itself in gratitude to and in contentment with God. Moses warns Israel not to be ungrateful and not to develop a self-sufficient life-style. Instruction in redemptive history is an antidote against self-sufficiency because it teaches each generation to see what God has done in the past.

6:10–12 Moses warned the people not to forget that their possessions were God's gifts. God had not only saved their ancestors from slavery, but He had also given them a good land. The Israelites needed continually to praise and thank God for His mercy toward them.

6:13–15 serve: The Lord demanded absolute commitment to Himself. Out of gratitude, the people were to do this willingly. **oaths in His name:** The fact that God had revealed His name assures the people of God's goodness to them. He wanted them to look to Him alone for refuge and sustenance. Jesus quoted this text when Satan was tempting Him (Matt. 4:10).

6:16–19 God may test His children, but they may never test or **tempt** Him by their rebelliousness or sin (Matt. 4:7; Luke 4:12). For the incident at **Massah,** read Ex. 17:1–7. **keep . . . do what is right and good:** Moses applied a lesson from the past and exhorted the new generation to be faithful to God (4:1, 5; 5:29; 6:1). **to cast out all your enemies:** Canaan's false worship and its immorality could no longer influence the Israelites if the Canaanites were entirely thrown out of the land.

6:20–24 your son asks: Moses commanded the Israelites to teach their children the significance of their ritual. In the same way, Christians should make sure their children know the meaning of their practices. The answer to the Israelite child's question would include four components. (1) **We were slaves . . . in Egypt;** (2) **the LORD** brought us out . . . with a mighty hand; (3) **to give us the land;** and (4) we have a challenge to responsible action. Clearly, the redemption and the privileges are the Lord's, but the responsibility belongs to His children. The rabbis interpreted this section in a wonderful way. They observed that it was not the present generation that had been delivered from Egypt, nor was it the children who would now hear the story. Yet each, the parents and their children, were to regard themselves as though they had personally been brought forth from Egypt. In each generation, each believing Hebrew was to regard himself or herself as a principal receiver of God's mercy.

6:25 Moses did not offer the people a works-righteousness by keeping the Law. **Righteousness** is a right relationship with God. God initiates this relationship, and His children respond to it as an expression of love.

7:1–26 The conquest of the land. Moses challenges the people to be responsible agents in God's judgment on the seven nations of Canaan. Israel has no inherent merit by which they are blessed, whereas the people of Canaan are cursed. Whatever Israel received and will

receive is because of God's love and grace. God will be present with Israel in the conquest. He expects them to act responsibly in eradicating every trace of the pagan religion, in not adapting to the pagan culture, and in waiting patiently for Him to give them the land little by little.

7:1 The Hittites came originally from Asia Minor (Gen. 23:10). **The Girgashites** are an unknown people mentioned also in Gen. 10:16 and 1 Chr. 1:14. **The Amorites** were the native population of Canaan that had settled in the mountains. **The Canaanites** were the native population that had settled in the coastlands. **The Perizzites** were the native population that had settled in the hill country. **The Hivites** were the native population settled south of the Lebanon mountains. **The Jebusites** (perhaps an offshoot of the Hittites) were the native population settled near what later became Jerusalem.

7:2 Covenant refers to any treaty with the Canaanite nations that might undermine God's covenant with Israel.

7:3, 4 Intermarriage with the Canaanite population would have tempted the Israelites to adopt Canaanite culture. This would have threatened Israel's ability to be a countercultural force. They were not to "blend in." Similarly, the Christian church is called to demonstrate God's love to the world like sheep in the midst of wolves (Matt. 10:6; Rom. 12:2; Phil. 2:14–16; 1 Pet. 2:9).

7:5 destroy . . . break down: The destruction of idolatrous sites was meant to keep the Israelites from imitating and borrowing false pagan practices (12:2; 16:21, 22).

7:6–16 Israel has no inherent merit by which they are blessed. Neither are members of Christ's church. If one is ever puzzled by the question of why God chose Israel to be His special people, let that person first answer satisfactorily why God has chosen him or her.

7:7 The Israelites had no reason for pride, for they were the **least of all peoples.** Whatever privileges or possessions they enjoyed were due to God's grace.

7:8 The biblical authors verbally paint a wonderful picture of God: the powerful God extending His **mighty hand** to save His people.

7:9, 10 faithful God . . . for a thousand generations: Throughout all time, God has remained true to His commitment made to Abraham, Isaac, and Jacob. He is a faithful God (Ex. 20:6; Heb. 13:5). **love Him and keep His commandments:** Loving God always finds expression in doing His will. The Lord is a God of justice. He will **repay** those who rebel against Him.

7:11, 12 Moses clearly affirms human

responsibility and divine sovereignty. The positive or negative response of God's people is related to the manner of fulfillment of the promises (Is. 48:18, 19).

7:13–16 bless the fruit . . . increase: God's blessings extended to the quality of life, with the assurance of children, health, food, drink, and peace.

7:16 The people's immediate responsibility was to **destroy** the Canaanites' wicked presence and influence in the land (2:34).

7:17–19 you shall remember: The past saving acts of God demonstrated His nature and power. The people were to remember the details of His actions so that they could face the present moment in the light of eternity.

7:20, 21 The hornet (Ex. 23:28; Josh. 24:12) may refer to a dramatic act of God, such as a violent storm or a plague of insects. It may refer to campaigns by other armies that weakened the Canaanites before the Israelites arrived.

God's power is different from human manipulation, power politics, competition, and other ways of getting ahead. God gives grace.

Since **the great and awesome God** made the nations fear, why then should His own people be terrified (Ex. 15:14; Josh. 2:10, 11)? God was on their side and was even **among** them!

7:22 little by little: The conquest of the land was in two stages: (1) a rapid, broad conquest under Joshua; (2) a gradual, area-by-area, city-by-city conquest that followed. God's plan was that not all of the Promised Land would fall to Israel at once. Indeed, much of the land remained to be conquered after Joshua (Josh. 13:1–6).

7:23–26 lest you be doomed . . . like it: The lot of the Canaanites (2:34) could befall Israel, who must be resolute in avoiding any attachment to the gods of the host cities. The evil was not something inherent in the material object, as though it were something magical. Rather, the danger was in the thoughts that these things might bring upon one's mind. Thus David said, "I will set nothing wicked before my eyes" (Ps. 101:3).

8:1–20 Yahweh alone is the source of blessing, whether in the wilderness or in the land. Moses exhorts Israel to **remember** what God has done for them, in Egypt and in the wilderness, and to remain grateful for His blessings that they will receive in the Promised Land, lest they forget and abandon the Lord.

8:1 Live, in this context, has the same meaning as saving one's soul in James 1:21; 5:20.

8:2 remember: Reflecting on the past acts of God encouraged loyalty and devotion to Him. **forty years . . . to humble you and test:** The Lord taught Israel to rely on Him alone during the wilderness journey. **know what was in your heart:** The response to God's testings helped determine the people's inner nature.

8:3 God supplied His people with food in the wilderness (Ex. 16) so that they would learn that **man shall not live by bread alone.** Humans have a spiritual nature that can be satisfied only by the spiritual nutrients of God's Word. **man lives by every word . . . from the mouth of the LORD:** Jesus affirmed this truth by using these words to resist Satan (Matt. 4:4; Luke 4:1–4).

8:4 In addition to providing manna and water, the Lord made the clothing and shoes of the people last for forty years!

8:5, 6 That **the LORD . . .** chastens is still true today (Heb. 12:5–11).

8:7–9 The land had everything necessary to sustain life and develop an economy: water, crops, and metals for industry (11:8–12). The various water sources contrasted with the Nile, the only source of water the people knew in Egypt (11:10). The varied forms of plant life were surprising to the people who came from the wilderness.

8:10–14 bless the LORD: The proper response to plenty is thanksgiving and worship. It is Jewish custom to pray *after* certain festive meals because of the phrase **when you have eaten and are full.** In the absence of proper worship, people would **forget,** become complacent and greedy, and even deny that God provided for them (v. 17). **your heart is lifted up:** In the enjoyment of God's blessings, the people to their own detriment might think that they were self-sufficient.

8:14–16 God who brought . . . who led you . . . who brought water . . . who fed: These four historical allusions recall (1) the redemption from Egypt, (2) the presence of God in the wilderness, (3) the provision of water, and (4) the provision of manna. **humble . . . test:** Through the whole experience in Egypt and the wilderness, the Lord was leading His children into decisions that would bring out their true nature. **to do you good in the end:** Difficult as the tests were, the Lord was a good teacher because He had the future of His people in mind.

8:17 Moses warned the people that prosperity and **wealth** often leads to an exaltation of self and a rejection of God.

8:18 God's **power** is different from human manipulation, power politics, competition, and other ways of getting ahead. God gives grace.

8:19, 20 The threat was that the people would **perish** in the same manner as the nations whom they had come to drive out.

9:1–3 Hear, O Israel: Moses called on the people to see the future occupation of the land as a gift of divine grace, not the result of any righteousness of their own. The future was open to them if only they could learn from the past. **understand today:** wisdom from above begins with a confession of dependence on the Lord.

9:4–6 possess their land: The reasons for the conquest of the Promised Land were (1) the immorality of its inhabitants and (2) the promises God made to Abraham, Isaac, and Jacob (Gen. 15:18–21). **stiff-necked people:** Israel's history demonstrated how often the people grumbled, complained, and disobeyed. Moses hoped they would not forget their unworthiness before God, or think that they deserved His gracious gifts (vv. 7–14).

9:7–29 Moses reminds the people of their past disobedience and rebelliousness, lest they be tempted to believe that they deserve the land and God's goodness.

9:7, 8 In addition to remembering the grace of God, the people also had to **remember** how vulnerable they were to apostasy (1:6—3:29). **rebellious:** The people were characteristically stubborn. They continued to test the Lord (v. 27).

9:9 A person cannot go more than about three days without **water** and survive. God supernaturally preserved Moses during the **forty days.**

9:10–13 the LORD delivered to me . . . finger of God: God initiated the covenant with His people and gave Moses His laws. With God's approval, Moses taught the Law to the people.

9:14–19 destroy: The threat of destruction was real, even as the future threat always remained an imminent possibility.

9:19–21 the LORD listened to me: For Moses' prayer, read vv. 26–29. Daniel's prayer for the nation resembles Moses' intercession (Dan. 9:3–23).

9:22, 23 See Num. 11; 13.

9:24–29 Moses took God's judgment seriously. Nevertheless, he did not resign himself to God's justice but appealed to God's faithfulness, mercy, and honor. He reminded God of (1) His redemption of the Israelites from slavery, (2) His promises, (3) His reputation among all the nations, and (4) His election of Israel.

10:1–11 God's gracious renewal of the covenant. The new tablets of the Law symbolized God's promise to be present with His people, knowing that they were rebellious in their hearts (5:29).

10:1 at that time: Subsequent to prayer (9:25–29).

10:2 I will write: The condescension of the Lord is almost beyond belief. He prepared the tablets a second time, even after the first set was broken.

10:3 The **acacia** tree is still found in the Sinai Peninsula, but in smaller numbers than when the Israelites passed through.

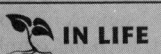 **IN LIFE**   ## The God Who Gives Wealth

There are two extremes today about the connection between God and wealth. One is that wealth and money are inherently evil and therefore God is opposed to them. The other is that God is just waiting to shower wealth on those who satisfy certain conditions or expectations that He has.

Moses' word to the Israelites that "God . . . gives you power to get wealth" (Deut. 8:18) helps to clear up both misunderstandings. On the one hand, it shows that ultimately wealth is a gift of God; therefore, it cannot be evil as such, or else God would not provide it (compare James 1:17). Numerous other passages reinforce the fact that whatever one possesses, one has God to thank for it (1 Sam. 3:7; Hos. 2:8).

On the other hand, Moses' statement shows that God is not a celestial Santa Claus. In the first place, no one today can claim this passage as a direct promise from God. These words were spoken to Israel because, as the text plainly states, the nation was involved in a covenant relationship with God. The terms of that covenant called for blessing on the nation (but not necessarily on individuals within the nation) if it kept the Law (Lev. 26:3–5). Moses was concerned that in the face of abundance, the people would forget the source of their wealth. For people today, who live outside that special covenant that God had with ancient Israel, Moses' words imply only the general truth that all that we have ultimately comes from God.

10:4, 5 He wrote . . . according to the first writing: The Lord did not add to or take away from the commandments.

10:6–11 Levi: The responsibilities of the Levites included: (1) care for the ark (Num. 3); (2) service in offering, worship, teaching, and legal matters (18:1–8); and (3) blessing Israel (Num. 6:22–27). The phrase **to this day** suggests that this explanation was written after Moses' death.

10:12–11:32 Moses challenges Israel to seek Yahweh, to love Him, and to keep His covenant, lest they fall subject to His judgment. This lovely and moving section has four challenges: (1) to love Yahweh, the source of all good, with one's whole being (10:12–22); (2) to remember what Yahweh has done in His judgment both on Egypt and on rebellious Israelites (11:1–7); (3) to practice the Law of God and receive His blessings (11:8–25); and (4) to remember that God is free in His blessing and in His curse (11:26–32).

10:13–15 Heaven and the highest heavens: The sky and the whole universe belong to God. **love . . . chose:** The Creator sovereignly and graciously involved Himself with Abraham and his descendants.

10:16 circumcise the foreskin of your heart: Circumcision was a *physical* sign of the covenant; faith and repentance were *spiritual* signs. Since the Canaanite worship system involved sexual excess, the distinctive sign on the body of the male Hebrew would be a significant reminder not to participate in the rituals of the Canaanites. But circumcision was to be done within as well as without. Marking the body as a sign of dedication to the Lord is unimportant unless there is a change of heart. The covenant administered by Moses required a spiritual change (30:6).

10:17, 18 Moses proclaims that the God of Israel alone is **God,** the sovereign Lord, the just and great King of all. The proper response to this God is awe, love, and service. **fatherless . . . stranger:** God uses His power to uphold justice—especially for those have no powerful ally (1:16; 24:17–22). **food and clothing:** God freely gives to all who are needy, even as He did to Israel in the wilderness (8:3, 4).

10:19 God's good provision for their own needs should have motivated the Israelites to **love the stranger** among them. To love and provide for the disadvantaged was in fact following God's example.

10:20 fear . . . hold fast: True faith expresses itself in awe, submission, and deep commitment to God.

10:21 He is your praise: Reflecting on the Creator-Redeemer—whose love, justice, and power extended beyond the covenant people—leads to worship, love, and obedience.

10:22 stars of heaven: God faithfully fulfilled His promise to Abraham (Gen. 15:5, 6).

11:1–7 Moses traced the mighty acts of God in order to encourage his hearers to respond to God's revelation. Acts and words go together, as do obedience and love.

11:6, 7 Dathan and Abiram rebelled against Aaron's priesthood and lost their lives (Num. 16).

11:8–25 This is a call to practice the God's Law and receive His blessings. Moses exhorts the people to respond to the Lord because He will give them a land so much better than Egypt. He exhorts them to love the Lord because He provides for them.

11:9–12 not like the land of Egypt: Agriculture in Egypt depended on irrigation, the annual flooding of the Nile (8:7–9). **land for which the LORD your God cares:** God would sovereignly control the seasons and rains to provide for His people (vv. 14, 15).

11:13–17 The early rain encouraged the sprouting of seed and new growth. **The latter rain** brought the crops to maturity. **Lord's anger:** God is gracious and loving, but also just when provoked by arrogant people. To **shut up the heavens** means "to withhold rain," as God did to Ahab (1 Kin. 17:1; 18:1).NSB]

11:18–25 This is an exhortation to treasure God's Word in the heart and to teach it to children.

11:26–32 Moses challenges the people to respond lovingly to the Lord because He is the source of life (blessing) and of death (curse).

11:26–28 The opposite of a blessing is a **curse.** As God's blessing brings vitality, so His curse takes it away. People become sick, suffer, and die (1 Cor. 11:30; James 1:13–15).

11:29–32 Gerizim . . . Ebal: See Josh. 8:30–35.

12:1–26:19 The development of the covenant fellowship is the concern of the Law of God (the statutes and judgments). The Law is God's revelation to Israel by which the great King teaches His people to develop a counter-culture, God's antidote against the autonomy of mankind.

12:1–16:17 This section surrounds the worship of God and a holy people. The distinctiveness of Israel is in her absolute allegiance to the one God, and this comes to expression in her worship, legal system, economics, society, family life, and individual and communal ethics.

12:1–31 One central place of worship would help them to maintain a certain faith. Moses stresses that God expects His people to focus on the one place chosen by God and to resist the attractiveness of the many pagan places and forms of worship. Israel in the land would receive many benefits from the Lord, and He in turn expected them to live responsibly.

12:1 giving you to possess: God was about to give the people the land. Yet He demanded their obedience as a condition for occupancy and enjoyment of it (chs. 28; 29).

12:2 mountains: The Canaanites built their temples on high places, believing that their gods resided in palaces on the mountains. These mountaintop shrines were considered gateways between heaven and earth. The Canaanites would worship at a **green tree** because they believed this would bring them success and prosperity.

12:3, 4 Sacred pillars were monuments dedicated to one of the gods. They represented the power of fertility. Archaeologists have found such pillars in excavations at Gezer and Hazor. **Wooden images** refers to the poles or trees dedicated to the goddess Asherah. The **worship** of the true God with any pagan ritual or reminder of paganism violated the Ten Commandments (5:8–10).

12:5 seek: Whatever one seeks is the object of one's desire and devotion (Ps. 122:9). **place where the LORD** your God chooses: The central place of worship was God's to choose (Ps. 132:13, 14). God blessed His people with His presence in the tabernacle in the wilderness and later at Shiloh, in the temple in Jerusalem, and

finally through Jesus Christ (John 2:18–22). **out of all your tribes:** The presence of God was for the benefit of all of the people without preference for any one tribe. God's **name** signifies His ownership. **dwelling place:** The Lord graciously agreed to live among His people.

12:6 The Hebrew word for **sacrifices** (*zebah*) always designates an offering of an animal. Often the word is used to describe a sacrifice offered to the Lord but eaten by the people. The **heave** offering was a communal offering, which the priest lifted up to signify that it was a gift to the Lord (Ex. 29:27, 28; Lev. 7:34). The priest took his due (Lev. 7:14, 32, 34), while the worshiper and his family ate the rest of the offering. A **vowed** offering was made in fulfillment of a vow (Lev. 7:16, 17; 22:21; Num. 6:21; 15:3–16; 30:11). A **freewill** offering was voluntary (Deut. 23:23; Ex. 35:27–29; 36:3; Lev. 7:16; Ezek. 46:12).

12:7 eat . . . rejoice: The communal offerings were to be eaten and enjoyed by those who offered them. It was a time of celebration before the Lord. **blessed:** God favored His people by giving them children, flocks, and the crops of the land. His blessing brought vitality, enrichment of life, and happiness to His people.

12:8 every man . . . own eyes: In the wilderness, the people did not develop a common focus on the Lord and become a body

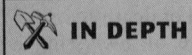 **IN DEPTH** | **A New Culture**

Israel was on the verge of a momentous occasion. Not only were they preparing to enter the Promised Land and conquer its inhabitants, they were also preparing to establish a brand new culture. The primary focus of this new culture would be on the living God. Every part of it would reflect His nature.

God's commandments gave the Israelites a concrete expression of how God wanted the people to live. In short, He wanted a people that loved and worshiped Him alone. By keeping a number of purity laws, the Israelites were to demonstrate their commitment to Him by keeping ritually clean. Ideally, this outward purity would reflect inward purity. Since God was perfect, He wanted His people to resist the immoral practices of the neighboring nations. But He not only wanted them to resist evil, He also wanted them to reflect His loving and compassionate nature by helping strangers, widows, orphans, and the poor. By following God's extensive instructions, the Israelites could establish their society on the just laws of the living God.

Many parts of the Israelite culture were distinctive in the ancient world, such as prohibitions against eating pork. These outward distinctions were a sign that the Israelites were set apart to God's holy purposes. However, the most prominent distinction was Israel's absolute allegiance to one God. Israel's entire society—its legal system, economic structure, family life, and individual and communal ethics—reflected this allegiance. While the nations that surrounded Israel worshiped a variety of gods at numerous shrines located all over the landscape, the Israelites (ideally) worshiped one God in one way at one place, the place He would choose. In the Promised Land, God planned to bless the Israelites abundantly. In turn, He expected the Israelites to live responsibly, in a culture unlike any that had preceded it.

of believers. Moses challenged the new generation to repent and return to the Lord.

12:9, 10 Moses envisioned a future state of **rest** for the people. Rest would mean that God's people would enjoy His blessings and live together in unity, free from fear of assault (Ps. 133; Jer. 31:2; Heb. 4:8–11).

12:11 The focus and guarantee of the promised rest are found in God dwelling with His people. In like fashion, God still has a "place" today (Heb. 10:24, 25).

12:12–14 You . . . and the Levite includes all Israelites—women and men, slaves and free, Levites and tribes with land. The Hebrew word for **rejoice** (*smah*) describes a deep enjoyment by the entire community of God's good gifts. God gave the Law to the people for their good, even for their enjoyment.

12:15 slaughter . . . meat: Butchering and eating meat was permitted wherever the Israelites settled. **gazelle . . . deer:** Many animals not suited for sacrifice to the Lord were still permitted for food.

12:16 The prohibition of eating or drinking **blood** in any form was an important restriction. Since blood represented life, the Israelites were to show respect for the vital fluids of animals (Gen. 9:4; Lev. 17:11).

12:17, 18 within your gates: Aspects of God's worship that were designed for community celebration were not to be done in the pri-

vacy of the home. Instead, God would designate the place where He would be worshiped. In a similar way, the NT places a strong emphasis on the community of believers. **rejoice:** God's prohibitions were designed for the mutual pleasure of God and the people.

12:19 The **Levite** received no tribal inheritance in the land and was dependent on the people for food.

12:20–27 enlarges your border: Moses emphasized the potential greatness of God's blessings on the people. The land might become so large that for many people frequent journeys to the central sanctuary would be impossible. In this case, provisions were made for the enjoyment of meat at home.

12:28 that it may go well: The Lord promised His blessing to all those who responded to His benevolent instructions. **and your children:** God's blessing extended to the succeeding generations (Gen. 1:27, 28; 9:1, 7; 17:19). Yet the Israelites did not gain their salvation through obedience, instead they found favor with God because of His mercy. He had chosen them to be His people.

12:29–31 The Lord would remove the temptation of the Canaanite nations, but the Israelites were responsible for not imitating their practices (Rom. 12:2; Phil. 2:14–16).

12:29, 30 God cuts off: The conquest was God's, but the Israelites were His responsible

---

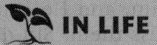 **IN LIFE**   ## Do-It-Yourself Religion

In a world in which the motto often is "do your own thing," people frequently develop self-styled religious beliefs and practices. For some this means a pick-and-choose, take-it-or-leave-it approach to established Christianity. For others it means coming up with outlandish ideas about God and eccentric ways of living. Either way, the ultimate authority becomes the individual, who assumes the prerogative of ignoring any demand or discipline that feels too limiting or imposing.

A somewhat similar attitude seems to have characterized the Israelites as they prepared to enter the Promised Land. Apparently they were doing whatever was right in their own eyes when it came to religious observance (Deut. 12:8). Not that they were necessarily turning away from God, but the lack of a permanently located worship center seems to have brought about a degree of laxness in regard to the ritual obligations of the Law. Moses warned them that that must change once they entered the land and God designated a site for worship (12:13, 14). They were to follow the detailed instructions of the Law concerning sacrifices, holy days, tithes and offerings, and other elements of religious life.

Is the same true for Christians today? In answering that, it is important to note that NT instructions and descriptions of worship are not nearly as detailed as those given to Israel in the OT Law. There seems to be a great deal more freedom given to individual believers and to their communities of faith. But that does not mean a do-it-yourself approach to religion. Scripture gives us an objective set of truths to be believed and behaviors to be lived. There may be latitude within those boundaries for cultural, ethnic, and geographic applications, but all believers fall into sin when they move outside the clear teaching of Scripture. In whatever manner we worship God, He still calls us to worship Him "in spirit and truth" (John 4:23).

agents (v. 2). **take heed:** Unfortunately, Israel did follow pagan religious ways.

12:31 God hated the Canaanite practices and was concerned that His children would be enticed by them (Lev. 18:21; 20:2–5). **Abomination** (Heb. *tô_bâ*) indicates the strongest form of revulsion and distaste. **burn . . . sons and daughters:** This is an example of one of the worst Canaanite practices, in which the Israelites later joined (2 Kin. 21:1–9; 2 Chr. 28:1–4).

12:32—13:18 Regulations guarding God's special revelation.

12:32 not add to it nor take away from it: The Word of God is not subject to whim, taste, or passing fancy.

13:1–5 The dangers of false prophets. The people of God had to be on the alert because false prophets would claim to be true. Thus the Israelites had to discern the intent of the message and the fulfillment of the prophetic words to understand whether it was a true prophet (18:21, 22). In the NT there are also warnings to "test the spirits" (1 John 4:1; compare Acts 20:28–31).

13:1, 2 a prophet or a dreamer: Both prophecy and dreams were legitimate forms of revelation. The fulfillment of a prophecy, **a sign,** or **a wonder** ordinarily validated the entire message of the prophet (18:22). **let us serve them:** Even if a wonder accompanied the message, a prophet who led the people away from the living God was a false prophet. Just like the Israelites, Christians today need to discern false teaching (Acts 20:28–31; Gal. 1:8; 1 John 4:1).

13:3, 4 The revelation of God through Moses was the test of any sign or message. When the message deviated from God's prior revelation, Israel had to discern the false teaching. **testing:** Just as the Lord had tested the people in the wilderness, He would continue to see whether they believed Him (8:2). **love . . . heart and . . . soul:** True faith is a commitment of one's whole being to the true God.

13:5 The offense was serious and so was the punishment, **death.** It was better for a false prophet to be executed than for one to escape judgment and mislead the people. **So you shall put away the evil from your midst:** Discipline, punishment, and testing were God's means of keeping His people pure. Having withstood the test, they could more easily resist the temptations of other evildoers.

13:6–11 The dangers of family pressures. Even when a close relative exerted pressure to leading one astray, the individual had the responsibility to not give in, and to bring it to public trial even if that meant the execution of the offender.

13:6–8 your brothers: Jesus speaks of unnatural hatreds that would pit brother against brother (Matt. 10:21). And He also said that He did not come only for peace. The believer must love Christ more than the members of the family, if there is a conflict within that family that would tend to drive one from Christ (Matt. 10:34–39).

13:9, 10 your hand shall be first: The relative who brought the charge would lead in the capital punishment of the relative who suggested the idolatrous practices. **to entice you away:** With unforgettable words, Jesus emphasized the severity of this offense. Such a person should not have been born. He would be better off if he were thrown into the sea with a millstone around his neck (Matt. 18:6, 7).

13:11–13 The term translated **corrupt men** denotes wicked, depraved people who oppose the will and work of God.

13:14 inquire . . . ask diligently: Proper investigation before a public trial guaranteed justice for everyone.

13:15, 16 strike the inhabitants: The people of the city, who were responsible for letting evil get out of hand, became subject to punishment. They were no better than the immoral Canaanites who were under God's present judgment (7:2; 12:2, 3).

13:17, 18 compassion . . . to keep all His commandments: The seemingly harsh judgment of evil was an act of obedience. God required the harsh punishment of evildoers so that immoral practices would not spread throughout the land. Then the Israelites could be completely devoted to Him, and He could remain among them and bless them. Sin disrupted this relationship with the Holy God.

14:1 children of the LORD: The motivation for Israel's distinct ethics and practices lay in the nation's special relationship to the Lord (1:31; 8:5). **cut . . . nor shave:** Pagan mourning rituals encouraged physical abuse. These practices were a form of magic by which people sought to exercise control over their well-being and over the gods (1 Kin. 18:28).

14:2 As a **holy people,** the Israelites were set apart to the Lord, separated from the nations, and chosen to practice the will of God on earth. The Hebrew word translated *holy* (*qdôsh*) means "to be separate" or "to be distinct." **chosen . . . special treasure:** Compare 1 Pet. 2:9.

14:3 not eat: The dietary regulations set Israel apart from the nations (Lev. 11). Most likely, God prohibited certain animals from being eaten in order to distinguish the practices of Israel from those of neighboring nations. With this physical sign, God symbolized Israel's holiness. Israel was dedicated to His purposes, not the world's. God usually referred to pagan practice as **detestable,** a word indicating strong repugnance.

14:4–11 Animals prohibited for food either did not have cloven hooves or did not chew the cud (Lev. 11).

14:12–18 These unclean birds were mainly birds of prey and scavengers. They were associated with dead flesh and were likely carriers of disease.

14:19 Creeping thing that flies refers to insects that could not be eaten.

14:20 may eat: Some of God's laws prohibit, while others permit.

14:21 not boil . . . in its mother's milk: Unlike the Canaanites who boiled young goats alive in the milk of their mothers as a sacrifice to fertility gods, Israel was to practice a more

IN FOCUS "chosen"

(Heb. *bachar*) (Deut. 7:6, 7; 14:2; Neh. 9:7; Is. 14:1; Hag. 2:23) Strong's #977: The Hebrew word translated *chosen* implies a decision made after close inspection. In the OT, the word is used to describe the careful action of "selecting" or "accepting." Sometimes the word is used for the choice of an object (1 Sam. 17:40) or of doing good (Is. 7:15, 16). In the OT, it is often God who chooses. The Lord chose Abraham (Neh. 9:7), the nation of Israel (Deut. 4:37), and finally David's family (2 Sam. 6:21). He chose, or elected, these people so that He could accomplish His will, the salvation of the world, through them (Is. 49:6). This choice was founded on His own love (Deut. 4:37).

humane method of animal sacrifice. Israel was to be different from its neighbors—that is **holy.**

14:22–15:18 Concrete expressions of various concern for the poor.

14:22–29 The laws of the tithe covered all agricultural products. In giving a tithe (the gift of one tenth to the Lord), the Israelites acknowledged that the land was the Lord's and that the benefits of the land were theirs only because of God's blessing. The tithe was to be enjoyed in the presence of the Lord, unless the people had come from a great distance. Then they could exchange it for silver and purchase food and drink with it in Jerusalem.

14:25–27 Money refers to uncoined silver. Coins were not struck until the Persian period.

14:28, 29 Every third year the tithe was given to the Levites and the poor.

15:1 every seven years: God taught His people to think in cycles of holy time: six days of work and the seventh of rest; six years of business and the seventh of giving freedom to the poor; six years of agricultural cultivation and the seventh of rest (Ex. 23:10, 11; Lev. 25:1–7). **Debts** were suspended as described in vv. 2–6. All of this shows a humane treatment of people regarding business relations.

15:2, 3 creditor . . . release it: The debtor could not repay in the seventh year because the fields could not be cultivated (Lev. 25:1–7). If creditors demanded repayment, the poor would sink even further into debt. In this, God showed His care and concern for the poor.

15:4, 5 no poor among you: God promised to bless every individual among His people. **only:** This promise was conditional. The Israelites had to obey.

15:6 lend . . . not borrow: God's blessing would bring a surplus. Israel's wealth and prominence among the nations would grow. This occurred during the reign of Solomon. **reign over many nations:** Instead of being subject to other nations, Israel's position would be that of leader among the nations (Is. 55:4, 5).

15:7, 8 not harden: The people's attitude toward the poor should have been a reflection of their gratitude for God's gifts to them.

15:9, 10 The creditor might have been wary of lending anything to the poor because the seventh year was approaching, the year that all debts were erased. Even though the creditor would not benefit from the loan, he was encouraged to lend to those in need.

15:11 The poor will never cease is a realistic statement compared with the ideal expressed in v. 4 (Matt. 26:11).

15:12, 13 When a poor man lost all his property, he could sell himself for work for **six** years. **let him go free:** The year of release canceled debts and freed the debtor (Ex. 21:2).

15:14 supply him liberally: The debtor-slave had been an instrument by which God had blessed the master. Upon the slave's departure, the slave would receive his or her due. In this way, the master acknowledged both the work of the slave and the sovereignty of the Lord.

15:15–18 remember that you were a slave: God's grace to the Israelites in freeing them from Egyptian slavery was a model for all Israelites to follow in relation to the poor. Only when the Israelites remembered their former poverty, thanked God for their riches, and assisted the poor would they be able to enjoy God's gifts to them.

15:19–16:17 Regulations concerning firstborn animals and the three annual pilgrimages. Moses explains how Israel was to be different in their celebrations from the nations around them. These celebrations were reminders of what God had done for them in the past, and they were ways of teaching children the history of redemption. Naturally children asked questions, such as, "Why are we doing this?" And the parents would have a wonderful opportunity to explain God's dealings and goodness toward them.

15:20–23 if there is a defect in it: God expected the best from the Israelites. He was their King, their Father, and their God (Mal. 1:8). To sacrifice one's best to the Lord was a leap of faith. One had to believe that God would bless one's flock despite the absence of its very best.

16:1–17 The requirement of three annual pilgrimages: the Passover and the Feast of Unleavened Bread (vv. 1–8), the Feast of Weeks (vv. 9–12), and the Feast of Tabernacles (vv. 13–15). Read Ex. 23:14–19; 34:18–26; Lev. 23:4–44; Num. 28:16—29:40.

16:1–5 Passover was observed on the fourteenth day (Ex. 12:18) of **Abib** or Nisan, which corresponds to our March-April. Read Ex. 12:1–28; 13:1–16; Lev. 23:5–8; Num. 28:16–25.

16:6, 7 The **twilight** sacrifice was in commemoration of the Exodus, which had occurred at that time (Ex. 12:29).

16:8–12 The last day of the Feast of Unleavened Bread was marked by a final **sacred assembly** of God's people. Putting **the sickle to the grain** took place on the second day of the Feast of Passover.

16:13–15 The Feast of Tabernacles was a harvest festival (Ex. 23:16; 34:22). During this pilgrimage, God's people joined together to celebrate God's goodness and to remember how they had once lived in tents (tabernacles or booths) during the wilderness wanderings. Today this festival is known as Succoth, from the Hebrew word translated *booths.* The feast lasted seven days, with a closing ceremony on the eighth (Lev. 23:36).

16:14, 15 rejoice: Sometimes modern people perceive the Israelites' worship as excessively burdened with details, ritual, and regulations, and imagine that the Israelites' worship experience must have been unpleasant. But sincere worshipers rejoiced in God's detailed instructions and enjoyed the symbols and ritual which reminded them of God's delightful characteristics. Then as now, worshiping God was a celebration.

16:16, 17 These verses summarize the regulations for the three annual pilgrimages to the central place of worship (Ex. 23:17; 34:23).

16:18–17:13 The administration of justice, the counter-culture, and the revelation of God. This section has several connected and loosely connected threads that bind it together: (1) jus-

tice, (2) leadership, and (3) the worship of God.

16:18 in all your gates: The areas framed by the towers in the gateways of ancient cities were the centers of community life and the places where the judges of the city would sit. **just judgment:** The Lord loves justice and hates discrimination.

16:19 Justice is the quality of dealing with people fairly. Judges particularly were expected to reflect God's just nature (32:4) by not dealing with the accused on the basis of discrimination, false witness, or hearsay. A **bribe** is any gift that might change the balance in favor of the giver, thus tipping the scales of justice (Ex. 23:8).

16:20 follow: Godliness is to imitate God in a love for what is just and true. **Altogether just** in the Hebrew is *sedeq sedeq,* repeated twice to stress its importance here. **live and inherit:** God's intention in all His instructions was for the good of His people.

16:21, 22 The Canaanites used certain trees and wooden images as representations of fertility gods. The Hebrew word translated **wooden image** is the Hebrew name for the Canaanite goddess of fertility, Asherah.

17:1 Sacrifice in Israel was never to be regarded as a means of dumping the unwanted or the unneeded. It showed faith that as one gave one's best to the Lord, He would make what remained suitable and plentiful for one's needs.

17:2, 3 The Hebrew verb for **transgressing** (*'abar*) is used elsewhere to indicate the crossing of a border or a stream. Here the word is used to indicate "crossing over" the boundaries that God had set for His people. Someone who served other gods had crossed over the boundary set by the first commandment.

17:4–6 inquire diligently: An investigation, rather than gossip, determined the truth of any report of idolatry. The guilty was condemned to death only after guilt was established by **two or three witnesses** (compare Matt. 18:16; 2 Cor. 13:1; 1 Tim. 5:19; Heb. 10:28). The First Commandment was not limited by gender. Either a **man** or **woman** could be executed for this crime against God.

17:7 hands . . . first: The witnesses participated in the stoning of the guilty because they were responsible for the person's condemnation. Jesus' words about throwing the "first stone" referred to this practice (John 8:7).

17:8 The more complex cases were sent to a higher court. **Degrees of guilt** refers to cases of manslaughter or murder—that is, accidental or intentional homicide.

17:9–11 The descendants of the family of Aaron were the **priests** of Israel. The **Levites** were the other descendants of Levi, who served in the tabernacle.

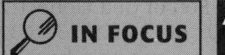

IN FOCUS **"write"**

(Heb. *katab*) (Deut. 6:9; 11:20; 17:18; 27:8) Strong's #3789. This verb literally means "to engrave or inscribe." Many different types of writing are mentioned in the OT. Stone tablets were inscribed on by God Himself (Ex. 34:1), scrolls were written (Jer. 36:2), stone and wood monuments often had writing carved on their surfaces (Josh. 8:32; Ezek. 37:20), even metals and gemstones were engraved (Ex. 28:11; 39:30). Since writing was a way to preserve the memory of historical events (Esth. 6:2; 10:2) and to give authority to human speech (2 Sam 11:14, 15), writing also suggests permanence. Thus the fact that Moses was commanded to write down God's words implies that those words are unalterable and fixed (Ex. 17:14; 34:27). The writings of Moses and the prophets were to be lasting reminders of God's revelation to both Israel's kings (as in 17:18) and all of God's people throughout the centuries.

17:12 The man who acts presumptuously is one who knows, but turns away from priestly instructions.

17:13 To **hear** God is to acknowledge Him, to respond to Him, and to obey Him (6:4). To **fear** God is to reverence Him and to worship Him (6:2). The idea here is *responsible reverence* (13:11; 19:20; 21:21).

17:14–18:22 Leadership and the revelation of God. In these various laws, Moses defines the place of the community officers, judges, priest-levites, kings, and prophets in the covenant fellowship. He foresees potential problems in the people's willingness to submit to the Lord. The laws provide a broad framework within which the community could develop under good leadership.

17:14 The regulations that follow anticipate the request that the Israelites would make for **a king.** At the time of Moses, Israel was privileged in being different from the **nations** because God was their King (Ex. 15:18; Num. 23:21). As problems arose during the period of the judges, some attempted to establish a kingship (Judg. 9:1–6). Gideon refused such an offer (Judg. 8:23). With Saul's kingship, God finally granted Israel's request for a national king (1 Sam. 8:4–9). Although Saul's reign ended in disaster, the Lord chose to anoint David and promise him a lasting kingship (2 Sam. 7:16; Ps. 89:3, 4).

17:15–17 These regulations limited the power and splendor of the future king. He would not be dependent on military power and riches. He was exhorted not to entangle the nation in political alliances that would expose Israel to pagan worship. Instead, he was exhorted to guide the nation into obedience to God's Law.

17:18 a copy of this law: The true king of Israel would be bound to God's instructions. He would not be a tyrant, but a king who ruled in accordance with God's revealed will.

17:19, 20 fear: Only if the king lived in proper reverence of God would the people follow suit. If the king were impious, the people's decline into evil practices would be accelerated. **heart may not be lifted:** By reading and obeying God's law, the king would be reminded that he was to be a man of the people. He was no different than anyone else, except that God had chosen Him to guide the nation in righteousness.

18:1 A portion of the dedication **offerings** was taken by the priests for their sustenance.

18:2–4 Unlike the other tribes, the Levites did not have a land **inheritance** in Canaan. They were to regard God as their inheritance. In other words, they had a special relationship with God that would be better than any grant of property. (Obviously, the Levites enjoyed the benefits of the lands surrounding the Levitical villages, v. 8.)

18:5 to minister: The priests were God's servants mediating between Him and the people (10:8; 21:5).

18:6 All the desire of his mind indicates wholehearted devotion. The suggestion is that there might have been people from the tribe of Levi who were not worthy to minister before the Lord. Their ancestry alone could not qualify them.

18:7 To serve in the name Yahweh was to experience more of the fullness of deity, His nearness, His goodness, His grace, and to be more aware of His holiness.

18:8 equal portions: The priests and Levites, who served before the Lord, were honored for that noble work.

18:9–14 False forms of revelation can come in the form of mantic and magic practices. Mantic (the use of animal divination) is an attempt to control the future by inquiring about the meaning of a particular sign, object, or dream. Mantic divination is an attempt to control people or events by special powers or rituals. All forms of mantic and magic were rejected as abominable because they sought guidance apart from God's revelation and manipulated people, and because in the end they encouraged an independent lifestyle with little regard for God. The most notable of the mantics of the ancient world was Balaam (Num. 22—25; 31).

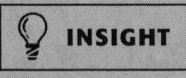

💡 INSIGHT   Seduction by Spirits

It is often said that "curiosity killed the cat." One curiosity not worth risking one's life over is the mystery of magic and the spirit world. God's Law spoke very clearly about the attraction of divination, witchcraft, mediums, oracles, and soothsayers: it called them "abominations" (Deut. 18:9–12].

18:10, 11 Some ancient pagan customs demanded that a **son** or **daughter** be offered as a sacrifice in order to learn about the future or to seek favor from a supposed deity. **calls up the dead:** Apart from His revelation, God prohibited any attempts to know the future. Saul's attempt to seek guidance apart from God's Word resulted in God's judgment of him (1 Sam. 28).

18:12 The pagan practices were **an abomination to the Lord** because they were based on an attempt to circumvent His revelation. The Lord is never a god among others; He alone is God!

18:13 Blameless indicates integrity and dependence on the Lord alone. Blamelessness characterized Abraham's life (Gen. 17:1) and is still the standard for Christians today (Eph. 1:4; 5:27).

18:14 Israel was to be distinct among the **nations,** a holy people, not only in what they ate but also in their faith toward God.

18:15–22 Regulations pertaining to the prophets. The Lord promises Israel that He will send them another prophet like Moses. This applies to all true prophets in that they were all God's spokespersons. The prophets were characterized by seven qualities: he or she was (1) an Israelite; (2) called by the Lord; (3) empowered by the Holy Spirit; (4) God's spokesperson; (5) authorized to speak in the name of the Lord; (6) a good shepherd over God's people; and (7) authenticated by signs. Yet, Jesus Christ was the true fulfillment of this prophecy. Jesus like Moses was the mediator between God and man

(vv. 16, 17; Heb. 9:15; 12:24). But Jesus was unlike Moses, being the Son of God (John 1:21, 25, 45; 5:46; 6:14; 7:40; Acts 3:22, 23; 7:37). When Moses died, there was the hope for another like him, yet greater than him (34:9–12).

18:15 All true prophets among the Hebrew people were raised up by **the Lord.** None could become a true prophet by self-will or desire.

18:16–22 does not happen: The test of a true prophet was the fulfillment of his words. However, there was one type of prophecy announced by a true prophet that might not occur. A prophecy of divine judgment might be averted because of the people's repentance in response to the proclamation. Both Jonah and Micah experienced this.

19:1–21:14 The administration of justice and the rules of war. God teaches His people to reflect justice in all situations, private, communal, and national.

19:1 Deuteronomy was written in anticipation of the conquest of Canaan, God's gift to His people. The **cities** of the land would become the possession of the people of Israel. The Israelites were not to destroy the cities in conquest, but to destroy the people who lived in them by waging war on the battlefield. Only Jericho and Hazor were to be burned. The burning of Ai was a consequence of sin.

19:2 Three cities of refuge would be selected in Canaan, to be added to the three that were east of the Jordan.

19:3, 4 The cities of refuge were intertribal cities. Anyone from any tribe could flee to the city that was closest to him. **manslayer:** Use of these cities for refuge was restricted to cases of unintentional homicide.

19:5 goes to the woods: An example is given of a situation that might lead to unintentional homicide.

19:6, 7 The avenger of blood was possibly a relative commissioned by the elders of the city to execute justice. This Hebrew word sometimes translated *kinsman redeemer* and here translated *avenger* means "protector of family rights." This was the individual who stood up for the family, either to redeem property and persons or to obtain vengeance. The glory of Israel was that its Avenger and Kinsman Redeemer was God Himself (Is. 41:14).

19:8, 9 enlarges your territory: God placed before the people not only the immediate prospect of the conquest of Canaan, but also the expansion of territory beyond the initial borders (12:20).

19:10 The shedding of **innocent blood** brought the **guilt of bloodshed** on the land. As in the case of Abel, whose innocent blood cried out to the Lord from the ground (Gen. 4:10), a nation of murderers would come under the judgment of God.

19:11, 12 For a person guilty of premeditated murder, there was no provision for refuge in the cities. He would be delivered over to the **avenger of blood.**

19:13 That it may go well with you indicates that God's concern was for the good of the community.

19:14 Removing a **landmark** was far more than moving a stone. It was changing a property line and in effect cheating some family out of the inheritance of land that God had given them.

19:15 Requiring **two or three witnesses** was a safeguard against the dangerous lies of an individual.

19:16, 17 The prospect of **a false witness** was chilling, particularly if it was a matter of one person's word against another's. **before the LORD:** At the tabernacle, the place of the higher court, the God of all truth would reveal the liar (17:8–13).

19:18–21 life . . . for life . . . foot for foot: The law of retribution established the principle that the punishment should fit the crime (Ex. 21:23–25; Lev. 24:17–20). The greater the crime, the harsher the penalty.

20:1–9 The exemptions indicate God's compassion for people whose minds are somewhere else (home, vineyard, wife) or whose hearts are not with Him (fear). This is a principle of understanding.

20:1–3 The Lord's presence is much greater than the enemy's military advantage of **horses and chariots** (Ps. 20:7). God the Divine Warrior would fight for His people (Ex. 15:3).

20:4 The use of the covenantal name for God, **the LORD,** Yahweh, along with the relational phrasing, **your God,** is designed to give the people confidence and assurance.

20:5 The owner of a new house was exempt from battle duty. **dedicate it:** This was not a formal ceremony, but the act of occupying a house.

20:6 The vinedresser was exempt from battle. It took as many as five years for a **vineyard** to begin to produce. A man who had waited for several years for the first produce from his vines was allowed to oversee the vines until they produced grapes.

20:7 betrothed: Betrothal was a commitment to be married; it was more binding than an engagement today. The betrothed man was exempt from battle. This exemption also applied to the newly married (24:5).

20:8, 9 fearful and fainthearted: The man who was nervous or who did not trust the Lord (v. 3) was exempt from battle. Since the battle was God's, the number of warriors was

not nearly as important as the army's belief that God was fighting for them.

20:10–15 Policy for cities far away. These laws detail the process of negotiations, subjugation, war, and spoils.

20:10, 11 This **offer of peace** specified that the people surrender, open up the city, and accept whatever conditions were laid down. **serve you:** The people of the city would become second-class citizens, on whom the Israelites could impose taxes and labor requirements.

20:12 not make peace: Some cities would refuse the terms of the treaty and come out in battle, as Sihon did.

20:13, 14 The reprisals for refusal were severe. **strike every male:** The men of war of the city were to be killed, for they posed a threat as long as they were able to bear arms. **Women** and **little ones** were to be spared, though they would become the property of the victors.

20:15, 16 The rules of the spoil (vv. 13, 14) applied only to distant **cities.** Different rules applied to the cities of Canaan (vv. 17, 18). They were to destroy the people of Canaan as part of God's judgment on those immoral peoples. **But of the cities of these peoples:** The people who lived in Canaan had practiced disgusting religious and social perversions for centuries. God had given them time to repent, but their judgment had come.

20:17, 18 utterly destroy: The Hebrew text uses two forms of the same verb to emphasize complete destruction of the Canaanites. This was not just a symbolic war; the entire Canaanite population was to be destroyed.

20:18 lest they teach you: The principal concern of the Lord was for the welfare of His people. The Canaanite population in the land was like a deadly tumor that eats away at the body. If the tumor was cut out, the body could live. So it was with the Canaanites. If the Canaanites were cut out of the land, the Israelites could thrive in the land by obeying God. Otherwise, the immoral Canaanite practices might slowly spread throughout the land.

20:19, 20 Trees, a part of God's creation, were useful for food, shade, and building material. In a long siege, the armies of Israel were not to cut down the trees and destroy the land. Only non-fruit-bearing trees were to be used for making siege machines.

21:1, 2 killed: The death may have been due to accidental or intentional homicide. This is a case of unsolved murder. **measure the distance:** As in our own day, the question of jurisdiction was important in criminal cases.

21:3, 4 heifer: The people of the nearest city were responsible for initiating a rite that established the people's innocence of the murder.

21:5–7 The **elders** of the city bore the

responsibility for the murder, even though they were not personally guilty. It was up to them to seek atonement for the murder.

21:8 Breaking the heifer's neck did not **provide atonement.** It was symbolic of the horrendous crime. God Himself graciously forgave.

21:9 Killing an **innocent** person was an extremely serious offense in ancient Israel. Unless the crime was solved or the rite was performed, there would be no real rest for the community.

21:10–14 Taking wives from among captive peoples was a common practice the world over. But in Israel God regulated the practice, working toward a principle of human dignity.

21:10, 11 Presumably the **enemies** were from distant cities (20:13–15), since the Israelites took **captives.** God had commanded the utter destruction of enemies within the Promised Land.

21:12 shave her head: This ritual was intended to give the woman time to adjust to the new culture and to mourn over the forceful separation from her family. It was also a symbol of cleansing. She was preparing to become part of a new community.

21:13 Since a foreign woman's distinctive clothes might have associations with the idolatrous practices of her former family, these clothes were taken from her. The woman was about to become part of God's covenant community. She was not allowed to keep anything that she might use to tempt the Israelites to worship false gods. **your wife:** After these precautions, the captive woman was given the status of any other married woman in Israel.

21:14 if you have no delight in her: The reason is not stated. The man might have experienced rejection in the marriage relationship. Perhaps the woman would not convert to the true worship of the Lord. Perhaps she was unable to conceive a child. In any event, the man was given permission to divorce her or **set her free. you have humbled her:** The woman had been dishonored by removal from her country and compulsory marriage. She was to be treated with some dignity in the event of an incompatible marriage.

21:15–25:19 In these regulations Moses summarizes and develops the place of the individual in relation to the community. The individual is responsible for the preservation of purity, justice, and compassion of the community.

21:15 two wives: Polygamy was commonly practiced in the cultures of the ancient Middle East and was assumed in the Law of Moses. In some cases, polygamy may have been a necessity in ancient Israel (25:5–10).

21:16 A father was expected to show consideration for the **firstborn** child, regardless of his attitude toward the child's mother.

21:17 Ancient Middle Eastern custom approved preferential treatment of the firstborn son. The **double portion** was a mark of the father's blessing. Among the sons of Jacob, it was actually Joseph who received the double portion (Gen. 48:8–22; 49:22–26). Reuben had forfeited his right as the firstborn by his disreputable behavior (Gen. 49:3, 4).

21:18 The **stubborn and rebellious son** was not an "ordinary" rebellious youth, but one who had been immoral over a long period of time.

21:19 his father and his mother: The parents were responsible to the community for their children. The **elders** bore the responsibility for the actions of the community as a whole.

21:20 they shall say: The parents presented the charge, though the behavior of the child would undoubtedly have been widely known. **A glutton and a drunkard** is an expression for "a good-for-nothing."

21:21 All the men of the community shared in the responsibility for executing the rebellious youth. Capital punishment seems harsh to the modern reader. Yet the community could not allow the rebellious youth to spread his immoral practices. They were God's holy people.

21:22, 23 hang: The guilty person was not hanged by the neck; this form of execution was not practiced in ancient Israel. The hanging was actually an impaling of the corpse for public viewing after death by stoning. Everyone would know that individual had brought guilt on the community. The exposure of the corpse was limited to one day. For **that day,** it reminded people of God's judgment on the sinner.

22:1–4 Love is shown in taking care of a neighbor's property and providing help.

22:1 hide yourself from them: Israelites could not ignore problems or misfortunes of their neighbors. Every individual in the community bore a responsibility to uphold justice within that community (compare Gal. 6:2).

22:2, 3 it shall remain with you: Community responsibility included taking care of lost property, whether animals or objects. **Hide yourself** means to ignore the problem or turn away.

22:4 Rendering assistance demonstrated a concrete expression of covenant life. The verbal construction translated **surely help** is emphatic in the original.

22:5 Cross-dressing was forbidden by God in ancient Israel. In the ancient Middle East, dressing in the clothing of the opposite sex was a magical practice intended to bring harm to people. For example, a transvestite male would predict that the soldiers of another army would be as weak as females.

22:6, 7 The **eggs** or young of a **nest** could be eaten for food. But the mother had to be freed because she perpetuated the species.

22:8 A **parapet** was a barrier erected on a roof to keep people from stepping or falling off. The **roof** of an ancient Israelite house was used like another room, particularly during warm weather.

22:9–12 Most likely, these regulations were based on the same principle as that of dietary restrictions. The Israelites were to be different from their neighbors in all aspects of life in order to show their separation to the living God.

22:13 Detests indicates a loathing following the consummation of the marriage because the husband found out that his new bride was not a virgin.

22:14 Charges her indicates a public accusation. In ancient times, virginity was highly regarded. The indisputable legitimacy of children was vital to ancient society and inheritance rights. Joseph's actions when he learned of Mary's pregnancy can be explained by these laws (Matt. 1:18–25). Because of Joseph's love for Mary, he did not want to make a public accusation. At the same time, he was not prepared to marry a woman who he thought had been immoral.

22:15–17 The **father and mother** would come to defend the girl and protect their name.

22:18, 19 A false accusation would be punished. A man was not permitted to bring a frivolous charge against his wife. Compare the penalty for a false accusation with the penalty recorded in v. 29.

22:20, 21 If the woman was not a virgin, she would be punished for her immorality. **the door of her father's house:** The parents also shared in her punishment. They were publicly disgraced because they did not dissuade her from such actions.

22:22 Both the man and the woman had to **die** (Lev. 18:20; 20:10).

22:23, 24 bring them both out: Both parties were presumed guilty in this instance. In this situation, the woman could have screamed for help since she was in a city. **The gate** of **the city** was the place for legal proceedings and executions.

22:25–27 no sin deserving of death: The woman was presumed innocent by virtue of the isolated place where she could not receive help

> *The Israelites were to be different from their neighbors in all aspects of life in order to show their separation to the living God.*

no matter how much she resisted.

22:28, 29 This law warned young men that they would be made responsible for their actions. A **young woman** was not freely available merely because she was not betrothed.

22:30 Uncover his father's bed is a euphemism for sexual relations (Lev. 18:8). This was the sin of Reuben, who slept with the mother of his brothers (Gen. 35:22).

23:1 Emasculated means that all or part of the sexual organs had been removed. This was done to men who were put in charge of harems to prevent intercourse with the women. It was also a pagan religious practice. Genital mutilation was prohibited in Israel. **Assembly of the Lord** indicates the people on whom the Lord had bestowed His special grace, with whom He had made a covenant, and to whom He had given the promises. In Deuteronomy, the word often refers to those gathered before Sinai (5:22; 9:10; 18:16). Exclusion from the assembly means restriction from full participation in religious rites.

23:2 Illegitimate birth may refer to the offspring of an illicit cultic union, such as the child of a temple prostitute (vv. 17, 18). **The tenth generation** most likely means "forever."

23:3–5 Since the Ammonites and Moabites showed hostility to the Israelites, they were not allowed to become citizens and participate in the worship of the Lord (Num. 22—24). **curse you:** God's loyalty to His people would not allow Him to listen to Balaam. Instead, the Lord turned Balaam's curse into His own blessing on the Israelites. Here, the Lord excluded those who had sought to curse the Israelites from full participation in the community of faith.

23:6, 7 You shall not seek their peace is a prohibition against making any treaty with these nations. Moab and Ammon were persistent enemies of Israel.

23:8 third generation: While the people of Moab and Ammon were excluded from the congregation, the people of Edom and Egypt had an opportunity to join the true worshipers of the living God. The provision for the Egyptians might have been due to their initial kindness to Jacob's family in letting them move to Goshen (Gen. 47). The provision for the Edomites was based on the close ties they had with the Israelites. They were descendants of Jacob's brother, Esau.

23:9–11 A **wicked thing** was a cause for

individual and communal uncleanness. Soldiers had to maintain their purity, for the Holy One was in their camp. **Unclean by some occurrence in the night** possibly refers to an involuntary emission (Lev. 15:16) or urination. Even though God's standards for purity were high, He provided a way for an unclean person to become clean. The person could go outside the camp until the next evening and wash.

23:12, 13 Digging latrines was a part of military life. Such attention to cleanliness not only promoted ritual purity, but also proper hygiene to prevent disease from spreading through the camp.

23:14 your God walks in the midst of your camp: The Holy One was present with Israel's soldiers whenever they went to war. It would never do for His soldiers to tolerate unhealthy living conditions in camp.

23:15, 16 The **slave** presumably entered Israel's territory from another country.

23:17 The Hebrew word translated here as **ritual harlot** (*qedsha*) is a form of the word meaning "holy" or "separate" (*qdash*).The ritual harlot was regarded by the Canaanites as one "set apart" for the worship of gods and goddesses of fertility. In Canaanite religious fertility rites, men lay with cultic prostitutes. The Canaanites believed that this act would bring fertility to their families, fruitful fields, and growth of their herds. This debased system of worship was evidently one of the reasons God brought such strong judgment against the Canaanites. The **perverted one** was a male prostitute.

23:18 Harlot here (Heb. *zônâ*) describes a common prostitute.

23:19, 20 Interest in the ancient Middle East was very high. Borrowing inevitably led to greater debt and sometimes to the enslavement of the debtor (Ex. 22:25–27; Lev. 25:36). **Your brother** refers to a fellow Israelite.

23:21, 22 A **vow** was a commitment to show one's love for the Lord in a particular way. Though a vow was voluntary, one was obligated to fulfill it once it was made. God expected His people to keep their commitments (compare Matt. 5:37). A failure to fulfill a vow was regarded as **sin** (Eccl. 5:4–6). But **vowing** was purely voluntary and not necessary for the development of godliness.

23:23–25 A traveler was permitted to eat **grapes** or **grain** while passing a field, but harvesting or storing the food for use at a later time was clearly prohibited. When Jesus and His disciples picked grain in open fields, they were following the common practice allowed by this regulation. However, the Pharisees challenged Jesus because they did it on the Sabbath (Mark 2:23–28).

24:1–4 The case involves a divorcee's return to her first husband after she had been married to a second man.

24:1, 2 uncleanness: The nature of the problem is not specified, though it would have been clear in the original context. It could have been a physical problem, such as the inability to bear children. The **certificate of divorce** was a legal document that provided rights to the divorcee (Lev. 21:7, 14; 22:13; Num. 30:9; Matt. 19:3–9). Such a certificate allowed the woman to remarry.

24:3, 4 defiled: Returning to her first husband after an intervening marriage might have placed the woman in the same position as an unfaithful wife.

24:5, 6 A **millstone** was a stone used for grinding grain into flour. The combination of the two stones constituted an essential household instrument for the daily provision of food. The principle is clear: A family was not to be deprived of the necessities of daily life.

24:7–9 Leprosy refers to a variety of infectious skin diseases. The disease known today as leprosy, Hansen's disease, is different from the diseases referred to here.

24:10–13 A **pledge** was a token that a debt would be repaid. Since this involved the poor within the covenant community, the regulations protected the debtor's privacy (vv.

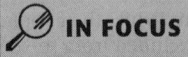 **IN FOCUS** | *"divorce"*

(Heb. *kerithuth*) (Deut. 24:1, 3; Is. 50:1; Jer. 3:8) Strong's #3748: This legal term signifies "a bill of divorce" and is related to the verb *karat* which means "to cut down" or "to cut off." The OT teaches that God hates divorce because it severs the oneness of the marriage relationship and the covenant between the husband and wife (Mal. 2:14–16). Jesus indicates that God permitted divorce in OT times only because the people were stubborn and sinful (Matt. 19:8). The divorce regulations in the OT protected the divorced woman. They allowed her to return to her parents with dignity or to seek a legal remarriage, instead of resorting to slavery or prostitution for her livelihood.

10, 11) and ability to provide for his family (vv. 12, 13).

24:14, 15 The following laws allowed property owners and laborers to receive a due profit from their properties and their labor. At the same time, both the owners and the laborers were to resist any greedy actions that would prevent a reasonable provision for the disadvantaged people in their communities. For instance, the poor needed daily payment of wages for daily subsistence. To be able to pay their wages and not do so was a **sin** against the Lord.

24:14–22 These regulations concerning these people—**the stranger, the fatherless, the widow**—are the three classic cases of the disadvantaged in the OT period. Each needed a defender. The righteous person should regard himself as an agent of God to protect the disadvantaged.

24:16, 17 Ezekiel applied this principle to the exilic community (Ezek. 18:4).

24:18–22 The passage exhorts the Israelites to **remember** their people's own slavery in Egypt (v. 22). Just as God showed compassion on them when they were oppressed (15:15), they were to show compassion on those who were now disadvantaged. **God may bless:** Ultimately, it is in one's own best interest to have a concern for the interest of others.

25:1–3 A rod was probably used for the beating (Ex. 21:20). **Forty blows:** Later Jewish law restricted the number to forty minus one (2 Cor. 11:24) to make sure that the authorities remained within the set limits. **brother be humiliated:** The offender was still a brother whose dignity in the community was to be preserved.

25:4 not muzzle an ox: Muzzling kept the animal from eating while it worked. This law encouraged kindness and consideration for animals. Later the apostle Paul used this law as an analogy to the principle of supporting ministers of the gospel (1 Cor. 9:9, 10; 1 Tim. 5:17, 18).

25:5–10 This law assured the perpetuity of the family name and of family property. This is an example of a custom in ancient Near Eastern law that was adapted for Israel and incorporated into the divine instructions for Israel.

25:5 The ancients greatly feared having no heirs to carry on the family's name. Furthermore, a widow with no children to take care of her would quickly become a beggar. Taking a brother's widow as a second **wife** protected her and preserved the name, memory, and interests of the deceased brother. The **dead brother** would be acknowledged as the legal father of the firstborn son of that marriage. This practice is called levirate marriage, from the Latin word for brother-in-law.

25:6 The deceased brother would be acknowledged as the "official" father of the child. The preservation of one's name was of utmost importance in ancient Israel. Ultimately, the preservation of one's name was a part of the grand, over-arching Messianic hope that threads its way through all aspects of Israel's history.

25:7–10 For his own reasons, a **man** might decide not to fulfill these obligations (Gen. 38:8–10). **he will not perform:** Legally, the brother-in-law was bound to keep the family name alive. His refusal was not merely a private matter, but also a public issue. For his insistence on his rights over the widow's rights he deserved to be publicly disgraced.

25:8 The accusation of the widow had to be validated by **the elders** of the city.

25:9, 10 To **remove** one's **sandal** was a sign of the loss of one's rights in the community; perhaps it was also a loss of the right to walk on one's own land (Ruth 4:7). To **spit** in someone's **face** was an act of strong, public contempt. Such a public disgrace discouraged men from shrinking from their duty as a brother-in-law. Since the living brother refused to maintain the name of his deceased brother, he was in danger of losing the memory of **his** own **name** in the community.

25:11–14 A merchant could defraud a customer by using different-sized **weights,** depending on whether he was selling or buying, to tilt the scales to his advantage (Amos 8:5).

25:15 Perfect and just refers to weights that were exact.

25:16 The opposite of conforming to a standard is "unrighteousness."

25:17, 18 Israel was to tell the story of what **Amalek** had done and never forget it (Ex. 17:8–16; Num. 14:39–45). **He did not fear God** is a way of saying that he had no regard for the special status of God's people.

25:19 blot out the remembrance of Amalek: The Amalekites would in effect come under the ban which God had placed over the people of Canaan (Lev. 27:29; Josh. 6:17, 18).

26:1 into the land: The author of Deuteronomy is always anticipating God's gift of Canaan to the Israelites (19:1).

26:2 The Israelites were to offer to God the fruit that ripened **first,** even though there was always a possibility that the rest of the crop would not ripen or be harvested because of some unforeseen circumstance. By offering the first of the produce to the Lord, the people expressed their trust in God's provision and their gratitude for His good gifts.

26:3 I have come: During the years that the people were in Egypt, whatever they raised was on soil that did not belong to them. During the years that they were in the wilderness, they were away from fertile land on which to grow things. But in the land that God planned to give them, crops, orchards, and vineyards would be theirs to enjoy. God had exceedingly blessed them, and they were to express their thanks.

26:4 Even before the temple was built, there was always an **altar** for sacrifices.

26:5–8 These words became part of the litany of the Passover Seder service, the Haggadah (recitation). The recital of these words formed a wonderful celebration of God's great deliverance of Israel from Egypt, not unlike the Christian recital of a creed or confession of faith.

26:5 My father was a Syrian (Aramean) is a reference to Jacob, whose parents' ancestral home was in Aram (Gen. 24:1–10). **about to perish:** Jacob's family suffered from the famine that struck Canaan, and they survived by fleeing to Egypt (Gen. 46:3–7). **few in number:** Jacob's family numbered seventy when they moved to Egypt (Gen. 46:8–27; Ex. 1:1–5). **A nation, great, mighty, and populous** is a reference to the great increase God gave His people while they were in Egypt (Ex. 1:5, 7).

26:6, 7 the LORD heard: God's response to His people was one of the great manifestations of His grace, mercy, and care (Ex. 2:23–25). He cared enough to answer their cries.

26:8 mighty hand . . . outstretched arm: This phrasing celebrates the direct involvement of the Lord in the salvation of the Israelites from slavery. **terror . . . signs and wonders:** This phrasing is regularly repeated to describe God's miraculous works during the Exodus (4:34; 34:11, 12). God with His own hand demonstrated His power to the Egyptians and delivered the Israelites.

26:9, 10 I have brought the firstfruits: The worshiper needed to say aloud what he was doing as he did it. Doing this added solemnity and dignity to the offering.

26:11, 12 and the stranger: When people came to live with Israel in the land, they were instructed in the worship of God.

26:13, 14 you shall say: As in the case of the firstfruits (vv. 1–11), the spoken word accompanied the act to reinforce the significance and purpose of the offering. **I have not:** The worshiper was to acknowledge that nothing had been held back or used for selfish reasons.

26:15 Your holy habitation: People direct their prayers to heaven, acknowledging at the same time that God is everywhere (Is. 66:1, 2).

26:16–19 The final exhortation of Moses. These verses conclude the legal corpus of Deuteronomy (12:1—26:19) in which Moses developed and applied the laws of the Book of the Covenant to a new situation, as Israel was about to enter the land. It is also an appropriate anticipation of the next section with its focus on covenant renewal (27:1—30:20).

26:16 The demands of obedience are found throughout Deuteronomy. To **observe** or do the will of God was not meant to be the means by which a person would be made righteous before God. Instead it would be part of a loving response to God's gracious covenant. **all your heart and . . . soul:** This is also a regular emphasis in Deuteronomy, a command to the whole person to respond fully to God.

26:17 The first generation had declared their loyalty to God at Mount Sinai (Ex. 24:7). In this covenant renewal ceremony, the new generation confirmed their commitment to God. To confess that the Lord was their God implied a commitment to live by His revelation.

26:18 The Hebrew word for **special people** speaks of God's great delight and pleasure in His people. They are like a very special jewel, an adornment that He treasures. The word denotes an elect people, set apart by the Lord to Himself, committed to the Lord and His revelation, and exalted above the nations (Ex. 19:5; Mal. 3:17).

26:19 Closeness to the Lord meant separation from the **nations. in praise . . . in honor:** The future of God's people was in His hands. He had promised to bestow honor on them (compare Gen. 12:2, 3; Is. 60; Rom. 8:18, 19). In a similar manner, the Lord has lifted up the people of His church, separating them from the nations and regarding them as a holy people (1 Pet. 2:9).

27:1–26 The renewal of the covenant in Canaan under Joshua.

27:1 The elders of Israel joined Moses at

🔍 **IN FOCUS**   **"worship"**

(Heb. *shachah*) (Deut. 26:10; Gen. 23:7; 37:7, Lev. 26:1) Strong's #7812: The most common Hebrew word for *worship* literally means "to cause oneself to lie prostrate." In ancient times, a person would fall down before someone who possessed a higher status. People would bow before a king to express complete submission to his rule. Joseph's brothers recognized the cultural significance of "bowing down" when they reacted so vehemently against Joseph's dream (Gen. 37:5–8). Bowing down to Joseph meant they were submitting to his authority. Following the example of the ancient people of faith, true Christian worship must express more than love for God, it must also express submission to His will.

 **IN FOCUS** | **"burnt offering"**

(Heb. *'olah*) (12:6; 27:6) Strong's #5930: In Hebrew, this word means "holocaust," an offering that is completely destroyed by fire. By burning the best of their offerings on God's altar, the Israelites expressed their dedication and gratitude to God, who had supplied all their needs. Many different types of burnt offerings were offered: bulls (Lev. 1:3–5), sheep or goats (Lev. 1:10), and birds (Lev. 1:14). If the burnt offering was presented as a sin offering, the worshiper would place his hands on the animal's head to show the transfer of sin to the animal. The animal was then killed by the priest. The priest collected the animal's blood and presented it to the Lord by sprinkling it on the altar. Pieces of the sacrifice were then placed on the alter and completely burned. These sacrifices were necessary until Christ offered Himself as a sacrifice for the sins of all.

this point. This joint declaration demonstrated the validity of God's revelation through Moses, even after Moses' death.

27:2, 3 The **large stones** were memorial stones on which the Law of God was to be written (v. 8). **whitewash them with lime:** These stones were coated with a plaster background so that the writing would be more visible.

27:4 Mount Ebal was north of Mount Gerizim (vv. 12, 13). Between the two mountains was the city of Shechem (Gen. 12:6, 7;

33:18–20). Shechem and its two mountains are roughly in the center of the land of Canaan.

27:5 altar of stones: The Lord gave the Israelites specific instructions on how they could approach Him. Forging **iron** was not a skill as characteristic of Israel as of some other Middle Eastern peoples. The Lord rejected an impressive altar for a humble altar of **whole stones,** that is, uncut stones. Perhaps an impressive altar would have diverted the worshipers' attention from God (Ex. 20:25).

Photo: Levant Photo Service

Mount Ebal, where threatened curses were pronounced against the Israelites at Moses' command if they failed to obey the Lord (Deut. 27:11–26).

27:6–10 Whole stones refers to stones not cut by tools.

27:11–14 During the covenant renewal ceremony with the second generation of Israel, the Lord used the topography of the land for dramatic visual effect. **Mount Ebal,** because of topographical and climatic conditions, is normally a barren peak, while **Mount Gerizim** is usually covered with vegetation. Consequently, Mount Ebal was an ideal place for the curses to be recited, and Mount Gerizim was suitable for the blessings. The association of the place and the word would have been unforgettable. Furthermore, the two mountains are quite close, so they would serve as a natural amphitheater for the recitation of the curses and blessings by the **Levites.**

27:15, 16 The first curse pertained to idolatry. A **carved or molded image** defied the first or second commandment or both (5:7–9). **Amen** was an expression of approval and submission to God's Word. This Hebrew word, from a root meaning "to be established," likely has gone into all languages where the gospel has gone. The reader will observe that the people of Israel said "Amen" to each of the twelve curses (and, presumably, to each of the subsequent twelve blessings). This gives a biblical pattern for the use of "Amen" in our own public worship. At times we may hear people saying "Amen" frivolously, but the biblical use was a formal statement of assent to the living God.

27:17 The third curse pertained to justice and greed. **landmark:** Moving the stone with the intent of extending the boundary of one's land enhanced one's own personal prosperity at the expense of someone else (19:14).

27:18 The fourth curse required the humane treatment of disabled people. **blind:** The underlying assumption is that only a person of great cruelty and no love for God would take advantage of a disabled person.

27:19 The fifth curse had to do with compassion to those who were defenseless. The **stranger, the fatherless, and widow** did not have the legal and social resources to defend themselves.

27:20–23 The sixth through the ninth curses covered sexual morality. Sexual relations with animals (bestiality) and incest were strictly prohibited (Ex. 22:19; Lev. 18:23; 20:15, 16).

27:24, 25 The tenth and eleventh curses addressed justice when a homicide occurred. **secretly:** The murderer might have escaped detection, but God saw his vile act. **bribe . . . innocent person:** Both a hired assassin and the person who did the hiring would have been guilty.

27:26 The twelfth curse was an all-encompassing one. A curse was on anyone who broke any part of the **law.** The Lord expected not only full submission to the law, but also a love for Him. Paul quoted this verse to emphasize the impossibility of keeping the law (Gal. 3:10). The blessings that would have corresponded to these twelve curses are not recorded here.

28:1–9 This passage repeatedly emphasizes the Israelites' responsibility to obey. **if you diligently obey:** Israel could never earn salvation through obedience. God had already chosen to save them from slavery and make them His people. He had already promised to be their God and give them the Promised Land. Yet God demanded diligent obedience from the Israelites in order for them to receive all of God's rich blessings in the land (Is. 48:17–19). **overtake you:** The Lord's blessings would be the source of the people's joy (Ps. 23:6). **blessed:** The vitality of the Lord comes to expression in all areas of life: city and country (v. 3), offspring of man and animals (v. 4), preparation of food (v. 5), and in travel (v. 6). Further, the Lord assures them of a restful future: protection from enemies (v. 7) and secure storehouses (v. 8).

28:10, 11 afraid: The nations would see God's presence and His blessing on His people and would stand in awe of the greatness of the Lord. **name of the LORD:** Here the name Yahweh is used for God. This indicates God's unique relationship with the Israelites. He had revealed to them His glorious name.

28:12 God gave graciously to the Israelites from the **good treasure** that He had stored up for them. The people received God's blessings solely because of His grace. **rain . . . season:** The Canaanites believed that Baal was the giver of dew and rain (1 Kin. 17:1). But God assured Israel that He controlled the heavens and would make their lands fruitful (Ps. 104:3, 13). **lend . . . borrow:** God's blessing on Israel would be so great that Israel would become the leader of the nations.

28:13 The phrase **the head and not the tail** indicates that Israel will rise to a place of honor among the nations.

28:14 not turn . . . to the right or the left: Since the Lord alone was the source of blessing, the Israelites had to follow Him alone in the pursuit of their happiness. They could not look in any other direction for insight.

28:15–19 if you do not obey: God's promises of the fullness of His blessing were dependent upon the obedience of His people. His curses were His reluctant—but certain—punishment for disobedience.

28:20 cursing, confusion, and rebuke: The coming of God's curse would lead to despair. **hand:** The curse would affect all human activities so that they would come to nothing (Ps. 112:10). The fruitfulness that came

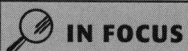 **IN FOCUS**   **"cursed"**

(Heb. *'arar*) (Deut. 27:15; 28:16; Jer. 17:5) Strong's #779: The word literally means "to bind with a curse." A curse is the opposite of a blessing. It wishes or prays for ill or injury on a person or an object. God cursed the serpent and the ground after the sin of Adam and Eve (Gen. 3:14, 17). Jeremiah, in despair, cursed the man who brought news of his birth (Jer 20:14, 15). The seriousness of God's covenant with His people is illustrated by the threat of a curse on any who violate it (Deut. 28:60, 61). In the NT, Paul taught that Jesus Christ became a "curse" for us, so that we might be freed from the curses of the Law (Gal. 3:13).

with God's overabundant blessings would disappear.

28:21, 22 Plague refers to devastations from pestilence and contagious diseases. **consumption . . . burning fever:** The diseases cannot easily be identified, but they have in common a fever or inflammation of body organs.

28:23, 24 Bronze and **iron** represent the harshness of God's wrath in withholding rain from His people (Lev. 26:19).

28:25, 26 carcasses: The idea of birds eating the flesh of the dead was particularly repugnant in ancient times. The lack of proper burial was a mark of terrible disregard for the person who had died (1 Sam. 31:11–13).

28:27, 28 boils of Egypt: The disease inflicted on the Egyptians (Ex. 9:10) would now be visited on the people of God for their disobedience. If the people obeyed God's laws, He promised to deliver them from such diseases (Ex. 15:26). **Tumors** may refer to hemorrhoids (1 Sam. 5:6, 12). **scab:** These skin diseases not only brought great distress, but also rendered a person unclean, unfit for the worship of God (Num. 5:1–4). **madness . . . confusion of heart:** These symptoms may indicate an advanced case of syphilis.

28:29–34 betroth a wife . . . build a house . . . plant a vineyard: The momentous events of life could not be enjoyed because of disasters and wars. **Your ox . . . Your sons:** Property and children alike would be taken from the people, and there would be **no strength** to recover what was lost.

28:36 Severe boils refers to skin diseases, such as Job experienced (Job 2:7).

28:37–43 The curses on the Israelites for disobedience were the direct opposite of the blessings the Israelites would receive for obedience. **an astonishment, a proverb, and a byword:** Contrast this repugnance of the Israelites with the honor promised in v. 13. **lower and lower:** Contrast this with the promise of v. 13; where the people of Israel

would once be exalted, they would now be debased.

28:44–47 The disasters would be **a sign** that would remind the people of their disobedience. **serve . . . with joy . . . for the abundance:** The expected response to God's goodness was joy and a heartfelt willingness to do His will. The absence of these responses incurred God's wrath.

28:48 Yoke of iron is an expression of servitude and enslavement.

28:49–51 The enemy **nation** is compared to a soaring eagle that swoops down on its prey (Jer. 48:40; Hos. 8:1). The enemy would show no compassion on the people whether old or **young.**

28:52–57 besiege you: Moses forewarned the people of the terrible stresses of sieges (2 Kin. 6:24–31; Lam. 2:20; 4:10). The horrors of siege, hunger, and deprivation would lead people to behave in ways that they otherwise could never imagine. **she will eat them:** Nothing could compare to the horror of a mother eating her own children.

28:58 The Hebrew words translated **glorious and awesome** together mean "overwhelmingly awesome." The **name** of the Lord inspired awe and fear because He had abundantly demonstrated His power in both Egypt and the wilderness. The phrase **THE LORD YOUR GOD** brought together God's awesome majesty and His personal care for His people.

28:59–68 The following verses are a summary of all the curses that would fall upon disobedient Israel. Many are reversals of the blessing list in vv. 1–14. Other curses are plagues that the Israelites had been spared from during the Exodus (vv. 60, 61). **back to Egypt:** This would be a tragic reversal of God's redemptive plan for Israel. God had saved the Israelites from slavery, but now God would send them back into Egyptian servitude.

29:1 The Hebrew phrase translated as **these are the words of the covenant** can be interpreted as a conclusion to the previous chapters or as an introduction to chs. 29—32. **In the land of Moab** is a reference to the beginning of Deuteronomy (1:1–5).

29:2–8 Once again, Moses reviewed the history of God's merciful acts to the people of Israel. For a more complete history read 1:30; 2:32—3:6; 4:34; 5:1; 7:18, 19; 8:2–4; 11:2–7.

29:2–5 Great trials . . . great wonders refers to the miraculous acts of God in Egypt, the wilderness, and the land east of the Jordan. Moses pointed out that God had supported the Israelites even in less dramatic ways, such as seeing that their **clothes** and **sandals** were **not worn out.**

29:6 Although the people did not eat **bread** in the wilderness, God had supplied them with bread from heaven, manna.

29:7, 8 The winning of the area east of the Jordan (2:26—3:22) was the glorious beginning of the conquest of the land. But there was still greater glory to come, the winning of the territory west of the river.

29:9–13 the words of this covenant: The members of the covenant community included all adults, children, and strangers who had joined the Israelites, as well as those yet to be born. **a people for Himself:** The central purpose of the covenant was to bind two parties, God and His people, together.

29:14, 15 not with you alone, but with: The covenant of Yahweh with Israel was not for one generation of people but for the nation through time. Thus, God's promises to Israel continue to our own day, and beyond, until the kingdom of the living Messiah is established on earth.

29:16–29 Moses warns Israel against apostasy and self-confidence and of God's judgment on all unrighteousness.

29:16, 17 for you know: Moses reminds them of the loathsome pagan practices.

29:18 Every individual **man** and **woman** was responsible to the community as a whole for his or her relationship to God. Since the entire community was covenanted to God Himself, every individual had to follow Him. **bitterness or wormwood:** Tolerance for idolatry and pagan practices would always corrupt the community, and therefore the covenant relationship with God.

29:19 he blesses himself: The self-absorbed person would consider himself worthy of the blessings of God; the righteous person would live by God's grace and gratefully obey His commands.

29:20, 21 For the memory of a person's **name** to be lost was considered a terrible fate in the ancient Middle Eastern culture. For God to record and remember their names was a glorious hope for the ancient Israelites (Ps. 87).

29:22, 23 God's judgments on a disobedient Israel would be a sign of His holiness for the future **generation** and for other nations. **Brimstone, salt, and burning** are images reminiscent of God's judgment of Sodom and Gomorrah (Gen. 19:24–29), with which **Admah and Zeboiim** were also destroyed (Gen. 10:19; 14:2, 8; Hos. 11:8).

29:24–27 The lesson of the faithless Israel would become known among the **nations,** even as the deliverance of Israel was to be known by them (2:25). The nations were supposed to learn about God's grace from Israel's example; what a shame if they were to learn of His wrath instead!

29:28 This day refers to the day of God's judgment on His people.

29:29 The secret things refers to the future, as well as the way in which the curses would come to pass. The will of God had been **revealed** in the Law. If these revelations were acted upon, the people would receive God's great blessing. To ignore the express commandments of God would be folly. Similarly, the Christian has God's revealed will in the Bible. To ignore that while chasing after the things God has left secret is pure folly.

30:1–20 Choose life or death, blessing or curse, God or self. In this last address, Moses challenges the people with a prophetic perspective on Israel's nature (rebelliousness), God's compassion and new act of grace, and Israel's responsibility.

30:1 When all these things come upon you refers to the blessings and curses detailed in ch. 28, particularly the curses. God allowed Moses to foresee Israel's future apostasy and God's dispersal of the people among the nations. These words should have been terribly upsetting to the people because they were spoken on the eve of their conquest of the land.

30:2–6 Not only did Moses foresee the future apostasy and **captivity** of Israel, he also saw Israel's future repentance and **return** to the land (Ezra). This passage could also await a future fulfillment.

30:6 circumcise your heart: God Himself would work in the hearts of His people so that they would love Him (10:16). God would extend the benefits of His work to the **descendants** of these people. He would create a community of faith that would worship Him from generation to generation. **all your heart and . . . soul:** God's intentions for His people have always been for the whole person to respond to Him. Outward symbols such as circumcision were always intended by God to be marks of inner realities.

30:7 God did not abandon His principle of reward and punishment for the nations (and for the individuals) based on their treatment of His covenant people (compare Gen. 12:3; 2 Thess. 1:5–10). He would repay Israel's **enemies.**

30:8, 9 The OT tends to focus on the disobedience of God's people to His revelation. But there were periods of national faithfulness to God, and there were always individuals who were faithful.

30:10 This Book of the Law is the Book of Deuteronomy (31:24, 26). God's blessing would come to those who obeyed the Law.

30:11–14 Mysterious means "difficult." Moses reminded the Israelites that obedience to God was not a complicated issue. **not in heaven . . . Nor is it beyond the sea:** Obedience to the Law did not require a superhuman effort, because God had revealed the Law to the Israelites (Rom. 10:6–10). **the word is very near you:** When God's Law was internalized by the working of the Holy Spirit, the believer loved God's instructions and sought to carry them out (Ps. 119:97–104). The believer would obey God's Law in response to God's love, not as a way of earning God's love or of deserving His forgiveness.

30:15–17 Moses challenged the people to determine what path they would follow. One way led to **life** (Ps. 1:6; John 14:6) because God's blessings rested on it (Ps. 23:6). The other way led to **death and evil** because God's curses rested on it. Likewise, Jesus in His ministry challenged the people to determine what path they would take (Matt. 7:13, 14).

30:18 The emphasis on **today** is remarkable in this passage. Moses establishes here the best pattern for the preaching of the Word of God. Responses to God should not be delayed. Assuming that there will be a later day to respond to Him is dangerous thinking.

30:19 heaven and earth as witnesses: All of creation witnessed Moses' instruction, his challenge to the Israelites to love and obey God, and the people's response (32:1). **choose . . . that both you and your descendants may live:** The present generation's choice would determine the direction of future generations.

30:20 If the people loved God they would find true **life,** because God is the source of all life. By rejecting God and His ways, the Israelites would by default choose the way of death. The people were on the verge of entering **the land** that had been promised them for so long. Before they made their way across the Jordan to begin their holy campaign of conquest, they needed to know what the stakes were and what was necessary not just to enter the land, but to remain in the land with God's enduring blessing.

31:1–3 Again Moses regretfully spoke of God's refusal to permit him to enter the Promised Land (1:37, 38; 3:23–29). Yet he

encouraged the people that **God Himself** would still protect them and fight for them. Instead of Moses, **Joshua** would lead the people into battle.

31:4–6 The Lord was the Divine Warrior, the commander-in-chief of Israel's forces. **He will not leave you nor forsake you:** Moses reminded the people that God had promised to remain with them, to protect them, bless them, and fight for them (Josh. 1:5; 1 Kin. 8:57). Joshua used the same language to assure the people of the continuity of God's Presence and of godly leadership (Josh. 1:6, 7, 9). Jesus made the same promise to His church (Matt. 28:20).

31:7, 8 With encouraging and challenging words, Moses publicly transferred his authority to **Joshua** (1:38; 31:14, 23; 32:44; 34:9). **He is the One who goes before you:** Moses applied the promise given to Israel (v. 6) to Joshua.

31:9 Moses wrote this law and delivered it: In accordance with ancient Middle Eastern practices concerning international treaties, Moses made provisions for the future reading of the Law and instruction in it. The ark

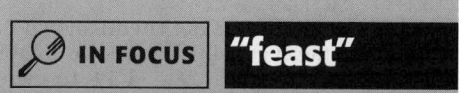

IN FOCUS "feast"

(Heb. *chag*) (Deut. 16:10, 13; 31:10; Ex. 12:14). Strong's #2282: The word *feast,* or "festival-gathering," is related to the verb that means "to make a pilgrimage" or "to keep a pilgrim feast" (Ps. 84:5). The Hebrews were commanded to observe three pilgrim feasts a year (16:16; Ex. 23:14). These sacred feasts were celebrated by all people and were joyous expressions of gratitude to God (2 Chr. 30:21). They included processions, dancing, and the enjoyment of food and drink (Lev. 23:40, 41; Judg. 21:19–21). God intended that Israel's religious feasts be worship events, a celebration of the joy God had given them (Lev. 23:7, 21, 24, 36). The OT prophets, however, condemned the feasts because the Hebrews were desecrating these holy convocations with sacrilegious behavior (Is. 1:12–15; Amos 5:21). Zechariah prophesied of a time in the future when all nations would keep the "pilgrim-feast" before the Lord (Zech. 14:16).

was called **the ark of the covenant** because it was the depository for the tablets of the Law.

31:10–13 you shall read this law: Specifically, the priests were given the responsibility of reading the Law and instructing the people (Neh. 8:1–6; Mal. 2:4–9). **men and women**

and little ones, and the stranger: The Word of God was for all to hear.

31:14 The words **the days approach** must have brought a renewed heaviness to Moses. He was ready to die, but his heart yearned to see the Promised Land. **I may inaugurate him:** The Lord's words to Joshua are recorded in v. 23 (compare Num. 27:18–23).

31:15 **The pillar of cloud** was the symbol of the presence of God during the wilderness journey (Ex. 13:21, 22).

31:16 The phrase **rest with your fathers** suggests that the body of the person would be laid to rest in a tomb. After the flesh had decayed, the bones would be placed with the bones of one's ancestors. Thus, the person's remains were "with his fathers." But the phrase may also refer to the intermediate state of the soul between death and resurrection. The Lord predicted Israel's future rebelliousness, apostasy, and breach of the **covenant.** The expression **play the harlot** speaks both of spiritual adultery and physical acts of sexual immorality that were performed in association with the worship of Baal and Asherah, the gods of Canaan (12:1–5).

31:17, 18 **I will forsake them:** Should the worst occur, the anger of God would be aroused as was described in chs. 28 and 29. **to other gods:** The principal reason for God's judgment on His people was their continual idolatry. They abandoned His grace and willingly embraced the evil religious practices of the Canaanites.

31:19–21 **This song** is the Song of Moses recorded in 31:30—32:43. God commanded Moses and Joshua to **teach** this song to the Israelites.

31:22 **Moses wrote . . . and taught it:** These words create an anticipation of v. 30. Psalm 90 is attributed to Moses as well.

31:23 **Be strong and of good courage:** God encouraged Joshua with the same words that Moses used to encourage the people (v. 6). **I will be with you:** God assured Joshua of His presence during the conquest (Josh. 1:5; Hag. 2:4).

31:24, 25 **when Moses had completed writing:** These words continue the subject of v 9. Those who deny that Moses wrote the Torah do so in the face of verses such as this (vv. 9, 22).

31:26–28 **This Book of the Law** is the Book of Deuteronomy. This book would be a witness against Israel when they turned from the living God to worship other gods. Then the book that originally had been a book of God's loving instructions to His people would unfortunately become a charter of His wrath.

31:29, 30 **For I know:** It is unclear whether Moses' words here were based on his own experience with the people or on a revelation from the Lord. Perhaps both were at work.

32:1 **O heavens . . . O earth:** Isaiah similarly called on heaven and earth to witness (Is. 1:2).

32:2 **my teaching:** The song is an expression of wisdom (Prov. 1:5; 4:2; 9:9). **rain . . . dew . . . raindrops . . . showers:** These four similes express the refreshing and invigorating nature of the instruction.

32:3 **Ascribe greatness to our God:** True wisdom and obedience always lead to the praise of God (Pss. 145:3; 150:2).

32:4 Unlike the powerless gods of the nations (v. 37), God gives life, stability, and happiness to His people (vv. 15, 18, 30, 31). The joyful life that He gives is based on His **perfect** works. Like a firm **Rock** that stands against the raging waters of a stormy sea, God and His works stand firm against the chaos produced by sinful lives. He is the sure foundation for all **truth** in a world of deception. Thus He will never let lies pervert justice (Zeph. 3:5). Instead, as a **righteous** Judge, He will protect those who have been oppressed. Right before the Israelites entered the land of Canaan in order to establish a new nation, Moses extolled the God who is the perfect foundation for any society.

32:5 **perverse and crooked generation:** Moses contrasted the Israelites with their faithful God. Compared to the perfect God of truth, they were corrupt, blemished, and deceptive (v. 20).

32:6 The ancient Israelites knew God was their **Father** (Is. 63:16; 64:8), but they rarely confessed this great truth. Thus these words are unusually striking because they express the Israelites' close relationship with God while at the same time castigating the people for abandoning their Father. God had chosen them, loved them, and cared for them. He had brought them out of Egypt and had even **established** them as a nation by giving them detailed instructions.

32:7 **Remember . . . they will tell you:** Here the song uses the language of wisdom literature to exhort the Israelites to search out God's ways. The Scriptures repeatedly emphasize that wisdom is based on the God of all truth.

32:8, 9 **Most High:** This designation for God's supremacy is unique to Deuteronomy. He is the sovereign God over all, even the **boundaries** of the nations. **the LORD's portion:** While it is the Lord's will for many nations to exist, He has favored Israel with His special grace, promises, and covenant.

32:10 **In a desert land** is a poetic reference to Egypt. **He instructed him:** God gave Israel His revelation and His laws in order to lead them in all truth. **Kept him as the apple** (or pupil) **of His eye** is a symbol of tender loving care for a precious object in need of protection.

32:11 The **eagle** is a bird of prey commonly found in desert regions. The song compares God's actions towards Israel with the care a mother bird showers on her young. God not only protected His children, He provided for them, got them moving, watched over them, and guided them to the Promised Land (Ex. 19:4). In all these actions He proved Himself to be a loving Father to the Israelites (v. 6).

32:12 the LORD alone . . . no foreign god: Deuteronomy is an extended argument against idolatry and paganism. Clearly the Israelites had no reason to abandon the God of grace and love who had given them all they needed.

32:13, 14 He made him ride in the heights of the earth: The Lord had great plans for His people (Is. 48:17–19). **produce . . . honey . . . oil:** The Lord had promised to supply His people with crops, rich food, olive oil, and even dairy products in the Promised Land, all of which the people lacked in the wilderness. **wheat . . . the blood of the grapes:** Grain and wine were also promised, symbols of God's mercy.

32:15, 16 Jeshurun, a pet name for Israel, means "Uprightness." This part of the song contrasts what Israel should have been and what they became. Since the nation had received God's revelation and His instruction, it should have become upright (v. 4). Instead, the nation would grow fat and rebel. **scornfully esteemed the Rock of his salvation:** Even though the Israelites would grow rich off God's blessing, they would reject the source not only of those blessings, but also of their salvation. Instead, they would embrace **foreign gods** that had done nothing for Israel (v. 12).

32:17 Rarely in the OT (Ps. 106:37; Amos 2:1) are references made to **demons** and demonic powers. Although the Scriptures make it clear that the false gods do not exist as such, this passage identifies the power behind these gods: demons.

32:18, 19 Fathered literally means "gave birth." This is one of several places where God is portrayed in terms that liken His role to that of a nurturing, life-giving mother (compare Is. 66:13).

32:20, 21 I will see what their end will be: Even though Israel would reject Him, God would be patient with His rebellious children.

> *God not only protected His children, He provided for them, got them moving, watched over them, and guided them to the Promised Land.*

32:22, 23 The expression **lowest hell** combines the word "Sheol" with a term meaning "lowest," suggesting gradations in perdition, even as there may be gradations in glory ("the third heaven," 2 Cor. 12:2).

32:24 hunger . . . pestilence . . . destruction: Instead of blessing His chosen people, God would send curses on them in order to discipline them. **teeth of beasts . . . poison of serpents:** Creation would also turn against the people.

32:25, 26 young man . . . virgin: The pairings of opposites in this verse indicate that God's judgment would be comprehensive. It would affect all of society. Similar pairings in Joel 2:28, 29 speak of the comprehensiveness of God's blessing.

32:27 Had I not feared: God will not completely destroy His people, lest the arrogant and autonomous nations boast in their prowess and abilities.

32:28 This verse anticipates God's judgment of Israel and Judah in the days of Isaiah (Is. 1:3; 6:9, 10).

32:29, 30 Often the phrase **latter end** is understood as "glorious future"; here it speaks of "ruinous future" for the rebellious Israelites. **Unless their Rock had sold them:** God's protection of His people was so certain that their conquest by enemies could occur only if it were He who gave them over.

32:31–33 The enemy nations were like the people of **Sodom** and **Gomorrah**—cruel, immoral, and oppressive.

32:34–36 laid up in store . . . Sealed: God's sure plan and purposes are hidden. **Vengeance is Mine . . . judge His people:** Only the God who is completely just can judge and make right all the wrongs committed (Rom. 12:19; Heb. 10:30). There will be a time for God's vindication. **compassion on His servants:** God would discern one day between the righteous and the wicked (Mal. 3:16). He would deal kindly with the remnant that loved and followed Him. This is the basis for all of the prophetic messages about the remnant of Israel.

32:37, 38 Where are their gods: The song mocks those who follow false gods. They abandoned the Rock of truth for a **rock** that was not even a pebble. When the **fat** was burned and the **wine** was poured out on the altars of the false gods, the gods were believed to eat and drink these offerings. Yet these gods did not even exist, so they neither **ate** nor **drank**.

32:39 I, even I, am He is a glorious affirmation of the incomparability of God (Ps. 113:4–6). God alone controls human existence. Because He is totally free to do what He wants, only He can either curse or bless, wound or heal, kill or give life.

32:40–42 I raise My hand to heaven: God made an oath to Himself that He would avenge His people (Gen. 22:16; Heb. 6:13–18). He would make right all wrongs.

32:43–45 Rejoice, O Gentiles, with His people: God in this song given to Moses invited all nations to join in the worship of the living God, to praise Him for promising to restore justice.

32:46 Law here may signify the Song of Moses or Deuteronomy as a whole (compare 31:26).

32:47 prolong your days: The intention of God's instruction was to show the Israelites the path that leads to fullness of life and rich blessing.

32:48–33:29 As Moses is about to die, the aged patriarch leaves a blessing for the tribes, framed by a testimony to God's kingship. The blessing particularly extends to Levi and to Joseph. The tribe of Judah gained prominence at a later time, after the tribe of Joseph

(Ephraim and Manasseh) had in the period of the Judges failed God time and again. Then He chose Judah and rejected Joseph (Ps. 78:67, 68).

32:48, 49 Mount Nebo is a mountain peak near Heshbon about ten miles east of the northern end of the Dead Sea.

32:50–52 you did not hallow Me: Moses did not completely obey God's instructions at Kadesh. Because of this, Moses could not enter the Promised Land (1:37; 3:23–26; 4:21, 22; 31:2; Num. 20:10–13). Yet God would graciously allow Moses to **see the land** (34:1–8).

33:1 Moses is to be remembered for his faithfulness in spite of his failure (Heb. 3:1–6). Scriptures describe him as a servant of God (Num. 12:6–8), a friend of God (Ex. 33:11), and a **man of God.**

33:2 came from . . . dawned . . . shone forth: These verbs reminded the Israelites of the awe-inspiring revelation of God in all of His glory. God came down to Israel and revealed His covenant and Law to them at Mt. **Sinai.** Poetically, Moses referred to **Seir** and **Paran**, located northeast of Mt. Sinai. With these references, Moses implied that God's revelation took place throughout the whole wilderness journey (Judg. 5:4, 5). **ten thousands of saints:** Angelic beings attended the

 **IN COMPARISON**   **The Gods of the Canaanites**

The Lord declared that "there is no God besides Me" (Deut. 32:39), a claim repeatedly made elsewhere in Scripture (Ex. 8:10; Deut. 4:35; 6:4; Mark 12:32). Yet the Hebrews were unique among the peoples of the ancient world in preserving their belief in one God (with certain lapses). Nearly all the other peoples believed in numerous gods.

The Canaanites, whom Israel was to dispossess, worshiped more than seventy deities. The ones shown below were the principal ones.

El	Highest of the gods, but remained in the background; conferred power and authority on lesser gods.
Baal	Name means "master," "possessor," or "husband"; a god over nature; often designated Hadad, the storm god; but also a name for other local gods such as Baal-Berith ("lord of the covenant," Judg. 8:33) and Baal of Peor (Num. 25:3).
Dagon	Exact nature unknown, but important to the Philistines (1 Sam. 5), who paraded blind, chained Samson in one of their temples to Dagon (Judg. 16:21–24).
Asherah	Wife of El (and sometimes of Baal) and mother to the other gods; goddess of the sea; often a favorite deity of women (probably Jezebel, 1 Kin. 18:19); often depicted by a wooden pole or cult pillar (1 Kin. 15:13).
Astarte or Ashtoreth	A goddess of the moon, sexuality, and fertility; sometimes worshiped as an idol by the Hebrews (Judg. 2:13; 1 Sam. 7:3, 4; 1 Kin. 11:5).
Anath	Baal's mistress; goddess of war, love, and fertility; may be the "queen of heaven" to whom Jews offered incense in Jeremiah's day (Jer. 7:18).

giving of the Law (compare Acts 7:53; Gal. 3:19; Heb. 2:2).

33:3 Saints could refer to Israel. It is also possible that the words beginning in the second line of v. 3 and concluding in v. 5 are Israel's response to Moses' opening words. If so, the Israelites confess that angelic beings were attending to Moses while he received the Law of God and instructed Israel in that revelation. This explains the reference to Moses and the use of the first person plural ("for us," v. 4).

33:4, 5 heritage: What made Israel unique was its reception of the Law of God mediated through Moses. God had chosen Israel alone to receive His instructions. The Lord alone was the **King** over His people. At the same time, He as the Creator ruled over all He had made.

33:6 Let Reuben live . . . men be few: Moses predicted that the Reubenites would have a future, but not a glorious one. Settled east of the Dead Sea, the Reubenites would eventually isolate themselves from the other tribes (Judg. 5:15, 16).

33:7 Moses prayed that **the Lord** would be present with **Judah** in its military leadership and would give it success in battle. **hands be sufficient:** Moses prayed that God would give adequate strength to the tribe.

33:8, 9 Moses prayed for God's guidance to rest on the Levites, who were responsible for judging cases. The **Urim** and **Thummim** (Ex. 28:30) were God's appointed instruments for deciding innocence or guilt and for guiding His people. **holy one:** A term for the Levites, who were separated from the other tribes to serve in the tabernacle. **Massah . . . Meribah:** The Levites passed the test when the other tribes failed to believe in the Lord's ability to provide and care for His people (6:16; 9:22). Moses commended the Levites for their loyalty to God's **word** and **covenant.**

33:10, 11 teach: The Levites were charged with the responsibility of instructing the Israelites. They had modeled loyalty (v. 9). Now they had to help Israel understand how to live by God's revelation. In this way, they continued the ministry of Moses. **incense:** The Levites were also responsible for the worship of God at the tabernacle (Ex. 30:7).

33:12–16 As the beloved son of Jacob, Benjamin was also **the beloved of the Lord** (Gen. 44:20). The Lord would give the tribe of Benjamin peace and **safety. shelters . . . dwell between His shoulders:** The Lord would provide Benjamin with His personal protection.

33:17, 18 glory . . . horns: God would give Ephraim and Manasseh prowess in battle and victory in warfare. Like oxen, these two tribes would **push** their enemies away from them. **ten thousands of Ephraim . . . thousands of**

Manasseh: In keeping with Jacob's blessing of Joseph's younger son Ephraim, Moses exalted him above Manasseh (Gen. 48:8–20).

33:19 The tribe of Zebulun would be located by the **seas.** The seas and their shores were God's appointed place for the tribe's prosperity.

33:20, 21 Moses compared Gad's military role to the power of a ravenous **lion** and predicted that this tribe would readily join the others in the conquest of Canaan (Josh. 22:1–6).

33:22 Lion's whelp may refer to the small size of the tribe of Dan. Though Dan's land inheritance was close to Judah by the coastal plains, the tribe would not be able keep their inheritance because of the hostility of the Philistines. Therefore, the Danites would one day migrate to the region of the **Bashan,** south of Mount Hermon (Judg. 18).

33:23 Moses' **blessing** on Naphtali indicates that this tribe would enjoy God's blessings of abundance. The tribe would inherit the land **west** and **south** of the Sea of Galilee.

33:24, 25 Dip his foot in oil is an image of God's rich blessing to Asher (Ps. 133:2). **Your sandals shall be iron and bronze:** Others read "your bolts shall be iron and bronze," referring to the mighty fortresses. (For Jacob's blessing, read Gen. 49:20). For reasons unknown to us, there is no blessing for the tribe of Simeon, as the text now stands (but compare the blessing of Jacob on Simeon, Gen. 49:5–7). Simeon seems to be absorbed early into the tribe of Judah in the time of the kings of Israel.

33:26, 27 There is no one like: This negative phrase is a Hebraic way of expressing a strong positive: "The God of Jeshurun alone will help." **rides the heavens . . . the clouds:** Like a soldier, the Lord is constantly on the lookout for ways to defend His people from attack. The Divine Warrior is always providing protection because He is **eternal.** God is a **refuge** or fortress for the people to flee to in times of distress (Ps. 90:1; 91:9). **everlasting arms:** The God who redeemed Israel with His strong arm will always be with His people in love and power.

33:28 Then Israel will dwell in safety: Moses affirmed the truth of the promise God gave through the pagan prophet Balaam (Num. 23:9).

33:29 Who is like you: The question is actually a declaration: "There is no people like you." **shield . . . sword:** These military images point to God, the source of all human protection. He would fight Israel's battles. **tread down their high places:** God would break down with His own feet the places of idolatrous worship, the pagan sites that defiled the nations (Mic. 1:3).

34:1 Moab was where Moses had given Israel an explanation of the Law (1:5) and had led them in a covenant renewal ceremony (29:1–28). **Jericho** was the first city in Canaan to be conquered. **And the LORD** showed him: Though he was still in Moab, Moses was granted

Photo by Ben Chapman

Michelangelo's statue of Moses, great lawgiver and leader of the Hebrew people. Moses died in the land of Moab before the Israelites entered the Promised Land (Deut. 34:1–8).

by God a close-up view of the land. How sad that his feet were not able to walk where his eyes danced! **Dan** was the territory below Mt. Hermon that was later conquered by the tribe of Dan (Judg. 18).

34:2 Judah refers to the highlands west of

Jericho and of the Dead Sea. The **Western Sea** is the Mediterranean.

34:3, 4 South refers to the Negev, the dry county south of Judah. **The plain** is the region around the Dead Sea, from the valley of Jericho to **Zoar,** the city in the southern plain where Lot escaped with his daughters (Gen. 19:22). **I swore:** God had promised this territory to Abraham long ago (Gen. 15:18–21; 17:1–8; Ex. 33:1).

34:5 Moses remained God's faithful **servant.** A servant of God is a person who has a close and trusted relationship with God, such as Abraham (Gen. 26:24) and David (2 Sam. 7:5).

34:6, 7 no one knows his grave: God took care of Moses' funeral. If his burial place had been known, some people most likely would have made it a shrine and begun to worship there. God graciously concealed the burial site of Moses. **not dim . . . diminished:** Moses died because it was God's will and not because of normal physical deterioration associated with old age (31:2).

34:8 Thirty days was the customary period of mourning. Though Moses was buried alone, he was not forgotten by his people.

34:9 Joshua was recognized for his **wisdom** as he followed the call of the Lord in his life.

34:10–12 a prophet like Moses: As important as Joshua was, he should not be confused with the One who would fulfill God's promise of a prophet who would have an even greater status than Moses (18:15). **Face to face** describes the unusual intimacy between Moses and the Lord (Ex. 33:11; Num. 12). Like Moses, Jesus of Nazareth performed **signs and wonders** when He began His ministry on earth (Matt. 4:23–25; John 5:46). **Moses performed:** The miraculous works accomplished by God were works through Moses' hand. In these engaging words of testimony to the significance of Moses as the servant of God, Deuteronomy comes to its grand conclusion.

The Book of

Joshua

HE BOOK OF JOSHUA DESCRIBES THE ISRAELITES' conquest of Canaan, from the initial invasion across the Jordan River to the final division of the land. Like most military histories, the Book of Joshua focuses on the commander. Yet for this unique war, the commander was God Himself (5:15). The book repeatedly emphasizes that the Israelites' victories were due to God's intervention (chs. 10; 11). The extraordinary victory

over Jericho dramatically demonstrated this (ch. 6). Now God was decisively acting on the promises that He had made to Abraham: He was giving the land of Canaan to His people! The Book of Joshua describes a God who faithfully fulfills His promises.

The events in Joshua occurred within a time span of less than a decade, forty years after the Exodus, probably around 1406 B.C. Caleb stated (14:7–10) that it had been forty-five years since he had been sent out from Kadesh Barnea to spy out the land (Num. 13). Since the Israelites spent thirty-eight years wandering in the wilderness (Deut. 2:14), the time from when they crossed the Jordan River till the time of Caleb's speech was seven years. Most of the events in the book probably occurred within that period.

Many scholars have suggested that the conquest of Canaan took place between 1250 and 1150 B.C. because there is archaeological evidence of the destruction of Canaanite cities around that time. However, there are problems with this view, the most significant of which is that the Israelites destroyed only three cities—

Jericho, Ai, and Hazor—during their conquest. God had promised that they would live in cities they had not built, enjoy fields they had not planted, and harvest fruit they had not tended (Deut. 6:10, 11). Therefore, the Israelites fought most of their battles in the fields outside the cities. The widespread destruction of Canaanite cities found by archaeologists may date to the time of the judges. During this period, God allowed many foreign invasions to devastate the countryside and the cities in order to discipline His rebellious people.

Brief summaries contained in Joshua often give the impression that the campaign of conquest was one in which the Israelites overwhelmed the Canaanites with a superior force, inflicting a series of total defeats. Chapter 10 is an example. But the Book of Joshua as a whole does not describe Israel as winning a frontal offensive attack by means of a superior force. Rather, under God's direction, Israel used various means such as ambushes and diversionary tactics to defeat its enemies. Furthermore, Joshua 16:10 and Judges 1 suggest that Israel's victory over the Canaanites was incomplete.

There were Canaanites still living in the land. Nevertheless, God did give the greater part of the land of Canaan into the Israelites' hands through a series of dramatic battles in a relatively short period of time. God was faithful to His promises.

The two most prominent themes in Joshua are the possession of the land and the covenant. God had repeatedly promised the land of Canaan to Abraham (Gen. 12:7; 13:14, 15, 17; 15:18–21; 17:8; 22:17), to Isaac (Gen. 26:3, 4), to Jacob (Gen. 28:4, 13; 35:12), and to the succeeding generations (Gen. 48:4–22; 50:24). The Book of Joshua emphasizes that the conquest of Canaan was a direct fulfillment of that promise. God was fighting for the Israelites and giving them the land in the process. Since God was demonstrating His faithfulness to Israel, He expected Israel to be faithful to His covenant with them. Possessing the land was based on their obedience to His Law (23:9–13, 15, 16; Deut. 4:1, 25–27, 40; 6:17, 18). In fact, the Book of Joshua portrays the complete possession of the land as the result of Joshua's obedience to God's commands (10:40; 11:20, 23; 23:9–13).

Conquering the land enabled Israel to experience God's *rest*, which He had promised to the Israelites from the beginning (1:13, 15; 11:23; 14:15; 21:44; 22:4; 23:1). "The LORD gave them rest all around, according to all that He had sworn to their fathers" (21:44). The author of Hebrews equates this Old Testament concept of rest with entering into Christ's rest, that is, His kingdom (Heb. 3; 4).

In addition to emphasizing the importance of faithfulness to the covenant (1:7, 8; 22:5; 23:6, 16; 24:15), Joshua records two ceremonies dedicated to the renewal of the covenant. The first was at Mount Ebal. There Joshua built an altar to the Lord, offered sacrifices, and copied and read the Law of Moses (8:30–35). The second was at Shechem (ch. 24), where Joshua wrote the words of Israel's covenant renewal in "the Book of the Law of God" and erected a large stone as a witness and memorial to the agreement (24:25–27). Both ceremonies impressed on the people's minds and hearts their responsibility to follow God alone and to keep His instructions. At the end of the conquest, the Israelites had a new challenge before them. The intensity of the battle was gone. Now the Israelites had to demonstrate their faithfulness to God in the ordinary activities of everyday life.

This book is named for the man who figures most prominently in it, Moses' successor and Israel's leader during the conquest of Canaan. Appropriately, Joshua's name in Hebrew means "The Lord Saves" or "May the Lord Save."

The Book of Joshua does not state who wrote it. Joshua himself undoubtedly wrote portions of the book, since 24:26 states, "Then Joshua wrote these words in the Book of the Law of God." But it is uncertain how much of the rest of the book he wrote. As for the date of composition, 6:25 reports that Rahab was living in Israel "to this day." This may indicate that portions of the book (if not all of it) were written shortly after the events recorded. But it could also mean that Rahab's descendants were still living in Israel at the time of writing.

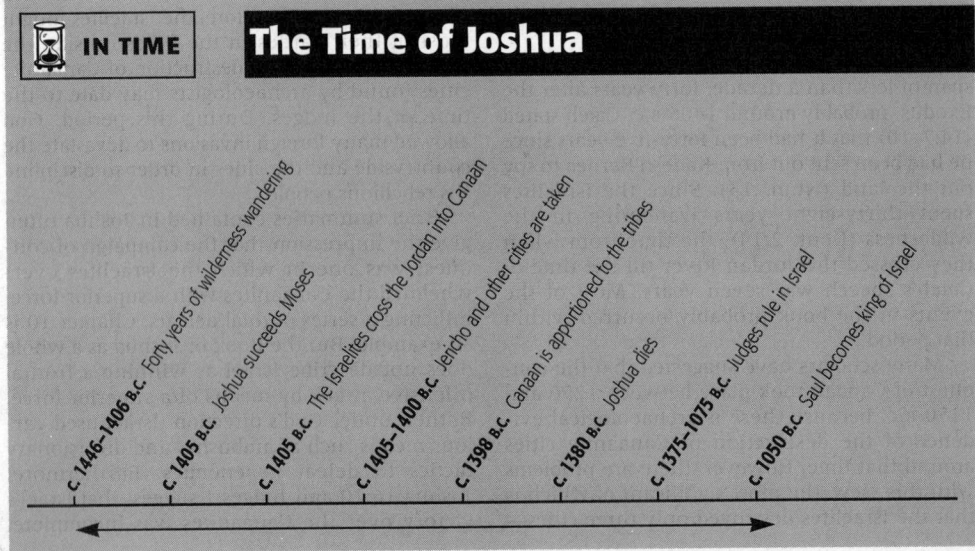

IN TIME **The Time of Joshua**

c. 1446–1406 B.C. Forty years of wilderness wandering

c. 1405 B.C. Joshua succeeds Moses

c. 1405 B.C. The Israelites cross the Jordan into Canaan

c. 1405–1400 B.C. Jericho and other cities are taken

c. 1398 B.C. Canaan is apportioned to the tribes

c. 1380 B.C. Joshua dies

c. 1375–1075 B.C. Judges rule in Israel

c. 1050 B.C. Saul becomes king of Israel

Outline

Commentary

1:1 Joshua begins where Deuteronomy ends, **after the death of Moses.** Moses is the central figure in the narrative spanning Exodus through Deuteronomy. He is called the **servant of the** LORD, a title that was first given to him at the end of his life (Deut. 34:5). In Joshua, Moses is called by this title fifteen times. In the Hebrew Scriptures it is a special title given only to Moses, Joshua (24:29; Judg. 2:8), David (Pss. 18:1; 36:1), and the Messiah (Is. 42:19). **Joshua the son of Nun:** Identifying someone by adding the name of his father was the Hebrew equivalent of a last name. Joshua was **Moses' assistant** (Ex. 24:13; Num. 11:28). The Hebrew word used for *assistant* usually refers to service in worship, but it can also mean service to an individual, as it does here (1 Kin. 19:21 for Elijah's assistant). Joshua is not identified as the "servant of the Lord" here, probably to show that he had not yet "filled Moses' shoes." He needed to grow into the job. Yet Deut. 34:9 hints that Joshua would do just that: "Now Joshua the son of Nun was full of the spirit of wisdom, for Moses had laid his hands on him; so the children of Israel heeded him, and did as the LORD had commanded Moses."

1:2–9 God's speech encouraging Joshua is a warmhearted, tender speech, assuring Joshua of His care, protection, and presence, and urging him to obey His Law. It is a model of God graciously encouraging His servants, and its exhortations are still of value today; true success in life cannot occur apart from knowing and doing the will of God.

1:2 the land which I am giving: The land of Canaan had first been promised to Abraham hundreds of years before (Gen. 12:7; 13:14, 15, 17; 15:18–21; 17:8; 22:17). Even though God would allow Abraham's descendants to be slaves in a foreign land (Gen. 15:13), He nevertheless promised to bring them back to their own land (Gen. 15:16). This promise was never rescinded. In fact, it was repeated many times (Ex. 6:4, 8; Deut. 1:6–8; 4:38, 40; 5:31; 7:13; 8:1–10; 9:4–6; 11:8–12, 17; 26:1, 9; 32:49, 52; 34:4).

1:3 You here is plural, referring to all Israel. Sometimes (as in v. 2), the land is pictured as in the process of being given to Israel ("I am giving to them"). In other places, as here, it is pictured as already having been given. This manner of speaking reflects the notion that Israel already had legal title to the land, even if the people had not yet actually taken possession of it. This is also the language of Gen. 15:18. **as I said to Moses:** God keeps His promises.

1:4 This description of the land gives its southern and northern extremities, and its western border; the eastern border is not mentioned, probably because it extended to where Joshua was standing on the plains of Moab, east of the Jordan River. The land of Canaan here is designated by one of its prominent ethnic groups, **the Hittites** (Deut. 7:1). A great Hittite kingdom in Asia Minor (modern Turkey), dating to around 1800–1200 B.C., has been identified. The relationship between the Hittites in Canaan and the ones in Asia Minor is unclear. **The Great Sea** is the Mediterranean Sea.

1:5 God's great promise to Moses **I will be with you** (Ex. 3:12) is now given to Joshua (1:9; 3:7). Of special comfort to Joshua would have been the fact that God would be with him in the same way He had been with Moses. Joshua had been present during the many demonstrations of God's presence in Moses' life and would have known how significant this promise was.

1:6 The command to **be strong and of good courage** was for Joshua's encouragement, and God repeated these words three times (vv. 6, 7, 9). The people later affirmed Joshua using these precise words (v. 18). David would later encourage his son Solomon with these words (1 Chr. 22:13; 28:20). **you shall divide:** This is the first notation of what Joshua's actual duties would be, that of giving the land to Israel on God's behalf.

1:7 very courageous: The instructions to Joshua here do not address military matters at all. This might seem surprising given the battles ahead. But his success depended more on his spiritual state and his degree of obedience to God than on any military strategy. The spiritual demands preceded the martial ones. **the law which Moses . . . commanded you:** Some scholars have questioned whether Moses gave the Law to Israel, arguing that the laws found in the Pentateuch come from a much later time. This passage, along with many others (Josh. 8:31–35; Deut. 31:24–26), states that Moses did indeed give the Law to Israel. The term translated **prosper** means much more than mere financial success. It includes spiritual well-being.

1:8, 9 To **meditate** means much more than just contemplation. The idea here is that one should reflect upon God's Word in a thoughtful way, appropriating its truths personally and applying them to life (Ps. 1:2, 3).

1:10 The **officers** were officials who helped

in the organization of Israel's affairs. The Egyptian pharaoh had appointed similar officials over Israel (Ex. 5:14, 15).

1:11 Provisions referred to the food needed for the next several days as the Israelites prepared themselves to cross the Jordan. **within three days:** During these three days, the Israelites prepared themselves to enter the land. These were the same three days that the spies hid in the hills outside of Jericho (mentioned in 2:16, 22). After the spies returned, the Israelites waited another three days before crossing the Jordan (3:2).

1:12–15 Joshua reminded the two and one half-tribes that were settling east of the Jordan that they had promised to fight with the rest of the Israelites for the land across the river. Here Joshua quotes Moses' words to these tribes almost verbatim (compare vv. 13–15 with Deut. 3:18–20). A change in v. 14, from Deuteronomy's "cities" to Joshua's "land," serves to highlight Joshua's special interest in the land. These tribes were granted the right to settle east of Jordan if they maintained covenant solidarity with their brethren by fighting beside them (Num. 32:1–42; Deut. 2:26—3:20). The account in Joshua indicates that they kept their promise. In fact, at the end of the book Joshua blesses them for their faithfulness in this matter (22:1–9). The story recounted in 22:10–34 illustrates their good faith in this matter.

1:13, 15 The promise of **rest** echoes Num. 32:20–22; Deut. 3:18–20. Read about the promises of rest in Ex. 33:14; Deut. 12:9, 10. This rest was God's gift to Israel. In Joshua, it primarily means rest from conflict with enemies. Other accounts in Joshua make mention of Israel or the land having rest (11:23; 14:15; 21:44; 22:4; 23:1).

1:14, 15 The Hebrew word for **armed** is related to the numbers five and fifty; it probably means "lined up in battle array in groups of fifty." **Mighty men of valor** were the elite of the military. Joshua chose 30,000 of these men to lie in ambush against Ai (8:3) and also took

 **IN FOCUS** "meditate"

(Heb. *hagah*) (Josh. 1:8; Ps 1:2; 77:12) Strong's #1897: The Hebrew verb for *meditate* conveys a variety of meanings in the OT. For example, it may refer to the "growl" of an animal (Is. 31:4) or the "moan" of a person in distress (Is. 59:11). It may also refer to "speaking" (Job 27:4), "muttering" (Is. 59:3), "planning deception" (Ps. 38:12), "studying" (Prov. 15:28), or "meditating" (Ps. 1:2). The word is related to a term meaning "to muse over." Thus God was commanding Joshua to remember His Law by "muttering" it to himself, "pondering" it, or "musing over" it. The Scriptures command people of faith to mediate on God's Law (1:8) and His works (Ps 143:5).

them into battle at Gilgal (10:7). Groups of
mighty men of 400 (1 Sam. 22:2) and later 600
(27:2) accompanied David, and later we read of
an elite group of thirty or more who were his
special warriors (2 Sam. 23:8–39).

1:16–18 The people affirmed Joshua
warmly and enthusiastically, echoing elements
of God's charge to Joshua in vv. 1–9. Compare v.
5 with v. 17 and note the fourth occurrence of
the exhortation to **be strong and of good
courage** (vv. 6, 7, 9). The pledges of obedience

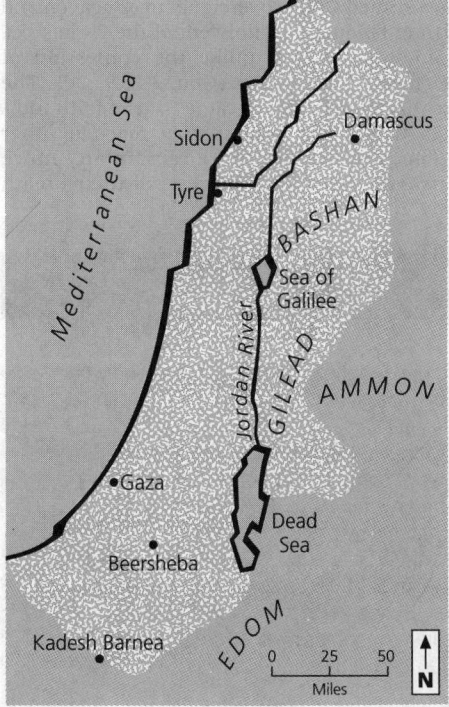

The Promised Land

From their camp in Moab, the Israelites prepared
to enter "the land which the LORD your God is
giving you to possess" (Josh. 1:11). This was the
land that God promised to give to Abraham's
descendants (Gen. 13:14–17). Its borders were
carefully defined by Moses (Num. 34:1–12). Now
under Joshua, the people were to go in and take
possession.

and loyalty to Joshua certainly must have been
encouraging to this new leader.

1:16 The text does not say clearly who
answered Joshua, the officers of the people (v.
10) or the tribes from east of the Jordan (v. 12).
From vv. 10, 12 it appears that Joshua's words
to the officers in v. 11 and to the tribes in vv.
13–15 are part of one event. The response in vv.

16–18 is therefore probably that of all Israel: In
this way, the entire nation affirmed Joshua's
leadership at the beginning of his duties as
leader.

1:17, 18 the LORD your God be with you:
The Israelites affirmed Joshua in the same terms
that God Himself used in promising to be with
him.

2:1–7 Joshua sent out two spies to explore
the land, especially Jericho. They went to a
place where news would be easily available, a
prostitute's house (v. 1). News reached the local
king, and he sent men to apprehend the spies
(vv. 2, 3). Yet Rahab protected the spies by
sending the king's men on a futile chase (vv.
4–7).

2:1 The **Acacia Grove** was the place east of
the Jordan River where the Israelites had been
encamped for some time (Num. 25:1). In some
translations of the Bible this place is called by its
transliterated Hebrew name Shittim, which
means "The Acacia Trees." Acacia Grove was
probably some distance from the Jordan
because it took a few days to get there. **Rahab**
was a Canaanite prostitute, and yet her story is
one of the most inspiring stories in the Bible.
Her actions in caring for the Israelite spies in
enemy territory demonstrated a faith in Israel's
God that is praised in the NT (Heb. 11:31; James
2:25). The term translated **harlot** (Heb. *zônâ*) is
the word for a common prostitute, not the word
for a cultic prostitute (*qedeshâ*). It is possible that
Rahab had been reduced to prostitution by the
death of her husband and by the needs of her
impoverished family (6:23 does not mention
her husband). In any case, out of all the populace of Jericho, only she reached out to the
living God, and He in turn saved her (6:25). The
name "Rahab," here, is to be distinguished from
the term that looks the same in English,
"Rahab," the name of the dragon, occasionally
used as a disparaging term for Egypt.

2:2, 3 it was told: Despite the secrecy of
the spies (v. 1), news of their arrival in Jericho
traveled fast. The **king of Jericho** ruled over a
small kingdom that included his city and the
territory around it. As is often the case in the
ancient world, his "kingdom" was actually a
city-state. Compare the reference to "Jabin king
of Hazor" in 11:1.

2:4–6 Rahab lied to the men searching for
the Israelite spies, but this does not constitute an
endorsement for lying as such. The Scriptures
clearly condemn lying (Lev. 19:11; Prov. 12:22).
Rahab did the best she could to save the men
sent by Joshua.

2:5 All major cities in Canaan were walled
and had a large **gate** for protection. Excavations
at Jericho have uncovered strong walls from different periods of the city's existence.

2:6 Like most houses, Rahab's had a flat **roof.** She hid the men there where she had laid out **stalks of flax** for drying. Flax is the oldest textile fiber known. It was used to make linen fabric for clothes.

2:7, 8 The River Jordan was nearly a hundred feet wide near Jericho, and from five to twelve feet deep. There were no bridges, and shallow **fords** were used for crossing.

2:9–11 Rahab's faith is visible in her words in these verses. She is a good example of a foreigner responding to Israel's God, and she was included with other women—Tamar, Ruth, and Bathsheba—in Jesus' genealogy in Matthew who were foreigners but who became part of Israel. This reflects the inclusiveness intended in the Abrahamic covenant (Gen. 12:2, 3).

2:9, 10 Rahab's use of God's personal name Yahweh, translated here as LORD, indicates that she had come to faith in the living God (v. 11).

God had graciously opened the heart and mind of a foreign prostitute to accept Him as Lord. **the terror of you has fallen on us:** Israel's reputation went before them. God already had dramatically delivered the Israelites in many ways, and the report had been spread throughout the nations. Rahab mentioned two miraculous deliverances: the crossing of the Red Sea and the victories over two kings east of the Jordan, Sihon and Og (v. 10; Ex. 14; Num. 21:21–35).

2:11 Here Rahab made a dramatic statement of her faith in **the LORD.** He is God in heaven: She affirmed God's sovereignty over heaven and earth in language reminiscent of the Psalms (Ps. 113:5, 6) and not unlike the confession of Melchizedek to Abram (Gen. 14:19, 20). The fact that non-Israelites came to true faith indicates that God's great mercy reached other nations. **neither did there remain any more courage:** The phrase suggests of their breath

---

 **IN DEPTH** | **Lying**

The Bible clearly condemns lying. Its commands forbid it, prophets condemn it, and godly people avoid doing it (Ex. 20:16; Jer. 9:4–9; Zech. 8:16; Eph. 4:25). Behind all these is God Himself, who cannot lie (Num. 23:19).

But what about Rahab? She lied to protect the spies of Israel who had come to scout out the city of Jericho. The story of her heroics paint her in a very positive light; Joshua praised her efforts, and both testaments of the Bible praise and honor Rahab for doing this (Josh. 6:22–25; Heb. 11:31; James 2:25). Her action made her part of God's people, ultimately placing her in the line of ancestry to David and Jesus. Her lie was also part of the conquest of Canaan, a task that God commissioned and blessed. Does her example mean that lying can sometimes be an acceptable course of action?

In Rahab's case, there are three possibilities. Either her lie was not a sin, or it was a sin but excusable, or it was a sin and inexcusable. Those who say her lie was not a sin will sometimes say they believe that "the loving thing" is all that matters; a "little lie" told in the name of love is no sin. In fact, it is the right thing to do.

Others have said that Rahab's sin was excusable because of a greater value, the lives of the spies. Those who hold this view believe that some sins are worse than others, and sometimes a person has to choose among them. In Rahab's case, the necessity of preserving the lives of the spies had a higher value than the truth. She did the right thing in misdirecting the king's men because it was more important to save their lives than to tell the king's men where they were.

The third possibility is that a lie is a lie, and that even Rahab's action was wrong. In this view, Rahab sinned no matter how noble her intentions. Of course, in her case, her sin is understandable because she lacked a complete knowledge of the living God. That is, what she did was wrong, but she did not know any better. We must be careful to make a distinction between Rahab's faith and the way Rahab expressed it. The Bible praises Rahab because of her faith in God, not because of her lying. That is, her actions would have been more noble had she protected the spies in some other fashion; as it is, she did the best she could.

Further, though the Bible calls Rahab a prostitute, we are not meant to take that as an endorsement for immorality. Rahab, like the rest of us, had a mixed character, but she believed in God and strove to honor Him and His people. That is what draws her praise. We should honor Rahab the way the Bible does. She was a great heroine of the faith, who came from the most surprising place. In time, her name would be honored not only for what she did for Israel, but for what she became: a mother in the line of Jesus (Ruth 4:18–22; Matt. 1:5).

was taken away; the people of Jericho were left breathless, and their **hearts melted** from fear of the Israelites!

2:12–14 Rahab asked the spies to **swear to her.** Even though to swear in God's name was a serious matter, the spies agreed to Rahab's request (vv. 14, 17, 20).

2:15 The Hebrew phrase translated **her house was on the city wall** suggests that Rahab's house was *in* the city wall rather than *on top of* it. The phrase might be rendered "in the double walls." This refers to a kind of defensive wall found around many cities in biblical times. The walls were built double and connected by cross-walls between them. The resulting spaces could be used for storage or as living quarters. Rahab's family may have lived in one of these residences. A dwelling in the wall would be a humble dwelling, just the spot for a poor prostitute . . . and for God's grace.

2:16, 17 Get to the mountain: The only hills near Jericho are to the west. This is the opposite direction from the route the pursuers had taken: they had gone east, down to the Jordan (v. 7).

2:18–21 The spies gave Rahab a line of **scarlet cord** to hang out the window as a sign of the agreement they had made. This is probably not the same rope she used to let the spies down, since the words are different. The cord's color is undoubtedly significant; it represents the color of the blood of atonement (Ex. 12:7, 13). It also alludes to the story of Tamar, since a scarlet thread was tied to the wrist of her first son (Gen. 38:28, 30). Both of these women were non-Israelite ancestors of Jesus (Matt. 1:3, 5).

2:22, 23 A "day" for the ancient Israelites could mean any portion of a day. Thus **three days** would refer to parts of three days, as in "part of today, tomorrow, and part of the next day."

2:24 faint-hearted: The spies reported to Joshua exactly what Rahab had said to them (v. 9).

3:1 The location of **Acacia Grove** is unknown today, but it was where Israel had been camped for some time after arriving at the plains of Moab, at the northern end of the Dead Sea (Num. 22:1; 25:1). It was where Israel was when Balaam came with the intent of cursing Israel (Num. 22—24), and where many Israelites had gone after prostitutes among the Moabite women (Num. 25:1–3). The day after the spies returned from Jericho, Joshua led the people from this place to the Jordan.

3:2 After three days, the **officers** went through the camp with instructions about the crossing itself. These instructions (v. 3) were different from the instructions given in 1:11, and this three-day period started on the day after the

spies returned from Jericho. The previous three-day period in 1:11 (and 2:22) began when the spies went into Jericho to begin with. After these two three-day periods, the Israelites crossed the Jordan on the next day, the seventh day after the book's action begins (3:5). This seven-day period immediately precedes the dedication of Israelite males in ch. 5. It is then followed by another seven-day period of marching around Jericho.

3:3 Chapter 3 emphasizes the significance of **the ark of the covenant,** mentioning it more than eleven times. The priests were responsible for carrying it (v. 3) in accordance with the rules given to Moses (Deut. 10:8; 31:9). They were to carry the ark with poles and not to touch it (Ex. 25:12, 13; 37:3–5; Num. 4:4–15). The ark symbolized God's presence. Everyone had to be careful to keep a healthy distance from it (3:4). The chapter refers to the ark in various ways, most commonly as "the ark of the covenant." The priesthood was restricted to **Levites** in general, and more specifically to Aaron's family (Num. 25:7–13; Deut. 18:1, 5). All **priests** were Levites, but not all Levites were priests. In later times Zadok, who was descended from Aaron through his third son, Eleazar (1 Chr. 6:1–8, 50–53), became a prominent priest. From that time on, Zadok's descendants became responsible for the temple service (Ezek. 44:15–31).

3:4 The Hebrew word for **yet** is emphatic and might be translated "be very sure." This emphasizes the importance of the command to keep one's distance from the ark. **Two thousand cubits** was more than half a mile. **that you may know:** The miraculous events are a source of emphasis in chs. 3 and 4, and their value in making the people "know" is important (compare v. 7).

3:5, 6 Sanctify yourselves: The Book of Joshua emphasizes the idea of holiness. The basic meaning of holiness (Heb. *qadash*) is "separation" from things that are unclean or common. **Wonders** translates the Hebrew word (*niphlaô't*) for what today are called miracles. These mighty acts of God astonished people and prompted them to praise Him (Pss. 9:1; 96:3). In ch. 3, God performs the miracle of stopping the waters of the Jordan (vv. 14–17).

3:7, 8 With the words **I will begin to exalt you,** God reaffirmed Joshua's place as successor to Moses (1:5, 9). **that they may know:** God performed miracles not only to bring about certain events but to reveal Himself to His people.

3:9 Here, Joshua functions as a prophet of God, even though he is never specifically called a prophet, because he stood before the people as spokesman for God.

3:10, 11 The miraculous events that follow not only brought the Israelites across the

Jordan; they also attested to the fact that the living God was with them (4:24). These wonderful acts testified to God's glorious presence among His people; God Himself was working on their behalf. **Canaanites . . . Jebusites:** This text mentions seven people groups. *Canaanites* sometimes denoted anyone living in Canaan,

INSIGHT · Parting the Jordan

The miracle of the Jordan River parting so that the people could enter Canaan on dry land (Josh. 3:14–17) recalled the miracle of the parting of the Red Sea (Ex. 14:21–31). It also helped to confirm Joshua as the successor to Moses. Centuries later, a similar miracle would confirm Elisha as the successor to the prophet Elijah (2 Kin. 2:14).

regardless of their ethnic identity (Gen. 36:2, 3; Judg. 5:19). Yet the present text distinguishes a specific group as Canaanites. In this case the Canaanites were probably the peoples living near the sea (5:1) who were known later as the Phoenicians. Their largest cities were Tyre and Sidon. As for the **Perizzites,** we know little about them. They appear to have lived in the forested areas of central Palestine (Gen. 13:7). **Amorites** is sometimes a synonym for *Canaanites* in its broader usage (Gen. 15:16; Judg. 1:34, 35). Sometimes the name refers to the peoples living in the cities in the central hill country of Canaan (Num. 13:29; Deut. 1:7), or to kingdoms east of the Jordan (13:10, 21). Here the name probably refers to inhabitants of the central hill country. The **Jebusites** lived in Jerusalem (15:8; 18:28).

3:12 twelve men: One man from each tribe was selected. The Hebrew emphasizes that it was to be only one from each tribe; it literally states "one man, one man per tribe."

3:13 The reference to **the ark** here parallels the phrase in v. 11. The reference to **the LORD,** the Lord of all the earth uses both His name and His title. Much as "Baal" was the name of the Canaanites' most important god, "the LORD" (Yahweh) is God's personal name. This was the name God revealed to Moses at the burning bush (Ex. 3:13–15; 6:2, 3). The term translated **Lord** means "master." It refers to God's status as sovereign of the universe.

3:14 The Hebrew reads "the ark, the covenant" here.

3:15 The parenthetical statement **for the Jordan overflows** is significant because it makes the point that a great miracle was involved. God did not merely slow the Jordan to a trickle during a time of drought; rather, He stopped the waters when the river was high. **during the whole time of harvest:** This phrase refers to the early summer harvest. At this time, the river was still swollen from the spring melting and rains. The Israelites crossed on the tenth day of the first month (4:19), which corresponds to March-April.

3:16 Adam: A city about eighteen miles north of Jericho, near where the Jordan and Jabbok Rivers converge. The Jordan flows between high limestone cliffs near Jericho. Sometimes parts of these cliffs collapse into the river causing the waters to back up. God could have miraculously caused such a slide to occur at precisely the moment when the Israelites needed to cross over. **The Sea of the Arabah** is the Dead Sea, into which the Jordan flows from the north. The Arabah itself is the region of the Jordan valley, running from the Sea of Galilee in the north to the Dead Sea in the south. The Dead Sea is the lowest place on earth, 1,286 feet below sea level. The phrase **Salt Sea** is added to the name because the sea has no outlet; it loses its water by evaporation. The concentration of salt and other minerals is so high that nothing can live in it.

3:17 A synonym for the term translated **dry ground** is found in 4:22, as well as in Ex. 14:16, 22, 29 where it refers to the dry ground of the bottom of the Red Sea. This crossing of the Jordan was similar to the crossing of the Red Sea. The miracle was so effective in both cases that the Israelites crossed on dry ground, not mud or shallow water.

4:1–9 This section is demarcated on either side by the references in 3:17 and 4:10 to the priests carrying the ark standing in the middle of the Jordan River until the crossing was completed. It introduces the important idea of making and observing memorials to what God has done.

4:1–3 The **twelve stones** (one stone per tribe) would mark the spot where God performed His wonderful miracle in stopping the waters of the Jordan so the Israelites could cross. The stones would remind the people of the great event and serve as conversation starters with their children, who would ask what they symbolized (vv. 6, 21).

4:4–6 The Hebrew term for **sign** (*'ot*) can mean "miracle" (Ex. 7:3), but here it means "memorial marker." The same idea is found in Ex. 12:13, 14; 13:8, 9, where there are instructions for celebrating the Passover and the Feast of Unleavened Bread. These observances were

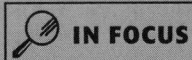 **IN FOCUS** "stone"

(Heb. *'eben*). (Gen. 35:14; Josh. 4:2; 1 Kin. 5:17; 2 Kin. 12:12) Strong's #68: The stones that littered the landscape of the ancient Middle East were used in numerous ways. They were the building material for houses, city walls, and fortifications (1 Kin. 5:17; 2 Kin. 12:12). Stones were also used for religious purposes, to build sacred pillars (Gen. 35:14) and altars (Deut. 27:5). Sometimes, stones were piled up as a memorial that marked the site of a divine revelation (Gen. 28:18, 22) or a significant event in the life of an individual (Gen. 31:46) or a nation (4:6). Because a stone was commonly used as a foundation for a structure, God Himself was called the "Stone of Israel" (Gen. 49:24). But Isaiah also described the Lord as a "stone of stumbling" for those Israelites who rejected Him (Is. 8:14). These same images are applied to Jesus Christ (Is. 28:16; 1 Pet. 2:4–8).

signs to the Israelites and their children that God had miraculously delivered them out of Egypt. **when your children ask:** The stones would inevitably stimulate a child's questions in the same way that the Passover and Feast of Unleavened Bread would. These questions would be opportunities for instruction (Ex. 12:26, 27; 13:8). An important principle is revealed here. In addition to remembering God's gracious work in our lives, we need to tell our children about it also (Deut. 6:20–24).

4:7 a memorial: The same word (Heb. *zikkarôn*) along with the word "sign" is found in connection with the Passover and Festival of Unleavened Bread (Ex. 12:14; 13:9).

4:8 the children of Israel did so: A standard feature of Hebrew narratives is repetition. This verse repeats almost verbatim the instructions given in v. 5. Far from being an unimaginative feature of a primitive storytelling style, such repetitions are a sophisticated literary device. Often they show that instructions, usually God's or those of His representatives, were carried out exactly, "to the letter." The pattern is for a character in the story to give the instructions and then for the narrator to confirm, using the same words, that the instructions were carried out. The phrase **as the LORD** had spoken to Joshua confirms the obedience of the Israelites even further. This literary device is used to highlight the importance of obedience to the words of God.

4:9 Joshua set up twelve stones: It is possible that there were two piles of memorial stones, one set up by the people on the banks of the Jordan River (v. 8) and one set up by Joshua in the middle of the river (v. 9), which would have been visible at low water levels. However, the Hebrew of the first part of v. 9 suggests that the activity described here took place earlier and could better be translated, "Joshua had set up twelve stones." Thus, he would have set up the stones in the Jordan itself before the people

crossed, and then after the crossing the people would have taken the stones out of the river (vv. 5, 8) and erected them on the banks. Verse 8 states that the people took the stones **from the midst of the Jordan**, which suggests that these are the stones that Joshua had erected there (v. 9).

4:10–14 These verses begin and end with references to Moses as he related to Joshua, picking up on the theme of Joshua as Moses' worthy successor. Their emphasis is on everyone's obedience to the words of God and to Israel's leaders.

4:10 the people hurried and crossed over: This paragraph represents something of a flashback, since 3:17 and 4:1 have already stated that the crossing was completed. The purpose is to look back and reflect upon the people's obedience.

4:11 The priests who were standing on dry ground in the middle of the river (3:17) were finally able to cross over themselves with the ark. This foreshadows the more detailed account of the priests' coming out of the water in v. 18.

4:12 The men of the Transjordan tribes acted exactly **as Moses had spoken,** that is, in direct obedience to the instructions Moses gave when Israel was still on the Plains of Moab (Num. 32:20–22; Deut. 3:18–20).

4:13 The number of warriors from Reuben, Gad, and half of Manasseh is **forty thousand,** much smaller than that listed in Num. 26. There the warriors from Reuben alone number 43,730 (Num. 26:7). The number here was most likely a portion of the warriors from the three tribes; the rest probably stayed with the women, children, and elderly to protect them. The reference to **Jericho** (the first in the book) foreshadows the dramatic events to follow in ch. 6. Jericho was six miles west of the Jordan, ten miles northwest of the northern end of the Dead Sea. It was near a large freshwater spring 825 feet below sea level.

4:14, 15 the Lord exalted Joshua: Once again, God affirmed Joshua's place as Moses' successor (1:5, 17; 3:7). In this context, **they feared him** indicates respect, reverence, or awe, not terror. The Israelites obeyed Joshua in the same way they had obeyed Moses.

4:16, 17 The Hebrew word for **Testimony** also means "reminder," and it is used in Ex. 31:18 to refer to the tablets on which the Ten Commandments were written, "the two tablets of the Testimony." "The tablets of the covenant" are mentioned in Deut. 9:11, which shows that "testimony" and "covenant" are closely related ideas. The ark is called "the ark of the Testimony" because it contained the two stone tablets on which were written the Ten Commandments (Ex. 40:20; Deut. 10:1–5).

4:18 This verse is a mirror image of 3:15. This neatly concludes the miraculous episode, showing the forces of nature resuming their natural course and reminding us of the marvelous nature of the miracle of God stopping the waters.

4:19 The crossing of the Jordan was on **the tenth day of the first month,** that is, the month of Nisan (Abib), corresponding to March-April. This was an important day because it coincides with the day that the Passover lamb was selected (Ex. 12:3). It foreshadows the keeping of the Passover in 5:10, on the fourteenth day of the month, when the lamb is actually killed (Ex. 12:6, 18). The location of **Gilgal** is uncertain; it was somewhere east of Jericho in the Jordan valley. At Gilgal, the Israelites celebrated several religious rituals, including circumcision and Passover (ch. 5). There also a sanctuary and an altar were built for God (9:23, 27).

4:20 The stones which the Israelites had brought up out of the Jordan River (v. 8) were now set up permanently at Gilgal.

4:21–24 The twelve stones were a memorial for them and their children, as had been stated earlier (vv. 6, 7). The crossing of the Jordan has many similarities to the crossing of the Red Sea.

The text makes this explicit in 4:23. **that all the peoples . . . may know:** The miracle was performed for a greater purpose than merely getting the Israelites across the Jordan River. It also was a sign to all peoples that God was powerful. Indeed the inhabitants of Jericho had heard about how great Israel's God was (2:10, 11).

5:1 God's drying up the waters of the Jordan caused the inhabitants of Canaan to fear Israel greatly. Such reactions of fear or opposition were common as Israel entered the land (9:1–4; 10:1, 2; 11:1–5). The language here especially recalls the same thought expressed earlier by Rahab (2:10, 11). This verse forms a transition between the Jordan crossing in chs. 3 and 4 and the adversaries to be encountered later in chs. 6—12. **we:** Most early translations and editions of the text read "they" here, including the earliest extant Hebrew manuscripts of Joshua (from Qumran), the earliest translations into Aramaic and Greek, and the marginal notations of the early Jewish scribes, the Masoretes.

5:2–5 Flint is a rock found in abundance in biblical lands, and its use is known from almost all periods of ancient history; many **flint knives** have been found in excavations. Flint was gradually replaced by metals, such as copper, bronze, and iron. Only in two places in the OT is the Hebrew word *flint* found, here and in Ex. 4:26, both in connection with circumcision. This they had to do **again the second time** (vv. 4, 5). The males of the generation that left Egypt in the Exodus had all been circumcised. However, that generation died in the wilderness and the practice had been neglected. Thus it was necessary to perform it again, especially before the important celebration of Passover. The original instructions for Passover had emphasized the importance of circumcising all participants before the ceremony (Ex. 12:44, 48).

5:6, 7 God would deny covenant benefits (Gen. 12:1–3; 15:18–21; 17:1–8) to individuals who did not obey Him. Anyone who was not circumcised was to be cut off from enjoying the blessings of God's people (Gen. 17:14). God's

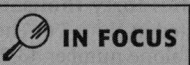 **IN FOCUS** "milk and honey"

(Heb. *chalab vedebash*) (Josh. 5:6). Strong's #2461; #1706: This phrase is frequently used in the OT to describe the land of Canaan, a land flowing with milk and honey (Ex. 3:8; Lev. 20:24; Num. 14:8; Deut. 6:3). The phrase depicts both the fertility of the land and its bounty (Num. 13:23–27). The land could support plenty of cows to supply an abundance of milk, and a variety of plants for bees to frequent. The expression also represents the two distinct lifestyles that the land of Canaan supported: the shepherd life of pastoral nomads (symbolized by milk) and the agricultural life of a more settled population (pictured by honey).

promises to Abraham's descendants would be fulfilled to the nation as a whole, but not every individual would automatically participate: faith and obedience were required. This truth is emphasized in 5:7 with the statement that God **raised up** another generation to replace the one He had consigned to perish in the wilderness. The land God had promised to Israel was

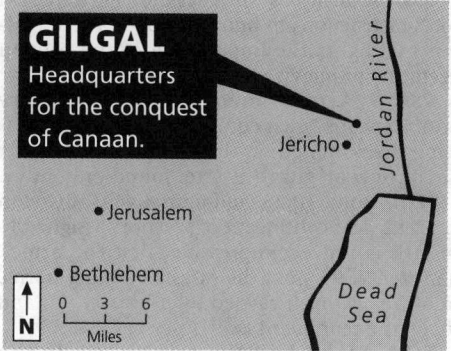

Gilgal was a site possibly located one mile northeast of Jericho where Israel first camped after crossing the Jordan (Josh. 4:19). The name meant "circle of stones" or "rolling," both of which fit two important events that took place there: the establishment of a monument from stones taken out of the Jordan (4:20), and the circumcision of uncircumcised Hebrews which "rolled away the reproach of Egypt" (5:8, 9). It was used by Israel as a base of military operations during the conquest of Canaan.

no wilderness, but **a land flowing with milk and honey,** a fertile land ready to supply all the Israelites' needs. God had described the land this way to Moses decades before (Ex. 3:8); the phrase appears fifteen times in the Pentateuch.

5:8, 9 **Gilgal** is related to the Hebrew word *galal,* which means "to roll." The name, therefore, was an apt reminder that the **reproach of Egypt** was now being **rolled away.** This reproach is to be understood as the reproach that was heaped upon Israel by Egypt (Egypt's scorn), in the same way as the "reproach of Moab" (Is. 51:7; Ezek. 16:57) is the reproach heaped upon Israel by Moab.

5:10 The Israelites celebrated the Passover on the **fourteenth day of the month,** four days after they crossed the Jordan River (4:19), **at twilight.** The Israelites scrupulously kept the instructions concerning the Passover (Ex. 12:6).

5:11, 12 The celebration of the Passover marked a significant turning point in Israel's life: right after this they began to live from the land

they were about to possess. The miraculous provision of **manna** in the wilderness stopped.

5:13 The capitalization of **Man,** here, indicates the translators' judgment that this was God Himself, or perhaps Christ. Hebrew has no capitalization scheme, so such decisions are left to scholars to make on other grounds. Many scholars connect the appearance here of this man, the commander of the Yahweh's army, with the Angel of the Lord spoken of elsewhere. Joshua's question **Are you for us** reflects a natural human concern with the immediate battles ahead and whether he could count on this man.

5:14 The stranger did not respond to Joshua's question, but instead identified Himself. He was the **Commander of the army of the LORD.** This elicited a response of humble worship from Joshua. Rather than any further questions about this Man's loyalties, Joshua asked how he could serve this One greater than him: **What does my Lord say to His servant?** The Book of Job ends in a similar manner. God did not answer Job's questions either. There as here it was the encounter with God that mattered most (Job 42:5, 6). Questions were silenced, and humble worship was evoked.

5:15 The command given to Joshua to **take your sandal off your foot** is virtually identical with the one given to Moses at the burning bush (Ex. 3:5). This reinforces the theme developed in the Book of Joshua about Joshua's filling of Moses' role as leader of Israel. Joshua was confronted with the living God, just as Moses had been (Ex. 33:9–11). John 1:18 strongly implies that appearances such as this were preincarnate appearances of the Savior Jesus, and not of God the Father, who cannot be seen (John 6:46).

6:1—8:29 The conquest of the first two cities is described in great detail, in contrast to the remainder of their conquests, which are described quickly and in a formulaic manner in chs. 10 and 11. Jericho was the gateway into Canaan from the east, a strong, powerful city just across the Jordan River, and its collapse via a miraculous intervention by God was a dramatic first step in taking the land (ch. 6). A crucial part taking Jericho was that the Israelites were to destroy everything in the city except for Rahab and her family. However, one man, Achan, disobeyed in this matter and as a result the entire nation suffered a defeat in their next encounter, at Ai. Israel's leaders were forced to discover and deal with this sin (ch. 7). After this, the Israelites successfully took Ai (ch. 8).

6:1, 2 The verb **have given** communicates that something has already happened, emphasizing the role of God in Israel's victories (2:24).

6:3 The site of Jericho measured less than half a mile in circumference, only about seven acres, so the **march around the city** would have been completed quickly. The phrase **men of war** (also found in 5:4, 6; 10:24) is essentially synonymous with "mighty men of valor" (v. 2). It is used several times in the Pentateuch to refer to the adult males who came out of Egypt but who were not allowed to enter the Promised Land (Num. 31:28, 49; Deut. 2:14,

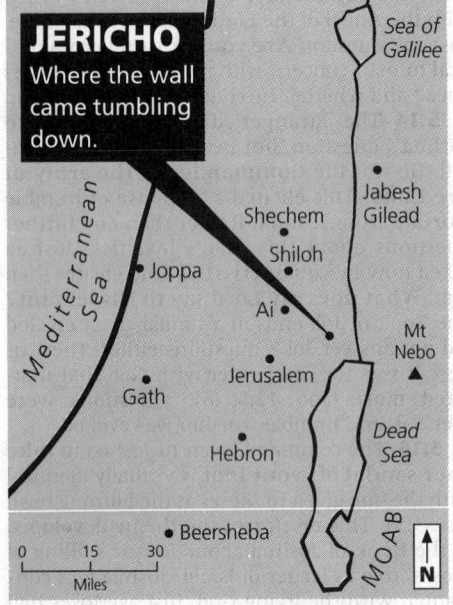

JERICHO
Where the wall came tumbling down.

Sea of Galilee

Jabesh Gilead
Shechem
Shiloh
Joppa
Ai
Mt Nebo ▲
Jerusalem
Gath
Dead Sea
Hebron
Beersheba
MOAB
Mediterranean Sea

0   15   30
Miles
N ↑

Jericho was one of the oldest cities in Palestine, located on the west bank of the Jordan River almost ten miles north of the Dead Sea. The site of a perennial spring which has attracted settlers since prehistoric times, it was the first Canaanite city taken by the Israelites after they crossed the Jordan (Josh. 6:1–21). It was virtually abandoned until the time of King Ahab, when Hiel the Bethelite rebuilt it at the cost of his two sons, fulfilling Joshua's curse (6:26; 1 Kin. 16:34).

16). Now a new generation of warriors, ready to fight the Lord's battles, was called by this phrase.

6:4 The number **seven** figures prominently in this passage: seven priests, seven trumpets, seven days, and seven trips around the city. Seven is a significant number in the Scriptures, beginning with the seven days of creation. It is a number that signifies completion. Its use here helps to demonstrate that the conquest of Jericho was part of a larger spiritual exercise that sanctified the people and the land for God. Another reminder of the spiritual significance of the event is the presence of **the ark** with the people. See ch. 3 for the impor-

tance of the ark in the crossing of the Jordan River.

6:5 The terms **ram's horn** and **trumpet** refer to the same kind of instrument. These terms refer to a horn that could produce only a few notes; it was used mainly as a signal. Here it both signaled God's presence and announced Jericho's impending doom. It is the most commonly mentioned instrument in the OT.

6:6, 7 Joshua's instructions here repeat God's instructions to him in vv. 2–5. The repetition highlights the importance of the solemn ceremony of marching around the city.

6:8, 9 Armed men is another military term. It means "men equipped for war," emphasizing their strength as they prepared for battle. The term **rear guard** is rare, found only in vv. 9, 13, in Num. 10:25, and figuratively of God in Is. 52:12. The contingent of warriors assigned to the ark is indeed impressive: first the armed men (vv. 7, 9), next the priests blowing horns, then the ark itself carried by priests (v. 8), and finally the rear guard (v. 9).

6:10, 11 he had the ark . . . circle the city: The narrative continues placing the ark in a prominent position. The people circled the city as well, but the focus is on the ark.

6:12 The phrase **rose early in the morning** is found in 3:1; 6:15; 7:16; 8:10; 8:14, as well as several times in Judges. "Rose early" (Heb. *shakam*) is related to the word "shoulder" (Heb. *shekem*). This thought here is that one would rise early and shoulder his burden for the day and then set off. It indicates a good start to a day. In this case, the task at hand would not consume much time, but it was of such spiritual significance that Joshua in his eagerness made an early start.

6:13–16 On the seventh day the Israelites marched around the city **seven times,** symbolizing completion of the task.

6:17, 18 The important Hebrew word translated as **doomed to destruction, accursed,** or **curse** occurs in these two verses five times. This word indicates that the city of Jericho, along with its inhabitants and everything in it, was to be completely destroyed as an offering to the Lord. This idea appears especially in the Book of Joshua. The concept was related to warfare; things would be offered to the Lord by being utterly destroyed. This was not limited to Jericho, however; it could happen anywhere, with respect to material wealth (7:1, 11), people (10:28, 35, 39, 40; 11:11, 20), or even entire cities (8:26; 10:1, 37; 11:12, 21). This practice, while referred to extensively in the OT, was not common in surrounding cultures. God wanted Israel to keep itself undefiled in order to reflect His holiness. In this particular circumstance, it was vitally important that the Israelites not be tempted by the pagan worship practices of the Canaanites. God's command that they devote the city of Jericho to Him was similar to His command to give Him the firstfruits of the harvest. Whenever Israel disobeyed this command, the effects were disastrous (ch. 7). The word **trouble** foreshadows the problems Achan would bring on the community (7:16–24).

6:19 The word translated **consecrated** means "holy." The valuable metal objects were not to be destroyed but set apart for the Lord.

6:21–23 The two **spies** who had visited Rahab's house went into her home and rescued her and her entire family. These two men rescued her so that there would be no mistake about whom they were to rescue. Remarkably, this prostitute, who was saved from utter destruction, became a member of the family line of Jesus (Ruth 4:18–22; Matt. 1:5).

6:24, 25 she dwells in Israel to this day: This may indicate that this portion of the Book of Joshua, if not the entire book, was written

Photo by Gustav Jeeninga

The mound of ancient Jericho, a walled city in southern Canaan captured by Joshua and the Israelites (Josh. 6:12–21).

The word **treasury** is also used of the treasuries in Solomon's temple (1 Kin. 7:51). However, no temple stood in Joshua's day, so the exact nature and location of this treasury is unknown. The "treasury of the house of the LORD" is mentioned in v. 24; it may have been associated with the "house of God" at Gilgal mentioned in 9:23.

6:20 With a great blast of the horns and a great shout from the people, God miraculously delivered Jericho into their hands: **the wall fell down flat** ("under itself"). The account of the taking of Jericho in vv. 8–20 is related in a slow, climax-building style. This first great obstacle to Israel's possession of the land fell merely at a shout of the people. The fact that it was utterly destroyed in a moment illustrates God's complete and effortless mastery over all His people's opponents.

within the lifetime of Rahab. The reason the author of the book included such a phrase was to authenticate his narrative; people could go and see Rahab living there, if they did not believe the story. This is true also with the account of the stone altar in 4:9, and the account of the stones that covered the cave where the Canaanite kings were buried in 10:27. These were tangible evidence that people could use to confirm what happened. These were not stories made up out of thin air to give Israel a "glorified" (but fictional) past; they told of real events, and the witnesses to these events still were living.

6:26 Joshua charged them: Literally "caused them to take an oath." The word **cursed** is one of the common Hebrew words for cursing; it is the opposite of *blessed*. Joshua

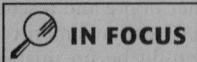

IN FOCUS | **"trumpet"**

(Heb. *shophar*) (Josh. 6:4, 5, 20; Ex. 19:16; Lev. 25:9) Strong's #7782: The *shophar* is an animal horn (typically from a ram or a goat) used as a trumpet (Josh. 6:6; Judg. 7:8). The word can also refer to a metal trumpet (Num. 10:2–10; 1 Chr. 15:28; 2 Chr. 15:14). The *shophar* was a signaling instrument used in warfare (Judg. 3:27) and for assembling the people at religious festivals, such as the Day of Atonement (Lev. 25:9; 2 Sam. 6:5; Joel 2:1). A trumpet blast announced God's descent to Mount Sinai to reveal His Law (Ex. 19:20). Both the OT and NT mention a trumpet announcing the day of the Lord, when He will come in judgment (Zeph. 1:16; Matt. 24:31).

cursed any attempts at rebuilding Jericho. The city was occupied sporadically after that (18:21; Judg. 3:13; 2 Sam. 10:5), but never to the previous extent. Joshua's curse found a dramatic fulfillment many centuries later when Hiel of Bethel laid its foundation and rebuilt its gates at great personal cost (1 Kin. 16:34). The language of the 1 Kings account consciously echoes that of this passage.

6:27 As a result of this first dramatic conquest in the land of Canaan, it was apparent that **the Lord** was with Joshua, and news of this spread far and wide.

7:1 This verse is a transition between the story of the conquest of Jericho and that of the defeat at Ai. It sets up the next chapter (especially vv. 20, 21). The phrase **committed a trespass** means "committed a treacherous vio-

lation." The names of **Achan** and his forebears in this verse are found again in 1 Chr. 2:6, 7. Usually whenever the **anger of the Lord** burned against Israel; He raised up an adversary against the nation to threaten and overpower it. Here God used the small army of Ai. The Lord's anger did not subside until Achan and his family had been punished (7:26).

7:2, 3 Ai, which is beside Beth Aven, on the east side of Bethel: That is, Ai was a small city west of Jericho. *Ai* means "ruin," and some have wondered if the name here may play some role in its interpretation in this text. **spy out:** The Hebrew word for *spies* (2:1) and *spying* is related to the word for "feet." The spies investigated the land by going through it on foot

7:4 Israel's force of **three thousand men** was a very small contingent indeed compared to the totals that they had available. According to 4:13, the number of warriors from east of the Jordan alone was 40,000.

7:5 Israel suffered **thirty-six** casualties before retreating. Although minor, this was Israel's first defeat in the land and a great surprise, especially after the inspiring events of the siege of Jericho. **the descent:** The topography west of Jericho rises sharply up out of the Jordan Valley. It appears that the men of Ai chased the Israelites eastward, down the steep hills, toward Jericho, from where they had come. **the hearts of the people melted:** In an ironic twist, the very words that Rahab used to describe the inhabitants of Jericho's fears in the face of the Israelites (2:11) are now used of the Israelites' fears of the men of tiny Ai. The effects of sin are often very demoralizing.

7:6 tore his clothes, and fell to the earth . . . put dust on their heads: The actions of mourning here are much more dramatic than typical mourning customs in the modern world. However, these were common actions in Israel

IN DEPTH | **Ai**

- Canaanite city probably located east of Bethel (Gen. 12:8) near Beth Aven (Josh. 7:2), and north of Michmash (Is. 10:28).
- Name meant "heap" or "ruin."
- Near where Abraham pitched his tent before journeying to Egypt (Gen. 12:8).
- Probably a small city at the time of the conquest, and thus said by Joshua's spies to be no match for Israel (Josh. 7:3). After a humiliating defeat caused by Achan's sin, 30,000 men tricked Ai's warriors into an ambush and took the city, burned it to the ground, and hanged its king (8:28, 29).
- Possibly the place later inhabited by the Ephraimites (1 Chr. 7:28, Ayyah).
- Taken over after the Babylonian exile by the Benjamites (Neh. 11:31, Aija).
- Exact location still a subject of some dispute.

and the ancient Middle East. Other mourning customs in Israel included weeping (Ps. 6:6), beating the chest (Is. 32:12), lifting up of the hands (Ezra 9:5; Ps. 141:2), lying or sitting in silence (Judg. 20:26; 2 Sam. 12:16), bowing the head (Lam. 2:10), fasting (2 Sam. 3:35), wearing sackcloth (Gen. 37:34), and sprinkling ashes, dust, or dirt (2 Sam. 15:32). However, the Israelites were strictly prohibited from practicing some pagan mourning rites, such as cutting the body or shaving the beard (Lev. 19:28; Deut. 14:1; Jer. 16:6).

7:7, 8 Joshua's bitter words echoed various complaints by the Israelites in the wilderness (Ex. 16:3; 17:3; Num. 11:4–6; 14:2, 3; 20:3–5). The certainty of the past was often preferable to the difficulties of the present and the uncertainty of the future. Joshua's desire to have remained **on the other** (east) **side of the Jordan** demonstrated his selective memory, since that spot had problems of its own. Indeed the Israelites had at times wanted to return to Egyptian slavery (Num. 11:4–6).

7:9 Despite Joshua's shortsightedness in v. 7, here he showed that he was aware of the larger issue at stake: God's **great name**—His reputation.

7:10–15 God's response to Joshua and the elders' mourning reinforced the importance of holiness. Israel—not just Achan—had sinned, and God would not tolerate it. This passage also shows that God had consistent standards for both Israel and the Canaanites. He had ordered Israel to exterminate the Canaanites because of their sin; He could not allow Israel to accommodate corruption, even that of one man, especially when the instructions concerning the infraction were so clear (v. 11; Deut. 7:26).

7:11 Hebrew has several words for sin. **Sinned** here means "missing the mark" of a standard set by God; **transgressed** means "crossing a boundary" set by God. This verse highlights the seriousness of Achan's offense, attributed here to the nation Israel, by referring to the sin in various ways: Israel had (1) **sinned,** (2) **transgressed** the Lord's **covenant,** (3) **taken some of the accursed things,** (4) **stolen,** (5) **deceived,** and (6) put the things **among their own stuff.** The quick, staccato accumulation of these verbs accentuates the severity of the action, since it was essentially one act. **My covenant:** The word *covenant* refers to many different dealings of God with His people at different times. Here the specific reference appears to be to the portion of the covenant that referred to the annihilation of the Canaanites (Deut. 20:10–20).

7:12 That God would declare the people of Israel **doomed to destruction,** as Jericho had been, because of their sin was a serious state-

ment. It meant God would no longer be with Israel until the sin was removed from the camp. God had specifically promised to be with His people (1:5, 9). This threat to withdraw His presence emphasizes once again God's absolute standards and His demand for holiness.

7:13, 14 The relationship between obedience and blessing and disobedience and cursing is well illustrated here: Israel would have no further successes until the sin had been uncovered.

7:15, 16 The Hebrew word translated **a disgraceful thing** denotes a blatant and senseless disregard for God's will. The text does not say by what method God indicated that **the tribe of Judah was taken** and the guilty party found out.

7:17–19 give glory to the Lord . . . and **make confession** . . . and **tell me:** These three actions commanded by Joshua are aspects of one event. By telling Joshua his sin, Achan was confessing to God, and by his confession, he was indeed glorifying God. We too dishonor God when we hide our sins from Him, and we honor Him when we confess them.

7:20, 21 a beautiful Babylonian garment: Literally, "one beautiful garment of Shinar." The land of Shinar is mentioned in Gen. 11:2 as the place where men built the Tower of Babel. **two hundred shekels of silver:** The shekel was the basic unit of weight for silver, and it was slightly more than four-tenths of an ounce. The total weight of the silver was considerable, more than eighty ounces. The gold Achan took weighed **fifty shekels,** or about twenty ounces. **coveted:** Achan's actions, besides violating God's instructions, also were a violation of the tenth commandment (Ex. 20:17). Achan had made fruitless attempts to hide his sin from God, from whom nothing can be **hidden** (Ps. 139:7–12).

7:22–24 Achan was brought out to be stoned, not only with each of the items he had stolen, but also with **all that he had** and his entire household. This was a severe punishment, but it illustrated God's firm insistence on holiness. Achan's sin had infected all Israel (7:1), and ridding Israel of the stain of this sin required the annihilation of everything with which Achan had intimate contact. Ironically for Achan, God allowed the Israelites to take the spoil in the next victory, at the second battle of Ai (8:2). Achan's greed was his own downfall.

7:25, 26 Achor is literally "trouble."

8:1–29 The victory over Ai was Israel's first true military victory in the land. God was no longer angry with Israel, since atonement had been made for its sin, and the task now was to get on with the conquest. Thus, He gave the city of Ai into the Israelites' hands, which they captured via an elaborate ambush.

8:1 The words **Do not be afraid, nor be dismayed** echo the words God used to encourage Joshua in 1:9. The sins of Achan had broken the special relationship God had established with His people, and so God reiterated His encouragement to Joshua. These words reinforce the statement of 7:26 that God had forgiven Israel, that He had "turned from the fierceness of His anger." **people of war:** The usual term is "men of war" (5:4, 6). This phrase seems to emphasize the unity of the entire nation in doing battle, even though it was most likely only the men who actually engaged in the battles. **I have given:** The conquest of the city was certain because God had willed it.

8:2 booty for yourselves: In contrast to the instructions concerning Jericho (6:17–19), this time the Israelites were allowed to take and keep spoils of war for themselves. Had Achan been less greedy, he could have participated in this as well. However, the Israelites were still to kill the inhabitants of Ai.

8:3–13 On the face of it, this section seems to describe two ambush forces sent out on two different days (vv. 3–9 and 10–13; especially vv. 3, 12). However, this is not according to God's instructions in v. 2, and it presents the particular difficulty of a first (improbably large) ambush force of 30,000 men (v. 3) being forced to spend two nights and a day in hiding near Ai without being detected by its inhabitants (vv. 3, 9, 13). Note also that the entire population of Ai, according to v. 25, is only 12,000. More probably, there was one ambush force. If so, the best way of understanding the section sees vv. 11–13 as a parenthetical aside, recapitulating the events already described in vv. 3–9. Thus the sequence of events would be as follows. Joshua commissioned a group of perhaps 5000 men to lie in ambush west of Ai, as Yahweh had instructed (vv. 2–4, 12, 13). He sent them out (v. 9), along with another fighting force ("the people of war") to be stationed north of the city (v. 11), and he himself spent the night with them (vv. 9, 13). He and the people went up to Ai the next morning (v. 10).

8:4–6 A select group of men was to **lie in ambush . . . behind** the city, that is, to the west. The main group of people would then be stationed north of the city (vv. 12, 13).

8:7 the LORD your God will deliver it into your hand: Here as elsewhere in the historical books, military victories are attributed to God. Israel was to depend completely upon Him for its successes.

8:8 commandment: After the disobedience in ch. 7, strict obedience was important here. Joshua urged obedience to God's commands, and the people complied (vv. 2, 8, 27).

8:9–13 The phrase **its rear guard** refers to the ambush forces stationed to the west of the city (vv. 3, 12). The largest contingent of warriors was stationed to the north. It appears that Joshua spent the night with the people, across the valley from Ai (v. 11), but late in the night he got up and went into the valley in preparation for the day's events (v. 13).

8:14, 15 the way of the wilderness: This may indicate merely that the men of Ai fled in disarray into the wilderness. The same phrase is found again in a similar context, where a coalition of Israelites set an ambush for the Benjamites at Gibeah (Judg. 20:42). The phrase occurs one other place, at Ex. 13:18, referring to the route that Israel took from Egypt through the desert.

8:16, 17 Bethel is an important city in the Bible. It has a fine pedigree that goes back to patriarchal times, when Abraham offered a sacrifice to God there (Gen. 13:3) and Jacob had a dream from God there (Gen. 28:10–22). Bethel was near Ai to the west (7:2), although its exact site is disputed. The inhabitants of Bethel came out of their city to help the men of Ai. Since the Israelite ambush was stationed between Bethel and Ai, they may have felt threatened by the Israelites. Or it may be that Ai was a small outpost for the larger city of Bethel (7:3) and an attack on Ai was understood to be an attack on Bethel. The text does not record Bethel's defeat, although its king is listed among those conquered by Joshua (12:16). It may be that in the defeat of Ai, Bethel was also defeated and no further reference was needed.

8:18 God told Joshua to **stretch out the spear** toward the city to begin the attack. Evidently this signal was relayed in some way to those lying in ambush (v. 19).

8:19 set the city on fire: Among all the cities that the Israelites captured, only three are said to have been burned: Jericho (6:24), Ai (8:19), and Hazor (11:11). The people of Israel were to live in and enjoy the cities of the land. Most of Israel's battles were in the field; they generally did not have to destroy the cities.

8:20–23 The Israelites were to treat **the king of Ai** exactly as they had the king of Jericho (v. 2). Chapter 6 does not specify what they did to the king of Jericho, but we can infer from 8:29 that they killed him and exposed his body in a humiliating way.

8:24–26 Joshua did not draw back his hand: This verse shows Joshua maintaining his arm outstretched, with his spear in hand, until the defeat of Ai was completed. The upraised spear was more than a signal to start the battle; it was also a symbol of God's presence and help in the battle (v. 1). This episode closely parallels that in Ex. 17:8–16, where the Israelites battled the Amalekites, and Moses stretched out his hand with "the rod of God" in it (Ex. 17:9). In that account, Moses' outstretched arm stood for God's presence, because the battle went in Israel's favor when Moses' hands were up, and against Israel when he tired and dropped his hands. This episode in Joshua shows yet another way in which Joshua was the worthy successor to Moses (1:1, 5; 24:29). Note that Joshua was the military leader when Moses stretched out his hand, and now Joshua was in Moses' position while others carried on the battle.

8:27 according to the word of the Lord: God had specified that the Israelites could take the city's possessions and livestock, but nothing else (v. 2), and this verse indicates that they carried out His instructions. This undoubtedly includes their treatment of the king of Ai (v. 29).

8:28 The word **heap** refers to a mound of ruins. Ancient cities were usually built on high points of land near water supplies, and when a city was destroyed a new city was built on the same site atop the packed and settled debris from the former city. Thus, over time, cities came to be on top of high mounds of compacted ruins. Ai was not rebuilt; therefore it remained a heap of ruins. The Hebrew word (*tel*) for *heap* is found in only a few places in the Bible (8:28; Deut. 13:16; 11:13; Jer. 30:18; 49:2), and in such place names in the Bible as Tel Melah and Tel Harsha (Ezra 2:59) or Tel Abib (Ezek. 3:15). The equivalent Arabic word *tell* is used today as part of the names of many sites in Israel. Ai's very name means "The Ruin," so the judgment implicit in its name is now made explicit in this wordplay.

8:29 As God instructed (v. 27), Joshua executed the king of Ai and exposed his body **on a tree** (see the similar action in 10:26). But he took down the body at sundown in accordance with the injunction in Deuteronomy that a body could not remain exposed overnight (Deut. 21:22, 23). In these texts, **hanged** means exposing the dead body on a sharpened stake as a mark of shame and horror, not hanging by the neck. **a great heap of stones:** A different Hebrew word for "heap" is used here from the one in v. 28, but the connection is clear. The king's fate here is exactly the same as Achan's fate in 7:26. God would not favor His own people when they blatantly disobeyed, any more than He would favor wicked Canaanites; for his sin Achan was expelled from Israel and treated like a Canaanite.

> *Here as elsewhere in the historical books, military victories are attributed to God. Israel was to depend completely upon Him for its successes.*

8:30–35 The victory at Jericho and the defeat and subsequent victory at Ai were significant events in taking the land, since they were "firsts." Later victories, while certainly just as dramatic, receive little individual attention in the telling (chs. 10; 11).

8:30 Mount Ebal is mentioned only here and in Deut. 11:29; 27:4, 13. It and Mount Gerizim, directly south of it, were the sites to be used for proclaiming blessings and curses when the Israelites came into the land; specifically, Ebal was to be the site of the curses (Deut. 11:29). Here it was the site of an altar. Ebal and Gerizim are two important peaks in central Canaan flanking an east-west pass through the north-central hill country. Almost the entire Promised Land is visible from the top of Mount Ebal.

8:31 Moses . . . had commanded this in Deut. 27:2–10. This is another example of the explicit fulfillment of God's words; the Israelites had disobeyed enough that they wanted to make doubly sure they did it right this time. **An altar of whole stones** refers to unfinished stones (Deut. 27:4), which was in accord with God's earlier instructions about making altars (Ex. 20:25). The unfinished stones would have contrasted with the finished stones found in many Canaanite altars. This was a reminder that, even in such rituals as offering sacrifices, the Israelites were to be different or distinct from their neighbors. **Burnt offerings** were sacrifices in which the animals were entirely consumed (7:1–10; Ex. 29:18; Lev. 1:1–17). **Peace offerings** were offerings in which portions of the sacrificial animals were to be joyfully eaten by the ones presenting them (7:11–21; Lev. 3:1–17).

8:32 Joshua publicly wrote **a copy of the law** on stones, which echoed the instructions for a king in Deut. 17:18. While Joshua was not a king, several indications in the book show him in a kingly light, acting with the authority of a king and in ways in which kings were supposed to act (1:5–9; Deut. 17:14–20).

8:33 This Hebrew word for **stranger** could more precisely be translated "resident alien." It refers to those foreigners who lived as permanent residents within Israel. These were different from foreigners or outsiders who had incidental contact with Israel, such as travelers or traders, who had few rights within Israel (Ex. 12:43; Lev. 22:10, 25). Resident aliens enjoyed certain rights even though they were not

Israelites by birth. They were allowed to take gleanings from the fields (Lev. 19:10; 23:22), and the Israelites were repeatedly instructed to give special care to them, along with the poor, the widow, and the orphan (Ex. 22:21; 23:9; Deut. 10:17–22). This special concern for aliens within Israel's borders was rooted in Israel's own alien status in Egypt, which God wanted them to remember (Ex. 22:21; 23:9; Deut. 10:17–22; 23:7). This is part of the missionary message of the OT: Israel was to treat aliens within its own borders in such a way that they would want a relationship with Israel's God. This is certainly a worthy model for Christians today, as well, in their contacts with friends,

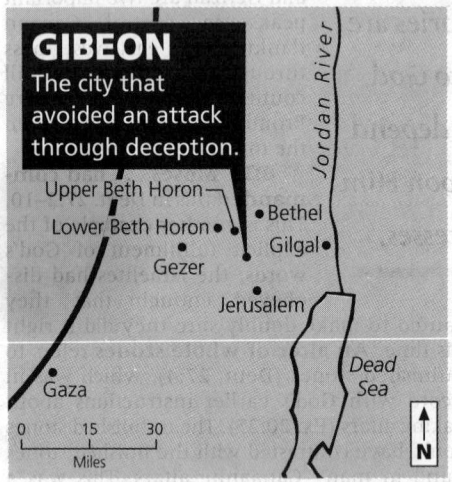

GIBEON
The city that avoided an attack through deception.

Upper Beth Horon
Lower Beth Horon
Bethel
Gilgal
Gezer
Jerusalem
Gaza
Jordan River
Dead Sea

0   15   30
Miles
N

Gibeon was a major Canaanite city located about six miles northwest of Jerusalem. Its name means "pertaining to a hill." In league with three other cities—Chephirah, Beeroth, and Kirjath Jearim—Gibeon used a deceptive strategy to make lasting peace with the Israelites (Josh. 9:3–27), though the Gibeonites were forced to work at menial tasks.

neighbors, and business associates; they are to conduct themselves in a manner that points people to their Lord (Matt. 5:16). In this passage we see aliens participating right along with the rest of the Israelites in the covenant affirmation ceremony.

8:34, 35 This was the first public reading of **the Book of the Law,** the entire body of the Law given by Moses, mentioned after Moses' death.

9:1, 2 Though a coalition of Canaanite kings banded together to oppose Israel, the text does not say whether this coalition ever actually fought Israel. It disappears from the scene after

v. 2. Six ethnic groups in Canaan, who often are mentioned together (3:10), are listed here. God told Israel to destroy these nations, and He did not want Israel to become allies with them under any circumstances (Ex. 23:28–33; Deut. 7:1–5; 20:16–18).

9:3 Gibeon was relatively close to Ai and about five miles northwest of Jerusalem. It is known mainly for the deceit of its inhabitants described in this chapter.

9:4–6 The Gibeonites went to great lengths to make it look as though they had **come from a far country.** Israel was allowed to make treaties with cities that were far from them (Ex. 34:11, 12; Deut. 20:10–18). Thus, if the Gibeonites' claim of v. 6 had been truthful, the treaty that the Israelites made with them would have been permissible. **A covenant** was a legal treaty. The literal wording in Hebrew is "cut a covenant," which may have referred to the ancient custom of sacrificing an animal to ratify it (Gen. 15:10).

9:7 The people of Gibeon are called **Hivites,** and were among the groups slated for destruction (Ex. 34:11; Deut. 20:17). Israel should not have made a treaty with them. This verse shows that the Israelites were initially suspicious of the Gibeonites.

9:8 Where do you come from is literally, "From where are you coming?" A subtle interplay between the Gibeonites' words in v. 6 and Joshua's in v. 8 reveals their differing perceptions of the situation. The Gibeonites state that they have "come from a far country," and the verb form makes it clear that, in their minds, they have reached their destination, that is, they have "arrived from a far country." When Joshua questions them, the verb form he uses makes it clear that he believes that they are merely passing by. We might paraphrase his words as, "From where are you coming as you pass by here?" The Gibeonites' deception was working; their own (secret) goal was the Israelite camp, but Joshua believed that they were on their way to someplace else.

9:9, 10 The fame of the Israelites' victories had preceded them among the Gibeonites, in the same way that it did among the inhabitants of Jericho earlier (2:9, 10).

9:11–14 The Israelites **took some of** the Gibeonites' **provisions** in order to inspect them, to confirm the Gibeonites' words. Significantly, the Israelites **did not ask counsel of the LORD,** contrary to God's explicit instructions to Joshua (Num. 27:21). The Israelites' confirmation of the Gibeonites' claim was purely in their own strength and on their own initiative. The mistake on Israel's part was not so much that they were deceived, but that they did not ask for the Lord's counsel. Similarly, many

Christians have found themselves in difficult or disastrous circumstances because they rushed to a decision without properly consulting the Lord, His Scriptures, and His people for guidance.

9:15 Joshua made peace with them: The treaty made in this chapter has much in common with typical ancient Middle Eastern treaties of the times. A subordinate group makes the agreement with a more powerful party in order to receive protection. Its binding nature (v. 18) forms the basis for the actions taken in 10:1–27, where the Gibeonites found themselves threatened by a Canaanite coalition and appealed to the Israelites for help.

9:16–21 The deceit is discovered and the Gibeonites are confronted. Despite the Gibeonite trickery, Israel was nevertheless bound by the oath, the seriousness of which is underscored by the fact that all of vv. 18–21a are devoted to it. The congregation was angry with its leaders for having done this, but their hands were tied by the oath the leaders had taken. This is stated explicitly and in repetitive detail.

9:17–19 Chephirah, Beeroth, and Kirjath Jearim were all towns near Gibeon. The first two were in Benjamite territory (18:25, 26), and the third was on its border (18:14, 15).

9:20–23 the oath which we swore: Oath taking and swearing were solemn affairs (the Hebrew words for "to swear" and "oath" are from the same root, *shaba'*). To take an oath was to give a sacred and unbreakable word to follow through on what was promised. From time to time, even God swore by Himself or His holiness or His great name to take certain actions (Gen. 22:16–18; Ps. 89:35; Jer. 44:26). Swearing falsely was a grave sin (Ezek. 17:16–21; Zech. 5:3, 4; Mal. 3:5). Because of the sacred, unbreakable nature of an oath, this covenant the Israelites made with the Gibeonites could not be revoked, even though it was obtained under false pretenses.

9:24–26 The report that reached the Gibeonites concerning the Israelites (v. 3) frightened them so much that they conjured up this deception. Their words **your servants were clearly told** bear witness to the great events of the Exodus that were not forgotten even forty years after the event (Deut. 1—3).

9:27 The phrase **the place which He would choose** is particularly important in Deuteronomy. It indicates that the Gibeonites were to serve only at sanctioned Israelite worship centers and not Canaanite ones. Until the Jerusalem temple was built, these centers included Shiloh (18:1) and Gibeon itself (1 Chr. 16:39). That they did so **to this day** (a phrase also found in 4:9; 5:9; 7:26; 8:29) shows that the Gibeonites did indeed continue this service for some time, although it is not specifically mentioned again in the OT. We may observe that in the deceit of this treaty, a people were brought into proximity with the true worship of the living God, who is able to bring good out of the worst of situations. Doubtless through this many Gibeonites came to faith in Him and became His worshipers.

10:1–11:23 These two chapters relate the accounts of Israel's conquest of northern and southern Canaan after it had gained a foothold in central Canaan. Several striking parallels can be seen between the two chapters. Both open with accounts of a coalition of kings who oppose Israel's invasion (10:1–27; 11:1–9). Both mention God's help in repelling the attacks (ch. 10 more than ch. 11, but see 11:8). Both open with descriptions of decisive battles (10:1–15; 11:1–9), and are followed by further military activity related to these (10:16–27; 11:10–15). Each shows one main instigator of the coalition. In ch. 10 it is Adoni-Zedek, king of Jerusalem; in ch. 11 it is Jabin, king of Hazor. And each chapter ends with a summary of the consolidation of power in each area (10:28–43; 11:16–23).

10:1–4 Once again Israel's reputation and victories had spread among the Canaanites, striking fear into their hearts. In contrast to Rahab, who turned to Israel's God in faith, and to the Gibeonites, who entered (by trickery) into a treaty with the Israelites, this coalition decided to resist Israel.

10:1, 2 Political and military calculations led the five Canaanite kings to conclude that if such **a great city** as Gibeon had to make peace with the seemingly invincible Israelites, their only option was to band together and attack (v. 5). **Ai** was a strong city, a fact to which Israel closed their eyes when they became overconfident in themselves (7:3).

10:3–5 The name **Amorites** probably refers to the inhabitants of the central mountain region of Palestine, although only **Jerusalem** and **Hebron** are really in the hill country. The king of Jerusalem was leader of a coalition of five kings against Gibeon. The events at Ai had struck fear into the kings' hearts, especially now that Gibeon, a prominent city, had made a treaty with Israel (ch. 9). Gibeon's treaty with Israel may have been a renunciation of one with Jerusalem. This could explain the special concern of the king of Jerusalem.

10:6, 7 Joshua ascended from Gilgal because Gilgal and Jericho were in the deep Jordan valley; he would have had to go up into the hill country in the central portion of Canaan to help the Gibeonites.

10:8 See 1:5, 9 for similar words of encouragement.

10:9 For Joshua's men to have **marched all**

night from Gilgal and then attacked speaks well of their stamina. Their night march covered about twenty miles up steep terrain, with gear, under stress, in the middle of the night, and with a battle still before them.

10:10, 11 This verse summarizes the victory; vv. 11–13 give the details. **the LORD routed them:** Despite Joshua's presence with his warriors (v. 7), it was God who gave the victory and God who received the credit. **the road that goes to Beth Horon:** One escape route for the Canaanite kings went northwest, down from the hill country toward the coast. **Azekah** was a town over the hills to the southwest of Gibeon, some distance away. That some were fleeing in this direction while others were fleeing toward Beth Horon indicates the completeness of the rout. The location of **Makkedah** is unknown, but presumably it was somewhere near Azekah.

10:12–15 The second section describing the battle is introduced with a Hebrew word for **Then** (*'az*) which reveals that important action took place at the same time as (not subsequent to) that of vv. 6–11. This means that somehow the hailstorm of v. 11 and the phenomena of vv.

12 and 13 either describe the same thing or (more probably) happened at the same time as part of the same miracle. The author's emphasis comes in v. 14. He marvels not so much at the miracle of v. 13 but that God heard and responded to the voice of a man (v. 14) who had been interceding miraculously for Israel (v. 12). The two previous miracles on Israel's behalf—stopping the waters of the Jordan and the victory over Jericho—had been God's initiative; this time, He moved in response to a man's petition. This again highlights Joshua's importance in the book, and it underscores God's faithfulness to His people.

10:12 In the sight of Israel, Joshua commanded the **Sun** and the **Moon** to **stand still over Gibeon** until the Israelites completed their task. The words of this verse form a two-part section of well-balanced poetry, and the words in v. 13 comment on them with a three-part echo.

10:13 The Book of Jasher (2 Sam. 1:18) confirms what the Book of Joshua reports here. It is not part of the Bible, and no part of it has survived.

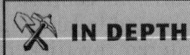 **IN DEPTH** | **Miracles**

Open the Bible wherever you like; you will soon find the mention of an event that only God could do. These stories of God's intervention in nature occur without apology throughout the Bible, and often only with the barest of details. The reader may be left wondering exactly what happened.

The account of Israel's victory over the five kings of the Amorites is a perfect example. Joshua 10:13 says that in response to Joshua's prayer, "the sun stood still, and the moon stopped." This miraculous event played a key role in Israel's victory that day. Even accepting this as a miracle, which the narrative surely bids us to do, leaves some questions unanswered. We know that the sun does not move around the earth, so it was not the sun that literally stopped, but what took place that day? And how did it help Israel?

Some take the text to mean that God stopped the earth's rotation. "The sun stood still" means that the position of the sun in the sky remained constant. Since the sun's position is determined by the earth's rotation, the earth's rotation must have stopped. This delay gave the Israelites the daylight they needed to finish routing their enemies rather than letting them escape.

Others suggest that God caused an unusual refraction of light in the earth's atmosphere that caused the sun to remain visible for a very lengthy period of time. The sun *appeared* to stop, but without any change in the rate of the earth's rotation. Again, this gave Israel time to finish their rout.

Others reinterpret the miracle. The verb translated "stand still" in vv. 12, 13 can also be translated "cease, stop." Some scholars therefore say that Joshua was asking that the sun stop *shining*, not that it stop moving. The long night's march, largely uphill and with full battle gear, left his troops tired. Joshua asked God to stop the sun from beating down on his troops before exhaustion overcame them. Joshua was seeking a cooler day, not a longer one.

Of course, we do not know exactly what happened. What we know for sure is that God intervened in the normal course of nature at exactly the right moment to give the Israelites victory over their enemies. As the writer of Joshua points out, the greatest marvel lies not in the occurrence of the miracle itself but that "the Lord heeded the voice of a man" (Josh. 10:14).

10:14 the LORD heeded: This is the climax of the section. The author of Joshua marvels (perhaps quoting from the Book of Jasher), not that a miracle happened, but that God listened to the voice of one man and fought on Israel's behalf so grandly. This is plain proof that one person can gain God's attention in prayer.

10:15–18 This verse is identical to v. 43 and appears to be out of place chronologically. It probably is part of the quote from the Book of Jasher, which omits the material intervening in vv. 16–42, between the account of the miracle involving the sun and the moon and Joshua's return. Some scholars see v. 15 as a scribal duplication, since the ends of vv. 14 and 42 are very similar. This too is possible, although perhaps not as plausible as the first option.

10:19 delivered them into your hand: Again Joshua gave God credit for the Israelites' victory. **enter their cities:** The fortified cities of Canaan offered some protection to their people. That is why the ambush at Ai was designed to draw the people out of the city (8:17). In v. 20, we see that some people escaped into the fortified cities.

10:20, 21 The slaughter of the Canaanites was great, but some escaped. This explains why there were still people in these towns later (vv. 31–37). **No one moved his tongue:** Literally, "sharpened his tongue." It means "to criticize" or "to slander."

10:22–24 Joshua told the captains to put their **feet on the necks of these kings** as a clear declaration of victory. See Ps. 110:1: "I [will] make Your enemies Your footstool"; and 1 Cor. 15:25–27, where God places Jesus' enemies "under His feet" (Ps. 8:6). Ancient sculptural reliefs show Assyrian kings doing this to their vanquished enemies.

10:25 be strong and of good courage: Joshua encouraged the people in the same terms God had used to encourage him (1:6, 9; 10:8). Now Joshua had the authority to give this exhortation to others.

10:26, 27 hanged them on five trees . . . until evening: Joshua did to these five kings what he had earlier done to the king of Ai (8:29). As before, he took the bodies down before sundown in accordance with Mosaic legislation (8:29).

10:28–43 After the in-depth account of the battle in 10:1–27, the narrative now moves quickly to summarize the Israelites' southern campaign in Canaan. The kings and people of seven southern cities are mentioned in a series of similar accounts. The Israelites had entered Canaan in the middle, at Jericho. Subsequently their campaigns went through the middle first, turning south (ch. 10) and then north (ch. 11). The fact that exactly seven cities are listed sug-

gests that this may be a summarizing account, describing the destruction of representative cities. Only bare details of their destructions are given, and the successive accounts contain many repeated phrases. Three of the cities (Lachish, Eglon, and Hebron) are ones whose kings had already opposed the Israelites (v. 3). The picture in this section is unequivocally one of complete and swift annihilation of the people throughout the entire region. However, the work was not complete.

10:28, 29 The first city mentioned is the one toward which the Canaanite coalition had fled, **Makkedah** (vv. 10, 16). The five kings had fled and hidden themselves in a cave.

10:30–32 Here and in vv. 32, 42, we are reminded that **the LORD** was Israel's warrior.

10:33–39 The account of the capture of **Gezer** is mentioned only incidentally to the account of the capture of Lachish. According to 16:10, Canaanites were still (or again) living in Gezer some time later.

10:40 This verse presents the first conclusion to the accounts that had begun in 9:1, 2. Here we see that Joshua was victorious over all who lived in **the mountain country** (the word is the same as "hills" in 9:1) **and the South and the lowland and the wilderness slopes.** The word for *South* is "Negev," which refers to the desert in the southern part of the land. The *wilderness slopes* are either the western slopes leading down to the *lowland* near the Mediterranean Sea or else the steep slopes going down to the Dead Sea to the east of the central mountainous area. This summary statement covers the central and southern portions of the land of Canaan, but it does not include the coastlands (13:2–6).

10:41–43 Neither **Kadesh Barnea** nor **Gaza** has been mentioned previously in Joshua; their inclusion here marks the southernmost limits of the land conquered. Gaza was a Philistine city, unconquered in 13:3. **Goshen, even as far as Gibeon** marks the southern and northern limits of this conquest. Goshen here is not the area in the northeastern Nile delta where the Israelites had lived before (Gen. 45:10; 46:28; Ex. 8:22; 9:26), but rather the city in the southern hill country of Canaan mentioned in 11:16; 15:51.

11:1–23 After conquering the southern coalition arrayed against them, Israel now faced a hostile coalition in the north as well, which it defeated (vv. 1–15).

11:1 Hazor was a large and strategic city in northern Israel; it is called "the head of all those kingdoms" in v. 10.

11:2 The geographical description here names areas rather than cities. **Chinneroth** is another name for the Sea of Galilee (12:3).

There was also a town called Chinnereth on the northwest side of the sea (19:35). **the heights of Dor on the west:** Dor was a seaport on the Mediterranean, and no hills are nearby; some commentators understand this to mean "the dunes of Dor."

11:3 The inclusion of **the Jebusite,** that is, the inhabitants of Jerusalem, is striking because Jerusalem was south of Jericho. Evidently, the Canaanites so feared the Israelite threat that they sought help from far and wide. Mount **Hermon in the land of Mizpah** was in the far north, the highest point in northern Palestine. Mizpah was a name of several cities in Israel's history, including one near Lachish (15:38), one

11:5 The site of **the waters of Mero** is not known with certainty. Earlier scholars identified it with Lake Huleh, the small lake that was situated north of the Sea of Galilee until it was drained in modern times. But most scholars today believe the better site was somewhere between the Sea of Galilee and the Mediterranean coast.

11:6, 7 God promised to deliver Israel's enemies into their hands by **tomorrow about this time.** This is especially significant in light of the impressive numbers arrayed against Israel. These are the same words used many years later by Elisha to predict the escape of Samaria from a siege imposed by the Syrians (2 Kin. 7:1). In

Photo by Howard Vos

In their push into northern Canaan, Joshua and his warriors destroyed the city of Hazor (Josh. 11:10, 11). This mound (center) marks the site of the city.

in Benjamin in the south (18:26), and another one in Gilead east of the Jordan (Judg. 10:17).

11:4 Horses at this time were for pulling **chariots.** These vehicles accompanied the infantry and carried a rider with a bow or a supply of spears. The Canaanite armies did not use mounted warriors. These armies came well-armed to fight the Israelites, but it did not matter. God still defeated them (vv. 6–9). Only in the battles of Jericho and Ai did the Israelites initiate the action. Here, as in the other battles described in Joshua, the enemy—usually well-armed and in great numbers—attacked the Israelites. God limited the size of the Israelite army so that the Israelites would not trust their military power. Similarly, the instructions for a king in Deut. 17:14–20 explicitly state that the king was not "to multiply horses for himself" (17:16); that is, not to depend on his military might, but rather on God.

both cases God's promise came true.

11:8 Greater Sidon was a Phoenician city on the Mediterranean coast, and the **Brook Misrephoth** was south of it. The defeat of the Canaanites described here shows them fleeing in all directions in a total rout.

11:9 as the LORD had told him: Joshua was careful to do exactly as instructed (v. 6).

11:10 Hazor was formerly the head: This is probably why Joshua struck at Hazor first, and why the text details its destruction. Excavation of Hazor has shown several destructions in the Late Bronze Age, one from about 1400 B.C. that could easily be attributed to Joshua.

11:11–13 Jericho and Ai were the only other cities burned. Most of the cities of Canaan were taken without being destroyed; their armies were defeated on the battlefield. In this way, most of the cities could be inhabited by Israel without rebuilding.

11:14, 15 Here, as with Ai, the Israelites were allowed to take **all the spoil** for themselves (8:2, 27). Their treatment of the inhabitants was the pattern for all their Canaanite targets: **They left none breathing,** but killed everyone (6:21; 8:22; 10:28, 30, 32, 33, 35, 37, 39, 40; 11:8, 11, 12). This complete annihilation of a population group has posed a significant problem for some people, who have felt that Joshua showed unjustified bloodthirstiness. Yet God had told Moses why Israel was to carry out this destruction in Canaan (Deut. 7:2–11; 20:16–18): the Canaanites were being judged by God for their wickedness.

11:16, 17 These verses summarize both the northern campaign and this entire section of the book (chs. 9—11). Verse 16 mentions many of the same territories as does 10:40, 41. The southern limit of the conquest is given here; **Mount Halak** is near Kadesh Barnea (10:41), and **Seir** is the hill country of Edom, southeast of the Dead Sea. **Baal Gad . . . Mount Hermon:** This is the northern limit of the conquest. Baal Gad was in the Lebanon valley, northwest of Mount Hermon.

11:18–20 to harden their hearts: The persons whose hearts God hardened were not good people, but were people already committed to doing evil (Ps. 14:1–3; Rom. 3:10–18). The marvel is that God has reached out to so many in order to graciously make them His children. See Rom. 9:14–24 concerning God's hardening of Pharaoh's heart.

11:21, 22 The destruction of the **Anakim** from the hill country was especially significant. Their fearsome presence had caused the Israelites to rebel against God's command to enter Canaan many years before (Num. 13:22, 28, 32, 33). But as this generation learned, their size did not matter.

11:23 This verse ends this section (chs. 9—11). It is a transitional verse, looking back to summarize the conquests and looking forward to anticipate the inheritance of the land. The statement **the land rested from war** draws the first section of the book to a close. The next section before the distribution of Israel's inheritance is the list of defeated Canaanite kings (ch. 12). The idea of rest for the entire nation is found in such passages as Deut. 12:10; 25:19, and it is echoed in the summarizing passages of Josh. 21:44; 23:1.

12:1–6 The Israelites' earlier conquests east of the Jordan are mentioned here, their victories over **Sihon,** king of Heshbon, and **Og,** king of Bashan. The Israelites defeated them under Moses' leadership and took possession of their land at that time (Num. 21:21–35). The detailed description of the territory they ruled makes more impressive the victory Israel had won.

Verse 6 confirms that this indeed had been given as an inheritance to the two and one-half tribes who settled there.

12:6, 7 The language of these verses makes it plain that Joshua succeeded Moses in his various roles, first as conqueror and second as giver of the land. The two men are described in the same way: As conquerors, **Joshua and the children of Israel** (v. 7), follow **Moses . . . and the children of Israel** (v. 6). As land-giver, **Joshua gave** (v. 7), as **Moses . . . had given** (v. 6).

12:7–24 The first major section of Joshua is now complete. The Israelites have been given the land, with God's help, and they have destroyed their enemies. The stage is set for parceling out the land and Israel settling into it, hundreds of years after it was first promised to Israel's ancestors.

13:1–21:45 The second half of the Book of Joshua is concerned with the distribution of the land. With its sedentary pace and relative lack of action, it is a sharp contrast to the action-filled first half. A major emphasis is Yahweh, the God of Israel, as the great land-owner and land-giver.

13:1–12 Despite the picture of complete victory in chs. 10; 11, God told Joshua that **there remains very much land yet to be possessed.** This included territories of the Philistines and their neighbors to the south, the Phoenician coastland to the north, and the northern, mountainous territories of Lebanon.

 IN FOCUS "inheritance"

(Heb. *nachalah*) (Josh. 13:7; Deut. 4:20; Pss. 16:5, 94:14) Strong's #5159: The word *inheritance,* meaning "possession" or "property," is linked to the promises of God, particularly those involving the Promised Land (Gen. 13:14–17). When this word is used of the Promised Land, it does not merely refer to what a person wills to his children. Rather God, the Owner of the entire world, had granted His people a specific parcel of ground. He had fixed its boundaries and promised to deliver it to them. However, the concept of Israel's inheritance transcends a simple association with the land. David and Jeremiah both affirm that God Himself is the real inheritance of His people (Ps. 16:5; Jer. 10:16). God's people can find joy and fulfillment in their relationship with God. Nothing this world can offer as an inheritance compares with God Himself (1 Pet. 1:4).

The famous five cities of the Philistines are mentioned (Gaza, Ashdod, Ashkelon, Gath, and Ekron). A hint that their territory remained to be taken appears already in 11:22, in the references to Gaza, Gath, and Ashdod. But Joshua was too old to command the remaining struggle for the land. God Himself would drive out the remaining inhabitants; Joshua merely had to apportion the land to the nine and one-half tribes west of the Jordan.

13:2, 3 the five lords of the Philistines: The word *lords* here translates a Philistine word, not a Hebrew word; it is the only clearly Philistine word recorded in the Bible. It is related to the Greek word that means "tyrant."

13:13 This verse shows that the comprehensive picture of the conquest in chs. 10 and 11 has another side to it, and that Israel had not driven out some peoples (the Geshurites and the Maacathites) and that these peoples would remain (as a contaminating presence) within Israel for many years.

13:14–21 to the tribe of Levi He had given no inheritance: This is an important concept in the Book of Joshua. Here, previous directives about the Levites' inheritance were obeyed (Num. 18:20–24; Deut. 10:8, 9; 18:1–5). Originally, the tribe of Levi was sentenced to be landless for its violent behavior (Gen. 49:5–7), but later the Levites redeemed themselves (Ex. 32:25–28) and were promised a blessing (Deut. 33:8–11). Of the original twelve sons of Jacob, Joseph's inheritance was divided between his two sons, Ephraim and Manasseh. This would make thirteen tribes, but excluding Levi from land inheritance kept the number to twelve (14:3, 4). The Levites did have cities in the territories of each tribe (21:1–42). Instead of a land inheritance, the sacrifices of God would be their privileged inheritance.

13:22 Balaam was the pagan fortune-teller who had been hired by Balak, king of Moab, to curse the Israelites in the wilderness (Num. 22—24). He found that he could speak only what God told him to, yet he sinned by inciting the Moabite women to seduce the Israelite men (Num. 25:1–9; 31:16). Hence, **the children of Israel also killed . . . Balaam.** This record of Balaam's death echoes the notice found at Num. 31:8. The story of how God turned Balaam's desire to curse Israel into a blessing instead is celebrated in several passages (Josh. 24:9, 10; Deut. 23:4, 5; Neh. 13:2; Mic. 6:5).

13:23–32 Large Canaanite cities such as Jericho were typically protected by walls. But there were many smaller villages around the cities. Thus, **the cities and their villages** made up the small city-states typical of Canaan at this time. The villages were permanent settlements without walls, outlying farming villages.

13:33 Levi . . . as He had said to them: This verse reiterates the information about the Levites' landless inheritance (v. 14); here, however, the inheritance is said to be God Himself and not the sacrifices. Because of their unique position, the Levites' relationship with God would be special.

14:1–5 The introduction to the land distribution emphasizes the Levites, who have just been mentioned (13:33). It also emphasizes God as the One who gives the land to Israel. It does this by mentioning His commands to Moses and by mentioning Eleazar, the priest's assistant in the land distribution. This shows that the inheritance of the land was a religious matter and not merely a real estate transaction.

14:2–5 God's place as the giver of the land is also highlighted by mention of the lot. God had commanded the casting of lots to determine Israel's inheritance (Num. 26:55). Thus, that **their inheritance was by lot** does not mean that it was by chance, but that God Himself determined who got what land (18:6, 8, 10; Prov. 16:33). The lot is also mentioned in 15:1; 16:1; 17:1.

14:6 Caleb is described here and elsewhere as **the Kenizzite** (v. 14; Num. 32:12). The Kenizzites were a non-Israelite group descended from Esau through Kenaz (Gen. 15:19; 36:11, 15, 42). Some of this group had apparently associated themselves with Judah at an early stage (Num. 13:6). It seems that Caleb, one of the most faithful to God of his time, was just a generation removed from a non-Israelite family.

14:7–9 These verses review events recorded in Num. 13; 14. The promise of Caleb's inheritance mentioned in v. 9 refers to God's words in Num. 14:24.

14:10, 11 The span of **eighty-five years** indicates the period of time covered by most of the Book of Joshua. According to v. 7, Caleb was forty when he was sent in to spy out the land. Now it was forty-five years later. Since forty years were spent in the wilderness, the conquest occupied five years.

14:12 It was **the Anakim** who had frightened ten of the Israelite spies forty-five years before, triggering Israel's rebellion against God (Num. 13). Caleb was no more afraid of them now than he had been then, even though he was now considerably older. As he says, **it may be that the LORD** will be with me—a use of understatement to express certainty.

14:13 Joshua blessed him: To bless others in the name of the Lord expresses the desire for them to experience God's best (Gen. 27:27–29; 47:10; 49:1–28; Judg. 5:24; Neh. 11:2). It is more than wishful thinking, because blessing in the name of God taps into the power and resources of God. In the Bible, blessings include

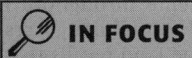

(Heb. *shaqat*) (Josh. 14:15) Strong's #8252: This Hebrew word translated *rest* means "to be at peace." It implies a freedom from anxiety and conflict. God had promised the Israelites *rest* in the Promised Land (Ex. 33:14; Deut. 3:1–20; 12:9, 10). For the nomadic Israelites, this meant freedom from wandering and fighting. In the Book of Joshua, the idea of *rest* is related specifically to the conflicts and hostilities Israel had with their neighbors. God promised His people a peaceful place to settle. Obtaining this *rest* depended on Israel's complete obedience to God's command to drive out the Canaanites (11:23; 14:15). The NT also speaks of the concept of rest. Christians are told that heaven will bring them rest from death, pain, sin, and all other earthly struggles (Heb. 4:1, Rev. 21:4).

children (Gen. 1:28; 28:3), land (Gen. 26:3; 28:4), wealth (Gen. 28:12–14), and a good reputation among others (Gen. 12:3; 22:18). When people are said to bless God, it means they are worshiping Him, ascribing worth to Him and His name (Ps. 104:1), and identifying Him as the source of their good (Ps. 103:1, 2).

14:14 Caleb's wholehearted devotion to God was never in question, even in the wilderness: **He wholly followed the LORD** (v. 8). As a result, he received the land that he requested. In the Bible, people are sometimes rewarded in this life for their faithfulness to God, but not always (Heb. 11:32–40). The believer's ultimate blessing will come in eternity. Those who set their hope on that promise will lose nothing, no matter what they suffer in this life.

14:15 Kirjath Arba: This was the former name of the city of Hebron (Gen. 23:2); it means "city of Arba." Arba was the founding ancestor of the Anakim and is mentioned only here and in 15:13; 21:11. **the land had rest from war:** This comment echoes 11:23, which concludes the account of the southern and northern campaigns.

15:1–12 The boundaries of Judah in southern Canaan are now described in detail. This reinforces the importance of the inheritance and the exact location that each tribe received.

15:13–19 This second passage about Caleb's inheritance (14:6–15) explains how he also took Debir, another city that originally had been taken by Joshua (10:38, 39) but which had evidently fallen back into Canaanite hands. This section closely parallels Judg. 1:12–15.

15:20–63 The cities that Judah inherited number more than a hundred and include their surrounding villages. The list has four parts: (1) cities in the south (vv. 21–32); (2) cities in the lowland (vv. 33–47); (3) cities in the mountain country (vv. 48–60); and (4) cities in the wilderness near the Dead Sea (vv. 61, 62).

15:63 The Jebusites, who inhabited

Jerusalem before the Israelites arrived, stubbornly held on to Jerusalem because the tribe of Judah did not follow through on its obligation to destroy them completely. God did not want Israel to make peace with the inhabitants of the land, but instead to drive them out and utterly destroy them (Num. 33:52–55; Deut. 7:1–5; 20:16–18). Judg. 1:21 repeats this verse almost verbatim, except that it states that Benjamin (not Judah) failed to drive out the Jebusites. This is because Jerusalem sat astride the boundary between Benjamin and Judah. In the early period, Jerusalem did not strictly belong to either tribe. The tribe of Judah did capture Jerusalem later (Judg. 1:8), but Benjamin did not drive out the Jebusites in their portion (Judg 1:21). Apparently Judah took the unfortified southwestern hill, while the tribe of Benjamin failed to take the walled city on the eastern hill. The details are not entirely clear, but it is stated that Jebusites and Israelites lived together (15:63; Judg. 1:21). The city effectively belonged to the Jebusites until the time of David (2 Sam. 5:5–10). Indeed, in Judg. 19:11, 12, the Levite from the hill country of Ephraim called Jebus (Jerusalem) an "alien city."

16:1–4 A single lot determined the inheritance of both of the tribes of Joseph—Ephraim and Manasseh. That these two tribes together received only one lot caused them later to complain (17:14–18).

16:5–9 The separate cities: Some of Ephraim's cities were actually part of Manasseh's inheritance (17:9). The reason for this is not clear, but it may have its basis in the greater blessing extended to Ephraim by Jacob (Gen. 48). Manasseh also inherited towns from the territories of two other tribes, Issachar and Asher (17:11).

16:10 they did not drive out the Canaanites: This previews the many statements about incomplete conquests in Judg. 1. **forced laborers:** The status of the Canaanites in Gezer was somewhat similar to that of the

Gibeonites (9:27), except that there was no treaty involved here, so the status of these Canaanites was somewhat lower.

17:1, 2 Manasseh's firstborn child **Machir** (Gen. 50:23; Num. 26:29) had already received

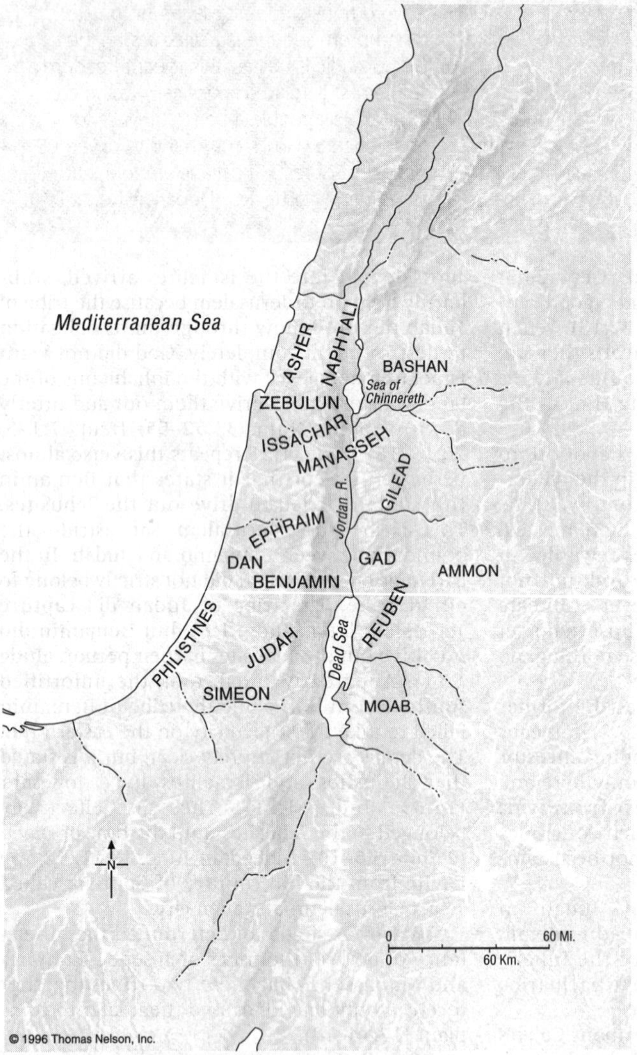

Mediterranean Sea

Division of Land Among the Twelve Tribes

© 1996 Thomas Nelson, Inc.

[Map labels: ASHER, NAPHTALI, BASHAN, ZEBULUN, Sea of Chinnereth, ISSACHAR, MANASSEH, GILEAD, Jordan R., EPHRAIM, DAN, BENJAMIN, GAD, AMMON, PHILISTINES, JUDAH, Dead Sea, REUBEN, SIMEON, MOAB, —N—, 0 60 Mi., 0 60 Km.]

a separate portion, Gilead and Bashan—that is, Manasseh's portion east of the Jordan (13:29–31). The rest of Manasseh's portion was west of the Jordan (vv. 2–13).

17:3–13 Here Joshua faithfully carried out the commands of God through Moses in the matter of the inheritance of Zelophehad, who had no sons (Num. 26:33; 27:1–11). Joshua made sure that the daughters received their inheritance as promised. This brief narrative

emphasizes once again how God keeps His promises, a persistent theme throughout the Book of Joshua. The faith of the daughters of Zelophehad in claiming the land recalls that of Caleb, who also claimed land on the basis of God's promise (14:6–15).

17:14–18 The episode here revives the complaint of the two tribes of Joseph that they together had received only one lot. Joshua encouraged them to take land in the hill country despite their fears of the Canaanites there (vv. 15, 17, 18; Num. 13:28–33). The episode presents a sharp contrast to Caleb's willingness to take the initiative in claiming his land (14:6–15). It also reminds us that plenty of land remained to be taken (13:1).

18:1, 2 Up to this point, Israel's central encampment in the land had been at Gilgal, near Jericho, where they had observed several religious ceremonies (4:19, 20; 5:2–12; 9:6). Now the entire congregation moved to **Shiloh,** about fifteen miles northwest of Jericho, where they set up the tent of meeting. This would remain an important Israelite religious center for several hundred years (19:51; 21:2; Judg. 18:31; 21:12; 1 Sam. 1:9) until the taking of Jerusalem in David's day. The ark was kept there (1 Sam. 3:3), and it was brought into battle against the Philistines, who captured it when Samuel was judge (1 Sam. 4). Soon after this, Shiloh was destroyed (Ps. 78:60; Jer. 7:14). **tabernacle of meeting:** This is the first of two references to the tabernacle in this book; the other reference is in 19:51. The tabernacle was an elaborate portable tent that served as God's "home" when the Israelites were in the wilderness. In it were the ark of the covenant and other holy items. It was made of wooden boards covered with layers of rich fabric (Ex. 26). The name *tabernacle* or *tent of meeting* usually means this tabernacle. However, there was another, different tent also called the tabernacle of meeting (Ex. 33:7). This was a tent that Moses used to pitch outside the camp, where he and the people could meet God. It was a temporary tent during the Israelites' days in the wilderness, and it was not used later in Israel's history.

18:3, 4 How long will you neglect to go: Joshua's rebuke of the seven tribes shows that it was not enough to defeat the inhabitants of the land; they also had to take possession of it. The Israelites had easily defeated the Canaanites (chs. 9—11) but they did not diligently follow up on their victories and occupy all of the land. This laziness disobeyed God's instructions in 13:1 and showed a lack of faith in His promises.

18:5-28 wrote the survey in a book: See 18:11—19:51.

19:1-46 Simeon did not get an independent inheritance, but rather inherited scattered lands within Judah's allotment. Their father Jacob had predicted this (Gen. 49:5-7). Later Simeon and **Judah** acted together (Judg. 1:3). In 1 Chr. 4:24-27 Simeon is described as a much smaller tribe than Judah.

19:47, 48 Dan's capture of **Leshem** is recounted also in Judg. 18, which gives more detail (in that account the city is called Laish). The Danites were forced out of their territory in the south (Judg. 1:34) and migrated north (Judg. 18:27-31), where they captured Leshem and renamed it **Dan.**

19:49, 50 The section ends, appropriately enough, with **Joshua** receiving his **inheritance** in Ephraim. **According to the word of the LORD:** The Bible does not record the command granting Joshua this particular inheritance, though the promise to Caleb and Joshua in Num. 14:30 did guarantee both of these faithful spies an inheritance in the land.

19:51 This is a summary statement about the allotments for each tribe, echoing elements from 14:1; 17:4; 18:6, 10. It is a fitting summary to the entire section of chs. 13—19. The involvement of **Eleazar the priest, Joshua, . . . and the heads of the . . . tribes,** as well as the mention of the tabernacle at **Shiloh,** all lend an air of importance and solemnity. The entire distribution of the land had taken place under God's watchful eye, decently and in order. The land was God's to give, and He had now given it.

20:1-9 The cities of refuge were to come from the Levitical cities, in fulfillment of the Mosaic legislation of Num. 35:9-28 (Deut. 4:41-43; 19:1-10). This legislation, the essence of which is repeated here, provided sanctuary zones where someone who had killed a person unintentionally could flee to live in safety.

20:1-6 accidentally or unintentionally: Literally, "through error and without knowing." God's Law made allowance for motives and intent just as modern criminal codes distinguish unintentional killing from murder. The word translated *avenger* (Heb. *go'el*) in **avenger of blood** is translated *close relative* in Ruth 3:13;

4:1. The basic meaning of the word is "protector of family rights." Num. 35 gives the demands and limitations on the avenger of blood, but it does not give license to take revenge. God clearly reserved that task for Himself alone (Deut. 32:35; Is. 34:8; Rom. 12:19). God's provision of the cities of refuge put a limit on private acts of vengeance.

20:7-9 The cities of refuge were evenly distributed so that none was more than a day's journey from any part of Israel's land. Golan, Ramoth Gilead, and Bezer were on the east side of the Jordan River, and Kedesh, Shechem, and Kirjath Arba (Hebron) were on the west. Despite their importance here and in the Pentateuch, cities of refuge as such are not mentioned again in the Bible.

21:1-42 Forty-eight cities were designated as the ones in which the Levites could live and graze their cattle nearby. These cities would remain the possession of the other tribes, but the Levites would have living and grazing rights therein, since they were to have no other land portion (13:14, 33; 14:3; 18:7). As teachers of the Law (Deut. 33:10; 2 Chr.. 17:7-9; 35:3; Mal. 2:6-9), the Levites could more easily teach all the people if they lived throughout the land.

21:1-3 The Levites came to Joshua to claim their rightful share of territory, which included cities throughout the territories God had promised (Num. 35:1-8). The **common-lands** refers to land that surrounded each city.

21:4-8 Here the Levitical cities are determined by the **lot.** The word *lot* occurs five times in these five verses; in this case it was a God-directed method of choosing the cities. God was in control of every aspect of the inheritance process.

21:4, 9-42 The priestly branch of the **Kohathites,** descended through Aaron, received thirteen cities from Judah, Simeon, and Benjamin. Thus the Aaronic priests were strategically located to serve in the temple and in the territory that remained in the hands of descendants of Judah through the years before and following the Babylonian Exile. Some of the cities were not actually in Israel's possession at this time (for example, Gezer, v. 21), and some appear never to have been in Israel's control for any length of time (for example, the Philistine cities of Eltekeh and Gibbethon, v. 23). These names may simply reflect the actual allotments in Joshua's day. Much land remained to be taken even after it had been allotted (13:1; 15:63; 16:10; 17:12, 13).

21:43-45 This glorious conclusion to these two chapters and to the entire section (chs. 13—21) celebrates the fact that **all came to pass** exactly as God promised. What has been visible all along is now said plainly: the God of Israel is

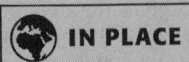 **IN PLACE**   # The Levitical Cities

In some Western nations today, religious institutions enjoy certain privileges such as tax exemption for church property and tax advantages for ordained clergy. Levites in ancient Israel enjoyed even greater benefits. One of the main ones was the use of forty-eight cities which are referred to as Levitical cities (Josh. 21:1–3).

Unlike the other eleven tribes, the tribe of Levi was not allotted any land in Canaan. Instead, God designated Himself as the Levites' "portion" (Num. 18:20–24). But because God considered the Levites a "gift" to the people to attend to the tasks of worship and sacrifice (Num. 18:5, 6), He commanded that each tribe set aside a proportionate number of cities and their surrounding pasture land for the use of the Levites (35:1–8).

Rights and Privileges

Levites were probably not the only people who lived in the Levitical cities, but they enjoyed special status as they lived alongside the other citizens. For example, Levites were allowed to graze their livestock on lands near their cities. Likewise, much of their support came from a ten percent tax of the people collected every three years (Deut. 26:12–15).

In addition, the Mosaic Law protected Levites from dispossession (Lev. 25:32–34), and they were granted an unlimited right of redemption, unlike other tribes. Still, as they were somewhat dependent on their communities for sustenance and protection, the Levites were accountable to local residents.

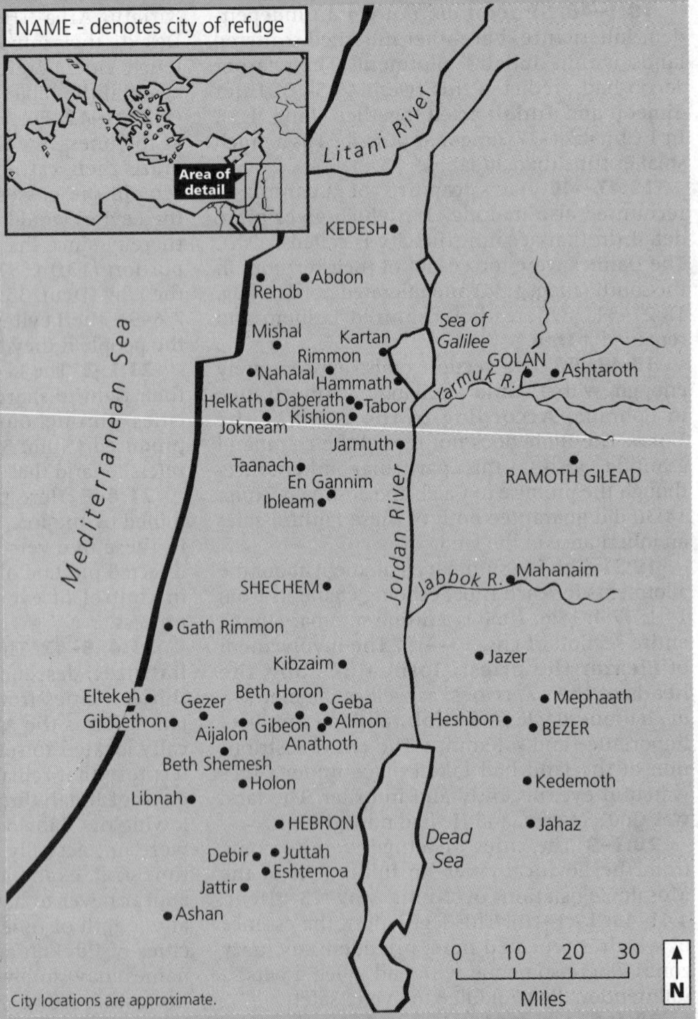

NAME - denotes city of refuge

Area of detail

Litani River
KEDESH
Abdon
Rehob
Mishal   Kartan   Sea of Galilee
Rimmon   GOLAN
Nahalal   Hammath   Ashtaroth
Helkath Daberath Tabor
Joknearn   Kishion
Jarmuth
Taanach
En Gannim   RAMOTH GILEAD
Ibleam
Mediterranean Sea
Jordan River
Yarmuk R.
SHECHEM   Jabbok R.   Mahanaim
Gath Rimmon
Jazer
Kibzaim
Eltekeh   Gezer Beth Horon   Mephaath
Gibbethon   Geba   Heshbon   BEZER
Aijalon Gibeon Almon
Beth Shemesh   Anathoth
Holon   Kedemoth
Libnah
HEBRON   Jahaz
Debir Juttah   Dead
Eshtemoa   Sea
Jattir
Ashan

0   10   20   30
Miles   N

City locations are approximate.

Strategically Located

The location of the Levitical cities, which tended to be on the borders between the tribes rather than at their centers, had the result of distributing the Levites throughout the country. This made the cities:

Mission stations for teaching. The Levites had a special ministry of teaching among the tribes (Deut. 33:8–10; 2 Chr. 35:3–6). Their cities were not to be places for shrines but bases from which

The Levitical Cities *cont.*

the Levites helped all the cities and tribes know and follow the Law.

Centers of justice and political influence. The Levitical teaching was more than just religious; it had significance for civil and political policy as well, as is evident in the reforms of King Jehoshaphat. He sent Levites along with governmental officials to teach the Law, so that peace might prevail over rebellion (2 Chr. 17:7–10).

One of the most important roles delegated to six of the Levitical cities was to be "cities of refuge" (Num. 35:11). Strategically located for accessibility, they provided protection from revenge for a person accused of manslaughter until the elders of the city could look into the matter and render a judgment. This placed the Levites in direct contact with matters of justice.

As a result of these influential responsibilities, some of the Levitical cities became major centers for Israel's civic and religious life, especially Gibeon, Bethel, and Gilgal.

a promise-keeping God, who gave Israel the land in accordance with the promises He had made with its ancestors, including Moses and the patriarchs. And in addition to giving them the land, He also granted them **rest.**

22:1–34 The chapter contains warm-hearted displays of spiritual devotion to God on the part of all the tribes. A central concern is the people's relationship with God and the unity of Israel's worship.

22:2, 3 The obedience to **Moses** and Joshua of the tribes settled east of the Jordan is commended here. The issue of the unity of the nation had arisen at the beginning, and these tribes had proven faithful.

22:4 rest . . . as He promised: This idea of rest as a gift from God is part of the fabric of the Book of Joshua. It had been promised by God (1:13, 15), and once again God fulfilled His promises.

22:5 The passionate exhortation to **take careful heed** captures the heart of this chapter. The words echo the call to faithfulness in Deut. 4:29; 6:5; 10:12, 13; 11:13. The verbs in this verse give a comprehensive picture of what a proper relationship to God includes: to **love** God, to **walk** in His ways, to **hold fast** (or cling) to Him, and to **serve** Him. This is the essence of the "first and great commandment," to love God wholeheartedly (Deut. 6:5; Matt. 22:37). Loving God is much more than an affirmation or a feeling; it is obedience, loyalty, and service to God above all else.

22:6–9 Joshua blessed them: The blessing here involves many riches from the spoils of the land (v. 7).

22:10–20 A crisis that tested Israel's unity now arose.

22:11 have built an altar: The account does not reveal why this altar was built until

after the events have developed into a full-blown crisis (vv. 21–29).

22:12 God had commanded Israel not to offer burnt offerings or sacrifices at any location except the tabernacle (Lev. 17:8, 9) and not to worship other gods (Deut. 13:12–15). The punishment for violating both laws was death, and this is why **Israel gathered . . . to go to war** against their brethren.

22:13, 14 Everything was done "by the book." First, the nine and one-half tribes west of the Jordan acted in perfect unity, carefully choosing one representative each, the highest ranking ruler from each tribe. Second, they sent the priest **Phinehas** to head up the delegation, reflecting their concern that true worship and ritual be maintained. All present probably remembered the tragedy at Baal Peor (Num. 25), when drastic actions had to be taken to stop the plague (v. 17).

22:15, 16 We know how serious Phinehas and his companions considered the offense—if it were indeed such an offense—from the term he used for it, **treachery.** This is the same Hebrew word used of Achan's sin in v. 20 (7:1).

22:17 The iniquity of Peor included the fact that the Israelites worshiped the Moabite gods and committed immoral acts with the women of Moab. The tribes west of the Jordan feared that this could happen again. The phrase **not cleansed till this day** implies that Israel had never completely rid itself of this sin, that it always flirted with, and at times participated in, the idolatry and attractions of neighboring pagan religious systems.

22:18–20 He will be angry with the whole congregation: No one can sin alone. If the tribes east of the Jordan were indeed sinning, then the entire nation would feel the effects, as in the case of Achan's sin (v. 20; 7:1).

22:21-29 The Transjordan tribes respond passionately that they are innocent of any rebellion or breach of faith. The section shows them innocent of anything malicious; they never intended to use this altar for sacrifices to God Himself, let along to other gods. Rather, they intended it only as a memorial or witness for their children, and their concern is the same as that of the tribes west of the Jordan: that the *unity* of Israel be maintained.

22:22 The repetition of **the LORD** God of gods reveals the deep emotion in the response of the tribes east of the Jordan. In an agitated state of mind, their words came out somewhat awkward, yet completely sincere. They firmly maintained their innocence and tried to convince their fellow countrymen of it.

22:23-25 The tribes from east of the Jordan were afraid that geographical distance would isolate them and in time cause the Israelites west of the Jordan to reject them. Thus they built the **altar** to prevent the existing unity from being lost.

22:26-29 Here is the replica: The eastern tribes chose their words carefully; the word *replica* clearly shows that they never intended this altar to be a substitute for the true altar at the tabernacle. Rather, they intended it only to serve as a **witness.** The same Hebrew word is used elsewhere for the pattern for the tabernacle given to Moses (Ex. 25:9, 40) and the "plans" of the temple that David gave to Solomon (1 Chr. 28:11).

22:30-34 The eastern tribes' impassioned defense quickly defused the crisis, satisfying the people's representatives. The representatives' response occupies only one verse, an abrupt ending to a crisis that is described in twenty preceding verses (vv. 10-29). The western tribes accepted the words of the Transjordan tribes on this matter, and the altar remained.

22:34 The climax of the chapter asserts that the altar was **a witness . . . that the LORD** is God. Previously, the chapter indicated only that it was to be a witness (vv. 27, 28), without saying what it would be a witness of. In a similar

vein, Jesus told His disciples that people would know they were His disciples by seeing their love for each other; that is, their love would point people to Christ (John 13:35).

23:1-16 This speech is reminiscent of the last speeches of Jacob (Gen. 49), Moses (Deut. 32, 33), and David (2 Sam. 23:1-7). In it, Joshua sums up all of the important motifs introduced throughout the book, passionately urging Israel to be steadfast in loving God, in obeying His Law, and in keeping itself uncontaminated by the religious practices of any of its neighbors. And he promises that Yahweh will be with Israel in the as-yet-unfinished task of driving out its enemies.

23:1, 2 a long time: The exact time intended here is impossible to know with certainty. The verse clearly echoes 13:1 (with its reference to Joshua's advanced **age**) and 21:44 (with its reference to **rest**). Some scholars believe that this "long time" is calculated from the beginning of the book (when God *began* to give rest to the land). However, more plausibly, it refers to the completion of the process. If this took place at the end of Joshua's life (he died at age 110: 24:29), and if he was anywhere near Caleb's age of eighty-five when the land was distributed (14:10), then his farewell speeches would have come some twenty-five years after the main events in the book.

23:3-5 He who has fought for you: A reminder that the land belonged to the Lord and that He gave it to Israel, even to the extent of fighting on their behalf (1:3; 8:7; 10:14, 19, 42).

23:6 be very courageous: Again, Joshua used the same words that God had spoken to him years earlier when He commissioned him (1:7-9). See also Joshua's words to the eastern tribes in 22:5.

23:7-9 That **no one has been able to stand** against the tribes of Israel was a fulfillment of God's promise in 1:5.

23:10 One man . . . shall chase a thousand: These words are similar to the promises in Lev. 26:7, 8. The power God's people had over their enemies was so dramatic it had to be miraculous.

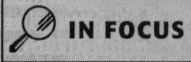 **IN FOCUS**   **"hold fast"**

(Heb. *dabaq*) (Josh. 22:5; 23:8; 2 Kin. 18:5, 6; Is. 41:7) Strong's #1692: The Hebrew word translated *hold fast* means "to cling tightly." Related Hebrew words mean "soldering" and "glue." The same Hebrew word is used to describe the intimacy between a husband and wife (Gen. 2:24) and Ruth's loyalty to Naomi (Ruth 1:14). When we are commanded to *hold fast* to God in the Scriptures (23:8), it means we must resolve to remain faithful to Him no matter what the circumstances. In other words, our devotion to Him must be stronger than any other loyalty.

23:11 The exhortation to **love the Lord** your God comes from Deut. 6:5.

23:12 The word translated **cling** is the same word translated *hold fast* in v. 8, bringing the different instances of clinging into sharp contrast. God wanted His people to cling to Him, not to the Canaanites they were driving out. This required, among other things, that they not **make marriages** with unbelieving foreigners under any circumstances (Ex. 34:11–16; Deut. 7:1–4). Years later Solomon ignored this command and proved how destructive the sin of intermarriage could be (1 Kin. 3:1; 11:1–8; 2 Cor. 6:14).

23:13, 14 they shall be snares and traps: See Ex. 23:33; Num. 33:55; Deut. 7:16. **not one thing has failed:** A strong affirmation of God's faithfulness, one of the book's main themes.

23:15, 16 you shall perish quickly from the good land: This indeed happened to Israel in its later history. This warning saw its most dramatic fulfillment when Judah was carried into Babylonian captivity because of its repeated rebellion against God (2 Kin. 25). But Israel's rebellion began almost immediately, during the period of the judges, when Israel began to do precisely what was warned against here (Judg. 2:16–23; 3:1–6).

24:1–13 This section reviews the past in terms of God's gracious provisions for His people. Verses 1 and 2 suggest the more formal nature of this chapter, since the leaders **presented themselves before God** and since the historical review is introduced with the traditional prophetic speech formula, **Thus says the Lord God of Israel.**

24:1 Shechem is a site with an ancient tradition of religious significance and covenant making in Israel, going back to Abraham's day (8:30–35; Gen. 12:6; 33:18–20; 34:1–31; 37:12–17; Deut. 11:26–32; 27:1–26; Judg. 9:31–57). Archaeological excavation has uncovered a series of temples, sanctuaries, and ceremonial standing stones from almost every period of its existence.

24:2–4 Israel's ancestors did not worship the true God at first; until God called them, Abraham and his relatives had **served other gods** (Gen. 31:1–4, 19, 34, 35). The words of this verse are used in the Passover celebration of the Jews all over the world today. When they recite these words, those who celebrate confess that the Lord's choice of their fathers was not because of an innate superiority in Abraham. Abraham and others were mere idolaters. But God chose Abraham and Sarah to be His special people for reasons known only to Him. Likewise in our case, it is not because of something wonderful in ourselves that God has reached out to us, but because of His loving, sovereign, gracious choice.

24:5–9 Afterward I brought you out: God's review of His gracious actions on behalf of His people (vv. 2–5) included Joshua's generation. God did not just make Himself known in ages past; He also worked mightily and graciously for the people of Joshua's day. Christians today are part of a long lineage of the people of faith (Heb. 11).

24:10 I would not listen to Balaam: For the full story on Balaam, see Num. 22—24.

24:11, 12 God's use of **the hornet** to aid Israel fulfilled the promise of Ex. 23:28. The hornet may be: (1) symbolic of the pharaoh of Egypt, whose symbols were a bee or hornet; (2) symbolic of God's terror or panic among the Canaanites (2:9–11, 24; 5:1; 6:27; Ex. 15:14–16); or (3) actual hornets. Whatever the case, the point is that God fought for Israel. The phrase **two kings** refers to Sihon and Og, whom Israel had defeated in the wilderness (Num. 21:21–35). These victories were God's, not dependent upon Israel's military power. The **sword** and **bow** are mentioned in connection with the first Israelite capture of Shechem by Jacob (Gen. 48:22).

24:13 A land for which you did not labor fulfills the promises given by Moses in Deut. 6:10, 11. The land was God's gracious gift to His people.

24:14–28 The proper response to these gracious dealings of Yahweh was for Israel to forsake other gods and follow Him, and Joshua himself would lead the way by example. The people's response was one of commitment, after which Joshua warned them about the consequences of this commitment, which the people then willingly accepted. The people ratified the covenant and were dismissed to their inheritances.

24:14, 15 Joshua's words in these verses contain a rare appeal to Israel to choose between God and the many false substitutes. If Israel would not choose to serve the Lord, they would have to choose between the gods that their ancestors worshiped and **the gods of the Amorites** (that is, the Canaanites). Of course, the appeal is rhetorical; from God's perspective there is only one option. With his famous words, Joshua clearly and unambiguously took his stand on the side of the living God. Joshua modeled a perfect leader's actions. A leader must be willing to move ahead and commit himself to the truth regardless of the people's inclinations. Joshua's bold example undoubtedly encouraged many to follow with the affirmations of vv. 16–18.

24:16–18 In their response to Joshua's challenge, the people acknowledged their debt to God for all their good fortune. This was a crucial point. As long as they remembered what God had done for them, they would be inclined to serve Him. Moses had said this many years before (Deut. 8:11–17).

24:19–21 Immediately after Joshua exhorted the Israelites to serve God (v. 14), he stated **you cannot serve the Lord!** This use of exaggeration emphasizes the gravity of the obligation to which the people committed themselves. Theirs was not to be a nominal, superficial faith. Subsequent history shows that Israel's record was poor in this regard. Joshua's challenge is also for Christians. Although salvation is God's free gift through Jesus Christ to those who believe, truly following Christ is the difficult way of the Cross (Matt. 16:24; John 1:12; 1 Cor. 15:1–5).

24:22–27 Joshua and **the people** sealed their covenant to serve the Lord by writing these words in **the Book of the Law of God** and by the erecting a **large stone** under an oak tree, the same tree that Jacob had encountered when he came to Shechem. This tree was near the Lord's **sanctuary,** which was probably not a formal building or temple but the "holy place" created at Shechem by the act of bringing of the tabernacle there. The reference to the people presenting themselves "before God" (v. 1) may indicate that the tabernacle was there. The stone under the oak tree functioned as a legal reminder or witness of the covenant just entered into by the people. Now the stone and the people were both witnesses. This echoes the function of the altar built by the tribes that settled east of the Jordan, which also was a witness (22:34). A large standing stone that dates to the Late Bronze Age (that is, roughly the time represented in this story) has been found at Shechem, and is possibly the stone mentioned here.

24:28 When Joshua dismissed the people, it was **each to his own inheritance,** fittingly closing this section with a reminder of one of the book's major themes.

24:29–33 The three burials signified the ends of eras: Joshua and Eleazar, the leader and priest of the people and the last recent links with Egypt, and Joseph, a distant link with Egypt and with the promises to the patriarchs.

24:29 This first reference to Joshua as the **servant of the Lord** shows clearly how Joshua had "grown into the job" that Moses had vacated. Now the book comes full circle, recalling the references in 1:1 to Moses as the servant of the Lord and to Joshua as merely Moses' assistant.

24:30, 31 Joshua was buried on his own land, in the city he had asked for and built, Timnath Serah (19:50). The Old Greek versions have a lengthy and fascinating addition in v. 30, stating that Joshua was buried in the tomb with the flint knives with which he had circumcised the Israelites years earlier, and that they were still there "to this day."

24:32 The brief account of the transfer of Joseph's body to Canaan from **Egypt** notes the fulfillment of Joseph's prophecy given hundreds of years earlier (Gen. 50:24, 25).

24:33 **Eleazar** the high priest had figured significantly in the land distribution, and now he too received a decent burial in his own land.

The Book of

Judges

T HE BOOK OF JUDGES IS A HISTORICAL NARRATIVE that contrasts God's faithfulness with Israel's apostasy. Despite the repeated falling away of His people, God provided deliverers—the judges—time and again. He did not do this unthinkingly or mechanically, nor was He manipulated by Israel's cries for help (3:9, 15; 4:3; 6:6; 10:10). He did not spare Israel from the consequences of its actions, as its constant trouble

with foreign oppressors indicates. Rather, God delivered Israel from oppression because of His promises to Abraham and his descendants. He remembered His vow to give the land of Canaan to Israel. Thus, the preservation of God's people was not due to their merit or goodness, nor even to their willingness to repent. Rather, God demonstrated His compassion and pity on a wayward people who grieved Him continually (2:16, 18) by providing bold leaders to rescue them. In fact, the real hero of Judges is God Himself, who alone remains faithful despite the failings of His people—and even of the judges.

The book was written to show the consequences of disobedience to God and the necessity of summoning a righteous king who would lead the people to God. In contrast to the serene way in which the Book of Joshua ends, with Israel in harmony with God's commands, Judges reveals that Israel began to disobey God even in the time of Joshua, and that this disobedience grew more serious—and more debased—over time. Judges 2:16–23 establishes the

cyclical pattern of sin, slavery, and salvation that would dominate the time of the judges. However, the book makes clear that the cycle had a downward spiral. Each new outbreak of disobedience and idolatry took Israel further away from God and deeper into sin and misery. By the end of the book, it is clear that Israel had violated its covenant with God in almost every imaginable way.

The purpose of the message is supported by the structure of the book itself. A close examination of chs. 17—21 leads to the conclusion that they are out of sequence with the events in the earlier chapters. Clues within the text support the theory that the events described in these latter chapters actually took place early in the period of the judges. For instance, we see the near unanimous action of Israel's tribal convocation, which successfully unites to take punitive action against Benjamin in ch. 20. This tribal league was clearly active during the time of Phinehas and in Joshua's day (Josh. 22:9–34). In these chapters, the Philistines are not mentioned as a military threat; the military campaigns described in chs. 20 and 21 would have been unlikely in later times, when the Philistines dominated much of Israel's territory. Furthermore, Bethel and Mizpah are both named as sites of a major religious sanctuary (20:1, 18, 31; 21:1) rather than Shiloh, which was a more prominent religious center in the Philistine period (1 Sam. 1:3, 9; 3:21; 4:4).

This arrangement of the narrative, while not strictly chronological, reinforces the theme that the period of the judges was one of steep decline. The sordid events in these last chapters, while they may have occurred early in the period, are purposely placed at the end of the book as a fitting epitaph to a degenerate time.

The author of this collection of historical writings about the judges, who ruled Israel during a span of several centuries, is never identified. Neither are there any clues elsewhere in Scripture. Late Jewish tradition ascribed its authorship to Samuel. This is certainly possible, but there is no way of knowing for sure.

Certainly the book was written after the last events recorded in it (about 1050 B.C.). The reference in 18:30 to "the day of the captivity of the land" refers most likely to the Babylonian exile (sixth century B.C.). This suggests that a later version of the book may have been compiled during the Exile or afterward. However, the reference to Jebusites living in Jerusalem "to this day" (1:21) suggests that a portion of the book may have been written prior to David's capture of Jerusalem around 1000 B.C. It would seem likely that Jebusites who survived the battle would have left voluntarily or

been expelled. Yet a few scriptural references suggest that some Jebusites remained in Jerusalem after David's conquest (2 Sam. 24:16), so this is not a conclusive argument. If one believes that Judges was written sometime late in the eleventh century B.C., then it becomes more credible to suggest that Samuel wrote most or all the book. Yet, like the question of authorship, the approximate date of the composition of Judges remains cloaked in uncertainty.

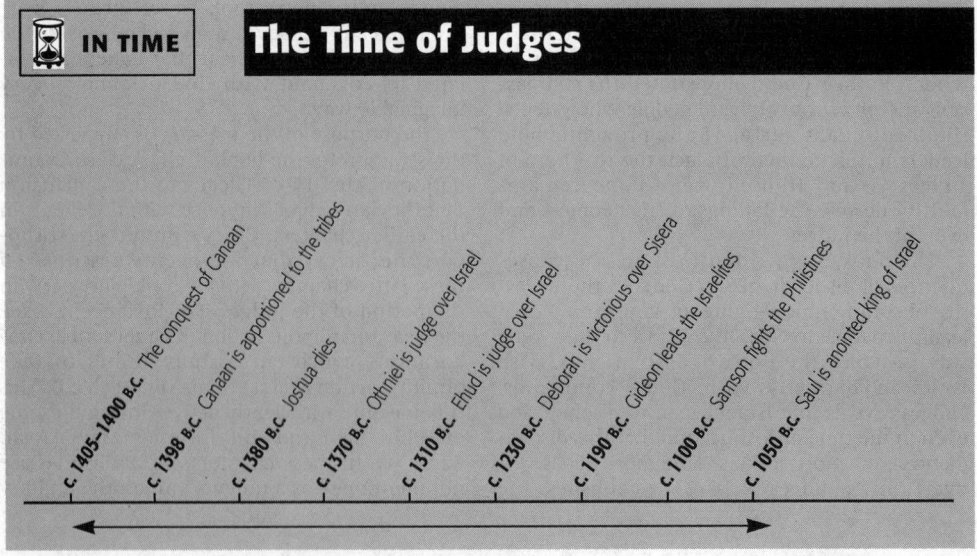

IN TIME

The Time of Judges

c. 1405–1400 B.C. The conquest of Canaan

c. 1398 B.C. Canaan is apportioned to the tribes

c. 1380 B.C. Joshua dies

c. 1370 B.C. Othniel is judge over Israel

c. 1310 B.C. Ehud is judge over Israel

c. 1230 B.C. Deborah is victorious over Sisera

c. 1190 B.C. Gideon leads the Israelites

c. 1100 B.C. Samson fights the Philistines

c. 1050 B.C. Saul is anointed king of Israel

Commentary

1:1–2:5 The introductory passage of Judges shows continuing military activity (1:1–26), which indicates that all military conquests had

not been completed during Joshua's day. It then explicitly details the incomplete conquests of several tribes (1:27–36). That Israel had disobeyed God's directions for conquest is evident in 2:1–5, where the Angel of the Lord makes such an accusation. In sharp contrast to the peaceful and unified picture of Israel at the end of the Book of Joshua, the breakdown of Israelite society is already evident. In Judg. 1, the conquest was somewhat incomplete (vv. 21, 27–36 give detailed accounts of land that various tribes had left unsubdued). This contrasts with the picture of the conquest in Joshua, especially Josh. 10. For example, Josh. 10:40 states, "Joshua subdued the whole region, including the hill country, the Negev, the western foothills and the mountain slopes, together with their kings. He left no survivors. He totally destroyed all who breathed." The contrast, however, is not merely between Josh. 10 and Judg. 1. Even in the book of Joshua, we have indications that the conquest was not complete. This is especially evident in Josh. 11:22; 13:2–6; 15:63; 16:10; 17:12, 13, all of which speak of people in the land who survived and who were not driven out. Also in contrast to the picture in Josh. 10 about a quick sweep, Josh. 11:18 states, "Joshua waged war against all these kings for a long time."

1:1–21 Judges begins with a record of conquests in southern Palestine. The tribe of Judah assumed leadership and allied with Simeon in campaigns against the Canaanites who had not been driven out of their respective territories. They fought a series of successful campaigns, "going up" against Bezek and Jerusalem, "going down" against Hebron, Debir, and Zephath, and concluding with an invasion of Philistine territory. They had mixed success against the Canaanites, but their successes (vv. 4–18, 20) outweighed their failures (vv. 19, 21).

1:1 Now after the death of Joshua it came to pass that: Judges begins as the Book of Joshua does, with reference to the death of the previous leader—Moses in Josh. 1:1, Joshua here. Yet no new leader was commissioned to lead Israel after Joshua; rather, the tribe of Judah was designated to lead in the fight against the Canaanites (1:1–4). The choice of Judah was the first hint that Jacob's prediction for Judah (Gen. 49:8–12) was coming to pass. The prophecy would come to fruition with the establishment of the monarchy under David and his descendants; David was from the tribe of Judah.

1:2 Judah shall go up: Judah's leadership had been anticipated as early as Jacob's blessing, in which he promised that kings would come from the line of Judah (Gen. 49:8–12).

1:3 History bound the tribes of **Judah** and

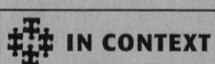 **IN CONTEXT** | ## From Conquest to Chaos

Periods just after great national victories can be times of great vulnerability. When people have overcome huge obstacles, survived grave threats, or defeated dangerous enemies, they tend to let down their guard and relax. That puts them at great risk, not just for external attack but also for internal decay.

This was the experience of Israel during the period of the judges. Having achieved impressive military victories under Joshua, the Israelites succumbed to moral and civil anarchy after Joshua's death. The root of their troubles was chronic disobedience in regard to the Law, and repeated departure from the Lord.

Judges makes for troubling reading because it shows a nation in moral and spiritual decline. This period has been called Israel's Dark Age.

Simeon together. They were both descended from the same mother (Gen. 29:33, 35), and Simeon had inherited land in Judah's territory (Josh. 19:1, 9). Theirs was a natural alliance.

1:4, 5 the Canaanites and the Perizzites: See Josh. 3:10. The site of the battle of **Bezek** between Israelites and Canaanites is unknown. Many scholars believe that it took place near present-day Khirbet Bezqa, about three miles northeast of Gezer, northwest of Jerusalem. However, 1 Sam. 11:8–11 mentions a town called Bezek northeast of Shechem in the territory of Manasseh, where Saul took a census of the people. Considering that Judah was leading a campaign on behalf of all Israel (vv. 1, 2), a battle in Manasseh's territory is quite possible. Later, Judah spearheaded a campaign in its own territory (vv. 8–19).

1:6, 7 Adoni-Bezek: The name of this minor king means "Lord of Bezek." To **cut off his thumbs and big toes** would prevent Adoni-Bezek from ever engaging in battle again, since a thumb was needed to hold a sword and the big toes were necessary for running. The practice of mutilating vanquished enemies is recorded in ancient sources found in Mesopotamia and Greece and was practiced by Adoni-Bezek himself. As a result of his wounds, however, Adoni-Bezek died.

1:8, 9 After the battle at Bezek, Judah pressed the campaign against the Canaanites elsewhere in **Jerusalem** and the **mountains,** the southland, and the **lowland.** Jerusalem was captured and burned, but not settled. Verse 21 states that Benjamin did not drive out the Jebusites from the city. For more on this differing account, read Josh. 15:63. The complete conquest and settlement of Jerusalem was not accomplished until David's day (2 Sam. 5:6–10).

1:10–15 The capture of Hebron and Debir appears as a new conquest, but these victories had already been recounted in Josh. 15. This passage is probably a reference to the earlier victory (or else the passage in Joshua is anticipating the victories to come). The account in vv. 11–15 is taken almost verbatim from Josh. 15:15–19, and it is the third account of Caleb's inheritance (the other account is found in Josh. 14:6–15).

1:10 The name **Hebron** means "Confederacy." This city's name was formerly **Kirjath Arba** (literally "city of four"). Arba was also the name of a leader of the Anakim (Josh. 14:15). From the names it is conjectured that Hebron was originally a close-knit alliance of four cities. Hebron, about twenty miles southwest of Jerusalem, was where Abraham settled and built an altar (Gen. 13:18). **they killed Sheshai, Ahiman, and Talmai:** Caleb drove these three men out of Hebron (v. 20; Josh. 15:14).

1:11 Debir was the next city captured by the Israelites. Its former name Kirjath Sepher means "City of the Book"; it may have been an administrative center where records were kept. However, the modern archaeological site, Tell Beit Mirsim, has not yielded any great library or records. Nevertheless, archaeologists have uncovered a strongly fortified city, which was destroyed close to 1200 B.C.

1:12, 13 Caleb offering his daughter in marriage as a prize is similar to Saul requiring one hundred Philistine foreskins of David as the price for his daughter Michal (1 Sam. 18:25).

1:14, 15 As a dowry, Caleb's daughter asked for springs of water in addition to the land he had given her. Land without fresh water was almost worthless, so her request was an astute one.

1:16, 17 References to the **South** (that is, the Negev) in vv. 9; 15 included mention of the descendants of **the Kenite,** Moses' father-in-law, Jethro (Ex. 3:1). This family connection

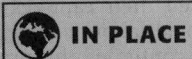 **IN PLACE** **Unfulfilled Expectations**

The Israelites departed from Egypt with high hopes. They had set out on a journey that would bring them into a land "flowing with milk and honey" (Ex. 13:3–5). Their first exposure to Canaan went badly (Num. 13; 14), but a new generation under Joshua finally crossed the Jordan to take possession of Canaan (Josh. 1:11).

Yet by the end of Joshua's life, major portions of the Promised Land remained unconquered, and many of the Canaanite and Amorite inhabitants, whom Israel was supposed to displace, remained in the cities (Judg. 1:27–36). This failure meant that Israel would go through several generations of civil, political, and spiritual unrest (2:11–23).

It was not until God raised up David as a unifying king that the extent of Israel's borders would begin to match the expectations originally laid out by God (Num. 34:1–12).

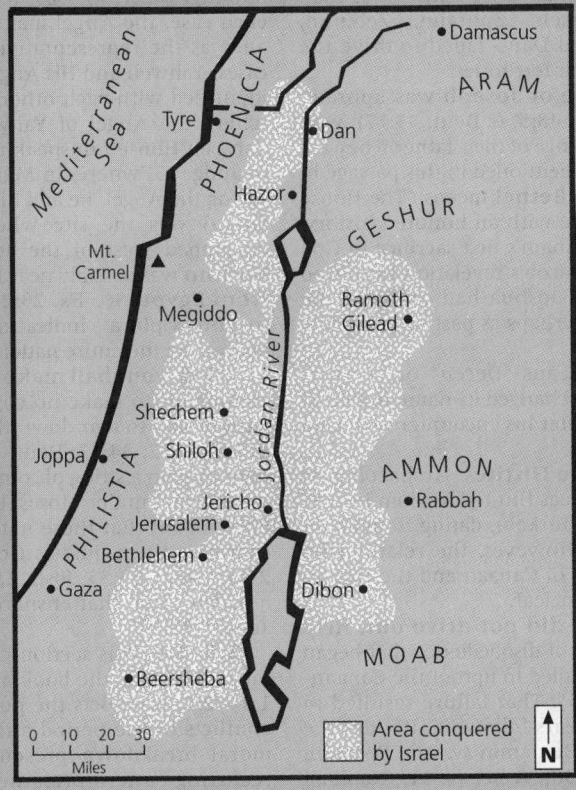

had led to friendly relations between the Israelites and the Kenites, who were Midianites, in the wilderness (Num. 10:29–32). Their harmonious settling with Judah fulfilled Moses' words of Num. 10:29. **City of Palms** is a reference to Jericho (Deut. 34:3; 2 Chr. 28:15), nestled deep in the Jordan Valley, northeast of Jerusalem.

1:18 Gaza ... Ashkelon ... Ekron were three of five major cities in the Philistine kingdom (the other two were Ashdod and Gath, Josh. 13:2, 3). Israel was not able to hold these cities for very long. By Samson's day, all three cities were in Philistine hands again (Judg. 14:19; 16:1; 1 Sam. 5:10).

1:19, 20 they could not drive out the inhabitants of the lowland: Since the three Philistine cities mentioned in v. 18 were in the lowlands, this verse must mean that the Israelites had no success beyond these three cities, and perhaps even means that they lost control of them very quickly. **Chariots of iron** were effective on the flat coastal plains but not in the hill country of Canaan. Thus the Israelites, who did not have chariots, were better matched against the **mountaineers.**

1:21 Benjamin did not drive out the Jebusites: This verse duplicates Josh. 15:63 almost exactly, except that the tribe of Judah is held responsible there for not driving out the Jebusites from Jerusalem. Note also that, in 1:8, the account states that Judah did capture Jerusalem (Josh. 15:63).

1:22–36 In contrast to their successes in the south (vv. 1–21), the Israelites suffered more failures in the north. They initially seized Bethel (formerly Luz), a major city in Ephraimite territory (vv. 22–26), but advanced little after that. Six tribes—Manasseh, Ephraim, Zebulun, Asher, Naphtali, and Dan—failed to drive the Canaanites from their territories.

1:22 The house of Joseph was Ephraim and Manasseh (Gen. 48:5, 6; Deut. 33:17), who had split the inheritance of their father. They are the next two tribes mentioned in this passage in Judges (vv. 27, 29). **Bethel** means "The House of God." It was a site with an honored history, beginning with Abraham's first sacrifice to God (Gen. 13:3, 4) and Jacob's revelation from God there (Gen. 31:13). Joshua had captured the city (Josh. 12:16), perhaps as part of the defeat of Ai (Josh. 8:17).

1:23–25 Luz means "Deceit" or "Perversion," but Jacob had changed its name to Bethel many years earlier after his encounter with God there.

1:26 land of the Hittites: Archaeologists have unearthed a great Hittite kingdom in Asia Minor (present-day Turkey), dating from about 1800 to 1200 B.C. However, the relationship between the Hittites of Canaan and the Hittites of this discovery is unclear.

1:27 Manasseh did not drive out: Here begins a long record of disobedience that began when the Israelites failed to uproot the Canaanites (Josh. 10:28–43). That failure resulted in much grief in the years following. Besides the tribe of Manasseh, Benjamin (v. 21), Ephraim (v. 29), Zebulun (v. 30), Asher (v. 31), Naphtali (v. 33), and Dan (v. 34) also did not do as God had commanded. We then see in ch. 2—and indeed throughout the rest of the book—the effects this had on Israel's life: the people turned to the gods of the Canaanites and abandoned the Lord. Moreover, **the Canaanites were determined to dwell in that land** and relied on their superior weaponry (v. 19) to intimidate the Israelites. Yet that difficulty could have been removed had the Israelites exercised their faith more completely.

1:28–33 They put the Canaanites under tribute means they forced their captives to work as involuntary, unpaid laborers. David, Solomon, and other kings continued this practice (2 Sam. 20:24). The Israelites enslaved the Canaanites in many areas (vv. 30, 33, 35; Josh. 16:10; 17:13).

1:34–36 Amorites were Canaanite peoples living in the central hill country of Canaan, and they blocked Dan's entry into this region. Eventually, the Danites were forced to migrate northward (18:1; Josh. 19:47). For more on the Amorites, see Josh. 3:10.

2:1 The Angel of the LORD appears as God's representative here, speaking authoritatively to the people about their covenant disobedience. This Angel appears several other places in Judges (2:1, 4; 5:23; 6:11–22; 13:3–21). In each case, the Angel makes a sudden appearance as the representative of the Lord. In all cases, Yahweh and His Angel seem to be closely identified with each other, such as in Judg. 6, where the Angel of Yahweh alternates with Yahweh Himself in speaking with Gideon, and in Judg. 13, where, in Manoah's judgment, in seeing the Angel, he and his wife had seen God. **Gilgal** was the site where Israel had first encamped west of the Jordan (Josh. 4:19). **Bochim** was possibly near Bethel. **I led you up from Egypt:** See Ex. 23:20–23. The reference to **you** is plural, indicating that the Angel is addressing the entire nation.

2:2–5 you shall make no covenant: God's commands to make no covenants with pagan nations and to tear down their altars are found in Ex. 23:32; 34:13; Deut. 12:3. Verses 1 and 2 here contain a string of commands that God had given Israel under Moses, but Israel's disobedience meant that these nations would become snares to them, just as God had warned (Ex. 23:33; Num. 33:55; Josh. 23:13). An example of a pagan ritual that ensnared Israel is given in Judg. 8:27.

2:6–3:6 This section constitutes a second introduction to the book after the prologue in 1:1—2:5. It depicts the political and spiritual conflicts of the period and elaborates on the moral breakdown presented in ch. 1. The recurring pattern presented in 2:16–23 owed much to the disobedience chronicled in ch. 1; each time the nation lapsed, it found itself oppressed by enemies. The final section (3:1–6) emphasizes God's purposes in testing Israel (2:22; 3:1, 4).

2:6–10 The author identifies the death of Joshua as a starting point for the trouble to come. This passage closely follows Josh. 24:28–30, in some places word for word, which suggests that the proper paragraph break here should be between vv. 5 and 6. Joshua's death is

mentioned in v. 8, although according to 1:1 it
has already occurred. The grammatical construction in 1:1 is a common one, and it is clear
that the events of ch. 1 are events that *followed*
Joshua's death. Most likely the reference to
Joshua's death in 1:1 is correctly placed and this
subsequent passage has been inserted by the
author out of sequence. It is a "flashback" that
leads into the second major section of the book
(2:6—3:6). Its resemblance to Josh. 24:28–30 is
meant to tie the events of Joshua's era to the
those of the next generation.

**2:10 Another generation arose . . . who
did not know the Lord:** The peaceful resolution that characterized the end of the Book of
Joshua gave way to an ominous future. The
meaning of *did not know* is that the people deliberately refused to acknowledge God's authority.
It is not simply that they were ignorant, but that
they were in unbelief.

**2:11, 12 The children of Israel did evil in
the sight of the Lord** is a statement also found
in 3:7, 12; 4:1; 6:1; 10:6; 13:1 and in 1 and 2
Kings. Israel would stray frequently from the
Lord. Only God's grace and the leadership of a few
godly men and women spared the nation from
complete corruption. **served the Baals:** See 3:7.

2:13 This verse is almost identical to the
second half of 3:7. **the Ashtoreths:** Ashtoreth
(Astarte) was a female fertility goddess and a
goddess of love and war, closely associated with
Baal (10:6; 1 Sam. 7:4; 12:10). She is not mentioned very often in Canaanite texts, but she
appears by the name of Ishtar in Mesopotamian
texts. The Ashtoreths mentioned here were
local shrines of this far-flung cult (3:7).

2:14 the anger of the Lord was hot:
When God's anger burned against the Israelites,
His pattern in Judges was to hand them over to
their enemies.

2:15 As the Lord had sworn refers to God's
promise to deliver Israel into their enemies'
hands if they forsook Him (Deut. 28:25; Josh.
23:13).

2:16 The Lord raised up judges: The judges
of Israel did not normally hold court, listen to
complaints, or make legal decisions (except for
Deborah, Judg. 4:4, 5). Rather, they were political leaders who delivered Israel from foreign
threat or oppression. Yet the message conveyed
is that the Lord alone is the true Judge of His
people (11:27), and He hands out blessing and
punishment. Six of the judges (Shamgar, Tola,
Jair, Ibzan, Elon, and Abdon) are known as
"minor" judges because of the few details given
about them in the narrative. The "major"
judges—Othniel, Ehud, Deborah, Gideon, Jephthah, and Samson—were distinguished by their
military prowess or heroic deeds. Many scholars
have suggested that the major judges rescued
Israel from enemies, while the minor judges
worked in the court as magistrates. However,
this judgment is misleading. For instance, the
two minor judges Shamgar (3:31) and Tola
(10:1, 2) clearly were military heroes. Deborah,
a major judge, was a war leader but settled disputes between the Israelites as well.

2:17 Played the harlot is a powerful and
familiar metaphor used to describe Israel's
unfaithfulness to God. Ezekiel and Hosea, in
particular, would later use this comparison to
describe Israel's unfaithfulness.

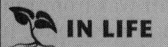 **IN LIFE**   ## Thorns and Tears at Bochim

God commanded the Israelites to dispossess the Canaanites by taking over their cities,
destroying their idols and altars, and refusing to enter into agreements with them (Judg. 2:2).
Apparently the citizens of Bochim failed to carry out those instructions. No one knows the exact
circumstances, but the offenses were serious enough for the Angel of the Lord to come up from Gilgal
to this village near Bethel and cry against it (2:1).

The timing of the sermon was important. The days of Israel's conquest of Canaan were drawing to
a close, yet many cities remained in the hands of, or at least were still influenced by, the Canaanites
(1:27–35). Joshua's life was over (2:8), and a new generation was coming into power (2:10). So
Bochim's spiritual failures were a serious matter. They set a dangerous precedent of idolatry that persisted from that day forward (2:3), as the Book of Judges shows. Apparently the people of Bochim
tearfully repented of their wrongs and, in the presence of Joshua, offered a sacrifice to atone for their
sins (2:5–6). But the pattern of spiritual adultery was established.

God's people cannot worship whatever gods they will. Like Israel, believers today may need to limit
their neighborliness if necessary to preserve their own faith and godliness. They must allow nothing to
distract them from unswerving allegiance to the Lord, lest they unwittingly invite a host of thorny
issues and a legacy of tears.

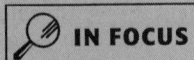 **IN FOCUS** **"judge"**

(Heb. *shaphat*) (Judg. 2:16; 15:20; 1 Sam 7:15) Strong's #8199: The Hebrew word for *judge* means "to deliver" or "to rule." The judges of Israel had a wide range of responsibilities. Like their modern counterparts, OT judges could decide controversies and hand down verdicts (Ex. 18:16). These judges were also involved in the execution of their judgment in both vindicating the righteous (Ps. 26:1) and destroying the wicked (Ex. 7:3). Many judges were God's appointed military leaders who, empowered by God's Spirit (6:34, 15:14), fought Israel's oppressors and thereby delivered the people. Later, Israel's king functioned as the national judge (1 Sam. 8:5). Ultimately, Israel's perfect Judge is God. He alone is capable of perfectly judging the wicked and delivering the righteous (Is. 11:4).

2:18 The Hebrew verb translated **moved to pity** is elsewhere translated *relent* (1 Sam. 15:29; Jon. 3:10). Here, the idea is that God changed His course (that is, relented) because of His compassion for the suffering Israelites (10:16).

2:19 Their fathers refers to those of the preceding generation, whereas in v. 17 *fathers* refers to those of Joshua's day.

2:20 this nation: Hebrew writers rarely used the word *nation* to refer to Israel. The phrase here has a contemptuous ring. Usually the word (Heb. *gôy*) was used for Israel's neighbors, while Israel itself was called *the people*. The choice of the impersonal word *nation* reflects the distance between God and His people.

2:21–23 I also will no longer drive out . . . any of the nations: This fulfilled a promise that God had made to the Israelites through Joshua (vv. 15, 23).

3:1–6 This concluding passage demonstrates that God intended to test Israel (2:22; 3:1, 4). The ultimate result of being approved after testing (2 Tim. 2:15) is the reward of His kingdom (2 Tim. 2:12; James 1:12). The stage is now set for the accounts of the judges who would deliver Israel.

3:1, 2 that He might test Israel: This trial was a testing by fire, so to speak. The idea of testing implies difficulty and adversity; elsewhere the same word refers to God's testing of Abraham (Gen. 22:1) and Hezekiah (2 Chr. 32:31). Here God was testing Israel to refine it.

3:3 five lords of the Philistines: See Josh. 13:3. **Sidonians:** Sidon was a port city northwest of Israel, in what today is Lebanon. These people were part of the broader Canaanite culture and worshiped the same gods. Little is known about the **Hivites.** From the geographical description in this verse, it appears that they lived in northern Palestine (Josh. 9:7). **Mount Lebanon** was beyond the northern borders of Israel. Evidently, hostile nations surrounded Israel on every side.

3:4–6 Canaanites: On the various peoples in this verse, read Josh. 3:10.

3:7–16:31 The main part of the Book of Judges concerns twelve people whom God appointed to deliver Israel from various crises.

3:7–11 The first judge was **Othniel,** who delivered Israel from Cushan-Rishathaim, king of Mesopotamia. Verses 7 and 8 repeat much of the material from 2:11–14. Because of the Israelites' sin, God allowed them to slip under foreign control for eight years.

3:7 the Baals and Asherahs: The plural is used for both gods because each was worshiped in different forms in the different local communities. In Num. 25:5, the Baal of Peor is mentioned. Place names such as Mount Baal Hermon (3:3); Baal Gad (Josh. 11:17), Baal Hazor (2 Sam. 13:23), and Baal Hamon (Song 8:11) occur with some frequency. Baal-Berith (that is, "The Baal of the Covenant") was another Baal manifestation worshiped by the Israelites (8:33). On Ashtoreth, another Canaanite goddess, see 2:13.

3:8 Cushan-Rishathaim was from much farther away than Israel's other enemies. It is remarkable that Othniel, who was from Judah, a region far to the south, was chosen to lead in this campaign. Cushan-Rishathaim's name means "Cushan of Double Wickedness"; this may not have been his actual name, but instead a name pinned on him by the author of Judges for ridicule. Note that this name is found four times in two verses (vv. 8, 10), which may support the point that the author was mocking the king.

3:9, 10 Othniel was the hero who captured the city of Kirjath Sepher (1:13; Josh. 15:17). He was from Judah and was Caleb's near kinsman and son-in-law. The Spirit of the Lord came upon him, and he prevailed against Cushan-Rishathaim.

3:11 The land had rest for forty years is the first of several references to forty-year or eighty-year periods of peace in the Book of Judges (3:30; 5:31; 8:28).

3:12–30 The second judge was **Ehud,** who delivered Israel from Eglon king of Moab. Verses 12–14 give us the familiar background, beginning with Israel's apostasy and the resulting conquest by Eglon, lasting eighteen years (v. 14 echoes v. 8). The story of Eglon's death is both graphic and hair-raising, reflecting the violence and chaos of this period in Israel's history. Yet it is also a literary masterpiece, skillfully weaving details together in a compelling narrative.

3:12 Moab was a plateau southeast of the Dead Sea. It was populated by nomadic herders and farmers in small agrarian settlements but had no large cities. It sat on either side of the King's Highway, an important north-south trade route. The ancestor of the Moabites was the offspring of Lot's incestuous relationship with his older daughter (Gen. 19:37), so the Moabites and Israelites were distantly related. The Bible frequently mentions conflict between the two peoples, except for the Book of Ruth, the events of which occurred during a time of stable rela-

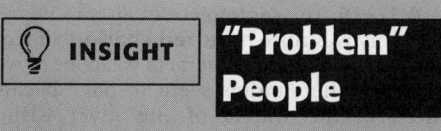

INSIGHT

"Problem" People

The Israelites shared the Promised Land with entire nations with whom they were in constant conflict (Judg. 3:1–4). Israel was supposed to displace these groups as it took possession of Canaan (Deut. 7). But for various reasons, many Canaanites were left. During the period of the judges, God used them to challenge His people, to punish them for violating His laws, and to turn them back toward Him.

tions between Moab and Israel. The Moabites worshiped Chemosh and his consort Ashtar, as well as Baal.

3:13–18 The City of Palms was Jericho (1:16). It is the only city on record that Eglon captured, although he ruled the Israelites eighteen years (v. 14). The reference to Jericho is surprising since one might assume the city had been completely destroyed by Joshua. However, the Israelites may have rebuilt the site because of its plentiful water supply and strategic location, advantages that Eglon certainly would have noticed.

3:19 The Hebrew word for **images** is used many times to refer to idols made of wood, stone, or metal (Deut. 7:5, 25; Is. 10:10; Hos. 11:2). These images were clearly important in

this passage—and prominent enough to be landmarks—since they appear again in v. 26, bracketing the account of Ehud's murder of Eglon. **Gilgal** had been the site of the Israelites' first encampment in Canaan and was an important religious center (Josh. 4:19).

3:20–23 upstairs in his cool private chamber: In ancient cities, the coolest place in the house was on the roof (compare the small upper room that a Shunammite woman and her husband made for the prophet Elisha, 2 Kin. 4:10).

3:24, 25 Attending to his needs is a euphemism for defecating (1 Sam. 24:3).

3:26 Seirah is mentioned only here in the Bible, and its location is unknown.

3:27–30 The trumpet described here is the ram's horn, which could sound only a few notes. Ram's horns were used to signal others (Josh. 6:5).

3:31 Shamgar is mentioned only here and in 5:6. This short passage does not fit the pattern usually associated with the rise of the judges. Missing is the customary prelude of apostasy and sin. Chronologically this verse may be out of place. The next chapter begins with the death of Ehud, the previous judge. Moreover, Shamgar delivered Israel but did not *judge* it. Even the name Shamgar is not Hebrew. Yet he was the **son of Anath**—clearly a Semitic name. This may mean that he was from the town of Beth-Anath in Galilee; more probably, however, Anath is derived from the name of the Canaanite warrior goddess. If so, then it is ironic that God used a foreign warrior to deliver Israel.

4:1–5:31 The fourth judge was **Deborah**, whose triumphs—along with Barak's—make up the first extended account in the Book of Judges. Unique to this episode is the poetic victory hymn (ch. 5) that follows the narration of the Israelite victory.

4:1–3 This new chapter follows the pattern of the Book of Judges by echoing the events of ch. 3. Again the people sinned and suffered oppression, this time enduring twenty years of Canaanite rule.

4:2, 3 Jabin king of Canaan, who reigned in Hazor: Years earlier Joshua had defeated a king of Hazor named Jabin (Josh. 11:1–15). Probably Jabin was a title rather than a proper name, resembling the use of the title Abimelech among the Philistines (Gen. 20:2; 26:1) or Ben-Hadad among the kings of Damascus. The name Jabin has been found in a text from Mari, an archaeological site on the Euphrates River. The system of small rival kingdoms prominent in Joshua's day still prevailed during the period of the judges (Josh. 2:2), but Jabin was clearly more powerful than most.

Hazor, having been destroyed earlier (Josh. 11:11), had now been rebuilt. The site of Sisera's headquarters, **Harosheth Hagoyim,** is unknown, but the ensuing battle was played out in northern Israel around Mt. Tabor (v. 6) and the River Kishon (v. 7).

4:4–10 The campaign of the Israelite tribes began with the introduction of Deborah. This episode also demonstrated widespread cooperation between the tribes. In response to the threat in the north, Deborah, who lived in the south of Ephraim near the territory of Judah (v. 5), ordered the Israelites to send troops against Sisera. At least six tribes contributed soldiers: Naphtali, Zebulun, Ephraim, Benjamin, western Manasseh (Machir), and Issachar (v. 6; 5:14, 15).

4:4 Deborah is one of five women to be called a prophetess in the OT. The others are Miriam (Ex. 15:20), Huldah (2 Kin. 22:14; 2 Chr. 34:22), Isaiah's wife (Is. 8:3), and Noadiah, a false prophetess (Neh. 6:14). She also judged Israel (vv. 4, 5) by deciding cases under a palm tree, which shows the judicial dimensions of her judgeship.

4:5 Ramah and Bethel were in the southern part of the land, near Judah. Ramah was in the territory of Benjamin (Josh. 18:25), and Bethel was near the border between Benjamin and Ephraim (Josh. 8:17; 18:13).

4:6, 7 Deborah summoned Barak from **Kedesh in Naphtali,** a settlement southwest of the Sea of Galilee. The soldiers were to gather at Mt. Tabor, where the territories of Issachar, Naphtali, and Zebulun met (v. 6). The battle would be fought along **the River Kishon,** which flows northwest into the Mediterranean, south of Mt. Tabor.

4:8–10 Barak hesitated to lead the Israelites in battle. His lack of nerve forced Deborah to go with him, and subsequently the glory for the victory would go to a woman. We naturally assume that Deborah would be this woman, but we discover later that Jael, a Kenite woman, killed the notorious Sisera (vv. 17–22). Both women were heroines in a time when Israel's leadership was mostly bankrupt. In fact, Deborah is shown in the best light of all the judges in the book. She is called a prophetess (v. 4), and many sought out her decisions (v. 5). For this reason, she is called "a mother in Israel" (5:7). She is probably included among the "leaders" in Israel (5:2), and she instructed Barak in the strategy of the battle (4:9, 14). She also was a prominent author of the victory song (5:1) and gave her name to a place in Israel, the palm tree of Deborah (v. 5).

4:11–16 The details of the victory are now recounted. Verse 11 anticipates the narrative in vv. 17–22 by introducing Heber, Jael's husband, who lived near Kedesh and who was distantly related to the Israelites. The emphasis in vv. 12–16 is on God's power and His work.

4:12–16 The centerpiece of Sisera's impressive army was **nine hundred chariots of iron;** they were swift, maneuverable weapons of war. However, the chariots seem to have become mired in the waters of the River Kishon (5:19–22).

4:17–24 The details of Sisera's death are told in the slow, suspenseful manner that characterized the story of Eglon's death (3:12–30). The story's conclusion is that God Himself subdued Jabin.

5:1–31 This chapter contains the victory song of Deborah and Barak. The hymn praises God for His triumph over the Canaanites and bears the hallmarks of very archaic Hebrew. Its vivid

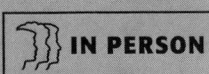 **IN PERSON**   ## Willing Leaders

While it is always easy to find people who want to be "in charge," it is difficult to find people of character and ability who are willing to step into roles of leadership. Israel faced a chronic crisis of leadership during the days of the judges, when "everyone did what was right in his own eyes" (Judg. 21:25). Few could be found who were willing and able to offer moral and spiritual direction.

Perhaps that's why Deborah, in her song of praise composed after Israel's victory over Jabin and Sisera, celebrated *willing* leaders followed by *willing* people (5:2, 9). Apparently the people were willing to follow if they could find leaders who would lead rather than despots who would dominate, such as Abimelech (ch. 9).

Deborah and Balak were good models of leaders willing to lead. Their stand for God and integrity before the people were profoundly inspiring, so much so that even common people such as the woman Jael were emboldened to grab whatever was at hand to strike down the enemy (4:17–22; 5:24–27).

descriptions of the events seem as if they might have come from eyewitnesses to them, which Deborah and Barak were. It is reminiscent of the victory song of Moses and Miriam in Ex. 15.

5:1 The verb **sang** here is in a feminine singular form, which supports the point made earlier about Deborah's prominence over Barak (4:8, 9).

5:2–9 The introduction to the hymn is set off by calls to worship at the beginning and end—**Bless the LORD!** (vv. 2, 9). Verse 3 also contains a call to worship similar to that found in many psalms.

5:2, 3 When leaders lead: The phrase literally means "the long-haired ones who let their hair hang loose." The precise meaning of the phrase is obscure, but it may mean that loosed locks or flowing hair were signs of great strength or leadership. **People willingly offer themselves** tells of the glad cooperation of the Israelites. The Hebrew term is related to the noun for "freewill offerings" (Lev. 7:16; 22:23). The spirit of willing involvement here is reminiscent of Ex. 36, where the people volunteered to give so much for the building of the tabernacle that Moses told them to stop giving, or Ezra 1, where a similar outpouring is found. Note also the NT churches of Macedonia who freely and willingly gave liberally out of their poverty (2 Cor. 8:1–4).

5:4, 5 A brief historical review now follows the calls to worship in vv. 2, 3. These verses refer to the Lord's marching from Seir and Edom, which likely refers to God's transferring His "abode" from the wilderness (Mt. Sinai, v. 5) into Canaan, by way of the land of Edom. This corresponds to the movement of His people from Sinai (Kadesh) northward into Canaan (Num. 10:12; 20:22).

5:6–8 Another historical review now follows the first one, detailing the bleak state of affairs before the battle until Deborah arose as a deliverer (vv. 6, 7). Israel had even chosen new gods, resulting in divine judgment (v. 8; 10:14).

5:7–9 The phrase **a mother in Israel** occurs twice in the OT, here and 2 Sam. 20:19. The title is given to Deborah as one of honor, respect, and prominence.

5:10–18 This section begins again with calls to worship in vv. 10–12. Verse 13 describes the battle in very general terms. Verses 14, 15, 18 praise the tribes who heeded Deborah's call. Ten of the twelve tribes are mentioned here, five and a half favorably, because they responded to Deborah and Barak's summons. Four and a half tribes are criticized because they did not join their countrymen: Reuben (vv. 15, 16), Gad and eastern Manasseh (Gilead), Dan, and Asher (v. 17). Judah and Simeon are not mentioned in the song or in ch. 4.

5:10–13 This verse calls all classes of society to bear witness to the mighty acts of God, from the ruling classes, those riding on **white donkeys,** to the lowest classes, those **who walk along the road.**

5:14–16 Machir is identified here with western Manasseh, in whose territory the battle

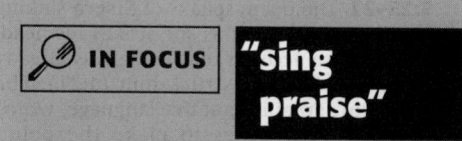

IN FOCUS "sing praise"

(Heb. *zamar*) (Judg. 5:3; 2 Sam. 22:50; 1 Chr. 16:9; Pss. 47:6, 7; 147:1) Strong's #2167: This Hebrew word usually refers to singing which exalts God, sometimes to singing accompanied with a musical instrument (Pss. 98:5; 149:3). In the Scripture, such singing is frequently addressed to the Lord and is an expression of gratitude for something He has done for the worshiper (Pss. 9:11; 105:2) or for His mercy and justice (Ps. 101:1). This word often is used as a summons for God's people to praise Him (5:3; Is. 12:5). The English word *psalm* is derived from the Greek translation of this Hebrew word.

took place. Elsewhere Machir is identified with eastern Manasseh (Josh. 13:30, 31). Machir was a noted warrior (Josh. 17:1).

5:17, 18 The reference to Dan remaining **on ships** probably reflects the location of their original inheritance, which was along the south-central coastal plain where they would have had access to the sea (Josh. 19:40–46). Later they migrated northward, having been forced out of their territory (1:34; 18:1; Josh. 19:47). Some scholars connect this tribe with the Danunians, a sea people who invaded the eastern Mediterranean shortly after 1200 B.C. However, the Bible clearly establishes the existence of the tribe of Dan many years earlier (Gen. 30:6; 49:16–18).

5:19–23 The victory proper is now described in vivid terms, and a curse is pronounced on Meroz, a site otherwise unknown (v. 23). The **stars** themselves were fighting against Sisera (v. 20), a vivid metaphor of God's intervention. The prose account says, "And the LORD routed Sisera and all his chariots and all his army with the edge of the sword before Barak" (4:15). The frantic pounding of the horses' hooves, their **galloping, galloping,** suggests the chaos caused by the waters of the River Kishon (vv. 21, 22; 4:7).

5:24-30 The poem now contrasts the two women who waited on Sisera: **Jael,** who killed him (vv. 24–27), and his mother, who longed for his return (vv. 28–30). Sisera's mother appears for the first time; in her futile waiting, she and her companions delude themselves as they dream up imagined glories that he was taking part in.

5:25-27 The poem speaks of **Sisera** sinking and falling at Jael's feet as she strikes his head, while the prose account tells us he was already lying down when she struck him (4:21). The poem is using graphic, emotive language, which it repeats several times to make the point.

6:1-8, 32 The fifth judge was **Gideon,** who twice fought the Midianites, first under God's instructions and later on his own initiative. Gideon's story is the second major account in the Book of Judges. In this narrative—along with the subsequent tragedy of Abimelech that follows in ch. 9—we can see, in ways not evident previously, the continuing deterioration of Israel's spiritual state. First, God now rebuked Israel when it called upon Him (6:7–10). Second, the judge himself contributed to the spiritual decline (8:24–27). Third, Israel's tribes fought among themselves for the first time (8:16, 17; 9:23–54), prior to an even worse dis-

Photo by Howard Vos

Remains of the city walls on the mound of Taanach, where Deborah and Barak defeated the Canaanites under Sisera (Judg. 5:1, 19–23).

Sisera's death probably was a bloodier affair than the prose account indicates.

5:28-30 The point of this pathetic story of Sisera's mother is not to elicit sympathy for her, but rather to remind us of Jael's stunning accomplishment. Sisera's mother expected her son to shower his people with great plunder; instead, Sisera lay dead at Jael's feet. Three times in the OT we read of women who looked through the window: Sisera's mother, Saul's daughter Michal (2 Sam. 6:16), and Jezebel (2 Kin. 9:30). All three opposed God's will and suffered accordingly.

5:31 The hymn concludes with praise to the Lord, as many psalms do. The prose account resumes with another period of forty years of rest (3:11).

sension later (12:1–6; 20:1–48). Despite God's continued intervention and Gideon's flashes of righteousness, Israel eroded spiritually and politically.

6:1-10 The pattern of continuing apostasy is resumed, with Israel sinning and falling under foreign oppression and then crying out to God for deliverance. However, rather than automatically sending a deliverer-judge, as previously, God this time sends a prophet, who condemns Israel. God would indeed deliver Israel through Gideon, but it is clear He would not respond mechanistically to any and all Israelite appeals, regardless of circumstances.

6:1 **Midian** was located in the Arabian peninsula, southeast of Israel and east of the Sinai peninsula. The Midianites were descendants of Abraham through his wife Keturah (Gen. 25:1, 2), so they were distantly related to the Israelites. Midianites bought Joseph from his brothers (Gen. 37:25–36), welcomed Moses in the wilderness (Ex. 2:15–21), and hired Balaam to curse Israel (Num. 22:7). Generally speaking, Israel counted Midian among its foes. In this account, the Midianites were menacing Israel, burning, looting, and leaving many near starvation (6:4, 5).

6:2 the dens, the caves: Caves were not used for permanent dwellings in OT times. That the Israelites were forced to abandon their homes and live in caves indicates the desperate straits they were in.

6:3, 4 The **Amalekites** were a nomadic people who lived in the Sinai desert and the Negev, the desert south of Israel. They were descendants of Esau (Gen. 36:12) and here joined the Midianites against Israel. **People of the East** were unspecified nomads who also plundered Israel. These easterners are also mentioned in several prophetic contexts (Is. 11:14; Jer. 49:28; Ezek. 25:4).

6:5–7 as numerous as locusts: Locust plagues were—and still are—a fairly common occurrence in the Middle East. In the prophet Joel's day, such an attack would be prophesied as a punishment upon the land (Joel 1:4, 15–17; 2:1–11).

6:8–10 the Lord sent a prophet: This prophet reminded the Israelites of God's faithfulness and how the people had nevertheless rejected Him (vv. 8–10).

6:11–40 Gideon's call is the centerpiece of ch. 6. It begins with the appearance of the Angel of the Lord to Gideon (vv. 11–24), followed by an account of Gideon's destruction of an altar of Baal (vv. 25–35), after which we see Gideon's wavering faith (vv. 36–40). Through it all, Gideon was ambivalent about being called to deliver Israel, much as Moses had been years earlier.

6:11, 12 The Palestinian **terebinth tree** is a large tree with a thick trunk and heavy branches, sometimes confused with the oak. It can grow as high as twenty-five feet. The terebinth figures in the stories of Abraham, who pitched his tent near the terebinth trees of Mamre (Gen. 13:18; 18:1), and of Jacob, who hid a treasure beneath a terebinth tree (Gen. 35:4). The exact location of **Ophrah** is unknown, but it was a city somewhere in the territory of Manasseh. It is not the same as the Benjamite city of the same name (Josh. 18:23; 1 Sam. 13:17). **Abiezrite:** See v. 24. A **winepress** was a square or circular pit carved into rock in which grapes were crushed (Is. 16:10; Jer. 48:33). Wheat was usually separated on open threshing floors so the wind could carry away the chaff in the winnowing process (2 Sam. 24:18). The fact that Gideon was forced to thresh wheat hidden inside a winepress—despite the fact that he had access to a threshing floor (v. 37)—shows again the desperate state the Israelites were in.

6:13, 14 My lord was a polite form of address, but **the Lord** is the personal name of God (Yahweh), the full meaning of which was revealed to Moses at Mt. Sinai (Ex. 3:13–16). The Hebrew word for **miracles** means "wonderful things," and it is translated elsewhere as *wonders* (Ex. 3:20; Josh. 3:5).

6:15 I am the least in my father's house: Gideon's objection is reminiscent of the words spoken by Moses (Ex. 3:11) and Jeremiah (Jer. 1:6).

6:16 I will be with you was God's great promise of His presence that He had given to Moses and Joshua previously (Ex. 3:12; Josh. 1:5, 9). This should have greatly encouraged Gideon, but he still expressed doubts (vv. 17, 36–40). Often we are quick to judge those who doubt God even when they have firsthand evidence of His mighty works. But we all fail to trust God fully at times. God accomplished His will despite Gideon's weakness, and He can do the same through us.

6:17, 18 Gideon's faith needed such bolstering that he asked God for **a sign.** Here as elsewhere, Gideon was slow to respond to God (vv. 39, 40).

 **IN FOCUS**   **"clan"**

(Heb. *'eleph*) (Judg. 6:15, 1 Sam. 10:19) Strong's #504: The word *'eleph* has several distinct meanings in Hebrew. It may represent the number 1,000 (Num. 35:4, 1 Chr. 18:4), or it may be rendered *tribe* or *clan* (6:15, 1 Sam. 10:19). Occasionally it designates a "region" or "district" (1 Sam. 23:23). This ambiguity has led to differing opinions over the number of people involved in certain OT events, whether they involved literally "thousands" or simply "units" composed of an unspecified number of people (Num. 1; Josh. 7:3–5).

6:19–21 An ephah of flour was two-thirds of a bushel, or about twenty pounds of flour.

6:22, 23 Gideon perceived: When the Angel of the Lord vanished, then Gideon realized (literally, "saw") who it was and feared for his life. This reaction of fear appears to have been rooted in the knowledge that anyone who gazed upon God would die. In Ex. 33:20, God, speaking to Moses, says, "You cannot see My face; for no man shall see Me, and live." The context of Ex. 33:18–23 suggests that it was the fullness of God's glory that Moses could not see, since Moses did speak with God and know Him "face to face" (Ex. 33:11; Num. 12:8; Deut. 34:10), and he even beheld the form of God Himself (Num. 12:8). Yet Gideon's fear was a proper response for those who found themselves in the presence of God's Angel. This was also Manoah's reaction when the Angel visited him (13:21, 22).

6:24 To this day: This expression, especially common in the books of Joshua and Judges (Judg. 1:21, 26; 15:19; Josh. 4:9; 5:9; 6:25; 7:26), lends authenticity to the account. It is the author's way of declaring to later generations that they could verify the story by going and seeing this altar themselves. **Abiezrites** were descendants of Joseph through his son Manasseh. They were part of the tribe of Manasseh that settled west of the Jordan River (Num. 26:30 [Jeezer]; Josh. 17:1, 2).

6:25–35 Gideon's first test was to topple the local shrines to Baal and Asherah, replacing them with an altar to the Lord. Gideon obeyed, but his fearfulness caused him to do this by night (v. 27). His forthcoming military tests are foreshadowed in the text (vv. 33–35). The battle he would lead would take place in the central highlands of northern Israel (Ophrah, Gideon's hometown, was in the Jezreel Valley, southwest of the Sea of Galilee).

6:25 The Hebrew word for **wooden image** here is Asherah, the name of the Canaanite goddess. Sacred wooden poles were erected at places where she was worshiped. The widespread worship of this goddess is attested to in 3:7 and elsewhere (1 Kin. 15:13; 18:19). **The second bull** is not a second animal, but a phrase by which the Lord was specifying more clearly to Gideon which bull should be sacrificed. The need to specify the bull underscores Gideon's continued reluctance (v. 17).

6:26, 27 The wood of the image means literally "the wood of the Asherah" (vv. 28, 30). The proper sacrifice that Gideon was to offer would be burnt with the wood of the destroyed idol.

6:28 The phrase **early in the morning** occurs in Judges at 6:28, 38; 7:1; 9:33; 19:5, 8, 9; 21:4.

6:29–31 Would you plead for Baal: Joash's questions are rhetorical. He refused to put his son to death, arguing that Baal should be able to take care of himself if he were indeed a god. Other examples of rhetorical questions in Judges are found at 9:2, 28; 11:25; 18:3; 20:28.

6:32–34 Gideon's father **called him Jerubbaal** to deride those who would put their trust in Baal. The name means "Let Baal Plead," and it echoes the question of v. 31. Thus Gideon became a living reminder of Baal's impotence. Second Samuel 11:21 refers to him as "Jerubbesheth," substituting the word "besheth," meaning "shame," for "Baal." Such changes also occur with other names that incorporate Baal's name, such as "Eshbaal," whose name means "man of Baal" (1 Chr. 8:33; 9:39), by the name of "Ishbosheth," which means "man of shame" (2 Sam. 2:8), and "Meribbaal," whose name means "Baal contends" (1 Chr. 8:34; 9:40), by the name "Mephibosheth," which means "utterance of shame" (2 Sam. 9:6). Thus is any sanction, or even any appearance of, an endorsement of Baal worship avoided in the text.

6:35 Gideon sent messengers through the territories of four northern tribes adjacent to each other: Manasseh, Asher, Zebulun, and Naphtali.

6:36–40 Before the fight itself, Gideon asked for signs to "test" God's guidance once more.

6:39 Let me test: The word translated *test* is the same one used when God tested Israel (2:22; 3:1). Gideon's desire to test God's sign could have been a violation of the law which prohibited people from testing God (Deut. 6:16; the Hebrew word translated *tempt* is the same word translated *test* here). Gideon himself was aware that he was doing something unwise, if not sinful, since he asked God not to be angry with him.

6:40 Despite Gideon's lack of faith, **God did so that night.** That is, He accommodated both of his requests. Many people have relied on Gideon's example as a way seeking guidance from the Lord, "putting out a fleece" in some way. Occasionally God has chosen to answer such requests, even as He did for Gideon. Nevertheless, Gideon already knew God's will for his life (vv. 14–16, 36). His requests only made evident his weak faith. Isaiah modeled a proper response to God's clearly revealed will: he said "Here am I! Send me" (Is. 6:8). So too did the disciples, who dropped their nets immediately and followed Jesus (Mark 1:18–20).

7:1–8:3 God figures prominently in Gideon's victory over the Midianites, especially in the amazing story of the 300 men who would subdue their numerically superior foes. The

🌱 IN LIFE | Determining God's Will

The example of Gideon is frequently cited as a model for godly decision-making. Before acting, Gideon carefully considered whether the Lord wanted him to rally an army and attack the Midianites. Twice he set out a fleece (a clump of wool) to make sure of God's intentions (Judg. 6:36–40). On this basis, some have argued that before Christians make major decisions with long-range consequences, they should "put out a fleece before the Lord," seeking some tangible sign that indicates His will with certainty.

Is that an appropriate way to know God's will? In considering the question, it is important to note that this is the only occasion in the Bible when God revealed His will through a fleece. It is also worth noting Gideon's extreme hesitation, doubt, and fear. The Lord had already told him what to do through the Angel of the Lord (6:11–16). In fact, the Angel had already given Gideon a confirming sign (6:17–22). In light of these facts, Gideon's use of the fleece would appear to demonstrate a lack of faith more than any zeal to be certain of God's will. Fortunately, God was patient with him and granted his request for a confirming sign. But it seems that using a fleece to determine God's will was the exception rather than the rule, and thus does not serve as the best pattern for how we can depend on God for guidance.

Is there a more reliable way? Yes, God has clearly and objectively told us what He wants throughout the Bible. For example, the Ten Commandments give straightforward instructions to guide our behavior in numerous areas. Likewise, Thessalonians says plainly, "This is the will of God" (1 Thess. 4:3) in regard to sexuality. Thus when it comes to making choices in life, God calls us to clear thinking, thinking based on our relationship with Him and our allegiance to His values, which are clearly spelled out in Scripture.

God has made us to be thinking, discerning, analytical persons who assume responsibility for working our way through life in accordance with His general plans and purposes. He challenges us to learn all that we can about any situation, relationship, responsibility, or opportunity that we have, weigh it in light of His precepts and principles, and only then to act. And as we act, we can take comfort from the fact that He is at work within us, "both to will and to do for His good pleasure" (Phil. 2:13).

reassurances from God that Gideon had received before the encounter were now reinforced by a dream (7:9–15). The battle itself did not involve any significant combat, for God Himself provided the victory (7:16–25). The Israelites blew horns, broke jars, and shouted, causing the enemy to kill each other in their confusion. The survivors fled across the Jordan with the Israelites in pursuit.

7:1, 2 lest Israel claim glory for itself: Right from the beginning, God made it clear that the glory for this victory was to be His. This makes even more incredible the Israelites' request that Gideon rule over them because he had "delivered us from the hand of Midian" (8:22, 23).

7:3 When Gideon allowed those who were **fearful** to leave, more than two-thirds departed, leaving only 10,000. Mosaic law allowed military exemptions for several classes of people, including those who had just built a home, those who had just planted a vineyard, those engaged to be married, and those who were fearful (Deut. 20:5–8).

7:4–9 Gideon thinned his army even more

by employing a strange distinction, namely, how his men drank water from a brook. Some commentators have suggested that the men who did not get down on their knees were maintaining a higher degree of military readiness by drinking out of their hands. However, they may be reading too much into the account, for the text does not indicate any reason for Gideon's preference. The reference to the way **a dog laps** might even be derogatory since dogs were despised creatures in the ancient world (1 Sam. 17:43; 2 Kin. 8:13; Matt. 7:6). If so, God's role in the victory becomes even more apparent, since the 300 who were left were the ones who did not even have the common sense to drink in a normal fashion. God's comment in v. 7 seems to reinforce this suggestion.

7:10, 11 Ironically, Gideon himself was afraid, but he had not been dismissed to go home as had the other men (v. 3).

7:12 This verse notes again the strength of Israel's enemies, including their intimidating numbers and their innumerable camels (6:3–5).

7:13 Tumbled in this context literally means "overturned." The word is also used in

Genesis to describe the sword "which turned every way" at the entrance to the Garden of Eden (Gen. 3:24) and the destruction of Sodom and Gomorrah (Gen. 19:25, 29). Here, the loaf "overturned" the Midianite camp.

7:14, 15 The sword of Gideon is the key to the interpretation of the dream. Coming from the mouth of one of Israel's enemies, it provided the confirmation that Gideon needed, in light of his earlier fear (v. 10). As a result, **he worshiped** God for being so patient with his wavering faith (v. 15).

7:16–18 The ram's-horn **trumpet** was used as a signal call (3:27; Josh. 6:5).

7:19 middle watch: According to Jewish tradition the nighttime hours were divided into three watches, which would put the time of this attack at roughly 10:00 P.M.

7:20–22 The sword of the LORD and of Gideon: Here the full version of the war cry is given. A more literal rendering of the Hebrew is "A sword for the Lord and for Gideon!"

7:23 The same tribes mentioned in 6:35 now pursued the Midianites, with the exception of Zebulun, which is not mentioned. Ephraim also joined in the pursuit (v. 24).

7:24, 25 The watering places probably refer to small tributaries that flowed into the Jordan River. Seizing them would seal off the enemy's escape routes. **The other side of the Jordan** is the east side of the Jordan, where the Israelites caught the enemy (Josh. 13:32; 18:7).

8:1–3 The men of Ephraim complained to Gideon that they had been called out late (v. 1). Gideon's flattering response had a calming effect on these men.

8:4–28 Gideon followed up the victory with a second military campaign, one which contrasts dramatically with the first. He pursued the two Midianite kings until he caught and killed them, and he punished the towns of Succoth

and Penuel. In this account, there is no indication of God's involvement as there had been previously; rather, Gideon is merely settling a private score (vv. 18, 19).

8:5–10 Succoth was east of the Jordan, near the Jabbok River. **Zebah and Zalmunna** are unflattering names meaning "Victim" and "Protection Refused." They may be wordplays on the real names of these kings, much like the name Cusha-Rishathaim (3:8). Yet the author of Judges may have had more sympathy for these two kings than for Cushan-Rishathaim, since Gideon is cast in a poor light in this chapter.

8:11, 12 Gideon's aggression contrasts sharply with the caution and fear so evident in ch. 6.

8:13, 14 he wrote down for him the leaders: Literacy in early civilizations was at first limited to an educated elite, as in Mesopotamia and Egypt. Their writing systems were complex and only a tiny portion of the population could read and write. However, the spread of alphabetic systems vastly simplified the task of reading and writing. Hundreds of potsherds from throughout Palestine have simple inscriptions on them, indicating that some degree of literacy had become widely accessible by Gideon's day. Even a youth whom Gideon happened upon wrote down for Gideon the names of seventy-seven men.

8:15–17 Gideon's actions here fulfill his pledges in vv. 7 and 9.

8:18 The killings to which Gideon refers do not appear anywhere else in the text. The answer from the two kings was flattering: **As you are, so were they;** they compared Gideon to the son of a king. Gideon, despite his refusal of a kingship, was not immune to the vanity that royalty encouraged. By naming one of his sons Abimelech, which means "My Father Is King" (v. 31), he may have succumbed to the

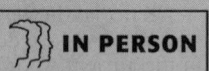 **IN PERSON**   **A Shrewd Politician**

Whatever fear Gideon may have felt prior to the battle with the Midianites, he displayed shrewd political instincts when he dealt with the men of Ephraim. His allusion to gleaning after a quality harvest (Judg. 8:2) was designed to soothe the Ephraimites' resentment that they had not been mustered for the main battle but only given the mop-up operation (7:24—8:1).

Gleaning was a custom of Israelite law that required landowners to leave a portion of their harvests in the fields or on the vines for the benefit of the poor. After the harvesters had completed their work, the poor were allowed to go through the fields and vineyards to gather what was left (Lev. 19:9, 10).

Thus Gideon praised the men of Ephraim by saying that the gleanings, or leftovers, of their vineyards was superior to the firstfruits of his own clan of Abiezer. This was quite a compliment, since the Valley of Jezreel, where the Abiezrites lived, was one of the most productive vineyard regions in all of Israel.

temptation of exalting himself as a king over Israel.

8:19–21 As a man is, so is his strength was a challenge to Gideon's manhood, and Gideon responded by killing the two kings himself. **Crescent ornaments** have been found at many sites in Palestine, but they are mentioned again only one other time in the Bible (Is. 3:18).

8:22 Immediately following his execution of the two kings, Gideon's men asked him to **rule over** them. This request, while understandable from a human perspective (v. 18), failed to acknowledge that it was God, not Gideon, who had delivered His people.

8:23 Gideon's answer was theologically correct: **the LORD shall rule over you.** The word order of the Hebrew makes it clear that God's claim was exclusive; it might be paraphrased, "It is the Lord, and no one else, who shall rule over you." This statement is widely assumed to indicate that God intended that Israel should never have a king, but that He would be their only King. However, God had promised Abraham and his descendants that they would count kings among their descendants (Gen. 17:6, 16; 35:11; 49:10). When the people of Israel asked Gideon to rule because of his military success, Gideon could only refuse, since his motivation was flawed and shortsighted. A king's true role was to lead people to God; he would leave the issues of warfare to God. This was the critical mistake of the people when they asked for a king in Samuel's day: they asked for a king to "judge us and go out before us and fight our battles" (1 Sam. 8:20). They wanted a king to do what the judges had done: lead them in battles. Yet the period of the judges was one of failure.

8:24–28 Despite Gideon's theologically correct answer in v. 23, these verses show that he was not careful to lead Israel in true worship of the Lord. By making the ephod, he encouraged idolatry. The total weight of the offerings brought for making the ephod—**one thousand seven hundred shekels**—was impressive. Assuming the unit of weight here to be the shekel (it is not specified in the Hebrew text), the total weight was more than forty-two pounds of gold (a shekel was about two-fifths of an ounce). The original **ephod** was an ornate ceremonial garment worn by the high priest (Ex. 28; 39). Some scholars believe that the ephod made by Gideon resembled an idol, but there is no clear indication here that this was the case. By placing the ephod in his own city, Gideon might have been "playing" at being judge. Perhaps tellingly, nowhere are we told that he "judged" Israel, whereas we read this of several of the other judges. After Gideon another man also made an ephod, with equally dismal results (17:5). **It became a snare** recalls the narrator's introductory comment in 2:3.

8:29–32 This transitional section tells of Gideon's death, but also introduces Gideon's fateful legacy: his son Abimelech, whose violent story is told in ch. 9.

8:31, 32 Although Gideon had seventy sons (v. 30), only **Abimelech** is mentioned by name. The name means "My Father Is King." Some scholars argue that Gideon did, in fact, become king, at least in practice if not in name, for he gave his son a royal name and acted as the people's leader (vv. 24–27).

8:33–35 Baal-Berith means "Baal of the Covenant," an ironic contrast to the covenant God of Israel whom the Israelites should have been worshiping. This god is also called "El-Berith" (9:46).

9:1–57 Abimelech's violent grab for power

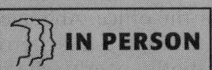 **IN PERSON** | ## The Man Who Would Be King

After Gideon defeated the Midianites, the people of Israel wanted to make him their king, but he refused the title (Judg. 8:22, 23). Apparently his son, Abimelech, was not so humble. Even though it meant the brutal murder of his seventy half-brothers, he arranged to have himself crowned king of Shechem.

Abimelech's glory was as limited in scope as it was in duration. His influence probably never extended more than ten miles, even though he was said to have reigned over Israel (9:22). And after three years he was driven from Shechem by troubles with the very people who had aided his rise to power. He sought safer quarters several miles south at Arumah (9:39–41).

As Abimelech's grasp on the region slipped, he resorted to more violence in a desperate bid to retain control (9:42–52). In the end, having been rejected by Gideon's family, by his mother's family, and by the citizens of his "kingdom," he died in shame. True to form, he made one last request. To preserve what little reputation he had left, he compelled one of his men to run him through with a sword (9:53, 54).

is the theme of ch. 9. The seeds of his offense were sown in Israel's persistent infidelity to God, which led to another rejection of the Lord (8:22, 24–27, 33–35).

9:1–6 Abimelech killed his own brothers to strengthen his royal claims. He began by traveling to Shechem, where ironically, Israel had reaffirmed the covenant years earlier (Josh. 24). He earned the trust of the Shechemites (v. 2) and hired men to kill all his brothers but one. Abimelech was then made king at Shechem (v. 6).

9:4, 5 The temple of Baal-Berith was a pagan sanctuary, a vivid sign of Israel's continuing apostasy (8:33). **worthless and reckless men:** Abimelech's character can certainly be judged by the company that he kept. The same can be said of Jephthah (11:3).

9:6 Sadly, the coronation took place at the **terebinth tree** where Jacob had put away his foreign gods many years before (Gen. 35:4). Here too, Joshua had commemorated his covenant with God (Josh. 24:26).

9:7–21 Jotham, the only brother of Abimelech who escaped, condemned Abimelech's treachery publicly by telling a fable—a story in

IN FOCUS "sincerity"

(Heb. *tamim*) (Judg. 9:16, 19; Gen. 6:9; Deut. 18:13) Strong's #8549: This word means "unblemished," "blameless," or "perfect." The Lord required that offerings dedicated to Him be unblemished (Lev. 22:21; Num. 6:14). The term can also be used to describe a people (2 Sam. 22:24; Ps. 119:80) or a course of action (Prov. 11:20; 28:18) that is blameless. The Bible describes Noah this way (Gen. 6:9), although he was not completely without fault (see Gen. 9:21). In declaring His covenant to Abraham, the Lord commanded His servant to be blameless (Gen. 17:1). In his farewell discourse, Moses gave the charge to the children of Israel to be blameless (Deut. 18:13). Many years later Joshua did likewise, exhorting the people to serve the Lord in sincerity and in truth (Josh. 24:14).

which creatures take on human characteristics. In this fable, the noble trees of the forest reject a call to kingship, which is finally conferred on the lowly bramble bush (vv. 8–15). The fable indicts the Shechemites for choosing the ignoble Abimelech as king. The story is not an indictment of kings in general (8:23).

9:20, 21 let fire come: Jotham issued a

warning to the people of Shechem—fire would devour them and Abimelech too if they had not acted properly. The threat was fulfilled when fire devoured a large number of Shechemites and Abimelech was killed by a Shechemite woman (vv. 49, 54).

9:22–55 Very quickly the harmony between the Shechemites and Abimelech disintegrated. Abimelech, who relied on the Shechemites to rise to power, now became the target of their lawlessness (vv. 22–25). This discord spread into open revolt under Gaal son of Ebed (vv. 26–33). Abimelech quelled the revolt and leveled Shechem in the process (vv. 34–45). He also burned Shechem's stronghold, its tower (vv. 46–49). Abimelech himself came to a violent end at nearby Thebez (vv. 50–55).

9:22 The Hebrew root for **reigned** here is one whose noun is usually translated "prince" or "commander." It is undoubtedly significant that the narrator does not use the normal Hebrew word for "ruled," which had been used in 8:22. 23, or for "reigned." The ignoble Abimelech, who had been "made king" by the people (v. 6), could only rule in reality as a secondary "commander," not as a true king.

9:23–27 A spirit of ill will can be translated literally "an evil spirit." The only other person in Scripture whose affliction is described with these words is Saul (1 Sam. 16:14, 15, 16, 23; 18:10; 19:9). Here, the spirit causes dissension between Abimelech and the Shechemites. Some scholars think God sent a demon to possess Saul and to afflict Abimelech and the Shechemites, but this goes against our understanding of God's nature. The most probable explanation is that God was responsible for the estrangement between the two sides, because both parties had sinned (9:1–6) and merited judgment. It is noteworthy that evil spirits afflicted Israel's first two kings, who were both unworthy candidates for the office. Abimelech had made himself king through a treacherous act, and he exercised authority poorly when in power. Saul, too, came to power because of the ill-advised wishes of the people of Israel, and he quickly demonstrated his unsuitability for the office despite his clear anointing. Significantly, it is the next king, David, who holds up the standard for Israel's future rulers. He is the first king who heeded the Lord's wisdom and was favored by the special presence of God's Spirit from the day of his anointing onward (1 Sam. 16:13).

9:28–36 Gaal asks a series of scornful rhetorical questions about Abimelech.

9:37, 38 the Diviners' Terebinth Tree: On trees as landmarks, read 6:11. **Where indeed is your mouth now** is Zebul's challenge to Gaal, taunting him to back up the boastful words he had uttered earlier (v. 28).

9:39–43 Interestingly, Abimelech divided his forces into **three companies** to attack Shechem, perhaps in conscious imitation of his father's success with three companies of men (7:16).

9:44, 45 Sowing Shechem **with salt** turned it into a barren, uninhabitable desert. See the association of salt and barrenness in Jer. 17:6.

9:46, 47 The Hebrew word from **stronghold** here is a rare one and may mean "fortified room" or something such as underground chamber. It occurs again only in v. 49 ("stronghold") and 1 Sam. 13:6 ("holes"). **the temple of the god Berith:** In Hebrew, the last phrase reads "El-Berith." *El* can be translated "god," but it was also the name of a well-known Canaanite god, the father of Baal. The "god Berith" means El-Berith, the Baal-Berith named in 8:33.

9:48–52 The location of **Mount Zalmon** is uncertain. Some scholars identify it with Mount Ebal, just northwest of Shechem. Others identify it with Mount Gerizim, also near Shechem. The snow-covered Mount Zalmon mentioned in Ps. 68:14 appears to be a different place.

9:53 an upper millstone: Mills used for grinding grain were typically made with two large stones. The upper one was moved back and forth or rotated on the lower one, and the grain was ground between them. An upper millstone would have easily crushed Abimelech's skull, as this verse asserts.

9:54, 55 kill me: Being killed by a woman was a disgrace to a warrior.

9:56, 57 The key to understanding Abimelech's fate may be found in the comments in vv. 23, 24, 56, 57. He was not a true king; he had established his reign through murder. God actively intervened against Abimelech, repaying his evil act of murdering his brothers. Note that his sin was murder (v. 56), not declaring himself king. Jotham's use of the fable proved to be prophetic: The fire that devoured the cedars (vv. 15, 20) would burn up both Shechem and Abimelech (vv. 49, 53).

10:1, 2 Tola was the sixth judge, the second of the minor judges (Shamgar was the first). He arose to **save** Israel, perhaps a necessary deed after the reign of Abimelech. This brief account echoes the time of Deborah in several ways (4:4, 5; 5:7).

10:3–5 Jair was the seventh judge, the third minor judge, and he judged Israel for twenty-two years. He was rather well off (v. 4), and he lived in Gilead, east of the Jordan, as would the next judge, Jephthah (11:1). Jair's abundance of children forms a sharp contrast with Jephthah's childlessness in the next chapter and in 12:8–10.

10:4, 5 thirty donkeys . . . thirty towns:

Literally, the Hebrew has "thirty donkeys . . . thirty donkeys." However, the word (*'ayarim*) used here for *donkeys* is an unusual one that resembles the Hebrew word (*'arim*) for *towns*. A later scribe mistakenly repeated the word for donkey.

10:6–12:7 Jephthah was the eighth judge. Like those of Deborah and Gideon, his story is relatively detailed. Jephthah freed Israel from Ammonite oppression, but suffered a personal tragedy of his own making in the process.

10:6–18 A lengthy introduction precedes the story of Jephthah. These verses repeat the themes of apostasy and God's unfailing mercy. A new theme here is the emphasis on Israel's confession and repentance (vv. 10, 15, 16).

10:6 The gods of Syria . . . Sidon . . . Moab . . . Ammon . . . the Philistines demonstrate the extent of Israel's idolatry. Not only did the people worship the major Canaanite gods (Baal, Asherah, Ashtoreth), but they also absorbed the religions of other groups. The more extensive list here indicates the depths of Israel's decline. The lists earlier in the book merely mention the Baals, Asthoreths, and Asherahs (2:13; 3:7). Seven gods are mentioned here, a symbolic number that forms a counterpoint to the seven nations mentioned in vv. 11, 12.

10:7–10 The Philistines and the people of Ammon were the Israelites' principal adversaries at this time. The next two major judges—Jephthah and Samson—were God's instruments against these two groups, Jephthah against the Ammonites and Samson against the Philistines.

10:11, 12 In these two verses, we find seven peoples from whom God had delivered the Israelites: **Egyptians:** God had dramatically saved Israel from Egyptian oppression (Ex. 14; 15); **Amorites:** God had rescued His people from Sihon and Og, kings of the Amorites (Josh. 2:10); **Ammon:** The Ammonites had been part of a coalition under Eglon, whom Ehud defeated (3:13); **Philistines:** Shamgar had already won a victory over the Philistines (3:31); **Sidonians:** There is no record of a previous triumph, but these people were among Israel's oppressors (3:3), and they might well have been part of the Canaanite coalition mentioned in 4:2. **Amalekites:** They had already opposed the Israelites in the time of the judges (3:13; 6:3), and their enmity with Israel went back much further (Ex. 17:8–16). God had given relief in each case. The **Maonites** appear later in Israel's history as adversaries (2 Chr. 20:1; 26:7, Meunites), but they are not mentioned earlier. Possibly what is meant is the Midianites, a people who had been defeated by Gideon (chs. 7; 8). This list of seven is probably not intended to be exhaustive, since neither the

Moabites nor the Canaanites are mentioned. The symbolic number seven, representing completeness, is probably the most important element here, especially when we note that seven groups of gods are mentioned in v. 6.

10:13, 14 The gods which you have chosen is a response of confrontation. The Israelites "chose new gods" at the time of Deborah (5:8). When Israel cried out to God, He reminded them again of their faithless ways. Other examples in Judges of confrontation include the Angel's indictment (2:1–5) and the prophet's message (6:7–10).

10:15–18 Not only is God a God of great justice; He is a God of great mercy, as the phrase **His soul could no longer endure the misery of Israel** reminds us. Despite their constant sinning and backsliding, God still loved the Israelites and shared their misery, much as parents are moved by their children's suffering.

11:1–3 Jephthah, like Jair before him (10:3), was from Gilead. He was a "mighty man of valor," but he was illegitimate, which caused his half brothers to expel him from his father's house. Like Abimelech before him (9:4), he attracted "worthless men" (v. 3), which did not bode well for his future. The territory of **Gilead** was in northern Transjordan (Josh. 17:1, 3; 5:17). The **Gileadites** were descended from a man named Gilead (Num. 26:29, 30; 27:1; 36:1), as was Jephthah himself. In this passage and in Josh. 17:1, 3, the term refers both to a region and a person. **mighty man of valor:** See Josh. 1:14. **The land of Tob** is probably an area east of Gilead. Ironically, its name means "Good," a quality that Jephthah frequently lacked.

11:1, 2 The territory of **Gilead** was in northern Transjordan (Josh. 17:1, 3; Judg. 5:17). The people in this region were descended from a man named Gilead (Num. 26:29, 30; 27:1; 36:1). Jephthah himself was the son of a man named Gilead. In this passage and in Josh. 17:1, 3, the term refers both to a region and a person.

11:3 Tob is probably east of Gilead. Its name means "good," a quality that Jephthah certainly lacked.

11:4–7 After negotiations and consultation with God, Jephthah was commissioned as head and

© 1996 Thomas Nelson, Inc.

The Judges of Israel

The Book of Judges lists a total of twelve judges who served in a variety of roles during a three-century era. (Barak served as a military leader under the judgeship of Deborah and was not technically a judge himself.) While some of them are major figures about whom much is known, others are only minor figures, mentioned briefly without a geographical or tribal affiliation. The significance of the era of the judges is that no one tribe or region seemed to dominate in producing these leaders. God called and equipped the necessary persons from throughout the land to lead Israel during this turbulent period.

commander over Israel. **after a time:** We return to the narrative left off in 10:17, 18 (11:1–3). **Come and be our commander:** Here we see a leader for Israel being commissioned by the people. God is given little place in the proceedings other than to confirm the choice (v. 10), another sign of spiritual deterioration. A **commander** was someone who performed some of the functions of a judge, but it is perhaps significant that the word *judge* is not used here since God was the only One who raised up judges.

11:8, 9 **That you may go with us and fight** is almost the same phrase that the Israelites used when they asked Samuel for a king in 1 Sam. 8:20: "that our king may . . . go out before us and fight." In both cases, even though God gave them the permission they sought, the request was improper.

11:10 **The Lord will be a witness:** Literally, "The Lord will be listening." This is not the normal Hebrew word for "witness" used in covenant-making ceremonies (Deut. 30:19; Josh. 24:22), but the sense is the same. God is called to be a witness to the covenant agreement (1 Sam. 20:12).

11:11 The people made Jephthah **head and commander** because he had demanded somewhat opportunistically to be their "head" as the price for helping them as "commander," so in the end he was made both. Jephthah's **words before the Lord** are a strange mixture of faith and foolishness. While Jephthah did acknowledge God here and later (11:21, 23, 27, 30, 31; 12:3), his self-interest and foolishness often overruled his faith. The Book of Hebrews has a more positive view of Jephthah than does Judges: Gideon, Barak, Samson, and Jephthah, along with others, are listed as examples of those "who through faith subdued kingdoms, worked righteousness, obtained promises,

stopped the mouths of lions" (Heb. 11:32, 33). Undoubtedly they demonstrated faith that allowed God to "subdue kingdoms" through them, but just as clearly the Book of Judges reveals some of their less-than-admirable characteristics.

11:12–28 A lengthy account now covers diplomatic negotiations between Jephthah and the Ammonites, consisting largely of an impressive speech from Jephthah through messengers to the king of Ammon, answering the king's charges against Israel. In this speech, Jephthah's verbal gifts are readily apparent. Interestingly enough, Jephthah's name means "He Opens." **Israel took away my land:** The Ammonites claimed that Israel had taken their land. Jephthah responded with a careful rebuttal. He declared that **the Lord** God of Israel Himself had dispossessed these peoples (vv. 21, 23, 24) and that Israel was not an aggressor but merely a recipient of the Lord's generosity. The Ammonites had brought their misfortune upon themselves by hindering Israel's advance into the Promised Land. Israel would not have taken Ammonite land, since God had expressly commanded them not to (Deut. 2:19). Later, Sihon king of the Amorites had taken some Ammonite territory (Num. 21:26), and then Israel had taken Sihon's land (Num. 21:25). Thus the Ammonites were only indirectly affected by Israel's expansion. In addition, the Ammonites never really had true claim to the land to begin with; it was in fact the land of the Amorites (vv. 19–22). The limits of the Amorite land in v. 22 are precisely what the Ammonites claimed as theirs in v. 13 (Num. 21:24 also rebuts the Ammonites' claim). Also, Israel had occupied the land in dispute for at least 300 years, long enough to make a legitimate claim on it (v. 26). Jephthah ended his speech with an appeal to God to judge the opposing claims (v. 27).

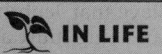 **IN LIFE** | **Overcoming a Tough Start**

Societies tend to have low expectations, sometimes downright hostility, for children born out of wedlock. Such was the case for Jephthah (Judg. 11:1).

The product of his father's dalliance with a prostitute, Jephthah was not only excluded but also expelled from his more "respectable" family (11:2). He led the life of a criminal (11:3), though he and his gang of raiders may have harassed the Ammonites more than the Israelites.

The irony of Jephthah's life was that when Israel faced war with Ammon, the leaders of his hometown came looking for Jephthah to deliver them. They offered no apology; they merely appealed for help. Jephthah agreed to help them after negotiating his terms (11:9–11), and God gave him the victory (11:33).

Jephthah's life illustrates that God can overcome any background and use any set of circumstances to accomplish His purposes.

11:13–17 The review of the past in this and the following verses recalls the events in the wilderness described in Num. 20:14–21.

11:18–24 Whatever Chemosh your god gives you was a derisive jab at the Ammonites' deity. Jephthah's point was that Israel's God had given His people much territory, whereas Chemosh, the god of the Ammonites, had done very little for them. The reference to Chemosh as an Ammonite god is unexpected, since elsewhere the Ammonites' god is named Molech (1 Kin. 11:7) or Milcom (1 Kin. 11:5, 33; 2 Kin. 23:13). Chemosh is customarily associated with the Moabites (1 Kin. 11:7, 33). However, Ammon and Moab lived side by side and shared a common heritage, both nations having descended from Lot (Gen. 19:37, 38). The two are often mentioned together (3:12, 13; 11:15; Deut. 2:18, 19; 23:3–5). It is likely that the two nations shared cultural and religious ideas, including the worship of Chemosh.

11:25, 26 Three hundred years may be an approximation, but it still gives us an important clue for determining the date of the Exodus and understanding how long the period of the judges lasted.

11:27, 28 the LORD, the Judge: This is the only place in Judges where a single individual is specifically called a judge. Significantly, it is a

INSIGHT — Following the King's Highway

As Jephthah prepared to battle the Ammonites, he traveled from the northern territory of Manasseh in Gilead south to Mizpah of Gilead (Judg. 11:29). Mizpah was probably the Levitical city of Ramoth Gilead, an important commercial center. It was located on a well-traveled highway called the Road to Bashan, which was the northern extension of the major north-south route known as the King's Highway (Num. 20:17).

name of God. He ultimately was—and is—the source of all justice. He has the right to judge every man and woman. With His divine authority and power, God always judges with justice, while at the same time He is loving, compassionate, and perfect.

11:29–40 The conflict with the Ammonites escalated, ending with Jephthah's victory aided

by the Spirit of the Lord (vv. 29, 32, 33). However, the narrative focuses on his rash vow (vv. 30, 31, 34–40). To induce God to help him, Jephthah promised to sacrifice to the Lord whatever came out of his house to meet him upon his victorious return. This misguided pledge demonstrated a clear lack of faith, since earlier Jephthah had indicated that he believed God would intervene on his behalf (vv. 9, 27). Note that the Spirit of the Lord had come upon him before he made his vow (v. 29). The tragic result of Jephthah's vow was the sacrifice of his only child—his daughter.

11:31–34 Some have interpreted Jephthah's vow **whatever comes out of the doors** as a clear intention to offer a human sacrifice. His surprise then is not that he had to sacrifice a human being, but that the unfortunate person was his daughter. The phrase **to meet me** seems to refer more appropriately to a human than to an animal, and it is difficult to see why Jephthah would try to persuade God by offering a common animal sacrifice. Undoubtedly, Jephthah knew that human sacrifice was strictly forbidden in Israel (Lev. 18:21; 20:2; Deut. 12:31; 18:10; Jer. 19:5; Ezek. 20:30, 31; 23:37, 39), but his foolishness and lack of faith impelled him to make a reckless vow in order to try to manipulate God (11:39).

11:35 I have given my word is literally "I have opened my mouth." In light of his eloquent speech to the Ammonites (vv. 15–27), it is ironic that he "opened his mouth" once too often in making this vow. But did Jephthah have to follow through on his vow? Ordinarily the answer would be yes. Vows were made only to God, and they were solemn pledges that had to be kept. People were not forced to take them, but if they did, they had to be honored (Deut. 23:21–23; Ps. 15:4; Eccl. 5:4, 5). But Jephthah had vowed something sinful in itself if his intent was to make a human sacrifice in the literal sense.

11:36–40 Those who believe that Jephthah intended to sacrifice a human being must also ponder whether Jephthah carried out his vow. The text does not explicitly say that he killed his daughter, only that **he carried out his vow.** When the verse goes on to say that **she knew no man,** some take this to mean that she was "sacrificed" by being dedicated to a life of perpetual virginity. Several arguments can be made for this interpretation. First, human sacrifice was contrary to the Law of Moses (Lev. 18:21; 20:2–5; Deut. 12:31; 18:10). Until the wicked reigns of Ahaz and Manasseh centuries later (2 Kin. 16:3; 21:6), there is no record of human sacrifice in Israel, even by those who followed Baal. Second, the great respect that Jephthah had for God surely would have prevented him

🌍 IN PLACE | The Philistines

The conflict between the Israelites and the Philistines that preceded the birth of Samson (Judg. 13:1) was one of many between the two peoples throughout biblical history. Probably no other group was as much a thorn in the side of the Israelites as their neighbors along the southwestern Mediterranean Coast in the land known as Philistia.

It is hard to say for sure where the Philistines originated. They were descendants of Noah's son Ham through his son Mizraim and grandson Casluhim (Gen. 10:13, 14). The name "Philistines" was used by the Egyptian pharaoh Ramses III to describe one of the "sea peoples," a coalition of invaders that he repelled in a naval battle in about 1188 B.C.

The Bible regularly associates the Philistines with the land of Caphtor, believed to be Crete, and its inhabitants, the Caphtorim (1 Chr. 1:12; Jer. 47:4; Amos 9:7). This is consistent with the view that as the Greeks moved into the Aegean area beginning in about 1500 B.C., the Philistines and other "sea peoples" migrated south and east. Some eventually settled on the southwestern coast of Canaan. Apparently this migration occurred in two waves. An early Philistine king, Abimilech of Gerar, was known to Abraham and Isaac (Gen. 20; 21; 26). By the time of the Exodus, a second wave had arrived and established five principal city-states that made up Philistia: Ekron, Ashdod, Gath, and Ashkelon, and Gaza.

Possessing weapons of iron, which were superior to those of the Israelites, the Philistines hacked away at Israelite territory after the conquest under Joshua. In fact, God used these attacks to discipline His people and to attempt to return them to the covenant (Judg. 3:1–3). But the revivals were usually short-lived. In the days of Eli the judge, the Israelites foolishly carried the ark of the covenant into battle, and the Philistines captured it (1 Sam. 4). The ark was eventually recovered, but the Philistine threat continued for centuries, right up to the fall of Jerusalem in 586 B.C.

---

from making such a perverse offering. Third, the fact that Jephthah permitted his daughter to bewail her virginity (vv. 37, 38) for two months fits an explanation of perpetual virginity better than human sacrifice. Fourth, the indication that his daughter "knew no man" also seems to be a detail that would support the idea of celibacy. Fifth, the Bible provides evidence that such devoted service for women did exist at the central sanctuary (Ex. 38:8; 1 Sam. 2:22; Luke 2:36, 37). In ancient Israelite society, the father had the power to prohibit a daughter to marry. Sixth, the conjunction in Jephthah's pivotal statement in v. 31, that whatever or whoever came out of

the door "shall be the LORD's, *and* I will offer it" could be translated *or*. Thus, if a person came out first, he would dedicate that person to the Lord, or if an animal came out first, he would offer the animal as a burnt sacrifice.

12:1–7 A final episode, in which the tribe of Ephraim sulks because they were left out of the battle, is similar to an incident when the same tribe challenged Gideon (8:1–3). However in the first incident, Gideon placated Ephraim, whereas in the second, Jephthah did not, and a civil war erupted. The Ephraimites were defeated, and that tribe does not play an important role in Israel's subsequent history.

12:2–4 You Gileadites are fugitives of Ephraim is the taunt that triggers the civil war. The insult may have its roots in the division of the nation into eastern and western groups (5:17; Josh. 1:12–15). Despite the emphasis in Joshua on the unity of all the tribes (Josh. 1:12–15; 22:1–34), the practical reality in the period of the judges was dramatically different. As in so many other ways, the life of the tribes deteriorated here also.

12:5 The fords of the Jordan were crossing points of strategic military value. Earlier on, the Israelites under Ehud had seized the fords and held them against the Moabites (3:28, 29). Under Gideon they had seized the "watering places," another name for the same place (7:24).

12:6, 7 Shibboleth . . . Sibboleth: This test devised by the Gileadites to catch the Ephraimites is the most famous example in the Bible of linguistic differences between the tribes. Today the English word *shibboleth* means an otherwise minor difference that becomes a sticking point because it distinguishes one side from another. The Gileadites chose this word because the "s" sound at the beginning was pronounced "sh" by one side and "s" by the other.

12:8–10 Ibzan was Israel's ninth judge. He allowed his thirty sons and thirty daughters to marry foreigners (v. 9). It is interesting to note that the judges who immediately preceded and followed the childless Jephthah both had thirty sons.

12:11, 12 Elon was the tenth judge.

12:13–15 Abdon was the eleventh judge, and like Jair and Ibzan had many children. He too possessed some wealth (vv. 13–15).

13:1–16:31 Samson, the last of the judges, lived at the beginning of the eleventh century B.C. He was unusual among the judges in many ways. He did not lead an army, but carried on his campaign against the Philistines single-handed. He is mentioned in Heb. 11:32 in the list of judges who accomplished great things through faith. The Book of Judges, in contrast, paints a darker picture of a man who violates a number of the Ten Commandments as well as his Nazirite vow (13:5). Samson's story brings the accounts of the judges to an end. His checkered history of heroism and moral failure resembles Israel's troubles during the time of the judges. Although we can find instances of obedience and humility in his life (15:18; 16:28, 30), for the most part his life was a string of careless adventures, with no true concern for following the Lord.

13:1–25 The story of Samson opens typically with a statement about sinful conditions in Israel, but the rest of ch. 13 continues with a long introduction to the life of Samson. The chapter details the encounter between Samson's parents and the Angel of the Lord, who announces Samson's birth and mission. The Angel emphasizes the requirements of the Nazirite vow that Samson is to observe in his life. It is as if the narrator wants to make sure the reader understands that Samson's life and accomplishments were under God's protection, provision, and guidance.

13:1, 2 Zorah was in the foothills west of Jerusalem, near Philistine territory, in the lowlands that separated the Philistine plain from the hill country of Judah. Manoah, Samson's father, was from the tribe of Dan, in whose territory Zorah lay (Josh. 19:41). Zorah is also mentioned among the inheritance of Judah (Josh. 15:33), indicating that it was along the border between the two tribes.

13:3 The Angel of the LORD made a supernatural appearance, described here as "very awesome" (v. 6). Manoah's wife recognized Him as "a Man of God" (v. 6). However, His essential character, embodied in His Name, was not to be revealed to them (vv. 6, 17, 18). This could mean that the Angel was God Himself (Ex. 3:14, 15) or His divine representative (2:1).

13:4, 5 The Angel declared that the woman's son should be a **Nazirite** from birth and for the rest of his life. The regulations of the Nazirite vows are found in Num. 6:1–21. Any man or woman could take a vow of separation to God. The vow was voluntary (Num. 6:2), had limited duration (Num. 6: 5, 8, 13, 20), and included three provisions: (1) abstinence from wine, strong drink, and the fruit of the vine; (2) not cutting the hair; and (3) no contact with the dead (Num. 6:3–8). A Nazirite who became unclean went through elaborate cleansing rituals (Num. 6:9–21). Note that both Samson's mother and Samson himself were to follow the regulations (13:4, 5, 7). Samson's Nazirite service was remarkable in three ways. First, he did not take his vow voluntarily; it was his before birth (vv. 5, 7). Second, his service was to be lifelong, not temporary (vv. 5, 7). Third, he eventually broke every one of its stipulations: his head was sheared (16:17, 19); he associated with the dead (14:6–9; 15:15); and he drank at his wedding feast (14:10–20). (The Hebrew word for *feast* in 14:10 is related to the word that means "drink," and it refers to a great drinking banquet.) The announcement that **he shall begin to deliver Israel** was welcome news. The Philistines had been a thorn in Israel's side for many years. Yet Samson's successes would prove to be temporary, since the Philistines remained Israel's adversaries during the days of Samuel, Saul, and David (1 Sam.).

13:6–13 Man of God was a term used for prophets elsewhere in the OT, including Moses (Deut. 33:1; Josh. 14:6), an anonymous prophet who spoke to Eli about his sons (1 Sam. 2:27), Samuel (1 Sam. 9:6–10), Elijah (1 Kin. 17:18, 24), Elisha (about thirty-five times), and others. At first, Samson's mother may have thought she was talking to a prophet, but His radiant appearance convinced her otherwise. Throughout this entire episode the Man of God **did not tell . . . His name** (vv. 16–18).

13:14, 15 The requirements for Samson's Nazirite vow were somewhat irregular (v. 5). Samson's mother was also required to observe a strict ritual (v. 4).

13:16 An editorial comment here tells us more than the story's characters knew (14:4; 16:21).

13:17, 18 it is wonderful: The word used here is related to the word for "wonders" (6:13). The Angel's name is too wonderful to comprehend, and so He does not reveal it to Samson's parents. Immediately afterward, the Angel did a "wondrous thing" by ascending into the heavens in a flame (vv. 19, 20).

13:19–22 When **Manoah** discovered that it was **the Angel of the Lord**, he feared for their lives because he and his wife had **seen God**. Gideon expressed a similar fear when he recognized the Angel of the Lord (6:22).

13:23, 24 The name **Samson** is related to the Hebrew word (*shemesh*) for *sun*. The story makes no comment on the meaning of his name. The choice of name may have been influenced by the fact that there was a town named Beth-Shemesh near Samson's hometown of Zorah, or the name may be related to the name of a sun-god, Shamash. **The Lord** blessed him is one of the few editorial comments by the narrator of Samson's story. For the most part, the narrator is content to tell the story without comment, letting the details speak for themselves.

13:25 the Spirit of the Lord began to move upon him: The Hebrew verb translated *move* can also be translated *impel*. The Spirit of the Lord was pushing Samson toward doing the work that God wanted him to do (14:4). The verb here is different from the one in 14:6 that is translated *came mightily*.

14:1–16:31 The actual exploits of Samson fall into two parts (14:1—15:20 and 16:1–31), each climaxing with a mass destruction of Philistines. In the first part, the Spirit of the Lord comes "mightily upon him" three times. Significantly, this fails to happen in ch. 16, when Samson was acting more on his own and falling out of favor with God. We find ten specific feats of strength and heroism: (1) killing the lion (14:5–9); (2) killing thirty Philistines (14:19); (3) burning the fields (15:4–6); (4) another slaughter of the Philistines (15:7, 8); (5) escape from ropes and killing 1,000 Philistines (15:14–17); (6) the Gaza gate incident (16:3); (7) escapes the bowstrings (16:9); (8) escapes the new ropes (16:12); (9) escapes the loom

---

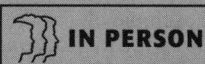 **IN PERSON**   ## God's Gifts Without God's Blessing

The Book of Hebrews lists Samson as a hero of the faith (Heb. 11:32), an honor that seems to conflict with the image of Samson in Judges. For example, he was notorious for his involvement with Delilah that led to his downfall. Likewise, as a Nazirite he was obligated to refrain from touching a dead body, to abstain from alcohol and other products of the vine, and to avoid the use of a razor. He clearly violated the first commitment (Judg. 14:8, 9, 19; 15:8, 15); in all likelihood violated the second, and ended up betraying the third (16:13–17).

Yet these failures must be put in perspective with the appallingly low moral and spiritual tide of Samson's day (13:1; 21:25). In the first place, he did act in faith at his death by praying to God for the strength to pull down the roof on his enemies (16:28–30). Thus he not only destroyed a temple of Dagon, he killed more Philistines than ever, most of which were probably members of the ruling class.

Samson also demonstrated that it is possible to experience the gifts and power of God without the blessing of God. God gives people abilities to accomplish His purposes, but that in no way guarantees that they will seek to know Him or follow His ways. Balaam, for example, was empowered by God to bless Israel, yet his own life remained spiritually bankrupt. For that matter, God could even speak through Balaam's donkey (Num. 22:28), but that hardly enabled the donkey to enjoy God's presence.

Samson is a sobering reminder that great abilities are not the same as great faith. As Paul pointed out, one can "speak with the tongues of men and of angels" yet live a life of loveless emptiness (1 Cor. 13:1).

(16:14); (10) destruction of 3,000 Philistines (16:28–30).

14:1–15:20 The episodes in this first section concern Samson's marriage to a Philistine woman and the cycle of offense and retaliation that surrounds it. Such marriages with foreigners were prohibited for Israelites (Ex. 34:16; Deut. 7:3). Samson's request for a wife defied the tradition that allowed the parents to arrange the marriage (14:2, 3). Despite Samson's disobedient and careless life, God intended to use him for His own purposes against the Philistines (v. 4), who were ruling over Israel at that time. It was the **Lord** (and no other) who ultimately was to rule over Israel.

14:1 Timnah was a town on the northwest border of Judah (Josh. 15:10) and was counted in the allotment of the tribe of Dan (Josh. 19:43). By Samson's day it was occupied by the Philistines. Samson's saga unfolds on the coastal plain where the Philistines lived, and in the lowlands and foothills near Jerusalem.

14:2 Such foreign marriages were against the Law.

14:3 The Philistines were Israel's neighbors but were almost always at war with them. They did not practice the ceremony of circumcision. Being **uncircumcised** appears as a cause for disdain or derision several times in Scripture (Judg. 15:18; 1 Sam. 14:6; 17:26, 36; 18:25; 31:4; 2 Sam. 1:20; 1 Chr. 10:4). **She pleases me well** is literally "she is right in my eyes." The phrase is usually used to describe a person or action that is right in the Lord's eyes (Deut. 6:18; 12:25). Samson's words revealed his self-centered attitude. Instead of seeking to serve God, he was seeking to please himself. Samson's comment here foreshadows the author's summary of the entire period of the judges in 17:6; 18:1; 19:1; 21:25.

14:4 The narrator adds that Samson's parents **did not know that it was of the Lord**. God would use Samson's defiant wish as a way of defeating the Philistines and providing relief for His people. For the five major cities of the Philistines and their rulers, see Josh. 13:3.

14:5–20 At his wedding feast, Samson challenged his 30 companions with a riddle. The riddle was based upon his astounding feat of killing a lion with his bare hands. When the guests could not solve it, they enlisted the help of Samson's wife, and she extracted the answer. In a rage, Samson killed thirty Philistines in Ashkelon to obtain the garments he needed to pay his companions. But in his absence, his wife was given to his best man.

14:6, 7 the Spirit of the Lord came mightily upon him: In the OT, there are thirty-nine references to "the Spirit of the Lord" or "the Spirit of God," as well as various other references such as "His Spirit" or "Your Spirit" or "the Spirit." The OT speaks numerous times of God's Spirit coming mightily upon individuals, usually to empower them physically for great feats of strength. Other judges received this power: Othniel (3:10), Gideon (6:34), and Jephthah (11:29). Yet the Spirit empowered others for the important task of speaking God's word (Gen. 41:38; Num. 24:2; 1 Sam. 10:6, 10; 19:20, 23; 2 Sam. 23:2). Probably the most important manifestation of the Spirit in the OT was the Spirit's ongoing presence. First Samuel 16:13 states that the Spirit lived with David from that day forward, and this is confirmed by David's statement in Ps. 51:11: "Do not cast me away from Your presence, and do not take Your Holy Spirit from me." This type of ongoing presence of the Spirit is something the NT emphasizes.

14:8, 9 Touching the dead lion violated Samson's Nazirite vow (13:5).

14:10, 11 The word translated **feast** denotes a banquet with considerable drinking, another violation of Samson's Nazirite vow (13:5).

14:12, 13 The Hebrew phrase **let me pose a riddle to you** literally reads "let me riddle you a riddle," using repetition to grab the reader's attention. The Hebrew word for **linen garments** is not the usual word for clothes, but appears only three times in the Bible, here and two others. In Prov. 31:24; Is. 3:23, it refers to fine linens worn or sold by women. Samson's offer was extravagant given the value of such finery. The Hebrew for **changes** of clothing is used in Gen. 45:22; 2 Kin. 5:22 in reference to valuable gifts.

14:14 This is the best example of a riddle in the Scriptures. The Hebrew word for *riddle* occurs twenty-one times in the OT, eleven of them in Judg. 14. The queen of Sheba posed riddles to Solomon (1 Kin. 10:1), and Daniel had skill in "interpreting dreams, solving riddles, and explaining enigmas" (Dan. 5:12).

14:15 the seventh day: Some other translations have "fourth day." The difference is only one letter in Hebrew, which could easily have happened as a scribe copied an early manuscript. "Fourth" fits better with the immediate context (v. 14 mentions three days of futile guessing about the riddle).

14:16, 17 Samson's wife pleaded with him for **seven days** to get the secret of the riddle, knowing the threat she faced from the young men.

14:18 The Hebrew word for **sun** is not the one commonly used. Perhaps the unusual word was chosen in order to avoid confusion with Samson's name, which resembles the common Hebrew word for *sun* (13:24). Samson's statement expresses his outrage that the men had not played fairly with him but had consulted his wife.

14:19 Ashkelon was one of the five main cities of the Philistines.

14:20 his companion . . . his best man: The Hebrew words here are the same, meaning "friend." The same man is referred to in 15:2.

15:1–20 When Samson could not gain access to his wife, he retaliated by burning the Philistines' fields, using 300 foxes (vv. 1–5). In response, the Philistines burned to death his wife and father-in-law. Then Samson killed more Philistines (vv. 6–8). The cycle of retaliation escalated, with the Philistines raiding Judah (vv. 9, 10). The men of Judah, not wanting to be involved in what they saw as a private dispute, delivered Samson to the Philistines (vv. 11–13).

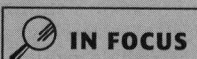

IN FOCUS "riddle"

(Heb. *chidah*) (Judg. 14:12, 19; Prov. 1:6; Hab. 2:6) Strong's #2420: The core meaning of this word is "an enigmatic saying." In Samson's story, the riddle is used in a contest of wits. Proverbs attributes enigmatic sayings to the wise (1:6). When the queen of Sheba tested Solomon's wisdom, her questions are described by this same Hebrew word (1 Kin. 10:1; 2 Chr. 9:1). In the Lord's confrontation with Miriam and Aaron, God describes Himself as speaking in "dark sayings" (the same Hebrew word) to the prophets, but to Moses face-to-face (Num. 12:6–8). Perhaps Paul had this last concept in mind when he admonished the Corinthians that even someone with the ability to understand all mysteries would not amount to anything if that person did not possess the love of God (1 Cor. 13:2).

The first section ends with the Spirit of the Lord coming upon Samson, empowering him to break his bonds and kill 1,000 Philistines (vv. 14–17). After this, Samson called upon the Lord for the first time, and the Lord answered his call, giving him water to drink (vv. 18, 19).

15:1–3 The time of wheat harvest was late May or early June. The wheat harvest was associated with the second of the three great festivals in Israel, the Feast of Weeks, also known as Pentecost (Lev. 23:15–22; Deut. 16:9–12). Samson came to visit his wife with **a young goat,** meant as a gift. Tamar also received such a gift before she had sexual relations with Judah (Gen. 38:17).

15:4 The **three hundred foxes** were probably jackals. The two animals are similar, and the same Hebrew word is used for both. Foxes are solitary animals, but jackals travel in packs and large numbers of them could be caught more easily.

15:5 the shocks and the standing grain: Shocks are bundles of wheat stacked together in the fields. Samson's jackals burned whole crops of grain, grapes, and olives. This damage naturally outraged the Philistines. According to the Law, anyone who burned someone else's fields had to pay restitution (Ex. 22:6). At another time, Absalom set fire to Joab's fields in order to attract his attention and gain an audience with the king; Joab reacted with anger (2 Sam. 14:28–32).

15:6 the Philistines . . . burned her: The Philistines held Samson's wife and father-in-law responsible for the deed and killed them both. Samson's wife had earlier escaped such a death by telling Samson's companions the answer to a riddle (14:15).

15:7, 8 The exact meaning of the phrase **he attacked them hip and thigh** is obscure. The following phrase—**with a great slaughter**—perhaps gets us closer to the meaning, suggesting that he not only killed but dismembered them. It may be that the expression *hip and thigh* originated in the art of wrestling, where brute strength like Samson's would have been a great help. **Etam** is otherwise unknown, but Samson obviously found a secure place to hide, perhaps a cave that was accessible only through a narrow fissure in the rocky crags near Zorah.

15: 9 Lehi means "jawbone," a name that the place received after Samson killed 1,000 Philistines with the jawbone of a donkey (vv. 15, 17).

15:10–13 two new ropes: Ropes were made of leather, hair, or plant fibers; one common fiber was flax (Josh. 2:6). The reference in v. 14 to the ropes becoming like burned flax suggests that this was the fiber. Being new, these ropes were the strongest possible.

15:14, 15 A fresh jawbone would have been tough, resilient, and virtually unbreakable.

15:16–18 Heaps upon heaps is a wordplay, since the Hebrew word for *heaps* resembles the word for *donkey*. A double expression similar to the one used here is found in Ex. 8:14, where the frogs of the second plague were piled in heaps.

15:19, 20 En Hakkore means "Spring of the Caller," a reference to Samson "calling out" to the Lord in v. 18 ("cried out" in v. 18 is literally "called out," and is the same word as is used in the name here).

16:1–31 Chapter 16 presents the conclusion

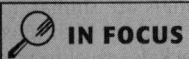 **IN FOCUS** **"deliverance"**

(Heb. *teshu'ah*) (Judg. 15:18; 1 Sam. 19:5; 2 Kin. 13:17; Prov. 21:31) Strong's #8668: The basic meaning of this term is "victory" or "safety." In the Scriptures, deliverance is almost always credited to God, who is frequently praised by the psalmists for His miraculous accomplishments (Pss. 51:14, 15; 71:14, 15). Elsewhere God's people are reminded that deliverance is not found in horses (Ps. 33:17) or in the capabilities of people (Pss. 108:12; 146:3); salvation is found only in the Lord (Lam. 3:26; Jer. 3:23). A day is coming when the Lord will provide everlasting salvation for His people (Is. 45:17). Placing our hope in the Lord and in that final day of justice is never inappropriate, for He will provide deliverance for His people.

of the Samson stories. Samson's involvement with two more Philistine women is detailed here. Verses 1–3 tell of a dalliance with a prostitute in Gaza, followed by another display of strength. Verses 4–22 chronicle his foolish affair with Delilah, which led to his downfall. Yet the story ends with Samson's destruction of the Philistines in their pagan temple.

16:1 Gaza is one of the five major Philistine cities, three miles inland from the Mediterranean coast. **a harlot:** Two Hebrew words are commonly used for prostitutes. One refers to priests and priestesses who performed sexual acts in the service of pagan gods (1 Kin. 14:24; Hos. 4:14). The other word refers to a common prostitute, such as the one Samson was consorting with.

16:2 At the gate reads literally "in the gate." The gates of the Early Iron Age were at least two stories high, with guard rooms on either side of a narrow opening. The Philistines waited in the recesses of the gate, hoping to trap Samson. He evidently slipped through unnoticed while they waited in one of the rooms.

16:3 Given the large size of city gates, Samson's feat was astounding. Hebron is forty miles east of Gaza. Samson's trip to the top of a hill that **faces Hebron** would have taken the better part of a day.

16:4–22 The account of Samson's downfall shows Delilah acting in cooperation with the leaders of the Philistines who were seeking to capture him. After three unsuccessful efforts, she succeeded in persuading him to reveal the source of his strength: his uncut hair. When he broke the final stipulation of the Nazirite vow by allowing his hair to be cut, the Lord left him (v. 20), and he was captured.

16:4 Delilah was the third Philistine woman that Samson entangled himself with (14:1; 16:1).

16:5, 6 Eleven hundred pieces of silver was a large sum of money; the same price would be paid to make two idols (17:2). This price was

multiplied by five (each of the five lords offered the same amount). The total reward probably weighed more than a hundred pounds.

16:7, 8 The first test of Samson's strength was breaking **seven fresh bowstrings** of animal gut. Newer animal strings would be stronger than old ones. Samson was showing contempt for his adversaries, who wanted to capture him quickly.

16:9–11 In this second test, Samson toyed with the Philistines, suggesting they use the **new ropes** that had proven worthless on an earlier occasion (15:13).

16:12, 13 The third test involving **the web of the loom** got closer to revealing Samson's secret, since his hair was involved. The loom that held Samson's hair was likely an upright one, supported by two posts that were firmly anchored in the ground. This was a more difficult test of strength for Samson, but he passed this one easily, too.

16:14, 15 she wove it tightly Samson was about to be fastened with a household implement, just as Jael had earlier "fastened" Sisera with a tent peg (4:21). Samson was able to free himself in this case, but like Sisera he eventually would fall victim to a woman's plot.

16:16 Delilah **pestered him,** just as Samson's wife had done earlier (14:17). Samson's foolishness prevented him from learning the lesson of his earlier experience.

16:17, 18 A **razor** in Samson's day would have been like a bronze knife with a handle of wood or bone. **a Nazirite to God:** See 13:5. **he had told her all his heart:** Delilah knew that Samson was finally telling the truth. This reference contrasts with the one in v. 15, where he withheld his heart from Delilah.

16:19–22 He did not know is another editorial comment by the narrator. See similar comments in 13:16; 14:4. **the Lord** had departed from him: See 14:6. They shackled Samson's hands or feet with a pair of **bronze fetters.** Samson became **a grinder,** forced to grind grain, most likely with a hand mill. Larger, animal-driven mills were not used until several centuries later. Grinding was typically a woman's job (9:53), so this only added to Samson's humiliation.

16:23–31 Samson's story ends with a measure of vindication: the Philistines and their gods were toppled at the hands of God. Samson's hair had begun to grow again (v. 22), and his second prayer to the Lord—his first was in 15:18—resulted in a great slaughter of his enemies, some 3,000 people, more than he had killed during his entire life. His call to the Lord is somewhat ambiguous; it appears to be more earnest than his first, but his motive—revenge for his blindness—is less than exemplary. Samson was buried with his father, following his twenty years of judging Israel (15:20). Samson's life is ultimately a story about God's faithfulness in spite of human weakness. God's hand can be seen throughout the story—in Samson's empowerment by God's Spirit and in God's professed desire to subdue the Philistines (14:4). It also can be seen in this last contest between the true God and the Philistine god Dagon. When the Philistines captured Samson, they attributed this to their god and celebrated his victory (16:23, 24). We know, however, that it was God who allowed it (v. 20), and that it was God who gained the ultimate triumph against Dagon and the Philistine rulers (vv. 27, 30).

16:23–25 Dagon was the principal Philistine god. He is known as Dagan in Syrian and Mesopotamian inscriptions. Temples dedicated to him have been unearthed at Ugarit in northern Syria, dating to the centuries just before Samson, and at Mari on the Euphrates River in Syria, dating to the eighteenth century B.C. A Philistine temple for Dagon was at Beth Shan, in northern Israel, in the days of Saul (1 Sam. 31:9, 10; 1 Chr. 10:10), and it was in another such temple that the Philistines stored the ark of the covenant for a time (1 Sam. 5:1–7). Dagon was once commonly thought to be a fish god, but modern excavations have shown that he was a god of grain. In fact, one of the Hebrew words for grain is *dagan*. **Our god has delivered:** The Philistine hymn of triumph reminds us of the language found in the Psalms.

16:26, 27 the pillars which support the temple: Numerous temples from this era with the supporting pillars described here have been excavated. Many were built around a courtyard. The roof, supported by the pillars, was where the spectators gathered. A crowd straining to see the spectacle of Samson would put considerable pressure on the structure of the building.

16:28–30 Samson demonstrated faith in calling upon God and in believing that God would help him. This is consistent with the praise of Samson in Heb. 11:32. Yet Samson's plea was basically a desire for revenge against the Philistines.

16:31 The story of the judges concludes with final editorial comments. Samson, the last judge, had been empowered by God's Spirit, just as the first had been. Despite the manifold failings of the judges themselves, God had delivered Israel and caused other nations to bow before Him. We can detect a general south-to-north pattern in the home areas of the judges and of most of the action. For example, Othniel, the first judge, was from Judah, in the south, and Samson, the last one, was from Dan, in the north. The judges' actions come full circle geographically, however, since Samson's exploits took place in the south. Despite the generally poor examples of the judges themselves, God had worked to deliver Israel and to protect His name and reputation.

17:1–21:25 The Book of Judges closes with two appendixes, the first in chs. 17; 18 and the second in chs. 19—21. They seem to be unrelated to the material preceding them and to each other. For instance, these chapters do not describe the cyclical pattern of sin, servitude, and salvation seen in the earlier chapters of Judges. While chs. 2—16 describe foreign threats to Israel, these last chapters show an internal breakdown of Israel's worship and unity. Furthermore, the events in these chapters appear to have taken place early in the period of the judges. Note that Phinehas, the grandson of Aaron who had figured in earlier events (Num. 25:6–15; 31:6; Josh. 22:30, 31), was still ministering before the ark at the time of the events of chs. 19—21 (20:28). The whole episode of the Danite migration (ch. 18) logically fits in the progression of events described in 1:34, during which the Amorites forced the Danites out of their allotted territory. Their migration in search of new land probably would have come soon after this, not some three centuries or more later. Thus, these chapters may have been written independently of the book's earlier chapters. Yet there is a certain logic to placing them at the end of the book. For one, the structure highlights the theme of the disintegration of Israel. The last chapters emphasize that "every one did what was right in his own eyes" (17:6; 21:25). The general tone of these last chapters is satirical and understated. The many violations of Mosaic law receive only minimal comments. However, a muted note of disdain for Israel's wanton behavior is evident in places.

17:1–18:31 The first of the appendixes concerns a man named Micah who created a private shrine. Migrating Danites seized Micah's priest and the symbols of his shrine, triggering the destruction of Laish.

17:1–3 These **eleven hundred shekels of silver** cannot help but remind us of the reward that the Philistine lords gave to Delilah. Micah, an Ephraimite, had stolen some silver from his mother, which he later returned to her. We learn that she had dedicated this silver to the Lord, but returned it to Micah so that he could make **a carved image and a molded image.** A carved image would be made of wood or rock. *Carved* is the same Hebrew word used in the Ten Commandments: "You shall not make for yourself a carved image." A molded image was one cast from a mold (2 Kin. 17:16). Micah's mother approved of his action, claiming that these images would be offered on the Lord's behalf. Today the temptation to mix elements of true worship of God with practices unacceptable to Him remains with us, albeit in different ways.

17:4, 5 a shrine: Literally "a house of God." This was a perversion of the true sanctuary where all worship was to take place. At this time, "the house of God" was at Shiloh (18:31). Micah also made an **ephod** (8:27) and various household idols. The word for *idols* is the same one used in Gen. 31:19, the story of Rachel's theft of Laban's household gods. Such idols are condemned in 1 Sam. 15:23. Micah further violated the law by appointing his own son as his private priest. Micah sinned because his son had not descended from Aaron (as priests were supposed to be) nor was he even a Levite (Ex. 28:1; 40:12–15; Num. 16:39, 40; 17:8).

17:6–8 what was right in his own eyes: This editorial comment is echoed in the last verse of the book (21:25). The author suggests that times were so bad that people did whatever they wanted, not what was right in the Lord's eyes (14:3). We may infer that a king who focused Israel's attention on the Lord would have prevented the outbreaks of sin and oppression so prevalent during the time of the judges.

17:9 The **Levite from Bethlehem in Judah** had been living there as a resident alien. Levites did not have a permanent land inheritance, but they had been granted forty-eight cities, scattered throughout the other tribes' territories (Josh. 21). However, Bethlehem was not one of these cities, and this Levite was seeking a place to settle down. He was only too happy to accept Micah's offer (vv. 10, 11).

17:10–13 be a father and a priest to me: To be called a father was a title of honor (see the reference to Deborah as a "mother in Israel" in 5:7). Micah wanted the Levite to be his priest, since his priestly background would lend legiti-

macy to his service. Micah thought this would bring him God's favor (v. 13). In later years, prophets were occasionally referred to as "fathers" (2 Kin. 6:21; 8:9; 13:14).

18:1 The **Danites** were looking for a place to settle because they had been unable to settle effectively in their allotted territory. Compare their allotment in Josh. 19:41–47 and their failure to capture it all in 1:34, 35.

18:2 The Danites decided **to spy out the land,** recalling the twelve spies who infiltrated Canaan in Moses' day (Num. 13) and the two spies that Joshua sent into Jericho (Josh. 2). The Hebrew word for *spy* is related to the word for *foot,* the idea being that spies went quietly on foot, scouting what they could see.

18:3 The Danite spies asked rapid-fire questions. Other places in Judges feature similar quick questioning (6:31).

18:4–7 The Danite spies found the city of **Laish** an attractive place to live and decided to seize it (vv. 7–10). The city was later renamed Dan (Josh. 19:47). **the Sidonians, quiet and secure:** On the Sidonians, see 3:3. The word for *quiet* is the same one that describes the "rest" that covered the land periodically (3:11). However, the word can also be rendered "unsuspecting."

18:8–14 Six hundred men was either a small part of the Danite army or a remnant that had survived recent fighting. Compare this figure with the 62,700 Danite soldiers in Num. 1:38, 39 and the 64,400 in Num. 26:42, 43.

18:15–20 Rather than condemning Micah's idolatry, the Danites took the gods for themselves. They then made Micah's Levite their tribal priest.

18:19, 20 The Danites' offer to Micah's Levite—**be a father and a priest to us**—was the same plea Micah had made earlier (17:10). Yet their offer was more attractive, for it allowed him to be priest over an entire tribe. The Levite's cynical acceptance of this opportunity for greater prestige indicates further how debased conditions had become. Even Levites were selling false spiritual services to the highest bidder.

18:21–29 As the Danites fled with Micah's priest and their stolen goods, they placed what they had stolen in front of them with the warriors behind them, as protection from being pursued. The Danites' power was too much for Micah and his neighbors, who turned back and did not attempt to recover what had been stolen from them. The Danites arrived at Laish, ruthlessly putting it to the sword and the torch, and they settled there, renaming the city **Dan.**

18:30 The Danites' priest and his descendants served the tribe for many years. This notice, written much later than the book's events, is a subtle reminder of Dan's later apostasy. Jeroboam I would establish idolatrous shrines in Dan and Bethel (1 Kin. 12).

18:31 Micah's image remained while the house of God was at Shiloh. Therefore, these events took place sometime before about 1050 B.C. when Shiloh was destroyed (Ps. 78:60; Jer. 7:12, 14; 26:6).

19:1–21:25 The concluding section of Judges is apparently unrelated to any preceding story. It concerns the brutal rape and murder of a concubine and the bloody events that followed. The story resembles that of the assault on Lot's home in Sodom (Gen. 19). A link here with the episode in Judges 17 and 18 is the Levite protagonist. In the former story, a Levite from Bethlehem travels to the hill country of Ephraim, while in the second, a Levite from the hill country of Ephraim travels to Bethlehem.

19:1, 2 A concubine was a female servant regarded as part of the family, often chosen to bear children. Several of the patriarchs had children with concubines: Abraham with Hagar (Gen. 16); Jacob with Bilhah and Zilpah (Gen. 30:4–13).

19:3–9 Obliged by custom, the Levite stayed in the home of his concubine's father for five days. Strict codes of hospitality still prevail in many Middle Eastern tribal cultures.

19:10, 11 Jebus (that is, Jerusalem): The city of Jerusalem was at this time in the hands of the Jebusites, and it is called "a city of foreigners" in v. 12. For more on the city and its early history, read Josh. 15:63.

19:12–14 Gibeah was four miles west of Jerusalem. Because it was in Benjamin, the Levite thought it would be a safer place to spend the night—a fatal misjudgment.

19:15–17 The open square of the city was a public area just inside the city gate. A traveler could expect an invitation to stay the night, but none was forthcoming from any inhabitant of Gibeah. an old man: The Levite received kindness from an outsider, an old man who was passing through Gibeah. Like the Levite, he was from the hill country of Ephraim.

19:18–21 The people of Gibeah were cold, even though the Levite had all that he needed with him, and even more than enough: he offered to take care of the old man and his servants, too.

19:22–26 The welcome offered by Gibeah

> *We may infer that a king who focused Israel's attention on the Lord would have prevented the outbreaks of sin and oppression so prevalent during the time of the judges.*

was no hospitality at all; it was the hospitality of Sodom (Gen. 19), an outrageous affront to the Levite and especially to his concubine. The men of Gibeah demanded to have sexual relations with the old man's guest. Offered the Levite's concubine instead, they assaulted her until she was half dead. This section closely resembles Gen. 19:4–9; indeed, the author may have written this story to make the comparison with Sodom unmistakable, as if to say, "Things are as bad now as they were in the days of Sodom and Gomorrah!"

19:22 Perverted men is literally the "sons of Belial," a phrase describing wicked or worthless people. The name Belial came to designate Satan, as it is used in 2 Cor. 6:15. That we may know him means that the men of Gibeah wanted to sodomize the Levite. The same expression is found in Gen. 19:5, where the men of Sodom wanted to force homosexual relations on Lot's guests.

19:27–30 The Levite's indifferent reaction to his concubine's collapse is followed by a gruesome deed: After carrying her away, he cut her body into twelve pieces, sending a piece to each tribe. This gesture was practically a call to arms; Saul did the same with oxen (1 Sam. 11:7).

19:30 The phrase no such deed has been done is ambiguous; it is uncertain whether they were horrified by discovering the dismembered body or by learning about the cruel rape and murder.

20:1–48 An assembly of all Israel convened at Mizpah and decided to unite against Benjamin (vv. 1–11). The Benjamites, who apparently were not at the assembly (20:3), responded by joining the men of Gibeah for battle (vv. 12–17). After withstanding two assaults, Benjamin was routed and its cities obliterated. The spiritual decay of Israel had resulted in the destruction of its own people with a vengeance once reserved for pagan peoples.

20:1 From Dan to Beersheba is a common expression for the full extent of the land of Israel from north to south (1 Sam. 3:20; 2 Sam. 24:2; 1 Kin. 4:25).

20:2–8 The assembly usually means the congregation of Israel as assembled for a religious event (Chr. 28:8) or a military campaign (Num. 22:4; 1 Sam. 17:47).

20:9–14 The tribes agreed to send a tenth of their men (v. 10), choosing them by lot. God's role is not mentioned here. To their credit, the Israelite tribes were **united together as one man,** a quality notably absent up to this point in the Book of Judges.

20:15 The Benjamite force of **twenty-six thousand men** was considerably smaller than the Israelite army of 400,000 (v. 17).

20:16, 17 The Benjamites counted on **seven hundred select men who were left-handed,** an advantage since their shots would come from unaccustomed angles. Ironically, the name Benjamin means "Son of the Right Hand."

fasting and sacrificing at Bethel, something done very rarely in this period. **The house of God** literally reads "Bethel," and probably the town is meant. Bethel was a Benjamite town that had been religiously prominent since Jacob met God there (Gen. 28:16–19).

20:28–30 Phinehas was the one who had stopped the plague at Peor (Num. 25:6–11). The fact that he was still alive shows that the organization of the Book of Judges is not strictly chronological. The author likely placed this account at the end of the book to make the

Photo by E. B. Trovillion

The Valley of Lebonah, situated between Shiloh and Shechem. This valley was mentioned in connection with a yearly feast celebrated at Shiloh (Judg. 21:19).

20:18–20 Judah first: The book begins and ends with Judah in this prominent position (1:1, 2). This is no accident, since the end of the book points toward the monarchy, whose true expression would come out of Judah.

20:21, 22 The Israelite coalition suffered an initial defeat, much in the same way that the men of Ai had defeated Israel some years earlier (Josh. 7).

20:23–25 Go up against him: The Lord graciously answered the Israelites twice when they called upon Him (v. 18).

20:26, 27 The Israelites suffered a second major defeat (v. 25). The result drove them to

point even more strongly about the spiritual deterioration of the nation.

20:31, 32 The highways were probably made of stone or gravel. The Hebrew word means "something raised," that is, a roadway elevated above the normal ground level (Is. 49:11).

20:33, 34 Baal Tamar: This is the only reference to this place, whose site is unknown. Its name means "Baal (lord) of the palm tree."

20:35–37 The LORD defeated Benjamin as punishment for the heinous crimes committed in Gibeah (ch. 19) and for disrupting Israel's unity, which He valued.

20:38–46 The burning of Gibeah and the

resulting rout of the Benjamites are almost an exact replay of the ambush of Ai (Josh. 8:17–22).

20:47, 48 Six hundred men of Benjamin survived the rout. They would become the remnant that would carry on the tribe's name (21:12–23).

21:1–25 After the devastating defeat of Benjamin, the remaining Israelites were struck with remorse because Benjamin faced almost certain extinction (vv. 1–7). Thus, ch. 21 tells of the provisions they made for the tribe's survival, though the means they chose were questionable or even brutal.

21:1–4 The details of an **oath at Mizpah** appear for the first time. It was presumably made when the people assembled at Mizpah before attacking Benjamin.

21:5–7 The **great oath** sworn by the Israelites provided the justification for punishing Jabesh Gilead and for providing wives for the Benjamites. Every tribe was expected to heed the Levite's call, since he had sent the concubine's corpse "throughout all the territory of Israel" (19:29).

21:8 Jabesh Gilead was a town east of the Jordan.

21:9–11 The phrase **utterly destroy** is found numerous times in the Book of Joshua in regard to the conquest of the Canaanites. However, there is no hint that God supported the bloodbath at Jabesh Gilead.

21:12–14 Four hundred young virgins were captured to become wives for the 600 survivors of Benjamin (20:47). Still, 400 were not enough, and the Israelites contrived to take more from Shiloh (vv. 19–22).

21:15–18 Void means "breach" and often refers to an outbreak of the Lord's anger (2 Sam. 6:8).

21:19 Some scholars believe that the **yearly feast of the LORD** in Shiloh was the Passover, held in the spring because of the dancing associated with it (vv. 21, 23); they point to the dancing of Miriam and the Israelite women after they had crossed the Red Sea as evidence for this practice (Ex. 15:20). However, the celebration was more likely the Feast of Tabernacles, celebrated in the fall, since vineyards are mentioned (vv. 20, 21). The grape harvest came in the early fall. This may have been the same event that drew Samuel's parents every year to Shiloh (1 Sam. 1:3).

21:20–23 The Benjamites were allowed to abduct enough women from Shiloh to supply every man with a wife. No justification is given except for the supposed needs of the Benjamites. To sidestep their oath, Israelites allowed the Benjamites to capture the young women. In this way, they could not be held responsible for giving brides to the 600, which they swore at Mizpah they would never do (v. 1).

21:24 every man to his inheritance: The Hebrew words here are the same as those found at the end of the Book of Joshua (24:28). However, the book's final comment (v. 25) indicates that times were far worse than they had been in Joshua's day.

21:25 The book ends with an editorial comment echoing the ones at 17:6; 18:1; 19:1. It is almost as if the author were weary and refused to dignify the state of affairs with more than, "Things are bad; they will get better under a king."

The Book of

Ruth

HE BOOK OF RUTH IS A BEAUTIFUL STORY OF love, loyalty, and redemption. One of only two books in the Bible named after a woman (see Esther), this narrative masterpiece tells the story of the salvation of Ruth, the Moabitess. Through her relationship with her mother-in-law Naomi, Ruth learned about the living God and became His devoted follower. Abandoning her family and homeland, she

demonstrated both her love for her widowed mother-in-law and her faith in Israel's God. Her faith was well placed, for God not only provided for her but also placed her in the messianic family line.

The account takes place during the time of the judges, a period of extreme spiritual and moral decay in Israel (c. 1380–1050 B.C.). The beautiful love story of Ruth contrasts strongly with the pervasive depravity of the period, giving a rare glimmer of hope in an otherwise bleak era.

The story itself reflects ordinary small town and rural life in Israel, specifically around Bethlehem. Details of cultural elements, such as the description of the barley harvest (1:22), the mention of the threshing floor (3:6), and the events at the city gate (4:1), add plausibility to the story. It is possible that the story was first circulated in Bethlehem by Naomi and her circle of women friends. Later, the author of Ruth retained some of the lovely feminine touches that grace this story.

The Book of Ruth underscores an overarching theme of the Bible: God desires all to believe in Him, even non-Israelites. This was

God's plan from the beginning. He had covenanted with Abraham and his descendants in order to bless other nations through the Israelites and draw all nations to Himself (Gen. 12:1–3).

While demonstrating this one significant theme, the Book of Ruth makes some distinctive contributions of its own. One is the important idea of loyal love that is evident in the book. The Hebrew word translated as *kindly* in 1:8 means "loyal love" or "covenantal love." This is a genuine love that keeps promises. When the word is used of God, it refers to God's loving faithfulness to His promises. Even though Ruth was a foreigner and was not familiar with God's Law, she displayed this type of love and loyalty to her mother-in-law Naomi. She left her homeland in order to be with Naomi in a time of need. Boaz also showed the same noble quality by protecting and providing for Ruth, a widow of one of his relatives. Yet the story of Ruth ultimately illustrates how God Himself demonstrated such love. He rewarded Ruth for her loyalty to Him by giving her an honored place in the community of faith. He blessed her with a child who would become the ancestor of King David and later of the promised Messiah.

The Book of Ruth also emphasizes redemption. God's providential hand in redeeming Ruth and Naomi from poverty is evident. He controlled circumstances so that Ruth and Boaz would meet, and He prompted Boaz to fulfill the responsibilities of the "close relative" or the kinsman-redeemer (3:9). The kinsman-redeemer was "the defender of family rights." This individual was a close relative who had the financial resources to rescue a poverty-stricken family member, stepping in to save that relative from slavery or from having to sell the family's ancestral land.

In the story of Ruth, Boaz redeemed the land that Naomi was about to sell. He also took on another of the kinsman-redeemer's responsibilities, the obligation of providing an heir for Ruth's deceased husband, Mahlon. Dying without an heir was considered a tragedy in the ancient Middle East. To rectify this situation, the brother of a deceased man was expected to marry the widow in order to produce a child, who would be considered the heir of the deceased. This was called a levirate marriage. Boaz willingly took on this duty, even though he was not the nearest relative (3:12, 13). He bought the land from Naomi, married Ruth, and carried on the family name through the birth of their son. Through all these actions, Boaz exemplified the compassion and love of a redeemer. His life is an illustration for us of the compassion of Jesus, who is our Redeemer (Gal. 3:13).

Traditionally, Samuel has been identified as the author of Ruth. However, some Jewish rabbis have ascribed the writing to Naomi. If the references to David in Ruth 4:17, 22 are an integral part of the original book and not a later appendix, then the book was not written by either since both died before David's was crowned king.

Some evidence in Ruth points to the conclusion that the book was written during David's or Solomon's reign. First, the genealogy of David in 4:18–22 indicates this. Second, the first verse of Ruth implies that the book was written after the time of the judges. Third, the fact that the narrator had to explain ancient customs to the intended readers in 4:7 indicates that the book was not written at the time of the events. All this evidence may point to the authorship of Ruth during Solomon's reign, a time regarded as the golden age of Hebrew writing.

Outline

I. Sojourn in the land of Moab 1:1–22
  A. Tragedy in Moab 1:1–5
  B. Friendship and faith in Moab 1:6–22
II. Ruth's first encounter with Boaz 2:1–23
  A. Boaz's introduction 2:1–3
  B. Boaz's discovery of Ruth 2:4–13
  C. Boaz's concern for Ruth 2:14–23
III. Ruth and Boaz at the threshing floor 3:1–18
  A. Ruth and Naomi's daring decision 3:1–7
  B. Boaz's delightful duty 3:8–18
IV. Redemption of Ruth by Boaz 4:1–22
  A. The relative's refusal to redeem 4:1–6
  B. Boaz's choice to redeem 4:7–12
  C. The reward of redemption 4:13–22

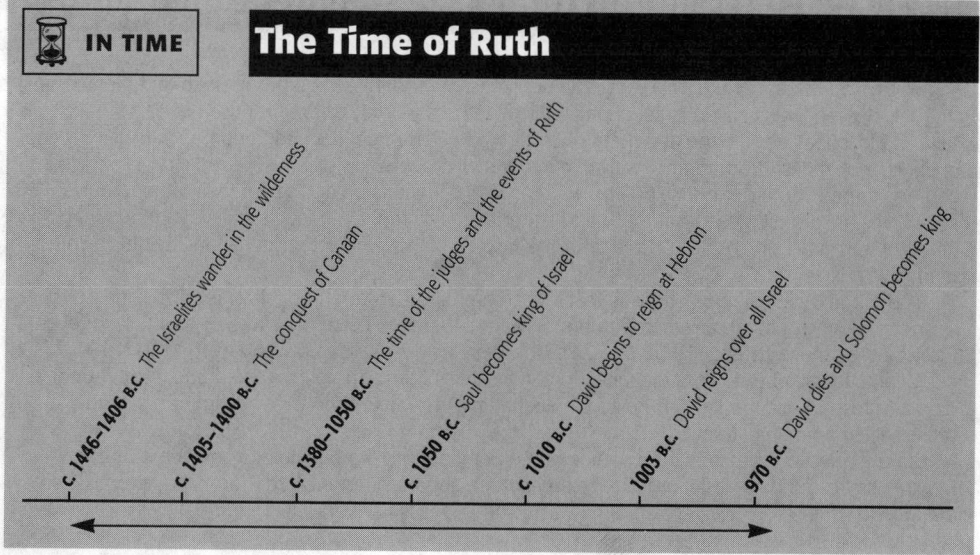

IN TIME — **The Time of Ruth**

c. 1446–1406 B.C. The Israelites wander in the wilderness

c. 1405–1400 B.C. The conquest of Canaan

c. 1380–1050 B.C. The time of the judges and the events of Ruth

c. 1050 B.C. Saul becomes king of Israel

c. 1010 B.C. David begins to reign at Hebron

1003 B.C. David reigns over all Israel

970 B.C. David dies and Solomon becomes king

Commentary

1:1 when the judges ruled: The events of
Ruth took place before the establishment of the
monarchy in Israel. The judges were God's servants, who established the teachings of God's
Law and righteousness during a time of political,
spiritual, and moral degeneracy. The story of
Ruth shines as a bright spot during a dark age in
Israel's history. **Moab** is located east of the Dead
Sea. The Moabites descended from Lot as a
result of his incestuous relation with his older
daughter (Gen. 19:30–37). The famine in Israel
extended to **Bethlehem** even though its very
name means "House of Bread."

1:2, 3 Due to the famine, **Elimelech,** whose
name means "God Is King," journeyed to Moab
with his wife and two sons. The names of his
wife and sons also carry significance. **Naomi**
means "Pleasant." She became bitter when
tragedy struck her family, but the story concludes with her bitterness being reversed (ch. 4).
The names of the two sons **Mahlon** and **Chilion**
mean "Sickly" and "Failing." The early deaths of
these two sons in Moab showed that their names
were appropriate (v. 5). **Ephrathites:** Ephrathah was another name for the region of Bethlehem (Gen. 48:7; Mic. 5:2).

1:4, 5 The Moabite name **Orpah** may mean
"Neck," a term of physical beauty in that culture. The Moabite name **Ruth** connotes
"Friendship." While the Law of Moses did not
prohibit Israelite men from marrying Moabite
women, it did exclude Moabites from the con-

gregation of Israel for ten generations (Deut.
23:1–4).

1:6, 7 the LORD: This is the first mention of
God's name in the story. God Himself is at the
center of the book. This verse illustrates the
mercy of the Lord, who supported even His disobedient people with food. He **visited** His
people both for blessing, as in this verse, and for
discipline (Ex. 20:5).

1:8 The Hebrew word (*hesed*) translated as
kindly is often used to describe God, and means
"loyal love." The word expresses both God's loyalty to His covenant and His love for His people.
Here Naomi expressed the hope that the Lord's
covenantal love would extend to her daughters-
in-law, who were outside the land of Israel and
were not Jewish.

1:9 The concept of **rest** referred to here is
the security that is found in marriage. Naomi
acknowledged in vv. 8 and 9 that it is the Lord
who intervenes in the lives of His people to
bring them gifts and blessings. His providence is
prominent throughout the Book of Ruth.

1:10–13 Naomi's daughters-in-law insisted
on returning with her. In response, Naomi
pointed out that she could not provide husbands for them and expressed concern for their
happiness. Her love for them is evidenced by
the use of the personal words **my daughters** in
vv. 11, 13.

1:13 grieves: Naomi was bitter (Heb. *marar*,
"grieves" here) that she was without husband
and sons and attributed her circumstances to
God's discipline.

✠ IN CONTEXT ## Can Anything Good Come from Moab?

The name "Moab" (Ruth 1:1) recalls two unpleasant incidents: the birth of Moab and the trouble
his descendants caused Israel during their wilderness journey to the Promised Land.

Moab was born in the aftermath of Sodom and Gomorrah. Lot fled Sodom with his family and,
in effect, took the sin from the city with him into the wilderness. His wife disobeyed God's instructions
and was turned into a pillar of salt (Gen. 19:26). Lot's daughters plotted to get their father drunk so
that he might commit incest with them and father their children. One daughter gave birth to Moab, the
other to Ammon (Gen. 19:30–38). In time, their descendants grew into rival nations that have contended with Israel to this day.

One of the most grievous offenses that Moab committed occurred during Israel's wilderness wanderings. The king of Moab attempted to hire Balaam the seer to curse the Israelites, but Balaam eventually blessed them instead (Num. 22–24). However, the seer came up with a plan to seduce God's
people into idolatry by sending Moabite women to entice them. The plan worked and 24,000 people
died as a result. Thus the Law prohibited a Moabite or Ammonite from ever becoming a member of
the Israelite community (Deut. 23:3).

But the question raised by the opening of the Book of Ruth—can anything good come from
Moab?—is a resounding yes! From Moab comes Ruth, and from Ruth, Obed; from Obed comes Jesse,
then David (Ruth 4:18–22); and through David comes Jesus Christ (Matt. 1:1, 5, 6).

1:14 In this verse, the responses of **Orpah** and **Ruth** are contrasted. Orpah did the expected thing and returned home. Yet Ruth unexpectedly stayed with her impoverished mother-in-law. Though understandable, Orpah's action meant that she had left the Israelites and their God. On the other hand, Ruth's action brought her into the Messiah's family line (4:18–22).

1:15 Naomi tried one last time to convince Ruth to return to Moab. The word for **gods** (*'elohîm*) refers to the deities of Moab. Here we are reminded that coming to Israel was also coming to the one Lord; remaining outside of Israel was remaining away from the covenant community.

1:16, 17 In a beautiful, emotionally charged poetic response, Ruth described her determination to remain with Naomi. Her assertion that Naomi's God would be her God is especially striking. This is an affirmation of faith in the Lord, the God of Israel. Ruth's use of the divine name Yahweh translated as **the LORD** in an oath indicates her commitment to the living God. She was choosing to cling not only to Naomi, her land, and her people, but also to her God. In effect, Ruth was forsaking all that she had ever known to follow the one true God. She was following in the footsteps of Abraham, who had forsaken his family and his homeland in response to God's command (Gen. 12:1, 4).

1:18–20 Naomi temporarily forgot or ignored the courageous and loyal commitment of Ruth. She wanted her name to reflect her bitterness over her circumstances so she named herself **Mara,** meaning "Bitter."

1:21 The concepts of fullness and emptiness appear here. Naomi left for Moab complete, with a husband and two sons. But now she returned to Bethlehem **empty.** She had no family except for Ruth. Her poignant question is an example of Hebrew parallelism, a device that heightens the expression of her emotion. Naomi was in utter despair over the Lord's dealings in her life. This makes it all the more remarkable that Ruth not only chose to stay with her but also to identify with her God.

1:22 The theme of *return* is prominent in this chapter. The word is even used of Ruth— an unusual word for the narrator to use since there is no indication that Ruth had ever been to Israel. **Ruth the Moabitess:** As the story explains, God extended His protection to Ruth even though she was a foreigner. Ruth and Naomi arrived at **the beginning of barley harvest.** Barley was the first crop to ripen, and this period would be the beginning of the harvest season. The fact that there was a harvest season indicates that the famine in Israel had ended (1:1, 6).

2:1 Boaz was related to Naomi's husband, **Elimelech.** This notice suggests the possibility of a solution for the distressed situation in which Naomi and Ruth found themselves. The status of a widow in the ancient Middle East was difficult at best. In times of trouble, the widow's situation was intolerable. That was why God

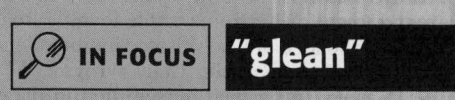

IN FOCUS "glean"

(Heb. *laqat*) (Ruth 2:2; Lev. 19:10; 23:22) Strong's #3950: The Hebrew word used here means "to gather together" or "to pick up." In the OT, people are described as gleaning a variety of objects: stones (Gen. 31:46), money (Gen. 47:14), manna (Ex. 16:4, 5, 26), and even worthless men (Judg. 11:3). The prophet Isaiah used this word to describe how the Lord would "gather up" His people from among all the nations and restore them to their own land (Is. 27:12). The verb occurs thirty-four times in the OT, with twelve instances in Ruth 2. In this passage, Ruth makes use of the stipulations the Lord gave to Moses. God had told the Israelites not to completely harvest their fields; instead they were to leave some unharvested so that the poor and strangers in the land could gather it up for their survival (Lev. 19:9, 10; 23:22).

commanded His people to care for the widow and the orphan (Deut. 24:19–22). As a relative, Boaz could stand up for the rights of these two women. He was described as **a man of great wealth,** a person of noble character and of high standing in the community. The name Boaz probably means "Swift Strength."

2:2 The Law of Moses allowed the poor to **glean** in the farmers' fields (Lev. 23:22).

2:3–6 happened to come: Though Ruth did not intentionally go to the field of Boaz, the Lord providentially directed her steps.

2:7 The **sheaves** refer to bundles of grain. Ruth was not presumptuous here but in gentleness asked for a favor that she might have claimed as an entitlement. Yet as an alien, her opportunities for gleaning in the fields of Judea may have been severely limited.

2:8, 9 Boaz demonstrated extraordinary concern for Ruth's provision and protection. He even thought of Ruth's need for water in the heat of the day.

2:10 Ruth was overwhelmed by the remarkable display of favor by Boaz toward her, especially since she was a **foreigner.** In the dark days of the judges, many in Israel would not be treating other Israelite families justly, much less those from other nations. Note Ruth's extreme act of submission and humility as she fell on her face before Boaz.

2:11, 12 Boaz explained that he favored Ruth because she had shown "loyal love" to her mother-in-law, Naomi. He then gave her a blessing, asking that God would abundantly **reward** Ruth for her remarkable loyalty. Boaz expressed the idea of God's protection by saying that Ruth had come **under** God's **wings.**

2:13 Now Ruth called herself the **maidservant** of Boaz. She no longer called herself a foreigner as she had in v. 10.

2:14–16 Boaz repeatedly demonstrated God's compassion toward the Moabite woman. Boaz went beyond the letter of the Law. He not only let Ruth **glean;** he also amply supplied her with food. Here we see how the Law could function in the lives of godly people. It was a guide to righteous living.

2:17–19 The amount of **barley** that Ruth gleaned was more than half a bushel, more than would normally be expected for a day's work. The generosity of Boaz and the labor of Ruth produced this substantial supply. Boaz exhibited the highest form of charity by giving in secret so as not to shame the recipient.

2:20–23 Naomi praised the Lord for His **kindness,** His "loyal love." God had not abandoned Ruth and Naomi. Instead, He had faithfully provided for their needs. After utter despair, Naomi once again placed her hope in God. **Close relatives** is the Hebrew word *go'el*, introduced into the story here, to be repeated many times.

3:1 Once again, Naomi returned to the subject of **security** or rest, which she addressed in 1:9. In the first instance, she had asked God to provide her daughters-in-law the "rest" of marriage. Now she was determined to seek this rest for Ruth.

3:2 The **threshing floor** was located in a public place. There animals would trample the husks in order to separate the grain. Then the mixture would be tossed in the air so the wind would blow away the chaff. Boaz had to stay the night to guard his grain from thieves.

3:3 best garment: This probably referred to an outer garment that Ruth wore to keep warm in the night. **eating and drinking:** Festivity accompanied the end of the harvest.

3:4 uncover his feet: Ruth would remove the edge of Boaz's outer garment from his feet and lie down by his uncovered feet. Touching and holding his feet was an act of submission. This was a daring and dramatic action that would call for a decision on his part to be her protector—and, likely, her husband.

3:5, 6 Ruth's trust in her mother-in law was implicit.

3:7, 8 Ruth came **softly,** that is, secretly, so that no one would see her. That she came at night was also a means of protecting Boaz from embarrassment in case he decided not to exercise his duty as a close relative.

3:9 your wing: Ruth deliberately used the same word that Boaz used in reference to God in 2:12. Though she spoke here of the edge of the garment of Boaz, she was clearly asking him for protection and security in the same way that Boaz spoke of Ruth seeking God's protection. The final phrase, **for you are a close relative,** shows that she was seeking his refuge in the sense of requesting him as her marriage partner. Since her husband had died without giving her a child, it was the responsibility of a close relative to marry her in order to provide an heir for her deceased husband.

3:10, 11 Boaz understood that Ruth was making a marriage proposal and praised her for not seeking younger men to marry. He knew that Ruth's initiative was in keeping with the Law. A levirate marriage would provide her deceased husband with an heir (Deut. 25:5–10). In the ancient Middle East, not having an heir was considered a tragedy for the family. The particular **kindness** that Boaz spoke of was Ruth's loyal love toward Naomi in choosing to

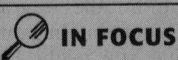 **IN FOCUS** **"close relative"**

(Heb. *ga'al*) (Ruth 2:20; 3:12; 4:1, 6; Is. 60:16) Strong's #1350: The Hebrew word refers to a relative who acted as a protector or guarantor of the family rights. He could be called upon to perform a number of duties: (1) to buy back property that the family had sold; (2) to provide an heir for a deceased brother by marrying that brother's wife and producing a child with her; (3) to buy back a family member who had been sold into slavery due to poverty; and (4) to avenge a relative who had been murdered by killing the murderer. The Scripture calls God the Redeemer or the "close relative" of Israel (Is. 60:16), and Jesus the Redeemer of all believers (1 Pet. 1:18, 19).

remain with her even though she faced poverty. **virtuous woman:** The high praise of Boaz shows that Ruth as a godly woman had not compromised herself.

3:12 The suspense in the narrative increases when Boaz announces that there is a **relative closer than** he. The nearest relative would have the opportunity to carry out that responsibility first.

3:13 Boaz wanted to take immediate responsibility for Ruth and Naomi, so he asked her to **stay** with him so she would not be exposed to any danger by returning to her home in the middle of the night. The statement **as the LORD** lives reinforces the resolve of Boaz to take responsibility for Ruth.

3:14 before one could recognize another: Ruth left at early dawn, in order to avoid anyone who might recognize her. Boaz probably did not want anyone to misconstrue what had taken place.

3:15 Again Boaz demonstrated loyal love or kindness by his gift of barley grain to Ruth and Naomi. **laid it on her:** Boaz probably helped raise the barley to Ruth's head in order for Ruth to carry it home to Naomi.

3:16 Is that you: These words are possibly a comment on the radiance of the woman who life was about to change so radically.

3:17 empty-handed: The theme of emptiness and fullness is repeated here (1:21).

3:18 Naomi was confident that Boaz would see the **matter** through to its conclusion the same day. Boaz had repeatedly demonstrated that he was an upright and compassionate man by his continuing provision for the two women.

4:1, 2 Official and legal business typically occurred at the **gate** of a city, so it was natural for Boaz to speak with the other **close relative** there in the presence of the elders of the community. During the time of the kings, a ruler might come to the city gate to proclaim a public judgment. **Friend** in the Hebrew is something of a joke, meaning "a certain so and so."

4:3 One of the duties of the **close relative** was to redeem land that had been sold by the family due to poverty. **sold:** This verb could be translated "about to sell." Verse 5 indicates that the sale was still in the future, and v. 9 states that Boaz purchased the land from Naomi. Thus we should probably understand that Naomi is about to sell Elimelech's land. The use of the tense of this Hebrew verb describes an act in the process of completion. Jeremiah seems to indicate that family members had the right to purchase a relative's land before it was sold to someone outside the family (Jer. 32:6–12). This is the likely scenario here.

4:4 Boaz offered the land to the closer relative first; this man initially agreed to purchase it.

The Law provided for land to stay within a family, even if it had to be sold temporarily due to poverty. The seller could redeem the land later, or a close relative could redeem it. If neither of these alternatives was possible, the land would be returned to the family in the Year of Jubilee, every fiftieth year. Land was not sold permanently because it ultimately belonged to God (Lev. 25:23).

4:5 To perpetuate the name of the dead makes it clear that the close relative was needed to buy the land but also to take Ruth as his wife. This was in accordance with the levirate law, which provided for an heir for the deceased. Here the **dead** relative was Mahlon, Ruth's husband (4:10). In carrying on the name of Mahlon, the line of Elimelech would continue.

4:6 When the close relative discovered that he was expected to marry Ruth, he declined his **right of redemption** because his **own inheritance** might be ruined. He apparently did not want the double responsibility of buying the field and supporting Naomi and Ruth. In addition, he did not want the field to be inherited by Ruth's future son instead of members of his own family.

4:7, 8 The removal of a **sandal** was part of a legal transaction in ancient Israel (Deut. 25:8–10). It would parallel the modern custom of concluding a transaction by signing a document or handing over a set of keys. By handing over his shoe, the **close relative** was symbolically handing over his right to walk on the land that was being sold.

4:9 The **witnesses** at the gate played a significant role in validating the transaction. **Chilion and Mahlon:** Elimelech's sons would have been the heirs of their father's land. **from the hand of Naomi:** The land was bought from Elimelech's widow, Naomi.

4:10 acquired: In addition to redeeming the land, Boaz also redeemed Ruth by taking her as his wife. In contrast to the land, Ruth was not bought. She did not require a purchase price nor was Boaz required to redeem her. He willingly chose to be her redeemer. Boaz was a blood relative of Elimelech, and he was financially able to take on the responsibilities of redemption. **Mahlon:** This verse adds the detail that Ruth had been the wife of the brother named Mahlon, a detail omitted from ch. 1.

4:11 The **people and the elders** affirmed the legal proceeding with their response, **we are witnesses.** Then the crowd gave Ruth a remarkable blessing by asking that **the LORD** make her like **Rachel and Leah,** Israel's founding mothers (Gen. 35:23–26). Even though Ruth was a Moabite, she was fully and eagerly accepted by the Israelites. The Law of

Moses demanded the exclusion of the Moabites from the congregation of Israel for ten generations (1:22). In this exceptional case we see a beautiful example of the spirit of the Law being maintained. Both the loyal love of Ruth and of God are demonstrated in this story. Ruth loyally loved Naomi by leaving her homeland and serving her mother-in-law even in the worst of circumstances. In turn, God rewarded Ruth by extending His loyal love to her. He gave this foreigner a godly husband, accepted her as one of His people, and gave her a child who would be an ancestor of King David and ultimately of Jesus (vv. 13, 22).

4:12 The Book of Ruth is replete with allusions to the Pentateuch. Here the name of **Tamar** refers to another story about the spirit of the Law (Gen. 38). Certainly Tamar's behavior would not normally be commended. Yet she was desperate because her husband's brothers would not fulfill their responsibility to her, and in the end Judah praised her as more righteous than himself (Gen. 38:26). Even in Tamar's deplorable situation, God mercifully blessed her with a son, and this son Perez was an ancestor to King David (v. 18). One more woman had an experience strikingly similar to Ruth's: That woman was Rahab, the mother of Boaz (Matt. 1:5). Like Ruth, Rahab was a Gentile woman. Yet God extended His loyal love to Rahab because of her faith in Him and included her in the messianic line.

4:13 the LORD gave her conception: Children are a gift from God. He fashions every person in the womb of the mother (Ps. 139:13).

4:14, 15 Here the **close relative** is not Boaz

but his newborn son, the grandson of Naomi. **The women** praised God for His provision for Naomi. They offered a blessing for the child, asking that his fame be extended throughout **Israel** and that he would comfort Naomi and nourish her in her **old age.** Naomi's emptiness had been replaced with fullness through the birth of this boy. Sons were considered a great reward, so for the women to state that Ruth **is better** to Naomi than **seven sons** was considerable praise for Ruth.

4:16, 17 The theme of Naomi's fullness continues to dominate as the **neighbor women** declared that a child was born to Naomi. His name was **Obed,** signifying "One Who Serves." The author at last reveals how Ruth, a Moabite woman, had become part of the royal Davidic line and, thus, the messianic line (Matt. 1:5). Her inclusion in the genealogy represents another beautiful illustration of Yahweh's loyal love (*hesed*) and His commitment to include Gentiles in the covenant community.

4:18–22 The story concludes with David's genealogy, beginning with **Perez,** the son of Judah and Tamar. This genealogy could have been added to the book long after the original writing was complete, but more probably the book as a whole was composed at a later date than the events described. The genealogy of David is not really an appendix but an essential element demonstrating the author's purpose, and the purpose of the Lord in the building of the family line of King David and the Messiah. The story of Boaz's redemption of a foreign woman points to Jesus' great redemption of all those who believe in Him.

The First Book of

Samuel

IRST SAMUEL RECOUNTS KING SAUL'S extraordinary rise to power and influence and his subsequent tragic fall. In this sense, the book reads like a classic Greek tragedy or Arthur Miller's *Death of a Salesman*. Saul's good looks, his physical size, and his success in war made him an obvious choice to be the first king of Israel. But the author of 1 Samuel highlights Saul's tragic flaw—his disobedience of God's commands (13:7–12; 15:10–26). Because of his disobedience, God rejected him. Abandoned by God, Saul quickly lost his courage, became jealous of David's success, and eventually lost his mind. From the ashes of this tragedy, God raised up another king who would obey the directives of the one true King, the God of Israel.

First Samuel is appropriately named after Samuel, the principal character of the early narratives and the one who anointed Israel's first two kings, Saul and David. First and Second Samuel were originally one book, "The Book of Samuel" in the Hebrew Scriptures. When these Scriptures were translated into Greek, around 150 B.C., Samuel and Kings were brought together into a complete history of the Hebrew monarchy. This unit of Scripture was divided into four sections: First, Second, Third, and Fourth Kingdoms. Samuel and Kings were later separated again, but the divisions of the Greek translation persisted. The result was a 1 and 2 Samuel and a 1 and 2 Kings.

At the beginning of 1 Samuel, the nation of Israel was at a religious low point. Even the priesthood was corrupt (2:12–17). To make things worse, Samuel's sons, who served as judges in Beersheba, were also dishonest (8:2, 3). With such evil leaders as models, the people of Israel showed open disdain for the word of God and refused to listen to His prophet Samuel (8:19).

Yet in the midst of widespread corruption and apostasy, there was a righteous remnant of Israelites who faithfully worshiped God (1:3). The worship center of Israel at this time was located at Shiloh, where the tabernacle was set up (1:3; Josh. 18:1). However, even the contents of the tabernacle were not left undisturbed during these tumultuous and evil times. The ark of the covenant was captured by the Philistines (4:11), and after a seven-month sojourn among the Philistine cities (5:1—6:16), it was returned to Beth Shemesh (6:19) and then kept at Kirjath Jearim (7:1) until David brought it to Jerusalem (2 Sam. 6:1–17).

During this time, the Israelites became dissatisfied with the abusive rule of the judges (8:3). The people longed for the glories of a monarchy such as they saw in the surrounding nations. So the Lord allowed the Israelites to have their way. He gave them a king like the other nations: the handsome and tall King Saul (10:1). Although Saul appeared to be well-suited for leading a nation, his reign ended in tragedy because he ignored the word of God. Much of the action of 1 Samuel is associated with the tumultuous life, reign, and decline of Saul, contrasted with the rapid rise of the young and faithful David.

During this early period of the Israelite monarchy (c. 1050–970 B.C.), the great empires of the ancient Middle East were in a state of weakness. The Hittites of Asia Minor had passed into insignificance. Assyria was in a state of decline, and Egypt was weakened by internal conflict. The Philistines constituted Israel's main threat during this period. Their skill in working iron had given them a decided military and economic advantage over Israel. Yet the threat of the Philistines had a positive impact on Israel's political situation. It caused the infant nation to unite under the leadership of its first kings, Saul and David.

The purpose of 1 Samuel is to provide an official account of the rise of the monarchy during the time of Samuel and the development of it under Saul and David. The book particularly focuses on the rise of David during this period. In fact, the second half of the book and first half of 2 Samuel amount to an apology for David's rise to the throne. The similarities of this section to the *Apology of Hattusilis*, a thirteenth-century B.C. writing, are remarkable. In this ancient document, a Hittite king outlined the reasons for the legitimacy of his rule. Such an apology was particularly important in the case of a king—like David—who founded a new dynasty. Hattusilis's dynastic defense included the following elements:

1. A detailed description of the disqualifications of the preceding ruler (compare 1 Sam. 15:1–35).
2. An extended history of events leading up to the new king's accession (compare 1 Sam. 16:1–2 Sam. 5:17).
3. A defense of the new king's ability to rule, as evidenced by military achievements (compare 1 Sam. 17:1–58).
4. A record of the new king's leniency on political foes, in contrast to usurpers, who typically assassinated the former king (compare 24:1–10; 26:1–9).
5. A report of the new king's interest in religion (compare 2 Sam. 6:1–19; 7:1–29).
6. A conclusion that included a summary of the new king's reign, demonstrating the divine blessing on his rule as evidenced by the expansion of his kingdom and the establishment of peace with surrounding nations (compare 2 Sam. 8:1–18).

The similarities between the *Apology of Hattusilis* and 1 Sam. 15:1 through 2 Sam. 8:18 illustrate clearly how that part of First and Second Samuel serves as an apology for David's reign. Part of the apology is the irrefutable evidence that God Himself had chosen David for the throne (16:1–13). Initially, David was a surprising choice, an undistinguished member of a rural family. Yet his remarkable faith in the Lord distinguished David from his fellow Israelites

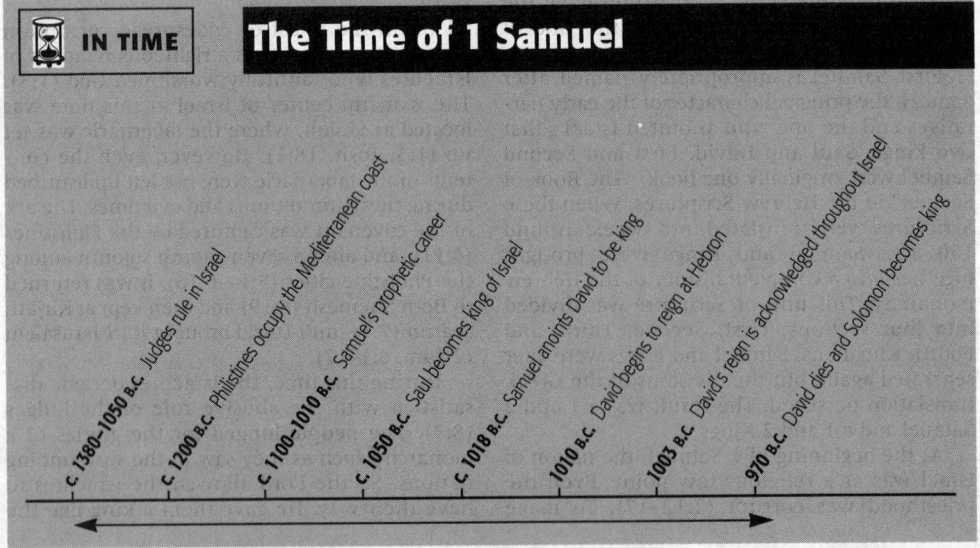

IN TIME

The Time of 1 Samuel

c. 1380–1050 B.C. Judges rule in Israel

c. 1200 B.C. Philistines occupy the Mediterranean coast

c. 1100–1010 B.C. Samuel's prophetic career

c. 1050 B.C. Saul becomes king of Israel

c. 1018 B.C. Samuel anoints David to be king

1010 B.C. David begins to reign at Hebron

1003 B.C. David's reign is acknowledged throughout Israel

970 B.C. David dies and Solomon becomes king

and from Saul (17:1–51). God shaped David's character while he was on the run from Saul's erratic wrath. In these distressing times, David learned to trust in God for deliverance. Although he made mistakes, he always turned back to God for mercy. For this reason, David was called the man after God's own heart (13:14).

The Jewish tradition suggests that Samuel was the author of the first part of the book (chs. 1—24), and that the prophet Nathan and the seer Gad were the authors of the remainder, including 2 Samuel. Another editor at a later date could have taken the memoirs of Samuel, Nathan, Gad, and others and woven them under the guidance of the Holy Spirit into the wonderfully unified book we have today.

A number of critical scholars have dated the book around the middle of the sixth century, much later than the lives of Samuel and Nathan (c. 1100–1010 B.C.). It is obvious that at least some parts of the book were written after the death of Samuel (25:1; 28:3), and perhaps even after the division of the monarchy (27:6). However, there is no reference to the fall of Samaria to the Assyrians (722 B.C.), and it is reasonable to assume that the book was complete by the last quarter of the eighth century B.C. The eighth-century author used documents dating back to David's reign or shortly after (1025–900 B.C.). The author included eyewitness accounts, and the antiquity of some linguistic features indicate that parts of the book were written at an early period.

Outline

I. The ministry of Samuel the prophet 1:1–7:17
  A. The birth of Samuel 1:1–2:11
  B. Samuel and the sons of Eli 2:12–36
  C. The beginning of Samuel's prophetic ministry 3:1–21
  D. The Philistine war at Aphek and the loss of the ark of the Lord 4:1–7:2
  E. Israel's victory over the Philistines under Samuel's ministry 7:3–17
II. The reign of Saul as the first king of Israel 8:1–15:35
  A. Israel's demands for a king 8:1–22
  B. Saul's anointing and public presentation by Samuel 9:1–10:27
  C. Israel's victory over the Ammonites 11:1–15
  D. Samuel's farewell address 12:1–25
  E. God's rejection of Saul 13:1–15:35
III. David chosen to succeed Saul as king 16:1–31:13

A. David's anointing and entrance into royal service 16:1–23
B. David's victory over Goliath 17:1–58
C. David's relationships with members of the royal family 18:1–20:42
D. David as a fugitive 21:1–31:13
  1. David's flight to Nob, Gath, and Moab 21:1–22:5
  2. Saul's punitive action against the priests of Nob 22:6–23
  3. David's rescue of the city of Keilah 23:1–14
  4. Saul's pursuit of David in the Wilderness of Maon and En Gedi 23:15–24:22
  5. Samuel's death and David's marriages 25:1–44
  6. Saul's pursuit of David in the Wilderness of Ziph 26:1–25
  7. David's flight to Philistia 27:1–28:2
  8. Preparation for the battle at Gilboa 28:3–29:11
  9. David's rescue of the inhabitants of Ziklag 30:1–31
  10. Saul's death 31:1–13

Commentary

1:1–7:17 The first seven chapters introduce the prophet Samuel, thought by many to be the greatest OT figure since Moses. Samuel is unique in ancient Israel in that he had three distinct roles, or offices, as a leader. He was been born into a Levitical family, so he served as a priest in Israel (10:8). He was also recognized as the last of Israel's judges and handled judicial decisions and disputes (7:6, 15; 12:11). And he was the first of a series of great prophets after the time of Moses (3:20).

1:1, 2 Ramathaim Zophim is another name for Ramah (v. 19), a village about five miles north of Jerusalem. **The mountains of Ephraim** refers to the hill country primarily occupied by the tribe of Ephraim. **Elkanah,** whose Hebrew name means "God Has Created," was a Levite (1 Chr. 6:26, 34). He is referred to as an **Ephraimite** since he lived in the territory of Ephraim.

1:3 yearly: The Law called for the Israelites to attend three annual pilgrim festivals in Jerusalem (Ex. 34:23; Deut. 16:16). **The LORD of hosts** is a military designation referring to God as the One who commands the angelic armies of heaven (1 Kin. 22:19; Luke 2:13; Rev. 19:14) and the armies of Israel (17:45). **Shiloh,** located about twenty miles north of Jerusalem, was the religious center for the nation at this time and the location of the tabernacle (Josh. 18:1). **Eli, Hophni,** and **Phinehas** served as priests at Shiloh, officiating at the sacrifices presented in the court of the tabernacle. Eli may mean "God Is High." Hophni means "Tadpole." Phinehas may come from an Egyptian word meaning "Black One."

1:4, 5 The **double portion** was designed to compensate Hannah for her lack of children and demonstrate Elkanah's love for her. **the LORD** had closed her womb: God is the One who provides the ability to conceive children (Gen. 33:5; Ps. 127:3).

1:6 Her rival refers to Peninnah, Elkanah's other wife, who took every occasion to flaunt her children before Hannah.

1:7 she went up: The Law demanded that the men of Israel appear before Him on three festival occasions. Many brought their families with them, but it was not required that they do so. This verse shows Hannah's devotion to the Lord in that she also made annual treks to Shiloh to worship God. **she wept and did not eat:** Peninnah's constant taunting drove Hannah to depression.

1:8 While Peninnah provoked Hannah, Elkanah sought to encourage her. He suggested that his love for Hannah was a greater blessing than having **ten sons.**

1:9, 10 eating and drinking: The worship of God involved not only the sacrifice of ani-

mals, but also lavish banquets of meat and wine. **Eli,** Israel's high **priest** and judge (4:18), was from the family of Ithamar, Aaron's fourth son (1 Kin. 2:27; 1 Chr. 24:1, 3). The last high priest mentioned before him was Phinehas, the son of Eleazar (Judg. 20:28). It is not known why or how the office of high priest passed from the house of Eleazar to that of Ithamar. **The door-post of the tabernacle** refers to the entrance of the place of worship, where people would approach Eli for judicial rulings. The term "tabernacle" (Heb. *hêkal*), here, is used elsewhere for the temple or for a palace and thus suggests that the structure at Shiloh was no longer merely a tent but a semi-permanent structure, which preceded the great temple built in Jerusalem by Solomon.

1:11 Within the context of her prayer, Hannah **made a vow** to God. She promised that if God would give her a son, the child would be given back to God. Levites customarily served from age twenty-five to fifty (Num. 4:3; 8:24–26). Yet Hannah dedicated her son for lifelong service (the Bible speaks of only one other Nazirite for life, the judge Samson; Judg. 13–16). The words **no razor shall come upon his head** refer to the law of the Nazirite (Num. 6:2–6). The Nazirite vow involved a designated period of time (usually no more than a few weeks or months) during which there was a commitment to refrain completely from wine, from cutting the hair, and touching any dead

---

⚒ **IN DEPTH**   **The Rise and Rule of David**

First and 2 Samuel were originally one book that gave an account of the transition between the period of the judges and the monarchy. First Samuel tells of the rise of David to the throne, and 2 Samuel deals with David's reign.

The demand for a king was based on the chronic moral and spiritual breakdowns that occurred under the judges. As 1 Samuel opens, Israel is again drifting under ineffective leadership. Eventually disaster strikes as the ark is captured by the Philistines. God graciously brings the ark back to His people and raises up Samuel as their judge. But as Samuel grows older, a debate ensues for and against a monarchy. Samuel's sons were not worthy to succeed him, and there seemed to be no other leadership on the horizon. Consequently, the people insisted on having a king, and God finally granted their wish. Yet Scripture says that this request was a "great wickedness" in that it was a denial of the Lord's right to rule over His people (1 Sam. 8:7; 10:19; 12:12, 17–20).

The problem was not that Israel did not need a king, but that the Israelites were not willing to serve the king that they already had—the Lord. How, then, would they follow a human king who had faults and failures? But God was already at work to produce a ruler of His own choosing. He allowed Saul to be anointed and reign temporarily, but His own plans called for David. First Samuel tells the story of how God brought David to the throne in spite of Saul's efforts to the contrary.

Second Samuel continues with an account of David's reign. At first he was king over Judah only, which he ruled for seven and a half years. During much of this period, he fought a war with the successors of Saul, until he finally gained control over all Israel.

body. Hannah promised that her son would be a Nazirite for life.

1:12–14 Eli watched her mouth: From a distance, Eli was unable to understand what Hannah was saying. Because of the long time she spent in prayer, Eli assumed that she had drunk too much wine.

1:15 Intoxicating drink is an older translation of the word (*shekar*) meaning "beer." **Poured out my soul before the Lord** is an excellent description of fervent prayer (Ps. 62:8; Phil. 4:6, 7; 1 Pet. 5:7).

1:16 The Hebrew for **wicked woman,** literally "daughter of Belial," means "without value." Belial was later used as a proper name for Satan (2 Cor. 6:15).

1:17, 18 Go in peace: Hannah's changed countenance seems to indicate that she experienced God's peace (Phil. 4:6, 7) as she waited for the answer to her prayer.

1:19 Elkanah knew Hannah means that he slept with her (Gen. 4:1). The word **remembered** indicates that God began to intervene on Hannah's behalf to answer her prayer.

1:20, 21 The birth of Hannah's son is part of a long history of godly women and men praying for a child as God's gift (Gen. 12:1–3). When Hannah gave birth, she named her son **Samuel,** which means "Name of God." She explained that she gave her son this name **because I have asked for him from the Lord.** There is a play on words in this verse, for "Samuel" sounds like the Hebrew words, "Asked from God" (v. 28).

1:22 until the child is weaned: Hebrew children were normally weaned when they were two or three years old.

1:23 According to the Law, Elkanah might have declared Hannah's vow a rash promise and prohibited her from fulfilling it (Num. 30:10–15). The fact that he did not do so shows his love and esteem for Hannah.

1:24, 25 three bulls: God's Law required that a burnt offering be given at the completion of a special vow (Num. 15:3, 8). Two of the bulls likely served as a present for Eli and the third one was sacrificed. **One ephah** was roughly five gallons. **A skin of wine** was for the drink offering.

1:26, 27 Hannah offered a testimony of what God had accomplished on her behalf. By telling others, she exalted God and praised Him for His gracious acts toward her.

1:28 lent him to the Lord: The Hebrew word translated *lent* has the idea of a complete giving up of the child to God. **they worshiped:** The Hebrew word for *worship* means "bow down." This is the humble response of grateful people who acknowledge the majesty of God.

2:1–11 Hannah's Psalm of Praise to the Lord. Hannah rejoiced and praised Yahweh in response to answered prayer. The scene stands in contrast to her previous visit to Shiloh (1:9–15). Her words of praise may have been delivered in song as a personal testimony before the congregation of worshipers at the tabernacle. This passage is written in the same type of poetry as other psalms in the Bible; metaphor and simile abound. The sovereignty of God and His providential rule in every aspect of life is the

✠ IN CONTEXT The Custom of Polygamy

Polygamy was an accepted social custom throughout the ancient Middle East. It was also a common practice among the ancient Israelites. Although it may seem that polygamy deviated from God's original plan for marriage (as illustrated in Gen. 2:24), the practice was permitted under God's Law, particularly in cases of a childless first marriage or a levirate marriage (Deut. 25:5–10).

In ancient Israel, failure to have children was regarded as a family tragedy, for several reasons. In an agrarian culture, children were needed to help with the work of everyday life. Without sons, the family name would not be preserved, and without an heir, the family would be unable to maintain its place in the tribal allotments. Finally, a woman without children would never be the mother—or an ancestor—of the promised Messiah (Gen. 3:15).

Elkanah most likely took a second wife, Peninnah, for a reason that was legitimate in the ancient world: his first wife was barren. At that time, the blame for not having children was always assigned to the woman, and barrenness was often the cause of divorce.

Even though polygamy was an accepted custom, God's Law warned rulers against marrying many women (Deut. 17:17). Furthermore, the Scriptures record the tragic results of polygamy: turbulent and divided families.

basic theme of this song. The prayer is a powerful affirmation of this woman's deep faith in the living God. Hannah acknowledged God's salvation (2:1), holiness (2:2), knowledge (2:3), grace (2:8), and judgment (2:10). We may learn to number Hannah among the great psalmists in ancient Israel, just as we may learn to number Mary in the NT (Luke 1:46–55). Indeed the Psalm of Hannah was twice reused in biblical poetry. It served as the basis for the lovely Psalm 113, and both psalms were used and developed further in Mary's psalm in Luke 1.

2:1 Hannah began her prayer by rejoicing in the Lord for having been given a child. **My horn is exalted:** Used figuratively, a horn represents power and strength, like that of an ox

Photo by Howard Vos

2:4, 5 Hannah mentioned three examples—military power, wealth, and the birth of children—of how God reverses human circumstances, humbling the proud and exalting the lowly. Mary made the same point in her song (Luke 1:46–55).

2:6 The word **grave** (Heb. *she'ôl*) refers to the place of the dead for both the righteous and the wicked (Gen. 37:35). The sovereign God who brings death also **brings up** from the grave. This verse may refer to God's power to resurrect the dead (Ps. 16:10; Dan. 12:2).

2:7, 8 dust . . . ash heap: These parallel terms describe the festering compost piles outside the city walls where people dumped their refuse, including the ash from ovens. It was

The modern village of Ramah, successor to the Old Testament city where the prophet Samuel was born (1 Sam. 1:19, 20) and buried (1 Sam. 28:3).

(Dan. 7:21; Zech. 1:18–21). With exalted horn means with head high, conscious of strength. Hannah's sense of strength was in God, who had answered her prayer.

2:2 No one is holy like the Lord: That which is holy (Heb. *qadôsh*) is marked off, separated, and withdrawn from ordinary use. *Holy* is the opposite of *profane* or *common*. The image of a **rock** when applied to God, speaks of His eternality, stability, and reliability (Deut. 32:4; 2 Sam. 22:2, 3).

2:3 Hannah addressed all the proud, not only Peninnah, but all who boast. Since **the God of knowledge** knows all things, He will appraise our performance along with our words and our promises.

there that beggars and lepers would sit and solicit alms. Hannah used the image to indicate the deepest degradation: God assists those in the worst circumstances (Ps. 113:7–9). **The pillars of the earth** is poetic imagery. Since the very "pillars" that uphold the earth belong to God, all creation is stable and secure under His care.

2:9, 10 In line with the pattern of ancient wisdom literature, Hannah contrasted the righteous and the wicked. The Lord would keep **His saints** from stumbling, but the **adversaries of the Lord** would face certain calamity. The Hebrew word for **anointed** means "Messiah." This phrase points to the ultimate **King,** before whom every knee shall bow (Phil. 2:10). Hannah saw the work of God in granting her a

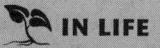 **IN LIFE** | # Hannah's Song: Praising the King

Many people today debate the potential as well as the limits of big government. The books of 1 and 2 Samuel make interesting reading in light of that discussion, for they offer an account of Israel's transition from rule by judges to a Jerusalem-based monarchy.

Under the judges, the nation went through periods of political and spiritual health. But for the most part, the people turned away from God (Judg. 21:25). Would they do better under the kings?

Hannah's song (1 Sam. 2:1–10) answers that question from the outset of the book: no matter who "rules" Israel, whether judge or king, the Lord is Israel's true King (2:3, 10), salvation is from Him (2:1), and God's concern is often for the outsiders, the poor—people on the "bottom of the heap" (2:4–9).

The rest of 1 and 2 Samuel, as well as 1 and 2 Kings, bear out these truths:

* When the people demanded a king (1 Sam. 8:4, 5), the Lord said that it was because they had rejected Him as their King (8:7).
* When the nation faced crises, it was not their king who delivered them, but the Lord (1 Sam. 11:13; 17:46; 2 Sam. 5:22–25).
* It was not Saul, the people's favorite, who firmly established the monarchy, but David, the eighth and youngest son of Jesse, a shepherd of Bethlehem (1 Sam. 16:7, 9–13; 18:23; 2 Sam. 7:12–16).

Hannah's song addresses our overconfidence in government of any kind. All government is ultimately established by God (Rom. 13:1–7). Ideally, governments should seek justice for all. But in the end, one's faith must not rest in the power of centralized control but in the power of God's justice, mercy, and salvation.

---

child as another step in the fulfillment of His promise to the mothers of Israel, that He would one day provide through them a Messiah.

2:11, 12 Were corrupt is literally "sons of Belial," persons of no value (30:22). **did not know the LORD**: They had no personal, intimate knowledge (Heb. *yada'*). The priests were teachers of God's Law and officiated at His sacrifices. How tragic for them to know so much about the things of God and yet not know Him personally.

2:13–15 The priests' rightful share of a sacrifice was the breast and the right thigh of the animal (Lev. 7:34). Eli's sons sinned by taking any part they wanted and demanding the meat immediately, before the part consecrated to God, **the fat,** had been burned on the altar (Lev. 3:3, 5).

2:16 if the man said: In this instance, the layperson knew God's Word and the importance of obedience better than the priests.

2:17 abhorred: Eli's sons dishonored God by doing their priestly duties with irreverence and disrespect. Those who regularly handle the things of God are sometimes in grave danger of carelessly and presumptuously performing the sacred duties entrusted to them.

2:18 The **linen ephod** was a sleeveless garment that was worn by priests, especially when officiating at the altar (2:28; 22:18; Ex. 28:6–14;). Occasionally it was worn by others engaged in religious ceremonies, such as David (2 Sam. 6:14), and here by Samuel.

2:19 The **little robe** made by Hannah is different from the ephod mentioned in v. 18. It

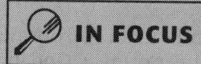 **IN FOCUS** | **"horn"**

(Heb. *qeren*) (1 Sam. 2:10; Deut. 33:17; Ps. 132:17; 2 Sam. 22:3) Strong's #7161: This word denotes the horn of an animal or even the tusk of an elephant (Gen. 22:13; Ezek. 27:15). Animal horns were used as instruments (Josh. 6:5) and as flasks for the prophets' anointing oil (16:1, 13; 1 Kin. 1:39). A horn was a symbol of power (1 Kin. 22:11; Mic. 4:13); consequently, the Lord is said to exalt the horns of the righteous and to cut off the horns of the wicked (Pss. 75:10; 92:10; Zech. 1:21). The wicked are told not to lift up their own horn (Ps. 75:4, 5). David in 2 Sam. 22:3 speaks of God as his "horn of salvation," the title Zacharias prophetically gave to Jesus (Luke 1:69).

was probably a long outer garment like those worn by people of rank or special status. The fact that Hannah made such a robe indicated her love for her son, whom she could visit only on rare occasions.

2:20 the loan that was given: The word *loan* here indicates a complete giving up of the child to God (1:28).

2:21 visited Hannah: God came to Hannah to grant her request, as He had to Sarah (Gen. 21:1). The Hebrew verb "visited" (*paqad*) speaks of God's gracious condescension: He comes near to His people to meet their needs (Ruth 1:8). In other circumstances, God's visit may be for the purpose of judgment (Hos. 1:4).

2:22 The joy of aged parents is in the godly success of their children. Few pains are greater in old age than to realize that one's children are living in spiritual ruin.

2:23, 24 Eli's protests seem weak in view of the enormity of his sons' sins.

2:25 Nevertheless may be translated "therefore" here, pointing to the severe consequences of their sin.

2:26 Compare the description of Samuel childhood with that of Jesus (Luke 2:52). The contrast between Samuel and Eli's sons is inescapable.

2:27, 28 The **man of God** was an unidentified prophet or spokesman for the Lord. **Your father** is a reference to Aaron, the brother of Moses and Miriam and the divinely appointed founder of the priestly house in Israel (Ex. 4:14–16; Num. 3:1–4).

2:29 Eli had warned his sons of divine judgment (v. 25), but he had never really rebuked them for their sins (3:13). By neglecting his parental duty, he was in effect favoring his sons above God.

2:30 I said: As descendants of Aaron, Eli's family benefitted from the promise God had given to Aaron and his sons that they would be a priesthood forever (Ex. 29:9). Eli is another example of godly men in Scripture who were unsuccessful in their parenting roles as "father."

2:31–34 The prophet predicted the destruction of the priestly family of Eli. The judgment was partially fulfilled in the massacre of the priests of Nob (22:11–19), and was ultimately fulfilled when the priesthood was transferred to the family of Zadok in the time of Solomon (1 Kin. 2:26, 27, 35).

2:34 The deaths of **Hophni and Phinehas** would validate the truth of the prophecy (4:17).

2:35 The **faithful priest** refers to Zadok, who was faithful to God and to the line of David and Solomon (1 Kin. 1:7, 8; 2:26, 27, 35). To **build him a sure house** means to guarantee a long line of succession for this faithful priest. **My anointed:** The household of Zadok would continue to serve alongside the divinely anointed kings, and ultimately before the Coming One (the Messiah). **Forever** here may mean to extend through human history. The sons of Zadok will serve in the messianic temple during the millennium (Ezek. 44:15; 48:11).

2:36 The impoverishment predicted here was probably fulfilled when Abiathar, a descendant of Eli, was dismissed from the priesthood by Solomon (1 Kin. 2:27).

3:1–18 After the time of Moses, the greatest of Yahweh's prophets (Num. 12), there were numerous true prophets of the living God (one is indicated in the phrase "a man of God," in 1 Sam. 2:27). But Samuel was the first of a series of named and celebrated prophets formally appointed by God to speak His word to the people of Israel. The first part of ch. 3 records his call to the prophetic ministry.

3:1 The word translated **boy** means "youth." It was used of David when he slew Goliath (17:33). **rare in those days:** Samuel

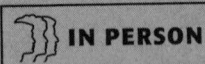 **IN PERSON** ## Eli, the Failed Leader of Shiloh

Eli served as a priest and judge of Israel for forty years (1 Sam. 4:18). It was not an easy time in which to exercise leadership. Israel had no centralized government, and "everyone did what was right in his own eyes" (Judg. 21:25), including Eli's own sons, Hophni and Phinehas. They abused the sacrificial system and committed immorality with the women at the tabernacle (1 Sam. 2:12–17, 22).

Eli was in a position to stop these abuses, but he was not equal to the task. He was unable either to restrain his sons or to remove them from the priesthood, and he and his descendants fell under the scathing judgment of God (2:27–36). Yet one bright spot of hope emerged from Eli's household, the boy Samuel, who in contrast to Eli's wicked sons followed the Lord and grew up to be one of Israel's greatest judges (2:17, 18; 3:1, 19, 20).

was called at a time of extremely limited prophetic activity, probably because there were so few faithful Israelites who would listen (Judg. 21:25).

3:2 lying down in his place: Eli apparently was quartered in the court of the tabernacle, where cells were built for the priests who served the sanctuary.

3:3 The lamp of God is the gold lampstand that was located in the holy place of the tabernacle (Ex. 27:20, 21; Lev. 24:2–4). The fact that it had not yet gone out indicates that Samuel's call took place just before dawn. The Hebrew text may be rendered, "Samuel was lying down in the temple of Yahweh," indicating that he slept as an attendant near the ark.

3:4–8 Three times Samuel mistook God's voice for the voice of Eli. Samuel had been assisting Eli in serving the tabernacle, but he did **not yet know the LORD** in an intimate and personal way. He had never heard God's voice. He had never received **the word of the LORD** by divine revelation.

3:9 Eli finally realized that God was speaking to Samuel and advised the young man what to do.

3:10 the LORD came and stood: These words reflect Samuel's very real sense of God's presence. This appears to have been a theophany, a visible appearance of God, as in Gen. 12:7. **Speak . . . hears:** Samuel voiced his readiness to receive God's revelation. "Hears" (Heb. shama') means "to hear with interest" and can be translated "obey." Samuel was listening for God's word and was determined to obey it.

3:11 I will do something: God is sovereign over judgment and calamity (Eccl. 7:13, 14; Is. 45:7).

3:12 from beginning to end: The judgment would extend from the death of Eli's sons and continue until the whole prophecy given by the man of God (2:27–36) was fulfilled.

3:13 I have told him: The message was given through the anonymous "man of God"

(2:27–36). **I will judge:** No descendants of Eli would serve as priest. **made themselves vile:** These were supposed to have been the esteemed priests of God, but they turned their privilege into disaster. **he did not restrain them:** Here we learn of Eli's personal failure as a father. The word translated *restrain* occurs only here in the Hebrew Bible. It suggests a rebuke that sets things right.

3:14 shall not be atoned: Eli and his sons were guilty of presumptuous sin (Num. 15:30, 31). For such a sin, there was no atoning sacrifice.

3:15, 16 The doors of the house refers to the entrance of the court of the tabernacle. After the people settled in Canaan, the tabernacle was set up permanently at Shiloh, and a walled enclosure with doors replaced the curtains which once surrounded the sanctuary. **Vision:** The term here applies to the message given to Samuel, since it came through divine revelation.

3:17 The phrase **God do so to you, and more also** is an oath. Eli was saying, "May God do something terrible, and worse, if you don't tell me the truth."

3:18 Let Him do: Eli submitted to God and accepted God's judgment. Even with all his failures as a father, Eli remained faithful to God.

3:19 the LORD was with him: This was the key to Samuel's success as a prophet (Matt. 28:20). God remained with him. **let none of his words fall:** All the prophecies God delivered through Samuel were fulfilled.

3:20 The expression **Dan to Beersheba** denotes the whole territory of Israel, from its most northern to its most southern point (Judg. 20:1). The term **prophet** (Heb. nab'î) means "spokesman" and refers to one who speaks for another (Ex. 7:1, 2).

3:21 The LORD appeared again in Shiloh: The idea here is that God was present in the midst of His people, both to receive their worship and to speak through His prophet. Samuel's

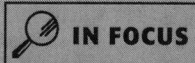 **IN FOCUS** **"hears"**

(Heb. shama') (1 Sam. 3:10; 17:28; Gen. 3:10, Ex. 2:15; Is. 6:9) Strong's #8085: The Hebrew word translated hears also means "to listen" or "to obey." This important OT word appears over 1,100 times. It implies that the listener is giving his or her total attention to the one who is speaking. In some cases, the word connotes more than listening and indicates obedience to what has been said. Abraham was blessed not only for hearing, but for obeying God's voice (Gen. 22:18, where the word is translated obeyed). In the present passage Samuel is listening for God's word and is determined to obey it. This young man is an example of the kind of person God delights to use—one who is always ready to receive His Word and follow it.

call at Shiloh provided the basis for an on-going prophetic ministry. The verse speaks of two means of divine revelation, visions and direct speech.

4:1 The **Philistines,** known in Egyptian texts as the "Sea Peoples," were Indo-Europeans who migrated from the Aegean Islands and Asia Minor to the eastern Mediterranean coastal region in the twelfth century B.C. Migrations had occurred earlier, for Abraham and Isaac had contact with the Philistines as early as the twentieth century B.C.. With their aggressive invasions and the fortress cities at Ashkelon,

Ashdod, Ekron, Gath, and Gaza, the Philistines established strong political and military control of the southern coastal plain of Palestine. With their iron weapons, the Philistines became a significant threat to Israelite security. The **battle** mentioned here took place between **Ebenezer** and **Aphek.** The name Ebenezer means "Stone of Help," and it commemorates Israel's victory at the same site about twenty years later (7:12). Aphek, located thirteen miles northeast of Joppa, was a strategic border city at the northern limit of Philistine territory (29:1).

4:2 **The field** refers to the flat coastal plain

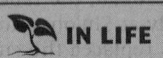 **IN LIFE**   # Who Is "Called"?

Are only certain people "called" by God (1 Sam. 3:20)? The issue of "calling" tends to be confusing today. Sometimes people talk about their day-to-day work as if that alone were their callings. "I'm John. I'm a chemist," or, "I'm Jane. I sell real estate." Others believe that occupations such as the pastorate or missionary work are true "callings." Pigeon-holing ourselves like this falls short what the Bible means by "calling."

A Task Set by God

The Reformation leader Martin Luther had a phrase that helps correct insufficient views of "calling." He said that a person's entire life was a "task set by God." In whatever we do—work or play, eating or sleeping, worshiping or relaxing—we have a responsibility to honor God, for He is Lord of all of life. From a biblical point of view, "calling" describes all of the responsibilities of all believers to serve God with all of their lives:

- Every believer is called to belong to God. Paul indicated to the Christians at Rome that both he and they had the same calling (Rom. 1:1, 6). Likewise, he wrote to the believers in Ephesus that just as there is one Spirit and one body (that is, the church), "you were called in one hope of your calling" (Eph. 4:4).
- Every believer is called a child of God. In His love, God brings us into His family (1 John 3:1), through faith in Christ Jesus.
- Every believer is called to accept the work of Christ on our behalf. Though we are sinners deserving of judgment, Christ's death on the Cross has "justified" us, made us able to stand before a holy God and receive His salvation and grace (Rom. 8:28–30; 2 Tim. 1:9). For this we have every reason to live lives of gratitude (1 Thess. 2:13).
- Every believer is called to become like Christ. Living the life God calls us to involves change in which we take on the character of Christ. That means resisting the temptation to turn away from Him, even though others may encourage us to do so (Gal. 1:6–9). It involves fleeing evil and pursuing good, fighting to maintain our faithfulness (1 Tim. 6:11, 12). Just as Christ is holy, so we are to develop holiness in everything we do (1 Pet. 1:15; 3:9). As we pursue Christlikeness, we can do so with the certainty that the Lord is helping us, equipping us for every good work (Phil. 2:12, 13; 2 Pet. 1:3–10).
- Every believer is called to serve God and other people. Christ has called us to Himself to live out our faith in a manner that is worthy of Him (Eph. 4:1–4). We have the privilege of declaring God's work through everything we do and say (1 Pet. 2:9, 10, 21).
- Every believer is called to become a citizen of the new heaven and new earth. The Christian life leads ultimately to the end of being "glorified," raised up to stand with Christ in eternal glory, pure and holy at last (1 Pet. 5:10; 2 Pet. 3:10, 11). In that day, we will celebrate the final coming together of Christ and all His faithful ones (Rev. 19:9, 10). Our obedience to the Lord right now confirms this ultimate calling (Matt. 5:19).

where the Philistines were able to use their chariots to great advantage (13:5).

4:3 The term **people** refers to the fighting men of Israel before there was a standing Israelite army. **Elders** refers to the family heads who gave leadership in politics and war before the creation of the monarchy. In preparation for their next battle with the Philistines, the Israelites brought the **ark of the covenant** from the tabernacle in **Shiloh** to the battlefield. It was the custom of ancient warriors to take symbols of their gods into battle so that their gods would deliver them (2 Sam. 5:21; 1 Chr. 14:12). This apparently was Israel's plan. They failed to recognize that God would be with them even if the ark was in Shiloh! **it may save us:** It seems that the Israelites viewed the ark superstitiously, believing divine power to be in the ark itself rather than in God.

4:4 who dwells between the cherubim: Cherubim are angels generally regarded as guardians of God's holiness (Gen. 3:24; Ex. 25:22; 2 Sam. 6:2; 2 Kin. 19:15; Pss. 80:1; 99:1; Is. 37:16; Ezek. 10:9). God revealed Himself to Moses from between the two cherubim mounted at opposite ends of the mercy seat of the **ark of the covenant** (Ex. 25:22; Num. 7:89).

4:5–7 the earth shook: The presence of the ark gave the Israelites a false sense of victory. **God has come into the camp:** The shouting of the Israelites at the sight of the ark struck fear in the hearts of the Philistines. They clearly viewed the ark as some sort of idol.

4:8–10 these mighty gods: The Philistines were polytheists, and they assumed that the Israelites also had many gods. The Philistines had heard the report of what God had accomplished for His people at the time of the Exodus (Deut. 2:25).

4:11 The loss of the **ark,** symbolic of God's presence among His people, was a great tragedy for Israel—even worse than the loss of life (v. 10). The ark probably never returned to Shiloh. The Lord destroyed Shiloh because of the wickedness of His people (Jer. 7:12), and archaeological excavations indicate that the city was destroyed around 1050 B.C., perhaps by the Philistines. The deaths of Eli's sons, **Hophni and Phinehas,** mark the first step in God's judgment on the house of Eli (2:34).

4:12 Torn clothes and dirt on the head were traditional signs of mourning (Josh. 7:6).

4:13–17 by the wayside: Eli was sitting by the city gate (v. 18), anxiously awaiting news of the battle.

4:18, 19 The loss of the **ark** was a catastrophic blow. In response, Eli fell off his chair and died—another sign of God's judgment on the house of Eli (2:33–36).

4:20 Like Rachel (Gen. 35:16–20), the wife of Phinehas died in childbirth. The words **you have borne a son** were spoken to comfort her as she was dying.

4:21 She possibly refers to the midwife attending the birth of Eli's grandson. The name **Ichabod,** meaning "No Glory" (Heb. *î-kabôd*) reflected Israel's circumstances. The loss of the ark meant the absence of God's glory in Israel.

4:22 The explanation of the name **Ichabod** is repeated, emphasizing what the godly wife of godless Phinehas sensed as the greatest tragedy, the loss of the ark. This truly was a day of ignominy, long to be remembered in Israel.

5:1–7:2 These chapters record "the wanderings of the ark" and its eventual return to Israel. Chapter 5 presents an amusing though grim story of the havoc the ark caused among the Philistines while it was in their possession. Although they thought that its possession would be to their benefit, the Philistines had to learn a hard lesson: the holy ark of the covenant was not a magical box to be use as a good-luck charm. It was a representation of the living God, and He would not allow His holy ark to be associated in any manner with their pagan worship or temples.

5:1 Ashdod, one of the five chief Philistine cities, was about three miles inland from the Mediterranean Sea and about twenty-two miles south of Joppa.

5:2 Dagon, the chief god of the Philistines, was thought to control the weather and the fertility of the land. This god appears to be a Philistine adaptation of the Canaanite god Baal, who is sometimes referred to in ancient literature as the "Son of Dagon." Philistia was an important grain-producing region; the worship of Dagon was thought to ensure a good crop.

5:3, 4 Twice the idol of Dagon fell prostrate before the ark—as if worshiping the Israelite God. The second time the head and hands were broken off. This was recorded in order to demonstrate the foolishness of worshiping an impotent god.

5:5 The destruction of Dagon's idol resulted in the foolish Philistine custom of stepping over the **threshold** of Dagon's temple (Zeph. 1:9). Apparently the threshold came to be regarded as taboo because of its contact with Dagon's hands and head (v. 4).

5:6, 7 The Hebrew word translated **tumors** (*'ophel*) literally means "swellings" and may refer to any kind of tumor, swelling, or boil.

5:8, 9 Lords (Heb. *saren*) refers to the rulers of the five cities of Philistia (6:4). To free themselves from the plague associated with the presence of the Israelite ark, they sent the ark to **Gath,** one of these cities.

5:10 The ark was sent next to **Ekron,** about

six miles north of Gath. **to kill us:** Having heard of the plague associated with the ark, the citizens of Ekron were less than enthusiastic about receiving the Israelite war trophy into their city.

5:11 The phrase **deadly destruction** (Heb. *mehûmat-mawet,* "a tumult of death") is particularly grim. Once again, the judgment of God followed the ark.

5:12 The Hebrew word **cry** means a cry for help (Ex. 2:23).

6:1, 2 Diviners claimed to be able to predict the future and determine the will of their gods by observing such omens as the flight pattern of birds or the liver of a sacrificed animal (Num. 22).

6:3 The priests and diviners (v.2) warned against returning the ark empty. They advised the Philistine leaders to present an offering to appease the God of Israel in order to end the plague. In their understanding, the God of Israel was another deity among many, who had won some sort of contest with their god Dagon. **trespass offering:** The gift was to be a compensation for trespassing against God by capturing the ark.

6:4 The offering of gold was fashioned to resemble the **tumors** and **rats** that plagued the people. **the number of the lords of the Philistines:** The offering corresponded to the number of Philistine cities and their respective lords or kings.

6:5 give glory to the God of Israel: By sending the gifts back with the ark, the Philistines acknowledged that it was God who had afflicted them with tumors. This recognition would add to His glorious reputation among the nations.

6:6 The Philistine priests and diviners recalled the experience of **the Egyptians and Pharaoh,** who **hardened their hearts** against God at the time of the Exodus. God's salvation of the Israelites was internationally known (Deut. 4). The words of the priests and diviners imply that the ark should be returned to Israel before a worse calamity befell the Philistines.

6:7 The use of a **new cart** and cows that had **never been yoked** was designed to show special reverence for God on the part of the Philistines. **take their calves home:** The natural inclination of cows would be to return home with their calves. This was a test as to whether God was behind the plagues.

6:8, 9 let it go: Where the cows went was going to be left up to God. **if it goes up the road:** If the two cows left their calves this would be a clear sign to the Philistines that the plague of tumors had been the judgment of Israel's God. **Beth Shemesh,** a Levitical city (Josh. 21:16), was close to the border of Philistia, about eight miles east of Ekron. The name Beth

Shemesh means "House of the Sun." It is likely that this ancient Canaanite city had been known for its temple to the sun god.

6:10–12 along the highway: The Hebrew literally reads "along one highway," indicating that the cows did not deviate onto any side roads. The **lowing** of the cattle was their plaintive crying for their calves. These cows were drawn by a strong power in the opposite direction from where their natural inclination would lead them. This would make an undeniable impression on the Philistine farmers, who knew the strong maternal instincts of cows.

6:13 wheat harvest: Wheat planted in the fall and harvested in the spring.

6:14 offered the cows as a burnt offering: Although Deut. 12:4–14 required that sacrifices be offered only at the central sanctuary, it seems that this law would not have been applied in view of the recent destruction of Shiloh. Since Beth Shemesh was a Levitical city (Josh. 21:16), there would have been priests available to officiate at the sacrifice.

6:15 Mosaic law stipulated that only the Levites could handle the ark, and even they could not touch it directly (Num. 4:5, 15). **offerings . . . sacrifices:** These were in addition to those mentioned in v. 14.

6:16 The **lords** or kings of the Philistine cities had followed the ark at a distance to see what would become of it.

6:17 Although there is no indication in the text that the ark was ever in **Gaza** or **Ashkelon,** these cities apparently fell under the same plague as the other Philistine cities; therefore, they contributed to the **trespass offering** (v. 3). Ashkelon, located on the Mediterranean coast about ten miles south of Ashdod, is one of the oldest, largest, and most important cities in the Holy Land (only Jericho is regarded as an older city in ancient Canaan). Archaeologists have found evidence of human occupation there that dates back to the Neolithic period (7500–4000 B.C.). The city covered some 160 acres. Herod was a native of Ashkelon, and in his later years he adorned the city with palaces, temples, and a large stoa. Gaza, another Mediterranean coastal city, was located about twelve miles south of Ashkelon. It was important commercially as the last stop on the Via Maris, or coastal highway, before entering the desert of northern Sinai. Samson once carried the city gate to a mountain top near Hebron (Judg. 16:1–3, and it was at Gaza that Samson ended his life by pulling down the pillars of the Philistine temple (Judg. 16:21–31).

6:18 Abel here is unrelated to the name of Adam and Eve's son (Gen. 4:2). This term may be a place or site name that more precisely locates the large stone.

6:19 The Lord brought judgment upon certain **men of Beth Shemesh** who were guilty of the presumptuous sin of gazing into the ark. They had shown a lack of reverence for the holy things of God and had directly violated Mosaic law (Num. 4:20).

6:20 Who is able to stand: Since God is holy, He requires those who minister or serve Him to be separated from all that is contrary to His holy character. The people responded in terror and frustration. They knew of the troubles that the ark had brought to the Philistines; now, they believed, they were next.

6:21 The people of Beth Shemesh were so disturbed by the tragedy that they requested the inhabitants of **Kirjath Jearim** to remove the ark from their city. Kirjath Jearim was about ten miles west of Jerusalem.

7:1 Eleazar, whose name means "God Is Help" or "God Is Power," was **consecrated** (literally, "set apart") to care for the ark. Eleazar was probably a member of the priestly family since there was no judgment on his ministry before the ark.

7:2 it was there twenty years: Most likely, it was twenty years before Samuel called the assembly at Mizpah (v. 5). The ark remained at Kirjath Jearim for about a hundred years. It was taken there just after the battle of Aphek around 1104 B.C. and remained there until David brought it to Jerusalem in his first year as king over all Israel, around 1003 B.C. (2 Sam. 5:5; 6:1–18).

7:3 If you return to the LORD: Repentance from sin and expressions of loyalty to God were prerequisites for the restoration of divine blessing (Deut. 30:1–10; 2 Chr. 7:14). The expression **foreign gods** is a general term for the idols of Canaan. **Ashtoreths** is the plural form of the name of the Canaanite goddess of fertility, sexuality, and war. The rites connected with her worship usually involved sacred prostitution. Sexual rituals in the Canaanite temples were designed to prompt the gods to make the earth fertile. **prepare your hearts . . . serve Him only:** They were not just to turn away from false gods but also to deliberately turn to the living God (1 Thess. 1:9). The constant teaching of Torah (Deut. 6:4) is that Yahweh is unlike the gods of the nations. He is not one of their number or merely one better than they. He and He alone is the living God, and He and He alone is to be worshiped by His people. He brooks no rivals, has no associates, tolerates no compromises with the gods.

> *The constant teaching of Torah is that Yahweh is unlike the gods of the nations.*

7:4 the Baals: In ancient sculptures, Baal was depicted with a horned helmet. In one hand he grasped a club or mace and in the other a shaft of lightning or a spear with leaves. In some sculptures, he stood on the back of a bull. The plurals **Baals** and **Ashtoreths** refer either to the many images of these gods or to the various local forms under which these gods were worshiped.

7:5 Samuel gathered the people for a prayer meeting at **Mizpah,** about eight miles north of Jerusalem. The city was the capital of Judah after the fall of Jerusalem (2 Kin. 25:22–25). **I will pray:** Samuel, like his mother (1:10–16; 2:1–10), repeatedly exhibited a commitment to prayer (8:6; 12:19, 23; Ps. 99:6; Jer. 15:1).

7:6 poured it out: The pouring of water was symbolic of repentance (Ps. 62:8; Lam. 2:19). **Samuel judged:** Samuel acted as chief magistrate, rendering decisions and settling disputes.

7:7 The Israelite gathering at Mizpah alerted the Philistines of a potential uprising. They immediately organized an attack.

7:8 Do not cease to cry out to the LORD: The Israelites did not want to engage in battle unless Samuel was praying for victory. In contrast to the debacle at Aphek (ch. 4), the Israelites were no longer depending on the ark as a magical talisman. They now wanted to depend solely on the power of God through prayer.

7:9, 10 a suckling lamb: According to Lev. 22:27, no animal could be sacrificed until it was at least eight days old.

7:11 Beth Car is not mentioned elsewhere in Scripture; it must have been a place of high ground overlooking Philistine territory.

7:12, 13 To commemorate the victory and acknowledge the Lord's intervention, Samuel set up a memorial stone on the battlefield and named it **Ebenezer,** meaning "Stone of Help." Samuel followed Joshua's practice of commemorating the victories of God for His people with stone markers (Josh. 4). The victory at Ebenezer was so decisive that the Philistines made no more attacks against the Israelites during Samuel's judgeship.

7:14 Ekron and **Gath** were Philistine cities near Israel (5:8, 10). The frontier settlements which the Israelites had been forced to evacuate could now be taken again. **Amorites** may refer to the original inhabitants of Canaan (Gen. 15:16), or to the hill dwellers of southern Canaan (Num. 13:29; Josh. 10:5).

7:15–17 This summary section speaks of Samuel's ministry in a positive manner. It is a necessary element because the next section will describe Israel's quest for a king in the manner of the other nations of the day (ch. 8). The narrator wishes the reader to know that this quest for a king was not due to any fault in the person or ministry of Samuel himself.

7:16 In addition to his religious duties as prophet, Samuel served as a circuit judge. **Bethel,** the "House of God," was where Jacob had his famous dream (Gen. 28:10–22). **Gilgal** was where the Israelites had first camped after crossing the Jordan River to conquer Canaan (Josh. 4:19, 20). It was about one mile from Jericho.

7:17 Ramah was about five miles north of Jerusalem.

8:1–15:35 The second major section of 1 Samuel brings a new personality, Saul, and a new institution, the Israelite monarchy. While Saul functioned as Israel's first king and military leader, Samuel continued to serve as the spiritual leader of the nation (1 Sam. 12:19–28).

8:1–22 Chapter 8 serves as a transition between the years of the judges and the institution of the monarchy. The chapter records Israel's demand for a king so they might be **like all the nations** (8:5, 20). Their demand for a king was in once sense their rejection of Yahweh as the ultimate ruler over Israel. But this also served to achieve the will of Yahweh in the ultimate selection of David, the king who would be the prototype of the Coming King, the Lord Jesus.

8:1 made his sons judges: It was highly unusual for Samuel to appoint his sons to assist him in judging cases. Judges were individually appointed by God, not by their fathers.

8:2 Joel means "The Lord Is God." **Abijah** means "My Father Is the Lord." **Beersheba** was at the southern extremity of Israel (3:20), about forty-eight miles south of Jerusalem. It was here that Abraham and Isaac had dug wells and formed alliances with Abimelech, king of the Philistines (Gen. 21:22–34; 26:1–33).

8:3, 4 One wonders if Samuel, like Eli, had not given proper attention to his family (notes at 2:22, 23, 29). God's standards and expectations for the judges is clear in Deut. 16:18–20. They were not to distort justice or take bribes. Samuel's sons missed the mark and dishonored God. They used their office and authority for personal gain and perverted justice. It is almost unbelievable that the sons of Samuel were as wicked as the sons of Eli, given the fact that Samuel's ascendancy was based in large part on the wickedness of Eli's sons.

8:5 make us a king: Two factors contributed to the elders' request for a king: (1) the corruption of Samuel's sons, and (2) their desire to follow the pattern of the **all the nations.**

8:6 There is nothing wrong with the concept of a monarchy. God had made provisions in His Law for the appointment of a king over His people (Deut. 17:14, 15). Yet Samuel was **displeased** because he felt that the demand for a king indicated a rejection of his own leadership. Samuel took the matter to God in prayer.

8:7, 8 they have rejected Me: The error of the elders of Israel was their failure to recognize God as their true King (12:12). **to you also:** The Lord drew a parallel between the Israelites' forgetfulness of His gracious acts and their lack of appreciation for Samuel.

8:9, 10 forewarn them: Samuel was called to warn the Israelites that a king would not solve all of their problems. In fact, having a king would create many hardships. The word **behavior** (Heb. *mishpat*, often meaning "judgment," "justice") refers to the "right" or "prerogative" that the king would claim. Israel's king would rule with arbitrary and absolute power.

8:11–17 First, a king would draft young men to serve in the military, farm his fields, and prepare for war. **Run before his chariots** is a reference to the king's state carriage. Runners would serve as messengers, announcing the king's coming. Second, a king would draft young women to work in his palace and serve in his court. Third, a king would tax the people's crops and flocks. He would take **the best** of

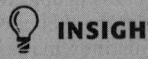 **INSIGHT** | **Wayward Children**

Scripture urges parents to raise up their children in the ways of the Lord (Prov. 22:6; Eph. 6:4), but it makes no guarantees as to how the children will turn out. Sometimes parents of the utmost integrity see their children utterly reject God. Such was the case for Samuel (1 Sam. 8:2, 3). No one knows how differently things might have turned out had Samuel confronted his sons and, as a last resort, taken them before the elders. The legacy of his family is a sober challenge to parents and their children.

their products. **take a tenth:** The proceeds of this tithe would be used to pay the salaries of the king's officers and servants. Fourth, a king would appropriate the servants of the Israelites and their **finest young men** and **donkeys.** Citizens would be forced into the king's service as well as slaves. Fifth, the king would take away the people's personal freedom.

8:18, 19 cry out . . . not hear: Since the Israelites were deliberately choosing their own path, they could not expect God to deliver them from the trouble that would inevitably result.

8:20 and fight our battles: The Israelites were looking for human leadership on the battlefield, instead of recognizing that God would lead them in battle—and win (Ex. 15:3).

8:21, 22 Samuel heard . . . and he repeated them: Samuel acted as mediator between the people and God.

9:1–10:27 This section records the commencement of the monarchy and how Saul was anointed privately by Samuel and then presented publicly before all Israel.

9:1 Saul's father, **Kish,** was from the tribe of **Benjamin.** The term **a mighty man of power** suggests that he was something like a feudal lord—a wealthy landowner and a leader in time of war. The same term is used of Boaz (Ruth 2:1).

9:2 Saul means "Asked For." **Choice** (Heb. *bachûr*) suggests that Saul was in the prime of manhood. Both his physical stature—**taller than any**—and personal appearance—**handsome**—were striking. Saul was endowed with what seemed to be great potential for leadership and service. In these respects, Saul was a king like those of "all the nations" (8:5).

9:3 The early history of Saul is rather endearing on many levels. Despite his great looks and physique, he is sent on a simple journey by his father, as any other son might have been sent. Further, the writer uses a journey motif to develop his theme. Saul went on a search for donkeys, quite unaware that *he* would be sought (as the meaning of his name; v. 2) for higher glory.

9:4 The search for his father's donkeys took Saul north from his home at Gibeah (10:26), through the **mountains of Ephraim.** Ephraim was the tribal inheritance of Joseph's son (Gen. 41:50–52), directly north of Benjamin (Josh. 16).

9:5 worried about us: These words speak of a person of responsibility and of sensitivity to the needs of others. The words also speak well of Kish, Saul's father. The story of Saul is a classic example of *tragedy* in the literary sense.

IN DEPTH | The King of Israel

Was it God's will for Israel to have a king? Certainly it was, for God had indicated that the kingship was part of His plan for Israel in a number of prophecies (Gen. 49:10; Num. 24:17; Deut. 17:14–20).

Although kingship for them was not wrong in itself, the way the Israelites were demanding it was wrong. The people clearly stated their motives for wanting a king. First, they wanted to follow the practices of the neighboring nations (8:5). Second, they wanted a king to lead them into battles (8:20). Both motives amounted to a rejection of the God of Israel as their King (8:7).

The Lord had demonstrated on numerous occasions that He would fight the Israelites' battles. From the miraculous collapse of Jericho's walls (Josh. 6:20) to Gideon's rout of the massive Midianite army (Judg. 7:19–22), God had delivered His people again and again from their enemies. Why did they need a king now to lead them into battles?

What is more, God had given the people His Word, the prophets, and the judges to guide them. But as the tragic history of Judges demonstrates, the people ignored God's guidance and followed the practices of their neighbors (Judg. 3:7). Now, once again, the people were following their neighbors instead of the living God and the Word He had given them. Although Samuel clearly communicated God's warning to the people, they stubbornly preferred their will to God's.

In the end, God allowed the Israelites to have what they wanted. He gave them a king like those of the other nations. The tall and handsome Saul would have been the perfect choice for a king. But through Saul's tragic reign, God taught the Israelites that they needed a king who was *not* like the kings of the other nations.

They needed a king who would obey God's word instead of following his own will, a king who would trust in God instead of himself. In the shadow of Saul's mistakes, God trained young David to walk in His ways so that He could eventually lead the nation in righteousness.

As in the stories of a great Greek king, Saul was an individual of enormous charm, great abilities, and splendid prospects, who rose to the heights of power in his nation but then, due to an inner flaw, declined into disaster.

9:6 **This city** refers to Ramah, Samuel's home after the destruction of Shiloh (1:1; 8:4). The term **man of God** refers to someone who was recognized for his prophetic ministry (1 Kin. 12:22; 13:1; 2 Kin. 23:17).

9:7 Saul was concerned that he had no **present** by which to honor Samuel for helping them find the missing donkeys. He recognized the principle of remuneration for services rendered (1 Cor. 9:5–14). Here, too, we find in Saul admirable qualities. When all the qualities of Saul described in these verses are put together, one is amazed to find how poorly he ended! We may also observe that many of the qualities that we so admire in his son Jonathan (chs. 18; 20), and perhaps also in his daughter Michal (chs. 18; 19), were imparted in his home, and under his direction. Is it possible that *he* is the good father we search for in the Bible?

9:8 Saul's servant unexpectedly produced **one-fourth of a shekel of silver,** which would serve as adequate compensation for the prophet's ministry. A shekel was about 11.4 grams.

9:9, 10 This verse is an explanatory note of an ancient custom to later Israelite readers. **Seer** (from the Heb. verb *ra'â,* "to see") refers to one who is able to see what is hidden from the eyes of ordinary people. **Prophet** (Heb. *naba,* "to prophecy") refers to one who speaks for God (Ex. 7:1).

9:11 **The city** is Ramah.

9:12–15 A **high place** (Heb. *bamâ*) was an elevated site of worship located on a hill or on an artificial platform in a temple. The Canaanites were known for building their places of worship on hills (Num. 33:52; Deut. 12:2–5). Nevertheless, pious Israelites appear to have used such facilities legitimately after the destruction of Shiloh and before the construction of Solomon's temple (1 Kin. 3:2). Sadly, the misuse of such high places to worship false gods eventually undermined the worship of God and contributed to the rise of idolatry in Israel (1 Kin. 11:7; 12:26–33).

9:16, 17 It seems significant that Saul is referred to here as **commander** (Heb. *nagìd,* also translated as "prince," "ruler," or "leader"), rather than as king (Heb. *melek*). The royal throne ultimately belonged to the line of Judah (Gen. 49:9, 10).

9:18 Asking **Samuel** directions to the **seer's house** at the entrance of the city was the final step in a remarkable sequence of events which

God sovereignly superintended to bring about the anointing of Saul.

9:19 **All that is in your heart** does not seem to refer to the matter of the donkeys, for Samuel immediately assured Saul that the donkeys had been found. Perhaps Saul was brooding over the problem of the Philistines.

9:20 **all the desire of Israel:** Samuel probably had in mind the honor and privileges that would come to Saul and his family through the monarchy.

9:21 **smallest of the tribes:** Benjamin was the second smallest tribe at the first census following the Exodus (Num. 1:36, 37). The tribe was reduced to 600 fighting men during the punishment of Benjamin for the atrocity at Gibeah (Judg. 19; 20). **the least of all the families:** If Saul's father was "a mighty man of power," these words contain a certain amount of self-depreciation (v. 1).

9:22 **The hall** was where local dignitaries sat for sacrificial feasts at the high place.

9:23 **which I gave you:** Samuel had been instructed by God to be prepared for this special encounter.

9:24 Giving Saul **the thigh** was intended to honor him in the presence of the other guests (Gen. 43:34).

9:25, 26 A **house** in ancient Israel usually had a flat roof which could be used for drying flax or as a place to relax. It appears that Saul slept on the roof (v. 26).

9:27 **Tell the servant to go on:** The anointing of Saul was private. Later, he would be publicly installed as king before all Israel (10:17–27).

10:1 A better new chapter break might have been at what is now 9:27. The use of olive **oil** in the anointing process has ancient roots. Ultimately all true anointings for special offices and functions point to the truly Anointed One, the Messiah Jesus. **kissed him:** Peoples of the ancient (and modern) middle East often greet one another with a kiss on the cheek. Here the kiss may have been one of genuine affection. **the Lord has anointed you:** There were two kinds of anointings in the biblical period. A ceremonial anointing involved pouring olive oil on the head or body of the person to be honored (Ps. 133:2). An official anointing used the same process but signified a consecration or setting apart for religious service (Ex. 29:7; 30:25; Lev. 8:12). The anointing of a ruler was actually a religious act. That is why David had such high regard for Saul, refusing to lift a hand against "the Lord's anointed" (24:6). **His inheritance:** The land of Israel was God's gift to His people, but it would return to God's direct control should the people prove unfit to manage it (Deut. 27—30).

10:2 Rachel's tomb: Rachel had died giving birth to Benjamin on a journey from Bethel to Bethlehem, and she was buried along the way (Gen. 35:16–20). **in the territory of Benjamin:** Rachel was buried near Bethlehem, which is in Judah (Gen. 35:16–20). Perhaps her burial site was very close to the border between Benjamin and Judah. **Zelah** is mentioned only here and must refer to a town then near Rachel's tomb. **father . . . caring:** This is a nice familial touch in the story. Saul's later estrangement from his son Jonathan (chs. 18—20) cannot be blamed on a lack of interest in him by his father.

10:3 The terebinth, sometimes translated oak or elm, refers to a strong tree, native to the land of Israel, which grows to a height of around thirty-five feet. **Tabor** is an apparent reference to Mount Tabor, in the Valley of Jezreel, where these trees were prominent.

10:4 For strangers to offer Saul **two loaves of bread** would have been a remarkable sign. Their bread would have been for use in the worship of God. For them, giving the bread to Saul substituted for a sacred act.

10:5 The Hebrew word translated **hill** (*gib'â*) probably refers to Gibeah, Saul's hometown (11:4). Gibeah **of God** was perhaps the full name of the city, due to its proximity to a significant **high place** (v. 13). **Philistine garrison:** The Philistines dominated the land and had set up a military outpost in Saul's home-

INSIGHT
Bands of Prophets

The prophets appear as religious ecstatics living in groups or bands (1 Sam. 10:5). "Prophesying" in this context was a recognizable form of abnormal behavior, like a trance. In Greek tradition also, the oracles of the gods were not delivered in a normal way. According to Heraclitus, the oracles were ambiguous, like riddles.

town. **A group of prophets** may refer to members of the "school of the prophets," which was probably instituted by Samuel for the purpose of preparing young men for prophetic ministry.

10:6–8 The Spirit of the Lord refers to the same Holy Spirit who came upon Othniel, Gideon, Jephthah, and Samson (Judg. 3:10; 6:34; 11:29; 13:25; 14:6, 19; 15:14). The expression **be turned into another man** may mean

spiritual regeneration or a marked advance in spiritual growth.

10:9 God gave him another heart: In Hebrew this expression literally reads, "God changed him for another heart." There is debate as to whether this refers to a work of God's Spirit which prepared Saul for kingship or to the act of spiritual regeneration. It may seem that Saul's subsequent attitudes and behavior do not reflect a genuine spiritual life. Yet Saul seems to have struggled with sin and desired to worship God (14:34, 35; 15:24–34).

10:10 God worked through His Spirit in Saul's life so that he was able to exercise a prophetic gift. This was not a vocation for Saul but an opportunity.

10:11 As a result of the Spirit's mighty working in Saul, the people asked, **Is Saul also among the prophets?** Some have taken this as an expression of contempt, but this implies a low view of prophets and prophecy. Rather, the question simply expresses surprise at Saul's sudden change in character.

10:12–16 But who is their father: The implication of this question is that the fathers of the prophets were not important people. The prophets in any case did not obtain their gift by inheritance, but by God's will.

10:17, 18 Mizpah was where the Israelites had gathered for a time of spiritual revival before their victory over the Philistines (7:5).

10:19 rejected your God: Samuel reiterated his earlier admonition (8:10–18), warning the people of their attitude—which was actually a rejection of God's kingship. **Clans** were a smaller family unit than **tribes.**

10:20, 21 The choice of Saul as Israel's first monarch was made by casting lots, a means of determining God's will in answer to "yes" and "no" questions. The lots were cast like dice. The principle underlying the use of lots was an active confidence in God's control of all events.

10:22, 23 hidden among the equipment: This may reflect Saul's modesty, or perhaps his hesitancy and self-doubt over assuming the position of national leader.

10:24 The phrase **him whom the Lord** has chosen reflects the sovereignty of God in the area of His permissive will. Although the Israelites decided to have a king, it was the Lord who selected Saul.

10:25 the behavior of royalty: Samuel taught the people what to expect from a king, possibly reviewing his instruction in 8:11–18 and God's laws for kingship in Deut. 17:14–20.

10:26 Gibeah, located just three miles north of Jerusalem, served as the first capital of the Israelite monarchy.

10:27 Some rebels questioned Saul's military leadership and refused to honor him with

 **IN FOCUS** "king"

(Heb. *melek*) (1 Sam. 10:24; Deut. 17:14) Strong's #4428: The term *king* may describe a petty ruler of a small city (Josh. 10:3) or a monarch of a vast empire (Esth. 1:1–5). An ancient king's jurisdiction included the military (8:20), the economy (1 Kin. 10:26–29), international diplomacy (1 Kin. 5:1–11), and the legal system (2 Sam. 8:15). He also functioned as a spiritual leader (2 Kin. 23:1–24), although Israel's kings were prohibited from some priestly functions (13:9–14). The Bible presents David as an example of the righteous king who set his heart on faithfully serving God (Acts 13:22). God's promise to give David an everlasting kingdom (2 Sam. 7:16) has been fulfilled in Jesus Christ, whose human ancestry is through the royal family of David (Luke 2:4).

the gifts customarily given a king. But Saul **held his peace** in order not to provoke the situation.

11:1–15 This section explains that the initial opposition against Saul (10:27) was overcome as he proved himself a capable military leader.

11:1 Nahash, whose name means "Serpent," was commander of the Ammonites, descendants of Lot who occupied the fringes of the desert east of the territories of Gad and Manasseh (Gen. 19:38). **Jabesh Gilead** is the Israelite city of Jabesh, located in the region of Gilead east of the Jordan. Gilead seems to be used rather loosely in the Hebrew Scriptures, being applied to regions between the Sea of Galilee and the Dead Sea, but always to the east of the River Jordan.

11:2 put out all your right eyes: The condition of surrender demanded by Nahash was not only cruel and humiliating but would have made the Israelite warriors unable to fight.

11:3, 4 The elders of Jabesh Gilead asked for **seven days** in which to find help before conceding defeat. Nahash agreed to the proposal, since he apparently was not prepared to take the city by force and wanted to avoid a long and costly siege.

11:5 Saul, coming behind the herd: Although Saul had been appointed king, he did not assume governmental authority at once. Saul continued farming until he could answer Israel's expectations of him as king by delivering the Israelites from their enemies (8:20).

11:6 the Spirit of God came upon Saul: The Holy Spirit empowered Saul to deliver the citizens of Jabesh.

11:7 Two **oxen** were customarily yoked together for work. Saul's call to arms was accompanied by a threat. His distribution of the pieces of the oxen throughout Israel is reminiscent of the grisly story of Judg. 19:27—20:1. **The fear of the LORD** begins with an awesome awareness of who God is (Prov. 2:5) and ends with a proper response to good and evil (Prov. 16:6).

11:8 Bezek was thirteen miles northeast of Shechem, due west of Jabesh Gilead on the other side of the Jordan. The distinction made between **Israel** and **Judah** in the numbering of the warriors (15:4; 17:52) may indicate that the book was either written or edited after the division of the monarchy in 930 B.C.

11:9 by the time the sun is hot: The sun becomes hot before noon.

11:10 The message to Nahash may have been designed to lull the Ammonites into a false sense of security.

11:11 Saul divided his forces into **three companies** so that he could attack at the same time from different directions (Judg. 7:16). **the morning watch:** The Israelites divided the night into three watches—nine to twelve, twelve to three, and three to six in the morning (Ex. 14:24–27; Judg. 7:19; Lam. 2:19). Saul's attack probably took place at dawn, before the Ammonites had armed themselves for battle.

11:12 Saul's victory over the Ammonites gave him the support and allegiance of the people of Israel. Some went so far as to suggest that those who had previously questioned his rule should be **put . . . to death** (10:27).

11:13 the LORD has accomplished salvation in Israel: Saul recognized that the victory over the Ammonites could be attributed to God alone and refused to heed the suggestion of his overly zealous supporters.

11:14, 15 It was to **Gilgal,** the first Israelite camp west of the Jordan at the time of the conquest (Josh. 5:10), that Samuel called the tribes to **renew the kingdom.** Although the monarchy had been inaugurated at Mizpah, there had been some question there about Saul's qualifications and abilities to lead in battle (10:17–27). As a result of Saul's victory over the Ammonites, the Israelites enthusiastically endorsed his kingship.

12:1–25 Chapter 12 records Samuel's farewell address at Gilgal as he relinquished the leadership of the twelve tribes to Saul. This is a bitter-sweet moment for Samuel, informing the reader of the inner heart and personal struggles of this man of God. It is noteworthy that leading characters in the Bible struggle with hope and doubt, with triumph and frustration, and with acceptance and challenge of the divine will.

12:1, 2 walking before you: Saul was leading Israel and attending to the nation's needs. Samuel referred to the two reasons cited by the elders of Israel in their demand for a king: (1) Samuel's **old** age and (2) his **sons,** who had demonstrated their unworthiness for public office (8:5).

12:3–5 Samuel began his charge to Israel by establishing his own integrity. **before the LORD** and before His anointed: Samuel asked whether anyone wanted to accuse him before God and His anointed king. The Israelites cleared Samuel of any impropriety or injustice in the administration of his duties as judge. Samuel's past record was established to inspire confidence in his present exhortation.

12:6, 7 Righteous acts refers to the benefits that God had bestowed on His people. These acts testified to the righteousness of God in blessing His people by fulfilling His covenant promises.

12:8 Samuel summarized the descent of Jacob's family into Egypt (Gen. 46), the Egyptian oppression (Ex. 1:8—22), the Exodus from Egypt (Ex. 2—15), and the conquest of Canaan (Josh. 1—12).

12:9 Samuel recounted the nation's apostasy and subsequent divine discipline. **Sisera** was a Canaanite general (Judg. 4:2–22). **Moab:** The Moabites were descendants of the incestuous relationship of Lot and his eldest daughter (Gen. 19:30–37). The Moabite oppression is recorded in Judg. 3:12–30.

12:10 After a period of oppression, the Israelites repented and cried out to the Lord for deliverance. The **Baals and Ashtoreths** were Canaanite fertility deities (7:3, 4).

12:11 Jerubbaal, also known as Gideon, delivered Israel from the Midianites (Judg. 6—8). **Jephthah** defeated the Ammonites (Judg. 11).

12:12 The threat of **Nahash** was probably felt long before the threatened attack of Jabesh Gilead (11:1–3) and was probably a factor in Israel's request for a king (8:20).

12:13, 14 The **fear** of **the LORD** is not merely a pious attitude but a serious and obedient response to the revelation of God's holy character.

12:15, 16 The consequences for disobeying God's covenant are outlined in Deut. 28:15–68.

12:17, 18 The season for **wheat harvest** in Israel is the months of May and June. **send**

thunder and rain: The land of Israel receives its rainfall during the winter season. For rain to fall during the wheat harvest would be most unusual. The miracle was intended to convince the people of their great **wickedness** in demanding a king. The miracle also served to enhance Israel's respect for both **the LORD** and Samuel.

12:19, 20 Do not fear: By this Samuel meant, "Do not fear the death penalty for disobedience."

12:21 Empty things refers to false gods and idols (Is. 44:9–20).

12:22 His great name's sake: In ancient times, one's name stood for one's character. The name of God speaks of His reputation and attributes. For God to abandon His people would be inconsistent with His reputation for faithfulness (Ex. 34:6; Deut. 31:6; Josh. 1:5; Heb. 13:5).

12:23, 24 Samuel assured the people that he would not forget **to pray** for them. For Samuel, a lack of prayer was a moral compromise, a sin. In fact, his life illustrates the importance of prayer (7:5; 1 Thess. 5:17; James 5:16). Although he was leaving his official duties as judge over Israel, Samuel promised to continue to **teach** the people.

12:25 The words **swept away** anticipate God's ultimate judgment of captivity and exile from the land (Deut. 28:41, 63, 64).

13:1–23 One of the reasons why the Israelites wanted a king was to provide military leadership (1 Sam. 8:20). The greatest threat to Israelite security in Saul's day was the Philistines, a powerful military people who ruled the coastal plain and had established several outposts in the hill country. Chapter 13 tells of the preparations for Saul's first encounter with the Philistines.

13:1 one year . . . two years: This verse provides a chronological note recording the date of this encounter with the Philistines relative to Saul's reign as king. Since Acts 13:21 reveals that Saul ruled over Israel forty years, the two years must refer to the period of reign up to a particular event—likely Saul's encounter with the Philistines described in this chapter.

13:2 Although Saul had raised a citizen militia to rescue Jabesh Gilead (11:7–9), here he selected and trained a regular, standing army. **Michmash** was seven miles north of Jerusalem. **Gibeah of Benjamin** was four miles southeast of Michmash.

13:3 While Saul was in Michmash, his son Jonathan attacked the Philistine garrison at **Geba,** about a mile southwest of Michmash. The two sites are separated by a deep ravine. The **trumpet** was a ram's horn used to signal and summon the military. **Hebrews** refers to the Israelites. The name may be connected with the name Eber, the ancestor of Abraham (Gen.

10:24), or it may be related to the Hebrew verb meaning "to cross over," since Abraham "crossed over" to the land of Canaan.

13:4 Saul had attacked: Either Jonathan had been acting under Saul's orders or Saul took credit for his son's victory. Saul withdrew his army to **Gilgal** in keeping with Samuel's instructions to him at his anointing (10:8).

13:5 Beth Aven was about a half mile west of Michmash.

13:6 the people hid in caves: The limestone of the hill country region contains many natural caves which could be used as hideouts in time of attack.

13:7 The land of Gad and Gilead refers to the region south and north of the River Jabbok, which flows into the Jordan from the east. **Gilgal,** located northeast of Jericho in the Jordan valley, was the appointed place of Saul's meeting with Samuel (v. 8).

13:8, 9 Waited seven days refers to the instruction given to Saul by Samuel after his anointing (10:8). Samuel had told Saul to wait seven days at **Gilgal** until Samuel came to offer sacrifices. Concerned that the people were losing courage and starting to scatter, Saul assumed priestly prerogatives and offered the **burnt offering** himself (Lev. 1). With this action, Saul tragically disobeyed both the Law of Moses and the instructions of God's prophet.

13:10-12 as soon as he had finished: Samuel's delay may have been intended as a test of Saul's obedience. Saul cited four justifications for his disobedience: (1) the soldiers were scattering; (2) Samuel had not come as promised; (3) the Philistines were gathering their forces at Michmash; and (4) there was imminent danger of Philistine attack.

13:13 Saul was soundly rebuked by Samuel. The Hebrew word **foolishly** here is a powerful play on words that serves to strengthen the contrast that the text will estab-

lish between Saul and David. It sounds like the word later used to describe David, but *with the opposite meaning* (18:5, 30). By this brilliant but subtle interchange, the contrasting characters of the two principals of the book are vividly demonstrated. Saul played the fool; David exhibited a wisdom beyond his years or experience. Saul's principal sin was failing to keep **the commandment** God had given through Samuel (10:8).

13:14 your kingdom shall not continue: Although Saul would retain his throne, his descendants would not carry on his dynasty. **A man after His own heart** is God's description of David, a man with many faults, but a man whose spirit was sensitive to God's will.

13:15, 16 Saul's army had dwindled from 3,000 (v. 2) to only **six hundred men.**

13:17 The Philistines sent their raiders to harass the Israelites in the hopes of weakening Israelite resolve or forcing a decisive engagement. **Ophrah** was located about seven miles north of Michmash.

13:18 The twin towns of **Beth Horon** (Upper and Lower) were located west of Geba, about two miles apart on a ridge guarding the approach to the hill country from the coastal plain.

13:19 no blacksmith: The Canaanites and Philistines learned how to forge iron from the Hittites. Although they were not great in numerical strength, the Philistines were able to dominate Israel. By the end of David's reign, the Israelites also had acquired iron technology (1 Chr. 22:3).

13:20 Sharpen may also be translated "to forge." The **plowshare** is the metal part of the plow that penetrates and breaks up the soil. A **mattock** is like a pickax but has blades instead of points. It is used for digging and breaking up soil that cannot be reached by a plow.

13:21 The **pim** was approximately two-

 **IN LIFE**   ## A Craving for Results

Saul lost his kingdom because of his craving for results. He wanted to defeat the Philistines so much that he offered a burnt offering, which it was not his place to do (1 Sam. 13:8–14). He was determined to do things in his way and according to his timing rather than God's. So God found a man "after His own heart" (13:14), a man who would get results, but do so by following God's plans.

Actually, getting results is not a leader's main job. The primary task is to create a climate where others can make things happen and accomplish goals. That climate has a variety of dimensions: technical (task-oriented), behavioral (relationship-oriented), political (power-oriented), and spiritual (God-oriented). If a leader concentrates on the immediate task at the expense of the other dimensions, the outcome may be short-term results but long-term losses.

thirds of a shekel. Based on what is known of ancient Israel's economy, the charge was exorbitant. **The points of the goads** refers to the sharp ends of prods used to direct cattle. The Israelites did not have the resources to forge iron implements for agriculture, much less for warfare.

13:22 The weapons available to the Israelite soldiers would have included slings, bows and arrows, and numerous instruments made of bronze.

13:23 **The pass of Michmash** is the deep gorge that separated Michmash and Geba.

14:1–47 This chapter tells the story of Israel's victory over the Philistines and Saul's rash vow, which nearly led to the death of his own son. The chapter also illustrates Saul's ongoing lack of wisdom and discretion in leadership.

14:1 **he did not tell his father:** Saul would have thought Jonathan's plan was reckless.

14:2 **Gibeah,** Saul's home, was about three miles southwest of Geba, where Jonathan was camped at the Philistine garrison he had captured (13:3, 16). **Migron** was located near Gibeah.

14:3–5 The genealogy of **Ahijah,** the high priest and descendant of **Eli,** is given in full. His name means "My Brother Is the Lord."

14:6–8 The term **uncircumcised** was an Israelite designation for the Gentiles, who did not share the distinctive mark of God's people under the Old Covenant (Gen. 17:10–14).

14:9–13 The assault of Jonathan and his armorbearer on Michmash was an act of faith, not a foolhardy adventure. The response of the Philistines, **come up to us,** was taken as a sign that God was leading and would grant them victory. The taunting words of the Philistines were turned into a challenge for the young men to display faith in God.

14:14 **about half an acre:** The Hebrew text reads "half a yoke of land." A yoke of land was the area a pair of oxen could plow in one day.

14:15, 16 The defeat of the garrison at Michmash left the Philistines in a state of panic. **The earth quaked** may refer to an actual earthquake, which added to the panic and confusion of the Philistines, or it may be a way of saying that the Philistines were shaking from fear.

14:17 **call the roll:** Saul had to have the troops mustered before he realized that his own son was not present.

14:18, 19 **Bring the ark of God here:** According to 7:2, the ark at this time was at Kirjath Jearim. There is no mention of its being moved before it was brought to Jerusalem by David. The ancient Greek translation of 1

Samuel reads "ephod," and this may be what is meant. The Urim and Thummim were kept in the breastplate of the ephod and were used to determine the will of God (Ex. 28:30; Num. 27:21; 1 Sam. 23:9–12). Furthermore, Ahijah was present and wearing the ephod (v. 3). **Withdraw your hand:** A disturbance in the Philistine camp distracted Saul from his consul-

INSIGHT | **A Foolish Order**

Some situations, such as war, call for tough-minded leadership that makes great demands on people. In Saul's war with the Philistines, he ordered his troops to forego food until they had vanquished the enemy (1 Sam. 14:24). Apparently Saul intended the command to be a noble challenge to his men. After all, why should they relax and enjoy a good meal when their longtime enemies, the Philistines, remained unbeaten? Yet the order was truly foolish, for it deprived the men of needed energy to fight the battle.

tation with **the priest** (that is, Ahijah), and he canceled the inquiry.

14:20 **against his neighbor:** There was such confusion in the Philistine camp that it was hard to tell friend from foe.

14:21 **The Hebrews who were with the Philistines** were deserters or mercenaries.

14:22, 23 The mountains of Ephraim refers to the mountainous region occupied by the tribe of Ephraim, just north of Benjamite territory.

14:24 **Cursed is the man:** Saul foolishly ordered that none of his soldiers should eat until he had **taken vengeance** on his **enemies.** Unlike Jonathan, he did not view the battle as the Lord's (v. 12).

14:25, 26 The bees had produced so much **honey** that it had flowed from their combs in the trees to the **ground.**

14:27 Due to his absence (vv. 1–17), Jonathan had not heard his father's oath. He did what any reasonable soldier would do and helped himself to some honey as he pursued the Philistines.

14:28–30 Jonathan recognized the foolishness of the unnecessary hardship imposed upon the soldiers by his father. Saul is marked by acting rashly, without thought of consequence—another unacceptable leadership failing.

14:31 Aijalon was located at the edge of the Philistine coastal plain, about eighteen miles west of Michmash.

14:32 ate them with the blood: The Israelite soldiers began to eat the captured Philistine livestock without first draining the blood, in violation of God's Law (Lev. 17:10–14).

14:33, 34 roll a large stone: Saul realized the serious nature of the offense and had a stone table set up to slaughter the animals and drain the blood properly.

14:35 Saul built an altar to thank God for his victory over the Philistines.

14:36–38 Let us draw near to God: Saul was anxious to finish off the Philistines but decided to ask for God's counsel about it. God's silence was taken by Saul as an evidence of sin in the camp.

14:39–45 he shall surely die: This was Saul's second foolish oath (v. 24).

14:46 their own place: As a result of Israel's victory, the Philistines left the hill country and returned to their settlements on the coastal plain.

14:47 Moab and **Ammon,** descendants of Lot (Gen. 19:30–38), occupied regions east of the Jordan and the Dead Sea. **Edom,** descendants of Esau (Gen. 36:8), occupied a region southeast of the Dead Sea. **Zobah** was the Aramean kingdom in the Bekah Valley. The **Philistines** occupied the coastal plain west of the hill country.

14:48 The victory over the **Amalekites,** nomadic desert tribesmen who lived south of the hill country, is recorded in 15:1–9.

14:49 In 1 Sam. 31:2 and 1 Chr. 8:33, the names of Saul's four sons are given as Jonathan, Abinadab, Malchishua, and Esh-Baal (Ishbosheth in 2 Sam. 2:8). **Jishui** is probably a second name for Abinadab.

14:50, 51 Ahinoam means "My Brother Is Pleasant."

14:52 took him for himself: Saul drafted the strong and brave young men into his army.

15:1–35 Israel's war with the Amalekites (14:48) is recounted in detail because it led to the breach between Saul and Samuel and Saul's subsequent rejection as king. Chapter 15 is significant in preparing the way of David's accession to the throne by demonstrating Saul's disqualification for kingship.

15:1 The LORD sent me: Samuel referred to his part in Saul's appointment to add weight and authority to the command that he was about to give.

15:2 The Amalekites were a nomadic people who lived in the region of the Negev, the dry land south of Judah (Num. 13:29).

15:3 The expression **utterly destroy** is literally "to put under a ban," similar to the ban placed on Jericho at the time of the conquest (Josh. 6:17, 18). The fact that no spoil was to be taken reflects God's judgment on the sins of the Amalekites (Deut. 7:2–6; 12:2, 3; 20:16–18). While such judgment is severe, it came at the command of a holy and just God. A holy God cannot let sin go unpunished.

15:4 men of Judah: Early in the period of the united monarchy, the distinctions between the northern tribes of Israel and the southern tribe of Judah began to be noted (11:8).

15:5 The Amalekites were a nomadic people. The term **city** must refer to their main settlement.

15:6 The Kenites, who had been loosely associated with the Israelites since Moses' marriage to the daughter of Jethro, a Kenite (Judg. 1:16; 4:11), were a nomadic offshoot of the Midianites (Num. 10:29).

15:7 Havilah refers to a district of northeast Arabia. **Shur** was the western part of the Sinai peninsula bordering Egypt. The campaign against the **Amalekites** covered extensive territory.

15:8 took Agag king of the Amalekites alive: This was a direct violation of the Lord's command (v. 3). Saul devoted the rest of the people to the ban but saved the life of the king.

15:9–11 By sparing **Agag** and the **best** of

 **IN FOCUS**   **"utterly destroyed"**

(Heb. *charam*) (1 Sam. 15:9; Ex. 22:20; Deut. 13:15; Josh. 6:18) Strong's #2763: In the ancient world, anything sacred or defiled was considered inappropriate for common use. This Hebrew verb refers to the "setting apart" of inappropriate things, usually because of defilement associated with idol worship. According to Deut. 13:12–15, Israel was to destroy everyone and everything that was wicked enough to be considered defiled. Violation of this command cost Achan his life (Josh. 7) and Saul his throne (15:9–11). Paul reminds us that we are all wicked, and as a result are defiled and deserve destruction. Yet God in His mercy has chosen to save those who place their trust in Jesus (Rom. 3:10–26).

the spoil, Saul was following his own desires instead of serving as an agent of God's judgment. Perhaps he wanted to gain prestige by bringing home the spoil of the Amalekites.

15:12 Carmel, located seven miles south of Hebron, would have been on Saul's route home. The **monument** that Saul set up was probably intended to commemorate the victory over the Amalekites. Saul then returned to **Gilgal,** where the Israelites had convened before their war with the Philistines (13:8–15).

15:13 Blessed are you was a form of ancient greeting (Gen. 24:31). Note that Saul's words **I have performed the commandment of the LORD** are the exact opposite of God's evaluation (v. 11).

15:14 this bleating: The words are almost humorous, were the situation not serious.

15:15–19 When confronted by Samuel, Saul excused his disobedience by blaming **the people.** He also sought to justify sparing **the best of the sheep and the oxen** by suggesting that he intended them for sacrifice.

15:20, 21 I have obeyed the voice of the LORD: Given another chance by Samuel to get things right with God, Saul persisted in affirming his innocence.

15:22 to obey is better than sacrifice: Samuel emphasized that sincerity and obedience were the prerequisites for worship that pleased God. There are those who have used this and similar verses to argue that God never intended that sacrificial worship be used to honor Him. Yet such verses do not undermine sacrificial worship; they place it in the true context of the importance of the heart of the person who comes to worship the living God.

15:23 Saul's independent, rebellious actions were as much a denial of God's authority as the recognition of Satan's supernatural power through **witchcraft.** Witchcraft (Heb. *qesem*) was condemned by the Law (Lev. 19:26, 31; Deut. 18:9–14) and was punishable by death (Ex. 22:18). Saul's stubborn disobedience was essentially an act of **idolatry** because it elevated his will above God's will. **He also has rejected you:** Saul failed to realize that he was not a sovereign and independent ruler like other monarchs. Instead, he was an agent and representative of the divine King. Saul's rejection of God's word resulted in the rejection of Saul as God's royal representative.

15:24, 25 I have sinned: In response to Samuel's rebuke, Saul confessed his sin and explained that because he **feared the people,** he **obeyed their voice.** Saul led the people by catering to their wishes.

15:26, 27 How sad the words of Samuel must have been. Saul had disobeyed God one time too many; for him, there was no return.

15:28 The accidental tearing of Samuel's robe (v. 27) served as a sign that God had **torn the kingdom** from Saul. For a similar incident, see 1 Kin. 11:30. The **neighbor** who would receive the kingdom was David (16:11–13).

15:29 the Strength of Israel: This designation of God occurs only here in the Bible. The phrase can also mean "the Glory of Israel." **will not lie nor relent:** God's decision to reject Saul was irrevocable.

15:30, 31 Saul's requests for forgiveness and desire to worship God suggest that, despite his flaws, he was a sincere believer in God. Samuel may have discerned that Saul's confession in v. 30 was more sincere than the one recorded earlier (v. 24).

15:32, 33 Bring Agag: Samuel determined to do what Saul had not done. He executed Agag in order to obey God's clear command (v. 3). The verb translated **hacked . . . in pieces** may simply mean "executed." **before the LORD:** The execution was an expression of divine judgment.

15:34, 35 See evidently means "to give attention" or "to regard with interest." The point is that God was through with Saul as king, and so was Samuel.

16:1–31:13 The next section records David's rise to the throne. David was known as a man after God's heart (13:14). His faith was so exemplary that centuries later God was pleased to be called "the God of David" (2 Kin. 20:5; Is. 38:5). David contributed to the worship of the Lord by planning the building of the temple (2 Chr. 28:11—29:2) and by writing many psalms (2 Sam. 23:1).

16:1 Fill your horn: The ram's horn served as a vessel for the anointing olive **oil** (10:1). **Jesse the Bethlehemite** was the son (or descendant) of Obed, the son of Ruth and Boaz (Ruth 4:21, 22). He is identified in relationship to his home town, Bethlehem, located about six miles south of Jerusalem, on the caravan route from Jerusalem via Hebron to Egypt. *Bethlehem* means "House of Bread," perhaps indicating that it was the grain center for its region. It is also possible that the name is an Israelite modification of an earlier, Canaanite name for the town, once dedicated to Lahmu, an old Canaanite deity of war. If so, the contrast is wonderful: the coming Prince of Peace (Is. 9:6; Mic. 5:2) would be born in a town that originally was devoted to a temple for the god of war! **I have provided Myself a king:** God made it clear to Samuel that this king would be of His choosing.

16:2, 3 Samuel's concern for his life was not unwarranted in light of Saul's suspicious nature and spiritual degeneracy (18:11). **A heifer** is a young cow. **say, 'I have come to sacrifice':**

God did not instruct Samuel to lie, but instead He provided a legitimate opportunity for Samuel to visit with Jesse and his family. By performing the anointing in Bethlehem while officiating at a sacrifice, Samuel would avoid arousing the suspicions of Saul.

16:4 Because Samuel's visit was unexpected, **the elders of the town** wondered if he had come to execute judgment (7:15, 16).

16:5 The Hebrew word for **peaceably** (*shalôm*, "peace") means "things as they ought to be." The word **sanctify** means "to set oneself apart" by means of ceremonial washings and purifications (Ex. 19:10, 14, 22). **he consecrated Jesse and his sons:** Apparently, Samuel personally supervised the purification of the father and his sons.

16:6, 7 Eliab means "My God Is Father." **said:** Samuel was probably saying these things to himself. The **appearance** and **stature** of Jesse's oldest son, Eliab, commended him to leadership. But these were the very things that had commended Saul (9:2). Instead of looking at appearances, God searched the **heart.** Thus, God gave Samuel a new perspective. The state of a man's heart was far more significant than natural ability and physical appearance.

16:8, 9 Abinadab means "My Father Is Noble." **Shammah** may come from the word that means "He Hears." The parade of sons began with the oldest, in a typical patriarchal manner. The assumption was that the firstborn would receive a higher rank than his brothers. Yet often God's way surprisingly reversed this expectation.

16:10 It is not clear in this verse if the number **seven** means in addition to the three already named or inclusive of them; 17:12 suggests the latter.

16:11 **Are all the young men here:** After looking at Jesse's seven sons, Samuel wondered if someone had been left out. In fact, **the youngest** was out in the field, caring for his father's flock. **keeping the sheep:** In ancient times, both divine and human rulers were frequently compared to shepherds (Ezek. 34). The famous Babylonian king Hammurabi described himself as a shepherd for his people. The fact that David was tending the sheep at this particular moment is something of a divine foreshadowing of his appointment as the king of Israel. **will not sit down:** The idea is that Samuel would not budge until the last son was brought before him.

16:12 **Ruddy** means "reddish," referring to complexion and perhaps hair color. **bright eyes:** The Hebrew words may also be rendered *beauty of eyes.* **good-looking:** God made it clear to Samuel that He did not choose David on the basis of his good looks (v. 7). This was a bonus to

David's inner worth. **the LORD** said: It is not clear whether anyone but Samuel heard these words of God. **anoint him:** David was anointed with olive oil. This religious ritual consecrated him to the kingship.

16:13 In Hebrew, **came upon** means "rushed upon." David was empowered by God's Holy **Spirit** for the work of ruling God's people, just as Saul had been (10:10). **David** means "Beloved."

16:14, 15 **departed from Saul:** After the Spirit of God came upon David, Saul was no longer empowered by the Spirit to serve as king. It appears that the ministry of the Holy Spirit was selective and temporary in the lives of OT believers. **distressing spirit from the LORD:** This affliction has been understood in various ways: (1) demon possession as divine punishment; (2) demonic attack or influence; (3) an evil messenger, like the one sent to entice Ahab (1 Kin. 22:20–23); or (4) a spirit of discontent created by God in Saul's heart (Judg. 9:23). Whatever it was, it was immediately noticed by Saul's servants (18:10).

16:16, 17 Whatever Saul's problem was, it was temporarily relieved by music (v. 23). It was generally believed in ancient times that music had a beneficial influence on those with sullen or morbid natures.

16:18 **a mighty man of valor, a man of war:** David the shepherd boy had not yet demonstrated his military abilities. The glowing description given by the courtier may have been exaggerated but was included here by the author because it anticipated what David would become in light of his reputation (17:34, 35).

16:19, 20 **Send me your son David:** Given the events in the first part of this chapter, this is an amazing turn of events, and the mark of a great story-teller.

16:21 David's appointment as Saul's **armor-bearer** may have taken place after his victory over Goliath (17:55–58). Perhaps it is mentioned here because it fits well with the theme of David's early service in Saul's court. Alternatively, it is possible that David was first in favor with Saul, then fell from favor only to be restored again.

16:22 **Stand before me** is an expression for entering the king's service (1 Kin. 10:8).

16:23 Empowered by the Spirit of God, David was able to drive away the **distressing spirit** (v. 14) with his soothing music (18:10). The verse suggests a lengthy period of time.

17:1–58 This section provides a major demonstration of David's right to rule God's people. In ancient Near Eastern thought, several elements worked together to form the ideal of kingship. Among them was the idea of the Warrior-Hero. This chapter shows Saul cowering in his tent with his armor and weapons in a useless heap, and it contrasts David marching out to war merely with a sling, but empowered by the living God. There are *two* battles here. One is the outer battle on the field; the other is the inner battle in the king's tent!

17:1 The Philistine and Israelite armies were gathered in the Elah Valley, about fifteen miles west of David's hometown of Bethlehem. The **Philistines** were camped between **Azekah** and **Sochoh,** on a hill (v. 3) south of the valley. Azekah, strategically located on a hill, was one of a string of fortresses built along the western boundary of Judah to guard the major roads penetrating the region. Sochoh was one of the cities that would later be fortified by Rehoboam (2 Chr. 11:7). The description, **which belongs to Judah,** reminds us that the Philistines were encroaching on Judean lands.

17:2, 3 The Valley of Elah is an east-west valley leading from the hill country of Judah toward the lowlands of the Philistines. The **valley** would have been suitable for the Philistine chariots had it not been for a steep ravine that extended up the middle of the valley. The war chariot of the Philistines had iron fittings and was the most advanced weapon of the day. Probably the ravine prevented a full-scale

stand-in for the entire army. His opponent needed to be as strong as he was. The most likely person to serve in this role was Saul. When he was chosen as king, it was noted that Saul stood head and shoulders over his countrymen (9:2). However, Saul made no move to oppose the braggart buffoon from Philistia. The **cubit** was about eighteen inches and **a span** was nine inches. Thus **Goliath** (the name may mean "Conspicuous One") stood nine feet, nine inches tall.

17:5, 6 bronze helmet: Ordinary troops had leather helmets. Goliath's **coat of mail** was made of overlapping plates of bronze sewn on leather. This armor weighed **five thousand shekels** or about 125 pounds. **Bronze armor** refers to the greaves that protected Goliath's legs. **bronze javelin:** This oversized weapon was designed for hurling. **Between his shoulders** means strapped to his back.

17:7, 8 The **spear** was a weapon designed for hand-to-hand combat, like a long sword. **six hundred shekels:** The head of Goliath's spear weighed about seventeen pounds. **shield-bearer:** There are two different Hebrew words for "shield." One (*magen*) refers to a small round shield usually worn on the left arm. The other (*sinnâ*), used here, refers to a much larger,

The Valley of Elah, site of the battle between David and Goliath (1 Sam. 17).

assault by the Philistines, causing the long delay before engaging in battle (v. 16).

17:4 champion: The Hebrew expression is literally "a man who is a go-between," meaning a warrior who will fight in single combat as a

oblong shield, often carried by the shield-bearer as the soldier moved into battle. Goliath was a veritable war machine.

17:9, 10 Defy is an unusually harsh word meaning "to put under reproach" (vv. 25, 26).

As the account later makes clear, the defiant taunts of Goliath were as much against the God of Israel as against the fighters (vv. 26, 36).

17:11 they were dismayed and greatly afraid: The army was sick with dread. Perhaps the Israelites had forgotten the victories God had given Israel in times past. Forgetfulness of God's past deliverance diminishes one's confidence in the face of present conflict.

17:12–15 that Ephrathite: Ephrathah was a family name in the tribe of Judah, the area where **Bethlehem** was located (Mic. 5:2).

17:16 The **forty**-day delay in the battle may have been due to the inability of the Philistine chariots to cross the deep ravine of the Elah Valley, which separated the armies. The number "forty" appears to play a significant role in biblical narratives. If a month is reckoned at thirty days, a period of forty days would be regarded as an extended, lengthy period of time. It certainly was a long period for Israel to hear the taunt words of this insufferable braggart!

17:17–19 In ancient times, soldiers usually lived off the land they conquered or depended on personal supplies that they or someone else brought from home. Jesse sent David with provisions—**grain, loaves,** and **cheeses**—for his sons and their officers. An **ephah** was a measure of grain, about five gallons.

17:20–23 rose early in the morning: These are the same words that were used of Abraham when he set out on his fateful journey to Moriah (Gen. 22:3). **going out to the fight:** The soldiers were going out to the battle line, but only to shout their taunts. **the supply keeper:** This wording suggests that what David did for his brothers was an ordinary service performed by families for their sons on the battlefield.

17:24 fled . . . afraid: The fear of the Israelite army was shameful. Perched on the fortified hillside, none of them was in immediate danger.

17:25 Saul promised riches, exemption from taxes and the duty of public service, and his daughter's hand in marriage to the one who would defeat Goliath.

17:26 Uncircumcised is used as an expression of contempt for a pagan person.

17:27, 28 David's oldest brother, **Eliab,** was rather abrupt with David. **pride . . . insolence:** This language is similar to that used to describe the rage of Joseph's brothers against him (Gen. 37).

17:29 Is there not a cause: David protested his innocence of the charges of pride (v. 28). There was reason to be agitated—not at David, but at the Philistine.

17:30–32 your servant will go: David weighed the difficulties from a divine perspective. Here was an opportunity for God to display His power.

17:33 Saul showed no evidence that he recognized David as the boy who had played the harp before him (16:23). There were probably many minor servants who waited on the king, and Saul may simply have not recognized David out of the context of the royal court.

17:34–37 David's past victories over **a lion** and **a bear** gave him the faith to trust God for victory over Goliath. For David, the issue was more a theological crisis—the Israelites' lack of faith—than a military one.

17:38, 39 Instead of putting on his own armor, trusting God, and going to the field of battle, Saul attempted to put the oversized armor on a young boy. Saul's armor was designed for a large man. David could not even **walk** in it, much less fight in it.

17:40, 41 his staff: Unprepared to face Goliath as an armed soldier, David prepared to face him as a shepherd. **five smooth stones:** David's experience had taught him how important shape, size, and uniformity were to achieve accuracy with a sling. A **sling** was the typical equipment of a shepherd. It was a hollow pocket of leather attached to two cords. Putting a stone in the pouch, the slinger would whirl it around his head to build up momentum. Releasing one of the cords would hurl the stone

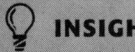 **INSIGHT** | **A Battle of the Gods**

Bible readers often focus on the human drama of the encounter between David and Goliath: A young shepherd boy confronts a seasoned man of war and kills him with a stone. But the contest was also between the gods of the Philistines and the Lord of Israel (1 Sam. 17:26, 36, 37, 43, 47). It was not uncommon in the ancient world for military "champions" to represent their armies in one-on-one combat. Victory was awarded to the side of whichever man prevailed. Goliath stood for the Philistines as well as for the gods of the Philistines. David represented both the people of Israel and the Lord.

at its target. Slingers were a regular part of armies in the ancient Middle East (Judg. 20:16).

17:42 David lacked the signs of age and the scars that one would expect of a battle-seasoned champion. Unlike most soldiers of Israel, he had not yet grown a beard.

17:43, 44 The appearance of a boy as his challenger offended the pride of Goliath. Further, Goliath saw the shepherd's staff (v. 40) and was angry because David appeared as if he were out to beat a **dog** instead of a giant. **cursed David:** Goliath treated David as contemptible. The word translated *cursed* is the same word used in Gen. 12:3. Since Goliath had cursed one of God's people, God was bound by His covenant to curse Goliath.

17:45 **Hosts** refers to the armies of heaven and of Israel, over whom God is Commander in Chief. **The name of the LORD** speaks of God's covenantal relationship with the Israelites. David was depending on the power of God as the Warrior and Defender of His people (Ex. 15:3).

17:46, 47 David intended his victory to demonstrate to **all the earth** that: (1) the God of Israel exists, and (2) that He delivers His own against overwhelming odds. David's words **the battle is the LORD's** put the contest into proper perspective.

17:48, 49 **hurried and ran:** Part of David's strategy was to rush the giant. Guided by the Lord, David skillfully hit the right spot on **his forehead** with a powerful blow.

17:50, 51 **cut off his head:** This was an indignity to a fallen foe and the decisive sign that he was dead. It filled the Philistines with terror.

17:52, 53 The Israelites pursued the Philistines north toward **Ekron** and east toward **Gath. Shaaraim,** meaning "Two Gates," is mentioned in Josh. 15:36 next to Sochoh and Azekah.

17:54 At this time, a part of **Jerusalem** was occupied by Israelites, but the citadel of Jebus was still in the hands of the Jebusites (Josh. 15:63). Later, it was captured by David when he became king over all Israel (2 Sam. 5:6–9). David took Goliath's **head** to the part of the city that was under Israelite control. David kept Goliath's **armor,** but the giant's sword was later deposited in the sanctuary at Nob (21:9).

17:55 **Abner,** one of Saul's generals, was also Saul's cousin (14:50). He was another seasoned soldier who was silent and inactive in the face of Goliath's taunting words. **whose son is this youth:** How does this question fit with the fact that David had been serving as a musician in Saul's court (16:18–23)? Saul's unstable mental condition (16:14, 15) may have affected his memory. Saul may have recognized David as his court musician but forgotten the name of David's father. He would need to know it in order to reward David's family (v. 25). It is also possible that in his question, Saul's principal interest was not David's identity, but the possibility that David was a contender for the throne of Israel.

17:56–58 **your servant Jesse:** In identifying his father, David likely intended to emphasize that Jesse was no threat to the king, that he was a loyal *servant* of Saul.

18:1 **soul of Jonathan was knit:** It has become customary today to speak of "male bonding." Perhaps the most interesting male friendship in the Bible is the story of Jonathan and David. As the story progresses, Jonathan's friendship to David would even make him (Jonathan) an enemy of his father.

18:2 Like his son Jonathan, Saul was captivated by David. He conscripted him anew to his court (16:19–23; 17:15).

18:3 This **covenant** was a mutual agreement in which David and Jonathan were bound to care for the needs and attend to the interests of each other. It was a treaty as between equals, yet these two men were not exactly equals. Such a relationship had to be initiated by Jonathan because he was a member of the royal household. **as his own soul:** These words, repeated for emphasis (v. 1), describe the unselfish nature of Jonathan's love for David.

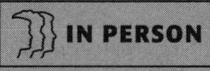 **IN PERSON** | ## Jonathan Transfers His Claim to the Throne

When Saul had offered David his armor and sword (1 Sam. 17:38, 39), David returned them. In 1 Sam. 18:4, Jonathan handed over to David his robe, military gear, and sword. With David's acceptance of the sword, he became who Jonathan was, the heir apparent to the throne of Israel. By his actions, Jonathan acknowledged God's decision that David should rule, and he stepped aside. Saul also knew what had happened with this transfer of the royal insignia (1 Sam. 20:30, 31).

18:4 sword . . . bow . . . belt: These were treasured items that would not have been casually surrendered. With these gifts Jonathan ratified his covenant with David. In retrospect, Jonathan's action was symbolic of a transfer of royal power from Saul's family to David.

18:5 behaved wisely: This description is a part of an ongoing subtle contrast between David and Saul. The phrase reveals that David was acting with skill and achieving success. It should be contrasted with the description of unwise actions of Saul (13:13). **set him over the men of war:** David did not replace Abner (17:55); he was simply acknowledged as a national military hero.

18:6 when David was returning: An event in the immediate aftermath of the famous battle of ch. 17 is mentioned here. **Women** came together from across the land to celebrate the national victory and their new national champion. **to meet King Saul:** The suggestion is that this was the usual pattern.

18:7 The popular song which celebrated David's military achievements became widely known, even among the Philistines (21:11). **thousands . . . ten thousands:** The poetic use of exaggeration is evident here. David had not yet slain even a dozen people, much less thousands. The women did not intend to offend the king; they were simply praising God for His ever-increasing benefits to the nation.

18:8 the saying displeased him: Saul saw David's abilities and achievements as undercutting his own prominence among the people. **the kingdom:** To Saul, there appeared to be no honor left for David except for him to take the throne. Ironically, this is exactly what God had determined.

18:9 eyed: Saul looked at David suspiciously, seeking any sign of betrayal or reason of mistrust.

18:10–13 The expression **he prophesied** can be used of legitimate prophecy or the erratic

prophetic ecstasy associated with the ravings of false prophets and pagan priests (1 Kin. 18:29; 22:12). Whatever the case here, God was judging Saul for his previous disobedience by allowing his mind to become troubled.

18:14, 15 behaved wisely: See 13:13. **the LORD was with him:** David's relationship with God was the key to his success.

18:16 he went out and came in before them: David's military activities elevated him to prominence before the people.

18:17–20 While Saul had previously promised to give his daughter to the man who killed Goliath (17:25), here he linked the marriage to future conquests, hoping that David would be killed by the Philistines.

18:21–23 that she may be a snare to him: Saul hoped that offering Michal in marriage would lead to David's death. **I am a poor . . . man:** David did not have the resources to bring a wedding dowry fit for a king (v. 25).

18:24, 25 In many cultures of the ancient Middle East, a **dowry** was paid by the bridegroom to the father of the bride as economic compensation for the loss of a daughter who helped around the home. **one hundred foreskins:** The foreskins would be proof that David had killed that many Philistines.

18:26, 27 the days had not expired: Apparently there was a time limit during which David had to fulfill the conditions of the dowry. **two hundred men:** David provided twice the number that Saul required.

18:28, 29 David's success in such dangerous exploits led Saul to believe that **the LORD** was with David. Significantly, the text adds that Saul' daughter **loved** David. With the marriage now in force, Saul had unwittingly placed a part of his family "in the enemy's hand." This brought a new element to Saul; he was now afraid of David.

18:30 The war with the **Philistines** continued, as did David's brave exploits. **behaved**

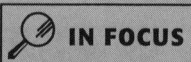 **IN FOCUS** **"dancing"**

(Heb. *mecholah*) (1 Sam. 18:6; 21:11; 29:5) Strong's #4246: The verbal root of this Hebrew word means "to whirl" or "to move in a circle." This is probably indicative of the type of dancing described here. When this word is used, there is regularly an association with joy, sometimes contrasted with mourning (Ps. 30:11; Jer. 31:4, 13; Lam. 5:15). Singing and playing instruments (especially the tambourine) are often mentioned in connection with dancing (Ex. 15:20; Judg. 11:34; Ps. 150:4). Although women usually do the dancing, men are also said to dance (Jer. 31:13). The ancient Israelites danced to celebrate the victories that God had given them (18:6; Ex. 15:20; Judg. 11:34). This was an exuberant expression of praise for their Creator and Deliverer (Pss. 149:3; 150:4; Jer. 31:4).

more wisely: This significant phrase meaning "to act with skill" is again contrasted with the phrase meaning "to play the fool," used of Saul in 13:13. David's successful military engagements gained him increasing honor and recognition.

19:1 When Saul's scheming efforts failed, he brought **Jonathan** and **all his servants** into the plot. Apparently, Saul did not know about the friendship of David and Jonathan. The Hebrew verb translated **delighted** (Heb. *haphes*) describes laughter, enjoyment, and pleasure.

19:2, 3 Loyal to his covenant of friendship, Jonathan pledged to intervene on David's behalf before his father (18:3).

19:4, 5 his servant: Jonathan's strongest argument was that David's actions demonstrated loyalty to Saul. **innocent blood:** Jonathan reminded his father of God's Law. By having David killed, Saul would incur the guilt of bloodshed (Deut. 19:10).

19:6, 7 Saul swore: Following the normal form for making such an oath, Saul says literally, "If he would die!" He means, "I will not allow him to die."

19:8–10 David's actions are contrasted with Saul's. Each time there was **war** with the Philistines, David had more opportunities for great exploits. Saul himself no longer went to war. He stayed at home sulking about David's victories.

19:11 tomorrow you will be killed: Because of her great love for her husband, Michal told David about Saul's plot. The story of David's escape is alluded to in the title of Ps. 59.

19:12 Window here may refer to an opening in the wall to allow in light and air or to the lattice work on a structure on the roof.

19:13 The Hebrew word for **image** is used elsewhere in Scripture to indicate household idols (Gen. 31:19, 30–35; Judg. 18:17–26; 2 Kin. 23:24; Ezek. 21:21; Zech. 10:2). Some have suggested that here the word means a life-sized object of a man. However, there is no evidence that ancient Israelites kept such objects in their homes. The **cover of goat's hair** and **clothes** was used to make it appear that David was still in bed.

19:14 He is sick: Michal loved her husband so much that she was willing to go against her father's wishes, to lie for David and even to die for him. The fact that she lied is a part of the drama of the story and does not necessarily endorse the practice of lying.

19:15–17 Saul's decaying mental and spiritual state is reflected in his words to his messengers. He feared and hated David so much that he was willing to murder a man lying sick in his bed.

19:18, 19 Facing a serious personal crisis, David **went to Samuel at Ramah** for help. Together David and Samuel went to **Naioth** ("Dwellings"), a community within the city of Ramah.

19:20, 21 The working of God's **Spirit** distracted Saul's messengers from their purpose and protected His servant David.

19:22, 23 Sechu is not mentioned elsewhere in the Bible. It was probably north of Jerusalem in the region of Gibeah and Ramah.

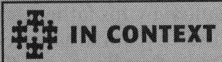 **IN CONTEXT** | **Wells**

In the ancient Middle East, wells like the one at Sechu (1 Sam. 19:22) were critically important to the life of cities and towns. Even in favorable locations, water tended to vanish at times during the summer months. Without a well to tap the water table or an underground stream, civilization was impossible to maintain.

Many different types of wells are mentioned in the Bible, though English translations tend not to distinguish between dug wells (John 4:11, 12), natural springs (Ps. 84:6), also called living springs (Neh. 2:13), and hewn cisterns (Gen. 16:14; 2 Sam. 17:18). Wells in Canaan were usually dug through solid limestone rock, sometimes to a great depth to keep them from running dry in the summer. Jacob's well, which still exists, is seventy-five feet deep and at one time may have been twice that.

Some wells had a curb or low wall of stone around the top to keep people and animals from falling in. The lip also formed a brace for users to use in letting down their buckets to draw water. Jesus probably sat on a curb of this sort when he talked to the woman at the well in Samaria (John 4:6). If a well was especially large, it was sometimes furnished with descending steps that allowed a person to dip directly from the pool of water (Gen. 24:16).

Because of their strategic importance, the ownership and use of wells tended to become a matter of dispute (21:25; Ex. 2:17–19). However, wells also served to bring people together and to remind them of important events in their heritage (Gen. 24:11, 20; John 4:6–14).

19:24 lay down naked: Ancient Israelite culture looked with disdain on nudity in public. It is probable that Saul removed his royal robe but retained his inner tunic. Here Saul's plan to kill David was totally thwarted by God's protective hand.

20:1, 2 You shall not die: Jonathan was certain that Saul would not kill David. It is possible that Jonathan was unaware of the events of 19:8–24 and was trusting in Saul's solemn oath not to kill David (19:6).

20:3 David impressed the seriousness of the situation on Jonathan with **an oath. Do not let Jonathan know this:** David suggested that Saul had kept his plans from Jonathan to avoid causing his son grief.

20:4 Jonathan's words reflected his covenant of friendship with David (18:3). He had vowed to help David.

20:5, 6 The first day of the month, **the New Moon,** was observed as a religious festival (Num. 10:10; 28:11–15). It was customarily celebrated with a sacrificial meal and rest from work (2 Kin. 4:23; Is. 1:13; Amos 8:5). **yearly sacrifice:** Apparently Jesse's family gathered for a special time of worship during the New Moon celebration (v. 5).

20:7–11 The words **deal kindly** may also be rendered "show covenant loyalty" (Heb. *hesed*). In other words, David was asking Jonathan to be faithful to his word. He had initiated a **covenant** of friendship (18:3). **if there is iniquity:** Since David had done no wrong, he was certainly not worthy of death.

20:12, 13 If the news was **good toward David,** Jonathan would send a messenger to inform his friend. If the news was **evil,** then Jonathan would inform David personally. All of this was couched in a solemn oath.

20:14, 15 the kindness of the Lord: Jonathan used the same Hebrew word meaning "covenant loyalty" that David had used earlier (v. 8). Both Jonathan and David were appealing to their covenant of friendship as a basis for acts of kindness. Whatever the outcome of the rift between Saul and David, Jonathan appealed to David to protect his own life and the lives of his descendants. Jonathan knew that David might someday take the throne, and he was well aware of the ancient custom of a new king killing the offspring of his predecessor (1 Kin. 15:29; 16:11; 2 Kin. 10:7).

20:16–18 Jonathan and David reaffirmed their covenant of friendship. **Jonathan made a covenant:** This refers to the agreement Jonathan sought from David in vv. 14, 15. **Let the Lord require it:** Jonathan prayed that the

Lord would hold David accountable to the obligations of the covenant. Out of love for David, Jonathan **again** requested that David reaffirm his **vow** (18:1; 19:1). David and Jonathan were holding each other accountable.

20:19 The stone Ezel was likely a familiar landmark.

20:20–24 Jonathan declared that **the Lord** would be a witness to the covenant of protection which he had arranged with David (vv. 14–16).

20:25–29 he is unclean: Noticing that David's seat was empty, Saul assumed that ritual uncleanness must have prevented his participation in the feast (Lev. 7:20, 21; 15:16). Since ritual uncleanness was only temporary, Saul's suspicions were aroused when David was absent on the second night of the feast. The reference to **Abner** suggests that David might have been threatening Abner's position as the general of the army.

20:30, 31 your mother's nakedness: Saul suggested that Jonathan and his mother with him were shameful because of Jonathan's apparently despicable behavior. Aware of David's increasing popularity, Saul knew that David would likely displace Jonathan from the throne. Here, Saul demonstrated his selfish concern for his family's welfare over God's sovereign will. Compare Eli's appropriate response to God's judgment (3:18).

20:32–34 his father had treated him shamefully: Jonathan, the loyal friend of David, was so upset he would not eat because of how David had been insulted by his father.

20:35–40 On the third day, Jonathan went to the field to signal to David that he should flee the court of Saul. However, Jonathan's love for David would not allow him to stop at a mere signal. He got rid of his servant on a ruse and at great personal risk went to meet David one last time.

20:41, 42 Before parting, David and Jonathan **wept together.** Both were valiant warriors but also men of tender hearts. They were loyal friends and committed to each other even in difficult circumstances. At their parting, the two friends reiterated their covenant of friendship (18:3; 20:14–16).

21:1–31:13 This third major section of 1 Samuel records the adventures of David as a fugitive. During most of this period he was fleeing from Saul and his army, and during these years suffered greatly. Through these difficult years David learned lessons on prayer, praise, and trusting the Lord. The "fugitive years" of David correspond to the "wilderness of

> *Jonathan knew that David might someday take the throne.*

Midian years" in the life of Moses. In both cases, the Lord used the perversity of man and the constrictions of condition and environment to shape, mold, and model His servants for greater work for His glory.

21:1 Nob was a priestly community; the tabernacle was relocated there after the destruction of Shiloh. **Ahimelech,** the great-grandson of Eli (1:9), was serving as high priest. His name means "My Brother Is King." **was afraid:** His fear may have been due to rumors of a breach between Saul and David. Since David was a respected soldier and a member of the royal court, it would be unusual for him to travel **alone.**

21:2 The king has ordered me: David deceived Ahimelech into believing that he was on a secret mission for the king. His lie unwittingly precipitated a tragedy for the priests of Nob (22:6–19). **I have directed my young men:** David apparently had arranged a rendezvous with a small band of men (21:4, 5; 22:2; Matt. 12:3, 4).

21:3–5 no common bread: In response to David's request for provisions, Ahimelech explained that the only bread available was **holy bread,** sometimes called the "showbread," which had been displayed before the Lord in the tabernacle (Ex. 25:23–30; Lev. 24:5–9). According to God's Law, this bread could be eaten only by priests. David explained to Ahimelech that his men had avoided ritual impurity, having had no contact with **women** for **three days** (Ex. 19:15; Lev. 15:16–18). **in effect common:** David argued that the bread was no longer sacred because new bread had replaced it before the Lord.

21:6 the priest gave him holy bread: The Talmud explains this apparent breach of the Law on the basis that the preservation of life takes precedent over nearly all other commandments in the Law (Lev. 24:9). Jesus referred to this incident in Matt. 12:2–4; Mark 2:25, 26, in His discussion with the Pharisees concerning the Sabbath. The spirit of the Law was kept by Ahimelech's compassionate act.

21:7, 8 Doeg, an Edomite, witnessed the encounter between David and Ahimelech and passed the word along to the king. Doeg was not at the tabernacle as a spy but as a man **detained before the LORD**—that is, under a spiritual vow.

21:9 Having fled Gibeah without weapons, David laid claim to **the sword of Goliath,** whom David had **killed in the Valley of Elah** (17:40–51). The sword was **wrapped in a cloth** to prevent the blade from rusting and had been placed **behind the ephod,** the high priest's ceremonial robes.

21:10 Achish ruled the city of **Gath,** one of the five major cities of the Philistines (6:17). Various sites have been proposed for the location of Gath. The most widely accepted is about twelve miles southeast of Ashdod.

21:11 David the king: This remark is an exaggeration of a rumored takeover of the throne by David. His military exploits certainly commended him to kingship. The popular song sung in his honor after his victory over Goliath had reached the ears of the Philistines (18:7; 29:5).

21:12, 13 These verses provide the background for Ps. 34 and perhaps Ps. 56. In Ps. 34, **Achish** is referred to as Abimelech, which was apparently a dynastic title used by the Philistine rulers (Gen. 20:2; 26:1). **very much afraid:** David's life was in jeopardy. If the superscription of Ps. 56 relates to this incident, David was seized by the Philistines. He had come for a place of refuge from Saul but found himself in the hands of the Philistines. **Madness** was associated in ancient times with being controlled by a powerful spirit. David changed his demeanor and behaved as though he were insane, writing graffiti on the doors of the gates and drooling.

21:14, 15 Achish had no interest in adding an insane soldier to his army. The title of Ps. 34 indicates the conclusion of this incident. The king "drove him away, and he departed."

22:1 After David's escape from Gath, he gathered his family and followers at a cave near the city of Adullam, about ten miles southeast of Gath and sixteen miles southwest of Jerusalem. **The cave of Adullam** was where David composed Ps. 142 and possibly Ps. 57.

22:2 David soon attracted a considerable following of those who were oppressed and discontented with Saul's rule. **Everyone who was in debt** apparently refers to those who were in danger of being sold into slavery by their creditors (2 Kin. 4:1). **Captain** is a general term for a political, military, or religious leader. The **four hundred men** soon grew to 600 (23:13). They were a group of drifters and debtors, troublemakers and those who were troubled. David expressed his disappointment when he realized that none of the men were there to support him (Ps. 142:4).

22:3, 4 The name **Mizpah** means "Watchtower"; this was probably a fortress in **Moab.** The region of Moab was located east of the Dead Sea. David's family connection with the Moabites is related in the story of Ruth (Ruth 1:4–18; 4:21, 22).

22:5, 6 Following the advice of the **prophet Gad** (2 Sam. 24:11), David left the **stronghold** and hid in **the forest of Hereth,** the location of which is unknown. The **tamarisk tree** is well-suited for hot, dry places, growing well on sandy, desert soils (Gen. 21:33).

 **IN PERSON** **A Watershed Event**

Certain decisions and incidents can be watershed events in the lives of ordinary individuals, authority figures, and even nations. The tragic massacre of the priests of Nob (1 Sam. 22:16–19) was such a moment.

When Saul instructed his followers to cut down Ahimelech and eighty-four of his associates, he was showing his true colors as to his religious convictions and commitments. Up until that command, most in Israel followed him out of respect for his position as king, even if they disagreed with his policies. But now he was crossing a line that even his own guard refused to cross (22:17). He was placing himself in direct opposition to the religious establishment in Israel. Thus, Saul began to lose a great deal of loyalty among his subjects on that day.

Not surprisingly, word of the slaughter quickly made its way to David (22:20–23). He was now perceived as the preserver of religion in the nation, as opposed to Saul, who had become the destroyer of God's people and priests.

22:7, 8 the son of Jesse: Saul perhaps was unwilling to refer to David by name (20:30, 31). Saul suggested that the Benjamites could not expect blessings under the rule of David, who was from the tribe of Judah.

22:9–13 Doeg sought to ingratiate himself with Saul by betraying **Ahimelech,** the high priest who gave David provisions and a weapon (21:1–9). **he inquired of the LORD** for him: This is not mentioned in 21:1–9, although Ahimelech seems to admit it in v. 15.

22:14–16 as faithful as David: In answering the charges against himself, **Ahimelech** inadvertently defended David. To hear the loyalty and faithfulness of David defended must have annoyed Saul considerably. **knew nothing:** Ahimelech made a case for his innocence by declaring his ignorance of the breach that had occurred between Saul and David.

22:17–19 would not lift their hands to strike the priests: The soldiers attending Saul knew better than to raise their weapons against the priests of the living God. They must have viewed the sentence as unjust or an act of sacrilege. Seeing a further opportunity to win Saul's favor, **Doeg,** a Gentile, carried out the slaughter of the eighty-five priests (21:7).

22:20, 21 Abiathar had not been among the eighty-five priests killed by Doeg at Gibeah. He escaped from Nob before the massacre. According to 23:6, he met up with David at Keilah.

22:22 I have caused the death of all the persons: David recognized that his deception led to the massacre of the priests and their families (21:1–9). In the sovereignty of God, the destruction of the priests of Nob was a partial fulfillment of the prophesied judgment on Eli's house (2:27–36). But the sovereignty of God never nullifies personal responsibility for one's actions (Acts 2:23).

22:23 he who seeks my life seeks your life: David and Abiathar were both regarded as enemies by Saul. **safe:** David offered Abiathar protection. The priest remained with David and provided a valuable service (23:9). He brought the ephod with him and inquired of the Lord for David (23:2, 6).

23:1 Instead of turning to Saul, their king, the people of **Keilah** appealed to **David** for deliverance from the **Philistines.** Located in a region of low hills about fifteen miles southwest of Jerusalem, Keilah belonged to the tribe of Judah (Josh. 15:44). **Threshing floors** were hard, flat surfaces where grain was trampled or crushed to separate it from the straw. Sometimes threshing floors served as storage areas. The Philistines raided the threshing floors after the Israelites had harvested and processed the grain.

23:2, 3 David inquired of the LORD: David sought the will of God concerning whether the Lord had called him to deliver Keilah. David recognized that need does not necessarily constitute a call to a particular ministry. **here in Judah:** The men had taken risks in associating themselves with David in Israelite territory, but they sensed that there would be increased risks if they left the hill country of Judah.

23:4–6 Abiathar did not join up with David until he was at **Keilah.** The account of this meeting was apparently included earlier to complete the narrative of what happened to the priests of Nob (22:20–23). The **ephod** was the outer vest of the priest. Its value was probably due to the Urim and Thummim attached to the breastplate. By means of the Urim and Thummim, God could be consulted and His will be determined (Ex. 28:30; Num. 27:21).

23:7, 8 a town that has gates and bars: Saul assumed that it would be easier to capture

David in a fortified city than to chase him all over the wilderness. Saul had not fought against the Philistines, the enemies of his people, for some time. But in an attempt to capture David, he was willing to destroy an entire Jewish town.

23:9–12 Bring the ephod here: David sought the will of God through the Urim and Thummim, which were attached to or inside the breastplate of the ephod (v. 6). David used the ephod to find out whether he was safe staying in Keilah. He asked two questions of the Lord: (1) Would Saul come to Keilah in pursuit of him? (2) Would the people of Keilah betray him to Saul? David received a "yes" answer to both questions.

23:13, 14 The number of David's followers had increased fifty percent, from 400 (22:2) to **six hundred. Strongholds** refers to the various hideouts where David and his followers found refuge. The **Wilderness of Ziph** is the barren region about four miles southeast of Hebron. This region had many ravines and caves in which David's men could hide.

23:15–18 Jonathan . . . went to David: This was the custom between the two; Jonathan initiated their friendship. To visit David, his father's archenemy, would have been risky for Jonathan. **his hand in God:** Both men had a fervent love for God, and Jonathan encouraged David to continue his obedient walk with the Lord. Jonathan recognized that David was destined to be Israel's next **king** and was content to take second place beside him because it was God's will. Finally, David and Jonathan renewed the **covenant** of friendship and protection which they had established earlier (18:3; 20:14–17).

23:19–29 While fleeing in the wilderness, David narrowly escaped being captured by Saul. This incident provides the historical background for Ps. 54.

23:19 Jeshimon may not be a proper name but a term meaning "waste" or "desert." The term is used here of the barren wilderness of Judah, which is in the vicinity of Ziph.

23:20–23 crafty: David's boyhood work as a shepherd gave him plenty of opportunity to learn the geography of the region and to become familiar with the hiding places of the wilderness.

23:24 By the time the Ziphites returned to **Ziph,** David and his men had moved to the **Wilderness of Maon,** a desert region to the south. Maon, a city of the Judean hill country (Josh. 15:55), was located about five miles south of **Ziph.**

23:25–28 Although Saul and his men managed to surround David's hideout, a report of a raid by the **Philistines** forced Saul to withdraw, allowing **David** to escape.

23:28 The place of David's near capture was

named **the Rock of Escape** to commemorate his deliverance.

23:29 En Gedi, meaning "Spring of the Kid," was an oasis east of Hebron, very near the shore of the Dead Sea. The site was noted in biblical times for the fresh water spring and lush vineyards (Song 1:14).

24:1, 2 The Rocks of the Wild Goats is another name for the area of En Gedi.

24:3 sheepfolds: At night, shepherds in this wild area would gather their sheep into a protective rock enclosure. A low stone wall would keep the sheep from wandering. The shepherd would position himself at the entrance of the sheepfold to guard against animals of prey and thieves. Often a cave with a wall built across its mouth served as a sheepfold in the wilderness. **Attend to his needs** (literally, "to cover his feet") is a euphemism for a bowel movement.

24:4 the Lord said to you: These words are not recorded elsewhere in Scripture. Perhaps they are given as the interpretation of the immediate events by David's men. **corner of Saul's robe:** Saul may have laid his robe aside, enabling David to cut off a piece unobserved. The piece of cloak would serve as proof that Saul had been completely at David's mercy.

24:5 David's heart troubled him: David was conscience-stricken. He knew it was wrong to assault the Lord's anointed king (vv. 6, 10). Even though David had not really done anything to hurt the king physically, the fact that he had reached out with his knife troubled him.

24:6 The Lord forbid: David had a high regard for the Lord's anointed king. To cut off a portion of Saul's robe constituted for David an act of disrespect for God's representative, even though that man was seeking to take David's life.

24:7 That David did not allow his men to slay Saul demonstrates that he was not an opportunist seeking a chance to take the throne through any means. David had a high regard for the office of kingship in Israel, even though the present ruler regarded him as a personal enemy.

24:8, 9 My lord the king: These words of respect from the voice that Saul knew well must have been quite stunning to him. **and bowed down:** This was not religious worship but an act of respect for Saul's position as king. **David seeks your harm:** Some people in Saul's court were falsely accusing David of trying to overthrow Saul.

24:10 the Lord delivered you today into my hand: David recognized God's sovereignty in bringing about the circumstances that gave him an opportunity to kill Saul.

24:11 My father is a warm term of affection and respect (2 Kin. 5:13; 6:21). It also reminded Saul that David was in fact his son-in-law. **your robe:** There could be no clearer evidence that David was not out to harm the king.

24:12 David dedicated to **the LORD** the matter of his relationship with Saul. God alone could settle the matter and bring about perfect justice (Deut. 32:35; Rom. 12:17–21).

24:13 Wickedness proceeds from the wicked: The meaning of the proverb is that only a wicked man would seek to do evil against another. Since David did not take advantage of the opportunity to kill Saul, he was most certainly a good man.

24:14, 15 David likened himself to a **dead dog** and a **flea** in contrast with **the king of Israel.** How could something as worthless as a dead dog or as insignificant as a flea be of any danger to Saul?

24:16–18 The words **my son** serve here as an expression of endearment. **Saul lifted up his voice and wept:** Saul's tears reflect his remorse at seeking to do David harm. However, it was a short-lived remorse (26:2). **more righteous than I:** For a similar admission, see the account of Judah and Tamar (Gen. 38:26).

24:19 may the LORD reward you with good: Saul prayed for God's blessing on David.

24:20, 21 swear now to me by the LORD: Saul asked David to commit himself by oath to (1) preserve Saul's family and (2) preserve Saul's name.

24:22 David swore to Saul: David agreed to Saul's requests and kept his promise (2 Sam. 9:1–13; 21:6–8). While Saul returned **home** to Gibeah (10:26), David remained in hiding. He

apparently had no great confidence in the lasting value of Saul's expression of remorse.

25:1 Then Samuel died: Samuel's death may have taken place while David was in the Wilderness of En Gedi (24:1). His death (or at least the recording of it) came at a propitious time. David had just been acknowledged as the successor of Saul by the king himself, and there was a short-lived truce between the two parties. Samuel's popularity was evidenced by the fact that the nation of Israel assembled at **Ramah** to honor him at his burial. After Samuel's death, David journeyed south to **the Wilderness of Paran,** a desert area in the northeast region of the Sinai peninsula.

25:2 Maon was located in the Judean hill country (Josh. 15:55), about eight miles south of Hebron. **Carmel** was located on the edge of the Judean wilderness, about a mile north of Maon. Like the times of harvest, the **shearing** of the sheep was a festive occasion.

25:3 The personal conduct of **Nabal** suggests that his name, meaning "Fool," was appropriate (v. 25). It is not known whether he used this name himself or whether it was something other people called him. Nabal was a descendant of the **house of Caleb,** which had occupied the area at the time of the conquest (Judg. 1:20). **Abigail,** a woman of wisdom and beauty, stood in stark contrast to the foolish nature of her husband. Her name may mean "My Father Is Rejoicing." The text also shows her wisdom (Prov. 31:10). **Good understanding** is a noun (Heb. *sekel*) related to the terms used to describe David in contrast to Saul.

IN LIFE   Pledging Allegiance

David spared Saul's life twice—once in the cave at En Gedi (24:1–7) and again in the Wilderness of Ziph (26:2, 7–12). Even though Saul was demented, unfit for office, and bent on destroying David, David refused to take his life, because Saul was the Lord's anointed (24:6).

David was even troubled in conscience for having cut the garment that Saul was wearing (24:5). It's similar to the way Americans "pledge allegiance to the flag of the United States . . . and to the republic for which it stands." To David, the robe of Saul represented the king.

David's respect for Saul's position serves as model for the high respect that God's people today should have for government and its officials. Like David, we may not care for the people in office or their actions, but we can respect the position, since government is ordained by God (Rom. 13:2).

All officeholders—whether they are Christians or not God-fearing people—deserve our respect and prayers (1 Tim. 2:1, 2). A governmental position invested by the prayers of God's people, anointed by God's representative, and confirmed with an oath of office invoking God's help—such an office is undeniably God-ordained.

Paul indicated that even "secular" governments, such as the autocratic Roman Empire, are God-ordained (Rom. 13:1–7). Likewise, secular governments carry out God's sovereign purposes. For example, He called Cyrus, the pagan king of Persia, His shepherd and His anointed (Is. 44:28—45:1).

25:4–9 Nabal lived in a wilderness area and owned thousands of sheep and goats, and so was a prime target for thieves. David and his men had generously protected Nabal's flocks and possessions (vv. 15, 16, 21). Since it was the time of sheepshearing, Nabal would have had plenty of cash from the sale of wool to reward David and his men for their services.

25:7 nor was there anything missing: David and his men had provided protection and had not taken advantage of their position or authority.

25:8, 9 David sent his men on a **feast day,** when most people display an extra measure of generosity. **Please give whatever comes to your hand:** Apparently, no price had been set for the services rendered.

25:10 Who is David: Nabal pretended not to know David. He added insult to injury by suggesting that David might be just another runaway servant.

25:11–14 Nabal lived in a region where **water** was scarce (Josh. 15:19).

25:15, 16 Nabal's own men testified to the care and protection they received from David and his men.

25:17 For he is such a scoundrel: The servants were so angry at their master that they spoke this way of him to his wife! The Hebrew phrase translated *scoundrel* is literally "son of Belial" or "son of worthlessness."

25:18 Taking matters into her own hands, Abigail gathered an abundance of goods to compensate David and his men. **skins of wine:** In ancient times, wine was carried in flexible containers made from animal skins. The Hebrew **seah** was a measure equivalent to one-third of an ephah or about one-fifth of a bushel.

25:19–21 Go on before me: Abigail wisely sent the provisions ahead to forestall any hostility caused by her husband's insulting behavior.

25:22 May God do so, and more also: David made an oath calling down God's judgment on his enemies should he fail to kill everyone who worked for Nabal.

25:23–31 Abigail's address to David is a masterpiece of charm, wisdom, and grace. She was able to avert a potentially disastrous situation in numerous ways: (1) by showing the respect for David that her husband had not shown; (2) by using humor concerning the name of her husband; (3) by acknowledging faith in the living God; (4) by confessing the wrong done to David; (5) by making restitution to David and his men; (6) by asking forgiveness for the transgression; (7) by recognizing David's right to the throne; (8) by helping David to put the present slight into a life-long perspective.

25:23, 24 Abigail's acts of humility were in strong contrast to the boorish behavior of her husband (vv. 10, 11). She did everything she could to show respect to David when he was angry and to obtain his forgiveness for the wrong Nabal had committed against him.

25:25 For as his name is, so is he: The name **Nabal** was quite fitting for a foolish man. Abigail's humor at her husband's expense was designed to save his life (vv. 21, 22).

25:26 as the LORD lives: Abigail showed herself to David to be a woman of truthfulness, piety, and faith.

25:27 This present means the provisions mentioned in v. 18. These gracious gifts expressed Abigail's desire to make things right.

25:28 an enduring house: Abigail's words indicate that she expected David to succeed Saul and enjoy a lengthy line of successors (v. 30).

25:29–31 bound in the bundle of the living: This metaphor reflects the custom of binding valuables in a bundle to protect them from injury. The point here is that God cares for His own as a man cares for his valuable treasure. **sling out:** This metaphor signifies God's complete rejection of David's enemies. **no grief to you:** Abigail sought to show David that the

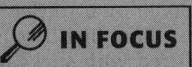

🔍 IN FOCUS   "forgive"

(Heb. *nasa'*) (1 Sam. 25:28; Gen. 4:13; Ps. 32:1, 5) Strong's #5375: This Hebrew word means basically "to lift up," "to bear," or "to take away." The word can apply to a person lifting up various objects including one's hand in an oath (Ezek. 20:5, 6), one's face to show favor (Num. 6:24–26), and one's voice in sorrow or joy (Gen. 27:38; Is. 24:14). The sense of "bearing" is often used in reference to sin or its punishment. Thus this Hebrew word was used to describe how the scapegoat "bore" the sins of Israel (Lev. 16:22) and how the Suffering Servant would "bear" the sins of the world (Is. 53:12). The idea of "taking away" is also frequently associated with sin. This activity is usually identified as a characteristic of God (Num. 14:18; Mic. 7:18). The NT describes God's forgiveness by stating that Jesus both bore our sins and took them away (1 Pet. 2:24; 1 John 3:5).

present slight was nothing compared to his future glory.

25:32–35 respected your person: A literal translation of this phrase would be "I lift up your face." This is the opposite of Abigail's bowing down before David when she first met him (vv. 23, 24).

25:36 Nabal's tremendous folly is seen in this scene. His wife has just saved his life, but he, unaware that he was even in danger, was engaged in an evening of excess! Abigail continued to show wisdom by not attempting to speak to her drunken husband that night.

25:37, 38 his heart died within him . . . like a stone: Nabal apparently suffered a stroke and became paralyzed. **the Lord struck Nabal:** Nabal's death was the result of God's judgment.

25:39, 40 David gave praise to the Lord, for it was God who had exacted justice and not David himself. This story is a splendid example of the biblical motif "'Vengeance is Mine, I will repay,' says the Lord" (Deut. 32:35; Rom. 12:19).

25:41, 42 to wash the feet of the servants: Washing the feet of others was a servant's task. Abigail expressed her willingness to do the most menial jobs. This was a genuine expression of her gratitude to David.

25:43 Ahinoam became the mother of David's oldest son, Amnon (2 Sam. 3:2). **Jezreel** is not the city in the north, but a town in the hill country of Judah (Josh. 15:56).

25:44 David was without **Michal,** his first wife (18:27). Saul had given her to another man during David's absence.

26:1 The Ziphites were from Ziph, four miles southeast of Hebron. They traveled about 25 miles north to report to Saul at **Gibeah. The hill of Hachilah** has been identified with a ridge about six miles southeast of Ziph (23:19). **Jeshimon** is probably not a proper name but a term meaning "waste" or "desert." The term is most likely used here of the barren wilderness of Judah, which is in the vicinity of Ziph and extends east toward the Dead Sea.

26:2–4 Apparently forgetful of the events of 24:16–22, Saul led his men into the wilderness in pursuit of David. The similarities between the events of ch. 24 and the events here are striking. **The Wilderness of Ziph** refers to the desert region around Ziph and eastward.

26:5 Abner the son of Ner had served as a very successful commander of Saul's army.

26:6 Ahimelech the Hittite was a non-Israelite who had joined David's force, probably as a mercenary soldier. The Hittites were a powerful, military people who ruled central Asia Minor during the second millennium B.C. **Abishai,** David's nephew (1 Chr. 2:15, 16), volunteered to go with David into Saul's camp.

Abishai became a leader among David's men (2 Sam. 23:18).

26:7 Saul's **spear** was a symbol of his authority (18:10; 19:9).

26:8 Abishai seems to have had a bloodthirsty nature (2 Sam. 16:9; 19:21). He promised not to strike Saul **a second time,** meaning that his first blow would be fatal.

26:9, 10 David once again refused to **stretch out his hand against the Lord's** anointed (ch. 24). He would not assassinate Israel's divinely appointed king (10:1). **the Lord shall strike him:** David knew that God would remove Saul from office according to His own perfect timing.

26:11, 12 take now the spear and the jug of water: These items would prove that David had been close enough to Saul to kill him but had refrained from doing so. David's visit to Saul's camp went undetected because the Lord had caused **a deep sleep** to fall upon the soldiers.

26:13, 14 calling out to the king: David did not shout directly to Saul; instead, he taunted Abner, Saul's general.

26:15, 16 The **spear** and the **jug of water** served as evidence of Abner's negligence and proof of David's goodwill.

26:17, 18 Is that your voice, my son David: Saul recognized the familiar voice, as he had near the cave at En Gedi (24:16).

26:19 If the Lord has stirred you up against me: David contemplated the possibility that God was using Saul as an agent of divine discipline. If this was the case, David expressed his willingness to offer an atoning sacrifice, **an offering.** On the other hand, he called for God's judgment on any evil men who had stirred up Saul against David. **Go, serve other gods:** This phrase reflects David's view that his exile was virtually equivalent to being forced to abandon the worship of God, since there were no sanctuaries to God outside Israelite territory.

26:20–22 David likened Saul's actions to pursuing **a flea** (24:14), hardly fitting for a royal figure. The **partridge** was known to flee for safety by running rather than flight. When fatigued, it could be captured with sticks or a net. Saul once again confessed his sin (24:17). He asked David to **return** home, promising not to make another attempt on his life.

26:23 Righteousness and **faithfulness** are characteristics of God Himself, which believers may share.

26:24, 25 David requested that his **life be valued** as much as he valued Saul's life. As the two parted, Saul recognized that David would eventually **prevail** (24:20). This was the last meeting between Saul and David.

27:1 Now I shall perish someday by the

hand of Saul: The evidence pointed to the contrary (13:14; 23:17; 24:20). Perhaps David was depressed. As he had done earlier in fleeing from Saul, David journeyed west toward the coastal plain and entered **the land of the Philistines.**

27:2 Various sites have been suggested for the location of **Gath.** The most widely accepted is about twelve miles east of Ashdod, or about twenty-four miles west of Jerusalem. **Achish** seems to have welcomed David. Perhaps he had heard of the split between David and Saul and was anxious to strengthen his own army with David's **six hundred** fighting men.

27:3, 4 David dwelt with Achish at Gath: David's move to Philistine territory delivered him from the immediate danger of Saul and provided him an opportunity to further develop his leadership and military skills (vv.

Photo: Levant Photo Service

the royal city: David suggested to Achish that it was too great an honor for him to continue to dwell in Gath, the city of the king. Perhaps David wanted to be free from constant surveillance by the Philistine authorities and from continued exposure to Philistine religious practices.

27:6 Achish established David as his vassal over **Ziklag,** one of the cities of the Israelite Negev. The city was originally assigned to Judah (Josh. 15:31) and was located about thirteen miles north of Beersheba. **Therefore Ziklag has belonged to the kings of Judah to this day:** This editorial note must have been added to the historical narrative after the division of the monarchy (930 B.C.). Before that time, there were "kings of Israel," but not of Judah.

27:7 Ziklag remained David's headquarters until Saul's death, when David moved to Hebron (2 Sam. 1:1–4).

The mound of Ziklag, a city which served as a base of operation for David's army during his years of struggle with King Saul (1 Sam. 27:6).

8–12). His time in Philistia also gave David knowledge of the geography of the region, which would serve him well during his later Philistine wars. As David had probably expected, his sojourn in Philistia put to an end to Saul's pursuit of him.

27:5 why should your servant dwell in

27:8 During his sojourn in Philistia, David convinced Achish that he was serving the Philistines. Yet he used Ziklag as a base for raids on desert tribes in the northern Sinai. These peoples were enemies of the Israelites. **The Geshurites** lived to the southwest of Israel (Josh. 13:2), between Philistia and Egypt. **The**

Girzites are mentioned only here. **The Amalekites** were a nomadic people who lived in the dry land south of the hill country (Num. 13:29). **Shur** was the border region separating Egypt from northern Sinai. The Israelites had wandered in this region after crossing the Red Sea (Ex. 15:22).

27:9, 10 Where have you made a raid today: Although David pretended to serve the interests of Achish, he was actually attacking the enemies of Israel. **The southern area of the Jerahmeelites** was the part of the Negev occupied by the family of Jerahmeel, one of the clans of Judah (1 Chr. 2:9). **The Kenites,** who were loosely associated with the Israelites since Moses' marriage into the family of Jethro, a Kenite (Judg. 4:11), were a nomadic offshoot of the Midianites (Num. 10:29). In fact, David was on friendly terms with both the Jerahmeelites and Kenites (30:29).

27:11 The complete destruction of human life seems to be the only way David was able to avoid discovery. David might also have reasoned that he was working to complete the destruction of the people of the land that had not been done fully during the time of the conquest (Josh. 23:4, 5).

27:12 he will be my servant forever: David's deception was so effective that **Achish** concluded that his switch in allegiance was permanent.

28:1–25 This chapter marks the spiritual low point for king Saul, recording one of the darkest hours of his reign. It also presents an incident that greatly troubles interpreters, the description of a man being summoned from the dead. Saul faced an imminent attack by the Philistines. With the prophet Samuel dead, and with heaven silent, Saul resorts to spiritism, only to learn of his own impending death and Israel's defeat. The tragedy of his life had nearly come to its bitter end.

28:1 in those days: The events of ch. 28 occurred during the time David was living at Ziklag as a vassal of the Philistine king. **gathered their armies:** All the time Saul was king, the Philistines were at war with Israel (14:52). **you will go out with me:** Since David was a vassal of **Achish,** the Philistines expected him to join them in their campaign against Saul. David faced a terrible dilemma.

28:2 Surely you know what your servant can do: The words of David were deliberately ambiguous. His life would have been at risk had he refused to join Achish so he was forced to wait for God's deliverance. **one of my chief guardians:** David found himself not only in the Philistine army but assigned as one of the king's chief bodyguards.

28:3 Samuel had died: He could no longer be counted on to bring forth a word from the Lord. The term **mediums** refers to necromancers, those who presume to communicate with the dead. **Spiritists** (Heb. *yidde'onîm*) is a general term for those who have contact with spirits. In keeping with God's Law, persons associated with necromancy and spiritism had been expelled from the land of Israel (Ex. 22:18; Lev. 19:31; Deut. 18:9–14). The medium at En Dor was one of the few such persons still known to live in the land (v. 7).

28:4 The village of **Shunem** was situated in the Valley of Jezreel, on the south slope of the Hill of Moreh. The Israelite forces were camped about five miles south of the Philistines on the mountain range of **Gilboa.**

28:5 Saul was so **afraid** of the forthcoming battle that his **heart trembled greatly.** Saul's persistent disobedience had left him completely without confidence in God's presence and protection.

28:6 In the midst of his fear and anxiety, Saul **inquired of the LORD**, but there was none that came. The comment in 1 Chr 10:14 that Saul "did not inquire of the LORD" is not a contradiction with this verse. It is rather a summary

---

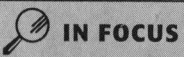 **IN FOCUS** | **"inquired"**

(Heb. *sha'al*) (1 Sam. 17:56; 28:6; Judg. 18:5; Job 8:8) Strong's #7592: The basic sense of this word is "to ask something of someone." One can ask for an object (1:20; Ps. 137:3) or for information (Gen. 43:7; Job 38:3). The Hebrew phrase translated "inquired of the LORD" occurs eleven times in the OT, all in Judges and 1 and 2 Samuel (Judg. 20:23; 2 Sam. 2:1). The Hebrew verb itself occurs a total of 172 times in the OT. On three occasions the context indicates the meaning "to lend" (1 Sam. 1:28 (twice); 2:20), and in another three passages it means "to borrow" (Ex. 22:14; 2 Kin. 4:3; 6:5). Thus when the children of Israel left Egypt they probably *asked,* not *borrowed,* the goods they took with them (Ex. 3:22; 11:2; 12:35). This Hebrew word is broad enough to encompass the idea of prayer, as in the famous verse: "Pray (ask) for the peace of Jerusalem" (Ps. 122:6).

that points to the fact that Saul went to the medium for counsel rather than *persistently* seeking a word from the Lord. God did not answer **Saul** by **dreams** as He had Joseph (Gen. 37:5–10); nor by the **Urim** and Thummim as He had the high priest (Ex. 28:30; Num. 27:21); nor by prophetic revelation as He had Samuel (3:10–21).

28:7 Find me a woman who is a medium: Rather than repent of his sin and continue to seek God's forgiveness, Saul turned to a forbidden source of counsel (Ex. 22:18; Lev. 19:31; Deut. 18:9–14). This tragic decision resulted in his death (1 Chr. 10:13). The Law of the Lord called for the death penalty on mediums (Lev. 20:27). **En Dor** was located in the Jezreel Valley, about a mile northeast of the Hill of Moreh.

28:8 Saul disguised himself: In light of his purge of mediums and spiritists from the land, Saul could not expect much help should his identity be known. **Conduct a séance for me** literally means "bring up for me."

28:9 Why then do you lay a snare for my life: The woman was aware of what Saul had done to those of her profession. She recognized the risk of being punished with death for practicing necromancy (Ex. 22:18) and sought to make sure that her visitor was not laying a trap.

28:10 Saul swore to her by the Lord: While engaging in a practice that was practically a denial of God's sovereign control of everything, Saul swore in God's name that he would protect the woman.

28:11 Saul sought the help of **Samuel** because he had anointed him as king and had spoken God's word to Saul before (10:1).

28:12 When the woman saw Samuel: When her séance really worked, the seer finally saw that her client was Saul. The appearance of Samuel has been interpreted in various ways. It has been suggested that the appearance took place in Saul's mind, as part of his psychological breakdown. The church fathers believed that a demon impersonated Samuel and appeared to Saul. Others have thought that the medium was a fraud who tricked Saul into thinking that he saw Samuel. It seems best to follow the early view that this was a genuine appearance of Samuel which God Himself brought about. Several points favor this interpretation: (1) The medium was surprised (v. 12). (2) Saul identified the figure as Samuel (v. 14). (3) The message Samuel spoke was clearly from God (vv. 16–19). (4) The text says that the figure was Samuel (vv. 12, 15, 16). There is no inherent difficulty with God bringing back the spirit of Samuel from heaven and allowing him to appear to Saul, in spite of the woman's evil profession.

28:13 What did you see? Apparently only the woman saw the spirit of Samuel. The word **spirit** is the term usually translated from the Hebrew Bible as "gods" or "God" (Heb. *'elohîm*). Here this word appears to have been used by the woman in her startled state to describe something she had never experienced before. It is, she said, as though a "god" has appeared, apparently referring to the unearthly appearance of the spirit. What a moment this must have been for her! Necromancers were either superb con artists or (rarely) in league with evil, demonic powers. Yet in this case the woman found herself unwittingly in league with Yahweh!

28:14 The **mantle** was a prophet's robe, such as the one Samuel had worn when he was alive. It was this robe that Saul once had torn (15:27).

28:15 The words **bringing me up** may be understood as meaning simply "up from the grave." This phrase indicates that the Israelites believed in life after death.

28:16, 17 the Lord has departed from you: These startling words are merely a restatement of what Saul himself acknowledged in v. 15. Samuel was not so much making an affirmation as he was pointing out the contradiction between Saul's words and actions. Even though Saul had said that God had departed from him, he was still seeking a word from the prophet of God.

28:18 Samuel traced Saul's disobedience and judgment back to his failure to destroy the Amalekites, particularly Agag (15:2–9).

28:19–23 Saul and his sons would die in the battle with the Philistines the very next day. The words **with me** simply refer to the grave. This text is not intended to provide a final answer concerning Saul's spiritual status. At the very least, it assumes the reality of life after death. **no strength:** Saul's sinful actions in seeking out a medium resulted in his complete collapse. He was terrified, sick, and totally weakened.

28:24, 25 Unleavened bread was baked without yeast and could be prepared without waiting for it to rise.

29:1, 2 Aphek was about thirteen miles northeast of Joppa. **a fountain which is in Jezreel:** The Israelites gathered at a prominent but unidentified spring in the Valley of Jezreel. **passed in review:** Apparently, the Philistine troops convened at an agreed-upon rendezvous to be reviewed and arranged in companies.

29:3 David was in a predicament, for he would not fight against his own people. He could do nothing but wait for the Lord to provide him with a means of escape from this dangerous situation. **Achish** came quickly to David's defense when the other princes questioned David's loyalty. Achish had **found no**

fault with David since his "defection" from Saul.

29:4 Make this fellow return: Achish was unsuccessful in persuading his fellow princes and soldiers to accept David and his men as part of the Philistine forces. They feared that David and his men might switch their allegiance back to Saul. See 14:21 for an example of what they feared.

29:5 Saul has slain his thousands: The popular Israelite taunt song (18:7) continued to echo in the ears of the Philistines (21:11).

29:6 Achish was thoroughly deceived by David's display of loyalty. **as the Lord lives:** Achish swore by the name of the God of Israel to impress David with the sincerity of his confidence in him. Achish had been close enough to David to know the language that David would understand best. The **lords** here are the Philistine rulers.

29:7, 8 go in peace: This farewell was much more than a courtesy. Achish was releasing David from any further obligation that he had incurred when Achish had made David a vassal king in Ziklag (27:6). **But what have I done:** David, who seems to have been a pretty fair actor, feigned surprise that Achish would dismiss him from the engagement.

29:9 Achish had been deceived by David. **Good** here means "blameless." The comparison with **an angel of God** appears again in 2 Sam. 14:17.

29:10 your master's servants: Achish was referring to Saul as David's master.

29:11 After the departure of David and his men, the Philistines marched north from Aphek (v. 1) to the Valley of **Jezreel.**

30:1 The attack on **Ziklag** took place **on the third day** after David and his men left the Philistine army at Aphek. **The Amalekites** were a nomadic people who roamed the Negev, the dry land south of the hill country (Num. 13:29). For their attack on the Israelites after the Exodus from Egypt (Ex. 17:8–13), they were placed under divine judgment (Deut. 25:19).

30:2–5 carried them away: Rather than kill the citizens of Ziklag, the Amalekites probably intended to make them slaves. Among those who were taken captive were David's two wives (v. 5), along with the wives and children of his men.

30:6 David faced a serious crisis in his leadership. He was **distressed** not only because of his personal grief but by the difficult situation pressing on him. **the people spoke of stoning him:** It is often the nature of unhappy people to vent their frustration through acts of hostility against their leaders (Ex. 17:4). **strengthened**

himself in the Lord his God: Unlike Saul, David knew where to turn in a time of crisis (Phil. 4:13). He had learned to wait on God, confident of God's eventual deliverance (Ps. 40:1–3).

30:7, 8 Abiathar, whose name means "The Great One Is Father," was the son of **Ahimelech,** the high priest from whom David had received provisions at Nob (21:1–9). The Urim and Thummim were attached to the breastplate of the **ephod** that David requested be brought to him (Ex. 28:30). By means of the Urim and Thummim, God could be consulted and His will determined.

30:9 The Brook Besor emptied into the Mediterranean Sea just south of the Philistine city of Gaza (6:17).

30:10 weary: The weariness of David's men was due to the fact that they had traveled about eighty miles from Aphek to Ziklag (29:1; 30:1), only to set off immediately in pursuit of the Amalekites.

30:11–13 found an Egyptian: A sick slave had been left by the Amalekites to die in the wilderness (v. 13). Life had been so devalued by the Amalekites that it was considered more economical to replace a slave than provide medical treatment for him when he was sick. **cake of figs and two clusters of raisins:** These foods were a regular part of the diet of David's men (25:18).

30:14 The Cherethites (2 Sam. 8:18; 15:18; 20:7, 23) were a clan closely related to, if not actually a part of, the Philistines (Ezek. 25:16; Zeph. 2:5). The **southern area of Caleb** refers to the part of Judah which was inherited by Caleb (Judg. 1:20).

30:15 In exchange for protection, the Egyptian agreed to lead David and his men to the Amalekites.

30:16 eating and drinking and dancing: The Amalekites were enjoying the booty they had taken from Philistia and Judah, including Ziklag.

30:17–21 Twilight here probably means just before first light in the morning. It is likely that David attacked the Amalekites in the early morning and that the battle continued through the next day. God was faithful to His earlier promise (v. 8); David's men were able to recover their wives and possessions. Not only did the men of David recover their own possessions, but they were able to capture the **flocks and herds** of the Amalekites. These animals were **driven before** the other livestock as they returned triumphantly to Ziklag.

30:22, 23 wicked and worthless men: These men insisted that the spoil captured from the Amalekites should not be divided with the men who stayed at the Brook Besor with the supplies. **with what the LORD has given us:** David pointed out that the booty captured from the Amalekites was actually a gift from God, who had given them the victory.

30:24, 25 For who will heed you in this matter: David questioned whether the men who waited at the Brook Besor would accept the proposal of the warriors who wanted to exclude them from any part in the spoil. **they shall share alike:** David's band of warriors were one, although they had different strengths and abilities. They would share equally in the fruits of victory.

30:26–31 David also shared the booty taken from the Amalekites with the elders of Judah. This goodwill gesture helped David reestablish his relationships among the leaders of Judah after his stay in Philistine territory.

30:27 Bethel is not the well-known city of Benjamin, but probably the Bethel of Josh. 19:4. **Ramoth of the South** may be the same city as Ramah of the South (Josh. 19:8), whose location is uncertain. **Jattir,** a Levitical city (Josh. 21:14) allotted to Judah (Josh. 15:48), was about thirteen miles southwest of Hebron.

30:28 Aroer was a village about twelve miles southeast of Beersheba. The village of

Photo by William A. VanGemeren

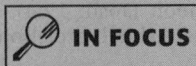

IN FOCUS | **"worthless"**

(Heb. *beliya'al*) (1 Sam. 30:22; Job 34:18; Prov. 6:12) Strong's #1100: This word has the basic sense of "unworthy" and "wicked." It occurs in the OT most frequently in phrases like "worthless men" (30:22; Prov. 6:12) and "worthless rogues" (2 Chr. 13:7). Worthless people are said to dig up evil (Prov. 16:27) and to plot wickedness (Nah. 1:11). This word became a proper name for Satan during the inter-testamental period. Thus Paul asked, "What accord has Christ with Belial?" (2 Cor. 6:15).

Siphmoth has not been identified. **Eshtemoa** was a Levitical city (Josh. 21:14) in the hill country of Judah.

30:29 Rachal is of uncertain location. The **Jerahmeelites** were one of the clans of Judah (1 Chr. 2:9).

30:30 Hormah was where the Israelites were first defeated by the Canaanites (Num.

The mound of Beth Shan, the city where King Saul's body was hung by the Philistines (1 Sam. 31:7–10), overlooks the ruins of a Roman theater in the foreground.

14:45). The location of the city, allotted to Judah (Josh. 15:30) and to Simeon (Josh. 19:4), is uncertain. **Chorashan** and **Athach** are also of uncertain location.

30:31 Hebron, also known as Kirjath Arba (Gen. 23:2), was soon to become David's capital (2 Sam. 5:3). Hebron was captured by Joshua and given to Caleb (Josh. 14:13). It was a Levitical city (Josh. 21:11) and a city of refuge (Josh. 20:7).

31:1 Mount Gilboa was a small mountain range in the eastern part of the Jezreel valley.

31:2, 3 Saul's fourth son, Ishbosheth, was apparently not present at this battle, since Abner promoted him to king after Saul's death (2 Sam. 2:8–10).

31:4 Saul took a sword and fell on it: This account of Saul's death is different from that given by the Amalekite in 2 Sam. 1:6–10. His story was probably a fabrication intended to win David's approval.

31:5 In a demonstration of loyalty, Saul's **armorbearer** joined his master in death.

31:6 all his men: This does not refer to the whole army (v. 7), but rather to men who were particularly associated with Saul, perhaps his royal bodyguards.

31:7 The other side of the valley refers to the Valley of Jezreel. **they forsook the cities and fled:** As a result of Israel's defeat, many of the cities of northern Israel were abandoned. The people fled to remote regions to escape the Philistine menace.

31:8, 9 the Philistines came to strip the slain: Battlefield looting was the rule in ancient times. The victors gathered clothes, weapons, and armor from the slain. **to proclaim it in the temple of their idols:** The victory of the Philistines was announced to assembled worshipers as a public testimony of the greatness of their gods in overcoming the Israelites.

31:10 The armor of Saul was placed in the **temple** dedicated to the worship of Ashtoreth, or Ishtar, the Canaanite goddess of fertility and war. **Beth Shan** was at the junction of the Jezreel and Jordan valleys, about four miles west of the Jordan. Although Saul's body was fastened to the wall of the city, 1 Chr. 10:10 records that his head was displayed in the temple of Dagon.

31:11 The inhabitants of Jabesh Gilead had been delivered from the threats of Nahash the Ammonite by Saul in his first military campaign as king of Israel (11:1–11).

31:12 the valiant men arose: Out of gratitude to Saul for delivering their city, the men of Jabesh Gilead risked their lives to recover the bodies of Saul and his sons and to give them a proper burial. **burned them:** Cremation was not the normal practice for disposing of the dead among the ancient Hebrews. The reason they burned the bodies of Saul and his sons may be that the corpses had been mutilated by the Philistines (v. 9).

31:13 Although the bodies of Saul and his sons were burned, the **bones** were recovered and **buried.** Later, David exhumed the bodies of Saul and Jonathan and had them reburied in Benjamin (2 Sam. 21:11–14). **fasted seven days:** In ancient Israel, fasting was a way of expressing sorrow in mourning. With their fasting, the men of **Jabesh** showed their respect for Israel's first king.

The Second Book of

Samuel

SECOND SAMUEL RECOUNTS THE TRIUMPHS
and defeats of King David. From his rise to the throne to
his famous last words, this biography describes a remarkable, divinely-inspired leader. As king, David took a divided and
defeated Israel from his predecessor King Saul and built a prominent nation. Like most political biographies, Second Samuel highlights the character traits that enabled David to succeed: his

reliance on God for guidance (2:1), his sincerity
(5:1–5), and his courage (5:6, 7). But the book
also describes the tragic consequences of David's
lust (12:1–23) and pride (24:1–17). By presenting both the strengths and the weaknesses
of David, the book gives a complete picture of a
very real person, a person from whom we can
learn.

Second Samuel is named after the prophet
Samuel, even though he does not appear in the
narratives of the book. This is because 1 and 2
Samuel were originally one volume. When the
Hebrew Scriptures were translated into the
Greek language (around 150 B.C.), the books of
Samuel and Kings were united as a complete
history of the Hebrew monarchy. This collection
was divided into four sections: First, Second,
Third, and Fourth Kingdoms. Samuel and Kings
were later separated again, but the divisions of
the Greek translation persisted. The result was a
1 and 2 Samuel and a 1 and 2 Kings, corresponding to the four sections of kingdoms in the
Septuagint.

Second Samuel covers the period from the
death of Saul (c. 1010 B.C.) to the end of David's
career (c. 970 B.C.). During the forty years of

his reign, David welded the loose-knit tribes together into a strong monarchy and transformed
the youthful nation into a military power able to
dominate surrounding nations. After capturing
the Jebusite fortress, Jerusalem, David made it
his capital. This new site became the powerful
geographical base for the establishment of
David's empire. Then David began to free the
Israelite territory from Philistine and Canaanite
domination. In doing so, David extended his
kingdom by military conquests to the north,
south, east, and west (ch. 8).

In addition to military conquest, David was
the first of Israel's kings to use marriage alliances
as an important dimension of the nation's foreign policy. Marriage alliances between royal
houses as a means of concluding treaties and
cementing relationships between states were
common occurrences in the ancient Middle
East. The first such marriage alliance is alluded
to in 3:3, where Absalom, David's third son, is
called "the son of Maacah, the daughter of
Talmai, king of Geshur."

David's conquests and alliances gave him
control of territory from the border of Egypt to
the Euphrates. This was largely due to David's

strong military presence in comparison with the general weakness that characterized Egypt and Mesopotamia at this time. For a brief period, Israel was as strong as any nation of the ancient world.

The unifying theme of 2 Samuel is the establishment of the kingdom of Israel, progressing from a diverse group of divided and warring tribes to a solidified kingdom under David. However the purpose for recording these events was not merely to have an "official" record of David's reign. Throughout the narrative, there is a continuing interest in the rule of God over His people. The book emphasizes that it was God who rejected Saul for his disobedience, chose David for the throne, and disciplined David for his pride. God was still the true King of Israel.

The key to David's successful reign was his relationship with the Lord. God had described him as a man after His own heart (1 Sam. 13:14). In his youth, David had demonstrated his strong faith in God by challenging a giant with only a few stones and his faith in God's strength (1 Sam. 17:45–51). In his adulthood, he continued to rely on God for guidance and strength (2:1; 5:19). Early in his reign, he demonstrated the importance of his religious convictions to all Israel by bringing the ark of the covenant to Jerusalem in the midst of a lavish celebration before the Lord (6:1–23). Following that, his eagerness to build a temple for the glory of the Lord was known to all (7:1–3). With such actions and the numerous songs he wrote in praise of God, David led the Israelites back to the true worship of God. Even when he

sinned, he demonstrated to the people his repentant heart before the living God (12:13–23; 24:17–25). In the final analysis, David's religious leadership was the most significant part of his reign.

Through all the triumphs and tragedies of David's reign, God was acting in the national and personal events of His people in order to accomplish His will. The Lord gave David a glimpse of His ultimate will in the promises He gave him, commonly called the Davidic covenant (7:12–16). In this unconditional covenant, God promised David an eternal dynasty, an eternal throne, and an eternal kingdom. Ultimately, a righteous King greater than David was coming. He would be David's son and would rule from David's throne forever (Is. 9:7). This promised King is Jesus (Luke 1:31–33; John 1:49).

Jewish tradition holds that the prophet Samuel wrote 1 Sam. 1—24, and that the prophets Nathan and Gad composed the rest of 1 Samuel and all of 2 Samuel. It is quite evident that some sections of 1 Samuel and all of 2 Samuel were written after the death of Samuel (1 Sam. 25:1; 28:3). Indeed, some notes may have been added even after the division of the monarchy in 930 B.C. (1 Sam. 27:6). In the absence of any reference to the fall of Samaria, the capital of the northern kingdom, it is reasonable to assume that the books were complete by 722 B.C. The majority of the composition of the Books of Samuel may have been done during David and Solomon's reigns (c. 1010–930 B.C.), with only a small number of notations coming from later periods.

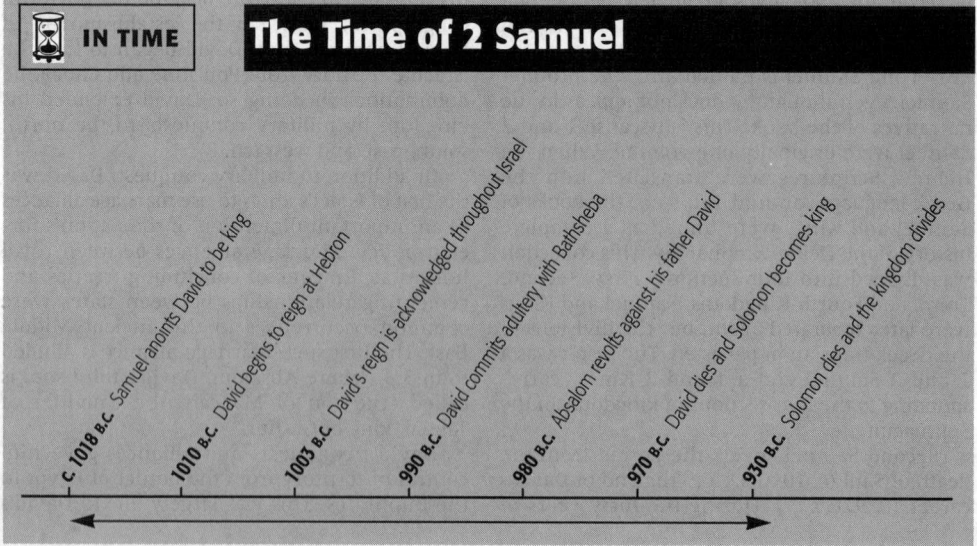

IN TIME

The Time of 2 Samuel

c. 1018 B.C. Samuel anoints David to be king

1010 B.C. David begins to reign at Hebron

1003 B.C. David's reign is acknowledged throughout Israel

990 B.C. David commits adultery with Bathsheba

980 B.C. Absalom revolts against his father David

970 B.C. David dies and Solomon becomes king

930 B.C. Solomon dies and the kingdom divides

Outline

Commentary

1:1–10:19 David's spiritual qualifications for his role as Yahweh's select king are highlighted by his concern for the ark and by his desire to build a temple for the worship of the Lord. His military qualifications are evidenced by his successful campaigns of conquest on the surrounding territories. These were glory years for David. During this time David served God well and enjoyed the evidence of God's blessing.

1:1 The death of Saul is recorded in 1 Sam. 31:3–5. **The Amalekites** were a nomadic, marauding people who roamed the southern part of Canaan. They were fierce enemies of Israel until they were brought under Israelite control in the time of David. **Ziklag** was one of the Israelite cities of the southern desert or Negev, originally assigned to Judah (Josh. 15:31). David was granted authority over the city when he served as vassal to Achish, king of Gath (1 Sam. 27:6).

1:2 clothes torn and dust on his head: The man was in mourning (1 Sam. 4:12). He **fell to the ground** to show his support for David as Saul's successor to the throne of Israel. In these actions of mourning and humility, the man attempted to demonstrate the one who was to become king.

1:3 escaped from the camp of Israel: The army of Israel had fallen in defeat to the Philistines, but the man had escaped from the battlefield.

1:4 The words **How did the matter go** lead the reader to anticipate the climax in the narrative, which comes to David from the messenger: the people have fled, many are dead, and so are Saul and Jonathan. The mention of Saul and Jonathon was the focal point for David in the rest of the encounter. Compared with their deaths, the loss of the battle was as nothing.

1:5 How do you know: David sought verification for the report. It is said that the first casualty in war is truth; rumors, lies, and distortions are not innovations of modern war. David needed to know the truth of the Amalekite's assertion.

1:6–10 The Amalekite's report of Saul's death is different from the account in 1 Sam. 31:4, which states that Saul died by falling on his sword. It appears that the Amalekite's story is a fabrication. Perhaps he sought recognition or reward from David by claiming to have slain Saul.

1:6–8 Mount Gilboa is a small mountain range located in the eastern part of the Jezreel valley.

1:9 In this context, **anguish** (Heb. *shabas*) refers to the agony of death.

1:10 I was sure that he could not live: According to the Amalekite's story, since Saul had no hope of recovery, there was justification in putting him to death. The **crown** was a mark of royalty. The **bracelet** was an ornament worn on the upper part of the arm. Apparently, it was the custom for kings to go into battle in royal regalia (1 Kin. 22:30). The Amalekite brought these items to David in order to substantiate his story.

1:11 tore them: Tearing one's clothes was a traditional expression of mourning in ancient times (3:31; Gen. 37:34).

A Survivor Arrives at Ziklag

INSIGHT

The survivor who arrived at Ziklag with news of Saul's death (2 Sam. 1:1, 2) must have been weary not only from battle with the Philistines but also from his long journey. Mount Gilboa, where the battle had been fought, was in the north of Palestine; Ziklag was about 90 miles to the south in the Negev, or southern Judah, near the boundary with Edom.

1:12 the people of the LORD: David and his associates mourned not only for the fallen king and prince, but also for those who had died from the ranks of Saul's army. This is surprising, for it was the same army that had been attempting to capture and kill David. He did not see them as enemies, but as members of God's family.

1:13 Where are you from: David's question might have been designed to determine whether the Amalekite resided in Israel or in Amalekite territory to the south. He might have been wondering how the man could be so ignorant of David's respect for Saul's life.

1:14 David's use of the phrase **the LORD's anointed** indicates that even though Saul was his enemy, David respected Saul's divine right to be king. With Saul's anointing, God had declared a sacred relationship between Himself and Saul (1 Sam. 10:1); Saul as king served as God's representative and ruler over His people. David repeatedly refused to harm him because of this (1 Sam. 24:6; 26:9).

1:15 execute him: David apparently believed the Amalekite's story and had him put to death on the basis of his own testimony. David's execution of the Amalekite was a strong statement to those under his command that he had no part in Saul's death and did not reward it in any way. Thus he exemplified respect for authority and distanced himself from the charge of being a usurper.

1:16 Your blood is on your own head: The Amalekite, not the executioner, was morally accountable for the shedding of his own blood.

1:17–27 David's eulogy over Saul and Jonathan is a highly poetic, intensely personal, and emotionally charged expression of sorrow over a national tragedy (compare 3:29). This is a psalm that reveals a great deal about David, the man after God's own heart (1 Sam. 13:14). The song focuses particularly on the loss of David's friend, Jonathan. It is arranged in three unequal movements (vv. 19–24; 25, 26; 27), which gradually diminish in force. Each strophe (section) opens with the exclamation, "How the mighty have fallen!" (vv. 19, 25, 27).

1:18 The Hebrew phrase **the children of Judah** means not young people but the descendants or tribe of Judah. **the Song of the Bow:** The words for "the Song of" do not appear in the Hebrew, leading some to suggest that the men of Judah were to be instructed in warfare and the use of the bow (Ps. 18:34; 144:1; 149:6). Others suggest that the poem was known as *The Song of the Bow,* based on the reference in v. 22. It is also possible the title refers to the tune for the song. **The Book of Jasher** was perhaps a collection of hymns about Israel's wars, in which important events and national figures were commemorated in poetry (Num. 21:14–18; Josh. 10:13).

1:19 The beauty of Israel refers to Saul and Jonathan. **High places** alludes to Mt. Gilboa (v. 6), where the warriors died.

1:20 Gath and **Ashkelon** are mentioned as representatives of the Philistine cities (1 Sam. 6:17) that would rejoice over the deaths of Israel's royal family. These two cities joined with Ekron, Gaza, and Ashdod to form the Philistine pentapolis, or five-city league.

1:21, 22 no dew nor rain: A curse was pronounced on the mountains of Gilboa, the scene of the military disaster (1:6; 1 Sam. 31:8). **not anointed with oil:** Shields were normally wiped with oil to cleanse, polish, and protect them. Saul's shield was declared useless because it had not protected him from death.

1:23, 24 Eagles and **lions** were poetic symbols of speed and strength. **weep over Saul:** David invited the women of Israel to lead in public lamentation for Saul, whose military exploits elevated the standard of royalty and enriched the nation (1 Sam. 14:47). David did not want the women of Philistia to sing (v. 20), but he invited the women of Israel to lament.

1:25 How the mighty have fallen: The poetic repetition of these words from v. 19 prepares the reader for the shift in focus of the poem to Jonathan.

1:26 The Hebrew word for **distressed** (*sar,*

often "trouble") means a tightness or constriction, as though life itself were closing in. **Your love:** David compared Jonathan's love with that of women in its depth and loyalty. David was not afraid to speak of his deep and genuine love for his friend.

1:27 How the mighty have fallen: The third repetition of this phrase (vv. 19, 25) brings the psalm to its painful conclusion. The phrase **weapons of war** is a figurative reference to the fallen warriors.

2:1–4:12 This section recounts the early history of David's kingship, when he reigned over Judah at Hebron. This was a period of conflict between two rivals—David, who took the throne of Judah, and Ishbosheth, Saul's surviving son, who took the throne of Israel. It is a record of treachery, betrayal and power-plays—all the painful ring of modernity.

2:1 David inquired of the Lord: Before taking an important step, it was David's custom to seek the will of the Lord (1 Sam. 23:2; 30:8). This was sometimes done by means of the Urim and Thummim which were attached to the breastplate of the priest's ephod (Ex. 28:30; Lev. 8:8; Num. 27:21; Deut. 33:8; 1 Sam. 23:6–9; Ezra 2:63; Neh. 7:65). The Lord directed David to **Hebron** (1 Sam. 30:31). Its central location—about 20 miles south of Jerusalem—and defensible position made it a suitable capital for David.

2:2 his two wives: David's marriages to Abigail and Ahinoam are recorded in 1 Sam. 25:2–43.

2:3 The ancient name for Hebron was Kirjath Arba (Gen. 23:2), meaning "Town of Four." Apparently, the town had four suburbs, one of which must have been Mamre (Gen. 35:27); hence, one may speak of **the cities of Hebron** (Josh. 21:11).

2:4 anointed David: This is actually the second anointing of David. The first had been performed by the prophet Samuel while Saul was still king (1 Sam. 16:13). The first anointing was a mark of God's intention; this second anointing was the recognition by the people of Judah that David was truly the Lord's anointed (5:3). **Jabesh Gilead** was on the north bank of the Jabbok River, about seven miles east of the Jordan. The men of Jabesh Gilead had risked their lives to provide Saul and Jonathan a proper burial (1 Sam. 31:11–13).

2:5–7 sent messengers: David's sincere action of appreciation for the kindness of the men also announced to them that he was ready to act on their behalf, because he was now the anointed king of the tribe of Judah. Translated **kindness** here, the significant Hebrew term *hesed* is elsewhere translated as "mercy" or "merciful kindness"; it may also be rendered as

"loyal love." It is the key term in the Psalms to describe the character of God. Here David prays that Yahweh will repay their act of loyal love by His own acts of "kindness and truth." **let your hands be strengthened:** David made an appeal to the men of Gilead for their strong support of his kingship. However, their loyalty to Saul's dynasty prevailed, and Jabesh Gilead became the headquarters of Ishbosheth, David's rival.

2:8 Ishbosheth means "Man of Shame." His original name Esh-Baal, meaning "Man of the Master" or "Man of the Lord," was changed because "Baal" suggested Baal worship (1 Chr. 8:33, 9:39). **Mahanaim,** the capital of Gilead, was north of the Jabbok (1 Kin. 4:14). It was named by Jacob when he saw the encampment of the angels of God around his own camp (Gen. 32:2). The name means "Double Camp."

2:9 Gilead usually refers to the central part of the Israelite territory east of the Jordan; here the term probably refers more generally to all of that territory. **Ashurites** is apparently a variant of the term Asherites (Judg. 1:32), referring to the tribe of Asher. The territory of Asher extended north from Mount Carmel along the Mediterranean coast and east into the foothills of the mountains of Galilee. **Jezreel** refers to the broad valley between the mountains of Galilee and the mountain range to the south. **Ephraim** and Manasseh occupied the central district north of **Benjamin,** the small plateau just north of Jerusalem.

2:10, 11 While David was king in Hebron for seven and a half years, Ishbosheth reigned for only **two years.** The difference may mean that Ishbosheth took about five years to recover the northern territory from the Philistines after Saul's defeat. His reign of two years would be his reign over "all Israel" (v. 9).

2:12, 13 Gibeon was about six miles northwest of Jerusalem. **pool of Gibeon:** Excavations at El-Jib—the site of Gibeon—uncovered a rock-cut pool 37 feet in diameter and 82 feet deep. A spiral staircase of 79 steps cut in the rock leads to the bottom. The pool was meant either to store rainwater or to provide access to the water table. **Joab:** David's nephew became a competent military commander of David's forces (10:7–14; 12:26–28).

2:14–17 Abner proposed a contest between champions to determine the outcome of the conflict between Ishbosheth and David (1 Sam. 17:38–54). This was not a friendly game that he proposed; it was a fight to the death in order to determine a victor. Yet the outcome of the contest would presumably save many lives. The two groups of **twelve** faced each other. Two champions contended at a time, each killing the other, until all twenty-four had died. Had one group of champions clearly triumphed over the other, the contest would have determined the future ruler of Israel. **fierce battle:** Since the contest between the champions was a draw, warfare between the two armies ensued, with David's men claiming victory.

2:18 Joab, Abishai, and **Asahel** were brothers, all sons of David's sister **Zeruiah** (1 Chr. 2:13–16). The **wild gazelle** was renowned in Israel for its beauty and swiftness.

2:19, 20 Asahel knew that if **Abner** was dead, Ishbosheth's power base would dissolve, and the tribes could be united under King David.

2:21, 22 Abner, confident that he could defeat Asahel, wanted to avoid the blood feud that would likely develop if he were to kill Joab's brother. It also appears that Asahel, renowned for his speed (v. 18), did not have on the body armor that would have made a fight with Abner a fair contest. Abner pleaded with Asahel to **turn aside** or at least to put on **armor.**

2:23 Unable to deter Asahel from pursuing him, Abner stabbed him with the **blunt end** of

his spear, which was the end opposite the spear head. It was probably pointed so that it could be stuck in the ground (1 Sam. 26:7).

2:24 The battle was turning in favor of David's supporters, and the brothers Joab and Abishai (v. 18) were in hot pursuit of Abner. They did not know at this time that their other brother, Asahel, had been killed (v. 30). The **hill of Ammah** and the town of **Giah** are mentioned only here and have not been identified.

2:25 the children of Benjamin: The men of Saul's tribe were among the strongest supporters of Abner and Ishbosheth.

2:26–28 devour forever: Recognizing that continued fighting would only result in further loss of life and deepened hostility, Abner and Joab agreed to call off the conflict. The use of silver trumpets to signal the army was established at the time of Moses (Num. 10:1–10). Here, the **trumpet,** a ram's horn or shofar, was used to mark a truce between the warring sides.

2:29–31 Abner's army retreated across the Jordan and returned to **Mahanaim,** Ishbosheth's headquarters (vv. 8, 12).

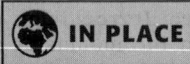 **Civil War Between North and South**

After the death of Saul, David did not immediately ascend to the throne of a united Israelite kingdom. First he was crowned king of Judah, which he ruled for seven and a half years from the city of Hebron (2 Sam. 2:1–7, 11). During much of this period, a civil war was fought between David and the heirs of Saul (3:1). One of these sons, Ishbosheth, (or Esh-Baal, 1 Chr. 8:33), pieced together a kingdom in the north, aided behind the scenes by Abner, one of Saul's generals (1 Sam. 2:8, 9). A great deal of blood was shed in determining whether David or Ishbosheth would ultimately rule Israel (2:12–4:12).

This tragic period in the nation's history was a reflection of the people's earlier insistence on having a king (8:4–9, 19–22). Had they waited for God to appoint a ruler in His own good time, the heartache of Saul's reign might never have happened and the years of civil war after he died could have been avoided.

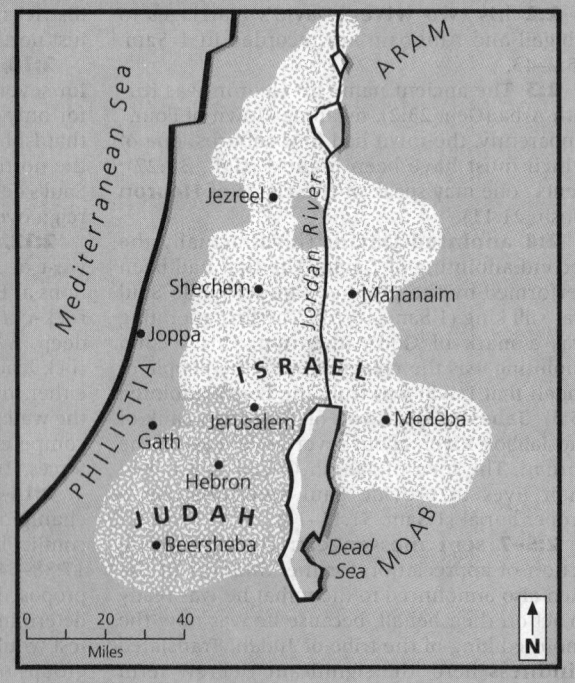

2:32 After burying Asahel at **Bethlehem,** six miles south of Jerusalem, Joab and his men marched another fourteen miles to **Hebron,** David's capital (v. 1).

3:1–39 The account of Abner's defection to David and his subsequent murder by Joab left Ishbosheth's kingship in a precarious state.

3:1 a long war: The conflict between the followers of Saul and the followers of David was not limited to the battle recorded in ch. 2. Hostilities continued between the two royal houses, with David gradually gaining ascendancy.

3:2 David began his reign in Judah with two wives, Ahinoam and Abigail. In Hebron, he married four more wives, each of whom bore him a son. This was despite the warning against polygamy in Deut. 17:17. **Amnon,** notorious for having violated his sister Tamar, was later murdered by Absalom (ch. 13). Amnon's mother, **Ahinoam,** is not the same as Saul's wife Ahinoam (1 Sam. 14:50).

3:3 Chileab is called Daniel in 1 Chr. 3:1. The story of his mother, **Abigail,** is found in 1 Sam. 25. She is not the same as Abigail the mother of Amasa (17:25). **Absalom** died at the hands of Joab (18:14). Absalom's mother, **Maacah,** is identified as **the daughter of Talmai, king of Geshur.** Geshur was the Aramean kingdom on the east side of the Jordan, northeast of the Sea of Galilee. David used marriage alliances to conclude treaties and cement relations between Israel and foreign nations. However, such alliances were forbidden by God's Law (Deut. 7:3).

3:4 Adonijah attempted to take his father's throne just before David proclaimed Solomon king (1 Kin. 1). **Shephatiah** and his mother, **Abital,** are mentioned only here and in 1 Chr. 3:3.

3:5 Ithream and his mother, **Eglah,** are mentioned only here and in 1 Chr. 3:3. **in Hebron:** These six sons, each from a different mother, constituted the royal family during David's reign over the house of Judah. The dynastic lists in Chronicles include four sons of David by Bathsheba (1 Chr. 3:5) and nine other sons whose mothers are not named (1 Chr. 3:6–8).

3:6, 7 The phrase **strengthening his hold** implies that Abner was usurping Ishbosheth's authority, becoming the power behind the throne. **father's concubine:** Ishbosheth's charge, that Abner was having sexual relations with one of Saul's concubines, was serious. The royal harem was the property of the king's successor. Taking a king's concubine was tantamount to claiming the throne (16:20–22). **Rizpah** plays out another tragic role in 2 Sam. 21.

3:8 Am I a dog's head: In the ancient Middle East, dogs were scavengers, living off dead animals and garbage, and were viewed with contempt (9:8; Deut. 23:18; 1 Sam. 17:43; 1 Kin. 22:38; 2 Kin. 9:36). **that belongs to Judah:** Since Judah was the enemy of Israel, this phrase intensifies the metaphor.

3:9, 10 The phrase **may God do so to Abner** is a prayer for divine judgment should Abner fail to keep his oath. The words **as the LORD** has sworn indicate that Abner knew that David had been divinely chosen to succeed Saul (vv. 17, 18). The expression **from Dan to Beer-**

IN LIFE ## Giving Birth to Trouble

David is an illustration of the fact that success in a career does not necessarily translate into success in personal and family life. While the "house of David {his position and stature as king-designate} grew stronger and stronger" (1 Sam. 3:1), his family life was headed for serious trouble.

Evidence for that can be found in the list of David's six sons born at Hebron (3:2–5). Each was born to a different wife, which indicates that David was strengthening his political ties through marriage, a common practice for ancient kings. But we see that in David's case it was a foolish practice. Not only did David's polygamy violate the Law (Deut. 17:17), it also led to enormous problems as he tried to blend his various families together. For example, David's son Amnon violated his half-sister Tamar, then was killed by her avenging brother, Absalom. That led to a bitter estrangement between Absalom and his father that resulted in the treason and, ultimately, the death of Absalom—all to David's great regret (2 Sam. 13–18).

David's polygamy also set a poor example for his successor, Solomon, who expanded his kingdom while marrying 700 wives and 300 concubines. Just as the Law had predicted, these women turned his heart away from the Lord to idols (1 Kin. 11:3). The Lord judged him for that sin by allowing the kingdom to be divided after his death (11:9–13). David demonstrates the biblical principle that the sins of the parents can extend "to the third and fourth generations" (Ex. 20:5).

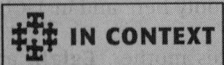 **IN CONTEXT**   **Abner's Outrage**

shbosheth's accusation that Abner, his father Saul's general, had sexually violated the late king's concubine outraged the seasoned veteran. The charge amounted to impugning the commander's loyalty and accusing him of attempting to steal the throne for himself (2 Sam. 3:7, 8).

It was common for wealthy and powerful men in the ancient world to own concubines, female slaves with whom they were free to have sexual relations. Concubines were not considered "full" wives, but they did enjoy certain rights that common slaves did not.

Had Abner actually intended to stage a political coup, he probably would have taken Saul's concubine for his own, the way conquerors commonly did in that era (compare 16:15–22).

sheba is used to refer to the whole territory of Israel from its northern to its southern border, a distance of about 150 miles (Judg. 20:1; 1 Sam 3:20).

3:11, 12 Whose is the land: The implication here is that the land could be David's if he entered into a binding agreement with Abner, because it was Abner who actually held all the power.

3:13 David's first wife **Michal** (1 Sam. 18:17–27) was left in Gibeah when David fled from Saul's court (1 Sam. 19:11–17). She was later given by Saul, perhaps out of spite, to a man named Palti (1 Sam. 25:44). This action may have been a burst of spite on Saul's part. David's request that she be brought back may have indicated his love for her. Certainly, we remember the notices of her love for him (1 Sam. 18:20, 28; 2 Sam. 3:5). A more cynical reading of the text may suggest that David needed to have Saul's daughter "in his camp," so to speak, to help to align the hearts of the northern tribes to his cause.

3:14, 15 David's request for Michal was formally addressed to Ishbosheth. This might have been a difficult demand for Ishbosheth since Michal was his sister. However, he was powerless to thwart Abner's plan. **a hundred foreskins:** David mentioned the number which Saul had originally asked for; David actually paid him double (1 Sam. 18:25–27).

3:16 Michal's second husband appears brokenhearted at her forced removal from his home. Nothing is said of Michal's feelings; however she grew to despise David (6:16). **Bahurim** was near Jerusalem, east of Olivet (16:5).

3:17, 18 For the LORD has spoken: The Bible does not record elsewhere the divine promise quoted by Abner and referred to in vv. 9, 10. It is possible that this was a revelation that God gave to him alone.

3:19 David faced the most opposition from Saul's tribe, **Benjamin.** Abner personally campaigned for David's kingship in this tribe. After

winning support for David in Israel, Abner proceeded to **Hebron** (2:1) to announce the people's decision to acknowledge David as king.

3:20, 21 The negotiations between Abner and David were productive. Plans were laid for David's rule to be extended over the northern tribes. The use of the **feast** as the setting for establishing their new political alliance has many parallels in ancient times as well as

 **IN FOCUS**   **"covenant"**

(Heb. *berith*) (2 Sam. 3:12; 23:5; Gen. 6:18; 15:18; Ex. 2:24; Jer. 31:31) Strong's #1285: Generally, the word *covenant* refers to an agreement between two or more parties. The term often refers to God's self-imposed obligation to reconcile fallen humanity to Himself. God's redemptive plans throughout history promise salvation and blessing to those who obediently serve Him. God made several covenants with His people in the OT. He made a covenant with Noah after the Flood (Gen. 9:9–17), a covenant with Abraham (Gen. 17:15, 16), and a covenant with David (2 Sam. 23:5). These covenants prefigure the supreme covenant made through Christ's sacrifice on the Cross. Jesus initiated the New Covenant which Jeremiah foresaw (Jer. 31:31–34).

modern. There is something about eating together that provides an occasion for forming and deepening friendships and for providing intimacy. The amicable conclusion was noted in the words **and he went in peace.**

3:22, 23 The words **gone in peace** are repeated (v. 21), to emphasize that the hostilities between David and Abner had been resolved.

3:24, 25 What have you done: Learning of Abner's visit, Joab challenged the king for allowing the commander of a hostile army and a cousin of Saul to come and go from Hebron without being apprehended and put to death. He insisted that Abner was trying to trick David with a display of good faith and sincerity, and that his real purpose was to gather intelligence.

3:26 The action of Joab is entirely his own at this point. The location of the **well of Sirah** is uncertain, but it may be identified with the spring and reservoir about a mile north of Hebron called 'Ain Sarah.

3:27 stabbed him: This was an act of treachery, especially in Hebron, a city of refuge (Josh. 20:7). In a city of refuge, a blood avenger could not slay a murderer without a trial (Num. 35:22–25). Joab wanted to avenge the death of **Asahel his brother,** who was killed in the course of a battle (2:18–23).

3:28, 29 My kingdom and I: David issued a public proclamation denying any involvement in the murder of Abner. The death of Abner was not only an act of treachery, but also a great blow to David's hopes for a peaceable unification of the nation under his control. **Let it rest on the head of Joab:** This verse forms a strong curse on the household of Joab. Both a discharge (Lev. 15:2–33) and leprosy (Lev. 13) made the afflicted person ritually unclean, an outcast from the community. The phrase **leans on a staff** describes one who is crippled, lame, or blind.

3:30 Abishai was Joab's other brother (2:18). His involvement in the murder of Abner is mentioned only here.

3:31, 32 Tear your clothes: These actions were associated in ancient times with mourning the dead (1:11; Gen. 37:34). **Sackcloth** (Heb. *saqqîm*) was coarse material, in contrast to more comfortable clothing. **followed the coffin:** David led the funeral procession.

3:33, 34 as a fool dies: Certainly a warrior like Abner deserved a more noble death. How much better for Abner to have died fighting than to have been stabbed to death while under a promise of safe passage. **Your hands were not bound:** Abner was not guilty of any crime that required him to be bound with chains and fetters.

3:35 The murder of Abner had the potential of breaking the fragile union of the twelve tribes. David refused to participate in the meal that was customarily served to mourners after the burial as evidence of his genuine remorse. In his oath **God do so to me, and more also,** David prayed that God would do the worst thing imaginable should he eat food before sunset (compare a similar oath by Abner in 3:9).

3:36, 37 All Israel refers to the people of the northern tribes and the Benjamites, who would be inclined to suspect David of plotting the murder of Ishbosheth's military commander. All the people became confident of David's innocence.

3:38 His servants refers to David's confidential servants or advisors. The words **a prince and a great man** reflect how highly David regarded Abner.

3:39 Weak (Heb. *rak*) means "tender" or "sensitive," in contrast with the term **harsh** (Heb. *qashîm*), used to describe Joab and Abishai. "Weak" may refer to David's emotional state due to the murder or Abner. He may also be alluding to his sense of inadequacy in dealing with the crime perpetrated by Joab. Unable to deal with the matter, he committed retribution to God (but see 1 Kin. 2:5, 6, 28–35).

4:1 Saul's son Ishbosheth lost the **heart** to act as king, since Abner, his primary supporter, was gone. **Israel was troubled** at the possibility of an attack by David's men.

4:2, 3 The fact that **Baanah** and **Rechab** were from the tribe of **Benjamin,** the tribe of Saul, makes their actions all the more reprehensible. **Beeroth** was one of the four cities of the Gibeonites (Josh. 9:17), with whom Joshua had made a covenant. For some reason, **the Beerothites fled to Gittaim** and their city was reoccupied by Benjamites (Neh. 11:33).

4:4 Merib-Baal, which means "The Master Is Advocate," was the original name of Jonathan's son (1 Chr. 8:34; 9:40). The author of Samuel changed it to **Mephibosheth,** meaning "He Scatters Shame," apparently to avoid the idolatrous implications of the word Baal.

4:5, 6 The **house of Ishbosheth** was at Mahanaim (2:8, 12). Ishbosheth was taking his midday rest, as perhaps were the members of the palace guard.

4:7 The murderers fled by way of **the plain,** meaning by way of the Jordan valley.

4:8–12 The account of the punishment of Ishbosheth's murderers is similar to the record of David's dealings with the Amalekite who claimed to have killed Saul (2 Sam. 1:1–16). The similarity between the two accounts provides an air of suspense. The reader knows how David will view this deed, but the assassins are in blissful ignorance of how the king will "reward" their actions.

4:8–10 Rechab and Baanah **brought the head of Ishbosheth to David,** perhaps in hopes of receiving a reward. They used the spiritual language **the Lord has avenged** to describe their despicable actions. Yet their lofty words did not fool David. The oath **as the Lord lives** implies that David was under God's protection. There was no need to kill Ishbosheth to defend David's life. **Someone** was the Amalekite who claimed to have killed Saul (1:2–16).

4:11 Ishbosheth was viewed as a **righteous person** since he was innocent of any wicked deed or crime. He had simply assumed royal power after the death of his father Saul.

4:12 The execution of the assassins was justified on the basis of Gen. 9:5. Their corpses were **hanged,** or impaled, **by the pool in Hebron,** which was frequented daily by the people of the city. Their bodies warned the people of the consequences of such foolish and evil actions. David demonstrated his respect for the slain son of Saul by having the **head of Ishbosheth** buried in Abner's grave at Hebron.

5:1 All the tribes refers to tribal leaders, such as elders and heads of clans (v. 3). **We are your bone and your flesh** means "we are your relatives" (Gen. 29:14; Judg. 9:2). The representatives of the tribes of Israel acknowledged their solidarity as a people.

both to God and to human rulers (Ps. 23:1; Ezek. 34:1–10).

5:3–5 before the LORD: Making a covenant was not merely a civil arrangement but a sacred occasion. **they anointed:** This was David's third anointing (2:4; 1 Sam. 16:13). His first anointing was in anticipation of his rule; his second was acknowledgment of his rule over Judah; his third was acknowledgment of his rule over the entire nation.

5:6–9 David's first move as king was to conquer Jebus, which came to be known as **Jerusalem.** The name Jerusalem may mean "Foundation of Peace." The city itself was strategically located in the hill country near the border of Judah and Benjamin, making it a foreign wedge between the northern and southern tribes. Although the city was attacked by men from both Benjamin and Judah, the Jebusites were not driven out of Jerusalem at the time of the conquest (Josh. 15:63; Judg. 1:21). The city had a long history. An earlier name of Jerusalem

Photo by Howard Vos

Modern Hebron, successor to the ancient city of the same name, which served as David's headquarters during the early years of his reign (2 Sam. 5:1–5).

5:2 The words **led Israel out** speak of David's service as a military leader during Saul's reign. The word **shepherd** is a vivid metaphor of the relationship between a king and his people. The Scriptures apply this metaphor

was Salem, known because of its righteous king Melchizedek (Gen. 14:18–20). Mt. Moriah— where Abraham had prepared to offer Isaac— was also located at Jerusalem (Gen. 22:2). Jerusalem would eventually become not only the site of the temple, but also the place where Jesus died and rose again.

5:6 The Jebusites were one of the Canaanite tribes living in the Promised Land (Gen. 10:16–18). Jerusalem was on a hill just south of Mt. Moriah, with steep cliffs on all sides except the north, making it a natural fortress. The defenders felt able to boast that **the blind and the lame** would be enough to defeat David.

5:7 Jerusalem is referred to as the **stronghold of Zion.** The word Zion originally applied to the Jebusite stronghold, which became **the City of David** after its capture. As the city expanded to the north, encompassing Mt. Moriah, the temple mount came to be called **Zion** (Ps. 78:68, 69). Eventually the term was used as a synonym for Jerusalem (Is. 40:9).

5:8 The **water shaft** extended about 230 feet up from the Gihon spring to the top of the hill where the Jebusite fortress was situated (2 Chr. 32:30). The tunnel gave the city a secure water supply in the event of a siege. The phrase **the lame and the blind** became something of a taunt, which David turned first into a challenge, and then into a victory song.

5:9 The term **City of David** is used in Luke 2:11 to refer to Bethlehem, the city of David's birth. Here the term refers to Zion, the city from which he ruled Israel. The term **Millo** is derived from the Hebrew "to fill," and means "mound" or "terrace." The "Millo" has been identified by archaeologists with the terraces built on the eastern slope of the city which formed supporting walls for the buildings above. Excavations at the city of Jerusalem continue unabated, hampered only by the twin facts that this is a living city and that these places have great religious significance. It is difficult to excavate in places where people live and work, and some religious authorities have objections to excavations in areas that may once have been sacred sites.

5:10 God of hosts may also be translated "God of Armies" (6:2). The hosts (Heb. *seba'ôt*) are the armies of angels that are at the Lord's command (v. 24).

5:11, 12 International recognition of David's rule came quickly. Because of the thirty-three year reign of David in Jerusalem (v. 5), some suggest that the **Hiram** mentioned here may have been the father of the ally who assisted Solomon in building the temple (1 Kin. 5:1–10). This would lead one to conclude that the name "Hiram" may have been a throne name in

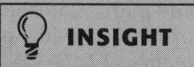 **INSIGHT** **An Invincible Fortress?**

The Jebusites assumed that they were invincible because of their strong fortifications (2 Sam. 5:6). But they failed to realize that God had determined to give David the victory, and so their well-defended citadel fell (5:7). Psalm 24 may recall this victory. As if mocking the defiant boast of the Jebusites, that "David cannot come in here," the psalm offers a ringing chorus, "The King of glory shall come in!" (Ps. 24:7).

Phoenicia, even as "Pharaoh" and "Abimelech" (Gen. 20:2; 26:1) were throne names in Egypt and Gerar. However, the wording of 1 Kin. 5:1 suggests that this is the same figure, for "he had always loved David." **Tyre,** located on the Mediterranean coast north of Israel, was a Phoenician city noted for its commerce, craftsmen, and wealth. Hiram's kindness toward David was probably prompted by economic interests, for he could profit from trade with Israel. The **house** that Hiram had built for David must have been sumptuous for the place and time. Most buildings in Israel were made of stone. The use of cedar wood added elegance to David's palace. Certainly he spoke of his home with reasonable pride (7:2).

5:13 These marriages reflect David's involvement in international treaties and alliances which were sealed with the marriage of a king's daughter to the other participant in the treaty. **Concubines,** wives who did not have the legal rights of a true wife, were part of a royal harem. The status of kings in ancient times was often

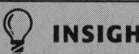 **INSIGHT** **The Start of a Long Friendship**

The initiative shown by Hiram of Tyre (2 Sam. 5:11) was perhaps the wisest investment he ever made. His trade with David blossomed into a friendship with David's successor, Solomon, which resulted in an extraordinarily lucrative contract for cedar and other resources for the temple.

measured in part by the size of their harems. Yet for Israel's kings, there had been a warning from God against acquiring many wives (Deut. 17:17).

5:14 Shammua is known as **Shimea** in 1 Chr. 3:5. Shammua, Shobab, Nathan, and Solomon were David's sons by Bathsheba (1 Chr. 3:5), the wife of Uriah. David planned Uriah's death so that he could marry Bathsheba (ch. 11). The child born of David and Bathsheba's affair died in infancy (12:15–23).

5:15, 16 The lists in 1 Chr. 3:5–9 and 1 Chr. 14:4, 5 record two additional sons, Nogah and another Eliphelet (Elpelet in 1 Chr. 14:4).

5:17–25 The **Philistines** were Indo-Europeans, actually, Mineon Greeks, who migrated from the Aegean Islands and Asia Minor to the eastern Mediterranean region about 1200 B.C. The Philistines established a strong political and military organization on Israel's southern coastal plain and were for many years a major threat to the Israelites. It was during one of Israel's wars against the Philistines that young David first became a national hero (1 Sam. 17). The Philistines may have ruled as a class of warrior-lords over the indigenous Canaanite populations in their areas. They were powerful warriors who made brilliant use of the chariot, the "tanks" of the ancient world. These then hi-tech military machines made them especially

INSIGHT

A Long-Overdue Victory

David's decisive defeat of the Philistines (2 Sam. 5:25) was a major break-through for the establishment of his kingdom. For years the Philistines had harassed the Israelites, who seemed unable to completely vanquish them. But by pushing them back as far as the Gezer, David was setting up the Philistines for the knockout punch they would soon receive from the Egyptians.

strong on the coastal plain, but these chariots were not as effective in the highlands of Judah. The Philistines are characteristically spoken of with great disdain by David and his compatriots as "the uncircumcised" (1 Sam. 14:6; 17:26; 31:4; 2 Sam. 1:20).

5:17 The Hebrew word translated **stronghold** means "mountain fortress," suggesting a fortress other than Jerusalem. Therefore, it is possible that these attacks took place between

the time when David was anointed over all Israel (v. 4) and when he captured Jerusalem (vv. 6–10).

5:18 The Valley of Rephaim, or "Valley of the Giants" (21:15–22), extends southwest from Jerusalem toward the coastal plain. The significance of the valley as a strategic approach to Jerusalem is evidenced by the fact that the Philistines made a second attempt to capture the city from this route (v. 22).

5:19, 20 As was his custom, **David inquired of the LORD** before engaging the Philistines in battle (2:1; 1 Sam. 23:2; 30:8). In matters of warfare, David was not presumptuous. He wished to know the will of God in choosing his battles and their timing.

5:21, 22 The idol **images** which the Philistines had taken into battle to assure them of victory were captured and carried away by David's men. This looting would have been regarded by the Philistines as a defeat of their gods by the God of Israel. According to 1 Chr. 14:12, David and his men burned the idols.

5:23 Mulbery trees (Heb. *beka'îm*) appears only here and in the parallel passage in Chronicles (1 Chr. 14:14). Some scholars prefer the rendering "balsam trees."

5:24 God was suggesting that the sound of rustling leaves in the treetops was in fact the sound of His angelic army going forth to attack (2 Kin. 6:17).

5:25 The **Geba** mentioned here is not the Geba of 1 Sam. 13:3, which was six miles north of Jerusalem. This Geba was most likely located south, in the Valley of Rephaim. **Gezer** was about 20 miles northwest of Jerusalem.

6:1–23 David was intensely interested in the worship of Yahweh and gave considerable attention to the ark of the covenant, which had lain neglected during the reign of Saul. Chapter 6 tells of the transfer of the ark to the new capital at Jerusalem. Since the loss of the holy ark had happened in an early battle with the Philistines (1 Sam. 4; 5), David's determination to restore the ark following his impressive defeat of the Philistines (2 Sam. 5) was most significant.

6:1 The **thirty thousand** men were not all the men of Israel capable of bearing arms, but the best of them.

6:2 Baale Judah, meaning "Masters of Judah," was also called Baalah and Kirjath Jearim (Josh. 15:9; 1 Chr. 13:6). It was a city on the border of Judah and Benjamin, about 10 miles northwest of Jerusalem. **The Name, the LORD of Hosts:** The personal name of God is revealed in Ex. 3:13–15, where the context reveals that the LORD is the mighty God of the patriarchs who intervenes on behalf of His people. At times the Name of God is accompanied by the designation "of Hosts" (5:10), referring to the angelic armies of the universe (1 Kin. 22:19; Luke 2:13) as well as the armies of Israel (1 Sam. 17:45). **Cherubim** are angelic beings generally regarded as guardians of God's holiness (Gen. 3:24; Ex. 25:22; Pss. 80:1; 99:1). God revealed Himself to Moses from between the two cherubim mounted at opposite ends of the mercy seat over the ark of the covenant (Ex. 25:22; Num. 7:89).

6:3, 4 they set the ark of God on a new cart: The Law was specific that the ark was to be carried by the sons of Kohath, not by a cart or any other vehicle (Ex. 25:14, 15; Num. 3:30, 31). David was doing what the Philistines had done (1 Sam. 6:7, 8). The ark had been taken to the **house of Abinadab** after its recovery from the Philistines (1 Sam. 7:1, 2). **The sons of Abinadab** should probably be understood in a broader sense as "the descendants of Abinadab."

6:5 Played literally means they "made merry" with dancing and music (v. 21). The worshipers had a variety of string, wind, and percussion instruments. **Sistrums** refers to Egyptian instruments consisting of rings hanging loosely on metal rods that make a rattling sound when shaken.

6:6 A **threshing floor** was a place for processing grain, separating kernels from the chaff (Ruth 3:2). In order to steady the ark when it

seemed as though it would fall, **Uzzah put out his hand.**

6:7 Although Uzzah's violation was unintentional, his error cost him his life. God had warned His people that not even the Levites could touch the holy objects of the tabernacle; the death penalty had been specified for violators (Num. 4:15).

6:8 David became angry—not at himself for the carelessness that resulted in this calamity, but at God. He named the place of the tragedy **Perez Uzzah,** recalling what had happened.

6:9 David was afraid of the Lord: The tragedy of Uzzah rekindled a necessary "fear of God" in the heart of David. Properly understood (Eccl. 12:13, 14), the fear of the Lord is essential to the pursuit of obedience and holiness.

6:10, 11 Obed-Edom was a Levite of the family of Korah, and later one of the doorkeepers for the ark (1 Chr. 15:18, 24; 26:4–8). He was called **the Gittite** because he was from the Levitical city of Gath Rimmon (Josh. 21:24).

6:12 That the ark had been a source of blessing to the house of Obed-Edom renewed David's interest in finding a way to bring it to Jerusalem.

6:13 This time the ark was carried (Ex. 25:14, 15), rather than transported by cart. Some interpreters think that the procession was halted and sacrifices were offered every **six**

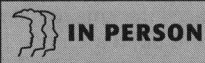 **IN PERSON**   ## A Love That Turned to Hate

Michal's story is tragic and bitter. She fell in love with the handsome David right after the young warrior defeated the giant Goliath (1 Sam. 18:20, 28). He further demonstrated his heroism by killing two hundred Philistines for her hand in marriage (1 Sam. 18:27). Michal's love for David must have only increased. Unfortunately, her love and her life turned sour.

As a result of Michal's feelings for David, she became estranged from her father King Saul. She risked her life in order to save David (1 Sam. 19:11–18), but the result was that she became separated from her first love. Perhaps in retribution for her protection of David, Saul gave Michal to another man, Palti. While living with her new husband, Michal saw her father and her brother Jonathan die in battle, and her other brother Ishbosheth was murdered by assassins.

It appears that Palti loved Michal deeply, for when she was forcibly removed from his home he wept uncontrollably (3:15, 16). We might conclude that she had grown to love him. Yet David demanded that she come back to him. Michal's reunion with David was hardly pleasant. David was no longer the young, courageous warrior who served her father's household. Instead, he was the man who replaced her father on the throne. Moreover, she would have to compete with at least six other women for King David's attention.

It is not likely that the mere actions of David, as he celebrated before the Lord at the return of the ark, brought about Michal's hatred of him (6:16). Her hatred had probably grown over the years. Her sarcastic words on David's great day of religious and spiritual joy came from a lifetime of pain (6:20). Unlike her brother Jonathan, Michal did not accept her God-given lot and trust God for her future happiness (1 Sam. 23:16–18). Instead, she became bitter not only at David but also toward God. Tragically, Scripture gives no indication that there was any healing for Michal. She died childless (6:23).

paces. It is also possible that the sacrifices were offered only once after the ark bearers had advanced the first six paces, thus consecrating the solemn procession.

6:14 The Hebrew word translated **danced** (*mekarker*) here literally means "whirled." The **linen ephod** was a short, sleeveless garment worn by priests (1 Sam. 2:18). David wore it to honor the Lord in view of his priestly activities that day (v. 13).

6:15 Shouting was an expression of celebration and triumph (Is. 44:23). The **trumpet** refers to the ram's horn or the shofar (2:28).

6:16 Michal, Saul's daughter, had been given to David in marriage (1 Sam. 18:27), and then to another man (1 Sam. 25:44) after David had fled from Jerusalem. Abner, Ishbosheth's military commander, had arranged her return to David (2 Sam. 3:13–16).

6:17 David erected a tent, no doubt patterned after the **tabernacle** of Moses, to serve as a temporary shelter for the ark until a more permanent building could be constructed. **burnt offerings:** See Lev. 1. **peace offerings:** See Lev. 3.

6:18 he blessed the people: David acted as a priest for the congregation; in this respect, he is a type of the Savior Jesus who is the great King and Priest.

6:19 A distinctive feature of the peace offering (v. 17) was that a portion would be eaten by the worshiper as a fellowship meal before the Lord. David shared this meal with those who participated in the celebration. **A cake of raisins** was a sweet treat (Song 2:5) sometimes used for religious offerings in Canaanite rites (Hos. 3:1) as well as in the worship of God.

6:20 to bless his household: At the moment of his greatest spiritual experience, David took pleasure in the prospect of bringing God's blessing to his home, only to be met by the curses of his wife. The scornful remark about David's **uncovering himself** no doubt refers to the priestly attire worn by the king instead of his royal robes (v. 14). Dancing about in this short garment, David had exposed more of himself than Michal thought appropriate. The term **base fellows** refers to empty persons, those of no value or worth.

6:21 David rebuked Michal by reminding her that God had chosen him in place of her **father** Saul, an evidence of divine blessing on his religious commitment and enthusiasm.

6:22 David declared that he would gladly be **even more undignified** and **humble** in his own sight to worship the Lord and to be **held in honor** by those who shared his spiritual values.

6:23 Michal's childlessness was the result of either estrangement from David, or perhaps divine punishment because of her refusal to join in the celebration of God's name. Thus there was no successor to the throne from the house of Saul. His sons were all dead, and his daughter remained childless. It is evident from this verse that Michal had not had children with Palti during her years as his wife.

7:1–29 This chapter records the establishment of the Davidic Covenant, which amplifies and confirms the nation or seed promises of the Abrahamic Covenant (Gen. 12:1–3). The issues of this chapter are of immense theological importance. They reach all the way to the coming of Savior Jesus and especially to His coming reign on the throne of David.

7:1 The **house** refers to the palace that the Phoenicians had built for David (5:11). **Rest from all his enemies** probably refers to the peace that prevailed after David's defeat of the Philistines (5:17–25).

7:2 Nathan was a personal advisor to David. As a **prophet** (Ex. 7:1, 2), he spoke for God, advising David on religious matters. Nathan later confronted David regarding his sins of adultery and murder (12:1–15). He helped Bathsheba secure the throne for Solomon (1 Kin. 1:10–45), aided in the establishment of music in the temple worship (2 Chr. 29:25), and chronicled the reigns of David and Solomon (1 Chr. 29:29; 2 Chr. 9:29). Although there was nothing immoral about dwelling in **a house of cedar,** David realized he had to give his attention to spiritual priorities.

7:3, 4 Nathan encouraged the king to follow the leading of his heart and build a temple for the ark. However, he spoke on the basis of his own understanding and not as a word from the Lord. His words **the Lord is with you** indicate in this context a general blessing and not a specific utterance of God.

7:5 Although Nathan had at first encouraged David to build a temple for the ark (v. 3), the Lord revealed that this was not His intention at all. The question **Would you build a house for Me to dwell in** implied a negative answer.

7:6 A tent was a traveler's dwelling. The **tabernacle** (Heb. *mishkan*) was the portable structure or the "dwelling place" of God in the midst of His people (Ex. 25:9, 22).

7:7 Throughout the history of God's dealings with the Israelites, never once did He reprove them for failing to build Him a permanent sanctuary. The word **shepherd** is a metaphor of leadership and was used throughout the ancient Middle East to refer to national leaders (Ezek. 34:2). The Great Shepherd is, of course, God (Ps. 23).

7:8 The formal and profound nature of the text is emphasized by the use of the name **Lord of hosts.** God reminded David of His gracious dealings in taking him from the humble role of a shepherd to serve as king over His people.

7:9 A great name or reputation was highly valued by the Hebrews. As God promised to make the name Abram great (Gen. 12:2), so He promised David that his name would be renowned.

7:10 God promised to provide Israel a secure dwelling place in the land of Israel. No longer would the Israelites be exposed to repeated attacks from their enemies, as had happened during the time of the judges.

7:11 house: David wanted to build God a house—that is, a temple (vv. 2–7). Instead, God intended to build David a house—that is, a dynasty of long duration.

7:12 The first provision of the Davidic covenant was that David would have a son for whom God would establish a **kingdom.** This son would be Solomon (1 Chr. 22:6–10).

7:13 House here refers to the temple (1 Kin. 6). God also promised **to establish the throne of** Solomon's **kingdom forever** (1 Chr. 22:6–10). This is not to say that Solomon would rule forever. Rather, the right to rule, represented by the image of the throne, would always belong to his descendants. Further, there would always be a male heir who would be able to rule.

7:14 iniquity: The sins of David's sons would require divine chastening (1 Kin. 11:1–13). The **rod of men** and **blows of the sons of men** would serve as instruments of chastening (1 Kin. 11:14, 23).

7:15 Although Solomon's sins would justify chastening, God promised that His **mercy** would not be removed, as was necessary in the case of Saul (1 Sam. 13:13, 14; 15:22, 23).

7:16, 17 Here God capsulized the provisions of the Davidic Covenant. The Lord promised that David's **house**, **kingdom**, and **throne** will endure **forever.** In other words: (1) the line, or house, of David will always be the royal line; (2) the right to rule will always belong to David's offspring; (3) the right to a literal, earthly kingdom will never be taken from David's posterity. The promise does not guarantee that the rule by David's posterity would never be interrupted (Hos. 3:4, 5). Indeed, it was interrupted when Judah was taken into exile (2 Kin. 25:1–21). However, the prerogative to exercise the privilege of ruling would always belong to the Davidic dynasty (Ps. 89:20–37). In Luke 1:32, 33 the angel Gabriel promised that Mary's son, Jesus, would receive the throne, house,

> *David wanted God's reputation to be magnified through the fulfillment of His promise.*

and kingdom promised David and his posterity. The ultimate fulfillment of this promise will be realized at the Second Advent when Christ returns to reign over His people (Rev. 20:1–6).

7:18 The words **sat before the LORD** indicate that David was in the tent which served to house the ark. **Who am I, O Lord GOD:** David's rhetorical question reflected his sense of unworthiness to have been extended such a gracious promise (vv. 12–16).

7:19, 20 David acknowledged that what God had done for him so far was far greater than anything he deserved. As if this were only **a small thing,** God now extended the promise concerning David's dynasty far into the future. All of human history leads inevitably to the rule of Christ on earth. This is its destiny, its prophetic fulfillment, the final meaning of all history.

7:21 For Your word's sake alludes either to earlier promises of God concerning Judah, the royal tribe (Gen. 49:10; Num. 24:17), or to the prophecy of David's kingship (1 Sam. 13:14).

7:22, 23 All that we have heard with our ears refers to the shared tradition regarding God's work in history (Deut. 4:32–40).

7:24 Your people Israel: At the heart of God's promise to David was the continuation of His promise to the nation of Israel (Gen. 12:1–3).

7:25 Having praised God for His gracious works, David prayed for the fulfillment of the promise. As David undoubtedly knew, God's will would be accomplished whether he prayed for it or not. But like David, when we pray *in* God's will *for* God's will, we became a *part* of His will. We also become an expectant people, ready to respond to God with great praise when He has accomplished His will (Ps. 142).

7:26, 27 The **name** of God refers here to His reputation. David wanted God's reputation to be magnified through the fulfillment of His promise.

7:28, 29 You are God, and Your words are true: David acknowledged that God could be trusted to fulfill His promise.

8:1–18 Chapter 8 records the expansion of David's kingdom as the Lord blessed and prospered him. The wars undertaken against surrounding lands were designed to protect Israelite settlements in Transjordan and the nation's frontiers against possible invaders. God gave David many great victories, which expanded both his empire and his fame. There was also within the military conquests of David

---

✠ IN CONTEXT   Being Remembered

David made a name for himself in the Valley of Salt (2 Sam. 8:13, 14), probably the wasteland plain southwest of the Dead Sea. But while his exploits greatly increased his reputation among his own people, they sowed lasting bitterness elsewhere, which would come back to haunt his successor, Solomon.

The "name" that David earned came at the expense of the lives of 18,000 Syrians, who probably were people of Edom. God explicitly commanded his people not to "abhor" the Edomites, since they were descended from the same ancestor, Jacob (Deut. 23:7, 8). Yet David's general, Joab, carried out a six-month campaign of genocide "until he had cut down every male in Edom" (1 Kin. 11:15, 16). This delighted the Israelites, who had long hated the Edomites.

However, an Edomite boy named Hadad watched the slaughter before his father's servants escaped with him to Egypt. He never forgot what he had seen. Years later, after David had died and his son Solomon had turned away from the Lord, God allowed Hadad to come back to Palestine, where he became a perennial thorn in Solomon's side (11:14, 19–22).

---

the fulfillment of the stated foreign policy for Israel in Torah; Israel was to eliminate the Canaanite peoples, who were under God's judgment, and they were to subjugate the surrounding nations to the rule of Israel and the rule of God (Deut. 20).

8:1 The Philistines seem to have migrated from the Aegean Islands and Asia Minor to the eastern Mediterranean region around 1200 B.C. They settled on the coastal plain of Israel and developed a relatively advanced culture and a powerful army. The Philistines were a major threat to Israel during the reigns of Saul and David (5:17; 1 Sam. 13:5; 17:1; 23:1; 28:1).

8:2 The Moabites were descendants of the incestuous relationship between Lot and his older daughter (Gen. 19:36, 37). These people occupied the land opposite Judah, east of the Jordan River and the Dead Sea. This verse may indicate that David spared the young Moabites (whose height was **a line**) and executed the adults (whose height was **two lines**). In any event, the survivors became vassals, or **servants** of David. Centuries later, the Moabites won their freedom from being vassals to Israel (2 Kin. 1:1).

8:3 David's campaign to the north resulted in the defeat of **Hadadezer,** who ruled the Aramean kingdom of **Zobah,** which extended north of Damascus.

8:4 hamstrung: David disabled the horses by cutting the back sinews of the hind legs to prevent them from being used for military activity (Josh. 11:6, 9).

8:5, 6 The use of the term **Syrians** is a common misunderstanding. The Hebrew text uses the term "Arameans." The existence of Syria as a political entity began in the Hellenistic Period (332–63 B.C.). At the time of David, the

region was called "Aram" and the people "Arameans."

8:5 Damascus, located at an oasis near the foot of the Anti-Lebanon mountains, was one of the most strategically located cities of the ancient world. Damascus lay at the crossroads of the two main international highways—the Via Maris, leading south and west to Egypt, and the King's Highway, leading from the east side of the Jordan south to Arabia.

8:6 The **garrisons** of Israelite soldiers were intended to keep the **Syrians** of **Damascus** under David's control.

8:7 Shields of gold were splendid trophies of war (1 Kin. 10:16, 17).

8:8 Betah, an Aramean city, was also known as Tibhath (1 Chr. 18:8). **Berothai,** also known as Berothah (Ezek. 47:16), was about 30 miles northwest of Damascus.

8:9 Hamath was about 100 miles northeast of Damascus.

8:10 The rich gifts of **Toi,** king of Hamath, reflect his desire to establish friendly relations with his powerful new neighbor. The gifts may also indicate that Toi voluntarily submitted to David and became his vassal.

8:11, 12 The **silver and gold** that David received from the nations he conquered were turned over to the priests to be used in building the temple (1 Kin. 7:51).

8:13 Name refers to the reputation **David** gained as a result of his military exploits.

8:14, 15 David reigned over all Israel: As a result of David's conquests, the sovereignty of Israel extended from the Gulf of Aqaba and the River of Egypt to the Euphrates River—the very region God had promised Abraham in Gen. 15:18. The words translated **judgment and justice** together mean "genuine justice." David

⚒ IN DEPTH | David's Cabinet

U nder David, the Israelite monarchy became firmly established. The description of David's cabinet gives a helpful picture of how the government was organized:

- Administrative duties were supervised by David's sons (2 Sam. 3:2–5; 5:13, 14). David also
  governed through garrisons, governors, and vassal kings (8:6, 14). This system was later
  streamlined by Solomon, who named twelve district governors, two of whom were sons-in-
  law.

Like other kings in the ancient world, David had an official recorder, Jehoshaphat, whose main role
was to keep a written record of David's exploits and decisions for history's sake.

A man named Seraiah functioned as David's scribe. In later years, scribes were mainly concerned
with copying, editing, and teaching the Law. But during the monarchy, scribes were similar to secretaries of state or chancellors.

- Legal matters were mainly David's responsibility. As king, he took over a role handled by the
  judges prior to the monarchy. It was his job to set the tone for administering justice by setting policy, deciding legal questions, prosecuting offenses, and appointing judges (1 Chr.
  26:29).
- The military was under Joab's command. However, Benaiah was placed over the Cherethites
  and Pelethites (2 Sam. 8:18), who probably acted as David's personal bodyguard.
- Religious matters were handled by Zadok and Ahimelech, the priests. The latter was the
  grandson of Ahimelech, the priest at Nob who had shown kindness to David, for which he
  and his fellow priests were massacred by Saul (1 Sam. 21, 22).

was careful to see that the decisions he made
and the laws he enforced were "fair and right"
for all.

8:16 Joab, the commander-in-chief of
David's army, had led the successful attack on
the city of Jebus, which became David's capital
Jerusalem (1 Chr. 11:6, 7). Joab was David's
nephew; **Zeruiah,** his mother, was David's
sister (1 Chr. 2:13–16). **Jehoshaphat** the
recorder kept track of state business, brought
appropriate concerns to the king's attention,
and advised him on official matters. His career
extended into the reign of Solomon (1 Kin.
4:3).

8:17 Zadok and **Ahimelech** are mentioned as the principal priests during David's
reign (15:24; 1 Sam. 22:20–23; 1 Kin. 1:7, 8).
The scribe served as secretary of state, drafting
official documents, handling correspondence,
and maintaining court records.

8:18 The Hebrew words Cherethites and
Pelethites have been variously understood as
referring to "executioners," "runners," "Cretans," or "Philistines." The form "Pelethites"
may have been created to avoid the suggestion
that the Philistines were too intimately associated with David's army. Whatever their identification, "the Cherethites and the Pelethites"
always appear as parts of David's army (15:18;

20:23). **Chief ministers** (Heb. *kohanîm,* and
usually meaning "priests") were confidential
advisors.

9:1–13 David displays his loyalty toward
Jonathan (1 Sam. 20:42) by ministering to the
physical needs of his crippled son, Mephibosheth. This incident must have taken place at
least fifteen years after Jonathan's death, for
Mephibosheth was five years old then (2 Sam.
4:4) and now he has a young son.

9:1 for Jonathan's sake: David and
Jonathan had entered into a covenant of friendship and protection that was to extend to their
offspring (1 Sam. 18:3, 4; 20:14, 15, 42).

9:2 Ziba was a servant of king Saul (16:1–4;
19:29).

9:3 The kindness of God recalls the words
of the oath that Jonathan had David swear (1
Sam. 20:14).

9:4 Machir the son of Ammiel was a
man, apparently of wealth and position, who
extended hospitality to David during Absalom's
revolt (17:27–29). **Lo Debar** was about 10
miles south of the Sea of Galilee just east of the
Jordan.

9:5, 6 Once he was made aware of Jonathan's
son, David did not hesitate to fulfill his covenant
commitment to his friend. He immediately sent
for Mephibosheth to be brought to Jerusalem.

9:7 Do not fear: Mephibosheth had good reason to be afraid. It was usual in the ancient Middle East for founders of new dynasties to kill the children of former rulers to keep them from trying to regain the throne in the name of their families. **The land of Saul** refers to the house and property at Gibeah which was claimed by David when he took the throne (12:8). To **eat bread** at the king's table was not a temporary honor; it meant that he would have a pension from the king. **continually:** These privileges and provisions would continue throughout Mephibosheth's life.

9:8, 9 such a dead dog as I: Dogs in Israel were regarded as unclean scavengers, and were generally viewed with contempt (2 Kin. 9:34–37; Prov. 26:11). Mephibosheth used the expression as a figure of speech. The remark reflects his low self-image and his astonishment at the grace being shown him.

9:10 your sons and your servants, shall work the land for him: The size of Saul's estate is reflected in the fact that Ziba had 15 sons and 20 servants. **that your master's son may have food to eat:** Although Mephibosheth would always have a place at David's table as a member of the royal court, the income from Saul's estate would provide for his house and family in Jerusalem.

9:11 In his dealings with Mephibosheth, David exemplified God's grace. Mephibosheth was wonderfully blessed, not because of anything he did, but because of David's faithfulness to a covenant promise. Likewise, believers are blessed, not because of any good work (Eph. 2:8, 9), but because of God's faithfulness to the New Covenant (Jer. 31:31–34) and the promises of the gospel. As Mephibosheth was regarded as an adopted son—**like one of the king's sons**—with attendant privileges and blessings, so believers have been adopted as sons and daughters into the family of God (John 1:12; Rom. 8:15; Eph. 1:5).

9:12 The family of Saul continued through **Micha** for several centuries (1 Chr. 8:34–40).

9:13 Mephibosheth had become **lame** as a

result of a fall that had occurred when his nurse was fleeing from Gibeah after the report of the deaths of Saul and Jonathan (4:4). For more on the story of Mephibosheth, read 16:1–4; 19:24–30; 21:7.

10:1–19 This section records the details of 2 Sam. 8:12 regarding David's campaigns against the Ammonites and Arameans. This war was the fiercest and most dangerous struggle that the Israelites experienced during David's reign. The story is told here as background for the account of David's sin with Bathsheba, which occurred while the Israelites were fighting the Ammonites (2 Sam. 11:1).

10:1 The king of **Ammon** was Nahash (v. 2), probably the same Nahash who was defeated by Saul at Jabesh Gilead (1 Sam. 11:1–11).

10:2 as his father showed kindness to me: The occasion of Nahash's kindness is not recorded. One possibility is that Nahash, an enemy of Saul, had given aid to David during his war with Ishbosheth (2:8–4:12). **to comfort him concerning his father:** David wanted to console Hanun over his father's death and to congratulate him on his new position as king.

10:3 David's gesture of kindness was met with suspicion by the king's advisors, **the princes.** They suspected that David had sent the men as spies for the purpose of planning an attack on **the city** of Rabbah (11:1).

10:4 David's servants were abused and humiliated. The beard was regarded in Semitic culture as a significant aspect of a man's appearance. Cutting off half the beard was a very serious insult. **Hanun** doubled the insult when he **cut off their garments,** leaving the soldiers indecently exposed.

10:5 To prevent their further humiliation, David ordered the messengers to remain in **Jericho** until their beards grew back. Jericho was just west of the Jordan and 15 miles northeast of Jerusalem.

10:6 Made themselves repulsive could be literally translated, "made themselves stinking." To protect themselves against Israelite revenge, the Ammonites hired 33,000 merce-

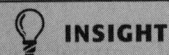 **INSIGHT**   ## Keeping Promises

Many people today have grown skeptical of the campaign promises of politicians. Scripture presents David as a leader who kept his promises. David had sworn that he would show "kindness" (Hebrew, *chesed*, "devotion") to Jonathan's descendants (1 Sam. 20:11–16, 42). So once he was installed as king, David asked whether any of Saul's descendants (and therefore Jonathan's relatives) remained alive (2 Sam. 9:1). Jonathan's son Mephibosheth was found, and David kept his promise (9:7–13).

nary soldiers from several Aramean states to the north. **Beth Rehob** and **Zoba** were Aramean citystates located north of Israel. **Maacah** was a small Aramean kingdom east of the Jordan whose territory was assigned to the half-tribe of Manasseh (Josh. 12:5; 13:11). **Ish-Tob** was a town at Et-Taiyibeh, 45 miles northeast of modern Amman, Jordan.

10:7 Although **mighty men** is used elsewhere to mean a select group of David's warriors (16:6; 20:7), the context here suggests that the whole army of Israel is intended.

10:8 The **gate** was an important part of a city's defensive fortification. The gates of fortified cities usually had towers which gave the defenders an advantage over enemies seeking to break through. Some cities had multiple gates. If attackers broke through one gate, they would find another gate in front of them. The Ammonites fought near the gate so they could retreat into the walled city if the battle turned against them. The mercenary soldiers were in more exposed positions **in the field.**

10:9 before and behind: Joab had allowed himself to become trapped between two enemy forces—the **Syrians** and the Ammonites. If he attacked either enemy separately, his rear troops would be exposed to the other. Joab decided to risk attacking both forces at the same time.

10:10, 11 Abishai, Joab's brother, was placed in command of the rest of the militia in order to attack the **people of Ammon.** Abishai was one of David's mighty men (23:18). He was a brave warrior (1 Sam. 26:6–9) and a successful commander (1 Chr. 18:12, 13), but was impetuous and perhaps even bloodthirsty (16:9; 19:21). He had played a part in the murder of Abner (3:30).

10:12, 13 Joab's exhortation, **be of good**

courage, and let us be strong, is reminiscent of God's charge to Joshua at the beginning of the conquest (Josh. 1:6, 7). **may the LORD do what is good in His sight:** Having done his best to prepare for the battle, Joab took confidence in the sovereignty of God.

10:14, 15 As the battle turned against the **Syrians,** the **people of Ammon** fled for shelter behind their city walls. **The city** refers to Rabbah (11:1), the capital of the Ammonites.

10:16, 17 Hadadezer ruled the Aramean kingdom of Zobah, which extended north of Damascus (8:3). **The River** refers to the Euphrates, designated by God as the northeast boundary of the Promised Land (Gen. 15:18). The 1780–mile-long Euphrates River rises in the mountains of Armenia in modern Turkey and eventually joins the Tigris to empty into the Persian Gulf. With some uncertainty, **Helam** has been identified with Alma, 35 miles east of the Sea of Galilee. **Shobach** is also spelled "Shopach" in 1 Chr. 19:16.

10:18 seven hundred charioteers: According to 1 Chr. 19:18, "seven thousand" charioteers were killed. One of these texts must be the result of a copyist's error. Probably seven hundred is correct.

10:19 All the kings who had been vassal rulers under **Hadadezer** transferred their allegiance to David. The word **served** indicates that they submitted to Israel's authority and brought them tribute (8:2).

11:1–27 This chapter marks a low point in David's career. He yielded to temptation and committed adultery with Bathsheba. This sin led to another, the murder of David's remarkably faithful soldier, Uriah, Bathsheba's husband.

11:1 Kings in the ancient Middle East went to battle **in the spring of the year,** when they

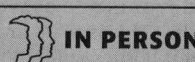 **IN PERSON** | **Joab, a Man Born to War**

The picture of Joab that emerges from the Bible is of a man who cared little for what a fight was about, as long as he was in it. Apparently he was a born fighter, and Scripture records only his many successes as David's military leader: against the Jebusites (2 Sam. 5:7; 1 Chr. 11:6), the Edomites (2 Sam. 8:13, 14; 1 Kin. 11:15, 16), the Syrians (2 Sam. 10:6–14), and the Ammonites (11:1, 2, 14–25; 12:26–29). During this last conquest, Joab became an accomplice in David's plot to kill Uriah.

Joab's political instincts seemed to be based on expediency and self-preservation. He functioned as a mediator between David and his estranged son, Absalom (14:1–33), but later killed the arrogant rebel (18:10–16). Afterward he urged David to reconcile himself to the loss of his son and avoid a mutiny of the army (19:1–8). On other occasions, Joab killed Abner (3:22–39) and Amasa (20:8–10) to advance his own prospects, and even supported Adonijah in his bid to succeed David (1 Kin. 1:7). This last treachery eventually cost Joab his job and his life (2:5, 6, 28–35).

could be assured of good weather and an abundance of food along the way. **David sent Joab** and his army to besiege the Ammonite capital of **Rabbah.** But instead of going off to war with his army, **David remained at Jerusalem.**

11:2 from the roof he saw a woman bathing: In ancient times, Israelite houses had an enclosed courtyard. Bathsheba was actually in her own house. **very beautiful:** Scripture rarely describes the physical appearance of people, but both Bathsheba and David (1 Sam. 16:12) are described as being of exceptionally fine appearance.

11:3 Bathsheba means "Daughter of Sheba." In 1 Chr. 3:5, her name is given as Bathshua.

11:4 she came to him: David was using his power as king to take advantage of Uriah's wife. It is difficult to know what Bathsheba's part was in all of this. **cleansed from her impurity:** Lev. 15:19–24 called for seven days of purification following a woman's monthly period.

11:5, 6 told David: In Lev. 20:10 the command is clear that both parties in an adulterous relationship were to be put to death. But in practice, a woman who became pregnant might be forced to bear the shame and guilt alone. Bathsheba's situation was precarious because it

INSIGHT

The Season of War

As any military strategist knows, the advantage is usually to the aggressor—the army that takes the offensive and uses the element of surprise. For that reason, ancient kings tended to make war in the spring of the year (2 Sam. 11:1), when road conditions were most favorable and troops could move quickly and without warning to an enemy. In Palestine, the rainy season occurs during the cool winter months. Summers are very hot, and the fall is marked by unpredictable thunderstorms off the Mediterranean. Thus the spring was the best season for kings to engage in warfare.

would have been known that her husband was off at war.

11:7 David's approach to Uriah was casual, ordinary—and entirely feigned.

11:8–10 Go down to your house and wash your feet: David encouraged **Uriah** to visit his wife. It is likely that David's words, "wash your feet," meant that Uriah should sleep

with his wife that night. The **gift of food** was given by David for Uriah and Bathsheba to enjoy together, to encourage them to be intimate.

11:11–13 The **ark** accompanied the army on their military campaign (15:24; 1 Sam. 4:3).

11:14–17 Whatever his thoughts, David is desperate now. One sin leads to another. Something unthinkable now becomes a possibility and a plan of action. David now acts in deceit and treachery.

11:14, 15 How sad that David would use the dangers of war to achieve his own ends, that he would send to his death an innocent man, and that he would have no thought of God, while Uriah was consumed with righteousness.

11:16–18 Valiant means outstanding in battle. David sent Uriah to where he thought the fighting would be fiercest.

11:19, 20 charged the messenger: Joab anticipated David's anger over the loss of life and the questions he would ask about why this was allowed to happen.

11:21, 22 Abimelech the son of Jerubbesheth refers to the son of Gideon. Jerubbesheth is also called Jerubbaal or Gideon (Judg. 6:32). Abimelech's death during the siege of **Thebez** is recorded in Judg. 9:50–55. **Was it not a woman:** For a soldier to die at the hand of a woman was regarded as practically a fate worse than death (Judg. 9:54).

11:23, 24 The report revealed that Joab did not follow David's orders exactly. David had told Joab to have Uriah killed by withdrawing soldiers from around him, leaving him to face the enemy alone. Perhaps Joab thought that this would be an obvious betrayal and would be difficult to explain to the other officers in the army. Instead, he devised a plan to have the soldiers fight near the wall. This maneuver endangered more soldiers and resulted in greater loss of life.

11:25, 26 the sword devours one as well as another: In other words, "This is war, some live and some die. Don't let it bother you." With this false bravado of nonchalance, David dismissed the messenger. What a contrast with David's responses to the message of the deaths of Jonathan and Saul (2 Sam. 1)! The pernicious work of sin works in the human heart.

11:27 when her mourning was over: Ordinarily, Israelites mourned a death for seven days (1 Sam. 31:13).

12:1, 2 There were two men: As king, David was the highest judge and the court of final appeal. The words **one rich and the other poor** present the story as a morality tale that would gain David's attention without raising his suspicions.

12:3 The poor man's **ewe lamb** was more a dearly loved pet than a farm animal. The details about sharing **food** and drink emphasize how precious the lamb was to the poor man.

12:4 he took the poor man's lamb: These words are reminiscent of 11:4, "David sent messengers, and took her."

12:5 David's anger was greatly aroused at the loathsome injustice that had been done. **the man who has done this shall surely die:** No capital crime had been committed; ordinarily, the rich man would not have been executed. Ironically, it was David who deserved to die for the crimes of adultery and murder (Lev. 20:10; 24:17).

12:6 he shall restore fourfold: David demanded that restitution be made to the poor man according to the Law (Ex. 22:1).

12:7 You are the man: It took courage and a strong commitment to the Lord for Nathan to speak these words to the king. David in his wrath could have retaliated against the prophet and had him executed. Nathan continued to present the words of God. It was the Lord who had made David king (2:4; 5:3; 1 Sam. 16:13), and it was He who had delivered David from Saul (1 Sam. 19:8–24).

12:8 your master's wives: Saul had had one wife, Ahinoam (1 Sam. 14:50), and one concubine, Rizpah (3:7). There is no indication that David married either of them after Saul's death. Since Ahinoam was the mother of David's wife Michal (1 Sam. 14:49, 50), the Law prohibited her from becoming David's wife (Lev. 18:17). The word translated *wives* (Heb. *neshê*) may also be translated "women," including the female servants and courtesans that became David's when he became king. **I also would have given you much more:** The grace of God to David was not something that was about to be exhausted; all David had to do was ask, and God would have granted him favor upon favor.

12:9 you despised the commandment of the Lord: David had broken the tenth, the seventh, and the sixth commandments (Ex. 20:1–17; Deut. 5:6–21), the ones about coveting, adultery, and murder. The word translated *despised* (Heb. *bazâ*) means "to think light of." This is the same term used of Esau, who despised his birthright (Gen. 25:34). **killed him with the sword of the people of Ammon:** Although David's own sword was clean, there was still blood on his hands.

12:10, 11 The judgment pronounced on

 **IN PERSON** | **An Innocent Victim**

Uriah the Hittite was one of David's mighty men (23:39). The name Uriah means "Flame of the Lord" or "The Lord Is Light." The fact that he is called a Hittite suggests that he may have been a foreign mercenary who had become a worshiper of Israel's God. Immediately, a contrast is set before the reader. On the one hand there was David, the Lord's anointed, the regent of God on earth. On the other hand there was Uriah, a convert—a man who was not born in the faith of Israel but who willingly chose it for his own.

David used his authority as king to take advantage of Uriah's wife Bathsheba while Uriah was fighting a war for Israel. As a result of David's sin, Bathsheba became pregnant. David attempted to cover things up by calling Uriah home from battle. If Uriah had relations with his wife while on leave, he might believe the child was his. However, Uriah, the ever-dedicated soldier, refused to enjoy the comforts of home while his comrades were on the battlefield. In this, he showed himself to be more righteous than David. Uriah's words in 11:11 must have stung David's conscience. He had neglected his duty. Moreover, he had stolen the wife of one of his best soldiers while his warriors risked their lives for him. Yet David persisted in covering up his sin; he attempted to break Uriah's resolve by giving him too much to drink. But even the effects of alcohol did not soften Uriah's determination. Once again, he refused to enjoy the comforts offered him.

Failing to cover up his sin, David plotted the loyal soldier's death. Perhaps David could not face the shame of seeing Uriah after the warrior had learned that David had slept with his wife. David's orders—which were carried back to the battle lines by Uriah himself—were for Joab, the commander of the army, to put Uriah in the heat of battle, and then to withdraw the other soldiers so that Uriah would be left alone and killed. So Uriah died in battle.

After Uriah's death, David took Bathsheba as his wife as soon as possible, to make it appear that the child was legitimate. However, "the thing that David had done displeased the Lord" (11:27). Although David had managed to conceal his sin from the people, God knew about it all. David's sin would not go unpunished (ch. 12). Even the King of Israel had to submit to God's discipline.

INSIGHT — You Are the Man!

Just as David was a man after God's own heart (1 Sam. 13:14), so Nathan was God's gift to the man after His own heart. Scripture introduces him suddenly, when David sought to build a temple to the Lord (2 Sam. 7:1, 2). Nathan revealed that God promised to establish David's dynasty, but that He wanted the construction of a temple to be left for Solomon (7:3–17).

Nathan's next appearance followed David's sin with Bathsheba. He pinpointed David's guilt with the stinging accusation, "You are the man!" Nathan's prophecy concerning David's house (12:10–12) came to pass with Amnon's rape of Tamar (13:1–20), Absalom's murder of Amnon (13:21–29), and Absalom's rebellion against his father and the violation of David's concubines (15:1–18; 16:20–23).

Nathan helped to prevent another of David's sons, Adonijah, from seizing the throne by reminding the king of his promise to make Solomon his successor (1 Kin. 1:11–27). He then assisted in the crowning of Solomon (1:32–40) before disappearing from the account.

David and his family was threefold. (1) Bloodshed would persist all the days of David's life. (2) David's own family would bring **adversity** against him. (3) David's wives would be taken by another. These predictions of judgment were fulfilled in the violation of Tamar (13:11–14), the violent deaths of Amnon and Absalom (13:28, 29; 18:15), and Absalom's public appropriation of David's concubines (16:22).

12:12 David's sin was private, but God's discipline and correction were public.

12:13 I have sinned against the LORD: David did not attempt to rationalize his sin or to make an excuse for himself. A fuller expression of David's confession is found in Ps. 51. **The LORD** also has put away your sin: God accepted David's confession and extended divine forgiveness. **you shall not die:** This is an evidence of divine grace. David was deserving of the death penalty for adultery and murder (Lev. 20:10; Num. 35:31–33). God's grace is able to circumvent His own plan for punishment.

12:14 Although David's sin was forgiven, **the child** born of his adulterous relationship with Bathsheba would die. David's actions had given an opportunity for **the enemies of the LORD** to blaspheme. The Lord could not ignore David's sins and give unbelievers an opportunity to say, "The God of Israel must not be very holy. Look how He tolerates sin in the life of the king!" While God forgives sin, He does not necessarily remove its consequences (Gal. 6:7).

12:15 The verb translated **struck** (Heb. *nagap*) is related to the noun (Heb. *negep*) used of the plague God brought to Egypt that caused the death of the first-born (Ex. 12:13). Here, in a sense, that plague that Yahweh had brought to Egypt so long ago now struck at the home of His king in Jerusalem. For David, like Pharaoh before him, had treated lightly the commands of God. **the child:** The baby seems not to have

lived long enough to be named. Normally a child would be named at the time of circumcision, the eighth day (Luke 1:59).

12:16 pleaded: In this verse, we sense the heart of David in anguish before the Lord. **fasted:** Fasting is an expression of the intensity of a petitioner's concern. It says, "This matter is more important to me than food."

12:17 The elders of his house were the senior officials and advisors of David's royal court.

12:18, 19 The child died: There is no more grievous a line than this for a parent to hear.

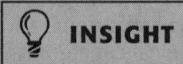

INSIGHT — Public Humiliation

God promised that David's wives would be publicly violated by a member of his own household (2 Sam. 12:11, 12). This prophecy was fulfilled when Absalom lay with David's concubines (16:21, 22). However, the punishment involved more than public humiliation. It would be perceived by the public as though David had been deposed by a conquering ruler.

the servants of David were afraid: Those who had observed the intensity of David's grief *before* the death of his child expected that his rage would be uncontrollable when he learned that the baby had died.

12:20, 21 So David arose from the ground: Usually, we think of the process of grieving as following the death of a loved one.

In David's case, his grieving began when the child became ill. Once the child was dead, there was nothing he could do but worship the Lord. **he went into the house of the Lord:** David left his palace and ascended Mount Moriah to worship at the tabernacle.

12:22 Who can tell: These words give us a remarkable insight into the meaning of prayer. As long as there is any possibility of God intervening in a new way, prayer should continue unabated. If one's hope is in God, then there is never the sense that it is too late until it *is* too late. God may intervene at the very last moment. Should He intervene and find us not still at prayer?

12:23 I shall go to him, but he shall not return to me: The child could not return to life, but David would someday join his son in death.

12:24 The name **Solomon** is related to the Hebrew word for *peace,* and means "Peaceable" or "Peaceful." **the Lord loved him:** God was not going to strike this child as He had the first one (v. 15). This child was God's choice.

12:25 Nathan the prophet was sent by the Lord to give Solomon the name **Jedidiah,** meaning "Beloved of the Lord" (v. 24). The Hebrew name is related to David's name, meaning "Beloved." The divinely sanctioned name, spoken by the prophet of the Lord, was the final symbol of God's forgiveness in the lives of David and Bathsheba.

12:26, 27 taken the city's water supply: Joab assured David that once he had done this the city could not hold out against a siege.

12:28, 29 lest I take the city: Joab wanted David to have the credit for defeating Rabbah and conquering the people of Ammon. So it was that David arrived with his elite corps and won the victory that was years in the making.

12:30 a talent of gold: The crown weighed about 75 pounds. It was an example of the opulence of the spoil from the city, which came **in great abundance.** It is possible that the crown was a symbol of the Ammonite god Milcom (1 Kin. 11:5).

12:31 saws and iron picks and iron axes: The foreign policy of ancient Israel was announced in Deut. 20. The Israelites were to exterminate the Canaanites and subjugate the other nations as God's judgment on the sins of those peoples. David punished the Ammonites in forced work parties with various tools and implements.

13:1 Absalom and **Tamar** were children of David and Maacah, daughter of Talmai, king of Geshur (3:3). **Amnon,** David's firstborn son, was the child of Ahinoam, the woman from Jezreel (3:2). **loved her:** Amnon's love for his half-sister was polluted by the passion of lust.

13:2 it was improper for Amnon to do anything to her: Marriage to a sister or half sister was forbidden by the Law of Moses (Lev. 18:11).

13:3 Jonadab was a cousin to both **Amnon** and Tamar. The Hebrew word translated **crafty** (*hakam*) is used elsewhere for those who are "wise," "technically skilled," or "experienced."

13:4–6 becoming thinner: Amnon's lust for his sister had made him obsessive; his was a self- destructive course of life. Sadly, he would destroy others as well. **pretend to be ill:** Jonadab, Amnon's shrewd cousin, devised a plan to lure unsuspecting Tamar into Amnon's bedroom. Feigning illness would be a means of gaining sympathy and avoiding the usual proprieties.

13:7–11 your brother Amnon's house: Apparently the royal princes had separate residences. This allowed Amnon to put his evil plan into action without the knowledge of the other members of the family. **made cakes in his sight:** Amnon was able to look from his bedroom into the courtyard where the baking was being done.

13:12 While Canaanites and foreigners might have condoned such practices, incest was forbidden among Israelites (Lev. 18:9, 11; 20:17). The words **disgraceful thing** translate a word (*neblâ*) used elsewhere to refer to a grave sin or sexual offense (Gen. 34:7; Judg. 20:6).

13:13 The word translated **fools** is related to the word translated *disgraceful thing* in v. 12. **he will not withhold me from you:** While the Law forbade incestuous marriage (Lev. 18:11), this regulation may not always have been strictly observed. It is also possible that Tamar made this suggestion as a way of escaping her immediate danger, with no real thought to the possibility of marriage.

13:14 he forced her: The word can also mean, "he humiliated her." Victims of rape sometimes speak more strongly of their humiliation than of the physical pain they were made to suffer.

13:15 Amnon hated her exceedingly: Amnon's lustful passion, once gratified, turned to hatred. Probably there was a measure of self-hatred as well.

13:16 The words at the end of the verse, **but he would not listen to her,** repeat the phrasing of v. 14.

13:17 It is difficult to translate the contempt which Amnon had for Tamar. Referring to Tamar, Amnon commanded his servant in a tone one might use to speak of dumping trash.

13:18 she had on a robe of many colors: The exact meaning of this phrase is debated; recent study suggests that it refers to a long garment with sleeves.

13:19 Tamar put ashes on her head, and tore her robe: These were traditional signs of grief and mourning among peoples of the ancient Middle East (Job 1:20; 2:12). **laid her hand on her head:** This is another expression of mourning (Jer. 2:37). Tamar had much to mourn. She had lost her virginity. Shamed by her own brother, she was as good as dead—the prospect of marriage and family was ruined.

13:20 hold your peace . . . do not take this thing to heart: Absalom's words seem cold and heartless. Apparently, he wanted to avoid a public scandal. Absalom planned to take revenge, but wished to conceal his plan at that time. **Desolate,** the term used to describe Tamar as she lived in the home of her brother Absalom, is used of ravaged cities and ruined lands (Is. 6:11). We have no idea what the later history of Tamar was; no further information on her life is found in the Bible. It is likely that she lived the rest of her life in desolation, for a time under Absalom's protection. Later, Absalom named his daughter Tamar (14:27), perhaps in honor of his sister.

13:21, 22 David was **very angry** over Amnon's violation of Tamar, but did nothing to punish his son. This may have been because Amnon was David's firstborn (3:2) and was expected to succeed him on the throne. Amnon deserved the death penalty (Lev. 20:17).

13:23, 24 Absalom delayed his revenge **two full years,** evidently to catch Amnon off guard. Absalom planned to murder his brother to avenge his sister's rape and perhaps to enhance his own chances of making a bid for the throne. Having carefully planned the murder of his brother, Absalom invited the **king's sons** to a sheepshearing festival at **Baal Hazor,** a mountain about 15 miles north of Jerusalem. **Ephraim** here is not the tribe but a city about two miles south of Baal Hazor (2 Chr. 13:19; John 11:54).

13:25 David declined the invitation, offering the excuse that he did not want to be a burden on Absalom. **he blessed him:** David wished Absalom well. Given the outcome of the story, David's memory of his blessing on Absalom must have been a grief to him (v. 36).

13:26, 27 Why should he go with you: Absalom's request seems to have aroused David's suspicions. After all, David knew about the blood feud between the two brothers (v. 22). Nevertheless, Absalom persuaded his father to allow Amnon and the rest of the king's sons to attend the celebration.

13:28 Absalom's servants planned to attack Amnon when his **heart** was **merry with wine**—that is, after the wine had dulled his senses and put him off guard. **Have I not commanded you:** These words indicate that Absalom would take full responsibility for the slaying.

13:29 Fearing for their own lives, the king's sons fled. A **mule,** the offspring of a donkey and a horse, combines the size and strength of the horse with the surefootedness and endurance of the donkey. Although the Israelites were forbidden to breed such hybrids (Lev. 19:19), mules were imported into Israel. The mule was the preferred mount of royalty during this period (18:9; 1 Kin. 1:33).

13:30 Absalom has killed all the king's sons: The report that reached David was greatly exaggerated. This news must have been utterly shattering to David.

13:31 tore his garments: Tearing one's clothes was a sign of grief and mourning (1:11; 13:19).

13:32 Jonadab, a cousin both of Amnon and Tamar, had helped Amnon plan his encounter with Tamar (v. 3). **Shimeah** was David's older brother, the third son of Jesse (called Shammah in 1 Sam. 16:9; 17:13; Shimea in 1 Chr. 2:13). Jonadab knew that Absalom's treachery had been brewing ever since the violation of his sister by Amnon.

13:33 only Amnon is dead: These words of Jonadab are strange solace. It was true that only one of David's sons was dead, not all of them (v.30). Nevertheless it was still one of David's sons, and the oldest one at that. Further, the words that David should not **take the thing to his heart** are reminiscent of what Absalom had said to his brutalized sister (v. 20). This is little comfort for a grieving person.

13:34, 35 The statement **Absalom fled** is repeated three times (vv. 37, 38) to contrast Absalom's flight with the return of the rest of David's sons. **The young man who was keeping watch** refers to the watchman on the city walls whose job was to alert the citizens of approaching danger (Ezek. 3:17).

13:36 wept: The festival had turned to mourning. The rape of a daughter had led to the murder of a son. The disintegration of the family of David continued. The sons and servants wept. David wept.

13:37, 38 Talmai was Absalom's grandfather, the father of David's wife Maacah (3:3). He ruled as king of the Transjordan territory of **Geshur,** northeast of the Sea of Galilee. **And David mourned for his son:** This mourning

> *Joab's long association with David enabled him to know the king's thoughts.*

must refer to Amnon, who had been killed. But it is somewhat ambiguous, placed in the context of Absalom's exile. It is possible that David's grief over the exile of Absalom was also an intense pain to him (v. 39).

13:39 As David's grief over Amnon's death gradually diminished, he **longed to go to Absalom:** Apparently, David wanted to see Absalom, but thought it inappropriate in view of the circumstances, or impossible due to the distance and royal commitments.

14:1–33 The subtle means whereby Joab coaxes David to call Absalom back from Geshur.

14:1 the king's heart: Joab's long association with David enabled him to know the king's thoughts. He was well aware that the king longed to be reconciled with his son, but that apart from some external prompting, he was not about to make the first move.

14:2 Tekoa, the hometown of the prophet Amos, was on the edge of the hill country, about six miles south of Bethlehem. **a wise woman:** Readers of the Bible are familiar with various vocations in ancient Israel, such as kings and priests, prophets and farmers. We know less about the wisdom movement. Along with other guilds, the "wise" were those who had particular skills and abilities in understanding human behavior, and they had insights into the ways in which God's world works (see the word in 13:3). The woman whom Joab brought from Tekoa must have been a well-known wise person in her region, but she was not among the wise counselors to the king, persons who would be easily recognized. The term "wise" (Heb. *hakamâ*, the feminine of *hakam*) suggests the idea of technical skill, aptitude, experience. This woman was experienced in dealing with human relations and skillful in reconciling differences (20:16). **do not anoint yourself with oil:** Olive oil was used in ancient times as a soothing lotion that made the skin and hair shine. Its use is associated with celebration and joy (Pss. 104:15; 133:2).

14:3–5 Joab gave the woman the story to tell to the king. As a wise woman (v. 2), she would know how to reply to David's responses and questions. **fell on her face:** The woman bowed before the king as a preliminary sign of her request for help. The same word is used for bowing before God when one comes into His presence for holy worship. **my husband is dead:** Although she had already described herself as a **widow,** these words may have been added for emotional effect.

14:6 The mention of **two sons** must have struck a chord in David; certainly he could not have been impassive when she described the one killing the other.

14:7 that we may execute him: The punishment for murder was death. The issue seemed clear, but the consequences for the woman were intolerable. **So they would extinguish my ember:** The woman used a graphic picture of the extinction of her family. The demise of a family name and the end of a surviving remnant or family line were crucial matters to the Hebrew people.

14:8 David apparently wanted to put the woman off with a promise of future action. Perhaps he was seeking to avoid having to defend the guilty son who was worthy of death. Perhaps he wanted to meet with his counselors or pray to the Lord for direction.

14:9, 10 let the iniquity be on me and on my father's house: The persistent woman expressed her willingness to bear any guilt if David would let the blood of her son go unavenged. David gave the persistent woman assurances of his protection, but was unwilling at this point to offer protection to her son.

14:11, 12 The Hebrew phrase **avenger of blood** joins the term sometimes translated *kinsman redeemer* to the word for *blood*. The kinsman redeemer is the protector of family rights. Here, the protector of the family would be expected to bring vengeance on one who had taken the life of a family member. Cities of refuge had been established under Moses for protection from the blood avenger in cases where the killing was accidental (Num. 35:9–34). In this case, the woman pressed David to the limit with respect to her son. David promised that **not one hair** of her son's head would **fall to the ground.**

14:13 you schemed such a thing against the people of God: She accused David of doing to the nation what her enemy was trying to do to her (v. 7)—taking away the heir to the throne. **his banished one:** Although not formally banished, Absalom was in his extended exile from Israel.

14:14 For we will surely die: The woman may be referring to Amnon (13:28–33). Amnon was dead, and no amount of punishment against Absalom would bring him back to life. **God does not take away a life:** God's will is to forgive sinners. The divine example is set in significant contrast with David, who had refused to forgive his son Absalom.

14:15 After speaking of David's treatment of Absalom, the woman returned to her story about her own family. **the people have made me afraid:** The woman said she was afraid that she would lose her own son to the avenger of blood (v. 7).

14:16 the man who would destroy me: Although the woman's life was not in jeopardy, the death of the son would mean the extinction of her family, depriving her of a future share in the workings of God among His people.

14:17, 18 as the angel of God: The woman suggested that the king had superhuman ability in the exercise of judgment. She used flattery and an appeal to piety to get David to act.

14:19, 20 David recognized **the hand of Joab** in the woman's charade. The woman explained that Joab was simply trying to be an agent for change in the relationship between David and Absalom. **my Lord is wise:** The wise woman knows she is not dealing with a fool. "Wise" here is the masculine term that corresponds to her as a "wise woman" (v. 2). She uses flattery to persuade David, saying that his wisdom is nearly divine: **according the wisdom of the angel of God**.

14:21, 22 the king has filled the request of his servant: Apparently, Joab had made other attempts to bring about the reconciliation of David and Absalom.

14:23 David's unwillingness to go himself may reflect some reluctance to forgive his son. **Geshur** was northeast of the Sea of Galilee. Talmai, Absalom's grandfather and the father of David's wife Maacah, ruled the region (3:3; 13:37).

14:24–26 do not let him see my face: David refused to grant an immediate audience to his son because he had not forgotten Absalom's heinous crime. **his good looks:** Absalom must have had the look of royalty. Many people must have viewed him as Israel's next king. By his charm and personal appeal, he later was able to lead the nation in a rebellion against his father (15:1–12). The reference to Absalom's long **hair** provides the background for the account of his death (18:9). **Two hundred shekels** was a considerable weight, about five pounds.

14:27, 28 In addition to three sons, Absalom

had a daughter whom he named **Tamar,** perhaps after his sister (13:1). Apparently, Absalom's sons died in infancy. When he set up a pillar in Jerusalem to memorialize his name, he mentioned having no sons (18:18).

14:29–31 Joab's failure to heed Absalom's summons seems inconsistent with his earlier effort to bring about Absalom's return (v. 22). Joab's refusal to go to Absalom no doubt contributed to Absalom's simmering resentment of the royal house.

14:32 Come here, so that I may send you to the king: Perhaps Joab resented being treated like Absalom's servant. **if there is iniquity in me, let him execute me:** Absalom pleaded that his offense either be punished or completely forgiven.

14:33 the king kissed Absalom: The kiss was the symbol of their reconciliation. Although David and Absalom were reconciled, the seeds of bitterness that had been sown would soon bear the fruit of conspiracy and rebellion. David's protracted delay in coming to terms with his son ultimately led to disaster. For the moment, though, there was peace.

15:1–18:33 This section records the conspiracy and rebellion of Absalom, and it relates how David was forced to flee from Jerusalem when his son usurped the throne. This is a classic illustration of "you reap what you sow." David reaped the fruit of his long delay in coming to terms with Absalom. David had been in the unhappy position of having to forgive one son whom he loved, for killing another son whom he loved, who had raped a daughter whom he loved. Nonetheless, his harsh and unforgiving treatment of Absalom (14:24–32) was regarded as an insult that led the son to an act of treason.

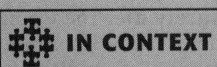 **IN CONTEXT** **A Sign of Strength**

Absalom seems to have taken great pride in his hair, which apparently was so long and thick that it weighed several pounds when he cut it each year (2 Sam. 14:26).

In ancient Israel, a full head of hair was considered a sign of strength and vigor. Thus Samson wore his hair long, though he did so because he was under a Nazirite vow and his hair was the secret of his strength (Judg. 13:3–5; 16:17). Baldness, on the other hand, was considered something of a disgrace (2 Kin. 2:23).

The deaths of both Samson and Absalom were related to their hair (and thus their strength). When Samson revealed to Delilah the secret of his strength, the Philistines cut his hair and paraded him in the temple of Dagon at Gaza, where he took his life in order to avenge himself (Judg. 16:15–30). Likewise, when Absalom fled from his army's defeat in the forest of Ephraim, his head caught in a terebinth tree, and he was dragged off his mule. Many believe that his hair was the cause of this accident, which made him easy prey for his pursuers (2 Sam. 18:9–15).

15:1–3 chariots and horses, and fifty men to run before him: This royal treatment was intended to attract attention to Absalom and to remind the people of his relationship to David as heir to the throne (1 Kin. 1:5). The runners would announce the coming of his chariot. Absalom would stand along the **way** leading to the royal palace, welcoming and showing interest in visitors who had come to Jerusalem to present their cases before the king. **good and right:** Absalom ingratiated himself to the people. Only those who really had a complaint would make the arduous trip to Jerusalem in the hope that they might find favor with the king. When they were told that they were right, but that the present administration would not help, their frustration was only increased. **no deputy of the king to hear you:** The implication of Absalom's remark was that David was too busy to hear the case, yet too jealous of his own authority to delegate someone to deal with the concern.

15:4 Administration of **justice,** the proper relationship between people in society according to God's standard of righteousness, was a major concern of OT rulers and prophets (8:15; 1 Kin. 3:28; 10:9; Is. 1:17; Amos 5:24). Absalom was playing on the people's emotions when he presented himself as the answer to their need for justice, but had none to give them.

15:5, 6 When anyone approached Absalom with a show of reverence or respect, the prince would extend **his hand,** as one would with an equal. In ancient times, a **kiss** could serve as a greeting—a sign of friendship, affection, and loyalty (19:39). **Absalom stole the hearts:** Through personal charm and promises, Absalom managed to win the affection and loyalty of the Israelites.

15:7, 8 Absalom sought David's permission to move to **Hebron,** about 20 miles south of Jerusalem, where he would have more freedom to start a rebellion. Since Absalom was born in Hebron (3:2, 3), it would probably not seem unusual to David that he would want to fulfill his vow there. **Geshur in Syria** was the region northeast of the Sea of Galilee.

15:9 How hollow the words **Go in peace** must have sounded later to David, as his memory cycled them in his mind. He sent his son with this blessing to Hebron for a recommitment to Yahweh and for His service. Actually, he had released his son to do his worst to effect his own destruction.

15:10 sent spies: Away from the attention of David and those loyal to him, Absalom began to enlist conspirators and sympathizers to join him in the forthcoming revolt. The slogan **Absalom reigns in Hebron** purposely alluded to David's kingship. David had been anointed king in Hebron (2:1–7; 5:1–5).

15:11 Absalom invited **two hundred** unsuspecting men to join him in Hebron for the supposed fulfillment of his vow (vv. 7, 8). No doubt he hoped they would give their support to him when they realized what was happening.

15:12 **Ahithophel** was from Giloh, a city in the mountains of Judah (Josh. 15:51).

15:13 The hearts of the men of Israel: By his deceptive practices, Absalom had gained the sympathy and support of the Israelites. One of the reasons he may have been able to do this was David's troubling rise to power. When David's power in Judah was confined to Hebron (ch. 2), he was resented by the supporters of Saul in the rest of the country. Old suspicions and resentments could be stroked again by a person who knew how to use people to his own advantage—a disreputable ability in which Absalom excelled.

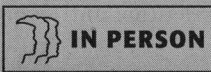 ## A Theft of Hearts at the Gates of Justice

One way to gain a following is to criticize a public system and then lead people to believe that you could fix the problem if given the power. This was the strategy by which Absalom "stole the hearts of the men of Israel" (2 Sam. 15:6).

Absalom chose Israel's justice system as his platform from which to attack his father, David. As king, David was ultimately responsible for overseeing legal matters in the kingdom. Apparently the system did not function as efficiently as it might have, a fact that Absalom exploited (15:3). He placed himself near "the gate" (15:2), which was either the city gate, where commercial, civic, and judicial business was transacted, or the palace gate. There he intercepted people coming to David seeking legal redress.

Absalom, perhaps fearing that true justice might assert itself against his treasonous scheme, employed fifty bodyguards, along with a contingent of chariots and horses. David should have suspected such a large battalion of men guarding a known rebel. Yet apparently he ignored the threat that was stalking his reign right outside, in the gates of justice.

15:14 Arise, and let us flee: David seems to have been taken completely by surprise. He was unprepared to thwart Absalom's rebellion. He fled from Jerusalem to avoid unnecessary risk of life and the tragedy of a military assault on the capital city.

15:15, 16 The loyalty of David's **servants** must have been a real encouragement in a time of such disloyalty from David's own family.

15:17 After leaving Jerusalem, David and the royal family stopped at the east edge of town before crossing the Kidron (v. 23), to allow his royal bodyguard to pass in review before him (v. 18). The need to flee the palace was immediate. But before those with him dashed off in head-long flight, David gathered them together to take stock of matters and to plan their next move.

15:18 The **Cherethites** and **Pelethites** were elite units of David's army. These trusted troops of David were not Israelites, but mercenaries from a variety of nations, possibly Crete and Philistia. They had been with David for years, owed him their loyalty, and would defend him and his family to the death. **Gittites** were either Philistine mercenary soldiers whom David had recruited during his stay in Gath (1 Sam. 21:10–15) or David's original followers from Gath (1 Sam. 23:13).

15:19 remain with the king: David gave his foreign mercenaries the chance to leave him. As foreigners, they were not obligated to fight in the coming civil war.

15:20 you came only yesterday: This is an obvious exaggeration, but reflects the fact that Ittai's association with David had been brief. He did not have the long-term relationship with David that the troops mentioned in v. 18 had. **Mercy and truth be with you:** David used the covenantal language of the biblical faith in his blessing on Ittai.

15:21, 22 As the LORD lives: With these words, the foreign military officer declared his abiding faith in and commitment to the God of Israel. These are words of the strongest oath, and they distinguish the true believer in various periods of Israel's history (1 Kin. 17:1, 12; 18:10). **whether in death or life:** Ittai's words are similar to those of another foreigner who came to faith in God—Ruth of Moab (Ruth 1:16, 17). Ittai's later appointment as commander of a third of the army (18:2) was David's way of showing his gratitude for such loyalty.

15:23 The **Brook Kidron** is a small stream that flows through the valley separating Jerusalem and the Mount of Olives during the rainy season (October through March). The **way of the wilderness** refers to the road leading through the wilderness of Judah to Jericho and down to the fords of the Jordan River.

15:24–26 Zadok and **Abiathar** were the main priests functioning during David's reign. They were loyal to David. They wanted to bring the **ark,** which David had brought to Jerusalem with a great celebration (ch. 6), **back into the city.** It was David who was going into exile, not the Lord; the symbol of God's presence with His people would remain in the place of worship for the entire community. **He will bring me back:** David committed the entire situation to the sovereign care and will of God. Contrast David's submission to the Lord's will to Absalom's deceitful words (v. 8). **His dwelling place** refers to the tabernacle that had been set up for the ark (7:6).

15:27 Are you not a seer: A prophet could come from any tribe, even from among the sons of Aaron. Thus, a priest could also be a prophet of the Lord (Zech. 1:1). David wanted the priests to remain in Jerusalem to minister in the tabernacle and intercede before God for him. Perhaps God would grant them a message that they could relay to him.

15:28 The plains of the wilderness refers to the Jordan valley near Jericho. **until word**

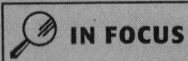 **IN FOCUS** **"ark"**

(Heb. *'aron*) (2 Sam. 6:2; 15:24; Ex. 25:10; 1 Sam. 4:3) Strong's #727: This Hebrew word can be translated "chest" (2 Kin. 12:9) or "sarcophagus" (Gen. 50:26), but usually appears in the phrase *'aron haberith,* which means "ark of the covenant." The ark was a wooden chest overlaid with gold (Ex. 25:10–22), housing the Ten Commandments (Ex. 40:20), Aaron's staff, and a pot of manna (Heb. 9:4). It sat in the Most Holy Place as a reminder of Israel's covenant with God and His presence among them. When the Israelites became careless with the ark (1 Sam. 4:1–11), God allowed it to be captured in order to demonstrate that His covenant relationship with them transcended symbols and superstitions. What He required was continual obedience to His covenant and a contrite heart surrendered to Him (Ps. 51:17; Is. 57:15).

comes from you to inform me: As vv. 35, 36 further explain, Zadok and Abiathar were to remain in Jerusalem to gather information for David. They could return a message from the Lord as well as news from the enemy camp.

15:29 back to Jerusalem: It was David who was going into exile, not the Lord. The symbol of God's presence with His people would continue to be in the place of worship for the community.

15:30 head covered . . . barefoot: These were outward signs of mourning (Jer. 14:3; Ezek. 24:17). The **Mount of Olives** was located east of Jerusalem.

15:31 Ahithophel was Bathsheba's grandfather (11:3). A wise counselor (16:23), he had been in David's service (v. 12) but had switched his allegiance to Absalom. David's prayer was for his enemy to be confused. The name Ahithophel may mean "Brother of Folly." If so, it may have been a name given to him later on account of his defection from David.

15:32–34 where he worshiped God: Prior to the building of the Jerusalem temple, there was apparently a place of worship located on the Mount of Olives. **Hushai** proved to be a loyal friend of David (15:37; 16:16). **Archite** was the name of a family living on the southern boundary of Ephraim, between Bethel and Ataroth (Josh. 16:2). Hushai's **torn** robe and the **dust on his head** were signs of grief (1:11; 13:19). Rather than joining David's followers, Hushai was directed to return to Jerusalem to thwart the counsel that Ahithophel would be giving to Absalom.

15:35, 36 Hushai was given a key role in relaying information about the enemy to David through **Zadok** and **Abiathar** and their sons, **Ahimaaz** and **Jonathan.**

15:37 The word **friend** can mean a counselor or an advisor (1 Kin. 4:5).

16:1 Ziba, a long-time servant of both Saul and **Mephibosheth**, assisted David and his party with provisions for their initial flight. **Summer fruits** probably refers to fresh figs (Mic. 7:1) or fig cakes (1 Sam. 25:18). **skin of wine:** In ancient times, wine was carried in animal-skin containers. The skin expanded with the liquid when it fermented (Matt. 9:17).

16:2 The donkeys are for the king's household: Since a couple of donkeys (v. 1) would not provide sufficient transportation for the royal family, they might have been intended for David's wives to ride in turn.

16:3 Your master's son is a reference to Mephibosheth. **Ziba** had been in the service of Jonathan, father of Mephibosheth (9:2, 9). **Today the house of Israel will restore the kingdom of my father to me:** According to Ziba, Mephibosheth was staying in Jerusalem in

hopes that Absalom's rebellion would result in his elevation to the throne. Even though David had shown special concern for Mephibosheth (ch. 9), the latter may have had some thoughts that this might be the time to advance the cause of the dynasty of Saul.

16:4 In the bleakness of David's experience when fleeing from his son Absalom, the loyal statements and actions of "outsiders" must have been comforting. First there had been the courageous action of Ittai, the Philistine from Gath, to align himself resolutely with David (2 Sam. 15:19–23). Now, with nothing to gain in the present circumstances, an aged servant of Saul brought donkeys, food, and wine as well as a warning concerning his own master, who was plotting to use the confusion of the present experience to his own advantage.

16:5 Bahurim was near Jerusalem, east of the Mount of Olives (3:16). **Shimei the son of Gera** was a distant relative of Saul (19:16–23; 1 Kin. 2:8, 9, 36–46). **cursing continuously:** These were not simple insults or merely the words of someone with a foul mouth. Shimei was asking God to destroy David (Num. 22:6).

16:6 threw stones: Throwing stones is a gesture of contempt, as if the fleeing king were merely a stray dog. Stones can also be dangerous weapons, as is shown by the fact that stoning was a normal means of capital punishment among the Hebrews (1 Kin. 21:13). **All the mighty men** refers to David's royal troops and bodyguards (17:8).

16:7, 8 Come out might be rephrased, "Go out" (into banishment and exile) or "Begone!" **You bloodthirsty man:** David was a man of war, and he was guilty of killing Uriah (11:14–27). But Shimei blamed the demise of Saul's family on David (v. 5)—an unjust charge (ch. 1). **You rogue,** literally "man of Belial," is an expletive against David that means worthless or useless. **The blood of the house of Saul** may refer to the murders of Ishbosheth and Abner, although David was completely innocent of their deaths (3:22—4:12).

16:9 Abishai was a nephew of David, the son of David's sister **Zeruiah** (1 Chr. 2:16). He was consistently devoted to David (19:21, 22; 1 Sam. 26:8). In the ancient Middle East, a **dead dog** was something utterly contemptible (3:8).

16:10 What have I to do with you: This idiom means that David did not share the feelings and views of Abishai. **sons of Zeruiah:** Apparently David considered that Joab, also a son of Zeruiah (1 Chr. 2:16), would share Abishai's willingness to kill Shimei. **the LORD has said to him, 'Curse David':** David might have remembered God's promise "to raise up adversity" for his sin with Bathsheba (12:11) and took Shimei's cursing as part of this discipline.

16:11 David argued that if his own **son** showed him no loyalty, there was no reason to expect respect from the **Benjamite,** that is, a person from the tribe of Saul.

16:12–14 the LORD will repay me with good: David hoped that the Lord would look upon his repentant heart and render a blessing to compensate for Shimei's curse.

16:15 Ahithophel, David's former counselor (15:12), had switched his allegiance to Absalom (15:31). In this context, **the men of Israel** refers to Absalom's followers.

16:16–18 Long live the king: Hushai deceptively professed loyalty to Absalom. In fact, these words could easily have applied to David for he was still the divinely sanctioned king. By using his words carefully, Hushai was able to lead his hearers to think he was praising Absalom, when in fact he was shouting for David. **your friend:** Absalom apparently was referring to Hushai's title, "David's friend" (15:37). **whom the LORD:** With these well-planned words, Hushai professed allegiance to whomever the Lord would choose as king. **his I will be:** Hushai's real allegiance was with David, who he knew was God's chosen one.

16:19–21 in the presence of his son: Hushai wished to imply that his allegiance to Absalom was the natural outgrowth of his loyalty to David. It was appropriate for a son to succeed his father, and for supporters of the dynasty to give their allegiance to the new king. Hushai was going to considerable effort to convince Absalom of his support. His words are capable of more than one meaning; David had other sons, and one would surely succeed him some day. Even the last phrase **so will I be in your presence** is capable of more than one meaning. Hushai was able to say, in these words, that he would continue to be loyal to David even while in Absalom's service.

16:22 Concubines were unofficial wives. In ancient times, taking over a king's harem was

a recognized means of claiming the throne. When Ahithophel advised Absalom to have sexual relations with David's concubines, he knew that this would finalize the breach between Absalom and David. It was an irrevocable action. Up to this point, Absalom would have been able to back away from all that he had done and still be reconciled to his father. But once he violated the harem of David, he was set on a course of sure and final alienation from his father. The **tent** that Absalom pitched **in the sight of all Israel** was probably a bridal tent. Absalom made the people of Israel fully aware that he was engaging in sexual relations with his father's concubines. Putting the tent on the roof of the palace was an insolent act that was guaranteed to stir the populace one way or another.

16:23 at the oracle of God: Ahithophel had acquired such a reputation that his counsel was taken to be equivalent to a word from the Lord. He was not a prophet, but his words were received as if they were prophetic.

17:1, 2 Ahithophel realized that the fleeing king was in a vulnerable situation. He counseled Absalom to pursue and kill David and his followers in order to eliminate any chance that David would regain the throne. The **twelve thousand men** that he asked for would likely have had an easy time defeating the weary troops of David. **I will strike only the king:** Despite his celebrated wisdom, Ahithophel underestimated the loyalty of David's crack troops. Ahithophel might have been able to defeat David in a surprise raid, but David's loyal warriors would not have scattered.

17:3, 4 I will bring back all the people: Ahithophel tried to persuade Absalom that if he killed only David, the people would align themselves with Absalom, and **peace** would be restored in the land.

17:5, 6 Although Absalom was pleased with Ahithophel's counsel (v. 4), he did not accept it

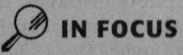 **IN FOCUS** | **"advice"**

(Heb. *'etsah*) (2 Sam. 17:7; Job 38:2; Ps. 1:1; Prov. 8:14) Strong's #6098: This Hebrew term has two primary meanings: "counsel" and "plan." Both senses are used of God (Jer. 32:19; Is. 5:19) and man (2 Kin. 18:20; Prov. 20:5). While the counsel of the Lord stands forever, He brings the counsel of the nations to nothing (Ps. 33:10, 11; Prov. 21:30). One of the psalmists prayed to be guided by God's counsel, a prayer not made by the rebellious people of Isaiah's day (Ps. 73:24; Is. 30:1). The Hebrew kings typically sought counsel from advisors who were old, experienced, and wise; however, Rehoboam tragically sought out the counsel of his peers (1 Kin. 12:8, 13; Ezek. 7:26). Solomon describes those who heed counsel as being wise (Prov. 12:15; 19:20), and the psalmists proclaimed their reliance on God's counsel (Pss. 16:7; 73:24).

immediately. He summoned **Hushai** (16:16) to get a second opinion on the matter.

17:7 Hushai, David's confidant, set about to frustrate Ahithophel's wise counsel. He realized that the plan proposed by Ahithophel would prove fatal for David. The words **at this time** leave room for an appreciation of Ahithophel's past counsel and might have been intended to deter suspicion over his critical evaluation.

17:8 Mighty men (Heb. *gibborîm*) are heroic fighting men. **like a bear robbed of her cubs:** Hushai used a strong simile to depict the ferocity of David and his men. There is no more dangerous foe in the woods than a mother bear who believes her cubs to be in danger. **will not camp with the people:** Hushai suggested that David, as an experienced warrior, would not camp with the civilian refugees. He would know that doing so would leave him vulnerable to attack and capture.

17:9 hidden in some pit: The countryside of Judah was riddled with caves, ravines, and hiding places. **a slaughter:** Hushai suggested that David could not be taken without some loss of life, and this would give rise to the rumor that Absalom was suffering a severe defeat.

17:10 Valiant (Heb. *hayil*) means well-trained and able to fight. **will melt completely:** Hushai suggested that even the bravest of Absalom's soldiers would yield to panic when facing David and his veterans.

17:11, 12 all Israel: Hushai advised that Absalom was going to need a larger army than he presently had, and that Absalom himself should lead the force into battle. **Dan to Beersheba** means the whole country, from Dan in the north to Beersheba in the south, a distance of about 150 miles. **like the sand:** Hushai used this figure of speech to describe the army that would be needed to destroy David's forces. Hushai knew it would take time to gather so many men, and that time was what David needed the most. **in some place:** The implication of this remark is that Absalom did not know where David was hiding. **as the dew falls on the ground:** Because of Israel's proximity to the Mediterranean, the land is noted for having a significant and consistent dewfall, which falls on everything that is exposed. In that way, Hushai promised, the vast new army will be able to overwhelm all their enemies.

17:13 The river means any river, not necessarily the Jordan.

17:14 For the LORD had purposed to: This is a rare example of the narrator "intruding" into the story line to explain specifically how God worked in these events. Often we are left to draw our own conclusions.

17:15 Zadok and Abiathar the priests had stayed in Jerusalem at David's request

(15:24–29). David had arranged for them to gather information about Absalom's activities and forward it to him through their sons (15:35, 36).

17:16 The plains of the wilderness means the Jordan valley in the vicinity of Jericho (15:28). Hushai told David to cross the Jordan since he could not be sure that Absalom would act on his counsel.

17:17, 18 Jonathan and Ahimaaz were the sons of Abiathar and Zadok. **En Rogel** was a spring or well south of Jerusalem at the junction of the Hinnom and Kidron valleys (Josh. 15:7; 18:16). **a female servant:** The young men would arouse suspicion by coming into the city, so a woman servant served as an intermediary. **a lad saw them:** The efforts of Jonathan and Ahimaaz to avoid detection were unsuccessful. **Bahurim** was on the east side of the Mount of Olives (16:5). The word translated **well** may also refer to a pit or cistern. Apparently, there was no water in it at this time.

17:19–22 Although **the Jordan** was not a large river, crossing it could be dangerous, even at the fords. David was safer once he got his family and followers across that barrier. There is a certain sadness in what David had to do. While the tribal allotments of ancient Israel included land on both sides of the Jordan, there was always an emotional understanding that the "real" land of Israel was west of the Jordan. David was truly in exile. Later, his enemies would charge him with having "fled from the land" (19:9).

17:23 Ahithophel committed suicide when he learned that his advice was not being followed. He apparently realized that Absalom's cause was doomed, and that when David returned he would be put to death as a disloyal subject.

17:24 Mahanaim was formerly Ish-bosheth's capital (2:8). It was east of the Jordan and north of the Jabbok.

17:25 Absalom put his army under the command of **Amasa,** since Joab had remained loyal to David. **who had gone in to Abigail:** This is not the usual phrase for marriage, perhaps indicating that Abigail did not leave her father's authority completely.

17:26 Gilead refers to the mountainous region east of the Jordan and between the Yarmuk valley to the north and the Jabbok valley to the south. Gilead was famous in biblical times for its forests (Jer. 22:6), pasture lands (Num. 32:1–4), and the medicinal balms made from its plants (Jer. 8:22; 46:11).

17:27, 28 When David arrived in the fortified city of **Mahanaim,** he found a gracious reception. **Shobi** was a vassal king under David who ruled **Rabbah,** the capital of **Ammon. Lo**

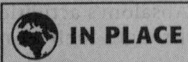 **IN PLACE** **Why Ahimaaz Outran the Cushite**

Knowledge about the geography near Mahanaim, where David awaited word of the battle with Absalom (2 Sam. 17:27; 18:4–6), helps to explain how Ahimaaz arrived before the Cushite messenger (18:24–31).

The Cushite, probably an Ethiopian (2 Chr. 14:12), was apparently a swift and powerful runner. In fact, he may have been retained in Joab's army as an experienced herald (foot runner bearing a message). But he chose the direct route from the battlefield to Mahanaim. This took him over rugged terrain, as the city lay in a steep gorge carved out by the Jabbok River.

Ahimaaz was also a renowned runner (2 Sam. 18:27) and an experienced messenger, having already shut-

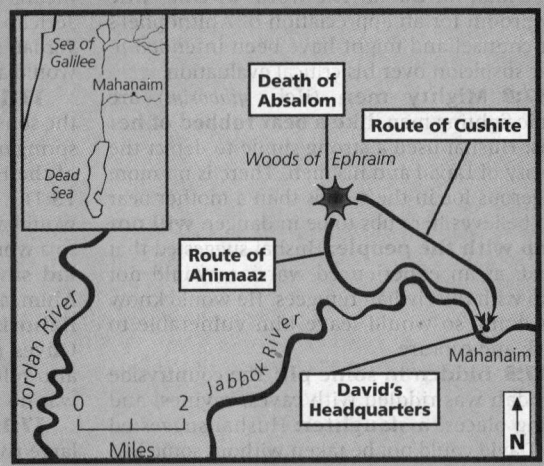

Why Ahimaaz Outran the Cushite

tled messages to David from Jerusalem during the rebellion (15:27, 36). Perhaps Ahimaaz was more familiar with the terrain, for he chose the "way of the plain" (18:23), the smooth riverbed of the Jabbok. The route was less direct but easier to run than that of the Cushite. As a result, Ahimaaz arrived first. Even so, he failed to tell David the sad news of Absalom's death.

Debar was about ten miles south of the Sea of Galilee, east of the Jordan river in the Jordan valley (9:4). **Barzillai** was an old man of great wealth (19:31–39; 1 Kin. 2:7).

17:29 The rulers showed compassion to David and his **weary** followers. Jesus taught that kindness done to others in need would not be forgotten (Matt. 25:34–36).

18:1 To prepare for battle, **David** counted and reviewed his fighting forces. **captains of thousands:** Although only a small contingent of troops left Jerusalem with David, other loyal followers soon rallied to his cause.

18:2 David divided his men into three companies—a frequent military tactic in ancient times (Judg. 7:16; 1 Sam. 11:11). **Abishai,** the oldest son of David's sister **Zeruiah** (1 Chr. 2:16), was noted for his brave but impetuous spirit (3:30; 16:9; 1 Sam. 26:6–9). **Joab,** the younger brother of Abishai, had become commander of David's army as a result of his heroic leadership in the capture of Jerusalem (1 Chr. 11:4–6). Little is known of **Ittai** except that he was strongly committed to serving David and the Lord (15:19–22).

18:3, 4 You shall not go out: Although David wanted to accompany his men into

battle (v. 2), he was persuaded not to go, both for his own protection and for the safety of Mahanaim (17:27). **you are worth ten thousand of us:** The Hebrew text underlying this phrase is somewhat cryptic. It may be a comparative statement, as in our translation, saying that David is worth more than the army (compare Ruth 4:15). The phrasing could also be read as an exaggerative flourish: "(David need not go because) now there are ten thousand like us."

18:5, 6 the woods of Ephraim: The battle took place in a dense forest north of the Jabbok river, east of the Jordan.

18:7, 8 Absalom's newly organized army, **the people of Israel,** were no match for the experienced soldiers of David. **the woods devoured:** Because of the rugged nature of the terrain and dense growth in the forest, more deaths resulted from the pursuit than from actual combat.

18:9, 10 The **terebinth,** sometimes translated *oak* or *elm,* was a strong tree, native to the land of Israel. It grows to a height of around 35 feet.

18:11 ten shekels: The shekel was the basic unit of weight, equal to 11.3 grams or

---

IN PERSON | A Royal Turns Out Wrong

The tragic account of David's son Absalom is a story of . . .

- *appearance.* Apparently he was the most handsome man in all Israel. His most notable feature was his thick, long hair, which he cut annually. Its weight was said to be 200 shekels, or several pounds (2 Sam. 14:25, 26).
- *affluence.* As a son of the king, he enjoyed the benefits of a royal family whose empire was on the rise. For example, Hiram of Tyre had built David a palace of cedar (5:11; 7:1, 2). Absalom may have had his own home at Baal Hazor, several miles north of Jerusalem, where he employed sheepshearers (13:23).
- *advantage.* He was next in line to the throne after his half brothers Amnon and Chileab. He also must have had a special place in his father's heart, for even after Absalom took Amnon's life, David longed to be with his son (13:39).
- *anger.* When Amnon violated Absalom's beautiful sister, Tamar, Absalom took revenge by luring Amnon to his country home, where he had his servants kill him after dinner (13:1–29).
- *ambition.* Reinstated after two years of exile, Absalom began building a power base among the people, right under the nose of David (15:1–6). When the time was right, he launched a rebellion to depose his father and rule in his place (15:7–18). His ultimate act of defiance was to violate his father's concubines, which in effect meant that he had assumed the throne (16:20–22).
- *anguish.* Under the seasoned command of Joab, David's troops severely defeated Absalom's army and, through an odd set of circumstances, ended Absalom's life tragically (18:6–15).

---

about a half ounce. The **belt** was part of a soldier's equipment (1 Sam. 18:4; 1 Kin. 2:5).

18:12–15 against the king's son: The soldier had not forgotten David's command not to harm **Absalom** (v. 5). Since the spears did not kill Absalom immediately (v. 15), the word translated **heart** may refer to Absalom's trunk.

18:16 Joab blew the trumpet to signal the army to stop its pursuit. The death of Absalom meant the end of the rebellion. The trumpet was a ram's horn or shofar (2:28; 6:15).

18:17 Rather than returning Absalom's body to Jerusalem for honorable burial, Joab had it buried in **a large pit** in the forest. The heap of stones that covered the grave may have been symbolic of a stoning, the legal penalty due a rebel son (Deut. 21:20, 21).

18:18 The King's Valley was near Jerusalem (Gen. 14:17). **to this day:** The great monument that Absalom had erected for himself was still in existence when the narrator wrote this section of Second Samuel.

18:19, 20 Ahimaaz with Jonathan had carried the message from Zadok and Abiathar, urging David to flee across the Jordan (17:20, 21). The word **avenged** is used here in the sense of "delivered."

18:21–23 Cushite means someone of the land from Cush, the remote region of what is today southern Egypt and Sudan. **let me also run:** Ahimaaz could not be restrained from also

running to David with the good news of victory. **The plain** was the floor of the Jordan valley. Ahimaaz took a longer route, but avoided the hilly terrain on the road taken by the Cushite.

18:24 two gates: The city of Mahanaim evidently had a double gate. Between the outer and inner gates there were probably stone benches. **The roof over the gate** refers to the gatehouse or fortress located on the wall over the city gate. The **watchman** at the gate was responsible to warn the city of an approaching army and to announce the arrival of important visitors. **Lifted his eyes** is a common Hebrew idiom that means "looked" (Gen. 22:4).

18:25, 26 If he is alone: The fact that only one runner was approaching led David to assume that the news was good. Perhaps he assumed that a group of men running toward the gate would have indicated a rout. Yet the approach of **another man** complicated the picture.

18:27, 28 All is well: The messenger's greeting was *shalom,* the word usually translated *peace.* **your God:** Ahimaaz recognized God's strong association with David.

18:29, 30 Is the young man Absalom safe: David expressed his first concern, his interest in the welfare of his son. Ahimaaz did not give a straight answer to David, though he knew that Absalom was dead (v. 20).

18:31, 32 the Lord has avenged: Like

Ahimaaz (v. 28), the Cushite gave God credit for delivering David. Furthermore he gave an honest answer to David's question about Absalom, although his words were carefully worded so as to soften the blow.

18:33 Was deeply moved (Heb. *ragaz*) can mean "quaked" or "quivered." David was overcome with sorrow. **O Absalom my son, my son:** The repetition of these words expresses clearly David's anguish.

19:1–3 the victory that day was turned into mourning: David's unrestrained expression of grief over the death of his son turned the well-deserved victory celebration into a day of mourning, not so much for Absalom himself, but for the grief brought upon David by his death (18:33). **the people stole back into the city:** What a description for the return of victorious warriors! Like cowards who had fled from battle, David's soldiers crept back into the city of Mahanaim (17:27), hoping to escape notice.

19:4 David **covered his face** as an expression of mourning (15:30). **my son:** His words, which were so touching when first announced (18:33), take on a grating sound when repeated many times.

19:5, 6 you have disgraced all your servants: Joab argued that by honoring his rebel son and neglecting his loyal soldiers, David had shamed and embarrassed those who had served him well. The words **your enemies** is literally "those who hate you." The words **your friends** is literally "those who love you." **Princes** refers to the captains of the army.

19:7 Speak comfort may be rephrased "speak to the heart." David would have to speak words of encouragement if he expected his troops to continue their support of his kingship.

19:8 The gate was the primary meeting place in ancient cities. **So all the people came before the king:** Although not directly stated, the context implies that David followed Joab's counsel by expressing appreciation to his loyal troops and faithful followers. **For everyone of Israel had fled to his tent:** This parenthetical note indicates that the rebellion ended and Absalom's followers returned home.

19:9, 10 The movement to restore David to power was not unanimous. Some Israelites thought that because he had **fled from the land,** David lost his right to rule. There may also have been some fear that David would avenge himself on those who had supported Absalom.

19:11 Zadok and Abiathar were priests who had remained in Jerusalem at David's request during the rebellion (15:24–29). The **elders of Judah** were reluctant to call David back to Jerusalem, perhaps because of their part

in Absalom's insurrection (15:10, 11). David asked his friends, the priests, to begin the movement to invite David back to his throne. Apparently, he did not want to come into Jerusalem without public support for his rule.

19:12 My brethren refers to the elders of Judah (v. 11). David knew that he needed the support of his own tribe and its leaders to resume his leadership over the nation. Without their full support there was no hope for the renewal of his kingship.

19:13 Amasa, David's nephew, had commanded the army of Absalom (17:25). David offered him Joab's position as commander-in-chief of David's army. This offer was intended to secure the allegiance of Amasa and the rebel army, as well as to discipline Joab for killing Absalom against his orders (18:14, 15).

19:14 David's acts of diplomacy were effective; he was invited to return as king. The fact that David was the anointed of the Lord meant that God would ensure that David would be restored. But David could not simply wait in exile in a foreign land. He had to act on the belief that God would continue to work His will.

19:15 Gilgal, the first place the Israelites camped after they crossed the Jordan (Josh. 4:19, 20), was about a mile from Jericho.

19:16 Shimei, who had cursed David when he was forced to leave Jerusalem, no doubt feared that David would punish him for this outrageous behavior (16:5–8). He hurried to meet the king so he could make amends.

19:17 a thousand men of Benjamin: This large contingent was a very good sign to David that his old hostilities with the family of Saul were over at last. **they went over the Jordan:** Ziba and his sons forded the Jordan to assist David and his family in crossing.

19:18 Another interpretation of **ferryboat** is "ford," with the idea, "They crossed at the ford of the river."

19:19 what wrong your servant did: Shimei's confession showed genuine repentance and godly sorrow. He added no excuse, self-justification, or explanation (compare Saul's behavior in 1 Sam. 13:11, 12; 15:20, 21).

19:20 The designation **house of Joseph** was sometimes applied to the northern tribes (Ps. 78:67; Ezek. 37:16) since Ephraim, the tribe of Joseph's son (Gen. 48:5, 13–20), was the largest and most powerful tribe in the north.

19:21 Abishai once again (16:9, 10) called for the death of Shimei for cursing God's **anointed** (23:1).

19:22, 23 What have I to do with you: David often had to quell the fiery spirit of his nephew (16:10). David had spared Shimei's life once before because of the timing of his attack on him; here he spared his life again because of the timing of Shimei's repentance. **You shall not die:** The amnesty granted Shimei was apparently conditioned on his continued loyalty. When David was near death, he ordered that Shimei be put to death by Solomon (1 Kin. 2:8, 9, 36–46). David could not put Shimei to death himself because of his oath; however, his son could do it if there were just cause.

19:24, 25 **Mephibosheth** was actually the **son** of Jonathan and the grandson **of Saul** (4:4; 9:1–13). Ziba claimed that Mephibosheth, in the turmoil of Absalom's revolt, sought to advance the cause of the house of Saul (16:1–4). **cared for his feet:** The personal neglect of Mephibosheth must have been striking. He intended his personal appearance to be a sign of mourning David's absence.

19:26–31 Mephibosheth claimed that Ziba had taken advantage of him, since he was not able to saddle or mount his donkey without help. **he has slandered your servant:** At this point, David faced a dilemma. Who was telling the truth—Mephibosheth or Ziba? **Why do you speak anymore:** David found the whole issue too complex to sort out. **divide the land:** In this way, both Ziba and Mephibosheth would be provided for in a generous manner (16:14). **let him take it all:** Mephibosheth's final words indicated his submission to David's decision.

19:32–34 **very aged:** The eighty-year-old Barzillai had proven himself to be an extraordinary help to David during David's exile. This was an opportunity for David to repay his kindness. **very rich:** Barzillai did not need money; David's offer of a royal pension was based on his loyal friendship.

19:35, 36 Can I discern between the good and bad: There was no effective contrast between the opportunity David offered and Barzillai's present living situation at Mahanaim.

What real difference would the change make in his life, since he was too old to enjoy the pleasures of the court? In going **a little way across the Jordan** with David, Barzillai fulfilled his duty as a gracious host.

19:37, 38 Chimham was later identified by the historian Josephus as Barzillai's son (1 Kin. 2:7). **I will do for him:** Because of his love for Barzillai, David promised to give a royal patronage to Chimham. This was similar to the provision David had made for Mephibosheth because of his love for Jonathan (ch. 9).

19:39, 40 The term **all** is figurative. It means that as a whole Judah supported David. **Half** means that the people of Israel were less enthusiastic.

19:41, 42 stolen you away: The people of Israel were annoyed by the fact that David's supporters in Judah had the greater part in bringing the king back from exile in the Transjordan. **The men of Judah** pointed out that even though they had a tribal relationship with David, they had never taken advantage of their privileged position.

19:43 The people of Israel were claiming a greater share in David's kingship since Israel's northern territory was formed by **ten** tribes. **fiercer:** This bitterness between the tribes of Israel and the tribe of Judah would lead finally to the division of the nation at the time of the death of Solomon, David's son (1 Kin. 12). In the present situation, it threatened to erupt into civil war, which would take place under the leadership of Sheba (ch. 20).

20:1 Sheba was from Benjamin, the same tribe as Saul. The term **rebel,** which also means "worthless person," suggests that Sheba was a scoundrel. **trumpet:** As was usual for military signals (2:28; 15:10; 18:16; 20:22), Sheba sounded a shofar or ram's horn. **We have no share in David:** These three lines of poetry form a campaign slogan or song of rebellion.

 **IN FOCUS**   **"Jerusalem"**

(Heb. *yerushalaim*) (2 Sam. 5:5; 20:3; Is. 40:2; Zech. 2:12) Strong's #3389: The name Jerusalem is related to the word for "peace" (see the psalmist's prayer for "the peace of Jerusalem"; Ps. 122:6). During the reign of king David, Jerusalem was made the political and religious capital of Israel and became central to the unfolding of God's redemptive plan. Jerusalem is described variously in the OT as: the city of God (Ps. 87:1–3); the place where God has put His name (2 Kin. 21:4); a place of salvation (Is. 46:13); the throne of God (Jer. 3:17); and a holy city (Is. 52:1). The prophets foresaw an approaching time when Jerusalem would be judged because of its iniquity (Mic. 4:10–12), but in pronouncing judgment they could also see its glorious restoration (Is. 40:2; 44:25–28; Dan. 9:2; Zeph. 3:16–20). This vision of a restored Jerusalem included the hope of a New Jerusalem in which God would gather all His people (Is. 65:17–19; Rev. 21:1, 2).

Every man to his tents may be paraphrased, "Let's go back home, and from there we can resist the king."

20:2, 3 every man of Israel: There was a general rebellion among the northern tribes. **From the Jordan as far as Jerusalem:** The people along David's route to Jerusalem expressed their loyalty to the king.

20:4 Amasa, who had commanded Absalom's army (17:25), had been offered Joab's position as commander in chief of David's army (19:13). Apparently, he accepted the offer and was commissioned to put down Sheba's rebellion.

20:5, 6 But he delayed: Amasa's delay in carrying out David's order to gather forces against Sheba's rebellion could have resulted in a disaster like that of Absalom's revolt. **Abishai,** Joab's older brother (1 Chr. 2:16), was enlisted to take command of the soldiers of Judah and put down Sheba's revolt. David knew that Sheba's revolt was potentially more dangerous than Absalom's, since Sheba's rebellion was based on long-standing tribal animosity between Israel and Judah.

20:7 Joab's men are distinguished from the rest of David's army. Apparently, Joab maintained his own group of elite soldiers.

20:8, 9 Gibeon was about six miles northwest of Jerusalem. Joab apparently adjusted his sword so that it fell from the sheath as he stepped forward to greet **Amasa** (v. 4). Assuming a mere accident, Amasa did not pay attention to the weapon in Joab's left hand (v. 10). **Are you in health, my brother:** The term translated *health* is the Hebrew word *shalom,* meaning "peace." *Brother* is not just a formality here; Joab and Amasa were cousins, sons of two of David's sisters (1 Chr. 2:16, 17). **Joab took Amasa by the beard:** This friendly greeting, a preliminary to a kiss, was now a preparation for killing him.

20:10–12 wallowed in his blood: The bloody spectacle of Amasa lying on the road caused the soldiers to stop and think about what it might mean to follow Joab. One of the soldiers finally covered the corpse so that the shocking scene would not impede the movement of the soldiers any further.

20:13, 14 He probably refers to Sheba, who traveled the land attempting to raise popular support for his rebellion. **Abel** and **Beth Maachah** were cities in northern Galilee so closely connected that they became identified with each other. They were four miles west of Dan (1 Kin. 15:20; 2 Kin. 15:29).

20:15 A siege mound was used in ancient warfare to allow soldiers to reach the top of a city wall. The mound consisted of dirt and debris placed against the wall.

20:16, 17 a wise woman: See note at 14:2.

20:18, 19 The wise woman explained to Joab that **Abel** was famous for the wisdom and counsel offered by its citizens. In addition to being **peaceable and faithful,** Abel was noted as a **mother** city, or a recognized leader in the region. The citizens had done nothing to deserve the city's destruction.

20:20–22 his head will be thrown to you: Convinced that the death of **Sheba** would end the siege, the people of Abel cut off his head and threw it **over the wall** to Joab.

20:23 Joab was the overall commander of David's army, while **Benaiah** was in charge of **the Cherethites and the Pelethites,** foreign mercenaries who fought for David.

20:24, 25 Revenue may refer to forced labor (1 Kin. 12:18). The **recorder,** meaning "one who causes to remember," was responsible for keeping official records. The **scribe** was the king's official secretary.

20:26 Ira replaced David's sons (8:18) as **chief minister,** a word customarily translated *priest.*

21:1–24:25 This section forms an appendix recording several incidents that occurred earlier in David's life. They are presented to show other problems David faced, including famine and plague (chs. 21; 24), military exploits (chs. 21; 23), and how he learned to praise God in the midst of his trials (ch. 22).

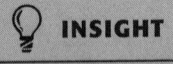 **INSIGHT** | **A Spiritual Cause to a Natural Event**

The three-year famine in the days of David was the result of Saul's violation of the standing peace treaty that Israel had with the Gibeonites (2 Sam. 21:1; Josh. 9:15, 19–21). This suggests two things: (1) Political commitments, such as peace treaties, have spiritual implications. God takes people's words—including the words of governments—seriously and expects people to honor their commitments. (2) Natural events may have spiritual causes. Scripture offers many illustrations that God may sovereignly allow and ordain such events for spiritual reasons.

21:1 Famine was a means of divine chastening intended to lead God's people to repentance (Deut. 28:47, 48). **he killed the Gibeonites:** About 400 years earlier, the Gibeonites had deceived Joshua and the Israelites into making a treaty that guaranteed their protection and security (Josh. 9:3–27). Saul had broken that agreement by putting some Gibeonites to death (v. 9). This incident was not recorded elsewhere.

21:2 The Gibeonites were Canaanites living near the site of present-day El-Jib, about six miles northwest of Jerusalem. **Amorites** is used here as a general designation for the original population of Canaan (Gen. 15:16). Saul's

ites for the wrong that was done. **Nor shall you kill any man in Israel for us** may also be translated, "It is not for us to put a man to death in Israel." The implication would then be that they had no authority, as a subject people, for taking blood vengeance. The Gibeonites sought justice in keeping with the principle of Num. 35:31, that a life demands a life. They asked David for royal authority to execute **seven** of Saul's **descendants.** The term **hang** suggests some form of solemn execution, followed by the public exposure of the dead body, which was impaled on a post (Num. 25:4). The words **before the Lord** indicate that the judgment was intended to satisfy divine justice (v.

Photo by Howard Vos

The mound of Gibeah, a city where David allowed several of King Saul's descendants to be executed and displayed in humiliation because of Saul's slaughter of the Gibeonites (2 Sam. 21:1–9).

zeal for the children of Israel and Judah led him to attempt to exterminate the foreign element from the land of Israel. Righteous zeal can be an act of heroic faith (Num. 25). But when zeal is misdirected, it can have serious consequences (Rom. 10:2; Phil. 3:6).

21:3 The word translated **make atonement** (Heb. *kaphar*) means to remove sin or defilement by offering a substitute or paying a ransom. David offered to make a settlement with the Gibeonites for the wrong Saul had done. **that you may bless the inheritance of the Lord:** David wanted the Gibeonites once again to look with favor upon the people of Israel.

21:4–6 No amount of monetary compensation, **silver or gold,** would satisfy the Gibeon-

1). **Gibeah,** about three miles north of Jerusalem, had been Saul's capital (1 Sam. 10:26).

21:7 because of the Lord's oath: Because of David's covenant of friendship with **Jonathan,** his son **Mephibosheth** was **spared** (1 Sam. 18:3; 20:8, 16). For the story of Mephibosheth, read 4:4; 9:1–13; 16:1–4; 19:24–30.

21:8 Mephibosheth, the son of **Rizpah,** is not the same as Jonathan's son of the same name (v. 7). Rizpah was Saul's concubine (3:7). The **Barzillai** mentioned here is not the same as David's loyal friend of 17:27.

21:9 they hanged them: God's Law explicitly prohibited the punishment of a son for the sins of his father (Deut. 24:16; 2 Kin. 14:6; Ezek. 18:1–4, 14–17). Since there is no condemnation of David in the text and since God apparently honored the action and ended the famine (v. 14), it is possible that those who were executed had been implicated in the killing of the Gibeonites.

21:10, 11 Rizpah remained near the bodies, protecting them from scavengers, from the barley harvest to the early rains (late April to October).

21:12, 13 Beth Shan was at the junction of the Jezreel and Jordan valleys, about four miles west of the Jordan. **from the street:** Apparently the bodies of **Saul** and **Jonathan** had been suspended on a wall along a main street of the Philistine city (1 Sam. 31:10). **Gilboa** is a small mountain range in the eastern part of the Jezreel valley (1 Sam. 31:1). **Those who had been hanged** refers to the seven sons in vv. 8–10.

21:14 Zelah was a town allotted to **Benjamin** (Josh. 18:28). **God heeded the prayer for the land:** Divine justice had been satisfied. God responded to the prayers of His people, bringing an end to the famine.

21:15–22 This section records the exploits of David and his men against the Philistines. The word translated **giant** throughout this section (vv. 16, 18, 20, 22) means one of the Rephaim, a people living in Canaan who were noted for their large size (Gen. 15:19–21; Num. 13:33; Deut. 2:11).

21:16 The **spear** of **Ishbi-Benob** weighed **three hundred shekels,** or approximately seven and a half pounds.

21:17 Abishai was Joab's brother (3:30; 16:9–11; 20:6; 1 Sam. 26:6–9). **You shall go out no more with us:** David's men did not want him to risk his life in battle. The **lamp of Israel** refers to **David,** whose life and leadership provided righteous guidance for the people of Israel.

21:18 Sibbechai the Hushathite is listed in 1 Chr. 11:29 with David's mighty men.

21:19–22 Jonathan was David's nephew, the son of **Shimea.**

22:1, 2 While this psalm later became part of the congregational worship of Israel (Ps. 18), it began as David's personal and earnest expression of praise **to the Lord.** This song was composed when God delivered David **from the hand of Saul** during David's wilderness exploits. Perhaps an incident such as the one recorded in 1 Sam. 23:24–28 provided the impetus for David to write this "song of testimony."

22:3 the horn of my salvation: The horn of an animal was used for protection and defense. Hence, the horn stands for might and power.

22:4, 5 To be praised means "to be boasted about joyfully." God is not only worthy of our contemplative worship, but also to be celebrated for what He does for us.

22:6 Sheol is used in Hebrew poetry as a synonym for death. Many believe the word is derived from the Hebrew word meaning "to ask" or "to enquire." In the OT, Sheol is described as a place of "dust," referring to death (Job 17:16), as a place of "corruption" (Ps. 16:10), and as a "Pit" (Is. 14:15).

22:7–15 These verses describe God's active intervention in terms reminiscent of His appearance to Moses at Mt. Sinai, with earthquakes, thunder, darkness, and lightning (Ex. 19:16–20; Ps. 68).

22:16–19 The imagery used here recalls the miraculous parting of the Red Sea (Ex. 14).

22:20–28 David acknowledges six reasons for Yahweh's gracious deliverance: (1) because God **delighted** in David (v. 20); (2) because of David's **righteousness** (vv. 21, 25); (3) because of David's obedience to God's **ways** and **statues** (vv. 22, 23); (4) because David kept himself from **iniquity** (v. 24); (5) because God is **merciful** (v. 26); (6) because God saves the **humble** (David) and humbles the **haughty** (Saul; v. 28).

22:21 according to my righteousness: David believed that God would deal with people according to their conduct, punishing the wicked and blessing the righteous (Deut. 30:15–20). These words may appear self-righteous, but they must be compared with David's own confessions of sinfulness (12:13; Ps. 38:1–10). His righteousness was based on God's unfailing kindness to him (v. 51; Ps. 38:15).

22:22, 23 I have kept the ways of the Lord: One thinks of David's rash action of adultery with Bathsheba and his sending Uriah to die. How then could he say these words? Perhaps this psalm was written before those events had taken place. Yet, there were doubtless many other sins in David's life even before the sins of great notoriety. In any event, David was forgiven those sins when he acknowledged them to the Lord. As is the case with believers today, David could stand in a *position* of righteousness even as he strove, by the power of God's Spirit, to *live* in righteousness.

22:24–29 David did not claim sinless perfection. The word **blameless** is used of a person who is sound, wholesome, and has integrity (Gen. 17:1).

22:30, 31 run against a troop: David refers to a successful military pursuit (1 Sam. 30:8).

22:32, 33 who is God: The rhetorical question emphasizes the reality of God in contrast with false gods and idols (Is. 40:25).

22:34 Deer are noted for their swiftness, agility, and surefootedness. They are also a picture of graceful beauty.

22:35–40 It would take unusual strength to **bend a bow of bronze** (Job 20:24).

22:41–43 the necks of my enemies: This metaphor is taken from the custom of a victorious king putting his foot on the neck of a defeated foe as a sign of complete overthrow (Ps. 110:1).

22:44–46 as the head of the nations: Through his military exploits and international agreements, David was able to exercise control over many surrounding nations.

22:47–49 The Lord lives: This shout of faith became a motto in biblical times, particularly when shouted in contrast to the false gods of other nations, who had no life. Like a **Rock,** God is strong, steadfast, and a place of refuge (Ps. 91:1–3). Perhaps this metaphor recalled to David the many times he had taken refuge in rocks to elude his pursuers (1 Sam 23:25).

22:50 Because God delivered His own (vv. 48, 49), David vowed to praise Him. The word translated **give thanks** means "to confess publicly" or "to give public acknowledgment." It is the primary Hebrew word for praise in the Book of Psalms.

22:51 His anointed: David referred to himself as God's royal representative on earth. But the word *anointed* also points to David's descendant, King Jesus. He is the ultimate Anointed One, the meaning of the name Messiah. The name derived from the Greek word for *anointed* is Christ. It is not just the "last name" of Jesus, but His great title: He is the Anointed One who is anticipated by the promises of the OT.

23:1 The Hebrew word for **thus says** is a stylized term that is often used in prophetic speech. It adds significance to what is said and may be translated "the solemn utterance" or "a revelation." This is a very impressive term in Hebrew poetry; here it is used twice in one verse. **raised up on high:** David recalled his humble origins as a son of Jesse, whom God sovereignly exalted to the throne of Israel. **the sweet psalmist of Israel:** Of 150 psalms in the Book of Psalms, 73 are attributed to David by the text. No person in the Scriptures is more closely associated with music in the worship of the Lord than King David.

23:2 The Spirit of the Lord spoke by: David claimed to speak the words of God through his inspired poetry (Ps. 139:4). This is a claim to the divine inspiration of the Scriptures, just as much as are the NT passages 2 Tim. 3:16; Heb. 1:1, 2; 2 Pet. 1:19–21.

23:3, 4 He who rules over men: David voiced God's expectations for rulers. Bringing blessing like the light dawn after the rain, like a clear morning, like tender grass—each of these similes speaks of new life, purity, and refreshment. The function of the king was not to

impoverish the nation. Instead, the king was to ennoble the people as he presented to them the refreshing will of God.

23:5 The establishment of the **everlasting covenant** that God made with David is recorded in 7:12–16. Here and in Ps. 89 are David's celebrations of the covenant in song. **Will He not make it increase:** This rhetorical question expresses David's faith that God would carry out His promise. The covenant was based on God's sovereign, unchangeable will.

23:6, 7 sons of rebellion: The Hebrew word used here is one of contempt and scorn. It is the word that wicked Shimei hurled at David when the latter was fleeing from the rebellion of his son Absalom (16:7). The word was also used to describe Sheba, the scoundrel from the tribe of Benjamin (20:1). David anticipated God's judgment upon the ungodly, who are likened to **thorns** fit only to be **burned.**

23:8–12 The term **mighty men** suggests that these were the elite of David's troops, possibly his personal bodyguards. These men were heroes in the full sense of the word. Their listing must have inspired others to attain to such

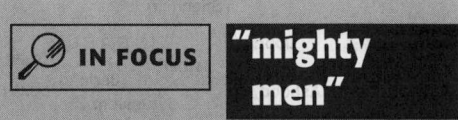

(Heb. *gibbor*) (2 Sam. 23:8; Joel 3:9) Strong's #1368: This word emphasizes excellence. In the OT, it is used for the excellence of a lion (Prov. 30:30), of good or bad men (Gen. 10:9; 1 Chr. 19:8), of giants (Gen. 6:4), of angels (Ps. 103:20), or even God (Deut. 10:17; Neh. 9:32). The phrase "mighty God" is used three times in the OT, including Isaiah's messianic prophecy of the birth of Jesus (Is. 9:6; 10:21; Jer. 32:18). The Scriptures state that the mighty man is not victorious because of his strength (Ps. 33:16) but because of his understanding and knowledge of the Lord (Jer. 9:23, 24).

accomplishments. **eight hundred:** Although 1 Chr. 11:11 records three hundred, this figure is probably accurate (v. 18).

23:13, 14 The Valley of Rephaim was a route to Jerusalem (5:18). **Bethlehem,** David's hometown (1 Sam. 16:1–13), was about six miles south of Jerusalem.

23:15, 16 poured it out to the Lord: The water had been provided at such great risk that David regarded it as too precious to drink, and offered it as a sacrifice. Ordinarily, wine was used for a drink offering (Lev. 23:13, 18, 37); here, water more costly than the finest wine was poured in celebration before the Lord.

23:17 David calls the water **blood** because it was brought to him at the risk of life.

23:18, 19 The exploits of **Abishai,** the

HAMATH

(ZOBAH)

Mediterranean Sea

PHOENICIA

Damascus

Tyre • Dan

Megiddo •
Beth Shan •

Shechem

Joppa •   I S R A E L

Bethel •   Jericho •   Rabbah

Ashdod •   Gath •   Jerusalem •   (AMMON)

Ashkelon •

Gaza •   Hebron •   Dead Sea

• Raphia   Beersheba •

(MOAB)

Zoar •

• Bozrah

• Kadesh Barnea

(EDOM)

N

0   60 Mi.
0   60 Km.

• Elath

© 1996 Thomas Nelson, Inc.

The Davidic Kingdom

David's military exploits successfully incorporated into the Israelite kingdom the powers of Edom, Moab, Ammon, and Zobah.

brother of Joab, are detailed in the record of the life of David (2:18; 10:10; 1 Sam. 26:6–9).

23:20–23 Benaiah served as commander over the Cherethites and the Pelethites (8:18). He was in charge of David's personal bodyguards. The term **his guard** means "his obedi-

ence"—that is, those who were bound to obey and protect David. **snowy day:** A light snowfall is not unusual in the Judean hill country during the winter.

23:24–39 thirty: The list actually contains thirty-one names. Apparently, the number of active soldiers in this unit was kept close to thirty. With minor variations, this list is also recorded in 1 Chr. 11:26–41.

23:39 thirty-seven: This figure includes **the three** (vv. 8–17); **Abishai** and **Benaiah** (vv. 18–23); the thirty-one (vv. 24–39); and David's commander, **Joab** (v. 37).

24:1 the anger of the Lord: This is an ominous note with which to begin the last chapter. That the chapter is an appendix and not the last act, as it were, is the saving grace. **He moved David:** This comment indicates that David's actions were prompted by the Lord, while 1 Chr. 21:1 reveals that he was prompted by Satan. These remarks reflect two aspects of the same incident. Satan instigated the independent spirit that led David to number the people, but God permitted Satan to exercise this influence so that His divine plan might be accomplished (compare Gen. 50:20). Yet God's sovereignty never annuls human responsibility for one's actions.

24:2 The expression **from Dan to Beersheba** denotes the whole territory of Israel from its northern to its southern extremity, a distance of about 150 miles.

24:3, 4 why does my lord the king desire this thing: Joab, for all his faults, saw the error in David's plan (1 Chr. 21:3) and raised his protest in the form of a question. Why was this census considered sinful when God had commanded a numbering in the time of Moses (Num. 1:1–3)? David may have been trusting in military strength rather than God's protective care (Deut. 17:16). Verse 9 suggests that this census was the first step in preparing for a military draft. God's plan seems to have been for Israel to have a citizen army rather than a large standing army, so that Israel would trust in His protection.

24:5 The numbering began in the territory east of the **Jordan. Aroer** was about 14 miles east of the Dead Sea on the north bank of the Arnon River. **Jazer** was east of the Jordan, about six and a half miles west of present-day Amman.

24:6 Gilead was east of the Jordan between the Jabbok and Yarmuk rivers. **Dan Jaan** is thought to refer to the city of Dan, about 23 miles north of the Sea of Galilee. **Sidon** was on the Mediterranean coast north of Tyre.

24:7, 8 Tyre was on the Mediterranean coast about 35 miles northwest of the Sea of Galilee. **The Hivites** were Canaanites who occupied the region of Lebanon (Judg. 3:3), Shechem (Gen. 34:2), and Gibeon (Josh. 9:3). **Canaanites** is a general term for the non-Israelite inhabitants of the land. **Beersheba** was in the desert parts of Judah about 28 miles southwest of Hebron.

24:9 men who drew the sword: The numbers given refer only to men of military age. It is impressive that the division of Israel and Judah was so well established. This division would in the end result in a divided kingdom. The numbers—800,000 in Israel and 500,000 in Judah—are clearly rounded figures.

24:10 David's heart condemned him: David fell into sin on several occasions, but his heart was always sensitive to God's righteous will. He quickly confessed his wrong and sought restoration with the Lord. The text still does not state precisely what the sin was. However, we may surmise that David's intent in numbering the people had some sinister aspect to it—perhaps pride in the size of his empire.

24:11, 12 Gad, David's prophet or **seer,** is first mentioned in 1 Sam. 22:5. He may have been one of the writers or contributing editors of 2 Sam.

24:13 David was given a choice of three punishments for his sin: (1) **seven years of famine,** (2) **three months** of flight, or (3) **three days** of **plague.** Moses warned of all of these punishments for those who broke God's covenant (Deut. 28:15–68).

24:14 let us fall into the hand of the LORD: David calculated that God would be more merciful than a person. He apparently took the third option, a plague. **Mercies** speaks of a mother's tender compassion for her child. Even in the exercise of His wrath, God has mercy on those he disciplines (Hab. 3:2).

24:15 The nature of the **plague** is not specified, only that its origin was from the Lord. The number of those who died was very high, over three times the number of soldiers of Absalom's army who perished in his abortive rebellion (18:7).

24:16 The judgment was carried out by **the angel of the LORD** (Judg. 6:11–22). In a demonstration of divine grace, God withheld the plague from destroying the people of Jerusalem. A **threshing floor** is a hard, flat surface where wheat is crushed to separate the kernels from the straw. **Araunah,** called Ornan in 2 Chr. 3:1, was a **Jebusite,** one of the original inhabitants of Jerusalem.

24:17–21 David interceded on behalf of the people—**these sheep**—regarding the plague. He once again confessed his sin (v. 10) and asked God to hold him, rather than the people, accountable.

24:22 Threshing implements refers to the heavy, wooden sleds which were dragged over wheat during the threshing process to break it up.

24:23, 24 Araunah wanted to *give* David the threshing floor and the oxen for sacrifice. David was unwilling to offer to the Lord that which cost him nothing. This is a powerful principle for all worship and service before the Lord. If there is no cost, there is no real sacrifice. David understood and practiced the principle of sacrificial giving to the Lord (2 Cor. 8:1–4). **the threshing floor:** The threshing floor was located on Mount Moriah, where Abraham had bound Isaac (Gen. 22:2). Later, Solomon would build the temple at this site (1 Kin. 6; 1 Chr. 21:27—22:1; 2 Chr. 3:1). **Fifty shekels of silver** paid only for the threshing floor, the oxen, and the implements. The land that surrounded the threshing floor would cost considerably more—600 shekels or 15 pounds of gold (1 Chr. 21:25).

24:25 The **burnt** offering was the principal atoning sacrifice for unintentional sins (Lev. 1:1–17; 6:8–13). It was completely consumed upon the altar, except for the hide, which was given to the officiating priest. The **peace** offering was an optional sacrifice, which did not form any part of the regular offerings required in the tabernacle or temple (Lev. 3:1–17; 7:11–34). It was a voluntary expression of thanksgiving or worship. The preservation of Jerusalem and the purchase of the temple site prepared the way for the coming of David's successor, King Solomon. He would build the temple for the true worship of Israel's God.

The First Book of

Kings

———————————————— ■ ————————————————

IRST KINGS RECORDS THE LIVES OF A NUMBER of famous people, both good and evil. King David, King Solomon, and the Queen of Sheba are famous examples of righteous people searching after God's wisdom. On the other hand, Ahab and Jezebel are two notorious examples of wicked people discarding God's Law and rebelling against Him. To confront a man as wicked as Ahab, God sent someone more than equal

to the task, the prophet Elijah. Often described as Israel's greatest and most dramatic prophet, Elijah displayed at Mount Carmel in an unforgettable way the power of God over the false god Baal and his four hundred prophets.

In the final analysis, 1 Kings is the story of one people headed down two different paths. It is a story of good kings and bad kings, true prophets and false prophets, and of disobedience and loyalty to God. Most importantly, it is a story of Israel's spiritual odyssey and God's faithfulness to His people.

The author of 1 and 2 Kings was heir to a long history of God's dealing with His people. In the two Books of Kings, the narrator presents a selected rehearsal of the events of the nation covering the period from the death of King David in the early tenth century B.C. to the fall of Jerusalem around 586 B.C. The author's focus is on the spiritual successes and failures in Israel's history.

First Kings begins this narrative with a detailed account of the great Solomonic era (971–930 B.C.; chs. 1—11). The narrative highlights Solomon's godly wisdom (1 Kin. 3; 4), his building projects, the temple and palace com-

plex (1 Kin. 5—8), and then Solomon's spiritual failures toward the end of his reign. After Solomon's demise, the book addresses the division of the kingdom into a northern kingdom (Israel), made up of ten tribes under Jeroboam I, and a southern kingdom, centered in Judah under Solomon's son Rehoboam as king (12:1–24). Thereafter, the different fortunes of the two kingdoms are traced in terms of the blessings and punishments that come as a result of the people's obedience or disobedience to God's Law. The sorry picture of Israel's growing apostasy is sketched up to the accession of Ahaziah in the northern kingdom (853–852 B.C.) and the reign of Jehoshaphat in the south (872–847 B.C.). During this period, the two kingdoms had to face the rising imperialism of Assyria, particularly during the reigns of the Assyrian kings, Ashurnasirpal II (883–859 B.C.) and Shalmaneser III (859–824 B.C.).

Thus, the narrative of 1 Kings stretches from the high prosperity of the Solomonic kingdom in the tenth century B.C. to the insecurity of the mid-ninth century B.C. During this period, the internal spiritual weakness of the two Israelite kingdoms that would one day spell their defeat was beginning to take shape. The book covers an era of dramatic change.

The author's purpose in writing 1 and 2 Kings was not primarily to provide historical information. Instead, the author wanted to evaluate Israel's spiritual odyssey that resulted in God's chastisement (2 Kin. 17:7–23; 24:18–20). As a result, the author devotes considerable attention to evaluating the kings according to the way they responded to the responsibilities detailed in the Mosaic and Davidic covenants. The author notes specifically those who handled such responsibilities well, such as Hezekiah and Josiah. Moreover, the ministry of the prophets as God's authoritative messengers is highlighted. Particular attention is given to the ministries of Elijah (1 Kin. 17—19; 21; 2 Kin. 2:1–11) and Elisha (2 Kin. 2:12—8:15).

In the entire account, the necessity for a genuinely godly walk—one in obedience to God's Law—is underscored. Particularly in the accounts relating to Elijah, true worship of the living God is contrasted with the false religion of the Canaanites (1 Kin. 17; 18). The main difference between the true God and the false gods is that the living God faithfully fulfills His promises (1 Kin. 8:20, 23–26). Hence, special attention is given to God's promises in the Davidic covenant. In that covenant, God had promised to bless Israel (1 Kin. 2:4, 5, 45; 3:6, 14; 6:12, 13; 2 Kin. 8:19). Yet this blessing was tied to obedience: Israel's only hope for God's blessing and true success lay in obedience to God's word (1 Kin. 2:2–4). The failures of the Israelites to walk in God's ways and their subsequent chastisement can serve as a warning to us. At the same time, the prophets, who stood up for God's truth in a period of decline, can motivate us to stand for truth and righteousness in our time.

First and Second Kings were originally one book in the Hebrew canon, as were the Books of Samuel. The translators of the Septuagint, the Greek Old Testament of about 150 B.C., joined Samuel and Kings together and divided the resulting book into four parts. When Samuel and Kings were separated later, these four parts became 1 and 2 Samuel and 1 and 2 Kings.

Traditionally, Jeremiah was identified as the author of 1 and 2 Kings. However, contemporary critical scholarship has suggested that the books were the result of a compilation process that began with its initial composition in the late seventh century B.C. and concluded in the middle of the sixth century B.C. The proponents of this view have identified a Deuteronomic school of writers as the source of 1 and 2 Kings because of the emphasis in these books on religious orthodoxy (the Law and the temple), the ministry of the prophets, and the central place of the Davidic dynasty.

Evangelical biblical scholars have largely rejected the idea of a Deuteronomic school of writers. Many continue to endorse the traditional view that Jeremiah wrote the books of the Kings. They cite as evidence for his authorship his priestly origin, his prophetic activity, his access to governmental authorities at the highest level, and his great personal involvement in the complex religious, social, and political activities that occurred during the collapse and fall of Judah in the early sixth century B.C. Certainly no other single person would have been in a better position to know the spiritual

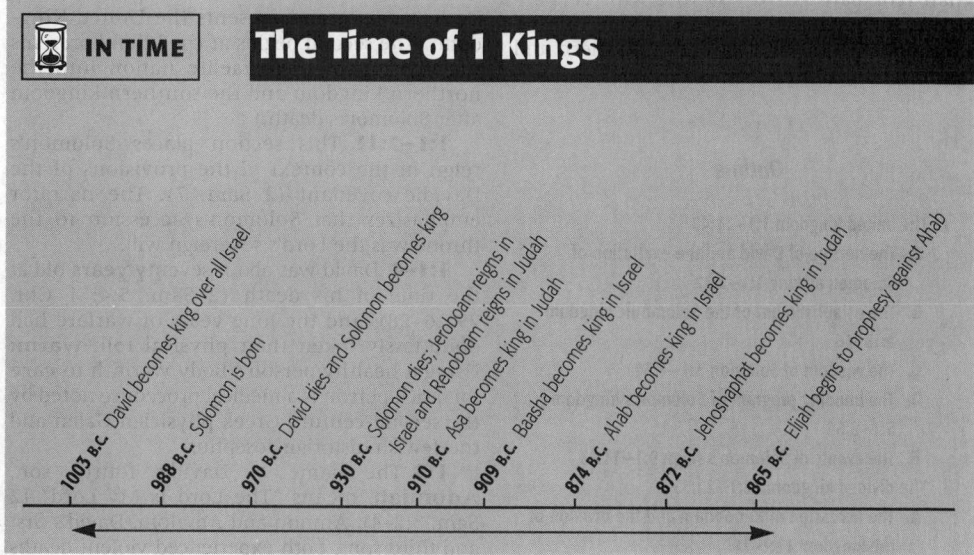

IN TIME   **The Time of 1 Kings**

1003 B.C. David becomes king over all Israel

988 B.C. Solomon is born

970 B.C. David dies and Solomon becomes king

930 B.C. Solomon dies; Jeroboam reigns in Israel and Rehoboam reigns in Judah

910 B.C. Asa becomes king in Judah

909 B.C. Baasha becomes king in Israel

874 B.C. Ahab becomes king in Israel

872 B.C. Jehoshaphat becomes king in Judah

865 B.C. Elijah begins to prophesy against Ahab

situation of the day and to have access to the state records, historical information, and source material necessary for writing 1 and 2 Kings.

Nevertheless, differences in writing style between the books of Jeremiah and Kings, as well as distinctions in the use of the names of Judah's kings make any final determination of the authorship of the books of the Kings uncertain. If due weight is given to the long section dealing with Judah (2 Kin. 18:1—25:26), it may reasonably be said that both books of Kings, except the final appended historical notice (2 Kin. 25:27–30), are the work of an author who lived through the last days of Judah and the fall of Jerusalem in 586 B.C. Perhaps the spiritual reform that followed the recovery of the Book of the Law during Josiah's reign (c. 622 B.C.) provided the necessary impetus for the author to gather up his sources and write an account of Israel's faithfulness to the covenant from the days of David until his own time.

To compose a work covering nearly four hundred years, the author of the Book of Kings would need excellent source material. Three sources are specifically named: (1) The Book of the Acts of Solomon (11:41), which detailed the events of the Solomonic era; (2) The Book of the Chronicles of the Kings of Israel (cited seventeen times in 14:19—15:31), which were the court records of the northern kingdom; and (3) The Book of the Chronicles of the Kings of Judah (mentioned fifteen times in 1 Kin. 14:29—2 Kin. 24:5), which were court records of the southern kingdom. Furthermore, the author might have had biographical accounts of David (1:1—2:11), Elijah, and Elisha (1 Kin. 16:29—2 Kin. 9:37), and access to the Book of Isaiah (compare Is. 36—39 to 2 Kin. 18:13–20:19). Such material was preserved in priestly and prophetic centers in both the northern and southern kingdoms.

Outline

I. The united kingdom 1:1—11:43
   A. The decline of David and the exaltation of Solomon as king 1:1—2:12
   B. The establishment of the Solomonic kingdom 2:13–46
   C. The wisdom of Solomon 3:1—4:34
   D. The building program of Solomon's kingdom 5:1—8:66
   E. The events of Solomon's reign 9:1—11:43
II. The divided kingdom 12:1—22:53
   A. The accession of Rehoboam and the division of the kingdom 12:1–24

   B. The early kings of the two nations 12:25—16:14
      1. The reign of Jeroboam in the northern kingdom 12:25—14:20
      2. The reigns of Rehoboam, Abijah, and Asa in the southern kingdom 14:21—15:24
      3. The end of the first dynasty in the northern kingdom: Nadab 15:25–32
      4. The second dynasty in the northern kingdom: Baasha 15:33—16:14
   C. The third dynasty in the northern kingdom: Omri 16:15—22:53
      1. The reign of Omri in the northern kingdom 16:15–28
      2. The reign of Ahab in the northern kingdom 16:29—22:40
         a. Elijah and the drought 17:1–24
         b. Elijah on Mt. Carmel 18:1–46
         c. Elijah's flight to Horeb 19:1–21
         d. A prophet's condemnation of Ahab 20:1–43
         e. Elijah's condemnation of Ahab 21:1–28
         f. Micaiah's prophecy of Ahab's death 22:1–40
      3. The reign of Jehoshaphat in the southern kingdom and the accession of Ahaziah in the northern kingdom 22:41–53

Commentary

1:1—11:43 First Kings has two large sections. The first focuses on Solomon's reign, following David's death, and presents the United Kingdom. (The second begins at ch. 12 and presents the division of the Israelite nation into the northern kingdom and the southern kingdom after Solomon's death.)

1:1—2:11 This section places Solomon's reign in the context of the provisions of the Davidic covenant (2 Sam. 7). The narrator emphasizes that Solomon's accession to the throne was the Lord's sovereign will.

1:1–4 David was about seventy **years** old at the time of his death (2 Sam. 5:4; 1 Chr. 29:26–28), and the long years of warfare had doubtlessly taken their physical toll. **warm:** Using a healthy person's body warmth to **care** for a sick person is a medical procedure noted by the second-century Greek physician Galen and the Jewish historian Josephus.

1:5 The name of David's fourth son, **Adonijah,** means "The Lord Is My Lord" (2 Sam. 3:2–4). Amnon and Absalom, David's first and third sons, both experienced violent deaths

(2 Sam. 13:28, 29; 18:14). Chiliab, his second son, apparently died at an early age. **I will be king:** Adonijah, the oldest surviving son, might have assumed that he would inherit the crown even though Solomon had been designated as successor (1:13, 17, 30; 2:15; 1 Chr. 22:9, 10). Adonijah evidently knew of the intended royal succession, because he deliberately avoided inviting those who would support the king's choice (vv. 8, 10). Adonijah thus **exalted himself** against God's will.

1:6 rebuked: While David had been a most capable leader and a man of deep spiritual sensitivity, he had not exercised proper parental discipline of his children (2 Sam. 13:21–39; 14:18–24).

1:7 In gaining important allies to support his quest for the crown, Adonijah sought the assistance of **Joab,** David's general, and **Abiathar,** the high priest.

1:8 Zadok was descended from the priestly line of Eleazar (2 Sam. 8:17). **Benaiah** served as the commander of the king's bodyguard and was considered one of David's mighty men (2 Sam. 23:20–23). The prophet **Nathan** had long been David's confidant, spiritual advisor, and conscience (2 Sam. 12:1–25). **Shimei** is probably the man who later became Solomon's district governor (4:18); he should not be confused with David's foolish enemy, Shimei the son of Gera (2:8; 2 Sam. 19:18–23).

1:9, 10 Zoheleth means "Serpent." Perhaps this was the shape of an outcropping of rock that was a well-known rendezvous point. Adonijah's ceremonial meal was held at **En Rogel** near the intersection of the Hinnom and Kidron valleys, a place well situated for Adonijah's purposes. En Rogel had positive associations with David (2 Sam. 17:17).

1:11 It is a mark of David's integrity that **Nathan,** who had confronted him with his terrible sin, was still welcome in the royal household (2 Sam. 12:1–15). Nathan went to

Bathsheba because she would not want to see Adonijah displace her son Solomon as heir to the throne. As David's wife, Bathsheba had immediate access to him, and she also had considerable influence in civil and social matters (15:10–13; 19:1–3; 21:5–15, 25). If Adonijah became king she and Solomon could probably expect to die in a royal purge of all potential claimants to the throne (15:29; 16:11; 2 Kin. 9:30–37; 10:1–17; 11:1).

1:12–27 Nathan and Bathsheba planned together (v. 14) how Nathan could confirm Bathsheba's report to the king. Nathan knew of David's solemn oath to Bathsheba (vv. 13, 30; Lev. 19:12), but was concerned that David might fail to act quickly against Adonijah's attempted usurpation of the crown. Bathsheba's report of the crisis was couched in terms that would provoke in David a proper sense of alarm.

1:25, 26 Giving the names of **Abiathar,** who was with Adonijah, and of **Zadok, Benaiah,** and **Solomon,** who were not, helped David see the situation that was developing.

1:27, 28 Has this thing been done: Nathan's question was both respectful and tactical. David had to act, even though he was reluctant to oppose his rebellious son (read the story of the rebellion of Absalom in 2 Sam. 15—18).

1:29, 30 An oath in the name of **the LORD** was the strongest oath a faithful Israelite would take (17:1). During the OT period, Israelites would use very strong language in oaths (Ruth 1:17). Jesus told his followers to avoid oaths completely (Matt. 5:33–37). **who has redeemed my life:** In these words of praise, David celebrated the innumerable times that the Lord had acted on his behalf, to deliver him from his enemies and from his own sins. Some of David's psalms were written in connection with those times of God's deliverance (Pss. 40; 142).

1:31 King David live forever: Bathsheba

 **IN CONTEXT** **Political Infighting**

Anyone who laments the state of politics and government today might pay careful attention to the account of Adonijah's bid for the throne of Israel (1 Kin. 1:5). With a dynasty in the making, the question was, who would succeed David? Adonijah enjoyed popular support, but David named Adonijah's half-brother, Solomon, as heir to the throne (1:11–14, 28–30, 38, 39).

Solomon extended grace to Adonijah (1:50–53), but the older brother refused to accept a lesser role. Desperate to maintain a foothold in the power structure, he enlisted Solomon's mother, Bathsheba, in a ploy to marry David's mistress, Abishag (2:13–18). The marriage would have implied to the public that Adonijah was the rightful heir to the throne, since a king's harem normally went to his successor. Solomon saw through the scheme and called for Adonijah's execution (2:22–25).

put her seal on the occasion by bowing before him and expressing the hope that his kingdom would never end.

1:32, 33 David summoned the recognized leaders in Israel who had not been party to the conspiracy (vv. 8, 10, 26) to lend their support to the coronation of Solomon. Solomon's prestige would be enhanced by riding upon the royal mule (2 Sam. 13:29; 18:9; Zech. 9:9; Matt. 21:5). **Gihon** was a spring, the principal water supply for Jerusalem. It was in the Kidron Valley east of the city. By means of a shaft leading from this spring, Joab had aided David in the capture of Jerusalem (2 Sam. 4:8; 1 Chr. 11:6), and it would be from this spring that King Hezekiah would have his famous water tunnel constructed to the pool of Siloam during the threat of the Assyrian invasion of 701 B.C. (2 Kin. 20:20).

1:34–37 The plans for public proclamation, with David's sanction and with a priestly blessing, were designed to let the people of the city know that Solomon was to be the next king of Israel.

1:38 The **Cherethites** and **Pelethites** were David's bodyguard (2 Sam. 8:18; 15:18; 20:7). Their association with David stretched back to his days among the Philistines, with whom both groups are usually identified (1 Sam. 30:13, 14; Ezek. 25:16; Zeph. 2:5).

1:39, 40 Solomon's anointing by the priest **Zadok** was normal procedure for an uninterrupted succession to the throne. When there was an interruption in the dynastic line, the anointing was performed by a prophet (19:15–18; 2 Kin. 9:1–10). Every priestly anointing would recall the words of Ps. 2, in accordance with the words of the Davidic covenant of 2 Sam. 7. The anointing announced that the anointed one was now the adopted son of the living God. Every anointing in the OT points forward to the ultimate Anointed One, the Messiah Jesus. The blowing of the **horn** celebrated and announced the anointing of a new king. The joy of the people seemed boundless, as **the earth seemed to split with their sound.**

1:41–49 The **noise** first, and then the news of the anointing of Solomon at Gihon, quickly reached Adonijah and his party at En Rogel just a few hundred feet further south (v. 9). This led to the complete demoralization of the coconspirators of Adonijah.

1:45–49 The clamor of the royally sanctioned coronation of Solomon **at Gihon** easily reached the ears of those gathered with Adonijah over the hill at En Rogel, which was just a few hundred feet south.

1:50–53 Adonijah's quest for mercy at the bloodstained (Lev. 4:7, 18, 25, 30) **horns of the altar** (v. 50) was in keeping with the traditional function of the altar as a haven of refuge for those who had committed unintentional crimes (Ex. 21:12–14). Later Joab also would try to find safety there (2:28).

1:53 Even though David was still alive (2:1–12) and the coronation had not yet taken place, the public celebration at his prophetic anointing at Gihon (1:38–40) was basically the same as declaring **Solomon** Israel's king. The name Solomon is related to the Hebrew word for "peace" (*shalom*) and the verb meaning "to be complete" (*shalem*). **Go to your house:** Solomon gave temporary clemency to his half brother, likely out of respect for his father.

2:1–3 he charged Solomon: David was following spiritual precedent as well as the custom of the ancient Middle East by passing on instruction to his son (1 Chr. 28; 29). David's charge to Solomon was reminiscent of Moses' words to the Israelites (Deut. 31:6) and the Lord's admonition to Joshua (Josh. 1:6, 7, 9). The specific instructions given here echo the standards of righteousness associated with the Mosaic covenant (Deut. 5:33; 8:6, 11; 11:1, 22).

2:4 not lack a man: God had made an unconditional covenant with David (2 Sam. 7:12–16; 1 Chr. 17:11–14), granting to him a continual posterity and a royal dynasty. Although the Davidic covenant was an everlasting sacred promise, individual kings through their evil behavior could fail to receive the benefits of the covenant (Ps. 89:3, 4, 14–24, 27–37). The line of promise would be preserved and Israel "would not lack a man," but there would come a time when the promised Ruler would not be on an earthly throne (Hos. 3:4). God's prophets predict that the heir of the throne of David will yet reign over a repentant, regathered, and restored Israel (Jer. 33:19–26; Ezek. 34:22–31) in fulfillment of the promises contained in the Abrahamic, Davidic, and new covenants (Ezek. 37:21–28; Mic. 7:18–20). The NT reveals that all this will be realized in Jesus Christ, the Savior King (Acts 3:25, 26; 15:16, 17; Gal. 3:26–29; Rev. 3:21), who is David's Heir in the ultimate sense (Acts 2:22–36).

2:5–9 David's parting advice singled out some problems that had not been solved. One concerned Joab. The bold, headstrong Joab had murdered two generals (2 Sam. 3:27; 20:10), and he had killed David's son Absalom (2 Sam. 18:14). He had joined Adonijah's ill-fated conspiracy (1:7, 19). Another problem concerned Shimei, who had treated the king shamefully on a previous occasion (2 Sam. 16:5–13; 19:16–23). **gray hair:** Both Joab and Shimei had lived a long time without requital for their wicked deeds. The aged king knew that these men would likely continue to be a problem to Solomon even as they had been to him.

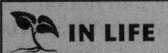

A Father's Final Charge

A farewell charge like David's to Solomon (2:1–9) was a fairly common way for fathers in the ancient world to pass on a legacy to their successors. David's last words provide a useful model for parents today to give final instructions to their children. David's charge contained several elements:

- A blunt recognition and acceptance of death (1 Kin. 2:2).
- A challenge to Solomon to act responsibly (2:2).
- A review of God's covenant with the nation of Israel (2:3) and with the house of David (2:4).
- Instructions about serving justice and honoring David's commitments (2:5–9).

2:7–9 David also included directions of kindness for the household of Barzillai, who had stood by him throughout the period associated with Absalom's rebellion (2 Sam. 17:27–29; 19:31–39). To **eat at** the king's **table** carried with it not only distinct honor, but royal favor (2 Sam. 9:7; 2 Kin. 25:29). It meant that the royal household would make provision for this family in perpetuity.

2:10–12 David's obituary will be recalled throughout Israel's history. His death, and the fact that he left a successor in his son Solomon, were the twin facts that showed that the Lord was going to accomplish His plan to establish the Davidic House and the coming rule of the Savior King.

2:10 There is a so-called tomb of David today on Mt. Zion in Jerusalem marking approximately where he might have been **buried.**

2:12 Solomon sat on the throne: By these words both his coronation as well as the establishment of his reign are indicated. The dramatic anointing marked him out as his father's true and only successor (1:38–40).

2:13–17 come peaceably: Adonijah would have Bathsheba believe that his request for Abishag was simply compensation for not receiving the crown that all had expected to go to him. Yet Adonijah's plea carried with it serious ramifications. Taking a member of the king's harem would normally be interpreted as a claim to the throne (2 Sam. 3:7–10; 12:8; 16:21–22). **Abishag** had cared for David in his old age (1:1–4, 15).

2:18–22 the kingdom also: Solomon not only saw through Adonijah's plot, but recognized Joab and Abiathar as fellow conspirators. All three were dealt with severely (vv. 23–35).

2:23, 24 Solomon's actions, though severe, were what he believed to be the means whereby he would be able to maintain faith with Yahweh, who had made him the king.

2:25, 26 hand of Benaiah: This mighty man of David did not participate in Adonijah's plots (1:8, 26). Furthermore, he participated in the anointing of Solomon at Gihon (1:38).

2:27 When **Abiathar** was **removed** from office as a priest, his influence was greatly restricted. Solomon spared Abiathar's life in recognition of his past service to God and David (2 Sam. 15:24, 29; 1 Chr. 15:11–15). With this act God's word to Eli came to fulfillment. Eli's descendants were removed from serving the Lord (1 Sam. 2:30–33).

2:28–31 Because Joab was a murderer (2 Sam. 3:27; 18:14; 20:10), he could not claim the protective sanctity of the **horns of the altar** (1:50). Therefore, he could not escape execution (vv. 29–31).

2:32–34 The recital of Joab's evil deeds brought about the reason for his execution, to remove the innocent blood from the head of David and his household.

2:35 Solomon then decisively appointed his two loyalists to the positions vacated. **Benaiah** became the captain of the army and **Zadok** the high priest. **Zadok** was a descendant of Eleazar, the son of Aaron (1 Chr. 6:4–8).

2:36–46 At first Solomon placed **Shimei** under an extended house arrest rather than executing him outright for his shameful treatment of David (2:8, 9). However, Shimei felt he must pursue **two slaves** that had run away. This disobedience led to his death. **all the wickedness:** Shimei had openly opposed and cursed David (2 Sam. 16:5–13; 19:16–23). He openly violated the terms of the agreement with Solomon (vv. 36, 37). By executing Joab and Shimei and removing Abiathar, Solomon fulfilled David's instructions to him (vv. 5, 8) and also solved the problem of a hostile high priest.

3:1–4:34 This section emphasizes God's approval of Solomon as David's successor by noting the divine bestowal of wisdom upon him, that he might rule the kingdom effectively. This section has four divisions: (1) Solomon's desire for wisdom (3:1–15); (2) Solomon's judicial wisdom (3:16–28); (3) Solomon's administrative wisdom (4:1–28); (4) Solomon's fame for wisdom (4:29–34).

3:1 married: In the ancient Middle East, political alliances were often ratified by the marriage of the son of one king to the daughter of another. Except in unusual circumstances, the pharaohs of Egypt did not observe this custom (but see 1 Chr. 4:17, 18). Therefore, the giving of Pharaoh's daughter to Solomon attested to the Israelite king's growing prestige and importance to the Egyptian king. Pharaoh gave the important town of Gezer to the couple as a wedding present (9:16). The moral and spiritual failure of Solomon in his later years was a by-product of his many marriages with foreign wives. Each of these would come with her own retinue of pagan servants and priests of her pagan religion. See ch. 11 for a development of this sad theme. **house of the LORD:** Both Solomon's palace and the temple are called a house. Just as Solomon occupied the palace, the Lord was considered uniquely present with His people in the temple.

3:2, 3 Whether the worship ceremonies took place in specially constructed enclosures or at an open-air sanctuary (13:32), such hilltop areas or **high places** provided a setting where Canaanite religious rites could be infiltrated into Israel's worship (11:7; 2 Kin. 16:4).

3:4, 5 Gibeon is a hill about six miles northwest of Jerusalem.

3:6, 7 The term for **child** often refers to a servant or to an inexperienced person still in training for a profession (19:21; 20:14, 15; 2 Kin. 4:12). With proper humility, Solomon stressed his relative youth and inexperience.

3:8, 9 an understanding heart: The phrase suggested not only the willingness and patience to listen to all sides of an issue, but also the desire for the ability to reason.

3:10–12 God answered Solomon's request in abundant measure, granting him not only an **understanding heart,** but one that was **wise** for handling the crucial affairs of life in a fair and skillful manner. The abilities that God gave to Solomon were truly exceptional. Solomon's newly acquired wisdom (1 Kin. 4:29–34) would be tested often (vv. 16–28; 10:1–13, 23, 24) and much needed for the critical problems that would face his administration. The succeeding chapters will attest to Solomon's administrative skills in the political (ch. 4), architectural (chs. 5—7), and socio-economic areas (9:10–28; 10:14–29). Solomon's wisdom, however, would provide no guarantee of spiritual wisdom (1 Kin. 11:1–13).

3:13, 14 what you have not asked: Because Solomon chose a greater gift than riches and honor, God promised him everything else as well (Matt. 6:33).

3:15 a dream: Dreams were one of the ways that God revealed His will (Gen. 20:3; 37:5; Dan. 2:3). Although David had brought the **ark of the covenant** to Jerusalem (2 Sam. 6), the tabernacle and its furnishings remained in Gibeon, which served as an important worship center (v. 4; 2 Chr. 1:3–5).

3:16–25 The fact that **harlots** could appear before Solomon suggested that he made himself available to persons of all stations of life who had a legitimate claim for justice.

3:26, 27 yearned with compassion: Her love as a mother made her give up her own child rather than see it die.

3:28 wisdom . . . justice: These important qualities which marked Solomon's reign from the beginning would characterize the rule of Israel's Messiah in a far greater way (Is. 11:1–5).

4:1–6 Solomon's wisdom was also demonstrated in his appointment of proper officials for all the needs of state. For civil affairs, Solomon

---

 **IN PERSON**   ## The Gift of an Understanding Heart

Instead of asking God for wealth, health, or happiness, Solomon asked for "an understanding heart" (1 Kin. 3:9). The request itself showed remarkable wisdom, but it also made a great deal of sense given the circumstances in which Solomon found himself.

He was following in the footsteps of a remarkable man (1 Kin. 3:6). He was young and perceived himself to be inexperienced (3:7). He was saddled with the responsibility of leading God's people (3:8), a people who had shown themselves on frequent occasions to be stubborn, rebellious, and hard on their leaders. And he had just emerged from a messy fight over succession to the throne (1 Kin. 1; 2). Most of his enemies had been eliminated. But could he ever forget the intrigue surrounding those events? Likewise, could he ever forget the many attempts that had been made on his father's life? And what about the circumstances surrounding his own birth (2 Sam. 11; 12)? Given Solomon's heritage, he had many reasons to ask for the ability to "discern between good and evil" (1 Kin. 3:9).

appointed **scribes** and a chief officer over the district officials (Azariah). He chose **Benaiah** to replace Joab as commander for **the army** (2:35). As a part of his personal staff, he

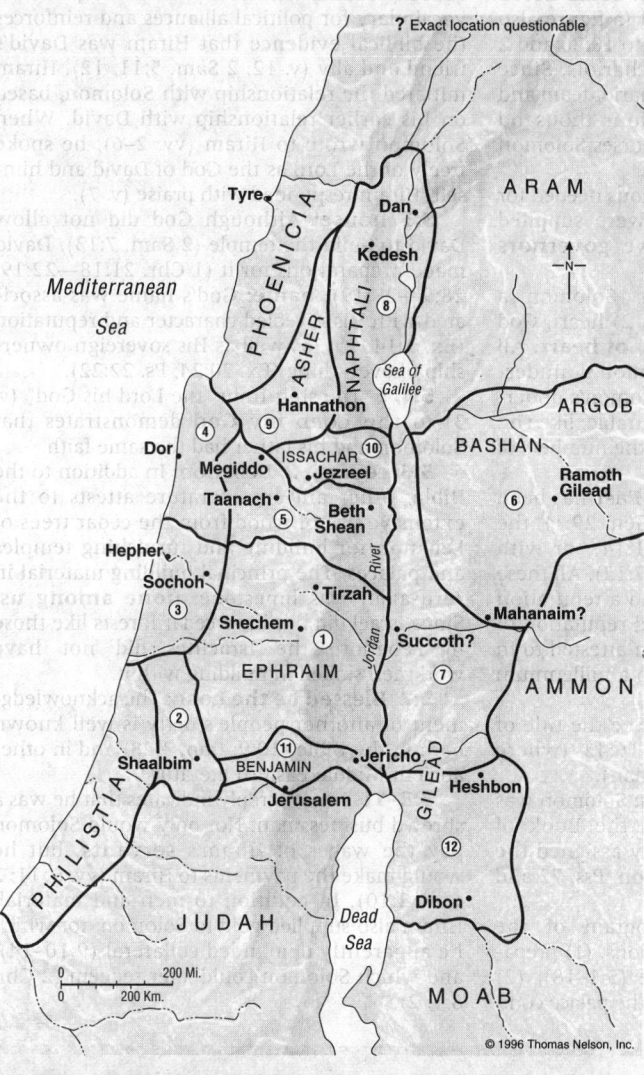

? Exact location questionable

Mediterranean Sea

Solomon's Administrative Districts

The growth and extension of Israel's borders under Solomon's leadership required extensive military expenditures. Coupled with this were ambitious building and commercial projects throughout his expanding kingdom. As a result, Solomon faced an urgent need for ever increasing revenues.

To address this need, Solomon divided Israel into twelve districts and appointed governors over each district. These governors were responsible for levying and collecting taxes to provide for the needs of Jerusalem and the royal palace. The increasingly heavy taxes upon Israel created major dissension because the region of Judah was exempted. Furthermore, the divisions of the districts violated the old tribal boundaries.

appointed a special advisor, **the king's friend;** a chief of protocol, **the recorder;** and a minister of palace and state, to be **over the household.** This last position became a powerful office in royal administration. Men who occupied this powerful position were Obadiah (18:3), Eliakim (2 Kin. 18:18), and Shebna (Is. 22:15).

4:7–19 These **twelve governors** were in charge of Solomon's districts. They were responsible for handling lesser administrative tasks and raising revenue for the crown. The districts did not follow tribal boundaries.

4:18, 19 Not the same person as the **Shimei** at 2:8. This Shimei may be the Shimei of 1:8—a supporter of Solomon.

4:20, 21 numerous as the sand: God fulfilled His promise to make Abraham's descendants numerous, a great nation (Gen. 15:5, 18). Solomon's empire extended far beyond the traditional boundaries of Israel. Through this greatly expanded empire, Jewish people not only traveled to far-flung regions, but they took with them their knowledge of the living God. **River:** The Euphrates. God's promise to Abraham (Gen. 15:18) was fulfilled in part in the hegemony of Solomon. By various trade arrangements, treaties, and power plays, Solomon extended his empire far beyond Israel's traditional boundaries. However, the complete fulfillment of God's words to Abraham in Gen. 15 still lies in the future.

4:22 kors: The kor was the same size as the homer (Ezek. 45:14), six and a quarter bushels, a normal load for a donkey.

4:23 oxen . . . fowl: Meat was a rare item in a person's diet, suggestive of a feast (Prov. 9:1).

4:24, 25 The name Solomon is related to the word **peace.** It is fitting for this name to be associated with the time of Israel's great reign of peace. The **vine** and **fig tree** are symbols of God's blessing for those who obey His covenant.

4:26 forty thousand stalls: Some Greek manuscripts read four thousand (a figure also found in 2 Chr. 9:25). According to 10:26 and 2 Chr. 1:14, Solomon had 1,400 chariots. Since three horses were considered a chariot team and would be quartered together, four thousand would be about the number of horses Solomon needed.

4:27, 28 The immense provisions needed for the royal house (vv. 22, 23) were supplied monthly by each of the twelve **governors** (4:7–19).

4:29 In addition to giving Solomon a hearing (3:9) and discerning (3:12) heart, God gave him **largeness** (or breadth) **of heart.** All three terms underscore Solomon's understanding. This verse describes Solomon's understanding as limitless and immeasurable, like **the sand on the seashore,** just like the numbers of the Israelites (v. 20).

4:30 The term **men of the East** has been associated with Mesopotamia (Gen. 29:1), the east bank of the Jordan (Is. 11:14), or with Arabia in general (Judg. 6:3, 33; 7:12). All these are places whose inhabitants had a reputation for wisdom (Obad. 8). The fabled reputation of **the wisdom of Egypt** had been attested to in Egyptian literature for more than a millennium before Solomon's time.

4:31 Ethan the Ezrahite: See the title of Ps. 89. **Heman:** See 1 Chr. 16:42 (where Jeduthun may be the same as Ethan).

4:32–34 proverbs . . . songs: Solomon was the author of a large part of the Book of Proverbs. He is also traditionally assigned the authorship of the Song of Solomon, Pss. 72 and 127, and Ecclesiastes.

5:1–8:66 The building program of the Solomonic kingdom has five sections: (1) preparations for building the temple (5:1–18); (2) building the temple (6:1–38); (3) the palace complex (7:1–12); (4) the temple vessels (7:13–51); (5) the dedication of the temple (8:1–66).

5:1, 2 Hiram: This Phoenician king ruled over Tyre for 34 years (978–944 B.C.). **Loved** reflects traditional Middle Eastern diplomatic vocabulary for political alliances and reinforces the biblical evidence that Hiram was David's friend and ally (v. 12; 2 Sam. 5:11, 12). Hiram initiated the relationship with Solomon, based on his earlier relationship with David. When Solomon wrote to Hiram (vv. 2–6), he spoke freely of the Lord as the God of David and himself. Hiram responded with praise (v. 7).

5:3 house: Although God did not allow David to build the temple (2 Sam. 7:13), David made preparations for it (1 Chr. 21:18—22:19; 28:9—29:19). **name:** God's name was associated with His revealed character and reputation (Ex. 3:14, 15), as well as His sovereign ownership of everything (Ex. 20:24; Ps. 22:22).

5:4, 5 The shift from "the Lord his God" (v. 3) to **the Lord my God** demonstrates that Solomon and his father had the same faith.

5:6 cedars . . . Lebanon: In addition to the Bible, other ancient literature attests to the extensive use of wood from the cedar trees of Lebanon for building and furnishing temples and palaces. The principal building material in Jerusalem was limestone. **none among us:** Since Israel did not have cedar forests like those in Lebanon, the Israelites did not have workmen skilled in building with it.

5:7 Blessed be the Lord: The acknowledgment of another people's deity is well known both in the Bible (10:9; Dan. 3:28) and in other ancient Middle Eastern literature.

5:8–11 Hiram's reply indicates that he was a shrewd businessman. Not only would Solomon pay the wages of Hiram's **servants,** but he would make the payments to Hiram (vv. 6, 11; 2 Chr. 2:10). In addition to men and material, Hiram also supplied gold to Solomon, for which he apparently demanded collateral (9:10–14), and which Solomon could later redeem (2 Chr. 8:1, 2).

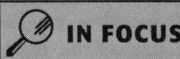 **IN FOCUS** **"understanding"**

(Heb. *tebunah*) (1 Kin. 4:29; Job 12:13; Prov. 3:13; 21:30) Strong's #8394: The verbal root of this noun means "to distinguish" or "to discern." Thus this noun conveys the idea of discernment. The Hebrew word is directly connected to the idea of wisdom in 22 passages, including Prov. 8 where they are both personified (Ex. 31:3; 1 Kin. 7:14; Prov. 8:1; 10:23). Due to its close association with wisdom, the word occurs often in Proverbs. Solomon contrasted *understanding* with folly (Prov. 14:29; 15:21; 18:2). He also exhorted his son to apply his heart to understanding (Prov. 2:2). Ultimately all discernment is from the Lord (Prov. 2:6), whose wisdom is infinite (Ps. 147:5; Is. 40:28).

5:12–14 labor force: The workmen were put to work as forced labor gangs on public projects. Solomon's long and extensive use of this type of social conscription to accomplish his vast building projects became a source of considerable difficulty for his successor Rehoboam (12:4).

5:15–18 quarried stone: Stonecutters were common laborers who cut and crushed rocks from a quarry.

6:1 four hundred and eightieth year: Many scholars take this date as the key date for establishing the time of the Exodus. The division of the kingdom at the death of Solomon can be dated at 930 b.c. (11:41–43). Allowing forty years for Solomon's rule (11:42), the fourth year of his reign would be 966 b.c. If the Exodus took place 480 years before 966 b.c., its date was 1446 b.c. Some consider this date too early for what occurs in the Book of Exodus and date the Exodus in the thirteenth century b.c. They suggest that the 480 years may be a round figure representing twelve generations, or that it may have been arrived at by adding the length of various concurrent or overlapping periods as though they were placed in one lineal string of eras.

6:2, 3 house . . . for the Lord: For the interior of the temple Solomon followed the floor plan of the tabernacle but doubled its dimensions. **sixty cubits:** The standard cubit was about 18 inches. The dimensions here are approximately 90 feet long, 30 feet wide, and 45 feet high. Solomon's temple was constructed on Mt. Moriah (Gen. 22:2; 2 Chr. 3:1) at the threshing floor of Ornan (or Araunah, 2 Sam. 24:24). Like the tabernacle, the temple was divided into the Most Holy Place, the holy place, and an outer courtyard. The outer court contained a bronze altar for sacrifices and a brass basin set on the backs of twelve bulls. On the east end of the temple there was a porch. Before the entrance to the porch were two freestanding pillars: Jachin (to the right) and Boaz (to the left; 7:21). Passing over the front porch one would enter the holy place. Here was the holy furniture so symbolic of Israel's religious experience: the gold plated table of the bread of the presence, ten golden lampstands, and the portable altar of incense. A veil separated the holy place from the Most Holy Place, in which were housed the ark and the mercy seat guarded by two cherubim. Only the priests could enter the temple itself to minister before the Lord.

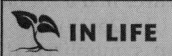 **IN LIFE**   # Sparing No Expense

Whenever modern-day churches draw up plans and budgets for buildings in which to worship, they face an age-old tension: what is appropriate in terms of size, materials, beauty, and expense? For Solomon, there seems to have been only one answer to that question as he proposed to build God's temple: spare no expense!

A more lavish building project has rarely been seen. The cost of such a venture today would be virtually incalculable. Was Solomon justified in incurring such an expense? The question is not easily answered.

On one hand, the project contributed to a number of economic and other problems of Solomon's reign such as heavy taxation, a growing underclass of foreigners, and the depletion of the forests of Lebanon. The temple was by no means the sole cause of these troubles (9:15–19), but it was built with a policy of "only the best," which seemed to typify the Solomonic empire. Even "silver . . . was accounted as nothing in the days of Solomon" (10:21).

On the other hand, Solomon apparently recognized that architecture is not neutral; it makes a statement. In fact, to the extent that temples and church sanctuaries follow (or sometimes dispense with) architectural forms and principles, they are works of art. Solomon's temple was a remarkable work of art, built to the glory of God (8:12, 13). Was it built to the glory of Solomon as well? Probably, since most great works of architecture are monuments to those who build them. Yet God apparently approved of Solomon's achievement, for He blessed the sanctuary with His presence (8:10, 11).

Yet even as the construction went forward, the Lord reminded His builder that what mattered was not a house of cedar and gold, but keeping the Law (6:11–13). Perhaps that is the most important architectural principle of all when it comes to houses of worship: it is not the size, beauty, or costliness of the structure, but the sincere devotion and obedience of those who worship in the structure. After all, the Lord does not dwell only in sanctuaries built by people, but in the people themselves (8:27; Acts 7:48; 17:24; 1 Cor. 6:19, 20).

6:4 This was long before the use of glass panes, of course. The **windows** were openings for light and ventilation. Often there might be lattice work for decoration and for protection against falling from the openings (2 Kin. 1:2).

6:5, 6 Three-storied **chambers** were built along the temple's outer walls. A series of **ledges** served as resting places for the beams of the floors. This meant that the three floors were progressively wider as one went up.

6:7–10 The rock was precut at the quarry for its proper fit in the temple building, so **no . . . tool was heard** at the temple itself. This required a high degree of skill in measuring, cutting, and fitting the immense stones in place.

Solomon constructed the temple on Mount Moriah, north of the ancient City of David. The temple was built according to plans that David

 **IN FOCUS** | **"gold"**

(Heb. *zahab*) (1 Kin. 6:20; 2 Sam. 21:4; 2 Chr. 9:1, 9; Job 23:10) Strong's #2091: This word almost always denotes the substance of gold, although occasionally it represents an alloy of gold (1 Kin. 10:16) or the color gold (Zech. 4:12). Gold symbolized wealth and was quite often mentioned along with silver, both of which were abundant during Solomon's reign (Gen. 13:2; 2 Chr. 1:15; Ezek. 16:13). In the OT, most references to gold relate to the tabernacle or to Solomon's temple and palace (Ex. 25:3; 2 Chr. 2:7; 9:13–27). Although gold was valued highly and continues to be, the Scripture asserts that certain qualities are to be valued more: wisdom (Job 28:17), loving favor (Prov. 22:1), and the judgments, law, and commandments of the Lord (Pss. 19:9, 10; 119:72, 127).

received from the Lord and passed on to Solomon (1 Chr. 28:11–13, 19). The division into a sanctuary and inner sanctuary corresponds to the division of the tabernacle into the holy place and Most Holy Place.

6:11 word of the Lord: This message to Solomon might have come by means of a prophet. On other occasions, Solomon had more personal encounters with the Lord (3:5; 9:2; 11:11).

6:12, 13 The most important work of Solomon was certainly the building of the temple. God promised to bless Solomon and his work if he faithfully obeyed His commands.

6:14–19 The ark of the covenant of the Lord (Deut. 10:8; Josh. 3:11) is so named because it housed the two stone tablets of the covenant—the Ten Commandments (Deut. 10:1–5). The ark symbolized the presence of the sovereign God in the midst of His people (8:10, 11; Josh. 3:13).

6:20–22 the inner sanctuary: The Most Holy Place was a cube of thirty feet. **with pure gold:** The amount of gold is given as six hundred talents, or about 21 tons, in 2 Chr. 3:8.

6:23–28 A great deal of attention was given to the placement of the **cherubim**, with special reference to their immense wings. This room symbolized the presence of the living God, and special care was necessary in construction. With all the care given here, only one person would enter the room, and that was the high priest, on one day of the year. The cherubim represented the glorious, wondrous angels that serve God in heaven. But they were never venerated. They were only symbols of a Greater Presence.

6:23–26 The two **cherubim** were overlaid with gold and set so as to face the door to the holy place (2 Chr. 3:12, 13). These cherubim were large, standing fifteen feet high. They were in addition to the two cherubim on the mercy seat (8:6–8). A cherub was probably similar to the winged sphinxes common in ancient Middle Eastern sculpture. These creatures had a human face, a lion's body, and wings (Ex. 25:19).

6:27, 28 The **inner room** symbolized the dwelling place of the living God among His people. Only one person would enter this room, and that was the high priest on one day of the year.

6:29, 30 The decoration of the temple must have been exquisite. **cherubim, palm trees, and open flowers:** These same three figures are mentioned in vv. 32, 35. The temple was decorated with beautiful carvings, even in places most people would never see. The beauty of the building was a symbol of the beauty of God's presence.

6:31, 32 The **entrance** to the inner sanctuary was two doors made of olive wood. A veil or curtain hung there as well (Ex. 26:31–36; 2 Chr. 3:14).

6:33, 34 Double-leaved, foldable doors made of cypress wood gave access to the holy place.

6:35, 36 The use of the **inner court** was restricted to the priests.

6:37, 38 seven years: The period of time was necessary because of the greatness of the task. Solomon had immense crews engaged in building the temple (5:13–18).

7:1, 2 Solomon's desire to complete the Lord's house before building his own **house** is commendable. **House of the Forest of**

Lebanon: Rows of cedar pillars as well as the free use of cedar throughout this building, gave a forest-like appearance to it. The building apparently was used at least in part as an armory (10:16, 17; Is. 22:8).

7:3–7 The **Hall of Pillars** was a colonnaded entry hall to the Hall of Judgment. The **Hall of**

His father was a Phoenician artisan who had married a widow from the tribe of Naphtali (2 Chr. 2:14). Like his father, Huram had become a master craftsman; his contributions to the work on the temple were extensive (7:40–47).

7:15–22 Among the major works of Huram were the freestanding **pillars of bronze** near

---

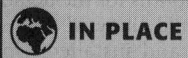

The Cedar Trade

The parched and war-torn landscape of modern-day Lebanon makes it difficult to imagine, but 3,000 years ago the area was flourishing with massive cedar trees. The timber was so plentiful that Solomon sent thousands of laborers to cut and transport cedar wood to Jerusalem, where he built numerous structures with it, including his impressive residence, appropriately called the House of the Forest of Lebanon (1 Kin. 7:2).

Cedar was also used for the construction of the temple (5:6–10; 6:9, 10, 15–18). It was used again many years later in the construction of the second temple, after the Babylonian exile (Ezra 3:7). Solomon was by no means the only ruler to import the fragrant, durable, and attractive cedar, as well as cypress and fir. Lebanon is known to have traded these woods with Syria, Egypt, and the nations of Mesopotamia. Yet something happened to this lively economy between the time of Solomon and the time of Christ. In fact, a massive change occurred in the overall ecology of the Palestine area. Scripture suggests that it was part of God's judgment of Israel for turning away from Him.

The forests of Lebanon were decimated by over-cutting. Solomon contributed to that, yet even his demand for cedar was apparently exceeded by that of the Babylonian ruler Nebuchadrezzar, according to extra-biblical sources and possibly the biblical prophets as well (Hab. 2:17). As a result, the ancient cedar forests vanished within generations, never to be replaced, despite attempts to reforest the land.

Map showing Mediterranean Sea, Forest of Lebanon, Tyre, Hazor, Megiddo, Jordan River, Joppa, Jerusalem, with compass pointing N.

Judgment was where the king could hear and decide cases too difficult for lesser officials.

7:8 house where he dwelt: Solomon's own house and that of Pharaoh's daughter are mentioned last. The gate between the palace complex and the temple area is called "the gate of the escorts" (2 Kin. 11:19).

7:9–11 costly stones: Exquisitely dressed blocks of the best quality limestone.

7:12 The **great court** was an outer court enclosing the entire temple and palace complex.

7:13, 14 Huram was of mixed parentage.

the entrance of the temple. These were objects of great beauty and gave the appearance of formidable strength. These pillars spoke of the power and might of God.

7:15, 16 A cubit was usually reckoned at about eighteen inches in length. Thus these pillars were about 27 feet high. In addition, each had a capital of another 7 1/2 feet. They must have been unusually imposing, wonderfully ornate structures.

7:17–22 Jachin . . . Boaz: Giving symbolic names to the pillars helped teach their meaning in the true worship of the living God. Jachin means "He Will Establish." Boaz may mean "In Him Is Strength." Another possible meaning is "He Is Quick." These two free-standing pillars were placed near the porch in front of the temple (2 Chr. 3:17). There is a question about the height of the capitals. Verse 16 records it as five cubits (as does Jer. 52:22), but 2 Kin. 25:17 as three cubits. This apparent discrepancy may involve simply a difference in what was measured, with 2 Kin. 25:17 recording the size of only the upper portion of the capitals.

7:23–26 Cast in one piece and set upon twelve bronze oxen, the **Sea of cast bronze** replaced the laver of washings for the tabernacle (Ex. 30:17–21). While the quantity of water held by the Sea is given here as two thousand baths (about 11,500 gallons), three thousand baths (17,500 gallons) is recorded in 2 Chr. 4:5. The figure in 2 Chronicles could be an error of copying (in the previous verse the number three occurs four times), or possibly it is an example of using different standards for the length of the cubit.

7:27–38 The **ten carts** each containing a bronze laver (v. 38) were arranged beside the molten Sea, five on either side, and were used for rinsing the burnt offerings (2 Chr. 4:6). These carts were both functional and ornamental. A biblical view, as represented here by the elaborate artistry associated with the furnishings of the temple, seems to be quite different from a common idea in which people speak distastefully about art and design in the context of worship, believing that such things "distract" from worship. But as our God is a God of great beauty, objects of beauty that are devoted to His glory may be used in association with His worship. All the while, we recognize that there is no object of human crafting that may *truly* represent His inexpressible loveliness.

7:39–48 The **furnishings** of the temple were designed to correspond with similar furnishings in the tabernacle. The golden altar replaced the altar of incense (Ex. 30:2–4), ten golden tables (2 Chr. 4:8) took the place of the table of the presence (Ex. 25:23–30), and ten lampstands were substituted for the one golden lampstand (Ex. 25:31–40). Although there were ten tables and lampstands where before there was one, their functions remained the same, all ten being considered one unit (2 Chr. 29:18).

7:49–51 The gifts of **David** dedicated to service in the temple were probably stored in one of the side chambers. David's personal example of giving (1 Chr. 29:1–9) provided a high model of godly concern in leadership.

8:1, 2 Having been brought to Jerusalem previously (2 Sam. 6), **the ark of the covenant** was now put in its place in the temple. With the erection of the temple and the placement of the ark, the division of spiritual activities between Gibeon, the location of the tabernacle, and Jerusalem, where the ark had resided in a temporary shelter, was now at an end. From now on the Deuteronomic ideal of centrality of worship could be realized (Deut. 12:1–14). Because the temple was completed in the eighth month of Solomon's eleventh year of reign, Solomon must have waited some eleven months for the dedication of the temple. This would allow all the furnishings to be completed and installed, final touches to be added, and ample preparation to be made for this solemn yet joyful event. The Feast of Tabernacles, occurring at the conclusion of the ceremonial year and commemorating God's granting of rest in the Promised Land to His people would provide a particularly appropriate occasion. Moreover, the covenant renewal observed in connection with this great feast (Deut. 31:10) made this time all the more appropriate. Accordingly, the festal season was lengthened to two weeks to allow the sacredness and joy of these days to have their full effect (2 Chr. 5:11–13).

8:3, 4 The holy **ark** was carried by the priests; all was done as God's Law demanded.

8:5–7 The joy of the people is seen in the abundance of sacrifices of **sheep and oxen.** The placement of the holy **ark** in its proper place without incident was truly a reason to celebrate. They had brought the symbol of the living God into the shrine which had been built to honor Him.

8:8 poles could be seen: This statement probably means that the carrying poles of the ark, which were not to be removed from their rings (Ex. 25:15), were so long that if one were to attempt to see their length, one would have to look into the Most Holy Place to see their ends. The ark with its poles was thus aligned crosswise to the door (or north to south).

8:9 The **two tablets of stone** upon which the Ten Commandments were inscribed were known as the "tablets of the covenant" (Deut. 9:9) and were kept in the ark (Deut. 10:1–5, 8) along with the jar of manna (Ex. 16:33, 34) and Aaron's rod that budded (Num. 17:10).

8:10, 11 As a **cloud** had covered the tabernacle and God's glory had filled it when it was inaugurated (Ex. 40:34,35), so now a cloud filled the temple. This visible presence of God's dwelling with His people—sometimes called the "shekinah glory"—gave the people assurance and incentive for obedient and holy living.

8:12, 13 Then Solomon spoke: God's dwelling in dark clouds is often mentioned in the Scriptures (Ex. 19:9; 20:21). This is a sign of His transcendence. Yet He is both near and far, both immanent and transcendent. God is

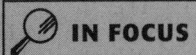

"supplication"

(Heb. *techinnah*) (1 Kin. 8:28; Jer. 42:2, 9; Dan. 9:20) Strong's #8467: This word signifies a petition for favor or mercy. Supplication is almost always directed to God, but Jeremiah used the word twice to represent a formal petition he made to a king (Jer. 37:20; 38:26). Of the twenty-four occurrences of this word in the OT, thirteen are in connection with Solomon's prayer dedicating the temple (8:23–9:3; 2 Chr. 6:14–42). Other words with the same root (and indicating supplication) occur seven times in the same context. Supplication is generally a petition for God to be merciful in the impending distress; thus personal enemies are cited on several occasions (Pss. 55:1–3; 119:70; Jer. 36:7). The Bible specifically records that God heard the supplications of David (Ps. 6:9), Solomon (9:3), and of wicked King Manasseh, who humbled himself before God (2 Chr. 33:12, 13).

obscured by a dark cloud; but at the same time He chooses to be present in His exalted house.

8:14–21 Here is a model for public declaration in a formal setting. Throughout there is glory given to the Lord, as well as a fair assessment of the work of His people in accomplishing His will.

8:20, 21 the LORD has fulfilled: Israel's God is a keeper of promises. His promise to give Abraham's descendants a land (Gen. 15:13, 14, 18–21; Josh. 14:12–15) had been provisionally realized (Josh. 21:43–45). Solomon also appropriated God's promise to David (2 Sam. 7:12–18). Subsequent kings in the Davidic line could likewise by faith enjoy the blessings of God promised in the Davidic covenant (Pss. 2; 89:3, 4, 19–24, 27–37). Ultimately the continuing promises in the Abrahamic and Davidic Covenants will come together in the New Covenant (Jer. 31:31–34), and all will be fulfilled in Israel's Greater David (Ezek. 37:24–28), Jesus Christ (Acts 2:29–36; 3:25, 26).

8:22–30 Solomon had begun his reign with a conscious dependence on God (3:9). His long public prayer (vv. 22–53) recognized that continuing need in his life (vv. 26, 28) and the lives of his people (vv. 30, 31, 33, 35, 38, 44, 46–48). In his prayer Solomon stressed God's faithfulness, and the need for similar faithfulness on the part of Israel, rulers and people alike, if God's full blessings were to be realized.

8:27–29 heaven . . . temple: The God of Scripture is infinite; all that He has made, vast as creation may be, finally has its limits. No mere building, no matter how wonderful, can be thought of as the dwelling place of God. Yet in His grace the Lord condescends to be viewed as having His dwelling among men. God's dwelling in a temple prefigured the Incarnation when the Creator became man, born in a stable in Bethlehem.

8:30 Since God was present in the temple in Jerusalem, prayer was to be directed toward **this place** (Ex. 15:17; Dan. 6:10).

8:31, 32 Solomon's first request asks for righteous judgment. In such situations where there was insufficient evidence to establish a charge, the accused was obliged **to take an oath** declaring his innocence.

8:33, 34 sinned against You: Solomon's second request asks for forgiveness of sin, where sin against God has caused Israel to be defeated.

8:35–40 Solomon's third and fourth requests deal with healing the land after distress or drought due to the people's sin (Deut. 28:21–24, 38, 42, 52, 59–61). The remedy in such cases of judgment is repentance and prayer for forgiveness, followed by renewed faithfulness to the standards of God's covenant.

8:41–43 Solomon's fifth request deals with prayer by a **foreigner.** Unlike God's people or resident aliens within the commonwealth of Israel (Deut. 10:18, 19), foreigners have no particular claim on the ear of God. But God's people expected foreigners to be drawn to Him through the worship of His people.

8:44–53 Solomon's sixth and seventh requests concern matters relative to wartime situations. **Battle** (v. 44) was to be waged in accordance with divine directions (Deut. 20; 21:10–14) and could be lost by disobedience (Deut. 28:64–68; Josh. 7). Believers must face all of life's crucial encounters with trust in God and faithful adherence to the standards of His word (Pss. 91; 119:57–61, 161–168, 173–176).

8:54–59 he arose . . . from kneeling: The parallel account of 2 Chr. 6:12–42 records that Solomon knelt on a tall platform that he had built for the occasion in order that all might see him praying before God. Chronicles reports that Solomon closed his prayer with a plea (Ps. 132:8–10) that God would continue residing with His people and remembering His promises to David (2 Chr. 6:41, 42). The writer of Kings records Solomon's dedicatory blessing on the congregation of Israel, in which Solomon praises God for giving the people their present rest (vv. 54–66; Deut. 12:9–25), invokes God's continued presence and direction of His people (vv. 57–60), and challenges the people to be loyal to God and His laws (v. 61). Chronicles adds that Solomon's prayer and blessing were accompanied by heavenly fire that consumed the sacrifice on the altar (2 Chr. 7:1–3).

8:60 all the peoples: This verse does not limit God to the Jews only but includes Gentiles as well.

8:61 The Hebrew term translated **loyal** basically means "at peace with," hence, "complete" or "perfect" (11:4; 15:3, 14).

8:62–66 The ceremony concluded with many special **sacrifices** (v. 62) and ended on a high note of **joyful** (v. 66) praise and thanksgiving to God for His goodness.

9:1–11:43 The account of Solomon's rule closes by relating the socio-economic successes of the era, coupled with the attendant apostasy and growing secularism that such attachments often bring. Solomon's kingdom had begun well but would be brought low by his own spiritual failures. This section has four subsections: (1) special relationships and activities (9:1–28); (2) the visit of the queen of Sheba (10:1–10); (3) the splendor of the era (10:14–29); (4) closing details relative to the era (11:1–43).

9:1–9 the second time: God had appeared previously to Solomon in Gibeon (3:4–15). The Lord's warning was a necessary reminder for Solomon, who would come to compromise the conditions required for enjoying God's blessing.

Solomon would have to endure the consequences of disobedience (11:1–11).

9:10–14 These **twenty cities** (v. 11) lay east and southeast of Acco in the tribal allotment to Asher. Apparently they had been ceded to Hiram as collateral for the gold necessary for furnishing the temple and palace complex. Hiram's displeasure with them would later result in Solomon's redeeming the towns by repaying the debt in some other manner (2 Chr. 8:1, 2).

9:14 one hundred and twenty talents of gold: This is an immense amount (see also the gift of the queen of Sheba in 10:10). **A talent** was said to be the full load one man could carry (2 Kin. 5:23). It was equal to three thousand shekels, or about 70 pounds.

9:15 The identification and location of the **Millo** are uncertain. Probably the word refers to architectural terraces and buttressing on the slope of the eastern hill of Jerusalem. **Hazor, Megiddo, and Gezer:** These three cities were important commercial, administrative, and military centers for Solomon. Archaeological excavations have uncovered common design elements in the walls and gates of all three.

9:16 Gezer, which had been a strong Canaanite city, was part of Ephraim's territorial assignment. Ephraim had never taken Gezer; however, Egypt had conquered the city. Its key location on the edge of the lowlands west of Jerusalem made it a splendid gift for Pharaoh to give on the occasion of his daughter's marriage to Solomon.

9:17–19 Three cities were key to Solomon's defensive strategy. **Lower Beth Horon** and

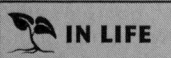 **IN LIFE**   ## A House of Prayer for *All* Nations

Solomon's prayer of dedication for the temple at Jerusalem showed that Israel's God was a God for all nations. The king anticipated that foreigners from all over the world would be drawn to the house of worship. So he asked God to honor their prayers in order that "all peoples of the earth may know Your name and fear You" (1 Kin. 8:41–43).

One early answer to Solomon's prayer was a visit by the queen of Sheba (10:1–13), who had heard of the splendors of Solomon's kingdom but wanted to see them for herself. After reviewing his accomplishments, she praised God for what he had done for Israel (10:9). Other visitors had similar reactions.

The temple was located at Jerusalem, but as Jesus pointed out (quoting Isaiah), it was meant to be "a house of prayer for all nations" (Is. 56:7; Mark 11:17). Likewise, Israel was to be a blessing to the nations and a light showing the way toward the one true God (Gen. 12:1–3; Is. 51:4).

Similarly, Jesus teaches His followers to be a light to the nations (Matt. 5:14–16). Rather than bringing people to a central place of worship, believers—who are themselves temples of the Holy Spirit (1 Cor. 6:19, 20)—are to go to the ends of the earth, taking the Good News of God's grace to all the peoples of the world (Matt. 28:19).

Baalath served to defend Judah's western front. **Tadmor** is probably the important commercial city in Syria, later known as Palmyra.

9:20, 21 The five nations listed here are peoples who constituted the early inhabitants of Canaan. Several such lists are given in the OT (Josh. 3:10). **Solomon** assigned their sur-

(present-day Yemen), **Sheba** was the homeland of the Sabeans, a people whose far-flung commercial enterprises stretched from Syria to east Africa to distant India. The Sabeans dealt in such precious commodities as gold, gemstones, perfumes, and rare spices. The **queen of Sheba** came to ask Solomon **hard questions** (Heb.

Photo by Howard Vos

A model of the ancient city of Megiddo, showing its impressive defensive wall built by King Solomon (1 Kin. 9:15).

viving members to work on public projects in accordance with the principle of compulsory labor (5:13).

9:22–25 These **three times a year** included the Feasts of Unleavened Bread, Pentecost, and Tabernacles (Deut. 16:16). Not only did Solomon show himself a faithful spiritual shepherd by leading His people in worship, but continual attention to prescribed religious duties would keep the temple **finished,** or properly maintained.

9:26, 27 **Ezion Geber** was at the head of the modern Gulf of Aqaba. Its key location as an outlet to the Red Sea and the regions beyond made it commercially important to Solomon and to Hiram, his Phoenician trading partner (2 Chr. 8:17, 18).

9:28 One of the main commercial sites reached via Ezion Geber, **Ophir** may have supplied gold for Solomon to repay his debt to Hiram (5:8–11; 9:11–14). Solomon also received a generous gift of gold from the queen of Sheba (10:10).

10:1, 2 Located in southwestern Arabia

hîdôt, meaning "riddles," enigmatic issues," "perplexing sayings"; Prov. 1:6) to satisfy her own mind and to examine his wisdom. She serves as an example of what must have happened on a lesser scale throughout the reign of Solomon. His wisdom, which became proverbial (4:29–34), was an attractive force. Wise men and sages from other cultures came to Jerusalem and learned of the wisdom that is rooted in the fear of God (Prov. 1:7). This suggests a lively intellectual climate in Jerusalem during the reign of Solomon the Wise.

10:3–9 Solomon's brilliant replies to the queen of Sheba's difficult **questions** (v. 3), as well as the skillful use of his wisdom for the needs and interests of his kingdom convinced her that such wisdom must be divinely bestowed. Her acknowledgment of Solomon's God and the Lord's covenant faithfulness toward Israel does not necessarily mean that she made a commitment of personal faith in the Lord. Such recognition of foreign deities was common in the literature of the ancient world. However, the possibility exists that she

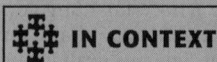 **IN CONTEXT** **Storage Cities**

Solomon's storage cities (1 Kin. 9:17–19; 2 Chr. 8:4–6) were essentially supply depots that warehoused government supplies such as food, building materials, and military equipment. They also were a measure of a kingdom's prosperity, prestige, and power.

Solomon's kingdom was divided into twelve administrative districts (1 Kin. 4:7–19), and many of the revenues collected by the governors were probably channeled through the supply cities before delivery to Jerusalem (4:21). Excavations at Beth Shemesh (1 Sam. 6:12) and Lachish have uncovered long, rectangular rooms used for storage. Likewise, a large underground silo dating to Solomon's era has been found at Megiddo, with capacity for almost 13,000 bushels of grain.

Solomon was not the only ancient ruler to build storage cities. As slaves in Egypt, the Israelites built the supply cities of Pithom and Raamses for Pharaoh (Ex. 1:11). Likewise, King Jehoshaphat and Hezekiah of Judah built storage cities during their reigns (2 Chr. 17:12; 32:27–29).

experienced a spiritual awakening as a result of her time with Solomon (5:7).

10:10–15 one hundred and twenty talents: Solomon used the gold not only to furnish the temple (6:20–35; 7:49–51) and palace (10:18–21) but also to make five hundred ornamental shields, which were placed in the House of the Forest of Lebanon (10:16, 17).

10:16, 17 Made of wood (or basketwork) and covered with gold plating, these **shields** were intended for ceremonial occasions. These shields would be carried off after Solomon's death by Sheshonq I of Egypt's twenty-second dynasty. Rehoboam would replace them with bronze shields (1 Kin. 14:25–28).

10:18–21 The **throne of ivory** was probably made of wood inlaid with ivory, as well as being overlaid with finest gold. Solomon received ivory as a result of his trading ventures with Hiram (v. 22).

10:22, 23 Solomon's **merchant ships** are linked to his commercial arrangements with Hiram.

10:24, 25 all the earth: This phrase refers to the international reputation of Solomon's wisdom.

10:26 one thousand four hundred chariots: The reasonableness of the figure given here may be seen in that Shalmaneser III of Assyria reports that at the Battle of Qarqar (853 B.C.) he faced a combined enemy chariot force of 3,900, some two thousand of whom were supplied by Israel.

10:27 silver . . . cedar: The point is that Israel under Solomon enjoyed its greatest period of prosperity. This time of prosperity and peace also must have allowed for the growth of scholarship and for arts and music.

10:28, 29 Keveh is probably the city of Que attested in a ninth century B.C. inscription found in southern Asia Minor. Que is probably also the

Cilicia of classical literature (Acts 6:9). Solomon's wide-ranging dealing in horses from Que to Egypt brought him perilously close to, or in actual violation of, breaking the prohibition of acquiring great numbers of horses (Deut. 17:16). Evidently Egyptian horses and chariots were highly prized, so that Solomon could make a tidy middleman's profit in selling them to Syrian and Hittite kings.

11:1–43 This chapter is the sad close to a brilliant reign. It presents the sin of Solomon in his many wives (11:1–13) and describes the decline of Solomon through his adversaries Hadad the Edomite (11:14–22), Rezon of Zobah (11:23–25), and Jeroboam of Israel (11:26–40). The chapter closes with the death of Solomon and the end of the Solomonic Era (11:41–43).

11:1 many foreign women: The word order in the Hebrew text emphasizes the word *foreign,* with a secondary emphasis on the adjective *many.* Solomon had committed two egregious sins. Taking foreign wives violated the Lord's prohibitions against marrying Canaanite women (v. 2; Ex. 34:12–17; Deut. 7:1–3); taking many wives violated the standard of monogamy established at the beginning (Gen. 2:24, 25), and resulted in rampant polygamy, something God had also forbidden to Israel's future kings (Deut. 17:17). Doubtless many of Solomon's marriages were in accord with the common ancient Middle Eastern convention of sealing alliances by marriages between members of the royal houses contracting the alliances. Solomon's yielding to the customs of the day would have serious spiritual consequences for himself (vv. 3–13) and his people (2 Kin. 17:7–20). David also had more than one wife (2 Sam. 3:2–5). David's early marriages were prompted by love (1 Sam. 18:17–28) and compassion (1 Sam. 25:2–42). Yet some of David's later marriages may have been prompted by the same

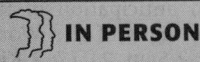 **IN PERSON** **The Wise King**

A list of Solomon's political, administrative, military, and architectural achievements would be one of the most impressive of the ancient world. Under his leadership, Israel expanded its influence from the Euphrates to the Mediterranean, and from Asia Minor to the Gulf of Aqaba and Egypt. Yet underlying all of Solomon's accomplishments was a God-given wisdom for which he was renowned in his own day and is remembered today (1 Kin. 3:6–14):

- The judgment that he rendered in the case of the harlots and the child won the respect of the entire nation (3:16–28).
- His wisdom was said to surpass that of all other known wise men of his day (4:30, 31).
- He gave 3,000 proverbs (4:32), many of which are contained in the Book of Proverbs.
- He composed 1,005 songs (4:32), including Pss. 72 and 127.
- He demonstrated competencies in botany, horticulture, zoology, and ichthyology (4:33; compare Prov. 30:24–31; Eccl. 2:4–6).
- Visitors from throughout the world traveled to Jerusalem to hear his opinion (1 Kin. 4:34), including the queen of Sheba (10:1–9).
- He was the originator of most of the Book of Proverbs and all of Ecclesiastes and the Song of Solomon; several pieces of extra-biblical literature are attributed to him as well.
- Folktales from ancient Israel, Arabia, and Ethiopia celebrate Solomon's wisdom and even ascribe magical powers to him.

acquisitiveness that later motivated his son Solomon (2 Sam. 5:13–16).

11:2 clung to these in love: Our harsh assessment of Solomon's many wives is mitigated somewhat by the use of this phrase (v. 1).

11:3 seven hundred . . . three hundred: If the reference to 60 queens and 80 concubines in Song 6:8 is to Solomon's wives, it represents a much earlier period in Solomon's reign.

11:4 Although it is true that David did not always live up to God's standards, he was **loyal** to God and trusted Him implicitly, even when he was rebuked for his sins (2 Sam. 12:13; Pss. 32:1–5; 53:1–5). Because of the influence of his many wives, Solomon compromised his faith by worshiping foreign gods.

11:5, 6 Ashtoreth was a Canaanite goddess of love and war. **Milcom** was the national god of the Ammonites.

11:7, 8 The use of a **high place** in association with the worship of foreign gods shows the terrible danger that the high places presented to Israel (3:2–4; 14:23; Mic. 1:3). **Chemosh** was the national god of Moab. His worship was practiced repeatedly by God's people (2 Kin. 23:13). The veneration of this deity is also attested in the recently discovered Ebla Tablets in a form that suggests his association with the city of Carchemish along the upper bend of the Euphrates River. **Molech** is associated with human sacrifice and with Baal (Jer. 7:31, 32; 19:5, 6; 32:35).

11:9–13 God appeared twice before to Solomon (3:5; 9:2). Solomon's spiritual odyssey may be seen in the details of his three audiences with God. While God graciously postponed the division of Solomon's kingdom until after his death, internal troubles appeared while he was still alive (vv. 14–40).

11:11–12 your servant: That is, Jeroboam the son of Nebat (11:26; 12:20).

11:13 one tribe: The tribe is Judah, the principal tribe of the southern kingdom. Simeon had assimilated with Judah by this time (12:17, 20, 21).

11:14–22 Hadad the Edomite was one of the survivors who had escaped when David defeated the Edomite army (2 Sam. 8:13, 14). Pharaoh's ready reception and favorable treatment of Hadad probably had political ramifications, the pharaoh seeing in him a potential future ally on Israel's border.

11:23–25 Having escaped David's earlier campaigns against the Arameans (2 Sam. 8:3–6), **Rezon** would later become king of Damascus and his people would remain a constant threat to Israel.

11:26 The meaning of the name **Jeroboam** is in some doubt. It may mean, "The People Increase" or "The People Contend." The second meaning would have been very fitting for Jeroboam I, as the rebellion of the northern kingdom, rooted deeply in ancient jealousies, was based immediately on reaction to the oppressive taxation policies announced by Rehoboam, Solomon's son (2 Kin. 14:23). While the name of his father, **Nebat**, is well-known, his father must have died when he was young, for his mother is called **a widow**. The plight of widows was quite difficult in the ancient world. The Ephraimite Jeroboam, a highly gifted and at first trusted official for Solomon (v. 28), would come under Solomon's wrath (v. 40). Like Hadad the Edomite (v. 17), he fled to Egypt where he found refuge. Eventually Jeroboam

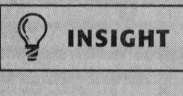 **INSIGHT**

Hadad, Solomon's Sworn Enemy

Solomon had never met Hadad the Edomite (1 Kin. 11:14), or had contact with him. Yet Hadad was Solomon's sworn enemy. The source of his hostility was the slaughter of his father and other Edomite males by David's general, Joab (11:15–17). That tragedy was largely the result of a feud between the Israelites and the Edomites, which had gone on for centuries.

was instrumental in bringing about the prophesied schism of the country (12:2–19). He became the first king of the northern kingdom (12:20).

11:26, 27 this is what caused: The phrasing suggests that there was a problem in the building projects that led to Jeroboam's rebellion. These two verses explain something about Jeroboam's background. He was a major officer of one of the large work groups. Among the projects to which Jeroboam had been assigned were the building of the **Millo** (9:15), and the repair of the **City of David.**

11:28, 29 The prophecy of **Ahijah** of Shiloh was fulfilled literally (12:1–20). Ahijah, whose name means "My Brother Is the Lord," would remain God's loyal prophet down into his old age (14:1–18).

11:30–32 God had already warned Solomon that all but **one tribe** would be taken away from Solomon's heir (v. 13; 12:20). Only ten tribes, however, are promised to Jeroboam. The twelfth tribe might be Simeon, which was absorbed by Judah. Possibly Benjamin existed as a buffer state between Israel and Judah, at times linked with the southern kingdom (2 Chr. 11:3; 14:8) and at times with the northern kingdom.

11:33–35 they have forsaken Me: See the list of particulars in vv. 4–8.

11:36 This is a biblical image of one of the divinely intended functions of Davidic kings in ancient Israel. In the midst of the darkness of a

pagan world, the Davidic kings were to be **a lamp** to the nations, in anticipation of the Coming One who is the Light of the World (John 1:1–9; 1 Kin. 15:4; 2 Sam. 21:17; 2 Kin. 8:19; 2 Chr. 21:7).

11:37, 38 an enduring house: Although God gave Jeroboam the opportunity to establish a lasting dynasty, he proved unworthy (12:25–33; 14:10–18). Jeroboam's name would forever be associated with the spiritual infidelity that would ultimately bring the northern kingdom to ruin (2 Kin. 17:21–23).

11:39, 40 Solomon, whose reign was characterized by peace more than that of any other king in Jerusalem (4:24), ended his life in strife as he sought **to kill Jeroboam. Shishak** (or Sheshonq I, 945–924 B.C.) was the first pharaoh of Egypt's strong twenty-second dynasty. Ironically, this future destroyer of Israel appears here as a protector of one of its future kings.

11:41–43 Because of his considerable sin, the golden era that Solomon initiated would die with him. Had he lived out his life in righteousness, and had he taught his son Rehoboam to succeed him in true justice, the golden era might have endured for generations.

11:41 The book of the acts of Solomon is mentioned only here; compare the references to the book of the chronicles of the kings of Israel (14:19) and the book of the chronicles of the kings of Judah (14:29). It is likely that the author of the present Book of Kings drew on these sources.

11:42 The symmetry of the **forty years** (2:10–12) of the reigns of David and Solomon may be a providential congruity, speaking of God's blessing on each of their reigns.

11:43 rested with his fathers: The meaning of this idiom in the Hebrew Bible is burial in the same place as one's ancestors. There may also be an indirect reference to life after death. **Rehoboam his son:** It is usual in a royal obituary to state who it was that followed the deceased on the throne. This provides a sense of continuity.

12:1–22:53 The second major part of 1 Kings, the divided kingdom, begins here. The story continues in 2 Kings.

12:1–24 The accession of Rehoboam and the division of the kingdom into the northern and the southern. The kingdoms would remain divided until each was overrun by foreign invaders, the northern kingdom in 722 B.C. and the southern kingdom in 586 B.C.

12:1–3 Rehoboam: His name may mean "The People Are Wide," referring to the expansion of the nation of Israel under the hand of God. Unfortunately, Rehoboam became a means of harming the expansion of God's people, even prompting civil war and the secession of the ten northern tribes. Situated in Ephraim, **Shechem** was an important center of Israelite activity. It was the first place mentioned in Canaan with reference to Abraham (Gen. 12:6). By going for his coronation to a place with ancient ties to the history of his people, and which was situated in the region of the northern tribes, doubtless Rehoboam believed that he was making a strategic move. The term **all Israel** refers to representatives of the northern tribes who had convened to consider the confirmation of Rehoboam as king of all the land.

12:4, 5 A system of forced labor had been imposed by Solomon to accomplish and maintain his building projects (see 5:13–18). Because this **burdensome service** was especially hateful to the northern tribes, relief from it was a crucial issue.

12:6, 7 By **elders** is meant the chief government officials who had advised Rehoboam's father Solomon (4:1–19). Their advice was to show moderation and temperance.

12:8, 9 The **young men** were men of Rehoboam's generation whom he had appointed to government office.

12:10, 11 little finger . . . father's waist: The advice of Rehoboam's own advisors was that the system of forced labor should be intensified until their sting become like that of a scorpion. **Scourges** were leather whips that could

have more than one tail to which barbed points or metal spikes were attached.

12:12–14 Foolishly, Rehoboam followed the advice of the hotheaded **young men.**

12:15 from the LORD: Even at this crucial time of national schism, God was sovereignly working through human events to accomplish His will, which had been made known through earlier prophecy (11:29–39).

12:16 What share have we in David: The ancient rivalry felt by the northern tribes now came to a peak in resentment against the tribe of Judah and the house of David. Saul was from the tribe of Benjamin and had been regarded as "one of their own." David, from the south, had seemed distant. Rehoboam's insensitivity to the volatile situation led to a division of the nation.

12:17 cities of Judah: The southern section also included the tribal allotment of Simeon. But Simeon was absorbed by Judah; their allotment was "within the inheritance of the children of Judah" (Josh. 19:1).

12:18 The resistance of the northern tribes to the king's agent **Adoram** was forceful and decisive—they killed him!

12:19 That is, to the **day** of the narrator. In the end, Israel's rebellion was its own destruction.

12:20 Jeroboam . . . king: The coronation of Jeroboam had been prophesied by Ahijah the

---

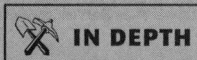 **IN DEPTH** | **The Divided Kingdom**

Tensions had existed between the tribes since the time of the judges, especially between Judah in the south and Ephraim, the most influential tribe in the north. Many of Israel's leaders, such as Joshua and Samuel, had come from the tribe of Ephraim. But David was from the southern tribe of Judah. These factors, along with the moving of the capital and the center of worship to the southern city of Jerusalem, strained the relationship more. Solomon's taxation to fund building the temple and palace in the southern city of Jerusalem alienated the northern tribes even further.

After Solomon's death, his son Rehoboam was approached by the people of Israel with a request that the taxes that they had been forced to pay under his father's numerous building programs be lessened. Rehoboam rejected his elders' advice to be lenient, and he insulted the people by threatening to make their burden even heavier (12:14). This was the final event that split the nation into two kingdoms. Rehoboam remained king of the southern kingdom while Jeroboam became king of the northern kingdom.

Citing the example of the calves created by Aaron near Mount Sinai, Jeroboam erected statues of two golden calves for worship so that his people would not be forced to travel the great distance to Jerusalem. With these idols, Jeroboam led his people away from the worship of the one true God, by combining true worship with the false worship of their neighbors.

The northern kingdom, known as Israel, and the southern kingdom, known as Judah, existed separately for another two hundred years. At times, the two fought each other; at other times, they cooperated in a friendly alliance against threatening neighbors. However, the period would become known more for the great prophets who rose up during times of spiritual instability than for either side's political success.

prophet of the Lord (11:29–31). Nonetheless, the actual coronation apparently was done apart from priest or prophet of the Lord; there was no divine anointing, no true religious ceremony. Only the kings of the southern kingdom would have the sanction of the Davidic covenant (2 Sam. 7).

12:21 Rehoboam's first inclination when he arrived in Jerusalem was to lead a war of reprisal against Israel. **Benjamin:** People of the border tribe might have gone either direction.

12:22 According to 2 Chr. 12:15, Iddo the prophet and **Shemaiah** together wrote a history of Rehoboam's reign. His name means "Yahweh Has Heard." The chronicler also reports that Shemaiah prophesied Judah's humiliation in the invasion of Shishak (2 Chr. 12:5–8). The Septuagint indicates that Shemaiah was the prophet who had predicted the division of the kingdom (1 Kin. 11:29–39). **Man of God** is one of the several terms used for God's prophets (1 Sam. 13:1).

12:23, 24 this thing is from Me: The foolish behavior of Rehoboam brought about God's judgment in dividing the nation into two new kingdoms.

12:25–16:24 This section traces the early kings and early history of the divided kingdom.

The northern kingdom's first king established spiritual compromises that would characterize Israel's spiritual condition throughout its existence. God's cause would fare little better in the southern kingdom, where only Asa receives divine commendation in this period.

12:25 built Shechem: That is, he fortified the ancient site (12:1). This strategic and historic city became the first capital of the northern kingdom. In fortifying this site, and **Penuel** (Gen. 32:30, 31), Jeroboam seems to have wanted to associate his reign with classic religious sites from the early history of Israel.

12:26, 27 However, Jeroboam knew **in his heart** that merely having a new presence in Shechem and Penuel would not in itself make the people of the northern kingdom forget the glories of the temple in **Jerusalem.**

12:28 Not only would they strike a familiar chord from Israel's history, but the **two calves of gold** would arouse the interest of the remaining Canaanites in the northern kingdom. The result of Jeroboam's action was religious confusion and apostasy; it would bring God's sure condemnation (14:9). It should be recognized that this is the first time the Scriptures mention any deliberate attempt to establish a heterodox doctrine, a substandard cult as an

---

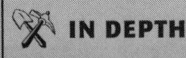 **IN DEPTH** | # A Chicken in Every Pot

When a nation enjoys the blessings of peace and prosperity, it has much for which to be thankful. But with affluence and power come temptations to forget that God is the source of every good thing. We see this in Israel's history.

Under Solomon, Israel briefly emerged as a powerhouse of wealth and military might. Its influence extended from the Euphrates to Egypt (1 Kin. 4:21) and its affluence to a majority of its citizens, whose prosperity is summarized as "eating and drinking and rejoicing" (4:20). As Solomon's reign put a temporary stop to threats from without and strife from within, everyone lived in safety, "each man under his vine and his fig tree" (4:25). In twentieth century terms, David's successor put "a chicken in every pot."

Yet storm clouds were brewing. The cost of maintaining Solomon's court was enormous (4:22, 23). His many building projects, including his gilded temple and his even more lavishly appointed palace, required increased taxes that created unrest and ultimately led to a tax revolt (10:14, 15; 12:4, 18). The system also created a two-class society of privileged citizens and menial workers, an underclass made up mostly of foreigners (9:15, 20–23). And while trade was lively (9:26–28; 10:22, 23), it contributed to the depletion of natural resources.

However, these problems remain in the background of 1 Kin. 4–10, which describes the general peace and prosperity that Israel enjoyed after so many years of turmoil. Glowing reports of the empire's power and prestige cascade from the text until the beginning of ch. 11, where the good news suddenly comes to a halt with the transition, "But King Solomon loved many foreign wives" (11:1).

Things head downhill from there as Solomon turns away from the Lord to idols (11:4–8). God pronounces judgment on him (11:9–13) and raises up adversaries against him (11:14–25). Jeroboam rebels (11:26–28), and the kingdom divides after Solomon's death (12:1–19).

official practice for the nation of Israel. While judgment was announced on this apostasy (ch. 13), the execution of this judgment would not take place for over two hundred years (the schism came in 930 B.C.; the destruction of the northern kingdom did not come until 722 B.C.). Jeroboam appealed to the people in several ways. (1) Traveling all the way to Jerusalem was too far, and unnecessary. (2) These calves were gods. (3) These calves were worshiped by their ancestors.

12:29 Bethel was north of Jerusalem in Benjamite territory, although its precise location is uncertain. It has been identified with Beitin; recent archaeological discoveries suggest Tell Bireh. Ai was nearby. In any case, Bethel had enjoyed a prominent place in Israelite history throughout the earlier patriarchal (Gen. 28:10–21) and post-conquest (Judg. 20:26–31) eras. **Dan** was in the northern portion of Israel. It was known as Laish and Leshem (Josh. 19:47; Judg. 18:7) until its capture by the Danites (Judg. 18:29). By that time it had already achieved a reputation as a center for pagan worship (Judg. 18:30). Jeroboam's choice of these two sites was a brilliant move. He had one site in the northernmost part of his kingdom and another in the southernmost part; both had long ties to Israel's past. No longer must the people make the long, arduous, and dangerous trip to Jerusalem. Jeroboam said, in effect, "We have brought religion to you."

12:30 The divine declaration is simple: **this thing became a sin.** The exclusive claim of Jerusalem as the central place of the worship of God in the holy temple (6:1) was now being ignored by the people of Israel.

12:31–33 Jeroboam's new religious institutions included starting a new religious order that did not include the Levites; setting up shrines at high places (3:2, 3); and replacing the Feast of Tabernacles with a fall festival in the eighth month. His various attempts at religious innovation would quickly incur God's denunciation (ch. 13) and earn him a reputation that would live in spiritual infamy (13:33, 34; 22:52).

13:1, 2 man of God: This prophet is unknown to us. The phrase **by the word of the LORD** occurs seven times in this chapter (vv. 1, 2, 5, 9, 17, 18, 32) and emphasizes that the man of God was functioning at the command of God and in God's power. **Jeroboam . . . altar to burn incense:** Having established his own deviant religion and his apostate priesthood, Jeroboam hardly had compunctions about serving priestly functions.

13:3 The word **sign** indicates something miraculous (Ex. 4:21; Jer. 33:20, 21). Miraculous signs may indicate either the intended pur-

pose of the deed or its wondrous effects, both ideas often occurring together (Deut. 6:22; Ps. 78:43).

13:4, 5 Unlike David, who confessed his sin when he was accused by Nathan the man of God (2 Sam. 12:13), the wicked Jeroboam sought to **arrest** his accuser. Instead he found his own arm "arrested" and the altar destroyed.

13:6–10 In mercy, the prophet was used by God to heal the hand of the king, but he would have none of his hospitality or reward.

13:6, 7 the LORD your God: This language may be simply deferential to the prophet, but here it may indicate a recognition by Jeroboam that he was no longer really serving the living God.

13:8–10 not go in: In biblical times, sharing a meal was more than just a social custom. It implied an intimate fellowship. Great religious ceremonies from the Passover to the Lord's Table center on people eating together. The prophet did not want his act of mercy to suggest that God accepted Jeroboam's deviant worship.

13:11 Besides being an important cult center (12:29), **Bethel** may have had one of the early prophetic schools (2 Kin. 2:3–7). **an old prophet:** Perhaps the aged prophet had been previously associated with such a group. Whatever his status then, at this point he clearly tells lies (v. 18).

13:12–18 The **prophet** was clearly an apostate. He had not spoken against Jeroboam; instead, he boldly lied to the Lord's true prophet.

13:19 went back with him: The man of God had withstood Jeroboam's attempt to save face by having the prophet stay with him (v. 7), yet now the prophet failed to discern the deception and plainly violated God's clear instructions (v. 9). The prophet would pay a terrible price for his disobedience (v. 24).

13:20–23 Whatever his motives were for bringing the man of God to his house, the aged **prophet** now received a true word from God. He realized too late his awful part in the condemnation of the man of God. The divine sentence (v. 22) would be speedily executed (v. 24).

13:24–28 The way **the lion** stood by both the man of God and his donkey shows that the lion did not kill for food but was God's executioner (vv. 25, 26, 28).

13:29–32 The old prophet (v. 11) was brought back to biblical faith at the sight of the death of the true prophet from Judah. The true but disobedient prophet had paid a terrible price for his disobedience to what he knew to be the word of God (vv. 20–24).

13:32 the saying . . . will surely come to pass: This confession proclaims renewal of faith in God's word by the prophet who had become deceitful. The mercy of God is at His disposal! The Lord had healed the hand of Jeroboam (v. 6) because of His mercy, and the Lord restored the faith of the deceitful prophet because of His mercy as well.

13:32 cities of Samaria: The city of Samaria did not in fact come into being for nearly a half century (16:24), but the author mentions it here from his own later perspective.

13:33, 34 Rather than learning from the report of this incident, Jeroboam became even more set in his **evil way.** His apostasy would earn for him his reputation as the one who "made Israel sin" (16:26).

14:1 Abijah: The name means "My Father Is the Lord."

14:2 In a time of distress Jeroboam turned not to one of his own prophets but to the true prophet of God who had predicted his kingship (11:29–39). Although **Ahijah** was now old (v. 4), his spiritual insight was not so dim that he could not see through disguised human intentions (v. 5).

14:3 ten loaves: The gifts that Jeroboam's wife took along are not those customarily given by a king (2 Kin. 8:7–9) but rather were common fare (1 Sam. 9:6–8). Jeroboam no doubt was hoping he could deceive the prophet by sending a simple gift.

14:4 Located about twenty miles north of Jerusalem, **Shiloh** had been the religious center for the nation during the time of the judges and was the location of the tabernacle (Josh. 18:1; 1 Sam. 1:3). The city was destroyed by the Philistines after the loss of the ark (1 Sam. 4:1–11; Jer. 7:12–15).

14:4–6 Although he **could not see,** Ahijah could "see" by means of the revelation of the living God.

14:7–16 Despite the prophetic sanction of the establishment of his kingdom (v. 7), Jeroboam's sins were severe enough to prevent his house from staying on the throne of Israel (vv. 8–10). Worse news still would come for his family. The child would die just as his mother returned to her city Tirzah (vv. 12, 13, 17). Moreover, an enemy would rise to destroy the household of the king (vv. 14–16).

14:10 bond and free: Like "heaven and earth" in Gen. 1:1, the two opposites together mean totality, or all kinds and classes of people (2 Kin. 14:26).

14:11, 12 Dogs were scavengers in the ancient Middle East and came to symbolize the dregs of society (2 Kin. 8:13).

14:13 something good: Abijah's character receives special divine consideration. Although the age of Jeroboam's son is not certain, he may have been quite young.

14:14 cut off the house: As prophesied

here, the end of Jeroboam's line would soon be accomplished (15:27—16:7).

14:15, 16 God had promised that He would **uproot** Israel should it violate its covenantal obligations (Deut. 28:63, 64). **wooden images:** The worship carried on here concerns the goddess Asherah. She had become associated with Baal (Judg. 3:7; 2 Kin. 23:4). Her worship would become one of the sins that would bring about the downfall of the northern kingdom (16:33; 2 Kin. 17:9–11).

14:17 Famed for its beauty (Song 6:4), **Tirzah** was a royal retreat and the capital of the northern kingdom's first two dynasties (15:33).

14:18 all Israel mourned: The sorrow of the people was also part of Ahijah's prophecy (v. 13).

14:19 The book of the chronicles of the kings of Israel is mentioned often in 1 Kin. as an early source book for the history of the northern kingdom. These chronicles should not be confused with the biblical books of 1 and 2 Chronicles.

14:20 Each of the subsequent kings of Israel would be judged against the example of the wickedness of **Jeroboam** (15:34). Only with Ahab (16:31) was a worse pattern set.

14:21–31 The greater attention was given to Jeroboam I in the northern kingdom in this document (compare 13:28—14:20). Despite his foolishness and wickedness, Rehoboam the son of Solomon was the divinely designated heir of the Davidic promise (2 Sam. 7). He and each of his successors would be measured in terms of faithfulness to Yahweh in the pattern established by David. In contrast, the kings of the northern kingdom would be measured in terms of their unfaithfulness to God as established by Jeroboam I. Some of the kings of the southern kingdom demonstrated a relative faithfulness to Yahweh, such as Asa (15:11). Others followed the pattern of folly and wickedness that Rehoboam established. None followed the Lord to the same degree or in the same manner as did David. Hezekiah (2 Kin. 18:1—20:21) and Josiah (2 Kin. 22:1—23:30) were the best of the series.

14:21 the city which the LORD had chosen: These words celebrate not only Jerusalem (Deut. 12:1–19) but also the Davidic kingship.

14:22 Judah did evil: Although Rehoboam apparently began his reign well (2 Chr. 11:5–17, 23), his spiritual condition soon deteriorated (2 Chr. 12:1). Despite the fact that Judah had several spiritually sensitive kings, apostasy ultimately took its toll in the southern kingdom, just as it also did in the northern kingdom (2 Kin. 17:18–20).

14:23 The **high places** were a problem

throughout the history of Judah and Israel (Mic. 1:3). At times, the worship offered on them might have been done sincerely, in the true worship of God (3:2–4; 2 Kin. 12:3). But these were also the places in which Canaanite worship rites were practiced in honor of Baal and where other foreign gods were worshiped as well. **Sacred pillars** refers to standing pillars of stone or wood. God had prohibited Israel from setting these up (Deut. 16:22).

Wooden images is literally "Asherahs" (v. 15), and refers to obscene wooden symbols that were associated with the sexual worship of the Canaanite deity of that name.

14:24 perverted persons: Male prostitutes were part of the fertility rituals of ancient Canaan (Deut. 23:18). Here the word is a term that means "devoted to sacred service." **abominations:** This is an exceedingly strong term; it describes perverted activities that impelled God to dispossess the Canaanite peoples from their land (Deut. 18:9, 12).

14:25 Shishak: Although Jerusalem and Judah were spared total annihilation at this time because Rehoboam repented, Jerusalem was looted as a result of the sins that took place "on his watch" (2 Chr. 12:1–9). Egyptian records confirm that Shishak's invasion was widespread and highly successful.

14:26–28 The sacking of **treasures of the house of the LORD** (v. 26) is particularly shocking, when we think of the long and detailed description of Solomon's greatest accomplishment, the building and furnishing of the holy temple in Jerusalem (chs. 6—8).

14:27, 28 bronze shields: A compelling symbol of the ruin of the temple treasures is seen in the change from shields of gold (v. 26; 10:16, 17) to bronze.

14:29 The book of the chronicles of the kings of Judah is mentioned 15 times in Kings. Apparently it was an official record of events in the southern kingdom down to the days of Jehoiakim. Neither this work nor "the chronicles of the kings of Israel" (v. 19) is to be confused with the biblical books of Chronicles.

14:30, 31 The early history of Rehoboam and Jeroboam (11:26—12:17) led to their continuing enmity and **war.**

15:1 Although it may reflect a popular name for Abijah (2 Chr. 12:16), **Abijam** is a strange name for a king of Judah, as it ties together the Hebrew word for "Father" with the Hebrew word for "Sea"—normally a deity of Canaan. It is possible that this name reflects the Canaanite influence that had come even into

the royal family this early in Judah's reign. The alternative name Abijah is a standard name of praise to God. It means "My Father Is the Lord."

15:2 The daughter of Uriel of Gibeah (2 Chr. 13:2) and Tamar (2 Sam. 14:27), **Maachah** was the granddaughter of Abishalom and the favorite of Rehoboam's eighteen wives. A woman of strong will, she wielded a good deal of influence during the reign of her son Abijam and her grandson Asa. The mothers of the kings of Judah are named to show that the claims to the throne are legitimate.

> *The deposing of Maachah took place in the fifteenth year of Asa's rule.*

15:3 The word translated **loyal** here (Heb. *shalem*) denotes one who is wholly devoted to God. Contrast this negative assessment of Abijam with the positive use of the same term when Asa is evaluated (15:14).

15:4 for David's sake: That is, because of God's love for David and the promise He had made to him (2 Sam. 7). **lamp:** This is one of the lovely images of God's intended blessing on the Davidic house.

15:5 The quality of David's reign is celebrated. **Uriah:** At the same time, his most grievous sin is not omitted (2 Sam. 11; 12).

15:6 Because Rehoboam reigned until his fifty-eighth year (14:21), Abijam probably knew little respite from **war** (14:30). Abijam did at least trust God during the war against Jeroboam, and God gave him a decisive victory (2 Chr. 13:2–20).

15:7, 8 This follows the pattern established for recording the obituaries of the kings of Judah.

15:9–11 Asa: The meaning of his name is perhaps "Healer."

15:12 perverted persons: This term is used for sacred prostitutes in the Canaanite religious practices (22:46; 2 Kin. 23:7).

15:13 removed Maachah: Asa's many spiritual activities (2 Chr. 14:2–5; 15:1–18) are telescoped into a few statements here (vv. 11–15). Although the reforms mentioned in vv. 11, 12 took place early in Asa's reign (2 Chr. 14:2–5), the chronicler indicates (2 Chr. 15:16) that the deposing of Maachah took place in the fifteenth year of his rule (895 B.C.). Maachah's removal came as a result of a time of covenant renewal (2 Chr. 15:1–15) and a consequent reaction against her vile idolatry.

15:14, 15 In some instances the **high places** were intended as places where the Lord was worshiped (3:2; 1 Sam. 9:12); in other cases they were used for pagan purposes (2 Chr. 14:2, 3).

15:16 war: There were periods of peace

between the two nations (the league of Ahab and Jehoshaphat, ch. 22). But this was a period of warfare, particularly in the border areas.

15:17 Ramah was about five and a half miles north of Jerusalem on the main north-south commercial route through the land, and it was therefore of great importance to both kingdoms. It gave east-west access to both the foothills of Ephraim and the Mediterranean coast, so it was of strategic military importance as well. Baasha was striking a blow for control of the center of the land.

15:18 To stave off the penetration of Israel into Judah, King Asa plundered the temple for money to try to make a military alliance with Damascus. Since the campaign mentioned here took place in the first decade of the ninth century B.C., the king involved was **Ben-Hadad** I (900–860 B.C.). **Tabrimmon:** There is a deliberate change in the Hebrew spelling of this name, based on an antipathy toward the god who is represented in the original name. Instead of writing *Tab-Ramman*, meaning "Thunderer," an epithet of the storm god Hadad (Zech. 12:11), the author wrote *Tab-Rimmon*, the Hebrew word meaning "Pomegranate."

15:19, 20 Asa apparently suggested that for all practical purposes **a treaty** between the house of David and Damascus had been in effect since the days of Solomon.

15:21 The retreat of **Baasha** from Ramah was due to the renewed treaty between Asa of Judah and Ben-Hadad of Damascus.

15:22 Asa's swift action in taking Ramah allowed him to dismantle its fortifications and the use of the material to fortify two nearby strategic Benjamite towns, **Geba** and **Mizpah.** The control of these three sites afforded advanced defensive protection for Jerusalem and northern Judah.

15:23, 24 diseased in his feet: Here is another case of a godly leader who did great exploits for the Lord but ended badly. The exact nature of Asa's malady is uncertain. Some scholars suggest gout, others dropsy, and still others some form of gangrene or venereal disease (the Heb. word for "feet" may at times be a euphemism for the genitals).

15:25, 26 Nadab: His name means "Generous" or "Noble," but he did not live up to his name.

15:27, 28 Baasha killed him: As Baasha, a military commander for Nadab, had done to his master, so it would be done to his own house. Zimri, one of the commanders of his chariot corps, would conspire against Baasha's son Elah and kill him (16:9, 10).

15:29, 30 The death of Nadab was in line with prophetic fulfillment, an act of God's judgment on the **house of Jeroboam** I (14:9, 16).

Nonetheless, the manner of his death was condemned by God through His prophet Jehu (16:2, 7).

15:31, 32 This follows the pattern established for recording the obituaries of the kings of the northern kingdom.

15:33 Baasha . . . in Tirzah: The second capital of Israel (14:17) was located in the highlands of Ephraim between Shechem (the first capital, 12:25) and Mount Gilboa.

15:34 did evil: Political exchange had not signaled any improvement in the spiritual climate of Israel.

16:1–7 As the son of the prophet Hanani whom Asa had executed (2 Chr. 16:7–10), **Jehu** (not to be confused with Jehu the king of Israel, 2 Kin. 9:2) came from the southern kingdom. His long prophetic ministry lasted into the days of Jehoshaphat. Like his father before him, he confronted sin fearlessly—even in the royal house.

16:2–4 In the ancient Middle East considerable attention was given to the proper care of the body of the diseased. Usually the body was interred on the day of death. When a body was left to the **dogs** and the **birds,** an intolerable feeling of shame extended to all family and friends of the deceased. For examples, see the ignoble ends of King Ahab (22:38) and Queen Jezebel (2 Kin. 9:33–37).

16:5–9 The first two dynasties of Israel ended in tragedy. Like Jeroboam's son Nadab (15:28), Baasha's son **Elah** was assassinated. There were three more claimants to the throne before the year 885 B.C. was finished: Zimri, Tibni, and Omri. With the advent of Omri, Israel's third dynasty would be established.

16:10–12 The assassination of Elah and the annihilation of his house by **Zimri** (v. 12), while treacherous, had prophetic sanction because of the wickedness of Elah and his father Baasha.

16:13, 14 idols: Here the plural of the term for "vapor" is used. This is a contemptuous term describing the deities of false, pagan theology.

16:15–22:40 The era of the third dynasty in the northern kingdom, the house of Omri. This section deals with especially the wicked king Ahab. Despite God's patience and repeated efforts to warn Ahab and bring him and his nation back to righteousness, especially through the great prophet Elijah, this king went stubbornly on in his sin and thus incurred the terrible judgment of God for himself, his posterity, and his nation.

16:15–17 As Baasha had done (15:29), so **Zimri** also fulfilled prophecy against a royal house (vv. 8–14).

16:18–20 Because he **burned the king's house** in Tirzah, Zimri may have contributed to

Omri's building of a new capital city and royal residence (v. 24), perhaps one that could be defended better.

16:21, 22 The source of Omri's political base is not certain. According to Josephus, **Tibni** was killed in the dynastic power struggles that brought in the dynasty of Omri.

16:23–28 The short reign of twelve years is not indicative of what **Omri** accomplished. He was one of the more impressive of the kings of

Photo by Howard Vos

verses given to the account of his reign. Ahab receives more than five chapters! This is for two reasons. First, Ahab followed his father Omri in intensifying evil over the kings who had lived before him. But then he accelerated the process to an almost unbelievable degree by making the worship of Baal the official cult of the northern kingdom. Second, Ahab was not allowed by God to promote his wickedness without a challenge. That challenge came in the person of Elijah, one

The hill on which King Omri of the northern kingdom built the city of Samaria (1 Kin. 16:24). It remained the capital city of Israel until the nation fell to the Assyrians in 722 B.C.

Israel in terms of his accomplishments. He invaded Moab and figured prominently in an alliance aimed at stopping the westward advance of the rising power of Assyria. Omri's exploits are commemorated in the Moabite Stone and the Assyrian annals. Indeed, he was so important to the Assyrians that they called Israel the "The House of Omri" long after his death. Yet the author of Kings describes little of Omri's achievements, because he **did evil in the eyes of the LORD."**

16:24–28 Omri's choice of **Samaria** as the site for his new capital city was doubtless motivated by several factors: its central geographic setting, its commercial location, and its defensive potential. As a Canaanite territory, it had political, ethnic, and religious independence from all previous allegiances.

16:29–22:40 The reign of Ahab. Whereas Omri was an exceptionally gifted king in terms of military, commercial, and strategic gifts and accomplishments (v. 23), there were only six

of the most courageous, powerful, and enigmatic figures in the pages of Scripture.

16:29 The name **Ahab** is a combination of the Hebrew words for "brother" and "father." The term "father" likely refers to God, and "brother" speaks of a relationship with God. Thus the meaning, "{My} Brother {Is} Father." By his life, Ahab gives the lie to his name.

16:30, 31 The first level of evaluation of **Ahab** is the same as that given to his father (compare v. 30 with v. 25). **a trivial thing:** By these words we realize that in Ahab we come to the very lowest point in the degeneration of the spiritual life of the kings of Israel. Each of the kings of the northern kingdom from Nadab (15:26), Jeroboam's son, to Omri (16:26), Ahab's father, had been guilty of walking in the perverse pathway of Jeroboam I. Ahab acted as though the sins of Jeroboam were a trivial thing. He did this in two ways: first, in his marriage to Jezebel; second, in his promotion of Baal worship as the state religion. Ahab's marriage to the Phoenician princess **Jezebel** was politically important and demonstrated the rising prominence of Israel's third dynasty. As in the case of the foreign wives of Solomon before him (11:1–13), Ahab's mar-

IN FOCUS   **"Baal"**

(Heb. *ba'al*) (1 Kin. 16:31; 18:21; Judg. 2:13; 2 Kin. 10:20) Strong's #1168: Baal was a pagan god of storms and fertility, worshiped throughout the ancient Middle East because of his association with powerful forces. His name literally means "Owner," "Master," or "Husband." In Canaanite literature, Baal is often associated with the fertility goddess Asherah, whose sacred "Asherah poles" are mentioned numerous times in the OT (2 Kin. 21:7). Worship of these pagan deities involved self- mutilation, ritual prostitution, and infant sacrifice. Despite these despicable practices, the Israelites themselves adopted Baal worship—a factor which eventually led to God's punishment (Judg. 2:11–15; Jer. 19:4–6).

riage produced tragic results. Jezebel was an exceedingly competent, highly gifted, powerful person—and she was exceedingly evil. She could influence Ahab to be wicked (ch. 21). However, when she was absent from Ahab, he had moments of relatively good behavior (ch. 20). Her father was both king and priest of Baal in Sidon; similarly, Jezebel was princess and priestess of Baal. Her Phoenician name was Abizebel, meaning "My Father (Baal) Is Noble." The Hebrew scribes deliberately dropped a letter from her name. Thus she would be known forever as Jezebel, a dishonorable name meaning "Lacking Honor." **he went and served Baal and worshiped him:** The outrage is that Ahab had gone quite beyond a mere combining of beliefs. He became a full-fledged worshiper of Baal, the Canaanite deity, for whom his wife Jezebel was a priestess.

16:32, 33 Further, Ahab established an **altar for Baal,** a **temple of Baal,** and a **wooden image.** In these actions Ahab went a considerable distance in establishing the Baal cult as the state religion of Israel. The worship of Baal in Israel would ultimately spell the end of both kingdoms (2 Kin. 17:16–23; Jer. 2:1—3:25). The sin that Ahab and Jezebel brought into the nation of Israel was a total rejection of the living God.

16:34 In defiance of Joshua's curse (Josh. 6:26, 27), Hiel **built Jericho.** Jericho had been occupied at various times (see Judg. 3:13), but not as a permanently occupied fortified city. Either Hiel offered his sons as foundation sacrifices (following ancient custom) or they died in some mishap. One way or the other, Joshua's curse was carried out.

17:1–4 No prophet had arisen since Moses (Deut. 18:15–19) like **Elijah.** His name means "The Lord Is My God." Elijah would speak for God fearlessly in the midst of the spiritual vacuum that gripped the northern kingdom throughout the days of Ahab, Ahaziah, and Jehoram. A prophet par excellence, his ministry and his stand against the rampant Baalism of the land reached the highest circles of government in Israel. Malachi would predict Elijah's return before the coming "great and dreadful day of the Lord" (Mal. 4:5). **Tishbite** has been understood traditionally as referring to a town named Tishbe or as designation for the settlers in Gilead. A formal, solemn oath (see David's words in 1:19), **as the Lord God of Israel lives** was also a brilliant declaration. Elijah, who stood unafraid before the king of Israel, unannounced and uninvited, could do so because he stood before One whose glory, majesty, and power were infinitely greater than Ahab's. **dew nor rain:** Because the Canaanite belief was that only Baal could govern the dew and the rain, Elijah's pronouncement was as an immediate challenge: Who is really God, Baal or the Lord? (see 18:21; Deut. 28:12; 33:28).

17:5 The Brook Cherith was across the Jordan, far from the palace in Samaria.

17:6–8 The Lord of all creation may use any means He wishes to feed His prophet, even **the ravens.**

17:9–11 Zarephath was in Phoenician territory, seven miles south of Sidon, the stronghold of Baal. The Lord's sustaining Elijah first by a raven and then by a **widow** provided the prophet with a dramatic test of faith at the outset of his ministry. The widow, too, would be taught the value of trusting in God alone (v. 24). Many widows were exceptionally poor, as they had few options in an agrarian culture. This one was in a desperate plight when she encountered God's prophet.

17:12 the Lord your God: The widow of Zarephath was a woman of faith in the living God, even though she lived in a foreign land. **Bread** here denotes a round cake. The flour **bin** was a large earthenware container (Gen. 24:14), while **jar** denotes a smaller, portable container such as a jug or flask.

17:13 me . . . first: Elijah's challenge to the widow would call for faith in the midst of her desperate circumstances.

17:14 The Lord God of Israel acknowledges the woman's identification of the Lord as Elijah's God (v. 12), but also points the widow directly to Him who is the Sustainer of all.

17:15-17 While an apostate Israelite nation suffered because of the drought, God supplied the daily necessities to a non-Israelite who willingly took Him at His word. The fresh supply of oil and flour each day would be a reminder to both the prophet and the widow of the value of personal trust in Him who alone is sufficient to meet every need (Phil. 4:19).

17:18 Sin is not always the immediate cause of suffering (John 9:3; Heb. 12:7-11).

17:19, 20 Elijah stayed in an **upper room,** temporary quarters on the roof accessible from outside the house. This arrangement that preserved the privacy of all parties and protected the widow's reputation in the community.

17:21 Elijah's action in the stretching out of himself on the dead lad **three times** may symbolize the power of the thrice holy God (Num. 6:24-26; Is. 6:3). Elisha later would perform a similar act (2 Kin. 4:34; Acts 20:10).

17:21, 22 cried . . . heard: The scriptural motif of crying and being heard or calling and being answered, is a theme that emphasizes intimacy of fellowship or communion (Pss. 22:24; 91:15; 102:1, 2).

17:23, 24 now . . . I know: The widow's belief had now grown into fullness of faith. That Elijah was indeed a "man of God" (v. 18) had been proved by word and deed. The entire incident demonstrates that the Lord is the God of Israelite and Gentile alike (Acts 10:34-35; 11:18; Rom. 3:29), and that He is the author of life itself (Luke 20:38; John 11:25, 26).

18:1, 2 The NT indicates that the drought ended in the fourth year (Luke 4:25; James 5:17). If the point of reckoning here is late **in the third year,** the end of the drought may well have not occurred until some three and a half years after its inception.

18:3 Although Jewish tradition has identified them, this **Obadiah** is probably not the author of the Book of Obadiah. Nothing in that book points to so early a date as this time. The Obadiah here is a highly sympathetic figure, whose great faith in God and heroic actions help us gain a more balanced picture of the situation of people of faith in Israel at the time. **in charge of his house:** This phrase reflects an official title (4:6). Obadiah was Ahab's palace official and

minister of state, in both cases serving as the king's personal representative.

18:4 That there could be **one hundred prophets** for Obadiah to hide may be seen from the fact that associations of prophets who met and may even have lived together are known from this period onward (1 Sam. 10:5; 2 Kin. 2:3-7; 6:1, 2). Over twenty thousand caves have been found in the vicinity of Mt. Carmel, many of them capable of holding fifty men.

The fertile plains surrounding Mount Carmel, site of Elijah's victory over the prophets of Baal (1 Kin. 18:1-40).

18:5-11 Keeping **horses** alive was important to maintain military preparedness in a world where there was nearly always the threat of new hostilities.

18:12-14 Obadiah was not quite sure whether he could trust the Lord's prophet. Obadiah recognized that God's Holy Spirit might come upon His servants (Judg. 6:34; 11:29) in such a way as to **carry** them to other places (Ezek. 8:3; 11:1). Obadiah had already jeopardized his life in hiding God's prophets. Reporting Elijah's presence without producing him to an already infuriated Ahab might well cost him his life (vv. 9, 14).

18:15-17 Hosts means "armies," a title for **the Lord** to designate God's control of a vast heavenly army ready to act at his command (Rev. 19:11-21) and His place as the commander of Israel's forces (Judg. 1:3), and also His universal sovereignty (Is. 37:16). Elijah acknowledged that he was standing before his supreme commander.

18:18 Baals: The wording indicates that Ahab had a practice of attending services at various local shrines where this deity was worshiped.

18:19–21 The wife of Ei, **Asherah** was a fertility goddess whose exploits and veneration were linked with Baal (14:15). The worship of Baal and Asherah held a constant fascination for Israel from earliest times (Ex. 34:13; Num. 25; Judg. 2:13) and eventually caused Israel's demise (2 Kin. 17:16–18).

18:22, 23 Although there were other prophets alive at the time (v. 13), Elijah focused on the fact that he **alone** stood ready to confront the 450 prophets of Baal.

18:24–26 The contest between the Lord and Baal would reveal who was the true god of storm. Such a god would have lightning in his arsenal of weapons (Ps. 18:12–14; Hab. 3:11). Sending **fire** for the wood and the offering would be a reasonable test of the power of the rival deities.

18:27, 28 The sharp words **for he is a god** were mocking and derisive. Perhaps their god was lost in thought, **meditating,** and simply needed them to call louder. **Is busy** is a euphemism. In his harsh attack on the folly of idolatry, Elijah suggested that the reason their god did not answer was that he had gone to a celestial men's room.

18:29 no voice: Nothing the priests did elicited a response from their supposed god.

18:30 repaired the altar: This was an earlier altar that had been used by the true people of God on a legitimate high place (3:2–4). Elijah avoided all contact with the altar that was associated with Baal.

18:31 The numerical symbolism of **twelve stones** cannot be missed. The people of Israel had descended from twelve tribes.

18:32 Rebuilding the **altar in the name of the Lord** would be a reminder that the Lord had not abdicated His position; He was still the God of all Israel, including the northern kingdom, where pagan syncretism and full Baal worship prevailed.

18:33–35 third time: The three applications of water not only made the sacrifice thoroughly soaked and beyond human trickery but may again attest the power of the thrice holy God (17:21).

18:36 The phrase **Lord God of Abraham, Isaac, and Israel** so characteristic of worship in the early period (Gen. 50:24; Ex. 3:6, 15, 16), reminded Elijah's hearers of the inviolability of the Abrahamic covenant. The God of Abraham, Isaac, and Jacob, was still the God of the northern kingdom, and the nation's only hope of life, protection, and blessing in the land of promise (Deut. 30:20; 2 Kin. 13:23).

18:37 Elijah's prayer had two elements. First, he wished that the Lord would demonstrate clearly to the **people** that He alone is the living God. Second, he prayed for the full revival of God's people. The first prayer would be answered in a dramatic manner.

18:38 Showing who really was the god of storm, Baal proved impotent, while **the fire of the Lord** destroyed everything on the site.

18:39 God's power over fire, water, and rain (v. 45) demonstrated that He, not Baal, is **the Lord, He is God!**

18:40 The prophets were **executed** because of their blatant sin and the ruin they had brought upon the nation.

18:41, 42 The respective reactions of the king and the prophet are enlightening. A compromising king, as bidden, gladly celebrated, while a faithful prophet **bowed down** and prayed for the promised result of the Lord's miraculous victory.

18:43, 44 This cloud may have seemed **as small as a man's hand** when it was first visible

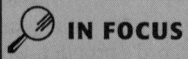 **IN FOCUS** | **"name"**

(Heb. *shem*) (1 Kin. 8:20; 18:24; Ex. 6:3) Strong's #8034: The Hebrew word *shem* may be related to a root meaning "to mark," but this is uncertain. In Bible times, a person's name not only served as a means of identification but could also describe a person's character, position, or destiny (read 1 Sam. 25:25 for the meaning of Nabal's name, "Fool"). Sometimes a person was renamed, reflecting a change in that person's character or status (Gen. 35:10). The various names of God are especially important. Each name reveals a particular aspect of His nature (for example, God Most High or the Lord of Hosts). For this reason, His name is to be honored and should never be used irreverently (Ex. 20:7). By sharing His name with Israel, God indicated the intimacy of His covenantal relationship with them (Ex. 3:13–15).

from Mount Carmel's height, but Elijah sensed the approach of the growing storm and warned Ahab that he had better hurry.

18:45 Elijah had announced more than three years earlier that there would be no more **rain** unless it came from the hand of the living God (17:1).

18:46 girded up his loins: Elijah tucked his garment into his sash, enabling him to run freely the 13 miles to Jezreel.

19:1–3 The aftermath of a great victory may become a new time for defeat. This was what happened with Elijah, following what he thought was his greatest moment. With the clear vindication of Yahweh, the living God, on Mount Carmel, and with the shameful defeat and execution of the wicked prophet-priests of Baal, surely he must have thought that there would now come a national revival (see his prayer in 18:37). But he found that nothing had really changed.

19:1, 2 The report **Ahab told Jezebel** did not cause her to repent or to turn from Baal to God. Ahab merely reported the facts that led to her personal embarrassment. Her response was to issue a death warrant for Elijah.

19:3 Elijah understood Jezebel's intentions **when he saw** her response, and he realized dejectedly that the Lord's victory on Mount Carmel would not necessarily bring a quick end to the paganism that was rampant in the land. Some ancient translations read "he was afraid" instead of "he saw." However, Elijah was not a man of fear, and he certainly had no reason to be afraid of Jezebel since he knew the living God and His power. What he faced was profound disappointment. He saw that nothing really had changed. He saw that despite the tremendous demonstration of the reality of God's power on Mount Carmel, the people would soon forget and would revert to their old evil ways. **He . . . ran for his life,** not from fear, but from a desire that Jezebel not be the one to kill him. Actually he wished for death, but he prayed that his death would be at the Lord's hand.

19:4 The **broom tree** has sufficient foliage for shade and often grows to a height of ten feet. It grows abundantly in Israel.

19:5, 6 God brought Elijah a **cake** and **water,** even as He had provided for him in earlier days (ch. 17).

19:7 Although **the angel of the Lord** can at times refer to God Himself (Ex. 3:2–6), in the Book of Kings it means a supernatural messenger (2 Kin. 1:3; 19:35).

19:8 As it frequently does in the Scriptures, **Horeb** refers to Mount Sinai itself, "the mountain of God" (Ex. 3:1).

19:9 The Hebrew text has "the" **cave.** This use of the definitive article here may be specific,

suggesting that this was "the cave" in which Moses had hidden when he experienced the presence of Yahweh on the mountain of God (Ex. 34).

19:10 zealous: Like Phinehas of old (Num. 25:7–13), Elijah had a passion for God that made him stand against the idolatry he saw all around him. **I alone am left:** In his depression, he thought he alone was faithful to God. When he was killed, there would be no one left to serve God.

19:11, 12 the Lord was not in: Although each of the things mentioned in vv. 11, 12 could signal God's presence (Ex. 40:38; Zech. 14:4, 5; Acts 2:2, 3), Elijah learned that God is not just a God of the spectacular. At times, the work of God is experienced in **a still small voice,** "the sound of a gentle stillness." Elijah had called for lightning, and he had called for fire and national revival. What Elijah did not see was that God was at work in the lives of many people (v. 18).

19:13, 14 What are you doing here: In the first instance (v. 9), the question invited Elijah to consider his reasons for coming to this particular place. Based on his reply and God's self-revelation, the second question may imply something like: it is time to be elsewhere, serving God both in the normal routine of life and in accordance with His specific commissions.

19:15, 16 Elijah's work for God was far from complete, but it would now take a new direction. Elijah would **anoint** Elisha (vv. 19–21), Elisha would anoint **Hazael** (2 Kin. 8:7–15), and Jehu would be anointed by Elisha's servant (2 Kin. 9:1–10). The importance of Elijah's task may be seen in that Elisha became Elijah's designated successor, and Jehu and Hazael became kings.

19:17 The three individuals, **Elisha, Jehu,** and **Hazael,** were instruments of God. One would follow the other in works of judgment on God's hard-hearted people.

19:18–20 There were still many people who were faithful to the living God. **Seven thousand** had not stooped to worship Baal. Although in each generation there are great spiritual leaders who do the work of God, there is a community of God among everyday people whose lives are not spectacular but who live faithfully for God.

19:21 Unlike those whom Jesus would mention in his teachings (Matt. 8:18–22; Luke 9:57–62), **Elisha turned back** to his home only to break fully with his past. As Joshua had faithfully served Moses in a period of training for a position of great responsibility, so Elisha would humbly serve this later "Moses" until Elijah was taken into heaven (2 Kin. 2:1–12). The use of the word **servant** for Elisha matches the use of this word for Gehazi, the servant of Elisha in 2 Kin. 4:12.

20:1 The **king of Syria** was **Ben-Hadad** II (860–842 B.C.). Although there is a modern nation called Syria, the ancient name for the people who had their capital in Damascus was *Aramean,* and their land was *Aram* (2 Kin. 5:1). One of the distinctive features of the ancient Middle East was the practice of forming alliances. Coalitions such as the **thirty-two kings** were common in times of war (Gen. 14:1–16).

? Exact location questionable

20:2 When he is associated with his wicked wife Jezebel, **Ahab** appears as thoroughly evil. But in this chapter he appears as a capable leader in a time of international turmoil, and as a person who had some sense of the power and presence of God (vv. 13, 14).

20:3, 4 Taken by themselves, Ben-Hadad's words **are mine** meant no more than that Israel was a client state to the more powerful Aramean state. Ahab's reply **All . . . are yours** would then have been acceptance of such a treaty, in which Israel was the subservient party.

20:5, 6 The language was no longer that of political formalities; this was a demand for complete surrender of everything of value, of any person of worth, of **whatever** was **pleasant** in Ahab's eyes, to be handed over to the foreign monarch.

20:7, 8 Ahab apparently held out little hope of withstanding so vast an enemy host. His **elders** (v. 8) counseled him against submitting.

20:9 first time . . . this thing: The distinction may be in the admission of a subservient status of Israel to Aram, as against the actual surrender of persons and goods to the suzerain nation.

20:10 Ben-Hadad's boast was that his striking power was so great that Samaria would be ground to a powder, yielding barely enough for each of his soldiers to carry away a **handful.**

20:11 Ahab's proverbial reply reminded Ben-Hadad that a **boast** alone would not get the job done.

20:12 The notice that **Ben-Hadad** was **drinking** during the time he should have been

Elijah and Elisha

Elijah's victory on Mount Carmel ended with the slaying of 450 prophets of Baal (18:20–40). His ministry spanned Canaan from the Brook Cherith near his birthplace (17:1–7) to Zarephath where he performed the miracle that sustained the widow and her son, and to as far south as Mount Horeb (not shown). In Samaria, Elijah denounced King Ahab's injustice against Naboth of Jezreel (21:17–29). Near Jericho, he separated the waters of the Jordan River to cross over and subsequently was carried to heaven in a chariot of fire (2 Kings 2:1–12). Elisha healed Naaman of leprosy in the Jordan River (5:1–19) and led the blinded Syrians to their defeat at Samaria (6:8–23). In Damascus, Elisha prophesied the death of Ben-Hadad and the succession of Hazael as king of Syria.

preparing for battle shows his arrogance. He was celebrating victory before he had begun fighting (v. 16).

20:13 This **prophet** is not named. We are reminded that there were many true prophets of the Lord at that time (18:13; 20:35). **I will deliver . . . you shall know:** Just as God had demonstrated His person and power on Mount Carmel (ch. 18), He would now make Himself known to Ahab in the coming battle.

20:14, 15 The prophet revealed the outlines of the strategy Ahab should use. To his credit, Ahab obeyed the divine command and **mustered** his force.

20:16 This was an alliance of **thirty-two kings** from small areas in Aram and the surrounding territories. But they were all **getting drunk**—an arrogant act before the battle had even begun.

20:17–21 Ahab followed up his probing skirmish with a well-timed charge by his main striking force. Ben-Hadad, the king of the Arameans, barely **escaped** (v. 20) with his life. The resulting **great slaughter** (v. 21) was a tremendous victory for the army of Ahab.

20:22 This is likely the same **prophet** through whom God had given an encouraging message (v. 13; contrast v. 35). Ahab ultimately trusted in human wisdom rather than divine standards (v. 42). The period of late **spring** to

early summer was one of the two main seasons for military expeditions. Provisions were readily available for men and cattle. The end of the rains allowed the movement of troops and provisions to be made more easily.

20:23–25 The Aramean advisors reflected traditional ancient Middle Eastern theological conceptions. Their gods' powers, such as their **gods of the hills,** were limited to particular locations. But the living God is not limited by time (Ps. 90:2) or space (Ps. 139:7–12). This is a fact beyond the imagination of these pagan "theologians."

20:26–30 This **Aphek** is not the Philistine city where the ark was lost (1 Sam. 4:1), but another location just east of the Jordan in northern Gilead. Apparently the Arameans were launching their second campaign in the Jordan valley. The Arameans would learn that the living God can deliver His people in the valley as well as the hills (Ps. 23:4; Joel 3:12–14).

20:31 Ben-Hadad now appealed to Ahab's **merciful** nature. The Aramean king sent his servants to Ahab in the traditional attire of submission and repentance.

20:32–34 The term **brother** was commonly used when relations between kings were cordial (9:13). Ben-Hadad might have been implying, "We are both kings."

 **IN PERSON**   **Ahab**

Generally recognized as the most evil king of Israel, Ahab did at times display courage and even real humility before God (21:29). Unfortunately, he never served the Lord wholeheartedly.

Like many today, Ahab struggled with an indecisive nature. All too easily he could be led into wickedness by his wife, the infamous Jezebel. His marriage to this Phoenician princess was politically important and demonstrated the rising prominence of Israel's third dynasty. But as in the case of the foreign wives of Solomon before him, Ahab's marriage to a pagan produced tragic results.

Jezebel's influence over her husband was much stronger than the godly influence of the prophet Elijah. It is only fitting that the most evil king in the history of Israel should have as his contemporary the most famous and dramatic of Israel's prophets. Ahab's feelings toward Elijah show through in his comments to him: "Is that you, O troubler of Israel?" and "Have you found me, O my enemy?"

Despite seeing the fire of the living God consume Elijah's godly sacrifices at Mount Carmel, Ahab still listened to his wife instead of listening to Elijah and obeying God. Ahab went beyond merely combining the worship of the true God with the worship of the false gods of the Canaanites. He rejected the living God by openly serving Baal and worshiping him. Ahab even built an altar for Baal, a temple for it, and a wooden image. By rejecting the true God, Ahab was also rejecting God's Law as a guide for his life. Hence, nothing stopped him from coveting his neighbor's vineyard and allowing his wife to murder Naboth in order to steal his land. Ahab's life of disobedience led to a tragic end. He died in battle and his blood was licked up by the dogs, as had been foretold.

The only legacy that Ahab left was negative. He is remembered to this day by the words, "Ahab the son of Omri did evil in the sight of the LORD, more than all who were before him."

20:35–41 This **certain man** is probably a different prophet than the one mentioned earlier in the story (vv. 13, 22). **sons of the prophets:** Although this term first occurs here, prophetic associations were known at least from Samuel's time (1 Sam. 10). Obadiah had only recently been instructed about rescuing such groups of prophets from Ahab's purge (18:13–14).

20:42–43 The prophet's dramatic tale is symbolic; as Ahab had judged the case, so he would be judged (22:29–37).

20:43 Sullen here connotes stubbornness as well as a downcast spirit. Rather than being grateful to God for the victories, Ahab resorts to human reason and adamantly refuses to change his ways.

21:1 Samaria was Ahab's capital city; its name is used to represent all of Israel (2 Kin. 1:3; 2 Chr. 24:23; Jon. 3:6).

21:2, 3 Technically, all land was the Lord's, who granted it in perpetuity to each Israelite tribe and family (Lev. 25:23–28). Accordingly, the property belonged to **Naboth** (Num. 36:2–9). Even the king was obliged to obey the Law (1 Sam. 10:25). Ahab therefore negotiated with Naboth for his property.

21:4–6 sullen: Once again (1 Kin. 20:43) the king's displeasure at not having his own way makes his spirit downcast.

21:7 In reminding Ahab that he was king and could do as he pleased, **Jezebel** reflected her Canaanite background where kings ruled absolutely (Deut. 17:14–20; 1 Sam. 8:11–18).

21:8–12 Such **letters** would be written by royal scribes on scrolls or tablets and then **sealed** with the sender's personal sign.

21:13, 14 two men, scoundrels: The charge against Naboth was serious (Ex. 22:28). Although two witnesses were required in capital cases (Deut. 17:6), these **two men** were **scoundrels**, easily bribed into giving false testimony (Prov. 19:28). Naboth was executed **outside the city** as the Law required (Lev. 24:14). God's Law was followed in the manner and place of his death, though his execution was an outrage against the whole spirit of the Law. As in the case of Achan (Josh. 7:24, 25), Naboth's sons were stoned to death with him (2 Kin. 9:26), preventing any successor of Naboth from seeking to undo the illegal land seizure.

21:15–18 Because **Naboth . . . was dead,** the property was confiscated by the throne. Although Ahab apparently was unconcerned about how this took place, he could not escape his guilty conscience (v. 20).

21:19–24 Soon Ahab's blood would be licked by **dogs** at the pool in Samaria (22:37, 38). Ahab had lost all sense of God's Law, the basic teaching of which was always love for God and for neighbor (Matt. 22:37–40). Ahab's consistent idolatry demonstrated that he had no whole-hearted love for God (18:18). Taking Naboth's vineyard showed he had no love for his neighbor either.

21:25–29 The vacillating nature of Ahab's complex character is seen here. He could all too easily be led into **wickedness** by his **wife.** Nevertheless, he could at times display courage (22:34, 35) and even real humility before God (v. 29). Unfortunately, he never really entered into a genuine spiritual relationship with God. The result was that he, like all who despise God's mercies (2 Pet. 3:5–10), would perish and leave his ill-gotten gain behind him (Ps. 49:5–14).

22:1–3 Faced with the rising threat of Assyria, Ahab had failed to press his advantage of three years before. He had not reoccupied the strategic highlands of **Ramoth in Gilead.** In the days of Solomon this area served as an administrative center (4:13), but apparently it was lost during the reign of Omri. Now that Aram and Israel as allies had successfully turned back Shalmaneser III of Assyria at Qarqar (853 B.C.), control of Ramoth Gilead was crucial.

22:4 Jehoshaphat was the fourth king of the southern kingdom. He was related to Ahab through the marriage of his son Jehoram to Ahab's daughter Athaliah (2 Kin. 8:18, 27). Jehoshaphat's relation to Ahab now placed him in the precarious position of going to war with Ahab against the Arameans.

22:5–8 Kings in the ancient Middle East commonly sought the will of the gods before entering battle (Judg. 20:27, 28; 1 Sam. 23:1–4). Jehoshaphat did not rely on Ahab's false prophets; he desired a true **word of the Lord.**

22:9 The prophet **Micaiah** is not known except in connection with this incident (2 Chr. 18:8–27).

22:10 A threshing floor was often used by the Canaanites for holding court. Threshing floors could also be scenes of spiritual importance (Judg. 6:36–40; 1 Chr. 21:15—22:1).

22:11–16 Zedekiah tried to validate his prophetic pronouncement with symbolic magic. The **horns** symbolize great strength (Num. 24:8; Ps. 18:2), an idea reinforced by the use of **iron.** A goring horn is used elsewhere in Scripture to symbolize victorious power (Dan. 8:7).

22:17–22 The imagery of **sheep** and **shepherd** was familiar to Micaiah's hearers (Ezek. 34:12; Mark 14:27). Micaiah's words are dramatic, emphasizing the gravity of Ahab's projected venture and counteracting Zedekiah's lies.

22:23–29 lying spirit: These prophets prophesied under the influences of evil, but their false predictions were just what Ahab wanted to hear.

🔍 IN FOCUS | "burn incense"

(Heb. *qatar*) (1 Kin. 13:1; 22:43; Num. 16:40; 2 Chr. 13:11) Strong's #6999: This Hebrew word has the basic meaning "to produce smoke." It is used only in reference to religious offerings. The offerings are sometimes made to the Lord and sometimes to other gods (9:25; 12:33; 2 Kin. 22:17). In Leviticus, the word is used to speak of true worship that the Lord had ordained. But in the historical books of 1 Kings through 2 Chronicles, the word is primarily used for the rituals of false worship. Even many of the "good" kings of Israel failed to abolish improper burning of incense (22:43; 2 Kin. 12:3; 14:4; 15:4, 35). Jeremiah often used the word to denounce the errors of his people, though he used it once to prophesy of a time when Israel would perpetually worship the true God (Jer. 1:16; 11:13; 33:14–18).

22:30–33 By hiding himself behind a **disguise,** Ahab hoped he could thwart Micaiah's prophecy of doom. Jehoshaphat's participation in royal regalia in a battle where he did not even belong (2 Chr. 19:1–3) nearly cost him his life. Ben-Hadad tried to shorten the battle by finding and killing Ahab. Jehoshaphat's life was spared not only by his timely cry but by God's direct intervention (2 Chr. 18:31).

22:34–37 The phrase **at random** indicates that the bowman did not realize that he was aiming at Ahab. The shot itself was well placed, striking the king in the gap between the breastplate and the lower armor. Ahab's wounded body was propped up in his chariot so his soldiers would keep on fighting, and not give up immediately as Ben-Hadad hoped.

22:38 The fulfillment of Elijah's grisly prophecy (21:19–24) concerning the house of Ahab unfolds here as **the dogs licked up his blood.**

22:39–42 Archaeological excavations at Samaria have illustrated the nature of Ahab's **ivory house,** a house with luxurious decorations made of ivory. The palace contained objects of ivory, and the walls and furniture were inlaid with pieces of ivory.

22:43, 44 Jehoshaphat continued in his father Asa's spiritual footsteps. These **high**

places were often used in the worship of Israel's God (3:2–4).

22:45 made war: In addition to the campaign at Ramoth Gilead, Jehoshaphat's military ventures included strengthening his forces and borders (2 Chr. 17:14–19), repelling an invasion (2 Chr. 20:1–30), and conducting an Edomite campaign (2 Kin. 3:6–27).

22:46, 47 perverted persons: See 14:24 for a description of these Canaanite cultic prostitutes, who were a part of the debased religious practices of Baal worship.

22:48–50 The destruction of the **merchant ships** sponsored by Jehoshaphat and Ahaziah ended the projected commercial enterprise. The prophet pronounces God's displeasure with the whole project (2 Chr. 20:35–37).

22:51–53 A wicked king of the northern kingdom, **Ahaziah** followed in the path of his father Ahab, much as Amon of Judah would later follow in the path of his wicked father Manasseh (2 Kin. 21:19–22).

22:52 Ahaziah thus continued in the spiritual course laid out for him by his **father.** The story does not end here but is continued in 2 Kings. The division of Kings into two books was done for convenience when the Bible was translated into Greek in the second century B.C.

The Second Book of

Kings

■

FROM THE ASCENSION OF THE PROPHET ELIJAH to heaven through the eventual fall of Israel and Judah, Second Kings continues the history begun in 1 Kings, of one people and two kingdoms. The narrative does not merely celebrate the Israelites. Instead, it displays both high and low points in the history of Israel and Judah. While it is true that few of the kings of the northern kingdom of Israel are spoken of

highly, the kings of the southern kingdom of Judah do not fare much better. First and Second Kings are more than a recounting of names and facts. The books describe a people without direction, leaders who failed to lead, and a God who was forced to discipline His rebellious people.

Second Kings continues the history of the divided kingdom from the point where First Kings ends, with the reigns of Ahaziah in the northern kingdom (853–852 B.C.) and Jehoshaphat in the southern kingdom (872–847 B.C.) It traces the events in the rest of Israel's third dynasty, together with corresponding details in Judah during the reigns of Jehoram and Ahaziah. In so doing, it describes details especially relevant to the prophetic ministries of Elijah and Elisha (1:1—9:37). During this period, the northern kingdom faced continued pressure from Aram (Syria) under its kings Ben-Hadad II and Hazael, as well as new threats from the rising state of Assyria with its powerful King Shalmaneser III (858–824 B.C.).

The account of the fourth dynasty in Israel begins with a purge of the rampant Baal worship that had plagued the first three dynasties (10:1—15:12). Unfortunately, the founder of

this dynasty, Jehu, was an opportunist who used the attack on Baal worship to further his own causes. Rather than keeping the Law completely, he perpetuated the apostate state religion initiated by Jeroboam I—the worship of the calves at Bethel and Dan. His successors in the fourth dynasty proved little better. The corresponding rulers of the southern kingdom ranged from the wicked Athaliah to Josiah and Amaziah, who received mild divine commendation. Externally, the Aramean menace was ended by the military campaign of Adad Nirari III of Assyria. Yet Assyria itself passed into a period of decline that spanned the first half of the eighth century B.C.

With the death of Zechariah in 752 B.C., the northern kingdom entered a time of rapid decline that mirrored its spiritual condition. The combined effects of spiritual apostasy and moral debauchery, together with unwise political entanglements with Assyria, ultimately brought the northern kingdom to its end in 722 B.C. Meanwhile, Jotham and his wicked son Ahaz were ruling the southern kingdom of Judah. Ahaz was so evil that even the godly Isaiah had little effect on the king's spiritual condition. The

Scriptures attribute Judah's ultimate demise to the idolatry of this king (2 Chr. 28:23).

The remainder of 2 Kings deals with the varying fortunes and spiritual pilgrimage of the southern kingdom, tracing Judah's history from the righteous Hezekiah (chs. 18—20) to the wicked sons of Josiah, under whom Jerusalem faced three invasions and deportations, the last in 586 B.C. Thus Judah was increasingly caught up in the complex international events that took place from the late eighth to the early sixth century B.C.

Judah's ability to maintain its identity in the midst of its powerful neighbors was due on the one hand to God, who was faithful to His covenant with the house of David, and on the other hand to the spiritual gains made during the reigns of its two faithful kings, Hezekiah (729–699 B.C.) and Josiah (640–609 B.C.). However, the forces of apostasy that had brought about the collapse of the northern kingdom also took their toll in the southern kingdom. Judah was led away captive, and their exile would last seventy years. Second Kings ends on this tragic note. Only the final word of Jehoiachin's release provides a ray of hope in the darkness of captivity (25:27–30). The symbolic message is clear: the Lord would still fulfill His promise to restore His people (1 Kin. 8:46–53).

Like 1 and 2 Samuel, 1 and 2 Kings were originally one book in Hebrew. The book was divided into two parts when the Old Testament was translated into Greek in about 150 B.C.

Hence debate over the authorship of First Kings applies equally to the authorship of 2 Kings. Many evangelical biblical scholars continue to endorse the traditional view that Jere-miah wrote the books of the Kings. They point to Jeremiah's priestly origin, his prophetic activity, his access to governmental authorities at the highest level, and his close personal involvement in the complex religious, social, and political activities that occurred during the collapse and fall of Judah in the early sixth century B.C. Jeremiah was certainly in an ideal position to know the spiritual situation of the day and to have access to state records, historical information, and other source material necessary for writing such a book. Jeremiah could well have written and compiled the book during the period of religious reform led by King Josiah (22:8).

Outline

(Continued from the outline of First Kings)

I. The divided kingdom 1:1—17:41

  A. The third dynasty 1:1—9:37

    1. The reign of Ahaziah in Israel 1:1–18

    2. The transition from Elijah to Elisha 2:1–25

    3. Elisha's ministry 3:1–8:15

    4. The reigns of Jehoram and Ahaziah in Judah 8:16–29

    5. The anointing of Jehu and the massacre of Ahab's family 9:1–37

  B. The fourth dynasty 10:1–15:12

    1. The reign of Jehu in Israel 10:1–36

    2. The reigns of Athaliah and Jehoash in Judah 11:1–12:21

    3. The reigns of Jehoahaz and Jehoash in

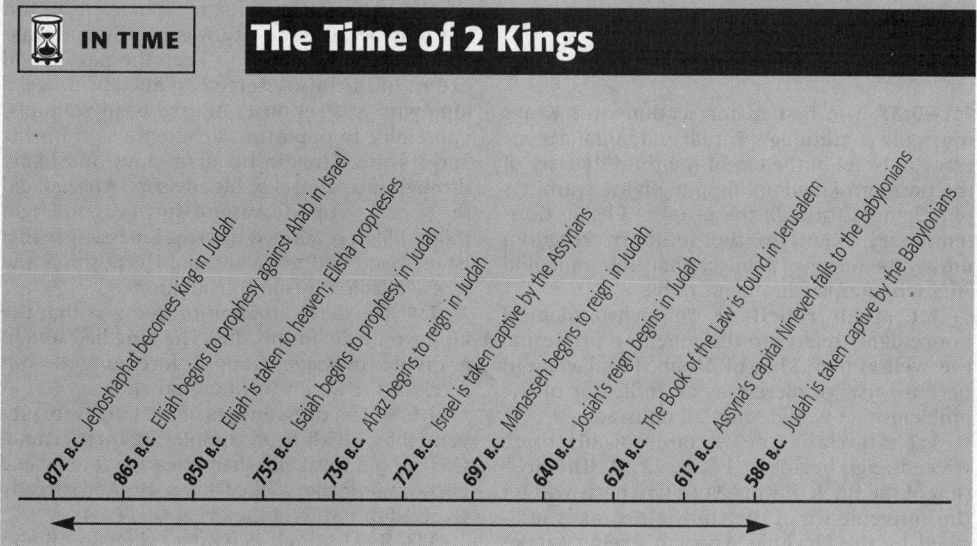

IN TIME

The Time of 2 Kings

872 B.C. Jehoshaphat becomes king in Judah
865 B.C. Elijah begins to prophesy against Ahab in Israel
850 B.C. Elijah is taken to heaven; Elisha prophesies
755 B.C. Isaiah begins to prophesy in Judah
736 B.C. Ahaz begins to reign in Judah
722 B.C. Israel is taken captive by the Assyrians
697 B.C. Manasseh begins to reign in Judah
640 B.C. Josiah's reign begins in Judah
624 B.C. The Book of the Law is found in Jerusalem
612 B.C. Assyria's capital Nineveh falls to the Babylonians
586 B.C. Judah is taken captive by the Babylonians

Commentary

1:1–9:37 The first major section of 2 Kings traces the continuing spiritual and moral degeneracy of Israel in the era of the third dynasty of the northern kingdom, despite divine warnings of judgment through the prophet Elisha. Contemporary events in the southern kingdom during the reigns of Jehoshaphat, Jehoram, and Ahaziah interplay in the narrative.

1:1 Moab rebelled: This chronological notice likely relates to the rebellion of Mesha, the well-known king of Moab. Its placement here may serve merely as an indicator of the problems that would soon fall on Israel.

1:2 Ahaziah: The account of his brief, wicked reign begins in 1 Kin. 22:51. The division of the Book of Kings into two parts was for the convenience of the translators, as is indicated by the fact that Ahaziah's reign carries

over from one book to the other without a break. **lattice of his upper room:** Houses in ancient Israel usually had one story. Palaces and grander houses would have had a second level. The upper stories commonly had balconies enclosed with latticework, allowing for the flow of air while maintaining protection from the sun and a certain privacy. Such latticework could easily be broken. **Baal-Zebub:** While the name "Zebub" is known in the Canaanite texts from Ugarit, here it may reflect a deliberate corruption of an original "zebul" (prince). If so, Hebrew scribes have transformed "Baal-Zebul" (Baal is prince) into "Baal-Zebub" (lord of flies). The scribes also wrote "Baal-Zebel" (lord of dung) at times. This deliberate change of the names of persons or gods associated with Baal worship shows the tremendous contempt with which these ideas were held by the Israelite scribes. See also the deliberate change in the names "Jezebel" (1 Kin. 16:31) and "Rimmon" (2 Kin. 5:18). The name Baal-Zebub would later be applied to Satan (Matt. 10:25; 12:24).

1:3 the angel of the LORD: At times this phrase is used as a way of referring to God. But often, and possibly here, this phrase speaks of one who is the Lord's messenger, but who is somehow distinguished from Him. The dramatic story of **Elijah** begins in 1 Kin. 17:1. **no God in Israel:** The contempt of the Lord for the errant behavior of the king is palpable in these words. **king of Samaria:** A king was identified by his country or by his capital city (1 Kin. 21:1; 2 Chr. 24:23; Jon. 3:6). This is just another title for the king of Israel. **god of Ekron:** Ahaziah followed the Baal worship of his father. The cult of Baal was strongly identified with Ekron, a city well known for its practice of divination (1 Sam. 6:2; Is. 2:6). Ahaziah sent his messenger to Ekron not only because the city was nearby but probably because he hoped to keep the nature and extent of his injury secret. In ancient times, a king who was seriously injured or ill would be vulnerable to opportunistic attempts on his life and throne. Thus in his own view, and likely through the counsel of his advisors, Ahaziah did the "smart thing." It was not, however, the right thing. Elijah reminded the royal messenger that Israel's God had not abdicated His position and was available for true consultation.

1:4 The determination of God was that the king would die for his sins. The king had sought a divine message from a foreign god, but received the Lord's word nonetheless.

1:5, 6 The **messengers** of the king were prevented by Elijah from completing their errand. God did not want any sham message coming and encouraging the wicked king. He had already received the word of the living God (v. 4).

1:7, 8 Although *hairy* may refer to Elijah's

💡 INSIGHT | **Mentoring in the Old Testament**

The relationship between Elijah and Elisha resembles what we today would call mentoring a prospective leader. Eventually, when Elisha literally took up the mantle of Elijah (2 Kin. 2:13), he was taking over Elijah's role as the main prophet of Israel, a role for which Elijah had helped to groom him (1 Kin. 19:16).

Mentoring involves a voluntary investment in others for their growth, development, and success. It is rooted in faith in the value of the other person. The goal is the gain of the one being mentored, whether or not the mentor benefits. Thus mentoring often requires loving sacrifice.

---

garments, the usual translation **hairy man** is supported by the ancient versions. Ahaziah knew the man was his opponent, **Elijah the Tishbite** (1 Kin. 17:1).

1:9, 10 fire . . . from heaven: Heavenly fire could signal divine judgment (Gen. 19:24). Elijah had already called down such fire in his contest with the prophets of Baal (1 Kin. 18:36–38). This fire was likely lightning. Baal was not the god of the storm he was reputed to be. The God of Israel was—and is—the Lord of creation.

1:11–13 Fifty men were a military unit attested elsewhere in the literature of the ancient Middle East. Each **captain of fifty** approached Elijah with a growing fear of the power of God associated with this great prophet.

1:14–17 So Ahaziah died: The prophetic word was fulfilled as announced. **no son:** This meant that the dynasty had ended. A king named **Jehoram** thus ruled in both kingdoms.

1:18 the rest of the acts: This follows the usual pattern for recording the obituaries of the kings of the northern kingdom.

2:1–4 Gilgal . . . Bethel . . . and Jericho were probably centers of prophetic activity that looked to Elijah for leadership. Gilgal and Bethel would become centers of pagan idolatry in the following century (Hos. 4:15; 9:15; 12:11; Amos 4:4; 5:5)—places where a true worship of God degenerated into centers of false teaching and apostasy.

2:1 about to take up Elijah into heaven: The story that follows is so extraordinary that the narrator introduces its subject early.

2:2–6 Stay here: The tripling of these incidents is similar to the tripling of the incidents of ch. 1 (the three bands of fifty soldiers who came to seize Elijah). **As the Lord lives:** Elisha made a solemn promise three times in these same verses; he determined that he would remain by his master Elijah no matter what might occur.

2:3–7 take away: The same Hebrew verb is used for Enoch's entrance to heaven (Gen. 5:24). The work that God was about to do had

been divinely revealed to many of God's servants (vv. 3, 5). This widespread knowledge of God's purpose would protect against later denials by cynical persons that the event had ever taken place. **keep silent:** It is not clear what prompted Elisha's harsh words here (and in v. 5).

2:8 The **water** was the Jordan River (vv. 7, 13), somewhere near Jericho. Elijah was like Moses in that his life and ministry show many parallels to that of Israel's greatest prophet. As Moses had divided the waters of the Red Sea in the final act of the redemption of Israel from Egypt (Ex. 14), so now Elijah replicated this miracle by dividing the waters of the Jordan. The difference is that Elijah did not use the power of God as a great redeeming miracle as Moses had done, but as an almost casual demonstration of God's wonders as he was walking on his way.

2:9 double portion: Although the narrative reports twice as many miracles for Elisha as Elijah, that was not the point of Elisha's request. His real request was that he would be Elijah's spiritual successor (Deut. 21:17). It was not a double portion of Elijah's goods that Elisha wanted but a double portion of his *spirit*. In material things, the principal heir received a double portion of his father's goods. Elisha wanted the principle of primary inheritance to apply to spiritual things. Nearby were all sorts of prophets. All of them would be his heirs. Any one of them might become the leading successor of Elijah. We may assume from the life he lived that Elisha's request was not due to pride. He simply wanted to be the man of God who would follow Elijah's model. Far from being a selfish request, Elisha's petition reflects his humble acknowledgment that if Elijah's ministry were to continue through him, it would take specially God-given spiritual power.

2:10 if you see me: We have no answer as to why this was important. Perhaps it spoke of persistence (vv. 2, 4, 6).

2:11 In one of the most dramatic scenes in

the Bible, heaven opened, a fiery chariot with fiery horses appeared, a whirlwind blew, and the prophet of God vanished alive into heaven. The **fire** associated with the **chariot** and the horses indicate the presence of God, much as the fiery angels do that Isaiah saw stationed around the throne of God (Is. 6:2).

2:12 The term **my father** underscores Elijah's relationship to Elisha as his spiritual mentor as well as the greatness of Elijah's reputation. The whole phrase is repeated at Elisha's passing (13:14). While these words were a tribute to Elijah on this great occasion, Elisha's accompanying actions indicated his personal sorrow at the loss of his spiritual master and friend.

2:13 **took up the mantle:** Elijah had once laid this mantle on Elisha as a symbolic action (1 Kin. 19:19); now Elisha took up the prophetic status and ministry that the mantle symbolized.

2:14 The **mantle** was only a symbol, but in the hands of Elijah it had been an instrument for the power of the living God. The mantle had been for Elijah what the rod had been for Moses and Aaron (Ex. 4:1–9; 7:9). It became the symbol of God's power in the hands of Elisha.

2:15 **the spirit of Elijah:** The prophets witnessed both the miracle of Elijah (v. 8) and the similar miracle of Elisha. In this way there would be common agreement that Elisha was

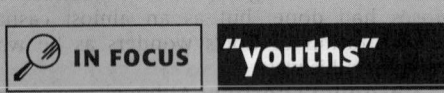

IN FOCUS   **"youths"**

(Heb. *na'ar*) (2 Kin. 2:23; Gen. 22:5; 1 Kin. 20:19) Strong's #5288: The noun *na'ar* always refers to males but can include different ages. It can refer to anyone from an infant (Ex. 2:6) to a young boy (Gen. 22:5) to soldiers (1 Kin. 20:17–20). It sometimes denotes a household servant (1 Sam. 9:3) or a royal official (19:6). The word can have the nuance of "rebellion," implying that the 42 youths killed by bears should be understood as "ruffians" or "delinquents," rather than young children.

the successor of Elijah. They **bowed,** not in worship, but in respect and submission to the will of God.

2:16 **fifty strong men:** Groups of fifty men were often called upon to perform an arduous task (1:9–15). The men decided they needed a search party. Even though they had received a revelation from God that Elijah would be taken to heaven (v. 3), still they checked things out.

2:17, 18 **he was ashamed:** Although these words may indicate Elisha's sense of shame on behalf of his disciples for their disbelief, the use of the phrase elsewhere indicates that it means Elisha was worn out, no longer willing to resist (8:11; Judg. 3:25). He came to the point where he gave in to their request.

2:19–22 Elisha's first miracle authenticated his calling as the principal successor to Elijah (v. 14). His second miracle, the cleansing of the waters of Jericho, was purposeful and ameliorative. It also demonstrated the power of God with respect to water, so necessary for life (1 Kin. 17:1).

2:20 Elisha performed a purification ceremony (Lev. 2:13; Num. 18:19). The **salt** taken from a new bowl and cast into the water symbolized the cleansing of the water for new use.

2:21, 22 The miracle was done in the name of God; Elisha was only His instrument. **to this day:** That is, at the day of the writing of the account.

2:23–25 Elisha's third miracle was punitive and judgmental. Prophets were instruments both of God's grace and His wrath.

2:23, 24 **Go up, you baldhead:** While the severity of the sentence has been questioned, the words of the youths indicated their disbelief of Elijah's "going up" into heaven (v. 11) and their disrespect for God's prophet. God did not tolerate blasphemy against Himself by the demeaning of Elijah's departure, or the abuse of His prophet, whom He had called for an important task at a critical period in Israel's history.

2:25 Elisha made his home on **Mount Carmel** (4:25), as well as in **Samaria** (5:3).

3:1–8:15 Elisha's prophetic ministry during the perilous times of Moabite and Aramean warfare with Israel.

3:1, 2 **sacred pillar of Baal:** Probably this was a stone pillar or statue erected by Ahab and bearing an inscription and image of the god Baal. Although it was put away temporarily, it apparently was not destroyed, because it later became one of the objects of Jehu's purge (10:26, 27).

3:3, 4 **Mesha king of Moab:** The existence of this Moabite king is confirmed by an inscription on a pillar known as the Moabite Stone. The inscription indicates that Omri had conquered the plains of Moab north of the Arnon River and that the area remained under Israelite control throughout Ahab's reign. Thus the events of this chapter probably took place after Jehoram's accession and shortly before Jehoshaphat's death in 847 B.C. (1:1). **sheepbreeder:** This Hebrew word (*noqed*) is used only of Mesha and of Amos the prophet (Amos 1:1). As for Mesha, his business must have been enormous if he could pay such an exorbitant tribute.

3:5, 6 The rebellion of Moab provoked **Jehoram** into a punitive war.

3:7, 8 Will you go with me: Because Jehoshaphat was related to the throne of the northern kingdom through the marriage of his son Jehoram to Ahab's daughter Athaliah, it could be presumed that he would be available as an ally. Because Edom had been added to the orbit of Judah as a result of an earlier war, Jehoshaphat proposed that they march through Edom to attack the Moabite territory. This route for their forces would avoid Moabite border fortresses and bring the attack from their rear.

3:9, 10 The route was very difficult. **no water:** In such a military campaign as this, both men and animals needed more water than they could carry with them.

3:11, 12 prophet of the Lord: A prophet or diviner often traveled with armies on their campaigns. While the account apparently focuses on the military campaign as such, the crucial role of Elisha in the story emphasizes the importance of the prophetic office in ancient Israel.

3:13 prophets of your father: Elisha spoke scathingly about the wicked kings of the north consulting with prophets of Baal (1:2, 3).

3:14 As the Lord of hosts lives . . . I stand: This is the same language used by Elijah (1 Kin. 17:1). **I would not look at you:** As a devotee of Baal, Jehoram had no claim on the favor of God. Nevertheless, he would enjoy the benefits of God's grace toward Jehoshaphat.

3:15 Elisha's call for a **musician** is an effort to achieve an atmosphere free of war and strife so that he might concentrate on the anticipated divine revelation.

3:16–19 As in connection with many OT miracles, the prophet's words carry instructions for human participation (4:3, 4, 41; 6:6), in order that man's faith and the divine provision may each have their proper part.

3:20–22 filled with water: The dry streambeds can easily overflow their banks in downpours of rain. Even distant areas can be flooded by water from faraway mountain streams swelled by heavy rains.

3:23–25 This is blood: The red water looked like blood and the Moabite king assumed falsely that the former enemies had once again fallen out with each other. It was a tragic miscalculation.

3:26 break through: It is uncertain if the Moabite king wished to retaliate against the Edomite king for joining the allied kings from across the Jordan, or if he considered the Edomite army the least formidable, or if he was attempting to establish an escape route. Perhaps all three are true.

3:27 offered him: Such desperate acts are frequently attested to in the literature of the ancient Near East. Scholars are divided as to whether the resultant indignation was God's, Moab's, or Israel's. The withdrawal of the armies may suggest that the disgust here was that of Israel's army.

4:1–7 The power of God through Elisha multiplies the widow's oil. It is customary to speak of "the miracles of Elisha." In all these cases, the miracle is the Lord's, of course. Hence, we speak of "the power of God through Elisha."

4:1 A certain woman: The fate of widows was perilous in the ancient Middle East. A practical test of biblical piety was to observe how those in power treated widows and orphans (Job 24:21; Ps. 146:9). **creditor:** Both the Bible (Lev. 25:39–45) and other ancient laws permitted selling one's family members into slavery for payment of debts. God's Law worked toward

---

🌱 **IN LIFE**   **The Widow's Oil**

I n the days immediately following the departure of Elijah, God empowered Elisha to perform a number of miracles. One of them was to increase oil for a poor widow (2 Kin. 4:1–7). This incident confirmed Elisha as a true prophet of God and the successor to Elijah. In fact, the increase of oil recalled the miracle that Elijah performed for the widow of Zarephath (1 Kin. 17:8–16).

In addition to what the miracle revealed about Elisha, it illustrated an important aspect of God's character: His concern for the poor and disadvantaged. Both Elijah and Elisha dealt with kings, commanders, and other powerful leaders. But they also helped the powerless. In this case, the widow was about to lose her sons to pay for a debt left by her late husband. That meant that she would be left with no means of support. God provided for her needs through the intervention of Elisha (compare Ps. 68:5).

James reminds us that true religion involves action, such as caring for "widows in their trouble" (James 1:27). Elisha was a true prophet practicing true religion.

limiting the abuse and the length of time in such a situation.

4:2–7 This miracle is similar in some respects to the miracle God did through Elijah in providing for the widow of Zarepath (1 Kin. 17:14–16). In both cases, Yahweh demonstrated that He alone is Lord of Creation (1 Kin. 17:1).

4:2–6 The small flask held olive **oil** intended for anointing, rather than food or fuel. Such a small flask was not very valuable.

4:7 Elisha is called **the man of God** throughout this section (vv. 16, 21, 22, 25, 27). The word God in Hebrew is literally "the God," meaning the true or genuine God. **sell . . . pay . . . live:** Elisha met not only her immediate needs but the long-range ones as well.

4:8, 9 The friendship of Elisha with the woman at **Shunem** is also similar to the friendship of Elijah with the widow of Zarephath (1 Kin. 17:8–16). **holy man of God:** The adjective describes Elisha, a man she perceived was truly set apart for the ministry of God.

4:10 upper room: Such quarters were commonly on the roof and could be reached from the outside. This accommodated the guest while providing privacy. Recognizing Elisha as one of God's choice servants, the Shunammite woman was especially concerned that the normal measures of hospitality be applied even more fully.

4:11, 12 The term for **servant** (Heb. *na'ar,* frequently "youth," or "attendant") often means a person engaged in a period of training. Rather than looking down upon this role, such a servant could consider the position an opportunity. Often these were responsible duties. The same word was also used of Elisha's own relation to Elijah (1 Kin. 19:21). Unfortunately, Gehazi would not prove as worthy of his master's trust as Elisha had been of Elijah's.

4:13–16 Elisha decided that the best thing he could do for the woman was promise her the birth of a son, despite her years of frustration about this. **do not lie:** The Shunammite woman felt that even Elisha could not fulfill such a promise.

4:17 The birth of the son to the **woman** was similar to the fulfillment of the promise of God in the birth of Isaac (Gen. 21).

4:18–21 the bed of the man of God: The Shunammite's action speaks strongly of her faith. Despite her overwhelming sorrow, she placed the fate of her child close to Elisha, through whose word, and by means of God's mercy, she had gained her son in the first place. Placing the body on the bed of the man of God also kept his death a secret until she could reach Elisha, from whom she had once seen the impossible accomplished. Again, compare the story of Elijah and the son of the woman of Zarephath (1 Kin. 17:17–24).

4:22, 23 New Moon . . . Sabbath: There was no work on these days and so they would be most suitable for seeing the prophet (Ex. 20:9–12; Amos 8:5).

4:24–27 Elisha knew that something was wrong by the furious way she drove (v. 24), but God had not made the particular issue known to the prophet. **the LORD has hidden:** The prophets did *not* know everything. They only knew what God made known to them (5:26). **caught him by the feet:** This action is a mark of humility and reverence (Matt. 28:9).

4:28 Did I ask: Her pain in the death of her child was worse than the emptiness she had felt before he was born. It was the prophet's fault, she charged. Yet it was to the prophet she had come for help.

4:29 Elisha's **staff,** like Elijah's mantle (2:13, 14), was symbolic of the power of God and the authority of the prophet. Laid upon the body of the child, the staff would signify that the prophet intended to come, and that he had faith that God would restore the boy.

4:30, 31 As the LORD lives: With this oath, the woman asserted her faith in the living God (1 Kin. 17:1). Elisha had used similar language when he refused to leave Elijah (2:2, 4, 6). Now he heard these words from her.

4:32–37 Elisha's actions demonstrate that his faith was in the person and power of God alone, and not in the staff that symbolized his prophetic office. Although he repeated the symbolic actions learned from Elijah his teacher (1 Kin. 17:17–22), his faith transcended mere symbol and ritual. He sought God who alone can grant life and perform the miraculous (Pss. 36:9; 49:7–9). The restoration of the boy's life is a demonstration that life itself is in the hands of God (1 Kin. 17:23).

4:37 bowed to the ground: The action of the Shunammite woman was a mark of humility and gratefulness to God and to His prophet. Although it is not recorded that a word passed between her and Elisha, as had been the case with Elijah and the widow of Zarephath (1 Kin. 17:24), her reverential action spoke strongly of her deep gratitude.

4:38 Gilgal was the first place the Israelites camped after crossing the Jordan into Canaan (Josh. 4:19, 20). Gilgal was probably about one mile northeast of Jericho. **sitting before him:** Elisha sat at the head of the sons of the prophets.

4:39, 40 The **wild gourds** were poisonous. **death in the pot:** The reaction of the hungry men was immediate and frightening.

4:41 The **flour** had no magical properties, of course. Elisha's faith in the living God effected the miraculous cure.

4:42–44 Baal Shalisha was near Gilgal.

The **firstfruits** were to be presented to God and His priests (Lev. 23:15–17, 20). With an entrenched false priesthood and a debased state religion prevailing in the northern kingdom, the man brought his offering to Elisha. The faithful prophet miraculously multiplied the loaves—with some left over.

5:1–19 The account of Naaman the Aramean is fascinating for several reasons. (1) A foreign national comes to faith in the living God. (2) The story provides aspects of the inter-cultural dimensions of spreading the gospel of Israel's great Savior God. (3) It contrasts the characters of Elisha and his servant Gehazi.

5:1 This Aramean general **Naaman** was a remarkable figure in biblical history. This verse is filled with phrases describing his character, his honor, and his ability. Surprisingly, we read that his military victories were granted by **the Lord**. The Hebrew word translated **leper** refers to any of several serious skin diseases (Lev. 13:1–46; Num. 5:1–4), including certain fungi (Lev. 13:47–56; 14:33–57). The **king of Syria** was Ben-Hadad II (860–842 B.C.). He was a constant

Aramean king had for his general that he granted his unusual request. Naaman's gifts are a measure of his wealth—and of his great personal need.

5:6, 7 While such letters of introduction were common in the ancient Middle East, Ben-Hadad's frequent forays against Israel made the **king** suspicious that the Aramean king was seeking a pretext for yet another invasion of Israelite territory (v. 2).

5:8 torn his clothes: Tearing a robe could be a sign of grief or agitation (11:14), as well as a mark of the sorrow that leads to repentance (Joel 2:13).

5:9 at the door: For some reason Elisha did not meet with the general face to face. Perhaps it was because contact with one with skin disorder would render the prophet unclean and therefore cut off his ministry with others (Num. 5:1–4).

5:10 Elisha's instruction for Naaman to wash **seven times** in the Jordan emphasizes that the full cure for Naaman's condition could be effected solely by the power of Israel's sover-

Photo by Howard Vos

The Abana River in downtown Damascus, Syria—known today as the Barada River. Naaman considered this river and the Pharpar River of his native land superior to the Jordan River in Israel (2 Kin. 5:11, 12).

threat to the northern kingdom and would lead an invasion against it later (6:24—7:20).

5:2 captive . . . young girl: God used the testimony of an Jewish servant girl and brought the commanding general of Israel's greatest military foe to biblical faith.

5:3 the prophet . . . in Samaria: Although Elisha traveled frequently and may sometimes have lived at Mount Carmel (4:25), he apparently maintained a residence in the capital city of Samaria (vv. 9, 24; 2:25; 6:9—7:20).

5:4, 5 It is a measure of the respect that the

eign God. The proud Aramean needed a lesson in humility and putting his personal trust in God alone (v. 15). The issue was obedience.

5:11, 12 Understandably, Naaman's initial response was one of disbelief and anger. This seemed a very strange and humiliating command for a general in the army of Aram. What, after all, was the Jordan compared to the greater **rivers** of Aram?

5:13, 14 Naaman listened to his advisors, did as he was commanded, and was healed. **clean:** The word suggests that the problem of skin diseases causing *uncleanness* was an issue in his country as well. The wonderful thing about Naaman is that once he gave it thought, he would have done whatever God commanded him through His prophet.

5:15, 16 stood before him: Now that Naaman was clean, he could stand in the presence of the prophet Elisha (vv. 9, 10). **no God in all the earth:** Naaman stands as a wonderful example of a foreigner who came to faith in God. **take a gift:** What Naaman had received could not have been purchased, nor would Elisha take advantage of the situation.

5:17 earth: Although ancient Middle Eastern custom associated the identity of a god with the location where he was worshiped, Elisha might have felt in this instance that Naaman's newly-gained acquaintance with Israel's God might be benefitted with this tangible reminder of the land of his cure. Elisha thus allowed Naaman an accommodation to his faith. He will also grant him such concessions as diplomatic protocol may dictate (vv. 17–19). In the latter case, Naaman might even plan to sprinkle some of Israel's soil under his knees when forced to bow in pagan temples, that in his own heart he may be bowing to the one true God.

5:18, 19 The name **Rimmon** is an example of a deliberate corruption of a name of a foreign god by the Hebrew scribes. Instead of writing *Ramman*, meaning "Thunderer," a name for the storm god Hadad (Zech. 12:11), they wrote *Rimmon*, meaning "Pomegranate."

5:20–22 Gehazi: The sad story of Gehazi's greed serves as a contrast to the principled behavior of his master Elisha (vv. 15, 16).

5:23 talents: A talent was an enormous amount of silver—equal to 3,000 shekels, or about 70 lbs. **two of his servants:** Each would have been carrying a heavy load.

5:24 the citadel: The Hebrew word can refer to a hill or mound, or a building such as a citadel (2 Chr. 27:3,4; Mic 4:8). Gehazi dismissed the men before coming to a place where his greedy gain might be observed by people who would know about Naaman and Elisha.

5:25 Since he had lied first to Naaman (v. 22), now he must lie to **Elisha.**

5:26 Did not my heart go: The use of the term *heart* suggests not only Elisha's knowledge but also his strong feeling for Gehazi.

5:27 The irony of justice punished Gehazi's sin with the **leprosy of Naaman.**

6:1 It is unclear whether **the place** refers to where the prophetic community lived, or to an assembly hall where they gathered, or to the houses in the general area. In any case, the present building situation proved inadequate. Apparently there were several prophetic communities (2:1–5). In some cases the prophets lived in separate houses or quarters (1 Sam. 19:18–22). Elisha had his own house in Samaria (2 Kin. 5:9). The precise arrangement may have varied according to local needs.

6:2–5 The details of this building program set the stage for the loss of the **iron ax head.** In a time when most tools were still made of bronze, an iron blade was valuable.

6:6, 7 he . . . took it: The man must have been tremendously impressed with what he saw, but the ax head could be of no use to him until he actually reached out and took it.

6:8–12 This remarkable narrative takes the reader into the tent of Ben-Hadad, the king of Aram, and to the meetings he had with his general staff. It turned out, much to the king's consternation, that his plans were known to the king of Israel and his staff. Ben-Hadad suspected a spy, and he was right. The spy was Elisha, who had never left Israel.

6:13–15 Dothan was in the central highlands of Israel. It is mentioned only here and in Gen. 37, when Joseph was sold to the Midianites (Gen. 37:17).

6:14 Ben-Hadad's great consternation is indicated by the fact that he sent **a great army** to size just one man.

6:15 the servant of the man of God: Since Gehazi had become a leper (5:27), it is possible that this is another servant. However, Gehazi is mentioned again in 8:4 as one who was still faithfully representing the miracles done through Elisha.

6:16 those who are with us: Elisha knew that God's unseen army was far more powerful than any visible army.

6:17, 18 horses and chariots of fire: In answer to his prayer, Elisha's reassuring words to his servant (v. 16) were validated by letting him see the spiritual realities that lay beyond normal human sight. Such a fiery scene had accompanied Elijah's translation into heaven (2:11).

6:19, 20 I will bring you: Elisha's words are technically true, although he employed tactics common in times of war to lead the Arameans to Samaria rather than Dothan. Such wartime measures are noted elsewhere in the Scriptures (Josh. 2:4–6; 1 Sam. 27:8–12).

6:21–23 The end of this story is even more amazing than the beginning. The blind soldiers were brought within the capital city of Israel where they easily might have been slaughtered. Instead, they were given a banquet and were sent back to Ben-Hadad unharmed.

6:21, 22 The term of deference **my father** was used earlier by Elisha to Elijah (2:12), and to Naaman by his servants (5:13). Its use here by King Jehoram (3:1) for Elisha is a clear indication that Jehoram knew he was not in charge.

6:23 bands . . . came no more: That is, for

a period of time. The wars between the two nations revived after a period (6:24).

6:24 The siege of **Samaria,** the capital of Israel, was Ben-Hadad's final attempt to destroy his rival Jehoram of Israel.

6:25–27 The desperate conditions in besieged Samaria had made even once common food and commodities scarce and expensive. The **dove droppings** may have been used for fuel or even as a substitute for salt.

IN PLACE | The Hittites

The Syrian army's fear at the prospect of facing a combined army of Hittites and Egyptians (2 Kin. 7:6) was understandable. Camped outside Damascus, the Syrians would have been pinched between the Hittites from the north and the Egyptians from the south. Panic-stricken, the Syrians fled into the night (7:7).

The Hittites of this period were the remnant of an empire that dominated northern Canaan between 1800 and 1200 B.C. Their ancestors had migrated from Asia Minor, where they were called Hittites from the name Hatti, another name for Anatolia, the capital of which was Hattushash. In northern Syria they populated cities such as Aleppo, Carchemish, and Hamath.

As the Hittites pushed south over the years, they came into conflict with the Egyptians, who tended to use Canaan as a buffer between their country and Mesopotamia. In 1286 B.C., a decisive battle was fought at Kedesh, on the Orontes River. The Hittites waited in hiding until the Egyptians had made camp, then released their chariots on the unsuspecting Egyptians. The northerners would have won the day had Egyptian reinforcements not arrived from the west, eventually forcing a retreat. Still, the Egyptians suffered heavy losses, and soon a treaty was signed designating the Orontes River as a border between the two powers.

Over the next few decades, relentless attacks by enemies from the west slowly brought the Hittite empire to a close. In Syria, seven city-states remained in a coalition. They were friendly with David and Solomon (2 Sam. 8:9, 10; 1 Kin. 10:28—11:1). But they came under the domination of the Assyrians and eventually passed into oblivion when their principal cities of Hamath and Carchemish fell (720 and 717 B.C., respectively; 2 Kin. 18:34; Is. 10:9).

The northern Hittites are not to be confused with another group called the Hittites, who lived in the Judean hills near Hebron. These Hittites were descended from Heth, the son of Canaan, and thus were a tribe of Canaanites. It was from a member of this group of Hittites that Abraham purchased the field of Machpelah as a burial ground for his family (Gen. 23:10—20). Years later, Abraham's grandson Esau married two Hittite women, much to the displeasure of his parents (26:34—35).

The Hittites of Canaan were among the people to be driven out of the land when Israel entered Canaan under Joshua (Ex. 3:8, 17; Deut. 7:1; Judg. 3:5). However, they were not completely done away with. Centuries later, several Hittites were among David's closest associates and most loyal soldiers (1 Sam. 26:6; 2 Sam. 11:6—11).

6:28, 29 eat him: Israel had been warned that national disobedience could reduce the people to such a loathsome deed (Lev. 26:29; Deut. 28:53, 57).

6:30 The king was not unmoved by the plight of his people. He tore his garments and wore **sackcloth** to attest to his concern.

6:31–33 if the head of Elisha: The phrase is an oath expressing the enraged king's will to kill Elisha, whom he blamed for the severe conditions.

7:1 Public business was conducted at the city **gate** (Gen. 19:1; Ruth 4:1). Elisha's words were good news: Although costly, food would once again be available.

7:2 an officer: The Hebrew term for *officer* originally designated the third man in a chariot, who held a large shield. By this time it meant a high military official serving as adjutant (9:25; 10:25). The officer's doubt brought judgment on him. Although the food did come, this officer ate none of it.

7:3, 4 Because **leprous men** were excluded from the city (Lev. 13:4–6; Num. 5:2, 3) and avoided by all, they probably were ignored by the invaders and had been left to their fate. If the ordinary people of the city were suffering from hunger, how much more must these men have been suffering. They concluded that they had nothing to lose by going to the other side.

7:5, 6 the noise of a great army: Doubtless, the army was God's (6:16–18). By the **kings of the Hittites** is meant the descendants of the earlier Hittites of Asia Minor who now inhabited various Aramean states. Assyrian documents routinely mention Palestine as "Hittite Land."

7:7, 8 In their joy, the **lepers** took advantage of their good fortune.

7:9–11 Good news and good fortune had to be shared (Prov. 15:27; 21:17, 18), and the men feared that failure to do so might merit divine **punishment.**

7:12 what the Syrians have done: The Israelite king suspected that another military trick was being played on him. He did not connect the good news with Elisha's prophecy of good times.

7:13–16 At last the king sent a scouting party, which confirmed the good news. The prophecy concerning the restoration of food for the city was fulfilled (v. 1).

7:17–20 you shall not eat of it: All of Elisha's prophecy came true. The sudden miraculous flight of the Arameans had provided goods aplenty, but the doubting officer would not enjoy them.

8:1 As had happened in the days of Elijah (1 Kin. 17; 18), God again instituted a **famine.** Such cases of divinely induced calamities were intended to chastise His people and bring them to repentance (Joel 2:12–14; Zeph. 3:5–7). God in His kindness spared the family of the Shunammite woman to whom Elisha had had such a significant ministry (4:8–37). It appears that she may have become a widow by the time of this incident.

8:2 Her sojourn in Philistia contrasts with the move of Elimelech's family to Moab in Ruth 1. The Shunammite woman went at the command of God for a temporary residence abroad. The family of Elimelech moved out of the covenant land on their own decision, and set about to live abroad permanently. The marriage of the two sons of Elimelech to Moabite women indicates that their family was in the process of becoming a settled Moabite family. Only the deaths of father and sons led Naomi to such a desperate state that she was forced to return to Bethlehem (with Ruth) and into the center of the divine plan for her life.

8:3 to make an appeal: The Shunammite woman had not renounced or sold her property, but merely had left during the previous famine. Moreover, she had returned within seven years (Deut. 15:1–6; Ruth 4:3, 4). Since the property was still legally hers, she pressed her claim to the king himself.

8:4, 5 Just as the Shunammite woman arrived, **Gehazi** was telling Jehoram about her. At this point, Gehazi was still faithful to the ministry of Elisha.

8:6 Restore all: We get a complex picture of King Jehoram. At times he was so angry at Elisha that he wished him dead (6:31), yet even then he was in mourning for his people. He acknowledged Elisha's spiritual leadership at other times (6:21), but he knew that Elisha did not hold him in high regard (3:14). In this section, his righteous judgment should be contrasted with the wretched behavior of the wicked Ahab with respect to the land of another farmer (1 Kin. 21:1–16).

8:7 Although Ben-Hadad felt that Elisha's arrival was accidental, God's prophet had come to **Damascus** in fulfillment of the instructions originally given by God to Elijah (1 Kin. 19:15–17). The instructions concerning dynastic change in Israel would soon be carried out (9:1–13).

8:8, 9 Ironically, a sick king of Israel had inquired of a false god concerning the nature of his illness (1:2); here, the pagan king of a foreign nation inquired of the living God concerning the nature of his illness.

8:10 You shall certainly recover: Left to natural circumstances, Ben-Hadad would recover. Yet Elisha knew that Hazael would seize both the opportunity of the king's illness and fulfill Elisha's prophecy by assassinating the king and taking the throne. Hazael chose his own method of carrying out the issue of dynastic succession in Damascus, not God's (v. 15).

8:11, 12 ashamed: He had reached the end of his ability to resist his emotions. **the man of God wept:** Elisha wept over the suffering that Hazael would bring upon Israel.

8:13, 14 In the ancient Middle East, the **dog** was despised because it was a scavenger (1 Kin. 14:11; 21:23). Appropriately, Hazael would similarly be held in disdain. Shalmaneser III of Assyria notes Hazael's accession to the throne with the words: "Hazael, son of nobody, seizes the throne." By these contemptuous words, we learn that Hazael was not the son of Ben-Hadad, but an opportunistic usurper.

Ahab's unlawful seizure of the land of Naboth was regarded as one of his most heinous crimes.

8:15 Having succeeded Ben-Hadad as king, **Hazael reigned** for about 40 years (842–802 B.C.). He remained an inveterate foe of God's people (10:32, 33; 13:3, 22). Yet like Elisha and Jehu, Hazael was an instrument of God's judgment on His sinful people (1 Kin. 19:15–17).

8:16–18 Jehoram: With Jehoram's accession to the throne of Judah, kings by the same name now ruled in both kingdoms. The name Jehoram means "The Lord Is Exalted" and can be spelled Joram. **eight years:** Joram of the northern kingdom ruled from 852–841 B.C.; Jehoram of the southern kingdom from 848–841 B.C. Although he had served alongside his father Jehoshaphat for the previous four years, Jehoram now ruled in his own right. With his father's death, he killed all his brothers and any claimant to the throne (2 Chr. 21:2–4), actions that would be repeated by his wicked wife Athaliah at the time of his death (11:1). A wicked ruler (2 Chr. 21:11), he was greatly influenced by Queen Athaliah (2 Chr. 21:6). Wickedness and spiritual bankruptcy in the royal house would bring about God's judgment on Judah in three separate military engagements with Edom, Libnah, and a combined Philistine-Arabian incursion (2 Chr. 21:16, 17), as well as a severe plague that would eventually take the life of the king (2 Chr. 21:12–15, 18, 19).

8:18 the daughter of Ahab: Most shocking was that the same source of evil that had brought God's judgment against the northern kingdom was now being brought into the southern kingdom. Ahab had been a wicked king, but his wickedness had been greatly accelerated by the actions and attitudes of his pagan wife Jezebel (1 Kin. 16:31). Now their daughter Athaliah (11:1) was established as the queen of Judah and the wife of a descendant of David. From the vantage point of international relations, the marriage of a daughter of the king of Israel to the king of Judah was a strategic event that could ease hostility between the two nations. But from a spiritual standpoint, this marriage was a grim omen of disaster for Judah.

8:19 Despite Jehoram's infidelity and wickedness, God remained faithful to the Davidic covenant (2 Sam. 7:12–16; Ps. 89:30–37). **a lamp:** This was a figure of the hope of the Davidic promise in the darkest of times, and the fulfillment in Him who is the light of the world (1 Kin. 15:4; John 1:1–13).

8:20–24 Judah's struggles with **Edom** were often accompanied by trouble with the Philistines (2 Chr. 21:16; Joel 3:4–8). Edom would remain a constant menace with the result that although Amaziah would later defeat Edom (14:22), they would renew armed hostilities against Judah in the days of Ahaz (2 Chr. 28:17, 18). Edom's constant enmity against God's people served as a focus of attention for Israel's prophets, who often predicted Edom's ultimate defeat and destruction (Is. 34:5–15; Jer. 49:7–22).

8:25 Ahaziah means "The Lord Has Grasped."

8:26 twenty-two years old: This figure is correct; compare 2 Chr. 22:2. **granddaughter of Omri:** The Hebrew word translated *granddaughter* is literally "daughter." Athaliah, Ahab's daughter, is the person meant (v. 18; 2 Chr. 21:6).

8:27 the way of the house of Ahab: The lowest point of Israel's religious apostasy was reached in the reign of Ahab and his wicked wife Jezebel (1 Kin. 16:31). Most likely due to the role of Athaliah, the evil that had spoiled Ahab affected the house of the king of Judah.

8:28 Here began the troubles with **Hazael** (v. 12). Ahaziah's grandfather Jehoshaphat had been drawn into war at **Ramoth Gilead** by Ahab (1 Kin. 22), and now Ahaziah was led by Joram to war in the same area. Ramoth Gilead means "Heights of Gilead." It was about 25 miles east of the Jordan. Hazael had recently been crowned in Damascus, and the year 841 B.C. would witness a change in the royal houses of both Israel and Judah.

8:29 Ahab had one of his palaces at **Jezreel,** a site between Megiddo and Beth Shan (1 Kin. 18:45). Both the injured Joram and Ahaziah came to Jezreel for a most fateful meeting (ch. 9).

9:1–3 The selection of **Jehu** as the next king of Israel was by prophetic designation; contrast 1:17. The name Jehu means "The Lord Is He." The instructions given by Elisha to one of his associates were marked by secrecy and intrigue. The action of the prophet was seditious in the eyes of the current king.

9:4, 5 for you: The servant was obedient to Elisha and was daring in his approach to Jehu.

9:6 poured the oil: As in the case of Hazael (8:7–13), the third part of the Lord's threefold command to Elijah (1 Kin. 19:15–18) was carried out by another. First, Elijah personally fulfilled the divine directive concerning Elisha (1 Kin. 19:19–21). Then he set in motion the process that would effect the other two commands. Elisha carried out the order with respect to Hazael. Third, one of the sons of the prophets serving under Elisha handled the case of Jehu. In the OT, an anointing was customarily reserved for a king (2 Sam. 2:4) or the high priest (Ex. 40:13).

9:7–10 The prophetic words to Jehu indicate that he would destroy the evil of the house of Ahab. **Jezebel:** The wicked wife of Ahab is given special attention; her gruesome end is predicted. **fled:** Once the young prophet gave the Lord's stern message to Jehu, he fled, just as Elisha had commanded him (v. 3). His life was in danger; at this time only he knew what had transpired with Jehu.

9:11 madman: The derogatory attitude of Jehu's soldiers toward one of God' prophets has often been repeated by unbelievers with regard to God's servants (Jer. 29:24–28; Acts 17:16–18). This verse has frequently been cited as evidence that Israel's prophets were ecstatics whose excesses mirrored those of heathen diviners. However, it seems best to regard their words as reflective of their contempt for the servants of the Lord.

9:12 A lie: Jehu's attempt to brush off the questions of his servants was not successful. He finally reported to them the fact of his prophetic sanction and divine anointing.

9:13 Placing a **garment** under a person is a mark of homage fit for a king (Matt. 21:8). The actions taken here are like those performed at the anointing of King Solomon (1 Kin. 1:34).

9:14, 15 Jehu lost no time in planning the assassination of the king. These verses also remind the reader of the situation at Jezreel (8:28, 29).

9:16–18 The question about **peace** was a standard step in ancient negotiations. Jehu's reply indicates that he refused to negotiate.

9:19, 20 The phrase **the son of Nimshi** actually refers to the grandson of Nimshi. This way of abbreviating genealogies was common in the ancient world (8:26; 10:1).

9:21 Make ready: The two kings rather foolishly prepared to meet Jehu in their chariots. They might have done better to have remained in the city. Joram was still recovering from wounds from his battle with the Arameans (v. 15). **the property of Naboth:** Ahab's dynasty ended on the very stolen property that occasioned the divine sentence of judgment (1 Kin. 21:17–24). Ahab's unlawful seizure of the land of Naboth was regarded as one of his most heinous crimes.

9:22 Is it peace . . . What peace: To his credit, the battle-weakened king came out and faced his possible opponent. Surely Joram knew something was up. He may have feared a military attack from his hotheaded captain. Perhaps the king met Jehu with the thought of making him realize that his plans would be acts of sedition against the legally constituted king. **harlotries . . . of Jezebel:** Jezebel's spiritual adultery had brought heinous demonic practices into the kingdom and sealed its doom (1 Kin. 21:25, 26). As God had threatened, such activities would surely bring about the nation's

---

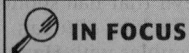 **IN FOCUS**   **"witchcraft"**

(Heb. *kesheph*) (2 Kin. 9:22; Is. 47:12) Strong's #3785: This Hebrew word usually appears along with other words that denote various forms of magic or divination (2 Chr. 33:6; Jer. 27:9; Mic. 5:12). The word used here seems to have the basic sense of "witchcraft" or "sorcery." Sorcerers interpreted dreams, prophesied, and performed miracles (Ex. 7:11; Jer. 27:9; Dan. 2:2). They had access to the royal courts of Egypt, Israel, and Babylon (9:22; Ex. 7:11; Dan. 2:2). Sorcery was forbidden in the Law, with capital punishment prescribed for a sorceress (Ex. 22:18; Deut. 18:10, 11). Many of the OT prophets directly linked divine judgment with sorcery, even expressly citing it as the cause (Is. 47:9; Nah. 3:4; Mal. 3:5). The Lord did not want His people to look to such deceptive sorcerers for direction. Instead He promised to raise up a prophet like Moses, which He did: His Son, Jesus (Deut. 18:10–15; Acts 3:22, 23).

demise (Deut. 28:25, 26). Jehu justified his actions as a judgment on Jezebel's sins.

9:23, 24 The frightened Joram shouted to Ahaziah, **Treachery.** But it was he and Ahaziah who were the true traitors. And they would be executed by Jehu, a man who served as the "terrible swift sword" of the Lord. **between his arms:** That is, in the middle of his back, as he was driving his chariot away.

9:25, 26 remember: Jehu rehearsed to Bidkar the gist of the curse against Ahab's house (1 Kin. 21:21–24). In this way, Jehu cited this curse for justification of his actions. He proclaimed himself God's avenger.

9:27–29 The wounded Ahaziah apparently made it to Samaria where he at last was apprehended by Jehu's men (2 Chr. 22:8, 9) and taken to **Megiddo** where he died. His body finally was buried in the royal tombs in Jerusalem (v. 28).

9:30, 31 Jezebel knew that her end was near; she had heard about the deaths of the kings of Israel and Judah. Yet she brazenly spent time putting on her makeup and adorning herself. Defiant to the end, Jezebel called Jehu a **Zimri,** a traitor who had killed his master in order to seize the throne (1 Kin. 16:11, 12).

9:32, 33 Jehu had a couple of Jezebel's servants throw her out the window. Her death was particularly gruesome. **Eunuchs** (Heb. *saris*) refers to males who have been castrated. Typically they were assigned to the harems of kings in the ancient Middle East. The word can also refer to officers in general.

9:34–37 bury her: After Jehu had Jezebel killed, he entered the palace to eat and drink. But then, because of Jezebel's rank, he ordered that her body be given a proper burial. However, she had become food for **dogs.** This was the grisly fulfillment of Elijah's prophecy (1 Kin. 21:23). Although Jezebel wanted Elijah dead (1 Kin. 19:1, 2), her own life was taken. **as refuse:** There was to be no marker, no mourning, no memorial, no sadness for this evil woman.

10:1 Ahab's **seventy sons** included children and probably grandchildren. Jehu wanted to eliminate all rivals to his kingship. The **rulers of Jezreel** were Samaritan officials, who often visited the royal residence in Jezreel. Such an understanding eliminates the necessity of emending the word Jezreel to Israel, as is often suggested. It is these officials, together with the elders (state officials closely related to the tribes) and those charged with educating and raising the royal children, who replied to Jehu (v. 5).

10:2–5 Jehu's first **letter** was written in order to determine who might be the greatest risk to his reign. **two kings:** The deaths of Joram (9:14–26) and Ahaziah (9:27, 28) were fresh in the rulers' minds, so the response of the leaders was a fearful submission to Jehu's power.

10:6–9 killed all these: Jehu pretended that his message was misunderstood and that in any case it was Ahab's wickedness that ultimately had brought about the divine judgment of these men.

10:10 Evaluating Jehu is difficult. His praise for the ministry of the prophets of God and his stated respect for the word of God commend him to us. But he did not balance his judgmental actions on Ahab's family with mercy and

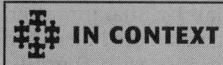 **IN CONTEXT** | ## A Missed Opportunity

While Jehu (10:1) is remembered as one of the great kings of the northern kingdom, he did not entirely follow God's ways. His bloody rise to power fulfilled Elijah's prophecy to Ahab twenty years earlier (1 Kin. 19:16, 17). His killing of Ahab's seventy sons and of his wife Jezebel placed him firmly on Israel's throne.

The northern kingdom from its beginning had been syncretistic in religion (1 Kin. 12). Jeroboam I had combined the worship of the living God with the worship of Baal and other Canaanite deities. Under Ahab, the religion of Israel reached its lowest point, practicing official, state-sponsored Baal worship (1 Kin. 16:31). Jehu's merciless purge of the official Baal priesthood was a major step in eradicating evil from the northern kingdom. However, the purge only brought Israel back to the syncretism established by Jeroboam I and his successors.

God rewarded Jehu with a reign of twenty-eight years, the longest of any northern king so far, and allowed his sons to rule Israel for four more generations, the longest dynasty in Israel's history. Jehu had an opportunity to be one of the greatest kings, but he did not follow God's Law completely or lead God's people completely back to it. He did not stop the worship of the golden calves left at Dan and Bethel. While not as overt as during the time of Ahab, the slide to Baal worship in Israel continued even after Jehu's purge of the worshipers of Baal.

justice for the poor and the oppressed. He was God's instrument of judgment, but he himself also stood under God's judgment (10:31).

10:11 Jehu . . . left him none remaining: In killing the house of Ahab, his supporters, as well as the surviving descendants of Ahaziah (vv. 13, 14), Jehu exceeded God's judgment. But he used the power God had given him for his selfish ends. Accordingly, no contradiction exists between the divine commissioning of Jehu (9:6–10) and the divine condemnation of him (10:31; Hos. 1:4).

10:12–14 Beth Eked means "Binding House," a site near Mount Gilboa. Here Jehu slaughtered **forty-two men** of the house of Ahaziah.

10:15, 16 Jehonadab means "The Lord Is Noble." He came along with Jehu as an observer. **son of Rechab:** Jehonadab was an ascetic, nomadic Rechabite. These people were known for their faithfulness to God and to the austere regulations laid down by Jehonadab (Jer. 35:1–16).

10:17 according to the word of the LORD: Jehu's action was by prophetic sanction (v. 10).

10:18–28 The last works of "Jehu the Eradicator" were to mount a frontal attack on overt Baal worship. The northern kingdom from its inception had been syncretistic in its religion (1 Kin. 12). Jeroboam I had combined the worship of Yahweh with many elements of Baal worship and other Canaanite deities, and this continued until the advent of Ahab, when the religion of Israel reached its nadir with official, state-sponsored Baal worship (1 Kin. 16:31). Jehu's purge of the official Baal priests, described in this section, was a major step in eradicating the evil of the northern kingdom. However, the purge only took things back to the level established by Jeroboam I and his successors (v. 31). Thus, while not as overt as under the time of Ahab, the slide to Baal worship in Israel continued even after Jehu's purge.

10:18–20 Finally, Jehu attacked overt Baal worship. With a lie, Jehu gathered all the principals of Baal worship to one place, the temple of Baal in Samaria (v. 21; 1 Kin. 16:32). He pretended that he was an even more ardent champion of Baal than Ahab. He issued a royal decree for a national **solemn assembly for Baal.**

10:21–23 temple of Baal: The temple that had been constructed by Ahab (1 Kin. 16:32). **vestments:** By having the Baal worshipers wear distinctive clothing, Jehu marked them for death. **no servants of the LORD**: Jehu carefully distinguished the enemy, in case some of the Lord's true priests might have gathered with the priests of Baal.

10:25–28 as soon as he: It is not clear whether a Baal priest or Jehu himself was making the offering. If it was Jehu, it would have been the most effective way of keeping the priests from suspecting any danger. **kill them:** Jehu followed Elijah's example on Mount Carmel (1 Kin. 18:40). Yet Jehu's executions were more thorough, for he had gathered all the priests and prophets of Baal in the nation. **to this day:** That is, at the time of writing. The suggestion is that even after the fall of Samaria one could see the foul place where the temple to Baal once had been. **destroyed Baal:** This summary statement refers only to the overt forms of Baal worship.

10:29 Jehu's destruction of Baal worship (vv. 18–28) was a political act. His continuing the state worship policies established by Jeroboam I clearly shows his disregard for true spiritual revival in Israel.

10:30, 31 done well: The evaluation of Jehu is one of limited obedience (v. 31). Nonetheless, he accomplished a great deal and received God's commendation for his work. Most likely, a prophet communicated God's message to Jehu.

10:32, 33 Because Shalmaneser III was occupied with political pressures in the east, Hazael took advantage of the situation, harassing Israel throughout his long reign. After Jehu's death, Hazael marched freely into Israel and even into Judah (12:17, 18; 13:22). The important point of these verses is that the attacks of Hazael were part of God's judgment on Israel.

10:34–36 The record of **Jehoahaz** is given in 13:1–9. He was followed by Joash (also called Jehoash; 13:10–13), Jeroboam II (14:23–29), and very briefly by Zechariah (15:8–12). The assassination of Zechariah by Shallum after a reign of only six months ended the line of Jehu in the fourth generation, just as the Lord had said (10:30).

11:1 Athaliah means "The Lord Is Exalted." Sadly, she did not live up to her name. **all the royal heirs:** Jehu had executed King Ahaziah of Judah, Athaliah's **son,** shortly after he had executed Joram of Israel (9:27–29). Ahaziah's older brother had been killed in an Arabian raid (2 Chr. 22:1). Further, Jehoram had killed his brothers and other royal relatives when he took the throne (2 Chr. 21:4), while Jehu had slain still more of the royal house (10:14). Therefore, Athaliah's destruction of all of the royal heirs must have concentrated on her own grandchildren. None of the usual details relative to accession to the crown in Judah are given here; Athaliah clearly usurped the office, setting aside the precepts of the Davidic covenant (2 Sam. 7:12–16; Ps. 89:35–37).

11:2, 3 Josephus says that **Jehosheba** was

IN LIFE | Called to Give an Account

Jehoash's dealings with the priests concerning temple repairs is a useful lesson in accountability:

- Jehoash delegated specific responsibilities to the priests with clear instructions concerning the collection and use of money (2 Kin. 12:4, 5).
- He personally confronted the priests, including their leader, Jehoiada, for their non- performance (12:7).
- He suggested a course of remedial action (12:7, 8) and then saw to it that an alternative solution to the problem would be carried out (12:9–12).

Accountability involves far more than simply telling someone what to do and then coming back later to see if instructions have been carried out. It means that a leader commits to overseeing the worker's performance and making sure that the project is completed.

Ahaziah's half sister (*Antiq*. 9.7.1). As the wife of the high priest Jehoiada, her marriage and her relation to the royal house made it possible for her to rescue and hide the young Joash. **Joash** (or Jehoash; 12:1) was the son of Ahaziah. He apparently was an infant at this time. Athaliah might not have known of his existence and for this reason have failed to kill him in her purges. Yet Joash was to inherit the promises of the Davidic covenant. His righteous reign (12:2) may be attributed in part to his early years spent **in the house of the LORD** and to the godly instruction and protection of his aunt Jehosheba and his uncle, the high priest Jehoiada. Meanwhile, the unthinkable was happening: The daughter of Jezebel was now the queen of Judah. A worshiper of Baal was in power in the nation of God's promise. She built in Jerusalem a temple to Baal (v. 18).

11:4–8 The **seventh year,** that is, of the reign of Athaliah and the life of Joash (v. 21). **Jehoiada:** The name of the high priest means "The Lord Knows." Other details about Jehoiada's careful preparations are given in 2 Chr. 23:1–11. Jehoiada's plan included the royal guard: the presentation and crowning of the legitimate royal heir coincided with the changing of the guard on the Sabbath.

11:4 bodyguards: The men of the royal guard are identified as the Cherethites and Pelethites in 2 Sam. 20:23; 1 Kin. 1:38. **showed them the king's son:** The revelation of this young prince was the critical moment. A zealous guard might easily have put him to death at once. There must have been a great deal of preparation on Jehoiada's part—and considerable prayer—for this moment.

11:5–9 The fact that the men of the royal guard followed the commands of Jehoiada the

priest was remarkable. It must have been because they were utterly disgusted by the wickedness of Athaliah.

11:10, 11 spears and shields: David had dedicated these weapons to the temple after his campaigns against Hadadezer (2 Sam. 8:11). Since they were not gold or silver, they had apparently been ignored by Shishak when he looted the temple and palace in the days of Rehoboam (1 Kin. 14:26).

11:12 Deuteronomy prescribed the duties of the king with regard to the preservation of God's Law (Deut. 17:18). By putting a copy of the Law in Joash's hand and the **crown** on his head, Jehoiada presented him as the rightful heir to the throne. The term **Testimony** recalls the covenant, emphasizing that Joash's coronation was given both its scriptural warrant and its rightful connection to the Davidic covenant.

11:13–16 The execution of Athaliah is described in this section. **in the temple of the LORD:** The temple was the appropriate place to crown the king of God's appointment. It was also probably a good place to hide from a queen whose god was Baal. **there was the king:** What a shock this must have been to Athaliah. There stood a little boy that guaranteed the end of her reign. Her words **Treason! Treason!** were technically correct. But it was she who had committed treason by murdering all the survivors of the Davidic house—except for the one who was now king. **killed:** The priest would not allow her execution in the temple, but her death was necessary. With her dead, the young Joash was safe.

11:17 Covenant renewal was particularly necessary after the unholy usurpation by the wicked Athaliah.

11:18 As Jezebel had seen her wicked husband Ahab build a **temple** to **Baal** in Samaria (1

🔍 IN FOCUS | "silver"

(Heb. *keseph*) (2 Kin. 12:13; Gen. 24:35; Job 22:25; Mal. 3:3) Strong's #3701: This word is related to a verb meaning "to become white or pale," thus silver is called "the pale metal." Since silver was the common medium of exchange in ancient times, the word is often translated *money* in the OT (1 Kin. 21:6; Is. 55:1). There is no reference to silver coins in the OT because silver was valued by weight in ancient times (Is. 46:6; Jer. 32:9, 10). Silver was one of the valuable materials collected to build the tabernacle and the temple (Ex. 25:1–9; 2 Chr. 2:7). As a precious metal, its value depended upon the economy; during Solomon's reign it was not as valuable, but during Ben-Hadad's siege of Samaria it became more precious (6:25; 1 Kin. 10:21, 27; 2 Chr. 1:15; 9:20, 27). In Ecclesiastes, Solomon gives us a warning about silver: "He who loves silver will not be satisfied" (Eccl. 5:10).

Kin. 16:32), so her daughter Athaliah was behind the building of a temple to Baal in the holy city of Jerusalem. **Mattan the priest of Baal:** The very fact that there was a priest of Baal in Jerusalem is astonishing. If Athaliah and her associates had not been stopped, the sins of Samaria would have paled beside the sins of Jerusalem.

11:19–21 The young child was established as king before the nation. **rejoiced . . . quiet:** The joy of the people and the peacefulness of the land were marks of God's blessing to the restored Davidic dynasty.

12:1 Jehoash (spelled "Joash" in 11:2) means "Yahweh Is Strong."

12:2 All the days in which Jehoiada the priest instructed him has an ominous tone. After Jehoiada's death, the king's activities would take a different turn, for Jehoash would become dependent upon counsel of a different sort (2 Chr. 24:17–19). Nonetheless, among the kings of Judah, he was one of the few who showed some signs of righteousness.

12:3 Although God Himself might be worshiped in such **high places,** the setting provided an association with Canaanite religious rites that could too easily lead to spiritual compromise (1 Kin. 3:2–4; 14:23). Apostasy would become a besetting sin later in Jehoash's reign (2 Chr. 24:17–19, 24).

12:4–16 One of Jehoash's significant accomplishments was an ambitious plan to raise funds to repair the temple. This section describes this accomplishment in elaborate detail. A big impetus for this beneficent work was Jehoiada the high priest.

12:5 Money collected from special taxes and voluntary offerings was designated for repairing **the temple.** Thus, renewed concern for spiritual things was evidenced after the neglect and abuse of the previous seven years (2 Chr. 24:7).

12:6–9 a chest: When the priest failed to do the work (vv. 6, 7), the king took a personal hand in seeing to its accomplishment. The chest

he prepared was set against the wall at the entrance facing the right side of the altar. Because the people responded generously (2 Chr. 24:10), the work proceeded and was soon completed (vv. 11, 12; 2 Chr. 24:11–13).

12:10–13 At first no funds were used for fashioning the sacred vessels, but there was **money** left over at the completion of the building repairs, and with it the sacred vessels could be completed as well (2 Chr. 24:14).

12:14, 15 dealt faithfully: Joash had commissioned such trustworthy men that no accounting of their use of the funds was necessary.

12:17, 18 The Aramean invasion recorded here took place late in Joash's reign. The **king** fell into apostasy after the death of his godly counselor, the high priest Jehoiada (2 Chr. 24:17–19, 23, 24), and this invasion came as a judgment of his wickedness.

12:19–21 Joash was severely wounded in Hazael's invasion (2 Chr. 24:24, 25), then he fell victim shortly afterward to the dissent and unpopularity that culminated in his assassination. Because of Joash's apostasy and murder of Zechariah, Jehoiada's son (2 Chr. 24:17–22), the king was not laid to rest in the royal tombs (2 Chr. 24:25).

13:1 The name **Jehoahaz** means "The Lord Has Grasped." Two centuries later another Jehoahaz would become king of Judah following the death of his father, the godly Josiah (23:31). The 17–year reign of Jehu's son Jehoahaz lasted from 814 to 798 B.C.

13:2, 3 evil . . . sins of Jeroboam: After the end of the house of Ahab in Jehu's purge (chs. 9; 10), the kings of Israel reverted to the level of syncretism that had been established by Jeroboam I. The mention of Hazael's son **Ben-Hadad** III (802–780 B.C.) may refer to his serving as a commander in his father's army or to his growing prominence in his father's later years (v. 24).

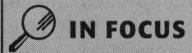

(Heb. *'aph*) (2 Kin. 13:3; Deut. 6:15; Ps. 18:8; Prov. 11:22; 29:8) Strong's #639: Depending on the context, this word signifies either "nose," "nostril," or "anger" (Gen. 2:7; Prov. 15:1). This term occurs about half of the time with words referring to burning. Thus these figures of speech typically depict anger as the fierce breathing of a person through his nose: "a burning nose" (Ex. 32:10–12). Most of the references describe God's anger. God is said to be slow to anger, but can be provoked into exercising judgment (Ps. 103:8; Deut. 4:24, 25). He is compassionate, but His wrath is reserved for those who break His covenant (Deut. 13:17; 29:25–27; Josh. 23:16; Judg. 2:20; Ps. 78:38). Although God's wrath is righteous, human anger is almost always evaluated in negative terms in the OT (Gen. 49:6; Prov. 14:17).

13:4 Although Jehoahaz did not follow the Lord exclusively (v. 6), God graciously heard his genuine plea for help. In His long-suffering mercy, God often deals patiently with people and blesses them despite their failures (1 Kin. 21:25–29; 2 Pet. 3:9).

13:5 Israel's **deliverer** (Heb. *môshîa'*, also rendered "savior") has been variously identified. Probably it was the Assyrian king Adad-Nerari III. Referring to an Assyrian king as a divinely commissioned deliverer of Israel is similar to the words of God in Isaiah describing the Persian King Cyrus as "His anointed" (Is. 45:1; compare Is. 44:28).

13:6–9 the wooden image: The Hebrew word for *wooden images* is a reference to the Canaanite goddess Asherah. The image itself was a sacred tree or pole that was perceived perhaps as some sexually-oriented symbol of the fertility religion of Canaan.

13:10 the thirty-seventh year of Joash: This notice seems to be at variance with 13:1 (the seventeen years of the reign on Jehoahaz began in the twenty-third year of Joash). The apparent discrepancy is resolved by noting that the author here has shifted to using the accession year scheme in the northern kingdom. Under this system, a new king's first year was assigned in accordance with the beginning of the new year in the fall after his enthronement. With due allowance made for the differences between the systems of reckoning in the northern and southern kingdoms, the year 798 B.C. marks the date when Jehoash became king in Israel. Some manuscripts, however, read "thirty-ninth year" here, suggesting a correction to a scribal slip in the traditional Masoretic text. Some scholars also suggest a two year co-regency between Jehoahaz and Jehoash.

13:11–13 At first, the 16-year reign of Jehoash of Israel appears to be recorded without further elaboration (vv. 10–13). But three stories are added: the death of Elisha during his reign (vv. 14–21), his military victories over the Aramean forces (vv. 24, 25), and his war with Amaziah of Judah (v. 12; 14:8–14).

13:14 O my father: Jehoash's cry over the aged Elisha repeats the words of Elisha spoken when Elijah was taken up to heaven (2:12). Thus, both at the beginning of his ministry and at its conclusion, Elisha is unmistakably linked to his mentor Elijah. The grief of Jehoash at the impending death of Elisha shows that, like his father Jehoahaz (vv. 4, 5), this Israelite king possessed some genuine spirituality. The line of Jehu had its good moments and received some reward from the Lord (10:30). However, none of this line or any other of the kings of Israel served God with all their heart (10:31).

13:15–19 This section describes a symbolic act that Elisha had Joash perform to ensure victories over his enemies; the king was only partly successful in completing the task. Elisha's symbolic act of putting his hands **on the king's hands** should have alerted the king that the aged prophet was conveying a divine blessing on him. Jehoash's halfhearted compliance with Elisha's instructions exposed his weak faith and illustrated God's unfavorable evaluation of his character (v. 11). God's dying prophet was rightly disturbed. Although god would allow Israel to defeat the Aramean army three times, their victory would be incomplete.

13:20 Elisha died: The supernatural translation of Elijah (ch. 2) was an unusual example of God's power; Elisha died a normal death. **bands from Moab:** This prepares for the miracle in the grave of Elisha (v. 21), but the mention of invasions such as this reminds us of how perilous life was during so much of Israel's history.

13:21, 22 the man . . . revived: Even in death the mere presence of Elisha's body was sufficient for a miracle. There was no magic in Elisha's bones, but a demonstration of the power of God associated with His servant. This miracle should have reassured Jehoash that God intended to rescue Israel from the deadly grip of Aramean domination (v. 25).

13:23 This verse is one of those dazzling lights that burst from the pages of the Bible, describing the wonderful mercy of the living God (14:26, 27). It draws in part on the imagery of Ex. 34:6. **His covenant:** God's faithfulness to His own promise is a regular theme of the OT (Ex. 2:23–25).

13:24 This **Ben-Hadad** is the son of Hazael (v. 3). After his father's death, he reigned as Ben-Hadad III (802–780 B.C.).

13:25 In accordance with Jehoash's striking the ground **three times** with arrows (v. 18), God gave Jehoash victory over the Arameans only three times. Yet God graciously overruled Jehoash's inadequate faith by granting Israel full victory over the Arameans during the reign of his son Jeroboam II.

14:1–3 The name **Amaziah** means "The Lord Is Mighty." **did what was right:** Amaziah was one of the few godly kings in the kingdom of Judah; the best kings were Hezekiah (18:1) and Josiah (22:1). **his father David . . . his father Joash:** Here is a good example of different uses of the Hebrew word for *father*. It can signify either remote or immediate ancestry.

14:4 Like his father Jehoash before him (12:3), Amaziah allowed worship at the **high places.** This practice would blossom into open idolatry in the reigns of subsequent kings (16:4; 21:3).

14:5, 6 executed his servants: The principals are named in 12:20, 21. These men were guilty of assassinating his father and might have been a threat to his own reign. **Book of the Law of Moses:** Amaziah followed the Law laid down in Deut. 24:16.

14:7 A more detailed account of Amaziah's defeat of the **Edomites** is given in 2 Chr. 25:5–13. Edom had regained its independence during the reign of Jehoram (8:20–22).

Amaziah's conquest of the formidable city of **Sela** atop the seemingly unapproachable cliffs of the Wadi Musa was a monumental accomplishment. Rather than recognize God's hand in this feat, Amaziah became proud and fell into spiritual compromise (2 Chr. 25:14–16).

14:8 let us face one another: Amaziah's pride over his accomplishment (v. 10) and his anger over the looting of Judean cities by Israelite mercenaries dismissed before the Edomite campaign (2 Chr. 25:6–10, 13) clouded his thinking.

14:9, 10 Jehoash replied to Amaziah in the form of a fable—a kind of story designed to teach a moral. By speaking of Amaziah as a **thistle** in comparison with the **cedar** of **Lebanon,** Jehoash tried to help Amaziah put a more realistic construction on his recent victory.

14:11 Beth Shemesh: The name of the city means "House of the Sun," indicating that there had once been a temple to the sun god there in Canaanite times. Beth Shemesh was in the Valley of Sorek, about 15 miles west of Jerusalem. This was the town where the holy ark was taken (1 Sam. 6:10—7:2) when it came back into Israelite hands after its "wanderings" among the Philistines. The tragedy of the battle between Amaziah and Jehoash was heightened by the fact that the proud Amaziah forced a battle in his own territory, **Judah.**

14:12 Judah was defeated: Jehoash's forces were seasoned warriors and had defeated the Arameans (13:25). Amaziah's pride spelled not only his own downfall (v. 13) but that of his capital city (14:13, 14). **fled to his tent:** This is an idiom for a complete rout (2 Sam. 18:17).

14:13 The damage to Jerusalem's northern walls extended from the **Corner Gate,** at the northwest corner of the city wall, east to the **Gate of Ephraim.** The northwest corner of Jerusalem had always been the city's most vulnerable point (18:17). A breach in the wall of **four hundred cubits** (600 feet) was a huge

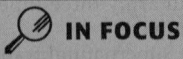 **IN FOCUS** **"high places"**

(Heb. *bamah*) (2 Kin. 14:4; 23:5; 1 Kin. 11:7; Jer. 19:5) Strong's #1116: This word often refers to a sacred area, an open-air sanctuary, located on top of a ridge. Before the temple was built, the Israelites could worship the true God at high places (see Solomon's worship of God at the high place at Gideon, 1 Kin. 3:2–4). But the Israelites soon began worshiping other gods, especially Baal, at these high places, copying the practices of the surrounding nations. The Israelites decorated these hilltops with pagan symbols, sacred pillars and stones, and these places were rallying points for pagan worship. They often were associated with Israel's religious rebellion and apostasy (1 Kin. 14:23; Jer. 19:5). Thus throughout the OT, the existence of *high places* and the worship that was practiced there was labeled as an affront to God (Ps. 78:58).

gap for the invading army to enter the holy city through.

14:14–16 gold and silver . . . articles: The looting of precious objects from the temple, as well as from the palace—**the king's house**—shows the humiliation that Judah suffered as the result of this disastrous war fueled by Amaziah's pride. **hostages:** People as well as goods were carried off by the king of Israel. **returned:** It had not been the intention of Jehoash to occupy foreign territory.

14:17, 18 The notice of **fifteen years** of life for Amaziah suggests he was released after the death of Jehoash for an additional period (782–767 B.C.). If so, he reigned alongside his son Azariah (or Uzziah), whose 52–year reign began in 792 B.C. (15:2).

14:19, 20 Amaziah not only reproduced his father's spiritual problems (14:3), he also died as his father had, at the hand of an assassin (12:20, 21). **Lachish:** This was one of the guard cities for Jerusalem, about 30 miles southwest of the capital. Lachish was seized by Sennacherib in 701 B.C., in the days of Hezekiah (18:13–17).

14:21 Young **Azariah** succeeded Amaziah (15:1–7). This king is also known as Uzziah.

14:22 Elath is the famous seaport on the Gulf of Aqaba. During the reign of Ahaz, Elath was captured by Rezin of Aram and became an Edomite holding (16:6).

14:23 Jeroboam: This is the second king of Israel to have this name. Jeroboam I was the founder of the northern kingdom at the time of the death of Solomon (930 B.C.; 1 Kin. 11; 12). **forty-one years:** Jeroboam II had a very long reign. His 41 years included ten years as co-regent with his father Jehoash (792–782 B.C.).

14:24 did evil: The assessment of his reign is like that of all the kings of Israel, except for the graver assessment given to the house of Ahab (10:29–31).

14:25 restored the territory: The first half of the eighth century B.C. was a period of prosperity and strength for the northern and southern kingdoms. Jeroboam II extended Israel's influence from the entrance of Hamath down the eastern side of the Jordan to the southern end of the Dead Sea. Since Azariah also campaigned in the southern territory, the two kingdoms must have been living in harmony and enjoying mutual cooperation. **Jonah:** Once again a prophet of God gave direction to a king. The reference to Jonah here provides the historical setting for the famous prophet.

14:26, 27 no helper: The living God saw that His people needed His help, and He became the helper of His people. God used Jeroboam II to bring Israel to a new period of greatness.

14:28 The Scriptures emphasize Jeroboam's military prowess. Yet Jeroboam's **might** may have also been economic. The well-known Samarian Ostraca, which may date from this period, record the delivery to Samaria of fine oil and barley produced on the royal estates.

INSIGHT   The Grief of Separation

The division in the kingdom that occurred in the days of Rehoboam (1 Kin. 12:19) left lasting scars and occasionally led to civil war between the northern and southern monarchies (2 Kin. 14:11–14). For many Israelites, particularly in the north, this separation from Jerusalem was grievous. Some believe that Pss. 42 and 43 were composed by a Judean in the north who was cut off from the temple at Jerusalem.

14:29 The brief reign of **Zechariah** is noted in 15:8–12. He was the fourth in the line of Jehu to reign in Israel, in fulfillment of God's gracious promise to Jehu (10:30).

15:1, 2 Azariah (or Uzziah, 2 Chr. 26:1; Is. 1:1) is credited with 52 years of reign. This figure includes 10 years during which his father Amaziah was held captive (792–782 B.C.), 15 years of coregency with Amaziah upon his release from captivity (782–767 B.C.), and 27 years of sole reign (767–740 B.C.). The latter part of Azariah's reign was tainted by his intrusion into the priestly office (2 Chr. 26:16–19), an act that resulted in his being stricken with leprosy (v. 5). This condition put his son Jotham on the throne to rule with him and handle public matters relative to the royal office. The nature of Jotham's duties (v. 5), the assigning of a full 52 years of reign to Azariah, and Isaiah's dating of his call to the year of Azariah's (or Uzziah's) death (Is. 6:1) may indicate that Azariah retained the power of the throne until the end. His name Azariah means "The Lord Has Helped."

15:3, 4 Azariah was another of the good kings in Judah and received some of the same evaluation that was given to Jehoash in 12:2, 3 and to Amaziah in 14:3, 4.

15:5–7 leper: The events that brought about this affliction are described in 2 Chr. 26:16–21. **over the royal house:** Jotham assumed the office of senior administrator. While the term *over the house* is used of the office of royal steward, this office grew in prestige, and the term came to designate a senior official of high standing. Jotham handled the business of state during his father's period of isolation.

15:8–12 The brief reign of **Zechariah,** the fourth in the line of Jehu, is described here. His name, which means "Yahweh Remembers," is the same as the prophet Zechariah. As in the case of many of the kings of Israel and Judah, he was assassinated (v. 10; 12:20; 14:19; 15:25).

15:12 fourth generation: Jehu had been promised a continuing posterity into the fourth

15:16 Because of its beauty (Song 6:4), **Tirzah** served as a royal retreat (1 Kin. 14:17). It also was the national capital during Israel's first two dynasties. **ripped open:** Such inhuman atrocities were all too common in times of warfare in the ancient world (8:12; Amos 1:13). Israel's sin repeatedly placed it in danger of such barbaric acts (Hos. 10:13, 14; 13:16).

15:17, 18 Menahem: This wicked king came to power by assassination and established his

Aerial view of the mound of ancient Hamath, a city controlled by Solomon and later conquered by Jeroboam II of Israel (2 Kin. 14:28).

generation as a reward for carrying out his divine commission (10:30). Unfortunately, Jehu and his house proved unworthy of their God-given opportunities so that they repeatedly earned the condemnation of God's prophets (13:18, 19; Hos. 1:4; Amos 7:9). After the death of Zechariah in 752 B.C. and the end of the fourth dynasty, Israel plunged into a period of degeneracy, bloody conspiracies, and international intrigue that would bring about its demise in 722 B.C. So Zechariah, whose name means "The Lord Remembers" (14:26, 27), was the last of the effective kings of Israel.

15:13–16 The short reign of **Shallum,** only one **month,** was indicative of the emerging collapse of the nation.

15:15 the rest of the acts: This follows the normal pattern for the obituaries of the kings of the northern kingdom. Even though Shallum was king for only one month, he still received the complete royal obituary.

authority by brutal acts against humanity (vv. 14, 16). Ironically, his name means "Comforter."

15:19–22 Pul is a second Babylonian name for the Assyrian king Tiglath-Pileser III (745–727 B.C.; v. 29; 1 Chr. 5:26). Although he came to the throne as a usurper from the ranks of the military, he would prove a competent king. Under Tiglath-Pileser III and his successors, Assyria became the dominant power in the Middle East for well over a century (747–612 B.C.). It was a period of repeated Assyrian interference in the affairs of Israel and Judah. The first such instance came quickly. In 743 B.C. Tiglath-Pileser III launched a western invasion that brought a great deal of Syria and Palestine under his control. The annals of this Assyrian king record that Menahem of Israel paid tribute to him, as is also recorded here (vv. 19, 20).

15:23–26 Pekahiah means "The Lord Has Opened the Eyes." After an evil reign of two years, a usurper "closed his eyes" for him.

IN PERSON   Azariah

While the account in 2 Kings summarily dismisses Azariah (15:1), the record in Second Chronicles presents a good deal of information about his considerable accomplishments. Known as Uzziah in Chronicles, Azariah is remembered for his domestic policies, his innovative measures for military preparedness (2 Chr. 26:9, 11–15), his attention to political and economic concerns relative to his southern and eastern borders (2 Chr. 26:2, 7, 8, 10–16; Joel 3:19; Amos 1:11, 12), and the settling of the perennial Philistine problem on his western frontier (2 Chr. 26:6, 7; Joel 3:3, 4; Amos 1:6–8). Like Jeroboam II in the north, Azariah led Judah in a time of national recovery and growth. The southern kingdom during his fifty-two year reign achieved a power and prosperity that had been unknown since the days of Solomon.

Although he pleased God during the early days of his reign, Azariah became proud due to his success. Like so many of the other kings of the northern and southern kingdoms, he did not remove many of the symbols of idolatry in the land. However, his ultimate mistake was going into the temple to burn incense on the altar. Only a divinely-appointed priest could perform this function. For this arrogance, God immediately struck Azariah with leprosy for the remainder of his days.

In the blink of an eye, a great and powerful king was transformed into a social outcast. The Lord gave Azariah a hard lesson in humility. No one is so great that he does not have to answer to God.

15:27, 28 Like Shallum and Menahem before him, **Pekah** sat on the throne through usurpation and bloody deeds. Because Hoshea's nine-year reign (17:1) began in 732 B.C., Pekah's **twenty years** must have included a time of kingship in his own district during the unsettled days of Shallum, Menahem, and Pekahiah (752–740 B.C.). Apparently Pekah rode the crest of anti-Assyrian sentiment. That same political stance ultimately brought about his downfall, during **Tiglath-Pileser** III's second western campaign (734–732 B.C.). It is this campaign in Galilee to which Isaiah alluded (Is. 9:1).

15:29, 30 Hoshea . . . killed him: Tiglath-Pileser III's campaign apparently caused a pro-Assyrian reaction within Israel that brought about both Pekah's death and Hoshea's ascension to the throne. The annals of Tiglath-Pileser III record Hoshea's heavy tribute and the Assyrian king's claim that he himself set the new Israelite king in office.

15:31–33 Jotham means "The Lord Is Perfect." Jotham's reign of **sixteen years** (752–736 B.C.) includes a 12–year coregency with his father Azariah. Since Jotham is earlier credited with 20 years (v. 30), it may be that he turned over the reigns of government to his son Ahaz in 736 B.C., even though he lived on for four more years.

15:34, 35 Jotham's reign was partly righteous. After the purge of Ahaziah and Athaliah (9:27–29; 11:13–16), the kings of Judah who reigned in relative righteousness were Joash (Jehoash) (12:2, 3), Amaziah (14:3, 4), and Azariah (Uzziah) (15:3, 4). A positive righteousness would be modeled by Hezekiah (18:3–6) and again by Josiah (22:2).

15:36 The author of Chronicles indicates that Jotham did extensive building in Jerusalem and Judah (2 Chr. 27:3, 4) and engaged in a war against the Ammonites (2 Chr. 27:5). Jotham

INSIGHT   The Lord Warns His People

God used several means to warn Judah of His impending judgment. One way was to send invaders from the outside (2 Kin. 15:37). Another way was to send prophets from within. One of these spokesmen was Micah of Moresheth (Mic. 1:1). He denounced Judah for adopting the idolatrous ways of Israel, and he criticized the leaders of Jerusalem for their oppressive policies toward the country's rural citizens.

apparently carried out the practices that brought Judah power and prosperity during the years of his father Azariah (Uzziah).

15:37, 38 Rezin . . . Pekah: These two adversaries were even more prominent in the time of Ahaz (ch. 16; Is. 7).

16:1, 2 The name **Ahaz** means "He Has Grasped." The **seventeenth year of Pekah** was 736/5 B.C. Ahaz's sixteen-year reign apparently ended in 720 B.C. If so, like Jotham before him, Ahaz must have lived on another four years after giving up his rule. Hezekiah's first year of independent rule began in 715 B.C., 14 years before Sennacherib's invasion of Judah and his siege of Jerusalem in 701 B.C. (18:13). If Ahaz was 20 years old at his accession in 736 B.C. (v. 2), he would have lived to be around 40. Since Hezekiah was 25 years old at his accession to coregency in 729 B.C., Ahaz was in his early teens when Hezekiah was born.

16:3, 4 After a series of kings in Judah who demonstrated a relative righteousness, Ahaz followed the evil ways of the kings of the northern kingdom. The author of Chronicles reports that the rite of making one's son **pass through the fire** was connected with the Baal worship practiced in the Valley of the Son of Hinnom (23:10; 2 Chr. 28:2, 3). Ahaz was an apostate who personally led his people in the religious worship practices of Canaan (v. 4; 2 Chr. 28:2–4).

16:5 Because of Ahaz's sin God delivered him into the hands of an alliance of the two kings **Rezin** and **Pekah** (15:37). A great slaughter followed, and a complete deportation of Judah was averted only by divine intervention (2 Chr. 28:5–15).

16:6 Azariah had recovered **Elath** for Judah (14:22). Now this major port city (1 Kin. 9:26) was taken from Judah. **to this day:** That is, the day of the narration of these events.

16:7–9 Ahaz's request of **Tiglath-Pileser** III coincides with the Assyrian king's second western campaign (734–732 B.C.) that eventually brought about the fall of Damascus in 732 B.C. and the replacement of Pekah with Hoshea on the throne of Israel in the same year. Tiglath-Pileser listed the tribute of both Hoshea and Ahaz in connection with his campaigning.

16:10–15 Having been summoned to Damascus by Tiglath-Pileser III, Ahaz saw a pagan **altar** that suited his tastes. His use of the altar to make sacrifices to God underscored Ahaz's essential paganism. His paganism was also evident in his many other religious innovations (vv. 14–18; 2 Chr. 28:2–4, 22–25). Ahaz went so far in his apostasy as to shut the doors of the temple (2 Chr. 28:24).

16:16 The participation of the high priest **Urijah** in the "new ways" of Ahaz is to be viewed as apostasy on his part.

16:17–20 cut off . . . removed: The exact purpose for dismantling the panels and removing the basins is unclear.

17:1, 2 twelfth year: Hoshea became king in 732 B.C., so the twelve years of Ahaz indicate a period of coregency with his father Jotham,

perhaps arranged due to the pressures of Tiglath-Pileser's first western campaign (744–743 B.C.). **Hoshea:** The name means "Salvation."

17:3 Shalmaneser V succeeded Tiglath-Pileser III as king of Assyria in 727 B.C.

17:4 conspiracy by Hoshea: Several elements of intrigue and international affairs may have entered into the picture here. Transitions in power were often occasions for rebellion or attempted overthrow. Further, a new strong man had appeared in Egypt—Tefnekht, a pharaoh of the twenty-fourth dynasty. The time may have seemed ripe for Hoshea to enter into an anti-Assyrian coalition.

17:5, 6 After a three-year siege, Samaria fell to the Assyrians in 722 B.C. Sargon, the field commander of Shalmaneser V who succeeded him to the throne, would later claim that it was he who **took Samaria.** It was ancient practice to deport large numbers of influential citizens of a conquered country or city to decrease the possibility of rebellion (25:11, 12; Ezek. 1:2, 3).

17:7–23 This remarkable piece of writing extensively describes the sin of Israel that led to the horrible calamity of 722 B.C. Perhaps the words of 14:26, 27 were on the writer's mind and he felt it necessary to describe what led to this downfall of Samaria and Israel.

17:7–9 Israel had sinned: The reason for the fall of Samaria and the end of the northern kingdom is clearly stated to be its spiritual failure, in turning from the living God to worship other gods that exist only in people's depraved imagination. The rehearsal that follows of Israel's spiritual adultery (vv. 9–17) makes it clear that Israel had grown thoroughly corrupt from the leaders on down (vv. 7–9, 21). Despite repeated warnings (vv. 13, 14, 23), Israel had persisted in every form of idolatry and licentious worship (vv. 10–12, 16, 17).

17:10, 11 pillars . . . images . . . high places: The pagan trilogy (18: 4; 1 Kin. 14:23).

17:12–21 Jeroboam . . . made them . . . sin: Jeroboam I had initiated the state worship that in effect set the standard for all of Israel's idolatrous activities. The worship of the calves at Dan and Bethel, and Israel's fascination with Baal (v. 16; 1 Kin. 12:28, 29; 16:32, 33), are repeatedly cited as the chief causes of Israel's spiritual defeat and political collapse. Jeroboam I's heresy was a standard of wickedness for the kings who followed him in the northern kingdom.

17:22–24 The **king of Assyria** was probably Sargon II (722–705 B.C.), although the practice described here was continued by later kings as well. Such a mixing of populations would break down ethnic distinctions and weaken the loyalties that the people had. It would also help create a sense of empire. The list of cities recorded here may indicate the order for a caravan of relocated people. Samaria was the whole region where the repopulation took place; the inhabitants would eventually be called Samaritans.

17:25–28 one of the priests: Although a deported Israelite priest was sent back to instruct the Samaritan population in the worship of the Lord, the end result was a mixture of various forms of paganism with the apostate religion of the northern kingdom (vv. 30–33, 40, 41). In the course of time, both the Samaritans and their religion were rejected by the Jews (John 4:9; 8:48).

17:29–41 A double charge is laid against the Samaritans: They did not worship the Lord, and they did not keep the laws and ordinances laid down by the Lord of the covenant. The author reminds all concerned that only the Lord is Israel's Redeemer.

18:1, 2 The third year of Hoshea is 729 B.C. The 29 years of Hezekiah's reign thus include a period of coregency with his father Ahaz before he ruled independently (715–699 B.C.). The name **Hezekiah** means "The Lord Has Strengthened."

18:3 The assessment of Hezekiah begins similar to that of his predecessors, but it goes on to transcend the evaluations of "relative righteousness" that are typical of the other kings of Judah (15:34, 35).

18:4 Consistently, the kings who preceded Hezekiah are criticized by the author for not destroying the **high places** (15:34, 35). While there were traditions of worship of the true God at these locations, far too often they became sites for the licentious worship of Baal and Asherah. Hezekiah's reforms included not only the destruction of the pagan cult objects introduced in the days of his apostate father Ahaz, but the **bronze serpent** that had been preserved since the days of Moses (2 Chr. 29—31). Symbols all too easily can be made into objects of veneration. Apparently such had become the case with this precious ancient object.

18:5, 6 none like him: Hezekiah's faith was unparalleled by any other king who had preceded him after the time of David; Josiah's adherence to the Law would be extolled in a similar manner (23:25). The fact of Hezekiah's faith forms the basis for the account that follows. Because Hezekiah trusted the Lord, he could courageously withstand Assyrian tyranny. The northern kingdom fell to King Shalmaneser V in 722 B.C. because it did not keep God's holy

---

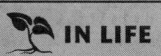 **IN LIFE**   **The Danger of Relics**

Jesus said that God is Spirit, and that those who worship Him must worship in spirit and truth (John 4:24). This means that we worship and serve a God whom we cannot see with our eyes, but must believe with our hearts. As a result, God is a bit of an abstraction for some people. One way that they have tried to make Him more real and present is through artifacts that they have associated with Him.

As understandable as the veneration of relics may be, it is a dangerous practice. It can easily tempt people to worship the object rather than the God whom the object is supposed to point to. In essence, the relic becomes a focus of idolatry.

That happened with a number of items that the Israelites venerated, including the bronze snake that Moses had made during the Exodus journey (2 Kin. 18:4; Num. 21:8, 9). Originally, the serpent on the pole served as a means of healing for snake-bitten people, by causing them to look to the Lord for help. But after the people settled in the Promised Land, they apparently turned this standard into an idol, as if the bronze snake itself had power to heal. They burned incense to it and even gave it a name, Nehushtan.

In a similar way, the Israelites turned a ceremonial robe, or ephod, that Gideon made from the spoils of his victory over the Midianites, into an idol (Judg. 8:25–27). Later they tried to use the ark of covenant as a charm against the Philistines, with disastrous results. And in Jeremiah's day, the citizens of Jerusalem cared more about their temple than they did about the Lord of the temple (Jer. 7:12–15).

These examples show the dangers of making too much of objects and places that have had a close association with the work of God. As human beings, we live in the natural world, but we worship a supernatural God. Therefore, we need to treat shrines and relics merely as means toward that end, never as ends in themselves.

standards (vv. 9–12), but Hezekiah's trust and faithfulness would let him face the later invasion of King Sennacherib (701 B.C.) and receive divine help (19:32–36).

18:7, 8 In addition to refusing to serve any longer as a vassal of **Assyria,** Hezekiah also conquered the **Philistines.** This helped establish Judah as an independent nation and new power in the region. No longer was Judah under the threat of military incursions from neighboring states simply because of its weakness.

18:9–23 That the siege lasted for **three years** suggests that the people suffered unspeakable horrors. The reason for the fall of Samaria is not because of a weaker army or its unstable walls. The principal issue was that they had rebelled against God.

18:13 Hezekiah's **fourteenth year** of sole rule was 701 B.C. The details of the generally rebellious situation that provoked Sennacherib to invade the western portion of his empire are recounted in his annals, where Hezekiah is particularly mentioned for his involvement in the whole affair.

18:14 I have done wrong: Literally, "I have sinned." Hezekiah had refused to be a vassal of Assyria and was now threatened by their army. The annals of Sennacherib report how he made a wide-ranging invasion of Judah. With the Assyrian army already at Lachish, Hezekiah felt an overwhelming sense of doom. One of Sennacherib's inscriptions describes the siege of **Lachish** and reports the heavy tribute demanded from Hezekiah. His fulfillment of Sennacherib's demands (vv. 14–16) doubtless whetted the conqueror's appetite for additional booty. Therefore Sennacherib placed Jerusalem under siege (18:13—19:36).

18:15, 16 This removal from the temple of immense amounts of **silver, gold,** and precious objects followed an earlier despoiling in the days of Amaziah (14:14).

18:17 Tartan . . . Rabsaris . . . Rabshakeh: These titles suggest persons of high station in Assyria. **a great army:** The accounts of the Assyrian kings suggest that they had mounted the largest armies known in the ancient Middle East. This huge army was stationed in the land of Judah. **Fuller's Field** was in the northwest corner of the city, the area most vulnerable to attack.

18:18 Eliakim was the senior palace administrator (15:5), and **Shebna** was the royal scribe. This verse indicates that Eliakim had already replaced Shebna in the office of senior palace administrator, as mentioned in Is. 22:15–25.

18:19 In the literature of the ancient Middle East, the term **great king** was reserved for a king of a major power. Here the Assyrian delegation delivered an ultimatum from the "great king" of Assyria to Jerusalem.

18:20 The Rabshakeh questioned the object of Hezekiah's **trust.** Perhaps Hezekiah's reputation for trusting in God was already widely known (v. 5). Trusting became the focal point of the Assyrian's psychological warfare (vv. 19–22, 24, 30).

18:21 Because Egypt depended upon the life-giving Nile with its reeds, the figure of a **broken reed** is most appropriate. Actually Sennacherib's warning against confidence in Egypt was well taken, the point having been made previously by Isaiah (Is. 30:3–5; 31:1–3).

18:22, 23 if you are able: The Assyrian official's taunt is that the Israelites do not have enough men and that the men they have are not trained for the coming conflict.

18:24, 25 The LORD said: The Assyrians may have been aware of prophecies concerning the judgment of Judah and Jerusalem and Assyria's own role as God's avengers (Is. 10:5–11). The remark was intended to introduce stark terror into the hearts of the people of Jerusalem (2 Chr. 32:18) by pointing out that now even their God was against them.

IN FOCUS   **"done wrong"**

(Heb. *chata'*) (2 Kin. 17:7; 18:14; Lev. 4:27; Judg. 20:16) Strong's #2398: The meaning of this verb is "to miss (a target)" or "to fall short (of a goal)." The word expresses this basic meaning in Judg. 20:16, where it is translated *miss:* "every one could sling a stone at a hair's breadth and not miss." When applied to ethics, the word implies falling short of a moral requirement. The word is the most common OT expression for sin. Several nouns are derived from the verb, including *chet,* "sin" or "guilt" (Is. 53:12); *chatta',* "sinful men" (Num. 32:14); and *chatta't,* "sin offering" (Lev. 4:3). In the NT, Paul also defined sin as "falling short": "for all have sinned and fall short of the glory of God" (Rom. 3:23). But then Paul offered the perfect remedy for our fallen condition: salvation through Jesus Christ (Rom. 3:24).

18:26 Since **Aramaic** was by this time the language of international communication, it might be expected that the Rabshakeh would carry on diplomatic negotiations with officials in Judah and avoid speaking the Hebrew of the common citizens. But the Assyrians loved speaking to people in their native dialect to make the intimidation more effective.

18:27, 28 their own waste: The Rabshakeh portrayed the potential horror of the coming siege by using an obscene expression. The words were drawn from street language.

18:29–32 trust in the Lord: The matter of trust (vv. 19–24) continued as an issue. The Rabshakeh tempted the Israelites to abandon their trust in the Lord and trust in Sennacherib instead. Then the promised covenantal blessings (vv. 31, 32; Deut. 8:8; Mic. 4:4; Zech. 3:10) could all be theirs. The repeated use of the words **Do not listen to Hezekiah** (vv. 22, 29, 30) was designed to lead the people to rebellion against their king. Moreover, he presented his land as a wonderful place for them to live in.

18:33–37 The Rabshakeh's assertion that none of the **gods of the nations** who had opposed Assyria had withstood the Assyrian king is both another aspect of the continued psychological warfare and another evidence of the Rabshakeh's awareness of Isaiah's prophetic words (v. 25; Is. 10:7–11).

19:1 he tore his clothes: Tearing of clothes was often a sign of grief (6:30) or of sorrowful repentance (Joel 2:12, 13). The humility of the king was evidenced in this action, one already performed by his trusted servants (18:37). In addition to humbling himself, the king **went into the house of the Lord.** That is, he sought guidance from the living God.

19:2 The ministry of the great prophet **Isaiah** had begun in the year that Uzziah or Azariah died (Is. 6:1), nearly four decades earlier (740 B.C.). Once Isaiah had sought out Judah's godless King Ahaz to minister to him (Is. 7:3); now the prophet was being sought by the godly Hezekiah. Isaiah participated in the events of Hezekiah's reign, and the details of 18:13—20:19 are also recorded in Is. 36—39.

19:3 day of trouble: The Hebrew phrase translated here indicates not only the great danger of the present Assyrian crisis, but the distress that Hezekiah felt. Hezekiah realized that the Lord's corrective chastisement had come upon Judah and Jerusalem. The closing proverb using the imagery of **birth** (Hos. 13:13) stresses the need for God's intervening strength if Jerusalem were to be delivered.

19:4, 5 hear . . . reproach: The first verb does not suggest that God might not be aware of the words of the Rabshakeh. Rather, the words describe God as determining to redress the wrong.

19:6, 7 Isaiah's prophecy was one of comfort. Not only would Sennacherib fail to conquer Jerusalem, but he would face a violent death upon his return home. Both points of the

prophetic message would come true, although Sennacherib was not assassinated until 20 years later (c. 681 B.C.). In his annals Sennacherib boasts of five more campaigns; however, he makes no mention of any other invasions of Judah.

19:8 returned . . . departed: The Rabshakeh had been doing everything in his power to persuade Jerusalem to surrender without being attacked. But when he returned with his report, he found that his king was already distracted with another war and had already moved his army away. Still, the Rabshakeh did not give up, as v. 9 describes.

19:9–11 Since **Tirhakah** did not become **king** until 690 B.C., there is an apparent problem in the chronology of this verse. However, it is possible that the biblical author merely calls Tirhakah by the title he was best known by at the time of writing.

19:12, 13 This is not the **Eden** of Genesis, but an area known today as Bit-Adini, south of Haran (Ezek. 27:23; Amos 1:5).

19:14 In a great act of faith, Hezekiah brought Sennacherib's threatening letter **before the Lord**. Of course, Hezekiah understood that the Lord already knew the contents of the letter. But by this symbolic action, Hezekiah expressed his own utter dependence on God for deliverance.

19:15–19 Hezekiah prayed: Hezekiah knew that there is a greater King than the king of Assyria (18:19). Hezekiah's trust in the Lord was demonstrated in his habit of prayer (20:2), and his prayer was answered favorably (vv. 20–34).

19:20 Isaiah gave him a direct answer from the Lord. This helps explain one of the ways in which the Lord spoke to the kings during the monarchy. Prophets could communicate the message from God to the king. **Because you have prayed:** The Lord rewarded His king with a promise of deliverance based in large part on his practical faith in God.

19:21–34 Isaiah's words here are also found, with slight variations, in Is. 37:22–35. The addressee of this oracle is not Hezekiah; it was given to him for his encouragement. It is addressed to the Rabshakeh, who had brought a message to Hezekiah from the "great king of Assyria." Now Hezekiah would be able to respond with a message that came from a much higher authority!

19:21 The virgin: Here we sense God's approval of Jerusalem. When God speaks to His people concerning their sin, His speech can be direct, confrontational, and sometimes scathing. But when He speaks to others about His people and His City, He uses favorable language. They are, on the ideal level, like a virgin daughter to

Him. **the daughter of Zion:** As elsewhere in the OT (Zeph. 3:14), this phrase should be written "daughter Zion," without the "of." Zion does not *have* a daughter; rather, Zion *is* the daughter. Zion (Jerusalem) is God's daughter whom He will guard and protect as only a father would.

19:22–24 God's answer to Hezekiah's prayer came once again (vv. 6, 7) through Isaiah (vv. 20, 21). **Holy One of Israel** is characteristic of Isaiah's own manner of referring to God. He uses the phrase 26 times (Is. 6:3). Sennacherib needed to know that his boastful pride blasphemed the sovereign and holy God of all nations. The verses that follow indicate that God knew not only the boasts, but the most inward thoughts of the Assyrian king.

19:25, 26 Did you not hear: Here the Lord answered the sarcasm of the Rabshakeh (18:17–25). In the manner of an ancient insult, God both asserted His own work on behalf of Judah and ridiculed the enemy who seemed completely unaware of reality.

19:27, 28 But I know: The Assyrians had a great gap in their understanding of reality; they did not include the living God in their processes. But they, in turn, were fully known. **Hook** and **bridle** are used to restrain animals (Ps. 32:9; Ezek. 19:4). Because the Assyrian kings often treated their prisoners of war in such fashion, Sennacherib would understand the threat only too well.

19:29 God graciously gave Hezekiah a **sign** (20:9–11) of His good intentions for His people. Despite the fact that the Assyrian invasion had adversely affected the crops for that year and the next, by the third year the fields would again yield a plentiful harvest. Even as a natural growth would remain for the two years preceding the harvest of the third year, so God left in Israel a spiritual remnant that would in a future day swell into a mighty harvest of souls (Joel 2:12–14; Mic. 2:12, 13; Zeph. 3:8–20).

19:30, 31 The promises in these verses were both for the immediate situation, for more remote times of regathering, and ultimately the final regathering of the Jewish people into their land in the time of the coming Messiah. **zeal:** The authenticating sign for the accomplishment of this promise is the solemn oath of God Himself (Is. 9:7).

19:32–34 The promises concerning the remnant (vv. 30, 31) have several phases in their fulfillment, leading up to and including the coming of the Messiah. In vv. 32–34, however, the message of Yahweh was specific and direct to the current issue, the bragging words of the Rabshakeh. Yahweh stated strongly that the Rabshakeh and the Assyrians would not find it possible to shoot even one arrow against Jerusalem.

19:32, 33 not come into this city: While Sennacherib later boasted of taking some 46 Judean cities, with reference to Jerusalem he could only report that he made Hezekiah "prisoner in Jerusalem, his royal residence, like a bird in a cage." God's defense and deliverance of Jerusalem demonstrated his faithfulness to the Davidic covenant (v. 34) in the face of blasphemous insults (vv. 22, 23, 27, 28; 18:34, 35).

19:34, 35 I . . . My own sake: As in the case of the redemption of Israel from Egypt at the time of the Exodus, so in the deliverance of Israel from the present trouble, God Himself would do it. He would not delegate the work of salvation to a lesser power.

19:36 departed: As God had promised through His prophet Isaiah (vv. 32–34), Sennacherib did not come against the city of Jerusalem.

19:37 The name **Nisroch** has been identified as the god Nusku or a corrupted form of Marduk, the traditional god of Mesopotamia. The events depicted here took place 20 years after God's deliverance of Jerusalem. When his father was assassinated, Esarhaddon took the throne and ruled from 681 to 668 B.C.

20:1 This phrase **in those days** simply designates the period of Hezekiah's reign. While some scholars believe that the events of ch. 20 took place after those of 18:13—19:37, the mention of Merodach-Baladan (v. 12) tends to favor an earlier time. The author of Kings often writes thematically rather than by arranging details chronologically. Thus, before talking of other events, and having mentioned the Assyrian invasion that brought the demise of the unfaithful northern kingdom (18:9–12), the author may have chosen to discuss the famous deliverance of the southern kingdom from the Assyrian threat due to Hezekiah's trust (18:13—19:37).

20:2, 3 Contrast the action of the sick Hezekiah with that of Ahaziah in 1:1, 2. Hezekiah was a great man of prayer (19:1, 14, 15). **I have walked before you:** Hezekiah's prayer recognized that although all of life is in God's hands, God is also a Rewarder of those who faithfully serve Him (Deut. 5:30–33; 30:15, 16). Hezekiah's habit of prayer would once again serve him well (vv. 5, 6; 19:14–19).

20:4–6 The pattern of divine revelation to Hezekiah was through His prophet Isaiah (19:20); compare also the word of God through Jonah to King Jeroboam II (14:25). **defend this city:** The Lord promised deliverance for Jerusalem.

20:7, 8 The practice of applying **figs** to an ulcerated sore is well attested in the records of the ancient Middle East, being mentioned as early as the Ras Shamra (Ugaritic) tablets of the second millennium B.C.

20:9–10 Once more the Lord provided a **sign** of His superintending intervention (19:29–31). Unlike his father Ahaz who cared little about a divine sign (Is. 7:12), Hezekiah welcomed it (vv. 10, 11). Hezekiah's underlying trust in the Lord (18:5) surfaced repeatedly throughout his reign.

20:11, 12 Berodach-Baladan, or more properly Merodach-Baladan, was a Chaldean king who twice ruled in Babylon (721–710, 703 B.C.). A perennial enemy of Assyria, he was twice defeated by them and cast out from Babylon. His search for allies in his resistance to Assyria may have occasioned the embassy to Hezekiah, especially because he had heard of Hezekiah's miraculous deliverance from the Assyrian army (2 Chr. 32:31).

20:12–15 One of the remarkable features of the Bible is that it does not gloss over the faults of its best heroes and heroines. This is a case in point. This account of the foolishness of Hezekiah follows immediately on the narrative of his great trust in the Lord (vv. 1–11).

20:16–18 Isaiah's messages of judgment were as important as his messages of mercy (ch. 19; 20:1–11). **all . . . shall be carried to Babylon:** Hezekiah's enthusiastic reception of Merodach- Baladan's ambassadors and disclosure of his wealth to them would be remembered in a future time when Babylon was no longer Judah's friend. Even before the fall of Jerusalem to Babylon (586 B.C.), Hezekiah's son Manasseh was carried off to Babylon by an Assyrian king (2 Chr. 33:11). Isaiah pointed out Hezekiah's foolishness.

20:19 The word . . . is good: Although Hezekiah recognized that Isaiah's dire prophecy was for a future day, he humbly acknowledged his folly in putting his people in danger.

20:20, 21 a pool and a tunnel: Hezekiah dug a tunnel between the spring of Gihon and the Pool of Siloam to bring a ready supply of water within the eastern wall of Jerusalem, a deed that would prove especially helpful in time of siege. It was a remarkable feat. The workmen excavated from opposite ends through 1777 feet of rock, following a double-"s" pattern. The engineering, which involved following the seams in the limestone, is still astonishing to modern visitors of the site.

21:1, 2 Manasseh: This wicked king bore the same name as the older son of Joseph (Gen. 41:51). His reign of **fifty-five years** (697–642 B.C.) was the longest of any of the kings of the divided kingdom. Externally, the period was one of political stability. It is known as the Assyrian Peace, an era in which the kings Esarhaddon (681–668 B.C.) and Ashurbanipal (668–626 B.C.) reigned and brought the Assyrian empire to its zenith. However, the length of Manasseh's reign

does not indicate a good rule, but rather God's persevering mercy and faithfulness to the Davidic covenant (2 Chr. 33:10–13).

21:3 high places . . . Baal . . . wooden image: All that Hezekiah had done removing the wickedness of Canaanite religion from Israel was reversed by his son. The wording suggests not simply that he allowed the rebuilding of these obscene images, but that he actively directed their construction. **host of heaven:** Worship of heavenly bodies was strictly forbidden in the Law of God (Deut. 4:19; 17:2–7) and was condemned strongly by Israel's prophets (Is. 47:13; Amos 5:26). Yet Manasseh

Bronze likeness of Baal, Canaanite fertility god. King Manasseh of Israel encouraged idolatry by building altars for worship of this pagan deity (2 Kin. 21:3).

paid no attention to either the Law or the prophets (vv. 7, 8; 2 Chr. 33:2–10).

21:4–9 The list of religious outrages of Manasseh seems unbelievably perverse. He even brought objects of pagan worship and obscene symbols of the fertility religion of Canaan into the temple itself (vv. 4, 5, 7). All that had been accomplished by the relatively godly kings following the purge of Jehu (15:34) and by the very godly king Hezekiah (18:4–6) was undone by this reprobate. But wicked as Manasseh was,

God heard his prayer when he repented and did good (2 Chr. 33:12–16).

21:10, 11 The author of Chronicles (2 Chr. 33:10, 11) reports that Manasseh's failure to heed **the prophets** of God led to his being taken prisoner by the Assyrian king. The chronicler also reports Manasseh's repentance, restoration, and subsequent reform efforts (2 Chr. 33:12, 13, 15, 16), all of which came too late to stop Judah's ongoing apostasy. As a result, with the accession of Manasseh's son Amon (642–640 B.C.), Judah's spiritual wickedness surfaced again (vv. 20–22).

21:12 his ears will tingle: The announcement of such a fearsome judgment was designed to bring the king to repentance. If God's purpose were merely to bring judgment, He would have done so without an announcement.

21:13 the measuring line of Samaria: The figures in this verse are marvelously powerful. If the people had any realization of the horrors that had befallen their sister city to the north, they would not want to be "measured" by the same implements that had designed Samaria's destruction. **as one wipes a dish:** God would soon bring a judgment so terrible that it would never be forgotten.

21:14 God's declaration that He would **forsake the remnant** does not mean He would abolish the Davidic covenant (Ps. 89:30–37). Rather, the meaning of God's word here is that Judah, the political remnant of God's kingdom (17:18), would also know chastisement for its sin.

21:15 since the day: The story of the OT is not a record of God's anger, but of the *delay* of the exercise of His wrath.

21:16, 17 innocent blood: In times of deep wickedness true believers often lose their lives (Joel 3:19). Innocent blood may also refer to human sacrifice (v. 6; 2 Chr. 33:6).

21:18 garden of Uzza: His burial place apparently was not among the other kings of Judah. Some have suggested that the garden of Uzza was a sacred shrine to an astral deity.

21:19–22 Amon: This wicked king followed in the path of his father Manasseh, much as Ahaziah of Israel followed in the path of his father Ahab (1 Kin. 22:51–53).

21:23–26 conspired against him: No reason is assigned for the conspiracy that brought about Amon's assassination. While it may have had some connection with the international crisis that precipitated Ashurbanipal's renewed attention to the west, Amon's own wickedness may have provided a sufficient cause. The assassins were themselves executed.

22:1 The name **Josiah** means "The Lord Supports." Like the name of Cyrus (Is. 44:28; 45:1) and of the city of Bethlehem (Mic. 5:2), the name Josiah was announced by a prophet long before the time of his birth (1 Kin. 13:1, 2).

22:2 what was right: The young Josiah apparently was in the hands of godly advisors, one of whom may have been the prophet Zephaniah. In any case, his own concern for righteousness led to reform early in his reign (2 Chr. 34:3–7).

22:3 In his **eighteenth year** of reign (c. 622 B.C.), Josiah began extensive repairs on the temple (vv. 4–7; 2 Chr. 34:8–13).

22:4 Hilkiah the high priest: This man was a major figure in the revival of true religion that young Josiah accomplished. The work of restoring the temple was under his direction.

22:5–7 The careful accounting for the money used in the restoration of the temple is akin to that in the time of King Joash of Judah and of the high priest associated with him, Jehoiada (12:9–16).

22:8, 9 By **the Book of the Law** may be meant either parts or all of the Pentateuch. This

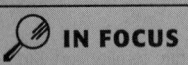 **IN FOCUS**   **"wooden image"**

(Heb. *'asherah*) (2 Kin. 17:10; 21:7; 23:6) Strong's #842: This word is both the name of a Canaanite fertility goddess (Asherah) and the designation of a wooden object representing her. In the OT, the word is rarely used as a proper name (21:7; 23:4; 1 Kin. 15:13; 18:19); far more often it is used for a carved image (21:7; 1 Kin. 14:15). Asherahs were placed on hills. Frequently altars and other images were next to these wooden images (1 Kin. 14:23; 2 Chr. 31:1; 33:19). The Lord warned His people before they entered the Promised Land that this false religion would snare them if they did not banish it from the land (Ex. 34:12–16; Deut. 7:2–6; 12:3; 16:21). Nevertheless, the problem persisted during much of the periods of the judges and kings (Judg. 3:7; 1 Kin. 16:33), although occasional reforms did seek to eliminate these images (18:4; Judg. 6:25–30). The prophets consistently sounded a clarion call to abandon such false worship, for God's judgment was coming (Is. 17:8; 27:9; Jer. 17:2; Mic. 5:14).

book, though placed by the side of the ark of the covenant (Deut. 31:26), may have been lost, set aside, or hidden during the wicked reigns of Manasseh and Amon.

22:10–13 read it before the king: This is the dramatic event that shaped Josiah's reign. Imagine what it must have been for the young king to hear the Word of God read for the first time. **tore his clothes:** Once again (19:1) a godly king tore his clothes in genuine remorse. Josiah's great qualities are seen in his desiring prophetic sanction for his new walk. He did not wish to move on with his own plan without a clear confirmation from the Lord.

22:14 Although **Huldah the prophetess** is mentioned only here (and in 2 Chr. 34:22–28) in the Scriptures, some have suggested that her husband Shallum was related to Jeremiah (Jer. 32:7–12).

22:15 Huldah takes her place beside several prophetesses recorded in the Scriptures, such as Miriam (Ex. 15:20) and Deborah (Judg. 4:4). This woman was an authoritative agent for the transmission of the word of God to the highest authorities in the land of Judah. She served at the same time as other godly prophets, such as Jeremiah and Zephaniah.

22:16 all the words: The threat of calamity for apostasy that the king heard may have been intended to reinforce the message of the parts of the Book of the Law that were found when the temple was being repaired and were read to the king (Deut. 28:15–68).

22:17–19 First was the bad news, addressed principally to the wicked who had forsaken God. Second was the good news, that Josiah would be delivered from impending judgment, basically due to his piety in a very difficult time.

22:20 in peace: Huldah's good word for Josiah personally was that he would not see the calamity that God was going to bring upon the people. Josiah's subsequent death in battle (23:29, 30) was not at issue in Huldah's prophecy. Like his godly grandfather Hezekiah, the righteous Josiah would not live to see God's future judgment of Judah (20:19).

23:1 all the elders: We may contrast Jehu's great gathering of the priests and prophets of Baal, in anticipation of his great "sacrifice" (10:18–31).

23:2, 3 he read . . . the Book of the Covenant: Like Moses (Ex. 24:3–8) and Joshua (Josh. 8:34, 35) before him, Josiah followed the ancient standard for godly leadership (Deut. 17:18–20; 31:9–13) and assembled the people to renew the covenant (Josh. 24). The king's own spiritual reaction and the reforms that he enacted (2 Chr. 35:1–19) suggest that the texts dealing with covenant obligations and sanctions (Lev. 26; Deut. 28) were a part of the public reading.

23:4 Articles of pagan worship had been taken to the **fields of Kidron** in the reforms of Asa (1 Kin. 15:13) and Hezekiah (2 Chr. 29:16; 30:14). **to Bethel:** Carrying the remaining ashes of pagan religious articles to Bethel was a bold condemnation of both the pagan religious rites and the place associated with them (1 Kin. 12:28–30; Amos 4:4, 5). Thus Josiah's reforms spilled over into the northern kingdom as well.

23:5 idolatrous priests: The term used here is also used by Zephaniah, who employs it of those priests who led the rites associated with Baal and with star worship of various kinds (Zeph. 1:4). These priests had been appointed by Judah's past kings but functioned outside the divinely established priesthood. Hosea had condemned the idolatrous priests who officiated in the calf worship at Bethel (Hos. 10:5).

23:6 Although destroyed by Hezekiah (18:4), **wooden images** associated with the worship of Asherah had been reintroduced by Manasseh (21:7) and also by Amon (21:21; 13:6).

23:7–9 perverted persons: Sacred prostitution was part of the debased practices of Canaanite religion (1 Kin. 14:24; 15:12; 22:46). The horrible thing here is not just that these perverted persons were practicing their trade in Jerusalem, but that they actually had places for their **booths** in the temple precincts.

23:10 Topheth . . . Molech: Some scholars equate Molech with a pagan deity such as the Ammonite god Milcom (1 Kin. 11:5) or an individual Canaanite god (Lev. 20:1–5), whose worship was carried on in Jerusalem. Other scholars think that Molech was the name of a type of child sacrifice associated with Baal (Jer. 7:31, 32; 19:5, 6; 32:35). Evidence of child sacrifice has been found in the excavations at the Phoenician city of Carthage. **Valley of the Son of Hinnom:** The heinous rites carried on in this place, and the later custom of utilizing the area as a dump where refuse was burned, furnished a basis for applying its Hebrew name (*gê hinnom*) to the site (Gehenna) in the NT, where it refers to the sinful, worthless works of believers who are not walking with the Lord. The context of Matt. 10:28 and Mark 9:43 is the teaching on *reward* (Matt. 10:41, 42; Mark 9:41). The ideas of Gehenna are latent in James' warning against the misuse of the tongue (James 3:6).

23:11–14 horses . . . dedicated to the sun: Excavations at Jerusalem have uncovered a sacred shrine used in solar worship and dating from the time of Jehoshaphat. Small horses with solar disks on their foreheads have been found both at Jerusalem and Hazor.

23:15–17 Josiah's actions were prophesied long ago by a prophet who denounced Jeroboam I's **altar that was at Bethel** (1 Kin.

13:26–32). The literal fulfillment of that prophecy confirms that this earlier man of God was a true prophet (Deut. 18:22).

23:18, 19 the prophet . . . from Samaria: The prophet from Samaria was the old prophet of Bethel (1 Kin. 13:11). Samaria is the name for an entire area, not just the city that was later the capital of the northern kingdom (1 Kin. 13:32; 16:23, 24). After the death of the man of God who had denounced Jeroboam I's altar at Bethel, the aged prophet of Bethel requested that at his death he should be buried in Bethel beside that prophet of Judah.

23:20 priests of the high places: Because these priests were not Levites, they were executed as God's Law demands (Deut. 17:2–7). True priests of the Lord who officiated at the high places in Judah were spared. The shrines were demolished (vv. 8, 9). Finally, these priests could not officiate at the temple in Jerusalem. They were treated much as priests with bodily defects (Lev. 21:17–23).

23:21, 22 the Passover: The restoration of religious places was part of the revival of spiritual worship. **since the days of the judges:** Although Hezekiah had held a Passover (2 Chr. 30), he had done so with some modification of the Law (2 Chr. 30:13–20). Accordingly, Josiah's meeting of the strict requirements of the Law (2 Chr. 35:1–19) was truly unparalleled since the days of the judges. Moreover, God's Law was observed by believers from Judah and Israel alike (2 Chr. 35:18). This last notice reminds us that we overstate things when we speak of the "lost tribes of Israel." It is correct that there was never a general return of the people who were depopulated from the northern kingdom as there was of those who returned to Judah from the captivity of the southern kingdom. Nonetheless, there were numerous people from the northern kingdom who drifted down to Judah in the years following the fall of Samaria. Others must also have made their way back to the land of Israel in various ways over a period of time. In the NT period there is evidence of peoples from all of the original twelve tribes.

23:23–25 no king: Josiah's following of the Law was unparalleled among the kings of Israel and Judah. Like his grandfather Hezekiah, who was famed for being without equal in his trust of the Lord (18:5), Josiah was truly a righteous king. Because of their outstanding examples of godliness, the authors of Kings and Chronicles devote considerable space to their reigns (chs. 18—20; 22:1—23:30; 2 Chr. 29—32; 34; 35).

23:26, 27 Despite their efforts, Judah's sin was so entrenched that judgment was inevitable (17:18, 19; 23:26, 27; Lam. 1:5). Even though Manasseh repented, he still reaped the results of his sin.

23:28–30 Pharaoh Necho (609–594 B.C.) was the recently crowned king of Egypt's twenty-sixth dynasty. During the long years of Josiah's reign (640–609 B.C.), Assyrian power had steadily crumbled until, as Nahum had predicted, Nineveh itself had fallen (612 B.C.) to a coalition of Chaldeans, Medes, and others. The surviving Assyrian forces had regrouped at Haran. Because Egypt was a long-standing ally of Assyria, Necho journeyed northward to help the beleaguered Assyrians. Josiah's deployment of his forces in the Valley of Megiddo was an attempt to prevent the Egyptians from aiding the Assyrian forces at Haran. Although Pharaoh Necho would be delayed sufficiently so that Haran would be lost to the Assyrians, Josiah's action ultimately cost him his life (2 Chr. 35:20–25).

23:31–36 Jehoahaz (called Shallum in Jer. 22:11) was Josiah's third son (24:18; 1 Chr. 3:15). The name Jehoahaz means "The Lord Has Grasped." This is the same name as the king of Israel, the son of Jehu (10:35). Johanan, Josiah's first son, apparently had died and Eliakim (or Jehoiakim), the second son, was bypassed. A fourth son, Mattaniah (or Zedekiah), would eventually ascend to the throne and rule as Judah's last king (598–586 B.C.). Jehoahaz's reign of **three months** came to an end with the return of Pharaoh Necho from Haran. Jehoahaz was summoned to Riblah, Necho's headquarters in Syria. Then he was led away to die in Egypt. His brother Eliakim was installed on the throne with his name changed to Jehoiakim. Judah thus became no more than a vassal of Egypt. The curse for Judah's disobedience was about to fall (Deut. 28:64–68).

23:37 did evil: Jehoiakim's short reign (608–598 B.C.) was noted for its extreme wickedness (2 Chr. 36:5, 8). Jeremiah depicts him as a despicable monster who took advantage of his people (Jer. 22:13, 14, 17), filled the land with every sort of vice and violence (Jer. 18:18–20), and opposed all that was holy (Jer. 25:1–7). Unlike his father Josiah, who led the nation in reformation at the hearing of the Word of God (22:11; 23:1–25), Jehoiakim went so far as to cut up and burn a scroll of Scripture (Jer. 36:21–24) and to kill Urijah, a true prophet of God (Jer. 26:20–23).

24:1 After defeating the Assyrians and Egyptians at the Battle of Carchemish (605 B.C.), Nebuchadnezzar invaded Judah and made the country his vassal. He took Daniel and other notables to Babylon as spoils of war. Nebuchadnezzar, who succeeded his father as king of Babylon in 605 B.C. and reigned until 562 B.C., boasted in his annals of 605 and 604 B.C. of the subjugation and submission of all Syria and

Palestine. Jehoiakim served Nebuchadnezzar **three years** and then rebelled, perhaps finding courage to do so when Pharaoh Necho succeeded in turning back the Babylonians at the Egyptian border in 601 B.C.

24:2 The name **Chaldeans** originally applied to certain inhabitants of southern Mesopotamia. But by the neo-Babylonian period, the term Chaldean had become identified with Babylonians, and Babylonia was called Chaldea. After the fall of the Chaldean or neo-Babylonian empire, the term Chaldean was used to mean "soothsayer" (Dan. 2:2). In this verse the ethnic sense of the term is meant. Not only Chaldeans but raiding parties from nearby countries harassed Judah.

24:3–7 Because Jehoiakim and Judah had reproduced **the sins of Manasseh** (21:1–17), God's judgment was inevitable. Jehoiakim himself would die soon, even as Nebuchadnezzar was launching a second campaign into Judah (598 B.C.).

24:8–11 The name **Jehoiachin** means "The Lord Has Appointed." **eighteen years old:** Because the scriptural descriptions of Jehoiachin seem to represent him as a mature young man (Jer. 22:24–30; Ezek. 19:6), Jehoiachin's age at accession was probably eighteen rather than eight, as given elsewhere in some manuscripts (2 Chr. 36:9).

24:12, 13 Jehoiakim apparently had died before Nebuchadnezzar arrived at Jerusalem, because it was **Jehoiachin** who was carried off captive with other leaders of Judah (such as Ezekiel; Ezek. 1:1). He had reigned only three months (v. 8); the year was 598 B.C. Jeremiah called him "Jeconiah" and "Coniah" (Jer. 22:24, 28).

24:14 Ten thousand is probably a round number for deportees of all types from Judah and Jerusalem. The figure probably includes various categories of exiles, such as those mentioned in v. 16.

24:15 carried Jehoiachin captive: Jehoiachin's captivity (2 Chr. 36:9, 10) was prophesied in Jer. 22:24–27. Unlike Jehoahaz, who was carried off into Egypt previously (23:33) and disappears from the pages of sacred history, Jehoiachin's eventual release is recorded twice (25:27–30; Jer. 52:31–34).

24:16, 17 Mattaniah is Josiah's youngest son. His name means "The Gift of the Lord." All three of Josiah's sons who succeeded him as king reigned under a throne name: Shallum (1 Chr. 3:15; Jer. 22:11) ruled as Jehoahaz (23:31); Eliakim as Jehoiakim (23:34); and Mattaniah as Zedekiah. Likewise, Jeconiah (1 Chr. 3:16; Jer. 24:1), Jehoiakim's son, ruled as Jehoiachin (24:8).

24:18, 19 Mattaniah, who reigned under

the name **Zedekiah,** came to the throne in 598 B.C. This was the year of Jehoiakim's death and Jehoiachin's captivity. Zedekiah reigned until the fall of Jerusalem in 586 B.C.

24:20 Zedekiah rebelled: The king of Judah foolishly relied on the Egyptians under Pharaoh Apries (or Hophra, Jer. 44:30) for help (Ezek. 17:15–18). Apries had recently succeeded Psamtik II (594–588 B.C.) on the throne. He had great plans for Egypt's renewed glory. Unfortunately, his plans were not realized. Although Apries challenged Nebuchadnezzar by attacking Phoenicia and coming to Zedekiah's assistance (Jer. 37:5), he was not able to deliver Judah (Jer. 37:7, 8). His own reign ended in a coup d'état that ultimately cost him his life.

25:1, 2 eleventh year: The siege of Jerusalem lasted for nearly two years (v. 1). A comparison with other OT texts provides the

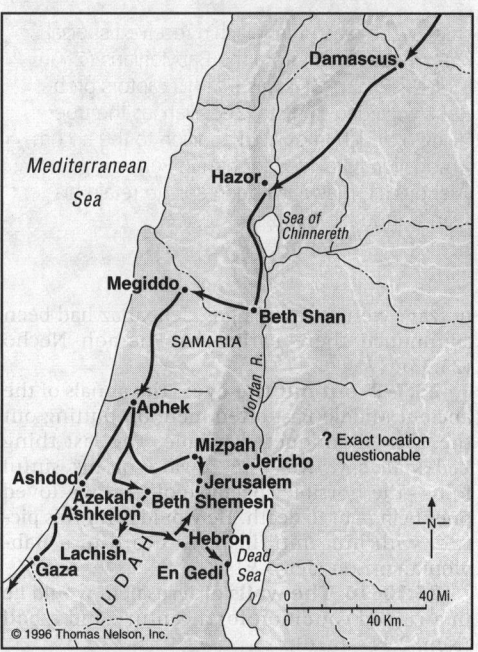

Nebuchadnezzar's Campaigns Against Judah (605–586 B.C.)

Nebuchadnezzar became king of Babylon in 605 B.C. and conducted several campaigns in Palestine. He squelched Jehoiakim's rebellion in about 602 B.C., deported Jehoiachin in 597 B.C., and destroyed Jerusalem in 586 B.C.

following information concerning the last days of Jerusalem: breaching Jerusalem's walls by the Babylonians and Zedekiah's flight (vv. 3–7; Jer. 39:2–7; 52:6–11); capture of Jerusalem and its citizens (vv. 8–12; Jer. 39:8–10; 52:12–16; 2 Chr. 36:19); looting the city (vv. 13–17; Jer.

52:17–23; 2 Chr. 36:18); executing the officials and deporting the citizenry (vv. 18–21; Jer. 52:24–30; 2 Chr. 36:17, 20, 21), sparing Jeremiah (Jer. 39:11–14).

25:3, 4 Zedekiah's escape route lay between **two walls** near the royal garden at the southeastern corner of the city.

25:5, 6 After his capture, Zedekiah was taken to **Riblah** on the Orontes River in Syria, which was the field headquarters for Nebuchad-

INSIGHT

Jehoiachin's Special Treatment

One reason Jehoiachin received special treatment from the Babylonians (2 Kin. 25:27–30) was that his captors probably regarded him, not Zedekiah, as the true king of Judah in exile. In addition to the accommodations provided for him in Babylon, Jehoiachin may have been able to retain his lands in Judah through a trustee.

nezzar's western campaigns. Jehoahaz had been summoned there earlier by Pharaoh Necho (23:33).

25:7–9 put out the eyes: The annals of the ancient Middle East often mention putting out the eyes of conquered people. The last thing Zedekiah saw was the reward of his sinful folly—the horrible spectacle of his own loved ones being put to death. He would carry this picture with him until his own death in a Babylonian prison (Jer. 52:11).

25:10–16 The walls of Jerusalem would lie in a ruined condition for a century and a half (Neh. 2:11—6:16).

25:17 Three cubits may be the height of the capitals not including the upper portion of ornamental work, for 1 Kin. 7:16 and Jer. 52:22 record the height of the capitals as five cubits.

25:18–20 Although **Seraiah** was executed at Riblah (v. 21), his son Jehozadak was simply deported (1 Chr. 6:15). Through Jehozadak's line would come Ezra, the priest and great reformer, who one day would return to Jerusalem and take up Seraiah's work (Ezra 7:1). The second martyred priest **Zephaniah** may be the priest mentioned by Jeremiah (Jer. 21:1; 29:5). Jerusalem would be less prone to future rebellions with the chief religious and civil officials gone.

25:21 Like Israel before it (17:18), Judah was **carried away** captive because of its sinful apostasy.

25:22 Gedaliah: Gedaliah's father Ahikam had supported Jeremiah in his struggles with the apostate officials of Judah (Jer. 26:24). Gedaliah's training and his descent from a family noted for its antiestablishment stance doubtless made him acceptable to the Babylonians. The prophet Jeremiah, spared by the Babylonians (Jer. 39:11–14; 40:1–5), was allowed to stay and assist Gedaliah in the process of reconstruction in Judah (Jer. 40:6). There is confirmation of Gedaliah's importance in a seal impression recovered at Lachish mentioning him as "over the house," that is, a senior administrator.

25:23–26 Mizpah had long been a center of spiritual and political prominence (1 Sam. 10:17; 1 Kin. 15:22). It was an ideal location for the provincial government. **Jaazaniah:** This name appears on a seal impression found in Mizpah. The murderous deeds of **Ishmael** and the role of **Johanan** in the events are detailed by Jeremiah (Jer. 40:7—43:7).

25:27 Evil-Merodach succeeded Nebuchadnezzar and reigned a short time (561–560 B.C.). Tablets from the reign of Nabonidus (555–539 B.C.) record the daily rations of Jehoiachin who is called "Yaukin, king of the land of Yahud (Judah)."

25:28–30 spoke kindly: Evil-Merodach's kindness toward Jehoiachin brings the Book of Kings to an end—on a ray of hope. Exile is the end neither of Israel nor of the Davidic line.

The First Book of

Chronicles

■

FIRST CHRONICLES IS AN INSPIRATIONAL HISTORY. Writing after the Exile, the author sought to inspire the remnant of Israelites with their extraordinary spiritual heritage. Appropriately, the book focuses on David. He was not only Israel's great king, but also one of Israel's greatest spiritual leaders. When he became king, one of his first priorities was to establish the worship of God as the center of Israel's national life.

Amidst a great celebration, David brought the ark of the covenant to Jerusalem and appointed priests to minister regularly before it (chs. 15; 16). His actions demonstrated his concern that all of Israel would "give to the LORD the glory due His name" (16:29). This was Israel's extraordinary spiritual legacy: true worship of the living God.

It is evident that Chronicles is the result of a compilation process. The chronicler made use of the books of Samuel and Kings for about half the narrative. Also, the genealogies in the beginning of the book are largely derived from the Pentateuch. The compiler even cites some of the sources. Among these are the genealogical records of the various tribes (7:9, 40), the book of the kings of Israel (9:1), and the books of Samuel, Nathan, and Gad (29:29).

A number of accounts in Chronicles parallel parts of Samuel and Kings. The fact that these accounts do not match word for word has led some scholars to assume that the chronicler was not concerned about accuracy in citation, or that the authors of all the books drew upon another common source. In any case, the inspiration and authority of 1 Chronicles is not at stake. Writing about the same events, the compiler of 1 Chronicles simply emphasized a different perspective on them than did the authors of Samuel and Kings. The synoptic Gospels function the same way. Each Gospel presents some of the same stories of Jesus in a different way. Each gives us new details and a new perspective on the event.

This chronicler's different emphases explain many of the differences between the narratives of Chronicles and Samuel. Some of the other apparent contradictions, especially in matters of spelling and numbers, can be explained as inadvertence in copying and text transmission. Numerals appear to have been written in notations that could easily be confused, and most of the deviations between Chronicles and Samuel can be accounted for in this manner. In many instances, the discrepancies are only apparent and suitable ways have been suggested to harmonize them. In any case, none of them threatens the inspiration and inerrancy of the original text.

Writing approximately when the Israelites returned from captivity, the chronicler wanted to emphasize the Israelites' continuity with their past. The remnant was returning to Jerusalem to rebuild the temple because of the promises God had given to David many years before (Ezra 7:10–23). God's promises were still in effect, even though the people had been in exile.

The long genealogical section in First Chronicles emphasizes this continuity with the past (chs. 1—9). The genealogies point out that the promises to David were founded on God's ancient promises to the patriarchs. God had pledged to Abraham that He would make him the father of a great nation, one through which He would bless the whole earth (Gen. 12:1–3). God had also promised that a king would rule over this special nation (Gen. 17:6). It was revealed to Jacob that the king would descend specifically from Jacob's son Judah (Gen. 49:10). Finally, the genealogy in the Book of Ruth explains the link between the promise and the fulfillment by tracing the line of Judah through his son Perez to King David (Ruth 4:18–22). God had faithfully fulfilled His promise.

First Chronicles recounts the lineage of the people of God's promise and emphasizes the connection between Perez and King David (2:5–15). God would establish His reign upon the earth through David's royal line (17:7–15; Gen. 17:7, 8; 2 Sam. 7). The kings God had promised to Abraham would begin with David and culminate in the One who would reign forever, Jesus (17:14; Matt. 9:27; 12:23; Mark 10:47, 48; Luke 18:38). God had given the promise to David, and the faithful remnant inherited that same promise.

Since the chronicler wanted to encourage the returning Israelites, he focused on the glories of David's reign—his conquest of Jerusalem (11:4–9), his heroic soldiers (11:10–47), his victories over the Philistines (18:1–12), and his celebration when bringing the ark to Jerusalem (15:25–29). On the other hand, the author of Samuel told the story of David as an objective, realistic biography that did not overlook David's sins and failures. While it does not depict David as spiritually and morally perfect (13:9–14; 21:1, 8), Chronicles surprisingly omits the stories that reveal David's weakness—his affair with Bathsheba, his murder of Uriah (2 Sam. 11), and his estrangement from his son Absalom (2 Sam. 15). These are not omitted to give a false impression of David's character, for the books of Samuel recount these incidents in detail. Instead, Chronicles was written to inspire the remnant to follow in the spiritual footsteps of David.

At a time when the Israelites were rebuilding the nation and the temple (Ezra 3:7–13), the chronicler painted a picture of David's kingdom as a kingdom founded on the true worship of God. Not the throne but the tabernacle and temple were the focus of David's kingdom. Chronicles extensively describes how David moved the ark of the covenant to a suitable place of worship (13:1—16:3), appointed appropriate religious personnel (16:4–6, 37–43; 23:1—26:32), and made plans for building a permanent temple (chs. 22; 28; 29). The theme of Chronicles is that God Himself established David's kingdom (29:10, 11) in fulfillment of His promises to Abraham, Isaac, and Jacob. Through the Davidic covenant, David's kingdom

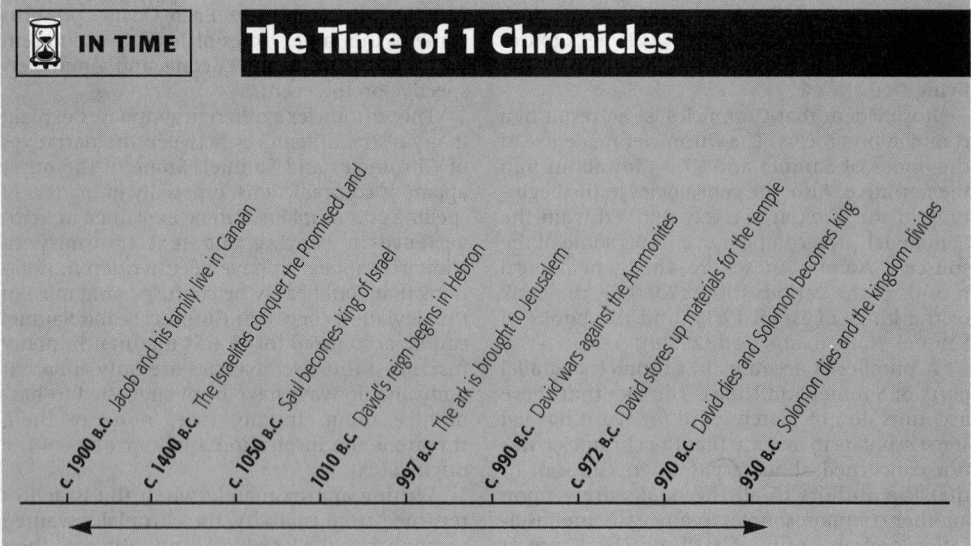

IN TIME | **The Time of 1 Chronicles**

c. 1900 B.C. Jacob and his family live in Canaan
c. 1400 B.C. The Israelites conquer the Promised Land
c. 1050 B.C. Saul becomes king of Israel
1010 B.C. David's reign begins in Hebron
997 B.C. The ark is brought to Jerusalem
c. 990 B.C. David wars against the Ammonites
c. 972 B.C. David stores up materials for the temple
970 B.C. David dies and Solomon becomes king
930 B.C. Solomon dies and the kingdom divides

itself embodies the promise of the future kingdom whose ruler is the great Son of David, Jesus Christ.

Originally both 1 and 2 Chronicles were one book. The overall consistency of style in the book indicates that although several contributors might have worked on it at various stages, one editor shaped the final product.

Jewish tradition identifies the editor as Ezra. This view finds support in the common themes and emphases of Chronicles and the Book of Ezra. Both books focus on the building and dedication of the temple. However, some have argued that the genealogies in 3:17–24 preclude Ezra's authorship because they include as many as eleven generations past Zerubbabel. To include such information, the book would have to have been written as late as the middle of the third century B.C.

On the other hand, it is possible that 3:17–24 may embrace only three generations. If so, a date of approximately 425 B.C. for the completion of Chronicles is quite reasonable. Ezra was active between 460 and 430 B.C. and thus could have incorporated this particular genealogy into the book. In short, the traditional Jewish view that Ezra wrote Chronicles can be accepted if it is remembered that Ezra was a compiler. He used sources and documents that account for the stylistic differences between the Book of Ezra and Chronicles.

Outline

Commentary

1:1–5 Adam, Seth, Enosh: The names of these ancient, pre-Flood characters were included in the genealogical record with people whose historical identities have never been questioned, such as David (2:15) and Zerubbabel (3:19). This indicates that the chronicler had no question as to their historicity.

1:6 Diphath: The genealogy in Gen. 10:3 has "Riphath" here, perhaps resulting from the fact that the Hebrew letters rendered into English as "D" and "R" look virtually the same in the Hebrew script.

1:7, 8 Rodanim referred to the Rhodites, natives of the Greek island of Rhodes. **sons of Ham:** Great nations were indicated by some of the names here: **Cush** referred to the Ethiopians, **Mizraim** to the Egyptians, **Canaan** to the Canaanites.

1:8, 9 Great nations are indicated in the names of the **sons of Ham:** Cush is Ethiopia; Mizraim is Egypt; Canaan is the Canaanites.

1:10, 11 Cush begot Nimrod: It seems that the chronicler used the genealogy of Gen. 10 as the primary source for this genealogy. However, he used it selectively. For example, Gen. 10:9–12 was not included. The apparent purpose of this genealogy was to establish the line between Adam and David, and between David and the reigning Davidic monarch.

1:12 Caphtorim: These people lived in Caphtor (Deut. 2:23), known in ancient Akkadian texts as Kaptara and probably to be identified as Crete. The Caphtorim were related to the Philistines, or the two terms might even be interchangeable (Jer. 47:4; Amos 9:7).

1:13–17 Heth founded the nation of the Hittites, a people in what is now central Turkey who achieved great power and prominence in

IN COMPARISON | How Chronicles and Kings Differ

In 1 and 2 Chronicles we see repeated much of the information found in 1 and 2 Kings. The following chart shows how the books differ:

	First and Second Kings	First and Second Chronicles
Style	realism	idealism
Viewpoint	civil and political	spiritual and moral
Purpose	indictment; to document the failures of God's people	incitement; to encourage the Jews returning from captivity
Focus	northern and southern kingdoms; all kings whether good or evil	southern kingdom of Judah; King David, King Solomon, and the godly kings of Judah
Discussion of the temple and worship	five chapters (1 Kin. 5—8; 2 Kin. 12)	twenty chapters (1 Chr. 13:15; 16; 22—26; 28; 29;2 Chr. 2—7; 24; 29; 30; 34)

the middle of the second millennium B.C. After the Hittite kingdom fell to the Sea Peoples around 1200 B.C., many Hittites settled in enclaves in Syria and Palestine.

1:18 Eber was the ancestor of Abraham, Isaac, and Jacob. The name Hebrew, a derivative of Eber's name, was applied to the Israelites. The central place Eber occupies in the genealogies of Abram in Genesis and 1 Chronicles suggests a connection between the names Hebrew and Eber (1:24–27; Gen. 10:21; 11:10–26). Indeed the name Hebrew may simply mean an "Eberite."

1:19–27 the earth was divided: This refers to the division of the earth's population by the scattering of the human race following the judgment of God on the Tower of Babel. Chronologically, **Peleg** apparently fits about halfway between Shem and Abram (1:24–27), a most suitable place for the Tower of Babel episode.

1:28–31 Isaac was the son of the covenant, so his name occurs first when the names Isaac and Ishmael are mentioned together, even though **Ishmael** was born first. Moreover, Ishmael was the son of Abraham's concubine Hagar—not of his wife Sarai.

1:32, 33 Both Ishmael and **Midian** were descendants of Abraham, Ishmael by a concubine and Midian by another wife Abraham married after Sarah's death (Gen. 25:1, 2). The Ishmaelites and Midianites were tribes that lived in the Arabian deserts: They were frequently associated with each other and even mistaken for one another (Gen. 37:25–28).

1:34–36 Timna was Eliphaz's concubine

(Gen. 36:12). Timna's son Amalek was the founder of the Amalekites, a people that became one of Israel's most persistent enemies (Ex. 17:8–16; Deut. 25:17–19; 1 Sam. 15:1–3).

1:37, 38 Seir was the patriarchal name of the pre-Edomite population of the region east and south of the Dead Sea (Gen. 36:20–30). Esau's daughter-in-law Timna (vv. 35, 36), was the sister of Lotan and daughter of Seir. Thus the people of Seir and the descendants of Esau were related by marriage, and together these two people groups became the kingdom of Edom (v. 43).

1:39–43 the kings ... of Edom: Compare Gen. 36:31–39. These kings were apparently descendants of Esau. The Edomites were ruled by kings several centuries before the Israelites. This fact helps explain Israel's later demand to have "a king to judge us like all the nations" (1 Sam. 8:5). Although the Edomite kings ruled in succession, they were not parts of a dynasty, as the reference to their particular cities makes clear. Apparently Edom did not have a capital, and its kings ruled from whatever place they considered home.

1:44–54 The Hebrew word translated **chiefs** ('allupim) usually referred to military leaders. Compare Gen. 36:40–43. It is not clear if they succeeded the previously mentioned kings, thus suggesting a new and different form of government, or if they served perhaps as military officials along with the kings.

2:1, 2 Compare the order of the **sons of Israel** with Gen. 35:23–26.

2:3 Though he was the fourth son of Jacob (v. 1), **Judah** appears first in the detailed genealogy because the messianic promise was to be channeled through him (Gen. 49:10). Thus the chronicler reveals that his genealogy and his presentation of the events are controlled by theological concerns rather than strict chronology.

2:4, 5 Unlike Genesis but true to his theological purposes, the author does not mention the details of Judah's shameful treatment of his **daughter-in-law** or his subsequent exposure (Gen. 38:12–26). He wants only to establish the lineage between Judah and David. But, of course, he cannot wholly avoid the implication of impropriety, in that he must at least identify who **Tamar** is.

2:6–9 Though the line to David passed through Zerah's brother Perez, Zerah's descendants are mentioned here because of the prominence of Achar (v. 7), called Achan in the narrative of Josh. 7:10–26. **Ethan, Heman, Calcol,** and **Dara** are mentioned because of their role in temple music under King David and their distinction as poets and sages (15:16–19; 1 Kin. 4:29–31).

2:10–14 This genealogy is selective, focusing on only those members important to the lineage. For example, **Nahshon** was head of the tribe of Judah at the time of the wilderness march from Sinai to Kadesh Barnea (Num. 1:7, 2:3; 7:12). He was more than five generations removed from Judah himself (2:4–10), since the time between Judah and Nahshon was over 450 years.

2:15 Jesse had seven sons, **David** being the youngest (compare 1 Sam. 16:10, 11 and 17:12 where it appears that Jesse had eight sons).

2:16, 17 Sisters are rarely mentioned in ancient genealogies. However, this genealogy pays particular attention to the family of David and thus to David's sisters.

2:18–24 This **Caleb** was not the famous companion of Joshua (Num. 13:6; Josh. 14:6, 7), who lived several centuries later, during the conquest of Canaan. In fact, one of this Caleb's descendants Bezalel (v. 20) was a craftsman charged with constructing the wilderness tabernacle (Ex. 31:2).

2:25–41 The sons of Jerahmeel would eventually occupy the Negev, the desert area of southern Judah.

2:42–48 This was the same **Caleb** as that of vv. 18, 19. Here his genealogy is much longer, apparently transmitted through other wives.

2:49, 50 The Caleb of Joshua's time had a **daughter** named **Achsah,** who became the wife of Israel's first judge, Othniel (Judg. 1:12, 13). It might appear that the **Caleb** here in Chronicles must be the same as the later Caleb, but this is ruled out by the consistent use of Caleb throughout the chronicler's genealogy to refer to an earlier individual by that name. The

meaning probably is that Achsah is the "daughter" of the earlier Caleb in the sense that she is his descendant. The later Caleb was doubtless a descendant of the early one, a conclusion supported by the record that both were from the tribe of Judah (2:4, 5, 9, 18, 42; Num. 13:6).

2:51–54 The chronicler recorded Caleb's genealogy because of the significance of Bethlehem, the birthplace of King David. One of Caleb's descendants, Salma, was the founder or **father of Bethlehem.**

2:55 Since the compiler of Chronicles was obviously a scribe, he was interested in tracing, if only briefly, various **families of the scribes.** These families are otherwise unknown, as is **Jabez,** the place they lived. They were **Kenites,** a people related to Israel through Moses' marriage to a Kenite, sometimes referred to as a Midianite (Judg. 4:11). Naming the Kenite scribes here suggests that they were descended from Judah, since the whole context of the passage is the genealogy of Judah. The genealogy also connects them with **Rechab,** the saintly founder of a line of pious Israelites who obeyed the commands of their fathers (Jer. 35:1–19).

3:1–5 The fact that David had six **sons** by six wives in Hebron does not condone polygamy. David had fallen into the ancient custom among kings of marrying the daughters of neighboring kings in order to create allies. Negative results inevitably followed such multiple marriages. David's first son, **Amnon,** raped his half sister Tamar (2 Sam. 13:14)—a deed for which he paid with his own life at the hands of his half brother **Absalom.** Later **Adonijah** tried to usurp the throne from **Solomon** to whom it had been promised (1 Kin. 1:5–10).

3:5 Bathshua: The spelling is confused for Bathsheba.

3:6–9 Tamar: The fact that only one daughter of David is named does not mean that he had no other daughters. Tamar appears in this genealogy because of her prominence in the story of King David's family (2 Sam. 13:1–39). The chronicler included those people who had particular relevance to the narrative and its theological purpose.

3:10–18 Shenazzar was probably the same man as Sheshbazzar, leader of the first group of Jews to return from Babylonian captivity (Ezra 1:8, 11) and builder of the foundation of the second temple (Ezra 5:15–17).

3:19 Zerubbabel here is designated as a son of **Pedaiah,** but elsewhere (Ezra 3:2, 8; 5:2; Neh. 12:1; Hag. 1:12, 14; 2:2, 23) as a son of Pedaiah's brother Shealtiel (v. 17). It is likely that Shealtiel had died while Zerubbabel was young and that the youth was reared by his uncle Pedaiah, thus becoming Pedaiah's son.

This relationship may explain Luke's statement that Zerubbabel was "the son of Shealtiel" (Luke 3:27), who was in turn a descendant of David through his son Nathan. Thus in the Gospels, the line of Jesus was traced back to David through David's two sons, Solomon and Nathan. These two lines met in the marriage of Jeconiah's daughter to Shealtiel. Luke traced Jesus' line through Zerubbabel and an otherwise unknown son Rhesa (Luke 3:27). Matthew, whose interest is particularly in Joseph, traced Jesus' ancestry back to Zerubbabel through still another son of Zerubbabel, Abiud (Matt. 1:13). Thus Luke reconstructed Mary's genealogy, Matthew did the same with Joseph's, and Chronicles traced yet a third line of David. Yet all of these genealogies passed through Zerubbabel and originated in David.

3:20–24 Pelatiah and **Jeshaiah** seem to be the only two **sons of Hananiah. Rephaiah . . . Shechaniah:** These names were detached from the Zerubbabel genealogy and may be other Davidic families. **The sons of Shechaniah:** Four generations of Shechaniah, ending in **Anani,** are listed. Hence the genealogy of vv. 17–24 presupposes about seven generations. Since Jeconiah reigned around 598 B.C. (v. 17), a date of approximately 425 B.C. for Anani is reasonable. Anani is the latest generation recorded in Chronicles, and any dating of the book should take this into account.

4:1–3 Although the genealogy of **Judah** leading up to David has already been recorded (2:3–17), the chronicler here refers to other persons and events relative to that genealogy. In the list of this verse, only **Perez** is Judah's own son. **Hezron** is his grandson, **Carmi** his nephew (2:5, 6), **Hur** the grandson of Hezron (2:18, 19), and **Shobal** the grandson of Hur (2:50).

4:4–8 Ephrathah has already been identified as Ephrath, a wife of the early Caleb (2:19) and mother of Hur. She was therefore the "great grandmother" of **Bethlehem,** since her son Hur was the "grandfather" of Bethlehem (2:50, 51).

Elsewhere the names Bethlehem and Ephrath are closely connected. When Jacob was on the way to Mamre, his wife Rachel died near Ephrath, identified also as Bethlehem (Gen. 35:19). In Ruth 4:11, Ephrathah is synonymous with the town of Bethlehem, and in Mic. 5:2 the birthplace of the anticipated Messiah is called Bethlehem Ephrathah.

4:9–12 Inasmuch as **Jabez** is mentioned in the context of the Judah genealogy, he was probably of that tribe. However, his precise connection to the tribe is not indicated. It may also refer to the man who founded the place called "Jabez," referred to in 2:55 as the home of a caste of scribes. In the present passage he is honored for his desire to enlarge the territory God had given him (v. 10). Even more noble was his wish not to cause pain to others, even though his name means "he will cause pain." Though his birth was painful to his mother, his life was a source of blessing to others, for "God granted him what he requested" (v. 10).

4:13 Othniel, the first of Israel's judges (Josh. 15:17; Judg. 1:13; 3:9), was son-in-law of the later Caleb—the friend and colleague of Joshua.

4:14, 15 Kenaz was the name of Othniel's father (v. 13) and Caleb's brother (Josh. 15:17), as well as of Caleb's grandson. It is clear that Othniel had married his own first cousin, a practice that was common in the OT (Abraham and Sarah in Gen. 11:29) and one not prohibited in the Law of Moses.

4:16–18 In a remarkable statement, told almost in passing, the chronicler identifies the wife of **Mered,** son of the otherwise unknown Ezrah (v. 17), as **Bithiah the daughter of Pharaoh.** It is impossible, however, to determine which king of Egypt is in view or how such an arrangement ever was made.

4:19–21 The fact that **Shelah** named his son **Er** indicates that he followed the levirate custom of raising up a child in the name of a deceased brother. Er, son of Judah, had died

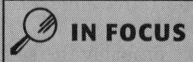 **IN FOCUS**   **"sons"**

(Heb. *ben*) (1 Chr. 4:1; 7:14; Ex. 12:37; 1 Kin. 2:1) Strong's #1121: The Hebrew noun *ben* is probably related to *banah*, which means "to build," as in "to build" a family (Ruth 4:11). The ancient Hebrews considered sons the "builders" of the next generation. *Ben* can either refer to a literal son as in 1 Kin. 2:1, or to one's descendants, as in 7:14. The word may also pertain to an attribute of an individual, as in Ben-Oni, meaning "Son of My Sorrow," and Benjamin, meaning "Son of the Right Hand" (Gen. 35:18). In the plural, the Hebrew word for *sons* can be translated *children* regardless of gender, as in the phrase "children of Israel" (Ex. 12:37). Perhaps the most significant use of the Hebrew word is for Israel's relationship to the Lord. God Himself declared: "Israel is My son, My firstborn" (Ex. 4:22).

because of some unspecified sin, but had left no children by his wife Tamar (Gen. 38:6–11). His brother Onan refused to honor the levirate practice on Er's behalf, so Tamar seduced Judah, her father-in-law, and bore the twin sons Perez and Zerah (Gen. 38:27–30). Shelah, the third son of Judah, apparently did honor his oldest brother by taking the widow Tamar as his wife and rearing a son in Er's name.

4:22 The chronicler made the point that his documentation rested on **ancient** texts. Even in the chronicler's own day, there were skeptics who questioned the accuracy of the genealogies.

4:23, 24 The genealogy of **Simeon** appears next because the Simeonites were a small tribe (v. 27) and had no land allocated to them (Josh. 19:1–9). They settled in the territory of Judah, and their genealogy is attached to his.

4:25–38 Because the tribe of Simeon was so small and had settled within Judah's territory, the tribe lost its identity and was considered a part of Judah when **David** became king.

4:39–41 The chronicler describes how the Simeonites lived as shepherds in Gedor. This was an area next to Egypt, possibly the same as Gerar (Gen. 26:17–20). The Hamites, who were Egyptians, had lived there at one time (v. 40), but were replaced by **Meunites.** The Simeonites expelled these people in the days of Hezekiah.

4:42, 43 The Simeonites pursued the Amalekites into Mount Seir, or Edom. **to this day:** That is, to the time Chronicles was written. The Simeonites had lived in Edom from Hezekiah's time.

5:1, 2 In this verse, the chronicler explains why he does not trace the genealogies of Jacob's sons in birth order. Usually the oldest son of an ancient family became head of the family upon his father's death and also received a larger share of the inheritance than the other children. But Reuben, the firstborn of Jacob, had slept with his father's concubine—perhaps hoping in this way to guarantee his rights as the firstborn son (Gen. 35:22). Because of this despicable act, he lost the **birthright.** Instead, Jacob blessed the **sons of Joseph,** Ephraim and Manasseh (Gen. 48:15–22), thereby transmitting the birthright to Joseph and his sons. The birthright assigned to Joseph did not carry with it the right to rule the tribes and nation; that privilege was granted to Judah. **Judah prevailed** in the sense that God freely chose them as the tribe through which His messianic Deliverer and King would come (Gen. 49:10). The **ruler** from Judah was David and his dynasty, a fact well known to the ancient Israelites.

5:3–6 Again a genealogy is brought forward to a later time, to part of the Israelite deportation by the **Tiglath-Pileser king of Assyria**

(745–727 B.C.). Though the tribe of Reuben virtually disappeared from the historical record by the time of the monarchy, there still remained people who identified themselves as **Reubenites,** as this verse makes clear.

5:7–9 Part of the reason for the absence of Reuben in the historical account was the tribe's need to seek greater pasture lands for their animals. They had pushed east into the wilderness as far as the **River Euphrates.** For this reason, the Reubenites were the first to be deported by the Assyrians (v. 6).

5:10, 11 Gad lived near Reuben and the half tribe of Manasseh. Gad was one of the tribes that sought permission from Moses to settle east

INSIGHT — An Overdue Judgment

The defeat of the Amalekite groups living in the pasturelands near Gedor (1 Chr. 4:39–43) fulfilled a promise of judgment that the Lord had made centuries before. King Saul had been told to carry out this sentence (1 Sam. 15:2, 3), but he failed to obey in full. As a result, it was not until the days of Hezekiah that the Simeonites were finally able to rid their land of the Amalekite enemies.

of the Jordan rather than west (Num. 32:1–42). Reuben occupied the area just east of the Dead Sea and the lower Jordan valley; Gad, the **land of Bashan** due east of the river; and Manasseh, the land to the east and north of the Sea of Galilee.

5:12–17 Once more the chronicler alludes to his sources, this time to genealogical records from the time of **Jotham** (750–735 B.C.) and **Jeroboam** II (793–753 B.C.). He wanted to emphasize that the genealogies are based on solid documentary research in texts that preceded his own time by more than 300 years.

5:18, 19 The **Hagrites** and their allies were probably desert peoples who felt increasing pressure from the expanding Israelite population. Their efforts at resisting the Israelites took place in the days of Saul (v. 10), though the narratives of Saul do not mention them.

5:20 they were helped: The help here came from God Himself in answer to their prayers. The people of Reuben, Gad, and Manasseh fielded an army of more then 44,000 men (v. 18), but ultimately it was God who brought success.

5:21, 22 the war was God's: This confirms the statement about God helping the Israelites in v. 20 and goes beyond it by referring to a practice of OT times known as "The Lord's War." At times, God commanded an offensive war as a means of achieving His purposes of conquest and occupation of the Promised Land (Deut. 20:1–20). At those times, God made it clear that the battle was by His initiative and that He would ensure its success. **the captivity:** In the light of vv. 6, 26, the captivity must be that of Tiglath-Pileser of Assyria, who carried off a significant portion of the Israelite population (2 Kin. 15:29).

5:23–26 The famous king **Tiglath-Pileser,** who reigned around 745–727 B.C., has gone down in Assyrian annals as one of the most powerful rulers of the neo-Assyrian period. The chronicler's reference to him as **Pul** (2 Kin. 15:19), once thought by some to be a sheer invention or a historically unfounded device of the biblical writers, has in recent decades been found in Tiglath's own records as "Pulu," a throne-name used alternatively with his more familiar one. **Gozan** is Guzanu or Tell Halaf on the Habor River.

6:1 Levi: All religious personnel involved in tabernacle or temple ministry had to be members of the tribe of Levi. Aaron was himself a Levite, and from the beginning of the priesthood his descendants were designated as the only ones who could serve as priests (6:16–25; Ex. 28:1). Later the Levites were especially set apart for service in the tabernacle in a role subsidiary to the priests (Num. 18:1–7). Anyone who wanted to serve in the temple had to establish his Levitical credentials. The present genealogy was designed at least in part to meet that need.

6:2 Kohath: This son of Levi was the one to whom the office of priest became exclusively

connected. Hence, every priest had to be a Levite, but not every Levite could become a priest.

6:3, 4 Beginning with **Eleazar,** the genealogy traces the line of high priests through Jehozadak, the priest who went into Babylonian exile with his people (v. 15). Including Eleazar and Jehozadak, there were at least 22 high priests in unbroken succession. Another line of priests began with **Ithamar,** including such persons as Eli, Ahimelech, and Abiathar. In the days of David, priestly service was divided between the Eleazar and Ithamar priests, with the Eleazar serving two-thirds of the time and the Ithamar one-third because of the difference in their numbers (24:1–5). Solomon rejected the Ithamar priesthood, reserving the honor of the priesthood exclusively for the priests descended from Eleazar (1 Kin. 2:26, 27).

6:5–8 Zadok: This priest, not the same person as the Zadok of v. 12, was the one selected by David to serve along with Ahimelech the son of Abiathar as high priest (2 Sam. 8:17). Eventually Zadok became sole high priest because of Abiathar's rebellion against Solomon (1 Kin. 2:26, 27).

6:9, 10 The detail that this **Azariah** ministered in Solomon's **temple** distinguishes this priest from his grandfather of the same name (v. 9).

6:11–14 Jehozadak: This last priest in the list was carried into exile in Babylon (v. 15). He was the father of Joshua, the priest who returned from Babylon with Zerubbabel to rebuild the temple and reestablish the Jewish community (Hag. 1:1, 12, 14).

6:15–17 Gershon: The purpose of the following genealogy was to list the principal offspring of the sons of Levi who were not priests, but regular or "ordinary" Levites.

6:18–21 Amram was the father of Aaron

 **IN FOCUS** | **"generations"**

(Heb. *toledoth*) (1 Chr. 5:7; Gen. 10:1; Ruth 4:18) Strong's #8435: The Hebrew *toledoth* is derived from the verb *yalad,* meaning "to give birth." *Toledoth* usually introduces an extended genealogical list, such as those in Gen. 5:1, 10:1 and 1 Chr. 5:7, 26:31. Ancient Hebrew culture depended on detailed genealogical lists to determine questions of inheritance and land use rights. After the conquest of Canaan, each tribe received its portion of the Promised Land to divide between its clans (Josh. 13–19). Land rights remained in the clans, passed down as part of the inheritance from father to oldest son, or daughter if there was no son (Num. 27). Other matters, such as service in the temple and royal succession, were also determined by genealogy. Old Testament genealogies attest to God's faithfulness in fulfilling His promise to make Israel a "great nation" (Gen. 12:1–3), and the genealogy of Matt. 1 shows Jesus as the legitimate heir to David's throne.

and the whole line of high priests. All other priests had to trace their lineage to Kohath through his other sons **Izhar, Hebron, and Uzziel.** Descendants of Levi who were not sons of Kohath could not be priests at all.

6:22 Amminadab is another name for Izhar (v. 18), who otherwise appears as the father of Korah (6:37, 38; Ex. 6:21; Num. 16:1).

6:23–27 The Levite **Elkanah** was the ancestor of Samuel the prophet. His line here, which reads **Zophai, Nahath, Eliab, Jeroham, Elkanah,** appears in 1 Sam. 1:1 as Zuph, Tohu, Elihu, Jeroham, and Elkanah. A parallel genealogy in 1 Chr. 6:34, 35 reads in reverse order: Elkanah, Zuph, Toah, Eliel, Jeroham, Elkanah. That these names varied in spelling and even in form was an accepted practice and does not make false the historicity of the persons or the lists. **Nahath:** This ancestor of Samuel is otherwise known as Toah (v. 34) or Tohu (1 Sam. 1:1).

6:28–32 Samuel: Samuel's ancestors were described elsewhere as Ephraimites (1 Sam. 1:1). Although Samuel was an Ephraimite by virtue of his residence in Ramathaim Zophim, a city in the tribal territory of Ephraim, this genealogy makes it clear that he was in fact a Levite. This explains why he could be trained in the tabernacle under Eli the priest (1 Sam. 2:11) and later officiate at public services that included sacrifices (1 Sam. 9:13; 10:8).

6:33–47 The temple musicians also were Levites and were divided up into three groups according to their descent from Levi's three sons. The **Kohathites** in David's time were led by **Heman,** grandson of **Samuel;** the Gershonites by **Asaph** (vv. 39, 43); and the Merarites by **Ethan** (vv. 44, 47). Ethan was otherwise known as Jeduthun (25:1). A glance at the genealogies of the three Levitical leaders, all of which trace back to Levi, reveals that the lists are selective with many names, particularly in the lineage of Asaph and Ethan, being omitted.

6:48, 49 In contrast to the Levites just listed, Aaron and his descendants had the privilege and responsibility of the office of the high priest. What set them apart from the other Levites was their access to the **altar of burnt offering** and **incense** and their work of making **atonement for Israel.** Levites could assist in this ministry and could officiate at local sacrifices. See the actions of the Levite Samuel (1 Sam. 7:9; 9:12, 13; 16:2–5). However, only priests in the line of Aaron could present sacrifices at the tabernacle or temple.

6:50–53 sons of Aaron: The genealogy of vv. 50–53 is the same as that in vv. 4–8, but this list ends with Ahimaaz. This list recites the line of Aaron only until the time of David (v. 31). Zadok and Ahimaaz were the last of the priests in the line of Eleazar under David's administration (2 Sam. 15:35, 36).

6:54 dwelling places: The remainder of the chapter describes the allocation of cities and towns to the priests (vv. 54–60), the rest of the Kohathites (vv. 61, 66–70), the Gershonites (vv. 62, 71–76), and the Merarites (vv. 63, 77–81).

6:55 Because the priests were all Kohathites, the cities of the priests were within the districts assigned to Kohath. **Hebron,** located in Judah, is the first of these cities. **surrounding common-lands:** The priests and Levites occupied not only houses within the city walls, but they owned and worked fields immediately adjacent to the cities as well. These common-lands extended out from the perimeters of the city walls for a thousand cubits (about 1,500 ft.) in every direction (Num. 35:4, 5) and could be used for farming and grazing (Num. 35:3). This does not mean that the priests and Levites supported themselves by farming, for the Law is clear that they were to live on the tithes and offerings of the other tribes (Num. 18:21–32). The produce they received from the common-lands was a bonus.

6:56 Hebron had originally been assigned to the faithful spy Caleb as part of his inheritance (Josh. 15:13). However, Caleb's inheritance was further defined as not the city proper, but the nearby **fields** and **villages** (Josh. 21:11, 12). Caleb's fields were outside the thousand-cubit

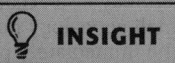 **INSIGHT** | **The Service of the Levites**

From the time of the Exodus, the Levites served as custodians of Israel's religious life. At first they were primarily responsible for the tabernacle (1 Chr. 6:48), Israel's mobile worship center (Ex. 27:9). Later they took on additional responsibilities for teaching among the tribes, which they did from certain designated centers known as Levitical cities (Josh. 21:1–3). After Israel became a monarchy and David came to power, the ark was relocated to Jerusalem and the Levites' duties changed (1 Chr. 23:24–32).

circumference that belonged to the priests of Hebron.

6:57–59 The Law specified that in the event of an unintentional killing, the perpetrator could find sanctuary in one of six **cities of refuge** scattered throughout the land (Num. 35:9–15). He or she could remain there in safety until the case came to trial (Num. 35:16–28). These six cities were included among the 48 Levitical cities, and **Hebron** was one of them.

6:60 The number **thirteen** refers to the original allotment of cities in Josh. 21:13–19. The chronicler was listing the priestly cities that existed in his own day, nearly a thousand years after the original distribution. This accounts not only for two missing cities, Juttah and Gibeon, but also for the variation in the spelling of some of the names as well. The priestly cities were concentrated in the areas of Judah and Benjamin, conveniently located near the temple in Jerusalem.

6:61–65 rest of . . . the Kohathites: These were the Levites who were not priests. Their cities were situated mainly in the **half tribe of Manasseh** on the west of the Jordan (v. 70), just south of the plain of Jezreel.

6:66 Beginning here, there is a continuation of the description of non-priestly Kohathite cities begun in v. 61. Some of these cities were in **Ephraim,** with Manasseh to the north and Benjamin to the south.

6:67–70 Like Hebron, **Shechem** was both a Levitical city and a city of refuge. Shechem was especially significant in Israel. It was the site of Abraham's first altar in Canaan (Gen. 12:6, 7), the place where Jacob bought a piece of land (Gen. 33:19), and the location of the first capital of the northern kingdom (1 Kin. 12:25).

6:71–75 Gershon: The tribal areas containing the cities of the Gershonite Levites were East Manasseh; Issachar, north of West Manasseh (v. 72); Asher, on the Mediterranean coast north of Mount Carmel (v. 74); and Naphtali, west and north of the Sea of Galilee (v. 76). **Golan:** This city in Bashan east of the Jordan was a city of refuge.

6:76 Kedesh was another of the six cities of refuge. It was the most northern of the three west of the Jordan.

6:77 The third Levitical order, that of **Merari,** occupied cities in Zebulun. Reuben was east of the Dead Sea (v. 78), and Gad was east of the Jordan from the Dead Sea almost to the Sea of Galilee (v. 80).

6:78–79 Bezer was also a city of refuge, the farthest south of those east of the Jordan.

6:80, 81 Another city of refuge, **Ramoth in Gilead,** was directly east of the Jordan. In this way the cities of refuge were distributed throughout the land so that any Israelite would

be within a few miles of one of them. All six cities of refuge were assigned to the Levites, with Hebron designated for the priests (v. 55). The cities of refuge were assigned this way because the priests and Levites had judicial responsibilities in the cases involving unintentional homicide (Num. 35:25, 28; Deut. 17:8–13; 19:17–21).

7:1, 2 The total here was limited to the **sons of Tola.** Undoubtedly there were thousands of other tribesmen of Issachar at that time, descendants of the three other sons of Issachar (v. 1).

7:3, 4 thirty-six thousand: These appear to be the offspring of Uzzi (v. 3), the son of Tola (v. 2). Since the figure is much greater than the 22,600 of v. 2, it must reflect the population of a much later time, perhaps as late as the period just before the fall of Samaria in 722 B.C. At that time, Issachar would have had its largest population.

7:5 This is the grand total of all the fighting men of Issachar at some unspecified time. This may also reflect the population at its greatest, some time just prior to 722 B.C.

7:6–12 The chronicler recounted the genealogies of **Benjamin** in some detail because King Saul was a Benjamite (7:6–12; 8:1–40; 9:35–44). Saul was an important figure even though his reign ended tragically. The complexity of the biblical genealogies can be illustrated by comparing the list of Benjamin's sons here with that in 8:1, 2; Gen. 46:21; Num. 26:38, 39. The differences in these genealogies are most likely due to the listing of principal descendants of different time periods.

7:13 The unusual brevity of the genealogy here may reflect the greatly reduced size and importance of **Naphtali** following the maraudings of the Assyrians under Tiglath-Pileser III. Naphtali's tribal area was specifically pointed out as the object of the Assyrian campaigns (2 Kin. 15:29). **sons of Bilhah:** Technically it was Naphtali who was son of Bilhah, Rachel's handmaid (Gen. 30:7, 8). The fact that the sons of Naphtali are here called sons of Bilhah points to the flexibility and latitude of the word "sons" and, indeed, of the genealogies themselves. These offspring of Bilhah were, in fact, her grandsons. This little notation may also account for the location of the Naphtali genealogy here, for Benjamin, the head of the immediately preceding one, was the son of Rachel, mistress of Bilhah.

7:14 Manasseh was the son of Joseph. **Machir:** Machir's daughter became the wife of Judah's grandson Hezron, thus joining the two tribes of Manasseh and Judah (2:21).

7:15–19 If the **Huppim** and **Shuppim** here are the same as in v. 12, the tribe of Manasseh and the tribe of Benjamin were connected

through the marriage of Machir and **Maachah.**
Zelophehad: Apparently a grandson of Gilead
(Num. 26:30–33), this man had no sons. This
situation prompted Moses to announce God's
provision for the inheritance rights of daughters
in such cases (Num. 36:1–9).

7:20–22 The genealogy of **Ephraim** follows
the genealogy of his brother Manasseh. **Tahath:**
This name and **Shuthelah** both occur twice,
illustrating the custom of sons
being named for their grandfathers or more remote ancestors.
The men of Gath were
probably the pre-conquest Philistines (Gen. 21:32, 34; Ex.
13:17). Since the story involves
Ephraim's sons in particular and
not just the tribe of Ephraim,
this verse establishes that
Jacob's family before the
Exodus had not completely lost
contact with the land of
Canaan.

7:23, 24 Lower and Upper Beth Horon:
These places were in Ephraim near the border
with Benjamin.

7:25–27 The fact that there were nine generations between **Joshua,** the famous successor
to Moses, and Ephraim (vv. 23–27) supports the
view that the story in vv. 21, 22 occurred before
the Exodus.

7:28, 29 children of Joseph: As this
phrase makes clear, vv. 28, 29 include the cities
of both Ephraim and Manasseh. The cities of
Beth Shean, Taanach, Megiddo, and Dor were
located in Manasseh.

7:30–39 Asher: This is the last tribal
genealogy in 1 Chronicles. It may be compared
with the genealogies of Asher in Gen. 46:17 and
Num. 26:44–46.

7:40 twenty-six thousand: This number
of fighting men would place the completion of
this genealogy in the period of David, as stated
in v. 2.

8:1, 2 The reason for this second and much
more detailed genealogy of **Benjamin** was its
climactic focus on the genealogy of King Saul
(vv. 29–40).

8:3–5 Addar is spelled "Ard" in Num.
26:40 and Gen. 46:21. Comparison with those
passages indicates that what appear here to be
sons of Benjamin are in fact grandsons and even
later generations.

8:6–8 A grandson of Jediael (7:10) or
Ashbel (7:6), **Ehud** apparently was the link
between Benjamin and Saul. The sons of Ehud
moved the Benjamites from **Geba** to **Mana-
hath.** The former town was a Benjamite site on
the border of Judah, about six miles northeast of
Jerusalem.

> *Jerusalem remained under Jebusite control until David conquered it.*

8:9–11 There was a well-known Moabite
king named **Mesha.** Both the Scriptures (2 Kin.
3:4) and the Moabite Stone attest to this fact.
The reference here to Mesha as a son of Sha-
haraim and Hodesh, a Moabite wife (v. 8), suggests that the illustrious Moabite king may have
had a Benjamite father, but the evidence is not
conclusive.

8:12 Ono and Lod were ancient towns
about twelve and seven miles
southeast of Joppa. The sons of
Elpaal probably rebuilt these
ancient cities.

8:13–27 Aijalon and
Gath were two places in the
western lowlands of Israel,
about seventeen miles apart.

**8:28 These dwelt in
Jerusalem:** This means that
the last generation in the preceding genealogy lived in
Jerusalem. This city was not
taken by David until approximately 1004 B.C.,
so the line of Benjamin was traced to at least
that time. Moreover, the fact that David succeeded Saul did not mean that all Benjamites
were excluded from Jerusalem or for that
matter from David's favor. For example, David
was careful to attend to Jonathan's survivors (2
Sam. 9:1–13), and he gave other Benjamites
positions of responsibility in his new government (11:31; 12:1–7, 29).

8:29 A comparison of this genealogy (vv.
29–40) with that of 9:35–44 shows that the
father of Gibeon was Jeiel. The city of **Gibeon**
was a prominent city that existed long before
this time, as the conquest narrative makes plain
(Josh. 9:1–27).

8:30, 31 Kish was the father of Saul (v. 33;
9:39). In this passage the relationship between
Jeiel and Kish is unclear, because Kish is also
named as the son of Ner (v. 33). However, in
9:35–39 the lineage is clearly traced from Jeiel
to Ner to Kish and finally to Saul.

8:32 Since Saul was not yet born at this
point in the genealogy, the **Jerusalem** here is
the city of pre-Davidic times. Jerusalem remained under Jebusite control until David conquered it (2 Sam. 5:6–10). Perhaps at this time
the Benjamites lived among the Jebusites.

8:33 Abinadab was eventually killed with
his father on the battlefield at Gilboa (10:2; 1
Sam. 31:2). **Esh-Baal** evidently was Saul's
youngest son, since he was not named in the
genealogies of the beginning of Saul's reign (1
Sam. 14:49). He succeeded Saul as king of the
northern kingdom after the five-year period in
which Abner was in charge (2 Sam. 2:10; 5:4,
5). The pagan name Esh-Baal (meaning "fire of
Baal") demonstrates the degree to which Saul

Early Temple Servants

The Nethinim (1 Chr. 9:2) were a group of temple servants who assisted the Levites. They performed menial chores such as cleaning the temple, carrying water and wood to the altar, and scrubbing utensils used in the sacrificial ceremonies. The name Nethinim means "those who are given."

Ezra's list of the returnees from the captivity mentions the Nethinim in conjunction with "the sons of Solomon's servants" (Ezra 2:43–58). Because the names used are not Hebrew, some have suggested that both groups were Gentiles, possibly descendants of the Canaanites or some other group that the Israelites had conquered. David and the leaders of Israel had appointed these groups to serve the Levites (8:20).

The Nethinim were not the first group of foreigners to be given servile positions among the Israelites. During the conquest of Canaan, Joshua made peace with the men of Gibeon, and they became woodcutters and water carriers (Josh. 9).

---

had succumbed to religious syncretism. The author of 2 Samuel attempted to downplay the pagan connotations of Esh-Baal by calling him Ishbosheth, meaning the "Man of Shame" (2 Sam. 2:8).

8:34–40 The same pagan tendency appears in the name of Jonathan's son. **Merib-Baal** means something like "Baal Is My Advocate."

9:1 The **book** or scroll mentioned here was not the canonical books of Kings, because those contain no genealogies. The reference must be to genealogical sources compiled and collected by the scribes of the kings of Israel. **carried . . . to Babylon:** This reference to the Babylonian captivity prepares the way for the genealogies and lists that follow (vv. 3, 4). As v. 3 points out, the evacuation of the cities and towns of Judah provided dwelling places for the returnees whose names follow.

9:2 Israelites: The deportation of Israel by the Assyrians from 734 to 722 B.C. resulted in Israel's dispersion throughout the eastern Mediterranean world. However, it is apparent from this verse that some of them joined their Judean brethren in the return from Babylon after 539 B.C. The word **Nethinim,** derived from the Hebrew verb "to give" and thus meaning "the ones given," refers to temple slaves. Since the Nethinim were distinct from the **priests** and **Levites,** these temple slaves must have been from other tribes (Ezra 2:43; 7:7; Neh. 7:46, 60, 73; 10:28).

9:3 Ephraim and Manasseh: These two tribes descended from Joseph and were especially blessed by the Lord (Gen. 49:22–26; Deut. 33:13–17). However, these two tribes did not belong to the nation of Judah. This is another confirmation that the community included Israelites as well as Judeans.

9:4–10 Uthai and the following names (vv.

4–9) are otherwise unattested, even in the lists of Nehemiah 11:4–24, which seem to allude to the same post-exile restoration. It may be that neither list is exhaustive and that the chronicler and Nehemiah respectively chose names as they did to suit particular purposes that are no longer evident to the modern reader.

9:11–13 Azariah: The list of priests that follows (vv. 11, 12) is greatly abbreviated when compared with the list in 6:3–15. This again indicates that biblical genealogies, while accurate when testable, are not always complete.

9:14–16 The normal pattern of dividing the genealogy of the **Levites** according to the three sons of Levi is not followed here (6:1). Rather, there are seven families listed in vv. 14–16, six of them living in Jerusalem and the seventh in Netophah. **Merari** is mentioned, but not Kohath or Gershon. In place of Gershon stands his descendant **Asaph** (6:39–43). **Jeduthun:** This is another name for Ethan, descendant of Merari (6:44–47). Both vv. 14 and 16 appear to list Merarites. **Elkanah:** The presence of this name suggests that this family is Kohathite (6:33–38). **Netophathites:** This refers to the inhabitants of the village of Netophah, a little over three miles southeast of Bethlehem. The Gershonites and Merarites evidently lived in Jerusalem in the post-exilic period, while the Kohathite or the Korahite Levites lived in Netophah.

9:17, 18 King's Gate on the east: This was the famous gate just east of the temple (Ezek. 46:1, 2). After the days of the wilderness tabernacle (Num. 3:27–31), and since the time of Zechariah and the temple of Solomon (v. 21; 26:1, 2, 14), the Korahites had been responsible for keeping the gates and attending to the place of worship.

9:19–21 As descendants of Kohath (Ex.

IN LIFE | The Value of Fasting

Responding to modern society's obsession with image and appearance, some weight-loss programs prescribe fasting. In ancient Israel, fasting was observed for more purposes than that. For example, the gallant men of Gilead fasted for seven days to express their grief over King Saul's death (1 Chr. 10:12). Rather than hide their sadness and feelings of loss, they openly expressed it by using fasting as a cleansing discipline.

Other purposes for fasting among the Israelites included:

- commemorating special occasions of God's deliverance (Zech. 8:19)
- repenting of and grieving for disobedience and sin against the Lord (Judg. 20:26; 1 Sam. 7:6)
- expressing humility before God (Lev. 16:29; Ps. 69:10)
- seeking guidance from the Lord by clearing out the senses and focusing on Him (Ex. 34:28; 2 Chr. 20:3, 4)

Today one hears much about "focus," "concentration," and "working the program" in areas such as sports, the workplace, and psychotherapy. Fasting is a means toward spiritual focus by concentrating on God rather than on food and other personal needs.

6:18, 21), **Korah** and his line had close connections with the priesthood. However, they could not be priests since they were descended from Izhar rather than Amram. Their close connection explains why these particular Levites ministered within the precincts of the temple.

9:22–24 The **gatekeepers** had been appointed in the days of **David and Samuel** (26:1–19). Since Samuel died long before David made his appointments, the chronicler must be saying that David was encouraged and instructed by the prophet from the days of his youth. In a sense, Samuel **appointed** the gatekeepers through David.

9:25 The gatekeepers lived in villages surrounding Jerusalem (v. 22). They came to Jerusalem on a rotating schedule to attend to their temple duties, serving for periods of **seven days.**

9:26 chief gatekeepers: Since there were four sides to the city and temple (v. 24) and four main gates, there must also be four **Levites** responsible for the oversight of these portals. They opened and closed the gates and provided security (v. 27). However, they also oversaw all the various rooms and other facilities of the temple. **treasuries:** This referred to the places where money was kept and to storage rooms in general.

9:27–29 they lodged: Whereas the Levites who tended the gates lived in surrounding villages, those in charge must have lived in the city, probably near the gates of the temple. They had to be nearby in order to supervise temple affairs, including the **opening** and closing of the gates.

9:30–32 Although the Levites could handle

such matters as the serving vessels (v. 28), furnishings, implements, and even materials for an offering (such as flour, wine, incense, and spices, v. 29), they were not allowed to prepare the **ointment of the spices.** This was reserved for the priests alone, as Ex. 30:23–25, 33, 37, 38 states.

9:33, 34 The head **singers,** like the chief gatekeepers (vv. 26, 27), lived in Jerusalem to be constantly on hand to supervise the ministry of the temple musicians. **They dwelt at Jerusalem:** In fact, it was the general policy that all the heads of the various Levitical classes would live in the capital.

9:35, 36 Ner is rendered "Zechar" in 8:31.

9:37–44 The interest the chronicler has in the genealogy of **Jonathan** probably springs from Jonathan's close friendship with David (1 Sam. 18:1).

10:1 Some 1,700 feet in elevation, **Mount Gilboa** lies in the southeastern part of the plain of Jezreel. This was Philistine territory from the time they arrived there in about 1200 B.C. The following account of Saul's final battle closely parallels the account in 1 Sam. 31:1–13.

10:2, 3 Saul's sons: There was a fourth son, Ishbosheth. He survived this battle and became king of Israel five years after Saul's death.

10:4, 5 Most Semites practiced circumcision for either hygienic or religious purposes, but for the Hebrews it was the sign of God's promise through Abraham to them. The **uncircumcised** were those outside, often their enemies the Philistines. **abuse:** The Philistines could not only harm Saul personally, but bring shame on the nation that had him as their leader. Saul was driven to an extreme course of action. Suicide was a rare occurrence among the Hebrews of OT times (v. 5; 2 Sam. 17:23; 1 Kin. 16:18).

10:6 all his house died: This statement was written in anticipation of the death of Ish-bosheth, the last of Saul's sons. With Ish-bosheth's death (2 Sam. 4:5, 7), Saul's dynasty came to an end.

10:7, 8 Though the **Philistines** had long dominated the Jezreel-Esdraelon Valley, there were Israelite cities in the region for some time. With Saul's death, even these were lost to the Philistines, who took them over when the Israelites abandoned them.

10:9 They stripped him: The parallel passage in 1 Sam. 31:9 adds, "and they cut off his head."

10:10 Dagon was worshiped by the Philistines and other peoples in Syria and north-west Mesopotamia as the god of grain. A hundred years earlier, the Philistines had placed the

people of this town took in retrieving Saul's corpse from Beth Shan was doubtless in memory of Saul's quick response to their cry for help early in his reign (1 Sam. 11:1–11). In the life of Saul, Jabesh Gilead may go back even further, for in the early days of the judges the tribe of Benjamin had been nearly annihilated in a bloody civil war brought about by the murder of the concubine of the Ephraimite Levite (Judg. 19:1–30), a murder in Benjamite territory which the Benjamites refused to punish (Judg. 20:1–48). A result of the intertribal warfare was the depletion of the women of Benjamin to such a degree that the surviving men had no wives by whom they could repopulate the tribe. To provide such wives, women from Shiloh and Jabesh Gilead were forcibly brought to Benjamin for that purpose (Judg. 21:1–25). It is likely that one of these was an ancestress of Saul himself, which could also explain his quick

Photo by Willem A. VanGemeren

Mount Gilboa, site of the battle in which King Saul and three of his sons were killed by the Philistines (1 Chr. 10:1–7).

captured ark of the covenant in the temple of Dagon at Ashdod (1 Sam. 5:2). Later Samson stood between the central pillars of a temple of Dagon, where he was mocked by the assembled Philistines (Judg. 16:23–31). Apparently the Philistines celebrated military victory by bringing a trophy of their success back to their temple, where it could be displayed as a tribute to the might of their god.

10:11 Jabesh Gilead was just east of the Jordan, not far from Beth Shan. The care the

response to their call for aid and their confidence in making their appeal in the first place.

10:12 This strange turn of events requires attention to 1 Sam. 31:12, which states that the people of Jabesh burned the bodies of Saul and his sons. This, of course, left only **bones**.

10:13 Saul's untimely death was the result of disobedience to God's **word.** He had disobeyed God by not waiting for Samuel to perform a sacrifice and by not utterly destroying the Amalekites (1 Sam. 13:1–15; 15:10–23).

consulted a medium: Before the battle, Saul had asked for Samuel's advice through the witch of En Dor (1 Sam. 28:3–25).

10:14 He killed him: This statement is shocking in its bluntness. In the final analysis, Saul's death was not by his own hand but by the hand of God. The Lord let Saul pursue a course that led to death. **turned the kingdom over:** This statement confirmed Samuel's earlier word to Saul, "The LORD has torn the kingdom of Israel from you today, and has given it to a neighbor of yours, who is better than you" (1 Sam. 15:28).

11:1, 2 Made famous because Abraham lived (Gen. 13:18) and was buried there (Gen. 25:9), **Hebron** was a Levitical city as well (6:54, 55). David made it his capital following Saul's death (2 Sam. 2:3) and reigned there until Ishbosheth's death seven years later (2 Sam. 4:1–12; 5:5). David's legitimacy as successor to Saul was confirmed by the support he received from **all** the tribes. **You shall . . . be ruler:** The crowds were very much aware of the promise God had made to David (1 Sam. 16:12; 24:20; 28:17).

11:3 The **covenant** refers to mutual pledges made between a king and his people, ensuring stable and successful government. The Law of Moses made provision for such a covenant (Deut. 17:18–20). Hints of the king's covenant guidelines may be found in the accession of Solomon (29:19; 1 Kin. 2:3) and Joash (2 Kin. 11:4), and in Josiah's promise to obey the statutes of the Book of the Covenant (2 Kin. 23:2, 3). **according to . . . Samuel:** Years before, Samuel had anointed David (1 Sam. 16:1, 3, 12, 13). This second anointing confirmed the first one.

11:4 Jebus was another name for Jerusalem. The name was coined by the Israelites because the city belonged to the **Jebusites.** The name does not occur outside the OT (Josh. 15:8; 18:16, 28).

11:5 Another name for Jerusalem was **Zion.** The original Canaanite city, surrounded by high, thick walls, was considered a stronghold. After David took the city and made it his capital, it became known as **the city of David.** When the temple was built on Mount Moriah (2 Chr. 3:1), a hill just north of the city, that area and sometimes the whole city was called Mount Zion.

11:6, 7 The stronghold of Zion (11:5) seemed impregnable until **Joab** found a means

---

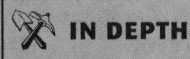 **IN DEPTH** | **David at Hebron**

While First Chronicles describes David's ascension to the throne in three verses, Second Samuel describes it in three chapters. The fundamental difference between the two accounts lies in the purposes of the authors.

The author of 2 Samuel goes to great lengths to describe the rocky course that David had to travel before unifying the entire nation. Although the Judeans anointed David king immediately after Saul's death, the rest of Israel crowned Saul's son Ishbosheth as king. Abner, Saul's cousin and military commander, supported Ishbosheth's kingship vigorously and confronted David's army in battle.

When it became apparent that Ishbosheth had no ability to rule, Abner recognized the inevitability that David would rule over all Israel. Thus Abner set in motion a plan whereby the northern tribes would submit to David, and Abner would be rewarded by becoming the leader of David's armies. The northern tribes submitted, but Joab, jealous about his own role as general, assassinated Abner. Ishbosheth too was murdered by some of his own countrymen. During these tumultuous events, David maintained his integrity. By genuinely mourning for the fallen leaders and by punishing those who had acted treacherously against them, he not only pleased God but also gained the affections of his people (2 Sam. 2:8–5:5). The author of Second Samuel lets us observe David's life up close so that it can become both a model and a warning to us.

The writer of 1 Chronicles emphasizes the unity of all Israel in support of God's anointed, King David. Three short verses in Chronicles stress that *all* the elders of Israel came to Hebron to covenant with David (11:3), something 2 Samuel only hints at by suggesting that Benjamin as well as Judah recognized David's kingship over the nation (2 Sam. 3:17–21, 37; 5:1–3). Thus the Chronicles narrative gives the impression that the shift of loyalty from Saul to David went without any opposition. For the chronicler's purposes, this was all that was significant about David's accession to the throne. In these events, the chronicler wanted to stress both the unity of the nation and God's choice of David as king.

of access. As a result, Joab was rewarded with the command of Israel's army. He already enjoyed a close relationship with David because he was a **son of Zeruiah,** David's sister (2:15, 16).

11:8, 9 The Hebrew noun **Millo** derives from a verb meaning "to fill" and therefore suggests "filling," "terracing," or the like. Once David occupied Mount Ophel, the original and very small area of Jerusalem, he greatly enlarged it by building retaining walls along the Kidron valley to the east and south and the Tyropoeon valley (or the Valley of Maktesh) to the west. Between these walls and the top of the hill he built terraces, so that various buildings could be constructed there.

11:10–12 the mighty men: This phrase applied to three persons, Jashobeam, Eleazar (v. 12), and Shammah (2 Sam. 23:11, 12). They were distinguished for their bravery and their service to David. Joab, already singled out as "chief" (v. 6), was above them in rank. **Jashobeam:** This first of the mighty men, known in 2 Sam. 23:8 as Josheb-Basshebeth, showed his heroism by slaying **three hundred** of the enemy single-handed. This event is recorded only here.

11:13, 14 If **Pasdammin** is the same as Ephesdammim, this may be the campaign against the **Philistines** in which **David** slew Goliath (1 Sam. 17:1). Eleazar, the second mighty man (v. 12), could then trace his association with David back many years. If this is the same battle, the chronicler adds certain details such as the **piece of ground full of barley** and the Israelites standing **in the middle of that field.**

11:15 Another elite group of **three,** not named in this episode, penetrated the defenses of the Philistines. **The cave of Adullam** was about 12 miles southwest of Bethlehem and was one of David's favorite hiding places in the days of his flight from Saul (1 Sam. 22:1). **The Valley of Rephaim** is southwest of Jerusalem in the direction of Adullam.

11:16, 17 It was particularly galling to David that the Philistines had come to occupy his hometown, **Bethlehem**. The occasion seems to have been David's conflict with the Philistines after he had been anointed king of Israel at Hebron but before he took Jerusalem (2 Sam. 5:17–25; 23:13–17). How the Philistines managed to seize Bethlehem is not clear, though their motive may have been to demoralize

---

IN PERSON   **David's Mighty Men**

David's rise to power was assured from the outset by the promises of God (1 Chr. 11:10; 1 Sam. 13:14; 15:28; 16:12). Nevertheless, the journey from the pastures near Bethlehem to the palace in Jerusalem was long and difficult. Along the way, David attracted a growing movement of loyal supporters who helped him attain the throne. Some of the most important of these followers were known as "mighty men."

These warriors or champions are celebrated for their military victories (2 Sam. 23; 1 Chr. 11), many of which were won after David was crowned king of Israel. But the nucleus of this group came from humble beginnings. When David was fleeing from Saul, renegades from Israelite society began gathering to the young Bethlehemite. Scripture gives three reasons why they found their way to David: distress, debt, and discontent (1 Sam. 22:2). Apparently having nothing to lose, they sided with David, who was also in trouble with the king.

Saul quickly learned of this band, which at first numbered about 400. Suspicious that his own people might defect, Saul chided his servants, "Will the son of Jesse give every one of you fields and vineyards, and make you all captains?" (22:7). In fact, the answer to this question was yes. Under David and his successor Solomon, the land prospered exceedingly (2 Sam. 6:19; 7:1; 1 Kin. 4:25), and many of David's followers became renowned as "mighty men."

During the days of David's flight from Saul, he and his followers acted as raiders, attacking Israel's enemies (1 Sam. 23:5; 27:8–12). These skirmishes served as training exercises for the days ahead. As soon as Saul was dead, David began his ascent to the throne and his mighty men rose to positions of power along with him. He was crowned king of Judah and his men followed him to Hebron (2 Sam. 2:3). From there they helped him fight a seven-year civil war with the house of Saul (3:1).

Finally, after David had been crowned king over all Israel, his men distinguished themselves by helping him capture Jebus, or Jerusalem, which then became his capital (5:6–10). The mighty men became the nucleus of a powerful army (5:17–25; 8:1–18).

David, who, perhaps in a whim of nostalgia or personal frustration, longed for a **drink of water from the well of Bethlehem,** a place so familiar to him that he describes its location to his men.

11:18, 19 David would not drink it: This was not an act of ingratitude. To the contrary, David expressed the utmost sense of appreciation. His men had risked their lives to bring water to David, and now in the face of their selflessness he felt unworthy to drink it. He **poured it out to the LORD** as though it were an offering of blood (v. 19).

11:20 Abishai was a brother of **Joab** and a son of David's sister Zeruiah (2:16). Like Joab, Abishai was chief over other warriors because of his great exploits.

11:21, 22 the first three: This refers to Jashobeam, Eleazar (vv. 11, 12), and Shammah. Chronicles does not mention the third one by name (2 Sam. 23:11, 12) but does acknowledge his existence (v. 12). For reasons not spelled out, Abishai was not qualified to be in the ranks of the first three.

11:23 Five cubits was about seven and a half feet.

11:24 three mighty men: Only Abishai and Benaiah were named as members of this group.

11:25 The next level below Joab, the commander, and the two groups of "three mighty men" was **the thirty.** Their names appear in vv. 26–47 and also in 2 Sam. 23:24–39. The term *thirty* may denote an elite military unit that consisted of approximately thirty men. The term does not indicate a literal number, because the list in vv. 26–47 includes more than thirty names.

11:26–38 Asahel was the third son of David's sister Zeruiah (2:16). Apparently he was not one of the "three mighty men," but his position as first in the list of "the thirty" suggests that he had a high rank. He may have failed to achieve greater prominence because of his untimely death at the hand of Abner (2 Sam. 2:18–23).

11:39, 40 Ammonite: Some of David's heroes were not Israelites. They may have been immigrants or mercenaries.

11:41 Uriah the Hittite: The irony of including this warrior in the list is obvious from the story of his death at the hands of David and Joab (2 Sam. 11:6–17). With remarkable candor, both Samuel and Chronicles include Uriah's name among the thirty.

11:42–47 Adina the Reubenite also appears to have led a group of the **thirty.** Though there are only sixteen names from Zabad through Jaasiel (vv. 41, 47), these sixteen might have formed the nucleus of such a mili-

tary unit. The others were no longer known, or the list was drawn up before the unit was complete.

12:1 About 25 miles southwest of Gath, **Ziklag** became David's private possession. He received it after he had crossed over into Philistia to get away from Saul and had placed himself under the lordship of Achish, the ruler of the city-state of Gath (1 Sam. 27:1–7). As an ally and vassal of Achish, David was required to pay tribute and show his loyalty and submission. Therefore, he made raids from Ziklag against various desert tribes, seizing their properties and bringing some of the plunder back to the Philistines. The rest he distributed to his own countrymen without the Philistines' knowledge. Meanwhile, David was joined at Ziklag by many other "outlaws" and refugees from Judah until he had a sizable number of **mighty men** there (1 Sam. 27:8–12).

12:2, 3 Included among his warriors were ambidextrous Benjamites, some of Saul's own fellow tribesmen. This shows the extent of dissatisfaction with Saul's rule. That these Benjamites could use the **right hand** as well as the **left** was ironic, because the name **Benjamin** means "Son of the Right Hand" (Judg. 20:16).

12:4, 5 This may suggest that the Benjamites listed here formed a unit known technically as **the thirty** (11:25), although not exactly thirty names are recorded here.

12:6, 7 Since the other heroes such as the Gibeathite in v. 3 were listed by their place of origin, Korah was probably the name of a place in Benjamin. These **Korahites** should not be confused with the Levites of that name (9:19).

12:8–13 David had attracted a following from all over Israel. The **Gadites** came from the far northern and central areas east of the Jordan (5:11–17) to join him. **The stronghold** was the cave of Adullam, David's principal place of refuge in the Judean wilderness (11:15; 1 Sam. 22:1).

12:14 hundred . . . thousand: These were terms for military units which may or may not have had precisely that many men. The Gadites were so famous for their valor and leadership skills (v. 8) that they rose to high ranks in David's army.

12:15–17 According to the agricultural calendar, the **first month** was Nisan, corresponding approximately to April. This was the time of the spring rains (Deut. 11:14), when the rivers were often at flood stage (Josh. 3:13; 4:18, 19). Ordinarily a person could not cross the Jordan at such times, but the Gadites were not deterred by such obstacles. As a testimony to their unusual courage, the chronicler states that they crossed the flooded Jordan pursuing their enemies in all directions.

12:18 Amasai was probably an alternative spelling of Amasa, the son of David's sister Abigail (2:17). He became David's army commander after Joab had fallen from favor (2 Sam. 19:13), but he held the post for only a short time before being assassinated by Joab (2 Sam. 20:4–13). The murder was all the more reprehensible because Joab and Amasa were first cousins.

12:19, 20 Manasseh defected: This incident reveals how compromised David's position was when he, as vassal to Achish of Gath (see v. 1), was pressed into joining the **Philistines** against Saul at Gilboa (1 Sam. 29:1–11). As it turned out, the other Philistine rulers outvoted Achish and sent David back to Ziklag before he had to go to war against his Israelite countrymen.

12:21 When David returned to Ziklag, he found that Amalekites had attacked the city and carried off his family with other prisoners (1 Sam. 30:1). Those who had abandoned David in his march to Gilboa (v. 19) now joined him in his pursuit of these **raiders** (1 Sam. 30:2–25).

12:22–27 The **army of God** refers to the angelic hosts, too vast to count. David attracted so many recruits while he was in the wilderness in flight from Saul and at Ziklag that they were beyond counting.

12:28 This **Zadok,** apparently an Aaronite (v. 27) and therefore a priest, was probably the same Zadok who was first appointed by David as priest at Gibeon (16:39), and then by Solomon at Jerusalem (1 Kin. 2:26, 27, 35). The office of priest was not incompatible with that of warrior, as Phinehas clearly demonstrated (Num. 25:6–9; Josh. 22:30).

12:29, 30 loyal to . . . Saul: Here is a subtle hint that the transition from Saul to David was not as smooth as a superficial reading of the account might suggest. There had to be a shifting of loyalties, something that usually is difficult, taking time and diplomacy.

12:31 These names represent delegates only and not the entire populations of the tribes. The support David enjoyed would have been even more enormous than the figures alone suggest.

12:32–37 understanding of the times: What the tribes were doing in appointing David king was not a historical fluke. It was the best and only thing to do in light of the present circumstances. The people of **Issachar** had some among them who understood clearly that God's time had come for His purposes to be put into effect.

12:38 keep ranks: This qualification (vv. 33, 36) pertains certainly to military formation as a skill or mark of discipline. But in the context of David's inauguration it also speaks of undivided loyalty, of **one mind.** No one was out of step when it came to recognizing that David was God's man and that the hopes of the nation as a theocratic community lay in **loyal** support of this.

12:39 eating and drinking: Besides the normal festivity that accompanied such a grand occasion as the installation of a king, this phrase alludes to a covenant meal (Gen. 31:43–55; Ex. 24:11)—a meal that solemnized a covenant between David and the people (11:3).

12:40 Issachar, Zebulun, and **Naphtali** were geographically the most distant of the tribes. The phrase **near to them** was a way of speaking of the common identity of God's people.

13:1, 2 David consulted: Though David was king and therefore could have acted independently, he understood the importance of godly counsel. Before he undertook the next major step, he sought the advice of his subordinate leaders.

13:3 This **ark** was the ark of the covenant that contained a copy of the Ten Commandments (Ex. 25:10–22). In the days of Eli, the ark had been captured by the Philistines, in whose hands it remained for several months (1 Sam.

 **IN FOCUS** **"peace"**

(Heb. *shalom*) (1 Chr. 12:18; Gen. 43:23; Num. 6:26; Is. 54:13) Strong's #7965: This word conveys the idea of completeness and well-being—of being a perfect whole. The word denotes an absence of discomfort, whether physical ailments or strife, internal or external (Gen. 43:28; Is. 26:3; Eccl. 3:8). It is used as an ordinary greeting, as a word of assurance, and as a term of blessing (Gen. 43:23; 1 Sam. 25:5, 6; 2 Kin. 5:19). The prophets Jeremiah and Ezekiel spoke out against the false prophets of their day for erroneously prophesying peace (Jer. 6:14; 8:11; Ezek. 13:10, 16). After God's judgment fell, Jeremiah proclaimed that God's thoughts toward the captives were for peace and not evil (Jer. 29:11). The word occurs in two important messianic prophecies identifying the Messiah as the Prince of Peace and the One who would assure our peace (Is. 9:6; 53:5).

4:11; 6:1). Next it remained at Beth Shemesh for a short time (1 Sam. 6:13–15) and finally it resided at Kirjath Jearim (1 Sam. 6:20—7:1). **since the days of Saul:** During Saul's reign, the people of Kirjath Jearim kept the ark in their city for safekeeping. Besides holding the Ten Commandments and serving as a throne for God, the ark represented the presence of the living God among the Israelites. David wanted to unify the Israelites around their God, so he brought the ark to the nation's new political center, Jerusalem. The city was already the seat of David's government (11:4–9); now it would become the dwelling place of God. Israelites from as far away as Beersheba and Dan would come to Jerusalem to worship their living Lord.

13:4 Again the chronicler highlighted the unity of the whole nation by saying that **all the people** agreed with David's decision to bring the ark to Jerusalem.

13:5 Shihor in Egypt: This was another way of referring to the Wadi el-Arish or "River of Egypt" that marked the boundary between Egypt and Canaan. This was Israel's most southwestern point (Num. 34:5; Josh. 13:3). **entrance of Hamath:** This was the most northern point of the kingdom under David, about one hundred miles north of the Sea of Galilee. It was also known as Lebo Hamath (Josh. 13:5; Judg. 3:3; 2 Chr. 7:8). **Kirjath Jearim**, otherwise known as Baalah, was a village about eight miles west of Jerusalem. It became the home of the ark of the covenant for more than 100 years (v. 3). It lay within the territory of **Judah**, just south of the border with Benjamin (Josh. 15:9, 10). While there it was in the custody of a certain Abinadab, who placed it in the cave of his son Eleazar (1 Sam. 7:1). Kirjath Jearim was not a priestly or Levit-

ical city, so it is not likely that this Abinadab was a priest.

13:6 A major feature of the Most Holy Place in both the tabernacle and temple was the **ark.** Above and behind the ark of the covenant, **cherubim** extended their wings over the cover (also called the mercy seat) of the ark (Ex. 25:17–22). The glory of God was perceived as sitting upon the top of the ark as a king sat on a throne. **His name:** In Deuteronomy, the presence of God is often spoken of as the presence of His name (Deut. 12:1–14).

13:7, 8 Only the Levites **carried the ark.** They carried it on their shoulders with poles passing through rings on the ark's corners (Num. 4:1–16).

13:9 Chidon's threshing floor is also called "Nachon's threshing floor" (2 Sam. 6:6). A threshing floor was a flat rocky surface on which grain was crushed by threshing sledges drawn by oxen. The floor was probably in or near Kirjath Jearim, for it is unlikely that the cart had gone far before God exposed to them their error in transporting the ark in a way contrary to His commands.

13:10 God struck Uzza dead because of the sacred inviolability of the ark. It was a holy object, representing the presence of God Himself (Ex. 25:21, 22), so it had to be handled in accord with the strictest regulations (Num. 4:5). Handling the ark in any other way, even with the best intention, invited God's anger (Num. 4:15). The narrative dramatically demonstrates God's holiness. His people had to approach Him with respectful awe.

13:11, 12 The threshing floor of Chidon was renamed **Perez Uzza,** meaning "Outburst Against Uzza." From that time forward, the name of this place would remind people that

---

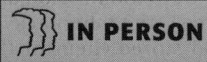 **David: The Rest of the Story**

The Chronicles were probably written at or just after the return of the Jews from exile. They tend to present King David positively and to pass by his foibles and failings. For example, the report of David's wives and family (1 Chr. 14:3–7) excludes the tragic details of his family life. Some of the other incidents omitted from the Chronicles account of David's life include:

- David's conflict with and flight from Saul (1 Sam. 18–30).
- Negotiations with Abner, Saul's general (2 Sam. 3:6–21).
- The murders of Abner and Ishbosheth (3:22–4:12).
- David's immorality with Bathsheba and the murder of Uriah, her husband (2 Sam. 11–12).
- The turmoil in David's family as a result of Amnon's rape of Tamar and Absalom's revenge (2 Sam. 13).
- Absalom's rebellion and death, and his father's grief (2 Sam. 15; 18).
- The disputed transfer of power to Solomon following David's death (1 Kin. 1; 2).

violating God's holiness meant inviting His wrath.

13:13, 14 A **Gittite** means someone from Gath, the name of several cities. Since **Obed-Edom** was a Levite (15:18, 24), he was probably from the Levitical city of Gath Rimmon in Dan (Josh. 21:25).

14:1, 2 A powerful ruler of the Phoenician city-state of Tyre, **Hiram king of Tyre** is mentioned in the Scriptures and in other sources. He was a contemporary of both David and Solomon. His work for David, constructing a royal palace, must have begun late in David's reign. Moreover, Hiram supplied material for the temple and other buildings, a project not completed until Solomon's twentieth year (1 Kin. 9:10). All this indicates that the chronicler was not writing in chronological order about the building of David's palace and the arrival of the ark. These did not take place early in his reign, but toward the end. **build him a house:** Once a king in the ancient Middle Eastern world had firmly established himself, he built a palace to publicize that fact. As v. 2 explicitly states, David built his palace with the understanding that God alone had put him in power and **exalted** him.

14:3 In addition to the wives he had taken in Hebron (2 Sam. 3:2–5), **David** married others in **Jerusalem.** Although the Bible never justifies polygamy, ancient kings frequently undertook multiple marriages for political reasons—a king would marry the daughter of another king in order to create a stronger alliance. The larger a king's harem, the more prestige the king enjoyed (3:1–5).

14:4 The four **children** listed here were all sons of Bathshua (Bathsheba; 3:5).

14:5–9 Extending southwest from Jerusalem and marking the northern border of Judah (Josh. 15:8), **the Valley of Rephaim** was the scene of many battles between Israel and the Philistines (11:15, 16; 2 Sam. 5:17–22; 23:13–17). The conflict here was a preemptive strike by the Philistines designed to prevent David from taking Jerusalem and making it the capital of Israel (11:4–9). God demonstrated that He was with David by granting him victory over the Philistines.

14:10, 11 Baal Perazim: There may be a reference to this place and event in Is. 28:21.

14:12–15 God has gone out before you: The strategy for this battle was different (vv. 10, 14) because God wanted David to understand that the battle was His, not David's. People often attribute their success to their own intelligence or strength, overlooking the fact that God is the source of all victories.

14:16, 17 Gibeon was about six miles northwest of Jerusalem, and **Gezer** was about sixteen miles west of Gibeon. The Philistines evidently left the Valley of Rephaim, fled north to Gibeon, and then were pursued all the way to Gezer, a town close to their own territory.

15:1 The **place for the ark** was in the tabernacle in the City of David. The original tabernacle built in Moses' day had been placed at Shiloh, in central Manasseh (Josh. 18:1). It remained there until the capture of the ark by the Philistines (1 Sam. 4:1–11), when it evidently was moved to Nob, just two miles from Jerusalem (1 Sam. 21:1–6). Next, the tabernacle was moved to a high place at Gibeon (2 Chr. 1:3), about two miles north of Saul's city Gibeah. When David became king, he left the Mosaic tabernacle at Gibeon and appointed the priest Zadok to attend to its ministry (16:39). Even after he had built a new tabernacle on

Stone carving of the ark of the covenant. David relocated the ark from Gibeon to Jerusalem soon after he made Jerusalem his capital city (1 Chr. 15:1–28).

Mount Zion and brought the ark into it, the original tabernacle remained at Gibeon. Finally, Solomon brought the ark from Mount Zion and the "tabernacle of meeting" (the tabernacle of Moses) from Gibeon and stored them in the new temple Solomon had built on Mount Moriah (2 Chr. 5:4, 5). In other words, the **tent** of David was a transitional home for the ark between the wilderness tabernacle and Solomon's temple.

15:2–4 Having learned his lesson from the incident with Uzza (13:10), David commanded that the **ark of God** be moved this time according to the provisions of the Law. It was to be carried by **Levites** by means of poles inserted through corner rings (Num. 4:14, 15).

15:5–7 David divided the Levites into divisions according to their genealogies. **Uriel** was head of the Kohathite clan (6:24), Asaiah was chief of the Merarites (6:30), and Joel was leader of the Gershonites (23:8).

15:8–10 All three of the following families were subclans of the Kohathites. **Elizaphan** was a grandson of Kohath (Ex. 6:18, 22), **Hebron** was a son of Kohath (Ex. 6:18), and **Uzziel** was another son of Kohath (Ex. 6:18).

15:11–16 The transition from the rule of Saul to David involved a transition from the old Mosaic tabernacle to the new place David had established on Mount Zion in preparation for the temple (v. 1). The father of **Abiathar,** the priest Ahimelech, was in charge of the old tabernacle when it left Shiloh and was moved to Nob (1 Sam. 21:1). Ahimelech (also known as Ahijah; 1 Sam. 14:3; 22:9) was Eli's great-grandson. Eli must have been a descendant of Aaron's son Ithamar, for the priesthood was taken from his line and given to the line of Eleazar, another son of Aaron (6:3, 4; 1 Sam. 2:22–36). The line of Eleazar produced **Zadok** (6:8). During David's time, representatives of both the Ithamar and Eleazar high-priestly lineages served concurrently. Zadok, who descended from Eleazar, served at the tabernacle at Gibeon. Abiathar, a descendant of Ithamar, was chief priest at Jerusalem. When Solomon came to power, Abiathar was deposed and Zadok ministered as high priest at the temple (1 Kin. 2:26, 27, 35).

15:17 The musician **Heman** was the grandson of the prophet Samuel (6:33), a Kohathite. He is probably the same Heman who appears in the superscription of Ps. 88. **Asaph** was leader of the Gershonite Levites (6:39, 43). Asaph and his sons ministered primarily as singers (25:1, 2; 2 Chr. 20:14) and composers, as their superscriptions suggest (Pss. 50; 73—83). **Ethan** was the head of the Merarite division of musicians (6:44). Ethan might be the same as "Ethan the Ezrahite," composer of Ps. 89 and known as a wise man (1 Kin. 4:31).

15:18, 19 second rank: The musicians

apparently occupied a place of higher status than the gatekeepers, who are mentioned next (9:17–27).

15:20 strings according to Alamoth: The musicians listed here are the same as the gatekeepers of v. 18. Since gatekeeping was on a rotating basis and might not have required full-time attention, these two responsibilities could have been combined.

15:21, 22 The word **Sheminith** might be derived from the Hebrew word for "eighth," referring to the musical scales.

15:23 The responsibility of the **door-keepers for the ark** appears limited to the task of moving the ark from the house of Obed-Edom to the Davidic tabernacle.

15:24–26 It is likely that **Obed-Edom** in this verse was the same person who had custody of the ark in the months just before it was brought to Jerusalem (13:13, 14). He apparently was a Levite (13:13) and was certainly a righteous man (v. 25; 16:38).

15:27, 28 linen ephod: This garment elsewhere in the OT is part of the attire of the high priest alone (Ex. 28:40) or, in its simpler pattern, of priests in general (1 Sam. 22:18).

15:29 David had married **Michal the daughter of Saul** at the beginning of his time of service in Saul's court (1 Sam. 18:27). Their relationship had been stormy, perhaps in part because David had spent at least ten years in flight from her father. In fact, Saul had annulled the marriage and had given Michal to another man (1 Sam. 25:44). One of the conditions of David's peace agreement with Abner and the reunification of the nation under David's kingship was that Michal be returned to him (2 Sam. 3:13–16). Michal was one of the few links remaining between David and the dynasty of Saul. For the transfer of government from Saul to David to be complete, it was necessary for

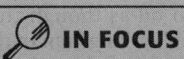 **IN FOCUS**   "cymbals"

(Heb. *metseleth*) (1 Chr. 13:8; 15:16; 16:42; 25:6; Neh. 12:27) Strong's #4700: The verbal root of this Hebrew word means "to tingle"; thus the noun form indicates some kind of cymbals, described on one occasion as made of bronze (15:19). Cymbals are always listed with other instruments, and they are regularly associated with singing (15:19; 2 Chr. 5:12, 13; Neh. 12:27). On one occasion cymbals accompanied the exercise of prophecy (25:1). David and Nathan established a Levitical order of musicians which included those who played cymbals, stringed instruments, and harps to glorify God (15:16; 2 Chr. 29:25; Ezra 3:10, 11). The Levitical cymbal player led these musicians in the worship of God (16:5). Cymbals were played during joyful celebrations to the Lord at such times as the dedication of Solomon's temple, Hezekiah's consecration of the house of the Lord, the laying of the foundation for the second temple, and the dedication of the wall of Jerusalem (2 Chr. 5:11–14; 29:25–31; Ezra 3:10, 11; Neh. 12:27).

Saul's daughter to be transferred back to David—even against her will. When Michal saw David rejoicing at the return of the ark, she despised him out of loyalty to her father and anger that she had been forced to return.

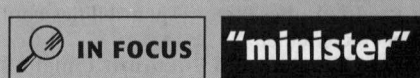

IN FOCUS "minister"

(Heb. *sharat*) (1 Chr. 16:4; Num. 3:31; Ps. 101:6) Strong's #8334: This Hebrew word means "to serve." It can denote honorable, high-level service, either secular or sacred. The secular sense of the term refers to the work of personal attendants, usually those who would succeed the office of the one served (Gen. 39:4; Josh. 1:1, 5). The sacred use of the word applies primarily to the work of priests, although occasionally Levites, and once even angels (15:2; Deut. 17:12; Ps. 103:21; Heb. 1:14). Most of the time the ministering is described as to or before the Lord, but the Levites are also said to minister to the priests (Num. 18:2), to the people (Num. 16:9; Ezek. 44:11), and to the tabernacle (Num. 1:50). Ministering before the Lord occasionally involved music and song (6:31, 32; 16:4, 5).

16:1–3 he distributed: David's distribution of food was in line with the nature of the peace offerings of vv. 1, 2. Such offerings often accompanied occasions of praise and thanksgiving such as this one. They were unique in that they provided a common meal in which all participated—the offerer, his family and friends, the priests, and even God (Lev. 7:11–14, 28–34; Deut. 12:17–19).

16:4–6 The appointment of **Levites** described here was of a more permanent nature than that of 15:1–24, which concerned the immediate task of moving the ark into Jerusalem. Some of the same persons were involved, as vv. 5, 6 make clear.

16:7–11 This strongly implies that David himself composed the **psalm.** David's musical abilities were well attested (2 Sam. 22:1; see the superscriptions of Pss. 3—9). This psalm consists of three different parts. Each portion correlates with part of another psalm, as follows: 16:8–22 with Ps. 105:1–15; 16:23–33 with Ps. 96:1–13; and 16:34–36 with Ps. 106:1, 47, 48.

16:12 His marvelous works: David appealed to the nation to reflect upon God's faithfulness as manifested in the nation's history. The God who had proved Himself in the

past was the One upon whom the unified nation could depend in the years to come.

16:13, 14 servant . . . chosen ones: These words reflect the role of Israel as an elect nation called by God to serve Him as "a kingdom of priests and a holy nation" (Ex. 19:6). David was very much aware of the importance of God's calling of Israel and of his responsibility as leader of this privileged nation.

16:15 The instrument that bound God and Israel together legally and formally was the **covenant.** This was an arrangement between two parties—in this case, a superior party and an inferior party—by which the two made solemn pledges of mutual loyalty and commitment. God's promises in the covenant were based on His faithful character.

16:16–18 To **Abraham,** God promised land (Gen. 12:7) and innumerable descendants (Gen. 15:5; 17:5–8). God designated Abraham's descendants as the people through whom He would bless all nations (Gen. 12:2, 3). In his psalm, David was reflecting on the reliability of God's promise to Abraham—a promise renewed to Isaac and confirmed to Jacob. Having just become king over all Israel, David was very much aware of God's faithfulness in granting the Israelites the land over which he had dominion.

16:19 very few: This refers to the time of the patriarchs. When Jacob went to Egypt, his extended family amounted to only seventy persons (Gen. 46:27).

16:20, 21 one nation to another: In patriarchal times, God's people moved about in Canaan and occasionally dwelt among other peoples such as the Egyptians (Gen. 12:10), Philistines (Gen. 20:1; 21:34; 26:1), and even the Hittites (Gen. 23:4, 17–20). **reproved kings:** This is a reference to God's judgment on Pharaoh (Gen. 12:17) and particularly his rebuke of Abimelech, the Philistine king of Gerar (Gen. 20:3–7).

16:22–24 Abraham and the patriarchs were not literally anointed with oil as though they were entering the priesthood or kingship. In this context, **anointed ones** means those set apart for God's service. **prophets:** Though the office of prophet as a "professional" calling began with Samuel, there were individuals from the earliest days of biblical history who were known as prophets. The reference here is specifically to Abraham, who is called a *prophet* in Gen. 20:7, the first occurrence of the word in the Bible.

16:25 above all gods: This does not admit the real possibility of other gods. Instead it refers to the various "gods" in which the pagans believed. The heathen might fear nonexistent gods, but the living Lord was to be feared more than them all, for He is alive and demands accountability.

🌱 IN LIFE | God above All Gods

Some people object to Christianity's claim that its God is the one true God. But the Bible states emphatically that the Lord is above all other gods, which are idols (1 Chr. 16:23–27). He alone deserves worship, for He is the Creator and Sustainer of life.

Most ancient cultures worshiped many gods, almost all of which were associated with nature. For example, the gods of the Canaanites were part of what was essentially a fertility cult designed to increase their harvests and the birth rate of their women. The Hebrews were virtually unique in their belief in one supreme God.

Today, too, people worship and serve a variety of gods, as well as a variety of often conflicting ideas about God. Meanwhile, the belief that there is one supreme God seems to be less and less popular, especially in an age that holds tolerance and religious pluralism to be among the highest of values. Yet God has not changed. He still invites—indeed, commands—all the families of the world to give Him the glory due His name (1 Chr. 16:28–30). Doing so need not be a statement of intolerance, simply a response to what is true.

16:26–30 idols: The poet here puts things into proper perspective and shows how foolish it is to fear gods who are manufactured products of human creativity.

16:31, 32 The phrase, **the LORD** reigns, is an appeal for the universal recognition of the sovereignty of the God of Israel. The Lord had called Israel into a special covenant relationship with Himself, but He did not thereby reject the other nations. Indeed, the whole purpose of Israel's election was that Israel might be the light to the nations that would cause them to turn to the one true God (Is. 42:5–7; 43:8–13).

16:33–36 trees . . . rejoice: This is a figure of speech called "personification," in which inanimate things are spoken of as if they had human characteristics. Because the whole creation was negatively affected by the fall of humanity into sin, it could not be restored to perfection and could not truly **rejoice** until humanity was redeemed. **He is coming:** This consummation of the ages will make all creation burst out in praise.

16:37 David appointed **Asaph** to be overall supervisor of worship before the Lord (v. 5).

16:38 Obed-Edom: There are two men by this name in this verse. The first is the Obed-Edom whose house sheltered the ark for three months (13:14) and who was a chief doorkeeper (15:24). The second, also a gatekeeper, was a **son of Jeduthun** (perhaps the one known as Ethan; 6:33, 39, 44).

16:39 Until the temple of Solomon was completed, there were two legitimate places for community worship—the Mosaic tabernacle at Gibeon and David's tabernacle on Mount Zion. **Zadok,** a descendent of Eleazar, served at Gibeon, while Abiathar, a descendant of Aaron, served at Jerusalem (15:11).

16:40 There must have been such an **altar** on Mount Zion, but the one at Gibeon was apparently considered more "official," no doubt because it had been built under Moses' leadership (2 Chr. 1:3, 5, 6). Zadok and his fellow priests officiated at the regular morning and evening sacrifices in Gibeon. Early in his reign, Solomon also went to the high place at Gibeon to offer sacrifices—an act completely acceptable to God, who blessed him there (1 Kin. 3:4, 5, 10–13; 2 Chr. 1:3, 11, 12).

16:41 Jeduthun: This was probably another name for the musician Ethan, who is usually named together with Asaph and Heman (15:17, 19; 6:33, 39, 44).

16:42, 43 instruments of God: This brief expression refers to instruments that play songs or praises to God. It is difficult to overemphasize the importance of music in OT worship. The Book of Psalms in itself and constant references to choral and orchestral ministry demonstrate the significance of music (9:33; 15:16–24; 16:4–6; 25:1–31). Music was an important way in which the people worshiped their Creator.

17:1–4 Nathan the prophet: This is the first time in this book that a prophet's name appears. Nathan apparently served David and Solomon as a private chaplain or counselor (2 Sam. 7:2, 3; 12:1–15; 1 Kin. 1:8–30, 32–38, 45; 2 Chr. 29:25). One of his written works, "the book of Nathan the prophet," provided a source for the composition of the books of Chronicles (29:29; 2 Chr. 9:29). A **house of cedar** indicates David's wealth, because cedar paneling was too expensive to be used in ordinary homes.

17:5 from tent to tent: This is a reference to the movement of God from the provisional "tabernacle of meeting" (Ex. 33:7), to the

Mosaic tabernacle (Ex. 40:34–38), and then to the tabernacle David erected on Mount Zion (16:1).

17:6 In addition to having "lived" in modest surroundings, God had also "lived" like a nomad, as the house of worship moved from one place to another. In the time of the **judges,** the tabernacle was at Shiloh (Josh. 18:1) and possibly Nob (1 Sam. 21:1). Before that, it had wandered with Israel through the Sinai desert before being set up at Gilgal (Josh. 4:19; 5:10). At this time it resided at Gibeon.

17:7 In the ancient Middle East generally, as well as in the OT, kings were often compared to shepherds (Is. 44:28; Zech. 10:3; 11:4–17). It was most fitting that David, who had literally shepherded **sheep,** should be called by God to shepherd His flock, Israel.

17:8 made you a name: David's reputation as a leader had become internationally known. He ranked with the great rulers of other nations.

17:9 appoint a place: This phrase did not suggest that Israel would move to a land other than Palestine, for that was the land of promise from the beginning (Gen. 13:14–17; 15:18–21; 17:8; Ex. 3:16, 17; 6:8; Deut. 1:8; Josh. 1:2–5). **sons of wickedness:** This was a general term for the Israelites' enemies—those who had persecuted them and taken them from their homeland.

17:10–12 As used here, **house** meant dynasty. David had said that he would build a house—that is, a temple—for God, but God told David that He would build a house—that is, a dynasty—for David. A human monarchy blessed by God was already apparent in the promise God had made to Abraham (Gen. 17:6). In addition, when Jacob blessed his sons, he asserted that a scepter and lawgiver—that is, a king—would arise out of Judah (Gen. 49:10). Samuel anointed David as king (1 Sam. 16:1, 12, 13) and David received assurances that he would rule over Israel (1 Sam. 23:17; 24:20; 26:25; 28:17). But God's promise to establish

David's dynasty forever was unprecedented. **your seed:** This is a reference to Solomon. Here **house** can only mean temple, because God has no dynasty. The temple was the dwelling place of God among His people (1 Kin. 8:10, 11).

17:13 Father . . . son: This remarkable statement affirmed that the dynasty of David had such an intimate relationship with God that its kings would be considered God's sons in an extraordinary way. **him who was before you:** This was a reference to Saul, from whom God had removed His blessing (10:14).

17:14, 15 The focus clearly shifts here from David's immediate successor, Solomon, to the entire succession of kings in David's line. It was the **kingdom** and **throne** of the dynasty that would endure **forever**, a promise made possible only by the reign of Jesus Christ, the Son of David (Luke 1:32, 33). Such a shift in reference is common in prophetic texts where the blending between the immediate and remote is so subtle as to be nearly imperceptible. Other clues must therefore be sought, as in this case, where Solomon is in view in v. 12, because he actually did build the temple, but Christ must be in view in v. 14, because only He qualifies to reign forever.

17:16–18 David responded to God's blessing with praise. **house:** David asked what made him the object of God's grace. He did not have any credentials to deserve God's amazing promises of an eternal kingdom. **small thing:** David's lack of pedigree and royal ancestry were of no consequence to God, because He was not impressed by such things. **What more can David say:** Once the truth of the promise sank into David's understanding, he found himself speechless.

17:19, 20 any God besides you: This is a clear assertion of the uniqueness of Israel's God. Statements such as "all gods" and "the gods of the peoples" in David's song of thanksgiving (16:25, 26) must be understood in light of this clear confession that there is only one living God.

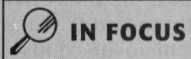 **IN FOCUS**   **"throne"**

(Heb. *kisse'*) (1 Chr. 17:12; Ps. 103:19; Is. 66:1) Strong's #3678: The Hebrew word can refer to any kind of seat or chair (Ps. 1:1), but usually it refers to a seat of honor (Is. 22:23), especially a throne (Esth. 5:1). Frequently the word is used to denote royal position or authority (1 Kin. 16:11). To "set up" or "establish" a throne is to establish or confirm a king and his dynasty. David's throne was particularly important in this respect, for in His covenant with David, God promised that the throne of David's son would be "established forever" (17:12; Ps. 89:4). Although Solomon and the succeeding kings of Judah sat on David's throne (1 Kin. 2:12; Jer. 22:2, 4), it is Jesus, the Son of David, who will fulfill this prophecy, reigning "upon the throne of David" forever (Is. 9:7).

17:21 David's observation here was not blind nationalism. As David continued to praise God, he expressed like Moses a theology of the election of Israel. God had chosen Israel, His treasured possession, by His will alone. The Israelites had nothing by which they could commend themselves to God. In fact, they were an insignificant and enslaved people (Deut. 7:6–11). Israel's prominent place among the nations was due to the Lord's abundant mercy. David's reference to Israel as **the one nation on the earth whom God went to redeem** does not preclude the eventual redemption of others. He is speaking here not soteriologically but in terms of servanthood. The redemption of Israel was not to save her so as to make her His people—that was already an accomplished fact (Ex. 3:7, 10; 4:22, 23)—but to deliver her so as to make a covenant of servanthood with her (Ex. 19:6). It also would provide occasion for the nations to marvel at Yahweh's power and thus to magnify His **name.**

17:22 Your very own people: This expression is clearly based on Ex. 19:5; Deut. 7:6; 14:2, where Israel is described as "a special treasure." The statement lies at the very center of the Mosaic covenant. At Mount Sinai, God had become the God of Israel; and Israel, in turn, had become the people of God.

17:23, 24 the word which You have spoken: David referred here to the covenant God had just made with him concerning his dynasty (17:7–14). David's appeal to God to establish His word came immediately after his reference to the Exodus and the Mosaic covenant. David knew that God's covenant with him was founded on God's previous promises to Abraham.

17:25, 26 Your servant . . . to pray: David here does not assert that he has now become a man of prayer because of God's promises to him. Rather, he has found the boldness to pray (vv. 16–24) because of the encouragement afforded by the promises.

17:27 blessed forever: David seems to allow no room for a temporary, conditional understanding of his kingship. He is convinced by the plain language of God's promise that he and his descendants will continue forever in the blessing of Yahweh (vv. 9, 12, 14).

18:1 This is the only record of David taking a Philistine city, although he had defeated the **Philistines** many times in battle. **Gath** was the Philistine city closest to Israelite territory, so it offered the greatest threat to Israel.

18:2 It must have been with mixed feelings that David undertook a campaign against the Moabites, for he had strong emotional links with **Moab.** His great-grandmother Ruth came from Moab (Ruth 4:13–17) and David had sent his own family there for protection when he was hiding from Saul (1 Sam. 22:3, 4). The technical expression for the relationship described here, in which the Moabites became **David's servants** and paid him **tribute,** is "suzerainty." This means that Moab was not part of the kingdom of Israel and did not have an Israelite governor. Native rulers were allowed to stay in office, but they had to show their submission to David by making a suzerain treaty with him.

18:3, 4 The campaign here may be connected to the Aramean war more fully outlined in 19:1–19, because **Hadadezer** is mentioned in both places. His kingdom, **Zobah,** lay immediately north of Damascus. David pursued him as far as Hamath, a hundred miles beyond Damascus, in an effort to extend the Israelite empire all the way to the River Euphrates. David's justification may have been God's promise to Abraham that the land He was giving him would extend "from the river of Egypt to the great river, the River Euphrates" (Gen. 15:18).

18:5 The capital of the Aramean kingdom just north and northeast of Israel was **Damascus.**

18:6, 7 servants . . . tribute: These technical terms, as in the case of Moab (v. 2), suggest that Damascus became a vassal state under Israel. Very quickly, Moab and Damascus became client states and Zobah an occupied territory.

18:8, 9 To the two cities **Tibhath . . . Chun,** Samuel added a third Berothai (2 Sam. 8:8). All three are referred to in Egyptian texts. They were northeast of Baalbek in central Lebanon.

18:10 greet . . . bless: This apparently casual language covers a more formal situation in which **Tou,** king of Hamath, was approaching David in willing submission to him as king. In other words, what Moab and Damascus did involuntarily, Hamath was doing voluntarily, making itself a vassal state under Israel.

18:11 The fact that David **dedicated** all the spoils of war to God suggests that he viewed the battles as campaigns of holy war. In such war, initiated and led by God, all proceeds of the victory belonged to Him. Such spoils were said to be "doomed to destruction" or "accursed" (Josh. 6:17, 18), meaning that they could not be used for secular purposes but were consecrated to God. When Solomon built the temple, he brought all the dedicated things into the temple treasuries (2 Chr. 5:1). The spoils of Amalek may have included some from Saul's conquest of the Amalekites (1 Sam. 15:9), but more likely the reference is to David's raids against them when he was living at Ziklag as a vassal of Achish of Gath (1 Sam. 27:8, 9).

18:12 One of David's nephews (2:15, 16), **Abishai,** was included in one of the groups of

David's "three mighty men" (11:20). **Valley of Salt:** This was a few miles east of Beersheba.

18:13, 14 The term **servants** suggests that Edom became not just a defeated foe, but also a vassal state under Israel's control. This allowed Edom to retain its own leadership, but it was

were elite companies of soldiers, probably mercenaries. They were commanded by Benaiah, a member of one of the groups of "three mighty men" (11:24). There were Philistines known as Cherethites (Ezek. 25:16; 1 Sam. 30:14), and the connection between Pelethites and Philistines

Photo: Levant Photo Service

Excavations at Ashkelon, one of the five chief cities of the Philistines. King David conquered the Philistines and captured all their cities (1 Chr. 18:1).

under David's close supervision, as the reference to Israelite garrisons makes clear.

18:15 David awarded his nephew **Joab** (2:15, 16) the rank of commander of the **army** for his success in penetrating the walls of Jerusalem (11:4–9). **recorder:** Jehoshaphat was the keeper of the royal archives or records. The chronicler himself may have had access to such documents when he composed the present work (27:24).

18:16 Zadok descended from Aaron through Eleazar (16:39). **Abimelech:** Abiathar, a descendant of Aaron's son Ithamar, had served as David's priest in the wilderness (1 Sam. 22:20) and later at Jerusalem (15:11). But he was disloyal to Solomon and was removed from office, leaving Zadok alone as high priest (1 Kin. 2:27, 35). It seems that David must have suspended Abiathar as well from service at some earlier point, for in the present passage his son Abimelech was priest with Zadok.

18:17 Cherethites . . . Pelethites: These

elsewhere (2 Sam. 15:18) leads to the conclusion that they were all from Philistia. **chief ministers:** These were David's sons who served in his government. They are called by the Hebrew word usually translated "priests" in 2 Sam. 8:18.

19:1 Since **Nahash** was reigning in Saul's earliest years (1 Sam. 11:1), the present incident must have occurred early in David's reign at Jerusalem. **Nahash** evidently reigned for over 50 years (40 years of Saul, plus seven of David in Hebron, plus whatever years had passed in Jerusalem).

19:2 I will show kindness: What David has in mind is not apparent. The word translated "kindness" is *hesed*, a Hebrew term rich in covenant significance. Perhaps David is saying that he will now make a covenant with Hanun inasmuch as Nahash had made a covenant with him. This would be particularly appropriate inasmuch as the death of one of the covenant parties would necessitate that it be renewed with his successor.

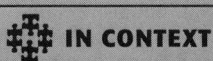 **IN CONTEXT** | **Gates and Fortified Cities**

B attles were often fought near the gate of a city (1 Chr. 19:9), which was its most vulnerable defensive feature. City gates were made of wood, so it was easier for enemies to gain access by beating them down or setting them on fire, rather than by storming or undermining a city's stone walls. For this reason a number of improvements were added to make a city's gate(s) more well-fortified (2 Chr. 8:5).

One development was to make the approach to the city a long narrow ramp, which would run parallel to one of the city's walls. These ramps were often built along the walls from the right to the left, that enemy soldiers (most fought right-handed) would be forced to turn nearly backward to defend themselves. The ramp also meant that enemy soldiers had to run the length of a wall to reach the gate, a process exposing them to observation and attack from the wall.

Cites also had more than one gate in the gatehouse or gate complex. The outer gate was built well outside the city and at a right angle to the city. It was placed directly in front of the approach ramp and was the first major obstacle for attackers.

These gatehouses were part of a castlelike building similar to towers. Defenders were stationed on the roofs of these complexes and behind doors. If attackers succeeded in gaining entrance, they would find themselves confined in a narrow passage that made a sharp right turn toward the main gate. Defenders both blocked this passage and were stationed above it on the walls. If attackers survived this gauntlet, they still faced the city's primary gate and its defenses.

The main gate was a multichambered structure resembling an extra large tower. It comprised four separate sets of gates, behind which were chambers for defending soldiers. The roofs of these gate structures were designed for defenders to have clear aim at the attackers.

19:3 search and . . . spy: The suspicions of Hanun's advisers may not have been totally unjustified, in light of David's ambitious plans to carve out an empire (11:9; 14:2).

19:4, 5 shaved . . . cut off: Ancient Semitic men were inordinately proud of their beards and scrupulously modest in their attire. The Ammonites humiliated David's men in the most offensive way possible.

19:6 made themselves repulsive: The Ammonites realized that David would surely retaliate for the way they had offended his delegation. **thousand talents of silver:** A talent was 75 pounds. **Mesopotamia:** This was not the great land between the Tigris and the Euphrates inhabited by the Assyrians and Babylonians, but a district on the upper Euphrates known as Aram Naharaim. **Syrian Maachah:** This was a small kingdom located between Damascus and the Sea of Galilee.

19:7 The parallel account in 2 Sam. 10:6 does not mention **chariots** but says there was a total of 33,000 men. The chronicler does not mention the number of men, but only of the chariots. Both writers gave different sources of the manpower and material, so clearly they were arriving at their totals from different perspectives or with different purposes in mind. **Medeba** was 20 miles southwest of Rabbah, the capital of Ammon. It is called Madaba today. **Ammon gathered:** The Israelites were appar-

ently between the Aramean armies and the city of Rabbah (v. 10), so when the Ammonites attacked from the city, the Israelites were pinned between two forces.

19:8–10 Completely surrounded, Joab split up his forces so that half faced those **before** and half faced those **behind.** Joab led the section that opposed the Syrians, and Abishai commanded the section that opposed the Ammonites (v. 11).

19:11–13 may the LORD do what is good in His sight: This may look like the resigned statement of a fatalist, but it was anything but that. Joab understood enough of the sovereignty and omniscience of God to know that after all human effort and energy had been expended, the battle was still God's.

19:14, 15 The Syrians were mercenaries and had no real commitment to the task at hand. When it appeared that they were in danger of defeat, they **fled.** Their retreat so demoralized the Ammonites that they withdrew into the safety of their city.

19:16 Syrians . . . beyond the river: The identity of these trans-Euphratean Arameans cannot be further established. They apparently were either treaty allies of Hadadezer of Zobah (18:3; 2 Sam. 10:16) or his vassals (2 Sam. 10:19). In any case they were under the command of Hadadezer's general **Shophach.**

19:17, 18 Samuel located the setting of the

battle at Helam (2 Sam. 10:17), about 40 miles east of the Sea of Galilee.

19:19 The defeat of Hadadezer and all his vassal kings brought about a shift in allegiance, so that all the Aramean states that had paid tribute to Zobah came under tribute to Israel. In this context, **servants** did not signify household slaves but national subservience to a greater power, in this case Israel. This effectively eliminated all the Arameans as allies of Ammon and precluded their being a further threat to Israel. With the subjugation of everything from Aram Maachah to the Euphrates, David occupied all the boundaries of the land of promise as outlined in the Abrahamic covenant (Gen. 15:18–21).

20:1 Great military operations were conducted **in the spring of the year** for two main reasons: (1) the latter rains were over and the dry months of summer, most suitable for military activity, were at hand; and (2) the barley harvests were in and the wheat harvests sufficiently well along to free men of military age for battle. **besieged Rabbah:** Having defeated the Aramean allies of Ammon at Helam (19:17, 19), Joab led Israel's armies against the main enemy and principal objective, the capital of the Ammonite kingdom, Rabbah. The modern city of Amman, Jordan, occupies the ancient site.

David stayed at Jerusalem: This agrees with Samuel's account, but Samuel also related the sordid story of David's adultery with Bathsheba, the plot to kill her husband Uriah, and the birth of David's son—all of which took place while Joab was laying siege to Rabbah. The chronicler was not trying to deceive his readers, since the truth was well known from the books of Samuel, which the chronicler himself cited. The chronicler omitted the material because it was not relevant to his literary and theological purposes. He was showing how the Davidic dynasty was the fulfillment of God's promises. **Joab defeated Rabbah:** In the chronicler's truncated version, this appears to have happened coincident with the launching of the spring campaign and a brief siege. The version in Samuel, however, makes clear that the campaign lasted several seasons.

20:2 David did not participate in the initial attack on Rabbah, but he did join Joab when it fell, because Joab earnestly entreated him to come share the credit for the victory (2 Sam. 12:27, 28). The **crown** David took was ceremonial and not for wearing, since it weighed a **talent** (about 75 pounds). **set on David's head:** This was only for this ceremonial occasion. David put the crown on his head to demonstrate that he had vanquished the

---

⚔ IN DEPTH   The Arameans

Some of the forces opposing general Joab were Syrians (1 Chr. 9:10), members of an ethnic group also known as the Arameans. They controlled the region northeast of the Sea of Galilee, from the Lebanon Mountains on the west to the Euphrates River on the east and northward. Their principal city was Damascus.

The Arameans were among the ancient peoples believed to have migrated into the Middle East from the west as early as 2250 B.C. They became fully established as a kingdom during the period of the Israelites' conquest of Canaan (c. 1200 B.C.). During the period of the judges, they overran Israel and oppressed it for eight years (Judg. 3:8–10). However, after David became king of Israel, he extended his nation's boundary north to the Euphrates River (2 Sam. 8:1–13). It was at this time that an Aramean official named Rezon fled to Damascus and founded a strong Aramean city-state there (1 Kin. 11:23, 24). This kingdom remained a bitter foe of Israel for many generations.

One strategy that the Arameans used to advantage was to side with one Israelite state or the other during the divided monarchy (15:18–20; 2 Kin. 16:5). However, when Judah eventually joined with Assyria against Israel and Aram in the eighth century B.C., the result was the downfall of Damascus (c. 732 B.C.; 16:7–18). Many Arameans were exiled to other lands, as was the Assyrian policy, and the kingdom of Aram came to an end.

Nevertheless, through their language the Arameans left behind a legacy that can still be felt today. Aramaic, which had been spoken from at least 2000 B.C., eventually became the language of trade, commerce, and diplomacy throughout the ancient Middle East. As a result, Aramaic (a language closely related to Hebrew) came to have an important influence on the Bible. Portions of the Book of Daniel were written in Aramaic, and it was the language commonly spoken by Jews in Palestine during the time of Jesus.

Ammonites and now reigned over them as well.

20:3 It was common in OT times for **people** defeated in war to be consigned to forced labor, particularly if they had been coerced into some kind of vassal relationship (Josh. 9:22–27; 1 Kin. 9:20, 21).

20:4, 5 The city of **Gezer** was on the frontier between Israel and Philistia and was constantly a bone of contention between them. **Sibbechai the Hushathite:** He was one of the thirty warriors who formed an elite corps (11:29). **the giant:** This apparently did not refer to a single individual, but to a giant race indigenous to the country east of the Jordan (Deut. 2:10, 11, 20, 21).

20:6 The same genetic aberration that produced giants may also have led to such mutations as described here.

20:7 Shimea: This was David's older brother, the third son of Jesse (2:13).

20:8 the giant: As in v. 4, this likely referred to a giant race living in and around **Gath,** though it is possible that a particular giant was in view. The Goliath killed by David was from Gath (1 Sam. 17:4).

21:1 The word **Satan** means "Adversary." While at first he was called "the Satan," this later came to be used as a proper name, Satan (Zech. 3:1, 2). The NT identifies him as the evil one, the devil, and the dragon, thus linking him to the serpent in the Garden of Eden (Gen. 3:1). **moved David:** Samuel attributed David's impulse to number the people to God Himself (2 Sam. 24:1). The apparent contradiction can be resolved by recognizing that though Satan is the author of all evil, he cannot exercise his evil intentions apart from the permission of God. Moreover, God could use him to accomplish His own purposes of judgment (1 Kin. 22:19–23) or discipline (as here with David).

21:2 Go, number: David's plan to take a census was not evil in itself, for the Lord Himself at other times had commanded the Israelites to be counted (Num. 1). What was wrong with David's census was David's attitude—his pride. He wanted to **know** the number of the Israelites so that he could glory in the extent of his reign (2 Sam. 24:1). **Beersheba to Dan:** This was the traditional way of describing all of Israel from south to north. The distance is about 150 miles.

21:3–5 Joab was concerned that David's arrogant command for a census would bring punishment, not only on the king but on innocent citizens, whom Joab described as David's **servants.** David's position as king and shepherd of his people implicated them in whatever he did. **cause of guilt:** In a courageous appeal, Joab pointed out that if David's decision was put

into effect David would be personally accountable for whatever followed.

21:6, 7 The men of **Levi,** dedicated as they were to priestly service, were ordinarily exempt from military conscription (Num. 1:47–49). **Benjamin:** The reason this tribe was excluded may be that the judgment of God commenced before the task was completed (27:24). Perhaps Joab simply abandoned the task before he finished, his sense of revulsion growing more and more as he carried it out.

21:8 I have sinned: To his credit, David blamed no one but himself for the judgment of God that fell on the nation. He rightly believed that if God would forgive him, the affliction of the nation would also cease.

21:9 Gad is the second prophet named in the book (17:1). He also produced a composition to which the chronicler refers (29:29). Here the chronicler calls Gad a **seer,** a person who sees or receives revelations from the Lord. The author of Samuel refers to him by the more familiar term *prophet* (1 Sam. 22:5).

21:10, 11 I offer . . . three things: This is the only place in the Bible where God offers someone a choice of punishments.

21:12 The formulaic phrase **the angel of the Lord** is used elsewhere in the OT to speak of Yahweh in an anthropomorphic if not human form. Thus, when an angel visited Abraham at Mamre, it was Yahweh Himself (Gen. 18:3, 16, 17, 22), as was the angel of the Lord who appeared to Gideon (Judg. 6:11, 15, 22) and to the Samson's parents (Judg. 13:3, 6, 16, 18, 21, 22). The combination of an angel with a **plague** here is reminiscent of the Passover story.

21:13, 14 David knew that the Lord is merciful—a God who forgives. David's willingness to fall into **the hand of the Lord** demonstrated his complete trust in the grace of God. Even when God was punishing him, David trusted God rather than **man**—God's forgiving nature over any leniency people might offer.

21:15 The Lord requires certain conditions people must meet in order for Him to act one way or another. One aspect of this is prayer, for often God chooses to act in specific cases according to whether and how His people pray. This is clearly the case here, since **God sent an angel to destroy Jerusalem,** but when He saw David's repentance and heard his intercessory prayer (v. 17), He **relented. Ornan the Jebusite** was a member of the native population of Jerusalem that remained to share the city with the Israelite conquerors (11:4; Judg. 1:21). That Ornan owned a piece of property, a **threshing floor** (13:9), suggests that he was wealthy, an interesting fact in light of the generally despised lot of the Jebusites (Ex. 13:5; 23:23; 33:2; 34:11; Deut. 7:1; 20:17; Josh. 3:10).

21:16 Sackcloth was a rough garment usually made of goat's hair (Is. 50:3), worn by mourners to express grief (1 Kin. 21:27; Is. 32:11). David and the elders of Israel were dressed in such a manner because of the terrible calamity brought on the nation by the plague.

21:17 By calling his people **sheep,** David was acknowledging himself as their shepherd (17:7). Since that designation first arose in the context of God's covenant promises, David's reference to his people as sheep very likely attested to his feelings of covenant unfaithfulness and irresponsibility. He was supposed to be the one who guided the flock to safety and security, but by his arrogance in numbering the people he had brought them harm.

21:18, 19 Building **an altar** in a time of judgment or impending judgment was for the purpose of offering propitiatory sacrifices. Sin had caused a breach between God and His people. The presentation of appropriate burnt offerings and peace offerings (v. 26) would be the occasion for reconciliation, as the Law explained (Num. 15:1–10). **threshing floor:** The altar was located precisely where the angel of the Lord stood with sword in hand to destroy Jerusalem (v. 15). This place of judgment would thereby become the place of grace and forgiveness.

21:20, 21 Ornan continued threshing not because he was indifferent to the appearance of the **angel** but because his **sons** saw the angel first and **hid themselves,** whereas Ornan was in the process of threshing when he first became aware of the angel's presence.

21:22, 23 Grant me . . . this threshing floor: David wanted the altar at precisely this place because this is where the angel stood with drawn sword (v. 15), and as was certainly known to David, this was where Abraham had prepared to offer Isaac as a sacrifice to God (Gen. 22:1, 2; 2 Chr. 3:1). It is fitting that this holy place should be the site of an altar where David could make atonement for his sins and thus effect the withdrawal of the plague.

21:24 David again showed a clear perception of the essence of sacrifice. Until he owned what Ornan had, and until he had expended his own resources for it, he could not use it as an offering to God. **which costs me nothing:** While David could have rightfully accepted these gifts without paying for them, he felt that this would not suffice as sacrifice. A true sacrifice to God required labor and investment on David's part.

21:25 The chronicler referred to the price for the whole **place,** probably several acres of valuable property. The fact that the temple was later built here suggests a large area.

21:26, 27 Just as a three-year drought ended in the days of Elijah when the prophet called down **fire** on a sacrifice at Carmel (1 Kin. 18:38, 41), so the three-day plague God brought on Israel ended with the sacrifice at Ornan's threshing floor.

21:28 he sacrificed there: Once David saw that God had sanctified the spot by setting fire to the sacrifice, he continued to use the altar as a regular place of offering.

21:29 This verse teaches explicitly that the original **tabernacle** and **altar of the burnt offering** had not been destroyed when the ark was taken from Shiloh. The OT account does not trace their movement fully after Shiloh, but they did end up at Nob and finally at Gibeon (15:1).

21:30 David could not go before it: It was David's custom to offer burnt offerings on the altar at Gibeon rather than on the one in Jerusalem. He did not dare go to Gibeon this time because of the judgment that God was about to pour out on the land. He understood that his offerings had to be offered where he was—at the threshing floor of Ornan.

22:1 This observation by David marks a significant turning point in the history of the central sanctuary. As long as the ark remained at Kirjath Jearim and the Mosaic tabernacle was at Nob and Gibeon, it was impossible for worship to be carried out in the manner originally intended. David had taken the first steps toward remedying that by bringing the ark to Jerusalem and placing it in a tent that he provided on Mount Zion. At last, and in a way totally unforeseen by anyone, the resolution of the problem was at hand. The **house of the LORD** God and the **altar of burnt offering** would be built on the threshing floor of Ornan.

22:2, 3 The fact that David could not **build** the temple did not prevent him from providing building materials for the use of Solomon's craftsmen.

22:4 Cedar trees came from Lebanon, the principal supplier of timber in the ancient Middle Eastern world. The most expert builders also hailed from Lebanon, and from cities like Sidon and Tyre.

22:5–7 Solomon was born about halfway through David's reign. He reigned with his father for about two years (23:1; 28:1; 29:22). Since David was only beginning to gather building materials for the temple, Solomon could not have been over 18 years old. It was precisely because Solomon was so **young and inexperienced** that David found it necessary to provide guidance for his son.

22:8, 9 You have shed much blood: The reason that God did not allow David to build the temple comes to light—David was a man of war. Until the enemies of Israel were subdued and an era of peace inaugurated, God determined that He would not "live" in a temple. The sign that a king in the ancient world had truly achieved dominion over his realm was his construction of a magnificent palace for himself. As long as he was at war and was contending for sovereignty it was inappropriate to build such a structure. David's son Solomon would **be a man of rest;** that is, a king whose reign would be free from constant warfare. At that time of peace, God had resolved that a temple would be built for Himself. God's actions here reflected the practice of many ancient kings: a king would construct a palace only after he had established peace in his land.

22:10–12 Having just observed the youth and inexperience of Solomon (v. 5), David knew that his son needed **wisdom** more than any other single gift. **the law of the LORD**: This cannot be limited to only the sections of the Law pertaining to kingship (Deut. 17:14–20), although this is the central focus. David must have had in mind the covenant of kingship to which he himself had subscribed when he became king at Hebron (11:3).

22:13, 14 These are staggering amounts. At $300 per ounce, the gold today would be valued at $36 billion. At $5 per ounce, the silver today would be valued at $80 million.

22:15–18 Rest, or peace, was a precondition for building the temple (22:8, 9). **subdued before the LORD**: In the final analysis, the conquest of the land begun in Joshua's time and completed under David, was a divine and not a human matter. The land was the Lord's and His people were His tenants. Therefore, only when God Himself brought the land into subjection would He authorize construction of a temple.

22:19 David's dreams and desires are encapsulated in this brief verse. At that time, the **sanctuary** was divided—at Gibeon and Mount Zion—and the ark was not united with the altar

at Zion (v. 1). More than anything else, David wanted the Israelites to worship the Lord as He had instructed them.

23:1, 2 made . . . Solomon king: The phrasing suggests that this is an official appointment of Solomon to be coregent with David, a choice that had to be accepted and later ratified by the whole nation (29:22). David seems to have been afraid that death was at hand and thus concerned to make the succession of Solomon a foregone conclusion and as smooth a process as possible. The amount of activity that took place between this appointment and the formal ratification presupposes the passing of a year or more, a suggestion supported by other chronological considerations (1 Kin. 1:35, 39; 1 Chr. 23:1; 29:22, 23).

23:3 A Levite normally entered service at age 25 (Num. 8:24, 25). However, exceptions were made (Num. 4:3) to answer the needs of various time periods and ministries. Evidently in David's time enough Levites could be found aged **thirty** and over that there was no need to call younger Levites into service.

23:4–7 the work of the house of the LORD: The work clearly involved anything around the temple except the work of gatekeepers and musicians, who had their own divisions (v. 5). **officers and judges:** To provide ready access to the Levites in matters of religious questions and activities, six thousand Levites were distributed throughout the land (26:29–32), presumably in the Levitical cities (6:54–81).

23:8 Jehiel . . . Zetham . . . Joel were evidently descendants of **Laadan** (or Libni, 6:17) who lived in David's time. For some of the genealogical links between Laadan and these three, see 6:20, 21.

23:9 Shimei: This is not the brother of Laadan (v. 10; 6:17) but probably an important descendant. This seems certain in that all the

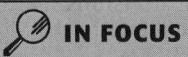 **IN FOCUS** "Levites"

(Heb. *levi*) (1 Chr. 23:26; Num. 3:9) Strong's #3881: The Levites were the descendants of Levi, one of the twelve sons of Jacob. The name is related to the verb *lavah*, meaning "to join," implying that the Levites were "joined" to God (Gen. 29:34). The tribe had three branches, named after the three sons of Levi: the Gershonites, the Kohathites, and the Merarites (Num. 3). At Mount Sinai, God chose Aaron, Moses' brother and a Kohathite, to be the nation's high priest (Ex. 28:1). No one but a descendant of Aaron could serve as a priest, but the other branches of the Levites shared many of their privileges and responsibilities (Num. 18:2). Originally the non-priestly Levites helped care for the tabernacle (Num. 4), but when David began preparations for building the temple, he created new duties for these Levites, making them singers, gatekeepers, treasurers, and royal officials (24:1–26:19).

Levites of vv. 8 and 9 are Laadanites, a total of six Gershonite divisions.

23:10 Shimei: This is the brother of Laadan (v. 7; 6:17). His sons constituted the leadership of **four** more divisions of Gershonites, making ten in all, it seems.

23:11, 12 one father's house: Since two of Shimei's sons had small families they combined to make one division.

23:13 give the blessing: This referred to the priestly benediction of Num. 6:24–26.

23:14 sons of Moses: Because the priesthood was limited to Aaron, brother of Moses, and his descendants, Moses and his sons could not have served as a priests. However, they could assume other responsibilities of Levites (Judg. 18:30).

23:15 Gershon was an immediate son of Moses (Ex. 2:22), as was **Eliezer.**

23:16 Shebuel cannot be the grandson of Moses but a distant relative, since he is a contemporary with David (24:20; 26:24).

23:17 Rehabiah was the first: This could be Eliezer's actual son, but more likely "first" here means "most important." Moses, then, gave rise to two Kohathite divisions of Levites.

23:18 Izhar was the second son of Kohath (v. 12).

23:19 Hebron was the third son of Kohath (v. 12).

23:20, 21 Uzziel was the fourth son of Kohath (v. 12). There were nine Kohathite divisions of Levites: two from Amram, one from Izhar, four from Hebron, and two from Uzziel.

23:22 Eleazar, son of Mahli, left no sons, so his **daughters** married their cousins, **the sons of Kish.** This resulted in a merger of the two lines of Mahli into one, so there was only one Levitical division through this branch of the Merarites.

23:23 The Mushi branch of Merarites produced **three** Levitical divisions in David's temple organization, making four in all, including the one traced to Mahli.

23:24–26 These were the sons of Levi: All three Levitical lines resulted in a total of twenty-two divisions, nine Gershonite, nine Kohathite, and four Merarite (24:18; 25:31). **twenty years and above:** At the beginning of the lists of divisions, the minimum age of the Levites was thirty (v. 3). The number *twenty* here was not a contradiction, for as v. 27 makes clear, the lower age was set by David in his last words. It seems that as time went by even 38,000 Levites were not sufficient, so that within two years or so it was necessary to lower the minimum age requirement.

23:27 by the . . . words of David: This remarkable statement made David almost a second Moses, in the sense that he was free to change a Mosaic legislation without challenge or reproof.

23:28 That **their duty was to help** is a clear statement of the role of the Levite with reference to the priest. It was a call to assistance in every aspect of ministry. Specifically it had to do with purifying **of all holy things** (Num. 3:31) and other tasks appropriate to conducting the services.

23:29 To free the priests for the work of offering sacrifices, the Levites prepared elements for the sacrificial ritual, such as **fine flour** and **unleavened cakes,** and in other ways assisted the prescribed services.

23:30 thank and praise: This ministry fell to the Levites engaged in choral and orchestral duties (25:1–31).

23:31 burnt offering: Though Levites outside the priestly line could not officiate at the sacrifices of the central sanctuary, they could assist the priests, for example by helping to skin the animal and cut it up. **Sabbaths:** The reason for the plural was not only because there were many Saturdays in a year, but other days as well could be called a "Sabbath." For example, the eighth day of the Feast of Tabernacles was considered a Sabbath no matter what day of the week it was (Lev. 23:39). **New Moons:** This referred to the first day of every month, otherwise known as the Feast of Trumpets (Num. 28:11–15). **set feasts:** These would be Passover and Unleavened Bread (Lev. 23:4–8), the Feast of Weeks or Pentecost (Lev. 23:9–22), and the Feast of Tabernacles (Lev. 23:33–43).

23:32 tabernacle of meeting: At this point the temple had not yet been built, so David's regulations for the Levites pertained to their service in the intermediate tabernacles at Gibeon and Mount Zion. **holy place:** This referred to the outer room of the tabernacle as opposed to the Most Holy Place, to which only the high priest had access.

24:1 In order for the priests to serve in rotation and have time off from their duties, they were assigned to shifts or **divisions.** For this rotation, David divided the priests by their lines of descent from Aaron (v. 3).

24:2 Nadab and Abihu died: This referred to the incident in which these two sons of Aaron incurred the wrath of God by offering up incense kindled with improper fire, that is, fire that did not originate from God (Lev. 9:23—10:2).

24:3 The **Ahimelech** here was the son of Abiathar (v. 6), the young priest of Nob who had joined David in the wilderness many years before (1 Sam. 22:20). There is not a complete genealogy of Abiathar in the OT, but it is clear from this passage that his ancestry was from Aaron through **Ithamar.**

24:4, 5 When the descendants of the two

lines were identified there were **sixteen** family divisions from Eleazar and only **eight** from Ithamar. This complicated the process of dividing the service assignments fairly. The solution was to assign the duties by casting lots. Evidently the priestly lines would each serve in turn, but the order of succession within each was determined **by lot.**

24:6 Shemaiah . . . wrote them down: In order to arrange the schedule for the priests' service and to keep it functioning properly, it was necessary that records be kept of all the names of the Levites by family and the shifts they were to fill in their rotation.

24:7–9 first lot: Since Eleazar and Ithamar are mentioned in that order in v. 6, it may be assumed that this list of names gives first someone from Eleazar, next someone from Ithamar, and so on alternately through the list.

24:10–19 This **Abijah** may be the ancestor of Zacharias, father of John the Baptist, who is named in Luke 1:5.

24:20, 21 sons of Levi: The non-priestly Levites also were divided by clan to determine their service rotation. The first division is Kohath, whose name does not appear but is implied in the mention of his son Amram. **Jehdeiah** and **Isshiah,** who were direct descendants of Moses (23:14–17), were omitted from the earlier list of Levites (23:16, 17).

24:22–24 The **Izharites** were Kohathites (23:12). **Hebron** was the third of the Kohathite clans (23:12). **Uzziel** was the last division of the Kohathites (23:12).

24:25, 26 Founder of the entire clan that bears his name (23:6), **Merari** was the third son of Levi. **Jaaziah:** This descendant of Merari appears for the first time here.

24:27–31 To assure the fairness of the Levites' assignments, they were selected by their divisions through the casting of the sacred **lots** (v. 5). **fathers . . . younger brethren:** There was no age discrimination in the work and shifts allocated to each. All served equally no matter what their age or status.

25:1 The involvement of **captains of the army** in the selection of Levitical musicians may at first appear strange. However in the conduct of God's battles against those who opposed His people, music was frequently an important element. **prophesy:** The role of a prophet was not limited to prediction or proclamation in words. Any divinely authorized utterance or deed from a prophet was a form of prophesying. Vocal and instrumental music could be a kind of prophetic message, usually in the form of praise (1 Sam. 10:5, 6; 2 Kin. 3:15).

25:2 according to the order of the king: This underscored the leading role David took in the religious life of the nation (23:27). Even as king, David ordered that proper worship be given to the Lord.

25:3, 4 prophesied with a harp: This illustrates the possibility of prophecy apart from a human voice.

25:5 Like Nathan (17:1) and Gad (21:9), **Heman** enjoyed a close relationship to David. **fourteen sons and three daughters:** The sons

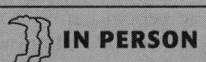

IN PERSON   The Sons of Asaph

The name Asaph (1 Chr. 25:1) probably would have been as important to worshipers in ancient Israel as the names Bach and Handel have become for many Christian worshipers today. Asaph (1 Chr. 15:17) was one of the principal musicians appointed by King David (16:4, 5). Others mentioned in Scripture included Heman, Jeduthun, Ethan (15:17), and Chenaniah (15:22, 27). But it was Asaph whose name became attached to the guild of temple musicians and singers that led Israel's worship throughout the kingdom period and after the return from exile (Neh. 7:44).

Apparently Asaph was more than a talented musician, though he was particularly known for playing bronze cymbals, as for example on the return of the ark of the covenant to Jerusalem (1 Chr. 15:19; 16:5). He was described as a seer (2 Chr. 29:30) who "prophesied according to the order of the king" (1 Chr. 25:2). In other words, Asaph was gifted and called to proclaim the Lord's message to His people through song.

Scripture contains examples of what that holy anointing produced. Twelve psalms (Pss. 50; 73—83) are ascribed either to him or to his descendants, some of whom also received the prophetic gift (2 Chr. 20:14). It appears that Asaph lived long enough to help dedicate Solomon's temple (5:12). He left a powerful legacy that dominated Israel's worship under Solomon, helped revive Judah's spiritual life under Hezekiah (29:30), and still echoed in the days of the second temple built by Zerubbabel and Ezra (Ezra 2:41; 3:10).

were accounted for in vv. 4, 13, 23–31. The daughters were not named but clearly participated along with their brothers in the public worship of God.

25:6, 7 the authority of the king: Once more the chronicler insisted that even the religious life of the nation was under the king's supervision. Israel was a theocracy in which God was the ultimate King and therefore head over all aspects of national life. As God's son (17:13), the king not only oversaw civil affairs, but also the worship of the Lord, the true King of Israel.

25:8–31 small . . . great . . . teacher . . . student: The equality of all these servants of God is seen in the equal distribution of their assignments, a principle that had determined the nature of the ministry of the priests as well (24:31).

26:1 There were four **divisions of the gatekeepers,** but they came from only two of the Levitical clans, Kohath and Merari.

26:2, 3 In both 9:21 and here, **Zechariah** is the son of Meshelemiah. This means that the lists of 9:17–27 and 26:1–19 refer to the same time and circumstances.

26:4, 5 This **Obed-Edom** was probably not the Obed-Edom of 13:14, but a gatekeeper, the son of Jeduthun (16:38).

26:6–9 The oldest son of Obed-Edom (v. 4), **Shemaiah,** gave rise to a subclan of gatekeepers whose total number is given in v. 8.

26:10, 11 The only other clan represented is **Merari**, whose descendant **Hosah** had four sons and nine other offspring who served as gatekeepers (v. 11). The grand total of all the leaders of the gatekeepers was ninety-three.

26:12, 13 The foregoing list appears to have identified the head gatekeepers only, that is, the **chief men.** Like their Levitical brethren in music (25:7) and the priests (24:31), these officials served right along with the four thousand others who made up the whole contingent of gatekeepers (23:5). They were not excused from such work because of their leadership positions.

26:14 The **East Gate** was the most important because it led straight into the main entrance of the temple. It was therefore assigned to Shelemiah (or Meshelemiah, v. 1) himself. **North Gate:** This was the responsibility of the oldest son of Shelemiah.

26:15 South Gate: Obed-Edom was in charge of the gate itself, and **his sons** (vv. 4, 5) took charge of the **storehouse.** This was undoubtedly the same as the treasuries (v. 20). Because these sons were gatekeepers, it is likely that their involvement with the storehouse was limited to its gates or doors. This position required utmost honesty and integrity, for the precious metals and other trophies of war that were dedicated to Yahweh were kept there (18:7, 8, 11).

26:16 Shuppim: This individual is otherwise unknown, but it is reasonable to assume that he, with Hosah, was a Merarite (v. 10). **Shalleketh Gate** appears to be based on the Hebrew verb meaning "to cast forth," which may refer to the portal through which the refuse of the temple was carried.

26:17 Two by two probably refers to two on each side of the storehouse gate, or four in all. If so, there were eight on the **south** side.

26:18 Parbar is usually left untranslated, but it likely refers to a place, perhaps a roadway or an open space, on the **west** side. The context here favors the view that it was a **highway** leading from a space adjacent to the temple. There were two gatekeepers at the entrance to the space itself (the Parbar) and four on the roadway leading to it. Depending on how one takes the "two by two" of v. 17, there were either twenty-two or twenty-four gatekeepers all told. These, of course, would be only the head gatekeepers, because there were 4,000 in all (23:5), no doubt several hundred serving in each shift.

26:19 Korah . . . Merari: This makes explicit the inference from vv. 1–11 that only the descendants of Kohath and Merari served as **gatekeepers**. The reason for the exclusion of the Gershonites is not stated, but it may be that they simply could not provide the manpower. They were also short in supplying musicians (25:2).

26:20 house of God: This likely referred to the storage area where regular tabernacle or temple paraphernalia were kept at hand for the worship services (9:28, 29). **dedicated things:** The second storehouse would contain the items taken as spoils of war that were used exclusively for holy purposes. David had already obtained a great amount of these (vv. 26–28).

26:21–24 The Levites listed in vv. 21–23 were in charge of the regular storehouse (v. 22; 23:8). **Shebuel** seems to have had general oversight of the regular storehouse. The Gershonites and other Kohathites of vv. 21–23 were under his direction.

26:25 The descendants of **Eliezer** became directors of the second storehouse, that of "the dedicated things" (v. 20). All the Levites who attended to the affairs of the tabernacle and temple treasuries traced their lineage back to Moses.

26:26, 27 The **treasuries of the dedicated things** fell under **Shelomith's** jurisdiction. These spoils of war were kept in storage until they could be used in the building and decoration of the temple (22:14; 29:2; 2 Chr. 5:1).

26:28 Showing the long-standing commitment of the nation to build and furnish the house of God, the chronicler listed leaders of the past who had **dedicated** spoils of war as readily as David had done.

26:29 Kohathites of the clan of **Izhar** provided **officials and judges** for conducting legal and religious affairs **outside Jerusalem**. This probably was restricted to questions pertaining to the Law of Moses and not to normal civil or political cases (23:4). Their leader was **Cheraniah**, not likely the music master of 15:22.

26:30 This third Kohathite clan was responsible specifically for Israel **on the west side of the Jordan.**

26:31 Since Hashabiah directed the Hebronites on the west (v. 30), **Jerijah** took charge of those on the east. He must have been over Hashabiah as well because he is called here **head of the Hebronites. fortieth year:** David reigned for 40 years (29:27), so these arrangements were completed in his very last year. **Jazer of Gilead:** This Levitical city (6:81) was located in the tribal territory of Gad, about seven miles west of Rabbah.

26:32 Reubenites . . . Gadites . . . half-tribe of Manasseh: These were the tribes of Israel who occupied the east side of the Jordan, often called the Transjordan.

27:1 heads of fathers' houses: This probably referred to tribal units, since the order appears to be in decreasing size through thousands and hundreds. **month by month:** The view that *fathers' houses* meant *tribes* is strengthened by the fact that there were twelve divisions, one for each month. Apparently a professional standing army is being described here, one broken up into twelve corps that served a month at a time on a rotating basis. **twenty-four thousand:** The total available manpower throughout Israel would be 288,000.

27:2, 3 A connection can be made here to the list of David's mighty men, which is also headed by **Jashobeam** (11:11). He was one of "the three," which meant he was regarded as unusually heroic.

27:4 Dodai's son Eleazar was the second of the mighty men included in the first trio along with Jashobeam (11:12).

27:5, 6 As the son of a priest, **Benaiah** was from the tribe of Levi. In the earlier list of mighty men he was celebrated for having killed a lion and a gigantic Egyptian (11:22, 23). Because of this kind of courage, he became part of the second group of "the three" (11:24). Later he was named commander of the entire

Israelite army (1 Kin. 4:4). His son served with him (v. 6).

27:7 David's nephew **Asahel** (2:15, 16) was among the thirty mighty men but did not achieve a position among "the three" (11:26). His son also served with him.

27:8 If, as some scholars believe, **Izrahite** is the same as "Zerahite," then this **Shammuth** is also a man of Judah. In the list of heroes he is called "Shammoth the Harorite" (11:27), Haror perhaps being the name of his home city (Harod in 2 Sam. 23:25).

27:9 A **Tekoite** was a person from the village of Tekoa, some five or six miles southeast of Bethlehem. This would make Ira a member of the tribe of Judah. It is clear that even if the military divisions were made up along tribal lines, their commanders were often David's own fellow Judeans. This appears to be so for Jashobeam (v. 2), Asahel (v. 7), Shamhuth (v. 8), and now Ira.

27:10 Helez: The leadership of the army was not limited to Judeans (27:9), since Helez was an Ephraimite in such a position.

27:11 Since Husha was a Judean (4:4), **Sibbechai** also came from the tribe of Judah. **Zarhites** likely referred to descendants of Zerah, a son of Judah (2:4; Num. 26:20). The present passage apparently placed the Hushathites in a position subsidiary to the Zarhites. In any case, Sibbechai was one of the thirty heroes, having distinguished himself by killing a Philistine giant (11:29; 2 Sam. 21:18).

27:12 A Benjamite commander, **Abiezer** came from the Levitical town of Anathoth, just north of Jerusalem. He was also a member of the elite thirty (11:28).

27:13 Since Netophah was a village near Bethlehem, **Maharai** was still another of David's fellow tribesmen named as commander of a **division** and member of the valorous thirty (11:30).

27:14 Another Ephraimite, this **Benaiah** (v. 5) came from Pirathon, five miles south of Samaria. Like the others he was one of the thirty mighty men (11:31).

27:15 Like Maharai (v. 13), this captain came from Netophah. Besides being one of the thirty (11:30), **Heldai** could claim descent from Israel's first judge, **Othniel.**

27:16 officer: The list that begins here (vv. 16–22) is clearly nonmilitary and tribal in nature. The description of these officers is much more political than the descriptions of the captains and officers of the military divisions (v. 1).

27:17 Aaronites: This is not a separate tribe

> The total available manpower throughout Israel would be 288,000.

but the priestly division of the tribe of **Levi**. **Zadok** the priest was naturally the leader of this segment of the tribe. The reason the tribe of Levi is listed here (contrary to many tribal lists) is to make up for two missing tribes and to bring the total to the ideal number of twelve.

27:18, 19 Elihu: This brother of David is usually called Eliab (1 Sam. 16:6).

27:20–22 This **Manasseh** and the one in v. 21 are counted as separate tribes here to make up for two missing tribes (v. 17). Levi was not normally counted, so with Levi and the other two tribes lacking there would be only nine. When Levi and two Manassehs (rather than one) are added, there are eleven. The twelfth was Simeon (v. 16), usually not counted since it was considered to be a sub-tribe of Judah (4:31; Josh. 19:1–9). The two missing tribes are Asher and Gad. The reason they are not included may be that they were dominated or occupied by the Phoenicians and Ammonites respectively at this particular time (2 Sam. 17:27–29). But this is speculative.

27:23 take the number: This ties in the previous list of tribes and leaders with David's ill-fated census near the end of his reign (v. 24; 21:1–17). So confident was David that his military might would be sufficient for any encounter, he omitted from his census all **those twenty years old and under.** Even so, the result of this census was over a million men (21:5), a multitude very much like **the stars of the heavens**—the words of God's promise to Abraham (Gen. 12:2; 15:5).

27:24 Joab's count included all the tribes except for Levi and Benjamin (21:6). Although these two tribes are included in the present list (vv. 17, 21), nothing is said of their being counted. On the other hand, Asher and Gad, missing in this list (v. 16–22), must have been included in Joab's **census.**

27:25 As opposed to the "treasuries of the house of God" and the "treasuries of the dedicated things" (26:20), the **king's treasuries** were the royal storehouses. They contained the revenues of the state in the form of precious metals (29:3–5) and other goods and commodities gained through taxation, tribute, and other means (2 Chr. 9:13, 14). **storehouses:** These were regional collection facilities ranging no doubt from granaries to warehouses to places of safe deposit of valuables. According to the following list, their primary purpose was to store agricultural produce.

27:26 Tilling the ground speaks of the production and storage of field crops such as wheat, barley, and vegetables.

27:27 vineyards: This industry was in two divisions, one to grow the grapes and the other to make **wine.**

27:28 sycamore: This word refers to a tree that yielded figs. It could also be a kind of mulberry.

27:29 A fertile plain between Israelite and Philistine territory, **Sharon** was ideal for grazing cattle and sheep. It is appropriate that someone from Sharon, who knew the land and all its seasonal changes, should be in charge of the livestock of that region.

27:30 Inhabitants of the desert were at home with the breeding and use of camels (Gen. 37:25), so naturally an **Ishmaelite** would be in charge of such animals.

27:31 Since there was no essential difference between the king and his state, the **property** of the king consisted of the assets of the nation.

27:32 The Hebrew word translated **uncle** here might be better translated "kinsman."

27:33 The only other **Ahithophel** mentioned in the Bible is the well-known **counselor** of Absalom, who advised him to attack his father David at the time of Absalom's rebellion. When his advice was spurned, he took his own life (2 Sam. 15:12; 16:15–23). If the counselor here is that Ahithophel, the list must be describing an office held some years earlier. However, it is entirely possible that the earlier counselor had a son by the same name, who eventually succeeded his father in that role. **king's companion:** This is likely a technical term signifying the king's closest confidant. It is interesting that he appears in the narrative of Absalom's rebellion as the counselor who contradicted Ahithaphel's advice and who evidently went on to replace him as chief adviser to the king (2 Sam. 17:5–23; 15:37; 16:16–19).

27:34 Jehoiada the son of Benaiah: In the list of military officers there was also a "Benaiah who was a son of Jehoiada" (v. 5). This is probably an example of the custom in which a man is named after his grandfather. The counselor Jehoiada was probably the grandson of Jehoiada the priest and son of the famous warrior Benaiah (v. 5). **Joab:** From the days of David's conquest of Jerusalem, Joab held the position of commander of the army of Israel (11:6), a post he kept until Solomon became king (1 Kin. 2:28–35).

28:1 These were the individuals of 27:1–34, plus others no doubt, who were **the leaders** of all the branches and extensions of Israel's government. The occasion was of such significance that a total assembly of dignitaries was essential.

28:2–4 The word **footstool** is a metaphor describing either the ark of the covenant or the tabernacle as the earthly base of God's activity. He sits on a throne in heaven, and His connection with the earth is focused in his earthly dwelling place, the tent or the ark. Elsewhere, the whole earth is described as God's footstool (Is. 66:1).

28:5 The call to rule was not limited to David, but included his descendants (17:11). Since only one of his **sons** could reign in his place, a choice ad to be made (14:3, 4), and God chose Solomon to succeed David as the king of Israel (22:9, 10; 2 Sam. 12:24; 1 Kin. 1:13, 30).

28:6 My son . . . his Father: This remarkable statement not only shows that the Davidic kings enjoyed unparalleled access to the Lord as His adopted sons (17:3; Ps. 2:7), but it anticipates the absolute sonship of the Son of David, Jesus Christ (Acts 13:33; Heb. 1:5).

28:7, 8 The conditional aspect of the covenant with David and his dynasty is real, not hypothetical. Not one of the kings, including David, was able to **observe** the **commandments** and **judgments** perfectly. Therefore they were unable in themselves to reign forever or even set the stage for an everlasting rule. But One would come who would be able to do so and who would fulfill the covenant perfectly. This One was Jesus, the Son of David (Matt. 5:7; 21:9).

28:9, 10 True service of God is more than rational and intellectual. It requires a commitment of the emotions as well. This was precisely where Solomon failed. Even though he had great wisdom (2 Chr. 1:12; 9:3, 22, 23), he allowed his **heart** to turn aside from God because he loved foreign women (1 Kin. 11:1–4). Loyalty of heart is essential for faithful, effective service.

28:11 The **plans** for the temple, as v. 12 makes clear, were not from David's own creative imagination but from the Spirit of God. **vestibule:** This was a porch in front of the temple (2 Chr. 3:4). **treasuries:** These, also called storehouses (26:15, 17), included "treasuries of the house of God" and "treasuries of the dedicated things" (26:20). **upper chambers:** Besides the main temple building, there were rooms of all kinds attached to it to accommodate the priests, the Levites, and all the equipment and items they needed to carry out the temple worship (Neh. 13:4, 5). Some of these chambers were built high on the outside of the temple walls (1 Kin. 6:6, 8). **the place of the mercy seat:** This was the Most Holy Place, the inner room that housed the ark of the covenant, the cover of which was known as the mercy seat (Ex. 25:17).

28:12, 13 by the Spirit: Moses had received the plans for the tabernacle by direct

revelation from God (Ex. 25:8, 9). David explained that he received the plans for the temple in the same way. David wanted it to be known that even the assignments he gave to the **priests and the Levites** (23:1—26:32) were revealed to him by God.

28:14–18 The chariot was a way of referring to the cherubim who hovered over the ark with outstretched wings, symbolizing the holiness of God. Cherubim appear in the story of the expulsion of man and woman from the Garden of Eden (Gen. 3:24) and as guardians of the "throne" of God in the tabernacle (Ex. 25:18–20) and temple (2 Chr. 3:10–13). They overshadowed the mercy seat of the ark of the covenant, enhancing its glory and protecting its holiness.

True service of God is more than rational and intellectual.

28:19 David asserted that **all the works of these plans** existed in written form from the hand of the Lord. David himself may have been the scribe, for he said that God's hand was upon him in the production of the plans. The detailed precision of the temple plans (vv. 11–18) attests to the clarity of the revelation and to its faithful recording by David.

28:20, 21 Be strong and of good courage: David's charge to Solomon is very similar to the charge given to Joshua when Moses handed over the leadership of Israel to him. For Moses' charge to Joshua, read Deut. 31:7, 8; for God's charge to Joshua, read Josh. 1:6–9.

29:1, 2 God Himself had **chosen** David out of all his brothers (28:4). Now He chose Solomon out of all of his brothers to succeed David on the throne (28:5). **the work is great:** The project was great not only because of its size and complexity, but because it was for God Himself. Since the very plans and specifications had been revealed to David by God (28:19), David was fully aware of the significance of his charge to Solomon. God's work could not be undertaken lightly. Solomon himself was aware of his limitations in this respect and of his need for supernatural direction (2 Chr. 1:10; 2:2–7).

29:3, 4 Because David loved God, he loved the work of God. **my own special treasure:** As a testimony to his professed affection for the house of his God, David pledged generous gifts from his own resources.

29:5, 6 This magnanimous gesture by David gave him the boldness to solicit a similar response from those under him. It is important to note that David asked the others to **consecrate** themselves, not their treasures. David knew that those who first consecrated themselves to God would have no difficulty in being generous to the work of God.

29:7 five thousand talents: About 190 tons. **ten thousand darics:** About 185 pounds of gold. **eighteen thousand talents of bronze:** This was equivalent to about 675 tons. **one hundred thousand talents of iron:** This was approximately 3,750 tons.

29:8 These **precious stones** provided the adornments worn on the shoulders and breastplate of the high priest (Ex. 28:9–12, 17–21).

29:9 loyal heart: The Hebrew is literally "with a fullness of heart." This parallels the word **willingly,** and the two words together suggest that coercion played no part in the offering.

29:10 David blessed the LORD: Upon the completion of the offerings, David offered praise, using a song no doubt composed especially for this occasion (vv. 10–12), followed by a prayer of confession and petition.

29:11 The purpose of the temple was to exalt the LORD and to acknowledge the universality of His **kingdom.** David modeled before the people the worship of the living God. It typically starts with praise for God's eternity, His complete control over the universe, and His great power. He is the glorious Master over all (Ps. 134:3).

29:12–14 David confessed that the **riches and honor** he enjoyed had come from God's generosity. The offerings he and his people had just made were possible only because God first had given to them. **able to offer so willingly:** Not only the ability to give, but the willingness to give, is a gift of God (2 Cor. 9:7, 8).

29:15 aliens and strangers: David asserts that life on earth is transitory and even nomadic. Only when a person becomes conscious of his or her place within the care and blessing of a sovereign God does life become more than a **shadow.** Suddenly the **hope** of a future with God illuminates that person's journey on this earth (Heb. 11:13–16; 13:14).

29:16 all your own: Once more David reiterates that he has nothing that did not first come to him from Yahweh. Therefore, it is impossible in the strict sense to speak of giving him anything.

29:17 If people truly can give nothing of value to God, why does He ask His people to give? David answers this question. God enjoys a person's **uprightness** or righteousness. With

gifts, offerings, and sacrifices, a person tangibly demonstrates not only gratitude to God, but trust in Him (1 Sam. 15:22). A righteous life always produces a generous spirit. For this reason, David could proclaim that his giving was only out of the uprightness of his heart. Moreover, his **joy** was heightened all the more when he saw that his people also understood this principle of true giving.

29:18 This formula LORD God of Abraham, Isaac, and Israel was associated with God's covenantal promises to the Israelites (Ex. 3:6, 15; 6:3, 4; Deut. 6:10). With this name of God, David was petitioning God to keep His people always in covenant fellowship with Himself.

29:19 In his prayer, David used the language of the covenant—**commandments, testimonies,** and **statutes** (Deut. 6:1, 2, 20; 8:11; 11:1). Unlike v. 18, David uses this language not as much for the nation as a whole as for his son Solomon. God had already made a covenant with David (17:7–14) and promised to renew it with his descendants. As with giving (v. 14), zeal for faithfulness to God's covenant must also come from God Himself (v. 14). Therefore, David prayed that God would give Solomon a **loyal heart** to be obedient. In Solomon's case, David's particular concern was that his son would keep his pledge **to build the temple.**

29:20, 21 the LORD and the king: David's special role as covenant son of God and theocratic mediator (17:13) meant that in the eyes of the people there was little practical or functional difference between prostrating themselves before God or the king. This does not mean, of course, that they failed to see the essential difference between the two, for in Israelite thought there was never any confusion about the utter dissimilarity and distance between the Divine and the human (Ps. 8:3–5).

29:22 ate and drank before the LORD: The scene here is one of covenant communion and confirmation as the participation of Yahweh and the people in a common meal here and elsewhere makes clear (Ex. 24:3–11; Gen. 26:26–30; 31:53, 54). **the second time:** This unusual phrase can only refer to the ratification of Solomon's kingship, not to its original establishment. David had appointed his son to be king at least two years earlier (23:1), an appointment that made Solomon a coregent rather than a true king, since he ruled alongside

> *The purpose of the temple was to exalt the LORD and to acknowledge the universality of His kingdom.*

his father David. **Zadok . . . priest:** Zadok had remained loyal to David and Solomon. But Abiathar defected to Adonijah, David's other son who attempted to overthrow Solomon's succession (1 Kin. 1:1–8).

29:23, 24 Once more the chronicler ties the kingship of David and that of God closely together. As God's son (17:13), Solomon would sit on the throne as God's representative. In that sense, the royal throne was also **the throne of the LORD** (v. 20). Eventually, Jesus as the Son of David and the Son of God would sit on that throne and reign forever (Luke 1:32).

29:25, 26 any king before him: Obviously this included only Saul and David, but it is still a remarkable statement in light of David's widely recognized power and magnificence (11:9; 14:2; 18:1–13; 29:28).

29:27, 28 In comparison to the patriarchs and even to such men as Eli and Samuel, David's 70 years seem short. However, in his time this was a **good old age.** Moses used it as the standard for reasonable longevity (Ps. 90:10).

29:29, 30 Here the chronicler revealed three sources he used in writing, and the reader interested in more information about **the acts of King David** is referred to those books. This note shows that the author of Chronicles did not invent the account or depend on oral tradition. Instead the chronicler cited texts available in his day.

The Second Book of
Chronicles

■

WHEN IT WAS FIRST WRITTEN, 2 CHRONICLES brought a ray of hope to a people desperately in need of encouragement. The Israelite community, reduced to a tiny minority in exile among the Babylonians, was struggling to understand its place. Had God's promises to Abraham and David been revoked because of the nation's sins? Was there any hope of reviving David's dynasty? Could Judaism survive without the temple? Second Chronicles addressed questions like these. Its answers came in a historical review of God's faithfulness to the Israelites. Although the nation had steadily declined over the centuries, God had always been faithful to those who remained true to Him. The good that God had done in the past would be the pattern for His future acts. God would keep His glorious promises to the Israelites.

The details of the history of Israel and Judah in 2 Chronicles communicate the great message of redemption—particularly God's blessing on David and his successors. First Chronicles focuses on the Davidic covenant during David's time; 2 Chronicles continues that theme in the period after David's death. Even though 2 Chronicles relates the experiences of Solomon and his successors, it continues to emphasize God's promise of an everlasting dynasty to David. Successors to David came and went. Some were true to the requirements of that covenant—they "walked in the former ways of their father David" (17:3)—and others were not. But God's commitment to the household of David continued throughout, even after the exile to Babylon.

Because of this emphasis on covenant, 2 Chronicles makes frequent mention of priests, Levites, the temple, and other elements of Israel's religious life. It tells how Solomon's temple was built and furnished (2:1—8:16) and includes a thorough description of the temple and its ministry (20:5–13, 24–30; 23:12–21; 24:4–14; 29:2—31:21; 34:2—35:19).

The centrality of the Davidic covenant also explains why 2 Chronicles devotes more attention to Judah than to Israel. Ever since the division into southern and northern kingdoms (10:16–19; 1 Kin. 11:9–13), Judah had become the inheritors of God's promises to David. Though David's successors ruled only the smaller kingdom of Judah, God had remained faithful to His unconditional covenant with David. Judah was the nucleus through which God would accomplish His work of redemption.

First and Second Chronicles were at first a single book (see Introduction to 1 Chronicles). The book itself does not state who wrote it, but the overall consistency of viewpoint and style indicates that it was probably the work of one person. Most commentators refer to this person as the "chronicler." One Jewish tradition identifies him as Ezra (c. 460–430 B.C.) because

Chronicles and Ezra share common themes like extensive lists, the Levites, and the temple.

The chronicler had access to many official documents, which he often mentions by name. These include (1) the Book of the Kings of Israel and Judah (27:7; 35:27; 36:8); (2) the Book of the Kings of Judah and Israel (16:11; 25:26; 28:26; 32:32); (3) the Book of the Kings of Israel (20:34; 33:18); (4) the annals (commentary) of the Book of the Kings (24:27); (5) the Book of Nathan, the prophecy of Ahijah, and the visions of Iddo (9:29); (6) the history of Shemaiah (12:15); (7) the annals of Iddo (13:22); (8) the writings of the prophet Isaiah (26:22); (9) the sayings of Hozai (33:19); and (10) the Laments (35:25). The chronicler also cites the canonical books of 1 and 2 Kings.

Outline

Commentary

1:1, 2 exalted him exceedingly: The repetition here of the wording 1 Chr. 29:25 shows how 1 and 2 Chronicles were originally one book, even though it is customary to print the two parts separately.

1:3, 4 The term **high place** comes from the fact that many ancient worshipers used hills for their sacred rites, thinking that such places were good "meeting points" between heaven and earth. Over time, *high place* came to mean any worship center, whether it was on a hill or not. In the OT, the high places were usually associated with pagan, particularly Canaanite, religion, but there was nothing inherently evil about using a hilltop as a place of worship. Thus

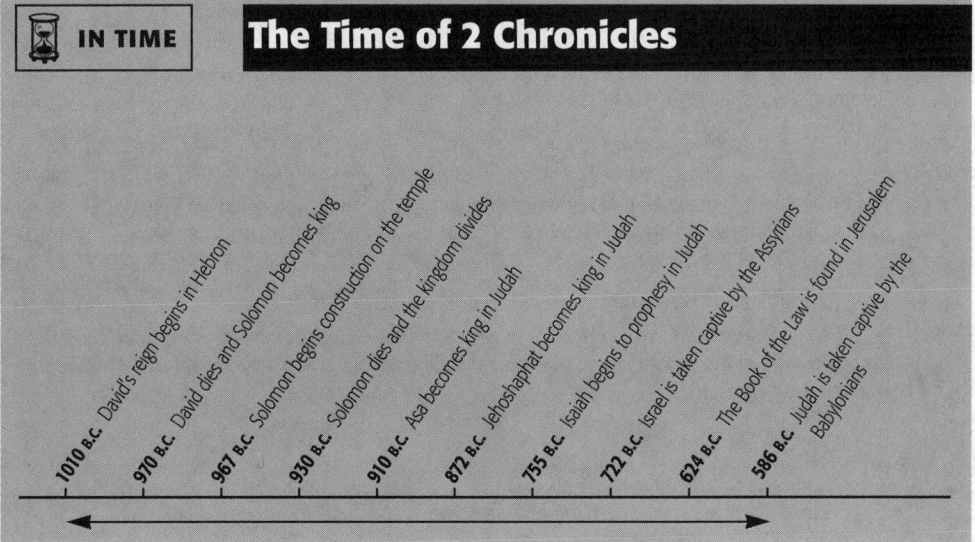

IN TIME — **The Time of 2 Chronicles**

- 1010 B.C. David's reign begins in Hebron
- 970 B.C. David dies and Solomon becomes king
- 967 B.C. Solomon begins construction on the temple
- 930 B.C. Solomon dies and the kingdom divides
- 910 B.C. Asa becomes king in Judah
- 872 B.C. Jehoshaphat becomes king in Judah
- 755 B.C. Isaiah begins to prophesy in Judah
- 722 B.C. Israel is taken captive by the Assyrians
- 624 B.C. The Book of the Law is found in Jerusalem
- 586 B.C. Judah is taken captive by the Babylonians

the patriarchs (Gen. 12:8; 22:2) and other worshipers of God offered their sacrifices on high
places (1 Sam. 9:12; 1 Kin. 18:19, 36–38). The
evil was not in the place itself but in the pagan
rituals that were usually practiced there. The
high place at Gibeon was the location of the
Mosaic **tabernacle** after Saul destroyed Nob
(1 Sam. 22:19). It seems that the Israelites
moved the tabernacle to Nob after they had
stopped using Shiloh as the religious center of
Israel (1 Sam. 4:21, 22; Jer. 7:12). The tabernacle remained in Gibeon together with the
great bronze altar throughout David's reign.

1:5 Bezalel was one of the two men chosen
especially by God to build the tabernacle in the
wilderness (Ex. 31:1–11). Aholiab was the other.
The text here mentions Bezalel alone apparently
because he was the master craftsman, while
Aholiab was his assistant. **the assembly sought
Him there:** This phrase is important because
Solomon and the people, as a congregation,
usually worshiped God at Gibeon.

1:6 went up: Solomon's worship at Gibeon

affirmed the covenant that bound God and the
Davidic dynasty together (1 Chr. 17:7–14) and
showed that Solomon accepted the religious
responsibilities of his office (v. 3). Solomon had
been appointed vice-regent by his father two
years earlier (1 Chr. 23:1). He had been elevated
to full kingship ("made king the second time")
in a service of anointing and public acclamation
(1 Chr. 29:21–23), and now his selection as the
Davidic heir was being sanctioned by the community as a whole, in line with already established precedent (1 Sam. 10:1, 24, 25; 11:14, 15;
16:13; 2 Sam. 5:3; 1 Chr. 11:1–3; 12:38–40).

1:7–9 Solomon knew about the Abrahamic
covenant and God's promise to make Abraham's
descendants like **the dust of the earth** (Gen.
13:16). Solomon believed that the promise had
come to pass, and he was confident that God
would fulfill His **promise to David** as well.
This meant that he saw his own succession
(1 Chr. 17:11) and the building of the temple as
fulfillment of God's promises (1 Chr. 17:12, 13).

1:10 wisdom and knowledge: These

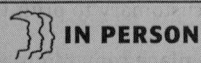

IN PERSON | Solomon: Successful But Not Satisfied

Thanks to the Lord's help, Solomon apparently became the wealthiest and wisest man of his era
(2 Chr. 1:1). No one, it seems, accumulated or accomplished as much as he did (Eccl. 2:1–9).
Yet by his own admission (assuming that Solomon wrote Ecclesiastes), his life was far from satisfying (2:11, 16).

Solomon is a case study in how a person can be successful in terms of power, wealth, and prestige, yet lack the true success that comes from knowing and honoring God the way someone should.
Notice how those who came after him remembered his legacy:

- Nehemiah (a leader of the returning Babylonian exiles): Presented Solomon as an illustration of
  disobedience through his intermarriage with foreign—and therefore idolatrous—wives (Neh.
  13:26, 27; compare 1 Kin. 11:1–8). In effect, Nehemiah warned that just as God had punished
  the nation for Solomon's sins, so he would punish His people again if they continued in
  Solomon's ways rather than God's.
- Jesus: Used Solomon and his splendor as an illustration of how His followers needed to concentrate on trusting, loving, and serving God rather than on material gain or even the problems
  of day-to-day life (Matt. 6:28–32). Later, Jesus challenged His enemies with the fact that the
  Queen of Sheba, a Gentile, had shown more faith in coming to Jerusalem to inquire of
  Solomon than they had shown after seeing His miracles and hearing His teaching (12:42).
- Stephen (a leader in the early church): In detailing the history of Israel, mentioned Solomon as
  the one who built a house for God, but praised Solomon's father David as the one who "found
  favor before God" (Acts 7:45–48).
- Paul (also a leader in the early church): In reviewing the history of Israel from the OT, mentioned several of the great leaders of Israel, including Samuel, the judges, Saul, and David—but
  not Solomon (Acts 13:22).
- The author of Hebrews: Catalogued the great models of faith from Israel's history (Heb. 11),
  but did not include Solomon.

Solomon wasn't all bad, but his life shows us that great achievements and success—whether in
business, government, academia, or any other field—pale in comparison to being faithful to God.

words are frequently in parallel and are essentially synonymous. However, Hebrew *hohmah*, translated "wisdom," denotes insight, usually of a spiritual kind, whereas *madda'*, "knowledge," pertains to the accumulation of information or facts and their proper use. Solomon knows already of his limitations because of his youth and inexperience (1 Chr. 29:1), but he also knows that "the fear of the LORD is the beginning of knowledge" (Prov. 1:7). **go out and come in:** This figure of speech refers to the totality of Solomon's life. As king he would lead by example as well as by edict.

nation located primarily in hilly terrain where chariots were of limited value.

1:15, 16 Keveh was probably an ancient name for what later came to be known as Cilicia. This city was on the northeast Mediterranean coast, a region famous for horses. The **horses imported from Egypt** were larger horses bred in Nubia and used mainly for pulling chariots.

1:17 six hundred shekels of silver: It is often impossible to assign a price in a modern currency to the goods and services of the ancient world. But this verse suggests that a

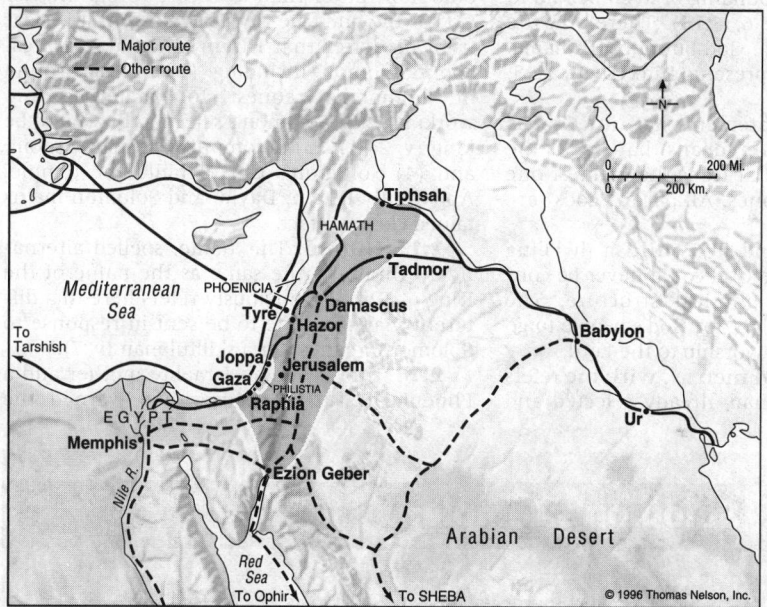

The Spread of Solomon's Fame

Solomon's influence in economic and political affairs was enhanced by the transportation and trade routes that intersected his kingdom. That Solomon acquired much through trade is suggested by the response of the queen of Sheba on her visit to Solomon, and by the mention of traders and merchants (9:14) in the account of his wealth. Solomon may have fortified Tadmor (8:4) in order to have a safe and direct trade route from Asia Minor to Damascus.

1:11, 12 Solomon's request for wisdom centered on God's **people** and how he could best serve them, not on his own gain. Once Solomon had demonstrated this spirit of servanthood, God granted many unsolicited blessings.

1:13, 14 Solomon located his **chariots** in other **cities** besides Jerusalem, possibly in Hazor, Megiddo, and Gezer (1 Kin. 9:15, 19). The 1,400 chariots and twelve thousand horsemen here compare to four thousand stalls for horses and chariots and twelve thousand horsemen in 9:25. A chariot force of 1,400 units was a significant achievement for Israel, a

chariot cost as much as four horses. **they exported them:** Solomon had a thriving business in horses and chariots. Because Israel was on the route between Asia and Africa, such goods would go through Israel and become subject to Solomon's heavy import and export taxes. **Hittites** were the peoples of the ancient nation of Hatti in central Asia Minor. They reached the height of their power at about 1350–1300 B.C., but were nearly exterminated by the Sea Peoples in about 1200 B.C. There were pockets of Hittites in Solomon's day, mainly north of Israel among the Syrians.

2:1, 2 a royal house for himself: It was customary for a new king to build a palace as a physical and visible sign of his newly won sovereignty, though this usually was done right after a military conquest (1 Chr. 14:1, 2).

2:3 Hiram king of Tyre was the same Phoenician ruler who had provided men and materials for David's palace (1 Chr. 14:1).

2:4 a temple for the name: This is a round about way of saying that he is **building** the temple for Yahweh. Solomon is very much aware of the holiness and transcendence of God and of the impossibility of imagining that God can be confined to a building or even be said to live in a building (v. 6; 6:18). Therefore, the temple does not house God but only His name, that is, that which represents Him (Deut. 12:5, 11, 21).

2:5 Solomon's statement that **our God is greater than all gods** means that God is the only true God, not that He is the greatest one among many lesser ones. All pagan "gods" are actually imaginary.

2:6 Solomon could not **build** a dwelling place for God because God could never be contained within any physical structure. The **temple** provided a place for God's people to go and offer sacrifices of worship to the Lord.

2:7, 8 The skillful men . . . with me refers to the ones **David** had already selected and

organized for the purpose of building the temple (1 Chr. 22:15, 16). The chronicler emphasized David's intense interest in the temple and the elaborate steps he took to prepare for its building (1 Chr. 22:1–19). **Algum logs** probably refers to a kind of exotic tree imported from Ophir—south Arabia, perhaps Yemen.

2:9, 10 The amount of **ground wheat** here is about 125,000 bushels or 3,750 tons. **Twenty thousand baths** is approximately 115,000 gallons.

2:11, 12 Blessed be the Lord God of Israel: Most likely a polite salutation to Solomon rather than a sincere recognition of God as the one true God. **a wise son:** It is clear from his letter that Hiram knew a great deal about Solomon, including: (1) the background of Solomon's request for materials and workmen, (2) Solomon's selection by God to be king (v. 2:11), (3) Solomon's unusual wisdom, and (4) Solomon's call to build the temple. Apparently Hiram, David, and Solomon maintained close contact.

2:13 Huram: This name, spelled alternatively Hiram, is the same as the name of the King of Tyre but obviously refers here to a different man, the one to be sent in response to Solomon's request for a skillful man (v. 7).

2:14 Hiram had an Israelite mother and a Phoenician **father.** Moses had warned the

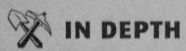 **IN DEPTH** **Solomon's Temple**

Solomon's temple was the first of three temples that Israel built in its long history. David wanted to build it, but as a man of war he was unqualified to build such a holy place. So with the plans that God gave David and which David passed on to him, King Solomon built the house of God. As God had instructed, Solomon built it on Mount Moriah just north of the ancient City of David.

Solomon wanted to build a temple worthy of being the center of worship for the entire nation, so he used only the best craftsmen and materials. The materials included cedar and algum logs, gold and silver, cut stone, and fine linen. Most of the temple's beams, posts, walls, and doors were overlaid with gold, decorated with carvings of palm trees, garlands, and cherubim. The Most Holy Place alone was overlaid with twenty-three tons of fine gold. In this room two giant gold cherubim, with seven-and-a-half-foot wings overshadowed the ark of the covenant. A veil of crimson and fine linen separated the Most Holy Place from the holy place. The temple's furnishings included ten lampstands of gold, ten tables, and one hundred bowls of gold. Only the most skilled craftsmen worked on these details. The temple was sixty cubits long and twenty cubits wide or ninety by thirty feet.

It took seven years for Solomon's workers to complete this grand building, and the finished structure dazzled all who saw it. Yet for all its beauty, Solomon knew that no manmade building could contain God, as heaven itself could not contain Him (6:18). The temple served mainly as a reminder of God's covenant. To all who came and worshiped there, God held out his promised presence. However, the temple was no guarantee of that presence. God had promised to live among the Israelites forever, and the temple was God's so-called "dwelling place," but for the Holy God to live among His people they had to remain faithful to Him. Unfortunately they did not remain faithful, and consequently the temple was looted and destroyed as were the second and third temples after it.

Israelites not to take spouses committed to pagan religions (Deut. 7:1–5).

2:15, 16 Joppa, now known as Jaffa, was the only seaport on the Israelite Mediterranean coast between Dor on the north and Philistia to the south. Jonah sailed from Joppa to escape God's call to Nineveh (Jon. 1:3). Though Hiram's rafts helped transport the timber from

the very site that he had purchased from Ornan, and where he had already built an altar, should be the location of the future temple (1 Chr. 21:18, 26). Mount Moriah is known today as the temple mount and the site of the Muslim Dome of the Rock. It is a hill directly north of Mount Zion, the location of David's tabernacle (1 Chr. 15:1).

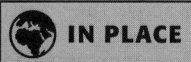 **IN PLACE** ▐ **Mount Moriah**

Mount Moriah was the name the hill just north of the City of David on which Solomon built the temple (2 Chr. 3:1). The name Moriah is used only one other time in the Bible, in connection with "the land of Moriah," where God told Abraham to take Isaac and sacrifice him as a burnt offering (Gen. 22:2). Presumably the temple was located at that site. David purchased the land that was later used for the temple from Ornan (Araunah in 1 Sam. 24:15–25) following David's sin of numbering Israel (1 Chr. 21). Apparently the purchase, and perhaps the census as well, was part of David's abiding desire to build the temple, which God delayed until Solomon's time (17:1–6; 22:1–10).

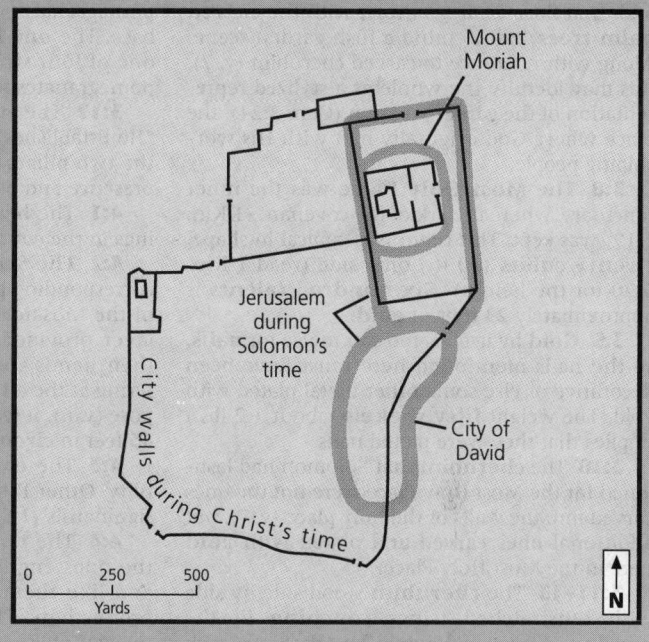

Lebanon to Israel, the route from Joppa to **Jerusalem** was not so easy—it was a winding, steep ascent of nearly 40 miles.

2:17 Solomon's policy of forced labor drafted **aliens** first into the hard work of carrying loads and quarrying stone (v. 18). The term suggests any persons living in Israel who were not native Israelites. **The census** refers to David's ill-advised count in the closing years of his reign (1 Chr. 21:1–5).

3:1 Mount Moriah was sacred and therefore an appropriate place for the temple not only because the **threshing floor of Ornan** was there (1 Chr. 21:18–30), but also because it was the "land of Moriah" to which Abraham took Isaac for sacrifice (Gen. 22:2). David had received explicit instructions from the Lord that

3:2 The **second day of the second month** fell in April of the modern calendar. Making arrangements for the building, amassing building materials, and clearing the site could easily have required four years. This explains why Solomon did not begin the project in his first year. Also, 1 Kings indicates that Solomon was busy in his early reign putting down potential insurrection and dealing with other problems attendant to his succession (1 Kin. 1; 2).

3:3 The Israelites had two standard **cubits,** one about 17.4 inches long and the other about 20.4 inches. Probably **the former measure** mentioned here was the 17.4–inch cubit, making the temple **foundation** about 90 feet long and 30 feet wide. The Mosaic tabernacle was 45 feet long and 15 feet wide (Ex. 26:15–37).

3:4 vestibule: This was a porch in front of the temple building proper. It was thirty feet long, thus stretching across the whole width of the temple, fifteen feet wide (1 Kin. 6:3), and 180 feet high (120 cubits) according to the Hebrew text here. Other ancient versions read twenty cubits (thirty feet) for the height, bringing that measurement more in line with the height of the temple itself as recorded in 1 Kin. 6:2, namely, thirty cubits or forty-five feet.

3:5–7 The **larger room** was the holy place or "sanctuary" (1 Kin. 6:17). The parallel account in 1 Kin. 6:18 suggests that the **chainwork** may refer to an interlocking design of buds and flowers. If so, these, with the **carved palm trees,** call to mind a lush garden scene. Along with reference to carved cherubim (v. 7), this may identify the whole as a stylized representation of the garden of Eden (Gen. 3:24), the place where God originally met with His worshiping people.

3:8 The Most Holy Place was the inner sanctuary, where the ark of the covenant (1 Kin. 6:19) was kept. This room was cubical in shape, **twenty cubits** (30 ft.) on a side (read 1 Kin. 6:20 for the height). **Six hundred talents** is approximately 23 tons of **gold.**

3:9 Gold by itself is too soft to use for **nails,** so the nails mentioned here must have been decorative or else some other metal plated with gold. The weight **fifty shekels** (about 1.2 lbs.) implies that they were plated nails.

3:10 The **cherubim** that Solomon had fashioned for the Most Holy Place were not the ones carved into the walls of the holy place (v. 7), but additional ones carved and plated with **gold** here in the Most Holy Place.

3:11–13 The **cherubim** stood side by side with outstretched wings **touching** in the middle and overshadowing the ark. Since each wing was **five cubits** long and the room was twenty cubits across, the cherubim's wings spanned the entire width of the room. Facing **inward** meant that the cherubim were facing the veil and the holy place.

3:14 The veil was a heavy curtain between the holy place and the Most Holy Place. It shielded the ark and cherubim from view (5:9). Cherubim were woven into the fabric of the veil. The materials and colors used here—**blue, purple, crimson, and fine linen**—are the same as those of the veil of the tabernacle.

3:15 The **two pillars** in front were free-standing and did not support any part of the temple. **Thirty- five cubits** was about 53 feet, and with the **five cubit capitals on top,** the pillars were about 60 feet tall. Because of the aesthetic and architectural problems caused by this, many prefer the measurements of the parallel 1 Kings account, which attributes eighteen

cubits to each column plus the capital (1 Kin. 7:15). This yields a total height of thirty-four-and-a-half feet for each, making the pillars about four and a half feet higher than the temple porch but lower than its roof.

3:16 As in v. 5, **chainwork** appears to be a network of fruits and plants, as the presence of **pomegranates** indicates. First Kings expands the description (1 Kin. 7:17–20). There were seven wreaths of chainwork on each capital and two rows of pomegranates above the wreaths. The capitals seem to have been in the form of lilies four cubits high with a one-cubit width band at their base. The wreaths and strands of pomegranates were intertwined around the base. The **one hundred pomegranates** were one of four strands, two to each pillar, or 400 pomegranates in all.

3:17 The names **Jachin** and **Boaz** mean "He Establishes" and "In Him Is Strength." Thus the two pillars were constant reminders of the presence and power of God.

4:1 The **bronze altar** was for burnt offerings in the courtyard of the temple.

4:2 The Sea was a large receptacle for water corresponding to the much smaller bronze laver of the Mosaic tabernacle (Ex. 30:17–21). That laver provided water for the priests to wash their hands and feet in preparation for ministering at the altar. The Sea served the same purpose (v. 6). It was huge—15 feet in diameter and 45 feet in **circumference.**

4:3 The **oxen** stood for strength and fertility. Other Bible passages use the ox's horn to signify this (1 Sam. 2:10).

4:4 The **twelve oxen** were in addition to the ones engraved on the outside of the Sea, and like them they symbolized strength and productivity. Their number corresponds to the twelve tribes of Israel.

4:5 The Sea was very heavy even when empty. When filled with **three thousand baths** (about 27,000 gallons) of water, it would have weighed about 110 tons more.

4:6 The **ten lavers** were arranged in two rows of **five,** on the north and south sides of the Sea. According to 1 Kin. 7:38, each held 40 baths or about 230 gallons. They could accommodate large animals such as oxen. The law of **burnt offerings** required that certain parts of the animal be washed in water before being placed on the altar (Lev. 1:9, 13).

4:7 Whereas the wilderness tabernacle had only one lampstand, this temple had **ten** (Ex. 25:31), five on the north side of the holy place and five on the south. They probably had the same form as the one in the tabernacle—a central stand with three branches extending from each side, making a total of seven lamps per unit (Ex. 25:32, 37). They symbolized the light of

God's creation (Gen. 1:3–5) and the fact that God Himself is light (John 8:12).

4:8 There had been only one **table** in the tabernacle (Ex. 25:23), but the temple had **ten.** They held the loaves of showbread (Ex. 25:30). **bowls of gold:** The word for bowls here is derived from the Hebrew verb meaning "to sprinkle." The priests used the bowls to hold liquids that were sprinkled.

4:9 There were areas in and about the temple that only the priests could enter. One of these was the area immediately surrounding it and enclosed by a separating wall, the **court of the priests.** The **great court** was an outer area where the people in general could go.

4:10–13 The **Sea** was placed to one side of the entrance to the temple, to the **southeast.** The temple faced east.

4:14–16 **Carts** were mobile stands designed as bases for the ten **lavers** referred to in v. 6. They were four cubits on a side and three cubits

uncovered evidence of this work in an area where the **clay** is suitable for bronze casting.

4:19–21 This is the first mention of the **altar of gold** in Chronicles (Ex. 30:1–10; 1 Kin. 7:48). This altar was used for offering incense. It was in the holy place just in front of the veil (3:14).

4:22 **inner doors:** The tabernacle had only a veil between the holy place, here called **the sanctuary,** and the **Most Holy Place** (Ex. 26:31–33). Solomon's temple had a set of doors there as well.

5:1 **The treasuries of the house of God** listed here were dedicated by David in the sense that he had allotted them to the building and maintenance of the temple (1 Chr. 18:7, 8; 29:3–5). Solomon put them in the regular temple treasuries.

5:2 Though David had built a tabernacle on Mount Zion to house the **ark** (1 Chr. 15:1), it was still separate from the original tabernacle at

Photo by Ben Chapman

The modern city of Jerusalem, showing the Dome of the Rock mosque (upper left) on the site on which Solomon's temple once stood (2 Chr. 5:1).

high, had four bronze wheels, and were covered on the sides by richly decorated panels (1 Kin 7:27–37).

4:17, 18 Many bronze products were made at a place in the Jordan valley about 35 miles north of the Dead Sea. Archaeologists have

Gibeon and thus was not yet in a permanent location. Completing Solomon's temple made it possible at last to place the ark in its proper setting.

5:3, 4 Since this was in the **seventh month** (that is, Ethanim or Tishri; 1 Kin. 8:2), the feast was Tabernacles. This feast was an appropriate occasion for moving the ark to a permanent location, because the Feast of Tabernacles commemorated Israel's wandering in the wilderness, when the ark had no permanent place (Lev. 23:39–43).

5:5 The term **tabernacle of meeting** refers to the Mosaic tabernacle. Solomon ended worship at the high place at Gibeon by dismantling the Mosaic tabernacle located there (1:3) and by bringing it and all its **furnishings** to Jerusalem.

5:6, 7 Like David before him, Solomon, a priestly **king,** exercised the privileges of his office by offering sacrifices (1 Chr. 16:1–3).

5:8 According to Moses' instructions (Ex. 25:12–15; Num. 4:6), the ark had rings attached to each corner, through which **poles** were inserted to carry it. These poles were about 20 cubits (30 feet) long, since those who ministered in the holy place could see them at either end of the veil (v. 9).

5:9 to this day: This statement would be charged with emotion for any Israelite who lived through the Babylonian exile years later, when Nebuchadnezzar's army destroyed Solomon's temple and carried away many of its furnishings.

5:10 The passage in Heb. 9:4, which states that the **ark** also contained the golden pot of manna and Aaron's rod that budded, seems to contradict the chronicler here. It may that all of these items were in the ark in Moses's time but that everything but the **two** stone **tablets** had been removed some time later. The chronicler, then, is relating the situation in Solomon's day.

5:11 On this day of inaugurating the temple **all the priests** participated in the services regardless of their priestly **divisions.** From then on they would serve in rotation according to their division (1 Chr. 24:1–19). **The Most Holy Place** was normally restricted to the high priest

only (Lev. 16:15; Heb. 9:7); on this occasion the regular priests had entered it to bring in the ark (v. 7).

5:12 Asaph, Heman, and Jeduthun were the heads of the divisions of Levitical musicians (1 Chr. 6:33, 39, 44; 15:17; 16:37, 42; 25:1). The **east end of the altar** was between the east gate of the inner court and the great bronze altar. Altogether there were far more than **one hundred and twenty priests;** the ones numbered here were probably a select group of instrumentalists.

5:13, 14 As v. 14 suggests, the **cloud** was a manifestation of God's glory. In a sense, the cloud both revealed and concealed the glory of God, which is too awesome for human eyes to see (Ex. 19:16, 18; 20:18, 21; 24:16–18; 33:9, 10, 22; 40:34–38).

6:1, 2 The dark cloud which had represented the glory of God now filled the temple (5:14). This was in line with God's own promise to David when He said, in response to David's decision to build a temple, that He had lived in a portable tabernacle (1 Chr. 17:5). Although David's son built a temple for God, the time would come when God would build David an eternal **house** or dynasty. With David's permanent dynasty would come God's permanent relationship with His people (1 Chr. 17:7–14). Thus Solomon built the "house" in which God could live among them.

6:3, 4 fulfilled with His hands: A direct reference to the covenant that God had made with David, when He promised him an everlasting house (1 Chr. 17:11, 12). Solomon, as David's chosen heir, had lived to see God's words of promise come true. God had made Solomon king and built the temple. Solomon may have hired Phoenician craftsmen, but he knew that the project's success lay with God, and that "His hands" really had done the work.

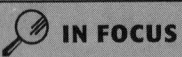 **IN FOCUS**   **"assembly"**

(Heb. *qahal*) (2 Chr. 6:3; Deut. 18:16; Judg. 20:2) Strong's #6951: The Hebrew term denotes a gathering of people for any type of occasion. It is used in a secular sense to designate civil meetings, war counsels, a gathering of evildoers, and even an assembly of the dead (1 Sam. 17:47; 1 Kin. 12:3; Ps. 26:5; Prov. 21:16). But the word is also used to speak of the gathering of individuals for religious purposes, such as the receiving of the Mosaic law and the celebration of religious festivals before the Lord (30:23; Deut. 5:22). Sometimes the term applies to groups of men only—most frequently with assemblies for war, but once, apparently, for those gathered to hear Joshua's reading of the Law (Josh. 8:35). During the time of Ezra, women, children, and even servants were specifically included in one religious assembly (Ezra 2:64–65; 10:1). The expression "assembly of the LORD" occurs several times in the OT to indicate a gathering of God's people for religious or secular purposes—including once to grumble against Moses (Num. 20:4; Deut. 23:1–3; 1 Chr. 28:8; Neh. 13:1).

6:5, 6 I have chosen Jerusalem: This refers not so much to Jerusalem as a political capital, as it was for David and Solomon (1 Chr. 11:4–8), but as a place for God's name. This emphasis is unmistakable in the narrative about Ornan's threshing floor (1 Chr. 21:18—22:1). Only Jerusalem would be acceptable as a place for God's earthly dwelling. **I have chosen David:** In His grace God chose David long before David actually took the throne, as Samuel's anointing of him in his youth made clear (1 Sam. 16:1, 12, 13).

6:7–11 The covenant of the Lord refers to the stone tablets of the Ten Commandments (5:10).

6:12 Solomon's **presence . . . before the altar** in the inner court, the place barred to any but priests and Levites, shows once more the priestly role and privileges of the Davidic monarchy. As a king-priest "according to the order of Melchizedek" (Ps. 110:4), he was entitled to be there as a theocratic mediator between God and the nation (1 Chr. 15:25–28; 2 Chr. 1:3).

6:13 The **bronze platform** was not a regular feature of the temple but a stage constructed for Solomon's speech, so the assembly outside the walls of the courtyard could see him. It was seven and a half feet square and four and a half feet high.

6:14 no God . . . like You: God is different from all other "gods." He alone made and kept a **covenant** with His people, something unheard of in the religious traditions of the nations. Solomon's acclamation makes sense to every child of God who reflects on God's faithfulness. **covenant and mercy:** The word for *mercy* here connotes loyalty; it means that God is faithful to His **servants**—to those who **walk before** Him **with all their hearts.**

6:15, 16 Solomon's very position as king attested to God's having fulfilled His **promise** (v. 10). But portions of God's promise depended on God's people obeying God's law. **Only if** David's **sons** took **heed to their way** would they enjoy the full benefits of God's favor. So Solomon prayed that his people would stay faithful. God would be faithful to them—would they be faithful to Him? No matter what their choice, however, God would carry out his ultimate plan to send the Messiah (Ps. 89:30–37).

6:17, 18 will God . . . dwell with men: God is altogether separate from humanity (2:6), but He accommodates Himself to the low position of human beings in order to fellowship with them (Gen. 2:8; 11:5; 18:1, 2; Ex. 23:20–26). He did this in an ultimate sense in the incarnation of Jesus Christ (John 1:14).

6:19, 20 The resolution of the tension between God being high and lifted up above all His creation (transcendence; Is. 6:1–4) and His nearness to each one of us (immanence) lies in such acts of God as localizing His **name**. Rather than contemplating the actual localizing of God in one place, even the **temple**, Solomon, along with an ancient preceding tradition (Deut. 12:5, 11; 16:2, 6), speaks of His presence in terms of the objectifying of His name. This is an early stage of the development of such doctrines as the personality of God, the being of God, and the union of God with humanity in the person of Jesus Christ.

6:21 The temple was God's **dwelling place** in the sense that it gave God's people a place to pray to the living God. Yet God could not be contained within the four walls of a building (v. 18).

6:22 comes and takes an oath: A reference to legal oaths in which people swore their innocence before God (Ex. 22:8–11; Deut. 17:8, 9). Such oaths had to be sworn in the temple and before the **altar,** symbolic of God's presence among His people.

6:23, 24 Solomon's request that God **hear from heaven** underscored God's transcendence. Although God had chosen to be present on earth at the temple, He also transcended the temple building.

6:25–28 bring them back: A hint of the future captivity and deportation of God's disobedient **people** (Deut. 28:29, 30). When the exile to Babylon became a reality, the temple was destroyed and no one could pray at that place as before. But even in those days, God's people directed their prayer toward Jerusalem. This is what Daniel did (Dan. 6:10).

6:29–31 Israel was a community and could pray together as a nation. But each member was also responsible for his or her own sin (Ezek. 18:1–4) and each needed to seek God's forgiveness. Prayer toward the temple could be national or individual.

6:32, 33 God made His covenant exclusively with Israel, the nation descended from Abraham, but He did so for the purpose of attracting the nations to Himself, the Creator of all people. A **foreigner** who embraced the Lord as God would be numbered among God's people.

6:34–36 there is no one who does not sin: This statement is repeated in the New Testament (Rom. 3:23; 1 John 1:8–10). All people sin and are guilty before God. **take them captive:** Solomon's speech anticipated the possibility of exile (v. 25), something that had already taken place by the time Chronicles were written.

6:37–40 Let Your eyes be open: God is Spirit (John 4:24) and doesn't have physical eyes and ears, but He is a Person who intimately knows us and hears our prayers. Solomon was praying that God would not ignore His people.

6:41 In light of Ps. 132:8, 9 (the passage quoted by Solomon), the **resting place** is the temple. **Ark** is a synonym for the presence of God.

6:42 Your Anointed: A reference to Solomon, which shows that he understood his unique role as one set apart by God for royal service (1 Chr. 22:10, 11). Like David, Solomon, was a messianic figure who anticipated the goal of his royal line, the true Anointed One, Jesus Christ (1 Sam. 2:10; Pss. 2:2; 18:50; 89:38, 51; 132:17).

7:1, 2 God responded positively to Solomon's prayer by igniting the sacrifices with heavenly **fire,** an act of approval recorded in other parts of the Bible as well (Judg. 6:21; 1 Kin. 18:38). **Glory . . . filled:** This was in the form of a thick cloud that filled the **temple** with darkness. The **priests** could no longer minister because of their awe and reverence before the glory of the Lord.

7:3–5 The people saw in God's **glory** His acceptance of the king and the temple, two central elements in His covenant promise to David (1 Chr. 17:11, 12).

7:6, 7 It is not clear as to how the musicians arranged themselves in this service of **praise,** but the use of the refrain **for His mercy**

🔍 **IN FOCUS**   **"pray"**

(Heb. *palal*) (2 Chr. 7:14; Gen. 20:7; Num. 21:7; 1 Kin. 8:44; Is. 16:12; Jer. 7:16) Strong's #6419: The Hebrew verb translated *pray* in God's promise concerning the revival of Israel (7:14) can also mean "to intervene," "to interpose," "to arbitrate," or even "to judge." The Lord was asking His people to intercede for others in their prayers. During the dedication of the temple, Solomon modeled intercessory prayer (6:3–42). He pleaded with God on behalf of the people and continued to pray with determination until the Lord answered. According to the Lord, this type of prayer would be the catalyst for revival and restoration in the future (Dan. 9:3–19).

---

endures forever (v. 3; 5:13) may suggest some kind of antiphonal or choral participation by some of the Levites or by the congregation.

7:8 The **feast** was the Feast of Tabernacles, which began on the fifteenth day of the seventh month and continued through the twenty-

second day (Lev. 23:34–36). **Hamath** and **Brook of Egypt** specify the extent of Solomon's early kingdom from north to south. The Brook of Egypt is probably the Wadi el-Arish, a seasonal stream about 40 miles southwest of Gaza.

7:9 The Feast of Tabernacles ended with an **eighth day** assembly, which fell always on the twenty-second day of the seventh month, Tishri. The seven-day **dedication of the altar** is the one referred to in 5:3.

7:10 he sent them away to their tents: Probably a reference to the huts or booths in which people stayed as part of the Feast of Tabernacles (Lev. 23:42, 43). Few if any Israelites used tents for their housing at this time.

7:11 The king's house refers to Solomon's own palace, a project much more elaborately explained in 1 Kings (1 Kin. 2:1; 7:1, 8). Since it took Solomon 13 years to build his palace and 20 years in all to build it and the temple (8:1), these events too are halfway through Solomon's 40-year reign.

7:12 In the next several verses (vv. 13–15), the Lord reviews and answers the petitions of **Solomon** (6:14–42). Solomon's prayers had been **heard** and would be answered, but there were conditions (v. 14).

7:13, 14 If God's people would do three things, God would respond in three ways. The Lord's people needed to become **humble,** that is, confess; they needed to **pray,** or repent; and they needed to **turn,** or come back to Him. If they did, God would **hear, forgive,** and **heal** them.

7:15–18 if you walk: The Lord challenged Solomon to remain faithful to Him and to the laws of the covenant so that he could enjoy the full benefit of God's blessing (vv. 17–20). **I will establish the throne:** The conditions for God's blessing on David and his line did not extend to the ongoing existence of that dynasty. The covenant promises to David were unqualified. The Lord had told David that if his son—that is, Solomon—sinned he would be disciplined, but "my mercy shall not depart from him," and "your house and your kingdom shall be established forever before you" (2 Sam. 7:15, 16; 1 Chr. 17:13, 14). Solomon might sin and be disciplined, but God's promises would stand—David's dynasty would go on.

7:19 if you turn: Here the word for *you* is plural. The Lord was speaking to the nation as a whole. The reference to **statutes** and **commandments** places this warning solidly within a covenant framework. Covenant disobedience, especially apostasy from Yahweh and the adoption of false **gods,** will bring dire consequences. Again, the covenant with David holds firm, but

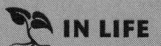 **IN LIFE** | **National Renewal**

As we struggle with the moral and spiritual chaos that seems to characterize life today, the promise that God will bring healing to the land (2 Chr. 7:14) looks attractive. Is this a verse on which Christians should base efforts at national renewal? In answering that question, it is important to notice that God was speaking to Israel, as indicated by the phrase, "My people who are called by My name" (6:5, 6, 33). Israel enjoyed a special covenant relationship with the Lord that no other nation has ever had. The words of the Lord (7:12–22), of which the promise of healing the land was a part, were essentially a restatement of the covenant (Lev. 26; Deut. 29).

It was not long after Solomon's death that this conditional promise saw its first test. Solomon's successor Rehoboam turned away from the Lord. As a result, God raised up the Egyptians to attack Israel. However, when Rehoboam and the leaders of Israel humbled themselves and turned back to God, the Lord heard their prayers and partially delivered them from the threat of the Egyptians (2 Chr. 12:1–12).

How, then, should Christians today regard this promise of God? It related directly to Israel. Does it relate at least indirectly to believers today? Yes, but only to a certain degree. Unlike Israel, Christians have not been called as a nation. Therefore, God's promise of healing the land cannot be applied universally to all national and international arenas of public life today. Nevertheless, the principle still applies that when believers humble themselves by praying and confessing their individual and corporate sins, God hears them, forgives their sins, and brings a measure of healing (James 4:7–10).

to enjoy its benefits his people must remain true to their God.

7:20, 21 proverb: The nation of Israel would become an object lesson to other nations, who would see the temple lying in ruins and understand the clear message about sin and its cost.

7:22 embraced other gods: Idolatry would be the downfall of the nation (Deut. 28; 29).

8:1, 2 This compressed account of transactions between Solomon and **Hiram** is more fully spelled out in 1 Kin. 9:10–14. In payment for the timber and gold that Hiram provided for Solomon's construction projects, Solomon gave twenty Galilean cities to Hiram. The Phoenician did not like the cities, but he took them anyway and even paid 120 talents of gold for them. Eventually Solomon took back the cities, rebuilt them, and settled Israelites in them once more.

8:3, 4 Solomon **built** and fortified cities such as **Tadmor** because they were on vital caravan routes. These fortified cities provided protection to his own caravans and became the customs points at which Solomon collected taxes. **storage cities:** Facilities were scattered throughout Solomon's outlying provinces to provide warehouses for his armies and merchantmen, as well as to store produce and other tribute paid by the vassal states (1 Kin. 9:19).

8:5 Upper Beth Horon and **Lower Beth Horon** were strategically located near the border between Judah and the northern tribal districts, along a major mountain pass to the Mediterranean (Josh. 10:10; 1 Sam. 13:18).

8:6 Baalath: Otherwise known perhaps as Baalah, this may be none other than the village at or near Kirjath Jearim, where the ark of the covenant was kept prior to its later location in **Jerusalem** (1 Chr. 13:6). This too lay on a major route from Jerusalem to the coastal plain. If not the same as Baalah, it was probably the Baalath listed as one of the cities of Dan (Josh. 19:44).

8:7, 8 The people groups named in this verse were remnants of the population of Canaan who survived the conquest. **Israel** reduced many of them to **forced labor** (2:17).

8:9–11 The daughter of Pharaoh is not named here. Solomon had married her early in his reign (1 Kin. 3:1) and had provided her housing near **David's palace** on Mount Zion. She had been forbidden to live in the palace, presumably because she was neither Hebrew nor God-fearing.

8:12, 13 The daily rate refers to the morning and evening sacrifices of lambs, one on each occasion (Ex. 29:38–42).

8:14, 15 Solomon, like all kings in David's line, had jurisdiction over **the priests and Levites,** as well as over civil, military, and political affairs.

8:16, 17 Ezion Geber and **Elath** were cities located close together at the northern end of the east branch of the Red Sea.

8:18 The Phoenicians were world-famous mariners, so when Solomon undertook a merchant marine enterprise he called once more on his good friend **Hiram,** the King of Tyre. The land of **Ophir,** located apparently in South Arabia (1 Chr. 29:4), was a source of finest **gold.**

9:1–3 Sheba was more than a thousand miles south of Israel, at the southern end of the Arabian peninsula. **hard questions:** Solomon was known for his great wisdom (1:10–12; 1 Kin. 4:29–34), a trait much prized and admired in the ancient Middle East.

9:4–7 No more spirit may refer to an attitude of pride or arrogance with which the queen had approached Solomon, or, more

9:14 The **gold and silver** that the **kings** and **governors** brought to Solomon was tribute—a form of taxation on vassal states, not a voluntary gift.

9:15, 16 The **shields of hammered gold** were for decorative or ceremonial purposes, not the armory. Gold was too expensive, too heavy, and too soft to use in battle.

9:17–20 Most scholars take this to be a **throne** inlaid with **ivory,** since there are no sources of ivory sufficient to yield a block of the

---

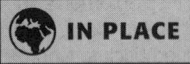 **IN PLACE**

The Queen of Sheba and International Trade

The queen of Sheba (2 Chr. 9:1; 1 Kin. 10:1) came to Jerusalem not only because she had heard of the fame of Solomon, but also because she had heard of Solomon's God (1 Kin. 10:6–9). However, even though her ultimate purpose in coming was spiritual, she might also have negotiated political and economic agreements during her visit.

Sheba was probably located in the mountainous region of southwest Arabia (now Yemen). Its strategic placement on the Gulf of Aden at the southern end of the Red Sea enabled it to control much of the trade from India and east Africa with the Middle East. Caravan routes along the coast connected Sheba with trading centers to the north, such as Tyre, Damascus, and Babylon. Solomon's growing shipping industry out of Ezion Geber (1 Kin. 9:26) and his ties to the Phoenicians may have brought the kingdoms of Sheba and Israel into direct competition for business. Thus a visit to Jerusalem would have been a timely trade mission.

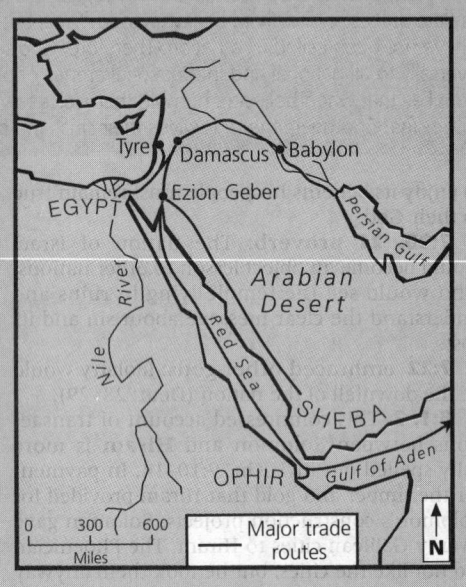

likely, a way of saying that what she saw and heard was breathtaking.

9:8–12 Blessed be the LORD your God: This was the language of politeness in the ancient world and does not suggest that the queen of Sheba was converted. Visiting dignitaries customarily praised the god of the host nation. Still, the queen's statements about God's love of **Israel** and election of **Solomon** were true enough (1 Chr. 17:11–14).

9:13 Solomon's annual income in **gold** through taxes alone amounted to 25 tons. Since king and state were identified, this figure reflects the annual revenues of the entire nation through taxes.

material that large. The throne, then, may have been of wood covered with **gold** plate into which ivory was embedded. Ivory, a product primarily of elephant tusks, certainly was available to Solomon (v. 21).

9:21, 22 To Tarshish is possibly a figure of speech, meaning "a great distance" or "to the ends of the earth."

9:23 In the context of Solomon's own time and place, **all kings** referred to the kings of the eastern Mediterranean world.

9:24, 25 each man brought his present: Ordinary presents are not given and received at a **set rate** so these presents were tribute paid to the king by vassals.

9:26, 27 Most of the kings of Israel had continuing trouble with the **Philistines,** even though they were able to subdue every other surrounding neighbor. David had some success against the Philistines (1 Chr. 18:2), and later Jehoshaphat managed to exact tribute from some of them (17:11).

9:28, 29 Nathan the prophet had rebuked David for his adultery and murder (2 Sam. 12:1) and had become a confidant and counselor to both David and **Solomon** (1 Kin. 1:8, 11). **Ahijah the Shilonite** would select **Jeroboam** as the first king of the northern kingdom of Israel (1 Kin. 11:26–40) and later would announce God's judgment on him (1 Kin. 14:1–16). **Iddo the seer** was a contemporary of Ahijah who compiled accounts of both Jeroboam and Rehoboam (12:15).

9:30, 31 Rehoboam was a son of Solomon by his wife Naamah of Ammon (12:13). Rehoboam was 41 when he began to rule, so he must have been born during the period when Solomon ruled alongside David (1 Chr. 29:22, 23).

10:1 Why did Rehoboam go **to Shechem** to be crowned? First, Shechem had a rich history dating back to Abraham's travels in the land (Gen. 12:6, 7; 35:4; Josh. 24:1–28). But more importantly, a rift had begun to develop between the northern and southern tribes (1 Kin. 11:26–40), and Shechem would be a more neutral place than Jerusalem.

10:2, 3 As head of all of Solomon's forced labor in the district of Ephraim, **Jeroboam** enjoyed great favor with the king. But the prophet Ahijah informed him that he would become ruler of the ten northern tribes because of Solomon's idolatry (1 Kin. 11:26–33). When Solomon heard of this he tried to kill Jeroboam (1 Kin. 11:40), but Jeroboam fled to **Egypt.**

10:4, 5 Solomon's heavy **yoke** included taxation and forced labor (1 Sam. 8:11–18; 1 Kin. 4:7; 9:15).

10:6–9 The term **elders** here should be taken not only to mean Solomon's physically aged counselors but also a technical way of referring to his official cabinet (1 Kin. 4:2–6). Both in the policy decision and the manner of arriving at his decision, Rehoboan clearly lacked the wisdom of his father, Solomon.

10:10, 11 Rehoboam promised that even the lesser evils of his reign—his **finger**—would be as hard as anything they knew under Solomon. The young men compared Solomon's rule to a **whip** and Rehoboam's to a **scourge,** a whip with sharp bits of metal that cut the flesh and caused excruciating pain.

10:12–15 the turn of events was from God: Human foolishness and decisions achieved God's purposes. Solomon's defection from God

late in his reign had already disqualified his descendants from ruling over all Israel (1 Kin. 11:9–13). Rehoboam initiated the split with his own foolish actions.

10:16, 17 In the people's poem, **Israel** referred to the ten northern tribes, **David** to the southern kingdom of Judah. **Tents** here can be figurative—the dwelling places of **Israel** in general, even though few people actually lived in tents in that era—or it may be a reference to literal tents in which the delegates to the Shechem assembly were staying while they were there.

10:18, 19 Hadoram, called Adoniram in 1 Kin. 4:6, was Jeroboam's counterpart in Judah as officer in charge of forced labor.

11:1 Shortly after the kingdom divided, the tribe of **Benjamin** joined **Judah** to form the southern kingdom. This is ironic because Saul was a Benjamite. However, Benjamites had shown great loyalty to David many years before (2 Sam. 19:16–20, 40–43). Also, Benjamin was closer geographically to Judah than to the northern tribes.

11:2–4 Like Nathan, Ahijah, and Iddo (9:29), **Shemaiah** was a prophet who wrote. The writer of Chronicles depended on Shemaiah's writings for some of his information (12:15).

11:5–12 cities for defense: Turning from an offensive strategy, **Rehoboam** decided to defend the small kingdom he had left by building fortifications throughout his land. They extended from Aijalon in the north (v. 10) to Ziph in the south (v. 8), and from Tekoa in the east (v. 6) to Gath in the west (v. 8).

11:13, 14 all their territories: Though Israel and Judah had split into two kingdoms, **the priests and the Levites** of Israel sided with Judah. One reason for this was that they knew that Rehoboam was David's offspring, and therefore the heir of God's covenant promise to David. Another reason was that Jeroboam had established his own religious cult which had no need for the true priests of God (1 Kin. 12:25–33).

11:15 The **calf idols** were the golden calves that Jeroboam had installed at Bethel and Dan.

11:16 Once the legitimate religious leaders had **left** Israel, the worshipers of God in the northern kingdom could no longer worship in good conscience, so they made pilgrimages **to Jerusalem** three times a year (1 Kin. 12:27, 32, 33).

11:17 Jeroboam's program of establishing a new religious structure in Israel apparently took at least **three years.** Meanwhile, the pilgrimage of godly Israelites from the north to Jerusalem **strengthened** Rehoboam and weakened Jeroboam (1 Kin. 12:27).

11:18, 19 Mahalath may have been David's

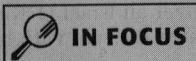 **IN FOCUS** | **"transgressed"**

(Heb. *ma'al*) (2 Chr. 12:2; Lev. 6:2; Ezek. 14:13) Strong's #4603: The principle sense of this word is "to break a trust," most often willfully but in some cases unintentionally (Lev. 5:15). The term is used in association with the word *sin* on several occasions (Lev. 5:15; 6:2; Ezek. 18:22–24). Transgression is almost always against the Lord and may be committed by individuals or communities, especially the covenant community (Num. 31:16; Neh. 1:6, 7; Ezek. 14:13). Also a wife can transgress against her husband, or a king can transgress by not rendering a true judgment (Num. 5:12; Prov. 16:10). The word occurs predominantly in the exilic and postexilic books. There death, military defeat, and exile are all viewed as divine judgments on Israel's transgressions (12:1–9; 1 Chr. 10:13; Ezek. 39:23; Dan. 9:7).

great-granddaughter. **Rehoboam** was David's grandson, so in any case this marriage was within the larger royal family.

11:20 Rehoboam's claims to legitimacy took further support from his marriage to **Maachah,** granddaughter of David's son Absalom. Their son **Abijah** would eventually succeed Rehoboam (12:16).

11:21, 22 Rehoboam named his son Abijah to be the next **king** to ensure a smooth succession following his death. Abijah probably served under or alongside Rehoboam, just as Solomon had served under David (1 Chr. 23:1).

11:23 In the context, **dealt wisely** pertains to how Rehoboam handled his many **sons.** He had selected one to be king, and to pacify the rest he gave them important assignments throughout the kingdom. The pampering extended even to generous material allowances and large harems.

12:1 the law: The normal Hebrew word for the Mosaic covenant, the Ten Commandments.

12:2, 3 Egypt was beginning to recover from a long period of decline and wanted to reestablish control over Palestine. God used their ambitions to discipline Rehoboam for abandoning the Lord. **The Lubim** were the Libyans. **The Sukkiim** were other desert tribes, perhaps from western Libya. **Ethiopians:** Sometimes referred to as Cushites, these famous warriors originated in the lands south of Egypt.

12:4–8 In order that the Judeans might understand how privileged they were to serve God, He would allow them to become **servants** to the Egyptians. Only then would they appreciate again the joy of being God's servant people.

12:9–11 The **treasures of the king's house** that the Egyptians seized had been spoils of war captured by David and dedicated to God (1 Chr. 18:6–8; 22:14). Judah was now a vassal state of Egypt.

12:12, 13 The king's conduct had inevitable consequences on the nation. When a king obeyed God, the Lord would bless the nation. When the king turned away from the Lord, his subjects would suffer. But when the king repented and **humbled himself** before God, God's forgiveness and restoration would cover both him and his kingdom.

12:14, 15 did not prepare his heart to seek the LORD: Note the differences between David, Solomon, Rehoboam, and Abijah (ch. 13). David, a man of God (8:14), died at a very old age with riches and honor. Solomon died wise, rich, and powerful. But Rehoboam **did evil.** As a result, he fought wars throughout most of his troubled reign. Abijah followed Rehoboam's example of not honoring God (13:8–18).

12:16 Abijah: Apparently Rehoboams eldest son (11:20, 22), who had already been appointed by his father as king-elect. Now he assumed kingship on his own.

13:1–4 Mount Zemaraim was a few miles southwest of Bethel (Josh. 18:22).

13:5 covenant of salt: Salt was a preservative and symbolized durability—an apt description of the eternal Davidic covenant (Lev. 2:13; Num. 18:19). **Israel** refers to the whole nation, not just the northern kingdom.

13:6 Abijah blamed the division of the kingdom on **Jeroboam,** not Rehoboam, or even Solomon (10:16). But Jeroboam's rebellion was fueled by Solomon's disobedience to the covenant and his harsh policies. Moreover, Rehoboam's foolish plan to increase the severity of those abuses infuriated the Israelites even more. The blame lay with all three—Jeroboam, Rehoboam, and Solomon.

13:7, 8 Abijah's version of the nation's division put his father in a relatively good light. According to Abijah, if Rehoboam had made any mistakes, it was merely because he was **young and inexperienced.** Abijah further equated the kingdom of Judah with **the**

kingdom of the LORD, making the victory of Judah over Israel sound like a foregone conclusion. This was a misrepresentation of the truth (v. 6) designed to scare the Israelites.

13:9 Jeroboam's illicit religion filled the priestly ranks with anyone who had the means to purchase the office. Thus Abijah asserted that all a person had to do to **consecrate himself** was to come with the appropriate sacrifices (1 Kin. 12:31; Lev. 8:2). But Abijah's words were hypocritical, for the same evil deeds were going on in his own kingdom (14:2–5).

13:10, 11 The **priests** of Judah were true priests, who traced their ancestry to **Aaron** as the Law required (1 Chr. 6:1–15). Throughout the passage the contrast is between the authorized worship at Jerusalem and the illicit practice of religion at Dan and Bethel. In summary, Abijah argued that Judah had remained true to God while Israel had **forsaken Him.**

13:12–16 The declaration that **God** is with them as their **head** and that the **priests** are there with **trumpets** is an assertion that the battle is being fought by God's people on His behalf. As in days of old when Joshua marched his armies out against Jericho in a procession headed by the ark of the covenant and accompanied by trumpets (Josh. 6:8, 9), so, Abijah says, would Yahweh lead the armies of Judah to victory now. In such a war it was useless for the enemy to resist, for the triumph of Yahweh was inevitable. In the **shout** are overtones of Joshua's hosts surrounding Jericho on the seventh day (Josh. 6:20). That **God delivered them** is also a way of affirming that the battle was the Lord's and not Judah's. They may have been His agents, but He gave the victory (Josh. 6:16). Yahweh did this for His people Judah in spite of their sin of inconsistency.

13:17–19 Among the Israelite cities that fell to Judah was none other than **Bethel,** the southern center of the false religious cult that Jeroboam had established (1 Kin. 12:29). **Jeshanah** may have been some six miles north of Bethel. **Ephrain,** otherwise known as Ephron, lay four miles northeast of Bethel.

13:20 Though there are no further reference to the details of Jeroboam's death, the verb **struck** here refers to a violent death either by sickness or by some outward act such as murder or assassination.

13:21, 22 One of the gauges of a king's power and prosperity was the size of his family.

14:1, 2 Abijah's son **Asa reigned** for 41 years, until 870 B.C. (16:13). **ten years:** This suggests that during the first ten years of Asa's reign there was peace between Judah and Israel (v. 6).

14:3–5 **Sacred pillars** were stone posts associated with Canaanite fertility rites.

Wooden images were fashioned from live evergreen trees, which were regarded as a fertility symbol, since they retain their leaves throughout the year. Eventually, cut poles took the place of live trees, because they could be erected anywhere, even in places where trees did not grow.

14:6–8 Rehoboam had **built fortified cities** in his time, but Shishak of Egypt had destroyed them (11:5–12; 12:2–4). It is likely that Asa merely rebuilt them. The phrase **in those years** refers to the first ten years of Asa's reign, the years of peace (v. 1).

14:9 Since Egypt was strong at this time (12:3) and fully in control of its own territory, it is likely that **Zerah** and his large army were mercenaries of the Egyptian king Osorkon I (914–874 B.C.), successor to Shishak. **Mareshah** was one of Asa's important fortified cities, about 25 miles southwest of Jerusalem (11:8). It was near the Via Maris, the coastal highway connecting Egypt and Canaan, making it strategically important.

14:10 The **Valley of Zephathah** was on the north side of Mareshah.

14:11, 12 **it is nothing for You to help:** Asa showed great faith in his prayer before the battle against Zerah's huge army. **in Your name:** Asa believed that God was on his side and that Zerah's attack was aimed at the Lord as well as at God's people (13:8, 12, 14, 15).

14:13–15 **Gerar** was at the frontier between Egypt and Canaan and might have been in Egyptian territory at this time.

15:1–5 **For a long time:** Much of what Azariah said to Asa could be said of the era of the judges, a time marked by long years of apostasy, ignorance, and lawlessness (Judg. 18:1; 21:25). **in their trouble:** These times were difficult. The Israelites were constantly being invaded and harassed. But when circumstances looked most hopeless, the people cried out to God in repentance, and He delivered them (Judg. 2:11–19). **no peace:** Beside the dangers of war, the continual perils of robbery and crime plagued the nation, a point expressly made in the Song of Deborah (Judg. 5:6, 7).

15:6, 7 **City by city** probably alludes to the civil strife that existed in Israel in the days of the judges, especially in connection with the abortive kingship of Abimelech (Judg. 9:1–57) and the lack of moral responsibility in Benjamin (20:18–35).

15:8 **The altar** had either suffered damage from some internal struggle or, more likely, had simply deteriorated from heavy use and lack of maintenance (compare 4:1).

15:9 Along with godly priests and Levites (11:13–17), many of the ordinary citizens of Israel **came over to** Judah when they saw Asa's zeal for God, and God's blessing upon him.

15:10 The **third month** quite likely locates this festival at the time of the firstfruits, the Feast of Pentecost (Lev. 23:15–21; Num. 28:26–31).

15:11 Spoil likely refers to the animals taken from the Ethiopians after Asa's victory over Zerah (14:15). If so, the battle of Mareshah (14:9, 10) must have taken place right before this event.

15:12, 13 Asa gathered an assembly to reaffirm Israel's **covenant** (or promise) to seek the Lord. The nation had assembled before to renew their commitment to God (Deut. 27:9, 10; 29:1; 31:10–13; Josh. 8:30–35; 24:1–28).

15:14 Taking **an oath** was an essential part of covenant-making (Ex. 24:7, 8; Deut. 27:11–26; 29:12). The people declared their determination to keep the covenant and agreed to accept God's judgment if they broke it.

15:15 The conflict with Zerah the Ethiopian (14:9) had broken the ten-year period of peace at the start of Asa's reign (14:1). After winning the war and renewing the covenant with God, Judah once again had **rest all around.**

15:16 Maachah is called Asa's **mother,** a Hebrew word that can also mean *grandmother.* Maachah was the mother of Asa's father, Abijah (13:2). Still, Asa demoted her **from being queen mother** because she had set up pagan idols—a courageous and delicate task for anyone, even a king.

15:17 high places were not removed from Israel: Asa destroyed the high places of Judah, but not those of Israel (14:3, 5).

15:18, 19 silver and gold and utensils: These items were taken as spoils of war and **dedicated** to the worship of God; they could not then be used for any other purpose (1 Chr. 18:8; 26:20).

16:1–3 The **treasuries of the house of the Lord** were items of value stored in the temple as ordinary revenue (1 Chr. 26:20). They did not include things dedicated to the Lord

(15:18). Asa used these treasuries to secure Ben-Hadad's assistance against **Baasha king of Israel.**

16:4 Ijon was in the tribal territory of Naphtali, some ten miles north of **Dan** and thirty-five miles north of the Sea of Galilee. **Abel Maim** was only three miles west of Dan. **Naphtali** was the most northern tribal territory of Israel, very close to Damascus.

16:6 Diverted by attacks from the north, **Baasha** left **Ramah** unfinished (v. 5). Asa, the king of Judah, took advantage of the situation and built his own fortifications at **Geba,** just east of Ramah, and at **Mizpah,** between Ramah and Bethel. Ramah ended up between Asa's fortresses and the Israelites could not rebuild it.

16:7–9 Hanani the seer was probably the father of another prophet Jehu, who once challenged King Jehoshaphat of Judah (19:2; 20:34).

16:10, 11 This **book** no doubt includes the biblical Book of Kings but much more besides. The chronicler cites his sources so that the skeptic can check for himself and that further information may be gained.

16:12, 13 diseased in his feet: Asa may have been suffering from gout, a common disease in the ancient world. For his malady Asa **did not seek the Lord,** but the physicians. The problem was not that Asa used doctors, but that he failed to turn to God during his sickness.

16:14 great burning: This had nothing to do with cremation, but was the burning of spices and perfumes to mourn a king's death (21:19).

17:1, 2 cities of Ephraim: Ephraim is a synonym for Israel. The cities referred to here are mentioned also in 15:8; they could include Ramah, Geba, and Mizpah as well (16:6), depending on fluctuations of the border between Israel and Judah.

17:3–8 Jehoshaphat was the first king since David who **walked in the former ways of his**

 **IN CONTEXT**   **Convicts with Conviction**

In an unjust society, it is often the righteous who are imprisoned. A number of leaders in the Bible, such as Hanani the seer (2 Chr. 16:10), spent time behind bars. Their loyalty to God's calling, to biblical convictions, and to genuine faith sometimes made them vulnerable to persecution or required them to resist laws or rulers in ways that landed them in jail.

The Bible shows us many cases where imprisonment has been used to persecute the innocent. Christ Himself, who was without sin, became a prisoner and was executed for our sakes. But even in cases where wrongs have been committed, the fact remains that Christ's good news is for captives and prisoners too. Forgiveness, restoration, and reconciliation are at the heart of the message of the Cross (Luke 4:18; Heb. 13:3).

father David. He obeyed God's commandments and took delight in the Lord's ways.

17:9 The Book of the Law refers to the five books of Moses, the Pentateuch. When Moses passed the leadership of Israel on to Joshua he instructed him never to let "this Book of the Law" depart from his mouth (Josh. 1:8). Unfortunately, Jehoshaphat's initiative in sending out teachers to instruct the nation in God's laws was not the norm (15:3).

17:10, 11 There is no record of Jehoshaphat conquering Philistia, but he was powerful enough to compel at least some of the **Philistines** to pay **tribute** to his sovereignty. Up to this point, only David had obtained such respect (1 Chr. 18:2).

17:12–18 Jehoshaphat's **men of war** were grouped into three divisions of Judeans with a total number of 780,000 (vv. 14–16), and two divisions of Benjamites numbering 380,000 (vv. 17, 18). The Hebrew word for **thousand** can also mean "clan" (as in Judg. 6:15; 1 Sam. 10:19) or "village" (as in Mic. 5:2), and possibly "company" in a military context. Thus, 780,000 may refer to 780 companies and 380,000 to 380 companies. The totals would then be nearer to 78,000 and 38,000.

17:19 Jehoshaphat's troops were stationed at Jerusalem. He had additional forces **in the fortified cities throughout** the countryside.

18:1 Jehoshaphat **allied himself with Ahab** by arranging for his son Jehoram to marry Ahab's daughter Athaliah (21:5, 6; 22:2).

18:2 Ahab died in battle a few days after Jehoshaphat's **visit** (v. 34). **Ramoth Gilead:** This important city some 35 miles east of Beth Shan was controlled by the Arameans. It was also one of the Israelite cities of refuge (Josh. 20:8; 1 Chr. 6:80).

18:3, 4 I am as you are: Jehoshaphat was referring to the intermarriage of their families (v. 1).

18:5 The prophets were probably prophets of Asherah, the Canaanite goddess worshiped by Ahab's wife Jezebel (v. 6; 1 Kin. 18:19).

18:6 There is some humor in Jehoshaphat's remark as he looks over the crowd of 400 prophets and asks if there **is not still a prophet of the Lord** here. He knows immediately that the prophets of Ahab are charlatans, unable and unwilling to speak the truth. The true prophet stands apart from them in his integrity and is therefore easily distinguished from them.

18:7, 8 he never prophesies good: Ahab means that this prophet of the Lord never says what Ahab wants to hear.

18:9 The **entrance of the gate** often led to a large open place in Israelite cities. Public assemblies could convene there or in rooms built into the sides of the gateway. The **threshing floor** was a large, flat area where grain was separated from straw (1 Chr. 21:15). The threshing floor of Ornan was just outside the walls of Jerusalem, where the winds could blow away the chaff. This is probably where the kings had set up their thrones.

18:10 In the OT, horns symbolize strength, so **horns of iron** would represent great strength (Zech. 1:18–21).

18:11, 12 In this context, **prophesied** suggests rantings and ravings typical of the demon-possessed false prophets of Canaan (1 Kin. 18:26–29), not true prophecy.

18:13, 14 whatever my God says: The true prophets' prophecies come directly from God. Their words are God's words.

18:15 Ahab knew from experience that his prophets told him what they thought he wanted to hear, not **the truth.** Because their prophecies agreed with Micaiah's, he knew that Micaiah must have been lying when he prophesied success.

18:16, 17 The Bible often uses **sheep** and **shepherd** as metaphors for the people of a nation and their king (1 Chr. 17:6, 7). **no master:** This is a prediction of Ahab's death (v. 34).

18:18, 19 Micaiah saw the **Lord** in heaven. Here we see God's sovereignty over all. The spirits who stood before Him were both angels and demons, and none could act without God's permission.

18:20–22 A lying spirit was a demon whom the Lord allowed to deceive the prophets. God cannot lie (Num. 23:19), but He does allow others to do so. In this sense, God **put a lying spirit in the mouth of** Ahab's prophets.

18:23–26 The term **governor** in Hebrew is literally "prince" **of the city. Amon** was probably the chief official of Samaria, a mayor in modern terms. **King's son** could be taken to mean the actual son of the king but more likely it is a technical expression referring to the king's representative (28:7; Jer. 36:20; 38:6). **bread . . . water of affliction:** Micaiah is to be punished for his insubordination by being denied any of the benefits of ordinary life.

18:27, 28 A real prophet's predictions always came true (Deut. 13:1–3; 18:22). Micaiah staked his reputation on the fact that Ahab would not come home **in peace**—that is, alive.

18:29 Ahab obviously does not want the Arameans to recognize him, so he puts aside his royal dress and goes incognito. **put on your robes:** The Arameans are not after Jehoshaphat but only Ahab. Therefore the king of Judah would be safer in his distinct royal apparel than he would even in **disguise** because the enemy would go out of its way to avoid hitting him if they knew who he was. It is not likely that Ahab is only trying to divert attention from himself, for surely Jehoshaphat was not so naive or unselfish as to set himself up as a sacrificial lamb.

18:30-32 What is suspected in light of v. 29 is put beyond doubt here. Jehoshaphat can feel free to openly identify himself, for he is not the target of Aramean hostility. Ahab and Jehoshaphat must have come to know this Aramean strategy by means of their intelligence network.

18:33, 34 at random: This is the human perspective. The wounding of Ahab, disguised as he was, appeared to be an accident. But from God's perspective, chance had no part in it. The arrow reached its true destination. Ahab's disguise could not foil God's plan. Micaiah's prophecy had come true (v. 16).

19:1, 2 The prophet Hanani had once chastised King Asa for depending on the Arameans to defeat Baasha, king of Israel (16:7). **Jehu the son of Hanani,** also a prophet, now went on a similar mission to Jehoshaphat.

19:3, 4 Originally the land of Israel stretched "from Dan to **Beersheba**" (Judg. 20:1). Dan refers to the town of Dan just north of the Sea of Galilee, not the tribe of Dan near Judah. But after the division into two kingdoms **the mountains of Ephraim** became the northern border of Judah. Thus this verse asserts that Jehoshaphat restored the people of Judah to more faithful observance of the covenant. This was admirable, but it was also a basic duty of the Davidic monarch (14:4; 15:9; 17:7-9). Jehoshaphat was only doing his job.

19:5, 6 The role of Jehoshaphat's **judges** differed from that of the heroic leaders who led Israel before David's time (Judg. 2:16). The judges that Jehoshaphat appointed served as local officials in the **fortified cities.**

19:7 The secret of success for fulfilling public office is a healthy **fear of the Lord**, for He is the supreme Judge to whom officials must ultimately give account.

19:8 Matters too difficult for the local judges or those that required appeal went to the high court **in Jerusalem** where the **Levites, priests,** and **chief fathers** sat.

19:9-11 As chief priest, **Amariah** (mentioned only here) held jurisdiction over all **matters of the Lord,** that is, religious cases. **Zebadiah,** the **ruler of the house of Judah** (1 Kin. 4:7), ruled over **all the king's matters**— that is, civil cases.

20:1 Moab went **to battle against Jehoshaphat** under the leadership of Mesha, who had gained Moab's independence from the Omri dynasty of Israel soon after Ahab died

(18:34). The battle mentioned here took place when Ahab's son Ahaziah was king of Israel (20:35). The defeat of Jehoshaphat's enemies in Israel only meant the rise of other enemies outside Israel. This situation would test Jehoshaphat's faith.

20:2 Hazazon Tamar is on the western shore of the Dead Sea, a few miles south of Qumran. It was David's hiding place in the days of Saul (1 Sam. 23:29).

20:3, 4 seek the Lord: Jehoshaphat's reforms (19:4) were not hollow religiosity, and they did not break under the strain of sour circumstances. As soon as he heard of bad news from the north, Jehoshaphat sought God and **proclaimed a fast.** He knew that success required God's favor. And if God was for them, they could not lose (vv. 6-12; 13:5, 12).

20:5-7 Jehoshaphat recalled God's care for His **people Israel** in the past, when He had led them to victory over their Canaanite foes.

20:8-10 Mount Seir is another, more original, name for Edom (Gen. 32:3). Listing Mount Seir with **Ammon** and **Moab** supports the view that Syria in v. 2 is actually Edom. These were all "brother nations" to **Israel,** and for that reason Moses and the Israelites were forbidden to **invade** them in the days of Israel's journey to Canaan from Egypt (Num. 20:17-21). Edom was another name for Esau, Jacob's brother (Gen. 25:30); Ammon and Moab were sons of Lot by his two daughters (Gen. 19:36-38).

20:11-14 As a member of the Asaph division of the Levites (1 Chr. 6:39; 15:17, 19; 16:7), **Jahaziel** was probably a musician. Music was an important part of Israel's religious life (13:12). The people would go into battle praising God with instruments and voices (vv. 19, 21, 22, 28).

20:15-17 The **ascent of Ziz** was a dry stream bed just north of En Gedi. The **Wilderness of Jeruel** lay between Hebron and the Dead Sea.

20:18, 19 The **Kohathites** were members of the Levitical division of Heman (1 Chr. 6:33). The **Korahites** were a subclan of the Kohathites (1 Chr. 6:37, 39), who were employed as gatekeepers to the temple (1 Chr. 26:1-19). Their positive response to Jahaziel's speech and their praise to God (vv. 15-17) was as important as any military preparation.

20:20 Tekoa was a town about 10 miles south of Jerusalem. The **Wilderness of Tekoa** was between the town and the Ascent of Ziz (v. 16). **believe . . . believe:** Success in serving God requires complete trust in Him (John 14:1).

20:21, 22 sing . . . praise: The battle was the Lord's and its outcome was certain. The people celebrated God and His victory (Ex. 15:1, 20, 21; Judg. 7:18-20; Pss. 47; 98).

20:23, 24 Before Judah's armies could even reach the battlefield, the Ammonites and Moabites attacked their Edomite allies and destroyed them, then they turned against each other. As a result, Judah won without even having to fight. God had demonstrated that the battle was His (v. 15) and that He could accomplish His purposes without even using an army.

20:25 Spoils of war like **valuables** (precious metals) and **jewelry** became God's property, because God Himself had triumphed and therefore deserved the fruits of war (15:18; Josh. 6:24; 1 Chr. 18:7, 8).

20:26–28 After they experienced God's blessing and protection in the wilderness, the Judeans renamed Ziz (Heb. *tsits*) the **Valley of Berachah,** meaning "Blessing," to remind themselves of God's goodness.

20:29–33 the LORD had fought: The spectacle of Jehoshaphat's enemies in defeat, like the battles that Joshua had led years before, struck fear in the hearts of enemy nations

(Heb. *yashar*) (2 Chr. 20:32; Ex. 15:26; Deut. 12:25; Judg. 17:6) Strong's #3477: The Hebrew word frequently translated *right* (as when used in Chronicles and Kings to assess the reigns of the kings of Israel and Judah) derives from a Hebrew word meaning "to be level" or "to be upright." By extension it carries connotations of being just or righteous. The word is not only used to speak of the perfect righteousness of God (Deut. 32:4; Ps. 111:7, 8) but also of the integrity of one's speech (Job 6:25; Eccl. 12:10) or the righteous quality of a person's lifestyle (Prov. 11:3, 6). The word even implies pure and faithful motives (as in Deut. 9:5; 1 Kin. 9:4). As Israel's second king, David exemplified these qualities in his life (1 Kin. 3:6), becoming a standard for assessing all the kings that followed him (2 Chr. 17:3; 34:2).

(17:10; Josh. 2:9–11; 1 Chr. 14:17) because it involved an obvious miracle. No human army could prevail over God's omnipotence.

20:34 For a complete account of Jehoshaphat's reign the chronicler recommended the **book of Jehu,** which itself was cited in **the book of the kings of Israel.** Jehu was the son of the prophet Hanani and was a prophet himself (19:2). He is mentioned in 1 Kings in connection with the kings of Israel (1

Kin. 16:1, 7). He was therefore a good source of information about both the northern and southern kingdoms.

20:35 Ahaziah was the son of Ahab; he succeeded his father and reigned for two years (1 Kin. 22:51). Ahaziah was injured in a fall and turned to the Philistine gods rather than to the Lord for healing (2 Kin. 1:2).

20:36 Tarshish was in the western Mediterranean. The name also came to represent any place far away. Ships of Tarshish were large vessels able to transport heavy cargo over long distances (8:17, 18; 9:21). **Ezion Geber** was a port on the Gulf of Aqaba (or Elath), the eastern arm of the Red Sea (8:17).

20:37 In **the ships were wrecked** is the implication that it was a natural disaster, suhc as a typhoon, behind which was the retributive hand of God.

21:1, 2 The names of Jehoram's **brothers** highlight Jehoram's choice as king emphatically, as if to say, "Not these brothers, but this one." We soon learn how significant for all of them this choice turned out to be (v. 4).

21:3 gifts . . . fortified cities: Jehoshaphat did what his great-grandfather Rehoboam had done. He gave the kingdom to his firstborn and then distributed extravagant gifts to his other sons (11:23). The purpose evidently was to satisfy each of his sons, since only one of them could succeed him as king.

21:4–6 princes of Israel: Jehoram extended his bloody purge as far as his distant relatives in Israel (18:1). He was so evil that not even blood ties restrained his lust for power.

21:7 Individual kings such as Jehoram committed evil and scorned **covenant** obligations, but the promise of God to **David** (Ps. 89:30–37) concerning his house remained intact (1 Chr. 17:7–14). **a lamp:** This is a figurative way of describing a descendant of David (1 Kin. 11:36).

21:8, 9 Edomites revolted: Jehoram's father Jehoshaphat had conquered Edom (20:22, 36).

21:10 In the western lowlands of Judah, **Libnah** was close to the border with Philistia.

21:11 commit harlotry: Israel's covenant with God was like a marriage relationship, and to violate it was to commit spiritual unfaithfulness (Ezek. 16:15–43; 23:1–21; Hos. 4:11–19). Like Solomon before him (1 Kin. 11:1–8), Jehoram failed to provide godly leadership. He **led Judah astray.**

21:12 Though 1 and 2 Kings pay considerable attention to **Elijah the prophet** (1 Kin. 17:1; 2 Kin. 2:18), the books of the Chronicles mention him only here. He had been taken up into heaven after King Ahaziah's death (2 Kin. 1:17; 2:1).

21:13–16 The Arabians were from the

southwestern part of the Arabian peninsula, probably near present-day Yemen. They lived across the Red Sea from the **Ethiopians.**

21:17–19 no burning: Part of the rituals of death and burial was the lighting of bon fires, the meaning of which is unclear (16:14). Because of his wickedness and the displeasure of his subjects, Jehoram was not honored according to custom.

21:20 The tombs of the kings was a royal cemetery in Jerusalem where most of David's dynasty were buried (Asa was an exception; 16:14). Jehoram was not buried there, but in Jerusalem, the **City of David.**

22:1–4 Ahaziah of Judah was the namesake of his uncle from Israel. Ahaziah's father Jehoram had married a sister of Ahab's son Ahaziah (1 Kin. 22:40; 2 Kin. 1:17; 8:18).

22:5 Jehoram the son of Ahab succeeded his brother Ahaziah because Ahaziah had no sons of his own (2 Kin. 1:17). He is also called Joram, a short form of Jehoram, to distinguish him from his brother-in-law Jehoram who was king of Judah. **Hazael** was the king of Damascus who came to power after assassinating Ben-Hadad (2 Kin. 8:7–15). Elijah had prophesied that this would come about and had even commissioned Elisha to anoint Hazael to his new position (1 Kin. 19:15). **Ramoth Gilead:** Ahab and Jehoshaphat had tried to recover this city from Aramean domination 12 years earlier (18:3, 28–34). Ahab's son Jehoram persuaded Ahaziah king of Judah to join him in a renewed effort to accomplish that objective.

22:6 Jezreel was a royal city located in the Plain of Jezreel and frequented by the kings of Israel. It was about 10 miles west of the Jordan and 25 miles west of Ramoth Gilead (1 Kin. 21:1–4). In this instance **Ramah** is an abbreviated form of Ramoth Gilead.

22:7, 8 Ahaziah's visit to his dying uncle turned out to be **God's occasion for Ahaziah's downfall.** Jehu was an officer in Israel's army who participated in the campaign against Ramoth Gilead and who was anointed there as king by a servant of Elisha (2 Kin. 9:1–6). Elijah had prophesied that Jehu would become king of Israel (1 Kin. 19:16). Elisha carried out the commission through his servant, telling Jehu to remove Joram from the throne and to eradicate the entire Omri dynasty (2 Kin. 9:7–10).

22:9 When Ahaziah became aware of the slaughter of the northern dynasty and even some of his own relatives who happened to be in Jezreel (v. 8), he fled to Israel's capital, **Samaria.** But Jehu found him there and murdered him. In one day, both kingdoms lost their rulers. **they buried him:** The people honored him in this way only because Ahaziah was the grandson of the godly Jehoshaphat.

22:10 Most of **the royal heirs** Athaliah murdered were her own grandchildren. She wanted to stamp out the Davidic dynasty and bring Judah back under Israelite control. But this could not happen as long as Jehu was in power in the north.

22:11 It was Ahaziah's own sister **Jehoshabeath** who rescued her nephew Joash from her mother Athaliah.

22:12 Though **Athaliah reigned** for **six years,** she was not a descendant of David and therefore was never listed among the kings of Judah. Meanwhile, her grandson Joash remained the sole survivor in the Davidic line.

23:1, 2 The **Levites** were the religious leaders of the nation; the **chief fathers** were the civil leaders. Jehoiada needed support and help from both civil and religious leaders to overthrow Athaliah.

23:3 covenant: This was a solemn pledge to restore the throne to Joash and to submit to him as David's rightful heir (1 Chr. 29:21–24). **he said:** The speech was given by Jehoiada, not Joash (vv. 3, 8).

23:4 one-third: Jehoiada was referring to the changing of **priests and the Levites** for the week to come (1 Chr. 24:3). The coming and going of so many men at once would disguise the plot.

23:5 gate of the foundation: This portal, called the Sur Gate in 2 Kin. 11:6, cannot otherwise be identified, but it must have been in or near the temple complex.

23:6–8 Though one division of priests and Levites would normally replace the other, both **divisions** remained at the temple so they would have enough men to place Joash, the true heir, on David's throne.

23:9, 10 The temple contained **spears** and **shields** that David himself had assembled over 150 years before (9:15, 16; 12:10, 11; 2 Sam. 8:10, 11; 1 Chr. 18:7, 10, 11; 29:2). Jehoiada distributed these among the soldiers, who could not have carried their own weapons into the area without arousing suspicion.

23:11, 12 The Testimony was a copy of the Law of Moses, part of which outlined the king's covenant privileges and duties (Deut. 17:18–20; 1 Chr. 29:19). **anointed him:** An anointing was the sign and seal of the king's appointment by God and a symbol of the Spirit of God upon him (1 Sam. 16:13; 1 Kin. 1:39).

23:13 The **pillar** was probably one of the two that stood in front of the temple (3:15).

23:14 not . . . in the house of the LORD: The temple was regarded as a place of sanctuary from violence.

23:15 The Horse Gate in the temple provided access to the royal palace. There was another Horse Gate in the city wall.

23:16 This appears to be only a more public, all-inclusive statement of the same **covenant** made in the temple area to the nation's leadership (v. 3).

23:17–19 killed Mattan: The Law required that leaders in the worship of false gods be put to death (Deut. 13:6–11). This sort of execution had been carried out before (1 Kin. 18:40; 2 Kin. 10:25–28).

23:20, 21 The Upper Gate joined the temple to the royal palace on the north side of the temple (27:3).

24:1, 2 Joash could not rule alone at the age of **seven,** so his uncle Jehoiada acted as his guardian and counselor (v. 3). As long as his Jehoiada was alive, **Joash did what was right** (but see vv. 17, 18).

24:3, 4 Repairing the house of the LORD was necessary because of the neglect it had suffered during the evil reigns of Jehoram, Ahaziah, and Athaliah (v. 7).

24:5, 6 the collection: This was the "atonement money" that the Levites collected for the temple and its services (Ex. 30:11–16).

24:7, 8 The **dedicated things** included gold, silver, and other valuables collected as tribute from defeated enemies and presented to God as spoils of war (2 Sam. 8:10, 11).

24:9–12 The priests and Levites who supervised various ministries such as music, gatekeeping, and maintenance did **the work of the service.** They knew best what the needs were, so **the king and Jehoiada** gave the money to them.

24:13, 14 The people had been so generous (v. 11) that **money** remained after all the work had been done. This extra money allowed for a complete restocking of the temple with the **gold and silver** implements needed for its services. The daily **burnt offerings** were a sign of spiritual vitality and faithfulness to God. As long as **Jehoiada** remained alive, Judah enjoyed a revival of the true worship of God.

24:15 This lifespan of **one hundred and thirty years** is so out of keeping with age-span during that period of history that many scholars suggest a corruption in the text or some other way of explaining it. Some have proposed that "one hundred and thirty" may refer to the amount of time that had elapsed since the division of the kingdoms, which had taken place in 931 B.C. One hundred and thirty years later would be 801, the approximate date of this passage. The figure, then, would be marking the era from the last important chronological benchmark to this one, the revival under Joash. While attractive in some respects, this interpretation is not sufficiently attentive to the emphasis that the chronicler is otherwise putting on the great age of the priest.

24:16 Jehoiada was buried **among the kings** because of his service to God and to Joash.

24:17–19 The extent of Jehoiada's positive influence on Joash became obvious soon after the priest's death. King Joash became a proponent of idolatry and **would not listen** to God's rebukes. Because of this, God abandoned the Judeans to their evil ways (v. 20).

24:20, 21 Jesus spoke of "Zechariah, son of Berechiah" as one of a series of prophets who was murdered in the temple court (Matt. 23:34, 35). This could be the Zechariah who wrote the Book of Zechariah (Zech. 1:7), which says nothing about his death. **Zechariah the son of Jehoiada** also died a martyr in the temple court, as described here. Either (1) the chronicler's Zechariah was actually the grandson of Jehoiada and the son of an unmentioned Berechiah, or (2) the prophet who wrote the Book of Zechariah was also slain in the temple precincts, a fact recorded only in the Gospels.

24:22 killed his son: Besides forgetting all the good Jehoiada had done for him, Joash had killed his own cousin (22:11; 24:20). This once-good king had sunk to the level of his evil grandmother Athaliah (22:10), despite decades of past faithfulness to God. The weakness of his own convictions did him in. As long as he received good advice, he did well. But all depended on the quality of that counsel. Once it was gone, he abandoned God.

24:23–27 God arranged for Israel's defeat and Joash's death in fulfillment of Zechariah's dying cry for justice (v. 22). **Judgment** for evil does not always come so quickly, but it is just as inevitable no matter how long it is delayed. **tombs of the kings:** Like his grandfather Jehoram, Joash was excluded from the royal cemetery because he fell far short of the Davidic ideal (21:20). Ironically, Jehoiada, who was not a king at all, was buried among the kings because of his faithfulness to God and to God's chosen king (v. 16).

25:1–3 Amaziah had to bide his time until he was well enough **established** to be able to take such matters in hand as to punish those who had slain **his father.**

> *God arranged for Israel's defeat and Joash's death in fulfillment of Zechariah's dying cry for justice.*

25:4 Amaziah did what was "right in the sight of the Lord" (v. 2) by obeying the **Book of Moses** with regard to the innocent children of lawbreakers (Deut. 24:16).

25:5, 6 The king of **Israel** was Jehoash (or Joash; v. 17). The hiring of Israelite mercenaries here, though judged evil (v. 7), implies that good relations existed between the two kingdoms.

25:7 As the breakaway kingdom that no longer stood within the Davidic covenant, **Israel** had disqualified itself as the people of the Lord. It was therefore improper for Judah to form alliances with the northern kingdom (19:2; 20:36, 37; 22:7). Because **Ephraim** was the dominant tribe in Israel, the whole kingdom at times was known as Ephraim (Hos. 4:15–19).

25:8, 9 If this war had been sanctioned by the Lord, victory would have been certain. But Amaziah had made his own decision to go to **battle** (v. 5) and had no assurance of God's help.

25:10 Amaziah heeded the prophet's advice and sent the Israelites back without even demanding the return of the hundred talents of silver he had paid them (v. 9). This **greatly aroused** the Israelite mercenaries because they thought their share of the spoils would have been much more than that.

25:11, 12 The **Valley of Salt** probably refers to the desert south of the Dead Sea. The **people of Seir** were the Edomites (20:10). Amaziah wanted to recover Edom as a Judean province, but he only succeeded in part (21:8, 10; 26:2).

25:13 The **soldiers** who attacked and sacked cities of Judah were those from Israel whom Amaziah had hired and then released (vv. 6, 10). Having been denied a part in the spoils of Edom, they set out to get them from Judah.

25:14 Amaziah had listened to the prophet of God, but then he turned around and worshiped the **gods of the people of Seir.** This is why the chronicler said that Amaziah served God, "but not with a loyal heart" (v. 2).

25:15, 16 could not rescue: Apparently it never occurred to Amaziah that it was foolish for him to worship a god who was powerless to defend his **own people.**

25:17, 18 The **thistle** here represents Amaziah, and the **cedar** Joash. The point is that it was arrogant for the weak, insignificant Amaziah to suppose that he could defeat Joash. The **wild beast** that passes by and tramples the thistle represents the war that Amaziah was so eager to pursue. Such a war would crush him.

25:19, 20 it came from God: As we find several times in 2 Chronicles, what appears to be a purely human decision or action turns out to be part of God's plan of blessing or judgment (22:7).

25:21 Of the three places named **Beth Shemesh,** this one was 18 miles west of Jerusalem. The ark of the covenant came here when it returned from Philistia (1 Sam. 6:12–14).

25:22, 23 Since Ephraim lay north of Jerusalem, the **Gate of Ephraim** was probably in the northern wall of the city, perhaps the same as the later Damascus Gate. The **Corner Gate** was at the east or west end of the north

---

 **IN LIFE**   # Following the Lord— but Not Wholeheartedly

Demographers today classify roughly one-seventh of the world's population as Christian. However, church leaders are quick to point out that many adherents of Christianity, particularly in the West, can only be classified as nominal Christians—that is, Christians in name only. They attend church sporadically and show little if any spiritual commitment.

The faith of Amaziah of Judah was nominal. He generally followed the Lord, but not wholeheartedly (2 Chr. 25:2). Apparently he practiced the Law, but probably did so more out of tradition than out of heartfelt commitment to the Lord. So it is not surprising to learn that Amaziah took ethical shortcuts when it was convenient. For example, he spared the lives of Israelite children of murderers, in accordance with the Law (25:3, 4). But then he killed 10,000 innocent Edomites (25:11, 12).

Amaziah's legacy is a sobering reminder that nominal faith is almost as bad as no faith at all. A person can lead a fine, upstanding life, yet have little or no relationship with God. If the main point of life is to know, love, and serve God, then merely following a noble religious tradition is of little value, and dangerously self-deceiving.

wall. **Four hundred** cubits was about six hundred feet.

25:24 One reason Joash's forces demolished the north wall was to gain access to the temple and its treasures. Obed-Edom's sons had been put in charge of the storehouse of the temple, probably meaning both the treasuries of the house of the Lord and the treasuries of the dedicated things (1 Chr. 26:15, 20). The **treasures of the king's house** refers not only to the king's private wealth but also to the state coffers, for there was no difference in principle and practice between the two (9:13; 1 Chr. 29:3). **hostages:** These might have included Amaziah himself.

25:25–27 They must refer to those who decried the defection of Amaziah from the Lord and who wanted to restore a godly regime. Thus Amaziah, like his father Joash (24:25), was assassinated. The fact that Amaziah reached the city of **Lachish** on the border with Philistia, some 25 miles from Jerusalem, suggests that he may have been seeking sanctuary among the Philistines.

25:28 City of Judah: This is an unusual way of speaking of the City of David. Since there is no note that he was buried with his **fathers** in the royal tombs, he probably was not.

26:1, 2 On the eastern arm of the Red Sea, **Elath** was technically in Edomite territory (8:17) but regularly was under Israel or Judah throughout OT times (20:36; 21:8–10). Some time after Amaziah's death, Uzziah rebuilt Elath.

26:3–5 The **Zechariah** named here may have been the son of Jehoiada (24:20, 21).

26:6 Also known as Jabneel (Josh. 15:11), **Jabneh** lay near the Mediterranean coast, less

than 10 miles north of **Ashdod.** The geographical pattern of Uzziah's campaigns suggests that he was trying to gain access to the Mediterranean Sea and neutralize Philistine influence.

26:7 Gur Baal was most likely at present-day Tell Ghurr, about eight miles east of Beersheba. The **Meunites** were a desert tribe living mainly in Edom, south and west of the Dead Sea (1 Chr. 4:39–41).

26:8 The last recorded contact of Judah with Ammon was almost a hundred years earlier, in the days of Jehoshaphat. The **Ammonites** and Moabites had defeated the Edomites, but then began to fight each other (20:1, 22, 23). Evidently they still had not recovered sufficiently to prevent **Uzziah** from dominating them and extracting tribute from them.

26:9 The **Corner Gate** was at one end of the north wall of **Jerusalem** (25:23). The **Valley Gate** was on the west side of the city near the temple mount (Neh. 2:13, 15).

26:10–14 Archaeological research has uncovered many **towers in the desert** that date from the time of Uzziah. **Carmel** was a region south of Hebron, not the famous mountain where Elijah confronted the prophets of Baal. David often went to Carmel when he was fleeing from Saul (1 Sam. 25:2, 5, 7).

26:15 devices: This is one of the earliest references to catapults, which seem to have been defensive weapons, since their users were **on the towers and the corners.**

26:16 Uzziah, swollen with pride, entered **the temple.** Uzziah was a descendant of David, but there were strict limits on his role in worship. Evidently Uzziah chafed at the restrictions.

✠ IN CONTEXT   No King-Priests in Judah

The Law of Moses stipulated that only the priests could perform the ritual sacrifices (Num. 3:5–10). The interior of the temple in Jerusalem was forbidden to all except certain orders of Levitical priests. Unlike the kings of neighboring nations, the king of Judah was not allowed into his own private temple, for he was not a priest, as most kings in the ancient Near East were.

The common ancient Near Eastern belief was that the most significant person in the community, the king, should also be the one representing the people before the god. Egyptian kings were considered embodied gods and had religious responsibilities withing the cult. Mesopotamian and Syro-Phonecian rulers were seen both as vice-regents of their patron deities and as high priests of the deities' cults. Certain public holy days could be carried out only by the king serving as high priest. One of the reasons Nabonidus, king of Bablyonia (556–539 B.C.), was so unpopular was because he did not perform the New Year's rituals for several years but left them to his son, which made the ritual improper and without value to the citizens.

Judah's king Uzziah was trying to act like these other kings by burning incense on the altar of the temple (2 Chr. 26:16–20), and by his action usurped the priest's role. The antagonistic encounter between Uzziah and the 81 priests (26:17, 18) probably reveals one of the many power struggles that went on between the kings and priests in Judah's politics.

26:17 The **Azariah** named here may be the same as Azariah the son of Johanan (1 Chr. 6:10).

26:18 the priests, the sons of Aaron: Uzziah sinned when he exercised priestly privileges that were reserved for the Aaronic order (Num. 16:39, 40).

26:19 Leprosy was any kind of serious skin condition (Lev. 13:1—14:32). Today, *leprosy* refers technically to Hansen's disease, a disease not known in Biblical times.

26:20 The urgency of the priests to **thrust him out,** as well as Uzziah's own haste to leave, came from the strict requirements of the Law (Lev. 22:2–6; Num. 12:10, 15). The Law viewed leprosy as a breach of God's own holiness; it was a graphic symbol of defilement.

26:21 isolated house: Because of his uncleanness, Uzziah had no access to the temple either as a worshiper or as king. **was over the king's house:** Control of the temple and the state now passed to Jotham. This implies a coregency. As long as Uzziah lived, Jotham exercised power on his behalf.

26:22 Isaiah was the prophet who wrote the Book of Isaiah (Is. 1:1). He witnessed the last years of Uzziah but wrote virtually nothing about him in his book that has survived.

26:23 reigned: This simply means that Jotham made the transition from coregent (v. 21) to full and independent king.

27:1 Jotham's **sixteen years** began eleven years before Uzziah died. This suggests that Uzziah had leprosy for more than a decade before he died.

27:2 did not enter the temple: Jotham, who took his father's place as regent because of his father's rashness in offering incense, certainly learned from that experience and did not seek to move outside the priestly limitations inherent in his office.

27:3 The **Upper Gate** connected the temple and the royal palace (23:20). Jotham repaired or rebuilt it. **the wall of Ophel:** Ophel was the original Jebusite area of Jerusalem. Its walls dated back hundreds of years and must have required regular maintenance.

27:4 cities . . . fortresses and towers: From the earliest days, the kings of Judah had built defense works and facilities for storing food and supplies (8:2, 4–6; 11:5–12; 14:6, 7; 17:12; 26:9, 10). In Jotham's time the Assyrians and other potential enemies were becoming a threat, so this building was necessary.

27:5–9 Uzziah had reduced the Ammonite **people** to tributary status, but evidently they had broken free. Jotham therefore reasserted his control and forced renewed payments. **second and third years:** After three years the tribute ended, suggesting that Ammon once more regained its independence.

28:1, 2 Ahaz's reign of **sixteen years** could mean that he came to the throne about four years after the sixteen-year tenure of his father Jotham (27:1).

28:3 The **Valley of the Son of Hinnom** was just outside the western wall of Jerusalem. It was a dumping ground for all kinds of refuse, much of which was burned. The valley itself became a symbol of impurity. It was used as a site of pagan worship, including human sacrifice (2 Kin. 23:10; Jer. 7:31, 32; 19:2–6; 32:35). **the abominations of the nations:** Worshipers of the Ammonite god Molech practiced human and child sacrifice (Lev. 18:21; 20:2–5; Deut. 12:31).

28:4 every green tree: Canaanite nature cults focused on evergreens, probably as symbols of perpetual fertility. Whereas other trees grew and shed their leaves, thus speaking of the cycles of life and death, these trees stayed green and spoke therefore of ongoing, uninterrupted life. Ritual prostitution conducted under these trees was thought to enhance the fertility of plant, animal, and human life.

28:5 king of Syria: Rezin (2 Kin. 16:5).

28:6 Pekah, who assassinated Pekahiah son of Menahem so he could become king of Israel (2 Kin. 15:23–25), reigned for 20 years (2 Kin. 15:27). He was murdered in a plot headed by Hoshea, the last king of Israel. **because they had forsaken the Lord** God: Pekah was not offended by Judah's godlessness and did not himself initiate this purge. Rather, God used Pekah to carry out His judgment.

28:7 The **officer over the house** was a manager of the palace and all of its staff and activities.

28:8, 9 This prophet **Oded** is mentioned only here. **killed . . . in a rage:** God used the Israelite armies to carry out his judgment on Judah (v. 6), but He never intended for the Israelites to enjoy it. Oded condemned their malicious and self-serving attitude.

28:10–12 The Israelites intended to make the survivors of Judah their **slaves,** although this was forbidden by the Law of Moses (Lev. 25:39–46).

28:13, 14 offended the Lord: This admission by Israel's leaders applies not only to the outrageous slaughter of their brethren from Judah (v. 6) but also to the whole course of their history until then. The Israelites could see from the rise of the Assyrians and their encroachment on Israel that the end was near. Within ten years, the Assyrians would capture Samaria and deport all of the Israelites. The Israelites brought this judgment on themselves (2 Kin. 17:7, 18).

28:15 anointed them: They applied balms and oils to the wounded.

28:16 The **kings of Assyria** were Tiglath-Pileser III, Shalmaneser V, and Sargon II.

28:17 The relationship between **Judah** and the **Edomites** changed often. Judah usually dominated Edom and was never under its control, but the extent of domination varied from one generation to the next (8:17; 20:2, 22, 36; 21:8–10; 25:11; 26:2). Now Edom was independent once again and powerful enough to invade Judah and take prisoners. Ahaz solicited help from Assyria (v. 16).

28:18, 19 lowland: This region between the hill country of Judah and the coastal plain is commonly called the Shephelah. **The South** was the Negev. **Beth Shemesh** was eighteen miles west of Jerusalem near the Philistine border. **Aijalon** was in the Aijalon valley seven miles north of Beth Shemesh. **Gederoth** was possibly the same as Gederah, located about three miles west of Aijalon. **Sochoh** was in the southern lowlands, about ten miles southwest of Hebron. **Gimzo** was eight miles northwest of Aijalon. All these places were near valleys that led up to central Judah from the surrounding plains. Control of them meant control of Judah itself. Because Ahaz understood this, he appealed to Assyria.

28:20–22 Tiglath-Pileser brought Mesopotamian influence over the countries of the eastern Mediterranean to its highest point. He undertook a campaign against Arpad in Syria and terrorized Menahem of Israel so much that Menahem paid him a huge bribe to be left alone (2 Kin. 15:19). Tiglath returned to the west again, and Ahaz scrambled for protection against Syria and Israel (2 Kin. 16:5–7; Is. 7:1, 2). The Assyrians overran Damascus and replaced the assassinated Pekah of Israel with Hoshea (2 Kin. 15:30), but they **did not assist** Ahaz. The king of Judah's troubles with the Edomites, Philistines, Arameans, and even Israelites (Is. 7:1) were over for the time being, but at great cost.

28:23 King Ahaz's idolatry and unfaithfulness to God (v. 19) led to God's judgment. Rather than repent, Ahaz sought to appease the gods who **had defeated him,** the **gods of Damascus.** Not only was he being idolatrous, he was ignoring the fact that Damascus itself had fallen to the Assyrians.

28:24 The account in 2 Kin. 16:10–18 relates how Ahaz, having seen an altar in Damascus, ordered one like it to be built in Jerusalem. On this altar he offered regular burnt offerings. He used the great bronze altar of Solomon as a means of divination. He disman-

tled the carts supporting the lavers (4:14) and took the great bronze Sea from its pedestals (4:2, 3). These must have been among the **articles** that he destroyed. **Shut up the doors** signifies the absolute repudiation of Yahweh worship and the wholesale adoption of heathen religion.

28:25 If destroying **high places** is a sign of a godly reign (14:3, 5; 15:16; 16:6), then constructing them is a clear sign of the opposite. The phrase **God of his fathers** calls attention to God's covenant relationship with both Israel and Judah.

28:26, 27 The term **kings of Israel** refers not just to the northern kingdom, but to the entire nation under God.

29:1, 2 Hezekiah was the only king of Judah who was as faithful to the Lord as **David** had been.

29:3 The **first year** of Hezekiah's independent rule began in 715 B.C. Hezekiah had ruled alongside Ahaz since 729 B.C. The fact that Hezekiah began his work on the restoration of the temple in his **first month** testifies to his zeal for God's work. Hezekiah **opened the doors** of the temple as a step toward spiritual renewal. Ahaz had closed the doors as an expression of hostility to God and the covenant (28:24). Hezekiah wasted no time in dealing with the sins of his predecessor.

29:4 The **East Square** was the courtyard directly in front of the portico of the temple (4:9, 10; 6:13; 7:7).

29:5 carry out the rubbish: It is impossible to know all that this involved, but it may be that Ahaz had used the temple as a sort of warehouse. Clearly more is in view than the temple furnishings themselves, because these were repaired and sanctified and put to use again (v. 19).

29:6–9 captivity: This could refer to the fall of Samaria and deportation of the northern tribes just seven years earlier (2 Kin. 17:6). But under the wicked leadership of Ahaz, many of the people of Judah had been taken captive by Rezin of Damascus and Pekah of Israel (28:5–8). Hezekiah's reference to Judah and Jerusalem (v. 8) suggests that he might have been referring to this.

29:10, 11 Hezekiah's **covenant** placed him and his people under the authority of God. Hezekiah pledged himself to lead the nation in faithfulness, as the terms of the original Davidic covenant demanded (23:3, 11, 16; Deut. 17:18–20; 31:9–13; 1 Chr. 28:9).

29:12 Kohathites . . . Merari . . . Gershonites: Hezekiah summoned the leaders of

> *Hezekiah was the only king of Judah who was as faithful to the Lord as David had been.*

the three major Levitical clans, two leaders from each clan.

29:13 The family of **Elizaphan** was part of Kohath (1 Chr. 15:8).

29:14 Asaph was the father of a division of Levitical musicians (1 Chr. 25:1, 2). **Heman** and **Jeduthun** were musicians (1 Chr. 25:1, 3–5). Jeduthun was also known as Ethan (1 Chr. 15:17, 19).

29:15 The phrase **at the words of the Lord** means that Hezekiah undertook his reformation at God's direction. His instructions to the nation in this case had unique authority (see 1 Chr. 28:11–19; 29:23, 24).

29:16 The **inner part** apparently refers to the Most Holy Place, and the term **temple** must refer also to the larger chamber, the holy place (3:5–7; 4:7, 8). The **court** was the inner court just outside the temple, the area restricted to the priests and Levites (4:9). The work of temple repair and restoration began in the Most Holy Place and then continued until it reached the courtyard. The **Brook Kidron** was the wadi just east of Jerusalem where debris was burned (15:16).

29:17, 18 The work began on the **first day of the first month** of Hezekiah's reign, not of the calendar month (v. 3). The **vestibule** was a porch across the front of the temple. **Sanctify** means to "cleanse or purify" or "to set apart for a holy purpose."

29:19 articles: Ahaz had destroyed some but not all of the temple implements (28:24).

29:20, 21 bulls . . . rams . . . lambs: The Law required the sacrifice of these animals for atonement of **sin** in general (Lev. 1:3–13). On the other hand, the sacrifice of goats atoned for specific sins (Lev. 4:1—5:13). Here the priests offered **seven** of each kind to signify the wholeness of their repentance. The **kingdom** refers to the nation as a political entity, **Judah** to the people. Both the state and the people needed atonement. The **sanctuary** refers to the temple itself.

29:22–24 The repetition of **all Israel** here suggests that Hezekiah meant to include all twelve tribes, including the northern kingdom (30:1–9).

29:25 King David was responsible for religious as well as civil and political matters. He had exercised that responsibility by appointing Levitical musicians and instructing them about their temple ministries (1 Chr. 23:2, 27; 25:1–31). He was guided and advised by two of God's faithful prophets, **Gad** and **Nathan.**

29:26 The **instruments of David** were those deemed appropriate for temple worship (1 Chr. 25:1, 3, 5, 6).

29:27–30 The words of David and of Asaph refers to the psalms of David and Asaph (1 Chr. 6:39; 15:17; 16:5), many of them in the Book of Psalms. The people of Judah used these psalms for community worship and private meditation.

29:31, 32 Sometimes called "peace" or "fellowship" offerings, **thank offerings** celebrated the relationship gained by the offerings of atonement (vv. 21–24; Lev. 3:1–17; 7:11–36). **willing heart:** People gave these gifts to God not out of compulsion but as a joyful responses to the grace of God.

29:33 The thank offerings included people, priests, and God Himself. In effect, the **consecrated things** made up a banquet at which everyone gathered before the Lord for fellowship and communion.

29:34, 35 Under Ahaz the **priests** and **Levites** had been stripped of their duties. Now, 20 years later, there were not enough priests. Hezekiah had to reconsecrate the older priests

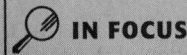 **IN FOCUS** **"cleanse"**

(Heb. *taher*) (2 Chr. 29:16; Lev. 14:48; Ps. 51:2, 7; Is. 66:17) Strong's #2891: This Hebrew term means "to make free from blemish," almost always in a ritual or spiritual sense (although once the word is used for the wind's cleaning away of clouds and once for the refiner's purifying of silver; see Job 37:21; Mal. 3:3). Almost half the occurrences are in Leviticus, where ritual cleansing is related to sanctification and is opposed to the moral filthiness of the Israelites (Lev. 16:19). Objects and people involved in the worship of the Lord—such as the temple, the furniture in the temple, and the Levites—needed cleansing because the Lord is a holy God (Num. 8:5–22; 1 Chr. 23:28). The ritual external cleansing of people was a symbol of internal purity (Gen. 35:2; Zech. 3:3–5). Jeremiah and Ezekiel prophesied of the future cleansing of the people from their sins so that they could truly be God's people, both outside and inside (Jer. 33:8; Ezek. 36:25, 33; 37:23). The idea of cleansing carries through into the NT. The Book of Revelation pictures the Lamb's bride—the church—in clean linen which symbolizes the righteous acts of believers (2 Cor. 7:1; Eph. 5:26; 1 John 1:9; Rev. 19:8).

and commission new ones. His reforms took place so quickly (v. 3) that the priests received a special dispensation to assign Levites to areas of ministry otherwise closed to them, such as skinning sacrificial animals (Lev. 1:5, 6).

29:36 so suddenly: This partially explains the unavailability of persons involved in religious worship (v. 34), and it testifies to Hezekiah's zeal in bringing about reformation as soon as it was within his power. One must not overlook the fact, however, that renewal came fundamentally because **God had prepared the people.**

30:1–3 Though the kingdom of **Israel** had split more than two centuries before, **Hezekiah** never lost sight of the fact that God's covenant was made with all twelve tribes and that His promises included them all (Ezek. 37:15–28). **The Passover** was ordinarily celebrated in the first month of the religious year (Ex. 12:6, 18). But this year the repair and consecration of the temple was still underway (29:1–17). The Law made provision for the Passover to be postponed if a person was absent on an important journey or was ritually defiled (Num. 9:9–12). Hezekiah interpreted this Law to include the priests who, had not yet consecrated themselves to ministry (29:34). All the people of Israel had not had time to gather **together at Jerusalem** in any case, so they delayed the celebration until the **second month.**

30:4, 5 The fact that **all Israel** was included reveals that there were many followers of God left in the northern kingdom, despite more than 200 years of backsliding and the Assyrian conquest (29:24).

30:6, 7 the LORD God of Abraham, Isaac, and Israel: Hezekiah appealed to the nation on the basis of the ancient Abrahamic covenant (29:5). Even though the kingdom was divided and many of its people languished in exile far from home, God's promise could not change, and it bound them all together as God's people. They still had time to return to the Lord. **the remnant:** In some places the word *remnant* means the godly elect from among the Israelite people as a whole (Is. 46:3; Mic. 2:12; 5:7, 8). Here it means those Israelites who had survived Assyrian slaughter and deportation.

30:8 People who were not priests were not allowed to enter the temple, so **enter His sanctuary** is a figure of speech for serving the Lord.

30:9 The **brethren** and **children** were Israelites who had been carried away into Assyrian captivity. Hezekiah pleaded with the remnant left behind to repent, promising that this would result in better treatment of those in captivity and would guarantee their return to the **land.** According to the covenant (Deut. 28—30), obedience would lead to blessing

in the land, and disobedience would result in exile.

30:10 Zebulun was probably the northernmost territory of Israel at this time because Naphtali had been taken by Tiglath-Pileser III (2 Kin. 15:29).

30:11, 12 In Judah the reaction to Hezekiah's invitation was totally different from Israel's (vv. 10, 11), because God had put His **hand on Judah.** God's grace is always a part of a person's efforts to please Him.

30:13 Because the **Feast of Unleavened Bread** immediately followed the Passover and was connected to it (Lev. 23:4–8), the Feast of Unleavened Bread sometimes referred to the Passover as well (Ezra 6:22). **second month:** A postponement of the feast from the first month was possible under certain circumstances (v. 2).

30:14 The debris removed from the temple had already been hauled off to the Brook Kidron for burning (29:16), but the burnt offering and **incense altars** still remained in Jerusalem until the time of the Passover.

30:15 The priests and the Levites were **ashamed** because they had been derelict in not consecrating themselves to their ministries earlier (29:34; 30:3). The cause for the delay of the Passover, in fact, was this tardiness on their part.

30:16 The Levites killed the animals and then handed the **blood** over to the priests to apply it. Usually burnt offerings were sacrificed by the individual worshipers who gave the blood to the priests (Lev. 1:4, 5).

30:17 Traditionally the **slaughter** of the Passover lamb was performed by the head of the family (Ex. 12:3–6). But on this occasion many were not ritually purified, and the Levites acted on their behalf.

30:18–20 not cleansed . . . yet they ate: Those who came from distant parts of Israel were disqualified from sacrificing and did not do so. Still, they ate the Passover meal, in violation of the Law of Moses (Ex. 12:43–49). They felt it more important to obey the spirit of the Passover than its letter. Hezekiah prayed for them, asking God to observe the desire of their hearts. In response, God **healed the people;** that is, He healed their relationship with Him. Genuine seeking after God is more important than adherence to ritual (1 Sam. 15:22).

30:21, 22 taught the good knowledge of the LORD: Because of Ahaz's many years of wicked rule (28:23–25), the people of Judah must have become ignorant of the truths of their faith. The people from the north (v. 18) had virtually no preaching of God's revelation for 200 years, apart from the witness of the prophets such as Hosea and Amos. But the Levites' ministry included teaching (17:8–10; Deut. 17:18; 31:9–13; 33:10), and this great

Passover was an opportunity to explain the history and purpose of God's covenant with Israel. The people **ate throughout the feast** because a meal was the central feature of the thank or **peace offerings** (29:31; Lev. 7:28–36; 9:18).

30:23 Like Solomon before him (7:8–10), Hezekiah found it impossible to limit the festivities to eight days (including the Passover). Their common consent to celebrate **another seven days** was a sure sign of renewed spiritual vitality.

30:24 Hezekiah . . . gave: As an extraordinary act of generosity and personal commitment, the **king** took shared his own resources with the people. Possibly this was somewhat necessary also in light of a second, unanticipated week of sacrifice.

30:25, 26 The **sojourners** were aliens who lived in Israel and Judah and who could come to the festivals because they adhered to God and the Law (Deut. 16:11; 26:11; 29:11; 31:12).

30:27 blessed the people: This may have been the formal blessing of Num. 6:24–26.

31:1 The phrases **all Israel** and **all the children of Israel** refer to the entire nation, north and south, Israel and Judah.

31:2 The long interruption (28:24) of Judah's official worship in the time of Ahaz brought chaos to their religious life. They abandoned the system of priestly and Levitical **division.** Just as David had originally organized the Levitical system (1 Chr. 23:1–26:28), so now Hezekiah had to reorganize it.

31:3 The **New Moon** celebrations came at the appearance of the new moon, the beginning of another month (Num. 28:11–15). Though there were many **set feasts** by the end of the OT period, the ones in view here were the Passover and Feast of Unleavened Bread (Lev. 23:4–8); the Feast of Firstfruits or Pentecost (Lev. 23:15–22); and the Feast of Tabernacles (Lev. 23:33–43).

31:4 The Law stated clearly that the people were to **contribute support** by their tithes and offerings so the work of the temple could go on (Num. 18:8–24).

31:5 The early harvests of grain, particularly barley, were being reaped at this time. The Passover had been held in the second month (30:2) and it was now already the third (v. 7). The **firstfruits** began appearing at the time of the Feast of Passover and Unleavened Bread— that is, in early April or so, and the harvests were fully gathered in some 50 days later, at the time of the Feast of Weeks or Pentecost (Lev. 23:9–22). **the tithe:** A tenth of the harvest belonged to the Levites, whose sustenance depended on it (v. 4; Num. 18:21–24). There were three tithes—two every year and one every third year.

31:6 The **holy things** were likely metals and other nonperishables (24:10, 11; 1 Chr. 29:2, 7, 8) which were **consecrated to God** for use in worship and service.

31:7–9 The **third month** was the month after the delayed Passover (30:2) and the time of the early harvest (v. 5). The **seventh month** was Tishri, the month of the final annual harvest of fruits. The Feast of Tabernacles celebrated the year-end harvest (Lev. 23:39; Deut. 16:13) at this time. There was a continual ingathering from the third to the seventh month, and the people brought their tithes to the temple as an expression of renewed devotion.

31:10 The **chief priests** from Solomon's time onward were Zadokites (1 Kin. 2:27, 35).

31:11 prepare rooms: Places already existed in the temple for storing food supplies and other materials (1 Chr. 26:15, 20).

31:12, 13 had charge of them: In order to ensure a fair and efficient distribution to the priests and Levites, certain persons were appointed to the task of supervision. Two persons were in charge of the distribution and ten others worked with them.

31:14 At the front of the temple the **East Gate** led to the great courtyard and the Kidron valley beyond (1 Chr. 26:14).

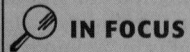 **IN FOCUS**   **"tithe"**

(Heb. *ma'aser*) (2 Chr. 31:5, 12; Gen. 14:20) Strong's #4643: The Hebrew word translated *tithe* is derived from *'eser,* the Hebrew number for *ten*. In Gen. 14:20, Abraham gave the priest Melchizedek a tenth of his wealth. This set the precedent throughout the OT for what was considered an appropriate portion of one's wealth to give to the Lord. According to the Law, Israelites were to set aside a tenth of their annual produce for God (Deut. 14:22–28). Whatever was given to the Lord was considered holy (Lev. 27:30–33) and was to be used to support the ministry of the priests and Levites (Num. 18:21). The prophet Malachi proclaimed that the failure to bring a tithe to God was the equivalent of robbing Him (Mal. 3:8).

31:15 Because most of the priests lived in the cities allotted to them and not in Jerusalem (1 Chr. 6:54–60), Kore and his **assistants** took provisions to them (v. 14).

31:16 three years old: The boys described here were young apprentice priests dedicated to the office by their parents. Samuel had such a ministry (1 Sam. 1:24, 28; 2:18).

31:17 All religious personnel had to descend from Levi, but the priests as such had to trace their **genealogy** specifically to Aaron (1 Chr. 6:49–53).

31:18 all who were written in the genealogy: This is an all-inclusive way of designating both priests and Levites. Anyone whose lineage was Levitical could draw upon the tithes and offerings raised for their support.

31:19–21 The preceding arrangements pertained to the maintenance of the priests and Levites who came to Jerusalem to minister when their divisional assignment dictated such a schedule (vv. 15–17). Those back in their own **cities** would require ongoing provision as well, so there were distributors there for that. Thus, whether "on the job" or not, all of God's servants could count on the people's support.

32:1–23 In this significant war, human responsibility blends with divine sovereignty. **Hezekiah** made careful preparations by stopping external access to the water source, repairing the broken wall and building a second wall, repairing the Millo, making weapons and shields in abundance, and organizing the army. Only after making thorough preparations does Hezekiah say that they could count on the Lord **to fight our battles.**

32:1, 2 In Hezekiah's fourteenth year, **Sennacherib** invaded Judah and eventually laid siege to Jerusalem (2 Kin. 18:13–17). One of the most imperialistic of Assyria's kings, Sennacherib undertook many military campaigns to the west. In his own inscriptions he boasts of having taken many of Judah's cities, a claim supported by the parallel account in 2 Kings. The **fortified cities** that he took had first been built and equipped by Solomon (8:2–6), and then rebuilt and enlarged by Solomon's successors down to the time of Hezekiah (11:5–12; 14:6, 7; 17:12; 26:9, 10; 27:4; 32:29).

32:3 With the help of 2 Kin. 20:20 we learn that Hezekiah managed to **stop the water** by concealing the springs **outside the city** and then digging a tunnel to bring them to the Pool of Siloam inside the city walls. Hezekiah hid the source of water and made it unavailable to the enemy. The Siloam Inscription describes how workmen constructed the 1,800-foot tunnel connecting the springs of Gihon to the Pool of Siloam.

32:4 The brook was the Wadi Kidron, east of Jerusalem.

32:5 Millo means landfill and refers to extensive terracing that surrounded the ancient hills of Ophel and Mount Zion. The work of extending the hills of Jerusalem was first undertaken by **David** (1 Chr. 11:7, 8) and continued by Solomon (1 Kin. 9:15).

32:6 The main **city gate** was where the population could assemble and where court and other official functions were held (6:12; 29:4).

32:7 more with us: This is not Judah's army; Hezekiah meant the armies of heaven (2 Kin. 6:14–17).

32:8 fight our battles: This terminology speaks of Yahweh as a warrior. Hezekiah sees the present struggle as a battle not just between nations but also between competing religious systems and ideologies (v. 19). Therefore, armies of **flesh** will be of no avail, for the conflict is spiritual and spiritual hosts will be led by the omnipotent God of Israel.

32:9 Both the OT and Assyrian inscriptions document the **siege against Lachish,** an important fortified city west of Jerusalem and near the great coastal route (11:9). Its capture by Assyria would cut off access to Jerusalem from the west and would give Assyria control of the coast.

32:10, 11 The **siege** of **Jerusalem** had not actually begun, but Sennacherib's envoys spoke of it as already underway. Jerusalem was under siege psychologically.

32:12 What should have been taken as a sign of religious reformation and exclusivity—the removal of pagan religious centers (31:1)—is taken by the Assyrians as evidence that Hezekiah has undermined his own cult.

32:13–16 Sennacherib's messengers tried to destroy the peoples' faith in God by pointing out that the other nations, despite their many gods and many altars, had been powerless to resist the Assyrians. The Assyrians thought the true God was no different than the **gods of the nations** they had already subjugated.

32:17 Sennacherib **also wrote letters** because he wanted to avoid a long and costly siege.

32:18, 19 Aramaic had become the language of international communication and diplomacy. The Judean negotiators wanted the matter discussed in Aramaic because they felt that they deserved to be addressed in regular diplomatic language. The Assyrians continued the dialogue in Hebrew to **frighten** and **trouble** the **people.**

32:20 By now **the prophet Isaiah** had been involved in public ministry to the kings of Judah for nearly 40 years (26:22; Is. 6:1). He had considerable prestige and was especially important as a counselor of young Hezekiah (Is. 37:1–7).

32:21–23 Sennacherib **returned shamefaced to his own land,** Assyria, and its capital Nineveh. The same Sennacherib who had mocked God's ability to preserve Hezekiah and Judah (vv. 17, 19) now died a violent death while in the very act of worshiping **his god. his own offspring:** Sennacherib's sons were Adrammelech and Sharezer. His two sons assassinated him 20 years after the siege of Jerusalem and fled for their lives. Then a third son Esarhaddon became king.

32:24 Hezekiah was sick: His sickness struck shortly after Sennacherib's defeat (2 Kin. 20:1, 12) and involved affliction with boils (Is. 38:10–21). **a sign:** When Isaiah told Hezekiah he would recover, the king wanted confirmation. The sundial moved backward for him ten degrees, adding forty minutes to the day (Is. 38:8).

32:25–29 God had given Hezekiah an extraordinary **favor**—15 additional years of life (2 Kin. 20:6). But his **heart was lifted up:** Hezekiah had received Babylonian envoys who had come to congratulate him on his recovery and probably to enlist his support in their struggle against Assyria (2 Kin. 20:12–19). Their visit ignited his desire to show off all the treasures of his kingdom. Because of this indulgence in pride, God's **wrath was looming.** The account in Kings reveals Isaiah's response to Hezekiah's pride. The time would come, the prophet said, when all the wealth that **Hezekiah** had used to impress his visitors would be seized by the same Babylonians and taken to their distant land (2 Kin. 20:16–18; Is. 39:6, 7).

32:30 Upper Gihon was a spring in the Kidron valley near the Water Gate. The **tunnel** meandered from Gihon south and then west for over five hundred yards (vv. 3, 4). It ended at the Pool of Siloam, then on the southwest side of Jerusalem.

32:31 The **test** was not for God's benefit but for Hezekiah's.

32:32 The vision of Isaiah is the prophetic Book of Isaiah (Is. 1:1).

32:33 The term **upper tombs** probably refers to the royal cemetery where all the godly descendants of David were buried. Others were entombed in the City of David, but not in the same area (28:27). **honored:** This would include such rites and ceremonies as public lamentation and ritual fires (16:14).

33:1, 2 Manasseh was not the only king who lived according to the **abominations of the nations.** Ahaz did too (28:3).

33:3 The host of heaven were the gods of the sun, moon, and stars. The Babylonians espe-

cially revered these deities (Deut. 4:19; Ezek. 8:16).

33:4 In Jerusalem shall My name be: The point was that God had the exclusive right to inhabit the temple, as opposed to the deities Manasseh introduced (v. 5).

33:5 In addition to altars inside the temple (v. 4), Manasseh erected altars to his astral deities in the **two courts**—that is, the court of the priests and Levites and the one open to the public (4:9; 1 Kin. 7:9–12).

33:6 Valley of the Son of Hinnom: Like Ahaz, Manasseh practiced human sacrifice, going so far as to offer up his own children

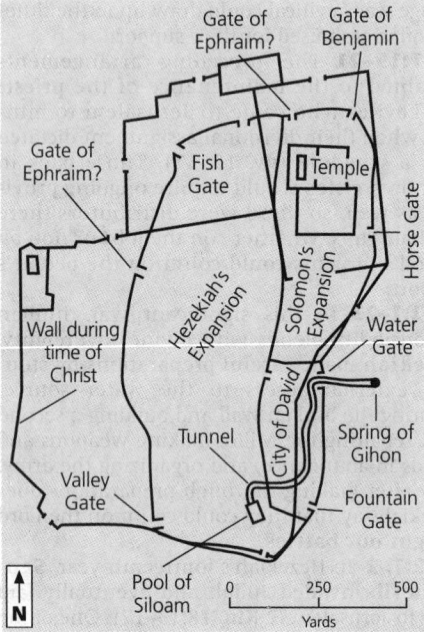

Hezekiah's Waterworks

In his efforts to fortify Jerusalem against Sennacherib and the Assyrians, King Hezekiah ordered the construction of a tunnel to bring water from the spring of Gihon to inside the city walls (2 Chr. 32:30). The tunnel was excavated through solid rock 60 feet underground for a distance of almost 600 yards. Workers started at opposite ends and dug with hand tools until they met in the middle of the shaft. When it was completed, Hezekiah's tunnel emerged at a spot that later came to be known as the Pool of Siloam.

(28:3). **Soothsaying** is divination, an attempt to determine the plans and purposes of the gods so as to avert their hostility or take advantage of their favors. Soothsayers and diviners inspected animal entrails, smoke, oil in water, the flights of birds, and heavenly phenomena (Is. 2:6; Jer.

27:9). **Witchcraft** and **sorcery** attempt to bring about desired results by employing magical or mystical rituals. **Mediums** are those who claim to contact and consult with the dead. The witch of En Dor appears to have done this, for she feared for her life when she realized that Saul had condemned necromancers to death (1 Sam. 28:3, 9). **spiritists:** These are "knowing ones" whose specialty also is communication with the dead in the hope of acquiring information inaccessible to the living. All such practices were common among Canaanite and other pagan religions and were to be strictly avoided by God's people (Deut. 13:1–6; 18:9–14).

33:7 The nature of this **carved image** or the god it represented cannot be determined, but that is almost irrelevant in light of the enormous blasphemy associated with it. This exceeded the wickedness of even Ahaz, who closed the temple to any use, placing his altars and **idols** elsewhere (28:23–25). But now the place reserved exclusively for Yahweh's name (v. 4) had become usurped and prostituted to most abominable purposes.

33:8, 9 God's ancient promise never to remove the people of Israel from the land they had inherited was conditioned on their obedience to all the covenant stipulations—**law, statutes, and ordinances**—to which they had sworn (Gen. 17:7, 8; Lev. 26:27–35, 46). Manasseh's behavior had greatly jeopardized the presence of the people in the land.

33:10, 11 For some time **Babylon** had been part of the Assyrian empire, though it had broken free on occasion, especially under the leadership of Berodach-Baladan, Hezekiah's contemporary (2 Kin. 20:12). Ashurbanipal brought Babylon back under Assyrian domination. He was the king who took Manasseh to Babylon as a prisoner.

33:12, 13 then Manasseh knew: The punishment Yahweh inflicted upon Manasseh for his sin was not retributive alone but produced repentance and fresh understanding of the absolute sovereignty of God.

33:14 The term **City of David** originally referred to Mount Zion alone (1 Chr. 11:5) but eventually designated the entire city including Mount **Ophel,** the original Jebusite settlement. **Gihon** was the spring that was the main source of water for Jerusalem (32:3, 4, 30). It was in the Kidron valley near the northeastern brow of Mount Zion. The **Fish Gate** was in the center of the wall north of the temple. Manasseh's construction began at Gihon and went north past Mount Ophel to the northeast corner of the temple mount. Then it went west to the Fish Gate. This was a total distance of about 750 yards. These **fortified cities** were the same ones that had been captured by Sennacherib.

33:15, 16 Manasseh **took away** the old idols—a sign of true conversion and devotion to God (v. 13).

33:17–19 The sin of worshiping at **high places** was in their association with paganism (Deut. 12:2, 3). The temple represented the dwelling place of God among His people. At this time, God wanted all worship by the people as a community to take place there. This is what is meant by the exclusiveness of the central sanctuary (Deut. 12:5–28).

33:20 in his own house: Manasseh had truly converted (v. 13), but his prior sin had been so heinous that he was denied burial in the royal cemetery (32:33).

33:21, 22 The **carved images** were in addition to the wooden images he had made (v. 3). The images were representations of deity carved from wood or stone. The carved image to which **Amon sacrificed** had been set up in the temple as an idol (v. 7). It was later removed from the city (v. 15) but apparently not destroyed, since Amon set it up again.

33:23–25 At this time **people of the land** was a technical term that indicated a certain level of leadership, perhaps a council of elders. In crises like the assassination of Amon they could assume interim powers until proper government could be restored (22:1; 26:1; 36:1).

34:1–3 The **wooden images** were poles dedicated to Asherah, the Canaanite fertility goddess (33:3). The **molded images** were like the **carved images** except that they were made of molded metal (Ex. 32:4, 8; Is. 42:17; Hos. 13:2).

34:4 Josiah's destruction of the altars and idols built by his grandfather Manasseh and father Amon recall Moses' grinding up the golden calf and scattering its **dust** upon the waters (Ex. 32:20).

34:5 burned the bones of the priests: This act of Josiah, which took place at Bethel, fulfilled the words of the prophet of Judah in the days of Jeroboam I, king of Israel (1 Kin. 13:1, 2; 2 Kin. 23:15, 16). The prophet had mentioned Josiah by name three hundred years before.

34:6, 7 Josiah's purge of the idolatrous cults was not limited to Judah and Bethel but extended from the south—**Simeon**—to the north—**Naphtali.** Israel had been subject to Assyria for a century, and new religious movements such as that of the Samaritans had gained a foothold in the region (2 Kin. 17:24–31; 23:19).

34:8 Shaphan was a scribe or secretary of the king (v. 15). He was responsible for state records that must have included the original temple plans and specifications. The temple was repaired strictly according to its original pattern.

The office of **governor** was like that of the modern mayor (18:25). A **recorder** kept the royal diaries. Official happenings were duly noted and recorded for posterity. The work of men like **Joah** provided sources for later historians such as the author of Chronicles (1 Chr. 18:15).

34:9 Hilkiah was probably the **high priest** of the genealogy of 1 Chr. 6:13 (Ezra 7:1).

34:10, 11 Josiah's work of restoring what was destroyed included not only repairs to the temple and related buildings, but repairs to the fortifications (15:8; 24:5; 28:24; 29:6, 7; 32:5).

34:12 The **sons of Merari** and the **Kohathites** were two of the three clans of Levi (1 Chr. 6:1, 16; 23:6).

34:13–16 Shaphan delivered the scroll because he was the king's scribe. He would know how to assess the authenticity of the text and tell the king whether it was important.

34:17–19 the king . . . tore his clothes: One gets the impression that this is the first time Josiah had ever seen a copy of the Scriptures and had ever heard it read. This does not mean that he was unaware of the Mosaic writings, for surely their teachings had been preserved through the apostasy, at least in oral form. In a day of mass production of literature, it is difficult for the modern reader to envision a time when any composition, even the Bible, existed in only a few dozen copies at most. This was the case throughout the ancient world, however, and it is entirely possible that an entire literary tradi-

tion could be lost. Josiah's reaction must be explained not in terms of the novelty of what he had heard but because he had seen and heard a copy of the Word of God with his own senses. Its impact is shattering because he knows how far his nation has drifted from its principles.

34:20, 21 Josiah knew that the scroll contained the Book of the Law of the Lord, but he did not know what to do about the words of **wrath** and judgment that it contained. **our fathers have not kept . . . all that is written:** Josiah wanted to know what God demanded of him because he fully intended to comply.

34:22 Huldah the prophetess is one of four female prophets named in the OT, the other three being Miriam (Ex. 15:20), Deborah (Judg. 4:4), and Noadiah (Neh. 6:14). **Shallum's** job was to supervise the storage and distribution of garments worn by the priests and Levites in the course of their duties. The **second quarter** was probably a suburb of Jerusalem near the Fish Gate north of the city (Zeph. 1:10).

34:23 Thus says the Lord indicates that Huldah's words were a prophecy.

34:24, 25 written in the book: Both Deuteronomy and Leviticus have long lists of blessings and **curses** attached to the covenant with Israel (Deut. 28; 29).

34:26–28 gather you to your fathers: In the context of the whole message, this was a promise that Josiah would die and be buried among his own people, not in a foreign land.

✠ IN CONTEXT   The Book of the Law of the Lord

Hilkiah's discovery of "the Book of the Law of the Lord" (2 Chr. 34:14) began a great revival in Israel. King Josiah's response to the book inspired him to initiate a reformation and refocus attention on Jerusalem as the center of worship (2 Kin. 23:4–20). It was one of the nation's greatest moments.

What was this "Book of the Law of the Lord"? The reforms that Josiah introduced reflect many of the themes of Deuteronomy, so it seems clear that Josiah's book must have included at least Deuteronomy. But the Law that was "given by Moses" (34:14) technically includes the whole Pentateuch, the first five books of the Bible (Ex. 24:4), and there seems no reason to doubt that this was the case in Josiah's day.

This copy of the Law somehow survived the long period of religious suppression under Manasseh and Amon. We may never know who put it in the temple or why, but God saw to its preservation and discovery.

Josiah's humble, obedient response to the book was and remains a model of how all people should respond to God's revealed Word. Josiah listened to the Scripture, allowed its words of truth to judge him, and humbly confessed that he had neglected God's commands (34:18, 19). After learning more about its truths (34:21), he shared the Scripture with others and led them in following it. He had the book read before the entire nation and led the Israelites in recommitting their lives to the Lord (34:29–31).

Huldah's promise that Josiah would die **in peace** meant that he would be spared the **calamity** by which Judah would be judged. Josiah died in a time of war (35:23, 24), but that war was not the time of calamity. The calamity came later when Babylonian forces captured Jerusalem (36:17–20).

34:29, 30 The term **Book of the Covenant** refers to the Book of the Law of the Lord (v. 14), the Pentateuch. Josiah was about to lead the community in renewing the covenant. His reading of the scroll was part of his duties as king (Deut. 17:18–20).

34:31 Very few of the kings of Judah promised to **follow the LORD** as Josiah did. After David, only Joash, Hezekiah, and Josiah made such public commitments (23:3; 29:10; 1 Chr. 17:7–14). They stand head and shoulders above the other kings of Judah and Israel. The terms **commandments, testimonies,** and **statutes** were all technical terms referring to the covenant (Deut. 4:40, 45; 5:31; 6:1, 17).

34:32, 33 We know that Josiah's commitment to the Lord was real because he **removed all the abominations.** This included any and all idols that had been introduced by earlier kings.

35:1–3 Josiah's command to **put the holy ark in the house** means that the ark of the covenant had been removed from the temple. Who removed it and when is not known, but there were plenty of wicked kings who could have done so. **no longer . . . on your shoulders:** The only proper way for transporting the ark was by means of poles thrust through corner rings of the ark and borne on the shoulders of the Levites (Num. 4:5, 6; 1 Chr. 15:2). The fact that they were carrying it about shows that it had no regular place of storage. Manasseh's vehement opposition to God must have kept the ark in constant jeopardy. But once the temple had been cleansed and repaired, the ark could be returned to its place.

35:4 In preparation for the Passover the priests and Levites had to organize themselves by their assignments within **divisions.** The divisions were determined by the genealogical registers (1 Chr. 6:1–30). **David** set up the divisions before the temple was built (1 Chr. 23:3—26:32) and **Solomon** confirmed them (8:14).

35:5 The term **holy place** here refers to the whole temple area. The **lay people** could not enter the area where the great bronze altar stood, so the Levites represented them there by tribe, clan, and family units. In former times the heads of families offered their own Passover lambs and thus had access to the altar (Ex. 12:3), but by Josiah's time the responsibility for slaughter rested upon the Levites alone (30:15–20).

35:6 prepare them for your brethren: The Levites were standing in for the people in the sacrifice of the **Passover** lambs. This became the tradition from that time on, with the result that the priests gained influence and power.

35:7 Normally the people provided the Passover **lambs and young goats** from their own flocks (Ex. 12:3, 5), but Josiah was being generous (30:24). That Josiah gave **thirty thousand** of them means that the total number of people must have been 150,000 or more, as each household offered its own lamb or goat. The **cattle** were for the burnt offerings that went with this particular Passover (v. 12).

35:8 Hilkiah was the chief priest under Josiah (34:9).

35:9–11 The way the **priests** and **Levites** prepared **the animals** was in accord with Moses' instructions (Ex. 12:4, 8, 9, 21, 22).

35:12 This particular Passover included a time of fellowship and praise. The **cattle** were used for **burnt offerings** (vv. 7–9) for the celebration of the thank or peace offerings (Lev. 3:1–5). The offerer, his family, and the priests and Levites could all eat any Passover animals and burnt offerings that were sacrificed as thank offerings. The Passover of Josiah was an occasion for recalling the deliverance of Israel from Egypt (Ex. 12:24–27), and a time of great festive celebration of God's goodness in bringing reformation and renewal. The **Book of Moses** was probably the scroll that Hilkiah found in the temple (34:14, 15); Josiah's desire to conduct the Passover sprang from the discovery and reading of the book.

35:13 The **other holy offerings,** distinguished from the Passover offerings, were the cattle slaughtered for thank or peace offerings (v. 7).

35:14 Themselves refers to the **Levites,** who had helped the priests.

35:15 Asaph, Heman, and Jeduthun headed up the Levitical musical divisions in the days of David (1 Chr. 15:17; 25:1). The day-long Passover celebration was accompanied by music.

35:16 It was most unusual to have such a combination of festivals and offerings all on **the same day.**

35:17 The Passover was held on the fourteenth day of the month Nisan (v. 1) and was followed for the next **seven days** by the Feast of Unleavened Bread, up through the twenty-first day of Nisan (30:21–23; Lev. 23:4–8; Num. 28:16–25; Deut. 16:1–8).

35:18 It had been almost four hundred years since the **days of Samuel the prophet** (1 Sam. 7:15–17). **None of the kings** had held so great a Passover in all that time (30:26).

35:19 Josiah was twenty-six years old (34:8) in the **eighteenth year** of his reign.

35:20 Located on the upper Euphrates River, **Carchemish** was one of the last strongholds of Assyria to resist the onslaught of the rising neo-Babylonian kingdom. The Babylonians and Medes were on their way to subdue Haran and Carchemish. Necho, more afraid of the Babylonians than the Assyrians, was hoping to get to Carchemish in time to assist his Assyrian allies in their time of peril. Josiah was an ally of Babylon, so he went to Megiddo (v. 22) to intercept the Egyptians and allow for the Babylonians to attack Haran and Carchemish without Egyptian interference.

35:21 The house is a reference to the Babylonians. **God commanded me:** God sometimes spoke to pagan rulers about a course of action He wanted them to take (36:22; Gen. 20:6; 41:25; Dan. 2:28). Necho did not know that the source of his divine leading was the God of Israel and not one of his own Egyptian deities. But God did direct him, displaying His sovereignty over even the wicked and unbelieving powers of this world (Is. 44:28—45:1).

35:22 The major route from Egypt to the upper Euphrates was the Via Maris or the Way of the Sea. This route went up the coast of Palestine before turning inland through the mountain pass at **Megiddo.** It crossed the Plains of Jezreel or Esdraelon, crossed the Jordan near the Sea of Galilee, and passed through Damascus where it joined the north-south route to upper Syria. Josiah's objective was to control the pass at Megiddo and dictate the movement of traffic through that vital point.

35:23, 24 As a godly successor of David, Josiah was buried with full honors in the royal **tombs of his fathers** in the City of David (32:33).

35:25–27 The book of the kings of Israel and Judah may have been the canonical book of 1 and 2 Kings.

36:1, 2 The people of the land was a technical term that referred to a body of leaders such as a council of elders or a kind of informal parliament (33:25). This group acted in time of crisis, such as the death of Josiah in battle. His loss was made worse by the fact that he had at least four sons who could succeed him. Josiah may not have made his choice of successor clear. Johanan was the oldest son, followed by Jehoiakim, Zedekiah, and Shallum (1 Chr. 3:15). Shallum was the same as **Jehoahaz** (Jer. 22:11).

36:3 The **king of Egypt** was Necho (35:20). After Assyria's defeat at Haran and Carchemish, the Egyptian army withdrew south of the Euphrates to dominate Syria and Palestine. Judah became an Egyptian vassal state, which explains why Necho could depose Jehoahaz and require **tribute.** Judah had become a poor and weak nation, smaller by far than at any other time in its history. Josiah left them richer spiritually, but poorer financially.

36:4 Necho required the change of name in order to display his power over **Eliakim.**

36:5, 6 Nebuchadnezzar was the son of Nabopolassar, founder of the Neo-Babylonian or Chaldean empire. He was leading a campaign against Carchemish when he succeeded his father. He drove Egypt out of Syria and Palestine and took some Jewish captives, including Daniel, back to Babylon (Dan. 1:1). At the same time, Jehoiakim changed his loyalty from Necho to Nebuchadnezzar and remained a trusted vassal for three years (2 Kin. 24:1). But then Jehoiakim rebelled against Babylon, and in about 602 B.C. Nebuchadnezzar returned to Jerusalem to punish him. Nebuchadnezzar **bound** Jehoiakim **to carry him off to Babylon.** He did not actually take him away, since Jehoiakim reigned until about 598 B.C. and died of natural causes in Jerusalem (2 Kin. 24:6; Jer. 22:18, 19).

36:7–9 Nebuchadnezzar . . . carried off:

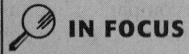 **IN FOCUS** **"Passover"**

(Heb. *pesach*) (2 Chr. 30:1, 35:1; Ex. 12:11, 43; Ezek. 45:21) Strong's #6453: The name Passover is derived from the Hebrew word meaning "to pass" or "to leap over." The festival was named in this way because it commemorated the time when God spared the firstborn of the Israelites, who sprinkled the blood from the Passover lamb on their doorposts. The Lord "passed over" the families so designated, not visiting their households with death (Ex. 12). So that the Israelites would not forget God's mercy on them, the Law of Moses prescribed in detail the ritual for commemorating the Passover (Lev. 23:5–8; Num. 28:16–25; Deut. 16:1–8). King Hezekiah's great Passover signaled spiritual renewal in Judah, including the removal of sin and impurity (30:14), joyful praise for God's pardon (30:21–22), and a prolonged celebration of God's blessing (30:23–26). Later Jesus celebrated this feast with His disciples (Matt. 26:2, 18), and in His death and resurrection He became its fulfillment, the ultimate Passover Lamb for our sins (John 1:29, 1 Cor. 5:7; 1 Pet. 1:19).

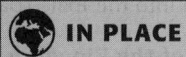 **IN PLACE** | # The Babylonians

Judah at its weakest was overrun by Babylonia at its strongest, when Nebuchadnezzar's troops captured Jerusalem dragging away Judah's young king in chains (2 Chr. 36:6). This attack, which occurred in about 599–597 B.C., was one of three major invasions of the land by the Babylonians.

Sargon and Hammurabi

Babylonia was an ancient empire located between the Tigris and Euphrates Rivers in southern Mesopotamia. Its capital, Babylon (Gen. 11:9), is said to have been founded by Nimrod, the son of Cush and the grandson of Ham (Gen. 10:8–12). Some believe that this ruler was King Sargon the Great, who united the people of Mesopotamia under his rule about 2300 B.C., establishing an empire that stretched from the Mediterranean coast and Asia Minor to Persia.

Around 2000 B.C., a king named Hammurabi emerged as the ruler of this region. One of his chief achievements was to establish a written system of laws, known today as the Code of Hammurabi. It was about this time that Abraham's family (Gen. 12:1) left Ur, a city in lower Babylon, and moved to Haran, a city in northwestern Mesopotamia. It was from Haran that the patriarch later migrated to Canaan in obedience to God (Gen. 12:4).

Babylonia itself was a long, narrow country, only about 40 miles wide at its widest point, but covering a total area of about 8,000 square miles. It was bordered on the north by Assyria, on the east by Elam, on the south and west by the Arabian desert, and on the southeast by the Persian Gulf.

From Assyria to Babylonia

Assyria's development was closely connected to Babylonia's history. In about 1270 B.C., the Assyrians overpowered their southern neighbors, and for the next 700 years, the Assyrians dominated

the ancient world. But in about 626 B.C., a Babylonian leader named Nabopolassar finally won his nation's independence from Assyria, and Babylonia again began to become a great empire. The Babylonians finally overthrew their rivals in 612 B.C. by capturing the Assyrian capital of Nineveh (Jon. 1:2). This opened the way for Nabopolassar's son Nebuchadnezzar to turn Babylon into the world's next great empire, and to expand the capital city of Babylon into one of the world's leading cities.

Nebuchadnezzar ordered the destruction of Jerusalem in 586 B.C., and carried away the leading citizens of Judah to exile. But during this period of captivity, the Persians emerged as a world power, and the Babylonian empire passed from the scene.

The Babylonian king looted the temple of much of its treasure, fulfilling the prophecy made to Hezekiah a century earlier (32:31; 2 Kin. 20:17). **His temple** was the Esagila, the temple of Babylon's patron god Marduk.

36:10, 11 Zedekiah was the youngest of the four sons of Josiah and the third to rule over Judah (see v. 1). He became king by Nebuchadnezzar's appointment, showing Judah's status as a Babylonian vassal (v. 3).

36:12 Jeremiah was the famous **prophet** who composed the Book of Jeremiah, which includes his words to Zedekiah (Jer. 21:3–7; 32:5).

36:13 By 588 B.C. Zedekiah **rebelled against King Nebuchadnezzar** and, like his brother and nephew before him, invited swift Babylonian retribution. Nebuchadnezzar captured Jerusalem after a two-year siege (2 Kin. 25:1–3).

36:14 The abominations of the nations refers primarily to idolatry and all the immorality and perversity that went with it. God's covenant with Israel required them to be different from the nations in this key respect (Ex. 23:24; Lev. 26:1; Deut. 4:15–20, 25–28, 18:9–14; 27:14, 15).

36:15 God's **messengers** were the prophets He had sent from the beginning of Israel's history.

36:16 no remedy: This does not mean that God had run out of options and had exhausted His ability to save. It suggests, rather, that He operates within certain predetermined parameters of response. Within that framework He forgave and restored His people over and over again. Finally they had stepped across the boundaries of His grace in history and had disqualified themselves from any further consideration. The point of no return had been reached. What did remain, however, was a final expression of divine initiative in days yet future, one hinted at in the decree of Cyrus (v. 23) and more fully spelled out in the prophets (Lev. 26:40–45; Isa. 40:1, 2; 49:14–23; Jer. 31:1–40; Ezek. 36:16—39:29; Zech. 14:1–21).

36:17–19 The **king of the Chaldeans** (Babylonians) was Nebuchadnezzar, who reigned from 605 to 562 B.C. He became an instrument of God's judgment all through Judah's last years and well into the Exile (Dan. 2:37, 38; 5:18, 19).

36:20 until the rule of the kingdom of Persia: Cyrus conquered Babylon in 539 B.C. and allowed the Jews to return to Jerusalem the following year.

36:21 In two places (Jer. 25:12; 29:10), **Jeremiah** predicted the Exile and its length (Dan 9:2). **Sabbaths:** According to the Law of Moses the land was to lie fallow every seventh year (Lev. 25:4). This became known as the sabbatical year. Judah's exile in Babylon allowed the land to enjoy the Sabbaths it had missed (Lev. 26:33–35).

36:22 The **first year of Cyrus** refers to his first year of rule over Babylon, not his first year over Media and Persia. He began to rule Media and Persia in 550 B.C. Twelve years later he brought Babylon under his control and issued his famous decree, known from the OT (here and Ezra 1:2–4) and from the Cylinder of Cyrus. This was his first year of involvement with the Jewish people. Jeremiah's seventy years were from about 609 to 539 B.C. **the LORD** stirred up: Cyrus was both a mighty monarch and the instrument by whom God delivered His people from exile, returned them to their land, and rebuilt the temple (Is. 44:28—45:1).

36:23 the LORD God . . . has given me: According to his own account on the Cylinder of Cyrus, the god who called and blessed Cyrus was Marduk, chief deity of the Babylonian pantheon of gods. Since that document was for Babylonian readers, his reference to Marduk is understandable. The Bible attributes his success to the living Lord. It was God Himself who gave Cyrus sovereignty, who commanded him to rebuild the **Jerusalem** temple, and who had inspired him to release the Jews to their own country. It is not likely that Cyrus was a convert to Judaism. Like Nebuchadnezzar (Dan. 2:47; 3:28, 29; 4:34–37) and Darius the Mede (Dan. 6:26, 27), Cyrus was willing to include Israel's God among the gods he recognized and extolled. The temple and the holy city lay in ruins, but God was not done yet. He was about to bring His people back to the land and to revive His promises to save and restore them.

The Book of

Ezra

T

HE BOOK OF EZRA IS A REMARKABLE WITNESS
to God's faithfulness to His people. With Nehemiah,
Ezra describes the events leading to the Judeans return
from captivity in Babylon and the discouraging experiences of
that small community in the harsh world of the Promised Land.
But through every experience God proved Himself faithful.
Through the leadership of Ezra and Zerubbabel, God fulfilled His

promises announced by His prophets to restore
His people from Babylon, to rebuild the temple
at Jerusalem, and to renew their hope that the
Davidic kingdom would be restored.

In 539 B.C., Cyrus of Persia defeated the
Babylonian empire. Unlike the Babylonian
kings before him, Cyrus allowed captive peoples
to return to their homelands and live by their
traditions and reestablish the worship of their
own gods. At the same time, all these peoples
remained an integral part of the Persian empire,
subject to the emperor.

The Jewish people had been exiled to
Babylon in three stages, and they returned with
the permission of the Persians in three stages.
Zerubbabel led the first group of returning
Israelites (538 B.C.) and started to rebuild the
temple (chs. 1—6). The priest Ezra led the
second group (458 B.C.) and instituted a number
of reforms (chs. 7—10). Finally, Nehemiah led
the third group (444 B.C.) and rebuilt the wall
around Jerusalem (Neh. 1—6).

Work on the restoration of the temple began
in the reign of Cyrus (536 B.C.), extended
through the time of Cambyses, and was com-

pleted in the sixth year of Darius I (515 B.C.).
The reforming careers of Ezra and Nehemiah
spanned the reigns of Artaxerxes Longimanus
(464–424 B.C.) and Darius II (423–405 B.C.).

The books of Ezra and Nehemiah are one
work in the Hebrew Bible and should be studied
together for a better understanding of the return
of the Babylonian exiles to Jerusalem. The combined narrative presents the story of the exiles'
return in two time periods, each marked by two
prominent leaders: rebuilding the temple under
Zerubbabel and Joshua the priest (538–515 B.C.)
and restoring the worship of God and rebuilding
Jerusalem's walls under Ezra and Nehemiah
(458–420 B.C.).

Yet the Book of Ezra is not simply a string of
historical facts about the returning exiles, for
the narrative shows how God fulfilled His
promises announced by the prophets. He
brought His people back from Babylon, rebuilt
the temple at Jerusalem, restored the patterns of
true worship, and even preserved the reassembled community from fresh relapses into heathen customs and idolatrous worship. Through
the prophets and leaders He had called, the Lord

had preserved and cultivated a small group of returning exiles, the remnant of Israel.

The extraordinary reality of God's promised restoration of His people (Jer. 27:22) is recorded in detail in the Book of Ezra. The remnant did not merely return to the devastated ruins of Jerusalem; they came back with a hope, placed in their hearts by God, to rebuild the nation. With godly determination, they rebuilt the temple. Then the Lord sent Ezra and Nehemiah to exhort them to obey His Law wholeheartedly. While the people were rebuilding Jerusalem's walls, God was rebuilding their hearts so that they would truly obey and worship Him. The restoration of the remnant was a complete restoration. The message for Ezra's day—as well as for our own—is that the God of Israel is faithful to His promises. He will completely restore His people when they come back to Him.

The Book of Ezra does not name its author, but Jewish tradition ascribes the book to Ezra along with the books of Chronicles and Nehemiah. Modern scholars generally agree with this tradition. Despite some dissimilarities, Chronicles, Ezra, and Nehemiah form a connected work. The themes of the temple and the Levites, and the focus on lists, appear in all three books. In the Hebrew Bible, Ezra and Nehemiah are one book. Thus it seems that one author compiled all three books.

The fact that Ezra is the principal character of major sections of Ezra lends some credibility to his authorship of this book. Ezra participates in the events described in the second half of Ezra (chs. 7—10), as well as in events described in a portion of the Book of Nehemiah (chs. 8—10). Both passages are written in the first person and provide detailed descriptions. Such vivid descriptions point to an eyewitness as the author. It is generally agreed that these chapters at least were drawn directly from Ezra's memoirs.

On the other hand, the first half of Ezra records events that occurred nearly sixty years before Ezra returned to Judah. If Ezra compiled the book, he had to consult other sources for those passages. In fact, much of the Book of Ezra consists of information obtained from other official sources: (1) the decree of Cyrus (1:2–4), (2) the list of the articles of the temple (1:9–11), (3) the list of those who returned to Jerusalem (2:2–58), (4) the letter to Artaxerxes (4:11–16), (5) the reply of Artaxerxes (4:17–22), (6) the report of Tattenai (5:7–17), (7) the decree of Cyrus (6:2–5), (8) the reply of Darius (6:6–8), (9) the genealogy of Ezra (7:1–5), (10) the authorization of Artaxerxes (7:12–26), (11) the list of the heads of the clans (8:1–14), and (12) the list of those involved in mixed marriages. Over half of the Book of Ezra consists of official documents and lists.

Moreover, the book is written in two languages. Most of the royal correspondence in the book is written in Aramaic, the international language of the Persian world, while the narrative sections are in Hebrew. In conclusion, the Book of Ezra is the work of a compiler, and that compiler certainly could have been the scribe Ezra.

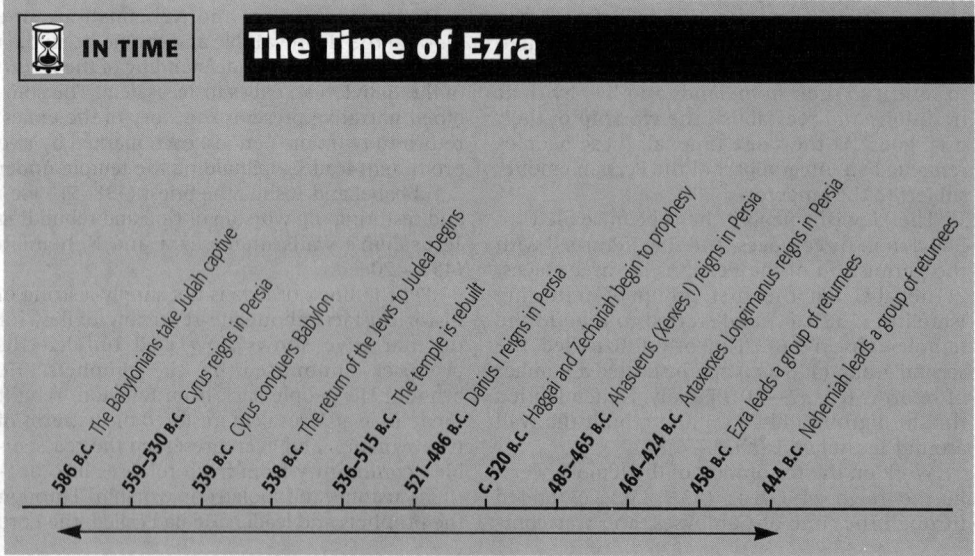

IN TIME   **The Time of Ezra**

586 B.C. The Babylonians take Judah captive

559–530 B.C. Cyrus reigns in Persia

539 B.C. Cyrus conquers Babylon

538 B.C. The return of the Jews to Judea begins

536–515 B.C. The temple is rebuilt

521–486 B.C. Darius I reigns in Persia

c. 520 B.C. Haggai and Zechariah begin to prophesy

485–465 B.C. Ahasuerus (Xerxes I) reigns in Persia

464–424 B.C. Artaxerxes Longimanus reigns in Persia

458 B.C. Ezra leads a group of returnees

444 B.C. Nehemiah leads a group of returnees

Outline

Commentary

1:1 The first year of Cyrus is the first year of his rule over Babylon. In 539 B.C. Cyrus the Great, founder of the greater Persian empire, conquered Babylon without a struggle. He ruled as king of Persia from 559–530 B.C. **the word of the LORD** by . . . **Jeremiah:** Jeremiah had prophesied that the Babylonian captivity would last 70 years (Jer. 25:11; 29:10), after which the Lord would judge Babylon (Jer. 25:12–14). Cyrus's **proclamation** was probably shouted by heralds in the principal towns of the empire and posted in public. **put it in writing:** The proclamation was also preserved in the official records in Persia (6:1).

1:2 the LORD God of heaven: After the destruction of Jerusalem, God was no longer identified with the temple as the One who dwelt between the cherubim (1 Sam. 4:4; 2 Sam. 6:2). The Persians could understand that there was a particular "God of Israel," but they would have recognized Him as simply one god among others. However, the phrase *God of heaven* indicates that the Lord is not just another god, but that only He is God. The fact that Cyrus used this title for the Lord suggests that He was prompted by Jewish advisors. **He has commanded me to build Him a house at Jerusalem:** Over one hundred years before Cyrus issued this decree, Isaiah prophesied that the king would make such an order (Is. 44:28; 45:1).

1:3 He is God: It is likely that Cyrus was speaking as a polytheist who merely recognized that the **God of Israel** should be worshiped **in Jerusalem.**

1:4 let the men of his place help him: The assistance that the Israelites were to receive from their non-Jewish neighbors in rebuilding the temple is reminiscent of the help an earlier

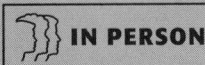 **IN PERSON**

Cyrus, The King of Persia

One hundred forty years before Cyrus issued the decree allowing the Israelites to return to their homeland, Isaiah prophesied that a man named Cyrus would issue such an order (Is. 44:28; 45:1). More than a century before Cyrus the Great, the founder of the Persian empire and the Achaemenid dynasty, was born, Isaiah called him by name! Indeed, Isaiah reported the word of God to this effect: "I have even called you by your name; I have named you, though you have not known Me" (Is. 45:4). Josephus, a first-century Jewish historian, would later assert that Cyrus was shown the prophecy of Isaiah recorded in Is. 44:28—45:1 and "an earnest desire and ambition seized upon (Cyrus) to fulfill what was written." (*Antiq.* 11.1). If this story is true, it is possible that Daniel was the one who showed Cyrus Isaiah's prophecy (Dan. 6:28; 9:1, 2; 10:1).

Certainly Cyrus's decrees might have been part of a clever military strategy. At this point, he had not yet conquered Egypt. A strong settlement of loyal people between him and the Egyptians would have been wise. This was a novel political policy; for the first time in hundreds of years a king permitted a subjected people to return to their homeland. But the point of Scriptures is to assert that God was at work through this powerful ruler of the ancient world. He spoke to Cyrus through His Word (v. 2) and moved Cyrus in his inner spirit (v. 1). Through Cyrus, God was accomplishing His own will: to graciously deliver His people from captivity.

generation received from the Egyptians before the Exodus (Ex. 12:35, 36). In a sense, the return to Jerusalem to rebuild the temple was a second Exodus (Is. 43:14–21; 48:20, 21).

1:5 Moved here translates the same Hebrew word as *stirred* in v. 1. The verb means "to rouse" or "to stir up" (Is. 45:13; Hag. 1:14; Zech. 4:1).

1:6 All those who were around included non-Jewish neighbors (v. 3) as well as Jews who wanted to stay in Babylon.

1:7 King Cyrus also brought: The people who returned to Jerusalem were helped not only by their neighbors, but by the king himself. Cyrus ordered the return of the temple articles that had been taken by **Nebuchadnezzar** (2 Kin. 24:1–7, 11–13; 25:8–17; 2 Chr. 36:5–7, 9, 10, 13–19; Dan. 1:2).

1:8 Mithredath the treasurer: not the same as the Mithredath in 4:7. The name

bazzar was a name by which Zerubbabel was known in Persian circles. There are two other possibilities. (1) Some suggest that Sheshbazzar died and his work was continued by Zerubbabel. (2) Others suggest that Sheshbazzar is another name for Shenazzar (1 Chr. 3:18), an uncle of Zerubbabel. **The prince of Judah** means he was in the Davidic royal line. Zerubbabel was the grandson of King Jehoiakim. In 1 Chr. 3:17–19 he is called the son of Pedaiah instead of Shealtiel. It may be that Shealtiel died childless and his brother Pedaiah married his widow, following the custom of levirate marriage (Deut. 25:5–10; 1 Chr. 3:18).

1:9–11 The separate items listed in vv. 9, 10 total 2,499. However, the total for **all the articles** given in v. 11 is 5,400. Probably vv. 9, 10 list only the larger and more important items that were transported back to Jerusalem.

2:1–70 Here are the names and numbers of

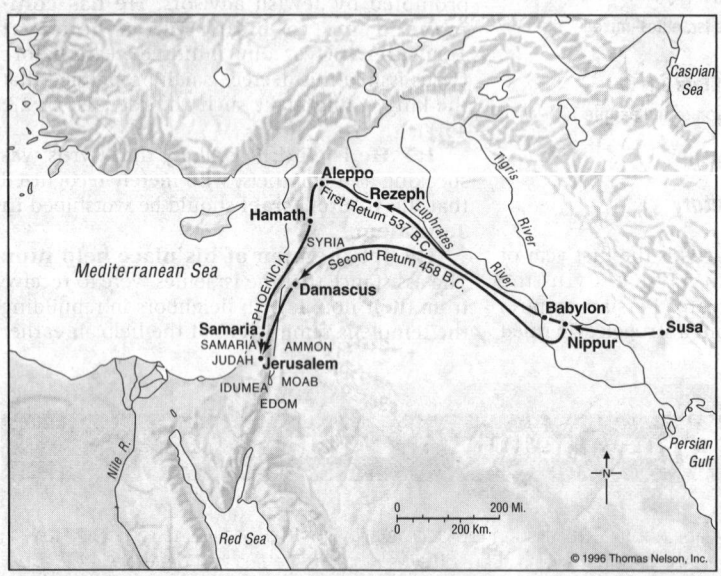

The Return from Exile

When Cyrus the Persian captured Babylon in 539 B.C., the way was opened for captive Judah to begin the return to her homeland. The edict of Cyrus in 538 B.C. allowed Jewish exiles not only to return to Judah, but also to rebuild the temple. While there were probably several caravans of returning exiles, two major expeditions are reported. The first led by Sheshbazzar occurred soon after the edict, possibly in 537 B.C. The traditional date of the second return led by Ezra is 458 B.C.

Sheshbazzar occurs only in two passages (vv. 8–11; 5:14–16), both related to official Persian actions. On the other hand, the name Zerubbabel is used in passages related to Jewish activity. Ezra 5:2, 16 appear to identify Sheshbazzar and Zerubbabel. It is possible that Shesh-

the Jewish people who decided to return to Jerusalem (vv. 1–67), as well as the offering and occupancy of the returnees (vv. 68–70). Except for a few variations the content of this chapter is reproduced in Neh. 7:6–73 (vv. 1, 2, 64, 69 for differences).

2:1 The people of the province refers to the Jewish people of Judah (5:8; Neh. 1:2, 3; 11:3). The use of this phrase probably indicates that the register of ch. 2 was compiled in Babylon. Nehemiah's list in Neh. 7:4–73 would have been compiled after he arrived in Jerusalem, which could account for some of the differences between the two registers. **His own city** means the city where a person's family had lived.

2:2 The men listed in this verse were the leaders of the expedition. **Jeshua** was Joshua the high priest (Hag. 1:1; Zech. 3:1). **Nehemiah,** listed as a leader here, was not the same man who rebuilt the wall of Jerusalem ninety years later. **Mordecai** was not the man of the same name who figures so prominently in the Book of Esther. Nehemiah gives a similar list (Neh. 7:7), with some differences of spelling and an extra leader Nahamani on the list. Those who returned to Jerusalem are called **the people of Israel** and not Judah, because all twelve tribes of Israel were represented.

2:3–20 These verses contain the names and numbers of the families who returned to Jerusalem. It may be that these were the people whose homes were in the city of Jerusalem itself.

2:21–35 These verses list the returnees according to their cities. Note that Jerusalem is not listed. Perhaps the registry dealt first with the inhabitants of Jerusalem (vv. 2–20) and then focused on those outside Jerusalem.

2:36–39 The total number of **priests** listed is 4,289. This was about ten percent of the returning remnant. As teachers of the Law and as the ones who led worship in the new temple, the priests were indispensable to the reestablishment of the temple services. If God's work was to be restored, there had to be religious instruction and there had to be true worship.

2:40 The **Levites** assisted the priests in the temple and in teaching the people the Law (Neh. 8:7–9). Compared to the number of priests who returned to Jerusalem (vv. 36–39), it is striking how few Levites were with them (other Levites are included in the special lists of vv. 41, 42). According to 1 Chr. 23:4, 24,000 Levites were involved in the worship of God during the time of David.

2:41 The **singers** were Levites who had the responsibility of praising God with music (1 Chr. 15:16). Though only 128 singers returned to Jerusalem, at one time there had been as many as four thousand people who "praised the Lord with musical instruments" in Solomon's temple (1 Chr. 23:5).

2:42 The **gatekeepers,** who were also Levites (1 Chr. 26:1–19), prevented unauthorized people from entering the restricted area of the temple. There were 139 gatekeepers in the return to Jerusalem under Zerubbabel; compare that figure to the four thousand gatekeepers who guarded the temple during the time of Solomon (1 Chr. 23:5).

2:43–50 Nethinim means "Given Ones" or "Dedicated Ones." In 1 Chr. 9:2, the Nethinim are distinguished from the priests and the Levites. Jewish tradition identifies the Nethinim with the Gibeonites who had been assigned by Joshua to assist the Levites in more menial tasks (Josh. 9:27).

2:51–55 The sons of Solomon's servants are linked with the Nethinim (v. 43). The numbers of the two groups are totaled together (v. 58; Neh. 7:60). The sons of Solomon's servants were probably descendants of the inhabitants of Canaan at the time of Solomon—that is, descendants of the Amorites, Hittites, Perizzites, Hivites, and Jebusites whom Solomon had hired to build the temple (1 Kin. 5:13).

2:56–63 Although these people could not prove their Jewish origin, they were permitted to return to Jerusalem. But without genealogies they were **excluded from the priesthood,** according to the Law of Moses (Num. 16:1–40). **The governor** Zerubbabel was careful to follow the Law by declaring that the would-be priests **should not eat of the most holy things,** meaning that they should not participate in priestly functions. **The Urim and Thummim** were sacred lots that were used to determine God's will (Ex. 28:30).

2:64 forty-two thousand three hundred and sixty: The individual numbers listed in ch. 2 add up to only 29,818. It is possible that the larger total includes women, who are not named in the lists.

2:65 The **singers** listed here were not the temple choir of v. 41. These were professional singers employed for banquets, feasts, and funerals (2 Chr. 35:25; Eccl. 2:7, 8). Their presence could be an indication of luxury (2 Sam. 19:35). It appears that many of the Jewish people had achieved some prosperity while living in Babylon. The Jews had not been enslaved in exile; they had only been restricted from returning to their land.

2:66 The large number of **horses** listed here also suggests affluence among those who returned to Jerusalem. Prior to this time, horses in Israel had been used only for war and ceremonies. Only the very rich and well-armed owned horses. The rich also rode **mules,** for they were scarce in Israel.

2:67 The beasts of burden were **camels** and **donkeys.** Camels were expensive; the poorer classes rode donkeys.

2:68 when they came to the house of the Lord: The first thing that many of the returnees did when they reached Jerusalem was

New Reasons for Taking a Census

IN CONTEXT

Census data has been used by governments throughout history for a variety of purposes: for example, to draft soldiers for military service, to collect tax revenue, and to conscript laborers for public works projects. When a census was taken of the Jews who returned to Palestine from Babylon (Ezra 2:1), the results were put to several new and interesting purposes:

(1) To return properties to their rightful owners. Generations earlier, Moses had taken a census of the Israelites as they prepared to enter Canaan, to obtain data to be used to divide the land among the tribes of Israel (Num. 26). Later, when the people took possession of the land, they settled in their allotted territories (Josh. 13–19).

From that time forward, each family's land was intended to stay in the family. In fact, an intricate set of laws was established to ensure that no family lost its land permanently. Thus when the exiles returned, it was important that they be able to trace their lineage in order to verify their claims to family lands or, in the case of priests and Levites, to Levitical cities (Ezra 2:3–58). Certain priests who could not prove their heritage were made to wait until a priest could consult God as to their status (2:59–63; Neh. 7:61–65).

(2) To collect resources for rebuilding the temple. Indirectly, the census became an occasion for the returnees to give a freewill offering that was used toward the building of a new temple (Ezra 2:68, 69).

(3) To redevelop and repopulate Jerusalem. Several years after this census was taken, Nehemiah reviewed it when he realized how empty Jerusalem was (Neh. 7:4, 5). Then the people cast lots in such a way that one-tenth of the population of Judah was relocated to the capital city in order to reclaim its public life (11:1, 2).

to contribute to the rebuilding of the temple. Offerings were brought even before the people settled in their houses (v. 70).

2:69 Ezra records the amount of gold, silver, and garments given for the rebuilding of the temple, as does Nehemiah (Neh. 7:70–72). However, the two sets of figures do not match. Apparently Ezra's list rounds off the figures, while Nehemiah's list presents them in more precise detail. It is also possible that the two lists give totals from different times of collection—perhaps in Babylon and then later in Jerusalem. **Drachmas** were Persian gold coins that weighed about two-tenths of an ounce, the weight of a quarter. Five thousand minas were about 6,300 pounds of silver.

2:70 priests . . . Levites . . . and all Israel: This indicates that representatives from the whole nation (the twelve tribes) were now back in the land. The process was in motion whereby God's promises could begin to be fulfilled. There is messianic hope in the expression "all Israel."

3:1 The seventh month was sacred to Jewish people. The first day of the month was the Feast of Trumpets (Num. 29:1–6), the tenth day was the Day of Atonement (Num. 29:7–11), and the fifteenth day was the Feast of Tabernacles (Num. 29:12–38). **as one man:** The people had come with the common desire of worshiping God (v. 9).

3:2, 3 Jeshua was the same person as the priest Joshua (Hag. 1:1; Zech. 3:1); his father's name **Jozadak** was also spelled Jehozadak (1 Chr. 6:14; Hag. 1:1).

3:4 In obedience to God's Word, the Israelites observed **the Feast of Tabernacles** or Booths, which commemorated the earlier generation's wanderings in the wilderness (Num. 29:13–38).

3:5, 6 The regular burnt offerings were the daily burnt offerings, the morning and evening sacrifices (Ex. 29:38–42). The offerings for the **New Moons** were not a set feast in Lev. 23, but they were part of Israel's worship (2 Kin. 4:23; Amos 8:5). **The appointed feasts** of Lev. 23 included: (1) the Sabbath (v. 3), (2) the Passover (v. 5) followed by Unleavened Bread (vv. 6–8), (3) the Feast of Firstfruits (vv. 9–14); (4) the Feast of Weeks (vv. 15–22), (5) the Feast of Trumpets (vv. 23–25), (6) the Day of Atonement (vv. 26–32), the Feast of Tabernacles (vv. 33–44). According to 2 Chr. 8:13, the appointed feasts were the three great annual Feasts of Unleavened Bread (along with Passover), Weeks, and Tabernacles; likely it is this listing that is what is intended here. The **freewill offering** was made on the feast days (Deut. 16:10, 16, 17) and whenever any of the Jewish people desired (Num. 15:3).

3:7 When Solomon built the first temple, he

purchased materials from **Sidon and Tyre,** had them shipped to **Joppa,** and paid for them with grain, wine, and oil (2 Chr. 2:10–16).

3:8, 9 The construction of Solomon's temple had begun in the second month of the year (1 Kin. 6:1). Likewise, construction of the second temple began in the second month. **from twenty years old and above:** The Law had required that Levites be at least thirty years old before they entered into service (Num. 4:1–3). Later, the minimum age was reduced to twenty-five (Num. 8:24). Finally, David lowered the minimum age to twenty (1 Chr. 23:24, 27). The lower minimum age allowed more Levites to enter into temple service. This provision was vital in view of the small number of Levites who made the trip back to Jerusalem (2:40).

3:10, 11 The returnees to Jerusalem celebrated laying the temple's foundation in almost the same way that the previous generation had celebrated the first temple (2 Chr. 5:13). Two choruses were sung **responsively.** One group sang **For He is good;** the other group responded with **For His mercy endures forever** (Neh. 12:31).

3:12, 13 Solomon's temple had been destroyed in 586 B.C., and this scene took place fifty years later. The **old men** could remember the grandeur of the first temple, and they **wept.**

4:1 The adversaries of Judah were the Samaritans. Esarhaddon (v. 2), who ruled Assyria from 681–669 B.C., had transported the conquered people of the northern kingdom to other lands. He then brought people from other lands into Palestine. These foreigners intermarried with the Hebrews who were left in the land. Their offspring became the Samaritans. **Judah and Benjamin:** The southern kingdom of Judah is called the nation of Judah and Simeon. The southern kingdom also included land from Benjamin, in which Jerusalem was located.

4:2 we seek your God as you do: The Samaritans did not use the proper name for God—that is, Yahweh—perhaps suggesting that their understanding of the Lord was still quite poor. As a result, they presented the threat of syncretism, or mixing true worship of God with the worship of false gods. This was the sin that had led to the deportation of the Israelites in the first place.

4:3 You may do nothing with us is not a rude rebuff; it is a righteous refusal. The people offering help were not friends, but adversaries (v. 1). They may have sacrificed to the Lord, but they were idolatrous at the same time (2 Kin. 17:29–35).

4:4, 5 The people of the land is another way of referring to the Samaritans, who became active enemies of Israel's rebuilding program for the next several years. The Samaritans trou-**bled** the Jewish people, perhaps with threats and attempts to cut off their supplies. The Samaritans then **hired counselors,** or lawyers, probably to represent them against the Jewish community at the Persian court. The Samaritans persisted in these attacks **until the reign of Darius** as much as fourteen years later.

4:6 When Darius I died (486 B.C.), his son **Ahasuerus** reigned (485–465 B.C.). Ahasuerus's Greek name was Xerxes. He is the same king who appears in the Book of Esther. At the beginning of his reign, the Samaritans wrote him a letter hoping to stop the Jews from completing work on the temple. Apparently nothing was accomplished by the letter.

4:7, 8 Artaxerxes Longimanus (464–424 B.C.) succeeded his father Xerxes. He too received a letter from the Samaritans against the Jews (v. 6). The letter was **written in Aramaic script, and translated,** or read aloud in Aramaic. Like the Samaritans' letter to Ahasuerus, this letter evidently was ignored.

4:8–6:18 This passage was written in Aramaic.

4:9, 10 The point of these two verses is that the Samaritan letter reflected the views of the whole province. The beginning of the letter, filled with rhetoric and flourish, was designed to bring political pressure on the Persian king. **Osnapper** was probably another name for Ashurbanipal, the king of Assyria (669–626 B.C.) who completed the transplanting begun by Esarhaddon (v. 2). **The River** is the Euphrates.

4:11 Your servants is a technical term for vassals. By including this term in the introduction of the letter, the men were assuring the king of their allegiance and were reporting the rebellion of the Jewish people. **And so forth** may mean "and now" (v. 10).

4:12, 13 the rebellious and evil city: The rebellion to which the Samaritans referred was the long period of siege the armies of Babylon were compelled to undertake against Israel. **finishing its walls:** The Jews perhaps had begun construction on the walls but were nowhere near completing them. They were not finished until many years later (Neh. 6).

4:14, 15 The Samaritans suggested that the king search his official records to see if Jerusalem had been destroyed in the past because of rebellion. Indeed it had. Nebuchadnezzar had conquered Jerusalem years before because it had rebelled against him.

4:16 The Samaritan letter concluded with a warning that if the king did not stop the Jews, he would lose not only income, but also dominion over Jerusalem and the region beyond the Euphrates **River.**

4:17 In this context, the word **peace** is used

of the treaty relationship that existed between the king and his vassals (5:7).

4:18 clearly: Here the Aramaic word *meparash* is close to the Hebrew word *meporash* in Neh. 8:8, translated "distinctly." A nuance of this word means "to explain more fully." The letter therefore was read and explained quite fully to the king.

4:19 A search of the king's official records confirmed the Samaritans' allegation of **rebellion** and **sedition** on the part of the people of Jerusalem, no doubt referring to the revolts under Jehoiakim, Jehoiachin, and Zedekiah (2 Kin. 24:1–20). The fact that these revolts were against the Babylonians and not against the Persians was not important. The Persians had become the heirs of the Babylonian empire, and they would take such a report seriously.

4:20 The Persian king also found out that Jewish kings had **ruled over** a large region. David and Solomon had both possessed a great sphere of rule. Subsequent kings had aspired to the former glory of David and Solomon.

4:21, 22 The Persian king Artaxerxes ordered the Jewish people to **cease** their work on the temple. However, he left open the possi-

---

🔍 IN FOCUS   "Jews"

(Heb. *yehudi*) (Ezra 5:1; 6:7; Dan. 3:8) Strong's #3062: The name "Jew" is popularly associated with the verb *yadah* (meaning "to praise" or "to give thanks"), on the basis of Jacob's blessing upon his son Judah in Gen. 49:8: "Judah you are he whom your brothers shall praise." Thus a Jew may be a person from the tribe of Judah (Num. 10:14). Later the name Jew was applied directly to those Israelites living in the geographical region known as Judah (Jer 7:30). The use of the name Jew for the Israelites as a people group became prominent during the postexilic period. This use is found in the NT as well: Jesus is called "the King of the Jews" (Matt. 27:29). In his letter to the Romans, Paul states that the true Jew is a person marked by "circumcision of the heart" (Rom 2:28, 29).

---

bility of a future change in policy. Years later at the request of Nehemiah the decision was reviewed (Neh. 2:1–8).

4:23, 24 By force may suggest that the enforcers of the king's edict demolished the part of the wall that had been repaired. This would

have been part of the rubble that Nehemiah discovered when he arrived in Jerusalem (Neh. 2:12–16).

5:1 Haggai, who wrote the OT book that bears his name, began his ministry in August, 520 B.C. (Hag. 1:1). **Zechariah,** a prophet who also wrote an OT book, began his prophetic ministry in October or November of the same year (Zech. 1:1). The Jews had been forced to stop working on the temple (4:24). Now years later, God revived His work. He instructed His prophets to prophesy, and He expected His people to respond in faith and action. The phrase **who was over them** is a reminder of the sovereignty of God. No king other than the Lord Himself commanded His people.

5:2 Zerubbabel the civil governor and **Jeshua** (also known as Joshua) the high priest led the people once again in rebuilding the temple. The prophets Haggai and Zechariah joined in this call to action.

5:3 When the temple rebuilding resumed, resistance renewed. **Tattenai** was a regional **governor.** Since there were only twenty regional governors called satraps in the Persian empire (8:36), it may be assumed that Tattenai was a very powerful man. Zerubbabel, as governor of the small district of Judah, was under the authority of Tattenai (1:8). The position of **Shethar-Boznai** is not described, but he was probably an aide or a secretary to Tattenai. The regional governor and his staff personally visited Jerusalem.

5:4 The official delegation of Tattenai asked who had commanded the work on the temple to be done (v. 3). The answer in this verse gives **the names of the men who were constructing** the temple, but not the name of the one who commanded the work to be done.

5:5 The eye of their God is a way of speaking of the sovereignty and providence of God (v. 1): God was protecting and watching over those who obeyed His command. The governor decided that he would not stop the work on the temple until an **answer was returned** from the king. In other words, Tattenai checked out the Jewish leaders' version of what was taking place.

5:6 The governor sent his inquiring letter to King **Darius** (who ruled from 521–486 B.C.). The fact that Tattenai contacted the emperor shows that despite his own considerable power, he still had to proceed under the process of Persian custom and law.

5:7, 8 The walls described in Tattenai's letter were the walls of the temple, not the walls of the city. **Timber** was used for the beams of the temple floor and roof. Most of the temple construction was done with massive stones, but beams and slats were also used.

5:9, 10 The officials had originally asked

two questions (v. 4). They wanted to know who was responsible for the construction, not just the names of the people doing the work.

5:11 In his report to Darius, Tattenai indicated that he had learned a great deal from the Jews about their history and destiny, including a reference to a **great king,** that is, Solomon.

5:12 Though the Jewish people acknowledged that **Nebuchadnezzar** destroyed the first temple, they traced the cause not to his power, but to their sin and ultimately to God's judgment. Tattenai's use of the title **God of heaven** is perhaps an unwitting acknowledgment of the reality and sovereignty of God.

5:13–16 This portion of Tattenai's letter to King Cyrus describes the events that led to the official Persian decree to rebuild the temple (1:1–4). Note that the delay described in ch. 4 is not mentioned here. **Sheshbazzar** may have been the Persian name for Zerubbabel. Alternatively he may have been the Jewish prince who was first appointed to lead the temple rebuilding efforts, but who did not survive and was replaced by Zerubbabel (1:8).

5:17 Apparently **the king's treasure house** contained the official records as well as the treasury. Tattenai's request to find the original decree **issued by King Cyrus** delayed the rebuilding. The trip from Jerusalem to Babylon (7:9) took eight months. The search for official documents also took time. The entire process could have taken as long as a year.

6:1, 2 At the suggestion of Tattenai and his aides (5:17), **King Darius** ordered his staff to search the official records in the **archives,** or "house of the books," to see whether Cyrus had authorized the rebuilding of the temple at Jerusalem. Apparently nothing was found in **Babylon,** and the search moved on to **Achmetha,** the summer residence of the Persian kings.

6:3–5 King Darius began his reply to Tattenai by quoting from the **decree** of **King Cyrus.** Cyrus's public proclamation can be found in 1:2–4. **its height sixty cubits and its**

width sixty cubits: Though the complete dimensions are not given, it is likely that the second temple was built on the foundation stones that were still in place from the time of Solomon (1 Kin. 6:2). The **three rows of heavy stones and one row of new timber** describes the construction of the wall of the inner court (1 Kin. 6:36). The heavy stones that had aroused Tattenai's suspicion (5:8) were expressly authorized.

6:6, 7 therefore: Based on the discovery of the decrees of Cyrus, King Darius issued an order of his own. He concluded that what the Jewish people were doing was legal and that the regional government should stop opposing them.

6:8–10 Moreover: King Darius endorsed Cyrus' order and added his own decree. **taxes on the region beyond the River:** Not only could Tattenai not stop reconstruction of the temple, he also had to fund its completion.

6:11, 12 Also I issue a decree: To ensure obedience, Darius decreed that violation of his order would be punished by death. **Hanged** does not mean hanged by the neck from a rope. It refers to impaling the dead body of the condemned on a pole as a public display and a grim warning to others.

6:13 Tattenai **diligently** carried out the king's orders. There is no indication that Tattenai mistreated the Jews in any way.

6:14 and they prospered: God blessed the people because they listened to the prophets and the preaching of the Word of God. **Artaxerxes** (464–424 B.C.) did assist the rebuilding of the temple, although it was completed years before Artaxerxes came to power. Artaxerxes contributed to the welfare of the temple by issuing a decree regarding its maintenance (7:15, 21).

6:15 The temple was completed in 515 B.C. in **Adar,** the month of February-March.

6:16 celebrated . . . with joy: Some people have suggested that Pss. 145—148 was used to celebrate the completion of the rebuilding of the temple.

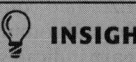 **INSIGHT** | ## State-Established Religion?

In many countries, Christians are a minority and struggle with how to live under unsympathetic or oppressive governments. By contrast, the Jews of Ezra's day, who were a minority in the Persian empire, enjoyed enough freedom to return to their homeland and rebuild their temple (Ezra 6:3, 6, 7). The Persian state officially sanctioned their religion and contributed resources toward the temple project (6:4, 8–10). There are quite different opinions worldwide on the issue of state-supported religion. But whether or not governments support Christians, Scripture exhorts Christians everywhere to pray for the governments under which they live (1 Tim. 2:1, 2).

6:17 As was the case with the dedication of the first temple, this dedication was celebrated with an abundance of **sacrifices.** Although there were more than 200 times as many sheep and oxen offered in Solomon's dedication (1 Kin. 8:63), it should be noted there were more people—and more wealthy people—participating in Solomon's dedication.

6:18 The Law laid down the duties of the **priests** and **Levites** (Num. 18). Later the **divisions** of priests and Levites were instituted by David.

6:19 This celebration of **the Passover** must have been exceptionally memorable; it was the

INSIGHT | **Hanged on a Timber**

The idea of hanging a violator of Darius' decree on a timber from the person's house (Ezra 6:11) may be a reference not to rope hanging but to something like crucifixion. The Persians were known to use impalement as a means of execution, a cruel practice that they inherited from the Assyrians, who were vicious warriors even for those days.

first time since the captivity that the people were able to celebrate according to the Law— with sacrifices offered in the temple (v. 20).

6:20 The priests and the Levites . . . purified themselves so that they could perform the duties of their office. The Levites **slaughtered the Passover lambs** for themselves and others. Originally the Passover lamb was killed by the head of each household (Ex. 12:6). In the days of Hezekiah, the Levites killed the Passover lambs for everyone who was not clean (2 Chr. 30:17). In the days of Josiah, the Levites killed all of the Passover lambs for everyone (2 Chr. 35:10–14). Thus, the observance of Passover was slightly modified over the years, though it was still observed on the original day (compare Ex. 12:6 with Ezra 6:19).

6:21 The nations of the land evidently refers to the people who had been transplanted into Palestine by the Assyrians (4:4). Those **who had separated themselves** were Israelites who had remained in the land during the captivity. The **filth** from which they separated themselves was the idolatry practiced by the pagans and perhaps their intermarriages with foreigners.

6:22 The Feast of Unleavened Bread

immediately followed the Feast of Passover. **The king of Assyria** is a reference to Darius. Even though he was actually the king of Persia, Darius could be called the king of Assyria because he was the ruler of the former realm of Assyria. The title **God of Israel** was probably effective in helping the Jewish people recapture a sense of their true heritage and rekindle their true hope.

7:1–5 after these things: The events of ch. 6 took place during the reign of King Darius; more specifically the temple was completed and dedicated in 515 B.C. Chapter 7 jumps forward many years to the reign of **Artaxerxes** (464–424 B.C.), for Ezra returned around 458 B.C. Thus between chs. 6 and 7 there is a gap of approximately 60 years. During this period, the events of the Book of Esther took place. **Ezra,** the leader of the second return to Jerusalem, is introduced with a long genealogy, demonstrating that he was from a priestly family—the family of **Aaron. Seraiah** saw the fall of Jerusalem (2 Kin. 25:18), and his son Jehozadak went into exile (1 Chr. 6:15). The phrase **son of Seraiah** indicates Ezra's line of descent rather than the name of his father.

7:6, 7 Ezra was not only from a priestly family, he was also **a skilled scribe**—one who copied and studied the Law. After the Exile, the office of scribe came into prominence, in some ways replacing the prophet in importance, and eventually eclipsing even the role of the priest. **The Law of Moses** actually refers to God's law. Moses may have been the person most closely associated with the Law, but it was the Law that **the LORD** God of Israel had given. The latter is by far the more significant designation (John 1:17). The phrase **according to the hand of the LORD** his God upon him is used repeatedly throughout this chapter and the next one (7:9, 28; 8:18, 22, 31; Neh. 2:8, 18). The phrase depicts God's grace working on Ezra's behalf.

7:8, 9 The first month is March-April; the **fifth month** is July-August. The route traveled by Ezra was dangerous because a rebellion had broken out in Egypt and spring was the time when ancient armies began their campaigns.

7:10 Throughout his life, Ezra had concentrated fully on the study, practice, and communication of the Word of God. **Heart** indicates the whole of one's being. Ezra diligently searched the Scriptures so that he could live by them and teach them to Israel. Because of this, the gracious hand of God empowered him (v. 9).

7:11 the priest, the scribe, expert: These words describe Ezra with exceptional praise. Ezra is referred to as "the scribe's scribe" or the teacher of scribes.

7:12 Ancient Middle Eastern monarchs commonly took self-aggrandizing titles such as

INSIGHT   The Skill of a Scribe

The skills that qualified Ezra to be a scribe (Ezra 7:6) were a detailed, technical knowledge of the Law and the ability to teach it (7:10). Officials called scribes had been known during the monarchy, but they were mostly recorders and secretaries. The era of scribes as custodians of the Law began with men like Ezra on the return of the exiles to Palestine.

king of kings (Ezek. 26:7; Dan. 2:37). The Persian kings were literally kings over many kings because the Persian empire included many conquered kingdoms. **Perfect peace** describes a treaty relationship between the Persian emperor and the vassal state of Judah.

7:13–19 Earlier, Ezra had requested permission to return to Jerusalem (7:6). Now the details are given.

7:14 Ezra desired to return to make sure that **the Law** was being observed. His burden was to teach his people God's Law (7:10). **the king and his seven counselors:** The authorization for Ezra came in suitable pomp and circumstance; unknown to the king of Persia was the hand of a greater King at work in the affairs.

7:15–19 Three sources of offerings for the temple are listed: (1) **the silver and gold** of **the king and his counselors,** (2) **the silver and gold** of the people of Babylon, and (3) **the freewill offering** of the Jewish **people** who remained in Babylon. Note that God accepts the gifts of those who do not know Him, as well as the gifts of those who know and serve Him in truth. The only gifts God rejects are those given by people who appear to know Him but whose hearts are far from Him (Is. 1:10–15). The **dwelling** of God **in Jerusalem** is a reference to the temple.

7:20 And whatever more may be needed: Ezra had what amounted to a royal blank check.

7:21–23 The decree of Artaxerxes included an order to the provincial **treasurers** to allow Ezra to claim extra supplies from them. However, there were limits on the supplies. Ezra could take no more than one hundred talents of silver (nearly four tons), one hundred kors of wheat (about 625 bushels), and one hundred baths each of wine and oil (about six hundred gallons each).

7:24 All temple officials were exempt from every form of **tax.** Artaxerxes, like Cyrus (1:2–4) and Darius (6:1–10) before him, wanted to win the goodwill and avoid the wrath of the gods that were worshiped throughout the empire.

7:25, 26 Ezra was given authority to set up a judicial system with the power to punish.

Although the **magistrates and judges** had authority over only Jewish people, their authority extended beyond Jerusalem to Syria, Phoenicia, and Palestine. Ezra later used his authority to punish sin in the community (10:8).

7:27, 28 To beautify the house of the LORD is a reference to the reestablishment of moral, spiritual, and religious life. **I was encouraged:** With renewed vigor, Ezra gathered **leading men of Israel** to return to Jerusalem with him.

8:1 These are the heads of their fathers' houses: The list of people who returned to Jerusalem recalls the list of the men for war at the time of the anticipated conquest of the land of Canaan (Num. 1; 26).

8:2–14 In this list, twelve families are represented by their chiefs and the number of males in each family is given. The total number of the heads of families who accompanied Ezra back to Jerusalem was 1,496.

8:15, 16 Ezra discovered that there were no **sons of Levi** among the returnees who accompanied him back to Jerusalem. Zerubbabel had faced a similar problem. Over four thousand priests returned with him to Jerusalem, but only 74 Levites were among the returnees (2:36–42).

8:17 The location and significance of **Casiphia** is uncertain. It has been suggested that this is Ctesipon on the Tigris River, near modern Baghdad. The Hebrew word for **the place,** a synonym for the holy place (Deut. 12:5), may mean that there was a Jewish sanctuary or temple in Casiphia.

8:18 Sherebiah, a particularly outstanding teacher, means "the burning heat of Yahewh."

8:19–21 On the road to Jerusalem, the large Jewish caravan would have been an easy target for robbers. Knowing that the returnees needed the Lord's help, Ezra **proclaimed a fast** as a symbol of their submission to God.

8:22, 23 To persuade the king to let him return to Jerusalem, Ezra had told him about the **power** and **wrath** of God. So when Ezra received the king's permission to return, he was **ashamed** to ask for an armed **escort.** Later Nehemiah would accept a military escort for his return to Jerusalem (Neh. 2:7–9).

8:24–30 Before the returnees departed, Ezra entrusted the load of valuables to twelve people. Although v. 24 reads as though **Sherebiah, Hashabiah,** and their **brethren** were **priests,** v. 18 indicates that they were Levites. Verse 30 confirms that the treasure was entrusted to priests and Levites. Ezra followed the Law, which taught that the priests were to handle the sacred objects and the Levites were to carry them (Num. 3:8, 31, 45). **the silver, the gold, and the articles:** One talent was about 75 pounds (7:22). The 650 talents of silver weighed nearly 25 tons. The one hundred talents of gold weighed over three tons. These figures do not include the numerous other valuable objects of exquisite artistry.

8:31 According to 7:9, the returnees began their journey on the first day of the first month. According to v. 15, the returnees camped at the river for three days. Yet this verse speaks of the departure on **the twelfth day of the first month.** These time discrepancies may be explained as follows: The people began to assemble at the river on the first day of the first month. During the course of the first three days, Ezra discovered that there were no Levites among the travelers. During the next eight days, Ezra enlisted Levites (vv. 15–20), entreated the Lord (vv. 21–23), and entrusted the travelers' considerable load to the priests and Levites (vv. 24–30). The returnees then departed from the river on the twelfth day. So from their point of view, the journey to Jerusalem began on the first day of the first month, when the people left their homes in Babylon. The group departed from the river on the twelfth day of the first month.

8:32 The returnees arrived in **Jerusalem** on the first day of the fifth month (7:9). The trip took about three and a half months (compare 7:9 with 8:31).

8:33, 34 After three days rest, the returnees deposited their treasury in the temple (Neh. 2:11). Four men—two priests and two Levites—counted and **weighed** everything. A **written** inventory was then put on file.

8:35 The **sin offering,** which consisted of **twelve male goats,** one for each tribe of Israel, was for the atonement for sins. The **burnt offerings** signified the surrender of the entire nation to the service of the Lord.

8:36 The **king's orders** were the authorization for Ezra to administer the Jewish law among the Jewish people of the province. Satraps, or "protectors of the realm," were highly placed individuals who ruled under the emperor in various regions of his empire (5:3).

9:1 When these things were done: These words seem to imply that **the leaders came** to Ezra immediately after the events of ch. 8. Actually, over four months passed between the events of ch. 8 and those of ch. 9. Ezra arrived on the first day of the fifth month (7:9) and he deposited the treasure in the temple on the fourth day of the fifth month (8:33). The assembly that took place soon after the leader's report occurred on the twentieth day of the ninth month (10:9). The delivery of the royal orders to the regional governor (8:36) may have taken weeks or even months. Ezra did not just deliver the decree, he secured the support of the king's satraps and governors. It was after Ezra had delivered the decree and returned to Jerusalem that he received the report from the leaders. **The people . . . have not separated themselves from the peoples of the land:** Both the leaders and the people of Israel had failed to remain separate from the Gentiles who lived in the land. The same kind of problem existed in Zerubbabel's day (6:21). **the abominations of the Canaanites:** The language here reflects that of the Law (Gen. 15:16, 19–21; Deut. 18:9–12). The term *abominations* occurs often in the first five books of the Bible (Deut. 17:1; 18:12; 22:5; 23:18) and in the prophets (Jer. 7:10; 44:22).

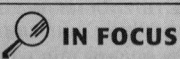 **IN FOCUS**   **"remnant"**

(Heb. *sha'ar*) (Ezra 9:8, 15) Strong's #7604: To be a *remnant* means "to remain" or "to be left over." A remnant is what survives after a catastrophe. In Ezra, the word frequently refers to those Israelites who survived the Exile and returned to resettle the Promised Land (9:8). The prophets use the word to speak not only of a group of Israelites who survived a particular calamity but to those Israelites who remained faithful to God (Amos 5:14, 15). The concept of the remnant is central to Isaiah, who prophesies that the Root of Jesse, the Messiah, would one day gather the remnant of Israel from all the nations, even attracting some Gentiles to Himself (Is. 11:10, 11, 16). The *remnant* therefore becomes a powerful OT theme of covenant faithfulness and salvation, for in sparing His people God maintained a nation through whom all the world would be blessed (Gen. 12:3).

9:2 The Jewish returnees were marrying the pagan peoples of the land, a practice that the Law of Moses expressly prohibited (Ex. 34:16; Deut. 7:3).

9:3–4 Ezra's response demonstrated tremendous grief. Using every immediate symbol he had available to him, he represented the anguish he felt: **tore . . . plucked . . . sat down astonished.** Compare Neh. 13:25.

9:5 knees . . . hands: Physical postures of prayer are often described in the Bible. Kneeling is a sign of humble respect. Raising one's hands is a sign of openness to God and recognizing that all gifts are from the Lord's hand.

9:6 ashamed and humiliated: Ezra felt an overwhelming sense of shame. His prayer was one of confession. Though Ezra had not participated in this sin himself, he identified with the sins of the people.

9:7 Ezra further acknowledged that the people's sinful actions were part of their history. The whole nation—**kings** and **priests,** as well as the people—had sinned in the past, and they had suffered for it at **the hand of the kings of the lands.** This suffering had included **the sword,** loss of life; **captivity,** loss of freedom; **plunder,** loss of property; and **humiliation,** loss of honor.

9:8, 9 a peg in His holy place: This metaphor refers to a peg in the wall on which a utensil is hung (Eccl. 12:11). God's mercy had permitted the remnant to be fixed in the place God had chosen. **enlighten:** God had given the light of His will to those who were in the darkness of sin. **bondage:** The people were no longer slaves; they were free. **repair the house of our God:** The temple had been rebuilt. **wall:** The people had a wall of protection in the form of the king's decree (7:12–26).

9:10–12 Ezra confessed the sins of the nation by referring to what **the prophets** had preached. The prophets (Moses is called a prophet in Deut. 18:15; 34:10; Hos. 12:13) prohibited intermarriage with Gentiles (Deut. 7:1–3; 23:7; Mal. 2:10–16).

9:13–15 Ezra ended his prayer not by asking for forgiveness, but by declaring that God was **righteous** (Deut. 32:4; Ps. 119:137; Zeph. 3:5). Israel was guilty and deserved whatever justice God gave them. God would have been just in consuming them, even to the point that there was **no remnant or survivor.**

10:1–44 This chapter describes what Ezra did to deal with the sin reported to him (9:1). From this point on, Ezra writes in the third person, putting himself in the background.

10:1, 2 Many people in Israel were concerned about the sin in their midst. So while Ezra wept, prayed, and confessed, these people **gathered** around him and **wept very bitterly.**

10:3 Making a **covenant** with God means binding oneself by an oath to God to do something. It was the most binding form of commitment a person could make.

10:4 Arise: Shechaniah (v. 2) reminded Ezra that it was his **responsibility** to teach Israel the Law of God (7:25).

10:5, 6 Jehohanan (a common name) is not the person mentioned in Neh. 6:18.

10:7, 8 within three days: This was a reasonable demand because Bethel (2:28), Lod (2:33), and Jericho (2:34) were some of the more distant Jewish cities, and they were all within three days' journey. According to the Law, the money from the sale of **confiscated** property went into the temple treasury (Lev. 27:28, 29, where *devoted* means "confiscated").

10:9 The ninth month (Chislev; Neh. 1:1) is November-December.

10:10–12 Ezra simply and briefly confronted them with their sin, indicating that these fresh offenses added to the black, bleak account against the nation. He urged them to confess to the Lord and comply to the Law. By a unanimous proclamation all the people agreed.

10:13, 14 The people faced two problems. (1) There were too many of them for the investigation to be done in a day or even two days. (2) The weather would not permit them to stay in Jerusalem. The people who had traveled from a distance could not stay in the city, living and sleeping in the open air, during the cold, rainy period. Therefore they requested that the investigation be organized by their officials.

10:15–17 Two men, with the support of two Levites, opposed Ezra's plan. The reasons for their opposition are not given. Apparently their objections had no effect (vv. 16–18). **Meshullam** is likely the same man who was part of the group of learned teachers that Ezra had recruited (8:16); however, he is not the same man who is mentioned among the repentant offenders in v. 29.

10:18–44 The list of those who had taken pagan wives included 113 men: 17 priests, 10 Levites, and 86 others.

10:19–24 They gave their promise may also be translated "they gave their hand." The symbol of raising a hand to take an oath is still practiced in many cultures. With this sign, the Israelites agreed to put away their unlawful wives and offer a sacrifice according to the requirements of Lev. 5:14–19. Although this promise and sacrifice are mentioned only in connection with the priests, it is likely that everyone on the list fulfilled these requirements.

10:25–44 Others of Israel refers to the people, as opposed to the leaders.

10:44 Even though some had had children with their pagan wives, they still separated themselves from them.

The Book of

Nehemiah

—•—

TIMES OF TRIAL REQUIRE GODLY LEADERSHIP. This book is principally the story of such gifted leadership in the person of Nehemiah. Facing criticism and opposition, Nehemiah resolutely led the small Israelite community as they rebuilt the walls of Jerusalem for its physical protection.

Whereas Ezra was the religious leader in Jerusalem, Nehemiah became the secular leader, the official governor of the Persian

province of Judah (Neh. 5:14). His great concern was the ruined state of the city, left without walls since Artaxerxes I had halted the repairs (Ezra 4:21). Using his position as a trusted servant in the inner court of Artaxerxes, Nehemiah obtained permission to resume the labor and complete Jerusalem's walls. But Nehemiah also did not hesitate to guide the Israelites spiritually. By demanding that the Israelites obey God's Law, Nehemiah pursued their spiritual as well as their physical welfare.

The historical setting of Nehemiah is that of the second half of the Hebrew book of Ezra-Nehemiah (458–420 B.C.). During this period, the Persian emperor Artaxerxes I Longimanus allowed the Jews to return to their land and rebuild Jerusalem. At that time Nehemiah occupied a prominent position in the emperor's court: he was the trusted cupbearer of Artaxerxes I. In Artaxerxes' twentieth year on the throne (444 B.C.), he allowed Nehemiah to go to Jerusalem and rebuild its walls.

Nehemiah stayed in Jerusalem for twelve years and then returned to Persia in Artaxerxes' thirty-second year (432 B.C.). Around 425 B.C., Nehemiah left Persia and returned to Jerusalem

for the last time (13:6). Nehemiah's memoirs could not have been completed until after his second visit to Jerusalem. Thus, the earliest that the Book of Nehemiah could have been completed would be around 425 B.C.

There has been considerable discussion about the order of the returns of Ezra and Nehemiah to Jerusalem. The Bible clearly presents the return of Ezra as preceding that of Nehemiah: Ezra returned in the seventh year of the reign of Artaxerxes (Ezra 7:8) and Nehemiah returned in the twentieth year (2:1). However, based on the way the revival of Ezra appears in the middle of the story of Nehemiah (chs. 8—10), many have argued that Nehemiah returned before Ezra.

The arguments for reversing Ezra and Nehemiah in this way are generally not convincing. Nevertheless, the inclusion of part of the Ezra story in the middle of the Nehemiah memoirs still needs explanation. It could be that Nehemiah's rebuilding the walls of the city was only part of the reconstruction needed among God's people. Even more necessary was the reinstitution of the Law. Certainly Ezra had used the Law previously in his dealings with the people, but at this time the great priest and scribe Ezra partnered with Nehemiah in order to thoroughly teach the people God's Law (8:9). Apparently, the compiler of Nehemiah wanted to show that the wall of the city would mean nothing without the wall of the Law surrounding the people.

In His covenant with Israel, God had spoken of a place where He would establish His name. In fact, Moses had told the Israelites to "seek the place where the LORD your God chooses, out of all your tribes, to put His name for His dwelling place" (Deut. 12:5). Later, it was revealed that this place was Jerusalem. When the temple was built during Solomon's reign, Jerusalem was at the height of its glory. Its fame helped to spread the glory of God's name throughout the nations. But God allowed Jerusalem to be destroyed because of the faithlessness of the Israelites. Even though Jerusalem lay in ruins during Nehemiah's time, it was still God's purpose to establish His name there.

The Book of Nehemiah records the restoration of Jerusalem under the leadership of Nehemiah. In the book, the returning Jews showed spiritual lethargy and a coldhearted indifference toward God. This problem continued, for the Book of Malachi denounces the Israelites for the same attitudes. It took a determined, godly leader like Nehemiah to motivate this group to act on God's promises and rebuild Jerusalem's walls.

However, the completion of Jerusalem's walls is only half the story of Nehemiah. The walls are rebuilt by chapter six, but the book has seven more chapters. These last chapters record a revival and describe the repopulation of the city. The subject of the book is not merely the rebuilding of the walls, but the complete restoration of the people of Jerusalem.

The Book of Nehemiah makes it clear that God did not restore His people only one time; rather, He repeatedly and continually restored them. He sent a number of prophets and leaders to teach, motivate, and guide the people into righteousness. Zerubbabel led a group of exiles to Jerusalem and began to rebuild the temple (Ezra 1—6). Then Ezra led a second group of exiles back to Jerusalem and helped restore the people to obedience to the Mosaic law (Ezra 7–10). Then Nehemiah returned and motivated the people to rebuild the walls of Jerusalem (chs. 1–6). Finally, Nehemiah returned a second time and exhorted the people to adhere closely to God's Law (ch. 13).

The pattern is clear: God continually restored His people. In spite of their unfaithfulness, God accomplished His will. The restored walls of Jerusalem, the repopulation of Jerusalem, and the repeated reformation of the Israelites was clearly God's work. In the end, His name would be glorified.

Many readers naturally conclude that the book was written by Nehemiah because of the words of the first verse, "The words of Nehemiah the son of Hachaliah." In fact, it is widely believed that Nehemiah originated the following passages: 1:1—7:5; 12:27–43; 13:4–31. But there are two different views the authorship of the rest of Nehemiah. Some believe that Nehemiah wrote the whole book, relying on his own memories. Others believe that Ezra wrote the book, using Nehemiah's memoirs, for the passages listed above. As evi-

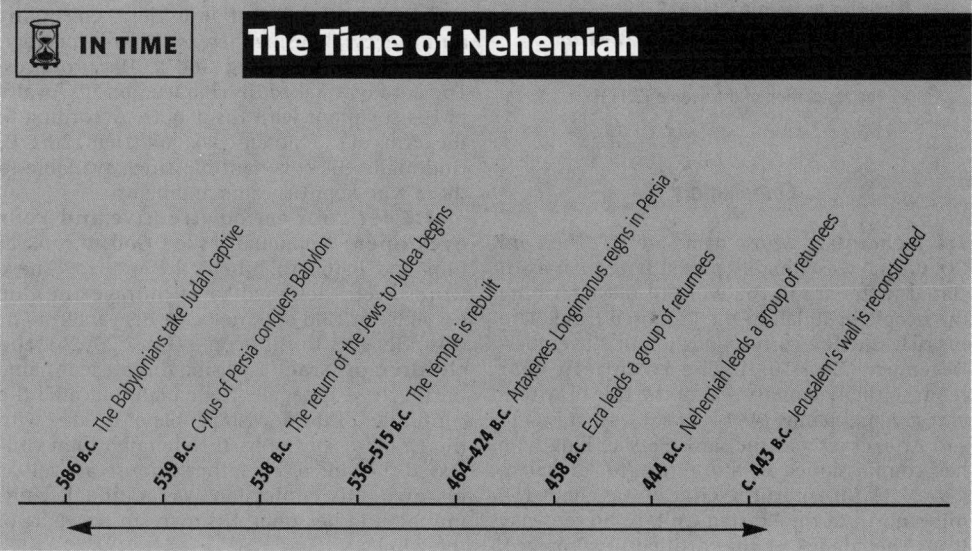

IN TIME

The Time of Nehemiah

586 B.C. The Babylonians take Judah captive

539 B.C. Cyrus of Persia conquers Babylon

538 B.C. The return of the Jews to Judea begins

536–515 B.C. The temple is rebuilt

464–424 B.C. Artaxerxes Longimanus reigns in Persia

458 B.C. Ezra leads a group of returnees

444 B.C. Nehemiah leads a group of returnees

c. 443 B.C. Jerusalem's wall is reconstructed

dence for the second view, it is noted that Neh. 7:5–73 and Ezra 2:1–70 are almost identical.

The similarities of Nehemiah and Ezra can be explained partly by the fact that they are only one book in the Hebrew Bible (see the Introduction for Ezra). In fact, many scholars argue that Chronicles, Ezra, and Nehemiah were compiled by the same person. All these books exhibit similar themes, such as a focus on the Levites, the temple, and extensive lists. With such priestly interests, the one who masterminded this long document may well have been a priest—like Ezra (see the Introduction to First Chronicles).

Outline

Commentary

1:1 Nehemiah, whose name means "The Lord Comforts," was a highly placed statesman associated with Ezra in the work of reestablishing the people of Judah in the Promised Land. **The month Chislev** corresponds to our November-December (Ezra 10:9). **The twentieth year** refers to the twentieth year of the rule of Artaxerxes I Longimanus (464–424 B.C.)—that is, 444 B.C. Artaxerxes was the same Persian king who had commissioned Ezra to return to Jerusalem (Ezra 7:1). **Shushan the citadel** was about 150 miles north of the Persian Gulf, in present-day Iran. The citadel, or the fortified royal palace,

was built on an acropolis. The city served as a winter residence for the monarchs of Persia. Shushan is also notable in biblical history as the place where Daniel received his vision of the rams and goats (Dan. 8:2), and as the home of Mordecai and Esther (Esth. 1:2).

1:2 Nehemiah's brother **Hanani** (7:2) had visited Jerusalem and returned to Shushan. This journey, which covered nearly a thousand miles one way, would probably have taken at least four months. It had taken Ezra and his caravan four months to make a similar round trip from Babylon to Jerusalem (Ezra 7:9). Nehemiah was concerned about the Jewish people and Jerusalem.

1:3 Life was difficult for the people in Jerusalem. This difficulty was due in large part to the condition of Jerusalem's **wall.** In the ancient Middle East, a city wall provided protection for the inhabitants. The condition of a city wall was also seen as an indication of the strength of the people's gods. The ruined condition of the wall of Jerusalem reflected badly on God's name.

1:4 wept . . . mourned: Nehemiah was deeply disturbed. Without a wall, Jerusalem was vulnerable to attack. The riches of the temple treasury (Ezra 8:15–36) would have been quite a temptation for Israel's enemies. **God of heaven:** This title for God is used frequently in the books of Ezra and Nehemiah.

1:5 LORD: Nehemiah called on God by using His covenant name (Ex. 6:2–9). Nehemiah's use of this title is similar to our use of the phrase "in Jesus' name" in our prayers. **God of heaven:** Nehemiah acknowledged God's government of the world, including His sovereignty over the pagan king who was over Nehemiah, the Jewish people, and the city of Jerusalem. **covenant and mercy:** By using these two words together, Nehemiah was holding God to His promises. The Lord had staked His character on His loyalty to His covenant with His people. According to the terms of the Mosaic covenant (Deut. 28; 29), God made His covenant blessings available to those who kept His commandments.

1:6 let Your ear be attentive and Your eyes open: Nehemiah asked God to look at him and listen to him as he prayed. These words were designed to encourage the one praying, for God does not turn His ears from or close His eyes to His people (Ex. 2:23–25). **the children of Israel:** By using this ancient name for the Jewish people, Nehemiah indicated the continuity of the Jewish people of his day with the Israelites of the past: Nehemiah then confessed the sins of his father's house as well as his own. His confession was national, communal, and personal. His own sin was part of the whole.

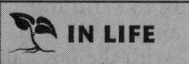 IN LIFE

Leadership Principles from Nehemiah, Part 1

Leaders Have a Sense of Mission (1:5).

Almost by definition, leaders have an end to which they are headed. This sense of mission helps to guide their decisions and determine their strategy.

Nehemiah's mission grew out of his knowledge of the Law and his awareness that the destruction of Jerusalem had come about through God's judgment of his people's sins (Neh. 1:5–8). At the same time, he knew that God was willing to forgive their sins and restore them to the land (1:9). Therefore Nehemiah determined that he would see to the rebuilding of Jerusalem, in accordance with the Lord's promises, and he began to devise a strategy toward that end (1:10, 11).

Nehemiah did not dream up a sense of mission out of his own agenda or self-interest. He responded to the news of Jerusalem's plight with tears, prayer, fasting, humility, and seeking the Lord's will (1:4). As he prepared to go before the king, he probably did not know exactly what he should say or do, only that he needed to go to Jerusalem. Nor could he have known all that he would encounter once he arrived at the ruined city. Nevertheless, convinced that God wanted the Holy City to be revived, Nehemiah stepped forward as a change agent, and his leadership proved strategic.

1:7 Israel had sinned against the Lord and against His **commandments.** By using the word **we,** Nehemiah included himself among the sinful people. **commandments . . . statutes . . . ordinances:** These words describe the totality of God's Law (9:13, 14).

1:8 Remember: After confessing his sin and the sin of the people, Nehemiah reminded God of what He Himself had said. **I will scatter you among the nations:** This is an allusion to God's covenant in Lev. 26:27–45 and Deut. 30:1–5. Nehemiah himself was born in Persia, a distant nation, because of God's fulfillment of this promise.

1:9 The Lord had promised that if the nation of Israel would **return** to Him in obedience, He would regather them to their land. Nehemiah addressed the Lord as a covenant-keeping God. He confessed his and the people's sin because the Law demanded confession (Lev. 16:21). Then he held God to His covenant to return Israel to the land. **bring them to the place which I have chosen as a dwelling for My name:** The ultimate intent of God's covenant was not just to return the people, but to return them to the place where God had established His name. For that to be accomplished, much needed to be done. So while it was true that some people had returned to the land and that the temple had been rebuilt, the fact remained that Jerusalem's wall was in ruins and the people were under reproach (5:9). In that sense, Jerusalem had not yet been restored.

1:10 Your servants and Your people: By using this phrasing, Nehemiah was suggesting to the Lord that the time was right, the people were right, and the task was right to restore Jerusalem. **Your strong hand** is one of the phrases associated with God's deliverance of Israel from Egypt (Ex. 6:1; 13:14; 15:6; Deut. 6:21).

1:11 Your servant . . . Your servants: Nehemiah and the godly people of Israel shared common concerns before God. **let Your servant prosper:** Nehemiah requested per-

 IN FOCUS **"confess"**

(Heb. *yadah*) (Neh. 1:6; Lev. 5:5; Num. 5:7; Pss. 92:1; 106:47) Strong's #3034: This Hebrew verb conveys two distinct meanings. The first is related to the offering of thanksgiving or praise to God (2 Chr. 5:13; Ps. 92:1; 106:47). The second is that of confession, such as the confession of God's greatness (1 Kin. 8:33, 35) and the confession of sin before God (Neh. 1:6; 9:2; Dan. 9:4). The basic meaning *yadah* is "to throw" or "to cast off." In one sense, confession is the "casting off" of sin by acknowledging our transgressions of God's commandments for holy living (Ps. 32:5; Prov. 28:13). In another sense, confession of sin is thanksgiving because it recognizes that forgiveness of sin is accomplished only by the grace and goodness of God (2 Chr. 30:22; Dan. 9:4).

mission to return to Jerusalem, rebuild the wall, and restore the community. He enjoyed the comfort and convenience of a royal palace and a position of honor and responsibility. There were many compelling reasons for him to stay where he was, but he asked for permission to do God's work. As **the king's cupbearer,** Nehemiah held an honored position. His constant proximity to the king of Persia made him privy to the state secrets and personal affairs of the king.

2:1 Nisan corresponds to March-April. **sad in his presence:** Four months after hearing the report from his brother concerning Jerusalem, Nehemiah was still grieving over the conditions in Jerusalem.

2:2 The king noticed Nehemiah's sad expression and concluded that it was caused by **sorrow of** heart rather than physical illness. **I became dreadfully afraid:** Persian monarchs believed that just being in their presence would make any person happy. Yet, Nehemiah was about to request the emperor's permission to go to Jerusalem, suggesting that he would rather be somewhere other than in the emperor's presence. On top of that, it was Artaxerxes himself who had ordered the work on the wall to be stopped (Ezra 4:21–23). Nehemiah had reason to be afraid.

2:3 live forever: Addressing the king with proper respect, Nehemiah related the burden of his heart. **the place of my fathers' tombs:** It is possible that this phrase was designed to catch the king's attention. In many Asian cultures, a connection with the burial places of one's ancestors was a matter of great importance.

2:4 I prayed: Even though Nehemiah had come into the presence of **the king,** he had never left the presence of the true King of kings.

2:5 After his silent prayer (v. 4), Nehemiah spoke boldly, asking for permission to leave the king's palace to travel to Jerusalem to rebuild the wall. Again Nehemiah spoke of his **fathers' tombs** (v. 3). Though this was not his principal concern, it must have been something he thought would be important to the king.

2:6 the queen: It is possible that Nehemiah implied by this parenthetical phrase that her presence influenced the king's decision. She may have looked on Nehemiah with a special grace. It is also possible that he had waited for a time when she would be present (v. 1). **How long will your journey be . . . when will you return:** In responding to Nehemiah's request (v. 5), the king might have had Nehemiah executed on the spot; or he might have dismissed Nehemiah with a laugh. However, his questions implied that the request was already granted. **I set him a time:** The fact that Nehemiah responded quickly to the king's request for spe-

cific details indicates that he had been planning the trip. **it pleased the king to send me:** The king not only sent Nehemiah to Jerusalem, he made him governor (5:14). With the possibility of unrest in Egypt and in Cyprus, the king might have decided that Jerusalem needed a wall after all (Ezra 4:21).

2:7 Nehemiah knew that he needed safe passage for his journey to **Judah,** so he requested **letters** from the king to show to **the governors of the region beyond the** Euphrates **River.**

2:8 Nehemiah's plans were detailed. He asked the king for permission to go to Jerusalem (v. 5), for letters to ensure safe passage (v. 7), and also for provisions. Nehemiah requested a letter addressed to **Asaph,** the man in charge of **the king's forest,** to enable him to obtain supplies of lumber for three projects: (1) the **gates of the citadel,** (2) **the city wall,** and (3) his personal **house.** Jerusalem had plenty of limestone for building projects. But timber, necessary for making roofs and other parts of large building projects, was scarce. The citadel was a fortress situated just northwest of the temple. It overlooked and protected the temple area. **according to the good hand of my God:** The king graciously granted Nehemiah all that he had requested, but Nehemiah knew that the ultimate source of his provisions was God.

2:9 captains of the army and horsemen: Nehemiah had a military escort to Jerusalem. In 458 B.C. Ezra had journeyed to Jerusalem with 1,800 people carrying valuable treasures, and had refused a military escort (Ezra 8:22). Fourteen years later, Nehemiah made the same trip with a smaller company and no valuables, but the king sent an escort with him.

2:10, 11 Some have suggested that since he traveled lighter than Ezra had, Nehemiah may have taken the shorter route from Shushan to Tadmor through Damascus, thus following the Jordan Valley to Jericho. He and his party would therefore avoid the Samaritan community and arrive in Jerusalem with no opposition. If that was their intention, it did not work. **Sanballat** was the governor of Samaria. **Horonite** refers to Sanballat's city Beth-Horon. **Tobiah** was probably Sanballat's secretary and confidential advisor. **Ammonite:** At the time of Nehemiah, the Ammonites (Gen. 19:38) had pushed west into the land vacated by Judah. The prospect of a strong Jewish community in newly fortified Jerusalem would have seemed threatening to the Ammonite power.

2:12–15 Since Nehemiah had arrived in Jerusalem from the north, he would have seen that side of the wall as he approached the city. If he lived in the southwestern part of the city, he would have had ample time for viewing the western wall. Nehemiah seems to have been concerned with inspecting the southern and eastern walls of Jerusalem. With a few servants, he passed through **the Valley Gate** into the Valley of Hinnom. He then traveled along the south wall. When the piles of stone and heaps of rubble obstructed his passage, he dismounted his animal and continued on foot

up the Kidron valley in order to view the eastern wall.

2:16 the officials did not know: The only people who knew Nehemiah's plans were the few men who had made the secret night ride with him (v. 12).

2:17 we: Nehemiah encouraged all of the people to assist in rebuilding the city's walls.

2:18 Nehemiah emphasized that it was not

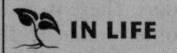 **IN LIFE** | # Leadership Principles from Nehemiah, Part 2

Leaders Leverage Their Power (2:5)

Management has been defined as the ability to get things done through other people. However, that can happen only if the people involved are in a position to get things done. Thus leaders must use their influence to get people of means participating in their efforts.

Nehemiah followed this principle in his plan to rebuild Jerusalem. He was in a key position of influence as the cupbearer to Artaxerxes (Neh. 2:1). He had the king's ear, and he leveraged his proximity to power for the advantage of his people. He requested and was granted a leave of absence (2:5, 6), letters of reference (2:7), and a government grant for building materials (2:8).

Today, the ability to leverage power is an indispensable requirement of leadership, especially for those who work in community development and urban ministry. There are plenty of resources to help the poor, for example, but it takes wise and disciplined leaders to align themselves with the powerful on behalf of the powerless. Tasks such as grant-writing, resource development, and asset distribution require careful cultivation of relationships with those in the networks of power.

Leaders Conduct Research (2:12)

A missile without a guidance system is a dangerous thing—all power and no direction. In the same way, leaders who don't know where they are going can wreak havoc. That's why it pays for people in leadership positions to gather the right kind of information, so that they can make wise choices about which path to pursue.

Before he launched his plan to rebuild the walls of Jerusalem, Nehemiah conducted careful research about the task at hand. He quietly walked around the city by night, without fanfare, surveying the extent of the problem and perhaps formulating some tentative strategies (2:11–15). Nehemiah's low profile was especially appropriate given that he was a new member of the community. As a representative of the king, he could have come in with trumpets blaring and declared what his expectations were. Instead, he kept his thoughts to himself and avoided attracting attention until he had formulated a plan.

Leaders Build Community (2:17, 18)

In many Western countries of the twentieth century, the labor force often has been sharply divided between management and labor. One problem of this rigid distinction is that it tends to create a mentality of "us" versus "them." History shows that most of the greatest achievements of humanity have been accomplished by teams and communities of people working together toward common ends.

Nehemiah understood the power of community as he undertook the task of rebuilding Jerusalem's walls. After surveying the situation, he gathered the people and gave a speech in which he mobilized the community around the rebuilding project. First he raised their awareness that something should be done, then he instilled confidence in them that something could be done—by them (2:17, 18).

It is interesting to notice that Nehemiah spoke in terms of "we" and "us," even though in his written account he used "they" and "them." Clearly he saw himself as a participant in the dire circumstances, even though he had just arrived from the royal palace. In fact, he bridged the class division between himself and his people by sharing the discussion he had had with the king, thereby showing that the people had a friend in the emperor's court.

just *his* idea to rebuild the wall of Jerusalem. Rather, the idea had come to him from the Lord (vv. 8, 12). In response to Nehemiah's challenge, the people replied, **Let us rise up and build.**

2:19 In v. 10, Nehemiah here mentioned two men who were unhappy about his coming—Sanballat and Tobiah. Here the opposition grows to three. **Geshem** was the leader of a company of Arab troops maintained by Sanballat. In v. 10, Nehemiah's opponents were grieved; here **they laughed.** They accused Nehemiah of false motives, of plotting rebellion against the king. The same charge had been directed against the Jewish people in Zerubbabel's time (Ezra 4).

2:20 Nehemiah ignored his opponents' accusation that he was rebelling against the king. He asserted that God was involved in what he was doing. Nehemiah's motive was not rebellion against the king, but submission to God. **you have no heritage:** Nehemiah indicated that Samaritans and foreign people had no place in Jerusalem (Ezra 4:3).

3:1–32 The people work to rebuild Jerusalem's wall. This chapter has four parts: (1) rebuilding the northern portion (vv. 1–7); (2) rebuilding the western portion (vv. 8–13); (3) rebuilding the southern portion (v. 14); (4) rebuilding the eastern portion (vv. 15–32). Approaches to studying this chapter vary. Some readers move through it quickly. Others use it for a detailed study of the topography of Jerusalem, for this chapter gives the most detailed specifications of the wall to be found in the Bible. Others approach this chapter by spiritualizing the gates. For example, the Sheep Gate is said to represent the Cross, where Christ the Lamb of God died for the sins of the world; the Fish Gate reminds allegorists of Christ's statement, "I will make you fishers of men," suggestive of soul winning. And so on. Nevertheless, one salient point of this chapter, which must not be missed, is simply that the people rolled up their sleeves and went to work.

Nehemiah is not mentioned one time in the whole chapter, but the people are named. The Hebrew word translated **build** occurs seven times and **repair** thirty-four times. Many other words and phrases for construction are also used. The point being that the people built the wall, and they worked as hard as they said they would (2:18).

3:1 Eliashib the high priest and the other **priests** were the first people to start rebuilding Jerusalem's walls. At this point in Israel's history, the priests were the leaders. There were no kings or judges, so the people looked to the priests for leadership. It is significant that the high priest and the priests **built the Sheep Gate.** The Sheep Gate was on Jerusalem's northeast side, just north of the temple and was used for bringing sheep to the temple for sacrifice. **they consecrated it:** The priests dedicated the repaired gate, wall, and tower to the Lord. They knew that unless God blessed the city with His presence, no walls and gates would keep the people safe (Ps. 127:1).

3:2–4 Next to: The idea here is that the people worked together—not just in the same place, but in cooperation.

3:5–7 God also took notice of those who did not work.

3:8–13 These verses detail the rebuilding of the western portion of Jerusalem's wall.

3:8 The Broad Wall was probably built in the seventh century B.C. by Hezekiah to accommodate the influx of refugees from the fall of Samaria in 722 B.C. (2 Chr. 32:5).

3:9–14 These verses describe the rebuilding of the southern portion of Jerusalem's wall.

3:15–32 These verses detail the rebuilding of the eastern portion of Jerusalem's wall.

3:15 The Fountain Gate probably faced the En Rogel spring. **The Pool of Shelah** is also known as the Pool of Siloam or Shiloah.

3:16–20 Carefully prepared translates the Hebrew verb *heherâ*, meaning "to burn." In other words, Baruch had a burning zeal for the work. He is the only person of whom this is said.

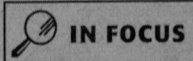 **IN FOCUS**   **"carefully"**

(Heb. *charah*) (Neh. 3:20; Ex. 32:10; Jon. 4:1) Strong's #2734: The Hebrew verb translated *carefully* here usually means "to burn with anger" (Gen. 39:19; Jon. 4:1) and depicts anger as a burning fire. This is the type of intense anger the Lord displayed when the Israelites worshiped a worthless idol of a calf instead of their Deliverer (the word is translated *burn hot* in Ex. 32:10). In the present passage, the word denotes burning with zeal, not anger. In other words, Baruch earnestly wanted to repair the walls of Jerusalem because he knew it was God's city and God's work. His repairs were for the glory of the living Lord.

3:21–28 In the easternmost part of the city, **the Horse Gate** was the gate leading to the Kidron valley.

3:29–32 **Goldsmiths** and **merchants** also labored on the wall. They were not bricklayers, but they worked just the same.

4:1 furious . . . indignant: These two words together mean "burning with rage."

4:2 Sanballat gathered men from the **army of Samaria,** his local militia, and then mocked the Jewish people with sarcastic questions. **these feeble Jews:** The verb from which the adjective *feeble* is derived is used of a woman who is no longer able to bear children (1 Sam. 2:5), of a fisherman whose trade fails (Is. 19:8), and of the inhabitants of a defeated land (Hos. 4:3). **fortify . . . offer sacrifices . . . complete it in a day . . . revive the stones:** Sanballat poured contempt on the Jewish people and on their God. The reference to reviving the stones came from the fact that the stones of the former wall had been **burned.** When limestone is subjected to intense heat, it becomes unsuitable for building.

4:3 Tobiah, the aide of Sanballat (2:10, 19), carried Sanballat's jest (v. 2) even further. Tobiah declared that if a small creature like **a fox** jumped on the wall, the wall would collapse because of its flimsy construction.

4:4, 5 Nehemiah did not respond to his opponents (vv. 2, 3). Instead, he prayed that the Lord would not forgive them. Nehemiah believed that when the people of God were involved in the work of God, any assault on them was an assault on God. In this case, to despise the Jewish workers was to despise God Himself.

4:6 Nehemiah went back to work immediately, and the people followed because they **had a mind to work.**

4:7, 8 When their ridicule did not stop the work on the wall, Nehemiah's opponents tried a threat of attack. The opposition against Nehemiah had started with two people (2:10) and had grown to three (2:19). Here it had become a multitude, one which surrounded Jerusalem. **Sanballat** was a Samaritan; Samaria was north of Jerusalem. **The Arabs** were to the south, **the Ammonites** to the east and **the Ashdodites** to the west.

4:9 Prior to this verse the prayers recorded in the Book of Nehemiah are individual prayers. This one was a group prayer. Nehemiah's spirit had affected the entire group of workers. They not only prayed, but they set a **watch** and did what was humanly possible to protect themselves from attack.

4:10 Under the circumstances, some of the workers became discouraged. The wall was half finished (v. 6), but the task was taking its toll. The words of the fatigued **laborers** appear as a song or poem in the Hebrew text.

4:11, 12 While the Jewish workers became discouraged (v. 10), the opposition intensified. The **adversaries** began a whispering campaign among the Jewish people to stop the building of the wall. These enemies used fear as a weapon, and they used the Jewish people to do their dirty work.

4:13 I positioned men: Because there was no Jewish army, the people had to defend themselves. Nehemiah placed men strategically on the wall. From the high places on the wall, men could see the approaching enemy. Other men defended the low places of the wall.

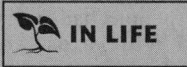 **IN LIFE**

Leadership Principles from Nehemiah, Part 3

Leaders Adapt to Adversity (4:8, 9)

Many people run from adversity; wise leaders expect it to happen occasionally. Wherever change and progress are underway, competing interests inevitably rise to challenge them. At that point, leaders must decide whether they will accept the challenge and meet it, or turn tail and let their opponents set the agenda.

Nehemiah's adversaries were a group of Jews from racially mixed backgrounds and Gentiles who had a vested interest in seeing that Jerusalem remained unprotected (Neh. 4:7). During the seventy years of Judah's exile, they had established dominance over those left behind. Therefore, Nehemiah's plan to rebuild the walls and revitalize the city threatened to end their monopoly on control.

Nehemiah responded to their opposition with resolute faith and prayer and measured resistance. Rather than escalate a touchy situation, he defended against attack and kept on working. Thus he adapted to adversity rather than run from it or overreact to it. God eventually rewarded Nehemiah's perseverance with the completion of the wall (6:15).

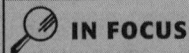 **IN FOCUS** | **"awesome"**

(Heb. *yare'*) (Neh. 1:5; 4:14; Gen. 32:11) Strong's #3372: The Hebrew word translated *awesome* is derived from the Hebrew verb meaning "to fear." In this context, the word does not mean "frightening." Rather it suggests the quality that inspires reverence or godly fear. In some Bible passages, "fearing" and godly living are so closely related that they are almost synonymous (Lev. 19:14; 25:17; Deut. 17:19; 2 Kin. 17:34). Thus while ordinary fear paralyzes a person, godly fear leads to submission and obedience to God. The person who properly fears God avoids evil (Job 1:1) and walks in God's ways (Ps. 128:1).

4:14, 15 nobles . . . leaders . . . rest of the people: Nehemiah's strategy was to address both leaders and laypeople. In this way, all the community would have "ownership" of the same ideals. **fight for your brethren:** Nehemiah reminded the Jewish people that they were not mercenary soldiers earning a salary or hoping for loot. Not only were their own lives at stake, but so were the lives of their loved ones. God answered Nehemiah's prayers. The people were inspired by his wise words and **returned** to their tasks.

4:16–18 Nehemiah armed the workers and divided his own **servants** into two groups. Half of them worked on the wall and half of them stood guard. Since the builders needed both hands to work, their swords were hung on their sides. Those who carried baskets of debris on their heads held their weapons in one hand and supported the load with the other.

4:19, 20 Nehemiah instituted an alarm system for those who worked on the wall. Apparently the workers were scattered all over the wall and separated so far from each other that some were beyond the reach of the human voice. For that reason, a trumpeter with a ram's horn stood near Nehemiah wherever he went. If the wall was attacked, the alarm would gather all of the people quickly to the danger spot. **Our God will fight for us:** These words evoked the spirit of the Exodus (Num. 10:1–10). God had fought for their ancestors, and now God would fight for them.

4:21–23 Nehemiah instituted a twenty-four hour work and watch program. The people worked during the day and stood guard at night. Workers living out of town were asked to remain in the city rather than return home. Except for **washing,** Nehemiah and his men never took off their **clothes.** They worked day and night. Chapter four illustrates three types of opposition to Nehemiah and the people of Jerusalem: opposition by ridicule, opposition by threat of attack, opposition by fear. Nehemiah ignored the ridicule; he prayed and he persisted.

He met the threat with prayer and by putting up a watch. He handled the fear by pointing to the Lord and by preparing the people for battle. His approach might be stated in two words: prayer and persistence, bound together.

5:1–5 The prolonged period of working, watching, fear, and weariness inevitably led to trouble among the people in Jerusalem. There were three groups of complainers, each introduced with the phrase **there were those who said.** The first group had large families, and did not have enough food to eat. The second group had large mortgages to pay and could not buy food. The third group had large taxes to pay and had been forced to mortgage their land and even to sell their children. While hunger, shortages, taxes, and money were the immediate results of the people's circumstances, they were not the heart of the problem. The people's basic problem is pinpointed in the words **against their Jewish brethren.** The people were not complaining merely about poverty and high taxes; they were grumbling about each other. In v. 1 the **people** refers to the poor; the *brethren* refers to the rich rulers (v. 7). In short, this was a class conflict. The poor people had **mortgaged** their **lands and vineyards and houses.** They had **borrowed money** and even had sold their sons and daughters into slavery. From the perspective of the Law, there were two problems here: (1) usury, lending money and charging interest, and (2) slavery. It was not wrong for a Jewish person to lend money with interest to a non-Jewish person (Deut. 23:19, 20), nor was it wrong for a Jewish person to lend money to a fellow Jew. However, the Law did prohibit usury (Ex. 22:25). Interest rates were exorbitant and could easily lead a person into poverty and enslavement. This leads to the second problem. According to the Law of Moses, a Jewish person could hire himself out to someone, but not as a slave (Lev. 25:35–40).

5:6 I became very angry: Nehemiah's first response to the sins of the Jewish people was anger. Deliberate disobedience to the Word of

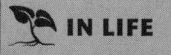 **IN LIFE** | # Leadership Principles from Nehemiah, Part 4

Leaders Resist Underhanded Politics (6:5–9)

Having failed to intimidate Nehemiah into stopping the work, Sanballat and his followers tried smear tactics to shut the project down (Neh. 6:5–7). Frustrated opponents often resort to that approach when other methods have proven useless.

The Bible does not explain why Nehemiah so easily dismissed their accusations (6:8) and apparently took no steps to prevent their letters from reaching the king. However, it seems plausible that he was relying on his years of trustworthy service as the king's cupbearer. He might have known that he had the full trust of King Artaxerxes, who would quickly see through the deception of anyone who accused Nehemiah of sedition. He also knew the process by which letters such as those Sanballat had written would be read and evaluated.

In short, Nehemiah had a clear conscience and an impeccable reputation. Therefore, no amount of "mud" could cause him to lose heart. He knew that none of it would stick. Further, Nehemiah did not resort to slinging mud himself. He probably could have come up with plenty of counter-accusations against his adversaries. But rather than waste time on a verbal exchange that would have distracted him from the wall, he prayed and ignored the politics swirling outside the city.

Leaders Serve People (7:1)

Some people regard leadership primarily as the art of getting results. Great leaders, they say, are those who get the job done. It matters very little how they operate, as long as they achieve their goals. But when we examine the great leaders of Scripture, we find that they not only accomplished much, but served people in the process.

Nehemiah illustrates the point rather well. His project of rebuilding the wall of Jerusalem was never an end in itself. The ultimate objective was to revitalize the people of Israel and return them to their covenant with God. To that end, after the wall was completed, Nehemiah turned the city's management over to local government leaders (7:1, 2). He did not create dependency on his own skills, nor did he use the project to gain wealth or fame for himself (5:18). Instead, right from the start, Nehemiah began the process of turning over management of Jerusalem to others.

Nehemiah also helped the people trace their roots by reviewing the census taken twenty-five years earlier in Ezra's time (7:5). That set the stage for repopulating the city (Neh. 11:1, 2) and continuing the initiative of urban revitalization.

God ought to make a person indignant toward the sin—but not toward the sinner.

5:7–10 After getting angry at the sins of the Jewish people (v. 6), Nehemiah spent some time in **serious thought.** He then confronted the guilty people. **rebuked:** This term is used often by the prophets to speak of legal cases brought against guilty persons (13:11). After rebuking the guilty parties privately, Nehemiah confronted them in public with the same charges. **not good:** Two issues were at stake here—**fear** of God (1:5) and **the reproach of the nations.** When Israel, a nation called by the Lord, stopped honoring and obeying Him, it became a scandal because God's name was being dishonored.

5:11, 12 Nehemiah challenged the lenders to **restore** what they had taken with interest. The **hundredth of the money** is probably a reference to the interest they had been charging.

5:13 Nehemiah **shook** his **garment** as if he were getting rid of what he was carrying. In doing so, he dramatized what God would do if the people broke their promise. God would shake them loose from their houses and their possessions.

5:14–19 This section summarizes Nehemiah's time as governor. What he did, as recorded here, contrasts to what the nobles had done (vv. 1–13). They had been selfish; he was unselfish. They were out for what they could get; he was there for what he could give. They were thinking of themselves; he was thinking of God and God's people. Nehemiah contrasts his own fear of God (v. 15) with their lack of this fear (v. 9). He contrasts his behavior with that of governors who had preceded him (v. 15). He had not come for self-serving reasons (v. 16) but to serve others (v. 17). His table was heavily loaded with wonderful foods and wine (v. 18) but not at the expense of others. Indeed, he managed not to use the provisions he might have exacted from the people as their governor (vv. 14, 18) because he knew their troubles were already many. And, in all, he desired the sense of God's pleasure (v. 19).

5:14 During his twelve-year administration (444–432 B.C.), Nehemiah did not collect taxes from the people, although as governor he had that right.

5:15 Several **former governors** had paid their own expenses with the people's taxes. **laid burdens:** The former governors had made life difficult for the people. **Rule** here indicates an arbitrary, oppressive rule—the abuse of power through extortion.

5:16–18 Nehemiah had not acquired mortgages on **land.** As governor, he could easily have acquired real estate and sold it at great profit. But instead of making money for themselves, Nehemiah and his servants worked on the wall of Jerusalem for the protection of the people and the glory of God.

5:19 Nehemiah's motives were pure. He was not doing **good** for the praise of men, but to please God. His prayer is repeated at the end of the book (13:31).

6:1, 2 Nehemiah's enemies, realizing that open opposition had not worked and that the wall was close to being finished, suggested a conference. **The plain of Ono** was about twenty miles northwest of Jerusalem. Somehow, perhaps by a word from the Lord, Nehemiah was warned of his enemy's intent.

6:3–6 an open letter: In those days, a letter to a leader might be folded in a silk bag and sealed, and only opened by the person to whom it had been sent. The letter here, however, was for public display. In it, the Jewish people were accused of wanting **to rebel.**

6:7 The evidence that was used to accuse Nehemiah of rebellion was the assertion that **prophets** were proclaiming Nehemiah to be king. Zechariah had prophesied that a king was coming (Zech. 9:9). With all the activity of rebuilding of the wall, people were probably talking about what Zechariah had said. Nehemiah's enemies threatened to take the matter to the king of Persia. They used this threat as leverage to force Nehemiah to attend their proposed meeting. Although they had no real intention of going to the king (v. 9), they hoped their threats would ruin Nehemiah's reputation so that the workers would lose their resolve.

6:8, 9 Nehemiah would not allow himself to get sidetracked. Instead, he committed his enemy's accusations to the Lord (Ps. 31:13, 14). His enemies wanted to weaken his hands, so he prayed for the Lord to **strengthen him.**

6:10 Evidently **Shemaiah** was a priest.

When Nehemiah visited him, Shemaiah proposed that they enter the holy place to be safe from assassins. Shemaiah's suggestion was for Nehemiah to flee into the sanctuary. It was lawful for an Israelite to seek refuge at the altar outside the temple (Ex. 21:13, 14), but only a priest could enter the holy place. Nehemiah's enemies were subtly tempting him. If they could trap him in sin, this would discredit him and the work. Then the people would cease to follow him, and the work on the wall would stop.

6:11–16 God gave Nehemiah the wisdom to discern the error in Shemaiah's counsel. **Tobiah and Sanballat** were the principal instigators behind Shemaiah. Nehemiah indignantly rejected Shemaiah's counsel for two reasons. First, a man such as himself should not **flee.** Nehemiah was the governor, a leader of the people. He was responsible to the king and ultimately to the King of kings. A man in his position should not run and hide out of fear. Second, Nehemiah refused to go to the temple to save his life. The Law prohibited him from entering the Most Holy Place under penalty of death (Num. 18:7).

6:17–19 Here is a postscript. It turns out that during the building of the wall, a number of personal letters had been exchanged between some of the **nobles of Judah** and **Tobiah.** Tobiah and his son **Jehohanan** had married Jewish women. Some of the nobles sang Tobiah's praises to Nehemiah and then reported back to Tobiah everything they learned from the governor. With these letters, they hoped either to entrap Nehemiah in his own words or to intimidate him.

7:1 The Levites were assistants to the priests (Num. 18:1–4) and guarded and cleaned the sanctuary. Nehemiah **appointed** the Levites to their duties in the temple. **The gatekeepers** and **singers** were numbered among the Levites. The gatekeepers kept watch over the house of God and opened and closed the gates of the temple court (1 Chr. 9:17–19; 26:12–19). The singers led the people in their musical worship of God. The number of Levites, gatekeepers, and singers is given in vv. 43–45.

7:2 Nehemiah appointed two guards over the city as municipal officers in charge of security, each guard responsible for half of Jerusalem (3:9–12). One of the guards was Nehemiah's brother **Hanani,** who had visited Jerusalem and brought back a bleak report to Nehemiah in Shushan (1:2). The other guard was **Hananiah.** Nehemiah put him over **the citadel** because he was **faithful** and because he **feared God.** "Faithful" (Heb., literally, "a man of truth"), means "firm," "reliable." Hananiah was a God-fearing man, which means that he knew the Lord and walked with Him. The fear of God dreads God's displeasure, desires His favor, reveres His holiness, submits cheerfully to His will, is grateful for His benefits, sincerely worships Him, and conscientiously obeys His commands.

7:3 Nehemiah not only established guards over Jerusalem (v. 2), he also established guidelines for protecting the city. **The gates** of a city

Photo: Levant Photo Service

Excavated section of the defensive wall built under Nehemiah's supervision around the city of Jerusalem (Neh. 4:6; 6:15).

normally opened at sunrise, but Nehemiah ordered Jerusalem's gates to be kept closed until the sun was high. This extra precaution would have discouraged enemies from mounting a surprise attack at sunrise. Gates were critical to the defense of an ancient city. Nehemiah also ordered the citizens of Jerusalem to organize a civil defense, with people taking turns standing guard at night outside their own houses. This was a clever strategy. The people would have been more alert in guarding their own homes than they would have been in guarding a general part of the city.

7:4 For the size of the **city,** Jerusalem was underpopulated. Even though it was 90 years since people had returned under Zerubbabel to live there, there was still much undeveloped space within the walls renewed by Nehemiah.

7:5 my God put it into my heart: Nehemiah attributed to the Lord the idea of a

census that would show the distribution of the population. If he knew the population pattern in the capital and the countryside, he could then determine which districts could best afford to lose a portion of their inhabitants to Jerusalem.

7:6–73 Nehemiah discovered a list, recorded by families, of the names of the Jewish people who came from Persia to Judah in 536 B.C. under Zerubbabel. This long list consisted of the names of leaders (v. 7), people by families (vv. 8–25), people by cities (vv. 26–38), priests (vv. 39–42), Levites (vv. 43–45), Nethinim or temple servants (vv. 46–56), Solomon's servants (vv. 57–60), returnees without a genealogy (vv. 61–65), the total number of people (vv. 66, 67), their animals (vv. 68, 69), and the gifts given for the support of the work (vv. 70–72). This same list is found in Ezra 2 with some minor variations.

7:70–73 One thousand gold **drachmas** would weigh about nine pounds.

8:1 The phrase **all the people** indicates that people gathered together from the cities and the countryside of Judah. The **open square** was presumably located between the southeast part of the temple and the eastern wall. The leader—in this case, the reader—was **Ezra.** This is the first time Ezra is mentioned in the Book of

Nehemiah. The people instructed Ezra to get the Book of the Law, which Ezra had brought to Jerusalem as much as 13 years before. What had been confined to private study among learned men was made public to everyone.

8:2 In Scripture, **women** are often presumed to be present in group gatherings; here they are mentioned explicitly. Everyone **who could hear with understanding**—that is, older children as well as adults—gathered **on the first day of the seventh month.** The wall had been completed on the twenty-fifth day of the sixth month (6:15) so this event took place just a few days after the completion of the wall.

8:3 morning until midday: This would have been a period of about six hours.

8:4 Apparently these men stood alongside Ezra to assist in the long time that it took for the reading.

8:5 As Ezra unrolled the scroll, **the people stood,** signifying their reverence for the Word. This gesture later became characteristic of the Jewish people in synagogue services.

8:6, 7 Before reading the Book of the Law, Ezra led the people in prayer. **Blessed** here indicates identifying God as the source of the blessing of the people (Ps. 103:1). The people answered **Amen** and lifted their hands, indicating their participation with Ezra in prayer. Then they bowed their heads and worshiped the Lord with their faces to the ground, indicating their willing submission to their Lord and Creator.

8:8 they read distinctly: The Levites explained fully the meaning of the Law of God. **they gave the sense:** The Levites explained the Law so that the people got the sense and insight of what was being read.

8:9–11 Once the people understood the Word of God, they **wept.** They had heard the high standard of the Law and recognized their low standing before the Lord, and were convicted. Nehemiah, Ezra, and the Levites were undoubtedly glad to see the people's conviction. However, they urged the people to stop crying and reminded them that this **day** was **holy to the Lord.** The first day of the seventh month (v. 2) was the Feast of Trumpets. It was not a time to weep, but to celebrate. The people were instructed to celebrate the feast with eating, drinking, and sharing. **The joy of the Lord** could refer to the joy that God has, but the context indicates that this is something the people also experienced. The joy of the Lord is the joy that springs up in our hearts because of our relationship to the Lord. It is a God-given gladness found when we are in communion with God. When our goal is to know more about the Lord, the byproduct is His joy. **Strength** here means "place of safety," a "refuge," or "protection." The people's refuge was God. They had built a wall and they carried spears and swords, but He was their protection.

8:12 The people went to their houses **to eat and drink,** to share and **rejoice,** because they took to heart the words of Nehemiah, Ezra, and the Levites (vv. 1–9). They obeyed the Word of the Lord and celebrated the Feast of Trumpets.

8:13 The **heads** of families, **the priests,** and the **Levites** came back the next day to hear more teaching from God's Word. **understand:** Even the leaders gathered to gain the sense of the Scriptures and how they should act.

8:14, 15 By this time, the reading of the Law had advanced to Lev. 23. The listeners discovered that they were to observe the Feast of

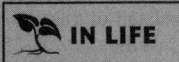 **IN LIFE**

Leadership Principles from Nehemiah, Part 5

Leaders Celebrate Often (8:1)

Effective leaders appreciate the value of celebrating the great things that God has done in and through their organizations. When the task is completed, when results have been achieved, when people have been served, then it is appropriate to take time to celebrate.

That is what Nehemiah did when the people completed the rebuilding of the wall (Neh. 8:1, 10). First he had Ezra read from the Law—the motivation for Nehemiah's mission in the first place. The words kindled not only a godly sorrow (9:1–3) but also genuine joy (8:10–12). Thus with heartfelt praise, choice food, and even an "amen" chorus (8:6), the community rejoiced in the Lord for the work it had accomplished.

One interesting sidelight to the celebration was Nehemiah's instruction to "send portions to those for whom nothing is prepared" (8:10). In other words, bring the poor to the party! Share the wealth. No one should be deprived of the joy.

Tabernacles from the fifteenth to the twenty-second day of the seventh month. During this time, the people were to live in **booths** made of fresh branches of fruit and palm trees. The booths would be set up in courts, streets, public squares, and housetops. No secular work was to be done during this festival. This feast was observed in memory of the their ancestors' living in booths—that is, tents—after the Exodus (Lev. 23:40). The booth was not a symbol of misery, but of protection, preservation, and shelter.

8:16 The people observed the Feast of Tabernacles according to the Law. Those who lived in cities built their **booths** on the flat tops of their houses or **in their courtyards.** The priests and Levites built their booths in **the courts** of the temple. The people from the country constructed huts in the street before the **Water Gate** and the **Gate of Ephraim.**

8:17 since the days of Joshua . . . the children of Israel had not done so: The reference here is to the construction of booths. The people of Israel had certainly celebrated the Feast of Tabernacles since the days of Joshua. In fact, those who had returned with Ezra kept the feast the first year of their return (1 Kin. 8:65; 2 Chr. 7:9; especially Ezra 3:4).

8:18 The reading of the Law was required during the celebration of the Feast of Tabernacles, which occurred on the Sabbath year (Deut. 31:10, 11).

9:1–38 This chapter is arguably one of the most significant in the whole of Hebrew Scripture. It presents a compelling recital of the basic OT story line, with a glorious focus on the work of Yahweh in the lives of His people. The passage does not end with history but with response. Any true understanding of the person and work of God leads to actions of righteousness and attitudes of worship. Most of the chapter (vv. 5–38) is often regarded as a prayer to God. If it is a prayer, it may be the longest prayer recorded in the Bible. But in its form and content, it appears more like a psalm, showing affinities particularly with Pss. 105 and 106. The text does not record who wrote these words, but we may cite the tradition that Ezra wrote them, and call this "Ezra's Grand Psalm."

9:1 the twenty-fourth day of this month: The people's public worship had begun on the first day of the seventh month (8:2). More than three weeks later, the people were still engaged in public worship. **Fasting, sackcloth,** and **dust** were traditional signs of mourning; here these signs were preparation for the confession of the people's sin (v. 2).

9:2 Of Israelite lineage means "the seed of Israel." The separation **from all foreigners** was a sacred separation from foreign persons who worshiped other gods and whose practices might have brought harm to the integrity of the Lord's worship by His people. **their sins and the iniquities of their fathers:** The confession of the people's own sins was for personal and corporate forgiveness; the confession of their father's sins was for remembrance, that they might not continue in past evil actions and attitudes.

9:3, 4 As in 8:5, the people **stood** in reverence at hearing the reading of the Scriptures. **one-fourth of the day:** Approximately three hours (compare 8:3) were spent in public reading and three hours were spent in corporate worship. **confessed:** When this word is used with God as its object, as in this verse, it refers to the praise of God.

9:5 Stand up and bless the Lord your God: These words were shouted by **the Levites. Forever and ever:** The Lord of Hosts will be praised through all eternity. **Your glorious name:** The importance of the name of God can scarcely be overestimated. This psalm is solidly based on the theology of the Law (the Books of Moses) as would be expected following the three-week reading of the Scriptures (8:1, 2). Thus this poem's exaltation of the Lord's name is based on God's own revelation of His name recorded in the Book of Exodus (Ex. 3:14). The prophet Isaiah also praised the Lord's "glorious name" (Is. 63:14).

9:6 One of the fundamental teachings of Scripture is that God is not one among many; He **alone** is the living God (Deut. 6:4). **heaven . . . earth . . . seas:** God alone has made all things, and He alone preserves all things. Therefore, worship is due Him. The first section of this psalm (vv. 5, 6) establishes the mood for the whole poem: God is incomparable (Num. 23:8, 9; Deut. 4:32–40; Ps. 113:4–6).

9:7–31 Here is a recital of Yahweh's faithfulness to His people despite their checkered history. This lengthy section is the heart of the Psalm. The poet dramatically contrasts the faithfulness of Yahweh to the sorry record of Israel's disobedience to His commands, disregard for His wonder, and disdain for His chastening actions. Yet He remains faithful.

9:7, 8 You are the Lord God: The word order of the Hebrew text is striking: "You are He, Yahweh (the) God." The use of the definite article on the word God marks Him as "the true God." **Abraham:** The story of the election of Abraham begins in Gen. 12:1–3. The point here is to emphasize God's grace. Abraham did not seek out the Lord. Instead God sought him. **You found his heart faithful:** None of the people of biblical history was without sin except Jesus. Still, there were some whose faithfulness to God was constant. Among were

Abraham and Sarah (Heb. 11). The subsequent history of the people of Israel was not marked by the steady faithfulness seen in Abraham, much to the displeasure of the Lord. The Promised Land, **the land of the Canaanites,** was populated by diverse groups of people who had all lost their right to the land because of their sinfulness (Gen. 15:18–21; Ex. 3:8, 17; 23:23; 33:2; Deut. 7:1; Josh. 3:10). **You have performed Your words:** This is the essence of the psalm. God's faithfulness to His people cannot be challenged. **You are righteous:** One of the greatest reasons to celebrate the character of God is His conformity to His own standard of perfection (v. 33).

9:9 The Book of Exodus tells about the plight of the Israelites in Egypt and their complaint to the Lord for deliverance. It then speaks of God's mercy in His response to the people's need. This verse suggests that before the people expressed their hurt, the Lord was already aware of their troubles.

9:10 The **signs and wonders** were the ten plagues of Ex. 7—12. These great acts of God were directed primarily **against Pharaoh. acted proudly:** In Ex. 18:11, Jethro, the father-in-law of Moses, used this same phrase to describe the presumptuous actions of the Egyptians. It was the proud actions of the Egyptians that brought God's judgment on them.

9:11, 12 You divided the sea refers to God's acts of deliverance at the Red Sea (Ex. 14; 15). Note the simile of Pharaoh's troops sinking **as a stone** (Ex. 15:5). **cloudy pillar . . . pillar of fire:** The continued presence of God in the lives of His people was indicated by these symbols (Ex. 13:21, 22; Num. 10:11, 34; Deut. 1:33).

9:13, 14 The significance of the **Sabbath** in God's Law for Israel is celebrated here (Ex. 20:8–11; 23:10–13; 31:12–18). **By the hand of Moses:** The Law came from the Lord, but it was given by the agency of Moses (John 1:17).

9:15 The gifts of **bread,** or manna (Ex. 16:9–35), and **water** (Ex. 17:1–7) demonstrated God's care for His people in their journey to the Promised Land.

9:16, 17 But they: These words stand in shocking contrast to the description of God's actions in vv. 9–15. The sin of the Israelites was that they **acted proudly**—that is, they behaved toward God in the same way that the people of Egypt had behaved toward them. The primary reference here is to the rebellion of Israel against the Lord at Kadesh (Num. 13; 14). The people's rebellion went so far that they **appointed a leader** to take them back to Egypt. **But You:** These words contrast the words "But they" at the beginning of v. 16 (Ex. 34:6). **Ready to pardon** means abounding in forgiveness. **Slow**

to anger: This phrase translates a Hebrew idiom ("long of nose") that has the same meaning as the English expression "to have a long fuse." **Kindness,** from a word that means "loyal love," is used often in the Book of Psalms (Ps. 13:5). Because of the God's loyalty and steadfastness, He **did not forsake** His people.

9:18–21 In these verses, the poet describes the faithfulness of God to the Israelites in the wilderness despite their wretched behavior. **Molded calf** is a reference to the act of rebellion described in Ex. 32. **Manifold mercies** describes deep feelings like those of a mother for her child. **You did not forsake them** is repeated from v. 17. God would have been justified in abandoning His people because of their extreme sinfulness and wicked rebellion; yet He was compelled by His character not to do so. **You also gave Your good Spirit:** God not only gave gifts to His people, He made Himself known in their midst. **Forty years:** The wilderness experience (Deut. 2:7) is viewed in two ways in the Bible: (1) as a period of prolonged punishment because of rebellion; and (2) as a period of continued mercy because of God's unchanging character. **clothes . . . feet:** God's provisions were daily experiences of divine miracles (Deut. 8:4; 29:5).

9:22–25 The poet describes the mercies of God in Israel's conquest of the Promised Land and in God's continuing provision for them. **kingdoms and nations:** The Bible celebrates the conquest of the land east of the Jordan, as well as the conquest of Canaan itself. **as the stars:** The miraculous growth of the people is described in this familiar hyperbole (Gen. 15:5; 22:17). **the people went in:** The conquest of the land as described in the Book of Joshua is indicated here. **strong cities . . . rich land . . . houses:** With few exceptions, the people of Israel conquered the inhabitants of Canaan in such a way that they were able to move into the Canaanites' undamaged homes and cities. The Israelites were also able to enjoy crops and wells for which they did not have to work. All of this is testimony to God's **great goodness.**

9:26–29 The rebellion of the people was expressed during the period of the judges and throughout the period of the kings. **Cast Your law behind their backs** is a graphic metaphor for rebellion. **killed Your prophets:** Jesus also directed this charge against the rebellious people (Matt. 23:31). **You delivered them into the hands of their enemies** refers to the experiences of the Israelites during the period described by the Book of Judges. **he shall live by them:** Salvation in any period is only by grace through faith (Eph. 2:8, 9). Keeping the Law was never a means of salvation, but a guide for living a life that pleases the Lord.

9:30, 31 God continued to be faithful to His disobedient people. **For many years** refers to the history of the people of Israel from Saul to the last of the kings. **Your spirit in Your prophets** speaks of God's work in inspiring the words of the prophets of Israel (Jer. 1:9). **You gave them into the hand of the peoples of the lands** refers to the captivity of Israel. **nor forsake them:** For the third time in this psalm (vv. 17, 19), this reality is affirmed.

9:32–35 On the basis of the Lord's continuing mercy through the centuries, the poet now turns to the present situation and asks that God's faithfulness will continue to be experienced by His people. This is a marvelous demonstration of the manner of biblical prayer. On the basis of God's past actions, the beleaguered believer requests in faith God's continuing mercy.

9:32 Now refers to the time of the great revival under Ezra (8:1, 2). **covenant and mercy:** God's covenant loyalty is unbreakable (Heb. 6:17, 18). **Do not let all the trouble seem small:** In view of the unspeakable wonder of God, the hardship of His people might seem too small a matter to be noticed. **kings . . . people:** The effects of Israel's trouble were all-inclusive. **From the days of the kings of Assyria:** The incursions of the Assyrians, beginning with Tiglath-Pileser III, began a period of oppression for the Jewish people.

9:33–35 You are just: The poet affirms the righteousness of God. **You have dealt faithfully . . . we have done wickedly:** This is the basic reality not only of this chapter, but of the history of God and His people.

9:36, 37 Servants is used as a term of irony here. The people of Israel had been called to be the servants of God (Lev. 25:55), but here they were servants of foreign rulers. The produce of the land did not belong to them; it went to **kings.** The people were taxed by Persians for the produce of the land that was God's gift to them.

9:38 The psalm ends in action, not just sentiment. The intent was changed behavior. The pledge was to mirror God's faithfulness. The new **covenant** community desired to demonstrate the faithfulness of Abraham and Sarah.

10:1 The way someone "signed" a **document** in the ancient world was similar to the use of a wax **seal** in more recent times. A distinctive seal was pressed into soft clay. The pattern of the seal showed what authority issued that document.

> *The people took an oath to live by the Word of God.*

10:2–8 The **priests** who sealed the covenant are listed here. Some of these names appear in a later list as heads of priestly houses (12:11–20). Twenty-one priests who were heads of households signed the agreement in the name of the houses and families of their respective classes. Ezra's name does not appear, perhaps indicating that he was not the head of a household.

10:9–13 The **Levites** also signed the covenant. Some of these names appear later as heads of the orders of Levites (12:8).

10:14–27 Forty-four **leaders** also signed the covenant. In contrast to the religious leaders, these were the political leaders of the Jewish community (compare 7:4–63; Ezra 2).

10:28 Not only leaders, but laypeople signed the covenant. **The Nethinim** were temple servants who did menial work in the sanctuary (Ezra 2:43). **Those who had separated themselves from the peoples of the lands** were the descendants of those Israelites who had been left in the land and who joined the returning remnant. Men, women, and children of sufficient age signed the covenant.

10:29 entered into a curse: The phrase points to the penalties for failure to comply with the covenant. The people took an oath to live by the Word of God. **God's Law:** The Law was a gift of God, **given by Moses.** The Israelites swore that they would observe the Law of God. **commandments . . . ordinances . . . statutes:** This is a way of speaking of the whole Law of God (1:7).

10:30 The Israelites' decision to obey the Word of God in every area of their lives (v. 29) was not just a general statement. The people specifically vowed to obey the Word of God in their marriage relationships. Marriage with non-Jewish people was clearly forbidden in the Scriptures (Ex. 34:12–16; Deut. 7:3; Josh. 23:12; Judg. 3:6). **We would not give our daughters . . . nor take their daughters:** The parents of Israel decided that they would not permit their children to marry non-Jews. In the ancient world, marriages usually were arranged by the parents.

10:31 Other areas of life were included in the people's dedication to God's Law. This verse deals with **Sabbath** observance. Three particulars regarding the Sabbath are mentioned. First, the people promised to stop all buying and selling from foreigners on the Sabbath. Second, they pledged to observe the Sabbatical year—

that is, to leave their fields uncultivated during every seventh year (Lev. 25:1–7). Third, they decided not to collect debts during the Sabbatical year (Deut. 15:1–6). The people were dedicating themselves to observe the Word of God in their business life.

10:32–39 The remainder of the chapter covers the people's promise to obey the Word of God concerning the temple. In this area, the people made four promises. (1) They promised to pay a temple tax to defray the expenses of the worship services in God's sanctuary. Verse 33 lists the objects that the tax would supply. (2) They promised to provide a **wood offering.** The Law prescribed that wood should be constantly burning on the altar (Lev. 6:12, 13). Nehemiah made this the business of the congregation. (3) They promised to offer their **firstfruits** at the temple. The firstfruits of the ground were given to the Lord as an acknowledgment of His status as landowner (Ex. 23:19; 34:26; Deut. 26:2). The people promised the firstfruits of **all trees,** which means that they were going beyond the requirements of the Law. The firstborn of the animals also belonged to the Lord (Num. 18:15, 17–19). (4) They promised to pay **the priests.**

11:1–3 Nehemiah **cast lots** to repopulate Jerusalem. We do not know for certain the nature of casting lots in the Bible. The most common suggestion is that stones were marked and put into a vase or urn, or into the lap or the fold of a garment. Then they would be mixed and one stone drawn out. Numerous uses for drawing lots are recorded in the Bible: (1) to determine which goat should be sacrificed on the Day of Atonement (Lev. 16:7–19); (2) to divide the land among the tribes (Num. 26:55); (3) to detect who had committed a crime (Josh. 7:14–18; Jon. 1:7); (4) to decide who should go to war (Judg. 20:9); (5) to determine who should be the first king of Israel (1 Sam. 10:20, 21); (6) who had offended God (1 Sam. 14:41, 42; (7) who would serve in the temple (1 Chr. 24:5); (8) who should burn the wood (Neh.

10:34; (9) who should replace Judas (Acts 1:26). Here in Nehemiah, lots were cast to determine God's will. Solomon wrote, "The lot is cast into the lap, but its every decision is from the Lord" (Prov. 16:33). **one out of ten:** This was the proportion demanded in order to bring the population of Jerusalem to the level deemed necessary for its strength and viability.

11:4–1 **Four hundred and sixty-eight** men from the tribe of Judah lived in **Jerusalem; nine hundred and twenty-eight** men from the tribe of **Benjamin** also lived there. According to 1 Chr. 9:3, descendants of Ephraim and Manasseh also made their home in Jerusalem.

11:12, 13 The **work of the house** refers to the work of the temple—specifically, attending the sacrifices of the temple.

11:14, 15 **Mighty men of valor** refers to the men who guarded the city of Jerusalem.

11:16–18 The **oversight of the business outside of the house of God** refers to the maintenance of the temple, including repairs.

11:19 The **gatekeepers** were also defenders of the city.

11:20–22 the overseer of the Levites: Uzzi was a principal administrator of the temple.

11:23, 24 The **king's deputy** was the representative of the people. This individual may have received and forwarded petitions and complaints to the king.

11:25–36 These verses record the residents outside Jerusalem—namely the tribes of Judah (vv. 25–30) and Benjamin (vv. 31–36). The people of Judah lived in 17 towns and their surrounding villages. The descendants of Benjamin occupied 15 sites.

11:25 **Kirjath Arba** is another name for Hebron.

12:1–8 The return of **Zerubbabel** is recorded in Ezra 1—6. **Jeshua** is Joshua the priest. **Ezra:** This is not the priest who wrote the book of the same name (Ezra 7:1).

12:9 stood across from them: The singing

 INSIGHT | **The Ten Percent Solution**

Nehemiah came up with a novel solution to revitalize a dying urban area, Jerusalem: let the outlying suburbs donate one-tenth of their people to move into the city (Neh. 11:1, 2). In effect, the districts surrounding Jerusalem tithed people for the purpose of community redevelopment. Nehemiah's recruitment for the repopulation program involved casting lots to determine who would relocate (11:1; compare Josh. 18:8–10). Those who were selected were "blessed" (Heb. *barak,* Neh. 11:2), or ordained, to the task by their fellow citizens. This suggests a formal commissioning of these families to carry out the redevelopment of Jerusalem.

was conducted with two choirs standing opposite each other.

12:10, 11 The listing of the descendants of **Eliashib** all the way to **Jaddua** may indicate that someone who lived after Ezra and Nehemiah added some of these names.

12:12–21 In vv. 1–7, the names of twenty-two **priests** are listed. Here only twenty names are recorded. Hattush (v. 2) and Maadiah (v. 5) are not mentioned in this list.

12:22 **Darius** refers to Darius II (Nothus), who ruled Persia from 423 to 405 B.C.

12:23–26 **The book of the chronicles** was not the biblical book, but an official record of **the heads of the fathers' houses.**

12:27–29 After the completion of Jerusalem's wall (ch. 6), a revival of the people broke out (chs. 8–10). After the revival, Nehemiah took steps to repopulate the city (7:4, 5; 11:1, 2). These two factors explain why **the dedication of the wall** was delayed. The word "dedication" (Heb. *hanukkâ*) is transliterated in English as "Hanukkah." The festival of Hanukkah developed from the experience of the Jewish people in rededicating the temple after its desecration by the Syrians and the subsequent revolt of the Maccabees in the second century B.C. The people celebrated **with gladness,** referring not only to their festivity but also to the worship of God. **Thanksgivings,** a term commonly found in the Book of Psalms (Ps. 147:7), means "public acknowledgment," "to declare aloud, in public, to another." This word, along with **singing** and **instruments,** suggests the use of the Psalms in musical settings with words of praise and instrumental accompaniment.

12:30–35 The method of purification is not stated, but the order is—**the priests and Levites,** followed by **the people, the gates, and wall.** Those who bore the vessels of the Lord had to be cleansed first.

12:36–42 The association of the name **David** with **musical instruments** was a reference to Israel's glorious past.

12:43 The **sacrifices** offered at the dedication of the wall probably were not burnt offerings but peace offerings, in which the people shared a common meal. The dedication was an occasion for great rejoicing. Everyone, including wives and children, took part.

12:44–47 After the dedication of the wall, the people took steps to provide for the **priests, Levites, singers,** and **gatekeepers** who served in the temple. The joy of the Lord should produce service for the Lord. In this case, the people's joy overflowed into providing for the temple. Men were appointed as custodians of the firstfruits and tithes. **the days of David and Asaph:** The times of the great music of Israel were never forgotten; they served as a model for the days still to come.

13:1–31 This chapter is a sort of "surprise ending" to the book. To understand it, one must know that between chapters twelve and thirteen Nehemiah returned to Persia. At first sight, the phrase **On that day** (v. 1) may seem to refer to the day of dedication just pictured. But 13:6 and 7 make that impossible, as does v. 10, which states that on the "day" of chapter thirteen, the Levites were not being given their portion, whereas that had just been done at the time of dedication (12:47). So, Nehemiah returned to Persia between chapters twelve and thirteen and on the day after his return, he discovered what became the surprise ending of his book; namely, that those devoted and dedicated people had tripped over temptation, fallen into sin, and lain down in disobedience. This chapter deals with five issues: foreigners (vv. 1–3), the temple (vv. 4–9), the Levites (vv. 10–14), the Sabbath (vv.15–22), and marriage (vv. 23–31). More specifically, the chapter records separation from foreigners, the cleansing of the temple, the

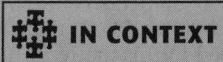 **IN CONTEXT** **Nehemiah's Religious Reforms**

Although Nehemiah is usually remembered for what is considered his greatest accomplishment, rebuilding Jerusalem's wall, he was also a religious reformer.

Like Ezra, Nehemiah was a purist in religious matters. True worship was only possible to the undefiled, and to Nehemiah that disqualified all of the people who had remained in the land during the Exile. Only the returned exiles, who had kept the faith pure while in captivity, were acceptable. When Nehemiah found that Tobiah, one of his enemies and an Ammonite official (Neh. 2:19), had been given rooms in the temple itself, he was aghast and removed Tobiah promptly (13:7–9). Nehemiah also restored official support of the Levitical ministers (13:10–14) and resumed enforcement of the Sabbath laws (13:15–22).

restoration of the Levites, the enforcement of the Sabbath, and the condemnation of mixed marriages.

13:1–3 The first area of backsliding for the **people** was their relationship with foreigners. Even though 9:2 states that "those of Israelite lineage separated themselves from all foreigners," the people once again allowed foreigners into the congregation. Relationships between the Jewish people and the foreigners in the land had caused them to violate God's command (1 Cor. 15:33).

13:4–9 The second major area of backsliding dealt with in this chapter (vv. 1–3) was that the high priest was allowing God's enemy to live in God's house. **Eliashib** was the high priest (vv. 4, 28). **Tobiah** was one of the men who had tried to stop the building of the wall (2:10, 19; 4:3; 6:10–12, 17, 19). Eliashib allowed Tobiah to stay in the large room of the temple that had previously been used for storing grain and the like. In fact, Tobiah had been given access to several rooms of the temple.

13:6, 7 Nehemiah returns to Jerusalem.

13:8, 9 When Nehemiah returned to Jerusalem, he immediately initiated reforms. He removed Tobiah's furniture from the chamber and then ordered that the room be cleansed. When the washing, scouring, and sprinkling with blood were completed, the chamber was once again filled with **grain** and the other items that had been there before.

13:10, 11 Contended is a term used often in the prophets to refer to God bringing a legal case against His errant people (Jer. 2:9). Nehemiah was acting like a prophet, bringing a legal case against an apostate person. He contended for what was right. Note the pointed question he asked: **Why is the house of God forsaken?**

13:12, 13 Then all Judah brought the tithe: The gifts that should have been brought earlier were finally being brought by the people. **treasurers:** Nehemiah chose faithful men (7:2; 1 Cor. 4:2; 2 Tim. 2:2) to make sure the gifts were distributed properly.

13:14 Normally prayer is offered to the Lord before or during an event. In this case,

Nehemiah's prayer followed his **good deeds.** Nehemiah was saying, "What I did, I did in accordance with Your will; now preserve it and protect me."

13:15–22 Another difficulty that Nehemiah faced concerned **the Sabbath.** The Jewish people in Judah were working on Saturday. People were buying and selling produce in Jerusalem. **Men of Tyre** brought fish and other things to be sold both in **Judah** and **Jerusalem.** These were all violations of Ex. 20:8–11 and of the people's own oath (10:31). The people had put their business ahead of obedience to God's command concerning their day of rest.

13:19–22 I commanded the gates to be shut: Nehemiah took charge, ordering the gates to be closed from Friday evening to Saturday evening and even posting his own servants as guards. When the **merchants** set up outside the wall, Nehemiah **warned** them that if they stayed around again **on the Sabbath,** he would himself attack them. Awed by the threat of the one-man army, the merchants left.

13:23, 24 The problem of Jews marrying foreigners had been dealt with thirty years before by Ezra (Ezra 9:1–4). The people had then made a covenant, vowing that they would not do this (10:30). In this case Nehemiah found children of the mixed marriages who could not speak Hebrew, the **language** of Scripture. Without knowing Hebrew, these children could not learn the Law in their homes or worship in the holy temple. The Jews were raising children who did not know or worship the living God.

13:25–27 Nehemiah's attack on the Jews who had married non-Jews was confrontational, direct, and even brutal. **contended . . . cursed . . . struck . . . pulled out their hair:** It is unnerving to read this list of verbs and imagine the scene. These were not the dispassionate remarks of someone giving a seminar. Nehemiah used everything he could, including his hands, to enforce obedience to the Law. **made them swear:** Nehemiah forced them to comply to the will of God in this matter. After all, this was the principal issue that had led to

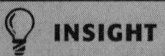 **INSIGHT** ## Ashdod and Its Implications

The name "Ashdod" (Neh. 13:23) was notorious among the Israelites as it indicated a group that had long been their enemies, the Philistines. Ashdod, located near the Mediterranean Sea, was one of five principal cities of the Philistines. It was an important military and commercial center because of its strategic location on the Via Maris, the main highway between Egypt and Syria.

Israel's captivity in the beginning. Nehemiah simply could not allow such a disaster to happen again. **Solomon:** Despite his greatness and God's love for him, even Solomon had sinned greatly in this regard (1 Kin. 11:4–8). How then, with the great lessons of the past so clearly before them, could the people repeat these sins?

13:28, 29 I drove him from me: This action was taken against the most prominent offender, the grandson of the high priest Eliashib. This young man had married the daughter of Sanballat (2:10), the governor of Samaria and the archenemy of the Jewish people. The marriage was particularly offensive because it formed a treasonable alliance with

Israel's enemies and compromised the purity of the high priesthood (ch. 12). Because of the seriousness of this offense, Nehemiah took dramatic action. He expelled the young man from the community, praying that God would remember those who had defiled the priesthood.

13:30, 31 I cleansed them of everything pagan: Nehemiah's testimony was that he had done everything he knew how to bring about righteousness in the priesthood and among the Levites, including their offerings and service. Nehemiah's last recorded words (5:19), **remember me, O my God, for good,** would serve well as the last words of any person of faith.

The Book of
Esther

THE BOOK OF ESTHER HAS ALL THE ELEMENTS of a great novel: a beautiful young orphan girl rises from obscurity to become queen. She even hides a secret that could bring about her demise. There is also the ambitious villain, whose passion is to destroy the innocent. Finally the story line involves a power struggle, romantic love, and a startling exposé. But in the end, the point of this true story is clear: once

again the Israelites' God had miraculously saved His people from certain destruction.

The events of Esther span a decade during the reign of Ahasuerus, or Xerxes, who succeeded his father Darius as ruler of the Persian empire in 486 B.C. During his reign (486–465 B.C.), Xerxes continued his father's campaign against Greece for its role in the Ionian revolt. After suffering defeat, he retired to Shushan, one of the four capitals of the Persian empire. Around 483 B.C. he threw an extravagant feast in Shushan to celebrate his achievements. Ten years later he executed Haman for his evil schemes (1:3; 7:9).

Some critical scholars question the historical accuracy of Esther on various counts. One difficulty is the passage that describes the royal feast (1:3–5). The passage appears to indicate that the feast lasted a particularly long time: "one hundred and eighty days in all" (1:4). However, a better interpretation is that this long period of time was the period of preparation for the military campaign in Greece, during which Xerxes displayed his power and wealth to his officials. The feast itself lasted seven days—a lengthy time for a feast but not an incredible period (1:5).

Another difficulty is that neither Vashti nor Esther is mentioned outside the Bible. However, historians do note that following his unsuccessful campaign against Greece (482–479 B.C.), Xerxes sought refuge in his harem. This coincides with the elevation of Esther (2:17). Furthermore, the word translated *queen* (1:9; 2:22) may refer merely to a principal wife rather than to a woman who ruled beside the king. Thus the obscurity of Esther and Vashti would be understandable. Even so, some still balk at the idea that a Persian ruler would marry a Jewish woman rather than choosing someone from the aristocratic Persian families. However, the Book of Esther makes it clear that Esther initially hid her Jewish identity. She used her Persian name Ishtar or Esther instead of her Hebrew name Hadassah. The climax of the story involves her surprising revelation that she was a Jew.

The Book of Esther has held an important place in the canon due to its strong testimony to God's providence and protection of His people. However, the book has been challenged by some. One of the main points in the dispute is the remarkable fact that neither the word God nor God's name Yahweh is found in the book.

There are two explanations that may account for this. First, it may be a result of the author's chosen point of view. The author might have viewed the Jewish people who remained in Persia and did not return to the land of Israel (Ezra 1:1) as a people cut off from the principal blessings of God. Thus, the absence of God's name in the book might be a way of expressing God's distance from the exiles. At the same time, the book clearly reveals God's surprising protection of them.

Second, the author may have written the book in the form of a Persian state chronicle in order to explain to the Persians the Jewish celebration of Purim. In accordance with this style, the author emphasizes the king's name, titles, and lists, but he writes about the Jewish people in a detached tone. This could help explain why the Book of Esther is the only book in the Bible that does not directly mention God.

Through the twists and turns of the story line, the author weaves an underlying story about God's character. The narrative demonstrates God's providence and sovereignty in a situation that seemed hopeless. The Israelites were living among foreigners who did not fear God and who did not care about them. An implacable enemy of the Israelites had gained power at court and was laying a plan to destroy the Jews. But at a time when God seemed so distant, He was actually preparing to deliver His people. God was in control of every event, even the sleeplessness of a foreign king (6:1).

Thus in the Persian capital, God demonstrated His covenant loyalty to the Israelites. Long ago, God had promised Abraham that He would curse any individual who cursed the Israelites (Gen. 12:2, 3). The downfall of Haman dramatically illustrated God's faithfulness to His promise. Even to the Israelites who remained in a foreign land, God remained true to His word, for they were still His people. Thus, the author of Esther clearly illustrates what the Israelites were celebrating at the Feast of Purim: God's faithful protection of His people.

The identity of the author of Esther is unknown. However the writer was probably Jewish and lived in Persia. A strong Jewish spirit pervades the book, particularly evident in the account of the establishment of the Jewish festival Purim. Moreover, the author was acquainted with Persian culture, as the extensive descriptions of the palace complex at Shushan (also called Susa) and the domestic details about the reign of King Ahasuerus indicate. For these reasons, some Jewish rabbis have ascribed the authorship of the book to Mordecai, one of its principal characters.

Whoever the author was, Esther was probably written shortly after the reign of Ahasuerus, no earlier than 465 B.C. The author writes of the rule of Ahasuerus and the deeds of Mordecai (10:2) in the past tense, indicating the book was not composed during Ahasuerus's reign. Yet the fact that Greek words do not appear in the book rules out a date after about 300 B.C., when the Greek language became more prominent in the ancient Middle East. On the other hand, the numerous words of Persian origin in the book point to its being composed during the latter half of the fifth century B.C. For example, the book calls Xerxes by the Hebrew name Ahasuerus, a spelling derived from the Persian Khshayarsha. If it had been written after

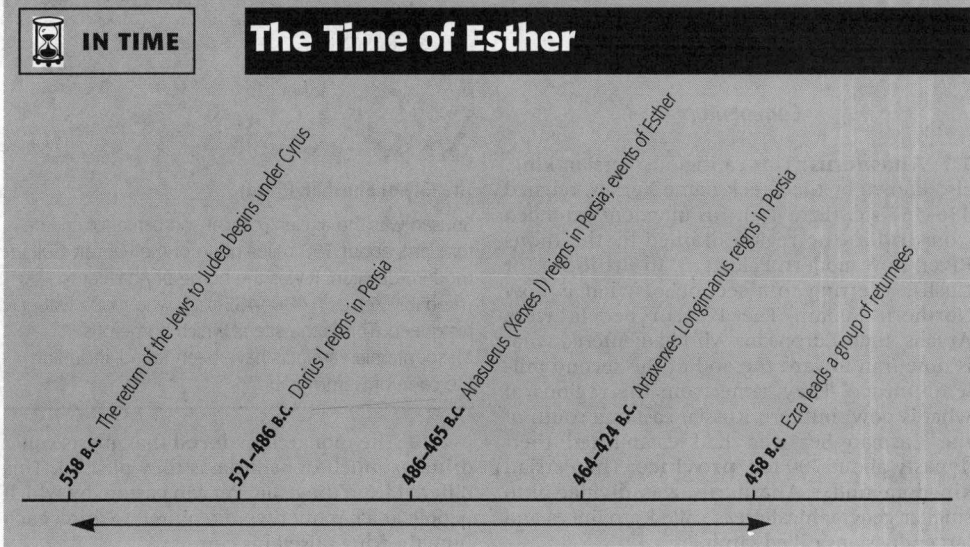

IN TIME

The Time of Esther

538 B.C. The return of the Jews to Judea begins under Cyrus

521–486 B.C. Darius I reigns in Persia

486–465 B.C. Ahasuerus (Xerxes I) reigns in Persia, events of Esther

464–424 B.C. Artaxerxes Longimanus reigns in Persia

458 B.C. Ezra leads a group of returnees

300 B.C. a spelling closer to the Greek form Xerxes would be expected.

Outline

I. A dethroned queen and a discovered queen 1:1–2:23
  A. The grand banquet 1:1–9
  B. Vashti's reluctance to expose herself to the drunken crowd 1:10–12
  C. Vashti's demotion as the chief of wives 1:13–22
  D. The search for a new queen 2:1–4
  E. The discovery and approval of Esther 2:5–18
  F. Mordecai's revelation of a plot 2:19–23
II. Haman's schemes against the Jewish people in Persia 3:1–7:10
  A. Haman's hatred of Mordecai 3:1–6
  B. Haman's decree 3:7–15
  C. Mordecai's reminder to Esther 4:1–17
  D. Esther's two banquets 5:1–7:10
    1. The first banquet 5:1–8
    2. The scheme against Mordecai 5:9–14
    3. Mordecai's reward and Haman's humiliation 6:1–14
    4. The second banquet and Haman's hanging 7:1–10
III. The deliverance of the Jewish people 8:1–9:32
  A. A royal reversal 8:1–14
  B. Rejoicing among the Jewish people 8:15–17
  C. Two days of deliverance 9:1–17
  D. The Feast of Purim 9:18–32
IV. Mordecai's preeminence 10:1–3

Commentary

1:1 Ahasuerus: This capricious Persian king, also known by the Greek name Xerxes, reigned 486–465 B.C. (Ezra 4:6). His kingdom extended from **India** (the region drained by the Indus River, now modern Pakistan), to **Ethiopia** (or Cush), referring to a section of what is now Northern Sudan. The Persian people were Aryans, Indo-Europeans who had entered what is now Iran toward the end of the second millennium B.C. They came from the regions of what is now southern Russia, east and south of the Caspian Sea and had established their dynasty about 700 B.C. **province:** The Persian kingdom under Ahasuerus was divided into smaller geographical areas called provinces and larger divisions called satrapies.

1:2 The capital of ancient Elam, **Shushan** (or Susa) was one of four royal residences for the Persian emperors. Shushan was 150 miles north of the Persian Gulf. It was the location of one of Daniel's visions (Dan. 8:2), and it was where Nehemiah served as cupbearer to King Artaxerxes I (Neh. 1:1, 2). **citadel:** The capital city had a palace fortress on the highest point of the city, the acropolis.

1:3–5 In **the third year** of his reign, Ahasuerus displayed the riches of his kingdom for six months. **made a feast:** There is some uncertainty about whether the king gave one feast or two. It is possible that v. 3 introduces the idea of the grand banquet and v. 5 records the specifics of what turned out to be a seven-day festival. It is not likely that the feasting itself extended for 180 days. **Persia and Media:** Previously the Medes had been the stronger of the two nations. Beginning with the reign of Cyrus, the Persians dominated the kingdom. Together they established a powerful empire (Dan. 5:28).

1:6, 7 white and blue: These were the royal colors of the Persians. The Persian custom was to recline on couches at the table.

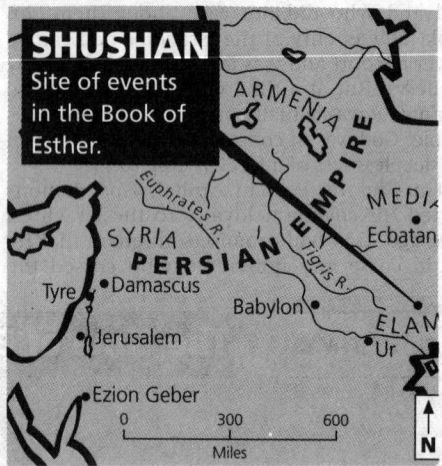

The City of Shushan (Susa)

Shusan was the ancient capital and center of culture for Elam, about 150 miles north of the Persian Gulf in modern-day Iran. It was the home of Ahasuerus (probably Xerxes I, 486–465 B.C.), who made Esther his queen. This is the site at which numerous Mesopotamian artifacts have been found, including the code of Hammurabi.

1:8 The monarch **ordered** that guests could drink as much or as little as they pleased. This differed from the usual Persian custom by which people at a banquet were required to drink each time the king raised his cup.

Photo by Gustav Jeeninga

Clilffside tomb of the Persian king Xerxes I, the ruler generally identified as King Ahasuerus of the Book of Esther (Esth. 1:1).

1:9 Vashti: The queen gave a separate banquet for the women guests. This verse serves to introduce the scene in vv. 10–12 and to establishes for readers the important distinctions between the status of women and men in the Persian court.

1:10–12 Castrated men, or **eunuchs,** were assigned to act as harem attendants and as agents of communication between the king and his harem (6:14). Because of the level of trust these men could attain, they might also function as administrators in the kingdom as well. **Harbona** plays a significant role later in the story (7:9).

1:13 men who understood the times: Court astrologers and magicians gave advice and predicted the future on the basis of what they pretended to know about the supernatural. The prophets often looked upon such charlatans with derisive scorn (Is. 44:24, 25).

1:14, 15 The **seven** counselors of Ezra 7:14 were probably the same group of men. These men enjoyed the unusual privilege of speaking personally with the king.

1:16–18 Acting as spokesman for the others, **Memucan** responded shrewdly by enlarging the offense beyond a personal affront to the king.

1:18 contempt: The Hebrew word used occurs only here in the OT. It is related to the verb translated *despise* in v. 17.

1:19–21 royal decree: Memucan urged the king to take immediate action against Vashti. The queen would be given what amounted to a divorce. This would have the effect of demoting her from her privileged position as the chief wife of the king.

1:22 sent letters: The Persians were known for their excellent postal system. **speak in the language of his own people:** This suggests the respect that was held for local languages and dialects in the Persian empire.

2:1–3 It was customary for the virgins of the king's harem to spend a year in **beauty** treatments and purification rites before going to see the king (v. 12). Again we see the exaggerated sense of power of the king contrasted with the fragile status of women. **Beautiful young virgins** were seen to exist merely to bring pleasure to the king.

2:4, 5 The name **Mordecai** is related to the name of Marduk, the principal Babylonian deity. The phrase **a certain Jew,** along with the genealogy and the tribal name Benjamite, prepares us for the upcoming conflict with Haman in ch. 3. **Shimei** may refer to the man from the family of Saul who cursed David (2 Sam. 16:5–13). **Kish** may be the father of Saul (1 Sam. 9:1, 2). If these figures are the ones intended, they are Mordecai's remote ancestors from the tribe of Benjamin.

2:6 This verse is difficult to interpret, as the

Hebrew text does not indicate the subject of the verb **had been carried away.** The subject could not be Mordecai. If he had been among those carried away into captivity, he would not

palace. She was brought into the palace complex, but not yet into the living quarters of the king. As custodian of the king's harem, **Hegai** was a eunuch (2:3).

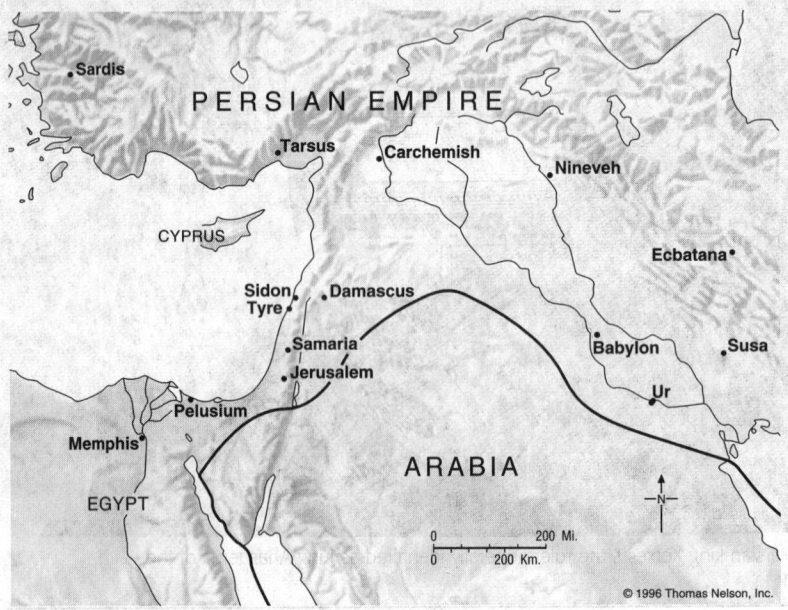

The Persian Empire (500 B.C.)

By Esther's time the Persian empire stretched from India in the east through Asia Minor to Greece in the west and included Egypt and some of coastal Africa to the south.

likely have lived until the time of Ahasuerus. The subject might be Mordecai's ancestor Kish, understood to be a different person than the father of Saul. It is also possible that the original phrasing merely means that Mordecai and his family were among those descended from the captives who were taken to Babylon in the days of Nebuchadnezzar. In this case, the person who was brought to Babylon is not specifically mentioned; only the more well-known ancestors are noted.

2:7 Hadassah is a Hebrew name that means "Myrtle." Esther is a Persian name meaning "Star." Like the name of her cousin Mordecai, the name **Esther** was related to that of a local deity, the goddess Ishtar. Jewish people in antiquity customarily had two names when they lived in regions distant from Israel. One would be their secular name, a name understandable in their adopted culture, and the other would be their sacred name given in Hebrew. **lovely and beautiful:** The two words complement each other to mean "supremely lovely" or "exceedingly beautiful."

2:8 We cannot determine whether Esther went willingly or reluctantly to the king's

2:9 obtained his favor: This phrase characterizes Esther's relationships with all who knew her, including the king (v. 17). Esther found favor with many, as is demonstrated throughout the chapter. The Hebrew word for *favor* is a term used regularly in the Bible to describe the character of God. This word may be translated "loyal love." The frequency of this concept with regard to Esther in this book may be a subtle way of suggesting the presence of the Lord without actually mentioning His name.

It was common in the ancient world for powerful rulers to have sizeable harems of concubines (Esth. 2:14; 1 Kin. 11:3). These women were often the captured wives of conquered rulers and their nobles. Kept as virtual slaves, they were used as wives to bear children, especially sons.

her allowance: Hegai made certain that Esther received choice food in liberal portions. He also gave her seven personal attendants and the most desirable place to live within the quarters of the harem.

2:10–13 Many reasons have been suggested concerning Esther's hesitation to **reveal** her national origin. The time does come when Esther would identify herself and her people (ch. 8). In fact, her self-disclosure would come at the point when the danger to her person was highest.

2:14 concubines: These women lived unfortunate, though highly pampered, lives. If the king never **called for** them again, they were destined to live as though they were widows for the remainder of their years (2 Sam. 20:3). The point made here emphasizes how courageous Esther was when she later made her appearance before Ahasuerus (4:11; 5:1).

2:15 Again we see the providence of God at work. Esther found favor with everyone she encountered. Here we learn her father's name, **Abihail** (2:7).

2:16 Esther became the principal wife of the king four years after Vashti was divorced. This period harmonizes with what we know from other historical accounts of the period. The account suggests that Ahasuerus (Xerxes) sought solace in his harem after his military trouncing in his disastrous campaign in Greece, a story is told by the Greek historian Herodotus. The month **Tebeth** corresponds to our December-January.

2:17 The king apparently was so delighted with Esther that he **made her queen** right away. The nouns **grace and favor** together mean "abundant favor."

2:18, 19 sat within the king's gate: This phrase has a special significance; it means that Mordecai had an official position. Shortly after Esther became queen, she gave Mordecai a position within the king's gate where official business took place (Deut. 22:13–15). In this strategic position, Mordecai was well placed not only in terms of his personal status but also to discern the various winds of power and intrigue that might endanger his cousin Esther. This is the kind work of God's providence. Mordecai was also able to use his position to discover the plot of the doorkeepers to kill the king (2:21). Mordecai's motivation was principally one of loyalty to the king, not a selfish desire to gain information that would be personally helpful in instances of palace intrigue.

2:20–23 Mordecai learned of a plot by **two** angry **eunuchs** to take the king's life. Mordecai not only used this information to save the king, but eventually his own people.

3:1 Some believe **Agagite** as a reference to the historical district of Agag within the Persian empire. Others believe this term more likely linked Haman's descent with the Amalekites. These people, descendants of Esau (Gen. 36:12), were ancient enemies of the Hebrews (Ex. 17:8). Agag, a king of the Amalekites, was captured by King Saul (1 Sam. 15:8). If Mordecai descended from Saul, and Haman from the Amalekites (as many rabbis believe), then what follows is the continuation of a long-standing hostility between their families.

3:2–4 All the officials of the king were on duty within the king's gate. **Mordecai would not bow or pay homage:** To comprehend the force of this verse, we need to look at v. 4. There Mordecai reportedly told the king's servants that he was a Jew. It is not known whether the bowing was required as an act of worship to the king's man or merely as an overt sign of deep respect. The Hebrew verbs in this passage usually describe the worship of God. There were occasions when Hebrews bowed before kings or high officials (1 Sam. 24:8) without any violation of the prohibitions of false worship. It may be that in Mordecai's case also, the bow was not to be a religious act, but one of honor. As a Jew, Mordecai may have not been able to bring himself to show this sign of respect to one who was an ancestral enemy.

3:5, 6 Mordecai's daily refusal to bow down to **Haman** filled the official with such rage that he sought to kill all Jewish people in the Persian empire. Haman's Amalekite ancestry would account for his deep hatred.

3:7 Nisan: This, the first month of the ancient lunar calendar, corresponds to March-April. The twelfth year of the king's reign was 474 B.C. **they cast pur:** The word *pur* was the basis for the name of the Feast of Purim in ch. 9. The casting of lots was common in ancient times. The fact that the lot was cast at the beginning of the year to determine the best time to destroy the Jewish people fits with the culture of the day. The Babylonian religion maintained that the gods gathered at the beginning of each year to establish the destiny of human beings.

3:8, 9 Haman did not identify the **people** at first. He may have played on the Persian emperor's native sense of superiority to other peoples. Haman acted as if his motive were no more than proper concern for the welfare of the king. He implied that this unnamed group was rebellious, a present danger to the king.

3:10 The king's **signet ring** symbolized his authority. When he gave this ring to Haman, he was passing to him a symbol of his own royal person. This meant that Haman could proceed with his plan.

3:11 It might seem that the king was refusing

to accept **the money.** However, this is difficult to harmonize with Mordecai's words to Esther in 4:7 and her comments about being "sold" in 7:4. More likely, the king was engaging in the common method of bargaining (Gen. 23:7–18).

3:12 scribes: The king had secretaries who put into writing the official documents. This verse gives us a picture of the comprehensiveness of the decree. It was given to officials in the provinces, making sure it was distributed everywhere. It was also written in the language of each people group within the realm. The mark of a signet ring was similar to an official signature in our own day (1 Kin. 21:8).

3:13, 14 The **couriers** were royal messengers stationed at various spots along the main roads who would carry messages on horseback. The plot to **kill** the Jewish people included the slaughter of those of all age groups and both sexes. The month **Adar:** This corresponds to February-March (3:7; 8:12).

3:15 The contempt of the king and Haman who **sat down to drink** while this message was being delivered cannot help but strike a responsive chord of empathy for the Jewish people among the readers of this book. The text notes that even the people in the city of Shushan were perplexed. The severe brutality of the decree is emphasized by the utter unconcern for human life expressed in this line. On the other hand, God's providence is certainly seen in the allowance of eleven months' time before the decree will go into effect.

4:1, 2 In the ancient Middle East **sackcloth and ashes** were used as a visible sign of mourning, indicating a sense of desolation.

4:3 In this book **fasting** connotes a strong but veiled appeal to God to intervene in a time of severe crisis. In v. 16 Esther commanded a three-day fast among Shushan's Jews. The queen herself, along with her maids, undertook a fast at this time before she approached the king. Even the Feast of Purim, which was established to commemorate the Jewish people's deliverance, incorporated fasting (9:31).

4:4 The verb **distressed** is strong, suggesting the idea of writhing in severe pain or anguish. Certainly Esther was deeply disturbed by Mordecai's appearance and agony, though she did not as yet understand what had happened (v. 5).

4:5, 6 city square: Many events took place in the plaza of a city, including gatherings, proclamations, and public lamentation.

4:7 If Mordecai had not been appointed as a high official at the **king's** gate, it is unlikely that he would have known about Haman's bribe to the king. He was providentially placed by God in an exalted position in a foreign government, as were Joseph (Gen. 41), Daniel (Dan. 2:48), and Nehemiah (Neh. 1:11). This is one of the many ways God used the descendants of Abraham to be a blessing to the nations (Gen. 12:2).

4:8, 9 Mordecai recognized the decree as a threat to the very existence of his people, so he boldly commanded Esther to intercede for her people before the king, knowing that this could only be at the risk of her life (v. 11). If she was not identified as a Hebrew woman, she might possibly escape the fate of her people—but only if her association with Mordecai (2:7, 15) was not remembered by their enemies. In any event, she would be in a most risky position. **make supplication:** The word means to ask for a gracious response. It is a term that often is used of coming to the Lord for deliverance; here it is used of coming to a king for mercy.

4:10, 11 Esther understood that Mordecai was asking her to risk her life. She was understandably fearful. Her fear was compounded by

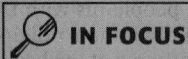 **IN FOCUS**   **"fasting"**

(Heb. *tsum*) (Esth. 4:16; 2 Sam. 12:23) Strong's #6684: The Hebrew root word simply means "to abstain from food." At times fasting meant abstaining from drinking, bathing, anointing with oil, or sexual intercourse. In essence, fasting acknowledges human frailty before God and appeals to His mercy. Fasting was a common practice in the ancient world, associated with mourning for the dead (2 Sam. 12:21, 22), intercessory prayer (4:3, 16), repentance and contrition for sin (Jer. 36:9; Jon. 3:5), and times of distress (Judg. 20:26; Neh. 1:4). Fasting was required for the Day of Atonement ("afflict your souls"; Lev. 16:31). There were also four fast days that commemorated the destruction of Jerusalem by the Babylonians (Zech. 8:19). Fasts varied in length from one day (1 Sam. 14:24; Dan. 6:18) to seven days (1 Sam. 31:13) and could even last up to forty days on extraordinary occasions (Ex. 34:28). The strict fasts lasted from sunset to sunset, whereas the more lenient fasts lasted from sunrise to sunset. But no matter what type of fasting was performed, the prophet Isaiah admonished His people to participate in acts of righteousness and social justice with their fasting (Is. 58:3–9).

the fact that the king had not summoned her for **thirty days,** implying that she had not been enjoying the king's favor recently. Who knew if he would still have regard for her at all?

4:12–14 This verse constitutes the classic reference to the providence of God in the book. Mordecai, by his confidence that **relief and deliverance** would come from **another place,** was strongly asserting his faith in God and His promised protection of the Jewish people. God controls all that happens in His world and would intervene with or without Esther. If she refused to help, she would perish, along with her **father's house.** Mordecai may be referring to divine judgment here. In the closing appeal, Mordecai suggested a providential reason for her becoming queen at this precise time in history; that is, Esther was acting as God's agent in delivering the Jewish people. **who knows:** Since Yahweh is in control of human history, and since He regularly uses His people to work out of His purposes, these wonderful, well-known words can extend to the lives of God's people everywhere.

4:15–17 Esther agreed to intervene with the king on behalf of her people. The fasting **for three days** implies a period of earnestly seeking God in prayer at this critical juncture. But even at this point, the narrator did not use the name of God—something that is most remarkable. Esther was also looking for the support of the Jewish community by asking them to join in this fast. Esther understood fully that she was breaking the law of the land and that she might have to suffer the ultimate consequence; she might **perish.**

5:1 A part of a **day** in Hebrew culture was counted as a whole day (read 4:16, where Esther speaks of three days and three nights). Apparently from the **inner court,** the king could see Esther from his throne room (5:2).

5:2 she found favor in his sight: Again we are struck by the providence of God, demonstrated by the king's response to Esther. To indicate his approval, the king held out the **golden scepter** to her.

5:3 The king, knowing that Esther must have had an unusual reason for daring to approach him, asked her what she wanted. He promised her **up to half** his **kingdom.** A similar promise was given to the daughter of Herodias by King Herod in Mark 6:23. Perhaps the phrase was a common form of exaggeration among royalty. Although it probably was exaggerated, the statement certainly showed the king's favorable attitude toward her.

5:4, 5 If it pleases the king: This expression is found frequently throughout the book. It was a formula of polite address. Esther made her initial request; she invited the king and Haman to come to her **banquet** that same day.

5:6–8 The king continued examining Esther for the real **request.** She delayed and asked the two back for a second banquet the following day. One may ask why Esther waited instead of disclosing what was on her mind. The delay providentially allowed time for the king's sleepless night and the events that followed (ch. 6).

5:6 The Persian feasts incorporated considerable consumption of **wine** (note at 1:8). Even the origin of the noun translated "banquet" is derived from the verb meaning "to drink." The author pointedly observes the wanton lifestyle of the Persian kings.

5:7–9 Haman's good spirits on the way home from the banquet were from the wine he had drunk and from the honor of being invited along with the king to the feast at Esther's table. However, his mood changed quickly when he encountered Esther's cousin. This time **Mordecai** did not even rise in his presence. Further, Mordecai showed no sign of fear before him, despite the death decree against the Jewish people.

5:10–12 Haman's vanity matched that of the king he served. He bragged to his wife and friends about his wealth, his sons, and his status in the kingdom. It was considered a great blessing among ancient Semitic peoples to have many sons. In Persia, the man with the most sons would receive presents from the king himself.

5:13, 14 gallows: This word is the usual word for wood, the material the gallows were made of (2:23). Its height, **fifty cubits,** was about 75 feet.

6:1 This verse marks the turning point of the book. Within this chapter we observe a series of events that unmistakably point to God's sovereign hand controlling all events. Only because of his sleepless night did the king learn of Mordecai's past bravery on his behalf. **the book of the records of the chronicles:** This would be the official record of the events of the Persian empire. It is referred to in 2:23 and again in 10:2. Ezra 4:15 also mentions such a work. Apparently the chronicles **were read before the king** for an extended period.

6:2, 3 The king might have been aware to some extent of Mordecai's deed when it originally occurred. In 2:23 the author says that the events were written down "in the presence of the king." Now the Lord led the king to this very text. It was customary for the Persian kings to reward promptly those who performed some noteworthy act of service. There are records of Darius and Ahasuerus bestowing such honors on deserving recipients. The two nouns **honor** and **dignity** mean "great honor."

6:4, 5 Again we see the hand of God sovereignly at work on behalf of his people. No sooner had Mordecai's reward been discussed than Haman appeared in the king's **court.** Ironically, Haman, who knew nothing of the recent discussion, was coming to recommend that Mordecai be hanged.

6:6–11 One cannot miss the irony and humor of this turn of events. In his arrogance, Haman presumed that the king desired to honor him. He suggested a course of action that he would most enjoy, a royal parade through the city plaza so that everyone could see and hear about the king's delight in him. The king obliged, but was planning the reward for a man Haman regarded as his enemy. Worst of all, it was Haman who had to lead Mordecai through the square and proclaim the king's pleasure in Mordecai.

6:8, 9 The **royal crest** on the head of the horse was a crown that formed from the forelock of the horse. Stone carvings of horses with this type of crest have been found at Persepolis, another Persian capital (1:2).

6:10 The term **Jew,** derived from Judah, came into use during the exile because the people were principally from the southern kingdom of Judah.

6:11, 12 That Mordecai was elevated instead of Haman, who had plotted his destruction, is an example of several dramatic reversals in the Book of Esther. For instance, Haman is hanged on the very gallows which he had built for Mordecai (7:10), and on the very day the enemies of the Jewish people hoped to overpower them, they were overpowered by the Jewish people (9:1). The hand of God in may bring about many such reversals for His people (compare 9:20–25).

6:13 The issue of the ongoing survival of the Jewish people is the point of this verse. Haman's wife and friends told Haman that he would **not prevail,** for the very reason of Mordecai's Jewish descent. The Hebrew wording is quite strong: the meaning is that he will most certainly fall.

6:14 The role of **eunuchs** as royal messengers is portrayed again in this verse (1:10). They were the ones who came to take Haman briskly to Esther's second banquet.

7:1, 2 This is an introductory element for the events to follow.

7:3, 4 Esther repeated her address of 5:8 and now added her request. **let my life be given:** Esther asked the king to spare her life and the lives of her people. This latter appeal was an impassioned plea to the king in which she also disclosed her true identity to him for the first time. Esther told the king that she and her fellow Jewish people **have been sold,** referring to Haman's bribe to the king in 3:9.

7:5 Esther's speech had a dramatic effect on the king. She had aroused more than his curiosity. He was angry. The life of his own queen was in danger because of a plot by one of his trusted men. The phrase **dare presume in his heart** reflects the depths of the king's passion here.

7:6 Esther finally exposed the culprit. It was none other than Haman, the **adversary** and **enemy,** "the fierce enemy." It is no wonder that Haman was **terrified** before Esther and the king. In his evil plan to kill his enemy, he had unwittingly threatened the queen's life.

7:7 The king was astonished and furious. He left the room and went out to the **palace garden.** This must have been a very unusual act for an autocrat. Usually, he would be expected to respond immediately and rashly. However, this time he was so taken aback by the turn of events that he needed time to think. The king's enraged response alerted Haman to the precariousness of his situation.

7:8 Haman was draped over the queen's **couch** in a compromising position. Presumably, he was grasping at her with a desire to implore her favor. The king, on discovering this outrageous situation, wondered aloud if Haman intended to ravage the queen. The Persians had strict rules about contact with the harem by any male other than the king. The eunuchs were the only persons who had access to the rooms of these women. Haman was in danger merely by being near her. This sight enraged the king. As he spoke, **they covered Haman's face.** It is likely that it was the eunuchs who came and did this. The covering of his face signified that he was condemned to death.

7:9, 10 Harbonah: This eunuch, first mentioned in 1:10, spoke at a critical moment to the ruler. He disclosed the story of the **gallows** which Haman had prepared for Mordecai and told the king where it was located. He reminded the monarch of Mordecai's bravery on behalf of the king. Ahasuerus took Harbonah's cue and commanded his servants to **hang** Haman on those very gallows.

8:1 On the same day as Haman's execution, the king gave his queen **the house of Haman.** The term *house* here refers to his estate. This was in keeping with Persian law, which put the estate of a traitor into the custody of the crown.

8:2 Mordecai was given Haman's position as the prime minister. He received the full authority of the king, as evidenced by the transfer of the **signet ring** to him. Esther also put Mordecai in charge of Haman's estate, which gave him great wealth.

8:3–6 Esther, knowing that danger still lurked ahead for her people, pleaded passionately for their lives before the king. The queen continued to receive the blessing of the monarch as he again extended the **golden scepter** to her. Courageously Esther implored the king to **revoke** Haman's hateful decree against all the Jews in the empire. The parallel statements in v. 6 reinforce Esther's poignant and personal plea to her king. The queen, by speaking in the first person, demonstrated her deep attachment to her people.

8:7 Mordecai had heard Esther's entire presentation to the king. Ahasuerus, by reiterating what he already had done, communicated his support for Esther and her people.

8:8 In the Persian empire, a royal **decree** could not be altered, but a second one could invalidate it. Thus, the king instructed Mordecai and Esther to write a second decree. The second decree would carry all the weight of the former one—but would reverse the expected results.

8:9, 10 Sivan: This would be May to June. The date would give the Jewish people approximately eight months of preparation for any attack (3:13).

8:11–14 These verses have occasioned controversy about whether the Jewish people were unethical toward their enemies. Some commentators understand these verses to mean that the Jewish people were given permission to slaughter even the wives and children of any people that would attack them. Another view is that the Jewish people may not have carried out what was permitted, but killed only the men who attacked them (9:6). There is another possibility, that these verses refer to the women and children of the Jews. That is, the assault mentioned here was expected to be directed against the men, women, children, and possessions of the Jews. Against such assault, the Jews were to arm themselves and make proper defenses (9:5, 6). **plunder their possessions:** This phrase could be a citation of Haman's decree (3:13). If so, it would explain why the Jewish people did not take any plunder (9:10), but simply defended themselves against their enemies.

8:15, 16 Mordecai, dressed in royal attire, received a joyful welcome from the **city of Shushan,** which included both Gentiles and Jews. The residents of this city **rejoiced** that Mordecai had been appointed as prime minister. The word **light** conveys the sense of happiness.

8:17 Note the marked contrast of the reaction of the Jewish people to this second decree as compared to the first one (4:3). The reality of

What an amazing outcome of Haman's hate— the evangelization of many Persians.

their deliverance influenced the Gentiles in the empire as well. **became:** This is the only place in the OT that this Hebrew word is used of conversion to Judaism. The unexpected turn of events in favor of the Jewish people greatly moved their neighbors.

The power of the God of Israel is implied here in the triumph of Mordecai over Haman, in the reversal of Haman's decree, and in the response of these pagan peoples. If the people truly became Jewish people, then they would share with the Jewish people faith in Yahweh, participation in the community as proselytes, and partake of Israel's blessing. What an amazing outcome of Haman's hate—the evangelization of many Persians!

9:1, 2 The Jewish people assembled throughout the kingdom to **lay hands on** or kill (2:21) their foes. The enemies of the Jewish people could not succeed in their assault against them due to a **fear** of them. This may have included a fear of the God of the Jewish people.

9:3, 4 In addition to a fear of the Jewish people, there was also a **fear of Mordecai** among the leaders, which caused them to assist the Jewish people. Their motive may have been to protect themselves politically in light of Mordecai's power and popularity.

9:5, 6 The defense of the Jewish people against their enemies was strong and certain. They **killed** five hundred of their enemies in Shushan alone.

9:7–10 The author returns to the conflict with Haman by recording the death of his ten sons. The patterns of reprisal and vengeance were so deeply ingrained in the cultures of the ancient Middle East that the survival of even one of these sons might mean trouble for the next generation of Jewish people. By listing each of the vanquished sons of their mortal enemy, the Jewish people celebrated the fact that the victory was complete.

9:11–14 Esther renewed her original request (8:11) for the Jews to have the authority to protect themselves against attack. The king assented. He also ordered **Haman's ten sons** to be exposed on the gallows. The men were already dead (v. 10). Their bodies were displayed as a warning to anyone who planned evil toward the Jews.

9:15, 16 In Deut. 25:17–19, Moses linked the people's continued **rest from their enemies** with the command to "blot out the remembrance of Amalek from under heaven."

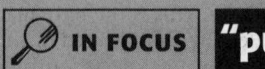

"pur"

(Heb. *pur*) (Esth. 3:7; 9:24, 26) Strong's #6332: *Pur*, originally a Babylonian word meaning "lot" or "fate," is used in Esther as a synonym for the normal Hebrew word for "lot." Lot casting, similar to rolling dice, was a common way to make a random selection (Neh. 11:1) or to discern the will of a god (Jon. 1:7). Believing that his gods controlled the fall of the *pur*, Haman cast lots to determine the right day to destroy the Jews (3:7). What he failed to realize was that God is sovereign and cannot be manipulated by superstition (Prov. 16:33). By casting lots, Haman inadvertently chose the day of the Jews' deliverance, a day that is still celebrated in the festival of Purim (9:28).

In this chapter, the blessing of rest for the Jewish people is associated with the destruction of their enemies (vv. 18, 22). This similarity with Deuteronomy reinforces the argument that Haman was a descendant of the Amalekites. This group may have been quite large by the time of King Ahasuerus.

9:17–19 These verses summarize the days of deliverance for the Jewish people. In Shushan, they had two days of fighting, then they rested and celebrated on the fifteenth day of **Adar** (February to March; 3:7, 12). The Jewish people in the remainder of the Persian provinces fought for one day and fasted on the fourteenth day of that month.

9:20–25 In light of the difference of timing between the Jews in Shushan and Jews in the rest of the kingdom, Mordecai told the people by **letter** that they should designate both the fourteenth and the fifteenth of Adar as annual holidays. These verses summarize the events of the book.

9:25 The subject of the verb **came** is not clear in the Hebrew. It is possible that the subject is some reference to the **wicked plot**. If so, the word "it" makes sense as a substitute for the word **Esther** here.

9:26–32 Purim: These verses explain the name of the two-day festival. The name is derived form the word *pur*, meaning "lot," the lot that was cast to determine the day of the Jewish people's death. Purim reminds the Jews of God's deliverance from their day of destruction. The feast was established as an annual festival.

10:1 tribute: This word may refer both to taxation and forced labor that the king imposed on all his territory.

10:2, 3 The Book of Esther concludes with high praise of Mordecai, whose deeds were recorded in the official chronicles of the Persian empire. Mordecai held the **second** highest rank in the land, a note that recalls Joseph's ascendancy in Egypt (Gen. 41:37–45).

The Book of

Job

A T ONE TIME OR ANOTHER, ALMOST EVERYONE HAS felt like Job. While going through trials and times of suffering, we are often overwhelmed by self-pity. We want an explanation for why God allows trials to happen to us. The Book of Job records the troubling questions, the terrifying doubts, and the very real anguish of a sufferer. The Book of Job can help us in the time when we are surrounded with troubles by

giving us a glimpse of God's perspective on our suffering.

Numerous details in the Book of Job indicate a patriarchal setting for its events: (1) Job's wealth is measured in livestock (1:3; 42:12), the same way Abraham and Jacob's wealth is measured (Gen. 12:16; 13:2; 30:43; 32:5). (2) The Sabeans and Chaldeans are portrayed as nomadic marauders (1:15, 17), indicating an early date. (3) The Hebrew word for *piece of silver* in Job (42:11) is otherwise found only in conjunction with the patriarch Jacob (Gen. 33:19; Josh. 24:32). (4) Without a priesthood or a sanctuary, Job offered sacrifices to God in a patriarchal fashion (1:5). (5) Job's longevity is consistent with the life spans of the patriarchs (42:16). (6) The preference in the poetic sections of the book for the divine name Shaddai over the divine name Yahweh may indicate a period before the Exodus (Ex. 3:14, 15).

The text indicates that the events of Job occurred in the land of Uz (1:1), but the location of Uz is unknown. That Job was the greatest among the people of the East (1:3) indicates that Job lived east of the Jordan River. Some have concluded that Uz was located in Syria or north-

west Mesopotamia. However, most writers think Uz was located near Edom, because many of the proper names in the Book of Job occur in the genealogy of Esau, the father of the Edomites (Gen. 36).

The basic structure of the Book of Job consists of a prose framework in the prologue (chs. 1; 2) and epilogue (42:7–17) enclosing the poetic body of the book (3:1—42:6). There are significant differences between the poetic body and the prologue and epilogue. The prologue and epilogue present Job as a patient "saint" who righteously endured suffering. On the other hand, the poetic body presents Job as despairing of fair treatment by God (9:1–3, 13–21). According to some critics, these differences indicate that the two sections are separate works by different authors. According to this view, the compiler of Job simply failed to reconcile the "two Jobs."

The apparent contradictions within Job should not be considered an indication of poor editing but the deliberate work of an accomplished author. The tension between the "patient" Job and the "impatient" Job contributes to the overall message of the book. It shows Job as a real person. He was no "plaster saint" who suffered stoically. Instead, he struggled with his emotions and feelings as we do today. The Book of Job teaches that it is not wrong for a person to ask the question *why*, as Job did repeatedly (ch. 3). But these questions must not grow into accusations against the sovereign Lord.

The Book of Job explores all the traditional Middle Eastern explanations of the problem of the "righteous sufferer." These include: (1) the inherent sinfulness of the human race (5:6, 7; 15:14, 16); (2) the accusation that God is unjust (9:22–24); and (3) the limitations of human understanding (11:7–9). But the main difference between the Book of Job and other ancient texts that address this same problem is God's direct intervention in Job's life. Thus the uniqueness of the Book of Job is not in its approach to the problem of suffering but in its revelation of the sovereign God to whom everyone must properly relate. Sufferer and nonsufferer alike must humbly trust in God's sovereign grace. Because Job and his friends were ignorant of Satan's challenge to God, the Book of Job contains much bad theology and misapplied truth. It is important to read passages in the Book of Job in light of the message and purpose of the entire book. The only proper response to the omnipotent God is submission and faith.

The Book of Job repeatedly emphasizes the sovereignty and omnipotence of God. For instance, the Hebrew divine name *Shaddai*, usually translated as "Almighty," is employed by all characters in the book. Eliphaz describes the Almighty as controlling the destiny of everyone (5:17–20) and as independent of humanity (22:2, 3). Bildad argues that the Almighty is just (8:3, 4) and sovereign in His rule over the universe (25:2, 3). Finally Zophar describes the ways of the Almighty as beyond human comprehension (11:7–10). Hence, Job's friends use the name *Shaddai* to speak of God's transcendence as well as His sovereign power.

This emphasis on the sovereignty of God refutes a simplistic understanding of divine retribution, which assumes that there is an automatic connection between one's spirituality and prosperity on earth. Such was the basis of Satan's accusation in the prologue that Job served God only for his own profit (1:9–11). Moreover, it is the basis for Eliphaz and Bildad's advice to Job. Both claimed that Job's suffering pointed to a hidden sin in Job's life, because God certainly would not punish an upright person (4:7–11; 8:11–22; 18:5–21). But God's answer to Job refuted this false belief (38:1—39:30). The Lord declared Himself completely sovereign. He is not obligated to bless those who obey Him. All His actions are based on His gracious nature and His own free will. In this way, the Book of Job is an extended refutation of Satan's challenge that prosperity is connected to people's goodness, and consequently that people's suffering is connected to their sin.

In this way, the Book of Job teaches that the Lord is not bound to anyone's preconceived theological system. Elihu's speech on God's greatness and His sovereign majesty over nature (36:1—37:24) serve as a prelude to the climax of the book: the Lord's answer to Job (38:1—

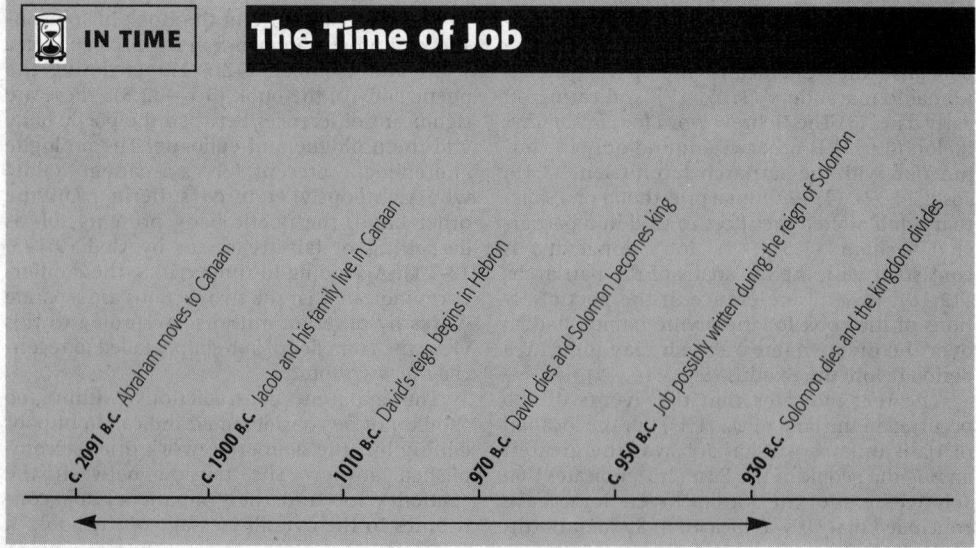

IN TIME

The Time of Job

c. 2091 B.C. Abraham moves to Canaan

c. 1900 B.C. Jacob and his family live in Canaan

1010 B.C. David's reign begins in Hebron

970 B.C. David dies and Solomon becomes king

c. 950 B.C. Job possibly written during the reign of Solomon

930 B.C. Solomon dies and the kingdom divides

42:6). In His speech, God lowers Himself to Job's level in order to answer Job's questions. In the process, He reveals to all people that He is completely free but also truly good. He is the sovereign and benevolent Creator who continues to determine the course of the universe according to His own hidden plan. Just like Job, we must learn to submit to the Almighty God and accept by faith that He has a good plan for us.

There is no consensus about who wrote the Book of Job or when it was written. Suggestions for an author include Job, Elihu, Solomon, and even Moses.

As for the time of writing, there is strong literary evidence that the Book of Job was compiled and written during the time of Solomon, when wisdom literature flourished. The mention of iron tools and weapons (19:24; 20:24; 40:18) and even mining (28:2) implies a date during the Iron Age (after 1200 B.C.). Moreover, the description of a horse in a military context (39:19–25) may indicate the mounted warhorse, which was used at the earliest around the tenth century B.C. Furthermore, at least two passages in Job may allude to biblical passages from the Solomonic era (compare 7:17, 18 with Ps. 8:4; compare 28:28 with Prov. 3:7; 9:10). These various strands of evidence may indicate that Job was written around the time of Solomon's reign.

Outline

I. Prose prologue 1:1–2:13
   A. Job's piety and prosperity 1:1–5
   B. Job's perseverance during two tests 1:6–2:13
II. Poetic body 3:1–42:6
   A. Job's initial monologue 3:1–26
   B. A dialogue in three cycles 4:1–27:23
      1. First cycle of speeches 4:1–14:22
         a. Eliphaz's first speech 4:1–5:27
         b. Job's response 6:1–7:21
         c. Bildad's first speech 8:1–22
         d. Job's response 9:1–10:22
         e. Zophar's first speech 11:1–20
         f. Job's response to Zophar and friends 12:1–14:22
      2. Second cycle of speeches 15:1–21:34
         a. Eliphaz's second speech 15:1–35
         b. Job's response 16:1–17:16
         c. Bildad's second speech 18:1–21
         d. Job's response 19:1–29
         e. Zophar's second speech 20:1–29
         f. Job's response 21:1–34
      3. Third cycle of speeches 22:1–27:23
         a. Eliphaz's third speech 22:1–30
         b. Job's response 23:1–24:25
         c. Bildad's third speech 25:1–6
         d. Job's response 26:1–14
         e. Job's response to the three friends 27:1–23
   C. Interlude: a poem on wisdom 28:1–28
   D. Job's concluding monologues 29:1–31:40
   E. Elihu's speeches 32:1–37:24
   F. God's speeches and Job's responses 38:1–42:6
      1. God's first speech 38:1–40:2
      2. Job's initial response 40:3–5
      3. God's second speech 40:6–41:34
      4. Job's final response 42:1–6
III. Prose epilogue 42:7–17
   A. God's rebuke of Job's three friends 42:7–9
   B. God's restoration of Job's prosperity 42:10–17

Commentary

1:1 The dramatic events of the prologue of the Book of Job set the stage for the intricate dialogues of the main body (3:1—42:6). **Uz:** The precise location is unknown but may have been near Edom. Two aspects of Job's character and actions are highlighted. **Blameless** and **upright,** meaning "straightforward" and "ethically straight," emphasize his spotless character. Like Daniel (Dan. 6:4), Job was blameless before his human critics, but not completely sinless before God. He later testified of his personal integrity (31:5, 6). Job **feared God and shunned evil,** an indication that his right relationship with God motivated him to turn away from evil. This descriptive phrase indicates that Job was the epitome of wisdom (28:28; Prov. 3:7; 14:16; also Prov. 1:7; 9:10).

1:2, 3 Job had an ideal family consisting of **seven sons and three daughters.** The number seven was the biblical number of completeness. In the ancient Middle East, having many children was generally considered a sign of God's blessing (Ps. 127:3–5).

1:4 Each of Job's sons would participate in a feast with his siblings on **his appointed day.** The term could refer to a birthday celebration. However, the context of v. 5 may indicate a regular, perhaps weekly or seasonal, cycle of celebration and feasting.

1:5 When Job undertook to **sanctify** his children through **burnt offerings,** he performed an intercessory role that corresponds to what he did when he prayed for his friends in the epilogue (42:10). **cursed God:** The Hebrew text has "blessed God," which is probably a euphemism—a reverent substitution of a milder word by a Hebrew scribe because he could not bear to have the word *cursed* next to the divine name.

1:6 The sons of God are celestial beings or angels who were created by Him and who serve Him (4:18; Ps. 103:20, 21) as his "holy ones" (5:1). Compare the expression "sons of God" in

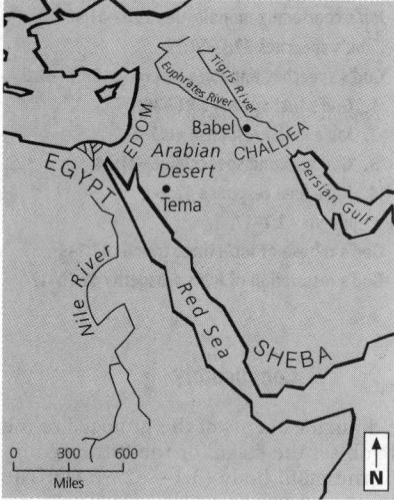

The Land of Uz

No one knows the exact location of Job's homeland, the land of Uz (Job 1:1). However, the Bible states or suggests several things about Uz. It was located in the East (1:3). This probably means somewhere east of the Jordan River. Job's friend Eliphaz came from Teman (2:11), known to be in Edom (Gen. 36:8; Jer. 49:20). Teman was the grandson of Esau (Gen. 36:11), and the region of Teman probably was named for him. It seems appropriate that Eliphaz was a Temanite, for apparently the Temanites had a reputation for wisdom (Jer. 49:7). ("Temanite" could also refer to Tema in the Arabian Desert; compare Job 6:19).

Gen. 6:1, where the phrase is used of angels who were enemies of the Lord. The imagery seemingly indicates a heavenly council over which the Lord sits as Supreme King (Ps. 89:5–7; Dan. 7:9, 10). Strictly speaking, **Satan** may be a title rather than the personal name of the leader of all evil forces. The Hebrew word was not clearly used as a proper name until 1 Chr. 21:1, chronologically one of the last OT books written. Nevertheless, the characteristics of the "Adversary" in the Book of Job imply that he was in fact Satan. He answered God's questions in an antagonistic manner and accused Job of ulterior motives. That Satan **came among** the hosts of heaven at this time suggests that Satan still had access to God's court, and that his final banishment was still in the future.

1:7 The Hebrew word Yahweh, usually translated **the Lord**, is the personal name of the true God of the OT (Ex. 3:14, 15). It is the particular name of God in covenantal relations with His people Israel (Ex. 6:1–6; 19:3–8). This indicates that though Job was not an Israelite, he had a relationship with the true God (read v. 21 where the Lord's name is employed). **From where do you come:** God's inquiry does not imply an ignorance of Satan's behavior but was part of the conversation with Satan. See the similar function of the question posed to Adam after the Fall (Gen. 3:9).

1:8 My servant refers to the proper relationship every person should have with God—that is, a joyful and reverent trust in God. Job was a model of this type of relationship with the Lord in the prologue and the epilogue (2:3; 42:7).

1:9 Satan, always "the adversary," questioned Job's motives for fearing and serving God. The expression **for nothing** is emphatic in the Hebrew text. The question may be paraphrased, "Is Job really free of ulterior motives?"

1:10 God had placed a **hedge** of protection **around** Job and **his household.** No harm could come to him unless the Lord permitted it

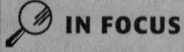 **IN FOCUS** | **"blameless"**

(Heb. *tam*) (1:1, 8; 8:20; 9:21; Ps. 37:37; Prov. 29:10) Strong's #8535 The verbal root of this Hebrew word means "to be complete." Thus, this word signifies an individual's integrity—a wholeness and wholesomeness. The word is used as a term of endearment for the Shulamite bride in the Song of Solomon ("perfect" in Song 5:2; 6:9). In the OT, the blameless are frequently associated with the upright (1:1, 8; 2:3; Ps. 37:37; Prov. 29:10) and contrasted with the wicked (9:22; Ps. 64:2–4). Job's claim to be blameless agrees with God's assessment of him, but it is not a claim to absolute perfection (1:8; 9:21; 14:16, 17). The Psalmist writes that the future of the blameless man is peace—as was the case for Job (42:10–12; Ps. 37:37).

(vv. 12; 2:4–6). Believers today should take great comfort from the biblical teaching that the Lord protects His people—whether by a cloud (Ex. 14:19, 20) or by a wall of fiery hosts (2 Kin. 6:17) or through guardian angels (Heb. 1:14).

1:11 Satan ignored customary court etiquette that would not permit him to address God directly as **You,** or use the personal references **Your hand** or **Your face.** Such irreverence was part of his constant strategy to demean God. **curse:** The sin of cursing God is a pivotal issue for the Book of Job. Job feared that his children might think or speak irreverently of God (v. 5). But Satan asserted that Job would **surely curse** God if his prosperity and blessings were removed. Even Job's wife would urge him to "curse God and die" (2:9).

1:12 That **Satan** must receive permission from the Lord to **lay a hand on** Job (v. 11) indicates that God limits Satan's power. Believers can find strength and assurance from the fact that Satan's actions are limited by God's sovereign control. After the prologue, Satan is never mentioned directly again in the Book of Job; he is only a minor character compared to the Lord of the universe.

1:13–19 In one **day** Job plummeted from the pinnacle of prosperity to the pit of poverty. He must have felt that all heaven and earth had turned against him. The four rapid disasters that struck him came alternately from earth and heaven. First was the raiding of his livestock and **servants;** then from heaven, **the fire of God;** then again from earth, the loss of his **camels** and **servants;** and then the climactic blow again from heaven, **a great wind** that demolished his **house** and killed his children.

1:14–16 The **Sabeans** were nomadic raiders from Sheba. They were probably the people of the queen of Sheba (1 Kin. 10:1–13). Her homeland was probably southwestern Arabia, present-day Yemen.

1:17–19 The Chaldeans were part of various west Semitic marauding tribes active in the middle Euphrates from the twelfth to the ninth century B.C. They migrated eastward into Assyria and then into Babylonia, and were the forerunners of the Chaldean or neo-Babylonian dynasty established by Nebuchadnezzar's father.

1:20 Finally the spotlight focuses on Job's reaction to his trials. Did he serve God for profit as Satan had alleged (1:9)? Job passed the first test with a model response. He showed intense grief according to the accepted custom of his day

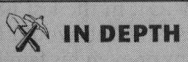

IN DEPTH | The Adversary

While the Book of Job teaches us much about human suffering, we also learn a great deal about Satan and his relationship to God. The first two chapters of Job demonstrate that although Satan is in rebellion, he is still accountable to God.

Originally an angel of God, Satan became corrupt through his own pride (2 Pet. 2:4; Jude 6). Ever since his rebellion against God, Satan has been God's enemy as well as ours. In fact, the Hebrew word for Satan means "Adversary." In the story of Job, Satan remained true to his name by accusing Job and afflicting him with all kinds of suffering. However, Satan's power is not equal to God's. Although Satan attempts to hamper God's work, he is limited by God. As much as he may wish to be a god, Satan still remains answerable to God.

In addition to being accountable to God (1:6), Satan, as a created being, is finite. He is not all-powerful, and he can be in only one place at one time (1:7). Therefore, his fellow fallen angels must aid him in his evil work. Of course, Satan can tempt us, but he cannot know what is in our minds or foretell our future (1:9–11). Most important, he can do nothing without God's permission (1:6–12). Because God actively restrains Satan (1:12; 2:6) and promises that He will not allow us to be tempted beyond what we can bear (1 Cor. 10:13), we can be confident that with God's power we can overcome Satan. Although we live in a fallen world, Satan does not have free reign to do whatever evil he wishes. God is still, and always will be, sovereign.

It was Satan who planned and implemented Job's suffering. God may have allowed Satan to test Job for a time. But in His time God Himself delivered Job from suffering, restored him, and blessed him even more than before (42:10). Even through Satan's evil plan, God had accomplished His good purposes. The relationship between Job and God was tested, and it withstood the test. God's love had won; Satan's accusations were answered. It was finally clear to all that God was both sovereign and compassionate. Through the experience, Job learned to appreciate God's gifts to him even more (42:1–6).

✠ IN CONTEXT — About the "Sons of God"

The term "sons of God" (Job 2:1; compare 1:6; 38:7) refers here to the angels, heavenly beings who are superior to humans in power and intelligence. According to the Book of Job, these beings would periodically present themselves before God, though we know little about the gatherings.

It may seem odd to find Satan mentioned as one of the "sons of God." Elsewhere Scripture describes him as an angel who was cast out of heaven for rebelling against God. Now he seeks to undermine the cause of righteousness in the world. In fact, the name Satan means "Adversary." So in what sense is Satan a "son of God"?

The Hebrew word for "son" (*bar*), can refer not only to an immediate male offspring but to a member of an entire class or category. For example, the OT speaks of the "sons of Israel" (Ex. 28:9) to refer to the descendants of Israel (Jacob), the Israelites. Likewise, the "sons of Asaph" (1 Chr. 25:1) refers to the temple musicians descended from Asaph, King David's principal musician.

In Job, the term "sons of God" is a descriptive term meaning "from or made by God," in the sense that angels, fallen or not, are spirits and inhabit the supernatural realm.

(v. 20). Then he humbly accepted God's will without complaining or blaming God for his tragedies. Job acknowledged God's sovereign control over all circumstances when he **fell to the ground and worshiped.** The context indicates that Job's fall was not an involuntary reflex of despair but a deliberate act of humility before God. Job's initial response was an ideal example of how to respond in time of crisis. Job is not only an ancient biblical hero but also an example for us when we face trials that test the mettle of each person's faith (1 Pet. 1:6, 7).

1:21 Having fallen on the ground, Job uttered words that were consistent with his posture. First, he gave a realistic appraisal of his status: just as he came into the world **naked,** so would he leave it **naked.** Then he repeatedly acknowledged the control of **the Lord** over all circumstances. The name Yahweh is used three times in this verse to emphasize Job's dependence on the true God. Except for 12:9, this is the only place where Job mentions the covenantal name of God. Though Job was not an Israelite, having lived in Uz centuries before the nation of Israel came out of Egypt, he worshiped the God of Israel.

1:22 Job had passed the test. He did not lash out at God, accusing him of doing **wrong** by permitting the tragedies.

2:1–3 The first sentence of this verse repeats 1:8 verbatim, emphasizing that Job's character had remained flawless despite Satan's assaults. In the second sentence the Lord affirms that Job had maintained **his integrity** (the same Hebrew root as *blameless* in 1:1, 8), although **Satan** had **incited** Him to destroy Job **without cause.** "Without cause" translates the same Hebrew word Satan had used in insinuating that

Job did not serve God "for nothing" (1:9). Now the Lord throws it back in his face.

2:4 The origin of the proverb **skin for skin** utilized by **Satan** is disputed. Some think it may have originated from the practice of bartering animal skins. Others believe that the phrase is similar to the proverb "life for life, eye for eye, tooth for tooth" (Ex. 21:23–25). In the last half of the verse Satan charges that Job would be willing to lose his possessions or even his family, as long as **his life** was spared.

2:5 bone . . . flesh: Satan sought to afflict Job's entire body with a debilitating disease.

2:6 When the Lord placed Job into Satan's **hand,** it is extraordinary that He commanded Satan to **spare his life.** Ironically, the word *spare* normally refers to God's role in His providential care of people (29:2).

2:7 The disease that inflicted Job with **painful boils** from head to toe is difficult to identify. The term for *boils* was used to describe the plague of boils in Egypt (Ex. 9:9–11). The same phrase *painful boils,* as one of the covenant curses for the disobedient (Deut. 28:35), denoted an incurable illness.

2:8 Again Job expressed his grief in the customary way (Jer. 6:26). **potsherd:** A piece of broken pottery. **ashes:** The town's trash heap.

2:9 The words of Job's wife—**curse God and die**—were probably Job's most severe trial. Ironically, her question **do you still hold fast to your integrity** employs almost exactly the same wording the Lord had used (v. 3). The wording emphasizes Job's perseverance, which his wife misconstrued as religious fanaticism—she thought he was blindly refusing to face the reality of his desperate situation.

2:10 Job's response to the second test, the

Insecurity in Job's World

Job doesn't explain what "the thing I greatly feared" was (Job 3:25). But there was little security in the world in which he lived. The dangers were many:

- diseases that struck livestock and people;
- famine, drought, and crop failure;
- destructive pests such as locusts and worms, and predators such as lions and wolves;
- weather-related calamities such as thunderstorms and lightning, floods, hail, windstorms, and tornadoes;
- bandits, raiders, and foreign invaders; and
- stillbirths and death to women due to complications in labor.

Job had lost his wealth, family, and health due to a number of these perils. The suddenness and enormity of his fall is a reminder that the people of the ancient world lived on the edge, never far from complete ruin. There was little they could do to protect themselves.

For example, the catastrophic loss of Job's wealth points to the fact that there were no banks. Most of Job's riches were on the hoof in the fields, extremely vulnerable to danger and loss.

loss of his health and alienation from his wife, was once again commendable. His rhetorical question, urging the acceptance of both **good** and **adversity from God,** anticipates one of the central messages of the Book of Job: the person of faith will trust in God through prosperity or adversity, even while unable to understand why bad things happen.

2:11 Eliphaz the Temanite was apparently an Edomite from Teman in northern Edom (Gen. 36:11). The term **Shuhite** may refer to Bildad's ancestry, or more likely to his geographical origin, since the other two friends seem to be identified by their home towns. **Zophar the Naamathite** may have come from Naameh, a mountainous area in northwestern Arabia.

2:12-13 These friends truly cared for Job because they **wept** and stayed close by him for **seven days and seven nights.** Yet later they would fail Job miserably by not listening to him (8:4-6; 13:5-13).

3:1, 2 When **Job cursed the day of his birth,** he came close to blasphemy. The Hebrew word for *cursed,* meaning "to hold in contempt," is elsewhere employed of cursing God (Ex. 22:28; Lev. 24:15) or cursing one's parents (Ex. 21:17). Job's pain had driven him to express a very strong malediction against the day of his birth and the night of his conception, which were personified as those responsible for his existence (vv. 3-6). However, Job did not commit blasphemy. He did not curse the Chaldeans or Sabeans, much less God. Neither did he express thoughts of suicide.

3:3-10 Job's wish that he had never been

born because his life was full of **sorrow** (vv. 3, 10) reflects a serious misunderstanding about the basic meaning of human existence. The Bible teaches that the purpose of life is not happiness but the praise of God's glory (Eph. 1:3-14).

3:8-19 Job employed two separate Hebrew words translated **curse,** different from the Hebrew term in v. 1. He wished that the popular magicians who cast spells on the day for their clients could have cast a spell on his day so that he would never have been born. Job's belief in one God (31:26-28) indicates that he was speaking poetically and dramatically. He was not endorsing any kind of pagan magic but employing vivid and forceful language to express the intensity of his agony and despair.

3:20-22 Even though Job longed for **death,** he was not considering suicide. The context of other passages indicates that Job merely wished that the Lord would let him die (7:15-21; 10:18-22).

3:23-26 Job bemoaned that God had **hedged** him **in** so that he could not die. The irony is that Job perceived God's protective hedge around him as keeping him from a desirable death. This is a typical feeling of those who suffer.

4:1 Since **Eliphaz the Temanite** spoke first, he was probably the oldest and therefore presumably the wisest of the three. Eliphaz was a little more courteous to Job than were his other two friends. However, his observations were distorted. Eliphaz firmly believed that God would never punish the righteous and would not preserve the sinner. He concluded that since

Job was suffering, he must be a sinner (22:4–11, 21–30).

4:2–6 Though Eliphaz seems surprised at Job's response (ch. 3), his initial remarks are complimentary and courteous. The content of vv. 7–11 suggests that v. 6 probably contains at least a mild rebuke.

4:5, 6 The phrase **you are weary** translates one word in the original Hebrew and repeats the same root word found in the phrase "will you become weary" in v. 2. This repetition indicates that Eliphaz had already recognized the apparent contradiction between the patient Job of the prologue and the impatient Job of the dialogue.

4:7–9 Eliphaz highlights the retribution doctrine—that is, God supports the righteous but abandons the wicked—with two rhetorical questions. He supports his belief by an appeal to his experience; that is, "you reap what you sow." Because the word **trouble** is the same word used by Job to describe his own plight as full of "sorrow" (3:10) and "misery" (3:20), Eliphaz may be equating Job with the wicked **who plow iniquity.**

4:10, 11 To the reader it may seem that Eliphaz suddenly adds illustrations of God's retribution on animals. But probably these are proverbial sayings with a double meaning. Eliphaz may have been implying that Job's "groanings" or "roaring" made him comparable to the old lion, symbolizing the wicked, whose sins were now being repaid with suffering.

4:12–18 Eliphaz appeals to a vision to authenticate his theology. He claims that he **heard a voice** that told him that no one was **righteous** compared to **God,** implying that Job was not righteous. But contrast the Lord's unqualified commendation of Job in the prologue (1:1, 8; 2:3).

4:19, 20 The description of people as living **in houses of clay** with their **foundation in the dust** emphasizes the mortality and fragility of human existence. Like the temporary houses they live in, people can perish without anyone knowing. Elsewhere Job uses the same two Hebrew words in parallel to describe the fragility of the human body. Since the body is fashioned from clay, God the potter who fashioned it can easily turn it back to dust (10:8, 9; 33:6).

4:21 The Hebrew word for the phrase **their own excellence** may mean "tent cord." Thus the text may be stating that humanity's existence is as precarious as a tent in the midst of a windstorm.

5:1 Eliphaz's warning against appealing to **holy ones,** or angels, anticipates Job's later desire for a "mediator" (9:33).

5:2 foolish man: An arrogant person seeking his own purpose regardless of God.

5:3–7 Eliphaz begins another appeal to personal observation and experience. Eliphaz uses a play on the words **ground** and **man,** along with the repetition of the word **trouble,** to aid his argument that Job's trouble did not come out of nowhere—that is, **spring from the ground.**

5:7 The word **sparks** may allude to the Ugaritic god of the underworld who was supposedly responsible for plagues and lightning. A reference like this to mythology does not imply or endorse a belief in other gods. Eliphaz is saying, "Just as a plague springs up from the demonic forces of hell, so does trouble come from person's nature."

5:8–16 Eliphaz suggests that Job commit his cause to **God** rather than arguing it himself. This is the wise course because God is absolutely good and fair.

5:17 Eliphaz insinuates that since Job's suffering was a result of God's **chastening** for his sin, he should **not despise** or reject what God was trying to teach him. Though it is true that God sometimes disciplines people for their sin through pain and suffering (32:1–37:24; Prov. 3:11; Heb. 12:7), Eliphaz was wrong to suggest that this was necessarily so in Job's case. The divine title *Shaddai,* translated **Almighty,** is used in Job thirty-one times, but only seventeen times in all the rest of the OT.

5:18–22 Eliphaz states that God is the author of both pain and healing. God would heal the **wounds** he inflicted for discipline. When God does allow pain to come into our lives, it is not to harm us but to make us better.

5:23, 24 The presence of stones in a field could make land impossible to farm (2 Kin. 3:19, 25). Thus the expression **covenant with the stones of the field** would mean being **at peace** and harmony with even the destructive forces of nature—including **the beasts of the field** (vv. 22).

5:25–27 your descendants shall be many (vs. 25); **you shall come to the grave at a full age** (vs. 26): These are the most highly regarded blessings in Job's day, a numerous and fine family and good health until finally one dies in **full age** with his loved ones gathered around. Job was to be blessed by God with just such a later life and death (42:10–17) because of his faithfulness and eventual humility (42:1–6).

6:1 When Job **answered,** he did not respond directly to Eliphaz. This may be the reason the text does not specify a name here. Job usually responded to all three of his friends, not to one individually (6:24–30). His friends in turn did not respond point by point to what Job said. Consequently the dialogue is not so much a conversation between friends as it is a speech contest in which one speaker tries to win a debate and impress his audience with his rhetoric.

6:2, 3 Job may be utilizing a proverbial expression in his belief that if his **grief** and **calamity** were **fully weighed** (by being placed on one side of a giant scale balance) his *grief* would outweigh all **the sand of the sea.** (The last word, plural in Hebrew, emphasizes the massive weight.) When he stresses his burdensome *grief* (Heb. *ka'as,* "vexation," "grief"), he employs the same term used in Prov. 27:3 ("sand is weighty but a fool's *wrath* is heavier"), and by Eliphaz in 5:2 when he argues that "wrath (Heb. *ka'as*) kills a foolish man." Though he admits that his *grief* is oppressive, he implicitly denies that he is a fool because his **words have** not **been rash** without cause (vv. 4, 5).

6:4 Job's suffering was so intense that he portrayed it as caused by **arrows of the Almighty** that were dipped in **poison.** The arrows of the Lord are generally symbolic of His judgment (Deut. 32:23, 42) or wrath (Ps. 38:1, 2). Job also assumed that God was required to reward the obedient and punish the guilty in this life, and he may have presumed that the Lord was punishing him unjustly.

6:5–7 Job **refuses** (v. 7) Eliphaz's "tasteless counsel" by two rhetorical questions that point out the absurdity of his overreaction to Job's words. In v. 5 he suggests that his loud cries of complaint are not without cause (like the *braying* of a **donkey** or the bellowing of an **ox**). In v. 6 the phrase **in the white of an egg** reflects a Hebrew clause of uncertain meaning that may be part of a proverbial expression. Some think it refers to the slimy juice of a plant.

6:8–10 Though the exact translation is disputed, the overall context of this verse seems to indicate that Job was more concerned to preserve his relationship to **the Holy One** than to have God remove his pain and **anguish** through death (vv. 8, 9).

6:11, 12 is my flesh bronze? In his misery, Job forgot a great truth: "He knows our frame; He remembers that we are dust" (Ps. 103:14).

6:13 The discouraged person feels there is no way out for him; all his resources are gone— he has no **help.**

6:14 The exact meaning of the Hebrew word translated **afflicted** is disputed. It may mean "to melt"; thus the idea could be "failing" or "despairing." Verse 14 seems to be transitional, linking Job's despair of vv. 8–13 with his disappointment of vv. 15–21.

6:15–17 Since the friends are called **my brothers,** Job apparently at one time had a close relationship with them. This only intensified his feelings of disappointment. He compares them to **the streams of the brooks,** the torrents of water that fill the ravines during the rainy season and **pass away** in the summer.

6:18 The word **paths** in this verse concludes the imagery of empty ravines left by the seasonal streams called "wadis" (vv. 15–18) and links this section to the next (v. 19).

6:19, 20 Job compares his intense disappointment with his friends to the thirsty **caravans of Tema** and **the travelers of Sheba,** whose hopes for water were dashed by reaching the dry stream beds. Tema was located in northern Arabia and Sheba in southwestern Arabia. These caravans and travelers would

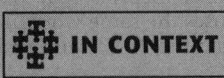 **IN CONTEXT** | **A Disappointing Oasis**

Water was the lifeblood of ancient caravans. That made the oasis of Tema (Job 6:19) a popular and indispensable rest stop for Sabean traders traversing the major north-south highway across the Arabian Desert. Their camels could travel up to a week without water, but sooner or later they had to have refreshment. If a caravan came to the watering hole and for some reason found it dry, disaster loomed.

Job was probably quite familiar with the caravans of Sheba. As the wealthiest man in the Middle East (1:3), he probably had traded with them on numerous occasions. Perhaps he had even arranged caravans himself. Likewise, he may have visited Tema; the site was only about 300 miles to the southeast from Edom, where some believe he lived.

In any case, Job described his disappointment over the lack of kindness shown by his friends (6:14) as like a caravan arriving at a dried-up oasis. Not only expecting but desperately needing water, the weary travelers find only dust. Their hopes dashed and their situation perilous, they face the terrorizing prospect of dying of thirst (6:21).

In a similar way, Job turned to his friends in his hour of need, expecting to find much-needed comfort. To his shock, they responded with rebuke and criticism.

have been familiar to his friends, since the story of Job most likely occurred near Edom in northern Arabia.

6:21 When Job hoped to receive help from his three friends, they offered **nothing.** This was like a desert wadi, a seasonal stream that vanishes in the time of greatest need.

6:22, 23 The answer to each question is no. Job had asked his friends only for understanding and concern, but they had disappointed him.

6:24–26 Job pleads with his would-be counselors to have understanding rather than an argumentative spirit. The friends' demeanor degenerates into arguments and reproofs as they overreact to Job's words, which even Job admits belonged to the **wind.** A counselor must be willing to make allowances for overreaction in someone who suffers and not respond with similar emotion. The sufferer often needs someone to be a friend who will listen with understanding, rather than a judge who simply wishes to give reproof.

6:27, 28 The Hebrew verbs are difficult to translate in this verse. The point seems clear, however. Job perceives his friends are attacking him when he is down, much like those who would take advantage of orphans. An alternative translation, with the same idea: "Oh, how you cast lots for the fatherless, / And how you barter for your friend."

6:29, 30 The repeated word **injustice** in these verses is the same term used by Eliphaz in 5:16. Eliphaz argued that God "saves the needy" from the unscrupulous tactics of the wicked (5:12–15), so "that the poor have hope and injustice shuts her mouth." Job responds by implying that the words of Eliphaz deal injustice to him in his time of need (6:14–21) by assuming that he is not righteous.

7:1, 2 Job argues that his own lot is worse than the **hard service** of the hired laborer or the common slave. Job's use of the word **servant** is an ironic indicator that his life as God's servant (the same Hebrew term in 1:8) has now become full of drudgery and slavery rather than joyous trust in the Lord.

7:3, 4 Although the Book of Job does not record how long Job suffered, the phrase **months of futility** implies that it was a considerable time.

7:5 Worms bred in Job's sores. The scabs on his ulcers broke and seeped.

7:6–8 Job's choice of the word **hope** in the context of the **weaver's shuttle** may convey a double meaning (11:18). The Hebrew word for *hope* sounds like the Hebrew word that means "thread" or "cord" (Josh. 2:18, 21). Not only did Job believe his days were without *hope* but that he had not even a *thread* of hope left. As if he

were regarding a thread in a weaver's shuttle, Job could not see the design that God had for his life through the suffering that he was experiencing. Though sometimes we may question the Lord as Job did, we must realize that the great Weaver has a design that we may not be able to see until He is finished with our lives.

7:9, 10 Job describes **the grave** (sometimes rendered Sheol) as a place from which one **shall never return** (10:21). The focus here is on death. Though the dead person would **never return to his house** on earth, there was a belief in a meeting "house" in the underworld for those who had been on earth (30:23).

7:11 Job speaks frankly with God as he begins to pour out his **anguish** and to **complain** in **bitterness.** He had no fear that the Lord would misinterpret him as his human counselors had. The Lord did not reprimand Job for this but instead commended Job for speaking "what is right" (42:7).

7:12–14 The **sea** and its terrifying inhabitant the **sea serpent** symbolized chaos and the forces of evil and were even considered gods in the pagan religions of the ancient world. Once again Job employs mythological imagery to express his frustration and deep anguish. Although Job interprets the Lord's **guard** as an invasion of privacy (vv. 13, 14, 17–20), God has designed it for a benevolent purpose (3:23).

7:15, 16 Job is not considering suicide when he states that he would choose **strangling and death rather than** to live in his **body** (3:20–22). Strangling may refer to the symptoms of his disease, such as coughing or choking, that he wishes God would use to kill him.

7:17–19 These verses sound similar to Ps. 8:4. Whereas the psalmist marvels that God should "visit him," Job uses the same word in a negative sense to complain that He **should visit him** all the time.

7:20, 21 Job appeals to God to show him what he has done to deserve being made a **target** for God's persecution. When Job calls God the **watcher of men,** he employs a participle that normally describes God in a positive role as one who preserves His people (Ps. 31:23).

8:1, 2 Bildad twists Job's words of 6:26. Job had acknowledged that he had overreacted with words that belonged to the **wind.** To paraphrase Bildad's sarcastic response: "Yes, you're right, Job! All your **words** are like a mighty wind; you are full of hot air!"

8:3 Bildad argues that God could never **pervert justice.** The only possible conclusion was that Job and his children received what they deserved as sinners (vv. 4–7, 20).

8:4–6 The repetition of the word **if** in these

three successive verses illustrates the presumptive nature of Bildad's statements (vv. 8–22). In his zeal to defend orthodox doctrine, he fails to listen to Job's pain.

8:5, 6 Bildad admonishes Job to **seek God** now so that God will restore Job's prosperity, rather than talking about how God will seek him unsuccessfully once he is dead (7:21). Bildad uses the words **pure and upright,** the same words the Lord has already employed in affirming Job's blameless character (1:8; 2:3).

8:7, 8 The advice that Job's **latter end would increase abundantly** anticipates Job's restoration in the epilogue (42:10–17), though it came about in a way quite different from what Bildad envisioned.

8:9, 10 When Bildad states that "we **know nothing**" compared to the wisdom of the past generations, the reader can laugh with the author of Job, since we know how very little Bildad really knows in light of the whole story. One purpose of the Book of Job is to challenge the traditional dogmas of the past—particularly the retribution dogma.

8:11–19 Bildad uses illustrations from nature to support his belief that God punishes only the wicked and always rewards the righteous in this life. He falsely deduces that one can always determine the cause by looking at the effect. Oversimplification resulting in pat, inadequate answers is a common error of Job's counselors.

8:14, 15 The metaphor of the **spider's web** implies that Job had trusted in his house and riches, which were no more permanent than the web.

8:16–22 Bildad's dogmatic statement about how **God will not cast away the blameless** is undermined by the fact that he uses the word *blameless* in the same way the Lord used it in the prologue (1:1, 8; 2:3) to describe Job.

9:1, 2 Job apparently agrees that Bildad has made some valid points (such as the dogma of retribution, which Job accepts). Then he rephrases a question Eliphaz had initiated in 4:17 concerning whether **a man** could be **righteous before God.**

9:3–7 The verb **to contend** indicates that Job was considering the idea of entering a legal case against God. The prophets often used this word when speaking of God bringing a legal case against Israel (Is. 1:2; Mic. 6:1). The Hebrew for *contend* is almost always used metaphorically in Job, referring to a "lawsuit" between Job and God. Job's legal dilemma before the Lord, who served simultaneously as Job's judge and legal adversary (13:20–28), underscores the urgency and hopelessness of Job's call for a mediator to hear his case (v. 33). Job calculates that the chances of answering

God's interrogation are very slim, **one** in **a thousand**—something God later verifies (38:1—42:6). The legal term **answer** means to respond to an accusation in court, particularly under cross-examination.

9:8 spreads out the heavens: Job attributes this phenomenon to God **alone.** The fact that the Lord **treads on the waves of the sea** shows his unique control over the alleged forces of evil (38:8–12). The word *waves* emphasizes that the Lord **treads** the supposed sea god Yamm under his feet (v. 13). This verse emphasizes that the sea is merely a natural force under the control of the omnipotent God.

9:9, 10 the Bear, Orion . . . the Pleiades: God's creation of the wonders of the heavens is also celebrated by Amos (Amos 5:8). Indeed, these words come back on Job's head (38:31–33). **great things . . . wonders:** The works of God are so amazing and numerous that the human mind simply cannot comprehend them.

9:11, 12 God's presence may not be perceivable by the human eye (v. 11), but His works may not be resisted by the human will (v. 12).

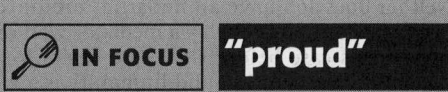

IN FOCUS   **"proud"**

(Heb. *rahab*) (9:13; 26:12; Is. 30:7) Strong's #7293 The verbal root of this word means "to act stormily" or "to behave tempestuously." The derived proper noun designates a mythological, primeval sea monster. Later it became a designation for Egypt. Isaiah reports the Lord Himself calling Egypt by this name (Is. 30:7); elsewhere Isaiah uses the word in a context that suggests a double reference—to both the sea monster and Egypt (Is. 51:9). When referring to the sea monster, this word is always couched in language depicting God's cosmic power (9:1–13; 26:12–13; Ps. 89:8–12; Is. 51:6–11). The ancient Middle East had many mythological tales of powerful primeval sea monsters. The Bible uses this image of Rahab, not to endorse mythology but to demonstrate the Lord's supremacy over all powers—even the ones in people's imagination.

9:13–16 the proud (Heb. *rahab;* 26:12) should be rendered by a proper noun, Rahab, another name for the mythical sea monster, and an equivalent of Leviathan, the cosmic sea monster (compare 87:3).

9:17–20 This verse teems with possible ironic innuendoes. Job's statement that God crushes him **with a tempest** anticipates the appearance of the Lord "out of the whirlwind" in 38:1, but with a different result. Job blames God for crushing and wounding him **without cause,** when actually it was Satan who had sought to destroy him without cause (2:3). The Hebrew word translated *crushes* in this verse is translated *bruise* in Gen. 3:15 and describes the conflict between Satan and humanity.

9:21 The phrase **I do not know myself** means "I do not care for myself" according to the clarification given in the rest of the verse.

9:22–24 Job contradicts Bildad's claims of 8:3, 20 by accusing God of unjustly destroying both the blameless and the wicked (8:20, 21). Thus Job accuses God of being an unjust Judge who blindfolds earthly judges (v. 24).

9:25–28 Job desires to stand before God as an **innocent** man—not absolutely sinless but innocent of any sin comparable to his suffering.

9:29–31 Even if Job cleansed himself to his own satisfaction, God could plunge him into **the pit** (literally, "corruption")—a filth so vile that his clothes would refuse to cover him.

9:32–35 Job complains that God is **not a man** who would **go to court** with Him (9:3). Neither does Job have an impartial **mediator** between God and himself—a mediator who can present his case before God. The desire for a mediator between God and humanity is a key theme in Job (16:19; 19:25), and it anticipates the NT emphasis on Jesus as the true Mediator between God and all of humanity (1 Tim. 2:5).

10:1, 2 Show me: Job dares to speak to God as an equal. Again using legal language (9:3), Job demands that God give him a fair trial through proper court protocol. Here Job comes close to unjustified indignation at God's sovereign will for his life.

10:3–7 This verse serves as a transition from Job's complaint (vv. 1–6) to his brief description of how God had lovingly created him (vv. 8–12). Job knows that he is **not wicked,** and he thinks that God is unjust in oppressing him. Yet Job also realizes that there is **no one who can deliver** him from God's **hand.**

10:8–17 In these verses, Job paints a portrait of the apparently contradictory nature of God, contrasting His loving character with His judgment. Job wonders how the God who had so carefully **fashioned** him in the womb can turn against him like a **fierce lion.** This is the desperate cry of a sufferer blind to the fact that God is working good out of all the tragic events of his life (42:12).

10:15, 16 Not being able to **lift up** his **head** expresses Job's shame and **disgrace** (Judg. 8:28; Lam. 2:10). Job's **misery** was so deep that although he believed he was innocent, he felt like a criminal with no self-esteem or dignity.

10:17 The phrase **you renew your witnesses against me** is a legal metaphor that may refer to each new aspect of Job's illness. In the equivalent **war** metaphor, the Lord was sending **changes** or troop reinforcements against him.

10:18–22 Job asks why he was ever born (vv. 18, 19; 3:3–10). Then he wishes the Lord would **leave** him **alone** to die (vv. 20–22; 3:20–26; 7:16–21). In contrast to 3:17–19, where the grave is described as a place of rest and freedom, the grave here is **the land of darkness** lacking **any order.** Job amplifies his wish that he could have gone straight from **the womb** to the tomb by linking the darkness of the grave with the dark day of his birth (3:3–9). Four different words for darkness in vv. 21, 22 stress the gloom and dreariness of the grave.

11:1–20 Zophar the Naamathite (2:11) was even more rude than Bildad (vv. 2–6; 8:1–13). He was a brash dogmatist who based his arguments on misapplied theology coupled with simplistic reasoning.

11:2–6 Zophar exaggerates what Job has said about his innocence (9:14–21) to make Job look foolish. Job never stated that his **doctrine** was **pure.**

11:7–9 When Zophar interrogates Job about the impossibility of comprehending the **deep things of God,** he employs for **search out** the same term Job used to describe God's wonders as beyond "finding out" (9:10). Thus Zophar may be trying to turn Job's words against him by saying that Job's actions are inconsistent with his theology. Since these verses anticipate portions of the Lord's speeches (38:16–18, 34–38), Zophar's doctrine is correct but the application is wrong. Biblical truth misapplied perverts the intent of the Scriptures and misleads. Sound doctrine without love does not please the Lord (Rev. 2:2–5).

11:10–12 Zophar's rhetorical question about God, **who can hinder Him,** echoes Job's sentiments in 9:12 verbatim. However, Zophar denies Job's allegation that God does not know the difference between the righteous and the wicked (v. 11; 9:22). As a retort to Job's rhetorical question (6:5) in which he compared his own cries to the braying of the "wild donkey," Zophar employs what may be a proverbial statement about the wild donkey. He could be implying that Job's "empty talk" indicates that he is **empty-headed** (vv. 3, 12).

11:13, 14 stretch out your hands: Stretching out the hands was a posture of prayer as well as of praise (Ps. 134:2). Assuming that Job is suffering because of his **iniquity,** Zophar rudely repudiates Job's assertion that he has no "injustice" on his tongue (6:30) by alleging that, in fact, it is Job's **tents** that are full of **wickedness** or injustice. The implication may be that

Job had acquired his wealth by wrong means or had tolerated evil in his household.

11:15, 16 as waters . . . passed away: This is similar to our expression "water under the bridge."

11:17–20 The phrase **dig around you** is a literal rendition of a Hebrew root that may mean "to look carefully about" with "eagle eye" scrutiny (the usage of the same Hebrew term in 39:29).

12:1, 2 Wisdom will die with you! What bold, delicious sarcasm this is! The two personal pronouns **you** are plural in Hebrew, indicating that Job responds to all three friends who concur that he is guilty and needs to confess his sin.

12:3 Using the word **understanding** (Heb. *lebab*, "heart" or "mind," the noun from which the verb translated "will be wise" in 11:12 is derived), Job states that his mental capacity is **not inferior** to his friends (13:2).

12:4 mocked by his friends: The verb Job uses is also found in a similar negative context in Ps. 2:4. In those contexts the verb indicates ridicule. But in other passages this word expresses joy and laughter (Gen. 21:6).

12:5 The translation **lamp** is a basically literal translation of the Hebrew term (Heb. *lappîd*, "torch"). However, since this yields little sense, perhaps the word should be understood as the preposition (Heb. *le* "to/for") plus the noun (*pîd*, "ruin, disaster," 30:24; 31:29) as the NKJV footnote implies.

12:6 The phrase **in what God provides by His hand** may be the proper rendition of a difficult Hebrew phrase. However, it could also be translated "those who bring their god {i.e. idols or a sword} in their hands."

12:7–9 The pronoun **you** (v. 7) is singular that may indicate that Job now addresses Zophar (who had compared him to a "wild donkey") to emphasize that even the dumb animals instinctively understand that **the hand of the Lord** (Heb. Yahweh) is responsible for calamities. A few Hebrew mss. read *'Elôah*, "God" instead of "Yahweh."

12:10–12 Job responds to Bildad's assertion of 8:8 (most likely in sarcastic fashion). It is nonetheless true that wisdom comes with age, a truth widely accepted in the ancient East.

12:13–25 It is possible that this is stated somewhat "tongue in cheek," but this section may also be read as a splendid confession of the unsurpassable wisdom of Yahweh. The words **wisdom and strength** and **counsel and understanding** (v. 13) form a double hendi-

adys (a hendiadys is where two words are used to express one idea; Gen. 1:2). This section is not unlike the confession of trust within a psalm of lament (for example, Ps. 13).

12:17–21 Job may be saying that God plunders **counselors** (such as his friends) and **makes fools of judges** such as himself. The word **plundered** could also be translated "make barefoot."

12:22, 23 God's reversal of **darkness** to **light** was precisely what Job needed (10:21, 22).

12:24, 25 God's coming reversal of human wisdom is desired by all who presently suffer the arrogance of people who prate their knowledge with no fear of the living God (Prov. 1:7).

13:1, 2 what you (Heb. plural) **know, I also know** (at 12:3). The irony is that neither Job nor his friends know very much because they all assume an inflexible dogma of retribution. The point should not be lost that the wisdom of the friends, although misapplied in this instance, is true wisdom—wisdom of God. There is a valid concept of retribution. It is just that it is not inflexible.

13:3, 4 Job desires to **reason** or argue his cause before God. He rejects the incompetent counsel of his three friends who, like **worthless physicians,** have made a wrong diagnosis concerning the cause of his disease and suffering. In fact they were **forgers of lies,** literally "falsehood-plasterers." Job's friends were smearing his sores with a sham concoction of dogma. Instead of piously accusing their unfortunate friend, they should have been praying with him.

13:5–13 In response to Zophar's derisive question concerning Job's words (11:3), Job expresses the desire that his friends would be absolutely **silent.** Indeed, that would have been the friends' wisest action (Prov. 17:28). Job's sarcasm reflects his earlier words to them in 12:2. Using the vocabulary of a wisdom teacher, Job explains his reason for insisting on silence. He wants them to **hear** and pay attention to his words. He urges them to listen diligently to his words instead of trying to defend God. Their pious **platitudes** are as worthless as **proverbs** composed of **ashes.**

13:14 The latter half of the verse seems to clarify **take my flesh in my teeth** to mean risking loss of one's **life** like an animal who tries to defend itself while carrying its prey in its mouth.

13:15–17 trust Him: While these verses are widely known as a powerful statement of

> *Job's friends were smearing his sores with a sham concoction of dogma.*

Job's trust in God, they are not without difficulties. The Hebrew word translated *Him* is similar in sound to the Hebrew word for *no*. Thus some have translated these verses as follows: "Behold, He will slay me; I have no hope." Yet the positive translation of these verses as it is here seems preferable because it follows the flow of the section (vv. 13–19), which has other positive elements (vv. 16, 19). It also makes wonderful sense within these verses. Job believes that God is in the process of slowly taking his life. But in a bold declaration of faith, Job declares his absolute trust in God. For when he would be brought into God's presence, he would plead his cause directly with God. And then, if not before, Job would rediscover what he had never really lost: God's love and salvation (v. 16).

13:18, 19 I shall be vindicated: Job's strongest statement of confidence so far in the book that God will declare him innocent.

13:20–28 Since Job is still in this life of pain (v. 15), he turns to God as best he can and appeals his case directly to Him. Job requests that God, as plaintiff, list the specific charges He has against him rather than continue being his Judge.

13:24–26 The Hebrew terminology resembles vv. 20, 21. Job asks **why** does God **hide** His **face,** a Hebrew idiom indicating the absence of God's favor and blessing.

13:27, 28 In a portrait of God's "malevolent activities," Job uses the verb **watch.** The word normally describes God's benevolent care over a person's life, but in the Book of Job it depicts the role God gives to Satan (2:6).

14:1–6 Job agrees with Eliphaz's assessment that a person is born for trouble. He stresses life's misery and brevity through two vivid metaphors: a fading **flower** and a fleeing **shadow.**

14:5, 6 That God has **determined** the length of a person's life (Ps. 90:10) emphasizes God's sovereign power and wisdom, and conversely the impotence of human beings, who are under divinely set **limits.**

14:7–9 hope for a tree: Job implies that life is better for trees than for people. When a tree falls, it can sprout again. This is precisely the point of Isaiah's beautiful prophecy (Is. 6:13). The house of Jesse—that is, Israel—will be cut off, as one might cut down a great oak tree. But in God's great mercy, that tree will sprout new growth. The "holy seed" is in the stump. That new growth is the beautiful Branch (Is. 11:1), the Savior King whose name is Jesus.

14:10–13 Job's wish for **the grave** to be a temporary hiding place from God's **wrath** differs dramatically from his earlier remarks concerning the grave (7:9, 10; 10:18–22). He attributes the cause of his suffering to God's

---

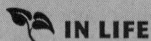 **IN LIFE** | ## Life after Death

Throughout history people have wondered whether this life is all there is. Is there a heaven or hell? Or does it all end here?

Job asked that same question as he contemplated his sufferings (Job 14:14). He believed that death would end his pain (14:13); but would it also end his existence? Elsewhere Job described death as the "way of no return" (16:22) and the "king of terrors" (18:14). At times it appears that Job did not have a particularly positive outlook as he faced the end of life.

Yet in reading about Job's perspective on death, it is important to remember that he was working from a smaller knowledge base than God's people have today. He probably had no written portion of Scripture, and he was unfamiliar with the work of Jesus to deliver people from sin and death (Rom. 6:23; 1 Cor. 15:20–28).

Yet even without these important truths, Job had a certain confidence that he would see God after death. In fact, his stirring declaration of faith, beginning with the words, "I know that my Redeemer lives" (Job 19:25–27), has provided hope for generations of believers (helped in no small measure by George Frideric Handel, the eighteenth-century composer who set Job's lines to music as part of his masterpiece, "Messiah").

Whatever questions about death may have lingered from the days of Job, Jesus answered them when He declared, "He who believes in Me, though he may die, he shall live" (John 11:25). For that reason, Jesus' followers can celebrate even in the midst of grief and mourning over the loss of friends and loved ones. Jesus has promised eternal life to believers, free from all tears, sorrow, and pain (Rev. 21:4). That is why when it comes to death, Christians are a people of hope.

wrath because he assumes the retribution dogma that the righteous are always blessed and the wicked will eventually experience God's judgment.

14:14–17 Job's question **if a man dies, shall he live again** is answered with an emphatic yes by Jesus and the NT authors (John 11:23–26; 1 Cor. 15:3–57; compare Is. 26:19; Dan. 12:2). But Job responds to his own question by a determination to **wait** for his **change** to come. Since Job considers life hard (7:1), perhaps he is implying that he will wait for relief from his suffering through death to find out the answer.

14:18–22 You destroy the hope of man (v. 19): Despite the hope against hope of vv. 13–17, the OT believer admits that he sees little evidence for a blessed afterlife. This is the importance of Jesus' resurrection. He promises, "Because I live, you will live also" (John 14:19).

15:1–3 The insinuation that Job had filled himself **with the east wind** is an allusion to the violent and scorching wind from the desert that brought no rain. Thus Eliphaz is implying that Job's arguments were destructive (vv. 12, 13) and without beneficial substance (the context of v. 3).

15:4–6 Eliphaz's statement **your own mouth condemns you** expresses ironic agreement with Job's earlier words (9:20). But Eliphaz deliberately twists Job's words to say that Job no longer needs a day in court since his own mouth has already incriminated him.

15:7 Are you the first man who was born: This sarcastic question anticipates a theme developed in the Lord's speeches (38:4–21).

15:8–11 wisdom . . . know: Eliphaz throws Job's words of 12:3; 13:2 back into his face. He counters Job's sarcastic rebuttal to Bildad that wisdom comes only with age (12:12) by saying that people **much older than** Job's **father** are on their side. Since Job was already a mature man who had raised ten grown children, this may be an exaggeration for effect.

15:12 wink: Although the precise meaning of the Hebrew word is not certain, it may mean "flash (with anger)" (context of v. 13).

15:13 The Hebrew word translated **spirit** may also be translated "temper" or "anger," as in Prov. 16:32.

15:14, 15 Eliphaz rephrases his thought of 4:17, 18 by interweaving an apparent gibe at Job's complaint of 14:1 about man "born of woman."

15:16–18 The phrase **what I have seen** shows that Eliphaz bases his instruction on experience and observation (4:1). He also appeals to the wisdom tradition as Bildad has done in 8:8–10.

15:19, 20 hidden from: The Hebrew could also be translated "stored up for."

15:21, 22 dreadful: Eliphaz begins his subtle argument to prove that Job is a wicked man. He alludes to Job's *dread,* the same word translated *feared* in 3:25, as an implicit indicator that Job is wicked.

15:23, 24 By using the phrase **make him afraid** in the context of **a day of darkness,** Eliphaz twists the words of Job's lament about the day of his birth (3:4, 5) to fit the dark day of his death (10:18–22). Then in contrast to 14:20 where Job blames God for *prevailing* against people, Eliphaz says that the wicked man's own fears **overpower** him.

15:25–33 The imagery of the **fat** man who eventually loses his **wealth** and **possessions** by divine punishment for his wickedness insinuates that Job's calamities have occurred because of his own self-indulgence.

15:34, 35 In mentioning the **fire** that **will consume** the tents of the wicked, Eliphaz employs the same two words that describe the fire of God that devoured Job's sheep and servants (1:16).

16:1, 2 I have heard many such things: Beginning with a rare direct allusion to what the previous speaker just said, Job belittles his friends as **miserable comforters.** To paraphrase Job: "Speaking of trouble, rather than comforting me in my troubles as a good counselor should, you have increased my trouble despite your claims to the contrary."

16:3 The phrase **words of wind** is a caustic comeback to Eliphaz's words in 15:2 and Bildad's in 8:2. Both had twisted Job's words of 6:26 (8:2; 15:2, 3).

16:4–18 The phrase **shake my head at you** indicates a mocking posture (as in Ps. 22:7). However, the word **comfort,** meaning "to nod the head sympathetically," is used in 2:11 of the friends who came to console him. In effect, Job is saying: "Please nod your head with understanding instead of mocking and ridiculing me."

16:19–21 The identity of Job's **witness** is disputed. One's understanding about Job's "Redeemer" in 19:25 will affect one's understanding of Job's *witness* (19:25). Some argue that Job was referring to God. However, the context of 9:33, where Job wished for an impartial mediator between God and himself (9:32, 33), and the immediate context of v. 21 suggest that Job was using a legal metaphor to express his wish for an advocate who would **plead for** him **with God, as a man pleads for his neighbor** on earth. This anticipates Jesus Christ, who is our Intercessor (Heb. 7:25) and Advocate (1 John 2:1).

16:20–22 The difficult Hebrew phrase rendered **my friends scorn me** might also be translated "my interpreter is my friend." What a powerful image this is!

17:1–11 In another legal metaphor, Job appeals to God to act as his advocate by laying down **a pledge,** that is, providing bail. The use of the same metaphor in Ps. 119:121, 122 to indicate the psalmist's request for relief from his "oppressors" may suggest that Job was pleading for God to demonstrate confidence in his innocence.

17:12 This verse may be a caricature of the friends' false assurances that if he would repent, his **darkness** would soon become **light.**

17:13, 14 Job counters the false assurances of his friends with a facetious statement about waiting for **the grave** as one who longingly desires to go home to his **house** and his long-lost relatives, **corruption** (or "the pit") and the **worm.**

17:15, 16 The plural verb **they go down** may refer back to the words *corruption* and *worm* (v. 14).

18:1–3 When Bildad asks why he and his friends are **counted as beasts,** he apparently resents the implication of Job's words in 12:7–9.

18:4 The phrase **you who tear yourself in your anger** seems to be Bildad's answer to Job's allegation that God had torn Job in His anger (16:13).

18:5–10 net . . . trap: Six different Hebrew synonyms for various types of nets and traps emphasize the many imminent dangers that God has designed for the wicked to ensure that they will be caught in their wickedness.

18:11–14 Bildad cruelly attributes Job's disease to **the firstborn of death,** a reference to the demon of plagues and disease (3:8). **The king of terrors** is probably death personified as a king. Others suggest that this may refer to Satan.

18:15–19 In describing **roots** as being **dried** or withered, Bildad contradicts Job's previous argument about the tree that is cut down but sprouts up from its roots (14:7, 8). There seems to be no hope for Job's family tree because God, who is about to wipe **the memory** of Job **from the earth,** has already removed his descendants or **posterity.** In ancient times this was a sign of a divine curse. Once again Bildad manifests great insensitivity toward Job over the loss of his children (8:4).

18:20, 21 In this summation of the evidence, Bildad uses the word **wicked,** in Hebrew literally the "unjust one," to suggest that he is refuting Job's allegation that God has turned him over to the "ungodly." Bildad believes that the evidence he has exhibited in vv. 5–20 implicates Job himself as the culprit, the wicked one.

19:1, 2 How long will you torment: Job is tired of hearing Bildad's rude questions and the tormenting words of all his friends.

19:3–8 Job's friends have used the **disgrace** associated with his disease to **plead** the case that he is guilty of sin (10:17; 16:8; 17:3). With the statement **God has wronged me,** Job responds to Bildad's implication in 8:3 that God does not subvert justice. He argues that Bildad's theory about God does not fit the facts. Instead he asserts that God has wrongly entrapped him as though he were a wild animal or criminal. In describing God as surrounding him **with His net,** Job continues the imagery of the divine hunter initiated by Bildad. Essentially, Job feels **fenced** in by God when it is really Satan who has been mistreating him (1:10; 3:23).

19:9, 10 Job compares his removal from the respected position of judge or city councilman (29:7–25) to being dethroned like a king whose **crown** is taken from his **head.** Job's **hope,** which had once sprouted up like a new tree from a stump (14:7–9), has been totally **uprooted.**

19:11–17 The mention of **the children of** Job's **own body** is problematic since the book seems to document the loss of all ten of his children (1:2, 18, 19). It is possible this is a rhetorical statement: "I would be repulsive even to my children" (compare v. 18).

19:18–20 The meaning of the phrase **skin of my teeth** is uncertain. It may imply that his body was so devastated by disease that his teeth had fallen out and only the *skin* or gums of his teeth were left intact.

19:21, 22 That Job believed **the hand of God has struck** him is ironic, since in fact, God had refused Satan's request to "stretch out His hand" against Job (1:11; 2:5).

19:23, 24 The irony of this verse in the context of the present book is wonderful. More significantly, some of Job's words would best have *not* been written!

19:25, 26 Job expresses his confidence in his living **Redeemer,** which in this legal context may be translated "Vindicator" or "Protector of the Family Rights" (Ps. 119:154; also Ruth 4:1 where the word is translated *close relative*). Some interpreters believe that Job was referring to God, a view supported by the context of 17:3 and possibly by the mention of **God** in v. 26. However, the context of the Book of Job—Job's longing for a mediator (9:33) and his desire for someone to plead on his behalf with God (16:19–21)—may suggest that he was thinking of someone other than God. Here is a strong, resolute hope for a mediator between God and humanity. Ultimately Job's longing for a vindicator or mediator was fulfilled in Jesus Christ (1 Tim. 2:5).

19:27 Again, the redundant, emphatic pronoun **I** in the Hebrew text (as in v. 25) indicates a strong belief and deep conviction. This is a wonderful example of a sufferer passionately expressing his resolute faith even in the middle of a horrible situation.

19:28 The NKJV translation **in me** follows the Masoretic Text, but several Hebrew manuscripts and versions indicate the translation **in Him**. The difference is basically one of deciding where the quotation in the first part of the verse ends.

19:29 Job's warning to his friends to be **afraid of the sword for yourselves** may have been his rebuttal of Eliphaz's remarks about the wicked person watching in dread for the sword (15:22).

20:1–3 The word **therefore** alerts the reader that Zophar will respond to Job's speech. He reacts angrily to Job's strong warning in his last statement (19:28, 29). Furthermore, when he speaks of having **heard the reproof that reproaches** him, he notifies Job that the hard feelings about being reproached (19:3 has the same Heb. root *kalam*, "to insult," "to humiliate") were mutual, since he also had felt the sting of Job's insults. The tragic results of venting one's emotions to others through sarcasm and insults illustrates that a war of words is a lose-lose situation. How tragic that these wise men failed to apply the wisdom principle that a "soft answer turns away wrath" (Prov. 15:1)!

20:4–6 Zophar confronts Job's confident statement in 19:25 with a sarcastic rebuke. Since Job supposedly knew so much about his Redeemer, surely he knew the wisdom teaching that the **wicked** prosper only for a **short** time.

20:7 The word **refuse** may also be translated "dung." This would be a scathing comment.

20:8–19 Though **evil** may be **sweet** to the wicked for a while, the certain consequences of their behavior will bring about their downfall.

20:20, 21 In stating that the wicked person **knows no quietness,** Zophar implies that Job has received what he deserves. Zophar's statement that the **well-being** or "prosperity" of the wicked **will not last** fits Job's circumstances: Job has lost everything. In essence, Zophar is confirming Job's complaint in 7:7 that he will "never again see good."

20:22–26 The phrase **fire will consume** echoes Eliphaz's searing words of 15:34 (same Hebrew words). The translation **shall go ill with him** could also be rendered "shall feed on him."

20:27, 28 Zophar apparently reverses Job's appeal to the earth and heavens (16:18, 19) for vindication. He argues that the **heavens** and **the earth** will bear witness not to Job's innocence but to his **iniquity.**

20:29 In this summary verdict, Zophar suggests that it is too late for Job to repent (contrast his previous words in 11:13–20). God would have no clemency for such a **wicked** person.

21:1, 2 your consolation: Job tells the three friends that if they will **listen carefully,** they will finally be of some consolation, or comfort, to him.

21:3–6 keep mocking: Perhaps Job turned directly to Zophar to rebuke the most offensive of his friends. Zophar had not only claimed that Job mocked (Zophar used the same Hebrew word for *mocking* in 11:13), but he mocked Job's words (20:9).

21:7 Why do the wicked live: With a rhetorical question, Job begins exposing the loopholes in the retribution dogma—the belief that suffering always indicates God's punishment of a person. The prosperity of the wicked is still a mystery for believers today. Other biblical writers agonized over it (Ps. 37; 73; Jer. 12:1–4). But the Scriptures affirm that God is controlling everything to accomplish His good purposes (Rom. 8:28).

21:8 In saying that sometimes the **descendants** of the wicked **are established,** Job defends himself against the corollary that even if a wicked man prospers for a while, his children will be devastated (18:19).

21:9–16 Job reacts to Eliphaz's argument in

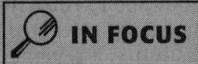 **IN FOCUS** **"behold"**

(Heb. *ra'ah*) (19:27; Deut. 3:27; Eccl. 11:7; Is. 26:10; Lam. 1:9) Strong's #7200: This is the common term used in reference to the natural function of the eyes and is thus most often translated as *see* (Gen. 48:10; Deut. 1:8; 2 Kin. 3:14; Mic. 7:9, 10). The word also has a number of metaphorical meanings, such as acceptance (Gen. 7:1; Num. 23:21) and provision (Gen. 22:8, 14; 1 Sam. 16:1). It can even convey the notion of assurance and salvation, as is the case here. In 42:5 the word means "to see" in the sense of "to come to recognize" or "to experience fully" something previously known or understood. At times the word is associated with a prophetic message, as a prophet is described as seeing a vision from God (Is. 6:1; Jer. 1:11–13; Ezek. 1:1).

15:21–24 that although the wicked live peacefully for a while, they live in terror of inevitable destruction. Job contradicts this by saying that the wicked even live in their **houses** safe—without **fear.** The wicked simply deny God's existence, so they live without any fear of His judgment.

21:17 The rhetorical questions introduced by **how often** expect the answer "not very often." With the first question about **the lamp of the wicked,** Job challenges Bildad's belief that the wicked person's light does go out (18:5, 6). The second question opposes Zophar's dogmatic statement in 20:23 that God will judge the wicked before they find enjoyment in life.

21:18 This verse may also be construed as a question (being subordinate to v. 17).

21:19–27 Job denies the dogma that even if a wicked person prospers temporarily, his children will be punished. Job's position is sustained by other passages in the Bible (Deut. 24:16; Ezek. 18:1–28; John 9:1–3).

21:28 Where is . . . the dwelling place of the wicked? Job's friends imply that it is destroyed in this life. This is the point of view which Job is denying (v. 30).

21:29 Those who travel give additional testimony to support Job's position that there are wicked people who prosper, and by inference, righteous people who suffer.

21:30–32 Job may be quoting his friends' position that the **wicked** are doomed. However, the Hebrew words translated **reserved for** could also be rendered "spared from," which would indicate Job's own contrary belief. This latter view is supported by the Hebrew word translated **brought out.** This word reappears in v. 32 in the context of a wicked person being *brought* to the cemetery without being repaid for what he has done (v. 31).

21:33 shall be sweet: Job uses the same Hebrew word Zophar employed (20:12) in arguing that evil is sweet to the wicked person but will become bitter in his stomach (20:14). Job contradicts this by saying that things are sweet for the wicked even in the grave.

21:34 Job concludes his speech with a rebuke for their failed efforts to convince Job of their theological views. Again, we observe that the failure in the friends of Job was not one of concern or of conviction. It was in their inability to anticipate such a glaring exception to the expected pattern of retribution that they believed drives like an unwavering moral force through the universe. To Job, their words were *vapor* (Heb. *hebel*; Eccl. 1:2).

22:1, 2 The implication of Eliphaz's rhetorical question—that a human being cannot put God under any obligation that God must repay—is a valid theological principle that the Lord Himself corroborates in 41:11. However, his application of that principle to Job's circumstances (vv. 3–5) was invalid, for it was based on the faulty assumption that the righteous are always blessed and the wicked always experience God's judgment on earth.

22:3, 4 The same Hebrew root words for **blameless** and **fear** had earlier been used by Eliphaz in his courteous remarks about Job's "reverence" and "integrity" (4:6). In these verses, Eliphaz is being sarcastic.

22:5–9 naked . . . weary . . . widows: Eliphaz lists some trumped-up charges concerning the way Job gained his great wealth: greedy exploitation of the poor in business dealings; lack of hospitality or charity; and lack of compassion to the bereaved. Job categorically denied these charges (29:11–17; 31:13–22) and God's own witness to Satan reveals to the reader that the charges were false (1:8).

22:10–14 Can He judge: Eliphaz misrepresents Job's position. Although he accuses Job of not understanding God, it is Eliphaz who has the greater misunderstanding.

22:15–17 Eliphaz twists Job's words recorded in 21:14–16 to support his own view that Job was walking in **wicked** ways. Because of this, Job's prosperity was only temporary.

22:18 The phrase **but the counsel of the wicked is far from me** (quoting Job in 21:16) may be an example of innuendo, mocking Job for what he was saying and also expressing Eliphaz's own sentiments.

22:19, 20 In stating that the **innocent will laugh** the wicked **to scorn** (Heb. *la'ag,* "to mock"), Job's friend mocks his suggestion to **keep mocking** (the same Hebrew verb). The **righteous** will be **glad** when the wicked (including Job) are judged.

22:21 The Hebrew word translated **acquaint yourself,** or sometimes "yield," is derived from the same root as "be profitable" in v. 2. This might be a play on words: "Although you cannot be profitable to God through your efforts, you can acquaint yourself with or yield to Him."

22:22, 23 Eliphaz issues another call for repentance (5:8–17) by asking Job to **return to the Almighty.** Then he suggests that Job **remove iniquity from** his **tents,** a reiteration of Zophar's words (11:14).

22:24–29 Eliphaz implies that Job has been trusting in his riches rather than in God, something Job would deny in 31:24, 25. Then he urges Job to trust in **the Almighty** God as he does in **gold.**

22:30 Eliphaz's prediction that God would **deliver one who is not innocent** through the **purity** of Job's **hands** would be fulfilled ironically through Job's prayer for the three friends (42:8–10).

23:1, 2 Job is **bitter** because of his suffering and the false accusation of his friends. **Even today**: Probably means "even now."

23:3 More than anything else, Job seeks to **find** God. At God's **seat** (throne), he is sure he would find justice because the reign of God is based on righteousness (Ps. 97:2).

23:4–9 After he **presents** many persuasive arguments, Job will rest his case because he knows God will be just. Job desires to **know** and **understand** rather than win an argument. Above all, he seeks to restore his communion with God.

> *Job protests against God ignoring those who cry out for help.*

23:10–12 Job's use of the metaphor about **gold** to express his assurance of being found pure from guilt may be a rebuttal to Eliphaz's brazen words of 22:24, 25. When Job asserts that he has **kept** God's **way,** he rejects Eliphaz's accusation that he has kept the way of the wicked (22:15).

23:13–16 When Job contemplates the **unique** power and sovereign freedom of God, he is **terrified.** To him, God seems to be a capricious despot who does as He pleases (9:12, 34).

23:17 This verse likely describes Job's **deep** depression, not only because of his losses, but also because of his failure to understand God's purpose.

24:1 Since times are not hidden from the Almighty might also be translated, "Why are not times stored up by the Almighty?" The parallelism of the second line may indicate that the word *times* alludes to the set **days** for God's judgment.

24:2–8 Removing **landmarks** in the ancient Middle East was tantamount to stealing land. It was a serious crime that placed a person under a divine curse (Deut. 27:17).

24:9–11 It is ironic that Job complains about God allowing people to **snatch** an infant from its mother's **breast.** Previously he had complained that God had not taken him from his mother's breasts after his own birth (3:12).

24:12, 13 In this transition between lists of social crimes and criminal acts, Job protests against God ignoring those who **cry out** for help, since God was supposedly ignoring his own cries for help.

24:14, 15 the murderer rises with the light is a good literal translation of the Hebrew text. The most natural meaning of the word *light* is "at dawn," but it may denote "at dusk" (context of vv. 14–16).

24:16 Thieves would **break,** literally "dig," **into houses** by night. The walls of houses were built of mud bricks through which thieves could dig. **Marked for themselves** may mean "shut themselves up" by day.

24:17 The words **if someone recognizes them / they are in the terrors of the shadow of death,** may also be rendered, "For they are acquainted with the terrors of deep darkness." On the words *shadow of death*, read 3:5.

24:18–25 These verses about the ultimate fate of the wicked are problematic. They sound more like the friends' words than Job's (15:1—21:34). Therefore, critics usually assign them to Zophar, who has no speech in the third cycle of dialogues, or to Bildad, whose last speech is very short (25:1–6). However, they should be considered as Job's words, for he was probably quoting his friends' viewpoint in order to refute them.

25:1, 2 In referring to God's **dominion and fear,** Bildad seems to be responding to Job's comments (23:13–17) that the very thought of God's sovereignty made him afraid.

25:3, 4 Bildad repeats the previous rhetorical questions posed by Job (9:2) and Eliphaz (4:17; 15:14) to emphasize that a person cannot **be righteous** or **pure** before the Lord.

25:5, 6 Bildad's view of God's dominion and majesty in the heavens causes him to devalue mortal **man** as a **maggot.** He responds insensitively to Job by suggesting that Job does not need to wait until he dies to be grouped with the maggots (the same Hebrew word that Job used in 17:14). This was caustic sarcasm, for Job was in fact covered with worms (7:5).

26:1–4 How have: Rather than presenting genuine questions, these verses are probably sarcastic exclamations by Job to imply how little Bildad has helped him. To paraphrase Job: "You've really been a big help to me! How encouraging that you tell me I'm nothing but a worm (25:6)! Finally my cries for help have been answered."

26:5, 6 The words of these verses echo the thoughts of God's omnipotence found in the Psalms (Ps. 139:7–12). While **Sheol** and **Destruction**—that is, death or the place of the dead—were fearful, hidden concepts to Job and his contemporaries, they caused no fear and held no secrets for the all-knowing God.

26:7, 8 the north over empty space: The Hebrew word translated *north* probably does not refer to a geographical designation (the same Hebrew term describes God's mountain in Ps. 48:1, 2) but to God's dwelling place in the heavens (v. 9 mentions God's throne). If the statement that God **hangs the earth on**

✠ IN CONTEXT | The Place of the Dead

The understanding of the afterlife in Judah and Israel resembled that current in Mesopotamia and Syria-Palestine. Under the earth, in a dark muddy realm, was Sheol—the netherworld where all the souls of the dead go, whether good or evil. The popular notion in Egypt of an afterlife with a touch of hope for a good eternity did not influence Palestine, despite Egyptian control of Canaan for a millennium. In Palestine, Sheol was understood as a place of darkness, meaninglessness, and hopelessness. Once entering the netherworld, one had to stay there. The prospect of eternity in a most unpleasant place made a long life in this world quite desirable.

The dead retained their individuality in the netherworld, and one could have contact with them. Tubes have been found in the tombs of Palestine from the Bronze Age through the Hellenistic period which allowed food or wine to be dropped into the netherworld. The living sought information from the dead through necromancy, as Saul attempted to consult Samuel's spirit rising from Sheol (1 Sam. 28:11–19). This form of inquiry was forbidden by Israelite law (Deut. 18:10, 11).

The cultures surrounding Judah and Israel had deities who ruled the netherworld. In Mesopotamia the divine couple Nergal and Ereshkigal hanged the corpses of the dead on butchers' hooks like slabs of meat. Egypt's afterlife under the rule of Osiris was more appealing, if you survived the journey to the land of the blessed dead. Syria-Palestine had the god Mot (meaning "death") who was hungry to devour the living. The voraciousness of the netherworld and the mercilessness of its ruler, Mot, is reflected in the "devouring" and "king of terrors" of Job 18:11–14.

nothing (Gen. 1:2) refers to the suspension of earth in space, it preceded Newton's concept of gravitational attraction by thousands of years. Though this may ultimately be the divine intent, it is not clear that Job himself would have understood the complete meaning of his own words. He probably thought, as did other ancients, that the earth was a circular disk (v. 10) supported by nothing. In other words, he thought of the earth as floating on the vast subterranean waters.

26:9 The translation **throne** (Heb. *kisseh*, an alternate spelling of the word, *kisse'*, "throne") follows the Masoretic Text, which is probably correct. However, some translate "full moon" (changing the word to *keseh*, an alternate spelling of *kese'*).

26:10, 11 Job's graphic description of the **circular horizon** and the pillars of heaven—probably the mountains that held up the heavens in ancient cosmology—pictures the way the earth appears to the human eye.

26:12, 13 With his power God controls **the sea,** which was a symbol of evil and chaos. The highly figurative language may express the power of God over creation in a wide variety of ways. Here the sea and **storm** are merely creatures under the control of the Creator.

26:14 This is one of the most stunning of all the verses in the Bible that describe the **power** of God. Job asserts that if we truly considered God's great power, we would know that what we observe of creation represents **the mere edges** of His garment—just His **whisper.** What

would happen to us if ever He were to **thunder?**

27:1 Moreover Job continued his discourse: The different editorial formula for introducing the speaker (as in 29:1) suggests something unusual. Perhaps Job had paused briefly to wait for Zophar before he continued speaking.

27:2, 3 As God lives: These words reflect part of an oath formula used in ancient courts. Job paradoxically combines these words with two accusations against God. According to Job, the living God is the very one who has denied him **justice**—his legal right to due process. Job swears in the name of the divine Judge who, as his opponent, has perverted justice in His own favor. He alleges that God has **made** him **bitter.** Though Job repeatedly complained of a bitter spirit (7:11; 10:1), the Lord did not cause him to respond that way. Job's responses only exposed the attitude that lay deep within his being. The message of the Lord for Job was that no matter what the circumstances, one should resolutely trust in God (40:8; 42:1–6).

27:4, 5 Job denies that he would use the tactics of his so-called friends (13:7). He not only refuses to **speak wickedness,** he will not lie nor attempt to defend himself. **you:** This Hebrew plural (vv. 11, 12) refers to all of Job's three friends. Job maintains that they are erroneous in their reasoning, and to agree with them would be to compromise his integrity.

27:5, 6 Job's determination to **hold fast** his **righteousness** and **integrity** was remarkable.

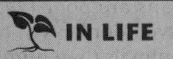 **IN LIFE**   ## The Fairness of God

Fires. Floods. Earthquakes. Famine. So many people seem to suffer from "acts of God" that strike without warning. Like Job, they appear to be relatively innocent of wrongdoing that might explain their pain. People wonder, "Is God fair to let these things happen?"

This was one of the questions with which Job and his friends wrestled. Calamity struck Job and his family for no apparent reason. Why? His friends took the view that God was punishing him, that he must have done something wrong to deserve such evil. Job disagreed, not only because he felt certain of his own integrity, but because the wicked actually seemed to prosper, not suffer (Job 12:6).

Yet that only brought Job back to the original question: Is God fair? If the wicked prosper, where is justice in the world? Job concluded that the seemingly easy life of the wicked is very temporary; sooner or later it will all fall apart (27:13–23). In the end, Job maintained, God will humble the proud, those with integrity will inherit their possessions, and justice will be served.

Ultimately God is indeed fair (36:6; 37:23, 24)—a fact for which we can be thankful, because life is not fair. In this life, people do not always get what they deserve. But this life is not the end of the story. God Himself will write the final chapters.

The Hebrew word translated *hold fast* also occurs in 2:9. Though Job believed that God had taken away a fair trial (v. 2), he would not **put away** his integrity. He persevered despite the discouraging words of his wife and friends.

27:7–12 In this imprecatory prayer, Job wishes that his **enemy** would receive the fate reserved for the **wicked.** Since he turns the words of his friends back against them, he may be alluding to his friends collectively as an enemy who **rises up against** him and deserves the fate of the wicked.

27:10–12 Job returns Eliphaz's own advice back to him (22:22–27). Whereas Eliphaz counseled Job to turn to the Almighty for instruction and to delight in Him, Job denies that a godless person would turn to God, much less **delight himself in the Almighty.** Therefore, Job insists that Eliphaz and his friends should turn to the Almighty and receive instruction.

27:13–23 Since these verses sound more like the friends' words than Job's, some scholars assign them to Zophar or Bildad. However, since Job had a fondness for turning the words of his friends back in their faces, these verses may be a satirical paraphrase of the friends' teaching about the fate of the wicked (24:18–25).

27:17 Job's prediction that the **innocent will divide the silver** may foreshadow what happens to Job himself in 42:11.

28:1–28 This is a magnificent wisdom hymn that is naturally divided into three stanzas by the refrain of vv. 12, 20, with v. 28 serving as a conclusion. The rhetorical questions in the initial refrains (v. 12) link the first two stanzas which provide a negative answer: (1) Though human ingenuity can discover precious metals, it cannot find true wisdom (vv. 1–11). (2)

People cannot find wisdom because they cannot fathom its value, which is beyond silver or gold (vv. 12–19). The final stanza (vv. 21–28) supplies a positive answer to the questions of the refrain (v. 20): Only God knows true wisdom, the wisdom He has placed in the fabric of creation (vv. 21–27) and has revealed to humanity (v. 28).

28:1–5 The mention of **iron** being mined **from the earth** implies a time after the beginning of the Iron Age (around 1200 B.C.) for the writing of the Book of Job.

28:6 The term translated **sapphires** probably means lapis lazuli.

28:7, 8 The **bird,** the **falcon,** and the **lions** represent all animals of every kind. No animal is familiar with the treasures hidden in the earth that human beings can discover (vv. 2–11).

28:9–11 The streams from trickling may be rephrased "the sources of the rivers."

28:12 The word **wisdom** (v. 20) may emphasize the true wisdom that only the Lord knows (vv. 23–27) and that people may learn in relationship with Him (v. 28).

28:13–19 Every verse in this whole stanza has the Hebrew word for **not** at least once, stressing the absence of wisdom and even the desire for wisdom. Thus the rhetorical questions concerning the whereabouts of wisdom and understanding (v. 12) receive an emphatic answer: **not** anywhere in **the land of the living** or of the dead (v. 14 and its parallel in vv. 21, 22).

28:20–27 Only **God understands** the **way** of wisdom and **knows** the **place** of understanding. Though people surpass the animals in knowing the place of precious metals (v. 1), and the "source" of gems (v. 6), God alone is the master and source of wisdom (vv. 27, 28).

28:28 This verse vindicates Job's stance and marks a transition from the dialogue to the discourses. The words **He said** may introduce a reference to the Book of Proverbs (Prov. 3:7; 9:10).

29:1, 2 Job's wish for the prosperity of **months past** suggests how long it was since his suffering began (7:3).

29:3–5 The picture of God's **lamp** shining on Job's **head** symbolizes divine blessing and success (contrast 18:5, 6; 21:17; also Ps. 18:28, 29).

29:6 The abundance of **cream** (or curds) and **oil** indicates wealth.

29:7 The gate of **the city** with its nearby **open square,** similar to the modern courthouse square, was a place where town business and court proceedings were held (Ruth 4:1).

29:8–11 saw me and hid: Job describes the respect he had received from young and old alike because of his position in the city.

29:12, 13 Job rejects Eliphaz's allegations of 22:6–9.

29:14, 15 The vivid portrait of Job being **clothed** in **righteousness** and wearing **justice like** a judicial **robe** is a stark contrast to his present condition, with his flesh being "clothed" with worms and dust (7:5). He will emphasize this in ch. 30.

29:16 Job was a **father to the poor** (i.e., a benevolent protector of their rights). Similarly King Hammurabi (in the epilogue to his famous Code) describes himself as "a true father to the people," whose words helped the cause of the oppressed.

29:17–19 broke the fangs: Job had rescued the poor (v. 12) and the helpless from the wicked. Functioning much like a judge, Job had established justice and righteousness (v. 14). This explains his frequent use of legal metaphors in his speeches (9:3).

29:20–25 Job reminisces about his past days of **glory.** While undergoing severe trials, he did what many of us do: he longed for "the good old days" when he still had prowess or "glory" with the bow. The phrase **bow is renewed** apparently symbolizes a rejuvenation of vigor and might (Gen. 49:24). Bows were usually unstrung when not in use, allowing the wood to retain its strength.

30:1–6 But now introduces Job's lament (ch. 30) about the complete reversal of his former prosperity (ch. 29). Rather than everyone respecting him (29:8–11, 21–25), even young ruffians were daring to **mock** him (29:24). These young people were so base that Job had **disdained to put** their **fathers,** who were presumably better than they, with his **dogs.** His words not only stress how low they are but also how humiliated he feels as an outcast among outcasts (vv. 9–11).

30:7 brayed: Job's use of this verb emphasizes not only that the ruffians are poor (24:5, where the poor are called "wild donkeys"), but also that they act more like animals than human beings.

30:8–10 Job denigrates the families of the outcasts as **vile men** (Heb. *benê-nabal,* literally, "sons of a fool"). Ironically Job had already used the latter word in warning his wife.

30:11–15 When Job says God **loosed** his **bowstring,** he apparently expresses a meaning opposite to that in 29:20. Here the words mean that God had put him "on the shelf," as a bow is set aside when it is unstrung.

30:16, 17 When Job says that his **soul is poured out** like water, he means being emotionally and physically drained of strength (Lam. 2:11, 12) because of his **days of affliction** (vv. 1–31). These words are much like those of David, as found in Ps. 22:14, 15.

30:18, 19 Job compares the terrible effects of his suffering and disease (vv. 16, 17) to being choked by a powerful **force.** Then he identifies God as the One who abuses His great power by harming Job for no apparent reason (9:19; 24:22). To the suffering Job, God seems like a gangster who grabs a person by the neck and flings him into the **mire.** He blames the Lord for throwing him in the **ashes** (2:8), even though Satan was in fact the cause of his suffering (2:4–6).

30:20, 21 Ironically, Job blames God's strong **hand,** which Satan could not move, for calamities that have actually been caused by the hand of Satan (1:11, 12, 18, 19).

30:22, 23 I know: Job declares his frustration with God almost as directly as he had expressed his confidence in the Redeemer (19:25). Just as surely as he knows that God will vindicate him, he also knows that God will **bring** him **to death.**

30:24 The meaning of this verse is disputed because the Hebrew text does not identify whether God or a human is the subject of the clause **stretch out his hand.** Yet if we assume that this verse refers to God, the point is potent. If the rubble could speak out, God would hold His hand. How can He not stay His hand when it is a man who calls out to Him?

30:25 Job builds on the image of the helpless (v. 24) by remembering his own compassion for the **poor.** Now that he is downcast, why does God not sympathize with him?

30:26, 27 By utilizing the same two Hebrew verbs used in 29:21, Job contrasts the demeanor of his constituents who waited (Heb. *yahal*) for him silently (Heb. *damam*), with his own stance before God. When Job **waited for light,** his disappointment with the **darkness** would not allow him to **rest** (Heb. *damam,* "be still or silent") internally.

30:28–31 In light of the nearby reference to Job's dark, diseased skin (v. 30), the word **mourning** might mean "darkened," as in 6:16. When Job cries **out for help,** both God (v. 20) and people of all social classes ignore him. His loud cries for justice are as futile as the wails of **jackals** and **ostriches.** Because of his diseased condition (v. 30), Job feels ostracized, like these animal inhabitants of desolate places.

31:1–40 Job's oath of innocence (29:1—31:40) contains curses that he invites God to impose if He is to find Job guilty (vv. 8, 10, 22, 40). Thus ch. 31 corresponds structurally to Job's curse against his day of birth in ch. 3. It bears a general similarity to the oath of clearance, widely used in ancient Mesopotamia. In this oath, an accused person would swear his innocence at a trial. However, the ethical content of Job's confession, with its emphasis on inward motivation (vv. 1, 2, 24, 25, 33, 34) and attitude (vv. 1, 7, 9, 26, 27, 29, 30), is unique and unparalleled until Jesus' Sermon on the Mount (Matt. 5—7). Yet in this oath, a hint of pride creeps in (vv. 13, 16; ch. 37), setting the stage for the speeches of Elihu and the Lord.

31:1 This verse begins Job's oath of innocence (ch. 31). When Job made a **covenant with** his **eyes,** he wisely recognized that the eye is the main avenue for temptation (vv. 7, 9, 26, 27).

31:2–5 The word **if** was part of a formula used by accused persons to swear their innocence (vv. 7, 9, 13, 16, 19–21, 24–26, 29, 33, 38,

39). The full oath formula was, in effect, "If I am guilty of this crime, may God impose that curse." Because of hesitation about speaking a curse, the person swearing the oath would normally use an abbreviated version. By contrast, Job's daring use of the full formula four times (vv. 7–10, 21, 22, 38–40) demonstrates his confidence that he would be acquitted.

31:6–13 Job implies that he had been fairer in listening to the lawsuit or **cause** (Mic. 6:1) of his own servants than God was being with his complaint.

31:14–16 Job claims to have satisfied the **desire** of the **poor,** possibly in contrast to God's refusal to give Job a fair hearing before Him.

31:17–22 The loss of an **arm** in ancient society usually meant the loss of income, respect, and even life itself.

31:23–27 The phrase **my mouth has kissed my hand** reflects the apparent ancient custom of kissing the hand as a prelude to the superstitious and idolatrous act of throwing a kiss to the heavenly bodies.

31:28–34 God who is above: Job was resolute in his belief in the one, living God. Though he lived in a world filled with notions of many gods, Job believed in one God. This text expresses the monotheism of early biblical faith, in contrast to the prevailing polytheism of that time.

31:35 Job's wish for **one to hear** him seems to express his continued desire for an impartial mediator or judge (9:32, 33; 16:19; 19:25). Job's

---

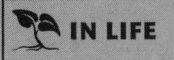 **IN LIFE**   # The Sin of Lust

Job's sufferings caused him to make a sweeping inventory of his inner life. One of the areas he evaluated was his attitude toward women and how he handled his own sexual drives (Job 31:1).

Job openly acknowledged the power of sexual appetites. He catalogued the steps of lust from "looking upon a virgin" (31:1), to allowing one's heart to follow one's eyes (31:7), to finally allowing oneself to be enticed by a woman and then scheming to have her (31:9).

Some may see this progression as normal, natural, or unavoidable. But Job viewed lust as a serious moral failure (31:11). He spoke of it in the same context with:

- falsehood and deceit (31:5);
- oppression of slaves (31:13–15);
- mistreatment of the poor (31:16, 19, 20);
- abuse or neglect of widows (31:16, 18);
- taking food out of the mouth of starving orphans (31:17, 18, 21);
- rejoicing over the misfortunes of others, even if they are one's enemies (31:29, 30);
- trusting in wealth (rather than in God, 31:24); and
- hypocrisy (31:33, 34).

Lust is a serious sin!

mark refers to his written signature attached to his oath of innocence (ch. 31). He seeks a sub-poena to compel God the **prosecutor** to **answer** him with specific charges, or perhaps an acquittal in a **book,** that is, a legal document. Hence, Job is arguing that God has not been fol-lowing proper court procedure (13:22).

31:36 Job believed that the written charges would be so few, if any, that he could wear the document proudly on his **shoulder.**

31:37–39 Job **would declare to** God **the number** his **of steps** or give account for his every act and thought (14:16; 31:4). His idea of approaching God **like a prince** shows his confi-dence that he will be vindicated but reflects a lack of humility, an attitude that the Lord Him-self will address (38:2, 3; 40:9–14).

31:40 the words of Job are ended: For the second time, the dialogue comes to a close (27:23), ending in a stalemate. Job has finished his words, and his three friends have nothing more to say. This leads to the voice of a new speaker, Elihu.

32:1 The phrase **these three men** seems to stress the distant relationship between Job and his so-called friends. A gulf existed partly because the trio had been accusing Job of self-righteousness.

32:2, 3 Elihu was of the tribe of Buz and of the **family of Ram,** perhaps an ancestor of King David (Ruth 4:19). His name means "He Is My God." Elihu was angry about what both Job and his friends had been saying. Like the other friends, Elihu thought that Job had only **justi-fied himself.**

32:4, 5 The editorial introduction (vv. 1–5) emphasizes the **wrath** of the young man against Job (v. 2) and against his three friends (vv. 3, 5). The word *wrath* is found four times in these verses.

32:6–22 I am young: Elihu introduces himself and his four speeches as he explains why he has waited to speak but feels compelled to speak out at the present time.

32:21, 22 As a reassurance to Job con-cerning his complaint that the friends are partial to God (13:7–10), Elihu promises not to **show partiality** in his voluntary role as an arbiter (vv. 12–14).

33:1–6 The translation **spokesman** (liter-ally, "as [or like] your mouth") may be sup-ported by the similar Hebrew wording of Ex. 4:16. However, the Hebrew text could suggest that Elihu was just like Job in that his mouth spoke to God in the same way Job's did. That he **also** had been **formed of** (Heb. *qaras,* literally, "pinched [from]") **clay** supports the latter view. An interesting parallel occurs in the Babylonian "Epic of Gilgamesh" where the goddess Aruru *pinched off clay* to form the man Enkidu.

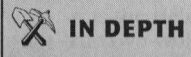 **IN DEPTH** | # Worshiping the Sun and Moon

A s Job takes an oath of innocence (Job 31), he swears that he has never been enticed to wor-ship the sun or moon (31:26, 27). Possibly worshipers threw kisses to these celestial deities, since kissing was part of idol worship (1 Kin. 19:18; Hos. 13:2). Job again swears that he has not gestured such kisses (Job 31:27). Job's oath reflects the popularity of both the sun and the moon as deities in Syria-Palestine.

Yareah, the moon good, is mentioned in the Ugaritic ritual and mythological texts, dating around 1400 to 1200 B.C. In one narrative Yareah is a guest at a drinking feast of the gods, but there is little mention of him otherwise. The moon god Sin of Haran was worshiped throughout Syria-Palestine and Mesopotamia from the third millennium through at least the Hellenistic period (332–37 B.C.). The characteristic crescent moon with dangling tassels, which symbolized this deity, has been found on numerous inscriptions and steles (stone slabs), including some discovered in Judah and Israel.

Much more is known about Shemesh. This deity, who could appear as either feminine (sun god-dess) or masculine (sun god), was important in all ancient Near Eastern pantheons. In Ugarit the god-dess Shapsu (meaning "sun") was the arbiter of divine judgment as proclaimed by the chief god El. In this she mirrored an image, found from Egypt to Mesopotamia, of the sun as a god of justice.[L&T, 1089]

People of the ancient Near East believed that the sun god rode through the sky by day and the netherworld at night, and thus saw and knew all human activity. Such knowledge made Shemesh useful for locating anyone who was to receive a message from El. In the Ugaritic texts, El sends Shapshu to order Baal and Mot to stop fighting. In Egyptian thought, the sun god (who had several names, including Re and Aton) was believed to be the creator of the universe each morning.

33:7, 8 Elihu responds to Job's **fear** of God (9:34; 13:21). Elihu reassures Job that he has nothing to *dread* since his **hand** will not **be heavy on** him.

33:9–13 In vv. 9–11 Elihu summarizes Job's position as he perceives it. Then he confronts Job by saying that Job is **not righteous** in attacking God. With great perception, Elihu cuts straight to the heart of Job's problem. Job has been treating God as though he were God's equal. Since **God is greater than man,** Elihu asks: **Why do you contend** or "file a lawsuit" against God? Job had been treating God as though He were merely a human who could be held accountable in court (34:23). Elihu continues this thought when he implies that Job has become proud—even while he sits dejected in the ashes (v. 17; 35:12–16).

33:14, 15 In response to 7:14 where Job complained of nightmares, Elihu suggests that God may have been trying to teach Job something through a **dream** or **a vision of the night.**

33:16–19 God seeks to keep mankind **from the pit** (Heb. *shahat*, the domain of the grave). The so-called "bottomless pit" (the shaft of the abyss), leading into the underworld or hell. Revelation 9:1, 2 may be a development of this concept. The point here is that God controls the length of our life.

33:20, 21 Elihu cites situations that fit Job's circumstances (6:17; 16:8).

33:22 the executioners are probably angels of death.

33:23–25 The precise identity of the **messenger** or angel is disputed. God may have employed this figure as **a mediator** to address Job's need for an impartial arbiter (9:32, 33; 16:19) and to contradict Eliphaz's counsel of 5:1. The intercessory role of this messenger to lead Job to repentance (v. 27) sounds much like the role that Christ would play (Heb. 7:25).

33:26 he (i.e., the sinner; v. 27) **will pray**.

33:27–33 This conclusion to vv. 14–30 succinctly states God's primary purpose in getting a person's attention through dreams and suffering: He wants to keep him from **the Pit**—that is, the grave and hell—and give that person **the light of life**—a meaningful life.

34:1–2 In vv. 2–15 Elihu addresses **you wise men,** probably a sarcastic reference to the three friends whose wisdom he had belittled in 32:12–16.

34:3–15 Surely God: Perhaps in response to Job's charges in 9:22–24, Elihu defends God's impartiality according to the traditional retribution dogma: God will justly punish the wicked. Elihu defends God's justice by siding with Bildad (8:3) against Job (19:6).

34:16 Elihu addresses Job directly in vv.

16–33, as indicated by the singular Hebrew verb translated **hear.**

34:17 The two rhetorical questions in this verse seem to rephrase Job's complaints of 9:14–31 and 24:1–17 in order to refute them. **Will you condemn Him who is most just:** The second question anticipates the Lord's own rebuke of Job in 40:8.

34:18–22 These verses emphasize God's omniscience (that He **sees** and knows all **the ways of man**).

34:23–28 Elihu responds to Job's complaints about God ignoring the plight of the poor and afflicted (24:1–12) by asserting that God does hear **the cry of the poor** and **the cry of the afflicted.**

34:29, 30 The sentence translated **when he gives quietness, who then can make trouble?** (supported perhaps by v. 30), may also be rendered "when He *exhibits* quietness, who then can condemn?" The parallelism of the next line (**when God hides his face**), and the context of Job's complaints, favor this latter translation.

34:31–33 The precise meaning of the Hebrew in this paragraph is unclear. Verses 31, 32 may be a caricature of Job's words.

34:34–37 Elihu's conclusion mixes sound analysis with an unfair representation of Job's position. His statement that Job's words are **without knowledge** anticipates the Lord's own words (38:2).

IN FOCUS **"right"**

(Heb. *mishpat*) (35:2; Pss. 1:5; 9:4; Prov. 12:5; Jer. 26:11) Strong's #4941: The Hebrew term translated here as *right* represents an important idea in the understanding of the judicial side of government, whether by humans or by God. The central idea of most uses of the term in the Bible is "justice" (Ps. 72:1, 2). The word can be used to designate the act ("judgment" in Josh. 20:6), the place ("the Hall of Judgment" in 1 Kin. 7:7), or the process ("judgment" in Is. 3:14) of a case of litigation, as well as the sentence ("deserves" in Jer. 26:11) or the time of judgment ("judgment" in Ps. 1:5). In the present passage, Elihu was asking whether Job had the legal right to question God's righteousness. Elihu correctly perceived that Job was implying that his ethical standards were higher than God's (29:12–17; 31:13, 16).

35:1, 2 Elihu asks: Is it **right** (a legal term; Heb. *mishpat*, "just") that Job acts as if his **righteousness is more than God's**. Building on Eliphaz's inquiry (4:17), he correctly perceives that Job has implied that his ethical standards are higher than God's.

35:3 By reading between the lines of Job's many complaints, Elihu exaggerates Job's position: "What benefit do I receive for being good?" Though Job had never made a bargain to serve God for mutual benefit, as in the religions of his day, Job's actions and words may have seemed to reflect that pagan attitude (read Job's own paraphrase of the sentiments of the wicked in 21:15).

35:4–8 God was not under any obligation to Job for any work or deed (41:11). Therefore, it was logically inconsistent for Job to demand that God must appear in court (31:35).

35:9, 10 People **cry out** (first verb, Heb. *za'aq*) **for help** (second verb, Heb. *shawa'*), because they need deliverance from the **oppressions** of the **mighty**, not because they acknowledge **God** as their **maker**. The nation of Israel during the period of the judges illustrated this principle. Their numerous cries to God were not always in repentance for sin but cries of desperation for deliverance from oppressors (Judg. 10:10–14, which uses Heb. *sa'aq* and *za'aq* interchangeably). This principle may explain many unanswered prayers today. However, this does not mean that all unanswered prayers are a result of pride. A general principle should not be made an ironclad rule; indeed, such was the very error of Job's friends in applying the retribution principle as a dogma.

35:11–16 One reason God **does not answer** when people **cry out** is that they are full of **pride** and devoid of pure motives (James 4:3). Elihu implies that Job's prayers have not been heard because of his pride (33:17). This accurate perception prepares the way for the speeches of God (chs. 38; 39).

36:1–4 Elihu's claim to be **one who is perfect in knowledge** is an arrogant statement. Unless he is being sarcastic, it borders on blasphemy (same phrase used of God in 37:16). Perhaps this statement illustrates the tendency in youth (32:4, 6) to think one has all the answers.

36:5–12 Elihu states his thesis: God is both **mighty** and just in His dealings with humankind (36:1—37:24). Elihu challenges Job's assertion that the wicked are not punished by God (21:7) and his subsequent arguments (21:27–33). Then Elihu counters Job's complaints of 24:1–17.

36:13–15 Affliction will also reveal the **hypocrites** who, because their hearts are incorrigibly wicked, **do not cry** to God **for help.** The warning is clear: Do not reject God's message by

failing to cry out to Him for help (Rom. 1:18–32).

36:16–29 Take heed: Elihu says that God intended to teach Job something through his affliction. Rather than trying to correct the Teacher, Job should **remember to magnify** God's **work** as Maker of all things. Thus, Elihu is setting the stage for the Lord, who will emphasize this concept in His speeches (38:1—42:6).

36:30, 31 light (the normal translation of the Heb. noun *'ôr*) could designate "lightning" as it does in v. 32 and 37:3. This translation is also probable for 37:21 (and possible for 37:11, 15).

36:32 God the sovereign warrior **commands** the thunderstorm as He dispenses **lightning** from **His hands** like arrows (16:12, 13). The Book of Job makes clear that God alone controls the unpredictable changes of the weather (38:22–30, 34–38).

36:33 The meaning of this verse is unclear in the Hebrew text.

37:1, 2 The plural Hebrew verb **hear attentively** indicates that Elihu appeals to Job and his friends and perhaps to any bystanders listening.

37:3, 4 The **voice** of God **roars.** The Hebrew word for *roars* seems to compare thunder to God growling like a lion, the majestic king of beasts.

37:5–7 He says: As God once spoke and brought forth light, land, and all manner of life (Gen. 1:3, 9, 14, 20, 24, 26), so now He speaks and controls all that He has made (Ps. 147:15–18). God uses the winter storms to stop **the hand of every man** so that he cannot work but instead **may** recognize the **work** of God.

37:8, 9 Elihu continues to praise the all-powerful God with a series of metaphors. He describes God as keeping the wind in a **chamber** just as He does the snow and hail (38:22, 23).

37:10 In a poetic figure of speech, Elihu speaks of the **breath of God** causing **ice** to form and **waters** to freeze. All of this is spoken with joyful delight, for Elihu is celebrating God's control of the world.

37:11 The phrase **His bright** (Heb. *'ôr*, "light") **clouds** may also be rendered as *His cloud(s) of lightning.*

37:12 The nautical term **guidance,** literally "steerings" or "rope-pullings" (the usage of this word in Prov. 1:5), portrays God as the wise Captain who skillfully charts the course for the clouds, which respond obediently to His hand at the helm.

37:13–17 God **causes** the storm **to come** for three specific reasons: (1) for punishment for people's wickedness, (2) for the nourishment of the earth (context of vv. 3, 6, 12), and (3) for supplying the needs of His people. **For correction** presents the idea of judgment by His rod or scepter. **for mercy:** The faithfulness and loyalty of God to His covenant promises are often tied to this word. This is the word that may be translated "loyal love" (Ps. 13:5). Thus God uses storms both to judge the earth and to bring the blessing of rain for His people (Ex. 15:7–10; Deut. 28:12).

37:18 Strong as a cast metal mirror: Ancient mirrors were firm and unbreakable because they were made of polished bronze.

37:19, 20 Resuming his role as arbiter, Elihu states (perhaps sarcastically): **teach us what** to **say to** God; **we can prepare nothing** (Heb. 'arak, "to set in order {a legal case}," as in 13:18), because you have kept us "in the dark."

37:21, 22 If people **cannot look at the bright light** of the sun **in the skies,** how much more difficult is it to approach God (v. 20), who appears in His own **golden splendor** and **awesome majesty?** See the experience of Moses described in Ex. 34. **the north:** In ancient times, north was viewed as the direction of God's abiding place (Is. 14:13).

37:23, 24 Elihu's concluding words offer praise to the living God who is at once elusive— **we cannot find Him**—and merciful—**He does not oppress. Judgment** means "justice." **Justice** means "righteousness." **fear:** Finally Elihu speaks of the reverential awe and worshipful wonder that all people should have for their omnipotent Creator.

38:1 out of the whirlwind: Though Job feared that God would crush him in a tempest (9:17), God does not come to destroy Job; rather God overwhelms Job into submission in order to restore him to his proper role as the Lord's servant.

38:2, 3 The theme of the first speech of the Lord is given here: Job **darkens** the **counsel** of the Lord—that is, God's plan or design for the universe. Ironically, God challenges Job to teach Him (v. 3; 40:7). These challenges are designed to alert Job to the consequences of his complaints and demands. Job's defiant attempt to meet God on equal footing in a law court (31:35–37) amounts to a rival claim to His throne (40:10–14).

38:4–7 Perhaps partially in reply to Job's words about the Lord shaking the pillars of the earth (9:5, 6), the Lord asks Job if he was an eyewitness when He laid the earth's **foundations.**

38:7 The joyful response of the **morning stars,** personified as singing, and **the sons of God** (1:6) as eyewitnesses to the earth's creation contrast with Job's complaints that were spoken in ignorance.

38:8–11 The Lord emphasizes His control of the **sea** and its **proud waves.** These forces, which ancient society considered to be chaotic and threatening, were allowed to exist only within divinely set limits (v. 10). Though Job knew this in theory (26:12, 13), he needed to apply this truth to his life.

38:12–15 The Lord answers Job's complaints that wickedness is rampant at night (24:13–17). Using personification, the Lord describes how He alone commands **the morning** to get out of bed and **the dawn** to pull off the covers of the night in order to shake out the wicked like bedbugs. God implies that only because of His control of the darkness are the activities of the wicked curbed at all. The Lord grants some freedom to humanity, but the wicked cannot go beyond His set limits. This section may be compared with the more familiar words of David in Ps. 19.

38:16–18 Has Job ever been to the bottom

✠ IN CONTEXT   Laying the Foundations of the Earth

Public building projects in the ancient Near East were begun with religious rituals, including liturgical singing in praise of the major deities. Kings ritually, if not actually, helped set the foundations of temples and symbolically aided the construction workers in laying walls and fastening gates. In Job 38:4–7, the universe is pictured as a great building project by God. All the inhabitants of heaven sing for joy as the foundations of the earth are laid (Job 38:7).

The heavenly beings who sing and shout are "the morning stars" and "the sons of God" (38:7). In the group of languages called Northwest Semitic, which includes Hebrew, "sons of God" is a standard way to describe the pantheon of deities. The specific mention of the morning stars may reflect Egyptian notions that creation begins anew each morning just as light appears along the horizon. Thus creation begins anew when the morning stars are in the sky. God reminds Job that he was not present, and cannot know what happened at creation when the heavenly choir sang (Job 38:4).

INSIGHT | **The Wild Donkey**

The onager (Job 39:5) is a name for the wild donkey. The onager was related to the Asian wild ass, called the kiang, but was generally smaller, with a broad stripe along its back. Onagers still exist throughout Asia.

Unlike domesticated donkeys, which were often used as beasts of burden, wild donkeys roamed freely throughout the wastelands of the Middle East. God used them as symbols of free-spirited independence in describing His ways to Job (Job 39:7–8).

of the sea or taken a trip through the **gates of death?** Perhaps in response to Job's desire for a respite in the darkness of Sheol (10:18–22), the Lord wants to know if he has ever been there.

38:19–21 Since Job had spoken intelligently about the distant horizons (26:10), the Lord exposes Job's limited knowledge by asking him to lead a guided tour to the abode of **light** and **darkness.** Since Job had stated that the wicked "do not know the light" or "abide in its paths" (24:13, 16), the Lord reveals the deficiencies of Job's secondhand knowledge. Had Job been there in person, he would have understood that the Lord has a **place** for both **darkness** and dawn, as well as for good and evil.

38:22–30 By asking if Job understands the seemingly unpredictable weather phenomena, the Lord reveals that His designs are not centered on humanity alone. Though God utilizes meteorological elements to intervene in human affairs (vv. 22–24), He also uses them to limit the chaotic wilderness and sea (vv. 25–30) that lie outside the human realm.

38:22, 23 The graphic metaphor of **the treasury** for **snow** and **hail** portrays these elements as weapons in the arsenal of God. He uses hail as sling stones (Josh. 10:11). He prepares other weapons, including snow (Ps. 68:14), thunderstorms, lightning (v. 24), and winds (37:9).

38:24–29 frost of heaven: Since frost is water vapor from the atmosphere that has condensed on cold surfaces, the word *heaven* may refer here to the atmospheric heavens.

38:30–32 The **Great Bear with its cubs** is a reference to the constellation known as Ursa Major.

38:33–38 In asking whose command the clouds obey, the Lord implies Job's impotence and ignorance of these matters, as well as His own sovereignty and omniscience. **voice:** The Lord alone controls the storms and lightning (36:32). The obedience even of lightning to God's command serves as another subtle rebuke to Job's complaints.

38:39–39:30 The Lord interrogates Job

concerning the animal kingdom to demonstrate Job's impotence to govern it and his ignorance of God's providential plan (38:1—40:5). The wild animals listed were either favorite game animals of kings or used by royalty. Before Job could validate his claims to be able to run the universe better than the Lord, he would need to prove that he could control these hostile forces.

38:40, 41 If the Lord provides for the young **raven** who cries out for help, how much more will He hear and provide for people when they genuinely cry out for help?

39:1–4 God, who provides the prey for the predators (38:39–41), also takes care of that prey, which includes the **mountain goats** and **deer.** By taking care of them in their most vulnerable moment of giving birth, the Lord provides for order and balance in nature.

39:4 The Hebrew word translated **with grain** may also be rendered "in the open field."

39:5–12 The **wild donkey,** the symbol of the exploited poor in 24:5, finds satisfaction where God has placed him on earth free from the **shouts of the driver** or "slave driver." This contrasts with Job's complaints about the voice of the oppressor (3:18). True freedom is found in being content where God has placed us (Phil. 4:10–12).

39:13–25 Job had identified himself closely with the **ostrich** (30:29). Therefore, the Lord ironically agrees that there are similarities. Both are deficient in knowledge (v. 17; 38:2). But although the ludicrous-looking ostrich is no doubt laughed at (as was Job; 30:1) and experiences misfortunes (vv. 14–16), the ostrich is not concerned about the situation. This contrasts with Job, who has been full of worry (3:25; 15:24).

39:26–30 God asks Job if he designed the majestic birds—the **hawk** and the eagle—by his aerodynamic genius. **eagle:** The context of v. 30, where the young birds feast on the blood of the slain, suggests that a vulture is in view. However, the traditional translation *eagle* conveys the royal and majestic qualities associated with the vulture in the ancient Middle East (vv.

26–30), in contrast to the revulsion its name brings to many modern readers.

39:30 The implication is that God allows the young vultures to feed on the **blood** of **slain** people to help prevent the spread of disease. This is an answer to Job's complaint about God's failure to stop the exploitation of the helpless (24:1–17) and His ignoring of the pleas of the

finished speaking. The words of v. 7 are repeated from 38:3, but the stakes are even higher now.

40:8 The Lord confronts Job with critical errors in his speeches. Job has dared to **annul** God's **judgment** or justice. The context of Elihu's speeches, where Elihu used this same word concerning the Lord's kingship over the

Photo by Amikam Shoob

The ostrich, which once lived in the Near East, is scorned in the Book of Job because of its haphazard nesting habits (Job 39:13–18).

dying. The Lord demonstrates to Job again that He limits evil.

40:1–3 Moreover the Lord answered: The Lord reinforces His initial thematic challenge (38:2, 3) with a dynamic question loaded with legal terminology. The word **contend** means "to bring a lawsuit" (9:3). God reverses Job's accusation that God has brought a lawsuit against him (the same Hebrew word is found in 10:2). It really has been Job accusing God, not the other way around. The Lord reprimands Job for his error. Who is Job to judge God? The Lord might be implying that Job has been trying to be his own "mediator" or "redeemer" (40:14).

40:4 vile: The context of vv. 4, 5 suggests that the Hebrew word for *vile* means "insignificant" or "unworthy." Job's placing his **hand over** his **mouth** is probably a gesture of respect (29:9) as God's subordinate.

40:5–7 prepare yourself: But God has not

universe (34:17; 37:23), suggests that Job has maligned God's justice by claiming that God rules without establishing moral or social order in the universe (24:1–17). Because Job had assumed the inflexible retribution dogma, which views suffering in this world as God's punishment for sin, Job had to **condemn** God in order to maintain his own innocence.

40:9–14 The absurdity of Job's defiant criticism of the way the Lord runs the universe (read 29:2–17 for Job's claim to be fair in his judicial duties) is forcefully brought to his attention by God's ironic invitation to become "king for a day" over the whole universe. If Job had the power, let him don the royal regalia of God's majestic attributes and **humble** the **proud** and **wicked** forces in the world. Job had criticized God for not doing this well enough (21:30, 31; 24:1–17).

40:15–24 The identity of **the behemoth,**

meaning the "great beast," is disputed. Suggestions include the elephant, some sort of dinosaur, or a purely mythical monster. The hippopotamus, which had overtones of cosmic evil, seems to fit the biblical and cultural evidence best. Job could not approach, much less subdue, this massive beast; how could he force his way to the Almighty with his case (40:15—41:34)? As the description of the beast continues, the elaborate language goes beyond any physical hippopotamus and presents the beast as a symbol of chaos. The same pattern is seen in the development of the Leviathan in the next section (ch. 41).

40:24 The clause **though he takes it in his eyes** is one possible translation of the Hebrew. However, it might also be construed as a question: "Can one take him by his eyes?" The phrase *in his eyes* may refer to the difficulty of capturing the hippopotamus when it is submerged, with only its eyes above the water. Also, because of the thick hide of the hippopotamus most weapons are ineffective unless they are shot through its eyes.

41:1 The identity of **Leviathan,** basically a transliteration of the Hebrew word for "sea monster" or "sea serpent," is disputed. The traditional view is that it is the crocodile. As in the case of the behemoth (40:15–24), the description of Leviathan begins as a grand, poetic description of a well-known, formidable beast. But by the time the description is complete (vv. 18–21), Leviathan has become a fire-breathing dragon, a powerful symbol of chaos, evil, and destruction. Ultimately, Leviathan's image is a portrait of chaos at the beginning of God's creation and of Satan at the consummation of the ages (Ps. 74:2–17; Is. 27:1; 51:9). Only God can control and destroy Leviathan; Job can only shrink back in humble fear. By means of ironic rhetorical questions, the Lord interrogates Job concerning his inability to confront, much less subdue, Leviathan.

41:2, 3 The **reed** indicates the material that was twisted or spun into a cord or rope, perhaps to "string" the Leviathan like a fish. However, the clause **pierce his jaw with a hook** may suggest the picture of Leviathan as a prisoner of war with a hook or ring in his jaw or nose (2 Chr. 33:11). This view is supported by the context of v. 4. This imagery is also used in Ezek. 29:3, 4, which describes the Lord capturing Pharaoh like a crocodile and putting hooks in his jaw.

41:4–9 The Lord continues to confront Job with a series of rhetorical questions. Can Job make Leviathan an eternal **servant** or vassal? The Lord's mention of the **covenant** implies that perhaps Job could offer it a peace treaty, like a great king subduing a lesser king in battle (v. 34).

41:10 When the Lord says **no one** would be so foolish as to **stir** Leviathan **up,** he is replying to Job's desire that this monster be roused (3:8). In effect, the Lord questions Job: "What would you do, Job, if he were provoked?" (vv. 8, 9).

41:11 **Who has preceded Me** could also be

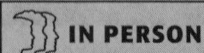 **IN PERSON** ## Job's Moment of Insight

After hearing from God, Job realized that he had been uttering "things too wonderful for me, which I did not know." The Hebrew word translated "know" implies more than a grasp of information; it suggests intimate knowledge of the sort that comes by personal experience. In effect, Job was admitting that all of his high-sounding talk had been so much blabber; he hadn't really known what he was talking about, certainly not the way God knows.

Likewise, Job had been pontificating on things that were "too wonderful" for him—literally incomprehensible or astonishing, things that only God could understand (compare Ps. 139:6). Job thought he was coming to terms with his troubles. Then he saw God, and he realized that he had no idea.

Job's response to this unexpected encounter with God was a sense of utter and absolute humility (Job 42:5, 6). The words, "I abhor myself" might be translated, "I reject what I have spoken"; "I cast away my words"; "I despise or disdain them." It's as if Job had written a journal or a book to detail and interpret his experience (19:23, 24), or a legal brief to make his case before God (31:35–37). But upon realizing who God was, he threw the book away.

As for Job's "repentance" (42:6), the word translated "repent" is not the term used for repentance from sin (*shub,* "to turn back or return"; compare 1 Kin. 8:47; Jer. 5:3), but a word meaning "to be sorry" or "to console oneself" (*nacham*). In other words, Job threw away his pretensions to wisdom and comforted himself "in dust and ashes," a common symbol of mourning or humility. He was satisfied with the humble knowledge that his sufferings were all part of the purposes of God—even if he could not understand those purposes with his finite mind.

rendered "who has confronted Me?" **that I should pay:** The Hebrew verb means "to pay a debt" or "to make restitution for something lost or stolen." The Lord confronts Job for implying that God owed him something for being righteous (34:5–8) or that God had to make restitution for the property and posterity He had allegedly stolen from Job (10:3). Thus the Lord plainly refutes Job's misconception that God is obligated to reward a person who is obedient. The idea that God does not have to reward us for what we consider good works is an essential part of the biblical doctrine of salvation by grace apart from our works (Eph. 2:8–10).

41:12–34 mighty power: The Lord reinforces the argument of vv. 1–11 by describing the invincibility and terrifying splendor of Leviathan's bodily features.

41:19–21 Using poetic exaggeration (v. 18), the Lord gradually transforms the physical Leviathan to the mythological dragon (7:12), which breathes **fire** and **smoke** (vv. 19–21).

41:22–34 The phrase **he beholds every high thing** could also be translated "he looks down on everything haughty." **King** Leviathan, who is **over all** who have **pride,** gazes with a look of superiority at the haughty. Therefore Job, whose pride had been exposed, could never succeed in subduing the mighty Leviathan or validating his claim to be able to rule the world better than God.

42:1–6 The phrase **I abhor myself** means "to reject" or "to recant." Job repents of his words and accusations that were based on the false belief that God always rewards the righteous in this life. Instead of accusing God of injustice, Job submits to the will of the sovereign Lord of the universe.

42:7, 8 In contrast to his friends, Job had **spoken** of God **what is right.** Unlike the friends, Job had recanted his false belief, repented of his pride (v. 6), and affirmed God's unconditional sovereignty over his life (v. 2). Job had been right in maintaining his innocence in the face of his friends' false accusations.

42:9–11 Since Israelite law required a thief to restore double for stealing "an ox or donkey or sheep" (Ex. 22:4), it was ironic that **the Lord** gave Job twice the amount of livestock he had before (v. 12). Clearly, the Lord was not admitting that He owed Job anything (41:11), but He was expressing His benevolent mercy.

42:12–17 The restored prosperity of Job should not be seen as compensation for his piety (41:11). After Job had given up his demand for his former prosperity, the Lord could give it to him as a free gift. This conclusion shows that the Book of Job does not totally reject the principle of divine retribution but only its false application. It concurs with the Book of Proverbs that the fear of the Lord normally leads to an abundant and long life. But we cannot presume that God will always operate in this manner, as Job's friends had done.

The Book of
Psalms

A S ONE OF THE GREATEST COLLECTIONS OF SONGS, prayers, and poetry, the Book of Psalms expresses the deepest passions of humanity. In these pages we can hear the psalmist's desperate cry in the midst of despair as well as his ecstatic praise of his Provider and Comforter. We can hear him pouring out his soul in confession but also bubbling over with joy. The Psalms lead us through the valleys and peaks of human experience, but in the end they guide us to the praise of our loving Creator.

Like the Pentateuch, the five books of Moses, the Book of Psalms is arranged in five sections: Book I (Pss. 1—41), Book II (Pss. 42—72), Book III (Pss. 73—89), Book IV (Pss. 90—106), and Book V (Pss. 107—150). Each book concludes with a doxology, an affirmation of praise to God found in the last verse or two of the concluding psalm. In the case of Book V, the entire last poem, Ps. 150, is the concluding doxology. The reason for this arrangement of the Book of Psalms is not clear. Most likely it had something to do with the use of the Psalms in the praise of God in temple worship. Books I and II are composed primarily of Davidic psalms; Book III includes the psalms of Asaph (Pss. 73—83) and the psalms of the sons of Korah (Pss. 84—88). Books IV and V include anonymous psalms, along with a few by David and others.

Many of the psalms can be identified as certain types by their theme.

The *royal psalms* emphasize God as King, often using the words "the Lord reigns." These psalms speak of His rule as Creator, as Savior of Israel, and as the Coming One. The royal psalms often point forward to the coming rule of the Savior King, the Lord Jesus.

The *psalms of Zion* focus on Jerusalem, using its endearing name Zion. These psalms rhapsodize on the city as God's choice for the site of His holy temple, the place for true worship of His name.

The *penitential psalms* are poems in which the poet confesses sin to the Lord, asks for and receives forgiveness, and then praises God for the renewed relationship that God's forgiveness provides.

The *wisdom psalms* focus on some of the same issues that are found in the Book of Proverbs. These psalms present sharp contrasts between the righteous and the wicked, address God's blessing and cursing, and often focus on righteous living.

One subcategory of the wisdom psalms is the *Torah psalms*. These are poems that focus on the beauty, truth, and sufficiency of the Law of God. Two other subcategories of the wisdom psalms are the *creation psalms* and the *history psalms*. In the creation psalms, the poet calls for the believer to praise God as the Creator of the universe and the Savior of His people. In the history psalms, the poet recounts the history of Israel and asks for a renewed commitment to God—even in the face of a history of rebellion.

Some of the most troubling psalms are those that contain prayers asking God to curse the wicked. These *imprecatory psalms* are sometimes thought to conflict with the sentiment of the gospel, but in fact they accurately reflect God's abhorrence of evil.

In contrast to the imprecatory psalms are the joyful and prophetic *Passover psalms* that became a part of the Passover celebration in Judaism. These psalms are a remarkable celebration of the great acts of the Lord in delivering His people from Egypt, the theme of the Passover celebration. They point forward to the deliverance that would come through the Savior, Jesus.

A final group of psalms is clustered at the end of the book. These are the *Hallel psalms*, named for the principal Hebrew word for praise, *hallel.* As their name suggests, these psalms praise God for His character and saving works.

In order to fully appreciate the Psalms, a certain number of their characteristics should be kept in mind.

First, the Psalms were written for singing. These were songs for public worship in the temple of ancient Israel. They are not merely poems but lyrics for music from the ancient world. As such they contain musical conventions peculiar to music and worship during that time.

Second, the poems in the Psalms were written over a period of a thousand years, from the time of Moses in the fifteenth century B.C. to the time of Ezra in the fifth century B.C. Although David is the main author associated with the composition of the Psalms, many other authors from various time periods contributed psalms to what would become the Book of Psalms.

Third, the Psalms were collected and arranged over a long period of time. This process involved some editorial additions to the poems, some cutting and expanding, and some rearranging and restructuring of various psalms. The Holy Spirit, who had inspired these poems in the first place, oversaw this process of restructuring them for temple worship.

Fourth, the Psalms were written in the language of the human spirit, the utterances of the soul. The Psalms are not cool, reasoned prose but deeply emotional works that use wrenching language, dramatic exaggeration, and figurative speech.

Fifth, psalms and the writing of psalms were part of ordinary life for the Israelites. The Scriptures record a number of times when the Israelites spontaneously responded to the Lord with a psalm of praise. Moses sang a psalm in praise of God (Ex. 15); Deborah and Hannah did the same (Judg. 5; 1 Sam. 2); and David blessed the Lord with a psalm (1 Chr. 29). Through a psalm the Israelites would express their devotion and thanks to their Lord. This tradition continued into the NT period, for Mary in Luke 1 responded to the angel's message with a psalm (Rev. 5). This Israelite tradition of psalm writing was confirmed by the discovery of a number of original psalms among the Dead Sea Scrolls discovered in 1947.

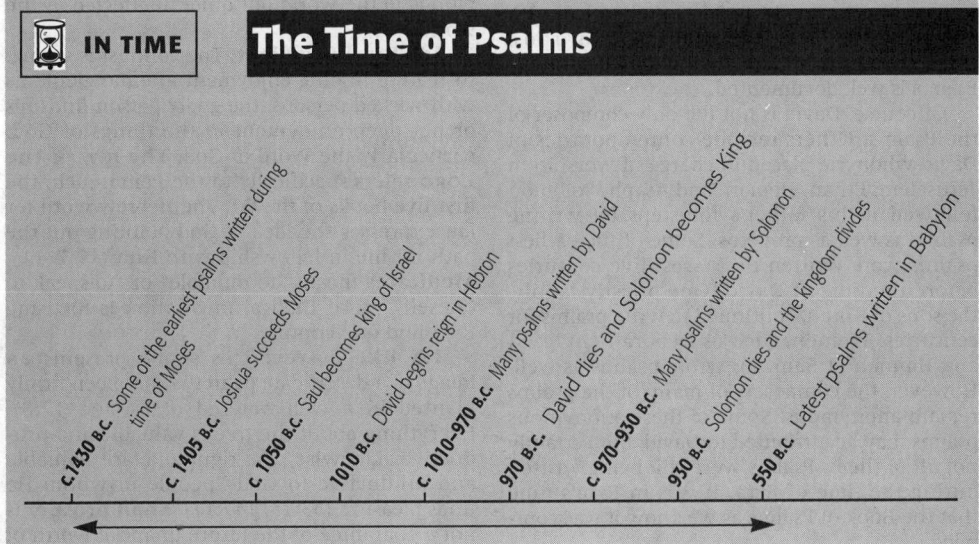

IN TIME

The Time of Psalms

c.1430 B.C. Some of the earliest psalms written during time of Moses

c. 1405 B.C. Joshua succeeds Moses

c. 1050 B.C. Saul becomes king of Israel

1010 B.C. David begins reign in Hebron

c. 1010–970 B.C. Many psalms written by David

970 B.C. David dies and Solomon becomes King

c. 970–930 B.C. Many psalms written by Solomon

930 B.C. Solomon dies and the kingdom divides

550 B.C. Latest psalms written in Babylon

Sixth, individual psalms were written for different purposes. Some began as works of private devotion, while others were designed from the beginning to be used in public worship. Ultimately, all the Psalms became the treasure of all the people in temple worship, for no matter what subject they addressed, they always led the people to the worship of the living God.

Finally, it must be remembered that the Psalms were written in the language of response. Each psalm records in powerful, poetic language one individual's response to God. From a desperate cry to an ecstatic shout of joy, each psalmist responds to God in the middle of a particular situation. Even though the Psalms became a part of the community's worship life, they remained a vehicle for individual expression as well. Even today, the Psalms are used both in public worship and in the devotional moments of individual Christians.

The superscription—the introductory words found before the first verse in most psalms—many times attributes the following psalm to King David, the "sweet psalmist of Israel" (2 Sam. 23:1). These superscriptions were probably not part of the psalms when they were originally composed but were added by editors to aid in the interpretation of the poems. Nevertheless, there is no reason to discount them. The historical books of the Bible speak of David's considerable accomplishments as a musician, singer, and composer of poems (1 Sam. 16:19–23; 18:10; 2 Sam. 1:17–27; 23:1–7; 1 Chr. 29:10–15). Moreover, one of David's psalms is recorded in 2 Sam. 22 and reappears with only slight variation as Ps. 18. Parts of the medley that David presented to Asaph in 1 Chr. 16:8–36 are taken from Ps. 105:1–15, Ps. 96, and Ps. 106:1, 47, 48. Thus, the connection between King David and the Psalms is well documented.

Of course, David is not the only composer of the Psalms. Others include contemporaries of David whom he placed in charge of worship in Jerusalem: Ethan, Heman, and Asaph. Solomon followed in his father's footsteps by writing psalms as well as proverbs. Some of the earliest psalms were written by Moses, five centuries before the time of David. One priestly family, the sons of Korah, continued to write psalms for centuries. Women, such as Deborah (Judg. 5) and Hannah (1 Sam. 2), wrote psalms as well. However, the composers of many of the psalms remain anonymous. Some of these anonymous psalms may be attributed to David, but certainly not all of them. Psalms were still being written during the time of Ezra. It was in Ezra's time that the Book of Psalms as we know it was compiled.

Outline

Book I: Pss. 1–41
Book II: Pss. 42–72
Book III: Pss. 73–89
Book IV: Pss. 90–106
Book V: Pss. 107–150

Commentary

Psalm 1, a wisdom psalm, presents a vivid contrast between the way of the righteous (vv. 1–3) and the way of the wicked (vv. 4–6). No author is named nor is any circumstance given for the writing of this poem. It was probably written late in Israel's history. With its focus on the distinctions of character and the different destinies of the righteous and the wicked, this psalm serves as an introduction to the entire Book of Psalms. The psalm is like a beacon of light piercing the darkness of a stormy night. It illuminates and points to the truth even when the falsehoods of our culture begin to cloud our thinking. The psalm affirms that there is one way to true life; to ignore this way is to foolishly accept death (Prov. 1:20–33).

1:1 The Hebrew word for **man** in this context means "person," without reference to gender. **Who walks not:** The parallelism in this verse speaks of an increasingly deeper involvement with wickedness: "walking beside," "standing with," "sitting beside." Similarly, the terms for the wicked are progressive: **ungodly, sinners,** and **the scornful.** The imagery of this verse presents an ideal righteous person—one who is *in* the world but quite unaffected *by* the world.

1:2 But his delight: The contrast is strong. Instead of finding enjoyment in entanglements with wicked persons, the godly person finds his or her deep enjoyment in the things of God, particularly the Word of God. **The law of the Lord** refers specifically to the Pentateuch, the first five books of the OT. The Hebrew word for *law* expresses the idea of God pointing out the path for life in fellowship with Him (19:7–11). **Meditates** means "to mumble" or "to speak to oneself" (4:4). Biblical meditation is focusing the mind on Scripture.

1:3 like a tree: This simile presents an image of a desert date palm that has been firmly planted in a well-watered oasis (Jer. 17:8). Everything about the tree is valuable and productive. Likewise, the righteous are valuable and productive to God—people in whom He finds pleasure (33:15; 147:11). **Shall prosper** is not a guarantee of the future financial worth of the righteous; rather, the righteous person is always useful and productive to the Lord.

1:4, 5 Like **chaff,** the refuse that is blown away by **the wind** after the grain harvest, **the ungodly** have no stability (35:5; 83:13). When

the judgment comes, the ungodly will no longer **stand** (5:5). This is similar to the picture of final judgment in the Olivet Discourse of Jesus (Matt. 25:31–46).

1:6 The Bible speaks of two ways (Prov. 2:8;

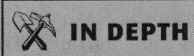

IN DEPTH | A Key to Understanding the Psalms

A fuller appreciation of the eloquence of the Psalms can be gained by understanding the basics of Hebrew poetry. The lack of a predictable rhythm and rhyme has confused some people about the poetic nature of the Psalms. Although Hebrew poetry contains some rhythm, it primarily makes use of repetition and recapitulation. One line of a verse is followed by another that gives a variation of the same idea. Not only do the psalmists use this poetic technique, but the authors of proverbs use it as well (see the Introduction to Proverbs). The second line of a proverb usually reinforces the meaning of the first line (Prov. 22:1). This reinforcement of the thought is not mere tautology, but the graceful artistry of a poet. The first line makes a statement that the second line sharpens or heightens.

A psalmist could modify this general pattern in a number of ways. First, the psalmist could use *synonymous parallelism* to make the two elements similar. For example:

But his delight is in the law of the LORD,
    And on His law he meditates day and night. (1:2)

Second, the psalmist could contrast the two elements. This type of parallelism, called *antithetical parallelism*, usually contains the word "but." For example:

For the LORD knows the way of the righteous,
    But the way of the ungodly shall perish. (1:6)

Third, the psalmist could develop the theme of the first line in the second line. This is called *synthetic parallelism*. For example:

Blessed is the man
    Who walks not in the counsel of the ungodly,
    Nor stands in the path of sinners,
    Nor sits in the seat of the scornful. (1:1)

A fourth improvement on general parallelism is *climactic parallelism*. In this type of parallelism, the first member of a couplet is incomplete and the second member partially repeats the first member and then completes the thought. For example:

Give to the LORD, O families of the peoples,
    Give to the LORD glory and strength. (96:7)

Finally, the psalmist could use *emblematic parallelism*. In this type, the first line contains a figure of speech and the following lines explain the figure by expansion or explanation. In the following example, the parallel lines of this verse explain the meaning of the expression "like a tree."

He shall be like a tree
    Planted by the rivers of water,
    That brings forth its fruit in its season,
    Whose leaf also shall not wither;
And whatever he does shall prosper. (1:3)

With poetic parallelism, the Hebrew psalmist powerfully expresses his praise of the Lord. By reading the psalms aloud and emphasizing the parallel elements, one can gain some sense of the harmonious poetic language from which the translation is derived.

4:19), only one of which leads to God. This is a consistent biblical theme, culminating in the celebrated words of Jesus, "I am the way" (John 14:6). The verb **knows** in this context refers not just to God's awareness but to an intimate, personal knowledge (101:4). God is intimately involved with the way of the righteous but has

The psalmist compared a righteous person to a desert palm tree flourishing in an oasis (Ps. 1:3).

no connection with the way of the ungodly, except in judgment (146:9).

Psalm 2, a royal psalm, focuses on the coming glorious reign of the Lord's Messiah. The author is anonymous in the Hebrew text, but the NT apostles assign it to David (Acts 4:24–26). This psalm should be read in conjunction with Ps. 110. Both psalms point prophetically to the coming rule of Jesus (Acts 13:33; Heb. 1:5, 6; 5:5; Rev. 2:26, 27; 12:5). Psalm 2 has four movements, each related to a different voice or speaker: (1) a description of the plans of the wicked (vv. 1–3); (2) the Father's derisive laughter from heaven (vv. 4–6); (3) the Son's declaration of the Father's decree (vv. 7–9); (4) the Spirit's instruction to all kings to obey the Son (vv. 10–12).

2:1 Why do the nations rage: This passage has multiple meanings. Originally it referred to the nations that confronted David and his legitimate successors. But the Davidic kings were mere shadows of the coming great King, the Savior, Jesus. Consequently, the verse also refers to any attack on Jesus and His divine kingdom. This assault by the nations occurred in its most dramatic form at the cross, but resistance to God's kingdom has continued. Throughout history, nations have resisted the claims of the gospel, the foundation of Jesus' kingdom.

2:2 Lord refers to the Father. **His Anointed** (18:50; 132:10) refers to the Son. The word conveys a sense of royalty, for kings were anointed (1 Sam. 10:1; 16:13). **The kings of the earth** would attempt to withstand the very King of the universe.

2:3 let us break their bonds: This is ultimately an end-time scenario that is described more fully in the NT (Rev. 19:11–21; Ps. 110). Here the kings of the earth make their last stand in their rebellion against heaven's King, Jesus.

2:4, 5 hold them in derision: God laughs scornfully at an attack on His Son (37:13). The idea of "fighting off" the will of God is truly preposterous. **He who sits in the heavens:** God is King of the universe (Ps. 93). What are the puny kings of the earth compared to Him?

2:6 My King: David and his legitimate heirs were given a divine promise that they would rule the Israelites under the Lord's blessing. Any attack on the king of Israel was an assault on God's promise. **Zion** is another name for Jerusalem. **My holy hill:** The site of Zion was "holy," for it was declared to be so by God. It was the place where Abraham bound his son Isaac (Gen. 22), where the holy temple was built (2 Chr. 3), and where the Savior would die (Matt. 27).

2:7, 8 You are My Son: Each time a legitimate son of David was crowned king as the successor to his father in the city of Jerusalem, these words could be used of him. The new king was adopted by God as his "son"; he would look to God as his "Father" (2 Sam. 7:5, 14). This formula of adoption was announced in a solemn ceremony of coronation attended by priests and prophets, with pomp and celebratory worship of God. In the NT, the Son of God is also declared to be the King, the true Anointed, the Christ (Matt. 3:17; Mark 1:1, 11; Luke 3:22; John 1:18; Acts 13:33; Heb. 1:5; 5:5).

2:9 rod of iron: The future rule of the royal Son would be absolute. There would be no rebellion.

2:10, 11 be wise: Potentially rebellious kings would avoid terrible judgment only by submitting to the Anointed of God. **rejoice with trembling:** Only with the proper fear, adoration, reverence, and awe of the Most Holy God could there be genuine joy in the coming kingdom.

IN CONTEXT — The King's Relationship to Divinity

The position of king in the ancient Near East was the point at which heaven and earth came together. The Egyptians believed their pharaoh was divine and returned to the gods when he died. From about 1500 B.C. the pharaoh was thought to be the son of the god Amon-Re, as well as the "image of god," both physically and in his actions. Egyptian kings had their own priests, and their palace was treated as a temple. The pharaoh counted on the help of the other gods in ruling his kingdom. As long as he did not alienate the other deities, they would fight with him to protect or expand the kingdom of Egypt.

In Mesopotamia, rulers were not considered divine, but they were understood to have been appointed king by the patron deity of their city or empire. Since the god had chosen him, the king ruled as vice-regent of the god and was accountable to the god for all his actions. As long as the king did what was expected of a good ruler, the gods would protect him and guarantee victory over his enemies.

Such ancient Near Eastern theology was used by Judah to celebrate the crowning of Davidic kings in Jerusalem. The psalmist describes Yahweh speaking to Judah's new king in words parallel to the Mesopotamian royal texts: "You are My Son, today I have begotten You" (Ps. 2:7). The early Christians understood Psalm 2 to refer to Jesus as the Messiah (Acts 4:25, 26; 13:33). But originally Psalm 2:7 meant that Judah's king was the legitimate heir to the throne (other rulers were "adopted"). The king was the vice-regent of Yahweh, seated at His right hand, and Yahweh would guarantee victories for the king over Judah's enemies.

2:12 Kiss the Son: In this passage, the kings and all peoples were presented with a clear choice. They could either love and respect the Lord's Anointed and so experience His great blessing, or they could refuse to submit, and incur God's wrath.

Psalm 3 is a lament psalm ascribed to David. The superscription indicates a precise setting: the period of David's flight from his son Absalom (2 Sam. 15). This is one of the few psalm titles that ties a psalm to a specific incident in the life of David. The brief poem has four movements: (1) David's opening lament (vv. 1, 2); (2) his strong confession of trust (vv. 3, 4); (3) his determined act of faith (vv. 5, 6); (4) his continuing plea (vv. 7, 8).

3:1, 2 Many: At this point in David's life there was one specific foe who troubled him greatly—his son Absalom. However, David's friends had also become his foes because they were advising him that no one would help him, not even God. **Selah:** This is a musical term, perhaps indicating a pause in the lyrics for a musical interlude.

3:3, 4 The phrase **but You, O LORD** changes the mood of the psalm from dejection to confidence. David says three things of the Lord: (1) When no one would help David, God was his **shield.** (2) When David had nothing to treasure, God was his **glory.** (3) When no one would encourage him, God Himself would encourage him and lift his **head. Holy hill** is a poetic reference to God's dwelling in heaven;

the place of Israel's worship was but a physical symbol of this dwelling.

3:5, 6 I lay down and slept: Given the stress that David faced, it is remarkable that he was able to enjoy a night's rest. This was possible only because of God's sustaining power. God's gift of rest may be given even in the most troubling times. **I will not be afraid:** When God is one's protector, there is no need to fear (23:4; 27:3; 118:6).

3:7, 8 In the language of the lament psalms, David calls out for God to **arise,** to move on his behalf, to incline to his prayer (40:1). **on the cheekbone:** In the poetic imagery David uses, his enemies are like powerful beasts whose strength is in their jaws and whose terror is in their teeth. God's strike at the source of their strength means that they are no longer a threat. **Salvation,** in this instance, refers to deliverance from the immediate pressure that the psalm has already described. One meaning of the Hebrew word translated *salvation* is "room to breathe." **Your people:** As is the pattern in Psalms, the experience of the individual becomes the template for the community.

Psalm 4 is linked to Ps. 3 in mood and concept. Both speak of the possibility of finding such peace in God's presence that even when torn by physical and emotional pain, a person may still have restful sleep (3:5; 4:8). This is a lament psalm of the individual, but one in which there is an unusual degree of confidence. To the wicked there is a proclamation of hope

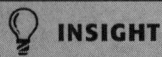

INSIGHT   Mysterious Musical Notation

The term *Selah* (Ps. 3:2) is used seventy-one times in Psalms and three times in Habakkuk, yet its exact meaning remains obscure. Perhaps the best guess is that it indicated a musical interlude or transition.

The root word from which Selah is thought to come means "to lift up." That has led some to believe that Selah marks a climax in the music in which the singers and musicians are to "lift up" their praise to God. Another suggestion is that Selah is an acronymic shorthand for a musical direction, somewhat similar to modern-day notations such as *mf* for *mezzo forte* (moderately loud) or *pp* for *pianissimo* ("very soft"). According to this theory, Selah supposedly means "change of voices" or "repeat from the beginning."

rather than a pronouncement of doom. Psalm 4 is the first of the psalms to have a superscription that focuses on its musical nature. **To the Chief Musician** is a notice that indicates that this psalm is from an early collection of psalms used in temple worship. **With stringed instruments** specifies the musical setting for the psalm. **A Psalm of David** serves not only as a notice of authorship, but also as a reminder that the poem was to be sung. The structure of the psalm is as follows: (1) a petition for deliverance (v. 1); (2) an address to the wicked, encouraging them to turn from falsehood and to trust in God (vv. 2–5); (3) an assertion that only God is able to provide genuine joy, deep peace, and abiding safety (vv. 6–8).

4:1 O God of my righteousness can also be translated "O my righteous God." The phrase has two meanings: (1) only God is righteous; and (2) all of a person's righteousness is found in Him alone. The psalmist is facing a very pressing need, but his confidence in God remains especially strong. He addresses God in terms of His character—His "righteousness." Then he speaks of God's earlier saving works in his life: **You have relieved me in my distress.**

4:2 How long: The psalmists often use these words to question God (13:1, 2). Here they are addressed to the wicked. **my glory:** For the believer, one's sense of glory or honor is found in relationship to the Savior.

4:3 set apart: This is the central point of this psalm. God has identified the **godly**—those who are devoted to God and His ways. He exercises special care over them and listens to their prayers.

4:4, 5 Be angry, and do not sin: These words are cited by Paul in the NT to describe "righteous indignation" (Eph. 4:26). Here the psalmist exhorts his reader not to let anger or anxiety erode complete trust or faith in the Lord. **Offer the sacrifices of righteousness:** These words speak of the salvation experience.

put your trust in the LORD: Those being addressed here are the wicked (1:4–6). Thus in this psalm, the poet calls his neighbors to put their faith in God (Ps. 67).

4:6 any good: Although our lives often seem to be filled with uncertainty, there is never uncertainty with God. **light of Your countenance:** This phrase recalls the Aaronic benediction (Num. 6:26) and indicates God's favor. Those on whom the Lord shines His face are truly blessed.

4:7 grain and wine: The joy God gives transcends the joy of the harvest. Agricultural produce, the result of abundant rain on fertile soil, was a blessing of God on His people. But there is something greater than full barns and overflowing cisterns—the joy of God's presence.

4:8 The peace that God gives is far from a relaxation technique. It is a peace that enables an anxious person to lie down **and sleep** (3:5).

Psalm 5, a lament psalm, speaks of an unspecified but distressing period of David's life, a time marked by enemies who verbally opposed him and his rule. In the culture of the OT, a blessing or a curse was an appeal to God to *do* what the curse or blessing specified. So when David's enemies hurled curses at him, they believed that those curses called on divine power to destroy him. In this psalm, David is in distress because of the lies and boasts of his adversaries (101:7). He identifies his own cause with that of the Lord, so that attacks on him became attacks on God Himself. The "righteous" in v. 12 ultimately points to Jesus, as is common in the Book of Psalms (1:6). The psalm has three movements: (1) a prayer to the Lord for deliverance in a time of trouble (vv. 1–6); (2) a desire to worship the Lord in a time of trouble (vv. 7–9); (3) a longing for final judgment by the Lord in times of trouble (vv. 10–12).

5:1–3 Give ear: As in 4:1, this is the language of a person who believes from experience that God has forgotten his plight. The sufferer

---

| IN DEPTH | **Does God Hate?** |

We know from Scripture that God is a God of love who shows mercy to sinners (Ps. 103:3; Matt. 9:12–13). Yet the Psalms declare that He "hates" people who commit iniquity and wickedness (Pss. 5:5; 11:5). How can we reconcile these seemingly contradictory pictures of God?

When the Bible speaks of "hatred," it does not mean the normal human reaction of retaliation or "getting even" for wrongs suffered. Nor does it mean a mad, irrational response to wrong or injustice. Rather, biblical "hatred" describes a studied expression of anger rooted in a commitment to justice. God does get angry at sin that injures and destroys His creation, especially human beings made in His image. He will not tolerate that which violates His "very good" work (Gen. 1:31).

But God's righteous indignation is not a fit of anger. It is rather a carefully considered application of a just disapproval and penalty against wrongdoing. It is godly wrath against evil (Ps. 2:5, 12).

---

calls on the Lord to listen, even though the Lord has been continually listening and caring. **Meditation** here refers to incessant groaning. **My King:** The psalmists often address God in heaven as King, the ruler over all. At times, the psalms focus on prayer **in the morning** (88:13)—a commendable habit that helps a person to dedicate all the activities of the day to the glory of God.

5:4–6 Takes pleasure means to find enjoyment or reason for laughter. There is no enjoyment to be found in evil. The Hebrew word for **boastful** is the same one used to describe the praise of God. The praise of God is the focus of the psalms, but praise of self—a mere boast—is a twisted, human perversion of true praise. **not stand:** This psalm speaks of final judgment on the wicked (compare 1:5). They will not be allowed to stay in His glorious presence. **You hate:** God's hatred is not merely a feeling but an action of His will. The phrase **workers of iniquity** occurs often in the psalms to describe those who characteristically practice evil (14:4).

5:7, 8 But as for me: In the Hebrew text, these words indicate a sharp contrast with the previous description of the wicked. The Hebrew word **temple** can be used of any very large structure—"palace" or "big house." David was a leader in reforming the worship of God in Jerusalem, and he established a structure for the worship that would take place in the temple to be built by Solomon. David uses the word *temple* in anticipation of the future glorious building; all later generations of Hebrew worshipers would understand their own worship better because of the use of this word in these psalms. **Make Your way straight:** David prayed that God would make clear His will for him.

5:9, 10 Their throat is an open tomb: These words describe the perverse language used by people in opposition to God. Paul used the words of these verses to argue for depravity of all people (Rom. 3:13).

5:11, 12 rejoice: Here the psalmist describes the joy of the saved, the ecstasy of the ones whom God saves from their own deserved destruction. Our joy must always be focused on our Savior (Phil. 4:4).

Psalm 6 is a lament psalm that shares elements of the penitential psalms. David was experiencing what he feared to be a mortal illness. He sensed that this illness may have fallen on him because of his own sinfulness. The title of the psalm is similar to those of Pss. 4 and 5. The specification of instruments is a reminder that this very personal psalm became part of the worship of the community when the temple was built. The psalm has four movements: (1) a petition for the Lord's mercy at a time of great pain (vv. 1–3); (2) an affirmation that the praise of the Lord comes from the living (vv. 4, 5); (3) a description of the psalmist's suffering (vv. 6, 7); (4) a rebuke of the psalmist's enemies, for the Lord has heard his prayer (vv. 8–10).

6:1–3 in Your anger: The psalmist suffers from a grave physical illness, one from which he fears he might not recover (v. 5). His principal concern is not only that his suffering might be more than he could stand but also that it comes as a result of God's severe anger. In his mourning, David cries out to God (as in 38:1). **My bones** is a poetic way of describing a deeply troubling illness; David's entire being is in torment.

6:4, 5 Return: This is a typical part of a petition in the psalms of lament (Ps. 13). The call for God to act is based on faith, even during a period of great stress. **Your mercies' sake:** Perhaps the most significant single term in the Hebrew text regarding the character of God is the word rendered *mercies* here. The Hebrew word describes what some prefer to call the loyal love of God. The translations vary because the word has much depth. Aside from the personal name of God (Yahweh), it may be the single most important term describing Him as the object of praise in the Book of Psalms (36:5). **In the grave:** When a believer dies, his or her voice is lost from the singers of God's praise in temple worship. The reasoning is clear: If God still desires to hear David's voice in worship, He must keep David alive. David would be of no use to God dead; alive he could sing, shout, and testify to God's love and His mercy (94:17).

6:6, 7 make my bed swim: This language of exaggeration is a way of emphasizing the reality of his pain. He seems to be weeping so profusely that he is about to drench his bed, drain his ducts, and die of grief.

6:8–10 Depart: Psalm 6 is a lament psalm in which the Lord answers the prayer of the afflicted David. The change of mood in the psalm is due to the Lord's response. David who has been so ill is now healed. The Lord has answered David's prayer. **workers of iniquity:** See 14:4; 101:8. **Let all my enemies be ashamed:** The psalmist speaks in righteous indignation against those who have reviled him, and more importantly have ridiculed his God.

Psalm 7 is a lament psalm, featuring David's protestations of innocence. In some psalms, the psalmist indicates that his suffering is deserved. Such cases lead to confession of sin. But in other cases, psalmists, like David in this psalm, do not believe they deserve the suffering or the feeling of being abandoned by God. Hence this psalm expresses David's extreme sorrow. Of course, none of us is exempt from sin and guilt. Ultimately all of us deserve God's wrath (Rom. 3). But when we become children of God, we anticipate mercy. Often we are shocked when we face suffering. But the dominant message in the Book of Psalms is twofold: (1) God is good; and (2) life is difficult. The life of faith is lived between these two realities. Although the title of the psalm refers to "Cush, a Benjamite," the Scriptures do not identify who this person was or what event in David's life prompted this psalm. The psalm has several brief movements: (1) an initial appeal for deliverance (vv. 1, 2); (2) a protest of innocence (vv. 3–5); (3) an appeal for God's judgment, part one (vv. 6–8); (4) an appeal for God's judgment, part two (vv. 9, 10); (5) a picture of God's judging work (vv. 11–13); (6) a portrait of the wicked (vv. 14–16); (7) a vow of praise (v. 17).

7:1, 2 I put my trust: The verb here can describe the action of a bird seeking refuge in the wings of its mother. This picture is found in the Book of Psalms (11:1; 17:8) and in the historical books (Ruth 2:12). **Tear me like a lion** vividly conveys the psalmist's fear. David had witnessed a lion who had captured its prey, and he compares his own fate to being captured and torn apart.

7:3–5 if I have done this: David protests that he is innocent of whatever charge his enemy has brought against him (Ps. 94). **let him trample my life:** These solemn words are spoken to God. The Lord can enact His judgment through David's enemies if his protest of innocence is false.

7:6–8 in Your anger: This is a plea for God to display His anger against the psalmist's adversaries, to judge them for their slander against David. **Lift Yourself up:** David implores the Lord to rise from His throne to intervene on his behalf, to bring justice in the intolerable situation (3:7). **Judge me:** Only someone confident of his own innocence would dare to pray these words before the Lord. David was innocent of the charges. He had not attacked someone without cause (vv. 3–5).

7:9, 10 In the Hebrew, **hearts and minds** is literally "hearts and kidneys"—an ancient way of describing the innermost person. **My defense** means "my shield." God hovers over the believer like a military shield, an invisible defense (33:20).

7:11–13 God is angry: The indignation of God is directed at the enemies of His people. **sharpen His sword:** The imagery in vv. 12, 13 is of a great warrior preparing for battle: the Warrior is the Lord and the battle is against the wicked (37:9; 118:10).

7:14–16 conceives trouble: The wicked become "mothers" to trouble. They will give birth to their own destruction.

7:17 Most High is a term often used to describe God's authority over the nations (47:2; 78:35; Deut. 32:8). The God of Israel is not just another national deity—He rules all nations.

Psalm 8, a psalm of praise with wisdom connections, is a poetic reflection of the great creation text of Gen. 1. This psalm expresses wonder at the majestic and sublime nature of God. However, the center of the psalm focuses on human beings, a rarity in Scripture. But even this focus leads to the praise of God, the Creator of humanity. Thus the psalm sets to music the significance of the phrase "in His image" in Gen. 1:26–28. The structure of the poem is: (1) a prologue in praise of God's excellent name (v. 1); (2) the praise of God from children (v. 2); (3) the praise of the Creator of humanity (vv. 3–8); (4) an epilogue in praise of God's excellent name (v. 9).

8:1 How excellent is Your name: The name of God and the glory of God are alternate ways of describing who He is. See the description of the meaning of the name of God in Ex. 3:14, 15 and the focus on the name of God in

113:1–3. This psalm ends with the same words it begins with. These words of praise to the name of God form a frame for its central subject—the praise of man as male and female, whom God has made to reflect His majesty.

8:2 mouth of babes: This verse was quoted by Jesus (Matt. 21:16) to the priests and scribes who wanted to squelch the people who were speaking the words of 118:26 in praise of Jesus.

8:3, 4 Your heavens: David is in awe at the splendors of creation; the wonders of nature lead him to praise its Creator. Even the universe with its infinite distances was the work of the Lord's fingers (19:1). **What is man:** In view of the vastness of creation and the surpassing glory of God the Creator, who are we to presume upon Him? Here *man* refers to all human beings regardless of gender.

8:5–8 You have made him a little lower than the angels: The response to the rhetorical questions of v. 4 is stunning. Man, as male and female, stands at the summit of God's creation. The Hebrew text is "You have made him to lack little of God." The Septuagint, the ancient Greek translation of the OT, translates the Hebrew word meaning "God" as *angels.* The author of Hebrews bases his argument in Heb. 2:5–9 on the Septuagint. So both readings are true. God made human beings in His image, just a little lower than angels. The words **crowned him with glory** fill out and explain the parallel phrase "a little lower than the angels." God created human beings as majestic creatures who

were to rule over His creation. But in our fallen state, we are profoundly disfigured, a perversion of the majesty God has intended (9:20). However, Jesus restores those who put their trust in Him. In Christ, we recover majesty; in Him, we become the people that God wants us to be. Whenever we feel worthless, the words of this psalm should encourage us. We and all other human beings are valuable because God Himself created us in His own glorious image.

8:9 O Lᴏʀᴅ, our Lord: The first word is the divine name Yahweh. The second Hebrew word translated *our Lord* speaks of the One in control: "our Sovereign."

Psalm 9 may have been originally one poem with Ps. 10. Indeed, there is evidence that several of the psalms have been restructured in varying ways (Pss. 42; 43). Note that Ps. 10 does not have a new superscription and that the two psalms deal with the same theme. Moreover, the psalms in the Hebrew text form a partial acrostic pattern. Ten of the initial letters of verses in Ps. 9 follow the order of the Hebrew alphabet, and seven initial letters in Ps. 10 continue the same pattern. In Hebrew, this pattern is pleasing to the listener and attests to the skill of the poet. Although Pss. 9 and 10 are psalms of lament, they present a triumphant determination to praise God. The structure of Ps. 9 is as follows: (1) a determination to praise the Lord (vv. 1, 2); (2) a rehearsal of God's saving deeds (vv. 3–5); (3) a rebuke of God's enemies (vv. 6–8); (4) a statement of confession (vv. 9, 10);

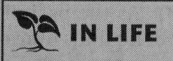 **IN LIFE**   **God the Judge**

However nations might justify and judge their actions, the ultimate Judge of their conduct is God. His righteousness, which flows from His very character, is the final standard against which right and wrong is measured (Ps. 9:4). This righteous Judge rebuked the nations of David's day for failing to do what David had done in Psalm 8—acknowledge God (8:1, 9).

The kingdom of Israel quickly rose to a place of prominence and power under David and his successor, Solomon. This window of opportunity opened during a period in which no one empire dominated the Middle East (c. 1000 B.C.). Egypt was in decline and Assyria had not yet become a major power. The two Israelite kings seized the moment by strengthening Israel's defenses, expanding its borders, increasing its trade, and storing up enormous wealth.

Meanwhile, many of Israel's neighbors continued to ignore God and govern with wickedness. Instead of ruling their people with justice and compassion, they often oppressed them. They also attacked other nations without provocation, destroying innocent people (Ps. 9:6). But God responded by destroying the destroyers. He pledged not to forget the needy and helpless, and avenged the injustices they had suffered by blotting out the wicked (9:7–18).

The same righteous God sits in judgment on the world today. He watches what nations do, and will not leave their sins unpunished. Nations and their leaders are still accountable to the Lord for their programs and policies. This fact should kindle a healthy fear of the Lord and a humble recognition that human leaders are only mortal (9:20).

(5) an ascription of praise to God (vv. 11, 12); (6) a petition for deliverance by God (vv. 13–16); (7) a vision of the judgment of the wicked (vv. 17, 18); (8) a call for deliverance by God (vv. 19, 20). The title of the psalm, which ascribes the poem to David, may also indicate the tune to which it was to be sung, "Death of the Son."

9:1, 2 with my whole heart: Real praise is not halfhearted; it involves one's whole being (146:2). The words of these two verses are characteristic of the praise of God in the Psalms. He is to be praised for His works and His name. His name represents who He is; His works stand for all He does. **Most High** is a designation for the Lord, especially as He rules the nations (47:2; 78:35; Deut. 32:8).

9:3–5 The **enemies** are not identified; this is common in the Psalms. All subsequent readers can fill in their own list of those who trouble them. The poet has confidence that God is in control (v. 4) and that He executes judgment (v. 5). Therefore in the middle of trouble, the psalmist is able to foresee the end of his enemies (vv. 17, 18).

9:6–8 One day even the names of the enemies of God will be forgotten. But the name of God will **endure forever.** One day there will be a final judgment when God will make right every wrong and establish His peace based on justice (96:13).

9:9, 10 Refuge speaks of a secure height, something inaccessibly high. David was often outdoors, and he used images from physical geography to describe the wonder of God's protective care (91:1, 2). **who know Your name:** To know the name of God was the OT equivalent of saving faith in the NT. **have not forsaken:** This is a further explanation of the meaning of God's name. Since the Lord is God, He cannot abandon those to whom He has bound Himself. He is a faithful God—a God who never gives up on His people.

9:11, 12 He avenges blood: God is the Avenger, not any person (Deut. 32:35). One day God will judge the wicked. In the end, He will establish His just rule.

9:13–16 David asks that his life be spared **from the gates of death** so that he might praise the Lord in the **gates** of the temple. David moved from the gates of death to the gates of life. Only God could accomplish such a sudden reversal; only the Lord could lift him from such depths. **Daughter of Zion** was an endearing term for Jerusalem. As Jacob was God's "son," so Jerusalem was God's "daughter" (Ps. 48). **In the net:** David prays that the evil the wicked intend for him will become their own trap (7:15, 16; 35:7, 8).

9:17, 18 hell: Just as the Psalms speak of heaven as the destiny of the righteous (23:6), so they also speak of hell as the destiny of the wicked (1:6). It is a place from which the righteous want to be delivered (86:13). Passages like this one confirm the NT affirmation of a day of final judgment in which the righteousness of God will be displayed and the wickedness of unrepentant humankind will finally receive punishment (Matt. 25:31–46). **The expectation of the poor** describes the often fruStrated hope that the oppressed may feel in this life. One day, however, they will be vindicated, for God Himself is their Protector (140:12).

9:19, 20 Do not let man prevail: Although human beings are made in God's image as described in Ps. 8, the wickedness of fallen humanity is profound. Humanity in rebellion against God is a gross perversion of God's plan. The Lord cannot allow this arrogance to go unchallenged.

Psalm 10 was originally part of Ps. 9. The two are found as one psalm in the Septuagint, the ancient Greek translation of the Hebrew Scripture. Psalm 10 reiterates the desire expressed in Ps. 9, that the Lord would deal with the wicked enemies of the psalmist. This psalm reflects a sense of urgency: the psalmist pleads for immediate deliverance from his enemies. The structure of Ps. 10 is: (1) an inquiry into the Lord's inaction (vv. 1, 2); (2) a description of the actions of the wicked (vv. 3–11); (3) a renewed call for the Lord to rise in judgment (vv. 12, 13); (4) a confession of trust in the Lord's final judgment (vv. 14, 15); (5) a presentation of praise to God who is King (vv. 16–18).

10:1, 2 Stand afar off are classic words of lament or mourning (13:1–3). As the psalmist views the actions of the wicked, he finds himself angry at wickedness and wondering how God can remain apathetic and inactive. But even with his doubts, he continues to pray to the only God who can deliver him from his troubles.

10:3, 4 God is in none of his thoughts: For the psalmist, this is the most difficult part of his circumstances (14:1). With no thought of God, his wicked enemies are able to boast in themselves. They turn reality upside down by praising evil and spurning God.

10:5, 6 Only those who stand on the sure foundation of God's Word can confidently say, **I shall not be moved** (15:5). The wicked who have lost all sense of God assume that they can use these words themselves. But eventually they will be swept away by the turmoil and troubles of this world (Prov. 10:25; Matt. 7:24–27).

10:8–10 sits in the lurking places: The psalmist views the wicked as oppressors. They are similar to lurking beasts, ready to pounce on their prey.

10:11 God has forgotten: The wicked behave the way they do because they doubt that the Lord knows, cares, or will act. They want to believe that there will be no final judgment, so they feel free to do as they please. But the truth is that God will establish justice (vv. 14, 15).

10:12, 13 Arise, O Lord: The psalmist returns to his call for God to act (9:19, 20).

10:14, 15 You have seen is the classic confession of trust in God in the psalms of lament. God does know; He does see; and He will act. God protects those like **the fatherless** who have no other protection (27:10). **Break the arm:** As in 3:7, this is a call for God to destroy the power of the wicked. This impassioned curse on the wicked displays the righteousness of God.

10:16–18 The Lord is King: These words suggest that Pss. 9 and 10 are royal psalms. Usually the royal psalms have a more positive viewpoint. They take the stance that God is King and the world is established and will not be moved. On the other hand, Pss. 9; 10 question how there can be such distress in the world with God as King. But since God *is* King, this psalm concludes with the fervent prayer that the will of God may be done on earth as it is in heaven (Rev. 19:1–6).

Psalm 11 is a psalm of trust. The title ascribes the psalm to David. In the middle of the psalms of lament (Pss. 9; 10; 12), this psalm expresses great trust in the Almighty Lord. It is the context of adversity that makes this psalm of trust all the more impressive. This brief poem has three movements: (1) an affirmation of trust in the Lord even during the assaults of the wicked (vv. 1–3); (2) an affirmation of trust in the Lord who reigns above and who will judge the actions of the wicked (vv. 4–6); (3) an affirmation of trust in the Lord because of who He is (v. 7).

11:1–3 The phrase **I put my trust** describes seeking refuge, similar to a bird under the wings of its mother (Ruth 2:12). **Flee as a bird:** Here is the contemptuous challenge of the wicked. They are like their father, the devil (John 8:44; 2 Cor. 11:13–15). They view the righteous as helpless birds flying to their mountain home. They do not realize that their mountain home is protection in the Lord Himself. **bend their bow:** This is a picture of the wicked on the hunt for the righteous (10:8–10). **foundations are destroyed:** These verses are the taunt of the wicked to the righteous. They are a false charge; the words are untrue. The foundations are *not* destroyed; there is a great deal the righteous *can do* (Eph. 6:10–18). Most important, the righteous can keep trusting in God, their true foundation.

11:4–6 The words **in His holy temple**

prove that the charge of v. 3 is false. God *is* in control; the foundations are not destroyed. **His eyes behold:** It may appear that God is not involved (10:11), but He does see and He will act (Ex. 2:23–25; 3:6–15). **tests the righteous:** There are times when the Lord allows trials to come into the life of the righteous as a test. But God's actions are more severe toward the wicked, whom He **hates.** The Hebrew word for

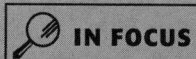

IN FOCUS   **"nations"**

(Heb. *goy*) (2:1; 10:16; Judg. 2:21) Strong's #1471: The Hebrew word *goy* basically means a body or group of people and is usually translated *nation*. Although *goy* can be used to designate the people of Israel, especially before their settlement in Canaan (Josh. 4:1; 5:6), the term generally refers to neighboring pagan nations (Deut. 4:38; Judg. 2:21, 22). These nations, characterized by wickedness (Deut. 9:4, 5), were considered enemies of God (2:1; 10:16). Yet the nations were not without hope, for the OT also speaks of the grace of God extending to all people through the coming of the promised Messiah (Is. 2:2; 11:10; 42:6).

hates is a strong term that speaks primarily of rejection (5:5). **rain coals:** The source for "fire and brimstone" judgment is the story of God's judgment on Sodom and the other cities near the Dead Sea in Gen. 19.

11:7 Because **the Lord** is righteous, the believer who is under stress can continue to trust in Him. Such faith allows one to ignore the taunts of the wicked. The believer needs only to return to the enfolding wings of God to renew strength and purpose in the midst of a troubled day.

Psalm 12, a psalm of lament, begins with a focus on the power of the wicked's perverse mouth (Pss. 52; 120). It concludes powerfully with an assertion of the power of the pure and truthful words of God. The title ascribes the poem to David. The psalm has five movements: (1) a description of the language of the wicked (vv. 1, 2); (2) a prayer for God's intervention (vv. 3, 4); (3) the intervention of God to deliver His own (v. 5); (4) a characterization of the language of God (vv. 6, 7); (5) a reminder of the continuing presence of the wicked (v. 8).

12:1–3 godly man ceases: David wonders if there are any righteous people left. **speak idly:** This psalm charges the wicked for using words to destroy and hurt others.

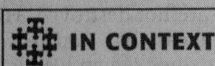 **IN CONTEXT** **Where God Lives**

ome passages of Scripture seem to declare that God lived in the inner sanctuary (or Most Holy Place) of the tabernacle, and later of the temple. Other passages appear to speak of God living in heaven. So where exactly does God live?

The answer is that God is pure spirit who is infinite and therefore not bound by time or space. He cannot be said to live in a place, in a way that would imply that He is limited to a specific location. At best, God can be said to live everywhere, though that is a very human way of looking at things. God lives in eternity, which is beyond human understanding.

Psalm 11 reflects that mystery by referring to God's dwelling place as "heaven" (Ps. 11:4). His presence in the temple, while real, was not exclusive.

God has made Himself known at certain times and locations in our world. He revealed Himself to the Israelites at Mount Sinai (Ex. 19:16–20), and later in the tabernacle (Lev. 9:23–24) and temple (2 Chr. 5:14). He also revealed Himself in His Son, Jesus (John 1:14; 14:9). Paul wrote that Christ lives in believers (Gal. 2:20), as does the Spirit of God (1 Cor. 3:16).

The point for us to apply is that God is not limited to buildings. That is not to say that houses of worship such as church sanctuaries have no value. But they are more a refuge for us than a residence for God.

12:4 With our tongue: Because the wicked do not submit to any authority over them, much less God Himself, they believe they can say anything they want.

12:5–7 Now I will arise: With these dramatic words, God speaks to David and reveals His righteous character. He will not linger; He will judge the speech of the wicked. **pure words:** In contrast to the idle words of the wicked (vv. 1–4), the words of God are altogether trustworthy. The eternal and steadfast nature of the Lord Himself stands behind His words. He will establish justice just as He has promised to David (v. 5).

12:8 The wicked prowl: Even with God's words of judgment, there are still wicked people looking for those whom they might destroy. One day there will be full punishment (10:16–18). For now, we still struggle with the help of the Holy Spirit against the evil in our own souls and the pervasive wickedness in our world.

Psalm 13 is a psalm of lament, an impassioned cry to the Lord for help. It is ascribed to David. The psalm is brief, even terse; but it is remarkably powerful in its tone and imagery. There are similarities between this psalm and Ps. 142. This psalm has three movements: (1) a lament of the forsaken (vv. 1, 2); (2) a petition for deliverance (vv. 3, 4); (3) a confession and a vow of praise (vv. 5, 6).

13:1, 2 These two verses present all three pronouns that occur in a typical lament psalm: (1) *I* am hurting; (2) *You* have forgotten; (3) *they* are winning. Four times in two verses David screams out **how long** (4:2; 6:3). The Lord

allows David to pour out his anxiety before Him. But by the end of David's prayer, the Lord has granted him a correct perspective on his situation. David's only option is to trust in the sovereign mercy of his loving God.

13:3, 4 Enlighten my eyes: As a person who is nearing death might sense the dimming of his vision (38:10), David also senses his death and pleads with God to intervene before he dies. **Lest my enemy say:** If God does not intervene, not only will the psalmist be lost from the community that praises the living God (6:5), but his enemies will also claim a victory over him and his God. Fundamentally, the Lord's honor is at stake. **rejoice:** The enemies' rejoicing would be intolerable because it would be aimed in part against God in whom the psalmist has trusted (35:19).

13:5, 6 This is the turning point of the psalm. The tone of the psalm abruptly changes from despair to hope. In this verse, David recalls his commitment to trust God completely. The term **mercy** describes God's *loyal love*, His faithfulness to His commitment to take care of His people. **I will sing** was the psalmist's vow to praise God in the worshiping community. Based on the assurance that God will deliver him, David resolves to tell the people about it—this is the essence of praise (40:1–3).

Psalm 14, which is closely allied with Ps. 53, is a wisdom psalm attributed to David. It speaks of the foolishness of living as if God did not exist. The psalm has three movements: (1) a description of the pervasiveness of evil (vv. 1–3); (2) an assertion that final judgment is coming (vv. 4–6); (3) a prayer for God's kingdom (v. 7).

IN DEPTH   Lament Psalms

I n the lament psalms, we hear the strong, emotional words of sufferers. These are words written by real people in very difficult situations. Sometimes the forcefulness of the psalmists' complaints against God is shocking. But these godly sufferers know that God will not be angry with their honesty, for even when they scream at God, it is a scream of faith.

The following is the basic structure of the psalms of lament:

1. An introductory cry
2. The lament proper
   • I am hurting
   • You do not care
   • The enemy is winning
3. A confession of trust
4. Reasons for God to act
5. Petitions
   • Hear me
   • Save me
   • Punish them
6. A vow to praise God

The introductory cry can be very brief—just an "O God," as in 79:1. This is the psalmist's cry of distress to the living God who will act on his behalf once again—even as He has done in the past.

The lament proper often consists of three parts. The first part introduces the pain and hurt that the psalmist is experiencing (6:6). The second part of the lament is the most astonishing, for in this part the psalmist addresses God directly. Often, God is accused of inattention, forgetfulness, or no longer caring about the psalmist and his plight (13:1). In the third part, the psalmist describes the success of the wicked (10:3–11). The wicked present two intolerable problems to the psalmist: one is the personal attack upon the psalmist, a friend of God; and the other is what this evil attack means for the reputation of God.

In the lament psalms, these complaints are followed by statements of trust. The confession of trust shows that the psalmist still believes in God—even when his faith is under assault by the evils of the world, the pressures of advisors, and nagging doubts. In the middle of his painful situation, the psalmist reminds himself of God's care for him in the past (13:5).

Many of the lament psalms contain a section giving further reasons for God to act. Here the psalmist describes in more detail his own situation, the acts of the wicked, or the consequences to his life and to the community of believers if the Lord does not deliver him from his distress.

On the basis of a renewed trust in the Lord, the psalmist presents his petitions. He calls out to God to listen to him, to deliver him (71:2), and to punish his enemies, who mock his faith in God (71:13). Finally, the psalm concludes with a vow of praise. The psalmist promises to praise God before the congregation when God delivers him from his plight (9:14).

The psalms of lament are a model of godly response to suffering. The Lord does not expect us to remain stoic when we face suffering. We can pour out our souls to the Lord. However, in the middle of our cry, we must remember God's loving care for us in the past so we can willingly trust Him with the future. With this type of response, we can renew our hope in the living Lord.

14:1 The word **fool** refers not to mental inability but to moral and spiritual insensitivity. The phrase **no God** suggests "practical atheism," the view that if there is a God, it really does not matter to one's life. This is the viewpoint stated in 10:4, 11; 12:4. The Hebrew word for **corrupt** has the idea of soured milk. Those who cease to believe in God will eventu-ally "sour"; they will degenerate into doing evil.

14:2, 3 The Lord looks down: Here the Lord's inquiry leads to judgment (as in Gen. 6:12). The pictorial language is a way of describing the omniscience of God, the fact that the Lord knows everything. **No, not one:** The biblical teaching on depravity is not that each individual is as evil as he or she could possibly be, but that sin is present in every individual (Rom. 3). Since no one is perfect, all must ask God for His forgiveness—something He freely gives to those who place their trust in His son Jesus (Eph. 1:7; 1 John 1:9).

14:4, 5 The wicked lack **knowledge** of God's truth. Although people may be brilliant in their chosen fields, they can still be morally insensitive and spiritually closed to the issues that have eternal consequences. **My people** refers to those who are faithful to God. God has delivered a group of people from the prison of wickedness. These people are His people and must follow His ways. They may become special targets of the wicked because they are different. **There** is an adverb of place that alludes to the final judgment.

14:6 His refuge speaks of shelter, as in the shadow of a tree. David as an outdoorsman had experienced the urgent need of shelter from the fierce elements. He uses this common experience to describe the various ways in which God protects His people from the storm of evil that surrounds them (9:9).

14:7 The salvation of Israel refers to a future salvation, the coming reign of God (Pss. 2; 89).

Psalm 15 may be a wisdom psalm, but its principal focus is on the proper approach to the worship of God. Although all of the psalms were used in the worship of God, we might call this poem a worship psalm because of its special focus on this subject. The psalm asks the question, Who is righteous enough to approach God? Certainly no one is except Jesus, the Messiah. But there have always been those who stand before God as forgiven sinners, whose righteousness comes as a gift from God. We who are in Christ learn to come boldly into the presence of the Father because we come on the

authority of His Son (Heb. 4:16). Jesus makes us feel at home in the presence of the Father. This psalm, ascribed to David, is posed in question-and-answer format. There are three movements: (1) the question of who may approach the holy God (v. 1); (2) the response (vv. 2–4); (3) the blessing (v. 5).

15:1 who may abide: Except for priests, people did not live in the precincts of the temple. These words describe an approach to God's presence in which one might feel accepted, even "at home." **holy hill:** As in 3:4, this phrase is used of the presence of God in the temple or the tabernacle. The Hebrew term is a general one that refers to wherever the tabernacle was in David's day; later readers and singers of this psalm appropriately applied the word to the temple built in Jerusalem.

15:2–4 He who walks uprightly speaks of relative righteousness, not absolute righteousness, for no one is innocent before God. The Lord commands us to be holy (1 Pet. 1:15, 16), and He also gives us the power to become holy (2 Thess. 2:16, 17). **vile person is despised:** The righteous hate what God hates (vv. 4, 5). The point is not so much the emotion of hatred as the deliberate rejection of wicked ways (1:1). **swears to his own hurt:** When a righteous person takes an oath, it must be honored even if it requires suffering.

15:5 never be moved: The promise of God for the righteous is for this life and for the life to come. The Lord is the righteous person's sure foundation.

Psalm 16, a psalm of lament, has a remarkable prophetic aspect that parallels many of the messianic prophecies concerning the Suffering Servant (Is. 53). This poem of David became central in the preaching of the apostles in the early church (Acts 2:22–31). The psalm has four movements: (1) a petition to God for deliver-

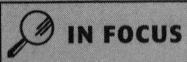 **IN FOCUS** **"joy"**

(Heb. *simchah*) (16:11; Neh. 8:12, 17; Prov. 21:15; Jon. 4:6) Strong's #8057: This Hebrew word is one of several frequently occurring Hebrew words that express exceeding gladness or rejoicing. Like its synonyms, this word can apply to a disposition of the heart (Prov. 14:10; Jer. 15:16). It is frequently set in a context of feasting (Neh. 8:12) and singing (137:3; 1 Sam. 18:6), as it is in a prophecy concerning God's singing over Jerusalem (Zeph. 3:17). The word is also used for the senseless happiness of the enemies of God's people (Judg. 16:23; Ezek. 35:15; 36:5), of the foolish (Prov. 15:21), of the lazy (Prov. 21:17), and of the hypocrites (Job 20:5). However, joy in the Bible is usually associated with the people of God, who celebrate God's blessing at a number of occasions—feasts, coronations of kings, victories in battle, and the dedication of the rebuilt walls of Jerusalem (Num. 10:10; 1 Kin. 1:40; 2 Chr. 20:27; Neh. 12:27). In fact, Moses exhorts the Israelites to serve God with joy, so that they would not lose their blessing (Deut. 28:47).

ance (vv. 1–3); (2) a condemnation of the wicked and their practices (v. 4); (3) an exaltation of the psalmist's relationship with God (vv. 5–8); (4) a confident assertion that God will spare the psalmist's life and bless it (vv. 9–11).

16:1–4 I put my trust: David uses the expression of a bird seeking refuge under its mother's wing to indicate his complete trust in the Lord (compare 7:1; 11:1). From this strong stance of confidence, he is able to boast that his goodness comes only from God. He shares with the people of God the enjoyment of God's presence.

16:5–8 My inheritance refers to the Promised Land. God had given this inheritance to His people (Deut. 6:1–3). However there was a greater inheritance for the Levites, who did not receive a share in the land (Num. 26:62); their share of the inheritance was in the Lord. David had an ancestral inheritance in the land. As king, he also had extensive royal holdings. But he realized that no inheritance was greater than his relationship with Almighty God.

16:9–11 path of life: With this phrase David speaks of his escape from death at a critical point, but he also indicates the eternal life given by the resurrected Savior to all who trust in Him.

Psalm 17 is a special use of the psalm of lament; it is a protest of innocence (Pss. 26; 35; 43; 69). The psalm is ascribed to David. At times, David suffers under the heavy hand of God's anger because of unconfessed sin in his life. But there are other occasions where he insists that his present troubles are not caused by any fault in his life. In such a case, he calls upon God to vindicate him. God indicates through these psalms that He has a special concern for people who experience undeserved suffering, even though He allows the trouble to come for reasons that may never be known in this life. The poem has six movements: (1) a plea for vindication (vv. 1, 2); (2) an acknowledgment of God's testing (vv. 3–5); (3) a plea for God's mercy (vv. 6–9); (4) a description of the wicked (vv. 10–12); (5) a renewed plea for vindication (vv. 13, 14); (6) a statement of resolute faith (v. 15).

17:1, 2 a just cause: With these words, David sets the tone of the psalm. By protesting his innocence, he hopes to convince God to move on his behalf and deliver him from his trouble. He asks for God to search him thoroughly and to declare his **vindication,** often translated "justice" or "judgment."

17:3–5 tested my heart: David knows that God has done what he is requesting even before he asks. That is, God knew David's needs and what was in his heart. David's prayer helps David to focus on the source of his strength and

reaffirm his determination to live a pure life (1:1–3; 19:14).

17:6–9 Incline Your ear is pictorial language describing the mercy of God (40:1): God will stoop down to earth to hear David's plea. **lovingkindness:** This significant term for God's loyal love is enhanced by the Hebrew term for **marvelous,** a word used in the Bible only with reference to God. **The apple of Your eye:** Just as a person has an instinctive response to protect the eye, so God cares instinctively for His servants. **shadow of Your wings:** Here God is described as a "mother hen" in a positive sense. Chicks who flee for protection to the wings of their mother find not only safety but warmth and love as well. In the same way, God protects us.

17:10–12 The words **fat hearts** are a description of insensitivity, similar to the language of Is. 6:10. **As a lion:** This language is similar to that of 10:8–10. The point is that the wicked are insensitive to human needs; they are like lions who wait for the right opportunity to destroy their prey.

17:13, 14 Arise, O LORD: The same language is used in 9:19, 20; 10:12, 13. **their portion in this life:** The wicked live their lives with only the pursuit of the pleasures of this world in mind. The righteous should not try to obtain what this life can offer, but instead pursue God and His ways.

17:15 when I awake in Your likeness: This verse is a key text on biblical immortality in the OT. Having rejected the idea that the pleasures of this life are ultimately fulfilling, David anticipates the day when he will awake in glory and be made in the likeness of God.

Psalm 18 is attributed to David. The text of this psalm is found in 2 Sam. 22 with some variations. The superscription indicates that this psalm was David's hymn of celebration to the grace of God. This may be a psalm of trust (Ps. 23), but it is unique. The lengthy poem has several movements: (1) a statement of faith and a description of deliverance (vv. 1–6); (2) a poetic description of God's battle for David's deliverance (vv. 7–19); (3) a recital of the blessings of God on the righteous (vv. 20–27); (4) an offering of praise to the person of the Lord (vv. 28–36); (5) a recounting of battles and victories in the Lord (vv. 37–45); (6) concluding praise for God's work of deliverance (vv. 46–50).

18:1 I will love You, O LORD: Twice in the Psalms the poet declares a love for God (116:1). Here an unusual word for *love* is used, referring to compassion as deep as a mother's love.

18:2, 3 The Hebrew word for **my rock** is balanced by its parallel Hebrew word **my strength,** meaning also "my rock." References to God as a mountain fortress that protects the believer are found many times in the Psalms (91:1–3; 144:1). This is a particularly apt image for David, who many times had to hide in the mountains for security (1 Sam. 26:1, 20). The words **strength** and **stronghold** reinforce the image of God as Protector. The **horn** symbolized strength.

18:4–6 In these verses, David describes how his life is endangered. Using very strong language, he expresses the pain he feels as he watches death come near: **sorrows of Sheol.** But even in the great depths of his trouble, David makes his distress known to God. He cries out to the LORD and the faithful God answers him.

18:7–9 the earth shook . . . He bowed the heavens: Underlying these poetic words is the understanding that the Almighty will turn the universe inside out, if necessary, to deliver His servant.

18:10–14 The language **He rode upon a cherub** is similar to the descriptions of Baal in Canaanite poetry. Thus David is taking the words typically used to praise Baal and applying them to the living God, the only One who truly deserves such praise. The *cherub* is a royal symbol and thus speaks of God's power and glory (80:1). The references to **darkness** speak of the hiddenness of God. He cannot be completely understood by those whom He has created. The references to **brightness** speak of God's holiness.

18:15 the channels of the sea: This culminates the picture of God's turning the universe upside down (v. 7). Even the most hidden passages of the sea are exposed, as are the elements that hold the earth together. The Lord God does all this to rescue His servant David (v. 16). All of the Lord's fearsome power is used to save the one who worships Him. The passage vividly

illustrates why the believer has no reason to fear (Heb. 13:6).

18:16–19 He drew me out of many waters: Again, David draws from the language of the Canaanites, turning it to the praise of God. The *waters* were regarded as dark gods in Canaan. But according to David, God is Lord of all, and the waters are His creatures. He delivers His servant David from any power that might hold him. Why David might ask, would God tear apart all of creation to act on his behalf? Because God takes pleasure in those who serve Him.

18:20–24 cleanness of my hands: David pleads his integrity, as in Ps. 17. Contrast this language with the description of the bloodied hands of unfit worshipers in Is. 1:15. **blameless:** As in Ps. 15, these are descriptions of relative righteousness. No one is completely innocent before God. But God enables His servants to pursue godliness in this life.

18:25–30 With the merciful: The poet describes the actions of God in terms of the people to whom He relates. God deals with each person according to his or her attitude. He opposes the proud but delivers the **humble,** for the humble turn to Him for strength.

18:31 who is God: With a question, David confesses that he cannot compare God to any person, god, or object (113:5; Is. 40:25).

18:32–36 The use of battle armor, such as a **shield,** as an image of God's provision for the righteous, is found in both the Old and New Testaments (Eph. 6:10–20).

18:37–41 pursued my enemies: God gives David strength to complete the battle against his enemies. God Himself is a Warrior (Ex. 15:3) and He outfits His servants for battle. **to the LORD:** Apparently in the extremes of battle, the enemies of David found no help from their gods, so they screamed aloud to David's

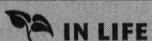 **IN LIFE** ## How We Know about God

Our understanding of God comes from three levels of His self-disclosure: the general revelation of Himself through nature, which He created (Ps. 19:1–6), the special revelation of His Word (19:7–11), and the particular work of God in one's individual life (19:12–14). After looking first at the firmament of God's world and then at the Word, which is the foundation of that world, David focuses on his own infirmities in his inner world.

Psalm 19 is typical of many psalms that look back and forth, up and down, outward and inward (compare Ps. 139). David realized how much he needed God to provide an integrated understanding of life. We can gain similar insight by using these multifocused psalms first to consider God's glorious universe, then to apply the spiritual disciplines of confession, Bible study, and prayer to our own lives, and finally to bear public witness to what we have come to know, see, and experience of God above, God around us, and God within.

God for deliverance. But God would not answer them. There is only one prayer from the wicked to which He gladly listens—the prayer of repentance.

18:42, 43 Head of the nations is language that prophetically speaks of the reign of the Messiah. David gained his empire by the work of the Lord on his behalf. But David's empire was only a picture of the kingdom of God that will one day be governed by David's greater Son, the Lord Jesus.

18:44–50 Ordinarily, praise to the Lord was given in the congregation of the Israelites. On occasion the poets speak of God's victories **among the Gentiles** who still worship other gods (138:1). This is a form of mission activity during the OT period (117:1). By proclaiming the victories of God to the nations, the poets were calling for the nations to respond in faith. How fitting that Paul would cite this verse (or its parallel in 2 Sam. 22:50) in Rom. 15:9 as a indicator of God's ongoing intention to bring His salvation to all people. **to His king:** David's victories are prototypes of the victories of the great King to come. The use of the word **anointed** is appropriate for David, but it points forward to the Savior who is *the* Anointed One (2:2). The words **to David and his descendants forevermore** connect the previous promises to the only Son of David who inherited an eternal kingdom, the Savior Jesus (2 Sam. 7).

Psalm 19, a wisdom psalm, celebrates the Word of God in the context of creation. Thus it is both a creation psalm and a Torah psalm. Both the creation psalms and the Torah psalms are regarded as subgroups of the wisdom psalms. The poem begins with the heavens, centers on the Word, and culminates in the heart of the servant of God. The poem has three movements: (1) a celebration of the greatness of God's creation (vv. 1–6); (2) a celebration of the purity of the Word of God (vv. 7–11); (3) a contemplation of the life of the person of God (vv. 12–14).

19:1–6 All of creation including the **heavens** reveals God's glory and majesty (Rom. 1:18–20). **Firmament** is another word for heaven (Gen. 1:6). The vast expanse we see is testimony to the craftsmanship of God (8:3). From the vantage point of earth, there is no heavenly body so wonderful as **the sun.** In the ancient Middle East the sun was often thought of as a god. In this poem, the sun is but a stunning symbol of the Creator. **Like a bridegroom,** it is pictured as celebrating its Creator.

19:7–11 The law is the Torah, which means "instruction" or "direction." This passage (vv. 7–9) presents six words for the Law of God—**law, testimony, statutes, commandment, fear,** and **judgments;** six evaluations of the law—**perfect, sure, right, pure, clean,** and **true;** and six results—**converting the soul, making wise the simple, rejoicing the heart, enlightening the eyes, enduring forever,** and **righteous altogether.** The value of the Scripture cannot be compared with any other desirable thing—even **gold.** It provides the key to wisdom, joy, and most importantly, eternal life.

19:12–14 his errors: The discussion of the nature and perfection of the Law of God leads the psalmist to consider his own imperfection. He is aware of both hidden **faults** and **presumptuous sins;** he asks to be delivered from both. His final prayer corresponds to 139:23, 24. **My strength** means "my rock" (18:1). **My Redeemer** describes God as the One who purchases our freedom from any bondage or slavery. The principal meaning of the word is "defender of family rights."

Psalm 20, a royal psalm, is a psalm of trust ascribed to David. The tone of the psalm is one of blessing, such as a king might bestow on his people, perhaps on the eve of battle. The brief poem has three movements: (1) God's blessing in battle (vv. 1–5); (2) the assurance of God's deliverance (v. 6); (3) an assertion of faith in God the King (vv. 7–9).

20:1–5 The day of trouble likely refers to

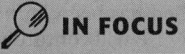 **IN FOCUS** | **"pure"**

(Heb. *bar*) (19:8; 24:4; Prov. 14:4) Strong's #1249: This Hebrew term appears only seven times in the Bible and always in the poetic books. Possibly it derives from a verb that can mean (1) to purify, (2) to choose or select, or (3) to make shine or polish. In 19:8, the word is associated with the eyes, suggesting radiance (compare Prov. 4:18). The concepts of "selectness" and "radiance" may fit the use of this word in the description of the chaste and pure Shulamite (the word is translated as *favorite* and *clear* in Song 6:9, 10). The term appears with other words denoting cleanness and purity (19:7–9), especially purity of the heart (24:4; 73:1).

the day of battle. But it has wide application for any troubled day in the life of the believer. **sanctuary:** Help from God was perceived to come from the temple in Jerusalem. Ultimately it comes from God's dwelling in heaven, of which the earthly sanctuary was a symbol. **your offerings:** The soldiers who were about to go to war would have completed the necessary sacrifices for confession of sin (Lev. 1—7). In the immediate context, **salvation** is used to describe daily deliverance from the rigors of the battle and the victory over the enemy. But the Lord's deliverance of us from our spiritual troubles should prompt the same type of praise.

20:6 King David was the **anointed** of the Lord (18:50). **His right hand:** This is a slogan that describes God's powerful deliverance of the Israelites from Egypt (17:7; 44:3; 118:16; Ex. 15:6).

20:7–9 Chariots were the leading weapon on the ancient battlefield. The implements of warfare are mere tools in God's hand—the wise trust in God because the battle belongs to Him. **May the King answer:** Above King David was God the Great King; moreover, one day King Jesus would rule from sea to sea.

Psalm 21 is another of the royal psalms of David. Psalm 20 is a prayer of the king for God's blessing on his army. Psalm 21 is an assurance of God's blessing on the king. Both psalms, as is the case with all the royal psalms, speak ultimately of the great King to come, the Lord Jesus. Psalm 21 has four movements: (1) a declaration of praise to God by the king (vv. 1, 2); (2) a review of God's blessing on the king (vv. 3–7); (3) an expectation of the final destruction of all enemies of the king (vv. 8–12); (4) a renewed commitment by the people to praise God (v. 13).

21:1, 2 joy in Your strength: An ancient king would tend to find joy in his own strength and power (20:7, 8). But a wise king would find pleasure in the Almighty, for all power comes from Him. **Your salvation:** Ultimately, spiritual salvation may be in view, but the immediate issue is more mundane. One meaning of the Hebrew word *salvation* is "room to breathe." God had given King David a release from the pressures and constraints that bound him. Jesus speaks of this kind of salvation in Matt. 24:13, as does Paul in Phil. 1:19 (James 1:21). **his heart's desire:** The Lord gives people their aspirations when they are derived from a fundamental desire for God's honor and glory (20:4; 37:4; 145:19).

21:3–7 blessings of goodness: King David acknowledges that all he has is God's gift; his kingship itself (the **crown**) is a gift from the Lord. But God's greatest gift is **life**—temporal and eternal. In response to God for His many gifts, David trusts **in the LORD**, for he knows

that this trust is not misplaced (15:5). These words of this passage should not be limited to King David, for they also speak generally of God's blessings on all believers. Each of us shares in the blessings of true royalty when we place our trust in the Lord, the Great King.

21:8–12 As is customary in the Psalms, the **enemies** of the king are the enemies of the Lord. Therefore the curse on the enemies is provoked by holy zeal for the glory of God (Num. 25). **The time of Your anger** may refer to any period of God's judgment, but compare to "the day of the Lord" (Joel 2:1; Zeph. 1:14). **Their offspring:** The wicked intend evil against the Lord; but He will prevail, causing them to flee from His anger.

21:13 Be exalted: The psalmist concludes with a shout of joy as he leads the faithful people in praising God for the promise of His final victory.

Psalm 22 is a profound lament psalm that concludes as a triumphant psalm of praise for God's deliverance. Although this psalm speaks of David's own distress and the Lord's deliverance of him, it also prophetically describes in remarkable detail Jesus' crucifixion and resurrection. The language David uses to describe his own predicament is prompted by the Holy Spirit. Thus it could span a thousand years to describe precisely the experiences of the Savior Jesus—both His excruciating death and victorious resurrection. See also Ps. 69, which predicts the emotional and spiritual suffering of Jesus. The title of Psalm 22 indicates that it was sung to the tune "The Deer of the Dawn." This lengthy poem has two main sections: (1) a description of the agony of impending death—an interplay of lament, confession, and petition (vv. 1–21); (2) an ecstatic celebration of great victory—a series of vows to praise God in the congregation (vv. 22–31).

22:1–3 With the words **My God, My God,** David expresses a painful sense of separation from God at a time of great trouble (38:21). These words were quoted by Jesus while in agony on the Cross (Matt. 27:46; Mark 15:34).

22:4 Our fathers trusted in You: Even in the midst of great pain, David confesses His faith in the God of his fathers. God has been faithful to earlier generations; surely He will continue to be faithful to those who call upon Him (v. 21 for God's faithful answer).

22:5–8 David's suffering makes him feel as though he were no longer human—instead he feels like a **worm.** When David was at his lowest, his enemies ridiculed his faith in the Lord. These words also describe the experience of the Savior who endured the verbal abuse of His tormentors (Matt. 27:27–31, 39–44).

22:9, 10 You made Me trust: With troubles and taunts swirling around him, David places his trust in the Lord—the One he has trusted throughout his whole life. David's response to difficult circumstances is instructive. Instead of doubting God's goodness, David reaffirms his lifelong faith in the Almighty.

22:11 Be not far from Me: David repeats his original plea (v. 1) for emphasis (vv. 19–21). He cannot endure his suffering without divine support.

22:12–15 David uses striking imagery to describe his distress. He is surrounded by animals—**bulls** and **lions.** Moreover, David's distress is so profound that he feels as if his life has been drained from him, as one might empty a jug of water. These words become even more poignant when they are applied to the sufferings of Jesus on the Cross (John 19:34). **My tongue clings to my jaws:** Jesus' words "I thirst" (John 19:28) expressed the pain of terrible thirst. **the dust of death:** For David, death would be avoided at this time (as in 16:9, 10). For the Savior, however, there was no reprieve.

22:16, 17 dogs: This is the third animal portrayal of the psalmist's enemies (vv. 12, 13). **They pierced My hands and My feet** explicitly predicts the crucifixion of the Lord Jesus Christ. The words are merely a figure of speech for the terrifying experiences of David; but as a prophet (Acts 2:30), David spoke accurately of the sufferings of Jesus.

22:18 The soldiers at Jesus' crucifixion gambled for His **garments,** in direct fulfillment of this text (Matt. 27:35).

22:19–21 Up to this point, the focus of this psalm has been on the suffering of the psalmist. The Lord God, who seemed so distant (vv. 1, 11), is now petitioned to draw near, to **help, deliver,** and **save.** The Lord is the only source of **Strength** to help David fight off the attacks of his tormentors. The use of animal imagery is now given in reverse order: **dog, lion,** and **wild oxen**—in contrast to bulls (v. 12), a lion (v. 13), and dogs (v. 16).

22:22–24 Not only does the psalm describe David's pain and prophetically Jesus' suffering on the cross, it also depicts God's deliverance. The Lord has answered, and David who has suffered so much promises to sing the praises of the Lord, his Deliverer. **Nor has He hidden His face:** The psalm begins with a sense of desperation based on a feeling of separation from God (v. 1). But the psalm ends with praise and gratitude: in reality God is near, He has answered, and He does save. David's hope has not been misplaced.

> *God refreshes His people with His quiet voice and gentle touch.*

22:25, 26 David promises to praise the Lord for His miraculous salvation among other believers—in the **great assembly** at the temple (13:6). This public proclamation would encourage others to place their trust in the faithful Lord who rescues His people.

22:27–30 All the ends of the world: For David, these words refer to the spread of the news of his deliverance to places far outside of Judah. For the Savior Jesus, these words speak of the eventual spread of the gospel of redemption to **all the families of the nations,** a fulfillment of God's promise that He would bless all nations through Abraham's descendants (Gen. 12:3). **Those who go down to the dust** is a common biblical expression for physical death and the resulting decay.

22:31 to a people who will be born: The gospel message of the death and resurrection of Jesus will spread not only geographically but also throughout all time. All people will hear the clear message of what **God has done.**

Psalm 23 is a psalm of trust. Within the six verses there is a development of the single theme of the first verse: David has no fear or concern, for the Lord is his Shepherd. This psalm of trust presents David in two ways. On the one hand, he is the "sheep" whose Shepherd is the Lord. At the same time, one of the most common descriptions of kingship in the ancient world is that of shepherd. In this sense, David as king was shepherd over the flock of Israel. This means that Ps. 23 is also a royal psalm. Even though the word "king" does not appear in it, this psalm is a description of what it means to be a good ruler. Moreover, the psalm prophetically speaks of Jesus. He is the Good Shepherd whose flock trusts in Him (John 10) and the King whose perfect rule will be established (Luke 23:2, 3; Rev. 17:14). The psalm has two movements: (1) a description of the Lord as Shepherd caring for the psalmist's every need (vv. 1–4); (2) a description of the Lord as Shepherd extending His mercy to all (vv. 5, 6).

23:1 The LORD is my shepherd: The word pictures David uses for God come from his own life and experience. He had been a shepherd in his youth (1 Sam. 16:19).

23:2 Any disturbance or intruder scares sheep. They are very fearful animals and **cannot lie down** unless they feel totally secure. **green pastures:** David uses eloquent language to express his view of the abundant care God gives to His people. **still waters:** Sheep are afraid of fast-flowing streams. God's provision of *still waters* has a soothing effect and calms the sheep.

23:3 He restores my soul: God refreshes His people with His quiet voice and gentle touch. For this reason, the sheep know the Shepherd and are known by Him (John 10:14). **For His name's sake:** The loving actions of the Shepherd proceed from His nature.

23:4 The valley of the shadow of death can refer to any distressing time in our lives. The awareness of our own mortality often comes with sickness, trials, and hardship. But the Lord, our Protector, can lead us through these dark and difficult valleys to eternal life with Him. There is no need to fear death's power (1 Cor. 15:25–27). **You are with me:** The Good Shepherd is with us even in what seem the most difficult and troubling situations. **Your rod and Your staff:** Ancient shepherds used the *rod* and *staff* to rescue, protect, and guide the sheep. Thus, they become symbols of the Good Shepherd's loving care over His flock. The sheep are not alone, their Shepherd is standing over them, guiding them into safety—just as the Lord stands over us and protects us.

23:5 a table before me: God's provision is so luxurious, it is as though He has prepared a banquet. **anoint:** Typically an honored guest in the ancient Middle East was anointed with olive oil that contained perfumes. **My cup:** God's provision is as abundant as the wine offered to a guest by a generous host. The lavish treatment of the guest is indicative of the loving care of God for His people.

23:6 The use of both **mercy** and **goodness** to describe God's loyal love intensifies the meaning of the two words. What is described in v. 5 is God's overabundant mercy—love that is in no way deserved. The Hebrew verb **follow** describes an animal in pursuit. When the Lord is our Shepherd, instead of being stalked by wild beasts we are pursued by the loving care of the Lord. **the house of the LORD forever:** God's promise for the Israelites was not just for the enjoyment of this life in the land of promise (6:1–3); it was also for the full enjoyment of the life to come in His blessed presence (16:9–11; 17:15; 49:15).

Psalm 24, a psalm of David, is one of the royal psalms. The psalm describes the Lord's entrance into the holy city. It may have been sung when David brought the ark of the covenant to Jerusalem (2 Sam. 6:15). This psalm is often linked with Pss. 22; 23, for all three psalms speak prophetically of the Lord Jesus. Psalm 24 also has some affinities with Ps. 15, for both ask and answer the question of who is fit to come into the presence of the Lord. The answer in Ps. 15 focuses on a person's righteousness; the answer in Ps. 24 focuses on the King of glory. Psalm 24 should also be read with Pss. 2; 110, which share a focus on the return of the Lord Jesus Christ to establish His kingdom on earth. This psalm has three movements: (1) praise to God the Creator and Sovereign of the world (vv. 1, 2); (2) an inquiry concerning the appropriate approach to the Lord (vv. 3–6); (3) an anticipation of the King of glory (vv. 7–10).

24:1, 2 The earth is the LORD's: The psalmist praises God as Sovereign over all He has created. These words also set the stage for the question of vv. 3–5: If God is Lord over all,

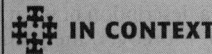 **IN CONTEXT** **Shepherd Boy**

Psalm 23, the shepherd's psalm, was composed by David, who himself was a shepherd in his youth:

- David was out keeping sheep when Samuel the judge came to his father Jesse's home to find a king of God's choosing (1 Sam. 16:11).
- The youngest of eight sons, David was left behind to tend sheep when his three oldest brothers went to battle. However, he occasionally visited them (17:12–20, 28).
- David used skills honed during years of shepherding to kill Goliath (17:34–37, 40–51).
- David is remembered as having been chosen by God and taken from the sheepfolds to shepherd the people of Israel (Ps. 78:70–72).

Psalm 23 reflects David's career shift. While the first four verses paint a pastoral picture, the last two have David sitting at a banquet table, most likely as king, while his enemies—those over whom God has made him triumph—look on. Having grown up in rural places, David had come to the city to exercise authority and power.

who then may approach Him? **those who dwell therein:** God's rule extends to all people, even those who do not acknowledge His power. **founded it upon the seas:** Drawing on the language of Gen. 1 in which God calls the dry land to rise from the watery abyss (Gen. 1:2, 9), David describes God's continued control over the waters.

24:3 Who may ascend: As in Ps. 15, those who approach the Holy One to worship Him in the temple in Jerusalem—**His holy place**—must approach Him in righteousness. This verse highlights the inability of any person except the King of glory to stand before God.

24:4, 5 Clean hands refers to a person's actions; pure heart refers to inner attitude.

24:6, 7 Lift up your heads: The gates of the city seem to sag; the doors appear loose. But they must rouse themselves for **the King of glory.** One is coming who is worthy to stand in the holy place. As He nears, the gates raise themselves to honor His entry.

24:8 Who is this King: This is praise for the King who is fresh from battle. This is the One who may enter the city, the Lord Himself. Only with the coming of Jesus did the meaning of this ancient poem become clear (Matt. 21:1–10; Rev. 19).

24:9, 10 The LORD of hosts: The repetition in these verses is for effect and emphasis. This is praise for the coming King.

Psalm 25 is a psalm of lament. But in the middle of his sorrow, David petitions the Lord to forgive him. Although the psalm contains elements of a lament psalm and a penitential psalm, the mixture of the two forms makes the psalm unique. The psalm is an acrostic, with one poetic line for each successive letter of the Hebrew alphabet. The structure of the psalm is as follows: (1) an introductory appeal that David will not be ashamed before his enemies (vv. 1–3); (2) a call for God to forgive David (vv. 4–7); (3) a focus on the character of God (vv. 8–10); (4) a renewed call for God to forgive David (vv. 11–18); (5) a concluding appeal that David will not be ashamed before his ene-

mies (vv. 19–21); (6) a concluding prayer for Israel (v. 22).

25:1–3 Let me not be ashamed is the opening and closing appeal of Ps. 25 (v. 20). Shame is the intended end of the enemies of God (35:26), but not of the faithful. **who waits:** Waiting on the Lord is the equivalent of hoping in Him (25:5; 40:1).

25:4–7 Show me is an appeal to God to enter into David's life more directly, to help him become conformed to the character of God (Rom. 12:1, 2). **sins of my youth:** Both the sins of immaturity and the **transgressions** of adulthood need forgiveness (1 John 1:9).

25:8 Good and upright is the LORD: In the midst of David's plea for forgiveness, he praises God by speaking of two of God's characteristics. God *must* be both good and upright. Because He is both, the Lord extends mercy to repentant believers and at the same time promises not to allow the guilty to go unpunished. God will bring justice to this fallen world.

25:9–14 Pardon my iniquity: David returns to the subject of his own sinfulness, summarizing vv. 4–7 as well as expressing his desire for the Lord to teach him. **fear Him:** Those who fear the Lord pay attention to His instructions and thus learn the secrets of God's wisdom (111:10; Prov. 1:7; 3:32).

25:15–20 Let me not be ashamed is a reprise of the opening verses, with emphasis both on David's **enemies** (v. 2) and on his continuing stance of waiting in expectant hope (v. 5).

25:21, 22 Redeem Israel: This concluding verse is outside the general acrostic pattern of the psalm. Here David petitions the Lord to be compassionate with the nation Israel just as He has been with David. The Lord was not only the personal Savior of David, but also the Savior of all the Israelites.

Psalm 26 is a psalm of lament in which there is a protest of innocence (Pss. 17; 35; 43; 69). The structure of the Psalm is as follows: (1) a prayer for vindication (vv. 1, 2); (2) an assertion of integrity (vv. 3–5); (3) a vow of praise

---

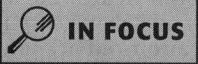 **IN FOCUS**   **"remember"**

(Heb. *zakar*) (25:6, 7; 106:45) Strong's #2142: This Hebrew verb has as its basic meaning "to contemplate" or "to call to mind." When it refers to recalling past ideas or events it is translated *remember* (Gen. 42:9; Num. 11:5). In other passages, it pertains to thinking about the future and is translated *dwell on* (Eccl. 5:20), *consider* (Lam. 1:9), and *mention* (Jer. 20:9). The psalmists frequently call on God to remember His people (106:4) or His mercy (25:6, 7). This does not imply that God has forgotten, but instead it is a request that God would take action according to His promises.

(vv. 6–8); (4) a prayer for discrimination (vv. 9, 10); (5) an assertion of integrity (vv. 11, 12).

26:1, 2 The Hebrew word for **vindicate** usually means "to judge"; however, here it means "to declare righteous." **my integrity:** This is the prayer of a forgiven sinner who is living in the fear of God but whose life has been plagued by undeserved evil. **My mind and my heart** refer to the innermost person.

26:3–5 Your lovingkindness: The loyal love (13:5) of God is the recurring focus of the Book of Psalms. **have not sat:** As in the description of righteousness in 1:1, David declares that he has no part with men of wickedness or idolatry. Instead he has continually sought the Lord.

26:6–8 go about Your altar: The heart of this psalm is the desire to worship God in integrity. In this regard, the poem shares the spirit of Ps. 15. **where Your glory dwells:** The place where God chose to reveal His glory to His people. The priests interceded for the people with the required offerings. Today "the Most Holy Place" is in the presence of God, where our Savior pleads our case (Heb. 7:25).

26:9–11 Do not gather: On the basis of his protests of integrity (vv. 1, 2), David prays for divine discrimination (4:3). God distinguishes those who have responded to His grace from those who have not.

26:12 As always in the Psalms, praise is a public and vocal action that has its proper place in the **congregations** of believers.

Psalm 27, a psalm of trust (Ps. 23), begins with David's affirmation of the reality of God in his life. The poem presents a strong desire to live in the presence of God and points to the ongoing need for believers to continue to "wait" on the Lord. The psalm has six movements: (1) a determination not to fear enemies because of God's presence (vv. 1–3); (2) a desire to live in the presence of the Lord (vv. 4, 5); (3) an affirmation of praise in God (v. 6); (4) a prayer for God's continuing presence (vv. 7–10); (5) a prayer for continuing trust in the midst of a life of stress (vv. 11–13); (6) a word of instruction (v. 14).

27:1–3 Light indicates deliverance from darkness (Gen. 1:3), which is a biblical symbol of evil. The word **salvation** combined with the word *light* means "saving light" (3:8). **to eat up my flesh:** David pictures his enemies as ravenous beasts who would shred his flesh (10:8–10; 22:12–16).

27:4, 5 The phrase **dwell in the house of the Lord** expresses David's desire to be always nearer to God's presence. **The beauty of the Lord** speaks of God's "pleasant nature." The name Naomi in the Book of Ruth is related to the Hebrew word for *beauty*.

27:6 Sacrifices of joy are praise offerings

the believers bring to God to celebrate the blessings He gives them (Heb. 13:15).

27:7–13 Throughout this psalm, seeking the presence of God (His **face**) was the psalmist's highest purpose. **Enemies** might dissuade the righteous from seeking the presence of the Lord. But the psalmist wants to know God's presence in this life—**in the land of the living.**

27:14 To **wait on the Lord** is to demonstrate confident expectation. The Hebrew word for *wait* may also be translated "hope." To hope in God is to wait for His timing and His action (40:1; Is. 40:31).

Psalm 28, a psalm of lament, is attributed to David. The psalm includes a prayer against David's enemies and a royal invocation of praise to the Lord. The psalm has four movements: (1) an appeal to God that He not be silent (vv. 1, 2); (2) a petition to be distinguished from the wicked and their deserved punishment (vv. 3–5); (3) a blessing of the Lord for His work in the psalmist's life (vv. 6, 7); (4) praise for the Lord who delivers His anointed and His people (vv. 8, 9).

28:1, 2 my Rock: For further references to God as a fortress and refuge, see 91:1, 2. **Do not be silent:** One of the ways David senses the distance of God is His "silence" (13:1; 22:1). David might be referring merely to his lack of a sense of intimacy with God (27:4, 5), but it is also possible that he is awaiting a specific word from the Lord through a prophet or a priest. **The pit** is one of the terms for death in the Psalms (9:17, 18; 16:10; 143:7). As in 6:5, David asks to be rescued from death so that he might live to praise God. **lift up my hands:** One of the standard postures for prayer in the Bible (134:2).

28:3–5 Do not take me away: Again, the psalmist is asking to be delivered from death (6:5). **according to their deeds:** David pronounces his curse on the wicked, from whom he wishes to be distinguished (4:3). **they do not regard:** The language here is similar to that of Paul in Rom. 1:18–32. One day even the wicked will have to acknowledge God as their Creator and give Him the glory He deserves.

28:6, 7 Blessed be the Lord: See 103:1, 2 for a development of this theme. **Because** the plea of the psalmist has been **heard,** the last section of the poem is a hymn of praise (138:1).

28:8, 9 The term **His anointed** acknowledges God's covenant with David, His promise that He would be David's God and David would be His representative. This passage became a heritage of the monarchy, a treasure for each godly king in the Davidic line to go back to for strength and encouragement. **Shepherd them:** As in Pss. 23; 80, the comparison of God with a shepherd is an image of the loving care of a great king (Eccl. 12:11). This image also foreshadows Jesus, the coming King and the Good Shepherd (John 10:11).

Psalm 29 is a worship psalm (Ps. 15). But it is also a royal psalm that uses striking language to assert the sovereign reign of the Almighty. David has taken over some of the vocabulary and poetic style of the Canaanites and used it to praise the living God. As in the case of Ps. 93, the result is both a debunking of Baal and an unusual way of praising the true God of Israel. The psalm has three movements: (1) a call to

scathing attacks on idolatry in 115:4–8; Is. 41:21–29. Here the poet takes a treasured image of Canaanite thought—Baal with other gods bowing before him—and turns it inside out. It is not Baal, but the true God who is worshiped. He is worshiped not by gods who do not even exist, but by His own angels.

29:3, 4 The voice of the LORD: Both the language and the parallelism of this verse directly reflect Canaanite poetry. Baal was believed to be the god of the storm who thun-

Photo by Gustav Jeeninga

Even the sturdy cedars of Lebanon could not stand before the Lord's might and power, the psalmist declared (Ps. 29:3–7).

the angels and all people to acknowledge the supremacy of God (vv. 1, 2); (2) a description of the living God as Lord over storms (vv. 3–9); (3) a blessing from God, who is enthroned as King on high, to His people (vv. 10, 11).

29:1 Give here means "to ascribe." **O you mighty ones** means "O sons of gods." This Hebrew phrase refers to spiritual beings who are in the presence of God. We know these beings to be angels. The Hebrew words are similar to those of Job 1:6, which also describes the angels who are in the presence of God.

29:2 glory due to His name: The call is for the angelic hosts to acknowledge fully the wonder of God. The poets of the Bible delighted in taking the ideas of the Canaanites and then stripping them of their essentials. See the

dered in the heavens. Here the sound of thunder is a symbol of the voice of God. The phrase "the voice of the Lord" occurs seven times in the passage (vv. 3–9), like rapidly succeeding peals of thunder.

29:5–9 cedars of Lebanon: There is a dramatic energy to these verses as they trace the movement of the storm from the north of **Lebanon and Sirion,** an ancient name for Mount Hermon (Deut. 3:9) to **Kadesh** in the south. Nothing stops the advance of the storm; its effects reach from sea to land, from north to south, from animals to trees. As at the beginning of the psalm, all the angels in the heavenly sanctuary acknowledge the surpassing **glory** of the omnipotent God.

29:10, 11 As Baal was supposed to have

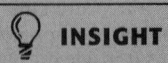

INSIGHT | To Crown the King

Psalm 29 is a coronation anthem composed for the enthronement of a king. Perhaps it was performed on formal occasions of state, much like "God Save the Queen" or "Hail to the Chief" today.

Like other royal psalms, such as Ps. 2, this one points beyond David, the earthly king, to the heavenly King, the Lord. He is seen sitting on His throne, from which He has ruled the world since before anyone can remember, and will until the end of time (Ps. 29:10–11).

been victorious over the waters, here it is God who is the true victor over all. He even controls the waters at the height of their destructive power, the **Flood.** There is no one to oppose His glorious rule; He is King forever. **The LORD** will give strength: Since He is the true God, there is none other. Only He can empower His people.

Psalm 30, a psalm of declarative praise, commemorates a time when God delivered David from mortal illness. The psalm has five movements: (1) a determination to praise the Lord (v. 1); (2) a report of deliverance (vv. 2, 3); (3) a call for others to join in the praise of the Lord (vv. 4, 5); (4) a report of the psalmist's mortal illness (vv. 6–10); (5) a presentation of the psalmist's praise to the Lord (vv. 11, 12).

30:1 I will extol You: David begins his song with a strong determination to praise God.

30:2, 3 up from the grave: David is not reporting a resurrection, but a deliverance from a nearly fatal illness. As in 28:1, the psalmist describes death as a great **pit** into which a person drops into the enveloping darkness of the unknown.

30:4, 5 Possibly David judges his illness to be in some way related to God's **anger. in the morning:** For a sick person, nothing is so long as a painful, sleepless night; few things are as desired as the coming of morning (5:3; 130:6; 143:8).

30:6–10 As in 6:5, the psalmist pleads with God to save his life so that he can fulfill his promise to **praise** God in the worship of the community. The emphasis is on singing praise to God in this life. **Helper** can be translated "power" or "strength" (33:20). What a sick person needs is strength for recovery: God is that powerful force.

30:11, 12 mourning into dancing: The psalmist has been transformed and renewed because of God's blessing on his life. He boasts in God as he fulfills his vow of praise. **My glory** refers to the psalmist's inner being (16:9).

Psalm 31 is a psalm of lament, but it has such a strong element of trust that it can also be classified as a psalm of trust (Ps. 23, for

example). The psalms of trust grow out of the confession of trust that occurs in the psalms of lament. In this psalm, the relationship between the two classifications is apparent. There are two major sections: (1) the presentation of lament in the context of trust (vv. 1–18); (2) the presentation of praise in the context of lament (vv. 19–24).

31:1–3 The phrase **I put my trust** pictures the action of a bird seeking refuge under its mother's wings (11:1; 17:7; 91:1–4). A different word for *trust* occurs in vv. 6, 14, which has the connotation of leaning on someone or something (Prov. 3:5, 6). The imagery of God as the **rock** and fortress for the believer recurs often in the Psalms (91:1–3).

31:4, 5 With the words **into Your hand I commit my spirit,** David expresses a complete dependence on God—his life is in God's hands to do with as He pleases. These words were spoken by Jesus on the Cross shortly before His death (Luke 23:46) and by Stephen before his death (Acts 7:59).

31:6–11 I am in trouble are classic words of lament and thus begin the lament section of this psalm. **My eye wastes away:** David uses similar language in 6:7 to express his sorrow. **a reproach:** As in the case of Ps. 30, it is possible that what faces the psalmist is a terrible illness—perhaps a physical condition that makes him repulsive to others.

31:12–18 With the words **my times are in your hands,** David reaffirms his earlier expression of complete dependence on the Lord (v. 5). David petitions the Lord, who is in complete control of his life, for deliverance. **Your face shine:** As in 4:6, this expression grows out of the words of the Aaronic benediction in Num. 6:24–26. It is a plea for God to "smile" in favor on David.

31:19–22 This verse begins the praise section of the psalm. David affirms that the delights of knowing God far outweigh any other kind of pleasure. **the secret place:** God makes His people safe in the intimacy of His friendship (27:5). **I said in my haste:** The psalmist says

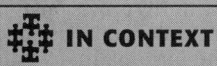 **IN CONTEXT** | Walled Cities

David was thankful for the protection God gave him through a strong city (Ps. 31:21). We do not know which city David had in mind, but several mentioned in the OT were refuges for him.

For example, the powerful Philistine city of Gath became a hiding place for David when he was fleeing from Saul (1 Sam. 27:1–4). Later he was given the Philistine city of Ziklag to use as his headquarters (27:5–6; 1 Sam. 30:1). Following Saul's death, Jerusalem became David's capital after he captured the supposedly impregnable stronghold of Zion from the Jebusites. David strengthened the city's defenses, but was forced to flee during Absalom's rebellion (2 Sam. 15:14–18).

In the ancient world, walled cities were one of the few protections against marauding bands of raiders and the sudden invasions of foreign armies. David praised God for the safety and protection of a walled city. In a similar way, believers today can be grateful to God for the means of protection He affords them.

things in his pain that he would not say under normal circumstances.

31:23, 24 David encourages the community to join him in praising God. Of all the sacrifices offered in the OT period, only the sacrifice of praise continues in NT worship (Heb. 13:15). **All you who hope in the LORD** is a characteristic term of piety in the Bible.

Psalm 32, a wisdom psalm, is also one of the great penitential psalms. It is generally believed that this psalm—like Ps. 51—has its origin in David's response to God following his infamous affair with Bathsheba (2 Sam. 11). It is one of the marks of the integrity of Scripture that the low points as well as the triumphs of its principal characters are described. The structure of this psalm is as follows: (1) a description of blessing (vv. 1, 2); (2) a report of David's agony before he confessed his sins (vv. 3–5); (3) a lesson to others based on David's experience with the Lord (vv. 6, 7); (4) an oracle from the Lord on righteous living (vv. 8, 9); (5) concluding praise to the Lord for His mercy (vv. 10, 11).

32:1 Blessed, the word that begins the Book of Psalms (1:1), means "to be happy." It is appropriate that this term is used of both the righteous person of the first psalm and the confessed sinner in this psalm. **sin is covered:** The poet describes God's dealing with sin in various ways. Sin can be taken away, the basic meaning of the word **forgiven,** and covered, the basic meaning of atonement.

32:2–5 I kept silent: The silence was a stubborn resistance to admitting guilt, a hope that in time the sin and its penalty would go away. The more David delayed his confession, the more he suffered. David realized it was not just his conscience or his feelings that were assaulting him, but the heavy **hand** of God

(38:1, 6–8). No matter who else is hurt, the principal offense of any sin is always against **the LORD.** You forgave: The consequences of David's sin with Bathsheba remained despite God's forgiveness (2 Sam. 12:13–20). But at this point, the greater news was God's forgiveness. God had restored His relationship with David.

32:6 who is godly: On the basis of his own experience, David instructs the congregation. They too can experience forgiveness if they will come to the Lord in faith as David has.

32:7 The psalm has quick and dramatic shifts. After addressing the congregation, David speaks directly to God: **You are my hiding place.**

32:8, 9 I will instruct you: The speaker changes. The Lord "comes into the psalm" to instruct the people. He exhorts the people not to be like a **horse** that will not go where its rider wants it to go; it has to be disciplined because it is stubborn. God does not want to muzzle or bridle His people like a horse. He expects His servants to respond promptly to Him of their own accord.

32:10, 11 The psalmist resumes his song by contrasting the **many sorrows** of the wicked with the joy of the forgiven sinner. He then calls for all the righteous to join him in public praise of the wonder of God's mercy.

Psalm 33, a psalm of descriptive praise, calls for all people to join Israel's faithful in praising God and waiting on (trusting in) the Lord. This is one of the few anonymous psalms in Book I (Pss. 1; 2; 10). The structure is as follows: (1) a call for the righteous to praise God, in view of His righteous acts in creation (vv. 1–7); (2) a call for the nations to praise God, in view of His sovereign work in creation (vv. 8–12); (3) a call for the people to praise God, in view of His care of creation (vv. 13–19); (4) a concluding affirmation of confidence in God (vv. 20–22).

33:1–3 God sees the praise from believers as **beautiful** (147:1). **harp:** Throughout the Psalms, many instruments are employed to praise the name of the Lord (98:5; 150:3–5). **to Him:** Praise is always directed to One who deserves all praise, the Lord Almighty.

33:4, 5 Although the world is filled with evil and with people who have no thought of God (Ps. 14), believers must look beyond the apparent confusion of the world to see God's **goodness**—the goodness that manifests itself every time the sun rises, a bird sings, and a mother lovingly embraces her child. Out of His goodness, God holds together the earth and provides for the sustenance of all people. One day God's goodness will prevail over all evil (98:2).

33:6, 7 The reference to God's control of the **waters of the sea** has a twofold origin (24:2; 93:3, 4). It grows out of the creation story in Gen. 1, in which God brings dry land from the waters and establishes His place for the waters that remain (Gen. 1:6–10). The idea also grows out of Canaanite religious ideas, for the Canaanites considered the seas as malevolent deities. But the Lord alone is God. No power—no matter how evil—is a threat to His control (Job 26:10; Prov. 8:28, 29).

33:8, 9 The Bible presents the **fear** of the Lord as a mark of reverence and awe on the part of those who recognize Him as Lord (40:3). **He spoke:** The account of creation in Gen. 1 describes God's word as the sole source of creation. This psalm emphasizes God's word as the controlling element in creation (vv. 4, 6). It was by God's "breath" (v. 6) that He made all things.

33:10–12 In contrast to the ineffective **counsel of the nations,** the counsel of God is wise counsel that lasts forever. **Blessed** means to be manifestly happy; the same word is used at the beginning of Ps. 1. Those who listen to God's counsel will be happy.

33:13–15 The **Lord** looks on humankind with a sense of discriminating pleasure. The emphasis of this section is not condemnation, but discrimination.

33:16, 17 army: People should not rely on physical strength or material resources to save them. Salvation belongs to the Lord (3:8), both for spiritual deliverance and for physical strength.

33:18, 19 eye of the Lord: This is a particularly warm image of God's care for His people. God watches all people, but He looks with delight on **those who fear Him** and **hope in His mercy** (147:11).

33:20–22 waits: To wait on God is to adopt a stance of resolute faith (40:1). **Just as we hope:** The psalm concludes with a phrase similar to "Amen." This is a "yes" to God's mercy, a statement of agreement with His provisions.

Psalm 34 is a wisdom psalm and a psalm of praise. It is written in the form of an acrostic, with one verse for each letter of the Hebrew alphabet. One verse appears to have dropped out at some point; there is no verse for the Hebrew letter *waw,* that would otherwise appear after v. 5. The title of the psalm ascribes it to David and specifies that it was written to commemorate his escape from Abimelech the king of Gath (1 Sam. 21:10–15). The name of the king in 1 Sam. 21 is Achish. It is believed that Abimelech was a throne name and Achish a personal name. The experience of David in the city of Gath (1 Sam. 21:10–15) must have been profoundly disturbing. David could easily have died in this Philistine city. He escaped by pretending to be insane. Afterward, the one who had appeared to be a "fool" wrote this psalm of wisdom and praise in honor of the Lord. The structure of the poem is as follows: (1) a call for the congregation to join the psalmist in praise (vv. 1–3); (2) a declaration concerning the psalmist's deliverance from trouble (vv. 4–7); (3) instruction about the fear of the Lord (vv. 8–14); (4) a declaration of praise to the Lord (vv. 15–22).

34:1–3 at all times: The determination of David to praise God is similar to the words of Paul in 1 Thess. 5:18. **Exalt His name together** is David's call for the congregation to join him in his praise of God.

34:4–7 He heard me is a classic statement of praise in the psalms. God is praised for the deliverance He provides in response to the prayers of His people (40:1). **were radiant:** Those who came to God in prayer as David did found themselves transformed; it was as if they also experienced what Moses had on Mount Sinai (Ex. 34:29; 2 Cor. 3:18). **Poor man** refers to the needy as well as the humble, whom the Lord delights to deliver (147:6). The phrase **the angel of the Lord** and the name of God are often interchanged. With the sense of God surrounding or hovering over the believer in this manner, there is no need to fear—even in the most desperate times.

34:8, 9 The center of biblical mission in the OT is found in the words **taste and see.** The task of Israel was to attract the nations to their God. For their faithfulness to Him, God had promised to bless them abundantly, and when the nations saw this blessing they would see that the living God was with them. In the midst of a world of gods who were not good at all, there was one living God, and He was altogether good (100:5). **Fear** is a call to awe, wonder, worship, and reverence (Prov. 1:7). To fear God is to respond to Him in piety and obedience.

34:10 People who live by their wits may eat as infrequently as **young lions. shall not lack:** As is true of 23:1, this is not a categorical statement. Time after time, however, the believer is able to attest to the ways God has met needs.

34:11–14 Come, you children: David took on the role of a wisdom teacher addressing the young people who are in his charge (Prov. 3:1–12). **Depart from evil:** The same sentiment is found in 37:27.

34:15, 16 In this context, **the eyes of the Lord** symbolize His care and protection.

34:17–19 the Lord hears: With slight variations, this is a reprise of v. 6. **The Lord is near:** When the Scriptures speak of God being near, it is to comfort the believer with a sense of His care.

34:20 guards all his bones: This verse, which speaks of the Lord's preservation of the righteous, notes that not a bone is broken. John 19:33–36 shows that the words of this verse were fulfilled in detail in the death of Jesus. Despite the terrible suffering the Savior endured, none of His bones were broken. When the Roman soldiers came to break Jesus' legs to hasten His death, they found that He had already died.

34:22 This verse is outside the acrostic pattern; it summarizes the psalm, giving appropriate praise to the Lord who saves those who put their faith in Him (1 Tim. 4:10).

Psalm 35 is a psalm of lament and a protest of innocence (Pss. 17; 26; 43; 69). Like Ps. 94, this poem by David places an unusual emphasis on the role of his enemies. Sometimes it is called an imprecatory psalm. The structure of the psalm is as follows: (1) an appeal to God the Warrior and Judge to plead the psalmist's cause (vv. 1–3); (2) a series of petitions for God to dishonor His enemies, deliver His servant, and glorify Himself (vv. 4–10); (3) a second series of petitions and promises (vv. 11–18); (4) a third series of petitions and promises (vv. 19–28).

35:1–3 Plead my cause is the classic protest of innocence (Pss. 17; 26; 43; 69). David has been wrongly attacked, so he prays that God will deliver him from these assaults (Ps. 94). **stand up for my help:** David is not afraid to ask God to take up arms like a soldier and fight for him. The psalmist does not shrink from asking the Lord to comfort him by saying the words **I am your salvation.** All these demands demonstrated David's complete dependence on the Lord.

35:4–9 David's first petition calls for **shame** on his enemies (v. 26). This is not just a call to embarrass them; it is a call for final judgment. In this instance, **the angel of the Lord** is a scourge (contrast 34:7). **without cause:** Here is the heart of David's position: he has not done anything to cause this evil attack upon himself.

35:10 These two verses are the first prayer of confidence in this psalm (vv. 17, 27). **All my bones** refers to the inner being, the total person. **who is like You:** There is nothing in all the universe to be compared with God.

35:11–17 The psalmist begins his second cycle of petition with reference to treacherous **witnesses,** like the false witnesses in the story of Jezebel and Naboth in 1 Kin. 21. The actions of these witnesses are even more shameful because they had received the help of the psalmist in their own times of need. **they rejoiced:** The ferocity of these witnesses is appalling. The psalmist finds that they are like animals in the way they treat him, rejoicing that troubles have come upon him.

35:18 give You thanks: This is the second of the vows of praise that follow each cycle of petition in this psalm (vv. 9, 10, 27, 28). The Hebrew word for *thanks* means "to make public acknowledgment," to praise God in the community (122:4; 136:1).

35:19–21 The enemies would **rejoice** if someone like David fell, who had trusted in the Lord. **hate me without a cause:** Again, David asserts his innocence (v. 7). The fact that he is hated for no cause is baffling and discouraging.

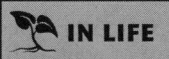 **IN LIFE** **God and the Poor**

The God we worship is deeply concerned that the poor and needy receive justice, deliverance, and vindication (Ps. 35:10). These deserve to be high on the agenda for any nation or public servant seeking to honor God and receive divine blessing.

The psalms mention "the poor" more than twenty-five times, usually either in terms of what the wicked are doing to them or what God is doing for them. Thus, to be on the side of God is to take up the cause of the poor. Doing so rescues the perishing (35:17), silences unjust critics (35:19–25), and magnifies the Lord (35:18, 27–28)—assuming that the spirit behind one's efforts is a genuine concern for justice and righteousness.

The passage also predicts the suffering of the Savior Jesus (John 15:23–25). **peace:** Far more than simply an absence of war, the biblical *peace* has the idea of wholeness, things as they ought to be. Note that the contrasting opposite here is not war, but deceit. **Aha, aha:** These contemptuous sneers are similar to the assaults in 22:7.

35:22–25 You have seen: The wicked were not the only ones who have seen David's grave distress (v. 21); God has also seen his pain. **Stir up Yourself:** The people of Israel know that God, unlike the false gods (1 Kin. 18:27), never sleeps (121:4; Is. 40:28). Yet for David, it seems as though God is napping (44:23).

35:26–28 The phrase **be ashamed** refers not to simple embarrassment, but to the revelation of the complete emptiness of wickedness before the judgment seat of God (14:5; 31:17; 36:12). **Who favor:** Only here do we learn that David has defenders: those who are on his side will share his joy when he is saved.

Psalm 36 is a wisdom psalm that gives a revelation of the nature of sin and an exaltation of God's unfailing love (Pss. 14; 53). The structure is as follows: (1) a revelation of the nature of sin (vv. 1–4); (2) praises to God, centering on His loyal love (vv. 5–9); (3) a prayer for God to continue His loyal love to His people even in the context of His final judgment (vv. 10–12).

36:1–4 The term **oracle** was used by the prophets of the OT to mean a divine utterance. In Mic. 4:6 the same Hebrew word is translated "says the Lord." In this psalm, David "the prophet" (Acts 2:30) has received a prophetic revelation as striking as any among the sons of the prophets. He has received divine insight into the nature of wickedness. **no fear of God:** Underlying wickedness is a complete disregard for the reality of God in a person's life and in the world. The word translated *fear* in this psalm is the same word used for "terror" at the final judgment (14:5). **flatters himself:** With no sense of God or of final judgment, the wicked become egotistical. **words of his mouth:** The theme of the wicked mouth is developed in Ps. 12. **ceased to be wise:** The wisdom that the psalmist observes here is the practical outworking of the skill of sound living. **Wickedness** is crookedness and perversity.

36:5, 6 The contrast of these verses with the previous ones is extreme. Just as the revelation of depravity in vv. 1–4 is awful, the revelation of the Lord's love is even more wonderful. **great mountains . . . great deep:** The contrasts continue with David ranging from the highest mountains to the depths of the sea to describe the perfect character of God. The height of the great mountains can be compared to how great God's righteousness is; the depth of the seas can be compared with how mysterious and inacces-

sible God's true judgments are. The word **deep** is also used in Gen. 1:2.

36:7–9 their trust: Because of God's nature, righteous men and women come to Him like nestlings seeking shelter under the wings of the mother bird (7:1; 11:1; 16:1; 31:1). Although the wicked are never **satisfied** (Prov. 27:20), the one who trusts in the Lord can find ample satisfaction. **fountain of life:** God's salvation and continuing mercy to His people are often described in terms of life-giving water (Is. 12:3; Jer. 2:13).

36:10–12 continue: On the basis of two of the revelations this psalm presents—the nature of the wicked (vv. 1–4) and the nature of God's loyal love (vv. 5–9)—David prays that God's loyal love will continue in the lives of His people. **There the workers of iniquity have fallen:** This is the third revelation in this psalm. David is given a glimpse of the horror of divine judgment on the wicked. In effect, the psalmist "sees" the judgment scene and shudders.

Psalm 37 is a wisdom psalm written as an acrostic. Its simple message is to maintain patience in the midst of troubles. God's people can have such patience because they know that their eternal reward will abundantly surpass any temporal troubles. The structure of the poem is as follows: (1) the need for patience in light of the apparent success of the wicked (vv. 1–11); (2) the need for patience in light of the final judgment of the wicked (vv. 12–22); (3) encouragement for the righteous in view of the role of the wicked (vv. 23–33); (4) a renewed call for patience in view of the apparent success of the wicked (vv. 34–40).

37:1–4 Do not fret is the theme of this psalm. When the wicked seem to prosper, the psalmist calls for patience, a renewed sense of dependence on the Lord, and a new sense of pleasure in knowing Him. **the desires of your heart:** When the righteous have desires that spring from the Lord, the Lord will surely fulfill those desires.

37:5, 6 To **commit your way** means "to roll in or on" the Lord. What a splendid picture of trusting in Him.

37:7, 8 Rest . . . wait patiently: These commands reemphasize the major point of the psalm, "do not fret" (v. 1). This is not a call to be inactive, but to depend actively on the living Lord. The psalm gives us a commandment to cease from worry.

37:9–12 The wicked sometimes appear to prosper; but constantly throughout this psalm the writer reminds his listeners that they will **be cut off. yet a little while:** From God's vantage point, the flourishing of the wicked is short (Eccl. 3:16, 17). **the meek shall inherit the earth:** Jesus quoted these words in Matt. 5:5, confirming the OT and showing the importance of the Psalms in His life.

37:13–17 The LORD laughs: These words recall the scornful laughter in 2:4. What sheer horror for the wicked to hear God's laughter directed against them! Contrast this laughter with the delight that the Lord finds in the ways of the righteous (v. 23).

37:18–20 The phrase **the LORD** knows the days of the upright has several meanings: (1) God knows our circumstances and provides for us; (2) God knows how long we will live and will sustain us to the end (90:12); (3) God knows that our days on earth are only the beginning of our days with Him in eternity.

37:21–23 the righteous shows mercy: There are many contrasts between the wicked and the righteous in the wisdom psalms; this one is based on contrasting attitudes toward possessions (15:5; 112:5). Of all the things on earth that God has created, only one will last—people. All material things will pass away (2 Pet. 3:10–12).

37:24 upholds him: The righteous know that when they fall, they are never left lying there; when they stumble, they are never completely forsaken.

37:25 begging bread: These words may be viewed from two perspectives: (1) The hunger of the righteous is temporary and will be replaced by fullness in the days to come; and (2) there is a hunger that the righteous never need

to suffer: they are never deprived of the Lord's presence (John 6:35). Perhaps this is also a call to help the righteous when they do suffer hunger in this world.

37:26–29 The same command to **depart from evil** is found in 34:14. In this life people must choose either to cling to God and righteousness, or to pursue evil. The way of God leads to everlasting life. **the LORD loves justice:** Because God stands opposed to injustice, to support injustice is to become His enemy. God's people ought to love the things that He loves and detest the things that He hates.

37:30, 31 in his heart: At numerous places in the Psalms, the poet declares his love for God's Law and his effort to make it integral to his life (1:2; 19:7–11; 119:1–176).

37:32–35 To **wait on the LORD** is an act of faith; not to wait on Him is foolishness. **like a native green tree:** David admits that the wicked might prosper, but he also affirms that they will not enjoy success forever.

37:36, 37 In this context **peace** suggests "everything as it ought to be." The destiny of the righteous is in sharp contrast to the fate of the wicked (1:4–6).

37:38–40 salvation: The principal issue here is not regeneration but sanctification—the daily deliverance of God's people from temptation and evil. **they trust:** The psalm concludes with the trusting God, like chicks running to the wings of their mother (17:8; 36:7).

🌱 **IN LIFE** | **Reacting to Suffering**

David saw his family torn apart by choices he had made (Ps. 38:11–12), even as his body was ravaged by sickness, possibly an acute skin disease (38:3, 5, 7). Yet however serious his physical problems may have been, they were overshadowed by the pain of his troubled heart (38:8, 10). Worst of all, he was unable to communicate his true thoughts and feelings (38:13–14).

Have sin and its consequences created distance between the members of your family? Has someone been abandoned to suffering because of anger or disapproval by the others? Psalm 38 offers several insights for redeeming the situation.

First, the psalmist who cries out is willing to confess his own sin and foolishness (38:3–5, 18). This is crucial in cases where someone's sickness or suffering is the result of sin. That sin needs to be acknowledged, confessed, and repented of (compare James 5:13–16).

But the psalm offers hope in the certainty that God sees and hears, even if family members cannot or will not (38:15). This hope in the Lord is available not only to the sufferer, but to innocent bystanders as well, such as parents, spouses, or children. By trusting in God's goodness, they can see themselves no longer as victims but as victors.

Finally, Psalm 38 challenges all of us not to abandon anyone to silent suffering in sin and sickness. The psalm may express David's predicament, but it also reminds us of the plight of everyone who has ever been brought low by their own foolishness. Rather than stand aloof from someone with the attitude, "You made your bed; now lie in it," we can draw near with understanding and compassion. Psalm 38 can help us respond to the plea of a lonely sinner, "Remember me."

Psalm 38 is a psalm of lament, specifically a penitential psalm. In it, David pleads earnestly for the mercy of God even when he senses God's discipline. All believers face times of distress, some of them the result of sin. The psalms of penitence are a model for our own prayers of confession and a warning against the type of behavior that will lead to God's correction. The structure of the Psalm is as follows: (1) a plea to God to stop rebuking (vv. 1–5); (2) a description of David's suffering (vv. 6–8); (3) a second plea based on the actions of David's friends and foes (vv. 9–12); (4) a commitment by David to trust solely in the Lord even in the time of His anger (vv. 13–16); (5) a third plea for deliverance based on David's weakening condition (vv. 17–20); (6) a concluding plea based on David's certainty that there is salvation in the Lord alone (vv. 21, 22).

38:1–5 As in 6:1, David has two concerns. His first concern is the painful distress he feels during the time of God's discipline on his life

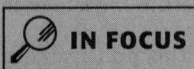

IN FOCUS "hope"

(Heb. *yachal*) (38:15; 130:5, 7; 131:3; Lam. 3:21–24) Strong's #3176: This Hebrew word signifies "to wait with expectation." Almost half of its occurrences are in the Psalms, and it is especially frequent in Ps. 119. Sometimes the idea of hope is expressed with confidence (Job 13:15; Is. 51:5), and sometimes hope is clearly in vain (Ezek. 13:6). The Bible describes Noah as waiting for seven days to send out the dove (Gen. 8:12) and men as waiting to hear the counsel of Job (Job 29:21); but by far the main object of "expectant waiting" or "hope" is God, His word, His judgment, and His mercy (33:18; 119:43; Mic. 7:7). That hope is not misplaced, for the One in whom we hope is completely faithful to His promises (Heb. 10:23).

(32:4). David's second concern is that God might be placing His heavy hand on him in **wrath,** as He does on the wicked (37:22). **my iniquities have gone over my head:** David uses expressive language to describe his loss of control: he cannot free himself from the burden of sin (69:5). This is similar to Paul speaking of himself as the "chief" of sinners (1 Tim. 1:15).

38:6 I am troubled: David feels he is carrying an immense load. In this case, the heavy load is guilt.

38:7–12 light of my eyes: As in 13:3,

David complains that he is about to lose his vision: probably he means that an oppression like death seems about to overcome him. **My loved ones:** David expresses sorrow because even those closest to him are leaving him. See Job's similar experience in Job 2:9, 10.

38:13–17 David is determined, even in the gravest suffering, not to present an opportunity for his enemies to condemn the name of the Lord. In this, David's silence foreshadows the silence of the Savior Jesus before His accusers (Mark 14:61).

38:18–20 I will declare: David's silence is only before his enemies (vv. 13–16); to the Lord he willingly confesses his sins. He expects that the merciful God will forgive and restore him (Ps. 32).

38:21, 22 be not far from me: These words echo the sentiment of 22:1. All that is left for David is to trust in God. In that sense, David was in the right place, for confidence in any person or thing other than God Himself is misplaced trust.

Psalm 39 is a wisdom psalm in the form of a psalm of individual lament. The title indicates that this is a psalm of David composed for Jeduthun. Psalm 39 is unusual in many respects. It speaks of a determination to be silent against foes, whereas most psalms speak boldly against enemies. Moreover, it ends with a request that God leave the psalmist alone, a stance that is remarkably like sections of the Book of Job. The structure of the poem is in four movements: (1) a determination by the psalmist to be silent before his foes (vv. 1–3); (2) a petition to God for help in view of the brevity of life (vv. 4–6); (3) a petition for forgiveness and deliverance (vv. 7–11); (4) a petition for God to leave him alone (vv. 12, 13).

39:1 I will restrain my mouth: David determines to be silent in suffering so that he will not speak out foolishly. See 32:3 for another reason to be silent.

39:2–5 Make me to know my end is an appeal to God to deliver the psalmist before his life passes him by (90:7–12). **Vapor** refers to something that passes quickly, not something that has no meaning.

39:6–8 My hope is in You: David knows that his only chance of deliverance is in God. But he also believes that his trouble has come from God. He is in a quandary. Should he ask for God's help or should he ask God to leave him alone? Unlike most of the psalms of lament, there is noticeable difficulty in moving into a posture of praise. **my transgressions:** David acknowledges his sin and throws himself on the mercy of the Lord (Ps. 32).

39:9–13 Hear my prayer: David has been silent for a period of his distress (vv. 2, 9) but can remain silent no longer. Here he cries for God not to be silent, but to deliver him. **Remove Your gaze:** If God is not going to deliver him, the despondent psalmist asks God to just leave him alone. It is rare outside the Book of Job to find language such as this (Job 7:19; 10:20, 21; 14:6). Sometimes the pain of the psalmist was so far from being resolved at the time when he composed his poem that he remained on the edge of despair to the last verse. Yet the fact that God saves those who call upon Him is described again and again in the Book of Psalms (22:21; 118:21).

Psalm 40 is a psalm of declarative praise that moves into a psalm of lament. This psalm is a remarkable example of how troubles and difficulties forced David to depend continually on the Lord. The structure of the psalm is as follows: (1) a report of deliverance (vv. 1–3); (2) instruction to the people to commit their lives to the Lord (vv. 4, 5); (3) a confession about worship (vv. 6–8); (4) a report to God of the fulfillment of the vow of praise (vv. 9, 10); (5) a renewed lament (vv. 11, 12); (6) a set of petitions for deliverance (vv. 13–15); (7) continuing praise in the midst of trouble (vv. 16, 17).

40:1 The Hebrew translated **I waited patiently** is literally "waiting I waited." The emphasis of this phrase is not really on patience, but on the fact that David waited solely on the Lord. The verb "to wait" expresses a confident trust or faith in the Lord (130:5). David knows that salvation comes only from the Almighty (3:8). The words **He inclined to me** present the image of the Creator of the universe, the King of heaven, stooping from His throne to save the helpless.

40:2, 3 horrible pit: David writes this poem during a period of terrible stress; he feels as if he is stuck in a pit or swamp. No matter how hard he tries, he cannot get out. But David turns his frustration over to the Lord and trusts in His strength. **a new song:** The Lord's salvation prompts David to praise God. The music is new because God's salvation is fresh and new to David.

40:4, 5 The proud refers to idolaters who will not bow in humility before the Lord (147:6). **Lies** refers to idols. Not only are the works of God directed toward the people of faith, but so are His **thoughts.** He is thinking about us.

40:6 The Lord takes pleasure in those who obediently come to Him with praise on their lips (1 Sam. 15:22, 23). **My ears You have opened:** The Lord not only gives us ears to hear His word, but also grants us understanding so that we can truly obey Him.

40:7, 8 Behold, I come: David brings his sacrifice, but his focus is on presenting his own

life to the Lord (Rom. 12:1, 2). According to the Book of Hebrews, Jesus spoke these words to the Father (Heb. 10:4–6). **Delight** is related to the word *desire* in v. 6. What brings pleasure to God will also bring delight to His people.

40:10–12 Do not withhold: Even after the experience of deliverance with which the psalm begins, David has another reason to turn to the Lord in renewed prayer. The Hebrew for **your tender mercies** (which can also mean "womb") refers to God's affection for us. In effect, David is asking the Lord to surround him with warmth and comfort that is practically maternal.

40:13–15 deliver me: David does not ask for forgiveness of sin here (contrast 51:3, 4), but for deliverance from powerful enemies. **Aha, aha:** David's enemies are all around him, taunting him mercilessly (35:21).

40:16, 17 The LORD be magnified: With these great words of praise, David encourages others in the community to glorify the Lord (35:27). **poor and needy:** The psalmist is still in trouble, pleading with God to deliver him anew.

Psalm 41 is a lament psalm. Since it begins and concludes with words of praise to God, it may also be called a psalm of praise. The poem is ascribed to David and speaks of the plight of a person suffering from serious physical illness. Ultimately, it presents the victory of the Savior Jesus over His enemies, especially the great enemy Satan. There are four movements in the psalm: (1) an affirmation of confidence in the Lord's power to deliver the godly from distress (vv. 1–3); (2) a description of David's distress (vv. 4–9); (3) a renewed expression of hope in the Lord (vv. 10–12); (4) a coda of praise marking the end of Book I of the Psalms (v. 13).

41:1 Blessed is the same word that begins Ps. 1. The same word introduces the first and last psalms of Book I (see Introduction). When the verb *blessed* is used with God as its object (as in v. 13), it serves as a word of praise (103:1, 2). To bless God is to identify Him as the source of our blessings. **The poor** refers not only to those who do not have enough money, but also to those who suffer illness or misfortune through no fault of their own. For such persons, God is Defender, Deliverer, and Sustainer (10:2, 9; 35:10; 69:33; 109:16; 140:12).

41:2, 3 Blessed on the earth refers to the acts of God's goodness in a person's life, including health, wealth, longevity, spiritual vitality, and harmony with God and people (Prov. 3:1–4). **bed of illness:** The distress in this psalm is the psalmist's serious physical illness.

41:4 for I have sinned: In the context of the psalm, this is a general acknowledgment of sin and the need for God's forgiveness and restoration (1 John 1:9).

41:5–8 At times, the psalmist's **enemies** are indicated (3:1), but more often these enemies are left unspecified in the psalms, allowing others to think in terms of their own situations. **his name perish:** In ancient cultures, for a person not to be remembered was like saying that he or she had never existed. The righteous in Israel hoped that their names would endure after them, that they would have a "great name" (Gen. 12:2). **he speaks lies:** David charges his enemies with visiting his sickbed on the pretext of mercy but with malice in their hearts.

41:9 Familiar friend describes a close, intimate relationship. The outrage of betrayal by one so close is nearly unbearable (Matt. 26:14–16). The fulfillment of this verse in the experience of Jesus and Judas is remarkable. Not only did the two eat a meal together (Matt. 26:21–25; Mark 14:18–21; Luke 22:21), but Jesus also called Judas a "friend" at the moment of betrayal (Matt. 26:50). Moreover Jesus quoted this verse, noting its fulfillment in Judas (John 13:18).

41:10–12 Raise me up was David's prayer for healing from the disease that had him bedridden (v. 3). In another sense, these words look forward to Jesus' resurrection (16:10, 11; 118:17, 18). **does not triumph:** The failure of David's enemy to destroy his life was an indicator of God's pleasure in David's life. **my integrity:** These words suggest that it is the righteous person who is suffering in this psalm, not an unrepentant sinner (26:1). **before Your face forever:** David prays not only for a long life on earth (v. 2), but also for eternal life in God's presence (23:6). His ultimate hope is to glorify and praise God in His presence forever.

41:13 Blessed: This psalm begins with a blessing of God on the righteous; it ends with the righteous blessing their Lord. The word here

for *blessed* is different from the word in v. 1. Here the word identifies the Lord as the source of our blessing. The word **Amen,** meaning "surely" and "let it be," is an affirmation of faith in God. It is simply saying "yes" to God. The repetition of the word parallels the repetition of the word *everlasting* and expresses enthusiastic agreement with the praise in the psalm.

Psalm 42 and Ps. 43 were probably originally one poem, like Pss. 9; 10. Note that Ps. 43 does not have a superscription and that 43:5 repeats the refrain of 42:5, 11. Apparently a longer psalm was divided into two sections for use in temple worship. As an independent poem, Ps. 42 is an individual lament with a strong emphasis on trust (Ps. 23). The psalm's two movements both conclude with a refrain of encouragement to hope in God (vv. 5, 11), even though the psalmist was in exile far from the temple. The psalm is attributed to the sons of Korah, a musical family in Israel. They descended from the priest who had led an abortive rebellion against the leadership of Moses and Aaron (Num. 16). God's judgment came upon Korah and his companions, but Korah's family continued for hundreds of years to be some of the premier leaders of worship music in Israel. The structure of the poem is as follows: (1) a description of the psalmist's longing for God's presence (vv. 1–4); (2) a description of the psalmist's fear that God might no longer remember him (vv. 5–11).

42:1–4 pant: The verb "to pant" is unusually expressive of a spiritual thirst for God. The poet describes his experience of being cut off from the worshiping community. He feels distant from God's presence among His people and he longs for intimacy with God (v. 4). For the believer who lived during OT times, there was only one place where the true worship of the Lord was possible—the temple in Jerusalem. **go**

⟩⟩ IN PERSON | **From Rebels to Praise Singers**

The sons of Korah (Ps. 42, title) had an infamous past on which to look back. Their ancestor Korah, of the tribe of Levi, led at least 250 of Israel's most important leaders in one of the worst rebellions against Moses and the Lord during the Exodus. God severely judged Korah's coalition by causing the earth to split open and swallow them and their possessions (Num. 16).

However, Korah's family survived (26:11), and years later his descendants were among the Levites appointed by David to oversee music in the worship of the Lord (1 Chr. 6:37). Their responsibilities included composing, arranging, and performing, and in this connection eleven of the psalms bear the heading, "of the sons of Korah."

The sons of Korah illustrate how a tragic legacy can be overcome. It need not determine the destiny of a family. By honoring the Lord, Korah's descendants became known, not for their ancestor's rebellion, but for their musical responsibilities.

with the multitude: The psalmist was consumed with thoughts of the worship of God that he had experienced at the temple in Jerusalem among throngs of joyful believers (Ps. 100). Generally the focus of worship in the Book of Psalms is on the community worshiping together (compare Acts 2:40–47; Heb. 13:15, 16).

42:5 Why are you cast down: These words are repeated in v. 11 and 43:5. The psalmist reminds himself that one day he will experience anew the presence of God. In the end, his hope in the Lord will not be misplaced. **praise Him:** As is common in the Psalms, the poet is not describing an act of private devotion, but of public praise of the goodness of God. This is praise in words and songs that would be repeated in the midst of the congregation (22:22; Eph. 5:19; Heb. 13:15).

42:6 The land of the Jordan and **the heights of Hermon** refer to the Promised Land, from which the people were exiled.

42:7–11 Why have You forgotten me: The psalmist asks these troubling questions in faith, for he remembers that God is his **Rock,** his protector and foundation. He cannot help but **hope** in Him in the middle of difficult circumstances.

Psalm 43 is a continuation of Ps. 42. The original poem was separated into the two psalms we have today so they could more easily be used for worship in the temple. As it stands, Ps. 43 shares features of a psalm of lament and a psalm of trust. The structure of the poem is as follows: (1) a call for vindication from the Lord (vv. 1, 2); (2) a prayer for the psalmist's return to the temple to worship God (vv. 3, 4); (3) a renewed call for hope in God (v. 5).

43:1, 2 Vindicate me is a protest of innocence (Pss. 17; 26; 35). The psalmist takes the stance of one wrongfully attacked. **Why do You cast me off:** More hurtful than the words of the psalmist's enemies is the sense that God has rejected him (Ps. 13).

43:3, 4 Your light and Your truth: The psalmist asks God for deliverance. See 104:2 for the significance of *light;* see 100:5 for the significance of *truth.* Only the "true light" of God could save the psalmist from the lies and darkness all about him. **Your tabernacle:** More than anything else the psalmist desires to rejoin the worshiping community in praising God (149:1).

43:5 Why are you cast down: These words are the refrain of this and the previous psalm (42:5, 11). In time of doubt and stress, the poet urges his inner being, by the power of God, to keep believing. He knows that one day, by God's grace, he will return to the place of praise to God, the center of worship in Jerusalem.

Psalm 44 is a lament of the community, a collective sigh of the people of Israel for God to help them in a time of great national stress. The psalm also presents an occasion for a rehearsal of God's great deeds in the Exodus, the major saving action of the Lord in the OT period (Ps. 105). This psalm is attributed to the sons of Korah, the descendants of the rebellious priest mentioned in Num. 16. The structure of the poem is as follows: (1) a rehearsal of God's deliverance of Israel in the past (vv. 1–3); (2) a statement of confidence in God the great King (vv. 4–8); (3) a lament of the people (vv. 9–12); (4) a protest of innocence of the people (vv. 13–22); (5) a petition of the people (vv. 23–26).

44:1–3 heard with our ears: God's marvelous intervention in history to deliver the Israelites from Egypt was the cornerstone of OT faith (17:7; 118:16; Ex. 15:6). Each generation of Israelites was obligated to tell the next generation about what God had done for them. The story that they told was not merely a national history, but also a description of the loving character of God (Deut. 8). **Your right hand** became a slogan of redemption in Israel. **You favored them:** The selection of Israel as the people of God came by His grace alone (4:3; Rom. 11).

44:4, 5 my King: In this community lament, it is striking that here the speaker is singular. It may be that these words are spoken by Israel's king to the King of glory. As the king of the nation, it was appropriate for him to lead the people in asking for God's renewed favor. **through Your name:** The king affirms that victory will be won only by God's Spirit.

44:6–12 The words **cast us off** begin the lament section of the psalm. The army of Israel was not to be regarded as merely a group of warriors—they were the warriors of the Almighty (Ps. 144). Their victories were the victories of God and their defeats were losses that He allowed them to endure. **You sell Your people:** When the people suffered loss, it was as though God had "sold" them. But God's deliverance of them from suffering is depicted as His purchase of His people—the meaning of the word *redemption* (v. 26).

44:13–20 we have not forgotten: The people protest that they have not rejected God. The implication is that their troubles would be deserved if they had rejected him. **Stretched out our hands** refers to a posture of prayer (Ps. 134). They protest that they have not prayed to the idols of the nations, but have been faithful to the only living God.

44:21, 22 as sheep: These words predict another beloved Son of the Most High who would also feel cast off by the Lord (Is. 53:7; Rom. 8:36).

44:23–26 Israel's God does not sleep (121:3,

4; Is. 40:28). The cry to **awake** is an appeal for God to act on behalf of His people. The cry is based on the people's faith that the Lord will forgive. **redeem us:** In v. 12, the people suggested that God had sold them; here they ask Him to redeem them—to buy them back for Himself.

Psalm 45 is a royal psalm—a royal wedding song that celebrates human marriage in such a grand manner that the NT writers applied it to the great King Jesus as well (compare vv. 6, 7 with Heb. 1:8, 9). Like many other psalms, this one not only portrays the joy of human marriage, but also describes prophetically the glorious reign of Jesus (Pss. 2; 22; 69). This psalm was composed by the sons of Korah. The structure is as follows: (1) introduction of the "good theme" (v. 1); (2) wedding wishes for the great king (vv. 2–9); (3) wedding wishes for the beautiful bride (vv. 10–15); (4) concluding blessings on the king (vv. 16, 17).

45:1–5 You are fairer: This poem's cultural setting is the opulence of an ancient eastern royal court. The profuse description of the royal groom would be appropriate in that culture. **O Mighty One:** In the ancient Middle East the king was supposed to be a great warrior. The model in Israel was David, the celebrated champion who defeated the giant Goliath (1 Sam. 17). The term Mighty One is also a messianic title. **Your glory and Your majesty** can be rephrased as "Your majestic glory." **right hand:** The victories of the king's hand would be awesome, a symbol pointing back to Exodus and forward to the works of the Savior Jesus.

45:6–9 The words **Your throne** indicate the messianic direction of the psalm. Here the King is addressed as **God,** yet it is "God, Your God" who anointed Him. Thus these verses describe the interaction of the Father and the Son, for both are called "God." The writer of Hebrews used these verses to assert Jesus' deity (Heb. 1:8, 9). **anointed You:** Anointing set aside a particular person for special service to God. In OT times, those who were anointed for

special service foreshadowed the Anointed One, the meaning of *Messiah* and *Christ.* As symbols appropriate for divine service, the **garments** of a priest or king had to be clean and luxurious. The king was surrounded by radiant women; his bride the queen was resplendent in her precious golden garments. This is a portrait of heaven, with God as King and the church as His radiant bride (Rev. 19:1–10). **Ophir,** possibly located in southern Arabia or on the east coast of Africa (2 Chr. 8:17, 18), was known in the OT world as a source of fine **gold.**

45:10–17 O daughter: The beautiful bride forsakes her own family and relationships as she becomes part of the family of her king and husband. **worship Him:** The bride is to give homage and worship to the great King. **robes of many colors:** In the ancient world, the beauty of the bride's gowns might be an expression of her family's wealth, their pride in her, and their love for her.

Psalm 46 as a psalm of trust (see Ps. 23) rejoices in the deliverance that the Lord gives His people in the midst of a fearsome battle or siege. There is reason to believe that Pss. 46—48 form a trilogy that focuses on God's special love for Jerusalem. Psalm 46 was Martin Luther's basis for the Reformation hymn "A Mighty Fortress Is Our God." The poem has three movements, each indicated by the closing word *Selah,* a musical notation perhaps indicating a musical interlude (vv. 3, 7, 11). The psalm is also called "A Song for Alamoth," a word that may refer to soprano voices. The structure of the psalm is as follows: (1) a celebration of God as our defense even though the earth is moved (vv. 1–3); (2) a celebration of God as our defense even though the nations rage (vv. 4–7); (3) a celebration of God as our defense even when the Lord brings His judgment (vv. 8–11).

46:1 Our refuge and strength may be rephrased "our impenetrable defense." The psalms regularly use imagery of a fortress to describe God. In the ancient Middle East, cities were built on heights with high walls for

---

✠ IN CONTEXT **Tunnel of Gladness**

The "river whose streams shall make glad the city of God" (Ps. 46:4) may allude to the tunnel that King Hezekiah built to guarantee a continuous water supply for Jerusalem in times of war (2 Chr. 32:30). The tunnel carried water from the Gihon spring outside the city to a cistern inside the walls. So when invading armies besieged Jerusalem, the unstoppable stream of water made the whole city glad.

Likewise, God makes His people glad through His continuous presence. His protection flows like a river out of His lasting commitment to those who honor Him.

defense. Yet there was no city and no defensive structure that was impenetrable. However, the psalmist describes here the One who is a sure defense.

46:2, 3 earth be removed: The wording of vv. 2, 3 moves the action to a cosmic level. What if the struggle were not just an ordinary war with ordinary weapons? What if the war involved even shaking the mountains and causing the seas to roar? It makes no difference. God is a refuge for His people against everything actual or imagined.

46:4, 5 God is in the midst of her: The people do not have an absentee deliverer, a defense that is only sometimes present. The Lord lives with His people. Consequently, His protection can be counted on.

46:6, 7 The LORD of hosts is with us: These words form a refrain (v. 11). The pairing of the words "the Lord of hosts" with "the God of Jacob" is notable in both this verse and v. 11. This refrain praises the Almighty, the Commander of heaven's armies, for choosing to live with the descendants of Jacob, His people. Who could protect His people better? See 9:9; 48:3 for other uses of the word **refuge.**

46:8–11 desolations: The picture here is of final judgment (Pss. 1; 110). **Be still:** The call for stillness before the Lord is not a preparation for worship, but for impending judgment (Hab. 2:20; Zeph. 1:7; Zech. 2:13). God will be exalted. All the earth will bow before Him.

Psalm 47, a royal psalm attributed to the sons of Korah, presents the grand ascent of the King of kings to His throne. The psalm also presents the joy of the people over the fact that the great King's rule means the end of all iniquity, warfare, and trouble (Is. 11:3–5). The poets of Scripture knew that God is King as Creator of the world (Ps. 93), that He is King of His people because He is their Savior (Ps. 99), and that He is the coming King in the prophetic future. This last is the focus of Ps. 47. The structure of the poem is as follows: (1) a call to shout in triumph at the coming of the King (vv. 1–4); (2) a call to shout in triumph at the enthronement of the King (v. 5–7); (3) a call to rejoice in the rule of the King (vv. 8, 9).

47:1–3 clap your hands: There are many ways in which the people of God express their joy in Him; one is the clapping of hands in joyful adoration. **all you peoples:** It is principally the people of God who will praise the great King; but the call for the nations was always a part of the larger picture in the theology of the psalms (Pss. 67; 117). **the LORD Most High:** The divine name usually translated "the LORD" is buttressed by the term *Most High*, which speaks of God's power over all nations (7:17; 77:10; 78:17, 35, 56; 82:6; 107:11; Deut. 32:8). **Awesome** is

related to the word for "fear" and suggests reverence for Almighty God (147:11). **Great King** is the key phrase of this psalm. All kings have derived authority; only one King, the great God of heaven, is absolute in power and righteousness. **He will subdue:** The promise of the eventual victory of God's people under the leadership of their great King is a basic focus in the Bible (Pss. 2; 110; 1 Cor. 15:24–28). The outcome of the final battle was determined long ago by God.

47:4 The words **whom He loves** are perhaps the most significant contribution of this poem to our understanding of God's purposes. To love means "to make one's choice in." God had chosen the Israelites to be His holy people and in that way He loved them. In his dialogue with Nicodemus, Jesus explained that God's love extended to all the nations as well as to Israel (John 3:16).

47:5–7 God has gone up: This psalm speaks of an anticipated enthronement of God. As He seats Himself on the throne, all who see Him in heaven and earth shout aloud in triumph. **Sing praises:** The repetition of this command in vv. 6, 7 is similar to the angelic voices singing of the holiness of God in Is. 6:3. The reason for the call to sing is clear: **God is the King of all the earth;** He deserves our praise. This psalm speaks of the coming great reign of Jesus when He establishes His holy rule.

47:8, 9 God reigns: We know that God is King over the earth. There are other forces clearly at work, but they function only by His permission. One day there will be an end to all evil, to all acts of rebellion, and to all acts of oppression. **The people of the God of Abraham:** This is the prophetic picture of the ultimate fulfillment of the Abrahamic covenant (Gen. 12:1–3). One day all the peoples of the earth who have come to faith in God through Jesus will discover that they are one people. They are all the true seed of Abraham, because they, like Abraham, believed in God (Gen. 15:6; Gal. 3:5–8). Then all **shields** will belong to God; there will be no other power on earth or in the universe apart from the power of God. **Greatly exalted** comes from the term meaning "to go up," the same root used in v. 5. God's ascent to His throne will come with the enthronement of Jesus and His coming rule in the New Jerusalem (Rev. 20).

Psalm 48 unites with Pss. 46; 47 to form three great psalms of praise to God for His kingship and His love for the holy city of Jerusalem. This emphasis on Jerusalem has led many scholars to speak of these psalms as "Songs of Zion." Attributed to the sons of Korah, this psalm calls the people to offer reverent praise to their Lord. The structure is as follows: (1) a celebration of God's greatness in the holy city of Zion (vv. 1–3); (2) a description of the gathering of the kings and the peoples to witness God's rule (vv. 4–11); (3) a celebration of God's greatness in the holy city of Zion (vv. 12–14).

48:1 Great is used often in the Psalms to describe the person of God (21:5; 77:13; 95:3; 96:4; 145:3; 147:5). **city of our God:** The city of Jerusalem had a particularly dear place in the heart of God's people (1 Kin. 14:21). The city was holy because of the presence of God in the temple.

48:2, 3 The joy of the whole earth: As is strongly established in the Book of Psalms, the purpose of God's work in Israel was to draw all nations to Himself (117:1). **sides of the north:** This phrasing is likely borrowed from Canaanite poetry. In Canaanite thought, the great gods resided in some remote northern location. For Israel, God's dwelling was the physical city of Jerusalem. **The city of the great King:** Jesus quoted these words in Matt. 5:35 and identified the city as Jerusalem. **God is in her palaces:** These words express a prayer for the present and hope for the future. The point is clear: the beauty of the city of Jerusalem comes from the presence of the Lord, who has made His dwelling there.

48:4–7 This section describes from a different point of view the final battle referred to in Pss. 2; 110. Psalm 48 describes the approach and hasty retreat of the errant **kings.** The con-

nection between this text and Ps. 2 is heightened by the use of an unusual Hebrew word for **fear**—a term meaning "trembling" or "quaking terror"—which is found in both places (2:11).

48:8 as . . . we have seen: The people who first sang this song knew the presence of God in temple worship. They knew that they were in the city where God had chosen to establish His blessing.

48:9 We have thought: The verb is an unusual one in Hebrew. It refers to making comparisons and looking for similarities, thinking and considering with discrimination. The point is that nothing can be compared to the loyal love of God.

48:10–14 Praising the city of **Zion** is another way of praising God, whose dwelling was there. To be a **guide** describes the work of a shepherd (78:52).

Psalm 49, a wisdom psalm attributed to the sons of Korah, has many similarities with Proverbs and Ecclesiastes. The psalm calls for the wise person to realize that there is nothing to fear from the oppressive rich: like animals, they too will die. But the righteous will live forever. This psalm is quite different from a psalm of praise; it is an instruction text set to music. Its structure is: (1) a call for understanding (vv. 1–4); (2) a declaration of the vanity of trusting in wealth (vv. 5–9); (3) a declaration of the worthlessness of possessions after death (vv. 10–12); (4) a description of God's redemption

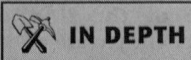 **IN DEPTH** | **Winds East, West, North, and South**

The ancient Hebrews described their climate in terms of four winds determined by the four points of the compass.

The east wind (Ps. 48:7) came from the desert and was notoriously violent. Called winds of the wilderness, these blasts were probably what struck the home of one of Job's sons, killing all of his children (Job 1:19). Likewise, an east wind caused by God parted the Red Sea (Ex. 14:21). So it is not surprising that Jeremiah would compare war to the east wind (Jer. 18:17).[WIL]

Hot and dry, the east wind had the potential to scorch grain and other crops (Gen. 41:6, 23, 27; Ezek. 17:9; Jon. 4:8) and to dry up springs of water (Hos. 13:15). An east wind also brought a plague of locusts (Gen. 10:13).

By contrast, the west wind carried moisture in from the Mediterranean Sea between November and February. A west wind blew away the locusts in Egypt (Ex. 10:19), and rain-bearing wind from the west also ended a severe drought in the days of the prophet Elijah (1 Kin. 18:43–44).

The dry north wind was the coldest. Modern-day Arabs call this wind the Simoom (from *samm*, "poison"). It can cause headache, fever, and neuralgia.

The gentle south wind "quiets the earth" (Job 37:17). It blew Paul's ship gently (Acts 27:13) until a fiercer wind demolished it. Coming from the highlands of Sinai and Arabia, the south wind blows for about one day at a time during the spring (February to June).

(vv. 13–15); (5) the conclusion that there is no need to fear the rich (vv. 16–20).

49:1–5 Hear this, all peoples: The call for wisdom and understanding goes to all, similar to the calls for universal worship of the Lord (Ps. 117). **Dark saying,** which may be translated "riddle" or "enigma," refers to a perplexing moral problem: how do the righteous come to terms with oppressive rich people who seem to have no thought for God?

49:6–9 Those who trust in their wealth: As in the teaching of Jesus (Mark 10:24), there is a warning against trusting in wealth, for wealth can achieve nothing of lasting value in this life or the life to come. **Nor give to God a ransom:** Wealth cannot buy redemption. **Pit** refers to the power of death in its dark aspect (16:10). Only God has the power to deliver us from death and hell.

49:10 The theme that **wise men die** is developed in Ecclesiastes. The rich and the poor, the wise and the fool, all have the same fate—physical death.

49:11–20 These verses vividly describe both the power of death and the greater power of God. **their beauty shall be consumed:** Death is the great leveler. People who have beauty, riches (vv. 16, 17), and power in this world will lose them all at death. They will be stripped of everything except their character or soul. This is why the Scriptures exhort us to pursue character development—God's law, holiness, wisdom, and knowledge—more than anything else. Each use of the word **grave** in these two verses is a translation of the Hebrew word Sheol, meaning death (16:10). **God will redeem my soul:** The psalmist trusts in God to deliver him from the power of death.

Psalm 50, a wisdom psalm, is the first of twelve poems attributed to Asaph, one of the music leaders appointed by David. This psalm contrasts the distinctions of the righteous and the wicked in the eyes of God, a constant theme of the wisdom writers. True wisdom in biblical thought is based on the "fear of the Lord," a proper response to the awesome nature of God. In this psalm, God is portrayed as the great Judge (Pss. 96—98). The structure of the psalm is: (1) the praise of God who shines forth from Zion (vv. 1–3); (2) a vision of the coming of God, the great Judge (vv. 4–6); (3) the instruction of the great Judge to His people concerning sacrifice (vv. 7–15); (4) the rebuke of the great Judge to the wicked (vv. 16–21); (5) the words of the great Judge on condemnation and salvation (vv. 22, 23).

50:1, 2 The Hebrew text uses the three terms **the Mighty One, God,** and **the Lord** as a stunning introduction to this poem. This language suggests a grand display of God Himself in the midst of His people (18:7–9). **Out of Zion:** The glory of God shines from His sanctuary in Jerusalem.

50:3–6 Our God shall come: This prophetic language speaks of the coming kingdom of God (Pss. 96—98). **God Himself is Judge:** See 75:7 for a powerful development of this idea. This is the point of this psalm; God is the great Judge. When used of God, the Hebrew word for Judge has connotations of royalty (94:2). Thus this wisdom psalm is also a royal psalm, because it speaks of the coming of the great King who both rules and judges.

50:7–10 not rebuke you: The sacrifices were commanded by God in Leviticus, but the people had difficulty keeping a godly perspective on the nature of sacrifices. **every beast of the forest:** The people were not doing God a favor by bringing their animals, for everything belonged to Him anyway. He knows every bird and beast.

50:11–15 If I were hungry: The God of Israel does not hunger for food; however, He does "hunger" for righteousness of His people. **Call upon Me:** Sacrifice in the Bible was for the good of the people. The Lord designated the sacrificial system as a the place when He would shower His mercy on those He loves.

50:16–21 As in the case of 1:4, the attention of the psalm turns from the righteous who need instruction to the **wicked** who merit judgment. This section announces God's judgment not against the nations, but against the people of Israel who heard but spurned God's word. **You give your mouth to evil:** God offered truth, but these people chose falsehoods. They had seen the light but preferred to live in darkness (John 3:16–21). **your own mother's son:** There was no sense of decency remaining in these wicked persons; even normal bonds of family relationships were disregarded.

50:22, 23 In the climax of the revelation of the coming judgment in this psalm, the Lord offers an opportunity to repent and receive forgiveness. This is an indicator of His grace. The Lord wants to save; His warnings are another expression of His mercy.

Psalm 51 is associated with one of the hardest experiences of David's life, the aftermath of his affair with Bathsheba. This is one of several psalms of David in which the title specifies the incident that inspired the poem. For the account of David's sin and Nathan's rebuke, see 2 Sam. 11; 12:1–15. David's response to Nathan was immediate: "I have sinned against the Lord" (2 Sam. 12:13). Sometime later, he wrote this memorable, penitential psalm. The structure of the poem is as follows: (1) a plea for God's mercy in the context of David's confession (vv. 1, 2); (2) an acknowledgment that David's sin

---

IN PERSON | A Positive Brokenness

For King David, there was ultimately only one way to deal with sin: face it, confess it, and be forgiven. Psalm 51 shows him doing precisely that. In total contrast to the pretense of confession practiced by so many today, David's prayer expresses utter brokenness.

What exactly was the sin to which David was admitting? The Bible tells us plainly that he committed adultery with Bathsheba, the wife of Uriah the Hittite, and that when she became pregnant David tried in vain to cover his sin, eventually engineering Uriah's death (2 Sam. 11). Yet Psalm 51 does not mention the adultery, and it only touches upon the murder (51:14). Instead, the main transgression confessed is, "Against You, You only have I sinned, and done this evil in Your sight" (51:4).

David was not evading responsibility for the sexual immorality and murder, but he recognized that ultimately sin is an offense against a holy, righteous God. Even when other people are hurt by our sins, it is God whose standards have been violated. Thus, while sinners owe apologies and restitution to people, they owe contrite confession to God. He alone is able to forgive sins (Mark 2:7).

---

was against the Lord (vv. 3, 4); (3) a confession that sin pervades David's being (vv. 5, 6); (4) a series of pleas for forgiveness (vv. 7–13); (5) a vow of praise by the forgiven sinner (vv. 14, 15); (6) a statement on the meaning of true worship (vv. 16, 17); (7) a plea for God to restore the fortunes of the people (vv. 18, 19).

51:1, 2 David 's call for **mercy** is the only appropriate request for a confessing sinner. No sinner should ask for justice, for that would mean judgment and ruin. Mercy and forgiveness is God's gift to the confessing sinner. Even when the Lord forgives, He does not tarnish His just character: confessed sins are covered by the sacrifice of His perfect Son on the Cross (2 Cor. 5:21). The phrase **according to Your lovingkindness** expresses God's loyal or covenantal love to His people (13:5).

51:3, 4 The months of agony that David suffered because of his guilt are expressed in the striking words—**my sin is always before me.** See the development of these ideas in Ps. 32. **Against You:** David had sinned against Bathsheba, Uriah, and the nation he was called to rule. But none of these indictments were as serious as David's offense against God. The first few verses use several different words to describe sin—"transgression," "iniquity," and "sin." The words for forgiveness are all pictorial words: "blot out" (v. 1), "wash," and "cleanse" (v. 2). All these words express the seriousness of sin and the great lengths God goes to in removing our sin. **be found just:** The Lord deals with sin in two ways: The wicked receive God's just condemnation; the righteous receive His undeserved mercy.

51:5, 6 brought forth in iniquity: Sin was found in David from the beginning; from birth he was inclined towards sin (Rom. 5:12). **Inward parts,** a rare word in the Hebrew Bible, indicates something clouded over, difficult for anyone but God to see. The Lord's penetrating gaze searches the innermost recesses of a person's mind and heart.

51:7–9 hyssop: Here David refers to the ritual acts of cleansing described in the Law of Moses (Lev. 14:4; Num. 19:6). David repeatedly calls for his cleansing (v. 9). By this, he expresses his profound sense of guilt.

51:10 This verse is significant in two areas, repentance and creation. The verb translated **create** is the same one used in Gen. 1:1 and refers to what only God can do. David was asking that his heart be renewed, restored, and transformed. God is the only source of such a renewal.

51:11–15 David calls **sinners** to salvation in this verse. He vows that he will use his experience of God's grace as a renewed motivation to bring others into the knowledge of the love and mercy of God (40:3). **my tongue shall sing:** David desires to be forgiven for several reasons: (1) for his own peace, (2) for the message of hope that he could communicate to others, and (3) for the praise he would be able to give in the community of the faithful.

51:16, 17 You do not desire sacrifice: The key term here is the verb *desire,* which means "to find pleasure in." God's pleasure is not in the sacrificed animal, but in the restored person. He demanded sacrifices, even from David; but His pleasure is in the person who comes obediently to Him (Gen. 4:1–7; John 4:21–24; Rom. 12:1, 2). Actions not accompanied by a contrite heart are not acceptable to God (Is. 1:12–20).

51:18, 19 Do good: David declared God's goodness to the whole community in their collective worship (125:4). The Hebrew verb translated **pleased** is the same verb translated *delight* in v. 16. God took pleasure in those whose hearts were humble before Him. Their sacrifices were a source of joy.

Psalm 52, a psalm of lament, strongly emphasizes judgment of David's enemies. The title of this psalm specifies the incident in David's life that prompted him to write it. Doeg, an official of Saul, had spied on David when he fled to Ahimelech, the priest at Nob, for provisions and guidance (1 Sam. 21:7). Doeg's report angered Saul so much that he destroyed the priestly family at Nob (1 Sam. 22). This incident must have been disheartening to David. His actions had caused the death of others, and his enemies were determined to destroy him. The structure is: (1) the question of why the wicked boast in evil (vv. 1–4); (2) a proclamation that God will destroy the wicked (vv. 5–7); (3) a vow to praise the Lord (vv. 8, 9).

52:1–4 Boast is related to the word meaning "praise"; however, boasting in evil is no more than a perversion of praise. **Mighty** is likely used here sarcastically; the only Mighty One is the Lord. **The goodness of God** is His "loyal love." The contrast is between a wicked man who boasts in evil and the Lord who is constant in His supreme character. **Your tongue** refers to more than just words. These people used language as a weapon, for they believed that the gods could empower their words to a devastating effect.

52:5–7 God shall destroy you forever: The poet uses the strongest terms to describe divine judgment on those who practice evil. **Uproot you from the land of the living** refers to death, but not eternal death. **The righteous also shall see and fear:** This fear is a deepened respect for God and a sense of awe before His throne. **Here is the man:** The righteous laugh at the wicked because of their foolishness. A reference to *man* often means man in his strength; but this "man" has no real strength at all. He seeks strength in himself instead of seeking the source of all strength, the Almighty.

52:8, 9 A green olive tree is a symbol of beauty. In Rom. 11, the olive tree is used as a symbol of the Gentiles who are grafted into the root, the people of God or the church. The Hebrew word for **mercy** is the same term, meaning "loyal love," that is translated "goodness" in v. 1. The Hebrew word for **praise** is the same word sometimes translated "give thanks" (105:1); it typically refers to vocal and public praise.

Psalm 53 is a recasting of Ps. 14 with only slight differences, particularly in the ending. Its structure is as follows: (1) an announcement of the judgment of the fool (v. 1); (2) the Lord's examination of people (v. 2, 3); (3) the judgment of the Lord (vv. 4, 5); (4) a prayer for the salvation of Israel (v. 6).

53:1 In the Bible, the term **fool** does not mean mental incompetence, but moral and spiritual insensitivity. The fool is the one who ignores God.

53:2–6 God has scattered the bones: This is a prophetic pronouncement of the final judgment on the wicked. Those who did not fear God will be filled with **great fear,** for God will come in His glory and power. One day there will be no more wickedness to contaminate the earth or to compromise the people of God.

Psalm 54 is a psalm of lament in which the answer to the prayer is declared before the end of the poem. The prayer's answer may have come through a priest or prophet. The psalmist

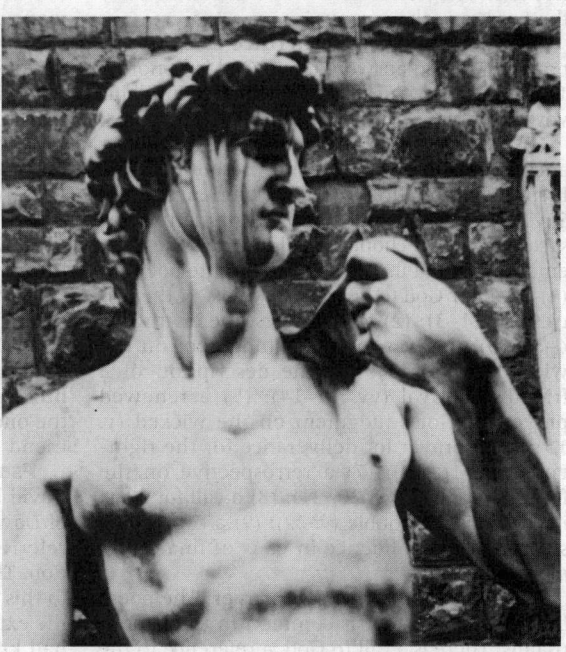

Statue of David, beloved king of Judah, who poured out his heart to God in sincere repentance and a plea for forgiveness in Psalm 51.

knew that he was being answered, and he sought immediately to make God's goodness known. Psalm 54 is another of David's psalms in which the title indicates the specific situation that gave rise to the poem (Pss. 51; 52). Twice the people of the Wilderness of Ziph had informed Saul that David was hiding in their region (1 Sam. 23:19–23; 26:1–3). David's distress is understandable; yet from the Ziphites' viewpoint, their actions were warranted. After all, Saul was the king and David was a fugitive. The structure of the poem is as follows: (1) a call for God's help in the midst of persecution from many foes (Ps. 54:1–3); (2) a declaration that God is David's Helper (vv. 4, 5); (3) a vow of praise (vv. 6, 7).

54:1–3 Save me, O God, by Your name: The poets of the Bible knew the significance of God's name even when they did not use it. The people of Ziph probably are indicated by the words **strangers** and **oppressors.** David makes the point that they are not pious people. Since he is God's servant, he expects that God will deliver him.

54:4, 5 Helper could also be translated "power." The Lord was David's strength in his time of need. **Cut them off** is David's curse on his enemies, an imprecation. Even so, David did not take vengeance into his own hands. Only the Lord can take revenge.

54:6, 7 I will freely sacrifice to You: The prayer has been answered, and God is honored. Thus David expresses his willingness to fulfill his vow.

Psalm 55 deals with life and death, deliverance from hell, and the abiding presence of God. It speaks prophetically of the experience of the Savior Jesus. This psalm consists of many short sections, and its choppy quality shows the deep emotion behind it. The structure of the poem is: (1) a call for God to hear in the midst of the distress (vv. 1–3); (2) a wish to escape death (vv. 4–8); (3) a prayer for God's judgment on the wicked (vv. 9–11); (4) the description of a friend's betrayal (vv. 12–14); (5) a renewed prayer for God's judgment on the wicked (v. 15); (6) a prayer for deliverance for the righteous (vv. 16–19); (7) a retrospective on the friend's betrayal (vv. 20, 21); (8) a call for hope in the midst of trouble (v. 22); (9) a concluding statement of confidence in view of final judgment (v. 23).

55:1–3 Give ear to my prayer: The poem begins in a way that is common in the lament psalms. There is a call to God, a reference to the psalmist's distress, and a notice concerning his enemy. David's shock is not that he is in distress again or even that he has more enemies. The great shock is that the enemy is his own friend (vv. 12–14).

55:4–8 David's intense pain can be felt in his strong language. The phrase **terrors of death** is unusual. The Hebrew word for *terror* or "dread" is first used in Scripture to describe the horror that Abraham felt in the unnatural darkness that seized him as God was about to come

near (Gen. 15:12). The word also described the horrors that would fall on the people of Canaan when the Lord gave the land to the Israelites (Ex. 15:16). To strengthen this feeling, David speaks of a "trembling fear" and an overwhelming **horror** (Ezek. 7:18).

55:9 David calls for God's judgment on the wicked; he renews this call in vv. 15, 23.

55:10–14 Here is the reason for David's terrible pain in this psalm. It was not an ordinary enemy who had risen up against him; it was his **companion,** his confidant and friend. The one who betrayed him was not only a close friend, but a person with whom David had worshiped the Lord.

55:15 In rage, David cries: **Let death seize them.** His words are directed against the wicked generally, and not personally against the one who had distressed David (vv. 13, 14). David could express his emotions to God in prayer, but judgment or revenge was in God's hands (Rom. 12:19).

55:16–19 The words **as for me** mark a dramatic turning point in the psalm. David reverts to a stance of faith; He declares his trust in the omnipotent Lord. **God will hear:** David reminds himself of the great acts of deliverance that God has done on his behalf in the past and the work that God will continue to do in the future. In a similar way, we should also remind ourselves of God's faithfulness in times of distress.

55:20 He has put forth his hands: David turns to describe of his former friend, now his enemy (vv. 13, 14). He had been completely taken in by the man's lies.

55:21–23 To anyone who has experienced grief or desolation, the command to **cast** one's **burden on the Lord** is refreshing. The Lord is the one constant in life (v. 19) and the one true friend (27:10). He can always bear the burden.

Psalm 56 is a psalm of lament. This poem of David has the same setting as Ps. 34—the flight of David to Achish at Gath. In Ps. 34, Achish is referred to as "Abimelech," his royal designation. The fact that two of David's psalms are tied to this one event demonstrates how devastating the experience was to David. Cut off from all he had known, David tried to find refuge among the Philistines. When they turned on him, he nearly lost his life. He escaped by pretending to be insane (1 Sam. 21:10–15). This psalm was sung in corporate worship, for it is addressed to the "Chief Musician" and is set to the tune "The Silent Dove in Distant Lands." The structure of the poem is: (1) a cry to God who alone is David's help (vv. 1, 2); (2) a confession of trust in God (vv. 3, 4); (3) a description of the work of David's enemies (vv. 5–7); (4) a confession of why David trusts in God during his time of distress (vv. 8–11); (5) a vow to praise the Lord (vv. 12, 13).

56:1 Be merciful to me: David cries out to God because of his overwhelming sense of loss during his time as a fugitive in a foreign land (1 Sam. 21:10–15).

56:2–4 I will trust are words of abiding confidence, even in times of distress. Alternating passages of pain and faith are a characteristic of the lament psalms (Ps. 13). **I will praise His word:** This insert is also found twice in v. 10. The idea of **what can flesh do** is repeated in v. 11 and is developed more fully in 118:6. These words are also an OT basis for the apostle Paul's confidence expressed in Rom. 8:31.

56:5 All day they twist my words: In lament psalms, the poet typically complains about lies, the misuse of language, and deceitful speech (Ps. 12).

56:6–11 You number my wanderings: The psalmist is confident that God has a particular interest in his every pain, even his every tear. He also knows the great truth that comes from the meaning of God's name, that the Lord is *for* us. See 118:6, 7 for a further development of this idea. **I will praise His word:** The double insert of this shout of praise shows the psalmist's great enthusiasm for the praise of God. **In God:** The poet repeats the words of v. 4 as a refrain of confidence.

56:12, 13 Vows made to You: The poet takes very seriously His determination to praise the Lord. **You have delivered my soul:** Here is the psalmist's report of deliverance. In the congregation of believing people, David rejoices in the Lord.

Psalm 57 is another of David's poems in which the title gives the specific setting of the psalm. The narrative of David's life indicates that he twice hid in caves—once in Adullam (1 Sam. 22:1–5) which was the setting of Ps. 142, and once in En Gedi (1 Sam. 24:1–7), the setting of this poem. In En Gedi, David spared Saul's life even though Saul had become an easy target. While pursuing David, the king had entered a cave to relieve himself. It so happened that he chose the very cave in which David was hiding. Rather than killing Saul while he had the chance, David cut off a piece of the king's garment. David later repented even of that act against Saul. This psalm is one of four that were set to the tune "Do Not Destroy" (Pss. 58; 59; 75). The structure of the poem is as follows: (1) a call for mercy in the midst of calamities (vv.

⚒ **IN DEPTH**   **Lessons in Music**

The Book of Psalms is the hymnal of ancient Israel. The psalms are ancient lyrics preserved with occasional musical notations. Most of these musical notations are found in the superscriptions or titles. For instance, many are directed "To the Chief Musician" (Pss. 51–62). Others call for musical accompaniment. For example, Ps. 4 calls for stringed instruments, Ps. 5 for flutes, Ps. 6 for the eight-stringed harp, and Ps. 8 for the instrument of Gath. The titles sometimes specify the tune to be used, such as "Death of the Son" in Ps. 9 and "The Lilies" in Ps. 45. In this way the superscriptions contain hints of the musical nature of the psalms.

The psalms present a balanced picture of the use of music in worship. In particular, the first three verses of Ps. 33 are instructive. As v. 1 suggests, the purpose of godly music is to rejoice in the God who has given us new life. As the psalmist notes with his directive to the "righteous," this type of praise can come only from those who have been cleansed by God's grace and renewed by His Spirit. Indeed the psalmist describes this praise from the righteous as "beautiful," for God enjoys receiving praise from His people. For this reason, worshipful music is always directed "to Him" (vv. 2, 3). That is, God is always the audience for the music performed in His name.

What kind of music can we present to God? The psalmist describes a variety of instruments, such as the harp and the instrument of ten strings, that join the human voice in giving praise to the Lord. But his exhortation to sing "a new song" (v. 3) is not merely a call for new music and new hymnals. The phrase new song means to sing to God with a renewed sense of wonder at all He has done for us. The worship of God should never degenerate into something that we just do; we should always approach God with rejoicing. With the phrase play skillfully (v. 3), the psalmist exhorts us never to approach our worship with a casual attitude. We are to "play skillfully" because we are playing to the Lord, and we must offer Him only our best. But skill is not the only criterion of worship music, for the psalmist's final exhortation in v. 3 is to play "with a shout of joy." Since God always considers our attitudes, genuine joy in the presence of our caring Lord is required for music to be truly worshipful.

1–3); (2) a confession of trust in the midst of trouble (vv. 4–6); (3) a determination to praise God in the midst of the people (vv. 7–11).

57:1–3 The opening cry **be merciful to me** is similar to many in the lament psalms, but here it is followed immediately by a confession of trust in the Lord. **in the shadow:** The picture of hiding under the wings of a mother bird is a familiar theme in the Psalms (91:1–4). Here the psalmist vows that he will pray only to his God, for God alone can deliver him from trouble. The Hebrew word for **performs** is translated "will perfect" in 138:8; the point is that God acts on behalf of His servant.

57:4–6 The psalmist's foes are like **lions** prowling about for prey. **Be exalted:** In the midst of his distress, the psalmist shouts his praise to God (v. 11). One of the ways in which God exalts Himself is by graciously delivering the needy. **They have prepared a net:** The psalmist is like a bird that is easily caught; yet by God's mercy, his enemies will fall into their own pit.

57:7 Near the end of his life, Paul was able to say that he had kept the faith (2 Tim. 4:7). With the words **my heart is steadfast,** David is assuring God of much the same thing: he has remained faithful to the God who has provided for Him from the beginning.

57:8–11 I will praise You: As is common in the Psalms, the conclusion is a vow to praise the Lord. Such praise would be centered on the Lord's saving acts. In this poem, the praise of the Lord revolves around His **mercy** and **truth** (86:15). The words of v. 11 serve as a refrain, a repetition of the words of praise in v. 5.

Psalm 58, an imprecatory psalm, might have been provoked by a very strong attack on David. This is one of the four psalms set to the tune "Do Not Destroy" (Pss. 57; 59; 75). It has four parts: (1) a description of wicked judges who wreak havoc on the earth (vv. 1, 2); (2) a description of the wicked who continue in evil (vv. 3–5); (3) a prayer for divine vengeance against the wicked (vv. 6–9); (4) a promise that the righteous will be vindicated (vv. 10, 11).

58:1, 2 You silent ones is a derisive term for the wicked judges. Although they were merely humans, they were behaving as though they had divine power. **wickedness . . . violence:** Instead of establishing righteousness, these wicked judges were producing havoc. They thought they had all power **in the earth.** But they would soon learn that God "judges in the earth" (v. 11).

58:3–5 The effects of the wicked in powerful places are as deadly as the effects of poisonous snakes that are out of control. The word **charmers** refers to those who have the ability to "control" the behavior of snakes; but in this

case, not even the equivalent of charmers could control the destruction and evil that resulted from wicked people in high places.

58:6, 7 In 57:4, the wicked are described as having powerful **teeth,** as though they were carnivores, eating the righteous alive. Here David asks God to shatter their teeth, symbolizing the destruction of the power of the wicked over the poor and defenseless (3:7).

58:8 The ancient Israelites desired children so much that a live birth was considered extremely precious. Alternatively a **stillborn child** would cause great sorrow.

58:9 In this verse, David speaks of the certainty of divine judgment. **Before your pots can feel:** It takes some time for a pot to boil. But the judgment of God will come suddenly—even before a pot would feel the heat. **as with a whirlwind:** The image speaks of sudden destruction. **As in His living and burning wrath** may also be translated "As He lives, so real is His anger."

58:10 The destruction of the wicked brings sadness at the thought of the waste of human dreams, lives, and hopes. But there is great joy for **the righteous** in the recognition that the Savior King has won the victory (Rev. 19:11–21). There is also joy in knowing that wickedness will no longer anger the Lord of the universe (68:3). Justice will be established forever.

58:11 a reward for the righteous: See 1 Cor. 3:11–15 for further development of this theme. **in the earth:** This is the fitting arena of divine judgment, for the wicked judges thought they possessed all authority on earth (v. 2).

Psalm 59, a psalm of lament, contains strong assurance of the final judgment of the wicked. The superscription refers to the story found in 1 Sam. 19:9–17: David escaped Saul's anger with help from his wife Michal. She showed unusual heroism and great devotion to David—actions that resulted in a strained relationship with her father Saul. Psalm 59 has four parts: (1) a prayer for deliverance (vv. 1–5); (2) a confident hope (vv. 6–10); (3) a renewed prayer for deliverance (vv. 11–13); (4) a renewed hope (vv. 14–17).

59:1, 2 The repetition of the phrase **deliver me** is for emphasis, meaning "to bring one out" of trouble and distress. The verb translated **defend** means "to set on high" or "to place out of reach of trouble" (91:14). **Save me:** This is the most common of the Hebrew verbs for salvation. It suggests "to give room to" or "to expand an area to breathe."

59:3, 4 they lie in wait: Enemies become like wild animals on the hunt or enemy soldiers lurking along one's paths. **Not for my transgression:** There were times in David's life when he knew that he was suffering because of sin in his life (Ps. 32). There were other times when he believed himself to be innocent of sin, but still he was hounded by wicked persons. Here he shouts his protest aloud: **through no fault of mine.** He was guilty of no wickedness that would cause such merciless attacks on him.

59:5 David's call for the Lord to **awake** is another way of asking God to pay attention to his plight (7:6; 35:23; 44:23; Is. 51:9). To ensure God's reception of his bold shout, David uses the "full name" of God: **LORD** God of hosts, the God of Israel. The Commander of the armies of angels is also the Protector of His people. **Do not be merciful:** The righteous constantly experience the mercy of the Lord, but His mercy is not extended to those who constantly oppose Him. The **wicked transgressors** were those who engaged in constant acts of treachery.

59:6, 7 A dog in the ancient Hebrew culture was considered a semi-wild scavenger, not the beloved pet of our own day. **Who hears:** Like those described in Pss. 9; 10, the wicked here believe that they will face no punishment for their evil. They are profoundly mistaken (75:7, 10; 92:6).

59:8 But You: This is a complete turnaround in the psalm—from thoughts about the wicked to an acknowledgment of the reality of God in human affairs. **shall laugh . . . in derision:** The wording is the same as in 2:4 (Job 9:23; Prov. 1:26). There is the pleasurable laughter of God in joy with His people (147:11; Zeph. 3:17). But this is the laughter of contempt.

59:9 Wait can also mean "watch." The enemies of David had come to watch for him; but David was determined to "watch" for God. **His Strength** may also be translated "My Strength" or "O My Strong One." The noun **my defense** means "a high place of refuge" and is related to the verb in v. 1. The same word is used again in vv. 16, 17 (62:2).

59:10 My God of mercy: The term *mercy* is sometimes translated "loyal love" (13:5). The Lord is the "God of my loyal love."

59:11 This verse begins the second round of the petition in the psalm. The imprecation or curse in this verse is unusual. Instead of asking for the destruction of the wicked, the psalmist asks for them to be scattered, to be made fugitives. This would be a constant reminder of the consequences of evil.

59:12, 13 The repetition of this verbal phrase **consume them** is similar to the repeti-

tion of the phrase *deliver me* in vv. 1, 2. **that God rules in Jacob:** The idea is similar to 58:11.

59:14–17 But I: The words of these verses capture the positive thrust of this psalm. David sings with joyful abandon of his relationship with God, despite the presence of wicked persons. There are two verbs translated **I will sing;** together they capture the idea that singing in the name of the Lord is a wonderful act of faith (Ex. 15:2).

59:17 You, O my Strength is repeated from v. 9. In God, the believer finds strength, **defense,** and **mercy.** This psalm ends in a grand manner with bold faith in the living God.

Psalm 60, a psalm of community lament (Ps. 80), expresses David's great faith in the eventual victory he would find in the Lord. In this psalm, we hear the voice of God breaking into the poem itself and pronouncing His judgment on David's enemies (vv. 6–8; Pss. 12; 75; 87; 91). Since the tone of the psalm is military in nature, it is possible that this poem was used in military training. Along with training in weapons and tactics, David gave ongoing instruction to his soldiers about how to trust their Lord. See 144:1; 149:6 for further examples of psalms in military training. The heading and content of this psalm add additional information to the account in 2 Sam. 8:3–8. The campaign of David and his general Joab against Hadadezer, the king of Zobah, did not succeed at first. This psalm describes the feelings of David and his army at the time of their defeat. But it also records their confident expectation that they would eventually succeed, something celebrated in the heading of the psalm and confirmed in 2 Sam. 8. The psalm has four movements: (1) a lament of the people when they experienced defeat (vv. 1–3); (2) an expression of confidence and a prayer for deliverance (vv. 4, 5); (3) the voice of God giving assurance of ultimate victory (vv. 6–8); (4) an expression of confidence in the Lord (vv. 9–12).

60:1–3 David accuses God of having **broken** them **down.** This is a poetic description of an otherwise unknown defeat of the armies of Israel in a battle that was part of the campaign against Aram of Zobah and Mesopotamian allies (2 Sam. 8). The defeat was so startling that it caused the people of Israel to feel as though God had **made the earth tremble,** a metaphor for devastation. **wine of confusion:** The defeat sent the people reeling; they could not understand how it could have happened.

60:4, 5 a banner: Despite the recent defeat,

> ## The Commander of the armies of angels is also the Protector of His people.

the people still had reason to hope in a final victory for Israel over its foes. The term **beloved** (127:2; Is. 5:1; Jer. 11:15) is particularly endearing. God had a reason to act on behalf of His people: He loved them.

60:6–9 At this point in the poem, God speaks (75:2–5, 10; 91:14–16). The Lord affirms that He is in charge, that the land belongs to Him, and that He will give victory to His people. **In His holiness** can also mean "in His holy place." **I will rejoice:** It gives God pleasure to grant His people success. **Shechem** and **the Valley of Succoth** represent regions west and east of the Jordan River in the central parts of the land. **Gilead** and **Manasseh** are also regions east and west of the Jordan; **Ephraim** and **Judah** are regions in the north and south. The Lord was asserting His sovereignty over the entire land of Israel. **Moab . . . Edom . . . Philistia:** These traditional enemies of Israel were also enemies of God. The Lord would not allow them to disturb His people.

60:10 Is it not You: The very One the people thought had **cast** them **off** (v. 1) would lead them to final victory.

60:11, 12 Ultimately, true **help**—the Hebrew word means "salvation"—comes only from God. **we will do valiantly:** As the title records, this was what happened. David's general Joab led the battle, and under God's hand Israel's enemies were soundly defeated. This psalm presents a strong encouragement to all believers who are presently experiencing difficulties in their lives: When **the help of man** proves **useless,** often God dramatically provides strength and power so that our boast is solely in Him.

Psalm 61, a royal psalm attributed to David, has elements of lament (Ps. 13) and trust (Ps. 23). In this psalm, the king of Israel points to the great King who is to come. The title includes the words "On a stringed instrument" (see the titles of Pss. 4; 6; 54; 55; 67; 76). The psalm has four parts: (1) a petition to God (vv. 1, 2); (2) an affirmation that God is David's refuge (vv. 3, 4); (3) an affirmation that God provides (vv. 5–7); (4) a vow to praise God (v. 8).

61:1 Hear my cry is classic language of a lament psalm. David calls on the Lord to hear the prayer of the troubled believer (5:2, 3; 17:1; 55:2; 66:19; 86:6; 142:6).

61:2 From the end of the earth: David describes his sense of being far from God's presence in his time of need. His prayer is that he might be brought back to **the rock that is higher** than he. The imagery of God as a Rock for the believer was introduced by Moses (Deut. 2:4) and is developed elsewhere in the Psalms (62:2; 71:3; 91:1, 2; 144:1).

61:3 The idea of God as one's **shelter** or

refuge is seen in a number of passages in the Psalms (14:6; 46:1; 62:7, 8; 71:7; 91:2, 9; 94:22; 142:5). Such verses present the psalmist's strong affirmation of the protection and deliverance to be found in God.

61:4 I will abide implies strong determination. It is used of a worshiper in God's house in 15:1. Elsewhere, the psalmist compares himself to (1) an everlasting guest in the tent of the Lord (Ps. 15) and (2) a chick who has complete **trust** under its mother's wings (63:7; 91:4).

61:5 The pronoun **You** is emphasized in this verse as David celebrates the work of God in his life and in the life of his people. **the heritage:** God had given the nation to David for him to rule responsibly. These words also refer to the greater reality of the Savior King who would receive the nations as His inheritance to rule forever. **who fear Your name:** This is standard language describing biblical piety. To *fear* is to hold the name of God in awe and wonder, in worship and obedience (147:11; Ex. 20:20).

61:6, 7 The terms **many generations** and **forever** refer to David's long rule but more literally prophesy the eternal rule of Jesus, the King of kings. **Mercy and truth** together mean "loving loyalty" (see John 1:14 for an equivalent expression: "grace and truth"). Psalm 23 presents the believer pursued by God's "goodness and mercy" (23:6); but here the king is guarded by God's loving loyalty.

61:8 My vows refers to the vows of praise to God mentioned in v. 5 (22:22–26; 66:13; 76:11).

Psalm 62 is a wisdom psalm that eloquently urges silent confidence in the victory of God over all enemies because salvation is found only in Him. Jeduthun in the superscription was the chief of one of the choirs in the temple (1 Chr. 9:16) whose descendants founded a temple choir (1 Chr. 16:41, 42). The superscription "To Jeduthun" is also found in Pss. 39; 77. This psalm consists of seven brief sections: (1) a statement of confidence in God (vv. 1, 2); (2) a direct challenge to the wicked (v. 3); (3) a description of the ways of the wicked (v. 4); (4) a renewed statement of confidence in God (vv. 5–7); (5) a direct challenge to the righteous (v. 8); (6) a further description and warning of the ways of the wicked (vv. 9, 10); (7) a final statement of confidence in God (vv. 11, 12).

62:1, 2 In these two verses, David declares his complete dependence on God. **silently waits:** David expresses silent resignation before the sovereign will of the living God. **My defense** is from the word also used in 59:9, 16, 17. **not be greatly moved:** See the development of David's confidence in God in the wording of v. 6.

62:3 How long: David addresses his tor-

| 🌱 IN LIFE | **The Shadow of God's Wings** |

One of David's favorite symbolic expressions was the word-picture of sitting in the shadow of God's wings (Ps. 63:7; compare 17:8; 36:7; 57:1; 61:4; and 91:4). The wings of a bird were a symbol of protection, defense, and refuge. For example, faced with a forest or range fire, a mother grouse or prairie chicken would gather her chicks together under her wings, settle down, and let the flames sweep over her. If necessary, she would die in order to save them. After the fire, the chicks would crawl out from under their mother's burnt body. They enjoyed life and safety because of her sacrificial devotion.

In a similar way, David was shielded from numerous attempts on his life, especially by King Saul and later by his own son Absalom. David knew by experience what it meant to have nothing standing between him and death but the gracious protection of God.

The Lord still offers the same refuge and protection today. For one thing, having voluntarily died on the Cross for our sins, He can deliver us from the penalty of sin (Rom. 5:6–10). Furthermore, He watches over His children with diligent care (Heb. 13:5–6; 1 Pet. 5:7). Thus we can rely on a God who loves us and acts on our behalf when we cannot help ourselves.

---

mentors directly, expecting that they will soon be judged. **attack:** The word means to threaten or shout at someone.

62:4, 5 wait silently: A different Hebrew word is used here, but the concept of v. 1 is restated. **My expectation** may also be translated "hope" (71:5).

62:6, 7 Verse 6 is a restatement of v. 2, but strengthened by dropping the word *greatly.* Verse 7 restates v. 6. **My salvation and my glory** may be rephrased "my glorious salvation."

62:8–10 Trust: David addresses the righteous (contrast v. 3) with his lesson of reliance on God (40:3). What is true for David (v. 7) is extended to all in the believing community.

62:11 once, Twice: It is a convention of wisdom literature to use a number and then raise it by one (Prov. 30:11–33). The point here is that David has heard the message with certainty.

62:12 Mercy can be translated "loyal love," the covenantal love of the Lord (13:5). **to each one:** God is the true Judge; He will repay and reward every person (Eccl. 12:13, 14).

Psalm 63 is a royal psalm with elements of the psalms of trust (Ps. 23). The brief biographical note in the title "when he was in the wilderness of Judah" possibly refers to an incident during the period when Saul was chasing David (1 Sam. 22–24). The pattern of the psalm is as follows: (1) a search for a renewed sense of God's presence (vv. 1, 2); (2) a confession of David's faith in God (vv. 3–5); (3) an expression of confidence in the Lord even during the lonely night watches (vv. 6–8); (4) a prediction of the end of David's enemies (vv. 9, 10); (5) a renewal of David's confession of trust in God the great King (v. 11).

63:1, 2 O God, my God: The opening words indicate faith in God, but they also suggest a time of trouble (22:1). **thirsts . . . longs:** The poet is away from the place of God's worship and feels the distance keenly (42:1, 2). **The sanctuary** had been at Nob (1 Sam. 21:1), and it was there that David had sought the presence of the Lord. Later it was moved to Jerusalem (76:1, 2).

63:3–5 The psalmist expresses his joy in knowing God and his determination to continue praising God throughout his life. **Lovingkindness** may also be translated "loyal love" (13:5). **Praise** is a vocal, public act in the Psalms (Heb. 13:15). **bless . . . hands:** Praise (the meaning of *bless* here) and raising the hands in worship are often associated in the Psalms (134:2). To lift the hands to the Lord expresses dependence on Him, coupled with an acknowledgment of His power, wonder, and majesty (77:2). **be satisfied . . . with joyful lips:** In coming to the Lord in praise, the poet finds the refreshment he has sought (v. 1).

63:6 From his **bed,** David continues to fix his thoughts on God (77:6). **night watches:** The Israelites counted three watches to the night. Evidently David is having difficulty sleeping, and he directs his thoughts to worship. **Meditate** means "to speak" about the things of God or to fill one's mind with the knowledge of God (1:2; 77:12).

63:7, 8 in the shadow of Your wings: See 91:4 for this expression of faith in God. **Your right hand:** The same power of God that delivered Israel from Egypt (Ex. 15:6) would support David—and all other believers in their daily life (74:11).

63:9, 10 David predicts the destruction of

his enemies. They will be driven to barren places where only **jackals,** wild dogs of the desert, roam.

63:11 The king refers to David. When he finally became king, David would find his true pleasure in God. **Everyone who swears by Him** refers to those who believe in the Lord.

Psalm 64 has elements of lament (Ps. 13) and imprecation (Ps. 137), but it appears to be basically a wisdom psalm. It contrasts the righteous and the wicked, compares their destinies, and is itself a "meditation" (v. 1). The structure of the poem is: (1) an appeal for protection from the wicked (vv. 1, 2); (2) a description of the evil activities of the wicked (vv. 3–6); (3) an expectation of the defeat of the wicked by God (vv. 7–9); (4) a description of the joy of the righteous (v. 10).

64:1 The initial cry of the psalmist expressed with the verbs **hear** and **preserve** resembles the psalms of lament (Ps. 13), but the term **my meditation** suggests that this is a wisdom psalm. This observation is confirmed in the rest of the psalm, which contrasts the destiny of the wicked with that of the righteous, a theme of wisdom psalms. In other passages the term *meditation* has the idea of "complaint" (55:2; 102:2; 142:2). But in this psalm the word indicates contemplation, for David contemplated the wicked and their end (73:17).

64:2–6 The arrogance of the wicked in their plots against the righteous is a continuing theme in the Psalms (Pss. 9; 10; 12). **Who will see:** The wicked do not know, or do not care, that there is One who sees (73:11), and who will repay (75:7).

64:7–10 The joy of confident **trust** in God cannot be overstated. By placing our problems into God's hands, we can rest in His sovereign will for our lives. Concerns about the future can be cast aside, for the Lord controls our future and has good plans for us (Rom. 8:28). **All the upright in heart** is another designation for **the righteous** or "the blameless" (v. 4). Their **glory** is their exuberant praise to God (63:11).

Psalm 65 is a wisdom psalm and more particularly a creation psalm (as Ps. 19). It celebrates rainfall, sharing the mood of Ps. 104 in this regard. But this is also a prophetic psalm, although it is not always recognized as such. The prophetic element is signaled in the first verse, the vow of praise yet to be paid—that is, all creation is waiting to praise the Lord when He finally appears in glory (Rom. 14:10, 11; Rev. 19:5). The psalm has five movements: (1) a vow of praise yet to be performed (vv. 1–3); (2) a blessing pronounced on the redeemed (v. 4); (3) a celebration of God's power that extends throughout the earth (vv. 5–8); (4) a celebration of God's provision of rain (vv. 9, 10); (5) a cele-

bration of God's coming blessings in the year of His goodness (vv. 11–13).

65:1 Praise is awaiting You: There is still a vow of praise to be performed (v. 3). In the background of this psalm is an idea not far from that of Paul in Rom. 8:22, the groaning of creation for its release from the curse brought on it by humanity's fall (Gen. 3:17). The point of the psalm is twofold: (1) Every good rain and every full harvest is a blessing from God, showing His delight in His creation. (2) A day of God's goodness is coming in which good rains and harvests will be greater than ever before.

65:2, 3 atonement: David speaks of a coming day when sin will be dealt with fully, when redemption will be completely paid. This took place in the death and resurrection of Jesus Christ (Eph. 1:7).

65:4 shall be satisfied: In other psalms, David expresses his desire to live in the presence of God (27:4, 5). The fulfillment of this desire in David's day came through the sacrificial services of worship in Israel.

65:5–8 The **awesome** power of God at creation in the beginning (Job 26) will one day be seen anew in the restoration of all things. **noise of the seas:** God's power over the "dark powers" of the seas is a regular theme in the royal psalms (Ps. 93).

65:9, 10 You visit the earth: Rainfall is seen here as a gracious visitation of God. This is in keeping with the provisions of God's covenant with Israel (Deut. 28:12). These words have some fulfillment every time the rains bring productivity to the earth.

65:11–13 Your paths: The picture is of wagon tracks across the heavens, where the "cart" of God's mercies sloshes abundance on the earth below. **they also sing:** The "singers" here are the pastures and the valleys. The coming of God's kingdom to earth will be a magnificent time of productivity (67:6). This is the vow that remains to be performed (v. 1).

Psalm 66, a psalm of praise, offers significant contributions to our understanding of the values of biblical worship. In the course of the psalm, the poet offers *descriptive praise*, praising God for who He is and what He does, as well as *declarative praise*, praising God for specific answers to prayer. The structure of the psalm is as follows: (1) a call for all the earth to join in the celebratory worship of God (vv. 1–4); (2) an enumeration of reasons to worship God (vv. 5–7); (3) a call for the peoples to join the psalmist in descriptive praise of God (vv. 8–12); (4) the psalmist's decision to participate in holy worship (vv. 13–15); (5) declarative praise of God (vv. 16–19); (6) a final blessing of the Lord (v. 20).

66:1, 2 As in 100:1, the call is not only for

the people of Israel, but for peoples of **all the earth** to join in the praise of the living God, the Most High (Pss. 87; 96; 117). **Sing out the honor of His name:** The Lord is pleased with music that praises His glorious name (Ex. 15:2). The Lord's name describes His character, so honoring God's name is honoring God Himself (Ex. 3:14, 15).

66:3, 4 How awesome: The **works** of God are designed to bring a sense of awe to people (19:1, 2). In this context, **submit** means "to cringe" before God. The term translated **worship** means "to kneel" or "to bow down." The opening verses of this psalm present a call and an expectation that one day all the earth will worship God, with a particular focus on the glory of God's name.

66:5–9 To **bless** God is to identify Him as the source of our blessing (103:1, 2). **you peoples:** The call is to all the nations of the earth (vv. 1, 4, 5). God's preservation of His people is one of many reasons to bless Him.

66:10–15 Your house refers to the temple in Jerusalem where God lived among His people. During periods of distress in his life, the poet made **vows** that when God brought him out of distress, he would publicly acknowledge God's deliverance (40:1–3; 61:5, 8; 76:11). Each of the **sacrifices** would be accompanied by the heart attitude of the true worshiper (John 4:23, 24). The psalmist speaks very personally of his intent to bring abundant sacrifices in his worship of God.

66:16–19 You who fear God refers to those who respond in awe and wonder to the Lord (v. 4). **iniquity:** Among the things that can block effective prayer is ongoing sin in a believer's life (Ps. 32). But the psalmist here confesses that God **has heard.** The psalmist appeals to the "peoples" in vv. 8, 9; he calls out to believers in vv. 16–19.

66:20 The concluding words of the poem are an affirmation of the psalmist's blessing of the Lord (v. 8) based on his realization of God's continuing goodness in his life.

Psalm 67, a psalm of praise, serves as a marvelous invocation and doxology in worship. The poem calls the nations of the world to praise God, to join Israel in honoring the Creator. There is: (1) a call for God's blessing for the purpose of world evangelization (vv. 1, 2); (2) a call for the nations to bless the Lord in view of His righteous judgments (vv. 3, 4); (3) a call for the nations to bless the Lord in view of His coming kingdom (vv. 5–7).

67:1, 2 cause His face to shine: In the language of the Aaronic benediction (Num. 6:24–26), the psalmist calls for God to smile on His people (Ps. 80). From the beginning, God had intended to bring His blessing to **all nations,** in fulfillment of the provisions of the Abrahamic covenant (Gen. 12:3). This passage anticipates the thrust of world mission that is found in the NT (Matt. 28:18–20; Acts 1:8). The point in this psalm is clear: May God bless His people Israel in such a manner that the message

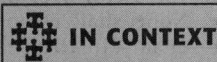 **IN CONTEXT** ## Blessings to Africa

With the relocation of the ark of the covenant to Jerusalem—the occasion for which Psalm 68 may have been composed—the Israelites must have felt that they were finally coming into their own as God's people. They were settled in the Promised Land. They were led by a good and righteous king. The Lord was their God, and His presence was assured as the holy ark was brought to Zion.

But in the midst of the celebration, David reminded his people that God's blessings would eventually extend far beyond Israel and its immediate circumstances. Nations throughout the world would learn about the Lord and come to worship Him (Ps. 68:32). These would include even such warlike peoples as the Egyptians and Ethiopians (68:31; 2 Chr. 14:12) who, during the days of the Israelite monarchy, were vying for power.

The promise of Psalm 68 was at least partially fulfilled in the first century A.D. when the treasurer of Candace, queen of Ethiopia, came to Jerusalem. After worshiping during the feast of Pentecost, he started out on his way home when he met a Christian named Philip. Philip explained to him the way of salvation in Christ, and the treasurer believed and was baptized as a Christian (Acts 8:26–40).

In this way, the message of Jesus reached into Africa. In fact, many modern-day Christians in Ethiopia view the treasurer's conversion as the beginning of their spiritual heritage. Through him, they feel directly linked to David, who foresaw the day when Ethiopians would "stretch out{their} hands to God."

of God's way would become known throughout the earth.

67:3, 4 Let the peoples praise You: God's desire is for all people to praise Him, for He is their Creator and their Provider (2 Pet. 3:9). This should also be the desire of God's people.

67:5–7 yield her increase: As in the prophetic aspect of Ps. 65, the coming of God's kingdom on earth will be marked by a magnificent increase in production. The curse on the land (Gen. 3:17–19; Rom. 8:22) will be lifted in "the year of God's goodness" (65:11).

Psalm 68 is based in part on the Song of Deborah in Judg. 5. It speaks with great power of the glory of God. The first and last verses of the psalm (vv. 1, 35) capture its essence. The title refers to it as both a "Psalm" and a "Song," indicating its musical nature. The structure of the psalm is as follows: (1) a call for God to rise in judgment against the wicked (vv. 1–3); (2) a call for the people of God to praise Him for His wonders and mercies (vv. 4–6); (3) a review of the works of God on behalf of His people (vv. 7–14); (4) a celebration of the city of God and His saving works (vv. 15–20); (5) an anticipation of the final victory of God over all His enemies (vv. 21–27); (6) an anticipation of the worship of God by the peoples of the earth (vv. 28–35).

68:1–3 Let God arise . . . flee before Him: The presence of the wicked on the earth is an assault on God's holiness and a constant threat to the righteous. Only God's mercy compels Him to delay His judgment (75:2). But when God awakes, His enemies will be scattered; they will disappear like **smoke. Let the righteous rejoice exceedingly:** The joy of the righteous will be great when there is an end to all evil (58:10).

68:4 Extol Him who rides on the clouds: A well-known description of Baal was as "the rider of the clouds." Here the title is stripped from the supposed "god" Baal and given to the living God of Scripture. The fact that the Lord is the Rider of the clouds indicates that He is the One who brings rain and controls the powerful forces of a storm (147:8, 9, 15–18). Yah is a shortened form of the divine name Yahweh (Ex. 3:14, 15). There is a significant emphasis on the name of God in this section (122:4; 135:1–3).

68:5 The Lord is not limited to clouds and storms; He also meets the needs of the helpless. For all people, He is **in His holy habitation,** dispensing justice.

68:6–10 The poet describes the work of God on behalf of His people in poetic terms that recall the Exodus events and draw on the Song of Deborah (Judg. 5:4). The language of this section is also an expansion of the description in v. 4; this is the march of God as the true God of the Storm.

68:11 The term translated **word** refers to a command rather than a revelation. The command was that God's works would be made known among the peoples. **Those who proclaimed it** translates a feminine participle. Thus the people who made the proclamation were women, most likely the women who gave praise to God under the direction of Miriam (Ex. 15:20, 21).

68:12–14 The Almighty is the name Shaddai, a title that refers to the majesty and strength of the Lord (91:1). The scattering of **kings** refers to the early battles won by Israel during the wilderness period and at the time of the conquest of the land of Canaan.

68:15, 16 Bashan was a very fertile area northeast of the Sea of Galilee, a part of the former territory of Og. It is possible that the connotation of Bashan as a place of plenty is transferred poetically to Jerusalem in these verses, for it was only in Jerusalem that the Lord had sworn that he would **dwell.**

68:17, 18 When God delivered His people from Egypt, He brought them out with great treasures from the Egyptians (Ex. 12:35, 36). These gifts were used by the people of Israel to build the tabernacle (Ex. 35) **that the Lord** God might dwell there.

68:19, 20 This section is a benediction, a blessing on the Lord, for His **daily** mercies in the lives of the people of faith. **The God of our salvation** is a great title for the One who saved Israel from Egypt, who saved Israel from their sin, who continues to save His people in their daily lives, and who will glorify His people in the future.

68:21, 22 The Lord is the Victor over the **enemies** of His people. None shall escape, whether near—**Bashan**—or far—in **the sea.** Like grapes they will be crushed, and justice will finally be served (58:10)

68:23–28 The **procession** of God could refer to one of three things: (1) carrying the ark of the covenant through the wilderness during the time of the Exodus; (2) God leading as the Commander of His armies in Israel; (3) the grand procession of the Savior King as He comes to establish His reign on earth (Rev. 19:14–21). **Timbrels,** or tambourines, often played by women, were used for both sacred and secular occasions. Associated with dance, they suggested joy (81:2; 149:3; 150:4; Judg. 11:34; 1 Sam. 18:6, 7; 2 Sam. 6:5; Is. 30:32). **The fountain of Israel** is a poetic term for the people as they rise to praise God. **little Benjamin:** The role of Benjamin, one of the smaller tribes, was significant. Saul was from this tribe, and the city of Jerusalem was located within its borders.

68:29, 30 Kings . . . presents: The term *presents* means "gifts offered in homage." Royal guests came to Solomon with gifts (1 Kin. 10:1–10); but the ultimate prophetic fulfillment of this verse was in the kings who came to Jerusalem to bring gifts to the infant Jesus (Matt. 2:1–12). One day all kings will show their obedience and humility before Jesus, the great King (2:10–12; 76:11). Egypt, Assyria, and Canaan may be indicated by the phrases **the beasts of the reeds, the herd of bulls,** and **the calves of the peoples.** The point of these verses seems to be general submission to the royal house in Jerusalem.

68:31–35 The psalm ends with a celebration of the presence of God in the midst of His people. This section looks forward to the reign of Jesus the Savior King (Zeph. 3:14–17). **Him who rides on the heaven of heavens** is a development of the phrase found in v. 4. The Lord's **voice** is the thunder; God is the true God of storm (77:16–20) and Creator of the universe. When all things are considered, there is nothing in the universe that can be compared with God. Thus the poet says **You are more awesome than Your holy places.**

Psalm 69, a psalm of lament, is more specifically a protest of innocence. This highly messianic psalm presents a remarkable description of the suffering of Jesus Christ. Whereas Ps. 22 describes Jesus' physical sufferings, Ps. 69 focuses more on His emotional and spiritual suffering. Yet like Ps. 22, this psalm was written by David approximately a thousand years before the events it describes. Both psalms begin with the sufferings of David but have their full meaning in the sufferings of Jesus. For these reasons, the apostles in the NT acknowledge that David was a prophet of God (Acts 2:30). Its structure is as follows: (1) a cry for deliverance that expresses the psalmist's weariness (vv. 1–3); (2) a description of the psalmist's enemies (v. 4); (3) a lament that expresses the psalmist's sense of alienation (vv. 5–12); (4) a cry for deliverance from the mire (vv. 13–18); (5) a lament that expresses the psalmist's reproach (vv. 19–21); (6) a petition for God to bring His judgment on the wicked (vv. 22–28); (7) a determination to praise the Lord (vv. 29–36).

69:1–3 I sink in deep mire: The opening words of this psalm of anguish use the strong image of a person about to drown—not just in deep waters, but in muck (40:2). This powerfully descriptive language expresses extreme mental anguish. **I am weary:** As a drowning man might exhaust his voice entirely, so David is worn out from praying and crying out to the Lord (6:6).

> *David praised God in exuberant joy when the Lord saved him from the depths of despair.*

69:4 hate me without cause: These words describe David's experience in a difficult period of his life. It seems that his foes are innumerable; but more devastating to him than their number is the fact that he has not caused their attack. Any attack is difficult; an unprovoked attack is intolerable. Yet these words also are prophetic of the sufferings of Jesus (35:19; 109:3–5; John 15:23–25).

69:5–12 zeal for Your house: Like Phinehas in Num. 25, David describes himself as a zealot for the house of the Lord. Jesus' cleansing of the temple was a fulfillment of these words (John 2:17). **When I wept:** Even the piety of David has become a reason for his enemies to chide him. **Those who sit in the gate:** The elders of the cities looked with contempt on David; similarly, many of the elders of Jerusalem held Jesus in disdain.

69:13–19 The words **deliver me out of the mire** tie the psalm together; compare the words of vv. 1–3. **Hear me:** This renewed plea to God is based on the character of the Lord; His lovingkindness or loyal love, and His tender mercies compelled David to keep looking to the Lord for deliverance.

69:20, 21 for my thirst: At one point during Jesus' suffering on the cross, He was offered vinegar to soothe His thirst (Matt. 27:34; Mark 15:23; Luke 23:36; John 19:28–30).

69:22–28 Pour out Your indignation upon them may refer to the Lord's judgment on His foes in this lament over Jerusalem. The words of v. 25 were fulfilled in Judas Iscariot. See Acts 1:20, in which the words of this verse are joined to the words of 109:8.

69:29–36 The phrase **I am poor** refers to a brokenness of spirit and sense of worthlessness caused by the assaults of the wicked. The *poor* in the psalms become a portrait of the Savior, illustrating the magnitude of Jesus' humility (described by Paul in Phil. 2:5–7). **I will praise:** David praised God in exuberant joy when the Lord saved him from the depths of despair. All humble people, especially those who suffer the indignities brought about by the wicked, will join in praise and joy before God their Savior.

Psalm 70, a psalm of lament, is a reprise of 40:13–17. The description of the poor and needy was such a necessary element in the encouragement of people enduring troubles that this section was selected for individual use as a freestanding poem.

70:1, 2 Let them be ashamed and confounded: David prays that those who rejoice in his misery will be proven wrong in their assumption that the Lord is unable to help His people. In this way, the Lord's deliverance of David will result in God's name being glorified—both by the joy of God's people and the shame of His enemies (vv. 3, 4).

70:3–5 The last three words of the psalm **do not delay** indicate the near-desperation of David. The cry echoes David's plea in v. 1 for the Lord to "come quickly" to save him. Even in panic-stricken despair, David does not forget to praise His Lord. He reminds Himself that the Lord is his only source of strength, help, and deliverance.

Psalm 71 is a psalm of lament with a major focus on the psalmist's trust in God. The psalm alternates between expressions of desperate need and resolute trust in the Lord. In this interplay, the psalmist models the way believers should react to suffering. A believer should completely trust the Lord in a difficult situation, but at the same time cry out to Him for deliverance. The poet describes himself as an old man who has trusted in God for a long time (vv. 5, 18). In his great time of need, he asks God to be faithful to His servant. The structure of the psalm is as follows: (1) a confession of the psalmist's resolute trust in God (vv. 1–3); (2) petitions for God to deliver the psalmist from trouble (vv. 4–6); (3) a determination to praise God even in the midst of trouble (vv. 7, 8); (4) petitions for deliverance (vv. 9–11); (5) a call for judgment on the psalmist's enemies (vv. 12, 13); (6) a commitment to trust and praise God (vv. 14–16); (7) a renewal of the psalmist's petitions based on his experience of God's faithfulness (vv. 17, 18); (8) a renewal of trust in God (vv. 19–21); (9) a determination to praise God (vv. 22–24).

71:1 The theme of the psalm is stated in this verse. On the basis of resolute **trust** (61:4; 91:3), the psalmist asks that he **never be put to shame.** Trusting in God is never foolish (4:2; 119:31).

71:2, 3 in Your righteousness: The psalmist is concerned not only with his own plight but with the character of God (vv. 15, 16, 19, 24). The psalmist's point is that God could display His righteousness by answering the needs of the psalmist, whose life had been lived in constant trust in God. **strong refuge:** The Hebrew words mean literally "rock fortress." The Lord is the only source of continual protection for the psalmist.

71:4 The Hebrew root of **deliver me** means "to cause to escape" (17:13; 37:40; 144:2). After asking for deliverance, the poet reasserts his strong faith in God, calling Him his **hope** and his **trust,** the One who has sustained him from his birth (22:10). He prays in faith, not allowing his circumstances to cause him to doubt the goodness of God.

71:5–7 a wonder: The poet declares that the work of God in his life has made him a special sign to the people, similar to the great miracles of God through Moses and Aaron in Egypt (Ex. 7:3; 11:9).

71:8–11 The poet uses familiar images in the psalms of lament (Ps. 13) to encourage God to respond to his need. **in the time of old age:** The psalmist has trusted in God his entire life (v. 6); it would be sad if he were dismissed by the Lord late in life (v. 18). Not only was the psalmist's own life and comfort at stake, but so was the reputation of God. If the enemies concluded that **God has forsaken him,** then the reputation of the Lord would be tarnished in the world.

71:12, 13 do not be far: These words evoke the language of 22:1, 19. **confounded:** The language of this verse is imprecatory (Ps. 137); the poet calls for justice and vengeance

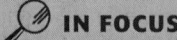 **IN FOCUS**   **"wondrous works"**

(Heb. *pala'*) (71:17; 107:8; 118:23; 119:27) Strong's #6381: The core meaning of this word is "to do something extraordinary." In reference to people, the word is used to describe an action or understanding beyond the normal capacity of humans (Deut. 17:8; 30:11; 2 Sam. 13:2; Prov. 30:18) or beyond normal obligations (Lev. 22:21; 27:2; Num. 6:2; 15:3, 8). However, the highest sense of the word is reserved for God alone, especially in the Psalms in which it occurs most frequently and always in reference to God (72:18; 136:4). God is wonderful in counsel; nothing is too marvelous for Him (Gen. 18:14; Is. 28:29). His wondrous works are cosmic (107:24; Job 37:14), national (Ex. 3:20; Is. 29:14), and personal (31:21; Job 10:16). Not everyone understands them (106:7; 78:32), but the Bible exhorts believers to remember these wonderful works of God and publicly praise Him for them (96:3; 105:2, 5; 1 Chr. 16:9, 12, 24).

against his enemies, for they are in fact enemies of the living God (v. 24).

71:14–16 I will hope: The Hebrew text has an emphatic pronoun meaning "as for me," bringing determination to the poet's words. The Hebrew verb translated *hope* describes a confident expectation that God will intervene and deliver (147:11).

71:17, 18 youth . . . old and grayheaded: The poet has trusted in God all his life. In his old age, he faces a crisis. He fully expects that God in His righteousness (vv. 2, 15, 16, 19, 24) will respond favorably to his request to deliver him and preserve him from shame (v. 1). For his part, the psalmist will continue to praise the Lord.

71:19, 20 The poet speaks of the **great things** that God had done, for which He is worthy of praise. He also speaks of the **great and severe troubles** that he has experienced at God's hand, and from which he seeks relief. **Depths of the earth** is a metaphor for the psalmist's despondency (40:2); he feels as though he has already dropped headlong into a pit.

71:21–23 The poem concludes with a bold vow of praise, in confident expectation that the psalmist's prayer will be answered. The poet praises God with **the lute,** but also with his **lips.** At the same time, his inner being, his **soul,** is filled with praises to the living God.

71:24 brought to shame: The psalm comes full circle with the word *shame*. The poet begins by asking the Lord to prevent him from becoming shamed (v. 1), and he ends the poem with a declaration that the wicked have been shamed. The Lord has answered his prayer; He has protected His righteous servant.

Psalm 72, a royal psalm, is one of two psalms (Ps. 127) ascribed to Solomon, the son of David. King Solomon might have arranged David's psalms in something like their present order, then appended his own psalm to the group (v. 20). This psalm is intensely messianic, speaking in ideal terms of the coming of the great King. On the basis of the ideals of ancient Middle Eastern royalty, the psalm calls for a good king to govern Israel under God's blessing. Ultimately this King is the Savior Jesus. The psalm has the following structure: (1) a call for a reign of judgment (vv. 1–4); (2) anticipation of a reign of righteousness (vv. 5–7); (3) a vision of a universal reign (vv. 8–11); (4) a vision of a reign of compassionate justice (vv. 12–14); (5) a prediction of a reign of great blessing (vv. 15–17); (6) praise for the God who will establish this glorious reign (vv. 18–20).

72:1–7 Fear You is an expression of wonder, awe, reverence, worship, and obedience. **He shall come down:** The great King is pictured as the gentle rains of God's blessing on the earth. His reign will lead to true **peace,** the state of things as they really ought to be.

72:8–12 The promises of God to Abraham included a promise that his descendants would have **dominion** over the land of Canaan (Gen. 15:18–21). These verses expand the geographical dimensions to include the entire earth. **The River** refers to the Euphrates—a distant, significant waterway that many Israelites hoped would become the extent of their kingdom. The glorious coming King will have the river as a *near* border; His territory will extend **to the ends of the earth.** No one will escape the power of His reign, not even those **in the wilderness. lick the dust:** The King's enemies will have their faces to the ground in forced submission to His majesty. **Tarshish** and **Sheba** were the most distant places known to the Israelites; they suggest distances beyond Solomon's imagination. As Solomon had received **gifts** from the queen of Sheba (1 Kin. 10:1–10), so he predicted that the coming King would receive gifts from rulers all over the earth.

72:13, 14 This section emphasizes the work of the King on behalf of the **poor** and **needy. precious shall be their blood:** The blood shed by the needy points to the blood the Savior shed on the Cross (Heb. 12:24). No wonder Jesus finds the shed blood of others to be precious.

72:15–17 The promise of life in the words **He shall live** is a messianic theme (16:10, 11; 91:16; 118:17, 18), for the coming Savior is the only One who grants true life (John 11:25). **gold of Sheba:** This is a reference to v. 10. The **name** of the great King will be regarded as the greatest name in the universe; Paul speaks this way of Jesus' name in Phil. 2:9–11.

72:18, 19 These magnificent words of benediction mark the conclusion of the psalm, as well as the conclusion of Book II of the Psalms. The repetition of the word **blessed,** the focus on the **name** (as in 89:16), and the double **Amen** all indicate that this psalm was used in the worship of God in His temple.

72:20 The prayers of David: The superscription of Ps. 72 attributes the psalm to Solomon. It is possible that Solomon wrote this poem in honor of his father David at the end of an early edition of the psalms so far collected. Other psalms were added later to this original collection.

Psalm 73 is a psalm of trust with some features of the wisdom psalms. the psalm is unusual in that it tells a story about the psalmist's struggle with envy, doubts, and his faith in God. But through his struggles, the psalmist Asaph learned to trust in God. The structure of the poem is as follows: (1) the temptation to be envious of the wicked (vv. 1–3); (2) a description of the wicked (vv. 4–14); (3) the realization that the end of the wicked is the balancing factor (vv. 15–20); (4) the psalmist's regret over his uncertainty (vv. 21–24); (5) a renewed resolve to trust in God alone (vv. 25, 26); (6) the destruction of the wicked (v. 27); (7) a renewed trust in God (v. 28).

73:1–4 In the opening verses Asaph describes the crisis of faith he experienced. He begins with one of the basic elements of biblical theology, that **God is good to Israel** (100:5; 106:1; 107:1). But then he confesses that he almost **stumbled** when he became **envious** of the success and wealth of the **wicked.**

73:5, 6 Asaph observes that the attitudes and actions of the wicked seem to place no constraints upon them. They appear not to have **trouble.** Their **pride** and **violence** are not hidden but are displayed like jewelry. They fulfill their lustful appetites and boast about their wicked accomplishments.

73:7–12 Asaph describes the apathy about God characteristic of the wicked, who had concluded that God—if there was a God—was disengaged from people's lives. Asaph is bothered by the fact that with this aberrant view of life the wicked are still able to enjoy life, drink their fill, and live **at ease.** Thus the psalmist feels that his own acts of righteous living are without meaning or purpose.

73:13–18 untrue: Asaph realizes that if he continued on this path, he would be abandoning the faith. He finds the issue **painful** to consider until he comes to a new sense of enlightenment in **the sanctuary,** the temple in Jerusalem. He rediscovered something he probably knew but had not really considered: the prosperity of the wicked will not last. Their wealth will have no value in the next life.

73:19 Asaph remembers that the wicked are just a step away from disaster. **In a moment** they could find all of their wealth valueless and their pleasure vanished as they face an eternity separated from the presence of their Creator.

73:20–24 Asaph **was grieved** because of his own lapse of faith (vv. 1–3). In the manner of a wisdom psalm, he speaks of his own **foolishness. like a beast:** An animal has no sense of eternity and a divine perspective. The poet was making an animal-like decision when he began to wonder about the wicked (vv. 1–3). But God had never left him, even when he struggled with doubts. **And afterward:** What helped the psalmist gain a proper perspective on this life was the afterlife. The righteous will have the glorious privilege of living with God forever.

73:25–28 The contrast between the words **shall perish** and **draw near to God** explains the heart of the psalm. There are those who may enjoy great wealth and notoriety today, but nothing they have or do will last forever. Therefore, Asaph concludes he has **put** his **trust in the Lord God.** Only those who place their trust in God will find eternal life and eternal peace.

Psalm 74 is a lament psalm of the community (as is Ps. 80) and a powerful presentation of Hebrew poetry at its best. The poem describes God's actions in the past and the desire of His people for Him to act in the present. In some ways, Ps. 75 may be regarded as the Lord's answer to the difficult questions of Ps. 74. This is one of eleven psalms attributed to Asaph (Pss. 50; 73–83). The outline of the poem is: (1) a community lament over a foreign invasion (vv. 1–8); (2) a community complaint that there appears to be no hope (vv. 9–11); (3) a recounting of God's historic victories against evil powers (vv. 12–17); (4) a petition for God to remember His covenant and deliver His people (vv. 18–21); (5) a call for God to act on His own behalf against His enemies (vv. 22, 23).

74:1, 2 O God, why is a classic lament in the Psalms (13:1). The invasion of a foreign power into Judah and Jerusalem had devastated the people. The foreign invader is viewed as an expression of the **anger** of the Lord. The principal call of the psalm is for the Lord to **remember** His people and the foolish ridicule of their enemies (vv. 18, 22). In his appeal to God the poet uses a series of endearing terms to describe the people of God: **the sheep of Your pasture, Your congregation, the tribe of Your inheritance,** and **this Mount Zion.** The psalmist also focuses on the loving actions of God for His people in the past: **You have purchased, You have redeemed, You have dwelt.** In the context of God's past faithfulness to the people He has chosen, the poet calls upon God to deliver His people in their time of need (vv. 20, 22).

74:3–10 Lift up Your feet is a call for God "to get up and walk" to see what is going on. The worst part of the enemy invasion was the desecration of the temple in Jerusalem. Several terms are used to describe this holy place: **the sanctuary, Your meeting place,** and **the dwelling place of Your name.**

74:11 The poet calls on God to fight against the enemy, to extend His **right hand** to protect and deliver the people as He had during the Exodus (63:8; Ex. 15:6).

74:12 The Lord is **King** by virtue of His creation of the earth (Ps. 93). He is King because of His special relationship with Israel (44:4; 99:1–3). And He is the coming King who will reign over all (96:13; 97:1–6; 98:6–9). **from of old:** The poet recalls the ancient victories of the Lord over the dark forces in a poetic recasting of the events of creation. **Salvation** here refers to God's deliverance of earth from the dark forces represented by the waters and serpents (vv. 13–15).

74:13 the sea . . . the heads of the sea serpents: In Canaanite mythology, the sea and its serpents joined together as enemies of Baal. Supposedly Baal was victorious over these enemies and subsequently became king. The poets of the Bible use the language of Canaanite myth to describe the victories of God in the formation of the earth, in the deliverance of His people from Egypt, and in future battles (77:16–20; 93:1–5; Is. 27:1; 51:9, 10). The division of the waters described in Gen. 1:6–8 is viewed as a battle in which God was victorious over both sea and serpents.

74:14 One of the enemies of Baal was the sea monster Lotan. In Hebrew literature this figure became the **Leviathan.** The name speaks poetically of various evil forces over which God has ultimate control and victory. Eventually the Leviathan became a symbol for Satan (Is. 27:1) who is "the dragon, that serpent of old" (Rev. 20:2). In this context, **the people** refers to beasts.

74:15 the fountain: The Lord gave water to the people of Israel in the wilderness (Ex. 17:5, 6; Num. 20:8–13). **mighty rivers:** He also enabled His people to cross over the Red Sea (Ex. 14) and the River Jordan (Josh. 3).

74:16, 17 In His great works of creation (Gen. 1) God established His rule over **day, night, light,** and **the sun.** In addition, He established the seasons and set **borders,** a reference to the limitations He placed on the waters (Prov. 8:27–29). Asaph's argument is that since God is in control, why was He allowing chaos in Israel?

74:18–21 Three times in this poem the poet calls upon God to **remember** (vv. 2, 22). In addition to appealing to the honor of God's **name** (v. 10), the poet uses endearing terms for God's people who are in distress: **Your turtledove, Your poor, the oppressed,** and **the poor and needy.** These were the people with whom the Lord Himself had chosen to make a **covenant.**

74:22, 23 The phrase **plead Your own cause** refers to a legal complaint and is often used by the prophets in contexts of impending judgment on Israel (Mic. 6:1). For the third time in this poem (vv. 2, 18), God is asked to **remember** His stake in Israel and His need to defend His own reputation against **foolish** people.

Psalm 75, a grand psalm of praise (Ps. 100),

> *God Himself is ready to intervene on the part of His people.*

contains a lively interchange between the people, the psalmist, and the Lord. For other psalms in which the Lord speaks, see Pss. 12; 75; 87; 91. In some ways this psalm may be regarded as God's answer to the questions presented in Ps. 74. The structure of the psalm is based on its varied speakers: (1) the people's praise of God for the sense of His presence (v. 1); (2) God's announcement of His sovereign determination to judge the earth at the proper time (vv. 2–5); (3) the people's declaration that God is the true Judge (vv. 6–9); (4) God's declaration of His intention to bring final judgment (v. 10).

75:1 Thanks indicates public acknowledgment of God. **Your wondrous works** speaks of the actions only God can perform, those that instill a sense of awe on the part of His people. **Your name is near:** God Himself is ready to intervene on the part of His people.

75:2 When I choose the proper time: God will not be rushed—not even by His people. **Uprightly** indicates the fullness and perfection of God's justice.

75:3 The earth . . . dissolved: In times of great stress, it may seem that the world is falling apart (60:2). God's response is **I set up its pillars firmly.** God has not abandoned His people, nor has He given up His authority.

75:4, 5 On the basis of God's determination to wait until the "proper time" (v. 2), there are strong warnings to **boastful** and **wicked** people who misinterpret God's delay and think there will be no judgment. **The horn** is an ancient symbol of strength. The wicked strut around like powerful animals, brandishing symbols of power with no thought of God. But the power of the wicked is feeble compared to the strength of the Almighty (v. 10).

75:6, 7 The words **God is the Judge** establish the fact that He is the true ruler of the universe (50:6; 58:11). **He puts down . . . exalts:** As Daniel declares in his prayer (Dan. 2:20–22), God is sovereign in the world's affairs.

75:8, 9 This is not a cup of blessing, but of the Lord's wrath. The biblical image of **wine** and judgment goes back to Jacob's blessing on Judah (Gen. 49:11) and is referred to in Christ's judgment as depicted in Rev. 19:13–15.

75:10 The psalm concludes with the words of God. Here God depicts the contrasting fates of the **wicked** and the **righteous. horn:** The wicked have proudly lifted up their horn (vv. 4, 5) by boasting in their strength. The Lord will take away the very strength in which they have boasted.

IN FOCUS — "glorious"

(Heb. 'or) (18:28; 76:4; 77:18; 97:4; Job 33:30; Eccl. 8:1) Strong's #215: This Hebrew word is the common word meaning "to give light." The author of Proverbs likens the life of the just to the light of the sun (Prov. 4:18). For one's eyes to be lit means that one has been revived or has received wisdom or understanding (13:3; 19:8; 1 Sam. 14:27–29; Ezra 9:8). The common prayer request that God would cause His face to shine upon someone was always, except for one possible early exception (Num. 6:25), a petition that God would grant mercy from distress (31:16; 67:1; 80:3, 7, 19; 119:135; Dan. 9:17). In the present passage, as elsewhere, the light is from the glory of God's presence, which is to be reflected by His people (Is. 60:1–3; Ezek. 43:2). One day, the light of the sun and moon will be completely replaced by the light of God's glory (Is. 60:19, 20; Rev. 21:23; 22:5).

Psalm 76 is a psalm of praise with a strong focus on the fear of God. The psalm has four movements: (1) a celebration of the center of worship in Jerusalem (vv. 1–3); (2) a celebration of the victories of God against His enemies (vv. 4–6); (3) a description of the fear of God at the anger of God (vv. 7–10); (4) an exhortation to the righteous to worship the Lord (vv. 11, 12).

76:1–3 The word translated **tabernacle** is literally a "lair," like that of a great lion. **Salem** is the shortened form of the name Jerusalem.

76:4–6 more glorious and excellent: Nothing in all the universe or in all eternity can ever be compared with God (77:13). His glory and beauty are unsurpassed and His power is unassailable. **Chariot and horse** refers to the defeat of the army of Pharaoh (Ex. 14; 15).

76:7 The repetition of pronouns **You, Yourself** is for emphasis: Only the Almighty is **to be feared.** For the righteous, the fear of God is a response of awe, wonder, adoration, and worship. For the wicked, the fear of God is terror, for there is no escape from Him (14:5).

76:8–10 judgment to be heard: In God's victories over the enemies of His people, word of God's glory and justice would spread to the entire world. Even the **wrath of men** will praise God because any anger against God is utterly futile. As Paul writes, "For who has resisted His will?" (Rom. 9:19). A person's futile hostility to God will only result in a demonstration of God's power and a subsequent glorification of His name. See the Lord's response to Pharaoh (Ex. 11:9).

76:11, 12 The psalmist instructs the righteous in the true worship of the sovereign Lord of creation. **Make vows:** These are vows of praise, sacrifice, and faithful living (61:5, 8; 66:13; Heb. 13:15). As one might **bring presents** to a king (72:10), so the righteous should bring their gifts to God—the ultimate gift being the dedication of their lives to the service of God (Rom. 12:1).

Psalm 77 is a psalm of a troubled believer. It is marked by a sense of inward trouble and reflection. Key terms in the psalm are the verbs "to remember" and "to meditate." The outline is as follows: (1) a cry to God (vv. 1–3); (2) doubts (vv. 4–6); (3) a question: Has God forgotten? (vv. 7–9); (4) focus on the goodness of God (vv. 10–12); (5) remembrance of the incomparability of God (vv. 13–15); (6) remembrance that God is Lord of the sea (vv. 16–20).

77:1, 2 stretched out: Asaph was in such need that he held his **hand** out before the Lord throughout the **night** (63:4; 134:1, 2). All the while, he groaned and complained as he remembered God. What he knew of God contrasted with what he was experiencing. The more the psalmist thought about these things, the more troubled he became.

77:3–6 You hold my eyelids open: Asaph could not sleep (63:6). Through the night he thought about his situation and his past (vv. 4–6), but most importantly he turned to God. First he cries out to the Lord in anguish (vv. 7–9). But then his focus changes; he reminds himself of the power of God and all the miraculous things the Lord has done (vv. 10–20).

77:7–9 Wondering if God is finished with him, Asaph asks if the Lord will ever show mercy to him again. Each of the verses presents painful questions; perhaps none as difficult as the one in v. 9: **Has God forgotten to be gracious?** Asaph was at the depths of despair.

77:10–13 I will remember the works of the LORD: Asaph made a conscious decision to turn from his pain and focus his thoughts on the person, works, and wonders of God. His first focus is on the incomparability of God. **Who is so great a God as our God?** With this question Asaph reminds himself that the living God cannot be compared to any other god or power. This wondrous God demonstrated His power in a variety of ways, but especially in the redemption of Israel from Egypt.

77:14–18 Asaph now turns his thoughts to God's sovereignty over the powers of the sea, His control over the **waters** and the **depths** (74:12–15; 93:1–5). Moreover, the Almighty controls the **skies,** for a storm as depicted in these verses is merely a response to His strength. **Your arrows** is a poetic description of lightning.

77:19 This verse presents images of God as the Lord of the storm (vv. 16–18) and the sea, walking on the waters. The term **great waters** may be rephrased "many waters" (18:16; 32:6; 144:7). The point is that the waters are no threat to God, for they are merely another pathway for Him to walk.

77:20 God is Lord of His people. He is the Shepherd who leads His **flock,** as He has done from the time of **Moses and Aaron.** Lost in contemplation of the greatness of God, the poet seems thoroughly distracted from his pain. He does not mention it again, not daring to compare it to the greatness of the Almighty.

Psalm 78, a wisdom psalm, relates the early history of Israel in a dramatic poetic alternation between reports of the faithfulness of God to His people and of their periodic outbreaks of stubbornness, willfulness, and rebellion against Him. Only Ps. 119 is longer. With his great command of Scripture, Asaph expresses an intense desire that the present generation not repeat the failures of so many past generations. The structure of the poem is as follows: (1) the lesson of the past works of God in Israel's history (vv. 1–4); (2) an exhortation for each generation to teach the next (vv. 5–8); (3) the rebellion of the people of Ephraim (vv. 9–11); (4) God's marvelous salvation of Israel in the Exodus (vv. 12–16); (5) the people's complaints (vv. 17–20); (6) God's anger against the ungrateful people (vv. 21–25); (7) God's judgment through the quail (vv. 26–31); (8) the continuing unbelief of the people (vv. 32, 33); (9) the people's remembrance of God's true character and God's remembrance of the people's weaknesses (vv. 34–39); (10) God's faithfulness and the people's unfaithfulness (vv. 40–55); (11) Israel's sins during the period of the judges (vv. 56–64); (12) God's victory over Israel's enemies (vv. 65, 66); (13) God's choice of Judah, Jerusalem, and David (vv. 67–72).

78:1, 2 The psalmist uses the vocabulary of the wisdom school to establish himself. **My law** is the familiar word *Torah*. The wisdom writers use this word to connote insight; their instruction is always in accord with the "instruction" of Moses (Prov. 1:8; 3:1; 4:2). The terms **parable** and **dark sayings** or riddles indicate sayings with "deeper meanings" or "teachings with a point" (Prov. 1:6). With the words **my people** the psalmist shows himself to be one with them even though he stands over them as their teacher.

78:3, 4 Asaph explains that the teaching was designed to be passed from one generation to the next, so that each generation would con-

tribute to **the praises of the LORD.** The phrase **His strength and His wonderful works** means "His extraordinarily wonderful works."

78:5, 6 The **testimony** God **established** was a lasting procedure, a means whereby one generation would pass on to the next the need to know the Lord. **the generation to come:** The psalm will make the point that the generations had not handed on the teaching as they should have.

78:7, 8 Because **their fathers** did not believe in God, the present generation needs to be different from their predecessors.

78:9 Asaph's first illustration of the faithlessness of previous generations is taken from an incident in which the people of **Ephraim** rejected God. The poet may be referring to Ephraim's conflict with Jephthah (Judg. 12:1–7).

78:10–16 The poet celebrates the **marvelous things** God did for Israel in delivering them from Egypt, especially at the crossing of the Red Sea (Ex. 14), the signs of God's presence with His people (Ex. 13:21), and the bringing of water from the rock in the wilderness (Ex. 17:1–7; Num. 20:1–13).

78:17, 18 The Hebrew word translated **rebelling** here is translated *provoked* in two other places in this poem (vv. 40, 56). **food of their fancy:** This derisive language is used to describe the outrageous ungratefulness of the Israelites as they clamored for food and water in the wilderness.

78:19–28 God's **anger** against His people centered on their lack of faith and **trust** in Him, evidenced by their contempt for the manna He gave them. The poet refers to God's manna as the **bread of heaven** and **angels' food.** The Israelites audaciously rejected the food of angels.

78:29–31 For He gave them their own desire: People of true faith will seek God's will and respond in grateful praise. Self-centered people will simply complain and suffer the result.

78:32, 33 In spite of this: The poet says that the people had suffered enough from their ingratitude to have learned the lesson of faith. Unfortunately, they had *not* learned. So God determined that they would not enter the land of Canaan but would spend their days **in futility.**

78:34–37 The people tended to remember the true character of God only when pressed to do so by His judgments; but God always **remembered** (v. 39) the frail nature of the people. The image of God as a **rock** is found in Moses (Deut. 32:4) and is developed elsewhere in the Psalms (61:2; 62:2, 7; 91:1, 2; 144:1). God as **Redeemer** is the Savior, who rescued

Israel from Egypt just as He also delivered them from their sins (19:14; Is. 41:14; 44:6). The title **Most High God** emphasizes the majesty and power of God. God surpasses all powers, all creation, and nothing can be compared to Him. It is utter folly for a person to shake a small fist at the Most High. This title is found three times in this psalm (vv. 17, 35, 56); it is also found in 7:17; 9:2; 18:13; 21:7; 46:4; 50:14; 56:2; 57:2; 73:11; 77:10; 82:6; 83:18; 87:5; 91:1, 9; 92:1; 107:11.

78:38 full of compassion: The awesome transcendence of the Lord is complemented in this section (v. 35) by an emphasis on His compassionate mercy.

78:39–42 The verb translated **provoked** here is used three times in this psalm (*rebelling* in v. 17; v. 56). Even though God had showered blessings on His people, they provoked Him with their contempt and ingratitude. **The Holy One of Israel** (89:18) is a phrase particularly favored by the prophet Isaiah (Is. 1:4; 5:24).

78:43–55 This section is a poetic retelling of the way God helped Israel in Egypt and during the wilderness years. Verses 43–51 recount the ten plagues of Ex. 7–12, and vv. 52, 53 speak of the deliverance of Israel at the Red Sea (Ex. 14). Verse 54 speaks of the experience at Mount Sinai, and v. 55 summarizes the conquest of the land of Canaan.

78:56 Tested and provoked may be rephrased "thoroughly provoked." The title **Most High** is used three times in this poem (vv. 17, 35), as is the Hebrew word for *provoked* (vv. 17, 40). The two words emphasize the seriousness of the Israelites' action; they were rebelling against their Creator, the Ruler of the entire universe.

78:57–67 A different Hebrew word from the one used in v. 56 is used for **provoked** here, but it conveys the same idea. **High places** refers to the places where the Canaanites worshiped Baal and other fertility gods. **Carved images** were fertility symbols from Canaanite cults. The reference to **Shiloh** places this period of Israel's apostasy in the latter period of the judges (1 Sam. 1:3). **His strength** and **His glory** are unusual ways of speaking of the ark of the covenant, which was lost to the Philistines during the battle of Aphek (1 Sam. 4:1–11). At this time the suffering of the people was acute, including even the deaths of **priests** (1 Sam. 4:17, 18).

78:68–71 The choice of **Judah** over the other tribes and of **Zion** over other cities is explained only in terms of God's sovereignty and love. The description of the **sanctuary** suggests that this psalm was written after Solomon's temple was built.

78:72 The words of praise for **David** in v. 72

are very close to 1 Kin. 9:4, suggesting some connection between the two passages. The shepherding attributed to David is an ideal; it will be fully realized in the Savior King, Jesus, the true Good Shepherd (Ps. 23; John 10).

Psalm 79, a lament of the community (Ps. 80), was written in response to an attack on the city of Jerusalem and the sacking of the holy temple. In these respects this psalm is similar to Ps. 74. It is possible that the event behind the psalm was the destruction of Jerusalem by the Babylonians; however, it may have been an earlier, less final devastation. The development of the poem is as follows: (1) a lament for the devastation of Jerusalem (vv. 1–4); (2) a call for God to punish the enemies of Judah and Jerusalem (vv. 5–7); (3) a plea for forgiveness and deliverance (vv. 8–10); (4) a prayer for God to help His people and judge their enemies (vv. 11, 12); (5) a vow of praise in anticipation of the Lord's deliverance (v. 13).

79:1 the nations have come: The words of this section are quite similar in tone to 74:1–8. **Your holy temple:** It is not clear whether the destruction described in this verse was what the Babylonians did in 586 B.C. The ruin of Jerusalem—it was **in heaps**—may indicate an invasion of the land prior to its total destruction.

79:2–4 The lament over the dead defenders of Jerusalem is similar to the words of Jer. 7:32–34; Lam. 4:1–10. **reproach . . . derision:** The wording is very close to 44:13.

79:5 The question **how long** is a standard element in the lament psalms (13:1, 2; 80:4). The question is based on the Lord's eternal character. Since God is eternal, Asaph asks, will He be **angry forever?**

79:6, 7 Pour out Your wrath: An imprecation or curse on one's enemies is often found in the psalms of lament (Ps. 137). Vengeance is left to the Lord, but such a call for vengeance is based in part on the covenant provisions God had established with Abraham. God had promised to curse those who cursed Abraham's descendants (Gen. 12:2, 3).

79:8–10 The appeal is based on the character of God as expressed by His name (Ex. 3:14, 15; 6:2, 3). Another basis for the poet's appeal is the international reputation of God (42:10). If God delivered the Israelites, His power would be demonstrated to all the nations.

79:11, 12 Groaning may also be translated *crying*. **Your power** refers to the powerful, outstretched arm of God that had delivered Israel from Egypt (Ex. 6:6). **Reproach** refers to an insult or taunt (74:10, 18, 22).

79:13 Sheep of Your pasture describes the Israelites. God's care for the Israelites was so great that they were called His sheep (77:20; 95:7; 100:3). The people vowed to bring

thanks, or public acknowledgment (35:18; 105:1), and **praise** to God.

Psalm 80, a lament of the community, has especially powerful imagery. The psalm is marked by two metaphors for Israel in its relation to God: (1) the flock of the Good Shepherd; (2) the vine of the True Vinedresser. Both of these metaphors are used by Jesus of His people in the NT (John 10; 15). This is one of Asaph's psalms (Pss. 50; 73—83) and is set to the tune "The Lilies" (Pss. 45; 69). The structure of the poem is as follows: (1) a call for the Shepherd of

was where Jerusalem was located; Manasseh was partly across the Jordan.

80:3 Cause Your face to shine is reminiscent of the priestly benediction, "The Lord make His face shine upon you" (Num. 6:25).

80:4, 5 Since their request for deliverance has seemed to go unanswered, the people ask whether God's anger is directed even **against their prayer.** The phrases **bread of tears** and **tears to drink** refer to the manna and water that God provided for Israel in the wilderness. The idea is that God had given the people of past

Mount Sinai (right), where God appeared to Moses and delivered the Ten Commandments in an act of self-revelation. The psalmist refers to this historic event in Psalm 81:6, 7.

Israel to restore the distressed (vv. 1–3); (2) a complaint concerning the Lord's anger against His people (vv. 4–7); (3) the metaphor of a vine (vv. 8–13); (4) an appeal for God to return, revive, and restore Israel (vv. 14–19).

80:1, 2 O Shepherd of Israel is reminiscent of the teaching of Ps. 23 and points forward to the teaching of John 10. God's pattern is to **lead** His people as a shepherd might lead **a flock. between the cherubim:** In the Most Holy Place, the ark of the covenant was topped by the mercy seat on which were two cherubim, heavenly symbols of the throne of God (Ex. 25:22). **shine forth:** After Moses had been in close proximity to the Lord, his own face was transformed by a resplendent glow (Ex. 34:29–35). Here the appeal means that the Lord should make His presence known in a saving manner. The tribes **Ephraim, Benjamin, and Manasseh** may be representative of the whole nation. Ephraim was in the north; Benjamin

generations nourishing food; but the people of this generation have only their tearful despair.

80:6–11 God's bringing the Israelites from **Egypt** to Canaan is compared to transplanting **a vine.** The vine grew phenomenally, so that it **filled the land** and reached to the Mediterranean **Sea** and the Euphrates **River.** These expansions of the Lord's vine occurred during the reigns of David and Solomon.

80:12 But then there came a dramatic change. The Lord broke **down her hedges**— that is, He removed Israel's protective walls. Israel became weak, subject to all kinds of assaults.

80:13–17 Look down from heaven: The appeal is for the heavenly Vinedresser to observe the sorry state of His vine. The Hebrew word translated **visit** can describe a gracious visit of the Lord (65:9) or a visit in judgment. Of course, the prayer offered is for a merciful visit from Israel's Protector. The appeal is for God to use His **right hand** (Ex. 15:6) to restore what He had **planted**. The Hebrew term for **vine-yard** is used only here in the Bible; it literally means "root-stock." **Branch** means "son"; it is the same Hebrew word translated *son of man* in v. 17. The nation of Israel was God's own son (Ex. 4:22).

80:18, 19 Revive us is a call for new life from God's Spirit. **We will call upon Your name:** In response to God's work of deliverance, the poet promises renewed praise centered on the *name* of God.

Psalm 81 begins as a psalm of praise and becomes a psalm of admonition (Ps. 50), in which the voice of the Lord Himself is heard (Ps. 75). The structure of the poem is as follows: (1) a call for the people to praise the Lord (vv. 1, 2); (2) a command for the people to celebrate the New Moon festival (vv. 3–5); (3) the Lord's report of His deliverance of His people (vv. 6, 7); (4) the Lord's admonition concerning idolatry (vv. 8–10); (5) the Lord's description of Israel's failure to obey Him (vv. 11, 12); (6) the Lord's lamentation of Israel's failure to obey (vv. 13–16).

81:1 Sing aloud . . . Make a joyful shout: The energy level of this psalm is similar to that of other psalms of praise (33:1–3; 35:27, 28; 66:1–4; 95:1, 2; 100:1, 2). The use of voices and instruments to praise God is a standard element of joyful worship in the Psalms (Pss. 149; 150).

81:2–5 The **New Moon** festival is mentioned in association with the Feast of Trumpets (Num. 29:6). Regulations for this festival can be found in the instructions to the Levites during the time of David (1 Chr. 23:31) and Solomon (2 Chr. 2:4). This psalm seems to be a basic instruction on the festival. **a statute . . . a law**

. . . a testimony: The language and regulations of this passage are as solemn as any in the Torah. The basis for the New Moon festival was the salvation of Israel from Egypt. **a language:** As in 114:1, there is a disdain for the history, culture, and language of Egypt.

81:6, 7 his shoulder . . . His hands: This is a poetic way of describing how God delivered His people from the Egyptian taskmasters (Ex. 1). **I answered you:** The Lord's appearance to Moses on Mount Sinai was God's great revelation of Himself (Ex. 19; 20).

81:8–10 The phrase translated **I will admonish you** is also found in 50:7, where it is translated "I will testify against you." The basic stipulation of the first commandment is repeated: there must be **no foreign god** among the Israelites (Ex. 20:3). God's great description of His own saving work for the Israelites is quoted from Ex. 20:2. Then the Lord invites His people to **open** their **mouth** so that He can meet their needs (v. 16).

81:11–16 The people's resistance to obeying God led to their punishment. God identifies the root of the people's problem as **their own stubborn heart.** They wanted to follow their own ways and refused to listen to God.

Psalm 82 is a wisdom psalm. The structure of the psalm is as follows: (1) God's call for the judges of the earth to appear in the heavenly assembly (vv. 1, 2); (2) God's review of His commands to the judges of the earth (vv. 3, 4); (3) God's hearing of the complaint of the oppressed (v. 5); (4) God's announcement of His judgment on the judges of the earth (vv. 6, 7); (5) the prayer of the people of the earth for divine justice (v. 8).

82:1, 2 The congregation of the mighty

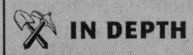 **IN DEPTH** | ## "Gods": Demons or Judges?

Psalm 82 presents modern readers with a puzzling reference to "gods" (Ps. 82:1, 6). We know that the ancient Israelites believed in one God. So what are we to make of this enigmatic allusion to other "gods" (Hebrew, *elohim*, "mighty ones")?

Two main suggestions have been proposed in answer to this riddle. One is that the "gods" mentioned here are demons, fallen angels who not only oppose God but harass human beings. The Book of Job tells of two occasions when "sons of God" met with the Lord, and Satan sought permission to oppress Job (Job 1:6–12; 2:1–7).

The second suggestion is that the "gods" are actually corrupt human judges who were either honored with or took upon themselves the title of "mighty ones." Some believe that they issued their rulings in the names of certain pagan gods in order to claim more authority for themselves.

Neither suggestion is without problems, but the second better fits the description in Psalm 82. The point of Psalm 82 is that ultimately all authorities are accountable to God. He is their final Ruler and Judge, as He is of the whole earth. He measures the integrity of those to whom He has delegated power according to their treatment of the poor, the fatherless, the afflicted, and the needy.

refers to an assembly before God. As a wisdom writer, the poet Asaph uses the language of Job 1, Ps. 110, and Is. 6 as a teaching device to present a morality tale. Asaph describes the wicked judges of all time gathering before God and His angels to give an accounting of themselves. **Gods:** The Hebrew word may refer to the true God or to false gods. Here it is the judges of the earth (v. 6). Asaph uses this honorific term sarcastically to express his contempt for the evil judges. **judge unjustly:** The unrighteous judges had perverted their calling, which was to represent God Himself by establishing justice on the earth.

82:3 God expects all judges to administer true justice. **do justice:** These words summarize the teaching of the Law and indicate God's basic desire that the defenseless would find a haven of justice in the courts.

82:4, 5 They do not know is the collective sigh of oppressed people of all ages. Wicked judges act as if they did not care about their official responsibility or the judgment they will face for abusing it. **All the foundations of the earth are unstable:** In 11:3, the taunt of the wicked is that the earth's foundations are destroyed. This is said to be untrue, for God is still in control. In this psalm, however, the situation *is* deemed unstable because of the profound wickedness of the judges.

82:6, 7 die like men: Jesus quoted these verses in His exchange with the religious authorities who wanted to stone Him for declaring Himself to be the Son of God (John 10:31–35).

82:8 Arise, O God: In view of the overwhelming disaster that wicked judges have created, the poor and afflicted of all time call out for the true Judge, God Himself to come. Their cry will not go unheeded. The righteous Judge is coming, and He will establish justice (96:13; 98:9).

Psalm 83 is a psalm of lament in which particular attention is given to the wicked. The curse that Asaph utters against the wicked puts this psalm in the category of the imprecatory psalms. When we read the strong words in this psalm, we need to keep in mind that the intent of the psalmist Asaph is to vindicate the glory of God. The psalm's structure is as follows: (1) a call for God to speak out in judgment on the wicked (vv. 1–4); (2) a recital of the acts of the wicked (vv. 5–8); (3) a recital of God's acts of judgment in the past (vv. 9–12); (4) a call for God to judge the wicked (vv. 13–18).

83:1 Do not keep silent: Calls for God to awaken, to rouse Himself, to turn and look, and to speak, are all ways the psalmists prayed for God to act. They believed that God as the Holy One would root out all evil. What they did not

always recognize was that God's delay in judgment was an expression of His mercy.

83:2, 3 Asaph feels revulsion against the **enemies** of the Lord. He hates what God hates (101:6–8). The attacks of the wicked are not only against God, but also against the **people** of God.

82:4 let us cut them off: God's attitude toward those who plots the destruction of His people is clear: His curse will rest on them (Gen. 12:2, 3). Asaph here is simply praying that God would act according to His promises.

83:5–8 consulted together: Throughout history, many nations have conspired to bring about the ruin of Israel and Judah. All such endeavors are condemned in this psalm. **against You:** In conspiring against the people of God, the wicked actually resist God Himself. **The tents of Edom:** The place names in this passage refer to nations on the borders of Israel and Judah. The **Hagrites** may have come from Arabia (1 Chr. 5:10, 19, 20). The people of **Gebal** may have lived in a mountainous region south of the Dead Sea; alternatively, Gebal may have been another name for Byblos, a city near Tyre.

83:9–12 Asaph recites God's great victories against the formidable foes of Israel. God's victory at **Midian** was accomplished through Gideon (Judg. 7). God's victory over **Sisera** was accomplished through Deborah and Barak (Judg. 4; 5). The same God who had battled Israel's enemies in the past would fight all those who might oppose His people in the future.

83:13–15 In a culture in which remembering a person was very important, an ultimate curse would have been to regard a person's memory as **whirling dust** or windblown **chaff.**

83:16–18 Shame is the opposite of dignity, an attribute of the righteous (25:2; 97:7). **seek Your name:** Asaph's first call for God to shame Israel's enemies is redemptive—that the nations might hear, feel shame, repent, and seek the face of the Lord. Yet if they continued in their wicked path, they would face further confounding and would one day face God in judgment. The title **Most High** is often used in the Psalms to speak of God's control over all the nations of the world (47:2; 78:35; 97:9).

Psalm 84 is one of the psalms of Zion. These psalms celebrate God's presence in Jerusalem, the city where His temple was built. Today it is not necessary to go to Jerusalem to draw near to God, for God is near those who trust in His Son (Matt. 28:18–20). This psalm was composed by the sons of Korah (Pss. 42; 44–49; 85; 87; 88). There are six movements: (1) the expression of the desire to be at home in Zion (vv. 1, 2); (2) the blessings of being at home in Zion (vv. 3, 4); (3) the blessings of those who make pilgrimages

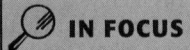 **IN FOCUS**   **"sun"**

(Heb. *shemesh*) (84:11; Josh. 10:12, 13). Strong's #8121: The Hebrew word for *sun* most often refers to the celestial body that illuminates the earth (136:7, 8). The idiom "before the sun" may describe an action done openly or in public (2 Sam 12:12). The sun is also a biblical symbol for righteousness (Mal. 4:2) and even a title for God in the Psalms (84:11). Many of the ancients worshiped the sun, moon, and stars (2 Kin. 21:3; Ezek. 8:16). But the psalmist understood that the sun, moon, and stars worshiped God because He created them (148:3). In the new creation, there will be no need of the sun because God Himself will be an everlasting light to the people (Is. 60:19).

to Zion (vv. 5–7); (4) a prayer for God's attention in Zion (vv. 8, 9); (5) the joy of being at home in Zion (vv. 10, 11); (6) the blessing of trusting in God (v. 12).

84:1, 2 Tabernacle is used here as a poetic term for the temple that was built by Solomon. **longs . . . faints:** For a similar expression of a psalmist's desire for the Lord's presence, see 42:1, 2. **the living God:** All other "gods" are nonentities; but He who created the universe, who chose Israel as His people, and who provided salvation for the world, lives forever in great glory.

84:3, 4 sparrow . . . swallow: By describing the approach of birds to the courtyards of the temple, the poet expresses his own great joy. **Blessed,** the same term used in 1:1, means "O, the great happiness of."

84:5–7 The phrase **whose heart is set on pilgrimage** refers to those who make their way to the temple not out of obligation, but out of a wellspring of joy. **The Valley of Baca,** or "Valley of Weeping," refers to the various difficulties that one might face on a pilgrimage. The person on a pilgrimage might discover that the once-dark valley is filled with springs, **rain,** and **pools**—all signs of God's blessing. **strength to strength:** As one nears the temple, the rigors of the journey become tolerable, for the joy of the approaching arrival strengthens the soul.

84:8 LORD God of hosts, literally the "God of armies," speaks of God's transcendence. The *hosts* are the angelic armies of the heavens. This title is balanced by the phrase **God of Jacob,** referring to the covenant relationship God established with the patriarchs of Israel.

84:9 The two phrases **our shield** and **Your anointed** both point to the same person, the king of Israel (89:3, 4). Each person who was anointed in the OT foreshadowed the coming Anointed One, the Messiah.

84:10, 11 a day . . . a thousand: Nothing in the pilgrim's daily experience can be compared to a day spent in the worship of God in the holy temple. **a doorkeeper . . . dwell in**

the tents: The role of a menial servant in the **house of** his **God** is more desirable than a life of luxury with those who practice **wickedness. Sun and shield** means "splendid shield." **Grace and glory** may be rephrased as "glorious grace." Whereas the anointed king was a "shield" (v. 9), the greater Shield is God Himself. **No good thing will He withhold:** This is the observation of a wise and righteous person; time after time, God gives good gifts to His people.

84:12 This lovely psalm ends as it began in the words **O Yahweh of hosts** (v. 1); this is termed an *inclusio*, a frame for the poem.

Psalm 85 is a prayer for restoration that is rooted deeply in trust in God. The setting for the psalm appears to be the restoration of the people of God following a great catastrophe—perhaps the Babylonian captivity. With this psalm, the people prayed for a revival of their spirits and a renewal in their land. The ultimate fulfillment of their prayer would be in the coming glorious kingdom of the Savior Jesus. This is one of the psalms composed by the sons of Korah (Pss. 42; 44–49; 84; 87; 88). The development of this psalm is in four sections: (1) a celebration of God's favor on the land (vv. 1–3); (2) a petition for restoration and revival (vv. 4–7); (3) an expectation that God will act soon (vv. 8, 9); (4) a description of the restoration (vv. 10–13).

85:1 You have brought back the captivity may refer to the return of the exiles from Babylon. But it also may be a more general reversal of fortune (14:7).

85:2–7 God of our salvation may be rephrased as "our Saving God." **Your anger:** The first section of this psalm already says God's anger has turned away from the people (v. 3). Yet until the restoration is complete, the people still feel the effects of God's wrath. This suggests an understanding that the people's troubles were due to their own sin disciplined by God. **revive us:** The people prayed for their own welfare and for renewed ability to praise God. **Mercy** may also be translated "loyal love."

85:8, 9 The speaker here may be a priest

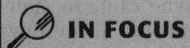 **IN FOCUS** | **"truth"**

(Heb. *'emet*) (86:11; 1 Kin. 10:6; Esth. 9:30) Strong's #571: This Hebrew term signifies truth that conforms to a standard—either to created reality or to God's standards. Truth is often associated with mercy, especially God's mercy (57:3; 117:2; Gen. 24:49). This word is also frequently used in the context of legal language: In secular contexts it is used in speaking of witnesses and judgments (Prov. 14:25; Zech. 8:16), while in religious contexts it is used in reference to the law and commandments of God (119:142, 151). Truth is precious, and its absence was lamented by the Prophets (Is. 59:14; Jer. 9:5; Hos. 4:1). God desires truth in the inward parts of His people (15:2; 51:6); thus it is the basis of a lifestyle that pleases Him (25:5, 10; 26:3).

expecting to **hear** a direct revelation from the Lord. Such a revelation would be consistent with God's character. **Peace** suggests wholeness, fullness, things as they ought to be. The word **saints** is related to the term translated *mercy* in v. 7; these are people who reflect the love of God in their own lives. **not turn back to folly:** God's blessing would continue only as long as the people remained faithful to Him. **His salvation** can describe any act of mercy on the part of God.

85:10–13 The words **mercy and truth** often appear together in the Scriptures to express one concept (25:10; 61:7; 86:15; 89:14). Here they are viewed as separate entities that come together, in the same way that **righteousness and peace have kissed.** The union of God's mercy and truth and His righteousness and peace describes the way things ought to be, or the state of *peace* spoken of in v. 8. The blending of the ideals of **truth** and **righteousness** in v. 11 suggests a vision of the kingdom of God (Is. 11). The fact that the word **righteousness** appears three times in the last four verses of this psalm alludes to the holiness of the coming kingdom of God and the sinlessness of the Savior and King who will rule over it.

Psalm 86 is a psalm of lament in which David expresses grave concerns about his lowly state, as well as joy in the God who alone is merciful. This poem is the only one in Book III of the Psalms that has David's name in the title. The structure is as follows: (1) a call for God to deliver David from distress (vv. 1–5); (2) a call for God to hear David's prayer (vv. 6, 7); (3) a statement that there is none other like God (vv. 8–10); (4) a petition for God to teach David about Himself so that he can praise Him forever (vv. 11–13); (5) a comparison of the assaults of the wicked with the character of the Lord (vv. 14, 15); (6) a renewed call for God to show His goodness to David in his distress (vv. 16, 17).

86:1–5 Bow down Your ear: As in 31:2, David uses a dramatic phrase that captures the grandeur of God on high and David's humble position on the earth below. Here the phrase **I am holy** does not speak of the transcendence of God, as in Is. 6:3. Rather it speaks of the faithfulness and godliness of a righteous person who, by God's grace, is living in accordance with God's law. It is another way that David describes himself as a **servant** of the Lord. **Rejoice:** God rejoices in those who serve Him, and His servants find their joy in Him.

86:6, 7 give ear: The verb is derived from the noun "ear." It means "make with the ears," a strong term to be used as a parallel term for the more expected verb "to hear." Often it is used for man (or nature) to listen to God (Is. 1:2), but sometimes as here it is used by man in an appeal to God to listen. There is a condescension of God in the very fact that He allows His servants to speak to Him in this manner.

86:8, 9 Among the gods: The ancient nations took their sense of identity in part from their ties to their supposed gods. When the nations found out that their "gods" did not exist, they would have to acknowledge that the Lord alone is God. Here David envisions other nations worshiping the true God and thus anticipates the missionary thrust of the NT (Ps. 117; Matt. 28:18–20).

86:10–13 Teach me Your way: David asks the Lord to teach him so that he will be able to praise God in the midst of the congregation. **Mercy** is the "loyal love" of the Lord. **depths of Sheol:** David describes the Lord as mercifully delivering him from certain death (9:17; 116:3, 4).

86:14 The Psalms consistently describe God as the enemy of **the proud** and the friend of the humble (138:6; 147:6).

86:15 The phrase **abundant in mercy and truth** is a precursor of the NT phrase "full of grace and truth" (John 1:14). The Lord upholds the truth so that He can mercifully free those caught in falsehoods.

86:16, 17 save the son of Your maidservant: The idea here may be that since David's mother was a pious woman, the Lord ought to save David from his lowly state (116:16).

Psalm 87, a psalm of Zion, is also an intensely evangelistic psalm that anticipates the NT mission to present the gospel to the entire world (Matt. 28:18–20). This psalm is one of the collection from the sons of Korah (Pss. 42; 44–49; 84; 85; 88). It has three movements: (1) a description of God's love for the city of Zion (vv. 1–3); (2) a description of the citizens of Zion coming from all nations (vv. 4–6); (3) a celebration of God's salvation (v. 7).

87:1 His foundation: God Himself established Zion or Jerusalem as the center of true worship. He ordained Solomon to build a temple there so that He could live among the Israelites (1 Kin. 6:13). Zion is holy because of God's declaration (1 Kin 11:13), His promise, the worship given Him there (1 Kin. 8:14–66), the future work of the Savior there (Matt. 21:4–11), and the future rule of the King there (Rev. 21).

87:2, 3 God has a special love for the place where His name is worshiped. **The gates of Zion** are the conspicuous entrance to the city. The verb **loves** includes the idea of choice (Deut. 6:5) as well as emotion. God chose Jerusalem; and He also has an enduring affection for the city. **City of God** may also be translated "city of the True God."

87:4 I will make mention: In this verse, God Himself speaks. **Rahab** is a symbolic name for Egypt (Is. 30:7) that has negative connotations. It alludes to the arrogance of the Egyptians. This is not the Rahab of Josh. 2:3–11, whose name is spelled differently in Hebrew. **Babylon** was the proverbial seat of apostasy and idolatry (Gen. 10:10). **To those who know Me** may be rephrased "*as* those who know Me." Thus the verse anticipates a time when foreigners would know and worship the living God. Among those who came to Zion to worship the Lord were people from Egypt, Babylon, **Philistia, Tyre, and Ethiopia.** At the time of the writing of this psalm, perhaps in the later period of Hezekiah's reign, foreigners were worshiping God in the temple along with Jews.

87:5 And of Zion: Despite their foreign heritage, the people who worshiped God were considered as having been **born in** Zion. Thus this psalm anticipates the NT teaching of the second birth (John 3). The title **Most High** is used particularly with reference to God's power over the nations (47:2; 78:35; 82:6). **shall establish her:** Zion would become the place where more and more people from other nations would come to worship the living God. This is prophetic of the coming of the gospel of Jesus, the spread of that gospel, and the culmination of the gospel in the rule of the Savior King (Is. 2:1–4).

87:6 The LORD will record pictures God making a register of the people of the nations. All believers will find their true identity in the Lord, to whom they will offer their worship in Zion.

87:7 The singers and the players are called to celebrate together the joy of the Savior God. The image of **springs** indicates salvation, which is found only in the Lord (Is. 12:3). This anticipated the salvation that God would offer through Jesus Christ (Titus 2:11).

Psalm 88 begins as a psalm of lament but never comes to the resolution of trust and praise that is the hallmark of those psalms. Thus Ps. 88 can be considered a psalm of complaint, a development of the lament portion of the psalms of lament. The title ascribes the psalm to the sons of Korah (Pss. 42; 44–49; 84; 85; 87), more specifically to Heman the Ezrahite. Heman is

---

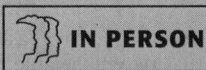 **IN PERSON** **Why Is Psalm 88 So Sad?**

Psalm 88 ends on a note of utter loneliness, as the psalmist feels cut off from loved ones and friends (v. 18). It may be that the troubles he was experiencing had isolated him from his community. However, it may also be that his troubles were largely the result of acquaintances who had turned away from God to spiritual darkness.

That was certainly the case for Heman the son of Joel, who some scholars identify with Heman the Ezrahite (title), the writer of this psalm. Joel was the son of Samuel the judge (1 Sam. 3:1), but he thoroughly rejected that great leader's godly ways. Samuel appointed Joel and his brother as judges in Beersheba, a city at the extreme southern end of Judah, perhaps where they could do the least harm. But in the end they did great harm, as their wickedness prompted the elders of Israel to demand a king. Over Samuel's objections, the king selected was Saul (1 Sam. 8:1–9; 10:23–25).

If Heman the son of Joel was indeed the composer of Psalm 88, his background may shed light on why this psalm is so dark and plaintive.

identified in 1 Kin. 4:31 as a gifted wise man, and in 1 Chr. 15:16–19 as one of the musically gifted Levites who ministered in worship during the time of David. The term Ezrahite may mean "native born." The name of the tune perhaps means "A Dance of Affliction." The structure is: (1) an opening prayer for deliverance (vv. 1, 2); (2) Heman's impending death (vv. 3–5); (3) a complaint about the Lord's attack on Heman (vv. 6–8); (4) God's delay in coming to the aid of Heman (vv. 9–12); (5) Heman's desperation as he senses no deliverance from the Lord (vv. 13–18).

88:1, 2 Even in the midst of despair, Heman confesses his faith in God's saving goodness—**O Lord, God of my salvation** (vv. 9, 13). **cried out . . . my cry:** This language of desperate weeping is not unusual in the psalms of lament. The Hebrew word for *cried* indicates a loud scream. The psalmist's appeal for God to listen—**incline Your ear**—has the same wording as in 86:1.

88:3–5 Grave here is the familiar word Sheol (86:13), which is often linked with the term **pit** as a symbol of death (30:3; 143:7; Prov. 1:12; Is. 14:15; 38:18). Heman feels so near to death that he describes himself as **adrift among the dead.**

88:6–8 Heman feels as though he were in **the lowest pit** and the deepest darkness. His most vexing problem, however, is his belief that God has brought this trouble on him. **put away . . . from me:** Not only does he feel troubled by God; he is also alone, separated from all of his friends.

88:9 Verses 9 and 13 are a reprise of v. 1. Heman continues to pray. Even though his eyes are strained and bloodshot from constant weeping, he continues to call out to the Lord for salvation.

88:10–16 The context of these verses is the worshiping community in Jerusalem (Ps. 6). If God allows Heman to die, Heman's voice will never again be heard in the temple giving praise to God. The word translated **place of destruc-**

tion is also found in Job 26:6; 28:22; Prov. 15:11; 27:20.

88:17, 18 In this psalm, Heman renews his complaints from earlier sections. However, he does not come to any resolution. As a person adrift at sea is aware only of the engulfing **water,** so Heman knows only the terrors of his life, which he believes come from the Lord. **Loved one:** In v. 8, Heman describes himself as removed from his friends; now he says his friends are removed from him. At the close of the psalm, Heman still feels alone, even though the psalms consistently describe a Lord that hears and answers those who call on Him (28:6).

Psalm 89 begins as a psalm of praise but ends as a psalm of lament. It celebrates God's covenant with David (2 Sam. 7) and then laments how David's descendants had not remained faithful to the provisions of that covenant (2 Sam. 7:14). Yet even in the face of unfaithfulness, this psalm reaffirms God's faithfulness to His covenant and its ultimate fulfillment in David's greater Son, the Messiah (vv. 33–37). The title attributes the psalm to Ethan, who was also known as Jeduthun (1 Chr. 25:1, 3, 6). The structure of the psalm is: (1) praise to the Lord for His everlasting covenant with David (vv. 1–4); (2) a celebration of God who established His covenant with David (vv. 5–18); (3) a review of the covenant with David (vv. 19–37); (4) consternation at a time of national distress (vv. 38–45); (5) a complaint to the Lord to provoke Him to remember His covenant and restore the fortunes of His people (vv. 46–51); (6) an appendix of blessing (v. 52).

89:1, 2 The **mercies** of the Lord in this psalm center on the covenant He made with David, promising him an eternal dynasty (2 Sam. 7). **Mercy,** which may be translated "loyal love," refers to the exact words of God's promise to David (2 Sam. 7:15). The Lord had promised that His mercy would always rest on David's son.

89:3, 4 Ethan quoted God's words to David

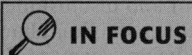 **IN FOCUS** "law"

(Heb. *torah*) (1:2; 89:30; 119:97; Ex. 24:12) Strong's #8451: Although usually translated *law*, the noun *torah* is derived from the verb *yarah*, meaning "to teach," and should be understood as carrying the idea of "instruction." The term can refer to any set of regulations, such as the instructions of parents (Prov. 1:8) or of a psalmist (Ps. 78:1). But usually the word refers to God's law. The writer of Ps. 119 expressed great love for God's law, because it led him to wisdom and righteousness (119:97–176). In the NT, Paul also praised God's Law because it pointed out his sin and made him realize his desperate need for a Savior (Rom. 7:7).

in 2 Sam. 7. David is referred to as **My chosen** and **My servant** (v. 20)—names that describe his intimate relationship with the Lord (2 Sam. 7:7). **Your seed . . . your throne:** God had promised David a line of descent and an enduring throne (2 Sam. 7:12, 13).

89:5, 6 All praise in heaven and earth belongs to God, who is incomparable. No one, not even the supposed gods, can match His strength and love. This is the point of the question, **Who in the heavens can be compared to the LORD?** The Hebrew phrase for **the sons of the mighty** may mean "sons of gods" or "heavenly beings." The reference could be to other supposed gods or to angels, members of the heavenly court (Job 1:6.).

89:7–10 Rahab is a title for Egypt (87:4). **The sea** and Rahab refer to God's great victories: in the beginning, His control of His creation; in the historic past, His victory over Egypt; and in the future, His complete triumph over Satan, sin, and death (Is. 27:1; 51:9). The psalmists regularly assert God's complete control of creation (24:1). Nothing can challenge God's majestic rule over the entire universe.

89:11, 12 The strong control of creation by the living God is asserted regularly in the psalms (24:1). He is victor over all His creation; there is nothing that can challenge His authority, power, or majestic rule.

89:13, 14 God is the great Deliverer; He brandished His **arm** and **hand** in delivering His people from Egypt (Ex. 6:6; 15:6). **Righteousness and justice** means "utter righteousness." **Mercy and truth** may be rephrased as "unbreakable loyalty."

89:15–18 Blessed, the same word used in 1:1, means "manifest happiness." To exalt the **horn** of the people (75:4, 5; 92:10; 132:17) means to give them power and eventual triumph. **The Holy One of Israel** (78:41) is the title Isaiah uses to describe God, following his experience of God's holiness in his memorable vision of God's throne (Is. 6).

89:19 The psalm recounts God's remarkable intervention in the life of David and the specifics of His covenant with David. **Your holy one:** David had been singled out as holy to the Lord. Yet his beginnings were not spectacular, for he was **from the people:** he had been an ordinary shepherd (2 Sam 7:18). In these respects and in many others, David was a type, or a divinely intended portrait, of the Savior. In a similar way, Jesus came from humble origins as the son of a carpenter. Yet He was the Holy One, the Son of the Most High.

89:20–23 These verses use highly poetic language to describe God's promise of protection for His king. Since the king was so closely allied with the living God, an attack on David (or his successor) was tantamount to an attack on God.

89:24, 25 My faithfulness and My mercy: The usual order of this common phrase is reversed here (vv. 1, 2). But the point is the same: God will remain true to His word and demonstrate His love to His servant. **sea . . . rivers:** The possible reference here is to Israel's expansion of its borders. But note the language used to describe God's control over creation (vv. 9, 10). The Lord is extending to His servant the authority He has over creation.

89:26–33 Father . . . firstborn: This wording is derived from God's covenant with David (2 Sam. 7:14). **seed . . . throne:** These words are repeated from v. 4 (v. 36; 2 Sam. 7:12, 13). **his sons:** The provisions of the Davidic covenant in 2 Sam. 7 included the discipline of errant sons.

89:34–38 The words **my covenant I will not break** and the wording of v. 35 are strong, so as to assure the reader that the will of the Lord is quite settled in this matter. The people might become faithless, but God cannot deny Himself. In spite of errors, rebellions, sins, and apostasies in the lives of many of the kings of Judah, God is determined to complete, fulfill, and accomplish His grand plan for David's dynasty (2 Sam. 7:1–24).

89:39 After the long recital of the details of the Lord's covenant with David and God's sworn statement that He would not revoke it (v. 35), the psalmist questions whether the covenant had really been honored. Most likely the occasion of this psalm was the defeat of Israel's armies, accounting for the psalmist's strong sense of consternation before the Lord. With the repeated use of the pronoun **You,** he addresses his complaint directly to God. **You have renounced the covenant of Your servant:** As in the case of Ps. 60, the military defeat that likely sparked this psalm was a temporary situation; a victory was still to come. Nonetheless, the poet presses his claim to God: This is the covenant that the Lord has established, that He has sworn Himself to uphold.

89:40–45 As a result of the military defeat, the people were despondent and disillusioned. The psalmist voices their feelings and thus allows the process of healing to begin, even as the people wait for their deliverance from the Lord.

89:46–48 The psalmist now gives the first of two *complaints*. The first is that God seemed to be unaware of how little time the people have to finally realize victory. Unlike God (90:1, 2), the life span of His people is quite ephemeral (90:3–6).

89:49–51 The writer complains that God has not been keeping His promises to David (2 Sam. 7:1–24). As a result, His people are experiencing undeserved **reproach** from their enemies. There is no resolution to this psalm; it ends with the people, the king, and the psalmist in distress. Yet the inclusion of this psalm among the praises of Israel suggests that God *did* answer this prayer of His beleaguered people, just as He did in the case of Ps. 60.

89:52 This verse is an editorial addition to Ps. 89, the concluding line of praise for Book III of the Psalms.

Psalm 90 is a psalm of lament in which the community complains of God's judgment and the brevity of life. But even in the midst of sorrow, the people acknowledge the security they have in the Lord and pray for renewal. This is the only poem in the Book of Psalms attributed to Moses, who wrote two other poems recorded in the Pentateuch (Ex. 15; Deut. 32). Psalm 90 has four sections: (1) an affirmation of the security of a life lived close to the Lord (vv. 1, 2); (2) a complaint about the brevity of life (vv. 3–6); (3) a complaint about God's judgment on His people (vv. 7–12); (4) a prayer for restoration (vv. 13–17).

90:1, 2 Lord here is not God's personal name (Ex. 3:14, 15), but a Hebrew word celebrating His majestic authority. The word suggests a title similar to "my Supreme Master." **Dwelling place** refers to the Lord as the "refuge" of His people (71:3; 91:9). **in all generations:** Throughout history, people have found the Lord to be their refuge in life.

90:3 The turn in this verse is alarmingly abrupt. One would have thought from the opening words of this psalm that it was a psalm of trust (such as Ps. 23). But this is not the case! The key to the psalm is found in vv. 11, 12; see there. **return:** Based on the words of Genesis 3:19, here the poet rues the words of God that call a life to *return* to dust. See the pun on this word in v. 13.

90:4, 5 Even if people lived **a thousand years,** they would pass away like **a watch in the night.** A thousand years may seem long at the time, but not in comparison to God's eternal existence. **Grass** sprouts after the spring rains, but wilts quickly in the heat—almost in a single day.

90:6, 7 wrath: The allusion is to the anger of God against the unbelieving Israelites in the wilderness (Num. 13; 14). An entire generation spent their lives wandering in the wilderness because of their unbelief and rebellion.

90:8–10 seventy . . . eighty years: The point here is not to set a maximum, but to present a context for the brevity of human life. No matter how long people live, it is inevitable that they will **fly away** to death.

90:11, 12 These verses are the key of the psalm. Moses had experienced a sufficient measure of God's **anger** (Ex. 32; Num. 14:11–25; Deut. 3:23–28). **teach:** What Moses needed was a new understanding of the meaning of his own life. **number our days:** This is more than just having a sense of mortality; it means valuing the time we do have by using it for eternal purposes.

90:13, 14 Moses uses the word **return** in v. 3 to refer to God's call for his death. Here he asks God to *return* for a renewed sense of life. **compassion . . . mercy:** Moses is asking God for new meaning in his life in the days that remain.

90:15 glad . . . afflicted: The pain of living can be modified by a sense of God's presence. This is a remarkable verse, showing tremendous insight into what some call "the human condition," but expressed in the context of biblical faith.

90:16, 17 Your work . . . Your glory: Moses asks God to give him a sense of lasting meaning in life, something that will continue to the next generation. The same idea is expressed in the words **the work of our hands. Beauty** refers to the "pleasantness" of God.

Psalm 91, a psalm of trust, does not identify its author. The psalm is sufficiently similar to Ps. 90, a psalm of Moses, that it might also be by him. Alternatively, the experiences and ideas of Moses could have been used by an anonymous writer. This poem has a very strong messianic thrust, and God Himself speaks in vv. 14–16 (Pss. 12; 60; 75; 87). The development of the psalm is in four main sections: (1) a confession of confidence in the Lord (vv. 1, 2); (2) assurance that those who trust in the Lord need not fear evil (vv. 3–8); (3) promises of God's protection to the coming One (vv. 9–13); (4) a description of the Lord's protection of the coming One (vv. 14–16).

91:1, 2 in the secret place: The person who trusts in God is the one who lives close to Him. The title **Most High** emphasizes God's majesty (92:1) and is parallel to the term **Almighty,** a translation of the divine title Shaddai. Together the terms Most High and Shaddai speak of God as a mountain-like majesty, in whose presence there is a "secret place" or a **shadow. My refuge and my fortress** may be rephrased as "my secure fortress."

91:3 fowler . . . pestilence: The images of

> A thousand years may seem long at the time, but not in comparison to God's eternal existence.

a bird trap and various types of disease are a general description of dangers that might come to helpless people.

91:4 His feathers . . . His wings: God is described as a mother hen under whose wings the psalmist can come for refuge (61:4; 63:7). **Shield and buckler** indicates complete protection from all harm. God is an all protective shield for the believer.

91:5, 6 The interplay of words for **night** and **day** in these verses indicates the universal nature of God's protection. **Terror, arrow, pestilence,** and **destruction** together refer to evil in general.

91:7, 8 A thousand . . . ten thousand: Like the Israelites in Egypt who were spared the danger that touched their neighbors (Ex. 9:26; 10:23; 11:7), believers in the Lord are protected from any assault. **look . . . and see:** The punishment of the wicked is as sure as the deliverance of the righteous.

91:9, 10 In vv. 14–16, God describes directly the same person addressed by the psalmist in vv. 9–13. This person is the coming One. **My refuge** is the same word used in v. 2. **Dwelling place** is the same word used in 90:1. **Most High:** The psalmist indicates that the coming One's faith in God is the same as the psalmist's.

91:11–13 His angels . . . a stone: These words were used by Satan to tempt the Savior (Matt. 4:5, 6). **the lion and the cobra:** The animal and snake imagery in this verse pictures all kinds of evil that might threaten the coming One. The Father will protect Him no matter what the danger.

91:14 The verb used here for **love** is not the usual Hebrew word for love. It has the idea of "holding close to," even "hugging tightly in love" (Deut. 7:7; 10:15). **He has known My name** speaks of an intimate, experiential knowledge of the Father (John 1:18).

91:15, 16 The promises of Yahweh are to **deliver** the Coming One (v. 15), and to grant Him **long life** (v. 16). These words are a promise of the Father for the resurrection of the Son, and for the provision of His subsequent everlasting life (16:10, 11; 72:15; 118:17, 18). The **salvation** provided for the Coming One is not justification (as He is just in His person), but deliverance from death in the Resurrection (as in 118:21). Thus, Psalm 91 concludes in a dramatic manner, a direct promise from the Father to the Son concerning His ultimate victory over death itself (1 Cor. 15:20, 21).

Psalm 92, a psalm of descriptive praise (see Ps. 113), celebrates the person and work of God in an exuberant way. The psalm also includes several wisdom themes. The title is unusual in that it attaches the designation "for the Sabbath day." The poem has four brief sections: (1) an

encouragement for the people to respond to God in praise and worship (vv. 1–4); (2) a celebration of the wisdom of God in bringing judgment on the wicked (vv. 5–9); (3) an acknowledgment of the mercy of God who has established the believer's present life (vv. 10, 11); (4) an anticipation of the mercy of God that will continue in the life to come (vv. 12–15).

92:1–5 The wording of this section has similarities to Pss. 33:1, 2; 147:1; 149:1. **To give thanks** means "to give public acknowledgment" or to praise God verbally in a public setting (35:18; 105:1).

92:6 A senseless man . . . a fool: In contrast to the limitless wisdom of God is the shallow nature of the fool (14:1).

92:87–9 You, Lord, are on high forevermore is the central shout of this psalm of descriptive praise (113:4). The Lord's eternality is contrasted with the brevity of the lives of His **enemies.** Because of God's patience, He allows evil to occur (2 Pet. 3:9)—but He will not allow it to flourish forever.

92:10 My horn you have exalted (75:4, 5; 89:17, 24; 132:17) is a figure of speech for the psalmist's eventual triumph, the celebration of the psalmist's strength. **I have been anointed with fresh oil** is not just a general statement of God's interest in the poet, but a prediction of the coming One, the Lord's Anointed.

92:11–15 The language of this section speaks of God's continuing blessing on the believer not only in this life but also in the life to come (Ps. 23). The **tree** image recalls the words of 1:3.

Psalm 93, a royal psalm, focuses on the reign of God over the earth, making use of a distinctly Canaanite perspective. The psalmist denies Baal and shouts exuberantly in praise of God. God is King of the universe. What are humans compared to Him? God is King of heaven. What are the gods compared to Him? God is King of all. To whom may He be compared (Is. 40:25)? This focus is one of the most impressive ideas in the Bible. The structure of Ps. 93 is as follows: (1) the establishment of the reign of God as King of creation (vv. 1, 2); (2) the celebration of the stability of God as King of creation (vv. 3, 4); (3) the acknowledgment of the excellent nature of God (v. 5).

93:1, 2 The Lord reigns is the key of the royal psalms (96:10; 97:1; 99:1). The language **girded Himself with strength** describes the victor of one-on-one combat. God is dressed in the garments of victory. This is a celebration of God as the Creator. **cannot be moved:** There is no power on earth or in the universe that can wrench control of the earth from God. **from of old:** Unlike Baal, who was a recent "upstart" in the myths of Canaan, the rule of God is from antiquity. The living God is eternal.

93:3, 4 The floods: Baal was supposed to have been victorious over the waters; thus, this section of the poem is a continuing refutation of Baal worship while it joyfully celebrates the power of God. **The Lord . . . is mightier:** The Creator King is infinite in power; no force in the universe competes with Him.

93:5 While this psalm uses language resembling the worship of Baal to emphasize the greatness of God (Ps. 29), it also glorifies God with praises never attributed to Baal. None of the accolades of Baal speak of his **testimonies.** But God is superior to Baal, for He is faithful to His word. He is the gracious God who speaks to His people; He is the holy God of Scripture who is approached by His people; and He is the eternal God whom we worship, as did the people of ancient Israel.

Psalm 94 is a royal psalm, since the phrase "Judge of the earth" (v. 2) is equivalent to "King" (50:4–6). The righteous call for the divine Judge to punish evil in the world (82:8; 96:13; 98:9). Psalms 93—99 are a splendid set of psalms focused on the eternal reign of God. The order of the psalm is as follows: (1) a call for the Judge of the earth to punish the wicked (vv.

1–3); (2) a description of the senseless acts of the wicked (vv. 4–7); (3) a chiding of the wicked concerning their ignorance of God (vv. 8–11); (4) a blessing on the righteous (vv. 12–15); (5) a prayer for God's intervention in the psalmist's life (vv. 16–19); (6) a prayer for God's defense of His own purposes (vv. 20–23).

94:1–3 Even when the poets call out for divine **vengeance,** they recognize that God decides when to exercise His wrath and judgment. God's Law clearly states that vengeance belongs to Him (Deut. 32:35). **How long will the wicked triumph:** This question is based on a concern for the glory of God. How long would the wicked defy God? The answer, of course, is in God's mercy. The Lord may delay this judgment, but in His own timing He will come to establish true justice (2 Pet. 3:9).

94:4–6 The Psalms often describe the wicked in terms of their evil **speech** (Ps. 12). **They slay the widow and the stranger:** The Israelites had been commanded to comfort widows and orphans and to welcome strangers as long as those strangers obeyed the Law of God (Ex. 22:22). Thus the wicked were brazenly disobeying God's commands.

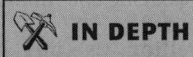 **IN DEPTH** | **Royal Psalms**

Some of the most inspiring psalms are the royal psalms. These are psalms that celebrate God as King. It is amazing that the first time Scripture refers to God as King is in one of the oracles of Balaam, the pagan seer who was blind to spiritual reality until God confronted him (Num. 23:21). Once God was revealed as the Great King, the psalmists made much of that fact.

The reign of God in the Psalms is presented against the cultural backdrop of Canaanite thought and religion. The Canaanites regarded their chief deity El as king of the gods. But according to Canaanite mythology, El's rule was attacked by Baal, a god of storm and fertility. He defeated a number of the followers of El. These were the gods Yamm (the god of the sea), Lotan (a sea monster), and Mot (the god of death). Baal himself was mortally wounded in this conflict and Anat, the wife-sister of Baal, was associated with his resuscitation. With this victory, Baal became king. But there was always a lingering question: How long would Baal rule? How long would his enemies remain defeated? Could not Lotan surge anew and threaten Baal's position? The Canaanites who believed in these stories lived their lives on the brink of a heavenly catastrophe. Their gods were fragile; they were easily established and easily deposed.

It is against this background that the words of Ps. 93 obtain their force. The living God is the King from the beginning of time; He is no recent claimant to power (vv. 1, 2). As King, He exercises authority over all. He does not have to fear a resurgent sea (vv. 3, 4). Not only is the Lord omnipotent, but He is truthful and holy, unlike any of the gods of the Canaanite imagination (v. 5).

In general, the royal psalms speak of the Lord as King in three different ways. He is King over creation, for He is the Creator (74:12–17). He is King over the Israelites (44:4), for He is their Savior. And He is the coming King, for He will eventually judge everyone (47:7, 8). Sometimes in people's minds God's kingdom is narrowly identified with the coming glorious rule of Jesus: God's present reign over creation is ignored. But sometimes the opposite is true. God's present rule can be emphasized so much that Jesus' coming is disregarded. The royal psalms consistently balance these two ideas: "The Lord reigns" (93:1), but the Lord is also coming to establish His permanent rule (24:9).

94:7 the LORD does not see: As in the description of the wicked in Psalm 10:11, these wicked persons are oblivious to the reality of God, scornful of His interest, derisive of His nearness. They shall rue these words and actions.

94:8–11 The command to **understand** is for fools to abandon their foolishness. Surely, the poet argues, the Creator of the earth is not deaf, nor is the Fashioner of the eye blind. Although idols do not have real eyes and ears (115:3–8), the God of heaven does see and hear. **The LORD knows:** The difference between the thoughts of God and the thoughts of human beings is beyond comprehension. **The thoughts of man** apart from God are **futile** or "quickly passing."

94:12 Blessed is the man: This beatitude uses the word with which the Book of Psalms begins, a term meaning "manifest happiness." These words are very similar to the ideas of 1:2.

94:13, 14 Pit is one of the words used as a synonym for Sheol (16:10). Digging the "pit" is a way of describing the preparations for the final judgment of the wicked (Rev. 20). **will not cast off His people:** God will not forget His people any more than He will forget or deny Himself (2 Tim. 2:13).

94:15 judgment will return: This verse seems to describe the way that the truly righteous will return to the Lord and to their walk with Him even after a time of disobedience. That is, those who truly know the Lord will be attracted back to Him; those who are not His may appear to belong, but in time will show that this is not the case.

94:16–19 Who will rise up for me is an appeal to the Lord who alone is the sure defense of the believer. **settled in silence:** The psalmist exclaims that if the Lord had not delivered him, he would have died. As in 6, if the psalmist had died, his voice would no longer be able to praise God in the temple. The **comforts** of God extend from His hearing the call of the righteous to His meeting their needs even when they are not aware of them.

94:20–23 Throne of iniquity is a description of the wicked who have great power. The holy Lord cannot tolerate evil in His presence. **The LORD . . . shall cut them off:** Final judgment will one day come to the wicked.

Psalm 95 places particular emphasis on the worship of God, making it a worship psalm. But it is also a royal psalm because of the way it acknowledges God as the great King (v. 3). The psalm has three movements, each reflecting a "mood" of the worshiping community: (1) the worship of God in a mood of celebration (vv. 1–5); (2) the worship of God in a contemplative mood (vv. 6, 7); (3) the worship of God in obedience (vv. 8–11).

95:1–5 Oh come: The psalm begins with energy and delight at the prospect of worshiping God in the temple (Ps. 100). The use of the **psalms** in worship is indicated in this passage. **In His hand** refers to God's control over all that He has made.

95:6, 7 Each of the key verbs in this sentence describes a physical posture of humility before the Lord. The Hebrew word translated **worship** means literally "to prostrate oneself." When **bow down, kneel,** and **worship** occur together as in this verse, they amplify each another and call for a reflective, humble approach to God. Worship is joyful and can be done with abandon (vv. 1–5); but at other times worship may be quiet reverence of the Almighty (Ps. 134). **people of His pasture:** These words seem to be an inversion of the wording of 100:3, expressing the loving care the Father has for His children.

95:7–11 The third movement of this psalm is a call for obedience in worship and a reminder of God's judgments in past times on people who did not take Him seriously. The entire section is quoted in its entirety in Heb. 3:7–11, with a notable introduction: "Therefore, as the Holy Spirit says" (Heb. 3:7). This phrase reminds us that the words of the psalms, which are the response of the worshiping Israelite community, are also the oracles of God.

95:8 The word **rebellion** is literally "Meribah," a word that would remind the Israelites of the times they had doubted the Lord's provision for them (Ex. 17:7; Num. 20:13). The event of Meribah was the rebellion of the first generation at Kadesh (Num. 14). By refusing to enter Canaan, the entire generation of Israelites lost their opportunity to enjoy the promises of God in the land of blessing.

Psalm 96, a royal psalm, is part of the set that begins at Ps. 93. This psalm emphasizes world mission, specifically the prophetic fulfillment of the mission provision of the Abrahamic covenant (Ps. 67). The structure of the poem is as follows: (1) a call to praise God (vv. 1–3); (2) a celebration of God the Creator (vv. 4–6); (3) a celebration of God the King (vv. 7–10); (4) a celebration of God the Coming One (vv. 11–13).

96:1–3 Among the nations is a bold declaration that one day the message of God's mercy will be known the world over. One day the message of God's salvation will be known **among all peoples.** This declaration depends on God's promise to Abraham that through his descendants all nations of the earth will be blessed (Gen. 12:1–3). It also anticipates Jesus' command to his disciples to spread the news of God's goodness to a desperate world (Matt. 28:18–20; Ps. 67).

96:4–6 The mention of other gods in v. 4 is

clarified by the words of v. 5: these gods are merely **idols. Honor and majesty** may be rephrased as "majestic honor." **Strength and beauty** may be rephrased as "beautiful strength."

96:7–9 families of the peoples: The allusion to the Abrahamic covenant continues (vv. 2, 3; Gen. 12:1–3). One day, the praise of God will come gladly from people of all nations. **Give to the Lord:** The words of vv. 7–9 are quoted from 29:1, 2, with the substitution of "O families of the peoples" for "O you mighty ones."

96:10 The Lord reigns is the key phrase of the royal psalms (93:1). It was the countercultural cry of ancient Israelites in a world that believed that gods could rise and fall. In contrast, the living God remains Ruler for all eternity. **He shall judge:** This verse answers the cry of the oppressed peoples of world history. God will restore justice (82:8; 94:1–3).

96:11–13 Let the heavens rejoice: This poem calls for all of creation to respond to the coming of the King of glory. **He is coming . . . He is coming:** Like the echo of approaching footsteps, the words echo each other. **judge the world:** See 98:9 for similar words; see Rev. 19—20 for their fulfillment.

Psalm 97, one of the series of royal psalms (Pss. 93—99), has a particularly apocalyptic tone in its description of God's final judgment on the wicked before He establishes His great kingdom. The structure of the poem is: (1) a call for the praise of God the King (v. 1); (2) a vision of the coming judgment of the wicked (vv. 2–6);

(3) a prophetic statement about the end of idolatry (vv. 7–9); (4) a promise of great joy for the righteous (vv. 10, 11); (5) a call for the praise of God the King (v. 12).

97:1 The Lord reigns is the key phrase of the royal psalms (93:1). **The earth** as a whole and its smallest parts—the **isles**—join together in rejoicing at the prospect of God's reign on earth.

97:2 Clouds and darkness may be rephrased "impenetrable clouds," an indicator of the final judgment and God's awesome power (Joel 2:2; Zeph. 1:15). **Righteousness and justice** may be rephrased as "absolute righteousness." The foundation of God's coming judgment will be His integrity; His judgments will be correct.

97:3–6 fire: The psalmist uses the imagery of the storm god Baal to describe God's judgment. This poetic language attempts to describe the final judgment of God upon the earth before He establishes His kingdom.

97:7, 8 The continuing practice of idolatry throughout world history is a grave offense against the Lord. Such behavior will finally end in **shame** and terror (14:5). **Worship Him:** Anything that serves as an object of worship will one day bow before the true God (115:4–10).

97:9–11 To **hate** means to reject; to **love** means to choose. Since both are an expression of the will and not merely an emotion, the Bible commands both love and hatred. **Light is sown:** The picture is that of someone sowing seed, with the seed being light and joy. This speaks of the restoration of the earth (Ps. 110).

✠ IN CONTEXT | Dismissing the "Gods"

Hymns of praise in the ancient Near East often declared the god being praised to be superior to all other gods. The Bible occasionally uses that kind of language, but more often goes beyond it and says that Yahweh is the only God.

One way of dismissing other gods was to say they were only statues. The supposed "gods of the peoples" are nothing more than the inanimate idols themselves (Ps. 96:5). Yahweh is declared the true deity because only He created the world—"the Lord made the heavens" (96:5). All other gods are impotent and unworthy of adoration; they should be ignored. People who could mistake stone, metal, or wood for a real god are foolish.

A second way of dismissing other gods was to leave open the possibility they existed, yet maintain that they had no serious power and therefore were not to be taken seriously. The prophet Jeremiah, for example, says that other gods did not create the world and will therefore cease to exist (Jer. 10:11). Their insignificance is stressed by their being placed lower than Yahweh in divine authority.

In this way the Hebrew poets were able to adapt the usual language of Near Eastern hymns into the worship of Yahweh. To Israel and Judah, only Yahweh mattered. The other deities either did not exist or were so meaningless that whether they existed was irrelevant. Yahweh was "to be feared above all gods" (Ps. 96:4).

97:12 rejoice: The psalm begins and ends on a note of rejoicing.

Psalm 98, one of the set of royal psalms that includes Pss. 93—99, is an exuberant psalm of praise This poem shares the same joy as Ps. 96. The outline is as follows: (1) a call to praise God as the Savior (vv. 1–3); (2) a call to praise God as the King (vv. 4–6); (3) a call to praise God as the coming Judge (vv. 7–9).

98:1–2 The term **marvelous things** is used only to describe the actions of God in the Bible. The **right hand** of the Lord is a way of referring to His great salvation of Israel from Egypt (Ex. 15:6; Deut. 4:34). The phrase is like a slogan for the Lord's redemption (118:15, 16). **sight of the nations:** God's salvation was designed to be a witness to the nations (Deut. 4:6).

96:4–6 above all gods: From time to time in the psalms, there is a tacit admission of the existence of other gods, only to allow the assertion that none of the supposed gods may be compared to Yahweh. **idols:** In this psalm, the admission of other gods in v. 4 is cut to the quick with the words of v. 5. Indeed, here is one of the great word plays in the Bible. The term translated *idols* is a pun on the regularly used word

---

🔍 **IN FOCUS**   **"psalm"**

(Heb. *mizmor*) (The titles of Pss. 98; 100; 103; 143) Strong's #4210: The Hebrew word *mizmor* is derived from the verb *zamar* "to make music." The word occurs only in the Psalms, in 57 of the psalm headings. It may designate a praise song or possibly a song accompanied by a certain type of instrumental music. In 34 psalm titles, *mizmor* follows the phrase "To the Chief Musician," perhaps indicating that the psalms were typically songs accompanied by instruments. Frequently the author of the psalm is also identified, such as the sons of Korah (Pss. 48; 84), of Asaph (Pss. 50; 82), and especially of David (Pss. 23; 29; 51).

---

for God. Here the word is *'elîlîm*, a word that sounds suspiciously like *'elôhîm* (God). But this word is a compound plural of the Hebrew term for "nothing"! The gods of the nations are "nothings." **made the heavens:** And Yahweh, the God who is, has created all that is. What great praise this is! **honor and majesty** (v. 6): These words form a hendiadys (25:8), as do the pair "strength and beauty" in the next colon.

The resultant pairs, "majestic honor" and "beautiful strength" are beautiful descriptions of the great King.

98:7, 8 In Canaanite thought, **the sea** represented a dark deity. In the Psalms, the sea is a part of creation that God completely controls (Ps. 93). The **clapping** of the **hands** of the **rivers** and the rejoicing of the **hills** represents the praise of creation at the establishment of God's kingdom on the earth.

98:9 He is coming: This verse and 96:13 answer the call for justice found at many points in the Psalms. The coming of the Judge is a reason for joy. At last the Lord will put an end to cruelty, evil, and injustice.

Psalm 99, the last of the set of royal palms that began with Ps. 93, praises God as the King of His people. The psalm has three movements, each ending with the words "He is holy:" (1) praise to the Lord in the greatness of His glory (vv. 1–3); (2) praise to the King in the justice of His rule (vv. 4, 5); praise to the Lord who answers the prayers of His people (vv. 6–9).

99:1, 2 The cherubim are the angels most closely related to the glory of God. Two gold cherubim graced the mercy seat of the ark of the covenant (Ex. 25:18–22). **Let the earth be moved:** Since God is the great King, the stability of the earth depends on Him; He can shake the world to demonstrate His power over it (Matt. 24:29). **great in Zion:** The holy temple in Jerusalem was the earthly structure for God's heavenly presence. But His reign extends throughout the entire world.

99:3 awesome name: The name of God is a blessing and comfort; it also evokes awe and wonder. **Holy** means to be "distant" or "distinct from." This is the principal Hebrew word used to describe the transcendence of God (113:4–6).

99:4, 5 The **footstool** of the Lord is sometimes said to be the earth (Is. 66:1); but more specifically, Zion is the Lord's footstool (132:7; Is. 60:13). When the Israelites came to the temple in Jerusalem to worship, they pictured themselves as being at the feet of the Creator.

99:6 The psalmists worshiped God by recalling His saving acts to their predecessors. **Moses** is mentioned by name in the Psalms several times (77:20; 103:7; 105:26; 106:16, 23, 32), as is **Aaron** (77:20; 105:26; 106:16; 115:10, 12; 118:3; 133:2; 135:19). This psalm is the only one to mention **Samuel** by name. **He answered:** The inference is clear—the Lord heard their prayers and did not remain silent. Since God answered the prayers of our ancestors, surely He will continue to answer the prayers of those who call upon Him.

99:7–9 His holy hill: As in 2:6, the site of Zion is "holy" because of the presence of the Lord. This holy hill is also His "footstool" (v. 5).

🔍 IN FOCUS | "thanksgiving"

(Heb. *todah*) (The title of Pss. 100; 69:30; 100:4) Strong's #8426: The Hebrew word *todah* is derived from the verb *yadah*. In its simplest form, *yadah* means "to throw" or "to cast," and common forms of this verb mean to "acknowledge," "confess," or "praise." Thus *todah* is an "acknowledgment" or "confession," either of one's own shortcomings (Josh. 7:19–21) or of God's goodness (100:4; 107:22). Another meaning of *todah* is "thanksgiving offering," which was an optional sacrifice made to express thanks to God (Lev. 7:12–15; 22:29). Psalm 100 is a typical psalm for use when giving such an offering, praising God's righteousness in contrast to the people's sin (as in Ps. 51:14) and confessing God's greatness through singing (as in Ps. 147:7).

Psalm 100 is a psalm of descriptive praise that follows a set of royal psalms (Pss. 93—99). Perhaps the ancient editors felt that the royal psalms demanded the response of worship provided by this psalm. The phrase "A Psalm of Thanksgiving" refers to public acknowledgment of the Lord.

100:1, 2 The Hebrew verb for **make a joyful shout** is a highly charged command for public praise. The command is addressed not just to Israel but to all the earth. The Israelites were to be a people who would attract the nations to worship God. **with gladness:** Joyful abandon was not the only mood of worship in ancient Israel (Ps. 95), but there was great emphasis placed on it.

100:3 The words **the LORD,** He is God reflect the great confession of faith in Deut 6:4–9. To **know** that the Lord is God is very similar to the command to "hear" in Deuteronomy. **And not we ourselves** is sometimes read "and His we are." **sheep of His pasture:** An inversion of these words can be found in 95:7.

100:4 Enter: The commands of vv. 1, 2 are reiterated. The people of the Lord may actually come into His presence and bring Him worship that pleases Him. **Be thankful** is a command for public expression of praise (106:1).

100:5 the LORD is good: The shout of the goodness of God in this verse is buttressed by an appeal to **His mercy** and **His truth.** The Hebrew word for *truth* comes from the root meaning "to be established" or "to be confirmed." From this root also comes the word *amen,* meaning "surely" or "truly." God's goodness is based on His loyal love and His truth.

Psalm 101 is a royal psalm. David the king declares his purposes and asks for God's help in maintaining righteousness. This brief psalm has a tone of strong judgment, indicating a desire not only to preserve the innocent and protect the needy, but also to maintain the reputation of God against the attacks of His foes. The outline of the poem is: (1) a determination to praise the

Lord (v. 1);2 a determination to behave wisely (v. 2); (3) a determination to abstain from wickedness (vv. 3–5); (4) a determination to discriminate between the righteous and the wicked (vv. 6–8).

101:1, 2 Mercy and justice may be rephrased as "gracious justice." There is a harshness to the tone of the psalm that might emphasize the *justice* element of this phrasing; but underlying the justice is God's "mercy" or "loyal love." **Behave wisely** means to act with skill. The strong form of the word indicates intense determination, not just a passing desire.

101:3, 4 The Hebrew expression for **wicked** implies utter worthlessness. The phrase **I hate** indicates utter rejection (5:5). David hated what God hated and loved what God loved. **not know:** The Hebrew verb for "to know" here has the idea of experience or intimate relationship with something or someone.

101:5–8 David made a covenant with his **eyes** (Job 31:1) to observe the righteous and sustain them in their walk. Alternatively, his eyes were also directed *against* the wicked. **the evildoers:** Elsewhere, this Hebrew phrase is rendered *workers of iniquity* (14:4).

Psalm 102, a penitential psalm, has an unusual inscription. The title describes a person in distress but does not name him. The structure of the poem is: (1) a cry to the Lord for deliverance (vv. 1, 2); (2) a description of the groaning brought about by guilt (vv. 3–7); (3) a description of suffering that results from the laughter of enemies (vv. 8–11); (4) praise to the Lord who rises to answer prayer (vv. 12–17); (5) praise to the Lord who stoops to the needs of His people (vv. 18–22); (6) a petition to the Lord to renew the strength of His servant (vv. 23–28).

102:1 In its entreaty for the Lord to **hear,** the beginning of the psalm reflects a pattern of lament (13:1, 2). The next section (vv. 3–7) reflects a pattern of penitence (32:3–5).

102:2, 3 my days are consumed: This description of the psalmist's sense of his own frailty is matched by the words of 144:4, "like a passing shadow."

102:4–8 The psalmist names birds—**a pelican, an owl,** and **a sparrow**—who live in distant, lonely places. The psalmist felt isolated, alone, and vulnerable, an isolation intensified by the harsh ranting of his enemies, who **deride** him for his decision to trust in the Lord.

102:9–12 Shall endure may also be translated "sits enthroned." God is King forever. He is gracious, loves His people, and promises to favor them. With these words of praise, the psalmist expresses his hope that God will deliver him.

102:13–15 The psalmist anticipates a time when the Lord will reign over all the **nations** (Pss. 96—98); but his prayer is for God's answer to his own cry for deliverance.

102:16–19 The psalmist realizes that the Eternal One has stooped from heaven to meet his need, that the King of kings has come to his aid. His joy is such that he wants people who have not yet been born to learn what God has done.

102:20–28 midst of my days: The psalmist remembers his troubling experiences and contrasts the brevity of his own life with the eternity of God. **Of old:** God is eternal and His works are from ancient times. The writer of the Book of Hebrews applies these words of creation and eternality to the Son (vv. 25–27; Heb. 1:10–12).

Psalm 103, a wisdom psalm attributed to David, is also a psalm of praise. The poem begins with the psalmist speaking in the singular (v. 1), but then moves to include the community, both angels and people (vv. 20–22). The structure of the psalm is: (1) praise of the Lord for His many benefits (vv. 1–5); (2) praise of the Lord for His ongoing mercy (vv. 6–10); (3) praise of the Lord for His transcendent glory and gentle care (vv. 11–14); (4) a comparison of the transitory nature of humanity with the everlasting rule of God (vv. 15–19); (5) a call for heaven and earth to bless the Lord (vv. 20–22).

103:1 To **bless the LORD** is to remember that He is the source of all our blessings. The psalmist blesses the Lord with his entire being (146:2).

103:2–5 heals all your diseases: There are godly people who suffer illness, despite repeated prayers for healing. Even though God is not bound to heal every disease, every healing does come from Him. **Who satisfies your mouth:** In addition to being a healer, God provides food as well as other blessings (111:5). His mercy enables the believer to rise up like an eagle (Is. 40:31).

103:6 God is *for* the helpless and the **oppressed.** He is not unfair, for He is the One who will restore justice to the earth.

103:7 made known His ways to Moses: God blessed His servant Moses in a special way by revealing the Law to him. **His acts:** During the Exodus and the wilderness wanderings, God acted on the Israelites' behalf. He saved them from Pharaoh's army, provided them with water and food, but most importantly revealed the Law to them.

103:8–14 The LORD is merciful: This is a basic description of God in the OT (86:15; Ex. 34:6, 7). If God dealt with us **according to our sins,** no one could stand before Him (130:3). There is no way to compare the divine with the mortal; the mercy of God is greater than **the heavens.** He removes our sins completely (Mic. 7:19) and cares for His people as a good **father** cares for his **children.** The fact that God remembers who we are and how He made us is another mark of His mercy, for **we are dust.**

103:15 as for man: The transitory nature of our lives is a regular feature of the thinking of the writers of the psalms; as with all thoughtful people, they were amazed at the brevity of life and its fragile nature. Our lives are as short-lived, it seems, as a spring flower that is beset by the summer wind.

103:16–19 Mercy may be rephrased as

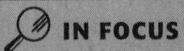 **IN FOCUS** | "soul"

(Heb. *nephesh*) (11:5; 103:1, 2; Lev. 26:30; Is. 1:14; 42:1; Jer. 5:9; 15:1) Strong's #5315: This Hebrew word occurs more than 750 times in the Bible. It has quite a number of meanings, but most of them can be reduced to the following four categories: (1) life or the life force, especially in connection with blood (Gen. 9:4, 5; Lev. 17:11, 14); (2) one's soul or the immaterial being, the seat of intellect and emotion (42:1, 2; 86:4; 1 Sam. 1:10; 2 Sam. 5:8; Prov. 23:7; Song 1:7); and (3) an individual or person (84:2; Gen. 2:7; Judg. 12:3; Ezek. 18:4). Originally the word probably referred to the breath (Job 41:21). The Bible typically considers a person as an interconnected whole. This is why the Bible tells us to love God with all our heart, soul, and strength—in other words, with our entire being (Deut. 6:4, 5; Josh. 22:5).

"loyal love." God's anger is for a moment (v. 8); His loyal love is forever. His blessing is on those who keep faith with Him (147:11). **His throne:** The Lord is King of all and King forever. His rule is the only rule that matters.

103:20–22 Bless the Lord: The poet began the psalm with a call to his own inner being to respond with praise to God (v. 1); he concludes the psalm with a call to heaven and earth to join him in joyful praise.

Psalm 104, a wisdom psalm, is also a creation psalm (Ps. 19). It is an exuberant poetic recasting of Gen. 1, a joyful celebration of the world as the creation of God. The poetry of the psalmists and the prophets often reflects upon God's work in creation. The structure of the poem is: (1) praise for God's great creation (vv. 1, 2); (2) the creation of the heavens (vv. 3, 4); (3) the creation of the earth (vv. 5–9); (4) the waters of blessing (vv. 10–13); (5) the fullness of the earth (vv. 14–18); (6) the patterns of life (vv. 19–23); (7) praise for God's great creation (vv. 24–26); (8) an acknowledgment that all life is dependent upon the Lord (vv. 27–30); (9) a prayer for God's glory (vv. 31, 32); (10) a personal response to God (vv. 33–35).

104:1, 2 God is Spirit (John 4:24), and descriptions of Him vary through the Bible. One strong description of Him is **light** (1 John 1:5). Here light is described as the garment that enfolds His wonder. The first act of God in Genesis was the command for light (Gen. 1:3).

104:3, 4 beams of His upper chambers: With these poetic words, the psalmist alludes to the heavenly dwelling place of God, a place beyond human understanding. **makes the clouds His chariot:** Idolaters used similar language of Baal. The psalmist strips Baal of these honors and applied them to the living God (Ps. 93). **Angels** are also spirit beings; they may appear as flames of fire (Is. 6:2).

104:5–7 You who laid the foundations of the earth is a poetic way of describing how God created the heavens and the earth. **The deep** is the same term used in Gen. 1:2. **At Your rebuke:** The poet recalls that God brought dry land from the watery abyss in Gen. 1:9, 10. The word of God is referred to as a "rebuke" or a "thundering."

104:8, 9 A boundary is a regular theme in wisdom literature (Prov. 8:29). God's control over the turbulent waters (Ps. 93) is proof that He, not Baal, is the true Sovereign.

104:10–13 the springs: From the exalted stance of vv 1–9, the poem now descends to the levels of valley springs and drinking donkeys. All is lovely, all in the blessing of God's great care (147:8).

104:11–15 vegetation: The basis for this section is Gen. 1:11–13, the creative acts of God on the third day. Here the psalmist indicates the

Photo by Gustav Jeeninga

Wild flowers near Jerusalem, in the Kidron Valley. The psalmist probably had flowers such as these in mind when he spoke of the fleeting nature of life (Ps. 103:15, 16).

specific purpose of God's creation: to provide for the needs of human beings. **Wine, oil,** and **bread**—staples of everyday life in Israel—are blessings of God to enrich life.

104:16–18 trees and **hills** each have their place in the divine ecology for manifold animal life. A Christian response to these verses includes a concern for animal habitat and the environment all about us. Such things God takes pleasure in; how may we ignore these altogether?

104:19 seasons: The events of the fourth day of creation are reviewed here (Gen. 1:14–19). The point is that God has established the patterns of life.

104:20–24 The Hebrew wisdom writers looked at the world with a sense of wonder and reverence because it reflected the **wisdom** of its Creator.

104:25, 26 References to the **sea** in the psalms are generally in the context of Canaanite ideas. The Canaanites said that Baal controlled the powerful gods of the seas. But the psalmist asserts in the face of this falsehood that God created the waters and everything in them—even Leviathan, the great sea monster (Job 41).

104:27–30 These all wait: All creation depends on the Creator for birth, life, and sustenance. Even death is controlled by the Sovereign One.

104:31 God continues to **rejoice** in His creative work on earth (Prov. 8:30, 31). The Lord considered His creation "good" from the beginning (Gen. 1:31), and His pleasure in it remains.

104:32–35 my meditation: The poet wants to respond properly to God's creation. **Bless the LORD** echoes the beginning of the psalm (v. 1).

Psalm 105, a psalm of praise (compare Ps. 113), focuses on the positive experiences of Israel in their early history. Contrast Ps. 106, which reviews the same period of history but with an emphasis on the faithlessness of the people. This poem celebrates God's faithfulness to His covenant with Abraham in the lives of His people. The people needed to remember to be faithful to God, who had never forgotten to be faithful to them. The structure of the poem is: (1) a call for praise to God (vv. 1–6); (2) God's covenant with Abraham (vv. 7–12); (3) the early experiences of God's people (vv. 13–15); (4) the experience of Joseph (vv. 16–22); (5) the experience of Israel in Egypt (vv. 23–25); (6) the great deliverance from Egypt (vv. 26–36); (7) the great provisions (vv. 37–41); (8) God's promise to Abraham (vv. 42–45).

105:1–6 The psalmist calls to memory what God did for His people in fulfillment of the covenant with Abraham (Gen. 12:1–3;

13:14–17; 15:13–21; 17:7, 8; 26:3, 4; 28:13–15). **Remember** is the key idea of the psalm: the psalmist wanted to remind God's people of His goodness.

105:7 His judgments: God's actions against the Egyptians (Ex. 6:6).

105:8 The psalmist assured his audience that even if they did not *remember,* God does remember. **He remembers:** The words of the original promise to Abraham set out the Lord's obligation in strong terms (Gen. 12:1–3). These ideas are reinforced by the dramatic encounter with Abraham in Gen. 15. In the story of the binding of Isaac in Gen. 22, the Lord undertakes an irrevocable oath of obligation (Gen. 22:16–18).

105:9–15 When they went: This section is an overview of the history of Israel, probably written after the return of the exiles from Babylon (Ps. 147). This is not a necessary conclusion, but it appears likely. The major theme of the poem is God's faithfulness to His people in their early history. **My anointed ones:** The parallel term **My prophets** suggests that these are the leaders of Israel—the kings and priests.

105:16, 17 The experiences of **Joseph** occupy a long section of the Book of Genesis (Gen. 37—50). Here Joseph's story is recounted as poetry and song.

105:18–25 Israel also came into Egypt: The descent of Israel to Egypt accomplished two things: they were spared from starvation during the period of great famine; they were kept from assimilation by the people of Canaan until they were large enough to be a cohesive people on their own. **He turned their heart:** When the time was right, God directed the attitudes of the Egyptians to turn on His people, to afford their redemption.

105:26–42 The psalmist recites the history

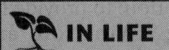 **IN LIFE** | **Looking Back**

Perhaps your pastor gives an annual report of your church in which he points out some of the ways in which God has been faithful to the congregation over the previous year. In a similar way, Psalm 105 takes a look back at Israel's history in order to praise the Lord for honoring His commitments to the Hebrews' ancestor Abraham.

The occasion for which this psalm was originally composed may have been one of the religious festivals, possibly the Feast of Tabernacles (Lev. 23:33), but more likely the Festival of Weeks or Pentecost (Lev. 23:15–21). The former celebrated the Lord's help during the Israelites' Exodus journey, when they resided in tents (or "tabernacles"). The latter was to show thanksgiving to God for the annual harvest.

Psalm 105, along with other psalms recalling Israel's history (for example, Pss. 78, 106), encourages God's people today to formally celebrate the promises that He has made and fulfilled for us. The habit of looking back at His gracious acts can stir up joy for today and new hope for the future.

of the plagues to demonstrate the Lord's power. The plagues took place within time and space; they were the action of God with humans in the real world. But the verses of this psalm are not historical prose; they are a poetic version of the events that capture the horror of it. The order of the plagues is not followed strictly, and only eight of the plagues are mentioned (Ex. 7—11).

105:43–45 with gladness: This poem celebrates the joy of the Lord in His acts of deliverance. **gave them the lands:** The psalm was probably composed after the exile in Babylon. A celebration of God's gift of land would have been a tremendous source of encouragement to the people who had just returned to the land.

Psalm 106, a wisdom psalm, rehearses much of the same history covered in Ps. 105. The two poems are companions, although their perspectives are different. Psalm 106 emphasizes the rebellion of the people despite the unflagging goodness of God. If Ps. 105 is about remembering, Ps. 106 is about forgetting—specifically God's people forgetting His mercies. This is a psalm of praise (as is Ps. 105), in that it calls for the praise of God despite the short memories of His people. The structure of Ps. 106 is: (1) a call to praise God (v. 1); (2) a report on the status of the present generation (vv. 2–15); (3) a recitation of the works of God on behalf of earlier generations (vv. 16–43); (4) a concluding appeal (vv. 44–47); (5) words of praise to conclude Book IV of the Psalms (v. 48).

106:1–5 Oh, give thanks to the Lord: The words of v. 1 and the general language of **praise** in v. 2 connect this poem with Ps. 105 as a set (105:1, 2). Possibly both psalms were written by the same poet and were designed to go together, since this psalm builds on the theme of remembering. **Remember me** seems to be a personal prayer based on the recitation of Israel's history in Ps. 105.

106:6 We have sinned with our fathers: The confession of sin comes without warning. This is a psalm of community penitence. The connection of the present generation to the sins of the fathers is ominous. Would the present generation have to suffer the misfortunes and judgments that God brought upon their fathers?

106:7–12 God knew that His people would be faithless repeatedly, yet He **saved them for His name's sake.** The crossing of the **waters** of the Red Sea was not mentioned in Ps. 105 but is included here. **Then they believed:** The people were often faithless; but they had moments of true faith and performed actions of true praise.

106:13–16 They soon forgot: These words contrast dramatically with the emphasis of Ps. 105, which may indicate that the two psalms were written by the same poet and designed to

go together. **He gave them their request:** Several times God gave the people what they thought they wanted, but with the gift came His judgment on their sin.

106:17 The rebellion of **Dathan** and **Abiram** is described in Num. 16.

106:18–23 The story of the gold **calf** is recorded in Ex. 32. **changed their glory:** In exchange for the living God, the people accepted an image of an ox.

106:24 The fact that **they despised the pleasant land** is regarded as a result of their unbelief and rejection of God's good gift. God's judgment (Num. 13; 14) was fully deserved.

106:25–30 Baal of Peor refers to the incident described in Num. 25, following the encounter of Balaam and Balak at Moab. However, this psalm adds a new detail to the story: eating sacrifices offered to the dead. **Phinehas,** one of the great champions of God in the OT, is celebrated in this poem. As Abraham's faith was accounted to him for righteousness (Gen. 15:6), so was the action of Phinehas (Num. 25).

106:31–33 Waters of strife is a reference to Meribah (95:8; Num. 20:1–13). Here the sin of Moses is called "speaking **rashly.**" In Num. 20:12, God specifically identified Moses' sin as dishonoring Him before the people by not trusting Him. By not following God's command "to speak" to the rock, Moses had not modeled proper obedience and respect for God's command.

106:34–39 God's judgment on Israel in Canaan was a result of the Israelites' failure to **destroy the peoples.** If the Canaanites had been driven out of the land, the people of Israel might never have succumbed to the idolatry that marked their existence for hundreds of years. Instead, the Israelites learned to worship the Canaanite idols. They participated in the worst aspects of their religion and **played the harlot** against God their Redeemer.

106:40–46 The wrath of the Lord must be viewed in the context of His long-standing mercy and forbearance. There was a long history of rebellion in the face of His gracious provision before God became enraged. Yet even in the midst of His wrath, God's merciful nature was evident. He remained faithful to His covenant with His people even during their rebellion.

106:47 The words of appeal **save us** are buttressed with the words **O Lord our God.** Though the people had been faithless, the Lord was still their God. If they would return to Him, they would have a home in His mercy and a promise of eventual triumph.

106:48 Blessed be the Lord God of Israel: This verse is an addition to Ps. 106 that forms the concluding verse of Book IV of the

⊕ IN CONTEXT | Ancestor Worship

The deification of ancestors was common throughout the ancient world. The mythological texts from Ugarit (1400–1200 B.C.) make reference to "rulers" in the netherworld who formerly had been monarchs in the human realm. These deceased humans were treated as minor deities, having religious feasts held in their honor. Even in ancient Palestine, the excavations of graves have sometimes uncovered tubes built into the ground so that communication and food could be delivered to the deceased.

Ancestor worship is not common in the Bible. There is one Canaanite practice mentioned, however, by which famous or important dead persons had become deities of the underworld. The psalmist reports that the Israelites "ate sacrifices made to the dead" (Ps. 106:28). The practice is associated with the "Baal of Peor" incident, indicating that the Israelites encountered the custom as they moved toward the Promised Land.

The Law of Moses made it unacceptable to treat any human as a god, whether living or dead (Ex. 20:2; Deut. 26:14). The Israelites who engaged in the regional religious belief of eating sacrifices for the dead were considered to have turned away from the one true God and "provoked Him to anger" (Ps. 106:29). To honor the memory of one's ancestors was desirable, but such honor must not pass over into worship.

Psalms. It is a beautiful liturgical call for the people together to bless their faithful God.

Psalm 107, a wisdom psalm, shares the form and many of the same themes as Pss. 105 and 106. The fact that this psalm begins Book V of the Psalms, however, suggests that it may not have been written as a companion psalm to the previous two psalms. Psalm 107 reviews God's actions in the experiences of His people, using illustrations not found in the narrative of the Pentateuch. The psalm begins and concludes with appeals to trust in the "loyal love" of God. The structure of the psalm is: (1) a celebration of God's enduring loyal love (vv. 1–3); (2) affirmation that God meets the needs of those who wander in the wilderness (vv. 4–9); (3) assurance that God delivers those in exile or in prison (vv. 10–16); (4) a declaration that God saves the foolish who call to Him (vv. 17–22); (5) God's salvation of those caught in storms (vv. 23–32); (6) God's provision for those in barren lands (vv. 33–38); (7) an affirmation that God multiplies peoples who are diminished (vv. 39–42); (8) a call to rediscover the loyal love of God (v. 43).

107:1 Oh, give thanks to the Lord: The beginning of this psalm links it to the two preceding poems (105:1; 106:1). The key point of this psalm is that God's **mercy endures forever.** He is always willing to restore those who call on Him.

107:2–9 They wandered in the wilderness: This may refer to the historical experience of Israel in the desert of Sinai. It also can apply to any group of dispersed Hebrew people away from the mercies of God. **Oh, that men would give thanks to the Lord:** These words are a

refrain throughout the psalm, exhorting the reader to thank God for His mercy (vv. 15, 21, 31). **He satisfies:** This is the point that every generation of believers needs to remember. We will never discover anything more satisfying than the Lord, who will meet all our needs.

107:10 Those who sat in darkness refers to prisoners. Those who know the Lord will call out to Him in their distress, even though it may have been their own rebellion that caused the distress. The mercy of God is demonstrated in His acts of deliverance, acts that call for renewed praise to Him for His goodness.

107:11–17 Fools is a harsh word that emphasizes moral failure (Prov. 1:7; 15:5). These people deserved the trouble they suffered. Yet they too may call upon the Lord, and He will deliver and restore them.

107:18–32 those who go down to the sea in ships: The words make us remember the idyllic description in Psalm 104:26; here the situation is not so pleasant. The people who are at sea find themselves in the storms and powers of the ocean over which they have no control. They suffer terribly (vv. 26, 27), and, as people in trouble everywhere, they cry aloud to the Lord (v. 28). Then God steps in, calms the storm and delivers them (v. 29). Why then do men not praise Him? (vv. 31, 32). Part of the answer may be seen in the failure really to focus on what God is like. The reward of practicing truth is the ability to discern good and evil and to make right decisions about our circumstances and environment (Heb. 12:13, 14).

107:33–35 He turns rivers into a wilderness: Because of the people's sinfulness, God may bring curses on the land and afflict people with harsh circumstances in order to drive them back into His loving arms (1 Kin. 17:1–7). **turns a wilderness into pools of water:** When His people cried to Him for assistance, God restored the fertility of the land (Deut. 30:1–10; Ruth 1:6).

107:36–42 when they are diminished: The poet now describes general upheavals. God is at work lowering the mighty (vv. 39, 40) and elevating the poor (v. 41). The question still remains: Why do people not praise the Lord?

107:43 Whoever is wise: There is no wisdom apart from centering in and responding to the love of God. The psalmist exhorts the readers to review God's history of delivering those in trouble, and to praise His great love.

Psalm 108, a psalm of trust, reveals the assurance a person can have when the Lord is his or her God. The psalm is actually a medley of two other psalms of David. Verses 1–5 are from 57:7–11, and vv. 6–13 are from 60:5–12. Since David is the author of both of these psalms, the verses of this psalm may be ascribed to him as well, even if the arrangement may have been the work of an anonymous editor. As this psalm shows, there was considerable reworking of some parts of the Book of Psalms so that the psalms could be used in the varying circumstances of temple worship.

108:1, 2 I will awaken the dawn: The psalmist wanted to sing to the Lord before the sun rose. The prospect of a sleepless night did not deter him from praise and thanksgiving.

108:3–13 The remarkable fact about the words **I will rejoice** is that they are spoken by God. The Lord has pleasure in delivering His people and giving them victory: He celebrates His deliverance of them.

Psalm 109, a psalm of lament, pays particular attention to the psalmist's enemies. As a result, this poem may also be regarded as an imprecatory psalm. The structure is: (1) a call for God not to be silent in the midst of the attacks from the psalmist's enemies (vv. 1–5); 2 a call for God to bring judgment on the wicked (vv. 6–20); (3) a call for God to come to the aid of the innocent (vv. 21–29); (4) a determination to praise the Lord (vv. 30, 31).

109:1–3 The call to **not keep silent** is a regular feature of the lament psalms. **fought against me without a cause:** The psalmist declares his innocence and insists that his enemies have rewarded his prayers with evil, his love with hatred.

109:4–8 Set a wicked man over him: Here the psalm takes a decidedly negative tone. The description of the wife of the enemy becoming an impoverished widow and the children becoming beggars seems particularly harsh. However, the psalmist directs these strong requests to the Lord; he does not actually take the sword into his own hand. He may feel compelled to vent his anger in words, but the psalmist understands that vengeance itself belongs to the Lord. **let another take his office:** These words (along with the words of 69:25) are quoted in Acts 1:20 as having been fulfilled in the replacement of Judas Iscariot.

109:9–16 Let the iniquity of his fathers be remembered: Although the psalmist's words may seem extremely hostile, he is simply asking that his enemy's evil actions be judged. **The poor** are not those without wealth so much as those without protection or defenders.

109:17–21 The poet asks for action that would befit God's **name**, a name associated with righteousness (23:3). His appeal is to God's **mercy** or "loyal love." The poet describes himself as a wasted, hollow shell of a man, as in 22:6–8. The intensity of the psalmist's attacks on his enemies can be explained in part by the intensity of his own afflictions, as described in these verses.

109:22–27 That they may know: Even in the psalmist's intense emotional state, he wants to see the name of God defended, proclaimed, and honored. The Psalms always lead to the praise of God, even from the depths of desperate circumstances.

109:28–31 The poet makes his vow of **praise** for the deliverance he knows that the Lord will provide. This vow to praise God is a characteristic of many of the psalms. **He shall stand at the right hand of the poor:** See 142:4 for a description of God as a shield at one's right hand.

Psalm 110, a royal psalm, is one of the most directly messianic of all the psalms. It should be read in conjunction with other messianic psalms such as Pss. 2; 24. Jesus Himself identified David as the writer of this psalm, as the title also indicates. Jesus' interpretation of this psalm is crucial for unlocking the psalm's meaning (Matt. 22:41–45; Mark 12:35–37; Luke 20:41–44; compare Peter's exposition of the psalm in Acts 2:34–36). The interpretive key to the psalm lies in the identification of "my Lord" in v. 1. Jesus asserted that in v. 1, David was speaking of someone greater than himself. Since no ordinary son of David could be greater than him, "the Lord" of v. 1 refers to the coming Messiah, God's Son. Hence this psalm describes a conversation between God the Father and God the Son (v. 1), in which the Father grants the Son royal and priestly honors. The structure of this brief psalm is as follows: (1) God's command to the Son to sit at His right hand (v. 1); (2) God's command to the Son to rule in the midst of His enemies (vv. 2, 3); (3) God's appointment of the Son to be a priest forever (v. 4); (4) God's description of the battle the Son must wage to win His kingdom (vv. 5–7).

110:1 The Lord is the Hebrew name Yahweh and refers to God the Father. **to my Lord:** According to Jesus' interpretation of the passage (Matt. 22:41–45; Mark 12:35–37; Luke 20:41–44), this is a reference to the Son of God in heaven in the presence of the Father. David himself confesses the Son to be his Lord, that is, his master or sovereign. **at My right hand:** This position of high honor beside the Father was given to the Savior upon His resurrection and ascension (Acts 2:33–36; 1 Cor. 15:20–28; Col. 3:1; Heb. 1:13). The Savior's placing His **feet** on His foes depicts the utter defeat of the enemies of Christ. Paul too describes this complete victory of Jesus (1 Cor. 15:25, 26; Eph. 1:22, 23).

110:2, 3 Rule: The Father commands the Son to take His kingdom back from His enemies. The outcome of this final battle was determined long ago (47:3). **your people:** The description

in vv. 2, 3 of the people who join the coming King in His great battle accords well with that in Rev. 19:14. **From the womb of the morning** describes the volunteer army in their robust and fresh vigor; they are ready for a holy battle.

110:4 priest: David himself had performed some priestly functions, especially when he led the worship surrounding the arrival of the ark of the covenant (2 Sam 6:12–19). He even exercised some authority over the priests by supervising the Levites (1 Chr. 23:1–6). But here David envisions God appointing the coming Messiah to be a priest (Heb. 7). This was a source of confusion for Jews, as evidenced by the questions the NT Jews had about the Messiah. Some Dead Sea Scrolls give evidence that more than one Messiah was anticipated. According to Scripture, the Messiah would be a descendant of David (Is. 9:7), but this prophecy presents Him as a priest. This might seem to be a contradiction because true priests had to be descendants of Aaron. The solution to this

---

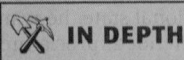 **IN DEPTH** | **Messianic Psalms**

For the Christian, perhaps nothing in the Psalms is more compelling than the prophecies that the book contains concerning the Lord Jesus Christ. Psalm 2 speaks of His coming reign; Ps. 22 describes His crucifixion; Ps. 16 speaks of His resurrection; Ps. 110 pictures the Savior at the right hand of the Father in heaven and as a Priest according to the order of Melchizedek. These and other celebrated passages have led many to speak of a category of messianic psalms.

Many psalms are messianic because they point forward to Jesus Christ. Some psalms are directly prophetic (Pss. 2; 110). Others prophetically foreshadow events related to Christ (compare the description of a wedding of a King in Ps. 45 with Heb. 1:8, 9; Rev. 19:6–8). But almost all the psalms point forward in some way to the coming Messiah and His eternal reign of righteousness (1:1–3; 41:9). For example, the words of 6:8, "Depart from me, all you workers of iniquity," do not seem to have a messianic thrust to them. Yet they are messianic, for Jesus is recorded to have used these very words in His prophetic pronouncement of the final judgment (Matt. 7:23). This indicates that David's experience recorded in Ps. 6 was in some manner prophetically linked to the experience of Jesus. In fact, David's language in the psalms regularly suggests the language of the great King to come—that is, Jesus Christ. Consider the words of 7:8:

The Lord shall judge the peoples;
Judge me, O Lord, according to my righteousness,
And according to my integrity within me.

These words are David's protest. Suffering without cause, he cried out to God to clear his name. But David, though innocent of the specific charge, was not innocent of every charge. There is only One whose innocence is absolute, whose freedom from sin is complete. Jesus is the One who can be judged on the basis of His righteousness alone. He alone could say these words without flinching, for these words depict His character.

The suffering of the poor (as in Ps. 13), the unjust attacks upon the righteous (as in Ps. 7), the idealization of justice (as in Ps. 15), the portrait of the righteous person (as in Ps. 1), the images of royalty (as in Ps. 45), even the pronouncements of curses on one's enemies (as in Ps. 6) are all motifs of the Messiah in the Psalms. Jesus is the coming One; many of the psalms are in fact His songs.

problem is that the Messiah was a priest by divine declaration—not human descent. **Melchizedek** is first mentioned in Gen. 14:18–20. He was a true priest of the Most High God, unrelated to Abraham and who lived hundreds of years before Aaron. He became a prototype of the Messiah, whose priesthood was not based upon connection with the line of Aaron, but was by divine decree (Heb. 5:5–11; 6:20; 7:1–28).

110:5–7 The Savior King is in battle (vv. 2, 3), and the Father is His shield at His **right hand** (16:8; 142:4). God the Father assists the Son in the battle. **execute kings:** The rule of the King will be absolute, dramatic, and forceful. **dead bodies:** This image is elaborated in Rev. 19:19–21. **He shall lift up the head:** As the great Victor, the Son will hold His head high in triumph over all His enemies (3:3).

Psalm 111, a wisdom psalm, also serves as a psalm of praise. This psalm and the next are written as acrostics. The structure of Ps. 111 is: (1) a determination to praise God in the midst of the congregation (v. 1); (2) a description of the praise of God for His wonderful works towards His people (vv. 2–9); (3) a concluding word tying the nature of true wisdom to the fear of the Lord (v. 10).

111:1 I will praise the Lord: The psalm begins in the standard manner, following the opening "Hallelujah." The determination to praise Yahweh is from his heart and before the congregation.

111:2–9 The distinctive message of this section of the psalm is an appreciation of the **works of the Lord** for the way they cause the psalmist to glorify God. Creation calls attention to the Creator (19:1–6; 104:1–35). **Gracious and full of compassion** may be rephrased as "wonderfully gracious." Faith understands **food** and all other provisions as gifts of God. **redemption:** The psalmists constantly look back to the Exodus, but they also speak of that which was still to come—redemption in the Savior Jesus.

111:10 The fear of the Lord describes an obedient response of wonder and awe before the Most High God.

Psalm 112, a wisdom psalm, is very similar to Ps. 111; together they form a matched pair of acrostic poems. The structure of the poem is: (1) a determination to praise God (v. 1); (2) the praise of God based on His works with His people (vv. 2–9); (3) the defeat of the wicked (v. 10).

112:1 Praise the Lord: Like Ps. 111, this psalm begins with the Hebrew word *hallelujah*. It then picks up where Ps. 111 left off. **Blessed,** a word meaning "one who is manifestly happy," is the same term with which the Book of Psalms begins.

112:2–9 His descendants will be mighty: Compare the blessings of vv. 2, 3 with the strong curses placed on the wicked in 109:6–13 to see the vivid contrast the Psalms make between the destinies of the wicked and the righteous. This black and white distinction is characteristic of the wisdom writers in Israel. The description of the **good man** in v. 5 is similar to the description in Ps. 15. The **horn** is a

---

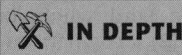 **IN DEPTH** | **Passover Psalms**

One of the most effective ways to teach spiritual truth is through song. Likewise, memories are often passed on most effectively through music. Aware of this, the ancient Hebrews composed Psalms 113–118 to be sung around the supper table during Passover.

The first two of the group were sung before the meal and the other four afterwards. Each of the psalms commemorated some aspect of the escape of the Israelites from their bondage to Pharaoh and the Egyptians (Ex. 12—15), and for that reason they are sometimes referred to as the Egyptian Hallel (*Hallel* means "praise"; compare Ps. 113:1). Jesus and His disciples probably sang these psalms at their last meal together in the Upper Room (Matt. 26:30; Mark 14:26).

The themes of these six Passover psalms are:

Psalm 113: Praising God for releasing the downtrodden.
Psalm 114: Escaping from Egypt.
Psalm 115: Praising God together as a people.
Psalm 116: Thanking God personally and giving oneself to Him.
Psalm 117: Calling non-Jews to praise God.
Psalm 118: Recalling God's steadfast, enduring love.

symbol of power. When used of a righteous person, it speaks of prominence and a lasting sense of worth in his or her life.

112:10 Here as in Ps. 1, the contrast between the righteous and the wicked is sharp and uncompromising. The desire of the righteous will prevail (v. 8), but the desire of the wicked will **perish.**

Psalm 113, a psalm of descriptive praise, begins and concludes with the words "Praise the Lord!" (in Hebrew, *hallelujah*). This psalm and Ps. 114 are regularly recited at the Passover Seder, a celebratory meal before the serving of the dinner. Pss. 115—118 are recited following the dinner. The structure of Ps. 113 is: (1) an exhortation to praise the name of the Lord (vv. 1–3); (2) a celebration of the transcendent glory and abundant mercy of the Lord (vv. 4–6); (3) illustrations of God's grace (vv. 7–9).

113:1–3 The name of the Lord refers to the person of God. In biblical times there was a close association between a person's name and his or her identity. The name symbolized the person. Therefore, praising the *name* of God centers one's thoughts on God's character. **The rising of the sun** is the east and its going down is the west. The verse does not mean at every time, from dawn to dusk, but in every place, from east to west, the name of God is to be praised.

113:4–6 high above all nations: Unlike the man-made gods of the ancient Middle East, the Lord is not limited to a certain tribe or territory. He is sovereign over all; He is Most High (7:17; 47:2). **glory above the heavens:** Not only is God supreme over all nations, His glory cannot be contained in the universe. His glory is not only beyond the universe, it is beyond the capacity of human language to fully describe. Perhaps this explains Paul's response to his visit above the heavens (2 Cor. 12:1–4). The rhetorical words **who is like the Lord** present the incomparability of God (Is. 40:25). **Who humbles Himself:** God draws near to us.

113:7 The poor might try to eke out their existence by scratching at rubbish heaps outside the city wall, that is, **out of the dust.** God's care for the poor and needy is a special interest in the Psalms. In this psalm we see a marvelous picture of salvation. While we scavenge about for significance, God's mercy in Jesus makes us citizens of heaven.

113:8, 9 No image better conveys human emotional suffering in biblical times than that of the **barren woman.** In that time and culture, a barren woman was without significance and without joy. Note that God stoops down to bring her the joy for which she craves—happy children. Salvation is like that. Not only does God fill us with significance, but also with joy.

Psalm 114 celebrates Israel's deliverance from Egypt. There is a light, lively spirit to this poem that balances the heavier pacing and stronger theology of the first song of deliverance in Ex. 15. This poem is recited with Ps. 113 at Passover before the dinner is served. This psalm has three movements: (1) a celebration of Israel's redemption from Egypt (vv. 1, 2); (2) a characterization of Israel's enemies (vv. 3–6); (3) a celebration of the Lord who redeemed Israel (vv. 7, 8).

114:1, 2 The newly freed slaves left Egypt still refusing the **strange language** of their long-term captors. With this slight, Israel affirmed that true values in life were not to be found in the "glories of Egypt," but in the presence of the Lord. **sanctuary:** This verse anticipates the NT sense of God living among His people rather than in a shrine (Ezek. 37:26, 27; 2 Cor. 6:16–18).

114:3–6 The sea and the **Jordan,** the **mountains** and the **hills,** all appear as frightened animals before the awesome presence of the Lord, who is not mentioned until v. 7.

114:7 tremble: At once we are arrested by the symbol of God's presence. While the sea and the Jordan, the hills and the mountains may gambol, people need to be startled. His judgment will be against errant man.

114:8 God not only delivered His people from Egypt, He also provided for their needs by bringing water from a **rock** (Ex. 17; Num. 20). Water was a physical blessing, but also a spiritual symbol of His salvation.

Psalm 115, a community psalm of praise, focuses on the glory of the Lord in the salvation of His people. Several sections of this psalm are used in Ps. 135. This poem has five movements: (1) a glorification of the Lord who alone deserves praise (vv. 1, 2); (2) a comparison of the false gods and the true, living God (vv. 3–8); (3) a litany of trust in the Lord (vv. 9–11); (4) a litany of blessing in the Lord (vv. 12–15); (5) a glorification of the Lord (vv. 16–18).

115:1, 2 Not unto us: People have a natural tendency to divert to themselves glory that belongs to God. This psalm redirects the glory to its proper focus, the Lord Himself. The **Gentiles,** who do not know God, are prone to insult believers in times of testing when God's activity is not apparent (42:3).

115:3, 4 Like the prophets (Is. 40; Jer. 10), the psalms are derisive toward the **idols** of the nations. The psalmist denies any reality to the false gods created by people (135:15–18). In contrast to these "gods" that have to be carried about, propped up, and coddled, Israel exalted the **God who is in heaven** and who **does whatever He pleases.** He is the only God who can demand our worship.

115:9–11 On the basis of the confession of the reality of God, the psalm commences a litany that encourages trust in God alone. With this litany the choir leader would exhort first **Israel,** then the **house of Aaron,** and finally all **who fear the Lord** to trust God. The refrain proclaims God's protective care over them: **He is their help and their shield.**

115:12–15 A second litany focuses on God's blessing. Not only is He the only God who is trustworthy, He also desires to bless all those who trust in Him.

115:16–18 The plural **heavens** may refer to the dwelling place of God (2 Cor. 12:2). **The dead:** As in 6:5, this is not a theology of death, but of praise. It is the work of the living to praise God. When anyone dies, that voice is lost from the living choir. **Praise the Lord:** Many of the Passover psalms (Pss. 115—117) conclude with word *hallelujah,* the Hebrew for "praise the Lord."

Psalm 116, a messianic psalm, is one of the Passover psalms (Pss. 113—118). This psalm most likely was recited by Jesus on the night of His arrest, the night He celebrated Passover with His disciples (Luke 22:15). The structure of the poem is: (1) a declaration of the psalmist's love for the Lord (vv. 1, 2); (2) an experience on the brink of death (vv. 3, 4); (3) praise for God (vv. 5–7); (4) the psalmist's deliverance from death (vv. 8–11); (5) a vow of praise to the Lord (vv. 12–14); (6) a reflection on the psalmist's deliverance (vv. 15–17); (7) payment of his vow of praise to the Lord (vv. 18, 19).

116:1, 2 The wording of **I love the Lord** in Hebrew suggests deep excitement and emotion. **He has inclined His ear to me:** As in 40:1, these words speak of the love of God: He bends from His place of glory to meet the needs of His people.

116:3–5 Pains of death describes the psalmist's harrowing experience of suffering that brought him seemingly to the brink of death (86:13). These words point prophetically to the Savior's anguish on the Cross (Matt. 27:27–35).

116:6 In this context, **simple** means innocent, clean, or untarnished. In the Book of Proverbs, the word usually means naive or untested (Prov. 1:22).

116:7–10 Paul quotes the words **I believed, therefore I spoke** in 2 Cor. 4:13, 14 as proof of the scriptural hope of the resurrection of the Savior Jesus. The belief in v. 10 is the hope, articulated in v. 9, that the psalmist would walk in the land of the living.

> *Jesus declared that He was the gate or door leading to salvation.*

116:11–13 With the phrase **what shall I render,** the psalmist vows to praise God in an audible and public manner among the people of faith. At Passover this psalm is read after the meal, immediately following the third cup of wine, called **the cup of salvation.** How appropriate that this Passover psalm would call to mind God's cup of salvation the very night that the Savior was betrayed (Matt. 26:27; Luke 22:14–22).

116:14–17 The psalmist declares that he is God's **servant.** As Jesus demonstrated in the Upper Room celebration of the Passover, every true follower of Christ must become a servant. Just as Jesus the Son of God became a servant to His disciples and washed their feet, so every believer needs to serve others (John 13:1–17). The words of the psalm were prophetically fulfilled when they were sung by Jesus on the night before He was crucified. The term **thanksgiving** basically means "public acknowledgment."

116:18, 19 I will pay my vows: These words are evidently the concluding words of the psalmist, declaring his intention to make good on his promise to bring his offering of praise to the temple court.

Psalm 117 is a descriptive psalm of praise. It is the shortest psalm and has a simple structure: (1) a call for the nations to praise God (v. 1); (2) an enumeration of reasons for the nations to praise God (v. 2).

117:1 Laud, which means "to speak well of," nicely parallels the term **praise,** which means "to be excitedly boastful about." The Hebrew word for Gentiles means all people except Jews; the word for **peoples** speaks of smaller groups of people, along ethnic and language lines.

117:2 Merciful kindness, or "loyal love," refers to God's faithfulness to His covenant promises to His people. The reason the nations are to give praise to God is found in His relationship with Israel. **Praise the Lord:** The concluding Hallelujah is an appropriate shout of triumph in God's mercy.

Psalm 118, a psalm of declarative praise, is the climax of the group of psalms called the Passover psalms or Hallel psalms, after the Hebrew word for praise, *hallel. Hallelujah* comes from this word. These psalms were probably sung by the Savior on the night before His death. The structure of the poem is: (1) a call for the praise of God in the community of the redeemed (vv. 1–4); (2) a report of confidence in the Lord (vv. 5–9); (3) a report of God's deliverance in a time of trouble (vv. 10–14); (4) the praise of the Lord by the righteous (vv. 15–18); (5) the declaration of the psalmist that he would enter the gate of the city to praise the Lord (vv. 19–21); (6) the picture of the rejected cornerstone (vv. 22–24); (7) the shout of "Hosanna" by the people in praise of God (vv. 25, 26); (8) the continuing determination of the psalmist to bring his praise to the Lord (vv. 27, 28); (9) the renewed call for the praise of God (v. 29).

118:1, 2 The liturgical instruction **let Israel now say** appears from time to time in the Psalms (Pss. 124; 129). This psalm was recited in antiphonal responses. The refrain praises God's mercy: **His mercy endures forever.**

118:3–8 The idea of **distress** in these psalms is a picture of constraint, constriction, or lack of room. Even when surrounded by impossible circumstances, the believer can proclaim **the Lord is on my side.** And if so, **what can man do to me?** See 56:4, 9; 94:17. If our trust is in the Lord's strength, we do not have to fear the reprisals of our enemies. **confidence in princes:** Although relying on other people is part of living, our ultimate trust can only be placed in the Lord God. Even powerful rulers are limited by their own mortality (146:3).

118:9–11 The poet feels that he is alone and that the whole world is arrayed against him. The words **I will destroy them** are used three times in vv. 10–12; the repetition is for emphasis and finality. Even though the psalmist is completely encircled by his enemies, he knows that God will help him triumph over them.

118:12–14 You pushed me: Translated literally, the Hebrew phrase means "pushing, you pushed me to make me fall." **But the Lord helped me:** Compare Paul's words in 2 Tim. 4:17, 18. Deliverance always comes from God. The Lord is not only our Helper, but also our **strength and song.** These words are a quotation from the "Song of Moses" (Ex. 15:2); they are also quoted in Is. 12:2. The God who delivered the Israelites by dividing the waters of the Red Sea was ready to deliver the psalmist from trouble.

118:15–17 The voice of rejoicing: The psalmist summons the people of God to join him in praise, just as in the days of the Exodus from Egypt. The slogan of redemption, **the right hand of the Lord,** is again a quotation from the Song of Moses (Ex. 15:6). It depicts God using His limitless strength to save the psalmist. **I shall not die:** The poet describes a near-death experience, as in 16:9–11.

118:18–21 Open to me the gates: The poet draws on the wording and imagery of Ps. 24. There is only One who can enter the gates of the Lord of His own accord—the perfect King of glory. **gate of the Lord:** It is possible that the literal reference is to the gate of Jerusalem, the city of God—or even to a gate of the temple. Jesus declared that He was the *gate* or door leading to **salvation** (John 10:9).

118:22 The Savior is pictured as a discarded **stone** that is then reused as the most significant stone of all, the **chief cornerstone.** This potent imagery depicts Jesus' rejection by many (Is. 53:3; Mark 8:31; Luke 9:22; 17:25). Jesus elaborated on this prophetic verse with the parable of the vineyard owner. In this parable, the rejection included the murder of the owner's son—a reference to God's only Son (Mark 12:1–12). But even though the Savior was rejected, He was elevated to the right hand of God (Acts 7:56). Only God could do this marvelous and unexpected work. The cross, the symbol of Jesus' rejection, has become the symbol of our salvation (1 Cor. 1:18; Heb. 12:2).

118:23–26 The words **save now** in Hebrew are more familiar in the transliteration "hosanna." These words are so significant that if the children had not shouted them aloud (Matt. 21:16) when Jesus entered Jerusalem, the stones would have had to shout them (Luke 19:40). The words **blessed is he who comes** are the words the people used to bless Jesus on his triumphal entry into Jerusalem (Matt. 21:9; Mark 11:9; Luke 19:38). As God's only Son, Jesus is the One who comes **in the name of the Lord;** He is the One who reveals God the Father (John 14:8–11).

118:27 God is the Lord: It is possible (and the fulfillment nearly demands this) that the words of this verse may have been recited by the disciples at the table with the Lord. They would have affirmed that God is their Savior and that He has sent His Light (who is Jesus). In their call for the sacrifice to be bound, they unwittingly would have called for the drama to proceed which would bring about their—and our—redemption.

118:28 You are my God: If the words of v. 27 were recited by the disciples, these words would come from the Savior. He is now about to leave the sanctuary of the celebration of the Passover Seder in the Upper Room. He will cross the Kidron, climb the Mount of Olives, pray in the Garden, then face His enemies in the power of the Lord.

118:29 The closing words call the community to end the psalm as it began (v. 1)—with praise for the goodness and love of the Most High God.

Psalm 119, a wisdom psalm, is the premier song about the Torah (Ps. 19). It celebrates the Word of God in a way that is almost exhaustive. This very lengthy poem is an acrostic: For each of the twenty-two consonants in the Hebrew alphabet, there are eight verses beginning with that letter. Within the psalm, eight words for God's Law occur again and again: law; testimonies; promise; precepts; statutes; commandments; judgments; word. The psalm uses the full meaning of all these words as it elaborates on the application of the Law of God to both daily life and Israel's destiny. The Law is specific and general, directive and restrictive, liberating and opening, gracious and solemn—it is as complex as the Lord who gave it. The Law is never considered a curse; it is always seen as a gift from God. The cumulative effect of this lengthy celebration of the Word of God is impressive: the psalmist cannot stop praising God for His mercy and goodness in providing His people with instructions for living.

> *To the one who delights to keep God's Law, God will give more grace to keep it.*

119:1–8 Then I would not be ashamed: Shame always follows transgression. In order to escape shame, we must be vigilant and constant in obeying the Word of God.

119:9 How can a young man cleanse his way? The word rendered his way (Heb. *orach*) signifies a track, a rut, such as would have been made by the wheel of a cart. A young sinner has not beaten a broad path, but rather has transgressed again and again in the same manner, creating a sinful rut. How shall he escape? **By taking heed to Your Word.** Heeding the Word of God leads to a godly lifestyle. Ignoring the Word of God leads to a godless rut.

119:10, 11 With my whole heart: Because the psalmist has sincerely and genuinely sought the blessing of God through obedience to His Word, he prays that God would not permit him to deviate accidentally or deliberately from his commandments.

119:12–16 I have rejoiced in the way of Your testimonies: The psalmist has taken more delight in the doctrines of God's Word than he has in the dollars of the world. **I will meditate on Your precepts:** That which we have laid up in our hearts and upon which we have meditated ceaselessly will never be forgotten.

119:17–20 I am a stranger in the earth: Since the psalmist is not native-born but a sojourner here, he needs the road map of God's commandments in order to find his way back to his home with God.

119:21–24 As he winds his way through life, the psalmist had been slandered by even the rulers and captains of this world. He paid no attention to the calumnies and barbs hurled at him, but rather found comfort and solace in meditating upon the Word of God. **Your testi-** monies also are my delight. When the world went one way, the psalmist went the other as counseled by God's Word.

119:25–29 My soul clings to the dust: When in a state of depression, the psalmist recognized that his soul had adhered to the dust as if he were already dead and buried. Reading, meditating, and obeying the Word would raise him to life and health again.

119:30–32 I have chosen the way of truth. The psalmist contrasts himself with those who have chosen the way of lying (v. 29). By choosing the truthful path, the psalmist has had to cleave or cling steadfastly to the testimonies of God. Therefore, he prays, **O LORD**, do not put me to shame.

119:33–40 Teach me, O LORD, the way of Your statutes. If there is an underlying theme to this psalm, surely this is it. The psalmist is convinced that if the Lord will but teach him His law, **I shall observe it with my whole heart.**

119:41–48 God had pledged that He would grant mercy and salvation to all His faithful servants (Deut. 28:1–13). Armed with that promise, the psalmist was confident that he would be able to **answer for him who reproaches me**. Still, he recognized that it was God Himself that would put the word of truth in his mouth and thus prayed that God would not remove it when he was reproached. The goodness and mercy of God exhibited in answered prayer was enough to cause the psalmist to determine, **So shall I keep Your law continually.**

119:49–52 Remember the Word to Your servant. As the psalmist requests Yahweh to remember His promises to the faithful, he reminds Yahweh that he himself has remembered the very principles of God's government. It is the Word of God that brings him **comfort in my affliction**. Though **the proud** laughed at him in derision, nevertheless **I do not turn aside from Your law**. Having found comfort in the Law of God, the psalmist knew that there was no reason in turn aside from that Law when he was ridiculed.

119:53–69 The word **indignation** signifies a burning tempest or desert storm. Here it signifies the mental anguish that came over the psalmist when he contemplated the fate of the wicked who had forsaken God's Law. **I remember Your name in the night, O LORD**. To the one who delights to keep God's Law, God will give more grace to keep it. There is never a time in which it is improper to turn to God and meditate upon His name. His name, and it

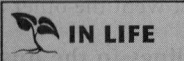

IN LIFE To Show the Way

I n OT times people used small lamps to furnish artificial light. Ancient lamps were essentially small ceramic bowls that were customized during construction to have a "nose" on one edge. The purpose of this extension was to hold a wick. Wicks of cloth were laid in the nose and extended into the oil in the lamp's bowl.

The light produced was not brilliant but necessary for finding one's way. In Psalm 119:105 the writer compares God's word with a lamp. While the light from that word does not blind the eyes, it does point the way for its hearers.

alone, will calm the mental anguish caused by the vision of horror from all that awaits those who forsake God's law.

119:70–72 Their heart is as fat as grease, i.e., insensitive to spiritual things. Nonetheless, the psalmist is convinced that **the law of Your mouth is better to me than . . . gold and silver.**[PRL]

119:73, 74 that I may learn Your commandments: Here is an acknowledgment from the psalmist that he has his existence from God. He reasons that since God has fashioned him, He will also teach him.

119:75–80 Fully aware that the judges of God are righteous, the psalmist recognizes that it is by those judgments that **in faithfulness You have afflicted me.** After affliction there was need for divine comfort. **Let Your tender mercies come to me.**

119:81 My soul faints for Your salvation. The psalmist is committed that regardless of the circumstances that cause him to faint in soul (not in body), he would continue to place his trust in the Word of God.

119:82, 83 like a wineskin in smoke: The simile here is very vivid. In the ancient Near East bottles were commonly made of animal skins and covered with dust and smoke. They were unsightly. This is a striking picture of the psalmist's own spiritual state. He had waited for the Lord to come and in spirit had become dried up by the pressure placed upon him.

119:84–88 Your Word is settled in heaven: Because of its perfect author, precise inscription, and permanent habitation, the Word of God is unsurpassable, undeniable, and unchangeable.

119:89–96 The wicked wait for me to destroy me, we must not again seek salvation but simply **consider Your testimonies**. When we look confidently to the Word of promise and daily trust the provision of God's grace, we are testifying not only to our salvation by God's grace but also to the face that *Your Word is settled in heaven* (v. 89).

119:97–104 The heavenly design of God's Word is not to confuse, camouflage, or cover over the kernel of truth, but to reveal the Word as truth.

119:105–112 I hate the double-minded: Simple dislike of evil is not sufficient for the man of God; perfect hatred against all manner and degree of evil is. Such hatred prompts the psalmist to say, **Depart from me, you evildoers.** There is no fellowship between light and darkness.

119:113–122 Be surety for Your servant for good: The word **surety** (Heb. *'arab*) means a pledge with which something is obtained, the full result of purchase to follow.

119:123–130 It is the **entrance** (lit, *opening*), i.e., the unfolding or unveiling, of the words of God that give light to the darkened soul. That which the human mind cannot comprehend by itself is comprehended through the aid of the Spirit of God.

119:131–133 The word **direct** (Heb. *kun*) means to make firm, to walk without halting. If no iniquity is to have dominion over us, our steps must be established by the Word of God.

119:134–144 Even though trouble and anguish had taken hold upon the psalmist, nevertheless he delighted in the commands of God; for **the righteousness of Your testimonies is everlasting.** His simple prayer to God is that Yahweh may give him full understanding of His commandments, their depth, their breadth, and their exceeding excellence.

119:145–149 So intense was his prayer that he confessed, **I rise before the dawning of the morning.** Before the light broke through the shadows of night, the psalmist was already prevailing upon God in prayer. **My eyes are awake through the night watches:** The Jews, like the Greeks and the Romans, divided the night into military watches instead of hours. Accompanying the prevailing prayer of the psalmist was a meditation in the Word of God. Prayer and reading the Word preceded the dawning of the day and continued unto the

✠ IN CONTEXT | **Meshech and Kedar**

Lamenting the fact that he was seemingly surrounded by warmongers, the psalmist compared his neighbors to two tribes renowned for their fierce, warlike ways—the people of Meshech and Kedar (Ps. 120:5).

The Meshechites were presumably descended from Meshech, a grandson of Noah through Japheth (Gen. 10:2; 1 Chr. 1:5). They were said to trade in slaves and copper (Ezek. 27:13), and may have invaded the Near East from the north. Often associated with the tribe of Tubal, they were infamous for their violence (32:26).

The tribe of Kedar, whose name may mean "black" or "swarthy," were Ishmaelites (Gen. 25:13; 1 Chr. 1:29). As nomads in the desert area to the east of Israel, they controlled the caravan routes between Palestine and Egypt, tending large flocks (Is. 60:7) and, it was said, living in black tents. One of Nehemiah's enemies may have been a king of Kedar.

watches of the night. That is the secret of getting a hold on God.

119:150–162 The psalmist could rejoice in the Word of God **as one who finds great treasure**. The riches of God's Word only come to those who have disciplined themselves to battle the enemies of time, apathy, and irregularity with regard to the reading of God's Word.

119:163–176 I long for Your salvation: It was the delight of the psalmist to meditate in the Law of God because he had received God's salvation. His soul had been made alive by God's Spirit, and it was now his responsibility to praise the living Lord. **Like a lost sheep:** This is a frequent figure in the Scriptures. Lost sheep never find their own way back to the shepherd; and thus, having admitted his depravity and person sin, the psalmist's final prayer is, **seek Your servant**. Thus, he ends his psalm with a note of dependency upon the grace of God.

Psalm 120 is the first of a group of psalms called the Songs of Ascent (Pss. 120—134). This group of hymns was likely used by pilgrims making their way to Jerusalem to worship the Lord during the three annual national feasts—Passover, Pentecost, and Tabernacles (Lev. 23). As pilgrim families made the arduous journey to the holy city for festive worship, they would use these psalms as encouragement along the way. It is also possible that once they arrived in Jerusalem, they would sing these songs anew as they drew near the temple, reenacting their journey and affirming God's blessing on their path. Ps. 120, a psalm of lament, focuses on the lies of the wicked that affect the righteous. The structure of the psalm is: (1) a report of deliverance and a prayer for help (vv. 1, 2); (2) a taunt of the adversary who attacks with lies (vv. 3, 4); (3) a lament concerning life in a hostile environment (vv. 5–7).

120:1–3 lying lips: In the context of these psalms, the lying lips belong to those who assault the believers for their trust in the Lord (40:4). **You false tongue:** As in Ps. 12, the poet is distraught at the seeming power of the words of the wicked.

120:5–7 This section of the psalm reveals the intensity of the psalmist's distress—**woe is me**. His environment was hostile even to his faith. **Meshech** and **Kedar** are random examples of the pagan peoples among whom the psalmist had to live. **I am for peace:** This may have set the stage for believers to make their pilgrimage to Jerusalem. In Zion they would be among the people of God. In Jerusalem they would hear the words of truth. In the temple they could pray for the peace of God (122:6; 125:5; 128:6).

Psalm 121 a psalm of trust (Ps. 23), is the second song of ascent. Ps. 120 sets the stage for the Israelites' journey to the Holy City; this poem is a song "for the road." The psalm may also have been designed for antiphonal response, like Pss. 118; 124; 129; 134; 135; 136. The structure of the poem is: (1) an affirmation that help is from God (vv. 1, 2); (2) a word of praise to God, who does not slumber (vv. 3, 4); (3) a word of praise to God who keeps His people (vv. 5, 6); (4) an affirmation that God will protect His people during their journeys (vv. 7, 8).

121:1, 2 The words **lift up my eyes** dramatically picture a traveler approaching the city of Jerusalem. On first sight of the city walls and the temple, the singer asks rhetorically where help is to be found. The answer is the strong affirmation: **Help comes from the Lord.**

121:3–7 He will not allow: It is possible that several sections of this brief poem were recited back and forth by small groups of pilgrims; there is an antiphonal quality to these verses (also Ps. 124). **will not slumber:** On the long journey to Jerusalem the people would have to stop and sleep, yet they would still be cared for by God. The language of confidence in this psalm indicates that it is about the psalmist's trust in the living Lord, his Protector. The phrase **nor the moon** indicates that at no time is God "off duty." The Keeper of Israel is always present.

121:8 and even forevermore: In what appears to be an antiphonal response to the words of vv. 6, 7, the poem concludes with a renewed affirmation of God's ongoing protection in this life and the life to come (23:6).

Psalm 122 a psalm of Zion, is the third song of ascent. This poem describes the joy of the pilgrim on arriving at Jerusalem to worship God. This is one of four songs of ascent attributed to David (also Pss. 124; 131; 133). The structure of the poem is as follows: (1) a description of the pilgrim's joy in coming to Jerusalem (vv. 1, 2); (2) a description of the beauty of Jerusalem (vv. 3–5); (3) a prayer for the peace of Jerusalem (vv. 6–9).

122:1 I was glad: The Hebrew verb for laughter and delight is used to describe the attitude of the pilgrim who arrives in Jerusalem to worship the Lord. The joy of the pilgrim in this psalm contrasts strongly with the sorrow of those who were not able to come to worship God, because of personal (42:1–3) or national exile (137:1–3).

122:2 within your gates: There is an almost childlike enthusiasm in these words; a sense of near unreality pervades the mood (see also the joy of discovery in 48:12–14).

122:3 The visitor is overwhelmed not just by the buildings of **Jerusalem,** but by the fact that the city was the place for the worship of God. **Where the tribes go up:** This refers to the

three annual feasts of ancient Israel (Lev. 23), as well as to any time that an individual or family needed to worship the Lord in the Holy City.

122:4 The Testimony of Israel may refer to the ark of the covenant (Ex. 16:34). **To give thanks** means "to make a public declaration" or "to give public acknowledgment" (105:1). The people of God would praise God for His goodness in their own lives. Their vocal praises would accompany their offerings of animals, grain, wine, and oil.

122:5 thrones: Jerusalem was not only the central place for worship, it was also the site where civil judgments and decisions were made. Religious and civil issues were closely intertwined in the Law of God.

122:6–9 peace of Jerusalem: In the process of praying for the good of the city, the people came under God's blessing. It is God's desire for the city to have peace (125:5; 128:6). True peace will only come when the Prince of Peace returns to establish His rule (Ps. 98). **Because of the house:** The determination of the pilgrim to seek the good of Jerusalem was based on the fact that the site was the central location for the worship of the Lord and the place God had chosen for Himself (1 Kin. 11:36).

Psalm 123 an individual psalm of lament, is the fourth song of ascent. This brief poem has two sections, as follows: (1) an affirmation that the people's eyes are fixed on the Lord (vv. 1, 2); (2) a petition for the Lord to direct His attention to His people (vv. 3, 4).

123:1, 2 who dwell in the heavens: The temple was considered God's dwelling place (132:5, 13, 14); yet the Israelites also knew that the One who made the heavens did not live in buildings made by hands (113:4–6). **As the**

🌱 IN LIFE | Seeking the Good of All

Psalm 122 is another song of praise on the theme of Mount Zion, site of the temple in Jerusalem. Pilgrimages to the house of the Lord were not only a regular obligation for the Israelites but joyous occasions as well. The march through the city gates and uphill to the temple complex was spiritually uplifting and communally bonding.

But one of the defining moments of this worship experience was a prayer for the peace and prosperity of Jerusalem (Ps. 122:6–9). This was actually an intercession for everyone involved in the life of the Holy City. It was essentially a request for God's blessing on the decision makers in government and their policies and programs.

But the pilgrims' concern for Jerusalem did not end with prayer. They also pledged to seek the city's good (122:9). This suggests that believers today do well to pray and work for the good of their own cities, in such a way as to benefit all the people of their communities. By promoting "peace within the walls" and "prosperity within the palaces" (122:7), God's people will be fulfilling Paul's admonition to "do good to all, especially {i.e., not only} to those who are of the household of faith" (Gal. 6:10).

eyes: True servants fix their eyes on their masters; similarly, our eyes should be fixed on God. The more we look to the Lord, the more we become like Him (2 Cor. 3:18). Not being distracted by the other things of this life causes us to win in the race of life (Heb. 12:1, 2).

123:3, 4 The people who prayed for God's **mercy** had to endure the **contempt** of their neighbors. Perhaps they were being mocked for their resolute faith in God at a time when it seemed that God was not answering their prayers.

Psalm 124 a psalm of declarative praise, is one of four songs of ascent attributed to David (Pss. 122; 131; 133). This psalm was likely designed to be read aloud as an antiphonal response (118:1–4; compare Pss. 121; 129; 134; 135; 136). The structure of the poem is: (1) a call for the people to confess God's deliverance (vv. 1–5); (2) a blessing on the Lord for His deliverance (vv. 6–8).

124:1, 2 The LORD who was on our side amplifies the meaning of the divine name of God (Ex. 3:14, 15). The wording of the Hebrew text is even more dramatic: "The Lord was for us." The priests may have spoken the words **let Israel now say** as encouragement for the people to rehearse aloud their national experience (Ps. 129).

124:3 swallowed us alive: The poet describes his enemies first as ravenous beasts, then as raging waters; but God has defeated them all. As in other psalms, the reference to raging **waters** has a double source—the story of creation and the Canaanite myths concerning evil gods who were believed to be water deities (Ps. 93).

124:4, 5 waters: As is common in the Psalms, the references to raging waters has a double source, the story of Creation and the Canaanite background of evil gods who were believed to be water deities (Ps. 93).

124:6, 7 Blessed be the Lord: Blessing God means identifying Him as the source of our blessing (103:2). **as prey:** The animal imagery of the enemies (v. 3) continues in this praise of God. The image of a helpless **bird** that has escaped a trap is common in the Psalms (11:1–3).

124:8 our help is in the name: The centrality of the name of God, Yahweh, is affirmed at many points of these Psalms. It is in His name that God reveals that He is for His people (the point of v. 1, above). The words **who made heaven and earth** are similar to the words in 121:2; 134:3. These liturgical phrases were recited by the worshiping community during their journey to Jerusalem and when they arrived for corporate worship.

Psalm 125 a psalm of trust (Ps. 23), is also a song of Zion. This anonymous poem is the sixth song of ascent. The structure of the poem is as follows: (1) a celebration of God's protection of the righteous (vv. 1, 2); (2) a declaration that the power of the wicked cannot endure (v. 3);

IN FOCUS "mercy"

(Heb. *chanan*) (102:14; 123:2; Ex. 33:19; Is. 26:10) Strong's #2603: This term signifies an act of graciousness to someone in need, from a person of superior rank or circumstance. The writers of wisdom literature frequently commend showing mercy to the needy (112:5; Prov. 14:21, 31; 28:8). But most of the references to *mercy* in the Bible have to God as the direct agent of mercy. The Scripture records God's mercy being sought on numerous occasions, often using the phrase familiar from the psalms of lament, "Have mercy on me" (4:1; 6:2; 25:16; 51:1; 86:16). God shows His graciousness in many ways, including the prevention of harm, the bestowal of family and possessions, and the communication of divine law (119:29, 124; Gen. 33:5, 11; 2 Kin. 13:23).

(3) a prayer for the upright (v. 4); (4) a curse on the wicked and a call for the peace of Israel (v. 5).

125:1, 2 As in the other songs of Zion (Ps. 48), there is a deep belief in the invincibility of the city of Jerusalem because of the Lord's choice of **Mount Zion** (1 Kin. 11:36). Likewise, the psalmist proclaims that those who trust in the Lord will endure. **the mountains surround Jerusalem:** Jerusalem is built on one of seven mountain peaks in the region. The mountains provide some protection for the city, since any invading army would have to march through arduous and dangerous mountain paths. Yet the city's true protection comes from the Lord.

125:3 The scepter of wickedness is a symbol of the power of evil. This verse recalls the Lord's promise that the gates of hell will not prevail against His church (Matt. 16:18). In this way, God in His mercy protects His people from participation in evil.

125:4 do good: Such is what we expect from God on those who are His own; His expectation in us is righteousness (51:18).

125:5 The phrase **workers of iniquity** is often found in the wisdom psalms (14:4); the

Lord will oppose those who do evil. **peace:** The psalm concludes with a prayer for God's peace to rest on His people. The same prayer appears at the close of Ps. 128; it may be a shortened version of the priestly benediction recorded in Num. 6:24, 25.

Psalm 126 a song of Zion, is the seventh song of ascent. The distinctive element of this poem is that it comes from the time of the restoration of Jerusalem following the Babylonian captivity (compare Ps. 137). The mood of this psalm is one of sweet joy following the sorrows of long separation. The structure of the poem is: (1) a description of the return from captivity (vv. 1–3); (2) a prayer for God to complete the process of return (v. 4); (3) a comparison of the return from captivity to a long-delayed harvest (vv. 5, 6).

126:1–3 The return from Babylonian **captivity** had been anticipated for so long that it seemed like a dream to the returnees. Some of the people had waited an entire lifetime. The joy of the people could not be contained; their praise to God was unstoppable. The mood of this section is one of laughter and joy, of rejoicing in God's salvation (Is. 12).

126:4 The people who returned were a small percentage of those who had been exiled. **Bring back** is the beginning of the prayer that God would complete the restoration of His people to their land. Ultimately, this is a prayer for the coming of Jesus, who will complete God's work among His people.

126:5, 6 The people of Judah had gone to Babylon in **tears.** Yet their sorrow reaped tremendous rewards; the Lord came to the rescue of His humbled people (34:18; Is. 66:2; Matt. 5:4). Upon their return to Jerusalem and Judah, they were reaping a harvest of rejoicing.

Psalm 127 a wisdom psalm and the eighth song of ascent, is one of only two psalms attributed to Solomon (the other is Ps. 72). The structure of the poem is: (1) an exhortation about the vanity of an endeavor in which the Lord is not active (vv. 1, 2); (2) a celebration of the value of an endeavor in which the Lord is glorified (vv. 3–5).

127:1, 2 With the words **unless the Lord builds,** the psalmist asserts that life lived apart from God is not worth living, a view that this psalm shares with the Book of Ecclesiastes. Even building a house is useless if the Lord is not in the process. The phrase **the bread of sorrows** captures the essence of those removed from a sense of the Lord in their lives. The food that should give them strength for life and a zest for living only maintains them in their miserable state.

127:3–5 children are a heritage: Children are God's gifts (128:3). **Like arrows:** In ancient

times, having many children was regarded as a symbol of strength. This was particularly true in an agricultural economy, since the extra hands of children increased the productivity of the farmer. A full **quiver** was a mark of God's blessing. The blessing of a home in ancient times gave a person a measure of pride in the community. **The gate** was the place where the elders of the city met and where citizens would convene (Ruth 4:1–12).

Psalm 128 a wisdom psalm, is also a psalm of Zion. Like Ps. 127, this poem addresses God's blessings in the home and family. The feasts of ancient Israel were family affairs. As families made their way to the holy city for the annual festivals, they would encounter other families and mutually celebrate the goodness of God in their lives. Psalm 128 is the ninth song of ascent. The structure of the poem is as follows: (1) a blessing on the righteous (v. 1); (2) a description of the blessing (vv. 2–4); (3) a prayer for the blessing (v. 5); (3) a blessing on the community (v. 6).

128:1 The word **blessed** describes the happiness of those who trust in the Lord and do His will (127:5). **who fears the Lord:** The fear of God is an attitude of respect, a response of reverence and wonder. It is the only appropriate response to our Creator and Redeemer.

128:2, 3 labor of your hands: There is a reward in work and a satisfaction in labor that is a blessing of God (Eccl. 3:9–13). **Your wife:** This psalm focuses on the godly man in ancient Israel. Bearing children was a mark of God's blessing on his wife. His children were regarded as precious provisions, like **olive plants,** in his home (127:3–5). In that time more children meant more people who could work in the fields and increase the general welfare of the family.

128:4–6 The Lord bless you: This is the psalmist's prayer for the man who desires for his own family the blessings described in the psalm. **children's children:** This priestly prayer of blessing includes a desire for longevity and for happy posterity in the land. Only when God grants His **peace** on His people will the ideal conditions of family life be realized. Therefore, whoever prays for the blessing of God on a family also prays for the blessing of God's peace on the community as a whole (122:6–9; 125:5).

Psalm 129 a psalm of trust (Ps. 23), has its roots in the psalms of lament, for those psalms contain a section proclaiming trust in the Lord. The psalm has an antiphonal quality, calling for response and counter-response (compare 118:1–4; 124:1–5). This is the tenth song of ascent. Its structure is as follows: (1) a rehearsal of the afflictions of Israel (v. 1–3); (2) an affirmation of the victory of God (v. 4); (3) a condemnation of the wicked who have afflicted Israel (vv. 5–8).

129:1–4 Many a time: The psalm begins with a liturgy of suffering, as the people of God acknowledge that throughout their history in the land they have been under constant assault by various peoples. With the words **let Israel now say,** the priest calls for the people to rehearse their history aloud (124:1). **The plowers plowed:** This imagery of the brutal treatment they suffered was especially vivid in an agrarian setting. Even in the midst of such cruel circumstances, the Lord was **righteous.** He remained faithful to His promises to His people and He fought for them.

129:5–8 those who hate Zion: This begins the imprecation or cursing of the foes of Jerusalem. **Shame** is the intended end of the wicked (35:26). This is not just a desire for their embarrassment but for complete humiliation before the Lord. **as the grass on the housetops:** Sod was sometimes used on the roofs of houses. After a spring rain, there might be grass growing on the housetop. But this was not grass that flourished; it soon withered under the summer heat. The curse here is strong: May the enemies wither as quickly as rooftop grass.

Psalm 130 is a penitential psalm. Its placement following a psalm of imprecation (Ps. 129) is fitting. After all, a person might take such joy in the destruction of the wicked that he or she no longer would consider his or her own heart before the Lord. This psalm is the eleventh song of ascent. The structure is as follows: (1) a call for God's mercy (vv. 1,Ps. 2); (2) a recognition of God's forgiveness (vv. 3, 4); (3) an expectation of God's forgiveness (v. 5, 6); (4) a call for God's mercy on all (vv. 7, 8).

130:1, 2 The poet shouts aloud to God from **the depths** of his own despair (Pss. 32; 51). In this case it was not enemies who were plowing his back (129:3), but his own sense of sin that was eating at the depths of his soul.

130:3, 4 God does not **mark** or keep count of our sins. Through the sacrificial system and ultimately in the provision of Jesus Christ, God dismissed His people's sins altogether (Mic. 7:19); He does not keep track—as an accountant would—of their sins. The grace of God in His provision for **forgiveness** is not to be taken lightly (Rom. 6:1, 2). The truly forgiven sinner realizes the magnitude of God's grace, remains grateful for Jesus' sacrifice for sins, and lives in the *fear* or awe of God (Ps. 128).

130:5, 6 I wait . . . I do hope: In these two verses, the poet repeats five times that his hope is in the Lord. This was a confident expectation in the God who was always faithful to His promises.

130:7, 8 The psalm moves from the experi-ence of an individual to that of the community. After proclaiming his own hope, the psalmist exhorts the community of **Israel** to **hope in the Lord.** God is not only capable of delivering the individual, He also delivers the community of believers who hope in Him (131:3). **He shall redeem:** In the OT, the redemption of God's people refers to God's deliverance of His people from Egypt and from all other national foes, as well as to God's forgiveness of sins through the sacrificial system. The final redemption of all God's people came only in the death and resur-rection of the Lord Jesus Christ (Gal. 3:13).

Psalm 131 a psalm of trust, is one of four songs of ascent attributed to David (also Pss. 122; 124; 133). The structure of the poem is as follows: (1) a statement of humility (v. 1); (2) a portrait of trust (v. 2); (3) a call for hope (v. 3).

131:1 my heart is not haughty: David presents himself with genuine humility, a deli-cate balance between self-abasement and arro-gant pride. From the life of David we know that he was not always able to keep this balance. But it was his desire, and at times—by God's grace—a reality in his life.

131:2, 3 Like a weaned child: The image is that of a child who is no longer unsettled and discontented, but one who is at peace and trusting in his mother, who is there to comfort and to meet his needs. The words **hope in the Lord** recall 130:7.

Psalm 132 a royal psalm, is the thirteenth song of ascent. Like Ps. 89, this poem reflects in poetry God's covenant with David (2 Sam. 7), in which He promised David a royal house—a promise that would be fulfilled in the coming of the great Savior King. It is possible that this psalm was written late in Israel's history, after the exile in Babylon. This would explain the people's call for God to remember His covenant with David. With no king on the royal throne of David, the people had great reason to call upon God to remember His promise. Psalm 132 is the longest of the songs of ascent and is sometimes classified as a messianic psalm. Its structure is as follows: (1) a call for God to remember His covenant with David (vv. 1–5); (2) the expecta-tion of the fulfillment of the promise (vv. 6–9); (3) a prayer for God's kingdom to come (v. 10); (4) a recitation of the promise yet to be fulfilled (vv. 11, 12); (5) an elaboration of God's covenant with David (vv. 13–18).

132:1 If this psalm was written during the postexilic period, the words **remember David** have a significant meaning. During the years between the return of the people to Jerusalem and the birth of Jesus, there would have been a growing desire on the part of godly people for the Lord to restore David's kingdom in fulfill-ment of the Lord's promise.

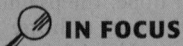 **IN FOCUS** | "shout for joy"

(Heb. *ranan*) (51:14; 132:9; Is. 35:6) Strong's #7442: This Hebrew word means "to utter loudly," with the vast majority of references being to shouts of joy or hearty, joyful singing (35:27; 59:16; 71:23). Twice the term is used of the summons of wisdom and once for the boisterous clamoring of a drunk (78:65; Prov. 1:20; 8:3). About half of its occurrences are in Psalms and about one fourth are in Isaiah. This word is associated with many terms for joy in the OT (32:11; Is. 49:13; Zech. 2:10). It is used to summon the heavens, the Gentiles, and most frequently the people of God—collectively and individually—to rejoice in God's blessings (33:11; Deut. 32:43; Is. 44:23; Zech. 2:10). Our loud rejoicing in the Lord is based on His greatness and His goodness to us (5:11; 145:7; Lev. 9:24; Is. 12:6).

132:2–4 The Mighty One of Jacob is a rare designation for God. Identical or similar expressions are found elsewhere in the Bible only in Gen. 49:24 and the Book of Isaiah (Is. 1:24; 49:26; 60:16). **a place:** The poet recalls David's desire to build a temple for the Lord (2 Sam. 7:1, 2).

132:5 a place: In these words, the poet recalls the desire of David to build the temple for the Lord (2 Sam. 7:1, 2). The poetic reworking of the narrative stories of Scripture is an old art in Israel (Judg. 4, 5).

132:6–9 Ephrathah refers to the region of Bethlehem (Ruth 1:2). The temple in Jerusalem was regarded as the **footstool** of God, whose dwelling is in heaven (99:5). In the context of this psalm, the call **arise, O Lord** is a prayer for God to fulfill His covenant promise to place a great king on David's throne (v. 1).

132:10 Do not turn away: Based on God's promise to David (2 Sam. 7), the psalmist calls for God to fulfill His word to send His Anointed. This is a clarion call for the coming of the Savior King, Jesus.

132:11, 12 The words **the Lord has sworn** are a poetic recasting of the central words of the Davidic covenant in 2 Sam. 7:8–16 (89:3, 4, 26–29). The ultimate fulfillment of these words is in Jesus Christ, the Son of David (Luke 1:32, 33; Acts 2:30). **your sons:** The promise to David was specific in terms of God's intended blessings on faithful sons, His chastening of wayward sons, and His ultimate fulfillment in the anticipated coming Son.

132:13 God's choice of the Davidic line was also a choice of **Zion** as His dwelling place.

132:14–16 my resting place: God's decision is to make Zion the place of His eternal dwelling place on earth (Heb. *menûhâ*, "a place of rest"). What choice words these are, and what condescension they suggest. He whose dwelling is beyond the heavens (113:4–6; 123:1), comes near His people to live among them (Zeph. 3:14–17), and to bless them with His presence (132:15, 16).

132:17 This verse celebrates God's covenant to send His **Anointed** One (v. 10). The words **horn** and **lamp** speak of the Messiah's authority and righteousness (Is. 11:1–5). **His crown:** The Messiah's kingdom will be established forever (Is. 9:7); His enemies will not withstand Him (Ps. 2).

132:18 His crown: The kingdom will be established forever (Is. 9:7); His enemies will not withstand Him (Ps. 2).

Psalm 133 is one of four songs of ascent attributed to David (Pss. 122; 124; 131). With its emphasis on the unity of the believers, this poem anticipates Jesus' prayer in John 17. The structure of the psalm is as follows: (1) a portrait of the beauty of unity (v. 1); (2) the blessing of unity (vv. 2, 3).

133:1, 2 Good and . . . pleasant may be rephrased as "great delight" or "good pleasure." There is a sense of serene wonder in these words describing the unity of God's people. **like the precious oil:** Priests were anointed with a fragrant oil as a symbol of God's blessing on their holy office (Ex. 30:22–33). This psalm pictures the oil in such large quantity that it flows from the **head** to the **beard** to the garment of **Aaron,** who represented the priests of God. When God's people live together in unity, they experience God's blessing.

133:3 like the dew of Hermon: This high mountain to the north of Israel received such large amounts of water that it seemed to be a source of moisture for the lands below. Similarly, the blessings of God flow to His people. **the blessing:** The intent of God is for the good of His people in this life and in the life to come. The people of Israel rarely achieved the level of unity—or the level of blessing—that the poem describes. Ultimately, this is a portrait of the kingdom of God. One day there will be the spir-

---

⊞ IN CONTEXT **The Old Testament View of Death**

Death is a universal dilemma. In one ancient Near Eastern story, the Gilgamesh Epic, the hero Gilgamesh is suddenly struck by the pain of death, when his friend Enkidu dies. Gilgamesh then begins a long journey in search of the secret of eternal life. Even when he finds it in a thorny plant, it is stolen from him, and Gilgamesh concludes that seeking immortality is useless because all must die.

The Israelites had a unique focus on the here and now. While the Egyptians prepared elaborate tombs, including paintings and figures that would supposedly benefit the dead one, the Hebrew Scriptures stressed the importance of living life to its fullness because death was the end of human activity. Hebrew wisdom offered this advice: Find joy in the daily rounds of life, "for there is no work or device or knowledge or wisdom in the grave where you are going" (Eccl. 9:10).

Death was often equated with a kind of sleep. Thus the psalmist uses the phrase the "sleep of death" (Ps. 13:3). When the kings of Israel died, we are told, they went to sleep or "rested" with their fathers (1 Kin. 2:10; 11:43; 14:31).

The Hebrews described death with visual imagery as the abode of the dead. A person who dies goes to Sheol (sometimes translated as "hell," "grave," or the "pit"), which clearly represents the grave (Job 21:13; Prov. 7:27). In Sheol there is no human activity, not even the praising of the Lord (Pss. 146:3, 4; 115;17). Or as the author of Ecclesiastes wrote, "For the living know that they will die; but the dead know nothing" (Eccl. 9:5).

Death was not to be dreaded; it was the expected, normal end of life. Indeed, death was considered good for the person who was "full of years" and had reached "a good old age" (Gen. 25:8; Job 42:17).

---

itual unity of God's people that this poem describes.

Psalm 134 concludes the songs of ascent. This psalm was likely read as a responsive poem of praise (Pss. 118; 121; 124; 129; 135; 136). The structure of this brief poem is as follows: (1) the blessing of the priests by the people (vv. 1, 2); (2) the blessing of the people by the priests (v. 3).

134:1, 2 To **bless the Lord** is to identify Him as the source of all blessing (103:2). In this context, **servants of the Lord** refers to the priests of Israel who conducted their ministry at all hours in the temple (135:1, 2). The idea behind this blessing was that the people who had come to worship at the temple were getting ready to go home. They had come for a great festival but had to return to their regular work and routine. However, the priests remained at the holy temple. It was their continuing worship of the Lord that allowed God's blessing to continue on the nation as a whole. **Lift up your hands:** One of the standard postures for prayer in biblical times was to stand with hands stretched out toward heaven (1 Tim. 2:8).

134:3 Bless you from Zion may have been the grateful response of the priests to the people, their own blessing on the people from the holy temple.

Psalm 135 a psalm of descriptive praise that recalls ideas and motifs from several earlier psalms, may have been composed after the exile in Babylon. The psalm presents God's saving works during the Exodus and contains a scathing attack on idolatry, taken from Ps. 115. The beginning and ending of this poem are written in the pattern of liturgical praise. The structure is as follows: (1) a call for the priests to bless the name of the Lord (vv. 1–4); (2) praise for the Lord who alone is the great and active God (vv. 5–7); (3) praise for the Lord's saving deeds (vv. 8–12); (4) praise for the Lord's saving name (vv. 13, 14); (5) contempt for the ineffective and powerless gods of the nations (vv. 15–18); (6) a call for the people to bless the name of the Lord (vv. 19–21).

135:1–5 you servants of the Lord: This psalm begins with a call for the priests of Israel to praise God in the temple (134:1, 2). The endearing term **special treasure** is used only here in the Psalms (Ex. 19:5; Deut. 7:6; 14:2).

135:6, 7 Whatever the Lord pleases: These words are adapted from 115:3. The words **lightning for the rain** appear to be a citation of Jer. 10:13, indicating that this psalm was written after the exile in Babylon The point of this section is clear: God is active in all creation. Conversely, the gods of the nations are impotent (vv. 15–18).

135:8 firstborn of Egypt: Like Ps. 78, this psalm rehearses the saving events of the Exodus, culminating in the events of the Passover (Ex.

12:12). The defeat of Egypt was solely the work of the Lord. Israel was merely His instrument; the battle belonged to Him (Ex. 15:3).

135:9–14 God's saving actions established His reputation. Because of them, His **name** and His fame spread throughout the world. **He will have compassion:** As in Ps. 147, those who faced the hardships of restoring themselves in the land needed to know of God's continuing promise of mercy (Ps. 132).

135:15 The idols of the nations: This verse is a citation from 115:4–8. It is a devastating satirical attack on pagan idolatry. The people who returned from Babylon had had their fill of the worship of idols; at long last, the

Painting of Babylon, the pagan city where citizens of Israel were held captive during the exile. Psalm 137 reflects the Israelites' longing for their homeland and the city of Jerusalem, referred to as "Zion" (Ps. 137:1–6).

people of Israel were ready to worship the only true God.

135:16–21 To **bless the Lord** is to identify Him as the source of all blessings (103:2) and to be grateful for all that He has given. This section is a sustained liturgy for the people to encourage one another to praise the Lord.

Psalm 136 is the quintessential psalm of descriptive praise. The worship leader, perhaps a priest, would read the first part of each verse. The people would then respond with their praise centering on the mercy of God: "For His

mercy endures forever." This psalm, known as the "Great Hallel," was often recited in the temple as the Passover lambs were being slain. Some include Ps. 135 and the psalms of ascents (Pss. 120—134) in the "Great Hallel." The pattern for the psalm is: (1) a call for the people to praise the Lord (vv. 1–3); (2) praise for the Lord who is the great Creator (vv. 4–9); (3) praise for the Lord who is the great Deliverer (vv. 10–22); (4) praise for the Lord who remembers His people forever (vv. 23–25); (5) a concluding call for the people to praise the Lord (v. 26).

136:1, 2 Give thanks means "to give public acknowledgment"; it is one of the principal words for praise in the Psalms (35:18; 105:1; 122:4). **Mercy,** which may also be translated "loyal love," is the most significant term used in the Psalms to describe the character of God. His mercy is "forever"; it is part of His eternal character. **God of gods:** The poet uses Hebrew superlatives to proclaim the Lord as the Supreme Deity.

136:3–5 In the OT, the term **great wonders** is used exclusively for the awe-inspiring actions of God. God's creation of the universe is the grand display of His **wisdom.** The heavens give a clear presentation of the glory of God (19:1–6). Romans 1:20 teaches that God's "invisible attributes" are clearly seen through the things He has made.

136:6–13 struck Egypt: The poet refers to God's great acts of deliverance in bringing Israel from Egypt at the dawn of Israel's redemption (Pss. 78; 105; 135:8–12). **strong hand:** This is a slogan of redemption (118:15, 16; Ex. 15:6). It has been said when God created the universe, it was the work of His fingers (8:3); but when He battled for the salvation of His people, it was with His strong right hand. **divided the Red Sea:** God brought Israel across the Jordan by dividing its waters, then used the same waters to destroy the pursuing army of Egypt.

136:14–20 The poet's recital of Israel's history includes the capture of the lands east of the Jordan, including the territories of **Sihon** and **Og** (Num. 21). The result was the gift of the land of Canaan to the people of Israel.

136:21–23 It is possible that the words **remembered us** suggest the return of the people of Judah and Jerusalem to their land following the Babylonian captivity. Like Ps. 135, Ps. 136 may have been written after the Exile.

136:24–26 Oh, give thanks: The psalm ends as it begins, with celebration of God's continuing faithfulness to His people Israel and a call to thank Him for His goodness.

Psalm 137 a song of Zion, is also a particularly impassioned imprecatory psalm. Although no author is named, the psalm clearly shares with the Book of Lamentations the despair of those who suffered the destruction of Jerusalem by the Babylonians in 586 B.C. This troubling psalm is one of deeply felt emotion. Its pattern is as follows: (1) weeping in Babylon at the memory of the destruction of Zion (vv. 1–3); (2) longing for Jerusalem and the restoration of song in praise of God (vv. 4–6); (3) desiring reprisals against Edom and Babylon for their destruction of Jerusalem (vv. 7–9).

137:1–4 Babylon was one of the great empires in world history. When this psalm was written, the Jews were living there in involuntary exile. **we wept:** The emotions of the psalm are clearly indicated. The memory of Zion was painful for those in a foreign land (42:1–3). **hung our harps:** Making joyful music to the Lord in a foreign land was so difficult that the captives refused to make music at all. They took the words of their captors as taunts.

137:5, 6 If I forget you: It is difficult for the modern reader to appreciate the love for Zion among the people of OT faith. As we observe regularly in the Psalms, this love was not just for a place but for its function in their lives. It was in **Jerusalem** that the temple had been built. The place was holy because of God's presence there (2:6).

137:7 Remember, O Lord: After speaking with great passion about his own remembering and forgetting (vv. 4–6), the psalmist calls upon the Lord to remember the abominable actions of the people of Edom in the day of Jerusalem's trouble (see Ps. 129 for a similar sentiment).

Raze it: The men of Edom leered and jeered as Jerusalem was shamefully leveled.

137:8 O daughter of Babylon: We have noted that the corresponding phrase, "Daughter of Zion," is better rendered "Daughter Zion" (see note at 9:14). That is, Zion does not have a daughter; she herself is God's "daughter," a term of great endearment. Is it possible, then, that in this place the words "Daughter Babylon" are used in a sarcastic manner? Zion is the Lord's daughter, not Babylon. She may be the offspring of some god, but not of the Lord.

137:9 Happy is the same term of blessing that begins the first psalm (1:1; 146:5). The blessing would come on the army that finally destroyed the wicked city of Babylon, that had itself been used as a tool of judgment in the hands of Almighty God (Hab. 1:12–17).

Psalm 138 is a psalm of declarative praise attributed to David. The mood of this psalm contrasts strongly with that of Ps. 137. Its structure is as follows: (1) a declaration of praise to God because of an overwhelming answer to the prayer of the king (vv. 1–3); (2) a prophetic vision of a future time in which all kings of the earth will join in the praise of God (vv. 4–6); (3) a determination to continually trust in God (vv. 7, 8).

138:1, 2 As in many psalms, the poet begins his praise with a determination to involve his **whole** being (146:1). **Before the gods:** David is so confident in his faith in the Lord that he is determined to take the name of God into foreign

---

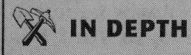 **IN DEPTH** ## By the Rivers of Babylon

Psalm 137 summarizes the question that perplexed not only the exiles of Judah in Babylon, but all of the Jews who were quickly being dispersed throughout the ancient world: How can we worship and serve the Lord in a foreign land? (Ps. 137:4).

Cut off from their homeland, they were without their magnificent temple. They had no king to guide them, no high priest to offer sacrifices, no ark of the covenant to signify God's presence. Spiritually speaking, they were cast adrift in the world without their familiar landmarks to guide them.

No wonder the people of Judah sat down and wept by the rivers of Babylon (137:1). Asked by their captors to sing songs of Zion, all they could think about was how their beloved city was now laid waste (137:3). Consequently, they sang a song—but not one that was expected. They sang a sorrowful, vengeful song calling for curses on the Babylonians who had destroyed Jerusalem (137:8) and on the Edomites who had celebrated the city's fall (137:7).

However, despite the sentiments expressed in this psalm, several positive things resulted from the Jews' dispersion. Lacking a temple, they invented the synagogue (Mark 1:21). They also collected their writings, which eventually led to the canonization of the OT. And because they were forced to learn new languages and adapt to foreign cultures, they eventually translated the OT from Hebrew into Greek, the common language of Christ's day.

Thus necessity became the mother of invention for the Hebrews. Many such gifts from the Lord came into the world because God's people were forced to "sing the Lord's song in a foreign land."

territory. **Your holy temple:** The use of the word temple does not rule out David as the author of this or similar poems (15:1). The Hebrew term is a general one that would fit whatever building was in use in David's day. The term was also proper for later readers and singers of this psalm when the actual temple had been built.

138:3–6 David, as a king who believed in God, looked forward to a day when **all the kings of the earth** would share his experience. **great is the glory of the Lord:** This is another way of expressing the reality of the living God. **regards the lowly:** God comes to the humble because they will have regard for Him. Conversely, He distances Himself from the proud (86:14; 147:6).

138:7, 8 Though I walk: The poet is well aware that new troubles will confront him. He has confidence that God, who has blessed him in the experience of this psalm, will continue to bless his path. **perfect:** The same Hebrew verb is translated "perform" in 57:2. The point of the word is that God acts on behalf of His servants. **Your mercy, O Lord, endures forever:** This is a slight rewording of the refrain in Ps. 136.

Psalm 139 attributed to David, is a wisdom psalm of descriptive praise. This mixture of wisdom and praise is not uncommon in the Psalms (Pss. 145; 146). This poem describes the attributes of the Lord not as abstract qualities, but as active qualities by which He relates Himself to His people. The structure of the psalm is: (1) a description of God's intimate knowledge of His servant (vv. 1–6); (2) a celebration of God's presence with David (vv. 7–12); (3) a celebration of God's creation of David from the moment of conception (vv. 13–16); (4) a declaration that God's thoughts toward David are innumerable (vv. 17, 18); (5) a prayer for the punishment of God's enemies (vv. 19–22); (6) a prayer that God might search and lead David (vv. 23, 24).

139:1–5 You have searched me: God is active to search and test His servants. He knows our motives, desires, and words before they are expressed. In short, He knows His servants completely. But as v. 5 makes clear, the purpose of His intimate knowledge of His servants is protective and helpful, not judgmental and condemning.

139:6 such knowledge: Here the poet gasps aloud at the wonder of the intimate relationship He has with God, and God with him. It is simply too much to comprehend; the human mind with all its ability is no match for the mind of God!

139:7 There are two different ways in which the words **where can I go** can be understood. One is that David *wanted* to flee from the pres-

ence of God, but could not. The second view takes the words as a celebration of God's mercy, that there was no place in all creation where David, the servant of God, would find himself separated from God's presence.

139:8, 9 heaven: The language is exuberant, expressive, and expansive. The point is clear, there is no place so high, so deep, so far, or so near that the servant of the Lord might find that there is a distance from God.

139:10–12 Your hand: The wording of v. 10 seems protective, suggesting that the psalm speaks of God's helpful presence. **darkness:** Here David stretches his imagination to the brink. Darkness refers to death or the "pit" (16:10). This is an expansion of the words of v. 8, "If I make my bed in hell." David suggests this as the one place in the universe where God would not be present. But even though God is opposed to all darkness, God would turn the darkness into light in order to find His servant David. As in 18:7–12, the Lord would overturn the structure of the universe to save the person who worshiped Him.

139:13–16 You formed my inward parts: David affirms that the work of God in his life extended back to his development in his mother's womb. **You covered me** may also be translated as "You wove me together," a description of the work of God creating the person in the mother's womb. **I am fearfully and wonderfully made** might be rephrased as "I am an awesome wonder" (Ps. 8). **skillfully wrought:** The development of the fetus was something quite mysterious to the ancients. To them, it was as though the fetus were being developed in the middle of the earth. The Hebrew word **my substance** indicates the embryo. **in Your book:** The idea is that the life of a person, and the structure and meaning of that person's life, are all established from the beginning by God.

139:17, 18 Your thoughts: Not only are the works of God in the life of the person of faith a thing of constant marvel, but so are the thoughts of God. They are directed toward the believer. They are more than can be numbered. If one were to attempt to count them, one would fall asleep. And the morning light would find God still near, His thoughts still new, and the marvel unexplainable.

139:19–21 slay the wicked: David desires a world in which there is no more evil, no more distraction, no more destruction. The enemies of God are David's own enemies because his life and thoughts are so closely tied to the Lord.

139:22 perfect hatred: These words may seem to be an oxymoron to some, but the idea of an enemy of God is so abhorrent to the psalmist that he faces such enemies as they really are.

139:23, 24 Search me, O God: These words are similar to those of 19:14. David asks God to examine his thoughts and purge him of sin so that he might enter into everlasting life.

Psalm 140 a psalm of individual lament ascribed to David, is particularly concerned with the wicked. David's desire for the judgment of the Lord to come upon the wicked identifies this poem as an imprecatory psalm. The structure of Ps. 140 is as follows: (1) a petition that David be delivered from the wicked (vv. 1–3); (2) a petition that David be kept from the wicked (vv. 4, 5); (3) a confession of trust in the Lord (vv. 6–8); (4) a prayer for the punishment of the wicked (vv. 9–11); (5) a declaration that the Lord will deliver the afflicted (vv. 12, 13).

140:1–3 Deliver me: David cries out to the Lord for deliverance from the wicked, who continually harm the innocent. The words **violent men** are repeated in v. 4. The word *violent* describes people who are harsh and ruthless, who plan the destruction of the righteous. They are purposefully evil and will be satisfied only if they can participate in the destruction of God's people. But God is always ready to deliver His precious ones from their grasp.

140:4, 5 from violent men: These words are repeated from the second colon of v. 2. The word "violent" (Heb. *hamasîm*) describes people who use harsh language, who behave in ruthless manners, who use acts of violence, who wield terrible weapons. In this psalm, the violent people are those who have set as their purpose the destruction of the righteous.

140:6–9 With the words **You are my God,** David confesses his complete trust in the Lord even though he is surrounded by people plotting his destruction. On the basis of his trust, he now pleads with the Lord to deliver him.

140:10 Let burning coals fall upon them: Here David recalls the judgment of Sodom and Gomorrah (11:6; Gen. 19:12–29) and asks God to use this particular judgment on his enemies.

140:11–13 The **cause** of the **poor** and the **afflicted** is of special interest to the Lord. He promises to uphold and comfort them (41:1; 72:4; 109:31; Luke 4:18; 6:20).

Psalm 141 an individual psalm of lament, is ascribed to David. In this case no particular event is cited as the cause for David's distress. Because this poem records David's desire for the judgment of his enemies, it falls into the category of the imprecatory psalms also. The structure is: (1) an introductory cry to the Lord (vv. 1, 2); (2) a prayer for a guard over David's mouth (vv. 3, 4); (3) an acceptance of righteous rebuke (v. 5a); (4) a vision of the punishment of the wicked (vv. 5b–7); (5) a statement of confidence in the Lord (vv. 8–10).

141:1, 2 Lord, I cry out to you: David asks to be heard as he prays in the assembly of the righteous. As the smoke and aroma of **incense** rises to the Lord as something sweet and compelling, so David desires that his prayer will not be ignored. **The lifting up of my hands:** With this impressive gesture David is asking God to pay attention to his plea.

141:3, 4 Set a guard: This is a prayer for wisdom, for restraining evil language, and for knowing the correct words to speak. David wanted to avoid any act of impiety, irreverence, or even idolatry; he did not want to offend God with anything he said.

141:5–7 With the words **let the righteous strike me,** David expresses his willingness to accept the judgment of the righteous; what bothers him is the instruction and judgment of the wicked. **against the deeds of the wicked:** As in Ps. 140, the wicked have brought David to his state of distress. He envisions a day when the wicked will be destroyed—their power will collapse and justice will reign in its place.

141:8–10 In light of the wicked's strength, it is easy for us to fix our eyes on, or worry about, the wicked. It is also natural to focus on ourselves: we either become self-absorbed in our difficulties or exalt ourselves in our victories. But David fixes his **eyes** only on the Lord (2 Cor. 3:18; Heb. 12:2, 3).

Psalm 142 a psalm of individual lament ascribed to David, provides a specific reference for the setting of the poem. The term *the cave* may refer to one of two occasions on which David hid from King Saul in a cave. One occurred in En Gedi (Ps. 57; 1 Sam. 24); the other at Adullam (1 Sam. 22:1, 2). The second may well be the setting for this poem of deep anguish. This was a time in David's life when it appeared that he was totally alone. In fact, he began to doubt whether even God was truly for him. But as the superscription indicates, David turned to the Lord in prayer. The structure of the psalm is: (1) David's cry for help from the cave of his despair (vv. 1, 2); (2) David's lament of distress that no one was on his side (vv. 3, 4); (3) David's confession of trust and petition for deliverance (vv. 5, 6); (4) David's vow of praise when God delivered him (v. 7).

> *The violent people are those who have set as their purpose the destruction of the righteous.*

142:1, 2 I cry out: There is a significant emphasis on the vocal and desperate nature of David's lament in this psalm. **With my voice** may also be translated "aloud."

142:3–5 In the midst of his distress, David makes his preliminary confession of trust—God **knew** his **path** from the beginning. **Look on my right hand:** With enemies on every path, David screams aloud to God that he is defenseless. The armed soldier in ancient Israel probably would have had his spear or sword in his right hand and his shield in his left. The shield of one man would protect the right side of his neighbor. David cries that there is no one on his right side; He expects to find God there (3:3, 4). **You are my refuge:** In the midst of his pain, David renews his confession of trust that somehow God must be near. He then pleads with God to deliver him from his foes.

142:6, 7 The cave that was intended as a place of refuge has become a place of confinement—**a prison.** The psalm ends with a vow that when God would deliver him from his awful experience, David would bring renewed **praise** to God in the worshiping community. Even though he is still in the midst of his distress, David is able to conclude with a prayer of faith: **You shall deal bountifully with me.**

Psalm 143 a psalm of individual lament ascribed to David, is similar in tone to other psalms of distress, particularly Ps. 6. Some scholars categorize Pss. 6 and 143 as penitential psalms. The structure of Ps. 143 is as follows: (1) a presentation of great personal distress (vv. 1–4); (2) a longing for former days of delight (vv. 5, 6); (3) prayers for deliverance (vv. 7–12).

143:1–3 David asks God not to bring him **into judgment,** yet he does not confess his sins as in Pss. 32; 38. **no one living is righteous:** This is not so much a confession of sin as an observation that everyone is sinful. **in darkness:** The biblical metaphor of light and darkness begins in Gen. 1:2, 3. To live in darkness is similar to being in the pit (v. 7); this is the reason for the parallel to those who are already dead (Job 10:21, 22).

143:4–6 the days of old: This is similar to 42:4, in which the psalmist remembers rejoicing in temple worship in times gone by. **spread out my hands:** This was one of the traditional postures for prayer in biblical times.

143:7, 8 the pit: Without a renewed sense of God's presence, described by the words, **Your face,** David believes that he is as good as dead. **in the morning:** Often in the psalms there is an expectation that an answer from God might come with the morning light (5:3; 30:5; 130:6).

143:9, 10 Your Spirit is good: This is a rather unusual statement of praise to the person of the Holy Spirit in the Hebrew Bible (Neh. 9:20).

143:11, 12 for Your name's sake: The requests of the psalmists are often tied to various character traits of God. When we pray "in Jesus' name," we pray both in the authority of His name and in the character it represents. **I am Your servant:** To be a servant of the Lord is a position to which even kings might aspire. Since there is no greater Lord, there is no greater position than to be aligned with His purposes.

Psalm 144 a psalm of descriptive praise with overtones of lament and petition, is ascribed to David. This poem is similar to Ps. 18 in that it describes the salvation acts of the Lord in terms of great heavenly phenomena. It is also possible that this psalm was used in the training of the army (as was Ps. 149). Warfare in ancient Israel was tied closely to the worship of God. Deliverance from the enemy was not just a task for tough soldiers, it was a matter of active piety. The structure is as follows: (1) a confession of praise to God the great warrior (vv. 1, 2); (2) a description of the frailty of human beings (vv. 3, 4); (3) a description of the saving acts of God (vv. 5–8); (4) a determination to praise the Lord (vv. 9, 10); (5) a call for God's continual deliverance of His people (vv. 11–15).

144:1, 2 The Lord my Rock is often used

 **IN FOCUS**   **"extol"**

(Heb. *rum*) (30:1; 34:3; 145:1; Ex. 15:2; Is. 25:1) Strong's #7311: The Hebrew word translated *extol* here is one of the many Hebrew words for praise in the Psalms. The specific meaning of this word is "to hold high" or "to esteem greatly." In contrast to King David's praise of the Lord as the exalted One (2 Sam. 22:47; Ps. 99:9), Lucifer's downfall came in trying to exalt himself above God (Is. 14:13). Thus in a negative sense, the word *rum* can mean "haughty" (2 Sam. 22:28). The psalmist's strong determination to honor and esteem God in 145:1 is indicated by the highly energized verb he employs in this passage, a verb which indicates a command directed to himself.

in the Psalms to describe God as the fortress of His people. At times, the word is translated *strength* (18:1). David found in the Lord the protection and preparation he needed in times of battle.

144:3, 4 what is man: This is a quotation from 8:4, but without the stunning answer presented in 8:5. Here the rhetorical question is used to speak of the frailty of humans who are in need of God's help. **passing shadow:** The sense of human frailty is illustrated dramatically in these words (102:2, 3).

144:5 bow down Your heavens: We understand language like this to be an exuberant use of terms for effect. Nonetheless, we may come to these words (which remind us of the descriptions in 18:7–12); we may call this the language of apocalyptic epiphany. The idea of God coming near is a concept of such power that the poets do everything they know to do to give us a sense of this awesome idea.

144:6 The **lightning** of the Lord is a symbol of His judgment (97:4). Here David celebrates God's righteous judgments, which he prays will be exercised against his evil foes.

144:7–10 I will sing a new song is David's vow to respond to God's deliverance with renewed worship and praise (149:1). **David:** It is rare for these poems to mention the psalmist by name (18:50). David's use of his own name indicated to later generations that this psalm arose out of actual experiences in his life.

144:11 lying words: The principal lie of the enemy was that the Lord could not save His people (Ps. 12).

144:12–15 The image of **pillars** seems to indicate health, beauty, and dignity. **barns:** Agricultural productivity was possible only in times of peace and would be meaningful only in times of national freedom. **Happy** is often translated "blessed" (1:1). Its use twice in v. 15 is dramatic. The happiness that David describes refers both to external well-being—**in such a state**—and to internal peace—**whose God is the Lord.**

Psalm 145 a wisdom psalm, is also a psalm of declarative praise. The poem is written in the form of an acrostic, with one verse for each letter of the Hebrew alphabet. The structure of the psalm is: (1) a focus on the greatness of the Lord (vv. 1–3); (2) an expectation of the ongoing praise of the Lord (vv. 4–7); (3) a focus on the character of the Lord (vv. 8, 9); (4) an expression concerning the kingdom of the Lord (vv. 10–13); (5) an acknowledgment of the grace of the Lord to all (vv. 14–16); (6) a focus on the righteous grace of the Lord (vv. 17–21).

145:1–3 The familiar words **great is the Lord** express God's grandeur in the universe and remind us of how small we are in His presence. The fact that frail humans are used to praise God is a marvel to the psalmist.

145:4–6 One generation . . . to another: The expectation is that the message of God's wonder and mercy will be known throughout the land and will be taught for generations.

145:7 The word **memory** may refer to the divine name of God. The Hebrew term for *memory* is translated "memorial" in Ex. 3:15.

145:8 God had described Himself as **gracious and full of compassion** (Ex. 34:6, 7; Num. 14:18). David uses God's own words to praise Him for His merciful character (86:5, 15; 111:4; 112:4).

145:9–13 All Your works echoes the words of 19:1–3. All that God has made bears the marks of His wonder (111:2). **They shall speak:** The task of the righteous is to declare the works of the Lord to all people. **an everlasting kingdom:** Because the rule of God is eternal, the message of His wonders needs to be delivered to all people in the present time.

145:14 The words **upholds all who fall** describe the ongoing actions of God on behalf of the needy in a way that may suggest that these words are absolute and invariable. Yet the same people who sang the songs of praise also cried out to the Lord with the psalms of lament. In a world in which life is tough, the psalms delight in affirming that God is good and that there is no limit to His power, His love, and His concern for His people. The psalms celebrate each example of God's saving mercy and each example of His grace. Time after time, instance after instance—the whole becomes a beautiful tapestry of His ongoing grace.

145:15–17 The pairing of **righteous** and **gracious** is a powerful demonstration of the character of God. His righteousness leads to His discriminating judgment; His grace leads to His saving works and forgiving actions. God both preserves and destroys based on His infallible insight into human intent and purposes.

145:18–21 My mouth: David resolved to be faithful in praising the Lord (146:1), but he also saw his praise as one part of the praise of all creation—that is, **all flesh.**

Psalm 146 a psalm of descriptive praise, is part of the grand pinnacle of praise in this book of praises. Each of the last five psalms begins and ends with the Hebrew word "Hallelujah!" This final set of praise psalms forms an exuberant ending to Israel's orchestrated responses to the wonder of God and His gracious works on their behalf. Psalm 146 also shows some similarities with wisdom literature. The structure of the poem is as follows: (1) a call for a life of praise to God (vv. 1, 2); (2) a warning against putting one's trust even in good people (vv. 3, 4); (3) a blessing on the one who finds help in God (vv.

5–7); (4) a description of the wonderful works of God in the lives of His people (vv. 8, 9); (5) a call to praise God the great King (v. 10).

146:1, 2 My soul is another way of speaking of one's inner being and is often used as a substitute for the pronouns "I" or "me." **while I live:** The poet makes a strong vow to praise the Lord for the rest of his life.

146:3 in princes: The point is that even the best of people are not adequate help in times of terrible stress. Even princes are mortal, and are not able even to help themselves (118:9). In contrast is the individual who finds ultimate help in God who lives forever (vv. 5–7).

146:4–6 Happy indicates a deep and abiding pleasure, a manifest joy. This is the proper description of one whose help and hope is in God. **Who made heaven and earth:** Creation themes pervade the hymns of Israel (Ps. 104); here the point is that the Creator of the universe is the One who comes to the aid of the righteous.

146:7 who executes justice: The descriptive phrases in v. 7 remind us of the praise of God in Psalm 103:3–6 and Psalm 107:8–10. These are the regularly recurring acts of God in response to the needs of His people (113:7–9).

146:8, 9 the eyes of the blind: In these two verses there is a special focus on the gracious actions of God on behalf of the impaired, the helpless, the lonely, and the needy (38:6). **But the way of the wicked:** The contrast in God's treatment of the righteous and the wicked is as pronounced in this psalm as it is in other psalms (1:4, 6; 147:6).

146:10 The Lord shall reign forever: The Bible presents several dimensions of the rule of God: He is King as Creator (Ps. 93); He is King as Savior of His people (Ps. 99); and He is King as the Coming One (Ps. 98). This verse speaks of God's present and eternal reign rather than specifically of His coming rule at the end of time. **Praise the Lord:** The use of the Hebrew term *hallelujah* at the end of the psalm balances its use at the beginning.

Psalm 147 a psalm of descriptive praise, places a strong emphasis on creation themes. This anonymous poem was likely written following the return of the Jewish people to Jerusalem from the Babylonian captivity (also Pss. 126; 132; 135). The structure is threefold, with each section introduced by a command to praise the Lord: (1) a command to praise the Lord for His restorative mercies (vv. 1–6); (2) a command to praise the Lord for the joy He finds in His people (vv. 7–11); (3) a command to praise the Lord for His Word (vv. 12–20).

147:1 The sentiment **praise is beautiful** is also expressed in 33:1. The people of God may bring their offerings of praise and worship to the Lord.

147:2, 3 builds up Jerusalem: The few people who had returned from captivity faced an immense task. But they needed to know, as do all subsequent people who do the work of the Lord, that because the work was God's, He would see that it was accomplished. It is a privilege for God's people to be counted as part of the fulfillment of the task, but the glory belongs to Him. **He heals the brokenhearted:** God's principal work is within the human heart (51:10–12).

✠ IN CONTEXT | Singing with the Universe

Hymns from Egypt to Mesopotamia are filled with praises to the deity. On the feast day of any given deity, the hymns named the god as the highest god of the pantheon on that particular day. Whether it was a hymn to Amon of Egypt or to Ishtar of Babylon, the singers praised that deity for creating the world, for ruling over the other gods, for unsurpassed wisdom, and for the blessings which the worshipers had received from the deity. Always, the deity to whom the song was directed was called the greatest of the gods.

Such a hymn is Psalm 148, possibly composed for a day set aside as holy to Yahweh. After the Exile this psalm could have been sung daily since, at least in Judah's later years, all days were thought holy to Yahweh. In the hymn, the residents of heaven are joined in their praise of Yahweh by inanimate objects, all of creation from heaven to earth (Ps. 148:7–10). Moreover, the song assumes that all peoples everywhere praise God who created them (148: 11, 12). Language and motifs that are used elsewhere in the ancient world for other gods are reserved in Psalm 148 exclusively for Yahweh.

The ancient world understood that one never sings hymns of praise alone, but always with the entire universe. This idea of solidarity with the entire created order was carried over into the early church and still remains a central aspect of Orthodox Christian liturgy.

147:4–6 He counts the number of the stars: Quoted from Is. 40:26, these words describe the infinite knowledge of God. But the words signify more: God's principal interest is not in stars or insects; God's interest is in His people (v. 11). **lifts up the humble:** God's greatness may be approached only by the humble; He resists the proud, but He comforts the lowly (86:14; 146:9; James 4:6).

147:7–9 Sing praises: The second movement of the psalm begins with a new call for the praise of God (vv. 1, 12). **rain for the earth:** A regular part of God's covenantal mercies is the bringing of rain for produce and livelihood (Lev. 26:1–13). More than that, God sends rain on the just and the unjust because of His continuing mercy to all. We may describe the actions of these verses as God's "regular mercies." **beast:** Jesus describes God's care as extending even to sparrows (Matt. 10:29).

147:10, 11 He does not delight: The enjoyment God finds in His people is greater than any pleasure He may find in horses or runners. Forms of the verb *delight* and **takes . . . pleasure** are found in 40:6–8; 51:16. These are God's responses to true piety; He enjoys people who respond rightly to Him (86:4). To **fear** God is to be properly responsive to Him in awe and wonder.

147:12 The words **praise the Lord** introduce the third movement of the psalm. This section was a reminder to the new settlers in the land of promise that God had blessed them in numerous ways. He had given them protection, posterity, peace, and productivity.

147:13–18 His word: The point of this section is that the command of God goes throughout His world; whatever He commands, the creation obeys. As in the celebrative words of Psalm 104; we sense in these words God's enjoyment in His creation. The very term "nature" is too passive a word, too removed from God. "Creation" is that which the Bible writers would understand, for it is responsive to the Creator.

147:19, 20 God's word goes throughout His creation, causing snow, frost, hail, wind, and every other aspect of weather to obey His command. Here He gives His word to His people. Shall we obey as does the wind? Or shall we be the only element of creation that is unresponsive to the divine will? **not dealt thus:** Israel confessed the unique revelation that it had received from God and acknowledged their unique responsibility. Our responsibility is as profound as Israel's, for we too have heard the testimonies of the Creator through Scripture.

Psalm 148 is a complex psalm. Because of its many references to the creation, it can be labeled a wisdom psalm, and more particularly a creation psalm (Pss. 19; 104). It is also highly charged with praise. Like Ps. 19, this psalm moves from the heavens to the human heart. The structure is as follows: (1) a call for the heavens to give God praise because He is the Creator (vv. 1–6); (2) a call for the elements of the earth to give God praise because He is also their Creator (vv. 7–12); (3) a call for the people of God to give God praise because of His wonder in their midst (vv. 13, 14).

148:1–6 Praise Him: All of the universe is called to boast of the wonder of God. In this first section, praise is commanded from all aspects of the heavens above, including the angelic hosts. The language **waters above the heavens** comes from the creation story in Gen. 1:7. **He commanded:** Genesis 1 describes creation as a spontaneous response to the word of God (33:9; 147:15).

148:7, 8 The focus of the psalm switches to **the earth.** All hosts above and all creatures below are to praise our great God. **great sea creatures:** This includes real sea creatures that inspired awe and wonder, as well as creatures of mythology that the Canaanites had made into gods. Israel called on all creatures to praise God—both those that are His creation and those that their neighbors believed to be gods. In this way, every principality and power, every creature known and unknown, was called to worship God. **Fire and hail:** All natural phenomena are at God's command (147:15–18).

148:9–14 the horn of His people: The people are pictured here as an animal whose strength is in its horn. **near:** When we consider the meaning of God's holiness (99:1; Is. 6:3), the marvel that He approaches us to mercifully provide for us becomes overwhelming.

Psalm 149 an exuberant call to praise God, was used by the army of Israel as well as by the people in their worship of God. The structure of the psalm is: (1) a call for a new song of praise (v. 1); (2) a call for the joyful worship of praise in the congregation of the Lord (vv. 2–5); (3) a call for the joyful worship of praise in the army of the Lord (vv. 6–8); (4) a concluding shout of praise (v. 9).

149:1 The call for **a new song** comes at several points in the Psalms (33:3; 40:3; 144:9). These words encourage more than just novelty; they call for freshness and integrity in performing music. **in the assembly of saints:** One of the primary emphases in the Book of Psalms is that the praise of God is to take place in the center of the worshiping community. Praise unites the people of God (33:1–3).

149:2–5 Maker: Not only is God the Creator of the universe (8:3; 19:1; 104:1–35), He is particularly the Creator of His people (100:3) and their great King (Ps. 93). In the temple of

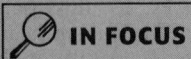 **IN FOCUS** **"praise"**

(Heb. *halal*) (146:1, 10; 147:1; 149:3; 150:1, 6) Strong's #1984: The verb *halal* is a common Hebrew word for *praise.* It may be used to exalt human beauty (Song 6:9), a virtuous wife (Prov. 31:30), or a wise man (Prov. 12:8), but most frequently *halal* is used to praise God. It often occurs in the imperative, expressing an exhortation or command: "Praise!" (135:1) or "Praise Him" (150:2). The most familiar example of the imperative is *halleluyah* (meaning "Praise the LORD!"; 146:1; 150:6), a combination of *halal* and the divine name *Yah.* The last five psalms present a climax to the praises contained in the Book of Psalms, commanding believers (145:10), the Israelites (149:2), the angels (148:2), Jerusalem itself (147:12), the heavens (148:1), and finally every being that has breath (150:6) to praise the Almighty God, the Creator of the universe.

the preexilic period, sacred **dance** was an integral aspect of worship (150:4). **Saints** refers to the redeemed who have been made God's people by His grace. The Hebrew word is related to the term meaning "loyal love" (13:5). The *saints* are those who demonstrate in their lives the characteristics of God whom they serve. **on their beds:** In some of the festivals of Israel, such as Passover, the people would recline at feast tables as a vivid symbol that they had been redeemed. In the first Passover (Ex. 12), the people were to eat standing, ready to travel. The custom that developed for the people to recline at the table, symbolizing their redemption and enjoyment of God's work in their lives.

149:6–8 two-edged sword: The focus of the psalm switches from the congregation at worship to the army in training. Israel's army was to be the vanguard for the battle of the Lord. Their training was to have a strong component of praise and worship to God.

149:9 the written judgment: It is likely that this is a direct reference to the Law (perhaps Deut. 7:1, 2) in which God decreed His judgment on the peoples of the land of Canaan.

Psalm 150 a psalm of praise, is a development of the Hebrew word *hallelujah,* meaning "Praise the Lord." How fitting that this book of

praises—the meaning of the name of the Book of Psalms in Hebrew—ends in repeated commands to praise the Lord. The structure is as follows: (1) a call for the praise of God in heaven above (v. 1); (2) a call for the praise of God for His great works (v. 2); (3) a call for the praise of God with all instruments (vv. 3–5); (4) a call for the praise of God from all creatures here below (v. 6).

150:1 in His sanctuary: The intent is for praise to come to God in His dwelling in heaven (148:1–4).

150:2 excellent greatness: This grand phrase (Deut. 3:24) is a splendid way to summarize all that the Psalms present of the wonder of God.

150:3–5 The varied instruments in this section include horns, reeds, strings, and percussion, encompassing many of the instruments known in Israel at that time (33:2, 3; 98:4–6).

150:6 everything that has breath: The very breath that God gives us should be used to praise Him. As long as we live we should praise our Creator (146:1, 2). By His breath God created all things (33:6), and by our breath we should adore Him. The Book of Psalms begins with God's blessing on the righteous (1:1) and concludes with all of creation blessing its loving Creator.

The Book of

Proverbs

EVERYONE KNOWS THE VALUE OF GOOD ADVICE.
Listening to those who are wiser than we are gives us the
benefit of their hard-won experience. Growing up, getting
along with others, and holding a job all would be impossible
without guidance from folks who have been there before. The
Book of Proverbs gives that kind of help.

But the book is more than a collection of "tips and tricks." It

passes on a core of knowledge and experience
that God says we *must* have if we are to live successfully. These proverbs are not merely old sayings that concern people in far-off lands but
universal principles that apply to all people of all
times. They speak to modern problems as much
as to ancient ones because they concern human
nature and God's ways. Human nature has not
changed since Solomon's time; neither has God's.
Only the landscape around us has changed.

Proverbs is cast in Hebrew poetry, a rich pattern of rhetoric that shares with poetry of many
cultures a special use of words for effect, sound
and sense, vivid imagery, and concise language.
In contrast to other types of poetry, Hebrew
poets—from the psalmists to the authors of
proverbs—use parallelism, the repetition of
related thoughts. A common type of parallelism
is *synonymous parallelism*, in which a second line
restates the first line in slightly different terms:

> A good name is to be chosen rather than
> great riches;
> Loving favor rather than silver and gold.
> (22:1)

Both lines say nearly the same thing; but the

restatement drives the point home. The pattern
is: "A is so; so is B."

Antithetical parallelism is also quite common
in Proverbs. Here the second line expresses the
thought negatively, again reinforcing the positive idea:

> A prudent man foresees evil and hides
> himself,
> But the simple pass on and are punished.
> (22:3)

This proverb contrasts the prudent person
with the simple person. The antithesis goes
both ways. Each line amplifies and explains the
other.

In another type of parallelism the second line
completes the thought of the first line. This is
called *climactic parallelism*. An example is:

> The rich and the poor have this in
> common,
> The Lord is the maker of them all. (22:2)

The two lines are incomplete without each
other.

Finally, many of the proverbs are based on
comparisons between two parallel lines. These are
the "better than" proverbs:

Better is a little with righteousness,
Than vast revenues without justice.
(16:8)

All these examples illustrate the heart of Hebrew poetry: parallelism. Each verse sharpens and heightens the thought by use of restatement, comparison, and building to a climax. These subtle devices draw us in and cause us to see and understand the point of each proverb more clearly.

Solomon's 375 proverbs (10:1—22:16) appear as a large collection with no particular organization to the whole. In places a few sentences on one theme appear together, but other sentences on that theme often appear elsewhere as well. We might expect all proverbs on poverty to be in one section and all on child rearing in another, but these and many other topics are interspersed throughout the collection. Sometimes repeated words or sounds are the link between separate sentences. Or it may be that phrases repeat, suggesting a new linking of ideas.

In addition to the proverbs that stand alone, at the beginning and ending of the book sections of extended instruction appear together (chs. 1—9; 30; 31). These chapters contain some of the same proverbs as the rest of the book, but as units they differ greatly from the main section of Solomon's proverbs (10:1—22:16). Unlike the scattered arrangement of Solomon's main section, these chapters develop themes.

The prologue states the book's purpose and theme (1:1–7): it is to give a course of instruction in wisdom, preparation for life, and the ways of life in God's world. Many topics, such as riches, success, and social relations, appear in other collections of wisdom literature that have survived from the ancient Middle East, but they are treated differently. Israel's contribution to wisdom literature was to place all wisdom in the context of faith in the Lord. The words "The fear of the LORD is the beginning of knowledge" (1:7) set the record straight, so to speak. This is the foundation on which all other wise sayings stand. It is the Book of Proverbs's central idea: fear of the Lord motivates us to obey God's commandments, and obedience to them constitutes true wisdom.

King Solomon wrote many proverbs, more than those that have survived to this day. The title of the Book of Proverbs (1:1) and two collections of maxims within it (10:1; 25:1) identify him as their author. First Kings confirms this by attributing three thousand proverbs and more than a thousand songs to him (1 Kin. 4:32). In fact, the writer of Kings boasted that Solomon's wisdom exceeded that of all the wise men in the East and in Egypt (1 Kin. 4:30). Solomon's interests and research covered nearly every aspect of knowledge, from zoology and botany to grammar and theology. To think of wisdom in Israel was to think of Solomon, who was granted wisdom by God's gracious gift (1 Kin. 3:12).

Although Solomon was the main writer of the Book of Proverbs (10:1—22:16), some proverbs were written by other writers, and some of Solomon's were not added to the book until after his death. Agur wrote ch. 30, and Lemuel wrote 31:1–9. Moreover, it is not clear whether Solomon wrote the first nine chapters; they may have been contributed by someone else as an introduction to the book. Proverbs 25:1 tells us

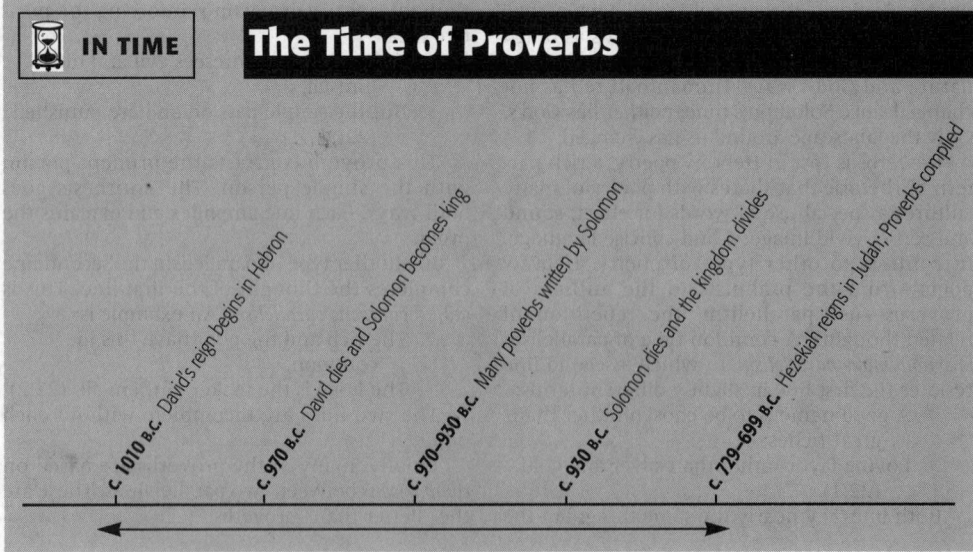

IN TIME   **The Time of Proverbs**

c. 1010 B.C. David's reign begins in Hebron

c. 970 B.C. David dies and Solomon becomes king

c. 970–930 B.C. Many proverbs written by Solomon

c. 930 B.C. Solomon dies and the kingdom divides

c. 729–699 B.C. Hezekiah reigns in Judah; Proverbs compiled

that a group of assistants to King Hezekiah (who reigned about 729–699 B.C.) compiled and added the proverbs of Solomon contained in chs. 25—29. The Book of Proverbs as we know it may well have been completed during Hezekiah's time, but we cannot be certain, because we have no information about Agur (ch. 30) or Lemuel (31:1–9) besides their names.

Outline

Commentary

1:1 The proverbs of Solomon: The *prologue* to the Book of Proverbs (1:1–7) is in three parts: (1) title (v. 1), (2) purpose (vv. 2–6) and (3) theme (v. 7). The title, "The proverbs of

Solomon son of David, king of Israel" (v. 1), may suggest three things: (1) Solomon is the author of the book, (2) Solomon is the one who made the principal contributions to the book, or (3) Solomon is the patron of wisdom in Israel, so his name is honorific in this heading. Since there are other authors (e.g., Agur {ch. 30} and Lemuel {31:1–10}), and even some of the material from Solomon was edited considerably later than his lifetime (25:1), it seems best to understand the opening words of the book as some combination of the second and third options. Solomon cannot be the author of the complete Book of Proverbs, but Solomon is its most notable contributor and is the model upon which the wisdom ideal was built in Israel.

1:2, 3 Verses 2–6 explain the purpose of the Book of Proverbs. The verbs **to know, to perceive,** and **to receive** refer to the ways we acquire wisdom. **Wisdom** refers to skill. **Instruction** could also be translated *discipline;* it refers to the process of receiving knowledge and then applying it to daily life. A person develops discipline in life by applying words of insight.

1:3 The word for **wisdom** in this verse is different from the word used in v. 1. This word denotes applied skill, such as that of an artisan or a musician. That is, wisdom affects living much the way the skills of artists affect the practice of their craft. The words **justice, judgment, and equity** give wisdom, discipline, and words of insight a moral context. Biblical wisdom involves all of life; it involves a change of behavior and a commitment to justice.

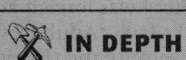 **IN DEPTH**   **What Kind of Wisdom?**

The purpose of Proverbs is straightforward: "to know wisdom" (Prov. 1:2). It is common to conceive of wisdom as either an advanced form of knowledge or learning, or else as a rare sense of deep understanding and insight. This view of wisdom has a touch of the mystical about it, as if those who possess it had in some way tapped into profound, enigmatic truths from ages past.

However, there is no mystery about the wisdom talked about in Proverbs, nor is it necessarily limited to a privileged few. The wisdom that Proverbs mentions more than forty times and that Ecclesiastes mentions twenty-seven times is the Hebrew *chokmah*, which means something like "the skill of living." This wisdom is practical, not esoteric. It means that a person knows how to live in a responsible, productive, and prosperous way.

From that standpoint, the wisdom of Proverbs has a lot in common with what we might call common sense, or even "street smarts." It is an understanding of the way the world works. The issue is not so much what one knows intellectually but what one does practically. It is truth applied.

That is why Proverbs deals with so many day-to-day issues of life, especially those involving moral choices and other decisions that affect the future. The wise person (Hebrew *chakam*) avoids evil and promotes good by observing what others have chosen and then pursuing a course of action based on the outcomes. Thus the Proverbs are not so much promises of God as they are observations and principles about how life works.

1:4 The simple or "naive" is young, inexperienced, and likely to make mistakes. The terms **prudence** and **discretion** include the harsh facts of life. A wise person has learned by experience how to distinguish what is true, praiseworthy, and good from what is false, shameful, and bad (Rom. 12:1, 2).

1:5, 6 increase learning: No one finishes the study of wisdom; there is always more to learn. Verse 6 speaks of the lessons that a more mature person gains from the study of a **proverb, an enigma, words of the wise,** and **riddles.**

1:7 The fear of the Lord is the most basic ingredient in wisdom. All wisdom depends on knowledge of God and submission to His will. To know something but not to know God overturns the value of having knowledge in the first place. **Fools** have rejected the fear of the Lord. The term **despise** packs a strongly negative punch—not fearing God is the same as rejecting wisdom outright (Dan. 11:32; John 17:3).

1:8, 9 The opening words of wisdom's instruction come as an appeal from parents to their **son** (a generic term for child)—a theme that continues throughout the book. Both **father** and **mother** teach.

1:10–14 if sinners entice you: This is the first of several texts in which wisdom teaches by means of a story.

1:15–18 The parents speak words of caution. One step on this precipitous path is a step toward destruction. Spreading a **net** in the sight of the bird one wishes to trap would be a fruitless task. Yet the fool is less sensible than the bird; he will watch the trap being set and get caught in it anyway.

1:19 It takes away the life: These words conclude the story and introduce a theme that the following passages develop further: the study of wisdom is a matter of life and death.

1:20, 21 The word **wisdom** is plural but the verb **calls** is singular. The plural is intensive—it calls attention to the word and heightens its meaning.

1:22–27 Wisdom addresses the **simple ones,** or "open ones," the naive. These are young people who have not yet made up their minds about life or the direction they will take. Wisdom ridicules those who reject her when they come to face the inevitable judgment of their foolishness (Ps. 2:4). Yet Wisdom laughs with joy at God's works and has delight in the people of God (8:30, 31).

1:28–33 I will not answer: When fools despise wisdom, they must face the results of their choice. Their hatred for wisdom arises out of a refusal to fear God (v. 29). Verses 31, 32 pick up the theme of v. 19 from the parents' instruction: fools bring about their own destruc-

tion. Rejection of wisdom **will slay them.** This dismal warning ends with a promise of life to the few who will **listen;** they will find safety and ease.

2:1–4 These verses begin the second of the **my son** passages and tie the concepts of wisdom and the knowledge of God more closely together. On the one hand, wisdom is near and available. Yet it is not easy to embrace.

2:5–8 When a person seeks wisdom, he or she finds it in **the fear of the Lord,** or **the knowledge of God.** Those who know God fear (revere) Him. Verses 6–8 resemble the words of a psalm (compare Ps. 91). **sound wisdom:** Here is another word for wisdom, a word that may be translated "abiding success" or "victory."

2:8–13 The phrase **paths of justice** (v. 8) contrasts strongly with **ways of darkness** (v. 13). This contrast introduces one of the dominant themes of Proverbs, the contrast of two roads. Jesus spoke of two roads, one narrow and the other broad (Matt. 7:13, 14). The right road is marked by demands of **righteousness, justice,** and **equity** (1:3). These demands come from God's law.

2:10, 11 enters your heart: These words stress the internalization of wisdom. The proverbs do not merely provide knowledge; they provide insight to be learned intimately and practiced.

2:12–15 The way of evil (v. 12) contrasts directly with the way of wisdom. It is characterized by **perverse things,** by lies and distortion, by twisting and deception, and by darkness and deviousness.

2:16–22 The immoral woman is literally "the strange woman." Adultery was foreign and strange to the ideal of God's law. "Adulteress" also connoted prostitution, because the "foreign women" of the ancient Middle Eastern fertility cults included sexual practices in their worship rituals.

3:1, 2 Law and **commands** are words that, as in 1:8, draw attention to the connection between wisdom and the Law of Moses. The proverbs are an application of the Law.

3:3, 4 Mercy and truth is an important pair of words in the Bible, describing God's character (Ps. 100:5) and the demands He makes of His people. The apostle John used the Greek equivalent of these words, "grace and truth," to describe Jesus' character (John 1:14).

3:5, 6 The words **trust in the Lord** echo the command of Deut. 6:5 to love God with all our being. The verb *trust* is complemented by the verb "lean." Trusting in God is a conscious dependence on God, much like leaning on a tree for support. The idea is reinforced here by the command to **acknowledge Him,** which means to observe Him and get to know Him in the process of living. In doing so, a person finds time and time again that God smoothes out paths.

3:7–10 The promises in these verses describe general patterns, not rules that have no exceptions. These are the results that often follow a full commitment to God. The command to honor God with wealth and to give to Him from the **firstfruits** of all income is a part of what it means to worship God. In God's covenant with Israel, fullness of **barns** and **vats** was God's blessing, a part of God's covenant promise.

3:11, 12 The discipline of the **Lord** is the other side of His grace. We should cherish God's correction in our lives, because God disciplines only those He **loves** (Heb. 12:7–10).

3:13–18 Happy: The beatitudes of Jesus in the Sermon on the Mount (Matt. 5:3–12) work much the way these verses do. The Hebrew term **blessed** is an explosive word: "O the manifold happiness of" (Ps. 1:1). It implies that God is truly pleased. The person who has discovered wisdom has found a priceless treasure. Adam

of wisdom with creation. Chapter 8 is devoted to this theme.

3:21 let them not depart: This verse encourages the **son** to keep faith with wisdom. The intent is much like that of the Shema (Deut. 6:4–9). It also resembles the basic ideas of Ps. 91 (compare v. 26 with Ps. 91:10–13).

3:22–26 The balance of ch. 3 contains sentences, much like the sentences of the later parts of the book. These sentences are something of a sampler of things to come, but they come now in the context of the blessing on the man who has come to the Lady Wisdom. As we think of these sentences, it is with a sure sense of direction. These sentences are not apart from a theological context. They are centered in the knowledge of God; they are based on the pathway of wisdom. As we read these sentences we will get our bearings for those that begin in ch. 10.

3:27–30 do not withhold good: The sentences of vv. 27–30 relate to the proper treatment of one's neighbor, one of the central

Photo by Gustav Jeeninga

"Hear, my children, the instruction of a father" (Prov. 4:1) reflects the close family ties of Bible times and the teaching function performed by the home.

and Eve were expelled from the Garden and forbidden access to the tree of life (Gen. 3:22–24), but wisdom is another **tree of life** and will begin to restore the lost happiness of Paradise.

3:19, 20 by wisdom founded the earth: One central theme in Proverbs is the association

teachings of Jesus (e.g., Luke 10:25–37). The point of the teaching of Jesus on relating to one's neighbor was to show mercy (Luke 10:37). Similarly, one is not to withhold good from one's neighbor when one has the power to do otherwise (Prov. 3:27). It is no kindness to

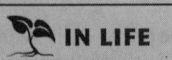 **IN LIFE**   ## A Parental Responsibility

As modern-day society is quickly discovering, there is no substitute for a solid, stable home life. Where parents are absent, negligent, or abusive, children will probably not learn to cope with the world in a healthy way. For that reason, Proverbs stresses that parents are given to children to impart wisdom (Prov. 4:3, 4). Out of their own seasoning, struggles, and suffering, parents can offer experience and insight that will help the next generation get started on the right course.

God's intention is that both parents are to be involved in their family's learning process. Fathers are to take the lead as sources of guidance and direction, and mothers are to offer governing principles based on God's Word (1:8; 4:1; 6:20). In addition, Prov. 4:3, 4 implies that grandparents play a role, largely through the parenting they have done with the parents of their grandchildren.

In this way, a family is to "train up a child in the way he should go" (22:6). That is the gift that the home gives. The child might not appreciate that gift until he is older, but parents are urged to give it nonetheless. Indeed, they cannot afford not to.

withhold payment when one is able to pay (v. 28), and mercy is not found in mercenary plots against peaceful companions (v. 29) or treacherous words (v. 30).

3:31–35 There is no benefit in feeling **envy** for **the wicked,** because God detests wickedness. Only a fool would wish to be detestable to God! The section ends with a contrast of God's blessing on the righteous and His curse on the wicked (Gen. 12:3).

4:1–4 In most of the ancient Middle East instruction in wisdom was primarily a matter of training for the court. The masters were regarded as "fathers" of the students. But in Israel, training in wisdom extended to the home. **Instruction of a father** implies warmth and affection, as well as a parent's concern and discipline. Verse 1 begins a little like the first parental section (1:8), but the addressee is now plural, **my children.** As his father had taught him, so the son now teaches his own sons, one generation instructing another. The call for parents to teach the things of God to their children is based on Deut. 6:7 and is reflected in the Psalms (as in Ps. 78:3, 4).

4:5–7 Verses 5–9 present an impassioned plea from the father to his sons to **get wisdom** whatever the cost. The presentation in these early chapters of Proverbs follows the pattern: statement, restatement, embellishment. By making generous use of creative restatement, the ideas come through all the more strongly. Particularly striking are the words of v. 7: **Wisdom is the principal thing.** The word *principal* is translated "the beginning of" in 1:7, but here it has the force of "first in importance."

4:8, 9 These verses emphasize the supreme value of wisdom. The person who holds wisdom in highest esteem and embraces it fully will be exalted and honored; its very presence becomes

an **ornament of grace** and a **crown of glory.** These metaphors are compelling calls for a heartfelt response (1:9; 3:3).

4:10–19 These verses present a renewed appeal from father to son to walk in **the way of wisdom** and to avoid **the path of the wicked** at all costs. The contrast of the two **paths** is profound. The way of wisdom is straight, unencumbered, and safe. The way of the wicked is tortuous, hazardous, and marked by violence. One road is a path of light, the other of darkness; one leads to promise, the other to a stumbling destruction.

4:20–27 This section demands constancy of **heart** and purpose, honesty in speech, steadiness of gaze, and a right goal in walk and **life.** Setting off on the path of wisdom is no casual thing. Much of this chapter reiterates and refines the themes found in chs. 1—3. The emphasis on virtue prepares us for the frightening warnings of ch. 5.

5:1–6 Chapter 5 returns to the theme of the **immoral woman** (2:16–19). This passage speaks strongly for marital fidelity against any and all pressure to the contrary. If you want to **preserve discretion,** heed these words, lest your **feet go down to death.**

5:7–14 The Bible teaches elsewhere that temptation in general is unavoidable, but some temptations should be avoided at all costs. A wise son knows this and will **not go near** an immoral woman. The apostle Paul's instruction to Timothy to flee youthful lusts (2 Tim. 2:22) teaches the same theme. Involvement with such sin dishonors and consumes all who fall into it.

5:15 In an arid country like Israel, a **well** was a prized possession and a privilege to be cared for. So was (and is) a spouse. **Drink water** is an oblique reference to sexual union (9:17), and **from your own cistern** is a clear call to marital fidelity—one man, one woman, together in marriage. The writers of the Bible sometimes speak of salvation as a spring (Is. 12:3); to call one's spouse a spring of water was a term of endearment (Song 4:15).

5:16, 17 Then he turns the tables a bit. How would it be, the teacher asks, if his own wife were to become the "strange woman" for other men? Should his springs flow down the streets? his waters be in the public squares? "No!" the teacher says. Let these waters be yours alone, not something you share with strangers (v. 17).

5:18–20 The words **rejoice with the wife of your youth** comprise a command and an encouragement to find pleasure in the mutual joy of married love. Indeed, pleasure in the marriage bed is **blessed** by God (Song; Heb. 13:4).

5:21–23 the eyes of the Lord: Here is the clincher: what one does in secret is never secret to God. The path of adultery is the course of ruin. A life of folly ends in bitter death. The secret path of an evil man is an open scandal in heaven; it ends in the loneliness of a private hell.

6:1–5 These verses warn against putting up **surety** (11:15), or cosigning a loan. This does not mean we should never be generous or helpful if we have the means, only that we should not promise what we cannot deliver. In Solomon's day, a cosigner who could not pay could lose all he had and be reduced to slavery besides. Even though laws differ today, inability

to pay a debt is still a form of bondage and can be a serious problem.

6:6–11 This passage warns against the trap of laziness. The **sluggard,** or lazy person, is held captive to leisure. He can learn all he needs to know by studying the **ant,** a humble creature that busies itself with storing food during the summer against the winter that lies ahead. Like the ant, a wise person works hard. By contrast, the lazy person is addicted to sleep and has lost all interest in work (26:13–16).

6:12–15 A wicked man is a troublemaker. Unlike the sluggard, whose only desire is another place to nap, the troublemaker cannot wait to cause more problems or to get into more mischief. Unlike the sluggard (v. 6), he is too busy, though he is doing the wrong things. He delights in bringing dissension. But like the sluggard, he does not realize that **calamity** awaits him.

6:16–19 This passage is a numerical proverb (30:15–31) that describes **seven** things that **the Lord hates.** The use of numerical progression—six, even seven—in these proverbs is a rhetorical device that embellishes the poetry, provides a memory aid, and builds to a climax. It gives the impression that there is more to be said about the topic. The progression involves not just the numbers but also the words that describe God's response; the word **hates** progresses to **abomination.** The word *abomination* is the Bible's strongest expression of hatred for

---

✠ IN CONTEXT | The Penalty for Theft

U nder the OT Law, a thief was ordinarily required to make restitution of twice the value of the loss. However, Proverbs indicates that if someone stole because he was hungry, he had to repay sevenfold, even if it meant losing his house and property (Prov. 6:30, 31). What accounts for this higher penalty?

The answer may be that the Law made numerous provisions to prevent poor people from starving. These included:

- The third-year tithe (Deut. 14:28, 29).
- Gleaning (Lev. 19:9, 10).
- The release of debts in the Sabbatical year (Deut. 15:1–3).
- The temporary sale of real property (Lev. 25:23–34).
- Mandatory charity loans (Deut. 15:7–11) at zero interest (Ex. 22:25).
- Voluntary indentured service (Lev. 25:39–55).

In light of these policies, there was no excuse for someone to steal in order to eat (unless the society failed to carry out these policies).

However, it is worth noting that each of these provisions involved a form of charity, and many people resist accepting charity for a variety of reasons such as pride, embarrassment, or a desire for independence. Perhaps the penalty of sevenfold restitution was intended to punish this prideful rejection of help.

wickedness (compare Lev. 18:22). In a list of this type, the last item is the most prominent. Thus, the reader knows that causing **discord among brethren** (v. 14) causes God's greatest disapproval. Contrast the blessing of God on brothers who live together in peace (Ps. 133:1).

6:20–24 This passage links the teaching of the father with that of the **mother** (1:8). The mother's instruction should be bound about one's **heart** and **neck,** a constant companion and a trusted guide—just like God's Law (compare Deut. 6:4–9; 11:18–21). **lamp . . . light:** Compare Ps. 119:105.

6:25 eyelids: Seductive glances.

6:26 The contrast emphasizes the utter devastation an adulteress brings into a man's life. Compared to the confusion a prostitute creates, an adulteress consumes the very life of her victim.

6:27–35 steals to satisfy: This passage does not condone theft. It merely contrasts theft, which can be an understandable course of action, with adultery, which never makes sense. Throwing away one's commitment to one's lifelong companion is pure folly. For the ancient Israelites, marital fidelity was a mark of one's fidelity to God.

7:1–5 The problem of immorality (2:16–19; 5:1–23; 6:20–35) does have a solution: **Keep my commands . . . as the apple of your eye.** People should guard wise words as instinctively as they protect the pupil of the eye. God cares for His people with the same diligence (Deut. 32:10).

7:6–13 The **young man** who gives in to the immoral woman is described as **simple,** a term that pegs him as naive, inexperienced, and **devoid of understanding** (1:4; 9:3). He has no idea how foolish he is. He thinks he makes his way to the **woman,** but she in fact seduces him.

7:14–21 All the adulteress does is perverse. She audaciously begins her proposition by talking about her supposedly righteous actions that day. Since the offerings she presented to the Lord were fellowship or **peace offerings,** she could bring part of them home for a feast before the Lord. But here she presents the offering as a feast for the young man she plans to entrap. Her preparations and her words of invitation might pass between a wife and husband and be honored by God. But in her mouth these words become evil. She overcomes her target's fear by assuring him that her husband will not come home and discover them together.

7:22, 23 The passage here uses several unflattering metaphors to describe how a young fool falls into immorality. The phrase **as a fool to the correction of the stocks** could be translated "as a stag prances into captivity." The

idea is that the young man is oblivious to his fate. Such a fool has no idea how foolish he is.

7:24–27 Now therefore, listen: The chapter ends in an epilogue (vv. 24–27) in which the lesson is driven home: Stay away from such a one! She is deadly, and has a great many victims.

8:1–11 Chapter 7 focused our attention on the fool and the traps that catch him; ch. 8 shifts to wisdom. It is a hymn of praise about how wonderful wisdom is. **Does not wisdom cry out:** Wisdom wants to reach everyone and therefore broadcasts her message publicly, unlike the immoral woman, who uses privacy and deception to achieve her goals. Wisdom's words can be trusted, and her offers of grace are beneficial. Her words of **truth** contrast with the lies of **wickedness** 7:21–23; wisdom will deliver on her promises; she is not a tawdry tease. What wisdom offers is of inestimable worth, far more valuable than **silver** and **gold;** no gems or other desirable things may be compared with it (a similar expression is found in 3:14, 15).

8:12, 13 The words **I, wisdom, dwell with prudence** introduce the second section of this passage about the excellence of wisdom (vv. 12–21). Again in this context we see wisdom tied directly to **the fear of the Lord.** The offer of wisdom is held out only to those who fear God. Coming to wisdom requires coming to God, and coming to God means turning away from all that God hates—evil, pride, arrogance, misbehavior, and perverse speech. Jesus said that the truth is found in Him (John 8:32).

8:14–21 princes . . . nobles . . . judges: Power and authority require the use of wisdom; this is one of its loftiest appeals. What's more, wisdom leads those who follow her to **riches and honor** (9:1–6). These contrast directly with the shameful fate of the fool (6:33, 35).

8:22–31 This section of ch. 8 describes wisdom's role in creation. **The Lord** possessed me at the beginning of His way: The Hebrew verb for *possessed* can mean "brought forth" or "created." Melchizedek used the same word to identify God as creator of the universe (Gen. 14:19). God, who is ever wise, produced wisdom; God, who possesses all knowledge, brought forth knowledge. Wisdom had a **beginning** only in the sense that God singled it out for special display at that time; insofar as it is one of God's perfections, it has always existed (v. 23). These verses provide part of the background for the NT portrayal of Christ as the divine Word (John 1:1–3) and as the wisdom of God (1 Cor. 1:24, 30; Col. 2:3).

8:30, 31 The term **master craftsman** speaks of an artisan or of a darling child. Wisdom is both. With wisdom's skill, God created the universe. A proper study of the universe is a progressive discovery of God's wisdom (Rom. 1:20). **delight:** In her playful, childlike exuberance, Wisdom is a darling child. And her greatest joy comes in the finest of the work of God—**the sons of men**—that is, humankind.

8:32–36 Now therefore, listen to me, my children: This section is the epilogue of the ch. 8 hymn of praise. It calls everyone to listen. Wisdom offers blessing and life to those who heed her, but cursing and death to those who hate her. Wisdom's gracious invitation is more desirable than anything and an invitation to a **blessed** life.

9:1 Here is the final contrast between wisdom and folly. Each holds a banquet, one for life (vv. 1–6) and one for death (vv. 13–18). Between the two banquet descriptions is a section (vv. 7–12) that speaks of consequences of the life of wisdom and of the plight of folly. **Wisdom has built her house:** Here as in 1:20, the term for *wisdom* is in the intensive plural rather than the singular. It calls attention to itself. **seven pillars:** The number seven represents completeness, as it often does in Semitic poetry. That is, it is not that there were precisely seven pillars so much as that the house of wisdom was solidly built and substantial in character.

9:2, 3 The meal at wisdom's banquet includes **meat** and **wine** and a lovely **table** (7:14). Freshly butchered meat was a mark of a feast in biblical times. **mixed her wine:** Wine was a staple in ancient Israel; but when a feast was special, a homemaker would add aromatic spices to the wine, enlivening the bouquet and improving the taste (Song 8:2). This all sets up a contrast with the foolish woman. While wisdom is busy, attending to every detail like a gracious hostess, the foolish woman sits at the entrance of her house with very little to do (v. 14). Wisdom sends her trusted **maidens** throughout the city, inviting people to come and dine.

9:4–6 Wisdom makes a point of inviting the **simple,** meaning those who have not yet made up their minds about their course in life (1:4; 7:6). **bread . . . wine:** Wisdom promises life. **Forsake foolishness:** The person who comes to wisdom has nothing to lose but naiveté. Read Heb. 5:14, which speaks of a mature person as one who is able to eat and to enjoy solid food, in contrast to the naive who is able only to drink milk (Heb. 5:13).

9:7–9 A **scoffer** or mocker is thoroughly set against wisdom (1:22) and scoffs at the things of

> *A wise man accepts correction and responds with gratitude to the one who points out his error.*

God (Ps. 1:1). How should a person respond to a mocker? It is best not to respond at all. By contrast, a **wise man** accepts correction and responds with gratitude to the one who points out his error. A wise person always welcomes constructive criticism; by implication, he or she is also humble (v. 10; 3:7; 11:2).

9:10–12 fear of the LORD: This is the central theme of the Book of Proverbs (1:7). The only appropriate way to approach the holy God is with fear, that is, reverence. The term **Holy One** is an intensive plural of the Hebrew word for *holy:* "the most Holy One" or "the quintessence of holiness." **for yourself . . . alone:** You will feel the effects of your wisdom or foolishness directly; you cannot escape them.

9:13–18 This section is a parody of vv. 1–6. Like personified wisdom, the **foolish woman** calls out an invitation. But she is brash, loud, undisciplined, and **knows nothing** (7:10–12). She cries out in the same words that wisdom has used (compare v. 16 with v. 4), but with a twist: she has no marvelous banquet for her guests, only shabby food, stolen and meager. Though she gets lots of attention, her appeal makes sense only to **him who lacks understanding.**

10:1 The proverbs of Solomon focus on the **wise son,** as in chs. 1—9, and contrast him with the **foolish son.** The term *son* is generic— the central issue is not that he is a son rather than a daughter, but that he is wise or foolish. The child's behavior affects both parents. Both parents find their joy or sadness in their child who demonstrates skill in life. The tense of the verbs suggests that time after time a wise child gladdens parents, and time after time a foolish child brings distress to parents.

10:2 Treasures: This verse is a warning against presumption on wealth apart from personal righteousness. The wicked may be wealthy but that wealth will not allow them to buy their way past death. In this type of saying, death is something to fear—if one does not know God. That righteousness delivers from death presages some hope of life beyond death.

10:3 This verse speaks of God's gracious provision of food for the **righteous** and His retributive justice on the **wicked.** Proverbs such as this emphasize (1) circumstances as they ought to be, and (2) the *end* of the wicked (Ps. 73:17). They do not necessarily indicate circumstances as they always are, nor what the wicked are experiencing right now.

10:4 slack hand . . . poor: Proverbs often

link laziness with poverty, and hard work with riches, but not always (v. 2). This proverb states the norm.

10:5 Gathers in summer contrasts a skillful person with a shameful person, based on whether he works hard during the harvest season. The description of the second person is particularly critical: "he who snores away during the harvest."

10:6 Blessings: The images this proverb present contrast an aura of blessing hovering over the righteous as against a spew of violence pouring from the wicked.

10:7 In biblical times, a person's **name** was significant and important. When a person's name was remembered by future generations for good, that person's life was believed to have been of great value. But when the memory of a name rotted away, it was as though that person had never lived.

10:8 The Hebrew verb for **will fall** means "is ruined" and comes from the same root as the verb *will rot* in v. 7. This type of poetic parallelism would have delighted the ancient Israelites.

10:9 Many of the proverbs contrast two paths of life. **Walks with integrity** means conforming to God's Law as a course of life. Choosing crooked paths is willfully to disdain the Law God so graciously provided.

10:10 winks with the eye: Although many proverbs contrast two behaviors, both units of this proverb speak of evil actions. Moreover, the second unit of this verse is identical with the second unit of v. 8; this is a connective link that ties the passage together.

10:11 a well of life: Another of the sentences dealing with the mouth (10:6, 8, 10), this verse presents speech as an outward product of an inward reality. The *phrase a well of life* is nearly a divine image, a particularly strong antithesis to the word *violence*.

10:12 Hatred . . . love: This verse describes interpersonal relationships, not salvation. When people respond in love to each other, they cover over the **sins,** or offenses, that would otherwise come between them.

10:13 This proverb tells of the positive role that speech can have—that of speaking wisdom. The **rod** refers to punishment, in this case deserved. The term **devoid of understanding** comes from the Hebrew idiom "lack heart." The one who "lacks heart" is contrasted with the one who is "wise in heart" (v. 8).

10:14, 15 To **store up** knowledge is a strong theme in the instruction section of chs. 1—9 (1:1–3; 3:1). This set of verses contrasts the wise person's pursuit of knowledge with the empty talk of a fool. **Wealth** is like a **strong city.** In biblical times only walled cities had any defense

against enemy armies; likewise, a wealthy person is able to withstand the assaults of others.

10:16, 17 These verses present the doctrine of the two ways: the righteous is on the **way of life,** but the wicked wander from it. The phrase **wages of the wicked** is similar to Paul's expression in Rom. 6:23: "the wages of sin is death."

10:18–21 These verses tell of the dangers of speech, particularly **lying** and **slander.** The way to avoid these sins is to exercise restraint.

10:22 The tie of wealth with the **blessing of the Lord** is made explicit in this verse. In this sentence there is Yahweh's provision of a lack of sorrow along with great wealth. Now, there is packaging!

10:23, 24 The word translated **sport** usually means "joyous laughter" (Job 8:21; Ps. 126:2). At times it means "hollow laughter" (14:13; Eccl. 7:3, 6). Here the proverb uses the word in a completely negative sense. For the fool, wickedness is only a game. He makes up the rules as he goes along; for him losing is only in getting caught. But a person who has understanding takes a longer-term perspective. In the end he gets his way while justice comes upon the **wicked.**

10:25 The short-lived nature of the wicked is contrasted with the stability of the righteous. As in Ps. 1:3, 4, where the righteous are compared to a tree and the wicked to chaff, so in this proverb the storm blows away the wicked but cannot dislodge the righteous. The **everlasting foundation** of the righteous is faith in God, much like the waters that nourish the tree of Ps. 1:3.

10:26 The **sluggard** person is a comic figure in the proverbs. Here the sluggard (Heb., `asel) is an irritant to the one who sends him on an errand. He is like the sour taste of **vinegar** in the mouth, the burning of smoke in the eyes.

10:27 This verse contains the first instance of the phrase **the fear of the Lord** in chs. 10— 22 (1:7, 29; 2:5; 8:13; 9:10). The tie of piety to long life, and of wickedness to an early death, is another common theme in Proverbs (3:1, 2).

10:28 hope . . . expectation: The **righteous** have something to look forward to; the **wicked** do not (v. 24).

10:29 Different people see the **way of the Lord** differently. Those who are innocent see it as a shelter from the storm and the heat of the day. Those who practice iniquity see it only as a source of terror. The viewer's perspective makes all the difference; the way of the Lord itself remains constant and true.

10:30 This proverb presents a confident hope in the ultimate survival of the righteous and the final judgment of the **wicked.** In our limited experience, we might see the wicked succeeding and the righteous only struggling to live. But the final judgment (Ps. 73) will reverse their fortunes.

10:31, 32 These verses form another pair of sentences about true and false speech. They may be compared to vv. 11, 13, 20, 21 and James 3. This repetition with variation indicates the significance of truth and falsehood in both ancient Israel and in the modern world as well.

11:1 Dealing fairly with one another is an outgrowth of the command to love one's neighbor as oneself (Lev. 19:18), which in turn is an outgrowth of the central command given to Israel, to love God alone (Deut. 6:4–9). That is why false balances are an **abomination** to God, a term that refers to stomach-wrenching hatred.

We all need to seek advice from wise and trustworthy people.

11:2 Many proverbs contrast the arrogant with the humble, as this one does. The Hebrew word for **pride** comes from a root that means "to boil up"; it refers to a raging arrogance or insolence. The image pictures the presumptuous or arrogant behavior of the godless person. Such behavior always leads to **shame.**

11:3–6 These verses form a series of proverbs that contrast the results of righteousness and perversity in people's lives. As pride and humility are contrasted in v. 2, so **integrity** and **perversity** are contrasted in v. 3.

11:4–6 From time to time the proverbs speak of **death** as a time of reward and punishment. **Riches** cannot help with this. Only righteousness has meaning and power beyond the grave.

11:7 As long as a person has life, there is an opportunity for hope. But hope dies when life passes if one has lived apart from God.

11:8 Final issues may be in view in this verse as well; the very troubles from which the righteous escape fall upon the wicked instead.

11:9 The profane man may trash his neighbor by his mouth, just as righteous ones are delivered by knowledge. The negative and positive powers of speech are among the most impressive concepts in these sentences.

11:10, 11 Truly **righteous** people bring justice to all the inhabitants of a **city,** and the city experiences true peace—that is, *shalom,* meaning "things as they ought to be." Many Psalm writers cried for vindication of the righteous and for a cessation of evil (Ps. 69:22–28). For the fate of a city without any righteous persons in it, see the story of Sodom and Gomorrah in Gen. 18:22–33.

11:12 Patience and control are part of wisdom. A person who is **devoid of wisdom,** who "lacks heart" (10:13), despises his neighbor. But the understanding person knows enough to control his passion and to keep silence (17:28).

11:13 A **faithful** friend **conceals** delicate matters that an unfaithful person reveals. "Love covers a multitude of sins" (10:12; James 5:20; 1 Pet. 4:8).

11:14 In modern times as much as formerly, leaders of nations need adequate **counsel.** So do all individuals. We all need to seek advice from wise and trustworthy people.

11:15, 16 These two proverbs balance each other. The first warns against rashly giving **surety** or a pledge for a stranger. The second praises generosity; generosity begets honor. One of the greatest virtues is to be freed of possessiveness. The members of the early church gave freely to those in need (Acts 2:44, 45; 4:32–35).

11:17 Yet another verse on generosity presents the good that redounds to the giver. Miserliness, on the other hand, tends to shrivel the cruel person to the size of his own niggardly heart.

11:18 Fraudulent work proceeds from wickedness; good work from righteousness. The righteous earn their wage; the wicked only steal.

11:19 Proverbs such as this remind us that the pursuit of righteousness is a matter of **life** and **death.**

11:20 The contrasting concepts of the **abomination** and delight of Yahweh (11:1) recur here with regard to the contrasting values of perversity and blamelessness of the inner man and his walk in life. It is possible to bring a smile to the Lord in the manner of one's life. It is also possible to prompt his revulsion.

11:21 The term **join forces** is literally "hand for hand." Collective opposition to God's purposes makes no sense at all (Ps. 2:1–4).

11:22 A golden **ring** would be ludicrous on a pig's **snout.** To the ancient Israelites, pigs were unclean and repellent. The immoral person is compared to such an animal, no matter what the outward appearance might be.

11:23 The term **desire** is used in some of the proverbs in a negative sense (13:12, 19; 18:1; 19:22), but here it has a positive meaning. The righteous desire good.

11:24–27 These proverbs should shape our attitudes toward wealth: it should be shared. Stinginess may lead **to poverty.** Generosity has the opposite effect. Selfishness is foolish because it only creates enemies and dishonors God.

11:28 This proverb addresses the folly of

trusting in **riches.** The second line can easily be misinterpreted to mean that righteousness always leads to success. The proverb actually addresses a person's attitude toward wealth. It is foolish to trust in riches instead of God.

11:29 Some acts of folly might be thought to be somewhat "iffy," but to bring trouble on one's **own house** is a sure thing. Here is a clear road to ruin, the inheritance of wind. Similarly, a fool is a servant of the wise, not his master.

11:30 As in 3:18, the image of the **tree of life** denotes the tree in the Garden of Eden (Gen. 2; 3). Righteousness and wisdom are ways of recovering the lost tree of life.

11:31 Here is a **how much more** proverb, one that argues from a premise to conclusion. Since the righteous will finally find their reward (2 Cor. 5:10), it follows that the wicked, who are defiant toward God and in conflict with His works, will certainly receive judgment.

12:1 The wise person knows that discipline and instruction will bring its own reward. Yet the person who hates a reprimand is **stupid,** literally "stupid as a cow."

12:2 He will condemn: John's Gospel speaks of one being condemned already because of evil deeds, and deliberately clinging to the darkness even though the light has come (John 3:16–21).

12:3 Contrasts such as the one in this proverb speak of a person's ultimate end; otherwise they would be proven false by countless examples of wicked persons who flourish while the righteous suffer. *In the end*, the righteous will stand sure, as in the image of the tree in Ps. 1:3.

12:4 Excellent wife, or "noble woman," are the same Hebrew words used in the famous acrostic in 31:10–31. A husband whose wife is like the woman described in ch. 31 should rejoice in her, because her noble character brings him honor.

12:5, 6 Our **thoughts** do matter. At the very least, they must not be **deceitful.** A person's thoughts determine what he or she says and does. The **words** of wicked persons are like a deadly ambush.

12:7 Here the poet says the wicked are no more among us, but the house of the righteous still stands. This means that all wicked persons in our own day, some who may be our antagonists, are living on borrowed time. Their days are numbered; the days of the righteous cannot be counted.

12:8 There is a proper praise that comes to one who displays wisdom, particularly when that wisdom is for the good of others. There is no proper praise of the wicked; their twisted hearts are suitable only for despising.

12:9 A **better . . . than** proverb, this verse contrasts a person who is a "nobody" but has a servant with a person who makes a great display but does not even have food on the table. Pretension and arrogance destroy those who indulge in them.

12:10 This is a proverb that moves from the lesser to the greater, comparing the smallest of the actions of a righteous man with the most grandiloquent acts of the wicked person.

12:11 tills his land: Many proverbs contrast hard work with laziness. Wise people work hard while fools waste time.

12:12, 13 yields fruit . . . is ensnared: Wickedness hurts the wicked; righteousness helps the righteous (v. 14). This is another way of saying "whatever a man sows, that he will also reap" (Gal. 6:7). The expression **the root of the righteous** also appears in v. 3.

12:14 Achieving satisfaction will not be

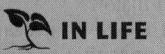 **IN LIFE**   ## Animals and Their Rights

One of the most complex issues of modern society is the impact that meeting the needs of people has on animals and their environment. Does the Bible have anything to say about this often divisive topic?

One principle that Scripture seems to affirm is that animals do, in fact, have certain God-given rights. For example, the Lord regards a person's care and concern for the life of an animal as righteousness, while cruelty to an animal is an act of wickedness (Prov. 12:10). The point is that animals have a right to be treated with wisdom and kindness, not cruelty. God pays attention to how we treat animals.

However, it is also true that God has given human beings dominion, or authority, over the other creatures (Gen. 1:26). Animals are a resource to be managed and used as humans see fit. Yet people are accountable to God for exercising this dominion. Wisdom, or the "fear of the Lord" (Prov. 1:7), suggests that we treat animals as God their Creator would treat them. For example, we know that God has an interest in the preservation of species (Gen. 7:1–5, 23, 24; 8:1, 17; Luke 12:6). Likewise, He is concerned that farm and work animals be cared for properly (Ex. 23:12; Deut. 22:4).

because of something exotic or strange; it is by speaking and dealing in righteousness. At this point, the reward of satiety is an abundant reward. The feeling that a job is done well is reward enough for the wise.

12:15 The self-delusion of the fool is notorious. Too rare is the one who seeks advice when he needs it. To seek help is an admission of need, something the fool is never able to request, due to his inflated sense of self.

12:16 at once: Careless words can make a fool out of us, so we are wise to think before we speak. King David showed such restraint (2 Sam. 16:5–12).

12:17 Righteousness and deception are the identifying marks, respectively, of the faithful and the lying witness.

12:18, 19 Many proverbs praise people who speak carefully and truthfully. Speech reflects a person's character. The words of a righteous person are faithful and true (v. 17), and soothe the listener.

12:20 The varied outward expressions of persons come from diversity of hearts. Those who plan evil have **deceit** in their hearts; those who counsel peace have joy in theirs.

12:21 The fear of harm is only valid for the **wicked;** the **righteous** have nothing to fear. Since we know that trouble does come into the life of the righteous, likely verses such as this relate to ultimate reality rather than immediate experience.

12:22, 23 An **abomination** is something that "nauseates" God (11:20). The term conveys extreme hatred. Thus it is better to remain silent than to have **lying lips.**

12:24 Anyone who wants to have a position of authority cannot dare to be **lazy** (vv. 11, 14).

12:25 Anxiety loses some of its force in the face of a positive, encouraging **word.** Barnabas's encouragement of Paul is a great example of this (Acts 4:36; 9:27; 11:2–30; Gal. 2:1).

12:26 Our **friends** help to determine who we will become (1 Cor. 15:33).

12:27 Lazy people do work, they just don't finish what they start. The cure for their laziness is **diligence**—to follow through to the end.

12:28 Fittingly, the last proverb of this chapter speaks again of **life** and **death** issues.

13:1 A **wise son** listens to instruction (10:1, 17) and is better off than the **scoffer**—the worst kind of fool (Ps. 1:1). Some fools are naive and inexperienced, but open to suggestions; sometimes even those established in folly may rethink their position. But scoffers laugh at righteousness. Such people are impervious to rebuke.

13:2, 3 When speech is what it ought to be, it may become a provision for gain and even a means of living; but when speech is evil, it may result only in an increase of violence. The wise person knows that at times to misspeak may endanger life itself. But for the wicked and the foolish there are no such inhibitions, and no such protection!

13:4 The slothful person is consumed by cravings that are insatiable because they are never realized. The industrious person may achieve his or her goals and find satisfaction.

13:5 The person who **hates lying** does not merely feel bad about it; he avoids it like the plague.

13:6 In the proverbs, **righteousness** is portrayed as a friend and **wickedness** as an enemy (11:27). Wickedness hurts us but righteousness helps.

13:7 rich . . . nothing: The paradox of greed causing poverty, and of generosity causing wealth, is a recurring theme in Scripture (11:24; Matt. 6:19–21). The point is not how much money you have, but what you do with it.

13:8 A person with great wealth may have to exhaust that wealth to pay a ransom. But a poor man is not likely to come under danger that would demand a ransom payment. Most of the poor might wish to run this risk, but there is some self-protective value in poverty.

13:9 For an ancient Israelite, an oil **lamp** would be the only source of light at night. Without it, a person had no way of seeing the path in front of him (20:20; 24:20).

13:10 The word **pride** (11:2) does not refer to self-esteem or to a positive mental attitude, but to arrogance and a refusal to glorify God. Such pride is self-serving and leads to conflict.

13:11 This proverb describes the natural long-term consequences of cheating. People who compromise their honesty to get rich merely postpone the inevitable need to earn their keep. The day comes when their cheating catches up with them, but by then their honest colleagues have become far better at obtaining **wealth.** Cheating doesn't work anymore, and the wealth of the dishonest is **diminished.**

13:12 The **tree of life** (11:30) symbolizes the achievement of a deeply felt desire. It is like coming back to the Garden of Eden.

13:13 will be rewarded: A person can either despise instruction or respond in reverence, understanding that the ultimate Giver of instruction is God. Correction is only for one's good.

13:14 fountain of life (10:11): In an arid land such as ancient Judah, a fountain provided water for oneself and for one's flocks. It was a necessity—a source of life. That is a very strong endorsement for **the law of the wise.** A fountain was also a picture of salvation (Is. 12:1–3).

13:15 Favor with God and other people—a good reputation—is highly desirable because it ensures that you won't be alone in life. It comes from **good understanding.** A good reputation was the first qualification listed by the apostles for deacons in the early church (Acts 6:3).

13:16 Many proverbs pit the **fool** against the **prudent** person.

13:17 A . . . **messenger** who acts wickedly will be discovered and his sentence will be harsh indeed. But a messenger who acts in faithfulness brings healing as he goes. In ancient times it was not unusual for a monarch to lash out against the bearer of bad news. This proverb is a lashing out against a wicked messenger.

13:18 Yet another proverb on the disdain of instruction (13:1), this verse speaks of **poverty** as the logical result of such intransigent behavior.

13:19 Few things are as **sweet** as accomplishment. But the folly of the fool is so deeply entrenched that he becomes ill if he leaves his self-destructive path. The term used of his revulsion, **abomination,** is the same word used of God in other passages (11:1).

13:20 **walks with:** The selection of friends (12:26) is extremely important. Pressure from peers is much stronger than many people realize.

13:21 **Evil** is a sinner's enemy (v. 6), not a friend; a pursuer, and not a companion.

13:22 In the Book of Proverbs, **wealth** is a topic with many themes. Wealth may come as a benefit of righteous living (v. 11; 10:22); but there is no guarantee of this (28:6). Wealth cannot make a person good (11:4), and in the end it matters less than God's favor anyway (11:28). **A good man** knows this and trusts in God to meet his needs; **the sinner** tries to acquire and keep wealth and in the end fails.

13:23 One of the first proverbs in this section to deal with injustice, this sentence observes that some who are poor actually might have possessions but have had it stolen from them by **lack of justice.**

13:24 **hates . . . loves:** This is the first of several proverbs on parental discipline. A parent's loving discipline is modeled after God's loving correction (3:11, 12).

13:25 In these sentences, genuine satisfaction is tied to righteousness; abject failure is linked to wickedness.

14:1 A **wise woman builds her house;** that is, she develops a peaceful setting for family nurture.

14:2 **Fears the LORD** contrasts starkly with **despises Him.** Love for **uprightness** will naturally coincide with love and respect for the most upright One of all, God Himself. Love for perversity will likewise result in hatred for Him. Fear of the Lord as the beginning of wisdom is the central theme of Proverbs (1:7).

14:3 **rod of pride:** This proverb addresses the dangers of foolish speech and the rewards of sensible speech. The words of the fool shape themselves into a rod that is ready for his enemies to use on him. This proverb calls to mind that many people are their own worst enemy; given enough rope, they prepare a noose for their own hanging.

14:4 **clean:** A farmer has to put up with some disorder in the barn if he wants the help of an ox. This is not an excuse to be slovenly, but an encouragement to work hard.

14:5 This proverb is a restatement of God's law: "You shall not bear **false witness** against your neighbor" (Ex. 20:16; Deut 5:20).

14:6 The image of the **scoffer** returns in this sentence (13:1) as a foil to display the validity of the pursuit of wisdom by those open to receive it rightly.

14:7 The fool is not just a nuisance; he is a hazard to the soul. Folly is not just an unpleasantness; it is a jeopardy to life itself. Hence, the prudent reaction to entrenched folly is to avoid it as one would any danger. Only the fool courts disaster by playing with folly.

14:8 This proverb contrasts prudent and

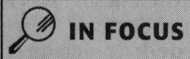 **IN FOCUS** **"foolish"**

(Heb. *'iwelet*) (14:1; 16:22; 17:12; 26:4, 5) Strong's #200: This Hebrew word signifies an absence of wisdom. Except for two occurrences in the Psalms, this term occurs only in Proverbs, where the foolishness of fools is frequently contrasted with the wisdom of the wise and prudent (13:16; 14:8, 18, 24). Foolishness characterizes the speech of fools and the reactions of the impulsive person (12:23; 14:17, 29; 15:2, 14; 18:13). Foolishness affects the lifestyle of a person, causing his or her heart to fret against God (15:21; 19:3). Indeed, foolishness is often identified with iniquity and sin (5:22, 23; 24:9; Ps. 38:4, 5). Although Proverbs does not hold out much hope for separating an adult fool from his foolishness, the rod of correction is identified as a remedy for children (22:15; 26:11; 27:22).

foolish people. Wise people know what they are doing and why they are doing it. They have wise reasons for what they do, based on a knowledge of their choices. **Fools,** on the other hand, deceive so often that they deceive themselves. They do not know where they are headed.

14:9 The extent of the depths of folly is seen in a mocking of sin and its consequences; this is self-deception of the worst sort. The wise, on the other hand, center on the pleasure of the Lord.

14:10 One of the most significant proverbs on the feelings and responses of an individual is this: no one really knows another's sorrows or joys. Empathy is an approximate art, never an exact science. Yet one is reminded of the words of the wonderful spiritual, "Nobody knows . . . but Jesus!"

14:12 Only when it is too late does the deluded person discover that he is on the crowded highway to **death.** The implication is not that he was tricked, but that he relied too heavily on his own "wisdom" rather than turning in humility to God. **a way . . . the way:** Many proverbs put their message in terms of two ways—one that leads to life and another that leads to death (16:25).

14:13 Rarely are deep emotions simple; complexities abound within the marvelous entity of human personality.

14:14 A person with a disloyal heart (Heb., *sug leb*) will be sated with the results of his wicked ways; similarly the good man will be sated with the results of his righteous paths. Good will out, and evil will be judged.

14:15 A characteristic of the naive person is gullibility. A **prudent** person is careful.

14:16 The phrase **fears and departs from evil** suggests fear of God (v. 2).

14:17 Both the **quick-tempered** and those of wicked intent are fools; wise persons shun them so that they are not involved in their folly.

14:18 The contrasts between the naive and the prudent (14:15) continue in this verse. The **simple** or naive person has a legacy of folly that he thinks is a gift to improve his life. The prudent person finds himself crowned with knowledge; that is, the most attractive thing about the prudent is the wisdom he shares.

14:19 In an ancient walled city, the gate area would normally be the weakest section of the wall. The city engineers of ancient Canaan developed complex structures to fortify this point. Controlling the gate of a city meant controlling the city; submitting at the gate meant an inability to overcome its defenses. In the end, the wicked will submit at the **gates of the righteous.**

14:20 Another witty proverb (14:11; 12:27),

this sentence speaks sardonically of the many friends that money attracts.

14:21 despises . . . sins: See Lev. 19:13, 17. Jesus identified the command to love others, and not hate them, as second only to loving God (Matt. 22:39).

14:22 One of the most significant pairings of words of piety in the Bible is the phrase translated **mercy and truth.** Together the words mean "constant faithfulness" or "true loyalty." In the NT, the Greek equivalent of this phrase is translated "grace and truth" (John 1:14) and is used of the Savior Jesus. Those who plot evil know nothing of this characteristic.

14:23 Talking about doing is never the same as doing. Only talking leads to poverty; only in doing is there the profit one seeks.

14:24 This present verse needs to be balanced with some of the more cautionary sentences. One sure thing: folly begets folly, and does so on a quick, sure breeding program.

14:25 We should expect no more from a false witness than deceit (14:5), but we may find that the true witness not only speaks that which is true—he may by his words deliver souls.

14:26, 27 These proverbs interject the central idea of the Book of Proverbs—the **fear of the Lord** (14:2). The fear of God provides both protection and a **fountain of life** (13:14; 18:10), an image that recalls the Garden of Eden.

14:28 There is not much to say for a king who has no subjects, except, perhaps, that he is a pretender to a throne. The greater the populace, the more glory to the king.

14:29 The development of a slow fuse is a not a mark of lethargy, but of wisdom. Fools fly off the handle easily and confirm their folly.

14:30 In the same manner in which a sound heart ensures the general health of the whole body, so envy may produce a rottenness in the bones.

14:31 oppresses . . . honors: The theme of "as you treat people, so you treat God" is central to Scripture (Ex. 22:22–24; Matt. 25:31–46; 1 John 4:20).

14:32 Some of the proverbs describe deliverance from **death** itself (11:4). The teaching of life after death is not a major teaching in the OT, but neither is it altogether neglected.

14:33 Another witty saying (14:20), this proverb observes that wisdom is not altogether unknown among fools, for she lets herself be known among them from time to time. Yet the true home of wisdom is with the one of an understanding heart. Among such ones wisdom rests. The contrast of an occasional glimpse of wisdom by the fool as against the reposing of wisdom with the understanding person is a delightful expression.

14:34 Righteousness exalts a nation: Although each individual is responsible for his or her actions, the effects extend to the whole community.

14:35 When the servant has done rightly, then the pleasure of the king basks on him. But the king also displays anger and personal animosity against the one who might bring him shame.

15:1 Often it is not so much what we say but the way we say it that prompts such varied responses as acceptance and **wrath.** For Abigail's gentle words to David when he was angry, see 1 Sam. 25:12–34.

15:2 Another comparison of contrasting uses of speech, this sentence poses the tongue of the wise against the mouth of fools. The one uses knowledge well; the other belches folly.

15:3 That the **eyes of the Lord** are in every place watching everything chills those who do evil and comforts those who submit to Him (Eccl. 12:14).

15:4 The soft answer of v. 1 is now a soothing tongue, and the hurtful word of v. 1 is now crooked dealing. The former is like a **tree of life,** taking us back to Eden (3:18; 11:30; 13:12); the other **breaks the spirit,** recalling the expulsion from the Garden (Gen. 3:23, 24).

15:5 The truly wise person profits from **instruction.** The term for the *prudent* in the second part of this proverb means "to be shrewd." Shrewdness can be evil, but here it has the positive sense of "street smarts" (1:4).

15:6 One **house** is a blessing and the other is ruinous; the reason for this lies in how the house was acquired and how it is being used. The house of the righteous contains great treasure because it is founded on wisdom and a proper response to God. On the other hand, the wicked never gain enough to suit them, and lose what they have because of their deceptive ways.

15:7 People reveal who they are by what they say. The **fool** cannot help but speak foolishness.

15:8, 9 From time to time the proverbs touch on the subject of worship (16:6). Worship from those who are not contrite or humble is an **abomination** to God (11:20). From Gen. 4 to John 4 Scripture contrasts good and bad worship (Is. 1:11–15). Verse 9 speaks of yet another **abomination to the Lord**—the course of life taken by the wicked.

15:10 This proverb promises **harsh discipline** for any person who **forsakes the way** of God. That is, discipline comes as a means of correction, not punishment. Only the person **who hates correction**—the one who stubbornly refuses to listen, time and time again—**will die.**

15:11 This is a "how much more" proverb (11:31), which impresses on the reader the clarity with which the Lord sees people's hearts. The Hebrew word *sheol,* translated **Hell,** in this proverb connotes the fear of the unknown (9:18). When used with the word for **Destruction,** *sheol* means "the mysterious realm of death," a dark and scary condition. Yet death is no mystery to the Lord. And if the mysterious realm of the dead is known to Him, then surely a person's heart is transparent to Him. Such arguments from the greater to the lesser appear in both Testaments.

15:12 The **scoffer** (14:6) is used as a foil or comparison in Proverbs to expose more sharply the character of the wise. Whereas the sluggard is a comic figure in Proverbs, the scoffer is a villain. He delights in scorning the things of God (1:22) and is incapable of responding to discipline (9:7), reproof (9:8), or rebuke (13:1). He cannot find wisdom (14:6) and should be avoided (Ps. 1:1). His basic problem is displayed in his response to correction. He does not learn from it nor does he seek it. The scoffer is adamant in his folly.

15:13 The point of the proverb is a reminder that we are whole persons, not just faces or hearts. What strikes the one will affect the other.

15:14 The person with an **understanding** heart, another description of the wise, is never satisfied with what he or she knows. The pursuit of wisdom and **knowledge** are life-long occupations—never fully realized in this lifetime. But fools, not knowing the extent of their ignorance, continue to pursue folly.

15:15 The happy-hearted person of 15:13 returns in this verse—a stark contrast between the perceptions of persons concerning their lots in life. For the cheerful person, life is a continual banquet. For the dour, each day is an affliction of evil.

15:16 Another of the "better than" proverbs (12:9), this one contrasts the net worth of the pauper with the rich in terms of one's holding or lacking a sense of the fear of Yahweh (14:26, 27). The idle rich may find they are beset with disquietude, while the pious poor may dwell at peace.

15:17 Hatred ruins even the finest feast; love ennobles the simplest fare.

15:18 A **wrathful** person can stir up strife where there is none; but a person who has a slow fuse—who is **slow to anger**—soothes contention (v. 1).

15:19 As against the highway of the upright, the path of the sluggard is a thorny hedge, constantly beset with prickly hurts. Because the path is so difficult, the sluggard decides to walk the path on another, easier day. Perhaps the thorns will drop off next Tuesday. Maybe Thursday.

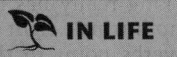 **IN LIFE** | **Between Parents and Children**

I f you come from a home background that left painful memories of childhood, you may find it hard to think kindly toward your parents. Yet Proverbs urges us as children to respect our parents, faulty though they may be. We need not like or approve of everything our parents did (and do), but only a fool despises his parents (Prov. 15:20).

It is important to add that the Bible sees parenting as a partnership between both the father and the mother, in which both are committed to each other and to the child's welfare. That is the ideal, and a child tends to thrive in that kind of home. But whether or not our parents have come even close to fulfilling their biblical responsibilities, they deserve a measure of respect and affirmation.

Proverbs includes a number of principles about how we and our parents ought to relate:

- We have life through the union of father and mother (Prov. 4:3; 23:25).
- As children, we have a significant impact on how our parents view their lives and evaluate their significance (10:1; 15:20; 17:25; 23:24).
- How we treat our parents displays our values and attitudes (19:26).
- Disrespect for our parents can have terrible implications for our own life (20:20).
- As our parents grow older, we should give them the gifts of listening and caring (23:22).
- By pursuing wisdom, we not only benefit ourselves but can bring great joy to our parents (23:25; 29:3).
- By pursuing evil and folly, we can be a destructive force in our parents' lives (28:24; 29:15).
- We will suffer greatly if we show no respect for our parents (30:11, 17).

15:20 despises his mother: This proverb is like the fifth commandment: "Honor your father and your mother" (Ex. 20:12; Deut. 5:16). Honoring and listening to parents is a favorite theme of Solomon's proverbs; this collection begins with the same exhortation (10:1).

15:21 The compounding problem of folly is that it feeds upon itself. Where there is folly, there will be delighted fools. Where there is folly, there is also an understanding man who is making tracks in another direction

15:22 The greater the decision, the greater the need for advice. Even wise, capable decision-makers—whether common people or rulers—need **counselors** (13:10).

15:23 Words are powerful: they can either build up or destroy. Solomon devoted many of his proverbs to the consequences of speech (v. 4; 14:23). Just as foolish words can bring about a person's own destruction (14:3), a wise **word** can bring joy to all who hear it. The apostle James wrote of the destructive power of words (in James 3:5, 6); the author of Hebrews also exhorted us to encourage one another (Heb. 10:24, 25).

15:24 The fright word **hell** (Hebrew, *she'ol,* 15:11) is used here as the destination of the fool, but not of the skillful. Whereas the path of folly is on a pronounced slant, descending into the abyss, the path of life points upward to glory and ultimately to God.

15:25 God will bring about justice in the

end. To the haughty, God will give a dose of humility. But for the **widow,** a completely defenseless person in ancient times, God will provide protection. Scripture in many places describes God as a Protector of the defenseless (Deut. 10:18; Pss. 68:5; 146:9; Jer. 49:11).

15:26 Many proverbs focus on what God hates (vv. 8, 9). Evil **thoughts,** for one, disgust Him. There is no such thing as "private thoughts." We should pray with David that our words and the meditation of our hearts would be acceptable in God's sight (Ps. 19:14).

15:27 The evil of bribes is in a perversion of justice, a distortion that ultimately brings distrust and dishonor to a populace.

15:28 A righteous (wise) person will ponder how best to respond; a wicked (foolish) person will simply bubble out evil. The fool attracts more folly by his behavior, and he is drawn in by foolish companions to wickedness and folly all the more.

15:29 Yahweh withdraws from the wicked, as though from a sense of a bad taste in the mouth or perhaps an unhealthy aura hovering over them. Yet he draws near to others; the prayers of the righteous are always welcome.

15:30 The salvational effects of good attitudes and positive feelings are presented in this verse even more strongly than in 15:16.

15:31, 32 He who disdains instruction despises his own soul: The natural instinct for self-preservation is dangerous when it is time to listen to a necessary rebuke. For the relationship between discipline and wisdom, see 1:7.

15:33 Knowledge alone does not make a person wiser; **the fear of the LORD** must accompany it. The same is true of **honor.**

16:1, 2 These verses contrast human limitations with the sovereignty of God. **Man** can plan, dream, and hope, but the final outcome is **from the LORD.** Rather than "resign ourselves to fate," we should trust in God. Our loving Lord is in control of our seemingly chaotic situations. Verse 2 elaborates on this theme. In addition to being sovereign, God is the final Judge. All the injustices of this world will be corrected some glorious day.

16:3 The verb **commit to** is from a word meaning "to roll." The idea is to "roll your cares onto the Lord." Trusting the Lord with our decisions frees us from preoccupation with our problems (3:5, 6).

16:4 This proverb speaks of the creative work of Yahweh in bold, comprehensive fashion. Then the verse encompasses even the wicked as being made for Yahweh's judgmental purpose. As Pharaoh was a foil for his saving work and the vindication of his glory, so the wicked in general are under his utter sovereignty.

16:5 proud in heart: Pride has everything backwards. It takes credit away from the Giver who gives graciously and awards it to the receiver who takes without thanking. That is why God sees it as an **abomination,** a word that throughout Proverbs refers to God's revulsion (15:26).

16:6 In mercy and truth can also be translated "by genuine piety." **Atonement** probably alludes to a sacrificial offering, but not apart from a contrite heart (as in Ps. 40:6–8). **fear:** Respect for God turns a person away from evil (3:7).

16:7 God's pleasure in a person's life may be boundless and may even lead to the benefit of one's enemies. This verse presents the hope of peace with God and man.

16:8, 9 The Book of Proverbs often speaks of wealth as the reward of wisdom and virtue (14:11), but not always. **Righteousness** is the real treasure.

16:10 This verse begins a section that relates to kings (vv. 10–15). The word **divination** refers to judicial decisions. Because the nation rested in the king's hands, his first responsibility was to obey God (King Josiah's reform of Israel, 2 Kin. 22; 23). Even the king had to submit to the dictates of justice.

16:11 Honest weights and scales matter to God because God is perfectly true. Falsehood and dishonesty do not merely cheat people, they also offend God.

16:12 A righteous king has as his model the divine Yahweh. A wicked king really has no model in God, and hence no intrinsic right to rule. Ultimately, such proverbs point to the reign of Jesus, as in Is. 9:7.

16:13 Yet another verse in an ideal of kingship (v. 12), this sentence pictures the rule of God from his gracious perspective.

16:14 An all-powerful king may have a consuming wrath that is as formidable as an angel of death to the unhappy offender. But as ferocious as this fury is, it can be appeased by the superior power of wisdom.

16:15 life . . . his favor: Successfully courting a powerful person's favor is like seeing rain clouds in a dry land. The phrase about the light of the face in this proverb helps us understand Aaron's benediction in Num. 6:24–26.

16:16 One of the "better than" proverbs (16:8), this one contrasts wealth and wisdom in much the same way as was done in 8:10, 11. Lady Wisdom may grant wealth, but she herself is ever better than anything else she might proffer to one who embraces her.

16:17 A **highway** is a thoroughfare, a metaphor for the way a person lives habitually. An **upright** person's "highway," or habit, is to **depart from evil.** He does not compromise; he consistently strives to do good.

16:18 These sentences are unrelenting in their attack on pride. A proud person feels he has no need for God. In fact, Yahweh has no need for the proud.

16:19 the proud: Destructive pride brings down many winners and is contagious.

16:20 The sentence could be read as a comparison: there is a good thing in demonstrating skill in a matter, but there is much more happiness in trusting the Lord. But it may also be taken as complementary: there is blessing in wisdom and there is also blessing in piety, for these are interchangeable ideas. One who is truly wise does trust in Yahweh; one who trusts in Yahweh has shown the finest wisdom. To know wisdom through trust in Yahweh is superior in every way.

16:21 This verse begins a small section of proverbs on the superiority of wisdom (vv. 21–24). Wisdom is never easily gained or quickly achieved; that is why a wise person **increases learning.**

16:22, 23 Those who possess **understanding** have access to a fountain of life that constantly renews itself and is available to everyone. The phrase **wellspring of life** is an image of salvation; water was essential for life in the arid regions of ancient Israel (Ps. 36:8–10; Jer. 2:13). The wise know they are ignorant, so they keep on **learning.**

16:24 The Hebrew word for **honeycomb** is

also used in Ps. 19:10, 11 with regard to the Word of God. The Israelites saw honey as a healthy food as well as a sweetener. Any comparison to it would connote positive, healthful effects.

16:25 Contrasts of God's **way** with the way of the wicked figure in the teaching of Jesus as well as the proverbs (Matt. 7:13, 14). This proverb likens the wicked to being on the wrong road. They think they are going the **right** way, but in the end it leads to **death** (14:12). Death refers to physical death (1 Cor. 11:29, 30; Rom. 6:23; 8:13; James 1:15; 5:20).

16:26 Hunger is, or ought to be, a powerful motivating force for hard work. In biblical times an able-bodied person who refused to work was not likely to be fed.

16:27–29 These verses all begin in a similar way, describing three different types of wicked people. The word **ungodly,** or "scoundrel," means "a man of Belial"; this person is a muckraker who uses bad information for evil purposes; he destroys people on purpose. The **perverse** person starts fights between friends. The **violent man** uses his power of persuasion to recruit others to join in his attacks.

16:30 Here is one who is so bent on evil actions that one can watch even his facial expressions. He squints his eyes as he considers perversity (same term in v. 28), and he purses his lips as he contemplates wickedness.

16:31 Old age becomes **a crown of glory** to those who walk the **way of righteousness**—one of the rewards of pursuing wisdom.

16:32 One of the most favored persons in the ancient Middle East was the military hero. Yet this proverb suggests that one **who is slow to anger** and **who rules his** speech is a greater hero than a returning warrior. Controlling one's rage is more impressive than completing a daring exploit (14:29).

16:33 The use of lots in ancient Israel (v. 10) could easily be confused with luck. But when a **lot** was cast as a means of determining God's will, the people knew it did not fall indiscriminately. God exercises sovereignty over human affairs (16:4).

17:1 The expression **a dry morsel** means "very little," especially in comparison to **feasting.** But the feasting in this verse is tainted by contention. *Feasting* could also be part of a sacrifice to God, but even such a feast could be ruined by angry disputes between believers.

17:2 Reversals of fortune could happen if the **wise servant** was sufficiently skillful and the **son** and his brothers were undeserving. Much of the Book of Genesis describes the rise of an unexpected younger son over his older brother (Gen. 25:23–34).

17:3 The refining of **silver** and **gold** is an exacting process, involving skill and considerable heat and stress. The refining work of God on His people often requires stress too.

17:4 This proverb presents the **evildoer** and the **liar** as a parody of the wise. As the righteous person listens with care to the instruction of a teacher, so the wicked person **listens** with care to the ruinous speech of the unrighteous.

17:5 Unprincipled humor at the expense of the unfortunate is an enticement to the wrath of God (14:31). Yahweh will not allow such a person to go unpunished, for in some mysterious way, when a person ridicules the poor he reviles his Maker.

17:6 Only a grandmother or grandfather can appreciate this verse fully. Yet all of us can see its central point: grandparents adore their grandchildren, and **children** adore their parents. It is this strong bond of family ties that keeps generations together.

17:7 It is a contradiction in terms for a **fool** to speak well or for a **prince** to be a liar. It is **not becoming** for such inappropriateness to exist.

17:8 The value of a gift to the receiver may be incalculable. Value is more than the cost of an item; value is perceived. One who is gifted by an extraordinary gift (Heb., *sahad*, "gift," "bribe") may become successful because of the new sense of worth he has received in this gift. An act of generosity may change a person's life around. Then again, a gift to the ungrateful may not even be noted.

17:9, 10 The covering of transgression in this sentence is not in the context of sin and salvation vis-a-vis one's relationship to Yahweh. The intention of this verse is to speak of the interrelations of friends, and the problems that may destroy that friendship. Faults observed and noted may be corrected by the offending party, but the offense produced in the revelation of the fault may break the friendship. Similarly, the breaking of confidences may break confidants apart.

17:11 The proper object for the Hebrew verb "to seek" is the person of God. But the obstinate **seeks . . . rebellion.** All the while he is on his disastrous course of action, he finds another is seeking him, a cruel messenger (perhaps the messenger of death).

> *Old age becomes a crown of glory to those who walk the way of righteousness.*

17:12 Nothing in the woods matches the rage of a mother **bear** who has been separated from her **cubs;** yet there is nothing in life more dangerous than the **fool** in the midst of his **folly.**

17:13 A perpetual entertainment of evil is granted to one who responds to goodness and kindness with evil.

17:14 A quarrel is like spilled water. It cannot be stemmed once it is released. The wise thing, then, is to dam up strife before it is too late.

17:15 abomination to the LORD (16:5): Since God is a God of justice, He detests those who pervert justice—both those who declare the innocent guilty and those who declare the guilty innocent.

17:16 As in the case of great speech in a fool, so wealth in his hand is a moral outrage. The fool should not be able to purchase what he is incapable to appreciate.

17:17 This proverb lauds faithfulness. Unlike fickle friends (14:20), a true **friend** is constant, and a real **brother** helps in times of stress.

17:18 Making a **pledge** for another person is not wrong, but this proverb does call for caution in such transactions (11:15). The one making the loan may lose his own independence.

17:19 One may love rebellion and exaltation only to find that rebellion leads to more trouble, and that any boasting of strength will be tested. As in the Old West in America, so in ancient and modern times, there is always a faster shooter who is on his way to town.

17:20 From perversion in heart and mind comes perversion in expression. These inure each other so that the person no longer even knows to look for good.

17:21 The foolish child is one of the hardest realities to face (10:1). There is no heartache so grievous as the pain of realizing that one's child is a **fool,** obdurate to God, and useless in life.

17:22 The role of attitude and feelings in terms of physical health and well-being is only recently being given consideration by standard medical practitioners in the West. This proverb asserts that there is a relationship between attitude and health.

17:23 Like false weights (16:11), skewed justice destroys a culture. A **bribe** is literally a "gift." In v. 8, the same Hebrew word is translated positively as *present,* but in this verse the meaning is negative because the purpose of the gift is to pervert justice.

17:24 Wisdom produces a satisfied life. The fool continues searching without finding any satisfaction.

17:25 As in 17:21 (10:1), this sentence amplifies the vexing nature of a foolish child to loving, believing parents. Both the father and the mother suffer. If they suffer apart (and not together), it is likely they will not only lose their wayward daughter or son, but each other as well.

17:26 Only a perverse population would **punish the righteous.** Like several other proverbs, this one describes what is to be recognized as an outrage.

17:27 Restraint in speech is a mark of wisdom. This cuts against the expectation we have. We usually look for the wise person to speak, not for him or her to listen.

17:28 A complement to v. 27, this sentence speaks of the value of restraint in speech, even in the case of the fool! When a foolish person restrains his or her lips, there may be folks who will regard this person as wise. That view will dissipate quickly when the fool begins to speak. But the illusion will have a chance as long as the fool holds back.

18:1 This proverb condemns any person who **isolates himself** from the community for selfish reasons. Such a recluse is so intolerant of anyone who disagrees with him that he finds fault with **all wise judgment.**

18:2 A compulsive talker never listens, only pausing to plan what he will say next. Every speech confirms what a **fool** he is.

18:3 The verse is a warning against trifling with evil. A person simply does not know what he may be getting involved with when he snuggles up to wickedness.

18:4 wellspring of wisdom: This image is similar to the phrase "a fountain of life" (10:11; 13:14; 14:27; 16:22).

18:5 show partiality: Distortion of justice is all too common; many proverbs condemn it (17:23).

18:6 A mark of the fool is his contentious personality. A battler may be a hero, a protector of persons. But the fool is merely a battler, constantly taunting others for a fight. How he does in the fight is any fool's guess.

18:7 Well, we needn't guess; his lips earn him the destruction for which they have called (14:3).

18:8 The words of a talebearer (16:28) are like delicious sweets. Although they are fun to eat, they ruin the person's health. Gossip is fun to listen to, but the stories damage the listener's **inmost body,** or soul.

18:9 The word **slothful** means a person who is "known to be slack." It refers to a lazy person (15:19). **Destroyer** means "lord of destruction."

18:10, 11 The phrase **name of the LORD** (v. 10) is a way of speaking of God's person. The **righteous** turn to God for security. Rich people,

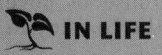 **IN LIFE** | **Cheap Talk**

Some people have a comment to make on virtually every subject. They never say, "I don't know," or just listen in order to learn something. They just spout off their uninformed opinions to any willing listener. Proverbs calls such persons fools (Prov. 18:2).

Talk is cheap partly because it is easily available. The Book of Proverbs offers some principles to help us evaluate the worth of our words:

- Sometimes the wisest course is to keep quiet. We need to weigh our thoughts and words carefully if we intend to be helpful (11:12; 17:27, 28).
- The one thing we never want to talk about is a confidence with which we have been entrusted (11:13).
- If we know how to use words, we can accomplish noble ends—for example, defusing a heated situation (15:1, 2).
- We need to watch what we say. Our mouth can get us in deep trouble (18:6–7).
- If we give our opinion on a matter before hearing the facts, we will tend to bring shame on ourselves (18:13).
- Talk is cheap, but easy talk can be expensive. Saying the wrong thing at the wrong time can lead to unfortunate consequences (18:21).

by contrast, tend to trust in their **wealth** (v. 11; Luke 12:13–21). **safe:** God's protection is a prominent theme in Scripture (Ps. 91:1–4).

18:12 The Hebrew word for **haughty,** ordinarily negative, can also be used positively to mean courage and daring (2 Chr. 17:6). The path to **honor,** which the proud so covet, is **humility.**

18:13 Communication skills are not just good interpersonal relations; they are actually moral issues of wisdom and folly. Responding before listening is stupid. It is also disgraceful.

18:14 This proverb affirms the value of coping skills. **Sickness** can be overcome, but there is no medicine for a **broken spirit** (15:13; 17:22; Is. 66:2).

18:15 The quest for knowledge is insatiable for the wise. Fools scarcely bother. The wise keep learning; the fool hardly begins.

18:16 There is power in a gift in the opening of a door that is invaluable. Once a person has entered the door, the rest is up to that person. But the door, at least, is open.

18:17 When one hears a story from one person, it seems credible. Then when a cross-examiner comes, the story seems to be significantly different. Everyone tends to present his best case, but not all will be able to withstand questions from the cross-examiner.

18:18 Whenever both sides agree on the method of settling a dispute, that method is a means to peace. The **casting** of **lots** was a biblical pattern for assistance in decision-making (16:33). Behind the lots was the sovereign power of God.

18:19 Here is another verse in which the term **contentions** is used (18:18), but here in the positive aspects of character that quarrels might produce. The strength of the fortifications of a city is less than the offenses taken by a wounded brother.

18:20, 21 **stomach . . . mouth:** Inner satisfaction comes from true and good speech. **Death and life:** The words people say wield great power (James 3:2).

18:22 **favor:** Problems in marriage arise from breakdowns in communication or mutual respect, not from some flaw in marriage itself (12:4).

18:23 The **poor man** petitions out of need and fear, the **rich** sneers out of a misguided sense of importance. In both there is error. But the error of the poor person is from need; that of the rich is from arrogance.

18:24 This is a difficult verse to translate because of confusion over an ambiguous Hebrew word translated here as **be friendly.** This translation takes it to mean "to make oneself pleasing" as in 1 Sam. 29:4. To have friends one must be friendly. But the word could also mean "to beat each other up" as in Is. 24:19. Then the verse could be translated, "Sometimes even friends destroy each other, but there is a Friend who loves more faithfully than a brother."

19:1 This proverb, one of the "better than" proverbs (17:1, 10), presents a **poor** person in a more favorable light than a rich person (28:6). In this case, the poor person's life is marked by **integrity,** whereas the successful person has gained his wealth through cheating and deception. The Book of Proverbs does not place a premium on health and wealth. It gives that honor to *integrity* (3:1–12)

19:2 A number of the proverbs use the phrase **not good**. This one says that there is no good in a person who is without knowledge; all there is in such a one are feet rushing to destruction. The feet of the fool are always ready to run to ruin (21:5).

19:3 How many times has a person wandered off in self-destructive folly, only to cry out to Yahweh for help to pull him out of his trouble? Time after time God may reach down in grace to extract a fool from his folly. But there is no guarantee that he will always do so.

19:4 This proverb speaks of the effects of **wealth** and poverty on friendship. It does not describe how friends ought to behave, but how many friends actually do. Like a faithful spouse, a faithful friend is priceless (14:20).

19:5 The need for truth is deeply important to an ordered society. Abuse of truth may not be tolerated if a people is to survive.

19:6 The use of a gift as an entree to gain a hearing is a time-worn grace, built upon a basic human pattern of response. It is clear that both the evil and the good person may use gifts to make their approach to another (17:8; 18:16). The presentation of a gift is not evil in itself, but the one making the presentation may well be evil.

19:7 The behavior of **brothers** and **friends** who abandon a friend because of poverty should be contrasted with the true friend in such texts as 17:17; 18:24.

19:8 Ultimately, to **find good** means to find the Lord in His Word (16:20).

19:9 A slight variation on 19:5, this verse is yet another jab at the evils of bearing a false witness, a breach of one of the Ten Words (Ex. 20:16; Deut. 5:20), and hence a breaking of faith with God and a breach of trust with God's people.

19:10 The phrase **is not fitting** might also be rendered "is not a pretty sight" (17:7). For the wrong people to rule is an outrage.

19:11 discretion: Patience and restraint are virtues of wisdom (16:32); rashness and violent outbursts of rage are not.

19:12 The descriptions of a lion's **roar** and **dew on the grass** are especially fitting when a monarch has all power. His rage may be violent and unpredictable, his pleasure gracious and restorative. A good king will display rage and spread favor for the right reasons.

19:13, 14 Continual dripping speaks of constant dissension within a family. **A prudent wife** is a woman who demonstrates wisdom or skill. Finding the right spouse is a blessing from God (18:22).

19:15 The proverbs have no kind words for **laziness,** the habit of the sluggard (6:6, 9). The

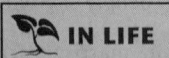 **IN LIFE**   ## Child Discipline

A popular belief today is that people are basically good. An extension of this belief is that children come into the world as morally pure and pristine creatures who are then "socialized" into harmful, hurtful patterns by parents and society.

The Book of Proverbs, along with the rest of the Bible, presents a very different picture of children and childrearing. Although children are seen as a blessing, they tend toward evil if left to their own nature (Prov. 22:15). For that reason, parents are urged to discipline their youngsters. Neglecting to do so amounts to condemning a child to death (19:18).

Opinions vary as to the best way to discipline children. But disagreements about means must never lose sight of what Proverbs says are the ends involved—to bring a child into adulthood with strong character and the ability to make wise choices (29:15). Whatever the term "rod" means to you as a parent, Proverbs encourages you to use discipline in raising your children (23:13).

Several principles of discipline are found in Proverbs:

- A child needs far more than discipline. In fact, discipline is only one part of a much broader home environment required to set a child on the path toward wisdom, self-appreciation, understanding, and humility (2:1–22; 4:3–9; 15:31–33).
- Punishment for wrongdoing is not only corrective but preventive in that it can steer a young person away from more powerful forms of evil and ultimate destruction (5:12–14; 23:14).
- Correction demonstrates love, whereas lack of it is a form of hate (13:24).
- Discipline is intended to purge children of the inherent "foolishness" that the Bible says they have (22:15).

proverbs call for mercy and compassion on the poor and the weak, but only contempt for the lazy (v. 17; 10:4, 5).

19:16 Wisdom and folly are life-and-death issues, as is amply demonstrated in the teaching of Prov. 1—9 (e.g., 1:32, 33). Hence, as in 19:8, the pursuit of wisdom is ultimately an act of genuine self-love; the pursuit of folly is an embrace of death.

19:17 Charity to the poor and needy is perceived in this verse as a lending to God. If one is to lend to anyone, then lend to Him. He will repay. Yahweh's concern for the poor is well-attested in Scripture (e.g., Deut. 10:18, 19).

19:18 on his destruction: Refusal to discipline dooms a child's future (13:24).

19:19 Unbridled rage is an act of folly, just as is intemperate discipline. Great rage has a price to pay. Nothing really changes when the hot-tempered person is delivered from his troubles. He will need to be delivered again.

19:20 Wisdom leads to the glorious future; it is a doorway to eternity. In the NT the idea that corresponds to the quest for wisdom in texts such as this is the goal of Christlikeness, to be conformed to His image. Ultimately, to be wise (in the biblical sense) is to be like Christ.

19:21 A wise person commits his or her **plans** to the Lord (16:3). A person whose plans oppose the Lord (as in Ps. 2:1–3) may actually become God's enemy. But the person whose ways are from God will certainly succeed (16:1, 9).

19:22 The poor person who has integrity has more honor than the successful person who has achieved his station or rank by deception (v. 1). **Kindness** may also mean "beauty." Faithfulness is beautiful, whereas deception is a disfigurement of character (3:14; 31:18).

19:23 This proverb emphasizes the lifelong nature of genuine piety and the abundant rewards that it gives. **The fear of the Lord** is contrasted with all other pleasures (15:16, 33),

because it alone keeps the believer innocent and provides lifelong satisfaction.

19:24 Here is one who is too lazy to keep bringing his hand to his mouth with the food he is eating! So there he slumps, head in the dish, hand at his side (26:15).

19:25 The **simple** person, the one who has yet to set his or her course in life, can learn by watching the **scoffer** suffer. The scoffer himself may not learn from his punishment, but anyone who is ready to learn surely can.

19:26, 27 The desire for a good **son**—or daughter—is the subject of several proverbs (10:1). A child who is abusive to his parents shames them and violates God's command (20:20; Ex. 20:12; Deut. 5:16). The juxtaposing of this proverb addressed to **my son** for the first time since chs. 1—9 with that of the abusive son in v. 26 is deliberate. As an abusive son is shameful, so an obedient son is faithful and successful.

19:28 Here is a proverb that ties together the false witness (19:5) and the **wicked** (the "man of Belial," 16:27). Such a one mocks (the verb is the same root as the term for the scoffer) at justice, and prates abroad all manner of iniquity.

19:29 Instead of necessarily prescribing physical beatings, this verse may describe the lot of the very stubborn. They bring punishment upon themselves. The verse may be read metaphorically as well as in a plain-literal sense. There is certainly no mandate here for thrashing children unmercifully.

20:1 This chapter begins with a warning against the abuse of **wine,** or excessive drinking (see this theme more extensively in 23:29–35). A wise person takes the danger seriously. There is no wisdom in drunkenness, only **brawling** and confusion.

20:2 Apparently this verse of warning against the furious **wrath of a king** is not unlike the warning against the unpredictable

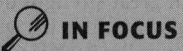 **IN FOCUS** "fear"

(Heb. *yir'ah*) (9:10, 16:6; 19:23) Strong's #3374: This Hebrew word signifies awe in regarding what is unknown or potentially dangerous. Sometimes it refers to fear or terror inspired by danger or one's enemies (Ps. 56:4). More often, it means "reverence," particularly for God (19:23). The use of this word does not imply that one needs to be afraid of God, but it does demand the appropriate recognition and respect for God's fearsome qualities, such as His righteous wrath (Ps 5:4–7). The fear of God—that is, the proper respect of God—compels us to abandon our evil ways (16:6) and teaches us wisdom (9:10). Perhaps somewhat ironically, fear of God leads to confidence in this life, for if we have submitted to the Almighty we do not have to fear any other power in this world. No one can harm us because the Almighty is our Protector (14:26, 27; Heb. 13:6)

nature of wine when abused (20:1). As wine, so the king; both may be agents for good, yet each can be a destroyer.

20:3 One who is a peacemaker is under the blessing of God (Matt. 5:9). A needlessly contentious person is but a fool. The man of peace has glory; the fool, only shame. Better to avoid the quarrel altogether (17:14).

20:4 Because the **lazy man** (19:24) does not plow his field on time, he has nothing to harvest (10:5).

20:5 draw it out: The wise of ancient Israel knew something that modern counselors rediscover in their training and experience, that motivation for behavior is complex. A gifted counselor is able to draw out from a person genuine feelings and motivations, just as someone draws water from a deep well.

20:6 The idea here is self-worth as against true worth, an inflated self-opinion as against the true nature of things. We each tend to present the best; but within we may know the worst.

20:7 The freedom and pleasure of **integrity** are magnified in this sentence (19:8). The idea is one of legacy. The **righteous** not only live well themselves; they also leave a happy legacy to their **children.** Conversely, the wicked (the foolish) leave a legacy of despair. A family's faith will engender family traits.

20:8 A good king uses his throne for justice. An evil or a weak king may be short-sighted when it comes to true justice.

20:9 Who can say: This proverb is a rhetorical question. Everyone sins, a theme that Paul addresses at length in Rom. 3:10–23. Anyone who claims never to sin is a liar (1 John 1:8, 9). But those who confess their sin obtain forgiveness (Rom. 4:7).

20:10 The repeated emphasis on crooked weights and **diverse measures** (11:1) reminds us that cheating is a chronic problem.

20:11 by his deeds: A pattern established early in life may continue to mark a person for his or her lifetime. Even at a very early age, a person's moral character may be revealed.

20:12 This proverb speaks of what **the LORD** has made. We can use both our ears and our eyes to learn about God's Law (Pss. 40:6; 119:18). They are physical means to getting the guidance we need. Contrast this verse with Moses' complaint of a stammering tongue and God's response (Ex. 4:10, 11).

20:13 Sleep is a gift from God that restores a person's energy and vitality. Yet sleep can also be a matter of excess and laziness. Hard work is necessary to make a living; laziness leads only to **poverty** (6:6, 9).

20:14 A "sharp buyer" complains how shoddy something is when he makes the purchase, then brags all the way home at what a deal he had made. There is not a moral here, but an observation. There is a lesson here . . . for the seller!

20:15 This verse is not a comment on the morality of wealth, but a statement about the comparative value of wisdom and money. Wisdom is simply worth more. Thus, being poor and wise is more **precious** than being rich and foolish (19:1).

20:16 It is foolish to lend to **a stranger** without securing a **pledge,** or promise, of repayment (11:15). The Israelites were not allowed to exact such pledges from other Israelites (Ex. 22:25–27).

20:17 afterward: The Scriptures do not say that there is no pleasure in sinning, only that the reward doesn't last (9:17, 18).

20:18 This proverb is a maxim that moves from the lesser to the greater (15:11). We should always think before we act, and serious matters like **war** require a maximum of forethought.

20:19 It is a form of slander to reveal confidential information. Such a person is a silly chatterer (11:13; 13:3). Loose lips not only sink ships; they ruin friendships as well!

20:20 This proverb is about breaking the fifth commandment, "honor your father and your mother" (Ex. 20:12; Deut. 5:16). The term **whoever curses** is based on a word that means "to treat lightly, to regard as insignificant." The statement **His lamp will be put out in deep darkness** is a symbol of eternal damnation.

20:21 at the beginning: Sometimes what seems to be sudden luck turns out to be a dismal turn of fortune. What seems too good to be true often is.

20:22 Because of our limited understanding and imperfection, we are not qualified to **recompense evil.** Instead we must commit our cause to God, whose vengeance is certain and perfectly just. God says "Vengeance is mine; I will repay" (Matt. 5:38, 39; Rom. 12:17, 19; 1 Thess. 5:15; 1 Pet. 3:9).

20:24 Even a man with great strength does not fully control his **steps,** his life; his very breath is a gift from God. Since life itself is God's gift, only a fool assumes he knows its full meaning.

20:25 Several proverbs warn against making rash promises about **holy** things, then withdrawing the promises later (Eccl. 5:1–7). It is better never to vow than to vow and then change one's mind.

20:26 This royal proverb (v. 8) presents discipline as a merciful act. To punish wickedness is entirely appropriate. When the **wicked** are sifted out and punished with the severity that their crimes demand, all of society benefits.

Verse 28 provides the balance to this principle. Ideally, the **king** in Israel mirrored God's character.

20:27 Here is an association of one's conscience with an activity of God.

20:28 The ideal of the king in Israel was to mirror the character of the rule of God. Ultimately, this ideal of rule would be found in the coming Messiah-King (Is. 9:6, 7).

20:29 Each stage of life has its own advantages. The **young** have their youth and vigor; the aged have their wisdom (16:31).

20:30 Suffering cleanses. No one wants to be **hurt,** but God can bring good out of any evil and make us better through hardship.

> *The pursuit of righteousness is its own reward.*

21:1 A person can look at a river and think that it is following a random pattern, but the water is following the direction of God's hand. So is the king. This world's apparent chaos is God's work.

21:2 in his own eyes: A person's own defense of his life, manner, or way may convince himself, but the final evaluation belongs to God (17:3).

21:3 The proverbs occasionally touch on the subject of worship (15:8; 16:6). This proverb affirms, as do Ps. 40:6–8; Mic. 6:8, and numerous other passages in the Bible, that righteous living is more important than **sacrifice** (1 Sam. 15:22).

21:4 haughty . . . proud: See 16:18. The second unit of the verse is difficult to translate. Some versions render the problematic Hebrew word for **plowing** as *lamp.*

21:5 Planning typically leads to **plenty,** and haste to **poverty** (20:21). It is not wrong to plan, but it is wrong to plan what the Lord has expressly forbidden (16:1).

21:6, 7 Some prosperity is good and some is bad. The difference lies in how one gets it. A **lying tongue** has a total return of zero.

21:8 The way: This antithetical proverb takes us back to the very beginning of the study of wisdom, the contrast between the righteous and the wicked (chs. 1—9; Ps. 1).

21:9 Ancient Israelite roofs were flat and could be used as a deck or terrace. On occasion people would build a temporary shelter on a part of the roof. Here, the harried husband finds he prefers to live on the **housetop** rather than below with the nagging words of his wife.

21:10 Here is a person whose passion is **evil;** hence, he has no compassion for anyone. Wicked persons typically refuse to think of anyone but themselves.

21:11 The fool in this text is the worst sort,

the **scoffer** (19:25); a person who is **simple** has enough sense to learn from seeing the scoffer punished. The **wise** always learn, the simple sometimes learn, but the scoffer is a lost cause.

21:12 Here is a verse that is quite difficult to translate. Some versions understand the word "the righteous" to refer to a righteous man or woman who learns from the fate of the wicked. Others understand the term "the Righteous" to refer to God who determines the fate of the wicked. It is likely that the verse does speak of God as the Righteous One, and the unusual expression in the second member describes his judgment as a twisting of the wicked, perhaps a wringing out of the wicked as one might wring out one's laundry.

21:13 cry himself: A person who is indifferent to people in need will find no one helping him when he calls out for help.

21:14 Proverbs 18:16 and 19:6 anticipate the ideas of this verse on the use of gifts to make way for a person, particularly a person of lower station desiring to be received by one of higher station. Gifts speak! And gifts given secretly speak pleasantly against all wrath, and soothe feelings.

21:15 Justice is not a heavy obligation that weighs a person down. For the righteous, promoting justice is a **joy.** For the wicked there is no joy in justice, nor will there be joy in their final end (10:29).

21:16 The assembly of the dead: The term *dead* is a frightful one, meaning "shades" (9:18). Death in these verses may speak of physical death rather than spiritual death (as is the case in James 1).

21:17 This verse is not a blanket indictment of wine or oil, any more than it is a charge against laughter. Excess is the issue that condemns the wicked; balance is the goal that animates the wise.

21:18 This difficult verse speaks in terms of final judgment. Ultimately, the righteous person will prevail and the wicked will not prevail. Finally, right will out.

21:19 This verse may have its other side: What a privilege to live at peace with a loving spouse (husband or wife!). See again the positive presentation of 19:14. To single out verses on the nagging wife is to bring a blanket disrepute to women that these verses cannot be said to sustain.

21:20 This proverb contrasts the prosperity of **the wise** with the poverty of the fool (20:15). The key lies in the way they treat their possessions. Fools abuse or neglect their own property.

21:21 **life, righteousness and honor:** It is possible that these three ideas go together to mean "a more abundant life." The pursuit of righteousness is its own reward. But added rewards are found in fullness of life, achieving righteousness, and receiving honor. All these things are gifts from the Lord (15:9).

21:22 Wisdom is a more potent force than brute strength, more formidable than a fortress. Therefore, pursue wisdom rather than mere bodybuilding.

21:23 This proverb has a pun on the word "to keep." If a person **guards** or "keeps" his mouth, he will **keep** or preserve his soul. The converse of this is seen in the many troubles a person brings on himself by careless speech.

21:24 This proverb applies four different Hebrew words for arrogance to the **scoffer** (v. 11). The first two words, **proud** and **haughty,** mean "profoundly arrogant" (v. 4). The second two, **arrogant** and **pride,** mean "boundless arrogance."

21:25 The longing of the lazy man **kills him;** he is devoured by his own passions because he will not expend the energy to fulfill them. Verse 26 describes further the insatiable greed of the lazy person by contrasting it with the generosity of the righteous.

21:26 This proverb may be paired with v. 25 as a further description of the insatiable lust of the lazy person. Conversely, the **righteous** is unceasing in his generosity. The lazy waits, and the righteous gives; the lazy has not, and the righteous has much.

21:27 When a wicked person brings a sacrifice, with no intention of changing from his wickedness, this is an abomination (Hebrew, *to'eba*). The abomination is in the eyes of Yahweh (as in 20:10), even though He is not mentioned in the sentence. But worse than bringing a sacrifice with wicked heart is to bring the sacrifice with a wicked intent.

21:28 A large number of proverbs focus on the **false witness** (19:28). The problem with a false witness is that his lies pervert justice for others. Even if he lies only once, the lie may be circulated by others.

21:29 There is a nice pun in the interplay between the words meaning "a fixed face" and "a fixed way." A **wicked man** is concerned with facial expression; an upright man is concerned with the course of his life (11:5).

21:30 Usually the proverbs use the word **wisdom** positively. But in this verse the word is paired with conjurers' tricks. These tricks have no power over God, as Balaam the pagan prophet discovered in his encounter with the Lord on the plains of Moab (Num. 22—24). True wisdom can be found only in God.

21:31 A soldier can do all within his ability to prepare for **battle** (20:18), but in the end no preparation can override God's power. Victory is in God's hands.

22:1 This proverb points out that a reputation has more value than possessions or wealth. A **name** cannot be replaced easily, not even with lots of money.

22:2 This sentence eloquently repeats the theme of riches (v. 1): God makes both **the rich and the poor.** This means that those who favor the rich over the poor (James 2). have not only missed the point of creation, they have insulted the Creator (14:31)

22:3 The term **prudent** means "shrewd" (a related word is in 1:4). There is no wisdom in being reckless.

22:4 The route to the good life—**riches and honor and life** (a similar triad is found in 21:21)—is humility (Mic. 6:8) and the fear of God.

22:5, 6 It is prudent to avoid the hooks and snares that line the path of life. A fool is the person who needlessly walks in threatening places, not knowing or caring what a dangerous position he is in.

22:7 When a person who is poor finds himself or herself indebted to the **rich,** that **poor** person is now in a position of being under the rule and dominion of the wealthy person. If the wealthy person is benevolent, then one may escape with little danger. If the wealthy person is a sadist, then the borrower may be reduced to pecuniary slavery.

22:8 The idea of just retribution is significant (21:7). Jesus' teaching on justice reflects the idea in this verse. A person who lives by violence is likely to die violently; a person who lives wickedly should not be surprised if he falls victim to crime (Matt. 26:52).

22:9 The words expressing the idea of generosity in this verse are "a good **eye.**" A good eye observes the needs of others first. A bad eye sees only its own self-interest.

22:10 The **scoffer** (21:24) should be expelled from the community because his influence is harmful to everyone. The wise know that the scoffer is not a laughing matter, because he is laughing at holy things, at God Himself.

22:11 A person who is marked by **purity** of speech and heart becomes the confidant of a good king. Compare this proverb with Ps. 15, which describes a person who wants to become a friend of the Lord.

22:12 **The eyes of the Lord** (15:3; 21:2) are the final arbiters of knowledge and justice. The eyes of human beings are simply not trustworthy. When the king takes his position seriously, he also makes decisions that are proper and upright (20:8).

22:13 The proverbs about **lazy** people

(19:15) provide comic relief by poking fun at how the lazy invent all sorts of excuses for avoiding work and risk. They will do anything to avoid doing anything.

22:14 This proverb takes us back to the **immoral woman,** or the "strange woman" (2:16). Her mouth is an open pit, destruction to anyone who falls there (9:18).

22:15 The idea here is to encourage a reluctant parent to discipline a foolish child. Folly is like a monster with its grip on the heart. It needs to be expelled.

22:16 The last of the proverbs of Solomon in this collection deals with social justice. Ultimately, all human affairs are in God's hands,

even though at times the wicked prosper. God made both the **poor** and the **rich** (v. 2) and He will justly determine their destinies (24:12).

22:17–24:22 The phrase **the words of the wise** marks a new section of the Book of Proverbs. The content changes at v. 17. Three elements distinguish this section: (1) the change from one-verse units to multiple-verse units, (2) section headings that are embedded in the text, and (3) the affinity of this section with ancient Egyptian wisdom texts, particularly the Instruction of Amen-em-opet.

22:17–21 **Incline your ear:** These introductory words call the reader to pay attention and to prepare to learn about and worship God.

 **IN DEPTH** | **Train Up a Child**

Doubtless 22:6 is one of the most often cited verses of the proverbs of Israel. There are three issues on which debates continue in its interpretation: (1) the meaning of the verb "to train," (2) the intention of the phrase "in the way he should go," and (3) the meaning of the verb "he will not depart" in the second half of the verse.

First, the word "to train" (Heb., *hanak*) is a term related to the familiar festival name, "Hanukkah," from the Hebrew for "dedication." The word *hanak* relates to a setting aside for special use, a dedication of a child to the Lord or to the path of God in his or her life. It includes the stimulation of proper responses (perhaps even the creating of a taste for something) and the (initial) guidance on right paths. This is the principal parental task, to receive children as a charge from the Lord, who are then to be dedicated to the way of God in their lives. In this manner, the verse presents the educational principle of readiness, as Paul does in 1 Cor. 3:1–3 (Heb. 5:12).

Second, the phrase "his way" in this proverb is said by some Bible teachers to refer to the natural path of the child, his gifting and interests. The phrase "in accordance with his way" is paraphrased by these teachers as "let him follow his natural bent." There is a great deal of good parental advice in this common view, but it may not be convincing exegesis. The phrase "the path" (or "the way") in the proverbs refers to correct morality in the eyes of Yahweh (15:10). Without further definition, one is hard pressed to say that the phrase "his way" refers to the natural bent of the child. The way of the proverbs is God's way. Likely, *the way* commended to the child is the way of God and His word.

Another tack taken by some is to suggest that the way of the child is his natural bent to depravity. We may paraphrase: Let a child grow according to his own way, and when he is old, he will be confirmed in wantonness. In this reading the verse is quite negative in tone. This approach can be justified on the basis of "his way," but not with due attention to the verb *hanak*.

Third, and most significant, the force of the verb "will not depart" is questioned. Many people come to the proverbs without any real sense of the genre of Scripture they are reading. These have absolutized the meaning of this verse, presenting it as some type of promise from the mouth of God. The idea is paraphrased: When the parent has done his or her job correctly, then there is a binding promise of God to spare that parent's child for eternity.

The problem, of course, is that there is no such guarantee in Scripture—in this verse or in any other. These verses are principles, not promises. A godly parent has no guarantee from God for faithful children. Each generation is responsible for its own relationship to God. To be brief: this verse is a proverb; not a promise. The verb in this proverb is imperfect (in the present sense). This verb form means that time after time one will observe the process and be aware of it.

The point of 22:6, then, is to present the task of parenting in a divine balance. The parents do their part and then God does His part. There is no magic; there are no guarantees. But there is at least a sense of participation, of excitement and fulfillment.

The advice emphasizes strongly that a person's **trust** must **be in the LORD**.

22:22, 23 Most violations of justice target **poor** and **afflicted** people because they are weak and defenseless. But anyone who does this makes an enemy of God, who **will plead their cause**.

22:24, 25 friendship with an angry man: Whereas the words of vv. 22, 23 are based on Hebrew faith, these ideas are derived from observation of human behavior and interaction. The Book of Proverbs includes both types of insight: revelation of truth about God, and observation of human experience (1 Cor. 15:33).

22:26, 27 If you have nothing: Should anyone give surety for more than he might be able to cover?

22:28 The ancient Israelites regarded respect for the posted **landmark** as more than a question of private property. They saw it as a basic part of civil life. People must feel a certain sense of public trust and fairness for society to function.

22:29 Excellent work still brings rewards from people and the approval of God. See also Eph. 6:5–8.

23:1–3 A big part of the training of the courtier would be in proper manners at state dinners and formal occasions. The comment on a **knife to the throat** is prompted by two concerns: (1) rude behavior was to be avoided at all costs, and (2) too many royal dainties would likely make one ill.

23:4, 5 These verses call for moderation in work. **Do not overwork to be rich:** Although the proverbs discourage laziness (22:13), they also discourage any overworking whose purpose is greater wealth.

23:6–9 bread of a miser: No real fellowship is developed by dining with a person who does mental calculations about what you are costing him while you eat his food.

23:10, 11 their Redeemer is mighty: The tendency of evil people in all ages is to take advantage of the helpless. But the destroyer of persons needs to know that the widow and the orphan have a Redeemer, a protector of family rights—His name is the living God.

23:12 The Hebrew word for **instruction** can also be translated "discipline."

23:13–16 he will not die . . . beat him: This language was designed to motivate overly permissive parents, who were afraid of damaging young children with any kind of discipline, or of making rules and enforcing them. There is no call here for abuse. Loving discipline does not destroy rebellious children; it does them a big favor.

23:17, 18 The first proverb here sharply contrasts the vain **envy** of **sinners** with the **fear of the LORD**, the expression of piety that the proverbs repeatedly encourage (1:7). The second gives the perspective that everyone needs: present success—or lack of it—is not the final outcome. There will be a future state fundamentally different from this world. The word **hereafter** can also be rendered "glorious future" (Num. 23:10).

23:19–23 The drunkard and the glutton have no self-control, and this fact plagues them. Hebrew culture gave a prominent place to eating and drinking, but it had little tolerance for drunkenness and gluttony.

23:24, 25 the father of the righteous: Joy comes to parents who see their children succeed. But when those parents have faith in the Lord, the greatest joy comes from seeing their children be faithful to Him.

23:26–28 The wise men of Israel never ceased warning against the prostitute and **seductress** (7:24–27). The corruption of character involved in debauchery was considered nearly fatal.

23:29–35 Who has woe: Along with Isaiah's celebrated description of debauchery (Is. 19:11–15), this section is one of the sharpest attacks on drunkenness in the Bible (vv. 19–21; 20:1). The satire is razor sharp and the imagery vivid.

24:1, 2 Do not be envious of evil men: Whereas 23:17, 18 tells about the future to discourage envy of the wicked, this set of verses simply points out how unworthy the wicked are of any admiration at all.

24:3–11 These verses speak with a certain confidence and understanding of life beyond the grave (23:17, 18). This verse is a prayer to God as **death** approaches.

24:12 according to his deeds: Jesus' words about eternal rewards open and close the NT (compare Matt. 5:11, 12 with Rev. 22:12). Yet Jesus' action on the Cross will deliver those who believe in Him from any condemnation (Rom. 5:18; Gal. 3:18; Rev. 22:17).

24:13, 14 Here is one of the associations in the Proverbs of **honey** and the **honeycomb** with wisdom (16:24). Wisdom and its pursuit, while rigorous, is good for the soul and can be pleasant.

24:15, 16 Ultimately the **wicked** will fall. The righteous can be assured of this not because they are strong, but because they have a Redeemer (23:10, 11).

24:17–22 fear the LORD and the king: The Hebrew text breaks the phrasing: "Fear God, my son, and the king" (Rom. 13:1–7; 1 Pet. 2:17). This proverb relates most fully to the Davidic kings, who were God's regents on earth; one way the ancient Israelites could show

---

IN PERSON | **Hezekiah, Preserver of Proverbs**

The proverbs collected in Prov. 25—30 reflect important reforms enacted by King Hezekiah of Judah (Prov. 25:1). Hezekiah's father and predecessor, Ahaz, had turned away from the Lord by serving idols and practicing child sacrifice (2 Chr. 28:1—4). As a result, Judah suffered devastating losses to the Assyrians and the Israelites of the northern kingdom.

But when Hezekiah assumed the throne, he removed the idolatrous practices and centers, restored temple worship, and resumed nationwide observance of Passover (2 Chr. 29—31). It was probably during this period that scribes found and copied these proverbs of Solomon, which were later included in the Book of Proverbs.

---

respect for God would be to respect the king. But the duty to honor civil authorities still applies to all people of all times (Rom. 13:1).

24:23–34 These things also belong to the wise is a sectional heading that corresponds to the one in 22:17. Verses 23–34 serve as an appendix to the preceding section (22:17—24:22).

24:23, 24 Israel's basic concern with equity in **judgment** was not unique; but in Israel a concern for equity was tied to God's character. Since God does not show partiality, neither should we.

24:25–27 afterward build your house: The matter of priorities is in view in v. 27. The diligent completion of labor in the fields must precede the building of one's house. Perhaps the starting of family life is in view here, as well. One ought to be certain that a well-ordered life has been established before embarking upon marriage.

24:28, 29 Verse 29 states the "Golden Rule" (Matt. 7:12) in terms of what we should *not* do. Jesus said this is our most important duty.

24:30–34 The lazy person is judged on the basis of the shambles of his field. From this sorry state of affairs the wise take a lesson. The only concern the lazy have is for **a little sleep.**

25:1–5 Silver is valuable only after the impurities have been removed. Similarly, wickedness needs to be removed from a king for his throne to be established rightly.

25:6, 7 Do not exalt yourself: Knowing your place is a recurring theme in the Bible. It is humiliating to be told to remove yourself from a seat of honor. Jesus spoke of the same need for deference (Luke 14:11). **Whom your eyes have seen:** This phrase reflects the custom in the ancient world of never looking directly into the eyes of a superior until told to do so (Is. 6:5).

25:8–15 hastily to court: In our own litigious age, this group of verses has unusual relevance. Seek to deal with complaints outside the court on a private level or even with an arbiter.

25:16 found honey: Too much of even a good thing can cause illness and distress.

25:17 neighbor's house: The issue is moderation. Too much "neighborliness" becomes an imposition.

25:18–26 The words of Jesus in Matt. 5:43–48 have direct ties to these verses. **Coals of fire** speaks of God's judgment (Pss. 120:4; 140:10); the idea is that an act of kindness to your enemy may cause him or her to feel ashamed. This is just one way to overcome evil with good (Rom. 12:20).

25:27 much honey: Moderation in good things (v. 16) goes with humility.

25:28 rule: Self-control is a key part of obedience to God (Gal. 5:22, 23).

26:1, 2 snow in summer: A most unlikely happening in Israel. **Rain in harvest** is not only unusual, but disastrous, because rain at that time would cause the crops to rot.

26:3 rod for the fool's back: The fool has no internal motivation to do anything. He is no better than a brute beast whom someone else has to motivate.

26:4, 5 Some people have called the two proverbs here contradictory, but that is not necessary. The phrase **according to his folly** appears twice as a play on words with two shades of meaning. On the one hand, it means "avoid the temptation to stoop to his level"; that is, don't use his methods, **lest you also be like him.** On the other hand, it means "avoid the temptation to ignore him altogether"; that is, respond in *some* way, or else he will become **wise in his own eyes** and his folly will get worse.

26:6–11 dog . . . vomit: A fool does not learn from his mistakes. The apostle Peter cited this verse and applied it to false teachers (2 Pet. 2:22).

26:12 Being haughty is even worse than being a **fool.** Egotism is the epitome of folly (28:11).

26:13–15 These proverbs about the **lazy**

man have a "can you top this" quality that provides comic relief; the lazy man is the object of many jokes in Scripture. This set of verses includes several (19:15). Each one belittles laziness and the many outrageous excuses people often use to justify it.

26:16, 17 The problem with taking a **dog by the ears** is that the dog will not like it and probably bite. The same is true of getting involved in another's quarrel. It's an invasion of privacy.

26:18–21 Fires do not burn without fuel; **strife**, or fighting, works the same way.

26:22 The slanderer looks upon his nasty words as **tasty** tidbits, delicious morsels of raw gossip. Many people have an insatiable hunger for malicious gossip.

26:23 The meaning of this proverb is not far from Jesus' remarks to His enemies that they were like whitewashed tombs (Matt. 23:27). No amount of painting on the outside changes the value of the rotten interior.

26:24–27 A person who hates says one thing but stores up anger **within.** He may find that his hatred hurts him, when in his life there is so much falsehood that no one believes him no matter how gracious and truthful he might be at times. **revealed before the assembly:** When we lament the unfairness of the prosperity of the wicked and contrast our own situation to theirs, we need to keep Ps. 73:17 in mind. Their end will more than compensate them for the evil they have done (Rom. 6:23).

26:28 A **lying tongue** results from hatred in the heart. It is kindled with the fire of hell (James 3:3–6).

27:1 As Jesus did in His teaching (Matt. 6:25–34), the wise of ancient Israel warned about a concern for **tomorrow** that overshadows the needs of today.

27:2–5 **Let another man praise you:** Self-praise is also out of place for the person of wisdom and reveals an insensitivity to the fitness of things. Praise is a comely garment; and though we may desire to wear it, it is always better if others place the garment upon us.

27:6 Correction given in love by a **friend** is better than insincere acts of affection (Ps. 141:5).

27:7 Those who are full do not appreciate what they have, while to those who are **hungry** anything tastes good.

27:8–10 **from its nest:** Straying from home can mean losing security and becoming open to new and powerful temptations (read the parable of the prodigal son in Luke 15).

27:11 This is the first **my son** proverb in this collection; it is very similar to those in the earlier parts of Proverbs (chs. 1—9). A child who grows up wise confirms that the parents who taught him or her were themselves wise (10:1).

27:12–16 Normally a **garment** given in **pledge** was only a symbolic collateral and was returned immediately, but not if the one making the pledge was unreliable or a stranger (20:16).

27:17 iron sharpens iron: A famous proverb, this verse may also be translated as applying to the will: "Let iron sharpen iron, and so let a person sharpen his friend." The idea is that people grow from interaction with one another.

27:18 keeps the fig tree: This proverb speaks of faithfulness and reward. The word **master** may refer to God.

27:19 a man's heart: Thoughts reflect a person's true character.

27:20–22 Hell and Destruction are used often in the Bible to describe the fearful aspect of death. They are like ravenous monsters. Compare this proverb with the image of Satan as a roaring lion (1 Pet. 5:8).

27:23–27 These verses affirm diligence and describe its practical rewards. The model is that of the farmer who cares for his **flocks and herds;** if he diligently cares for them, in time they will care for him.

28:1–3 The wicked flee when there is no cause (Ps. 53:5) because of guilt and the fear of getting caught that goes with it.

28:4, 5 When a person abandons God's **law,** he or she loses all sense of right and praises **the wicked** (Rom. 1:28–32). And since true **justice** is from God, the ungodly have trouble understanding it. This is why the fear of the Lord is the beginning of wisdom (1:7).

28:6 The proverbs balance their words on **poor** and **rich** people; they do not assume that godliness leads to wealth or that wealthy people are necessarily godly. As this proverb points out, sometimes we must choose between doing good and getting rich.

28:7 To be a **companion of gluttons** (23:20, 21) is to break God's law. This is why Jesus' enemies charged Him with associating with gluttons: such accusations were attacks on His faithfulness to God (Matt. 11:19).

28:8, 9 Profit taken by **usury** is unjust. God will help the poor eventually, at their exploiters' expense.

28:10–13 causes the upright to go astray: These words resemble Jesus' warning against leading his disciples astray (Matt. 18:6). Paul vividly captures this kind of evil: "If anyone defiles the temple of God, God will destroy him" (1 Cor. 3:17).

28:14 Happy is the man is a beatitude (Ps. 1:1) about the person who is in awe of God. The person who never thinks of God faces calamity.

28:15, 16 Like a roaring lion: The oppressive reign of a wicked ruler is compared to the viciousness of attacking animals. Lacking true understanding, these vicious persons fail to recognize that the security of the throne is related to the welfare of their subjects. The ruler who hates such senseless oppression will bring stability and length of days to his reign.

wisely: Security can only come by trusting God, not by relying on oneself.

29:1 The Hebrew phrase for **often rebuked** is "a man of rebukes." The judgment on a person who stubbornly rejects God's correction is swift and final.

29:2–4 The words **righteous are in authority** can also be translated "righteous are

Photo by Howard Vos

Mosaic of a lion, an animal known for its strength and courage. The writer of Proverbs declared that "the righteous are bold as a lion" (Prov. 28:1).

28:17–19 Tills his land is a call to hard work, a promise of reward, and a warning against **frivolity** or overindulgence in fun.

28:20 A faithful man succeeds. That is, faithfulness to God, not greed, determines success in life.

28:21, 22 To exercise **partiality** (literally, "to recognize faces") means to judge on the basis of favors or bribes instead of what is right.

28:23 rebukes a man: Constructive criticism has more value than flattery, which aims only to win people's affection.

28:24 robs his father: This proverb condemns breaking the fifth commandment, "Honor your father and your mother" (Ex. 20:12). Respect for parents as a duty is a common theme in the Book of Proverbs.

28:25–28 One of the main causes of **strife** is pride; trust in God leads to blessing. **walks**

great." People will always respond to good government and justice. Justice is not served by **bribes,** nor is good government established that way.

29:5, 6 Spreads a net: Lies entrap liars (10:8). Moreover, the evil one is trapped by his own actions. Both the liar and the wicked are contrasted with the righteous, who run happily because they are innocent of any wrongdoing.

29:7–12 Righteous people are concerned for **the poor** and help them (22:22); the wicked do not even consider the needy.

29:13, 14 God is responsible for giving life to both the **poor man and the oppressor.** Jesus attested that God causes rain to fall on the just and the unjust (Matt. 5:45).

29:15–17 The words **rod and rebuke** both speak of correction or discipline. An undisciplined child shames everyone, espe-

The final two chapters of Proverbs are attributed to men named Agur and Lemuel. Neither of these men are mentioned elsewhere in the Bible. Appearing in both attributions (Prov. 30:1; 31:1) is the Hebrew word *massa'*, which can be translated as "burden" or "utterance," as it is used by the prophets (Is. 17:1; 19:1). The word might also be the name of a place—Massa (Gen. 25:14; 1 Chr. 1:30). If so, the attributions might associate Agur and Lemuel with a country or a city named Massa. For instance, Prov. 31:1 would begin, "The words of Lemuel, king of Massa, which his mother taught him."

Even if these teachers are not from a place called Massa, they do not appear to be Israelites. There was no King Lemuel in Israel, and the name "Agur" is not formed in a typical Hebrew fashion. Agur's name does appear in Sabean inscriptions, and in light of that foreign source, it is interesting that the teachings of Agur include some of the most religiously oriented of all the proverbs in the book.

cially his or her parents (v. 17). Verse 17 places the burden of correction on the parents. The word translated **delight** speaks of rich, delicious food (Gen. 49:20).

29:18 Where there is no revelation: The Hebrew word for *revelation* speaks of revelatory vision, a word from God. Without God's revelation of the Law, the people flounder. True happiness is discovered within the constraints of revelation, in the counsel of the Savior.

29:19 A servant will not be corrected by mere words: The Septuagint reads "a stubborn servant." Verbal correction accomplishes little with men who deliberately refuse to obey commands. Sterner measures are needed, for it is only the fear of punishment that alters the resolve of these unprincipled and self-willed persons.

29:20–22 hasty in his words: Even a wise person may become foolish by speaking too quickly. It is better to be silent or to choose words carefully than to speak whatever first comes to mind.

29:23–25 See Ps. 147:6. God raises the **humble** and puts down the arrogant. Mary praised God for doing this marvelous thing (Luke 1:46–55).

29:26, 27 God controls human affairs. Therefore it makes more sense to **seek** the Lord first before stooping to seek the favor of human rulers.

30:1 An entirely new section of the Book of Proverbs begins with **the words of Agur.** Like Lemuel (31:1–9), Agur was a non-Hebrew contributor to the Book of Proverbs. He came to faith in the God of Israel in a foreign land. We know nothing about his father **Jakeh,** but the word translated **his utterance** may be a place name. **Ithiel and Ucal** were probably Agur's pupils. Since the back-to-back repetition of the name Ithiel is unusual, some construe the Hebrew letters differently and translate the text "I have wearied myself, O God; I have wearied myself, O God, and am consumed." This would fit the context of the following verses.

30:2, 3 more stupid than any man: Agur means he was at a loss. Similarly, his denial of **knowledge of the Holy One** is a rhetorical flourish as well (as is seen by comparison with his words of vv. 5, 6). Agur was stating with dramatic irony that he could not explain the puzzle before him.

30:4 This verse gives the riddle that perplexed Agur. The questions are enigmatic. They culminate in **What is His name, and what is His Son's name, if you know?** At this point, the riddle has no answer. The OT would answer that "His name" is the Lord God, but did not have a name for His Son. This riddle was to remain unsolved until Jesus answered it for Nicodemus (John 3:13). These verses form one of the most straightforward messianic texts in the Bible.

30:5–9 Two things: This was all Agur needed.

30:10 This proverb is unusual in warning against slandering a **servant.** Slaves in ancient times were often regarded as less than a full person.

30:11–16 Agur wrote about **a generation** plagued by social ills such as lack of respect for parents, self-righteousness, greed, and selfishness. Ironically, such evils have plagued every generation, not just Agur's.

30:17 mocks his father: The lack of parental respect spoken of in v. 11 leads to this curse. The language is strong and violent, as is the punishment of the one who abuses his or her parents.

30:18, 19 The term translated **virgin** could also read "young woman" in this context.

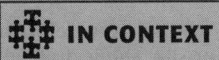 **IN CONTEXT** | **The Virtuous Wife**

Prov. 31:10–31 is an acrostic poem, in which the first word of each line begins with a successive letter of the Hebrew alphabet. This poem is part of the instruction that King Lemuel's mother gave to teach her son about wisdom (31:1). In describing the "virtuous wife," Lemuel's mother was showing what wisdom looks like when it is lived out in everyday life.

Why is the woman of Prov. 31 more valuable than rare jewels (31:10)? It is because of her wisdom, her ability to live life in a responsible, productive, and prosperous way (Prov. 1:2). The Book of Proverbs often personifies wisdom as a woman (8:1–11), and also describes wisdom as more valuable than any riches (3:15; 8:11).

Thus it is no surprise that the woman of Prov. 31 earns praise in the most public of places, the gates of the city (31:31), which in her day represented a combination of city hall and the marketplace. She is a woman whose hard work brings material rewards (31:13–16, 21, 22). Proverbs promises that whoever seeks and finds wisdom will also find wealth, happiness, honor, and long life. This woman is an example of how those promises are fulfilled.

It is worth noting that this woman pursues what are sometimes thought of as traditional female jobs, such as making clothes (31:13, 19), as well as nontraditional work, such as real estate investment, farming, and merchandising (31:16, 18). Furthermore, her energies are directed not only toward providing for her family and household (31:11, 14, 15, 27), but also toward meeting the needs of people in the community (31:20).

In short, the woman of Prov. 31 is a model, for both women and men, of a way of living that brings fulfillment and contentment. She exhibits a lifestyle of work and love, based on godly wisdom.

30:20 This verse contrasts with the way of v. 19; this **way** is awful whereas the former is wonderful. The **adulterous woman** regards her illicit sexual relations without remorse, as if she were finishing a plate of food.

30:21–23 Contrasting with the four wonderful things of vv. 18, 19 are four things that are grievous, an upsetting of order. Three are clear: the **servant,** the **fool,** and the **maidservant** are all in unexpected positions of power. The **hateful woman** describes the sorry lot of a woman whose husband hates her.

30:24–28 This numerical proverb speaks of **four** creatures that are small in size but amazing in behavior. Each of these small creatures has a behavioral trait from which wise people can learn.

30:29–33 The proverbs of Agur conclude with warnings against boasting and trouble-making. The phrase **put your hand on your mouth** means "stop it." The idea is if you are in the middle of making trouble and suddenly realize your foolishness, stop right then before things get worse.

31:1 This verse begins a new section of material from a non-Israelite source. Some have thought that the name **Lemuel,** meaning "Belonging to God," is a pseudonym for Solomon, but this is only a guess.

31:2–7 Lemuel's mother advised him not to **give** his **strength to women.** Often in the ancient world a king would amass a large harem or involve himself sexually with many women. The wisdom of Lemuel's mother was that such behavior destroys rulers. She likewise advised him to avoid **intoxicating drink** altogether, so that he could always have a clear enough head to rule justly.

31:8, 9 for the speechless: The duty of a king in the ancient world was to defend the weak, to uphold the helpless. These ideals were rarely realized in that age or even in our own. But one day a King who is the Defender of the helpless will establish his righteous reign (23:10, 11).

31:10–12 Proverbs 31:10–31 is an acrostic poem; each verse begins with a successive letter of the Hebrew alphabet. Some have thought that it continues the teaching of King Lemuel's mother (vv. 1–9), but it may also be an independent, concluding unit. As the Book of Proverbs begins with the Prologue (1:1–7), which gives the goals of wisdom in general terms, so now it concludes with this Epilogue (vv. 10–31), which presents them in a case study. The opening words **Who can find** position this woman as an ideal. The phrase **a virtuous wife** speaks of excellence, moral worth, ability, and nobility, not just marital fidelity (12:4). Such a woman is the ideal of wisdom in action.

31:13–15 These verses emphasize both hard work and skill. The woman they describe does things she enjoys, finding her fulfillment in varied tasks. The words **she also rises while it is yet night** describe her concern for others;

she gives of herself to care for her family and servants.

31:16, 17 She considers a field; that is, she buys and sells and builds her own resources. These words are remarkable in light of the many restrictions placed on women in the ancient world.

31:18, 19 her merchandise is good: One of the avenues the woman exploits is a "cottage industry" in which she acts independently.

31:20–22 The virtuous woman works not to get rich, but to give **to the poor.** She can be concerned for others because she has provided for her family.

31:23 The virtuous woman's husband has a position **in the gates** as an elder of the city; some of his status comes from his wife's reputation, not just his own.

31:24 Linen garments probably indicates clothing for women.

31:25 The virtuous woman's own **clothing** is far richer than linen or silk; she is dressed in strength and honor.

31:26, 27 Any woman who **opens her mouth with wisdom** deserves praise, given all the information on the use and misuse of speech in the Book of Proverbs. A virtuous woman takes care to speak well (James 3:2).

31:28, 29 The virtuous woman is blessed by her family—by her **children** as well as her husband. The words of v. 29 are the blessing of her husband.

31:30, 31 Charm may be used for good or for evil; it is not necessarily bad. But its good use requires the fear of the Lord—the main theme of the Book of Proverbs.

The Book of

Ecclesiastes

T HE BOOK OF ECCLESIASTES IS ONE OF THE most misunderstood books in the Bible. Christians have tended either to ignore the message of the book or to regard it as the testimony of a man living apart from God. This is unfortunate, for the book asks relevant, searching questions about the meaning of life, and it declares the utter futility of an existence without God. Like all Scripture, the Book of Ecclesiastes benefits and edifies God's people.

Negative descriptions such as "cynical," "fatalistic," or "existential" do not do the Book of Ecclesiastes justice. There is too much evidence of robust cheerfulness throughout its pages. "So I commended enjoyment" (8:15) is a recurrent theme that pervades the book; in fact, the Hebrew words for "gladness" and "being glad" appear seventeen times in Ecclesiastes. The underlying mood of the book is joy: finding pleasure in life despite the troubles that often plague it. Those who fear and worship God should experience this joy; they should rejoice in the gifts God has given them.

Solomon probably wrote this book toward the end of his life, after he had repented of idolatry and his pursuit of foreign wives. Thus the Book of Ecclesiastes is both a monument to Solomon's recommitment to the living God and a guide for others through the pitfalls and perils of life.

In fact, Solomon might have written this wisdom book as a tract for other nations. That would explain why he did not write about the Law, and why he used the divine title Elohim, meaning "Exalted God," instead of the covenan-

tal name Yahweh in the book (Ex. 3:14, 15). Solomon had entertained many dignitaries from other nations, including the queen of Sheba. The queen's questions concerning the basic meaning of life might have prompted him to write Ecclesiastes to teach the Gentiles about the living God and their need to worship only Him. Centuries before, Moses had called for this type of treatise to the pagan nations (Deut. 4:6–8). The nations that had heard of Israel's success needed to know about the living and exalted God who had blessed Israel with wealth and wisdom.

Sometimes it is better to read the end of a book to understand better the direction in which the book is headed. This is certainly true of Ecclesiastes. The book should be interpreted in light of its conclusion: "Fear God and keep His commandments, for this is man's all" (12:13). To fear God means to revere, worship, and serve God—to turn from evil and turn in awe to the living God. This was the attitude of Abraham (Gen. 22:12), Job (Job 1:1, 8, 9; 2:3), and the Egyptian midwives (Ex. 1:17, 21). It does not involve dread but instead a proper respect for and obedience to our Creator. Why should we respect and obey God? The Book of Ecclesiastes answers this question in its concluding verse (12:14): God will judge everyone—both the righteous and the wicked. Life cannot be lived with abandon, as if God will not see or remember the deeds of the past. For on the final day, He will call forth all men and women to account for their actions. The admonition to fear God and the expectation of divine judgment are the two great themes that conclude the book and provide an interpretative framework for the rest of it (12:13, 14).

The journey of Solomon to his conclusion "to fear God" is founded on the human search for meaning in life. In 3:11, Solomon eloquently expresses humankind's dilemma: God has placed eternity in our hearts. A search for true meaning in this life—in money or fame, for instance—will only leave us empty-handed, because our souls yearn for something that will last. Our frustration arises from a hunger to fellowship with our eternal Creator—the only One who can give meaning to our lives. In Ecclesiastes, Solomon takes us on a tour of all of life and concludes that all of it is vanity. Pleasures and riches lead merely to boredom and despair. Only a relationship with the One who created us and continues to care for us will truly satisfy. Troubles and uncertainty will continue to plague us, but even during these times we can find joy in a secure trust in our Father.

The writer says that he was "the son of David, king in Jerusalem" (1:1, 12, 16), words that have led many to assume that the writer was Solomon. Evidence in the book itself points to Solomon: (1) the author had "more wisdom than all who were before" him (1:16; 1 Kin. 3:12); (2) he gathered for himself "silver and gold and the special treasures of kings" (2:8; 1 Kin. 10:11–23); (3) he "acquired male and female servants" in great numbers (2:7; 1 Kin. 9:20–23); (4) he engaged in extensive building projects (2:4–6; 1 Kin. 9:1–19); (5) he developed a great understanding of plants, birds, and natural phenomena (2:4–7; 1 Kin. 4:33); (6) he declared, "there is not a just man on earth who does good and does not sin" (7:20; 1 Kin. 8:46); and (7) "he pondered and sought out and set in order many proverbs" (12:9; 1 Kin. 4:32).

Nevertheless, some scholars argue that Solomon is not the author. They point to two passages to make their case: 1:12 and 1:16. The past tense of the verb in 1:12: "I . . . *was* king over Israel in Jerusalem" may lead the reader to think that the author was no longer king when he wrote this work. But the verb can denote a state of action that began in the past and continues into the present. Hence 1:12 could be translated, "I have been {and am} king." Also, the phrase in 1:16 suggests there were many kings before Solomon in Jerusalem. Since David was the first Hebrew king in Jerusalem, the argument goes, the writer must have lived many generations after the time of David. Yet we should recall that the history of Jerusalem can be traced to early Canaanite settlements. The kings of Jerusalem may well have included Melchizedek (Gen. 14:18), Adoni-Zedek (Josh. 10:1), and Abdi-Khepa (mentioned in the Amarna Letters), to name just a few. Therefore, it can reasonably be asserted that Solomon is the author of this wonderful but unusual book.

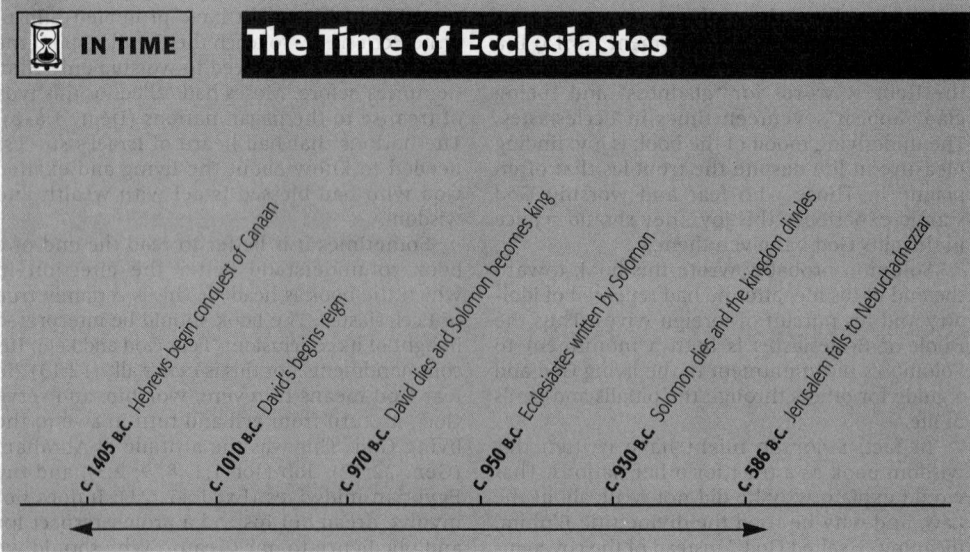

⧗ IN TIME

The Time of Ecclesiastes

c. 1405 B.C. Hebrews begin conquest of Canaan

c. 1010 B.C. David's begins reign

c. 970 B.C. David dies and Solomon becomes king

c. 950 B.C. Ecclesiastes written by Solomon

c. 930 B.C. Solomon dies and the kingdom divides

c. 586 B.C. Jerusalem falls to Nebuchadnezzar

Outline

Commentary

1:1 The title **Preacher** denotes a function or a profession. It literally means "one who assembles" or "one who gathers people together." Thus the word refers to Solomon as a person who convened an assembly of the wise in order to explore in a formal manner the meaning of life. It might be better to transliterate the Hebrew word *Qohelet* rather than to translate it, for it seems to be Solomon's pen name.

1:2 Vanity of vanities: This phrase translates the Hebrew superlative, familiar from such phrases as "song of songs" and "holy of holies." Here it might express "the ultimate absurdity" or "utter emptiness." This has led many to conclude that the Book of Ecclesiastes is a negative, cynical book that denies any meaning in life. Others have suggested that this book explains that life *apart from* God is "utter emptiness." However, the book itself does not say this, for there is no qualifying phrase such as "except when one is related to God." Instead, the book

clearly says that *life itself* is "vanity of vanities." The word *vanity* means "breath" or "vapor" and thus speaks of life as "quickly passing." Life is like a vapor; indeed, it is like the thinnest of vapors (the superlative of the word). Wherever we read the word *vanity* in Ecclesiastes, we should think not of what is "meaningless" but of what is "quickly passing" (v. 14; 6:12). This is one of the key terms in the Book of Ecclesiastes, for it is found thirty-eight times there but only thirty-four times in the rest of the OT. The teaching of the Preacher is to realize that life is a fleeting thing that needs to be savored and enjoyed as a gift from God.

1:3 The senses of the term **profit** are: (1) "advantage" and (2) "adequate gain." Here it refers to compensation or gains, usually in the commercial realm. The question is: What is left after all expenses are taken into account? **labor:** Both the noun and the verb carry negative connotations, referring to activities requiring exertion. **under the sun:** This phrase (also translated as "under heaven" in v. 13; 2:3; 3:1) describes *life* lived here on this earth, as God has been pleased to place us. In these two verses (vv. 2, 3), the Preacher has established one of his principal ideas: Life may seem pointless because it is quickly passing. It is the burden of the rest of his book to help the assembly of the wise understand how to truly value life because it does indeed pass so very quickly.

1:4 The term **generation** suggests both the human actors and the natural phenomena as well. With the verb **passes away** we have the first of a series of antitheses in Ecclesiastes. **the earth abides forever:** Only God is eternal and everlasting in the fullest sense. But compared to the lives of humankind, the earth abides with little change.

1:5–7 The sun . . . The wind . . . the rivers: These three elements of God's creation are seen to be going about in their expected courses, with little change and little effect.

1:8, 9 All things are full of labor: What is true of the sun, wind, and rivers (vv. 5–7) is also true of all other temporal things. The whole world is made up of what could be called "the restless ones." **The eye is not satisfied:** Here a proverb is quoted describing insatiable appetite (4:8; 5:10; compare Prov. 27:20) in depicting the seeming pointlessness of the courses of natural phenomena.

1:10, 11 If it appears that something **new** does happen from time to time, it is only because people's memories are short.

1:12 I, the Preacher, was king: There is a shift from the third person of vv. 1, 2 to the first person here. The writer, or perhaps a later editor, returns to the third person in the epilogue,

---

IN LIFE | **Life Under the Sun**

O ne way to understand the enigmatic Book of Ecclesiastes is to read it as a contrast between two very different outlooks on life—either acknowledging and depending on God, or failing to do so.

Failing to honor God is life "under the sun" (Eccl. 1:3, 9, 14; 2:11, 17), "on earth" (1:4; 5:2; 8:14), and "under heaven" (1:13). It is a life filled with pain, toil, disillusionment, and sadness. By contrast, living life in relationship to God is to live by the "hand of God" (2:24), which leads to harmony and joy (2:26; 3:13; 5:19).

These opposing lifestyles are similar to the contrasting lives that Adam and Eve lived before and after sinning. Originally, all of creation was good (Gen. 1:26–31) and there was no shame between man and woman (2:24–25). But after the first couple's rebellion (3:1–7), the history was filled with pain and toil (3:8–24), murder (4:1–24), rampant evil (6:5–7), drunkenness, shame, and curses (9:20–27), and ultimately worldwide confusion (11:1–9). The world that God had designed for people's good became evil and destructive.

12:8–14. This is most likely a reference to Solomon as the author of the book.

1:13 under heaven: This is a synonymous expression for "under the sun" (vv. 3, 9); it refers to life as it is lived by people on earth. **God:** Ecclesiastes does not use the divine title Yahweh, God's covenantal name (Ex. 3:14, 15). Instead, the book uses the word *Elohim* for God twenty-eight times, a word that stresses His sovereignty over all creation. The wisdom writers often use *Elohim* when they wish to speak of universal truth instead of truths that are peculiar to God's covenantal relationship to Israel. **sons of man:** This is a way of speaking of human beings in a very general sense. **may be exercised:** This verb is used only in Ecclesiastes and means "to be occupied with" or "to be busy with"; it is associated with the noun **task** (3:10).

1:14 grasping for the wind: This phrase does not occur in the Hebrew Bible outside of Ecclesiastes. Seven of its nine occurrences (v. 14; 2:11, 17, 26; 4:4, 6; 6:9) follow "vanity" statements. The phrase explains the nature of life according to the Preacher. Life is real but quickly passing; any attempt to seize it is as futile as grasping the wind.

1:15 Solomon is not claiming that there is no use trying to straighten out or change anything. Rather, he explains that no amount of investigating or using the resources of earth will ever straighten out all that is **crooked,** twisted, perverted, or turned upside down (7:13).

1:16 all who were before me in Jerusalem: This phrase does not rule out Solomon as the author of the book just because he was preceded in Jerusalem as an Israelite king only by his father, David. There were other kings, including Melchizedek (Gen. 14:18) and Adoni-

Zedek (Josh. 10:1). The city of Jerusalem had existed for hundreds of years before Solomon became its king.

1:17 It was not **wisdom** that Solomon judges absurd but rather becoming "more wise" (2:15) and "overly wise" (7:16).

1:18 much wisdom is much grief: For all of wisdom's other advantages, Solomon confesses that much wisdom and learning are the source of pain, chagrin, and sorrow. It is well known that the very process of learning is an expansion of the awareness of our ignorance. For mortals, an increase of wisdom may only increase pain (12:12).

2:1 The Preacher uses a literary device of conversing with himself as a way of describing his thought processes. **mirth:** A new test is proposed, following the test of wisdom. It is the test of "joy," or "pleasure."

2:2 Solomon labels the lighter side of pleasure and joy as sheer **madness,** but even the weightier aspects of laughter cause Solomon to ask if anything substantial is really achieved. As Solomon writes in Prov. 14:13, "Even in laughter the heart may sorrow, and the end of mirth may be grief."

2:3 flesh with wine . . . heart with wisdom: Here the test is an attempt to balance excess on the one side with learning on the other.

2:4–6 I built myself houses: Solomon worked for thirteen years building "the king's house" (1 Kin. 9:10); then he built "the house of the Forest of Lebanon" (1 Kin. 10:17) and another house for his wife, Pharaoh's daughter (1 Kin. 9:24). He also fortified the cities of Hazor, Megiddo, Gezer, Beth Horon, Baalath, and Tadmor (1 Kin. 9:15, 17, 18). **vineyards . . . gardens and orchards:** Solomon's interest in

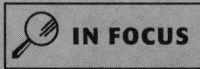

IN FOCUS | **"vanity"**

(Heb. *hebel*) (1:14; 2:1, 11; 6:12; 7:15; Ps. 78:33; Is. 49:4) Strong's #1892: This word basically means "vapor" or "breath," such as the rapidly vanishing vapor of one's warm breath in cool, crisp air. With this word, the Preacher described worldly pursuits—such as wealth, honor, fame, and various pleasures—as similar to desperately grasping at air (2:17). It is absurd and useless. Jeremiah used the same word to denounce idolatry as "worthless" (Jer. 18:15); and Job used it to bemoan the brevity of human life (Job 7:16). But the Preacher of Ecclesiastes used the word more than any other OT author. According to him, all of life is vanity unless one recognizes that everything is from the hand of God (2:24–26).

the natural world (God's creation) was prodigious (1 Kin. 4:33).

2:7, 8 Maintaining the various buildings and gardens of the king must have demanded an extensive staff of servants. **silver and gold:** Solomon's riches were unsurpassed by the kings of the ancient world (1 Kin. 10:14–29). **musical instruments:** The meaning of the Hebrew term so translated has long been debated. An Egyptian letter found at Amarna contains this word in Akkadian as an explanation of an Egyptian word meaning "concubine."

2:9, 10 my eyes desired: Solomon had limitless ability to fulfill any and all of his desires. **labor:** One of the Preacher's favorite words occurs here for the third time. It appears in the book about thirty-one times.

2:11 At the end of his grand quest for possessions and experiences, Solomon concluded that it was **vanity,** or "vapor," a **grasping for the wind.** That is, even with all he had done and experienced, there was still a sense that nothing lasting or enduring had been achieved.

2:12 madness and folly: This topic was introduced briefly in 1:17. The two words together express a single concept, "senseless folly."

2:13 There is a relative value of **wisdom** over **folly,** but both have their limitations (vv. 19, 21).

2:14 the same event: Some versions incorrectly render this Hebrew term, which means "happening" or "event," as the word *fate*. This is one of the Preacher's favorite words (vv. 14, 15; 3:19; 9:2, 3, 11). Here, the inevitable *event* is death. Both the wise and the foolish must die.

2:16 no more remembrance: Life in and of itself cannot supply the answers to the ultimate questions being asked here. Death will overtake both the wise person and the fool alike. In that sense, both life and death are cheats.

2:17–19 Such hatred of **life** is astonishing since the one who finds wisdom also finds life, according to Prov. 3:16; 8:35. But the Preacher's dissatisfaction was related to the quickly passing nature of everything (1:2), including even the good things; they were a **grasping for the wind** (1:14).

2:20 labor in which I had toiled: This could refer either to all the toil he had undertaken or, more probably, to the "earnings" he had gained.

2:21 The noun **skill** is found only in Ecclesiastes (v. 21; 4:4) It depicts one who is expert at a craft. **great evil:** The term *evil* often has a sense of moral evil; here, however, it may mean "calamity" or "ruin." There is a sense of sadness that runs through this section. Nothing that we gain in this life can be carried on into the life to come.

2:23 his work (i.e., his task).

2:24 This translation, with most interpreters, assumes that the comparative form— **better**—is to be supplied here, though it is missing in the Hebrew text; it is in agreement with later passages (3:12; 5:18; 8:15). The Preacher concludes that all good is located only in God. **eat and drink . . . good in his labor:** This repeated refrain marks one of the central affirmations of Ecclesiastes (vv. 24–26; 3:12, 13; 3:22; 5:18–20; 8:15; 9:7); in the midst of a world of trouble, a believer is able to seize the moment in joy from God. Only God supplies the key to the meaning of life. Without Him, genuine meaning, satisfaction, and enjoyment in life are ultimately elusive. **from the hand of God:** This figure of speech announces that even such mundane acts as eating, drinking, and earning a paycheck are gifts from God.

2:25 more than I: An alternative meaning of this phrase, "apart from God," may be more appropriate in this context. Believers pray before their meals in order to affirm that God is the great Giver of all good gifts. They can enjoy the food on their plates only when they recognize that fact.

2:26 God gives: One of the words used most frequently in Ecclesiastes to describe God's relationship to individuals is the verb "to give." It appears eleven times with God as subject.

3:1–15 This poem speaks with eloquence of the role of time in the life of the believer. Some regard the Book of Ecclesiastes as describing life apart from God, but clearly this text describes life that is lived in relationship with God. Through

IN PERSON | One Who Had It All

The writer's claim that he had more possessions "than all who were in Jerusalem before me" (Eccl. 2:7) is consistent with reports of Solomon's wealth (1 Kin. 3:13; 10:23). Furthermore, in addition to riches, Solomon possessed extraordinary wisdom (3:12; 4:29–34), which the writer of Ecclesiastes also had (Eccl. 2:9).

The irony is that Solomon, who enjoyed greater wisdom and wealth than any of the Israelite kings, came to great spiritual ruin because of his foolish choices regarding idolatry (1 Kin. 11:1–13). Ecclesiastes does not reflect that spiritual apostasy. However, is it possible that Solomon's disillusionment with pleasure and knowledge, which eventually caused him to "hate life" (Eccl. 2:1–17), might have been a contributing factor in turning his heart to other gods? Scripture does not say. But the tragic fact remains that one of the greatest of Israel's kings had his kingdom come to "vanity" because he forsook the God who had given him all that he possessed.

these words, the Preacher is not teaching that everything has an opportune time according to which one should choose one action or the other. Rather, he teaches that all events are in the hand of God, who makes everything happen in the time He judges appropriate. Illustrating this comforting assertion, the Preacher turns to fourteen pairs of opposites in vv. 2–8.

3:1 a season . . . a time: Both words are usually regarded as being specific points in time rather than a continuity of time. **under heaven:** That is, life "under the sun," the sphere in which human life is lived.

3:2 born . . . die: The pairs of words in these verses are natural events in human life, and all are under the hand of the living God.

3:3 A time to kill: In the plan of God, there is a time for executing murderers (Gen. 9:6) and for going to war against enemies designated by God. **A time to break down:** There is a time for dismantling walls, stone buildings, or even nations (Is. 5:5; Jer. 18:7, 9).

3:4 weep . . . laugh: God's plan includes both sorrows and joys. Believers do not mourn in the same way as unbelievers (1 Thess. 4:13), but we do mourn (Matt. 5:4). Dancing and leaping are natural ways of expressing laughter, pleasure, and joy in the presence of the Lord (Ex. 15:20; Pss. 149:2, 3; 150:4) and in times of personal happiness (Luke 15:25).

3:5 In times of peace, **stones** were cleared from the fields, allowing for cultivation. In wartime, the rocks were thrown on the fields to make them unusable (2 Kin. 3:19, 25). **to embrace:** In this context the words describe the sexual embrace.

3:6 to keep . . . to throw away: There is a period of life in which one wishes to accumulate things for enjoyment and memories; later in life one needs to work out ways to dispose of what has been accumulated.

3:7 When bad news came, it was customary to rip one's garments to show grief (2 Sam. 13:31). When the problem passed, it was just as well to **sew** the garment back together. **silence . . . speak:** See the two contrary ways of responding to a fool (Prov. 26:4, 5).

3:8 In this verse the first part names the positive **love** first, then the negative **hate.** The second part uses the reverse order, negative then positive, to end with **peace.**

3:9 What profit: This is the same question posed in 1:3. The answer here is that all of life unfolds the appointment of God. All the toiling of man cannot change the times, circumstances, and control of events that God has reserved to Himself.

3:10 One of the words that is unique to the Book of Ecclesiastes, **task** may have a neutral connotation as here (5:3; 8:16) or a negative connotation (something burdensome, as in 1:13; 2:23, 26; 4:8; 5:14).

3:11 All of God's creation is **beautiful.** The point is that God makes everything that way **in its time.** From the divine perspective, there is no ugliness in the events of our lives (3:1–8). **Eternity in their hearts** refers to a deep-seated, compulsive drive to transcend our mortality by knowing the meaning and destiny of the world. Because we are made in the image of God, we have an inborn inquisitiveness about eternal realities. We can find peace only when we come to know our eternal Creator. Even then, we know God only in part (1 Cor. 13:12). **from beginning to end:** All we see is the micromoment of our own existence in the grand span of eternity. Thus the Scriptures call people to live in robust faith during times of trial and pain; in the grand scheme of things, God will make **everything** beautiful.

3:12, 13 nothing is better: As in 2:24, the advice of the Preacher is to seize the day in the joy of God. **rejoice . . . enjoy:** Biblical faith is a call for joy, even when we live in a wicked world and under terrible stress; this is because we find true joy in the living God.

3:14, 15 God's works have a durable quality to them. As Deut. 4:2; 12:32; Prov. 30:6 advise, **nothing** may be **added** and nothing **taken** away. **should fear:** The "fear" of God in wisdom literature refers to true piety, not terror (5:7; 12:13).

3:16, 17 The term **judgment** may also be translated "justice," giving an even more striking contrast to these words. It was outrageous that in the very establishments where people should expect justice, they could find only **wickedness.** The Preacher warns the wicked judges that God, the final **judge,** will come, rectify all wrongdoing, and bring true justice. This theme is so prominent in the book that Solomon repeats it in the conclusion (12:14), and he raises it often in the course of his argument (9:1; 11:9).

3:18 tests them: The basic meaning of the verb is "to choose, select, purify, test." Death is the great leveler of all persons. In that regard, humans are no different than animals.

3:19 one breath: The Hebrew expression might be translated "one spirit" or "one wind." The phrase in this case describes breath as the sign and symbol of life (8:8; Gen. 6:17; 7:15, 22). In this, humanity and animals are alike (but read v. 21). **advantage:** This word appears only here in Ecclesiastes. It is also found in Prov. 14:23: "In all labor there is *profit*," and in Prov. 21:5: "The plans of the diligent lead surely to *plenty.*"

3:20, 21 All go to one place: Both humans and beasts die and go to the grave. But this is not the end for human beings—they will face eternal life or death. The rhetorical question **who knows** occurs six times in the Hebrew Bible outside of Ecclesiastes (2 Sam. 12:22; Esth. 4:14; Ps. 90:11; Prov. 24:22; Joel 2:14; John. 3:9) and four times in Ecclesiastes (2:19; 3:21; 6:12; 8:1). People and animals differ; their bodies go back to the dust from which they came, but the human spirit is immortal.

3:22 better: As in v. 12 and 2:24, there is a blessing given to humankind in terms of ordinary pleasures. **his heritage:** The allotment that God has designated may include material possessions (2:21; 11:2) or the pleasures that come from them (2:10; 3:22; 5:17, 18; 9:9).

4:1 Here is another complaint that threatens the plan of God. So much pain can come to the downtrodden that they may even despair of life (1 Kin. 19:4; Job 3:3–10). Only when the oppressed go into the house of God will they gain perspective for possible recovery (5:1–6; Ps. 73:17). **they have no comforter:** The absence of anyone to offer comfort only increases the pain and frustration.

4:2 I praised the dead: Being without a comforter is often worse than death itself.

4:3 he who has never existed: So powerfully wrong and so lonely is the suffering of the oppressed that Solomon, with a good deal of poetic license similar to Job 3:3–10, argues that nonexistence could be preferred over existence.

4:4 a man is envied by his neighbor: To the previous obstacles to accepting that God's plan encompasses everything is now added a fourth: the envy and cruel competition found in the world.

4:5, 6 Two proverbs follow. **The fool:** There are numerous statements in the Book of Proverbs about the self-destructive nature of laziness. **a handful:** Moderation is preferred to overexertion. In place of the sometimes cruel competition of the marketplace, Solomon recommended: "Better is a little with righteousness, than vast revenues without justice" (Prov. 16:8).

4:7, 8 The problem of sadness and loneliness is another obstacle to accepting the fact that God has a plan that embraces everything. Consider the person who has no family, not even an heir to whom he can leave all for which he has worked so hard. In 4:1 there is "no comforter." In 4:4–6 there is no rest. In 4:8 there is no companion. **grave misfortune:** This literally refers to an evil or burdensome task (3:10).

4:9–12 Throughout this section there is an emphasis on the obvious benefits of companions. The intimacy and sharing of life brings relief for the problem of isolation and loneliness. A companion can offer assistance, comfort, and defense. **threefold cord:** The Preacher uses this proverbial saying to clinch his case about the value of friends.

4:13, 14 Before the Preacher lists the final obstacle (vv. 14–16) to believing in God's good plan, he first places the answer in proverbial form. Popularity, even in the form of royal power, is elusive. In one case, an old **king** had been born to the throne but becomes so **foolish** and senile that he cannot discern that his days for ruling are over. In another case, a young man, like Joseph, may rise from prison to take the throne (Gen. 41:14, 37–41).

4:15, 16 those who come afterward: Even the young man who replaces his predecessor will share the old king's fate. Today's hero may become tomorrow's beggar.

5:1 Walk prudently: Literally, this phrase is "guard your feet" when you go to worship God. It means to behave yourself. The idea of righteous behavior is rephrased at the end of the section in the words: "But fear God" (5:7). **to hear:** As is common in the prophets, there is a warning

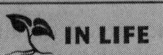 **IN LIFE** | **Four Benefits of Companionship**

People these days often celebrate the myth of rugged independence, praising the self-made, self-reliant individual. Yet whatever feats people may accomplish on their own, far greater achievements are won by dedicated, united teams working together toward common goals. The writer of Ecclesiastes recognized this. He placed a high value on companionship for four reasons:

- *Greater productivity.* No matter how hard a single person works, he can rarely do as much as two people working together (Eccl. 4:9). A team has to expend far less effort to achieve the same results, and a team can maximize results through increased efficiency.
- *Access to immediate assistance.* Sooner or later everyone fails. It is only human to do so. But if someone is alone in failure, the results can be devastating—not just to the product, but to the person. However, by working in partnership with others, people have a buffer against failure. It is less likely to occur, and when it occurs, companions are standing by to offer consolation and to help their friend get back on track (4:10).
- *Human comfort.* The world can be a cold place. It can tear people apart without a second thought. That's why it helps to have companions. They can offer comfort when life is harsh, not necessarily by anything they say, but just by being there (4:11).
- *Security.* The world can be indifferent, but it can also be dangerous. One need not even go looking for trouble; trouble can come stalking on its own. But wolves tend to attack the solitary sheep, not the entire flock. That's why it makes sense to travel through life in the company of others (4:12). There is safety in numbers.

Have you made the effort to establish a solid, lasting friendship with one or two other people? If not, you are missing out on some valuable benefits that God intended for you. It is not wrong to be alone or to be independent by nature. But all human beings need someone with whom to share themselves. That is how God has made us.

to be circumspect about sacrifice. God has no pleasure in those who do all the right things for all the wrong reasons (Is. 1:10–15). **the sacrifice of fools:** As the prophet Samuel warned Saul, "Behold, to obey is better than sacrifice, and to heed than the fat of rams" (1 Sam. 15:22).

5:2, 3 God is in heaven . . . you on earth: The essential contrast between God's righteous might and our sinful mortality should cause us to revere the Almighty (v. 7).

5:4, 5 One should not attempt to bribe God with a hasty **vow.** The first part of this verse is almost identical to Deut. 23:21. See the later example of the lie of Ananias and Sapphira (Acts 5:1–11).

5:6 A priest or prophet or one of God's angels is the **messenger of God** who would hear such excuses for unfulfilled vows (Hag. 1:13; Mal. 2:7).

5:7 To **fear God,** a central theme of the Book of Ecclesiastes, does not mean to be afraid of God (Ex. 20:2). It means to have reverence, awe, and wonder in response to His glory. For the wisdom writers (Job 1:1; Ps. 111:10; Prov. 1:7), "to fear God" means to respond to Him correctly, in true piety.

5:8 province: This term (2:8; Heb. *medînâ,* Esth. 1:1) is usually thought to be a Persian word, and hence is used by some to argue for dating the book to the postexilic period. But Solomon was acquainted with many languages and had contacts with a number of nations. His use of "exotic" vocabulary may simply be a demonstration of the remarkable sophistication that was evident in his speech.

5:9 for all . . . king: All people live by God's grace in His provision for the earth.

5:10 not be satisfied: The topic of an insatiable appetite is addressed for the third time (1:8; 4:8). Desire always outruns possessions, no matter how vast acquisitions may grow.

5:11, 12 There are few things so satisfying in life as **sleep** following a hard day's work, but the greedy rarely enjoy decent rest.

5:13, 14 Misfortune literally refers to a "worthless task" (compare 3:10).

5:15 naked shall he return: The maxim that "you can't take it with you" is affirmed here (2:21).

5:16 labored for the wind: The wording is similar to "grasping for the wind" (1:14).

5:17 darkness . . . anger: The frugal lifestyle

This gold mask of an Egyptian pharaoh represents wealth and extravagance. The writer of Ecclesiastes declared that such worldly possessions do not bring happiness and contentment: "He who loves silver will not be satisfied with silver" (Eccl. 5:10).

of the covetous prevents them from enjoying what they *do* have (contrast 2:24–26; 3:12, 13).

5:18, 19 God has separated the **gift** of enjoying something from the gift of the object itself so that we might be driven back to the Giver.

5:20 keeps him busy: The literal meaning of the verb is debated, but it appears to be a form of the verb meaning "to answer." God keeps a person occupied and delighted primarily with Himself and then with the gifts He gives. **joy of his heart:** The Preacher uses the word *joy* in two ways: (1) "enjoyment," an internal sense of pleasure (2:10, 26; 4:16; 9:7; 10:19), and (2) "pleasure," pleasurable actions (2:1, 2, 10; 7:4; 11:9).

6:1, 2 God does not give him power: Prosperity without the divine gift of enjoyment amounts to nothing (5:19).

6:3 Sometimes the achievement of the greatest of goals becomes hollow when there is no decent end to life. **stillborn child:** Ordinarily a great sadness, the child who does not live is considered to be better off than the person who has lived poorly. If life is nothing more than a meaningless journey to death, then a stillborn is better off, for that child reaches the end of the worthless journey with less pain (vv. 4–6).

6:4–6 That one **place** is, as 3:20 argues, the grave. If a long life terminates in death with no prospect of anything else, will that life have been worthwhile? Long life without knowing God and without the power to enjoy it is indeed frustrating and useless.

6:7, 8 The Hebrew word for **soul** can also be translated *appetite*. If it is meant to parallel the word *mouth* in the first line, then *appetite* may be appropriate in this context. Yet the translation *soul* fits well in the argument of the gift being kept separate from the power to enjoy the gift (5:10).

6:9 The meaning of this proverb is that it is

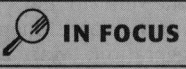 **IN FOCUS**   "labor"

(Heb. *'amal*) (2:11; 5:18; Ps. 105:44; Jer. 20:18) Strong's #5999: This noun means "toil," or work for material gain (Ps. 127:1; Prov. 16:26), but it can also mean "trouble" or "sorrow" (Job 3:10). The effort required for work and human achievement produces "sorrow" and "troubles" in the sense that it can never satisfy the deeper needs of the human soul (6:7). However, when believers recognize that their work is a gift from God, work can become a joy (5:18–20). Our work is part of God's plan to establish His eternal kingdom. In this sense, we can be assured that our faithful commitment to our work will have eternal consequences and reap eternal rewards (1 Cor. 3:8, 14; 15:58).

better making do with what we can look on and enjoy than fantasizing about desirable things that are beyond our grasp.

6:10 Whatever happens has been already known, because to name something is to know it (1:9–11). All things are foreknown and fore-ordained by God (1:9–11).

6:11 How is man the better? The word used for "better" is a synonym for the more common term in Ecclesiastes "profit" (Heb. *yitrôn*). The Preacher (Qohelet) does not mean that no one exists in the world, but that in a dis-putation with God (v. 10), what is to be gained from many words?

6:12 like a shadow: This phrase is a confir-mation of the meaning of the Hebrew word translated *vanity*. Life passes away quickly, like a vapor. **what will happen after him:** The implied answer is that only God knows what will happen to us after death. Rather than imply that nothing exists beyond the grave, this book teaches that each person's life will be reviewed by God after death.

7:1 A person's death may be **better** than the day of birth if the name of that person has merited a lasting reputation and influence.

7:2–4 These verses expand upon the idea of v. 1. We may learn more about the meaning of life in the **house of mourning** than in the **house of feasting.**

7:5, 6 Burning **thorns** will provide quick flames, little heat, and a lot of noise, just like the sudden outbursts of laughter among fools; there is more noise than substance.

7:7, 8 bribe: Another form of this maxim is found in Ex. 23:8; Deut. 16:19 (read Matt. 28:11–15; Luke 22:4–6).

7:9 See James 1:19.

7:10 The temptation to glorify the past at the expense of the present must be resisted. The pleasures or advantages of those **days** may be more imaginary than real.

7:11 Those who find **wisdom** find life, argues Solomon (Prov. 8:35). Wisdom is as good as an inheritance; in fact, wisdom is even more advantageous or profitable. **who see the sun:** This seems to be a variation on the more familiar phrase "under the sun."

7:12 The word translated **defense** literally means "shade" or "shelter," a kind of protection. The Hebrew word translated here as **excellence** is often rendered *profit* in Ecclesiastes.

7:13 The **crooked** that needs straightening (1:15) is the presence of afflictions and adversi-ties in life. Both prosperity and adversity come from the hand of God. For prosperity give thanks, but in adversity reflect on the goodness and comprehensiveness of the plan of God.

7:14 find out nothing: If mortals do not come to know God and His plan, they will not be able to discern anything about life (3:11) or about what will happen after they are gone.

7:15 just man: There are inequities in life that will always be a mystery (3:16–4:3; 8:14).

7:16 Do not be overly righteous: Few verses in Ecclesiastes are more susceptible to incorrect interpretation than these (vv. 16–18). This is not the so-called golden mean that advises: "Don't be too holy and don't be too wicked; sin to a moderate degree." The Preacher was warning instead about pseudoreligiosity and showy forms of worship. The Hebrew verb for "be wise" may be rendered "think yourself wise," and to "be overly righteous" would mean "righteous in your own eyes" (Prov. 3:7).

7:17 Do not be overly wicked, nor be foolish: Perhaps this could be more sharply translated as "Do not—multiply{your} wickedness and do not be a fool—why die before your time?"

7:18, 19 The **this** that Solomon refers to is the true wisdom that comes from the fear of God. The **other** is the folly of fools. **fears God:** True piety in reverence and awe is the best pro-tection against either absurdity.

7:20 not a just man on earth: This lan-guage recalls Solomon's prayer when he dedi-cated the temple (1 Kin. 8:46; Pss. 14:2–4; 143:2).

7:21, 22 take to heart: At times you may find another doing to you the same harmful thing that you have done to someone else.

7:23 proved by wisdom: The verb means "to put to the test."

7:24 The theme of wisdom's inaccessibility also appears in Job 28. The answer to this search for wisdom is that God **can find** wisdom (Job 28:23–28).

7:25 my heart: Here, as in 2:1, there is almost a personification of the "heart" as the Preacher talks to his heart.

7:26 Wisdom literature is filled with warn-ings about the loose **woman** (Prov. 7). How-ever, this is balanced by the Preacher's praise for a spouse as a gift from God (9:9).

7:27 Adding one thing to the other: The Preacher painstakingly added one thing to another to arrive at a sum total. This verse has the first two of six uses of the verb "to find"

7:28 The truth that all persons are sinners is put in a deliberate exaggeration. **Man** and **woman** mean "a good man" and "a good woman." In the Book of Proverbs, Solomon asked the same question: "Who can find a faithful man?" (Prov 20:6).

7:29 Even though God made everything beautiful (3:11) and **made** human beings **upright** (Gen. 1:31), Solomon's search for the "sum" had failed. Yet humankind's search for wicked devices and intrigues had succeeded wonderfully.

8:1 The idiom "to cause one's **face** to **shine**" (read the Levitical blessing of Num. 6:25) is an image of a person who is stable. Out of the depths of experience and understanding, that person is able to enjoy life and build up others.

8:2, 3 Subjects are obligated by an **oath** of allegiance to render their obedience to "the powers that be" (Rom. 13:1–5). **not . . . stand for an evil thing:** Even before a king, evil is to be resisted (Acts 5:29).

8:4, 5 What are you doing: This same question is asked of those who pretend to be able to rebuke God (Job 9:12; Dan. 4:32). The rhetorical question amounts to a firm denial of the king's power.

8:6, 7 time and judgment: The phrase means an "appropriate time of judgment." God will judge everyone; every matter, including judgment, has its set time (12:14).

8:8, 9 Since the word **spirit** is paralleled by the "day of death," the term *spirit* in this context means "life force" (3:19).

8:10 It was difficult to see the **wicked** receiving a funeral procession from the city to the cemetery while the righteous were **forgotten.**

8:11 sentence . . . is not executed: There are cases when God postpones punishment, letting the guilty person live longer.

8:12, 13 The sharp contrast of the righteous and the **wicked** in these verses is a hallmark of Hebrew wisdom literature (Ps. 1).

8:14 according . . . righteous: Although there seem to be some glaring inequities in this present life, we know that God is working out His good purposes (3:16—4:3; 7:15).

8:15, 16 In contrast to the mad search for the meaning of all things is the contentment that a wise, loving God gives to those who will receive His gifts of **enjoyment.** Here is one of the central themes of Ecclesiastes. **eat, drink, and be merry:** The Preacher marks the end of the third major section of his book with this refrain. The wicked person (the fool) decides that the best thing to do is to "eat, drink, and be merry" with no thought given to the living God. But the righteous person (the wise) can enjoy life while thinking of God and His good gifts.

8:17 Solomon equates God's work with the activity that takes place on earth. Therefore, it should not be surprising that humans cannot fathom God's activity (3:11; 7:25–29; 11:5–8). The Hebrew word translated **attempts** can also be translated *claims* or *thinks* in this context (the word is translated *think* in 2 Chr. 13:8).

9:1 In the hand of God means "in God's control and possession." **love nor hatred:** Sometimes in Hebrew two opposites together are a way of saying "everything." Love and hate

---

✠ IN CONTEXT   ## Death and Life

Ancient people reflected on the inevitability of death. As the Book of Ecclesiastes expresses: "No one has power in the day of death" (Eccl. 8:8). Similar reflections are found in the Gilgamesh Epic, the adventures of Gilgamesh, king of Uruk around 2600 B.C.

The Gilgamesh Epic, composed in Akkadian, has been preserved in two major versions, one from late in the Old Babylonian period (1750–1600 B.C.) and a second by Neo-Assyrian scribes (750–612 B.C.). The Neo-Assyrian version contains a scene in which Gilgamesh, in his search for immortality, passes by Siduri, the divine alewife (who is tending her beer stand on the seacoast). Her advice (in the Old Babylonian version) on the futility of his quest is quite similar to the advice of Ecclesiastes: "Live joyfully" (Eccl. 9:9).

Siduri begins by reminding Gilgamesh that it is impossible for humans to find eternal life, which the gods have reserved for themselves. Her advice to Gilgamesh is to eat, make merry, and rejoice in the feasting while he can. She tells him to enjoy the daily rounds of life: wear clean clothing, bathe himself, play with his children, and enjoy his wife. That is all, she tells him, that is allowed by the gods. Old age and death will overtake everyone. Gilgamesh continued on his search, but found that Siduri's words reflected reality.

The writer of Ecclesiastes offers readers much the same advice: eat and drink with joy, wear clean ("white") garments, attend to your body ("oil on your head"), and enjoy your wife (Eccl. 9:7–9). The passage in the Gilgamesh Epic shows that these ideas of Ecclesiastes were known in the ancient Near East as early as the Israelite and Judean kingdoms. Siduri's speech proves that the idea of resignation to mortality was pondered in the ancient Near East in almost the same terms as it was by the preacher of Ecclesiastes.

are best viewed as words for God's favor and disfavor.

9:2, 3 Some versions translate the word **event** as "fate" (2:14). However, there is no hint here of the power of fate as some people in antiquity believed. The word simply refers to an outcome determined by God.

9:4 In this verse, Solomon uses a proverb that says a living lowly creature is preferable to a dead exalted creature. The point is not that death is the absolute end of all things; instead, the point is that while there is life, there is **hope** of doing something to the glory of God.

9:5, 6 This, again, is not a flat denial of any hope beyond the grave. The point of view is limited to what can be known strictly from a human point of view, "under the sun." **they have no more reward:** The Preacher's point appears to be the same as that in the Gospel of John: One must work while it is still day (that is, while one is still alive), for the night will come when no one can work (John 9:4).

9:7 God meant for all His gifts to be enjoyed. The image of **bread** and **wine** is frequently used in Scripture as a symbol of the fact that God gives comfort and cheer to people (Gen. 14:18; 1 Sam. 16:20; 25:18; Neh. 5:15; Lam. 2:12).

9:8 It was difficult in ancient times to keep white **garments** clean (read the analogy in Is. 1:18). White garments and ointments—**oil**—were symbols of joy and purity.

9:9 Marriage is the gift of God. "Marriage is honorable" and the marriage bed should be kept "undefiled," instructed the writer of Hebrews (13:4). Marriage is to be cherished (Prov. 5:15–20) and unfaithfulness avoided (Prov. 5:1–14). **vain life:** That is, life that passes so quickly.

9:10 It is possible that the apostle Paul had this verse in mind when he wrote, "And whatever you do, do it heartily, as to the Lord and not to men" (Col. 3:23). **no work . . . in the grave:** This affirmation is not a denial of a personal future state after death. Yet in relation to this world, the possibilities of working and learning have ceased. If we plan to do anything to the glory of God in this world, we had better do it while we still have time (John 9:4).

9:11–13 We would like to think that the best always win, that the deserving are always rewarded. But our experience shows that these expectations are not always realized. **not to the swift . . . strong . . . wise . . . men of understanding . . . men of skill:** These five assets were enjoyed by individuals. But while some planned and counted on their assets, God in the end determined their lot. Who was speedier than Asahel (2 Sam. 2:22, 23), stronger than Samson (Judg. 16:19), wiser than Solomon (1

Kin. 11:1–25), more discerning than Ahithophel (2 Sam. 16:23; 17:5–14), or more learned than Moses (Ex. 2:11–15; Acts 7:22)? Yet each met his limit and was countered by God.

9:14–18 Here is a parable about how an unstoppable military operation against a small city was prevented by the wisdom of one **poor** but **wise man.** The conclusion is that wisdom is preferable to strength and should be heeded.

10:1 Just as one fly can ruin a whole batch of **ointment,** so an ounce of folly will spoil a pound of wisdom.

10:2 In ancient thought, the **right hand** was the place of honor and favor, while the left hand was the reverse.

10:3 There are times when even **a fool** acts appropriately, yet he remains a fool.

10:4, 5 conciliation pacifies: This proverb is similar to many ancient sayings that were used to train courtiers and diplomats.

10:6 Folly . . . dignity: Things are simply not always what we think they ought to be (9:11); but God is still in control and He works His good purposes through events we do not understand.

10:7 servants on horses: In the ancient Middle East, such a reversal of the normal roles of servant and master was felt to be an outrage against society.

10:8, 9 digs a pit (v. 8): The idea of just retribution is still the expectation (Prov. 26:27). **quarries stones:** There are certain risks attendant to certain occupations.

10:10 The wise person will sharpen the **ax.** A person of limited training will have to work harder, as though with a dull ax, than someone wiser whose tools are in order.

10:11 A serpent may bite: Along with the preceding verses, the point made here is that an unused skill is wasted.

10:12, 13 It is the inability of the **fool** to choose his words carefully that will bring about his own destruction.

10:14 who . . . after him: This rhetorical question about the fool's lack of knowledge about the future is one of the repeated themes of Ecclesiastes. The same question is asked in 3:22; 6:12; 8:7; in part in 9:12; and especially in the grand conclusion of 12:14.

10:15 go to the city: If **fools** are so untrustworthy in ordinary affairs, how can they be trusted when they express their opinion about the hereafter?

10:16 Pity those with leaders so young or inexperienced that they lose control over their areas of responsibility or who spend their nights banqueting into the early **morning.**

10:17 Useful nobility expresses itself in a sense of responsibility and deference to social order. This verse is an argument for propriety.

proper time: Here is Solomon's case for moderation and orderliness.

10:18 All forms of **laziness** bring houses and lives into disrepair.

10:19 money answers everything: Rather than being cynical or critical about wealth or the rich, this comment is to be taken in the context of the dissolute nobles (v. 16) and banqueters (v. 17). Wealth for them is only pleasure and a means of having fun.

10:20 a bird of the air: We should watch what we say, for we never know who is listening.

11:1 Cast your bread upon the waters: Verses 1–6 emphasize the element of risk and uncertainty in commercial and agricultural enterprises. Thus, if the preceding proverbs in ch. 10 deal with royalty and leaders, these in vv. 1–6 deal with common people. Men and women must venture forth judiciously if they are ever to realize a gain, even though there is always a certain amount of risk.

11:2 seven, and also to eight: This urges us to be generous to as many as possible—and then some.

11:3 Regardless of which way a **tree falls,** someone is going to get the use of its wood, so stop worrying that it did not fall on your side (or even hoping that it will).

11:4 will not sow: The person who is so cautious that he must wait for the ideal time before he makes a move is doomed to fail.

11:5 Some works of God defy explanation. **who makes everything:** The concept of God as Creator in Ecclesiastes is not limited to 12:1. The inability of humans to know God's works apart from knowing Him is one of the themes of this book (3:11; 8:17; 9:12).

11:6 which will prosper: Do not hold back from getting involved. Let the success or failure of a task rest in the hand of God—but get to the task.

11:7 light is sweet: An affirmation of the joy of life, despite all the troubles that the book has presented.

11:8 remember the days of darkness: In appreciating the opportunities of life, we must think more seriously about death. This is contrasted with the joy of working while it is still light.

11:9 If Solomon was the author of this book and wrote it late in his life, then the point becomes even more clear. He was speaking to young people (Prov. 1:8; 2:1; 3:1), encouraging them to learn the lessons that he had learned over the course of his extraordinary life. **Walk**

> *Let the success or failure of a task rest in the hand of God— but get to the task.*

in the ways of your heart: This verse is not an invitation to live sinfully in sensual pleasure (as Num. 15:39 describes). Instead, it urges young people to enjoy themselves completely while not forgetting that God will review the quality of their life (3:17; 12:14).

11:10 Tragically, **youth** does not last; it too passes like a vapor. We all seem to discover that "we get old too soon and smart too late."

12:1–8 Most interpreters have argued that this poem is an allegory of old age. This is the view advocated here. Other views include: (1) a description of a winter's day as a metaphor of old age; (2) a description of people's reaction to a fearful thunderstorm; (3) the figure of a ruined house representing the failure of human efforts; and (4) the decay of a house representing death and human frailty.

12:1 Remember now your Creator: Solomon does not call for mere mental cognizance of the person of God; in robust biblical terms he calls for the appropriate actions that go along with that recollection of the living God. For example, when the Lord "remembered" Hannah (1 Sam. 1:19), He did more than call her to mind; He acted on her behalf and she conceived a child. Our "remembering" of Him is to be in thought, word, and act.

12:2 The person is losing his sight.

12:3 Verses 3–6 list the bodily infirmities that increasingly hinder an older person from serving God. If the **house** stands for the aging body, then the **keepers** are the arms and hands. **strong men bow down:** The legs are bent in feebleness and the knees cannot be depended on for support. **grinders cease:** The teeth, now fewer than before, cannot chew the food as well as they once did. **those that look through the windows grow dim:** The eyes begin to lose their sight.

12:4 doors are shut in the streets: Just as the jaws of Leviathan are called the "doors of his face" (Job 41:14), so the lips and jaws are possibly intended here. **sound of grinding is low:** A depiction of toothless old age when eating only soft foods makes little or no noise. **daughters of music are brought low:** The ability to hear—and thus the ability to make and enjoy music—wanes.

12:5 afraid of height: Things that used to be a regular part of life now become threatening. **almond tree blossoms:** Hair turns white. **grasshopper is a burden:** This may refer to the halting step of the elderly as they hobble along on their canes. **desire fails:** This is

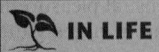

IN LIFE   Old Age Comes to All

Young people commonly think and act as if they were going to live forever. For that reason, Eccl. 12 paints a picture of old age and introduces it to young people with the warning, "Remember your Creator in the days of your youth."

Certainly there are many elderly who defy this portrait. Yet in the main, the conditions mentioned are typical. Ecclesiastes warns the young to remember God before earthly life ends. Several images convey the coming of death and mourning: a silver cord is loosened, a bowl is broken, a pitcher is shattered, a wheel ceases to turn (12:6), the "dust" of the body returns to earth (12:7; compare Gen. 3:19; Job 34:15), and the spirit goes to God, presumably for judgment (Eccl. 12:7, 14).

This is the fate of every human being. No matter how young or old we are, every day each of us is a bit closer to death. Given that reality, Ecclesiastes challenges young people to live unto God, for life is empty and meaningless without Him.

---

generally understood as a reference to a vanishing sexual desire. Then comes death: **eternal home.**

12:6 Some suggest that **silver cord** refers to the spinal cord. **golden bowl is broken:** This may refer to the brain. **pitcher shattered at the fountain:** One suggestion is that this is a failing heart. **wheel broken at the well:** The system of veins and arteries radiating out from the heart might have appeared to the ancients like the spokes on a wheel. An alternative explanation of this verse is that each of the four images represent death. That is, there is no physical representation intended in these images as in those of vv. 3–5. Instead, this verse describes the destruction of four significant objects—a demonstration of the finality of this life.

12:7 dust will return: These words refer clearly to the universal fate of the descendants of Adam and Eve. **spirit will return:** This is a clear allusion to Gen. 2:7. The term *spirit* is the same used in earlier passages (3:19, 21; 8:8).

12:8 The refrain of **vanity**—the brevity of life—is here repeated. It is possible that the book originally ended with these words.

12:9 Early on in his book, **the Preacher** speaks of his pursuit of wisdom (1:12–2:26). It is possible that he speaks of himself here in the third person (as in 1:1, 2). Probably it was an editor under the guiding hand of God who wrote these evaluations of Solomon, much as Joshua or some other editor wrote an evaluation of Moses under the influence of God's Spirit (Deut. 34). **pondered . . . sought out . . . set in order:** The three verbs that describe Solomon's activity may also be translated "weighed . . . examined . . . and arranged."

12:10 The Preacher devotes special care to write **acceptable** words—pleasant words, words

of grace—and **words of truth.** The truth referred to here is the truth from God.

12:11 Just as an ox goad prods an animal in the right direction, so will the words of this book when they are properly understood. **well-driven nails:** The nails, or "pegs," referred to here are the same as in 2 Chr. 3:9; Jer. 10:4. These are hooks in tents where families hung the clothes and pots needed for everyday life. Here they refer to mental hooks giving stability and perspective to life. **by one Shepherd:** Kings were typically compared to shepherds, and Solomon is claiming that the source of his ideas is God, the Shepherd of Israel (Ps. 80:1).

12:12 Many other **books** may weary their readers. Careful study of Ecclesiastes will have the opposite effect as it instructs, warns, and admonishes its readers.

12:13 To **fear God** is one of the major themes of this book and of wisdom literature in the OT. To fear God is to respond to Him in awe, reverence, and wonder, to serve Him in purity of action, and to shun evil and any worship of anything else in His universe. **keep His commandments:** The commandments of the Law are in view here. Jesus summed them up as to "love the LORD your God" and "your neighbor as yourself" (Matt. 22:34–40). **man's all:** We are whole or complete only when we fear God and obey His commandments. What profit is there in living? If we follow what this book has said, we will have a relationship with God and find life in Him.

12:14 judgment: This same teaching is echoed by the apostle Paul in 2 Cor. 5:10. Death is not the end. All of life will be reviewed by our righteous Lord (3:17). Life must be lived through faith with the values of the eternal God in view.

The
Song of Solomon

THE SONG OF SOLOMON IS A MOVING LOVE story between a young country girl and King Solomon. In delicate poetry, the lovers express intense passion and deep longing for each other. The young girl compares her love for her husband to the anticipation of a frantic search, while Solomon likens his bride's beauty to picturesque gardens and delicious fruit. Yet even in this eloquent expression of the passion

between a bride and bridegroom, there is an exhortation to remain sexually pure before marriage (2:7). In this way, the book celebrates human sexuality within the context of marriage.

The book has not always been understood in this way. Jewish scholars around the time of the birth of Christ interpreted the book allegorically, stating that it describes the love of God for Israel. Similarly, some Christians have taught that the book speaks of the mystical relationship of the Lord Jesus Christ and His bride, the church.

However, one does not need to get into allegorical meanings to understand this book. The Song of Solomon celebrates the beauty and intimacy of married love in a narrative poem. It teaches that a lasting marriage requires dedication, commitment, and strong loyalty between husband and wife. The Song also presents an idealized picture of how human love can be expressed under God's blessing. This is a very important issue. Some critics have claimed that Christianity's standards for marriage ignore or undervalue sexual relationships. But the Song of Solomon refutes this. It reiterates the biblical

admonition against sex outside of marriage, but it also affirms that God not only approves of, but also encourages, sexual pleasure within marriage.

Perhaps nowhere in the Bible is the literary culture of the Middle East more apparent than in this book. The genre or literary form of the Song of Solomon is unique in the Bible. It is a lyric idyll, a type of love song. As in the case of the Book of Job, the Song of Solomon reveals its treasures to the patient reader who approaches the book on its own terms, searching for and meditating on its meaning. The form of the lyric idyll displays two features. The first is that speeches and events do not necessarily follow in chronological order. At times the story line remains suspended while the audience views scenes from earlier or yet untold incidents.

A second feature of the lyric idyll is the use of the chorus. In addition to the two characters that carry the story line—the Shulamite and King Solomon—a group of women interrupt certain scenes with brief musical speeches or warnings. Solomon uses the chorus to make transitions from one scene to another, as well as to add emphasis to important themes.

The Song of Solomon retells the romance between King Solomon, the richest king ever to rule Israel, and his beloved bride, who came from a small village in the region of Galilee. Solomon owned vineyards all over the nation. One was close to Baal Hamon in the northernmost part of Galilee near the foothills of the mountains of Lebanon. On one of his visits to this vineyard, Solomon met a young woman. Strangely we never learn her name. She is called simply the Shulamite. For some time he pursued her and made periodic visits to her country home to see her. Finally, he proposed. The Shulamite gave much thought to whether she really loved Solomon and could be happy in the palace of a king. Finally she accepted.

If the Bible is the book about God, then one may well ask what a narrative about human sexuality has to do with theology. This is an even more potent question when one observes that God is never mentioned in the entire text (except possibly in 8:6) nor are there any references to prayer, worship, or piety. In this respect it bears similarities to the Book of Esther, which also does not mention God. Nevertheless, Esther is a story of the redemption of God's people and includes episodes of prayer, fasting, and thanksgiving. Such themes are notably absent from Solomon's poetic story, making it unique among the books of the Bible.

To resolve this difficulty, it is important to remember that the Bible not only describes who God is and what God does; it also tells us what God desires for His people. The Song of Solomon provides an example of how God created male and female to live in happiness and fulfillment. People are created as sexual beings. It would be wrong to suggest that the full experience of our humanity is impossible apart from sexual union in marriage, since this would disqualify the widowed, divorced, and celibate—including our Savior, who was celibate. At the same time, God ordained marriage from the beginning of creation: man and woman were to become one flesh (Gen. 2:25).

Because of its emphasis on human love, this book presents an extraordinary variety of expressions for love, perhaps the richest selection in all Hebrew Scripture. But within this celebration of love, the book condemns unchaste relations outside of marriage—and in particular, sexual experimentation before marriage. Indeed, this book may contain the Bible's strongest argument for chastity before marriage. Ironically because of its explicit language, ancient and modern Jewish sages forbade men to read the book before they were thirty (and presumably kept women from reading it at all). We cannot ignore the sexual content of the book, but we can appreciate the context in which it is placed—a godly marriage. The Song of Solomon is necessary reading not only for the married but also for young people who want to understand God's design for marriage.

The author of the Song of Solomon is Solomon, the son of David and the third king of Israel. He is named as the author and his name appears seven times in the book (1:1, 5; 3:7, 9, 11; 8:11, 12). Even so, some have argued that the references to Solomon may be only a stylistic device and the author may have been from a later period. The arguments for this are incon-

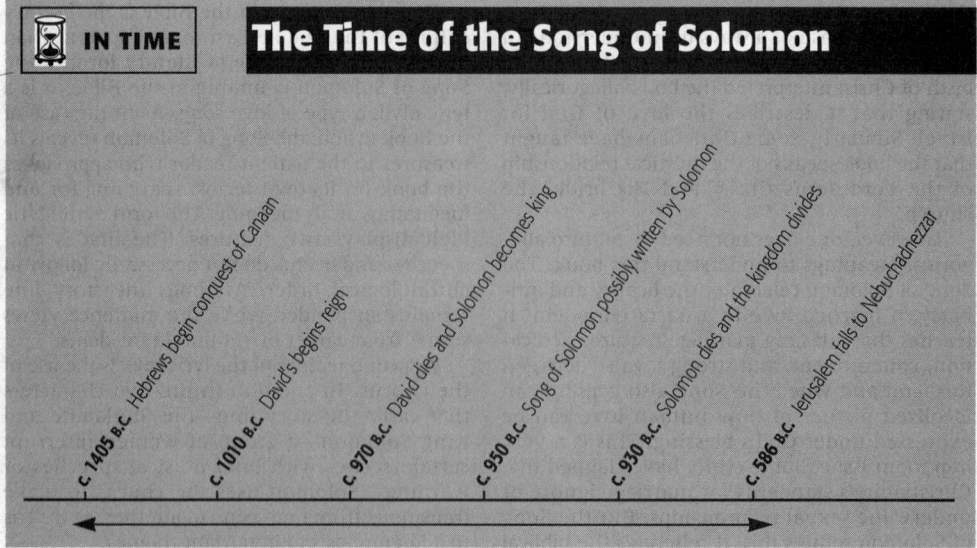

⧗ IN TIME

The Time of the Song of Solomon

c. 1405 B.C. Hebrews begin conquest of Canaan

c. 1010 B.C. David's begins reign

c. 970 B.C. David dies and Solomon becomes king

c. 950 B.C. Song of Solomon possibly written by Solomon

c. 930 B.C. Solomon dies and the kingdom divides

c. 586 B.C. Jerusalem falls to Nebuchadnezzar

clusive. But the fact that Solomon was known for his wisdom and poetry (1 Kin. 4:29–34) partially substantiates his authorship of this book.

Outline

I. Three reflections on the wedding day 1:2–2:7
  A. In the palace 1:2–8
  B. At the banquet table 1:9–14
  C. In the bridal chamber 1:15–2:7
II. Three reflections during the courtship days 2:8–3:5
  A. A springtime visit 2:8–14
  B. Catching the little foxes 2:15–17
  C. A dream of separation 3:1–5
III. Two reflections on the wedding day 3:6–5:1
  A. The wedding procession 3:6–11
  B. The wedding night 4:1–5:1
IV. Five reflections on adjustment to marriage 5:2–8:4
  A. A dream of love refused 5:2–8
  B. A change of attitude 5:9–6:3
  C. The return of Solomon 6:4–10
  D. The Shulamite in the garden 6:11–13
  C. The dance of the double camp 6:14–8:4
V. A final reflection: a vacation in the country 8:5–14

Commentary

1:1 Like the superlative expressions "holy of holies" or "king of kings," **song of songs** means "the loveliest of songs." **which is Solomon's:** There are two principal speakers in this book, the woman (the Shulamite) and the man (Solomon). Even though Solomon wrote this book, the point of view is largely that of his bride.

1:2 This prologue to the book forms the emotional setting for all that follows. **love:** The Hebrew noun used here means sexual love, as it clearly does in Ezek. 16:8 (Prov. 7:18; Ezek. 23:17). This is the Hebrew word that most closely approximates the Greek word *eros*. In the Song of Solomon, this plural word (a mark of intensity) speaks of divinely blessed lovemaking (used also in v. 4; 4:10; 7:12; compare 5:1).

1:3 ointments: It was customary in biblical times to rub the body with fragrant *ointments* (oils) after a bath in preparation for a festive occasion (Ruth 3:3). **your name:** The Shulamite speaks of her beloved's reputation as akin to a lovely aroma; he was an object of desire to young women everywhere. The term **virgins** is the same word used at Is. 7:14. The word means women of marriageable age (they are the same

as the "daughters of Jerusalem" in v. 5). **love:** Here the common Hebrew verb meaning "to love" is used of romantic feelings (as in Gen. 24:67); in other passages this verb means to choose someone (an act of the will; Deut. 6:5). Thus this Hebrew verb shares some, but not all, of the meanings of the Greek verb *agapao*.

1:4 The complexity of the interchanges in this book are illustrated in this verse. The headings help sort out the speakers. **The king:** This is Solomon; yet aside from the title (v. 1), he is not identified by name as a protagonist until 3:7, 9, 11 (his name in v. 5 is part of a descriptive phrase). **chambers:** This means the bridal chamber. The verse ends with the thoughts of the young woman as she gazes at her lover: **Rightly do they love you** employs the verb for *love* found in v. 3, indicating romantic feelings.

1:5 The Shulamite compares her **dark** coloring, acquired from long hours working in the vineyards (v. 6) with the lighter complexion of the city maidens. The point here is her class and station in life. Unlike the young women of the court in Jerusalem who had been raised in comfort and conditions of ease, this woman had worked as a field hand under the blazing sun. **but lovely:** She knows that her beauty is not diminished by her more rugged manner of living. Her groom assures her that this is truly the case (v. 8). The rare term *lovely* is used to describe physical beauty in this book (v. 10; 2:14; 4:3; 6:4; compare the word in v. 8); in the Psalms this word speaks of the beauty of true worship to the living God (Pss. 33:1; 147:1). **O daughters of Jerusalem:** These are women who serve as the attendants of the bride. These woman also serve as the chorus in the book. They are the same as the "virgins" of v. 3.

1:6 Her **own vineyard** refers to her appearance. Unlike the beautiful women of the royal court, the Shulamite had not had the lifestyle or the resources to take much time for her appearance. Still, it was she who swept away the king's heart. The Shulamite uses the word *vineyard* again with a different twist in 8:12.

1:7 you whom I love: A more literal rendering might be, "whom my soul (my inner being) loves." Here the young woman mentally addresses Solomon, her husband. She pictures him as the shepherd of Israel. **one who veils herself:** Solomon, as king, was busy with affairs of state. The young bride does not want to veil herself as a prostitute would in order to get his attention, nor does she want to be left alone. She desires to be his true companion.

1:8 If you do not know . . . feed your little goats: It would be better if she returned to the borders of Lebanon and the life of the farm rather than live alone and anxious in

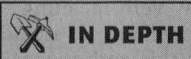 **IN DEPTH** | **The Sweet-Smelling Aroma of Love**

Smell is the most evocative of the senses, and so it is not surprising that the Song of Solomon, like many romantic poems, alludes to numerous scents and fragrances. All have to do with the sweet-smelling aroma of love:

- *Spikenard* (Song 1:12; 4:13–14), a fragrant, costly oil derived from the dried roots and stems of nard, an herb of Asia. It could be used either as an ointment or made into expensive perfume.
- *Myrrh* (1:13; 3:6; 4:14; 5:5, 13), an aromatic, resinous extract of a stiff-branched tree with white flowers and plum-like fruit. Myrrh was an ingredient in anointing oil (Ex. 30:23) and perfume (Ps. 45:8; Prov. 7:17), and was used in purification rites for women (Esth. 2:12).
- *Henna* (Song 1:14; 4:13), a large plant whose fragrant white flowers were often exchanged as a token of friendship. Solomon was known to have henna vineyards at En Gedi. The plants were used to make an orange-red dye valued as a cosmetic.
- *Cedar* (1:17), the aromatic wood of the massive evergreen trees which in Solomon's time covered the hills and mountains of Lebanon (hence the "fragrance of Lebanon," 4:11). Solomon imported enormous quantities of cedar in order to build the temple and other projects, including his palace complex known as the House of the Forest of Lebanon (1 Kin. 5:1–10; 7:1–8)—perhaps the location of the scene described in Song 1:17.
- *Frankincense* (3:6; 4:6, 14), an aromatic gum resin obtained from the Boswellia tree in northeast Africa and Arabia. The highly fragrant substance was used in the Hebrew religious rites (Ex. 30:7, 34; Lev. 2:1; 24:7) and was considered a symbol of religious fervor. Frankincense was a valuable item of trade in the ancient world.
- *Saffron* (Song 4:14), a product of crocus blooms which were dried and pressed into cakes. The product was used as a coloring for curries and stews, or as a perfume for floors and especially for weddings.
- *Calamus* (4:14), or sweet cane, a fragrant, reed-like grass that grew along streams and river banks. The leaves are ginger-flavored when crushed. Calamus is listed as an ingredient of the anointing oil used in Hebrew worship (Ex. 30:23).
- *Cinnamon* (Song 4:14), a product of the cinnamon tree native to Ceylon. The oil of the tree was used as a perfume both for secular (Prov. 7:17) and religious (Ex. 30:32) purposes.
- *Aloes* (Song 4:14), the highly valued wood of the large eaglewood tree native to India. It was made into perfume and incense.
- *Apples* (2:5; 7:8), or possibly apricots, which may have been imported from groves in the Caucasus region to the north of Canaan.
- *Mandrakes* (7:13), perennial herbs with dark green leaves and small bluish-purple flowers in winter. The plant's spring-time fruit is yellow, fragrant, and sweet. Said to have narcotic qualities, mandrakes were called "love apples" and were used as a love potion (compare Gen. 30:14–16).

Solomon's palace. The point of this verse is that one should always count the cost of marriage to a particular person *before* the marriage. **O fairest among women:** The term *fairest* is the usual Hebrew word for "beautiful."

1:9 Here is yet another term for **love** in the book, the rarer word meaning "dear companion" (compare at vv. 2, 3). **my filly:** In Solomon's time the horse was the companion of kings. Solomon loved horses, particularly those from Egypt. Eventually he had a stable of twelve thousand horses with 1,400 chariots (1 Kin. 10:26).

1:10 Steeds were ornamented with costly harnesses and the most elegant of headgear. In return for her affirmative response to his advances, the king promises costly gifts. She is indeed beautiful, but with the expensive adornments that he will give her she will have an unsurpassable beauty. She is to have necklaces of silver discs and gold beads. Such jewelry is to replace the poor ornaments worn by the maiden.

1:11 ornaments: These are kind words from the women of the court (1:4). Their kindness is remarkable, since each of these women may have hoped to be chosen by the king (as v. 3 indicates).

1:12 his table: That is, the setting of the wedding banquet.

1:13, 14 This verse refers to an oriental custom for a woman to wear a small bag of **myrrh,** a perfumed ointment, around her neck at night. All the next day a lovely fragrance would linger about her. The young woman says that beginning that night, it would be her husband who would lie with her. **my beloved:** Here the noun *beloved* is related to the word translated "love" in v. 2, referring to sexual love. **En Gedi:** David, Solomon's father, had found refreshment and protection from the vindictive king Saul in this oasis on the eastern shore of the Dead Sea (1 Sam. 24).

1:15 Behold, you are fair: The word *fair* means "beautiful" (as in v. 8). **my love:** This term is used for the first time in the book; it means "dear friend." **dove's eyes:** The idea is purity, innocence and beauty (4:1; 5:12; compare 2:14; 5:2).

1:16 The word **handsome** used here is the masculine counterpart of the term translated "fair" in v. 15.

1:17 beams of our houses are cedar: *Houses* may mean "grand house" or "mansion." As the Shulamite lies on their wedding bed (v. 16), she observes the marvelous cedar beams above her head. The opulence of Solomon's personal and public buildings in Jerusalem is well documented (1 Kin. 7:1–12).

2:1 I am the rose of Sharon. The Plain of Sharon was famous for its flowers and pasturelands. The maiden is saying, I am merely a flower of the plain. I am only one among a host of others.

2:2 Solomon takes the young bride's words (v. 1) comparing herself to a simple flower and assures her that, beside her, the fancy women of the city are but **thorns.**

2:3 The **apple tree** and the raisin cakes (v. 5) are symbols for sexual passion in ancient love songs.

2:4 the banqueting house: The literal meaning of the phrase is "the house of wine," used because of the role that *wine* plays not only in feasting, but especially in weddings in biblical cultures (1:2). In the Bible, wine is a symbol of joy (Ps. 104:15) and the drinking of wine is associated with joyful occasions. **his banner:** This may be the same term as used in Num. 1:52, meaning "standard" or "flag." Even today, Jewish weddings take place under a "banner" or covering. **love:** This is the first use in the book of the common noun for *love* related to the verb in v. 3. This noun corresponds somewhat to the well-known Greek noun *agape*, which refers to a self-sacrificial love for others (1 Cor. 13).

2:5, 6 These verses describe the joy of sexual expression between a husband and wife. **raisins . . . apples:** Ancient symbols of sexual passion (v. 3). **lovesick:** These are the words of one overwhelmed with love.

2:7 Here the Shulamite speaks to her attendants in their virginity and entreats them (**I charge you**) to maintain their sexual purity until marriage (3:5; 8:4). **by the gazelles. . . does:** She beseeches the young women by all things that are beautiful. **love:** This is the noun used in v. 4, demonstrating that this word may also be used of sexual passion. The association of this charge with the description of sexual intimacy in v. 6 suggests that the warning is against awakening such desires before **it pleases**—that is, at the proper and appropriate time within the bounds of marriage. While the Book of Proverbs

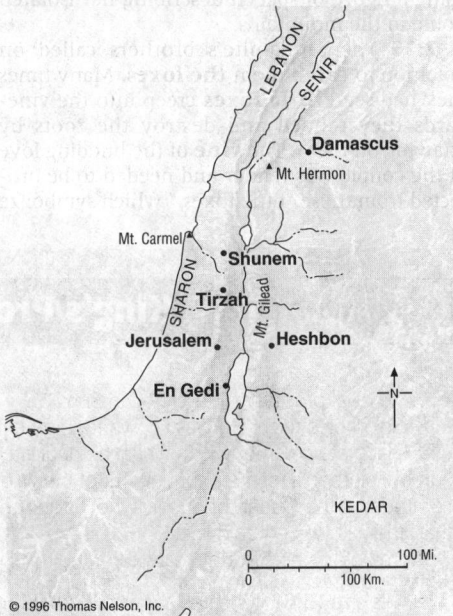

Places Named in the Song of Solomon

From the peaks of Lebanon to the streets of Jerusalem (4:8; 6:4), the love story in the Song of Solomon takes place in a variety of settings. The lovers speak of, and to, each other with several word pictures, including "the rose of Sharon" (2:1), "the lily of the valleys" (2:1), and "the vineyards of En Gedi" (1:14).

frequently exhorts young men to live in sexual purity (Prov. 7), the Song of Solomon frequently addresses its warnings to young women.

2:8, 9 leaping . . . skipping: This is the young bride's imaginative way of recalling the joy *she* experienced at her husband's arrival. The same is true of her words for him: **gazelle . . . stag,** animals that symbolize virility. **windows . . . lattice:** That is, Solomon was looking at *her* through an opening in the wall.

2:10 my love: A term of endearment meaning "my dear friend" (1:15). **my fair one:** Solomon describes his bride as "beautiful" (1:8, 15).

2:11–13 the winter is past: By this Solomon means that the time of joy has come; it is the summer of their love. Solomon may have come at a time of great beauty in the fields and forests where the young woman lived; he uses the beauty of creation to describe the ripeness of time for their love.

2:14 Solomon's great find in this young woman is occasioned in part by her shy charm. **in the clefts:** Solomon speaks of the Shulamite using a figure of speech describing her isolated home in the mountains.

2:15 The Shulamite's brothers called on Solomon to **catch** them the **foxes.** Many times they had seen **little foxes** creep into the vineyards they tended and destroy the roots by gnawing on them. The **vine** of the budding love of the couple was tender and needed to be protected from these "little foxes," which symbolize the problems of life that may gnaw away at a relationship.

2:16 My beloved is mine, and I am his: The expression describes the mutual intimacy that a married couple experiences. Both belong to each other (6:3; compare 7:10).

2:17 Until the day breaks: Here the woman wishes the king to leave for the night. The book is pervaded with the sense of doing what is right at the appropriate time. Here, she wishes him to flee like a **gazelle.** Later, she will want him to rush to her like one (8:14).

3:1 on my bed: This is a dream that took place before they were married. The young woman was becoming concerned about what she would be getting into in this royal marriage.

3:2, 3 Her frantic search for her beloved is initially unsuccessful. Twice in these verses she describes him as **the one I love.** In each case, the wording is "the one whom my soul (or my inner being) loves."

3:4 At last she finds him, using the same phrasing (**the one I love**) of vv. 2, 3. In her dream she takes him to her mother's **house.** That is, the worry of his absence is intolerable to her; she wants him to move back with her to her familiar home and lifestyle.

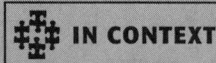 **IN CONTEXT** | **A King's Procession**

The royal procession described in Song 3:6–11 reflects the splendor and pageantry that marked Solomon's reign. He was known for his wealth (1 Kin. 3:13; 10:23), and Scripture reports on the elaborate ceremony with which he dedicated the temple (1 Kin. 8; 2 Chr. 6). The poem's depiction of Solomon's retinue "coming out of the wilderness" on its way to the royal wedding recalls the comment of the Queen of Sheba, who, having seen the magnificence of Solomon's court, admitted that "the half was not told me."

Some of the noteworthy features of the royal procession include:

- Its size (3:6). It creates a great cloud of dust along the road, "like pillars of smoke."
- Its attractiveness (3:6). The dust of the procession is mingled with fragrant wafts of myrrh, frankincense, and other aromatic powders. The observer is drawn toward the spectacle by its delightful scent.
- The royal guard (3:7, 8). Sixty hand-picked men surround Solomon as an escort.
- The elaborate litter (3:9, 10). Solomon's "couch" (3:7) or "palanquin," like so many other furnishings of his court, is made of cedar, imported from Lebanon. The wood is either covered, decorated, or used in conjunction with supports of silver and gold. The cushions, and perhaps the curtains as well, are made from purple, a costly cloth as valuable as gold in the ancient world.

Perhaps on this special occasion the chair is adorned with flowers—"paved with love by the daughters of Jerusalem." The palanquin is probably borne by a detachment of slaves, though the text does not mention them.

- A throng of cheering women (3:11). The women of Jerusalem greet the procession, perhaps singing and dancing as on other festive occasions (Ex. 15:20; 1 Sam. 18:6–7).

3:5 do not stir up: Again there is a strong warning against premarital sex. People should not allow sexual passion to stir before they have gotten to know each other in other ways (2:8–17), until they have worked out the problems of their relationship (the "little foxes," 2:15–17), and until they have counted the costs of marriage (3:1–4).

3:6 Who is this coming: Contrast the bold, royal journey here with the earlier, playful approach in 2:8. **pillars of smoke:** This is language reminiscent of a divine visitation (Ex. 19:18). **perfumed:** The precious ointments here are marks of luxury and royalty; later, on the woman, these elements would be symbols of love (4:6).

3:7, 8 The **couch** was a sedan chair with poles projecting from the front and back so that a person could be carried by several bearers (vv. 9, 10). The Shulamite was being carried to the wedding and to her groom on Solomon's own couch. **valiant men:** The term describes war heroes, as v. 8 explains. **fear:** That is, these warriors were prepared for any threat.

3:9, 10 Apparently Solomon had ordered this couch (vv. 7, 8) to be designed and built especially for the wedding. To the Shulamite, the couch's rich ornamentation of **silver** and **gold** is less significant than the fact that the couch represents Solomon's **love** and care for her (2:4).

3:11 O daughters of Zion: These are the Daughters of Jerusalem (1:5). **and see:** For a wedding to be recognized in ancient Israel, it had to be a public event. Such a day has always been regarded as a day of **gladness** (Ps. 19:5). **the crown:** Solomon's royal symbol was appropriately worn at this wedding.

4:1 Solomon lavishly praises his bride's great beauty. He uses verbal symbols of loveliness to paint a picture of the breathtaking charm of the Shulamite. **Dove's eyes** (2:14) are a picture of purity, innocence, and beauty (as in 1:15). The bride's **veil** would have covered the rest of her face, leaving only her beautiful eyes to be seen (2:14; 5:7). The king compared the movement of her flowing **hair** to the graceful movement of **a flock of goats** in their descent **down from Mount Gilead.**

4:2–5 The king rhapsodizes on the perfection of his bride's **teeth,** her **lips** and facial features, her **neck,** and at last her **breasts. Scarlet** (v. 3) describes luxuriance and beauty; the **pomegranate** speaks of sweetness; the term **lovely** is the same rare word used first in 1:5. The **tower of David** (v. 4) pictures strength and grace; the **fawns** (v. 5) have exquisite loveliness.

4:6 Until the day breaks: The couple's first night together was a precious time (8:14).

the mountain of myrrh . . . the hill of frankincense: These playful names again give us a glimpse into their passionate love for each other (1:13, 14; 2:6).

4:7 fair: The king has used this term for beauty before (v. 1). However, the difference here is in the word **all.** Now he rhapsodizes on how perfect his bride is; every part of her is attractive.

4:8 These words demonstrate Solomon's sensitivity to his new bride's emotions at this point. He calls her mind back from thoughts afar off. He says, "**Come** back **with me.**" His use of the word **spouse** for the first time is appropriate here on their wedding bed (vv. 9, 10, 11, 12; 5:1).

4:9 My sister, my spouse: This strange pairing of words was based on the idea that in marriage a couple became "related." The woman was dignified as a member of the king's family.

4:10 your love . . . your love: That is, erotic love.

4:11 lips . . . honey and milk: The sweetness of his bride's kisses are like food to him (5:1; compare 1:2).

4:12 spring . . . fountain: Solomon evokes thoughts of refreshment and delight. His use of the words **enclosed . . . shut up . . . sealed** indicate, in a poetic manner, his wife's virginity on their wedding night. This was the treasure she brought to him, and which she adjured the other young women in the court to maintain for their wedding nights as well (2:7).

4:13–15 pleasant fruits: These verses expand the images of the garden and the fountain for sexual love from v. 12.

4:16 The bride is now ready to accept her lover for the first time to her **garden.** She calls on the **wind** to blow through. That is, she is ready to make love to her husband for the first time.

5:1 drunk my wine: This verse is a necessary part of the preceding chapter. At the conclusion of their lovemaking, the groom speaks of his complete satisfaction in his beautiful bride.

5:2–7 I sleep: These words begin a section (vv. 2–8) that most likely is another dream sequence (3:1–5). The bride dreams that her lover is coming to her, but she has already washed, removed her **robe,** and gotten into bed (v. 3). She finally goes to the **door** to let him in, but he is gone. Her sorrow at this drives her into the **city** to search for him. The **watchmen** find her and are hostile toward her.

5:8, 9 The bride asks the **daughters of Jerusalem** to help her in her search. But they question what is so special about the one for whom she seeks.

🔍 IN FOCUS | "beloved"

(Heb. *dod*) (4:16; 1 Sam. 14:50; Prov. 7:18; Is. 5:1) Strong's #1730: In Hebrew love poetry, *dod* is a term of endearment used for a male loved one, usually translated beloved (Is. 5:1). The writer of the Song of Solomon uses this word 32 times. The name David is derived from *dod* and carries the same sense, meaning "Beloved One." When *dod* is used in narrative, it means "uncle" or another close male relative (1 Sam. 14:50).

5:10 My beloved is white and ruddy. The bride responds to the question of v. 9 with a poem extolling the handsomeness of her husband.

5:11–16 His head is like the finest gold (literally, gold of gold). Gold that has been doubly refined. His **eyes** with irises surrounded by clear white were perfectly spaced and are set as gems in a ring. His beard upon his **cheeks** is compared to beds of aromatic plants. His lips are pictured as the dispensers of spices and myrrh. His **hands** resemble golden cylinders, and his body reminds her of polished ivory. His legs are symbols of strength and stability. They are pillars of marble or alabaster set upon foundations of purest gold. **His mouth:** The members of Solomon have been described in striking terms. He is, however, no inanimate statue. Most pleasing of all is the voice that emanates from this noble and commanding man. His voice is altogether lovely (i.e., melodious).

6:1 The chorus members now join in the search. In the dream sequence, we suspect that the chorus is well aware of his location. It is only the bride who needs to discover his whereabouts.

6:2 his garden . . . his flock: This is a change of language from 4:12–16. On their wedding night, the bride presented herself to Solomon as his garden. But he has another "garden" to tend as well, and it is one in which he also takes great pleasure. This is the "garden" of his work, his responsibility as the king of Israel. The flock is the people; the lilies represent the produce of the land. This realization leads to the strong affirmation in the next verse that the husband and wife belong to each other. Another use of the word *garden* occurs in 6:11.

6:3 I am my beloved's, and my beloved is mine: These words are an inversion of the words of 2:16; compare also 7:10. **He feeds his flock among the lilies:** With these words the bride comes to terms with the reality that, as much as she and the king are in love, he still has other responsibilities and so does she. His work as king makes him the shepherd of his people, yet his love for her does not

necessarily diminish because of his devotion to his work.

6:4–7 beautiful . . . lovely: The first is the word usually translated "fair" (1:8, 15; 4:1); the second is the rarer word for beauty used first in 1:5. **Tirzah . . . Jerusalem:** Solomon idealizes the beauty of these cities, even as people speak of beautiful cities in our own day. **army with banners:** From a distance, there is a kind of beauty in the sight of an army, especially for a king.

6:8, 9 sixty . . . eighty: This use of numbers is a rhetorical device to emphasize that the bride alone is Solomon's love. **praised:** Here is a use of this verb in a context other than the worship of God.

6:10 morning . . . moon . . . sun: The king's rapture at the very thought of his wife lifts his soul to the heavens.

6:11 Here the term **garden** refers to the Shulamite's homeland.

6:12, 13 The chorus calls the bride back from her daydreams and reminds her that she is Solomon's queen. **Shulamite:** The term is not a name but a title. It may mean "a woman from the village of Shulam." However, the hometown of the woman is usually thought to be Shunem. Her title sounds very much like the Hebrew pronunciation for the name Solomon. Both words are related to the Hebrew word for peace (*shalom*). **the dance of the two camps:** In Hebrew, the word is Mahanaim, the town where David fled as a fugitive from Absalom (2 Sam. 17:24). The woman offers to dance before her beloved so that he might enjoy her beauty in lovely motion.

7:1–4 Solomon rhapsodizes on the beauty of his bride. In the eyes of love, one's lover has a beauty that transcends what others might see. **prince's daughter:** Although of common birth (1:2), the Shulamite has regal beauty. **the curves of your thighs:** The Hebrew wording suggests not only her form but the fluid motion of her dance (6:13).

7:5 Your head crowns you like Mount Carmel: The marginal reading *crimson*, from Heb. *karmil*, preserves the parallelism with the next

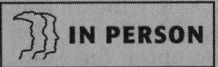 **IN PERSON** | **Who Was the Shulamite?**

I n only one instance does the Song of Solomon identify the bride in the poem as "the Shulamite" (Song 6:13), and no other references directly reveal her identity. Who, then, was this young woman who so passionately became the object of Solomon's affections? Several suggestions have been made:

- She may have been a woman from Shunem, a town in the territory of Issachar near Jezreel (Josh. 19:18). If so, she would have been known as a Shunammite, but by interchanging the Hebrew letters *lamed* ("l") and *nun* ("n"), which was commonly done, she could also have been known as a Shulamite.
- She may have been Abishag, the Shunammite maiden who was at David's side in his old age (1 Kin. 1:1–4, 15). Upon David's death, one of his sons, Adonijah, requested that he be given Abishag. But this was improper in that Solomon, David's named successor, was entitled to her along with David's other wives and concubines (2:17–22).
- It may be that "Shulamite" could also be rendered "Shelomith," which would make the name a feminine title related to the name Solomon, "the Solomoness."

clause better. Her flowing tresses and beautiful head are a source of greater delight to Solomon. The king is literally captivated by them.

7:6 This verse summarizes the king's joy in her beauty. **fair:** This term (here a verb) for beauty is used often in the book (1:8, 15). **love:** Here he uses the common noun for *love* as in 2:4.

7:7, 8 palm tree: This is a sexual image that has its basis in the pollination of palm trees. To fertilize a female palm tree, the gardener climbs the male tree and takes some of its flowers. Then he climbs the female tree and ties the pollen-bearing flowers among its branches.

7:9, 10 desire: This word is used only three times in the Bible. Here it clearly means "sexual longing."

7:11, 12 She was familiar with all the environs, but especially the **vineyards** (1:6; compare 8:12). **my love:** This refers to a sexual embrace (the same word is used in 1:2).

7:13 From early times, **mandrakes** were associated with fertility (Gen. 30:14).

8:1, 2 like my brother: The love of the bride for her beloved was so intense that she wished that she had known him dearly his entire life.

8:2 spiced wine: The wines of the ancient world were often flavored with aromatic spices on special occasions (Prov. 9:2).

8:3, 4 left . . . right: The repetition of 2:6, 7 punctuates both the joy of sexual intimacy within marriage and the warnings against sexual activity before marriage.

8:5 The king takes his bride back to her home country for a visit. The **apple tree** symbolizes the place where the Shulamite had been

awakened sexually and where her mother had given birth to her.

8:6 A **seal** is a symbol of possession or ownership. The Shulamite wants the king to feel a total ownership of her in his **heart.** She is committed only to him; and she wants him to be completely committed to her. As long as she

Photo by Gustav Jeeninga

A flowering pomegranate. In Bible times the juice of this fruit made a pleasant drink (Song 8:2).

resides in his heart, she feels secure. She knows that love deeply rooted in a heart commitment is intense—**strong as death**—and passionate—like **flames of fire.**

8:7 quench . . . despised: The point of this powerful verse is that true love cannot be destroyed, and neither can it be purchased.

8:8 The Shulamite came from a fatherless home where she had been raised by her mother and brothers (1:6). They alternated between protective concern for her and anger with her. But in her growing up, her brothers had protected her.

8:9 If . . . a wall: By this the brothers meant that they would praise her for virtue and strength during puberty. **if . . . a door:** However, if she were loose, like a swinging door, they would have to protect her from herself and from untoward advances by young men.

8:10 The woman explains that she has been virtuous in her youth—**a wall**—and she will remain faithful in her adulthood—**towers.** In this way she discovers **peace.** How unexpected to find this rich Hebrew word used here of sexual completion.

8:11, 12 Solomon owned many vineyards, some in areas remote from Jerusalem. **Baal Hamon** ("Lord of Hamon") was a site near Shunem, the town near where the Shulamite may have been raised. It was customary for an absentee owner to lease out a vineyard. As Solomon's vineyard had been entrusted to the Shulamite's brothers, so had the Shulamite. After caring for this vineyard, the brothers earned one thousand shekels profit. But they also cared for and protected the king's other "vineyard," the Shulamite. Now, she requests that her brothers be rewarded with two hundred shekels profit. **My own vineyard:** This phrase takes us back to 1:6 where the Shulamite makes a play on words with *vineyard.* Here she sees that vineyard of old (7:12), but indicates that she now has another "vineyard" to tend—her dear husband.

8:13 The companions: This may be a reference to the woman's friends living nearby.

8:14 Make haste: During the period of courtship, the young woman had asked her suitor to run away like a **gazelle . . . stag,** lest they become entangled with passion too soon. Now, in their married love, she wishes he would rush to her (4:6). **the mountains of spices:** That is, she wants him to return to her loving embrace (1:13; 4:6).

The Book of

Isaiah

◆

*I*SAIAH WAS A MAN WITH A MISSION. THE LORD had shown him a glimpse of His glorious throne and placed a call on his life. As a prophet, he spoke God's words. For the most part, these were words of confrontation, exhortation, and warning—words that made him extremely unpopular. But even when he faced opposition, Isaiah continued to stand up for the truth. The Lord had called him to warn the

people of their headlong rush into disaster. The Book of Isaiah records these prophetic words of warning, but it also records Isaiah's words of promise and hope. One day a Messiah would come who would save, comfort, and bless His people.

Isaiah is filled with prophecies. Understanding Hebrew prophetic literature involves recognizing and interpreting parallelism. The Hebrews used parallelism in poetry and prophecy as a literary technique to emphasize a particular thought. Here is an example: "The ox knows its owner / and the donkey its master's crib; / but Israel does not know, / My people do not consider" (1:3). In the first part of this verse, both the ox and the donkey intuitively know the objects on whom they depend, namely, the owner (provider) as well as the "master's crib" (provision). The second part of the verse contrasts the intuition of animals with the behavior of the Israelites. Israel does not know "its Owner," and even though they are God's "people," they "do not consider" God's provision. Thus the second half of the verse creates the analogy in parallel with the first half.

Prophetic poetry uses colorful images that

point to further meanings. Unlike prose, which addresses historical realities more directly, poetry draws its readers and listeners into spiritual realities with the use of evocative language. Thus, in 42:15 the images of "mountains and hills" represent all sorts of obstacles—both physical and spiritual—to the exiles' return to Jerusalem. The promise that the Lord would "dry up" these obstacles means that He would eliminate all impediments to the exiles' return, just as He had dried up the Red Sea for the Israelites long before. Similarly in 41:18, that the Lord would "open rivers" and make "the dry land springs of water" means He would miraculously provide for the returning exiles in the same way He had provided water from a rock (Ex. 17:1–6).

Another major element in understanding prophetic literature is recognizing that the prophecies themselves and their arrangement often lack chronological perspective or have multiple fulfillments. For example, the same prophecy may speak of both Jesus' First and Second Comings (63:1, 2). Likewise, one prophecy may speak of both the virgin birth of Jesus as well as the birth of Isaiah's son during

Pekah's invasion. Moreover, an oracle about the servant Cyrus, the Persian emperor of the sixth century B.C. (41:1–29), may stand next to a prophecy concerning the Servant Jesus (42:1–9). Ultimately, the interpretations of Jesus and the New Testament authors provide a guide for interpreting Old Testament prophecies.

As a prophet, Isaiah spoke to three historical epochs. In chs. 1—39, he delivered his message of condemnation to the eighth-century Israelites, pronouncing judgment on their immoral and idolatrous lifestyles. This judgment came quickly, for during Isaiah's ministry, Tiglath-Pileser III (745–727 B.C.) set out to extend Assyria's rule into the west, and in doing so put pressure on Israel and Judah. In 722 B.C., another Assyrian king, Sargon II, conquered the northern kingdom. Only the nation of Judah was left. But Isaiah predicted that even Judah would fall—as much later it did, in 586 B.C.

In chs. 40—55, Isaiah comforted the future generation of weary exiles—the Jews who thought that God had forgotten them (40:27). In a brilliant series of prophecies, Isaiah presented the case that Israel's captivity was not due to the superiority of Babylon's idols, but to the disciplining rod of Israel's Lord (42:23–25). He predicted the exiles' return and encouraged them to rouse themselves (52:1–10), to flee Babylon (48:20, 21), and to entrust their future to the Almighty (41:14–20).

Finally in the third section (chs. 56—66), Isaiah exhorted the Jews who had returned to the land. This was the period before the temple was rebuilt (58:12; 61:4; 64:10) or perhaps while it was being rebuilt (66:1). Isaiah encour-

aged these Jews to put away greed (56:9–11), self-indulgence (56:12), idolatry (57:3–10), cynicism (57:11–13), and hypocritical self-righteousness (58:1–5). But he also predicted that the community would be split between true and false worshipers (chs. 65; 66). The complete restoration of Israel was still to come (49:8–26). The promised Messiah would appear in the future (61:1–3). Then Gentiles would join Israel's godly remnant to become the "servants" of the Lord (56:3; 65:1, 15, 16) in a new nation (65:1; 66:8). The ultimate triumph of good over evil would have to await the new heaven and the new earth (65:17–19).

Concerning the authorship of the book, Isaiah the son of Amoz has traditionally been identified as the writer of the entire document that bears his name (1:1). However, since the rise of historical criticism in the late nineteenth century, debate has surrounded the authorship of Isaiah. The book addresses three different historical time periods, and some critical scholars have concluded that there were three different authors for the book.

Because chs. 1—39 address Israel when it was confronting Assyrian invasions during the second half of the eighth century B.C., most scholars have agreed that these chapters were composed by Isaiah the son of Amoz, the so-called Proto-Isaiah (or "First Isaiah"). But chs. 40—55 speak to the discouraged exiles in Babylon in the first half of the sixth century B.C., two centuries after the prophet Isaiah lived. For this reason, some have assumed an anonymous author called Deutero-Isaiah (or "Second Isaiah") for these chapters. The rest of the book,

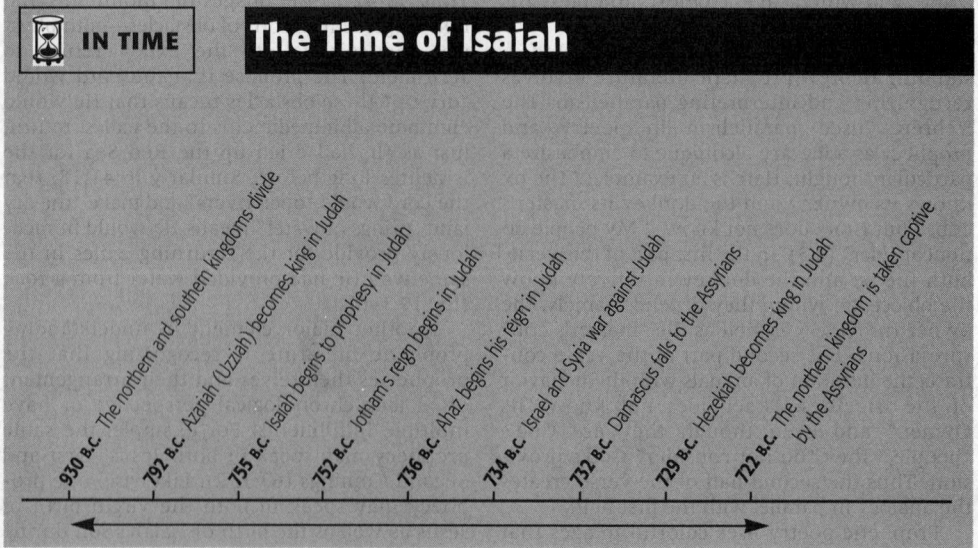

IN TIME   **The Time of Isaiah**

930 B.C. The northern and southern kingdoms divide

792 B.C. Azariah (Uzziah) becomes king in Judah

755 B.C. Isaiah begins to prophesy in Judah

752 B.C. Jotham's reign begins in Judah

736 B.C. Ahaz begins his reign in Judah

734 B.C. Israel and Syria war against Judah

732 B.C. Damascus falls to the Assyrians

729 B.C. Hezekiah becomes king in Judah

722 B.C. The northern kingdom is taken captive by the Assyrians

chs. 55—66, addresses the controversies that surrounded the postexilic community in the second half of the sixth century B.C. Thus this last section has been identified as the work of either Deutero-Isaiah or another anonymous author called Trito-Isaiah (or "Third Isaiah").

The basis for this elaborate analysis of the Book of Isaiah is the assumption that a Hebrew prophet could only address his contemporaries and not distant generations. According to these critics, a prediction of a future event, such as Isaiah's prophetic naming of Cyrus two hundred years before that ruler came to power (44:28; 45:1), is simply impossible.

Contrary to the critics' assumption, a prophet would commonly ask one generation to participate in the future events of another generation. For instance, Moses spoke this way when he addressed the new generation of Israelites at Moab as though they had participated in the events at Mount Sinai (Deut. 5:3); yet none of Moses' audience, with the exception of Joshua and Caleb, had actually been there (Deut. 1:35–38). Isaiah, who began his career in 740 B.C. and ended it around 681 B.C., also used this technique. He commanded the Israelites to "go forth from Babylon" (48:20) many generations before the Exile in 586 B.C. and the return in 538 B.C. This was a miraculous prophecy of the Israelites' return from Babylon, a prophecy that would sustain the faith and hope of the exiles, such as Ezra and Nehemiah.

The internal evidence of the Book of Isaiah points to one author, namely, the prophet Isaiah. Unlike books that have multiple authors, such as the books of Psalms and Proverbs, no editorial notices in Isaiah indicate a change of author (2:1; 13:1). Moreover there are numerous linguistic similarities throughout the book, such as the use of relatively rare titles for God, "the Holy One of Israel" and "the Lord of Hosts." Variations in style between chs. 1—39 and chs. 40—66 may be due to differences in subject matter, changed perspectives, and perhaps even the prophet's growing maturity. The New Testament confirms the view that Isaiah authored the entire book. For example, the apostle John attributed prophecies from 53:1 as well as from 6:9, 10 to the prophet Isaiah (John 12:38–41). Thus there is no convincing reason to discount Isaiah's authorship of the entire book.

Outline

I. The Syrian and Assyrian background 1:1–39:8
    A. Introduction 1:1–31
    B. A condemnation of the people's pride and a
       promise of the Lord's exaltation 2:1–5:30

C. Isaiah's call to be the Lord's prophet 6:1–13
D. A condemnation of fear of the nations rather than fear of God 7:1–12:6
E. The day of the Lord: oracles of doom against the nations 13:1–23:18
F. The "little apocalypse": judgment and restoration 24:1–27:13
G. Six woes and promises of salvation 28:1–35:10
H. The history of Hezekiah and Isaiah 36:1–39:8

II. The Babylonian background 40:1–55:13
    A. Introduction 40:1–31
    B. The nations on trial 41:1–46:13
    C. Oracles of salvation and oracles concerning the Suffering Servant 47:1–55:13

III. The postexilic background 56:1–66:24
    A. Identifying the true people of God 56:1–8
    B. A condemnation of Israel 56:9–57:13
    C. The Lord's dwelling with the contrite 57:14–21
    D. Condemnation of hypocritical fasting 58:1–14
    E. The restoration of repentant Israel 59:1–8
    F. Israel's lament 59:9–15
    G. The Lord's vindication of His people 59:16–21
    H. Jerusalem's glorious future 60:1–62:12
    I. Israel's lament 63:1–64:12
    J. The contrast between true and nominal Israel 65:1–66:24

Commentary

1:1 God mediated His message through the godly **Isaiah** to **Judah,** the people of the southern kingdom—specifically to their magistrates, priests, and prophets in **Jerusalem.** The nation of Israel had been divided into two parts: Judah (the southern kingdom) and Israel (the northern kingdom). While Isaiah's message was primarily for the southern kingdom, it was also for the northern kingdom—the entire nation was heading down a path of sin and idolatry that would end in destruction. Thus in this book, the word *Israel* sometimes refers to both the southern and the northern kingdoms. Isaiah lived to see the nation of Assyria take the northern kingdom into captivity in 722 B.C. Therefore this record of Isaiah's visions contains the revelations that God graciously gave during the reigns of **Uzziah** (792–740 B.C.), **Jotham** (752–736 B.C.), **Ahaz** (736–720 B.C.), and **Hezekiah** (729–699 B.C.). Because God never changes, this revelation is still relevant for His people today.

1:2, 3 The indictment against Judah has two parts: (1) Isaiah summons heaven and earth as witnesses to the trial (v. 2) and (2) the

Lord, as Plaintiff, indicts Judah, here called **Israel** (vv. 2, 3).

1:2 Moses, who mediated God's covenant with Israel at Sinai, summoned the **heavens** and the **earth** (that is, the entire creation) as a witness that he had duly warned the Israelites that they would be judged by the Lord for their disobedience (Deut. 4:24; 30:19; 31:28). As Jacob and Laban set up a heap of stones as a witness of a treaty between them (Gen. 31:43–55), so the creation is a fitting witness between God and Israel. God's relationship with His people is personal; He compares Judah to ungrateful **children** (63:8; Ex. 4:22; Hos. 11:1). The Hebrew term translated **rebelled** means "to refuse to submit to someone's authority and rule" (63:10; 66:24).

1:3 Even an **ox** and a **donkey** recognize the **owner** who feeds them, so they do not rebel against him. But Israel, God's own children whom He "nourished and brought up" (v. 2), had rebelled against Him. Judah's rebellion was incomprehensible and inexcusable.

1:4–9 Isaiah's indictment against Judah has three parts: (1) Judah had been rebellious (v. 4); (2) Judah remained unrepentant, though disciplined (vv. 5–8); and (3) only God's grace spared a small remnant from annihilation (v. 9).

1:4 sinful nation: Despite God's divine parenting, the people had turned to sin (5:1–7). **The Holy One of Israel** is Isaiah's favorite title for God. The Lord is holy because He is profoundly different from all of humanity (40:25). He alone is the Creator (45:11, 12) exalted in heaven (6:1–3) and without sin (6:4–7). He alone is the righteous Judge (v. 20) and the Protector of the faithful (10:20; 43:3). Yet the phrase "of Israel" describes the Holy One as sustaining a relationship with His people (Ps. 40:1).

1:5–8 Isaiah first compares the nation's affliction to a badly wounded soldier (vv. 5, 6) and then describes its land as ravaged by war (vv. 7, 8).

1:5 Isaiah answers his own indignant question, **Why should you be stricken again?** The people would only **revolt more and more.** More preaching would only make their hearts hard (6:9, 10). In 53:4–6, Isaiah reveals God's gracious response to their hard hearts: the Lord will strike His Servant instead of sinners (53:4–6). Such love can win over even the toughest rebel (Rom. 5:8).

1:6, 7 From **foot** to **head** means everyone and everything. Judah's wounds were not **closed, bound up** (bandaged), or **soothed,** because the people had refused to repent.

1:8 Daughter of Zion is a beautiful personification of Jerusalem (37:22; 60:14). Actually, the *of* in this phrase is somewhat misleading. "Daughter *of* Zion" seems to indicate that Zion *has* a daughter. In fact, Zion *is* the daughter—the daughter of the Lord. **Booth** and **hut** refer to lean-to shelters used by farmers and watchmen during the harvest.

1:9–17 This invitation to repent falls into three parts: (1) Isaiah's appeal to the rebellious rulers and people of Jerusalem to hear the Lord's instruction (vv. 9, 10); (2) the Lord's scathing indictment and rejection of the people's external, formalistic worship (vv. 11–17); and (3) the Lord's invitation to the people to repent and do justice in order to save themselves from death (vv. 18–20).

1:9 The title **LORD of hosts** describes God as ruler over all powers in heaven and earth through His command of His angelic armies. The title is a favorite of Isaiah, for it speaks of God's holiness and sovereignty. Judah's survival was not ultimately due to an enemy's weakness but to God's power. Though God punished His sinful people, He always preserved a **remnant** (6:13; 10:20; 11:16) because He was faithful to keep His promise to Abraham (Gen. 22:16–18; Ex. 34:6, 7; Mic. 7:19, 20; Rom. 9:29; 11:5). The word *remnant* basically means "survivor" (Num. 21:35; Josh. 8:22). **Sodom** and **Gomorrah** were regarded as the epitome of sinfulness; to say that Jerusalem had become like those cities was a scathing condemnation (Rev. 11:8). Elsewhere these words are used as symbols of God's final judgment upon sinners (Amos 4:11; Matt. 10:15; 2 Pet. 2:6).

1:10–15 God desired **sacrifices,** but not from people who disobeyed Him and mistreated others, even if the sacrifice presented was the best. "To obey is better than sacrifice," said the early prophet Samuel (1 Sam. 15:22, 23). Later prophets agreed (Hos. 6:6; Amos 4:4; Mic. 6:6–8), and so did the Lord Jesus (Matt. 23:23). God judges not only our outwardly pious acts, but more importantly the attitude of our hearts (1 Cor. 4:5).

1:13–15 Here is an itemized condemnation of the people's sacred seasons, **New Moons** (Num. 28:11–15), **Sabbaths** (Ex. 31:14–17), and **appointed feasts** (Ex. 23:14–17). These feasts are condemned as **futile** because the people did not celebrate them out of love for God.

1:14 God sarcastically refers to the feasts as **your** rather than "My" **New Moons** because the people had changed the spirit of God's ceremonial laws from love of Him to manipulation of Him.

1:15 God did not look with favor on the fervent **spread out . . . hands** of those who oppressed others, and He would not hear their **many** accompanying **prayers** (James 4:1–6).

1:16–20 The invitation to repent has two parts: (1) The people must wash themselves by seeking **justice,** by rebuking **the oppressor,** and defending **the fatherless** (James 1:27). (2) God Himself would wash the people if they were **willing and obedient** to meet this condition. As the righteous Judge, God both reproves the wicked and defends the innocent (11:4).

1:17, 18 Reason together means "to come to a legal decision." There is no call for a compromise here; the people were to come to an agreement with God concerning the enormous gravity of their sin. God was not declaring His people innocent of wickedness, but He was prepared to pardon their sins if they would repent and turn to Him. God offers us that same forgiveness. He does not deny our sinfulness. Instead, He can forgive us based on the payment for sin in the death of the Savior, the Lord Jesus Christ. **Says the LORD**: The verb form suggests a repeated offering of grace. **Scarlet** recalls the picture of "hands . . . full of blood" (v. 15). God's grace and power can make such bloodstains as **white as snow** (Rom. 3:21–26). The words **scarlet . . . white** also suggest the idea of soiled garments (64:6) that in ancient times were not capable of being cleansed (namely, to whiteness). But God can cleanse anything. He can do this and still maintain His righteousness because Jesus died for sinners (Rom. 3:21–26).

1:19, 20 There was another side to God's offer. If the sinful people did not repent, instead of the promise that they **shall eat the good of the land** (3:10) stood the threat that they **shall be devoured by the sword.** The promise and threat were certain because **the LORD** had spoken them. Here the verb **has spoken** indicates finality (contrast the verb *says* in v. 18). While God had graciously extended His offer of mercy over a significant period of time, this was the only offer God made. They could not "cut another deal" with Him (40:5; 55:11).

1:21–31 In these verses, God announced His intent to purify Israel. This announcement falls into two parts: (1) a prophecy of judgment (vv. 21–26) and (2) an elaboration of God's sentence (vv. 27–31). God's purpose for Judah was not final destruction, but purification from social injustice (vv. 25, 26) and redemption from idolatry (vv. 27–31). Idolatry and injustice are inseparable. When people turn from trusting the fair and loving God, they will start oppressing the poor and helpless (Jer. 23:13, 14; Hos. 4:1–14; Amos 2:6–8).

1:22, 23 The debased **silver** and **wine** refer to Jerusalem's unjust rulers.

1:24, 25 God's **hand** had effectively delivered Israel from Egypt. Now that same hand was against the people in judgment.

1:26 God's goal for Jerusalem was that it would become a **city of righteousness,** a city where the Lord would be faithfully worshiped.

1:27, 28 The Hebrew word for **redeemed** means "ransomed" or "freed someone from another's ownership through the payment of a price." Zion's **penitents,** those who turned their back on idolatry and injustice, would find freedom from sin and judgment. Ultimately, like all forgiven sinners, they have justice imputed to them through Jesus Christ and effected in them through the Holy Spirit. Of course, these realities become clear in the NT. Judgment passes, but Zion's beauty will never fade.

1:29 Idolaters **shall be ashamed** because the **terebinth,** a sacred tree, and the **gardens,** sacred groves for fertility rites or the worship of spirits, would fail to save them in the time of judgment (65:3).

1:30, 31 Terebinth represents both the sacred trees (v. 29) and the **strong,** dominating rulers of Israel. **The work of it** is perhaps a reference to the injustice of Israel's tyrants (v. 23), which was the opposite of the Lord's righteous work (5:12). **no one shall quench:** God will rid His creation of the proud through His gracious, purifying judgment.

2:1–5 Isaiah's prophecy about Zion's exaltation falls into three parts: (1) an introduction locating the vision "in the latter days" (v. 2); (2) a vision of Zion established as the chief mountain (vv. 3, 4); and (3) a conclusion exhorting Judah to obey the Law until the vision is fulfilled (v. 5).

2:2 Some have interpreted the phrase **in the latter days** as pointing to the new epoch initiated by the saving work of Christ and the coming of the Holy Spirit at Pentecost (Acts 2:17). According to this interpretation, this prophecy will be completely fulfilled in the Second Coming of the Messiah (1 Cor. 15:28). Others interpret this passage as referring to conditions in Christ's future kingdom. See the fuller development of this theme in Mic. 4:1–4. Just as **the LORD's house** (the temple) was a type of the heavenly sanctuary (Heb. 9:24), so presumably **the mountain** (Mount Zion) was a copy of a heavenly reality (Heb. 9:23, 24; 12:22–24). In the coming kingdom, the city of Jerusalem and its glorious temple will again become prominent. The false gods of pagans had sacred moun-

> *In the coming kingdom, the city of Jerusalem and its glorious temple will again become prominent.*

tains with temples; to raise the Lord's house to **the top of mountains,** or "as the chief mountain," is to establish Him among the nations as the only true God.

2:3 By quoting the people's words, **let us go up to the mountain of the LORD,** Isaiah vividly depicts their regenerated hearts, since the unregenerate do not seek God (Rom. 3:11). In OT times, only Israel went up to Mount Zion. But in the kingdom age, all nations go up to the glorious temple. Today the Lord Jesus has authority over all nations and gives eternal life to those who trust in Him (Matt. 28:18–20; John 17:2). When the fullness of the Gentiles has come in during this present age (Rom. 11:1–17), the literal dimensions of this present passage will be fulfilled. Then Israel will be grafted in again, and then the nations will come to Zion. Then the teaching of the Lord Jesus Christ, as King of the earth, will flow from Jerusalem as a beautiful, life-giving nectar.

2:4 Plowshares probably means "hoes." The nations of the earth have been caught up in warfare since the dawn of human history. From time to time throughout history, there has been an elusive dream of world peace. But that dream has never been realized. In the meantime, implements of warfare have become ever more sophisticated, so that in our present day the nations of the earth have weapons and delivery systems that are unimaginably horrific in their potential for the destruction of people and objects. Yet in a future glorious day there will be an end to all weapons and warfare. This will only be possible because of the reign of the Prince of Peace (9:6), the Savior King whose Name is Jesus.

2:5 Isaiah includes himself with the godly remnant and encourages them: **let us walk.** Even though they could not see the glorious future of Zion, they continued to place their faith in God's promises and obey His law. **Light** is a metaphor for God's law, which illuminates the path that leads to everlasting life (Ps. 119:105).

2:6–9 The condemnation of Judah for misplaced confidence is in three parts and in the form of a prayer: (1) a judicial sentence (v. 6); (2) a condemnation of Judah's misplaced confidence in witchcraft, pagan alliances, money, weapons, and idolatry (vv. 6–9); and (3) a concluding prayer that God should not forgive the people for substituting faith in the works of their own hands for faith in Him (v. 9). The Law prohibited the king from accumulating money, weapons, and alliances, in order to keep him dependent on God (Deut. 17:16, 17).

2:6 The exhortation to **the house of Jacob** was necessary (v. 5), for God had handed it over to destruction. **You have forsaken** was a present, but not a permanent, condition for the Israelites. To renounce **eastern ways** and **soothsayers,** the customs of Mesopotamia, was a hallmark of genuine faith in the God of Israel (Deut. 18:10). **They are pleased** could be translated "they clasp hands," suggesting political alliances with foreigners. See 2 Kin. 16:7 for Ahaz's dependence on the Lord for salvation.

2:7 Horses . . . chariots signifies "horse-drawn war chariots." Riding horseback by military forces was unknown in the time of Isaiah.

2:8 The work of their own hands refers to man-made idols in particular.

2:9 Each man humbles himself before things that are themselves debased—idols. Wanting God to uphold moral order, yet intimately knowing God's gracious character, Isaiah implored Him **not** to **forgive** those who had turned to idols.

2:10–22 Isaiah predicted that in the day of the Lord, the Lord alone would be exalted. The oracle is in three parts: (1) an introductory command to the proud to hide themselves from the terror of the Lord (vv. 10, 11); (2) a prediction that in the day of the Lord every pretension would be humbled (vv. 12–18); and (3) a concluding command to the righteous to separate themselves from the proud (v. 22). The refrain "the Lord alone shall/will be exalted" (in vv. 11, 17), the refrain "when He arises (vv. 19, 21), and

---

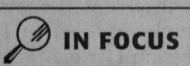 **IN FOCUS**   **"light"**

(Heb. *'or*) (2:5; 9:2; 58:8; Eccl. 2:13; 11:7) Strong's #216: This word refers to literal or symbolic light. The Hebrew word often denotes daylight or daybreak (Judg. 16:2; Neh. 8:3), but it can also be symbolic of life and deliverance (Job 33:28, 30; Pss. 27:1; 36:9; 49:19; Mic. 7:8, 9). In the Bible, light is frequently associated with true knowledge and understanding (42:6; 49:6; 51:4; Job 12:25), and even gladness, good fortune, and goodness (Job 30:26; Ps. 97:11). The Bible describes light as the clothing of God—a vivid picture of His honor, majesty, splendor, and glory (Ps. 104:2; Hab. 3:3, 4). A proper lifestyle is characterized by walking in God's light (2:5; Ps. 119:105; Prov. 4:18; 6:20–23).

the similarity of wording in verses 11, 17, unite the prophecy by highlighting its theme. In other words, the effect of self-exaltation is confrontation with the only Glorious One. Everything that vaunts itself before the Holy One must be humbled, just as soap bubbles burst in the sun's heat.

2:10 Dust symbolizes the abject humility of the defeated (47:1; Gen. 3:14; Ps. 44:25). The wicked among the Israelites would grovel in the dust before the righteous Lord.

2:11 Lofty looks are the outer manifestation of proud hearts. The refrain **the Lord alone shall be exalted** highlights the theme of this prophecy and describes the coming, glorious revelation of the risen and exalted Savior King. **In that day** the Savior will be exalted above all other proud contenders.

2:12–19 The body of this oracle has three parts: (1) a summary statement (v. 12); (2) an itemized account of the lofty pretensions to be humbled, from those in creation (vv. 13, 14) to those made by people (vv. 15–17), followed by a summary statement with an emphasis on idolatry (vv. 17, 18); and (3) a concluding prediction that people will hide themselves at the time of God's judgment (v. 19).

2:12 Lifted up is translated "exalted" in v. 2. Any rival to God's exaltation will be dwarfed. **The day of the Lord** is any time when the Lord of Hosts is victorious (1:9), be it against Babylon through Media (13:1—14:27), or against Egypt through Babylon (Ezek. 30:2–4),

or against Israel through Assyria (1:24; Amos 5:18). Zephaniah 1:14–16 is particularly graphic about that day. The phrase is also used of the past actions of the Lord when He brought about the great victory against Egypt in His deliverance of Israel in the Exodus (Ex. 15:3). Similarly, the day of the Lord's vengeance may also be the time of Israel's deliverance that is to come (34:2—35:10), which is represented as the Lord decisively defeating all the nation's opposition (Joel 3:14–16; Zeph. 2:2, 9; 3:8–20). The day of the Lord has two sides: (1) the night of God's judgment, and (2) the daylight of His salvation after judgment. Isaiah used the term to describe either or both aspects.

2:13–15 The cedars of Lebanon and **the high mountains**—the exalted things of creation—as well as the **high tower** and the **fortified wall**—the exalted things made by humanity—will be humbled so that the arrogant can see the greatness of God.

2:16, 17 The ships of Tarshish were large oceangoing vessels—prized objects that the arrogant made and considered to be more important than God.

2:18 The term **idols** means "worthless things."

2:19 holes . . . caves: People will scurry like frightened animals with no place to hide (Matt. 24:16). **Terror** refers to the dread of the wicked at the sight of God (Ps. 14:5).

2:20, 21 When the formerly precious idols

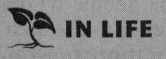 **IN LIFE**   **A Leadership Vacuum—A Public Crisis**

How important is the character and quality of a nation's leaders? Extremely important, according to Isaiah. At the time when Is. 3 was given, the nation probably was prospering under the wise, godly leadership of King Uzziah (around 792–740 B.C.) or his successor, King Jotham (around 750–735 B.C.).

However, Isaiah foresaw a time when God would remove the better leaders (Is. 3:1–3), leaving behind mere "babes" who would have no experience in running the institutions of society and no respect for the wisdom of the past. As a result, these "children" would become selfish oppressors (3:4, 5) who would run roughshod over the needs of the poor (3:14, 15). That happened when Jerusalem fell to Babylon (586 B.C.; 2 Kin. 25:11, 12, 22–26), though no one can say whether that exhausted the fulfillment of Isaiah's prophecy.

The lesson is that a leadership vacuum leads to public crisis. That being the case, we as God's people today do well to prevent that kind of vacuum from forming by:

- recruiting and appointing the best people available, leaders of high moral character and outstanding leadership skills;
- appropriately paying and rewarding people for their public service;
- supporting leaders and working together with them in their efforts to promote good government and prevent social, economic, and moral deterioration;
- praying for leaders as they exercise their authority; and
- raising up and training our children to be outstanding leaders for the coming generation.

fail the proud at the time of God's judgment, they will contemptuously throw them to **the moles and bats**, the small, unclean rodents that make people feel squeamish.

2:22 Sever yourselves: Since God will reject proud idolaters, it follows that the faithful should also reject them. How ludicrous to trust in transitory, impermanent man, whose **breath is in his nostrils,** instead of in the One who gives everyone breath.

3:1–9 This judgment against Jerusalem and Judah is in two parts: (1) a judicial sentence against anarchy (vv. 1–7); and (2) an accusation of arrogance (vv. 8, 9).

3:1 For links this oracle with the previous exhortation to sever a relationship with an arrogant man (2:22). God **takes away** Judah's leaders through the sword and exile. No historical reference is given because the truth is universal (2 Kin. 25:18–21).

3:2, 3 Judah's administration was organized around warriors—**mighty man, man of war, captain of fifty;** sages—**judge, elder, honorable man, counselor;** religious mediums—**prophet, diviner, enchanter;** and craftsmen—**artisan.**

3:4 Because of the Lord's judgment on Judah, the shrewd, ungodly leaders would be replaced by **children** and **babes,** meaning inexperienced and incompetent leaders.

3:5 For **every one** to be oppressed **by another** describes a state of anarchy. In such an upside-down world, **child** is against **elder, the base** against **the honorable.** In His judgment, the Lord has given over the wicked to their own evil ways.

3:6, 7 During this period of deprivation, society would be so deprived of leadership and possessions that people would qualify for leadership merely by having **clothing.**

3:8, 9 The people's **tongue** and **look** betray their arrogance against God.

3:9 Considered a horribly sinful city (1:9), **Sodom** had been destroyed by God (Gen. 19). Yet Judeans were parading their defiance against God just like the Sodomites.

3:10–15 This oracle against Judah's leaders is in three parts: (1) an affirmation that God repays good and evil (vv. 10, 11); (2) an accusation that Israel's leaders were leading people astray (v. 12), and (3) a divine lawsuit against the leaders for exploiting their subjects (vv. 13–15; 1:23).

3:10, 11 eat the fruit: Compare this idea with 1:19.

3:12 The lamenting words **My people** (v. 15) are reminiscent of David's pain over his erring son Absalom (2 Sam. 18:33). The profound difference, of course, was in the shared blame of David and his son. In the case of the

Lord and His people, the blame is solely their own.

3:13 to plead: This is a judicial term meaning to plead a case (Mic. 6:1).

3:14 The vineyard represents the nation (5:1–7), used here as a term parallel to **the poor.** The leaders had taken advantage of the weak in order to plunder them (v. 15).

3:15 Lord GOD of hosts: See the similar usage in 1:9.

3:16—4:1 This oracle against the vain women of Judah has three parts: (1) an accusation that the women were "haughty" and would be humbled (v. 16, 17); (2) a list of the pretentious trappings to be done away with (vv. 18–23); and (3) a depiction of Jerusalem's desolation (3:24—4:1). The oracle expands from the women of Zion (vv. 16–23) to the Daughter {of} Zion, a personification of the whole city (3:24–26), and then back to the women again (4:1). The expansion clarifies that the contrived glory of people is also in view. The oracle also moves from Jerusalem's vain beauty before the Exile, to the shameful conditions of the Exile (vv. 24, 25), to its desolation after the Exile (3:26—4:1).

3:16 The plural **daughters of Zion** suggests the women of the city as well as a personification of Jerusalem (1:8). **Mincing** probably means "childlike steps." The prophet shows his scorn for pretense and flagrant display.

3:17 The term **secret parts** and its parallel **head** may mean "forehead."

3:18–26 Rope . . . baldness . . . sackcloth refer to the conditions of the people who are going into exile. **Your men** refers to the men of Jerusalem. The **gates** of Zion **mourn** because its inhabitants have gone into exile for their sins.

4:1 in that day: This phrase connects this verse with the preceding unit (3:16–26). The once-proud women of Jerusalem (3:16–23) would have to beg a **man** to father their children and **take away** their **reproach**—the fact that they have no children. Most of the men of Jerusalem would have died in the process of defending the city (3:25).

4:2–6 The prophecy of Zion's restoration has three parts: (1) the Branch of the Lord will be glorious (v. 2); (2) the remnant will be sanctified (vv. 3, 4); and (3) the Lord will provide a protective covering over Mount Zion (vv. 5, 6).

4:2 In that day speaks of the future revelation of the glory of the Lord on the earth (2:2–4). **The Branch of the LORD** has the double sense of the **earth** yielding its **fruit** and of Christ yielding spiritual fruit (11:1–5; Jer. 23:5; Zech. 3:8; John 15:1–8). Because Christ humbled Himself, He will be crowned with glory (49:7; 52:13; 53:12; Phil. 2:9–11). **beau-**

tiful and glorious: Together the words indicate "dazzling beauty." The reign of Jesus the King of Creation will be marked by plenty. The earth will be released from its curse, producing all that God intended it to produce in the beginning (Ps. 65).

4:3 recorded: The record of births in Jerusalem (Ps. 87:5, 6) may be related to the "heavenly book" (Ex. 32:32; Ps. 69:28; Dan. 7:10; Rev 20:12).

4:4 Spirit could mean wind (the hot searing wind of fire), the human spirit, or the Holy Spirit. All three may be intended (11:2; 30:1; 42:1; 48:16; 59:21; 61:1; Luke 3:22). **The spirit of judgment . . . burning** means "a fiery judgment." Through the processes of a purging fire, which outwardly consumes the faithless and inwardly purifies the faithful, God will produce a holy city.

4:5 Create is something only God can do; the word also suggests a divine "refashioning." **Cloud and smoke** recalls God's protective presence at the Red Sea (Ex. 13:20–22), on the tabernacle (Ex. 40:34–38), and in the wilderness (Num. 9:15–23). Here the phrase symbolizes His protective **covering** over the restored and sanctified Mount Zion. The **glory** of Mount Zion in

the messianic age will be bestowed by God Himself (40:5; 60:2; John 17:10, 22, 24).

4:6 Over the cloud and smoke on each dwelling will be the overshadowing **tabernacle,** symbolizing God's protection of and communion with His people (Ps. 91:1; Rev. 21:3).

5:1–7 Isaiah's "Song of the Vineyard" is in three parts: (1) an introduction to the allegory (vv. 1, 2); (2) an accusation and sentence (vv. 3–6); and (3) an interpretation of the allegory (v. 7; see Ps. 80:8–16). The body consists of an accusation by Isaiah (vv. 3, 4) and the sentence handed down by the Lord Himself (vv. 5, 6).

5:1–3 Judah is compared to a vineyard that has every advantage. Its failure to produce justifies God's judgment (1:2, 3). **Well-beloved . . . my Beloved:** Isaiah speaks about the Lord in endearing terms.

5:2 The Lord, the true Vinedresser, had done everything possible to make the soil ready to grow fine grapes. The term **wild grapes** means "stinking things" (v. 4). This result was as unexpected as were the rebellious children of 1:2–4.

5:3 My vineyard: The pronoun indicates God's love and pride over His possession—the

 **IN PERSON** | **Isaiah the Prophet**

In some ways, Isaiah rejected all that his contemporaries considered valuable: wealth, alliances, military protection, and clever strategies. Though he was rebuffed, Isaiah remained true to his calling.

In an extraordinary vision of the heavenly court, God Himself called Isaiah to be a messenger to his people. His calling was glorious, but his task was a challenge. He had to confront the people of Judah with the truth: they had broken the Lord's covenant, rebelled against their God, and would have to face the consequences of their sins (6:1–13; Deut. 28).

Isaiah did not proclaim his message of gloom without feeling. With a broken heart, he cried out: "Lord, how long?" (6:11) How long would Israel remain rebellious? Israel's hypocrisy repulsed him, and he did not shrink from comparing them to the rulers of Sodom and Gomorrah (1:10–20). Yet while he warned the wicked of their tragic fate, he also encouraged the penitent and sorrowing to place their hope in God.

Even Isaiah's name, which means "the Lord saves," served as a sign to the nation (8:18), as did the names of his sons—Shear-Jashub, which meant "A Remnant Shall Return" (7:3), and Mahar-Shalal-HashBaz, which meant "Speed the Spoil, Hasten the Booty" (8:1–4). These names pointed to the Lord's coming salvation. Even though the nation faced the Lord's discipline, salvation would come. A remnant of the Israelites would return to the land and experience God's blessing. In fact, the whole Book of Isaiah revolves around this remnant theology—the judgment of the wicked and the salvation of the faithful.

In one crisis after another—the Assyrian invasions and war against Jerusalem—Isaiah maintained a steady grip on God. He considered human help vain and idolatrous, and he relied only on the Lord for his strength (30:1–5). As Judah's watchman he appealed to the Lord on the people's behalf (59:9–15; 62:6, 7; 64:1, 2). The same mouth that exposed the people's sins fervently interceded for them. Isaiah was not merely a messenger—he was also a watchman, a conscientious guard over the Lord's people.

nation of Israel. All the more reason for God's disappointment in its infertility.

5:4 What more could have been done: When there is a failure in human relationships, we usually expect that both parties bear part of the responsibility. When it comes to the failed relationship between God and His people, the blame falls solely on the people. The Lord did everything He could—from instructing His people to giving them the Promised Land.

5:5 Please let Me tell you may be translated more forcefully as "Now I *will* tell you." God was not asking for permission; He was warning His people.

5:6 Briers and thorns symbolize the anarchy described in 3:4, 5, which will overtake the land after the Exile. **clouds:** As God had promised in His covenant with Israel on Mount Sinai, sufficient rainfall would come to the people who were faithful to His commands, but the rain would be withheld if the people were rebellious (Deut. 28:12, 23, 24).

5:7 justice . . . oppression: These words have similar sounds in Hebrew, as do the words **righteousness** and **cry for help.** Choosing similar sounding words is a common technique of Hebrew poetry.

5:8–30 This prophecy consists of six accusations or "woes" that specify the sins of "the wild grapes" (vv. 2, 4) and the nature of their acts of oppression: greed (v. 8), debauchery (vv. 11, 12), cynical unbelief (vv. 18, 19), perversion (v. 20), arrogance (v. 21), and injustice (vv. 22, 23). To these sins are added prophecies of judgment: desolation (vv. 9, 10), captivity or death for the pompous leaders (vv. 13, 14), and humiliation for all (v. 15). The conquering army is depicted in vv. 26–30.

5:8 Till . . . land: The greedy land barons aimed to control all of the choice land of Israel. God gave the fields, which "shall not be sold permanently, for the land is Mine" (Lev. 25:23) as an inheritance to all His people (Num. 27:7–11). Deprived of these ancestral lands, Israel's citizens had become day laborers or slaves on what had formerly been their family inheritance.

5:9, 10 While invaders could destroy the mansions, only God could bring the drought implied in these verses. Yet both calamities were judgments from His hand.

5:9 without inhabitant: This phrase is also found in 6:11.

5:10 One bath is about six gallons. **A homer** is about six bushels. **One ephah** is one-tenth of a homer. The produce of the land would be extremely meager in the time of divine judgment.

5:11, 12 Greed (v. 8) is closely connected with indulgent, egocentric living.

5:11 This verse is a strong condemnation of the abuse of **intoxicating drink** (beer) and **wine** (v. 22). For a contrasting example of wine used in a positive context of the enjoyment of God's salvation, read 55:1. **inflames them:** The life-pattern of these wicked rulers is dissipation.

5:12 The harp and the strings: For a similar idea, read Ps. 33:2. Music was played in ancient Israel both in the worship of the Lord and in times of feasting. Wine was also a part of feasting in biblical times (Prov. 9:2; John 2:10). Here **their feasts** means "their drinking parties." **do not regard . . . consider:** The people were oblivious to the reality of the work of God in their midst (Ps. 10:4). **The work of the Lord** includes justice, entailing punishing the tyrants and saving the oppressed (vv. 24, 25).

5:13 have gone into captivity: Though the verb is in the past tense, here it refers to something still in the future—the Judeans had not yet gone into captivity. **Knowledge** refers to a personal involvement with someone or something. **thirst:** The judgment matches the crime of indulging in alcoholic beverages (vv. 11, 12).

5:14 Sheol is the poetic word for "grave," which is here compared to a gaping jaw that devours the elite rich and the common masses alike. Sheol is portrayed as a monster in Proverbs (Prov. 1:12; 27:20).

5:15, 16 For the exaltation of the Lord alone, see 2:9, 11, 17. The judgment of the wicked is one demonstration of His exaltation.

5:15 the eyes of the lofty: Proud people get little respect from God (Ps. 147:6).

5:16 The Hebrew term rendered **hallowed** is a form of the verb meaning "to make holy," which basically means "to be distinct," "to be removed," or "to be separate." These words speak of the transcendence of the Lord in His majesty and glory.

5:17 What were formerly mansions surrounded with lush vineyards would become **waste places,** where **lambs** and **fat ones,** those prepared for sacrifice, feed.

5:18, 19 Those who mocked Isaiah's proclamation of the day of the Lord were not simply "falling" into sin; rather, they labored to **draw iniquity** along, as on **a cart.** Isaiah named his son, "**speed** the spoil, **hasten** the prey" (8:3), perhaps partially in response to this taunt (5:26).

5:20 call evil good: Those who pervert God's evaluation of what is good by calling evil good are heading down a dangerous path—one that leads to judgment.

5:21 At the root of the moral, social, and theological corruption denounced in this prophecy is being **wise** in one's **own eyes**—an insensitive, arrogant egotism.

5:22 mighty at drinking wine: See v. 11 on the abuse of wine. The **intoxicating drink** was probably beer.

5:23 bribe: The perversion of **justice** by bribery is a serious evil that undermines society.

5:24 As the vineyard yielding only sour grapes is finally judged, so the wicked will finally be cut off without hope.

5:25 The hills—that seem most permanent—**trembled,** even as the sea "fled" before the anger of the Lord (Ps. 114:3, 7). **Their carcasses** is a grisly image of the defeated foes of God (34:3; 66:24). The Lord's **anger is not turned away** even after the horrible judgments of vv. 24, 25. **His hand:** Often in Scripture, "the hand of God" is a symbol of His grace and salvation (Ex. 15:6). How tragic that the same hand is stretched out to punish His people.

5:26 The Assyrian army, which included many mercenaries (Mic. 4:11–13), literally "trampled down" (v. 5) the pleasant land of Israel. **whistle:** The Lord would control this army of judgment, for He would give them their signal to invade (7:18).

5:27–29 The preparations of the Assyrian army were complete; the soldiers were thoroughly ready for war (40:30, 31).

5:29 like a lion: This means that the Assyrians will be prepared to dispatch their **prey** as easily as a **lion** might.

5:30 The clouds symbolize judgment.

6:1–13 Isaiah's call to be a prophet of God consists of five sections: (1) the historical setting (v. 1); (2) Isaiah's stunning vision of God (vv. 2–4); (3) his new insight into himself (v. 5); (4) his call (vv. 6–8); and (5) his commission (vv. 9–13).

6:1 King Uzziah died in 740 B.C., signaling the end of an age. This good king (2 Chr. 26:1–15) would be eventually replaced by wicked Ahaz (7:1); the relative prosperity of the first half of the eighth century would be replaced by the Syro-Ephraimite wars and the Assyrian campaigns into Israel. King Uzziah had been one of Judah's best rulers, but he had succumbed to pride (2 Chr. 26:1–5), leading to his leprous condition. When he became proud, God had to discipline him. The **throne** where **the Lord** is seated, **high** and exalted, represents His eternal, sovereign, and universal rule. He is high above all other kings, but at the same time He is concerned about the welfare of His people. **Temple** means "palace"—the Lord's throne on earth with its counterpart in heaven.

6:2 The **seraphim** used two of their **six wings** to cover **their faces** so that they would not gaze on the Lord's glory. With two of their wings **they covered their feet** in self-conscious humiliation. And **with two they were flying** to do the Lord's bidding. The behavior of the **seraphim** contrasts strongly with the pride of Uzziah (2 Chr. 26:16). All human pride is mocked by the behavior of these angels. They know that in the presence of God there is no room for pomp, no reason for pride.

6:3 Holy, holy, holy: To say the word *holy* twice in Hebrew is to describe someone as "most holy." To say the word *holy* three times intensifies the idea to the highest level. In other words, the holiness of God is indescribable in human language. To be holy means to be different, distant, or transcendent. Thus the song of the seraphim is a constant refrain that the transcendence of God is indescribable. Though the Lord is totally different from us—He is perfect—in His mercy He still reaches down to take care of us. **The whole earth is full of His glory:** The Hebrew word order is, "The fullness of all the earth is His glory." We know that the glory of God transcends the universe (Ps. 113:4–6); yet in order to balance the expression of the transcendence of God in the first half of this verse, the words of the second half emphasize God's closeness to His creation—His involvement with the earth and its people.

6:4 If even the doorposts of the heavenly temple shook in response to God's holiness, how much more will the whole earth (v. 3) shake when the Lord visits it (Matt. 24:29, 30).

6:5 Confronted with this vision of the Lord, Isaiah realized that he was under judgment—that he was **undone.** He must have thought that he had come to the end of his life. **I am a man of unclean lips:** Isaiah knew that he was a sinner. He realized that his lips were the only ones not giving God praise in that setting. **a people:** Isaiah's plight is the plight of every person. No one, in his or her present state, is capable of standing before the Holy One (Ps. 24:3). **the King, the LORD of hosts:** After contemplating the death of Uzziah (v. 1), Isaiah had seen the King who will never die.

6:6–8 Isaiah's call consists of his inward cleansing (vv. 6, 7), his call to serve (v. 8a), and his acceptance (v. 8b).

6:6 The **live coal . . . from the altar** symbolizes both the purification of blood and the fire of the Spirit that enabled the prophet to speak. From that point on, his words would be light to his hearers and power to those who would listen. The fact that a coal from the altar was used reminds us that ultimately all sin is forgiven because of a sacrifice. The sacrifices on the temple altar point to the ultimate sacrifice of the Savior Jesus. God sovereignly and graciously forgave Isaiah's sin.

6:7 Isaiah had a personal Day of Atonement before the Lord (Lev. 23:26–32). **taken away:** This word alludes to the Israelite practice of symbolically placing the sins of the

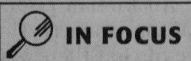 **IN FOCUS** | **"seraphim"**

(Heb. *seraphim*) (6:2, 6) Strong's #8314: This noun is probably related to the verb *saraph*, which means "to burn with fire." These angelic creatures belong to the heavenly host and are only mentioned twice in Scripture—both times in Is. 6. Apparently these beings conduct the worship of God in heaven and are different from the cherubim, who are described in Rev. 4:6–8 as surrounding God's throne instead of standing above it, as described here (6:2). The relation of their name to burning may be due to their flaming appearance (similar to the fiery serpents of Num. 21:6; Deut. 8:15). But their name probably relates to their role in purification. Fire is a symbol for purity; appropriately one of these fiery beings purified Isaiah's lips with a live coal (6:6).

people on a scapegoat and driving that goat into the wilderness (Lev. 16). The Hebrew word translated **purged** means "covered" and is the same term that is rendered "atonement." The word refers to the process of killing an animal and sprinkling the blood on the altar for atonement.

6:8 At times, the prophets would be invited to participate in the heavenly court (1 Kin. 22:19–22; Jer. 23:18, 22). Here the Lord uses the pronoun **Us** to mean Himself and His angels (Gen. 3:22; 11:7). **Send me:** In ancient Middle Eastern religions only divine beings are sent as messengers of the gods. Yet the God of Scripture uses human beings as a matter of course. Only at certain times does He use angels in a direct way to reveal His will to humankind. Isaiah's willingness proceeded from a grateful heart; he wanted to serve the God who had forgiven him (v. 7).

6:9, 10 Paradoxically, Isaiah's preaching to the religious and arrogant people who **keep on hearing** was destined to **make . . . their ears heavy** (42:20). Only the humble would **understand** the Lord's message. The more the prophet would proclaim the word of God, the less response he would get from the people. This was a call to a discouraging ministry. In truth, the call of God is for faithfulness to Him, to His word, and to the call itself.

6:11 Understandably, Isaiah's third expression to the Lord (compare vv. 5, 8) was one of incredulity. He wondered **how long** the people would continue to be unresponsive to his words of truth from God.

6:11, 12 The answer was grim. **waste . . . desolate:** These words describe the coming judgment of God on Judah that would lead to the nation's captivity under the Babylonians. **Removed men . . . forsaken places** describe the desolation that would follow the conquest by Babylon.

6:13 But . . . consuming: After the coming Babylonian invasion, the part of the land and the people who remained would be scorched again

(5:25). This describes the return from the Exile and the subsequent troubles of Judah in the land. **A tenth** is one of Isaiah's expressions for the "remnant"; it is only a small percentage of the Israelites. From Israel's blasted **stump,** God would produce a **holy seed** (11:1), for He cannot deny the nation He has chosen (2 Tim. 2:13). An immediate fulfillment of this prophecy occurred in Isaiah's time: King Hezekiah repented and showed himself to be part of the holy seed (ch. 38). Ultimately, the *holy* seed would issue in the Beautiful Branch (11:1). This is the promise of the Savior Jesus.

7:1—12:6 This major section of Isaiah contains a series of prophecies related specifically to the Syro-Ephraimite wars—the invasion of Judah by Rezin and Pekah. These prophecies aimed to call Judah back to faith in God.

7:1 This is an editorial heading to 7:2—12:6 (2 Kin. 16:5). The Book of Isaiah was written over the period of the prophet's lifetime; but chapters 7—12 were set in the context of the Syro-Ephraimite wars. **Syria** is the later name for the ancient nation of Aram.

7:2—8:10 This section consists of five prophecies (7:2–9, 10–17, 18–25; 8:1–4, 5–10) predicting both Judah's deliverance from the kings of Syria and Israel and its devastation (short of annihilation) at the hand of the Assyrian king.

7:2—9 The introduction to the command to trust the Lord, not Assyria, consists of the historical situation (vv. 2–6) and the oracle predicting the destruction of Ephraim (vv. 7–9). The historical situation consists of what was told to Ahaz (v. 2), what the Lord told Isaiah to say to Ahaz (vv. 3, 4), and what Syria and Ephraim counseled concerning Judah (vv. 5, 6).

7:2 The phrase **house of David** is a substitute term for the king of Judah, Ahaz. This phrase recalls the Lord's eternal covenant with David in which He promised to give to His servant an eternal seed, throne, and kingdom (2 Sam. 7:16; Ps. 89:19–37). The word **Ephraim**

represents the northern kingdom, Israel. The **heart** of the nation was **moved** because Syria had defeated Ahaz earlier (2 Chr. 28:5).

7:3 Shear-Jashub means "A Remnant Will Return." The name of Isaiah's son spoke of a coming Exile and then the salvation of the remaining faithful. All this would occur long after Isaiah's lifetime. Ahaz was probably standing at the **aqueduct** at the time of this encounter, seeking to secure Jerusalem's supply of water in case of the siege (2 Chr. 32:30).

7:4 God contemptuously dismissed the arrogant kings of Syria and Israel. What Ahaz greatly feared, God considered merely **stubs of smoking firebrands** drawn from a bonfire. The **son of Remaliah** is Pekah, king of Israel (v. 1).

7:5, 6 The plotting of Syria and Ephraim was no secret to God, who made it known to His servant Isaiah. **Tabel** means "Good for Nothing." Syria and Israel wanted to place an incompetent puppet king over Judah.

7:7, 8 It shall not stand: The plans of humankind are futile when they oppose the will of God. **Within sixty-five years** suggests that one must believe that God will fulfill His promises even beyond the time of one's own death.

7:9 You is plural. The prophet was speaking to the royal family and the nation. **Believe** and **established** are a play on the same Hebrew word from which we get our word *amen*. Believing entails having knowledge of God's Word, accepting that it is true, and placing our trust in the Lord to help us keep it. Believing the Lord is the key to receiving His promises (John 14:1).

7:10 While Isaiah's prophecy was principally addressed to King **Ahaz,** it was directed to others in v. 13.

7:11 The **sign** pertains to the prediction in vv. 7–9, the demise of the power of Samaria. **In the depth or in the height** indicates that Ahaz could ask for any sign he wished.

7:12 not ask . . . test: In the mouth of the wicked Ahaz, these arrogant words rang hollow.

7:13 The pronoun **you** is plural here (v. 14). Thus in this verse, Isaiah is speaking to the entire royal line of David. **weary:** God responded to Ahaz in indignation. This petty and arrogant king dared to refuse the Lord; he would not trust in God even when his enemies surrounded him (v. 12).

7:14 Again **you** is plural here. Isaiah turns from the king whom he has dismissed in judgment and addresses all who are present. The **sign** is for many. The word **Lord** speaks of the sovereignty of God, of His great control over all His creation. The pronoun **Himself** adds an absolute certainty to the impending sign. The

Hebrew word rendered **virgin** means "a young woman of marriageable age." But the word also connotes the idea of virginity, for the Septuagint, the Greek translation of the Hebrew Bible made in the second century B.C., renders the Hebrew word with a Greek term that specifically means "virgin".

7:15 Curds and honey contrast with "bread and wine" from cultivated lands and symbolically represent the Judean's simple diet after the Assyrian invasion. Thus the Child, similar to Isaiah's son Shear-Jashub (v. 3), would be identified with the remnant.

7:16, 17 For before: Similar prophecies were spoken of the Child's birth and Isaiah's

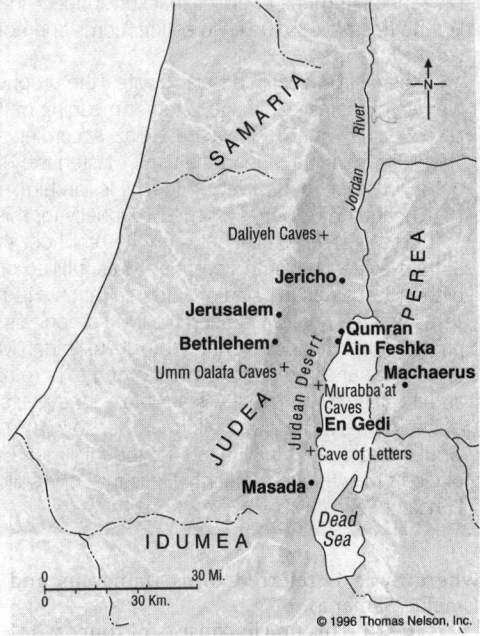

The Region of the Dead Sea Scrolls

In 1947 a shepherd looking for a stray goat in a cave near Qumran stumbled upon some clay jars containing ancient scrolls. Though these scrolls were all from the first century A.D. or before, the hot and dry climate of the Dead Sea region had preserved them remarkably well. One of the most significant scrolls in the discovery was a complete copy of the Book of Isaiah. Its contents amply confirm the authenticity of later manuscripts. Later searches of the Dead Sea region led to discoveries of scrolls containing the Minor Prophets, near En Gedi, and other biblical fragments in the Murabba'at caves.

other son Maher-Shalal-Hash-Baz (8:3): Israel and Syria would be destroyed before this child and Isaiah's son would reach maturity (8:4,

IN CONTEXT Immanuel—God with Us!

Behold, the virgin shall conceive and bear a Son, and shall call His name Immanuel." During the Christmas season, this verse becomes a part of our common vocabulary (7:14): Most Christmas pageants recite the verse, and pastors explain the meaning of Immanuel, "God with Us." How the prophecy was fulfilled in the birth of Christ is recorded in the Gospel of Matthew (Matt. 1:23). But there are still questions that surround this prophecy. For instance, how could the birth of Jesus be a sign to Ahaz?

Sometimes unraveling biblical prophecy can be difficult. This is one of those cases; Christians have interpreted this prophecy in several different ways. Some have thought the anonymous "virgin" may refer to a royal mother—more specifically Ahaz's wife. Thus the child would be Hezekiah, Ahaz's successor. Hezekiah would be a sign to Ahaz that God was in control: The Lord was with Ahaz; He would save Judah from the enemies that surrounded Ahaz, enabling his son to inherit the throne (7:1–3). Yet the reference to the child eating "curds and honey" was a prediction of Assyria's eventual domination of Judah.

Others have identified Isaiah's wife, "the prophetess" of 8:3, as the "virgin." She was a young woman of marriageable age, another meaning of the Hebrew word translated *virgin*. The child in this case would be Maher-Shalal-Hash-Baz. According to this view, the child's two names, Maher-Shalal-Hash-Baz meaning "Speed the Spoil, Hasten the Booty," and Immanuel meaning "God with Us," symbolize judgment and salvation. In fact, Isaiah himself described his children as "signs" to the nation (8:18), and he delivered a similar prophecy for this son (compare 7:16 with 8:4).

Some cite the parallel between the prophecy that a "virgin shall conceive" and Jesus' miraculous birth as evidence that this prophecy was fulfilled only in Jesus. Mary was the virgin mother; and the birth of Jesus was the sign of God's salvation. His name would be Immanuel, "God with Us," because Jesus was the Son of God and He lived among us (Matt. 1:23). According to this view, Isaiah's prophecy had no fulfillment prior to Jesus' birth (Matt. 1:18–25).

It is not uncommon for biblical prophecies to have one level of fulfillment in the immediate future, and a final fulfillment many years later in the person and work of the Savior, Jesus. Thus the pregnancy of Isaiah's new wife and the birth of her son (8:3) could have been a sign to King Ahaz. However, this would have been *a* fulfillment, not *the* fulfillment. The prophecy was completely fulfilled in the coming of God's only Son to the earth. He is the only Child who can truly be called Wonderful, Counselor, and Prince of Peace (9:6).

where Syria is referred to as Damascus and Israel as Samaria).

7:18–25 This oracle consists of four "woe" prophecies (18, 19, 20, 21, 22, 23–25), each of which begins with **in that day** (2:12). They reveal the details of the veiled threat in verse 17 of how the Lord will judge the unbelievers.

7:18, 19 The invading hordes are compared to swarming insects—**the fly** and **the bee**—blanketing Judah, a condition fulfilled in the Assyrian invasions.

7:20 shave . . . the hair: This was a symbol of humiliation. **Hired** refers to Ahaz's foolish idea of paying Assyria to save him from the alliance of Syria and Israel.

7:21, 22 in that day: This phrase can indicate times of trouble as here, or periods of blessing (as in 2:2). **A young cow and two sheep** out of what used to be herd indicates impoverishment in the time of trouble. The land would be so depopulated and impoverished

that the limited fare of **curds and honey** (v. 15) would look like an **abundance.**

7:23–25 vines . . . thorns: The productivity of the land would be greatly reduced in the period of God's judgment. The repetition of **briers and thorns** in vv. 23–25 is emphatic; in other words, the land would no longer be cultivated.

8:1 large scroll: This message from the Lord was intended to be read and pondered by many people.

8:2 Just as the wicked Ahaz was forced to be a party to the sign regarding the birth of Immanuel (7:10–17), **Uriah,** an apostate priest (2 Kin. 16:10–16), and **Zechariah,** presumably a false prophet (not to be confused with the prophet who wrote the Book of Zechariah), were forced to witness to this prophecy.

8:3 Isaiah's wife was a **prophetess** in her own right. It is possible that this was a new wife, following the death of the mother of Shear-Jashub (7:3).

8:4 spoil of Samaria . . . king of Assyria: This is a specific prediction of the fall of Samaria to the Assyrians in 722 B.C. This prophecy has to have been written shortly before that time, as the fulfillment would come before the new child would be able to speak.

8:5–10 This prophecy shifts from Syria and Israel's defeat before Assyria to Judah's defeat for unbelief. It consists of three parts: (1) the accusation of Judah's unbelief (vv. 5, 6), (2) Judah devastated but not annihilated by Assyria (vv. 7, 8), and (3) the doom of all Judah's enemies (vv. 9, 10).

8:5 The Lord also spoke to me again: This phrase introduces a new prophetic section and reminds the reader of the source of the prophetic images in the Book of Isaiah.

8:6 These people is "this people" in Hebrew, the same construction as in v. 11. The gentle waters of **Shiloah** picture the sustaining presence of the Lord; He had quietly supplied the Israelites their needs, such as pure water. Shiloah may have been a little stream that flowed through an aqueduct (7:3) to carry the water from the spring Gihon on Jerusalem's east side (2 Chr. 32:30) to the Pool of Siloam (Neh. 3:15) in the lower or southern end of the city. **rejoice:** The Judeans rejoiced because they thought they were going to defeat the kings of Israel and Syria through Ahaz's strategy of hiring the armies of Assyria. They looked for the salvation that a mere king could offer instead of appealing to the King of kings for protection.

8:7, 8 The River refers to the Euphrates, but also conveys the image of pagan gods. **neck:** Assyria would devastate Judah, but not completely annihilate it (ch. 37). **wings:** In the middle of v. 8, the image of Assyria as mighty waters changes to the image of a bird of prey. Isaiah bestows the name of the promised Child, **Immanuel** (7:14), on Judah, for it would be preserved only because God was with that nation (v. 10).

8:9 Far countries refers to the many nations that made up Assyria's international army (5:26; 7:18). **Gird yourselves . . . be broken:** The nations would do the will of God, but in turn would be destroyed.

8:10 It will not stand: The Lord would defeat the purposes of Judah's enemies; all their councils would come to nothing. This promise concludes the prophecies of 7:1–8:10. The Child whose name would mean **God is with us** (v. 8; 7:14), was a sign not only of the destruction of Syria and Israel (7:17), but of all of God's enemies, including Assyria.

8:11–9:1 After an introductory summary (v. 11), this prophecy consists of two cycles: (1) Judah is commanded to trust in the Lord or perish, a command reinforced by Isaiah and his children, who serve as signs to Judah (vv. 12–18). (2) Judah is commanded to walk in the light of Isaiah's prophecies or be thrown into utter darkness (8:19—9:1).

8:11 Strong hand signifies a powerful sense of the Lord's inspiration (Ezek. 1:3).

8:12 Do not say: The commands in vv. 12, 13, 15, 19 are in the plural. Perhaps Isaiah's adversaries were labeling his rejection of an alliance with Assyria a **conspiracy.**

8:13 Hallow means to treat as holy. **Your fear** indicates a sense of reverence, awe, and wonder. **Your dread** indicates fright and terror. If the people want to be frightened, they should be frightened of God. If they want to respond to God correctly, they should treat His name with awe and fear Him (Ex. 20:20).

8:14 God is a **sanctuary** for believers, but a **stone of stumbling** for unbelievers (Ps. 118:22; Luke 20:17, 18; Rom. 9:33; 1 Pet. 2:6–8). **Both the houses** designate both the northern and the southern kingdom, that is, both Israel and Judah.

8:15 stumble . . . broken: The wicked will not prevail for long (v. 10).

8:16 Testimony refers to a legal transaction. **Law** refers to God's instruction revealed through Isaiah. Isaiah's disciples put his prophecies in the form of a legal transaction probably to prove their authenticity when they were fulfilled (vv. 1, 2; compare Jer. 28:9; 32:12–14).

8:17 wait . . . hope: These words indicate a confident expectation that God would meet the needs of His people and deliver them from disaster (40:31; Ps. 40:1). Ultimately, the hope of Isaiah would be fulfilled in the Savior Jesus (Heb. 2:12, 13).

8:18 children: Isaiah, whose name speaks of the salvation of God, and his two sons, whose names speak of the impending judgment of God, were **signs and wonders in Israel**—that is, they were symbols (20:3). **Mount Zion:** The place of the holy temple was a mirror of God's dwelling in the highest heaven.

8:19, 20 In the fertility religions of Canaan, **mediums and wizards** would deliver divine revelations. **who whisper and mutter:** But the best one could get from these perverted "prophets" was garbled muttering. **Seek the dead** indicates that the people were involved in necromancy, namely, the practice of conjuring up the spirits of the dead in order to influence events (29:4; 65:4).

8:21 They refers to the wicked who refuse to revere God (v. 13). **It** refers perhaps to the implied **darkness** of v. 20. **curse:** For similar usage, see Ex. 22:28; Lev. 24:15, 16.

8:22 The prophets commonly used the imagery of **darkness** to indicate judgment (5:30). The synonyms for *darkness* in this verse describe not only moral and spiritual blight, but also the invasion of Assyria that took away liberty and brought foreign oppression.

9:1 Nevertheless the gloom: This line completes the thought of 8:22 and promises a dramatic change to come. That change would be the explosion of light found in the Good News: Jesus can free us from the darkness that comes from our sin (Eph. 5:8). The ancient tribal allotments of **Zebulun** and **Napthali** (Josh. 19:10–16, 32–39), which included **Galilee,** were the first to feel the brunt of the Assyrian invasions (2 Kin. 15:29). The three phrases at the end of the verse—**the way of the sea, beyond the Jordan, Galilee of the Gentiles** or "nations"—indicate administrative districts of the Assyrian conqueror Tiglath-Pileser III as a result of the three campaigns he waged in the west around 733 B.C.

9:2–7 This seventh prophecy in the context of the Syro-Ephraimite war is climactic: An ideal monarch will come who will bring an end to war and usher in universal peace. The light that will replace the darkness of Assyrian oppression will be a Child, God incarnate (7:14). His four compounded throne names (v. 6) depict His divine-human nature as well as His universal program of salvation.

9:2 Have seen: The future event is described by the prophet, under the impulse of the Spirit, as having already occurred. **Light** stands for God's blessings, presence, and revelation (2:5), that is incarnate in Jesus (58:8; 59:9; 60:1, 2, 19, 20; John 8:12). **Shadow of death** means "deep darkness" (compare 60:2; Ps. 23:4). Here this Hebrew word complements the more commonly used word for **darkness.**

9:3 joy of harvest . . . divide the spoil: The agricultural society knows no greater joy than that of harvest. A soldier knows no greater joy than that of a finished battle when his side has won, he is still alive, and there is now booty to divide. Contrast the joy of harvest in this verse with the lack of joy at harvest in 16:10.

9:4 yoke . . . staff . . . rod: These three images of oppression emphasize the suffering of the people during the period of foreign domination. The pronoun **his** refers to Assyria, which boasted of the heavy yokes it imposed on its captive peoples (10:27). **The day of Midian** refers to the defeat of Midian (10:26; Judg. 6—8).

9:5 warrior's sandal: Assyrian armies were marked by the noise of the marching of many feet. **Garments rolled in blood** from past battles was a deliberate scare tactic to frighten enemies in an impending battle. All of these emblems of warfare were to be burned in the coming day of the reign of the divine Child (v. 6).

9:6 Born speaks of the Child's humanity and **given** of His deity. **Wonderful, Counselor** is one name, meaning "wonderful divine Counselor" (11:1–5). **Mighty God** indicates that the Lord is a powerful Warrior (10:21). **Everlasting Father** describes a King and Father who provides for and protects His people forever (40:9–11; Matt. 11:27–30). Thus the word **Father** is used

---

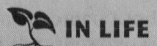 **IN LIFE**   # Be Careful of Counsel

As you make decisions and strategize plans, you'll do well to gain counsel from wise, trusted confidants. In fact, Proverbs says that utilizing input from many counselors offers safety (Prov. 11:14). Their variety of opinions tends to ensure success (15:22; 20:18; 24:6).

The people of Isaiah's day could have benefited by heeding wise counsel, but they had a hard time distinguishing good counsel from bad. So Isaiah contrasted the two. Reliable counsel . . .

- listens carefully to God (Is. 8:11);
- is not quick to identify "conspiracies" (8:12);
- avoids acting solely out of fear (8:12); and
- praises and respects the Lord (8:13).

Unreliable counsel . . .

- ignores God's Law and testimony (8:19, 20);
- allows anger to distort things (8:21); and,
- leads to trouble and anguish (8:22).

Can you identify the sources of good and bad counsel in your life? Would anyone be able to mention you as a source of wise counsel and advice?

here of the Savior's role as an ideal king. **Prince of Peace** is the climactic title (2:4; 11:6–9; 53:5; Luke 2:14; Rom. 5:1). The Child is the true Prince—the One who has the right to reign and who will usher in peace. The four double names combine aspects of Jesus' deity and His humanity. Together, these four double names assert the dual nature of the Savior: He is God become man.

9:7 Of the increase may be translated "to Him will increase." **Government and peace** may be rephrased as "peaceful reign." The risen Lord Jesus brings His rule of peace to the believer's heart in the present age. Moreover, He will establish the kingdom of God, which will be His reign of peace. The fact that this coming Child will occupy **the throne of David** forever fulfills God's promise to David (2 Sam. 7:8–16; Ps. 89:19–37; Luke 1:32, 33).

9:8–10:4 This passage contains a judgment against the northern kingdom: the Lord will destroy it and its capital, Samaria. The accusations and judicial sentences in this section indicate that the Lord is both Judge and Punisher (9:11, 14, 19; 10:4).

9:9, 10 Bricks refers to the mud brick walls common in ancient Israel. The people were planning to make their buildings more grandiose, not taking into account the fact that the Lord was about to destroy the buildings completely because of His judgment on their sins.

9:11 The adversaries refers to the Assyrians who were used by **the Lord** to punish the northern kingdom.

9:12 The Syrians were to the east of Israel and the **Philistines** to the west.

9:13 Turn indicates repentance and a desire for restoration.

9:14, 15 Head and tail is a figure of speech for all leaders.

9:16 cause them to err: For a similar usage, see 3:12.

9:17 Young men . . . widows denotes every person. Everyone had turned from the faithful worship of God. All of Israel had been contaminated with evil, hypocrisy, and foolishness (read 1 Cor. 5:6 for an exhortation not to let wickedness corrupt the church).

9:18, 19 The **fire** of **wickedness** is matched by the **fire** of **the wrath of the Lord**.

9:18 Wickedness refers both to the sin itself and to its destructive consequences.

9:19, 20 No man shall spare his brother refers to anarchy (3:4, 5). **right hand . . . left hand:** These figures of speech indicate an insatiable hunger and the consequent ruin that would occur in the day of judgment.

9:21 Manasseh fought **Ephraim** (Judg. 12:4); then together they fought **Judah** (but see 11:13).

10:1 Woe is a chilling word when spoken by God (5:8–23; 10:5; 18:1); here the Lord condemns the leaders who write laws that perpetuate evil in the community.

10:2 The **needy** are regularly seen in Scripture as those to whom the righteous should show true piety. When godly people reach out to help those who cannot help themselves, they display pure, biblical religion (James 1:27). Conversely, the mark of the ungodly can be seen in their oppressive actions against people who cannot help themselves. They set themselves up for the sure judgment of God (v. 3).

10:3 From afar refers to Assyria. **To whom:** The wicked could not turn to God, for they had refused to do so before and had ignored God's warnings (8:6).

10:4 Prisoners refers to the Israelites being led away into exile.

10:5–11:16 This section moves beyond the wasting of Israel to the subsequent destruction of Assyria and the deliverance of Judah.

10:5–34 This salvation oracle has two major sections: (1) Assyria's doom (vv. 5–19) and (2) the remnant's salvation (vv. 20–34).

10:5 And . . . indignation may also be translated "even the staff in My indignant hand." **rod of My anger:** Though God sovereignly uses sinners as instruments of His will (7:17; 13:5), they will be held accountable for their own wickedness. Thus God shows that He is just in all His ways (Hab. 1—3).

10:6 The **ungodly nation** is Judah (vv. 11, 12).

10:7, 8 in his heart: The purpose of the arrogant Assyrians was to continue their path of uninterrupted conquest. But God had different plans for them (v. 12).

10:9 Calno . . . Damascus: This is a list of cities that had already fallen to the Assyrians.

10:10, 11 idols . . . images: The Assyrians had conquered the nations who had false gods; surely, they believed, they would also have an easy time against **Jerusalem and her idols.** Though only the living God was to be worshiped by the Israelites, they had repeatedly broken that command (Ex. 20:4–6; Judg. 2:19).

10:12 The **fruit** is the king's speech cited in vv. 13, 14. **arrogant heart . . . haughty looks:** For a similar idea, see 2:11; 3:9; 9:9.

10:13 By the strength of my hand: The wicked are quick to take credit for their successes. The righteous correctly give praise to God for their accomplishments.

10:14 as one gathers eggs: That is, the conquests, the wicked brag, were child's play. The nations they had ravaged provided no more opposition than a hen when one gathers eggs.

10:15 An implement in the hand of its user has no reason for boasting; Assyria was merely a tool in the hand of God. It had no reason to **boast.**

10:16 leanness . . . burning: These words describe the coming judgment of the Assyrians, who had become **fat** because of their acts of conquest.

10:17, 18 The Light of Israel is a wonderful title for God (9:2; 58:8; 60:1, 19, 20). The Lord Jesus is described as a "Light" of Israel as

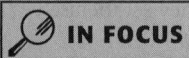

IN FOCUS "hosts"

(Heb. *tseba'ah*) (10:16; Gen. 2:1; Pss. 103:21; 148:2) Strong's #6635: This word comes from a verb meaning "to fight" or "to serve." Angels are said to be *hosts* because they serve God (1 Kin. 22:19; Ps. 103:20, 21; compare Luke 2:13). The heavens are under the command of God and render Him worship, thus they are also called *host* (45:12; Neh. 9:6; Ps. 33:6). The term also commonly refers to combat troops (2 Kin. 5:1; 1 Chr. 7:11, 40). "The armies of the LORD" is an expression used once for the children of Israel, and twice for God's army of angels (Ex. 12:41; Josh. 5:14, 15). Of the nearly five hundred uses of this word, almost three hundred are in an expression such as "the LORD of hosts" (1 Sam. 17:45), a title describing God's power. On two occasions, the NT writers transliterated this Hebrew title as "the Lord of Sabaoth" to describe the awesome might of God (Rom. 9:29; James 5:4).

well (John 1:1–13). **His thorns . . . his forest** refers to all persons and possessions in the Assyrian Empire. What people count as honorable or despicable will mean little before God's burning judgment.

10:19, 20 The remnant is the portion of Abraham's offspring that God preserved. The Hebrew word used here for remnant is different from the words used in 1:9; 6:13. **depend:** Finally there will be a people whose trust will be unchangeably in the Lord.

10:21, 22 as the sand . . . A remnant: Most of the people of the northern kingdom were carried off into captivity. But some Israelites made their way to Judah and became part of the southern kingdom. These people and their descendants would act as a remnant by preserving the names of the northern tribes among the people of God.

10:23 determined end: This powerful language contrasts with the vagueness of false prophecies among the nations.

10:24 Lord GOD of hosts: For a similar usage, see 1:9. **O My people:** The language here expresses the loving care of the Lord for His people. They need not fear the armies of the Assyrians.

10:25 a very little while: From the viewpoint of eternity, the period of trial is exceedingly brief.

10:26 slaughter of Midian: Despite its powerful and ruthless armies, Isaiah prophesied that Assyria would go down in Israelite history alongside the Midianites and the Egyptians, as a foe miraculously vanquished by the Lord (Is. 10:26). That is exactly what happened. **on the sea** refers to God's great triumph over Pharaoh at the Exodus (Ex. 14; 15).

10:27 in that day: For a similar idea, see 2:12. The meaning of **anointing oil** here is uncertain. If it means "fat," the image may be of a strong, fattened ox breaking its yoke.

10:28–32 These verses depict Isaiah's vision of the king of Assyria's relentless march south over difficult terrain from **Aiath**—that is, Ai. Ai was ten miles north of Jerusalem on a point overlooking the city.

10:28, 29 The cities as listed in these verses are closer and closer to the capital at Jerusalem. Each town conquered was another step toward the impending defeat of the holy city.

10:30, 31 Lift up your voice: The language turns to that of panic. The actions are those of a frightened people facing defeat and disaster.

10:32 daughter of Zion: The army was near **Jerusalem** itself. The pronoun **he** refers to Assyria, the enemy.

10:33, 34 The **bough** is the king of Assyria and the **thickets** are his army. The point is that God will bring judgment on the instruments that He used to judge Israel.

11:1–9 This celebrated salvation oracle about the King of Peace (4:2; 7:14; 9:6) consists of three sections: (1) His endowment (vv. 1, 2); (2) His righteous rule (vv. 3–5); and (3) His kingdom of peace (vv. 6–9).

11:1 A Rod from the stem of Jesse (1 Sam. 16:10–13) represents the new and greater David. As David inaugurated a kingdom of righteousness and peace, the new David, the "rod" or "root" from David's line (53:2), will establish an incomparably greater kingdom. The words Rod and **Branch** are messianic terms. They are figurative words for the great descendant of the household of David, the Seed of the Woman promised in Gen. 3:15, Jesus Christ Himself (Matt. 1:17).

11:2 Spirit: As in the case of David (1 Sam. 16:13), the Messiah would be empowered by the Holy Spirit (4:4; 42:1; 48:16; 59:21; 61:1; Luke 3:22), the Agent for establishing God's kingdom (Gen. 1:1, 2; Judg. 3:10; 6:34; 1 Sam. 10:6). The first readers of the Hebrew Scriptures likely thought that the term *Spirit* was just another way of speaking about God with awe or wonder. In the NT, we learn that the term refers to the third Person of the Trinity (Matt. 28:19). Solomon prayed for **wisdom and under-standing** (1 Kin. 3:9), the administrative skill to govern the people according to the principles of righteousness and justice (Deut. 1:15–17). The Messiah will embody all this; He will be the ideal King (33:6). The Holy Spirit's **counsel** is not advice, but authoritative plans and decisions. **the fear of the LORD**: The Messiah would demonstrate in all His life the correct response to God: He would honor and obey Him (Ex. 20:20). The people of God in all ages are under orders to respond to Him with reverential awe (Lev. 19:14; Prov. 19:23).

11:3 Delight refers to the sense of smell. There may be an allusion to the incense burned at a coronation ceremony. Whereas "fear of God" usually means a standard of moral conduct known and accepted by humankind in general, **the fear of the LORD** in this case may refer to the standard of moral conduct known through special revelation and accepted by the faithful.

11:4, 5 In this context, **judge** does not mean to bring people to account, but to act on their behalf. As the judge of His people, God sentences the wicked and offers protection and defense for the innocent and oppressed. **rod of His mouth:** The Messiah will conquer by His speech (49:2; Heb. 4:12; Rev. 19:15).

11:6–9 This picture of cruel beasts miraculously regenerated with a new nature that makes them protect their natural prey depicts a reign of peace and security. This can only be realized in the return of the Messiah to establish the kingdom of God (65:17–25). In God's peaceful kingdom, carnivores will become herbivores; natural enemies will become companions; and little children will play safely near the dwellings of formerly venomous snakes.

11:6–8 a little child shall lead them: In the coming kingdom, a youngster will be able to lead formerly wild animals. This is a way of emphasizing the end of terror, fright, and danger in the coming kingdom.

11:9 In ancient times, **the knowledge of the LORD** was limited and spotty; there is coming a glorious age in which there will be no limit to access to divine truth. **As the waters cover the sea** means "thoroughly." God will make Himself known throughout the earth.

11:10 in that day: This verse forms a single prophetic vision. The exalted **Root of Jesse** will attract the **Gentiles** to **His resting place** (2:3). This is a prophecy of the coming of people of all nations to the knowledge of God. Thus, in the OT, the Lord expresses His concern for the salvation of other nations (Gen. 12:1–3). World mission was not a new idea with the Great Commission (Matt. 28:18–20). **Banner** is a rallying symbol. Jesus the Messiah is the *banner* for the gathering of peoples from all over the earth.

11:11–16 This prophecy concerning the second Exodus (51:9–11) consists of the regathering of the exiles (vv. 11, 12), their unity in opposition to God's enemies (vv. 13, 14), and an allusion to the first Exodus to show how much greater is the second one (vv. 15, 16).

11:11 The **second time** may refer to the remnant coming back to the land in 538 B.C., in contrast to the first Exodus from Egypt. Beyond that, it could also refer to the remnant's coming to Christ in the present age (Rom. 11:5), or to its future return to Christ (Rom. 11:11–27). **From Assyria . . . and the islands of the sea** indicates the whole earth (v. 12).

 **IN DEPTH** | **God's Anger Brings Peace**

Critics of Christianity sometimes point to God's wrath as a contradiction in His supposedly loving character. "How can you say that God is a God of love when the OT says that He is going to 'strike the earth with the rod of His mouth'?" (Is. 11:4) they scornfully ask.

One response is to observe that God's wrath is not exactly like the anger that human beings often display. People often vent their rage in vindictive, selfish ways that may dissipate emotion but do little to promote true justice. By contrast, God's wrath is based in His just and righteous character (11:5). When He judges people and nations, it is not because He feels hurt, but because wrongs need to be righted. His wrath comes against evil and wickedness.

Furthermore, God's anger results in a righteous outcome—peace (11:6–9). When human beings vindicate themselves, their wrath often leads to more violence, suffering, and bitterness. But God's judgments will ultimately produce peace on earth because they serve true justice and do away with those who are committed to injustice and unrighteousness.

11:12 the four corners of the earth: This figurative expression is similar to the words of Acts 1:8: "to the end of the earth." The Messiah will gather disciples from all over the world.

11:13 Ephraim . . . Judah: Not only will God destroy the enemies of the Israelites and Judeans, but He will also remove their ancient enmities (9:20, 21).

11:14 upon the shoulder: The image is that of a bird of prey attacking another bird. **The Philistines, Edom, Moab,** and **Ammon,** Israel's traditional enemies, may represent the adversaries of the Messiah's kingdom (a similar use of the word Assyria is found in Mic. 5:6).

11:15 Mighty wind is an allusion to Ex. 14:21–27. **The River** refers to the Euphrates. **dry-shod:** As God had provided a dry passage across the Red Sea in the first Exodus, so in the second Exodus He would remove any physical barrier that would hinder the return of His people.

11:16 A highway symbolizes the certainty of the return, for no obstacles would hinder the Lord's returning exiles (35:8–10; 40:3, 4; 57:14; 62:10). **In the day:** The reference here is to the first Exodus (v. 11).

12:1–6 This hymn of praise for God's salvation by the restored remnant after the second Exodus (11:12–16) resembles Moses and Miriam's hymn of praise after the first Exodus from Egypt (Ex. 15). The song consists of a hymn of thanksgiving by the remnant for their salvation (vv. 1–3), and a hymn of thanksgiving proclaiming His salvation among the nations (vv. 4–6). Ultimately, this is an end-time psalm of praise (as is 42:10–17), a poem to be sung in the future kingdom by the redeemed of the Lord in His glorious presence.

12:1 in that day: For a similar idea, see 2:12. The first **you** is singular, representing the remnant as an individual. **angry:** The anger of God had caused the people to be dispersed among the nations (5:25; 9:12); His grace would lead to their regathering.

12:2 God is my salvation: This psalm of redemption is based on the first psalm of redemption in Exodus (Ex. 15:2; Ps. 118:14). YAH, the LORD, by its repetition, emphasizes that Israel's covenant-keeping God—and not the nations—brings salvation (26:4). **My strength and song** may be rephrased as "my strong song" or "my song of strength" (Ex. 15:2).

12:3 You in vv. 3–5 is plural. The Hebrew poets often associate the concept of **water** with salvation (Ex. 17:1–7). In an arid land, the provision of **wells** and springs was regarded as a divine gift (55:1).

12:4 As in the Psalms, this hymn uses several terms for the praise of God. **Praise** means "to give public acknowledgment" or "to declare aloud in public." **Call upon His name** may be rephrased as "proclaim in His name." **Declare** means "to make known." **Make mention** means "to cause to remember." Each of these verbs designates public, vocal acknowledgment of the wonders and works of God. **among the peoples:** Like Ps. 117, this is a poem of international evangelism.

12:5 Sing to the LORD: The principal audience of sacred songs is God Himself (Ps. 33:1). **excellent things:** In Ex. 15:1, the root of this term is translated "triumphed gloriously." **all the earth:** This emphasis fits the same line of thought found in Ps. 19:1.

12:6 Cry out and shout may be rephrased as "shout aloud in great joy." **Inhabitant of Zion** originally referred to the people who returned from captivity in Babylon. The future singers of this psalm will be the people in the kingdom of the Messiah. They will celebrate Him and His salvation. **in your midst:** In the coming age of the reign of King Jesus, He will be in the **midst** of His people (Zeph. 3:16–18).

13:1—27:13 The Book of Isaiah takes a major turn at 13:1. The focus in this extended section is first on the Lord's judgments against the nations (chs. 13—23): Babylon and Assyria (13:1—14:27), Philistia (14:28–32), Moab (15:1—16:14), Damascus (17:1–14), Ethiopia (18:1–7), Egypt (19:1—20:6), Babylon (21:1–10), Edom (21:11, 12), Arabia (21:13–17), Jerusalem (22:1–25), and Tyre (23:1–18). This prophecy of judgment is followed by an end-time prophecy that is sometimes called "the little apocalypse of Isaiah" (chs. 24—27).

13:1—14:27 The oracle against Babylon consists of seven sections: (1) the assembly of the army of the Lord of Hosts (13:1–5); (2) the announcement of the day of the Lord (13:6–18); (3) the annihilation of Babylon (13:19–22); (4) the salvation of Israel (14:1, 2); (5) Israel's mocking dirge for the king of Babylon (14:3–21); (6) the destruction of Babylon (14:22, 23); and (7) the destruction of Assyria (14:24–27).

13:1, 2 The word **burden** comes from the root meaning "to lift up" or "to bear." It is as though the prophet were heavily laden with a message from God that he must deliver due to its sheer weight (Nah. 1:1; Hab. 1:1). **Babylon** was the crown jewel of the Assyrian Empire. This oracle may refer to its destruction around 689 B.C. when Sennacherib quelled a rebellion there. Yet the Lord's overthrow of **Babylon,** "the glory of kingdoms" (v. 19), symbolizes His triumph over the world (v. 11). Babylon is the epitome of religion and culture in the ancient Middle East. Thus the oracle is indirectly against all nations, especially Assyria (14:24–27). Peter uses the term Babylon symbolically in the NT (1 Pet. 5:13) as does John (Rev. 14:8; 18:2, 10–21) to refer to any enemy of God's kingdom.

13:3, 4 Sanctified ones refers to the victorious armies of the earth **who rejoice,** wittingly or unwittingly, in the Lord's **exaltation** (45:1–7; Joel 2:11). **Many people** represent all nations, who will be instruments in God's hands for judging sinful nations, though they themselves are sinners.

13:5 Far country . . . end of heaven refers to the whole earth (11:11, 12). **His weapons of indignation:** The nations are the tools God will use to vent His wrath against Babylon.

13:6 The day of the LORD refers to a time of unusual activity of God in the lives of people, for judgment or for mercy. **At hand** is also translated "near." The basic idea of the term is not that of approaching a fixed date, but that the day of the Lord is about to burst into one's world. The day of the Lord is imminent—able to happen at any time—not because people have almost reached it as a destination, but because it may burst in upon people without further warning. The title **the Almighty** is the Hebrew name Shaddai (Ex. 6:3; Ps. 91:1).

13:7, 8 limp . . . melt . . . afraid: These images describe the depth of the people's fear. **a woman in childbirth:** This is a familiar image of stress in the poetry of the Bible.

13:9, 10 Will not give their light symbolizes the dark aspect of God's judgment. It is as though heaven blushes at the thought of the awful wrath of the Lord against wickedness. The imagery in vv. 10 and 13 may be drawn from and or merged with the final destruction of the cosmos (34:4).

13:11 iniquity . . . arrogance . . . proud . . . haughtiness . . . terrible: The common element is pride, which brings the nations down (2:6–22).

13:12 mortal: The Hebrew word speaks of the inherent weakness of humanity (Ps. 8:4).

13:13, 14 heavens . . . earth: The shaking of the cosmos, including the sun, moon, and stars—which were worshiped by the pagans—symbolizes the overthrow of all that unbelieving humans exalt as rivals to God (2:12–18).

13:15, 16 Everyone . . . children . . . houses . . . wives: In the ancient Middle East, the brutality of war extended to everyone, regardless of age, gender, or station.

13:17, 18 The Medes, who lived in what is today northwest Iran, were fierce enemies of the Israelites. Significant for dating this prophecy is the fact that Persia, which conquered the Medes in 550 B.C. and in conjunction with the Medes conquered Babylon in 539 B.C., is not mentioned. **silver . . . gold:** The point is that the Medes will not be bought off with bribes.

13:19 In 4:2, the same Hebrew word translated **glory** here is translated "beautiful" to describe the Branch of the Lord. The ascriptions of beauty to Babylon are not exaggerations; the city at its zenith must have been spellbinding.

13:20 It will never be inhabited: The fulfillment of this prophecy should not be sought in a specific event, but in the general principle that the kingdoms of this world would not endure. Places that once were fabled for their great structures will become so desolate that even desert peoples would not **pitch tents there.**

13:21, 22 The language of these verses is that of the ancient Middle Eastern curse. The animals named in these verses ominously represent that which is unclean, unholy, uncivilized, and unsettled (34:14, 15; Rev. 18:2). The godly people of ancient Israel would have no associations with such animals.

14:1, 2 These verses relate the salvation of

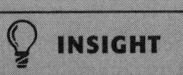 **INSIGHT** | **The Failure of the Stars**

Isaiah predicted that the heavenly bodies would fail to give light when the day of the Lord came against Babylon (Is. 13:10). This suggested the catastrophic destruction that God would bring on this evil empire. Darkness would descend on a nation that exalted itself above all others (14:12–15).

Isaiah's prophecy may also have been mocking the Babylonians' reliance on astrology and astronomy to make plans and interpret history. Calendars surviving from the Assyrians and Babylonians show that they linked important events such as battles, floods, famines, and the death of kings to the movement of the stars and planets. (These artifacts have helped modern-day researchers carefully estimate the dates of these events and construct a fairly accurate timetable of ancient history.)

Thus, if the stars were to fail, the Babylonian worldview would fail as well, leaving the nation in utter confusion.

Israel in the midst of the judgment on the King
of Babylon. The judgment of sinners, represented by Babylon, was necessary for the Lord
to establish Immanuel's kingdom (7:14; 9:1–6;
11:1—12:6). These two verses form an oracle of
blessing on Jacob in the context of the Lord's
burden of wrath against Babylon (chs. 13; 14).

14:1 Still may also be translated "again," in
which case it refers to the second Exodus, the
return of the remnant from Babylonian captivity (11:15, 16). **choose:** The Lord will make
His choice in Israel. **Strangers** will join the
returning Israelites as they did in the first
Exodus (Ex. 12:38). But in this case, the
strangers will be loyal adherents of the Lord.

14:2 people will take them: For the
development of this idea, see Ezra 1:1–8. **captive:** For the development of this theme, see
Eph. 4:8.

14:3–21 These verses are Israel's mocking
dirge for the King of Babylon.

14:3 Hard bondage is an allusion to the
first Exodus (ch. 12). **Rest** recalls the freedom
from Egyptian servitude (Deut. 5:12–15).

14:4–23 This taunting lament has four
stanzas presenting four scenes: (1) the earth's
rest now that the tyrant of Babylon is gone (vv.
4–8), (2) Sheol's astonishment when Babylon
arrives there (vv. 9–11), (3) heaven's expulsion
of Babylon after he ascends there (vv. 12–15),
and (4) the people of Babylon's consignment of
him to an shameful burial for his tyranny against
them (vv. 16–21). The first and last scenes are
more literal; the middle ones draw their imagery
from ancient Near Eastern mythology. Chronologically the third stanza precedes the first two.

14:4 the king of Babylon: No particular
king of Babylon is indicated (13:1). **Proverb**
refers to a highly figurative poem. **oppressor:**
This is the same term used in 9:4 of an unnamed
Assyrian tyrant.

14:5, 6 The staff and **the scepter** were
symbols of authority and power in the ancient
Middle East (9:4). **struck:** The Babylonian kings
had paraded their tyranny in order to intimidate
any who dared to oppose them. But now the
Lord in judgment was breaking their instruments of oppression. **cypress:** The Babylonian
kings boasted of the splendid trees they carted
off from the lands they pillaged to build their
own palaces.

14:7, 8 At rest and quiet may be rephrased as "utterly quiet." This is the security
that comes after the tyrant is dead. **cypress
trees rejoice:** The trees are personified,
describing the joy of the formerly oppressed
people (35:1; 44:23; 55:12). **No woodsman:**
The trees would no longer be cut down to construct machines of war.

14:9–11 excited: The commotion in hell

when the king of Babylon arrives contrasts
sharply with the rest on earth when he is gone.
The Hebrew word for **the dead** is similar in
connotation to our word *ghost:* it speaks of the
dead in a frightening manner (Prov. 9:18). The
defeated subjects of the Babylonian tyrants are
pictured as sitting on **thrones,** while the king is
given a blanket of **worms.**

14:12 Fallen from heaven is a figure of
speech meaning cast down from an exalted
political position. Jesus said, "And you, Capernaum, who are exalted to heaven, will be
brought down to Hades" (Luke 10:15), and
apparently with the same meaning, "I saw Satan
fall like lightning from heaven" (Luke 10:18).
The name for **Lucifer** in Hebrew literally means
"Day Star," or the planet Venus. The poetic language of this verse describes the aspiration of
this brightest star to climb to the zenith of the
heavens and its extinction before the rising sun.
This is an apt summary of the failed goal of the
king of Babylon (v. 4), who wanted to grasp
universal and eternal domination. Tertullian,
Milton, and others have linked this passage to
the career of Satan on the basis of Luke 10:18,
but the text does not specifically make this connection.

14:13 above the stars of God: The
description is of a star that wanted to be grander
than other stars. In this highly poetic language,
Isaiah describes a king whose longing for glory
was unlimited. **Mount of the congregation** is
an allusion to a mythological mountain where
the heavenly deities were thought to assemble.
Farthest sides of the north probably refers to
Mount Casius in northern Syria, the mountain
believed by the Canaanites to be the realm of
the gods (Ps. 48:1, 2).

14:14 I will be like the Most High is the
most outrageous of the arrogant desires of this
Assyrian or Babylonian king. He wanted to surpass the Most High, a term for the Lord that is
often used in connection with the nations of the
world (Pss. 87:5; 91:1, 9; 92:1).

14:15 Sheol: See the reference to hell in v.
9. The word **lowest depths** renders the same
Hebrew word translated "farthest sides" (in v.
13). This is an example of comic justice for this
king who wished to ascend to the heights of the
gods and even the Most High Himself. **The Pit** is
a synonym for Sheol often used together with it
(Jon. 2:2, 6).

14:16 man . . . tremble: Isaiah compares
this king to the One who can truly shake the
earth (13:13).

14:17, 18 The house of his prisoners
refers to exile. Unlike Cyrus, who sent the exiles
home, the king of Babylon kept them captive.

14:19 out of your grave: The ancients
believed that a proper burial was exceedingly

important. The king's memory would be trampled by the people whom he abused in life.
abominable branch: Contrast this with the
Beautiful Branch, the Messiah (11:1). This is an
"anti-Messiah" figure.

**14:20 The brood . . . shall never be
named:** This evil king's posterity will not be
remembered.

14:21 his children: None would survive
the wicked ruler, lest they follow in his evil
steps.

14:22 I will rise: The Lord Himself is
behind the destruction of this arrogant king (v.
5). Whereas Israel will have a remnant (10:20),
Babylon will not have anyone left.

14:23, 24 porcupine . . . marshes: The
former beautiful city of Babylon (13:19) would
become a wild, inhospitable place.

14:25–27 My land . . . My mountains:
The Lord asserts His sovereignty. **yoke . . . his
burden:** In 9:4, these same terms are used of
the Assyrian menace.

14:28–32 After an introduction (v. 28), the
oracle against Philistia falls roughly into two
cycles: (1) the annihilation of the Philistines and
the preservation of God's poor and needy (vv.
29, 30) and (2) the destruction of Philistine
cities and the founding of Zion (vv. 31, 32).

14:28 King Ahaz died in 720 B.C.

14:29 Rod is probably a metaphor for the
Assyrian king (10:5). **its offspring will be . . .
serpent:** More trouble would come upon
Philistia; it would have nothing for which to
rejoice.

14:30 Like Babylon (v. 22)—but unlike
Israel—Philistia would have no future, for it
would have no **remnant.**

14:31 The **gate** of a walled **city** was its
weakest point. When the gate fell, the city could

be taken. The Assyrian army would come **from
the north. No one will be alone** speaks of the
close ranks of the Assyrian army.

14:32 founded Zion: The destruction of
Philistia would leave no refuge for the Philistines.
The only place they could go to be saved would
be Jerusalem, the city built by God. That would
be the place to which the **poor** of all nations
could come, becoming God's **people** (Ps. 87).

15:1—16:14 The oracle against Moab has
five parts: (1) an editorial superscript (15:1); (2)
the sudden, devastating destruction of Moab
(15:2–9); (3) a plea from Moab for shelter in
Zion (16:1–5); (4) a reflection contrasting Moab's former pride with its fallen state (16:6–12);
and (5) a postscript (16:13, 14).

15:1 For the origin of the people of **Moab,**
see the story of Lot and his daughters in Gen.
19:30–38 (Num. 22—25; Deut. 1:5). **burden:**
For similar phrasing, see 13:1. **Ar** and **Kir** were
cities of Moab (16:7, 11; Deut. 2:9; 2 Kin. 3:25).
This passage is marked by a lavish listing of cities
and settlements in Moab. These words reflect a
love of place, a focus on the contours of the
land. There are twenty-one sites or geographical
locations in Moab mentioned in chs. 15 and 16.
Further, Moab is mentioned by name seventeen
times in the two chapters. The verbs **laid waste
. . . and destroyed** are also repeated for dramatic emphasis.

15:2 He refers collectively to **Moab. High
places** were sites of pagan worship (16:12).
weep . . . wail: This refers to the mourning
over the destruction of the cities of Moab. **Baldness** and having one's **beard cut off** were
aspects of mourning rituals.

15:3 Sackcloth and **weeping** were part of
Middle Eastern mourning rites (Gen. 23:2;
37:34; 2 Sam. 1:11, 12).

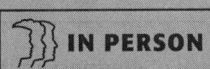 **IN PERSON** | ## King Hezekiah Heeds Isaiah

Upon the death of King Ahaz (Is. 14:28), the Philistines are believed to have sent representatives
to Judah to invite Ahaz's successor Hezekiah to join them in rebelling against Assyria. The offer
is interesting, given that only a few years before the Philistines had captured numerous cities
and villages in western Judah (2 Chr. 28:18). Furthermore, Ahaz had made Judah a tributary of Assyria
during the later years of his life (2 Kin. 16:7–9; 2 Chr. 28:21).

Apparently the Philistines perceived Hezekiah to be a different man who would be willing to throw
off the Assyrian yoke. As it turned out, they were right. For a while, Hezekiah quit paying tribute (2 Kin.
18:7) and strongly resisted the Assyrians, even when they sent a force to besiege Jerusalem (18:13–
19:37; 2 Chr. 32:1–21).

Nevertheless, the Philistines misread Hezekiah by apparently assuming that he would ally his
people with theirs. Instead, the new king consulted God, who used Isaiah to warn him against any
Philistine alliances (Is. 14:29–32). In fact, he eventually attacked the Philistines and recaptured much
of Judah's lost territory (2 Kin. 18:8).

15:4 armed soldiers: The weeping would extend even to hardened fighting men.

15:5 My heart refers to Isaiah, who felt sympathy for Moab (16:9–11). **Zoar** was a southwestern border city of Moab on the south end of the Dead Sea. **The Ascent of Luhith** is also mentioned by Jeremiah in his lament over Moab (Jer. 48:5).

15:6–8 The **waters** and **green grass** of the oasis could not survive the numerous refugees.

15:9 The term **Dimon** sounds like **blood** in Hebrew. **Lions:** Fleeing from one tragedy after another in their flight southward, the refugees

throne will be established (9:1–7; 11:1–5; Amos 9:11, 12; Acts 15:16, 17).

16:6 Pride is a regular target of the Lord's judgment (2:5–22; 13:11).

16:7 Kir Hareseth is another name for Kir (15:1).

16:8 Vine is a figure of speech for Moab (compare Israel's description as a vine in 5:1–7). **Sea** may refer to the Dead Sea because it is the nearest large body of water to Moab.

16:9 Heshbon and Elealeh were among the principal settlements in ancient Moab (15:4).

Photo by Gustav Jeeninga

A city wall uncovered in the excavation of Dibon, one of the leading cities of Moab. Isaiah predicted the destruction of the cities of Moab (Is. 15:1, 2).

turn to Judah in the west for asylum (16:1–5). As would be the case with Israel (1:9; 6:13; 10:20; 11:16)—but not with Assyria (14:22) and Philistia (14:30)—a **remnant** would survive in Moab.

16:1 The **lamb** is a collective for the thousands gathered **from Sela to the wilderness** and sent as tribute to the **ruler** of Judah (Num. 32:4; 2 Kin. 3:4).

16:2 Wandering bird is a sad description of the hopeless condition of the **daughters of Moab,** the women of the nation.

16:3 Take counsel may also be translated "make plans." Moab would find salvation in the **shadow** of Zion (2:2–4).

16:4, 5 Moab's salvation ultimately lies in the coming One, Jesus the Messiah, whose

16:10 Contrast the lack of **gladness** in this verse with the ecstatic joy of 9:3.

16:11 Kir Heres is an alternative spelling for Kir Hareseth (v. 7) or Kir (15:1). Isaiah the prophet expresses his determination to one day rejoice over Moab. This is a promise of its future restoration.

16:12 high place . . . sanctuary: As long as the people worshiped false gods, they would be doomed to pain, judgment, and recurring trouble (15:2).

16:13, 14 A former prophecy against Moab (15:1) would be realized **within three years,** perhaps referring to the quelling of a rebellion against Sargon in 715 B.C. However, a **remnant** would remain (15:9). Moab had far more hope for salvation than did either Babylon or Philistia.

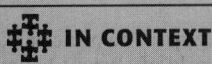 **IN CONTEXT** | **The Fall of Damascus**

Occasionally in the world's history, an individual city serves as the key to a particular region. For example, Hong Kong has become a gateway to and from China. Vancouver is a gateway for many Asians into North America. For years, Berlin was a tightly controlled place of passage between East and West.

In the ancient world, Damascus was the doorway to and from the area we know today as Palestine. Damascus, the oldest continually inhabited city in the world as far as we know, served as a front line of defense in the north for a league of allied cities to the south. Therefore, Isaiah's startling prophecy of Damascus's fall (Is. 17:1) must have shocked the Israelites who heard it. If Damascus were to fall, all its allies were likely to fall as well, like a series of dominoes.

That is exactly what happened. Damascus, the capital of Syria, had joined together with the northern kingdom to attack Judah in about 734 B.C. The southern kingdom hired the Assyrians to come to its rescue (2 Kin. 16:7, 8; 2 Chr. 28:21), and by 732 B.C. Damascus was captured and its ruler, King Rezin, was killed (2 Kin. 16:9)—just as Isaiah had predicted. The city never again regained the prominence it had previously enjoyed.

17:1—18:7 The oracle against Damascus falls into seven parts: (1) an editorial superscription (17:1); (2) the desolate ruin of Damascus (17:2, 3); (3) the ruin of Israel, which is left only a remnant (17:4–6); (4) the anticipation that in the future people will trust Israel's God (17:7, 8); (5) the accusation that Damascus replaced God with pagan deities (17:9–11); (6) a proclamation of doom upon the nations "who plunder us" (17:12–14); and (7) a prediction that a powerful nation will bring tribute to the Lord (18:1–7).

17:1, 2 burden: For similar phrasing, see 13:1. **cities . . . flocks:** Where people once lived, conditions would be suitable only for flocks (14:23).

17:3 Fortress may refer to Samaria, the capital city. **Ephraim** designates northern Israel. Since **Damascus,** the capital of Syria, was allied with Ephraim, the oracle of God's judgment was against both nations.

17:4 In that day: For a similar phrase, see 2:12.

17:5 harvests: The nation of Syria would be "harvested" of its people. The term **Rephaim** is the Hebrew word for "shades" or "ghosts." Thus the Valley of Rephaim is the Valley of Death.

17:6 A remnant would be **left** (10:20) even though it would be pitifully small. It is thus something of a misnomer to continue to speak of the "lost tribes" of Israel. The fact that God promised a remnant from Israel means that they were never all "lost."

17:7 The verb translated **look** means "to look with interest" or "to look with favor." **Holy One:** For a similar idea, see 6:3.

17:8 Altars refers to pagan worship. **work of his hands:** For similar wording, see 2:8;

31:7. Asherah was represented by **wooden images** (27:9), which were part of the sexual cults of Baal worship among the Canaanite peoples.

17:9 In that day: For a similar phrase, see 2:11. **His strong cities** (contrast the "Rock" in v. 10) will become as fragile as a little **branch.**

17:10 You refers to the northern kingdom. **forgotten:** For background, see Deut. 8:11–20. The people had committed the very sin that God warned them not to: they had forgotten the God who had saved them from slavery. The language recalls the first Exodus; the Lord is called **the God of your salvation** and **the Rock** (compare Ex. 15:2; Deut. 32:4).

17:11 Make your plant to grow may allude to the ancient practice of force-blooming potted plants and allowing them to die. Pagans believed that this reenactment of the life cycle would secure fertile fields. But even after performing this rite, **the harvest** would be in ruin. Just as the choice vines of the Lord's vineyard disappointed Him (5:1–7), so His errant people would find their harvest hopes shattered.

17:12 Many people refers to the nations that plunder Israel (v. 14). **Seas** and **mighty waters** speak of chaos and death (8:7; Ps. 46:3).

17:13 Chaff, which lacks life, value, and stability, was threshed and winnowed on windy **mountains** or hilltops. When God judges the unrelenting, roaring seas—the nations that plundered God's people—they will become mere tumbleweed **rolling** before **the whirlwind** of God's judgment.

17:14 Sennacherib's army would be destroyed between **eventide** and **morning** (37:36–38). **us:** Isaiah identifies himself with his plundered people.

18:1–7 This message, probably directed to the Ethiopians, consists of two parts: (1) a command to the Ethiopians emissaries to carry a message to a powerful nation, probably their own people (vv. 1, 2), and (2) the message itself (vv. 3–7). The message predicts that all nations will clearly perceive (v. 3) that God will quietly make His burning presence felt (v. 4) when He brings judgment at the perfect time (v. 5) and in an exhaustive way (v. 6), after which the powerful nation will bring tribute to Him (v. 7).

18:1 Ethiopia, called Cush in the Bible, was at the southern end of Isaiah's world. A Cushite dynasty took over Egypt in 715 B.C. and probably sent ambassadors to Jerusalem. Cush may have been a Hebrew term for black African peoples (Num. 12:1; Ps. 87:4).

18:2 Sea may refer to the Nile River, from which small **rivers** branched. **Tall and smooth** (v. 7) probably designates the peoples along the entire stretch of the Nile River. Perhaps the term *smooth* refers to the ancient Egyptian custom of shaving the whole body.

18:3 banner: For the use of this word to refer to salvation instead of judgment, see 11:10, 12.

18:4, 5 The figure of God working in **rest** speaks of His indescribable power and unlimited sovereignty. God is steady in His work. His judgment will be felt **like clear heat in sunshine.** This is another example of a bad **harvest** (17:10, 11).

18:6 God's judgment will be so extensive that the carcasses of His victims will be devoured in the **summer** and **winter.**

18:7 the place of the name: Note how closely the Lord identifies with Mount Zion. This was the one place for the true worship of God.

19:1–20:6 The oracle against Egypt falls into three parts after the historical superscription (19:1): (1) the collapse of Egypt before the Lord (19:2–15); (2) the salvation of Egypt in the Lord (19:16–25); and (3) a specific historic fulfillment of the collapse of Egypt at the time of Sargon (20:1–6).

19:1 the LORD rides on a swift cloud: For similar imagery, read Pss. 18:10; 68:4; Matt. 26:64.

19:2–15 After proclaiming the Lord as the ultimate cause of Egypt's collapse (v. 2), the oracle singles out (1) the failure of Egypt's many gods resulting in anarchy (vv. 2–4), (2) the failure of the Nile leading to economic collapse (vv. 5–10), and (3) the failure of its ancient and vaunted wisdom resulting in hopeless defeat (vv. 11–15). The language, in contrast to chapter 20, is not historically specific but stylistic and symbolic.

19:2 The political anarchy of **Egyptians** against Egyptians has religious roots; their many gods failed them.

19:3 The spirit of Egypt: The principal key for understanding the world of ancient Egypt is the concept of *ma'at,* an Egyptian word for "order." When God brought Moses to confront Pharaoh (Ex. 5—14), it was *ma'at* that was under attack. God would attack the Egyptians in the future as He had in the past.

19:4 Cruel master may be an allusion to Pharaoh's tyranny against Israel (Ex. 6:9).

19:5–10 The disruption of the **waters** and all that is related to them marks God's attack on the nation.

19:10 The **foundations** and those **who make wages** together may be a figure for the whole economic spectrum, from wealthy managers to day laborers.

19:11, 12 you . . . your: In verse 11, Isaiah addresses the scribes; in verse 12, he addresses the pharaoh.

19:11 Zoan was the capital of Egypt at this time. **Son** here refers to a member of a guild. Egypt was famous for its **wise** men (1 Kin. 4:30), who, as disciples, learned the wisdom of **ancient kings.**

19:12 Where are your wise men: The Lord taunts those who consider themselves wise and learned. True knowledge comes from the fear of the Lord (Prov. 1:7). For a similar idea, see 1 Cor. 1:20.

19:13, 14 Noph or Memphis was Egypt's ancient capital.

19:15 Nothing will **work for Egypt** to save it. Its deliverance is only in the Lord (vv. 16–25).

19:16–25 The prediction of Egypt's salvation in the Lord is divided into four parts by the phrase **in that day** (vv. 16, 18, 19, 23, 24), moving in an ascending order from (1) "fearing" Judah because of the Lord of Hosts, who works through it (vv. 16, 17), and so is the beginning of wisdom (Prov. 1:7); (2) to taking a pledge of allegiance to the Lord (v. 18); (3) to knowing God as Savior (vv. 19–22); (4) to becoming part of the one nation under God (v. 23), the blessed nation that brings blessing to the earth (vv. 24, 25). Interpreters differ over whether the prophecy is historically specific or metaphoric, drawing its imagery from Isaiah's world (11:14) and Israel's experiences. The former option is unlikely, for it would entail a contradiction between this prophecy that foretells Assyria's future salvation (vv. 24, 25) with other prophecies that predicted Assyria would be annihilated without a remnant (14:22). Egypt, representing the Gentiles, will recapitulate Israel's history of redemption (vv. 21–25). The prophecy probably finds fulfillment, though not its consummation, in the nations one day going to heavenly Mount Zion

(2:2–4) under the rule of Christ (4:2; 9:7; 11:4, 14; Rom. 10:11–20).

19:17, 18 Five cities will **speak the language of Canaan and swear by**—take an oath of allegiance to—**the Lord of hosts** (1:9). These new habits spring from the miracle of regeneration—a radical transformation of their nature. With the words **City of Destruction,** Jewish scribes were probably belittling the "City of the

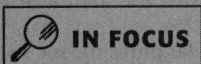

IN FOCUS   "blessing"

(Heb. *berakah*) (19:24; 65:8; Deut. 11:27; 33:1) Strong's #1293: The significant Hebrew word translated *blessing* expresses several ideas, namely to fill with potency, to make fruitful, or to secure victory. In Is. 19:24, the word alludes to God's promise to bless all nations through Abraham's descendants (Gen. 12:3). When people offer a blessing, they wish well or offer a prayer on behalf of themselves or someone else (Gen. 49; Deut. 33:1). OT patriarchs are often remembered for the blessing they gave to their children. When God gives a blessing, He bestows it on those who faithfully follow Him (Deut. 11:27), providing them with salvation (Ps. 3:8), life (Ps. 133:3), and success (2 Sam. 7:29).

Sun," known by its Greek name Heliopolis, by deliberately changing the word meaning "sun" to the word meaning "destruction." This is similar to the deliberate change of the name of Ahab's wife to the name Jezebel (1 Kin. 16:31).

19:19 Altar and **pillar** may allude to the patriarchs Abraham and Jacob respectively (Gen. 12:8; 28:22).

19:20 The words **oppressors** and **saviors** may allude to the Judges (Judg. 2:18).

19:21, 22 The Egyptians will know probably alludes to Israel's experience in the Exodus (Ex. 6:7; 7:5).

19:23, 24 A highway signifies the removal of alienation and separation (11:16). Historically, **Egypt** and **Assyria** were enemies.

19:25 My people and **the work of My hands,** titles for Israel (10:24; 60:21), are applied here to the converted Gentiles, symbolized by Egypt and Assyria (56:7; 65:1).

20:1 Tartan was one of the three chief officers of the Assyrian empire (2 Kin. 18:17). **Ashdod** was the leading city when the Ethiopian pharaoh, Shabako, fomented rebellion against Sargon II, king of Assyria, in 713

B.C. Ashdod fell to Sargon in 711 B.C. An inscription mentioning Sargon by name has been dug up in ancient Ashdod.

20:2, 3 Isaiah replaced wearing **sackcloth,** the garb of spiritual mourning, with walking **naked and barefoot,** signs of being exiled into captivity. **servant:** For a similar usage, see 41:8. **Three years** means "involving three years," a minimum of fourteen months. **a sign and a wonder:** For a similar usage, see 8:18.

20:4 Esarhaddon, **king of Assyria,** conquered Egypt and fulfilled this prophecy in 671 B.C.

20:5, 6 They and **this territory** probably refer to the nations bordering the eastern shore of the Mediterranean Sea, who looked to Egypt to save them from Assyria. This would include Judah.

21:1–10 The oracle against Babylon, after an enigmatic superscription (v. 1), consists of a dreamlike vision of Babylon's fall (vv. 2–9) and its significance to Judah (v. 10).

21:1 Wilderness means "desert." The phrase **Wilderness of the Sea** may be a sarcastic parody of Babylon, whose southern region on the Persian Gulf was called the "Land of the Sea."

21:2 Elam, a major part of Persia, and **Media** were allied in 700 B.C. Perhaps as part of the Assyrian army (5:26) they helped bring about the fall of Babylon in 689 B.C., since they certainly did so in 539 B.C. (11:11; 13:17). **Its sighing** may refer to the sighing Babylon inflicted on others, or to its own sighing under Assyrian oppression.

21:3 Perhaps Isaiah was **distressed** by the report of Babylon's fall because it meant that Babylon could not save Judah from the Assyrians.

21:4 Though Isaiah **longed** for the fall of Babylon, he feared its consequences to Judah.

21:5 Having summoned Babylon's princes to **eat and drink,** Isaiah summoned them again to **anoint the shield** in preparation for battle (Dan. 5).

21:6 Lord here means "Master." The **watchman** is probably Isaiah.

21:7 A chariot of donkeys probably means "donkey riders" and **a chariot of camels** probably means "camel riders." The Persian army used donkeys and camels.

21:8, 9 In the daytime . . . every night suggests "continually"—a display of Isaiah's faithfulness to his calling.

21:10 My threshing is a metaphor for the punishment coming on Judah.

21:11, 12 This brief oracle against **Dumah,** an oasis in northern Arabia, consists of an editorial superscription (v. 11), a question by sleepless Edom to Isaiah about how much of the night is left (v. 11), and Isaiah's enigmatic response that night accompanies the new day (v. 12).

21:11 Dumah was located at the intersection of the east-west trade route between Babylon and Edom and the north-south route between Palmyra and Edom. Dumah played a vital military and economic role in the relationship between Mesopotamia and Edom, and its fate greatly affected Edom. **Seir** is Edom (34:5–17; Gen. 32:3). **Watchman** refers to the night patrol, who kept watch on the city. The metaphor refers to the prophet Isaiah, who as a guard on the walls could see the dawn—the light of salvation—in the east before others. **What of the night** may be rephrased as: "What is left of the night?"

21:12 and also the night: Dumah's future was grim. Relief from Assyrian domination would be followed quickly by Babylonian domination.

21:13–17 The oracle against Arabia, after the superscription (v. 13), has three parts: (1) an address by Isaiah to Teman to provide for Arabian refugees fleeing from battle (vv. 13–15); (2) an address by the Lord to Isaiah confirming and elaborating upon Arabia's defeat (vv. 16, 17); and (3) an epilogue guaranteeing the prophecy (v. 17).

21:13 Dedanites may be the refugees described in v. 15. Dedan was about ninety miles southeast of Tema (v. 14).

21:14 Tema was about two hundred miles southeast of Dumah (v. 11).

21:15 The **drawn** swords are those of the Assyrians and Babylonians.

21:16 Kedar was a relatively fertile region in the northwestern part of the Arabian desert in which Dedan and Tema were located (60:7). Its refugees would be driven deeper into the desert.

22:1–25 After the superscription (v. 1), the oracle against Jerusalem consists of five parts: (1) a contrast between Jerusalem's blind revelry and Isaiah's appalling vision of its selfish rulers

having fled the city, leaving it to be plundered (vv. 1–4); (2) Isaiah's detailed vision of the city's fall (vv. 5–8); (3) Isaiah's indictment of Jerusalem for its misplaced confidence in its defenses instead of in the Lord (vv. 8–11); (4) Isaiah's indictment for its response of merrymaking instead of repenting (vv. 12, 13); and (5) a final vision confirming that this last apostasy sealed Jerusalem's doom (v. 14). The vision is followed by an example of Jerusalem's blindness in Shebna, the city's steward (vv. 15–19), whose weakness is contrasted with the ability of his successor Eliakim (vv. 20–25).

22:1 burden: For similar phrasing, see 13:1. **Valley of Vision** sarcastically describes Jerusalem. Mount Zion is ironically personified in its valleys from which it could see nothing. Instead of partying on **housetops,** the ailing city should have been in its prayer closets.

22:2, 3 In the prophet's vision, the rulers are **not slain with the sword** while heroically defending the city, but are **captured** while fleeing to save their own skins (2 Kin. 25:4–6).

22:4, 5 daughter of my people: For a similar reference see 1:8.

22:6, 7 Kir is **Elam.** The Elamites may have been part of the Assyrian army (5:26). **gate:** The same army that plundered Babylon (21:2) will arrive at Jerusalem's gates.

22:8 The House of the Forest is the nation's armory (39:2).

22:9–11 The defense of the city depended upon the availability of **water** within its **walls.** Hezekiah addressed this need by digging a tunnel beneath the city, connecting the **lower pool** in Jerusalem's southwestern valley with the **old pool,** the source of water in the eastern valley.

22:12, 13 Called for weeping and for mourning . . . But instead, joy and gladness: God demanded repentance and renewal; the people instead turned to pleasure and parties. **eat and drink:** At times, this is a proper response to adversity (Eccl. 2:24; 3:13); but to use food, drink, and sensual pleasures as a

---

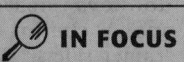 **IN FOCUS**   **"burden"**

(Heb. *massa'*) (23:1; 2 Kin. 9:25; Jer. 23:33) Strong's #4853: This noun is a derivative of the verb *nasa'* which means "to lift up" or "to carry away." *Massa'* refers to something that is taken or carried such as a present, tribute, or message. It is also translated *oracle* (Jer. 23:33) when God uses His prophets to convey judgment against someone or some nation. Isaiah frequently used this term in what are commonly known as the "oracles against the nations," where he spoke of God's judgment on different kingdoms (13:1; 15:1; 17:1; 19:1; 21:1, 11). Translating the word as *burden* emphasizes that Isaiah carried and delivered God's indictments against the nations.

means of shielding oneself from righteousness before the Lord is disastrous (Luke 17:26–29).

22:14 no atonement: When one rejects the salvation that comes from the living God, there is none other.

22:15–19 Isaiah's message against **Shebna**, a representative of blind, selfish leadership, falls into four parts: (1) an introductory prophetic formula in v. 15a; (2) an accusation against Shebna for attempting to memorialize himself in death (vv. 15, 16), followed by a judicial sentence to death in disgrace (vv. 18, 19); (3) a description of what a steward should be, as exemplified in Eliakim (vv. 20–24), followed by a proclamation that he too he must fall (v. 25a); and (4) a concluding prophetic formula (v. 25b).

22:15 Steward refers to a high government official who was responsible for caring for the king and his dominion.

22:16 Here refers to Silwan, on the eastern side of the Kidron valley, overlooking the City of David. By hewing himself **a sepulcher on high,** Shebna rivaled the king (2 Chr. 16:14), to whom he should have been a father (v. 21).

22:17 throw you away: An impressive grave is no defense against God.

22:18, 19 The **large country** refers to Assyria. **drive you out:** Shebna was demoted to a secretary by the time of the Assyrian siege (36:3, 22).

22:20 Eliakim was an official whom God would honor in place of the arrogant Shebna (v. 15).

22:21 The pronoun **your** refers to Shebna (v. 15). The word **father** suggests the self-sacrificing love of Eliakim for citizens of Jerusalem.

22:22 The steward had the **key** that gave him an audience with the king (Matt. 16:19; Rev. 3:7).

22:23 A peg suggests one who is firmly in place, namely, a reliable person (but see 22:25). **Glorious throne** suggests that Eliakim will bring honor to the memory of his **father's house** in contrast to the shame Shebna had brought to his master (v. 18).

22:24 All vessels is a metaphor for all of the inhabitants, both the influential and the insignificant.

22:25 the peg that is fastened in the secure place: The reference here appears to be Eliakim (v. 20). Even the noble Eliakim could not sustain the **burden** of government. Only Immanuel could do that (9:6, 7).

23:1–18 The oracle against Tyre consists of two main parts (following the superscription in v. 1): the fall of Tyre (vv. 1–14) and the restoration of it (vv. 15–18). As in ch. 13, the language is stylized, general, and symbolic, not historically specific.

23:1–6 The fall of Tyre is represented as a grim **report** (v. 5), spreading to the ships at sea expecting to dock at Tyre (v. 1), to Sidon on the Phoenician coast (vv. 2–4), to Egypt (v. 5), and finally to Spain (v. 6).

23:1, 2 burden: For similar phrasing, see 13:1. Tyre was besieged several times over a period of about four hundred years before it was finally **laid waste** by Alexander the Great in 332 B.C. **Cyprus** had close commercial ties with Tyre (Ezek. 27:6), as did Solomon (1 Kin. 5:1, 8–11). The pronoun **it** refers to the report that Tyre had fallen.

23:3, 4 Shihor, a synonym for Egypt (Jer. 2:18), brought its coveted **grain** to Phoenicia, bringing **revenue** to Tyre, the **marketplace for the nations. Sidon,** the other prominent city along with Tyre, depended on the Mediterranean **sea** for its livelihood, which is personified here as a bereft father.

23:5 Egypt would be in **agony** because its profitable trading partner was gone.

23:6, 7 Tarshish is Tartessus in Spain and represents the most distant place to the ancient Israelites (2:16). **Whose feet . . . to dwell** is a personification of Tyre's colonies. Tyre's large merchant fleet transversed the Mediterranean Sea. Their colonies were sprinkled throughout the Mediterranean world in support of their shipping empire.

23:8 crowning: Tyre crowned its trading merchants with wealth and prestige.

23:9 dishonor the pride: For a similar idea, see 2:12–19.

23:10–12 Oppressed suggests "crushed" in war. **virgin daughter of Sidon:** It is possible that this phrase is used as a parody. Jerusalem is the Lord's daughter; Tyre is merely a pretender.

23:13, 14 Since **the Chaldeans** had not escaped the siege **towers** of the Assyrians who **raised up** or laid bare the foundations of Babylon's **palaces,** neither would Tyre.

23:15 Seventy years symbolizes a full measure of time, a lifetime.

23:16 The **forgotten harlot** who, in her old age, sings **songs** to be **remembered** is a metaphor for the restoration of Tyre.

23:17 Will deal is a translation of the Hebrew verb "to visit." Though the verb can express God's merciful visitation on His people, here the verb is used to express God's judgment (24:21). **Commit fornication** is a metaphor for Tyre's forming economic alliances with anyone that enriched her, regardless of ethics.

23:18 Tyre's **pay** would be **set apart,** or "regarded as holy," **for the LORD** (18:7; 60:5–11). This was not a violation of Deut. 23:18, which forbade bringing a harlot's pay to the temple. Tyre's destruction was part of the Lord's war against the unrighteous. The spoils would belong to Him as the Victor (Deut. 2:35; Josh. 6:17, 19).

24:1–27:13 The section describing the Lord's "burdens" against particular nations (chs. 13–23) is now placed in a larger framework that depicts God's triumph over the entire earth for His elect. Chapter 24 focuses on God's overthrow of the corrupted earth; ch. 25 focuses on the responsive praise to His actions. Chapters 26 and 27 focus on God's efforts for His people.

24:1–23 Chapter 24 consists of five stanzas: (1) the desolation of the earth because of sin (vv. 1–6); (2) the end of revelry in the city (vv. 7–13); (3) glory to God, but grief over the earth (vv. 14–16); (4) the hopelessness of flight, for the whole earth shakes (vv. 17–20); and (5) the vision of God reigning on Mount Zion over the cosmos (vv. 21–23).

24:1 Scatters is an allusion to Gen. 11:9. The Lord had scattered the **inhabitants** of the earth in the past at the tower of Babel; He would do so again.

24:2, 3 As . . . debtor: Wealth and power will make no difference. Both will suffer for wickedness before God.

24:4 The earth mourns: For a similar idea, see Rom. 8:22.

24:5 laws . . . ordinance . . . everlasting covenant: The usual language concerning a breach of the covenant is applied more generally to the wicked nations. Perhaps these words speak of that innate sense of right and wrong— the conscience—that God has given to all humankind, but which everyone violates (Rom.

1:18–32; compare Acts 24:16).

24:6 Left may also be translated "remnant" (10:20, 21).

24:7 New wine is simply a synonym of the standard word for wine.

24:8, 9 Mirth and **joy** represent the same Hebrew word.

24:10 Confusion is translated "without form" in Gen. 1:2.

24:11, 12 cry for wine: For a similar image, see Zeph. 1:13.

24:13 shaking . . . gleaning: People in desperation continue to seek for a single **olive** or for **grapes.**

24:14 They refers to those who love God's Law and who have suffered for righteousness.

24:15 dawning light . . . the sea: The imagery suggests the east (the dawn) and west (the Mediterranean Sea). From east to west, everyone should give the Lord the praise that is due to Him.

24:16 But I said: The prophet could not join the oppressed's hymn of praise because he saw the awful treachery that would precede the rejoicing (33:1; Dan. 7:28; 8:27).

24:17, 18 Windows may be an allusion to the Flood (Gen. 7:11). In the OT the word means "openings."

24:19, 20 The earth shall reel: This is an end-time prophecy of coming doom, to be followed by renewal in the age of Messiah Jesus.

24:21 The Hebrew word for **punish** means "to visit" (23:17). The **host** of stars (Jer. 33:22) is identified with fallen angels (Matt. 24:29; Rev. 12:4, 9). **kings of the earth:** The idea is that all

---

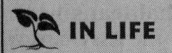 **IN LIFE** | **The Wasteland**

Damage to the earth's environment seems to be on the rise today. Yet current ecological difficulties pale in comparison to what the world will experience someday under God's judgment. Isaiah envisions a virtual wasteland in which nothing remains untouched (Is. 24:1).

Why will the earth be plundered, polluted, burned up, and destroyed? Because it languishes under the curse of a broken covenant (24:5, 6). Humanity has turned away from God, and the world must be destroyed before it can be made anew.

It will be made anew, but not before "the wine fails, the vine languishes, {and} all the merryhearted sigh" (24:7). In other words, joy will be turned to gloom. Society will break down, as evidenced by boarded-up houses (24:10), a depressing sight already common in many cities today. Likewise, the city "gate" will be destroyed (24:12), meaning that urban life and commerce—indeed, everything the city stands for—will be ruined. The world will be left like so many war-ravaged areas today: without government, police, hospitals, and food; wracked by disease, desolation, and death.

This somber outlook for the world leaves little room for comfort. It assures us that in the end God will reign (24:23), but the point seems to be that our world is ultimately headed for judgment. If we are sobered and saddened by that message, then perhaps Isaiah's words have had their intended effect.

of God's enemies, whether in the heavens or on earth, will face His judgment.

24:22 prisoners: For a similar idea see 2 Pet. 2:4.

24:23 reign: In the end times, the reign of the Father and the Son will be united (52:7; 1 Cor. 15:24; Rev. 4:1—5:14). **Mount Zion:** This anticipates the glorious reign of the Savior King in the age of renewal from Zion's throne. **His elders** may be a reference to angelic beings who attend God's majesty.

25:1–12 This poem celebrating God's destruction of the sinful earth falls into three parts: (1) a hymn of praise by Isaiah (vv. 1–5); (2) the Lord's feast on Mount Zion celebrating His destruction of death (vv. 6–8); and (3) a hymn of praise by the congregation (vv. 9–12).

25:1 Wonderful things refers to the wonders only God can do. **Faithfulness and truth** may be rephrased as "absolute truth."

25:2 Any proud **city** is in view here (24:10). **never be rebuilt:** For a similar idea, see 24:20.

25:3 The terrible nations are those addressed in chs. 13—23. The pairing of **glorify** (24:15) and **fear** speaks of the absolute submission to God of all people (Phil. 2:10).

25:4 The repetition of the word **strength** and the use of the terms **refuge** (57:13) and **shade** is similar to the listing of terms for protection in Ps. 91:1-3.

25:5 The use of the term **terrible ones,** or nations, three times in vv. 3–5 emphasizes divine judgment on the nations represented.

25:6 mountain: For a similar usage, see 2:2. **A feast of wine on the lees** refers to the best wine. **Fat things full of marrow** refers to the choicest food. The feast is similar to the one prepared by Wisdom in Prov. 9:1–6.

25:7 The surface of the covering and **veil** refer to a "shroud." This is a promise of the end of death (v. 8).

25:8 Death is often pictured as an "enlarged mouth" by the poets of the Bible. Paradoxically, the Lord **will swallow up death.** Lord is the title meaning Sovereign or Master; the word **God** represents the divine name Yahweh, ordinarily translated Lord. **wipe away tears:** This promise is given anew in Rev. 7:17; 21:4. **the Lord has spoken:** The promises are as sure as the eternal character of God (1:20).

25:9 Note the change from "my God" (v. 1) to **our God.** This verse is the faithful's song of praise. **Be glad and rejoice** may be rephrased as "be exceedingly happy." **Salvation** is deliverance from constraint, whether it is falling into a pit (Ps. 40:2) or the constraint of sin and death.

25:10, 11 Moab symbolizes the proud. **for the refuse heap:** This phrase refers to water mixed with dung—a very unpleasant image.

25:12 He will bring down: This will be the work of the Lord.

26:1—27:1 This poem consists of three sections: (1) a pilgrim's song celebrating the city of God (26:1–6); (2) a song of trust in God (26:7–19); and (3) an encouraging promise that God will punish evil (26:20—27:1).

26:1–6 After a superscription (the first part of v. 1), the song consists of the faithful pilgrims' celebration of their "strong city" (vv. 1–3), a command to trust in the Lord (v. 4), and an affirmation that the "lofty {earthly} city" on earth will be destroyed.

26:1 In that day: For a similar phrase, see 2:12. The pilgrim's **strong city** presumably is Mount Zion (2:2; 60:14).

26:2 Open the gates is the language of a pilgrim song (Ps. 118:19, 20).

26:3 The Hebrew expression translated **perfect peace** is literally "peace, peace"; compare the word *holy* in 6:3. Immanuel will inaugurate this superior kind of peace (9:6; 11:6–9).

26:4 Trust means "to commit oneself fully to." Yah, the Lord is an emphatic designation of God (12:2).

26:5, 6 Line after line asserts the destruction of the **lofty city** (v. 1) by the power of God.

26:7–19 The song of trust contrasts (1) the present trust of the righteous (vv. 7–9a) with the need of the wicked to learn righteousness through future judgment (vv. 9b–11); (2) the present oppression of the faithful (vv. 12, 13) with God's past judgment on the tyrants (v. 14); and (3) blessings on His nation (v. 15) and their present unfruitful labors (vv. 16–18), with their future resurrection from the dead (v. 19).

26:7 uprightness; O Most Upright: The relative uprightness of the righteous is put into the context of the absolute uprightness of the Holy One.

26:8 waited: For a similar idea, see 40:31 (compare Ps. 40:1).

26:9 in the night . . . early: The prophet describes his relentless search for God.

26:10 The wicked show contempt for God's **grace** (Rom. 2:4). **Majesty** is translated "excellent things" in 12:5.

26:11 Your hand: The works of God are ignored by the wicked (5:12). **The fire of** may also be translated "the fire upon."

26:12 True **peace** comes only from the Lord (26:3; John 14:27).

26:13 Other **masters** included rulers of Egypt in the past, rulers of Assyria in the present, and rulers of Babylon in the future. **Make mention of Your name** refers to God's character as learned through past experience.

26:14 They are dead: The prophet saw the

future demise of the enemies of God's people. In contrast to the faithful (v. 19), these people **will not rise.**

26:15 You have increased the nation: The repetition of this expression emphasizes both its certainty and its magnitude.

26:16 The pronoun **they** refers to the faithful nation.

26:17, 18 a woman with child: A woman can endure labor pains for the sake of the joy that follows. The faithful remnant of Isaiah's time endured oppression, but **brought forth wind,** a metaphor for meaningless labor.

26:19 Isaiah, addressing his faithful peers, assures them that their **dead** will rise in resurrection (Job 19:26; Dan. 12:2). **Dew** is a picture of new life and blessing (Ps. 133:3; Hos. 14:5). It is often alleged that the faithful in the OT period had no real hope for resurrection, that their hope was solely to enjoy living in the Promised Land in this life. Yet, here is a verse that clearly indicates otherwise (Ps. 23:6).

26:20—27:1 The prophet's encouraging promise consists of a contrast between the momentary distress for God's people (v. 20) and the future punishment for tyrants (v. 21) and a use of poetic imagery to underscore the punishment of all evil (27:1).

26:20 My people refers to the faithful, righteous remnant. Their sufferings under the Assyrian tyrants were but **for a little moment,** and were not worthy to be compared to the eternal joy that would follow (26:19; 54:7; Ps. 30:5; 2 Cor. 4:17).

26:21 Comes can also be translated "is about to come." When **the earth** discloses the **blood** of the poor and needy that it has swallowed from the hands of ruthless tyrants, it will bear testimony against those evil people; the Lord will avenge them (Gen. 4:10).

27:1 Punish links this verse with 26:21; this verse is the climax of the preceding section. As in the case of the serpent Lotan in the Ugaritic myths, **Leviathan** was a mythological, dragonlike deity who symbolized chaos and who battled unsuccessfully against God (Job 3:8; 41:1; Ps. 74:14). **serpent . . . reptile:** Isaiah borrows the imagery of this battle myth to teach that God will triumph over all who oppose Him. **in the sea:** See Ps. 93 for a development of this theme.

27:2–13 This prophecy is a song about the Lord's restoration of His vineyard, Israel (vv. 2–6); a contrast of the Lord's discipline of Israel (vv. 7–9) with His annihilation of its oppressors (vv. 10, 11); and a promise that the Lord will regather the exiles to Mount Zion (vv. 12, 13).

27:2 The **vineyard** is Israel (5:7; 27:6). **Red wine** contrasts with "wild grapes" (5:2). This was God's intention for His people—He

wanted them to produce, as it were, delectable wine.

27:3 I . . . keep it contrasts with "I will lay it waste" (5:6). **Water it every moment** contrasts with "no rain on it" (5:6). **Lest any hurt it** contrasts with "I will take away its hedge" (5:5). This passage is a complete reversal of the judgment recorded in ch. 5.

27:4 Fury is not in Me contrasts with "For all this His anger is not turned away" (5:25). **Who would set briers and thorns** contrasts with "there shall come up briers and thorns" (5:6).

27:5 peace: For a development of this theme, see 9:6; 11:1–16; 26:3.

27:6 Those who come refers to the regathered exiles (v. 13).

27:7 Has He: The two questions that begin with these words expect a negative answer. **struck Israel:** The Lord struck the nations fatally (14:22, 30), but not Israel (10:24–26).

27:8 Sending it away refers to the Exile (v. 13).

27:9 iniquity . . . covered: See 40:2 for another statement that Israel's punishment atoned for its guilt. **Wooden images:** For a similar usage, see 17:8.

27:10, 11 the fortified city will be desolate: For a similar idea, see 25:2, 10–12; 26:5, 6.

27:12 Thresh refers to harvesting a crop by flailing, such as beating an olive tree. **the River to the Brook of Egypt:** These geographical references mark out Israel's ideal homeland—from the Euphrates to the Wadi el-Arish (Gen. 15:18).

27:13 The great trumpet is a figure of speech for assembling troops (Ex. 19:16, 19; 1 Sam. 13:3; 2 Sam. 6:15; Matt. 24:31; 1 Cor. 15:52; 1 Thess. 4:16).

28:1—35:10 This section consists of six woes (28:1; 29:1, 15; 30:1; 31:1; 33:1), including woes to future rulers (28:1—29:24); woes for accepting foolish counsel (30:1—31:9), with an appendix promising salvation in God the King (32:1–20); and woes against Assyria, which give promise of Zion's future glory (33:1—35:10).

28:1–29 The woe oracle against the northern kingdom's rulers (vv. 1–13) was to serve as an example to Judah's rulers (vv. 14–29). Note the word *therefore* in v. 14.

28:1–13 The woe oracle consists of an indictment of the northern kingdom's drunken political leaders (vv. 1–4), contrasted with the ideal future King (vv. 5, 6); an accusation against its religious leaders for drunkenness (vv. 7, 8) and for debunking God's true prophets (vv. 9, 10); and the sending of a messenger (vv. 11, 12) with the announcement of judgment (v. 13).

28:1 The crown of pride refers to

Samaria. **drunkards:** The biblical writers regularly condemn the abuse of wine, drunkenness, and debauchery (5:11, 12). **Ephraim:** This name sometimes refers to all of Israel (7:2–9).

28:2 The **strong one** refers to Assyria, which is compared to **hail** that strips a plant of its leaves and **mighty waters** that sweep away the stalks (8:7, 8; 17:12, 13).

28:3, 4 crown of pride: This phrase is repeated from v. 1. The repetition of many phrases is for emphasis; but there is a sadness in this repetition. The people of Samaria and Ephraim ought to have enjoyed their **beauty** and **verdant valleys.** They were to lose everything, however, because of their incessant idolatry, namely, their refusal to acknowledge the Lord alone as the living God.

28:5 In that day: For a similar phrase, see 2:12. The true **crown of glory** (29:17–24; 30:18–33; 32:1—33:24) stands in contrast to the false one (vv. 1–4). **remnant:** For similar references, see 1:9; 10:19–23.

28:6 The **spirit of justice** will prevail in the messianic age (11:1–5; 42:1–4).

28:7 They also refers to the religious leaders, **the priest and the prophet.**

28:7 There is a natural limit to the strength of alcohol that can be obtained without distilling, a process unknown in biblical times. Great quantities of grain were used to make beer, which was more of a food or thin gruel than today's beer. Numerous warnings in Scripture show that drunkenness was a problem.

28:9, 10 Will he teach was spoken by the hardened leaders against Isaiah.

28:9 A child was **weaned** between the ages of three and five, the time for elementary moral education, which is described in v. 10.

28:10, 11 The **stammering lips** were those of the Assyrians, who would become the teachers of Israel because of Israel's own failed leadership (33:19).

28:12 In place of the **rest** that comes from faith, Israel's oppressors would teach with a rod.

28:13 The word of the Lord would take the shape of discipline in the form of foreigners with stammering lips teaching their morals to Israel, who should have learned from God.

28:14–29 Isaiah's prophecy against Judah's scoffing rulers has two parts, introduced by **hear** (vv. 14, 23): (1) first to the threatened judgment (vv. 14–22), and then (2) to a wisdom instruction showing that God has given the simple peasant more sense of right judgment (v. 26) than the scoffing rulers (vv. 23–29). The two sermons end with reference to the Lord of Hosts, first as the author of destruction (v. 22), then as the "wonderful in counsel" (v. 29).

28:14–22 The threat of judgment consists of an accusation against Judah's unrighteous rulers of cynical mockery of Isaiah's threats (vv. 14, 15), of a renewed threat (vv. 16–21), with a renewed appeal to them not to mock (v. 22).

28:14 Scornful men are worse than "fools"; beyond choosing what is bad, they despise what is good (Ps. 1:1).

28:15 covenant with death . . . lies . . . falsehood: These phrases are probably Isaiah's way of describing the people's covenant with Egypt. **Overflowing scourge** is likely the prophet's way of describing the Assyrian reprisals (10:26; 28:2). The scorners have sarcastically thrown Isaiah's warnings back in his face.

28:16–22 The threat of judgment has two parts: the Assyrian army will be the immediate cause (vv. 16–19), and Lord of Hosts will be the Ultimate Cause (vv. 20–22).

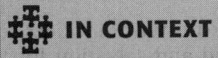 **IN CONTEXT** | **A Covenant with Death**

In the ancient world, worshipers prayed to both demons and deities of death to spare them, or they wore amulets to protect them from death by warding off the divine beings. Such amulets are commonly found in Middle Eastern archaeological digs, including Judah and Israel.

The god of death in Syria-Palestine was Mot. The Ugaritic myths from Ras Shamra, Syria, depict Mot as having an insatiable appetite for living beings and, in the end, devouring all life. In Canaanite thought, Mot, the bringer of death, struggles with Baal, the bringer of life. Mot's victories result in death and destruction on earth, while Baal's victories bring life-giving rains and good crops.

Isaiah confronts some leaders of Jerusalem who anticipated a coming destruction (Is. 28:14–22). The "overflowing scourge" (v. 2:15) pictures a "flood," a metaphor used throughout the ancient Near East for military destruction. These leaders believed that by making a covenant with Mot they would be safe. Mot, they supposed, would protect them when the devastation passed through. Isaiah answers that their "covenant with death," their bargain with Mot, offers no real security (vv. 18, 19). All Mot can deliver is death itself.

28:16, 17 Therefore: In response to the people's scoffing, **the Lord** promises to establish His future kingdom on the **sure foundation** of justice and faith. **I lay** refers to the future, "I will lay." The apostles identified the **stone for a foundation** as Jesus Christ (1 Pet. 2:4–6). **hail . . . waters:** For similar descriptions, see v. 2.

28:18, 19 As often as: The Assyrian army trampled through Israel many times.

28:20 The too-short **bed** and the too-narrow **covering** give a false promise of security and comfort, an apt figure for the people's ill-advised, obstinate alliance with Egypt.

28:21 At **Mount Perazim,** God broke forth like a mighty flood (2 Sam. 5:20; 1 Chr. 14:11; compare vv. 2, 15, 17, 18). In the **Valley of Gibeon,** He brought forth hail (Josh. 10:10, 11; compare vv. 2, 17). God's judgment on Israel was **unusual,** or "alien," in that He rarely struck out in wrath against His own sinful people. The Hebrew Scripture is not a record of the wrath of God, but of His long patience toward His erring people, whom He still desires to call "My people" (Ex. 6:2–8).

28:22 Mockers comes from the same Hebrew root as "scornful men" in v. 14. **Lord God of hosts:** For a similar usage, see 1:9. **upon the whole earth:** For a similar idea, see 24:1–23.

28:23–29 The sermon praising the wisdom of the peasant farmer, after an introductory admonition "to hear" (v. 23) has two parts: his wisdom in planting (vv. 24–26) and in threshing (vv. 27–29). Each concludes by pointing to the Lord as the Author of wisdom in right judgment (vv. 26, 29). The scoffing rulers, by contrast, have foolishly mocked the Lord.

28:24, 25 The idea being conveyed in these verses is that there is a pattern to farming, just as there is a pattern to life.

28:26–28 A **threshing sledge** would have been too large a tool for such a finely ground product as cummin.

28:29 wonderful in counsel: For a similar idea, see 9:6. The wisdom that the farmer uses in vv. 24–28 to tend his crops comes from God, the source of all good counsel.

29:1–14 The second woe is against Jerusalem for its hypocritical religion—specifically its empty worship (vv. 1–8) and its blind prophets (vv. 9–14).

29:1 Ariel probably means "altar hearth" (Ezek. 43:15, 16). The destruction and bloodshed in Jerusalem would make the city appear like an altar. The repetition of the term *Ariel* indicates the Lord's sorrow over the sorry state to which His city had fallen. **where David dwelt:** David made Jerusalem his capital and planned the temple that Solomon would later build in that city. These words show God's con-

tinuing love for His servant David, the prototype of the coming King Jesus. **Add year to year** is a sarcastic reference to repetitious, empty ritual (1:10–17).

29:2 Heaviness and sorrow may be rephrased as "grievous sorrow."

29:3 Siege refers to the Assyrian siege of the city in 701 B.C.

29:4, 5 Voice . . . like a medium's refers to the forbidden, deceptive "voices" for which the medium supposedly served as a channel. The strong voice of the city of Jerusalem would become merely a **whisper** (8:19).

29:6 Punished is literally "visited," a word sometimes used for bringing salvation. **thunder and earthquake and great noise . . . storm and tempest . . . fire:** The Lord's coming to His people is described using the imagery of the elements that accompanied Him at Sinai (Ex. 19:16–19) and when He fought for Israel (19:1; 30:27; Judg. 5:4, 5; Ps. 18:7–15; Hab. 3:3–7).

29:7, 8 all the nations: For a similar usage, see 5:26. **Ariel:** The term is also used in v. 1 for the city of Jerusalem. **As a dream** means "quickly passing," almost "unreal."

29:9, 10 Pause . . . Blind: Whereas the religious leaders of Israel were physically **drunk** (28:7), those of Jerusalem **stagger** not from intoxicating drinks, but from ignorance of the Lord and His ways. **Deep sleep** is from a Hebrew word used also of Adam's sleep (Gen. 2:21), a supernatural stupor. **prophets . . . seers:** The visions that God had given were not appreciated or obeyed.

29:11, 12 The **literate** represent the religious leaders who found Isaiah's prophecies **sealed** due to their own spiritual blindness (Rev. 5:1). The **illiterate** represent the common people.

29:13 The people's **mouths** and **lips** spoke the right things, but their inner nature was far from God.

29:14 God's **marvelous work** includes both judgment on the proud and salvation for the lowly (vv. 17–24). **wisdom . . . shall perish:** For a similar idea, see 1 Cor. 1:18–31.

29:15–24 The third woe oracle, directed against Israel's unbelieving counselors, consists of an accusation that the counselors had turned the religious world upside down by seeking to manipulate God rather than submitting to Him (vv. 15, 16), and the promise that God would turn the counselor's social world upside down by deflating the pretentious and elevating the lowly (vv. 17–24).

29:15 The word **counsel** refers to making alliances instead of running to God for assistance.

29:16 potter . . . clay: For a similar idea, see 45:9.

29:17 Lebanon is a symbol of the earth's might (2:13; 10:34; 33:9). **Fruitful field,** or "garden," is the opposite of Lebanon, a forest.

29:18 Those who were once **deaf** and **blind** to **the words of the book** will miraculously understand it (vv. 9–12).

29:19 poor: For a similar usage, see 61:1.

29:20 terrible one: For similar references, see 13:11; 25:3, 4; 49:24. **scornful:** For a similar reference, see 28:14.

29:21 By a word refers to false testimony. **Lay a snare** may include the miscarriage of justice through legal technicalities. **By empty words** refers to winning a case through lies or clever arguments.

29:22 redeemed Abraham: For additional information, see Acts 7:2–4. **Jacob shall not now be ashamed:** Based on God's covenant with the patriarchs, the Lord gave a renewed promise of deliverance and blessing to the Israelites.

29:23, 24 My hands: God Himself will bring about the redemption of His people. **Holy One of Jacob** refers to the One whom Jacob regarded as holy; it is a variant of the expression "Holy One of Israel."

30:1–33 In the previous chapter, Isaiah denounces those who seek human support, instead of depending on the Lord. In chs. 30 and 31, Isaiah addresses the specific folly of depending on Egypt. This woe oracle consists of a condemnation of dependence on Egypt (vv. 1–17) and a promise that the Lord will save Israel and destroy Assyria (vv. 18–33).

30:1–17 The "woe" to stubborn rebels of Judah for trusting Egypt, instead of the Lord,

consists of reproof for misplaced confidence (vv. 1–7) and of a judicial sentence for rejecting God's word (vv. 8–17).

30:1–7 The reproof consists of an accusation that they repudiated faith in God for faith in Egypt (vv. 1, 2) and a prediction that Egypt will fail them (vv. 3–7).

30:1 This is the fourth **woe** in 28:1—35:10. **The rebellious children** are Hezekiah's advisers. To the sin of injustice they **add** the **sin** of devising plans independently of God. **My Spirit** is another way of speaking of God (11:2).

30:2 the shadow of Egypt: The contrast, of course, would be trusting in the "shadow of the Almighty" (Ps. 91:1).

30:3 Shame refers to deep humiliation.

30:4 His ambassadors may be the people from Judah who went from **Zoan** (19:11–13) in the Delta to **Hanes,** some fifty miles south of Cairo.

30:5 Shame and **reproach** speak of an intolerable humiliation.

30:6 The burden against the beasts was due to the fact that they vainly carried Judah's gifts through the wilderness to Egypt (vv. 7–11).

30:7 Rahab, which literally means "Storm" or "Arrogant," was a dragon from pagan mythology who was pictured as resisting creation. Both the Rahab and Leviathan are symbolic of the forces of evil in the universe that God will destroy (51:9).

30:8–18 The sentence consists of two cycles: (1) reproof for rejecting God's word (vv. 8–11, 15), and (2) the report of His judgment (12–14, 16, 17).

30:8 The oldest writing tablets discovered so

IN LIFE   What's the Hurry?

Perhaps you feel rushed or caught on a treadmill, always focused on a deadline, always thinking about what is happening next rather than what is happening right now.

The people of Isaiah's time were consumed with anxiety about the Assyrians. They were busily making plans and preparations in case the enemy invaded. But God warned them the key to withstanding the threats of Assyria was not in frenetic activity, but in quiet, confident trust in Him (Is. 30:15). It was not that wise planning had no value; it did. But faith in God demands a certain amount of ceasing from work to reflect on one's situation and the Lord's ability to handle it.

Conventional wisdom urges us to pause and smell the roses occasionally. Scripture calls us to pause and worship the Lord regularly (Ex. 20:8–10). This principle of a balanced, measured approach to life was established at the end of the first work week in history, when God paused in His work to consider what He had accomplished (Gen. 1:31–2:2).

Why not spend time right now to reflect on your life—where it has come from, where it is, and where it is going. Reflect on your relationships—the conversations you have had, the memories you have gained. Are you willing to take the time to find God in your life?

far can be dated to about 1350 B.C. They were found in A.D. 1986 in a shipwreck off the coast of southern Turkey. Until this discovery, the oldest tablets were those found in a well at Nimrud, near Nineveh, dating from about 700 B.C. The original writing surface was a coating of wax.

30:9 That can mean "because." **Law** refers to the prophet's instruction, which is from the Lord Himself (v. 15).

30:10 Do not see: For a similar usage, see Mic. 2:6.

30:11 To cease: This was the most flagrant of the people's wicked words.

30:12 To not choose to obey the Lord is to reject Him, even to **despise** His message. **trust in oppression:** For a similar idea, see 1:15–17; 29:20, 21.

30:13, 14 A bulge in a high wall and **the breaking of the potter's vessel** signify that judgment would come **suddenly** and completely. **A shard** is a piece of broken pottery.

30:15 Returning entails repentance. **rest:** For a similar idea, see 28:12. **Quietness and confidence** may be rephrased as "utter trust." Trusting in God's strength instead of our own is the only way we can find true rest.

30:16 Instead of trusting in the Lord, the people were depending on Egypt for **horses** and chariots to defend the land (31:1).

30:17 One thousand shall flee: The point is that the nation will be utterly routed (Deut. 32:30).

30:18–33 This promise of salvation consists of (1) the basis for blessing found in God's justice (v. 18), (2) the promise of Judah's deliverance (vv. 19–26), and (3) the threat of Assyria's destruction (vv. 27–33).

30:18 God's **justice** demands that the Assyrian oppressors be punished (Judg. 2:16). God's **gracious** character and His **mercy** are balanced; they interact with His justice and the fact that He will be **exalted.**

30:19 You shall weep no more: A similar promise is given in 25:8. **the sound of your cry:** For a similar idea, see Judg. 2:18.

30:20 bread of adversity: The Lord was giving the Israelites meager rations as though they were in prison (1 Kin. 22:27). But after judgment the Lord would provide salvation: Israel's **eyes** would **see** (29:24). **Teachers** probably refers to the prophets (v. 10).

30:21 Walk in it contrasts with "turn aside" in v. 11. The people had been living in such a way that they were oblivious to their spiritual teachers (v. 20); now they would be taught by the Spirit of the living God.

30:22 Defile means "to desecrate by destruction" (2 Kin. 23:4–14). **Unclean thing** refers to something soiled by menstruation; the idea is to get rid of it.

30:23, 24 The promises that were part of the original Mosaic covenant were in force again. **rain:** Blessing would extend from field to flock (Deut. 28:11, 12).

30:25, 26 on every high mountain . . . light of the sun will be sevenfold: These phrases emphasize the magnitude of the coming salvation. **waters:** The coming of ample rainfall and strong streams are associated with the blessing that comes from trust in God (32:2; 41:17, 18). **When the towers fall** is associated with the collapse of human pride (2:12–17).

30:27–33 The prediction of Assyria's destruction consists of two cycles: (1) one of attack (vv. 27, 28 and 30, 31), and (2) one of rejoicing (v. 29 and v. 32), and then concludes with a notice about the king's funeral pyre (v. 33).

30:27 The name of the LORD refers to His character, as memorialized in His saving acts throughout history. **Comes** refers to the Lord's coming in a storm (29:6).

30:28 His breath describes the sound of the Lord's voice as a roaring, overflowing river. **neck:** For a similar image, see 8:8.

30:29 song . . . in the night: In times of festivals, singing would extend long into the evening. **The Mighty One** literally means "Rock" (Ps. 144:1).

30:30, 31 Here God's **voice** is compared to the thunder (Ps. 29:3, 4; contrast v. 28). **descent of His arm:** The strong arm of God had delivered the Israelites from Egypt, now His arm would descend in judgment (Ex. 6:6). **Assyria:** Only here in this section is the enemy nation mentioned by name.

30:32 tambourines: For additional references to this instrument, see Ex. 15:20; 1 Sam. 18:6. **And in battles:** These were soldier-musicians; they were to be ready to fight or to play music as the occasion demanded.

30:33 Tophet, located south of Jerusalem, was the place where the valleys of Hinnom and Kidron met. It was probably a deep, wide pit containing a bonfire of blazing wood, where children had at times been burned to death as offerings to pagan deities (2 Kin. 23:10; Jer. 7:31, 32; 19:6, 11–14). The area has filled in significantly through the centuries. **Brimstone** is a reminder of the fiery destruction of Sodom (34:9, 10; Gen. 19:24).

31:1–9 The fifth woe oracle reaffirms the fourth oracle (30:1–33); it too was addressed to those who replaced faith in the Lord with reliance on Egypt. This oracle consists of a condemnation of dependence on Egypt (vv. 1–3), and a promise that the Lord will save Mount Zion (vv. 4, 5) and destroy Assyria (vv. 6–9).

31:1 Woe to those who go down to Egypt: For a similar idea, see 30:2. **Look** means "to look with interest" or "to look with respect."

🌱 IN LIFE | Justice in the Wilderness

Perhaps like many people you think of the countryside as a gentle, quiet refuge from the complications of urban life. However, in Bible times, rural areas were generally places without law and order, where everyone "did what was right in his own eyes" (Judg. 21:25). It was the city that tended to offer peace and protection.

For that reason, Isaiah's vision of justice in the wilderness (Is. 32:16) was a remarkable promise. The key to the transformation would be the presence of the Spirit (32:15). However, the Spirit would not impose God's peace on unwilling people. Rather, peace would be the fruit of seeds sown in righteousness (32:17).

The Lord challenged the complacent women of Judah to wail for the woeful consequences that would befall their corrupt, escapist society (32:9–13). However, God promised to intervene. The city would be secure, not because of its walls, but because the Spirit would defend it.

Regardless of whether you live in an urban area, Isaiah's vision of God's peace is instructive. As you sow the seeds of righteousness in your community, you give the Spirit an opportunity to bring a blessing on you and your neighbors. Those "seeds" may involve feeding the hungry, shutting down a business based on immorality, or simply praying for civic leaders. Whatever action you take, know that the Spirit can multiply your efforts many times. "The fruit of righteousness is sown in peace by those who make peace" (James 3:18).

Seek the LORD here entails consulting His prophets for direction (29:9, 10; 30:1).

31:2, 3 The house of evildoers refers to Judah. Their **help** refers to Egypt. Both Egypt and Judah **will perish together.**

31:4, 5 Lion connotes the LORD of hosts (1:9) and His resolve to **fight** the enemy. The **multitude of shepherds** refers to the Assyrian officers. **Mount Zion** and **hill** are synonyms. **Birds flying about** pictures the Lord's passionate commitment to **defend Jerusalem. Passing over** is a technical term used for the destroying angel who "passed over" Israel in destroying the Egyptians and defending Israel (Ex. 12:13, 23).

31:6, 7 revolted: For an explanation of the rebellion, see 30:1. **throw away:** For a similar idea, see 30:22. **your own hands have made:** For similar wording, see 2:8; 17:8.

31:8 Not of man refers to the death angel that destroyed Sennacherib's vaunted army (37:36).

31:9 A banner was a rallying point for a battle. The **princes** would be too dispirited to rally for the cause. **fire:** For similar imagery, see 10:17, 18; 30:27, 30, 33.

32:1–20 The fifth woe (ch. 31) concludes with a prophecy about leadership (vv. 1–8) and its effects (vv. 9–20). Paradoxically, generous leaders (vv. 1–5) produce abundance and permanent security (vv. 16–20), whereas the miserly (vv. 6, 7) produce false security and desolation (vv. 9–14).

32:1 The prophecy concerning this **king** is fulfilled in the Lord Jesus Christ (7:14; 9:1–7;

11:1–5; 28:16; John 10:11, 16). The **princes** are His "undershepherds" (1 Pet. 5:2–4).

32:2 The four similes for the future King's protection and provision of His people contrast with Israel's present incompetent leadership (28:7; 29:9, 10; 30:1, 2; 31:1, 2).

32:3, 4 Clear **eyes** and listening **ears** are figures for the future sensible leadership, in contrast to the present senseless, foolish leadership. The people's eyes and ears would also be opened (6:9, 10; 29:18, 24; 35:5; 42:7); similarly, they would have a **heart** that is understanding and a **tongue** that speaks **plainly.**

32:5–7 The contrast between the way the noble and foolish **speak** comes from the person's **heart** (v. 4). If a person meditates on evil, that person will speak and act treacherously. **destroy the poor with lying words:** For a similar idea see 29:20, 21.

32:8, 9 The term **complacent** is used three times of these women (vv. 9, 10, 12); it is derived from the verb meaning "to trust." Thus the word can also be rendered as "assured" and "secure" (vv. 17, 19). Though the wicked erroneously relied on Egypt for their security (31:1), the righteous placed their trust in the Lord and obtained true security.

32:10–12 Mourning women in the ancient Middle East removed their clothing and wore **sackcloth** around their **waists** (Gen. 37:34).

32:13, 14 thorns and briers: For similar usage, see 5:6; 7:23. **palaces . . . pasture:** These images speak of the complete ruin of Jerusalem in the day of God's judgment.

32:15 The new age depends on the creative

work of **the Spirit** (11:2; 42:1; 61:1; Ezek. 36:26, 27; Joel 2:28, 29) who originates **on high,** in God's dwelling (33:5). This is in contrast to going "down to Egypt" (31:1).

32:16 fruitful field: This is a reversal of the judgment predicted in 29:17.

32:17, 18 The Hebrew words translated **assurance** and **secure** are related to the Hebrew word translated "complacent" in v. 9.

32:19, 20 Hail may refer to Assyria (28:2).

33:1–24 The sixth woe differs from the others in that it is addressed to Assyria, not to Judah. By focusing exclusively on Assyria's defeat and Judah's salvation, the prophecy magnifies Judah's exalted King (vv. 3, 5, 10). This woe oracle consists of an introduction of the main themes of the oracle (vv. 1–6); an emphasis on Judah's need for salvation, the Lord's provision of that need (vv. 7–13), and its spiritual impact on sinners (vv. 14–16); and a conclusion showing the majestic King in His beauty (vv. 17–24).

33:1–6 The introduction prophecies the destruction of the destroyer (v. 1), the Lord's response to the remnant's prayer (vv. 2–4), and the transformation of Zion (vv. 5, 6).

33:1 You refers to Assyria, who **treacherously** (21:2; 24:16) broke its treaties (2 Kin. 18:13–37).

33:2 be gracious: For a similar idea, see 30:18. The besieged remnant, including Isaiah, had **waited** for the Lord in prayer (37:14–20) and in confident expectation (40:31). **salvation:** For a similar reference to God as the only place to find salvation, see 12:2.

33:3 When You lift Yourself up speaks of an exaltation of the heavenly King (vv. 5, 10) as He rises to demonstrate His glory and vindicate His justice. **Scattered** is an allusion to Moses' song of praise (Num. 10:35).

33:4 The **plunder** of God's war with His enemies belongs to the Lord, the true Victor (23:18; 34:2). It will be **gathered** as swiftly and completely as **the caterpillar** and **locusts** can strip a field, since the Lord's judgment will come quickly without warning (1 Thess. 5:2).

33:5 exalted . . . on high: This chapter presents the "rising glory" of the Savior King over His people, defending them against Assyria and all others. **Justice and righteousness** may be rephrased as "true justice."

33:6 Wisdom and knowledge . . . fear of the LORD: The Messiah's characteristics (11:2) will also characterize His city.

33:7–13 With all of Judah's hope gone (vv. 7–9) the Lord responds (v. 10) by destroying Assyria (vv. 11, 12).

33:7, 8 Valiant ones may sarcastically refer to three officials of Judah who conferred with the Assyrians (36:3, 22). Judah's **ambassadors**

wept **bitterly** because Assyria took their gifts, but continued to besiege Jerusalem (v. 1). With the treaty between Assyria and Judah broken, the **highways** were not safe.

33:9 Sharon was on the western coastal plain. **Bashan** was on the east side of the Jordan. All of Israel's most verdant areas, from **Lebanon** in its far north (35:2) to **Carmel** in the northwest, are desolate after Assyria has ravaged the land.

33:10 Now . . . Now . . . Now: The King is about to assert His authority (vv. 5, 16).

33:11 You refers to Assyria (v. 1). **chaff . . . stubble . . . fire:** The grandeur of Assyria would be consumed quickly.

33:12 The burnings of lime—all that is left from burning lime is dust—and **thorns . . . in the fire** indicate the thoroughness and swiftness of Assyria's destruction (27:4).

33:13 Hear: For a similar call for all to acknowledge the Lord as Sovereign, see 34:1.

33:14 Who among us shall dwell: This is the language of a pilgrimage psalm (Pss. 15:1; 24:3). **burnings:** For a description of God as a consuming fire, see Deut. 4:24; 9:3; Heb. 12:29.

33:15, 16 walks righteously: For a similar description of the person who can approach the Holy One, see Pss. 1:1, 2; 15:2; Gal. 5:22–25; Eph. 5:1, 2. **Who stops . . . shuts:** These words do not advocate ignoring social evil, but refusing to take part in it. **On high** refers to God's dwelling (v. 5)—the place the righteous will go to live with God forever.

33:17 The **King** is the Lord (v. 22). The **land** of the Lord's dominion will stretch **very far off** (26:15).

33:18 The scribe . . . who weighs refers to those who took the tribute (2 Kin. 18:14).

33:19 stammering tongue: For a similar idea concerning Israel's enemies, see Deut. 28:49.

33:20 The **feasts** were celebrated from the heart (30:29), and not perfunctorily (29:1). **Not be taken down** implies that the Exile is over. Judah's immediate salvation merges with its ultimate deliverance.

33:21 Judah would be protected figuratively by **broad rivers,** like those at Tyre (23:1–3) and Thebes (Nah. 3:8). However, no intimidating ship would be on the rivers, because God Himself would defend Judah.

33:22, 23 Note that the **Lawgiver** is associated with other acts of mercy (Deut. 6:1–3; John 1:14–18); the giving of the Law was God's way to point out the correct path for the Israelites to follow. This was merely another expression of His mercy.

33:24 Sickness and sin will be removed in the coming kingdom of the glorious Savior.

34:1–35:10 Two prophecies form an appendix to the sixth woe (ch. 33): (1) the fertile land of the plundering nations will be transformed into a desert (ch. 34) and (2) the desert will be transformed into fertile land (ch. 35).

34:1–17 This prophecy of judgment consists of two parts: (1) judgment on all the nations (vv. 1–4) and then (2) judgment on Edom representatively (vv. 6–15; read 22:15–25, 25:10–12; 63:1–6 for similar specifications). The prophecy is followed by an epilogue guaranteeing the prophecy (v. 16, 17).

34:1 nations: For a similar reference, see 5:26. **Let the earth hear:** For similar calls for all the world to listen to Isaiah's prophecy, see 1:2; 33:13.

34:2 Indignation is a strong term used to describe the wrath of God. **Destroyed** means "to devote to destruction." Because the Lord had defeated His enemy, the spoils were to be devoted totally to Him by burning them (23:18).

34:3 The **blood** of the slain would be so great that it would create mudslides.

34:4 The host of heaven here refers to pagan deities (24:21; 2 Kin. 17:16). **be dissolved:** See the similar language of 13:10, 13. **heavens . . . rolled up like a scroll:** The old cosmos will give way to the new (51:6; Matt. 24:29; Rev. 6:13, 14; 21:1).

34:5–17 The Lord's judgment on Edom consists of (1) its becoming a sacrifice to God (vv. 5–7), (2) a desolation (vv. 8–12), and (3) a place for unclean, wild animals (vv. 13–17).

34:5 The Lord's avenging **sword** moves from demolishing the pantheon of **heaven** (v. 4) to **Edom** (63:1) in particular. **Curse** comes from the same root translated "destroyed" in v. 2. Edom is "devoted to destruction."

34:6 Blood and **slaughter** link Edom's destruction with that of the nations (vv. 2, 3). Sin must be atoned for by **sacrifice,** either of the sinner himself as here (Ezek. 33:10), or by the substitutionary sacrifice of Christ (52:13–15).

34:7 Oxen and **bulls** may represent Edom's troops or leaders.

34:8 vengeance: The Lord secures His sovereignty and keeps His community whole by saving His wronged subjects and punishing their guilty oppressors.

34:9, 10 Brimstone and **burning pitch** may be allusions to Sodom and Gomorrah (30:33; see Gen. 19:24; Ezek. 38:22).

34:11 The pelican, porcupine, owl, and **raven** are all unclean creatures of remote, uninhabited places (Deut. 14:14–17). In the day of God's judgment, Edom would become a wasteland. The Hebrew words translated **confusion and emptiness** are translated "without form and void" in Gen. 1:2. Edom will be returned to chaos.

34:12 There will be no **nobles** or **princes** in the desert.

34:13–15 For a similar description of these unclean desert creatures, see 13:21, 22.

34:16 The book of the LORD may refer to the prophecy found in vv. 1–15.

34:17 As God gave Israel the Promised Land

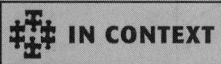 **IN CONTEXT** **A Deadly Demon**

The prophet Isaiah describes the total desolation that God would visit upon Edom for its hostility to God (Is. 34:2, 5). Among the descriptions of God's wrath is the sole reference in Scripture to a well-known Mesopotamian demon named Lilith. Later Jewish tradition connected the name *Lilith* with the Hebrew word for night, giving the traditional English translation "night creature" (v. 14). However, as a Mesopotamian name, *Lilith* comes from the Sumerian word *lil*, meaning "wind" or "spirit."

The earliest records and amulets from Mesopotamia show that people there feared the Lilu, a group of particularly malevolent demons. Lilith herself was believed to attack both babies and mothers in childbirth, eating their flesh and sucking their blood. The only protection from the Lilu was to call upon the king of demons for help.

Jewish inscriptions and amulets describe Lilith in a similar fashion, but with additional features. She was known as a woman with long hair and wings, attacking men who slept alone. Jewish incantation bowls have been found that petition God to defeat and bind Lilith as she seeks her human prey.

For Isaiah and his listeners, the threat of Lilith finding "a place of rest" (v. 14) among humans was nothing but terrifying. Where once the Edomite cities housed wisdom and life and cultured society, there would now be wasteland. Edom would become uninhabitable, the domain of wild animals and wild beasts. The nobility that once led the land would be gone (v. 12). No human would dare to dwell in the area (v. 10), for Lilith ensures its perpetual desolation.

by **lot** in the sacred assembly (Josh. 18:10), so in His judgment He **divided** Edom **among** the unclean animals.

35:1–10 The poem prophesies (1) the reversal of earth's barrenness to fruitfulness, giving encouragement to the fearful (vv. 1–4); (2) a reversal from infirmity to health and from wilderness to water (vv. 5–7); and (3) a secure, holy highway whereby the redeemed can come back to Zion (vv. 8–10). Physical and spiritual salvation are merged in terms of an earth free from fear, injustice, sickness, and death. Chapters 36—39 show that this is more than assertion. History began to reverse itself when God, in miraculous fulfillment of Isaiah's prophecies, supernaturally judged Assyria at Jerusalem's gate and saved the faithful remnant within it.

35:1 wilderness . . . desert: The Spirit of God will make the earth fruitful again (32:15). **rejoice:** The joy of the elements of creation is a reflection of the joy of God's people at the arrival of His salvation (14:7, 8; 44:23; 55:12).

35:2 glory of Lebanon . . . Sharon: This is a reversal of the judgment of 33:9. **The glory of the Lord** would be seen in the return of the captives from Babylon (40:5).

35:3 Strengthen the feeble hands: This phrase is cited in Heb. 12:12 (Josh. 1:6, 7, 9, 18).

We can reassure ourselves with the knowledge that our Savior is coming. In that day, justice will be restored.

35:4 save you: When the Lord comes, He will offer salvation (Luke 19:10). **vengeance:** See the use of this word in 34:8.

35:5, 6 eyes . . . ears . . . lame . . . tongue: This prophecy of healings was fulfilled in the physical and spiritual healings of Jesus (61:1; Matt. 12:22; Luke 4:18; 7:22). **opened . . . unstopped:** For similar usage, see 29:18; 32:3.

35:7 The habitation of jackals speaks of the coming reversal of the devastation God had brought on the land (34:14). **Reeds and rushes** speaks of the reversal of the destruction described in 19:5, 6.

35:8, 9 The promise of a safe **highway** is a reversal of the judgment in 33:8; 34:10 (11:16; 40:3, 4; 57:14; 62:10). **ravenous beast:** Ferocious animals could make traveling dangerous in the ancient world.

35:10 the ransomed: The restored Babylonian exiles symbolize political and spiritual exiles and the physically and spiritually blind, deaf, and lame of all times and places. The Lord would come to rescue them from their tragic predicaments. **come to Zion with singing:** For a description of this scene, see 12:1 (compare Ps.

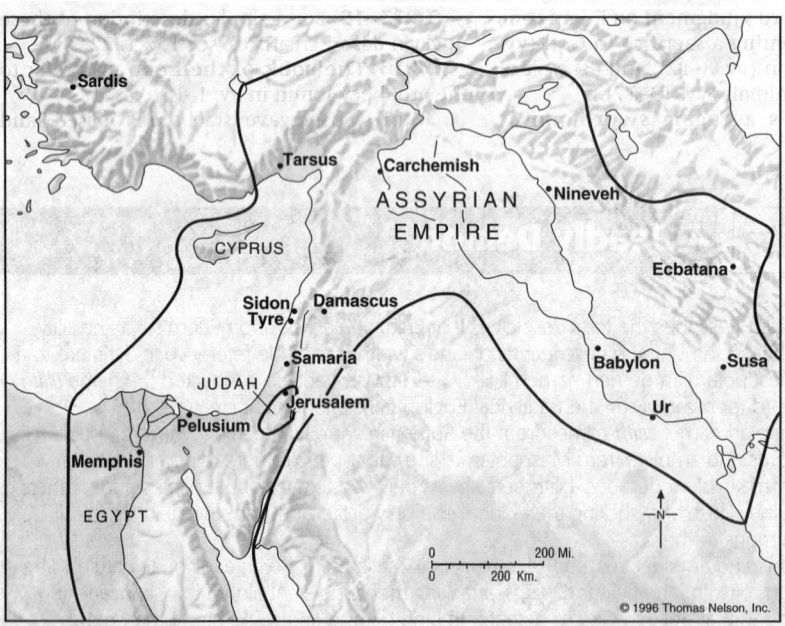

The Assyrian Empire (650 B.C.)

By 650 B.C. the Assyrian Empire, whose capital was Nineveh, stretched from the Persian Gulf in the east through the fertile crescent into Palestine and beyond, embracing for a short time all of Egypt in the southwest. Judah paid tribute to Assyria during the reign of Manasseh, even though it was technically a free zone.

126:1–6). **sorrow and sighing:** For more detail, see 25:7, 8.

36:1–39:8 This historical bridge between chs. 1—35 and 40—66 consists of two parts: (1) Hezekiah's faith in the face of an Assyrian threat (chs. 36; 37) and (2) Hezekiah's mixed faith in the face of illness (chs. 38; 39).

36:1–37:38 This section validates Isaiah's predictions that the Lord would (1) destroy Judah through Assyria (36:1), (2) besiege Jerusalem (36:2–22), (3) deliver the faithful remnant (37:1–35), and destroy the Assyrians (37:36–38). Isaiah proclaims that sin compounded with misplaced confidence brings defeat; conversely, repentance and faith in the Lord brings deliverance (2 Kin. 18:13—19:37; 2 Chr. 32:1–23).

36:1 The **fourteenth year** of King Hezekiah's sole reign was 701 B.C. **all:** In his annals, Sennacherib mentions forty-six cities that he attacked.

36:2 The Rabshakeh may have been the king's personal advisor. **great army:** For the defeat of this fighting force, see 37:36. **aqueduct:** For a similar reference, see 7:3.

36:3 Eliakim . . . Shebna: For further details, read 22:15–23.

36:4, 5 Only the Assyrian leader is referred to here as **king,** not **Hezekiah.** This is an indication of the Assyrians' perspective on their own status.

36:6 Judah had refused to listen to Isaiah's insistence that reliance on **Egypt** was worthless (19:14–16; 30:3, 7; 31:3). Here they were given the same warning from their enemy.

36:7 taken away: Hezekiah had destroyed the idolatrous high places and altars that his father Ahaz had built, see 2 Kin. 18:1–5; 2 Chr. 31:1–3.

36:8 riders: Micah referred to Jerusalem's soldiers as merely a "troop" (Mic. 5:1) compared to the enormous international army of Assyria (Mic. 4:11).

36:9 one captain of the least: Judah had no hope of defeating the force that surrounded him.

36:10 The LORD said to me: Ancient Middle Eastern conquerors liked to claim that the gods of their defeated enemies had joined their side (2 Chr. 35:21). These words about the Lord were no more than a boast.

36:11, 12 Aramaic was the language of international diplomacy during this period.

36:13, 14 The Rabshakeh spoke **in Hebrew** to be deliberately provocative: he wanted his words to be understood by the citizens of Jerusalem. **deceive you:** The Rabshakeh structured his speech so that he would quickly discourage those who heard it.

36:15–17 take you away: The Assyrians commonly exiled the people groups they conquered (2 Kin. 15:29; 17:6).

36:18–21 The Rabshakeh assumed that different gods were worshiped in **Samaria** than in Jerusalem, so he repeated some of the same sentiments articulated by the Assyrian king in

Photo by Howard Vos

This stone monument, known as the prism of Sennacherib, gives the Assyrian account of Sennacherib's invasion of Jerusalem (Is. 36; 37).

10:10, 11.

36:22 The words of the enemy would not bring pleasure **to Hezekiah.** The torn **clothes** indicated that the messengers were bearing bad news (37:1).

37:1 Sackcloth was a sign of mourning, repentance, and humiliation (20:2, 3; 1 Kin. 20:31; Neh. 9:1; Dan. 9:3). **went into the house of the LORD:** For a related passage, see 1 Kin. 8:33, 34.

37:2, 3 Eliakim . . . Shebna: One of Isaiah's prophecies condemns Shebna for his arrogance (22:15–23).

37:4, 5 For more references to the **remnant,** see 1:9; 10:20.

37:6–10 The Lord commonly reassured His servants with the words: **Do not be afraid** (7:4; 35:4; Gen. 15:1; Josh. 1:9). We have no reason to fear if our trust is in the all-powerful God (Heb. 13:6).

37:11 utterly destroying: See 34:2 for another use of this term.

37:12–15 Hezekiah prayed: Hezekiah had learned to turn to God for help in his times of need (30:1). For another of Hezekiah's prayers, see 38:2, 3.

37:16–21 Because you have prayed to Me: God's gracious response was a direct answer to the prayer of a godly king. Though God can certainly work His will without our prayers, He has chosen to faithfully answer the prayers of His people.

37:22 virgin: Cities are often personified as female in the Scriptures. This imagery speaks of Jerusalem as a "daughter" being threatened by an attacker. Yet Jerusalem prevails and overcomes her assailant. **Daughter of Zion** is an endearing term for the city of Jerusalem. Just as the Lord called Israel His son (Ex. 4:22), so He looked upon Jerusalem as His daughter (1:8).

37:23 reproached and blasphemed . . . raised your voice . . . lifted up your eyes on high: The folly of the wicked of all ages is epitomized here. Anyone who lifts himself or herself up against the living God deserves the same strong words from the Almighty (vv. 28, 29). **Holy One of Israel:** The Lord embodies perfect holiness: He is completely different or set apart from all of creation (40:25); He alone is entirely sinless (6:4–7). Yet God chooses to enter into a relationship with His people, the Israelites (Ps. 40:1).

37:24 Chariots were the most prized military hardware of the time. **height of the mountains:** See 2:12–16; 14:13, 14 for other occurrences of these arrogant words.

37:25 dug and drunk water: Deserts cannot stop Assyria's king; he presents himself as invincible. The king boasts that he has **dried up** Egyptian streams. But the Lord will dry up the Egyptian sea (11:15; 44:27).

37:26–29 your rage against Me: This accusation picks up the point of the indictment in vv. 23, 24. The Assyrians dragged prisoners away with a **hook in the nose**; soon *they* would get the hook! The Lord's judgment was coming. For another use of the image of a hook, see Ezek. 38:4.

37:30–32 Assyria had promised to feed the Judeans; but only God could guarantee that the people would **eat** (36:16, 17). The **third year** could have been as early as thirteen to fifteen months from that time; any part of a year was counted as a year.

37:33 thus says the LORD: God gives His final sentence against the Assyrian tyrant.

37:34, 35 defend: For similar expressions of the Lord's protection of Jerusalem, see 27:3; 31:5. **for My own sake:** The Lord would save and protect the city for His own honor, for He had established the city for the worship of His holy name. For similar wording, see 43:25; 48:9, 11; contrast 42:21. **for My servant David's sake:** God maintained His promises to David (9:7; 49:8; 2 Sam. 7:8–16; 1 Kin. 8:17–20; Ps. 89:19–37).

37:36 This verse is the fulfillment of God's promise to take vengeance on those who trouble His people (34:8). **the angel of the LORD:** Often a visitation from the angel of the Lord brought deliverance to God's people, as in the incident with Balaam (Num. 22) and the appearances to Gideon (Judg. 6:11, 12) and Manoah (Judg. 13). At other times the angel of the Lord came in judgment (2 Sam. 24:10–25). Here the angel of the Lord delivers His people by fighting for them (Ex. 15:3).

37:37 The Assyrian king Sennacherib returned home in defeat to his palace at Nineveh, located on the Tigris river. To the many relief sculptures that adorned the walls of his home, he added a scene of his victory over Lachish (36:2; 37:8). But he omitted the disaster at Jerusalem in his written record of the campaign.

37:38 Death **in the house of Nisroch** contrasts with life in the house of the Lord (37:14; 38:20). **Esarhaddon** began his reign in 681 B.C.

38:1–39:8 Although Hezekiah trusted in God to heal him (38:1–22), he failed when the Babylonian envoys visited him. After his recovery, he paraded his own glory, not the Lord's (39:1, 2). Thus he implicitly placed his confidence in military strength and political alliances instead of the strength of the Almighty God. Because of his unbelief, Judah would go into exile (39:3–8).

38:1 In those days refers to a time before the events recorded in chs. 36, 37 (v. 6). These earlier events are presented after Jerusalem's deliverance from Assyria, for that deliverance was not the last word for either Hezekiah or Jerusalem.

38:2 prayed: For another prayer of Hezekiah, see 37:15.

38:3–6 loyal heart: For similar descriptions see 2 Kin. 18:3–5. **Hezekiah wept bitterly** because apparently at that time he had no male heirs. Hezekiah lived an additional fifteen years (v. 5); Manasseh, the successor to his throne, was twelve when Hezekiah died (2 Kin. 20:21—21:1).

38:7 sign: For a related reference, see 7:11–14.

38:8 Bringing **the shadow on the sundial**

. . . **backward** symbolized the divine extension of Hezekiah's life.

38:9–20 Hezekiah's thanksgiving song celebrating his healing consists of (1) a report of his lament (vv. 10–14) and (2) a report of the Lord's deliverance (vv. 15–20). His personal deliverance modeled the future national deliverance (41:8–11).

38:9 the writing of Hezekiah: Scriptures attest to King Hezekiah's interest in devotional literature. Apparently he instructed his scribes to compile some of the proverbs of Solomon (Prov. 25:1). Furthermore, he ordered the Levites to worship God with the psalms of David and Asaph. The following song of praise (vv. 10–20) has some affinities with those psalms (2 Chr. 29:30).

38:10, 11 Sheol: For additional references to Sheol see 5:14; 14:9, 11; 38:18. Hezekiah was mourning the fact that he was dying at an early age.

38:12 Pulling up a **tent** represented impermanence (33:20; 2 Cor. 5:1). Hezekiah's life was quickly passing away.

38:13–17 for my own peace: Hezekiah models an exemplary attitude to hardship: he accepted trials as part of God's good plan for him. For a development of this theme, see Rom. 8:28. **sins:** The forgiveness of sin and healing are two different aspects of God's salvation (53:5; Matt. 8:14–17; Luke 5:17–26). Apparently Hezekiah's poor health was connected to his sin. Yet not all sickness is due to one's own sin (Job 42:7–11; John 9:2, 3).

38:18 cannot thank: Praise for healing can only be offered while a person is alive (Ps. 6:5). **Hope** for temporal life cannot be extended beyond death, but hope for eternal life remains beyond death (Ps. 22:22–31; 2 Tim. 1:10; Heb. 2:10–12; 1 John 5:11, 12).

38:19 father . . . children: For a similar idea of the righteous teaching their children of God's faithfulness, see Ps. 22:30, 31.

38:20 sing: For a song of praise to God our Savior, see 12:1–6.

38:21 Them may refer to the court physicians. **poultice:** All healing is of God, who may and often does mediate it through medicine and the skills of health care professionals.

38:22 Depending on one's attitude, the request for a **sign** may express either unbelief (Matt. 12:39; John 6:30) or faith (v. 7). The healing of a boil would be the sign that the Lord would save Hezekiah (v. 20, 21).

39:1 At that time . . . sick: For the background see ch. 38. The **letters** were probably

about rebellion against Assyria. **recovered:** The miracle of the sundial (38:8) would have held special interest for the astronomy-minded Babylonians (2 Chr. 32:31).

39:2–4 The fact that Hezekiah showed **his treasures** instead of praising God suggests that he was trusting in his might and the armies of the nations like Babylon, instead of in the Lord.

39:5, 6 LORD **of hosts:** This is the same title as used in 1:9. It describes the Lord as Commander in Chief of the angelic armies.

39:7, 8 Eunuchs were royal officials or servants. In ancient times, these servants were often castrated to keep them from being a threat to the king's harem. For further references to eunuchs, read 56:4; Dan. 1:3–6.

40:1—55:13 This section is addressed to the Babylonian exiles in a prophetic manner. This book of comfort, written about 150 years before the time of Cyrus, promised the exiles from Judah that they would return to Jerusalem (40:1, 2), where God would meet them in the form of the Suffering Servant (42:1–4)—the same One who would become a great King (7:14; 9:6, 7; 11:1–5). The restoration after the Exile pointed to the coming of the Lord's kingdom. In Isaiah's prophecy, this first taste of salvation merges with predictions of the full salvation that Jesus Christ would bring.

40:1–8 This prophecy consists of addresses by three heavenly heralds. The first calls upon the others to comfort the exiles because their time of servitude has ended (vv. 1, 2). The second calls for building a highway so that all may see the coming of the Lord (vv. 3–5). The third guarantees the vision (vv. 6–8).

40:1 Comfort is used to address all of the people of Zion (v. 9) with words of God's mercy. This verb, repeated for emphasis, denotes the announcement of an end to the people's suffering. The message reversed the exiles' complaint (Lam. 1:2). This consolation was fulfilled in the birth of Christ (Luke 2:25). **My people . . . your God** evokes the covenantal relationship between God and Israel (Ex. 6:7).

40:2 Here the word **Jerusalem** represents the exiles. The Lord would end their period of exile and restore them to the city of Jerusalem. **Warfare** refers to Israel's hard servitude in Babylon, from which they were about to flee (48:20, 21). **Double** may mean "the equivalent" or "the right amount."

40:3 crying in the wilderness: The voice is heard in the wilderness, calling the people there to ready themselves for the coming of the Lord.

> Hezekiah models an exemplary attitude to hardship: he accepted trials as part of God's good plan for him.

The analogy is based on the anticipated coming of a magnificent ruler from a distant land. The people who lived in the area of his intended visit would do everything possible to prepare the road for his arrival. **Prepare** means "clear away the obstacles" (57:14; 62:10). **Highway** represents the hearts of people who must be spiritually prepared by repentance for God's glory to be revealed on the earth (Luke 3:3–20).

40:4 valley . . . mountain: For a similar description, see Zech. 14:1–11. While the highway of v. 3 was to be prepared by the people of the Lord, the changes required in v. 4 could be accomplished only by divine action.

40:5, 6 The glory of the Lord began to be **revealed** in the restoration of the captives of Judah from the Exile (44:23). More grandly, the glory of the Lord would be displayed in the coming of the Lord Jesus Christ (4:2; Luke 2:29–32; John 1:14). The ultimate revelation of the glory of the Lord will be in His glorious kingdom (60:2; Zeph. 3:14–17), where the Savior King dwells in the presence of His people for all eternity (Rev. 22:1–5). **All flesh** refers to all humankind. **the mouth of the Lord has spoken:** The importance of this prophecy is underscored by the language of divine oath.

40:7, 8 breath of the Lord: This phrase pictures God's wrath on the wicked as the summer wind that blows on the grass and dries it up (40:24; Jer. 4:11). **But the word of our God stands forever:** These words offer full assurance of the reliability, stability, and eternal nature of the divine word. The Son of God fulfills the Word (Matt. 5:17, 18), *is* the Word (John 1:1–18), and lives forever.

40:9–11 Isaiah summons Zion to join the heavenly heralds (vv. 1–8) in proclaiming to the other cities of Judah the coming of the victorious Lord to shepherd His people.

40:9 In this section of Isaiah (40:1—55:13),

Zion is an endearing term for the remnant who have remained faithful to God. The **good tidings** are that God has come to rescue His enslaved people. **Behold your God:** Compare John 1:36; 19:5.

40:10 The Lord God might be rephrased "the Lord, the Master." The Lord's **strong . . . arm** figuratively brings His mighty acts of judgment and deliverance (48:14; 51:5, 9; 52:10; 53:1). **Reward** describes the spoils of victory—namely, the delivered people. The rescued exiles merge with the messianic community (65:15, 16). **Work** is a synonym for "reward."

40:11 In the ancient Middle East the ideal king was often depicted as **a shepherd** (Ps. 23; John 10). **Gather the lambs with His arm** is a description of the Father's love for His people (Mic. 5:4).

40:12–31 This oracle, proclaiming the Lord as the only source of eternal strength, addresses five questions: (1) Who is the Creator? (vv. 12–17); (2) To whom may He be compared? (vv. 18–20); (3) Who rules the kingdoms of this world? (vv. 21–24); (4) To whom may He be compared? (vv. 25, 26); and (5) Why are you despondent, Jacob? (vv. 27–31).

40:12 Who: The answer is "God, Creator of the cosmos, and Israel's Lord" (vv. 15–17). **A span** is the width of a stretched-out hand. The verse dramatically imposes images of God's might.

40:13, 14 directed: These questions are an attack against Marduk, a Babylonian deity, who needed the assistance of other gods in creating the world.

40:15 a drop in a bucket: Wicked nations have no power to thwart the purposes of God (Ps. 2:1–6). The word **scales** links the answer in this verse to the question in v. 12: Who has measured the dust of the earth? Its sovereign Creator has.

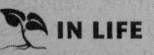 **IN LIFE**   ## God Helps Young People at Risk

Youth is supposed to be a time of energy and vitality. But what happens when extreme circumstances sap the life out of young people, robbing them of enthusiasm and rendering them too weak to go on?

God has pledged Himself to help young people at risk (Is. 40:30–31), as well as those who are lowly and despised, poor and needy, thirsty and hungry (41:17). This concern for people living on the margins of life is a theme that punctuates and permeates Isaiah's prophecy. And more often than not he urges people of power and means to do something about the needs of their at-risk neighbors.

If you work with young people at risk for "fainting" from the demands of life, or if you yourself are close to giving up because of the circumstances weighing you down, you can take comfort from God's promises for strength. The key is "waiting on the Lord" (40:31), expecting Him to supply what you cannot.

40:16 to burn: Lebanon's forests were proverbial in the ancient Near East (for example, see 33:9; 35:2; 37:24). As a measure of power to withstand the living God, however, the sum of them barely would make a sputtering pressed log.

40:17 Worthless is the same term used to describe the primeval chaos (Gen. 1:2).

40:18 liken God: The God of Scripture is incomparable; there is no one else like Him (40:25; 46:5; Ps. 113:4–6).

40:19 goldsmith: Many idols were made with wood, then overlaid **with gold** (41:6, 7; 44:9–20; 46:6, 7). **Silver chains** kept the idol from moving or falling.

40:20 too impoverished: The poor had to choose the best wood available and then hope it was good enough. Note the satire in these words. What is the value of the prayer of a poor man to a plain idol? What is the value of the prayer of the rich to one covered with gold? To both questions, the answer is "none."

40:21, 22 Have you not known: The questions here and in v. 28 express God's incredulity at worshipers of idols. Even though the worship of the Lord reached back to the **foundations of the earth** (Gen. 4:26; Rom. 1:19, 20), these people chose idols over the true worship of the living God. **The circle** refers either to the horizon or to the apparent hemisphere over the earth. The point is that God is not to be confused with His creation. **stretches out the heavens:** Creation is the work of the God of Israel: only He deserves our praise.

40:23, 24 nothing . . . useless: For a similar expression of the insignificance of entire nations before the might of the living God, see v. 17. **planted . . . blow . . . wither:** This imagery describing God's judgment is similar to that in vv. 6–8.

40:25 To whom then will you liken Me: This and the following question in this verse form part of an important biblical theme, namely, the incomparability of God (v. 18). Since God is **the Holy One,** He is distinct from all others.

40:26 Lift up: Human beings are responsible to discern the greatness of the Creator in His creation and are held guilty for suppressing such discernment (Rom. 1:18–32). **created:** For similar descriptions of God's creative work, see 4:5; 41:20; 43:1; 45:18; 65:17, 18. **These things** refers to the heavenly bodies. The Babylonian deities were identified with the heavenly bodies. The words here would have had particular relevance to Israel as they learned to say no to Babylon and yes to the Lord. **by number:** Each of the stars is known to the Creator; to each He has given a **name** (Ps. 147:4).

40:27 My way is hidden from the Lord does not question God's omniscience, but His good will. Would the Lord bless His people? The Israelites had a **just claim** because God had promised to make them a blessing to the nations (Gen. 12:3; 28:13–15).

40:28, 29 Have you not known: The Lord repeats this rhetorical question for emphasis (v. 21). God is not only **everlasting**—transcendent over time—but also **the Creator of the ends of the earth**—transcendent over space. He is omnipotent and inscrutable. **Neither faints nor is weary** refers to how God meets the needs of His people: the Lord will never let His people down (Ps. 121:3, 4). **power to the weak:** Strength is a gift of God (Jer. 9:23).

40:30 youths: The point is that human strength cannot compare with the power of God.

40:31 To wait entails confident expectation and active hope in the Lord—never passive resignation (Ps. 40:1). **Mount up . . . run . . . walk** depicts the spiritual transformation that faith brings to a person. The Lord gives power to those who trust in Him. **eagles:** The eagle depicts the strength that comes from the Lord. The Lord describes His deliverance of the Israelites in Ex. 19:4 as similar to being lifted up on an eagle's strong wings. In Ps. 103:5 strength of people who are nourished by God is compared to the strength of the eagle.

41:1—42:17 In this prophecy the Lord puts the nations on a trial to show them that He alone is God because only He can predict the future. The trial consists of two cycles (41:1–20; 41:21—42:9) followed by a praise hymn (42:10–17). In each trial cycle, there are three elements: (1) a call of the nations to trial (41:1, 21–24); (2) a prediction of the coming of Cyrus (41:2–7, 25–29); and (3) a celebration of the victories of the Servant (41:8–20; 42:1–9).

41:1 Keep silence: Divine calls for silence usually anticipate judgment (Zeph. 1:7). **Coastlands** includes Lydia in Asia Minor, which was conquered by Cyrus (51:5). **Renew their strength** contrasts strength that results from faith with unassisted human strength.

41:2 One from the east refers to Cyrus, king of Persia (559–530 B.C.; 46:11). Since God had made a covenant between Himself and Abraham (v. 8), He delivered the exiles in **righteousness,** a synonym for salvation in Isaiah (45:8; 46:13; 51:6; 56:1). God, who has authority over the nations, **gave the nations** to Cyrus as a ransom for Israel (43:3).

41:3 Cyrus advanced so fast it was as though **his feet** did not touch the ground.

41:4 first . . . last: For similar references concerning God's sovereignty over all of time, see 44:6, 10; Heb. 13:8; Rev. 1:8, 17. The Lord is eternal not only in that He is not bound by time, but also in that He is Master of time. **I am He:** For similar uses of this phrase, see 43:13; 46:4.

41:5 The pronoun **it** refers to the conquests of Cyrus (vv. 2, 3).

41:6, 7 This verse satirizes assistance from idols in contrast to the sure help from the living God (vv. 10–16). The **goldsmith** was working on the idol that presumably could save the people. For a similar reference to this occupation, see 40:19. Here the pronoun **it** refers to an idol (2:8).

41:8 Servant refers to one highly honored by the Lord. There is no higher position to which a person can aspire. The term was bestowed on the person **chosen** to administer and advance God's kingdom (Ex. 14:31; 2 Sam. 3:18). In chs. 40—55, the title of servant is bestowed implicitly on Cyrus (45:1–4) and explicitly on God's prophets (44:26), the nation of Israel (44:21; 45:4), and particularly on the Lord Jesus Christ (42:1–4; 52:13). **Abraham:** The Lord calls him **friend** (Gen. 18:17, 18; 2 Chr. 20:7; James 2:23).

41:9 The ends of the earth probably refers to Mesopotamia (Gen. 11:31; 12:1) and perhaps Egypt (Gen. 15:13). The term indicates God's sovereign rule over the earth (v. 4). The Lord had punished Israel (42:18–25), but had **not cast** them **away** (29:22–24).

41:10 The Lord's command to the Israelites to **fear not** contrasts with the fright of pagans in vv. 5, 6. God had bared His **right hand** at the first Exodus in order to destroy the power of Pharaoh (Ex. 15:6): the phrase indicates His sovereignty and strength over all who oppose Him (40:10).

41:11, 12 The people of God are given renewed assurance that their formidable enemies will be brought to **nothing** (40:17, 23).

41:13 The Lord will hold the exile's **right hand** (42:6) just as He held the hand of Moses (63:12). The Lord is with them; they have nothing to fear.

41:14 Exiled Israel seemed as feeble and despicable as a **worm** (Job 25:6; Ps. 22:6). **Redeemer** refers to the family protector of distressed relatives, who would avenge murders (Num. 35:19) and redeem indentured slaves (Lev. 25:47–49). A redeemer could also purchase land for a relative or marry a widow whose first husband was childless (the role of Boaz in the Book of Ruth). When the Lord is called the Redeemer the title highlights His zeal to defend, protect, and purchase back His people (49:26).

41:15 The lowly "worm" (v. 14) would be transformed into a **threshing sledge** (28:27) that removes **mountains,** the symbols of opposition and the location of pagan temples and palaces (Mic. 1:3–5).

41:16 winnow: As threshed grain is tossed in the air to separate the chaff, so the victorious people of God would have complete control over their enemies.

41:17 The poor and needy refers to the exiles moving homeward across the desert. **thirst:** God will meet the people's most basic needs. For a related reference, see 44:3.

41:18 rivers . . . fountains . . . pool of water . . . springs of water: In the first Exodus, the people of Israel were often con-

IN CONTEXT | A Second Isaiah?

One of the most impressive of the "near" prophecies of Isaiah is the specific, extended description of a monarch whose birth was 150 years in the future from Isaiah's time. This, of course, is regarded as quite impossible by many critical readers of the Bible. Thus, they argue that a "Second Isaiah" who lived after the events of Cyrus and the return from Exile must have penned the words of chs. 44—55.

However, what is one to say of Isaiah's words concerning the coming of the Savior King? Must these passages also be dated after the event? And what will one say concerning the passages that describe the millennium, heaven, and the eternal state? The unbelieving logic that denies Isaiah, the son of Amoz (1:1), the authorship of chs. 40—55 could also be used to argue that large portions of the book have actually not yet been written, for they discuss events still future!

The point of the extended references to Cyrus in ch. 41—46 is that only the living God could have made this specific prophecy before the fact (45:3). Those who suggest "Second Isaiah" wrote these sections after the fact have gutted the section of faith, wonder, and miracle. Heroditus could write of Cyrus after the fact; but only the living God could call him by name (as He gives names to the stars, 40:26) before he was born (45:3). The same God who named Cyrus also named the Messiah (9:6), and even the place of His birth (Mic. 5:2).

cerned about water (Ex. 17:1; Num. 20:2). The returning exiles would also need water in the second Exodus (v. 17), but God's provision would be bountiful.

41:19 in the wilderness . . . tree: The abundant water supply would also lead to the Lord's massive plantings of trees and vegetation (35:1, 2).

41:20 The people's reception of God's power and care is the primary concern. **the hand:** God's hand indicates His power and strength (40:10; 41:10). **created:** Only God can truly create (4:5; 40:26).

41:21 King of Jacob: This title for God pictures His special relationship with His people (43:15).

41:22 The former things probably refers to prophecies of judgment by earlier prophets, and some prophecies spoken by Isaiah in chs. 1–35 (42:9, 21–25; 43:9, 10; 46:8, 9; 48:3). **Latter end of them** may also be translated "their glorious future." The phrase **things to come** may refer to the mighty acts God would do through Cyrus. Ultimately, *things to come* refers to the gathering of God's people and the establishment of Christ's kingdom on earth. The point is that idols cannot tell the past or the future, but the Lord God can.

41:23 that you are gods: This is part of the satire (vv. 21, 22). **Do good or do evil** is a way of saying "do anything."

41:24 The word **indeed** assumes a period of silence between v. 23 and v. 24. The supposed "gods" were mute. An **abomination** is something that causes revulsion.

41:25, 26 from the north . . . From the rising of the sun: The conquest of Media by Cyrus (550 B.C.) made him master of the territories north of Babylon. Cyrus, who did not personally know God (45:4), nevertheless called on God's **name** when he released the exiles (2 Chr. 36:23; Ezra 1:1–4).

41:27 The pronoun **they** refers to the "former things" and "things to come" (of v. 22).

One who brings good tidings refers to the prophet Isaiah.

41:28, 29 These verses present the futility of the nations; they do not have any true understanding of reality, whether past, present, or future (41:26).

42:1 Behold: The Lord formally presents His Servant. The title **My Servant** is identified with Jesus Christ in the NT (Matt. 12:15–21). Isaiah may have foreshadowed Him, but only Christ brings universal justice (v. 4) and an everlasting covenant (v. 6). **uphold:** When God upholds a person, nothing can bring him down. For a similar idea, see 41:10. The Servant—that is, Jesus—possessed the Holy **Spirit** (4:4; 11:2; 48:16; 59:21; 61:1; Luke 3:22), who empowered Him to bring **justice** to the world.

42:2 The Hebrew word rendered **cry out** means "to cry out in distress." The phrase **cause His voice to be heard in the street** suggests the same idea; the Servant's rejection is heard for the first time (49:4; 50:5, 6; 53:4–9).

42:3 The phrase **a bruised reed** represents the poor and needy (41:17; 42:7). The phrase **not break** is an understatement for the positive equivalent: "mend" or "restore." A **smoking flax** represents those who have almost lost their faith and hope in the Lord. The Servant will come to restore the poor and needy and encourage people in the faith (Matt. 11:5).

42:4 law: The Servant will be more than another Moses (Deut. 18:15–18; Acts 3:22–26); He will mediate the New Covenant (2 Cor. 3:3; Heb. 8:7–13).

42:5 The Lord God introduces Himself as the source of all physical and spiritual life— **breath** and **spirit**—for He will enable the Servant to free people from death and spiritual darkness (vv. 6–9).

42:6 Called, hold, keep, and **give** are expressions parallel to the words of v. 1. In contrast to Cyrus, who brought political deliverance (41:2), the Servant **in righteousness** will deliver Israel from sin. The Servant will institute

 **IN FOCUS**   **"servant"**

(Heb. *'ebed*) (20:3; 42:1; 2 Sam. 10:19; Jer. 7:25) Strong's #5650: This noun is derived from a verb meaning "to serve," "to work," or "to enslave." While *'ebed* can mean *slave* (Gen. 43:18), slavery in Israel was different than in most places in the ancient Middle East. Slavery was regulated by the Law of Moses, which prohibited indefinite slavery and required that slaves be freed on the Sabbath (seventh) year (Ex. 21:2)—and the Year of Jubilee—the fiftieth year (Lev. 25:25–28). Sometimes the Hebrew noun can refer to the subjects of a king (2 Sam. 10:19). But usually the word is best translated *servant.* God referred to His prophets as "My servants" (Jer. 7:25) and spoke of the coming Messiah as His Servant, the One who would perfectly obey His will (42:1–4; 49:1–6; 50:4–9; 52:13–53:12).

INSIGHT | **Israel—Chosen for Service**

In what sense was Israel a "chosen" nation (44:1, 2)? As Isaiah makes plain, God chose the Israelites to carry out a mission. His choice was based on sovereign purpose and strategy. Israel's assignment was twofold: to serve as the family through whom the promise and blessing of the Messiah would come (compare Gen. 12:1–3; 15:5–7; 17:4–8), and through Him to be a spiritual light to the other nations of the world (Is. 42:6–7; 44:8; 49:6).

The Hebrews, beginning with Abraham, were given a missionary task to live in the light of what God had revealed to them. He placed them in a strategic locale, and enabled them to build a house of prayer for all nations (1 Kin. 8:41–43). Grateful obedience and faithful witness were the proper responses to God's call.

a new **covenant** binding Israel to the Lord (49:8). The prophets refer to this new covenant as a "covenant of peace" (54:10; Ezek. 34:25); an "everlasting covenant" (which is also associated with the Davidic covenant; 55:3); a "new covenant" (Jer. 31:31–34); and most often simply as a "covenant." **The people** refers to the **Gentiles** (60:3). Christ is the true **light** of the world (9:2; 49:6; 60:3; John 8:12; 9:5; Acts 26:17, 18, 23), and Christ's followers should reflect His light (Matt. 5:14).

42:7 To open . . . darkness is metaphorical language drawn from the Babylonian captivity; it indicates spiritual sight and salvation from sin's bondage (6:9, 10; 29:18, 24; 32:3; 35:5, 10; 61:1). Christ gave sight to the blind to show that He had the power to give everyone spiritual insight (v. 16).

42:8 My name: The fact that God reveals His name to His people is an indication of His wondrous grace (Ex. 3:14, 15). **My glory:** Here and in 48:11 this phrase is parallel to God's name.

42:9 former . . . new: For a similar idea, see 41:22. The former prophecies had come to pass; God through Isaiah was announcing new prophecies, and these too would come to pass.

42:10, 11 You who go down to the sea . . . the wilderness and its cities: The command is for all people to **sing.** The **new song** celebrated the second Exodus from Babylon, just as Moses' song celebrated the first Exodus from Egypt (Ex. 15:1–21). **ends of the earth:** For a similar use of this phrase to describe the honor and praise God will receive from all the world, see 41:5.

42:12 Glory links this hymn with the Servant's song (v. 8).

42:13 man of war: For a similar description of God as a Warrior, see Ex. 15:3. The Lord is completely sovereign: He will fight for His people even when they are exiles in a foreign land (vv. 14–17). The **zeal** of the Lord is also

described in 9:7. **He shall prevail against His enemies:** A similar promise that the Lord will eventually triumph is found in 41:11, 12.

42:14 The phrase **held My peace** describes the Lord's patient delay in acting (48:9; 57:11). **A long time** most likely refers to the seventy years of captivity (2 Chr. 36:21). **Now** indicates the introduction of a new age (43:1; 44:1). **woman in labor:** The words not only speak of her **cry,** but of the timely bringing forth of the new age begun with the restoration.

42:15 mountains . . . rivers: These words refer to all obstacles in the way of returning to the land from Exile. The word **dry up** is an allusion to the Exodus through the Red Sea (Ex. 14:16–29; Ps. 66:6) and entrance into the land through the Jordan River (Josh. 3:14–17).

42:16, 17 Blind refers to the state of the exiles, forming a link with the Servant's task (v. 7) and the Lord's accusation against Israel (v. 18). **Make darkness light** echoes the first Exodus (Ex. 13:21, 22). For similar references to darkness and light, see 58:8, 10; 59:9; 60:1, 2.

42:18–25 This prophecy, justifying the Exile as punishment, consists of (1) an address by the Lord to the exiles, accusing them of being blind and deaf to His mighty acts (vv. 18–22) and (2) an address by Isaiah accusing the exiles of sin (vv. 23–25).

42:18, 19 The people of Israel were **deaf** because they would not listen (vv. 23, 25) and **blind** because they would not see (vv. 7, 16). The Lord turned the exiles' implicit accusation that He was deaf and blind (40:27) against them (6:10). **My servant:** Isaiah uses the title *servant* for Israel (41:8) because that nation was supposed to be God's **messenger** (44:26) to the nations (Gen. 12:3).

42:20, 21 The LORD is well pleased: For a similar use of this phrase to express God's good will, see 53:10. **for His righteousness' sake:** In punishing Israel for its sin, the Lord exalted His **law.**

42:22–24 Israel was **robbed and plundered** first by the Assyrians (10:6) and then by the Babylonians (39:6). These words link the Lord's speech with Isaiah's in v. 24. No one said **Restore** until Cyrus commanded the exiles to return to Jerusalem (Ezra 1:2–4).

42:25 For similar descriptions of God's **anger,** see 10:5; 28:21.

43:1 Thus says the Lord emphasizes the Author of the prophecy and the certainty that it will be fulfilled (49:8; 50:1; 56:1). The words **created** and **formed** allude to the creation of the human race in Gen. 1; 2. The Hebrew verb translated *created* means "to fashion anew"—a divine activity, and is the same key word used in Gen. 1:1 (40:26; 41:20; 45:12, 18; 57:19; 65:17, 18). The second verb *formed* means "to shape," to fashion as a potter, and is used in Gen. 2:7 of God fashioning the body of the man from the dust of the earth. The use of these verbs here suggests that the Lord's creation of Israel as a people was as decisive an act as His creation of human beings at the beginning. In the same way, the NT describes Christians as new creations in Christ (2 Cor. 5:17; Eph. 2:10). **by your name:** The Lord's use of *name* demonstrates His intimate relationship with the Israelites. He had revealed His name to the people (Ex. 6:2–8) and declared their name to Pharaoh (Ex. 4:22).

43:2 Pass through the waters is an allusion to the crossing of the Red Sea (Ex. 14:21, 22) and the Jordan River (Josh. 3:14–17). **Walk through the fire** is a metaphor for protection in danger (Ps. 66:12); consider the Lord's protection of Shadrach, Meshach, and Abednego in the fiery furnace (Dan. 3:25–27).

43:3 Lord your God: The God of all creation declares Himself to be the God of the Israelites; He had every right to be their God and to call them His people, because He had saved them from the Egyptians. For more on this divine title, see Ex. 6:2–8. **Holy One of Israel:** For a similar usage of this divine title, see 1:4. The Hebrew word for **Savior** comes from the verb meaning "to save," the word from which the name Jesus is derived (Matt. 1:21).

43:4 Israel is considered **precious** because of God's sovereign grace (Deut. 7:6–8).

43:5, 6 Fear not: God's people are to *fear* Him—that is, hold Him in awe and reverence. Being sure of His presence, they need not be afraid of anything or anyone else. Israel's **descendants** are called by the Lord **My sons** and **My daughters** (Hos. 11:1). **east . . . west . . . north . . . south:** For a similar idea, see 11:11. **ends of the earth:** For similar phrases, see 11:12; 24:14–16; 41:25. The Lord will gather all His people together—all those who praise His name and follow Him.

43:7, 8 As a **blind** and **deaf** witness, the nation of Israel did not fulfill the prophecy of restoration (42:18–20).

43:9, 10 You is strongly contrasted by "I" at the beginning of v. 11. **witnesses:** The people of Israel had witnessed the great works of God in their midst (Ex. 4).

43:11–13 These verses form a magnificent celebration of the sovereignty of God (14:24, 26, 27; compare Num. 23:19). **no foreign god:** The Hebrew text contains merely the word **foreign;** the word *god* is implied. The point is that only the living God was at work in the Israelites' midst. **savior:** This same Hebrew term is used in v. 3. **before the day:** The Lord was always at work—saving, protecting, guiding, and disciplining His people. The concluding line of the song of praise—**there is no one . . . My hand**—is quoted from Deut. 32:39.

43:14 Thus says the Lord: The same phrase is used in v. 1 to emphasize the ultimate source of this prophecy: God Himself. The Lord is described as a **Redeemer** because He zealously defends, protects, and purchases back His people (49:26). In ancient Israel, a redeemer was a family protector of distressed relatives. For a similar use of this title, see 41:14. **Babylon:** For a description of Babylon's destruction, see Jer. 51:1–44. **The Chaldeans** were a people who settled in lower Mesopotamia and founded the Neo-Babylonian Empire.

43:15–17 With the titles of **the Lord** (Ex. 3:14, 15), **Holy One** (1:4), **Israel's Creator** (40:26; 41:20), and **your King** (41:21), the living God declared His intimate relationship with the Israelites. He was not only their God, but also the One who created their nation and ruled over them.

43:18 The Lord commanded the people not to **remember** the past (46:9, 10). The kingdom of Israel inaugurated at the first Exodus and the conquest of the Promised Land would be insignificant compared to the new kingdom God would establish. **former things** refers to the prophecies of judgment by Isaiah and other prophets (42:9, 21–25; 43:9, 10; 46:8, 9; 48:3). **the things of old:** For a related passage, see 65:16.

43:19, 20 A new thing refers to Cyrus' command for the exiles to return to Jerusalem; the fall of Babylon and Israel's restoration (v. 20); and the restoration of all things (65:17–19). For a similar use of this phrase, see 48:6. **a road in the wilderness:** The Lord would give the exiles an unobstructed route back to the Promised Land (40:3–5). **rivers in the desert:** Even in desolate regions the Lord would refresh His people (41:18, 19).

43:21–28 In this trial scene (41:1–42:13; 43:8–13) the Lord finds Israel guilty of sinning against Him by not worshiping Him (vv. 22–24), and instead making Him weary with their sins (v. 24), treating His forgiveness with complacency (v. 25), and sinning against Him from the beginning (vv. 26, 27). The verdict is clear: His destruction of the temple's leaders was deserved (v. 28; 42:18–25).

43:22 The Lord's accusation was that the people had not worshiped Him in the way He prescribed and with the motivation He demanded. **You** identifies the exiles with their fathers, since the exiles did not have any opportunity to offer sacrifices.

43:23, 24 The exiles' ingratitude—**Nor have you honored Me**—contrasts with the Lord's forbearance—**you have burdened Me.**

43:25 for My own sake: The Lord chooses to save and forgive. This arises out of His own character. For similar phrases, see 37:35; 42:21; 48:9, 11.

43:26 State your case: More than once through Isaiah, the Lord asks Israel to answer His charges (41:21; 45:21).

43:27, 28 First father refers to Abraham (51:2). Despite his many acts of faithfulness, Abraham also had **sinned** (Gen. 12:18, 19; 20:9). Israel's false religious leaders (Mic. 3:9, 10) are called **your mediators** in contrast to "My mediators." **Princes of the sanctuary** refers to the leaders of the priests in Jerusalem (1 Chr. 24:5).

44:1 Now: The call to listen immediately is featured in 42:14; 43:1. **servant:** For a similar usage of the title *servant* for the nation of Israel see 41:8.

44:2 Thus says the LORD: This emphatic statement emphasizes that God authored the prophecy and thus it is certain to come to pass (43:1). **made . . . formed:** The Lord demands an audience with Israel, for He is their Creator, see 43:1, 7. **Fear not:** Since the Lord is the all-powerful One, Israel had nothing to fear. This same encouragement not to worry is found in

43:5. **Jeshurun,** meaning "Upright One," is a poetic word for the nation of Israel (Deut. 32:15).

44:3 Pour water may refer either to miracles during the exiles' journey home (43:19–21) or to blessings on those who had returned to the Promised Land (41:17; 55:1). **pour My spirit:** Moses prayed for the Lord's Spirit to come on all Israel (Num. 11:29); the prophets foretold it (Joel 2:28–32), and Christ fulfilled it (32:15; Acts 2:14–36).

44:4 Luxurious **grass** symbolizes prosperity.

44:5 The repatriated would proudly identify themselves with the Lord. **The name of Israel** would no longer be associated with a worm (41:14).

44:6–23 This passage describes another fact-finding trial like the one in 41:1—42:17; 43:8–13. Between the command not to fear (v. 8) and the command to remember (v. 21) and return (v. 22), there is an extended, biting satire on idolatry (vv. 9–20). An exhortation to nature to praise Israel's redeeming Lord concludes the oracle (v. 23), which contains many allusions to the Song of Moses (Deut. 31:30—32:43).

44:6, 7 Thus says the LORD: This emphatic statement refers to the truthfulness of what follows (43:1). **King of Israel:** For background see Ps. 99. **Redeemer:** This term is also used in 41:14 and refers to the zeal with which the Lord acts to defend his people. **First . . . Last:** God is completely sovereign over time (41:4). **Besides Me there is no God:** For a similar idea see Deut. 32:39.

44:8 Do not fear: A similar command is given in 43:5. When God is on your side, you do not need to fear anything or anyone else. **You are My witnesses:** The people of Israel had already witnessed great miracles on their behalf (43:10). **Rock:** The image of a rock represents stability and protection (Ps. 62:2, 6, 7). For a similar description of God, see Deut. 32:4, 15, 31.

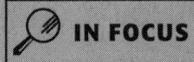 **IN FOCUS** | **"diviners"**

(Heb. *qasam*) (44:25; 1 Sam. 6:2; Ezek. 21:23) Strong's #7080: This term refers to people who attempt to foretell the future through occult practices. Diviners are often mentioned along with other practitioners of the occult—all of whom were forbidden in Israel (Deut. 18:10–22). False prophets, such as Balaam, practiced divination, and the penalty was death (Josh. 13:22; Jer. 27:9; 29:8; Ezek. 22:28). Diviners brought judgment not only on themselves but also on their nations (Deut. 18:10; 2 Kin. 17:17, 18; Mic. 3:6, 7). Divining was practiced by several methods: calling up the spirits of the dead, casting arrows as lots, consulting images, looking at the organs of a dead animal, or interpreting dreams and visions (1 Sam. 28:8; Ezek. 13:23; 21:21, 29; 22:28; Mic. 3:6, 7; Zech. 10:2). Diviners charged fees for their services.

44:9–20 This satire against idolatry consists of (1) an introduction condemning idols and those who make them (vv. 9–12), (2) the main section showing the absurdity of idolatry by describing how metal and wooden idols are made (vv. 12–17), and (3) a didactic conclusion against idol makers (vv. 18–20). The prophet Isaiah was speaking to the future generation, warning them of the foolishness of worshiping idols (40:19, 20; 41:21–29; 42:17).

44:9 an image: This is the term used in the Second Commandment to describe an idol (Ex. 20:4). **Useless** is translated "without form" in Gen. 1:2.

44:10 The Hebrew has the words **god** and **image** together, stressing the absurdity of worshiping an image molded by human hands.

44:11, 12 be ashamed: When all people come face to face with God, it will be a day of shame for those who rejected Him in this life.

44:13, 14 While people were made in the image of God (Gen. 1:26–28), idolaters made gods in **the figure of a man** (Deut. 4:16; Rom. 1:23).

44:15, 16 Isaiah was particularly struck by the absurdity of using one part of a log for burning and the other part of the very same log as an object of worship.

44:17, 18 you are my god: This is a scene of complete hopelessness (57:13); an idolater prays for deliverance from a powerless piece of wood. Worshiping and depending on any object made by human hands—such as money—is just as hopeless.

44:19 abomination: For another use of this word communicating revulsion, see 41:24. **a block of wood:** The awful truth was that people were worshiping objects made from God's creation instead of the Creator Himself.

44:20 He feeds on ashes: Compare the two banquets in Prov. 9:1–6, 13–18.

44:21 My servant: The nation of Israel is often described as God's servant (41:8). **formed you:** This verb suggests that the formation of the nation was a decisive act on the part of God (43:1). **not be forgotten:** Though the exiles might have thought God had forgotten (49:14, 15), the Lord unambiguously declared that He would remember the nation He had created.

44:22 blotted out: The idea of total forgiveness of sins is also found in 40:2; 43:25. The word **redeemed** describes God as buying back His people. For the Lord as Redeemer, see 41:14.

44:23 The songs (12:1–6) of the **heavens** and **earth** (1:2; 49:13), the **forest** (35:1, 2) and **every tree** (14:7, 8; 55:12) mirror the joy of God's people at the arrival of salvation. **glorified Himself:** The Lord honors Himself when He saves because it demonstrates to the world His mercy and His power (40:5; 42:8; 43:7).

44:24—45:13 This salvation oracle proclaiming Cyrus as the Lord's anointed to save Israel consists of an expanded introduction concerning its Author (44:24–28), a direct address to Cyrus summoning him to service (45:1–7), and concluding commands to the heavens to rain the Lord's blessings and to the earth to receive them (45:8). In a twofold epilogue, the Lord reproves anyone who faults His sovereignty (45:9, 10), and asserts His right as Sovereign to fashion His own tools.

44:24 Thus says the LORD: Because the Lord says this, it will come to pass (43:1, 14; 44:2, 6, 24). **Redeemer:** This same title is used in 41:14. It pictures the Lord's zeal to defend, protect, and purchase back His people. **who formed you:** That God *formed* Israel pictures His desire for them as a nation and His constant loving care on their behalf. For a similar idea, see 43:1.

44:25 Babblers refers to the **diviners** (2:6, 8; 8:19; Deut. 18:10, 11). **wise:** These were people wise in their own eyes, but not wise toward the Lord. For a similar description, see 29:14.

44:26 performs the counsel: This idea is explored in more detail in 41:1—42:13; 43:8–13; 44:6–8. Israel was to be both the servant (41:8) of the Lord, and His messenger (42:19) to the nations (Gen. 12:3). **You shall be inhabited:** This same promise is found in Jer. 32:15. **built:** The rebuilding of the temple and the resettlement of the land after the devastation by Babylon inaugurated the new age (58:12; 61:4).

44:27 Deep refers either to the moat protecting Babylon or to the obstacles blocking the returning exiles (42:15). This may be an allusion to the chaotic waters resisting creation (Gen. 1:2); the Red Sea blocking the first Exodus (43:16–19; 51:10); or the Jordan River opposing the entrance into the Promised Land (Josh. 3:14–17).

44:28 Cyrus: Here Isaiah mentions by name the king of Persia who would allow the Israelites to return to Jerusalem in 538 B.C. (Ezra 1:1–4). For a less specific reference, see 41:2. **Shepherd** is a title for an ideal king (40:11; Mic. 5:4).

45:1 To be **anointed,** literally to be "Messiah," indicates appointment to an office, usually as king (61:1). The bestowal of this unique and exalted title on the Persian king, after it had been used in Israel of such notables as the patriarchs (Ps. 105:15), David (Ps. 2:2), and the coming Messiah (Dan. 9:25), must have shocked the Israelite audience of Isaiah (vv. 9, 10). Why would the Lord appoint a foreign pagan to carry out His will? **The double doors,** which were part of the **gates** connected with

Babylon's defensive moat, were not **shut** when Cyrus captured Babylon (44:27).

45:2 I will go before you: This was the Lord's promise to Cyrus, similar to His promise to His people of old. Babylon had one hundred **gates of bronze.**

45:3, 4 have not known Me: Cyrus knew that the Lord had appointed him, but he did not know the Lord God personally (Ezra 1:2).

45:3 Treasures of darkness is an allusion to the fabled wealth of Sardis captured by Cyrus in 546 B.C. **Who call you by your name** refers to the specific naming of Cyrus by the Lord

power of our living Creator. He is sovereign over everything—both good and evil. The symbols of **light** and **darkness** (Ex. 10:21–23) are clarified by the words **peace** and **calamity** (47:11; Amos 3:6).

45:7, 8 Righteousness and **salvation** are used as synonyms in the Book of Isaiah (46:13; 51:6; 56:1). In the Middle East people commonly believed that the fertility of the earth and the maintenance of the social order depended on the king's right relationship with a deity. Because Cyrus was anointed by the true God, heaven would shower its blessings on earth.

Photo by Howard Vos

Ruins of the palace of one of the Persian kings at Persepolis. Isaiah declared that God would use King Cyrus of Persia as His "anointed" to return the Jewish people in exile to their homeland (Is. 45:1–7).

before Cyrus became king (compare 43:1). In this prophecy, the Lord had named Cyrus as both "shepherd" (40:11; 44:28) and "anointed" (v. 1).

45:4 For Jacob My servant's sake: God anointed Cyrus to establish again the people whom He loved (43:1).

45:5, 6 From the rising of the sun to its setting means everywhere (Ps. 113:3). No other person or object can compare to the holiness and

45:9–13 The epilogue counters the objections against the Lord's appointment of foreigner Cyrus as His anointed shepherd (44:28; 45:1). It develops in two parts: (1) from analogies of the sovereign rights of a creator over his creation and a father over his children (vv. 9, 10) and (2) to the Lord's sovereignty over Israel (v. 11), over all creation (v. 12), and finally over Cyrus (v. 13).

45:9, 10 Woe: For a similar use of this word

see 5:8. **Maker:** For similar references to God as Creator see 29:23; 43:1; 45:11. **potsherd:** Why should a created being question the Creator? A piece of pottery does not question the potter. For similar references see 29:16; Jer. 18:6.

45:11 Thus says the Lord: This emphatic statement points to the certainty of these words (43:1, 14; 44:2, 6, 24). **things to come:** For similar phrases, see 41:22, 23.

45:12 Created is the same verb used in Gen. 1:26–28 (43:1).

45:13 The pronoun **him** refers to Cyrus (44:28; 45:1). Though the Lord gave Cyrus a handsome **reward** (vv. 3, 4) to ransom His people (43:3), this was not the reason Cyrus sent the captives home.

45:14–25 These prophecies predict worldwide salvation through Israel (14:1, 2; 19:23–25; 49:23; 54:3; 60:11). The nations of Africa will join Israel in worship (v. 14). Idolaters will be ashamed, but Israel will be saved forever (vv. 15–17). The Creator and Redeemer will not be thwarted in His purposes (vv. 18, 19); only He can predict the future, for only He controls it (vv. 20, 21). All nations will eventually bow before Israel's God (vv. 22–25).

45:14 After the Lord handed over **Egypt, Cush,** and **the Sabeans** to Cyrus as a ransom (43:3, 4), they would hand themselves over to Israel and its Lord. **come over:** For a similar reference, see Ps. 68:31. **You** and **yours** are both feminine singular, referring to the Daughter of Zion (1:8; 40:9). **Bow down to you** indicates submission to the Lord and recognition of His presence with His people in Zion (2:2–4).

45:15, 16 God hides Himself in His wrath (8:17; 54:8; 55:8, 9), but He reveals Himself in the Scriptures (48:5–8).

45:17 an everlasting salvation: These words of divine promise are echoed in 51:6.

45:18 Created and **formed** are used as synonyms as in the Book of Genesis (compare Gen. 1:27; 2:7). Both verbs identify the Lord as the Creator and do not focus on the way He accomplished His grand act of creation. **In vain** is the same term used in Gen. 1:2. The Lord created the earth **to be inhabited,** not to be desolate, as the Assyrians and Babylonians had left the land of Israel (6:11; 7:18, 19; 27:10, 11; 33:9; 44:26, 28).

45:19 Pagan diviners pronounced their mysterious and ambiguous oracles **in secret** and **dark** places. The Lord's prophets proclaimed the truth openly to all who would listen.

45:20 Draw near together: For similar ideas see 41:1, 21, 22; 43:9; 44:7.

45:21 The pronoun **this** refers to the universal salvation begun with Cyrus's decree that Israel return home (44:24–45:13).

45:22 no other: For additional references to God's incomparability, see 40:25; 45:5.

45:23 I have sworn by Myself: The Lord's promise to Abraham was sworn by His own person (Gen. 22:16; Heb. 6:13). The certainty of the Word of the Lord is emphasized strongly in the Book of Isaiah (40:8). The Lord's promise **that to Me every knee shall bow** will be fulfilled in Jesus Christ (Rom. 14:11; 1 Cor. 15:24, 25; Phil. 2:10, 11).

45:24, 25 Those **who are incensed against** God will have no share in His eternal kingdom (50:11; 66:24).

46:1–13 This collection of salvation oracles are all spoken by the Lord, and all are addressed to the stubborn exiles. They begin with similar imperatives, "Listen" (v. 3); "Remember" (v. 8); "Listen" (v. 12); and they share the common theme that the Lord is truly God.

46:1, 2 Bel, meaning "Lord," was a title of Marduk, Babylon's chief deity. **Nebo,** Marduk's son, was the god of fate, writing, and wisdom. Ironically, each of these gods is said to **bow down,** to stoop along with their idols. In pagan thought, the idols and the gods that they embodied were inseparable. The heavy idols that were expected to bring deliverance were **themselves** dragged away into **captivity.**

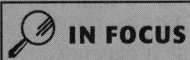 **IN FOCUS** | **"woe"**

(Heb. *hoy*) (5:8; 45:9; 55:1; Jer. 23:1) Strong's #1945: This interjection was primarily used by the prophets at the opening of a section where the evil practices of a particular person or group was denounced (Jer. 23:1). It is found at the beginning of judgment oracles against foreign nations, drawing attention to a threat by God (10:5). These judgment oracles frequently occur in a series, as in ch. 5 (5:8, 11, 18, 20, 21). A prophet could use the word *woe* to express personal feelings of despair or lament (24:16). Yet even then, the prophet was typically expressing God's lament and condemnation of wickedness (Jer. 22:13–17). Jesus used an equivalent expression (Gk. *ouai*) when He cursed Chorazin and Bethsaida (Matt. 11:21) and later the scribes and Pharisees (Luke 11:44).

46:3 An unbelieving **remnant** (1:9; 10:20) is likely being referred to here, judging by the parallel words, "transgressors" (v. 8) and "stubborn-hearted" (v. 12; see 1:2; 48:1–5; 57:4). **carried from the womb:** For a similar image of the Lord carrying the nation of Israel, see Deut. 1:31.

46:4, 5 Old age indicates the Lord's never-ceasing care. **I am He:** Note in this verse the emphasis God places on His activities on behalf of His people; the Lord Himself and no one else would save Israel (41:4). **liken Me:** This is the third time the incomparability of God is asserted in this section of Isaiah (40:18, 25).

46:6, 7 The pronoun **they** refers to the idol makers (40:19, 20; 41:6, 7; 44:9–20). **They bear it:** In contrast to the living God who carries and supports His people (v. 4), idols have to be carried by those who worship them.

46:8 Transgressors refers to the unbelieving remnant (v. 3).

46:9, 10 the end from the beginning: For a similar description see 41:4. As the Sovereign of the cosmos, God can do anything He desires. His **pleasure** (Ps. 147:10, 11) includes the salvation of His people (Zeph. 3:17) and the worship of their hearts (John 4:23, 24).

46:11 A bird of prey from the east refers to Cyrus (41:2) and to the speed and power of his conquests (41:3). The point is that God may use any tool He wants to accomplish His purposes on earth (Rom. 9:14–23).

46:12 As there were those in the first Exodus who longed to return to Egypt (Num. 14:3), so in the second Exodus there would be those who refused to leave the comfort and security of Babylon and Persia.

46:13 Righteousness is a synonym for **salvation** in Isaiah (41:2; 45:8; 51:6; 56:1). Salvation from the Exile was not only certain, but **near** (51:5). **Israel My glory:** In spite of the Israelites' long history of rebellion (Ex. 32), God loves His people Israel and has never utterly cast them aside (Rom. 11:1).

47:1–15 The humiliation and exile of Babylon's gods (ch. 46) left Babylon's inhabitants exposed to the same fate. Isaiah predicted Babylon's fall in a mocking funeral song aimed at discouraging Babylon and encouraging Israel. The poem has four stanzas (vv. 1–4, 5–7, 8–11, 12–15).

47:1 O virgin daughter of Babylon: The language is sarcastic. Babylon had acted as though she were "God's daughter." She was about to discover that she was the **daughter of the Chaldeans.** No longer would she be thought of as a heavenly princess—**tender and delicate.**

47:2, 3 Grinding **meal** was a usually work for female slaves (Ex. 11:5). **Uncover the thigh** suggests doing menial labor with overtones of the shame of indecent exposure. Babylon would lose its status and privilege. **Nakedness** indicates disgrace, impropriety, lack of dignity, and vulnerability (Gen. 9:22, 23).

47:4 In contrast to the humiliated Babylon, Israel had a **Redeemer** (41:14). **The Lord of hosts** (1:9) would deliver the nation of Israel.

47:5 The similar structure of vv. 1, 5 link the first stanza (vv. 1–4) with the second stanza (vv. 5–8).

47:6, 7 Babylon's cruel abuse of Israel when the Lord had **given them into** Babylon's **hand** would be avenged, as in the case of the Assyrians (10:1–19; 49:25). **a lady forever:** Babylon was arrogantly boasting that it would remain an empire, "the Lady of Kingdoms" (v. 5; compare Dan. 4:30), throughout all time. This amounted to blasphemy.

47:8, 9 Hear is addressed to the wicked "daughter," Babylon (vv. 1, 5; see 1:8). Babylon had deified itself with the statement **I am** (v. 10). They had tried to usurp the Lord's unique attribute: Only the Almighty has an existence that is not dependent on another (45:5, 6, 18, 21, 22; 46:9). This wicked self-deification mirrors the boasting of the king of Tyre (Ezek. 28:11–19). Babylon is no longer considered a virgin (v. 1), but instead is a **widow.** The imagery of **the loss of children** suggests the loss of hope in the future. Contrast Babylon's fate with that of Zion (49:21–23; 54:1–6).

47:10 Wickedness, wisdom, and **knowledge** refer to the same idea as "sorceries" and "enchantments" in v. 9 (Dan. 2; 5; contrast with 11:2). **No one sees me:** The selfish pride of the wicked is based in part on believing that there is not an all-knowing, all-seeing God in the universe.

47:11 The word **therefore** links Babylon's pretensions of "knowledge" (v. 10) with the just judgment that the nation did **not know.**

47:12–14 The command to **stand** matches the Lord's introductory commands in vv. 1, 5. The word **sorceries** links the final stanza with the earlier ones (vv. 9, 10).

47:15 Babylon's fate would also overtake those **with whom** it had **labored,** its ancient **merchants,** on whose trade it depended for its wealth. Compare the arrogance of the king of Tyre based on Tyre's successful trading (Ezek. 28:16, 18).

48:1–11 This passage, addressed to all Israel, condemns the people for hypocrisy (v. 1), idolatry (v. 5), arrogance (v. 7), and treachery (v. 8). At the same time, the oracle promises the people salvation for the sake of the Lord's name (vv. 9–11). The tone is similar to 42:18, 19; 43:22–25; 46:1–13. The oracle has four parts: (1) summoning Israel to hear the address (vv. 1, 2); (2) a

---

⚒ IN DEPTH | **The Purpose of Prophecy**

Perhaps you think of prophecy as having mainly to do with predictions about the future. That's understandable, since prophets in Bible times sometimes foretold what would happen in the future (for example, Is. 7:14–17; 45:1–7; Jer. 28:12–17). However, the purpose of prophecy goes beyond merely informing people about things to come. There are at least two additional reasons why God spoke through the OT prophets:

First, *prophecy shows that the Lord is God*. A god who cannot reveal himself to human beings is unlikely to command much respect. But through prophecy, the Lord has made Himself known in compelling ways. For example, He demonstrated His omniscience by revealing to the Israelites what would happen in the future, something no pagan idol could do (48:5). He also demonstrated His power through the prophets in ways that left no doubt about who He is (1 Kin. 18:36–39).

Second, *prophecy announces God's word*. Closely related to God's revelation of Himself through prophecy is His communication of truth that He wants people to know. Prophecy is often referred to as the "word of the Lord" (Is. 1:10; 28:14; 38:4); in fact, it is often prefaced by the words, "thus says the Lord God" (7:7; 10:24; 22:15). Thus prophecy is revelation from God. It brings to light truth that would otherwise would remain unexpressed.

The point of these revelations is not merely to inform, but to declare what is true, and then to tell people how they should live in light of what is true. Sometimes prophecy helps to warn people about the consequences of their actions, and sometimes it encourages them when circumstances appear to be desperate. But whatever its effect on people, the purpose of prophecy is to proclaim God and His word.

---

charge that Israel's unbelief is without excuse because the Lord had revealed that it was He who was helping them (vv. 3–5); (3) a prediction of future salvation (vv. 6–8); and (4) a promise that the Lord will defer judgment for the sake of His name (vv. 9–11).

48:1 Hear is an urgent appeal to "deaf Israel" (6:9, 10; 48:6, 8). **Jacob . . . Israel:** For a similar use of these names, see 41:8. **called by the name:** For related descriptions of Israel as called by God, see 43:1, 7; 63:8.

48:2, 3 The **holy city** is Jerusalem. The citizens of Jerusalem professed to **lean on the God of Israel** (Rom. 9:6).

48:4 Obstinate means "hard" (46:12; Ex. 32:9; Deut. 9:6, 13). **Iron and bronze** here are metaphors for rebelliousness (Jer. 6:28).

48:5 Despite Israel's knowledge that no **idol** had helped them, Isaiah anticipated that in the future they would attribute their salvation to some god other than the one Lord.

48:6 New things include the career of Cyrus (v. 14); the fall of Babylon and Israel's restoration (v. 20), which inaugurated the messianic age (v. 16); and the restoration of all things (65:17–19). To be able to **declare . . . hidden things,** the Lord must know and control the future.

48:7, 8 As God unfolded His plan of redemption, He **created** events that Israel had **not heard** about before. God knew that if the Israelites had possessed such knowledge, they

would have acted **treacherously,** claiming **"Of course I knew them."**

48:9 The Lord works out everything for His **praise** (42:8–12; 43:21). **Defer My anger** means to be "longsuffering" (Ex. 34:6).

48:10 Refined, a reference to judgment (1:25; 4:4), talks of the Babylonian captivity. **Furnace** is an allusion to Israel's suffering in Egypt (Deut. 4:20; Jer. 11:4).

48:11 For My own sake: The Lord shows His settled will to maintain the integrity of His great name (v. 9). God's acts of mercy are His own initiative, springing from the depths of His mercy (37:35; 42:21; 43:25). **My glory** is a parallel expression to "My name" (42:8), as is the expression "My praise" in v. 9. **profaned:** For descriptions of how Israel had desecrated God's name, see Ezek. 20:8, 9; 36:21–23.

48:12–22 This section, directed to all Israel, encourages the unrighteous to participate in the Lord's redemption of the nation from Babylon. The Lord (1) presents Himself as the sovereign Creator (vv. 12, 13), (2) shows that He alone predicted Israel's salvation through Cyrus (vv. 14, 15), (3) promises to come to the people in the form of His Servant (v. 16), and (4) promises peace and posterity to those who obey Him (vv. 17–19). Isaiah follows the divine speech with an exhortation to flee Babylon (v. 20) and participate joyfully in the second Exodus (vv. 21, 22).

48:12 called: For a similar reference to God's calling of Israel, see 42:6. **First . . . Last:**

For a similar description of God's sovereignty over all time, see 41:4.

48:13 Earth and **heavens** refer to the entire cosmos (13:13; 40:21, 22; 51:6, 13).

48:14 Assemble yourselves probably was addressed to the nations; the pronoun **them** likely refers to the idols of the nations (41:21–23; 43:9; 45:20, 21). The pronoun **him** refers to Cyrus (41:2, 25; 45:13; 46:11), a designation made explicit in 44:28—45:1.

48:15 I, even I draws attention to the source of this prophecy: the living God. **called:** For a similar reference to this calling, see 41:2.

48:16 Me refers to the Servant, Jesus (42:1–13; 61:1), who has **spoken** through His prophets (1 Pet. 1:10, 11). **Lord** here means "Master," suggesting that the speaker is the Servant (50:4). For additional references to God's **Spirit,** see 11:2; 30:1; 42:1; 59:21; 61:1; Luke 3:22.

48:17 The Lord **teaches** and **leads** through His servants (Deut. 5:27), His prophets, and His Son.

48:18 A river supplies abundant water to produce luxuriant growth (41:18; 66:12; Amos 5:24). **The waves of the sea** speak of power, constancy, and increase.

48:19 Sand recalls God's promise to the patriarchs that the Israelites would become very numerous (Gen. 22:17; 32:12).

48:20 By putting the command **declare** into the present tense, the future salvation is brought vividly into the present (40:9–11; 44:23; 46:1–4). **Go forth:** The people are told to leave Babylon, forsaking its comforts (Gen. 12:1; Ex. 12:31). **proclaim:** For examples of proclamations, see 12:1; 44:23; 49:13.

48:21 They did not thirst is an allusion to God's provision of water during the first Exodus (41:17–20; 43:16–21; Ex. 17:1–7; Num. 20:2–11). **waters . . . from the rock:** For a NT perspective on these miracles, see 1 Cor. 10:4.

49:1–13 This second song of the suffering Servant (42:1–13) consists of two parts: the Ser-

vant's soliloquy (vv. 1–6) and the Lord's oracles to Him (vv. 7–9). The song is followed by Isaiah's elaboration (vv. 9–12), and it concludes with a hymn of praise (v. 13).

49:1 coastlands: The Servant's mission pertains to the whole earth (41:1). **Matrix** means "womb" (Gen. 25:23; Ruth 1:11).

49:2 Through the preaching of His **mouth,** the Servant will conquer the earth (11:4). **like a sharp sword:** For similar descriptions of Jesus' speech, see Eph. 6:17; Heb. 4:12; Rev. 1:16. **Shadow** suggests protection (30:2, 3; 51:16). Because the Servant's mission was **hidden** until He was sent, it would be more effective (48:6–8).

49:3 Israel may refer to the quintessential Israel—the Savior Jesus—who would come to redeem national Israel (v. 5). **In whom I will be glorified:** In partial fulfillment of this prophecy, Jesus prayed to His Father, "I have glorified You on the earth. I have finished the work which You have given Me to do" (John 17:4).

49:4 The Servant's complaint that He **labored in vain** (26:17, 18) points to His rejection by the nation of Israel and His suffering (42:2). **reward:** The Servant will be vindicated (50:8) and will be rewarded after His death (53:8) and resurrection (53:10).

49:5 The political mission of Cyrus **to bring Jacob back** from Babylon (44:28; 45:13) foreshadows the spiritually redemptive mission of the Servant to free His people from their captivity to sin (42:7).

49:6 light to the Gentiles: The Servant fulfills the call of Abraham (Gen. 12:1–3) and the nation of Israel (Ex. 19:5, 6) to be a blessing to other nations. After Jesus' death and resurrection, the great commission of global evangelism is carried on by His apostles (Acts 13:47; 26:23) and those who succeed them to the end of the age (Matt. 28:18–20).

49:7 Paradoxically, the King who humbles Himself to become the **servant of rulers** will

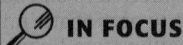 **IN FOCUS** | **"salvation"**

(Heb. *yeshu'ah*) (49:6; Job 30:15; Ps. 67:2) Strong's #3444: This word describes deliverance from distress and the resultant victory and well-being. The term occurs most often in Psalms and Isaiah, where it is frequently used along with the word *righteousness,* indicating a connection between God's righteousness and His saving acts (45:8; 51:6, 8; 56:1; 62:1; Ps. 98:2). This word can be used for a military victory (1 Sam. 14:45), but it is normally used of God's deliverance (Ex. 15:2; Ps. 13:5, 6). The expressions "the salvation of the LORD " and "the salvation of our God" speak of God's work on behalf of His people. The expression "the God of my salvation" is more private in nature, referring to the deliverance of an individual (12:2; 52:10; Ex. 14:13; 2 Chr. 20:17; Pss. 88:1; 98:3).

Himself receive homage from them (4:2; 45:24; 52:15). Kings will also bow down to His people (v. 23).

49:8 In an acceptable time, in contrast to the day of vengeance (34:8; 61:1; 2 Cor. 6:2), the Lord will hear the Servant's complaint that His mission toward Israel was in vain (v. 4). The Lord will crown His Servant as King **to restore** blessing on the famished earth (45:8). The pronoun **them** refers to Israel.

49:9 Go forth is an allusion to Isaiah's command for the exiles to leave Babylon (48:20). The imagery of feeding in pastures implies that the Servant would be Israel's Shepherd-King (40:11).

49:10 The word **thirst** is an allusion to 48:21. **Heat** and **sun** may be allusions to Ps. 121, a psalm of pilgrimage. The word **guide** may be an allusion to the first Exodus (42:16; 48:21; Ex. 15:13).

49:11 Mountains, which were once barriers (2:2, 13, 14; 42:15), will become **highways,** the means of salvation (vv. 22, 23). The pronoun **My** before both *mountains* and *highways* is significant: God the Creator is the sovereign Owner of all creation.

49:12 The north and the west indicates the universal salvation of all Israel (11:11, 12; 43:5, 6). These oracles are addressed to all Israel and all the earth (48:1; 49:1). **Sinim** was a district on the southern frontier of ancient Egypt.

49:13 Sing: The Lord is the Creator of music (12:1–6; 44:23).

49:14–26 This section consists of two complaints of Zion (vv. 14, 24), followed by the Lord's reassuring responses to them (vv. 15–23; vv. 25, 26). The aim of the two sections is to cause Israel and the nations to know that the Lord of Israel is the eternal God (vv. 23, 26).

49:14 Zion represents the exiles (40:1, 9). The complaint **The LORD has forsaken me** resembles that in 40:27–31. The Lord disciplined the Israelites briefly because of their sin (54:7; Lam. 5:20–22).

49:15 The Lord says: **I will not forget you.** The nuance of the verb suggests an even stronger assurance, "As for Me, I am *unable* to forget you."

49:16 inscribed: This may refer to the Lord's command for the names of the tribes of Israel to be inscribed on the stones of the priest's ephod (Ex. 28:9–12). When the priest was in the temple, the engraved names would remind God of His covenant with Israel. **Your walls are continually before Me:** The Creator God has His thoughts focused on the welfare of His people (Ps. 40:5).

49:17 Cyrus gave the edict to rebuild Jerusalem (44:28). The restored **sons** of Zion would carry out the decree. Zion's would-be

destroyers were the Babylonians (2 Kin. 25:8–10).

49:18 As I live: This is an oath formula. The Lord swears by His own eternal person (Gen. 22:16). Zion's returning "sons" were a splendid **ornament,** like the jewels of a **bride** (61:10).

49:19 Desolate means "childless" (54:1).

49:20, 21 The complaint that **the place is too small** is in fact a cause for rejoicing (54:1–3; Zech. 2:4, 5), because it means the Lord would cause His people to grow. This prophecy points to the return of the exiles to Jerusalem, for under Ezra and Nehemiah the exiles built a relatively small city (Ezra 2; Neh. 7). Some view the ultimate fulfillment of this prophecy to be the gathering of the Lord's people at the coming of Jesus' kingdom.

49:22 I will lift My hand in an oath: God swears by His own character. **Standard** is often translated "banner" (11:12). The return of the Israelites from **the nations** and not only from Babylon shows that the future salvation of all Israel is in view (Rom. 11:26).

49:23 The nations that had enslaved Israel had served Israel as **foster fathers** and **nursing mothers** (14:2; 43:6; 60:9).

49:24, 25 Israel asks rhetorically: **Shall the prey**—captive Israel—**be taken from the mighty**—Babylon? Apparently Israel expects a negative answer to this question, but the Lord responds affirmatively. He would **contend** with the mighty, terrible Babylon (Jer. 50:33, 34) and free His people.

49:26 oppress: Cannibalism was not unknown during the horrible famine of a siege (9:20; see Deut. 28:53–57; 2 Kin. 6:24–31; Lam. 4:10; Zech. 11:9). **I, the LORD . . . Mighty One of Jacob:** The last couplet is a celebration of the name and character of the living God. The Almighty asserts that He is the One who can powerfully save His people (Ex. 3:14, 15; 34:6, 7).

50:1–3 In this prophecy, the Lord defends Himself (42:18–25; 43:22–28) against the implied accusation brought by the unbelieving exiles of the second generation, that He was unwilling or unable to save them.

50:1 Though the Lord had put away Israel, as a husband might put away a wife, it was for only a short period of exile (54:5–7; 62:4) and not permanently. Permanent exile would have required a **certificate** of **divorce** (Deut. 24:1–4). If the Lord had issued one, He could not have taken Israel back (Deut. 24:1–4; Jer. 3:1, 8). No prophet suggested that God had completely broken His covenant; rather, they predicted God's faithfulness to a remnant who would return (Mic. 4:9, 10). **Your mother** refers to Jerusalem, more specifically, the inhabitants of the preceding generation that had gone into

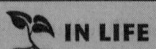 **IN LIFE** | **The Dangers of the Tongue**

People tend to be known by what they say. Words may strike fear in others, they may reveal the speakers to be foolish, or they may be a source of help or comfort to other people.

In a passage that probably pertains to the coming Messiah, Isaiah said the Lord's Anointed would "know how to speak" by receiving instruction from God (Is. 50:4). As a result of this divine tutelage, He would be able to speak appropriately to the weary. How much more do the rest of us need help in knowing what to say, given our sinful condition. Scripture repeatedly warns us about the power and danger of our words. As Scripture frequently shows, they can:

- cut like a sword (Pss. 57:4; 64:3);
- be as dangerous and poisonous as a snake (Ps. 140:3);
- convey lies with the impact of a bow (Jer. 9:3);
- strike down other people like an arrow (Jer. 9:8); and
- curse and demean others (Hos. 7:16).

What is the impact of your words on other people? Does what you say build others up or tear them down?

exile. If the Lord had sold Israel to **creditors** (Ex. 21:7; 2 Kin. 4:1; Neh. 5:5), He would not have any authority over their destiny. But the Israelites had sold themselves because of their own **iniquities** (42:23–25). Therefore God as their Redeemer could buy them back (41:14; 52:3).

50:2 God **came** to Israel at the time of the Exile through the prophets He sent. Later God came to this earth through His Servant and Son, Jesus (41:9). But no one answered Him (6:9, 10; 66:4). **Is My hand shortened:** For a variation of this rhetorical question, see Num. 11:23. **dry up the sea:** The Lord alluded to His parting of the Red Sea and the Jordan River to evoke images of His strength (43:16, 17; 44:27; 51:9–11).

50:3 Blackness may be an allusion to the ninth plague of Egypt, when the Lord made darkness cover the earth (Ex. 10:21).

50:4–11 The third Servant song consists of a soliloquy by the Servant (vv. 4–9), and the prophet's address to believing and unbelieving Israel (vv. 10, 11).

50:4 The title **Lord God** is emphasized in this section (vv. 5, 7, 9). The title *Lord* means "Master"; the word *God* represents the divine name (Yahweh). The Lord educated the Servant's **tongue** through suffering. The word **learned** is translated elsewhere as "disciple" (8:16). **weary:** Unlike unbelieving Israel (Jer. 31:25), the Lord **awakens** the Servant's **ear to hear** (contrast 42:18, 19).

50:5 opened: The idea is the same as that in Ps. 40:6—the opening of the ear canal as a symbol for hearing and obeying. **not rebellious:** Contrast 1:2.

50:6 People sometimes **struck** the **back** of a fool (Prov. 10:13; 19:29; 26:3). Jesus suffered this humiliation (42:2; 49:4; 53:12; Matt. 27:26; John 19:1). Pulling someone's **beard** was a sign of contempt and disrespect (2 Sam. 10:4, 5; Neh. 13:25). **shame and spitting:** This prophecy was fulfilled in the suffering of Christ (Matt. 27:30).

50:7 The Lord is the Servant's only source of **help** (41:10, 13, 14; 49:8). The phrase **not be disgraced** means to be honored (49:7; 52:13). **Like a flint** indicates determination in the face of opposition (Ezek. 3:8, 9). For this prophecy's fulfillment in Christ, see Luke 9:51.

50:8 justifies: God would view this One as completely righteous. This prophecy was fulfilled in Christ (1 Tim. 3:16).

50:9 the Lord God will help Me: See the same voice of confidence in the Lord in Ps. 118:6–12, another prophecy of the suffering of the Savior Jesus.

50:10 Who . . . fears the Lord: The fear of the Lord—that is, the reverence or awe of God—is the beginning of true wisdom (Prov. 1:7).

50:11 Those **who kindle a fire** means those who are self-reliant, instead of walking in the light of the Lord and His Servant (2:5; 42:6). When the Light comes into the world, some will choose darkness (John 3:17, 18). **Torment** indicates God's punishment for unbelief.

51:1–8 Three oracles (vv. 1–3, 4–6, 7, 8) are linked by the same imperative, "Listen" (vv. 1, 4, 7); the same speaker, the Lord (except v. 3); the same addressees, the faithful exiles; and the common theme of comfort as a result of the coming salvation.

51:1, 2 Look links the metaphor of v. 1 with its interpretation in v. 2. The metaphors **rock** and **pit** are interpreted in v. 2 as referring to **Abraham and Sarah**.

51:3 Zion replaced **Eden**. Both were walled-in places of fellowship with God, free from sin, and guarded by cherubim so that only God's people could enter (Gen. 3:24; 3:7).

51:4 The Servant is the **light of the peoples** (42:6; 49:6; John 3:17, 18).

51:5 The day of the Lord is always **near** (2:12; 56:1; Zeph. 1:14; 1 Thess. 5:4–11; James 5:8); here the reference is to the restoration from Exile (46:13). **The coastlands** (41:1), like the exiles, **wait** for the Lord. The verb translated *wait* has to do with confident expectation and active hope (40:31; Ps. 40:1).

51:6 Heavens and **earth** suggest the entire cosmos (13:13; 40:21, 22; 48:13; 51:13). The old cosmos will **vanish away** and **grow old** (34:4; Heb. 1:10, 11), **and those who dwell in it will die** (v. 8). Only God's people will inherit the new cosmos. **Righteousness,** a synonym for **salvation** in Isaiah (45:8; 46:13), will last forever (45:17; 56:1).

51:7 In whose heart is My law refers to those who are bound to God by the provisions of the New Covenant (42:6; Jer. 31:33). The **reproach** of the exiles anticipates the rejection of the Servant (50:4–11).

51:8 righteousness . . . forever . . . salvation: The interrelationship of salvation, righteousness, and eternality can also be seen in v. 6.

51:9–16 This oracle bases Israel's salvation on the Lord's past mighty acts at creation and the Exodus. It consists of three sections: (1) a call to the Lord to stir up His might as in days of old (vv. 9–11); (2) the Lord's response, recalling those acts and chiding the people for forgetting Him (vv. 12, 13); and (3) a recounting of His gift of prophecy (vv. 14–16).

51:9 Awake implies that the Lord appeared to be asleep (40:27; Ps. 44:23). The Lord's **strength** at creation in subduing the sea is the subject of Ps. 93. Isaiah's prayer is based on God's promise (50:2), and poetically addressed to God's strong **arm** (41:10; 51:5). **Rahab** was a mythical **serpent** that resisted God's creation of the universe (Job 7:12; Ps. 74:13, 14). This imagery, possibly borrowed from Canaanite myths, also represents the Lord's defeat of Egypt—the nation that resisted the creation of Israel (30:7). The language here associates the Lord's creative work in the first Exodus and in the second Exodus (the return of the exiles) with His creative act of transforming the chaos of Gen. 1:2 into the cosmos of Gen. 2:1 (27:1).

51:10, 11 dried up: For similar references, see 42:15; 50:2. The Lord's victory at the Red Sea (Ex. 14:21, 22) is probably represented by the imagery of a pagan myth in which the **sea** opposed the creating deity. The probable allusion is supported by **the . . . deep,** a term used for the primeval chaotic waters of Gen. 1:2. The Exodus is placed within the broader framework of God's power over evil.

51:12 The Lord responds to the double imperative of v. 9, "Awake, awake," with the doubled pronoun **I, even I.**

51:13 stretched out: For a similar description of creation, see 40:22. **oppressor:** For a graphic depiction of the punishment of Israel's oppressors, see 49:26.

51:14 Captive exile literally refers to the exiles in Babylon. The meaning extends to all who experience the darkness of sin and alienation from God (48:20; 49:9).

51:15 Who divided the sea . . . roared: The sea represents all that is evil and in opposition to the Lord (Ps. 93).

51:16 Your mouth refers to the words of the Servant (41:9; 44:26; 50:4). **shadow of My hand:** For a similar use of the phrase, see 49:2.

51:17–23 This salvation oracle urging Jerusalem to have faith in God consists of two parts: (1) Mother Jerusalem (49:20, 21; 50:1) must awaken herself from her staggering stupor (vv. 17–20), and (2) the prophet asks the people to hear the Lord's promise that He will transfer the cup of His anger from them into the hands of her enemies (vv. 21–23).

51:17, 18 Awake, awake: The same double imperative is found in v. 9 (contrast 40:1). **drunk . . . the cup:** For similar imagery see Jer. 25:15–29; Lam. 4:21; Ezek. 23:31–34.

51:19, 20 These two things refers to the desolation of the land and the destruction of the people. **at the head of all the streets:** A similar image of destruction is used in Lam. 2:19.

51:21–23 The cause of drunkenness was not **wine,** but the **cup of trembling,** the terror of God's judgment. **those who afflict you:** Israel's oppressors would be made to drink "the cup of . . . fury" (v. 22).

52:1 The double call to the Lord to **Awake, awake** is also used in 51:9, 17. **Holy city** (48:2) contrasts with **uncircumcised** and **unclean** Babylon. **Jerusalem** (1:8; 40:1, 9) is commanded to awake because she is forever free of her despicable oppressors. **Zion:** The exiles are identified by their home city (40:1, 9). Zion's **strength** is like **beautiful garments** that adorn a queen mother (61:10). The Babylonian hordes would not only be expelled (49:17), but would **no longer come** to Zion (Nah. 1:15; Rev. 21:27; 22:14, 15).

52:2, 3 Arise . . . sit down evokes the image of a queen ascending her throne. **Loose yourself:** For similar images of freed captives, see 42:7; 48:20; 51:14.

52:4 to dwell there: The wording suggests that Israel was dependent on Egypt's hospitality; but the text assumes the Egyptians betrayed that trust. **Without cause** does not mean that Israel was without sin (42:23–25), but that Israel had not wronged either **Egypt** or Assyria.

52:5 Here refers to Babylon. God's justice demands that those who make Israel **wail** will be punished and that Israel will be delivered. **My name is blasphemed:** For a similar charge, see 37:23, 24.

52:6 My people refers to the redeemed exiles. **Know My name** is an allusion to Ex. 3:13, 14; 6:2. The Lord glorifies His name by predicting and fulfilling the promise of redemption pledged in v. 3.

52:7 The vision is of the **feet** of the one who runs from the scene of battle across **mountains** to the city waiting for news (2 Sam. 18:26). The glorious message of this runner is **salvation,** meaning "victorious deliverance" (49:8). This is **good news** or **glad tidings.** The idea appears in the NT as "to tell the Good News." The message **Your God reigns** stands behind all history; the Lord controls every power on earth.

52:8 Your watchmen refers to those who long for salvation (21:11; 62:6).

52:9, 10 The Lord has made bare His holy arm in order to fight majestically (40:10; 51:9; Ex. 6:6). **the ends of the earth:** For similar uses of this phrase, see 45:22; 48:20.

52:11 Depart! Depart: For another use of a double word, see 51:9, 17. **Touch no unclean thing:** For other passages concerning separation, see 2 Cor. 6:17; Heb. 12:14; 13:13; 1 Pet. 2:1–12; Rev. 18:4. In the first Exodus, Israel carried out silver and gold from Egypt; in the second Exodus, the priestly nation would **bear the vessels** made from those elements (2 Kin. 25:14, 15; Ezra 1:7–11; 5:14, 15).

52:12 Before and **rear guard** are allusions to the pillar of cloud and fire that protected Israel in its flight from Egypt (42:16; 49:10; 58:8; Ex. 13:21, 22; 14:19, 20). **the Lord . . . the God of Israel:** The pillar of cloud and fire actually stood for the Lord Himself (Ex. 33:9–11).

52:13—53:12 The fourth of the Servant Songs forms the central unit of chs. 40—66, predicting the Servant's death for the sins of His people. The passage consists of three sections: (1) The Father praises the work of the Servant (52:13–15); (2) Israel confesses that it has despised Him (53:1–9); and (3) the prophecy expands on the significance of the Servant's death (53:10–12). This passage is cited many times in the NT, where the Servant is identified with Jesus Christ (Luke 22:37; 24:27, 46; 1 Cor. 15:3; 1 Pet. 1:11).

52:13 Exalted and extolled and be very high may refer to three successive events, describing the Servant's resurrection, ascension, and glorification (Rom. 4:24, 25). Or the three phrases might simply emphasize the great exaltation of the Lord's servant (Phil. 2:9–11).

52:14 So His visage was marred . . . more than the sons of men: People would be

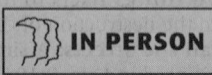 **IN PERSON** ## The Suffering Servant

Amidst a declaration of the Lord's coming salvation (52:7–12; 54:1–10), Isaiah places a portrait of the Suffering Servant (52:13—53:12). Despised and rejected (53:3), wounded and bruised (53:5), this unattractive Servant would know heartache and sorrow. What was the reason for His suffering? His life could not be the cause, for He was blameless, speaking only the truth (53:9). Yet the Servant would be led to prison and then to death for our sins (53:6–11).

Three other passages in Isaiah focus on the Servant and are called the "Servant songs" (42:1–4; 49:1–6; 50:4–9). The first song celebrates the Servant as the One who will establish justice for all (42:4). The second highlights the deliverance that the Servant will provide. He will restore Israel and become a "light to the Gentiles." The third emphasizes the God-given wisdom of the Servant. All this culminates in the description of the suffering and death of the Servant in ch. 53, the final Servant song.

Though at times Isaiah refers to the nation Israel as a Servant (49:3), the preeminent Servant of the Lord was clearly a unique person, a suffering Messiah yet to come (53:6). New Testament authors such as Matthew understood Jesus' teaching and preaching as a direct fulfillment of Is. 42:1–4 (Matt. 12:15–21). Philip used one of the Servant songs as a starting point for evangelism (53:7, 8). The Ethiopian eunuch asked him to explain the passage "He was led as a sheep to the slaughter" (53:7, 8; Acts 8:31–34). Philip introduced him to Jesus, the One who was led to His death for the sins of all humanity.

horrified at the Servant's appearance; He would be so disfigured that He would no longer look human.

52:15 The **nations** are represented by their **kings. Shut their mouths** is a token of stunned respect. **For what had not been told . . . they shall consider:** Romans 15:21 refers to this passage. **What** they are told is the report of ch. 53.

53:1 Who has believed: This rhetorical question, quoted in John 12:38 and Rom. 10:16, expects a negative answer. The word **report** is related to the verb "they heard" in 52:15. **Our** refers to the believing remnant in Israel. **Arm** refers to God's great work (40:10; 52:10; Ps. 118:22, 23).

53:2 Tender plant refers to a shoot rising from a plant's stem or root. **A root out of dry ground** suggests Christ's rejection by Israel (49:4; 50:6). **No form or comeliness** indicates that the Servant did not have a majestic manner.

53:3 He is despised and rejected: For related references describing the rejection of the Servant, see 42:2; 49:7; 50:6 (compare Mark 9:12). **Man of sorrows** does not indicate that the coming One would be humorless or dour, but He knew better than anyone the havoc that sin brings into human life. Because He is a "Man of sorrows," He is able to comfort those who experience sorrow.

53:4 He has borne: The Savior Jesus came to suffer and die for the sins of others (53:6, 11, 12; Matt. 8:17; Heb. 9:28; 1 Pet. 2:24). **Griefs**— or pain—and **sorrows**—or sickness—refer to the consequences of sin. The people considered Christ to have been **smitten by God** because the law said, "he who is hanged {on a tree} is accursed of God" (Deut. 21:22, 23; Gal. 3:13).

53:5 The repetition of the pronouns **He, Him,** and **His** for **our** and **we** underscores the fact that the Servant suffered in our place. **The chastisement . . . His stripes:** For a similar reference, see 1 Pet. 2:24. **Peace** sums up the Servant's ministry of reconciliation, justification, adoption, and glorification (2 Cor. 5:17–21). By saying that they were **healed** (v. 4), the remnant expressed its faith in what God had announced in 52:13.

53:6 All we like sheep have gone astray: For a NT perspective, see 1 Pet. 2:25.

53:7 Opened not His mouth speaks of the Servant's willingness to die for sinners; it also marks His dignity and authority (Matt. 26:67, 68; 27:12–14; 1 Pet. 2:23). **as a lamb to the slaughter:** For similar imagery, see John 1:29, 36; 1 Cor. 5:7; Rev. 5:6, 12; 13:8.

53:8 cut off from the land of the living: This language clearly indicates that the Servant would die.

53:9 Often in Hebrew poetry, **the rich** appear as synonymous with **the wicked.** Joseph of Arimathea was a rich man, but he was not wicked (Matt. 27:57–60). **at His death:** The Hebrew term rendered *death* is in the plural, as a focus on the deep significance of Christ's death.

53:10 it pleased the LORD: The OT pointed to the doctrine of the atonement long before Jesus died for our sins (1 Cor. 15:3 where Paul speaks of the doctrine coming from "the Scriptures"). The atonement was part of God's eternal plan (Eph. 1:4–7). The Father was *pleased* that His Son should die because it would cover up the sins of many and reconcile them to Himself (v. 11). **Offering** refers to the "trespass offering," the sacrifice of a ram in order to secure the Lord's atonement for sin (Lev. 5:6, 7, 15; 7:1; 14:12; 19:21). Here the prophet Isaiah describes the Servant Jesus as a trespass offering. **His seed** refers to the spiritual seed, born to the Servant after His death (Gal. 3:26–29).

53:11 Knowledge means having insight into one's mission (52:13). **Justify** means to acquit from guilt and to declare righteous (5:23).

53:12 As the great King, the Lord will **divide the spoil** of victory with His Servant (41:8; 52:13). **Great** and **strong** correspond to the Servant's condition after His rejection, suffering, and death.

54:1–10 In this salvation oracle (49:14–23), the Lord promises Zion that He has not forsaken her, but will give her many offspring. In vv. 1–3, Zion is a barren woman who gives birth to numerous children. In vv. 4–10, Zion is a forsaken wife who receives an everlasting covenant of peace.

54:1 Sing: For similar commands to sing, see 12:6; 44:23; 49:13. Zion (1:8; 40:1, 9) had **not labored with child** because Cyrus returned the exiles without any pressure from the Israelites. The increase that began in the restoration from exile (51:1–3) continues today, for the NT applies this verse to "the heavenly Jerusalem" (Heb. 12:22), "the mother of us all"—the church (Gal. 4:26, 27). Salvation depends on sovereign grace.

54:2, 3 The Arabs of the desert, known as the Bedouin, live in tents made of dark goat hair. The floor plan of these tents is rectangular with an interior curtain dividing the tent into two parts. A standard tent is made of 6 to 8 lengths of cloth held up by 9 interior poles. The overall size can be up to 6 by 10 yards. Large tents are made twice the size of a standard tent.

54:2 As a husband encourages his wife, the Lord encourages Zion, the mother of His people, to **enlarge** the family **tent** for her many children (49:19, 20).

54:3 Expand is an allusion to Gen. 28:14, where the same Hebrew word is translated "spread abroad."

54:4 The shame of your youth refers to Israel's infidelity, that led to the Egyptian and Assyrian oppression (52:4; Jer. 31:19; Ezek. 16:1–6). **The reproach of your widowhood** refers to the Babylonian exile (vv. 6–8).

54:5 The point of the titles **Lord of hosts** (1:9), **Redeemer** (41:14), and **God of the whole earth** is that God did not forsake Zion out of necessity or weakness (50:1–3). Neither did He forsake Israel permanently (v. 7).

54:6 The Lord calls Zion to be His wife (62:4, 5). **Like a woman forsaken . . . you were refused** refers to Zion's experience in exile (40:27; 49:14; 50:1).

54:7 God's anger against His elect is **for a mere moment** (26:20; Ps. 30:5). **Great mercies** speaks of the affections of God in nurturing, maternal terms.

54:8 Kindness may also be translated "loyal love." **I will have mercy:** That is, "I will love you as only a mother can love."

54:9, 10 As the Lord had sworn to **Noah** that **the waters . . . would no longer cover the earth** (Gen. 9:11), so He swore to Zion after the Exile that His **covenant of peace** (42:6; Ezek. 34:25) would not **be removed.** Contrast this with the **mountains** and **hills,** symbols of strength and permanence, that had been **removed** from sight in the Flood (Gen. 7:19, 20).

54:11–17 In this salvation oracle, the Lord addresses devastated Zion, first promising the rebuilt city greater glory than before (vv. 11–13) and then protection (vv. 14–17).

54:11, 12 walls of precious stones: For a more detailed description of the New Jerusalem, see Rev. 21:18–21. The **afflicted one** is Zion or Jerusalem (51:21).

54:13 The **children . . . taught by the Lord** include those taught by Christ (Jer. 31:34; John 6:45), who had "the tongue of the learned" (50:4).

54:14–17 The **tongue** that speaks propaganda is one of the weapons of war (ch. 36). The Lord will **condemn** the accusers of His people even as He equipped His Servant (50:7–9; Luke 21:15; 1 Cor. 1:20). Throughout the rest of Isaiah, the word **servants** refers to *all* saints, Jews and Gentiles (56:6–8; 63:17; 65:8, 9, 13–15; 66:14), the spiritual offspring of the Servant.

55:1–13 Chapters 40—55 conclude with two related invitations: (1) to come to the Lord and participate in the Davidic kingdom (55:1–5) and (2) to seek the Lord and find pardon (vv. 6, 7). The promise is sure because God's grace is unfathomable (vv. 8, 9) and His word will certainly be fulfilled (vv. 10–13). The invitations, first addressed by the Lord to the exiles, are now held out to everyone (Rev. 21:6; 22:17).

55:1, 2 Ho is an exclamation of pity. **Everyone:** The ones addressed at first are the covenant nation, the remnant who respond to God. But they will be the means for bringing the same message of God's salvation to the nations (v. 5). **Thirsts** is a metaphor for desiring what satisfies a person's spirit (41:17; 44:3; Pss. 42:1, 2; 63:1; Matt. 5:6). **Waters** is a metaphor for the enjoyment of salvation in God (John 4:10–14; 7:37). **Wine and milk** are symbols of complete satisfaction (v. 2). Not only does God's salvation supply what is necessary for life, but it also provides what brings joy. **You who have no money . . . buy** expresses that salvation cannot be bought, but is a free gift for those who desire it (52:3; Deut. 8:3; Rom. 6:23).

55:3 Incline your ear and **Hear** are synonyms for **come to Me.** The **everlasting covenant** (54:10) refers to the Davidic covenant and to the New Covenant. **The sure mercies of David** are God's promises of an eternal Offspring, throne, and kingdom (2 Sam. 7:12–16; 1 Kin. 8:23–26; Ps. 89:19–37). The pronoun **Me** includes the Servant of the Lord, Jesus the Messiah (48:16; 61:1). **you:** The promises of the Davidic covenant are extended to all who

---

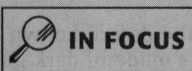 **IN FOCUS**   **"inherit"**

(Heb. *yarash*) (54:3; Deut. 5:33; Josh. 12:1; 19:47) Strong's #3423: The Hebrew word translated *inherit* means to "take something from someone else and possess it for yourself." The word is frequently used to describe the Israelite conquest of Canaan (Deut. 5:33; Josh. 12:1; 19:47). At times the word can be translated *dispossess* (Num. 33:53) and may even mean "impoverish" (1 Sam. 2:7). In 54:3, the prophet Isaiah uses this word to describe Israel's expansion. The nation would expand so much that they would take possession of the land of other nations (11:14). Isaiah was prophesying that Israelites would increase in number so much that they would be like a nomad who has so many children that he has to expand his tents to accommodate them all (54:2).

come to God; they are fulfilled in Jesus Christ (4:2; 7:14; 9:6; 11:1–5) and His church (Rom. 16:20).

55:4, 5 God's fulfillment of the promises to the house of David, climaxing in the resurrection of Christ, serves as a **witness** to the nations (43:10, 12; 44:8). Jesus Christ is a **leader . . . for the people** (42:6; 49:6; Dan. 9:25; Heb. 2:10; 12:2).

55:6, 7 To **seek the LORD** is to seek His word (Amos 5:6, 14; Acts 17:27).

55:8, 9 God's gracious **thoughts** exceed all human imagination (64:4; Rom. 11:33; 1 Cor. 2:9; Eph. 3:20). No one can fathom the depths of His wisdom.

55:10, 11 bring forth: For a similar reference, see 2 Cor. 9:10. God's **word** is similar to rainfall; it produces fruit (Ps. 147:15–20). Just as water enlivens and strengthens a withering rose, God's word produces life in the hearts of sinners.

55:12 The phrase **go out** refers historically to the Exodus from Babylon (48:20, 21; 52:11, 12). The **singing** of the elements of creation is a way of describing the singing of God's people. The rejoicing of the people at the Lord's salvation will be so full that it will seem that **mountains, hills,** and **trees** join in the chorus and applause (14:7, 8; 44:23).

55:13 Instead of the thorn shall come up the cypress tree: This expression symbolizes the replacement of God's judgments with salvation (compare 5:6; 32:13; 41:19). **Everlasting sign** recalls the rainbow after the Flood (19:20; Gen. 9:8–17).

56:1–66:24 The prophecies in these concluding chapters are addressed to those who returned to the land of Israel before the rebuilding of the temple in 520 B.C. The temple was still in ruins (63:18; 64:8–12), but its rebuilding was foreseen (56:6–8). The restored worshiping community faced the question of who would be admitted into the religious community (ch. 56). As before the Exile, Israel continued to struggle with idolatry (57:1–13), hypocrisy (ch. 58), injustice (59:1–8), and spiritual malaise (64:1–7).

56:1 about to come: God's salvation is always near (51:5; Phil. 4:5). **My righteousness** is a synonym for **My salvation** (41:2; 45:8; 46:13; 51:6).

56:2 Keeps from defiling the Sabbath (Ex. 20:8–11) epitomizes righteousness, for the Sabbath was the sign of the covenant (Ex. 31:13–17; Jer. 17:21–27; Ezek. 20:20, 21). Since keeping the Sabbath revealed clear commitment to the Lord, it was closely associated with righteousness and justice.

56:3 In speaking of the proselyte **who joined himself to the LORD**, Isaiah was not speaking of the foreign wives that returning exiles married. Ezra and Nehemiah would have to purge the restored community of these unconverted pagans (Ezra 9). Isaiah was prophesying of foreigners who would be converted to the worship of the true Lord (44:5). These were foreigners who would demonstrate saving faith and thus be counted among those "born in Zion" (Ps. 87).

56:4, 5 eunuchs: Probably some of the male exiles were castrated so that they could serve in the Babylonian and Persian courts (39:7; Dan. 1:3). **A place and a name** may be rephrased as "a memorial monument." For Isaiah, this memorial is **better than that of sons and daughters** because it symbolizes an **everlasting name,** or everlasting life, in the temple. **Not be cut off** is an idiom for preserving one's name through one's offspring. The phrase links this passage with 55:13.

56:6, 7 house of prayer: Inclusion in the covenant community involves intimate communion with God (Ps. 15:1; Matt. 21:13). **for all nations:** People of other nations who came to a living faith in God were met with a **joyful** welcome (2:2–4; 1 Kin. 8:41–43). Jesus also

---

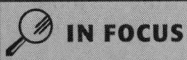 **IN FOCUS** | **"sign"**

(Heb. *'ot*) (7:14; 19:20; 55:13; Gen. 1:14) Strong's #226: The Hebrew word translated *sign* refers to something that is marked off or made distinct. God gave circumcision to Israel as a sign of their covenant relationship with Him, the fact that they were set apart for Him (Gen. 17:11). The word was also used to call attention to a particular event and God's promises surrounding that event. For instance, the rainbow is a reminder of the Flood and God's promise to refrain from destroying the earth with a flood again (Gen. 9:13). God promised to provide a clear sign of the coming Messiah in His virgin birth (7:14). The counterpart of this word in the NT (Gk. *semeion*) is used widely by the Gospel writers (Matt. 16:4; Mark 8:12; John 2:11) to refer to Jesus' miraculous signs, which confirmed His divinity.

spoke of joy in heaven over a repentant sinner (Luke 15:7).

56:8 Outcasts refers to the exiles (11:11, 12).

56:9 The unclean, ravenous **beasts** summoned to attack the ungodly community are hostile nations (18:6; Jer. 12:8, 9; Ezek. 34:5, 8, 25; 1 Cor 15:32). In ancient Eastern religions, demons and spirits were often believed to appear as animals.

56:10 The pronoun **His** refers to the Lord. **Watchmen,** those who ought to warn the city of approaching danger, refers to prophets (21:6; Jer. 6:17; Ezek. 3:17; 33:2–7) who do not fear God. The ungodly watchmen leave the people defenseless.

56:11, 12 greedy dogs: The dog was not highly regarded in biblical culture, and to the Jews they were unclean. **Shepherds** is a metaphor for rulers (40:11; Ezek. 34:1–6).

57:1, 2 Peace here refers to the final state of the righteous who **rest** in their deathbeds (3:10, 11; 53:5; Phil. 1:21–23). No one understood that the righteous were being spared the judgment to come (2 Kin. 22:19, 20).

57:3, 4 offspring: For similar references, see 1:4; Ezek. 16:3, 45. **Adulterer** and **harlot** allude to the perverse Canaanite fertility rites that threatened the culture of ancient Israel.

57:5 Green tree was associated with pagan fertility rites (1:29, 30; 1 Kin. 14:23; Jer. 2:20). **Slaying the children** was associated with the worship of Molech and with demon worship (30:33; 2 Kin. 23:10; Ps. 106:37, 38; Jer. 7:31).

57:6 Immoral idolatry was the people's **portion** or **lot,** instead of the Lord (Deut. 4:19, 20; Pss. 16:5; 142:5).

57:7 A **high mountain** refers to a place for idolatrous practices (Jer. 3:6; Ezek. 16:16; Mic. 1:3–5). The word **bed** is associated with sexual aspects of idolatry (Ezek. 23:17; Hos. 4:13). **sacrifice:** Animal and grain offerings were also part of pagan worship. There were enough similarities between true and false worship for people to be confused (compare "wisdom" and "folly" in Prov. 9).

57:8 Remembrance may refer to a pagan cultic symbol in the home. **made a covenant:** This phrase, which has so many associations with true religion, is here used in the context of obscene behavior associated with pagan worship. **nudity:** The Hebrew word is the regular term for hand. Here it appears to be a euphemism for the male genitals.

57:9 King probably refers to the Ammonite god Molech (1 Kin. 11:7), whose name means "king." **Sheol** here alludes to the gods of the underworld, perhaps associated with necromancy.

57:10 There is no hope: The people persisted in worthless idolatry. The people's **way** is detailed in vv. 5–9. They found a counterfeit **life** in immorality and idolatry that would only lead to permanent death (Rom. 1:18–32).

57:11, 12 of whom have you been afraid . . . not remembered Me: For a related passage, see 51:12, 13. **Lied** here refers to infidelity to the Lord. The Lord **held** His **peace** by not sending judgment immediately (42:14; 48:9; 2 Pet. 3:9).

57:13 Let your . . . idols deliver you: The thought is pitiful (44:17). The worshiper of idols was appealing to a work of his own hands for deliverance. **the wind will carry them all away:** The idols are like worthless chaff (Ps. 1:4). **But:** This word shows that there is an appeal in the denunciation. Each judgment text is a call for repentance. **puts his trust:** This verb is used of a little chick finding shelter under its mother's wings (4:6; 25:4; Ruth 2:12).

57:14 This verse is based on 40:1–4. The phrase **one shall say** resembles "The voice of one crying" (40:2). **Heap it up** resembles "Every valley shall be exalted" (40:4). **Prepare the way** repeats the appeal of 40:3 (11:16; 35:8–10; 62:10). **Stumbling block** probably refers to the idolatry described in vv. 3–13.

57:15 This verse matches Ex. 34:6 as a defining passage for understanding the biblical view of God: Though God is completely unapproachable, He reaches down to lift up those who humble themselves before Him. **High and Lofty** may be rephrased as "Exceedingly Lofty" (2:11; 6:1; 52:13). This is one of the ways in which Isaiah describes the transcendence and holiness of God. He is above everyone—perfect and holy. **inhabits eternity:** Not only is God eternal, without beginning or ending, He transcends time itself. In this way He is able to give all of His time to each of His people; He is not bound by the succession of moments that limits our experience. **High and holy** may be rephrased as "unsearchably high" (32:15; 33:5, 16). **Contrite and humble** may be rephrased as "genuinely humble," referring to those who submit and repent under God's judgment (Pss. 34:17, 18; 51:17; 1 Pet. 5:6).

57:16 God **will not contend forever**, for humans will always **fail.** Therefore, in His sovereign grace, the Lord "created" salvation (54:9; 57:19; Gen. 8:21, 22; Ps. 130:3, 4).

57:17 I hid: For a related reference, see 1:15. **I was angry:** For a similar reference to the Lord's anger, see 54:7, 8. **Covetousness** violates God's covenant (56:11; Ps. 119:36; Jer. 22:17).

57:18 I . . . will heal: The Lord is the Physician (30:26). **I will . . . lead him:** For similar imagery describing the Lord's guidance, see

40:11; 42:16. **Mourners** refers to those who lament the destruction of Jerusalem (66:10).

57:19 fruit of the lips: For an explanation of the fruit, see Heb. 13:15. **Peace, peace** indicates "genuine peace." Contrast the false use of this phrase in Jer. 6:13, 14; 8:10, 11. **far off . . . near:** For a similar reference, see 56:7, 8 (compare Acts 2:39; Eph. 2:13, 17).

57:20 cannot rest: Contrast v. 2. The fate of **the wicked** is also described in 56:9–12; 57:3–13. **troubled sea:** For a similar analogy comparing the wicked to turbulent waters, see Jude 13.

57:21 There is no peace . . . for the wicked: This phrase is also found in 48:22.

58:1 Isaiah was to alert the people as loudly and clearly as a **trumpet** (Ex. 19:19; 20:18; Hos. 8:1; 1 Cor. 14:8). **Transgression** is related to the Hebrew verb translated "rebelled" in 1:2.

58:2 They seek Me daily contrasts with the seeking called for in 55:6. **Ordinance** is translated "justice" in 56:1. The hypocritical religionists **delight in approaching God** in ritual worship (29:13).

58:3, 4 Formerly, the nation **fasted** in times of national calamity (Jer. 36:9; Joel 1:14); later, fasting became part of the liturgical calendar (Zech. 7:2, 3; 8:19; Luke 18:12). This sermon may have been delivered on the Day of Atonement when the people of Israel **afflicted** their **souls** (v. 10; Lev. 16:29). **You take no notice:** A similar attitude is expressed in Mal. 3:14. Paradoxically, Israel finds **pleasure** in

fasting, but not in keeping the Sabbath (vv. 13, 14). The accusations, **you . . . exploit all your laborers** and **you fast for strife and debate,** expose the hypocrisy of the people's worship. Instead of ceasing their normal pursuits and setting the day aside to fast and pray, they **strike with the fist** the laborer who does not work. **Will not** may also be translated "cannot."

58:5 Is it a fast that I have chosen: For related passages, see 1:10–15; Amos 5:21–23; Mic. 6:7. The people's fast was not **an acceptable day to the Lord** because it focused on self-righteousness and not on justice for others. **Bow down** and **spread out** refer to the mourning ceremonies that accompanied fasting (2 Sam. 12:16; Joel 1:13, 14). **Like a bulrush** is meant to signify humility (42:3).

58:6 To loose, to undo, to let . . . go free, and **break every yoke** are synonyms of genuine righteousness (Ezek. 18:16–18). *Yoke* is a metaphor for social oppression.

58:7 the hungry . . . the naked: For similar expressions of the duty to take care of the poor, see Job 31:16–23; Matt. 25:35, 36. **The poor who are cast out** refers to those whose lands and houses were confiscated in payment of debts.

58:8 The **light** dawned with the advent of Christ (v. 10; 9:2; 10:17; 59:9; 60:1–3; Luke 1:78, 79). **Righteousness** refers to salvation (56:1). **The glory of the Lord** probably alludes to the pillar of cloud and fire in the desert (4:5,

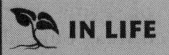 **IN LIFE**   **Worship *and* Service**

What is your concept of *worshiping* the Lord? Attending a church service at which you sing hymns, read Scripture, recite prayers, listen to a sermon, and partake of holy communion? All of these practices can lead to worship, but Isaiah shows that true worship goes beyond that (Is. 58:6, 7, 9, 10).

In Isaiah's day, there were apparently plenty of religious people, but not many responsive people. They "afflicted their souls" with fasting, "delighted" to know God's ways, inquired about "the ordinances of justice," and enjoyed their worship services (58:2, 3). But little if any of their piety translated into action. Yet they expected God to answer their prayers and bless them. Through Isaiah, God said that true worship is not just a weekly ritual, but a daily lifestyle. It may begin in a house of prayer, but it ends up in the public square.

What might that "public-minded" worship look like in today's world? What would it mean for believers as they respond to the hungry, the homeless, the prisoner, the wage-earner, the debtor, the poor, and the hopeless? There is no easy answer, but one fact is clear: as Isaiah told the people of his day, God cannot be expected to shower good things on His people as long as they withhold good things from others (58:8, 9, 11, 12).

So what starts with worship ends in service. Today that means that the church gathered for worship on Sunday becomes the church scattered for service on Monday through Saturday. Building believers leads to believers rebuilding their communities. Worship and service form a seamless robe.

6; Ex. 13:21; 14:20). **rear guard:** A marching army needs an alert rear defense (52:12).

58:9 The pointing of the finger was a sinister gesture (Prov. 6:13).

58:10 The afflicted soul here contrasts with the hypocritical affliction described in v. 3.

58:11 A watered garden and a perennial **spring** are similes for prosperity and the blessings of God's salvation.

58:12 Build the old waste places presupposes that the restored exiles had not found the spiritual and economic resources to rebuild Judah (44:26, 28; 61:2, 4; Ezek. 36:10; Hag. 1:2–9). The coming of Christ rebuilt the house of David (Amos 9:11, 12; Acts 15:15–17).

58:13 Doing your pleasure probably refers to commerce (vv. 3, 4; Amos 8:5). **Holy day** clearly indicates that in vv. 2–9 the Lord was not rejecting ritual altogether (66:23).

58:14 This blessing is based on the Song of Moses in Deut. 32:9, 13.

59:1, 2 the Lord's hand is not shortened: For related passages, see 40:10; 50:2. The Lord's **ear,** unlike Israel's (6:10), is able to **hear.**

59:3 your hands are defiled with blood: For similar passages on the people's guilt, see 1:15; 59:7; Ezek. 7:23. **Your lips have spoken lies:** For related passages, see 33:15; 59:13; Mark 7:21–23; Rom. 3:10–18; Gal. 5:19–21.

59:4 Calls for justice probably means to help the poor in the law courts (Job 9:16; 13:22). No one would **plead** the case of the poor fairly (1:17; 5:23; 59:14). **Conceive evil and bring forth iniquity** is translated "conceive trouble and bring forth futility" in Job 15:35.

59:5 Hatch . . . eggs and **weave the . . . web** signify the deliberate, calculated wickedness in the courts (32:7; 59:4).

59:6 Their webs will not become garments illustrates the futility depicted in v. 4 and the ultimate failure of the schemes depicted in v. 5 The wicked power structures would prove worthless (Job 8:14, 15).

59:7, 8 This passage is cited in Rom. 3:15–17 to document the universality of sin. **Their feet . . . make haste to shed innocent blood:** The people **run** without forethought into evil (Prov. 1:16). **thoughts of iniquity:** Contrast 55:7–9. Those who deny **peace** to others will themselves not know peace (57:21). **crooked paths:** For similar images of the wicked person's way of life, see Prov. 2:15; 10:9; 28:18.

59:9 Therefore links Israel's repentance with the prophet's reprimand. With the pronoun **us,** Isaiah identified himself with his people's sins (Ezra 9:6, 7; Dan. 9:5). The words **justice** and **righteousness** refer to God's salvation (46:13). **Light** and **darkness** refer to salvation and doom respectively (9:2; 42:16; 58:8, 10;

60:1–3). The Book of Isaiah, like the Gospel of John, makes much use of the words *light* and *darkness* as a way to contrast eternal life and death, truth and falsehood (John 1:4–9; 3:19–21; 8:12; 9:5; 12:35, 36).

59:10 The people **grope . . . like the blind** in fulfillment of the covenant curse on those who were disobedient (Deut. 28:29).

59:11–13 The people **growl** out of frustration. **moan:** For related images of the people's despair involving doves, see 38:14; Ezek. 7:16.

59:14 Justice and **righteousness** speak here of ethical conduct (v. 4).

59:15, 16 Justice refers here to **salvation** (vv. 9, 10). The Lord, using the first person, expresses the thought of this passage in 63:5. **no man:** God's salvation does not depend on humans (Ezek. 22:30). **no intercessor:** Contrast the intercession of the Servant in 53:12. **His own arm** figuratively represents the Lord as a warrior (42:13; 49:24, 25; 51:9; 52:10). **Righteousness** refers to the Lord's victorious salvation (46:13; 51:6, 8; 56:1).

59:17 The Lord's **breastplate** and **helmet** are taken up by His saints in their battle against the devil (Eph. 6:14–17). **garments of vengeance:** For a more detailed description of the Lord who comes to judge but also to save, see 63:1–3.

59:18 Recompense to His enemies is translated "fully repays His enemies" in 66:6. **Coastlands** indicates that the Lord's adversaries were distant nations (41:1). However, He judged wicked Israelites as well (65:6, 7). Only the repentant will be blessed (vv. 9–15, 20).

59:19 From the west . . . from the rising of the sun is another way of saying everywhere. **When the enemy comes** could also mean "when He comes as an enemy" (35:4).

59:20 The Redeemer will come in the person of Jesus Christ. For other prophecies of the Redeemer see 41:14. **turn from transgression:** For similar appeals to turn from sin in the prophecies of Isaiah see 1:17–19; 30:15; 31:6; 59:9–15.

59:21 Them refers to the repentant (v. 20). **My Spirit:** For similar references see 11:2; 30:1; 42:1; 48:16; 61:1; Luke 3:22. **You** and **your** in this verse are singular, probably with reference to Isaiah. God's Spirit and **words** would be given to all Israel so that all would become prophets of the living God (44:3).

60:1 Arise is addressed to Zion (v. 14). **shine:** Zion is both the recipient of God's light and the reflector of it. **light:** Isaiah's prophecies often emphasize the contrast between light and darkness to symbolize the contrast between eternal life and death, salvation and judgment (9:2; 10:17; 58:8; 59:9; 60:19, 20).

60:2 As was the case during the Exodus

from Egypt, **darkness** is on the wicked while God's light is on His people (Ex. 10:23). **Deep darkness** elsewhere describes a cloud enfolding the glory of God (Ex. 20:21), and serves as a warning of His impending judgment (Jer. 13:16).

60:3 Gentiles is translated "nations" in 2:2–4. In the earlier passage, they come to heavenly Zion to be taught of God; here they come to bring tribute (vv. 5, 11, 13). Isaiah foresaw a day when not only would the righteous remnant in Israel be devoted to God, but so would the redeemed from all peoples. Christ is the **light** to **kings** (42:6; 49:6).

60:4 Lift up your eyes . . . they come to you is cited from 49:18. **Your sons . . . your daughters** is cited from 49:22. Those verses were addressed to exiles and primarily concerned their return to the land, while this verse is addressed to the few restored exiles and looks to a greater return that is still in the future (11:11).

60:5 become radiant: See "shine" in v. 1. **wealth of the Gentiles:** For similar phrases, see Hag. 2:7; Zech. 14:14.

60:6, 7 Camels, animals of burden, carried **gold and incense. Midian** was famous as a caravan leader and trader (Gen. 37:28, 36). **Ephah** was one of Midian's sons (Gen. 25:4). The allusion to **Sheba,** renowned for its wealth, links this city with Solomon's (1 Kin. 10:1–13; Ps. 72:10). **proclaim the praises:** The nations would not bring just their wealth; they would accompany their gifts with public, vocal acknowledgment of the wonder of God (1 Kin. 10:9; Heb. 13:14, 15).

60:8 The ships' sails resemble a fast-moving **cloud** and **doves** returning **to their roosts.**

60:9 The reference to **the ships of Tarshish** (2:16) alludes to the wealth of King Solomon (1 Kin. 10:22).

60:10 Foreigners, such as Hiram king of Tyre, helped build the first temple (1 Kin. 5); today Gentiles are building up the church, the temple of the Lord (Eph. 2:11–22). **Wrath** is translated "indignation" in 34:2.

60:11 Zion's **gates shall be open continually** both because the city is secure and because the doors must be open in order to accommodate the great influx of the **wealth of the Gentiles** (v. 5). For the "gates of Zion," see Ps. 87:1–3. This verse is alluded to in Rev. 21:24, 25.

60:12 The nation and kingdom that does not serve Zion, where Christ now reigns (Acts 2:29–36), **shall perish** (John 3:18; Heb. 2:3; 9:27; 10:27). In the coming kingdom, there will be no opposition to the reign of the Savior-King.

60:13, 14 As **the glory of Lebanon**—its luxurious **cypress, pine,** and **box tree**—glorified the first temple (1 Kin. 5:10, 18) so it will **beautify** the temple again (vv. 5–7). Formerly, the **place of** the Lord's **feet** was the ark of the covenant (1 Chr. 28:2); later it was the temple (Ezek. 43:7), and then the whole earth (66:1).

60:15 The new sanctuary will be greater than the old one because it is **eternal,** rich, and spiritual (vv. 17, 18). **you have been forsaken:** For related ideas, see 49:14, 21; 50:1; 54:6.

60:16 This verse is modeled on 49:26. In the earlier verse, the nations serve Israel; here they enrich it. **milk the breast of kings:** This line, representing great wealth, demonstrates clearly that the prophet was using figurative language.

60:17 The new temple will be made of better-than-necessary metals—**gold, silver, bronze,** and **iron**—symbolizing by exaggeration its exceedingly great and enduring wealth. **Peace** and **righteousness** are personified as **officers** and **magistrates** respectively (26:3; 48:18).

60:18 Judging from the figurative language in vv. 15–22, especially v. 17, God's **Salvation** and Israel's **Praise** will be the city's defense (Zech. 2:4, 5).

60:19, 20 These verses form the basis for the description of the New Jerusalem in the new

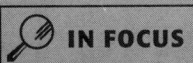 **IN FOCUS** **"everlasting"**

(Heb. *'olam*) (30:8; 60:19, 20; Ps. 89:2; Amos 9:11) Strong's #5769: This word is likely related to the one that means "to hide"; thus this term connotes "hidden, unknown time," usually referring to the future but sometimes to the past. The word may speak of time that is limited by a single life, that reaches through several generations (Gen. 6:3, 4; Deut. 15:17; Neh. 2:3; Mal. 3:4), or that extends to the beginning of the created order (64:4; Gen. 49:26). Sometimes the word refers to a period of time beyond death (45:17; Prov. 8:23; Eccl. 12:5; Dan. 12:2). Thus the term is quite naturally used of God, who is eternal and hidden (40:28; Gen. 21:33; Ps. 90:2). It refers to God's never-ending covenants, statutes, salvation, and love (Gen. 9:12; Lev. 16:29–31; Jer. 31:3). The Bible also describes the coming Messiah, His kingdom, and His priesthood as eternal (9:7; Pss. 45:6, 7; 110:4).

heaven and earth (Rev. 21:1, 23; 22:5; 65:17; 66:22).

60:21 In the new Zion, **people shall all be righteous** (4:3; Rev. 21:27). Though the exiles were back in the land (49:8; 54:3), they looked to a new Zion, when Israel would **inherit the land forever. The branch of My planting:** For similar references to God's people as a branch, see 4:2; 5:1–7; 61:3.

60:22 A little one shall become a thousand: The inhabitants of the new Zion will be prolific (54:3; Lev. 26:8).

61:1–11 This is the fifth of the Servant songs. In this song, the emphasis is on the Servant's mission.

61:1 The Spirit: For similar references, see 11:2; 30:1; 42:1; 48:16; 59:21; Luke 3:22. The **Me** featured so prominently here is the same Servant as in 42:1; 49:1; 50:4; 52:13. Several reasons point to this identification: (1) The Servant refers to God as His Master, the **Lord** (compare 50:4); (2) He has received the Lord's Spirit (compare 42:1); (3) He brings a word of healing and liberation (compare vv. 1–3 with 42:7; 49:9; 50:4); (4) He proclaims the "year of the Lord" (compare v. 2 with 49:8); (5) He is associated with an everlasting covenant (compare v. 8 with 42:6; 49:8); and (6) Jesus Christ inaugurated His ministry by identifying Himself as this Servant (Luke 4:17–21). The passage may also refer to Isaiah, but if so, he is only a pale shadow of Christ. **the Lord has anointed:** This phrase signifies that the Servant is more than a prophet, since only kings and high priests—with the exception of Elisha (1 Kin. 19:16)—were anointed (45:1). The name Messiah, or Christ in Greek, means the "Anointed One." **Poor** also means "humble," which like **brokenhearted,** indicates those who confidently hope in God in spite of their present distress (11:4; Pss. 34:18; 51:17). **Proclaim liberty** probably alludes to the official inauguration of the "Year of Release" or Jubilee (Lev. 25:10). **Captives** refers to those in

bondage to the wicked (58:6) or to wickedness in general—not to the exiles as in 51:14. **Those who are bound** is translated "prisoners" in 49:9, where it refers in part to the exiles; here it means "captives."

61:2 The acceptable year of the Lord corresponds to "the day of salvation" (49:8) and "the year of My redeemed" (63:4). **our God:** For a similar use of this term see 25:9. **To comfort all who mourn:** For related passages see 12:1; 49:13; Matt. 5:4.

61:3 A host lavished on a guest the **oil of joy** (Ps. 23:5; 45:7; Luke 7:46). **He may be glorified:** For similar references see 44:23; 49:5.

61:4, 5 They refers to Jews (58:12) and Gentiles (60:10). **desolations of many generations:** See 58:12; 60:10.

61:6 priests of the Lord: With Christ, they will make intercession for sinners (53:12; Ex. 19:6; 1 Pet. 2:9; Rev. 1:6). **Servants** here means "ministers," a synonym for "priests." (1 Kin. 8:11).

61:7, 8 Everlasting joy: For other references to eternal joy, see 35:10; 51:11; 60:19, 20.

61:9 Shall be known has the sense of "shall be renowned." **among the Gentiles . . . whom the Lord has blessed:** This section alludes to the fulfillment of the promises made to Abraham (41:8; 51:2; Gen. 12:3).

61:10 I and the parallel **My soul** refer to personified Zion. **Rejoice** is translated "joy" in v. 3 (65:18). **Clothed** signifies the Servant's new glorified status or condition (47:2; 52:1; 59:17). **Ornaments** is translated "beauty" in v. 3. **bride:** For a similar image, see 49:18.

61:11 spring forth: This phrase is also found in 42:9; 43:19; 45:8 to describe the coming of God's salvation. **Righteousness** here means "deliverance" (54:17). **before all the nations:** For related passages, see 52:10; 60:2, 3.

62:1, 2 The repetition of **righteousness** (v. 1) shows that the divine oracle and the prophet's comment are linked. **A new name,** like new clothing (61:10), signifies a new status

---

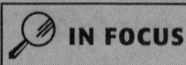 **IN FOCUS**   **"righteousness"**

(Heb. *tsedeq*) (62:1; Pss. 45:7; 85:10; 132:9; Prov. 1:3) Strong's #6664: This term denotes conformity to an ethical or moral standard. It occurs in reference to honorable business dealings (Gen. 30:33; Lev. 19:36; Deut. 25:15) and proper speech (Ps. 52:3; Prov. 8:8). The term is used most often in relation to one's standing with legal authorities, either human or divine. The word is frequently found in the context of other legal terms such as judgment or justice (Lev. 19:15; Pss. 23:3; 72:2; 119:6–8). Righteousness, judgment, and justice are declared to be the foundation of God's throne (Pss. 89:14; 97:2). God's righteousness is associated with deliverance. It is in this context that one of the divine names of God is revealed: "The Lord Our Righteousness" (41:10; 51:5; Jer. 23:6; 33:16).

(Gen. 17:5, 15; 32:28; Rev. 2:17). For the new names see vv. 4, 12.

62:3 Zion does not *receive* **a crown of glory,** or **royal diadem,** but *is* one **in the hand of the L****ORD****.**

62:4, 5 The name **Forsaken** is a symbolic name for Jerusalem (the symbolic name Immanuel in 7:14). It appears as the name of a person in 1 Kin. 22:42. For related references see 54:6; 60:15. **Desolate:** The term is also found in 49:8, 19; 54:1. **Hephzibah** and **Beulah** are symbolic names, though Hephzibah does appear as a personal name at 2 Kin. 21:1. The names are explained in the end of the verse.

62:6, 7 **I** refers to the Lord (vv. 1, 8). **Watchmen** refers to prophets (56:10). **You who make mention of the L****ORD** is Isaiah's synonym for "watchmen" and shows that the prophets were intercessors. The phrases **do not keep silent** and **give Him no rest** relate the prophets' prayer to the Lord's promises in v. 1 (64:12; 65:6).

62:8 **The L****ORD** **has sworn:** For other examples see 14:24; 45:23; 54:9. **no longer:** This phrase gives assurance that the covenantal blessings will outlast the curses.

62:9 **in My holy courts:** This phrase anticipates the rebuilding of the temple (Lev. 23:39, 40; Deut. 12:17, 18; 14:22–27; 16:9–17).

62:10 For the double imperatives **go through** and **build up,** see 40:1; 51:17; 52:11. The prophets not only prayed for the people (vv. 6, 7), they encouraged them to worship. **Gates** probably refers to those in the "holy courts" (v. 9). The prophet commanded the worshipers of v. 9 to pass through the gates in order to praise the Lord. **Prepare the way** means to encourage the people to come to the temple for worship (40:3, 4; 57:14). **Stones** refers to any impediment to worship (57:14). **Lift up a banner** (5:26; 11:10) is an encouragement to all **peoples** to worship God.

62:11 **Proclaimed to the end of the world** links this verse with "a banner for the peoples" in v. 10. The Hebrew verb rendered **say** is plural, indicating that a number of people will declare this announcement of salvation to Jerusalem. **your salvation is coming:** For similar references to the coming of the Lord's salvation, see 40:9; Zech. 9:9; Matt. 21:5.

62:12 The pronoun **they** refers to the Gentiles (v. 2). **The Holy People:** For similar descriptions of the redeemed, see 4:3; Ex. 19:6.

63:1 The word **comes** links this verse with 62:11. **Edom** epitomized Israel's enemies (Ps. 137:7; Lam. 4:21, 22; Ezek. 25:12; 35:1–15; Obad. 13, 14); it was famous for its winemaking (v. 3 for a reference to wine). Note that the text does not say God vanquished Edom, but rather the "peoples" (vv. 3, 6). **garments:** See

the warrior's garments in 59:17. **Bozrah** was the chief town of Edom (34:6; Jer. 49:13). The pronoun **I** refers to the Lord.

63:2 The **apparel** will be **red** from bloodstains.

63:3 The pronoun **I** is applied to Christ in Rev. 19:15. **trodden:** For this figure of judgment, see Lam. 1:15; Rev. 14:17–20. **The winepress** represents the battle.

63:4–6 **year of My redeemed:** This phrase alludes to the "law of redemption" of slaves and property (61:2; Lev. 25). A close relative of a slave had the right and duty to buy back the slave and rescue a family member from destitution.

63:7 **I will mention:** Isaiah, representing the people, publicly proclaims God's saving mercies (Pss. 77:12; 89:1). The plural words **lovingkindnesses** and **praises** refer to the Lord's many acts of love and loyalty to His people. The word *lovingkindnesses* is translated "sure mercies" in 55:3 (Ps. 89:1).

63:8 In the Hebrew Bible, the term rendered **My people** is used in two ways: (1) for those who were united nationally to God by blood and history through Abraham's flesh (48:1; Ex. 3:7) and (2) for those who were united to Him inwardly through Abraham's faith and obedience (Lev. 26:12; Deut. 29:13). The nation is in view here. **Lie** means "to deal falsely." Israel's rebellion was unexpected (1:2, 3). Just as godly parents *expect* godly children (Prov. 22:6), so God Himself *expected* godly spiritual children.

63:9 **Their affliction** probably refers to God's sympathy for His people in Egypt (Ex. 2:25; 3:7) and at the time of the judges (Judg. 10:16). **He was afflicted:** God shares the hurt of His people (Ex. 2:23–25). Paul's persecution of the members of the early church caused Christ to be afflicted (Acts 9:4). **Bore** and **carried** are allusions to Ex. 19:4 (Deut. 1:31; 32:10–12).

63:10 **rebelled:** The Hebrew verb means "to be contentious" (Num. 20:10; Pss. 78:40; 106:33, 43). The **Holy Spirit** is referred to from time to time in the Hebrew Scriptures, and several times in the Book of Isaiah (11:2; 42:1).

63:11 **Days of old** refers to the period of the Exodus and the Wilderness. **The sea** is an allusion to the Red Sea (50:2; Ex. 14:21–29). **Shepherd,** referring to Moses, is plural. Christ is the greater Shepherd (John 10:11; Heb. 13:20; 1 Pet. 5:4). **Put His Holy Spirit within them** is an allusion to Num. 11:17, 25.

63:12 **Glorious arm** is an allusion to Ex. 15:6 (41:13; 51:9). **Dividing the water** is a reference to Ex. 14:16, 21 (Ps. 78:13).

63:13, 14 The account of the Exodus and settlement of the land is concluded with two images.

The first is **a horse** moving surefootedly across the sea bottom as through a **wilderness**—that is, a "desert"; the second is **a beast,** meaning "a domesticated herd," returning from grazing on mountainsides **into the valley . . . to rest** (Deut. 12:9; Josh. 1:13; 11:23; 21:44).

63:15 Heaven refers to God's universal rule over space and time (Ps. 11:4–6). The pronoun **me** is a personified Israel (59:9–15).

63:16 The people of Israel are the Lord's children (v. 8). He is their **Father** because He created them as a nation (Deut. 32:6; Jer. 3:4, 19). It is rare in the pages of the Hebrew Bible to find the explicit statement of the Fatherhood of God, though it is often presented implicitly. **Abraham** and **Israel,** the people's human fathers (51:2), were limited in their knowledge by time and space—in contrast to the Lord, the people's **Father** and **Redeemer from Everlasting** (41:14).

63:17 us: Isaiah identifies himself with his people (59:9–15). The Lord, confirming the people in their sin, **hardened** their hearts (6:10; Ex. 4:21; Ps. 95:8).

63:18, 19 Called by Your name signifies the Lord's ownership of the people (Deut. 28:10; Jer. 14:9).

64:1, 2 Oh, that . . . You would come down: This appeal for the Lord to appear and strike terror in the enemy is based on His appearances at Sinai (Ex. 19:16–18) and for David (Ps. 18:7–15). The image of **fire** often symbolizes God's presence (10:17; 31:9; Ex. 19:18; Heb. 12:18), especially in judgment (Heb. 12:29).

64:3 Awesome things: The appearance of God is a fearsome event (Ex. 19:16–21; Deut. 10:21; 2 Sam. 7:23; Ps. 106:22). **for which we did not look:** God's saving acts surpass human expectations (Eph. 3:20). **The mountains shook:** For a similar description see Ex. 19:18.

64:4 Paul cites this verse with some changes in 1 Cor. 2:9. **Nor . . . seen any God besides You:** For similar ideas see 43:11; Deut. 4:35.

64:5 You meet him . . . Who remembers You in Your ways: These words reinforce the idea of v. 4. **does righteousness:** For a similar phrase, see 56:1. The word **indeed** provides a transition from the petition (63:15—64:5) to the confession of sin (64:5–7).

64:6 Unclean means the people were unfit for God's presence. **Filthy rags** refers to garments stained during menstruation ("sins . . . like scarlet" in 1:18), making a woman unclean (Lev. 15:19–24; Ezek. 36:17). **As a leaf** signifies the people's worthlessness and separation from God.

64:7 No one who calls is an exaggerated phrase calling attention to the people's apathy.

hidden: God is never really "in hiding," but He does obscure His presence because of human sin (1:15).

64:8 The prophet Isaiah, as a representative of the whole community, turned to God for aid. He called upon the Lord as **Father,** invoking the special relationship between Israel and God. The term **Father** should not be understood according to our modern conceptions of fatherhood. **Father** is not so much a term of endearment, as it was a word of authority and ownership. Under Israelite law, a parent's children where his or her property, over which he or she exercised much power. The covenant community was helpless before God as **Father** like clay in the hands of a potter. The prophet interceded for the people for forgiveness so that God's faithfulness might be revealed again in a restored Jerusalem.

64:9 Do not be furious claims God's promise in 54:7, 8. **Nor remember** claims God's promise in 43:25. **Please look** refers to God's "hiding" of Himself in v. 7.

64:10 cities . . . Zion . . . Jerusalem: The prophetic picture of the devastation of the land following the Babylonian invasion is used as a means of appeal to the heart of God.

64:11 Holy and beautiful may be rephrased as "exquisite beauty." **Our fathers praised You** suggests that the speakers are at least a generation removed from the fall of the temple.

64:12 Will You restrain Yourself: The people use the language of love, of remembrance, of family, and of shared values in this section (vv. 8–12) to implore God to act again on their behalf.

65:1 I was sought literally means "I allowed Myself to be sought." **I was found** literally means "I allowed Myself to be found." This promise links this oracle with Isaiah's lament (64:7). **Here I am** (58:9) is repeated for emphasis (the repetition of the word *comfort* in 40:1). The Lord's glorious presence assures salvation. **A nation that was not called by My name** includes the Gentiles (42:1; 49:6, 22; 52:15) and the remnant who "sought" God (v. 10). Together they are the servants who will be called "by another name" (v. 15). Paul saw his ministry to the Gentiles as a fulfillment of this promise (Rom. 10:20, 21). Peter calls the church "a holy nation" (1 Pet. 2:9).

65:2 I have stretched out My hands pictures God beckoning Israel to respond to Him. **All day long** suggests the Lord's long-suffering patience. **Rebellious** describes Israel (63:10). **Who,** repeated six times in vv. 2–5, introduces a sorry catalogue of Israel's abominable religious practices: arrogance (v. 2), open defiance (v. 3), idolatrous fertility rites (v. 3), divination (v. 4), eating unclean foods (v. 4), and blasphemous self-righteousness (v. 5). **their own thoughts:** Contrast the Lord's thoughts in 55:8, 9.

65:3 To My face means "openly." The people did not hide their shameful practices or restrain their evil habits. The Babylonians would commonly offer incense to the "host of heaven" on the **brick** or tile roofs of houses (2 Kin. 23:12; Jer. 19:13; Zeph. 1:5).

65:4 Spend the night in the tombs may refer to the practice of seeking an oracle from a god or from the dead. The Law prohibited eating **swine's flesh** (66:17; Lev. 11:7; Deut. 14:8). **Abominable things** refers to other foods that were prohibited to Israel (Lev. 11). When the people of Israel ate the same foods as their neighbors, they ceased to be holy or distinct.

65:5 I am holier than you: The idolaters were like the worst of the Pharisees in the NT times. Jesus called the Pharisees children of the devil (John 8:44), but they regarded themselves as better than others (Luke 18:9–14). **Smoke** and **fire** stand for things that provoke God's anger.

65:6 It is written refers to the heavenly book that records sin. Royal courts in the ancient world recorded unpunished crimes. **I will not keep silence:** For a similar phrase, see 62:1. **repay:** For similar references to the Lord's vengeance see 33:10–14; 34:8; 59:18.

65:7 the iniquities of your fathers: For related passages, see Ex. 20:5; Ezek. 18:20. **blasphemed Me:** The Israelites rejected and offended God by offering sacrifices to the false gods of other nations on the hilltops (Ezek. 20:27, 28). **Therefore:** The punishment matches the crime (47:11).

65:8 New wine represents the **servants** (54:17); the otherwise unproductive **cluster** represents all Israel (5:1, 2). The association of wine and **blessing** here is common in the Scriptures. *Servants* include "the remnant," as well as foreigners (56:6). **not destroy them all:** For a related passage see 1:8, 9.

65:9 I will bring forth descendants is fulfilled in Christ and in all those who are found in Him (Gal. 3:16, 26–29). **Jacob** and **Judah** represent all Israel. **An heir** involves the Messiah (Gen. 49:10; Matt. 21:38; Gal. 3:16). **My elect:** For a related passage see 41:8, 9 (compare Gal. 3:26–29).

65:10 Sharon, the coastal plain in the west, and **the Valley of Achor,** near Jericho in the east, represent the whole land.

65:11 The word **who** occurs four times in this verse, introducing more (vv. 2–5) of Israel's sins. These sins involved forsaking the Lord, forgetting His place of worship, worshiping **Gad,** a god of good luck, and worshiping **Meni,** a god of fate.

65:12 When I called, you did not answer contrasts with "Before they call, I will answer" in v. 24.

65:13 Therefore logically connects this stanza with the first two, vv. 1–7, 8–12. **Behold . . . But:** The pattern here recalls the blessings and curses on Mount Gerizim and Mount Ebal (Deut. 27), in the Beatitudes (Luke 6:20–26), and in Christ's picture of the Last Judgment (Matt. 25:31–46). **Eat** and **drink:** This is a festive meal accompanied by rejoicing.

63:14 Sing here develops the idea of rejoicing in v. 13 (12:1–6; 35:10; 61:7).

65:15 The **chosen** (v. 9) will use the apostates' **name as a curse** by invoking the terrible fate of the apostates upon others. The chosen will say, "The Lord make you like apostate Israel." See Jer. 29:22 for an example of how the Babylonian captives used the names of Zedekiah and Ahab as a curse. **Another name** signifies the launching of a new era (62:2); this name would be associated with blessing (v. 16), not with a curse.

65:16 He who blesses himself in the earth —Jew or Gentile—will invoke the Lord's name, because He is the **God of truth.**

65:17, 18 I create may also be translated "I am creating" or "I am about to create." **new heavens and a new earth:** As God fashioned the existing heavens and earth, so He will fashion a new cosmos that will be ready for His presence and for the enjoyment of His people. **Former** encompasses everything up to the creation of the new cosmos (Rev. 21:4). **Be glad and rejoice** means "to be openly, deliriously happy." Saints are called upon to celebrate by faith the coming glorious salvation (66:10). **Create Jerusalem** signifies that it will be entirely new, with no resemblance to the old city (62:7). John also links the "new heaven and new earth" with the New Jerusalem (Rev. 21:1, 2).

65:19 My people: This title for the citizens of Jerusalem is also used in 63:8. **weeping shall no longer he heard:** For similar ideas concerning God's coming salvation, see 25:8; 35:10; 51:11.

65:20 the child shall die one hundred

> *When the people of Israel ate the same foods as their neighbors, they ceased to be holy or distinct.*

IN LIFE | New Work for a New World

Did you know that in the world to come you will have work to do, and that your work will be gratifying, fulfilling, and enduring? According to the glimpse of the future that Isaiah was given, people will build houses and cultivate vineyards (Is. 65:21, 22), an indication that God's new earth will be filled with meaningful activity.

This should come as a comfort to you if your present occupation seems insignificant, boring, or dissatisfying. In the world to come, you will "long enjoy the work of {your} hands" (65:22). That is, you will see the results of what you accomplish and enjoy the benefits of your efforts. You will not "labor in vain" (65:23) the way so many workers do now. Isaiah's vision has reference to this world as it was originally created. It was "very good" in God's estimation (Gen. 1:31), and the work of the world was "very good" as well. In His new world, God will restore work to its original purpose.

In the meantime, we can serve God as His coworkers, using the abilities and resources that He has given us to wisely manage this earth and meet the needs of people. We can also anticipate our future with God by walking with Him through life and learning what He has in store for us. And we can share our future hope with others, encouraging them to place their lives and future in the loving hands of Christ.

---

years old: On one level, these words indicate a return in the coming kingdom to the extended life spans that are noted before the Flood (Gen. 5). It appears that people will not be affected by disease and aging in the same way as in our present world. **Sinner** can also mean "the one who fails" to live a long life.

65:21, 22 These verses imply meaningful work in both the coming kingdom as well as in the new cosmos, along with a reverse of the curse (Deut. 28:49–52). **houses . . . vineyards:** The life of blessing in the coming kingdom is presented in terms that would have been readily understood by the people of Isaiah's day (Mic. 4:4). Industry will not be limited to these twin pursuits, but the happy, blessed life is indicated by them. **As the days of a tree** indicates longevity and stability (v. 20). The words **long enjoy** reinforces the idea of longevity.

65:23 They shall not labor in vain: These words speak of God reversing the curse on this cosmos (Gen. 3:17–22) and removing the curse that came in the time of Moses (Deut. 28:30). The Hebrew word rendered *vain* means "empty."

65:24 Before they call, I will answer expresses the truth that there will be no sorrow between petition and praise (30:19; 58:9). Praise will be continuous.

65:25 This verse condenses the promises of 11:6–9. The figures represent the reversal of nature and the coming of universal peace. **Dust shall be the serpent's food** is an allusion to Gen. 3:14 to indicate that this specific curse will be consummated.

66:1 The Lord has no need for a man-made temple, for **heaven** and **earth**—the whole cosmos—is His sanctuary (40:22). **footstool:** The resting place for the "feet" of the Lord is extended beyond the ark of the covenant (60:13) to the whole earth. **Where is the house:** No place on earth can accommodate the transcendent God (1 Kin. 8:27). **The place of My rest** refers to the temple (1 Chr. 28:2; Ps. 132:8, 14).

66:2 Those things refers to everything in the universe. **I look:** God seeks true worshipers (John 4:24). **Contrite spirit . . . trembles at My word** is similar to Jesus' phrase "in spirit and truth" (John 4:24).

66:3 The term **He who,** used four times in this verse, refers to those who worship according to the letter but not the spirit of the Law. Their worship in God's estimation is as unacceptable **as if** it consisted of abominable pagan practices (1:11–14; 65:3–5). God's harsh criticism of false liturgy is tempered with His promise of the coming true liturgy (vv. 20, 23). **Slays a man** may refer to child sacrifice (57:5). **Breaks a dog's neck** may refer to a pagan practice; in any case, the dog was regarded as an unclean animal, a detestable scavenger. The sacrifice of **a bull, a lamb, a grain offering,** and **incense** was considered to be **their own ways** because the worshipers lacked a contrite spirit. It was as if **their soul** delighted **in their abominations.**

66:4 So will I choose their delusions: For a related passage, see 63:17. **their fears:** This is the judgment spelled out in vv. 15, 16, 24. **when I called . . . I do not delight:** This passage echoes 65:12.

66:5 You who tremble at His word:

These words link vv. 5–11 with vv. 1–4. **Your brethren who hated you:** These words intensify the opposition encountered in ch. 65. **Let the Lord be glorified** represents the false worshiper's hypocritical righteousness (v. 17). **Cast . . . out** of the temple, the true worshipers went into the world and brought back Gentiles (v. 18). **Joy** is spoken sarcastically (Ps. 22:8). The persecutors **shall be ashamed** and the persecuted shall "rejoice" (v. 10).

66:6 Isaiah heard the **sound of** battle **noise** proceeding from the **city** and the **temple** (13:4). **His enemies** refers to the self-righteous idolaters persecuting God's servants. This prophecy may find its fulfillment in the fall of the temple in A.D. 70. (Matt. 24:1, 2) or at the Lord's second coming (66:17; 2 Thess. 1:7–10).

66:7, 8 Before she . . . gave birth represents the birth of the community from the cast-out worshipers as coming so quickly that it will be without pain. At times, Zion is pictured as the daughter of the Lord (1:8); here she is the mother of His people. The **male child** and **her children** may refer to Christ and His church.

66:9, 10 The rhetorical questions introduced by the words **shall I** guarantee the prophecy of vv. 7, 8. God finishes what He begins (Phil. 1:6).

66:11 Through the joyful faith of v. 10, saints before Christ's coming ate figuratively at a banquet (65:13).

66:12 For links vv. 12–24 with vv. 5–11. The pronoun **her** refers to Mother Jerusalem (vv. 7, 8). **You** refers to true worshipers and their offspring (v. 22), the beloved children of Mother Jerusalem. **On her sides . . . carried:** For similar images see 49:22; 60:4.

66:13 I will comfort you: Here God Himself is the comforting "Mother" (2 Cor. 1:3, 4).

66:14 Heart and **bones** refer to mental and physical health (Pss. 6:2; 109:18).

66:15 For links the judgment with **rebuke.** This verse is a picture of God's judgment. The Lord's coming corresponds to Isaiah's prayer (64:1–3). **Fire** is the lightning; **His chariots** are the storm clouds (Deut. 33:26; Ps. 18:10). **Like a whirlwind** depicts the speed and strength of the Lord's coming (Jer. 4:13).

66:16 The Divine Warrior comes with **fire** (v. 15) and **sword** (27:1; 31:8; Luke 21:24; Rev. 19:11–15). **All flesh** refers to all of the false worshipers described in this chapter (Jer. 9:2).

66:17 This section summarizes the abominable practices of the false worshipers (65:2–5; 66:3).

66:18 Their works and their thoughts probably refers to the right acts and spirit of the true worshipers, on whom God looks with favor (v. 2), since reference is made to bringing salvation to the Gentiles (v. 19). **My glory** probably refers to God's presence in His temple (Ezek. 11:22, 23; 44:4).

66:19 The **sign** may be the deliverance of the true worshipers as judgment falls on the false. **Those . . . who escape** may refer to those who escape God's slaughter (vv. 16, 17), but more likely to those who escape persecution (Matt. 24:9–14). Those who escaped would bring God's glory to the nations (v. 18) and then give birth to the new age (vv. 7–11). **to Tarshish . . . the coastlands:** For similar references see 23:6; 60:9. **declare My glory among the Gentiles:** For another prophecy by Isaiah of the spread of God's glory throughout the world, see 24:14–16.

66:20, 21 an offering to the Lord: For a related reference, see Deut. 12:5–7. **horses . . . camels:** Animals represent the diverse countries from which they come. The Gentiles are compared to **a clean vessel** (56:6, 7; Acts 10:28), a striking reversal of the dominant attitude towards Gentiles in the OT (52:1).

66:22 A prediction of the coming of **the new heavens and the new earth** also occurs in 65:17. **Your descendants . . . remain** guarantees the continuity of true Israel (65:9; Rom. 11:1–36).

66:23 From one New Moon to another refers to all time. **All flesh** refers to the blessed—Jew and Gentile—in contrast to the rejected (vv. 16, 24). Through all time and from all the earth, true **worship** will be offered to God.

66:24 Corpses refers to the rebels (5:25; 34:3). The word for **transgressed** is related to the word for rebelled in 1:2. **Their worm . . . is not quenched** depicts eternal punishment (48:22; 57:20). The imagery derives from the Valley of Hinnom that was Jerusalem's garbage dump, where unclean corpses decomposed and were burned. This verse is cited by Jesus in Mark 9:44, 46, 48. Though the Book of Isaiah depicts God's coming salvation, it closes with a strong statement of the judgment of the wicked.

The Book of

Jeremiah

•

———————————————————————————————

*P*ERHAPS MORE VIVIDLY THAN ANY OTHER BOOK of the Bible, Jeremiah reveals the inner struggles of a prophet of God. In "confessions" such as those in 15:10–21; 20:7–18, Jeremiah candidly discloses his inner turmoil concerning his call to prophetic ministry. Indeed, the prophet's anguish over the message of judgment upon his people and the coming destruction of the land was at times overwhelming (4:19–22).

Yet despite his anguish, Jeremiah fulfilled his ministry of proclaiming God's judgment against the people of Judah for their idolatry, their unfaithfulness to the covenant, and their obstinate disobedience of His will. Long acknowledged as one of the great prophets of the Old Testament, Jeremiah serves to this day as an example of someone who remained faithful to the word of God despite countless hardships.

Jeremiah's ministry covered a critical time in the history of the ancient Middle East. When Josiah king of Judah died at the hands of the Egyptian army, Judah became subject to Egypt and its ruler Pharaoh Necho. The people of Judah chose Jehoahaz to succeed Josiah. However, three months later Necho appointed Jehoiakim (Eliakim) to rule as his vassal on the throne in Jerusalem. Having lost their freedom, the people of Judah turned not to God but to the idols they had worshiped in the days of Manasseh and Amon. This idolatry was the reason for Jeremiah's proclamations of God's judgment.

In 605 B.C., Nebuchadnezzar defeated Pharaoh Necho at Carchemish, and Jehoiakim immediately submitted to the Babylonian king, who permitted him to remain on the throne as a vassal. Three years later, Jehoiakim rebelled against Nebuchadnezzar and was deposed (2 Kin. 24:1, 2). Jehoiachin replaced Jehoiakim on the throne for a short time, but he was then exiled to Babylon by Nebuchadnezzar. Thousands of political and religious leaders were carried to Babylon with Jehoiachin in 597 B.C. (2 Kin. 24:14–16).

Nebuchadnezzar made Jehoiakim's brother Zedekiah the new ruler of Judah. In 589 B.C., Zedekiah led a rebellion against Babylon, and Nebuchadnezzar's reprisal was swift. His army entered Judah and destroyed all resisting fortified settlements. Nebuchadnezzar's army turned aside from besieging Jerusalem when the Egyptian army appeared in southwest Palestine in the summer of 588 B.C. But the Egyptians soon withdrew, and Nebuchadnezzar resumed his siege. Several times during the siege of Jerusalem, Zedekiah came to Jeremiah for counsel from the Lord. The prophet advised him to surrender, but Zedekiah would not listen.

Jerusalem's walls were breached in the fourth month of 586 B.C. One month later, the temple was burned, along with the palaces, houses, and other administrative buildings. An additional 4,600 Jerusalemites were deported to Babylon. Gedaliah was appointed governor of Judah at Riblah. Jeremiah, who had been imprisoned by Zedekiah, was released and sent to serve under Gedaliah. Gedaliah was assassinated, and his supporters fled to Egypt, fearful of Nebuchadnezzar's revenge. Jeremiah went with them to Egypt against his will, and there he continued to confront the Jews for their idolatry and unfaithfulness.

The structure and organization of the Book of Jeremiah have perplexed interpreters for generations. A brief examination of passages with explicit historical notes proves that the material is not ordered chronologically. Instead, the organization of the oracles, prose sermons, and other material is based on content, audience, and connective links. The division is as follows: (1) the call of Jeremiah (ch. 1); (2) the judgment of Judah and Jerusalem (chs. 2—24); (3) Jeremiah's ministry to the nations (chs. 25—51); and (4) an historical appendix recounting the fall of Jerusalem (ch. 52). This arrangement gives balance and unity to the lengthy prophetic text.

Jeremiah's prayers, confessions, laments, and dialogues reveal the depth of the prophet's understanding of the character of God and the nature of His relationship to people. For Jeremiah, the God of Israel was the incomparable God of all creation, the Lord over nature and history. He reigned not only over Judah and Israel but over all nations (25:13).

The thread that wove together Jeremiah's knowledge of God was his understanding of the word of God. It permeated the prophet's life and speech, for God Himself promised to touch Jeremiah's mouth and infuse His words into Jeremiah's mind and speech (1:9). From then on, God's words were like an unquenchable fire burning within the prophet's soul (20:9).

Jeremiah was keenly aware of the provisions of the covenant between God and Israel. The covenant bound Israel to God in a special relationship of love, faithfulness, and hope. But the covenant had two sides. Faithfulness to the Lord and the covenant would bring blessing; disobedience would result in punishment, destruction, and exile (Deut. 27:14—28:68). Jeremiah called the people to obey the words of the covenant and to turn from their idolatry and their unjust treatment of one another (11:6, 7).

Jeremiah's message of judgment also contained a word of hope: a righteous remnant would be restored. The land had been defiled by the people's idolatry. The leaders had brought the nation to the brink of disaster and the people were exiled. But based on His everlasting love for Israel, God promised to bring the people back from captivity and restore them to blessing (30:18—31:6). Israel's enemies would be defeated (30:16), and the people would sing joyfully of God's goodness (31:12).

Jeremiah was born in Anathoth, just three miles northeast of Jerusalem in the hill country of Benjamin. His father was Hilkiah. Jeremiah's ministry extended from 626 to 586 B.C., making him a contemporary of Zephaniah, Ezekiel, and Habakkuk. The prophet's writing ministry began in the fourth year of Jehoiakim's reign in 605 B.C. (36:1, 2), though portions of the book may have been written earlier. The book was completed sometime after the fall of Jerusalem in 586 B.C.

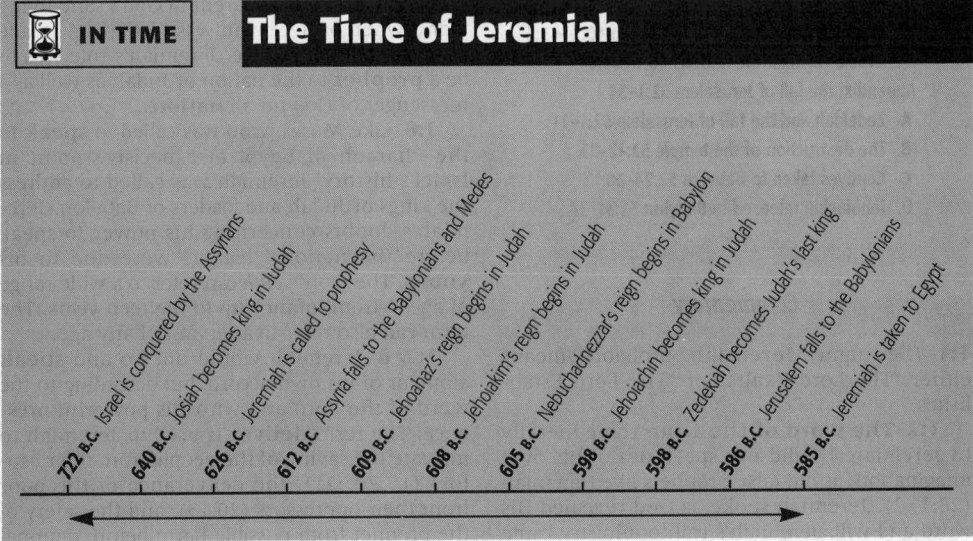

IN TIME

The Time of Jeremiah

722 B.C. Israel is conquered by the Assyrians

640 B.C. Josiah becomes king in Judah

626 B.C. Jeremiah is called to prophesy

612 B.C. Assyria falls to the Babylonians and Medes

609 B.C. Jehoahaz's reign begins in Judah

608 B.C. Jehoiakim's reign begins in Judah

605 B.C. Nebuchadnezzar's reign begins in Babylon

598 B.C. Jehoiachin becomes king in Judah

598 B.C. Zedekiah becomes Judah's last king

586 B.C. Jerusalem falls to the Babylonians

585 B.C. Jeremiah is taken to Egypt

Outline

Commentary

1:1 The name **Jeremiah** probably means either "The Lord Exalts" or "The Lord Establishes."

1:2 The word of the LORD came literally to Jeremiah. He did not speak out of his own imagination, as did false prophets like Hananiah (28:1, 2). Jeremiah spoke as God revealed His word and will. Jeremiah's call to ministry came in **the thirteenth year** of Josiah, who reigned thirty-one years.

1:3 Jeremiah's ministry as a prophet lasted from the beginning of the reign of **Jehoiakim** (608 B.C.) to **the eleventh year of Zedekiah** and the fall of Jerusalem (586 B.C.). Gedaliah was appointed governor over the peasant-populated Judah after the Babylonians, under Nebuchadnezzar, had deported the leading citizens of Jerusalem. Jeremiah continued ministering until he was taken unwillingly to Egypt following the assassination of Gedaliah.

1:4–19 These verses detail the call of Jeremiah. The record of his divine summons to the ministry is one of the most graphic of all the prophets, except perhaps that of Isaiah (Is. 6).

1:4 The word of the LORD came: A standard way of introducing a divine oracle at the beginning of a prophetic book (Ezek. 1:3; Hos. 1:1; Joel 1:1; Jon. 1:1; Mic. 1:1; Zeph. 1:1; Hag. 1:1; Zech. 1:1). We do not really know how the word of the Lord came to the prophets. It is possible that it would come in a variety of ways, such as visions, dreams, audible voices, visual impressions, or a deeply felt internal sense of things. Regardless of how it came, the prophets had a strong sense that the message was not their own; rather, it was the word of the Lord.

1:5 Jeremiah was keenly aware that the call of God in his life had been determined by the Lord from before the prophet's conception. As God's word became a reality in Jeremiah's life, he understood that God **knew** him and had called him to proclaim a critical message at a crucial point in the history of the nation. The Hebrew verb rendered *knew* refers to an intimate knowledge that comes from relationship and personal commitment. That intimate relationship was made apparent in God's sanctifying work, whereby Jeremiah was "set apart" (made holy) for special service. Jeremiah's role was to be a **prophet** to the nation of Judah as well as a messenger of God for all **nations.**

1:6 Like Moses, who was called to **speak** to the Pharaoh of Egypt at a decisive point in Israel's history, Jeremiah was called to address the kings of Judah and leaders of Babylon. Jeremiah's doubts concerning his power to speak before the nations' leaders were due to his **youth.** The word *youth* can refer to a wide range of ages—from infancy up to the teen years. The term can also refer to a servant of any age.

1:7, 8 Jeremiah would not **go** and **speak** alone or of his own accord, but according to the word of the Lord and with His powerful presence. The term **deliver** is used in Jeremiah to indicate the saving of the people from their captors (15:20, 21), the deliverance of the poor from their oppressors (20:13), and the safety of the prophet from possible harm before national leaders. **I am with you:** Twice in Jeremiah's call (v. 19), God reassured the prophet of His presence and protection. In moments of personal crisis, Jeremiah prayed these words back to God (20:11).

1:9 Jeremiah is commissioned for his task and the essence of his message is outlined. **I have put My words in your mouth:** The source of Jeremiah's message was clearly the Lord, but the message would be expressed

1:11, 12 God confirmed His call to Jeremiah with two visions. The first vision involved an **almond tree,** which blossoms when other trees are still dormant. The almond tree served as a harbinger of spring, as though it "watched over" the beginning of the season. In a similar fashion, God was "watching over" His word, ready to bring judgment on Israel.

1:13 The second vision God used to confirm Jeremiah's call involved a **boiling pot** that was

Photo: Levant Photo Service

Hills near the village of Anathoth, home of the prophet Jeremiah (Jer. 1:1).

through the personality, experience, and artistry of the prophet. This verse gives us an understanding of the dual nature of Scripture. The message is the Lord's; its expression is accomplished through His servants the prophets (Heb. 1:1).

1:10 I have . . . set you over the nations: The nations were instruments in God's purpose of revealing Himself. The Lord would use Babylon to punish Judah, and then He would use the Persians to punish Babylon. The phrasing here suggests the official appointment of a person to an authoritative position, as when Nebuchadnezzar appointed Gedaliah governor of Judah. With God's words in Jeremiah's mouth, the prophet had the authority to stand before any ruler. **To root out and to pull down . . . To build and to plant:** Judgment and restoration were the two messages of the prophet of God. The words *root out, pull down,* **destroy, throw down,** *build,* and *plant* are repeated at key points in the Book of Jeremiah to reaffirm Jeremiah's call (18:7; 24:6; 31:28; 42:10; 45:4).

tilted toward the south, indicating the direction in which the pot's contents would be spilled. The message of this vision derives from the common everyday meal preparation. It is also based on the fact that the principal direction of attack on Judah and Jerusalem was from the north. Occasionally the direction would be from the south (for instance, Egypt, Cush, Arabian tribes). To the west was the Great Sea, and to the east was the great desert. The north was the danger region. The world of the northern frontier was the homeland to little known tribes such as the Scythians, Cimmerians, and Urartu. The dark forces of Tubal and Meshech of Ezekiel were indigenous to this region. If they were not raiding villages and farmlands of the fertile crescent, they served as mercenary troops. Not until 20:4 does the prophet Jeremiah finally identify who the "terror from the north" will be against Jerusalem; it is Babylon.

1:14 The **calamity** suggested by this vision was an enemy attack on Judah and Jerusalem from **the north.** In 20:4, Jeremiah finally identifies this enemy as Babylon. Babylon itself was

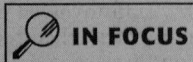 **IN FOCUS** **"build"**

(Heb. *banah*) (1:10; 24:6; Gen. 22:9; Is. 45:13) Strong's #1129: Things described as built using this word are "a new house" in Deut. 20:5, "the altar" in Deut. 27:6, and "the house of the LORD" in 1 Kin. 6:1. The expression "build a house" can also refer to establishing a family (Ruth 4:11) or a dynasty (Ps. 89:4). The word may also be used in the sense of "rebuilding" or "restoring" something that has been destroyed or is in disrepair (Neh. 2:17). Jeremiah's commission as God's prophet included the task of building and planting (1:10). In the present context the term is used figuratively of the prophetic ministry of restoring the people of God, or spiritually rebuilding Israel as the people of God, after the Exile (31:4).

east of Jerusalem, but the road went around the desert and approached from the north.

1:15 The calamity from the north (v. 14) would involve a siege of **Jerusalem** and **all the cities of Judah. I am calling:** The use of the first-person pronoun indicates that it was God Himself who was at war with His people. Which tribal or ethnic group from the **north** Jeremiah had in mind in the original setting of this oracle is unknown. Ultimately, most of Israel's enemies came from the north. Egypt was weakened, and the peoples to the east and southeast did not pose much of a threat to Judah. By the fourth year of Jehoiakim, the obvious identity of the "foe from the north" was Babylon. Babylon, of course, is located to the east of Judah. But the intervening desert demands an approach from the north

1:16 One of the main reasons for God's judgment on Judah and Jerusalem was Israel's worship of **other gods.** God is not one among many; He alone is God of Israel (Deut. 6:4). **Burned incense:** The Hebrew term meaning "to burn" or "to make smoke" is used nineteen times in Jeremiah, all in the context of burning sacrifices to other gods. **worshiped:** The term means "to cause oneself to bow down" in honor or service of God or man. The first and foremost commandment (Ex. 20:3) had been broken.

1:17 Prepare yourself is literally "gird up your loins," or "tuck your robe in your belt so you can run" (1 Sam. 2:4). **do not be dismayed:** If Jeremiah shrank back in terror before the men God had commanded him to confront, God Himself would bring terror into the prophet's life.

1:18 Jeremiah's position is phrased in military language, emphasizing the certainty that God would fight for him. God **made** Jeremiah an impregnable **fortified city** with **bronze walls.** Jeremiah's defense system could not be battered down or tunneled under by people and armies. **kings . . . princes . . . priests . . . people:** This list of the various types of people

in Israel suggests that the entire nation would be against Jeremiah.

1:19 The people and their leaders would **fight** against Jeremiah and his message, but they would not overcome, for God Himself protects and fights for the faithful.

2:1–3 Chapter 2 is presented in the form of a covenant lawsuit, that is, an indictment brought by God against His people (2:1–3:5). The lawsuit typically contained the following elements: (1) a recounting of the founding and benefits of the relationship; (2) a calling of witnesses of heaven and earth; (3) accusations and indictments versus the defendant; (4) a reference to futility of seeking aid from other sources; and (5) an announcement of threat of judgment and delineation of punishment. Jeremiah challenged the people of Judah to remember God. The **betrothal** period between God and Israel in the **wilderness** was a time when Israel **went after,** or worshiped, the Lord. The nation of Israel is referred to as the **firstfruits,** which rightfully belonged to God (Deut. 26:1–11) and **holiness,** something set apart for God's glory. In the time of Jeremiah, the people of Judah no longer remembered the days when their grandfathers and grandmothers had worshiped and obeyed God.

2:4 The message is addressed to **all the families of the house of Israel**. The message may have been proclaimed to the collective tribes late in the reign of Josiah, when reunification of Judah and the remnant of Israel had taken place (2 Chr. 34:6). Josiah's untimely death at Megiddo in 609 B.C. ended all hope of prosperity and unity.

2:5 Idols means "futility," "vapor," or "worthlessness." The Hebrew word translated **followed** is used in the books of Jeremiah and Deuteronomy to describe the worship of idols and other gods. **They . . . have become idolaters:** Those who serve idols, which are only vapor, become like vapor themselves.

2:6 In pursuing other gods, the people of

IN PERSON Jeremiah's Faith

Some might consider Jeremiah the model of faithfulness, while others might think of him as an example of failure and futility. He served as God's prophet for over forty years, yet the rulers and the people of Judah did not listen to his warnings. Jeremiah was put in prison, thrown into a well, and taken to Egypt against his will. He was not allowed to marry. He was rejected by his friends, neighbors, family, false priests and prophets, and kings. Jeremiah stood alone in his call for the people to repent and turn to God. He warned them time and time again of their impending punishment. And even though much of what he prophesied came true during his ministry, the people and the leaders continued to ignore him.

Yet through all the hardship and humiliation Jeremiah was forced to endure, he remained obedient and faithful to God. Though at first he questioned God's calling, once he accepted his position, he became a model of perseverance and devotion. After enduring decades of abuse, threats, and outright indifference, Jeremiah could easily have turned his back and walked away. But he knew that was exactly the problem God had told him to warn the people about. The people had turned away from God's will, and Jeremiah was not about to do the same.

Some may look back at Jeremiah's ministry and consider it a failure, for the people did not respond to the prophet's call. In reality, his life was a glorious success, for Jeremiah remained faithful to his God. He may not have seen immediate results, but his struggle to obey God in a world that had turned wholesale away from its Creator has inspired generations of believers.

Israel lost sight of their identity as the elect of God. They forgot how God had delivered them from oppression in Egypt and had given them food, water, and protection in the **wilderness** for forty years.

2:7 God's guiding hand had **brought** Israel out of the desert and into a **bountiful country,** the region of Carmel, with its luxurious trees and vineyards. Israel had enjoyed the bounty of the land flowing with milk and honey, but then turned God's beautiful **heritage** into a polluted **abomination.** The Hebrew word translated *heritage* refers to God's possession of the land that He bestowed upon the nation.

2:8 The people had not sought the Lord, nor had the **priests, rulers,** or **prophets.** Those who should have known God most intimately **did not know** Him at all. The rulers **transgressed against** God and His covenant. The prophets prophesied in the name of Baal rather than God.

2:9 Charges of apostasy and idolatry are formally presented in 2:9–13.

2:10, 11 The charges are more heinous than heaven and earth have ever known. In hyperbolic language, the prophet reveals the astonishing reality of the character of the people. The only nation whose god was truly God, was at the same time the only nation that exchanged its God for others. The hearer is challenged to search the world from east to west, from the coastlands of **Cyprus** and beyond, to the Arabian desert region of **Kedar** (49:28, 29) to see whether such an uncanny occurrence has ever transpired. The challenge is phrased in a negative rhetorical question: **Has a nation changed its gods, which are not gods?** Of course this has not happened among the nations. Each nation and city had its patron deity, whom the people served, even if other deities were incorporated into the local pantheon. Yet Israel, whose **glory** was the Lord, gave up her allegiance to Him to serve a host of pagan deities.

2:12 In the celestial court, the **heavens** stand appalled as witnesses to this unparalleled phenomenon. They are horrified and decimated. Frankly, the issue is simply unthinkable; yet it happened!

2:13 God's **people** had **forsaken** (1:16) Him and served worthless deities. God, **the fountain of living waters,** offered a limitless supply of fresh, life-giving sustenance. Instead the people chose **broken cisterns,** which were useless for storing water and useless for sustaining life.

2:14 Israel was not founded to be a **servant** or **homeborn slave.** Yet the nation that God set free from slavery and oppression had placed itself in the position of a servant, enslaved by Assyria and Egypt.

2:15 Assyria—**the young lions**—laid waste to Israel and Judah during several invasions between 734 and 701 B.C.

2:16 Egypt forced Judah into a vassal relationship. The Egyptians had **broken the crown of** Israel's **head** by killing Josiah. **Noph** is Memphis, the capital of Lower Egypt. **Tahpanhes** was in the eastern Nile delta.

2:17 The affirmative rhetorical question points to Israel's voluntary and forced submission that she has brought upon herself as a result of her forsaking the Lord. Seeking the ways of the world or those who claim allegiance to God will often have serious consequences.

2:18 **Sihor** means "Black" and refers to the Nile. The word **River** refers to the Euphrates, which is associated with Assyria. Tragically, the people of Judah had left the everlasting fountain of God for the broken cisterns of Assyria and Egypt (v. 13).

2:19 **Backslidings** means "turnings." Israel had turned in every direction for help except to the true source of safety and security. The phrase **says the Lord GOD of hosts** confirms the severity of the crime and the certainty of the punishment about to befall the people of God.

2:20 Israel had **broken** its **yoke** like a beast, even though the people had promised to be faithful when they came into the land (Josh. 24:24). Instead, idolatrous abandonment of God had pervaded the land: **on every high hill and under every green tree.** The term **harlot** is a figurative way of referring to unfaithfulness to God, and in addition it may refer to the ritual prostitution of Canaanite and Phoenician fertility cults.

2:21 **Noble vine** refers to the lush vines of the Sorek valley, which runs from Jerusalem to the Mediterranean through some of the richest farmland in the country. Judah became an **alien** vine, fertilized by foreign gods (Is. 5).

2:22 The imagery of a non-removable stain indicates the depth of Judah's sin. Her iniquity is indelibly etched.

2:23–25 The picture of the wild **dromedary,** a female camel in heat, and a **wild donkey** mad with lust vividly portrays the craving of Israel for foreign gods. Jeremiah warns the nation against this fruitless pursuit, but the response evidences the addictive, consuming passion of idolatry.

2:26 The accusation of idolatry is compared to catching a thief in the act of stealing. Several levels of leadership are delineated, conveying that the whole of Israel's leadership has disgraced itself.

2:27, 28 Jeremiah depicts the nation's leaders as so corrupt, that they confused sexual identities. The **tree** usually denotes the female deity (the Asherah) and the **stone** the male deity. But the Israelites addressed the female as **father** and the male as the one who gave them birth. (Confusion reigns when one rejects rather than seeks the Lord.) To these non-deities the people would seek refuge in time of despair, but the confusion will only intensify. They will seek help from innumerable gods, but there is no

safety, no security, and no deliverance apart from the Lord.

2:29, 30 The term **plead** recalls the charges made by God against Israel in v. 9. The people tried to *plead* their case, but Jeremiah repeated God's charge of rebellion (v. 8). God, the Sovereign Lord, **chastened** His **children** repeatedly, but they **devoured** His spokesmen the **prophets** like hungry mountain lions.

2:31, 32 A **virgin** bride could hardly forget the wedding sash that was the sign of her new status. Yet God's bride Israel had forgotten her wedding adornment, namely, God Himself.

2:33 **taught the wicked women:** This phrase implies that the people of Judah had become so skilled in adulterous ways that they could have instructed prostitutes in new methods of seduction.

2:34, 35 **The blood . . . of the poor innocents:** Provision for the poor was specifically commanded in the Law (Deut. 15:7–11).

2:36, 37 Israel turned every direction but to the Lord. Appealing to **Egypt** would have been as fruitless as appealing to **Assyria** had been in the past. **With your hands on your head:** This was a gesture of grief and remorse—in this case, over Israel's futile pursuits.

3:1 Deuteronomy 24:1–4 forbids a man to remarry his divorced wife if she has remarried and been divorced in the meantime. The implication is that the woman has been defiled by the second marriage. After forsaking God, Israel had taken many other **lovers**—that is, the nation worshiped many other gods. Yet the Lord in His mercy still extended His loving hand to His unfaithful bride. The word **return** implies repentance (5:3).

3:2 **desolate heights:** This term parallels the high hills of 2:20. Upon these barren heights Israel committed physical and spiritual adultery. The word **lain** has strong sexual connotations. Like Arabs who were known for ambushing caravans, Israel lustily sought other gods.

3:3, 4 **Showers** and **latter rain** refer to the two types of rain that fall in Israel in the spring, from March to early April. These rains are vital in the dry land. Even the punishment of drought did not soften Israel's **harlot's forehead.** This term may refer to a distinguishing mark of slaves, or it may describe a person's character (Ezek. 3:8). Israel was like a prostitute who was totally unashamed.

3:5 The plea for God's mercy was a shallow one because the people's deeds were **evil**.

3:6 The reign of **Josiah** (640–609 B.C.) followed the idolatrous reigns of Manasseh (697–642 B.C.) and Amon (642–640 B.C.). **On every high mountain and under every green tree** echoes the words of 2:20 (v. 2).

3:7 **Return** means to return to God in faith

(5:3). Judah had witnessed Israel's refusal to repent.

3:8, 9 Adultery is forbidden by one of the Ten Commandments (Deut. 5:18), the heart of the covenant. Because of Israel's adultery, the Lord presented her with a **certificate of divorce** based on Deut. 24:1–4. As a consequence, in 722 B.C. Israel was taken captive by

IN FOCUS   **"guide"**

(Heb. *'alluph*) (3:4; Prov. 2:17; 16:28; Mic. 7:5) Strong's #441: The Hebrew word translated as *guide* here means "friend." Israel's appeal based on God's friendship with them will avail them nothing due to their hardness of heart (v. 3). This word is translated *companion* in Prov. 2:17 and Mic.7:5, where the subjects are human. In Ps. 55:13, the treachery of a false friend is reproached.

Assyria, and Samaria was destroyed. Judah looked on but did not learn from Israel's example.

3:10 Judah pretended to repent in times of distress, but did not actually turn with its **heart** to the Lord (Deut. 6:5; 10:16). The *heart* means the people's will, mind, and emotion.

3:11 Because it had not learned from Israel's example, Judah was considered more **treacherous** than Israel.

3:12–4:4 This extended summons to repentance consists of a delicate interweaving of appeals, accusations, and promises: (1) summons 3:12, 13; (2) promise 3:14–18; (3) accusation 3:19–20; (4) confession of the people 3:21–25; and (5) recapitulated summons with promise 4:1–4. The final section also provides transition into the foe/nation cycle of 4:4—6:30. God made an appeal as the faithful Husband and Father to the faithless wife and children of Israel.

3:12 The cry **toward the north** may indicate a summons for the northern kingdom in the days of Josiah to repent. **Return, backsliding Israel:** If the people turned in repentance (3:1, 7; 5:3), God's **anger** would not come upon them. The basis of this appeal is that God is **merciful,** faithful to His covenant promise.

3:13 Iniquity refers to the breaking of the covenant commandments. Israel's rebellious iniquity is identified as the pursuit of **alien** gods, idolatry committed throughout the land.

3:14 To marry in this context means to become lord or master. In other words **married**

describes the covenant relation between God and Israel. **take you . . . bring you:** The remnant of Israel would be united with the remnant of Judah on Mount Zion in Jerusalem.

3:15 shepherds: Throughout the Bible the image of the shepherd is an important one. God provides shepherds for His people to watch over them, guide them, care for them, and lead them. From Moses in the OT to Jesus in the NT, God provides faithful, devoted leaders after His own heart. God rules with a heart of **knowledge and understanding,** not falsehood and deceit.

3:16 God ordained that His shepherds would lead Israel through a time of blessing, increase in numbers, and material prosperity. In that future time, the highest symbol of God's presence, the **ark of the covenant,** would no longer be central to the true religion of Israel. God Himself would be central to Jewish worship.

3:17 Jerusalem, not the ark of the covenant, would be **The Throne of the LORD** and the focal point of the world's religion. **The name of the LORD** summarizes the essence of His character and His relationship with His people (Ex. 3; 14; 15).

3:18 Restoration and reunification of Israel, unknown since the days of David and Solomon, would be brought about by God Himself. From the **north,** the direction from which Israel's enemies typically came, God would bring back His people and bless them in the **land** of promise, under the Lord's chosen Shepherd—the Messiah.

3:19, 20 The possession of the **land** was always dependent on the covenant faithfulness of Israel to their God. The Lord's desire has always been to bless His people.

3:21 The confessions and prayers of the people are voiced in the midst of their idolatry. Their cries were but idle words, because they had **forgotten** their God.

3:22 The call to repentance of v. 14 is reiterated in words strongly reminiscent of Hos. 14:1–4. The confession begins with acknowledgment of the Lord as God in accordance with the First Commandment (Ex. 20:2, 3).

3:23 The term **vain,** meaning "falsehood," is found thirty-seven times in Jeremiah, often in reference to idolatry and false prophecy (5:2; 7:4, 9). The mountains were centers of idol worship and thus were strongholds of falsehood. True **salvation** or deliverance could be found only in the true God of Israel.

3:24 Shame is a euphemism for idolatry, which had consumed Israel's thoughts, their flocks and fields, and even their children. The reference to children recalls the human sacrifices in the Valley of Hinnom in the days of Manasseh.

3:25 The people acknowledged the **shame** and **reproach** that they had brought upon themselves. They had **sinned against** God since their days of **youth** in the wilderness.

4:1 The term **abominations** or "detestable objects" is usually used in the context of idolatry in the OT (7:30). **You shall not be moved** implies that repentant Israel would be unwavering in its faith in God.

4:2 The LORD lives: This phrase was regularly used in oaths. When spoken by those faithful to the covenant it should have been a sign of **truth, judgment,** and **righteousness.** These three terms summarize the ultimate and ideal demands of the covenant. They are the standards by which all people, from kings to slaves, were and will be judged. **bless themselves:** The results of Israel's justice and righteousness would have international consequences. See God's promise to Abraham in Gen. 12:1–3 that other nations would be blessed through his descendants.

4:3 fallow ground: This is unused soil, not a regularly plowed field. Israel needed a new field in which to sow its seed of faithfulness, a radical departure from its ways of sin and idolatry.

4:4 Circumcise: Circumcision was a sign of the covenant relationship between Israel and God (Gen. 17:10–14). The intent of God was always that the outward symbol should be a

sign of an inward reality of total devotion to Him (Deut. 10:12–21). **fury:** Jeremiah's stern warning of judgment is given with the picture of an unquenchable fire (Joel 2:3). If the people did not repent of **evil,** destruction would come.

4:5 Jeremiah announced the judgment of Judah and Jerusalem with the alarming sound of a **trumpet,** literally a *shofar* made of a ram's horn. This was the instrument used to sound the alarm when an enemy attacked a city.

4:6 Standard may refer to signal fires that connected Jerusalem with the perimeter fortresses of Judah. Since the foe **from the north** was yet unidentified by Jeremiah, this prophecy probably dates from between 622 and 609 B.C. All of Israel's enemies except Egypt came from the north. Later on, Jeremiah identified this enemy as Babylon.

4:7 Destruction would come as a terrible surprise, like a **lion . . . from his thicket** pouncing suddenly upon its prey. The desolation of the land and the deportation of the people would be the result.

4:8 Sackcloth was a rough-textured fabric worn as a sign of mourning or distress (6:26). **fierce anger:** The burning wrath of God would come as an inextinguishable fire.

4:9, 10 Even Jeremiah was overwhelmed at what God was about to bring upon Jerusalem. This passage indicates the deep inner struggle Jeremiah faced in his proclamation of the divine

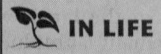 **IN LIFE**   ## Evangelism Through Repentance

Jeremiah's third chapter is a call for the nation of Judah to turn away from idols. In verses 9–13, the people are described as:

- committing spiritual harlotry and adultery;
- being treacherous;
- backsliding;
- transgressing against the Lord; and
- disobeying the Lord's voice.

Yet despite these sins, God extended an invitation to the nation to be reconciled to Him, and to find mercy and healing. The way back was through confession of and repentance from sin, and a wholehearted return to the Lord (3:13, 22).

In the middle of this call to repent, the Lord also revealed His heart for the other nations of the world. First, Israel would return to Him, and then all nations would be gathered around His name at Jerusalem (3:17). People from all over the world would serve Him rather than following the "dictates of their evil hearts."

God's offer of hope and salvation still extends to everyone on earth. As before, His primary strategy for drawing nations to Himself is through His people. In light of Judah's history, believers today do well to consider whether their sins may be keeping others away from the Lord. Is there a need for repentance and spiritual renewal among God's people before evangelism can take place in any major way?

message. Jeremiah challenged God's dealings with His people, claiming that God had **deceived** the people with a message of **peace.** False prophets like Hananiah foretold a time of peace when in reality despair was more in order.

4:11, 12 The sirocco **wind** comes from the deserts east and south of Israel, bringing scorching heat and whirling dust. The divine winds of judgment would bring destruction to Jerusalem, the **daughter** of God. This last phrase is particularly touching; Jacob is God's "son," and Jerusalem is His "daughter" (4:31; 6:2).

4:13 Judah had become the foe of God, and He would use the nation's international foes to discipline them. The imagery of **clouds** and **chariots like a whirlwind** portray the thoroughness and swiftness of God's judgment. The people would respond in horror to their fate.

4:14 The Hebrew word translated **wash** is used in Leviticus and Numbers to describe the cleansing of garments that had become defiled through contact with unclean objects or diseases. Cleansing of the **heart** is foundational to salvation (Is. 1:18–20).

4:15 Dan: The most northern city of Israel proper. Dan was conquered by Tiglath-Pileser III in 733 B.C. and was incorporated as part of an Assyrian province. The city continued to be occupied through the Assyrian period by remnants of the northern kingdom and by foreigners who had been settled there. **Ephraim** was in the southernmost region of the northern kingdom of Israel. The message is clear. Just as Israel had been subjugated, Judah was also in danger.

4:16, 17 Jeremiah, the prophet to the **nations,** announced the attack of foreign enemies who would raise their battle cries against Judah.

4:18 Recompense for **wickedness** that has been done is the order of God's just dealings with His people. Evil and bitterness reach to the **heart,** namely, the innermost depth of one's being. The heart of Judah needed cleansing and

transformation. So does the heart of all people. Judah is not alone here; she is just the Lord's prime example.

4:19–22 The "confessions" of Jeremiah recorded in these verses reflect his deep inner conflict. They present him struggling with the reality of sin and an understanding of the necessity God's judgment over against his personal identification with the people of Israel and Judah. After all, he is a part of the nation; what God was about to bring upon Judah and Jerusalem would affect Jeremiah, his people, and his associates.

4:19, 20 Soul here means "bowels" or "belly," a reference to the internal organs. In ancient Middle Eastern thought, the internal organs were the seat of emotions and feelings. The term describes Jeremiah's inward anguish over the coming destruction of Jerusalem. The phrase **makes a noise** depicts the "groaning" of the prophet's **heart** at the sound of the trumpet announcing Judah's destruction (v. 5). The **destruction** of Judah extended to the entire land, even to Jeremiah's own dwelling place, adding to his misery.

4:21 How long? The prophets often cried out, "How long?" (a phrase found also often in Ps. 13:1, 2). How long would God delay judgment? Jeremiah wonders how long he can endure the anguish of the battle cry. In this and in similar incidents we sense the deep feelings of Jeremiah. The prophets of Israel did not record words of judgment without feeling. The dire messages first affected them deeply; only then could they express these proclamations of doom adequately to the people.

4:22 Foolish describes the character of the people. The terms *foolish* and **silly** are contrary to the terms **knowledge** and **understanding.** God described His people as impudent children. They were **wise** in the ways of **evil,** but totally deficient in knowing how to **do good.**

4:23–28 Jeremiah compares the situation in Judah to a reversal of God's creation. Sin has turned the earth into a desolate waste, like a sea

---

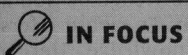 **IN FOCUS** | **"mourn"**

(Heb. '*abal*) (4:28; 12:4; Job 14:22) Strong's #56: This term is one of several Hebrew verbs that refers to the outward acts involved in ancient mourning rites for the dead. Mourning often involved the appearance of an individual: a mourner would frequently wear sackcloth and ashes as a symbol of mourning (6:26)—sometimes even the head would be shaved (Amos 8:10). In the Bible, this Hebrew verb is also translated *lament* (Lam. 2:8). Often the verb is used figuratively of objects that cannot really mourn. Here Jeremiah uses the verb to describe the earth as mourning in reaction to the broken covenant. God's people had neglected their obligations to the Lord's covenant.

without land, like a world without light, and like a desert without a creature.

4:23 without form, and void: This Hebrew phrase is the same one used in Gen. 1:2 to describe the chaos before the ordering of the cosmos. **no light:** The prophets spoke about darkness as part of God's judgment on the world. Here the lack of light describes the disastrous effects of sin on creation, particularly on the land of Judah.

4:24, 25 The symbols of stability and of strength would be shaken as by an earthquake. **Birds** would disappear as Hosea had proclaimed (Hos. 4:3). In Gen. 1, the creation of the birds of the heavens depicts the fulfillment of the creative process. In Jeremiah and Hosea, the removal of the birds symbolizes the reversal of creation.

4:26 The term **fruitful** refers to the region of Mount Carmel, where there were productive vineyards, olive groves, and oak trees. The term is used figuratively to symbolize the productivity of the land as a "garden of God." Yet this also would be turned to desert, namely, desolate and unproductive land.

4:27 Desolate refers to the uninhabitable devastation of Judah as a result of its unfaithfulness. Yet the land would not see total destruction. A slim ray of future hope still existed. God remembers His mercy in His wrath.

4:28 The **black** skies associate darkness with God's judgment. The term **relent,** meaning "to repent" or "to be sorry," parallels the term **turn back.** God's judgment on sin and rebellion is inescapable (Num. 23:19).

4:29 Destruction by foreign armies was concentrated on the cities, which were the centers of insurgence and economic activity. The cities would be left abandoned as the people fled in fear.

4:30 Instead of turning to the Lord in its time of despair, Judah would turn to the idolatrous activity that had caused its dismal plight. To **adorn** oneself in **crimson, gold,** and eye **paint** depicts the seduction of clients by a prostitute. The Hebrew word translated **lovers** describes Judah and Israel's history of physical and spiritual prostitution.

4:31 The voice of God called for repentance; but the **voice** of the people cried out in anguish and despair, but not to the Lord their Savior. **Daughter of Zion:** The term is an endearing way of describing Jerusalem as God's beloved daughter (4:11; 6:2). The use of this warm phrase in such a terrible context heightens our appreciation of the horror of the moment. **spreads her hands:** This phrase portrays the agony of the impending death of Jerusalem. **My soul is weary** suggests dying words of agony and despair. Judah's lovers had become her **murderers.**

5:1–9 These verses contain a description of wickedness. The depths of wickedness in Jerusalem have made her ready for judgment from God. The disintegration of the social, moral, ethical, and covenant life of the city provides the justification for the destruction that awaits.

5:1 Similar to Abraham's plea that Sodom be saved on account of the few faithful people among its inhabitants (Gen. 18:16–33), so Jeremiah summoned the people to search the city of Jerusalem for one just and righteous person. **Judgment** describes one who has done what is right and just before God and man.

5:2 Used at times by the prophets of Jeremiah's day to introduce divine oracles or by people in swearing oaths (4:2), the phrase **as the LORD lives** invokes God's name and character in the proclamation. **falsely:** This often used term in Jeremiah (3:23; 7:9) summarizes the total collapse of the covenant relationship between God and Israel. Instead of swearing in justice, truth, and righteousness, the people swear by falsehood.

5:3 God always looks for **truth** (v. 1) and faithfulness. When truth was found lacking in Judah, God punished the people of Jerusalem through foreign invasion. But rather than responding with remorse and repentance, the people reacted in rebellion. The Hebrew term translated **correction** means "chastisement" or "discipline." Sometimes it means "instruction." In the prophets it generally refers to God's attempt to teach His children faithfulness by means of discipline or punishment (7:28). But despite the words of Jeremiah and other prophets, Israel refused correction and continued down the path of self-destruction. The illustration of **faces harder than rock** emphasizes the rebellious attitudes of the people.

5:4 Here the term **poor** is paralleled by the word **foolish,** a rare term used by Isaiah (19:13) to refer to the nation as deluded and deceived. Thus the word *poor* refers to those who lack knowledge of God and are insensitive to His instruction and inattentive to His will.

5:5, 6 Greatness is achieved not by wealth and power but by the knowledge of God and obedience to Him. **known:** The word refers to intimate and practical knowledge. Here the knowledge is of the **way of the Lord**—the path characterized by truth, justice, and righteousness. Jeremiah paints a picture of Judah as oxen that have **broken** their **yoke,** wandering aimlessly through the field, guided by their own desires. Because they have broken the yoke, they are exposed to the elements and the wild animals of the forest and desert. The animals symbolize the foreign nations who would lay siege to their cities. The cause of the devastation is the many **transgressions,** meaning "rebellions," and **backslidings,** or "turnings," of Judah.

5:7 The message is still addressed to the leaders of Judah (v. 5). The word **pardon** means forgiveness that cannot be granted where there is no repentance, but only continual abandoning of the ways of the Lord. **not gods:** The use of this phrase, found also in 2:11 and 16:20, is tantamount to declaring the nonexistence of the foreign deities that Judah worshiped. The words **your children** refers to the children of the leaders, who are the leaders' children and not God's. **I fed:** The term means God had satisfied their every need. **adultery . . . harlots' houses:** These terms refer to physical adultery, though the source of this immoral sexual conduct may have been the presence of pagan cultic prostitutes. The prophets generally referred to cultic prostitution as adultery.

5:8 In the context of Josiah's reforms, the men may have turned from cultic prostitutes, whom the king had eradicated, to ordinary prostitutes. From the brothels they turned to one another's wives. Like **stallions,** their lust was uncontrollable.

5:9 The Hebrew word translated **punish,** literally meaning "to visit," can be used of the visitation of God in mercy (Ps. 65:9) or in wrath. Here it clearly refers to wrath.

5:10, 11 An unidentified adversary is called upon by the Lord to attack Jerusalem, but not to utterly destroy her. **her branches:** The degenerate, unfaithful limbs would be pruned because they were not His.

5:12 The people **lied** about the Lord, denying that **He** was about to inflict a horrible defeat. They had deceived themselves into thinking that God would not punish His own city and people, forgetting the negative effects of disobedience to the covenant (Deut. 27; 28).

5:13 False **prophets** like Hananiah (28:11) had foretold a time of peace and deliverance from the domination and destructiveness of their enemies. But their **word** was like an empty breeze. The very **sword** (v. 12) they denied would seal their fate.

5:14 Lord **God of hosts:** This phrase reminds the hearer that the true God of Israel controls all of the forces of heaven and earth. **this word:** This refers to the proclamation of Jeremiah, who voices the words of the Lord with the intensity of a blazing **fire.**

5:15 The true prophet Jeremiah announces the imminent coming of a **mighty nation** from

distant lands who will carry out the divine purpose. The nation is not named, indicating that the oracle predates the advent of Babylon under Nabopolassar and Nebuchadnezzar. The only identification is that the enemy speaks a tongue unknown to the people in Jerusalem.

5:16 quiver . . . open tomb: The enemy archers are deadly; their arrows bring sure death to their enemies.

5:17 The word **eat** is used four times in this verse to paint an image of the enemy as consuming field, flock, and fortifications.

5:18 In the middle of a prophecy of judgment, Jeremiah includes a word of hope. The phrase **in those days** is indicative of the judgment God would visit upon His people. God would not destroy His people, but He would make them suffer greatly. One of the notable themes of the Bible is the doctrine of the "remnant," which is the part of the people that God preserves. Only what remained of the people after the devastation of Jerusalem by the Babylonians in 586 B.C. was able to return seventy years later. But it was foretold that there would be a remnant to return (46:28).

5:19 In summary, Jeremiah repeats two key words describing the sins of Judah and Israel: **forsaken** (abandonment) and **foreign gods** (idolatry; see 1:16; 2:13). Since Judah persisted in worshiping gods from foreign lands, God would allow them to be deported and serve their enemies.

5:20–31 These verses provide further elaboration and reiteration of the sins of Judah. The people are slack of heart, rebellious against God, and abusive of others.

5:20 house of Jacob: Even after the northern kingdom had been destroyed, the prophets still spoke of Israel. There was not a complete destruction of the northern tribes, as is commonly assumed.

5:21 foolish: This term emphasizes the people's ignorance of the ways of God. The parallel phrase **without understanding** shows the waywardness of the mind of the nation. Judah's blind eyes and deaf ears were a fulfillment of Isaiah's prophecy more than one hundred years earlier (Is. 6:10).

5:22, 23 To **fear** God is to acknowledge His majesty and to submit to His will. The negative rhetorical questions highlight Judah's refusal to submit to and to serve God. Instead, they bowed to the many foreign gods who were entirely powerless. God controls the sea, the realm of the mythological Canaanite gods Yamm and Lotan

The prophets generally referred to cultic prostitution as adultery.

(Is. 27:1). The people of Israel feared the sea, so they hired Phoenicians (worshipers of Yamm) to captain their ships (1 Kin. 10:22). They were ignorant of their own God's power over the seas (Ps. 93).

5:24, 25 The **fear** of the **Lord** is associated here with His creation of the natural world. **our God:** This title indicates the covenant affinity between the Lord and His people, which was sadly lacking in their **heart** and mind. **Who gives rain:** In the Canaanite fertility cult, Baal was viewed as the provider of the rains that enriched the soil and brought productivity (1 Kin. 17:1). Elijah's victory over Baal and Asherah on Mount Carmel demonstrated that the God of Israel was the true provider (1 Kin. 18). **former:** The former rains descend in the fall of the year, beginning in September or October. The **latter** rains come in the spring, lasting until March or April. Because no rain falls in the summer months in Palestine, water is a precious commodity. **weeks:** The underlying Hebrew term is also the name of the pilgrim festival that followed Passover by seven weeks. The Feast of Weeks (known as Tabernacles and New Wheat) served as a time for the people to celebrate God's rich blessings in the harvest. In the Passover ritual, sheaves of barley grain are "waved" before the Lord. In the Feast of Weeks freshly harvested sheaves of wheat are presented before the Lord as a sign of His mercy in the crops of the field. Sadly, the wicked people had not been acknowledging the Lord; they had become enamored with Assyrian and Moabite substitutes (such as Baal and Asherah). The living God of Scripture will not be one among others; He alone is God (Deut. 6:4).

5:26–29 the wicked: Those responsible for the welfare of the whole populace had abused their positions by exploiting the lesser elements of Israelite society. The picture presented is one of **birds,** or the poor, being ensnared by **great** men who were building wealth at the expense of orphans and the **needy** (Deut. 10:18).

5:30, 31 Jeremiah describes the moral depravity of Judah's leaders as **an astonishing and horrible thing.** The deterioration of the leadership of the land reached to the **prophets** and **priests,** the same people who were to be the mainstays of righteousness among the people. The prophets were charged with the proclamation of the truth, justice, righteousness, and the will of God. The priests were the teachers of the Law as well as sacrificial overseers. Both offices had succumbed to the temptation of abusing of their power, rejecting their responsible roles as messengers and servants of the Lord.

6:1–8 These verses contain an announcement of impending disaster. The prophet sounds the alarm of the oncoming enemy siege from the north and describes the incursion. The inevitable judgment was at hand, and only a glimmer of hope remained for a reprieve from total annihilation for the people of God.

6:1 The siege alarm was sounded to the cities surrounding Jerusalem. Jeremiah called his own tribe of **Benjamin** in the north to abandon the city for more secure territory. To the south in **Tekoa,** the watchman's **trumpet** was blown; to the west in the **Beth Haccerem** region, communication signal fires were sent. The offensives of Sennacherib in 701 B.C. and of Nebuchadnezzar in 586 B.C. brought siege forces from both the north and the south. The origin of the **disaster** is the north, the direction from which most of Israel's enemies approached Jerusalem.

6:2, 3 Jerusalem is compared to a **lovely woman,** the beautiful **daughter . . . Zion** (4:11, 31), against which armies (**shepherds**) would come and lay siege walls and camps.

6:4, 5 Prepare or "make holy" speaks of ritual sanctification performed in preparation for battle. The words are overheard in the camps of the enemies who are about to come against Jerusalem. Sorcerers and diviners were called upon to perform sacrifices to determine the will of the gods and assure a successful outcome in battle.

6:6 The terminology implies that God Himself was the true combatant against Jerusalem. Though the enemies were calling on their supposed deities for help in their siege against Jerusalem, it was the Lord who would fight for them and assure the defeat of Jerusalem. **Cut down trees . . . build a mound:** A siege mound was a ramp of wood, stone, and sand that sloped toward the wall of a city. Armored siege machines could go up the ramp and attack the city walls. The reason for the assault was the **oppression** within the city. The leaders were abusing their power, especially against the poor, widows, and orphans (Deut. 14:29).

6:7 Jerusalem had become a well of bitter and polluted waters rather than fresh and pure **water. Violence and plundering** characterized the city that was once overflowing with peace, justice, and righteousness. **Grief and wounds** describe the sickness and injury that would continually plague the inhabitants. The horrors of the siege of Jerusalem by the Babylonians in 588–586 B.C. were unspeakable (the Book of Lamentations).

6:8 Instructed can also mean "disciplined" or "chastened." Jerusalem was advised to heed the discipline of the Lord or face imminent desolation as a result of His departure.

6:9 The Lord of hosts may also be translated "The Lord of armies" (2:19; 5:14). Those who cultivated grapes in ancient Israel were required by law to allow the poor to **glean** their vineyards. Gleaning was the process of going back over the vineyard after the main harvest to gather every last grape that the harvesters had missed. Jeremiah used this metaphor as a powerful image for what the Babylonians would do to the **remnant** of Israel. Not only would Nebuchadnezzar's army capture the city—the main harvest, in a sense—but would then come after the survivors to **thoroughly glean** what was left. Every person among the **remnant** of Israel would know God's judgment. **put your hand back:** Jeremiah had to return to his proclamation so that no one would be unaware.

The prophet was both angry and weary with the entire nation.

6:10–15 This section deals with the false hope of an unfaithful people and takes the form of a dialogue between God and Jeremiah.

6:10 Because their ears were **uncircumcised,** meaning that their lives were not devoted to the Lord, the citizens of Jerusalem were incapable of keeping the covenant. Furthermore, their rebellion had become so ingrained that the **word of the Lord** had become a disgrace to them. The revelation of God's divine will was no longer a **delight** to them.

6:11 Jeremiah's own emotions reveal his identification with God's feelings about Judah. The prophet was both angry and **weary** with the entire nation, from the youngest of **children** to the oldest of the **aged** men. God's judgment, as well as His blessing, has no special regard for age or gender, class or position. The wicked are wicked together; the righteous are righteous together. The ground is even both beneath the Cross of the Savior, and on the battlefield of the avenging Divine Warrior (Rev. 19).

6:12 The entire **land** and its contents would be given to others by the power of the **hand** of God. God's hand had saved the people; it would also bring about their judgment.

6:13 The accusation of **covetousness** suggests monetary gain by means of deception and fraud. Even those called to guide the nation in its covenant relationship had defrauded God and people.

6:14 The religious leaders sought to comfort the people with a message of hope and **peace.** But such words were not the word of God. *Peace* describes the wholeness of life, the safety, security, and tranquility of heart and mind that come from living by faith according to God's Word.

6:15 Nor did they know how to blush: The people had lost all sense of what was right before God. **they shall fall:** Everyone would experience the harsh hand of God's judgment.

6:16–21 This judgment oracle is structured as follows: (1) two indictments (vv. 16, 17); (2) the witness of the nations and the earth (vv. 18, 19); (3) the announcement of judgment (v. 19a); (4) a reiteration of cause (v. 19b); (5) a third accusation (v. 20); and (6) final judgment (v. 21).

6:16, 17 Old paths probably refers to the Sinai covenant and the Book of Deuteronomy, as Jeremiah called the people back to former days of steadfast devotion. The people obstinately refused to **walk** rightly and **find rest.** They also refused to **listen** to the alarming **sound of the trumpet,** denying that any danger existed.

6:18, 19 The **nations** and the **earth** are called to witness the stubborn character of Judah (Is. 1:2; Mic. 1:2). **My words . . . My law:** The revelation of God through Moses and the prophets was rejected by the people for whom it was prepared and given.

6:20 Even if the people used the most expensive offerings available in the markets of that day, their sacrifices were still neither **acceptable** nor **sweet.** The **burnt offerings** were the "holocaust" offerings, in which the entire animal was consumed by fire. The **sacrifices** were those that were partially consumed by the offerers. The people performed these sacrifices incorrectly, making themselves the primary beneficiaries of their own worship.

6:21 The entire nation will reap the judgment.

6:22–26 This section is the sixth oracle featuring the foe from the north (1:13; 4:5, 15; 5:10; 6:1); each is presented with growing intensity. The foe is depicted as cruel and merciless, bringing anguish and sorrow upon the people of Judah and Jerusalem.

6:22 The **people** from the **north** are as yet unidentified, except that they come from the **farthest parts of the earth.** From this phrase, some have identified the foe as the Scythians, a nomadic marauding tribe from the region of modern Ukraine. The Scythians were a powerful force in seventh and sixth centuries b.c., as Assyria declined and the Medes ascended.

6:23 This marauding foe is skilled at warfare with the **bow, spear,** and **cavalry,** striking with merciless cruelty. The divine pathos echoes from this verse. God loves His spiritual children, even though they are flagrantly disobedient.

6:24, 25 Anguish or distress overwhelmed the people. Their **pain** is compared to childbirth. The people were prisoners in their own city.

6:26 Daughter of my people may be rendered "O Daughter, My people" (4:11, 31; 6:2, 23). Jeremiah used an endearing word for Jerusalem even in the middle of this warning of coming judgment. The most dreaded loss for an ancient Israelite family was that of an **only son. Sackcloth** was a dark, coarse fabric of goat or camel hair (4:8). To **roll about in ashes** symbolically expressed sorrow and despair.

6:27 The Lord describes Jeremiah's role. The prophet would act as the nation's **assayer,** the one who tests or evaluates quality or purity. **fortress:** An alternative translation of this term is *tester* or *assessor,* which might fit this context better as a synonym for *assayer.*

6:28 Jeremiah gives his assessment of the people. **Rebels** speaks of their defiant attitudes. **Slanderers** refers to those who tell tales. **Corrupters** refers to those who destroy.

6:29, 30 Jeremiah assesses Judah as a refiner purifies **silver,** using **lead** to remove impurities (9:7). The lead is consumed, so the dross in the silver ore cannot be purged. This results in the refiner discarding the ore because it is so impure that the smelting process is not worth the energy it takes. Similarly, God rejects those whose wickedness cannot be refined.

7:1–15 This passage (called the Temple Sermon) marks the advent of a series of four prose oracles dealing with false religion, from the Jerusalem temple cult to the aberrant worship of foreign deities. The Temple Sermon counters the popular theology of Jeremiah's day that Jerusalem and the temple of the Lord were inviolable. We speak about this today as "the temple cult heresy." The sacrificial activity flourished, and prophetic activity was thriving. The people presumed that the copious cultic activity secured the sanctity and safety of Jerusalem and its worship center. But their ritual was devoid of heart devotion, as the ethical demands of the covenant were neglected. The date of this proclamation is generally accepted as 609 B.C., in the beginning of the reign of Jehoiakim (the parallel passage in 26:1–24). The passage is structured as follows: (1) introduction and setting (7:1, 2); (2) a call to repentance (vv. 3, 4); (3) stipulations (vv. 5–7); (4) an accusation (vv. 8–11); and (5) a warning of disobedience (vv. 12–15). With the death of King Josiah, Jeremiah recognized that the religious reforms initiated by the godly king were dead. The people returned to their idolatry.

7:1, 2 The word that came to Jeremiah was a direct message from God in His temple courts. **Stand in the gate:** The parallel in 26:2 suggests the proclamation was made in the outer court of the temple, where Jeremiah would have been guaranteed a large audience. **Worship** suggests bowing prostrate in service and obedience to a god, king, or priest. In bowing down, the worshiper pledged himself or herself to obedience in adhering to the demands of the one being honored (22:9).

7:3 The Lord of hosts can also be translated "God of armies" (2:19; 5:14; 6:9). **Amend:** The call to repentance here uses a different term (26:13) from the usual word translated "return" (3:1). A complete transformation of the people's **ways** and **doings,** lifestyle and beliefs, was necessary.

7:4 Trust conveys the sense of security and confidence that the people had in their holy place. They believed that since God had chosen Jerusalem as His dwelling, had promised that a Davidic king would remain on the throne forever, and had delivered the city from attack in the days of Hezekiah and Isaiah, He would never allow the city or the temple to be destroyed. **Lying words** may refer to the unfounded reliance on the temple as an idolatrous symbol or to the worship of foreign gods. **The temple of the Lord** had become a good luck piece to the Israelites. They believed the building guaranteed their security, regardless of whether they obeyed the provisions of the covenant. This false hope was a lie (3:23; 7:9; 8:8).

7:5, 6 The only true hope for dwelling in the context of the temple was a radical restructuring of Judah's society. **Thoroughly amend,** or "make good" or "do good," emphasizes the necessary transformation of Jerusalem's inhabitants. **thoroughly execute judgment:** The emphatic phrase form implies the depth of corruption that existed in the land; there was no justice. **Stranger** refers to resident aliens who were dwelling in the land. **The fatherless** and **the widow** were accorded special treatment in the Law, but they had been abused by the leaders of Jerusalem. **Innocent blood** refers to those convicted of capital crimes on false charges, such as Urijah the prophet (26:23). Humanitarian concern for all persons was a central element of the covenant. To **walk after other gods** is to serve and worship them.

7:7 I will cause you to dwell: This phrase emphasizes the will and work of God to establish the nation of Israel in the land. In order for the nation to dwell in the land, it had to be faithful to God (Deut. 7:6–11).

7:8 The refrain of v. 4 is complemented here by the phrase **cannot profit** (2:8, 11). The idea that the temple was inviolable was as profitless as the powerless gods that Israel idolized.

7:9 The covenant stipulations that Jerusalem's

inhabitants had violated are listed here (Ex. 20:1–17). **burn incense:** Jeremiah uses this phrase nineteen times in the context of worshiping deities other than God (1:16). **Know** refers to an intimate, purposeful relationship—like that between husband and wife.

7:10 Stand before means "to place (oneself) in submissive service to someone." Entering the temple of God in such a manner while worshiping other gods was incomprehensible. Furthermore, for the people to think that they were secure (**delivered**) enough to perform perverted **abominations** (2:7) was the ultimate hypocrisy. Paul builds on this concept in Rom. 6:12–16.

7:11 den of thieves: Like robbers hiding in a cave for safety, Judah attempted to hide behind the sanctuary of the temple for protection from the divine hand of judgment. But the Lord had **seen** the hypocrisy of Israel's ways. Jesus quoted this verse when He cleansed the second temple (Matt. 21:13).

7:12 Shiloh was the site of the tent of meeting and ark of the covenant in the days of the judges. Leaders in the family of Eli had abused their priestly position for personal gain, and idolatry was rampant in the land. When the Israelites attempted to use the ark as a victory-giving good luck piece, the ark was captured (1 Sam. 4) and the sanctuary was destroyed by the Philistines. The Philistines were instruments of divine punishment for the **wickedness** of God's **people.** God's love for His people does not prevent Him from chastising them for their wickedness.

7:13 All these works are the sins listed in vv. 6, 8, 9.

7:14, 15 The earlier dwelling place of the ark of God, **Shiloh,** served as an example of the impending destruction of Jerusalem. The temple had to be destroyed to vindicate the name of God; the people had to be removed from the land in order to purge it of wickedness.

7:16–20 These verses detail the idolatry of Ishtar (Astarte, the Assyrian goddess of love, fertility, and war). Condemnation of the decadent cultic practices of Judah continues with a judgment oracle set forth as an address from the Lord to Jeremiah.

7:16 God's instruction to Jeremiah, **do not pray for this people,** indicates the extreme depravity of Jerusalem's inhabitants (11:14; 14:11). No manner of **intercession** was to be made on behalf of Judah. God would **not hear** Jeremiah's appeals.

God's love for His people does not prevent Him from chastising them for their wickedness.

7:17, 18 The queen of heaven refers to Ishtar, who was worshiped in open-air cultic centers throughout the eastern Mediterranean region and Mesopotamia. Worship of Ishtar involved the preparation of special **cakes** that bore the goddess's image, as well as **drink offerings** (44:19). The family cooperation in the idolatrous worship of Ishtar stood in direct opposition to the covenant demands that a father instruct his children in the ways of the Lord (Deut. 6:4–9).

7:19 Provoke, meaning "to vex or irritate," describes the effects of Israel's continual unfaithfulness on God. Furthermore, they were bringing harm upon themselves.

7:20 God's judgment on the abominable idolatry of Ishtar worship is described in terms of a fire that cannot be **quenched.** The devastation of the fire would extend to **man, beast, field,** and **fruit.**

7:21–27 The keyword of this passage is **obey.** The psalmists and prophets were unanimous in declaring that God required obedience rather than sacrifice (Pss. 40:6–8; 51:16, 17; Hos. 6:6; Amos 5:21–24; Mic. 6:6–8). Sacrifice could never achieve communion with God apart from a repentant or devoted heart. On the other hand, sacrifice (rightly done) was an absolute necessity in the worship patterns the Lord demanded (Lev. 1—7).

7:21 Add your burnt offerings to your sacrifices: Because the people had missed the true meaning of the Lord's worship, they could multiply their offerings as much as they liked and it would do them no good. The Lord cared for none of their sacrifices. To Him they were simply **meat.**

7:22 All **sacrifices** were not rejected, only those offered without true repentance and a commitment to obey the Lord.

7:23 God required that His people **obey** His **voice. that it may be well with you:** Obedience would bring blessing. When the prophets lashed out against sacrifice, it was not against the sacrificial system as God had established it, but against the corruption of that system as the people practiced it. The same emphasis is found in the NT passages that seemingly speak against the Law. Both the NT writers and the Hebrew prophets denounce the abuses of divine systems in human hands.

7:24 The history of Israel is seen in terms of disobedience rather than faithfulness to the covenant, reflecting the people's **evil hearts** (4:14). The result was a worsening or **back-**

ward direction rather than an improving or forward walk.

7:25 From the days of Moses, God sent His **servants the prophets** to call the nation of Israel to obedience based upon the covenant. **Daily rising up early and sending them** indicates the persistence and urgency of God's message through His prophets.

7:26, 27 Incline their ear suggests eager listening and readiness to obey. **Stiffened their neck** suggests a cold rebuff to the will and work of God. Jeremiah, like Isaiah before him (Is. 6:9, 10), was told that the people would not respond to his message.

7:28 The people were stubborn, rejecting the laws of the covenant. They were persistently disobedient to the **voice of the LORD** revealed through His prophets. **Correction** refers to the instruction of the Law and the prophets (5:3). **Truth** refers to the faithfulness and fidelity that was characteristic of God but absent among His people.

7:29–34 This judgment oracle continues the theme of idolatry and takes the form of a lament, having the following outline: (1) introductory lament (7:29); (2) accusation (vv. 30, 31); and (3) judgment announcement (vv. 32–34).

7:29 To **cut off** one's **hair** was a way of expressing mourning and grief. The act may also have symbolized that Judah had rejected the covenant relationship just as if they had broken a Nazirite vow, a sign of personal devotion that required the hair not to be cut (Num. 6:1–21). **desolate heights:** The place of **lamentation** was the very place where Judah carried on its idolatrous practices (3:2). The Lord had **rejected** this **generation,** even as they had rejected His Law (6:19) and had been rejected by their "lovers" (4:30).

7:30, 31 The **evil** doings of this generation, which had continued since the days of Manasseh, included the placing of **abominations** or "detestable objects" such as idols and pagan altars in the temple of God. The **Tophet** sacrifices, adopted from Phoenician and Canaanite practices, involved the ritual sacrifice of children in times of national crisis or disaster. **burn . . . in the fire:** This took place in the Valley of Hinnom southwest of Jerusalem (called Gehenna in the NT). **I did not command:** In their perverted confusion of God's will, the people perhaps thought that they could alleviate foreign domination, famine, and disaster by sacrificing their children. **into My heart:** The awful concept was totally alien to the mind and will of the living God.

7:32 days are coming: This phrase signifies the advent of a divine intervention in history, usually in judgment. With the phrase **Valley of Slaughter,** Jeremiah uses the prophetic device of changing a name to express the Lord's assessment of the Valley of Hinnom.

7:33 Unburied **corpses** left to the elements and animals were regarded as a horrible desecration in the ancient Middle East.

7:34 Prayer would avail Judah nothing on account of its great sin. The nation would be devoid of all joy and **gladness.** The **land** would **be desolate.** The word *desolate* is used extensively in Isaiah, Jeremiah, and Ezekiel to refer to the devastation in Jerusalem.

8:1–3 In the day when Jerusalem's judgment was fulfilled at the hands of its enemies, the **bones** of its people and their leaders would be desecrated by being removed from their graves. **the sun and the moon and all the host of heaven:** The gods and goddesses to whom Jerusalem looked for deliverance would

---

🌱 **IN LIFE**   ## Which Way Are You Headed?

Faith is not a one-time, sensational event in one's life, neither is it a state of moral and spiritual perfection to which a handful of super-saints attain. Faith is a dynamic, lifelong journey that each believer is on. At any given moment, we are either moving toward God or turning away from Him.

The people of Jeremiah's day stood under God's judgment because they turned away from Him—they "went backward and not forward" (Jer. 7:24). Rather than cultivate a growing relationship with the Lord based on sustained, faithful obedience, they went their own way and followed the "dictates of their evil hearts" (7:23–24).

May that not be true of you! The only way to make progress in your journey of faith is to keep moving toward God as best you know how. You may fail and fall at times, but the main thing is to keep turning back toward God, not away from Him. Paul described this dynamic in his own spiritual experience: "Forgetting those things which are behind and reaching forward to those things which are ahead, I press toward the goal for the prize of the upward call of God in Christ Jesus" (Phil. 3:13–14).

stand over the people's desecrated corpses, which are pictured here as **refuse** or "dung" (9:22). Those who survived the siege and attack as exiles and slaves would prefer **death** over **life.**

8:4–17 In light of the people's continual disobedience, they are foolish to maintain a false

their instincts to migrate, the people of Israel refused to follow God's promptings to obey His covenant. Note that God still refers to the people of Judah as **My people** even though they continued to rebel against Him. **do not know:** Like his northern counterpart Hosea (Hos. 4:6), Jeremiah identified the people's major deficiency as

Some of the people of Judah in Jeremiah's day had fallen so deeply into idolatry that they actually practiced child sacrifice to the pagan god Molech. This despicable practice, condemned vehemently by Jeremiah, was conducted at this site known as the Valley of Hinnom, southwest of Jerusalem (Jer. 7:30–34).

hope of peace. This ill-founded confidence is framed around a series of rhetorical and absurd questions, known as a disputation speech.

8:4, 5 The questions in these verses emphasize the absurdity of Judah's lifestyle. Instead of correcting their erroneous behavior, the people were engaged in **perpetual backsliding,** falling deeper and deeper into sin and despair. **hold fast:** In stubborn defiance, the people clung to their lives of **deceit** or "treachery."

8:6 No righteous or repentant person could be found in the city of Jerusalem. Rather than turning from sin, every person pursued his or her **own course,** a lifestyle leading to destruction. Judah is compared to a **horse** running mindlessly headlong into battle.

8:7 Jeremiah contrasts the citizens of Jerusalem with the birds **in the heavens** who understand the approach of the seasons and **appointed times.** Whereas the birds follow

their lack of knowledge of the Lord and His **judgment.**

8:8, 9 Jeremiah contended with fraudulent scribes and **wise men** whose understanding of the Law Jeremiah deemed **falsehood. False pen** describes the idolatry and errant beliefs of the Jerusalem's leadership. The wisdom of the scribes and wise men was folly and shame, for it was not founded on a true knowledge of God's word and law.

8:10–12 The people had interpreted the Law unwisely, believing that **peace** and prosperity would be granted to them. They were grossly mistaken (6:12–15).

8:13 No fruit can be found among desolate vineyards and trees that have been consumed by the Lord's judgment. In His wrath He has taken away the sustenance He had provided.

8:14 Assemble . . . enter: Judah's inhabitants would gather within the citadel and walls

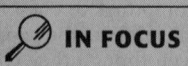

"falsehood"

(Heb. *sheqer*) (8:8; 23:25; Prov. 6:17; 31:30) Strong's #8267: This word refers to all actions meant to deceive others, such as fraud, lying, betrayal, and unfaithfulness. It is sometimes translated *lying* (7:4), *vain* (3:23), or *deceitful* (Prov. 31:30). One of Jeremiah's greatest tasks as a prophet was to speak out against the deceitful schemes of lying prophets (23:9–40). These prophets were prophesying relief for Judah from suffering when God was actually handing Judah over to the Babylonians for judgment (23:17–19). Their deceptive ways made them enemies to the truth, the truth of God's word (Ps. 119:20, 30).

of Jerusalem for protection from an oncoming army. **Silent** can also be translated "perish." The people believed that God was judging them with bitter, poisoned **water,** by which they would surely die.

8:15 The search for **peace** and **health** was hopeless and full of **trouble**—"terror" or "dismay." God's hand of judgment strikes terror in the hearts and minds of those who continue in sin and rebellion.

8:16, 17 Dan lies at the northern border of Israel. In 1:14, 15, Jeremiah warned that calamity would come from the north. The **snorting** of enemy horses would sound the fury of the impending invasion. **His horses:** The enemy's horses were instruments of divine judgment.

8:18–9:1 After the series of judgment oracles, Jeremiah is overwhelmed by his emotions in concern for God's people. The prophet's lament echoes the voices but not the heart of the unrepentant inhabitants of Judah. The outline of the lament is as follows: (1) the introduction (8:18, 19a); 2) an accusation (v. 9b); (3) judgment (vv. 20–22); and (4) the lament recapitulated (9:1). The dominant theme is that of healing.

8:18 The hopelessness of Judah was so overwhelming to Jeremiah that his **heart** was **faint.** The word *faint* describes an illness or sickness that results from great **sorrow.**

8:19 Cry refers to great grief resulting from God's rejection or foreign oppression (Ps. 18:6). **Far country** or **far places** probably refers to the outer reaches of the land of Judah. **Is not the Lord in Zion? Is not her King in her:** These rhetorical questions expect an affirmative response. God, the King, had not abandoned His people; it was the Israelites who had rejected the living God for other gods. **Provoked** vividly describes the defiant attitudes of the people toward the pure worship of God. **Carved images** generally refers to stone idols. The phrase **foreign idols** in Hebrew is "foreign futilities." The people were looking for deliverance in useless and motionless images. Excavations in

Jerusalem dating back to Jeremiah's time have uncovered numerous images and household idols.

8:20–21 Harvest and **summer** represent the two successive phases of the harvest season. The grain harvest was from April to June. The fruit harvest was later. If the former failed, the people could still look forward to the latter. But if both failed, famine was inevitable. For Judah, the harvest season was over; and no fruit had been stored for the winter ahead. Therefore, **we are not saved.** This proverb reflects the sense of helplessness in the early fall. The **harvest** was meager and the oppression persisted. Even Jeremiah was deeply **hurt**—this translates a Hebrew word derived from the verb meaning "to break" or "to shatter"; in other words, the prophet's spirit was broken over the fate of his people.

8:22 Is there no balm in Gilead: The region of Gilead was known for its balsam ointment (Gen. 37:25). There is no healing, physical or spiritual, for a people intent on rebelling against God.

9:1 my eyes a fountain of tears: Jeremiah, who is known as the "weeping prophet," identified personally with the suffering of his people. Here he expresses his desire for a reserve of tears that would flow without stopping.

9:2–11 This section presents judgment juxtaposed against the previous lament. Jeremiah was constantly torn between remorse and wrath, sorrow and anger over the impending destruction of God's people. The theme of this passage is **deceit**, which characterized interpersonal relationships among the people of Judah. This section probably dates to early in the reign of Jehoiakim, about 609 B.C.

9:2, 3 Jeremiah desired a **wilderness** refuge where he would be free from the agony, sorrow, bitterness, and degradation of Jerusalem. The word **adulterers** refers literally to unfaithful husbands or wives, but here to idolaters as those who are spiritually faithless.

9:4 take heed to his neighbor . . . do not trust any brother: The personal affairs of the people were characterized by deceit, slander, and mistrust. Ethical standards had collapsed. **Supplant,** which means "to defraud," is the basis of the name Jacob. As Jacob deceived his brother Esau, so the people of Judah defrauded their brethren (Gen. 27).

9:5, 6 They weary themselves to commit iniquity: The people had literally worn themselves out with perversions. **Deceit** here is the same term used of Jacob's trickery toward Esau (Gen. 27:35). The term refers to swindling by false speech or false scales. **they refuse to know Me:** The essence of Judah's problem was its lack of knowledge of God.

9:7 Jeremiah returns to the imagery of metallurgical refining (6:28–30). God would **refine** and **try** the people by fire to see if any were faithful to Him.

9:8, 9 Jeremiah returns to the imagery of bow and **arrow** to depict Judah's deceit (v. 3). The picture is of a person speaking **peaceably to his neighbor** while lying **in wait** to ambush him.

9:10, 11 weeping and wailing for the mountains: The entire land would be laid waste by destruction. Even the animals would abandon the land because not a crumb of food would remain for the **birds** and **beasts.** The holy city of Jerusalem would become a **den of jackals** where no man or woman lived. Jackals are desert creatures who live far from people. The only way Jerusalem could become home for jackals was for it to be no longer inhabited by God's people.

9:12–16 The explanation for the judgment and lament outlined in 9:2–11 is set forth in prose form in three parts: (1) the introduction (v. 12); (2) the accusation (vv. 13, 14); and (3) the announcement of judgment (vv. 15, 16).

9:12 The wise man observes and understands the natural order and the working of God in the world He has made. No wise person could be found among the inhabitants of Judah and Jerusalem.

9:13, 14 The people's lack of adherence to the covenant they had **forsaken** is indicated by the phrase **have not obeyed . . . nor walked.** The word obey, which comes from the Hebrew verb meaning "to hear," implies an active response to the hearing of God's word. Instead of walking according to God's law, the people walked according to the **dictates** or "stubbornness" of **their own hearts.**

9:15, 16 Water of gall, used in 8:14 to describe God's judgment, refers to some kind of poisonous or salty drink. **scatter them . . . send a sword:** The people of Judah would be exiled from their promised homeland and even

killed as they ran away because they rejected God.

9:17 Skillful wailing women refers to professional mourners, women who attended funerals to express the emotions of those in sorrow. Jeremiah called women to sing laments when Josiah died (2 Chr. 35:25). Here they are called to weep over the collapse of Jerusalem.

9:18 make haste: There is urgency in summoning the skilled mourners to lead the people in tearful lament over the imminent destruction of Judah.

9:19 plundered: This verb, which means "to devastate," is used frequently in Jeremiah to refer to the impending devastation of Jerusalem.

9:20–22 Teach your daughters wailing: The impending disaster in Jerusalem would be so great and the dead would be so numerous that multitudes of trained mourners would be needed. **Death has come** like the Canaanite god of death Mot, who was believed to enter a household through an open window to bring adversity, destruction, and death. **children . . . young men . . . men:** Death claims its victims without respect to sex or age. Corpses would remain in **the open field** like **refuse** or dung (8:2), or like **cuttings** left in the field to decompose.

9:23, 24 wise . . . mighty . . . rich: The people with whom Jeremiah contended were depending on their own capabilities rather than on God. **Glory** may also be translated boast, meaning "to praise oneself." The idea is that people should find their real meaning and true worth in the fact that they know God and may celebrate His attributes. True knowledge of God resulting from an intimate relationship with Him will be demonstrated in a person's character. Three attributes of God that He demands of people called by His Name are **lovingkindness,** meaning "loyal love"; **judgment,** meaning "justice"; and **righteousness,** meaning "uprightness."

9:25, 26 God would **punish** or "visit" Judah, along with its **uncircumcised** neighboring nations. Circumcision, the sign of God's covenant with Abraham, was meaningless without a **heart** faithfully devoted to God. Here Judah is listed as just another nation. In fact, it is not even at the head of the list. The point of this text is similar to the concept of temple inviolability (ch. 7). Just as God would destroy even the temple (7:12–14), so He would ignore even circumcision when it was merely an outward symbol (Deut. 10:12–22).

10:1–25 This text has two major sections: (1) the absurdity of idolatry (vv. 1–16) and (2) punishment by exile (vv. 17–25).

10:1–16 In this poetic satire, the prophet confronts the utter falsehood, absurdity, and futility of idolatry. There are some parallels between this passage and Isaiah 40:18–20, 44:9–20, and 46:5–7. The structure of the section is as follows: (1) introduction (vv. 1, 2a); (2) the powerless gods (vv. 2b–5); (3) the incomparable Lord (vv. 6, 7); (4) the vanity of the false gods (vv. 8, 9); (5) the living Lord (v. 10); 6) the perishable false gods (v. 11); (7) The Lord, the Creator (vv. 12, 13); (8) judgment on the makers of the false gods (vv. 14, 15); and (9) The Lord, the God of Israel (v. 16). The four polemical cycles serve to contrast the Lord and the foreign idols according to various attributes of deity. Idolatry is seen as a rejection of Israel's essential identity. Incidentally, Jer. 10:12–16 is duplicated in 51:15–19, in the oracle against Babylon, the city of innumerable idols.

10:1, 2 The way of the Gentiles was worshiping natural phenomena by means of handmade icons and symbolic imagery. **The signs of heaven** were the astral deities (8:1–3) worshiped in the days of Manasseh and reinstituted following the death of Josiah and the collapse of his reforms. **dismayed:** The heavenly realms held a certain awe or terror for the nations, but Israel was to worship God who held the heavenly realm under His control.

10:3, 4 Customs refers to the practice of constructing deities for worship. **Futile,** which means "vapor," "vanity," or "worthlessness," describes the utter uselessness of idol worship. The process for manufacturing idols begins with the felling of a **tree** for wood, which the **workman** carves. Then the wood is overlaid with **silver and gold** ornamentation to give it

"quality." **Nails** are utilized to provide stability, so that it would not **topple.** But the idols are not always stable. For example, the statue of the grain god Dagon toppled on successive nights before the ark of the covenant in the Philistine temple at Ashdod (1 Sam. 5:3, 4).

10:5 The **upright** idols were dumb and motionless; they required attendants to care for them and carry them from place to place. **Do not be afraid:** There is no reason to fear—let alone worship—objects that are completely powerless, unable to do **good** or **evil.**

10:6, 7 there is none like You, O LORD: This phrase expresses one of the great teachings of the prophets—the "incomparability of God." God is not simply "better" than other gods; He alone is the living God. He is **great in might,** not powerless and motionless like the fabricated gods of the nations. Furthermore, the answer to the rhetorical question expressed in v. 7 is that all would **fear** Him. The idols cause no one to fear them. **King of the nations:** This title reminds us that there is no power in all the universe that may compare to the power of the living God. A righteous king is a **wise** ruler, and none compares to God's understanding of nature and history.

10:8 Dull-hearted can mean " brutish," "stupid," or "unreceptive." The idea here is that instruction received from idolaters is as worthless as the idols themselves.

10:9, 10 Silver came from **Tarshish,** which some scholars have identified with Tartessus in southern Spain. The wooden and metallic idol was adorned with **blue and purple** fabrics,

---

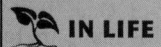 **IN LIFE   Sin Is Sin**

Jeremiah presents a sobering message, both to the people of his day as well as to people today: God is against all sin. His judgment of wrath falls on the sin of all individuals and all nations, without exception (Jer. 9:25–26). It doesn't matter whether one is Jew ("circumcised") or Gentile ("uncircumcised"). No group is exempt. No one has special privileges. As Paul put it, "The wrath of God is revealed from heaven against all ungodliness and unrighteousness of men" (Rom. 1:18). All have sinned and stand under God's judgment (3:10–18, 23).

Jeremiah leaves no room for bargaining. He says that God will punish Egypt, Judah, Edom, Ammon, Moab, and every other nation, even those living in the farthest corners of the earth. That includes all the nations that have ever existed or will exist. Apparently the Lord sees no difference between the sins of Judah and the sins of Egypt, the sins of ancient cultures or the sins of modern culture. Sin is sin. There are no good sins. The sins of one people are as evil as the sins of another.

This is the "bad news" that makes the message of Christ's work on the Cross good news indeed. Yet even the bad news shows that God is as evenhanded in His judgment as He is in His mercy and grace (Rom. 3:29–30). He warns of judgment on all, but He also offers life to all. No one can hide from the all-seeing eyes of the Lord. But no one needs to lose out on His salvation unless that person rejects God's provision, Christ.

whose dye probably originated with the Phoenicians. However, even the most **skillful** or "wise" craftsmen could not manufacture true gods for there is but *one* **true, living,** and **everlasting God.** The fabricated icons were lifeless, deteriorating, false gods who were no more powerful or wise than their makers.

10:11 This verse was originally written in Aramaic rather than Hebrew, the usual language of the OT, but the reason for this change of language is not known. (Aramaic also occurs in Ezra and Daniel.) The message is clear that the helpless so-called **gods** would be destroyed.

10:12, 13 Jeremiah emphasizes the creative power of God, drawing from the imagery of Job 38 and Ps. 8. By God's **power, wisdom,** and **discretion** or "understanding," **the earth** and **the heavens** were brought into orderly existence. By the command of **His voice,** at Creation (Gen. 1:1—2:4), the **waters, lightning,** and **wind** are summoned. Jeremiah reminded the people of Judah that their God not only created the universe but also governs its ongoing life.

10:14, 15 True **knowledge** is found only in relationship to God. **metalsmith:** The craftsmen who used silver and gold for the images they constructed were **put to shame** by their handiwork. The lifeless and useless objects that they fashioned showed that their efforts were **futile.**

10:16 The Portion of Jacob: The Lord is the portion or share of His people, sufficient for their every need. **His inheritance:** Israel belonged to God; God is the sufficiency of His people.

10:17–25 This section completes the collection of oracles addressing the problem of false religion, which has contrasted the wisdom and understanding of people with that of God. The passage moves from judgment (vv. 17, 18), to lament (vv. 19, 20), to judgment (vv. 21, 22), and finally to prayer (vv. 23–25).

10:17, 18 gather up your wares: The Assyrian stone reliefs of Shalmaneser III depict captives transporting household goods on their heads as they go into exile in the eastern reaches of the empire. Soon, this would be the fate of the people of Judah.

10:19 Woe is me: Jeremiah personally identified with Judah and the destruction of Jerusalem. **my hurt . . . My wound:** The injuries inflicted upon Judah were **severe;** the Hebrew text suggests "incurable wounds." **infirmity:** Supplementing the words *hurt* and *wounds,* the word *infirmity* completes the threefold imagery of the damage done to Judah. Writing in triplets was a Hebrew technique to symbolize fullness.

10:20 Like the Bedouin whose tent had been destroyed by marauding bandits, Judah lay **plundered** while its **children** were murdered or deported. No one remained to **pitch** the **tent** and reestablish the nation.

10:21 In the Book of Jeremiah, **shepherds** usually refers to the national leaders to whom God gave the responsibility of maintaining justice. Judah's leaders had become **dull-hearted,** dumbfounded by the chastisement that God had brought upon them. Because the leaders had not **sought** God with a whole heart, they would not **prosper** with the growth of their **flocks.** Instead the shepherds would lose their flocks. The people would be **scattered** like sheep.

10:22 The advance of the foe from the **north** is announced (1:14, 15; 8:16). The armies of this foe would destroy the towns of **Judah,** reducing it to a **desolate . . . den of jackals** (9:11).

10:23 The theme of humankind's limited understanding of the ways of God is renewed. The one who would **direct his own steps** stands to reap the fruitlessness of his labors.

10:24 The Hebrew verb rendered **correct,** which means "to discipline" or "to instruct," has as its goal conformity to the word and will of God. Jeremiah pleaded with the Lord to deal with the nation according to His **justice,** but to withhold His **anger.**

10:25 The passage ends with a prayer to God to bring judgment upon those who destroyed Judah. Though the Gentile nations were not heirs to God's covenant, they would be judged according to His ethical standards.

11:1–17 This section evidences Jeremiah's knowledge of the Deuteronomic covenant and its stipulations for blessings and curses. A covenant is a legal treaty or relationship between individuals, between nations, or—in the case of Israel—between a nation and its God. The covenant specified rights, obligations, and responsibilities of the parties entering into the agreement. The outline of the passage is as follows: (1) exhortation to obedience (vv. 1–7); (2) Judah's disobedience (vv. 8–10); (3) judgment of Judah (vv. 11–14); and (4) the rejection of the Lord's beloved (vv. 15–17). The passage likely dates to the early years of the reign of Jehoiakim, or about 609–605 B.C., when the people ceased obeying the Mosaic covenant.

11:1, 2 Jeremiah's message from the Lord here is strongly associated with the Book of Deuteronomy. The term rendered **words** is the Hebrew name of the Book of Deuteronomy; it is also used to refer to the terms of the **covenant.**

11:3 Cursed suggests the negative provisions of the covenant as summarized in Deut. 27:26 (all of Deut. 27; 28).

11:4 iron furnace: This terminology comes directly from Deut. 4:20, which is set in a context of a warning against worshiping idols. **Obey:** Obedience is the key to blessing (Deut. 27:10; 28:1–14).

11:5, 6 that I may establish the oath: The blessing of the land, as promised to Abraham, was dependent upon the covenant loyalty of the people. The words **Judah** and **Jerusalem** are a standard way of referring to the entire nation of Israel. **Hear . . . and do:** These terms set forth the correct response to God's law.

11:7, 8 The emphatic form of the Hebrew phrase **earnestly exhorted** highlights the history of God's continual urgent—**rising early**—pleas for loyalty from His nation, from the Exodus until the present. The message had been the same from the beginning: **obey. Incline their ear** also means "obey." The Hebrew word translated **dictates** means "stubbornness" or "obstinance."

11:9, 10 A conspiracy is a plot with treacherous intent. **turned back:** The people had returned to the ways of **their forefathers,** who had rebelled against God and the covenant. **Gone after** means "to serve" or "to worship." Both the northern and southern kingdoms had practiced idolatry and broken the first of the Ten Commandments.

11:11 Because the heart of the nation was evil, God would **bring calamity** upon the people. God's justice is inescapable when sin is intrinsic to one's character. Even if the people were to **cry out** in distress, God would **not listen.**

11:12, 13 Rather than accept God's punishment and repent of their evil ways, the nation preferred to **cry out** to other **gods** for deliverance. The **altars** of their **incense** (1:16; 7:9) and sacrifices would become **shameful** objects.

11:14 Judah's status was decided. Jeremiah's **prayer** would be to no avail (7:16; 14:11).

11:15, 16 My house: The nation had no right to worship in God's temple while paying homage to other gods.

11:17 The term **planted** recalls the theme of 2:21, the idea that God had established Israel as His choicest vine. However, here the context is the impending **doom** that would result from the **evil** done by the Lord's people.

11:18–23 The disobedience and obstinacy of the nation is exemplified by the people from Jeremiah's hometown. The faithful prophet, who is rejected by his own, is echoed in Jesus' banishment from Nazareth (Matt. 13:53–58). In this section, Jeremiah typifies the life of our Lord. Jeremiah answers with a judgment oracle against the people of Anathoth. The oracle is then followed by Jeremiah's own reflective words of despair (12:1–6).

11:18, 19 the LORD gave me knowledge: God revealed to Jeremiah a plot against the prophet's life. **a docile lamb brought to the slaughter:** This imagery is reminiscent of Is. 53:7 and the sacrificial death of Jesus Christ. The fellow inhabitants of Anathoth had **devised schemes** for the assassination of the Lord's prophet. **destroy . . . cut him off . . . remembered no more:** The plot is delineated in a trilogy of phrases, which is typical of Jeremiah's literary style. Rejection by friends and the threat of murder are reasons for deepest depression.

11:20 Jeremiah appealed for vindication to God, as the one true righteous Judge. **Mind** is literally the internal organs of the body, and is a way of referring to the seat of human emotion. **Heart** refers to the seat of the intellect and will. **Vengeance** describes God's fury and anger against sin that demands punishment.

11:21–23 The death threats that the **men of Anathoth** made against Jeremiah must have been particularly alarming to the prophet, in that Anathoth was his hometown. Thus, he was betrayed by those who were probably closest to him. The **men of Anathoth** insisted that Jeremiah **not prophesy in the name of the LORD.** If Jeremiah had yielded to their demand, he would have repudiated his calling, his person, and his God. The threat of death to Jeremiah was answered by punishment of the **young men** as well as their children. The prediction of death by **famine** was fulfilled when the city was besieged by the Babylonians in the days of Zedekiah.

12:1–4 In this section, Jeremiah asked why the evil people of Judah prospered. This confession of the prophet reveals his deep personal struggle with one of the questions that faced the wisdom writers of the ancient world: Why do the wicked prosper? The soliloquy unveils the thinking and feelings of Jeremiah.

12:1 Plead means "contend legally." While no legal grievance can be brought against God, Jeremiah could pose legal questions to the righteous Judge.

12:2 The theme of God's establishing the nation of Israel is also found in 2:21; 11:17. The plant had **taken root,** but was producing bad **fruit. near in their mouth . . . far from their mind:** Pious phrases, such as "as the Lord lives," were often spoken by the rebellious leaders of Israel, but without a commitment of their mind (11:20). Sacrifices, oaths, and prayers are ineffectual without a full heart commitment.

12:3 You, O LORD, know me: God's intimate relationship with Jeremiah is evidenced here. The prophet had faced becoming like a

sheep for the slaughter (11:19); here he calls for his enemies to be judged in the same way.

12:4 How long: Jeremiah's question related to God's delay of judgment on the people of the land. **land mourn . . . herbs of every field wither . . . beasts and birds are consumed:** These three elements are recurring themes in Jeremiah and other prophetic texts (4:28; Is. 40:7; Zeph. 1:3). Despite past chastisement, the people believed that God would not bring their country to an end.

12:5, 6 God's response to Jeremiah's question (v. 4) comes in the form of two metaphorical questions. The first metaphor, foot racing, was designed to teach Jeremiah that the obstacles he faced in his hometown were meager compared to those he would encounter before the kings of Judah and Babylon (the **horses**). The second metaphor, **peace,** was designed to remind the prophet of the impending turmoil he would have to endure in proclaiming the message of judgment to an unrepentant leadership. The relatively peaceful setting of Anathoth, with its minor opposition from treacherous family members, served to prepare Jeremiah to struggle against greater antagonists.

12:7–13 The precise setting of this lament is unknown. Yet the context would fit the period after Nebuchadnezzar seized control of Palestine and the vassal kingdom of Jehoiakim. Edomites, Moabites, and others attacked the perimeters of Judah, plundering towns and fortresses and taking captives.

12:7 dearly beloved: God's love and concern for His people does not preclude discipline when their sin makes it necessary.

12:8, 9 Judah had become like a **lion** roaring against God, resulting in His beloved becoming His **hated.**

12:10, 11 Rulers here refers to the foreign kings who had come as agents of God to judge Judah. The repetition of the word **desolate** three times in v. 11 describes the complete devastation of Judah (Is. 6:11). Because of sin, the land that once saw God's bounteous blessing would experience His devastating judgment.

12:12 Destruction would come to the **desolate heights** where Israel and Judah performed their idolatrous deeds (3:2; 3:21; 4:11).

12:13 The imagery turns to the fields, which the Israelites believed were endowed with fertility by Baal. Because of the people's idolatry, their fields were overgrown with **thorns.**

12:14–17 Following the extensive condemnation oracles, the concluding section provides assurance to Jeremiah and the faithful remnant that God will judge even those nations that He has utilized against His own people. The exiled Judah is promised restoration, but is warned about the consequences of future sins.

IN PLACE — Anathoth, Jeremiah's Hometown

Located less than five miles northeast of Jerusalem, Anathoth was a Levitical city (Josh. 21:1–3). It was the hometown of Abiathar the priest (1 Kin. 2:26) and two of David's mighty men (2 Sam. 23:27; 1 Chr. 12:3).

As a Levitical city, Anathoth should have been a model of justice and righteousness. It

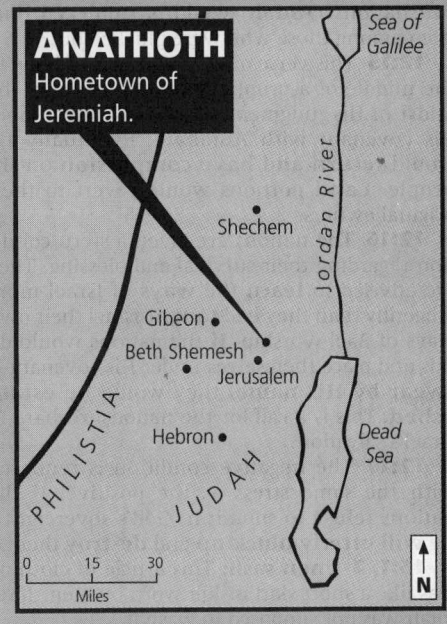

should have been among the first to respond with repentance to Jeremiah's warning of the Lord's impending judgment. In fact, the city had already been captured once before, by the Assyrians under Sennacherib, in fulfillment of God's judgment (Is. 10:30). Yet despite this history, Anathoth rejected both the message and the messenger of God.

12:14 Evil neighbors included the powerful nations of Babylon and Assyria, as well as opportunistic kingdoms like Edom, Moab, and Ammon. These latter kingdoms seized land, crops, and hostages when Judah was weakened by invasion. **The inheritance** refers to the

 **IN FOCUS** "forsaken"

(Heb. '*azab*) (2:13; 12:7; Is. 1:4; 54:7) Strong's #5800: The prophets frequently used this term to describe the people's relationship to the covenant God made with them. Israel is described as "forsaking" God and His covenant by turning to idols (22:9; Ezek. 20:8). Moses warned the Hebrews about breaking God's covenant and forsaking Him. Because of their unfaithfulness, God would in turn forsake His own people (Deut. 31:16, 17). Here the prophet Jeremiah indicates that this divine threat had become a reality for the nation of Judah (12:7).

land that God gave His people under specific conditions. **Pluck . . . out,** which means "to root out, destroy," is often used in the Book of Jeremiah in the context of God's retribution on evil nations. **Judah** would be "plucked out" from among those who were plucked out.

12:15 This verse offers a glimmer of hope in the middle of a prophecy of judgment. In the midst of His judgment, God would remember His covenant with Abraham. Eventually He would **return and have compassion** on His people. **Land** portions would revert to their original owners.

12:16 The nations are given a stern condition regarding their survival and blessing. They are advised to **learn** the **ways** of Israel more diligently than they had **taught** Israel their own ways of Baal worship. **If** the nations would do this and place themselves under His covenant— **swear by His name,** they would be **established.** This is a call for the nations to share in Israel's salvation.

12:17 The negative condition is rendered with the same stress as the positive. If the nations refuse to submit to God's sovereignty, He **will utterly pluck up** and **destroy** them.

13:1, 2 linen sash: This article of clothing was like a short skirt or kilt worn by men. Jeremiah was not supposed to wash it.

13:3–5 Jeremiah was commanded to take his linen **sash** to the **Euphrates** River and **hide** it between the rocks. Since this would have meant a round-trip journey of some seven hundred miles—a trip that would have taken two to three months—some scholars have suggested that the river, generally translated as Euphrates, was within Palestine, perhaps the springs at the head of the Wadi Farah.

13:6, 7 Because Jeremiah's sash was dirty and then was exposed to the elements, it was **ruined** and **profitable for nothing.**

13:8–11 As Jeremiah's waistcloth was ruined (v. 7), so Judah's **pride** would be reduced to **ruin.** *Pride* describes the self-exalting conduct that characterized Israel in its love for idols. This pride is explained in a triplet of verbal phrases:

refuse to hear . . . follow the dictates of their hearts . . . walk after other gods. Jeremiah's undefiled waistcloth in v. 1 symbolized unspoiled Judah in its early days of devotion to God, tightly bound to Him in covenant faithfulness. But as the waistcloth became ruined near the Euphrates, so Judah defiled itself by its allegiances to Assyria, Babylon, and their national deities.

13:12 Jeremiah's quotation of a well-known proverb on the blessing of plentiful **wine** would be met with a derogatory response. The **bottle** was a clay storage jar used for wine, water, and oil.

13:13 Blessing turned to debauchery among the leaders and citizens of Jerusalem. The listing of **kings, priests, prophets,** and **inhabitants** is a means of depicting the entire religious and political nation by listing the different parts.

13:14 The wine jars of God's wrath would be smashed and broken together, a picture of a devastated nation. The triplet of synonyms for compassion—**pity, spare,** and **have mercy**— heightens the effect of hopelessness in Judah's situation.

13:15 Proud here refers to self-exaltation and contempt for the **spoken** or revealed word of God.

13:16 To **give glory** to God is to exalt and worship Him. This verse warns of the consequences of failing to glorify God. Four Hebrew synonyms for darkness are found in this verse, deepening the impression of divine displeasure meted out against God's people. In the rugged **mountains** that dominate the landscape of Judah, where walking in the **dark** is hazardous, no hope or **light** would be discerned.

13:17 Jeremiah had been told not to pray for the rebellious and unresponsive people of Judah (7:16; 11:14; 14:11), but here he expresses **in secret** his deep lament for the **Lord's flock,** who had been carried away into exile.

13:18, 19 The king and **the queen mother** are Jehoiachin and his mother Nehushta, who were exiled by Nebuchadnezzar

(2 Kin. 24:8–12) after only three months on the throne in Jerusalem. **Humble yourselves:** Jeremiah advised the royal household to submit to Babylon. Judah had established a series of fortresses in the **South** that were an important line of defense from the days of Solomon to Zedekiah. They were a source of pride for the military but were destroyed by the Assyrians and again by the Babylonians.

13:20 Those who come from the north refers to the Babylonians.

13:21 you have taught them . . . to be head over you: This verse seems to indicate that Judah had cooperated with its enemies as they began to dominate the nation. The metaphor of childbirth portrays Judah reaping the fruits of its labors in pain and anguish.

13:22 Your skirts have been uncovered: Judah would be shamed by its conquerors in the same way that a prostitute was publicly disgraced.

13:23 The negative rhetorical question confirmed Judah's inability to change its own ways. The nation had reinforced its habit of doing **evil** (4:22) for so long that it did not know how to **do good.**

13:24, 25 The consequence of Judah's continual rebellion would be the scattering of its inhabitants like chaff or **stubble** driven by the desert **wind.** The word rendered **falsehood** is one of the key terms Jeremiah uses to refer to the fraudulent worship of foreign deities.

13:26, 27 Uncover your skirts refers to public exposure (v. 22). Since Judah had lustfully sought adulterous relationships with foreign gods and goddesses, God would expose and bring to **shame** its actions. **Adulteries** are literally sins against marriage. Applied to Israel the term means involvement with another nation's gods. **Neighings** refers to animals in heat pursuing mates. **The lewdness of your harlotry** describes both physical and spiritual prostitution.

14:1–15:21 This extended lament over Judah is composed of a series of short dirges, judgment oracles, and confessions, concluded by a word of assurance to the prophet from the Lord.

14:1–10 This lament over the drought and pestilence that have befallen Judah is outlined as follows: (1) an introduction (v. 1); (2) the drought situation depicted (vv. 2–6); (3) a cry to the Lord for deliverance (vv. 7–9); and (4) an accusation (v. 10).

14:1 Droughts were viewed as indicators of divine displeasure, as in the idolatrous days of Ahab, Jezebel, and Elijah.

14:2 Four short clauses using four words for lament profile the mourning of the country. The Hebrew word translated **mourns** is a general

term for grief over the dead. **Languish** means "to wither" or "to shrink back." The Hebrew word for **mourn** describes the dark gloom of weeping and wailing. Finally, **cry** describes a clamoring cry of joy or sorrow.

14:3, 4 nobles: The men of renown, who could have afforded any price for water, sent out servants to search in all the normal locations for water, but **no water** could be **found.** The rain-starved farmlands were scorched by the sun, and the farmers **covered their heads** in mourning.

14:5, 6 The drought of Judah affected even the wild animals. The doe abandoned its fawn for lack of forage. **Wild donkeys stood** on barren hills, sniffing the wind for the scent of moisture—to no avail.

14:7 Jeremiah echoes the sentiments of his people in his plea for forgiveness and deliverance for the nation. The Hebrew word translated **iniquities** refers to the accountable guilt that results from continual unconfessed sin.

14:8, 9 Jeremiah pleaded with God on the basis of His name and character, particularly His role as the **Hope** and **Savior** of His people. Instead of having an intimate relationship with Judah, God had become like **a stranger** or **a traveler** in the land, for the people worshiped other gods.

14:10 Unlike the troubled Jeremiah, the **people** were unrepentant and in need of correction. Jeremiah realized that judgment was inevitable because God offered no hint of deliverance. **they have loved to wander:** *Loved* describes voluntary desire. *Wander* describes a repetitive back and forth movement—in this case, of seeking every possible occasion for sin. Because no one displayed any restraint from sin, God could not violate His holy character and **accept** the people of Judah.

14:11, 12 Because divine discipline was inevitable, Jeremiah was instructed **not to pray** for the **good** of Jerusalem. **fast . . . offer burnt offering:** These methods of expressing penitence and establishing communion with God were ineffective because of the people's disobedience. The doom of Judah was sealed.

14:13 Jeremiah complained to the Lord about false **prophets** who were proclaiming a message of **peace** instead of war and pestilence. These pretentious prophets presumed upon God's mercy and promise of deliverance as demonstrated in the days Hezekiah and Isaiah, when Jerusalem was miraculously rescued from the siege of Sennacherib's army.

14:14 The prophet who truly speaks in the **name** of God will see his words come to pass. The false prophets who promised peace (v. 13) spoke **lies** of their own device (2 Pet. 1:19–21). **Divination** is prohibited in Deut.

18:14. **Worthless thing** is a degrading description of the idols that were worshiped in the days of Isaiah (Is. 2:8) but condemned by the Law (Lev. 19:4).

14:15, 16 God's condemnation would fall first on the false **prophets** because of their prophecies of peace (v. 13). Next in line for judgment would be the inhabitants of the city who had been deceived by the false prophets. Individual responsibility for one's sins is one of the key developments in Jeremiah. Destruction and desecration will befall them; none will survive to properly dispose of the bodies. This imagery of exposed corpses—the ultimate desecration—occurs earlier in 7:33, 8:3, and 9:22.

14:17–22 This section continues themes from vv. 1–16 of God's relentless judgment, lament of prophet and people, and the futility of intercession on behalf of the nation.

14:17, 18 The setting for this lament over the desecrated **city** may be either 597 B.C., when Judah was invaded, or 588–586 B.C., when Jerusalem fell. Jerusalem is **broken** by a great **blow** from the Lord. **field . . . city:** The entire region is laid waste. Corpses cover the fields, a continuation of the imagery of verse 16, and the city is filled with famine. The religious leaders wander aimlessly in an unidentifiable land.

14:19 A series of questions probes the issue of God's total rejection of Judah. The concept was foreign to the peoples' minds, evidencing an obliviousness to the potentiality of the covenant curses. The latter part of the verse is a duplicate of 8:15. The people begin to understand their hopeless situation.

14:20 The people of Judah acknowledged their **wickedness,** meaning "rebellion," their **iniquity,** meaning "perversity," and the fact that they had **sinned.** This triplet of terms indicates the pervasiveness of sin in the land.

14:21, 22 The people's plea for God's mercy was based on His character—His **name's sake,** His **glory,** His **covenant** relationship with Israel, and His power over creation. Entreaties based on divine character and attributes are common in the Psalms. At stake was God's reputation and the blessing that would come to the people, but here the obligations of the people to the Lord are disregarded.

15:1–9 The message of judgment is resumed, with the present oracle building upon the theme of the people's plea in 14:17–22. Despite the request for relief on the basis of the covenant, the Lord is bringing destruction and devastation based upon the same covenant.

15:1 When **Moses and Samuel** interceded with God on behalf of the nation, God responded favorably. However, not even these men of God could alter the Lord's intended purpose for the people of Judah—namely, that they should be driven from the land.

15:2 Death, sword, famine, and **captivity** would be the outcome of God's judgment. He would use foreign armies as instruments of judgment (14:11, 12).

15:3, 4 The **four forms of destruction** describe the complete judgment of Judah. The imagery of **dogs, birds,** and **beasts** devouring human flesh vividly illustrates not only death, but desecration. The basis for this desecration is the defilement of Jerusalem that took place during the reign of **Manasseh,** when idolatry reigned in the temple courts and children were sacrificed to Molech (7:31).

15:5 Rhetorical questions set the tenor for the mournful state of affairs in the once holy city. Desecrated and defiled, Jerusalem is a town without pity; there is none to console her.

15:6 Forsaken means "cast down" or "rejected." The people threw off the yoke of the covenant and went **backward** instead of for-

 IN PERSON　**The Persecuted Prophets**

Throughout his ministry, Jeremiah had to endure intense persecution because of his stand for the Lord (Jer. 15:15). In this he was not alone. Another prophet named Urijah also spoke out against the wicked policies and practices of the leaders in Jerusalem. For this he was sentenced to die, but fled to Egypt. However, King Jehoiakim was able to have him extradited back to the city, whereupon he was put to death (26:20–23).

Later the leaders turned on Jeremiah, launching a campaign of verbal attacks against him and plotting ways to destroy him (18:18). Eventually they put him on trial for speaking against Jerusalem, a charge for which they demanded the death penalty (26:10–11). Fortunately, an official named Ahikam intervened and was able to spare the prophet's life (26:24). Nevertheless, Jeremiah was imprisoned for his message. Yet eventually he was vindicated when his prediction that Jehoiakim would not die peacefully in Jerusalem (22:18–19) came to pass in about 598 B.C. (2 Chr. 36:5–6).

ward in obedience. **My hand** indicates the active power of God in accomplishing His will for His people (Deut. 26:8). **I am weary of relenting:** *Relenting* refers to God's restraining from totally demolishing Israel and Judah. For hundreds of years, the Lord had refrained from fully punishing Israel for its idolatry and unfaithfulness.

15:7, 8 Like wheat chaff that is scattered by the **winnowing** fork and the wind, the people of Judah would be dispersed. The population would be decimated. The further ravaging of the land is revealed in the numerous **widows** who would be left in the wake of the death of the men of Judah.

15:9 The blessing of **seven** sons was the ultimate hope for ancient mothers and fathers. But the utmost horror was to lose all seven in death, resulting in the loss of an heir.

15:10, 11 Every one of them curses me: To curse someone in ancient Israel was to invoke condemnation on that person with a prescribed formula. Jeremiah now comes to the lowest point in his career. Friendless, forsaken, discouraged, frustrated, he even despairs of life itself. But God had not forsaken him. Eventually good would come of this hopeless situation.

15:12 Iron here may symbolize Jeremiah, who was called an "iron pillar" in his call in 1:18. The iron of the north could then refer to the high quality iron from Asia Minor or the Balkans. Otherwise the imagery is that of a powerful foe from the north.

15:13, 14 Judah would be taken captive and exiled to an unknown **land,** as had happened to Israel a century before. **Fire** is often used in the books of the prophets as a symbol of divine wrath and judgment (4:4; 11:16).

15:15 God's **patience** was shown in the way He endured for a long time the sin of His people. Jeremiah requested God to be patient with him and not **take . . . away** his life because of his own rebellion (Jeremiah's lament in v. 10).

15:16 Eating the **words** of the Lord means to internalize them and allow their meaning to become a reality in one's life. Inner **joy** and **rejoicing,** or "abundant joy," are the endowment of the one who knows and is known by the Lord. To be **called by** the Lord's **name** is to be recognized as belonging to Him as a servant.

15:17 Jeremiah's isolation and **indignation** were the results of his obedience to the word and calling of God.

15:18 My pain refers to Jeremiah's internal agonizing over his prophetic role. The **unreliable stream** is a vivid picture of the arid regions of the Middle East, where water is at a premium and streams can run dry without warning.

15:19 The Lord responded to Jeremiah's

impassioned inquiry (vv. 15–18) with a message of repentance and reassurance of Jeremiah's call. **return:** Jeremiah is admonished to "repent" (3:1, 7, 12), after which God would restore him to his prophetic position as God's spokesman. **Stand before** means "to serve"; repentance and divine appointment are necessary for genuine prophetic service.

15:20, 21 I will make you . . . a fortified bronze wall . . . they shall not prevail: Jeremiah was recommissioned with words similar to those of his original calling (1:18, 19). The term **deliver** suggests bringing out from danger, bondage, and oppression. **Redeem** means to rescue from danger. **The wicked** refers to people such as Jehoiakim and the people of Anathoth who had opposed Jeremiah so vehemently (11:18–23). God promises His presence in times of opposition, persecution, and imprisonment for His sake.

16:1–13 Jeremiah's own life became a symbolic act representative of the nation's struggle. This section is an autobiographical message from the Lord evidencing the prophet's own self-understanding. The message is formulated around three prohibitions to Jeremiah (vv. 2, 5, 8), each followed by an explanatory word about the people, and concluded by a standard judgment oracle against the rebellious and idolatrous acts of the people.

16:1, 2 In the case of Jeremiah, the prohibition against marriage was both a sign to the nation and a blight against his name among the people. Celibacy was abnormal; large families were indicative of God's blessing upon a household. Jeremiah faced life with God as his sole comfort and support.

16:3, 4 Had Jeremiah married and had children, they might have experienced the terrifying horror of destruction, famine, death, and desecrated corpses. Death would reach such proportions that mourners would be lacking. **Sword, famine,** and exposed **corpses** are three of the common means of judgment in Jeremiah (7:33; 14:11, 12). The ultimate desecration and abuse of humanity in the ancient Near East was to allow a body to go without proper burial.

16:5 God's prohibition against participating in the customary grief process reveals the abnormal nature of Jeremiah's life. The trio of terms for sorrow—**mourning, lament,** and **bemoan**—is followed by a trio of terms referring to God's faithful care—**peace, lovingkindness,** and **mercies**—from which Judah had been removed.

16:6, 7 The pagan mourning practices of cutting oneself and shaving oneself **bald** were strictly forbidden in the Law of Moses (Lev. 19:28; 21:5; Deut. 14:1). The **bread** of **mourning** and **cup of consolation** probably refer to food and drink brought for the family of the deceased.

16:8, 9 The **house of feasting** was a banquet hall often used for wedding celebrations. Jeremiah was restricted from participating in all meaningful family ceremonies. Jeremiah's life was symbolic of the state of **Israel** and the estrangement between God and Judah.

16:10 The trio of questions posed by the people indicates their lack of understanding of God's word. The people of Judah had missed the purpose for which they were chosen, to manifest to the world the nature and character of God by living as the people of God.

16:11, 12 Judah had **forsaken** its covenant **LORD** and pursued other deities. Abandoning God and His **Law** or "instruction" led to disaster. **listens:** This term is foundational to the nation's existence; it recalls Deut. 6:4, the central creed of Israel's biblical faith.

16:13 The blessing of devotion to God was freedom, prosperity, and large families in the land. Blessing was dependent on obedience; the consequence of disobedience was a dreaded life **out of** the **land,** in a world the people did **not know.**

16:14, 15 the days are coming: The future restoration of Israel would surpass the ancient deliverance from Egypt (23:7, 8).

16:16, 17 The **fishermen** and **hunters** refer to the Babylonian armies that would scour the land for Judah's rebels. Hunting and fishing imagery as a metaphor for deportation is also found in Ezek. 12:13; Amos 4:2.

16:18 Defiled is used sometimes to refer to combined ethical, physical, and spiritual uncleanness. God's **land** or **inheritance** had been profaned by numerous cultic objects, which Jeremiah scathingly refers to as **the carcasses of their detestable and abominable idols.**

16:19, 20 A message of hope begins with a trio of honorific terms for God: **strength, fortress,** and **refuge.** *Strength* and *fortress* are related words in Hebrew, like the English "strength" and "stronghold." A *refuge* is a place of

safety from danger. Jeremiah knew that his only place of strength and safety was in God. The scope of Jeremiah's hope is universal. The Gentiles, among whom the people of Judah would be exiled, would come to the God of Israel in fulfillment of the promise of Gen. 12:1–3.

16:21 know: The message of the collected oracles of chapter 16 is the revelation of the will and work of God. He will personally cause the people to **know** Him and thus enter into an intimate relationship with Him. To know His **name** is to understand His nature and His ways.

17:1–18 This section is composed of four miscellaneous sections (vv. 1–4, 5–8, 9–11, 12, 13) centered on the word **heart**, with a literary bracket formed on the word **written**. Like the collection in chapter 16, the section is concluded by a personal heart confession of Jeremiah (vv. 14–18).

17:1, 2 Judah's **sin** had become so deeply **engraved** that it could not be removed. The **point of a diamond** on **a pen of iron** indicates the permanence of the engraving. The **heart** of the people, the center of their spiritual, emotional, and mental well-being, was inextricably entangled in stubborn rebellion against God. **horns of your altars:** Excavations in Israel have uncovered horned altars at sites such as Dan, Beersheba, and Arad. On some altars bloodstains can still be detected after more than 2,500 years.

17:3 Jerusalem and the other cities of Judah were demolished and plundered by the Babylonians. The remaining **treasures** of the temple of God were carried by Nebuchadnezzar's army to Babylon. Even the idolatrous cultic centers were destroyed (15:13, 14).

17:4 let go: This phrase, when used in the context of land, usually refers to letting the land lie fallow during the sabbatical year (Ex. 23:10, 11). Judah's captivity would provide rest for the land from the idolatrous activities of its people.

17:5, 6 cursed: This term is used extensively in Deuteronomy. Two different words for

 **IN FOCUS** **"heal"**

(Heb. *rapha'*) (17:14; 2 Chr. 7:14; Is. 19:22; 53:5; 57:18) Strong's #7495: This word applies literally to the work of a physician. Occasionally it refers to inanimate objects and can be best translated *repair* (1 Kin. 18:30). But more commonly this word connotes the idea of restoring to normal, as in 2 Chr. 7:14, where God promises to restore the land if His people pray. In the Psalms, God is praised for His role in healing disease (Ps. 103:3), healing the brokenhearted (Ps. 147:3), and healing the soul by providing salvation (Pss. 30:2; 107:20). Isaiah declared that the healing of God's people results from the sacrificial wounds of His Son (53:5–12).

man are used in this passage. The first refers to a strong and capable male; the second is a generic term for humankind as made in the image of God (Gen. 1:26–28). One cannot trust in both God and humankind; to turn one's **heart** toward people is to turn away from God.

17:7 The term **blessed** is used often in the Psalms and Deuteronomy to describe the benefits that accrue to one who is devoted to the Lord and His word. The words translated **trusts** and **hope** are related in Hebrew.

17:8 planted: The imagery of a fruitful tree derives directly from Ps. 1:3. This verse teaches that one who trusts in God will not be free from trials and adversity, but that God will bring fruit and blessing in and through those difficulties (14:1–9; 15:19–21).

17:9, 10 The heart refers to the mind, the source of thinking, feeling, and action. It can betray a person in basic issues concerning the reality of God, His will, and His word. The **heart** can belie the truth. No one can comprehend its true character but God Himself, for only He can discern the motives and the reasoning behind it. God can **know** the **heart,** for only He may **search** and **test** the **mind**. This is a most powerful statement about the process of God's discernment of the inner person. The Lord's justice is evidenced in all His ways, giving people just recompense for all their **ways** and **doings**. God rewards or punishes according to faith, namely, trusting in Him and His name.

17:11 The teaching of vv. 1–10 is supported by a proverb based on the common belief that the **partridge** hatched eggs other than its own. When the young birds recognized that the partridge was not their mother, they would leave her. Similarly, a person who unjustly gains wealth will be abandoned by that wealth and then be known as a **fool.** *Fool* here refers to a person without moral, ethical, or spiritual character.

17:12, 13 A glorious high throne refers to the temple in Jerusalem and the ark of the covenant, the symbol of God's presence and sovereignty over the nation. **The hope of Israel** refers to the expectation of deliverance and the restoration of the faithful (14:8). Judah had nowhere to turn because it had **forsaken** God and His lordship. There is only one source of life and hope for Israel and all nations—the LORD, **the fountain of living waters.**

17:14 Though Jeremiah struggled with difficulties, including persecution and loneliness, he continually turned in **praise** to the Lord who can **heal** and **save.** Likewise, the only hope of healing and salvation for the nation of Judah was divine intervention.

17:15, 16 Some scoffers dared to defy God and the message revealed through Jeremiah,

taunting the Lord to bring the judgment threatened by His spokesman. Jeremiah pointed out that he took no pleasure in proclaiming judgment. He remained a devoted **shepherd** who was intimately concerned for his own people.

17:17 Terror may refer to physical, emotional, or mental horror. The Hebrew word translated **hope,** meaning "refuge" or "shelter," refers to a position of safety and security in the face of danger and helplessness, such as Jeremiah faced in Judah and Jerusalem.

17:18 Jeremiah called for his persecutors to be **ashamed** and **dismayed,** to be dishonored and demoralized. The prophet also called upon the Lord to confirm the message of judgment in the **day of doom** and **double destruction.**

17:19–27 The tenor of the chapter changes abruptly with a specific message on the sanctity of the Sabbath. Unlike many of Jeremiah's oracles, this one is conditional upon the people's response. But in light of previous judgment passages, the likelihood of repentance is remote. The outline is as follows: (1) instruction to Jeremiah (vv. 19, 20); (2) a call to keep the Sabbath (vv. 21, 22); (3) the example of the disobedient ancestors (v. 23); (4) blessings of obedience (vv. 24–26); and (5) the curse of disobedience (v. 27).

17:19, 20 The particular **gate** is not mentioned, though the description would place it in the area of the Davidic citadel. Jeremiah's message was to be proclaimed throughout the city. From **kings** to peasants, all of the **inhabitants** of the city were to **hear**—and obey—the word of the Lord.

17:21, 22 Take heed: This same phrasing is used in Deut. 4:15 in a warning against idolatry. The sanctity of the Sabbath was a most serious matter. The Sabbath stood as a sign of creation and the covenant relationship between God and Israel. To **hallow** it is to set it apart, to distinguish it from other days.

17:23 Abuse of the Sabbath was apparently commonplace throughout the history of the nation.

17:24, 25 If the **Sabbath** was kept holy, signifying the covenant faithfulness of Israel, the nation would retain its sovereign **kings and princes.** In other words, the promise of unending Davidic succession in kingship would be fulfilled (2 Sam. 7:16).

17:26 If the stipulations of v. 21 were followed, the temple would once again become the center of worship for the nation. People would travel from throughout the land to Jerusalem to worship God with their **sacrifices.**

17:27 The consequence of disobedience would be total destruction of the city. If the stipulations of 17:21 were not followed, the Lord of the covenant would bring an unquenchable, destructive **fire** against the city and its **palaces** (4:4; Hos. 8:14; Amos 1:4–2:5).

18:1–20:18 This extended section has three parts: (1) a judgment parable of the potter (18:1–23); (2) a symbolic act: the broken flask (19:1–15); and (3) Pashhur imprisons the prophet named Magor-Missabib (20:1–18).

18:1–23 This section is also divided into three parts: (1) the parable of the potter (vv. 1–12); (2) the people rejected by God (vv. 13–17); and (3) the persecution of Jeremiah (vv. 18–23).

18:1–12 The parable of the potter is the first of several prose autobiographical sign-actions,

Photo: Matson Photo Collection

A potter practices his craft at a revolving turntable. Jeremiah watched a potter like this at work as he refashioned a marred vessel, and he compared it to God's ability to remake the nation of Judah (Jer. 18:1–11).

similar to the symbolic act account, which provide further demonstration of Judah's rebellion against God. Those that are undated belong to the period between the beginning of Jehoiakim's reign to the fall of Jerusalem in 586 B.C. The potter is a symbol of the Lord, and Israel is the clay in His hands.

18:1, 2 Arise and go down is a common formula for divinely directed service.

18:4–6 The potter's **vessel** was **marred** and thus unsuitable for its intended purpose. The potter's remolding of the clay into an acceptable and unblemished work symbolized God's action in reforming Israel. The people had become marred and defiled and had to be

reformed into a vessel fit to be identified with the Lord.

18:7, 8 If a **nation** threatened with destruction would turn **from its evil,** God would **relent of the** promised **disaster.** God the Potter was more than willing to forgive the iniquity and stubborn rebellion of Judah. Unfortunately, the people continued in their stiffnecked ways. In Gal. 4:19, Paul uses this imagery to depict the formation of the image of Christ in the obedient Christian.

18:9, 10 A nation to whom God has promised His blessing may forfeit its preferred status through disobedience. In such a case, God would **relent** of the **good** He had promised and bring calamity upon the rebellious people.

18:11 God was **fashioning a disaster,** a calamity, for **Judah** if it did not repent or **return** to Him and change its actions from **evil** to **good.**

18:12 The people's response to God's warning (v. 11) is similar to that in 17:23: They rebelliously pursued their own ways. **Hopeless** describes the despair the people felt concerning obedience to God. These feelings were the direct result of the **evil heart** that is characteristic of people who continually turn away from the Lord and His ways.

18:13–17 Building upon the rebellion theme of v. 12, Jeremiah emphasizes by means of lessons from nature how unnatural are Israel's actions. This approach develops further the role of the prophet as a wise person who observes and understands nature and humankind (1:11–13; 2:21; 5:22). The form of the passage is the disputation speech, which is composed of rhetorical questions, an indictment, and the delineation of judgment.

18:13, 14 Negative rhetorical questions show the absurdity of Israel's rebellion. **The snow water of Lebanon** describes the Mount Hermon watershed that erupts in numerous springs, providing most of the water for the Jordan River. God's blessing was often demonstrated in the provision of water from rocks in arid regions (Ex. 17:6). No one would trade cool spring water for **strange** or "alien" **waters.**

18:15 The principal indictment brought against Judah was idolatry, which had resulted in the people's wayward lives and the humiliating destruction of the land. **forgotten:** This term is used in the same way in 3:21; 13:25. **worthless idols:** Foreign deities such as Baal and Asherah were represented by empty and ineffective cultic figurines. **they have caused themselves to stumble:** The people had brought upon themselves the droughts and disaster that they faced because they had strayed **from the ancient paths,** the way of the Law and the covenant relationship to God.

18:16, 17 make their land desolate: For similar descriptions of the destruction of Judah, see 4:27; 6:8; 9:11.

18:18–23 Outward proclamation of God's truth can lead to strong opposition, even persecution leading to death. Jeremiah learns about a plot to slander and denigrate him because of his insistence on proclaiming a message of harsh judgment.

18:18 Similar to the situation in 11:18–23, the people devised **plans** to counter the words of **Jeremiah.** They reasoned that with their own priests, wise people, and prophets in Jerusalem, they did not need to listen to Jeremiah.

18:19, 20 Jeremiah reminded the Lord how he had interceded for the people and had asked God to **turn away** His **wrath** and judgment. But instead of showing their appreciation for Jeremiah's intervention, the people **dug a pit** in anticipation of his demise.

18:21, 22 Jeremiah's cry for personal revenge may not be as easily justified as those of the psalmists (Ps. 137). Nonetheless, he had been falsely charged with misrepresenting the truth of God. All the imprecations, or calls for divine cursing, in the Bible have one element in common: though strongly worded, they await the work of God rather than speaking of initiating revenge. **Famine** was one of the curses of breaking the covenant (Deut. 28:48).

18:23 You know: As God had known Jeremiah's heart (12:3; 15:15), so He was keenly aware of the people's plots against the prophet. The Hebrew word translated **atonement** is the same term used in Yom Kippur, the Day of Atonement. The word emphasizes total cleansing and removal of sin and its effects. The word **blot out** is also used to refer to the removal of sin and guilt by God. Jeremiah's appeal was for God to condemn in **anger** rather than to forgive his enemies.

19:1–15 This section has two parts: (1) the broken flask in Hinnom Valley (vv. 1–13) and (2) a message in the temple court (vv. 14, 15).

19:1, 2 A **flask** was a small, narrow-necked water bottle made of clay, six to ten inches tall. **The elders** were summoned to follow Jeremiah to the **Valley of the Son of Hinnom** (7:31, 32), a dumping area where children were ritually sacrificed in the days of Manasseh. The **Potsherd Gate** accessed the valley on the southern side of the city since the days of Hezekiah's expansion.

19:3 Hear: This key word of the Deuteronomic code (Deut. 6:4) calls for a decision regarding the content of the message. **his ears will tingle:** This expression is used to refer to a harsh, ringing judgment announcement (1 Sam. 3:11).

19:4–6 made this an alien place: The people, through their idolatry, had prevented the once-holy city of Jerusalem from being the place where God chose His name to dwell. The city had become a place of alien gods and goddesses. **neither they . . . nor the kings of Judah have known:** The word *know* speaks of an intimate, personal knowledge that it is impossible to have with inanimate physical objects. **The blood of the innocents** refers to the murderous act of child sacrifice (7:31). Human sacrifice was known among the Phoenicians, Moabites, and Canaanites. This abominable practice, performed in the name of religious worship, was explicitly forbidden in the covenant (Deut. 12:31).

19:7 Babylon was the agent who would **make void,** or "lay waste," **the counsel** of the elders who rebutted the Lord's message through Jeremiah and continued in idolatry. The desecration of **corpses** by allowing **birds** and wild **beasts** to consume the flesh would be the ultimate defilement among peoples of the ancient Near East (7:33; 9:22).

19:8 God would allow Jerusalem to be made an object of derision and humiliation in order to vindicate His name (18:16). **Plagues** would strike the city according to the covenant curse of Deut. 28:58–61 (Lam. 2:15; Zeph. 2:15).

19:9 The gruesome practice of cannibalism appears, recalling the words of Deut. 28:53. After years of siege resulting in severe famine, the people would resort to eating human **flesh** in order to survive. This prophecy was literally fulfilled in 586 B.C. when Nebuchadnezzar invaded Judah, and again in A.D. 70 when Titus destroyed Jerusalem.

19:10 After the proclamation of this horrifying message of judgment, the symbolic act is performed before the summoned elders and other inhabitants of Jerusalem.

19:11 As pottery **breaks** into pieces when it is thrown on the hard ground, so God's judgment would shatter the city and scatter those dwelling there. Restoration would be impossible. The number of corpses would outnumber possible burial sites (7:32, 33).

19:12, 13 As the **inhabitants** of Jerusalem had made the Valley of the Son of Hinnom a place of death, so the Lord would make the entire city of Jerusalem a place of death (vv. 4–6).

20:1–18 This section has two parts: (1) Jere-

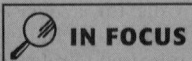

IN FOCUS   "word"

(Heb. *dabar*) (1:2, 13; 7:2; 20:8; 26:5; Deut. 24:5) Strong's #1697: This Hebrew word is derived from the verb "to speak," and it signifies the word or thing spoken. Often it refers to the idea or content of what is said, and is translated *matter* (2 Sam. 11:19), *thing* (Ex. 16:16), or *business* (Deut. 24:5). The phrase "word of the Lord" is used by the prophets at the beginning of a divine message (1:13). In the case of prophetic literature, *word* can be a technical term for a prophecy. In the Bible, the word of revelation is associated with prophets (26:5), just as wisdom is associated with wise men and the law with priests (18:18). Jeremiah used *dabar* more than any other prophet in order to clarify the authority given to him by God.

miah's message to Pashhur (vv. 1–6) and (2) Jeremiah's complaint and lament (vv. 7–18).

20:1 Pashhur . . . chief governor: A person in this position had to be a priest. He had oversight of the temple, the temple guards, entry into the courts, and so on. Jeremiah's proclamations against the city and the temple were of grave concern to Pashhur because of the threat to the continuation of the cult in which he was involved.

20:2 Jeremiah was beaten and confined to a stockade by **Pashhur.** This was not a normal prison or dungeon, but a holding cell for those who might defile the area by uncleanness or aberrant behavior. **The high gate of Benjamin** was also called the Upper Gate, to distinguish it from another city gate of the same name. This portal provided access into the temple court-yards from the north, the direction of Benjamin's territory.

20:3, 4 The name **Magor-Missabib** means "Terror on Every Side." As Pashhur had been a **terror** to Jeremiah, so he would become a terror to himself, his family, and his associates. The foe from the north described in earlier passages (1:13–15) is here identified as **Babylon.**

20:5 The four resources of Jerusalem that would be transported with the exiles to Babylon were **wealth, produce, precious things,** and **treasures.** This list is balanced by four terms for the confiscation of Jerusalem's valuables: **give, plunder, seize,** and **carry.** The use of these terms for both the plunder and the confiscation indicates comprehensiveness.

20:6 Pashhur, his family, and his close associates who had opposed Jeremiah would be deported to **Babylon** because Pashhur had **prophesied lies.** Pashhur apparently had announced that Jerusalem would not suffer destruction.

20:7–18 Jeremiah's despair deepens as he accuses God of luring him into this position of ridicule (vv. 7–10), then breaks into an expression of faith and praise (vv. 11–13), followed by

a relapse into despondency over his birth and call (vv. 14–18). This outline follows closely the form of the individual lament that is found in the Book of Psalms.

20:7 induced . . . persuaded: A play on words is intended by using two forms of the same Hebrew verb, which means "to entice." Jeremiah claimed that the Lord had seduced him and that he had succumbed to the temptation.

20:8 Jeremiah had faithfully proclaimed the Lord's **word** of judgment and destruction, but the prophecy had not been fulfilled, thus opening the prophet up to **reproach** and **derision.**

20:9 Jeremiah decided to refrain from declaring God's word or speaking **in His name.** But the divine message could not be held within or in any way hindered from accomplishing God's purpose (Is. 46:10, 11; 55:11). God's **word** was like a consuming **fire** in Jeremiah's **heart** and **bones;** unless the word was unleashed, the prophet would perish. Unlike the heart of the people, Jeremiah's mental, physical, emotional, and spiritual life was overwhelmed by God's word and will for His people.

20:10 Jeremiah was mocked with his own words, **fear on every side** (v. 3, 4). **Report . . . and we will report it:** Whatever Jeremiah announced or denounced, the leaders of Judah turned back against him until he was devastated and demoralized.

20:11 Most psalms of individual lament contain a confession of trust in God (Ps. 13). Jeremiah turned to God in prayer and praise in his hour of deepest need. **with me:** In his call, Jeremiah was promised God's presence to deliver him (1:8, 19). **mighty, awesome One:** God was Jeremiah's powerful warrior. Jeremiah's enemies would **not prevail** (vv. 7, 10), but would **stumble** and fall before God. Their punishment would be shame and **everlasting confusion** (23:40).

20:12 You who test: God tests (6:27;

17:10) and judges **the righteous,** those who walk uprightly in His ways and truth. **see the mind and heart:** God can see the innermost being of a person and discern his or her attitude and spirit. **vengeance:** Jeremiah cried for the Lord's promised judgment and destruction to be fulfilled without delay.

20:13 Jeremiah's confession of trust turns to praise as he quotes or paraphrases a psalm or hymn. The context and content of the psalm closely parallel Ps. 35:9, 10 (Ps. 109:30, 31).

20:14–18 This section is an expansion of the **woe** lament 15:10.

20:14, 15 In ancient Israel, to curse God or one's parents was an offense punishable by death. Jeremiah avoided committing a capital offense by cursing his conception and birth, and hence his call from God.

20:16, 17 Jeremiah's intense dejection caused him to call for the death of the man who told Jeremiah's father the good news of his son's birth. **did not relent:** Jeremiah, in his distress, thought it would have been more merciful for him to die before birth than to endure the hardship of rejection, persecution, and imprisonment that he faced.

20:18 Jeremiah's crying question goes unanswered in this context. The explanation would be found in the words of his call and the imminent fulfillment of the words he had faithfully and diligently proclaimed.

21:1–23:40 This section begins a series of oracles based upon Jeremiah's encounters with the kings and religious leaders of Judah, concluded by a vision account (24:1–10) parallel to the previous section, which ended with a symbolic act account.

21:1–10 This chapter is linked to the previous by the name **Pashhur** (21:1; 20:1), though not the same person. The date of the prose judgment oracle is 589 B.C. or 588 B.C., when Nebuchadnezzar began the siege of Jerusalem in reprisal against the rebellion of Zedekiah. In conjunction with promised support from Egypt, Zedekiah sought freedom from its vassalage to Babylon. But as Jeremiah declared, the rebellion would result in the final devastation of Jerusalem.

21:1 Pashhur the son of Melchiah had Jeremiah cast into a dungeon for the prophet's alleged disloyalty to the kingdom (38:1–6). **Zephaniah the son of Maaseiah** was a temple officer who, with others, sought divine guidance through Jeremiah's counsel (37:3, 4).

21:2 To **inquire** of the Lord means to seek His will. **Nebuchadnezzar** was king of Babylon from 605–562 B.C. **wonderful works:** This phrase is primarily used of God in His cosmic activity and mighty acts in history on behalf of Israel (Ps. 40:5). God had delivered Jerusalem

from destruction during the siege of Sennacherib of Assyria in 701 B.C.; King Zedekiah was hoping for a similar divine deliverance.

21:3, 4 Jeremiah's response to **Zedekiah** was demoralizing. Instead of turning back the forces of the Babylonians, God would thwart what little strength Jerusalem could muster against them.

21:5 Because the people of Judah had become God's enemies, the Lord would **fight against** them. **outstretched hand . . . strong arm:** The divine instruments by which Israel had gained freedom from Egypt (Ex. 15:6; Deut. 6:21) and deliverance from their enemies would be used against them.

21:6, 7 The **pestilence** that would strike **man and beast** recalls one of God's plagues on the Egyptians prior to the Exodus (Ex. 9:1–7). **Nebuchadnezzar . . . enemies . . . those who seek their life:** Not only did the Babylonians inflict damage upon Judah, so did constant enemies like the Edomites, who raided and then settled in the dry regions to the south. God would not **spare** or **have pity** on the stubborn and rebellious inhabitants of Judah and Jerusalem.

21:8, 9 way of life . . . way of death: *Death* would come to those who attempted to survive the siege of Jerusalem; *life* was possible through surrender to the **Chaldeans** (Babylonians). **Prize** usually refers to the booty and spoils of war. Those who submitted to the Babylonians were on the side of God, and their "booty" would be their lives (38:2). In some ways, the Book of Jeremiah reads like a political tract. There were two parties competing for attention in Jerusalem. There was the pro-Egypt party, who believed that an alliance with Egypt would protect Judah from the threat of Babylon. Then there was the pro-Babylon party, who believed that the fall of Jerusalem was inevitable. Indeed it was the will of God. Thus, the best thing to do was to prepare for the inevitable. Jeremiah, who advanced the cause of the latter group, found himself as an enemy of the state when the pro-Egypt party gained the dominant hearing.

21:10 I have set My face: This phrase describes the fixed intention of God, which in this context was against Jerusalem. The result would be **adversity** rather than **good.**

21:11–14 This oracle in language reminiscent of 7:6 and Deut. 17:18–20 establishes the basis for judgments against the kings of **Judah** in subsequent chapters. The **king** was to be devoted to the commandments of God and was to mete out **judgment,** or justice. The ultimate test of the king was measured in his judicial response to those who were oppressed and **plundered** (Is. 1:17; Amos 4:1–3).

21:13, 14 inhabitant of the valley . . . rock of the plain: These phrases refer to Jerusalem. **come down:** Attacking armies generally approached Jerusalem from the north along an elevated ridge. **Punish** means "to visit in judgment" in this context.

22:1–10 This section expands upon the seed oracle in 21:11, 12 concerning royal justice. It anticipates the direct messages to the three kings Shallum (Jehoahaz), Jehoiakim, and Jehoiachin in 22:11–30.

22:1 One goes **down** to Jerusalem by coming from the north in Anathoth and descending slightly in elevation. **The house of the king** was the royal palace located just south of the temple courtyards.

22:2 Jeremiah's prophecy was addressed to three groups: kings who sit upon the **throne of David** and thus are of David's lineage, the kings' **servants** (royal officials and attendants), and the **people who enter these gates.** The last phrase may refer to the citizens in general or to personnel who regularly entered the palace gates.

22:3 According to Is. 11:1–5, the ideal Davidic king would **execute judgment,** or justice, **and righteousness,** or uprightness, fairness, and conformity to standard. This description anticipates the "Branch of righteousness" in 23:5. The wisdom and prophetic writers echoed the same sentiment concerning the righteousness of kingdoms—that they must be measured according to their protection of the three segments of society who were unable to defend themselves: the **stranger,** the **fatherless,** and the **widow.**

22:4, 5 If justice and righteousness characterized the leadership of the land, the continued prosperity of the Davidic dynasty would be assured. However, if the Lord's **words** were not heeded, the house of David would be made a **desolation**—that is, a ruin or waste.

22:6, 7 Gilead and **Lebanon** were sources for timber for the royal palaces. These luxurious residences would be reduced to deserted **wilderness** and set ablaze if the kings disobeyed the covenant.

22:8 Even the **nations**—the Gentiles—would recognize that the punishment described in vv. 5–7 was the work of the Lord, the result of His displeasure with His people.

22:9, 10 The pagan nations would recognize that the destruction of Jerusalem was the result of Judah's violation of its **covenant** with God. The people of Judah had exchanged their God for alien deities, whom they **worshiped** and **served.**

22:11–30 Three messages to kings of Judah and a lament over Jerusalem are found in this section: (1) a message concerning Shallum (vv.

11, 12); (2) a message concerning Jehoiakim (vv. 13–19); (3) a lament concerning Jerusalem (vv. 20–23); and (4) a message concerning Coniah (vv. 24–30).

22:11, 12 This is the first of three messages directed at specific kings of Judah. **Josiah** died at Megiddo in 609 B.C. while attempting to block Pharaoh Necho of Egypt from coming to the aid of Assyria. **who went from this place:** This is a reference to Jehoahaz, also called **Shallum.** This fourth son of Josiah was placed on the throne by the people of Judah, but he was dethroned after three months by Pharaoh Necho. Shallum was imprisoned and taken captive to Egypt (2 Chr. 36:1–4). Eliakim (Jehoiakim), Shallum's brother, was placed on the throne as an Egyptian vassal. Necho maintained control of Palestine until Nebuchadnezzar defeated Egypt at the Battle of Carchemish in 605 B.C. Shallum (Jehoahaz) died without returning from Egypt, in fulfillment of Jeremiah's words (2 Kin. 23:34).

22:13–23 The second message is directed at Jehoiakim, who embellished his palace with forced labor, according to the content of this message. The prophecy is to be dated between 609 and 605 B.C., while Jehoiakim was under Egyptian control. His actions are characterized by the qualities opposite to a faithful Davidic king: unrighteousness and injustice.

22:13, 14 unrighteousness . . . injustice: The key terms for true, biblical leadership quality—righteousness and justice—were negated by the king's actions. **uses his neighbor's service without wages:** The king was supposed to be the guardian of his people, but Jehoiakim enslaved his fellow Israelites to build his self-aggrandizing palaces.

22:15, 16 Did not your father . . . do justice and righteousness: This rhetorical question identifies Josiah, father of Jehoiakim, as a model king. **knowing Me:** Israel perished because of its lack of knowledge of God (Hos. 4:6). Knowledge of God here is related to concern for **the poor and needy** (20:13).

22:17 Jehoiakim did not follow in the footsteps of Josiah. **covetousness . . . shedding innocent blood . . . practicing oppression and violence:** This triad of sins characterizing the reign of Jehoiakim would hammer home a resounding message to Judah concerning the collapse of its kingship. Covenant violations would not go unpunished.

22:18, 19 A king of such despicable character as **Jehoiakim** deserved no **lament. burial of a donkey:** Instead of proper funeral rites due a king, Jehoiakim would receive an ignoble burial, like an animal, alone and unlamented.

22:20–23 In this lament over the holy city,

Jerusalem is depicted as an abused and humiliated woman with many foreign lovers.

22:20 Jerusalem was called upon to mourn its destruction in the mountainous regions of the north—**Lebanon,** in the northeast—**Bashan,** and in the mountainous regions of the southeast—**Abarim. Lovers** here probably refers to Judah's past and present political allies, such as Phoenicia, Aram, Moab, and Egypt.

22:21 God had spoken to Israel and Judah in times of **prosperity,** as in the days of Azariah, Jeroboam II, and Josiah, but the people would not **hear** and **obey** the words of the prophets, righteous kings, priests, and other leaders.

22:22, 23 The wind shall eat up: The winds of adversity and invasion would carry off Judah's leaders and allies alike. The nation would be **ashamed** that it had entered into such futile associations. **Lebanon** refers to Jerusalem here (in contrast to v. 20). **Cedars** refers to the luxuriant royal palaces in the city (Ezek. 17:1–10).

22:24–30 Coniah, also known as Jehoiachin, succeeded his father in 598 B.C. under the threat of siege from Babylon as a result of

Jehoiakim's rebellion. The king's **signet** ring, a symbol of his power and authority, was used to seal official court documents. Jehoiachin could not serve God in such a capacity because of his evil reign (2 Kin. 24:9). Jehoiachin reigned for three months until he and his family were exiled to Babylon by Nebuchadnezzar (2 Kin. 24:6–16). **Your mother** refers to Nehushta, the queen mother of the eighteen-year old Jehoiachin. Eventually Jehoiachin was released from prison, after the death of Nebuchadnezzar (2 Kin. 25:27).

23:1–8 The kings of Judah had failed to live up to the Davidic and divine standards for kingship, so deliverance and restoration could only come through divine intervention. The first section (vv. 1–4) provides a transition from the condemnation of the kings (shepherds) of Judah (22:11–30), to the proclamation of a coming Righteous and Just King (vv. 5, 6), and the restoration of the remnant to the Israelite homeland (vv. 7, 8).

23:1, 2 Woe usually introduces a harsh message of judgment. **shepherds:** In the ancient Middle East, the ideal of kingship was often presented in the imagery of a shepherd.

✠ IN CONTEXT | Knowing God

People speak about "knowing God." But what does that mean? Scripture seems to suggest two related ways in which a person can "know God." The first is to have a personal relationship with Him. We can know God in that sense because of what Christ did on the Cross to remove the barrier of sin that separated us from God (Gal. 4:3–9; Heb. 8:11–12). However, knowing God in the sense of having a relationship with Him goes hand in hand with another sense of "knowing" Him—living a godly lifestyle. If we say that we "know" God, then our actions should show it (1 John 1:6; 4:7). It was on this point that Jeremiah challenged King Jehoiakim (Jer. 22:15–16).

Jehoiakim was appointed king by the Egyptians, who deposed his brother Jehoahaz after only three months on the throne (2 Kin. 23:31–34). Judah became a tributary of Egypt, paying one hundred talents of silver and one talent of gold, probably annually. To raise that sum, Jehoiakim levied taxes (23:35), which apparently were particularly hard on the poor (Jer. 22:16–17). Meanwhile, he launched extravagant building projects, again in a way that oppressed the working class (22:13–14).

In addition to these sins, Jehoiakim brought back the idols that his father Josiah had removed (Ezek. 8:5–17), and even hunted down a prophet of the Lord and had him executed (Jer. 26:20–23). In general, God's assessment of this king was that he was committed only to his own covetousness (22:17).

Perhaps Jehoiakim thought that because he was an Israelite and because his father had known the Lord that he automatically "knew" the Lord as well. If so, he was mistaken. Josiah had matched his words with actions, actually doing justice and righteousness and not just talking about them. In that sense, he truly "knew" the Lord (22:15–16).

How about you? Do you have a personal relationship with God on the basis of faith in Christ? If so, does your life reflect that relationship through what you do—especially the way you treat others, particularly those who are at a disadvantage? Would your life and character influence an unbeliever toward God, or drive them away from Him? Be careful of claiming to "know" the Lord if you act as if you've never even heard of Him (Luke 6:46–49).

For Israel, the ideal of the Good Shepherd was found in its Great King (Ps. 23) and was reflected in the reign of David, the shepherd-king. But instead of protecting and nurturing the nation, the shepherd kings of Israel had **scattered** and **not attended to** or "visited" the people.

23:3 The kings of Israel had caused the dispersion of the nation; but the Lord would mercifully bring about the restoration of the **remnant.** The concept of a reestablished remnant is prominent in the prophets (Is. 1:9; 10:20–23; 11:16; 46:3). The blessing of restoration and prosperity as a consequence of repentance is outlined in Deut. 30:1–10.

23:4 God would raise up a new generation of kings who would place the people's welfare and God's will above all other considerations.

23:5 **Branch:** Beginning with Is. 4:2, this term is used of the promised Messiah (33:15; Zech. 3:8; 6:12). This great king will reign with **judgment,** or justice, and **righteousness.** This ideal was founded on God's promise to David (2 Sam. 7:16). The necessity for the Lord to send His own king is based on the failure of Israel's monarchs to live up to the standards of kingship (21:11, 12; 22:1–4).

23:6 The **days** of the Messiah's reign would bring salvation. Both **Judah** and **Israel** would be restored. The **name** that characterizes this ideal king is **THE LORD OUR RIGHTEOUS-NESS.** Contrast that to the name Zedekiah, which means "The Lord Is My Righteousness" (21:1). Zedekiah's name was a gross misnomer compared to the One who would establish the true, righteous rule—God's appointed king (Is. 9:7; 11:1–10). This verse is one of the texts in the Hebrew Bible that speaks specifically and surely of the coming of the glorious Savior and King.

23:7, 8 the days are coming: The future restoration of Israel would exceed anything in the past; it would surpass even the first Exodus, the deliverance from Egypt. A similar text is found in 16:14, 15, following a judgment oracle.

23:9–40 Jeremiah's thematic addressing of the leaders of Judah now turns to the prophets who abused their divinely appointed position and proclaimed false hopes of peace and deliverance. Because these false prophets had associated themselves with foreign cults, they knew not the counsel of God. Comparison with the extended oracles against the false prophets in 26:1—29:32 would suggest a date during the reign of Zedekiah. This lengthy section has four parts: (1) the adulteration of leaders and land (vv. 9–15); (2) a false message of peace (vv. 16–24); (3) hopeless dreams (vv. 25–32); and (4) oracles of reproach (vv. 33–40).

23:9, 10 Heart here refers to the mind more than the emotions. Jeremiah's dismay over the false **prophets** weakened him mentally and physically, so much so that he felt **drunken** from the inner turmoil. The prophet also felt unrest from his being consumed by the **holy words** of God. **adulterers:** This term could apply to those who practiced immoral sexual behavior, those who committed spiritual adultery by pursuing other gods, and those who were involved in cultic prostitution. The effects of the adultery reached to the **land.** Instead of experiencing the God-given fertility and productivity of crops, the **pleasant places** were **dried up. Wilderness** refers not to the desert in this context, but to pasture land. **Might** here refers to royal power.

23:11, 12 Prophets were to be spokespersons for God in directing the nation. Priests were to teach the Law, to distinguish between the clean and the unclean, and to oversee religious ceremonies (Lev. 10:8–20). **Profane** means "unclean" or "corrupt." **My house:** Like the **prophet and priest,** the temple of God had become polluted by the **wickedness** of the spiritual leaders.

23:13, 14 The **prophets of Samaria,** rather than speaking in the name of God, **prophesied by Baal.** They **caused** the **people of Israel to err**—that is, to stray morally, mentally, and spiritually from God's norms. Samaria had been the capital city of the northern kingdom of Israel. Founded by the Israelites, it almost immediately turned to what Jeremiah called its **folly,** namely, the wholesale worship of idols. Eventually, God let the Assyrians conquer it. **Horrible thing** here refers to "something utterly disgusting" (5:30). God found that the **prophets of Jerusalem** were committing **adultery** (v. 10) and walking **in lies.** The term *lie* is used commonly by Jeremiah to refer to idolatry. The leaders of Judah had supported **evildoers** who, like the kings, had abused the power of their position. The nation had become like **Sodom** and **Gomorrah** and thus deserved the same judgment those cities suffered (Gen. 19:12–29).

23:15 Wormwood and **water of gall** refer to bitterness and death by poison. According to Deut. 18:20, the consequence of false prophecy was death.

23:16 Worthless is used to describe the futility of listening to those who **speak a vision of their own heart.** Visions were commonly understood to be a means of receiving a message from God (or the gods). The term *vision* used here and in 14:14 is also found in Daniel (Dan. 1:17; 8:1); plus it is used in other prophetic books to describe a divine revelation (Is. 1:1; Mic. 3:6).

23:17 The false prophets proclaimed a false

hope of **peace** and security to those who despised Jeremiah. However God's intention was to bring **evil** or calamity (6:14).

23:18 God's **counsel** is available to one who walks in the fear of the Lord according to **His word,** who understands God's working in nature and history.

23:19, 20 God's counsel to Jeremiah's audience was not peace but harsh judgment. **Whirlwind** is used as a symbol of God's judgment (Is. 29:6). **thoughts of His heart:** This phrase denotes God's plans and purposes by which He was bringing punishment (contrast Ps. 40:5).

23:21, 22 A true prophet must be **sent** by God with a word from God. A true prophet of God calls people to repentance of sin or **evil** and to renewed faith.

23:23, 24 The section closes as it began (vv. 18–24), with rhetorical questions that contrast the nature of God with the errant views of the people. God is not a distant unconcerned deity, like Baal (2 Kin. 18:27), but one who is ever **near** to His people. Nothing can be hidden from Him; nothing goes unnoticed.

23:25–32 The content of this oracle is rooted in Deuteronomy 13:1–6, in which the "dreamer-prophet" is condemned to death for leading the people away from God and His Law.

23:25–27 **Lies** here is singular, referring to the quality of the word the false prophets spoke. **I have dreamed:** Dreams were prized among the Assyrians, Egyptians, and Babylonians as a means of divine revelation. But in Israelite law and tradition, dreams were received cautiously. **the heart of the prophets:** The character of the false prophets was based on **lies** and **deceit.** Their deception was apparent because their goal was to draw the people into idolatry with their fanciful dreams, leading people to **forget** God and follow **Baal** (2:8).

23:28, 29 This poetic interlude compares **dream** and **word.** A dream is fleeting, like **chaff** in the wind. God's word has the force of **fire** and a **hammer.**

23:30, 31 **steal My words:** Lacking true knowledge and a word from God, the false prophets repeated false hopes and twisted God's words. **use their tongues and say, "He says":** The false prophets spoke on their own, lacking a true word from God.

23:32 The counterfeit spokespersons of God prophesied **false dreams,** deluding the people. **Recklessness** further indicates the perverse character of the false prophets.

23:33–40 This section consists of an ex-

The character of the false prophets was based on lies and deceit.

tended pun (play on words) centered upon the term **oracle** and the question of divine or human origin. The Hebrew rendered term **oracle** denotes a harsh prophetic speech that was a burdensome issue to the prophet.

23:34–36 No true **oracle** would come from the false prophets. The sharing of oracles among neighbors (v. 27) would involve perverting **the words of the living God. Perverted** means "overturned." The false prophets turned God's words around to their own desired benefit.

23:37 Jeremiah belittles with biting sarcasm those claiming to have received a word from God.

23:38–40 Speaking **the oracle of the LORD** was forbidden for the false prophets. **everlasting reproach . . . perpetual shame:** The disgrace that resulted from the false prophets would last for an extended period of time; its memory would endure forever (20:11).

24:1–10 The first major cycle of Jeremiah's oracles (2:1—24:10) is concluded with a vision reminiscent of those that confirmed his call (1:11–16). The message is concerned with the interpretation of two baskets of figs, one ripe and ready for consumption, the other inedible.

24:1–3 **The LORD showed me:** This phrase suggests a visionary experience like those of Amos and Joel. The historical setting is the 597 B.C. exile of **Jeconiah** (Jehoiachin).

24:4–7 The **good figs** are identified with the deported exiles, including Jeconiah's royal household, whom God set apart **for good.** God would **bring . . . back** the captives, establish them in the **land,** and multiply their crops. Above all, God would **give them a heart to know** Him. This verse anticipates the new covenant message of 31:31–34.

24:8–10 According to chs. 28, 36—38, the people who remained in **Jerusalem** treated Jeremiah harshly, subjecting him to beating and imprisonment. **Zedekiah** and his entourage, along with Jews who fled to Egypt, would see the **trouble,** meaning "trembling fear" or "horror," and **harm,** meaning "calamity," from the Lord.

25:1–51:64 The second half of the Book of Jeremiah begins at this point. In chs. 2—24, Jeremiah spoke principally against the sins of Judah and Jerusalem. Beginning in ch. 25, he speaks not only to Judah and Jerusalem, but to the nations of the earth.

25:1–38 The entire chapter serves as a transitional passage between the two major collections of the oracles of Jeremiah. Many scholars see this chapter as a summary discourse of the first section (chs. 2—24) of judgment oracles against Judah. But it also introduces the second section (chs. 26—51) of oracles against the nations, beginning with Judah. Chapter 25 has two parts to it: (1) the seed oracle: judgment versus Judah and Babylon (vv. 1–14) and (2) judgment on the nations (vv. 15–38).

25:1–14 Judgment against Judah and Babylon functions in chs. 25—51 in the same manner that 2:1–3 functioned for chs. 2—24, namely, to provide in kernel form the essence of the larger context. The key themes in seminal form are: (1) the Lord's judgment against Judah (vv. 1–11), which anticipate chs. 26—45 and (2) the Lord's judgment against Babylon (standing for the nations; vv. 12–14, 15–38), which anticipates chs. 46—51. The date is given as the fourth year of Jehoiakim (the first year of Nebuchadnezzar), or 605–604 B.C.

25:1, 2 the first year of Nebuchadnezzar: In 605 B.C., Nebuchadnezzar succeeded his father on the throne of Babylon. He quickly moved his army to Carchemish and then defeated the Egyptians and some Assyrians. The following year Nebuchadnezzar's forces gained control of all of Palestine, reaching southward to the Brook of Egypt.

25:3 Starting from the time he was called in 626 B.C., Jeremiah faithfully proclaimed the message of the Lord for twenty-three years. The idiom **rising early and speaking** describes Jeremiah's diligence and persistence.

25:4, 5 Other **prophets,** such as Habakkuk, Zephaniah, Urijah (26:20), and those of previous centuries, had persistently proclaimed the message of repentance so that the nation might remain **in the land.** Security, prosperity, and long life *in the land* were directly related to the nation's covenant faithfulness to God (Deut. 28; 29).

25:6, 7 The phrase **go after** is used throughout Jeremiah to mean resorting to **other gods** in worship. **The works of your hands** refers to the man-made idols used in pagan worship, a breach of the covenant (Ex. 20:3–5) that provoked God **to anger.**

25:8, 9 behold, I: The Lord was the One bringing judgment; the Babylonians and tribes from the north were merely agents of His destruction. **families of the north:** The Babylonian army employed Scythian and Cimmerian mercenaries from Asia Minor. **Nebuchadnezzar . . . My servant:** This expression does not imply that the Babylonian monarch worshiped Israel's God, but simply that he was used by God to fulfill His purposes (as in the case of Cyrus, who is called the Lord's "anointed" in Is. 45:1).

25:10, 11 take: This term means "cause to perish" and indicates harsh judgment. Life as

they knew it would cease. **These nations** refers to Judah and the surrounding nations, such as Moab and Phoenicia, who would be subjected to enslavement and captivity. **Seventy years** is the approximate length of the Babylonian captivity. According to 2 Chron. 36:17–22, it marks the period from the destruction of the temple (586 B.C.) to the proclamation of Cyrus for the restoration of the temple and the return from exile (538 B.C.), a period of forty-nine to fifty years. In Zech. 1:12–17, it marks the period between the destruction of the first temple (586 B.C.) and the building of the second temple (520–515 B.C.), or about sixty-six to seventy-two years. The period between the accession of Babylon under Nebuchadnezzar (605/604 B.C.) and the fall of the city to Cyrus (538 B.C.) also approximates the number. In the Book of Daniel, the period is reinterpreted as seventy weeks of years until God's plans for the nations are fulfilled. Attempts to force the exactness of this number have proved unsuccessful. The phrase "seventy years" is best viewed as an approximate period for the Babylonian captivity; it is a number with potent elements: ten sevens. It is also a number that caught the attention of Daniel in captivity (Dan. 9:2).

25:12–14 punish the king of Babylon . . . nation . . . land of Chaldeans: Jeremiah's role as a prophet to the nations (2:5) is fulfilled in the seminal form of an address to the mightiest nation known in his day. Like Judah, Babylon will be brought to **desolation. in this book:** After a short period of approximately seventy years, Babylon under Nabonidus and Belshazzar would fall to Cyrus and the Persians, and then Alexander the Great would conquer the city. **according to their deeds . . . the works of their own hands:** Babylon is condemned because of her immoral and unethical treatment of people in conquered lands and because of her multitudinous idols (51:33–50).

25:15–38 This section has three parts to it: (1) the cup of judgment (vv. 15–29); (2) a lawsuit against the nations (vv. 30, 31); and (3) a lamentation over desolation (vv. 32–38).

25:15–29 The oracles against the nations served a dual purpose: to deliver a warning to the nations against injustice to Israel and other nations and to provide Israel assurance that God cared for her and would punish her enemies. The key word in this section is the term **cup** containing God's **wine,** a symbol of **fury** that was about to be poured out upon the nations. This imagery occurs in Is. 51:17–22, Hab. 2:15–17, and Jeremiah's oracle against Edom (Jer. 49:12).

25:15–17 The triad sequence **drink . . . stagger . . . go mad** depicts the judgment process by which the **sword** of the Lord subdues those opposed to Him. The state of drunkenness was condemned in the OT; to drink the cup and stagger was to display one's guilt (Num. 5:19–28). **Then I took the cup:** Jeremiah responded faithfully to God's commands.

25:18 The list of nations that would be made to drink from the cup of the Lord's judgment begins with **Judah** and **Jerusalem,** which would be made a source of derision (19:8; 25:9).

25:19 The first foreign nation condemned by God through Jeremiah was **Egypt.** The expanded oracle is found in ch. 46.

25:20 The **land of Uz** is generally interpreted as the region of Edom or northern Arabia. **Ashkelon** was captured by Nebuchadnezzar in 604 B.C. **Gaza** and **Ashdod** are also mentioned in Nebuchadnezzar's Babylonian chronicles (ch. 47).

25:21, 22 The states of **Edom, Moab,** and **Ammon,** and the Phoenician coastal territories of **Tyre** and **Sidon,** suffered heavily under Nebuchadnezzar's attacks (48:1–49:22; Ezek. 27; 28).

25:23, 24 The Arabian desert kingdoms of **Dedan, Tema,** and **Buz** were condemned. Dedan and Tema were in Edomite territory (49:7, 8). The location of Buz is unknown.

25:25, 26 **Elam** and Media were located east of Babylon (49:34–39).

25:27, 28 The triad of terms for progressive inebriation—**drink, be drunk,** and **vomit**—emphasizes the extent of judgment that would flow from God's cup of wrath. Those who refused the cup would be forced **to drink.**

25:29 God's judgment would **begin** with His own people and their holy city. God would **bring calamity** on the city that was called by His **name.** In doing so, God would vindicate His name and His holiness. From Jerusalem, God's **sword** of judgment would go forth to the ends of the earth.

25:30–32 The universal judgment of God is depicted in poetic imagery of a mountain lion roaring from the hill tops. The contention with the nations is described in terms of a covenant lawsuit with introduction and setting (v. 30), indictment (v. 31), and announcement of judgment (vv. 32, 33).

25:30 on high . . . from His holy habitation: Generally these phrases refer to God's abode on Mount Zion (Joel 3:16; Amos 1:2).

25:31 **A noise** refers to a thunderous judgment resulting from God's **controversy** or "covenant lawsuit" against the nations. Though they had not received the Law like Judah and Israel, the Gentiles would be judged, for they were **wicked.** The word *wicked* refers to the guilt associated with the breach of ethical standards, including violating the poor and needy and abusing the oppressed.

25:32, 33 As with Judah's horrifying calamity of unburied corpses (7:33), the nations would experience massive death and extensive destruction. The neglect of the dead is described in a triad of terms: **not be lamented . . .** (not be) **gathered . . .** (not be) **buried.** This desecration would be finalized by the decay of bodies into **refuse** or "dung" (8:2; 9:22; 16:4).

25:34–36 The triad of lament, **wail . . . cry . . . roll,** serves to stress the seriousness of the coming judgment, which will result in **slaughter** (death) and **dispersion** (captivity and exile).

25:37, 38 Homes and pastures that once were **peaceful** and secure would be devastated. **The Oppressor** is a surprising designation for the Lord.

26:1–24 This section has four parts to it: (1) a call to repentance at the temple (vv. 1–11); (2) a reiteration before Jerusalem's leaders (vv. 12–15); (3) the example of Micah the prophet (vv. 16–19); and (4) the example of Uriah the prophet (vv. 20–24). The circumstances of this account of Jeremiah's temple sermon and subsequent confrontation with Judah's leaders is the accession of Jehoiakim to the throne following the deportation of Jehoahaz to Egypt by Pharaoh Necho (thus, late 609 or early 608 B.C.). The sermon in the temple (vv. 2–6) is an

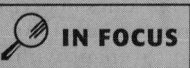 **IN FOCUS** **"shepherd"**

(Heb. *ra'ah*) (23:1; 25:34; 31:10; Gen. 49:24; Ps. 23:1) Strong's #7462: The Hebrew noun for *shepherd* refers to someone who feeds and tends domestic animals. David spoke of God as His shepherd, for God provided, sustained, and guided him (Ps. 23). Kings and other leaders were also seen as shepherds of their people, and the title "shepherd" was frequently applied to kings in the ancient Middle East. David was a true shepherd-king, responsibly leading and protecting his people (2 Sam. 5:1, 2). Jeremiah rebuked the leaders of Israel, who were false shepherds and failed in their responsibility of caring for the spiritual well-being of God's people (23:1–4).

abbreviation of 7:1–15, perhaps the work of Baruch, which is part of a series of oracles against Jerusalem and set in the context of idolatry (7:1—8:3). The temple sermon here serves to introduce the conflict between Jeremiah and the religious and political leadership in Judah and Jerusalem.

26:1 In the beginning: This expression technically refers to the part of the year between the day the king ascended to the throne and the beginning of his first full year of reign, which began in the spring month of Nisan (March through April), 608 B.C.

26:2 The **court** of the temple may refer to one of the inner courts connected by the gate mentioned in 7:2. **Come to worship** describes the normal worship there or perhaps more specifically the pilgrimages to Jerusalem for festival and fast days. **Do not diminish:** Jeremiah was told to speak unsparingly with unwavering boldness.

26:3–5 The introduction to the judgment oracle is expressed in conditional terms. If the people repented of **evil,** the Lord would relent from the **calamity** He was threatening to bring on them.

26:6 Shiloh was not far from Jerusalem. The people could see the effects of its destruction by the Philistines in 1050 B.C.—a destruction that overtook it even though it was the first resting place of the ark of the covenant. Jeremiah uses Shiloh as an illustration of the coming judgment of Jerusalem even though the temple of God had been built there.

26:7 The account of the hearing of Jeremiah's message by the three constituent elements of Judah's society serves to anticipate the confrontations to follow.

26:8, 9 The priests and the prophets and all the people refers to the collective worship assembly. The religious leaders responsible for overseeing the temple considered Jeremiah's words blasphemy, for he spoke of the destruction of the temple itself. The people rejected Jeremiah's prophecy and tried to kill him (see John 8:59 for the similar rejection suffered by Jesus).

26:10, 11 Jeremiah's words were reported to the **princes,** the royal administrators and kingdom officials, who came to the **New Gate** to carry out an official inquiry. The prophets and priests presented an accusation against Jeremiah, calling for the death sentence for speaking **against** Jerusalem.

26:12, 13 Jeremiah called the assembly to **amend,** or make good, their evil **ways** and to **obey** God's **voice,** here referring to the covenant and the words proclaimed by Jeremiah.

26:14, 15 Held captive by the hostile crowd, Jeremiah pointed to the potential sin of shedding

innocent blood. Jeremiah had already accused the leaders of Jerusalem of shedding innocent blood with child sacrifices in the Hinnom valley (2:34; 19:4). **truly the LORD has sent me:** Sentencing God's prophet to death would result in greater judgment, in addition to the people's other offenses against heaven.

26:16 This man does not deserve to die: Jeremiah's self-defense gained acceptance from the crowd, against the objections of the wicked religious leaders.

26:17–19 After Jeremiah's hearing, one of the **elders** from the people cited the precedent of the eighth century prophet **Micah of Moresheth.** In the reign of **Hezekiah,** Micah had announced the impending destruction of Jerusalem by the Assyrians (Mic. 3:12). Yet because of the repentance of Hezekiah and the inhabitants, the city was spared from the onslaught of the Assyrian army under Sennacherib (701 B.C.).

26:20–23 Urijah, whose name means "My Light Is the Lord," was from Kirjath Jearim, about fifteen miles west of Jerusalem (1 Sam. 7:1, 2). Like Jeremiah, Urijah had **prophesied in the name of the LORD** about judgment against Jerusalem. When **Jehoiakim** and his administrators heard of Urijah's declarations, they sought to seize the "blasphemous" prophet, who escaped by fleeing to **Egypt.** Since Jehoiakim was a vassal to Necho of Egypt, Urijah was extradited and executed. **Elnathan the son of Achbor** was among the princes in Jehoiakim's court who heard the reading of Jeremiah's first scroll of oracles (36:11–19) and protested Jehoiakim's burning of the scroll (36:20–26).

26:24 Jeremiah was sheltered by **Ahikam the son of Shaphan** who, along with his father, served as a scribe under Josiah when the Book of the Law was found in the temple (2 Kin. 22:8–14). Ahikam's brother Gemariah also opposed Jehoiakim's burning of Jeremiah's original scroll (36:25). This faithful family was supportive of Jeremiah and was instrumental in saving his life.

27:1–29:32 In the days of the monarchy and divided kingdoms, court prophets like Nathan and Isaiah guided the kings in decision making with a counsel from the Lord. As the nation departed from the covenant with the Lord, prophets arose claiming divine inspiration, but in fact their words might have been of their own initiative, self-interest, politically and religiously. Conflict with a true prophet of God like Jeremiah was inevitable. These three chapters contain such confrontations with Zedekiah and some unnamed prophets (ch. 27), Hananiah (ch. 28), and Ahab, Zedekiah, and Shemaiah (ch. 29).

27:1–22 This section has four parts to it: (1)

yokes sent to nations allied against Babylon (vv. 1–11); (2) a message to Zedekiah of Judah: submit to Babylon (vv. 12–15); (3) beware of false prophets of peace (vv. 16–18); and (4) the deportation of the temple vessels (vv. 19–22).

27:1–11 The form and setting of the first address is the symbolic act account of an ox yoke sent to the Transjordan kings of Edom, Moab, and Ammon, and the Phoenician kings of Tyre and Sidon. The performance of the instructions from the Lord by Jeremiah is implicit, for Jeremiah has faithfully fulfilled each divine charge in the past.

27:1–3 Bonds and yokes are wooden bars or beams that attach to a pair of oxen with leather bands. The symbolic act of wearing the yoke would communicate bondage, restraint, and enslavement. The **messengers** were foreign ambassadors in Jerusalem.

27:4, 5 The foreign ambassadors were to announce to their **masters** that the God of Israel is the true sovereign Lord over creation and the affairs of humans. The whole of creation is summed up in the triad **earth . . . man . . . beast.** Unlike the gods of the nations, whose power was often believed to be geographically limited, the God of Israel reigned over all the earth, granting territorial rights and power to nations and kings as **it seemed proper** to Him.

27:6, 7 My servant: With all of his military might and conquests, the king of Babylon was still a servant of the God of Israel, carrying out the Lord's purposes—namely the judgment of Judah. **son's son . . . time of his land:** Following the death of Nebuchadnezzar in 562 B.C., his heirs and successors retained control of Babylon for only twenty-four years. Babylon fell without a battle to Cyrus and the Persian armies in 539 B.C., and later to Alexander the Great of Greece.

27:8 The symbol of the **yoke** is explained to the foreign ambassadors. Those who would not submit as vassals to Babylon would be punished.

27:9, 10 The way kings summoned various prophet-diviners to give them direction is well known from the Book of Daniel (Dan. 2:2; 5:7). Besides **prophets,** there were **diviners,** like Balaam (Num. 22—24), who were prohibited from practicing their craft in Israel (Deut. 18:9–14); **dreamers,** a class of fortune-tellers prohibited by the Law (Deut. 13:1–5); as well as **soothsayers** and **sorcerers,** both common among the nations but forbidden to practice their trades in Israel (Deut. 18:9–14). The collective effort of these diviners to determine the future of their nations failed. Like the false prophets of Judah, they heralded a message of rebellion and resistance against Babylon. Only Jeremiah stood for the truth: the Lord would punish Judah through Nebuchadnezzar.

27:11 bring their necks under the yoke: To submit to Babylon was to submit to the will and purposes of God.

27:12–14 Jeremiah's message to **Zedekiah**

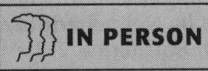 **IN PERSON**   ## "Nebuchadnezzar, My Servant"

Who is the most treacherous, dangerous world leader you can think of? Who would you say is the greatest threat to world peace and stability today? Whoever it is, you probably cannot regard that person with greater suspicion and disdain than the people of Judah had for Nebuchadnezzar of Babylon. Yet God described this pagan king as His own "servant" (Jer. 27:6; compare 25:9). That had to be unimaginable for the people of Jeremiah's day. To them, Nebuchadnezzar was a great evil. He ruled a ruthless superpower that was poised to overrun their lands and destroy their cities. How could he possibly be God's servant?

Interestingly, the description of Nebuchadnezzar sounds a lot like the description of Cyrus, the Persian king, given through Isaiah: "My shepherd" and "His anointed" (Is. 44:28—45:1). Both of these rulers had power over vast territories in the ancient Middle East. Their decisions determined much of what happened in history at that time. From the human perspective, they were the ones in charge.

But the prophecies of Isaiah and Jeremiah show that ultimately these rulers were not in control of the final outcomes. Whether they knew it or not, they were only finite human beings placed in positions of authority by the hand of God. As such, they were God's servants, God's agents. Through their decisions, they ended up serving God's purposes—even if they didn't realize they were doing so!

God is the King of all the kings—then and now. Because that is so, what does it say about the leaders of the world today? Perhaps the ones we dislike the most are in fact "servants" of the living God! And like Nebuchadnezzar and Cyrus, God seeks not merely to use them, but also for them to know Him. Are you praying and working toward that end (1 Tim. 2:1–2)?

was the same as his message to the foreign ambassadors (vv. 4–11): submit to Nebuchadnezzar and the Babylonians and **live,** or rebel against Nebuchadnezzar—and God—and **die.** The message of death is delineated in the same triad of destruction as that of v. 8 to the foreign nations. Jeremiah spoke against not only the religious leadership but also the political leadership, espousing a position tantamount to treason. Despite the opposition he faced, he stood firm in his understanding of the message of God.

27:15 I have not sent them: Divine call and commission are prerequisites to fulfilling a true prophetic role. False prophets such as Hananiah (ch. 28) gave hope to Zedekiah's aspirations for freedom from Babylon's yoke, but Jeremiah calls their words a **lie**, spoken in the **name** of the Lord. Because they had profaned His name, both the king and his prophets would **perish**. When Jerusalem fell in 586 B.C., Zedekiah attempted to flee to the desert by means of the road to Jericho. He was captured and taken to Riblah, where his sons were killed in front of him, and then his eyes were put out (2 Kin. 25:4–7). This particularly barbaric act meant that the last sight he had in this life was of the deaths of his boys.

27:16–22 Jeremiah's third address is given as a warning to the **priests** and **people** who listened to the false prophets concerning the future of themselves and the temple.

27:16, 17 Do not listen: For the priests to listen to the false words of the prophets concerning the inviolability of the temple was to seal their own doom and that of the temple. Many **vessels** (v. 19) had been carried off by Nebuchadnezzar in the exile of Jeconiah (Jehoiachin). The false prophets said that Babylon would be defeated and the temple furnishings would be returned.

27:18–20 Jeremiah proposed a test to verify the words of the contentious prophets. **if the word of the LORD is with them:** If the prophets truly spoke for the Lord, their **intercession**—the survival of the remaining temple implements—would come to pass. **vessels which are left:** Many of the furnishings of the temple of the Lord were transported to Babylon in the exile of Jehoiachin and his entourage (2 Kin. 24:13). According to Jeremiah, the vessels that remained would be taken in the final destruction of the city. Events would demonstrate whose word was from the Lord.

27:21, 22 Jeremiah's message from the Lord is presented in detail. The remaining **vessels** in the temple, as well as in the king's palace, would be **carried to Babylon** until the Lord restored His people. In the midst of a prophetic message against the false prophets, Jeremiah spoke a message of hope and restoration. Destruction was imminent, but God does not forget His people. He would restore the righteous remnant.

28:1–17 The oracles against the false prophets turn to focus on the confrontation between Jeremiah and Hananiah, which took place not long after the events outlined in the previous chapter, perhaps immediately after. The autobiographical account consists of four movements: (1) Hananiah's prophecy of deliverance (vv. 1–4); (2) Jeremiah's response: judge the results (vv. 5–9); (3) Hananiah's rejoinder: two years until deliverance (vv. 10, 11); and (4) Jeremiah's response: Babylon comes, Hananiah dies (vv. 12–16), and the epilogue concerning the death of Hananiah (v. 17).

28:1 The same year refers to the time of ch. 27 (593 B.C.). **The fifth month** was the month of Ab (July/August). **Hananiah** was from **Gibeon,** six miles northwest of Jerusalem and about five miles west of Jeremiah's hometown, Anathoth. Hananiah's name means "The Lord Is Gracious."

28:2–4 Hananiah spoke in the name of the **LORD of hosts,** using the name of God as Jeremiah did to introduce a solemn message of judgment against Babylon. Building on Jeremiah's imagery of the yoke (ch. 27), Hananiah proclaimed the contradictory message that the **yoke of . . . Babylon** would be **broken** by God. Hananiah believed that God's message for Judah was one of imminent deliverance—**within two full years**—from servitude to the king of Babylon. Hananiah also prophesied the return of the holy **vessels** taken by **Nebuchadnezzar** from the temple of God. Furthermore, Hananiah espoused the popular belief that the kingship of Zedekiah was illegitimate and that God would restore **Jeconiah** (Jehoiachin) to the throne in Jerusalem.

28:5, 6 Jeremiah's words may seem sarcastic, but he truly would have wished that Hananiah's **words** were God's words. Jeremiah longed that the temple of the Lord would not be destroyed and that its furnishings would not be carried away into captivity. The burning message inside though was contrary.

28:7–9 war and disaster and pestilence: Hananiah's message of peace and prosperity ran contrary to the long tradition of the genuine Hebrew prophets. Amos, Hosea, Micah, Joel, and Nahum spoke words of judgment and destruction against **great kingdoms** like Assyria and Egypt. **Peace** in this context refers to the well-being and wholeness resulting from God's restoration of the nation.

28:10, 11 Seizing the **yoke** from Jeremiah's **neck** (ch. 27) and breaking it before the people, Hananiah made a resounding proclamation:

Even so I will break the yoke of Nebuchadnezzar . . . from the neck of all nations within the space of two full years. This announcement reversed every statement by Jeremiah and advanced the cause of rebellion against Babylon by Judah and the surrounding nations, something King Zedekiah had desired all along.

28:12, 13 After an indefinite period of time, the **word of the LORD came to Jeremiah.** God's prophet was instructed to return to Hananiah with a new interpretation of the yoke motif. Because Hananiah had broken the original **yokes of wood,** God would replace them with **yokes of iron** that could not be broken.

28:14 All these nations against which Jeremiah originally had spoken (in 27:1–11) would serve Nebuchadnezzar.

28:15, 16 Hananiah had not been **sent** by God, but he had led the people astray with a **lie.** As a result, Hananiah would be **cast . . . from the face of the earth** and **die** that very year.

28:17 The seventh month: Two months after Hananiah prophesied about Judah's captivity (v. 1), the false prophet was dead.

29:1–32 Various letters comprise this assemblage of correspondence with the exiles who were taken captive in 597 B.C., including Jehoiachin and the royal household. The grouping of these letters with the oracles against false prophets of chs. 27 and 28 would suggest a similar date, or 594 B.C. The Babylonian Chronicles and other contemporary documents indicate that territorial unrest was plaguing Nebuchadnezzar's empire. Jeremiah advises the exiled Jews to settle down and not expect an immediate return to their homeland. The chapter has the following sections: (1) an introduction (vv. 1–3); (2) settle down and be content (vv. 4–7); (3) beware of false prophets of early return (vv. 8–10); (4) seek the Lord and He will restore (vv. 11–14); (5) destruction and plague against Judah (vv. 15–19); (6) false prophets in exile to be executed (vv. 20–23); and (7) a word against Shemaiah the prophet (vv. 24–32).

29:1 words of the letter: A written document was carried from Jerusalem to the Jews in Babylon. **remainder:** This may imply that some of the **elders** were executed in the 594 B.C. revolt alluded to in vv. 21–23.

29:2 This parenthetical passage provides background from 2 Kin. 24:12–16 concerning the deportation of Jeconiah (Jehoiachin), the royal family, and chief artisans of Judah to

> *Jeremiah had proclaimed a period of seventy years of Babylonian exile.*

Babylon in 597 B.C. This method of eliminating leaders and leaving the peasant population to pay taxes to the kingdom was learned from the Assyrians and was designed to reduce the likelihood of rebellion.

29:3 The messengers were **Elasah the son of Shaphan,** perhaps a brother of the sympathetic Ahikam (26:24), and **Gemariah the son of Hilkiah,** a member of Jehoiakim's administration (36:10). The purposes of the visit may have been several: normal official business, to bring tribute from Judah, and perhaps to assure Nebuchadnezzar of Judah's allegiance to Babylon in the light of the rebellion of the states in Transjordan and Phoenicia.

29:4 Jeremiah reminded the exiled community that ultimately it was **God,** not Nebuchadnezzar, who had caused them to be **carried away captive . . . to Babylon.**

29:5, 6 Jeremiah had proclaimed a period of seventy years (25:12) of Babylonian exile. For the meantime, he counseled the people to settle in and carry on their normal daily activities. The terms **build** and **plant** are significant because they fulfill the particulars of Jeremiah's call (1:10). Exile did not necessarily mean imprisonment or enslavement, but displacement and resettlement in unknown lands. **be increased . . . not diminished:** If the people were faithful in the circumstances of captivity, God would cause them to prosper with children and with fertile crops.

29:7 The exiles were instructed to **seek** and **pray** for the **peace,** or well-being of Babylon and the other towns where they were deported. As a result, they themselves would live in peace as beneficiaries of God's gracious sovereignty over the nations (27:5, 6).

29:8, 9 Jeremiah issued a warning against following the advice of **prophets, diviners,** and **dreams.** A similar warning was issued to the nations surrounding Judah in 27:9, 10 and to Judah in 27:14, 17.

29:10 The concept of the **seventy years** of Babylon captivity is reiterated from 25:12. The number *seventy* symbolizes completion and fulfillment of God's sovereign plans for creation and human history. The completion of the years of the kingdom of Babylon would also be the completion of Judah's exile.

29:11 I know the thoughts that I think: The Lord here places considerable emphasis on His unchangeable plan to bring **peace** and not **evil. a future . . . a hope:** God had not terminated His relationship with Judah; He

 **IN FOCUS** | **"hissing"**

(Heb. *shereqah*) (29:18; 2 Chr. 29:8; Mic. 6:16) Strong's #8322: The Hebrew word translated *hissing* is from a verb meaning "to whistle" (Is. 5:26) or "to play a pipe" as a signal for flocks (Judg. 5:16). This word may refer to a superstitious practice among ancients: they would shake their head and whistle when passing by the ruins of a village or a deserted city, as a charm against suffering the same fate. The OT prophets used this word to warn the Israelites of the ridicule and scorn they would endure as part of God's judgment on their sins (Lam. 2:15, 16; Zeph. 2:15). Jeremiah often used this word in connection with "astonishment" over a calamity (19:8; 29:18; 51:37). Zechariah used the same word to describe God's gracious regathering of the Israelites from the Exile (Zech. 10:8), using the image of a shepherd whistling for his sheep.

remembered His covenant promises of restoration (Deut. 30:1–10).

29:12, 13 The promised response of the Lord to the people's prayers stands in contrast to His refusal to hear in 7:16. **all your heart:** The picture here differs greatly from the usual depiction of the heart of the people of Judah as stubborn and wicked (3:10; 4:14; 7:24). God would search the people's heart and reveal its true character (11:20).

29:14 I will be found: Those who seek God with a whole heart will find Him and experience His renewal. **I will bring you back . . . gather you . . . bring you to the place:** God was the captor, and He would restore His people from captivity.

29:15–20 The cause of Jerusalem's shame was its failure to heed the **words** of God, revealed through the covenant stipulations and the diligent—**rising up early**—proclamation of the prophets (25:3; 26:5).

29:21 Ahab the son of Kolaiah, and Zedekiah the son of Maaseiah were the prophets spoken of in 29:15. The two were accused by Jeremiah of a deplorable crime: prophesying **a lie** in God's **name.** Their lie was prophesying the imminent collapse of Babylon and the restoration of the captives to Jerusalem. Such false prophecy urging rebellion against God was a capital offense (Deut. 13:5–10). The prophetic punishment of Ahab and Zedekiah was death by command of **Nebuchadnezzar.**

29:22, 23 This term **curse** may be a play on the name Kolaiah ("called of the Lord"; v. 21). He claimed to be called of God, but was cursed along with those who supported his position. These Jewish leaders had compounded their sin by doing **disgraceful things** (Deut. 22:21).

29:24–28 Jeremiah addressed **Shemaiah the Nehelamite** concerning his correspondence with **Zephaniah the son of Maaseiah** and the Jerusalem priesthood. Shemaiah had challenged Zephaniah's apparent leniency in

dealing with the problem of Jeremiah's prophecies about the exiles' immediate future.

29:29, 30 When **Zephaniah** received the **letter** from Shemaiah, he read it to Jeremiah, who then received a word of judgment from God against Shemaiah and his family.

29:31, 32 prophesied . . . caused you to trust in a lie: The accusation against Shemaiah parallels that of numerous judgment oracles in Jeremiah (5:31; 14:14; 23:16; 27:10). The ensuing sentence against Shemaiah is like those against Pashhur (20:6), Jehoiachin or Coniah (22:30), and Hananiah (28:16).

30:1–33:26 This collection of oracles has been called the Book of Consolation or Comfort. It contains two sections, the first dealing with the physical and spiritual restoration of Israel and Judah (chs. 30, 31), and the second with the faith and assurance of God's future blessing of His people (chs. 32, 33). The first twenty-nine chapters contain primarily oracles of harsh judgment against Israel, Judah, their leaders, and the nations. The precise setting and date of chapters 30, 31 is not readily evident. Chapter 32 dates to the end of the reign of Zedekiah.

30:1, 2 The oracles of Jeremiah were recorded by the scribe Baruch (ch. 36). **Book** refers to any type of writing medium, from a clay tablet to a parchment scroll. Jeremiah's oracles were recorded on a scroll (36:2).

30:3 they shall possess it: Possession of the land, as in the original possession under Joshua's leadership, would be the responsibility of the faithful remnant living according to the covenant relationship.

30:4–11 This poetic section recounts the travail of God's people in exile and the impending act of deliverance from captivity. A date of 588 B.C. has been suggested, but any precise dating remains inconclusive. Verse four heads the collection of oracles from vv. 5–24.

30:5, 6 voice of trembling . . . fear . . . not of peace: Jeremiah's audience was the whole nation of Israel and Judah, which had experienced the dread and horror of the day of the Lord (Joel 1:1—2:11; Amos 5:18–20). **Hands on his loins** symbolizes the agony of God's people, who had become like defenseless pregnant women in the midst of delivery before their enemies (4:31; 6:24).

30:7–9 The incomparable **day** of God was an ordained time of horror and distress for Israel and Judah, out of which the Lord would save them. Jeremiah expressed the hope of release from the bondage of the **yoke** of Babylon according to the Lord's timing (25:12) and not that of people (28:11). Then Israel would no longer serve foreigners in foreign lands or in their own. Instead, the people of God would **serve the LORD their God, and David their king.** God would **raise up** a messianic king from David's line to rule over the nation (Is. 9:7; 11:1; Hos. 3:5).

30:10, 11 My servant: The use of this terminology for Israel and Judah parallels that of Is. 42:1; 44:1. The hope of the nation was **rest,** tranquillity in the absence of external and internal distress, and **quiet,** security and ease resulting from trust in the Lord.

30:12 Your affliction is incurable, Your wound is severe: God's hand of judgment had brought serious harm to the nation, a mortal wound unless God intervened.

30:13 Healing here refers to the growth of new skin over an open wound.

30:14 Israel's **lovers** were nations like Assyria, Egypt, Phoenicia, Ammon, and Edom, with whom it had made political and religious alliances. These nations had quickly **forgotten** Judah; they shrank back or were defeated by Nebuchadnezzar. Egypt, for example, had supported Zedekiah's rebellion, but was defeated in 588 B.C. by Nebuchadnezzar. When the Egyptian army retreated beyond the Brook of Egypt, the army of Babylon laid siege to Jerusalem and destroyed it, in 586 B.C. (37:1–5).

30:15 iniquities . . . sins: These terms are repeated from v. 14, emphasizing the character of the people and echoing the reasons for harsh judgment. The lament applied to both the sin and its results.

30:16, 17 Restoration and healing of Israel came in two forms, retribution against its enemies and healing of its wounds. Four sets of terms designate God's retributive justice: **those who devour** would **be devoured; adversaries** would **go into captivity; those who plunder** would become **plunder; and all who prey** would become **prey.** Healing was promised in response to the people's repentance (3:22; 33:6), a reversal of their incurable position (8:22; 30:12).

30:18–22 Restoration is described in more concrete terms than in previous contexts. Recovery is outlined as to dwellings (v. 18), much joy and thanksgiving (v. 19), community (v. 20), and local leadership (v. 21). Israel will be the Lord's again (v. 22).

30:18 Jacob's tents . . . dwelling places . . . city . . . palace: These phrases emphasize God's work in rebuilding the homes and cities of His returning exiles, from the peasant population to the administration.

30:19 Instead of the voice of lament, fear, and trembling echoing throughout the land (4:31; 30:5), the sound of **thanksgiving** and merrymaking would reverberate. The word *thanksgiving* refers to a manner of appreciative praise. **Merry** suggests the joy of laughter and play.

30:20 The collective community with **children** and **congregation** will be reassembled for carrying out their purpose as God's chosen. Any oppressor who violates the societal order will be chastised.

30:21, 22 Israel's leaders would no longer be appointed by foreign kings, and foreign rulers would not preside over Israel's lands.

30:23, 24 These verses are essentially a reiteration of 23:19, 20. In this context, they attest to Israel's new understanding of its God and assure the people of God's judgment on their enemies and oppressors.

31:1–22 The section is composed of several restoration oracles with the northern kingdom Israel (**Ephraim**) in focus, though they are applicable to Judah as well. Some have suggested that certain portions may date to Jeremiah's early ministry in 626–597 B.C., and were combined with later oracles during the early exilic period.

31:1 Coinciding with the restoration of the nation to its land would be the fulfillment of the covenant between God and His people, **all the families of Israel.**

31:2 survived the sword . . . found grace in the wilderness . . . give him rest: These phrases describe Israel's deliverance from Egypt and God's victory over the army of Pharaoh. God's grace, or favor, was manifest in the desert as He provided sustenance, shelter, and rest for His people.

31:3 Of old, which may also be translated "from afar," may refer to the betrothal days of Israel in the wilderness (2:1–3) or to the distant lands of Assyria and Babylon to which Israel and Judah had been exiled. The phrase **everlasting love** is paralleled with **lovingkindness,** which means "loyal love" or "covenant loyalty." Out of His faithfulness to the covenants He established with Abraham and Moses, and out of His great love, God established the nation Israel for His glory and for hers. The Lord would also deliver

His people from captivity and reestablish them by His love.

31:4 There will be rejoicing as village life is restored. **I will build:** In Ps. 127:1, the psalmist says that unless God builds a house, the labor is in vain. **O virgin of Israel:** Earlier in Jeremiah, this expression was used sadly in depicting the departure of Israel from faith in God (2:32; 14:17). Here the image is reversed; Israel is rebuilt in the manner of her former betrothal (2:2), having become again like a virgin bride to God. **adorned . . . go forth in the dances:** Joyful celebration of marriage and festival throughout villages is in view here (v. 13).

31:5 Originally **Samaria** was the name for the capital of the northern kingdom of Israel. The city had been built by King Omri in the early ninth century B.C., presumably to establish his kingship after a period of civil war and unrest in Israel. Previous Israelite kings had ruled from Tirzah. Later the name **Samaria** would also be associated with the northern kingdom itself. **The mountains of Samaria:** The hill country of Samaria is a harsh, mountainous land full of fissures and valleys. Mountain passes make Samaria's hills accesible. Jeremiah declared that the hill country, which was ravaged by the Assyrians in 733–722 B.C., would be replanted with vineyards. The hills would produce fruit for consumption rather than tribute for foreign powers. The plantings would be for regular, normal enjoyment—a gift of God in the lives of His people.

31:6 The **day** would come when the nation would be united once again, with northern kingdom Israelites making pilgrimages to **Zion** (Jerusalem) for worship, instead of continuing to visit the rival sanctuaries of Dan and Bethel (1 Kin. 12:27–29). The purpose of the **watchmen** would be not to warn the people about oncoming armies but to call them to come with joy to the holy city.

31:7–14 The joyful homecoming of Israel from the many lands to which she was exiled is in view. The poetic elements often constitute a reversal of the situation in the early periods of Jeremiah's ministry. Terms for praise, rejoicing, and gladness emanate throughout.

31:7 The **chief of the nations** would be **Jacob,** meaning Israel. In 15:9 the **remnant** is described as all but vanquished. Here the restored community shouts for joy.

31:8 In 6:22 and 25:32, Israel's enemies came from the **north country** and the **ends of the earth.** Now Israel herself is brought back by the Lord, with even the infirm, weak and fragile.

31:9 weeping . . . supplications: Phrases from the Songs of Ascents (Ps. 120—134) are found here. In Ps. 126, those who are weeping

are filled with gladness at the Lord's return of exiles from captivity. **rivers of waters:** This imagery of God's provision of life-sustaining water through the desert is like Is. 35:5–7. The reference to the **straight way** parallels Is. 40:3–5. **Father:** This text is one of the few cases in the OT where the fatherhood of God is portrayed directly (Deut. 32:6; Is. 63:16). Israel was familiar with the idea of God as Father, but it was not until the teaching of Jesus that the phrase took on the importance that we understand it to have in our lives today. **Firstborn** conveys the concept of preeminence (31:7; Deut. 32:9).

31:10–12 God would be the people's good **shepherd,** unlike past kings (23:1–4). **redeemed . . . ransomed:** These two terms for redemption describe the transfer of ownership of Israel from the mighty Babylon to the incomparable God. Israel's freedom was gained by God, its great "kinsman redeemer" (Is. 51:10, 11).

31:13 The theme of joy in the restoration continues with jubilation in the **dance** (Ps. 149:1–4). The "dance" in Hebrew culture is a world away from what many people think of in contemporary western culture. Dance is movement of the body in response to music; it is music made visual. To dance in joy before the Lord was regarded as a natural, spontaneous response of the people of God in the culture of ancient Israel.

31:14 The theme of joy is summarized in God's intention to fill the **priests** and the **people** with **abundance.** Jeremiah gave the people hope and comfort in facing the poverty and oppression of exile and captivity.

31:15–22 Joy turns to lament among the exiled of Ephraim over her chastisement from the Lord. The oracle is clearly intended for the northern kingdom of Israel, with references to Rachel, Ramah, and Ephraim. The passage outline is as follows: Rachel's lament (v. 15); God's call to cease lamentation (vv. 16, 17); Ephraim's repentance (vv. 18, 19); and God's compassion for Ephraim (vv. 20–22).

31:15, 16 According to 1 Sam. 10:2, 3, Rachel's tomb was near Zelzah, which was near **Ramah** in Benjamin. This may have been a memorial for Rachel, located in the tribal allotment of the descendants of her son Benjamin (Gen. 35:16–20). Genesis says that Rachel was buried in Ephrath, near Bethlehem (Gen. 35:19; 48:7). Rachel was the mother of the northern Israelite tribes of Benjamin and Joseph, whose sons were Ephraim and Manasseh. Rachel's **bitter weeping** was caused by the exile and captivity of her children. She refused **to be comforted** in her sorrow and loss.

31:17 Hope describes a faith that waits

expectantly for God's redemptive and eternal blessing. **their own border:** Ephraim would be restored to its God-ordained territories.

31:18, 19 struck . . . on the thigh: This indicates an outward demonstration of remorse over sin and change of life (Ezek. 21:12).

31:20 My heart yearns: This phrase describes the Lord's deep love and concern for the welfare of His children.

31:21 The **signposts** and **landmarks** would point out the way to the people's homeland. More importantly, Israel was instructed to **set** its **heart** toward the **way** that is the path of faith in its God.

31:22 Backsliding was a major theme in 3:6—4:4, describing the continual waywardness of the nation. Here the Lord was bringing about the re-creation of His people. **A new thing** probably refers to the fact that virgin Israel would **encompass** or cling to her divine Bridegroom.

31:23–26 Mountain of holiness refers to the ideal city of Jerusalem, the holy mountain home of God, the Righteous One, and Judah, His righteous remnant. As with Israel, Judah's reestablishment would see renewed productivity of its crops and flocks (31:5, 12). The people would be **satiated** (31:14).

31:27, 28 sow: God would plant and multiply the **seed of man** and animal in the land of Judah. **To build and to plant** are the same terms used in Jeremiah's call (1:10).

31:29, 30 The proverb in this passage is also found in Ezek. 18:2. The contexts in both books indicate that this proverb is not original to Jeremiah or Ezekiel. In Israel and other ancient Middle Eastern communities, corporate responsibility was emphasized in legal and moral matters (Deut. 5:9), though individual accountability was not overlooked (Deut. 24:16; 2 Sam. 12:1–15). In Jeremiah and Ezekiel, focus is placed on the responsibility of the individual for his or her **own iniquity.**

31:31 days are coming: In Jeremiah, this phrase usually introduces a special occasion of divine intervention in history. **new covenant:** As contrasted with the Mosaic and Deutero-

nomic covenant. One problem that we encounter in both the OT and the NT is the mistaken idea that merely keeping the law (in an external manner) may bring about justification. But according to the NT as well as the OT, the law could not accomplish salvation and forgiveness of sins apart from a heart of faith and humility (Mic. 6:6–8; Rom. 4:1—5:2; 7:13–25). The Law of God was never designed as a means of justification, but rather as a pathway for the redeemed to walk (in other words, a means of their sanctification). **house of Israel . . . house of Judah:** According to 11:10, both kingdoms had broken God's covenant by rejecting His words and by worshiping other gods.

31:32 The old **covenant** demanded adherence to stipulations (Ex. 19:1—23:33) that the people were unable to keep. Above all other commandments, the people were commanded to love and serve God and abandon all others (Ex. 23:33; Deut. 6:4, 5). This they did not do. **fathers:** From the wilderness period (Ex. 32:1–10; Num. 25:1–9) until the days of Manasseh, the history of Israel was permeated with idolatrous activity, only occasionally broken by periods of true faithfulness to God. The people seemed incapable of acting in sustained obedience to the covenant. **husband:** As Hosea was to Gomer, the Lord had been a faithful and devoted husband to Israel.

31:33 I will make: The new **covenant** would be initiated by God Himself, assuring its effectiveness. **after those days:** This expression looks forward to the time of fulfillment of the New Covenant, which found fruition in the life, death, and resurrection of Jesus Christ. **put My law in their minds . . . write it on their hearts:** Together the *mind* and *heart* describe the total inner motivations of mind, will, emotion, and spirit.

31:34 No more shall every man teach: No longer would intermediaries like priests or prophets be needed to show the people how to **know the Lord**. From youngest to oldest, from peasant farmer to kings and princes, all would know God. Knowledge of God is a major theme

---

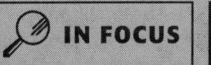 **IN FOCUS**   **"plant"**

(Heb. *nata'*) (1:10; 18:9; 31:28; 2 Sam. 7:10) Strong's #5193: Aside from references to the planting of crops (Gen. 9:20), this verb is used to describe the placement of tents and other objects on the ground (Dan. 11:45). Jeremiah uses this word to testify of God's sovereignty not only over Israel but over the establishment and eventual overthrow of all powers great and small on earth (12:2). Since God planted and established every nation, He could also uproot them whenever He wished (1:10).

of Jeremiah (2:8; 4:22; 5:4; 8:7) as well as of other prophets (Hos. 5:4). This knowledge is an intimate relationship with God evidenced by faith, obedience, and devotion. God will **forgive** and will purposefully not **remember** the **sin** and **iniquity** of His people who come to Him in repentance and faith. Jesus the Messiah fulfilled this promised New Covenant through His work on the Cross (Matt. 26:26–28; Mark 14:22–24; 1 Cor. 11:25).

31:35 sun . . . moon . . . stars: God, the Creator of all things, entered into covenant with His people. **sea . . . waves:** The Hebrew people learned from their Canaanite neighbors to fear the sea (Ps. 93). But God is Master of the sea, as He is Master of all things (Is. 51:15).

31:36, 37 Ordinances here are the natural laws that govern creation. The foundation of the New Covenant is as sure as the God who maintains creation. **measured . . . searched out:** At the peak of Judah's apostasy, shortly before the destruction of the nation by Babylon in divine judgment, the Lord emphatically reaffirmed His

covenant relationship with the Jewish people in such strong terms that the promise was unbreakable, even by Him. When we see a rainbow in the sky, we should recall God's promise to Noah, even as God does (Gen. 9:16). When we observe the sun, moon, or stars in the sky (v. 35), we should remember God's promise to the Jewish people, even as God does.

31:38–40 days are coming: This expression introduces a new era in the history of God's dealing with His people. A survey is made of the environs of the new Jerusalem, a city **built for the Lord** in its entirety. The **Tower of Hananel** (Neh. 3:1) was located at the northeast corner of the city. The **Corner Gate** (2 Kin. 14:13) was to the northwest. Expansion of the northwest side of the city took place under Uzziah and Hezekiah. The **valley of the dead bodies** is probably a reference to the Valley of Hinnom, where children had been sacrificed in times of terrible apostasy (7:32). **The fields as far as the Brook Kidron** are the slopes of Mount Zion bordered by the Valley of Hinnom.

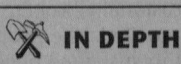 **IN DEPTH** **The New Covenant**

Jeremiah is the only OT prophet who speaks about the New Covenant that Jesus inaugurated (Matt. 26:28). Some readers, desiring to celebrate what is "new" in the New Covenant, might be tempted to disparage the former covenant, the Mosaic covenant. But we should be careful to avoid any implication that there was something wrong in the covenant God had graciously bestowed on Israel.

God had never designed the Law of Moses as a means to obtain salvation. Instead, forgiveness of sins has always been God's gracious gift to those who have humbled themselves before Him in faith (Gen. 15:6; Mic. 6:6–8; Rom. 4:1–5:2; 7:13–25). The Law was God's way of pointing out the pathway that believers should walk. Thus, the problem with the covenant at Mount Sinai was not in God's provision, but in Israel's response.

The Israelites had continually broken the covenant. Time and again through priests and prophets God called His people to repent, but any change of heart they underwent they soon abandoned. In the days of Jeremiah, King Josiah destroyed the idols that were in the land. But soon after this godly king died, the people turned back to worshiping the idols of the neighboring countries. The *hearts* of the people remained unchanged. Only God Himself could change hearts and minds: thus a new covenant was needed.

The announcement of a new covenant by the prophet Jeremiah would have been alarming to godly Israelites. After all, the old covenant had come from the hand of God and had been accompanied by miracles and wonders. But the New Covenant would also be accompanied by the miracle of changed hearts and lives. The Spirit of God would enter people's lives in order to assure their adherence to the covenant (31:34; see Acts 2). No longer would intermediaries such as priests or prophets have to stand between the people and God. The Spirit would teach the people the knowledge of God—a knowledge that would demonstrated by faith, obedience, and devotion to the Lord.

Jesus fulfilled Jeremiah's prediction of the coming of a New Covenant through His work on the cross. By His death, the giving of His blood for many, redemption and forgiveness of sins were attained (31:34). While Jesus was on earth, He instructed His disciples in His Father's ways (Luke 24:13–27). But after Jesus ascended to heaven, the Sprit of God was poured out on the believers gathered in Jerusalem, fulfilling the promise spoken by Jeremiah.

plucked up . . . thrown down: The destructive terms of Jeremiah's call are employed again (1:10). No longer would the city see devastation, for it would be **holy to the LORD.**

32:1–44 The hope for restoration is solidified in the symbolic act of Jeremiah's purchase of a field in his hometown of Anathoth. The chapter has these divisions: (1) Jeremiah's purchase of a field (vv. 1–15); (2) Jeremiah's confessional prayer (vv. 16–25); and (3) God's answer of assurance (vv. 26–44).

32:1, 2 This verse relates the chronologies of Israel and Babylon. Nebuchadnezzar's **eighteenth year** was 588 B.C., at the beginning of the siege of Jerusalem. The siege resulted from Zedekiah's revolt against Babylonian rule. The insurrection was instigated in part by Egypt under Psammetichus II and Hophra (or Apries), as well as Tyre and Ammon, in mid-589 B.C. By January, 588 B.C., Nebuchadnezzar had established his Levantine headquarters at Riblah in Syria and began to attack the Shephelah fortresses of Azekah and Lachish. Then Jerusalem was blockaded from the south and the north, cutting off all supplies to the city. In the summer of 588 B.C., the Egyptian army advanced to the coastal plain and the Babylonian army suspended its assault long enough to drive back the Egyptians. This brief respite may have afforded Jeremiah the time to complete the deed transfer, and Zedekiah the reason for questioning Jeremiah, who had been placed in a guardroom of the palace court.

32:3–5 Jeremiah was imprisoned for his declaration that Jerusalem would fall to the **Chaldeans** and **Zedekiah** would be taken captive. **face to face . . . eye to eye:** The one-on-one confrontation with Nebuchadnezzar would result in the removal of Zedekiah's eyes (39:5–7).

32:6–8 The Lord instructed Jeremiah to purchase a field in his hometown of **Anathoth,** three miles north of Jerusalem, when Jeremiah's cousin **Hanamel** came to visit. **right of redemption:** According to Lev. 25:25–30, a person had the right to redeem property when a relative found it necessary to sell land because of debt or financial failure.

32:9–11 The land transaction was conducted according to the legal customs of the day. The price of **seventeen shekels** would amount to about seven ounces of **silver.**

32:12 Baruch the son of Neriah: This friend of Jeremiah is first mentioned here (ch. 36); he may have brought the silver for the land to Jeremiah in prison.

32:13–15 earthen vessel: Examples of storage jars that served as safety-deposit vessels have been excavated Judah. The Dead Sea Scrolls were also stored in ceramic vessels, aiding their preservation for almost two thousand years. The illustrated message of the purchase was assurance and confirmation that restoration of the land was certain. **shall be possessed again:** Jeremiah realized that the end of the city was near (v. 2); his action in purchasing land was a remarkable demonstration of faith in God that the people of Judah would return one day to their land.

32:16–25 Jeremiah's prayer of praise concludes the deed transaction. The prayer consists primarily of a rehearsal of God's past deeds in creation, the Exodus, and the conquest, leading up to Jeremiah's reminding God of the present Babylonian siege and the prophet's own recent purchase of property. The prayer expresses both confidence in God's power and bewilderment at His purpose.

32:17 There is nothing too hard for You: Affirming God's power in creation (27:5) bolstered Jeremiah's faith in God's ability to deal with the siege of Jerusalem.

32:18, 19 The Lord's mercy and devotion to His people was demonstrated in His extending **lovingkindness,** or loyal love, to **thousands** (Deut. 5:9, 10). The Lord's faithful love far outweighs His punishing judgment, but the seriousness of sin is not to be overlooked (Ex. 20:5, 6; 34:7). **everyone according to his ways:** Every person will be judged individually on the basis of their own actions (17:10).

32:20, 21 The great historical demonstration of God's loyal love was the exodus of Israel from **Egypt.** This was accomplished **with signs and wonders** (Ps. 78:43) by which the name of God was made known among nations such as Moab (Num. 22—24), and peoples such as those in Jericho (Josh. 2:8–14). **strong hand . . . outstretched arm:** These expressions are found in Israel's confessional statement regarding the Exodus (Deut. 26:8). The addition of **great terror** indicates the mighty acts done against the Egyptians.

32:22, 23 The final step in this rehearsal of history was the gift of the Promised Land. **not obeyed:** The nation responded to God's grace with disobedience and breaking of the covenant, resulting in the **calamity** of the Babylonian siege and the eventual destruction of Jerusalem.

32:24, 25 You see it: What Jeremiah had prophesied in the name of God, the attack of the Babylonian foe from the north and the ensuing **sword, famine,** and **pestilence** (21:7), was now being fulfilled. Buying a field in a disintegrating land seemed out of line with Jeremiah's previous messages of destruction. Why buy land in a region overrun by Babylonians?

32:26–44 The answer to Jeremiah's bewilderment comes in the form of a speech from the

Lord. The structure is closely parallel to that of Jeremiah's previous prayer but is lengthier. The history portion (vv. 26–35) contains extensive terminological parallels to several earlier judgment oracles. The restoration section (vv. 36–44) likewise derives much of its phraseology from earlier restoration oracles. In this speech there is a dramatic contrast of Israel's sinful past and the future of God's blessing in restoration.

32:26, 27 God of all flesh: God was Lord over Israel and Judah, and Lord over the nations (27:1–11)—including mighty Babylon (25:15–26). **too hard**: Nothing is impossible to God. This expression connects the present section with the previous one.

32:28–31 The Lord reassures Jeremiah of His intentions in judging Judah and Jerusalem with fire and destruction, for they had worshiped **other gods**. Condemnation of the worship of foreign gods is one of the key themes in the Book of Jeremiah, with the phrase "other gods" occurring eighteen times, along with numerous references to specific deities such as Ba'al, Milcom, Nabu, Chemosh, and Marduk.

32:32–35 kings . . . princes . . . priests . . . prophets . . . men of Judah . . . inhabitants of Jerusalem: This exhaustive list indicates the rebellion of the entire nation against God.

32:36–38 This verse serves as a summary of the situation in Jerusalem, described by the regular triad of devastation: **sword . . . famine . . . pestilence.**

32:39 one heart . . . one way: Because the Lord had written on the heart of the people a New Covenant (31:33), no longer would they worship other deities and turn to foreign nations for help. The word *way* is often used in Jeremiah to denote the character of a person's life, whether evil (4:18; 7:3, 5; 10:2; 18:11) or good (7:23). **fear Me:** To fear God is to submit to His sovereign majesty and walk according to His way.

32:40 The expression **everlasting covenant** is also found in Is. 55:3; Ezek. 16:60; 37:26. In Ezekiel it is equated with a "covenant of peace" that God will establish with His people. This covenant will be everlasting, unlike the Sinai covenant that had been broken and ignored for so long. **My fear in their hearts:** This phrasing closely parallels in meaning and purpose that of the New Covenant of 31:31–34.

32:41 plant: This term from Jeremiah's call (1:10) depicts God establishing His people back in their homeland with a restoration of peace and prosperity. **My heart . . . My soul:** These terms describe God's total devotion of heart, will, and emotions to His faithful children.

32:42–44 calamity . . . good: God would act to reverse the manner in which He dealt with His people after they had been punished by the Babylonians. **Men will buy fields:** Final assurance is given to Jeremiah, who had purchased a field in perilous and disastrous times. Fields would be bought and sold again throughout the land when the **captives** had been brought home.

33:1–26 This section is composed of two collections of restoration speeches, the first (vv. 1–13) describing the healing and cleansing of Judah and Jerusalem, and the second (vv. 14–26) composed of messianic teachings related to the Jerusalem leadership.

33:1–13 The setting of this speech is the court of the guard, where Jeremiah was kept during the Babylonian siege in 588 B.C. The contents closely parallel chapter 32. Here the emphasis is placed upon the joy and glory of restored Jerusalem. This section is outlined according to the three occurrences of the messenger formula: (1) restoration and cleansing of Jerusalem (vv. 1–9); (2) the joy in the restoration (vv. 10, 11); and (3) the restoration of Judah (vv. 12, 13).

33:1 while he was still shut up: A chronological tie is made to 32:2 (588 B.C.). Jeremiah had been placed under palace **court** guard because of what his enemies regarded as "seditious speeches," announcing the fall of Jerusalem and giving advice to Zedekiah to surrender to Nebuchadnezzar.

33:2 Jeremiah appealed to God's power in creation as the basis for his proclamation about the coming demonstration of power in restoration. Previously the creative power of God provided the foundation for the authority of the Lord to announce the destruction of the nation (2:12; 4:23–25), as well as the future restoration (32:17). The renewal of the nation is tantamount to a new creation.

33:3 Jeremiah urged the people to call out to the Lord, pointing out that this time the Lord would hear and **answer** (7:16) their cries. **Mighty things** has the abstract meaning of "inaccessible" or "unfathomable." God had done **great** things in creation; here the people were invited to observe anew the unfathomable greatness of God's work on their behalf.

33:4, 5 Houses that were built along the city walls could be torn down and filled with rubble to produce a wider, more solid wall. This was one means of combating the sloping earthen siege ramparts that armies constructed opposite domestic quarters rather than at heavily fortified towers or gates.

33:6–8 Three beneficent acts of the Lord will bring renewal to Judah: healing, rebuilding, and cleansing.

33:6 Judah and Jerusalem in their idolatry and rebellion were without peace and **health**

(8:15, 22). The Lord promised **healing** in response to their repentance (3:22; 30:17).

33:7 as at the first: Return and rebuilding will bring security to both Israel and Judah, as well as restore the glory of their former days.

33:8 Forgiveness is described with two terms, **cleanse** and **pardon**. The word *cleanse* describes ritual purification of what is physically or spiritually unclean or defiled, such as Israel and Judah (2:23; 7:30). *Pardon* means "to forgive" and in the OT is used only with God as the subject as He forgives people. This fact helps us understand the reaction of the scribes when they heard Jesus forgiving sins (Mark 2:7).

33:9 As the citizens of Moab (Num. 22:1–6) and Jericho (Josh. 2:8–14) were full of fear and trembling before the nation that had benefited from the Lord's mighty works, so all would **fear and tremble** in amazement at God's new masterwork.

33:10, 11 Jerusalem would be made an object of derision, humiliation, and horror (25:9), but after the years of judgment and abandonment were fulfilled, the voices of sorrow would be turned to joy. This prophecy was partially fulfilled when Ezra and later Nehemiah led exiles back to rebuild, beginning with the temple and the city walls. However, Jerusalem's joy would come about ultimately as a result of a new covenant (31:31), which would be initiated at the coming of Christ (Heb. 8:6–13). That New Covenant would provide a lasting basis for hope and joy—knowing God.

33:12, 13 The focus turns to the regions within the nation of Judah that would experience God's mighty restoration. **desolate:** Note the parallel judgment in 7:34; 25:9. The regions listed are similar to those in 17:26. The six locations are organized around two triads: one introduced by the words **mountains** (the hill country), **lowland** (the Shephelah), and **South** (the Negev); and the second moving in a north-south direction: **Benjamin, around Jerusalem, Judah.** The term **flocks** is used to depict the Israelites as they returned from captivity into the fold of the holy city of Jerusalem.

33:14–26 This section is a collection of messianic oracles outlining the benefits that will accrue to the nation of Israel from her kingly and priestly leadership (vv. 14–18) and from the Davidic covenant (vv. 19–26).

33:15, 16 These verses closely parallel 23:5, 6, which has as its focus the royal leadership of the nation, the combined restored Israel and Judah. **Branch of righteousness:** God would raise up a messianic king of Davidic lineage who would rule according to the divine ideal, with **judgment,** meaning justice, and **righteousness. saved . . . dwell in safety:** Following the devastation of the Babylonian onslaught, Jerusalem would exist under divine protection.

33:17, 18 The Davidic covenant of divine succession is reiterated (2 Sam. 7:12–16). The Levitical priesthood would likewise be heirs to a divine succession in overseeing the sacrificial system in the Jerusalem temple. Jesus, as Priest and King, fulfills both offices in the New Covenant.

33:19–26 Assurance of the continuance of the Davidic covenant is conveyed through comparison to the divine order of the universe (an argument from the absurd). Davidic succession on the throne is as certain and constant as the cycle of day and night.

33:20, 21 My covenant: The divine order in the universe is readily evident in the day and night cycle from creation; it was confirmed in the covenant with Noah and again in the Decalogue (Gen. 1:14–18; 8:22; Ex. 20:8–11). This covenant is immutable for as long as earth exists. So also is the covenant with David and the Levites. As the Levites demonstrated their faithfulness in the wilderness and their leadership was confirmed (Ex. 32:25–29), so their descendants would have dominion over the sacrificial system.

33:22 The promise to Abraham and Jacob of innumerable posterity is confirmed to the Davidic throne and Levitical leadership (Gen. 13:16; 15:5; 28:14).

33:23, 24 The two families in this context are the houses of David and Levi (Zech. 12:12,

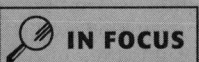 **IN FOCUS**   **"cast away"**

(Heb. *ma'as*) (8:9; 33:26; Lev. 26:43). Strong's #3988: This Hebrew verb means "to despise," "to hold without regard," or "to refuse, reject" (Lev. 26:43; Job 30:1; 1 Sam. 16:10). Like the Hebrew verb *'azab* (meaning "to abandon"), this term has reciprocal connotations when used in covenant contexts. When the people of Judah rejected God's Law (6:19), the Lord rejected that generation (7:29). As part of the New Covenant, the Lord promised that He would never again reject His people, but would forgive their sin and remember it no more (31:34, 37).

13). Because of their sins of rebellion against the covenant and their idolatry, Israel and Judah were **despised** (6:30; 7:29) by God and ridiculed among the nations.

33:25, 26 Ordinances refers to the laws that govern the divine order of the cosmos (5:22; 31:35, 36). If day and night should cease, only then would God **cast away** the great multitude of **the descendants of Jacob.** The promise of leadership succession is extended to the nation in terms of its existence as the people of God. The evidence of that promise and God's **mercy** would be the **return** and restoration of the exiles to the land of God's inheritance.

34:1–39:18 This collection of material dates from the reigns of Jehoiakim and Zedekiah, concluding with the fall of Jerusalem in 586 B.C. The section is organized in a chiastic structure (an inversion of order), beginning with Zedekiah (ch. 34), moving toward back in time to Jehoiakim (chs. 35, 36), and then returning to the reign of Zedekiah (chs. 37—39). The high point of the chiasm is the burning of Jeremiah's first scroll by Jehoiakim, an act tantamount to rejection of the Lord as God of the nation and assuring the fulfillment of Jeremiah's judgment oracles against Judah. The section begins with a judgment oracle against Zedekiah during the Babylonian siege, and it ends with the destruction of Jerusalem by the Babylonians.

34:1–22 This chapter commences with the judgment against Zedekiah in the midst of Nebuchadnezzar's attack upon the fortified cites of Judah. The Babylonians' assault on Judah in late 589 B.C. was the result of Zedekiah's alliance with Egypt and Phoenicia in rebellion against Nebuchadnezzar. In the spring of 588 B.C., when only the two Shephelah fortifications of Azekah and Lachish remained, Pharaoh Hophra of Egypt brought his army across the northern Sinai to fight against Nebuchadnezzar. When Nebuchadnezzar temporarily withdrew his siege to go out to meet the Egyptians, there was a brief respite for the inhabitants of Judah and Jerusalem. When the Egyptians had been driven back, the siege was renewed with even greater intensity.

34:1 all his army . . . all the kingdoms . . . all the people: Jeremiah pictured all the armed forces of Babylon and its vassals arrayed simultaneously against Judah and Jerusalem.

34:2, 3 you shall not escape: Though Zedekiah attempted to flee to Jericho, Nebuchadnezzar's forces captured him and brought him to Riblah for a **face to face** meeting with Nebuchadnezzar (32:3, 4).

34:4, 5 In 21:4–7, Jeremiah proclaimed the destruction of Jerusalem and the death of its inhabitants by sword, pestilence, and famine. The particular implications for **Zedekiah** are

outlined here. The king would **die in peace** in Babylon, meaning that he would not be executed by the **sword.** According to 2 Kin. 25:6, 7, his sons were killed before his eyes and then his eyes were put out.

34:6, 7 The background of the siege of Judah and Jerusalem is outlined. The fortifications at **Azekah** and **Lachish** in the lowlands were the avenue through which possible aid from Egypt would have come. They were the last to fall before Jerusalem was destroyed.

34:8–22 During the siege of Jerusalem in the spring of 588 B.C., Zedekiah proclaimed the freedom of slaves according to the message of the Lord through Jeremiah and the teaching of Law (Deut. 15:12–15). But when the Babylonian siege was temporarily halted, the policy was reversed and those set free were taken back by their masters. Jeremiah condemned Zedekiah for this breach of the covenant.

34:8, 9 covenant: A legal agreement was made between Zedekiah and the people of Jerusalem during the Babylonian siege to release from bondage all Hebrew slaves. **Liberty** is a technical word for the release of Hebrew slaves every fifty years in the Year of Jubilee (Lev. 25:8–10), when slaves were freed and indebted land was returned to its original owners. In Deut. 15:1, 12–15, a similar release during the sabbatical year is outlined.

34:10, 11 The **princes** concurred with the king's covenant (vv. 8, 9) and released Jews in bondage to them, but then reversed their decision when the siege was briefly withdrawn (vv. 21, 22). This opportunism in a moment of crisis demonstrated the leaders' contempt of the covenant.

34:12–14 Jeremiah, a faithful steward of the **word** of God, began his attack against Judah's leaders by recounting the teaching of the Law on the matter of emancipating slaves (Ex. 21:2–6; Deut. 15:12–15). He reminded the people that their ancestors were slaves in **Egypt,** and that God had freed them from slavery and oppression.

34:15, 16 When the princes of Judah emancipated their Hebrew slaves, it demonstrated their covenant faithfulness and devotion to God (v. 10). But when the righteous decision was reversed (v. 11), the **name** of God was **profaned.** The name of God sums up and represents His attributes, character, and work. That name had been defiled by the breach of covenant in the same way that the people had defiled the land with their idolatry (16:18).

34:17 Because the leaders of Judah had disobeyed the covenant by revoking the **liberty** granted to Hebrew slaves (v. 11), the Lord declared that He would grant liberty to the leaders—liberty from their disobedience and lib-

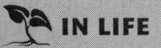 **IN LIFE** | **Everybody's Doing It!**

People sometimes excuse or justify their immoral behavior with the attitude that "everybody's doing it." But that notion is false. Not everyone is doing it. Not everyone is giving way to popular opinion. Some people maintain their moral convictions—even those that are not based on specific biblical teachings.

For example, the Rechabites showed that it is possible to remain faithful and obedient to God, no matter what other people may be doing. After all, if this family could remain loyal to convictions that were not even prescribed by God, then surely the rest of the people could hold fast to beliefs and standards that God had commanded (35:12–16).

The same principle applies today. Here and there in modern society, we find groups of people who steadfastly maintain traditions or lifestyles that they have inherited from their ancestors. They go about their business seemingly undeterred by the fads and fashions of the surrounding culture. But if these groups are able to hold onto their convictions, is there any reason why those of us who claim to follow Christ should not maintain the moral standards and doctrinal truths that the Lord has established in Scripture?

erty **to the sword, to pestilence, and to famine.**

34:18, 19 The covenant ceremony is outlined. The main ritual of the two-party covenant began with cutting the sacrificial animal in half, after which the two participants would walk together between the **parts** (Gen. 15). The divided animal portrayed the potential fate of one who broke the covenant stipulations.

34:20 I will give them into the hand of their enemies: The slaves who had been wronged by the leaders of Judah would be vindicated by God, using the Babylonian army as His instrument.

34:21, 22 gone back: Nebuchadnezzar had withdrawn from Jerusalem to meet the Egyptian army of Pharaoh Hophra. **Zedekiah** had hopes that Hophra would be successful in delivering Israel from its impending doom. However, Nebuchadnezzar soon renewed the siege of Jerusalem and destroyed the city.

35:1–19 The setting of Jeremiah's encounter with the Rechabites, as indicated by v. 11, is near the end of the reign of Jehoiakim who died in December, 598 B.C. Nebuchadnezzar had ordered troops from the Ammonites, Moabites, Aramaeans (**Syrians**), and Chaldeans to attack the rebellious Judah under Jehoiakim (2 Kin. 24:2). These raids provide the background for the Rechabites leaving their territory and seeking refuge in Jerusalem. The account is similar in form to the symbolic act account. The placement of the Rechabite encounter in connection with the account of Zedekiah's reversal of freedom of the slaves (ch. 34) was to illustrate covenant faithfulness with a concrete example.

35:1 in the days of Jehoiakim: Jehoiakim reigned from 609 to 598 B.C.

35:2 The Rechabites were a tightly knit group of descendants of the Kenites (Judg. 1:16; 1 Chr. 2:55). This group is known first from the story of Jehonadab the son of Rechab, who assisted Jehu in purging the Baal prophets from Samaria (2 Kin. 10:15–28). The Rechabites lived as nomads, rejecting all forms of urban and agrarian life. They refused to drink wine or strong drink and would not cultivate vineyards. They also would not plant any other crops. Many scholars believe that they were a clan of metalsmiths. The Rechabites were invited by Jeremiah into one of the **chambers** surrounding the courtyard of the temple of God for a symbolic demonstration.

35:3–5 Man of God refers to a number of named and unnamed prophets, emissaries from God who delivered specific messages (1 Sam. 2:27; 1 Kin. 12:22; 13:1; 2 Kin. 1:9). **Hanan** was apparently sympathetic to Jeremiah's preaching. In the temple and in the presence of leading temple personnel, Jeremiah tested the Rechabites' faithfulness to their tradition by putting **wine** in front of them and telling them to drink.

35:6–10 The faithful Rechabites refused to drink wine, on the basis of the teaching of **Jonadab** their forefather. **obeyed the voice:** This is the language of faithfulness, often used in the negative by Jeremiah to refer to Judah's failure to obey the covenant (3:13; 7:23, 24).

35:11 The present military threat from Nebuchadnezzar had brought one change. Though not in keeping with their tradition, the Rechabites had now sought protection from the Babylonians within the confines of the walls of Jerusalem.

35:12–15 receive instruction . . . obey My words: This phrasing comes from the words of the Rechabites (v. 8) and from Jeremiah's oracle in 7:28. The Rechabites had obeyed the instructions of their ancestor Jonadab. In the case of Judah, though God Himself had instructed the Israelites in the covenant and had presented His message repeatedly through many faithful prophets, the people had not obeyed Him. **Rising early and speaking . . . sending** describes the persistence of the many prophets in the Israel's history.

35:16, 17 The Rechabites had not wavered in keeping the **commandment** of Jonadab, but the Israelites had continually rebelled against the teaching of God.

35:18, 19 Blessing is pronounced over the faithful household of the Rechabites. Their complete obedience is outlined in a triad of verbs: **obeyed . . . kept . . . done.**

36:1–32 The Book of Jeremiah provides more insight into the nature, recording, composition, and history of the word of God in its formative periods than perhaps any other book of the Bible. There are more than 250 references to the word of God in Jeremiah in phrases like "the word of the Lord," "My word(s)," and "the Lord spoke," Jeremiah the prophet was the vocal instrument in the revelatory process, speaking as God revealed His message to him. In this chapter, Jeremiah's early oracles are recorded on a scroll (vv. 1–4); Baruch was instructed to read it in the temple (vv. 5–8); the scroll was read during the fast (vv. 9, 10); Micaiah reported the pronouncement to the royal palace (vv. 11–13); Baruch read the scroll in the palace (vv. 14–19); the scroll was read before Jehoiakim, who then burnt it (vv. 20–26); the scroll was rewritten (vv. 27, 28); and the resulting judgment oracle was pronounced against Jehoiakim and the royal household (vv. 29–32).

36:1 The narrative recounts the interaction with Jehoiakim concerning the word of God during the king's fourth year, 605–604 B.C. In late spring as the year began and the river was "at flood stage," Nebuchadnezzar crossed the Euphrates and defeated the Egyptians at Carchemish. **it came to pass:** The original scroll of Jeremiah's oracles, which had been prepared with the scribal assistance of Baruch, was read in the temple in the ninth month of the fourth year of Jehoiakim in November through December 604 B.C. (v. 9). This was at the same time as the attack of the Babylonians on Ashkelon.

36:2 scroll of a book: The usual material for a scroll was parchment (a kind of leather), though Egyptian papyrus was also available. The contents of the scroll were the oracles dating from the **days of Josiah**, at the advent of Jeremiah's ministry (626 B.C.), to **this day** (604 B.C.).

36:3 The reasons for Jeremiah's dictation to Baruch are several: (1) divine instruction; (2) Jeremiah was prohibited from speaking in the temple so that an emissary was needed to transmit the Lord's message to the people; (3) Jeremiah was compelled to proclaim the message of God by any means possible in hope of Judah's repentance; and (4) the precedent of the scroll discovery in the days of Josiah that resulted in national reformation.

36:4 Baruch the son of Neriah was a trained scribe and close friend of Jeremiah (32:12). **at the instruction:** This phrase refers to the process of dictation from Jeremiah to Baruch.

36:5 Confined can refer to physical imprisonment, being placed under guard (33:1; 39:15); a mental or spiritual constraint; or some other form of restriction. No prison is mentioned in this chapter. It is possible that Jeremiah was somehow prohibited from entering the temple courts, perhaps after his temple sermon (7:1–15; 26:1–19).

36:6, 7 The **scroll** of Jeremiah's early oracles against Israel and Judah was to be read on a **day of fasting,** a time aside by official declaration of the king or priests (v. 9) in a period of national crisis.

36:8 Baruch, a faithful disciple like Jeremiah, read from the **book** of God's words in the temple of the Lord. This act closely parallels the reading of the Book of the Law in the temple of God after it was discovered there (2 Kin. 22; 23).

36:9, 10 The official proclamation of the **fast** came in November through December of 604 B.C. People from all over Judah assembled in the temple of the Lord for the fast, providing Baruch and Jeremiah a sizable audience. **Gemariah** was **the son of Shaphan,** the scribe who read the scroll found during Josiah's reign (2 Kin. 22:1–20). It seems Gemariah was sympathetic toward Jeremiah, allowing the use of the room in the **upper court,** a room overlooking the temple courts and giving access to those gathered for the fast.

36:11–13 Gemariah's son **Micaiah** reported the occasion and words to the royal **princes,** including **Gemariah** and **Elnathan.** Elnathan's father **Achbor** also played a role in the reading of the scroll in the days of Josiah's reform. The parallels between Josiah's reform and Jeremiah's desire for national revival were included by Baruch deliberately, to remind the people of the earlier event.

36:14 Jehudi: The list of three ancestors is unusual. The last name **Cushi** may indicate that Jehudi was a Cushite, thus of foreign ancestry. Jehudi was the messenger appointed to summon Baruch to the court of the princes.

36:15–19 looked in fear: Alarmed at the words of the scroll, the princes felt impelled to inform the king. **wrote them with ink:** Baruch told the princes how and when the scroll was written. The leaders told Baruch to **go** with Jeremiah and **hide** until the matter could be investigated.

36:20–24 Baruch and Jeremiah would have learned later that the original scroll was destroyed, since they were in hiding when it happened. **winter house:** The royal palace had rooms with fireplaces for use in the winter. As the scroll was read, Jehoiakim showed no signs of fear or lamentation, unlike Josiah when the Book of the Law was read in his hearing (2 Kin. 22:11–13).

36:25, 26 The king's son could mean: (1) the literal son of **Jehoiakim;** (2) the son of a man named Hamelek, which means "the king"; or (3) an office title for a person with the function of a deputy or policeman. The third view seems to be indicated in this context.

36:27, 28 The Lord told Jeremiah and Baruch to prepare a second **scroll** of the earlier oracles. Verse 32 notes that additional material was included.

36:29–32 Indictment and judgment against Jehoiakim is pronounced. The indictment was declared because he destroyed the scroll of the word of the Lord. First, the Davidic lineage would not continue through him. His son would rule for only three months before Nebuchadnezzar deported Jehoiachin to **Babylon,** where he died. Second, the king's body would be treated disgracefully after his death. As the king had **cast** the scroll into the fire, so his body would be cast from the royal palace. Third, the royal household would experience the destructive judgment that had been proclaimed in the words of the original scroll.

37:1–21 The text returns chronologically to the period of the respite from the Babylonian

siege in 588 B.C., when Nebuchadnezzar went out to meet the Egyptian army under Pharaoh Hophra. Jeremiah's interaction with Zedekiah during this period began with the abuse of Hebrew slaves. In chapter 37, two further encounters with Zedekiah are recounted: (1) the prophecy that the Babylonians would return and besiege the city (vv. 1–10) and (2) the accusation and imprisonment of Jeremiah for treason (vv. 11–21). The chapter begins the series of narratives recounting events leading up to the fall of Jerusalem (ch. 39).

37:1, 2 Zedekiah, like **Jehoiakim** and so many other kings before him in Israel and Judah, had rejected the word of God and its warnings of judgment, though it was communicated tirelessly and faithfully by God's messengers the prophets. The end of rebellion was in sight. Jerusalem would soon fall to the Babylonian armies, the instruments of divine discipline.

37:3, 4 Jehucal was a friend of Pashhur (21:1). Together they eventually called for Jeremiah to be executed (38:1). **Zephaniah the son of Maaseiah** was a member of the delegation who had sought a word from God at the beginning of the Babylonian siege (21:1–10). He was sympathetic toward Jeremiah, as reflected in the letter from Shemaiah (29:24–28).

37:5 In late spring or early summer 588 B.C., Pharaoh Hophra led the Egyptian **army** into southern Palestine. The Babylonian forces withdrew their siege of Judah and Jerusalem to confront the Egyptians. Zedekiah hoped the Babylonians would be defeated, but his hopes proved to be in vain.

37:6–8 Jeremiah's response to Jehucal and Zephaniah (vv. 3, 4) was the same unchanging **word** from **the Lord** he had always proclaimed. The Babylonians would soon return to destroy Jerusalem.

37:9, 10 Do not deceive yourselves: To

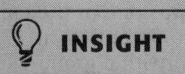 **INSIGHT** | **Children of Rebellion**

While Scripture urges parents to raise their children "in the training and admonition of the Lord" (Eph. 6:4), it makes no guarantees about how one's children will turn out. Nor can it: each individual decides whether to follow the Lord or depart from His ways. Parents can point their children in the right direction, but once young people become adults, they determine which way they will go.

That helps to explain why some godly parents have children who are spiritually rebellious. By the same token, people of great faith and compassion have been known to come from homes where God was dishonored or even unknown. Josiah was a man of faith and a conscientious ruler of Israel (2 Chr. 34:1). Nevertheless, all three of his sons, including Zedekiah (Jer. 37:1–2), turned away from God, and paid a tragic price as a result.

🔍 IN FOCUS "prophet"

(Heb. *nabi'*) (37:6; Deut. 13:1; 1 Sam. 3:20; 2 Kin. 19:2) Strong's #5030: The probable root word for *nabi'* means "to announce" or "to proclaim" (19:14; Ezek. 37:4). Another possible derivation is from a Hebrew word meaning "to bubble up" or "to pour forth." Prophecy can be compared to the "bubbling up" of the Holy Spirit in a person who delivers a divine message (compare Amos 3:8; Mic. 3:8). In OT times, prophets were heralds or spokesmen who delivered a message for someone else (1:5; 2:8; 2 Kin. 17:13; Ezek. 37:7). In the case of the Hebrew prophets, they spoke for God Himself. This is the reason the prophets introduced their messages with "thus says the LORD of hosts" on countless occasions (9:7, 17).

think that the brief respite caused by the Egyptian appearance in the southern coastal plain was proof of imminent deliverance, as the false prophets declared, was an exercise in self-deception and futile imagination.

37:11, 12 The lifting of the **siege** by the Babylonians afforded the people in Jerusalem some opportunity for movement outside the city. The precise chronology of events associated Jeremiah's intended visit to Anathoth, three miles to the north and in the direction of one of Nebuchadnezzar's original siege camps, and the purchase of the field from Hanamel (32:1–14) is not clear. A possible interpretation of parallel events in 32:2 ("in the court of the prison") and 37:21 ("commit Jeremiah to the court of the prison") would seem to indicate that Jeremiah may have had prior knowledge of the availability of the property in Anathoth before he was arrested.

37:13 Irijah, **a captain of the guard** and a royal military official, arrested Jeremiah at the **Gate of Benjamin** on the north side of the city. The charge of defection was not unreasonable. Jeremiah had advised the people of Jerusalem to defect to the Chaldeans so that their lives would be spared (21:9). A number of them followed his advice (38:19).

37:14–16 Jeremiah denied the accusation of defection but to no avail. Irijah arrested the prophet and arraigned him before the court of **princes.** Prison space was lacking in Jerusalem due to the crowded conditions of the siege, so a prison was devised **in the house of Jonathan the scribe. the dungeon and the cells:** Jeremiah's prison seems to have been a cistern with vaulted ceilings in Jonathan's house.

37:17–19 Fearing possible exposure and opposition from his courtiers, Zedekiah **secretly** summoned Jeremiah and asked of him a message from the Lord. The several encounters between Jeremiah and Zedekiah indicate the weak character of Zedekiah. He seems to have earnestly desired a message from God but could not come to grips with the reality and respond appropriately.

37:20, 21 Jeremiah appealed to Zedekiah's sense of justice and decency and asked to be released from prison. Zedekiah consented and committed the prophet to the **court of the prison,** a place near the royal palace where limited mobility was possible, such as in the transaction to purchase the field (32:1–15; Neh. 3:25).

38:1–28 Based on a general comparison of the contents, scholars are divided as to whether this chapter is a duplicate of the Jeremiah-Zedekiah encounter of 37:11–21. Both contain similar outlines of arrest scenarios with charges of treason, arraignment before the court princes, imprisonment in a cistern structure, a private meeting with Zedekiah, and subsequent confinement to a less inhumane, alternative prison facility. Differences include several personnel involved, the name of the place of confinement to the cistern, and numerous details exclusive to either account. Since variant duplicate accounts of events are not uncommon in the Book of Jeremiah (for instance, the temple sermons in 7:1–15 and 26:1–15), these could well be the same event with different emphases.

38:1 Jucal (Jehucal) was one of the emissaries sent by Zedekiah to Jeremiah in 37:3. **Pashhur** came to Jeremiah with a group when the Babylonian siege began in January 588 B.C.

38:2, 3 Verse 2 is almost an exact duplicate of 21:9. Jeremiah said the choice was between **life** under the Babylonians and death among the ruins of Jerusalem. Such a statement was treasonous, as was the statement that Jerusalem must fall.

38:4 The **princes** accused Jeremiah of demoralizing Judah and seeking the harm of Jerusalem. **weakens the hands:** This expression describes the discouragement or demoralization of soldiers (Ezra 4:4).

38:5 the king can do nothing: Zedekiah

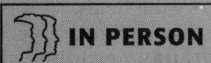 **IN PERSON** | # Africans in the Bible

E bed-Melech the Ethiopian, the official who unexpectedly came to Jeremiah's aid (Jer. 38:7), was one of a number of Africans mentioned in the Bible. The fact that Africans often played a significant role in biblical history was largely the result of Israel's location at the intersection between Africa and Asia.

The majority of Africans with whom the Israelites had contact were Egyptians. This began when Abraham visited Egypt to find food during a severe famine (Gen. 12:10). Later, the family of his grandson Jacob would relocate to Egypt for the same reason (41:53—47:31). The Israelites remained there for 430 years before returning to Canaan (Ex. 12:41). Throughout the rest of Israel's history, Egypt served alternately as either a resource or a menace.

Other Africans mentioned in the Bible represented Ethiopia (or Cush or Nubia), a term that designated both the country and the unknown lands south and southwest of Egypt; and Libya, probably the same as Put, the lands west of Egypt. The land of Ophir, renowned for its gold, may also have been located on the African continent (1 Kin. 9:28).

Beginning after the fall of Judah, many Jewish colonies were started in Africa, mostly in Egypt, but also at Cyrene. This led to the recruitment of numerous proselytes to Judaism, some of whom were present at Pentecost (Acts 2:10). The gospel probably came into Africa first by way of the African Jewish colonies. For example, tradition holds that John Mark (Acts 15:37) was the first evangelist to Alexandria, Egypt, and the first bishop of that city.

was powerless before the court of princes. The fate of Jeremiah was placed in their hands.

38:6 Jeremiah was imprisoned in the basement cistern of **Malchiah the king's son.** Probably due to the length of the Babylonian siege, the cistern had no water sufficient for drinking, only **mire** of muddy lime clay. This particular cistern had a narrow circular opening, and could be entered and exited only by means of ropes. The court princes probably expected Jeremiah to die a slow and quiet death in an unpleasant environment.

38:7–10 Ebed-Melech the Ethiopian: The name means "Servant of the King." **Gate of Benjamin:** Jeremiah had entered and left the city many times through this northern gate. The king was likely performing his normal function of mediating disputes and settling legal questions. **no more bread:** A siege cut off water and food supplies from a city, hoping starvation would force a surrender.

38:11–13 Ebed-Melech took special care to obtain **rags** for Jeremiah to cushion his armpits, preventing the **ropes** from cutting his skin. A foreigner, a once-despised Cushite, cared more for the prophet of God than did the king and princes of Jeremiah's own people.

38:14 This meeting between Jeremiah and Zedekiah is parallel to the account in 37:17–21. The location of the **third entrance** is unknown. The secrecy of the meeting may indicate that it was a private access for the king from the royal palace into the temple courts. Zedekiah's request to ask Jeremiah **something** is asked

with sincerity. He wanted the prophet to be honest and open in his answer.

38:15, 16 will you not: Jeremiah was fearful of being returned to the dungeon, of being turned over to the Egyptian courtiers who would do him further harm, or of being executed for speaking boldly against the king. Zedekiah swore by the name of God that no harm would come to the prophet from any source.

38:17, 18 Jeremiah repeated to the king the message recorded in vv. 2, 3. **Surrender** would spare the life of the king and the city; failure to surrender would bring death and destruction.

38:19 I am afraid: Zedekiah revealed he was afraid to surrender to the Babylonians because he feared retaliation by early deserters (21:9; 39:9; 52:15) from Jerusalem. His unfitness to be king is proven by his concern for his personal safety above that of the city and its inhabitants.

38:20–23 Jeremiah tried to settle Zedekiah's fears and to resolve his moral and ethical dilemma by reassuring him that surrender would result in his personal safety. But if the king refused **to surrender** to Nebuchadnezzar, the **word** of judgment would fall. **Women** and **children** would be handed over to Nebuchadnezzar, and Jerusalem would be destroyed.

38:24–26 Zedekiah instructed Jeremiah not to tell the pro-Egyptian **princes** about their conversation lest the prophet be executed. Together they constructed an account of their meeting that might be used if Jeremiah was questioned about what had been **said.** It is clear that Zedekiah was afraid of a revolt from within his royal court.

38:27, 28 As expected, **the princes** questioned Jeremiah. The answer he and Zedekiah had prepared proved satisfactory.

39:1–10 The fall of Jerusalem in 586 B.C. was one of the most lamentable events in the history of the nation. On the Fast of the ninth of Ab the Book of Lamentations is read in the synagogue during the special service commemorating the fall of the city in 586 B.C. under the Babylonians and the second time in A.D. 70 under the Romans. With the exception of v. 3, this section is duplicated or adapted in 52:4–16 and in 2 Kings 25:1–12.

39:1 The Babylonian siege began in the **tenth month** of the **ninth year** of Zedekiah's reign, that is, in December 589 or January 588 B.C. Today the tenth of Tebeth is a fast day in the Jewish calendar.

39:2 eleventh year of Zedekiah . . . fourth month . . . ninth day: The walls of Jerusalem were breached about the time food supplies were exhausted, in June or July 586 B.C.

39:3 sat in the Middle Gate: The Middle Gate was probably in the north wall of Jerusalem, the direction from which the city was taken. The Babylonian princes sat in the gate to assert their authority in the conquered city. **Nergal-Sharezer** ruled Babylon from 560 to 556 B.C. **Nebo** may be a short form of Nebushasban. When combined with **Sarsechim,** the resulting name is probably a variation of the name Nebushasban Rabsaris (v. 13). **Rabmag** and **Rabsaris** are titles.

39:4 When **Zedekiah** saw the Babylonian officers enter the gate on the north side of Jerusalem, he and his men left at night through a **gate between the two walls,** probably near the union of the Kidron and Tyropoeon valleys on the south side of the city. **Plain** refers to the Jordan valley.

39:5–7 Zedekiah and his military escort were captured near Jericho and taken to **Riblah,** a city in Aram. **Hamath** was a region of Aram. There Zedekiah met Nebuchadnezzar face to face, as Jeremiah had prophesied (34:3). Zedekiah's sons and his men were **killed** before his eyes just before he was blinded. **Bronze fetters** refers to the pairs of shackles placed on his wrists and ankles. Zedekiah died in prison in Babylon (52:11).

39:8–10 In addition to the royal palace and homes of the inhabitants, 52:13 includes the "house of the Lord" among the buildings burned in Jerusalem. **poor:** Typically the Babylonians deported the upper classes, such as court officials, merchants, artisans, and craftsmen, and left behind peasants to work the fields.

39:11 Nebuchadnezzar had given special instructions to **Nebuzaradan** regarding the treatment of Jeremiah. The positive teaching of the prophet regarding the king of Babylon had come to his attention in some way, perhaps through deserters or spies.

39:12–14 During the destruction of Jerusalem, Jeremiah was released from the court of the prison and brought to Mizpah to be under charge of **Gedaliah,** whom Nebuchadnezzar had appointed governor over the peasant population of Judah and Benjamin. A more detailed account of Jeremiah's trip from Jerusalem to Ramah to Mizpah is found in 40:1–6. One way of harmonizing the accounts is the suggestion that Jeremiah was gathered by the soldiers along with others in Jerusalem for transport to Babylon, taken to the holding camp at Ramah, and then released from Ramah by Nebuzaradan.

39:15–18 Ebed-Melech, who had carefully rescued Jeremiah from the muddy cistern in the prison court (38:11–13), was promised safety and deliverance by the Lord because of his assistance to Jeremiah and because he had **put** his **trust in** God.

40:1–6 The destruction of Judah and Jerusalem by the Babylonians was massive and complete. Cities lay burned, the leading citizens had been exiled, and a peasant population of farmers, herders, and the like was left to produce an agrarian tax base for the empire economy. A new district capital was established at Mizpah, and ruled by the puppet governor named Gedaliah. The material in 40:1—43:13 relates to the rule of Gedaliah, from the release of Jeremiah to the assassination of Gedaliah, and then to the aftermath leading up to the Jews' flight to Egypt. The present section provides an introduction to this Gedaliah material.

40:1 Ramah was about five miles north of Jerusalem, along the ancient road leading from Jerusalem to Shechem. With the destruction of Jerusalem still in process, Ramah served as a way station for captives going to the eastern provinces of the Babylonian Empire.

40:2, 3 Nebuzaradan knew about Jeremiah's predictions regarding the demise of Jerusalem and the victories of the armies of Babylon. Prophets whose words were deemed verified were generally treated well by peoples of the ancient Middle East. **The LORD your God has pronounced this doom:** Consider the irony of a foreigner stating the truth concerning the reason for Jerusalem's destruction.

40:4, 5 Jeremiah was released from bondage and given three options: (1) to go with Nebuzaradan to Babylon and enjoy special treatment and protection there; (2) to **remain**

in the care of Gedaliah, the district governor at Mizpah; or (3) to live in the land as he chose. Nebuzaradan gave Jeremiah rations and gifts because of the prophet's proclamations about Babylon and Nebuchadnezzar (25:9; 27:6).

40:6 Jeremiah chose to go to **Mizpah** to serve under **Gedaliah son of Ahikam,** staying with his people not far from his hometown and the property he had purchased while in the court of the prison (32:1–15). Mizpah was about eight miles north of Jerusalem.

40:7–10 The captains of the armies refers to the surviving Jewish commanders of the armies in the towns throughout Judah who had fled into the rugged hill country. Among the list of escaped leaders was **Ishmael,** a member of the royal family and a court officer (41:1); **Johanan,** who would become the leader of the assembly (vv. 13–16); and **Jezaniah** (Jaazaniah) whose father was a **Maacathite.**

40:11, 12 The Jews who had escaped the Babylonian onslaught into neighboring states returned home and began working the fields, vineyards, and orchards.

40:13, 14 Johanan led a group of leaders to Gedaliah to warn him of a plot by **Ishmael** and the Ammonite king **Baalis** to assassinate the governor.

40:15, 16 Johanan **secretly** asked **Gedaliah**

permission to kill **Ishmael** secretly, fearing reprisal from Babylon that would surely destroy the reconstruction efforts and lead to further bloodshed. Unfortunately, Gedaliah was far too trusting of Ishmael, the royal descendant who seems to have coveted Gedaliah's position.

41:1–3 The year of the assassination of Gedaliah is not given, only the month—**the seventh** month or Tishri, September through October. The murder of the **governor** could have taken place as soon as three months after the fall of Jerusalem. Others associate the third deportation of 582 B.C. with this rebellion. Ishmael's act was especially despicable since it took place during a banquet.

41:4–7 Two days after Gedaliah's death a group of faithful pilgrims were on their way to Jerusalem, probably with grain rather than animal offerings. Ishmael and his followers falsely led the worshipers aside, massacred them, and **cast** their bodies into a **pit.**

41:8 Ten men with **treasures** of agricultural goods were spared at their own request. Why these ten were not slain is unknown. Perhaps Ishmael left them to tell the story, or perhaps they bargained their goods for their lives.

41:9–12 When **Johanan,** who had warned Gedaliah about the assassination plot (40:13–16), heard of the atrocities of Ishmael, he mustered

Photo by Howard Vos

The great pool, or water well, in Gibeon (Jer. 41:12) has been uncovered by archaeologists. About thirty-seven feet in diameter, it extends thirty-five feet deep through solid rock.

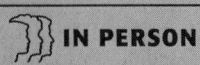 **IN PERSON** | ## The Reluctant Refugee

Terrified of the Babylonians after the fall of Jerusalem, and fearful of the Ammonites after the assassination of the appointed governor Gedaliah, the survivors of Jerusalem made preparations to flee to Egypt (41:16–18). Before departing, however, they made a pretense of asking Jeremiah for a word from the Lord (42:1–3).

Despite Jeremiah's warnings to remain in the land (42:9–22), the people insisted on leaving (43:1–7). Apparently Jeremiah and his secretary Baruch were compelled to go along, reluctant though they were. Jeremiah may have spent his final days in Egypt, for there is no record that he returned to Jerusalem.

his captains and forces and confronted the rebel army at **Gibeon.** The **pool** at which Johanan and his men found Ishmael was a large, circular pit cut into solid rock to a depth of about thirty-three feet. The **pool** was six miles northwest of Jerusalem and three miles from Mizpah, and was the site of the famous battle between Joab and Abner's men (2 Sam. 2:12–29).

41:13–15 When they saw **Johanan,** the captives Ishmael had taken from Mizpah ran over to join his forces. **Ishmael** and **eight** of his men escaped to Ammon.

41:16–18 Fearing imminent reprisal from the Babylonians on account of the rebellion, Johanan gathered the inhabitants of Mizpah, including Jeremiah, together with those he had rescued and began a trek toward **Egypt,** seeking a place of safety. Egypt was the only country in the region that was free from Babylonian control. Johanan and his group went south toward Bethlehem, camping at **Chimham.**

42:1–6 After the initial stage of the flight from Mizpah, Johanan and other leaders consult Jeremiah for a word from the Lord with regard to their future direction.

42:1–3 said to Jeremiah: The people asked Jeremiah to intercede with the Lord on their behalf. The small remnant had a leader, but needed direction and guidance.

42:4–6 I will pray: Jeremiah cautiously agreed to pray to God. He asked the people to agree to abide by the answer he received. The people responded with an oath of obedience, calling upon the Lord as witness.

42:7–10 after ten days: God's response to Jeremiah's prayer on behalf of the people did not come immediately. Jeremiah convened the assembly and declared the answer from God in terms reminiscent of his call: **build you . . . not pull you down . . . plant you . . . not pluck you up** (1:10).

42:11, 12 Jeremiah assured the people with the same words the Lord had used to give him assurance in his call: **I am with you, to save**

you and deliver you (1:8). God's promise to bring His people through a time of trial to experience His restorative power would show His great **mercy.** God had promised this restoration in earlier oracles (12:15).

42:13, 14 If the people disobeyed God and fled to Egypt, they would suffer the consequences. The people's hope for safety in Egypt is presented in a triad of phrases: **see no war, nor hear the sound of the trumpet, nor be hungry.** The people seem to have had their minds made up before they sought the word from the Lord (vv. 2, 3).

42:15–17 set their faces: This expression indicates the fixed intentions of the people. The announcement of judgment against the disobedient evacuees echoes Jeremiah's earlier pronouncements against Judah. The very thing they were trying to escape from would meet them in Egypt. **sword . . . famine . . . pestilence:** This common triad indicates the completeness of God's judgment upon the disobedient.

42:18–22 The message was succinct and clear: **Do not go to Egypt!** Again Jeremiah felt he had been deceived by a people speaking words of empty oaths and promises. He reiterated the triad of judgment terms of v. 18 that describe the end that would befall the rebels in Egypt.

43:1–3 The people had already intended to go to Egypt to escape the perceived danger of Babylon. **Azariah** and **Johanan** spoke out against the counsel given by Jeremiah in 42:9–22. As the leaders of Jerusalem had spoken before the fall of the city, the new leaders of the remnant indirectly call the message of the Lord "false" as revealed through His prophet. Baruch is accused of influencing Jeremiah to declare a deceptive message that would lead to their capture. Baruch is seen in a different light than in earlier passages, where he was simply a scribal agent or legal emissary. Here the faithful scribe Baruch is portrayed in his own right as an influential and effectual leader.

43:4–9 Johanan led the migration to Egypt, against the direction of the Lord through Jeremiah. The caravan journeyed **as far as Tahpanhes,** a city on the eastern edge of the Nile Delta (2:16).

43:10, 11 This judgment oracle echoes earlier pronouncements against Judah, with Nebuchadnezzar identified as the **servant** of God (25:9; 27:6). The **stones** symbolized the strong foundation of Nebuchadnezzar's empire, the point from which he would spread his **royal pavilion** (tent, or canopy). **death . . . captivity . . . sword:** Severe judgment is pro-

god Re. The temple was known for its two rows of **pillars,** or inscribed obelisks.

44:1–30 This chapter consists of an extended prose discourse concerning the Jews in Egypt. The chapter outlines as follows: (1) judgment oracle against Jews living in Egypt (vv. 1–14); (2) the response of the Jews living in Egypt (vv. 15–19); and (3) Jeremiah's rejoinders in condemnation of idolatrous practices among the Jews (vv. 20–30). The language derives from earlier prose sermons such as the Temple Sermon in 7:1–15. Jeremiah's messages from the Lord had become highly stylized, reflecting consistency from the beginning of his ministry under Josiah to the exilic period. Idolatry and

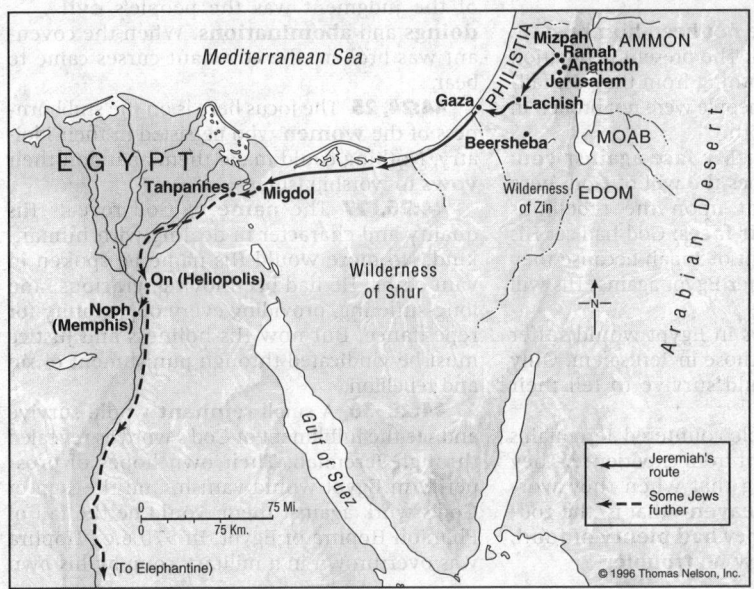

Jeremiah's Journey to Jerusalem

When Jerusalem fell to Nebuchadnezzar, Jeremiah was taken in chains to Ramah and then released. He went on to Mizpah to support the people left in the land. When the governor was killed, Jeremiah prophesied that people should not leave the land, but he was taken against his will to Tahpanhes in Egypt. His further prophecies to Jews living in Migdol, Noph, and Tahpanhes may have contributed to establishing Jewish settlements in other parts of Egypt, as far as Elephantine.

nounced on Egypt, including judgment on the disobedient people of Judah.

43:12, 13 The destructive judgment was extended to the temples of Egyptian gods and goddesses. Destruction of Egyptian temples was carried out by Esarhaddon of Assyria in the seventh century B.C., and again by Cambyses of Persia in the sixth century B.C. **Beth Shemesh** ("House of the Sun") was the temple of the sun

covenant rejection remain the center of his proclamation of the word of God. These are the last known words of Jeremiah.

44:1 Migdol is a common Semitic term meaning "Watchtower." Here the term is identified with a small fortress twenty-five miles east of Tahpanhes. **Noph** is another name for Memphis, the capital of Lower Egypt. **Pathros** is Upper Egypt. Since Jehoahaz had been deported to Egypt in 609 B.C., a number of Jews had settled there in the fertile lands along the Nile.

44:2, 3 Jerusalem was brought to **desolation** because the people broke God's covenant by worshiping other gods, rejecting the lordship of God, and thus provoking Him to anger.

44:4–7 prophets, rising early and sending: Jerusalem had been warned time and again by faithful and tireless messengers from God (7:25; 25:4; 26:5). **they did not listen or incline their ear:** The reference here is to the people's disobedience in continually worshiping foreign deities.

44:8 provoke: This term indicates willful, stubborn rebellion against God, which roused His anger.

44:9, 10 They have not been humbled . . . nor have they feared: The present generation of Jews had learned nothing from the past failures of the nation. The people were not broken in heart, only more stubborn.

44:11, 12 I will set My face against you: This expression describes the will of God, here pronouncing judgment upon the rebellious Jews in Egypt. **set their faces:** God had set His face against the remnant of Judah because they had set their face to enter Egypt against His will (43:7).

44:13, 14 The Jews in Egypt would suffer the same judgment as those in Jerusalem. Only a small **remnant** would survive to tell their story.

44:15–17 The people countered Jeremiah's words with an argument from experience. They rejected God by saying that when they worshiped the **queen of heaven**—that is, the goddess Ishtar or Astarte, they **had plenty of food, were well off, and saw no trouble.**

44:18 Queen of heaven refers to Ishtar, a goddess of war and fertility who was worshiped with explicit sexual activity. The people reasoned that when they stopped worshiping the queen of heaven in the days of Josiah's reform, their king was killed and their land was overrun and destroyed.

44:19 Women were leaders in the Ishtar rites, which included incense burning, drink offerings, and special ceremonial **cakes** marked with the symbol of the goddess (7:18).

44:20, 21 remember: This term is often used in contexts describing the basis for God's judgment.

44:22, 23 no longer bear it: The long-suffering of the Lord had reached its end. The cause of the judgment was the people's **evil . . . doings** and **abominations.** When the covenant was broken, the covenant curses came to bear.

44:24, 25 The focus here is on the stubbornness of the **women** who persisted in their idolatry. Nothing could make them abandon their **vows** to worship Ishtar.

44:26, 27 The **name** of God reveals His quality and character in dealing with humankind. No more would His name be spoken in vain oaths. He had been loving, gracious, and long-suffering, providing every opportunity for repentance. But now His holiness and justice must be vindicated through punishment of sin and rebellion.

44:28–30 A small **remnant** would survive and see the fulfillment of God's word as revealed through Jeremiah. Their own hopes of prosperity in Egypt would vanish, and the sign of God's work against them would be the fall of Pharaoh Hophra of Egypt. In 570 B.C., Hophra was overthrown in a military coup by his own

---

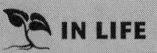 **IN LIFE**   # Words of Judgment, Words of Hope

Jeremiah announces specific judgments that the Lord vowed to bring on nine nations (chs. 46–51). In reading these sobering words, it is important to remember two truths:

(1) *God's wrath was not without cause.* There was definite justification for God's wrath: every single one of the nations listed had turned away from their Creator to worship and serve false gods. Every one of them was guilty, and God's holy nature required judgment on their sin.

(2) *God's wrath was not without remedy.* Even as the Lord had called Judah to repent of its sins throughout the years of Jeremiah's ministry, so He had called the nations to turn to Him and be saved. Tragically, they had refused God's gracious offer. Now they faced His wrath.

Yet even the Lord's judgment is redemptive in its purpose. He is willing that no one should perish (2 Pet. 3:9), and repentance is always available as an alternative to wrath, right to the end. There was always the possibility that the nations listed in Jer. 46–51, or even a handful of individuals in those nations, would fear the judgment of the Lord and turn toward Him.

general Amasis. Three years later he was executed in fulfillment of Jeremiah's prophecy.

45:1–5 The importance of Baruch in the life of Jeremiah and in the proclamation and preservation of the word of God has been noted earlier. In this passage, allusion is made to the actual words of Baruch. They form a confessional lament, to which the Lord responds with words of blessing upon his livelihood, in spite of the disastrous circumstances he experiences.

45:1 Baruch assisted and encouraged Jeremiah when he was imprisoned. In this passage Jeremiah replies with a personal word of encouragement from the Lord for his scribal friend. The date of the passage, 604 B.C., identifies it with the circumstances of ch. 36. Baruch had read Jeremiah's oracles before the temple crowd and the princes of Judah, before Jehoiakim burned the original scroll. A second scroll was prepared by Baruch, and he remained an assistant to Jeremiah throughout his ministry, including the journey to Egypt.

45:2, 3 Jeremiah addressed Baruch in light of the scribe's sorrow. **Woe:** Baruch lamented his plight in the same manner that Jeremiah had done (15:10). **added grief to my sorrow:** Baruch suffered mental anguish and personal rejection from his people due to his association with Jeremiah (36:15–19; 43:3).

45:4 The judgment against the land that had persecuted the faithful scribe and prophet is presented in telescopic fashion. The words echo the adverse terms of Jeremiah's call (1:10).

45:5 great things: Baruch apparently had hopes for position, honor, and distinction. However, these dreams were lost through his association with Jeremiah. Yet Baruch would be spared the judgment that would befall the land, for the Lord would give him his life as a **prize,** or booty (21:9; 38:2).

46:1, 2 This verse introduces a collection of oracles **against the nations.** The text moves generally from the west—Egypt—to the east—Elam and Babylon. Scattered throughout the oracles are brief messages of the restoration of Israel and Judah. Internal evidence indicates a date prior to the fall of Jerusalem for most of the material. In v. 2, the first oracle is dated specifically to 605 B.C. In other oracles, the contents reflect events dating from Nebuchadnezzar's southern campaigns (604 B.C.) to his subsequent campaigns in 586 or even 582 B.C. The main message of these oracles is the sovereignty of God over all the nations of the earth. He rules over them, and they are responsible to Him for their sins against His Law and order in the cosmos. Those nations that do not adhere to ethical and moral standards of justice and righteousness will be judged severely. Those who do exercise righteous quality in leadership and rule will profit from His grace and beneficence.

46:3, 4 Buckler and shield are two different sizes of shields (1 Kin. 10:16, 17).

46:5, 6 The strong Egyptian army was overpowered suddenly by the mightier Babylonians. **fear . . . all around:** This expression was also the name given to Pashhur by Jeremiah in 20:3, 4, and to Jeremiah's persecutors in 20:10.

46:7–9 Egypt had been weak for three hundred years (1 Kin. 14:25), but was still known for producing and exporting chariots. **Ethiopians, Libyans,** and **Lydians** were apparently mercenaries under Necho.

46:10–12 The day of the Lord is described here as **a day of vengeance** in which Egypt is punished for the death of Josiah. The imagery of a devouring sword is also found in 2:30. Egypt's demise is pictured as a sacrificial feast. As there was no healing **balm** for sinful Judah, so now Egypt was mortally wounded, stumbling to its death.

46:13 This verse is a prose introduction to a poetic description of Nebuchadnezzar's attack on **Egypt.** After the battle at Carchemish, the Babylonian march through Palestine was resumed in 604 B.C. They attacked Ashkelon and then pursued the Egyptians.

46:14–17 Why are your valiant men swept away: The fall of the gods before God in judgment is a prominent theme in the oracles against the nations (v. 25). **the LORD drove them:** Babylon is depicted as the instrument of God's judgment.

46:18, 19 King . . . LORD of hosts: The term *hosts* can also be translated "armies." God is the true and sovereign King over all the armies of heaven and earth. **Tabor . . . Carmel:** The mountains stand for the certainty of God's kingship. Like Judah, Egypt would face God's destructive judgment.

46:20–24 Egypt's destroyer invaded **from the north,** the same direction from which Judah's adversary attacked. **fat bulls:** Egypt's well-paid **mercenaries** were frail before God and the Babylonians, who came like lumberjacks cutting down the forest and chopping the fleeing serpents, the Egyptians. Egypt's demise is parallel to Israel's; the virgin daughter had been violated and stood **ashamed** (2:26), soon to be taken captive by Babylon.

46:25–28 do not be dismayed: Israel would be preserved. These verses are like 30:10, 11 with only slight variation.

47:1–7 The setting of the oracle against the Philistines is problematic. From the description of the judgment, it seems clear that the agent is Babylon. The reference in v. 1 to an attack of Pharaoh on Gaza is problematic. Gaza may have been assaulted by Psamtik about 611/610 B.C., prior to his capture of Ashdod, or by Necho in 609 B.C. on his way to aid Assyria at Haran, the same campaign in which Josiah died at Megiddo. This would place the oracle in the reign of Jehoiakim, like the previous proclamation against Egypt. Nebuchadnezzar destroyed Ashkelon in 604 B.C., after which Philistia was no threat as an independent state. The text may refer to Necho's attack on Gaza about 601 B.C., before Nebuchadnezzar returned in reprisal attack against Judah.

47:1, 2 The metaphor of rising **waters** is found in Is. 8:7, 8; 28:17 in reference to the Assyrian army; here the foe is Babylon (1:13; 4:6; 6:1, 22; 25:9). The destructive **overflowing** of the river is more typical of the Euphrates in the north than of the Nile floods, which bring beneficial nutrients to the fertile valley.

47:3 Lacking courage is literally "from weakness of hands," describing the paralyzing terror felt by parents as they abandon their children in flight.

47:4, 5 Philistines and Phoenicians are associated through their origins among the sea peoples who came from the northern Mediterranean and Aegean islands to the coastlands of Palestine in the twelfth century B.C. **Caphtor** is identified with Crete. **Tyre and Sidon** were the largest Phoenician ports. **Gaza** and **Ashkelon** were the last of the Philistine strongholds to fall, along with Ashdod, which is not mentioned. **Baldness . . . cut yourself:** Shaving the head and self-inflicted wounds were mourning customs forbidden in Israel (16:6).

47:6, 7 The image of the **sword of the Lord** is often used to portray divine judgment (12:12; 46:10, 14, 16). **quiet . . . Rest . . . be still:** The judgment had long been withheld; the long-suffering of the Lord had reached its end.

48:1–47 This chapter is composed of several poetic sections broken by short messenger formulae: **thus says the Lord** (vv. 1, 8, 40) and **says the Lord** (vv. 12, 25, 30, 35, 44, 47). There are a number of parallels with Is. 15:16, 24, indicating a possible dependency by Jeremiah on thematic characterizations there. Sections of this poetic discourse are adaptations of older material. The unifying theme is the destruction and humiliation of Moab, a nation known for its great pride. The contents highlight the major cities and towns of the Moabite plateau, which extended along the eastern side of the Dead Sea from Heshbon and Mount Nebo southward toward the Wadi Zered. The location of several of the cities is unknown, though extensive archaeological surveys have been carried out. Contemporary records of Babylon's involvement in Moab are meager, though it is generally assumed that Moab submitted to

Babylonian rule about 604 B.C. Moab sent mercenaries for Babylon into Judah during the rebellion of 598/597 B.C. (2 Kin. 24:2). In Zedekiah's rebellion of 588–586 B.C., Moab pondered the idea of joining Judah, but refrained.

48:1, 2 The name of the Moabite capital, **Heshbon**, means "stronghold." It was not especially appropriate, in that the city changed hands numerous times throughout its history, from the Amorites to the Israelites to the Moabites (Num. 21:26).

48:3–10 The juniper ekes out its stunted growth in the wilderness, hiding in crevasses of rock. As the apostate people of Judah trusted in the queen of heaven (44:17, 18), Moab trusted in its patron deity **Chemosh,** a god of fertility and storm. **captivity:** Taking a deity captive was a well-known Middle Eastern custom. The national statue of the patron deity was seized and it was believed that the captured god could no longer protect its people.

48:11–13 not been emptied from vessel to vessel: Though Moab was subject to Israel in the ninth century B.C., it had never experienced exile and had become complacent in its security. God would **empty** Moab's **vessels,** causing the Moabites to be taken captive. **break the bottles:** Moab's cities would be destroyed. **Chemosh** (v. 7), the great protector of Moab, would become powerless before God, as **Bethel** fell with **Israel** (Amos 3:14).

48:14–17 Jeremiah assured Moab that there is but one true **King, Whose name is the Lord of hosts,** the all-powerful "God of armies." **Bemoan:** A note of sarcasm is communicated. The nations around Moab, like Judah, who was attacked by Moab's mercenaries, were called upon to lament Moab's destruction.

48:18–20 Dibon was the capital from which King Mesha ruled (2 Kin. 3:4–27). The haughty **Moab** was **shamed** by the destruction of its mighty fortresses.

48:21–25 Mephaath was one of the Levitical cities (Josh. 21:37). **Bozrah** refers not to the capital of Edom, but to Bezer, one of the cities of refuge (Josh. 20:8). **Kerioth** is mentioned in Amos 2:2. **Horn** and **arm** are symbols of the power and strength that was broken.

48:26–29 Make him drunk: Judgment is portrayed in the form of drunkenness to the point of vomiting, the result of Moab's mockery of Israel (25:15–29). **Pride** refers to the self-indulging, self-honoring haughtiness by which one thinks of oneself as greater than others.

48:30–33 The scene in Moab turns to mourning and intense lamentation over the failure of the crops and vineyards. **Kir Heres,** also called Kir Haraseth (2 Kin. 3:25; Is. 16:11), may be a name for the capital city of Moab (Kir of Moab; Is. 15:1). The **joy** once heard echoing from the vineyards and winepresses had vanished before the horrifying sound of horses' hoofbeats and clashing weapons.

48:34 The waters of Nimrin empty into the Jordan opposite Jericho. A lament from **Heshbon** and **Elealeh** to **Horonaim** and **Zoar** would cover all the Moabite plateau from north to south, from the Dead Sea to the desert.

48:35–39 offers sacrifices . . . burns incense: Idolatry would end; the people could no longer worship Chemosh and other deities. **head . . . beard . . . hands . . . loins:** Every kind of lament would be used to mourn for Moab, as the proud Moab became **a derision and a dismay** like Judah.

48:40–44 The imagery is that of Babylon spreading its ravaging armies over Moab like an **eagle** spreading its **wings** (49:22; Deut. 32:11; Ezek. 17:7). **exalted himself:** Moab's chief sin was pride, considering itself greater than the God of Israel. Its pride would be turned to fear and terror, and then the nation would be taken captive.

48:45, 46 The last view of Moab is that of fire destroying her cities as she flees in terror. Chemosh has fallen to defeat.

48:47 Bring back means "restore the fortunes of." Moab would see its people restored to their homeland. Their crops and vineyards would once again be productive. Moab, Judah, and Israel returned home in 538 B.C., during the reign of Cyrus.

49:1–6 The setting of the oracle against Ammon is based on the historical conflict between Israel and Ammon, particularly over the territory of the tribe of Gad. The oracle probably dates to the period before the fall of Jerusalem in 586 B.C., but after the raids of Moab, Ammon, and others into Judah (2 Kin. 24:2).

49:1, 2 Milcom, the patron deity of the Ammonites, is pictured as taking **possession** of the land formerly belonging to the Gadites, a process that began in the days of the judges.

49:3 Heshbon (48:2) was at one time possessed by the Ammonites, but later lost to the Moabites. **Ai** is not the Israelite city of the same name. **Rabbah** was the capital city of the Ammonites. The **captivity** of the patron deity **Milcom** was tantamount to his defeat, visible in the exile of leaders and people, together with his statue, from their homeland.

49:4 Valleys . . . flowing valley may be a reference to the Jabbok valley on the northern border of Ammon.

49:5 no one will gather those who wander off: Those who fell by the wayside during the flight from Ammon would be abandoned.

49:6 The restoration of Ammon, as in the case of Judah, Israel, Egypt, and Moab, is alluded to briefly in stereotyped fashion.

49:7–22 The oracle against Edom is closely related to the Book of Obadiah and to portions of the oracle against Babylon (ch. 50). The territory of Edom extended from the Wadi Zered (modern Wadi al-Hasa) in the north to the Gulf of Aqaba in the south. The capital city was Bozrah, modern Buseira about twenty-five miles southeast of the Dead Sea. Strife between Israel and Edom dates to the conflict between Jacob and Esau. The oracle is based upon the events leading up to and following the Babylonian invasion of Judah, during which Edom took the opportunity to move into the Negeb region in southern Judah, eventually dominating the region south of Hebron by the end of Nebuchadnezzar's reign.

49:7, 8 Edom was known in the Bible for its wisdom (Obad. 8). **Teman** was the name of a city or district of Edom in which the capital city Bozrah was located.

49:9–11 grape-gatherers: This imagery derives from 6:9, but there was no real remnant left in Edom. The nation had been totally ravaged and stripped bare, with only women and children left alive to work the land. These workers were invited to **trust in** God.

49:12, 13 drink of the cup: The imagery of the cup of divine wrath is found in 25:15–29.

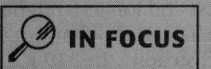 **IN FOCUS** **"cup"**

(Heb. *kos*) (25:15; 49:12; Ps. 23:5; Is. 51:22) Strong's #3563: The Hebrew word translated *cup* refers to a drinking goblet. In the OT prophetic books, the word is usually associated with imagery of God's wrath, such as "the wine cup of fury" or "the cup of horror" (25:15; Ezek. 23:33). In other places the cup can have a positive significance: it indicates a close relationship with a powerful person. Moreover in both the OT and NT the cup can be symbolic of fellowship because of the cup's association with togetherness. The cup is an important image in the NT, especially in the celebration of the Lord's Supper (1 Cor. 11:25–28).

Here it is particularly applied to Edom and more specifically to its capital city, **Bozrah.**

49:14–16 The imagery in these verses is that of **the nations** being mustered by God to besiege Edom. Edom would be reduced from a proud people of mighty mountain fortresses to one that was **small among** the nations.

49:17–19 an astonishment . . . hiss: Like Israel, Judah, Egypt, Moab, and Ammon, Edom would be destroyed and would become an object of derision. Like the **lion** that emerges from the thickets along the lower Jordan and seizes its prey, God would attack the Edomites through His appointed instrument.

49:20–22 The two things on which Edom most prided itself, its wisdom and its fortresses, would vanish before the judgment of the Lord. As the strongholds collapsed, the earth would quake; its tremors would be felt all the way to the Red Sea. The imagery of the broad wings of the **eagle,** representing the all-encompassing power of God and His agents of destruction, is also found in 48:40, 41.

49:23–27 The oracle against Damascus, the chief city of the Aramaeans, is brief probably due to the fact that its last period of strength was in the last half of the eighth century B.C., one hundred years before Jeremiah's ministry. Apparently Damascus experienced a brief period of independence like Judah after the collapse of Assyria in 612–610 B.C., and before the incursion of Nebuchadnezzar in 604 B.C. In the days of the kings of Israel and Judah, Aramaean kings like Ben-hadad II and Hazael raided their villages. Amos (1:3–5) condemned their inhumane practices.

49:23–25 Hamath and Arpad were major towns located west and north of the capital of Damascus.

49:26, 27 The same themes occur here as in other oracles against the nations: fear and weakness like a woman in childbirth, war and destruction, and lamentation and shame. **Ben-Hadad** was the name (or title) of several earlier kings of Aram-Damascus (Amos 1:4). No restoration is envisioned here.

49:28–33 The oracle against the Arab tribes of Kedar and Hazor is introduced by the messenger formula, **thus says the Lord** and is composed of three short sayings.

49:28 The region of **Kedar** was the most important Arab tribal group in the biblical period. Kedar was in northern Arabia and was known for its sheepherding and merchant caravans (2:10; Is. 60:7; Ezek. 27:21). The phrase **men of the East** is associated with the Arameans, Midianites, Amalekites, and other nomadic desert tribes (Gen. 29:1; Judg. 7:12).

49:29 The various items listed in this verse are typically those of nomadic peoples. The panic-filled shout, **fear is on every side,** is common in Jeremiah's oracles (6:25; 20:10; 46:5; 49:5).

49:30–33 Nebuchadnezzar's destructive army would attack the tent villages of Kedar and **Hazor.** The oases would be left to the **jackals** for habitation (9:11; 10:22). The Bedouin peoples would be scattered afar, as if by the hot desert winds.

49:34–39 The final oracle of the collection is against **Elam**, dated to the accession year of Zedekiah, in the spring of 597 B.C. The capital city of Elam was Susa, about 250 miles east-southeast of Babylon.

49:34–36 break the bow: The Elamites were famous for their skilled archers (Is. 22:6), who became an important part of the Persian army under Cyrus. The expression **four winds** indicates the military might that the Lord musters against His enemies (Ezek. 37:9; Dan. 8:8).

49:37–39 I will set My throne: This expression depicts the establishment of the kingdom of the God of Israel, the great conquering King in the land of the Elamites (1:15; 43:10). Elam would experience the restorative power of God, as its people were returned and its fortunes restored (48:47; 49:6).

50:1—52:64 The last oracle is against the greatest nation of the day, Babylon of Nebuchadnezzar. The extended treatise is composed of numerous short poetic proclamations against the nation that on one hand was the servant of the Lord (25:9), and on the other hand was the archenemy of God's people. The previous chapters focused upon the role of Babylon as servant of the Lord in judgment on the nations. These two focus upon: (1) the imminent overthrow of Babylon and the defeat of her many gods, particularly Marduk, the patron god of the city and nation and (2) the restoration of the Jews to their homeland.

50:1 The Chaldeans, or Babylonians, were vassals of Assyria until the revolt of Nabopolassar, who gained control of Babylon in 626 B.C. Nebuchadnezzar, the son of Nabopolassar who succeeded his father to the throne in 605 B.C., was the strongest and longest-reigning Chaldean monarch. After Nebuchadnezzar died, the nation declined steadily. In 539 B.C. it was conquered by Cyrus, apparently with little effort.

50:2, 3 Bel was a title like Baal, meaning "Lord," for **Merodach,** another name for Babylon's patron deity Marduk. **idols . . . images:** The oracle begins with a defamation of the gods of Babylon. The term translated *images* means animal droppings. The Hebrew prophets are openly contemptuous of idols and speak of them with ridicule. **out of the north:** The invading nation is not defined, yet from historical records it is known that Cyrus attacked Babylon from the north after defeating the city of Sippar.

50:4, 5 Israel and **Judah** would be restored as they sought the Lord in mournful repentance, looking for help to return home. They would enter into a **perpetual covenant** with the Lord that they would not forget or reject (Ezek. 16:60).

50:6, 7 Shepherds refers to the national princes, priests, and prophets who led the people to sin against the Lord, their true source of hope and sustenance (23:1–4).

50:8–10 The train of thought turns to the Jews, who should flee from Babylon like **rams** of a flock.

50:11–13 Babylon's plunder would be its punishment for gloating over Judah's demise and the abuse of God's **heritage.** Great Babylon would be reduced to the **least of the nations.** Defamation, drought, dehabitation, desolation, and derision were Babylon's destiny (18:16; 19:8; 49:17).

50:14–16 against her all around: Assault forces would press hard on every side, as what had been the instrument of God became the object of His wrath.

50:17–20 The Lord had used Babylon to punish **Assyria** for deporting Israel; He would use another foe from the north to inflict punishment on **Babylon.** The result would be the restoration of Israel and Judah and the pardoning of their iniquities and sins, the very reason for their demise (5:25; 16:10, 18; 31:34; 33:8).

50:21–28 utterly destroy: The tables would be turned on Babylon, the soon-to-be-broken **hammer** and future **heaps of ruins.** The LORD **God of hosts** had launched His vengeful weapons upon the city through His anointed servant Cyrus (2 Chr. 36:22, 23; Is. 45:1).

50:29–34 The wise and righteous Ruler would **plead** the **case** of the oppressed children of Judah and obtain their redemption. A redeemer was one who secured the freedom of a kinsman, protecting family rights. Here God, the **Redeemer** of Israel (Is. 47:4), offers to obtain the legal freedom of His people from captivity.

50:35–46 The **sword** of God would overturn all elements of Babylon's greatness—its leaders, its weapons, and its wealth. **A drought is against her waters:** Babylon was built on

The scroll that Jeremiah gave to Seraiah contained a list of the various evils that would befall Babylon as a result of God's judgment.

both sides of the Euphrates, and the region of southern Mesopotamia was networked with irrigation canals. The Lord would carry out His judgment against Babylon as He had in the days of Elijah.

51:1–14 The oracle against Babylon continues amassing image after image of destruction, bringing to bear upon the mighty nation every form of judgment possible within the language. The message is occasionally broken by a message of hope for the exiles of Israel and Judah.

51:1–5 Though **Israel** and **Judah** had **forsaken** the lordship of God, He had not forsaken His sinful people.

51:6–10 The imagery of Babylon's **cup** of fury from 25:15–29 is reversed. Here Babylon's cup is broken by the Lord. **balm:** As in the case of Judah (8:22), decadent Babylon was beyond healing and had to be abandoned. The destruction of Babylon was the vindication of the justice of God. Jeremiah's prediction (25:12–14) would be realized: Israel would be made righteous through God's work.

51:11–14 vengeance: The Lord would avenge Babylon's fierce abuse of Israel and other conquered nations. The **covetousness** of Babylon is typified in the taking of temple treasures from Jerusalem (2 Kin. 25:13–17). **locusts:** The locust plague depicts the swarm of enemy soldiers pouring into the magnificent city.

51:15–19 These verses are almost verbatim from 10:12–16. The text is inserted here to demonstrate the futility of Babylon's idols against the power of the Lord, the God of Israel.

51:20–26 Babylon had been God's **battle-ax** for judgment against the nations, and Judah in particular. **I will repay:** Babylon would experience God's battle-ax of punishment for the **evil** it inflicted on Jerusalem. The seemingly invincible **mountain** of Babylon would be crumbled by the power of God's outstretched arm.

51:27–32 Babylon's enemies from the north (50:3) are summoned by the trumpet to prepare for the assault on the heavily fortified city.

51:27, 28 Ararat, Minni, and Ashkenaz were mountain tribes from what is today eastern Turkey and Armenia. **The Medes** were from the Zagros mountain region in present-day central Iran.

51:29–32 The mighty men of Babylon have ceased fighting: The Nabonidus Chronicle, a text describing the fall of Babylon, reports that "Cyrus entered Babylon without a battle." By the time Cyrus reached Babylon, he had conquered all of Babylonia except for the capital city, cutting off roads and supply routes.

The (Medo-)Babylonian Empire (560 B.C.)

In 605 B.C. Nebuchadnezzar successfully concluded a two-year siege of Carchemish, and most of the Assyrian Empire rapidly became the Babylonian Empire. In 586 B.C. Nebuchadnezzar conquered all of Judah, besieging and destroying Jerusalem and the Jewish temple. At its zenith in 560 B.C., Babylon ruled the entire fertile crescent and Arabia as well, although Egypt regained its autonomy.

51:33–35 The harvest **threshing floor** depicts the punishment of Babylon. Nebuchadnezzar had become like a gluttonous warrior, devouring the nation of Judah and the temple and people of Jerusalem.

51:36–40 plead your case: The imagery here involves a legal proceeding. Babylon had been arraigned, indicted, and convicted. Here it is sentenced to punishment by the Lord. The **lions** of Babylon would be slaughtered like **lambs.**

51:41–48 This section continues the theme of the overthrow and denigration of the proud and mighty city of Babylon.

51:41–44 The primeval **sea,** conquered by Marduk according to the Babylonian creation myth, would overflow Babylon in the form of enemy nations. **Bel** is an honorary title for Marduk, the patron deity of Babylon. **I will bring out . . . what he has swallowed:** Nebuchadnezzar had swallowed up nations like a glutton (v. 34); those very same nations would be returned.

51:45–48 The release of Israel from captivity is foreseen. The people would be called upon to flee the city because of its impending destruction. In Jeremiah, the expression **days are coming** usually introduces a message of divine intervention into history. **carved images:** Babylon was known for its thousands of images of its numerous gods and goddesses. As the king claimed to conquer nations in the name of his patron deity, so the gods of the defeated would be punished along with their worshipers. The devastation of decadent Babylon would be no cause for mourning among the nations. Instead, the nations would sing joyfully of Babylon's fall.

51:49–58 The Hebrew term rendered **plunderer** provides a link from v. 48 to this section, in which emphasis is placed upon the plunder of the city known for its merciless plundering of others, particularly Judah and the temple of the Lord. Several themes recur here: the crushing of idols (v. 52; see v. 47; 50:2); tumultuous waters (v. 55; v. 42); broken bows (v. 56; 49:35); and drunkenness (v. 57; v. 7; 48:26).

51:51 The prophet expresses feelings of **shame** for himself and his people as he recalls how their sin was ultimately responsible for

Nebuchadnezzar's destruction of the LORD's house in 586 B.C.

51:59–64 The oracles against the nations are concluded by a symbolic act that was enacted after the deportation of the Jews. The scroll **Jeremiah** wrote probably had contained many of the individual oracles of chapters 50 and 51, or material from earlier chapters (25:12–14). Jeremiah instructed **Seraiah,** a brother of Baruch who was about to be taken captive to Babylon, to read a scroll within the walls of Babylon. (Babylon was proud of her great and numerous walls, built with the slave labor of her captives, which made the city almost impregnable. Today the city lies in ruins of stone, mudbrick, and rubble.) The scroll that Jeremiah gave to Seraiah contained a list of the various evils that would befall Babylon as a result of God's judgment. After reading the contents of the scroll, Seraiah was to tie a stone to it and cast it into the Euphrates, which bisected the city. Notably, it was by means of the river that Cyrus conquered the city in 538 B.C. The message of the symbolic act was that as the scroll and stone sank in the river, so would Babylon sink in the silt of the river and surrounding desert sands.

52:1–34 The closing chapter of the Book of Jeremiah is an appendix of historical material related to the fall of Jerusalem, the destruction of the temple of Lord, the subsequent deportation of leading citizens of Judah to Babylon, and an epilogue recounting the release of Jehoiachin from prison. The contents are based upon 2 Kings 24:18—25:30, excluding the portion in Kings concerning Gedaliah's brief governorship. The purpose of the chapter is to relate the fulfillment of many of the prophecies included in the previous chapters.

52:1–3 Zedekiah reigned as king of Judah from 598 to 586 B.C., until God finally cast him out of Jerusalem for doing **evil in the sight of the Lord** (23:1–4).

52:4–6 The siege of Jerusalem began on the **tenth day** of the **tenth month** (Tebeth)—probably in December 589 B.C. The siege of Jerusalem lasted over two years. In June through July 586 B.C., as food supplies were exhausted, the walls of Jerusalem were breached (39:2).

52:7–11 The attempted escape, capture, and ultimate fate of **Zedekiah** are also described in 39:1–10.

52:12–23 The destructions of Jerusalem, the royal palace and the temple of the Lord are described in 2 Kings 25:8–17. Jeremiah provides additional details.

52:13–16 The entire city of Jerusalem was burned, from the temple to the royal palace to the **houses.** The city **walls** were demolished. Leading citizens and some of the poor were deported under Nebuzaradan's command, leaving only a remnant of peasant farmers to work the fields, vineyards, and orchards.

52:17–23 Sacred implements and furniture from the temple of God were taken as booty to Babylon. Most of these items are described in 1 Kin. 7:15–51. The **bronze bulls** had been removed by Ahaz and presented to Tiglath-Pileser III (2 Kin. 16:10–18), but apparently had been returned or remade.

52:24–30 Certain persons were chosen for execution. **Seraiah** was the grandson of Hilkiah, the faithful priest under Josiah. **Zephaniah** is possibly the person of the same name in 29:25. **Doorkeepers** were key temple personnel. Leaders of Judah's forces were executed.

52:31–34 Jehoiachin was released from prison soon after Nebuchadnezzar died in 562 B.C. Nebuchadnezzar's son **Evil-Merodach** became king but reigned only two years (562–560 B.C.). **lifted up the head:** A Hebrew phrase expressing the kindness and good will that Evil-Merodach showed toward Jehoiachin in pardoning him. Jehoiachin was provided food and given a seat of honor in Babylon. This restoration was symbolic of the future restoration of Israel and Judah to their homeland.

The Book of
Lamentations

THE BOOK OF LAMENTATIONS REVEALS THE broken heart of the prophet Jeremiah. In forceful poetry, Jeremiah expresses his grief over the national tragedy that had unfolded before his eyes: Jerusalem, God's city, had fallen to the Babylonians. Jeremiah's sorrow and tears were not for his own personal loss, however, but for the sinfulness of the Israelites. The people of Israel had chosen to reject God. Yet

even in this time of suffering there was hope. The Lord would not discipline His people forever; He would eventually restore those who waited on Him.

The five chapters of Lamentations are five poems with ch. 3 as the midpoint or climax. Accordingly, the first two chapters build an "ascent," or crescendo, to the climax, the grand confession in 3:23, 24: "Great is Your faithfulness. The LORD is my portion." The last two chapters are a "descent," or decrescendo, from the pinnacle of ch. 3.

Chapters 1 and 5 provide summaries of the siege and fall of Jerusalem, while chs. 2 and 4 offer more detailed and explicit descriptions of the devastation. Chapter 3 moves from a mixture of lament and hope in vv. 1–24 to colorful praise of the compassionate and faithful Lord in vv. 25–39. This is followed by the confession of vv. 40–54 and the accompanying prayer of vv. 55–66. Then ch. 4 relaxes the emotional intensity of the earlier chapters, dispassionately describing how suffering affected all classes of the populace of Jerusalem. The final chapter is a prayer that begins with "Remember, O LORD" (5:1) and ends with "Turn us back to You, O

LORD" (5:21). In this way, Jeremiah's lament moves from mourning to praise and then from praise to a prayer for restoration.

The poetry of the book enhances its purpose and structure. Chapters 1 through 4 are composed as acrostics of the twenty-two letters of the Hebrew alphabet. Each verse or group of verses begins with a word whose initial letter carries on the sequence of letters in the Hebrew alphabet. This would be similar to an English poem in which the first line begins with A; the second line begins with B, and so on. One purpose of this device was probably to aid in memorization of the passage. The acrostic also suggests that the writer has thought things through and is giving a complete account of the subject.

Like the Book of Job, the Book of Lamentations addresses human suffering. Unlike Job, Lamentations focuses on national suffering—specifically, the suffering of Judah. Along the way, the book tackles some of the toughest questions faced by God's people: How can God's love and justice be reconciled with our pain? If God is in control of history, how could a nation suffer so much so soon after it had been led by such godly leaders as King Josiah and those involved in that revival? Where was God during His people's unhappiest hour?

The Book of Lamentations offers some practical theological reflections on the purposes and results of suffering. Rather than explaining away pain, the book helps us face pain. By avoiding cheery cliches, the Book of Lamentations provides companionship for those who are suffering and plants seeds of hope for rebuilding after the suffering is over.

In fact, the anger of God is a sign that He cares. The Lord's anger is never capricious or unreasonable. His discipline is a sign that He has not abandoned us. Even in His display of anger, God is still full of mercy and grace. The beacon light in the midst of disintegration is found in 3:22–24. Come what may, God remains faithful. His faithfulness is the greatest comfort to those who suffer; His compassions are new every morning.

Though no author is named in the book, the prophet Jeremiah has been traditionally identified as the writer of Lamentations. In fact, some copies of the ancient Greek Septuagint translation begin the book with these words: "And it came to pass, after Israel had been carried captive, and Jerusalem became desolate, that Jeremiah sat weeping, and lamented this lamentation over Jerusalem." Crediting Lamentations to Jeremiah is based on the following considerations: (1) Jeremiah was known as a composer of laments (2 Chr. 35:25). (2) Jeremiah was the prophet who mourned, "Oh, that my head were waters, and my eyes a fountain of tears, that I might weep day and night for the slain of the daughter of my people!" (Jer. 9:1).

(3) In 3:1, the author seems to identify himself with Jeremiah when he says, "I am a man who has seen affliction by the rod of His wrath." (4) There are many linguistic similarities between Lamentations and Jeremiah.

Outline

I. Grief after the destruction of Jerusalem 1:1–22
II. Personal suffering after the destruction of Jerusalem 2:1–22
III. Hope in the face of adversity 3:1–66
IV. The pain of the destruction of Jerusalem 4:1–22
V. Remembering that God still reigns 5:1–22

Commentary

1:1–22 The first poem in Lamentations has four movements to it: (1) in its loneliness (vv. 1–7); (2) in its causes (vv. 8–11); (3) in its purposes (vv. 12–17); and, (4) in its confession (vv. 18–22).

1:1 How: This exclamatory word is used frequently in laments and funeral songs. It expresses astonishment, sorrow, and dismay (2:1; 4:1; Is. 1:21; 14:4; Jer. 9:19; 48:17; Ezek. 26:17). **lonely:** This is a stranded individual, one who is **like a widow.** Jerusalem is personified, or portrayed as a person (Is. 1:21). Beginning in v. 12, Jerusalem "speaks" of her own troubles in the first person. **princess . . . slave:** This is a terrible reversal of fortune.

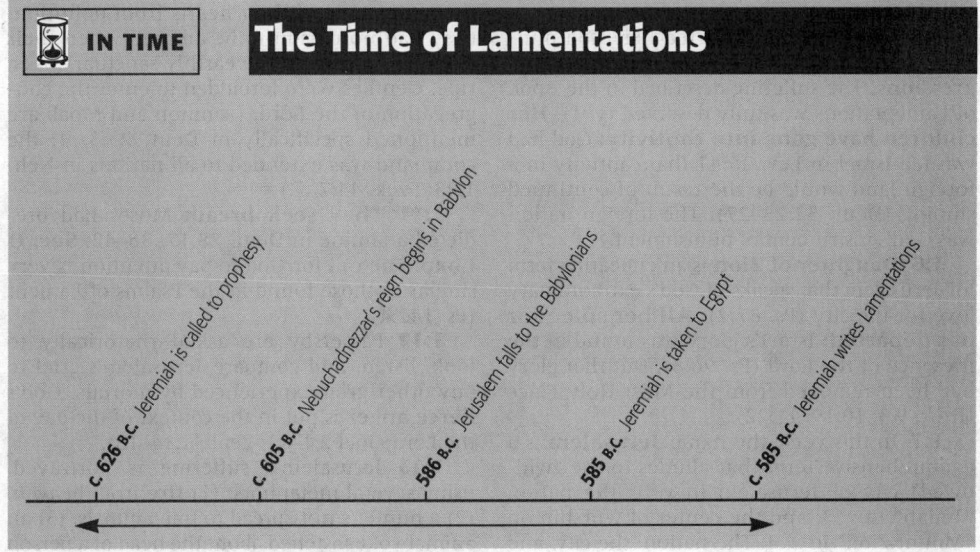

IN TIME

The Time of Lamentations

c. 626 B.C. Jeremiah is called to prophesy

c. 605 B.C. Nebuchadnezzar's reign begins in Babylon

586 B.C. Jerusalem falls to the Babylonians

585 B.C. Jeremiah is taken to Egypt

c. 585 B.C. Jeremiah writes Lamentations

IN FOCUS   "weeps"

(Heb. *bakah*) (1:2, 16; Job 30:31) Strong's #1058: This verb describes the act of wailing, which expresses emotions ranging from grief to happiness. While the word is often associated with lamentation, the "bitter wailing" of ancient people who were mourning their dead (2 Sam. 1:12), it is also used with expressions of joy (Gen. 29:11). The ancients wept when saying farewell (Ruth 1:9), over impending doom (Jer. 9:1), to express their joy over the rebuilt temple (Ezra 3:12), and at the burial of an individual (Gen. 50:1). In Lamentations, Jeremiah weeps over the sins of the people, the sins that would eventually result in the destruction of Jerusalem (1:1, 16).

1:2 Among all her lovers (v. 19) describes Judah's sin of turning away from God and toward the gods of Canaan (Jer. 3:1–6). Also, the sins of Judah often involved the sexual forms of pagan worship that characterized the Canaanite people.

1:3 The southern kingdom **Judah** is personified here as Jerusalem was in v. 1. **captivity:** The implications of v. 1 are made clear. The reference here is to the Babylonian captivity suffered by Judah following the destruction of Jerusalem in 586 B.C.

1:4 When the temple was built, **Zion** was used to describe the hill on which the temple was located. Later the name came to stand for the whole city. **mourn:** The roads "mourned" because there would no longer be throngs of pilgrims traveling to Jerusalem to worship at the temple. **her gates:** The image of sad gates is also found in Ps. 24:7–10, which indicates that the gates would not always mourn. **priests . . . virgins:** These two words indicate people from all elements of the city; everyone in the city experienced **bitterness.**

1:5 the LORD has afflicted her: God punished Jerusalem because of the people's **transgressions.** The suffering described in the Book of Lamentations was fully deserved (v. 1). **Her children have gone into captivity:** God had warned Israel in Lev. 26:41 that captivity in a foreign land would be the result of continued sinning (Deut. 32:23–27). The foreign nation was God's instrument of punishment.

1:6 Daughter of Zion is an endearing term for Jerusalem that speaks of God's extraordinary love for the city (Ps. 87:2). **All her splendor has departed:** Israel's glory was found in the presence of the Lord (Ps. 96:8). But that glory had been removed from the Most Holy Place (Ezek. 9:3; 10:19; 11:22).

1:7 In this verse the name **Jerusalem** is a comprehensive term that alludes to the "widowed" city of Jerusalem in v. 1; the nation "Judah" in v. 3; and the center of worship on "Mount Zion" in v. 4. The nation, the city, and

the temple were ravaged by the invading Babylonian armies in 586 B.C. The emphasis is on Jerusalem's utter helplessness as her enemies ridiculed her miseries (v. 21). **Her pleasant things** refers to objects of value in the temple (v. 10), and perhaps objects in the people's homes as well (v. 11).

1:8 they have seen her nakedness: It was an extreme humiliation for a woman to be stripped of all her clothing in public. Such exposure was reserved for prostitutes (Ezek. 16:35–39; 23:29), which Judah had become in a spiritual sense (vv. 2, 8, 9).

1:9 Judah is pictured as a "dirty harlot" because of her involvement with the sins of Canaanite worship. In fact, Judah was so engaged in dishonorable behavior that she had lost her sense of decorum and would not clean **her skirts. She did not consider her destiny** despite Moses' warning, "Oh, that they were wise, that . . . they would consider their latter end!" (Deut. 32:29).

1:10 Since God's people had not preserved the **sanctuary** of their hearts from pollution, they had no reason to be amazed when their enemies desecrated the earthly sanctuary. As a rule, Gentiles were forbidden to enter the congregation of the Lord. (Ammon and Moab are mentioned specifically in Deut. 23:3, 4; the command was extended to all nations in Neh. 13:3; Ezek. 44:7, 9.)

1:11 They seek bread: Moses had predicted a famine in Deut. 28:17, 38–42. **See, O LORD:** The call for God to pay attention is very similar to those found in the Psalms of Lament (Ps. 142:4).

1:12 Passersby are asked rhetorically to look, listen, and compare Jerusalem's grief to any other grief experienced by mortals. God's **fierce anger** is put in the context of the day of the Lord (Joel 2:1–11; Zeph. 1:14–18).

1:13 Jerusalem's suffering is portrayed, using several metaphors: (1) **fire** from heaven, (2) a hunter's **net** spread to trap animals, (3) an animal yoke fastened about the head of a person

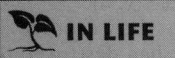 **IN LIFE** | **The Peril of Ignoring Consequences**

From time to time newspapers carry tragic stories of people who have fallen into serious trouble by failing to consider the consequences of their actions. Often they admit to the error of their ways with a statement such as, "I didn't think anyone would get hurt"; "I didn't know it was loaded"; "Things just got out of hand"; "I guess we didn't think it through."

The people of Judah failed to think through the consequences of their choices (Lam. 1:9). For generations they ignored the Law's warnings against idolatry, oppressing the poor, cheating in business, relying on foreign governments (especially Egypt) for security, and other sins of public life. They maintained a pretense of worshiping the Lord by keeping up temple rituals, but the reality was that they had turned their backs on God. The Lord sent numerous prophets to warn His people of impending disaster, but the Judeans routinely ignored them (2 Chr. 36:15–16). As a result, they were shocked when the Babylonians finally came and destroyed their way of life.

As you consider your own life, what consequences are you perhaps ignoring? Is there a relationship that needs healing, a problem that needs to be solved, a habit that needs to be broken or established, or a decision that needs to be made? Procrastination will only invite sudden disaster and ruin. Why not get started today on making changes—before it's too late?

(v. 14), and (4) the crushing of grapes in a winepress (v. 15). **turned me back:** The purpose of Jerusalem's suffering was to bring about a turning or repentance.

1:14 yoke of my transgressions: The idea here is sinful patterns of life becoming compulsive, burdening people like a yoke on a beast of burden. **woven together by His hands . . . He made my strength fail:** God imposed a yoke until all of Zion's strength failed. With no power of their own left, weary people are more likely to listen to God. **Those whom I am not able to withstand** refers to the Babylonians.

1:15 The virgin daughter of Judah: Jerusalem (Judah) was supposed to be the chaste bride of God. Instead she had become a polluted harlot because her people worshiped other gods than the God with whom they covenanted (vv. 2, 8, 9).

1:16 The people of Jerusalem wept because the fate Jeremiah had prophesied had come to pass. **comforter . . . Is far from me:** The real Comforter of Judah is God. But because of Judah's sin, God would not come to their assistance.

1:17 Spreads out her hands is a reference to prayer (2:19). **an unclean thing:** The Israelites were supposed to be God's holy people (Deut. 7:6). However, they had become worse than their pagan neighbors.

1:18 The Lord is righteous: Verses 5 and 17 establish that ultimately it was the Lord who permitted Jerusalem's collapse. Yet God remained just and right in what He did (Ex. 9:27; Ezra 9:15; Neh. 9:33; Jer. 12:1). **virgins . . . young men:** Pairs of opposites usually indicate totality in Hebrew ("priests . . . virgins" in v. 4);

these particular groupings suggest the "best of the nation" (2:4, 21).

1:19 priests . . . elders: The people who should have been a help were themselves in trouble.

1:20 While the roads leading to Jerusalem "mourned" because there would be no more pilgrims traveling to the city (v. 4), the **sword** of Judah's enemies mourned because there were no more Jews to kill.

1:21, 22 All my enemies: Those who previously had been friends of Judah (v. 2) became Judah's enemies. **Bring on the day:** Several times the "day" of God's wrath is mentioned in the Book of Lamentations (2:1, 21, 22). The term is used to refer not only to the time of Jerusalem's fall in the past, but also to a future day when God would rectify all of the wrongs that the nations had committed against Israel and God.

2:1–22 The second poem of the book has four movements to it: (1) because it comes from the Lord (vv. 1–10); (2) because it affects God's messenger (vv. 11–13); (3) because it provokes such personal responses (vv. 14–19); and, (4) because it makes its complaint to the Lord (vv. 20–22).

2:1, 2 His anger is a firm expression of God's displeasure with wickedness and sin. Yet God's anger never shuts us off from His compassion (Ps. 77:9). **The beauty of Israel** was found in its temple (Is. 64:11) and its ark of the covenant (1 Sam. 4:21, 22; Ps. 78:60, 61). In 1 Chr. 28:2 God's **footstool** is identified with the ark of the covenant. Occasionally God was pictured as enthroned and seated between the cherubim that were over the ark (1 Sam. 4:4; 2 Sam. 6:2; Pss. 80:1; 99:1, 5; 132:7). This passage says that God, in His wrath, had abandoned His footstool.

2:3 The **horn** was a symbol of strength and power (1 Sam. 2:1; Pss. 75:5; 92:10; 148:14; Jer. 48:25). **drawn back His right hand:** Usually the right hand of God is understood as the instrument of help for God's people stretched out against their enemies (Ex. 15:6; Ps. 20:6). Here God's hand is withdrawn from the enemies, leaving the people of God at their mercy.

2:4 like an enemy: The Lord did not simply relax His protection of Judah (v. 3). He purposely worked against His people **with His right hand. All who were pleasing to His eye** refers to virgins and young men—the pride of the nation (1:18).

2:5 swallowed up: Sheol, or death, is sometimes portrayed as "swallowing up" people (Prov. 1:12; 27:20; 30:16); here God is described as doing the swallowing (v. 2).

2:6, 7 Tabernacle means "booth" or "hut," a structure found in a **garden.** The point seems to be that the glorious temple of God had become similar to the dilapidated house of David (Amos 9:11). The temple of God had become a booth of branches similar to those used for the Feast of Booths (Succoth). **altar . . .**

sanctuary . . . walls . . . house: Each of these terms refers to the holy temple (v. 6).

2:8 Four weeks after the capture of Jerusalem, Nebuchadnezzar had destroyed the temple, the palace, the homes of the people, and the city **wall** (2 Kin. 25:9, 10; Jer. 52:13, 14).

2:9 The Law is no more: These words do not suggest the end of the Law, but rather the ceasing of the work of the Law in the lives of the people for their blessing (Deut. 6:1–3). **her prophets find no vision:** Divinely appointed instruction ceased for both the nation and the individual. This is not to say that the Law or prophecy were no longer available. God spoke to Jeremiah ten days after the prophet requested a word from God (Jer. 42:4–7); furthermore Ezekiel and Daniel prophesied during the 70 years of the Exile.

2:10 Throwing **dust** on the head (Job 16:15; Is. 29:4; Mic. 1:10) was a common sign of mourning in Israel and in other countries of the ancient world. **virgins of Jerusalem:** Their sadness was increased by the knowledge that this was not a time for marriage and family. Even though their lives had been spared, they had lost their futures.

2:11 My eyes fail with tears: This is the

 **IN CONTEXT** **How Far Will God Go?**

The destruction of Jerusalem revealed an astonishing fact about God: He will go to great lengths to draw His people back to Himself.

The people of Judah strayed far from the Lord. It was not that they were irreligious. On the contrary, they were pious and devout. For the most part they maintained the religious rituals detailed in the Law, gathering in the temple week after week to offer sacrifices and observe the Sabbath. But during the rest of the week, they ignored the Law. They forgot what Jesus later called the "weightier matters" of the Law—justice, mercy, and faith (Matt. 23:23; compare Mic. 6:8).

In essence, the people confused means with ends. They forgot that the sacrificial system, the Sabbath, the temple, and even the Law were all merely means to a far more important end—the end of knowing and serving God (Jer. 22:15, 16). So eventually God took these means away (Lam. 2:5–9), important and valuable as they were:

- God destroyed Jerusalem.
- God pulled down the temple and its furnishings.
- God did away with the religious rituals.
- God removed the king and the high priest.
- God allowed the written Law itself to be destroyed.
- God stopped giving visions to the prophets.

The removal of these things must have been unthinkable to the ancient Israelites. But God took them away in order to regain His people's attention and affection.

God's people today must also beware of confusing means with ends. Religious activities and resources have value, but they are not what life is all about. God Himself is what matters, and He will go to whatever length is necessary to help us remember that.

response of the author Jeremiah who suffered with the afflicted (1:2). **Bile** is literally "liver," a symbol of deep emotion.

2:12 Grain and wine are used here merely as a synonym for food.

2:13 How shall I console you: Jeremiah had no words to help the grieving women of Jerusalem as they looked helplessly on their dying babies.

2:14 false and deceptive visions: False **prophets** spewed forth their "utterly valueless" lies.

2:15, 16 Shake their heads was a common expression of derision (Pss. 22:7; 109:25; Jer. 18:16; see also 1 Kin. 9:8; Job 27:23; Jer. 19:8; 49:17; 50:13; Ezek. 27:36; Zeph. 2:15). Losing face in the ancient Middle East was a terrible evil. In the Psalms (Pss. 48:2; 50:2), Jerusalem was **the joy of the whole earth,** the source of spiritual blessings for all the nations of the earth (Gen. 12:3). Now Jerusalem was profaned (v. 2) and unclean (1:17).

2:17 The Lord has done what He purposed: God had promised Moses that He would judge sin (Deut. 28:15, 16). The destruction of Jerusalem was a fulfillment of that promise. Jeremiah used the same language to affirm that God had planned to deal with Babylon as well (Jer. 51:12).

2:18, 19 The **wall** of the people's hearts was more impenetrable than the wall of the city of Jerusalem (2:7, 8).

2:20 Should the women eat their offspring: So desperate were the scenes of starvation in Jerusalem that women actually fought over whose deceased child would be eaten next (4:10). **priest and prophet:** Many godly people in Jerusalem perished.

2:21 Young and old: The punishment of Jerusalem affected everyone. **virgins . . . young men:** The punishment of Jerusalem extended even to the "pride of the city" (1:18; 2:4).

2:22 The terrors that surround me: The people mocked Jeremiah with the slogan "terror on every side," for in the people's eyes he saw catastrophe everywhere.

3:1–66 The third (and climactic) poem in Lamentations has three parts to it: (1) the Lord's love and mercy to us are unending (vv. 1–24); (2) the Lord's goodness and control of all our lives are reassuring (vv. 25–39); and, (3) the Lord's forgiveness and answers to our prayers are encouraging (vv. 40–66).

3:1 I am the man: Jeremiah's personal testimony paralleled the experience of the city of Jerusalem as a whole (2:11). **The rod of His wrath** here refers to the Babylonians as instruments of God's judgment (2 Sam. 7:14; Job 9:34; 21:9; Ps. 89:32; Prov. 22:8). In Is. 10:5, Assyria is referred to as "the rod of (God's) anger."

3:2, 3 The imagery of **darkness** in this verse represents adversity and God's judgment (Job 12:25; Is. 9:2; Amos 5:18).

3:4, 5 He has aged my flesh: This imagery suggests the ebbing and wasting away of Jeremiah's life and that of the nation.

3:6, 7 like the dead of long ago: So hopeless did the situation seem that he felt like he had died long ago. **Dark places** may imply the grip of death itself (Ps. 88:6, where the same Hebrew word is used in parallel to the word *pit*).

3:8 He shuts out my prayer: On occasion, God had forbidden Jeremiah to pray for the deliverance of Judah (Jer. 11:14; 14:11).

3:9 He has blocked my ways with hewn stone: A common practice of the Assyrians was to wall up prisoners in extremely confined places and leave them to die.

3:10, 11 Jeremiah compared God to a **bear** or **lion** waiting to ambush (Hos. 13:8; Amos 5:19). God had permitted Judah to be attacked and mangled.

3:12, 13 He has bent His bow: This verse echoes Job 16:12, 13, in which Job compares God to an archer who makes human beings His target (2:4).

3:14 I have become the ridicule of all my people: Jeremiah was made the butt of scoffing and mockery (Jer. 20:7).

3:15 Wormwood was a bitter herb used to flavor some drinks.

3:16, 17 He has also broken my teeth with gravel: The people had sensed that they were so associated with dust and sackcloth— symbols of mourning—that it was as though they fed on dirt. The dust became gravel that broke the people's teeth. The people were also **covered** with **ashes,** another symbol of mourning (Jer. 6:26).

3:18 My strength and my hope have perished from the Lord: All of vv. 1–18 could be summed up by the impression that everything seemed to be lost. There was nothing but mourning, anger, and disappointment.

3:19, 20 Remember: Jeremiah attempted to change his mood by recalling his past experiences. However, what he remembered only made him feel worse.

3:21 This I recall to my mind: Jeremiah's remembrance of God's faithfulness brought about a change in the prophet's emotions. As long as we contemplate our troubles, the more convinced we will become of our isolation, our hopelessness, our inability to extricate ourselves from the present trouble. But when we focus on the Lord, we are able finally to rise above, rather than to suffer under, our troubles.

3:22 This verse seems to contradict all that had been written up to this point (2:1–5). Yet the fact that there was a prophet left to write these words and a remnant left to read them show that not every person in Jerusalem had been **consumed.** The fact that there was a remnant at all was due to the **mercies** and **compassions** of God. Even in His wrath (2:1–4), God remembers to be merciful.

3:23 new every morning: Every day presents us with a new opportunity to discover and experience more of God's love. Even in the midst of terrible sorrow, Jeremiah looked for signs of mercy. **Great is Your faithfulness:** Here is the heart of the Book of Lamentations. The comforting, compassionate character of God dominates the wreckage of every other institution and office. God remains "full of grace and truth" in every situation (Ex. 34:6, 7; John 1:14).

3:24 The Lord is my portion: This expression is based on Num. 18:20, in which Aaron was denied an inheritance in the land but was told instead that the Lord Himself was his portion and inheritance. The same idea is also found in Pss. 16:5; 73:26; 119:57; 142:5. **I hope in Him:** Hope is not a wishful thought, but a confident expectation in Lord. The Hebrew verb rendered *hope* suggests the idea of a "waiting attitude" (v. 21).

3:25 those who wait: The idea here is the acceptance of God's will and His timing (Ps. 40:1; Is. 40:31). The Hebrew word for *hope* here translates another verb meaning "to hope," "to wait" than the one in v. 24 (Ps. 40:1; Is. 40:31).

3:26 good: Not only is God good to those who wait and hope on Him (v. 25), but it was also good for the people. **hope and wait quietly:** A quiet confidence in the **salvation of the Lord** is always in order. Verses 22–26 focus on the renewal of hope in the midst of terrible distress.

3:27, 28 Youth here refers not to age, but the sense of still-unbroken strength, as opposed to diminished vitality.

3:29 Put his mouth in the dust is a figure of speech for conquest. The phrase pictures a captive lying face down with the conqueror's foot on his back. **Hope** refers to the confident expectation that the Lord will deliver (v. 26).

3:30 give his cheek: Submission to the Babylonian oppressors is advised; the troubles will not last forever.

3:31, 32 The promises that God made to the patriarchs (Gen. 12:1–3; 15:13–21; 22:15–18) were not **cast off,** but were still in force. The wickedness of God's people delayed but could not frustrate the complete fulfillment of His promises.

3:33 He does not afflict willingly: It is not God's purpose to bring trouble to humankind (Is. 28:21). Yet one may ask a question: What about the evil that comes from the malice of individuals and not from God? It is this question that the next two triads answer, vv. 34–36 and 37–39. There is no wrong done on earth that falls outside the control of God.

3:34–36 before the face of the Most High: God is offended when a person deprives another human being of his or her rights. God is omniscient and notices everything.

3:37–42 These verses present a plan for repentance and renewal. **turn back:** Repentance in the OT prophets is often expressed by the verb meaning "to turn" (5:21; Jer. 3:1). **lift our hearts and hands:** Lifting hands was a common posture in prayer (2:19).

3:43–46 So long as sin festered, God's wrath

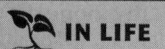 **IN LIFE**   **God's Unfailing Mercy—Our Only Hope**

What has been the deepest, darkest experience in your life, the time when you felt the worst emotions, perhaps to the point of utter despair? For Jeremiah and his contemporaries in Judah, it was the destruction of Jerusalem. The death of the city was absolutely crushing. The Israelites' magnificent temple was reduced to ashes, the city walls were pulled down, the main part of the populace had been either killed or deported, and only starving elders, women, and children remained (Lam. 2:10–12).

Only one truth kept hope alive—the knowledge of the mercies of the Lord (3:22–24). God's mercy (Hebrew *chesed*; see Deut. 7:9) involved His undying love and loyalty toward His people. Having committed Himself to Israel through His covenant with them, the Lord could be expected to follow through on that commitment. He might discipline His wayward people, allow them to be ravaged by their enemies, and even let their temple and the Law be destroyed (Lam. 2:9), but He would never ultimately forsake His people.

Neither will God forsake His spiritual children today. His mercy and grace have been extended to those who are in Christ Jesus (Rom. 8:1), and nothing can separate us from His love (8:31–39). As a result, we can have hope (5:1–5; 1 Pet. 1:3–5), even in the midst of the gloomiest circumstances (2 Cor. 1:8–11).

was a **cloud** (2:1) or veil through which no prayer could penetrate—including the prayers of the people (Jer. 14:12) and the prayers of Jeremiah (Jer. 7:16; 11:14; 14:11).

3:47, 48 Desolation and destruction may be rephrased as "utter devastation."

3:49–51 The imagery of weeping continues from v. 48 (1:2; 2:11). **Daughters of my city** refers to the people of Jerusalem.

3:52–54 silenced my life in the pit: Jeremiah speaks not only of his own experience of being cast into a pit (Jer. 38:4–6), but also of his pain and grief over the wretched condition of his fellow countrymen. The *pit* is a metaphor for the grave or extreme danger (Pss. 28:1; 30:3; 40:2). **The waters** is another danger symbol (Ps. 69:2).

3:55–57 The Lord's **name** is the term by which He delights to reveal His mercies to His people (Ex. 3:14, 15).

3:58–60 pleaded the case: Jeremiah used the terms of God's formal accusation (Jer. 2:1–3:5); however, here the words are used *for* the people rather than *against* them. **You have redeemed my life:** Here is a hint of the light of the NT gospel in the dark pages of the Book of Lamentations. The only way that God would be able to *plead the case* of His people was if He Himself paid for—or redeemed them from—their sinfulness.

3:61–63 Jeremiah here turns to the **enemies** who treated God's people so poorly during their weakened state (1:21).

3:64–66 Repay them, O Lord: The request for divine vindication is an expression of a longing for God's righteousness and the success of His kingdom and His truth.

4:1–22 The fourth poem of Lamentations has three movements to it: (1) in its costs (vv. 1–11); (2) in its causes (vv. 12–20); and, (3) in its conclusion (vv. 21, 22).

4:1, 2 The Babylonian army looted the temple and overturned all its huge **stones. precious sons:** The people of Jerusalem were of more value than the temple. Elsewhere these people are referred to as "My son, My firstborn" (Ex. 4:22) and "a special treasure to Me . . . a kingdom of priests and a holy nation" (Ex. 19:5, 6). The bodies of the brave defenders of Jerusalem were thrown out like broken pieces of **clay pots.**

4:3 Jackals were the dogs of the desert, disreputable beasts. However, even these animals cared for their young. **Ostriches,** on the other hand, seem to care little for their young.

4:4 The tongue of the infant: The theme of thirsting and starving children is revisited (2:11–13).

4:5, 6 People who formerly could have eaten any **delicacies** they wanted groveled in refuse **heaps** during the terrible days of the Babylonian siege of Jerusalem.

4:7, 8 Nazirites were men and women who specifically committed themselves to God for periods of special devotion (Num. 6:1–21). **Like sapphire . . . soot:** The siege of Jerusalem was so terrible that no one was exempt, not even the truly godly people like the Nazirites.

4:9 Dying early in the siege was perhaps **better** than living through all of its horrors.

4:10, 11 This verse describes the horrible effects of the long siege that were alluded to in 2:20. The women who were forced to eat their own children began as **compassionate women. cooked their own children:** This unimaginable horror could only have occurred in the most inhumane conditions of human suffering.

4:12 Would not have believed: Jerusalem had been entered by conquerors before, but none had wrecked the havoc Babylon did. This

---

🌱 IN LIFE | **Feeling Wicked Satisfaction!**

Do you celebrate the misfortunes of your enemies, especially when you feel that they are only getting their "just deserts"? It's a natural human tendency to gloat over the downfall of the high and mighty. But is that an attitude that God desires?

The people of Edom, Judah's neighbor to the south, were delighted to hear the news of Jerusalem's fall (Lam. 4:21; compare Ps. 137:7). But God rebuked the Edomites for their derisive attitude. His exhortation to "rejoice and be glad" (Lam. 4:21) was spoken ironically. In effect, the Lord was saying, "Enjoy your gloating while it lasts"—because it won't last for long. Soon it will be Edom's turn for judgment (compare Jer. 49:17, 18).

Scripture never encourages God's people to be happy when others suffer, even if they deserve to suffer. The love that God calls us to "does not rejoice in iniquity, but rejoices in the truth" (1 Cor. 13:6). Instead of gloating over the misery of our enemies, we should pray that somehow their circumstances will turn them toward the Lord and away from evil (Rom. 12:14–21).

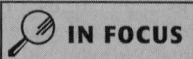 **IN FOCUS** | **"renew"**

(Heb. *chadash*) (5:21; 2 Chr. 24:4; Ps. 103:5) Strong's #2318: As a verb, the term can mean "to renew" (Ps. 51:10) or "to repair" (Is. 61:4). As an adjective, the word identifies something new in contrast to something old (such as the "old harvest" versus the "new harvest"; see Lev. 26:10), or something different when compared to the status quo (such as "a new spirit"; Ezek. 11:19; 18:31). The Bible teaches that God alone is the One who makes things new, whether a new song in the heart of the faithful (Ps. 40:3), a new phase in His plan of redemption (Is. 42:9; 43:19), a new name (Is. 62:2), or a new heaven and earth (Is. 65:17).

was something so horrible that neighboring kings would gasp in wonder.

4:13, 14 The same people who should have been agents of righteousness became agents of sin (Jer. 8:10; 14:18).

4:15, 16 Wherever the wicked wandered, they were treated as lepers, people who were not welcome in any place. **the Lord** scattered them: The priests and prophets were separated from **the face of the Lord** because they had helped cause the people of Judah to stumble.

4:17–19 a nation that could not save us: After the fall of Jerusalem in 586 B.C., the survivors in Judah turned to Pharaoh Hophra of Egypt to deliver them, thereby breaking covenant with Nebuchadnezzar and the specific word of God (Jer. 42—44; Ezek. 29:16).

4:20 The heir to the Davidic line was **"the breath** of life" to the nation. But King Zedekiah was captured while trying to escape, put in chains, blinded after watching his sons massacred, and marched off to Babylon to die.

4:21, 22 It is possible that the phrase **daughter of Edom** is a sarcastic, judgmental phrase. Edom may have thought so highly of herself (Obad. 3) that she believed she could assume the place of privilege her father Esau had lost, once Judah was destroyed.

5:1–22 The fifth poem (and last) in Lamentations has four movements to it: (1) our condition (vv. 1–9); (2) our individual suffering (vv. 10–14); (3) our feelings (vv. 15–18); and, (4) our questions (vv. 19–22).

5:2, 3 The Promised Land had been a gift from the Lord to Abraham. This **inheritance** was a kind of "down payment" on the future reign of God that would include the restoration of His people to that land. God demonstrated that He owned all nations and that Israel was to be His instrument for blessing all the nations on the earth. Yet in their present condition, the people of Israel seemed to be the most helpless of all peoples.

5:4–7 The survivors of the Babylonian siege were reduced to servitude, caught between **the Egyptians** and **the Assyrians** (4:17–19).

5:8, 9 The small harvests that were obtained from the land after the destruction of Jerusalem were vulnerable to nomads from the desert who occasionally took the **lives** of the people of Judah as well.

5:10 Our skin is hot: Disease would have been rampant during the siege.

5:11–13 The suffering of Jerusalem left no one unscathed—**women, princes, elders,** and **young men.**

5:14 gate . . . music: Ordinary events and pleasures were no longer appropriate or even possible for the people of Jerusalem.

5:15 joy . . . dance: This verse illustrates Eccl. 3:4. This was a time to weep and mourn, not to laugh and dance.

5:16 The crown has fallen from our head expresses the loss of Judah's position of honor.

5:17 our heart is faint . . . our eyes grow dim: The normal zest for life was gone. Death would be better than a horrible existence during the siege of Jerusalem.

5:18 foxes: The idea of wild animals roaming the holy city where the people of God once came in glad worship was the final indignity.

5:19, 20 You, O Lord, remain forever: God's eternal rule and reign are a hope and support during the bleakest moments of suffering and despair (Pss. 80:1, 2; 89:3, 4; 103:19).

5:21 The one word **turn** (1:13; 3:40) can summarize God's message to His rebellious people. In one of Jeremiah's earlier messages, he had exhorted the people to *turn* to God no less than seven times (Jer. 3:1, 7, 12, 14, 22; 4:1).

5:21, 22 Unless You have utterly rejected us: What is stated as a possibility actually emphasizes that the occurrence is completely out of the question: The Lord cannot reject His own people forever. The same literary technique is found in Jer. 14:19.

The Book of

Ezekiel

THE PROPHET EZEKIEL HAD THE THANKLESS JOB of proclaiming God's message on the crowded and hostile streets of Babylon. At the same time that Jeremiah was warning the citizens of Jerusalem about the coming destruction of that holy city, Ezekiel was preaching the same message to the exiles in Babylon. Though these exiles were hundreds of miles away from the promised land and the temple, God would not leave them in the dark. Instead He sent Ezekiel to warn, exhort, and comfort the weary exiles.

Unlike most biblical prophetic books, Ezekiel gives considerable attention to chronology and exact dates throughout his book. No other prophet provides so many dates (thirteen). By utilizing the data from archaeology and the most recent research into the calendar systems of the ancient Middle East, a precise dating of many events in Ezekiel is possible.

The key to dating the opening chronological notice and the other specific dates in Ezekiel is the reference in 1:2 to the "fifth year of King Jehoiachin's captivity." In 2 Kin. 24:12, this deportation is equated with the "eighth year of (Nebuchadnezzar's) reign" or 597 B.C. Ezekiel began prophesying in 593 B.C. calling attention to the Babylonian captivity of Judah. He ended in 571 B.C. with a message on God's coming judgment upon Egypt at the hand of the same Babylonian monarch. Ezekiel prophesied during four different periods: 593–588 B.C. (1:1—25:17); 587–585 B.C. (26:1—29:16; 30:20—39:29); 573 B.C. (40:1—48:35); and 571 B.C. (29:17—30:19). In all, Ezekiel prophesied from 593 to 571 B.C., a period of twenty-two years surrounding the climactic fall of Jerusalem in 586 B.C.

During Ezekiel's life and ministry, Israel (the northern kingdom) was corrupt politically and spiritually. Their idolatry led to captivity by Assyria in 722 B.C. The leadership of Judah (the southern kingdom) at that time was righteous; but eventually they too, though experiencing brief revivals at times, fell into the idolatry of the neighboring nations. The people refused to heed the prophets' reminders about the curses and blessings promised by God in the Mosaic covenant. Ezekiel prophesied that there would come catastrophe and captivity for Judah and Jerusalem. Yet he also had a message from God concerning eventual restoration and renewal, based on God's faithfulness to the promises of all the covenants made with His people since the Abrahamic covenant.

In speaking to his fellow exiles in Babylon, Ezekiel experienced and then employed visions (chs. 1—3; 8—11; 37; 40—48). These visions are similar in structure to "dream visions" known from Mesopotamian literature of the seventh and sixth centuries B.C. These texts have two main sections: (1) an introduction to the setting and general situation, including time, place, circumstances, and the person involved; and, (2) a description of the vision. In chs. 37; 40—48, Ezekiel uses such a format to introduce apocalyptic visions—revelations that symbolically describe the end times. Living in Babylon, both Ezekiel and his audience were familiar with this type of literature.

Elsewhere, Ezekiel employs themes and illustrations from the religious life and literature of the societies whose judgment he predicts. Typically the nations under God's judgment were those that had mistreated Israel or had led them into idol worship. The exiles and those Israelites still living in Judah knew the religious behavior and beliefs of their neighbors and would not be puzzled by the prophet's language. In addition to visions and religious themes, Ezekiel uses many literary techniques to communicate God's message to the exiles: both prose and poetry, parables and proverbs, lamentations and dirges, allegories and puns.

Ezekiel ministered in Babylon, at Tel Abib near the Chebar River. This is in the southeastern section of modern Iraq, northwest of the Persian Gulf. The Babylonians settled the Jewish exiles in this region to colonize them. Ezekiel's ministry was primarily to those Jews deported from Judah by the Babylonians and any Israelites that remained in exile from previous deportations by the Assyrians. Still his messages had great instructional and practical significance for the Hebrews remaining in Israel and for the surrounding pagan nations, whose future he foretold. Though Ezekiel was transported in

visions to Jerusalem (chs. 8; 11), those revelations were always for the benefit of him and those to whom he was speaking in exile.

Ezekiel's oracles of national calamity include warnings of disease, death, destruction, and deportation. Yet because of God's unconditional promises and through the people's repentance, God's spiritual and material blessings would return to the people. Ezekiel's purpose was to remind God's people about their spiritual unfaithfulness (ch. 16) and about God's faithfulness to His own promises. Ezekiel showed the people how judgment was a natural outcome of a holy God's wrath against sin. It was also a loving God's means of disciplining His people: to correct their beliefs, redirect their behavior, and restore intimate fellowship between Himself and them. Thus Ezekiel preached to the exiles the imminence of God's judgment and the need for individual and national repentance.

The Book of Ezekiel stresses the ultimate aim of God's charity and chastisement: that "they shall know that I am the LORD." This refrain is repeated 65 times in the book and emphasizes that the purpose of God's actions is always to bring about the spiritual renewal of all people. Ezekiel teaches both individual and corporate responsibility for sin before God (chs. 18; 23). While themes of idolatry, social injustice, public and private immorality, imminent judgment, and future blessings of restoration and redemption are not unique to Ezekiel, his prophecies relate these themes to the centrality of the temple and the influence of the sacrificial system in the life of Israel. Past defilement and disobedience by the priests and people had led

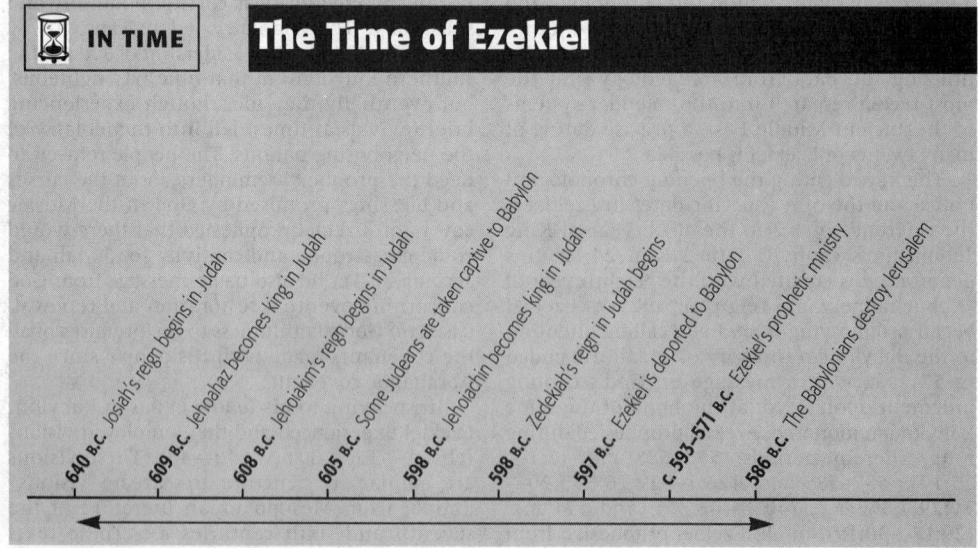

IN TIME | **The Time of Ezekiel**

640 B.C. Josiah's reign begins in Judah

609 B.C. Jehoahaz becomes king in Judah

608 B.C. Jehoiakim's reign begins in Judah

605 B.C. Some Judeans are taken captive to Babylon

598 B.C. Jehoiachin becomes king in Judah

598 B.C. Zedekiah's reign in Judah begins

597 B.C. Ezekiel is deported to Babylon

c. 593–571 B.C. Ezekiel's prophetic ministry

586 B.C. The Babylonians destroy Jerusalem

to the present dispersion and would lead to further judgment (chs. 4—32). The people's behavior was intrinsically connected to how they approached their God in worship. Insincere worship would led to immoral behavior and judgment; proper worship of the living God would led to moral behavior and blessings. Yet in the end, Ezekiel concludes with the comforting news that a day would come when God's rule and practical righteousness would return with a new temple and city and a renewed land and nation (chs. 33—48).

Ezekiel received and reported revelations from the living God as an exile in Babylon during 593–571 B.C. All that is known about this solitary prophet comes from his written prophecy, and no compelling data exist for the acceptance of any author other than the one named in the book itself: Ezekiel, son of Buzi (a priest), who was taken captive with Jehoiachin and other Hebrews in 597 B.C.

Since he was from a priestly family, Ezekiel was a priest as well as a prophet. Therefore he was well acquainted with the Levitical laws and rituals as well as the temple and its regulations. This becomes evident when he writes about his apocalyptic vision of the future messianic temple. Furthermore, he had a detailed knowledge of the Mosaic covenant, including the ethical, moral, and spiritual requirements of God's revelation and the inevitable results of obedience or disobedience to God's law. Though his exiled audience was cut off from the temple, the priesthood, and the related ceremonies and feasts, the prophet Ezekiel informed the exiles not only about these details, but also about the importance of obeying God's Law and seeking after Him.

The Book of Ezekiel reveals that the prophet was married (24:15–18) and had a house (3:24; 8:1). Overall, he enjoyed a large measure of freedom in captivity. The Babylonians had not captured the Jews in order to make them slaves in Babylon; instead they wanted to displace the population of Israel, especially its leadership and nobility, and settle their own citizens and other foreigners in the land. As for his personality and abilities, Ezekiel appears to have been articulate, intelligent, and dramatic. He was a person that could withstand great opposition in order to obey the demands God placed on his life.

Outline

Commentary

1:1–3:27 God's call and commission of Ezekiel to a prophetic ministry is set forth in three stages: (1) a revelation of God's character through a supernatural, symbolic vision (1:1–28); (2) a description of the chosen audience concluding the vision (2:1—3:15); and, (3) an explanation of God's charge and challenge to the prophet (3:16–27).

1:1 Ezekiel was preparing to become a priest when the Babylonians attacked Judah in 597 B.C. and carried him and many others into captivity (2 Kin. 24:10–14). **The thirtieth year** most likely refers to Ezekiel's age. At that age, a man could become a priest (v. 3) and begin serving in the temple (Num. 4:1–3). In this case, it was the time when God called him to be a prophet. **as I:** Of all the writing prophets, Ezekiel alone refers to himself at first with a pronoun ("I"), not using his name until v. 3 (Is. 1:1; Jer. 1:1; Hos. 1:1; Jon. 1:1; Zeph. 1:1). **River Chebar:** A branch of the Euphrates flowing southeast from Babylon. **heavens were opened:** As with all the true prophets of ancient Israel, the visitation of God was at His initiative, calling certain people to special responsibilities (Jer. 1:1–9). **visions of God:** The word *vision* is derived from the common Hebrew verb meaning "to see," rather than from

---

IN PERSON   Ezekiel's Obedience

Ezekiel resembles many of the other prophets of the Old Testament, for like them, he seemed strange to his neighbors and friends. It is one thing to prophesy about impending judgment and warn people to repent; it is quite another to lie on your side for 390 days to illustrate a point. But Ezekiel did not worry about how he looked to others, for he owed his obedience to God. So if God told him to do something he did it.

Some of Ezekiel's actions may have seemed peculiar, such as imprisoning himself in his own house. Others, like lying on his left side for 390 days and his right side for 40 days, may have appeared almost comical. Some, such as not mourning his own wife's death, must have appeared callous, even abhorrent according to the rituals and traditions of his day. But God had a purpose in having Ezekiel perform each of these acts. A point was illustrated and a lesson was taught. Some may have laughed at the prophet, and many ignored him—to their own peril.

Modern believers can relate to Ezekiel's being out of step with his contemporaries. Obedience to the will of God can be difficult in any generation. It is a struggle to live the way God wants you to live while the rest of society continues in its sinful ways. While our actions may not be as dramatic as Ezekiel's, their consequences can be important, both as examples to others, and as indications of our obedience to God.

---

the specific verb used for prophetic vision as in Is. 1. The plural of this word also calls attention to Ezekiel's visions, which were unparalleled both in nature and quantity.

1:2 This was the **fifth day** of the fourth month (v. 1). Ezekiel's "thirtieth year" was 597 B.C., when King Jehoiachin was deported to Babylon by Nebuchadnezzar (2 Kin. 24). The year 593 as the **fifth year of . . . captivity** is arrived at by using the Babylonian calendar, which begins in March. Jehoiachin's deportation to Babylon took place after he decided to surrender rather than subject Jerusalem to a Babylonian siege. He was imprisoned for 36 years (2 Kin. 25:27) before being released by Nebuchadnezzar's successor, Evil-Merodach. Throughout Jehoiachin's captivity, he received rations from the government. He may have even been able to retain his lands in Judah, which were placed under the management of a trustee.

1:3 Ezekiel uses the introductory phrase **the word of the LORD** came 50 times in this book. It always introduces a divine message and sometimes a new section. The name **Ezekiel** comes from the verb meaning "to seize," "to hold fast," coupled with the term meaning "God." Thus Ezekiel's name indicates that he was a man whom God had seized. See also 3:8 for another dimension of meaning in this name, "the one whom God has strengthened." **the hand of the LORD** was upon him: The divine origin of Ezekiel's message is emphasized in these first few verses.

1:4–14 This is a vivid and powerful image of God's all-powerful, all-knowing, all-seeing, and all-present characteristics. Bible students can be comfortable with such symbolic revelation (apocalyptic literature) if they remember to: (1) focus on the main thrust of the vision and not on the details; (2) be guided by any divine interpretations given in the immediate context and by parallel passages; and, (3) treat it as figurative language not to be taken in a rigid literal sense.

1:4 whirlwind . . . great cloud . . . raging fire: Compare the descriptions of divine appearance in Ex. 19:16–20; Ps. 18:7–15; Mic. 1:2–4. See also v. 13 below. **north:** quite frequently indicates the direction from which the majority of Israel's enemies approached them. For example, the Babylonian Empire extended from the land of the Chaldeans to the north of the holy land. The Hebrew term translated **amber** may also be understood as something like "glowing metal" (v. 27).

1:5 In ch. 10, these **living creatures** are related to the cherubim—celestial beings associated with God's holiness and glory and sometimes poetically with storm winds upon which God travels (Ps. 18:10). There are two basic approaches to understanding the *four living creatures:* as a highly symbolic representation of deity, or as highly symbolic representations of angelic beings who serve in God's presence. Probably they are angels, for God Himself is not revealed until the end of the section (v. 26). These stunning angelic creatures are dazzling attendants to God's majesty.

1:6 four faces: This image may suggest complete awareness; nothing is "behind" or "beside" these creatures. See vv. 8, 10. **four wings:** Contrast the six wings of the seraphim

---

🔍 IN FOCUS | **"son of man"**

(Heb. *ben 'adam*) (2:1; 3:1; 17:2; 24:16) Strong's #1121; 120: The expression *son of man* is used nearly one hundred times as a title for Ezekiel (2:1). It serves both to emphasize the difference between God the Creator and His creatures, and to mark the prophet Ezekiel as a representative member of the human race. Ezekiel's life was a living parable or object lesson to the Hebrew captives in Babylon (compare 1:3; 3:4–7). In word and deed, Ezekiel was a "sign" to the house of Israel (12:6). Jesus adopted the title Son of Man because He too is a representative person—the "last Adam" who became a life-giving spirit (Matt. 8:20; 1 Cor. 15:45). The title of Son of Man for Jesus also alludes to Daniel's vision of the heavenly being who is "like the Son of Man" (Dan. 7:13). Thus the title Son of Man for Jesus highlights the mystery of the Incarnation, the fact that Christ is both divine and human. As the God-man, Jesus became a glorious sign for all of sinful humanity (Luke 2:34).

---

in Is. 6:2; the wings are further described in vv. 9, 11.

1:7 legs . . . feet: The imagery portrays strength and beauty.

1:8 The "humanlike" representation includes **hands** and presumably arms.

1:9 did not turn: This seems to follow from the four faces (v. 6).

1:10 man . . . lion . . . ox . . . eagle: Composite fantastic figures in these classic combinations have been found in Mesopotamian and Egyptian iconography. The idealized strengths of each figure were thus presumed to reside in the living creature so described. The face of **man** may well represent the realm of intelligence among God's creatures; the face of the **lion,** the majesty of His creation; the face of the **ox,** the patient service that creation returns to Him; and the face of the **eagle,** swiftness to see and bring judgment where needed.

1:11, 12 One pair of **wings** was stretched upwards, as if in reverence; the other pair was used to cover the body as if in submission. Compare the description of the seraphim in Is. 6:2.

1:13–15 fire . . . lightning: These phenomena regularly attend descriptions of the appearances of God to His people (Ex. 19:16–20). See also v. 4. **Coals of fire** is used here as a symbol of judgment and holiness. By such means, Isaiah's lips were purged (Is. 6:7). Note the coals of fire upon the altar to burn the sacrifices as substitutes for the sinners. The fire of judgment seen here in the vision was soon to be exercised upon the unrepentant remnant still in the land.

1:16, 17 beryl: This may be chrysolite, a yellow or gold-colored stone. **wheel in the middle of a wheel:** The composite wheels were able to go in any direction without pivoting. A wheel symbolizes movement. In His government, God never is static, but is always

moving. The idolatrous remnant was saying judgment would not come. However, God's reward or judgment will never fail to come.

1:18 rims . . . full of eyes: The wheels had an exquisite beauty and an animate intelligence. **awesome:** The word means "compelling wonder."

1:19–21 The prophet stresses the association of the wheels with the living creatures, as well as the creatures' ability to travel wherever they wished. The mysterious phrase **the spirit . . . in the wheels** emphasizes the significance of the wheels. It appears that the wheels represented the flexibility and mobility of the living creatures. This is a pictorial representation of God's omnipresence.

1:22, 23 firmament: The same Hebrew word is used in Gen. 1:6. It means an "expanse" or "platform." Compare also the "sea of glass, like crystal" of Rev. 4:6. **An awesome crystal:** Like the brilliant sparkling of ice when the sun shines upon it.

1:24 Noise of their wings. The symbolism is that of unlimited strength and power. Nothing can deter God from accomplishing His plans of judgment, and even angels have frequently been used in executing His judgment (2 Kgs. 7:6; Dan 10:6). **Almighty:** This is the divine name *Shaddai*, most likely based on a Hebrew word meaning "mountain," to suggest God's omnipotence and majesty (10:5).

1:25 This **voice** connects with the "man" of v. 26. In Gen. 1 the voice of God summons light from the darkness (Gen. 1:3). Here above the din of angels' wings there is *a voice.* In John 1:1 is revealed the apostle's term for the Savior: the Word.

1:26 While Isaiah describes the elevation of the Lord's **throne** (Is. 6:1), Ezekiel focuses on its beauty. **sapphire:** This is precious lapis lazuli, a deep blue stone with golden specks. The same

Rev. 21:19. **The enthroned . . . pearance of a man** is the . . . vision.

. . . burning metal (**amber,** v. . . ., and rainbow-like **brightness** surrounded the One on the throne (v. 26). **the likeness of the glory of the LORD**: Human *likeness* here may reflect the personal nature of God's revelation of Himself. Further, it points forward to the plan of a more personal revelation of God coming as the Messiah (John 1:1–18). The *glory* indicates the wonder, majesty, and worthiness of the living God. Amid the wheels, the creatures, the colors, and the dazzling light was a figure who appeared like a man (v. 26). Compare the vision of Daniel who saw One "like the Son of Man" (Dan. 7:13). **I fell on my face:** The prophet's response was to fall down in worship and submission. All believers should recognize God's great glory and fall down in humble submission before Him (Phil. 2:10, 11).

2:1 Son of man: Ezekiel uses this phrase more than ninety times to refer to himself. It emphasizes his humanity in his God-given role as a spokesman for God. The meaning of the phrase is "human one." In the OT, only Dan. 7:13 and 8:17 also employ this phrase. In the NT, *Son of Man* is used frequently by Jesus for Himself. With this phrase Jesus was calling Himself "the Human One," the long-awaited Messiah who came as God in the flesh (Luke 21:27; John 1:14; 2 John 7). Thus the expression *Son of Man* is not a contradiction of Jesus' divinity, as is sometimes alleged. **stand on your feet:** Ezekiel had been bowing before the glorious One (1:28). Perhaps his initial thoughts were similar to those of Isaiah (Is. 6:5). The commandment to *stand* suggests that he had no reason to be afraid.

2:2 the Spirit: This reference to the indwelling of the Holy Spirit in God's prophet is of great importance. The visions and messages of Ezekiel revelations from the living God. In contrast to the Holy Spirit indwelling all believers of our present age, in OT times He came upon some individuals by sovereign choice for the divine enablement needed for superhuman tasks. It was not universal among those who trusted in God, nor was it a permanent indwelling.

2:3, 4 Ezekiel was called to speak God's message to the **children of Israel.** God describes them as **a rebellious nation** and more specifically **impudent and stubborn**— literally "stiff-of-face and hard-of-heart children" (3:7). The Hebrew term for *rebellious* indicates a breaking of the covenant relationship. **Thus says the Lord GOD**: GOD told Ezekiel to emphasize the divine origin of his messages by using these words. Like Moses (Ex.

3; 4), Ezekiel would speak in God's name only what God commanded him. The term *Lord GOD* combines a title indicating God's sovereignty (*Adonai*) and His personal name (*Yahweh,* conventionally translated with GOD or LORD in small capital letters).

2:5 If the rebellious people refused to listen to Ezekiel's message, Ezekiel would still prove himself a true **prophet** of God by continuing to proclaim God's messages (v. 7). Read 2 Kin. 21 for an example of the nature of the rebellion that had led to their captivity.

2:6, 7 briers and thorns . . . scorpions: These images vividly portray the nature of the rebellious opponents of Ezekiel's warnings. God told Ezekiel not to allow fear to hinder his message, whether or not the message was wanted (v. 7).

2:8, 9 eat: In contrast to rebellious Israel, Ezekiel was to set an example by being receptive and listening to God's message. **hand . . . scroll:** Compare Jer. 1:9.

2:10 The unusual feature of writing on both sides of a scroll indicates the magnitude of the nation's transgressions and its need for lengthy **lamentations** (Zech. 5:3; Rev. 5:1). Tough Ezekiel would later bring words of comfort and consolation (chs. 33—48), his first prophecies from God contained only sorrow and sadness.

3:1–3 eat: The symbolic act of eating the scroll demonstrated that Ezekiel internalized the message in preparation for speaking to the people.

3:5–7 Though no linguistic barrier existed between Ezekiel and the nation, Israel would pay less attention to the prophet than foreigners would. Israel's rejection of the prophet's message was the symptom of a prior and more fundamental revolt against God's rule (1 Sam. 8:7). All Israel was characterized as **impudent**— literally "hard-of-head"—and **hard-hearted** (2:4). Those who have had generous exposure to the truth and reject it can be harder than those who hear it for the first time.

3:8, 9 I have made your face strong: There may have been an intentional pun on Ezekiel's name, which means "strongly seized by God" (1:3) or "God strengthens." Double meanings in biblical names are common (Cain; Gen. 4:1). The prophet was adequately equipped by God for his calling.

3:10, 11 A necessary prerequisite to God sending Ezekiel as His messenger was Ezekiel's reception of all God's words. God told Ezekiel that he was to make it clear that his message and authority came from the Lord, and that he must continue to **speak** regardless of his audience's responses and reactions.

3:11 get to the captives: Two groups of exiles had already been brought to Babylon, one in 606 B.C., and another in 597 B.C. Ezekiel was sent to them to show God's justice in their being chastened. The fact of Ezekiel being sent to them indicates God's love and compassion by pleading with them to repent and turn to Him.

3:12, 13 Blessed . . . from His place: This **thunderous** acclaim in praise of the living God came from His myriad of angelic armies (compare Is. 6:3). **glory:** The word suggests "weight" or "significance," indicating the wonder, majesty, and worthiness of the living God.

3:14 Bitterness means "distress" and "anguish." Ezekiel's human perspective caused him to focus on the distasteful calling of delivering a message no one would listen to. The prophet was angry—**heat of my spirit**—and appalled. But the **hand of the LORD** was pre-

people about the beneficial consequences of turning from evil and the disastrous results of refusing to live by the stipulations of the Mosaic covenant, which would rescue them from a wasted existence.

3:17 The **watchman** stood on the city wall guarding against any external or internal threat. He would sound an alarm upon sighting impending danger (2 Sam. 18:24). God made Ezekiel a spiritual watchman over His people.

3:18, 19 his blood: Doubtless, this severe warning given to Ezekiel was similar to that given to a military watchman in ancient times. If the watchman failed to give the alarm to the city in a time of peril, the blood of the city would be required of him. But if the watchman sounded the alarm and the city did not respond,

Drawing of the ancient city of Lachish, showing its outer and inner defensive walls. Ezekiel compared himself to a watchman on such a wall who warned of approaching danger, but his task was to warn the people of moral and spiritual danger (Ezek. 3:17).

sent to help him deal with these feelings and then move him on to live and work among the captives (v. 15).

3:15 The Israelites who had been exiled to Babylon lived in **Tel Abib,** meaning "hill of flood." **Seven days** is the time normally taken for mourning the dead, as well as the time set aside for a priest's consecration (Gen. 50:10; Lev. 8:33). Ezekiel sat **astonished** with these captives for seven days as evidence that he had experienced a unique encounter with God (Job 2:13). At the end of the seven days Ezekiel would be ordained for the priesthood and would be ready to proclaim mourning for Israel.

3:16–21 Ezekiel's prophetic service was basically that of warning and reminding the

the watchman could hardly be blamed. **delivered your soul:** As a faithful watchman, Ezekiel would not have placed his own life in jeopardy by failing in his critical duty. A watchman who was "asleep at the switch" would forfeit his life. The word *soul* often merely means "life" in Hebrew. See also v. 21.

3:20, 21 The **stumbling block** is interpreted by some as a death sentence. If the person continued repeatedly in sin, then death would result. The reference to "life" and "death" in this section is to physical, not eternal, realities. **delivered your soul:** See v. 19.

3:22, 23 The word **glory** suggests "weight" or "significance." The emphasis is on the central significance and awesome wonder of the living God.

3:24 Ezekiel wrote more of the indwelling of God's **Spirit** than any of the prophets (2:2).

3:25–27 This God-ordained muteness was a restriction: (1) from moving about publicly to speak (v. 25); (2) from proclaiming just the theme of divine judgment (v. 26); and, (3) from communicating only in God's authority and when God opened his mouth (v. 27). A comparison of the dates in 1:1–3 with 33:21–22 shows the length of this silence to have been seven and one-half years, until the fall of Jerusalem in 586 B.C. Ezekiel clearly orated other messages during this time (11:25; 14:1; 20:1).

3:26 The phrase **not be one to rebuke them** qualified what was meant by Ezekiel's being **mute.** The idea may be better stated as "not be a legal mediator." During his "mute" period, Ezekiel would not be allowed to speak as a mediator on behalf of the people before God, their Judge.

3:27 He who hears, let him hear: Jesus used this warning often in His teaching (Mark 4:23). The phrasing emphasizes individual responsibility and readiness to accept the divine message.

4:1–3. This first of the symbolic and speechless demonstrations—probably enacted outside the prophet's house (3:15, 16)—portrays the success and certainty of the coming siege of Jerusalem by Babylon.

4:1 The **clay tablet** was unfired mud or clay soft enough to be inscribed with a stylus. The Hebrew term rendered **portray** means to scratch or mark on the tablet.

4:2 Lay siege: The city of Jerusalem would come under *siege,* meaning that the Babylonians would surround the city and cut off its outside supplies. The purpose was to starve the inhabitants into submission (vv. 9–12; 16, 17). By his symbolic drawing, Ezekiel may have been commanded to do what other "prophets" of the nations might do. That is, the hired "prophets" of the pagan nations might use such a drawing as a device for invoking the gods to bring about the event graphically described. In Ezekiel's case, the drawing was the opposite of what the people wanted. As they sat in captivity, the worst news would have been that the holy city had been destroyed. In this case, the drawing showed the people the horrible truth of what God already had sovereignly ordained.

4:3 The **iron plate** or pan was a utensil that Ezekiel possessed as a priest; it was for baking grain for the cereal offerings (Lev. 2:5; 6:21; 7:9). Here its purpose was to represent a wall between Ezekiel and the city. The first three verses of the chapter dramatize **to the house of Israel** the inevitable and inescapable siege that would come against the holy city.

4:4–6 bear their iniquity: The prophet represented Israel—the northern kingdom—and Judah—the southern kingdom—and the length of time each was going to be punished for its sin. Since Ezekiel set the deportation of Jehoiachin (597 B.C.) as his chronological reference point (1:2), the most straightforward interpretation of vv. 4–8 pictures the punishment of exile and Gentile rule inflicted upon the Hebrew nation over a 430–year period as extending from 597 to approximately 167 B.C. This was the time Jewish rule returned to Judah, through the Maccabean revolt.

4:7 The **arm . . . uncovered,** used in connection with God's command that Ezekiel **set** his **face toward the siege** (4:3), most likely refers to the siege as a set and certain event (Is. 52:10, and the modern idiom of "rolling up one's sleeves"). As horrible as it was, the siege ultimately showed God's faithfulness to His covenant established in the days of Moses: that idolatry and disobedience would bring curses, which would include being conquered, captured, and removed from the land (Deut. 28:15–68).

4:8 Restrain you more literally reads "place ropes on you." Ezekiel was bound while lying on either side for the entire 430 days; but the activities described in 4:9–17 show that his lying down and being tied up occurred only during parts of each day.

4:9–11 The recipe of six mixed grains for the bread indicates the limited and unusual food supply while in bondage in a foreign land. The small amounts of these grains vividly picture the short supply of food in a city under siege. Because a city under siege was cut off from outside supplies, the people had to ration their **food** and **water.** If it ran out, they would be forced to surrender. In Jerusalem, the people would be allowed daily only a half pound of bread (**twenty shekels**) and less than a quart of water (**one-sixth of a hin**).

4:12–15 The bread is called **defiled** (v. 13) in light of what is said in v. 12. In order to portray the fate of the unfaithful nation, God wanted Ezekiel to temporarily eat food made unclean by being cooked over a fire fueled by **human waste** (Deut. 23:12–14). God at first commanded Ezekiel to use human excrement because it would most accurately and forcefully symbolize the horror of the coming siege of the city. But **cow dung,** a common fuel then as now, was allowed as a substitute in light of Ezekiel's prayerful insistence and practical faithfulness to the ceremonial law (Deut. 12:15–19; 14:3–21).

4:16, 17 The terrible conditions of the siege of Jerusalem would fulfill Ezekiel's symbolic acts (vv. 9–12). Both **water** and **bread** would be rationed. **Anxiety** and **dread** (12:19) would be rampant. The Hebrew term for *dread* could also be rendered "horror" or "shuddering." All this would occur because of Judah's **iniquity**. The people had broken their covenant with God, and He had no choice but to bring upon them the promised consequences of their disobedience (Lev. 26:14–29; Deut. 28:47–53; 2 Kin. 25:1–3).

5:1 Shaving the **head** was an act showing shame or disgrace in Hebrew culture (7:18; 2 Sam. 10:4). It also represented a type of pagan mourning forbidden by the Law (27:31; Deut. 14:1; Is. 15:2; 22:12). Shaving the head was a mark of defilement, making a priest like Ezekiel ritually unclean, and so unable to perform his duties in the temple (Lev. 21:5). This message was telling the people that they were about to be humiliated and defiled.

5:2 Each citizen of Jerusalem would suffer one of the three fates depicted by each of the three mounds of the equally measured shorn hair: (1) some would be burned along with the city or would die from plague, famine, or other **siege** conditions (5:12; 2 Kin. 25:9); (2) some would be murdered by the **sword** during the attack (5:12; 2 Kin. 25:18–21); and (3) some would be scattered in the **wind**—referring to the Exile (5:12; 2 Kin. 25:11–17, 21).

5:3, 4 a fire will go out: A remnant from the group sent into exile would be saved from death and merged into the foreign culture. Other exiles would be killed.

5:5–7 This is Jerusalem: The words were being said in anguish. The personal God of the Hebrews had given them the city as an inheritance. God loved it and established it as the center of the world, because His temple was there. Here, however, He describes the extent of its people's abominations. **She has rebelled** refers to the people of the favored city who had not only stubbornly refused to keep the Law, but whose sin was even worse than that of the nations around them—they had failed to follow even the moral laws that were common among the pagans.

5:8 therefore: Here is the solemn announcement of the sovereign judge. **I, even I, am against you:** The solemn, emphatic pronoun is sad indeed.

5:9–17 The elements in God's judgment on the people for their sins can be enumerated in this way: (1) a judgment that will be worse in extent than ever before; (2) a terrible famine that will lead to cannibalism; (3) **pestilence,** meaning plagues and diseases associated with famine; (4) violent death by sword or wild beasts; and, (5) the scattering and killing of a remnant. These punishments would come as the result of the people's idolatry—they had **defiled** God's temple with **detestable things** and **abominations** (v. 11), evidencing their complete disregard for the Law (vv. 6, 7; 11:18). The Ten Commandments were the foundation of all Mosaic legislation, and they prohibited idolatry (Ex. 20:3). Further, these judgments would be accomplished: (1) without pity and with no hope of escape (v. 11), (2) with a full expenditure of God's wrath (v. 13), and (3) with the result of making God's people an object lesson of warning among the onlooking neighbor nations (v. 15). In His covenant with His people, God had promised to send these curses if the people chose to rebel against Him (Deut. 28:15–68). The disobedient and rebellious people should not be surprised at the horror they were soon to face.

6:1–3 The **mountains of Israel** may signify the land in general (36:1–6); however, the **hills** could be especially condemned because in their wooded areas the people had built altars and shrines to Canaanite idols (v. 13). **High places** were originally elevated locations for the worship of the god Baal and other deities of the Canaanite pantheon. The term *high place* could be used of any location, whether hilltop or valley (v. 6; Jer. 7:31) where Canaanite gods were worshiped (1 Kin. 11:4–10). The Israelites adopted the use of these and associated worship practices including sexual misconduct, sorcery, spiritism, snake worship, and child sacrifice.

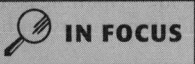 **IN FOCUS** **"idols"**

(Heb. *gillulim*) (6:4; 20:16; 30:13; 2 Kin. 23:24) Strong's #1544: This Hebrew noun is related to a verb that means "to roll" (Gen. 29:3; Josh. 10:18). The word refers to "shapeless things" like stones or tree logs of which idols were made (6:9; 20:39; 22:3; 1 Kin. 21:26). The prophet Ezekiel uses this Hebrew term for *idols* nearly 40 times, always contemptuously, for these false gods had led Israel away from the true God (14:5). The word *gillulim* may be related to a similar Hebrew expression meaning "dung pellets." Later Jewish commentators mocked the *gillulim* as the "dung idols," idols as worthless as dung.

IN LIFE | Then You Will Know!

Ezekiel was sent to the Hebrew captives in Babylon (Ezek. 2:1–5; 3:14–15). Despite the fact that the Babylonians had invaded Judah twice, fulfilling the warnings of the prophet Jeremiah, the exiles still did not understand why God had allowed these events to happen, nor why they had been deported to Babylon. They still had not grasped the fact that their nation's troubles were the result of their idolatry and other sins against the Lord.

God used Ezekiel to make this truth clear. Time after time, over a period of at least 20 years, the prophet spelled out the people's sins and warned them of the certainty of God's wrath. Nevertheless, the people remained willfully blind to their condition. This hardness of heart helps to explain why the phrase, "You {or they} shall know that I am the Lord," is repeated some 60 or 70 times in the book (6:7, 10, 13, 14). Quite often, these declarations can be found in the middle of a promise of God's wrath: "The slain shall fall" (6:7); "I would bring this calamity" (6:10); "thus will I spend My fury" (6:12); "I will . . . make the land desolate" (6:14).

We will either know the Lord in His grace and mercy, or in His wrath and fury. The choice is ours. But regardless of our response, God makes it clear that "You shall know that I am the Lord." God is determined to be heard. He is the Lord—and sooner or later, we will know that He is.

Before entering the Promised Land, the Hebrews had been commanded to abolish all the high places where idols were worshiped (Num. 33:52).

6:4–6 The phrases **cast down your slain, lay the corpses,** and **scatter your bones** refer to God's judgment. Dead people lying unburied and bones scattered around signify the ultimate defilement of the land. God would bring this upon them because they had defiled and desecrated themselves by worshiping in the pagan high places (2 Kin. 23:20; Ps. 53:5).

6:7 you shall know that I am the Lord: Ordinarily, one would come to *know* more to experience the reality of the living God through encounters with His mercy. But because of the evil path that the people of Judah had taken, they would experience His reality in a dreadful manner—through His judgment (Is. 28:21).

6:8–10 Not only would God prove His justice and faithfulness to His past promises and warnings about the consequences of idolatry (5:13), but He would **leave a remnant** of His people so they would **remember** the One true God **among the nations.** God had promised that, despite any future destruction of the nation that might occur because of sin, He would always preserve a portion from annihilation (Deut. 28:61–64). The chief purpose of even calamitous punishment was the production of a repentant and spiritually restored remnant.

6:11, 12 Alas: This word, also translated "Ah!" (21:15) and "Aha!" (25:3), is meant sarcastically. Either God was displaying His delight over the destruction of idolatrous places and practices (vv. 1–7, 13) or He was having Ezekiel enact the mocking role of a jealous neighbor nation, such as Ammon (25:1–7).

6:13, 14 Then you shall know that I am the Lord: As in vv. 7, 10, the Lord states the purpose of the coming destruction of His city and many of its people. The use of God's personal name further emphasizes the intent to bring His people back to a personal, intimate relationship with Himself.

7:1–4 The three uses of the key word **end** stresses that the fulfillment of the prophecy was at hand. The word **has come** denotes certitude. **The four corners of the land** suggests that all the people of Judah would be affected, not just those in Jerusalem.

7:5–7 As in vv. 2, 3, key words in these verses include **end** (used two times), in parallel with **doom.** There now is an added stress on **disaster** (used two times); the coming disaster will be unlike any other (5:9). The word *doom* is a rare term and may be better explained as "mourning."

7:8, 9 Again at the end of this oracle (vv. 4, 27), God states His purpose in disciplining Israel: to cultivate in His people a better understanding of Himself.

7:10–12 The flowering of the **rod** and **pride** indicates that the time to bring judgment was ripe. These words describe one whose time had come, a person marked by arrogance. In this case, it pictures the chosen instrument of God (Num. 17:5) with whom He would discipline Jerusalem and Judah—namely, Nebuchadnezzar, king of Babylon and the characteristic representative of the arrogant and evil Babylonians (v. 21). **Rod of wickedness**

refers to a stick or club (Ex. 4:20; Is. 10:5) used for punishing wickedness.

7:12, 13 Let not the buyer rejoice: The fact of coming judgment was so certain, and its effects would be so lasting and devastating, that transactions of buying and selling would be concluded improperly or not at all.

7:14, 15 No one goes to battle for Judah because the nation and land would be so devastated by death and diseases brought on by warfare and famine (5:8–17).

7:16–19 Those left alive would hide in the hills and be characterized by four things: (1) **mourning**—moaning **like doves** in **shame,** displaying their humiliation over sin by wearing **sackcloth** and shaving their heads (Is. 15:2, 3); (2) weakness; (3) **horror;** and, (4) disgust and disillusionment over wealth.

7:20–22 This section describes the judgment that would come on the people for taking the treasures of the temple to make pagan images. **Beauty of his ornaments** and **My secret place** both refer to Jerusalem and its temple. The people had sinned horribly when they crafted idols out of the temple treasures and then worshiped what their hands had made (Rom. 1:25).

7:23–27 The punishment will fit the crime—God promised to **do to them according to . . . what they deserve.** Because Judah had been so bloodthirsty, God would send **the worst of the Gentiles** to **possess their houses,** defile the temple, and bring **violence** to the land. This section predicts Nebuchadnezzar's desecration of the Jerusalem temple in 586 B.C. As a last resort, peace at any price would be fervently sought from false prophets, priests, and politicians, but without success. The deadline for decisive action would have passed.

8:1 sixth year: This second exact date given in Ezekiel is 592 B.C., when Ezekiel was acting out the siege of Jerusalem (1:1; 4:1–8).

8:2 The first word translated **fire** may also be read in Hebrew as the word meaning "man." In the second instance **fire** is the expected meaning. This description parallels 1:26, 27.

8:3, 4 The **north gate of the inner court,** called the "altar gate" in v. 5, was near the sacrificial altar (Lev. 1:11). There Ezekiel saw the **image . . . which provokes to jealousy.** All idolatry was forbidden, and any idol represented a violation of the loyalty that belonged to Israel's God. **the glory of the God of Israel:** See 3:12.

8:5, 6 to make Me go: The people thought that just because the temple stood among them, whatever wrong they might do could not bring ultimate disaster. They thought the temple guaranteed their security. They did not realize that their evil had actually caused God to leave His temple, which would then no longer be their protection. See ch. 10.

8:7–9 A view through a **hole** in the temple **wall,** this next scene of the vision gives a glimpse of even worse idolatrous acts. The people's **abominations** (vv. 6, 9, 10, 13, 15, 17) were not limited to a periphery. They extended deeply into the hierarchy of Israel's religious leadership.

8:10 all around on the walls: In conformity with surrounding pagan nations (primarily Egypt), God's people were worshiping images of clean and unclean creatures that represented various gods. Polytheistic idolatry was being practiced in Israel.

8:11 The **seventy** elders represented the nation's leaders (Num. 11:16–25). The **censer** each man carried (a vessel for holding burning incense) and the burning **incense** would not necessarily be evil, but here they were being used to worship idols. **Jaazaniah:** Nothing more is known about this person.

8:12 The emphasis is on the elders' pagan beliefs as well as their resultant secret behavior—**in the dark.** Ironically and inconsistently, they thought of God in limited, human terms, much as their neighbors viewed the gods of the nations. They thought He was not omniscient and omnipresent.

8:13, 14 Tammuz was a fertility god. The women were crying out to the idol because they had no children or because the crops were failing. In the sixth month, August-September, Tammuz was thought to "die" with the scorched land. Worshipers would wail over his death and cry for his resurgence.

8:15, 16 The location for the sun worship was in the **inner court . . . between the porch and the altar.** These 25 **men** must have been Levites if temple regulations were being followed; otherwise, the area was forbidden (Num. 3:7, 8; 18:1–7; 2 Chr. 4:9; Joel 2:17). Whether priests or not, they were turned in the wrong direction—their backs were to God's temple and they were **worshiping the sun.**

8:17, 18 trivial thing: There is similar wording in the Lord's condemnation of Ahab (1 Kin. 16:31). **put the branch to their nose:** This action is not mentioned elsewhere. In the context it appears to be (1) a ritualistic gesture used in idol worship, or (2) an action indicative of the extensive violence which was occurring in Judah as a result of idolatry.

9:1–11 The guilty idolaters are killed: a vision of the coming destruction of Jerusalem.

9:1 He is the God of Israel, who has been speaking since Ezekiel saw the glory of God (8:5). **those who have charge over:** This is the sense given to a Hebrew word that is frequently used of a vengeful visitation (Is. 10:3).

9:2 One man among them was probably one in addition to the six, making six men equipped as executioners and one representing the presence and purity of the holy God, who is worthy to mark out some for judgment and to omit others (vv. 3–7; Ex. 12:1–13; Rom. 9:14–29; Rev. 7:3; 9:4). **his battle-ax:** Literally, "the implement of his shattering" (compare Jer. 51:20). The **upper gate** from which these seven came was equivalent to the north gate of the inner court (8:3; 2 Kin. 15:35). The **bronze altar** was the sacrificial altar.

9:3 It is not clear whether the term **cherub** here indicates (1) the cherubim on the ark of the covenant in the Most Holy Place, or (2) the cherubim of the throne with wheels in 10:1–5, 18. Either way, this pictures the departure of God's glory from the temple, then from Jerusalem, and then from Judah, as seen in chs. 9—11. The **threshold** refers to the entryway.

9:4 Mark translates the Hebrew name for the last letter of the Hebrew alphabet, which in Ezekiel's time looked like an X. Those so marked are people who **sigh and cry** over the abominations of idolatry so far mentioned. Those who demonstrated a righteous attitude through true repentance and remorse were marked out from the hardened rebels. These would be the remnant (v. 8), the ones who continued to follow God's commands (Rev. 7:2–4; 9:4; 14:1).

9:5, 6 Go after him: The universality of this judgment is shocking to us; but this is in line with divine judgments from the time of the Flood in Genesis to the final judgment described in Revelation.

9:6, 7 My sanctuary: The corrupt spiritual leaders had been practicing idolatry and immorality in the temple itself (8:3–16). Judgment would begin with them because they had led the nation astray (1 Pet. 4:17). **Defile the temple:** This means to carry out the execution and leave dead bodies in the temple environs (Lev. 21:1; Num. 19:11).

9:8 The prophet was horrified by what he saw. The true servant of God always sorrows over the destruction that people bring on themselves by their rebellion. The word **Ah** was sarcastic in 6:11; here it is a sincere gasp of pain (as in 11:13). **The remnant,** a group chosen and saved from destruction by a sovereign God, is a recurring theme in the Bible (2 Kin. 19:31; Ezra 9:8; Is. 1:9; 10:20–23; Amos 5:15; Rom. 9:27–29; 11:1–8).

9:9, 10 Three reasons are given as to why the nation deserved this terrible outpouring of God's wrath—serious and undeniable (1) **iniquity,** or guilt of sinful offenses (4:4–8); (2) **bloodshed,** or violence (8:17); and, (3) **perversity,** or more precisely injustice. The people and especially rich rulers willfully chose to believe that God did not see or care what injustices went on.

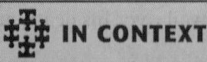 **IN CONTEXT** | **Mercy to the Repentant**

God's forgiveness has always required repentance on the part of sinners. It did in ancient times; it still does today.

In Ezekiel's vision of Jerusalem, the Lord commanded angelic executioners to place a special mark on the foreheads of those who were moved to repentance over the "abominations" being committed in the city. The rest were to be slain (Ezek. 9:4–7). The justification for this slaughter was that the sins of the wicked—bloodshed and perversity (idolatry)—were "exceedingly great" (9:9). By contrast, citizens who demonstrated a deep concern for holiness were shown mercy.

This vision recalls a similar judgment in Egypt, in which the Lord killed the firstborn children of the Egyptians, but spared the Hebrew households that had marked their doorposts with blood (Ex. 12:1–36). In both cases, God marked out those to whom He would show mercy on the basis of their heart attitude toward Him.

It is interesting to note that the "mark" referred to by Ezekiel is the Hebrew letter *taw*, the last letter of the Hebrew alphabet. Today, *taw* is the equivalent of "T," but in Jeremiah's day it was written like an "X" and was often used as a signature (Job 31:35). Early Christians pointed out the similarity between Ezekiel's "mark" and the sign of the cross. Both indicated God's mercy and redemption of sinners.

The judgment foreseen in Ezekiel's vision applies to people today. It demonstrates that God shows mercy, but He always looks for repentance. Those who resist Him and remain committed to sin can expect His wrath. But those who "sigh and cry" over their own sins and the sins of others will know His comfort and forgiveness (compare James 4:8–10).

9:11 I have done: The report of judgment was brought by one man (vv. 3, 4) appearing as a righteous accountant.

10:1 See ch. 1 for an understanding of the several terms in this verse. The **cherubim** here are the living creatures of 1:5. **sapphire stone:** This was probably lapis lazuli, a dark blue, opaque stone found mainly in Afghanistan. It was a most valuable gemstone in ancient times. The modern sapphire is a translucent blue aluminum silicate, chemically the same as ruby. It is extremely hard and could not have been cut or polished by ancient craftsmen. Lapis lazuli is approximately as hard as glass.[L&T]

10:2 Coals of fire (1:13) are sometimes related to a chastisement for cleansing (Is. 6) and at other times to judgment by fiery catastrophe (Gen. 19:24, 25).

10:3–5 The **cloud** represented God's glory (as in 1:4), which was seen moving from the **inner court** to the **threshold** of the temple. From there it filled the temple (**house**). **glory:** See 3:12, 23. **sound . . . Almighty:** See 1:24.

10:6 when He commanded . . . he went in: These words display the man's unquestioning obedience to God (v. 5; 1:24; 8:2–5).

10:7, 8 A particular **cherub** handed the coals to the man in linen (v. 2). Though not stated explicitly, it is implied that all the directives of v. 2 were now carried out. The coals were then scattered on Jerusalem.

10:9–17 Ezekiel describes the **wheels** (vv. 9–14) and then the **cherubim** (vv. 15–17). See ch. 1 for details in this vision. Only in v. 14 is something different from the description in ch. 1. Whereas one of the four faces in 1:10 is an ox,

here it is a **cherub.** There are ancient sculptures with animal bodies and wings but human faces, sometimes called "cherubs." The difference of the faces between 1:10 and 10:14 should not be called an error; it is possible that the images that Ezekiel saw were changing from time to time.

10:18, 19 God's **glory** continued moving gradually but progressively away from the temple (vv. 3, 4): from the entrance door of the temple to the wheeled cherubim throne, and then with the throne to the **east gate** of the temple. The Lord's departure suggests that He was reluctant to leave. Though His holiness had been rejected so that He would not stay, He left with sorrow over the end His people had brought upon themselves.

10:20–22 The cherubim sometimes serve as guardians (Gen. 3:24). They are associated with God's throne and presence (the mercy seat on the ark; Ex. 25:18–22; 1 Chr. 13:6). They are also associated with God's chariot-like throne (v. 1; 1:20–26; Ps. 18:10).

11:1–13 In this section, the public and political leaders, who should have modeled godliness in the community at home and work, have a judgment of death by sword prophesied against them.

11:1, 2 Ezekiel saw **twenty-five** civic leaders at the temple. **Princes of the people** denotes public and political officials often serving in judicial, military, or royal posts (2 Sam. 8:15–18; 20:23–26). **Jaazaniah:** Son of Azzur, and not the same Jaazaniah as in 8:11 (son of Shaphan). These men had been giving **wicked counsel,** and even stooped so low as to **devise iniquity** against their own people.

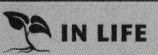 **IN LIFE**　　**The Ultimate Tragedy**

Readers of Ezek. 10 are likely to focus on the spectacular vision of the cherubim and the wheels within wheels. But the real story in this passage is the Lord's departure from His temple at Jerusalem (Ezek. 10:18). Given the history and significance of the temple, nothing could be more tragic for Judah.

The temple was designed by David and built by Solomon to be the "house of the Lord" (2 Chr. 5:1). When it was completed, God blessed the magnificent structure by filling it with His glory and presence (5:14). From then on, the temple was regarded as a hallowed symbol that stood for God (6:20). Yet now Ezekiel saw God departing from the temple. There is little wonder why. The people had turned the "house of the Lord" into a house of idolatrous abominations. As a result, God decided to leave His temple and go "far away" from His people (Ezek. 8:5–17; compare 11:23). Clearly, the end of Judah was at hand.

Can there be a greater tragedy—to enjoy the Lord's presence, only to have it withdrawn because of a willful, long-term commitment to sin and rebellion? If that is the picture of your life, then Ezekiel's vision should serve as a warning and an appeal to repentance. Nothing could be worse than to drive God away when He longs to bless you with His presence (Heb. 6:4–12).

Because they were trying to combine Hebrew and heathen religions, these leaders had deceived themselves and their followers into thinking that they were speaking for the true God. On **Pelatiah,** meaning "The One Delivered by the Lord," see v. 13.

11:3 The time is not near to build houses can be rephrased, "Is it not now time to build houses?" These officials were proclaiming that the inhabitants of Jerusalem were as secure behind the city's walls as meat was safe in its cooking pot (**caldron**). There was no impending doom, they said; therefore, new construction projects were encouraged.

11:4 prophesy . . . prophesy: The repetition is for emphasis, a literary technique common in Hebrew style. **Son of man** means "human one." This phrase appears 90 times in Ezekiel and emphasizes Ezekiel's humanity in his role as a spokesman for God. In the OT the phrase is used also for Daniel (Dan. 8:17) and for the coming Messiah (Dan. 7:13). In the NT the phrase *Son of Man* is used frequently by Jesus for Himself (2:1).

11:5–12 God's message to the corrupt officials of Jerusalem and Judah is declared, pinpointing the justifications for divine anger (vv. 5, 6, 12) and predicting a judgment of death (vv. 7–11).

11:6 slain: Jerusalem's official leaders had been accused of wicked activities and giving unrighteous advice (v. 2); here we discover that they had killed fellow countrymen.

11:7–12 The verdict of a death penalty is announced. Contrary to the leaders' false beliefs, the ones they killed were the godly people whose presence might have offered protection in the **caldron**—that is, Jerusalem. Those who had gained power by the sword, knowing the dread of such force, would experience defeat and death the same way. They would be dragged out of the city and slain by **strangers,** referring to the Babylonians.

11:13 Ezekiel's reaction showed that **Pelatiah,** one of the corrupt city leaders (v. 1), was struck dead by God as undeniable proof that the prophet's message would come true. Ezekiel himself was awestruck and asked whether this meant that God would not after all preserve a **remnant** (9:8).

11:14–25 In this section, God responds to Ezekiel's concern over a saved remnant. He tells Ezekiel that a remnant is being preserved that will be regathered to the land of Israel and will receive a new outpouring of God's Spirit (vv. 14–21). God's Spirit then leaves Jerusalem (vv. 22, 23), and Ezekiel's vision returns him to Babylonia, where he tells what has happened to the exiles (vv. 24, 25).

11:14–21. God gives promises to the remnant of Israel with present (11:14–16) and future (11:17–20) aspects.

11:15 Ezekiel's **brethren** were those in exile with him. The people in Jerusalem (representative of Judah) regarded the exiles as sinners because they had been deported to Babylon.

11:16 God explained to Ezekiel that the Hebrews taken captive and spread among foreign lands were actually the remnant whom God was protecting. God Himself would continue as their **sanctuary**—a word in Hebrew that literally means a "holy place" or a "set-apart place."

11:17 I will give you the land: God promises that Israel will be restored to the promised land. This is in keeping with the unilateral and unconditional nature of the covenant made with Abraham (Gen. 12:1–3; 15:13–21; Deut. 30:1–6), and renewed with David (2 Sam. 7:12–16) and Jeremiah (Jer. 31:31–34).

11:18–20 When the remnant returned to the land, they would abolish idolatry. At that time, God would establish a new covenant with them (Jer. 31:31–34). Then God would pour out His Spirit (36:26, 27; Joel 2:28, 29) so that His people would become united in purpose and empowered to maintain their righteousness—**walk in My statutes.** They would finally and truly become His people (Ex. 6:6–8).

11:21 As with Pelatiah, God promised to continue judging idolaters whose affections were for **detestable** objects—that is, idols. Such **recompense** was fully deserved because ample warning had been given; the people were personally responsible for the choices. From His giving of the Law at Mount Sinai, the Lord had continually expressed His abhorrence of idolatry (Ex. 20:1–6). Praise and worship belonged only to the Lord—their Creator and Deliverer.

11:22, 23 God's glory continued to move away from **the city** to the Mount of Olives—**the mountain.** See 10:3, 4, 18, 19. The Hebrew term for **glory** literally means "weight" or "significance" and refers to the wonder and majesty of the living God.

11:24, 25 the Spirit: Ezekiel's visions are not merely dreams; they were inspired by God Himself and thus were prophetic. **Chaldea:** This is an alternate term for Babylon. **So I spoke:** Presumably the telling and retelling of Ezekiel's visions (8:2–11:23) led to the more permanent record that makes up his book.

12:1–20 Ezekiel acts out a prophecy as if he were in Judah preparing to go into captivity after the fall of Jerusalem.

12:1, 2 The exiled community among whom Ezekiel was ministering was described twice as **a rebellious house.** This is further defined by

the phrases: **eyes to see . . . and ears to hear**
(Is. 6:10). The Israelites' hardness of heart was
sustained for over a year (1:1, 2; 8:1). They
would not listen to the prophet's words or his
dramatizations of coming judgment (chs. 4–6).

12:3–8 Ezekiel's next visual demonstration
warned the captives already in Babylon that they
should not expect a quick return to Jerusalem.
He had already shown that the city would soon
fall (chs. 4; 5); those not killed would be led into
exile. These exiles should have understood
Ezekiel's meaning, for they had done what he
was displaying only six years before, when they
had been brought into exile. **a sign:** The Hebrew
term here does not mean a miracle but a visible
symbol (v. 11; 24:24, 27). **I did as I was commanded:** In contrast to the inattention and disobedience of the people, God's prophet Ezekiel
was always obedient to Him (chs. 2—5).

12:9, 10 Ezekiel's audience was composed
of people who had already experienced exile;
but the people were so rebellious and so resistant to the message they continued disdainfully
to ask the prophet, **What are you doing? The
prince in Jerusalem** was Zedekiah (vv.

to Babylon six years later, and prophesied
exactly what would happen to their leader
Zedekiah. The king would attempt to escape by
night, secretly and in disguise (**cover his face**);
but he would be caught and blinded by the
Babylonians, then carried off to Babylon where
he would die (2 Kin. 25:1–7; Jer. 52:1–11).
Ezekiel was a **sign** to his audience already in
exile as he symbolically and verbally foretold
the fate of the Jews still living in Jerusalem. The
land of the Chaldeans is Babylonia.

12:15, 16 The LORD translates God's personal name. It appears in this prophecy to indicate God's special relationship to the Israelites.
Ezekiel instructed the exiles that their difficult
situation did have a purpose. God would use it
to demonstrate that He was a personal, caring
Lord. Its aim was corrective and instructive:
Then they shall know. Furthermore the Exile
would be a testimony or sign to **the Gentiles.**
The defeat of God's people would not indicate
the Lord's lack of strength, but the serious consequences of sin against Him. Yet He would
demonstrate that His purpose had always been
to restore His people to Himself (Heb. 12:1–11).

A stone carving from the palace of Tiglath-Pileser of Babylon, showing the deportation of conquered citizens of
Judah. The Lord declared through Ezekiel that His people would bear witness of Him to the Gentiles during their
years in exile (Ezek. 12:15–17).

12–14), the ruler of Judah (2 Kin. 24:17–20).
burden: The message a prophet proclaimed is
often called a burden (Is. 13:1; 15:1).

12:11–14 Speaking in 592 B.C., Ezekiel predicted the deportation of Jerusalem's population

Through the difficult experience, His people
would learn that their God was both holy and
loving. Sin offended Him, but He still would
reach out to restore the sinner.

12:17–20 A dramatized prophecy of the fear

and food shortages in Jerusalem during the siege.

12:18, 19 To the **people of the land** (that is, his fellow exiles), Ezekiel was to demonstrate and declare God's warning about the devastating conditions that would befall the people in Judah and Jerusalem.

12:20, 21 For the fulfillment of the prophecy that Jerusalem and Judah would be **laid waste,** see 2 Kin. 25:8–21; Jer. 39:8–10; 44:1–6; 52:1–30; Lam. 1:3, 4.

12:22 The **proverb** or popular saying among the exiles indicates how hardened they were to Ezekiel's prophecies. **The days are prolonged, and every vision fails:** Though already captive, the people were cynical and apathetic, mistakenly thinking that a delay in judgment meant no judgment, at least in their lifetime (vv. 25, 27, 28; 2 Pet. 3:3, 4).

12:23–25 The days are at hand, and the fulfillment of every vision: An antithetical proverb would replace the old one (v. 22), and false prophets opposing Ezekiel would cease to speak. **in your days:** The exiles would live to see the judgment on Jerusalem fulfilled.

12:26–28 The people still thought that judgment would be delayed; Ezekiel was told to assure them a second time that the judgment would not **be postponed any more.**

13:1–23 In this passage, Ezekiel prophesies judgment against false prophets, both male (vv. 1–16) and female (vv. 17–23). In each case he first vividly characterizes their sin (vv. 1–7, 17–19) and then gives God's verdict of condemnation (vv. 8–16, 20–23).

13:1–4 The false prophets were **foolish** and like **foxes in the deserts.** The Hebrew word translated *deserts* conveys the idea of open, desolate places. In the immediate context (v. 5), the foxes are pictured roaming amid the rubble of ruined city walls. The prophets were fools because they confused their own thoughts with God's. They were like foxes among the ruins because they scavenged for themselves while causing, ignoring, and profiting from the human wreckage surrounding them. They were racketeers instead of reformers.

13:5 to build a wall: Of spiritual protection. They contributed neither prayer, example, nor advice that would turn Judah back to God. The **day of the LORD** refers to times when God triumphs (7:19; 30:3). The phrase is particularly used by the prophets to describe those periods in which God is unusually active in the affairs of His people, either for deliverance or for judgment (Joel 2:1; Zeph. 1:7). In that day, God will actively bring about His purposes for the world: He will rescue the righteous and judge evildoers.

13:6, 7 The false prophets, such as Balaam, practiced **divination** (Josh. 13:22). This was the pagan art of finding "divine" guidance through such means as astrology, reading sheep livers and other animal organs, and consulting spiritists or witches to communicate with the dead (1 Sam. 28:3–19). These prophets hoped to receive some kind of revelation. But they did not find the truth for they were not searching for it where God had clearly pointed it out—in the Law and the prophets. By prefacing their predictions with **the LORD says,** these false

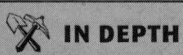 **IN DEPTH** | **Scattered and Gathered**

God always finds a way to assert His sovereignty and accomplish His purposes, regardless of whether we as human beings cooperate with His plans. The Israelites had to learn that lesson the hard way. They resisted God's intention of establishing them as His people in their own land, with His Law to guide them. As a result, He determined to "scatter them among the nations" (Ezek. 12:15).

This promise of dispersion was a major theme for the prophet Ezekiel. Several other times he declared that the Lord would scatter His people abroad (5:10, 12; 6:8; 11:16; 12:15; 20:23; 21:15; 34:6; 36:19). This began when the Assyrians captured Israel in 722 A.D., and continued with a series of deportations from Judah to Babylon in the early sixth century A.D. Yet the scattering of God's people was not the end of the story. Ezekiel also declared numerous times that the Lord would "gather" His people from the countries of the world and return them to the land (Ezek. 11:17; 20:34, 41; 28:25; 34:13; 36:24; 37:21; 38:8, 12; 39:27). Thus God demonstrates His sovereignty, whether scattering His people abroad or gathering them together again.

If God is going to accomplish His purposes one way or another, then the ultimate question we need to consider is how we can cooperate with His plans. To do otherwise is to miss out on what He is doing, or worse, to cause Him to proceed in spite of us.

prophets were deceitfully claiming that God had spoken to them when in fact He had not. God's prophets never sought visions through the methods of divination (Deut. 18:10; Mic. 3:6), instead they received their visions and prophecies through the Spirit of the Lord.

13:8 The divine judgment on all false prophecy and knowledge is given in this verse; it is **nonsense.** The Hebrew word for *nonsense* is translated "in vain" in Ex. 20:7.

13:9 Because these false prophets had prophesied messages that contradicted God's truth (v. 10), they were condemned. The Lord would separate them from God's people, from membership in the nation of Israel, and from life in the land. **enter into the land:** The false prophets would not participate in the future restoration of the people to the promised land.

13:10–16 These prophets would experience God's wrath—just as the walls of Jerusalem which were being constructed at that time would be destroyed. Jerusalem would be conquered and captured for the sins of its inhabitants. The preaching of a false **peace** had prompted people to build for a "certain" future; but only the opposite was certain. The false prophets had deceived the people with false hopes of comfort and prosperity (v. 10). Their deception placed them not only at odds with God's truth, but also with God Himself. Their destruction was certain.

13:17–19 the daughters: The Hebrew women who were false prophetesses were confusing their own ideas with God's and casting magic death spells through sorcery or witchcraft (Lev. 19:26). The **charms** and **veils** were elements used in occult rituals in the ancient Middle East.

13:20–23 These prophetesses were sowing discouragement and doubt among those not involved in demonic divination and were offering encouragement to those already initiated: **the righteous . . . the wicked.** They would be stopped through the same judgment that was to come on the rest of the false prophets.

14:1–3 God revealed to Ezekiel that this group of **the elders of Israel** consisted of double-minded people (1 Kin. 18:21; Matt. 6:24; James 1:5–8). Outwardly, they came to seek a message from God through His true prophet Ezekiel, but in their hearts they harbored loyalties to other gods. **let Myself be inquired:** God knows all hearts and minds (Ps. 139:1–6), and He asks Ezekiel a rhetorical question about whether He ought to give revelatory guidance to such religious hypocrites (vv. 4, 5).

14:1 In at least one respect, the Babylonian exile turned out to be a blessing in disguise by encouraging a new form of Judaism that was more mobile, cross-cultural, and knowledgeable than it had been in Judah. One of the key factors of this development was the invention of the synagogue. In Judah, the Israelites had looked to the temple at Jerusalem as the center of their cultural and religious life. But the loss of the temple in 587 B.C. called for a new approach to maintaining Jewish identity. Building a temple in Babylon was out of the question, so the captives began meeting in local assemblies for worship, education, and political discussion. It was probably leaders from one or more of these groups that gathered before Ezekiel. Before long, these groups, known to us by their Greek name as synagogues ("gatherings" or "assemblies"), began to take on formal responsibilities as they were vested with authority from the Jewish communities in exile.

14:2–4 answer . . . according to the multitude of his idols: God responded to these hypocrites by allowing them to experience the practical consequences of disbelief and disobedience. Their idolatry consisted not only of the theological error of worshiping other gods, but also the immorality that was a natural result of a heart turned away from the living God. Evil is

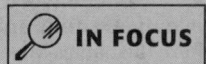

IN FOCUS **"repent"**

(Heb. *shub*) (14:6; 18:30; Gen. 8:3; Ps. 85:4) Strong's #7725: The Hebrew word translated *repent* means "to turn back" or "turn around." The word refers to a reversal or a change of direction, as when the word is used of the receding floodwaters (Gen. 8:3). The prophets commonly used this word to call the Israelites to a radical, conscious rejection of their past sin. A psalmist used the word to describe God's restoration of a believer (Ps. 85:4). Repentance implies a complete turnaround: to change one's mind about one's former sinful ways, to reject one's past conduct, and turn in obedience to the Lord (Deut. 4:30; Is. 10:22; Jer. 3:14; 22:10).

never caused by God (Ps. 5:4), but He permits the suffering it brings to the world (Job 1; Rom. 6:23). This process punishes the unrepentant, encourages sinners to repent (v. 5), and purifies the righteous (James 1:2–4).

14:5 seize the house of Israel by their heart: These words announced God's restorative purpose (Prov. 3:12; Rev. 3:19) in allowing sin to run its course.

14:6, 7 Idolatry was condemned whether practiced by an Israelite (one of God's chosen people) or by **strangers** (Gentiles) spending time in Israel. Anyone from any culture who had come into contact with specific revelation about the Hebrew God was held responsible for his or her response to the truth.

14:8 The unrepentant idolater would be separated not only from God but also from God's people (13:9). This experience would be a strong visual warning—**sign**—and an international example—**proverb**—of God's absolute honoring of His promise to punish disobedience with cursing (Lev. 20:1–7).

14:9–11 The relationship between God's sovereignty and human responsibility is implicit in these verses. God allows false preaching for His own inscrutable purposes, but the preacher is held accountable for the content of the message. These were Israelite false prophets who deliberately ignored the truth and mixed it with falsehood. Their punishment would be the same as **the one who inquired** (the elders; vv. 1–3). But they would also have the same redemptive plan (v. 5).

14:12–20 Jerusalem's "persistent unfaithfulness" was so offensive to God that the presence of spiritual giants could not stay judgment by famine, wild beasts, military invasion (**sword**), or disease (**pestilence**). **Noah, Daniel, and Job:** Compare Jer. 15:1, where the names Moses and Samuel are invoked in a similar manner to these names. In this list, Daniel seems out of place among the other two men of faith, Noah and Job. Daniel was a younger contemporary of Ezekiel in Babylon (Dan. 1), whose greatest exploits were likely still to come. The Hebrew

spelling of the name in Ezekiel is *Dan-El*, rather than Daniel, raising the question whether a different person is meant than the biblical Daniel. There are some stories preserved about an ancient hero named Dan-El, but he was a worshiper of Baal, and would not have had the **righteousness** about which Ezekiel speaks. It is possible that the first hearers of Ezekiel's message knew of a righteous Dan-El who is not known to us.

14:21 These **judgments,** though stated hypothetically so far, would actually come on **Jerusalem** (Lev. 26:22–26).

14:22, 23 A remnant would be **brought out** from Jerusalem. When the exiles observe **their ways and their doings**—that is, their wicked actions, they will be reminded of God's justice and grace. This is a remarkable use of the term *remnant*. Ordinarily the term is used of the righteous. Here it is used as a sample of the wicked people, whose deeds justified the actions of God in sovereign judgment: **I have done nothing without cause.**

15:1–5 The **wood of the vine** is depicted as useless. Unlike an olive tree, whose wood is also useful, the vine has only one use, to bear grapes. The regular use of *vine* imagery in the Bible (Ps. 80:8–19; Is. 5:1–7; John 15) demonstrates the importance of grapevine cultivation in Israel.

15:6–8 In this instance the vine is symbolic of the Israelites still in Jerusalem (Ps. 80:8–19; Is. 5:1–7). God had designed the people of Israel for a particular purpose, to bring glory to His name by living faithfully to His covenant and by bringing the nations to the knowledge of the Lord. Instead, Israel had become like the pagan

---

🌿 IN LIFE **Skeletons in the Closet**

Some people go to great lengths to hide their background. They feel ashamed of certain details about their origins which they regard as "skeletons in the closet," ugly facts that they feel would harm their reputation if brought out into the open. God rebuked the people of Jerusalem and the surrounding country by revealing three "secrets" about their past that called into question their proud self-image. The Lord said that:

• They were born to Canaanite parents (Ezek. 16:3).
• They were abandoned at birth (Ezek. 16:4–5).
• They were adopted (Ezek. 16:6–7).

The humiliating facts about Jerusalem's past are basically no different from the "skeletons in the closet" of any Christian today. We, too, were born outside the family of God. We, too, were once lost apart from His grace. We, too, have been adopted in God's family. Therefore, we, too, need to evaluate our lives and consider whether we are living with humility and gratitude, and honoring the Lord with our attitudes and behavior. Otherwise we raise questions as to whether we really belong to God.

nations around them. Israel had **persisted in unfaithfulness** and had failed to trust in God's power. Jerusalem, and by implication the entire nation, had not faced exile before but now would be disciplined with **another fire.** This refers to additional destruction and deportation to be brought by Nebuchadnezzar, whose armies burned Jerusalem in 586 B.C. (7:23–27). The Judeans had already endured two deportations to Babylon, in 605 and 597 B.C.

16:1, 2 to know her abominations: The Hebrew word translated *abominations* describes that which makes one physically ill. What follows is an animated development of the dreary story, designed to teach errant Jerusalem the real nature of her character in the eyes of God.

16:3 your father was an Amorite and your mother a Hittite: These shocking words refer to the cultural and moral origins of Jerusalem. Ancient Canaan was inhabited by Semitic and non-Semitic peoples. The Amorites and Hittites are associated in Scripture with the southern hill country, where Jerusalem is (Num. 13:29). The point is that non-Israelites founded this city. Jebusites controlled it when the Israelites entered the land under Joshua (Josh. 15:8, 63). Israel did not fully control the city until David conquered it (2 Sam. 5:6, 7).

16:4, 5 Rubbing a newborn baby with salt was a Palestinian custom. In caring for a baby during the first days of life, the parents and their society take possession of the child through traditional procedures, such as rubbing. In particular giving the child a name is highly important. In Israel, God took possession of the firstborn male children on the eighth day of life, through circumcision. God reminds Jerusalem that He had rescued them from being like an abandoned newborn child, unwashed, unsanitary (not **rubbed with salt**), and exposed to the elements to die. God alone had given her glory.

16:6 In contrast to Israel's apathetic disdain—which led to disobedience including idolatry (Judg. 1, 2)—God had wanted Israel to **live,** having purposed and planned to impart His life and glory to them.

16:7–9 breasts were formed: The city is compared to a young woman, mature and lovely. Yet the city was **naked and bare** until God covered it with a relationship of covenantal love. This began when David moved the ark of the covenant there and God established the covenant with David (2 Sam. 6:1–7:17; Ps. 132). Jerusalem became God's dwelling place (2 Sam. 7:12–17; 1 Kin. 5; 6).

16:10–14 The adornments listed here are gifts from a groom to his bride. Figuratively they express the beauty and bounty God gave to Jerusalem under Solomon. **badger skin:** The exact meaning of this Hebrew term is unknown, but it refers to a kind of fine leather. One suggestion is "dolphin skin." The idea is that God clothed Jerusalem in the finest materials available. During the reigns of David and Solomon, Jerusalem achieved significant status as the capital of a nation rich in wisdom and wealth (1 Kin. 10:23). But this was only because God **bestowed** it. **perfect:** This does not mean perfect in a moral sense, but complete, finished.

16:15 trusted in your own beauty: These words indict God's people for forgetting that their fame and fortune were God's gifts and not their own doing (v. 14). They relied on themselves and their gifts instead of on God. They came to believe that their material health and wealth as a nation absolutely demonstrated God's approval of their spiritual life, even through they were becoming spiritually corrupt. Solomon, who was king when Israel reached its zenith of power and prosperity, is a conspicuous example (Eccl. 2:1–11). **played the harlot:** This phrase refers to spiritual prostitution—idolatry, trusting in false gods. The metaphor works in a powerful way, however, because the worship of these gods often involved literal sexual misconduct (v. 16; Hos. 4:11–19) and other immoral acts (vv. 20–22).

16:16–21 These verses list the particular acts of idolatry engaged in by the spiritually unfaithful in Jerusalem and Judah. Mesopotamian and Canaanite pagan rituals are featured. The people's unfaithfulness to God consisted of: (1) building altars to idols and decorating the **high places** with their **garments** (1 Kin. 11:7, 8); (2) fashioning **male images** (phallic or sexually perverse statues) from **gold** and **silver** that God had provided; (3) giving what belonged to the true God to these false gods; and, (4) practicing human sacrifice to appease these gods (2 Kin. 16:1–4).

16:19 My food: This charge is an explicit denial of Baalism. Baal was the Canaanite god of fertility, who was thought to provide the grain in the field, the young of the flock, and even the children of the marriage. Israel forgot that God, not Baal, had **fed** them.

16:20–22 The Israelites **did not remember** how much God had done for them since rescuing them from a dirty, destitute, and dying condition (vv. 1–14).

16:23–26 Egypt is called a **fleshly** neighbor because that nation wanted alliances with Israel, who **committed harlotry** by eventually reciprocating (1 Kin. 10:28; 2 Kin. 17:4; 18:21; Hos. 7:11).

16:27–29 Jerusalem's kings had sought political alliances with Assyria (2 Kin. 15:17–20) and Babylon (2 Kin. 20:12–19) instead of relying on their God for security. Probably a part of the treaty-making ceremonies was to worship the other nation's gods. For Israel to do this would be a violation of the First Commandment. In fact, King Ahaz dared to replace the bronze altar of the temple at Jerusalem with a copy of an Assyrian altar (2 Kin. 16:5–18). In this way, foreign alliances led the Israelites away from God. The Lord judged the city for this: He allowed Sennacherib to give some of Jerusalem's lands to the Philistines (2 Chr. 21:16, 17).

16:30–34 Jerusalem was denounced as being less like a prostitute and more like **an adulterous wife.** She was deemed worse than the typical prostitute because instead of receiving payment for services rendered, she sought out **strangers** (foreign nations) and **hired** them for the privilege.

16:35, 36 Jerusalem was filthy spiritually because the city had soiled itself by worshiping foreign idols and practicing infanticide (vv. 20, 21; Deut. 12:29–32).

16:37–43 As a result of its sin (compared to harlotry, vv. 25–30), Jerusalem would be punished. God would use her foreign **lovers** to expose Jerusalem's hypocrisy and bring international shame (**uncover your nakedness**). According to the Law, adultery was punishable by death (Lev. 20:10). The people deserved death because they had committed spiritual adultery and had murdered their own children through child sacrifice. The city would be looted and burned, and its people slain. The tangible material riches gained as a result of God's favor (v. 8) would be lost. All this would culminate in the Babylonian invasion of 586 B.C. led by Nebuchadnezzar. During the ensuing captivity, Israel would abandon idolatry and polytheism, as Ezekiel predicted. God's anger over the people's sin would be satisfied. **My jealousy:** God's covenantal love and loyalty to His people would continue even though they had been unfaithful and forgetful of God's grace in their lives.

16:44–47 This allegory describes Jerusalem as the sister of two cities—**Samaria** and **Sodom.** All three were presented as the characteristic offspring of the religiously and morally corrupt cultures in Canaan (v. 3). Thus the proverb **Like mother, like daughter** applied to Jerusalem. The condemnation of the mother—that is, the Hittites—and the sisters—Samaria and Sodom—for **loathing husband and children** is difficult to explain. It probably refers to idolatry—God being the hated husband (Hos. 2:16)—and infanticide. Sodom no longer existed at this time—its evil had been so great that God had wiped the city off the face of the earth (Gen. 19:24–25). Samaria, the capital of the northern kingdom, had already faced

destruction and exile (2 Kin. 17:5, 6). Jerusalem, the very city of God, had become "more corrupt" than even Sodom and Samaria. Clearly this passage emphasizes the people's great sinfulness and the certainty of their punishment. **sister of your sisters:** This is a superlative statement like "King of kings" meaning "the greatest king." Thus with this phrase, Jerusalem is described as the "sister" most conformed to Canaanite corruption.

16:48–52 Ezekiel names the sins for which the cities of Sodom and Samaria were renowned. Jerusalem was pronounced even more guilty—the other evil cities **did not commit half** of Jerusalem's **sins.** Spiritual, moral, and social sins are all listed. Jerusalem **justified** the other cities because when they compared themselves to Jerusalem, and they were more righteous than her.

16:53–59 As Jerusalem had arrogantly poked fun at Sodom, so Jerusalem would be despised by Syria and Philistia. Hope and humiliation would be hers because when the people returned from captivity, they would return alongside others whom they considered horribly wicked. Although restoration was promised, the people still had to pay for their sins by living in exile. This punishment was consistent with God's past and persistent promises to repay disobedience with specific curses (4:16, 17; 5:8–17). **Syria** is rendered *Edom* in some translations because this alternative exists in the Syriac version and in many Hebrew manuscripts. Historically Syria (or more literally the ancient nation of Aram) no longer existed. Therefore that nation could not ridicule the exiles in Ezekiel's day. The people had **despised the oath by breaking the covenant** that God had made with Moses; thus they would receive the punishments for disobedience that were written in that covenant (Ex. 24; Lev. 26; Deut. 28; 29). Blessings or curses were dependent on Israel's obedience or disobedience.

16:60–63 Nevertheless: Despite Jerusalem's disobedience to the Mosaic covenant and the resulting punishment (v. 59), the covenant with Abraham—**My covenant**—would still be honored: **I will remember.** Fulfillment of the covenant with Abraham did not depend on the people's faithfulness; God had made the promise and He would keep it (Gen. 15; 17:7, 8; Lev. 26:40–45; Ps. 145:13; Phil. 1:6). The **everlasting covenant** had been made with Abraham before the Hebrew nation even existed. This covenant would be remembered and reestablished with the exiled Judeans. At that time, God's people would be ashamed by the contrast between their faithlessness and God's faithfulness and the fact that they were being exalted over those who were less sinful—Sodom

---

🔍 IN FOCUS | **"rebellious"**

(Heb. *meriy*) (2:5–8; 3:9; 12:2; Is. 30:9) Strong's #4805: This Hebrew noun is derived from a verbal root that means "to resist authority" or "to be contentious" (Deut. 1:26; Jer. 4:17; Neh. 9:26). It depicts someone opposing an authority figure out of stubborn pride (Deut. 21:18) and commonly describes disobedience (1 Kin. 13:21). Ezekiel identified Israel as a "rebellious house" a dozen times, meaning they were willfully disobedient, refusing to listen to the word of God (2:5–8). Ezekiel was addressing an audience chafing under God's authority (3:9). Samuel equated this kind of rebellion with witchcraft (1 Sam. 15:23).

---

and Samaria. The people of these other sinful nations would also inherit land, but only by God's grace, because no such covenant was made with them. Further, God would provide **atonement** through the New Covenant (Jer. 31:31–40), which pointed ultimately to the Cross of Christ.

17:1–21 In this section, the ways of kings and their people are revealed to be in the hands of the Lord.

17:1, 2 The Hebrew words translated **riddle** and **parable** can both be used to refer to allegory. The *parable* primarily refers to a comparison between two things. A *riddle* was sometimes used as political contests of mental competition between kings, in which the loser would submit to the winner and be killed. Some take the following riddle as a contest posed by God to Zedekiah, Judah's king.

17:3–10 This allegory is focused around a main point and is followed by an explanation to guide the reader (vv. 11–21). In light of vv. 11–21, the **great eagle** is the king of Babylon (v. 12); **Lebanon** symbolizes Canaan, of which Jerusalem (v. 12) is the major city; the **highest branch** is the king of Jerusalem and Judah (v. 12); the **topmost young twig** refers to the nobility of Judah (v. 12); the **land of trade** is Babylon (v. 12); the **seed** is a member of the royal family (v. 13); the **fertile field** is the land where this royal offspring would rule (vv. 13, 14); the other **great eagle** is the king of Egypt (v. 15); and the **vine** is the remnant and ruler left in Judah. This remnant failed to prosper because they made a treaty with the Egyptian pharaoh. As a result, even the remnant was slain and scattered by Babylon's army (vv. 15–21).

17:11–21 Since Ezekiel had preached earlier about Jerusalem's past abominations (ch. 16), the people were likely charging God with unfairness in punishing the present population. Ezekiel points out that present and past sins make God's actions just and fair. In this section, the LORD explains His grounds for using Babylon to judge Judah. The prophecy predicts that: (1) Nebuchadnezzar will capture Jehoiachin and the princes of Jerusalem and take them to Babylon (v. 12); (2) Zedekiah, Jehoiachin's uncle, will be made ruler of the Judean remnant as a result of a political alliance with Nebuchadnezzar, but this will stifle growth (vv. 13, 14); (3) Zedekiah will rebel against Babylon and God by making a treaty with Egypt (588 B.C.) leading to his unexpected defeat and death (vv. 15, 16; Is. 30:1–5); and, (4) Zedekiah will not be protected by Egypt but will be punished through Babylon according to the stipulations of the Mosaic covenant: death, destruction, and dispersion (vv. 17–21; 12:13, 14). The historical background of this story is found in 2 Kin. 24; 2 Chr. 36; and Jer. 37; 52.

17:22 I will take: The Hebrew is emphatic: "I Myself will take" In contrast to human kings, God declared that He personally would pick out, plant, and make prominent a **tender one**—that is, a twig or a sprig. Cedar branches are symbolic of rulers on the Davidic throne (17:3, 4, 12, 13), and elsewhere of a line of David's descendants prophesied to produce the Messiah (2 Sam. 7:16; Is. 11:1–5; Jer. 22:24–30; 23:1–6; Zech. 6:9–13; Matt. 1:1–17). If not directly messianic in intention, vv. 22–24 at least have strong messianic implications. Thus, with reference to His humanity, we discover a new title for the Savior Jesus. He is the Tender One.

17:23, 24 What was accomplished in the restoration under Zerubbabel was a fulfillment of this promise. But as is often the case in biblical prophecy, the greater fulfillment is still to come in the reign of the Savior King. The establishment of the cedar twig, the Messiah, over Israel will make the nation a fruitful and **majestic cedar** where diverse people will live in unity and harmony. all the trees of the field: All nations will realize that the LORD is their sovereign God and that He has accomplished what He said He would do.

18:1–3 The Hebrew word (Eccl. 10:10) rendered **set on edge** is literally "made dull" but can refer to a sour sensation. The main idea of the **proverb** is clear: children are affected by their parents' behavioral choices just as eating sour grapes produces a bitter taste. However, the people were interpreting and applying this proverb incorrectly; therefore, God said they should not use it any longer.

18:4 The exiles' problematic doctrines and attitudes became evident from God's corrective teaching. Apparently the exiles were filled with despair and had a fatalistic approach to such truisms as the proverb quoted in v. 2 (as also in 16:44) and to related Scriptures (Ex. 20:5; 34:6, 7; Deut. 5:9). Their false belief was that they were being punished for the sins of previous generations. Their sin was that of becoming insensitive and irresponsible, since they thought judgment would come regardless of what they might do. God's reply reminded them that it had always been otherwise: only the individual person **who sins** will **die.** In this verse, the physical, earthly consequences of sinful behavior are being addressed (3:16–21; 33:12–20; Deut. 30:15–20).

18:5–9 A righteous man—a father or the first generation—is **lawful.** He does what is morally right according to the Law of Moses. He does not participate in the following sins: (1)

idolatrous ceremonial meals, (2) sexual misconduct, (3) mistreatment of the poor, (4) theft, or (5) **usury,** charging interest on debts owed by fellow Hebrews (Deut. 23:20). His reward is life (Ex. 20; Lev. 18:1–5; Deut. 5; 11). **during her impurity:** In ancient Israel, intimacy during the woman's menstrual period was prohibited. The OT does not explain the reason for this, but it may be tied to the special role of blood for the atoning of sin (Lev. 15:19–33). The principal point in this passage is that the person was observing the standards laid down by the Law.

18:10–13 The unrighteous son of the righteous man of vv. 5–9 (the second generation) breaks and rejects the laws and ethics that defined his father's lifestyle. His punishment is death (vv. 13, 18; Rom. 6:23) and **his blood shall be upon him.** Clearly the point of this passage is personal responsibility for sin.

18:14–18 The grandson of the righteous man of vv. 5–9 (third generation) purposely chooses to live by God's laws, imitating his righteous grandfather and not his sinful **father.** The grandson, like the grandfather, **shall surely live** as a result of his own righteousness; but the father dies due to his own disobedience and depravity (vv. 9, 13, 18).

18:19–32 In this passage, Ezekiel further

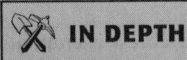 **IN DEPTH** | **Accountability**

Sometimes warnings get twisted into excuses. The people of Ezekiel's day, suffering from the consequences of a history of rebellion against God, found it easier to blame their ancestors for sin than to take responsibility for their own offenses. We can understand their predicament. Their immediate circumstances held little hope. News had reached Babylon about the fall and destruction of Jerusalem. Plans to return to the promised land would be marred by descriptions of devastation. The wreckage of God's judgment seemed too great to be restored. It was easier to sink into pessimism. The bitter proverb about sour grapes and teeth set on edge (18:2) became a slogan of resentment for the people. Instead of examining their own behavior before God, they excused their sin by blaming their parents.

The law of cause and effect may be obvious, but the exact connections sometimes elude us. Sin always has consequences. The second commandment (Ex. 20:4–6; Deut. 5:8–10) points out that the sin of idolatry (a sin from which flow many others) causes effects that can last generations. But Ezekiel had to remind the people that experiencing hardship as a consequence of the sins of ancestors was not the same as judgment for one's own sins. Suffering caused by another's sins does not excuse willfully sinful behavior.

God made it clear to the Israelites and also to us: We may suffer for someone else's misdeeds, but we will be judged for our own. "I will judge you, O house of Israel, every one according to his ways" (18:30). What should be our response? "Repent, and turn from all your transgressions" (18:30). This will lead to "a new heart and a new spirit" (18:31). Perhaps the clearest evidence of our fallen human nature can be heard in our quickness to blame others when we ought to examine ourselves and remember that we are accountable to God. His message to us is persistent: "Therefore turn and live!" (18:32).

clarifies his teaching on individual responsibility for sin by answering certain questions that reflect what his audience might be thinking in response to his previous message. God's response to their questions through Ezekiel is in part also composed of questions. **Live** and **die** refer to physical death and not eternal death, since this passage relates to the standards and stipulations of the Mosaic covenant (16:6; Lev. 18:5; Deut. 30:15–20; 2 Pet. 3:9). **turn . . . and live:** Everyone is judged equitably and individually. God never enjoys condemning a person, but is just and righteous in dispensing His judgments.

19:1 The **princes** were Judah's kings. Ezekiel likely turned his attention to these kings because he had just spoken (in ch. 18) of the relationship between fathers (leaders) and children (followers), and of the sins committed in Judah by powerful people.

19:2–10 Most likely the **lioness** and the **vine in your bloodline** (v. 10) both represented the nation of Israel since each was a "mother" of kings—the **cubs** and the **branches.** The vine and lion images are common symbols for Hebrew royalty and nationality (15:1–6; 17:1–10; Gen. 49:9; Num. 23:24; Ps. 80:8–16; Is. 5:1–7; Mic. 5:8). The first cub **brought . . . with chains to the land of Egypt** was Jehoahaz, who was captured and imprisoned by Pharaoh Necho in 609 B.C. (2 Kin. 23:31–34; 2 Chr. 36:1–4). The second cub that was **trapped in their pit** was the destructive Jehoiachin, who gave out false hopes of revival and was taken captive by **the king of Babylon** (Nebuchadnezzar) in 597 B.C. (2 Kin. 25:27–30; 2 Chr. 36:9, 10).

19:10–14 These verses mention the fruitful monarchical period of the past, but the focus was on the present distress and promised judgment. At this time, Judah had already experienced two invasions by Babylon, called the **east wind** (15:1–8; 19:5–9). Ezekiel and the other exiles were presently living in that desert land. Neither the current king Zedekiah (the **rod of her branches**) nor any other leaders were fit to

rule. Judah's rulers were responsible for the nation's horrible condition (Jer. 22:10–13). The immediate source of rebellion and the cause of imminent judgment was Zedekiah, who would be deported when Jerusalem was destroyed in 586 B.C. (2 Kin. 24; 25). **wilderness . . . dry and thirsty land:** To anyone who loved the covenantal promises focused on God's worship in Jerusalem, any alternative to Jerusalem was akin to living in the desert.

20:1 The chronological note suggests a date of July-August 591 B.C. and the start of a new section and series of messages (8:1, which was eleven months earlier). The political context of this prophecy was Zedekiah's foolish and sinful alignment with Egypt against Babylon in hopes of deliverance from Nebuchadnezzar's attacks. The social context was that of exiled elders coming to Ezekiel to obtain a divine explanation of current events. They wanted to know whether Egypt would save Judah from the Babylonians.

20:2–4 God explains to Ezekiel that the elders of Israel (v. 1) had forfeited any right to inquire of Him due to the **abominations of their fathers.** All people are responsible for their own sins, and this does not mean that these Hebrews were paying for sins their ancestors had committed. Instead, the present generation of Hebrews in exile had clearly shown their failure to learn practical lessons from history, and thus had condemned themselves to repeat many mistakes. These leaders came to God with questions, but the questions were foolish and demonstrated the people's sinfulness. They showed that they were oblivious to the inconsistencies between what they were asking, their past practices, and God's revealed promises and principles. In this chapter God gives a remedial review of their past.

20:5–9: In Egypt, God promised to make the Hebrew people into a nation (v. 5) and to move them to a specific homeland (v. 6), which involved management by law (v. 7) leading to the Mosaic covenant given at Sinai on the way from Egypt to Canaan. But the Israelites

 **IN FOCUS** | **"lamentation"**

(Heb. *qiynah*) (19:1, 14; 2 Sam. 1:17; Jer. 9:10) Strong's #7015: This Hebrew noun refers to a type of poetic song with a distinctive meter, a dirge that was sung to express grief over someone's death. It is derived from a Hebrew verb that means "to sing a song of lament" (2 Sam. 1:17). Such songs would be sung during funeral rites. The prophets' use of the word was intended to suggest the coming death of Israel and other nations because of the inescapable condemnation they had incurred for their sin (Amos 5:1).

rebelled by following false gods; so God judged them by prolonging their captivity (v. 8) in Egypt, which lasted over 400 years. Then God graciously released them as He had promised (v. 9; Gen. 15:13–16).

20:5, 6 I chose Israel: Here is the only use of this elective verb in Ezekiel. It signifies Israel's sovereign selection for God's eternal and temporal purposes. **raised My hand:** This image refers to the unconditional vows made by God to Abraham and later renewed with the nation He formed in Egypt from Abraham's descendants (v. 9). That God "raised His hand" reveals His determination to maintain His covenant promise.

20:7 abominations: Elsewhere in Ezekiel this Hebrew term is translated "detestable things." See vv. 8, 30; 11:18.

20:8 the idols of Egypt . . . in the midst of the land of Egypt: Here God spoke about something not explained in the Book of Exodus; that is, the Israelites had engaged in the idolatry of the Egyptians during their sojourn there. Thus, though not mentioned elsewhere, there was the threat of divine retribution against the people before the time of the Exodus (which is mentioned in v. 10).

20:9 acted for My name's sake: God vindicated His grace, power, and trustworthiness before the Egyptians by fulfilling His promises to defeat Egypt and deliver even His disobedient people (His people who were supposed to worship God). On God acting for the sake of His name and honor, see also Is. 48:9–11 (compare 2 Tim. 2:13).

20:10–11 Following their exodus from slavery in Egypt, God began to sanctify the Israelites by revealing to them a code of law and entering a covenant relationship with them on a Creator-creature basis. **if a man does, he shall live:** This does not teach that eternal salvation can be earned by good works, but that the quality of the believer's physical and spiritual life on earth are related to his or her obedience to the living God. God's **statutes** and **judgments** were given to His people as a means of maintaining their walk with the living God, not as the basis for establishing their salvation.

20:12–19 My Sabbaths: This is an important verse (emphasized again in v. 20) for understanding the Sabbath (Ex. 20:8–11; Deut. 5:12–15). Sabbath means "rest." In other words, the Sabbath was a day to cease all ordinary work or labor, as clearly emphasized in Ex. 20:8–11; Deut. 5:12–15. This verse explains the purpose of the Sabbath; it was to serve as **a sign** or a potent symbol of God's covenantal relationship with His people Israel.

20:20–26 hallow: This Hebrew word means "to treat as holy," "to observe as distinct," and "to consecrate." God commands that His **Sabbaths** be continually maintained by His people as sacred—distinct and separate from all ordinary days.

20:27 During the conquest and settlement of Canaan (the period described in Joshua and Judges), Israel inherited the promised land. Yet again God's people were obstinate and guilty of

---

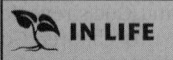 **IN LIFE** | **God's Reputation Is at Stake**

How does God make Himself known to the nations and people of the world? Aside from the witness of Scripture and the life and work of Jesus Christ, His primary means is through people who are dedicated to Him and live as He wants them to live. They are the light of the world, whose good works light the way to the Lord (Matt. 5:14–16).

That means that God's reputation is at stake when it comes to how His people conduct their lives. That was certainly true for ancient Israel. He made a covenant with them to be His people (Ezek. 20:5–6). Yet three times before they even got to the promised land, they reneged on their commitment and turned back to the idols that they had learned to serve in Egypt. Each time the Lord threatened to pour out His fury on them (20:8, 13, 21), but each time He spared them for one reason: He wanted the rest of the world's nations to know who He is (20:9, 14, 22).

If Israel were destroyed, the pagan nations would have lost an important witness to the living God. In fact, Moses pointed this out at Mount Sinai, when the Lord wanted to destroy the idolatrous Israelites and start a new nation from him. Moses argued that then the Egyptians and other nations would misinterpret God's purpose for bringing the people out of Egypt (Ex. 32:9–14).

In light of this history, believers today need to think about the reputation of our lives, and whether it is worthy of the Lord. Would people be attracted to God or repelled by our conduct? Are we winsome? Is God honored by unbelievers because of the things we do and say?

blasphemous disloyalty because they served false gods (Num. 15:30, 31).

20:28, 29 high hills . . . thick trees: These phrases refer to the locations of altars in Canaan for idol worship. Many of the exiles had visited such places in the past, and many in Judah were still doing so. **high place:** The name **Bamah** is a transliteration of the Hebrew word for *high place* (16:15–34).

20:30 defiling . . . committing: These participles stressed the continual, ongoing nature of Israel's disobedient disloyalty.

20:31, 32 like the Gentiles: Chosen to be a nation separate from sin and secular ways—a special instrument to reveal God's glory—Israel's consistent tendency was to identify with the neighboring, ungodly nations and to take on their idolatry (Ex. 19:5, 6; Deut. 17:14; 26:16–19; 31:21; 1 Sam. 8:5; Ps. 135:4).

20:33–36 The judgment of captivity in Babylon had begun in the deportations of 605 and 597 B.C. and would be continued with Jerusalem's fall in 586 B.C. However, God also promised to restore Judah and to judge her enemies with fury (Deut. 4:34). This refers to the Persian conquest of Babylon in 539 B.C. and to the three returns of the Jews to their land and the rebuilding of their homeland (538—c. 330 B.C.; see the books of Ezra and Nehemiah). Yet Israel would again be taken captive and made to wander throughout the nations: **wilderness of the peoples.** This section refers to the time of Roman domination, which began with Pompey taking Jerusalem in 63 B.C. **mighty hand . . . outstretched arm:** The language repeats the phrasings used in the Exodus from Egypt (Ex. 7:5; 15:6). **I will bring you out:** Leaving Babylon would be a second Exodus, celebrated prophetically by Isaiah as well (Is. 40:1).

20:37, 38 pass under the rod: This is the way a shepherd counts and controls his sheep (Lev. 27:32; Jer. 33:13). A rod sometimes speaks of discipline (Ps. 89:32), but here it is parallel to the idea of **bring you into the bond of the**

covenant. God's lordship of His people for personal, purposeful relationship is in view. This future bonding with God will be a time when Israel is cleansed of spiritual idolaters (v. 39; 16:15–34). At that time, the people will finally **know that** God is **the Lord** (16:63; 36:25–38; Jer. 31:31–34; Dan. 12:10).

20:39 The command **Go, serve every one of you his idols** is an ironic command; the rest of the verse indicates that God was giving the stubborn people over to what they had decided. God grants each one a destiny consistent with his or her decisions. Then God looks to an unspecified future time when Israel will glorify His name, meaning "His reputation" among the nations (vv. 40–44).

20:40–45 The future repentant, renewed, and regathered Israel will be characterized by: (1) a return to the land of Israel and an acceptable, sacrificial system of worship (chs. 40—48); (2) a revived, personal knowledge of its sovereign and faithful Lord; (3) a renunciation of former sins; and (4) a recognition that God's grace governs the nation's history of sin and salvation. **My holy mountain:** Reference is made to the glorious central location for worship in Israel—Mount Zion in Jerusalem (Pss. 2:6; 78:68; Is. 35:10; 60:14).

20:46–49 The **forest land, the South** refers to the land of Judah—the southern kingdom—which had more trees then than now. **from the south to the north:** This figure of speech expresses totality, meaning "everywhere."

21:1–5 both righteous and wicked: This pairing shows that God was going to allow the dreadful temporal consequences of sin to affect everyone in the land, both faithful and unfaithful.

21:6 breaking heart: The phrase translates words that literally mean "breaking loins," suggesting great emotional upheaval.

21:7 when they say: This means "when they ask" (12:9).

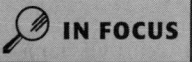 **IN FOCUS** **"abomination"**

(Heb. *shiqquts*) (20:7, 30; Dan. 12:11; Hos. 9:10) Strong's #8251: The Hebrew noun translated *abomination* is from the verb meaning "to detest" (compare Lev. 7:21; 11:11). Typically it refers to ceremonially unclean foods and animals (8:10; Lev. 11:23; Is. 66:17). But it may also describe the detestable practices associated with pagan idol worship, including child sacrifice and ritual prostitution (1 Kin. 11:5–7; 2 Kin. 23:13; Jer. 7:30; 13:27). Hosea rightly observed that those who love abominations become like the unclean practices they love (Hos. 9:10). But the Lord had called the Israelites to a different and higher purpose: they were to remain pure and holy, for their God was holy (Lev. 11:45).

21:8-11 The Babylonian army led by Nebuchadnezzar—the **sword**—is pictured as ready and moving swiftly. While vv. 9–17 are written as Hebrew poetry, the lines actually meant to be sung may have been limited to these in vv. 9–11. **My son:** In this context, the words refer to Judah ("My people" in v. 12). If the people reacted with **mirth,** it would show that they mistakenly believed that such judgment would never come on God's people and must therefore be meant for an enemy nation.

21:12 Cry and wail . . . strike your thigh: Ezekiel was told to add verbal groans and a physical gesture to his musical message. In that culture, these actions displayed great grief and sorrow (Jer. 31:19).

21:13 Israel failed a test. The **sword** would strike God's people, specifically the nation's rulers (the meaning of the word **scepter**). These words drew upon the messianic implications of Gen. 49:9, 10 and the promises of the Davidic covenant in 2 Sam. 7. The Jews had misinterpreted these promises to mean that their nation would never fall. Because of their sin, however, the Davidic line of kings would be interrupted. False messianic hopes related to Judah were corrected when Jerusalem was overthrown in 586 B.C. by Nebuchadnezzar (vv. 25–27).

21:14-18 Ezekiel was commanded to clap (6:11). The order **the third time let the sword do double damage** was a numeric device (Prov. 6:16) used here to emphasize the extent and effectiveness of the sword's (or Babylon's) employment against Judah. **I also will beat My fists** pictures God clapping along with Ezekiel. God would applaud the fact that even evil events can be made to serve His purposes and plans (Jer. 27:5).

21:19, 20 Ezekiel was instructed to draw a map to depict the path of the coming conquerors. The **king of Babylon** is Nebuchadnezzar; the **same land** is Babylon. **Make a sign:** Ezekiel was to place a signpost at a fork in the road leading to the capital cities of Ammon—**Rabbah**—and Judah—**Jerusalem.**

21:21 Three ancient pagan arts for seeking divine guidance would be used by Nebuchadnezzar to determine which city to attack. **shakes the arrows:** This was a method of casting lots using arrows inscribed with names. They were shaken about in the quiver and then dropped to the ground like throwing dice. **consults the images:** This refers to the teraphim or household idols (Gen. 31:19; Judg. 18:14; 1 Sam. 19:13; Hos. 3:4). **looks at the liver:** Sheep livers from sacrificed animals were studied. The shades and shapes of various sections of the organ were the basis for a positive or negative prediction.

21:22 That Nebuchadnezzar's answer coincided with God's promises and predictions for Jerusalem did not mean that his **divination** was acceptable. It merely demonstrated that God is sovereign while individuals remain responsible for all choices, good or bad (Gen. 45:4–8; 50:20; Job 2:10; Dan. 2:20–23; 4:34–37; Rom. 8:28).

21:23, 24 The Judeans in their pride and false sense of security in the treaties (**sworn oaths**) would conclude that the king received a **false divination** (vv. 21, 22; 2 Kin. 24:20). However, the verdict had been pronounced: Jerusalem would be **taken.** Nebuchadnezzar would be God's instrument to punish the people's rebellion (7:3, 4).

21:25 The **prince of Israel** Zedekiah would come to its **end** by being captured in 586 B.C. (7:27; 12:9, 10, 11–14).

21:26, 27 The **turban** (Ex. 28:4, 37–39) and the **crown** stand for the priesthood and the kingship. Both would be removed from Judah. **overthrown:** This word means "wrecked" or "ruined" and is used three times consecutively in the Hebrew text to underscore the comprehensive and intensive nature of the destruction. The priestly and kingly offices would not return until the coming of Him **whose right it is**—the Messiah (Gen. 49:10; Heb. 5—7).

21:28 Ammon was east of Judah between the Jabbok to the north and the Arnon to the south. While Jehoiakim was king (608–598 B.C.; 2 Kin. 24:2), the **Ammonites** joined other nations east of the Jordan in raiding Judean territory, in return for protection from Nebuchadnezzar. Later, during the reign of Zedekiah (about 593 B.C.), Ammon, Moab, Edom, and others conspired against Babylon, but with false hopes of help from Egypt (Jer. 27:3–11). **their reproach:** This was the Ammonites' ridicule of Judah and delight over the destruction of Jerusalem, especially the temple (25:3, 6; 36:15; Obad. 10–14; Zeph. 2:8). The **sword** bringing judgment was either Nebuchadnezzar's army (vv. 9, 10, 19, 20; 25:4) or the Ammonites who had been led to believe they would be involved in Judah's defeat (v. 29).

21:29 Ezekiel pronounced that Ammonite prophecies of victory and security from a fate similar to Judah's were **false visions.** The slain Judeans would be joined by Ammonite corpses.

21:30 I will judge you: This is God's prediction for Ammon and the Ammonites. How it would be done is the subject of vv. 31, 32.

21:31, 32 The **brutal men** are defined as "the men of the East" in 25:4. The fall of Jerusalem meant only that Judah would be judged first. Some Judeans took refuge in Ammon (Jer. 41:1–3). God remembered Ammon's animosity and foretold its future as a place that **shall not be remembered.** The events of Jer. 41 led to a Babylonian expedition against Ammon in which the capital city Rabbah was sacked and many inhabitants deported (25:1–7). Ammon was later invaded by Arabs and its autonomy ceased. Eventually it was absorbed into the Persian Empire.

22:1–5 These verses focus on the sins of Jerusalem, principally bloodshed (social sin) as a result of idolatry (spiritual sin). A problem in the vertical relationship with God inevitably leads to some degree of injustice and injury in horizontal, human affairs. **You have caused your days to draw near:** The city was ripe for judgment. When such hypocrisy is exposed and punishment is executed before the world, God's people become lasting objects of ridicule.

22:6–12 Jerusalem's **princes** had shed the blood of innocent people (7:27; 11:1; 12:10; 19:1; 21:13; 2 Kin. 21:16; 23:36–37; 24:1–4, 18, 19). These evil leaders had been: (1) taking advantage of parents and the weak (Ex. 20:12; 22:21–24; 23:9; Lev. 19:3; Deut. 24:17); (2) rejecting God and His covenant, leading to ungodliness and inhumanity (Ex. 20:8); (3) murdering the innocent by slandering them (Lev. 19:16); (4) preferring idolatrous religion and its immoral rituals (22:1–5; Deut. 12:1–2; 16:21, 22); (5) engaging in sexual immorality with **neighbors,** family, and relatives (Lev. 18:6–23; 20:10–21); and, (6) loving money and using it to get ahead of fellow citizens (18:5–9; Ex. 23:8; Deut. 23:19, 20; 24:6, 10–12; Matt. 6:24; 1 Tim. 6:5–10).

22:13–16 God reveals His planned actions against Jerusalem and Judah. The expression **beat My fists** (21:14–17) shows great anger. **Defile yourself** refers to the desecration and destruction of Jerusalem by the Babylonians (2 Kin. 24:13; 25:9, 13–21).

22:17–23 These verses are primarily about God's chastisement of His sinful people through the burning of Jerusalem by the Babylonians (2 Kin. 25:9). Yet the verses also point to the fiery ordeals and trials that force all of us into a more perfect relationship with our Lord (v. 22; Ps. 66:10; Jer. 9:7; Dan. 11:35; 12:10; Zech. 13:9; Mal. 3:1–3; James 1:2–4).

22:24, 25 This verse echoes the promises of Deut. 28:12, 24, where the abundance or absence of rain in the **land** is associated with obedience or disobedience to the Law.

22:26, 27 The **priests** were not examples of separation from worldly ways (Ex. 19:6; Lev. 11:44; 22:32). Some at least were motivated by monetary gain (Mic. 3:11).

22:28 plastered them: This probably refers to the prophets themselves. **untempered mortar:** The Hebrew word means "mud-plaster" or "whitewash." These prophets were involved in "whitewashing" the sins of the nation's leaders (Matt. 23:27; Luke 11:39). If the proper antecedent for **them** is "princes" (v. 27), then the priests were also guilty of approving murder. **divining:** The false prophets used sheep livers in the hope of finding the will of the gods (13:7; 21:21).

22:29 As go the leaders so go the followers (12:18, 19). The **people of the land** were average citizens or commoners.

22:30, 31 sought for: God could not find a spiritual leader to guide the people in godliness. Why not Ezekiel? (3:17–21; 33:1–6.) A qualified leader is useless if people refuse to be led. **stand in the gap:** The figure is of a wall with a section broken down by a siege. If no soldier stands in the gap to repulse the enemy, the city surely will be taken. God represented Himself as against His people. Unable to find anyone who, by life or by

---

🌱 IN LIFE | **The Go-between**

Perhaps as you look at some of the tragedies of the world—the armed conflicts, the political breakdowns, the crimes of injustice or indifference, the ethical compromises—you wonder why some good and strong person cannot be found to lead the way out of the trouble. The Lord wondered the same thing as He surveyed wicked Judah. Having enumerated the sins of the people, He told Ezekiel that He had searched in vain for someone who could "stand in the gap" between their guilt and His righteous wrath (Ezek. 22:30). No worthy go-between could be found.

Ultimately, only Christ is righteous enough to serve as the go-between to connect a holy God and sinful humanity (1 Tim. 2:5; Heb. 9:15). Apart from Him, none of us would be free of God's wrath, for all of us have sinned (Rom. 3:21–26). However, because Jesus took on Himself the judgment for our sin, we can have unimpeded access to God.

We can also act as go-betweens in the troubles around us, "standing in the gap" to bridge chasms of indifference and oppression. We can do what we can to stem the tide of evil and tell others of the opportunity to know God through Christ. And we can intercede for others in prayer.

intercession, could turn aside that judgment (14:13–20), He will pour out His **indignation** on the city.

23:1, 2 The **one mother** of the two **daughters** was the Hebrew nation—Israel. The two daughters are the northern kingdom—Israel, or Samaria—and the southern kingdom—Judah. Though they did not split apart until after the death of Solomon, the allegory speaks from that later time and perspective as it presents a pictorial review of Israel's past.

23:3 It was during the formative years of the Hebrew nation in Egypt (its **youth**) that the Israelites began practicing political and spiritual prostitution by conforming themselves to the ways of the world, worshiping idols, and trusting in an earthly instead of heavenly power (16:26; 20:7, 8).

23:4 In Hebrew, the names **Oholah,** meaning "Her Own Tabernacle," and **Oholibah,** meaning "My Tabernacle Is in Her," seem to refer to God's sanctuaries in each land or, in a distinct usage, to the tent shrines for Canaanite idols as opposed to God's true temple (2 Sam. 6:17). **Samaria** is the **elder** (literally the "greater") because she first made political and idolatrous alliances with foreign nations and was the first to be punished by foreign captivity. **They were Mine:** The Lord identified both cities as a part of His chosen nation. **sons and daughters:** This phrase refers to the growth of the nation of Israel. They would become a powerful nation, but with pagan allies and a proliferation of idolaters.

23:5, 6 played the harlot: This word may be used for any immoral sexual acts. Here it refers to the nation placing its faith in and seeking strength and security from alliances with political powers instead of God (2 Kin. 15:17–20; 17:1–4; Hos. 12:1–2).

23:7–10 Ezekiel reminds his audience of how God already had judged Samaria through Assyrian conquest and captivity in 722 B.C. (2 Kin. 17:5–41). **Uncovered her nakedness** means to be stripped bare and so put to great shame. **Became a byword** means people began using the name "Samaria" as a synonym for "immoral nation."

23:11–14 Judah **increased her harlotry** by engaging in political and spiritual intercourse with first the Assyrians (vv. 12, 13; 2 Kin. 16:7–9) and then the **Chaldeans** (a regional term used for the entire Babylonian Empire; vv. 15, 17, 23). The last two lines tell how Judean envoys to Babylon became enamored of Babylonian rulers and their power through pictures (Jer. 22:14) on their palace and temple walls. Vermilion is a red color.

23:15–18 alienated herself: This is an allusion to Judah's turning in disappointment and disgust from relying on Babylon to relying on Egypt (2 Kin. 23:28–24:1). God's alienation from Jerusalem is an allusion to the city's coming defeat by Nebuchadnezzar in 586 B.C.

23:19, 20 Judah renewed its alliance with Egypt (Jer. 37:5–7), which is strikingly symbolized in this verse as a lustful, illicit lover (v. 3; 16:26).

23:21–27 God's verdict was that He would judge Jerusalem through Babylon, formerly an ally but now an enemy. **Pekod, Shoa, Koa, . . . the Assyrians with them:** These were tribal vassals of Babylon that would join the assault on Judah. A **buckler** was a large rectangular shield. Removing the **nose** and **ears** was an ancient punishment for adultery.

23:28–31 This "lover" was one whom the Judeans came to **hate** as an enemy. God explains that He would use the Babylonians as an instrument of His wrath: (1) to expose the extreme unfaithfulness of Judah and (2) to punish Judah for its idolatry that had resulted from forbidden political alliances (Ex. 20:1–6; 34:10–17; Deut. 18:9–14). The **sister** is Samaria (vv. 4, 33) with whom Jerusalem would share a similar destiny of destruction—**her cup.**

23:32–34 The **cup** is often symbolic of God's judgment (Ps. 75:7, 8; Jer. 25:15–29; Matt. 20:22; Rev. 14:10). **break its shards:** The phrase vividly portrays how completely Judah would drink the cup of wrath, breaking what was already broken. **Tear at your own breasts** pictures the resultant agony and anguish.

23:35 This verse summarizes why God was going to punish Jerusalem with such vengeance: **you have forgotten Me.** The people had intentionally ignored God, pictured by the parallel phrase **cast Me behind your back.**

23:36–39 adultery . . . defiled . . . slain: These themes have been developed previously (v. 8; 16:20, 21; Ex. 20:3–13, 22–26; 22:20; Lev. 18:21; 19:30; 20:1–5; Deut. 4:15–40). The religion of Judah had become so adulterated that the people did not recognize that child sacrifice to an idol and worship of the Lord wee totally incompatible.

23:40–42 Sabeans: This Hebrew word may also be read as "drunkards." The nomadic peoples east and south of Israel were considered uncivilized and repugnant by the Hebrews.

23:43–49 Alarmingly, those God would use to judge Samaria and Jerusalem (Assyria and Babylon, respectively) are here called **righteous.** Obviously this does not describe their standing before God or their way of life. Instead, it underlines their role as instruments of God's just judgment (vv. 46, 47; Deut. 22:13–30).

24:1, 2 This is the fourth chronological reference given by Ezekiel (1:2, 3; 8:1; 20:1). The date is January 588 B.C., the **very day** that Neb-

✠ IN CONTEXT | **The City as a Melting Pot**

Many cities today are called "melting pots" because of their large number of immigrants and the tendency of ethnic groups to assimilate into the larger culture over time. Jerusalem was, and always has been a melting pot of cultures. But around 588 B.C., the city became a melting pot of a different kind.

The Babylonians began a siege then that lasted for about two years, with one brief respite, and culminated in the fall of the city. Hundreds of miles away in Babylon, the Lord told Ezekiel to utter a parable about a pot of stew (Ezek. 24:3–5). Jerusalem was portrayed as a stew pot full of water, choice meats, and spices, with "fuel bones" (logs) blazing underneath. Some believe that Ezekiel's parable was based on a folk song commonly sung by women as they prepared their food. The Lord may have turned a well-known ditty into a powerful spiritual lesson.

The illustration provided a recipe for cooking up a yummy stew. But the parable introduced a problem in the preparations. Scum (or rust) in the pot was spoiling the stew so that no one would want to eat it (24:6). By analogy, the sins of God's people in Jerusalem had made them odious and distasteful. The Lord's remedy was to "turn up the heat" (24:9), so much so that the water would eventually evaporate, the meat would burn up, the pot would turn red hot, and the scum would burn off (24:10–11). Thus God would cleanse the city of its impurities. That was essentially what the Babylonian siege accomplished.

In thinking about cities today, the image of the boiling pot is still appropriate. If a city is relatively healthy, it can stand a certain amount of "heat" and even profit from it. To some extent, heat and pressure necessary to fully cook the diverse ingredients and meld them together into an enjoyable, nutritious meal. On the other hand, when a city ignores its problems and allows spiritual and moral decline to go unchecked, an increase in heat can be explosive. In the worst case, it can lead to melt-down. That is what happened to Jerusalem when Babylon conquered it. What steps are you and your community taking to ensure that you avoid a similarly bad outcome?

uchadnezzar—**king of Babylon**—began his attack on Jerusalem (2 Kin. 25:1–3; Jer. 39:1, 2; 52:1–6). Ezekiel was commanded to **write down the name of the day.** This would be a bitter reminder of God's trustworthiness to do what He promised through the prophets. Nebuchadnezzar's siege was God's judgment on Jerusalem.

24:3–5 The subject of this **parable** is explained in v. 2. The audience was again **the rebellious house** (2:3–8; 3:5–7; 11:3–12; 12:2, 22–28). **Flock** was symbolic of God's chosen people (compare ch. 34). **Bones** were sometimes used as a fuel for fire.

24:6 Bloody city explains why Jerusalem—the **pot**—must experience the heat of God's wrath (v. 9; 22:2–12) through the Babylonian siege that had now begun. The remainder of this verse announces the verdict: exile. **Bring it out piece by piece** refers to individual inhabitants, the "choice cuts" of meat in vv. 4, 5. **no lot has fallen:** God does not play favorites; His judgment would fall equally on all inhabitants of the city, for they all had sinned.

24:7, 8 These verses elaborate on the city's sin of bloodshed (v. 6). The people failed to deal with the sin, so God declares that it would remain exposed to His judgment (Gen. 4:10; Lev. 17:13; Is. 26:21).

24:9–15 have cleansed you, and you were not cleansed: This probably refers to the deportations of 605 and 597 B.C., whose cleansing effects were incomplete.

24:16, 17 the desire of your eyes: This refers to Ezekiel's wife (vv. 18, 21, 25). **one stroke:** This phrase is used elsewhere of a plague reflecting God's wrath (Ex. 9:14; Num. 14:37; 16:46). **you shall neither mourn nor weep:** This solemn command of God may be one of the hardest ever given to one of His servants. The picture of Ezekiel's wife dying and Ezekiel not being allowed to grieve illustrated God's pain over the death of His wife—Jerusalem—and His inability to mourn because the nation deserved the punishment. Ezekiel was called by God to "be a sign to the exiles" by demonstrating what they should do (vv. 21–23) in response to the "death" (destruction) of their desire and delight—their nation and its capital city. What Ezekiel was commanded to accept and do illustrated the degree of personal sacrifice and separation from ordinary life that the prophetic ministry often required. A long period of mourning was the normal, ritual response to the death of a loved one in the ancient Middle East (1 Sam. 4:12; 2 Sam. 1:12, 17; 3:31, 35; 15:30; 19:4; Is. 58:5; Jer. 16:7; Mic. 1:8, 10). The expression of those in mourning was not to **bind** the **turban,** but to remove it and replace it with dust. **cover your lips:** This alluded to the practice of covering the lower half of the face with a veil. The **bread of sorrow** was food given to a mourner after fasting.

24:18 did as I was commanded: Ezekiel had been given a revelatory command that was extremely hard for him personally. He faithfully communicated it to the people. His absolute obedience to the harshest of God's commands contrasted with the disobedience of his fellow citizens.

24:19, 20 tell us: When obedience to God demanded unusual actions, the people's curiosity about the reasons for such behavior was aroused, creating an opportunity for verbal witness about God's revelation (12:9; 21:7 for the two previous times of similar response).

24:21 the delight of your soul: The meaning "affection" is likely intended here. The entire phrase means something like the "object of your affections." The Judeans had the wrong kind of pride about the temple. Instead of the temple being a place of worship and house of God—**My sanctuary**—the Judeans took pride in the building as a sign of their importance. Therefore, God was going to **profane** it by allowing the Babylonians to capture the city and destroy the temple (v. 25; 2 Chr. 36:15–21; Lam. 1:10, 11). With no city or temple to boast about, the humbled Israelites could boast only in God's mercy.

24:22–24 The Judeans should or would respond to the death of the nation as Ezekiel had been told to respond to the death of his wife (vv. 15–18): they would not mourn their loss. The consistent purpose of divine discipline is seen again: **you shall know that I am the Lord God** (6:8–10; 12:15, 16). The trials would prompt the Israelites to depend on the Lord and know that He is holy. **sign:** See 12:3–7; 24:16, 17. When Jerusalem fell, God would prove Himself as trustworthy and righteous, and Ezekiel as His true prophet (v. 27).

24:25–27 When the **one who escapes** on the day Jerusalem falls (586 B.C.) arrives to give Ezekiel the news (perhaps about three months later), Ezekiel would be relieved of his inability to speak anything except judgment, and would be allowed to preach hope (vv. 1, 2, 24; 3:25–27; 33:21–39:29; 2 Kin. 25:8, 9).

25:1–32:32 These oracles serve as an interlude between Ezekiel's prophecies of judgment upon Judah in chs. 1—24 and his prophecies of restoration in chs. 33—48. Similar oracles

appear in Isaiah (chs. 13—23) and Jeremiah (chs. 46—51). They are a reminder that though God would use the Gentiles to punish His people, those nations too must pass before the bar of divine justice.

25:1, 2 On **Ammonites,** see 21:20, 28. Ammon corresponds roughly to the present-day country of Jordan with its capital Amman.

25:3 For further background on the Ammonites and Ammon, see 6:11; 21:15; 26:2; 36:2; Neh. 4:7–9; Ps. 35:19–21; Jer. 49:1–6; Amos 1:13–15; Zeph. 2:8–11. **Aha!** An expression of mocking and delight.

25:4, 5 Men of the East is another title for the Babylonians (21:31). Ancient historical records mention Ammon's subjugation by Nebuchadnezzar five years after the fall of Jerusalem. Arab invaders came to dominate the territory, and Persian control began about 530 B.C.

25:6, 7 The Ammonites rejoiced at the destruction of Jerusalem and its temple; therefore, they would also be punished. The Ammonites were eventually to perish as a people.

25:8 Moab was south of Ammon, east of the Dead Sea and between the Arnon and Zered rivers. The Moabites descended from the incestuous relationship between Lot and his first daughter (Gen. 19:30–38). **Seir** (Edom) is mentioned because it was guilty of accusing Israel of being **like all the nations** (35:15; 36:5; Gen. 32:3; 36:8, 9). This accusation reflects Moab and Edom's malicious misinterpretation of Judah's misfortune as a proof that God was powerless (Gen. 12:1–3; Ex. 19:5, 6; Num. 22:12; Deut. 7:6–8; Jer. 48:27; Zeph. 2:8, 9).

25:9–11 the territory: This expression, literally meaning "shoulder" or "side," describes the northwest corner of Moab, the area most difficult to conquer due to its topography (a mountain plateau high above the Jordan valley). Apparently the attack would culminate in the ruin of Moab's **glory,** its frontier cities.

25:12 Edom was located south of Moab, from the Zered River south to the Gulf of Aqaba. The Edomites descended from Esau. On this **vengeance** of Edom see 35:10; 36:1–7 (compare Gen. 36:6, 7; Ps. 137:7; Lam. 4:21, 22; Amos 1:11, 12). The transgressions most characteristic of Edom were its perpetual animosity and repeated, vindictive acts of violence against Israel. The Hebrew words rendered **greatly offended** ("be guilty") may indicate continuous or repeated rather than intensive behavior.

25:13 The precise locations of **Teman** and **Dedan** are not known, but they probably are mentioned to convey the idea of Edom from one end to the other (Joel 3:19).

25:14 Since Edom had taken their revenge

on the Judeans and showed them hostility when they needed help, God would show Edom His **vengeance.**

25:15 The **Philistines** were in southwest Palestine along the Mediterranean coast. They had a long history (**the old hatred**) of constant competition for control of Judah (Judg. 13—16; 1 Sam. 4; 13; 31; 2 Sam. 5:17–21). The Hebrew verb meaning "to take revenge" is found three times in this verse, indicating the great vengeance of which Philistia was guilty.

25:16, 17 Cherethites: This term (probably meaning "Cretans") was used here as a substitute term for some or all of the Philistines, who migrated from Caphtor (understood to be Crete). Their more remote ancestors were Aegeans. See 1 Sam. 30:14; 2 Sam. 8:18; 15:18; Jer. 47:4; Amos 9:7; Zeph. 2:5.

26:1 The date places the prophetic pronouncements against Tyre, the Tyrian monarch, and Sidon somewhere in March or April of 587–586 B.C. (**the eleventh year**). This was at or just after the fall of Jerusalem (v. 2).

26:2 Tyre, in competition with Sidon (1 Kin. 16:31; Is. 23:2, 12), was a major seaport and leading city in Phoenicia (present-day Lebanon). **has said:** The past tense could refer to an event that had not yet taken place, using a Hebrew idiom which describes a future event as so certain that it can be expressed as having already been accomplished (Is. 9:6, 7; 52:13—53:12). **I shall be filled** was evidence of Tyre's greed and materialism, desiring any wealth of Jerusalem that could be found in its ruins after the Babylonian conquest.

26:3, 4 The armies (**many nations;** vv. 4, 7–14) that would attack Tyre are appropriately compared to waves of the sea, because the city of Tyre was an island fortress.

26:5 midst of the sea: Tyre was originally a rocky islet. Fortified, it proved impregnable for centuries, but now would be plundered.

26:6–14 The fulfillment of this prophecy of Tyre's fate began with the long siege of the city by the Babylonian army under **Nebuchadnezzar** (between 580–570 B.C.). Nebuchadnezzar ruled the Neo-Babylonian (Chaldean) Empire from 605–562 B.C. The second phase came with the Persian conquest in about 525 B.C., followed by the final and famous siege of 332 B.C. by the Greeks under Alexander, which completed the predictions of this passage (especially vv. 5, 14; 47:10). Note the switch from **he** to **they** (v. 12; v. 4) as well as the use of the pronoun "I" by God, which explains His sovereign

> *Tyre, in competition with Sidon, was a major seaport and leading city in Phoenicia.*

control over all the nations (28:7; 29:8). Alexander literally fulfilled the words **break down your walls** (v. 5) when his army built a causeway half a mile long between the shore and the city on its island. He tore down defensive walls to build the causeway.

26:15, 16 The **princes of the sea** (27:35) were the rulers of various settlements in Phoenicia that were connected with Tyre. They would surrender and submit to Babylonian rule when they saw what happened to Tyre: **be astonished at you.** They would mourn in song (vv. 17, 18) after they took off their **robes** and **embroidered garments** (Jon. 3:6).

26:17–19 The **deep** is the same Hebrew word as in Gen. 1:2. Imagery of the chaotic waters of creation picture the coming catastrophe.

26:20, 21 The **Pit** is probably a synonym for hell (Is. 14:15; 38:18). **never be inhabited:** Ancient Tyre would cease to exist.

27:1–3 perfect: The proud citizens of Tyre saw themselves as the finest example of a merchant "ship" in the ancient world.

27:4–11 A description of the building, outfitting, and manning of the trading vessels that symbolized Tyre's glory. Material came from many points in the eastern Mediterranean world. Her shipbuilders, sailors, and mercenary soldiers came from as far as Africa, Asia Minor, and Persia.

27:5 Senir is an Amorite term used for Mount Hermon or another peak in its range. **Fir** is rendered elsewhere "pine," "cypress," or "juniper."

27:6 Bashan (39:18) was the broad and fertile plateau east of the Sea of Galilee and the upper Jordan.

27:7 Elishah has coasts and is associated here with Egypt; therefore it may be Italy or Sicily.

27:8 Sidon was a Phoenician seaport about thirty miles north of Tyre. The two cities were rivals, but Tyre tended to dominate Sidon (28:21, 22; Gen. 10:15, 19; Judg. 18:28; Is. 23:2; Matt. 11:21, 22). Like Tyre, the city of **Arvad** was on an island off the coast of Phoenicia. It was Phoenicia's northernmost town (28:11; Gen. 10:18; 1 Chr. 1:16).

27:9 Gebal was another successful Phoenician port, between Sidon and Arvad (Josh. 13:5; 1 Kin. 5:18). It was called Byblos by the Greeks and Romans, and Gubla by the Assyrians and Babylonians.

27:10, 11 Lydia and **Libya** are literally Lud

and Put, usually understood to be in western Asia Minor (Lud) and Africa (Put).

27:12 Tarshish was possibly in Spain.

27:13 Javan is Greece (Gen. 10:4). **Tubal** and **Meshech** are thought to have been in eastern Asia Minor (modern Turkey).

27:14 On **the house of Togarmah,** see Gen. 10:3. This phrase may refer to the people of Armenia in eastern Asia Minor (38:6).

27:15 Dedan may perhaps be understood as "Redan" (Rhodes), because the written forms of the Hebrew letters for *d* and *r* are easily confused. Rhodes was a major trading center in the southern Aegean Sea.

27:16 The Hebrew term for **emeralds** may also be translated "turquoise."

27:17 Minnith was in Ammon (21:28) and presumably was famous for its fine wheat. **Millet** translates a Hebrew word that apparently stands for some type of food, but exactly what kind is not known today. **Balm** was an aromatic resin or other gummy substance that may have had medicinal value (Jer. 8:22).

27:18 Damascus was and is the capital of Syria (v. 16). **Helbon** is north of Damascus, a region still recognized for its wine production. The phrase rendered **white wool** is understood by some to mean "wool from Zachar," a place possibly associated with modern Sachra, also north of Damascus, where goat and sheep are common.

27:19, 20 Dan seems out of place in this context, so some transliterate the Hebrew as Wedan. Others argue that the name Dan is another title for Greece. **Cassia** (Ex. 30:24; Ps. 45:8; Song 4:14) was either a type of cinnamon tree or a plant from which perfume and incense were made. **Cane** refers to an oil-producing reed found in swamps.

27:21 Kedar was a nomadic tribe in Arabia.

27:22 Sheba and **Raamah** were located near Arabia (Gen. 10:6, 7).

27:23, 24 Ancient **Haran** was a merchant city along the important Euphrates trade route (Gen. 11:27–32), in what is now eastern Turkey. **Canneh** (Is. 10:9), **Eden,** and **Chilmad** were probably in Mesopotamia, most likely south of Haran (2 Kin. 19:12). The verse seems concerned with cities, so **Assyria** is better translated *Asshur,* a city of Nineveh; but the term could stand for the citizens of Assyria. On **Sheba,** see v. 22.

27:25, 26 The **east wind** was often powerful and potentially destructive (Gen. 41:6; Job 27:21; Ps. 48:7; Is. 27:8). Thus it symbolizes the destruction the Babylonian army would bring on Tyre. In 26:7, Babylon would come from the "north." This was the direction from which the army would invade Phoenicia.

27:27, 28 The **common-land** was the pastureland controlled by a city.

27:29–36 The final verses of the chapter present a remorseful and revengeful lament to be chanted, perhaps over and over, by Tyre's trade partners. Tyre's nearest neighbors (26:16–18) would be greatly troubled by Tyre's defeat, but soon they would turn against Tyre themselves in the vain hope of escaping a similar fate at the hands of the Babylonians.

28:1–10 Because Tyre's great splendor and sin were the by-products, primarily, of the influence and intentions of its king, Ezekiel is led by God to proclaim the reasons for (vv. 2–6) and means of judgment (vv. 7–10) against its chief ruler and most prominent citizens.

28:1–3 you are wiser than Daniel: The Hebrew name Daniel is spelled here the same way as in 14:14: *Dan-El.* It might refer to a different person otherwise unknown in Israel's ancient history.

28:4–7 The **strangers** are the Babylonians (7:17–19; 23:23; 30:11; 31:12; 32:12).

28:8, 9 The phrase **midst of the seas** parallels the word *Pit* and reinforces its meaning, for it too signifies the place and fact of death.

28:10 the death of the uncircumcised: This term denotes a disgraceful death (31:18; 32:19).

28:11–19 Interpretations of this difficult passage explain the unusual wording in one of three ways generally: (1) Satan being symbolized by the "king"; (2) the historical king(s) of Tyre being compared to Adam; or, (3) the king(s) being addressed with hyperbolic language and described through allusions to Phoenician religious, mythological literature and/or religious and social practices common in Canaan and the ancient Near East. The first approach is popular and sensational but satisfies the understanding of only a few pieces of the entire passage. The second and more so the third approaches answer the most questions about the nature and import of the language in light of: (1) the immediate and larger literary contexts (chs. 26—27; 28:1–10); and, (2) what has been learned about the historical, cultural, and mythological contexts. To see Satan is not the most normal, natural, logical, and expected reading of this text consistent with the various contexts.

28:12 Seal of perfection is more literally "the one sealing a plan" (the same Hebrew word for "plan" or "pattern" appears once more at 43:10). In effect, the king affixed the official seal of his signet ring to the plans that made Tyre one of the leading centers of commerce in that day. **wisdom . . . beauty:** These descriptions mark out the king of Tyre as an exceptional ruler, displaying the ideals of kingship in the ancient Middle East.

28:13 in Eden, the garden of God: This is

possibly an exaggerated comparison: this king invaded a place like Eden in its beauty. **created:** The Hebrew verb for *created* is the same as the one used in Gen. 1:1. Just as in Genesis, the word emphasizes God's active work in history. It was God's sovereign plan and purpose to allow this man to become king.

28:14 The holy mountain of God could be "the holy mountain of gods." According to Canaanite beliefs, the "seat of the gods" was in the "mountains," or the "mountains of the north" (Ps. 48:2). The focus here seems to be on the king of Tyre's attempt to enter into the council of the gods. So instead of the verse referring to the king's presence in Jerusalem, it could refer more logically to a Phoenician ritual, the celebration of their patron god Melqart's fiery resurrection. This king wanted to imitate Melqart.

28:15 The Hebrew term rendered **perfect** does not mean sinless, but complete or flawless. The king of Tyre had been in complete control and was unchallenged until he was filled with prideful **iniquity.**

28:16–19 The king's pride led to materialism, violence, and sinfulness in business and religion. **abundance of your trading:** The expression is most easily and appropriately applied to the human king who was the driving force behind the development of Tyre's commercial empire. The true God—the pronoun **I**—dethroned the king, derailed his unholy ambitions, and destroyed the source of his pride in order to make his example a deterrent to others. The king's commercial empire collapsed and his machinations to resemble a god were crushed in the sight of local rulers who would gaze in astonishment.

28:20–23 Sidon was Tyre's sister city, but its lesser importance may explain the brevity of treatment here (27:8). As commercial "sisters," the cities had similar characters and concerns, so they shared similar crimes. The LORD displayed justice through deserved judgment so the people would recognize that He is the true and righteous God.

28:24 God would free Israel. The **brier** and **thorn** refer to the nations around Israel who had been enemies and evil influences. When the judgments were executed fully, these nations would no longer be able to harass and oppress Israel.

28:25, 26 God promised that Israel will someday be gathered from its dispersion among the nations to return and **dwell in their own land,** the land that God had given to **Jacob** (the land of Canaan; 11:17; 20:41, 42; ch. 33—39; Gen. 12:7; 26:3; 28:10–13; 35:12; Jer. 30:10). The end of the foreign nations' ability to attack Israel will lead to a time of peace, prosperity, and protection.

29:1 tenth year . . . tenth month: This is December 588 or January 587 B.C. This introduction of another date by Ezekiel (his sixth) is a chronological break, but not a thematic break, with 26:1—28:26 (1:2; 8:1; 20:1; 24:1; 26:1).

29:2 The **Pharaoh** was Hophra (around 589–570 B.C.; Jer. 44:30). The prophecy against him was also a prophecy against all Egypt (30:22; 32:2), like the previous prophecy against Tyre and its king (28:1–19). The context suggests that literal, human kings were meant in chs. 28 and 29.

29:3 O great monster: The Pharaoh is pictured here as a crocodile. **My river** refers to the Nile. Pharaoh's arrogant pride is described by his words about the Nile River, **I have made it for myself** (compare with the words of the king of Tyre, 28:2). In the Egyptian religion the crocodile god Sebek was a protector (32:2).

29:4, 5 Whereas v. 3 explains why Pharaoh would be punished, these verses explain how the punishment would be accomplished. The imagery pictures a crocodile being caught, carried out of the water onto land, and left as carrion. The **fish** represent the Egyptians, who would be judged along with Pharaoh (v. 2). Pharaoh's destiny to be **food** may have been an intentional insult to the rulers famous for their burials and pyramids.

29:6, 7 God's purpose for judging Egypt was to encourage the nations and individuals to come to know Him (6:14; 7:27; 12:20; 14:11; 22:16; 23:49; 25:7, 11, 17; 28:24). **Staff of reed** refers to the people of Egypt. This alludes to Egypt's weakness as an ally and the worthlessness of that country's protection (Is. 36:6). Israel was foolish to rely on Egypt for protection. They should have turned to God for their security and strength.

29:8 sword: Here is another reference to the Babylonian army under Nebuchadnezzar, the predicted human instrument of God's coming wrath (21:1–7, 9–11, 19, 20; 26:7–14).

29:9 The nation was indicted as a result of what **he**—that is, Pharaoh—boasted. Often national monuments were inscribed in ancient times with the exaggerated and arrogant boasts of kings.

29:10 Migdol to Syene refers to places most likely near the northern and southern

> *In the Egyptian religion the crocodile god Sebek was a protector.*

boundaries of ancient Egypt, indicating the totality of the land (Judg. 20:1). The desolation would extend to the land south of Egypt—ancient Nubia which is modern Sudan.

29:11, 12 The Egyptians would experience a scattering to other lands for **forty years** (4:4–8). A Babylonian chronicle suggests that Egypt was conquered around 568 B.C. Forty years after this date, the Persians instituted a policy of resettlement for many of the peoples who had been dispersed by Babylon.

29:13–15 The **land of Pathros** is southern Egypt. This kingdom would thereafter be **lowly** and **the lowliest,** never again to dominate other nations.

29:16, 17 came to pass: Ezekiel received this oracle from God (vv. 17–21) and apparently the following message also (30:1–19) in March-April 571 B.C., the latest date in the book (v. 1).

29:18 labor strenuously: This recalls the difficult siege of Tyre. Heads were **made bald** and shoulders **rubbed raw** in the protracted siege, which took thirteen or more years. **yet neither:** The fact was that neither Nebuchadnezzar **nor his army received** much of a reward for their efforts.

29:19, 20 God affirms that He is sovereign over the coming fall of Egypt to Babylon to make up for the **wages** they had not received from their conquest of Tyre. God specifically named Nebuchadnezzar as his instrument (Jer. 43:8–13). The Babylonian chronicles imply that Babylon invaded Egypt in approximately 568 B.C.

29:21 In that day: This refers to the day when Egypt would fall to Babylon, and a prophecy about the Messiah should not be read into this text. **Cause the horn . . . of Israel to spring forth** means that the nation would renew its strength. Renewal and encouragement would come to God's people in exile when they heard about Egypt's downfall orchestrated by the hand of God, who is holy and sovereign.

I will open your mouth was God's promise to restore Ezekiel's speech (33:22) and therefore to magnify Himself and His ways: **know that I am the LORD**.

30:1–3 The phrase **the day of the LORD** here refers to the period of divine wrath on the nation of Egypt. This term suggests God's personal involvement in His judgmental work. In this context (vv. 4–19) God would use Babylon under Nebuchadnezzar to punish Egypt and her allies (Gen. 12:3; Jer. 25; 46). **the time of the Gentiles:** That is, the time of God's wrath on the nations.

30:4, 5 Ethiopia is the Hebrew Cush, and refers to the area south of Egypt toward modern Ethiopia; see 29:10. **Libya** and **Lydia** were in Africa and Asia Minor; see 27:10. **Mingled people** may be read as "all of Arabia." **Chub** is an obscure term that was understood as the "Libyans" by the Septuagint translators of the Hebrew OT. The **allied** lands were lands to the south, east, and west of Egypt that would also fall to the Babylonian army.

30:6, 7 Migdol to Syene means the whole land of Egypt; see 29:10.

30:8 Fire is often symbolic of judgment (20:47; Is. 4:4).

30:9 This **day of Egypt**—the day that Egypt and her allies would be conquered—was part of a larger period of God's judgment on the nations outside Israel by means of Babylon; in fact, Ezekiel describes the Babylonians as **messengers** sent from God Himself. No one could prevent the coming day of judgment, for the Almighty had ordained it: **for indeed it is coming.**

30:10–12 These verses add extra details to the more general predictions about Egypt's doom in the preceding verses (vv. 3–9). **Most terrible of the nations** was applied to the Babylonians, for their cruelty was legendary (2 Kin. 25:7; 2 Chr. 33:11; 36:17; Jer. 39:4–10).

30:13–19 This fourth and final message

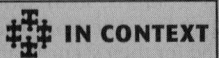 **IN CONTEXT** **Under Siege!**

From ancient times, large cities have often protected themselves by building massive walls that would be difficult if not impossible to breach. An enemy might try pushing down or burning the city gates or tunneling under the walls, but these strategies were not always prudent. An alternative was to build siege ramps and mounds next to the walls—an approach that Jeremiah predicted would be taken against Jerusalem (6:6).

A siege ramp was an earthen incline made by piling up dirt, boulders, trees, and other debris against the besieged city's wall. When preparations had been made for an assault, soldiers could march up the ramp to the top of the wall and fight their way over. An example of such a ramp built by the Romans is still in place at the ancient fortress of Masada in southeastern Israel.

adds more detail to the description of the coming destruction of Egypt. Emphasis seems to be placed on the fall of major cities. **Noph** was ancient Memphis, a significant city in Egypt. It was capital of the Old Kingdom in the third century B.C. On **Pathros,** see 29:14, 15.

30:21 I have broken the arm of Pharaoh: The prophecy refers to Pharaoh Hophra's unsuccessful attempt to relieve the siege of Jerusalem just a few months earlier (29:2, 6, 7). God used Nebuchadnezzar to defeat the Egyptian army. A muscular *arm,* as a symbol

Photo by Howard Vos

A portion of a pagan temple at Luxor, Egypt, a city referred to as No in the Bible. Ezekiel predicted that Egypt and its cities would fall to the Babylonians as a result of God's judgment (Ezek. 30:13–19).

Zoan, the classical Tanis, was a city in the northeastern delta. **No** was ancient Thebes, the capital of Upper or southern Egypt. Thebes was destroyed by the Assyrians in 661 B.C. **Sin** was ancient Pelusium, a fortress town on the northeastern border where the ruling Egyptian dynasty of Ezekiel's day had a residence: the **strength of Egypt. Aven** (or Heliopolis, "the City of the Sun") was ancient On, a center for worship of the sun-god Re. Aven was north of Memphis at the southern tip of the delta. **Pi Beseth,** or Bubastis in Greek form, was once the capital of Lower Egypt (the northern or Nile Delta area). **Tehaphnehes** was also a fortress town on the northeastern border, the place where the Babylonian army would enter Egypt to bring this dark **day. A cloud** would arise from burning the city, and its vassal villages— **her daughters**—would be attacked and set ablaze also.

30:20 first month: March-April 587 B.C. (29:1, 18–20). Ezekiel returns to a chronological sequence for the prophecies.

of the king's (and thus the army's) strength, often appeared in Egyptian art and architecture. Even Hophra took the title "He Who Is Strong-Armed." That God had broken Pharaoh's arm symbolized his complete defeat.

30:22–26 I will scatter: These verses predict the continued weakness of Hophra against Nebuchadnezzar and the coming catastrophe for all Egypt when its cities would be defeated and the people deported (beginning around 568 B.C.).

31:1, 2 third month: May-June, 587 B.C. See 1:2; 8:1; 20:1; 24:1, 2; 26:1; 29:1, 17; 30:20.

31:3 Egypt was compared to Assyria in greatness and presumably in its great pride over its achievements. Ezekiel uses another allegory (15:1–8; 17:1–10): **Assyria** as **a cedar in Lebanon.** This image pictures the nations as trees in a forest in Lebanon (a country prized for its cedar trees; vv. 15–18; 1 Kin. 5:7–10; 7:2, 3; Ps. 29:5). Assyria at one time was the highest tree, but it had been cut down. Its capital city Nineveh fell in 612 B.C., signaling the end of

Assyrian domination and the beginning of neo-Babylonian control of the ancient Middle East.

31:4 The **waters** were the Tigris and Euphrates rivers. These mighty rivers brought agricultural fertility and fostered the development of great cities along trade routes (vv. 8, 9; 15–18; Gen. 2:10–14).

31:5–9 The unparalleled greatness of Assyria is portrayed with vivid poetic images. There is both comparison and contrast with Egypt. Before turning to the mostly narrative explanation in vv. 10–18, the prophet indicates that though Egypt was great, it was not the greatest nation. If Assyria had fallen to Babylon, no hope would remain for Egypt (31:18).

31:10–14 Because Assyria gloated over her greatness, God sentenced this cruel nation to harsh treatment and subjection under Babylon, **the mighty one of the nations. I will deliver:** The past tense, "I delivered," would be more accurate for this context. The meaning is that Babylon, the **terrible** nation, had **cut** Assyria down. The picturesque conclusion to this second message of ch. 31 indicates that all the other nations (**birds, beasts,** and **trees**) that observed Assyria's **ruin** would share its destiny of **death, depths,** and the **Pit,** and would never attain its heights of power.

31:15–17 Hell renders the Hebrew word sometimes transliterated as *Sheol,* which often merely speaks of the grave or death (Gen. 37:35; Ps. 6:5; Jon. 2:2). God had dried up or devastated Assyria, and all the nations were caused to **mourn for it** and **shake** because of its death and burial, as it was cast into **hell, the Pit,** and **the depths of the earth.** Those nations, **the trees of Eden,** who were guilty of a similar, sinful pride in their achievements would receive the same punishment.

31:18 If Assyria, the greatest nation, had fallen to the Babylonians, surely a nation less great would also fall. This pointed to Egypt—**Pharaoh and all his multitude** (vv. 2, 3, 5–9).

32:1 twelfth month: February-March 585

B.C. (31:1), after the fall of Jerusalem in 586 B.C. (2 Kin. 25:8), but about twenty years before the Babylonian invasion of Egypt (29:19–20). However, the record of the fall of Jerusalem is given in 33:21. This section (32:1–33:20) is placed before 33:21, though it reports events that follow the fall of Jerusalem. Ezekiel's arrangement is thematic. He can first record his lament, and then explain the events that inspired it. Though the Egyptians arrogantly thought that they, unlike Judah, would not fall to Babylon's forces, they would eventually experience the same fate as the citizens of Jerusalem.

32:2 The words **lion** and **monster** depict Egypt as proud and powerful.

32:3–10 These poetic lines picture Egypt and its ruler, Hophra, as a crocodile who is going to experience the judgment ordained by God. Egypt will be caught, killed, and consigned to **darkness**—a recognizable element of the day of the Lord (30:1–5; Amos 5:18–20; Acts 2:20).

32:11–15 This section interrupts the flow of vv. 3–10. The **king of Babylon** was Nebuchadnezzar. **the most terrible of the nations:** That is, the Neo-Babylonian Empire (30:10–12). **rivers run like oil:** This phrase, not used elsewhere, pictures the time following massive killing when the Nile and its tributaries would experience a "deadly" calm. The **waters** will be **clear** because there will be no human or animal life.

32:16 Such a scene of judgment will produce mourning and great grief; but God is to be seen as just and doing what was necessary to stop the people's arrogance. **The daughters of the nations:** These were among the "many peoples" in vv. 9, 10 who shall **lament** and be astonished over Egypt's destruction.

32:17 This is fifteen days later than v. 1, still in 585 B.C.

32:18–21 Depths of the earth, the Pit, and **hell** refer to the grave or death, not the place of eternal punishment for God's enemies.

32:22, 23 Assyria was the master of the

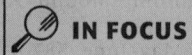 **IN FOCUS** | **"watchman"**

(Heb. *tsaphah*) (3:17; 33:2; 1 Sam. 14:16; Hos. 9:8) Strong's #6822: This Hebrew noun is derived from the verb meaning "to watch in anticipation." This verb is used to describe the actions of individuals waiting in ambush as they watch for their prey (Ps. 37:32). Watchman was an official military position. They were stationed on the towers of a city and were responsible for spotting approaching armies and sounding the alarm to warn the city (1 Sam. 14:16). The imagery behind the watchman is much like that of the shepherd, though *watchman* as a symbolic title was limited to the office of a prophet (Hos. 9:8). A watchman's failure was punishable by death. In the case of Ezekiel, punishment would come directly from God if he failed to report to the people the messages God gave him (33:8).

ancient Middle Eastern world until the rise of the neo-Babylonians around 612 B.C., early in Jeremiah's career and about 20 years before Ezekiel's first vision.

32:24, 25 Elam was east and southeast of Assyria, in what is now Iran. The people of Elam were descended from one of the sons of Shem (Gen. 10:22; 1 Chr. 1:17).

32:26, 27 Meshech and Tubal: These peoples were located in ancient Anatolia or Asia Minor, present-day Turkey. These names are mentioned as sons of Japheth (Gen. 10:2; 1 Chr. 1:5).

32:28, 29 Ezekiel switches suddenly to the second person singular—**you**—as a wake-up call or reminder to Pharaoh, the representative of Egypt. **Yes** is an emphatic use of the conjunction otherwise translated as "and."

32:30 The **princes of the north** are lands north of Israel such as Tyre and Sidon in Phoenicia. The **Sidonians** were from Sidon, a seaport on the coast about 30 miles north of Tyre (27:8).

32:31, 32 Pharaoh: Now the message (vv. 17–32) comes full circle. The point is that Egypt and Pharaoh will die like the other nations at the hand of the living God, who judges every nation with justice.

33:1–11 This passage is concerned with Ezekiel's responsibility as a watchman as it relates to the nation's depravity and captivity: (1) his call and culpability (vv. 1–6); (2) his commission (vv. 7–9); and, (3) his concluding words of conviction (vv. 10, 11).

33:1–6 The watchman is not responsible for the consequences of disobedience if he faithfully sounds the warning as God has instructed him.

33:1, 2 The **children of your people** refers to fellow Israelites in exile with Ezekiel, now including the people of Judah deported to Babylon after Nebuchadnezzar's third invasion.

33:3–9 Ezekiel's duty as a **watchman** is defined. Compare also the responsibility of the elders of the church in the NT to "watch" (Acts 20:31; Heb. 13:17; 1 Pet. 5:1–4).

33:10 pine away: This phrase means to rot, waste, or dwindle.

33:11–20 In punishing Israel, God was being faithful to the covenant stipulations. This covenant had been approved by the Israelites. They had agreed to its commands and accepted the consequences of breaking them, corporately and individually (5:8–17; 12:15, 16; 16:60, 61; 18:19–32; 20:5; Ex. 19:1–9; Deut. 27). God presents His rationale in these verses for deciding who would be rewarded with life and who would suffer death: He would save those who repent and turn to Him, but would condemn those who trust in themselves and do evil. After presenting His rationale, God declares that His judgment is just and fair—certainly more just than the practices of the Israelites.

33:21–48:35 The final, large collection of messages in Ezekiel communicates comfort and consolation to the exiles in Babylon following the shock of the destruction of Jerusalem. Until Jerusalem had fallen, Ezekiel's message was predominantly negative, insisting that the city would be destroyed. But after news about that event came (33:21), God's message immediately turned to hope: hope for a new leadership (ch. 34), a new spirit (chs. 36, 37) a new victory (chs. 38, 39), and a new temple (chs. 40—48).

33:21, 22 In January 585 B.C., Ezekiel received the news that Jerusalem had been taken. The city had been under siege by Nebuchadnezzar and the Babylonians for two and a half years (2 Kin. 25:1–10). These two verses introduce six oracles (33:23—39:29). Ezekiel received a message from **the LORD** and reported it to the exiles in Babylon.

33:23 Ezekiel's introductory formula—identical or similar to this verse—marks the beginning of the messages received from **the LORD** in this section of the book (33:21—39:29).

33:24 they who inhabit those ruins: This refers to the people who had remained in Jerusalem. They thought they were the remnant—the faithful ones. But they experienced the final siege of the city by King Nebuchadnezzar, for reasons God will give in the following verses.

33:25–29 Ezekiel confronted his people with specific examples of their past and present refusal to obey God's revealed will for their lives (18:6, 10; 22:11; Ex. 20:4, 5, 13–14; Lev. 7:26, 27; 17:10–14; 19:26; Deut. 12:16, 23). Was it not then reasonable that God would punish the present generation by removing them from the land, at least temporarily? The writer of Hebrews, after using the example of Israel's failure to enter the land (ch. 3), admonished the church in a similar way (Heb. 4:1).

33:30–33 This section contrasts the actions and attitudes of the exiles with the life of God's **prophet** Ezekiel. The exiles had claimed to go to the prophet to receive God's revelation, but their behavior was inconsistent with their stated beliefs. Their true desire was for entertainment, not for divine enlightenment. If the fall of Jerusalem failed to awaken them spiritually, nothing would. Yet it certainly would open their eyes to the divine truth of Ezekiel's preaching. In these verses then, God also comforted and consoled Ezekiel. The musical terms may relate to the lyrical nature, and Ezekiel's singing or chanting, of some of these oracles (19:1; 21:9–12).

33:31 hear . . . do not do: See James 1:21–25 for another condemnation of those who hear God's word but do not put it into practice.

34:1–31 In this section, God fingers the failures of Israel's leaders (vv. 1–6) and then forcasts: (1) their end (vv. 7–10); (2) His own shepherding style (vv. 11–16), which is marked by condemnation (vv. 17–19) and salvation (vv. 20–24); and, (3) a covenant of peace and prosperity (vv. 25–31).

34:1–6 The **shepherds of Israel** is a metaphor for Israel's political rulers, but it could include spiritual leaders also (even kings were supposed to be spiritual examples). The shepherds were accused of forsaking the key feature of godly leadership: selfless, sacrificial service (Is. 52:13—53:12; Matt. 23:11; Mark 10:45; Luke 22:24–30; Acts 20:17–38; Rom. 12:1–5; Phil. 2:1–11; 1 Tim. 3:1–7; 1 Pet. 2:18–25; 5:1–4). The results of self-serving leadership for Israel are seen in vv. 5, 6. **there was no shepherd:** This means that having leaders who seek to be served, rather than to serve, is tantamount to having no leader at all; therefore, the people of Israel were like sheep without a shepherd (Matt. 9:36). They were aimless—**wandered**—and easily attacked—**became food. Scattered** alluded to Israel's deportations and dispersion among the nations.

34:7–10 did not feed My flock: The crimes of Israel's leaders come under review before their punishment is pronounced.

34:11–16 Compare the Lord's persistent shepherding and guiding of His people with the faithlessness of Israel's leaders in v. 6 (vv. 25–31; Jer. 23:1–6; John 10:1–30). See also Ps. 23, where similar ideas pertain to God's shepherding of the individual rather than corporate Israel. The **cloudy and dark day** was the day Jerusalem fell (30:1–5; Zeph. 1:15). It may also speak of the future day of deliverance when God will **seek out** His **sheep** (36:16–36). Israel, though guilty and misguided, would eventually be rescued by the divine Good Shepherd and restored to the promised land (chs. 33—39).

34:17–22 The **rams and goats** were the leaders of Israel who had failed to lead properly. They had used their positions of power to their own advantage and to the disadvantage of the people.

34:23, 24 The change from the pronoun **I** to **he** in this verse indicates that God would continue operating as the Chief Shepherd through this chosen future ruler from the Davidic line. He is the Messiah—God's only Son and His **servant.**

34:25–31 The exiles were encouraged through this promise of a **covenant of peace** (37:26–28; 38:11–13; 39:25–29; Is. 54:10), which was characterized by these promises: (1) security from foreign aggressor nations, the **wild beasts;** (2) **showers of blessing,** meaning productivity and prosperity; and, (3) the cer-

---

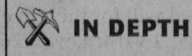 **IN DEPTH** | **Shepherds**

Throughout the Bible, the image of the shepherd is important. From David, the shepherd boy who became the first king of Israel, to Jesus Christ, who said of Himself, "I am the good shepherd" (John 10:11), the shepherd represents one who loves and cares for his flock just as a leader or ruler cares for those under his charge.

Some characteristics of a good shepherd include feeding the flock, tending the weak and sick, searching for the lost, guiding with love, gathering and protecting the sheep, and giving one's best to them. On the other hand, a bad shepherd is more concerned about feeding himself, worrying about his own health, guiding with a heavy hand, abandoning or scattering his flock, and keeping the best for himself.

It's easy to see in these comparisons why the Scriptures often exhort leaders to be shepherds to their people. A good leader is concerned that the people's physical needs are being met and that care is provided for the sick and injured. A true leader looks for those who have fallen away. He leads like a shepherd by providing direction and correction, not with a fist but with a loving hand. A good leader protects those under his care and does not leave them to the wolves—to those who lead them astray. And finally, a good leader gives of himself to those under his charge. He cares about them and their well-being.

Because Jesus called Himself the Good Shepherd, it's clear that He is the One about whom Ezekiel prophesied. He is the One who searches after His followers (34:11), saves them (34:12), guides them (34:13), and supplies their needs (34:14; John 10). Jesus' self-sacrificing life provides the perfect blueprint for making a good shepherd and leader.

tainty that **the LORD** is Israel's God and desires reunion with His people and a lasting relationship built on a new covenant (Jer. 31:31–34; Heb. 8:6).

35:1, 2 Mount Seir is Edom (v. 15; 25:8; Gen. 36:30; 2 Chr. 20:10). It was the rugged and mountainous area south of the Dead Sea inhabited by the descendants of Esau. The enmity between Esau and Jacob began with the selling of his birthright for a mess of pottage. However, he had been a rebel at heart before the incident. Edom's hatred against Israel continued until Jerusalem's destruction.

35:3, 4 God reveals the nature and the purpose of His judgment on Edom (**Seir**, v. 2). These verses are poetry and perhaps were used as a song.

35:5 at the time of their calamity: This refers to how Edom took advantage of the people of Judah during and after the Babylonian invasion (Obad. 11–14).

35:6–9 Having stated why Edom deserved judgment, Ezekiel explained how the nation would be punished. The punishment would include widespread death and unrelieved destruction (Is. 34:6–8; 63:1–6; Jer. 49:7–13; Obad. 18).

35:10 A second reason for God's revenge on Edom is given, in addition to that in v. 5—Edom expected to take over Judah and Israel after their destruction by the Babylonians. **These two nations** refers to Israel and Judah (37:15–28).

36:1–7 The land of Israel itself was addressed—**the mountains**—because the nations desired to own it and, in seeking possession, destroyed it physically and defamed it verbally. Israel was termed **the ancient heights** because of the hill country central to its geography. God is glorified and the exiles comforted by the following: (1) exposing the crimes of the enemies of His nation; (2) exonerating His land from false charges (vv. 13–15); and, (3) executing judgment and justice against the foreign nations. **Edom:** This nation was singled out because of its long history of animosity toward Israel (35:5). The **rest of the nations** were the others who in some way had mistreated Israel and thus received a sentence of judgment (chs. 25—32).

36:8, 9 they are about to come: This was spoken to the land, picturing it as eagerly awaiting the quick return of its rightful and most respectful owners. The first return from exile would come under the Persian king Cyrus, about fifty years later (538 B.C.).

36:10, 11 This restoration would involve **all the house of Israel.**

36:12–14 My people Israel: Despite all their sinfulness, which the book has taken enor-

mous pains to detail and describe, the nation was still referred to as the people of God. They would finally and forever take possession of their land, symbolized by the mountains and the central hills of Palestine, which are personified as **you** in this verse.

36:15, 16 The mountains addressed as **you** would no longer **cause** the **nation to stumble,** for God would make the nation secure from foreign armies. God Himself would reestablish the nation and place His prince on its throne (34:24).

36:17 like the uncleanness of a woman: The uncleanness of the blood of menstruation (not the woman herself) was compared to the past behavior of Israel in Canaan (18:6; 22:10; Lev. 12:2–5; 15:19–30).

36:18 Israel had defiled God's territorial gift in two main ways: (1) The nation had **shed** innocent people's **blood.** (2) The nation had worshiped **idols** by mixing the true worship of the Lord God with involvement in the idolatrous and immoral practices of pagan religions.

36:19 God **judged them according to their ways.** Israel had been hypocritical and unholy; they had not separated themselves or made themselves distinct from the pagan world around them (v. 18). God had given His people the promised land as a place where they could show the world the difference it makes to follow the true God (Deut. 7:1–11). They failed to follow God, so He forced them out of the land. Through either their obedience or their disobedience, God would demonstrate to the watching world His personality, power, and plans.

36:20, 21 The most tragic outcome of Israel's sin (vv. 18, 19) was that the nation **profaned** God's **holy name.** Defeat and dispersion, especially in the ancient world, were negative reflections on the character (or the *name*, see 20:9) of a nation's god. God's reputation as wholly set apart from other so-called gods in power and purpose was compromised by Israel's refusal to trust in His ways, whether in their own land or in exile. To rescue His holy reputation and His rebellious people, God remained faithful to His promises in the Mosaic covenant.

36:22–32 This section concerns the restoration of God's people to the promised land The same features and format of restoration seen in Deut. 29:1—30:10 also appear here: (1) preservation/restoration (vv. 22–24); (2) purification (v. 25); (3) regeneration/empowerment (vv. 26, 27); and, (4) abundant provision and production (vv. 28–30).

36:22–24 The preview of the return to the **land** in the Mosaic covenant is related to the promise of perpetual—but not necessarily uninterrupted—possession of the land of Canaan in the Abrahamic covenant (Gen. 12:1–3; 13:14–18; 15:12–21; Hos. 3:4).

36:25 Sprinkle clean water on you symbolizes cleansing from sin (v. 17; 11:18; 37:23; Jer. 33:8). This is God's forgiveness based on a blood atonement (Ex. 12:22; Lev. 14:4–7, 51; Num. 19:14–22; Ps. 51:7; Zech. 13:1; 1 Cor. 6:11; Heb. 10:22.).

36:26, 27 The ritual of purification from sin would be empty and meaningless apart from true repentance and the regenerating and empowering work of the Holy **Spirit** on the inner spirit of individuals. God would not only restore the people physically to the land, but would restore them spiritually, by giving them a **new heart** and **new spirit** to help them follow Him and do His will. (11:19–20; 18:31; 37:14; 39:29; Jer. 31:31–34; Joel 2:28, 29; Acts 2:17, 18; Rom. 7:7–8:11; 2 Cor. 3:3–18; Heb. 8:6—10:39.)

36:28–30 you shall be My people: See vv. 1–15; 34:29. The purpose of the Mosaic covenant would finally be realized (Deut. 26:16–19; 29:13; 30:8). The Israelites would become a people dedicated to God's ways.

36:31, 32 These verses restate the reasons

for the planned restoration and renewal of God's people. The restoration from the Exile would recover God's glorious reputation among the nations and erase the guilt of the Israelite's sin. This is all a product of God's favor on the Israelites—even though they had done nothing to merit such mercy.

36:33–35 The garden of Eden is mentioned here to suggest beauty, fertility, and productivity so great that people would be reminded of the "garden eastward in Eden" (Gen. 2:8; contrast 28:13).

36:36–38 Like a flock . . . flocks of men: Animals offered for sacrifice had to be free from any observable impurity or disfigurement. The returned people of God will be living sacrifices (Rom. 12:1, 2), pure and unblemished. **I am the LORD:** This is the constant refrain of Ezekiel; God would make Himself known as the one true God in both His judgment and His restoration of His people.

37:1–14 In this vision of the dry bones God reviews the method and and means of restoring and rebuilding His nation in their land. The vision illustrates the blessing and security promised in the covenant of peace and the new

---

✓ IN COMPARISON   The Visions of Ezekiel

Vision	Reference	Significance
God	1:1–28	Ezekiel is called, commissioned, and empowered with an overwhelming vision of divine glory.
Abominations in the temple	8:1–18	Ezekiel is transported to Jerusalem where he sees pagan idols in the temple and Israelites worshiping these false gods. God reveals His anger to Ezekiel over such sinful behavior.
People slain in Jerusalem	9:1–11	Ezekiel witnesses a violent vision in which Israelites of all ages are judged and killed because of their rebelliousness and idolatry.
The temple and the cherubim	10:1–22	Ezekiel watches God's glory and the mysterious cherubim deport from the temple because of the sinfulness of the people.
Twenty-five wicked rulers	11:1–12	Ezekiel is transported to the East Gate where he sees twenty-five Israelite leaders plotting evil. He condemns them for their evil ways.
Valley of the dry bones	37:1–14	Ezekiel is transported to a valley where he sees dry, bleached bones come together, recover flesh, and come to life. This vision depicts God's power and promise to restore and revive a dead people.
The temple	40:1—43:10	Ezekiel sees a detailed vision of a new temple and the return of the Lord. This vision encourages the Israelites that God will return to bless His people.

covenant. In vv. 1–6, God introduces the vision and instructs the prophet; in vv. 7–10, Ezekiel interacts with the vision; and in vv. 11–14, God interprets the vision.

37:1, 2 The wording recalls the past visionary experiences of Ezekiel (1:1, 3; 2:2; 3:12, 14; 8:1, 3, 7) though the word *vision* is not employed in these verses. **bones:** Not only do the bones speak about death, indeed about many deaths, but for bones to be left in the open was an indignity and indecency according to Jewish custom. To leave bodies unburied until the bones were exposed was unthinkable.

37:3 You know: The prophet placed his faith completely in the living God. Ordinarily, one would say "no" to the question God posed. But Ezekiel did not limit God; he knew the Almighty could make bones live.

37:4 Prophesy to these bones: Ezekiel's prophecies had often been directed to people as deaf as these old, dry bones.

37:5 The word rendered **breath** is translated in other places as *wind* or *Spirit*. The breath sent by God into the lifeless bodies symbolizes the Holy Spirit (v. 14), who brings renewal, regeneration, and rebirth (vv. 6, 9; John 3:5–8; 6:44; 7:37–39; 16:5–15; Rom. 8:9–11).

37:6 you shall live: This passage is not about resurrection from physical death, but rebirth from spiritual death brought about by divine power. Psalm 87 is another text in the Hebrew Scriptures that speaks about spiritual rebirth. The point of Jesus' words to Nicodemus in John 3:1–16 was that he should have known and understood the concept of a second birth.

37:7, 8 The dramatic **noise** and then coming **together** of the bones with new flesh must have been chilling and thrilling to the prophet. This was a prophetic portrayal of the rebirth of Israel (Rom. 9–11).

37:9 The Hebrew word rendered **breath** is the same as the one translated **winds**. It can also be translated "spirit."

37:10 an exceedingly great army: The dead bones in the valley (vv. 1, 2) must have looked like the aftermath of a horrible military defeat in which there were no survivors even to bury the dead. But now the army **stood upon their feet.**

37:11–15 The **bones** symbolize the **whole house of Israel.** This identification picks up on imagery already used: (1) those identified as **dry** or spiritually dead (vv. 2–5); (2) those identified as despondent and dejected, with no apparent **hope** of being "resurrected" as the people of the living God; and, (3) those described as disassembled and dispersed before being rejoined and rebuilt (vv. 6–10). The major thrust of this passage is the coming spiritual rebirth of God's chosen people through the agency of His Spirit (vv. 15–28; 36:22–32). The spiritual rebirth would miraculously revive and restore human beings to what God had intended them to be in the beginning. The same body-breath sequence occurs in the creation of Adam (Gen. 2:7).

37:16 a stick: This is Ezekiel's final symbolic drama employing an object (4:1, 3, 9; 5:1).

37:17–22 Many citizens of the northern kingdom had been carried into exile by the Assyrians nearly 150 years before. Yet some of their descendants too would join in the return, when the two nations again would become **one**.

37:22 mountains of Israel: This phrase represents the promised land (36:1–7, 12). The **one king** refers to the future ruler, the promised Messiah, also called Shepherd, Servant, and Prince (vv. 24, 25; 7:27; 34:11–31; John 10).

37:23 The Hebrew word translated **dwelling places** is *backsliding* in other ancient manuscripts. In Hebrew, the two words differ in the placement of one letter.

37:24, 25 The title **David My servant** refers to the Messiah and King who would come from David's line to save Israel (v. 22; 2 Sam. 7:8–16).

37:26–28 The Lord had made an **everlasting covenant** with Abraham, the nation of Israel, and David (16:60, 61; Gen. 9:16; 17:7; Num. 25:12, 13; 2 Sam. 7:13, 16; 23:5; Jer. 32:40). **My sanctuary in their midst:** The sanctuary or holy place of the living God is His dwelling place among His people (Zeph. 3:15–18). **My tabernacle:** This term meaning "dwelling place" is a synonym for *sanctuary*. Both can be used of God's dwelling in the midst of His people in the wilderness. Here they point to the future dwelling of the living God in the midst of His people **forevermore.** We may also compare the use Paul makes of these verses in 2 Cor. 6:16.

38:1, 2 Son of man is a title for Ezekiel emphasizing his humanity, even though his message was from God. The proper names in this prophecy do not have to be specifically identified for an understanding of the main message. The term **Gog** appears in only one other place in the OT (1 Chr. 5:4), but not in reference to the same person (compare Rev. 20:8). The term could be a name or a title. **Magog** (or the "land of Gog"; Gen. 10:2; 1 Chr. 1:5) is usually understood to be an area near the Black Sea or the Caspian Sea. In Gen. 10:2, Magog is one of the sons of Japheth, whose descendants occupied lands from Spain to Asia Minor, the islands of the Mediterranean to southern Russia. Some connect Magog with the Scythians. **Rosh:** There have been some expositors in recent years who have argued that the word Rosh means "Russia." However, this is highly unlikely, for usually the Hebrew word means "head" or "chief." The phrase could be read "the chief prince of Meshech and Tubal." Concerning **Meshech** and **Tubal** we also have no knowledge. Geographically, these last two are thought to be near Magog. All that is known is that Gog, from Magog, was the leader over two or three regions or countries located near the Caspian or Black seas.

38:3, 4 God is sovereign over the invasion (vv. 14–17). **hooks into your jaws:** Here Gog is portrayed as a huge animal, perhaps a crocodile, that will be controlled by hooks. **horses, and horsemen:** When the biblical prophets

(Heb. *gog*) (38:2; 39:1) Strong's #1463: Ezekiel prophesied God's judgment against "Gog, a prince of the land of Magog" (38:2). The land of Magog is named with Meshech and Tubal, regions near Asia Minor (38:2; Gen. 10:2). But more than as a specific person and territory, Ezekiel uses Gog and Magog as a metaphor for vast armies invading Israel from the north in the end times (38:8). They oppose God and seek to destroy His people Israel, but God promises to deliver them (38:14–23). In the Book of Revelation, Gog and Magog become symbolic names for evil nations deceived by Satan and opposed to God and the kingdom of Christ (Rev. 20:8).

speak of battles in the distant future, they use descriptions of weaponry and tactics known to them ("sword" in v. 8; "bow arrows" in 39:3).

38:5, 6 Nations will ally with Gog from all directions: from the east—**Persia;** south—**Ethiopia;** west—**Libya;** and north—**Gomer.** The people of Gomer were the Cimmerians, a people from what is now southern Russia. **Togarmah** was near the Black Sea (Gen. 10:3; 1 Chr. 1:6).

38:7–9 dwell safely: This phrase (vv. 11, 14) indicates that the Israel of this passage is secure; the nation is not safe from attack, but it is safe from defeat. The time of the invasion is suggested by two temporal phrases—**After many days . . . In the latter years**—and the overall context. The second phrase appears only here in the OT. The first phrase usually denotes an indefinite time period, sometimes extending

into the distant future or the end times (Dan. 8:26). See also v. 16, where "the latter days" is used, a phrase that frequently points to messianic times or to the times when Israel is regathered. From Ezekiel's viewpoint, he was predicting a time in the very distant future—the *end times.* Unless the passage refers to spiritual warfare, the invasion of Israel and the subsequent time of confident and carefree peace are still future events.

38:10–13 Gog's **evil plan** will be to attack an unsuspecting, unprepared, and peaceful people in **unwalled villages. I will go up** demonstrates that Gog will decide to attack Israel even though God foresees, predicts, and controls Gog's evil actions. On **Sheba, Dedan . . . Tarshish,** see 25:13; 27:12, 15, 22. **Young lions** represent their rulers; however, a few ancient versions translate the Hebrew as "villages."

38:14–17 On **far north,** see v. 2. **riding on horses:** In early biblical history, horses were not ridden in battle, but were used to pull chariots (v. 4). **may know Me, when I am hallowed in you, O Gog:** These words show that God is determined to bring glory to His name in this unusual battle and even in this evil person. The question **are you he** suggests that previous prophets had foretold Gog's invasion. The prophecies in mind could be general references to a time when enemies of God and His people would be defeated (v. 21; Deut. 30:7; Is. 26:20, 21; Jer. 30:18–24; Hag. 2:20–23; Zech. 14:12–15).

38:18–23 These verses speak about God defending His nation against Gog and his army with supernatural and earthshaking methods. Unusually strong language concerning the wrath of God is found in these verses. The piling up of intense phrases indicates more than an "ordinary" future battle. **fire . . . brimstone:** A rare phrase, reserved only for the greatest catastrophes (Gen. 19:24 when a similar phrase is used for the destruction of Sodom). This judgment would rival the magnitude of the judgment Sodom experienced. **Then they shall know:** This terrible battle will reveal God's might to the entire world and His concern for His people (39:6).

39:1–3 I will knock . . . out: This pictures God fighting for His people (38:21).

39:4, 5 mountains . . . open field: The rout will be total; there will be no place for the enemies of God to flee for safety.

39:6, 7 Fire from the Lord often refers to lightning bolts (1 Kin. 18:38). **they shall know:** There is a significant emphasis in chs. 38; 39 on God's purpose in demonstrating the central truth that He is **the LORD** (vv. 13, 21, 22, 28; 38:16, 23). God's battle with Gog will demonstrate His sovereignty and majesty in His universe.

39:8 Surely it is coming . . . This is the day: The language throughout this section seems unusually grave, and the outcome is announced with unusual solemnity and certainty.

39:9, 10 The **seven years** could be, but does not have to be, equated with the "seven months" of vv. 12, 14. If symbolic, the number would suggest the completeness and finality of the war. The point here is not that modern armored vehicles must be made of some combustible material. What is emphasized is God's utter destruction of Israel's enemies, despite their having soldiers and weapons so vast as to be humanly invincible.

39:11 That day is the time after Gog's defeat. Burial will be necessary for reasons of sanitation as well as consecration (Lev. 5:2, 3; 21:1; Num. 6:6). **East of the sea** is unclear, but because the valley will **obstruct travelers,** a likely candidate is the area of southern Galilee that leads toward the Dead Sea (called the Valley of Jezreel in Josh. 17:16).

39:12 cleanse the land: The Law of Moses prescribed the sacrifice of a heifer to cleanse the land if a murdered person was found in a region (Deut. 21:1–9).

39:13 gain renown: This verse implies that the burial of Gog would become a memorial day to glorify God. Consider the parallel in 1 Cor. 15:24–28, which speaks of the inauguration of the new heavens and the new earth after all of Christ's enemies are defeated.

39:14–16 A complete purification is emphasized (Lev. 11:45). **Hamonah** means "Horde," indicating a multitude of corpses.

39:17–20 A poem or song is addressed to the scavenging birds and beasts who come to the multitude of dead bodies (vv. 14–16). Whether figurative or not, the passage powerfully pictures God's sovereign control over the complete conquest of Israel's future and most ferocious enemies (Rev. 19:11–21). The meal would be a divinely prepared sacrifice served at God's table—the land or **mountains of Israel.** The main course would be the mighty rulers of the earth. The **fatlings of Bashan** portray the might of these men. The herds of Bashan—**rams and lambs, . . . goats and bulls**—were the strongest and most important animals of ancient Israel, fed in the rich pasturelands east of Galilee.

39:21, 22 My glory among the nations: The universal knowledge of the living God of Israel will be based finally on the outcome of the battle described in chs. 38; 39. Ezekiel followed the great theme of biblical theology begun in Gen. 12:3 that the ultimate purpose of God in His choice of Abraham and Sarah was to make His blessings known to all the families of the earth. God will demonstrate His glory both among the nations and among His chosen people Israel.

39:23–29 The Hebrew term rendered **captives** (Jer. 30:3) can also mean "fortunes" (Deut. 30:3).

40:1 This date is about 573 B.C., twelve years since the six messages of hope delivered the year following the fall of Jerusalem (33:21—39:29) and twenty-five years after the deportation of Jehoiachin (1:2; 33:21, 22; chs. 33—39).

40:2 Ezekiel was taken in a vision to a **very high mountain** from which he could see a city to the south. The sight seems somewhat vague, **something like the structure of a city.** Since the temple is there (v. 5), Jerusalem is suggested; but neither the mountain nor the city is named. Such a high mountain north of Jerusalem does not correlate with the geography of Israel, then or now. Mount Hermon, north of Galilee, is possible if the boundaries of the land are understood as extending that far.

40:3–5 The special circumstances of these final visions are noteworthy. Ezekiel saw a messenger with a **bronze** appearance (1:27, 28) who was equipped with tools for measuring. Ezekiel was commissioned to minister the complete revelation to **the house of Israel.** A **cubit** was about 18 inches, or the distance from fingertips to elbow. A **handbreadth,** the width of the hand across the widest part, was approximately three inches. Both a long cubit (a cubit of around 21 inches) and a short cubit (the standard 18 inches) existed. Based on these measurements, the **measuring rod** was six long cubits in length, about 126 inches or 10.5 feet, the height and width of the wall around the temple.

40:6–16 The thresholds of the eastern gate measure 10.5 feet wide; each gate-chamber or guard room is 10.5 by 10.5 feet, separated by a space 8.75 feet wide. The **stairs** apparently lead up to the outer threshold, and the rooms (three on each side) line a walkway to the inner threshold leading to a vestibule (or porch) that is 14 feet wide. The **gateposts** are 3.5 feet square; and the distance across the **gateway** of the outer threshold is 17.5 feet. The distance from the beginning of the gate through the outer threshold is 22.75 feet: 10.5 feet of this being the threshold. A space in front of each guardroom is 1.75 feet wide (21 inches or one long cubit). The overall dimensions of the east gate, and of the two identical north and south gates, are 43.75 by 87.5 feet. The gateposts are 105 feet high. These gates have some similarity to those excavated in Israel from the time of Solomon.

40:17–27 The lower pavement is equal in length to the gateway: 87.5 feet; and the distance between the outer gateway and the corresponding inner gateway (across the pavement) is 175 feet. **chambers:** Rooms, probably for storage or priests' quarters, line the inside of the northern, southern, and eastern walls.

40:28–37 The **archways** are 43.75 feet long by 8.75 feet wide (vv. 8, 9, 14; apparently the porches of the gate systems in the inner court have different dimensions, though these gates are said to be like the others). Also in contrast to the outer gates, these have their porches (vestibules) on the outward side (entrance), where seven steps go up (vv. 22, 26).

40:38–43 Ezekiel observes a room near the entrance of the northern gate of the inner court where animals are slaughtered and washed for sacrificial offerings. These sacrifices point to the ultimate sacrifice: the sacrifice of God's only Son on the Cross once for all. Christ's sacrifice of His own life paid for our sins and provides salvation to all those who believe on Him (Heb. 7:20–28; 9:23–28).

40:44–46 On the inner side (facing the inner court) of the northern and southern inner gateways are rooms for priests whose principal work is singing (1 Chr. 16:4–6; 2 Chr. 29:25–30). Those housed at the northern gate serve at the sacrificial altar. These **sons of Zadok** would be the only Levites permitted to serve God directly (44:15–31). The priests of the southern (inner) gate minister in the temple.

40:47–49 The inner courtyard is 175 feet square. On **altar** and **temple** see chs. 41–43. The width of the entrance—**vestibule**—to the temple sanctuary can be determined: twenty cubits (35 feet) with a three-cubit (5.25 feet) extension of the five-cubit (8.75 feet) **doorposts** on each side, leaving an entrance with a width of fourteen cubits (24.5 feet).

41:1–4 The outer area, the holy place (Ex. 26:33) and the inner area, the **Most Holy Place** (1 Kin. 6:16–20) of the temple itself are described. Overall, the outer room is 70 feet

 **IN DEPTH** | ## Measuring the Future

Ezekiel could be called one of the most visionary prophets. God showed him spiritual insights that still stir the imagination twenty-five centuries later. Like other prophets, Ezekiel's ministry among his people had two distinct phases: condemnation and consolation.

The first thirty-two chapters of Ezekiel catalog the sure and future judgment of God on His own people and seven other nations. Incredibly, though Jerusalem had been defeated and many of her people had been deported, the exiles clung to the vain hope that God would never let His city and temple be destroyed. They missed the point that God's ultimate commitment was to people—not places or buildings. In order to purify and preserve the people, God allowed the devastation of the promised land and the temple itself. Yet God also held responsible those nations that used their temporary domination of Israel as an opportunity to mock the living God. Ezekiel's early messages focused on the coming of God's judgment and the urgent need for repentance.

The last part of Ezekiel represents a sudden change of tone. With the fall of Jerusalem, God's terrible judgment had finally come. The weary and disillusioned exiles had lost all hope. But God filled Ezekiel with a new message. Though all immediate evidence pointed to hopelessness and despair, God invited His people to return to Him and to place their confidence in Him. Whatever their temporary setbacks and suffering, God was still in control. His purposes would win out, and His plans were specific. In fact, His plans were so definite they could be measured. Ezekiel received a vision of the dimensions of a new temple (recorded in 40:1—48:35) to demonstrate that fact.

Many efforts have been made to understand the details of Ezekiel's vision in such a way that the prophecy might be described as fulfilled. However, attempts to do this have failed. Those who eventually returned from exile did not use Ezekiel's plans to rebuild Jerusalem. It is also difficult to interpret this prophecy as a symbolic description of the church in our age. The most confident statement we can make about the vision and its accompanying instructions is that it is a prophecy yet to be fulfilled. At the same time, we can apply these chapters to the present as examples of God's planning, precision, and sovereignty. He maintains control of the events of history. When events seem chaotic, God reminds us to rest in His ability to bring order. Ezekiel's vision of a new temple when the temple in Jerusalem had just been destroyed reassured the exiles: God would create beauty out of ashes. The people in Ezekiel's day needed that vision of hope, and we still need it today.

long by 35 feet wide and has an entrance 17.5 feet wide. The inner **sanctuary** is 35 feet square with an entrance 10.5 feet wide. **Doorposts** for the outer room are 10.5 feet square and for the inner sanctuary 3.5 feet square. Walls on each side of each entrance protrude from the side walls 8.75 and 12.25 feet. The height of the entrance to the inner room is 10.5 feet.

41:5–11 Next the dimensions are given for the **wall** surrounding the **temple.** Its width is 10.5 feet. Running along the inside of the western, northern, and southern walls (but not attached) are three levels of ten rooms (90 total; perhaps these are storerooms), each 7 feet square with an outer wall 8.75 feet thick. They sit on a foundation 10.5 feet high. A space of 35 feet is apparently between these rooms and the priests' **chambers** north and south of the temple (42:1–14). A **terrace** that is 8.75 feet wide is on all three sides.

41:12 Behind the temple, between its western end and the western wall of the outer court is a **building** 122.5 feet wide and 157.5 feet long with walls 8.75 feet thick. Its purpose is not given.

41:13–26 Like the temple, the western building is 175 feet in total length (its inside length plus the width of the walls on each side plus 8.75 multiplied by 2; v. 12). The full width of the eastern side of the temple proper is the same, as is that of the inner courtyard and the courtyard separating the temple and the western building. Various decorations are described in vv. 16–20. Some likely have symbolic meanings (28:13, 14 regarding cherubs), but no explanations are given here. A wooden **altar** (v. 22), the only piece of furniture mentioned in this passage, is 5.25 feet high and 2 feet square (the dimensions of the stone tables of 40:42 and the altar of sacrifice in 43:13–17). The purpose and position of this altar is not known; but it is called **the table that is before the Lord,** to which some compare the altar of incense in the tabernacle (Ex. 37:25–28).

41:23, 24 The **temple** here means the holy place. The **sanctuary** means the Most Holy Place. Each door had **two panels,** but only one panel had to be opened to enter either room.

42:1–14 To the north and south of the courtyard separating the temple and the western building (41:12–14) is a building for the priests 175 feet long and 87.5 feet wide, with three stories (vv. 5, 6) and a door along the length facing the outer courtyard. The entrance has a **walk** 17.5 by 1.75 feet. Mainly the northern building is described, but apparently the southern building is the same or very similar. Parallel to the eastern wall (the width) and its door is a wall 87.5 feet long (vv. 7–9). These are places for certain priests ("sons of Zadok" in 40:46) to eat and change clothes, indicating that the rooms also provide storage facilities for the holy food offerings and priestly garments.

42:15–20 measured it all around: Ezekiel was taken through the eastern gates outside the entire temple and courtyard structure and shown the size of the land area prescribed for the temple complex. Whether **rods** in v. 16 is correct or whether "cubits" is meant is debated by many scholars. Five-hundred rods square is 5,250 feet per side, nearly a mile, which to some seems too large. The cubit is the most frequent measure used to this point, but the rod has been introduced as the standard for measuring the temple (in 40:5 the rod is equated with six cubits). It makes sense that the larger unit should be employed for the greatest dimensions. The large bordering area around the temple complex might be there in order to set it apart and to stress the temple's holiness (43:12).

43:1, 2 came from . . . the east: In 11:23, God's glory had left the temple and gone east over the Mount of Olives as His presence left the city. Here His presence is pictured as returning to the city from the east. See 1:24; 10:4 (compare Rev. 1:15; 14:2; 19:6; 21:11, 23).

43:3–6 I came is "He came" in a few Hebrew

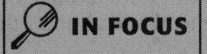 **IN FOCUS** | **"glory"**

(Heb. *kabod*) (43:2; Ex. 24:16; 1 Kin. 8:11) Strong's #3519: This word is derived from a Hebrew verb that is used to describe the weight or worthiness of something. It can refer to something negative. For example, in reference to Sodom, it depicts the severe degree of sin that had reached the point of making that city worthy of complete destruction (Gen. 18:20). But usually the word is used to depict greatness and splendor (Gen. 31:1). The noun form is translated *honor* in some instances (1 Kin. 3:13). God's glory is described in the OT as taking the form of a cloud (Ex. 24:15–18) and filling the temple (1 Kin. 8:11). The appropriate response to God's glory is to reverence Him by bowing before Him, as Ezekiel did (3:23; 43:3).

manuscripts, referring to God's judgment on Jerusalem.

43:7-9 This temple is God's residence from which He will rule and reign over **the children of Israel forever** (37:26–28). The second half of this verse appears to predict an absolute end of the idolatrous and immoral practices of the **house of Israel,** which had taken place around the temple (2 Kin. 23:1–20). **their harlotry:** This is either an allusion to their spiritual adultery in general or, more specifically and literally, to their participation in the religious prostitution of Baal worship (16:15). **carcasses:** This is taken by some as a metaphor ("lifeless idols," Lev. 26:30) because of the context, but it could refer to memorial graves of kings buried near the temple mount (2 Kin. 23:30), perhaps near the royal houses just outside the southern wall (v. 8; 1 Kin. 7:1–12). **high places:** This phrase came to refer to any place of idolatrous worship, whether on a hilltop or not.

43:10-12 God explains to Ezekiel the purpose of revealing the detailed description of the future **temple** (8, 9; 42:15–20; Lev. 20:7; Ps. 11:4; Is. 6:3).

43:13-17 The cubit described here is the long cubit—a **cubit and a handbreadth,** or 21 inches. The altar has a base 1.75 feet (21 inches) wide and high. A rim around the edge of the base is **one span,** or about 9 inches, wide. On top of the base is a lower section 3.5 feet high, having a 1.75-foot ledge. The distance between the smaller and larger ledges is 7 feet. The **altar hearth,** the top section of the altar where the sacrifice is offered, is 7 feet high. The **four horns** are on top of the corners (1 Kin. 1:50, 51). Overall the hearth is 21 feet square. Apparently the middle section is 24.5 feet square with a rim about 10.5 inches wide; and the lower section extends 3.5 feet beyond the middle one, 28 feet square (vv. 14, 16, 17 where—assuming the symmetry of the altar—the middle section extends two cubits beyond the top). The height of the altar is therefore about 11 cubits or 19.25 feet. Assuming an 18cubit square (hearth and middle section in vv. 16–17) and one-cubit-high base, the foundation is 31.5 feet square. **Steps,** previously forbidden for an altar (Ex. 20:26), are necessary for this altar because of the great size of the structure. The huge altar is positioned in the center of the inner court in front of the temple entrance.

43:18, 19 These **ordinances** relate to the cleansing and consecration of the altar. See Ex. 29:36–37; Lev. 8:14–17 regarding the tabernacle altar and 2 Chr. 7:9 for the temple altar.

43:20-27 **Atonement** and **sin offering** suggest purification and cleansing from sin. Because of the sinlessness—**without blemish**—of the sacrifice, the people for whom the sacrifice

is made are declared acceptable before God (v. 27; Ex. 29:14, 16, 36, 37; Lev. 3; 4:12, 21; 5:9; 8:14–17; Heb. 13:10–13).

44:1-3 The **outer gate of the sanctuary** is the eastern gate of the outer court (40:6–16; 43:1) which must remain **shut.** The eastern gate known today as the "Golden Gate" dates from several centuries after Christ. It is walled shut today in accordance with an Islamic tradition. **the prince:** The identity of this prince is unknown. The Hebrew term does not always mean a king or a member of royalty (Gen. 23:6). It is not the Messiah, for 45:22 indicates that this leader must make a sin offering for himself. He may be one of the Zadokite priests (vv. 15, 16).

44:4-9 Ezekiel experiences another awe-inspiring vision of God's glory leading him to bow in worship (1:28–2:1). God demands that His renewed people follow His regulations exactly. He emphasizes the necessity of holiness and righteousness, especially in light of Israel's past **abominations** related to rules regulating who was to enter the temple **sanctuary.** Specifically, they had allowed **foreigners** without evidence of faithfulness to God to serve in the sanctuary (Josh. 9:23–27; Ezra 8:20): these people were **uncircumcised in heart and uncircumcised in flesh.** This was in disobedience to God's commands (Ex. 19:8; Lev. 26:41; Num. 3:10; Deut. 10:16; 30:6; Neh. 13:8; Jer. 4:4; 9:25), but was in conformity with the practices of foreign pagan religions, which God's people had been forbidden to imitate (Ex. 34:12; Deut. 18:9; compare Rom. 12:1, 2).

44:10 See Lev. 21; 22 for a description of the duties of the **Levites.** Unfortunately, during the history of Israel, Levites had not obeyed the commands Moses had given them and had even encouraged idolatry (compare ch. 8; 14:1–11; Deut. 33:8–11; Judg. 17–19).

44:11-14 God explains to Ezekiel why the Levites would be limited to certain types of temple ministry. The Levites (with the exception of the sons of Zadok, v. 15) could not be priests but could be **ministers** (servants or attendants). They could not serve in the inner court or temple, where the **holy things** are located; but they could oversee the general operation of the temple complex.

44:15, 16 The **Levites, the sons of Zadok** were descendants of the priest Zadok in the Levitical line who remained faithful when others did not (1 Sam. 2:27–36; 2 Sam. 8:17; 15:24–29; 1 Kin. 2:26–35; 1 Chr. 6:7, 8, 50–53). While salvation is never earned (Rom. 3; 4; Gal. 2; 3; Eph. 2:8, 9), God does reward faithfulness and righteousness. Here He rewarded His faithful priests and Levites with the opportunity to minister before Him. Responsibility and recognition have to be deserved, but never demanded (1 Sam. 26:23; Matt. 5:12; 25:21–23; Rev. 2:10). Again there is an emphasis on holiness and righteousness. The Zadokites were honored for their special obedience. The **table** is not identified, but could be similar to the wooden altar of 41:22.

44:17–19 These verses speak of holiness as **linen garments** (42:14; Ex. 28:42; 29:37; 30:29; Lev. 6:11, 27; 16:4; 21:10; Hag. 2:12). Common things were to be kept distinct from what was consecrated.

44:20–22 These verses speak of holiness in conduct. These regulations continued practices already prescribed in the Law of Moses (Lev. 10:6, 9; 21:1–6, 7, 10, 14). Their aim was to help the priests avoid conformity to the immoral and idolatrous religious rituals and conduct among the pagan nations. The **priests,** then and in the future, have the responsibility of modeling and maintaining the highest standards of morality, self-control, self-denial, discipline, and obedience to God's will. In Israelite culture, shaving the head indicated mourning (7:16–19), and growing long hair could mean the taking of a special vow (sometimes connected with complete or controlled abstinence from wine; Num. 6:3, 4). The point is the priests' clear separation from the rest of society.

44:23, 24 they shall teach My people: The priests were to demonstrate verbally and visually before the people how to distinguish between what is godly and ungodly. They also served as judges in disputes and debates (22:26; Lev. 10:10, 11; 11:47; Deut. 17:9; 19:7; 21:5; 33:10).

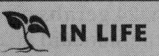 **IN LIFE** | # Holiness—It's Not Just a Place

For many, the word "holy" brings to mind special places such as cathedrals and temples. It would be easy to limit our concept of holiness to such concrete examples, especially when we see so many such cases in the OT. At various times throughout their history, God called the Israelites to dedicate various places (and persons) in a way that would remind God's people that they were His own. Certain monuments, the tabernacle, the temple, and even certain mountains, along with some of the leaders, the priests, and the prophets were designated as "holy," consecrated, or set apart to the Lord.

This pattern was continued in Ezekiel's vision of the new temple, access to which was to be highly restricted (Ezek. 44:1–19). Likewise, a certain "holy district" was to be established in the restored land (45:1–5). So holiness was attached to certain places, but we shouldn't forget that the call to holy living is not confined to one place or another. All of life is to be holy, no matter where one is. Ezekiel pinpoints some practical and even mundane dimensions of holiness:

- Stop the use of violence and oppression (45:9).
- Cease the pattern of evicting people (45:9).
- Restore honest dealing in business, using standards of value that have integrity and can be trusted (45:10–12).
- Donate a percentage of each business transaction to God, whether one is a prince or one of the common people (45:13–17).
- Mark all of life with monthly festivals and celebrations that include everyone (45:18–25).
- Restore the six-day work week, and protect the Sabbath rest, with the prince providing substantially for this observance (46:1–15).
- Follow careful guidelines in the matter of inheritances and boundaries, maintaining fair treatment of aliens and strangers (46:16–18; 47:13–23).
- Provide an area for the common people, for homes and common space (48:15–20).
- Name each of the commercial centers—the exits or gates of the city—after a portion of the citizenry (tribes) (48:30–35).
- Name the city itself "THE LORD IS THERE," reflecting a inclusive view of holiness: everything that goes on there pertains to the Lord (48:35).

All of life is to be holy. One might be more reverent in certain settings and on certain occasions, but one is made neither more nor less holy by entering or exiting a particular place. Christ has already invited us into the most holy place there is, so that we will live as His holy people in everything we do (Heb. 9:11–15; 10:19–25).

44:25-27 This section deals with holiness regarding death among the people (Lev. 21:1-3; Num. 19:11-19; Hag. 2:13). Contact with a dead body was forbidden; however, a partial exception was made for immediate family members. The act still defiled the person, causing ceremonial uncleanness for a certain time. God's concern over purity in practice and procedures is seen in that the priest was to submit to a cleansing ritual and then personally present a sin offering. He was to publicly declare and deal with his own uncleanness, though what he had done was not forbidden. The circumstances that allowed touching a dead body did not overturn its consequences according to the Law. God was preserving the sanctity of His temple and statutes.

44:28-31 These verses explain holiness in the priests' provisions (Lev. 17:5; 22:8; Num. 18:10-13, 20, 23-24; Deut. 10:9; 14:21; Mal. 3:8-12). **I am their possession:** God was to be the priests' possession in all respects; they were not to inherit land or cities. The **dedicated thing** (Lev. 27:21, 28; Num. 18:14; Judg. 11:29-40) was something wholly and irrevocably devoted to God as a sacrificial gift. The giver would be blessed in giving (Acts 20:35). God's laws are governed by His love and goodness, and they are given as guides to holy and healthy living (John 10:10). God is truthful and trustworthy; His codes of conduct are blessings, not burdens (Matt. 11:28-30). They can be followed with confidence because of His revealed character, even though all the specific reasons for His rules are not spelled out.

45:1-5 A distinct—**set apart, holy**—section was to be allocated for God. This area would be divided into two equal sections. One would be the portion for the Zadokites—**priests, the ministers of the sanctuary.** In the center of this part of the holy district is the holy square-mile environs for the temple—**the sanctuary, the Most Holy Place.** The other half of the holy district would be the portion given to the Levites. All this is holy; God owns it. The **twenty chambers** is read "towns to live in" in the Septuagint.

45:6 The **city** is not named, but Jerusalem is most likely. Its allotted property is 25,000 by 5,000 cubits. This area is located **adjacent** to and south of (according to 48:18) the Zadokite district—**the holy section.** See 48:15-19, 30-35.

45:7, 8 The identity of the **prince** is unknown (44:3). But his allotted area is on both sides (east and west) of the **holy district.** He will own this land bordering a tribal territory to the north and south, where the **west** and **east border** suggest respectively the Mediterranean Sea and the Dead Sea or Jordan River. The

prince and God's **princes** of messianic period—in contrast to previous leaders of Israel (11:1-13; 14:1-11; 20-22; 34:1-10)—will not be greedy for riches and real estate but will give the land that remains to the people (48:1-29; contrast the descriptions of the evil behavior of the rulers of Israel in 1 Sam. 8:10-18; 1 Kin. 20; 21; Is. 3:13-23; Mic. 3:1-4; 7:3; Zeph. 3:3).

45:9-11 The merchants were exhorted to use accurate measures of the **ephah** (estimated to be around a bushel) and the **bath** (from six to nine gallons), both defined as **one-tenth of a homer** (five to ten bushels or 60 to 90 gallons). Merchants must not cheat anymore when weighing produce (Lev. 19:35, 36; Amos 8:5; Mic. 6:10-12). God called for an end to dishonesty and deceit; a time is coming when all such scheming will end (vv. 16, 17; 37:15-28).

45:12 Ezekiel also demanded fair weights. The **shekel** weighed about 11.5 grams or four-tenths of an ounce. In Babylon, 24 **gerahs** made one shekel while Ezekiel sets the standard at 20; but 60 shekels made one **mina,** which conforms to the standard prescribed in this verse. In Ezekiel's system this mina is thought to weigh about 1.5 pounds.

45:13-17 These verses describe an **offering** to be given to the prince (v. 7) who, unlike previous rulers, will be just and truthful (v. 8). The prince, in turn, will make offerings to God in order to **make atonement for the house of Israel** (v. 17), symbolizing cleansing from sin (40:38-43). Instructions regarding the temple sacrifices can be found in Ex. 25:2-7; 30:13-15; 35:4-29; 36:2-7; Lev. 1:4; 9:7; 10:17. The Law of Moses also included extended instructions on **feasts** (Lev. 23:1-44; Num. 28; 29).

45:18-20 This is an annual day of purifying the temple sanctuary. In the light of Jesus' death on the cross, the actions of the prince symbolize and emphasize that God has made atonement for all through the sacrifice of the Messiah (vv. 15-17; 18-22). The forgiveness of individual sins is illustrated through daily sin offerings (vv. 23-25). The pronoun *you* in **you shall take** and **you shall do** is singular, while the pronoun in **you shall make atonement** is plural. The prince represents the people in these actions of worship (Lev. 16:15-17, 33, 34; 22:19-21; 2 Chr. 7:1-7; 29:20-24.) The way the **day** is specified suggests an act to be performed annually.

45:21-25 In this passage the feasts of **Passover** and Tabernacles are observed (Ex. 12:1-14; Lev. 23:5-8; 33-43; Num. 28:16-25; 29:12-38). The dates are in relation to the Levitical calendar, the Jewish religious year. The procedures as well are similar to those of the Mosaic system. These feasts commemorate God's faithfulness to His promises.

46:1-8 The prince shall enter: What the

rituals signified under the Law was fulfilled by the Messiah. At the time of this prince, certain promises were being fulfilled and the covenants consummated in the messianic age (40:6–16, 28–37; 43:18–27; 44:1–2; Ex. 20:8–11). **hin:** This was a liquid measure about one-sixth of a bath, approximately one gallon (4:11; Ex. 30:24; Lev. 19:36).

46:9–11 the people of the land: This phrase describes the citizens of the promised land during this messianic period (v. 3; 12:18, 19; 22:29; 39:13; 45:16, 22). The prescribed protocol was probably to ensure an orderly procession and service. Such regulations would be needed on the special feast days due to the participation of large numbers of people.

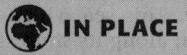 **IN PLACE**

Ezekiel's Vision of the Restoration of the Land

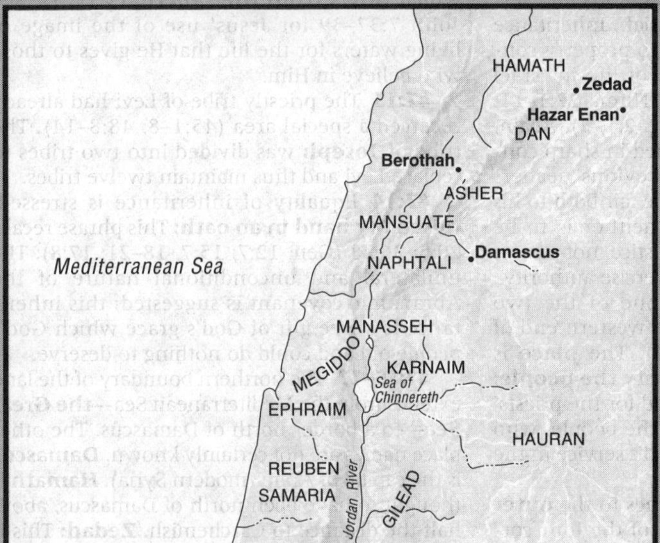

HAMATH
Zedad
Hazar Enan
DAN
Berothah
ASHER
MANSUATE
NAPHTALI   Damascus
Mediterranean Sea
MANASSEH
MEGIDDO
KARNAIM
Sea of Chinnereth
EPHRAIM
HAURAN
REUBEN
SAMARIA   GILEAD
Jordan River
JUDAH
AMMON
Jerusalem
BENJAMIN
Dead Sea
SIMEON
PHILISTIA
MOAB
ISSACHAR
ZEBULUN   Tamar
EDOM
GAD
Meribah of Kadesh
—N—
0   60 Mi.
0   60 Km.

© 1996 Thomas Nelson, Inc.

The boundaries of the restored nation of Israel approach the boundaries of the land as it was under David and Solomon. However, the area east of the Jordan—Gilead and Transjordan—will not be a part of this new inheritance. It was not part of the land that had been promised.

The tribes are not arranged as they were historically when the land was divided under Joshua (Josh. 13–19). God will do something new in the restoration. The central portion of the land around Jerusalem will be set apart for religion and government. To the north of the central district are seven tribes—Dan, Asher, Naphtali, Manasseh, Ephraim, Reuben, and Judah. To the south are the remaining five tribes—Benjamin, Simeon, Issachar, Zebulun, and Gad.

46:12 The preparation and presentation of this offering is the one exception to 44:1–3 (vv. 1, 2). The **voluntary** or freewill offering was given beyond what was required (Lev. 22:17–30).

46:13 shall daily make: This is a change from the provisions in the Law (Num. 28:3–8; 2 Kin. 16:15).

46:14 perpetual ordinance: This is a change from the provisions in the Law (Num. 28:5). God's people cannot be reminded too often of God's provisions for them; nor can they thank Him too much or too frequently.

46:16–18 The language of this passage speaks clearly and concretely about descendants, servants, and property, so a spiritual or allegorical meaning for this passage is difficult to defend (44:3). Likewise, the **prince** has sons and servants, so he cannot be the Messiah. Inheritance laws and family claims related to property continue as an important feature of life in Israel (Lev. 25:8–15, 23–34; 27:24; Num. 27:1–11; 33:54; 34:18; Josh. 14—21; Mic. 2:1, 2). Again, the prince's character is described in sharp contrast to many of Israel's previous leaders (34:1–10). This civil ruler is to be fair both to his children and to his subjects; neither is to be turned out of his inheritance. Justice, not power, should be the goal of all who exercise authority.

46:19, 20 The setting is one of the two buildings for the priests on the western end of the temple complex (42:1–14). The **place** is something like a kitchen. **Sanctify the people:** Food from the sacrifices reserved for the priests' use was not even to approach the people, who had not been consecrated to God's service in the same way the priests had been.

46:21–24 The setting switches to the **outer court** (40:17–19), where each of the four corners has an enclosed kitchen court. These kitchens are distinguished from those for the priests (vv. 19, 20); these belong to the Levites: **ministers of the temple,** see 44:11–14.

47:1 He is the "man" of v. 3 (40:3; 46:19).

47:2–6 One thousand cubits is approximately 1,750 feet (40:3–5). Four times the man uses the measuring **line** to mark off this distance across the stream, which progressively gets deeper from ankle depth, to knees, to waist, and finally too deep and wide to cross except by swimming. The water flows eastward from the south side of the temple.

47:7–12 The water becomes a river of healing and the source of abundant life for everything and everyone (Gen. 2:8–10; Zech. 14:8; John 4:13, 14; 10:10; Rev. 22:1, 2). It continues flowing southeast: through the dry, rocky region between Jerusalem and the Dead Sea— that is, the Arabah or **eastern region**—and south along the Jordan valley and the Jordan

Rift, as far as to the Dead Sea. When it **reaches the sea** (the Dead Sea), the salty sea becomes fresh and able to sustain life so that fishermen can fish there: **its waters are healed.** This is an amazing picture—the Dead Sea is the saltiest body of water (approximately 25 percent saline content) and is presently unable to support life. It is also the lowest point on earth, with its surface 1,300 feet below sea level and the water itself 1,300 feet deep. The living water that God will provide has immeasurable power to renew, restore, and resurrect life. This sea which is dead will teem with life all along its shores— **from En Gedi to En Eglaim.** Great volumes and variety of vegetation, everlasting and perpetually productive, will result from this river which **flows from the sanctuary** (v. 1). See John 7:37–39 for Jesus' use of the image of living waters for the life that He gives to those who believe in Him.

47:13 The priestly tribe of Levi had already received a special area (45:1–8; 48:8–14). The tribe of **Joseph** was divided into two tribes to replace Levi and thus maintain twelve tribes.

47:14 Equality of inheritance is stressed. **raised My hand in an oath:** This phrase recalls 20:5; 36:28 (Gen. 12:7; 15:7, 18–21; 17:8). The unilateral and unconditional nature of the Abrahamic covenant is suggested; this inheritance is a free gift of God's grace which God's people did and could do nothing to deserve.

47:15–17 The northern boundary of the land extends from the Mediterranean Sea—**the Great Sea**—to a border north of Damascus. The other place names are not certainly known. **Damascus** is the capital of Aram (modern Syria). **Hamath** is thought to have been north of Damascus, about half the distance to Carchemish. **Zedad:** This is believed to have been east of Hamath and Hazar Enan (the eastern point of this border). **Hauran** appears to be an Israelite region east of the Jordan River and north of Gilead.

47:18 The eastern border runs from the Damascus region southwest through Hauran to and along the Jordan River (Num. 34:10–12). **eastern . . . sea:** The Dead Sea.

47:19 The southern border goes from the eastern side of the Dead Sea to **Tamar** (a town to the southwest) to the **waters of Meribah by Kadesh** (Num. 20:13, 24; 27:14) **along the brook** (of Egypt; the Wadi el-Arish) and on to the Mediterranean Sea (Num. 34:3–5; 1 Kin. 8:65). This line runs from the Dead Sea southwest across the Negev to the Brook of Egypt, a river bed in west Sinai.

47:20 The western border runs along the coastline of the **Great Sea** (the Mediterranean Sea) north to a point directly west of Hamath (Num. 34:6; Rev. 21:1).

47:21–23 The treatment of **strangers** or aliens in the land is considered. Non-Israelites who married and settled within the Jewish communities were to be accepted as native Israelites, qualified to share in the territorial inheritance of whatever tribe they joined (Lev. 19:34; Is. 56:1–8).

48:1–7 From the northern district south to the priestly portions, the tribes in order are **Dan, Asher, Naphtali, Manasseh, Ephraim, Reuben,** and **Judah.** Each district is bordered north and south by another tribe. The east-west borders for each are the same as in 47:18, 20. The tribes resulting from the offspring of Jacob and his wives' servants are given lands farthest from the most holy areas (45:1–8), while the descendants of Jacob's wives occupy a central position (Gen. 35:23–26). The tribe of Judah is most favored, for it produced the Davidic and messianic line (37:18–28; Gen. 49:8–10; Is. 11). Historically, the tribe of Dan had occupied the northern limits of the land (Judg. 20:1). Its idolatry was well known—Jeroboam had placed a golden calf there (2 Kin. 10:29).

48:8–15 The district has the **city** in its **center** surrounded by housing, farming, and grazing lands for general use.

48:16–22 shall belong to the prince: See 45:7, 8. The tribal territories of Judah and Benjamin are immediately north and south of the **holy district** (vv. 1–7, 20). **Benjamin** like Judah is favored (Gen. 35:24).

48:23–29 Continuing southward in order are the tribal allotments for **Benjamin, Simeon,**

Issachar, Zebulun, and **Gad.** Gad is the southern border of the land.

48:30, 31 The gates are named after the original twelve **tribes** (Rev. 21:12, 13). The gate for Joseph represents the two tribes of Manasseh and Ephraim (v. 32; 47:13). The northern gates are **Reuben** (the firstborn), **Judah** (the tribe of the messianic line), and **Levi** (the priestly tribe)—all descendants of Jacob and Leah (Gen. 35:23).

48:32 On the eastern side the gates represent **Joseph, Benjamin,** and **Dan.** While the first two were children of Jacob and Rachel, the third was the child of Jacob and Rachel's servant Bilhah (Gen. 35:24, 25).

48:33 South of the city, the three other offspring of Jacob and Leah have gates named for them: **Simeon, Issachar,** and **Zebulun** (Gen. 35:23).

48:34 The three western gates are named after **Gad** and **Asher**—the sons of Jacob and Leah's maidservant Zilpah—and **Naphtali**—a son of Jacob and Bilhah (Gen. 35:25, 26).

48:35 The designated name for this city from **that day** is **THE LORD IS THERE** (Is. 60:14; 62:2–4, 12; Jer. 3:17; 33:15, 16). This return of the Lord and the regathering of His people is predicted by Ezekiel in 11:17; 20:33–44; 37:15–28; 39:21–29. The Lord was forced to depart from the city and the temple because of the wickedness of the Israelites (8:6; 10:18). But here, Ezekiel foresees the return of God in all His glory to His people, His temple, and His land.

The Book of

Daniel

■

*I*N 626 B.C., NABOPOLASSAR BECAME KING OF Babylon and altered the course of ancient history. He quickly overthrew the domination of long-standing rival Assyria, and by the time of his death in 605 B.C. he had eliminated the Assyrian Empire and swallowed it into what became known as the Neo-Babylonian or Chaldean Empire. This course of events had significant implications for Judah, the surviving

remnant of the nation of Israel. Judah had been largely under Assyrian domination from about 670 B.C., but now found itself serving a new master. In the same year as Nabopolassar's death, King Jehoiakim of Judah became a vassal of Nebuchadnezzar, the son of Nabopolassar (2 Kin. 24:1). Nebuchadnezzar brought his father's empire to even greater heights, eventually deporting many Jews to Babylon.

Daniel lived in the midst of all these momentous events. What direct impact he had on the community of exiles cannot be known, but he was a force for good as far as the Babylonians were concerned. Daniel was a close confidant of Nebuchadnezzar throughout the Babylonian king's reign (605–562 B.C.). Later Daniel served with equal distinction Cyrus, the enlightened Persian ruler who conquered Babylon. One of the first policies Cyrus implemented after subduing Babylon was to allow the Jews to return to their homeland and rebuild their way of life. It is more than likely that Daniel had some influence on Cyrus's decision. The Book of Daniel is a testimony to how God works out His purposes through His servants even in the courts of pagan rulers (2:21; 4:18).

Daniel wrote his book with two purposes in mind. First, he wanted to assert that the God of Israel was sovereign, even over the powerful nations that surrounded His people. God's chosen nation had been conquered and dispersed by a mighty empire that did not acknowledge the Lord. What would happen now? Would Babylon's yoke remain forever on Israel's shoulders? Would God's people never see their homeland again? Had God forgotten His promises? Daniel's answer was that Babylon would fall to another empire, which in turn would fall to yet another great kingdom. History would continue in this pattern until God judged all Gentile nations and established His everlasting rule. Daniel's message was obviously meant to uplift and encourage the weary hearts of the exiled Jews.

Yet Daniel also looked forward to the day when God would restore and reward Israel. Israel was suffering punishment for its disobedience; but when would the punishment end? Daniel's message was both discouraging and encouraging. He predicted trouble ahead; Israel would suffer under Gentile powers for many years. But the encouraging news was that the time of trials would also pass away. The time was coming when God would gather His children to Him again. He would establish His messianic kingdom, which would last forever. The God who directs the forces of history has not deserted His people. They must continue to trust Him. His promises of preservation and ultimate restoration are sure.

Daniel claims to have written the book that bears his name (12:4) and uses the first person singular from 7:2 to the end of the book. The Jewish Talmud agrees with Daniel's testimony. Christ Himself mentions Daniel by name in His predictions concerning the last days (Matt. 24:15). There is no reason to doubt either that Daniel was a historical person or that he wrote the book that bears his name. A well-educated Jew, chosen for special training in the palace in Babylon, Daniel possessed all the linguistic skills and the historical and cultural knowledge needed to write a book of this depth and complexity.

Since Daniel refers to the reign of Cyrus (6:28), a date of 530 B.C. or so is reasonable for the book's composition. Critical scholars, however, deny that this is possible mainly because the book appears to predict events that did not come to pass until the third and second centuries B.C. These predictions are so precise and detailed that some believe them not to have been prophecy at all but a record of the events after they transpired. Thus according to some, Daniel must date from the second century in order to account for at least those passages that predict later times.

If one concedes the possibility that Daniel was inspired to write prophetically about events two or three hundred years in the future, there is no reason to deny Daniel's authorship of the book in the sixth century B.C. The accuracy of its historical information, the form and style of its Hebrew and Aramaic passages, and the unanimous testimony of ancient tradition all confirm the witness of the book itself concerning its authorship and date.

Outline

I. Introduction 1:1–2:3
II. God's judgment on the Gentile nations 2:4–7:28
   A. Nebuchadnezzar's dream 2:4–49
   B. The image of gold 3:1–30
      1. The command to bow before the image 3:1–7
      2. The refusal to bow 3:8–18
      3. The deliverance of the faithful 3:19–25
      4. The reaction of the king 3:26–30
   C. Nebuchadnezzar's second dream 4:1–37
   D. Belshazzar's feast 5:1–31
      1. The writing on the wall 5:1–12
      2. The interpretation of the writing 5:13–29
      3. The fall of Babylon 5:30, 31
   E. The plot against Daniel 6:1–28
      1. The decree of Darius 6:1–9
      2. Daniel in the lions' den 6:10–23
      3. The reaction to Daniel's deliverance 6:24–28
   F. The vision of the four beasts 7:1–28
III. God's ultimate restoration of Israel 8:1–12:13

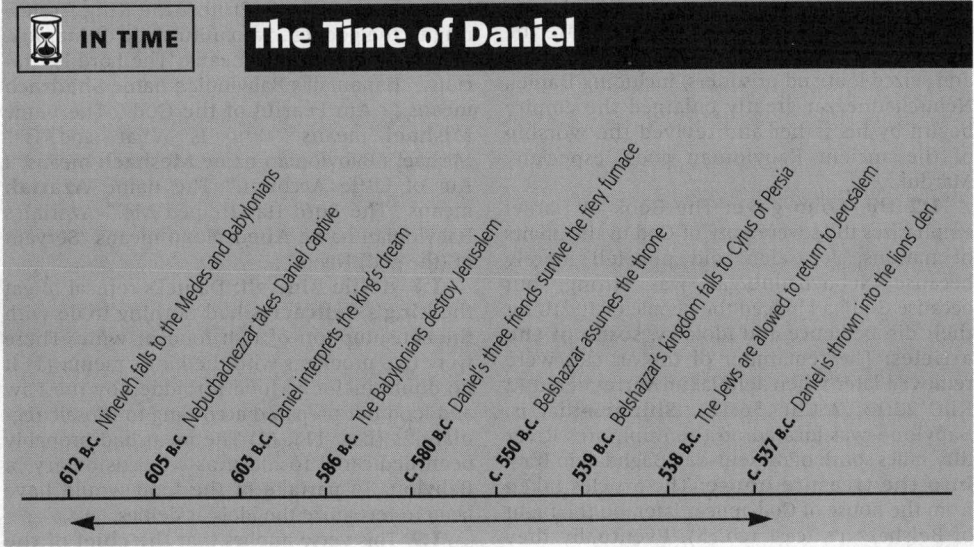

IN TIME — **The Time of Daniel**

612 B.C. Nineveh falls to the Medes and Babylonians
605 B.C. Nebuchadnezzar takes Daniel captive
603 B.C. Daniel interprets the king's dream
586 B.C. The Babylonians destroy Jerusalem
c. 580 B.C. Daniel's three friends survive the fiery furnace
c. 550 B.C. Belshazzar assumes the throne
539 B.C. Belshazzar's kingdom falls to Cyrus of Persia
538 B.C. The Jews are allowed to return to Jerusalem
c. 537 B.C. Daniel is thrown into the lions' den

Commentary

1:1 Jehoiakim king of Judah reigned from 608 to 598 B.C. **The third year** was 605 B.C., according to the chronological system used by Daniel in which only whole years were counted. Jeremiah, on the other hand, followed a system in which any part of a year was counted as a full year. Therefore, he designated 605 B.C. as the fourth year of Jehoiakim (Jer. 25:1; 36:1; 46:2). Jehoiakim was an evil king who sided first with the Egyptians and then with the Babylonians until 602 B.C. when he rebelled. His independence was short-lived, however, and Jehoiakim remained under Babylonian domination until his death. The son of Nabopolassar, the founder of the Neo-Babylonian (Chaldean) Empire, was **Nebuchadnezzar,** who reigned from 605 to 562 B.C. In the summer of 605 B.C. when his father died, Nebuchadnezzar was leading the Babylonian armies. He returned to Babylon to secure the throne, but not before he besieged Jerusalem and seized loot and prisoners, including Daniel. Nebuchadnezzar greatly enlarged the empire begun by his father and revived the worship of the ancient Babylonian gods, especially Marduk.

1:2 the LORD gave: The Book of Daniel emphasizes the sovereignty of God in the affairs of nations. Jerusalem did not fall merely because Nebuchadnezzar was strong, but because God had judged the people of Judah for their disobedience and idolatry. **some of the articles:** The remainder of the articles were removed later when Jehoiakim surrendered (2 Kin. 24:13; 2 Chr. 36:18). **Shinar**—that is, Babylon—was located on the Euphrates River fifty miles south of present-day Baghdad in Iraq. **into the treasure house:** The articles taken from the house of God appear later, on the night of Belshazzar's feast (ch. 5). Eventually they

were returned to Zerubbabel who brought them back to Israel (Ezra 1:7).

1:3 eunuchs: In ancient Middle Eastern monarchies, royal harems were typically superintended by men who had been emasculated and were considered reliable to serve in that capacity. A eunuch was often regarded as a privileged official. He enjoyed the personal friendship of the king, and his advice was frequently sought. Some have speculated that Daniel and his friends were eunuchs or at least that they were set apart to advise the king (v. 9), but there is no specific statement in the book to this effect. **The children of Israel** refers to the general population of the nation of Israel.

1:4, 5 Possessing knowledge refers to the young men's previous education. **the language and literature of the Chaldeans:** The language of most of Mesopotamia was Akkadian, which was written in cuneiform script, usually on clay tablets. Over the centuries the Babylonians and Assyrians produced a massive body of literature of all types. Though Aramaic had begun to replace Akkadian by 600 B.C., Babylonian scholars continued to study and even write literature in their classical tongue. For Daniel and his friends to be truly educated required that they be familiar with these literary traditions. The term Chaldeans was commonly applied to the Babylonians in general, and also to the guild of astrologers, diviners, and other practitioners of wisdom to which Daniel was being introduced (1:17; 2:2, 4, 5, 10; 3:8).

1:6 According to the first-century Jewish historian Josephus, all four of these young men were members of Zedekiah's royal family.

1:7 The name **Daniel** means "God Is My Judge." Daniel's Babylonian name **Belteshazzar** means "Lady Protect the King," referring to the goddess Sarpanitu, wife of Marduk. The name **Hananiah** means "The Lord Is Gracious." Hananiah's Babylonian name **Shadrach** means "I Am Fearful of the God." The name **Mishael** means "Who Is What God Is?" Mishael's Babylonian name **Meshach** means "I Am of Little Account." The name **Azariah** means "The Lord Has Helped Me." Azariah's Babylonian name **Abed-Nego** means "Servant of (the god) Nebo."

1:8 defile himself: Daniel's refusal to eat the **king's delicacies** had nothing to do with the consumption of rich food or wine. There were two problems with the king's menu: (1) It no doubt included food forbidden by the Law and food not prepared according to Mosaic regulations (Lev. 11). (2) The meat had probably been dedicated to idols, as was customary in Babylon. To partake of the food would have been to recognize the idols as deities.

1:9 This verse implies that **the chief of the**

eunuchs was over Daniel, leading some scholars to conclude that Daniel himself was a eunuch.

1:10, 11 In the Hebrew text, **your** is plural. Daniel's friends joined him in refusing to eat from the king's menu (vv. 7, 17, 19). **Endanger my head** suggests that the king might have had the chief of the eunuchs put to death for accommodating Daniel and his friends.

1:12, 13 Vegetables means things grown from seed and includes vegetables and grains. The request for **water** indicates that Daniel and his friends did not want to drink wine, probably because, like the food, it was dedicated to idols (v. 8).

1:14–16 Better and fatter indicates that Daniel and his friends were healthier than **the young men who ate . . . of the king's delicacies.**

1:17 God gave them knowledge and skill in all literature: As Moses was educated in the knowledge of Egypt, so Daniel and his friends acquired a Chaldean education. The **wisdom** of the Chaldeans consisted of sciences current at the time, including the interpretation of omens communicated through astrology, the examination of livers, kidneys, and other animal entrails, and the examination of the organs and flight patterns of birds. **Daniel** had the additional advantage of understanding **visions and dreams.** In the ancient Near East dreams were considered a source of divine reve-

lation, and thus their interpretation was highly valued. Daniel's gift from God in this area put him far beyond the abilities of the Chaldean interpreters (4:5–9).

1:18 The end of the days refers to the end of three years (v. 5). **The chief of the eunuchs** was Ashpenaz (v. 3).

1:19–21 Daniel served as counselor to the king from the completion of his training under Nebuchadnezzar (about 603 B.C., v. 5) until **the first year of King Cyrus** (539 B.C.). Thus Daniel held his position until the very end of the Babylonian Empire.

2:1 second year: Nebuchadnezzar's reign commenced in 605 B.C., so this is likely 603 B.C., given Daniel's preference for a "full-year" chronological system (1:1). The king was **troubled** because he did not know the future of his kingdom (v. 29).

2:2, 3 The Hebrew word translated **magicians** refers to those who use the pen—most likely, those learned in the sacred writings of the Babylonians. **Astrologers** studied the stars. **Sorcerers** received power from evil spirits. **The Chaldeans** were probably a class of wise men.

2:4 the Chaldeans spoke to the king in Aramaic: Daniel 2:4—7:28 is written in Aramaic, the common language of the day.

2:5, 6 Cut in pieces refers to the ancient practice of dismembering a body (3:29; 1 Sam. 15:33).

2:7–9 tell me the dream: Nebuchadnezzar

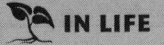 **IN LIFE**   ## Stand for What Is Right!

Perhaps in no other area do we as Christians today have as great an opportunity to influence people around us than in our ethics and morality in the workplace. How we behave on the job tells others everything they need to know about our values and commitments. The question is, are we standing for what is right?

Daniel and his three companions made up their minds to stand for godly values right from the start of their careers (Dan. 1:8). As ambassadors-in-training in Babylon, they declined to eat the specially prepared food provided by the government. The exact reasons why they found the food objectionable matter little. The important point is that once they realized that eating it would result in "defilement," they took a stand. They refused to just "go along to get along."

Therein lies the real challenge of workplace ethics today. Occasionally we may struggle to discern the right from the wrong, which is a matter of the intellect. But most of the time our need is to summon the conviction and the courage to do what we know is right, which is a matter of the will. Ultimately, ethics and morality have less to do with the head than with the heart. Daniel and his friends settled in their hearts what they needed to do and not do, based on biblical principles. As a result, they were able to carry out a plan with tough-minded resolve. In other words, they showed some moral backbone.

As you face ethical choices where you work, you can choose to stand for what is right. It may cost you, but God will give you the strength to deal with whatever consequences come your way. Furthermore, the cost of losing your integrity is infinitely greater than whatever it costs you to keep it.

reasoned that if the wise men could supernaturally interpret his dream, they should first be able to tell him the content of it.

2:10–12 Babylon here probably refers to the city, not the whole province.

2:13, 14 they began killing the wise men: Nebuchadnezzar's penalty was excessive and extreme (v. 15).

2:15 Urgent means sharp or severe (v. 13).

2:16–18 Daniel, despite his education and expertise, still knew that prayer to the omniscient God was the first step in a crisis situation. However, Daniel did not pray alone. He sought the counsel of friends who would raise petition to the Lord with him. **God of heaven** is a favorite title for the Lord in late OT literature (vv. 37, 44; 2 Chr. 36:23; Ezra 1:2; 5:11, 12; 6:9, 10; 7:12, 21, 23; Neh. 1:4, 5; 2:4, 20). The title emphasizes the universality of God's dominion over all nations.

2:19, 20 night vision: Normally visions occurred in the daytime (8:1–14) and dreams occurred at night.

2:21 Seasons here refers to the events of history.

2:22–27 Deep refers to something inaccessible (Ps. 92:5, 6). What is **in the darkness** is hidden from sight.

2:28–30 The latter days is an expression used frequently of the end times when God will intervene in human history to establish His eternal kingdom (Is. 2:2; Hos. 3:5; Mic. 4:1–3).

2:31–33 Image here means statue, not idol. **gold . . . silver . . . bronze . . . iron:** The metals are listed in descending order of weight and value. The strength of the metals, however, increases from head to legs.

2:34 Without hands signifies supernatural activity.

2:35, 36 In biblical imagery, a **mountain** is often a metaphor for a kingdom (Ps. 48:2; Is. 2:2; 11:9; Jer. 51:25; Ezek. 20:40; Zech. 8:3). The same is true in this case, as the later interpretation makes clear (v. 44).

2:37 God . . . has given you a kingdom: The God of Israel is the God of all nations. Though the rulers of those nations may not have recognized Him as Lord, that did not nul-

---

 **IN COMPARISON** | **Dreams and Visions in Daniel**

Daniel's God-given ability to interpret "visions and dreams" (1:17) served him well in his role as advisor to King Nebuchadnezzar of Babylon, a man noted for his mysterious and troubling dreams. The following brief comparison of a dream of Nebuchadnezzar and a dream and vision of Daniel reveals a common theme in the Book of Daniel—the successive rise and fall of four kingdoms.

Nebuchadnezzar's Dream	Daniel's Dream	Daniel's Vision	Interpretation
An image with a head of fine gold (2:32)	A beast like a lion with eagle's wings (7:4)		Babylon would establish itself as the first world empire (2:38; 7:17).
An image with a chest and arms of silver (2:32)	A beast like a bear with three ribs in its mouth (7:5)	A ram with two horns, one of which was higher than the other (8:3)	Medo-Persia would defeat Babylon and establish itself as the second world empire (2:39; 7:17; 8:20).
An image with a belly and thighs of bronze (2:32)	A beast like a leopard with four wings (7:6)	A male goat with a large horn, later replaced by four horns and a little horn (8:5–9)	Greece would defeat Medo-Persia and establish itself as the third world empire (2:39; 7:17; 8:21).
An image with legs of iron and feet of iron and clay (2:32)	A beast with iron teeth and ten horns (7:7)		Rome would defeat Greece and establish itself as the fourth world empire (2:40–43; 7:17).

lify God's ultimate sovereignty nor did it alleviate the rulers' responsibility to Him.

2:38 The **head** is a reference to the Babylonian Empire, personified in Nebuchadnezzar.

2:39, 40 The image that Nebuchadnezzar saw (vv. 31–35) represented four kingdoms that would **rule over all the earth.** The first worldwide empire—the head of gold (v. 32)—was Babylon (v. 38). The second empire—the chest and arms of silver (v. 32)—was Medo-Persia (5:28; 8:20; 11:2). As silver is inferior to gold, so Medo-Persia was inferior to Babylon, not in size but in its effectiveness in governing its people. The third empire—the belly and thighs of bronze (v. 32)—would be Greece (8:21). The **fourth** empire—the legs of iron (v. 33)—is the only one not identified within the Book of Daniel. Rome is the most likely choice, for it succeeded Greece. **Strong as iron:** The focus shifts from the value of the metals to their comparative strength. The Roman Empire was marked by strength, but it was destructive strength. Iron replaced bronze as the most common metal for tool and weapons, starting about 1200 B.C. The process of replacement lasted some time. For one thing, iron has to have some carbon in it; then it can be hardened by heating and quenching. Weapons were known to bend during use and the soldiers had to straighten them in the midst of battle. Yet in the end iron was recognized as the common symbol of war.[L&T]

2:41–45 The kingdom shall be divided may be a reference to the fourth kingdom, the Roman Empire (v. 40). Differences about what is meant by the ten toes (v. 42) and the kingdom that filled the earth (represented by the stone in v. 45) has resulted in widely varying interpretations. Some believe that vv. 41–45 point to future events that have not yet been fulfilled. In this scenario, the Roman Empire will one day be revived (v. 41), will be ruled over by ten rulers (the toes of v. 42), will feud over internal problems (v. 43), will witness the return of Jesus Christ (v. 44), and will be destroyed by Christ at the Second Coming (v. 45).

2:44 The **kingdom which shall never be destroyed** is the kingdom of God. There are at least two views as to what form this kingdom will take. Amillennialists suggest it is a spiritual kingdom introduced by Jesus Christ at His first coming. Premillennialists suggest that it is a literal kingdom to be established by Jesus Christ at the Second Coming, at which time He will destroy the kingdoms of this world (Rev. 19:15).

2:45–49 your God is the God of gods: One should not conclude from Nebuchadnezzar's confession that he had been converted. Since the Lord had enabled Daniel to interpret the king's dream, Nebuchadnezzar was willing to admit that Daniel's God was supreme, at least in matters of divine knowledge. The king gladly promoted Daniel as a result (v. 48).

3:1 sixty cubits . . . six cubits: A cubit in Israel was approximately 18 inches; in Babylon it was about 20 inches. Therefore Nebuchadnezzar's image was 90 to 100 feet tall. The 10:1 ratio of height to width, however, suggests that the image was standing on a high pedestal so that the proportions of the figure itself would be closer to the normal ratio of about 4:1. The image most likely served as a symbol of the cohesion and monolithic character of Babylon under the rule of its glorious king Nebuchadnezzar. Since the state and its king could not be separated from its gods, however, to bow down before the image was to worship it (vv. 5, 12, 14, 18, 28). **The plain of Dura** was probably about six miles southeast of Babylon.

3:2, 3 The officials of the kingdom are listed in descending order of rank. **Satraps** were the chief officials of the provinces of the empire. Daniel was one of the **administrators** (2:48). In later times, Zerubbabel (Hag. 1:1) and Nehemiah (Neh. 5:14) were appointed **governors.**

3:4, 5 harp . . . psaltery . . . symphony: These three words appear to be Greek in origin. Greek words of a cultural or technical nature appeared throughout the ancient Middle East well before 600 B.C.

3:6, 8 Accused means "ate the pieces of, devoured piecemeal." The term suggests slander and malicious accusations, which devour the accused piece by piece.

3:9–12 No explanation is given for Daniel's absence.

3:13–16 we have no need to answer you: Shadrach, Meshach, and Abed-Nego were not being arrogant; they were admitting their guilt.

3:17 God . . . is able: The response of the Jewish young men is a model of confidence in God and submission to His will. Shadrach, Meshach, and Abed-Nego recognized God's sovereignty and power.

3:18 But if not: While the faithful men knew that God could deliver them (v. 17), they were also aware that God may have chosen not to do so. Faith in God may not translate into victory in every circumstance (Heb. 11:32–39). To these men the outcome was irrelevant, for what was at stake was not God's ability or their own lives, but their faith and obedience to serve Him regardless of the cost.

3:19, 20 The **mighty men of valor** were Nebuchadnezzar's personal bodyguards.

3:21 bound in . . . garments: Criminals were normally stripped before execution. The fact that the fine clothes of the Jewish men were

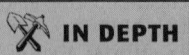 **IN DEPTH** | **The Trinity in the Old Testament**

When King Nebuchadnezzar exclaimed that the fourth man walking about in the fiery furnace with Shadrach, Meshach, and Abednego was "like the Son of God" (3:25), it may be an overstatement to say that he recognized Jesus. Yet even though he worshiped other gods, Nebuchadnezzar somehow knew that this mysterious fourth figure was divine (3:28).

Though the doctrine of the Triune God was not fully revealed until Jesus' time, we find clues that God was preparing humanity for this truth. In the OT, such foreshadowings of God or the preincarnate Christ in a visible form are called *theophanies,* meaning "appearances of God." These theophanies include the Angel who comforted Hagar (Gen. 16:7–13), the visitor who revealed to Abraham and Sarah that they would have a son (Gen. 18:1–15), the Lord's appearance to Moses in the burning bush (Ex. 3), the pillars of cloud and fire that led the Israelites from Egypt (Ex. 14:19, 20), and Moses' glimpse of God on Sinai (Ex. 33:11). Some people would also include as a theophany the appearance of Melchizedek, the priest-king of Salem, who gave wine and bread to Abram (Gen. 14:18–20).

The OT contains nearly eighty references to the Spirit of God and anticipates the arrival of God's Son, the Messiah, who would deliver His people. Daniel also calls Christ the Son of Man (Dan. 7:13). These theophanies were temporary, however. They were hints of the incarnation of Christ, fully human and fully divine, who would live among and redeem His people.

not removed implies that the king's command was carried out with great haste (v. 22).

3:22 killed those men: The price of Nebuchadnezzar's rage was the loss of capable men.

3:23–25 walking: The enormous number of bricks demanded in Babylon required kilns large enough to permit people to walk in them. **The fire** burned off the men's bonds (v. 21), but did not **hurt** them.

3:26, 27 the fire had no power: The God of Shadrach, Meshach, and Abed-Nego saved them completely, so that there was not the slightest evidence that they had ever been in danger. The salvation offered by the Lord is so effective and complete that nothing of the lost condition remains.

3:28–30 no other God: Pagan cultures did not deny the existence of other gods, even those of other peoples. Nebuchadnezzar declared only that the God of the Jews was a god who is able to deliver; the king forbade others to despise Him.

4:1–3 These verses are a royal proclamation by Nebuchadnezzar concerning the God of Israel in which the king celebrated what God had done for him and extolled His power and universal dominion.

4:4 rest . . . and flourishing: Nebuchadnezzar had peace at home and prospered in his work.

4:5, 6 This **dream** of Nebuchadnezzar occurred thirty years after the dream in ch. 2. **Troubled** means terrified.

4:7 I told them the dream: In ch. 2, Nebuchadnezzar did not tell his wise men the content of his dream (2:5).

4:8 My god refers to Marduk. Nebuchadnezzar was still a pagan at this point.

4:9 Daniel, also known as **Belteshazzar,** was **chief of the magicians,** a position given to him years earlier (2:48).

4:10–17 In ch. 2, Nebuchadnezzar dreamed of a great image, of which he was a part. His second dream involved a tree, which represented him (v. 22). A tree is often a symbol of towering strength, providing shade, food, fuel, beauty, and the raw materials for some buildings.

4:15 let him: At this point it becomes obvious that the tree is a symbol of a person.

4:16 Seven times could refer to years, months, weeks, days, or hours. Most take it to mean years, based on the usage of "times" elsewhere in Daniel (2:8; 3:5, 15; 7:25). Seven is the blbical number for completeness.

4:17 The point of Nebuchadnezzar's dream is that **the Most High rules** supreme in the world.

4:18 Spirit of the Holy God: The doctrine of the Triune God—the Father, Son, and Holy Spirit—is evident in the OT (Gen. 1:26; 11:7; Is. 48:16), but is not developed (3:25). Nebuchadnezzar was merely saying that Daniel's ability to interpret dreams was the result of God's giving Daniel the spirit of interpretation.

4:19 astonished . . . troubled: Having come to an understanding of Nebuchadnezzar's dream, Daniel was so upset by its content that he hesitated to divulge its meaning. **may the dream concern those who hate you:** Daniel wishes that the awful message of judgment were somehow intended for the king's enemies and not the king.

| 🔍 IN FOCUS | **"interpretation"** |

(Aram. *peshar*) (2:4; 4:6, 5:12, 16) Strong's #6591: This verb literally means "to untie" or "to loose." In other words, Daniel could unravel the mysteries of dreams and visions: he could explain or solve them. Yet he was always quick to give God the credit for his ability (2:28). By the time of Jesus, rabbinic Judaism had interpreted much of the OT allegorically. These "pesher" explanations of the Scriptures might have been what Jesus was addressing when He said, "you have heard that it was said" (Matt. 5:21, 27, 31, 38).

4:20 In the OT, a **tree** is a common symbol for a ruler (Judg. 9:7–15; Ezek. 31:2–14; Zech. 11:1, 2). Since few trees were present in Babylon, a tree of the gigantic proportions described here would have been impressive and unique.

4:21 leaves were lovely . . . fruit abundant: Daniel indicates that Nebuchadnezzar was the source of abundant blessing for all. The **beasts** and **birds** represent the happy citizens of Nebuchadnezzar's realm.

4:22 heavens . . . earth: These terms convey the idea of totality. Using deliberate exaggeration, Daniel says that Nebuchadnezzar's kingdom extended from heaven to the ends of the earth, and so was universal.

4:23, 24 Watcher means "a waking one," one who is constantly alert. The parallel **holy one** suggests that the watcher is either the Lord Himself or one of His angels (3:28; 6:22; 8:16; 10:13; 12:1). **stump and roots:** The tree—Nebuchadnezzar—would be cut down but not uprooted. The stump would produce suckers and the roots would produce new growth that would eventually give rise to a new tree, one as grand as before (v. 26). **Seven times** means seven years (7:12, 25).

4:25–28 beasts of the field: The affliction of Nebuchadnezzar is known technically as boanthropy, that is, man acting like animal. It is a disease well attested to in historical and scientific literature. Many critics view this account as a fable or tale without historical substance since nothing is known of this malady of Nebuchadnezzar apart from the account here in Daniel. It is important to remember, however, that there is virtually no information about the reign of Nebuchadnezzar from 594–562 B.C., the year of his death. His madness could easily have fallen within that period.

4:29–31 twelve months: The reference here is to a "grace period" between the prediction of Nebuchadnezzar's madness and its occurrence. Perhaps Nebuchadnezzar was allowed a full year in the hope that he might repent and avert the judgment of God for his arrogant pride.

4:32, 33 until you know: Nebuchadnezzar would become insane, animal-like in his habits and senses. Yet in that condition he would learn more of God than he ever had before. In fact, the purpose of the judgment was that Nebuchadnezzar might know who God is and how He sovereignly creates kingdoms and distributes them to whom He wills. Nebuchadnezzar had to be humbled before he could be exalted again. The chastisement of God is always for a holy and helpful purpose.

4:34–37 Nebuchadnezzar praises **the Most High**, recognizing that God **lives forever** and rules forever. The king unmistakably acknowledges Daniel's God as the omnipotent, eternal Sovereign of the universe.

5:1, 2 Belshazzar is called the **king** and the son of **Nebuchadnezzar** (v. 22). Other ancient records, however, seem to dispute both facts. These records indicate that Belshazzar was the son of Nabonidus, the last king of Babylon. Two possible explanations can reconcile these differing accounts: (1) Belshazzar served as vice-regent during his father's frequent absences from the capital. Thus he would have been in charge when Nebuchadnezzar's insanity began. Note that Darius the Mede was also called king even though he served Cyrus (5:31; 6:6). (2) Belshazzar was the grandson of Nebuchadnezzar; hence, the term *father* in v. 2 indicates that Nebuchadnezzar was an ancestor of Belshazzar.

5:3, 4 gold vessels . . . from the temple: Belshazzar's use of the sacred vessels at a drunken orgy was a blasphemous act of sacrilege (v. 23). **praised the gods:** Belshazzar's actions demonstrated deliberate defiance of the true God (v. 23).

5:5–7 Nabonidus the king was in Arabia. Belshazzar was his vice-regent. **The third ruler** would have been next in line to the throne.

5:8–10 The queen was not Belshazzar's wife, but the queen mother. She was either the wife of Nebuchadnezzar or the daughter of Nebuchadnezzar who had married Nabonidus, the current king.

5:11, 12 The Spirit of the Holy God is the same expression used by Nebuchadnezzar (4:8, 9, 18).

5:13–16 This event took place in 539 B.C. (v. 30). **Daniel** was an old man at this time, possibly eighty years old or older.

5:17–24 When Daniel refused Belshazzar's **gifts** and **rewards,** he was not being ungrateful or showing disrespect. He was simply saying that he would interpret the **writing** regardless of reward.

5:25–28 MENE means **numbered.** The repetition is for emphasis. God had numbered the days of Belshazzar's kingdom; its time was up. TEKEL means **weighed.** God had weighed Belshazzar, and the king did not measure up to God's standard of righteousness. UPHARSIN, the plural of PERES in v. 28, means **divided.** That very night (v. 30) Babylon would be divided and defeated by the **Medes and Persians.**

5:29, 30 That very night (October 12, 539 B.C.) Babylon fell to the Persian army commanded by Gubaru.

5:31 Darius the Mede is mentioned by name only in the Book of Daniel (6:1, 6, 9; 9:1). He is not the famous Darius I Hystaspes because Darius I was not a Mede and he lived too late (522–486 B.C.) to be a contemporary of Daniel. There are two principal suggestions as to the identity of Darius the Mede: (1) He was Cyrus

the king of Persia. However, it is unlikely that Cyrus would be called a "Mede" since he was in fact a Persian. (2) He was Gubaru, a governor appointed by Cyrus. Both Daniel and ancient literary sources indicate that a certain official ("Darius the Mede" in Daniel, "Gubaru" in Persian texts) took over immediately in Babylon until Cyrus appointed his own son Cambyses as viceregent around 538 B.C. This figure is most likely identified with Darius. Why he is called Darius is uncertain, though ancient rulers often took other names for themselves.

6:1, 2 Daniel had previously been appointed a governor in Babylon by Nebuchadnezzar (2:48). Here he was governor in the new Medo-Persian reign. **Suffer no loss** refers to taxes.

6:3, 4 Excellent spirit probably refers to Daniel's surpassing ability to do his job and perhaps includes a commendable attitude.

6:5–7 Daniel had been circumspect in obeying the laws of the land, but his enemies knew that when the law of the land conflicted with **the law of his God,** Daniel would break the former in favor of the latter.

6:8, 9 the law of the Medes and Persians: Once a royal decree had been issued, it could not be revoked—even by the king himself. It remained in force until its time of expiration. The practice of creating an unchangeable law may follow from the idea that changing a decree was an admission that it had been faulty.

6:10–12 Undeterred by the royal proclama-

⌘ **IN CONTEXT**　**The Medes and Persians**

The kingdom of Media is first mentioned in Assyrian sources describing the ninth-century campaign of Assyria's Shalmaneser III (858–824 B.C.) into the land of the Medes. Media was apparently situated in the area of modern west-central Iran and flourished for the next two centuries, according to the same Assyrian sources. In the Assyrian texts the Medes are pictured in these centuries as comprised of a group of small autonomous tribes. The Greek historian Herodotus (484–425 B.C.) gives a legendary account of a unification of Median tribes occurring during the seventh century B.C. By the late seventh century the unified Median tribes, led by Cyaxares (around 625–585 B.C.) were allied with the Chaldeans against Assyria. The united Medes thus contributed to the downfall of the Assyrian capital of Ninevah in 612 B.C.

The Median kingdom continued under Astyages (about 585–550 B.C.), successor of Cyaxares, until the middle of the sixth century B.C. In 550 B.C., Cyrus of Persia successfully united the Persian and Median tribes, though it is uncertain whether the Medes were conquered or were peacefully incorporated into the empire of Cyrus. The ruler was apparently related to the royal hourse of both Media and Persia. Thus the union of the two nations may have been accomplished as a result of the legal claim of Cyrus to the throne. Media continued to be geographically distinct even under Persian government, and the Medes were second only to the Persians in the empire. So even after Persian absorbed Media in 550 B.C., the Medes continued to be recognized as a distinct people. This situation is evident in the recurring phrase "the law of the Medes and Persians" (Dan. 6:8, 12, 15).

tion (vv. 6–9), Daniel resumed praying by the windows of his house that opened **toward Jerusalem**—that is, toward the west. His enemies were correct in assuming that if Daniel was forced to choose between the decree of an earthly king and the eternal word of the King of heaven, he would choose his God (v. 5).

6:13–15 Daniel's accusers did not describe him as governor (v. 2), but as **one of the captives from Judah,** in order to implicate him in a treasonous act.

6:16 The Aramaic word for **den** means "pit," implying that it was underground.

6:17–20 sealed it: To ensure that the den remained closed and that no effort could be made either by the king or his officials to intervene, the lid of the den was impressed with the royal seal and with the seals of the king's lords. The lid of the den could not be removed without breaking the seals.

6:21, 22 Though this is a standard way of greeting a king (2:4; 3:9; 5:10; 6:6), it is ironic here because Daniel, who has just been made alive by the God whom even Darius confesses as "the living God" (v. 20), blesses the king with the wish that he should **live forever.** That is literally possible for the king, of course, only if he comes to know Daniel's God, who is the source of life as the lion's den episode shows so clearly.

6:23 because he believed in his God: Daniel's faithfulness got him into trouble (v. 10); his faith got him out of it (Heb. 11:33).

6:24, 25 children . . . wives: The entire families of the wicked conspirators were destroyed because the Persians, like the Hebrews and other Semites, considered guilt a collective responsibility, especially in families. The examples of Korah (Num. 16:1–35) and Achan (Josh. 7) illustrate this principle well.

6:26, 27 I make a decree: Darius's original thirty-day decree (vv. 6–9) had probably expired.

6:28 Daniel prospered throughout **the reign of Darius** and **in the reign of Cyrus**. Gubaru, or Darius, served Cyrus for about one year (539–538 B.C.), after which Cyrus appointed his son Cambyses as vice-regent over Babylon. Cyrus himself continued as king until 530 B.C.

7:1–12:13 Here we find a series of visions that teach a similar truth to the experiences of the first six chapters. In chs. 1—6, God is portrayed as being in control of the present. In chs. 7—12, He is seen as also controlling the future.

7:1–28 Daniel has a vision of four beasts. The general tenor of this vision is much like that of the dream in ch. 2. There, Daniel was shown a vision of four successive empires that would rule the world in which God's people lived.

7:1 the first year of Belshazzar: Chapter 5 records Belshazzar's death, indicating that the

Book of Daniel is not arranged chronologically. The date of Belshazzar's first year cannot be stated precisely. However, since Nabonidus appears to have spent at least ten years in Arabia and since Belshazzar reigned for Nabonidus in Babylon during that time, a date of 550 B.C. for Belshazzar's first year cannot be far off. This date coincides with the inauguration of the Medo-Persian Empire under Cyrus, an occasion that may have prompted Daniel's vision.

7:2 Four winds seems to refer to winds from every direction, covering the whole earth. **The Great Sea** is probably a reference to the Mediterranean Sea (Josh. 15:12; 23:4; Ezek. 47:10, 19), here used figuratively of the nations of the world (Is. 57:20; Rev. 17:15).

7:3 The **beasts** represent kings (v. 17) or kingdoms (vv. 18, 23).

7:4 lion . . . eagle's wings: It is commonly recognized that these two animals are the king of the beasts and the king of the birds respectively, a fitting description of Nebuchadnezzar and the Babylonian Empire (Jer. 49:19, 22). There has been almost universal agreement from the early centuries until today that this beast represents Babylon. It is also agreed that the vision of ch. 7 and that of ch. 2 speak about the same four kingdoms. **Plucked off** is a reference to Nebuchadnezzar's humiliation (4:28–33).

7:5 If the lion with eagle's wings represents Babylon (v. 4), the **bear**—in line with Nebuchadnezzar's first dream—represents Babylon's successor, the Medo-Persian Empire (2:38, 39). **Raised up on one side** suggests that the Persians were greater and more powerful than the Medes. The **three ribs** represent the three kingdoms that the Medo-Persians devoured—Babylon, Lydia, and Egypt.

7:6 If the second beast of Daniel's dream represents the Medo-Persian Empire (v. 5), the **leopard** represents Greece (2:39). **Four** symbolizes universality (see "four winds," v. 2); **wings** are synonymous with speed. The Greeks under the leadership of Alexander the Great rapidly conquered the known world. **Four heads** describes "heads" of government. After Alexander's death, his empire was divided among his generals into four different parts.

7:7 The **fourth beast** did not look like any known animal. Since this beast follows Greece (v. 6), it may represent Rome (2:40).

7:8 The **horns** here represent rulers. Though the **little one** begins small, it would become the greatest of all (v. 20).

7:9 Ancient of Days is a reference to God the Father as certified by the submission of "the One like the Son of Man" to Him (vv. 13, 14) and His role in judgment (v. 22). **Fiery flame** symbolizes judgment. **Its wheels** refers to the chariot in which God rides to battle to exercise His sovereignty and to appear as Judge (Ezek. 1:15–21; 10:1–22).

7:10 A thousand thousands . . . Ten thousand times ten thousand: The reference here is to innumerable servants. **The books** record the names and deeds of those who will be judged (Rev. 20:12).

7:11 The horn here is the same as the one in v. 8. **the burning flame:** The idea that the end of the wicked is fiery destruction is apparent in the OT (Gen. 19:24; Is. 66:24; Mal. 4:1, 3),

Photo by Howard Vos

Bust of Alexander the Great, Greek military conqueror. Many interpreters believe the leopard in Daniel's prophecy (Dan. 7:6) refers to the future Greek Empire and its dominance under Alexander's leadership.

but reaches its fullest expression in the NT teaching about hell (Matt. 5:22, 29, 30; 10:28; 2 Pet. 2:4).

7:12 The rest of the beasts is a reference to the three beasts of vv. 3–6—Babylon, Medo-Persia, and Greece. **they had their dominion taken away:** Though these nations passed away, their "dominion" was inherited by their respective successors. **A season and a time** is an idiom for an indefinite period.

7:13 Son of Man is Semitic for "human being." Daniel saw **One like** the "Son of Man," indicating that He is not a man in the strict sense, but rather the perfect representation of humanity. Jewish and Christian expositors have identified this individual as the Messiah. Jesus Himself used this name to emphasize His humanity as the incarnate Son of God (Matt. 9:6; 10:23; 11:19; 12:8, 32, 40; Mark 8:31; 9:12; Luke 6:5; 9:22; John 3:13, 14; 5:27). **Coming with . . . clouds:** John uses the same expression to speak of Jesus coming in judgment (Matt. 24:30; Rev. 1:7).

7:14, 15 Him refers to the Son of Man (v. 13), who will reign over all things as the regent of Almighty God (1 Cor. 15:27, 28; Eph. 1:20–23; Phil. 2:9–11; Rev. 17:14; 19:16). In contrast to the vanishing nature of the previous empires, **His dominion is . . . everlasting.**

7:16 One of those who stood by refers to an angel standing by the throne of God (v. 10).

7:17 These **kings** represent kingdoms (8:21). Thus each beast represents both a king and a kingdom.

7:18–20 saints of the Most High: Saints means "holy ones," a term that can refer either to angels (Job 15:15; Ps. 89:5, 7; Zech. 14:5) or to redeemed men and women (Pss. 16:3; 30:4; 31:23; 37:28; Prov. 2:8; Rom. 1:7; 12:13; Rev. 5:8). The kingdom received and forever possessed by the saints must be the same as the dominion of the Son of Man, which is also everlasting (v. 14). The Son of Man thus rules through His saints, a fact proclaimed frequently in the NT (Rev. 2:26, 27; 20:4–6).

7:21–23 Daniel's vision reveals the hostility waged by the little horn **against the saints.** The little horn's militaristic character is seen also in 11:38, 39 and particularly in Rev. 13:1–10. There, in the guise of a beast, this blasphemous enemy of the saints prevails for forty-two months. The connection between Daniel's "little horn" and John's "beast from the sea" is unmistakable.

7:24, 25 There are three common interpretations as to the **ten kings who shall arise from this kingdom:** (1) The fourth beast is Greece and the ten horns are ten divisions of the Grecian Empire. (2) The fourth beast is Rome and the ten horns are the fragments of the Roman Empire. (3) The fourth beast is a revived Roman Empire and the ten kings are members of a future realm. **Another** refers to the little horn of v. 8 (vv. 20, 21). This king will **subdue three** others, blaspheme God (11:36; 2 Thess. 2:4; Rev. 13:5, 6), **persecute the saints** (v. 21; Rev. 13:7), attempt **to change times and law,** and dominate the **saints** for a limited time. **time and times and half a time:** Time can refer to a year, times to two years, and half a time to one half of a year, for a total of three and one-half years. Some suggest that the expression does not indicate a specific number of years but instead a period of time that God in His mercy would shorten.

7:26 The **dominion** of the little horn will come to a violent end when he submits to the **court** of God (v. 10).

7:27, 28 the kingdom . . . to the people, the saints: The kingdom of God, governed by His saints, will exercise rule over all the earth.

8:1 After writing in Aramaic from 2:4–7:28, Daniel returns to writing in Hebrew.

8:2 Shushan was about 230 miles east of Babylon. **Ulai** was an artificial canal located a few miles from Shushan.

8:3 The **ram** represents Medo-Persia (v. 20). The **two horns** symbolize the people of Media and the people of Persia.

8:4 Cyrus and his successors conquered **westward** including Babylon, Syria, and Asia Minor, **northward** including Armenia and the Caspian Sea region, and **southward** including Egypt and Ethiopia.

8:5, 6 The **goat** represents Greece (v. 21). The **notable horn** symbolizes Alexander the Great (v. 21), who launched his attack against Persia in 334 B.C. By 332 B.C., he had essentially subdued the Persian Empire. **without touching the ground:** Alexander's conquest was so rapid that it seemed as if he flew across the earth.

8:7 The Persian forces outnumbered the Greeks. But in two decisive battles, the Medo-Persian Empire collapsed.

8:8 the large horn was broken: Alexander the Great died at the height of his career, before he was thirty-three years old. **four notable ones:** After Alexander's death, four of his generals carved up the Macedonian Empire. Antigonus ruled from northern Syria to central Asia; Cassander ruled over Macedonia; Ptolemy ruled in Egypt and southern Syria, including Palestine; Lysimachus ruled over Thrace.

8:9 The **little horn** here is not the same as the little horn of ch. 7. The former horn comes out of the fourth beast, Rome, whereas this one comes out of Greece. The *little horn* here refers to Antiochus Epiphanes, the eighth king of the Syrian dynasty who reigned from 175 to 164 B.C. Thus, this prophecy skips from 301 B.C., the time of the division of Alexander's empire, to 175 B.C., when Antiochus became king. **toward the south:** Antiochus invaded Egypt. **The east** is Parthia and **the Glorious Land** is Palestine.

8:10 The host of heaven and **the stars** both refer to God's people (12:3; Gen. 15:5). **Cast down some** describes Antiochus's conquest.

8:11 The Prince of the host refers to God Himself. The little horn, like Lucifer (Is. 14:12), aspires to be like God. **sanctuary . . . cast down:** Antiochus desecrated the house of God by erecting a statue of Zeus on the bronze altar.

8:12 Truth is a reference to the Mosaic Law.

8:13 A holy one and **another holy one** both refer to angels (4:13, 23).

8:14 Two thousand three hundred days refers to the time between Antiochus's pollution of the temple and the Maccabees' cleansing of it.

8:15 the appearance of a man: This person is not identified. It could be the voice of God, or Christ, or and angel.

8:16 This is the first mention of the messenger **Gabriel** in the Bible. The angel is mentioned three other times in Scripture (9:21; Luke 1:19, 26).

8:17, 18 The time of the end is a reference to a time that may already be underway (1 John 2:18) in some respects, but will not find its fulfillment until the Second Coming of Christ (Matt. 24:14).

8:19 The indignation is that of the Lord against those who have rebelled against His dominion. **The end** (see "the time of the end" in v. 17) indicates that this judgment is against all those in rebellion against God, especially those living at the time just before the coming of Christ.

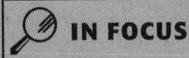 IN FOCUS | **"vision"**

(Heb. *chazon*) (8:1; Is. 1:1; Prov. 29:18) Strong's #2377: The Hebrew word for a dream or a vision is derived from a common Hebrew verb meaning "to see." Dreams and visions were often recognized by the ancients as revelations from the gods, or from God Himself in the case of the Hebrews (Is. 1:1). Daniel received a visionary message from God that spoke about the future of the kingdoms of Persia and Greece. His dream was encoded in symbols which required the interpretive assistance of the angel Gabriel (8:15–27). The author of Proverbs insists that revelation from God is essential to the well-being of a society. Without God's Law revealed in Scripture, the foundation of a society crumbles (Prov. 29:18).

8:20 The two horns represent the two countries of **Media and Persia.** It is significant that the two are regarded as one empire, represented by **the ram.**

8:21 The first king of Greece was Alexander the Great.

8:22 not with its power: None of Alexander's four generals ruled with the strength of Alexander (v. 8).

8:23 When the transgressors have reached their fullness means when the sinful actions of the Jews have reached the point where God cannot permit them to go any further without bringing punishment (Gen. 15:16; Matt. 23:32; 1 Thess. 2:16). **A king** refers to Antiochus IV Epiphanes, the king of Syria who made his capital at Antioch.

8:24 Not by his own power indicates that Antiochus would be energized by Satan, as will the Antichrist (2 Thess. 2:9).

8:25 Without human means: Antiochus died without human intervention. According to the apocryphal Book of Second Maccabees, Antiochus (v. 23) died of a painful disease.

8:26 seal up the vision: Most documents of Daniel's time were written on scrolls that could be rolled up and sealed to protect their contents. This document pertained to a time **many days in the future.**

8:27 I . . . fainted and was sick: Daniel suffered a severe emotional reaction to the vision of ch. 8, apparently even greater than the reaction he had experienced after his first vision (7:15, 28).

9:1 The first year of Darius was 539 B.C., the year he was appointed by Cyrus as administrator of Babylon.

9:2, 3 The books refers to Scripture, specifically the Book of Jeremiah, which states (Jer. 25:11, 12; 29:10–14) that the desolation of Jerusalem would be fulfilled in seventy years. Daniel's own captivity occurred in 605 B.C. It was now 538 B.C., some sixty-seven years after the conquest. The period of captivity was almost over. Zechariah refers to the seventy-year period as beginning with the destruction of the temple, which took place in 586 B.C. (Zech. 7:5). The temple was rebuilt in 515 B.C. (Ezra 6:15).

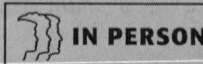 **IN PERSON**   **Responding to Prophecy**

Modern-day readers of the Bible have a variety of reactions to the prophetic passages of Scripture. Some find them fascinating and revealing, others puzzling and enigmatic. Some regard them as a clearly marked roadmap for the future, others as writings whose meaning generally remains hidden and mysterious. For quite a few, the question is this: What difference do these prophetic passages make?

In thinking about an appropriate response to biblical prophecy, it helps to understand that the prophets were less concerned with prediction than with revelation. That is, regardless of whether a prophecy pertains to the future, it is significant because it reveals something that the Lord wants His people to know. It has been said that prophecy is not just foretelling the future, it is forthtelling the Word of the Lord.

Daniel's response to the prophecies of Jeremiah is instructive. When the kingdom of Babylon was taken over by the Persians, Daniel recognized that more than political change was involved; he perceived the hand of the Lord. Apparently he had access to Jeremiah's prophecies (Dan. 9:2). Perhaps he had a copy of the letter that Jeremiah sent to the exiles in Babylon, telling them to expect a seventy-year captivity (Jer. 29:10).

As Daniel reflected carefully on this information, he was moved to repentance (Dan. 9:3–7). This is a remarkable response, given other reactions that one might expect. For example, he could have hailed the fall of Babylon as the prophetic event signaling the end of Judah's captivity. He could have taken the information to Darius and demanded his people's immediate release, in the style of Moses. He could have become complacent in his duties, figuring that he was on his way home.

Daniel did none of these things. Instead he repented. His focus was not on dates and timetables, but on his own heart attitude toward the Lord. He was less concerned with how soon the captivity was going to end than with why it had to happen in the first place. The question for him was not "When are we going to return?" but "Are we ready to return?"

Perhaps Daniel's response is worth emulating today. Prophecy can be a fascinating study, but the point is not to solve riddles; it is to hear what God has to say and respond accordingly. Daniel shows that one of our first responses to God's revelation should be repentance and remorse for sin.

Therefore, the **seventy years** has several beginnings and endings.

9:4–14 This is a prayer of repentance for Israel's past sinfulness, but it is also a prayer of confidence, for God was about to overthrow the Babylonians and allow the Jews to return to their homeland to rebuild it. The seventy years of captivity were almost up, and glorious things lay ahead. Daniel confessed that Israel had departed from the Word of God, had disregarded the prophets of God, and had despised the Lord Himself.

9:11–14 the curse and the oath: Covenant documents typically contained statements concerning the penalties for covenant violation. In **the Law of Moses,** such sanctions are found particularly in Lev. 26:3–45; Deut. 27; 28. In both passages the most feared and devastating curse of all—deportation from the land of promise—is emphasized (Lev. 26:33–39; Deut. 28:36–68). Daniel pointed out that the curse had come to pass.

9:15, 16 brought Your people out of the land of Egypt: Daniel reflected on the greatest redemptive event of Israel's history, the exodus from Egypt, and prayed that God would repeat what He had done long ago.

9:17 Your sanctuary is a reference to Solomon's temple, which had lain in ruins since 586 B.C.

9:18 Your great mercies: It is important to note that the only basis for Daniel's appeal was the grace of God.

9:19 Do not delay: These words must be understood in light of Daniel's reference to the seventy years (v. 2). Daniel knew full well that all of God's promises had not come to pass, nor had the blessings been conferred on the regathered and restored people (Lev. 26:40–45; Deut. 4:29–31).

9:20–23 while I was speaking: The angel was sent at the beginning of Daniel's prayer (v. 23). **The man Gabriel** is not a denial of Gabriel's angelic nature; the title simply serves to identify Gabriel with the vision of 8:15, 16. **evening offering:** Because the temple was in ruins, regular daily sacrifices were impossible. Nevertheless, Daniel observed the ritual of worship by praying at the hour of the evening sacrifice. Daniel's prayer was his evening offering.

9:24 Seventy weeks may also be translated *seventy sevens*. Many scholars agree that the "sevens" are years, as the seventy years of captivity addressed in v. 2 implies. Leviticus 25:8 speaks about "seven sabbaths of years"; Lev. 26:18, 21 implies that Israel's punishment would be multiplied sevenfold. Therefore, a seventy "week" exile would be expected to last for seven times seventy years. Second Chronicles 36:21 suggests that the captivity was to last long

enough to make up for seventy omissions of the sabbatical year, which occurred every seven years. This would amount to 490 years before God's people would experience perfect reconciliation with their God. There are many different interpretations of how these years account for the eras of world history before the Second Coming of the Messiah. Some interpreters have suggested that the use of the number seven in this verse is symbolic representing completeness—that is, the completion of all of human history.

9:25 The command to restore and build Jerusalem may be a reference to (1) the decree of Cyrus in Ezra 1, (2) the decree of Darius in Ezra 6, (3) the decree of Artaxerxes in Ezra 7, or (4) the decree of Artaxerxes in Neh. 2.

9:26 One commonly held interpretation maintains that **the sixty-two weeks** can be added to the seven weeks of v. 25, resulting in a total of sixty-nine weeks, or 483 years. If these years are added to the date of the decree of Artaxerxes in Neh. 2, 445 B.C., with an adjustment to allow for the use of a 360–day year, the end of the sixty-nine weeks coincides with the date of the crucifixion of Jesus. Various other interpretations of the time periods indicated by the sixty-two weeks have been presented, including one that asserts that the Messiah in this verse refers to Cyrus, who was also called the Lord's anointed (Is. 45:1). **Messiah shall be cut off** may be a reference to the crucifixion of Jesus Christ. The phrase *cut off* means "to destroy, to kill." The fact that Jesus Christ died **not for Himself** but for the sins of the world may support the view that the Messiah in this verse refers to Jesus Himself. **The prince who is to come** may be a reference to the Antichrist (v. 27).

9:27 He may be a reference to the Antichrist, who will **confirm a covenant** with Israel. **In the middle of the week**—that is, three and one-half years later—he will break the covenant. **abominations . . . desolate:** Antiochus committed an abomination of desolation by setting up an altar to the god Zeus in the temple in Jerusalem (11:31). The Antichrist will also commit an abomination of desolation against the living God (Matt. 24:15). **the consummation . . . is poured out on the desolate:** The fact that this abomination does not occur **until** the consummation suggests that this verse is describing the abomination of the Antichrist and not that of Antiochus.

10:1 The third year of Cyrus's rule over Babylon was 536 B.C.

10:2, 3 Daniel **was mourning** because he wanted to understand the vision (v. 12). **Three full weeks** refers to Daniel's observance of the Passover and the Feast of Unleavened Bread, which took place during the first month of the year (Ex. 12:1–20). The Passover was kept on the fourteenth of the month, and the Feast of the Unleavened Bread for the next eight days, with the whole festival ending on the twenty-first day of the month.

10:4 The twenty-fourth day of the first month occurs three days after the Unleavened Bread festival (v. 2).

10:5 A certain man is either an appearance of the preincarnate Christ or an angel. The

10:13 The prince of the kingdom of Persia cannot be a human ruler, for the conflict referred to here is in the spiritual, heavenly realm, as the allusion to **Michael** makes clear. The prince, therefore, must be understood as a satanic figure who was to supervise the affairs of Persia, inspiring its religious, social, and political structures to works of evil. Paul refers to principalities, powers, rulers of the darkness of this age, and "spiritual hosts of wickedness in the heavenly places" (Eph. 6:12). The "man" here

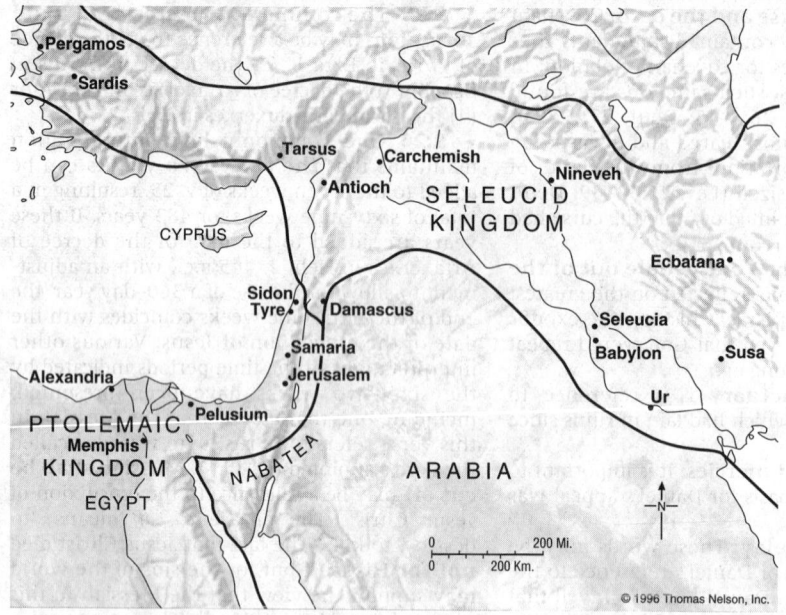

Ptolemaic Control of Palestine (270 B.C.)

Alexander's death resulted in the breakup of his empire into smaller kingdoms ruled by his generals. Two of these generals, Ptolemy and Seleucus, became established in the regions around Palestine. By 275 B.C. the Ptolemies were controlling Egypt, Palestine, Cyrene, Phoenicia, Cyprus, and the coast of Asia Minor. The Seleucids controlled Mesopotamia, Syria, and most of Asia Minor and Iran.

description that follows suggests that this individual is Christ (v. 6).

10:6, 7 The description of the man here is very much like Ezekiel's description of the glory of God (Ezek. 1:4–28) and John's description of the triumphant, risen Christ (Rev. 1:9–20).

10:8–10 Vigor suggests majesty, splendor, or beauty. **turned to frailty . . . no strength:** Humans are weak and frail in the presence of God.

10:11, 12 greatly beloved: God loves everyone (John 3:16); yet some, because of their special relationship to God, are objects of unusual divine love (1 Sam. 13:14; John 13:23; 14:21, 23; Acts 13:22).

says he was detained for **twenty-one days,** which equals the time of Daniel's mourning and fasting (vv. 2, 3). The wicked prince of Persia sought to detain the "man" so that Daniel would be prevented from hearing more of God's revelation (vv. 12, 14). **Michael** seems to be one of the most powerful angels. He is mentioned three times in the OT, all in Daniel (v. 21; 12:1), and twice in the NT (Jude 9; Rev. 12:7).

10:14, 15 latter days: This expression is used throughout the books of prophecy to refer to the future (Is. 2:2; Jer. 23:20; 49:39; Ezek. 38:16; Mic. 4:1). The messenger here is referring to the revelation of ch. 11.

10:16, 17 One having the likeness of the

sons of men may refer to the preincarnate Christ (v. 5) or to the angel of vv. 10–15.

10:18, 19 For the third time in this chapter Daniel is supernaturally **strengthened** by one who **touched** him (vv. 10, 16). The first touch enabled him to arise from the ground, the second to speak, and the third to carry on a conversation.

10:20 Just as Persia was under the ultimate dominion of an evil spirit from Satan (vv. 13, 14), so also was Greece. Once the **prince of Persia** was overcome, the messenger would enter into conflict with the **prince of Greece.** The succession of world powers follows the pattern of Daniel's second vision (8:20–22).

10:21 your prince: God chose Michael the archangel to be a prince in His kingdom on earth.

11:1 the first year of Darius: This is the same year as that of the revelation of the seventy weeks, 539 B.C. (9:1). At the beginning of the Persian administration, the divine messenger **stood up to confirm and strengthen** Darius. This suggests that though the kingdoms of the world are under demonic control, their human rulers can be delivered from that control and used for a higher purpose by God as He sees fit.

11:2–35 These verses contain prophecies concerning Persia (v. 2), Greece (vv. 3, 4), Egypt and Syria (vv. 5–35).

11:2 three more kings will arise in Persia, and the fourth ... against the realm of Greece: Darius (under Cyrus) was followed by Cambyses (530–522 B.C.); Gaumata (522 B.C.); Darius I (522–486 B.C.); and Xerxes (486–465 B.C.), who was the richest king of all due to his conquest and severe taxation.

11:3 The scene shifts to Greece (v. 2). The **mighty king** is Alexander the Great (v. 4).

11:4 The kingdom of Alexander was **divided** into **four** parts (8:22), **but not among his posterity**—that is, his heirs. **Others** refers to those outside Alexander's family—his generals ruled the empire he had conquered (8:8, 22).

11:5 Having predicted that there would be four divisions of the Greek kingdom (v. 4), the angel here speaks about two of them, the Syrian kingdom just north of Palestine and the Egyptian kingdom to the south. The first **king of the South**—that is, Egypt—was Ptolemy I Soter (323–285 B.C.). **One of his princes** refers to Seleucus Nicator (311–280 B.C.).

11:6 At the end of some years refers to the time period around 252 B.C. **The daughter** refers to Berenice, the daughter of Ptolemy Philadelphus (285–246 B.C.) of Egypt. **The king of the North** refers to Antiochus II Theos (261–246 B.C.) of Syria.

11:7–9 The **branch of her roots** refers to the brother of Berenice (v. 6), Ptolemy III Euergetes (246–221 B.C.), who conquered **the king of the North,** Seleucus Callinicus (246–226

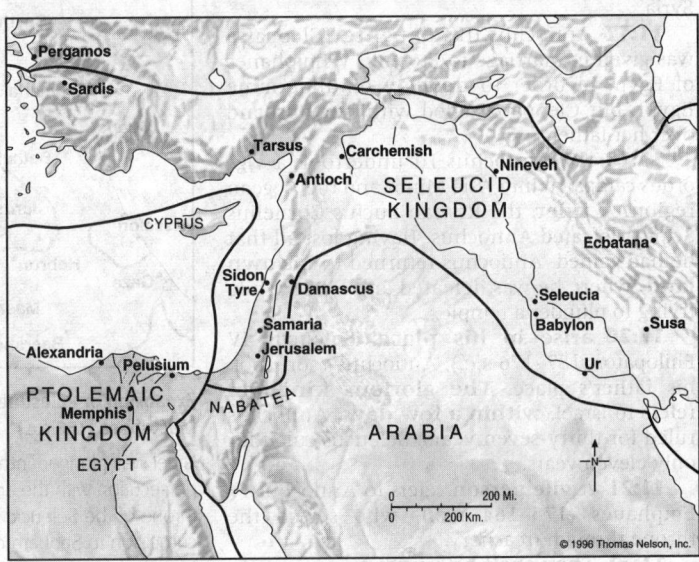

Seleucid Control of Palestine (190 B.C.)

Antiochus III, king of Syria, expanded the boundaries of the Seleucid kingdom in numerous battles with the Ptolemies. In 221 B.C. he captured part of Palestine, only to lose most of it in 217 B.C. Returning in 201 B.C. he finally defeated the Ptolemies in 198 B.C. with the aid and support of the Jews. Palestine enjoyed freedom from Egyptian domination until 175 B.C., when a new leader, Antiochus IV, became king of Syria. His oppression of the Jews led to the Maccabean Revolt of 167 B.C. and eventual Jewish autonomy in 164 B.C.

B.C.) of Syria. Ptolemy III returned **to Egypt** with great booty and outlived Seleucus by six years. Seleucus attempted an attack on Egypt but returned to Syria without accomplishing his purpose.

11:10 The **sons** of Seleucus Callinicus were Seleucus III Ceraunus (227–223 B.C.) and Antiochus III the Great (223–186 B.C.).

11:11, 12 The king of the South, Ptolemy

IV Philopator (221–204 B.C.), defeated **the king of the North,** Antiochus III the Great, at Raphia in 217 B.C.

11:13 The king of the North, Antiochus III, assembled a great army and attacked Egypt in 201 B.C.

11:14 Many shall rise up indicates that others like Philip V of Macedonia helped Antiochus fight **against the king of the South,** Ptolemy V Epiphanes (203–181 B.C.) of Egypt. The **violent men of your people** refers to Jews who tried to help Antiochus bring to pass what had been predicted in the vision of ch. 8, but failed.

11:15 The king of the North, Antiochus, defeated the **fortified city** of Sidon in 198 B.C.

11:16 The Glorious Land refers to Israel. The control of Palestine passed from Egypt to Syria.

11:17 Antiochus III's **daughter** Cleopatra was given in marriage to Ptolemy V Epiphanes of Egypt in order to **destroy** or undermine Egypt, but Cleopatra sided with her husband over her father.

11:18, 19 Antiochus III undertook a vigorous campaign into Asia Minor and the Aegean region. **A ruler,** the Roman Lucius Cornelius Scipio, defeated Antiochus. Having lost all that he had gained, Antiochus returned to **his own land,** where he was defeated and killed while trying to plunder a temple.

11:20 arise in his place: Seleucus IV Philopator (187–176 B.C.), Antiochus's son, took his father's place. **The glorious kingdom** refers to Israel. **within a few days:** Antiochus ruled for thirty-seven years; Seleucus ruled for only eleven years.

11:21 A vile person refers to Antiochus IV Epiphanes (175–164 B.C.), who seized the throne through treachery.

11:22 They shall be swept away is probably a reference to the Egyptians. **The prince of the covenant** refers to Onias III, the high priest in Jerusalem who bore that title.

11:23, 24 He refers to Antiochus IV Epiphanes (v. 21). **shall disperse:** Antiochus took from the rich and gave to the poor.

11:25, 26 The king of the South at this time was Ptolemy Philometor (181–145 B.C.) of Egypt. **those who eat . . . his delicacies:** The trusted counselors of Ptolemy Philometor who ate at his table betrayed him.

11:27 Both . . . bent on evil: Both Antiochus and Ptolemy resorted to deceit and betrayal in working out truce arrangements.

11:28 The holy covenant refers to Israel. **do damage:** On his way back to Syria, Antiochus looted the temple in Jerusalem and killed many people.

11:29 return and go toward the south:

After learning that Ptolemy VI and Ptolemy VII had formed a union against him, Antiochus returned to Egypt in 168 B.C.

11:30 Cyprus here refers to Rome. When the Romans forced Antiochus to depart from Egypt, he unleashed his frustration on **the holy**

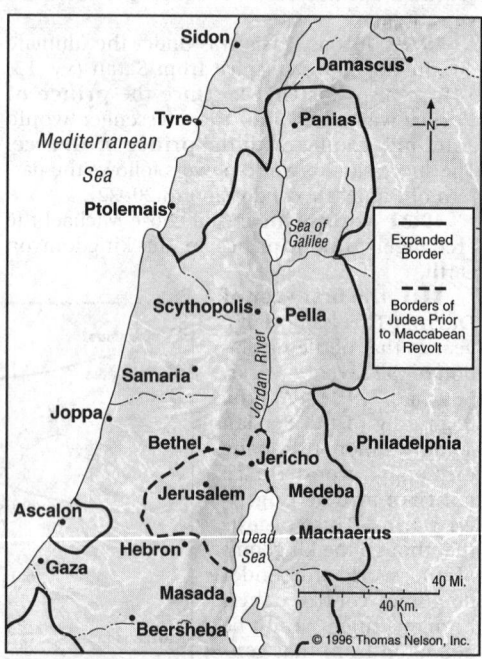

Expansion of Palestine under the Maccabees (166 B.C.)

Israel was plunged into an grueling period of religious persecution with the accession of Antiochus IV to the throne of the Seleucid kingdom in 175 B.C. From circumcision to Sabbath observance, many Jewish customs were outlawed. Opposition to Antiochus's policies centered around Mattathias's home in Modein, a town seventeen miles northwest of Jerusalem. In 167 B.C. Antiochus desecrated the temple itself by erecting a statue of Zeus and sacrificing a pig. A guerrilla war ensued. In 164 B.C. Mattathias's son, Judas Maccabeus, successfully recaptured Jerusalem and reconsecrated the temple. Judas's brothers, Simon and Jonathan, continued the struggle against Syrian tyranny until 142 B.C. After that date, Israel remained practically independent until the Romans invaded Palestine in 63 B.C.

covenant—that is, Israel (v. 28). **Those who forsake the holy covenant** refers to the apostate Jews (v. 32) who cooperated with Antiochus.

11:31 defile the sanctuary: Antiochus polluted the altar by offering a sow upon it. He declared **the daily sacrifices** and other Mosaic ceremonies illegal and committed an **abomination of desolation** by erecting an image of Zeus in the holy place (9:27; 12:11). Jesus said a similar thing would happen just prior to His return (Matt. 24:15).

11:32 the people who know their God shall be strong: Mattathias, father of five sons, refused to offer sacrifices in a profane manner and killed the king's agents. He and his sons then fled to the mountains and began the famous Maccabean revolt.

11:33 Many devoted Jews were killed in the Maccabean revolt (Heb. 11:37, 38).

11:34 As some Jews were killed in the Maccabean revolt, others provided **a little help. Many** joined **by intrigue**—that is, insincerely.

11:35 Some of those of understanding refers to those who understood God's Word and were allowed to go through troubled times so that they could be refined and purified.

11:36 the king: Many ancient and modern interpreters have concluded that at this point a new person, the Antichrist, is introduced. This king is distinguished from the king of the North (v. 40); therefore he cannot be Antiochus Epiphanes.

11:37 The king of v. 36 will cast aside **the God of his fathers,** the worship of his ancestors. **The desire of women** is usually taken to be either a female goddess or the desire of every Jewish woman to be the mother of the Messiah.

11:38, 39 god of fortresses: The king of v. 36 will not regard any god except the god of power. **A god which his fathers did not know** is probably a reference to self worship (v. 37; 2 Thess. 2:4).

11:40 The backdrop of this verse and the remainder of the chapter is the covenant the king of v. 36 will make with Israel. **The time of the end** refers to the period just before the return of Christ (Matt. 24:14).

11:41–43 The king of v. 36 will **enter the Glorious Land** of Palestine. **Edom, Moab,** and **Ammon,** the traditional enemies of Israel, will not be invaded. The king will then conquer **Egypt,** Libya, and Ethiopia.

11:44 The north here could be a reference to Palestine, a view which seems to be confirmed by v. 45.

11:45 The seas refers to the Mediterranean Sea and the Dead Sea. **The glorious holy mountain** refers to Mount Zion, the site of the temple. The **end** of the king of v. 36 is sealed at Christ's second coming (Rev. 19:11–21).

12:1 At that time refers to the "time of the end" (11:40), the end of the evil king (11:36) at the Second Coming of Christ (11:45). **A time of trouble, such as never was since there was a nation** refers to the period of tribulation just prior to the coming of Christ. Those who **shall be delivered** are those whose names are **written in the book** of life, God's record of those who have been justified by faith (Ex. 32:32; Ps. 69:28; Luke 10:20; Rev. 20:12).

12:2 Sleep is a euphemism for death, as the context **in the dust of the earth** illustrates. **Awake** is a reference to resurrection. Though this passage appears to refer to a general resurrection, other passages suggest that there is more than one (John 5:25). It is not unusual for prophecy in the OT to present events separated by a considerable span of time as if they occurred in immediate relationship to each other (Is. 61:1, 2). Daniel is simply saying that after the tribulation, **many**—both righteous and wicked—will be raised. This resurrection of many of the righteous seems to be a reference to the resurrection of Israel ("your people" in v. 1).

12:3 The **wise** not only understand salvation themselves (2 Tim. 3:15), they also **turn** many others to the way of **righteousness.**

12:4 Knowledge shall increase is a reference to knowledge that pertains to these prophecies.

12:5, 6 As Daniel stood beside the Tigris

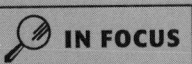 **IN FOCUS** **"sealed"**

(Heb. *chatham*) (12:9; Is. 29:11; Jer. 32:10) Strong's #2856: This word means "to affix a seal." To authenticate a document and assure its integrity, a king or official would close it with an application of clay or wax, stamped with an impression of his seal. The document then carried his authority and could not be altered without breaking the seal. Letters (1 Kin. 21:8), land deeds (Jer. 32:10), covenants (Neh. 10:1), and royal decrees (Esth. 3:12) were all authenticated with seals. Daniel's prophetic announcements were symbolically sealed (12:9), indicating that they were authoritative and could not be altered, until the day of their fulfillment. In Revelation, a seal of the scroll of judgment is broken, indicating that the time of its fulfillment has come (Rev. 5:1–10).

River, he saw three persons, one on each side of the river and one above the **river.** The **two others** refers to two angels, different from the ones Daniel had already seen. **The man clothed in linen** may be the preincarnate Christ (10:6). **How long** refers to the duration of the trials. Daniel was not asking when the events would begin.

12:7 A time, times, and half a time, which adds up to three and one-half years (7:25), may refer to the period immediately preceding the Second Coming of Christ (7:27). Others have suggested that this expression does not refer to a specific number of years but instead a period of time that the Lord would shorten because of His mercy.

12:8, 9 Daniel **did not understand** his own revelation (v. 4).

12:10 Many will be **purified, made white, and refined** (11:35). Suffering will refine the righteous, but the **wicked** will be continue in their evil.

12:11, 12 one thousand two hundred and ninety days: Various interpretations have been suggested for this number of days. One significant interpretation is that these days refer to the middle of a seven-year period of tribulation prior to the coming of Christ. At that time, the Antichrist will abolish the abominable and idolatrous sacrifices that he had established (9:27).

12:13 you shall rest, and will arise: Daniel would die and be resurrected.

The Book of

Hosea

LIKE OTHERS BEFORE AND AFTER HIM, HOSEA discovered that being a prophet had its occupational hazards. The Lord sometimes required His prophets to perform difficult and even humiliating object lessons to complement their messages. At the beginning of Hosea's prophetic ministry, the Lord told him to get married and announced that Hosea's chosen bride would be unfaithful to her marriage vows.

Her adultery would vividly illustrate Israel's unfaithfulness to her covenant Lord.

Hosea chose Gomer, the daughter of Diblaim, as his wife and they had three children, each of whom received a symbolic name from the Lord. The firstborn son's name *Jezreel* was a reminder of the atrocities that had occurred at Jezreel. God would soon judge Israel for these sins, appropriately through a military defeat at this same city. Their daughter *LoRuhamah's* name, meaning "Not Loved," announced that the Lord would temporarily withdraw His love from Israel. The third child's name *Lo-Ammi*, meaning "Not My People," anticipated the severe disruption of the Lord's covenantal relationship with His people.

Because of Gomer's adulteries, the marriage disintegrated, and she eventually became the slave or concubine of another man. However, the Lord instructed Hosea to buy back his wife. Hosea's act of mercy toward his wife was a striking picture of the Lord's great love for Israel.

Hosea began prophesying during a time of general prosperity. Jeroboam had extended Israel's borders through several military operations (2 Kin. 14:24–28). In the south, Uzziah

had strengthened Judah's armed forces and defeated the nation's enemies (2 Chr. 26:1–15). But despite the outward success of the two nations, signs of trouble were on the horizon. As the Book of Hosea makes clear, idolatry—especially worship of the Canaanite god Baal—was widespread in the northern kingdom. The assassination of Zechariah, Jeroboam's son and successor, in 753 B.C. ended Jehu's dynasty and introduced a new era of political turmoil.

Making matters worse, the mighty Assyrian Empire, after several decades of declining power, was once more flexing its muscles and looking westward. During the second half of the eighth century B.C., Assyria reduced Israel to a vassal state (required by treaty to pay regular tribute to Assyria), then a puppet state (ruled by a king chosen by Assyria), and finally a province (ruled by an Assyrian governor). Judah also declined spiritually and was torn by political dissension. King Ahaz rejected Isaiah's offer of divine protection and instead embarked on a pro-Assyrian policy that facilitated the Assyrian takeover of the Palestinian states, reduced Judah to vassal status, and drained the nation's economic wealth.

The Book of Hosea fluctuates between judgment and salvation. Each of the book's five major sections begins on a sour note but concludes with a positive affirmation of God's commitment to His people and the expectation that He will restore them. As a prophet and a poet, Hosea uses an arsenal of rhetorical and poetic techniques to communicate his message in a memorable and persuasive manner. He uses a variety of metaphors as he depicts a broad range of themes, including God's anger, judgment, devotion, and love, as well as Israel's waywardness and stubbornness. Hosea employs images that were familiar to his contemporaries, drawing extensively from agriculture and nature. Hosea paints some of the most moving, terrifying, and exhilarating word pictures in all of the Bible.

Hosea's purpose was to denounce sin, to warn of impending judgment, and to assure the faithful that God's love would win out in the end. Israel, the northern kingdom, is the primary focus of Hosea's prophecy. Hosea accused the nation of being unfaithful to its vows, just as his own adulterous wife had been unfaithful to her vows. By participating in the pagan fertility rites of Baalism, the people violated their covenant with the Lord. The Lord did not tolerate this rebellion and was prepared to bring against Israel the judgments threatened in the covenant (Deut. 28:15–68). God's purpose, however, was not entirely punitive; He intended these severe judgments to bring the nation to its senses. Hosea proclaimed that the Lord would eventually restore His marriage with His people and again pour His blessings upon them.

Israel's covenant relationship with God is at the heart of Hosea's message. God delivered His people from slavery in Egypt, established them as a nation, and took great delight in them. He looked for a favorable response to His love and obedience to the commandments He had given to regulate the people's worship and daily activities. However, the people were ungrateful, turning to other gods, violating the religious and social standards of God's covenant, and forming alliances with surrounding nations.

When God establishes a binding relationship, He demands absolute loyalty. Through Hosea, God announced that He would use severe judgment to free His people from their spiritual stupor and get their attention. This judgment would take the forms of drought, invasion, and exile. Though the severity of God's judgment might give the impression that Israel had been abandoned forever, the Lord intended to restore of His people. When they repented of their sins, He would return them to their land, reunite the north and south under an ideal Davidic king, and restore His rich blessings.

The Book of Hosea gives us a clear and balanced picture of God. He loves His people and desires an intimate and vibrant relationship with them. He is jealous of their affections and tolerates no rivals. When they sin, He will discipline them as severely as is necessary. While God's jealousy may seem inappropriate and His discipline may seem harsh, this divine response to His people's sin is actually evidence of His love and commitment. He will allow nothing to ruin the relationship He has established and will do everything to preserve it. In the end, His

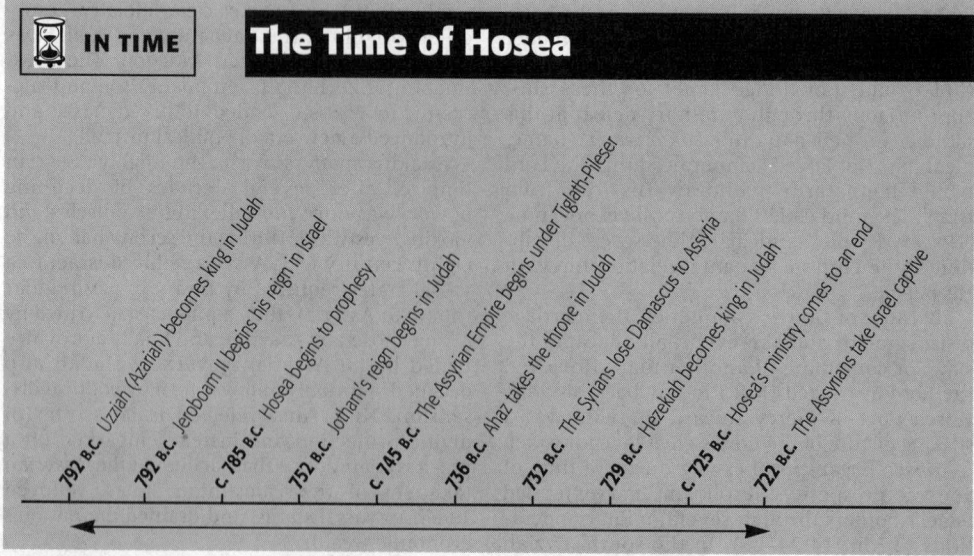

IN TIME **The Time of Hosea**

792 B.C. Uzziah (Azariah) becomes king in Judah
792 B.C. Jeroboam II begins his reign in Israel
c. 785 B.C. Hosea begins to prophesy
752 B.C. Jotham's reign begins in Judah
c. 745 B.C. The Assyrian Empire begins under Tiglath-Pileser
736 B.C. Ahaz takes the throne in Judah
732 B.C. The Syrians lose Damascus to Assyria
729 B.C. Hezekiah becomes king in Judah
c. 725 B.C. Hosea's ministry comes to an end
722 B.C. The Assyrians take Israel captive

devotion and mercy will win out, and His people will come to their senses, giving Him the love He fervently desires.

Hosea the son of Beeri prophesied during the eighth century B.C. His ministry began while Uzziah (Azariah) was king of Judah (792–740 B.C.) and Jeroboam II was king of Israel (792–753 B.C.). Hosea's prophetic career spanned the reigns of the Judean kings Jotham (752–736 B.C.) and Ahaz (736–720 B.C.) and ended during Hezekiah's rule (729–699 B.C.). Hosea also witnessed the reigns of the last six kings of Israel, though he did not name these kings in his prophecies.

Outline

Commentary

1:1–3 wife of harlotry: Gomer may have been a common prostitute at the time Hosea married her, or perhaps she had participated in a ritual sexual act as part of the Baal cult. However, it is more likely that the descriptive phrase anticipates what Gomer would become fol-

lowing her marriage to Hosea. **children of harlotry:** If Gomer was a prostitute when she married Hosea, this could refer to children that Gomer already had and that Hosea adopted at the time of marriage. A more likely possibility is that the title anticipates children born to a mother whose reputation and escapades would make their lineage suspect. Gomer's marital infidelity is a picture of Israel's idolatry and unfaithfulness to its covenant with God.

1:4 bloodshed of Jezreel: In 841 B.C. Jehu, with God's approval, destroyed the evil dynasty of Omri by slaughtering Jezebel, the sons of Ahab, and the prophets and priests of Baal (2 Kin. 9; 10).

1:5 To **break** the enemy's **bow** means to destroy his military strength (1 Sam. 2:4; Ps. 46:9; Jer. 49:35).

1:6 Lo-Ruhamah means "Not Loved," foreshadowing the Lord's rejection of Israel.

1:7, 8 Will save them: This prophecy looks ahead to the Lord's deliverance of Jerusalem in 701 B.C., when He would miraculously destroy the Assyrian armies outside the city's walls (2 Kin. 19:32–36). This emphasized that the end of pity or mercy was for the northern kingdom only. The prophecy was fulfilled during Sennacherib's invasion in 701 B.C.

1:9 Lo-Ammi means "Not My People," threatening the termination of the Lord's covenant relationship with His persistently unfaithful people (Lev. 26:12).

1:10 The Lord would not reject His people forever. God would fulfill His promise to Abraham and make the Israelites as numerous as the **sand of the sea** (Gen. 22:17; 32:12).

1:11 One head refers to the messianic king to come (3:5). **Jezreel** means "God Plants," picturing God as sowing seed that would germinate and grow abundantly (2:23).

2:1 brethren . . . sisters: God would mercifully restore His covenant relationship with His people, reversing the judgment symbolized by the names Lo-Ruhamah and Lo-Ammi.

2:2–17 The events of these verses summarize in capsule form the remainder of the prophecy—what Gomer has done, Israel has done. What happens to Gomer will happen to Israel. Three events are important: (1) her reprobation (vv. 2–5); (2) her retribution (vv. 6–13); and, (3) her restitution (vv. 14–17). These events constitute the background for the messages of the prophecy that follow in the next major division: (1) concerning Israel's reprobation (4:1—7:16); (2) concerning Israel's retribution (8:1—13:16); and, (3) concerning Israel's restoration (14:1–8).

2:2 Bring charges: The Lord formally accused Israel of unfaithfulness to the covenant. **Your mother** refers to the sinful nation of

INSIGHT   **There's Nothing *Minor* Here!**

It's unfortunate that the last twelve books of the OT are known today as the Minor Prophets. The name was intended to distinguish them from the four "major" (that is, longer) prophetic books, Isaiah, Jeremiah, Ezekiel, and Daniel. But in modern culture, where bigger is seen as better, and where celebrity is mistaken for significance, anything called "minor" is subtly thought of as less important. Thus the Minor Prophets are sometimes treated as the "minor league" prophets, as if those who wrote them were on God's "second team." That would be a grave misperception. There is nothing *minor* about these books. On the contrary, they play a *major* role in declaring God's Word not only to the Israelites and other nations of the ancient world, but to us as well. By reading them, we gain additional perspective on the sins God hates and the faith He honors.

Hosea's time, symbolized by Gomer (1:2, 3). **she is not My wife:** This may be a formal announcement of divorce or a realistic confession that the relationship between God and Israel had lost its vitality.

2:3 The Lord warned that He might publicly humiliate His unfaithful wife by stripping her **naked** (Ezek. 16:35–43). **dry land:** This simile pictures the loss of fertility, an appropriate punishment for a nation that had sought fertility by worshiping another god.

2:4, 5 **Her children** refers to the Israelites who lived in the land. Though the **mother** (the land) and the children (the inhabitants of the land) are distinct in Hosea's metaphor, both actually refer to the sinful nation. The Lord warned that He might disown the children because they were a reminder of their mother's unfaithfulness.

2:6, 7 **chase:** This word draws attention to the strong passion the people of Israel felt for Baal. These verses anticipate the Exile, when Israel would be separated from the idols of Baal.

2:8, 9 Since Israel refused to acknowledge the Lord as her source of agricultural prosperity, the Lord would **take back** His blessings and no longer provide for the nation's basic needs.

2:10 **uncover her lewdness:** The Lord would publicly expose Israel's unfaithfulness through judgment. **in the sight of her lovers:** The Baal idols would be unable to help Israel, proving their unworthiness to be worshiped.

2:11 **New Moons** were monthly celebrations (Num. 10:10; 1 Sam. 20:5, 18, 24). Sabbath celebrations were weekly.

2:12 The people of Israel believed that the Baal idols gave them agricultural prosperity in exchange for their worship. **forest . . . beasts of the field:** The Lord would break down the nation's defenses and turn them into overgrown thickets inhabited by wild animals.

2:13 The word **earrings** may refer to rings

worn in the ear (Gen. 35:4; Ex. 32:2, 3) or nose (Gen. 24:47; Is. 3:21; Ezek. 16:12).

2:14 Having separated Israel from her lovers, the Lord would seek to win her back by making romantic overtures and wooing her with tender words of love. **wilderness:** The coming Exile from the land is compared to the wilderness wanderings of Moses' time.

2:15 **Valley of Achor,** meaning "Valley of Trouble," was a reminder of the sin of Achan and God's discipline of the nation of Israel for his sin (Josh. 7:24–26). This place would be transformed into a **door of hope** when the returning exiles passed through it on their return to the land.

2:16, 17 Israel would call the Lord her **Husband,** not her **Master,** because the latter title might have reminded the people of their former devotion to Baal. The word *Baal* can mean "Master."

2:18 The land will experience peace. The Lord will protect its crops from hungry animals (v. 12) and prevent hostile armies from invading it.

2:19, 20 **betroth:** Betrothal was a binding commitment, the last step before the wedding and consummation. **forever:** The Lord emphasized that the new marriage between Himself and Israel would be permanent. **Lovingkindness** means "devotion, commitment." **you shall know:** Israel would respond positively to the Lord's love and acknowledge that He is her husband and benefactor (contrast vv. 8, 13; see Jer. 31:34).

2:21–23 **The heavens** would provide rain for the **earth**; the earth would produce its fruit in turn. Israel is called **Jezreel**, meaning "God Plants," because the Lord would replant Israel in the land.

3:1–3 This section divides into two parts: (1) the prophet's commission by God (v. 1); and (2) his compliance to God (vv. 2, 3).

3:1, 2 To illustrate His intention to redeem

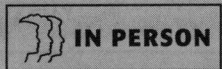

Love Is a Conscious Choice

Popular culture often describes love in terms of passion, sexuality, or blind devotion. By this measure, love is little more than an uncontrollable attraction toward another person that ebbs and flows unconsciously. This sort of "love" looks only for its own gain and can walk away if its demands and needs go unmet or unsatisfied. By contrast, God called Hosea to pursue a radically different kind of love, one based on a conscious choice to be committed to someone else for her benefit, regardless of her response to that gift (Hos. 3:1–3). That was how God was committed to Israel. Hosea's marriage was an illustration of God's marriage to the spiritually adulterous nation of Israel.

Israel, the Lord instructed Hosea to reclaim Gomer, his unfaithful wife. **raisin cakes:** These may have been used in the worship of Canaanite fertility gods. **I bought her:** Gomer had become the property of another man. The value of the **silver** and **barley** that Hosea paid was approximately equal to the 30 shekels required for a female slave (Ex. 21:32). Hosea's purchase of Gomer symbolized God's great devotion, which moves Him to seek reconciliation even if it means subjecting Himself to humiliation (Phil. 2:8).

3:3, 4 Gomer's isolation symbolized Israel's exile, when she lost her political independence and could no longer worship as she chose (2:6, 7). **sacred pillar:** These were stone pillars used by the Canaanites in their worship of Baal and other gods (2 Kin. 3:2; 10:26, 27; 17:10). An **ephod** was a priestly garment (Ex. 28); **teraphim** were idols (2 Kin. 23:24). Both were apparently used for divination.

3:5 seek: This word highlights the change that would occur in Israel's attitude (2:7). **David:** This is likely a reference to David's Son, the Messiah (Is. 11:1–10; Jer. 23:5; 33:15). Other prophets also refer to the Messiah as David (Jer. 30:9; Ezek. 34:23, 24; 37:24, 25). The northern kingdom of Israel rejected the Davidic kingship in their rebellion against Rehoboam (1 Kin. 1216–19). Their return to God would involve a reunion of Israel and Judah, along with the recognition of the divinely established dynasty of David.

4:1 charge: The Hebrew word refers to a formal complaint charging Israel with breaking the covenant. **Mercy** means "loyalty" or "devotion." **knowledge:** This word does not refer to intellectual awareness, but to recognition of God's authority as Israel's covenant Lord.

4:2 This accusation mentions five of the Ten Commandments. **Swearing** refers to the misuse of the Lord's name in oaths and curses (Ex. 20:7).

4:3 A drought would come upon the land and negatively impact the inhabitants of all three of the basic spheres of existence—the dry land, sky, and waters.

4:4 The people were rebellious and showed no respect for authority (Deut. 17:12).

4:5, 6 The failure of Israel's religious leaders, including most of the prophets, would bring about their downfall. **lack of knowledge:** The priests had failed to teach God's Law to the people (Mal. 2:7). As a result, the priests would be the special object of God's judgment. He would terminate the priestly line.

4:7, 8 their glory: Great honor was attached to the priesthood. However, Israel's sinful priests would forfeit their prestige. **eat up the sin of My people:** The priests greedily accepted the meat from the people's hypocritical and empty sacrifices (6:6; 8:11–13).

4:9 The leaders of God's people should be models and teachers of God's righteous standards, but these priests were at the same moral level as the sinful people.

4:10 The Israelites worshiped Baal in order to have good crops and many children, but they still would not have enough to eat, nor would they multiply in number. **Harlotry** here refers to religious prostitution associated with Baal worship, not to immorality in general.

4:11–14 Wine was apparently used in Baal worship, along with divination, sacrifices, and ritual sexual acts. **Their staff** refers to **wooden idols** that Baal worshipers consulted for guidance. The religion of Canaan was practiced in innumerable small shrines located on hilltops and in groves of trees. The idols consisted of stone pillars and wooden poles. **daughters . . . brides:** Many of Israel's young women had participated in the sexual rites of Baal worship, but **the men** were just as guilty.

4:15, 16 Hosea warned the people of **Judah** not to follow in the sinful footsteps of the northern kingdom **Israel. Gilgal** was an important religious center in the north, known in Hosea's time for its hypocritical religious practices (9:15; 12:11; Amos 4:4). **Beth Aven,** which means "House of Iniquity," is a sarcastic reference to the important religious center Bethel, which means "House of God" (Amos 5:5).

4:17–19 Ephraim, one of the largest tribes

✔ **IN COMPARISON** **Hosea's Heartbreak and God's Grief**

The tragic marriage of Hosea and Gomer painted a vivid portrait for the Israelites of how God viewed His relationship with them.

Hosea and Gomer	God and Israel
Hosea marries Gomer (1:3).	God is betrothed to Israel (2:19).
Hosea is a faithful husband (3:3).	God is a faithful "Husband" (1:7).
Hosea's love is unrequited (3:1).	God's love is unrequited (3:1).
The relationship disintegrates (3:1).	The relationship disintegrates (2:2).
Gomer pursues other men (3:1).	Israel pursues other gods (4:1).
Gomer is indifferent to the feelings of Hosea (3:1).	Israel is indifferent to God's feelings (11:1).
Hosea has a daughter whose name Lo-Ruhamah means "Not Loved" (1:6).	God will not have pity on His wayward children in Israel (5:6).
Hosea has a son whose name Lo-Ammi means "Not My People" (1:9).	God declares that the Israelites are not His people (1:9).
Hosea redeems and restores the adulterous Gomer (3:2).	God redeems and restores the unfaithful nation, Israel (14:4–8).

of Israel, is used here to represent the entire northern kingdom. **Let him alone:** These words have a tone of frustration and resignation, suggesting that Israel was hopelessly rebellious. The wind of divine judgment would sweep the Israelites away and leave them embarrassed by their idolatry.

5:1–6:3 In this section God's condemnation results in three things: (1) rebuke (5:1–7); (2) retribution (5:8–15); and, (3) repentance (6:1–3).

5:1 Mizpah here is probably a reference to Mizpah of Gilead, located in Israelite territory east of the Jordan. **Tabor:** Mount Tabor was in the northern kingdom, southwest of the Sea of Galilee. **snare . . . net:** The leaders of Israel,

especially the **priests,** had promoted pagan worship at Mizpah and Tabor and in this way led the people to destruction.

5:2 The revolters probably refers to the leaders and priests who had rebelled against God's authority by rejecting His commandments. **Slaughter** may refer literally to acts of violence or to pagan sacrifices.

5:3 not hidden: God's people could not hide their **harlotry,** for it had **defiled** them. According to the Law of Moses, adultery made a person spiritually unclean or *defiled* (Lev. 18:20, 24; Num. 5:20, 27, 28).

5:4 spirit of harlotry: The people had an uncontrollable desire to worship other gods.

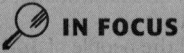 **IN FOCUS** **"stumble"**

(Heb. *kashal*) (4:5; 5:5; 1 Sam. 2:4; Is. 3:8) Strong's #3782: Literally this Hebrew verb means "to totter," "to trip and fall," or "to stumble." The prophets frequently used this word to describe the spiritual life of the Hebrews. For example, Hosea compares both false prophets and their followers to those who stumble in the dark: they are stumbling over the sin of idolatry and falling to their ruin (4:5; 5:5; Is. 3:8). Isaiah warns that those who rely on their own strength will stumble and fall (Is. 40:30), but those who are led by the Lord will not stumble (Is. 63:13). In fact, the Lord will provide strength to those who have stumbled in the past and now call upon Him (1 Sam. 2:4).

5:5 Israel's arrogant attitude was self-incriminating and self-destructive. **Judah,** the southern kingdom, had followed Israel's moral example and would experience the same consequences.

5:6, 7 Though Israel had rebelled against God, many Israelites still tried to maintain a semblance of outward devotion to Him. They had **dealt treacherously** with God by worshiping

The terebinth tree, also referred to as the oak tree by some translations, was considered sacred by some pagan worshipers of the ancient world (Hos. 4:13).

other gods and participating in **pagan** fertility rites. **Their heritage,** or "portion," refers to the people's landed property and fields, which God would allow wild animals and invading armies to overrun and **devour** (2:12; 11:6).

5:8–15 This section may refer to the period during the Syro-Ephraimite war (2 Kin. 16:5–9; Is. 7:1–9) when Israel's efforts to win independence from Syrian domination failed.

5:8, 9 Blow the ram's horn: This act signaled an emergency and mustered the fighting men to defend the land. The towns mentioned

here were north of Jerusalem, within or near the borders of Benjamin. The implication is that the enemy army had already swept through the north and was ready to invade Judah. **what is sure:** The Lord affirmed that the announced judgment was an unalterable decree.

5:10, 11 Stones were used to mark the boundaries of property. A thief could steal a part of someone's land by moving the **landmark.** The Law warned that altering a boundary in this way would bring a special judgment from God (Deut. 19:14; 27:17; Prov. 22:28).

5:12 As a **moth** slowly destroys clothing, so the Lord would destroy Israel (Job 13:28; Is. 50:9; 51:8). **Rottenness** elsewhere refers to bone or tooth decay (Prov. 12:4; 14:30; Hab. 3:16).

5:13 Both Israel and **Judah** sought protection through alliances with **Assyria,** but the cruel Assyrians were more interested in exploiting God's people politically and economically. **King Jareb** probably refers to Tiglath-Pileser III, with whom both Israel and Judah formed alliances (2 Kin. 15:19, 20; 16:7–9).

5:14, 15 Attacking like a ferocious, invincible **lion,** God would scatter His people as judgment for their treachery. But the purpose of the Lord's discipline was to drive the people to **earnestly seek** Him. The Hebrew verb for *earnestly seek* suggests eager longing and desire (Job 24:5; Ps. 63:1).

6:1 After being **torn** by the divine lion (5:14), the people would come to their senses and seek to renew their allegiance to the Lord.

6:2 two days . . . the third day: The reference here is to a short time period. When God's people truly repent, God is eager to restore His relationship with them. The people's hope for revival was consistent with God's ancient promises through Moses (Deut. 30:1–3).

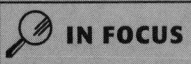 **IN FOCUS**   **"commit harlotry"**

(Heb. *zanah*) (1:2; 5:3; Jer. 3:3; Ezek. 16:35) Strong's #2181: The Hebrew verb *zanah* refers to having illicit sexual relations, especially involving prostitution. Two forms of prostitution were practiced in the ancient world: common prostitution and ritual, or "sacred," prostitution, which involved pagan fertility rites. Both forms were strictly forbidden in God's Law (Lev. 19:29; Deut. 23:17). The OT frequently uses prostitution as an image of the sin of idolatry. Israel was pledged to serve one God (Ex. 20:3), so idolatry was like marital unfaithfulness against the Lord. Jeremiah and Ezekiel develop this image in graphic detail (Jer. 3; Ezek. 16; 23), and Hosea actually married a prostitute as a living symbol of God's patience with Israel's infidelities (ch. 1).

6:3 God's restored presence and blessings would be like **the rain** that waters and renews the **earth. latter and former rain:** The *latter* rains of Israel came in the spring and caused the plants to grow. The *former* rains came in the autumn and softened the ground for plowing and sowing.

6:4–11:11 This section contains a further recital of Israel's sins with an emphasis on their perverted love. Again, however, the warning ends on a note of hope. Israel's love may be fickle, but God's love is unchanging.

6:4 Any apparent **faithfulness** that Hosea's generation displayed was short-lived and disappeared as quickly as fog or dew before sunlight.

6:5 words of My mouth: The **prophets** announced God's destructive judgments, which then fell on His unrepentant people. **your judgments are like light that goes forth:** This comparison suggests that God's judgment, like bright sunlight, was obvious to all; or that like a bolt of lightning or a blinding flash of light, it came swiftly.

6:6, 7 Mercy means "loyalty" or "devotion" (4:1). **Knowledge of God** does not refer to mere head knowledge, but to a genuine recognition of God's authority that produces obedience to His commandments.

6:8, 9 Even Ramoth-**Gilead** and **Shechem,** which were cities of refuge where manslayers could find asylum, had been contaminated by bloodshed.

6:10 horrible thing: A related Hebrew word is used in Jer. 29:17 of rotten figs.

6:11 The comparison of God's judgment to a **harvest** indicates that the judgment was inevitable and implies that it would be thorough in its destruction.

7:1–16 Israel's follies are enumerated in 7:1–7, and her floundering is portrayed in 7:8–16.

7:1, 2 Hardened sinners typically **do not consider** that God will hold them accountable for their deeds (Ps. 73:11).

7:3 While kings should promote justice and be appalled by **wickedness** (Ps. 101), Israel's rulers approved of the people's sin.

7:4–7 The background for these verses is the political turmoil of the northern kingdom. During a 20–year period (752–732 B.C.), four Israelite kings were assassinated (2 Kin. 15). The dangerous, uncontrollable perpetrators of these crimes are described here. These conspirators were like a large baker's **oven** that has been heating up for several hours while the bread dough rises. By morning, the **flaming fire** within can be quite destructive.

7:8 Instead of depending on the Lord for political stability, Israel formed alliances with surrounding nations. The destructive outcome of this policy is compared to a **cake** that has been placed over a fire and left **unturned.**

7:9, 10 gray hairs: Israel did not recognize that its power was declining and its freedom was slipping away, like an aging man who is gradually overtaken by the signs of old age.

7:11, 12 Israel was caught between the two superpowers, **Egypt** and **Assyria.** Israel tried to maintain its independence by playing one power against the other, but this vacillating policy was **without sense.** Israel was like a **silly dove,** flitting about from place to place. The Lord would trap them and **chastise** them for their spiritual unsteadiness.

7:13 Like a bird that flies away when frightened (Jer. 4:25), Israel **fled** from the Lord and His standards, despite His willingness to help the people.

7:14 God sent a drought that took away Israel's **grain and new wine.** Yet instead of turning to Him in repentance, the idolatrous Israelites demonstrated their devotion to Baal.

🌱 IN LIFE | **Foggy Faith**

Early morning fog can be a beautiful sight as it creeps over the mirrored surface of a lake or huddles over a silent meadow. Many a photographer has waited until just the right moment to capture a subject enshrouded in mists before the sunlight burns them away. Yet while fog may be impressive in the natural world, it can be utterly perilous in the spiritual, as Hosea pointed out. He used the image of fog as a metaphor of Israel's faithlessness (Hos. 6:4). The nation's commitment to the Lord was as empty and fleeting as a cloud. As soon as the people felt the "heat" of moral and spiritual conflicts, their loyalty to God evaporated.

This same "foggy faith" characterizes many people today. In an emotional moment they may pay impressive lipservice to loving and serving God, but as soon as their feelings of devotion fade, their "faith" is effectively vaporized. Clearly, as the Lord evaluates faith, what seems to matter is not whether it is beautiful, but how long it will last.

According to Canaanite religious beliefs, prolonged drought was a signal that the storm god Baal had been temporarily defeated by the god of death and was imprisoned in the underworld. Baal's worshipers would mourn his death in hopes that their tears might facilitate his resurrection and the restoration of crops.

7:15 Strengthened their arms probably refers to God's past military help, especially during the reign of Jeroboam II earlier in the eighth century B.C. (2 Kin. 14:24, 25).

7:16 A treacherous bow is a bow that is damaged or flawed in its workmanship and does not shoot effectively. Such a bow would be unreliable and therefore worthless to a warrior or hunter. Though the Lord had been faithful to Israel, Israel had not been loyal to Him (Ps. 78:57). **derision in the land of Egypt:** Note the irony in the fact that one of the nations to whom Israel had looked for help (v. 11) would make fun of Israel when judgment fell.

8:1–14 Five reasons are given for the trumpet call to retribution: (1) because of Israel's transgressions against God's covenant and Law (vv. 1–3); (2) because of her setting up kings and princes without God's direction (v. 4a); (3) because of her idolatrous practices (vv.

4b–7); (4) because of her alliance with Assyria (vv. 8–10); and, (5) because of Israel's multiplication of sacrificial altars (vv. 11–14).

8:1–3 Just as an **eagle** swiftly swoops down and snatches its prey, so Assyria would invade Israel and take its people into captivity. **The house of the LORD** refers to the entire land of Israel. **we know You:** Though Israel claimed to acknowledge the Lord's authority, it had violated His covenant and rejected the qualities the Lord regarded as **good,** such as justice, loyalty, and humility (Amos 5:14, 15; Mic. 6:8).

8:4 They set up kings: This phrase alludes to the political turmoil surrounding the throne of the northern kingdom during the eighth century B.C., when four kings were assassinated during a 20–year period (7:4–7).

8:5, 6 If the capital city **Samaria** stands for the northern kingdom in general, the reference here may be to the calf idols made by Jeroboam I (1 Kin. 12:28–30).

8:7 In its original context, this well-known proverb emphasizes the futility of Israel's alliances with false gods and foreign nations. Morally speaking, Israel had planted **wind,** symbolizing its moral bankruptcy, and would **reap** a **whirlwind,** symbolizing the coming judgment.

⁑ IN CONTEXT | **Corrupted and Half-Baked**

Those who speak about a moral and spiritual decline in society today might want to borrow a page from the Book of Hosea. The prophet denounced ancient Israel by heaping up metaphors that sound a lot like what is being said about modern culture. He described Ephraim (Israel) as:

- *Corrupted* (7:8). Israel "mixed" itself with surrounding nations by allowing their pagan religions to corrupt its religious and spiritual life. In doing so, God's people violated the First and Second Commandments (Ex. 20:3, 4). They also formed political alliances to prop up their defenses rather than relying on the Lord (for example, 2 Kin. 16:5, 6).
- *Half-baked* (7:8). An unturned cake was like a pancake that is burned on one side and gooey on the other. Israel was half-baked in that its prosperity under Jeroboam II was purely material and not at all spiritual. Its vapid, self-absorbed culture had nothing significant to offer.
- *Weakened and feeble* (7:9). The "aliens" (Hebrew, *zarim*) mentioned by Hosea were foreign "allies" such as Assyria and Egypt who seemed to be friends but were actually enemies (2 Kin. 15:17–20; 17:3, 4). These nations "devoured" Israel's strength by requiring heavy payments and tribute. Yet this "aging process" occurred imperceptibly over a period of about 40 years, so that the Israelites hardly even noticed their loss of power.
- *Arrogant* (7:10). Despite the many reversals that took place between the prosperous reign of Jeroboam II (between 793–753 B.C.) and the foolish reign of Hoshea, Israel's last king (between 732–722 B.C.), the nation lived with an illusion of strength and virility. The people arrogantly resisted the Lord right up to the end of their kingdom (2 Kin. 17:13–18).

No nation can survive for long when it actively turns away from God. The experience of Israel shows that material prosperity is not enough to sustain a culture. Without godliness at the core, a society has to keep propping itself up with expensive yet unreliable crutches. Sooner or later, though, moral weakness will bring it down—proud and foolish to the end.

8:8 swallowed up: This image vividly depicts the effects of Israel's foreign alliances, which drained the nation economically.

8:9, 10 like a wild donkey: This comparison draws attention to Israel's free-spirited attitude and desire to live unrestrained by God's standards. **King of princes** refers to the conquering Assyrian king.

8:11–13 altars for sin: The Lord regarded Israel's religious rituals as sinful because they were not supported by an obedient lifestyle. In fact, Israel treated God's **Law** as if it were something **strange** or alien to them. **return to Egypt:** Egypt symbolizes exile and slavery. The people would actually be taken to Assyria (9:3; 11:5).

8:14 True security comes from the Creator, but God's people trusted instead in their own efforts, symbolized by their **temples** and **fortified cities**.

9:1–17 There are five reasons why Israel is prohibited from rejoicing: (1) because of her immorality (vv. 1, 2); (2) because of her coming captivity (vv. 3–6); (3) because of her spiritual insensitivity (vv. 7–9); (4) because of her sterility (vv. 10–16); and, (5) because of her coming exile (v. 17).

9:1, 2 Because of their association with the harvest, **threshing** floors were the site of agricultural festivals in which Israel offered up sacrifices to Baal. The Lord would take away the **joy** of the harvest by destroying the crops and leaving the threshing floors and **wine** vats empty.

9:3 the LORD's land: Israel had forgotten that their land belonged to the Lord. He alone decided who would or would not live in it (Lev. 25:23).

9:4, 5 Because they had touched a dead body, **mourners** were ceremonially unclean and contaminated everything that came in contact with them (Num. 19:14, 15, 22). Living in a foreign land, Israel would be ceremonially defiled and unable to worship the Lord with sacrifices and offerings.

9:6 Memphis: This Egyptian city, known for its great cemeteries, tombs, and pyramids, symbolized the unclean land of exile (Assyria) to which God's people would be taken captive. **Nettles . . . Thorns:** The land of Israel would be abandoned, leaving the people's possessions and homes to be overrun by weeds and briers.

9:7 Sinful Israel disdained God's true prophets, regarding them as raving maniacs. The Hebrew word translated **insane** is used in 1 Sam. 21:15 of David when he pretended to be a madman before the Philistine king. **Enmity** refers to strong resentment that can give rise to violent behavior.

9:8 A **watchman** would look for approaching armies and then warn the people so that they could secure the city and prepare for battle (Ezek. 33:6). The prophets were like watchmen, for they were sent by God to warn the people of judgment and urge them to repent (Ezek. 3:17).

9:9 As in the days of Gibeah: The reference here is to the rape and murder of a young woman by men of Gibeah, an event that started a civil war (Judg. 19). Those who witnessed this violent deed remarked that it was the worst crime committed in Israel's history until that time (Judg. 19:30). However, the sins of Hosea's generation rivaled the infamous Gibeah murder.

9:10 At the beginning of Israel's history, God found great delight in His people. **Grapes in the wilderness** would be a pleasant surprise; **the firstfruits on the fig tree** were an irresistible delicacy (Is. 28:4; Jer. 24:2; Mic. 7:1). However, Israel had quickly fallen into sin. At **Baal Peor** the Israelites had participated in fertility rites with Moabite women, bringing God's judgment down upon the nation (Num. 25).

9:11 Their glory refers to Ephraim's (Israel's) population, especially its children. **like a bird:** Ephraim's population would dwindle as its women became barren. The punishment would be appropriate because this generation of Israelites, like an earlier generation at Baal Peor, promoted fertility by worshiping Baal.

9:12, 13 Any **children** who were born in Israel would be killed in the coming invasion. **Tyre** was an important economic center located at an advantageous spot on the Mediterranean coast.

9:14 miscarrying womb: Some women of Israel would be barren (v. 11); others would bear children, only to lose them to the invader's sword (vv. 12, 13). Still others would conceive, but miscarry.

9:15, 16 Gilgal had become a center of idolatry (12:11; Josh. 5). **hated:** Marriage and divorce provide the background for the language used here. The Lord would reject (hate) His unfaithful wife (Deut. 22:13; 24:3), **drive** her from His **house** (the land), and remove His protective care (**love**) from her. There may also be an allusion here to Gen. 3:24; 4:14, which tell how God drove away Adam and then Cain.

9:17 Wanderers may allude to the end of Cain (Gen. 4:12), who like Israel (v. 9) was guilty of murder.

10:1–13:16 In this section Israel's retribution is portrayed in six figures: (1) as a spreading or luxuriant vine (10:1, 2); (2) as in a state of anarchy (vv. 3–10); (3) as a trained heifer (vv. 11–15); (4) as a youth (11:1–11); (5) as one who feeds on wind (11:12—12:14); and, (6) as one who is spiritually dead (13:1–16).

10:1 Israel empties his vine refers to

God's blessings upon the nation, which contrast with the nation's ingratitude and idolatry.

10:2 divided: This verb refers to Israel's deceitful and hypocritical ways.

10:3 now they say: This verse anticipates the people's response when God's judgment came to destroy Israel's political stability and independence (vv. 7, 15).

10:4 like hemlock in the furrows of a field: This analogy refers to poisonous weeds sprouting up in a field and choking out the crops. In the same way God's judgment would replace His blessings.

10:5, 6 The Assyrians often **carried** off the idols of their defeated foes. **His own counsel** probably refers to Israel's foreign alliances, which would prove disappointing.

10:7 The comparison in this verse depicts Israel's **king** being swept away like a piece of wood in a stream.

10:8 thorn and thistle: This phrase may allude to Gen. 3:18, the only other passage in the OT where this wording occurs.

10:9 Israel had persisted in sin since the day when a young woman was raped and murdered by the men of **Gibeah** (9:9).

10:10 The imagery in this verse depicts the Lord binding His people, like oxen, to a yoke. The figurative yoke is comprised of **their two transgressions,** probably referring to the ancient crime at Gibeah (v. 9) and the collective sin of Hosea's generation. The yoke imagery suggests that the people could not escape the consequences of their deeds.

10:11 loves to thresh: Israel preferred to be unrestrained, like an unmuzzled heifer at the threshing floor that can simply lean down and eat the grain. **pull a plow:** Israel's rebellious spirit necessitated harsh treatment, compared here to a farmer binding his calf to the yoke and forcing it to do hard labor. Threshing in this context refers to Israel's service to the Lord; plowing refers to the discipline that Israel had to acquire through judgment and exile.

10:12 Hosea calls the people to repentance, reminding them that a decision could not be postponed, and that God's blessings could still be restored. In Israel's case, the people had to reestablish social justice—**righteousness**—and loyalty—**mercy**—in the land. **Break up your fallow ground:** Plowing and planting are necessary preliminary steps for growing a crop, which eventually sprouts when the rain falls in season. In the same way, repentance would set the stage for restored blessing, which God would eventually rain down on His people.

10:13 The process of repentance and restored blessing outlined in v. 12 contrasts sharply with reality. Israel had planted the seeds of sin and reaped the inevitable consequences. **Fruit of lies** likely refers to the people's lack of loyalty to God (v. 4).

10:14 The identity of the conqueror **Shalman** and the location of **Beth Arbel** are uncertain. At any rate, the **battle** referred to seems to have been well known to Hosea's audience because of its extreme violence.

10:15 Israel's defeat would be so swift that the nation's **king** would be **cut off** before the battle had scarcely begun.

11:1–12 No chapter in the OT more graphically depicts the suffering love of God for His people. He is a gracious Father, tenderly teaching His little child to walk (vv. 3, 4); a lamenting Husband, agonizing over the waywardness of His faithless wife (v. 8); and the loving Savior (vv. 9–11), not giving up on His people (Ps. 139:7–10).

11:1 The Lord regarded Israel as His **son** and treated the nation with special care, delivering the people from bondage in **Egypt** (Matt. 2:15).

11:2 they called them: The plural subject probably refers to God's prophets (12:10; Jer. 7:25, 26).

11:3 Like a father teaching his child to walk, the Lord patiently gave the people of Israel direction and cared for them tenderly when they experienced pain or injury.

11:4 The image of v. 3 changes as God is compared to a farmer and Israel to a beast of burden. The Lord had placed restraints—**cords** and **bands**—on Israel, but His regulations, rather than being overly strict or harsh, reflected His concern for the people's well-being. God did not drive them mercilessly but provided for their needs, like a farmer who periodically removes **the yoke** from an animal's neck so that it can eat.

11:5 Repent is the same Hebrew word translated **return** earlier in the verse. Israel could not remain stationary. It had to return either to the Lord or to bondage. Israel's refusal to return to the Lord would result in a return to slavery.

11:6, 7 Devour is the same Hebrew word translated *fed* in v. 4. The people of Israel had rejected the gentle Master, who fed them and provided for their needs. As a result, they would be devoured by the swords of the invading Assyrians.

11:8, 9 As the Lord contemplated the judgment of Israel, His **sympathy** moved Him to

At the beginning of Israel's history, God found great delight in His people.

⚒ IN DEPTH | **Back to Baal**

By Hosea's time Baalism had captured the minds and hearts of many Israelites. Baal was the most important deity in the Canaanite pantheon. Baal's followers believed that his blessing guaranteed the continuation of human life and the preservation of social order. As a fertility deity, Baal was the provider of children, a prized possession in the culture of the ancient Middle East. As the god of the storm, Baal brought the rains and made the crops grow. Baal's devotees trusted that with the elements of the storm at his disposal, he could defeat the enemies of his people. As the king of the divine realm under the ultimate authority of the high god El, Baal overcame the powerful and terrifying deities Yamm, the god of the chaotic sea, and Mot, the god of death and the underworld.

Recognizing the threat that Baalism posed for His people, the Lord actively opposed this false religious system from the beginning of Israel's history. He affirmed that He is the only living God (Ex. 15:11; Deut. 33:26; 1 Sam. 2:2) and Israel's rightful king (Ex. 15:18; 20:2–6). The Lord revealed His sovereignty over the elements of the storm (Ex. 9:23, 24; 19:16, 18; Deut. 33:26; 1 Sam. 7:10; 12:17, 18; 1 Kin. 17:1; 18:1, 45), demonstrated His authority over the chaotic sea (Ex. 15:8, 10) and the realm of death (Ex. 15:12; 1 Sam. 2:6; 1 Kin. 17:17–23), and proved that He alone could provide children to the infertile (1 Sam. 2:5). This attack on Baalism climaxed at Mount Carmel, where the Lord hurled a fiery lightning bolt down from heaven (1 Kin. 18:38, 39) to demonstrate beyond the shadow of a doubt that He is the living God. In contrast, Baal's prophets with their frenzied mourning rites could not provoke any response (1 Kin. 18:26–29). When Jehu later purged the kingdom of Baalism (2 Kin. 10:18–28), the Lord's victory seemed complete. However, less than a century later, Baalism had resurfaced as the religion of the people, forcing the Lord to confront Israel through Hosea the prophet.

How are we to explain Baalism's success? The Lord demanded obedience to strict moral and ethical standards as a basis for blessing. In stark contrast, Baalism appealed to the sensual nature. Baal's favor was gained through sympathetic magic in the form of ritual prostitution. Through these rites, young men and women supposedly could gain Baal's favor and ensure their ability to produce and bear children (4:12–14). Because of Baalism's attractions to the base side of human nature, it persisted in Israel. It promised an easy and even enjoyable road to prosperity, while God's way, the way of true life, demanded selflessness.

---

have compassion and stop short of totally annihilating the people. **Admah** and **Zeboiim,** sister cities of Sodom and Gomorrah, were destroyed by God's judgment (Gen. 10:19; 14:2, 8; Deut. 29:23).

11:10, 11 In the coming judgment, God would tear Israel like a lion (5:14); in the future, God's lionlike **roar** would summon His people to return from exile. In the past, the people of Israel had flown back and forth between the nations like a dove (7:11); in the future, the people would speed back to their homeland **like a bird.**

11:12 Ephraim has encircled Me: The northern kingdom had surrounded God as if He were under siege.

12:1 The prophet especially focuses on the nation's social injustice and foreign alliances. Israel's wicked behavior would lead nowhere. **Oil** may have been used in a ritual ratifying a treaty or given as a sign of loyalty.

12:2 according to his ways: God judges people and nations according to their deeds.

12:3, 4 Hosea draws a lesson from the life of Jacob, the father of the nation. Jacob's greedy, self-reliant, and deceitful character was evident from birth when he grabbed **the heel** of **his brother** Esau (Gen. 25:26). The climactic event in Jacob's spiritual growth was his wrestling match with God the night before he was reunited with his brother. Jacob acknowledged his dependence on God, begged for divine favor, and received a blessing (Gen. 32:24–30). **the Angel:** Making no mention of an angel, the Genesis account refers to Jacob's foe as "a Man" (Gen. 32:24 reflects Jacob's initial perspective), but then indicates that Jacob wrestled with God Himself (Gen. 32:28, 30). Since vv. 4, 5 seem to place **God** and the Angel in parallel, some understand the Angel of the Lord to be in view here. This Angel is sometimes equated with God in the OT (Gen. 16:9–13; Judg. 6:11–14; 13:20–22).

12:5, 6 Just as Jacob had come to his senses and recognized his dependence on God, so Israel was to repent (**return**), reestablish justice in society, and depend (**wait**) on the Lord.

12:7 The Hebrew word rendered **Canaanite** also means "merchant." Here the word may allude to Israel's dishonest economic activities. **Deceitful scales:** In violation of the OT law (Lev. 19:36), dishonest merchants sometimes rigged their scales so that they could give buyers less than what the buyers thought they were purchasing (Prov. 11:1; 16:11; 20:23; Amos 8:5; Mic. 6:11).

12:8 Ephraim's boastful self-sufficiency mirrors that of its ancestor Jacob and ignores the nation's history, which was a testimony to God's enablement and provision (vv. 9, 10, 13).

12:9–11 The Lord had given Israel direction **by the prophets,** but the people had rejected the message. To teach Israel dependence, God would drive them from their homes and send them into exile. This would be comparable to dwelling **in tents,** as the people did during the

Israel's ingratitude, made evident by its sin, angered the Lord and made judgment inevitable.

13:1 The tribe of Ephraim had gained a prominent position in the northern kingdom and could strike fear into the hearts of the other tribes. **Trembling** probably refers to the effect that Ephraim's speech had on the other tribes.

13:2 Kiss the calves refers to the idolatrous practice of kissing images as a sign of homage (1 Kin. 19:18).

13:3 God's judgment would sweep Ephraim away quickly, just as the sun dispels fog and dries up the **dew,** or as the wind blows away **chaff** and **smoke.**

13:4, 5 The Lord reminded Israel of who He is, what He had accomplished for His people, and what He expected from them. Because He alone was Israel's **God** and **savior,** the Lord

The prophet Hosea predicted that God would punish the tribe of Ephraim, which lived in these fertile hills north of Jerusalem (Hos. 13:1–3).

appointed **Feast** of Tabernacles that commemorated the wilderness wandering (Lev. 23:33–43). The towns that epitomized Israel's sin, such as **Gilead** (6:8) and **Gilgal** (4:15; 9:15), would be destroyed. The **altars** of Gilgal would be turned into **heaps** of stone.

12:12–14 God had always protected His people. He protected Jacob when he had to flee for his life to a foreign land. He used Moses to bring **Israel out of Egypt** and preserve the people on their way to the promised land.

expected the people's undivided loyalty. **know . . . knew:** The repetition of the verb "to know" correlates God's demands with His grace. Because He *knew* (cared for) Israel in the wilderness, He had every right to expect them to *know* (be loyal to) Him.

13:6–9 God provided for Israel's needs and richly blessed the people, like a shepherd leading his flock to lush pasture lands. In return, Israel **forgot** the Lord. God's relationship with Israel would change drastically from caring

Shepherd to ravaging Predator. Ironically and tragically, Israel's rebellion had turned its Helper into a Destroyer.

13:10, 11 These verses recall how Israel demanded from Samuel a king like those of the nations around them (1 Sam. 8). Though offended by the people's request, which implied their rejection of divine authority (1 Sam. 8:7), the Lord granted their wish. Israel's king could not protect the people from divine judgment; in fact, he himself would be swept away.

13:12 bound up . . . stored up: God had kept a careful record of Israel's sins, to be revealed as evidence of guilt in the day of judgment.

13:13 This metaphor of childbirth illustrates Israel's spiritual insensitivity. When the crucial time of judgment arrived, Israel would respond unwisely, resulting in death. The nation's failure to repent is compared to a baby that is not positioned properly during labor and jeopardizes the life of both mother and child.

13:14 God announces salvation for Ephraim, proclaiming to **death** and the **grave** that He will deliver His people from their grasp. Paul appropriated part of this verse to declare that the Christian will not be totally overcome by death (1 Cor. 15:55).

13:15, 16 Israel was like a fruitful, well-watered plant, but God's judgment would come like a scorching **east wind** and bring drought.

He shall plunder: The reality behind the imagery of the wind is the Assyrian army, which would plunder Israel's riches and mercilessly kill the people, including helpless infants and pregnant women.

14:1–3 The final section of Hosea's prophecy begins with a call to repentance that includes a model prayer. The people of Israel were to pray for God's gracious forgiveness and renew their allegiance to Him by renouncing foreign alliances, their own military strength, and artificial **gods.**

14:4–8 The Lord anticipates a time when He would restore repentant Israel. The Lord's renewed blessing is compared to **dew.** Revived Israel is compared to a beautiful **lily,** a deep-rooted and aromatic cedar of **Lebanon,** an attractive **olive tree,** and a fruitful **vine.** The Lord Himself would be like a **green cypress tree** that provides protective shade. **I have . . . observed:** This affirmation of God's watchful care stands in stark contrast to His judgment, which was compared to a leopard stalking its prey (13:7).

14:9 The book concludes with advice for those who read Hosea's prophecy. God's **ways,** His demands and principles, are completely true. The wise person will choose to obey them, but the foolish person will ignore them and consequently **stumble** into judgment.

The Book of

Joel

·

NATURAL DISASTERS—FROM RISING FLOOD WATERS TO violent earthquakes—provoke fear and dread. With all their ingenuity, people still cannot control these powerful and destructive forces. They can only watch in awe. Joel begins his book with a description of such a natural disaster—a plague of ravenous locusts. In the prophet's hands, the destructiveness of this plague becomes a vivid warning of the

power of God's coming judgment and a clear appeal to run to the Lord for mercy.

Others believe that the Book of Joel is so close in tone and idea to the Book of Zephaniah that it is likely that the two prophets were contemporaries. The primary evidence for this is the fact that both books prominently feature the concept of the impending "day of the Lord" (compare 2:2 with Zeph. 1:14–16). Since Zephaniah's book dates from around 627 B.C., a number of scholars assign a date of about 600 B.C. for the Book of Joel.

If we assume that the book was written early in the reign of Joash, then we can refer to 2 Kin. 11:1—12:21 for background on this period of Judean history. Joash inherited the throne of Judah as a boy. He had survived Athaliah's murder of all potential claimants to the throne only through the heroic efforts of his aunt Jehosheba, who hid him in the temple. Joash was crowned king at the age of seven by Jehoiada the high priest, who had enlisted the captains of the royal guard to dispose of the wicked Athaliah. Jehoiada advised the young king during the early years of his reign. It is possible that during these years the nation of Judah

was devastated by a great swarm of locusts. This catastrophe would have given the prophet Joel an occasion to call the people to repentance in view of an even greater judgment to come—the day of the Lord.

However, it is not unreasonable to place Joel's ministry during the twenty-five years before the Babylonians destroyed Jerusalem in 586 B.C. If Joel was a contemporary of Zephaniah, then his message of impending national disaster, using the natural calamity of a recent invasion of locusts, would have been a powerful announcement of the horrible events that soon were to come on Jerusalem.

Joel's prophecy had two purposes. First, Joel wrote to call the nation to repentance (2:12) on the basis of its experience of the recent locust plague. The recent disaster was but a token of a more devastating judgment to come. Yet that judgment could be averted by sincere and humble repentance (2:13, 14). In this, Joel shares a common message with other prophets. In the light of impending judgment, there is always a message of hope for those who will return in faith to God. Second, the prophecy was intended to comfort the godly with promises of future salvation and blessing (2:28–32; 3:18–21). Should the national disaster occur, Joel offered hope to the true believers that all was not over. God would keep His promise; the Savior would one day reign.

The author of the book is Joel, the son of Pethuel (1:1). Little is known about the author's life or circumstances. His name means "The Lord Is God," suggesting that he was reared in a home where God was honored. The references to Zion, Judah, and Jerusalem (2:15, 23, 32; 3:1) indicate that the prophet lived and prophesied in Judah and Jerusalem. His frequent references to the work of priests in the temple (1:9, 13, 14; 2:17) lead some to conclude that he was a priest. But Joel also displays considerable interest in agriculture in all of its forms. As a prophet of the Lord, he could have been knowledgeable about the temple in Jerusalem without having been a priest.

Scholars have offered various dates for the writing of the Book of Joel, from early preexilic times to as late as 350 B.C. Some believe that internal evidence indicates that the book was written during the reign of Joash king of Judah (835–796 B.C.), and in the time of the high priest Jehoiada. This view is based on the following considerations: (1) The location of the book between Hosea and Amos in the Hebrew canon suggests a preexilic date of writing. (2) The allusion to the neighboring nations as Judah's foes rather than Assyria, Babylon, or Persia points to an early date for the book. (3) The book does not mention any reigning king, which may suggest a time when the responsibility for ruling rested upon the priests and elders—as was the

case during the early reign of young king Joash (2 Kin. 11:4—12:21).

Outline

I. The devastation of the locust plague 1:1–20
II. The coming day of the Lord 2:1–32
   A. The desolation of the day of the Lord 2:1–11
   B. Exhortation to sincere repentance 2:12–17
   C. Deliverance of the land 2:18–27
   D. The promise of the pouring out of the Spirit 2:28–32
III. Judgment on the nations 3:1–17
   A. The time of the judgment 3:1
   B. The place of the judgment 3:2
   C. The basis of the judgment 3:3–8
   D. The preparation for judgment 3:9–12
   E. The execution of judgment 3:13–17
IV. The promise of future blessings 3:18–21
   A. The prosperity of the land 3:18
   B. The desolation of the nations 3:19
   C. The inhabitation of Judah and Jerusalem 3:20
   D. The presence of the Lord in Zion 3:21

Commentary

1:1–20 This section describes the devastating results of the locust plague that ravaged the country of Judah. Joel highlights the unprecedented nature of the calamity. The account

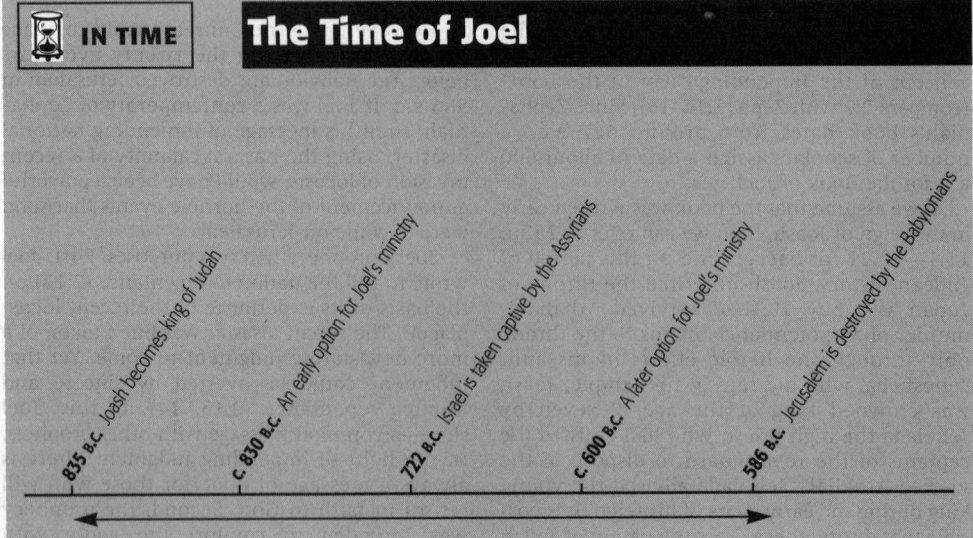

IN TIME

The Time of Joel

835 B.C. Joash becomes king of Judah

c. 830 B.C. An early option for Joel's ministry

722 B.C. Israel is taken captive by the Assyrians

c. 600 B.C. A later option for Joel's ministry

586 B.C. Jerusalem is destroyed by the Babylonians

serves as the basis for an appeal to national mourning and repentance.

1:1 The word of the LORD . . . came attests to the divine origin of the prophet's message. The presentation of the message was the work of the prophet. **Joel** means "The Lord Is God."

1:2, 3 Has anything like this happened: The calamity of recent days was unprecedented in the memory of the people.

1:4 Many interpreters have viewed this **locust** swarm as foreign armies that attacked Judah in successive waves—Assyria, Babylon, Greece, and Rome. Yet literal locust plagues were one of the judgments promised if the people disobeyed God and broke their covenant with Him (Deut. 28:38, 39, 42). Further, Joel's description of the damage done by the locusts compares with eyewitness reports. The impression given is one of overwhelming devastation.

1:5 Awake, you drunkards: The vineyards had been destroyed, and the wine had been lost.

1:6 Nation may refer to a literal or figurative swarm of locusts. They came in such numbers that they were like a vast army. Rains bringing an end to drought can trigger the

square miles, stripping vegetation, fouling the air with excrement, and triggering epidemics as they die and rot. It has been estimated that a single swarm of locusts could eat in one day what 40,000 people eat in one year.

1:7 Branches of trees stripped of bark by the rasping teeth of the locusts were left splintered and ghostly **white.**

1:8 The image here is of a young bride widowed on her wedding day. **Sackcloth** was worn by those in mourning in ancient Israel.

1:9 The drink offering refers to the wine offerings that accompanied the priests' morning and evening sacrifices (Ex. 29:38–41). The devastation of the locust meant that no sacrifice could be offered.

1:10 The **land** is personified as mourning because the three principle crops it produced— grain, grapes, and olives—had been destroyed (Deut. 7:13; Ps. 104:15).

1:11, 12 The people had anticipated the joy of harvest, but due to the disaster of the locust plague, their **joy has withered away.**

1:13–20 Joel reminds the nation's leaders that being restored to blessing requires repentance (Deut. 30:1–5; 2 Chr. 7:14). God will not

These before-and-after pictures of the same tree made 15 minutes apart show how a swarm of locusts can quickly devour all vegetation in its path (Joel 1:7).

hatching of dormant locust eggs and stimulate existing locusts to breed. The origin of these swarms is not fully understood even today. Some factors that may induce normally solitary locusts to swarm are high temperatures, low humidity, and population crowding. Adult locusts, with serrated jaws rasping from side to side, can consume daily their body weight in food. Yet they are able to live for four days without feeding, surviving on stored fat. A locust swarm can cover more than a square mile, with 50 million insects capable of devastating 100 tons of vegetation a day. Locust swarms have been known to blanket 2,000

withhold His favor and blessing from those who are truly repentant.

1:14, 15 The day of the LORD refers to a time of judgment and deliverance. Joel views the locust plague as a contemporary day of judgment that was serving as a token or forewarning of an even greater, future "day of the Lord."

1:16 Is not the food cut off . . . Joy and gladness: With the sudden loss of food, there was also a loss of joy at harvest (Is. 9:3).

1:17 The seed shrivels indicates further devastation in the land and an inability to replant the following year.

1:18–20 Not only did the people of Judah

suffer from the drought, so did the **animals, cattle,** and **flocks.** Joel depicts the animals poetically as joining in the lament, groaning in their hunger and distress (Rom. 8:22). **I cry out:** The prophet adds his own voice to the bellowing of beasts, the wailing of drunkards, and the mourning of priests. He was part of the suffering community, not an outsider looking on from a distance.

2:1 The **trumpet,** or ram's horn, was used in ancient times to signal danger or warn of a military attack (Jer. 6:17; Amos 3:6). God demonstrated His grace by warning His people beforehand and providing opportunity for repentance before He brought His judgment upon them. **Zion** refers to Jerusalem (Ps. 133:3). **coming . . . at hand:** The Bible presents the day of the Lord as an imminent reality. It is not something that we are gradually moving toward; rather, it is ever ready to burst in on us. At any moment, the day that is "near" may become present.

2:2 Darkness is used as a figure for misery,

distress, and judgment (Is. 8:22; 60:2; Jer. 13:16).

2:3–11 Joel describes the locusts and their destruction of the land in vivid, poetic terms.

2:3–5 The invasion that Joel prophetically envisioned was like a raging **fire** that transformed all that was beautiful into desolation. Joel compared the speed and strength of the invaders to galloping **horses.**

2:6–9 writhe in pain: The invading armies were locustlike in number and in their ability to penetrate any defense; but like men of war, they bring fear and death with them. The imagery of locusts (ch. 1) is used in this section to describe the overwhelming power of a military invasion.

2:10, 11 References to the **sun, moon,** and **stars** growing dim allude to a future outpouring of divine wrath (Is. 13:10; Matt. 24:29; Rev. 6:12, 13). **Who can endure:** Nothing will be able to withstand the wrath of God (Matt. 24:21, 22).

2:12–17 Having warned the Judeans about the nearness of a greater day of judgment than

---

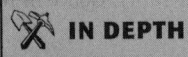 **IN DEPTH**   **The Day of the Lord**

One of the central themes of the Book of Joel is "the day of the Lord" (1:15; 2:1). This language describes a period of time in which God "comes down" in a dramatic way to bring wrath and judgment on the wicked and salvation to the righteous. God is Lord of time. There is no period that is not "the day of the Lord" in a general sense. But at times God enters the space-time arena to assert in bold, dramatic ways that He is in control.

The day of the Lord is a major theme of OT prophecy. Thirteen of the sixteen prophets address this subject. The concept of the day of the Lord probably originated with the conquest of Canaan—a conquest that was in fact the Lord's war (Deut. 1:30; 3:22; Josh. 5:13–15; 6:2); that is, a day of judgment for the wicked Canaanites (Lev. 18:25; Deut. 9:4, 5).

The day of the Lord is not an isolated phenomenon or a single event in human history. Periods in Israel's early history and latter history, the coming of Jesus, and His second advent are all called "the day of the Lord" in Scripture. The predictions of a coming day of the Lord can be fulfilled in a number of different events. The invasion of locusts in the historic events of the life of Joel was the day of the Lord (ch. 2). But the day of wrath and deliverance that soon fell on Judah in the Babylonian invasion was also the day of the Lord.

While most references speak about future events, five biblical texts describe the day of the Lord in terms of past judgments (Is. 22:1–14; Jer. 46:2–12; Lam. 1:1–2:22; Ezek. 13:1–9). These texts reflect circumstances of military defeat, tragedy, and judgment. Such events may have stimulated the development of the prophetic concept of a future "day" or time of judgment for the disobedient of Israel and all of the nations (1:15; Is. 13:6, 9; Zeph. 1:14–18).

However, the day of the Lord is not just a day of wrath and judgment on the disobedient. In some contexts, it also includes deliverance and restoration for the righteous. The day of the Lord speaks not only about future judgment, but also about future hope, prosperity, and blessing (Is. 4:2–6; Hos. 2:18–23; Amos 9:11–15; Mic. 4:6–8). Joel reveals that this day is to be heralded by heavenly phenomena (2:30, 31) that will bring sudden darkness and gloom on the earth (2:2). It will be a day of divine destruction (1:15) on the nations that have persecuted Israel (3:12–14) and on the rebellious and disobedient of Israel (Amos 5:18–20). Yet it will also be a time of deliverance and unprecedented blessing for God's people (2:32; 3:16, 18–21; 1 Thess. 5:2–5).

the one just experienced, Joel now calls the nation to repentance.

2:12 Turn to Me: As in Zephaniah (Zeph. 2:1–3), an opportunity for repentance, remorse, and renewal was offered to the people.

2:13 rend your heart: God is not satisfied with outward acts of repentance. Tearing one's garments was a customary way of expressing grief or remorse (Josh. 7:6; 1 Sam. 4:12). However, like all outward acts, the tearing of a garment could be done without true sorrow or repentance. God required more than mere external words or actions; He wanted a change of heart and sorrow over sin. The attributes of God that provided the basis of Joel's appeal were first revealed to Moses in Ex. 34:6. **slow to anger:** God is reluctant to punish. Judgment is God's "unusual" or "foreign" task, for He wants all to come to repentance (Is. 28:21).

2:14 Who knows: These words suggest that even at the last moment, the Lord would withhold His wrath and display His grace if the people would truly repent. As a result, agriculture would be restored and productivity would return. There would be food and drink, for the people and for offerings to the Lord.

2:15 Blow the trumpet in Zion: The repetition of these words from 2:1 ties the chapter together and renews the urgent appeal for a proper response to God.

2:16 The urgency of the situation is apparent, for all ages and classes of the population were summoned. According to Jewish tradition codified in the Mishnah, a **bridegroom** and **bride** could be excused from reciting daily prayers on their wedding day. But Joel excused no one from prayer at this time of spiritual emergency.

2:17 Spare Your people: If the leaders and the people would gather together with prayers of true repentance and genuine renewal, the horrible events that God was threatening might be averted. **Why should they say among the peoples:** This rhetorical question was designed to move God to intervene. Failure to come to Judah's aid might encourage the nations to make a mockery of Judah's God.

2:18, 19 zealous for His land: The deep love of God for the land of Israel is coupled with His abiding love (**pity**) for the people. On every occasion in which God brought judgment on the land, there was the hope that one day His zeal for the land would lead to a renewal of blessing. Genuine repentance is the prerequisite for God's blessing. In response to repentance, God would bring restoration and blessing.

2:20 The north was regarded as the direction from which misfortune generally came upon Israel. **The eastern sea** refers to the Dead Sea. **The western sea** refers to the Mediterranean Sea.

2:21 Fear not: There is coming a day (Ps. 65) when God's restoration of the earth will be complete.

2:22 open pastures . . . tree bears its fruit: The renewal of agriculture would be a sign that God had renewed prosperity and peace to His land.

2:23, 24 The former rain softened the soil for planting winter wheat. **The latter rain** fell in the spring, causing the grain to swell and ensuring a good harvest. If the rains failed, the crops would not grow.

2:25, 26 The same God who brings judgment is pleased to restore blessing to those who repent. This does not mean that sin leaves no scar, but that God can restore people to usefulness in spite of past disobedience.

2:27 I am in the midst of Israel: Ultimately, this is the promise of God's presence in the midst of His people in the coming reign of King Jesus (Zeph. 3:14–20). However, God promises to be present at all times with the individual who is at peace with Him.

2:28–32 After describing the physical blessings that would come upon his generation if they would repent, Joel describes the spiritual blessings that God would bestow upon His people in the future. This passage was quoted by Peter on the Day of Pentecost (Acts 2:17–21) to explain the miracle of speaking in tongues. There are three main viewpoints regarding how Joel's prophecy was used by Peter in Acts 2:17–21: (1) Some interpreters see a complete fulfillment of Joel's prophecy in the experience of the first believers on the Day of Pentecost. The outpouring of the Spirit ushered in the kingdom age. The wonders in the skies were fulfilled at the crucifixion, when darkness covered the land. (2) Some interpreters believe that Peter was simply using Joel's prophecy as an illustration of what was happening. In effect, Peter was saying, "This is that same Holy Spirit who was spoken about by Joel." According to this view, the prophecy will be fulfilled in the future when the remnant of Israel believes. (3) Some suggest that Joel's prophecy was partially fulfilled on the Day of Pentecost. The gift of the Holy Spirit was given, but the signs mentioned in vv. 30–32 will be fulfilled later in connection with the return of Christ in great glory.

2:28, 29 Afterward indicates the prophetic future; this word is a signal that the text was pointing to the messianic age. **Pour out** is derived from the imagery of Israel's heavy winter rains; it speaks here of abundant provision. **All flesh** anticipates the inclusion of both Jews and Gentiles in one body in Christ (Eph. 2:11—3:6). The ministries of the Spirit mentioned here were experienced in the early

 **IN FOCUS** **"spirit"**

(Heb. *ruach*) (2:28; Gen. 6:3; 1 Kin. 22:23; Pss. 32:2; 146:4) Strong's #7307: The noun *spirit* is related to a verb meaning "to breathe" or "to blow." It can signify breath (Job 9:18; 19:17), wind (Gen. 8:1; Ex. 10:13), air (Eccl. 1:14; Is. 26:18), the breath of life (whether animal or human; Gen. 6:17; 7:15), disposition or mood (Gen. 41:8; Ezek. 21:7), an evil or distressing spirit (1 Sam. 16:14–16), or the Spirit of God (Gen. 1:2; Ps. 51:11). The spirit of life is the gift of God to all creatures (Job 12:10; 33:4; Eccl. 12:7). The endowment of God's Holy Spirit is a special gift to believers, which brings spiritual life (Pss. 51:10, 11; 143:10), power (Judg. 6:34), wisdom and understanding (Is. 11:2), and divine revelation, which leads to a better understanding of God's Word and His perfect ways (2:28; Is. 61:1, 2).

church (Acts 11:28; 21:9; 2 Cor. 12:1–4; Rev. 1:1–3). **Your sons and your daughters:** The outpouring of the Spirit and the ministries done through His power will be accomplished without regard to gender, age, or class.

2:30, 31 The heavenly wonders described here will take place before the **great and awesome day of the LORD**, an apparent reference to the end times. **Blood and fire** correspond with Rev. 8:7, 8. **Smoke** corresponds with Rev. 9:18. **Darkness** corresponds with Rev. 8:12. **Moon into blood** corresponds with Rev. 6:12.

2:32 Anyone who **calls on the name of the Lord**—that is, repents and believes—will be **saved** from the judgment that will fall on the wicked and unbelieving. The judgment and deliverance referred to is that which will take place at the return of Christ (Zech. 14:1–3). At the same time, these words apply as well to spiritual deliverance of repentant peoples in any period of human history. It is with this gracious announcement of deliverance through the power of God that Joel ends this great section of his prophecy.

3:1–16 Joel now describes God's judgment on the nations gathered around Jerusalem (Zech. 14:1–3) at Christ's return. This is the counterpart to Judah's experience in the Day of the Lord. The nations that have persecuted Israel will themselves be judged.

3:1 In those days indicates a time in the prophetic future (2:28). The judgment will take place after the Lord has restored His people to the land (Matt. 25:31–46).

3:2–8 The Gentile nations must give a final accounting to God for what they have done to His people. Based on the experiences of the people of his day, Joel lists the kinds of things that the Gentiles will be accountable for: crimes against the land (v. 2), cruelty to the people (vv. 3, 6), and looting of the treasures of God's temple (v. 5).

3:2, 3 Valley of Jehoshaphat: The name

Jehoshaphat means "The Lord Judges." The location of this valley is not known. Perhaps this was merely a symbolic name for the location of the great battle in the end times.

3:4, 5 Tyre and Sidon were Phoenician cities on the Mediterranean Sea, north of Galilee. **Philistia** was on the Mediterranean coast south of Joppa.

3:6, 7 The mention of the **Greeks** has been used as evidence for dating the book to the Greek period (332–363 B.C.). However, Greek people were known in Assyria in the time of Sargon II (722–705 B.C.) and are mentioned in Egypt's Tell el-Amarna tablets (around 1300 B.C.).

3:8 Sabeans were people of Semitic origin who lived in the southwest Arabian peninsula.

3:9–12 With a note of biting sarcasm, the Lord calls the nations to prepare themselves for the judgment that is to take place at Messiah's coming (Rev. 19:11–15).

3:9, 10 The military weapons of the Gentile nations would not be sufficient to protect them against God's judgment. Therefore, they are exhorted to beat their **plowshares into swords** and their **pruning hooks into spears.** For predictions of the reverse, see Is. 2:4; Mic. 4:3.

3:11 Joel saw two armies assembling for battle. The one is made up of the **nations;** the other is made up of the **mighty ones** of the Lord (Mark 8:38; Rev. 19:14).

3:12, 13 The use of harvesting imagery in the Book of Joel is complex. It begins in terms of the great scarcity resulting from the locust plague (ch. 1). Then there is a promised renewal of agriculture with the return of God's blessing to His repentant people (2:18–27). Here, the riches of renewed agriculture serve as a mocking backdrop for a world in conflict. In 3:18–21, there is a final renewal of agriculture because of the blessing of the resident King.

3:14 The valley of decision may be a symbolic name for the Valley of Jehoshaphat (3:2), or it may refer to the option before the people to continue toward certain judgment or to turn to God in repentance (vv. 12, 13).

3:15, 16 These verses parallel 2:30–32 and describe the same heavenly phenomena (Matt. 24:29). In the midst of calamity, God was offering a **shelter for His people** (Zeph. 2:1–3).

3:17 Joel anticipates a day when strangers would no longer pass through Jerusalem to plunder and destroy. Instead, they would worship the Lord (Zech. 8:20–23).

3:18 In that day indicates the prophetic future (2:28; 3:1). Joel uses poetic imagery to describe the productivity of the land in the messianic age. The vineyards will be so productive that the **mountains shall drip** with wine (Ps. 65:11–13). The pasture land will be so rich and green that engorged udders of female goats will **flow with milk**. The abundance of **wine** is representative of the joy to be experienced in the messianic age (Amos 9:13, 14). **The Valley of Acacias** was the location of the last encampment before the Israelites entered Canaan (Num. 25:1; Josh. 3:1).

3:19, 20 **Egypt** and **Edom** are mentioned as representatives of the Gentile nations that God will judge before the establishment of the Messiah's kingdom. Note the stark contrast with the eternal destinies of **Judah** and **Jerusalem.**

3:21 The Lord dwells in Zion: The Lord's presence in Jerusalem is the key to the blessing of the whole land.

The Book of

Amos

T HE BOOK OF AMOS IS PERHAPS THE MOST familiar of the Minor Prophets, not in detail, but in its theme of justice and in some of its striking metaphors. The figure of Amos, a Judean sheepbreeder with a strong message for Israel delivered in the shadow of Jeroboam's pagan temple at Bethel, both attracts us and commands our respect. In this book we can read, just as the ancient Israelites heard, a masterful

literary creation given by God through a man of the people. But more importantly, we read and hear the Word of God, still ringing down the centuries with clarity and force.

God's passionate concern for justice is the main theme of the Book of Amos. Justice is not an abstract issue with God. Instead, justice is relational; it promotes good relations between people and between groups of people. Injustice breaks down good relationships and breeds anger, hostility, and violence. God created the human race to enjoy good relations with Him and with each other; therefore, injustice that breeds alienation in all of its varieties breaks God's heart.

The renewed prosperity of Israel based on the successes of Jeroboam II brought new wealth to the upper classes. They used that wealth to enlarge their landholdings and to build great houses for themselves. They violated the rights of the poor and the landed peasants, throwing many off their ancestral lands. Through God's provisions in the Mosaic covenant, the landed peasant class had been the foundation of Israel's society. But under Jeroboam's rule, this class virtually disappeared. As

the rich became richer, the poor became poorer and more numerous; many were sold into slavery. Israel's social structure became thoroughly unstable.

The immediate purpose of the prophetic ministry of Amos was to call the leaders of ancient Israel to repent and reform. Amos warned them that if they did not heed his call, their injustice against the poor and the weak would destroy the nation. God would not allow them to continue in their unrighteous, unjust course. Repentance or retribution were the only alternatives. It is no accident that what we often remember from Amos is his stirring call, "Let justice run down like water, and righteousness like a mighty stream" (5:24).

The Book of Amos is named after the prophet who delivered its oracles. Amos was from Tekoa, a town at the edge of the Judean wilderness, about five miles southeast of Bethlehem. Because of marginal and uncertain yearly rainfall, this area was suited more for raising sheep and goats than for cultivating crops. Amos specifically calls himself a sheepbreeder (1:1; 7:14, 15). The Hebrew term used indicates that Amos was not a hired shepherd, but rather the owner of one or more flocks of sheep.

Amos also describes himself as a "tender of sycamore fruit" (7:14). The sycamore fig tree bears thousands of figs much like the common fig, but smaller and not as good. Before this fruit could ripen properly, a small hole had to be pierced in the bottom of its skin. This piercing was done by hand and was a tedious and time-consuming task. Why was Amos obliged to tend the sycamore? Western Judah, the oasis of Jericho, and lower Galilee were the regions where sycamore figs grew most abundantly. The shepherds needed to bring their flocks to one of these regions in late summer, after the desert pastures had dried up. Since this was the time for piercing the sycamore fruit, landowners would exchange grazing rights for labor. A shepherd could watch his flock while sitting on the broad limbs of the sycamore, piercing its fruit. Thus Amos was not a wealthy man. Wealthy sheepbreeders hired shepherds to tend their flocks. Amos followed his flock himself (7:15), and when that meant piercing sycamore fruit, he pierced sycamore fruit.

Amos prophesied during the reigns of Uzziah king of Judah and Jeroboam king of Israel. Uzziah was king of Judah from 792 to 740 B.C., though from about 752 on, he was stricken with leprosy and shared power with his son Jotham. Jeroboam II was king of Israel from 792 to 753 B.C. Uzziah and Jeroboam formed an alliance for much of their reigns and together ruled for a brief time an area nearly as large as the empire of David and Solomon.

When it was written, the prophecy of Amos was dated to a time "two years before the earth-quake" (1:1). It is impossible to tell what earthquake is meant, for there are no other historical references to it. However, this dating, along with the dialogue of Amos with Amaziah, the priest of Jeroboam's temple at Bethel (7:10–17), indicates that the period of the prophetic activity of Amos was short, unlike many of the other prophets. Amos went to Bethel from Tekoa, delivered his prophetic oracles, and returned home. He probably stayed in Bethel only a few days. The spoken oracles of Amos should be dated around 755–754 B.C. Within two or three years after the prophet's appearance at Bethel, Jeroboam II died, and Israel's rapid decline began. Within thirty years, Israel was conquered by the Assyrians.

Outline

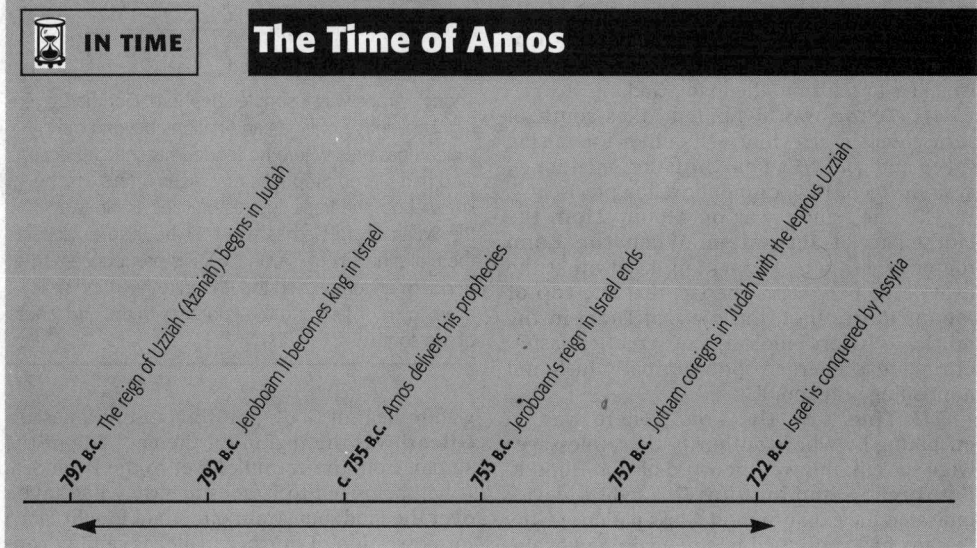

IN TIME   **The Time of Amos**

792 B.C. The reign of Uzziah (Azariah) begins in Judah

792 B.C. Jeroboam II becomes king in Israel

c. 755 B.C. Amos delivers his prophecies

753 B.C. Jeroboam's reign in Israel ends

752 B.C. Jotham coreigns in Judah with the leprous Uzziah

722 B.C. Israel is conquered by Assyria

Commentary

1:1–2:16 The Lord sent Amos, a Judean, to Bethel to prophesy of coming judgment on Israel. But in Bethel, Amos faced a hostile audience. Israel's first king, Jeroboam I, had made the town a center of pagan worship. Because the temple in Jerusalem was in Judah and not in the nation of Israel, Jeroboam had encouraged the Israelites to worship at Bethel instead of Jerusalem. Thus the Israelites who gathered at Bethel would regard Amos, a Judean, with suspicion. Yet Amos bravely condemned there the sins of Israel's neighbors—the Syrians, Philistines, Phoenicians, Edomites, Ammonites, and Moabites. Then he went on to point out the iniquity of Judah and Israel: they had rejected the God who had covenanted with them. They too stood before God condemned by their own evil ways. With a steady voice, Amos called the Israelites to return to the living God.

1:1 Tekoa was about ten miles south of Jerusalem, in a region well-suited for raising sheep and goats. **The earthquake,** mentioned again in Zech. 14:5, cannot be dated precisely.

1:2 The temple was on Mount **Zion,** the oldest part of **Jerusalem.** When **the LORD** roared from there, the nation dried up at the heat of the fiery blast. The fact that **the top of** Mount **Carmel,** on the coast of Israel in the north, **withers** indicates a great disaster. Carmel was a garden spot, normally lush and flourishing year-round.

1:3 Thus says the LORD: There was no mistaking by whose authority these messages were spoken: this was the word of God Himself. **For three . . . and for four:** This stylistic device indicated the exhaustion of God's patience—the Syrians had continued to sin, again and again.

This device is repeated as Amos speaks God's words against nation after sinful nation. The **transgressions** of the neighbors of Israel and Judah were against the general revelation, or "law of nature," that all people recognize and acknowledge. Since the neighboring nations had not received God's special revelation, as Israel had at Mount Sinai, Amos's oracles did not call them to account by that standard, but by the standard they *had* received. **Damascus** was the capital of Syria (also called Aram), a powerful kingdom that had been a frequent adversary of Israel throughout its history. Israelites listening to Amos would have been

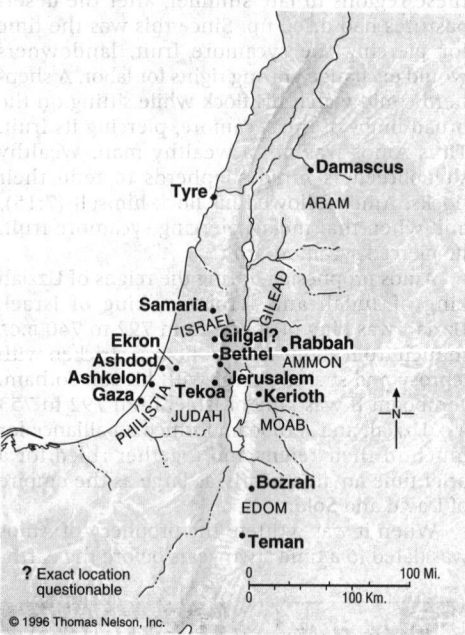

Damascus
Tyre
ARAM
Samaria
GILEAD
Ekron
Ashdod
Ashkelon
Gaza
PHILISTIA
ISRAEL
Gilgal?
Bethel
Jerusalem
Tekoa
Kerioth
Rabbah
AMMON
JUDAH
MOAB
Bozrah
EDOM
Teman

? Exact location questionable

0   100 Mi.
0   100 Km.

© 1996 Thomas Nelson, Inc.

Amos: Places Judged by God

Though Amos was a simple shepherd, God had given him knowledge of lands and nations beyond the Judean pastures where he tended his sheep. Because God had placed prophetic messages on his lips, he knew about the tragic futures of cities as far away as the Syrian city of Damascus (1:5), but also as close as the Philistine city of Gaza (1:6). His pronouncements of doom encompassed the Phoenicians in the seacoast town of Tyre and the Edomites in the arid lands of the south.

glad to hear of God's punishment of Damascus. **Gilead** was the region on the east side of the Jordan from the Yarmuk River to the Dead Sea. It had belonged to Israel since they had taken over the land, but Aram often had fought Israel for possession of northern Gilead, gaining control there in Israel's times of military weakness. **Threshed . . . with implements of iron** indicates extreme cruelty and inhumanity in warfare. After reaping, wheat or barley was laid out on the threshingfloor, a hard flat surface of bedrock or packed earth. An ox pulled a wooden sledge around the threshingfloor. The ox's hooves and the sharp stones imbedded in the bottom of the sledge beat out the grains from the heads of wheat.

1:4 I will send a fire . . . Which shall devour the palaces: Fire in an ancient city was a real threat. Cities were crowded with houses close together on very narrow streets; there was too little water to effectively fight raging fires. **Hazael** and **Ben-Hadad** were kings of Syria who had been particularly harsh in their treatment of Israel.

1:5 I will also break: Amos makes numerous references to the demolition of urban infrastructures that would occur in a coming day of judgment. He particularly mentions those that pertain to the defense of cities. Ancient city walls usually incorporated small fortresses or citadels at strategic points along their expanses, and particularly around the gates. These reinforced structures provided a perch for commanders and a secondary means of defense in the event the walls were breached. **The gate bar** was the large timber that barred the city gate from the inside. If it was broken, the city would lose its security and could be captured easily.

Aven . . . Beth Eden: Amos may have intended a play on words here. Aven means "Sin" in Hebrew; Damascus was a verdant oasis city on the edge of the desert that could be compared to Eden. However, Amos may also have been referring to the Beth Eden region on the north bank of the Euphrates River. **Kir** is where the Assyrian king Tiglath-Pileser III exiled the Syrians of Damascus in 732 B.C. Amos later referred to Kir as the place from which the Syrians had originally come (9:7).

1:6, 7 Gaza was one of the five principal cities of the Philistines, the traditional enemies of Israel who lived on the southwest coast of Canaan. **They took captive . . . to deliver:** The principal method of acquiring foreign slaves in the ancient Middle East was capturing them in war. There were many incidents of open warfare and small-scale raiding between Philistia and Judah and between Philistia and Israel in the long history of their animosity. **Edom** controlled important trade routes and had trading relations with many nations; they traded in slaves as well as in other precious goods.

1:8 Ashdod and **Ashkelon,** coastal cities located north of Gaza, were two of the five major Philistine cities. **Ekron,** also one of the five major Philistine cities, was situated inland.

1:9, 10 Tyre, the principal Phoenician city, was on the northwest coast of Canaan. The Phoenicians were master seafarers. Tyre and Israel had forged an alliance that was profitable

---

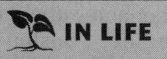 **IN LIFE**   # Led Astray by Lies

Have you ever tried to minimize the guilt of telling a lie with the attitude, "Of course I lied. Doesn't everybody? What's the big deal?" Part of the "big deal" is that if you assume you're joining the crowd by using deception, then who can you trust ultimately? How can you ever be sure that you are hearing the truth from anyone? Maybe everyone else has taken the same attitude you have: "Everyone lies. What's the big deal?"

Amos warned the people of his day that lies would always lead them astray; deception would always cause trouble. In fact, they were already in trouble largely because they followed the lies of their fathers (Amos 2:4). The prophet's statement and the history of Israel show that generations can suffer tragically from patterns of deception.

Yet people try many ways to deceive themselves about the true nature of lying. For example, we use euphemisms such as "shading the truth," "telling a little white lie," or "skirting the issue." We also try to justify lying by suggesting that it is normal, and even inevitable, as if sooner or later we have to lie. But the worst tragedy about this way of living may be that we end up telling lies and believing lies about God (Rom. 1:25), and about ourselves (1 John 1:10).

Lying is not an inescapable fact of human nature. God does not lie (Num. 23:19; Titus 1:2), and He tells us not to lie in the Ten Commandments (Ex. 20:16). Likewise, Paul exhorted believers not to lie to one another (Eph. 4:25; Col. 3:9). So it is possible to speak and live with honesty. But it is self-defeating to practice deception. In the long run, there is no integrity in the habit, and sooner or later one begins to distrust everyone—including oneself.

for both. However, Tyre ignored the long-standing **covenant of brotherhood,** and sought commercial gain by selling Israelite slaves to **Edom.**

1:11 The nation of **Edom,** located southeast of the Dead Sea, controlled important caravan trade routes, and thus was deeply involved in commerce. **his brother:** The Edomites traced their ancestry to Esau, the brother of Jacob. But several times in the history of their stormy relationship, Edom took advantage of Israel's (or Judah's) misfortune to help others attack them.

1:12 Teman and **Bozrah** were principal Edomite cities.

1:13 The nation of **Ammon,** located east of Gilead on the edge of the desert, was descended from one of the sons of Lot, Abraham's nephew (Gen. 19:36–38). Thus Ammon was related to Israel, though not as closely as Edom. **ripped open . . . enlarge their territory:** The Ammonites killed pregnant women in order to prevent the increase of the Israelite population in Gilead, which they were trying to wrest from Israel's control.

1:14, 15 Rabbah was the capital of Ammon.

2:1 Like Ammon (1:13), **Moab** (located southeast of Israel) was descended from one of the sons of Lot. **burned the bones:** This act was believed to desecrate the remains of a deceased person, a heinous act in ancient times and a great dishonor to the person's memory.

2:2, 3 Kerioth was a major town of Moab. It was the site of a temple of Chemosh, Moab's national god.

2:4, 5 Judah was Israel's neighbor to the south. Israel and Judah shared a common heritage, a language, a faith, and a covenant with the Lord. **the law of the LORD . . . His com-**

mandments: The basis of Judah and Israel's judgment was different from that of the nations Amos had just called to account before them (1:3—2:3). Judah and Israel had received God's special revelation at Sinai; they were in a special covenant relationship with Him and were held to a higher standard of accountability.

2:6 I will not turn away its punishment: Here the focus shifted to Amos's audience. This was Israel, God's people who had violated their covenant relationship with Him. God was calling them to account for violations of the covenant. **sell the righteous for silver:** In His law, God had instructed the Israelites to work off their debts through indentured service—administered humanely and for a strictly limited time (Lev. 25:39–43; Deut. 15:12). By Amos's day, those in power in Israel were taking advantage of the courts to sell debtors as slaves, termed **the righteous** here because they were the innocent victims of the corruption of the courts. **For a pair of sandals** means for little or nothing.

2:7 pant after the dust: Amos used deliberate exaggeration to portray the greed of those oppressing the poor. Not satisfied with gaining their victims' farms and selling the people into slavery for money, the greedy rich would not let the poor go until they had shaken the **dust** from their heads. The **humble,** those without power or influence, should have been able to depend on the justice due them. Instead, justice was denied them. As a result, their life was turned to poverty, oppression, and insecurity. **Go in to** means to have sexual intercourse with. **the same girl:** Several possibilities have been suggested: (1) Both father and son visited the same temple prostitute in their worship of pagan gods. (2) A man bought a slave girl, made her his concubine, then gave his son sexual rights to her. (3) A man married a woman, his

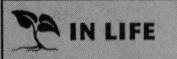 **IN LIFE**   **A Nation Loses Its Conscience**

Amos' description of Israel is sobering, if not downright frightening: "They do not know to do right" (Amos 3:10). Wickedness overflows the nation like a mighty river. As a result, the people are drowning in sin. They can no longer tell right from wrong. There is no longer any national conscience.

A nation is on the verge of collapse when good and evil look the same. If questions of right and wrong no longer even enter the people's minds, then that nation is in desperate trouble. In Israel's case, enemies were waiting just around the corner (3:11, 12).

Has your nation lost its conscience? Do people call good bad and bad good? Or can they even tell right from wrong? Or worse, do questions of morality not even concern them? If so, consider how you could act as an agent of conscience. Perhaps you could challenge people to consider their ways, and apprise them of their responsibility to fear God. You may not be received well, but God will honor you for standing up for righteousness.

father seduced her, and they became lovers. All of these practices were unlawful.

2:8 Clothes taken in pledge, as security for a loan, were to be returned in the evening, for clothes were the bedding of the poor (Ex. 22:26, 27). The powerful in Israel were spreading the clothes out as beds for themselves beside the altars, in a show of empty, merciless piety.

2:9, 10 Yet it was I: This emphatic statement underscores the fact that God had been Israel's Champion, and the nation's success had not been its own doing. **The Amorite** refers to the previous inhabitants of the land of Canaan. **Cedars** were proverbial for their height, **oaks** for their strength. **His fruit above and his roots beneath** means "totally, completely."

2:11, 12 Prophets were especially privileged; God spoke to them and gave them messages for the people. **Nazirites** dedicated themselves to God with a vow that entailed specific responsibilities and prohibitions, either for life or for a specified period (Num. 6:1–21). Total abstinence from **wine** was one of the prominent features of the Nazirite vow.

2:13 Weighed down by you is a powerful metaphor of the burden of Israel's sin on the Lord. This is the same God Isaiah describes as measuring the waters of the earth in the hollow of His hand, measuring the heavens with the span of His hand, and weighing the mountains in His balance (Is. 40:12).

2:14–16 No resources of personal strength, no skill with weapons of war, not even the help of the mighty war horse would suffice for the military **men of might** to save themselves in **that day,** when God would bring His judgment upon them. If the strong could not save themselves, what would become of the rest of the people?

3:1 The whole family which I brought up emphasizes the personal, intimate relationship that God had with Israel.

3:2 You only have I known, in this context, means "You only have I chosen." God's relationship with Israel was not only intimate, it was exclusive. God had been faithful to Israel; yet Israel had not been faithful to God. For this reason, the nation would be judged.

3:3–6 This series of rhetorical questions illustrates the seriousness, certainty, and righteousness of God's impending action against Israel. Each question is framed so as to require a resounding "no" as its answer.

3:7 This parenthetical statement interrupts, yet underscores, Amos's point that God is sovereign and does what He wills; therefore, Israel's judgment was certain.

3:8 Two more rhetorical questions complete the group of nine (vv. 3–6). It would do Israel

no good to forbid prophecy (2:12; 7:13, 16); the true prophet *must* prophesy, just as certainly as God's judgment must come to pass.

3:9, 10 Ashdod, one of the five principal cities of the Philistines, was on the Mediterranean coast southwest of Israel. For God to call Philistia and **Egypt** to witness His judgment of Israel implies that these pagan nations were relatively more righteous than Israel. They had not received God's revelation at Sinai; yet Israel, having received it, had violated it grossly and repeatedly.

3:11 This verse pictures a formal sentencing of Israel in the presence of the witnesses whom God had called (v. 9). Sapping Israel's **strength** was exactly what Assyria did in the years following Amos's prophecies, finally putting an end to the nation in 722 B.C.

3:12, 13 The hired **shepherd** was responsible to the owner for the safety of the sheep. He had to make good any loss, unless he could prove it was unavoidable. A **lion** taking a sheep was an unavoidable loss, but the shepherd had to prove that the lion had taken it. A couple of small bones or a piece of an **ear** was sufficient; the owner would recognize the lion's work. As complete as the destruction of a sheep by a lion would be the destruction of Israel that God would bring.

3:14 the altars of Bethel: Jeroboam I had erected sanctuaries in Bethel and Dan to prevent Israelites from traveling to Jerusalem to worship and possibly returning their political allegiance to the house of David. Those sanctuaries of false worship had tempted many Israelites to be unfaithful to God. **Horns** represent strength. If the horns of the altar were cut off, it would symbolize the altar's weakness and signal its destruction.

3:15 The four houses mentioned here were all symbols of oppression. Many small inheritances had been stolen to form the large estates of the wealthy and powerful, where they built their opulent houses.

4:1, 2 Bashan, the region east and northeast of the Sea of Galilee, was (and is) a prime grassland area renowned for its cattle. **Cows of Bashan** refer to the sleek, fat, well-fed women of **Samaria.** Amos was not condemning prosperity for its own sake, but the way these women and their men had gained their prosperity, by the oppression and robbery of the poor and powerless. These were the women of the powerful families who not only urged their husbands on to greater oppression so they could drink more and more wine at ever more elaborate social functions. They themselves oppressed **the poor** and crushed **the needy**. The biblical record is clear that Israelite women, at least of the upper classes, could engage in wide-ranging economic activities of their own, independently of their husbands (Prov. 31:10–31). Given the system-atic oppression of Israel's poor that Amos described, it is not surprising to find him indicting the women of the upper classes for their part in it.

4:3 Broken walls were a symbol of the thoroughness of the destruction of the city and the homes that the people held so dear. In an undamaged city, the usual way in and out was the one main gate. But Samaria would be so

This elaborate ivory carving discovered at Samaria recalls the words of the prophet Amos that Samaria's "houses of ivory" would be destroyed by God's judgment (Amos 3:15).

ruined that the deportees would be driven straight through the breaches in the walls of their houses and their city.

4:4, 5 This passage is a bitterly sarcastic call to Israel to worship. **Bethel,** a city on the central ridge road just inside Israel's border with Judah, was the site of the most important shrine in southern Israel. **Gilgal** refers to a site in the Jordan valley where Israel had encamped before and after the taking of Jericho (Josh. 5:10; 9:6). Thus, Gilgal had historical connections with Israel's early faith and early life in the land. **For this you love:** Ignoring God's desires, the Israelites did what they wanted. They loved the feasting that went with the festivals of sacrifice, but not God's calls for justice.

4:6–11 This passage describes a series of five calamities that God had already sent upon the Israelites in an effort to drive them to repentance. A striking feature of this narrative is God's emphatic claim that the Israelites had

brought these disasters on themselves. Each stanza ends with the tragic refrain, "Yet you have not returned to Me."

4:6 The first calamity was famine. **Cleanness of teeth . . . and lack of bread** indicated the exhaustion of all food supplies.

4:7, 8 The second calamity was drought. Lack of rain with **still three months to the harvest** meant the total ruin of the grain crops.

4:9 The third calamity was crop disease and locusts.

4:10 The fourth calamity was **plague** and warfare. **After the manner of Egypt** suggests that God was reminding Israel of the ten plagues that preceded their exodus from Egypt; these included epidemic diseases and other disasters. **The stench of your camps** resulted from lack of sanitation, from disease, from the putrefaction of wounds, and sometimes from corpses of men and of animals that could not be buried quickly enough.

4:11 The fifth calamity was the destruction of Israelite cities. The overthrow of **Sodom and Gomorrah** was the scale by which many subsequent disasters were measured. It meant total destruction, meted out in judgment by the hand of God Himself (Gen. 19:24, 25). **A firebrand plucked from the burning** refers to a stick snatched from a fire with one end already ablaze. Here it was a vivid metaphor for God's last-minute rescue of most of Israel from the fate He brought upon some of its cities and territories.

4:12 Because Israel had not returned to God through these five calamities, it would have to meet God Himself. To be confronted—inescapably—by the God it had scorned and rejected would be a fate more terrible than Israel could imagine.

4:13 Amos grounded God's right to exercise judgment upon Israel on His character as Creator and Sustainer of all the earth, a more fundamental basis than His deliverance of the Israelites from Egypt. God is sovereign over all the earth; on that basis He called Israel, and can call any nation, to account. **forms mountains:** The Hebrew word *forms* is derived from the word often rendered "potter." As easily as a potter forms vessels of clay, so God forms mountains. **Wind** also means "spirit." The ambiguity in this word may be deliberate. God creates both the wind and the human spirit; therefore, He is sovereign over both.

5:1, 2 The term **virgin of Israel** depicts the

🔍 IN FOCUS | "seek"

(Heb. *darash*) (5:4; Ezra 6:21; 7:10; Ps. 119:10; Is. 34:16; 55:6) Strong's #1875: This Hebrew verb can be correctly translated "to inquire of," "to ask," and "to seek." The term conveys the idea of "going to see" in the sense of personally verifying something said, or "searching for," in the sense of pressing for an answer to a question. Amos encourages his audience to seek life in the living God, not in the dead idols of Bethel and Gilgal (5:4). The psalmist found help in times of trouble by seeking the Lord (Pss. 34:4; 77:2). On several occasions, the Israelites were encouraged to seek God by preparing their hearts for God through humble repentance (1 Chr. 16:11; 2 Chr. 30:19).

---

nation as a young maiden, cut off from her life before it had really begun. **On her land** is a reminder that the land had been God's gift to Israel. By their faithlessness, the people had turned God's gift into the place of their death and burial.

5:3, 4 The lamentation continues with a different image of Israel's destruction: the troops Israel would send out to defend its territory. Rather than saving Israel, its armies would themselves be decimated.

5:5 Beersheba, about 50 miles southwest of Bethel, was the site of a temple in Amos's day.

5:6 The house of Joseph here refers to the whole nation.

5:7 Wormwood, a plant of the aster family with a bitter taste, is used several times in the Bible as a metaphor for sorrow and bitterness.

5:8 Pleiades refers to a cluster of stars within the constellation Taurus, one of the twelve signs of the Zodiac. One of Israel's idolatries was astral worship. Far from being deities, Amos asserted, the constellations also were God's creations. **Orion** refers to a prominent constellation in the southern sky in the shape of a hunter, containing two stars of the first magnitude. **He turns the shadow . . . dark as night:** God designed and sustains the daily cycle of light and darkness through His own servant, which was not a deity, the sun. **He calls . . . the earth:** God, not Baal, Tammuz, or any other fertility deity, designed and sustains the atmospheric water cycle by which the earth receives its necessary rainfall. **The LORD** is His name underscores the uniqueness of Israel's God. He is not just a national God; He is the *only* God.

5:9 The God who created and sustains the processes of all the universe surely can bring His judgment to bear, even upon the strong of the earth and their fortresses.

5:10 The gate was the location of the town court, where justice was to be upheld in all legal proceedings, whether civil or criminal.

5:11 Taxes were collected in kind from those with few resources of silver and gold. To **take grain taxes** from the poor was to put them at risk of starvation if the harvest had not been bountiful. Yet the rich and powerful had sufficient resources to build luxurious **houses of hewn stone** for themselves. God promised that the rich would not enjoy their luxury stolen from the lifeblood of the poor and powerless.

5:12 manifold . . . sins: Israel's leaders did not sin incidentally or furtively; they sinned brazenly and habitually, as though God had never revealed Himself and His standards of justice and mercy.

5:13 the prudent: Even those with knowledge that could ensure justice for the poor were intimidated into silence, knowing they would be targeted for violence if they spoke up against the rich and powerful.

5:14, 15 Seek good: The prophet interrupted himself, as it were, to plead with Israel to return to God and avoid the judgment He otherwise would bring upon them. **As you have spoken:** Worshiping in the Lord's name, the Israelites invoked the Lord's presence with them in their spoken prayers and blessings. If they began to live as God had taught them in the Law, He would indeed be with them.

5:16, 17 God's purposed action was that He would **pass through** the nation. A visit from God is a dreaded and mournful event for anyone not ready to meet Him. **In all vineyards:** A vineyard was typically a place of rejoicing and gladness.

5:18 The popular theology of Amos's day apparently looked forward to **the day of the LORD** as the time of Israel's restoration to military, political, and economic greatness, perhaps to the greatness of the reigns of David and Solomon. Amos declared such hopes futile, even pitiable. What the people looked forward to as a day of light and triumph would rise upon them instead as a day of darkness and ruin.

5:19, 20 The images of **a bear** and **a serpent** evoke the terror that follows when a person escapes a terrible danger and is exhausted and relieved, only to find a worse danger so close at hand that it is inescapable.

5:21–23 God had promised that if the Israelites honored Him with their lives, He would **savor, accept,** and **regard** Israel's sacrifices and **hear** their words. By stating He would no longer accept Israel's sacrifices or listen to them, God was rejecting Israel's worship as hypocritical, dishonest, and meaningless. **Feast days** and **sacred assemblies** refers, in general, to all of Israel's worship of God. **burnt offerings . . . grain offerings . . . peace offerings:** For more details on the sacrificial system, see Lev. 1—3.

5:24 After dismissing Israel's empty worship as noisy and tumultuous, God called for the honest tumult of the rolling waters of **justice** and the perennial **stream** of **righteousness,** the only foundation for true praise and worship of the Lord.

5:25 This verse is a rhetorical question with "yes" as the expected answer; Israel *had* worshiped God **in the wilderness.**

5:26 Israel had not worshiped the Lord exclusively, even in the earliest wilderness days. **Sikkuth** and **Chiun** are pagan deities; apparently Israel had made images of foreign gods. The true believer in the Lord understood, without question, that any gods **made** by human hands were not gods at all.

 **IN COMPARISON** **Pagan Gods of Bible Times**

One of Amos's primary responsibilities as a prophet of God was to announce the "day of the Lord," the time of God's judgment of wicked Israel. Idolatry, perhaps more than any other sin, was the reason for this impending punishment. The history of Israel is littered with apostasy, as the children of God pursued the false idols of their Canaanite neighbors. In 5:26, the prophet specifically identifies Chiun as the object of the people's worship. The following chart lists some of the pagan gods mentioned in the Old and New Testaments.

Pagan God	Description	Biblical Reference
OLD TESTAMENT		
Ashtoreths	Baal's wife or female counterpart.	Judg. 2:13
Bel	A god identified with Merodach (Marduk), chief Babylonian god.	Is. 46:1
Chemosh	God of the Moabites and Ammonites.	Jer. 48:7, 13
Chiun	A star-god, identified with Saturn	Amos 5:26
Dagon	Chief Philistine god.	1 Sam. 5:2–7
Merodach	Chief Babylonian god, connected with war. Also known as Marduk.	Jer. 50:2
Molech	Ammonite god connected with child sacrifice.	Lev. 18:21
Nebo	Babylonian god of wisdom and arts.	Is. 46:1
Rimmon	Syrian god of rain.	2 Kin. 5:18
Tammuz	Babylonian fertility god.	Ezek. 8:14
NEW TESTAMENT		
Twin Brothers	Castor and Pollux, twin sons of Zeus, the chief Greek god.	Acts 28:11
Zeus	Chief Greek god.	Acts 14:12, 13
Hermes	The Greek god of commerce and speed.	Acts 14:12,13

5:27 Since Israel insisted on worshiping other gods, including astral deities, God would send them into exile to lands where these deities seemed to rule supreme. Israel was exiled **beyond Damascus**, Syria's capital, to regions of Assyria and beyond.

6:1 **Zion** refers to Jerusalem, the capital of Judah (the southern kingdom). **Samaria** was the capital of Israel (the northern kingdom). At the time of Amos's prophecy, Israel and Judah together had enjoyed about a generation of military might and economic prosperity. It became natural for officials in Jerusalem and Samaria to regard themselves as **notable persons.**

6:2 It was the boast of Israel's elite that no other nation was greater than they were. Their boast came back upon their own heads, for just as Calneh, Hamath, and Gath were subjected to Assyrian rule, so Israel would also be subjugated by the Assyrians. **Calneh,** a city in northern Syria, was the capital of a small kingdom. **Hamath,** an important city in central Syria, was located north of Damascus. **Gath,** one of the five principal Philistine cities, was southwest of Israel.

6:3 You who put far off the day of doom refers to those who insisted that Israel was too strong for destruction to fall upon the nation any time soon.

6:4–6 This passage describes the extravagant living indulged in by the rich, and paid for with the wealth stolen from the poor. **Ivory** had been imported into Israel from the south since at least the days of Solomon, probably from the mysterious land of Ophir by way of Sheba. Much of it was used for fashioning idols. At Samaria, archaeologists have found numerous ivory plaques and inlaid wood portraying Egyptian and Syro-Phoenician gods and goddesses. **lambs . . . calves:** Meat was a luxury for most families of the ancient Middle East, consumed only on special occasions. Meat on a daily basis was the privilege only of the rich and powerful. The upper classes of Israel were so engrossed in their own privileges and luxuries that they cared nothing for the **affliction of** their fellow Israelites, though it was their transgressions that had caused it.

6:7 God's judgment would be both fitting and ironic. Those who had fancied themselves the leaders of the nation would lead their nation into exile.

6:8, 9 If God takes an oath, He takes it **by Himself,** for there is none greater than He. In his oracles against the seven nations (chs. 1; 2), Amos had prophesied the destruction of their palaces. Now it was Israel's turn. Luxurious palace strongholds represented both the **pride of Jacob** in their own strength and the oppression of the powerless, whose stolen wealth had

financed the construction of these palaces. **I will deliver up the city:** God personally would see to the destruction of Samaria and its proud inhabitants.

6:10, 11 These verses depict the aftermath of God's judgment, when relatives came around to carry out the bodies. **One inside the house** may refer to the last survivor, sick but not yet dead himself. In this context, such a person might have been expected to invoke the name of God for help after answering, **"None."** Before he could do so, however, the questioner would silence him, fearful of getting God's further attention by using His name. People who had not believed that God would come in judgment would now be afraid of what further disaster He might bring upon them.

6:12 By citing two obviously impossible actions in areas of life with which all Israelites would have been familiar, Amos hoped to get the people to see the moral impossibility of Israel's perversion of justice. As absurd and impossible in God's sight as horses running up vertical cliffs or oxen plowing the sea was Israel's—or any nation's—perversion of justice and righteousness. **Gall** is a bitter, poisonous herb.

6:13, 14 Israel's pride in its military strength would be its downfall. **Lo Debar** was a city east of the Jordan that Israel regained from Syria when Assyria crippled the strength of Damascus. **Karnaim,** a city east of the Jordan near the farthest limits of Israelite possession, was also regained when Assyria weakened Syria. God's punishment of Israel would fit its sin of pride. As the Israelites reckoned that they had extended their borders by their own military strength, God would allow them to be harassed and defeated from border to border. **The Valley of the Arabah** refers to the desert valley that was the southern limit of Israelite control. From north to south, from border to border, God would allow Israel to be defeated in battle; they would realize that their own strength was puny indeed.

7:1 locust swarms: Locusts are a kind of grasshopper. Joel 1:4—2:11 describes the devastation locusts bring to agriculture, stripping every green leaf and twig, and even killing trees. **The late crop** refers to the last growth of crops and pastures, evidently including hay, before the summer dry season. **The king's mowings** implies that the king took the first harvest of hay as a tax. Thus a swarm of locusts devouring the late crop would leave the people with nothing for themselves, inflicting a crippling economic blow.

7:2, 3 Oh, that Jacob may stand: If God carried out the threatened punishment, Jacob (the nation of Israel) might be destroyed. One function of the prophet was to serve as intercessor for the people before God. Amos prayed that the vision decreed in heaven might be halted before it was accomplished on earth. The basis of Amos's petition lay in the true assessment of Israel's position. They were not large and strong, as they thought; rather they were **small** and weak. In response to Amos's intercession, and out of His own love for Israel, God stayed His decree.

7:4–6 To call **for conflict** means to put on trial or to bring a lawsuit against Israel. To try **by fire** means that fire would have been both the instrument by which Israel's guilt would be judged and the instrument by which their punishment would be carried out. **The great deep** refers to the primordial waters that remained beneath the firmament after God fashioned it (Gen. 1:6–8). These include the oceans and seas, and the subterranean waters that are the sources of springs and wells. For the deep to be dried up by fire means that the land would be devastated beyond hope. **The territory** refers either to the portion of the earth God had assigned to Israel or to Israel as God's portion among the nations of the earth.

7:7–9 A plumb line is a string with a weight tied to one end, used to establish a vertical line so that a wall can be built straight. **What do you see:** Unlike the first two visions of natural disasters, the visions of the plumb line and the basket of summer fruit (8:1) were not self-explanatory. God asked Amos what he saw, then explained the vision's meaning. Also unlike the first two visions, God did not give Amos opportunity to intercede, nor did He relent. These judgments would be executed. The plumb line of God's revelation in the law had been set **in the midst of . . . Israel** for many generations. Now God would stretch a plumb line to demonstrate how "crooked" the people's observance of His commands had been. **The high places** refer to temples, groves, and other shrines dedicated mostly to pagan deities. **Isaac,** the father of Jacob, represent all Israel in Amos's day. **Jeroboam** may refer to Jeroboam I, the first king of Israel, who instituted idolatry in the northern kingdom (1 Kin. 12:25–33), or to Jeroboam II, the monarch during the time of these prophecies. If it is Jeroboam I, then **the house of Jeroboam** is a metaphor for the nation. If it is Jeroboam II, then the prophecy specifically concerns the royal household. In v. 10, the prophecy is taken by Amaziah to refer to the current king. Jeroboam II himself did not die by **the sword,** but his son Zechariah was assassinated after reigning only six months (2 Kin. 15:8–10).

7:10, 11 Amaziah, the priest in charge of the temple at Bethel, informed the king about the prophet who was making threats against the king's house. Amaziah was reacting to Amos's third vision, which ended with God's promise to bring the sword against the house of Jeroboam. Amaziah regarded Amos's words as a political threat, and reported them not as a prophecy from God, but as Amos's call to revolt.

7:12, 13 After sending his report to Jeroboam, Amaziah turned his attention to Amos himself. Since Amaziah was an official of the king, his command to Amos to return to Judah would have amounted to making Amos officially unwelcome in Israel. Amaziah was not concerned at all that Amos had proclaimed a message from God, only that the king's interests should be protected from this seditious prophet.

7:14–17 Amos's answer to Amaziah came in two parts. First he denied being a prophet by profession. **Nor was I a son of a prophet** indicates not only that Amos's father was not a prophet, but also that Amos had not been trained in prophecy. **the LORD took me:** Amos made it clear that he had neither desired nor sought his prophetic task. The second part of Amos's answer was directed against Amaziah personally. **Your wife shall be a harlot:** The only way the spouse of an important official like Amaziah would be reduced to prostitution would be if all her family and all her resources were taken away and she were left to fend entirely for herself. The rest of Amos's oracle predicted that such a situation would happen to Amaziah's family. **Your land shall be divided** indicated that it would be assigned or sold to new owners. As a high official of the king, Amaziah certainly possessed large land holdings; he would retain none. **Defiled land** refers to the land of pagans.

8:1–3 summer fruit: The fruits that came at the end of the harvest in late summer included grapes, pomegranates, and figs. **The end has come:** Amos could not have discerned the meaning of this vision until God's pronouncement. Israel's wickedness was about to result in a harvest of judgment. Most good harvests are times of rejoicing. But in this one, **the songs of the temple**—the songs of thanksgiving—would be turned to **wailing** because the harvest would be death.

8:4 Fail means essentially "to have no means of survival."

8:5 The New Moon, the first day of the month on the Hebrew calendar, was a day of special sacrifices, a feast day, and a **Sabbath** day (Num. 28:11–15; 1 Sam. 20:5). Rather than observing the New Moon and the weekly Sabbath with worship, thanksgiving, and rest, these people were impatient to resume their cheating and oppression of the poor. In biblical times, the ephah was the most common measure of dry volume. To make **the ephah small,** therefore, was to cheat the customer of value received for price paid. The shekel was a unit of money. To make **the shekel large** was to cheat the customer by taking too large a price (weight) of silver for value received.

8:6 Israel's system of indentured service for members of the covenant community was to be humane and limited in time (Ex. 21:2, 3; Lev. 25:39–55). The rich and powerful of Amos's day were making slaves of Israel's poor, the people they had dispossessed of their lands. **the bad wheat:** The chaff and other refuse of the threshing floor, perhaps even moldy or mildewed wheat, were mixed in with the good wheat to stretch it further and make a greater profit.

8:7 The form of the Hebrew oath marks its seriousness: God will not forget. **Their works** refers to the economic injustices Amos spoke against in vv. 4–6, as well as other sins, including unfaithfulness to God.

8:8 **The River** and **the River of Egypt** refer to the Nile River. **Heave and subside:** The Nile rises and falls several feet in its annual flood. Amos may have intended to portray a severe earthquake in which the land's rise and fall would be as dramatic as the rise and fall of the Nile. Though the Nile's flood usually was quite gentle in Egypt, an earthquake that reminded one of it would be violent indeed.

8:9, 10 God's judgment would be a great reversal—of light to darkness, and joy to mourning. **That day** probably refers to the "day of the Lord" (5:18). **Sackcloth,** a coarse cloth of goat or camel hair, was uncomfortable to wear. Thus it was worn next to the skin as a sign of mourning or great distress. Shaving the head to create temporary **baldness** was another mourning sign.

8:11 In 4:6, Amos reminds Israel that God had sent famine upon them, yet they had not returned to Him. Now the famine would be, not of food, **but of hearing the words of the LORD.**

8:12, 13 **From sea to sea** means from the Dead Sea to the Mediterranean. **to and fro:** Those in Israel searching for the word of God would have to circle all of Israel's territory, but in vain. **The fair virgins and strong young men** refers to those who are most vigorous and apt to survive.

8:14 **Dan** in the far north and **Beersheba** in the far south were the limits of significant

> *God would stretch a plumb line to demonstrate how "crooked" the people's observance of His commands had been.*

Israelite settlement. In Amos's day, Beersheba was in the kingdom of Judah. Israel could swear oaths by the Lord, claiming they loyally worshiped Him from the extreme north to the extreme south of His land, but that would not relieve the famine of God's word.

9:1 The people would have expected a vision of God **by the altar** to mean that He intended good for them, blessing them with His presence. Instead God would start at the altar, commanding that the destruction of the sinful nation begin there. **them all . . . the last of them:** The reference here is to faithless Israel.

9:2 **hell . . . heaven:** In this imagery, Israel's fugitives from God's judgment could escape neither up nor down; God would find them no matter where in the universe they fled.

9:3 If the universe could not hide the fugitives, neither could the earth. The **top of Carmel** represented the highest point on the earth. Whether as high as that, or as low as **the bottom of the sea,** the earth would provide no escape.

9:4–6 Even **captivity** in enemy lands would not provide a refuge from God's further judgment upon Israel. **I will set My eyes on them** usually is a formula that expresses God's blessing on Israel; here it alludes to the fulfillment of the curses for breaking the Mosaic covenant.

9:7 **Ethiopia** refers to the region near the southern horizon of Israel's geographical knowledge, south of Egypt. God's rhetorical question told Israel that they were not the only recipients of God's attention and care. God loves all peoples, even **the Philistines** and **Syrians. Caphtor** refers to Crete, a large island in the Mediterranean Sea.

9:8 **The sinful kingdom** is Israel. **I will not utterly destroy:** This was a glimmer of hope in a long passage of judgment and doom. God's judgment would be thorough, but a remnant would survive.

9:9, 10 Sifting grain **in a sieve** was the final operation in cleaning grain before gathering it into storage. In winnowing, all the chaff was blown away; only pebbles and small clumps of mud remained with the grain. The sieve was constructed with holes that were sized so the grain fell through when it was shaken, but pebbles and other debris were retained in the sieve. Thus the **smallest grain** refers to the smallest pebble; it would not fall to the ground with the clean grain.

9:11, 12 The tabernacle of David: Amos pictures the royal house of David metaphorically as a "booth" fallen in disrepair. Judah was a fallen, ruined shelter, incapable of protecting its people from any significant storm. **As in the days of old** reflects the nostalgia of Israel's people for the glory days of the kingdoms of David and Solomon, when they lived in strength, prosperity, and security. **Gentiles** refers to the peoples around Israel and Judah. **Called by My name** is a designation of sovereignty and ownership. **Says the LORD** who does this thing: God would take this task upon Himself.

9:13 Israelite farmers plowed at the beginning of the rainy season, from mid-October. They harvested the grain crop—first barley, then wheat—from late March to early June. For **the plowman** to **overtake the reaper** would mean such an abundant harvest that it would last all summer and would not be gathered until the plowing had started again. Grapes were harvested from midsummer to early fall. The grain crop was sown after the plowing in late fall. For **the treader of grapes** to overtake **him who sows seed** would mean the grape harvest would be so abundant that it would be extended for several weeks. The harvest of grapes would be so great that it would seem as though the **mountains** and **hills** themselves were flowing with rivers of **sweet wine.**

9:14 The promised restoration will be a total reversal of the punishment that God was bringing upon Israel.

9:15 As Israel planted vineyards, fields, and gardens, so God would **plant** the people **in their land**, never again to **be pulled up** in exile. **Says the LORD** your God are the final words of Amos's prophecy. God would do what He threatened through Amos—if Israel did not return to Him. God would also do what He promised through Amos in the last few verses of this book. God does not abandon His promises or His covenant, nor does He leave His people without hope. God's punishment is certain, but His restoration is just as certain. That word of hope for God's people of old is valid also for God's people of today.

The Book of

Obadiah

■

THE BOOK OF OBADIAH IS ONE OF ONLY TWO MINOR prophets that is addressed entirely to a nation other than Israel or Judah. It deals with the ancient feud between Israel and the nation of Edom, between the descendants of Jacob and those of his brother Esau. Through the prophet Obadiah, the Lord expressed His indignation at the nation of Edom. When they should have been helping their relatives, they were

gloating over the Israelites' problems and raiding their homes. A day was coming—the day of the Lord—when all these wrongs would be righted. The Lord would bring justice to the world.

In 586 B.C. Nebuchadnezzar's army crushed Judah and destroyed Jerusalem and Solomon's temple, ending Judah's existence as an independent nation. Edom, as a closely related nation, should have helped Judah's refugees. But instead of offering sympathy and help, Edom handed Judeans over to the conquering Babylonians. The Edomites even murdered some of the refugees. Such treachery to a related nation could not be overlooked. God gave Obadiah a stern message for Edom, a warning of God's judgment on them for their callous treatment of the fleeing Judeans.

The Edomites' pride and presumed self-sufficiency became their downfall. Their fortress capital of Sela, which they considered impregnable, became their tomb. Their Arab neighbors turned on them, taking over their land and their livelihood. The Edomites were pushed into what had been southern Judah. In the second century B.C., the resurgent Jewish kingdom

under the Maccabees conquered the Edomites and forcibly converted them to Judaism. At that time they were called Idumeans.

While Obadiah's short prophetic oracle was addressed to Edom, it is doubtful that Edomite leaders ever heard or read it. One purpose of the oracle was to comfort and encourage the surviving Judeans with the message that God had not abandoned them. Judah would be restored to its own land after the judgment of the Exile had been accomplished, and their enemies would be punished.

In the grand scheme of the biblical message of God's redemption of fallen humanity, the Book of Obadiah may seem to be of little importance. But its portion of that message is tremendously vital. God is sovereign over all nations, regardless of whether they acknowledge His sovereignty. God desires that we show mercy and favor to our neighbors in their time of distress. Treachery against a relative is never justified and will be judged by the God of justice.

The name Obadiah means "Servant of the Lord." It is not known whether this was the prophet's personal name or whether he used it as a title, preferring to remain anonymous.

Nothing is known about Obadiah's personal life or standing in Judean society. Some scholars date the book very early, in the mid-ninth century B.C., following raids by the Philistines and Arabian tribes during the period of King Jehoram of Judah (2 Chr. 21:16, 17). This would make Obadiah the earliest of the prophetic books. However, most scholars date the book immediately following the Babylonian destruction of Jerusalem in 586 B.C.

Outline

I. Edom's coming judgment vv. 1–9
  A. God's summons to the nations v. 1
  B. Edom's pride and disaster vv. 2–9
II. Edom's sin: violence against Judah vv. 10–14
III. Edom's judgment and Judah's restoration vv. 15–21
  A. The day of the Lord against Edom vv. 15–18
  B. God's restoration of Judah vv. 19–21

Commentary

1 Vision, a word common in the prophets (Is. 1:1; Nah. 1:1) indicates that the prophet "saw" the revelation. **Obadiah** means "The Servant of the Lord." **Thus says the Lord GOD**: This phrasing is a strong affirmation that the prophetic oracle did not originate in the prophet's own thinking; God was and is the Initiator. A national oracle is directed against

Edom, a country east of the Dead Sea and south of Moab. **The nations** is the standard biblical term for the larger national entities of western Asia and northeast Africa. See Jer. 49:7–22 for a passage with many similarities to the Book of Obadiah. Ezekiel also contains prophecies against Edom that are similar to the message of Obadiah (Ezek. 25:12–14; 35:1–15).

2 I will make you small: God would bring about a reversal of Edom's inflated self-importance.

3 the clefts of the rock: This may be a reference to the fabled Petra (Sela), which later became the capital of the later Nabatean kingdom (beginning in 312 B.C.). During the time of Obadiah, Petra was a stronghold of the Edomites. Petra was approached only through a mile-long cleft in the rock. This passage is so narrow in spots that one can reach out and touch both rock walls simultaneously. The magnificent ruins that one sees at Petra today in the country of Jordan are from a period later than ancient Edom. Undoubtedly, the Edomites had similar magnificent structures in the rocky face of this site during their own time. **habitation is high:** Some of the mountain peaks of Edom reach over six thousand feet; Jerusalem is about 2,300 feet above sea level. **Who will bring me down:** Edom's presumed physical safety led the Edomites to become haughty; this would be their downfall.

4 as high as the eagle ... among the stars: Edom's physical location became a metaphor for the proud and haughty spirit that the nation had displayed at the time of Judah's distress. Trusting in its high places and mountainous strongholds,

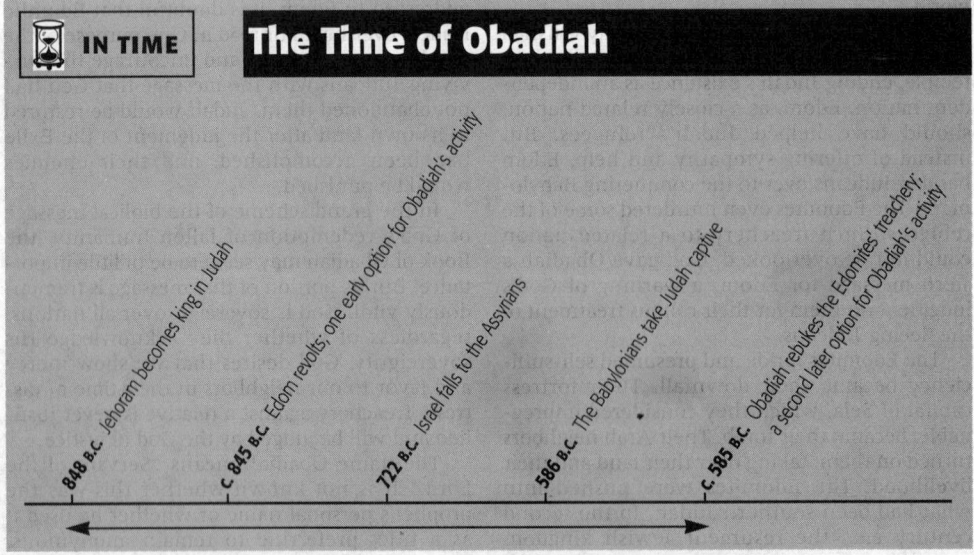

IN TIME   **The Time of Obadiah**

848 B.C. Jehoram becomes king in Judah

c. 845 B.C. Edom revolts, one early option for Obadiah's activity

722 B.C. Israel falls to the Assyrians

586 B.C. The Babylonians take Judah captive

c. 585 B.C. Obadiah rebukes the Edomites' treachery; a second later option for Obadiah's activity

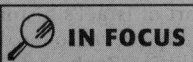 **IN FOCUS** "pride"

(Heb. *zadon*) (v. 3; Prov. 11:2; 13:10; Jer. 49:16) Strong's #2087: The Hebrew noun is related to a verb that means "to boil up." In the OT, the noun has the meaning of "acting proudly or presumptuously" (Deut. 18:22; 1 Sam. 17:28). The defining characteristic of the nation of Edom was pride (Obad. 3; Jer. 49:16). Interestingly, Jeremiah uses the word *pride* symbolically as a synonym for Babylon (Jer. 50:31, 32). Pride incites insolence and rebellion toward God, and it brings shame (Prov. 11:2) and destruction (Ezek. 7:10–12). The "pride of your heart" about which Jeremiah speaks is "presumptuous godlessness," the arrogance of those who think that they can thrive without their Creator (Prov. 11:2; 13:10; Jer. 49:16).

Edom assumed that no one could bring it to account for its actions.

5, 6 If thieves had come: The implication is that Edom would be stripped of everything. The nation would have been better off if thieves and robbers had come. **searched out:** Rather than being robbed randomly, the nation would be systematically pillaged (Jer. 49:7–10).

7 In your confederacy referred to the nations who were allied with Edom in a covenant relationship, **at peace** and eating **bread** with them.

8 Edom had a reputation for having many **wise men** among its citizens (Jer. 49:7).

9 The name **Teman** comes from a son of Eliphaz, who was the firstborn son of Esau (Gen. 36:9–11). The word is often used as a synonym for Edom (Jer. 49:7; Amos 1:12), and is thought to have been one of its principal cities. One of Job's friends, also named Eliphaz, came from Teman (Job 2:11).

10 your brother Jacob: Esau and Jacob were brothers, the sons of Isaac and Rebekah (Gen. 25:24–26). Edom was descended from Esau; Judah was descended from Jacob.

11 In the day refers to the time of Judah's distress. **strangers . . . foreigners:** These words, used to describe Judah's principal enemies, contrast with the words of v. 10, "your brother." It was one thing for the Babylonians to attack Judah; for a nation like Edom to join the Babylonians against their own brothers was unthinkable.

12 Judah's defeat and destruction should have brought sorrow to its neighbors. Instead, Judah's brother nation had laughed aloud. More than that, Edom had helped to complete Judah's destruction, taking spoil, capturing those who were trying to escape the Babylonian onslaught, and turning them over to Nebuchadnezzar's soldiers. **Nor should you have spoken proudly:** A literal translation would be, "You should not have made big your mouth."

13 The day of their calamity, repeated

three times in this verse, refers to the day of God's judgment upon Judah, carried out by the hand of Nebuchadnezzar.

14 stood at the crossroads: The phrasing suggests deliberate actions on Edom's part. **day**

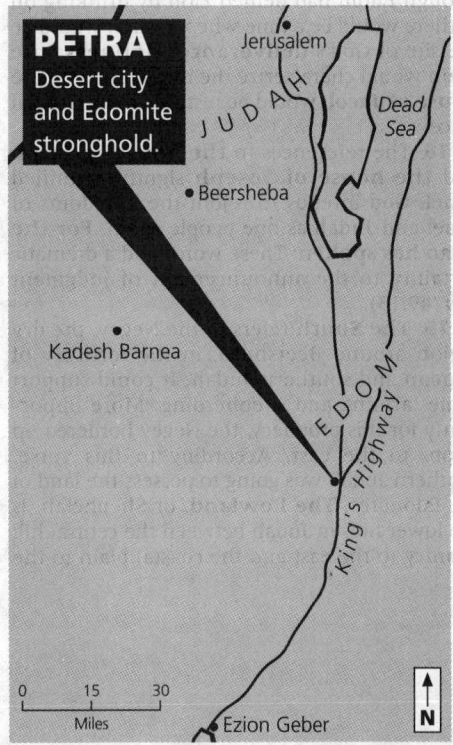

Petra, the capital of Edom, was located in a mountain stronghold some 5,000 feet above sea level. This virtually impregnable fortress produced an arrogant sense of security in the Edomites.

of distress: This phrase, repeated from v. 12, is a synonym of "day of their calamity" in v. 13.

delivered up those . . . who remained: The Edomites had captured those who were attempting to escape the Babylonian army and then had turned them over to their pursuers.

15 The **day of the LORD** is a technical term used by the prophets to indicate the day of God's judgment (Amos 5:18–20). Here the term likely refers to the time when God would judge **all the nations,** including Edom, that had participated in Judah's destruction. **As you have done:** The nature of God's judgment always reflects the nature of the sin being judged.

16 as you drank: The reference here is to the "cup of God's wrath" that was passed from Samaria to Judah, and finally to the nations— including Edom (Jer. 25:27, 32, 33). The Lord still viewed Jerusalem as His **holy mountain** because He intended to reestablish His presence there (Zech. 1:16).

17 Mount Zion and "My holy mountain" (in v. 16) refer to the same place: Jerusalem. Though Edom had defiled Zion by drinking on it, there would be a time when again it would be the site of God's **deliverance. Holiness** once again would characterize the mountain and **the house of Jacob** would be restored to its rightful place.

18 The references to **the house of Jacob** and **the house of Joseph** signify a unified Israel. God intends to rejoin the kingdoms of Israel and Judah as one people again. **For the LORD has spoken:** These words add a dramatic certainty to the announcement of judgment (Jer. 49:13).

19 The South refers to the Negev, the dry region around Beersheba, in the territory of Simeon and southern Judah. It could support some farming and shepherding. More importantly for this prophecy, the Negev bordered on Edom to the east. According to this verse, southern Judah was going to possess the land of the Edomites. **The Lowland,** or Shephelah, is the lower hills in Judah between the central hill country to the east and the coastal plain to the

west. Judah and Philistia fought fiercely over this region in the early part of Israel's history. But Judah would eventually prevail over the lands contested with Philistia (Zeph. 2:4–7). **Ephraim, Samaria,** and **Gilead** were parts of Israel during the period of the judges and most of the monarchy. Ephraim and Samaria were the heartland of the northern kingdom of Israel during the time of the divided monarchy. But at the time of Obadiah's prophecy, all three regions had passed under foreign domination and had experienced a significant influx of foreign population. In the day of the Lord of which Obadiah prophesied, these regions again would come into the possession of the Israelites. The land of Israel would be restored to its rightful inhabitants.

20 Zarephath was a Phoenician city 14 miles north of Tyre (1 Kin. 17:8–24). **Sepharad** was a city to which some Judeans were exiled. The restoration of Judah from exile, which these verses predict, was a sign to Judah and all nations that the God of Israel was not just a local God. The Babylonian god Marduk had not defeated the Lord. The fact that He could allow His people to be carried into captivity in a foreign land and then bring them back to their own land was proof of His power and sovereignty over all the earth.

21 Saviors means "deliverers" or "those who will bring about salvation" (Neh. 9:27). The Judeans who had been taken into captivity would come back as deliverers, and they would reign over the people of Edom. **the kingdom shall be the LORD's:** These were Obadiah's last words against all human arrogance, pride, and rebellion. Edom had thought itself indestructible; but the Lord humbled that nation and restored the fallen Judah. Many people are tempted to consider themselves beyond the reach of God. But God will bring them low, just as He will lift those who humble themselves before Him. And one great day, He will establish His just rule over all.

The Book of

Jonah

T HE BOOK OF JONAH HAS BEEN DESCRIBED AS a parable, an allegory, and a satire. The famous story of the "great fish" (often erroneously thought of as a whale) has led many to dismiss the book as merely a biblical "fish story." It is a mistake (based in part on the difficulty some readers have in coming to terms with the miraculous character of the story line) to assume that the events and actions of the book are not

historical in nature. While the story line is unusual, it is presented as normal history. Further, Jesus used the story of Jonah as an analogy of His own impending death and resurrection (Matt. 12:39–41). Jesus' analogy depends on the recognition of two historical realities: (1) the historical experience of Jonah in the belly of the great fish, and (2) the historical experience of the repentance of the people of Nineveh based on the preaching of Jonah (Luke 11:29–32). Indeed, the phrase "the sign of the prophet Jonah" must have been a recurring phrase in the teaching of Christ, for it is found on more than one occasion in Matthew's account of Christ's ministry (Matt. 16:4). Thus any view of the Book of Jonah that does not assume it describes historical events is obliged to explain away the clear words of Jesus to the contrary.

By the time of the ministry of Jonah, Assyria was preoccupied with the mountain tribes of Urartu, and did not continue its westward campaigns until Tiglath-Pileser III came to power in 745 B.C. Israel rejoiced at this preoccupation of Assyria, and they aggressively pursued a policy of defense by strengthening their fortified cities,

building up the army, and developing international relations.

The Book of Jonah challenges God's people not to exalt themselves over others. The Lord, the great King, is free to bless, to be gracious, and to be patient with all the nations of the earth. More than that, He may show compassion even on the wicked. Indeed, His mercy extends even to animals (4:11).

Jonah's view of God was too restrictive. He believed that God was the Creator of everything, but that He was compassionate only toward the elect of Israel. Jonah believed that since God had chosen Israel from among the wicked nations, He had to show mercy to Israel, even if the people were rebellious. Jonah had failed to appreciate that the Lord may be equally forbearing with other nations as He was with Israel.

The Book of Jonah affirms God's freedom, sovereignty, and power. God is sovereign because He is the Creator of everything (1:9). His power extends over all creation (the storm, the fish, the vine, the worm). God is free, and He can never be bound by human misconceptions.

The self-righteous make the grave mistake of rejoicing only in their own deliverance (2:9) and in God's answers to prayer (4:6). They miss out by narrowing God's grace and mercy to themselves. Like Jonah, they cannot share in God's delight in saving the sailors and the city of Nineveh, including infants and even animals (4:11). They confess that God is Creator and King of the whole cosmos, but restrict His involvement to judgment, justice, and retribution. In this manner they do not see His acts of compassion, righteousness, and forbearance. The Lord's final proclamation to Jonah (4:10, 11) sums up the prophetic message of the book: God is free to bestow His mercy on anyone and anywhere He wills. His concern and mercy extend to all creation.

Jonah's story contains a strong warning to all godly people. The elect may miss the blessing of seeing God's grace extended outside their own sphere because of their imposition of limits on God. While Jonah was praying anxiously for his personal deliverance, the sailors had already been experiencing the love of God for three days. Likewise, the people of Nineveh who repented of their sin rejoiced that the impending judgment had not come. Jonah, however, was miserable. As we laugh at him, we may need to wince at ourselves. Jonah's silly sin is finally no laughing matter. We are condemned along with him if we share in his provincial folly.

As already noted, the literary form of the Book of Jonah differs from that of other prophetic books. It has no prophecies. Instead, the book is largely narrative. Chapter 2 is a song of deliverance, a lovely, vibrant lyric prayer like many in the Book of Psalms.

It is best to understand the book as a prophetic parable. The events in the book are historical, but its place among the prophets leads us to interpret it as a prophetic writing. As a prophetic book, it is unique in that the message of the book centers on the negative interaction between the Lord and His prophet. As a parable, the book draws attention to the grace of God and to the folly of Jonah. The prophet's folly encourages the godly reader to avoid Jonah's negative example and to be a messenger of God's mercy and judgment to the nations.

The book does not specifically state who wrote it. But the tradition that it was written by Jonah as his own report of his foolish behavior and his final statement of coming to terms with the divine will is a likely possibility.

The prophet Jonah lived in the eighth century B.C., but we know little about him apart from this book. He is mentioned in only one other passage in the Old Testament apart from the book that bears his name. Second Kings 14:25 announces the fulfillment of a prophecy of the living God that came through "Jonah the son of Amittai, the prophet who was from Gath Hepher." This passage locates Jonah's ministry in the northern kingdom of Israel during the reign of King Jeroboam II (792–753 B.C.). The text suggests that through Jonah's ministry the Lord encouraged Israel and gave the nation a period of prosperity under Jeroboam. Yet we also know that during this period of political, geographical, and economic expansion, Israel forgot its past troubles, did not return to the

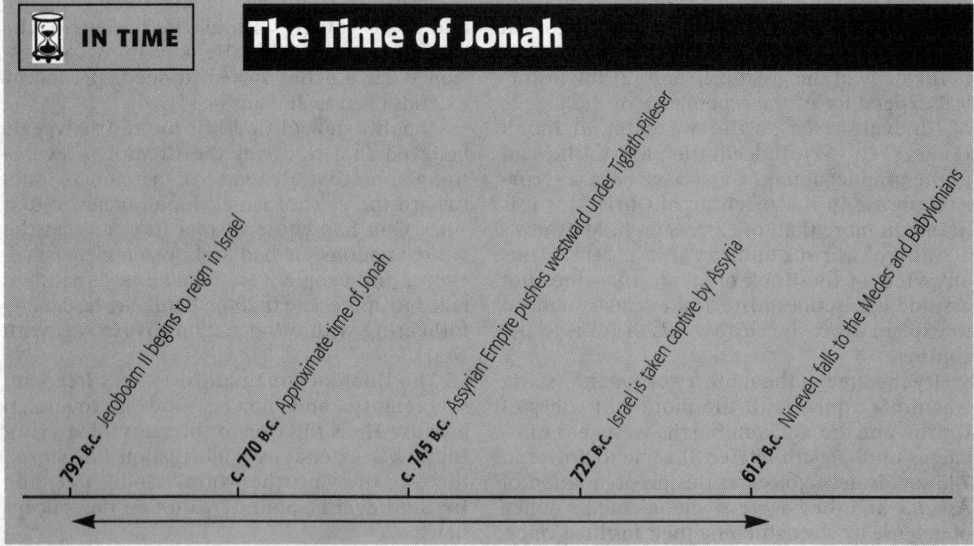

IN TIME — **The Time of Jonah**

792 B.C. Jeroboam II begins to reign in Israel

c. 770 B.C. Approximate time of Jonah

c. 745 B.C. Assyrian Empire pushes westward under Tiglath-Pileser

722 B.C. Israel is taken captive by Assyria

612 B.C. Nineveh falls to the Medes and Babylonians

Lord, and did not worry about Assyria's growing power. Clearly, the historical passage presents Jonah in a positive manner. The Book of Jonah, however, presents the prophet in a negative light as it highlights his disobedience to the Lord, leading the reader to reject Jonah's attitudes and actions.

The prophet Jonah was from Gath Hepher, a town in the territory of Zebulun (Josh. 19:10, 13; 2 Kin. 14:25), several miles northeast of Nazareth. Nothing is known about his father Amittai. The name Jonah means "Dove." We associate the dove with peace and purity; however, this positive meaning is not the only possible association. A "dove" could also be a symbol of silliness (Hos. 7:11), a description that sadly applies to this tragicomical prophet.

Outline

I. The prophet's flight from his commission to go to Nineveh 1:1–2:10

 A. The commission to go to Nineveh 1:1, 2

 B. The flight to Tarshish 1:3

 C. Jonah in a storm 1:4–8

 D. Jonah's proclamation of faith in the Lord 1:9

 E. Jonah thrown into the sea 1:10–16

 F. Jonah in the great fish 1:17–2:1

 G. Jonah's prayer of praise 2:2–9

 H. Jonah's deliverance from the great fish 2:10

II. The prophet's obedience to his commission to go to Nineveh 3:1–4:11

 A. A new commission to go to Nineveh 3:1, 2

 B. Jonah's proclamation in Nineveh 3:3, 4

 C. The deliverance of Nineveh 3:5–10

 D. Jonah's sorrow over Nineveh's deliverance 4:1–8

 E. Jonah's debate with the Lord 4:9

 F. The proclamation of the Lord to Jonah 4:10, 11

Commentary

1:1–2:10 The Book of Jonah contains two main sections (chs. 1 and 2, and 3 and 4). The first major section of the book (chs. 1 and 2) describes how Jonah, a true prophet of the Lord, attempted to flee from the commission that God had given him to bring the divine message to Nineveh. This section is composed of eight small units: (1) Jonah receives a commission to go to Nineveh (1:1, 2); (2) Jonah flees on a ship to Tarshish (v. 3); (3) Jonah and the sailors are caught in a storm (vv. 4–8); (4) Jonah proclaims

his identity and his faith in the Lord (v. 9); (5) Jonah is cast into the sea to save the sailors's lives (vv. 10–16); (6) Jonah is swallowed by a great fish (1:17—2:1); (7) Jonah's psalm of deliverance recounts his gratitude to the Lord for His amazing act of deliverance from the sea (2:2–9); and, (8) Jonah is delivered from the great fish (v. 10).

1:1 the word of the LORD came: This phrase affirms the divine source of the message to Jonah (1 Kin. 17:8; Jer. 1:4; Hos. 1:1; Joel 1:1; Mic. 1:1; Zeph. 1:1; Hag. 1:3). The name **Jonah** means "dove."

1:2 Nineveh, located on the Tigris River (Gen. 10:11, 12), was the capital of ancient Assyria (2 Kin. 19:36) for about a century (Zeph. 2:13–15; see also the Book of Nahum). Nineveh was over five hundred miles from Gath Hepher, Jonah's home near Nazareth in Israel. **Their wickedness** refers to Nineveh's pride, greed, brutality, and adultery (3:8; Nah. 2:11, 12; 3:1–4). **has come up before Me:** This figurative language pictures evil swelling up to confront the Lord (Gen. 18:21; compare Lam. 1:22).

1:3 flee to Tarshish: The location of this port city is uncertain, but it could be Tartessus on the southeast coast of Spain. The city represents the most distant place known to the Israelites. **Joppa,** a non-Israelite port town, was west of Jerusalem and about 50 miles southwest of Jonah's hometown of Gath Hepher. Note how sharply Jonah's faith contrasted sharply with the mariners' misdirected but sincere faith. Unlike Jonah, they had had little if any experience of the true God; nevertheless, they displayed more apparent spiritual sensitivity. They also showed more compassion toward Jonah than Jonah seemed to feel for the people of Nineveh.

1:4–16 Jonah's experience in the ship may be God's first effort to bring him around to the divine point of view. God used Jonah to make the pagan sailors aware of Himself.

1:4, 5 But the LORD sent out a great wind: Throughout the Book of Jonah, the Lord shows Himself sovereign over every aspect of creation. In this case, the storm at sea was so ferocious that even the experienced **mariners were afraid.** The Phoenicians were the primary mariners of the ancient Middle East, so this was probably a Phoenician ship. Jonah was so sure he had averted God's will that he **was fast asleep** in the ship's hold.

1:6 your God: The ship's captain, a pagan, urged Jonah to pray to whatever god he might believe in. Of course, Jonah's "god" was the true God, who had caused the storm in the first place (v. 4).

1:7 cast lots: The sailors turned to practices common among them in an attempt to find the

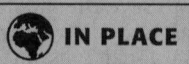

The City of Nineveh

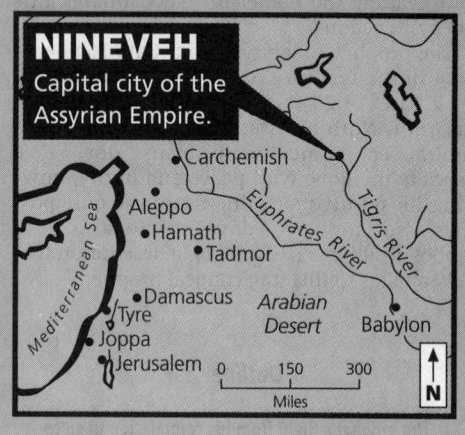

NINEVEH
Capital city of the Assyrian Empire.

Carchemish
Aleppo
Hamath
Tadmor
Damascus
Tyre
Joppa
Jerusalem
Arabian Desert
Babylon
Euphrates River
Tigris River
Mediterranean Sea

0   150   300
Miles
N

Nineveh was not only the capital of the Assyrian Empire but also a symbol of power and might. The city was detested by all peoples because of its heartless conquests. Founded by Nimrod, along with Rehoboth Ir, Calah, and Resen (Gen. 10:11, 12), the city was a massive urban quadrangle 60 miles across. Nineveh rivaled Babylon for beauty and splendor with its royal palaces, temples, broad streets, public gardens, and impressive library containing more than 26,000 clay tablets—one of the largest in the ancient world. It was destroyed in 612 B.C. by a siege of Babylonians, Scythians, and Medes, who penetrated its defenses when sudden floods eroded the walls (compare Nah. 2:6–8).

will of the gods. **the lot fell on Jonah:** Jonah was singled out as the guilty party (Josh. 7:12–18; 1 Sam. 14:40–42).

1:8 The sailors fired a series of questions at Jonah, seeking to discern the reason for the storm. In regard to Jonah's **occupation,** the sailors may have wanted to know the prophet's reason for being on board the ship.

1:9 I am a Hebrew: With these words, Jonah identified himself with the people of the Lord's covenant (Gen. 14:13). **I fear the LORD:** *Fear* here indicates an ongoing activity of awe before the Lord, of piety in His presence, of obedience to His word, and of saving faith (Gen. 22:12; Ex. 20:20; Prov. 1:7). Yet Jonah's actions contradicted his words. Many people say they have faith in God but live as if they did not. **God of heaven:** The Lord is not merely a local deity worshiped by an obscure people; He is the Supreme Ruler over all people and all creation (2 Chr. 36:23; Ezra 1:2; Neh. 1:4, 5; compare

also Gen. 24:3, 7; Deut. 10:14). Jonah may have intended to distinguish God from Baal, the Canaanite "god of the sky" whom so many Israelites worshiped (1 Kin. 18:20–29; 2 Kin. 21:3; 2 Chr. 17:3). **who made the sea and the dry land:** In the midst of the storm, Jonah proclaimed that his God is Lord over the sea (Ex. 15:1–8; Pss. 89:9; 93:3, 4; 95:5).

1:10, 11 exceedingly afraid: This is the same term for *fear* that Jonah used in his statement of piety (v. 9). But here the word means "to be in terror"; it refers to overwhelming dread (v. 16). God, the Creator of the universe, was after Jonah. And because God was after Jonah, He was after the sailors as well. They had every right to be afraid (Gen. 12:18; Judg. 15:11).

1:12, 13 throw me into the sea: Jonah knew that the only way for the storm to abate was for the sailors to toss him overboard. Jonah was ready to die (4:3, 8; 1 Kin. 19:4; Job 3:1;

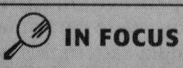

"prepared"

(Heb. *manah*) (1:17; 4:6–8; Ps. 147:4) Strong's #4487: This Hebrew verb basically means "to count" or "to assign." The psalmist uses this verb to praise God for knowing the number of stars and naming each one (Ps. 147:4). In the Book of Jonah, it signifies "to appoint" or "to ordain," amd describes God's intervention in natural events to bring about His will. By *preparing* the fish, the plant, and the worm, God made sure that Jonah's mission was not left to chance. God exercised sovereignty not only over the plant and animal world, but also over Jonah's life, using animals as small as a worm to teach Jonah about His great mercy (Jon. 4:6–8).

IN PERSON | Jonah: A Reluctant Missionary

Sometimes the prophets of the Lord tried to challenge His wisdom in calling them for divine service (Moses in Ex. 4; Jeremiah in Jer. 1). However, Jonah is the only case in the record of Scripture where a true prophet of the Lord (2 Kin. 14:25) tried hard to thwart the will of God by fleeing from the task that God had given him (1:3). In contrast to Elijah's obedience to the Lord (1 Kin. 17:8–10), Jonah tried to go as far as he could in the opposite direction from where God had commanded him. Jonah hoped that Nineveh would get just what it deserved. He was afraid that if he announced judgment the people of Nineveh might respond in a manner that would prompt God to change His mind (4:2). So, in an attempt to restrain God from being merciful to his national enemies, Jonah ran away.

There is something humorous in this account. How could a prophet of God hide from the Creator of the universe? (The location of Tarshish may have been the southeast coast of Spain. In any case it represents the farthest place known to the people of ancient Israel. It is similar to going "to the ends of the earth.") Yet there is also something frightening here: Were a prophet of the Lord directly to disobey the Sovereign God, he might place not only himself, but others connected with him, in dire jeopardy. Sadly, Jonah was not on a mission of mercy, even if he had achieved his goal. He was, in a way, an antimissionary, namely, one who resisted God's call to go to the nations. The repetition of the words "from the presence of the Lord" emphasizes Jonah's attempt to remove himself as far as possible from his service to the Lord.

When we remember that the people of Israel were not a maritime people, but rather had a great fear of the sea (Ps. 93), we are all the more amazed at Jonah's risky action. Jonah's natural aversion to the ocean was overcome by his greater distaste for the thought that Nineveh might escape God's threatened doom. Thankfully, God did not allow Jonah to succeed, so there is something reassuring here as well. God accomplished His work despite the resistance of His reluctant worker.

7:16). His words, **because of me,** are an admission of guilt and show a sense of resignation.

1:14 they cried out to the Lord: Ironically, the pagan sailors prayed to the Lord on behalf of the Lord's rebellious prophet. Jonah needed God's grace as much as Nineveh did. **as it pleased You:** The narrator skillfully uses the sailors' words to express one of the book's themes: the Lord is free to act as He wills.

1:15 The sailors did as Jonah had said (v. 12), but only when they saw there was no other option (vv. 13, 14). With a sense of permission from the God of heaven and Creator of the seas (v. 9), the sailors **threw** Jonah **into the sea.**

1:16 Then the men feared the Lord exceedingly: In the Hebrew text, the words of this part of v. 16 are precisely the same as in v. 10, with one exception: the object of the sailors' fear. In v. 10 these words described the sailors' overwhelming dread of the raging sea; in this verse they *feared the Lord,* indicating piety and believing faith. The sailors had the same reverential awe of God that Jonah had claimed to have (v. 9). In spite of Jonah's failure, the sailors became converts (Ps. 103:11, 13, 17). **offered a sacrifice:** The text does not say where this happened, but it may have been after the ship reached land. The important

point is that their sacrifice was made to the God of Israel.

1:17—2:10 This section relates God's second attempt to convert Jonah to the divine purpose. The prophet cannot escape God even in death. The prophet becomes an agent of evangelism to non-Hebrews despite his unwillingness to do so.

1:17 the Lord had prepared a great fish: God sent the fish—not a whale, as is commonly thought—to rescue Jonah from drowning, not to punish him (ch. 2). **Three days and three nights** may refer to one full day and portions of two more (3:3; Gen. 30:36; Ex. 3:18; 1 Sam. 30:12; Esth. 4:16; Luke 2:46; 24:21). Jesus said that His death and resurrection were foreshadowed by Jonah's experience (Matt. 12:39, 40; 16:4; Luke 11:29; 1 Cor. 15:4).

2:1 Jonah prayed to the Lord his God: In his psalm (vv. 2–9), Jonah acknowledges God's help and thanks him for it. The phrase *the Lord his God* shows that Jonah, even though he was disobedient, was a true believer in God.

2:2–9 Jonah's psalm of deliverance has four parts: (1) an introductory statement of the Lord's deliverance (v. 2); (2) an account of his trouble (vv. 3–6); (3) a report of his cry for help (v. 7); and, (4) a vow of praise (vv. 8, 9).

2:2 I cried . . . I cried: These terms come

from two different verbs. The first is a more general term meaning "to call aloud," with a wide range of usage in the Bible. The second is a term that means a "cry for help," particularly as a scream to God (Pss. 5:2; 18:6, 41; 22:24; 28:1; 30:2; 31:22; 88:13; 119:146). Jonah was terrified. **Out of the belly of Sheol:** When the sailors threw Jonah into the sea, he seemed to be "as good as dead." Thus for Jonah, the sea became like Sheol, the place of death (Gen. 37:35; Pss. 16:10; 88:4, 5; Prov. 9:18; Is. 28:15).

2:3 Jonah's use of the pronouns **You** and **Your** in this verse are not accusations, but acknowledgments of the Lord's sovereign control of his life (Ps. 88:6–18).

2:4 I will look again toward Your holy temple: The man who had run from God's presence (1:3) was alone, yet he clung to the hope that God would not abandon him. The temple, the sanctuary in Jerusalem (v. 7; Deut. 12:5–7; Pss. 48; 79:1; 132; Heb. 9:24), was the symbol of God's presence.

2:5 The deep: This is the same term used in Gen. 1:2 to describe the mysterious and terrifying sea. In the Bible, the sea is described as a part of God's creation (Gen. 1:10) that brings Him joy (Ps. 104:24–26), but it also appears as a

faith in the Lord and renews his commitment to Him (Pss. 22:27; 63:6; 106:7).

2:8 worthless idols: This phrase (also found in Ps. 31:6) condemns every alternative to God. *Idols* here means "vapor," that which passes away quickly. These vaporous gods (Ps. 86:8–10; Jer. 10:15; 51:18) were without value. **Mercy** (loyal love), the term that so often describes God's faithfulness to His covenant and to His people (Pss. 13:5; 59:10, 17; 89:1–3) is used as a name for the Lord (4:2).

2:9 I will sacrifice to You with the voice of thanksgiving: This vow of praise is common in the Psalms (Pss. 13:6; 142:7). **I will pay what I have vowed:** Jonah declares that he will keep his promise, a pledge both to sacrifice and to acknowledge God's help (Job 22:27; Pss. 22:25; 50:14; 66:13; 116:14, 17; see also Rom. 6:13, 19; 12:1; 1 Pet. 2:5). **Salvation:** It is the Lord who delivers His people. God acts on behalf of His creation and the redeemed community to insure a relationship with them (Ex. 15:2, 17, 18; Pss. 88:1; 89:26; 140:7; Is. 12:2). Chapters 1 and 2 both end with vows of sacrifice and thanksgiving.

2:10 the Lord spoke to the fish: The focus in the story of Jonah is on the Lord's sov-

Photo by Howard Vos

The mound of Kuyunjik is only one of the many mounds that mark the site of ancient Nineveh, an "exceedingly great city" where Jonah preached a message of judgment and repentance (Jon. 3:1–4).

symbol for hostile forces (Ps. 74:12–15; Is. 27:1) that the Lord nevertheless holds in His firm control (Ps. 93).

2:6 Jonah pictures himself so deep in the sea that it is as if he had found **the moorings of the mountains. pit:** This term, along with *Sheol* (v. 2), is used to describe the realm of the dead (Job 33:24; Pss. 30:9; 49:9).

2:7 I remembered: Jonah reaffirms his

ereign control over creation to bring about His purpose. It has been surmised that Jonah's experience in the belly of the fish would have had some effect on his skin. Perhaps the acids of the fish's digestive system would have produced blotches. If so, it may have been his physical features that enhanced his subsequent message to the people of Nineveh.

3:1–4:11 The second part of the Book of

Jonah (chs. 3—4) presents the prophet grudgingly obeying his divine commission to bring the
Lord's message to Nineveh. This section has
eight small units: (1) Jonah receives a new commission to go to Nineveh (3:1, 2); (2) Jonah
obeys and makes proclamation in Nineveh (vv.
3, 4); (3) Jonah's proclamation leads to the
deliverance of Nineveh (vv. 5–10); (4) Jonah
laments God's mercy to Nineveh and wishes for
death (4:1–4); (5) Jonah sulks under a shelter
(vv. 5, 6); (6) Jonah languishes and wishes
again for death (vv. 7, 8); (7) Jonah debates
with the Lord (v. 9); and, (8) Jonah hears the
proclamation of the Lord (vv. 10, 11).

3:1, 2 Jonah's new commission was essentially the same as the one he had received in
1:1, 2.

3:3 In contrast to 1:3, Jonah obeyed the
command of the Lord the second time and made
the journey to Nineveh. **a three-day journey
in extent:** The city wall of Nineveh had a circumference of about eight miles, indicating that
Nineveh was an exceedingly large city for the
times. But the reference to "three days" likely
refers to the larger administrative district of Nineveh, made up of several cities, with a circumference of about 55 miles.

3:4 Jonah proclaimed that there were only
forty days before the destruction of Nineveh.
Both the announcement and the specified delay
show God's mercy. It was this mercy that bothered Jonah (4:1–3). Evidently the prophet
wanted Nineveh to fall, rather than repent and
escape God's judgment. The Assyrians had long
been a menace to Israel. Perhaps Jonah recognized that if the Assyrians repented, they were
likely to restore their country to dominance,
probably to the detriment of Israel. So it is possible that the prophet fled in order to avoid
strengthening the hand of a potential enemy.
Moreover, how might his people have treated
him were they to learn that he had succeeded in
bringing their worst enemies to repentance?

3:5 believed God: The term used for God
here is the general term for deity. In contrast,
the sailors in ch. 1 proclaimed faith in the Lord,
using the personal, covenant name for God
(1:16). The fact that the writer does not use the
personal name for God here may suggest that
the Ninevites had a short-lived or imperfect
understanding of God's message. History bears
this out: We have no historical record of a
lasting period of belief in Nineveh. Eventually
the city was destroyed, in 612 B.C.

3:5–9 fast . . . sackcloth . . . ashes: These
are expressions of mourning and lamentation
(2 Kin. 19:1; 2 Chr. 20:3; Is. 58:5–9; Jer. 36:6–9;
Joel 1:13, 14; 2:12–18). The nationwide fast
decreed by the king of Nineveh was a remarkable display of humility before the Lord. The

decree shows that the king well understood the
nature of genuine repentance. Not only was
every man, woman, and child, and even their
animals, forbidden to eat, or even to drink
water (v. 7), but they were exhorted to turn
from evil and violence (3:8). Thus the fast was
not merely an external show of piety, but an
opportunity for a heartfelt change of attitude
and behavior.

3:6, 7 proclaimed and published: The
king's edict reached all of Nineveh.

3:8, 9 God will turn and relent: The
reversal of the threat to destroy Nineveh
depended solely on the grace and mercy of the
Lord. At times, the announced judgment of God
is *not* His real intent (4:2; Jer. 18:7, 8; Amos 7:3).
Such announcements usually include offers of
mercy and forgiveness (Zeph. 2:1–3).

3:10 God relented: The Ninevites', repentance moved the Lord to extend grace and
mercy to them.

4:1 Jonah . . . became angry: In contrast
to God, Jonah had no compassion on the people
of Nineveh. **displeased:** Jonah's irritation
belied the good news that the city would be
spared. Jonah himself had just been spared
God's fair judgment, but he was unable to
appreciate the parallel.

4:2 I know: Jonah himself had experienced
the excellencies of God. **Gracious and merciful** may be rephrased as "marvelously gracious." **Lovingkindness** can also mean "loyal
love." This is the same word that Jonah had
used in his praise of God in 2:8. **One who
relents from doing harm:** In this recital of
God's blessed character, Jonah built on the revelation of the Lord to Moses (Ex. 34:6, 7).

4:3, 4 please take my life: Contrast Jonah

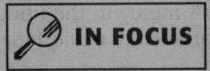

IN FOCUS **"slow to anger"**

(Heb. *'arek; 'aph*) (4:2; Num. 14:18; Prov.
14:29) Strong's #750; 639: The idiom for
anger in the Old Testament translated literally is
"the nose burns" or "the nose becomes hot"
(Gen. 30:2; Ex. 4:14). The Hebrew idiom for
"patient," or "slow to anger" is literally "long of
nose" (Pss. 86:15; 103:8). The nose is symbolic of anger because an angry person
breathes heavily or noisily. The Hebrew idiom
for *slow to anger* is frequently applied to God
to describe His great mercy and kindness (Ps.
145:8; Joel 2:13).

Why Nineveh Repented

Many factors may have accounted for the Ninevites sudden change of attitude. Yet we know that God has a way of drawing people, and of arranging events so people are more likely to turn toward Him. Financial pressures, political turmoil, natural disasters, sickness—such things often cause people to take stock of their relationship with the Almighty. The case of Nineveh shows that this is true for nations as well as individuals.

Nineveh's repentance is instructive for Christians today. Like Jonah, we have been commissioned to take the gospel of repentance and salvation to the nations of the world (Mark 16:15, 16). In doing so, it might be well to consider a strategy of targeted evangelism. Efforts would seem likely to be more effective in areas where recent political upheaval and natural disasters have created instability and more openness to a message of grace. If God has been preparing hearts beforehand, it is reasonable to expect greater success under such circumstances.

---

and Elijah: Jonah's death wish came from disgust at the people's repentance; Elijah's came from a yearning for the people's repentance (1 Kin. 19:4). Only a few days before Jonah had screamed for God to keep him alive.

4:5 till he might see what would become of the city: In his continuing stubbornness and lack of compassion, Jonah held out hope that God would judge Nineveh. This was God's chief complaint against him (Ps. 58).

4:6 the LORD God prepared: The same verb was used in 1:17 to describe the Lord's preparation of the great fish. The term is also used in v. 7 regarding the worm and in v. 8 regarding the east wind. The repeated use of *prepared* is a subtle reference to the sovereignty of God. **a plant:** The nature of this plant is unknown. Some have speculated that it was a castor-oil tree or a bottle-gourd vine. It may have been a species that grew especially fast. **to deliver him:** The Lord had rescued Jonah from drowning (1:17); now He wished to relieve His prophet from the misery of the sun. The reach of God's mercy to the undeserving is a theme that continued to elude Jonah even as he experienced it.

4:7 God prepared a worm: The Book of Jonah depicts the Lord as both sovereign and free to act in creation. God placed the worm in the plant to serve as His agent in Jonah's life.

4:8 vehement east wind: The scorching sirocco wind that blows in from the desert draws moisture from plants, causing them to wither (Is. 40:7, 8).

4:9 The word translated **is it right** comes from the verb meaning "to be good," "to do well," or "to be pleasing." Here, as in Gen. 4:4, the expression has to do with ethical behavior (Lev. 5:4; Ps. 36:3; Is. 1:17; Jer. 4:22; 13:23). Jonah's anger (v. 1) did not arise from a desire for justice but from his own selfishness. He continued to justify his rebellious attitude. And again, God was merciful.

4:10 Pity describes an expression of deeply felt compassion (Ps. 72:13; Ezek. 20:17; Joel 2:13, 14). However, Jonah pitied himself more than the plant.

4:11 pity: The same word used to describe Jonah's feeling toward the plant in v. 10 is used of God's feeling toward the people of Nineveh. People are of more value than animals, and animals of more value than plants, but the Lord has a concern that extends to all of His creation. The Lord's pity comes from His character (v. 2; compare Joel 2:13, 14). **livestock:** If Jonah could take pity on a plant, which is even less important than an animal, it only made sense that God would take pity on human beings, who are made in God's image. The Book of Jonah ends on this note of contrast between Jonah's ungracious heart and the kind heart of the Lord.

The Book of

Micah

O LD TESTAMENT PROPHETS ARE OFTEN THOUGHT of as providing not much more than "doom and gloom" predictions, but the Book of Micah presents an impassioned and artistic interplay between oracles of impending judgment and promises of future blessing on Israel and Judah. The peoples of both nations had broken covenant with their Lord. Through His messenger Micah, the Lord confronted His people,

but He also promised to bring future blessing through the One who would be coming. This One would be the true Shepherd of God's flock.

The career of Micah extended over the last third of the eighth century B.C., during the reigns of Jotham (752–736 B.C.), Ahaz (736–720 B.C.), and Hezekiah (729–699 B.C.). The Book of Micah centers on the threat of the Assyrian invasions that occurred throughout this period, beginning around 730 B.C. against Israel and culminating in 701 B.C. against Judah. Much of Micah's preaching warned Judah about an impending national disaster. Yet the religious leaders of Jerusalem were falsely confident that no evil would come to them because of the inviolable presence of the holy temple in their midst. Micah sternly confronted their arrogance and their mistaken notions of God: not even the temple on Mount Zion would be spared the onslaught of God's wrath (3:12).

The lengthy delay in Micah's prophecies against Jerusalem may be attributed to several causes. First, God may have decided to spare the city, even though it was He who had condemned it (Jer. 26:16–19; compare God's judgment on Nineveh in the Book of Jonah). The

significant delay in the judgment against Jerusalem may be attributed to the mercy of the Lord, much as the delay of the judgment of God against Nineveh is attributed to His mercy by the prophet Jonah (Jon. 4:1–3). Second, though the judgment of Jerusalem was postponed, it was finally realized in the destruction of the city by the Babylonians in 586 B.C.

The interplay of texts of wrath and mercy in the Book of Micah mirrors the character of God, for even in His wrath He remembers mercy. In the darkest days of impending judgment on the nations of Israel and Judah, there was always the possibility of a remnant being spared. Though the Lord was determined to maintain His holiness, He was equally intent on fulfilling His loving promises to Abraham (Gen. 12; 15; 22). The Lord would balance His judgment with mercy. Consequently Micah also balances his oracles of judgment with oracles of promise.

In doing so, Micah points back to the covenant and also forward to the coming One. The book begins with the language of a court. Micah calls the peoples of earth to come to hear the Lord's case against Israel, for the nation had broken the covenant (3:1; 6:1–3). The language recalls the language of the covenant or contract the Lord established with His people. The Lord was judging His people according to the terms of the covenant. But in the middle of the oracles of judgment, Micah reveals the Lord's wonderful promises of a glorious future. There would be a time when the coming King would gather His people together (2:12, 13), when He would establish peace (4:3), and when He would bring justice to the earth (4:2, 3). Remarkably, Micah prophesies that this coming Messiah would be born in Bethlehem (5:2). The fulfillment of this prophecy in Jesus' birth in Bethlehem gives us confidence that the prophecies of Jesus' glorious future will also be fulfilled (Matt. 2:1).

Little is known about the prophet Micah beyond his name, his place of origin, and the personal tone of his book. Micah was born in the rural village of Moresheth Gath in the lowlands of Judah, near the region of Philistia, setting him apart from his more illustrious contemporary Isaiah, who was from Jerusalem.

The Book of Micah has numerous points of similarity with the much longer Book of Isaiah. In fact, virtually the same passage is found in both books (compare 4:1–3 with Is. 2:2–4). Some attribute this unusual phenomenon to one prophet borrowing from the other, but it is difficult to argue for the priority of either Micah or Isaiah from the texts. More likely both prophets made use of the same source, perhaps a psalm of confidence.

It is often asserted that the Book of Micah was written by his disciples and followers many years after his ministry. However, the tone of Micah's prophecies against Jerusalem indicates that they had not yet come to pass. It appears that Micah prophesied that the Assyrians would destroy Jerusalem in the same way they had already destroyed the city of Samaria (compare 1:6 with 3:12). While the Assyrians under Sennacherib did lay siege against Jerusalem in the campaign of 701 B.C., they did not finally destroy the city. Jerusalem was not destroyed until over a century later by the Babylonians (586 B.C.). It is almost inconceivable that disciples of Micah would collect, record, and promote his prophecies long after the fact if those prophecies had not come to pass as anticipated. It is far more likely that the prophecies of Micah were compiled by the prophet as an anthology of his own lengthy preaching career.

Outline

I. **The first cycle of oracles 1:1–2:13**
    A. **The first set of oracles of judgment 1:1–2:11**
    B. **The first promise of blessing: the Lord will restore His remnant 2:12, 13**
II. **The second cycle of oracles 3:1–5:15**
    A. **The second set of oracles of judgment 3:1–12**
    B. **The second set of promises of blessing 4:1–5:15**
III. **The third cycle of oracles 6:1–7:20**
    A. **The third set of oracles of judgment 6:1–7:7**
    B. **The third set of promises of blessing 7:8–20**

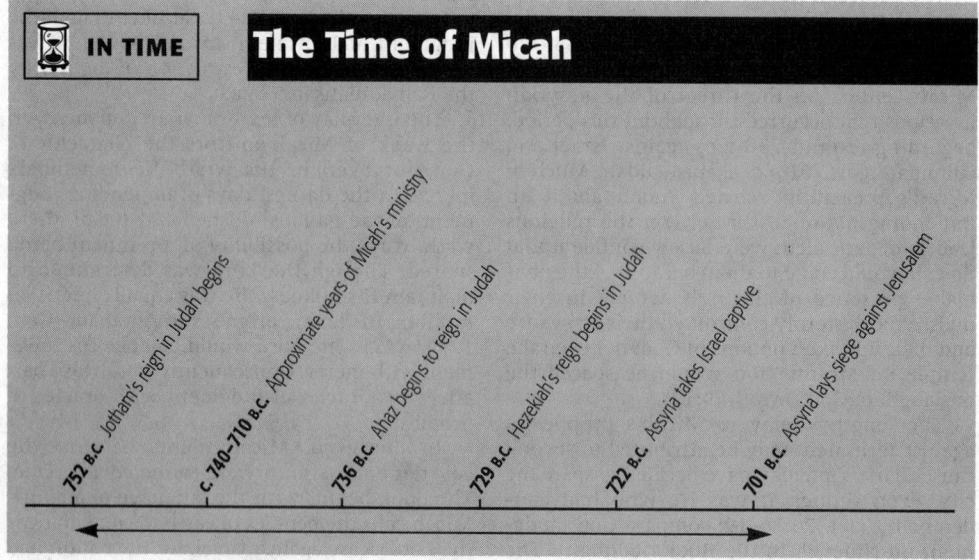

IN TIME

The Time of Micah

752 B.C. Jotham's reign in Judah begins

c. 740–710 B.C. Approximate years of Micah's ministry

736 B.C. Ahaz begins to reign in Judah

729 B.C. Hezekiah's reign begins in Judah

722 B.C. Assyria takes Israel captive

701 B.C. Assyria lays siege against Jerusalem

Commentary

1:1 Micah means "Who Is Like the Lord?" The question presents a major biblical theme, the idea that God is incomparable (7:18; Deut. 4:32–40; Ps. 113:4–6). **Jotham, Ahaz, and Hezekiah:** The reigns of these kings were particularly troubled by the Assyrian military threat. In three successive campaigns (734, 733, 732 B.C.), the Assyrian army under Tiglath-Pileser III brought much of Phoenicia, Philistia, Israel, Syria, and large tracts of Judah under its control. Micah's ministry centered on the Assyrian threat to **Samaria,** the capital of Israel that was destroyed in 722 B.C., and **Jerusalem,** the capital of Judah.

1:2—2:13 The first cycle of oracles are in five parts: (1) the Lord is witness and comes in judgment against His people Israel (1:2–7); (2) the prophet mourns the message of God's judgment (vv. 8, 9); (3) the cities of Judah are to prepare for a shameful disaster (vv. 10–16); (4) a woe oracle against the peoples because of their greed and violence (2:1–5), and, (5) the false prophets are judged for their lying words (vv. 6–11).

Though the first oracles of judgment are largely judgmental in nature (1:2—2:11), they end in a splendid promise of restoration of the Lord's remnant (2:12, 13).

1:2 all you peoples: All the earth was to know that God was witnessing **against** His people. This announcement of judgment is based on the people's breach of covenant. The faithlessness of the people provoked **the Lord God** to enter into a judicial dispute with them.

1:3, 4 the Lord is coming: This is the language of epiphany, the dramatic coming of God to earth, here in a solemn procession of judgment. In other texts the language of epiphany is used to describe God's dramatic acts of deliverance (Ps. 18:7–19). The expression **high places** is ironic. Jerusalem and Samaria were the "high places," or elevated capitals, of Judah and Israel; but "high places" were also sites of idolatrous worship.

1:5 Jacob is used to refer to the northern kingdom Israel, whose **transgression** was centered in its capital Samaria. Judah's sins were centered in its capital Jerusalem. In this verse, the intent of the term **high places** (v. 3) is

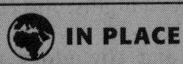 **IN PLACE** ## Geographical Puns in Micah

With skillfully written wordplays on the names of Judah's cities, Micah prophesied of the coming destruction of Judah (1:3–16). He turned around the meaning of a number of town names as a way of describing the world being turned upside down. Shaphir, meaning "Beautiful," would be shamed (1:11); and Jerusalem, a name suggesting "Peace," would be disrupted (1:12). Lachish, a name sounding like the Hebrew word for *swift steeds*, would flee on its horses. All this agitation was caused by God's judgment on Judah for worshiping other gods on the high places. In fact, idolatry was so rampant that Micah describes Jerusalem and Samaria, the capital cities of Judah and Israel, as high places themselves (1:5).

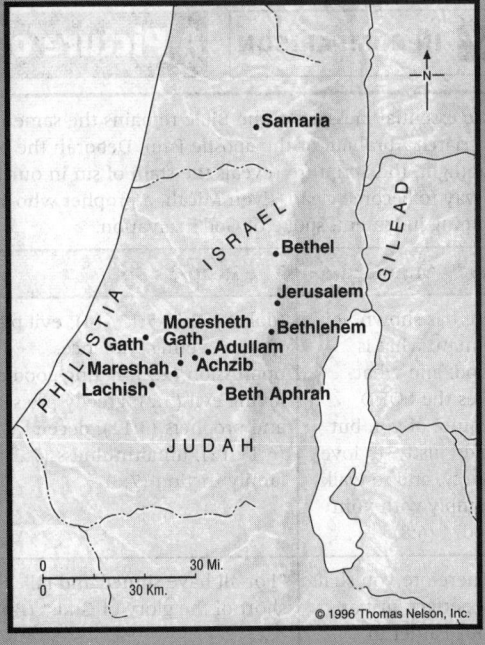

© 1996 Thomas Nelson, Inc.

made plain. Jerusalem, which was once "beautiful in elevation" (Ps. 48:2), was nothing more than another platform of pagan worship, like the "high places" of the Canaanites.

1:6 a heap of ruins: God's judicial decision was to destroy Samaria so thoroughly that it would be a place fit only for vineyards among the rubble.

1:7 Idolatry is often described in the Hebrew Bible as spiritual adultery (Jer. 3:1; Hos. 4:15). Israel is pictured as a wife who is unfaithful to her husband (Jer. 2:20). This is not just a metaphor, however; the worship system of Canaan was sexual in nature. The word **idols** here has the sense of "disgusting images," probably referring to the explicit sexual nature of these idols. But there is comic justice at the end of the verse. The pagan symbols of Israel's worship would be reused by the nation's conquerors (Assyria) in their own debased temples.

1:8, 9 I will wail . . . I will go stripped: Micah's immediate response to God's message was an overwhelming sense of dread (7:1). **naked:** Micah's words describe mourning rites in which outer garments were laid aside in deep humility. The mourning person thought no longer about himself but only about the calamity that had overcome his senses.

1:10 in Gath: The reference here is to the lament of David in his mourning over the death of Saul and Jonathan (2 Sam. 1:20). Just as it was unseemly then to have the bad news of God's people profaned in a foreign city, so it would be in the present circumstance. The Hebrew word translated **tell** in this verse sounds like the Hebrew place name Gath. **Beth Aprah** means "House of Dust"; appropriately, the inhabitants would **roll** themselves **in the dust,** an act of extreme mourning.

1:11 The name **Shaphir** means "Beautiful." Ironically, its inhabitants would be shamed by their nakedness. **Zaanan:** This name speaks of "sheep" who "go out on their own." However, this would no longer be the case for the citizens of Zaanan, who would no longer go out because of their fear.

1:12 Maroth means "Bitterness." The name **Jerusalem** suggests "Peace." Thus the inhabitants of the *town of bitterness* would be sickened with dread, and the inhabitants of *town of peace* would experience God's judgment.

1:13 Lachish: This famous guard city to Jerusalem was judged as being among the first places in Judah to adopt the sins of Baal worship. **daughter of Zion:** Jerusalem is the daughter of the Lord.

1:14 Moresheth Gath, which means "The Possession of Gath," was Micah's hometown (v. 1). The **presents** were farewell gifts; the city was soon to be lost.

1:15 The words **heir** and **the glory of Israel** might lead one to assume that this is a

---

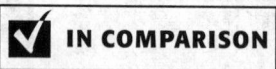 **IN COMPARISON** | ## A Picture of the Gospel

The essential message of the Bible remains the same no matter whether we are reading about the patriarch Abraham or the apostle Paul, Deborah the judge or Mary the mother of Jesus. Like a spotlight, the Scripture reveals the stain of sin in our lives. But it does not leave us exposed; it offers a way to become clean. Even Micah, a prophet who spent most of his time warning the Israelites of coming judgment, spoke of God's salvation.

God's Standard	The People's Sin	God's Salvation
"He has shown you, O man, what is good; and what does the LORD require of you but to do justly, to love mercy, and to walk humbly with your God?" (6:8)	Idolatry (1:7; 5:13, 14); evil plans (2:1); coveting, violence, oppression (2:2); hating good and loving evil (3:2); greedy priests and prophets (3:11); deceit (6:11,12); unfaithfulness (7:2); family friction (7:6)	"Who is a God like You, pardoning iniquity and passing over the transgression of the remnant of His heritage? He does not retain His anger forever, because He delights in mercy. He will again have compassion on us, and will subdue our iniquities. You will cast all our sins into the depths of the sea." (7:18, 19)
"Therefore you shall be perfect, just as your Father in heaven is perfect." (Matt. 5:48)	"For all have sinned and fall short of the glory of God." (Rom. 3:23)	"In [Christ] we have redemption through His blood, the forgiveness of sins, according to the riches of His grace." (Eph. 1:7)

messianic verse, a promise of hope in the midst of despair. Yet the context is judgment (v. 16). The point here may be that the situation would be so bad that the proper *heir* and *glory* of the nation—the members of the royal family— would have to flee in terror to remote hiding places. **Mareshah** is an alternative spelling for Moresheth Gath of v. 14.

1:16 In a culture in which a man's hair was highly valued, to **cut off** one's **hair** was the ultimate sign of mourning.

2:1–5 This is a woe oracle in which the Lord judges His people for greed and violence. Social injustice is presented as the reason for divine judgment upon the nation. But Micah's concern goes beyond economics to theological consider- ations, for the distribution of the land, by covenant provision, was irrevocable (Lev. 25:23–34). Mortaged land was to return eventu- ally to the original landowner either through redemption, or free in the Year of Jubilee. How- ever, the rich corrupted God's Law to acquire for themselves large landholdings, creating an unequal distribution of wealth, whereas God's provision was for a balance of possessions. He wanted all to have sufficient resources for a quality of life that would sustain dignity and self-respect.

2:1, 2 devise iniquity . . . covet: The eth- ical teaching of the prophets regularly included oracles of judgment against greed, theft, and oppression, actions of the powerful in attacking the weak. To *covet* is not just to have a passing thought; it is a determination to seize what is not one's own.

2:3 devising disaster: While the wicked devised iniquity (v. 1), God made some plans of His own. **your necks:** The idea here is that the disaster of God would be inescapable.

2:4 A *proverb* was a taunt song. **To a turn- coat:** God would take the property rights from those who had seized them illegally and give them to people who were even more reprobate than they were.

2:5, 6 no one to determine boundaries: Land-grabbers would no longer have a legiti- mate claim among God's people. God would dis- possess them even as they had dispossessed others. **Do not prattle:** These words may have been a strong warning to Micah not to be like the lying prophets who counseled that all was well in the land.

2:7–9 The **words** of God were different from the words of the lying prophets (v. 6). The words of God bring **good** to the righteous even as they bring judgment against the wicked.

2:10, 11 The lying prophets (v. 6) spoke about **rest** when **utter destruction** was decreed by the Lord. They spoke about **wine and drink** at a time of disaster. It is also possible

that the words of v. 11 speak about false prophets who were willing to prophesy "good words" in exchange for wine and beer.

2:12, 13 assemble . . . gather . . . put them together: The verbs are emphatic, demonstrating the certainty of God's determina- tion to bring to pass His good pleasure on His people (Deut. 30:1–6). **breaks open . . . break out:** These phrases speak about regathering Israel from wherever the people may have been scattered.

3:1–5:15 In this cycle of oracles, there are pronouncements of judgment (3:1–12), and promises of blessing (4:1–5:15), with the promises far more extensive than in the first set (2:12, 13).

3:1–12 These oracles of judgment have three parts: (1) the rulers of God's people should know justice (vv. 1–4); (2) the false prophets wrongly speak about peace (vv. 4–7); and (3) Zion shall be plowed like a field (vv. 8–12).

3:1 Is it not for you to know justice: The idea here is that one might not expect justice from pagan leaders in a faraway place. But the **rulers** of the people of God were expected to emphasize justice. Justice is one of the key con- cepts of the Law (Deut. 10:18; 32:4; 33:21). Per- verting justice was strongly prohibited by God (Deut. 16:19; 24:17). Yet this was precisely what the leaders of Judah were doing. They had used their authority to destroy justice rather than to establish it among the people.

3:2, 3 Micah used an image of barbaric can- nibalism to describe the horrendous actions of the leaders against the people. It was as if the leaders were eating **the flesh** from the people's **bones.**

3:4 He will not hear them: The wicked- ness of the people was so great that last-minute repentance would not suffice (Jer. 11:11).

3:5–7 This oracle of judgment was pre- sented against the false **prophets** who pro- claimed **peace,** causing the people to be unprepared for trouble. These prophets would have neither true prophetic insight (**vision**), nor help from the forbidden arts of **divination.** Finally they would have nothing to say, for there would be **no answer from God.**

3:8–10 full of power: Unlike the silenced false prophets (vv. 5–7), Micah was divinely empowered (1 Cor. 2:13; 2 Pet. 1:21). **Justice and might** may be rephrased as "powerful jus- tice," a contrast to the ineffective leaders of Israel (v. 1).

3:11 bribe . . . pay . . . money: The wicked leaders and prophets of Israel "worked" only when they could gain something from it. Need- less to say, if justice had to be paid for, it would not be justice. **Is not the LORD among us:** Many people of Jerusaiem believed that they would not be affected by God's judgment because God Himself dwelled in the holy temple in Jerusalem. They reasoned that despite their evils, as long as God was in His temple, they were safe—even from divine judgment. What the people refused to believe was that God might *leave* His temple because of the sinfulness of the people. The Book of Ezekiel describes a vision of the glory of God leaving the temple as a prelude to His judgment on the city (Ezek. 10).

3:12 This verse was quoted by Jeremiah (Jer. 26:18). While the false prophets and the wicked rulers believed that they were untouchable and that Mount Zion was inviolable, the prophet Micah announced that **Zion** (Jerusalem) would **be plowed like a field,** indicating complete devastation of the city.

4:1—5:15 Here we find four major sections of God's promises of future blessing on His faithful people and the destruction of their enemies: (1) the future exaltation of Zion (4:1–5); (2) the future restoration of the people (4:6—5:1); (3) the future coming of the Messiah in Bethlehem (5:2–5a); and, (4) the future judgment on the enemies of the people of God (vv. 5b–15).

4:1–5 This passage is one of the great prophecies of the Bible. It is remarkable not only in what it says, but in the fact that the same text is found as well in Is. 2:2–4. Various theories have been advanced as to who borrowed from whom, Isaiah or Micah. It is possible, however, that both Isaiah and Micah took these words, under the leading of the Holy Spirit from a third source, perhaps from a spiritual song.

4:1 The phrase **in the latter days** is an indication of a prophecy of end times. **The mountain of the LORD's** house describes the temple in Jerusalem. The text projects a future change in the topography of Jerusalem. Originally the temple site in Jerusalem was located on one of several hills that make up the general area. In the *latter days* the temple site will be elevated **above the hills** (Zech. 8:1–3; 14:1–11).

4:2 Many nations: When non-Israelites came to true faith, it would be in **the God of Jacob. He will teach:** As God spoke to Moses on Mount Sinai (Ex. 19; 20) so He will speak to all from Jerusalem. **we shall walk:** Unlike the people of Micah's generation who were strangers to justice (3:1), the peoples of the coming kingdom will be obedient to God.

4:3 judge . . . rebuke: These are actions of the Savior King who will rule with a rod of iron (Pss. 2; 110). **swords . . . spears:** All weapons

---

✠ IN CONTEXT The King's Hometown

Almost two years after Jesus was born, a dusty and majestic caravan made its way into Jerusalem. The members of the caravan stopped for directions. Their simple question shook the city: "Where is He who has been born King of the Jews?" (Matt. 2:2). A strange star had announced the birth. King Herod knew the wise men had no interest in him. But he also realized that if their quest was legitimate, his own reign was about to be eclipsed by the arrival of another King, the long-awaited Messiah. He was not going to give up his throne without a fight.

Among the prophecies of the OT, God had clearly revealed the birthplace of the Messiah. The Jewish religious leaders that Herod gathered to answer the strangers' question pointed immediately to Mic. 5:2 for the location of the Savior's hometown, Bethlehem. They knew. Micah had left written directions hundreds of years before. But they were not ready to believe. Curiously, no one volunteered to go with the wise men to look for the Messiah.

God offered a clear invitation to His people through Micah: Watch Bethlehem! The people remembered the invitation, but failed to take it seriously. Given an opportunity to discover truth, the people of Jerusalem let someone else take the risk of disappointment. Herod even killed the children of Bethlehem in a vain attempt to eliminate his rival.

Other prophecies of Micah surround the passage pinpointing Bethlehem as the Messiah's hometown. Some of the prophecies were fulfilled by the return of the Israelites from Babylon (4:10). Others have yet to be fulfilled (4:1–5). But Bethlehem remains a symbol of God's working out of His purposes in history.

Micah's invitation still rings true. But our response must be different from that of the people of Jerusalem. The people in Jesus' time were waiting for something to happen, but they missed it because of unbelief. We can look back at Jesus' death and miss it just as seriously through our own unbelief. A crucial chapter in God's story of salvation begins in Bethlehem. God gave more than a hint of that salvation in Micah.

of destruction will be recycled into tools of production. There will finally be an end to conflict. **War** will not even be a subject for study anymore.

4:4, 5 The **vine** and **fig tree** are symbols of peace and prosperity (Zech. 3:10). **no one shall**

threshing floor (v. 12). This is a way of speaking of the final victory over all of Israel's foes.

5:1 gather yourself in troops: The reference here seems to be to the assaults of the enemies of Judah on the people of God before their final defeat. **strike . . . on the cheek:** One day

The city of Bethlehem in southern Judah, the place where the prophet Micah predicted the Messiah would be born (Mic. 5:2).

make them afraid: Fear, like war (v. 3), will become a thing of the past.

4:6, 7 In that day: This wording connects this section with the end times referred to in v. 1. **lame . . . outcast:** Those who were abused by the wicked leaders of Israel would be exalted by the Lord. **afflicted:** Those whom God had driven from the land would be the people of His new kingdom. This is a remarkable surprise—a surprise of grace. **remnant:** The majority of people in Israel did not live their lives in faith and dedication to the Lord. However, true faith never really died out in Israel, even in the worst of times.

4:8 Tower of the flock is a description of Jerusalem in the ideal sense. A *tower* was a vantagepoint for protecting a flock of sheep. Likewise, Jerusalem is the **stronghold** or defense point for the flock of God (2:12).

4:9–12 Micah addressed the city of **Zion** (Jerusalem) as though it were a **woman in labor.** The troubles of the present moment would lead finally to the birth of a deliverer. **To Babylon you shall go** refers to the Exile.

4:13 Arise and thresh: The nations would be gathered by the Lord like sheaves on the

the enemies of the Savior would strike Him (Mark 15:19); but on a still-future day, He will strike all of His enemies (Rev. 19).

5:2 Bethlehem means "House of Bread" (Ruth 1:1). **Ephrathah** locates the village in a known region in Judah (Gen. 35:16). This prophecy figures significantly in the NT story of the visit of the wise men to the Christ child (Matt. 2:1–12). Governments would be overturned to make it necessary for Mary while still pregnant to make the journey from Nazareth to Bethlehem. The specific detail of this oracle about Bethlehem is similar to the Lord's prophetic announcements of the name of Josiah to Jeroboam I (1 Kin. 13:2), and of Cyrus to Isaiah (Is. 44:28—45:7). **goings forth:** The birth of this Savior King would be unlike the birth of any other, because He was preexistent. He is **from everlasting.**

5:3, 4 The future of Israel is pictured here in terms of the birth, life, and ministry of the Savior King. The two advents of the Savior are seen as one event by Micah. Whereas v. 2 speaks about the birth of the Savior in His First Coming, vv. 3–5 speak about the time of the rule of Jesus in the Second Coming. **She who is**

🔍 **IN FOCUS** | **"complaint"**

(Heb. *rib*) (6:2; Judg. 12:2; Prov 17:14; 18:6; Jer 11:20) Strong's #7379: This word can mean "dispute" or "quarrel" in the sense of a feud (Judg. 12:2), "controversy" or "strife" (Prov 17:14; 18:6) prompted by a rebellious spirit (Num. 20:13; Prov. 17:14; 18:6), or even a "legal case" or "lawsuit" (Job 31:13, 35; Jer. 11:20). The prophets frequently used this word as a technical, legal term in contexts pertaining to the Lord's covenant relationship with Israel (Jer. 25:31; Hos. 4:1; 12:2). In this chapter, Micah was informing Judah that God had registered a formal, legal complaint against His people. He was ordering them to stand trial for violating covenant stipulations forbidding idolatry and requiring social justice (6:2–16).

---

in labor probably refers to Zion (4:10). The metaphor refers to the deliverance in the end time of those who will be able to delight in the coming of God's kingdom (4:9—5:1). **the remnant:** This minority will never be forgotten by the Lord.

5:5, 6 And this One shall be peace: Isaiah 9:6 refers to this One as the Prince of Peace. **When the Assyrian comes:** The principal threat against Israel and Judah at the time of Micah was Assyria. Micah used the nation as a symbol of all of Israel's enemies and of God's final victory over each of them. **Seven shepherds and eight princely men:** These are in contrast to the wicked rulers that Micah condemned in ch. 3.

5:7–9 This section concerns God's blessing on **the remnant of Jacob.** The wickedness of the people would bring about God's judgment, but He would not cast them off completely. **In the midst of many peoples** describes the spread of the Jewish people throughout the earth in the time of God's judgment. Twin images are used to describe the effect of the Jewish people on the nations in which they lived. Verse 7 describes the Jewish people as **dew** and **showers**—that is, blessings from God on their neighbors. Verse 8 describes the Jewish people as a **lion**—that is, a powerful force that eventually would triumph.

5:10, 11 I will cut off: It was God's intention to destroy the evils in Israel's society. **Horses** and **chariots** represent the pride of Israel's military power. Israel's tendency was to rely on its own military power rather than on the Lord.

5:12–14 Both Israel and Judah were beset through their history with apostate rites, defiant participation in the dark arts of their neighbors, and in crude idolatry of all sorts. God's promise here is to eradicate from their midst any vestige of these wicked practices and rebellions.

5:12 Sorcery and soothsaying had been strongly condemned by God (Deut. 18:10).

5:13–15 The second commandment had forbidden the use of **carved images** in Israel (Ex. 20:4). **Sacred pillars** refers to phallic poles used in Canaanite sexual worship rites. **Wooden images** refers to the Asherah groves. Both of these items had been condemned strongly in the Law (Deut. 16:21, 22).

6:1, 2 God (the Judge) calls for the people (the defendants) to **plead** their **case. The mountains** and **hills** were among the witnesses to the covenant that God made with His people (Deut. 4:26; 32:1; Is. 1:2). **He will contend:** If the people were silent before the **mountains,** the Lord Himself would speak against their sin.

6:3 what have I done: The Lord was entirely innocent of misbehavior against His people (Jer. 2:5).

6:4, 5 The Lord summarized His great mercies to Israel, including His saving works in bringing the people from **Egypt** in the Exodus and His deliverance of Israel from the evils that **Balak** and **Balaam** had planned (Num. 22—24).

6:6, 7 Come before means "to make an approach in true worship" (Ps. 15). **burnt offerings . . . calves a year old:** These were among the divinely prescribed sacrifices of true biblical worship (Lev. 1:3; 9:3). The words of v. 7 go far beyond any demand of the Law, and even go *against* the Law in the suggestion that God may not be satisfied except by an offering of one's own child. Micah uses hyperbole (deliberate exaggeration) to emphasize the necessity of a right attitude in the true worship of God. **be pleased:** The idea of bringing pleasure to God through sacrifice is found elsewhere in the Bible. God is pleased with those who do as He commands (Gen. 4:1–8).

6:8 This verse speaks about the underlying attitudes that must accompany all true worship. **what does the LORD require of you:** The idea here is that God seeks certain characteristics of true worship from His people. **do justly . . .**

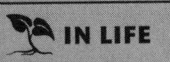 **IN LIFE** | **Marks of True Spirituality**

What does it mean to know God? What are the marks of true spirituality? Micah offers a summary by giving three primary virtues that are to characterize every one of God's people: to do justice, to love mercy, and to walk humbly with God (Mic. 6:8). This three-sided approach to life is balanced, unlike many of the fads and fetishes of modern spirituality. For example:

- To act with justice keeps one in the real world rather than getting bogged down in theoretical abstractions that actually ignore oppression and injustice.
- To love mercy keeps one in touch with the grace of a faithful God rather than succumbing to the tyranny of results-oriented spirituality, which tends to produce legalism, weariness, and burnout.
- To walk humbly with God keeps one dependent on the Lord's resources rather than trusting in merely human solutions, which creates unrealistic pressure on individuals and institutions.

love mercy . . . walk humbly: These phrases summarize biblical piety in true worship. The majority of the people of Israel had violated each of these standards repeatedly. The rulers did not know *justice* (3:1), had no interest in *mercy* (3:2, 3), and demonstrated no *humility* (3:11). **with your God:** It is the Lord who ultimately gives a person strength, courage, and ability to exercise the virtues of godly living.

6:9 The rod is a messianic image. It is possible that this verse is based on Ps. 2 (vv. 9, 11, 12).

6:10–15 The people of Judah were abusing others with false measures, with **violence,** and with **lies.** Such practices were far removed from the description of true worship in v. 8. This is the divine vindication of the Lord's determination to bring judgment on Jerusalem, despite the fact that His holy temple was there (3:11, 12). The worship that was being offered, though it followed the form of the Law, did not come from true biblical attitudes and practices of piety.

6:16 The spiritual history of the northern kingdom reached its lowest point under the rules of **Omri** and **Ahab.** Whereas Jeroboam I had combined the worship of God with the nature and sexual worship rites of Baal (1 Kin. 12:25–33), Ahab and his wife Jezebel (in a marriage arranged by Omri) brought about the state worship of Baal and Asherah (1 Kin. 16:21–34). For these reasons, and despite the presence of the temple, God was about to bring utter shame on His people.

7:1, 2 Micah was moved by the oracles of judgment that God delivered through him (1:8). **no cluster:** For Micah, the harvest was over. There was nothing around him but undesirable fruit. **The faithful man has perished:** The norms of society had broken down; everyone was out to destroy someone else.

7:3–6 with both hands: The people were pursuing **evil** with gusto. The leaders of the state were leading the way in evil (3:11). **The day of your watchman** refers to a time when people needed to be alert for the approach of an enemy army. In this context, judgment was imminent.

7:7 Therefore I will look: These words are a pun on the words of v. 4. While there would need to be a *watchman* for the coming of an

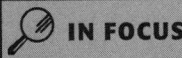 **IN FOCUS** | **"compassion"**

(Heb. *raham*) (7:19; Ex. 33:19; Prov. 28:13) Strong's #7355: The Hebrew word translated here as *compassion* means "to love from the womb" and is frequently translated *mercy* (Is. 14:1). The noun form of this verb means "womb," and consequently this verb depicts the tender love of a mother for her own helpless child (1 Kin. 3:26). "From the womb" speaks of the depth of emotion associated with this expression of love. God loves His people with a deep compassion and love that is almost beyond description. God used a form of this Hebrew word to reveal His character and name to Moses: "And the LORD passed before him and proclaimed: 'The LORD, the LORD God, merciful and gracious, longsuffering, and abounding in goodness and truth'" (Ex. 34:6).

enemy army, Micah was going to be a *watchman* for the advent of **the LORD**.

7:8, 9 The speaker in these verses is the nation Israel after it comes to repentance. **I have sinned** is the confession of the people in saving faith. **He pleads my case:** Here the Lord is speaking on *behalf* of the people (compare ch. 6). As God had delivered Israel in the past because of **His righteousness**, so He would deliver a repentant Israel in the future.

7:10 The people of Israel knew that they would suffer indignities at the hands of their enemies in the period of divine judgment. However, God's judgment of His people was designed to bring about their repentance.

7:11–13 In the day: These words call attention to a future day, the time of the end. **You** here is Zion (Jerusalem). This is a prophecy of the return of the remnant (2:12, 13; 4:1–4, 6–8; 5:3, 7, 8). **The River** is the Euphrates. The idea of these verses is a universal regathering of God's people in His land (Deut. 30:1–6).

7:14, 15 Micah prayed that God the **Shepherd** would care for His **flock.** Micah requested that the greatest wonders of the relationship between God and His people at the time of the Exodus would be realized anew.

7:16, 17 The response of the wicked **nations** to the renewed mercies of God on His people would be terror. The nations would be humiliated because they had taunted Israel in the day of its trouble (vv. 8–10).

7:18, 19 Who is a God like You: These words speak about the incomparability of God. There is nothing in all of creation to compare with God (Is. 40:25). **Pardoning iniquity:** These words come from the revelation of God to Moses in Ex. 34:6–9.

7:20 This last verse is reminiscent of God's promise to Abraham in Gen. 12; 15; 22 and His promises to Jacob in Gen. 32. The Lord had sworn to fulfill His promises to the patriarchs. He would not—He could not—leave His promise unfulfilled (Ps. 89:33).

The Book of

Nahum

THE BOOK OF NAHUM IS ONE OF TWO BOOKS OF the minor prophets that centers on Nineveh, the capital city of Assyria. In the Book of Jonah, written in the eighth century B.C., we behold a man of God who was called to preach to Nineveh. He was one of the few prophets who despaired when his listeners heeded his warning. The people of Nineveh repented, and God demonstrated His great compassion

by not judging the city. In the Book of Nahum, written in the seventh century B.C., we find another prophet called by God to preach to Nineveh. Evil again reigned in the capital. Tragically, the people of Nineveh this time ignored Nahum's warning.

The people of the northern kingdom of Israel had been sinning grievously against God and ignoring the warnings of punishment given through God's prophets. Finally God used the nation of Assyria, with its capital city in Nineveh, to destroy the nation and carry the people into captivity. A century after the fall of Samaria in 722 B.C., the Book of Nahum was written to express a major truth of the prophets. Even when God uses a nation for His own purposes of judgment, this does not excuse that nation from its own guilt before the Lord. It was Nineveh's turn to feel the wrath of God. The last great emperor of Assyria was Ashurbanipal (669–627 B.C.). After his death, the nation did not last much longer, for the Lord was against it (2:13; 3:3).

How does the mood of the Book of Nahum accord with the sentiment of the Sermon on the Mount? Though the Lord Jesus certainly spoke

about loving one's enemies (Matt. 5:43–48), He strongly warned about the inevitability of judgment (Matt. 5:21, 29, 30; 7:13, 23). He said that "all who take the sword will perish by the sword" (Matt. 26:52). If ever the words of Jesus concerning the sure destruction of those who live by violence had a direct application, it was to Nineveh.

In the conquest of the ancient world, the Assyrians were merciless and cruel. Their atrocities included everything from burning children to death to chopping off hands. In many ways, the Book of Nahum is a theology of the maxim of the sword. Nineveh had an international reputation for bloodthirsty acts of repression, destruction, and wantonness. God could not be good if He failed to call such an evil nation to account. The theology of the Book of Nahum is a theology of the goodness of God in bringing about the final destruction of those who oppose His will and abuse His people.

Nineveh was not only a city in the ancient world that received the promised judgment of God, it is also a prototype for the coming judgment of God on all workers of wickedness. Those who know that the Lord is good may rejoice in the fact that He avenges aggressive acts against His people (1:7, 8).

The seriousness of coming judgment is never a call for complacency among God's people. Implicit in any announcement of doom is a call for holy living on the part of God's people and an urgent call for them to bring the message of salvation to those who, apart from salvation, will experience the wrath of God. Judgment is God's "unusual act" (Is. 28:21), but it ultimately arises out of the goodness and justice of God.

Nahum, the author of this book, is not known apart from the three chapters of this prophecy. Even the location of the place of his birth, Elkosh (1:1), is in doubt. However, since Nahum wrote considerably after the destruction of Israel in 722 B.C., we may assume that Elkosh was in Judah.

The fall of Thebes in 663 B.C. (3:8) determines the limit for the earliest date of the book. The fall of Nineveh, which the book predicts, took place in 612 B.C., not long before the final destruction of the Assyrian Empire in 609 B.C. This means the Book of Nahum was composed sometime before 612 B.C, perhaps under the reform of Josiah in 622 B.C.

Outline

I. A psalm of praise for the avenging wrath of the Lord 1:1–2:2
  A. God's vengeance on His enemies as a sign of His goodness to Judah 1:1–11
  B. God's restoration of Judah dependent on His judgment of its enemies 1:12–2:2
II. Prophecies concerning the coming judgment of Nineveh 2:3–3:19
  A. The siege of the city 2:3–13
  B. A woe oracle concerning the siege 3:1–19

Commentary

1:1 Most of the biblical prophets directed their judgment oracles against the sinning peoples of Israel and Judah. **Nahum,** however, brought the word of God's judgment **against Nineveh.** The Hebrew term rendered **burden** was sometimes used by the prophets (Hab. 1:1; Mal. 1:1) to describe the "heaviness" of their message of judgment.

1:2–8 In Hebrew this poem is an alphabetic acrostic, namely, a writing in which the first word of each successive line begins with the succeeding letter of the alphabet. For instance, v. 2 begins with the Hebrew letter *aleph*; v. 8 concludes with the Hebrew *kaph.* Acrostics were possibly used to facilitate memorization and recitation.

1:2 avenges . . . furious: The repetition of words and the use of parallel terms are typical devices in Hebrew poetry for intensifying and sharpening the poet's message.

1:3 Slow to anger indicates the patience of the Lord (Ex. 34:6, 7). However, God's patience is not a reason to disbelieve His final judgment (Ps. 10). **whirlwind . . . storm . . . clouds:** The

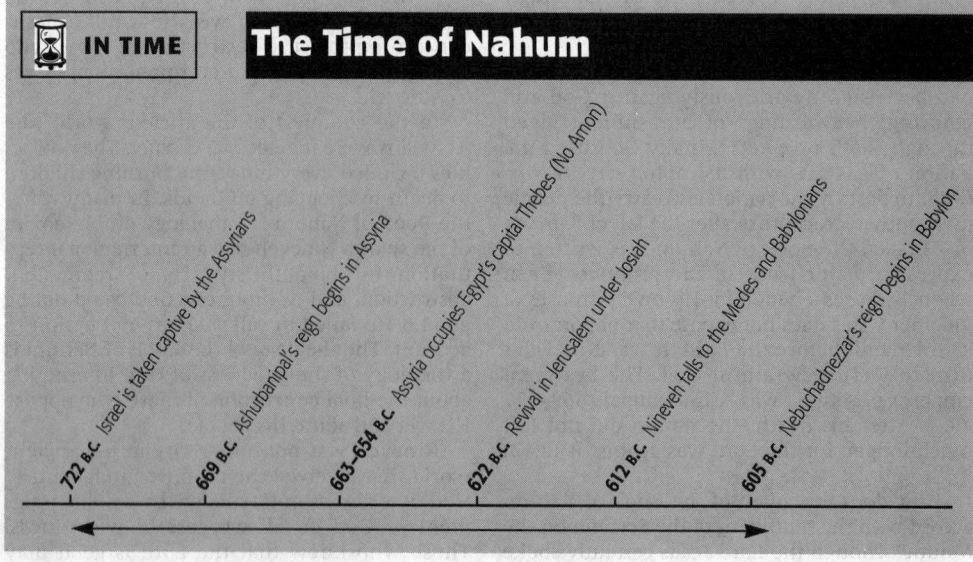

IN TIME   **The Time of Nahum**

722 B.C. Israel is taken captive by the Assyrians

669 B.C. Ashurbanipal's reign begins in Assyria

663–654 B.C. Assyria occupies Egypt's capital Thebes (No Amon)

622 B.C. Revival in Jerusalem under Josiah

612 B.C. Nineveh falls to the Medes and Babylonians

605 B.C. Nebuchadnezzar's reign begins in Babylon

peoples of the ancient Middle East worshiped nature gods, particularly deities associated with storms, clouds, and rainfall. In Canaan, this fixation on storms was centered in the worship of Baal and his consorts Anat and Asherah. The Scriptures testify that there are no gods but the Lord; it is He who rules and is above all creation.

1:4 sea . . . rivers: The Lord's control extends to all bodies of water and to places of lush vegetation—including **Bashan, Carmel,** and **Lebanon.**

1:5, 6 quake . . . melt . . . heaves: The people of God had experienced such demonstrations of God's presence at the foot of Mount Sinai when the Lord descended with His Law (Ex. 19). **indignation . . . anger. . . fury:** Grouping these three terms causes the force of the words to be felt more deeply. In other words, God's anger burned intensely against the sinful people of Nineveh.

1:7 The Lord is good: For the righteous, this is the best news of all. Because we know that the Lord is good, we can endure the tribulations of life.

1:8 flood . . . end . . . darkness: The judgment of the Lord will be inescapable. The word *flood* is both a poetic term for overwhelming devastation and a specific reference to the actual manner of Nineveh's fall. It is believed that the invaders of Nineveh entered the city through its flooded waterways (2:6).

1:9–13 In this section the prophet directly foretells the Assyrian defeat. He addresses them directly and shows that their resistance to the Lord is futile. In so doing, the prophet argues from the general to the specific.

1:9, 10 What do you conspire against the Lord: Who is wise enough, experienced enough, and strong enough to fight the power of God? No one, of course. At their very best, the enemies of God will be comic figures. Their best plans will be merely a tangle of **thorns;** their finest moves will be only the sloppy walk of **drunkards.**

1:11 Wicked is one of the harshest terms in biblical language, nearly a curse word. The term speaks of someone who is utterly worthless.

1:12, 13 Thus says the Lord: Here is an oracle of deliverance from God to His people. The present sense of safety and power that the enemy felt would not last; the past judgments of God on His nation would not continue. The Lord promised to **break off** the **yoke** that the enemy had placed on His people (Is. 9:4).

1:14 Here God spoke to His people's enemy—the nation of Assyria typified by its capital city Nineveh (v. 1). In destroying the nation's **name,** God would remove its power. Further, the Lord swore to destroy their false religious system, with its pagan temples, idols, and disgusting practices. **You are vile:** The only thing to be done with Nineveh was to **dig a grave** and bury it. This prophecy came true literally—the city was destroyed so completely that its very existence was questioned until its discovery by archaeologists in the nineteenth century (3:13–15).

1:15 Behold . . . The feet: The image is that of a herald of **peace** (Is. 52:7). **O Judah:** With the promise of future deliverance from oppression, the prophet called for the people to live in righteousness and expectation. There is nothing better for the people of God in any age than to live in obedience to Him and in anticipation of His coming deliverance.

2:1 Man the fort: These were sarcastic words to the people of Nineveh and its leaders, as if they would be able to protect themselves against the wrath of the Lord.

2:2 the Lord will restore: The wrath of God against the enemies of His people means that one day the enemies will be destroyed and the people of God will be restored. **Excellence** means "majesty," "beauty," or "wonder" (Is. 4:2). The ruin of Israel would not last forever.

2:3–13 This passage presents a description of the siege of Nineveh. The fall of Nineveh

---

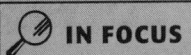 IN FOCUS   **"jealous"**

(Heb. *qanno'*) (1:2; Josh. 24:19) Strong's #7072: This Hebrew term is related to a root word that can mean "to be eager, zealous for" (1 Kin. 19:10, 14), or even "to be furious" (Zech. 8:2). One of God's names is *Jealous* (Ex. 34:14). When the expression "the Lord your God is a jealous God" is used in the OT, it is usually associated with an injunction against idol worship (Ex. 20:5; Deut. 4:24; 5:9; 6:15). God's jealousy for His people is a claim for exclusive allegiance rooted in His holiness (Josh. 24:19) and His role as their Creator and Redeemer (Pss. 95:6, 7; 96:2–5). We tend to associate jealousy with a self-serving emotion that usually results from feelings of inadequacy. God's jealousy, in contrast, proceeds from His holiness. Because He alone is the Holy One (Is. 6:3; 40:25), He will tolerate no rival (Ex. 20:5).

predicted by Nahum took place in only a few years after this prophecy—in 612 B.C., followed by the final destruction of the Assyrian Empire in 609 B.C.

2:3 red . . . scarlet . . . flaming torches: These images speak of blood, violence, and warfare. Isaiah refers to the custom the Assyrians had of rolling their outer garments in blood before a battle (Is. 9:5) to strike terror in the hearts of their opponents. Here the tables would be turned. While others would have **shields, chariots,** and **spears,** the people of Nineveh would be bathed in blood—their own blood. Unlike much of ancient literature, the Bible does not glamorize war. It paints a grimly realistic picture to show that war is an outcome of humanity's rebellion against God. The Lord takes no delight in watching human armies clash. However, sometimes in judgment He removes His restraining hand, exposing people

they would appear helpless in their actions. **Nobles** may be used with sarcasm here; these people do not seem very impressive.

2:6 gates of the rivers: The destruction of Nineveh is believed to have taken place when the besiegers entered the city through its flooded waterways. The attack came at flood time, when rivers undermined the walls and defenses of the city. Archaeologists have found evidence of flood debris that may be associated with the destruction of the city. Thus the words of Nahum were fulfilled exactly.

2:7, 8 She shall be led away: The nation that had made so much about taking captives would be made a captive by others. **Halt! Halt!:** No one would listen to their shouts of panic.

2:9, 10 spoil: Assyria had despoiled many nations, including Samaria and the cities of Israel. There seemed to be no end to the loot that could be found within its walls. Nonethe-

Photo by Howard Vos

Ruins of an ancient temple at Thebes, Egypt, a city referred to by the prophet Nahum as No Amon (Nah. 3:8).

and nations to their own unbridled destruction of each other. This was the case for Nineveh.

2:4 The chariots rage: The Assyrians used chariots as formidable war machines. The proficiency of the chariot drivers underlies the imagery of this verse. But as in the case of the shields and spears of v. 3, the chariots of Nineveh would not prevail no matter how fast they drove.

2:5 stumble: The people within the city would be so stunned to be under attack that

less, even Nineveh was exhausted of its treasures. At long last, it was **empty.**

2:11, 12 Nineveh was the city of **lions** (v. 13). Yet despite all the horrors that the *lion* of Nineveh had brought to other nations, it would no longer need to be feared by anyone.

2:13 Though the Babylonians conquered the city, they were only God's instruments. Nineveh's greatest foe was **the LORD** of hosts Himself.

3:1–19 Chapter three of Nahum is a woe oracle explaining the reasons for the siege and destruction of Nineveh.

3:1 the bloody city: Nineveh was known throughout the Middle East as a city that excelled in violence and bloodshed.

3:2, 3 Horses and **chariots** were instruments of war. Verse 3 describes the horrors of the nation's war machine, which resulted in **countless corpses.**

3:4 Harlotries refers to paganism. Any worship of gods other than the God of Scripture is an act of spiritual prostitution. Nineveh was so adept at pagan practices that the city earned the descriptive title, **the mistress of sorceries.** By this means the Assyrians "seduced" numerous rulers into dependence on them for military aid. In addition, Nineveh was a center for the worship of idols. The city was the site of temples to Ishtar, goddess of sexual love and war, and to Nabu, god of wisdom. Magical arts such as omens, fortune-telling, reading the entrails of animals, and the use of spells and incantations were all a part of Assyrian religion—practices strongly condemned elsewhere in Scripture (Deut. 18:9–14).

3:5 I am against you: This repetition of this phrase from 2:13 is more chilling each time it is heard. Who could survive the Lord's opposition? **lift your skirts:** The Lord would publicly humiliate Nineveh.

3:6, 7 The Lord described the fate of Nineveh as comparable to a person on whom unspeakable **filth** was cast. When Nineveh lay in ruins, no one would **bemoan her.** The nations would be glad that the city was gone.

3:8 No Amon . . . the River: The destruction of the city of Thebes near the Nile River in 663 B.C. was going to be a template for the destruction of Nineveh. No Amon is the Hebrew name for Thebes, derived from the Egyptian name meaning "City of (the god) Amon." The argument seems to suggest that before its destruction, no one would have even dreamed of the fall of Thebes. But the destruction *had* happened—not long before the writing of the Book of Nahum. The city of Thebes was rebuilt only to be destroyed later during the Roman period (29 B.C.). Nineveh, however, would never be rebuilt.

3:9, 10 The city of No Amon had many powerful allies, but they were not sufficient to protect her in her hour of need. Who would ally with Nineveh to fight off the Lord's attack?

3:11 drunk . . . hidden . . . seek refuge: Nineveh would be like a helpless drunk hoping for refuge but finding nowhere to turn for it.

3:12, 13 Nahum satirically describes the **strongholds** of Nineveh as being so easily defeated that they would be like fruit trees that drop their **figs** into waiting mouths.

3:14, 15 Nahum taunted Nineveh by telling the people to prepare for their siege. The actual siege of Nineveh continued over two years.

3:16, 17 Despite the great economic and military strength of Nineveh, there was nothing lasting in the city's power. **When the sun rises:** The people of Nineveh would be like nocturnal insects that disappear at daylight.

3:18 Your shepherds slumber: When the shepherds are not alert, the sheep cannot be saved from danger.

3:19 All who hear: Every nation and people that had suffered under the abusive power of Nineveh would shout and **clap** upon hearing of the city's destruction. There would be no mourning for Nineveh.

The Book of

Habakkuk

⬥

"O LORD, HOW LONG SHALL I CRY, AND YOU WILL not hear?" (1:2). Habakkuk was unique among the prophets in that he asked questions of God. Most prophets were filled with messages: "Hear the word of the Lord." Even if everyone doubted the Lord's word, the prophet would still believe. And if the prophet did have any misgivings, he kept them to himself.

But again, Habakkuk was different. To raise these questions was—for our sake—part of his message. His questions were, "Why does evil in Judah go unpunished?" "How can a just God use a wicked nation like Babylon to punish His chosen people?" Habakkuk wanted to know, just as we do, what God was doing and why. There seemed to be too much evil among the "righteous" and too much freewheeling power among the wicked.

God did not strike Habakkuk down for these questions. He answered. The Lord Himself will establish His kingdom. He will hold all people and nations accountable. The present may be filled with wickedness and chaos, but the future belongs to the righteous—the truly righteous. God will bring in His kingdom, give rest and salvation to His children, and judge His people's adversaries.

The Book of Habakkuk contains two prophetic laments (1:2–4, 12–17) in which Habakkuk questions God's righteousness. The Lord responds by explaining His plans to judge (1:5–11; 2:1–4). This is followed by five woes that taunt those who have committed evil with

their certain doom (2:6–20), as if to say, "Don't worry, Habakkuk—God is righteous; He will judge." The book ends with the prophet's prayer of praise and his acknowledgment of God's sovereignty over all outcomes.

Nations are given to greed, power, idolatry, and to immorality. People treat one another in an inhumane fashion. Often it seems as if power and success come to those who break God's laws and reject His legitimate claims on creation. Yet according to Habakkuk, the Lord remains sovereign; He sits in His holy temple watching the earth. He will eventually judge each person for his or her life (2:20).

While people may be seduced into wickedness by the allure of power and success (2:6–20), a glorious future awaits those who submit to God (2:4). Habakkuk's prophetic vision (2:2) and prayer (3:1) provide a proper perspective for viewing the injustices of this world. The Almighty is in control. He will establish His righteous kingdom in the end. In that day, all wrongs will be made right: The wicked will be judged for their sinfulness, and the righteous will be saved. Believers look forward to this day with great joy (3:18, 19).

We know little about the prophet Habakkuk. The reference to music (3:1, 19; 1 Chr. 25:1–8) may mean that he was a Levite associated with the temple singers. The designation *the prophet* is an official title, showing that others recognized him as a prophet of the Lord. His name Habakkuk appears twice in the book (1:1; 3:1). Some scholars have associated the name with the Hebrew word for *embraced*. Thus his name may mean "Embraced by God."

Habakkuk prophesied during the fall of Nineveh in 612 B.C. and the rise of Babylon as the Neo-Babylonian Empire. By 605 B.C., Assyria and Egypt had been defeated by Babylon at Carchemish. Judah's days were numbered, and Babylon's power was rapidly expanding. In addition, the death of King Josiah in 609 B.C. brought an end to an era of religious reform in Judah. It seemed that the wicked were prevailing both inside and outside Judah. Habakkuk cried out against the violence, lawlessness, and injustice he saw all around him.

Outline

I. Habakkuk's first complaint 1:1–4

II. God's first response 1:5–11

III. Habakkuk's second complaint 1:12–2:1

IV. God's second response 2:2–20

V. Habakkuk's prayer 3:1–19

Commentary

1:1 A **burden** refers to a prophetic oracle, usually addressed to a foreign nation (Is. 13:1).

1:2–11 The prophet observed how corrupt Judean society had become and how far the people had deviated from their Lord. They oppressed each other and reflected a society in which the rich and famous had power, succeeded, and got by with breaking the law. Habakkuk wondered how long the Lord would tolerate such evil. God's response was clear. He declared that He will send the Babylonians to deal with the apostasy of His people. This section has two parts: (1) The complaint of the prophet (vv. 2–4), and (2) God's response to His prophet (vv. 5–11).

1:2–4 In these verses, the prophet accused his people with being grave sinners and asked God why He remained so patient when the righteous were suffering.

1:2 Habakkuk spoke to God using His covenant name Lord (Ex. 3:14, 15). **how long:** This question is phrased as a formal complaint (Ps. 13:1, 2).

1:3 iniquity . . . trouble: The deterioration of society had become a cause of frustration and disappointment for the godly. **plundering and violence:** Abuse of power, acts of injustice, and oppressive deeds were common in Judah. **strife . . . contention:** The people of Judah argued with each other and were involved in destructive litigation.

1:4 the law is powerless: The revelation of God given at Mount Sinai had little impact on the hearts of people whose lives were focused

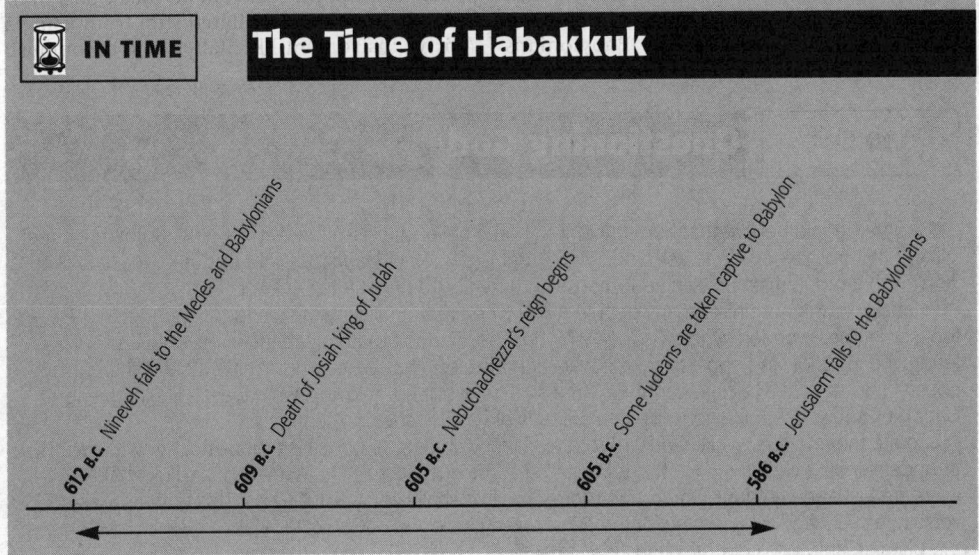

IN TIME

The Time of Habakkuk

612 B.C. Nineveh falls to the Medes and Babylonians

609 B.C. Death of Josiah king of Judah

605 B.C. Nebuchadnezzar's reign begins

605 B.C. Some Judeans are taken captive to Babylon

586 B.C. Jerusalem falls to the Babylonians

on material success. These people had little interest in living by God's definition of what is fair and humane. **wicked:** God's chosen people committed and tolerated heinous acts through corruption of the courts. **righteous:** There were always people who were faithful to the Lord, a righteous remnant. Here the godly were restricted in what they could say and do because of the evil that surrounded them. **perverse judgment:** The powerful people of Israel corrupted justice.

1:5–11 In these verses, the Lord answered Habakkuk's questions by revealing to him that judgment was imminent. But here is a surprise: the Babylonians would be God's instrument of justice.

1:5 Look among the nations: The international scene during Habakkuk's lifetime was full of turmoil, with Assyria on the decline and Babylonia on the rise. **work a work:** The Hebrew words suggest that something ominous and impressive was about to occur.

1:6 I am raising up: God controls the nations for His own purposes (Dan. 2:21), sometimes indirectly and at other times directly. **Chaldeans** is another word for Babylonians. **bitter:** The Babylonians were harsh and oppressive in their rule. **hasty:** Under Nebuchadnezzar, Babylon quickly had become the dominant power of the day.

1:7 terrible and dreadful: Far from being humane, the Babylonians prided themselves on their arrogant use of raw power. **Their judgment and their dignity proceed from themselves:** The Babylonian system of law and order had no regard for other legal systems.

1:8 The Babylonians' use of **horses** and chariots made them fearsome in the ancient world. **fierce . . . wolves:** The Babylonians

were powerful and tyrannical. **eagle:** The Palestinian eagle is a bird of prey, a vulture. These images from the animal kingdom present a vivid picture of the ferocious nature of this world power.

1:9 Habakkuk had observed **violence** in Judah (v. 2), but Babylon *relished* violence. **gather captives like sand:** The Babylonians resettled numerous conquered peoples with little regard for them as individuals.

1:10, 11 scoff . . . scorned: The Babylonians did not respect authorities and powers other than their own. **deride every stronghold:** The Babylonians mocked human systems of fortification, bursting through any defense they encountered.

1:12—2:5 Habakkuk followed up his first questions (v. 2) with a question concerning God's righteous rule over the nations. Then he awaited the Lord's response. God answered his question in an unsuspecting manner. This section has two parts: (1) the complaint of the prophet (1:12—2:1), and (2) the Lord's response to His prophet (2:2–5).

1:12—2:1 Habakkuk raised questions regarding God's justice in ordering the wicked and cruel Babylonians to be God's instruments for judging wicked Judah. The charges were: (1) How can the scale of justice be balanced when a more wicked nation destroys a wicked nation (1:13)? (2) How can the Lord reduce humans to the level of fish or reptiles (v. 14)? (3) How may God permit the Babylonians to deal so ruthlessly with humanity (vv. 15–17)? After the charges, Habakkuk awaited the Lord's response (2:1).

1:12 Are you not . . . my Holy One: Habakkuk's point seems to be that God's holiness should have prohibited Him from using a "dirty" instrument like Babylon to accomplish

---

🌱 **IN LIFE**   # Questioning God

Some people believe that human beings should never question the ways of God. Some even feel that it borders on sin to ask God, "Why?" But the Book of Habakkuk counters that idea. It is filled with a prophet's perplexing questions—and the Lord's penetrating answers.

Habakkuk was not unlike many people today who are troubled by the world around them. They, too, sometimes wonder: Where is God? Why doesn't He do something about all the pain and suffering, the injustice and oppression, the wars and diseases that destroy humanity? If He is there, why doesn't He speak? If He is powerful, why doesn't He act? If He is loving, why doesn't He intervene? Habakkuk shows that questions like these are as old as the seventh century A.D.

So are the answers. While God may not explain everything to our satisfaction—nor are we capable of understanding everything He has told us—He assures us, just as He assured Habakkuk, that His ways are just and righteous, and furthermore, "the just shall live by faith" (2:4). This truth applies universally, as Paul and other writers of the NT realized (Rom. 1:17; Gal. 3:11; Heb. 10:38). In the end, the ultimate answer to our questions is to trust God.

His purposes in judging and reproving His own people.

1:13 purer eyes: Habakkuk wondered how God could look on as the wicked Babylonians perverted justice. **A person more righteous than he:** This was the ethical dilemma that faced Habakkuk: The Judeans were less corrupt and idolatrous than the Babylonians, who were being used to judge them for their sins.

1:14, 15 Habakkuk's charges against the Lord became even more daring. The prophet charged the Lord with reducing humans to the level of **fish** or insects and with causing chaos among the nations.

1:16 they sacrifice to their net: This phrase speaks of the contemptuous pride of the Babylonians in their devices of destruction.

1:17 Habakkuk wanted to know how God could allow the brazen activity of the Babylonians to **continue** unabated. The prophet reasoned that God surely had a desire to punish the Babylonians for their pride.

2:1 my watch . . . on the rampart: Habakkuk stationed himself as a watchman to look at the nations, as God had commanded him (1:5). The prophet also waited expectantly for God's response to his three charges in 1:12–17. **what He will say to me:** Habakkuk's faith is seen in his anticipation of a response from God. **when I am corrected:** This phrase indicates the prophet's submission to God.

2:2 The command to **write** the revelation is unusual. Generally prophets *spoke* the word of the Lord first. The term **vision** here is related to the verb translated "saw" in 1:1. The noun speaks about a prophetic revelation (Is. 1:1). **he may run who reads it:** Messengers would proclaim the divine oracle.

2:3 An appointed time speaks of a determined time in God's eyes. **Though it tarries, wait for it:** God knows His plan and the outworking of all things in accordance with His purposes. The godly are responsible to study and proclaim His revelation while awaiting its fulfillment. **it will surely come:** The assurance of fulfillment lies in God Himself. **It will not tarry:** The fulfillment of the vision would not take any longer than God had planned.

2:4 The proud refers to the Babylonians, who exalted themselves and boasted of their conquests and power. **His soul is not upright in him:** The Babylonians had no regard for God, His commandments, or His people. **the just shall live by his faith:** True righteousness before God is linked to genuine faith in God. A proud person relies on self, power, position, and accomplishment; a righteous person relies on the Lord.

2:5 proud man: This arrogant and boastful person is a personification of Babylon (v. 4). The term **hell** is used here as a personification of death which, like a greedy person, is never satisfied (Prov. 30:15, 16). **all nations . . . all peoples:** These peoples of the earth should have been gathered together before the Lord in holy worship (Ps. 117:1); instead, they became morsels for the rapacious appetite of Babylon.

Photo by Howard Vos

Mosaic of a warrior with his bow and quiver for arrows. The prophet Habakkuk lamented that the Babylonian army, composed of such warriors, was on a mission of world conquest and God seemed unconcerned about the fate of His people (Hab. 1:5–11).

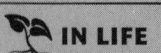 **IN LIFE**   **Living by Faith**

Few phrases of Scripture have had as far-reaching an impact as the Lord's declaration to Habakkuk that "the just shall live by his faith" (Hab. 2:4). If you are a Protestant today, this verse is an important part of your spiritual heritage: Martin Luther adopted it as his watchword during the Protestant Reformation of the early 1500s.

However, Habakkuk probably had little idea of the explosive truth contained in God's statement. It came as part of a prelude to a taunting song that the prophet was instructed to give against Babylon (2:1–6). The Lord was explaining why the Babylonians would be judged. Fundamentally, they were a "proud" people in the sense that they had no fear of God. By contrast, the "just" person—the individual deserving of God's approval and blessing—would find favor because of his "faith" in God.

Actually, the Hebrew word used for "faith," *emunah*, means "steadfastness" or "faithfulness." An Israelite who faithfully pursued the covenant by following God's Law was considered a "just" or righteous person (Ps. 15). The issue was not one's ethnicity as a Jew, but obedience to God. Thus the problem for the Babylonians was not that they were Gentiles, but that they were committed to a lifestyle of wickedness and idolatry. They arrogantly lived as if their own self-interests were all that mattered. For that reason, the Lord would humble them according to the five "woes" pronounced by Habakkuk (Hab. 2:6–20).

In the NT, Paul picked up on the idea of the just living by faith (Rom. 1:17; Gal. 3:10–12). Because of the coming of Christ, he was able to deepen the understanding of this phrase. "Living by faith" does not mean outward observance of the Law, as many of the Jewish leaders of his day had come to assume. Rather, it involves a heart commitment to the Lord and a recognition that Christ alone is able to make one righteous before God. This does not take away the need for "faithful," godly living; if anything, it establishes a proper basis for it.

2:6–20 This prophetic taunt (a use of sarcasm in the prophetic speech) is in the form of five "woe oracles." Its purpose is to assure the hearers of the "vision" (vv. 2, 3) that God will judge greed and oppression, that He will intervene on behalf of the righteous (v. 20), and that He will establish His glorious kingdom (v. 14). While the focus of the vision is on Babylon's fall (539 B.C.), the extent pertains to the fall of all human kingdoms. Babylon the Great will fall, never to rise again (Rev 17:1—19:4). The vision has five parts. Each is introduced by, or contains within, the Hebrew word translated "woe." These are the five sections: (1) the folly of extortion and plunder (vv. 6–8); (2) the folly of exploitation and injustice (vv. 9, 10); (3) the folly of murder (vv. 11–14); (4) the folly of drunkenness and immorality (vv. 15–17); and, (5) the folly of idolatry (vv. 18–20).

2:6 A **woe** oracle is an oracle of judgment consisting of two parts: a declaration of the wrong and a notice of impending judgment. The judgment usually applies the principle of the law of retaliation: a wrong would come back to haunt the wrongdoer. **increases . . . what is not his:** The Law prohibited lending for the purpose of charging interest (Deut. 23:19). **pledges:** The practice of pledging something as a guarantee for repayment was permitted under the Law, but with limitations to ensure the humane treatment of people (Ex. 22:26, 27; Deut. 24:10–13).

2:7, 8 The Hebrew term for **creditors** has the idea of "those who bite," suggesting sudden, hurtful attacks (Mic. 3:5).

2:9, 10 evil gain: Gaining property through extortion and the abuse of power was strictly prohibited in the Law of Moses (Deut. 16:19). **his nest:** As a bird builds a nest far away from people and wild animals, so the rich work hard at avoiding threats to their fortune.

2:11 the stone will cry out . . . the timbers will answer it: The whole structure of Israel's society called out for justice; every part reverberated with the need for righting wrongs.

2:12 Micah also spoke against the leaders of Judah, who were developing the **city** and kingdom at the expense of humane treatment of others, and of justice (Mic. 3:10).

2:13 LORD of hosts speaks of God as the commander of the armies of the heavens (Hag. 1:5).

2:14, 15 God's future kingdom on earth will feature a reign of righteousness (Is. 2:1–4; Mic. 4:1–5). All humanity on the renewed earth will know the Lord and live in accordance with His will. The structures of human systems, adequate as they are for the present, will fall under God's judgment because they encourage a spirit of independence from Him. **knowledge:** What

---

🔍 **IN FOCUS**   **"image"**

(Heb. *pesel*) (2:18; Lev. 26:1; Deut. 5:8; 2 Kin. 21:7; Is. 42:17) Strong's #6459: This term is related to a verbal root meaning "to hew out stone" or "to cut or carve wood" (Ex. 34:4). A *pesel* is an image or idol in the likeness of a human being or animal made from stone, wood, or metal. God prohibited the Hebrews from making such idols at Mount Sinai (Ex. 20:4). God intended the lack of images among the Hebrews to be one distinguishing feature of their true religion. Tragically, Israel followed the example of their pagan neighbors and worshiped carved images (Judg. 18:30; 2 Chr. 33:7). The psalmist describes such images as worthless and those who worship them as shameful (Ps. 97:7). Both Isaiah (Is. 40:19, 20; 44:9–20) and Habakkuk (2:18, 19) mock those who would put their trust in images made with mere human hands. They have no capacity to see, hear, speak, or do anything for their devotees.

Satan fraudulently promised in Gen. 3:5, God will deliver. **The glory of the LORD** speaks of the full manifestation of His person, significance, presence, and wonder. The true knowledge of God in the time of His kingdom on earth will be like **the waters**—all-embracing, inescapable, and fully enveloping.

2:16, 17 Only God's kingdom is glorious. The **glory** of human kingdoms, such as Babylon, will be transformed into disgrace. **be exposed:** In their nakedness the Babylonians would expose themselves as being **uncircumcised,** not part of God's people nor recipients of His mercy. **The cup of the LORD's right hand** represents the wrath of God (Is. 51:17, 22; Rev. 14:10; 16:19).

2:18, 19 teacher of lies . . . trust in it: Idolatry begins with deception, encourages deception, and calls for a commitment to deception (Is. 44:20).

2:20 the LORD is in His holy temple: These words are not set in a context of worship of God by His people. The Lord is sovereign and holy. He looks at the nations and holds them accountable. **keep silence before Him:** The call to silence is not an invitation to worship, but a command to reflect on the terrible state of all who fall into the hands of the angry God (Zeph. 1:7).

3:1–19 This chapter is a psalm in the form of a prophetic prayer. Habakkuk leads the righteous (2:4) to strengthen themselves while awaiting the glorious kingdom (2:14) by (1) meditating on God's acts in the past; (2) praying in present crises; (3) remaining faithful to the Lord; and (4) rejoicing in the future deliverance. After the superscription (v. 1), the psalm has two parts: (1) a prayer for the Lord's intervention (vv. 2–15); and (2) the triumph of faith and hope (vv. 16–19).

3:1, 2 I have heard: Habakkuk knew the stories of God's mighty acts as celebrated in song and in the feasts and festivals of Israel. These mighty acts included the Exodus from Egypt, the miracles by the Red Sea, and the conquest of the land. **Speech** here signifies the message of God's great acts, rather than the communication process. **afraid:** As he meditated on God's work in human affairs, Habakkuk was overcome with an aweinspiring sense of the greatness of the Lord. **revive . . . make it known:** Habakkuk prayed for God's renewed involvement in Israel. **In the midst of the years:** This was a way of calling for a quick response.

3:3 Teman is a poetic reference to God's appearance at Sinai (Deut. 33:2). **Selah** is probably a musical term, but its exact meaning is unknown. It may indicate a sudden shouting of "Amen," a moment of silence, or a musical chord.

3:4 Habakkuk compared the appearance of God at Sinai (v. 3) to a thunderstorm, with its darkness and flashing lights (Ps. 18:9–14). **His power was hidden:** While God reveals evidence of His power, its totality and greatness remain hidden.

3:5 pestilence . . . fever: These plagues are personified as messengers of judgment (Deut. 28:21, 22).

3:6 everlasting mountains . . . perpetual hills: The prophets often portrayed nature quaking, mountains shaking, and creation in turmoil at the coming of God (Is. 24:1–3; Jer. 4:24–26; Mic. 1:3, 4; Nah. 1:5).

3:7 Cushan . . . Midian: These tribes are representative of the quaking nations.

3:8–10 rivers . . . sea: The Lord had divided the Red Sea and the Jordan River for His people to cross (Ex. 14:26—15:5; Josh. 3:14–17). **chariots of salvation:** The appearance of the Lord was for the purpose of bringing deliverance to His people.

3:11, 12 The sun and moon stood still: This is an allusion to the battle of Gibeon (Josh.

10:12, 13). Habakkuk portrayed God as a Warrior armed with a bow, **arrows,** and a **spear** (Ex. 15:3; Ps. 18:14; 77:17).

3:13–15 The Lord's acts of vengeance against the nations would comfort His people, for those acts would lead to Israel's **salvation** (2 Thess. 1:7). The people of God as a nation were **anointed** (Ex. 19:6; Ps. 114:2). **The house of the wicked** is an allusion to Israel's redemption from Egypt.

3:16–19 Habakkuk turned finally to the future deliverance, as he awaited with hope and joy the new acts of God's judgment and salvation.

3:16–18 Habakkuk was overcome with a sense of awe at God, as well as a sense of his own weakness. **rest in the day of trouble:** The prophet encouraged the godly not to be anxious in adversity.

3:19 **The Lord God:** Here the divine name *Yahweh* is tied to the term *Adonai*, which means "Lord." **my strength:** God will strengthen those who trust in Him (Ps. 18:32, 39). He will give those who live by faith the same confidence that a surefooted **deer** has in climbing mountains (Mal. 4:2). Like a victorious army, the righteous with God's strength will occupy **the high hills.**

The Book of

Zephaniah

■

W E HAVE A WORD FOR PEOPLE WHO PREDICT terrible times ahead: *doomsayer*. It's an unflattering word, meant to poke fun at the bearers of bad news. We don't really want to believe their predictions of doom, so we caricature them. Maybe they will feel ashamed and go away. Sometimes it helps a little when the prophet of doom offers a solution. The unspoken question "Is there any hope?" is on everyone's mind.

Zephaniah's message had both halves of the bad-news-good-news equation. His first words were bad news indeed: the day of the Lord was coming and that meant terrible judgment. The Israelites had acted like their pagan neighbors—they had scorned God's law, worshiped false gods, and sinned without remorse long enough. Now it was time to repent: they had to turn back to their God or face the consequences. It was the "turn back to God" part of Zephaniah's message that offered a ray of hope. And to those who listened and responded to his call, the good news wiped out every line of bad. God would restore those who sought Him.

History tells us that it worked. The Book of Zephaniah tells about events that took place in Jerusalem in the late seventh century B.C., when Josiah was king. The northern kingdom of Israel had been destroyed nearly a century earlier by the Assyrians. The southern kingdom of Judah had suffered under the extraordinarily wicked rules of Manasseh (697–642 B.C.) and Amon (642–640 B.C.). The evils of their reigns had made doom appear certain. But the godly King Josiah led an important revival that affected all Judah. Scripture reports that this revival, though short-lived, delayed God's judgment, the invasion by Babylon (2 Chr. 34:27, 28). Zephaniah's message announced the day of the Lord—a coming day of doom—in the darkest of terms, but it also promised the blessing of future glory in a picture as bright as the doom was dark.

Many books of prophecy in the Bible speak about "the day of the Lord" (especially the Book of Joel). This day is a time of judgment that includes both God's people (Israel and Judah) and the surrounding nations. The prophet Zephaniah scolded Judah's leaders for countless acts of wickedness (3:1–7). His prophecies against the nations included Philistia (2:4–7), Moab and Ammon (2:8–11), Ethiopia (2:12), and Assyria (2:13–15). These nations were judged because of pride and arrogance against God's people and because of their continuing idolatry.

But the last section of Zephaniah's prophecy contains words of hope (3:8–20): promises of protection for the remnant and promises for the future of those who know Him truly. In a future day, peoples of all nations will come to worship the Lord (2:11; 3:9). His own people will be renewed in righteousness (3:11–13). And the King of kings Himself will rule in their midst (3:15; Rev. 21:1–6). That day of the Lord's return will be a day of song and gladness. Even God will burst out in joyful singing (3:16, 17). The raging anger of the Lord (1:1, 2) will be replaced by His happy singing, for salvation will finally have come to His people.

The prophet Zephaniah traced his ancestry back four generations to Hezekiah, most likely Judah's famous king. After the long and evil reign of Manasseh (697–642 B.C.) and his son Amon (642–640 B.C.), Josiah began his rule of Judah. Zephaniah began ministering as prophet in Jerusalem in the same year as the great prophet Jeremiah (627 B.C.). They and Hulda the prophetess (2 Chr. 34:14–28) witnessed the religious reform that Josiah started, a reform that unfortunately did not last. After Josiah's death, the people returned to their errant ways; less than fifty years later (around 586 B.C.), God used Babylon to discipline them.

Outline

I. A warning of impending judgment 1:1–18
  A. The judgment announced 1:2–6
  B. The judgment defined 1:7–13
  C. The judgment described 1:14–18
II. A call to repentance 2:1–3:8

  A. An invitation to repentance 2:1–3
  B. A detailed warning of judgment 2:4–3:8
III. A promise of future blessing 3:9–20
  A. The promise of conversion 3:9–13
  B. The promise of restoration 3:14–20

Commentary

1:1 The word of the Lord which came: The messages of the OT prophets did not arise from the prophets' own will, but from God Himself (2 Pet. 1:20, 21). **Zephaniah** means "Hidden in the Lord," a name that relates to the principal message the prophet presented (2:3). The names of the prophets were often significantly associated with the message that God gave them to present to the people. **Hezekiah** most likely refers to the notable king of Judah (2 Kin. 18—20). Thus Zephaniah the prophet was related to King Josiah.

1:2, 3 utterly consume: The message of Zephaniah begins with a pronouncement of universal judgment (Gen. 6—8). These words not only introduce the particular judgment that would be pronounced upon Judah (v. 4), but they also speak about the final judgment that will usher in the kingdom of God on earth (Rev. 19). **Stumbling blocks** here refers to idolatry, or substitutes for God in the life and affections of a person. Because there is nothing in the universe that really may be compared to the Creator (Is. 40:25), God abhors all forms of idolatry. **Says the Lord:** This phrase added gravity to

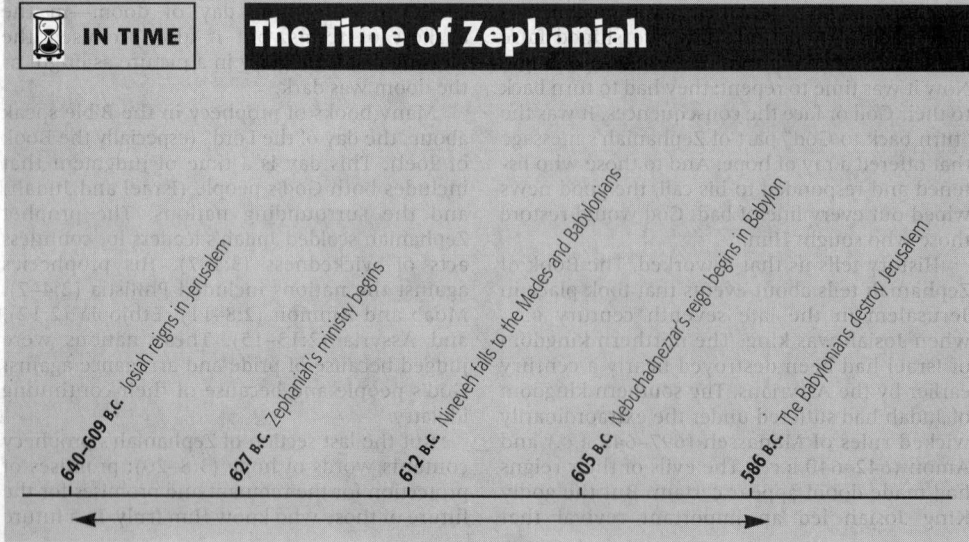

IN TIME — **The Time of Zephaniah**

640–609 B.C. Josiah reigns in Jerusalem

627 B.C. Zephaniah's ministry begins

612 B.C. Nineveh falls to the Medes and Babylonians

605 B.C. Nebuchadnezzar's reign begins in Babylon

586 B.C. The Babylonians destroy Jerusalem

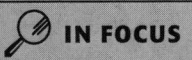 **IN FOCUS**   **"meek"**

(Heb.'*anav*) (2:3; Ps. 22:26; Is. 11:4) Strong's #6035: This Hebrew word may be translated *humble* (Ps. 34:2) or *meek* (Ps. 37:11; Matt. 5:5) and is derived from a verb meaning "to be afflicted" or "to be bowed down" (Ps. 116:10). Forms of this word occur twice in 2:3: first translated as *meek* and then as *humility*. The word frequently refers to the poor or oppressed (Prov. 14:21; Amos 2:7). But it also signifies strength of character in enduring suffering without resentment. Such character is rooted in a strong faith in God and His goodness and a steadfast submission to the will of God.

the prophetic oracle and assured the hearer of the source of the message.

1:4–6 The message of God's impending judgment on the nation of Judah and its capital city **Jerusalem** must have been startling to those who believed that God would never destroy the site of His holy temple (v. 12). **every trace of Baal:** Baal worship and its evils had led to the destruction of Israel and its capital Samaria in 722 B.C. Likewise, Baal worship and its associations would lead to the destruction of Judah and its capital Jerusalem in 586 B.C. **Milcom** is a reference to an Ammonite deity whose worship included acts of infant sacrifice (2 Kin. 23:10; Jer. 32:35). **turned back:** The people had experienced God and then turned away from Him.

1:7 Be silent: This prophetic call for silence was for solemn preparation for the horror of divine wrath (Hab. 2:20; Zech. 2:13). **The day of the Lord** describes a period of unusual activity on the part of God in the affairs of His people. **sacrifice:** The people of God were expected to prepare sacrifices for the Lord as acts of contrition and celebration. But rebels, scofflaws, idolaters, and apostates would themselves become God's sacrifice. **His guests** may be the birds of the heavens—vultures and buzzards who feed on carrion (Rev. 19:21).

1:8, 9 Foreign apparel here suggests two things: (1) acts of greed and extortion against the populace, amassing funds for exotic clothing; (2) participation in foreign religious rites associated with exotic clothing. **Leap over the threshold** may refer to a pagan practice like the one mentioned in 1 Sam. 5:5. The priests of Dagon would not step on the doorway of the temple to Dagon because the hands and the head of Dagon had fallen there.

1:10, 11 On that day is a common way of referring to the coming time of judgment (or blessing) on the day of the Lord. **Maktesh:** Zephaniah shows his familiarity with the various quarters of Jerusalem as he mentions certain gates, sections, and districts of the city.

Maktesh refers to a market district. Every area of the city would be affected by God's judgment.

1:12, 13 The Lord will not do good, nor will He do evil: The complacency of the wicked people led them to believe that God is similarly complacent. Foolishly these people believed that the Lord would be inactive, neither blessing nor cursing, neither benefiting nor punishing His people.

1:14–16 The language of this passage is quite similar to Joel 2:1–11, on which it may be based in part. **Near** describes the imminence of the coming judgment. The references to **clouds** and **darkness** resemble Canaanite poetry in which clouds and thunder are associated with the false god Baal. The poets of the Bible used this language to describe the true God, who would send forth His judgments like lightning bolts from a dark mass of clouds (Ps. 97:2–6). The references to **fortified cities** and **high towers** speak about the extent of God's judgment. There would be no adequate defense against the Lord's searing judgments.

1:17, 18 like blind men: God's judgment would be so sudden and so overwhelming that the survivors would be in a state of shock, stumbling around in the dark.

2:1–3 Having delivered a warning of judgment against Judah (1:2–18), the prophet now turns to implore the nation to repent nationally (2:1, 2) and personally (v. 3). The people doomed for judgment in the day of the Lord (1:14–18) were commanded to **gather together** in repentance. **Seek the Lord:** This is the language of true repentance, renewal, and regeneration. **you will be hidden:** Zephaniah used a play on words with the meaning of his own name, "Hidden in the Lord." Even in the midst of the most calamitous of judgment scenes, the mercy and grace of the Lord is still available to a repentant people.

2:4, 5 The focus of the book moves from the description of God's judgment on Judah and Jerusalem to a description of divine judgment on the surrounding nations. The judgment begins with the nation to the west, Philistia, and

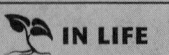 **IN LIFE**   **God's Warning**

I n Zephaniah's day, the people of Judah had grown deaf to the periodic warnings of the Lord concerning the imminent shipwreck of their nation. Occasionally He took extreme measures to shake them out of their complacency, to no avail. For example, he "cut off" entire nations and cities (Zeph. 3:6), including Israel, as an example of the judgment waiting for them. He felt that perhaps this would cause His people to "receive instruction" before it was too late (3:7). Yet despite the Lord's every effort, Judah remained stubbornly "rebellious and polluted," refusing to receive correction (3:1, 2). Princes, prophets, judges, and priests persisted in their evil ways, oblivious to God's urgent warnings of danger ahead (3:3, 4).

its major cities and seafaring industries. The five main cities of the Philistines were **Gaza, Ashkelon, Ashdod, Ekron,** and Gath. All but Gath are mentioned here. **Cherethites** is another name for the Philistines. **Canaan** is the ancient name for the land of the people of Israel, derived from its prior inhabitants. A later name of the land was Palestine, a term derived from Philistine.

2:6, 7 The seacoast shall be pastures: The coastal cities of Philistia and the coastal plain that the Philistines dominated for so long would one day become the possession of the Hebrews. The same God who brought destruction upon the people of Judah (1:14–18) would restore their fortunes.

2:8, 9 The peoples of **Moab** and **Ammon** to the east of Judah were hostile to the Hebrews from the earliest times. **Moab shall be like Sodom:** Here is God's promise of retribution (Gen. 19:12–29).

2:10, 11 The LORD will be awesome to them: There may be a double meaning in these words. For the righteous people of Judah and

Photo by E. B. Trovillion

A model of Jerusalem, showing its massive walls with fortified gates and defense towers. The prophet Zephaniah predicted that Jerusalem would be destroyed through God's judgment but that God would raise up His people and the city again in the future (Zeph. 3:14–17).

⊞ IN CONTEXT | Beyond the Rivers of Ethiopia

I f you are a Christian and of African descent, you may be interested in Zephaniah's prophecy that the Lord would restore His "dispersed ones" from "beyond the rivers of Ethiopia" (Zeph. 3:10). This was a remarkable promise, given the map of the world in Zephaniah's day. As far as we know, Ethiopia represented the southwestern limits of Judah's knowledge of the world. The interior of Africa, "beyond the rivers of Ethiopia," was literally "off the map" for the ancient Israelites. It was uncharted territory for them.

To what, then, was Zephaniah referring? The context shows that he was anticipating the day when the Lord would bring people from the ends of the earth to form a holy people who would worship and serve Him with true hearts (3:9, 12, 13). Among them would be people from "beyond the rivers of Ethiopia." The prophet called this new people "the daughter of My dispersed ones" (3:10) and "the remnant of Israel" (3:13). Thus Zephaniah's vision seems to tie in with Jeremiah's predictions of a scattering of the Jews throughout the world, followed by an eventual restoration (Jer. 30:10, 11, 18–22; 31:1–40).

Beginning in the sixth century, many Jewish colonies were established along the Nile and the Mediterranean coast of Africa. In fact, some have suggested that Zephaniah's prophecy pertains to the Jewish community in northern Abyssinia. However, the prophecy may look beyond a strictly Jewish restoration. It seems to correspond with a prediction by David that Ethiopians would someday "stretch out [their] hands to God" (Ps. 68:31). Likewise, Isaiah envisioned a day when distant lands which had not heard of God would be recruited to send representatives to the Lord at Jerusalem—a vision that appears to correspond with the mission of the church (Is. 66:18–21).

As far as we know, Zephaniah himself had no idea of the vast tribes of people living "beyond the rivers of Ethiopia." But every time one of their descendents turns to faith in Christ, Africa adds one more member to the "peoples {of} a pure language" who are called to serve the Lord "with one accord" (Zeph. 3:9).

Jerusalem, there would be a response of awe and wonder before God, who had responded to the prayer of His servant. But for the wicked there would be quite another response, one of terror and dread. **People shall worship Him:** Not only would there be a righteous remnant in Judah, there would also be people coming to God from the nations of the earth.

2:12 Ethiopians: Only one verse in this chapter is given to the message of the Lord to the peoples of the south, the Ethiopians. The message to them is indeed stark. Since God is speaking, their judgment is sure and certain.

2:13–15 Assyria was to the east. But the ancient armies could not march across the desert. Therefore they went around the desert and entered the land of the Hebrews from the **north. The pelican and the bittern** were birds found in remote areas (Is. 34:11). Their presence in the ruins of Nineveh attest to the severity of the destruction announced on these people. **the rejoicing city:** The rejoicing here is ironic, seen as an act of the city's complacency. Soon the judgment of God would descend suddenly, and the region would be useful only for herding animals.

3:1–4 The addressee of the prophetic word here is Jerusalem, the **city** of David. Jerusalem had become a center of oppression, rebellion, and apostasy. It would soon be marked by destruction. The expression of grief is reflective of God's own heart. The **princes, judges, prophets,** and **priests,** whom God had especially designated to work for righteousness, were more wicked than the "regular" citizens of Jerusalem. These leaders were destroying and defrauding the weak, the needy, and the helpless.

3:5–7 Because He is absolutely **righteous,** God had no place in the midst of such an evil people. **cut off nations:** God's punishment of Judah's neighbors should have brought the people to their senses.

3:8 the fire of My jealousy: God's response to the wickedness of Jerusalem was to declare His judgment. He would use other nations to punish the city for its rebellion.

3:9–13 The focus of the text moves to a time of national regeneration and restoration. **Pure language** refers to language used in the pure worship of God. One day human language will become a unifying element in the true worship of God. **My worshipers:** God's people would come from all nations to worship Him.

3:14–17 The people of God would be called to **sing** because their deliverance had come. **Daughter of Zion** is an affectionate title for the city of Jerusalem. **In that day:** The people are first commanded to abstain from fear, to keep from hanging their arms in a posture of resignation. Instead, they were to take encouragement and strength from the new reality that their God lived among them.

3:18–20 those who sorrow: God is going to make all things right. Those who are enemies of God's truth will be gathered and removed; those who are disenfranchised, God will restore. **I will give you fame and praise**: Ordinarily Scripture speaks about the praise that should be brought to God. Here we find the praise that God will bring to His people. As in the beginning of His dealings with Abraham and Sarah (Gen. 12:1–3), where God promised blessing, honor, and a renowned name, so here God promises *fame and praise* to each individual in His family. **Says the Lord**: This is a solemn vow of God to do what He has promised. Zephaniah begins and ends with the strong assertion that the Lord is speaking. The implication is clear: "Listen and live!"

The Book of

Haggai

---

*H*AGGAI WAS A PROPHET TO THE JEWS WHO HAD
returned from the Exile in Babylon. His first task was
to force them to see where their hearts and priorities
really lay. He urged them to do what they should have done from
the start: to rebuild the temple with a willing heart. To these
admonitions he added the promise of God to be with them. With
this promise, the people could return to their first enthusiasm

and carry out God's purposes for them. Then
their worship would be joyful and sincere.

When some of the Israelites returned from
the Babylonian captivity beginning in 538 B.C.,
they determined to restore the worship of God
to its rightful place at the center of their lives.
They planned to build a new temple in
Jerusalem (Ezra 1). Sadly, however, their
resolve seems to have vanished shortly after
their arrival in Jerusalem. They built an altar on
the original temple site and later laid the foundations for the new temple. But when enemies
who lived in the vicinity applied pressure, the
Persian king ordered the work on the temple to
cease. A later emperor of Persia, Darius I, lifted
the restrictions that had been placed on the
rebuilding of the temple and told them to proceed. But even when the barriers were lifted,
the people lapsed into spiritual lethargy. They
were not the idolaters that their ancestors had
been, but they had lost their early passion for
the worship of the living God. They explained
their behavior by advancing the time-honored
excuse of procrastination: it just doesn't seem to
be the right time (1:2).

When Haggai confronted the people, he
addressed the problems of his day: the infertility of the land and the hard economic times
(1:6). But he did not blame these problems on
poor fiscal planning. Instead, he exhorted the
people to focus on their spiritual condition.
They were focusing on insignificant matters
like the decoration of their homes, while every
day they ignored God's temple lying in ruins.
The temple was more than a building. It was
the site of the people's meeting with the living
God, the symbol of the abiding presence of the
Creator of the universe. If the people ignored
the physical ruin of the temple, they were
ignoring the spiritual wreckage in their souls
as well.

Zerubbabel the governor and Joshua the
high priest, along with the people of God,
responded quickly to the message of Haggai
(1:12). Three weeks after Haggai gave his first
message, they began their work on the temple
(520 B.C.). Anticipating a positive response,
Haggai came with another message. This was a
simple one, but it had profound implications:
Haggai assured them that the Lord was with

them (1:13). This was the same message that Moses had brought to the Israelites in Egypt (Ex. 3:8). Indeed this would be the name of the coming Messiah—Immanuel, God with us (Is. 7:14). When the people chose to make God the center of their lives, the Lord could Himself remain in their midst even without a physical building.

To emphasize some key points about the people's attitude towards God, Haggai posed a couple of questions. One of these was about the laws concerning what was clean and unclean (2:10–14). These laws had several purposes: (1) they protected people from diseases; (2) they taught certain spiritual lessons; and, (3) they created in the people an instinctive sense of right and wrong. In other words, they underscored the message that the Lord, and not any person, determines what is good or evil.

Haggai asked the priests whether cleanness or holiness might be transmitted through touch. The priests answered that it could not. Then the prophet asked whether uncleanness could be transmitted through touch. The answer was yes. Haggai applied this principle to the nation. An indifferent attitude toward the construction of the temple had polluted everything the people touched. Their attitude made the work of their hands unacceptable to the Lord. Though the temple work had begun, the people's hearts left them unclean in the eyes of the Lord. Even so, God in His great grace would still bless His people.

In a question-and-answer format (2:15–19), Haggai also encouraged the people to think about their circumstances before they started to build the temple. None of their past work had resulted in success: "Is the seed still in the barn?" (2:19). But from that day God would bless His people, because they had reordered their priorities. They had put the worship of the Lord before their own welfare (1:4, 14). Out of the bounty that the Lord would provide, the Israelites would be able to bring the proper sacrifices of true worship into the new temple.

Little is known about the prophet Haggai except what is in the book that bears his name. Ezra mentions him briefly in association with the prophet Zechariah (Ezra 5:1; 6:14) and the rebuilding of the temple. The name Haggai means "Festival," an appropriate meaning given the prophet's work in restoring temple worship. But what is most remarkable about Haggai's ministry is its brevity; his messages were given in the span of only four months in 520 B.C.

Outline

I. The call to rebuild the temple 1:1–15
  A. The people's indifference 1:1–11
  B. The people's repentance 1:12–15
II. God's greater temple and blessings 2:1–23
  A. Encouragement from God 2:1–9
  B. Holiness and the worship of God 2:10–19
  C. God's blessing on Zerubbabel 2:20–23

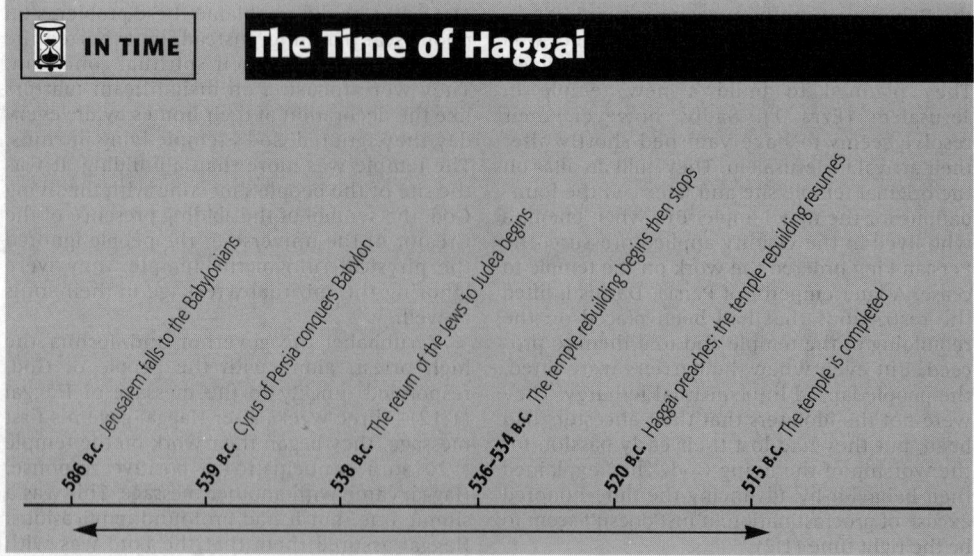

IN TIME   **The Time of Haggai**

586 B.C. Jerusalem falls to the Babylonians

539 B.C. Cyrus of Persia conquers Babylon

538 B.C. The return of the Jews to Judea begins

536–534 B.C. The temple rebuilding begins then stops

520 B.C. Haggai preaches; the temple rebuilding resumes

515 B.C. The temple is completed

🌱 IN LIFE	**First Things First**

'll pay more attention to religion as soon as my schedule lightens up." "I'll get back into a daily time of prayer and Bible reading as soon as I finish the project I'm working on." "One of these days I'll get around to helping that mission to the poor I've been thinking about."

If you've ever made comments such as these, then you have some idea of the situation in postexilic Judah. The people had started to rebuild the temple, but stopped after a year or two of work. They got involved in other commitments, and before they knew it, 16 years had gone by. The temple was still incomplete. "We'll get around to it," they apparently said. "It's just not time yet" (Hag. 1:2). However, God rebuked them for that attitude. Their priorities were distorted. They were putting God at the tail end of their commitments, rather than honoring Him as the Lord of their lives. The neglect of the temple was essentially a neglect of God.

God's word to the Jewish returnees also may speak to your priorities. If your spiritual life has been slipping, maybe it's time to put first things first and place God back at the center of your commitments.

Commentary

1:1–15 The Book of Haggai can be divided in two parts, as indicated by its two chapters. The first major section (ch. 1) focuses on the need for the people who have returned to Jerusalem to complete the rebuilding of the temple of God. The second major section (ch. 2) focuses on the need to reform the people and their worship of God in the new holy temple. The first section is comprised of two smaller parts, each presenting a dated message of the prophet Haggai (1:1–11, 12–15).

1:1 second year . . . sixth month . . . first day: The date for this first message of God through Haggai is August 29, 520 B.C. The prophecies of Haggai are among the most precisely dated in the OT. **Zerubbabel** was the governor of Jerusalem at the time of Haggai's ministry and the **governor** of the first group of returning exiles from Babylon (Ezra 3:2; Neh. 7:7).

1:2 The time has not come: The people had decided that rebuilding the Lord's dwelling among His people was not important.

1:3, 4 The principal building material in Jerusalem was stone. Those who wanted to make their **houses** elaborate installed wood panels. The people of Haggai's time were making their homes elegant, rivaling royal residences and the holy temple itself. But they still did not feel that the "time was right" to begin working on the renewed temple. While this verse is not a blanket condemnation of elegant living among God's people, it certainly calls for a reevaluation of priorities.

1:5 Consider your ways: The people were asked to mull over their habits and activities and to ask whether their attitude was sensible before the Lord.

1:6 God asked the people to take stock of their lives. Though they ate and drank, they never seemed satisfied. Though they put on clothes, they never felt **warm.** Wage earners constantly felt as though their pockets had holes in them through which their money was lost.

1:7, 8 The people were instructed to go to great lengths to get **wood** for paneling the temple of the Lord (v. 4). **that I may take pleasure in it:** God's joy in the temple is related to His pleasure in the people who would worship Him there. **be glorified:** Clearly God does not need to receive more glory (Ps. 24:7–10); however, He gladly receives the adoration of His people.

1:9 runs to his own house: Because of their preoccupation with personal comfort, the people were ignoring the central spiritual concerns of their lives. Their faulty principle of life was being shaken by the Lord. The Savior Jesus later proclaimed the true and abiding principle for the life of faith: "But seek first the kingdom of God and His righteousness, and all these things shall be added to you" (Matt. 6:33).

1:10, 11 The blessing and cursing formula of the Lord's covenant with His people comes into play here (Deut. 28). **Dew** is a poetic way of speaking of rainfall.

1:12 The remnant of the people were literally those who had made the trek back to Judah from their place of captivity in Babylon; it also refers to those within a larger population who are faithful to the Lord.

1:13 I am with you: God's promise to Moses was, "I will certainly be with you" (Ex. 3:12). God's promise to the people of Judah was that the name of the Coming One would be Immanuel, meaning "God is with us" (Is. 7:14). Here God repeated the same message of comfort and encouragement.

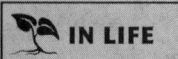

IN LIFE

Remember the Past, but Face the Present

As a new temple began to take form in the place where the old one had stood, some of the old-timers could remember the "former glory" of the first temple (Hag. 2:3). They remembered its beautiful cedar paneling, gold overlay, and other magnificent furnishings. By comparison, the new temple seemed "as nothing" in their eyes.

The Lord did not discourage them from honoring this gilded, glorious past, but He did exhort them to turn their eyes toward the present. He challenged the leaders and the people: "Be strong and work; for I am with you" (2:4). The new structure might not bring back the days of Solomon, but it would at least be a building of which they could be proud.

Scripture often encourages us to remember and honor the past, but it also urges us to face the reality of the present. God is at work today, just as He was at work yesterday. His Spirit remains with us (2:5; John 14:16, 17), just as He was with believers in times past. If we cooperate with what the Spirit is doing, we may bring even greater glory to God and accomplish even greater ministry than has yet been seen.

1:14, 15 This verse bears witness to the work of God's Spirit on the human **spirit** of His leaders and His people to accomplish His tasks. It is reminiscent of God's work in stirring up the people to build the original tabernacle (Ex. 35:29; 36:2). **remnant:** Always within Israel a remnant existed. Paul stated there was such a

remnant in Elijah's time (Rom. 11:2–4; compare 1 Kin. 19:18).

2:1–23 The second section of the Book of Haggai brings a focus on the people. Here, the people are prepared for the true worship of the living God. This chapter has three parts to it: (1) a promise of a future temple (vv. 1–9); (2) holi-

Photo by Gustav Jeeninga

A cylinder seal, used to validate decrees or legalize contracts. Seals like this were often engraved on rings. The prophet Haggai spoke of Zerubbabel as a "signet ring" who would guarantee God's presence and authority among His people (Hag. 2:23).

🔍 **IN FOCUS**   **"signet ring"**

(Heb. *chotham*) (2:23; Gen. 38:18; 1 Kin. 21:8; Jer. 22:24) Strong's #2368: The Hebrew noun *signet ring* is derived from a verbal root meaning "to affix a seal," "to seal up," or "to fasten by sealing." The signet in OT times was an engraved stone set in a gold or silver finger ring, bracelet, or armband (Song 8:6). When pressed upon wax or soft clay, the ring left the impression of the personal insignia of the bearer (Ex. 28:11, 21, 36; 39:6, 14, 30). The signet ring was like an identification card or badge in the ancient world (Gen. 38:18). It symbolized status or position and the binding nature of the authority attached to items sealed by the ring (1 Kin. 21:8; Job 38:14). Haggai's comparison of Zerubbabel to a signet ring (2:23) has messianic implications, since Zerubbabel would overturn the curse of Jeremiah on King Jehoiachin's dynasty and restore royal authority to the line of King David (Jer. 22:24–30).

---

ness in the life of the people (vv. 10–19); and, (3) blessing on Zerubbabel (vv. 20–23).

2:1 twenty-first of the month: By our calendar this would be October 17, 520 B.C. In the ancient Jewish calendar this day was the last day of the Feast of Tabernacles or Succoth (Lev. 23:33–44). During this holiday the people of Israel lived in booths, or temporary shelters, commemorating their departure from Egypt when they lived in temporary shelters in the wilderness.

2:2 Speak now: Haggai was called again to address the leaders Zerubbabel and Joshua (1:1) and the true people of God (1:12).

2:3 The **temple** of Solomon was one of the wonders of the ancient world (1 Kin. 6). The older temple would have loomed large and magnificent, far outstripping the present structure. So even though the building was completed, there may have been the sense among some of the people that it was **as nothing.**

2:4 I am with you: The Lord's words to the people (1:13) were the same as His great words to Moses (Ex. 3:12). The words of this verse draw a comparison between the events of this period and the events of the first Exodus. God brought the people back from Babylon as He had brought them back from Egypt. The message to the first set of leaders, Moses and Aaron, and to the second, Zerubbabel and Joshua, was the same: God would be present with them. Finally, the mission in the promised land was the same, to build a place for the true worship of God.

2:5 According to the word: The same covenant that related the people to God in their departure from Egypt bound them still. The events surrounding the decline of the nation and the people's captivity in Babylon had not rescinded the covenant relationship that insured God's presence with His people (Ex. 29:42–46).

2:6 I will shake: This is another way of

speaking of the day of the Lord. The purpose of the day of the Lord is to prepare the earth for the glorious reign of Jesus Christ on earth (Matt. 24:29; Rev. 6:12–17).

2:7 Desire of All Nations: Some interpret these words as a messianic title that speaks about the joy of the redeemed of the nations at the time of the rule of King Jesus. Others observe that the Hebrew word meaning *desire* is used principally for objects (as in 2 Chr. 32:27; Hos. 13:15; Nah. 2:9) rather than persons. However, the word is used occasionally for persons (1 Sam. 9:20).

2:8 silver . . . gold: God owns the cattle on a thousand hills, the gold in all coffers, and the wealth of all nations.

2:9 Peace includes good health, well-being, and an abundant life. The term refers to everything being as it ought to be.

2:10–19 In these verses the prophet speaks about ways that holiness in the life of the people related to their worship of God. This section has two smaller units in it: (1) issues concerning the clean and the unclean (vv. 10–14); and, (2) issues concerning cursing and blessing (vv. 15–19).

2:10 The twenty-fourth day of the ninth month corresponds to December 18, 520 B.C. on our calendar.

2:11 The responsibilities of the **priests** included leading public worship and instructing the people in the nature and meaning of God's **law.**

2:12 will it become holy: Since the role of the priest was to interpret God's law, it was reasonable that questions on holiness should be addressed to them. Haggai asked whether holiness could be transferred by contact. The answer was *no.*

2:13–15 It shall be unclean: The priests were asked whether a religiously unclean person, someone who had touched a corpse, could contaminate someone else by touch. The answer was *yes* (Num. 19:11–13). The **people** had worked hard to rebuild the temple, only to be told that their worship would be unacceptable in the new temple. The existence of the temple itself guaranteed nothing. The hearts of the people had to be in harmony with the sacrifices being made.

2:16, 17 you did not turn to Me: Despite God's acts of withholding His blessing, the people still had not turned fully back to Him.

2:18–21 from this day: God determined to bring His blessing on His people, but He demanded that they recognize Him as the source of their great productivity.

2:22 I will overthrow: Haggai focused on the power of God to do as He wills among the nations (Dan. 2:21). These words speak both in a general way about the sovereignty of God over the nations throughout history, as well as more specifically of God's final judgment on the wicked nations at the time He institutes the rule of His Son as King of kings (Pss. 2; 110; Rev. 19).

2:23 A signet ring was an item of great value in the ancient world. The owner used it much like we use our personal signature on checks or other important documents. God used this imagery to indicate that **Zerubbabel** was in His hand, that he was highly valued, and that he represented God's authority in his leadership of the people. Even though the people had been told they were still unclean in God's eyes (2:10–14), their leader Zerubbabel was encouraged to guide them through those spiritually trying times.

The Book of

Zechariah

—■—

ENCOURAGEMENT AND HOPE ARE THE UNDERLYING themes of the prophecies of Zechariah. The prophet Zechariah was one of the three prophets, along with Haggai and Malachi, who ministered to the exiles returning to Jerusalem. These exiles faced the ruins of what had once been a splendid city and a glorious temple. There was much to be sad about, but Zechariah encouraged the exiles with visions of judgment on

Israel's enemies and of the complete restoration of the city of Jerusalem. Yet the most thrilling vision of all was the prediction of a coming King—the Messiah who would bring eternal salvation and the promised eternal kingdom.

Zechariah lived and prophesied during the period following the Babylonian captivity (597–538 B.C.). Jeremiah had predicted that the Israelites would return to the promised land after seventy years of discipline in exile. God began fulfilling this promise when He raised up Cyrus king of Persia, whose military exploits brought about the capture of Babylon in 539 B.C. Following his victory, Cyrus decreed that all exiled peoples could return to their homelands. The people of Judah were among those who benefited from this reversal of Babylonian policy. The first group of Jews returned under the leadership of Sheshbazzar (Ezra 1:8) in 537 B.C. The altar for the temple was erected in the fall of that year, but construction of the temple itself did not begin until the spring of 536 B.C.

Opposition to the temple rebuilding by enemies of the Jews living in and around Judah resulted in the abandonment of the work until 520 B.C. During these sixteen years of neglect

the people of Judah lost their vision and sense of spiritual purpose. Their procrastination resulted in divine chastening (Hag. 1:11; 2:17). Though the crops failed and the people languished, they did not repent until God raised up two prophets to turn the people back to Himself. In 520 B.C., Haggai called for the Israelites to recognize their spiritual priorities and rebuild the temple. Zechariah began his prophetic ministry just two months after Haggai (compare 1:1 with Hag. 1:1).

The ministries of Haggai and Zechariah did not cease when work began in earnest on the temple. The prophets continued to encourage the people. Haggai's messages were delivered in 520 B.C.; Zechariah's last dated prophecy was given in 518 B.C. (7:1). With the people committed to restoring the worship of the Lord and the temple, God poured out His blessing on a repentant and spiritually revitalized people. The temple was completed in 515 B.C. and rededicated with great rejoicing.

Zechariah's prophecies had two purposes. First, they challenged the returning exiles to turn to the Lord, to be cleansed from their sins and to experience again the Lord's blessing

(1:3). Second, Zechariah's words comforted and encouraged the people regarding the rebuilding of the temple and God's future work among His people (1:16, 17; 2:12; 3:2; 4:9; 6:14, 15).

In the first several chapters, Zechariah encourages the people by focusing on God's choice of Jerusalem (1:17; 2:12; 3:2). The Lord had not set aside His ancient covenant people. Through Zechariah, God not only reaffirmed Jerusalem's divine election, but promised to come among His returning people and live in their midst (2:10, 11; 8:3, 23). It was through His personal presence among His people that God would accomplish a miraculous work. In the second half of the book, Zechariah details God's future dealings with His chosen people, revealing the overthrow of Israel's enemies, the future glories of Zion, and the universal reign of the Messiah. This is the overarching theme of the book: the complete restoration of God's people would occur in the redeeming and delivering work of the coming Messiah.

Zechariah teaches a great deal concerning the First and second comings of Jesus the Messiah. He refers to the Messiah as the "BRANCH" (3:8), God's "Servant" (3:8), and God's "Shepherd" (13:7). There is also an allusion to the Messiah's ministry as a Priest-King in 6:13 (Heb. 6:20—7:1). Furthermore, he prophesied the Messiah's entrance into Jerusalem on a colt (9:9; Matt. 21:4, 5; John 12:14–16), His betrayal for thirty pieces of silver (11:12, 13; Matt. 27:9, 10), the piercing of His hands and feet (12:10; John 19:37), and the cleansing from sin provided by His death (13:1; John 1:29; Titus 3:5). In fact, chs. 9—14 of Zechariah are the most quoted section of the Prophets in the narratives of the Gospels. Concerning the Messiah's second coming, Zechariah prophesied such future events as the conversion of Israel (12:10—13:1, 9; Rom. 11:26), the destruction of Israel's enemies (14:3, 12–15; Rev. 19:11–16), and the reign of Christ in a new Jerusalem (14:9, 16; Rev. 20:4–6).

Along with his emphasis on the Messiah, Zechariah appropriately gives an important message about God's plan for salvation. The importance of repentance and returning to the Lord of Hosts is emphasized in the introduction (1:3–6). And then in 3:1–5, Zechariah provides a striking illustration of the removal of sin and the imputation of righteousness. The removal of the high priest's filthy garments and the provision of clean festal robes illustrates the work of Christ. Through His atoning death, Christ strips us of our filthy sins and clothes us with His own righteousness. In this way we can approach our holy God.

True religion, according to Zechariah, is not found merely in external acts of religious piety, but is based upon a personal relationship with God (7:5–7). Such a relationship with God should change one's attitude to one's neighbors. Like the prophets before him, Zechariah condemned the oppression of the widow, the orphan, the stranger, and the poor (7:10). As a preacher of righteousness, he called God's people back to the virtues of justice, kindness, compassion, and truth (7:9; 8:16).

The name Zechariah means "Yahweh Remembers." This powerful phrase communicates a message of hope: the God of Israel will

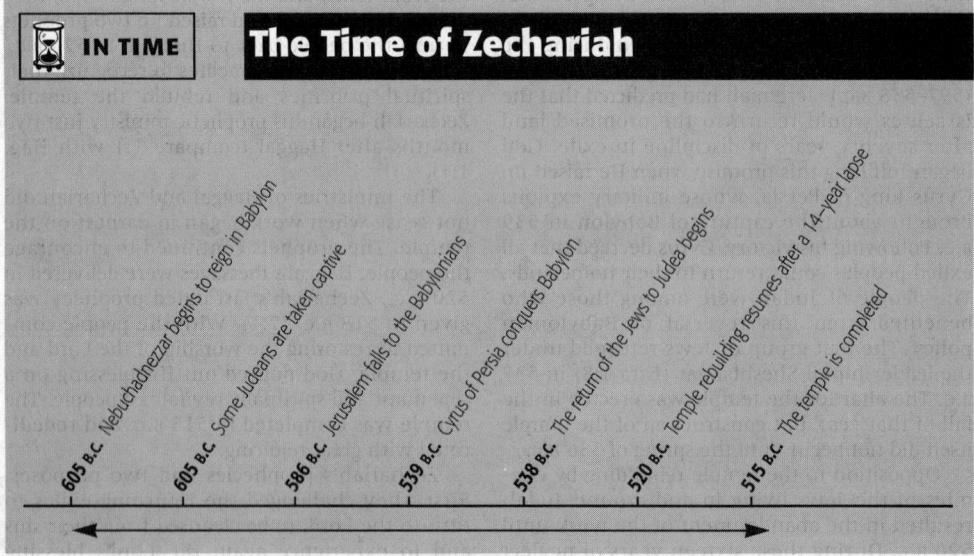

IN TIME — **The Time of Zechariah**

605 B.C. Nebuchadnezzar begins to reign in Babylon

605 B.C. Some Judeans are taken captive

586 B.C. Jerusalem falls to the Babylonians

539 B.C. Cyrus of Persia conquers Babylon

538 B.C. The return of the Jews to Judea begins

520 B.C. Temple rebuilding resumes after a 14-year lapse

515 B.C. The temple is completed

mercifully remember His people. The prophet is identified as "the son of Berechiah, the son of Iddo." Iddo was among the heads of the priestly families that returned from Babylon to Judah. Zechariah, then, was a member of the tribe of Levi and probably served as both a priest and a prophet. He entered his prophetic ministry two months after his contemporary Haggai had concluded his first oracle.

Those who question the unity and single authorship of Zechariah usually argue that chs. 9—14 date from the Hellenistic period (331–167 B.C.) or the Maccabean period (167–73 B.C.). The reference to "Greece" in 9:13 has often been cited as evidence for a late date, after Alexander's conquests (about 330 B.C.). However, Greek influence was strong in the ancient Middle East as early as the seventh century B.C. Greece is mentioned by the eighth-century prophet Isaiah (Is. 66:19, where Greece is referred to as Javan) and the sixth-century prophet Ezekiel (Ezek. 27:13, 19 for Javan). Those who hold to the unity of the book generally date its completion between 500 and 470 B.C. Zechariah began his prophetic ministry in the second year of the Persian king Darius (522–486 B.C.) and his last dated prophecy was delivered two years later, in 518 B.C.

Outline

Commentary

1:1–6 The first section of the book introduces the prophet (Zechariah) and his message (an invitation to return to the Lord of Hosts).

1:1 The **eighth** month corresponds to October-November on our calendar. **Darius** ruled Persia from 522 to 486 B.C. Thus his **second year** was 520 B.C. The name **Zechariah** means "Yahweh Remembers," emphasizing God's faithfulness to His covenant promises and to His people.

1:2 The **fathers** refers to the ancestors of the present generation who had disobeyed God and come under His judgment (2 Chr. 36:15, 16). These people formed the generations of Hebrews whose willful departure from the Lord of Hosts led to the destruction of Jerusalem by the Babylonians. Implied in Zechariah's words is the implicit warning: What God did in the past, He may do in the present. As in the sad experience of the wilderness generations (Num. 13; 14), God has time to raise up a people who will be faithful to Him!

1:3 The words **return to Me** remind us of the depth of God's unconditional love. **says the LORD of hosts:** The personal name translated LORD speaks about God's gracious nature as He relates to His people (Ex. 3:15); the *hosts* are the angelic armies that await His every command.

1:4 The **former prophets** refers to people like Habakkuk, Zephaniah, and Jeremiah, who had lived during the last years of the Judean monarchy and had warned of coming judgment.

1:5, 6 Their **fathers** had been killed or exiled and even the **prophets** had perished. The previous generation had been overtaken by God's judgment (Deut. 28:15–68).

1:7–6:15 This section contains a sequence of eight night visions concerning Israel's future, followed by the symbolic crowning of the high priest Joshua. Here Zechariah pursues the same end as Haggai, rebuilding the temple as the center of worship and world rule, and as a place of pilgrimage for the nations (8:20–23; Hag. 2:7–9). The eight night visions follow a general pattern. Zechariah describes what he sees, then asks the question, "What does this mean?" Finally he is given an explanation by an accompanying angel.

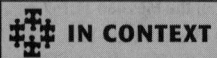

The Parables of Zechariah

A parable is a truth wrapped in a memorable story or word picture. It could be fictional, dramatized, or the result of a vision. Jesus gave much of His teaching through parables. So did several of the OT prophets, including Zechariah. He saw eight visions that can be understood much like parables.

- The Man and Horses Among the Myrtle Trees (Zech. 1:8–17)
  Indicated that the Lord would again be merciful to Jerusalem.
- The Four Horns and the Four Craftsmen (Zech. 1:18–20)
  Showed that the Babylonians and others who scattered Judah would be cast out.
- The Man With a Measuring Line (Zech. 2:1, 2)
  Promised that God would be a protective wall of fire around Jerusalem.
- The Cleansing of Joshuah's Garments (Zech. 3:1–10)
  Illustrated that the redemptive work that God would do for his people.
- The Golden Lampstand and Olive Trees (Zech. 4:1–14)
  Symbolized the way in which the Lord was going to empower His people by the Holy Spirit.
- The Flying Scroll (Zech. 5:1–4)
  Indicated that dishonesty is cursed.
- The Woman in the Basket (Zech. 5:5–11)
  Illustrated the removal of wickedness.
- The Four Chariots (Zech. 6:1–8)
  Revealed that the spirits of heaven would execute judgment on the whole earth.

1:7–17 This vision can be divided into three parts: (1) the time of the vision (v. 7); (2) the details of the vision (vv. 8–12); and, (3) the promise of the vision (vv. 13–17).

1:7 The **eleventh month** (**Shebat** is the Babylonian name) corresponds to January-February, 519 B.C. **the word of the LORD**: Here the phrase refers to a prophetic vision.

1:8, 9 Myrtle is an evergreen tree that was once common in the vicinity of Jerusalem (Neh. 8:15).

1:10 Darius had an elaborate network of imperial inspectors who went about the empire investigating complaints and dealing with disloyalty among the subjects. Similarly, the Lord has His patrollers to observe and report.

1:11 When Darius took the throne of Persia the empire was in an upheaval. Many provinces were in revolt. During his first two years of rule, Darius defeated nine kings in nineteen battles to secure his throne. Now all was quiet and peaceful.

1:12, 13 The prophet overhears a conversation between **the Angel of the LORD** and God. This may be a conversation between the preincarnate Jesus and the first Person of the Trinity, God the Father (Ps. 110). It is certainly an allusion to Jesus' role as Intercessor. As the author of Hebrews states, Jesus lives to make intercession for us (Heb. 7:25) at the right hand of the Father. The **seventy** years refers to the period of exile during which the temple lay in ruins (586–515 B.C.; Jer. 25:7–14).

1:14 the angel who spoke with me: This is the interpreting angel in the dramatic vision, not the Angel of the Lord (v. 11). **I am zealous:** The passion of the Lord can be seen in His defense of His special relationship with Israel and Jerusalem.

1:15 I am exceedingly angry: Here the anger of God was against the nations that He had used to punish His unrepentant people.

1:16 God promised to show compassion on His people and to rebuild the Jerusalem temple (**My house**). **A surveyor's line** was used to make measurements in preparation for new construction. The stretching of the line was a promise that the work would begin and that the completion of the task would follow.

1:17 again choose Jerusalem: Jerusalem's election is a prominent emphasis in Zechariah (2:12; 3:2). The word **Zion** describes Jerusalem in an affectionate way (Zeph. 3:14).

1:18–21 In the second night vision, Zechariah sees four horns (vv. 18, 9) and four craftsmen (vv. 20, 21). Here God promises to destroy those enemies who have scattered His people.

1:18, 19 Animal **horns** were often used by poets and prophets as symbols of powerful nations and their kings (Dan. 7:7, 8, 24). The horns that persecuted Israel and Judah included Assyria, Babylon, Medo-Persia, and later Greece.

1:20, 21 four craftsmen: The craftsmen or

"smiths" destroyed the **horns** (v. 19). Historically, Babylon destroyed Assyria, Medo-Persia conquered Babylon, Greece conquered Medo-Persia, and Rome overcame Greece. These are dominant themes in the prophecies of Daniel (Dan. 2; 7).

2:1–3 Taking measurements and establishing boundaries is the first step toward rebuilding the city. The Lord is about to take possession of His place.

2:4, 5 This young man refers to Zechariah. Here the words may indicate that Zechariah was young when he began his prophetic ministry (Jer. 1:6). **towns without walls:** Jerusalem will have no need for defensive fortifications because God's presence will guarantee its safety and security. These words refer ultimately to the future Jerusalem under the rule of its glorious king (Zeph. 3:15–19). **I will be the glory:** These words drive us to the vision of the new Jerusalem (Rev. 21:1–3, 10, 11, 22, 23).

2:6 Though Babylon was east of Israel, travelers typically followed the Euphrates River and approached Israel from **the north.**

2:7 The name **Zion** may have first applied to the Jebusite stronghold captured by David (2 Sam. 5:7). It was later used for the temple mount (Ps. 78:68, 69) and became a synonym for Jerusalem (Is. 40:9; Mic. 3:12). **Daughter of Babylon** signified the people living in the city of Babylon.

2:8, 9 The word **touches** refers to a touch that produces harm. The **apple of His eye** refers to the pupil. This is an endearing expression, suggesting how enormously important the Hebrew people are to God because of His covenant with them. Just as we protect our eyes from even the smallest particles of dust, so God protects and cares for His people. **Then you will know:** The fulfillment of this prophecy would authenticate Zechariah's commission as God's spokesman (Deut. 18:21, 22).

2:10 daughter of Zion: As elsewhere, we may think of this phrase as a particularly affectionate manner of addressing Jerusalem and its people as the daughter of the Lord (Zeph. 3:14).

2:11 Many nations refer to Gentiles who will enter into a relationship with God and become His people (Gen. 12:3; Joel 2:28; Amos 9:12; Rev. 21:24). The words **My people** are used elsewhere in the context of the renewal of God's covenant with His believing people (Jer. 31:33; 32:38; Hos. 2:23; Ex. 3:7; Deut. 4:20; 14:2; 26:19).

2:12 Surprisingly, the familiar phrase **the Holy Land** occurs in the OT only here. The land is *holy* because of the presence of God among His believing people.

2:13 God had **aroused** Himself from His heavenly sanctuary and was about to intervene on behalf of His people. Hence **be silent** was not an anticipation of worship, but calls for terror at the judgment that was about to be unleashed from God's glory (Zeph. 1:7).

3:1–10 The fourth night vision—the cleansing of Joshua the high priest—depicts how the nation of Israel will be cleansed spiritually by the Messiah's work.

3:1 Zechariah saw a heavenly courtroom where **Joshua,** representing the people of Judah, was standing before the **Angel of the Lord** and was being accused by **Satan.** This is not the Joshua who succeeded Moses, but the high priest who returned to Jerusalem with the exiles (Ezra 3:2). **Satan:** The Hebrew is literally "the Satan," meaning "the Accuser." The picture is not unlike that of Job 1, where Satan stands before the Lord making accusations against people who follow God.

3:2 The Lord rebuke you, Satan: These words presuppose an earlier conversation in which Satan made accusations against the people and their priest. We are reminded that Satan is not sovereign; he is subject to the Sovereign Lord who will handle him. The **brand plucked from the fire** refers to Judah, delivered from the *fire* of Babylonian captivity. Joshua, their priest, represented the nation, a people of God's favor.

3:3 The high priest represented the people before God (Ex. 28:29) and under no circumstances was to become defiled or unclean (Ex. 28:2; Lev. 21:10–15). Joshua's **filthy garments** were literally "befouled with excrement."

3:4, 5 The cleansing of Joshua was not complete with the removal of his sin-soiled garments. God replaced the dirty clothes, dressing Joshua in clean garments that represented the gift of God's righteousness. As sin is removed by the work of Christ, so His righteousness is placed in the believer's account (Rom. 5:18, 19; 2 Cor. 5:21). We are clothed in the garments of Christ's righteousness. The fact that Joshua had no part in his cleansing indicates that this work was totally by God's grace.

3:6–10 These verses give the application of the vision to Israel in three parts: (1) to Israel's restoration to the service of the Lord (vv. 6, 7); (2) to the coming of Messiah (vv. 8, 9); and, (3) to the millennial reign (v. 10).

3:7 Joshua was recommissioned as the nation's high priest. For his faithfulness he was promised the privilege of exercising authority over God's temple—**My house**—and its courts.

3:8 The coming Messiah is depicted as God's **Servant** (Is. 53:11). He is also referred to as **the BRANCH.** Isaiah used this word and a similar one to describe the Messiah who will grow out of the root of the family of Jesse as a tender sprout shoots up from the ground (6:12; Is. 4:2;

11:1; 53:2). Joshua and his companions were a **sign** because the reinstitution of the priesthood made public God's continuing intention to fulfill His promises to His people.

3:9 stone: Like the priest Aaron, who possessed a jeweled ephod (Ex. 25:7; 35:9), so the new priest possessed a lustrous stone, a symbol of the authority of his office. The **eyes** may be symbolic of wisdom and of the endowment of the Holy Spirit (4:10; Is. 11:2).

3:10 Sitting **under** the **vine** and **under** the **fig tree** is an image of peace and tranquillity characteristic of the messianic kingdom (Mic. 4:4).

4:1–14 The fifth night vision concerns the golden lampstand between the two olive trees. The lampstand is designed to show that the rebuilding of the temple will be accomplished not by human ingenuity but by divine power.

4:1 wakened me: It appears that these night visions came in the course of a single night.

4:2, 3 The **lampstand of solid gold** would remind the people of the lampstand in the tabernacle and the temple.

4:4–6 The rebuilding of the temple, which had at last begun in earnest (Ezra 5:1, 2; Hag. 1:14), would be accomplished not by human strength or resources, but by the power of God's **Spirit.**

4:7 The **great mountain** was a figurative reference to the great obstacles the people faced in rebuilding the temple (Ezra 5:3–17). The setting of the **capstone** would mark the completion of the project. The words **Grace, grace to it** may be understood as a prayer for God's favor, or as a cry of admiration over the grace and beauty of the newly built temple.

4:8, 9 His hands: The promise concerning **Zerubbabel** is significant; the task that he began he would also complete.

4:10 the day of small things: There is nothing wrong with a small work. Little can indeed be much if God is in it. **These seven,** a

number used symbolically to represent the idea of completeness, are identified as **the eyes of the Lord** ("eyes" in 3:9). The fact that these eyes will **rejoice** at the plumb line in Zerubbabel's hand suggests the delight of God over the rebuilding of the temple.

4:11–14 The **two olive branches** are identified as **two anointed ones,** representatives of the religious and political offices in Israel, or of priest and king. Many identify the two branches with the high priest Joshua and the governor Zerubbabel.

5:1–4 The sixth night vision of the flying scroll indicates that there will be severe judgment on those who neglect the basic provisions of the Law of God.

5:2 A **scroll** was made of rolled parchment or leather and was the ancient equivalent of a book (Jer. 36:1–8). A **cubit** was about 18 inches.

5:3 The writing on the scroll was a message of judgment. **The curse** refers to the judgments spoken of in the Mosaic covenant (Deut. 30:7). The message on the scroll warned that the curses described in the covenant as a result of the people's disobedience would be executed upon the whole land.

5:4 And consume it: God's great love does not preclude the exercise of His judgment on those who violate His will. The judgment upon the disobedient would be certain and severe.

5:5–11 The seventh night vision concerns a woman in a basket. From this vision the prophet learns that sin and wickedness will be removed from Israel and will center in Israel's nemesis, Babylon.

5:6 The word translated **basket** is literally *ephah,* a unit of dry measure of about half a bushel. The word translated **resemblance** was understood as *iniquity* in some ancient versions.

5:7, 8 The woman sitting inside the basket is **Wickedness,** a personification of sin.

5:9 Next Zechariah saw **two women,** God's agents, disposing of the wicked woman in the

---

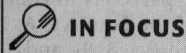 **IN FOCUS** **"angel"**

(Heb. *mal'ak*) (4:1; 2 Sam. 2:5; 24:16; Ps. 34:7; Is. 37:9) Strong's #4397: This noun may refer to angelic beings (4:1, 5; Gen. 19:1; Ps. 91:11), human messengers (Gen. 32:3; Deut. 2:26), or ambassadors (Is. 30:4; Ezek. 17:15). A special use is the manifestation of the Godhead known as the Angel of God in the OT (2:6; Gen. 21:17; Ex. 14:19). In the OT, prophets (Hag. 1:13) and priests (Mal. 2:7) function as messengers from God. In Zechariah, angels bring revelations from God about the future and interpret the meaning of dreams and visions (1:14; 6:4, 5). Jesus identified the messenger who prepared the way for the day of the Lord, forecast in Mal. 3:1, as John the Baptist (Matt. 11:10, 11).

basket. **the wings of a stork:** The stork is a migratory bird frequently seen traveling north along the Jordan valley in the spring of the year.

5:10, 11 Shinar was an ancient name for the district in which the cities of Babylon (Babel), Erech, Accad, and Calneh were located (Gen. 10:10; 11:2). Babylon was the place of Judah's captivity. The fact that a **house** was built for the woman suggests that the removal of wickedness (v. 8) from Israel was permanent.

6:1–8 The eighth night vision depicts four chariots coming from between two bronze mountains. The vision indicates that divine judgment will fall upon the Gentile nations.

6:1 chariots: In ancient times two-wheeled and fourwheeled horse-drawn carts served as vehicles for transportation and for warfare. The war chariots usually had a crew of two or three men including a driver, an archer, and a defender who used a shield to protect the others.

6:2–4 Some commentators have sought to find symbolic significance in the colors of the horses, but this involves unnecessary speculation. As in 1:8–11, the colors of the horses add a sense of intensity to our awareness of what the prophet saw.

6:5 These chariots and their teams represented **four spirits of heaven,** probably angels.

6:6, 7 The **horses** were **eager** to take the four spirits on their mission to bring divine judgment on the peoples of the earth.

6:8 The activity of the chariot teams would give **rest** to God's **Spirit** because His agents would be executing His judgment on the nations that threatened Israel. Cyrus's overthrow of Babylon in 539 B.C. may well have been a part of this judgment (Is. 13:1–22; 45:1–6).

6:9–15 Zechariah's eight night visions are followed by the symbolic crowning of Joshua the high priest. This vision serves as a fitting climax for this section (1:7—6:15).

6:10, 11 The **captives** refer to the new arrivals from Babylon, who brought gifts of silver and gold to help the restored community of Israelites. The **elaborate crown** was possibly a composite crown made up of several circlets. The crown was to be placed on the head of Joshua the high priest.

6:12 The Messiah Himself will **build the temple of the LORD.** Since the restoration temple (the second temple) was already being built and would be completed by Zerubbabel (4:9), the temple referred to here may be the future temple of the messianic kingdom (Is. 2:2–4; Ezek. 40—42; Mic. 4:1–5; Hag. 2:7–9). The temple of Zerubbabel was a prophetic symbol of the temple that is still to come.

6:13 He will **sit and rule** and **be a priest.** In the Messiah the two offices of king and priest will be united (John 1:49; Heb. 3:1).

6:14 The **elaborate crown** is to be kept in the temple as a memorial to those who brought the gifts from Babylon and as a reminder of the future union of Israel's king and priest in the coming Messiah.

6:15 Those from afar include Gentile peoples (8:22; Hag. 2:7–9; Eph. 2:13). Here again we hear the theme of God's purpose for bringing His blessing and His salvation to peoples abroad (2:11); there are those from the most remote nations of the earth who will join the faithful of the covenant community in the true worship of God. God's election of Abraham was designed ultimately to bring His blessing to all families of the nations (Gen. 12:3).

7:1–8:23 This section deals with a matter that was of utmost concern for the Jews living in Babylon—the observance of religious fasts. The issue is considered primarily in 7:1–7 and 8:18, 19. The text leads to insights in the nature of true religion.

7:1 The **fourth year** of Darius was 518 B.C. The **ninth month** or **Chislev** (the Babylonian name) corresponds to November-December.

7:2 The words translated **house of God** may also mean "Bethel," a town twelve miles north of Jerusalem. Over two hundred Jews from Bethel returned from Babylon in 538 B.C.

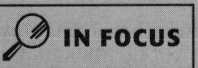 **IN FOCUS**   **"BRANCH"**

(Heb. *tsemach*) (3:8; 6:12; Is. 4:2; Jer. 23:5) Strong's #6780: The Hebrew term translated as BRANCH here means "Shoot" or "Twig." This is one title for the coming Messiah, the "Branch" who would "shoot" up from the royal stock of David, a dynasty that had been interrupted with the Babylonian exile (Is. 11:1). Many of the prophets promised that a King from David's line would reign in righteousness (Jer. 23:5, 6) and as a priest would reestablish true worship of the Lord (6:12, 13). In His ministry, Jesus Christ fulfilled these predictions by taking on both a royal (John 12:13–15; 1 Tim. 6:13–16) and a priestly role (Heb. 4:14).

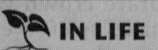 **IN LIFE** | **Fasting for the Upwardly Mobile**

You may think of fasting as something done only by people who have taken vows of poverty, or perhaps by the highly devout. But Zechariah discussed fasting for people who were prospering materially (Zech. 7:5). Largely because their community was in the middle of a building boom, they were moving up the ladder economically. In today's terms they might be called upwardly mobile.

It is interesting that Zechariah challenged these people with fasting in the context of community development and social justice (Zech. 7:6–10). This leads to at least three reasons why fasting can be a valuable practice for people who are recovering economically and moving up in the world:

(1) Fasting can help us remember what it was like to be hungry and to do without.
(2) Fasting can help us focus on the Lord and His spiritual resources that sustained us when we didn't have much.
(3) Fasting can help us open our hearts and identify with the poor and hungry in our world.

(Ezra 2:28; Neh. 7:32), and the city was reoccupied during the restoration period (Neh. 11:31). It seems most likely that the people of Bethel sent a delegation to ask a question about the priests in Jerusalem.

7:3, 4 The **house of the Lord** of hosts refers to the temple in Jerusalem. The **fast in the fifth month** (July-August) commemorated the destruction of the temple in 586 B.C. (2 Kin. 25:8). The delegation from Bethel wanted to know if it was necessary to continue this annual fast as it had been observed during the Babylonian captivity.

7:5, 6 did you really fast for Me—for Me: The rhetorical question was designed to confront the people and priests with the selfish motives of their self-righteous fasting. Biblical fasting is meant to be time taken from the normal routines of preparing and eating food to express humility and dependence on God during a time of prayer. There was only one required fast in the Law of Moses, the fast on the Day of Atonement (Lev. 16:29). The fast during the **seventh** month lamented the slaying of Gedaliah (2 Kin. 25:25). The **seventy years** (1:12; Jer. 25:11; 29:10) refer to the period of time while the people were in exile and the temple lay in ruins. **for yourselves:** Their fasting and their feasting were both motivated by self interest rather than a desire to honor God.

7:7 The **former prophets** were those who ministered before the Exile (1:4; 2 Chr. 36:15, 16). The **South** is the Negev, the dry region of Judah around Beersheba. The **Lowland** is the transitional region between the hill country of Judah and the coastal plain.

7:8–10 Zechariah's four admonitions highlight the practical social concerns that many of the prophets emphasized (Is. 1:11–17; Hos. 6:6;

Mic. 6:6–8). **Execute true justice:** Judicial decisions must be made without partiality or bias. **Show mercy and compassion:** Loving commitment and concern should guide our relationships with others. **Do not oppress:** No advantage is to be taken of the helpless and less fortunate. **Let none of you plan evil:** Evil scheming against others is prohibited. Sacrifices and worship are of little interest to God if they are not accompanied by practical piety.

7:11–14 Zechariah describes the response of the disobedient Judeans living in the land before the Babylonian exile. The consequence was God's judgment—they were **scattered.**

8:1–17 While 7:8–14 looks back to the consequences of past disobedience, this section looks ahead to the future and focuses on the restoration and blessings of Zion.

8:1–3 The Lord again states that He is **zealous** for Jerusalem (1:14; Nah. 1:2). This theme in Zechariah emphasizes the Lord's great passion for His people. He longed to bless them with His presence and in turn desired their worship. **Zion** is the poetic equivalent of **Jerusalem** (2:7). The label **City of Truth** will be valid only when the Messiah brings His righteous reign to that city. Then the land will be holy (2:12).

8:4, 5 Zechariah predicts that in the future messianic era, Jerusalem will be inhabited and secure. The longevity of the citizens and the presence of children at play **in its streets** suggests the city's future prosperity and divine blessing.

8:6 The rhetorical question implies that nothing is too **marvelous** or difficult for God.

8:7, 8 The terms **east** and **west** represent all parts of the earth. The expressions **My people** and **their God** (2:11) occur in the descriptions of God's covenant relationship with His people

(Ex. 19:5; 29:45; Lev. 26:12; Hos. 2:23). With these words, Zechariah anticipates a renewal of God's covenant with His people (Jer. 31:31–34).

8:9 The **foundation** of the second temple was laid in 536 B.C. (Ezra 3:8–13).

8:10 no wages . . . no peace: Zechariah recounts the desperate situation in Judea before the work on the temple resumed in 520 B.C. (Hag. 1:1, 6, 10, 11; 2:16, 17).

8:11–13 In the past, the people had been subject to God's discipline. In view of their recent obedience with regard to rebuilding the temple, they could now anticipate His blessing. **Let your hands be strong:** In view of God's gracious purposes and future plans for His people, they were called to be diligent in their present efforts to serve Him with sincere hearts (1 Cor. 15:58).

8:14, 15 These verses contrast God's past and present dealings with the people of Judah; they are retrospective of the beginning of the prophecy (1:3–6).

8:16, 17 Zechariah set forth the ethical obligations of a life of faith. He upheld the positive values of **truth** and **justice** and condemned evil plans and false oaths. The words **speak each man the truth** are quoted by Paul in Eph. 4:25.

8:18, 19 As a result of God's blessing on his obedient people, the former fasts will become feasts. The **fast of the fourth month** commemorated the breach of Jerusalem's walls (Jer. 39:2). The **fast of the fifth** commemorated the temple destruction (2 Kin. 25:8). The **fast of the seventh** commemorated the slaying of Gedaliah (2 Kin. 25:25), and the **fast of the tenth** commemorated the beginning of Nebuchadnezzar's siege of Jerusalem (2 Kin. 25:1, 2).

8:20–23 Here Zechariah announces a great turning of the nations to God. During the messianic era, a multitude of people from many cities will go to Jerusalem to **seek the Lord**. These Gentiles will be included among the people of God by faith (Eph. 2:13–19).

9:1–14:21 In this section Zechariah sets forth some end-time prophecies concerning Israel and the nations. Some scholars believe that these chapters are not original to the book and are anonymous prophecies dating from a later period. These arguments are based on supposed different style and vocabulary; however, the end-time thrust of this section may well account for these differences. No Hebrew manuscript of the book has ever discovered with this section of Zechariah missing from it.

9:1–8 The critical debate in this passage is in regard to the historical fulfillment of the prophecy. Many commentators identify this section with the campaign of Alexander the Great through Palestine (332–331 B.C.). Others have argued for a military campaign during the time of Josiah, Tiglath-Pileser III, Sargon, or the Maccabees. No one historical setting really answers exactly to the situation described in these verses. More recently it has been suggested that this section is set in the literary form of a "Divine Warrior Hymn," a poem which describes a warrior-god's battle and establishment of peace. According to this view, no specific historical situation lies at the background of the poem. Rather, Zechariah is poetically anticipating God's intervention among the nations with a view to the establishment of the blessing He has promised Israel. The use of place names does not record an actual battle march, but is suggestive of the lines a battle march might take.

9:1 The word **burden** suggests that a weighty judgment must be declared. **Hadrach** was north of Hamath on the Orontes River, southwest of Aleppo. **Damascus,** 60 miles northeast of the Sea of Galilee, was the capital of Aram (ancient Syria).

9:2 Hamath is mentioned in several places as the northern limit of the promised land (Num. 13:21; Josh. 13:5). **Tyre and Sidon** are port cities located north of Israel on the Phoenician coast.

9:3, 4 The complete overthrow of **Tyre** by Alexander the Great in 332 B.C. illustrates how even such a powerful city can come under God's judgment.

9:5, 6 Ashkelon, Gaza, Ekron, and Ashdod were Philistine cities located on Israel's coastal plain south of Joppa (1 Sam. 6:17). The city of Gath completed the "five principal cities" of the Philistines. Zechariah prophesied that the worst fears of the Philistines would be realized as the judgment of the Lord swept through their land**.**

9:7 The removal of **blood from his mouth** and **abominations** refer to the cessation of unlawful and idolatrous practices (Lev. 17:14; Is. 65:4; 66:17). **Ekron like a Jebusite:** The Jebusites were the old inhabitants of Jebus, the stronghold that became Jerusalem (2 Sam. 5:6, 7).

9:8 God will return as a victorious Warrior to the temple—**My house**—where He will set up a guard against any who would dare tramp through Judah's territory.

9:9, 10 The first coming of the Messiah is set against the background of God's victory march (vv. 1–8).

9:9 This prophecy was fulfilled on the day of the Triumphal Entry, when Jesus rode into Jerusalem on the colt of a donkey (Matt. 21:2–7; John 12:12–15). The **donkey** was the mount of princes (Judg. 5:10; 10:4; 12:14) and kings (2 Sam. 16:1, 2).

9:10 Instruments of warfare—**the chariot** and the **battle bow**—will be destroyed and universal peace will be established. **Ephraim** refers to the northern tribes of Israel. **The River** refers to the Euphrates, the northeast boundary of the promised land (Gen. 15:18).

9:11, 12 The release of **prisoners** announced here would serve as a great encouragement for the Jewish people still in exile. Though the prisoners were living in a well-watered place in Persia (Ezek. 1:1), they were in a place akin to a **waterless pit** in terms of their opportunity for spiritual nourishment. They were exhorted to **return to the stronghold** Jerusalem.

9:13 Zechariah used a bold metaphor likening Judah and Ephraim to a **bow** and arrow prepared by the Lord to be used against **Greece,** literally Javan (Is. 66:19).

9:14 whirlwinds: This description, patterned after God's appearance at Sinai (Ex. 19), reveals God's sovereignty and power to protect His own.

9:15 Zechariah describes the victory banquet of God's people in celebration of His victory over the nations and securing of Jerusalem. The people will **be filled** with drink like sacrificial basins were filled with blood, and they will be filled with meat like the corners of a sacrificial altar (Ps. 110).

9:16 As a shepherd cares for his flock, so God will save and care for His people. And the people whom He saves will be lustrous as jewels, like a banner over His land. Here we sense God's joy in the salvation He provides for His people.

9:17 The abundance of **grain** and **new wine** suggests the prosperity and blessing of this future day (3:10; 8:4, 5; Amos 9:13).

10:1–12 Here Zechariah describes how the Lord will restore His people to their land. The unifying theme of this section is the restoration of the Jewish people by divine power.

10:1 The **latter rain** (Deut. 11:14) refers to the rain that comes in late spring and is essential for an abundant grain harvest.

10:2 Idols refers to household gods (Gen. 31:19). **Diviners,** like Balaam, interpreted omens as a means of foretelling the future (Josh. 13:22; 1 Sam. 6:2). **no shepherd:** The metaphor of *shepherd* was often used in the ancient Middle East to represent a king or ruler (Ezek. 34:6–8, 23, 24). Here the emphasis was on the lack of spiritual leadership.

⚒ IN DEPTH │ The Coming King

Luke tells us that after Jesus ascended to heaven, the disciples returned to Jerusalem (Luke 24:52). They also went back to the Scriptures. The OT suddenly blossomed with good news. Everywhere they looked they found evidence that pointed toward the specifics of Jesus' life and ministry. When they wondered why they had missed the connections before, they must have also remembered Jesus' promise, "When He, the Spirit of truth, has come, He will guide you into all truth" (John 16:13).

When the Gospel writers recorded the details of Jesus' life, they often used references from the OT to illustrate how clearly Jesus fulfilled the character of the promised Savior and the prophecies regarding His ministry. They particularly enjoyed quoting OT passages that clearly predicted the suffering and rejection aspects of the Messiah's role. For them, it was the central theme that set Jesus apart from the popular ideas of a conquering and powerful political messiah.

Zechariah 9:9, 10 presents a prophecy whose fulfillment was clearly set in motion (though not completed) by Jesus' arrival in Jerusalem on a colt, the well-known Triumphal Entry. Both Matthew and John mention this passage. John even notes that the disciples saw no immediate connection between Jesus riding on the colt and His identity as the Messiah prophesied in Zechariah. After Jesus was glorified, "then they remembered that these things were written about Him" (John 12:16).

These verses in Zechariah include an important transition. The arrival of the saving King is followed immediately by a description of the effects of his long-term reign. This is an example of "prophetic compression." Viewed from the broader context of prophecy, Zechariah was mentioning together two stages in God's plan which are actually separated in time. The coming King would arrive twice. Jesus came first as a humble King of peace and salvation, accomplished in Jesus' earthly ministry and His death on the Cross. Second, Jesus will come as a victorious Ruler over all the world who will "speak peace to the nations." We should rejoice over Jesus' first coming and anticipate the complete fulfillment of Zechariah's prophecy at Christ's glorious return.

10:3 While Israel lacked national leadership, there were plenty of tyrants seeking to rule God's people. These **goatherds** will be judged. By way of contrast, God will strengthen **the house of Judah** as an instrument to overthrow these oppressors.

10:4, 5 The poetic metaphors in these verses reflect the strength, stability, and victory that God will impart to His people (vv. 3, 6). **Cornerstone** is an image of steadfast strength or stability, coupled with beauty and honor (Is. 28:16; Ps. 118:22). **tent peg:** A peg firmly in place suggests permanence and endurance (Is. 22:23). **battle bow:** This image pictures the strength necessary for military conquest (2 Kin. 13:17).

10:5 Some commentators have interpreted this verse with reference to the Maccabean victory over the Syrians, but the context is more general and eschatological. Nothing in the verse demands a report from a Maccabean battle; the verse may speak prophetically of a class of victories like those of the Maccabees.

10:6 The **house of Judah** indicates Israel's southern territory. The **house of Joseph** is Israel's northern territory, dominated by Ephraim (v. 7) and Manasseh, tribes named after Joseph's sons (Gen. 41:51, 52). The promise **I will bring them back** is a promise of restoration. The dispersed remnant of Israel would return to the promised land (Matt. 24:31).

10:7 What was promised to Judah in v. 5 is here promised to **Ephraim. as if with wine:** Wine is used here as a symbol of abundant joy (Ps. 104:15; Amos 9:13; John 2:1–11).

10:8–12 Zechariah develops God's promise to regather His scattered people from worldwide dispersion (Matt. 24:15–20). Some commentators suggest that these verses detail the future regathering of only the Northern Kingdom, represented by the tribe of Ephraim (10:7). The text, however, does not appear to limited the promise to Ephraim. Indeed, God will bring both "Judah" and "Joseph" (the southern and northern tribes) back to the land (10:6).

10:8 As a shepherd signals his sheep, so the Lord will **whistle** for His people to return to the land. **For I will redeem them:** God will deliver them from sin (3:4, 9) and from the bondage of captivity (Matt. 24:31).

10:9 Being sown **among the peoples** was God's punishment of the exiles for their disobedience (Deut. 28:63, 64). The words **they shall remember Me** anticipate their turning to the Lord in repentance. **Shall live** implies more than mere survival. God promises spiritual life and blessing to the repentant.

10:10 Assyria is the region of northern Mesopotamia. **Egypt** and **Assyria** had been lands where Israel was captive. **Gilead** is the territory east of the Jordan and southeast of the Sea of Galilee. **Lebanon** is the region north of Galilee. The future restoration will be so complete that the land will be filled with people.

10:11 God would remove any impediment to Israel's return. Zechariah used imagery from the Exodus—**the sea, the River**—to illustrate the kinds of obstacles God would overcome (Ex. 14:21–31; Josh. 3:14–17).

10:12 I will strengthen them: The regathering will be accomplished by God's power as He gives strength to His people. **they shall walk . . . in His name:** In the last days, Israel will return to the land as a believing nation (v. 8; 12:10—13:1; Rom. 11:26).

11:1–17 Zechariah records prophetically the rejection of the Good Shepherd and the acceptance of a worthless shepherd who brings ruin.

11:1–3 These verses introduce ch. 11, setting forth in vivid, poetic terms the devastation of the land of Israel due to Israel's rejection of the Messiah, the Good Shepherd (11:4–14; Matt. 23:37–39). The judgment anticipated here

---

🌱 IN LIFE   **Fortune-Telling: A Dangerous Delusion**

There were apparently droughts in Judah after the exile (Zech. 10:1), and some of the people were turning to diviners and false gods for help rather than the Lord (10:2). This was utterly foolish in light of the fact that Judah's exile had been a judgment for exactly these kinds of practices (compare Jer. 14:1–10).

The Lord condemns all forms of divining, fortune-telling, and sorcery (Deut. 18:9–14). Practices such as rain dances, consulting the stars, seances, and casting charms and spells, and the use of items such as divining rods, tarot cards, Ouija boards, and crystals are far from innocent. These arts and objects engage demons that are in opposition to the one true God. Their leader is a liar (John 8:44), and his strategy is to deceive people (2 Cor. 11:3, 4). The way of true wisdom is to be found in a relationship with God, not through dabbling in the occult.

was probably fulfilled in the destruction of Jerusalem by the Romans (A.D. 70).

11:1 Lebanon was known for its beautiful and fragrant cedars, trees used by Solomon in building his palace and the temple.

11:2, 3 The **cypress,** or juniper, will **wail** for the cedars of Lebanon. The **shepherds** will wail because the grazing lands will be ruined. The **lions** will roar because of the destruction of the **pride of the Jordan,** the jungle thicket that was their shelter.

11:4–14 These verses are regarded as among the most enigmatic in the Hebrew Scriptures. The passage describes a shepherd who cares for a flock doomed to be slaughtered. The flock represents Israel, and the shepherd represents a divinely appointed leader who was rejected by His people. The rejection results in severe judgment.

11:4 Zechariah was commanded to **feed** or pasture the **flock** of God's people Israel, knowing it was destined **for slaughter.**

11:5 God's people Israel were suffering under the oppression of leaders who were only interested in self-enrichment (Ezek. 34:1–10).

11:6 The petty tyrants and oppressors (v. 5) will fall victim to foreign kings who **attack the land.**

11:7 In obedience to God's command (v. 4), Zechariah pastured the flock doomed for slaughter. As shepherds carried implements to guide and protect the sheep (Ps. 23:4), so Zechariah had **two staffs.** Their names **Beauty** and **Bonds** suggest that he wanted the flock to enjoy God's favor and to experience national unity. According to Canaanite legend, the god Baal was given the two clubs named Driver and Chaser to battle the dark deities of the sea. It is appropriate that God's messenger Zechariah is given shepherd's staffs to guide the people, instead of clubs for fighting.

11:8 three shepherds: Some have suggested that the three shepherds represent classes of rulers in Israel: kings, priests, and prophets. Others suggest that they refer the last three kings of Judah or to certain high priests of the Maccabean era.

11:9 Let what is dying die: The judgment which God has decreed should be accepted, not resisted. **eat each other's flesh:** Cannibalism was one of the horrors of famine that resulted from siege warfare (Deut. 28:54–57; Lam. 4:10).

11:10 The breaking of the staff **Beauty** symbolizes the end of God's protection of His people. **break the covenant:** God's unconditional promise to Abraham (Gen. 12:1–3) or to David (2 Sam. 7:12–16) would never be broken. Like Ezekiel's covenant of peace (Ezek. 34:25), the *covenant* here may refer to an agreement with the Gentile nation on Israel's behalf.

11:11 Those who witnessed Zechariah's symbolic breaking of his staff (11:10) immediately realized that it had prophetic significance. They knew it was from the Lord.

11:12 Zechariah, taking the role of the messianic shepherd, requested his wages for service rendered. His wage was calculated as **thirty pieces of silver,** the price of a slave (Ex. 21:32). This was the price paid to Judas for betraying Jesus (Matt. 27:6–10).

11:13 The command **throw it to the potter** is further illuminated by Zechariah's action. He **threw them into the house of the Lord** for the potter. Potters may have been connected with the temple because of the continual need for sacred vessels (Lev. 6:28).

11:14 The rejection of the messianic Shepherd, represented by Zechariah, meant that the national unity the Israelites hoped for would not be achieved at this time. But one day the two nations **Judah and Israel** will be united (Ezek. 37:16–28).

11:15–17 The rejection of the good shepherd will result in a leadership vacuum that will be filled by a wicked shepherd who will actually destroy the flock.

11:15, 16 To take the **implements of a foolish shepherd** means to behave like one. **Eat the flesh** and **tear their hooves** expresses the savagery of a foolish shepherd.

11:17 The **worthless shepherd** will be judged. His **arm,** which should have been used to protect the sheep, will wither. **His right eye,** which should have watched over the sheep, will be blinded.

12:1–9 Zechariah looks to the future day of Israel's deliverance from her enemies, when the unbelieving Gentile nations are destroyed. The prophet is suggesting that the final establishment of God's kingdom will be preceded by a concerted, but unsuccessful, opposition to the people of God.

12:1 As in 9:1, the **burden** is a weighty judgment that the prophet must discharge. Three phrases are used here in describing the greatness of God as Creator of the **heavens,** the **earth,** and **the spirit of man.**

12:2 Jerusalem is depicted as a **cup** of wine or strong drink that causes **drunkenness.** The *cup* is a common metaphor for God's wrath (Is. 51:17; Jer. 25:15; Ezek. 23:33; Rev. 14:10; 16:19). **Siege** warfare involved encircling a city to prevent the inhabitants from fleeing and to cut off all supplies of food and water.

12:3 Jerusalem is compared to a **heavy stone** that brings injury to anyone who tries to remove it from its place.

12:4 God will confound both the horses and horsemen of the besieging army. The threefold judgment of confusion, madness, and blindness appear in the curses of the covenant (Deut. 28:28).

12:5 The **governors** or leaders of Judah would affirm God's power to deliver through His people. The people's **strength** would be **in the Lord** (Phil. 4:13).

12:6 Judah is compared to (1) a **firepan** used to carry hot coals for the purpose of starting a fire, and (2) a **fiery torch** that could quickly ignite a field of cut grain.

12:7 Tents of Judah alludes to Jews living outside Jerusalem in the rural districts of the land. The **house of David** means David's descendants.

12:8 With bold analogy, Zechariah compares David's descendants to God. The **Angel of the Lord** is clearly a divine being (Ex. 23:20; Num. 22:22; Judg. 2:1; 13:15–22).

12:9 All the nations that have attacked Jerusalem (v. 2) will be judged and destroyed (Matt. 25:31–46).

12:10–13:6 Zechariah goes on to describe the further deliverance of His people in terms of repentance and spiritual renewal. The events described here have their eschatological setting at the time of the Messiah's Second Advent.

12:10 pour: This metaphor is derived from the deluge of winter rains and speaks about abundant provision (Job 36:28; Is. 44:3; Lam. 2:19). **Spirit of grace** refers to the gracious working of the Holy Spirit that leads to conviction and repentance (John 16:8–11). **supplication:** The Spirit will stimulate an attitude of repentance and prayer for God's mercy. There are many significant ministries of the Holy Spirit in the period of the Hebrew kingdom. **Me whom they pierced:** Jewish commentators often regard this as a corporate reference to the Jews killed in the defense of Jerusalem (12:1–9). The Jewish Talmud views the text as referring to the Messiah, who will be *pierced* in battle. The messianic view is favored by the fact that Jesus was pierced with a spear after His death on the Cross (John 19:34).

12:11 Hadad Rimmon may have been the site of some tragedy whose grief was still vividly remembered. Or the place may have been associated with religious rites involving mourning.

12:12–14 All of Israel will mourn for the Messiah, including members of the royal family and the priests, **the house of David** and **the house of Levi. wives by themselves:** These words are quoted in the Talmud as an argument

for separating men and women in worship. But the verse seems to indicate that each mourner will face his or her sorrow alone, without the comfort of companionship. **Shimei** was Levi's grandson (Num. 3:18, 21).

13:1 The **fountain** is an image of abundant, overflowing provision. Christ at the Cross made available cleansing from the impurity of sin. At the time of Christ's second coming, the repentant and believing remnant of Israel will appropriate that provision and enter into the benefits of the New Covenant (Jer. 31:31–34; Ezek. 36:25–28). Paul anticipated this great day in Rom. 11:26.

13:2–6 Zechariah announces that there will be a day when God will purge false prophets from the land, along with idolatry and demonic influence.

13:2 cut off the names of the idols: In ancient times, a person's name reflected his or her reputation. Zechariah anticipated the complete removal of the reputation and acknowledgment of false gods.

13:3 According to the Law of Moses (Deut. 13:5; 18:20), a false prophet must be put to death. The startling thing here is that the false prophet's parents must confront the offender and carry out the penalty.

13:4–6 These verses reflect the shame and embarrassment of those who have been involved with false prophecy. They will shun every link with their past.

13:4 False prophets will deny that they are prophets for fear of punishment and will refuse to wear **a robe of coarse hair,** the traditional prophet's clothing (2 Kin. 1:8; Matt. 3:4).

13:5 Instead of laying claim to prophetic office, they will say they have been farmers from their **youth.** This seems to be a parody of Amos 7:14.

13:6 It is likely that the **wounds** betrayed the profession of an ecstatic prophet who slashed himself on the back or breast. The words **between your arms** refer to the body, either the back or the chest. Self-inflicted wounds were thought to gain the attention and blessing of the gods (1 Kin. 18:28). Under questioning, the man declares that the wounds were received from **friends** so that he will not be found out as a false prophet and be put to death (v. 3).

13:7–9 Zechariah resumes the shepherd motif (11:4–14) and returns to the theme of the Messiah's rejection.

13:7 The **sword,** an instrument of death, is

Zechariah concludes his great prophecy with a description of the worship that will take place in the Messiah's kingdom.

likened to a warrior being roused for action. The Lord commands the sword to strike the Messiah, **My Shepherd.** This clearly indicates that the death of Jesus was no accident, but was divinely determined. **My Companion:** This term is used elsewhere of one who is a near neighbor or close companion (Lev. 6:2; 18:20; 19:15). It suggests a relationship of equality. The **little ones** may be first-century disciples, unbelieving Jews of all ages, or a faithful remnant of the future. Since Jewish people have suffered throughout history (the Crusades, the Spanish Inquisition, the Nazi Holocaust), this passage may be taken as a general prophecy of persecution and suffering for the shepherdless people of Israel.

13:8 Zechariah revealed the devastating result of God's dealing with His errant flock. The scattered flock will face a great judgment in which only **one-third** will survive.

(Lev. 26:12) and speak here about a covenant renewal to a spiritually revitalized Israel (Ezek. 36:28; Hos. 2:23; Rom. 11:26, 27).

14:1–5 Zechariah describes events associated with the second coming of Jesus the Messiah at the end of the campaign of Armageddon (Rev. 16:16).

14:1 Some have suggested that this **spoil** refers to what is seized from Israel's enemies, apparently anticipating the victory mentioned in v. 14. The immediate context, however, indicates that the *spoil* was taken from Jerusalem by her enemies (v. 2).

14:2 The **remnant of the people** who survive the attack are evidently the one-third that will be brought through the refiner's fire (13:8, 9).

14:3 The Lᴏʀᴅ will turn Jerusalem's defeat into a victory. God the Warrior (Ex. 15:3) will

Photo by Howard Vos

The Spinx and the Great Pyramid of Egypt. The prophet Zechariah predicted that Egypt and other pagan nations would be punished and disciplined by the Lord (Zech. 14:16–19).

13:9 The remnant that survives will be purged, purified, and reestablished in a covenant relationship with God. **refined:** The smelting pot uses intense heat to separate the dross from pure metal. **tested:** Once refined, precious metal must be analyzed to determine its value. The expressions **this is My people** and **the Lᴏʀᴅ is my God** recall the covenant

intervene on Israel's behalf against the attacking nations.

14:4 Zechariah provides further details about how Jerusalem's deliverance will come about. The **Mount of Olives,** located east of Jerusalem and the Kidron Valley, is a north-south hill about 2,700 feet in elevation. The Messiah will return to the Mount of Olives, the same mountain from which He will have ascended after His time on earth (Acts 1:10, 11). On the day of Messiah's return, the mount will be split by a deep east-west valley.

14:5 The splitting of the Mount of Olives will provide a way of escape for the besieged and defeated people in Jerusalem. The site of **Azal** has not been identified but must be somewhere in the desert east of Jerusalem. The flight of the surviving remnant from Jerusalem is likened to what took place following the **earthquake in the days of Uzziah.** The **saints** are literally the "holy ones," angels who will accompany Jesus at His return (Mark 8:38; 2 Thess. 1:7).

14:6, 7 Cosmic upheaval is associated with the second coming. The glory of the Messiah's kingdom is preceded by dark days of judgment. **there will be no light:** The imagery of darkness as a portent of judgment is common in the prophets (Is. 5:30; 8:22; 13:9, 10; Ezek. 32:7, 8; Amos 5:18, 20; Zeph. 1:14, 15).

14:8–11 Zechariah describes the culmination of the great prophetic promise of a kingdom in which Israel's Messiah will rule on David's throne (2 Sam. 7:12–16; Lk. 1:31–33).

14:8 The term **living waters** describes running water from a spring or river, in contrast to the stale and stagnant water of a cistern (Jer. 2:13). The water will flow from Jerusalem toward the **eastern sea** (the Dead Sea) and the **western sea** (the Mediterranean). In contrast with the seasonal streams that flow only during the rainy season, these streams will irrigate the land **both summer and winter.**

14:9 Zechariah anticipates the glorious day when the LORD will reestablish His reign on this earth, where it was first challenged by Satan (Rev. 20:1–3; also Pss. 93:1; 97:1; 99:1). This will be the answer to the prayers of all those who pray Jesus' words, "Your kingdom come" (Matt. 6:10). The words **the LORD is one** speak about His unity and His uniqueness (Deut. 6:4).

14:10 Geba was 6 miles northeast of Jerusalem. **Rimmon** was about 35 miles southwest of Jerusalem. **Benjamin's Gate** was most likely the gate in the north wall of the city. The **First Gate** as not yet been identified. The **Corner Gate** probably marked the northwest limit of Jerusalem. The **Tower of Hananel** was probably a defensive fortification on the north wall.

14:11 people shall dwell in it: This is a contrast to the time of Nehemiah when the population of Jerusalem was sparse (Neh. 7:4; 11:1). In the Lord's coming kingdom, the city will be inhabited and its citizens secure.

14:12–15 These verses elucidate 12:4–9 and 14:3, providing further details about how God will fight against and destroy those nations attacking Jerusalem.

14:12, 13 plague: This word was used to describe the judgments of God upon the Egyptians (Ex. 7:17—12:30).

14:14, 15 As the attackers are destroyed, the people of **Judah** will join the citizens of **Jerusalem** in recovering the spoil taken by the enemy (v. 1) and capturing additional booty (Hag. 2:7, 8).

14:16–21 Zechariah concludes his great prophecy with a description of the worship that will take place in the Messiah's kingdom.

14:16 Repentant and believing people among those nations that had attacked Jerusalem (vv. 1, 2) will **worship the King** (Jesus, the Messiah) and celebrate **the Feast of Tabernacles,** a fall harvest festival that commemorated the wilderness experience of Israel (Lev. 23:33–43). This feast of thanksgiving is the only one of the many feasts that will still be appropriate in the new kingdom— the others will have been fulfilled, but thanksgiving will be a continual theme in Messiah's kingdom.

14:17–19 The nations that are unwilling to come to Jerusalem to worship King Messiah and celebrate the feast will be subject to divine judgment. **Egypt** is used as an example, since it was a traditional enemy of Israel.

14:20, 21 In Messiah's kingdom, the people of Judah and Jerusalem will fulfill their destiny as a holy, priestly nation (Ex. 19:6). The words **HOLINESS TO THE LORD** will be inscribed on the gold headband worn by the high priest (Ex. 28:36). Holiness will so permeate Messiah's kingdom that even the lowly cooking pots will be holy. The name **Canaanite** here refers to the merchants who frequented Jerusalem and the temple courts with their wares (Neh. 13:19–22; Matt. 21:12; John 2:14). None will profiteer in the worship of God in the coming age. God's search for true worshipers will be realized in a company of devoted, holy people.

The Book of

Malachi

∎

THE BOOK OF MALACHI IS ABOUT THE ERROR of forgetting the love of God. When people forget God's love, it affects their attitudes, home, and worship. With God's love and loyalty in doubt, sacred commitments no longer remain sacred. God sent Malachi to rouse the people from their spiritual stupor and to exhort them to return to the living God. But the Book of Malachi reveals a people who question the

reality of their sin and the faithfulness of God, a people hardened through and through. Thus the book ends on a poignant note, a confrontation between a disappointed God and a disappointed people.

In a sense, the Book of Malachi shows that the Old Testament comes to a chasm, with the bickering voices of the people on one side and the stern warnings of God on the other. Only the Lord Himself could provide a way out of this impasse. Malachi looks forward to this deliverance, for he speaks about the one who would prepare the way for the Messiah. The promised Messiah was the only One who could bridge that widening chasm between the people and their God.

Wide agreement exists that the Book of Malachi was written during the last half of the fifth century B.C. Some even pinpoint the date between 420 and 415 B.C. This would place the Book of Malachi about one hundred years after the ministries of Haggai and Zechariah. There are numerous ties in the book to the concerns of Nehemiah, who was governor in Judah around 440 B.C. These include marriages with foreign women (Neh. 13:23–27), not paying tithes

(Neh. 13:10–14), neglecting the Sabbath (Neh. 13:15–22), a corrupt priesthood (Neh. 13:7–9), and injustice (Neh. 5:1–13).

After the great turmoil of the wars of the Assyrians, Babylonians, and the Medes and Persians, a period of comparative peace came to Israel's part of the ancient world. The books of the preexilic prophets were formed in the flaming crucible of international wars and catastrophes. But under Persian rule the people were allowed to return to the land in peace. The constant threat of international conflict did not loom over their heads. The Persians collected taxes, but otherwise they were content to leave the Jews alone. Yet economic shortages were still common during this period.

The history of the Jewish people is a story of a recurring pattern of captivity, exodus, and restoration into which Malachi also falls. There are two captivities in the Old Testament story, and two accounts of an exodus of the Jewish people from captivity. The first captivity and the great Exodus is Israel's experience with Egypt at the beginning of Israel's history; the second is Israel's experience with Babylon.

In the account of the first Exodus, Moses and

Aaron occupy themselves to a significant degree with the issue of the proper worship of the living God, which was centered in the tabernacle. A significant portion of the Book of Exodus, the whole of Leviticus, and parts of Numbers and Deuteronomy provide guidance for worship at the tabernacle. The point of the Exodus was the creation of the people of God as a worshiping community (Ex. 5:1).

Similarly, two of the books of the second exodus, the return of God's people from Babylon, concern themselves with the proper worship of God. These two books, Haggai and Malachi, focus on worship centered on the rebuilt temple. Haggai exhorted the people to rebuild the temple in Jerusalem in 520 B.C. Thus this book parallels the Book of Exodus in which God gave instructions for the construction of the tabernacle. Similarly, Malachi parallels the Book of Leviticus in that both are concerned with how the people and the priests should act in the temple. Yet there are significant differences. Leviticus emphasizes what the people should do, what offerings they should bring, and what calendar they should keep in their worship of God. Malachi's emphasis is on the attitude of those who bring their worship to God. In Leviticus one reads about *how* to worship God; in Malachi the focus is on the *heart* of those who worship.

The priests of Malachi's time were indifferent to the rules of worship (1:6–14), and the people themselves had become apathetic about their offerings to God (3:6–12). Where did this neglectful attitude come from? In a critical introductory verse, God said to the people, "I have loved you." The response of the people was, "In what way have You loved us?" (1:2). The people's suspicion about the motives of God toward them resulted in their halfhearted response to Him. Their apathy toward God was also reflected in their relations with other people—especially their spouses. It had become common at this time for men to divorce their wives. Such men ignored the fact that the Lord was a witness to their marriages, and as a result God ignored their offerings. The prophecy of Malachi is God's response to this "loveless" condition.

Nothing is known of the prophet Malachi apart from this book. We are not even sure that Malachi was the name of the prophet. The word means "My Messenger," and it is possible that the first verse should be translated, "The burden of the word of the LORD to Israel by My Messenger." In any case, Malachi's name identifying him as a messenger of God highlights one of the major themes of the book. Malachi prophesies that God would send a "messenger," a prophecy of John the Baptist, and "the Messenger of the covenant," a prophecy of Jesus (3:1).

In 2:7 the role of a priest is described as "messenger of the LORD of hosts." Based on that description, a priest-prophet in the temple might have used the designation "My Messenger" for himself. Because of the writer's apparent concern with the priesthood, it may be argued that the author of the book was a priest to whom God also gave a prophetic message.

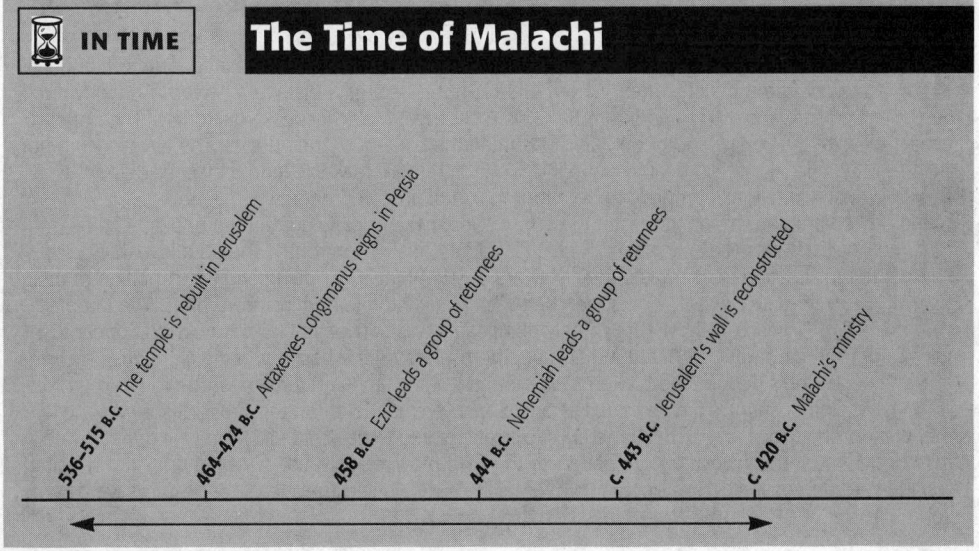

IN TIME — **The Time of Malachi**

536–515 B.C. The temple is rebuilt in Jerusalem

464–424 B.C. Artaxerxes Longimanus reigns in Persia

458 B.C. Ezra leads a group of returnees

444 B.C. Nehemiah leads a group of returnees

c. 443 B.C. Jerusalem's wall is reconstructed

c. 420 B.C. Malachi's ministry

Outline

Commentary

1:1 As in the case of Nahum (Nah. 1:1), the prophetic message of Malachi was like a **burden** from which he needed deliverance (Is. 13:1; Jer. 23:33–38; Hab. 1:1). **to Israel:** In the postexilic period, the use of the word Israel for the people of Judah expresses the hope that the Lord was in the process of reasserting the fullness of His original promises to His people. The name **Malachi** means "My Messenger."

1:2–5 A dispute over the love of God. Sadly, the Book of Malachi concerns a series of disputes between the Lord and His people. This section forms the first of six such disputes.

1:2 I have loved you: God is like a loving parent who speaks with fatherly affection. However, His chosen people were like rebellious children who challenged His words of love for them.

1:3 But Esau I have hated: The contrast between the words *love* and *hate* here and in v. 2 seems much too strong. But on many occasions in the OT, the verb *hate* has the basic meaning "not to choose." God's love for Jacob was expressed in His electing grace in extending His covenant to Jacob and to his descendants (Gen. 25:21–26; Is. 44:1–5). In His sovereign purpose, God set His love on the one and not the other. The term *hate* may carry the idea of indifference as well.

1:4, 5 Edom has said . . . we will return: Edom was a nation descended from Esau, and they shared Esau's unbelief and self-confidence. Destruction made Israel reexamine her relationship to God. But destruction for Edom resulted only in continued pride and self-effort. **LORD** of hosts: This expression describes God as the supreme commander of the universe. The *hosts* are His heavenly armies.

1:6 A son honors his father: Here the Lord uses truisms: A father and a master can expect honor from those beneath them, but God was not receiving the honor due Him. **I am the Father:** The image of God as Father is common in the NT but less frequent in the OT (Is. 63:16; 64:8). **who despise My name:** In ancient Israel, a name was a symbol of a person's character, works, and reputation. Therefore, this charge was

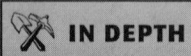 **IN DEPTH** | ## Blemished Sacrifices

Why should the condition of a sacrifice matter to God? He created all things, defective animals as well as the healthy ones. Why would He not accept gifts that were flawed? And why did God care about this enough to have his messenger Malachi speak so strongly? The imperfect sacrifices of the priests and people demonstrated the content of their hearts. The people were not sincere. To sacrifice a perfect, healthy animal looked to them like a waste, and they considered the work of preparing their gifts properly to be a foolish use of time and energy.

Malachi confronted this attitude with the Law of God, which clearly demanded unblemished sacrifices and sincere hearts (Lev. 1:3; 3:1; Deut. 17:1). Malachi also confronted the people with God's judgment of their actions. God was perfectly aware of what they were doing and the condition of their hearts. No sacrifices at all would have been better than second-rate and insincere ones. The people were not giving "sacrifices"; they were merely doing what was convenient, just enough to appear to obey God. Then they would turn around and pat themselves on the back for being righteous.

But though God's people had broken their covenant with Him, God remained true to His promises (Is. 53). He did not shrink from sending His only Son to a cruel death on the Cross. Jesus was the true, unblemished sacrifice to which the OT sacrifices pointed (Heb. 7:26–28). He was perfect—free from all sin. And through Jesus' sacrificial death the Lord provided salvation for all of our sins. In doing this, the Lord demonstrated His sincere love for us because He sacrificed the very best to save us (John 3:16).

most serious. But the people dare to ask: **In what way have we despised Your name?**

1:7 God's answer to the question posed in v. 6 was in terms of **defiled food.** The word *defiled* describes bread that was not prepared properly. The bread (Ex. 25:23–30) and the **table** on which it was displayed were holy symbols, but the priests were treating them like ordinary things.

1:8 the blind . . . lame and sick: The demands of holy worship of God had been made clear in the Law. Only the best should be presented as an offering to the Lord (Lev. 1:3); no one was to come with an offering that was blemished or unclean (Lev. 7:19–21).

1:9 The mercy of the Lord is seen in this verse. Despite their indifferent attitudes toward His commands, God still offered grace to His willful servants. Yet, clearly, there must be a change in both their attitude and actions. This is reminiscent of the mercy God extended to Cain when his worship was also inappropriate (Gen. 4:6, 7).

1:10 shut the doors: In a choice between service without gratitude and no service at all, God chose the second. **pleasure:** The word

---

 **IN COMPARISON** | **Malachi: A Portrait of Spiritual Indifference**

When the prophet Malachi began preaching to the Israelites, he found that the people had cold hearts. They were indifferent and apathetic. When he confronted them with their sin, they asked a series of questions that reveal volumes about their spiritual condition.

Question	Significance	Application
"In what way have You loved us?" (1:2)	This question reveals an alarming lack of trust in God. The Israelites were implying that God had been unfaithful to His covenant. "If You really love us, why are we still under foreign oppressors, waiting for the promised kingdom?"	Do we demand proof of God's love for us?
"In what way have we despised Your name?" (1:6); "In what way have we defiled You?" (1:7)	This question shows the halfheartedness and the rationalizations of the nation's religious leaders. They were saying, in effect: "We've been making the required sacrifices. What more do you want?" But as Malachi pointed out, the sacrifices offered to God were unfit animals (1:8–10).	Do we offer God our best in worship, or do we just go through the motions?
"In what way shall we return?" (3:7)	This question reveals an appalling blindness to sin and an arrogant attempt to floss over wrongdoing. "We don't know what You want us to do, because we don't see what we have done wrong."	When faced with our sin, do we make excuses?
"In what way have we robbed You?" (3:8)	This question underscores the people's greed. They did not view their possessions as God's possessions to be used for His glory.	Do we gladly give to God?
"What have we spoken against You?" (3:13)	This question displays the Israelites' callousness. They had said it was "useless to serve God" (3:14). But they continued to think that their external observance of religious ceremonies would satisfy God's demands on their lives.	Do we wholeheartedly serve God?

describes the desire of God to smile, even to laugh with joy at true worship from a godly people (Pss. 40:6–8; 147:10, 11).

1:11 great among the Gentiles: God would one day receive praise from all the nations. Even the despised Gentiles would offer praise, while God's own people were profaning His holy name (Pss. 87; 117).

1:12 you profane it: The people were treating God with contempt by their careless attitudes concerning their offerings.

1:13 The demands of God were neither understood nor appreciated; they seemed to be mere busywork. **stolen . . . lame . . . sick:** The gifts of the priests were not presentable; some were stolen goods, and others were animals that were useless. To sacrifice something of no value was not a sacrifice at all.

1:14 Can anyone really deceive the Lord? The deception is only in the eyes of the **deceiver. I am a great King:** The reputation of the Lord among His people was to have been the means whereby all the nations would be drawn to worship Him as well.

2:1–16 The prophet explores more deeply why the nation was treating God as it did. His conclusion is that God's treatment stems from a breaking of the covenant by three groups: the priests (vv. 1–9), the people at large (vv. 10–12), and individuals who divorced their wives (vv. 13–16). The word *covenant* is prominent in these verses.

2:1 The address to the **priests** shows that the section begun in 1:8 continues in this chapter.

2:2 If you will not . . . give glory: The behavior of the priests was defiling the name of God. **I will send a curse:** At the passage of the people into the promised land, the Levites spread before the people the blessings of obedience and the curses on disobedience (Deut. 27; 28). But the priests were not obeying the Law that they were supposed to uphold. They would therefore receive the curses.

2:3 Refuse was the dung in the sacrificed animal that should have been removed when the animal was prepared for sacrifice to the Lord.

2:4 My covenant with Levi: The Levites had been given the privilege of serving the tabernacle (Deut. 33:8–11).

2:5 The **covenant** of God was with Phinehas, a descendant of the tribe of Levi (Num. 25:1–14). **life and peace:** The basic meaning of the word *peace* is fullness, completeness, things as they really ought to be. **that he might fear Me:** The context here means holding God in reverential awe, responding properly to His wonder, and worshiping Him in spirit and in truth (3:5, 16; 4:2).

2:6 the law of truth: The priests of the OT period had a twofold responsibility—they were to represent the people in holy worship before the living God, and they were to teach and apply God's law to the people. **in peace and equity:** This refers to complete moral virtue in all things before the Lord.

2:7 In the OT, a prophet was commonly called a "**messenger** of the Lord." But this is apparently the only time in the OT that priests

---

🌱 **IN LIFE**   **Dealing Treacherously in Marriage**

The more a nation's divorce rate increases, the more God regards the situation as a national scandal. That seems to be the import of Malachi's words concerning divorce (Mal. 2:14–16). Apparently a substantial number of husbands in postexilic Judah were "dealing treacherously" by divorcing their wives. This treachery involved a retraction of their marriage vows, but it also represented treachery against the Lord.

What provoked this skyrocketing divorce rate? The books of Ezra and Nehemiah tell of those two leaders challenging the men of the land to "put away" the wives that they had married from among the Canaanites and other peoples of the land (Ezra 9; 10; Neh. 13:23–27). These divorces were regarded as a means of national cleansing and a return to the covenant.

But is it possible that this policy of dissolving mixed marriages helped to create a jaded attitude about divorce? Could it have contributed to a climate in which divorce became an easy alternative even when both partners were Jewish, evidence of which we continue to see in Jesus' day (Matt. 19:3–9)?

Malachi, a contemporary of Ezra and Nehemiah, spoke clearly about God's attitude: "I hate divorce" (Mal. 2:16). The prophet warned the people to "take heed to your spirit." A casual attitude toward divorce was a symptom of a problem with one's heart attitude toward the Lord. Loyalty to Him was what counted.

are specifically called the messengers of the Lord (3:1).

2:8 departed . . . caused many to stumble: The judgment on the departed religious leader would be more strict because of the ripple effect of that one person's sin. **the covenant of Levi:** God made this covenant with the tribe of Levi and specifically with Phinehas (v. 4). Other passages also presuppose a covenant (Neh. 13:29; Jer. 33:20, 21).

2:9 The priests had the truth but had not **kept** it or practiced it. When they acted as judges, they showed partiality, making their sin even worse (Deut. 17:9–11; 19:17).

2:10 one God created us: The use of the term *create* calls to mind the great creation text in Gen. 1:26–28. **deal treacherously:** Because God is the Creator of all humanity (Gen. 1:27), He requires that humans deal equitably with one another.

2:11 The term **abomination** is a strong word indicating a stomach revulsion; the people had done something so awful as to make one ill. **institution which He loves:** The term *institution* is supplied by the translation; a more literal rendering might be, "God's holy thing, that He loves." The text presents the ideas of affection and revulsion, which we usually think of in the verbs *to love* and *to hate*. Marriage is something God loves; divorce is something He hates (v. 16). The Lord's people had polluted something in which God takes great pleasure. **daughter of a foreign god:** The question of intermarriage in ancient Israel was not racial nor ethnic but spiritual: lack of faithfulness to God Himself.

2:12 cut off: The phrase may refer to banishment or even death. **being awake and aware:** The phrase is difficult but may refer to a deliberate offense against the Lord (Lev. 10:1–3).

2:13 the second thing: The prophets at times spoke of the compounding sins of the people (Jer. 2:13). **Tears** here seem to be judged as hypocritical acts of insincere repentance (Is. 1:10–15). **He does not regard the offering:** When right things are done for the wrong reasons or with the wrong attitudes, God does not accept them (Ps. 40:6–8). **goodwill:** The Hebrew suggests God's pleasure and enjoyment. God's pleasure is in sacrifices offered with attitudes of humility, faithfulness, and joy.

2:14 For what reason: The feigned surprise of the people fooled no one, certainly not the Lord. **witness:** There are some whose witness may be challenged, but the Lord is not among them (3:5). **wife of your youth:** These men had not only married pagan wives, but they had divorced their first wives to make room for their new ones. **Companion** describes a permanent partnership. **by covenant:** The union of a marriage is formal, public, legal, and sacred, a binding contract.

2:15 make them one: Here the prophet recalls the words from Gen. 2:24, "one flesh." **a remnant of the Spirit:** This somewhat difficult phrase most likely indicates the work of God's Holy Spirit in the life of the married couple. God has joined them, and by His Spirit He has worked on their behalf to strengthen them. **godly offspring:** God seeks godly children even as He seeks for true worshipers (John 4:23, 24). **take heed to your spirit:** We must control our attitudes so that they will be in line with those of God's Spirit.

2:16 treacherously: To the Lord, attitudes of indifference to marriage vows and duties are the actions of a traitor.

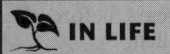 **IN LIFE** ## Robbing God, Robbing the Poor

As modern-day churches set budgets and allocate financial resources, it is worth noting that in the OT, the Israelites were commanded to give tithes ("a tenth part") of their produce or income for three reasons: to celebrate the abundance of the Lord's provision (Deut. 14:22–26), to support the Levites (14:27; Num. 18:20–24), and to provide for the poor (Deut. 14:28, 29).

In Malachi's day, the postexilic Israelites were withholding their tithes and offerings (Mal. 3:8–10). Apparently they preferred to keep more for themselves rather than give what God asked. In doing so, they were not only robbing from God, they were in effect robbing from the Levites and the poor.

Could the same be true among believers today? Malachi tried to reawaken a sense of corporate responsibility for the poor and for public worship. He knew that obedience to God was more than just private religion; there are social implications to one's relationship with God. One of those implications involves giving away a portion of one's income to those who need it.

IN FOCUS | "try"

(Heb. *bachan*) (3:10; Gen. 42:15, 16; Ps. 26:2; Jer. 9:7) Strong's #974: This Hebrew verb means "to try," or "to put to the test." (Job 23:10; Ps. 139:23; Zech. 13:9). The word can mean "to test" in the sense of separating or discriminating one thing from another (Job 34:3). When this word is used to depict God's "testing" of people, it means the proving of individuals in such a way that their faith becomes more established (Ps. 66:10–12; Jer. 17:10; 20:12). Malachi's challenge to the Israelites to *try* God is a rare instance in which people are encouraged to test the faithfulness of the Lord (3:10). This word for *try* can be contrasted with another Hebrew verb for testing, *nasah.* That latter word is frequently used in a negative sense, to describe the way Israel was testing God with their unbelief (Ex. 17:7; Pss. 78:18; 95:9). The Law of Moses warned the Israelites not to tempt God (Deut. 6:16; Ps. 95:9); it was a mark of spiritual adultery (Matt. 12:38, 39). According to James, God tests people in order to grant them the crown of life—but He tempts no one (James 1:12–14).

2:17 God is **wearied** by people who do not submit to Him but who argue their points against His revelation. When **justice** comes, they will be sorry they asked (3:5).

3:1 prepare the way: Here is one of the

Statue of the prophet Elijah. The Old Testament ends with God's promise to send "Elijah the prophet before the coming of the great and dreadful day of the Lord" (Mal. 4:5).

great, explicit prophecies relating to the messianic age. In its specific detail, this verse resembles the prophecy of Mic. 5:2 concerning the birthplace of the Messiah. Matthew and Mark identify the messenger of this verse as John the Baptist (4:5; Matt. 11:10; Mark 1:2, 3). **The Lord** refers here to Jesus Christ (as is the case in Ps. 110:1). There are three persons in view in this verse: The Father (the Lord) speaks about of sending a messenger (John the Baptist) who will prepare the way for the coming of the Lord (Jesus). **suddenly . . . His temple:** Both the righteous and the wicked will be surprised when the Messiah arrives. **Messenger of the covenant:** This is a messianic title, referring to the One who will initiate the New Covenant (Jer. 31:33, 34; Matt. 26:28; Heb. 12:24). **He is coming:** As in Ps. 96:13, this dramatic wording indicates something that was just about to occur. However, it would be four hundred years before these words would be fulfilled.

3:2 In this verse Malachi turns to the second coming of the Messiah. This second advent will be one of judgment and purification (Joel 2:11; Amos 5:18; Luke 21:36; Rev. 19:11–21). **refiner's fire . . . launderers' soap:** These two images are vivid illustrations of the purifying process. The Savior King Himself will sift all people to prepare for His reign.

3:3 purify the sons of Levi: Since the priests had come under such strong censure in this book (1:6—2:9), and since the prophet himself was likely a priest, these words would have had a special significance for him.

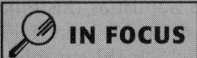 **IN FOCUS** | **"day"**

(Heb. *yom*) (4:5; Gen. 7:11; Prov. 25:13; Amos 5:8, 18) Strong's #3117: The Hebrew noun *yom* has a variety of uses in the OT. It can refer to the daylight hours in contrast to the night (Amos 5:8), or to a twenty-four-hour day, such as a certain day of the month (Gen. 7:11). It may also refer to a time period, such as the "time" of harvest (Prov. 25:13), or even to a year (2 Sam. 13:23). The word is used in the significant phrase "the day of the LORD" (Is. 2:12; Ezek. 13:5; Joel 1:15; Zeph. 1:14). For the prophets, the day of the Lord was the future day when God would decisively triumph over all His foes. That day will be a day of great rejoicing and blessing for God's faithful servants (Is. 2), whereas for God's enemies it will be a day of "darkness" (Amos 5:18).

3:4 The Hebrew word translated **pleasant** refers to things that are sweet and pleasing. God derives joy from the end result of His work.

3:5 judgment: The same word may be translated *justice* (2:17). The people had wondered where the God of justice was; now they will know. **Sorcerers** were people who made potions. **fear Me:** Holding God in reverence and awe also means obeying Him (2:5; 3:16; 4:2).

3:6 I do not change: We might expect these opening words to ensure the nation's doom; instead, they give assurance of God's continuing mercy.

3:7 The history of Israel is not a record of everincreasing obedience. Instead, it is a long, sad story of recurring departure from God. **Return:** This is the key term in the Hebrew prophets for repentance, renewal, and restoration (Is. 55:11; Jer. 4:1; Zech. 1:3).

3:8 The **tithes** were the gifts to the Lord that the Law required. There were three: two that were annual and one that came every three years. The tithe supported the priests and Levites, and also widows, orphans, and foreigners (Deut. 14:28, 29).

3:9–11 The people were **cursed** with poor production from their land and animals. A key verse from the Law of Moses reads that the curse will come "because you did not serve the LORD your God with joy and gladness of heart, for the abundance of everything" (Deut. 28:47). The forces that caused loss of production are pictured collectively as **the devourer.**

3:12 One of the ways in which **all nations** would be drawn to the worship of the Lord was by seeing how the people of Israel fared with the Lord as their God. **a delightful land:** The adjective indicates enjoyment, life that is genuinely pleasurable (1:10; the related verb is found in 3:1). Faithfulness to God would lead to fruitfulness in the land.

3:13 In this verse God addresses not just their **words** but the thoughts that prompted them.

3:14 What profit: The people secretly entertained doubts about the value of following the Lord. In fact, they had not really **kept His ordinance** anyway. The proper attitude is encouraged in 4:4.

3:15 the proud: This word refers to godless, rebellious people (4:1; compare Ps. 119:21; Prov. 21:24; Jer. 43:2).

3:16 There were other voices, those of people who did place themselves under the Law, those **who feared the LORD.** God did not ignore those who were faithful to Him. **a book of remembrance:** God never forgets His promises. God teaches us to remember and value the good that people do (Phil. 4:8); He does the same as He commands us. Those **who meditate** fear the Lord, think highly of Him, and ponder His significance as it relates to their lives.

3:17 The excitement of these words is that we can sense the pride God has in His children. The Hebrew word translated **jewels** could be rendered "special treasure." It is a wonderfully endearing term that is used in the OT only of the people of Israel as they are valued by the living God (Ex. 19:5; Deut. 7:6; Ps. 135:4).

3:18 one who serves God: Serving God means putting Him first, obeying His commands, and finding one's chief joy in life as the advancement of the glory of His name.

4:1–6 The last chapter of the Book of Malachi departs from the dispute pattern of the first chapters. Now there is the solemn voice of the living God giving warnings to the people based on the reality of the great and coming Day of the Lord.

4:1–3 The first set of warnings are based on the certainty of the coming Day of the Lord, while the second (4:4–6) focus on the coming of Elijah in that day.

4:1 Scripture consistently describes a **coming** day when God will arrive as a Judge and will deal with the wicked (v. 5; compare Is. 13:6–10; Joel 1:15; 2:1–11; Zeph. 1:2—2:3;

Zech. 14). **the proud:** What some people thought about the "blessedness of the proud" is exposed as a grave error (3:15).

4:2 you who fear My name: This is the righteous remnant who held God in wonder and awe, responded to Him in obedience, and lived for Him with constant faith. **with healing in His wings:** The prophet compares the Savior to a bird whose comforting wings bring healing to the chicks that gather underneath (Ps. 91:1–4).

4:3 trample the wicked: The victory of the righteous over the wicked is a promise of the living God that transcends the two testaments (Ps. 110:4–6; compare Rev. 19:11–21). **On the day that I do this:** The identity of the Victor is already known.

4:4 Remember: This word means more than simply "to recall." The command is to act on the teaching that had come from the living God. **the Law of Moses:** The Law had its origin in the Lord, and Moses was the divinely appointed transmitter of God's will and word to the people (John 1:17).

4:5 Elijah the prophet: The story of the prophet Elijah is found in 1 Kin. 17—2 Kin. 2. The NT identifies John the Baptist as this Elijah (Matt. 11:14; 17:10; Mark 9:11–13; Luke 1:17). There are three ways in which this prophecy might be fulfilled: (1) John the Baptist, whom Malachi had already prophesied (3:1), was the first to fill the promise of the Elijah figure. John, like Elijah, was a minister of the Lord calling people to repent and prepare for the coming of the Messiah (Matt. 11:14). (2) Elijah appeared in person along with Moses at the Transfiguration, a stunning vindication of the messianic role of Jesus (Matt. 16:28—17:8). (3) An Elijah-like figure will appear at the end times; he will call fire down from heaven just as Elijah did (1 Kin. 18:36–40; Rev. 11:1–7).

4:6 Malachi ends with both a promise and a warning. **fathers to the children . . . children to their fathers:** As in every act of God announcing judgment, there is also an offer of His mercy (Jon. 4:2). **a curse:** The term is one of the harshest in Scripture. The Hebrew word suggests complete annihilation. This is the term translated *doomed* in the account of the destruction of Jericho (Josh. 6:17).

The Intertestamental Period

THE READER OF THE NEW TESTAMENT QUICKLY becomes aware of having entered a world quite different from that of Malachi. New religious and political parties have risen to prominence. A new world power is in control. Even Jewish popular perceptions regarding the Law and God's promised Messiah have changed.

No canonical records exist for the 400-year period between the return from Babylon and the birth of Jesus, but an understanding of the historical and religious developments during this time is critical to our understanding of the New Testament world. Jesus' ministry and the development of the early church take place within this new context and are shaped, at least in part, by more recent events as well as by Israel's Exodus, kingdom, and the Exile.

One Period—Six Divisions

If the Book of Malachi was completed in about 450 B.C., then the period under consideration begins at that point and continues until the angel's announcement of the birth of John the Baptist (Luke 1:11–17). Six historical divisions are observable within this time span: The Persian Era, which actually dates to 536 B.C. but coincides with the Intertestamental Period from 450 to 336 B.C.; the Greek Era (336–323 B.C.); the Egyptian Era (323–198 B.C.); the Syrian Era (198–165 B.C.); the Maccabean Era (165–63 B.C.); and the Roman Era (63–4 B.C.). This study will look at these six divisions chronologically, giving attention to the historical situation and the religious developments within each segment.

The Persian Era (536–336 B.C.)

Historical Situation

The Persians were the dominating power in the Middle East as far back as 536 B.C. God had used the Persians to deliver Israel from the Babylonian captivity (Dan. 5:30, 31).

Persia's attitude was tolerant toward the Jewish remnant in Palestine, until internal rivalry over the politically powerful office of high priest resulted in partial destruction of Jerusalem by the Persian governor. Otherwise the Jewish people were left undisturbed during this period.

Religious Developments

The Babylonian captivity was used by God to purge idolatry from His people. They turned to Jerusalem with a new reverence for the Scriptures, especially the Law of Moses. They also had a firm grasp on the theological concept of monotheism. These two influences carried over into the Intertestamental Period.

The rise of the synagogue as the local center of worship can be traced to this period. Scribes became important for the interpretation of the Scriptures in the synagogue services. By the time Jesus born, the synagogue was well developed in organization and was spread throughout the Jewish communities of the world.

Another development that affected the spread of the gospel during New Testament times had its origin toward the end of the Persian rule. A temple was founded in Samaria, establishing a form of worship that rivaled Judaism. That event encouraged the ultimate social and religious separation between Jew and Samaritan.

The Greek Era (336–323 B.C.)

Historical Situation

Alexander the Great was the central figure of this brief period. He conquered Persia, Babylon, Palestine, Syria, Egypt, and western India. Although he died at the age of thirty-three, having reigned over Greece only thirteen years, his influence lived long after him.

Religious Developments

Alexander's cherished desire was to found a worldwide empire united by language, custom, and civilization. Under his influence the world began to speak and study the Greek language. This process, called Hellenization, included the adoption of Greek culture and religion in all parts of the world. Hellenism became so popular that it persisted and was encouraged by the Romans even into New Testament times.

A long and bitter struggle developed between the Jews and Hellenism's influence upon their culture and religion. Although the Greek language was sufficiently widespread by 270 B.C. to bring about a Greek translation of the Old Testament (the Septuagint), faithful Jews staunchly resisted pagan polytheism.

The Egyptian Era (323–198 B.C.)

Historical Situation

With the death of Alexander in 323 B.C., the Greek empire became divided among four generals: Ptolemy, Lysimachus, Cassander, and Selenus. These were Daniel's "four kingdoms" that took the place of the "large horn" (Dan. 8:21, 22).

Ptolemy Soter, the first of the Ptolemaic dynasty, received Egypt and soon dominated nearby Israel. He dealt severely with the Jews at first, but toward the end of his reign and on into the rule of Ptolemy Philadelphus, his successor, the Jews were treated favorably. It was during this time that the Septuagint was authorized.

The Jews prospered until near the end of the Ptolemaic dynasty, when conflicts between Egypt and Syria escalated. Israel again was caught in the middle. When the Syrians defeated Egypt in the Battle of Panion in 198 B.C., Judea was annexed to Syria.

Religious Developments

The policy of toleration followed by the Ptolemies, by which Judaism and Hellenism coexisted peacefully, seriously undermined the Jewish faith. It brought a gradual infiltration of Greek influence and an almost unnoticed assimilation of the Greek way of life.

Hellenism's emphasis on beauty, shape, and movement encouraged Jews to neglect Jewish religious rites that were aesthetically unappealing. Thus worship was influenced to become more external than internal, a notion that had a lasting impact upon Judaism.

Two religious parties emerged: the Hellenizing party, which was pro-Syrian, and the orthodox Jews, in particular the Hasidim or "Pious Ones" (predecessors of the Pharisees). A struggle for power between these two groups resulted in a polarization of the Jews along political, cultural, and religious lines. This same conflict led to the attack of Antiochus Epiphanes in 168 B.C.

The Syrian Era (198–165 B.C.)

Historical Situation

Under the rule of Antiochus the Great and his successor Seleucus Philopater, the Jews, though treated harshly, were nonetheless allowed to maintain local rule under their high priest. All went well until the Hellenizing party decided to have their favorite, Jason, appointed to replace Onias III, the high priest favored by the orthodox Jews, and to bring this about by bribing Seleucus's successor, Antiochus Epiphanes. This set off a political conflict that finally brought Antiochus to Jerusalem in a fit of rage.

In 168 B.C. Antiochus set about destroying every distinctive characteristic of the Jewish faith. He forbade all sacrifices, outlawed the rite of circumcision, and cancelled observance of the Sabbath and feast days. The Scriptures were mutilated or destroyed. Jews were forced to eat pork and to sacrifice to idols. His final act of sacrilege, and the one that spelled his ultimate ruin, was to desecrate the Most Holy Place by building an altar and offering a sacrifice to the god Zeus. Many Jews died in the ensuing persecutions.

Perhaps a reminder of God's way of working with man is needed at this point. He creates or allows a desperate situation, then calls upon a special, faithful servant. However, man often attempts to rescue himself and may seem almost at the point of success before winding up in worse shape than before. This was about to happen in the life of God's people the Jews. God was simply setting the stage for the coming of the true Deliverer.

Religious Developments

The Jewish religion was strongly divided over the issue of Hellenism. The groundwork was laid for an orthodox party, generally led by the scribes and later called the Pharisees, and for what we may call a more pragmatic faction of the Jews that became more or less associated with the office of high priest. This latter group's pattern of thinking later fostered the rise of the Sadducees.

The Maccabean Era (165–63 B.C.)

Historical Situation

An elderly priest named Mattathias, of the house of Hasmon, lived with his five sons in the village of Modein, northwest of Jerusalem. When a Syrian official tried to enforce heathen sacrifice in Modein, Mattathias revolted, killed a renegade Jew who did offer sacrifice, slew the Syrian official, and fled to the mountains with his family. Thousands of faithful Jews joined him, and history records one of the most noble demonstrations of holy jealousy for the honor of God.

After the death of Mattathias three of his sons carried on the revolt in succession: Judas surnamed Maccabeaus (166–160 B.C.), Jonathan (160–142 B.C.), and Simon (143–134 B.C.). These men had such success that by December 25, 165 B.C., they had retaken Jerusalem, cleansed the temple, and restored worship. This event is commemorated today as the Feast of Hanukkah (Dedication).

Fighting continued in the outlying areas of Judea, with several futile attempts by Syria to defeat the Maccabeans. Finally, under the leadership of Simon, the Jews received their independence (142 B.C.). They experienced almost seventy years of independence under the Hasmonaean dynasty, the most notable leaders of which were John Hyrcanus (134–104 B.C.) and Alexander Jannaeus (102–76 B.C.).

Religious Developments

The most significant religious development of this period resulted from a strong difference of opinion concerning the kingship and high priesthood of Judea. Over hundreds of years the position of high priest had taken on some obvious political overtones. Emphasis had not been upon the Aaronite line but upon political strength. Orthodox Jews resented and resisted this development. When John Hyrcanus became governor and high priest of Israel, he conquered Transjordan and Idumaea and destroyed the Samarian temple. His power and popularity led him to refer to himself as a king. This flew in the face of the Orthodox Jews, who by this time were called Pharisees. They recognized no king unless he was of the lineage of David, and the Hasmonaeans were not.

Those who opposed the Pharisees and supported the Hasmonaeans were called Sadducees. These names appeared for the first time during the reign of John Hyrcanus, who himself became a Sadducee.

The Roman Era (63–4 B.C.)

Historical Situation

The independence of the Jews ended in 63 B.C., when Pompey of Rome took Syria and entered Israel. Aristobulus II, claiming to be the king of Israel, locked Pompey out of Jerusalem. The Roman leader in anger took the city by force and reduced the size of Judea. Israel's attempt at freedom from oppression had paid off for a while, but now all hope seemed to be lost.

Antipater the Idumaean was appointed procurator of Judea by Julius Caesar in 47 B.C. Herod, the son of Antipater, eventually became the king of the Jews around 40 B.C.

Although Herod the Great, as he was called, planned and carried out the building of the new temple in Jerusalem, he was a devoted Hellenist and hated the Hasmonaean family. He killed every descendant of the Hasmonaeans, even his own wife Marianne, the granddaughter of John Hyrcanus. Then he proceeded to murder his own two sons by Marianne, Aristobulus and Alexander. This was the man on the throne when Jesus was born in Bethlehem.

Religious Developments

In addition to the Pharisees and Sadducees, two other parties joined the political mix of this time. The *Zealots* were even less tolerant of change than the Pharisees, and they added a strong nationalistic spirit to the Pharisee's devotion to the Law. The *Herodians* went a step further toward pragmatic politics than the Sadducees, openly supporting Herod's government and opposing any hint of rebellion. A fifth group, the *Essenes,* responded to cultural and political issues by withdrawing into a monastic lifestyle.

Despite their differences, all of these people shared a concern for the future of the Jews. And each group had its own expectations for the long-promised Messiah.

Conclusion

More than four hundred years after Malachi, the Intertestamental Period came to an end when God sent John the Baptist to announce

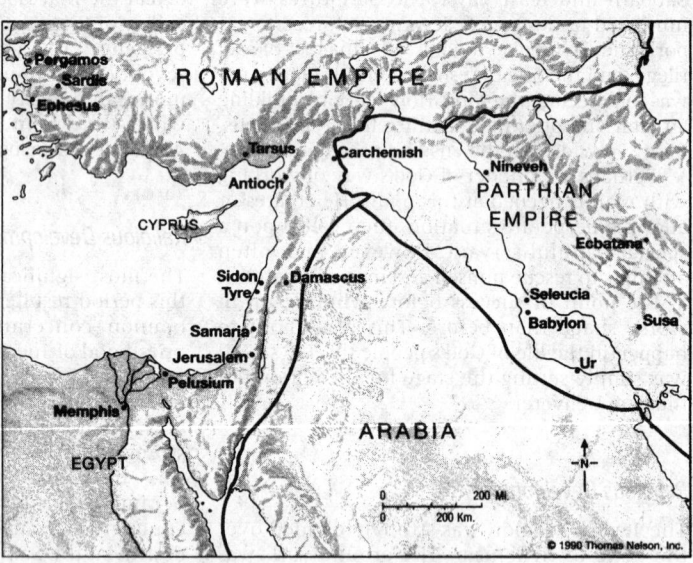

Roman Control of Palestine (63. B.C.—beyond NT times)

the coming of His Son, the faithful Servant of the Lord, the Christ—God's ultimate revelation to man.

THE
NEW TESTAMENT

■

The Gospel According to
Matthew

SUCCESSION TO A THRONE IS OFTEN A TIME OF conflict and uncertainty. David's son Absalom tried to usurp the throne (2 Sam. 15:1—18:18). Solomon's choice of successor lost more than half the kingdom to a traitor (1 Kin. 12:20). Menahem assassinated his predecessor in Israel (2 Kin. 15:14). Royalty is a dangerous business.

This is no less true when the heir is the King of kings. If ever

there was a high-stakes succession, this was it. A Man claims to be Israel's own Messiah; *of course* all Israel sits up and takes notice. Of course He must prove His credentials: Who wants an impostor? The Book of Matthew presents Jesus' credentials. It presents Jesus as the King, but King of a totally different kingdom—the kingdom of heaven.

The Gospel of Matthew has many Jewish overtones. For example, the term *kingdom of heaven* appears thirty-three times and the term kingdom of God four times. No other Gospel lays such stress on the kingdom; the restoration of the glories of David's kingdom was a burning hope for many Jews at the time. Matthew clearly identifies Jesus with that hope by using the Jewish royal title "Son of David" nine times in his Gospel. Furthermore, he calls Jerusalem "the holy city" (4:5; 27:53) and the "city of the great King" (5:35), both uniquely Jewish ways of referring to it. First-century Jews emphasized righteousness, and Matthew uses the words *righteous* and *righteousness* more often than the Gospels of Mark, Luke, and John combined.

Matthew also discusses the Law, ceremonial cleanness, the Sabbath, the temple,

David, the Messiah, the fulfillment of Old Testament prophecies, and Moses—all from a Jewish point of view. He has fifty-three Old Testament citations and more than seventy allusions to the Hebrew Scriptures. Thirteen times, the book emphasizes that Jesus' actions were a direct fulfillment of Old Testament prophecies. The genealogy of ch. 1 is recognizably Jewish, tracing the lineage of Jesus back through David to Abraham, the father of the Jewish people. Furthermore, the Gospel mentions Jewish rulers (2:1, 22; 14:1) and customs such as ceremonial washing (15:2) without explanation, indicating that Matthew expected his predominantly Jewish audience to be familiar with such practices.

Matthew's Gospel serves several purposes beyond presenting a mere biography of Jesus. One purpose is to prove to Jewish readers that Jesus is their Messiah and promised King. The genealogy in ch. 1 points to Christ as the One who inherited God's promises to David of an eternal dynasty. Jesus' use of a familiar messianic psalm in Matt. 22:41–44 would have clearly implied to any Jew that He was the heir of the Davidic throne. Even though many Jews of Jesus' time were blind to Jesus' identity, Gentiles (such as the wise men) identified Him as Israel's promised King when He was a baby. Finally, the charge that hung above Jesus' head on the Cross clearly highlights His royalty: THIS IS JESUS THE KING OF THE JEWS (27:37). But most important, the Book of Matthew proves Jesus' legitimate authority by highlighting His wise teaching and righteous life (7:28, 29).

Another purpose of the book is to outline the characteristics of the kingdom of God, both for Israel and the church. Orthodox Jews would typically scoff at any assertion that Jesus is their Messiah, let alone their King. They would retort, "If Jesus is King, where is the promised restoration of the kingdom of Israel?" Many Jews of Jesus' day rejected Him as Messiah, even though both Jesus and John the Baptist continually preached that the kingdom was "at hand" (3:2; 4:17; 10:7). This rejection of Jesus by the Jews is a dominant theme of Matthew (11:12–24; 12:28–45; 21:33—22:14). Because of this rejection, God postponed the fulfillment of His promises to Israel and subsequently extended His blessings to both Jew and Gentile in the church.

Matthew is the only Gospel writer who speaks directly of the *church* (16:18; 18:17). He points to the Gentile composition of this church by including several stories of the Gentiles' faith in Jesus: the wise men, the centurion, and the Canaanite woman. He records Jesus' prediction that the gospel will be preached to all nations (24:14), and the commission to the disciples to "make disciples of all the nations" (28:19).

Jesus' teaching pointed to the blessings of the kingdom being extended to Gentiles. But one day, Israel will be restored to its place of blessing (Rom. 11:25–27; 15:8, 9).

A final purpose of Matthew is to instruct the church. An obvious clue to this is in the Great Commission: "teaching them to observe all things that I have commanded you" (28:20). The discipling process involves instruction in the words of Christ, and the Gospel of Matthew revolves around five of Jesus' discourses (5:1—7:28; 10:5—11:1; 13:3–53; 18:2—19:1; 24:4—26:1). Instead of emphasizing a narrative of Jesus' life as Mark does, Matthew uses the narrative elements in his Gospel as a setting for Jesus' sermons.

This Gospel does not name its author, but it does contain clues. The author knew the geography of Palestine well (2:1; 8:5; 20:29; 26:6). He was familiar with Jewish history, customs, ideas, and classes of people (1:18, 19; 2:1; 14:1; 26:3; 27:2). He was well acquainted with the Old Testament (1:2–16, 22, 23; 2:6; 4:14–16; 12:17–21; 13:35; 21:4; 27:9). And the terminology of the book suggests that the author was a Palestinian Jew (2:20; 4:5; 5:35; 10:6; 15:24; 17:24–27; 18:17; 27:53).

Other details point specifically to Jesus' disciple Matthew as the writer of this Gospel. As a tax collector, Matthew would have been literate and familiar with keeping records of money. Appropriately, this Gospel contains more references to money than any of the others. Furthermore, Matthew's hometown was Capernaum, a village that is given special attention in this Gospel. When Capernaum is mentioned, some

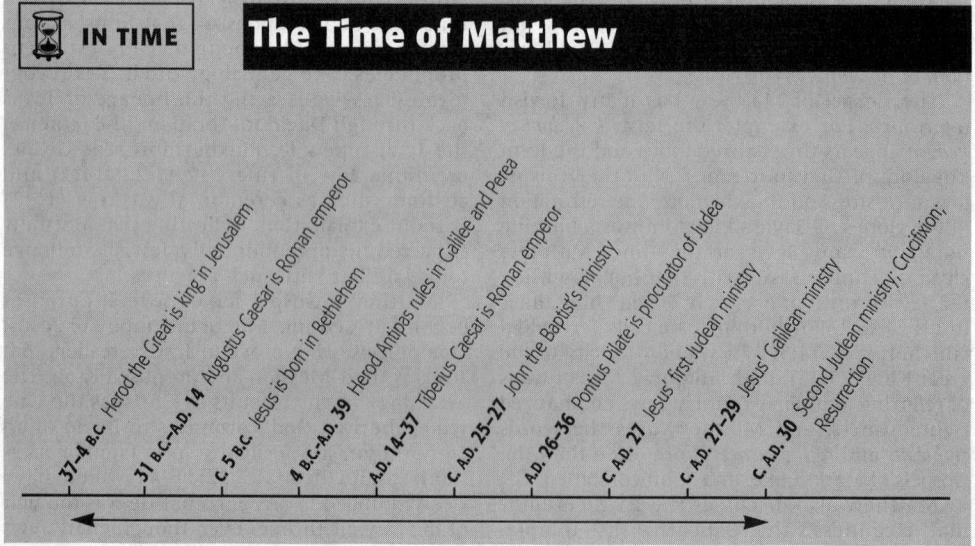

IN TIME

The Time of Matthew

37–4 B.C. Herod the Great is king in Jerusalem

31 B.C.–A.D. 14 Augustus Caesar is Roman emperor

c. 5 B.C. Jesus is born in Bethlehem

4 B.C.–A.D. 39 Herod Antipas rules in Galilee and Perea

A.D. 14–37 Tiberius Caesar is Roman emperor

c. A.D. 25–27 John the Baptist's ministry

A.D. 26–36 Pontius Pilate is procurator of Judea

c. A.D. 27 Jesus' first Judean ministry

c. A.D. 27–29 Jesus' Galilean ministry

c. A.D. 30 Second Judean ministry; Crucifixion; Resurrection

special description is usually attached to it (4:13; 11:23).

Matthew wrote the Gospel before the destruction of Jerusalem in A.D. 70. He describes Jerusalem in the book as the "holy city" and as though it was still standing (4:5; 27:53), and he speaks of the customs of the Jews as continuing until "this day" (27:8; 28:15). Furthermore, Jesus' prophecy (recorded in 24:2) of Jerusalem's destruction includes no indication that it had already occurred when Matthew wrote Jesus' words. In light of all of this, it is reasonable to conclude that the book was written sometime between A.D. 50 and 60.

Outline

I. **Jesus' birth and preparation 1:1–4:11**
   A. Jesus' birth and childhood 1:1–2:23
   B. Jesus' preparation 3:1–4:11
II. **The declaration of Jesus' principles 4:12–7:29**
   A. The beginning of Jesus' ministry 4:12-25
   B. Jesus' principles: the Sermon on the Mount 5:1–7:29
      1. The setting 5:1, 2
      2. The subjects of the kingdom of heaven 5:3–16
      3. The explanation of genuine righteousness 5:17–7:12
      4. Jesus' warnings 7:13–27
      5. The people's response 7:28, 29
III. **The manifestation of Jesus: His miracles and commissioning 8:1–11:1**
   A. Demonstration of Jesus' power: a collection of miracles 8:1–9:34
   B. Declaration of Jesus' presence: the commissioning of the disciples 9:35–11:1
IV. **Opposition to Jesus 11:2–13:53**
   A. Evidence of the rejection of Jesus 11:2-30
   B. Illustrations of opposition to Jesus 12:1–50
   C. Jesus' adaptation to His opposition: parables of the kingdom 13:1–53
V. **Jesus' reaction to opposition 13:54–19:2**
   A. Jesus' withdrawal 13:54–16:12
   B. Jesus' instruction to His disciples 16:13–19:2
VI. **Formal presentation and rejection of the King 19:3–25:46**
   A. Continued instruction of the disciples 19:3–20:34
   B. Formal presentation of the King: the Triumphal Entry 21:1–7
   C. The nation's rejection of the King 21:18–22:46
   D. The King's rejection of the nation 23:1–39

E. Predictions of the rejected King: the Olivet Discourse 24:1–25:46
VII. **Crucifixion and Resurrection 26:1–28:20**

Commentary

1:1 Genealogy means "origin." Genealogies were very important to first-century Jews. A genealogy (1) proved that a person was indeed an Israelite, (2) identified the tribe to which he or she belonged, and (3) qualified certain Jews for religious duties such as Levitical and priestly service (Ezra 2:61, 62). Christ's genealogy is crucial to historic Christianity. Matthew traced the lineage of Christ Jesus back to Abraham, Isaac, and Jacob to show that He was a Jew, but also back through David to inform the readers that Jesus is qualified to rule on the throne of David (2 Sam. 7:12), an event still in the future (19:28). That "the Son of David" precedes "the Son of Abraham" in the genealogical listing is significant. The order of names is inverted chronologically because Abraham preceded David by a thousand years. The reason Matthew reverses the order is found in the nature of the promises God gave to Abraham and David. The promises to David were more narrow than those given to Abraham. The promises to Abraham were personal, national, and universal (Gen. 12:1–3; 13:14–17; 15:1–21; 17:1–21; 21:12, 13; 22:16–18); on the other hand, the Davidic covenant relates to personal and national blessings (2 Sam. 7:13–16; Pss. 89:1–4, 19–37; 132:11–18). In the Gospel of Matthew the Lord Jesus first came to Israel (Matt. 10:5, 6) and then to the world (Matt. 28:19, 20). Just as individual salvation is dependent upon a person's response to the gospel, so the coming of the promised messianic kingdom to this earth is contingent upon Israel's acceptance of Jesus as its Messiah (Acts 3:19–21; Zech. 12:10—14:21). Though He was rejected by Israel as king, God in His grace also sent the message of the gospel to Gentiles (Rom. 11:11–24). This pattern of Christ first coming to Jews and then to Gentiles is a key to understanding the Gospels, Acts, and in fact the entire NT (John 1:11, 12; Acts 13:45, 46; 18:6; 28:26–28; Rom. 11:7–36; 15:8, 9, etc.) The very first words of this Gospel imply the worldwide responsibility of the church.

1:2–7 The mention of women in a Jewish genealogy is unusual. But in addition to Mary, four women are listed in this catalog of names. The extraordinary emphasis is underscored by the *kind* of women Matthew mentions: **Tamar,** who was involved in a scandal with Judah (Gen. 38); **Rahab,** the Canaanite harlot of Jericho (Josh. 2); **Ruth,** who was not an Israelite, but a Moabite (Ruth 1:4); and Bathsheba, **the wife**

of Uriah, a woman involved in a sin of horrendous proportions (2 Sam. 11:1—12:23), and who may have been a Hittite. At the beginning of his Gospel, Matthew shows how God's grace forgives the darkest of sins and reaches beyond the nation of Israel to the world. He also points out that God can lift the lowest and place them in royal lineage.

1:8–15 Joram . . . Uzziah: Between these two kings are three links that Matthew omitted (Ahaziah, Jehoash, and Amaziah), as well as Jehoiakim, the father of Jeconiah. Though Matthew obviously knew this, he listed three cycles of fourteen, perhaps for mnemonic purposes (see comment on 1:17). Though "all the generations" (1:17) from Abraham to David were fourteen, not "all the generations" are said to be listed in the last two cycles. Special mention needs to be made of Jeconiah. Joseph is identified as descending from this king of Judah. The problem is that a curse was put on the line of David through Jeconiah (he is called Coniah in Jer. 22:24, 28 and Jehoiachin in 2 Kin. 24:8, depending on whether his abbreviated name is used and whether the English is from the Hebrew or the Greek). Jeremiah 22:24–30 records the curse. He will be childless and no one will sit on the throne of David from his lineage. The reason for the curse is given in 2 Kings 24:9: "He did evil in the sight of the LORD." We are not given the specific sin or sins, but they were such that God cut his line off from the throne of David. Since the physical line of Jeconiah was forbidden to sit on David's throne, Jesus could not be Messiah and at the same time come from the physical lineage of Jeconiah through Joseph. Mary, however, came from the physical lineage of Nathan, son of David (1 Chr. 3:5). In view of this, Jesus could be physically of the line of David through Mary but legally be the son of David through Joseph.

1:16 Joseph the husband of Mary: The genealogy brings the reader to Joseph, a legal heir of David's throne. Matthew, however, is careful not to identify Jesus as the physical son of Joseph. The Greek term translated **of whom** is a feminine singular pronoun that can only refer to Mary. Had the gospel writer wanted to include Joseph as the father he could easily have used the same practice found in the previous genealogical listing (1:16a), which uses the word **begot**; so: **Jacob begot Joseph,** and Joseph begot Jesus. Or he could have used a plural pronoun, rather than the feminine singular, to include them both. Matthew, then, diligently avoided any idea that Jesus was born of any other but Mary and the Holy Spirit. The terms **Christ** and Messiah both mean "anointed one"; the first is a Greek noun and the second Hebrew. In the OT, anointing pointed to two things: God's choice and His gifting or enablement for the task. People were traditionally anointed to one of three offices: prophet, priest, or king. The Lord Jesus was God's anointed in all three senses: He was chosen by God to be the Savior; He was supernaturally enabled (Luke 4:18–21; Acts 10:38); He is prophet, priest, and king *par excellence*. (While Christ is prophet, priest, and king, the emphasis in Matthew's gospel falls on His royalty.)

1:17 Abraham . . . Christ: The genealogy is broken down into three groups of names with fourteen generations in each list. Undoubtedly this would make it easier to memorize. However, the reason for this breakdown may be more significant. The name **David** in Hebrew has a numerical value of fourteen. Because the heading of the list is "Son of David" (1:1), Matthew may be drawing particular attention to the Davidic thrust in these names. The fortunes of the Davidic throne are also seen here. In the first group the Davidic throne is established; in the second, the throne is cast down and deported to Babylon; in the third, the throne is confirmed in the coming of the Messiah. Further, a basic promissory covenant is set forth in each of these three periods: the Abrahamic in the first (1:3–6); the Davidic in the second (1:6–11); and the New in the third (1:12–16).

1:18 betrothed: Universally, the basic element of marriage is a contract (Mal. 2:14). In Jewish culture this covenant was made about a year before the consummation of the marriage. It was during the one year period of betrothal that Mary **was found with child**. The fact that Mary was a virgin at this time is clearly implied by **before they** (Joseph and Mary) **came together**, and the virgin conception, which is to be deduced from Matthew's account, is stated clearly in Luke 1:34, 35. The righteous quality of Joseph and his desire to divorce Mary when her pregnancy became known (1:19) shows that the discovery of Mary's pregnancy would have been a cruel shock to Joseph. Mary spent the first three months of her pregnancy with Elizabeth in Judea (Luke 1:36–56). Elizabeth understood the miraculous nature of Mary's conception; she also had a supernatural intervention in her pregnancy (Luke 1:39–45). When she returned to Nazareth, Mary's condition became known to Joseph.

1:19 In agreement with the popular Jewish understanding of Deut. 24:1 (Matt. 5:27–32; 19:3–9; Jer. 3:1, 8), Joseph wanted to divorce Mary on the grounds of infidelity. A divorce would be necessary because they had already made a marriage covenant, even though they had not yet known each other physically. Joseph could have made the divorce a public matter, or he could have gone through a private ceremony before two witnesses. Being a gracious and **just man,** Joseph decided to keep it private.

1:20 conceived . . . of the Holy Spirit: Verses 1–17 establish Jesus as a legal son of Joseph; vv. 18–25 deny that Joseph was Jesus' physical father. The first was necessary to establish Jesus' lineage to David and His royal right to be King. The second was necessary to establish His qualifications to be the Savior of all people: Jesus was God's Son, not Joseph's. Matthew elaborated on Jesus' kingship while Luke detailed His miraculous conception by the Holy Spirit (Luke 1:26–56).

1:21–22 call His name JESUS: "Jesus" means "Yahweh is Savior" and is the Greek equivalent of the OT Hebrew name "Joshua." That Joseph was to name the child ("you shall call" is second person singular) is significant. If the father named the child it meant he was claiming the baby as a member of his family. This gave the Lord Jesus legal rights to the line of David. Even if Joseph had difficulty in doing this, obedience to God demanded it.

1:23–24 Behold . . . Immanuel: This is a quotation from Is. 7:14, where the prophet Isaiah consoles King Ahaz of Judah. A coalition of two kings, King Rezin of Aram and King Pekah of Israel, was opposing Ahaz. Isaiah tells Ahaz not to fear, for the plans of his enemies would not succeed. As a sign to Ahaz, a son would be born of a woman, and before that boy reached the age where he could tell right from wrong, the two kings would no longer be a threat to Ahaz. There are several interpretations of Matthew's use of this OT prophecy. Some view Isaiah's prophecy as directly prophetic of Jesus' birth and nothing else. According to this view, only the miraculous birth of Jesus can be considered a sign that fits the qualifications of the type of sign with which Yahweh challenged Ahaz (compare Is. 7:11). Since the Hebrew noun translated *virgin* in Is. 7:14 can also mean "young woman," some have suggested that Isaiah was prophesying about a son born during the lifetime of Ahaz—perhaps Isaiah's son Maher-Shalal-Hash-Baz (Is. 8:3). Others have interpreted Isaiah's prophecy as a prediction that a virgin, a contemporary of Isaiah, would marry and have a child. The sign to Ahaz was the sudden dissolution of Rezin and Pekah in the face of Assyria. Even though uncertainty

⚔ IN DEPTH | The Birth of Jesus

No one knows precisely when Jesus was born. Even His year of birth is only an educated guess based on the information available. The intention of the medieval creators of our calendar was to set the date of Jesus birth at A.D. 1. They simply miscalculated. The Jewish historian Josephus places the death of Herod the Great in 4 B.C., and both Matthew (Matt. 2:1) and Luke (Luke 1:5) presume that Herod was king at the time of Jesus' birth. But it is not clear how much before Herod's death Jesus was born.

We know that Herod became king of the Jews in 37 B.C. Outside of Matthew (Matt. 2:16), no historical record mentions Herod's slaughter of the infants in Bethlehem. Josephus does write that Herod ordered the murders of members of his own family to protect his throne. So it is not surprising that a few peasant children in Bethlehem went unnoticed among Herod's many atrocities, leaving us with no help with dating. Since Herod's calculations led him to target children under two years old, Jesus' birth likely occurred one or two years before Herod's death—in either 5 or 4 B.C.

A date of about 5 B.C. would fit with Luke's note that Augustus, who reigned from 27 B.C. to A.D. 14, was the Roman emperor when Jesus was born (Luke 2:1). Luke's mention of Quirinius (2:2), however, creates a problem. After Herod died, Rome divided his territory among his surviving sons. Archelaus ruled in Judea (Matt. 2:22) until he was deposed by the Romans in A.D. 6. Only then was Quirinius appointed governor, after serving for more than a decade as commander of the Roman troops in the area. Perhaps Luke simply identified him by his later office.

Some have tried to specify Jesus' birth date by appeal to astronomical phenomena that might explain the star of Bethlehem (Matt. 2:2, 7–10). Halley's comet appeared in 12 or 11 B.C. and another comet in 5 B.C. But in antiquity, comets were thought to forecast evil, not blessed, events. In 7 B.C. a rare (once every 794 years) conjunction of the planets Jupiter, Venus, and Saturn occurred in the constellation Pisces. Whether Matthew's star was any of these is pure speculation. For ancient people the star confirmed again that Jesus was the Messiah who fulfilled Balaam's star prophecy (Num. 24:17; Matt. 1:18–25; Luke 2:1–20).

surrounds how this prophecy was fulfilled during Isaiah's lifetime, Matthew makes it clear that Isaiah's words find their ultimate fulfillment in the virgin birth of Jesus, a sign to people of all ages that God was with them, since he follows the Jewish translations of Isaiah in the Septuagint by using a Greek word (*parthenos*) which only means "virgin."

1:25 Joseph **did not know** Mary physically until after **she** gave birth to Jesus. The clear implication of this verse is that Mary was a virgin only until the birth of Jesus. The brothers and sisters of Jesus were younger siblings born to Joseph and Mary after Jesus' birth (13:55, 56). Joseph could not have had children by a previous marriage, as some suppose, for then Jesus would not have been heir to the Davidic throne as the oldest son of Joseph.

2:1 The events of ch. 2 probably took place some months after Jesus' birth. Several reasons may be offered to support this conclusion: (1) Joseph and Mary were living in a house (2:11); (2) Jesus is referred to as a child, not an infant (2:11); (3) Herod murdered all the male children *two years old and under* (2:16); and (4) it would have been strange for Joseph and Mary to offer the sacrifice of the poor, a pair of turtledoves or pigeons (Luke 2:24; Lev. 12:8), if the wise men had just given them gold, frankincense, and myrrh. Thus, the wise men must have arrived after the ritual sacrifice described in Luke 2:22–24, 39. **Herod the king** is Herod the Great, who reigned over Palestine from 37 B.C. until his death in 4 B.C. A crafty ruler and lavish builder, Herod had a reign marked by cruelty and bloodshed. Augustus, the Roman emperor,

 **IN COMPARISON** **The Prophecies of Jesus' Birth**

Jesus fulfilled hundreds of Old Testament prophecies. Many of these prophecies involved the circumstances surrounding His birth. Below is a list of numerous such prophecies. Note the irrefutable similarities between the Old Testament predictions and their New Testament fulfillment.

Prophecy	Old Testament Prediction	New Testament Fulfillment
The Messiah would be the seed of a woman.	Gen. 3:15	Gal. 4:4
The Messiah would be a descendant of Abraham.	Gen. 12:3	Matt. 1:1
The Messiah would be a descendant of Isaac.	Gen. 17:19	Luke 3:34
The Messiah would be a descendant of Jacob.	Num. 24:17	Matt. 1:2; 2:2
The Messiah would be from the tribe of Judah.	Gen. 49:10	Luke 3:33
The Messiah would be an heir to the throne of David.	Is. 9:7	Luke 1:32, 33
The Messiah would be anointed and eternal.	Pss. 45:6, 7; 102:25–27	Heb. 1:8–12
The Messiah would be born in Bethlehem.	Mic. 5:2	Luke 2:4, 5, 7
The Messiah would be born of a virgin.	Is. 7:14	Luke 1:26, 27, 30, 31
The Messiah's birth would trigger a slaughter of children.	Jer. 31:15	Matt. 2:16–18
The Messiah would also come from Egypt.	Hos. 11:1	Matt. 2:14, 15

🔍 IN FOCUS | "Jesus"

(Gk. *Iēsous*) (Matt. 1:21; Luke 1:31; Acts 2:36; 4:18; 13:23; 17:3) Strong's #*2424*: The Greek name *Iēsous* is the equivalent of the Hebrew name *Yeshua*, meaning "The Lord Shall Save." Although a common name among the Jews (Luke 3:29; Col. 4:11), the name expresses Jesus' work on earth: to save and to deliver. This is affirmed by the explanation the angel gives Joseph after telling him to name the virgin-born child Jesus: "for He will save His people from their sins" (Matt. 1:21). After Jesus was crucified for the sins of His people and raised from the dead, the early apostles proclaimed Jesus as the one and only Savior (Acts 5:31; 13:23).

---

reportedly said in a paraphrase of a Greek play on words that he would rather be Herod's sow ("pig," Gk. *hus*) than his son (Gk. *huios*). His craftiness and murderous ruthlessness are confirmed by Mathew's account in this chapter. The word translated **wise men** can refer either to fraudulent sorcerers (Acts 8:9, 11; 13:6, 8) or, as here, to a more honorable class of astrologers. Clearly they are the latter in this case. That they were from the East (probably Persia) may help to explain why they were interested in a Jewish Messiah. Perhaps these men learned about the Jewish Scriptures from Israelites who had been deported to Babylon and Medo-Persia. In particular, it is feasible that the writings of Daniel, a wise man in the Babylonian kingdom, would have been of special interest to these *magi*. Daniel has much to say about the coming of Israel's king, especially the time of his arrival (Dan. 9:24–26).

2:2–3 born King of the Jews: These words would have struck both terror and fury into the heart of Herod. **His star in the East** may refer to a star supernaturally introduced into the heavens. The star reappeared to guide the wise men to where Christ was (2:9). The fact that it was called "His star" indicates that the wise men identified the star with the arrival of the King of the Jews. It seems God literally moved heaven at the birth of the Savior of the world.

2:4 chief priests: This first mention of the Jewish council—**all the chief priests and scribes of the people**—reveals that the Jewish leaders were alerted early to the coming of the Messiah. Their quick recital of Mic. 5:2 showed their astuteness concerning the messianic prophecies (Matt. 2:6).

2:5–9 Matthew clearly records how the Jewish religious authorities, who became Christ's enemies later, unintentionally affirmed that Jesus had fulfilled a messianic prophecy in His birth. God can use the words of His opponents to speak the truth (John 11:49–52).

2:10 The wise men undoubtedly would have been discouraged by several things: their failure to find the King in Jerusalem, the lack of knowledge concerning the birth of the Messiah among the leaders, the disinterest among Israel, and their weariness from the long journey. The reappearance of the star must have brought them great joy and encouragement. It might be observed that *joy* is the mark of a positive response to God's revelation. This is evident in many places (1 Pet. 1:6, 8; Acts 2:46; 5:41; 8:8, etc.).

2:11 Everything in this passage centers on the Lord. Mary is a bystander; Joseph is not even mentioned; Christ is the recipient of the

---

💡 INSIGHT | What's in a Name?

Jesus was and is Immanuel, "God with us" (Matt. 1:23). In Jesus, God comes to people and lives in their world, rather than have them try the impossibility of going to Him. Jesus does not take people out of the turmoil and pain of daily life; He walks with them in it. Salvation is not an escape from the world but God's engagement with the world. That is where Jesus is, as His name indicates, and that is where He gives people power (Acts 1:8).

---

homage and the gifts. He is to have the preeminence in everything (Col. 1:18). **Gold** symbolized royalty; **frankincense** was a fragrance; **myrrh** was the ointment of death.

2:12–14 warned in a dream: Five dreams of divine guidance emphasize God's orchestration of these perilous events (1:20; 2:12, 13, 19, 22).

2:15 fulfilled: This is the second fulfillment of prophecy recorded in ch. 2. The first, in 2:6, is a direct fulfillment of Micah's prophecy about the birthplace of Jesus; this one in 2:15 is a

---

✠ IN CONTEXT | **A Poor Family Comes into Wealth**

What happened to the gifts presented to Jesus by the wise men (Matt. 2:11)? Scripture doesn't say. Clearly they reflected the magi's worship of Christ at His birth. Yet we can speculate that they may have provided the means for His family's flight to Egypt (2:13-15).

The angel's warning and instructions to Joseph were sudden and unexpected, and there was no time to save enough money for such a long journey—if saving was even an option. The family was poor, as is indicated by their offering of turtledoves or pigeons (Luke 2:24), and the costly gifts probably represented more wealth than either spouse had seen in a lifetime.

In this instance, therefore, the offerings of worship may have paid for their journey to Egypt and a new life in a strange land.

---

typological fulfillment. The prophecy quoted here, from Hos. 11:1, refers to the nation of Israel as God's son coming out of Egypt in the Exodus. Jesus is the genuine Son of God, and, as Israel's Messiah, is the true Israel (John 15:1); therefore, He gives fuller meaning to the prophecy of Hos. 11:1.

2:16-21 This prophecy comes from Jer. 31:15, in which Rachel, who had been entombed near Bethlehem some thirteen centuries before the Babylonian captivity, is seen weeping for her children as they were led away to Babylon in 586 B.C. In the slaughter of the male infants at the time of Christ's birth, Rachel once again is pictured as mourning the violent loss of her sons.

2:22 Like his father Herod, **Archelaus** was violent and cruel. The Romans tolerated his savagery for ten years and finally deposed him in A.D. 6, after a Jewish delegation took their protest to Rome. Joseph, aware of Herod Archelaus's reputation and guided by God in a dream, **turned** north to **Galilee.**

2:23 Nazareth: So obscure as never to be mentioned in the OT, the village was considered an unlikely place for the Messiah to be raised (John 1:45, 46). It was the location of the Roman garrison in northern Galilee. Those who lived there were suspected of compromise with the enemy.

3:1 As Christ's forerunner, **John the Baptist** preceded the Lord Jesus in birth, ministry, and death. Luke describes John's birth (Luke 1), but Matthew jumps directly into the account of John's proclamation about the coming of the kingdom of heaven. John is called **the Baptist** because he baptized people. Unlike the common practice of proselytes and Jews administering ceremonial cleansings to themselves, John baptized those who came to him professing repentance and identifying with his message.

3:2 The Greek verb translated **repent** indicates a change of attitude and outlook which well may result in sorrow for sins. But the basic idea is a reversal of thinking which changes one's life (3:8). **The kingdom of heaven** is most likely synonymous with "the kingdom of God." Both terms seem to be used consistently throughout the NT to refer to God's heavenly kingdom coming to earth in the person of Jesus Christ. This kingdom had drawn near in that it was being offered to Israel in the person of the Messiah. Nowhere does the NT say the kingdom was present. (Passages that may imply this will be dealt with in the course of Matthew's Gospel.) The actual coming and presence of the kingdom was contingent upon Israel's response to its Messiah (Acts 3:19-23). This contingency remains to this day (Zech. 12:10-14). The kingdom was **at hand** because it was being offered to Israel in the person of the Messiah. John's preaching assumed that judgment would precede the coming of the kingdom, a fact that was taught by the OT prophets (Is. 4:4, 5; 5:15, 16; 42:1; Jer. 33:14-16; Ezek. 20:33-38; Dan. 7:26, 27; Joel 1:14, 15; 3:12-17; Zeph. 1:2-18; 3:8-13; Zech. 13:2, 9; Mal. 3:1-5; 4:1-6). At this point, John assumed that the nation of Israel would repent and that the kingdom would come. John told the Jews of his generation to repent in order to gain entrance into Christ's kingdom.

3:3-6 As roads were repaired, smoothed, straightened, and leveled before a king came, so John was preparing a spiritual road for the Messiah before His arrival. The quotation is from Is. 40:3, where the prophet announces the need to prepare a highway for the return of the Jewish exiles from captivity to their homeland, Israel.

3:7-9 The Pharisees and Sadducees were two prominent groups in Judaism during the time of Christ. Both groups claimed to be true followers of Judaism, but their beliefs were considerably different. The Pharisees were primarily associated with the laymen of Israel. In doctrine, they held not only to the Law of

---

⚔ **IN DEPTH** **Jesus the Nazarene**

he politics of Jesus' day forced Joseph to move his family around. From Bethlehem they fled to Egypt. Their return to Israel found them skirting Judea and finally resettling in the relatively peaceful region of Galilee, in the town of Nazareth. Matthew sees God's providence in these moves. Micah 5:2 had predicted that the Messiah would come from Bethlehem (Matt. 2:6), and Matthew cites another prophecy, "He shall be called a Nazarene," as being fulfilled when Joseph moved to Nazareth (2:23). An exhaustive search of Scripture reveals that the specific words of this prophecy are not found in any OT prophet.

There have been two major explanations of this biblical mystery. Some have traced the origin of the word *Nazarene* to the Hebrew word for "branch" or "shoot." The word *Branch* is used by the prophets to speak of the coming Messiah. For example, Is. 11:1 states that the Messiah would come out of Jesse's "roots," as a "Branch" (Is. 53:2). Like a tree that had been cut down, the royal line of David had almost been destroyed in the Babylonian captivity; yet a twig would grow out of the stump. This is Jesus, a descendant of David and the King of kings. Others have pointed to the plural "prophets" in Matt. 2:23 as an indication that Matthew was not referring to a specific prophecy but to a concept that appears in a number of prophecies concerning the Messiah.

The town Nazareth housed the Roman garrison in northern Galilee. Jewish hatred of the Romans was so extreme that most Jews avoided any association with Nazareth. In fact, Jewish people who lived in Nazareth were thought to be "consorting with the enemy." At that time, calling someone "a Nazarene" indicated utter contempt for the person.

Having come from Nazareth, Jesus was despised in the eyes of many Jews. Even Jesus' disciples initially harbored bad feelings about people from Nazareth. When Nathanael heard that Jesus was from Nazareth, he scoffed, "Can anything good come out of Nazareth?" (John 1:46). That Jesus was despised because of His Nazarene background aptly fits several OT prophecies about the humble character of the Messiah (Ps. 22:6–8; Is. 42:1–4; Mic. 5:2).

Whether the word *Nazarene* is associated with the prophecies of the Messiah as the "Branch" or with the general prophecies of the Messiah's humble character, apparently Matthew's largely Jewish audience would have seen the association clearly. Otherwise Matthew would have provided further explanation.

Moses, the Prophets, and the Writings, but also to a whole body of oral tradition. Their activities were centered in the synagogue. The Sadducees were associated with the priestly caste, for whom worship was centered in the temple. Extremely conservative, they based their beliefs essentially on the Pentateuch—the books of Genesis through Deuteronomy (Acts 23:6–10).

3:10 the ax is laid to the root of the trees: John likened his ministry to the ax of God clearing His orchard of dead wood, especially that which did not bear the fruit of repentance.

3:11–14 He will baptize you with the Holy Spirit and fire: John identified people with himself and his message of repentance by water baptism; the One coming after him was so much greater that He would unite people to Himself by means of the Holy Spirit. John knew that the kingdom to come would be characterized by a great display of the Holy Spirit in the lives of God's people (Is. 32:15; 44:3; Ezek.

11:19; 36:26; 39:29; Joel 2:28; Zech. 12:10). It would be the work of the Messiah to accomplish this, to baptize His people in the Spirit. Those who rejected Him, the Messiah would baptize with fire, which is probably a figure for God's judgment (3:10, 12). In His first advent, Christ baptized in the Spirit. When He comes again, He will baptize with fire. The meaning of **fire** here is debated. It probably should be understood as a figure for God's judgment stated both before (v. 10) and after (v. 12). A careful comparison of the four parallel passages (Mark 1:8; Luke 3:16; John 1:33) reveals that baptism with fire is only used when judgment is in the preceding context.

3:15 to fulfill all righteousness: This phrase does not suggest that Jesus came for baptism because He had sinned, for the Lord Jesus was without sin (2 Cor. 5:21; Heb. 4:15; 7:26). Jesus' baptism probably served several purposes: (1) Jesus joined with the believing remnant of Israel who had been baptized by John; (2) He

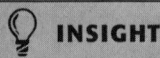

INSIGHT | John the Street Preacher

Would John the Baptist (Matt. 3:4) have been comfortable using today's media to proclaim his startling message? Probably not. He reflected none of the outward trappings of a successful ministry of his day or a willingness to employ the methods of the status quo. He was not the head rabbi of a large city synagogue. He did not dress in fine clothes, sport a hot chariot, or take sumptuous meals with leading citizens. Nevertheless, news about him spread far and wide, and people throughout the region around Jerusalem and the Jordan came to hear him.

John the Baptist illustrates the truth of Paul's words that "God has chosen the weak things of the world to put to shame the things which are mighty" (1 Cor. 1:27).

confirmed the ministry of John; and (3) He fulfilled the Father's will.

3:16, 17 the Spirit of God descending: This was God's official recognition of Jesus as the Messiah.

4:1, 2 Satan did not lead Christ to the temptation, the Holy Spirit did. At the very beginning of His ministry Christ is proven to be holy and beyond the clever testings of the devil. This temptation took place immediately after Jesus' baptism (compare Mark 1:12). Spiritual victories are often followed by testings (compare Elijah in 1 Kin. 19). Following His public baptism, Jesus was led up by the Spirit **into the**

wilderness, referring to the elevation of the Judean wilderness. The historical setting of the temptation, which was directed against Jesus' human nature, indicates that this was a literal experience which He really conquered, not merely a mental victory over His own thoughts. The reference to being **led up by the Spirit** makes clear the interrelation of these two members of the Godhead. In His earthly work, Jesus depended upon the ministry of the Holy Spirit to empower Him.

4:3, 4 It is written: Jesus' response to all three temptations was to quote the Word of God, showing His followers the power of Scrip-

Photo by Howard Vos

Traditional site of the baptism of Jesus in the Jordan River at the beginning of His public ministry (Matt. 3:13–17).

⚒ IN DEPTH   The Baptism of Jesus

In the synoptic Gospels, Jesus' baptism marks both His inauguration as the servant Messiah and the dawning of the new age of the Spirit. The Spirit is the agent of a new beginning. The open heaven, the descending dove, and the confirming heavenly voice highlight the ultimate revelatory significance of the baptism. Jesus was anointed by the Spirit of God as the Messiah and the Servant of the Lord described centuries earlier by the prophet Isaiah (Is. 11:2; 42:1; 61:1).

Mark's abbreviated account of Jesus' baptism left it open to several possible false interpretations. Readers of his Gospel might conclude that Jesus was a repentant sinner (Mark 1:4, 9), or that He was inferior to John who baptized Him (1:9), or that He became the Son of God at His baptism (1:10, 11).

The other evangelists denied such speculations early in their Gospels. The birth narrative in Matthew and Luke emphasize that Jesus was conceived of the Holy Spirit (Matt. 1:20) and that even as a baby Jesus was the Christ (Luke 2:11). He was neither sinful nor inferior prior to His baptism. John's prologue makes it clear that Jesus did not become the Son of God through baptism, but that He had been such through eternity (John 1:1–18).

Each evangelist further reformulates the baptism story to preclude any confusion that Mark's account might allow. Matthew introduces a conversation between John and Jesus in which Jesus explains His motive for receiving baptism ("to fulfill all righteousness," Matt. 3:15) and in which John the Baptist acknowledges his inferiority to Jesus (3:14). Luke reports the imprisonment of John the Baptist (Luke 3:19, 20) before describing Jesus' baptism (vv. 21, 22). Yet nowhere in his baptism narrative does Luke refer to John or describe the Spirit coming upon Jesus in response to His prayer.

The Fourth Gospel stresses John the Baptist's inferiority to Jesus (John 1:6–8, 19–37) and never mentions Jesus' baptism by John or John's preaching of repentance. John the Baptist served only as a witness to Jesus: (1) that Jesus received the abiding Spirit; (2) that He is the One who baptizes with the Spirit; and (3) that He is the Son of God (John 1:32–34). (Matt. 3:13–17; Mark 1:9–11; Luke 3:21, 22; John 1:29–34).

ture in battling the Evil One (Deut. 6:13; 8:3; Ps. 91:11, 12). There was nothing *morally* wrong with turning stones to bread; the devil was tempting Jesus to do a miracle outside of the Father's will. This explains why Jesus quotes Deut. 8:3. Bread alone does not sustain life; ultimately God is the One who sustains all life. Thus it is our responsibility to trust God and remain in His will. No matter how innocent an act may be, the ultimate question is one of faith (Rom. 14:23) and God's will.

4:5, 6 throw Yourself down: In quoting the protective promise of Ps. 91:11, 12 to Jesus, the devil omitted the words "to keep you in all your ways." The devil tempted Jesus to gain public attention through spectacle rather than through His righteous life and message. This is a danger that all of us must avoid, especially those who are often in the public eye.

4:7 Deuteronomy 6:16 emphasizes that no one should test God. The Lord asked the Israelites to put Him to the test in only one area: tithing. By giving to Him they could test whether He would fulfill His promises to bless them (Mal. 3:10).

4:8–10 Christ rebuked the devil for asking for worship, a temptation to do exactly the opposite of what every Israelite was called upon to do (Deut. 6:13, 15). Specifically in reference to Jesus, Satan was offering a crown without a cross. Jesus' experience serves as a pattern in spiritual warfare today: Jesus *resisted* Satan (Eph. 6:11, 13, 14; James 4:7; 1 Pet. 5:9), then He *defeated* Satan with consistent, meaningful use of the Scriptures (Eph. 6:17).

4:11 angels came and ministered: Having rejected Satan's offer of bread, assistance from angels, and earthly kingdoms, Jesus was immediately visited by angels who helped Him.

4:12–16 The passage quoted here, Is. 9:1, 2, foretells the reign of the Messiah in the coming kingdom. The ministry of Jesus in **Galilee** was a preview of what was yet to come. Galilee was a fertile, populous area with two major trade routes. **The way of the sea** was one of those routes.

4:17 The phrase **from that time Jesus began** occurs twice in Matthew (16:21), and both mark a crucial direction in the book. The one in 4:17 looks to the beginning of His earthly ministry, while 16:21 anticipates His crucifixion and resurrection. Jesus' exhortation to **repent**

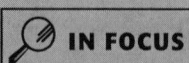 **IN FOCUS** "tempted"

(Gk. *peirazō*) (Matt. 4:1; Luke 4:2; Mark 1:13; Heb. 4:15) Strong's #3985: The word means "to try" or "to make proof of," and when ascribed to God in His dealings with people, it means no more than this (Gen. 22:1). But in Scripture, the word is chiefly used in a negative sense and means "to entice, solicit, or provoke to sin." Hence the name given to the wicked one in Matt. 4:3 is "the tempter." Accordingly, "to be tempted" (4:1) is to be understood both ways. The Spirit conducted Jesus into the wilderness to try His faith; but the agent in this trial was the wicked one, whose object was to seduce Jesus away from His allegiance to God. This was temptation in the bad sense of the term. Yet Jesus did not give in to it but passed the test (2 Cor. 5:21; Heb. 7:26).

was identical to that of John the Baptist's (3:2).

4:18–22 I will make you fishers of men: This allusion to Jer. 16:16 was used to call Peter and Andrew to discipleship and a life of ministry. This is not the Lord's first contact with Peter and Andrew (for the first, see John 1:35–42). Many lessons may be learned from this encounter: (1) God delights to use ordinary, even insignificant, people; (2) the lessons learned in life and occupation will prove valuable in serving Christ. The fishermen could use their experience in netting people for the Lord; and (3) genuine obedience is evidenced by immediacy (compare "immediately" in 4:20, 22).

4:23–25 Teaching...preaching...healing summarizes Jesus' earthly ministry. His teaching is illustrated by His discourses; His preaching is illustrated by the announcement in 4:17; His healing is illustrated by His many miracles.

5:1 The multitudes were found at the beginning and end of Jesus' Sermon on the Mount (the term is translated "the people" in 7:28). Yet this verse implies that Jesus left the multitude. Evidently He went away from the crowds so that He could instruct the disciples. As He taught the disciples, the crowds came to where He was. **when He was seated:** It was normal for a teacher or rabbi to sit while he taught, with his audience gathered around. The **mountain:** probably a high hill on the northwest shore of the Sea of Galilee, which would have served as a natural amphitheater. **disciples:** Jesus had many disciples in addition to the crowds who followed and listened to His

teaching. From the many disciples, He selected twelve to receive special instruction and power.

5:2 He . . . taught them: This Sermon on the Mount recorded by Matthew (chs. 5—7) is slightly different from the sermon preached to the multitude in Luke 6. The essence of this sermon was probably preached many times during Jesus' early ministry. The Sermon on the Mount was not given as the way of salvation for the lost, but as the way of life for true children of the kingdom. It was instruction for those who had responded to Jesus' invitation to "repent" (4:17). These disciples were probably confused as to the true nature of righteousness and God's kingdom. In this address, Jesus clarified both the heart of the law and the nature of true religion in God's kingdom (Mic. 6:8). In a sense, Jesus turned the law, which was mainly negative, inside out to show its positive core (v. 17).

5:3–12 The beatitudes (from Latin *beatus* meaning "blessed") are comprised of three elements: a pronouncement of blessing, a quality of life, and the reason why the recipient should be considered blessed. The pronouncement of blessing is found in the word **Blessed** which introduces each beatitude. In the Greek it literally means, "Oh, the happiness of _____" (Ps. 1:1). It was really a form of congratulations. The second element of the beatitudes does not describe different kinds of people but a composite picture of the kind of person who will inherit Christ's kingdom (1 Cor. 6:10; Gal. 5:21). The third part of each beatitude looks ahead to some aspect of the coming kingdom. Because an individual with the qualities described in these beatitudes will enter the kingdom, he is to be congratulated.

5:3, 4 Blessed are the poor in spirit: The idea of God blessing the humble and resisting the proud can also be found in Prov. 3:34 and James 4:6.

5:5 The meek . . . shall inherit the earth refers again to those who have been humbled before God and will inherit, not only the blessedness of heaven, but shall ultimately share in the kingdom of God upon the earth. **Earth** can also be translated "land" (Ps. 37:3, 9, 11, 29; Prov. 2:21). Here, in the opening statements of the Sermon on the Mount, is the balance between the physical and spiritual promise of the kingdom. The kingdom of which Jesus preached is both "in you" and is yet "to come." The Christian is the spiritual citizen of the kingdom of heaven now.

5:6 These future possessors of the earth are its presently installed rightful heirs and even now they **hunger and thirst for righteousness.** They experience a deep desire for personal righteousness, which is, in itself, a proof of their spiritual rebirth. Those who are poor and empty in their own spiritual poverty recognize the depth of their need and hunger and thirst for that which only God can give them. "To hunger" means to be needy. It is joined with "to thirst"; the born-again man has a God-given hunger and thirst (inner passion) for righteousness. This hungering and thirsting continues throughout the life of the believer. He continues to hunger and to be filled and to hunger and to be filled. God supplies his every spiritual need daily. This act of hungering and thirsting after righteousness is the by-product of a regenerated life. **They shall be filled** (Gk. *chortazō*) refers to a complete filling and satisfaction. The psalmist proclaimed: "He satisfies the longing soul, and fills the hungry soul with goodness" (Ps. 107:9). This filling comes from God, who is the total source of satisfaction of His people. It comes now and it will continue to come throughout eternity to those who hunger and thirst for it.

5:7 Those who are **merciful . . . shall obtain mercy** has reference to those who have been born again by the mercy of God. Because divine love has been extended to them, they have the work of the Holy Spirit in them producing a mercy which defies explanation by unregenerate men. Jesus Himself became the ultimate example of this when He cried from the cross, "Father, forgive them, for they do not know what they do" (Luke 23:34). The form of proverbial teaching should not confuse the order of these statements; for example, the

birth, saving faith, and holiness. The process of sanctification is ever conforming them to the image of Christ (Rom. 8:29), which image consists in "righteousness and true holiness" (Eph. 4:24). Purity of heart is both the end of our election and the goal of our redemption. We read in Eph. 1:4, "He chose us . . . that we should be holy," and in Titus 2:14, "who gave himself for us, that he might redeem us . . . and purify for Himself His own special people." To which we add Heb. 12:14, "Pursue peace with all people, and holiness, without which no one will see the Lord."

5:9 Peacemakers are the ones who are at peace with God and live in peace with all men (Rom. 5:1). They are called **the** peacemakers for these are not social reformers, but rather the ones reformed by the regenerating power of the gospel. They are peacemakers because they themselves are at peace with God. They have entered into the peace of Christ and thus are able ambassadors of God's message of peace to a troubled world. Hence, they shall be called **the sons of God.** These only shall be called the sons of God. Throughout the Beatitudes Jesus clearly underscores that only those who have the life-changing qualities herein described are citizens of His kingdom.

5:10–12 Blessed are those who have been persecuted: Jesus' promise of blessing for persecution appears the most difficult one to

---

 **IN FOCUS**   **"blessed"**

(Gk. *makarios*) (Matt. 5:3; Luke 6:20–22; Rom. 4:7, 8; James 1:12, 25) Strong's #*3107*: This Greek word is derived from the root *mak,* which means "large" or "lengthy," and means "fortunate" or "happy." The Greek word was used in Greek literature, in the Septuagint (the Greek translation of the OT), and in the NT to describe the kind of happiness that comes from receiving divine favor. The word can be rendered *happy.* In the NT it is usually passive; God is the One who is blessing or favoring the person.

---

believer does not show mercy in order to obtain mercy, he shows mercy because he has obtained mercy. In so continuing to show the evidence of the grace of God in his life he continues to receive that grace. In other words, he is not saved simply because he shows mercy and is kind to people. He shows mercy and is kind because he is saved.

5:8 Those who are truly saved shall **see God.** These are the **pure in heart.** Their lives have been transformed by the grace of God. They are not yet sinless but their position before God has been changed. They have the new

accept; it also promises the greatest rewards (the first of many such promises in the NT consummating with Rev. 22:12). It seems strange, indeed. When we see people experiencing this kind of persecution, do we think, "Blessed"? Hardly! Why? Because we are not truly kingdom oriented. If we can really believe what Jesus is saying here, it will revolutionize our attitude toward trials. The truth is that our positions of service and dimensions of glory that we will enjoy in the kingdom are being determined today by how we handle the experiences of this life. It seemed contrary, in fact, to the covenant promises of material blessing for righteous living, on which the Pharisees built their materialistic view of life (Deut. 7:12–16; Ps. 84:11). Jesus clinched His point by appeal to the persecuted prophets (Heb. 11:32–40). For the first time the Lord changes from the third person, "they," to the second person, "you." Perhaps He is saying that if the Beatitudes are lived out in life, the Lord's followers may expect persecution. Persecution is not unusual. Proper response is! The Beatitudes emphasize character. The Lord begins this discourse with this accent to show that *being* precedes *doing*. Sometimes it is said that a person's character should not be at issue but only his or her ideas, viewpoints, or actions. The Beatitudes belie such a perspective. Character stands behind each of our thoughts and beliefs.

5:13–16 Two similitudes follow the Beatitudes to point out this principle of *doing* following *being*. Some Christians emphasize *being* so much they never get to the goal of *doing* anything!

5:13 Pure **salt** maintains its flavor. In Israel, some salt was mixed with other ingredients. When it was exposed to the elements, the salt would be "leached out." Such leached-out salt was used for coating pathways.

5:16 Let your light so shine: Whereas salt passively affects its environment for good, light must be properly placed so as to best glorify the Father. As Jesus was "the light of the world" . . . "As long as I am in the world" (John 9:5), the believer now takes that place as the only "light of the world" to glorify the Father. The believer does not have inherent light; we have *reflective* light. As we behold the glory of the Lord, we reflect it. Therefore, we need to make sure that nothing comes between us and the Lord's light (2 Cor. 3:18; Phil. 2:14–16).

5:17, 18 I did not come to destroy: Jesus disclaimed the Pharisees' charge that He was nullifying the Law. The Law was both temporary (Gal. 3:19; Eph. 2:15; Heb. 7:12) and

eternal (Matt. 5:18; Rom. 3:31; 8:4). As a covenant system with Israel, it ended at the Cross when the temple veil was rent and a new priesthood was established; as a set of spiritual and moral principles, it is eternal. **Fulfill** (*pleroo*) means to fill out, expand, or complete, not to bring to an end (*teleo*). A great deal has been written on how Christ fulfilled the OT (Gal. 3:15–18). He did this in several ways: (1) He obeyed it perfectly and taught its correct meaning (compare vv. 19, 20); (2) He will one day fulfill all of the OT types and prophecies; and (3) He provided a way of salvation that meets all OT requirements and demands (Rom. 3:21, 31). **one jot or one tittle:** This statement by Christ provides us with one of the strongest affirmations in the Bible of the inerrancy of Scripture. The **jot** (Heb. *yod*) refers to the smallest letter of the Hebrew alphabet and the **tittle** (Gk. *keraia*) refers to a minuscule distinguishing mark at the end of another Hebrew letter. God's revelation as written by the authors of Scripture has absolutely no falsity even to the smallest detail. It is absolutely trustworthy.

5:19, 20 The **righteousness of the scribes and pharisees** was essentially external and activity oriented. Christ says God demands more than this, which must have shaken the disciples since the seemingly meticulous righteous deeds of the Pharisees and teachers of the law were viewed as far above that of the average person. In reality, though, the only righteousness that satisfies God's standard is faith in Jesus Christ (Rom. 3:21, 22). Christ's words are also a "declaration of war" against the cherished legalistic system of the Pharisees. Not only will good works, as taught by the Pharisees, not make someone great in heaven, but also the legalism could not get them into heaven.

5:21-48 In communicating the depth of His message, Jesus used a series of contrasts between the outward demand of the Law and the inner attitude of heart desired by God. Here we discover the practical application of genuine

---

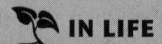 **IN LIFE**   **What about Old Testament Law?**

Jesus' critics claimed that His teaching encouraged people to violate the Mosaic Law, allowing them to get away with sin. Actually, He warned people to avoid the hypocrisies of the rabbis. While making an outward show of righteousness they took ethical shortcuts and carried out wicked schemes. In Matt. 5:17–20, Jesus turned the tables on His opponents by appealing to the Law as the basis for His moral code, not the Law as they taught it but as God intended it.

Jesus' words are crucial for Christians today. While God does not require believers to live by the specific regulations of the Law, He still expects them to honor OT morality, in both private and public life.

Christian character to true spiritual living. The Christian may live above the demands of the Law and the temptations of the world because he has an inner depth of character which is the product of the divine nature within him.

LAW	SPIRIT
(It has been said)	(But I say)
Murder	No anger
Adultery	No lust
Divorce	Commitment
Oath-taking	Speak the truth
Retaliation	Forgiveness
Hate your enemy	Love your enemy

5:21 You have heard refers to the teaching of various rabbis rather than to that of Moses. Jesus was questioning the interpretation of the Jewish scholars, not the OT itself.

5:22–24 The scribes and Pharisees said that a person who referred to someone as **Raca**, meaning empty head, was in danger of being sued for libel before **the council** (the Sanhedrin). On the other hand, Jesus said that whoever calls another a **fool** will have to answer to God. That is not to say that calling someone a fool will condemn a believer to eternal punishment in hell. Rather, using a figure of the destruction of garbage in the valley of Hinnom, Jesus was saying that to utter such words is to place oneself in a worse condi-

tion at the time of judgment (1 Cor. 3:12–15).

5:25, 26 It is wise not to have enemies. One should make peace as soon as possible because enemies are capable of doing great damage.

5:27, 28 to lust for her: A man who gazes at a woman with the purpose of wanting her sexually has mentally committed adultery.

5:29, 30 The hyperbole (exaggerated saying) about tearing out one's eye is similar to the phrase in Prov. 23:2, "put a knife to your throat if you are a man given to appetite." In striking overstatement, Jesus advises removing every temptation to evil, no matter what the cost. The warning of **hell** (v. 22) indicates that those whose lifestyle is characterized by uncontrolled immorality are not heirs of the kingdom (1 Cor. 6:9, 10).

5:31, 32 Sexual immorality is a general term that includes premarital sex, extramarital infidelity, homosexuality, and bestiality (19:3–12).

5:33–37 Do not swear at all does not forbid solemn, official oaths (Gen. 22:16; Ps. 110:4; 2 Cor. 1:23), but only oaths made in common speech. Such oath-taking suggests that a person's normal words cannot be trusted. God's law says, "Do not lie under oath" (Lev. 19:12; Num. 30:2). Jesus was telling His followers not to lie under *any* circumstances. The phrase **to the Lord** could be used as a cover-up for falsehood. Any oath with God's name in it

---

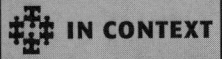 **IN CONTEXT** | **An Eye for An Eye?**

Jesus appears to make some stark, seemingly impossible demands: God's people should never use force in self-defense (Matt. 5:39); they should never contest a lawsuit (5:40); they should comply with every type of demand (5:41); and they should lend without reserve (5:42). Could Jesus possibly be serious?

In this part of the Sermon on the Mount, the Lord is addressing the issue of justice. He was alluding to the OT Law dealing with *public* vengeance. The Law limited damages in criminal cases to no more than the loss suffered—"an eye for an eye" (5:38; Ex. 21:24, 25). Nevertheless, as might be expected, people tended to justify *personal* vengeance by appealing to the same texts. We would call it "taking the law into your own hands."

Jesus' morality challenged that. To be sure, some circumstances call for resistance and self-defense. The Law specifically sanctioned self-protection when there was no other apparent recourse (Ex. 22:2). Likewise, Jesus Himself protested when He was slapped (John 18:22, 23).

But He warned against the needless use of force, particularly in revenge. In self-defense the alternative to resistance may be injury or death. But in vengeance one inflicts harm even though immediate danger is past. A slap on the cheek is little more than an insult. There's no place for violence in response to that. Furthermore, vengeance belongs to God (Deut. 32:35; Rom. 12:19–21), who often uses governing authorities to carry it out (Rom. 13:4).

Throughout Matt. 5:17–48, Jesus speaks in stark contrasts and strong hyperboles (overstatements for the sake of emphasis). The key to understanding this section is to keep in mind the major thrust of His teaching: good not evil, grace not vengeance, love not hatred. That is the morality of Christ.

was legally binding; however, an oath without God's name was not legally binding. This explains the emphasis of vv. 34–37.

5:38 This law is known as the *lex talionis* (the law of retaliation) and so important in the OT (Ex. 21:24; Lev. 24:20; Deut. 19:21). It was meant for punishment, but it also restrained or limited retribution and thus curtailed revenge! A person could demand no more than an eye or a tooth.

5:39–42 The Lord seems to be speaking in hyperbolic terms to teach the lesson of non-retaliation. Generally He commands us to have a generous and compassionate attitude toward the needy. He makes this application in four areas: physical attacks (v. 39), legal suits (v. 40), government demands (v. 41), and financial requests (v. 42).

5:41, 42 Compels is a technical term that refers to the law of impressment. The Roman government could press anyone into its service to carry a load as far as one mile. Matthew records a Roman officer doing this to Simon of Cyrene in 27:32.

5:43, 44 Hate your enemy is not found in Moses' writings. This was a principle drawn by the scribes and Pharisees from Lev. 19:18.

5:45–47 To be a "son of" was to be like someone or something. **That you may be sons of your Father in heaven** means "that you may be like the Heavenly Father who displays His love without discrimination."

5:48 This verse, which comes from Deut. 18:13, refers to completeness. In the context of 5:43–48, it seems to mean that Jesus' followers are to be as mature or perfect as God in the ways that they love. God does not lower the standard to accommodate our sinfulness. Rather, He gives us the power to keep His righteous standard. Thus, He says, "Be holy, as I am holy." And He chose us to "be holy and without blame before Him in love" (Eph. 1:4).

 **IN DEPTH** — **The Sermon on the Mount**

Repent, for the kingdom of heaven is at hand," Jesus warned as He began His public ministry in Galilee (Matt. 4:17). His message quickly spread, and huge crowds came to hear Him from Galilee, from nearby Syria and the Decapolis, and from as far away as Jerusalem, Judea, and east of the Jordan River (4:24, 25).

They came to hear about a kingdom. Instead, Jesus talked about a lifestyle—the lifestyle of those who intend to live in the kingdom. The Sermon on the Mount contains the core of Jesus' moral and ethical teaching:

The Beatitudes (5:3–12). True happiness comes from looking at life from God's perspective, which is often the reverse of the human point of view.

Salt and Light (5:13–16). Jesus wants His followers to influence the moral and spiritual climate of the world.

The Morality of the Kingdom (5:17–48). Jesus' listeners were familiar with the law and with the many traditions that generations of rabbis had added to it. But Jesus revealed a morality that went beyond the letter of the law to its spirit.

Spiritual Disciplines (6:1–18). Practicing religion certainly involves behavior, but it goes beyond an outward show of spirituality to the hidden quality of one's character.

Treasures on Earth (6:19–34). Our relationship to money and material possessions reveals much about our relationship to God. Jesus does not denounce worldly goods, but He urges His listeners to place ultimate value on the treasures in heaven.

Judging Right and Wrong (7:1–6). Most of us are quick to point out the moral flaws of others. Jesus warns us to pay more attention to our own.

Asking and Receiving (7:7–12). When we approach God with a request, we can expect Him to deal with us as a loving father deals with his child. And just as God deals with us in love, He expects us to deal with others in love.

A Challenge to Obedience (7:13–29). Jesus wraps up His message with a challenge to change. The alternatives are clear: living a lifestyle that is worthy of the kingdom, resulting in life and joy; or ignoring the way of Christ, resulting in death and disaster.

In this manner, Jesus described the lifestyle of the kingdom.

✠ IN CONTEXT   Praying to Our Father

Jesus cautioned His disciples not to pray "as the heathen do," using "vain repetitions" and "many words" (Matt. 6:7). When Greeks and Romans prayed, they often called deities by as many different names and titles as possible. Also, their prayers frequently reminded the deity of any favors he or she owed the worshiper because of sacrifices the worshiper had offered.

Jewish people were not supposed to barter with God or try to impress Him with titles. They were to approach God with confidence that He was their Father, as the OT taught them (Ex. 4:22; Is. 63:16). Most children in the ancient world saw their fathers as strong providers and protectors (with whom they did not need to bargain). Jewish prayers, therefore, regularly invoked God as "Our Father in heaven," and trusted Him to provide (Matt. 6:8, 9; 7:7–11).

Teaching His disciples to pray (Matt. 6:8–14), Jesus adopted a fairly common Jewish prayer called the *Kaddish*, which was prayed regularly in the synagogues and included the lines: "Exalted and hallowed be His great name . . . and may He cause His kingdom to rule." This was a prayer for the future kingdom. The Jewish people longed for the ultimate coming of God's reign, when He would rule the earth unchallenged and restore justice and mercy in all the world. At that time God's name would be "hallowed," shown to be holy (Ezek. 39:7, 27); people would no longer profane it by swearing oaths by it lightly or living in such a way as to dishonor it.

"Hallowing God's name" was a central principle of Jewish ethics: Live even among the Gentile in such a manner that people will honor God. The reverse of such honorable behavior, "profaning God's name," was considered so odious that some teachers insisted that those plotting to do evil should disguise themselves as Gentiles first.

6:1–4 they have their reward: The verb translated *have* was used in receipts and is similar to "paid in full." The only reward the hypocrites will ever receive is **glory from men** (vv. 5, 16). Contrast that with the heavenly rewards of Christ given to His followers (2 Cor. 5:10; Rev. 22:12).

6:5–8 Those who pray with improper motives **have their reward**—like those who do charitable deeds with improper motives (v. 2).

6:7 From the *motives* for praying (vv. 1–6), Jesus turned to *methods* of praying. *Why* one prays determines *how* one prays. Nothing is wrong with repeating prayers (26:39, 42, 44). Here Jesus was referring to the empty recitation of words.

6:7 It is not the length of prayer but the strength of prayer that prevails with God. Jesus Himself prayed all night prior to His crucifixion and on most other occasions prayed very briefly. He is not condemning lengthy prayers, although there is nothing particularly spiritual about them. He is merely emphasizing that prayer must be a sincere expression of the heart, not mere accumulation of verbiage. God is not impressed with words, but with the genuine outcry of a needy heart.

6:8 Many have questioned the meaning of the statement **your Father knows the things you have need of before you ask Him.** "Then why should we pray?" they ask. Prayer is not

man's attempt to change the will of God. God's method of changing our will is to bring it into conformity with His will. More than changing things, prayer changes people. Prayer is not conquering God's reluctance to answer, but laying hold of His willingness to help! Prayer, in the life of the true believer, is an act of total confidence and assurance in the plan and purpose of God.

6:9, 10 In this manner does not mean to pray using only these words, but to pray in this way. People often reduce this prayer to empty recitation—exactly what the Lord said *not* to do (v. 7). The prayer is composed of six requests. The first three ask for the kingdom to come (vv. 9, 10) and the last three are for God to meet the needs of His people until the kingdom arrives (vv. 11–13). **Hallowed be Your name** is not an ascription of praise to the Father. The verb is an imperative and means "May Your name be hallowed." This recalls Ezekiel's prophecy in Ezek. 36:25–32, where the prophet says Israel has profaned God's name among the nations. One day God will gather His people from the nations, cleanse them, and by this means vindicate the holiness of His great name. The hallowing of the Father's name means the arrival of God's kingdom.

6:11 Daily bread is a reminder of God's daily supply of manna to Israel in the wilderness.

6:12 This request, explained in vv. 14, 15, is not telling people how to be justified (compare

Rom. 3:21–26; Eph. 2:8–10), but how a justified person maintains his day-by-day walk with God. It is not positional, forensic (legal) forgiveness but family fellowship to be maintained (1 John 1:9).

6:13 The doxology at the end of the prayer is from 1 Chr. 29:11. Some ancient manuscripts of the Scriptures omit this doxology.

6:13–15 Do not lead us into temptation is a plea for the providential help of God in our daily confrontation with the temptation of sin. James 1:13, 14 makes it clear that God does not tempt us to do evil, but rather that we are tempted of our own lusts. However, God does test us in order to give us the opportunity to prove our faithfulness to Him. It is never His desire to lead us into evil itself. Therefore if we resist the devil, we are promised that he will flee from us.

6:16–18 When you fast is a reference both to fasting prescribed under the Mosaic Law in connection with the Day of Atonement (Lev. 16:29) and the voluntary fast of that day. The Pharisees added two fast days, on Monday and Thursday of each week, as a case of public display and piety. The true purpose of fasting was intended, however, for deep contrition and spiritual communion. Fasting was especially emphasized as an effective means of dealing with temptation (Is. 58:6). The Pharisees regarded the practice of fasting as meritorious and appeared in the synagogues negligently attired. Their sad disfigurement of face and the wearing of mourning garb gave them an opportunity to exhibit their superior ascetic sanctity before the people. The phrase **disfigure their faces** (Gk. *aphanizo*) means literally "covering their faces." It is also a figurative expression for mournful gestures and neglected appearance of those wanting to call attention to the fact they are enduring. This was often done with dust and ashes (Is. 61:3).

6:19, 20 Do not lay up . . . but lay up may be rephrased as "Do not give priority to this, but give priority to that." This passage does not mean that it is sinful to have such assets as insurance, retirement plans, and savings accounts. After all, parents are to save for their children (Prov. 13:22; 2 Cor. 12:14). **For yourself** makes it clear that the desire for reward in the kingdom is not sinful. The contrast is between the now and then. We cannot have it both here and there. We cannot take it with us, but we can invest it now in the future.

6:20, 21 The attention of the believer is directed toward **treasures in heaven.** The term "treasures" implies the addition or accumulation of things. The two kinds of treasures are conditioned by their place (either upon earth or in heaven). The concept of laying up treasure in heaven is not pictured as one of meritorious benefits but rather of rewards for faithful service, as is illustrated elsewhere in the teaching of Jesus. The ultimate destiny of our lives is either earthly or heavenly and the concentration of our efforts will reveal where our real treasure is.

6:22, 23 One of the world's leading architects has said, "No muscle of your body can relax if your eye is uncomfortable." Notice Paul's play on words in Gal. 3:1: "Who has bewitched (double-eyed) you . . . before whose eyes Jesus Christ was clearly portrayed." The concept here is based on the ancient idea that the eyes were the windows through which light entered the body.

6:24 Mammon refers to wealth, money, or property. No one can serve two masters because a time will come when they make opposing demands. Jesus advises us to invest in our future with Him by giving of ourselves. Mammon encourages us to collect material objects for our present enjoyment.

6:25, 26 Adding doubt to the danger of possessions, Jesus now deals with the equally dangerous tendency of those who have no possessions: worry! **Do not worry** (Gk. *merimnao*) means do not be anxious. Anxious care is an inordinate or solicitous concern or grief beyond our immediate needs. It is the direct opposite of carefulness, cautiousness, and faith. Therefore, even the poor are not to worry needlessly about what they should eat, drink, or wear. The question, **Is not life more than food and the body more than clothing?** indicates that inner mental stability must come from the spirit of a man and not from outward physical provisions. To set one's heart upon material possessions or to worry about the lack of them is to live in perpetual insecurity and to deprive one's self of the spiritual blessings of God.

6:27 Stature here probably means "length of life," or age. **Cubit** then means a "length" of time, not a distance.

6:28–30 little faith: These are followers of Christ who are anxious about material things (8:26; 16:8).

6:31–32 Gentiles refers to non-Jews or to the heathen—those who do not know God (3 John 7). The Jewish people, because of God's revelation to them, were supposed to think differently than the Gentiles.

6:33, 34 To seek . . . **the kingdom of God and His righteousness** means to desire God's righteous rule on this earth (vv. 9, 10).

7:1 This restriction does not mean that a disciple never judges. After all, some kind of judgment is required in order to obey the command in v. 6. The point of this verse is that a Christian should not have a spirit of carping criticism and fault-finding.

7:2–5 Every **judgment** that a person makes becomes a basis for his or her own judgment (James 3:1, 2).

7:6 **Dogs** and **swine** refer to people who are enemies of the gospel, as opposed to those who are merely unbelievers. Such enemies are to be left alone (Matt. 15:14; 2 Cor. 6:14–18). One example of such a person was Herod Antipas, who heard John the Baptist gladly (Mark 6:20) but then beheaded him (Matt. 14:1–12; Mark 6:14–28; Luke 9:7–9). Later when Christ stood before Herod, He said nothing (Luke 23:8, 9). In the context of this verse, Herod had become a "dog" or a "pig."

7:6 The connotation here is not that we should withhold our message to those who are the outcasts of society, for Jesus Himself went to the poor sinners among His people. Rather, the idea is that it is futile to continue to present

Everything that we need for spiritual success has been promised to us. The blessings and provisions of God are available to every one of His children.

7:12 The phrase **the Law and the Prophets** echoes 5:17. This so-called "golden rule" is the practical application of Lev. 19:18: "You shall love your neighbor as yourself."

7:13–27 The closing section of the Sermon on the Mount presents two choices to the listener. These are presented in a series of contrasts: two ways (vv. 13, 14); two trees (vv. 15–20); two professions (vv. 21–23); and two foundations (vv. 24–29). This was a common method of teaching in both Jewish and Greco-Roman thought.

7:13, 14 wide . . . broad: The vast majority of people in the world have the same attitude as the scribes and Pharisees. They simplistically

---

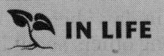 **IN LIFE**   **Judge Not!**

What was Jesus calling for when He ordered His followers to "judge not" (Matt. 7:1)? Did He want them to close their eyes to error and evil? Did He intend that managers forego critical performance reviews of their employees, or that news editors and art critics pull their punches? And what about juries? Should they stop judging? Or should people go even further and decline any assessment of others, since none of us is perfect?

No, those would all be misapplications of Jesus' teaching. He was not commanding blind acceptance but grace toward others. Since we are all sinners, we all need to stop bothering with the failings of others and start attending to serious failings of our own (7:3–5). His words here extend His earlier exposé of hypocrisy (6:1–18). Don't blame or put down others while excusing or exalting yourself, Jesus was saying.

Is there room, then, to assess others? Yes, but only in Jesus' way: with empathy and fairness (7:12), and with a readiness to freely and fully forgive (6:12, 14). When people must correct others, they should act like a good doctor whose purpose is to bring healing, not like an enemy who attacks.

---

truth to those who have refused what they have already heard.

7:7–11 Earlier a paralleling contrast was drawn between the outward acts of worship (giving, praying, fasting) and the inward attitudes of devotion (possessing, praying, judging). Since the opposite of judging is fasting, it seems fitting that Jesus here makes a lengthy statement on the importance of prayer. This statement is not out of place as some have assumed; rather, it is the Christian alternative to judging. If we would sincerely pray for those whom we are prone to criticize we would ultimately do them much more good. The three imperatives **Ask, seek, knock** are, in the original, in the present tense, suggesting both perseverance and frequent prayer to be made on behalf of those for whom we are concerned.

believe that their external works are what count. Jesus gives a much different interpretation to the law, which was the rule of life for His followers. He takes it to the heart and, in so doing, eliminates many from kingdom reign. **narrow . . . few:** Those who put their trust simply in external deeds (1 Cor. 3:12–15; 6:9–10).

7:15–20 Beware of false prophets: Deuteronomy 13:1–11; 18:20–22 provide information on discerning and responding to false prophets. The way to tell false teachers from teachers of truth is **by their fruits.** *Fruits* here refers to more than their deeds; it includes their doctrine (16:12; 1 John 4:1–3). A person speaking in the name of God is to be tested by the doctrines of Scripture. The same principle still holds true today. Speakers and teachers should be tested against the truths in God's Word (Jude 3; Rev. 22:18, 19).

7:21–23 Because so **many** people teach the wrong way, there is a tendency to ask how so many people could be wrong. Besides they do such good things which seem so right. For example, they **prophesied, cast out demons,** and did **so many wonders.** And they did these things **in Your name.** The threefold repetition strongly emphasizes this (compare Matt. 24:4, 5; 23–25). The question arises, "What is greater evidence of authority than these things?" Remember that Christ has been interpreting the law for them and the law was very clear that the word of God is superior to any miracle. Furthermore, even if the sign comes to pass, it is to be rejected if the message is not according to the Word of God and the false teacher was to be executed (Deut. 13).

7:24–27 The key difference in the two houses is not their external appearance. Pharisees and scribes may seem to be as righteous as the heirs of the kingdom. The key in the story is the foundations. The **house on the rock** pictures a life founded on a proper relationship to Christ (Matt. 16:18; 1 Cor. 10:4; 1 Pet. 2:4–8). It will stand the test of Christ's judgment, but the **house on the sand** will fail the test (1 Cor. 3:12–15).

7:28, 29 not as the scribes: Scribes would often cite authorities in order to lend credence to their statements. Jesus' words were self-authenticating. Note His phrase "I say to you" in 5:20, 22, 26, 28, 32.

8:1 In Matt. 8:1—9:38 ten miracles are recorded in rapid order. The logical connection to the Sermon on the Mount is obvious. The King, having presented His platform—the Manifesto of the Kingdom—now demonstrates His power to perform what He has said. Often we hear grand, swelling promises from potential political powers but we wonder, "Can he produce?" Christ the King is now going to demonstrate His ability to produce the projected program. The miracles are divided into three groups by two discussions regarding discipleship. All of the miraculous works authenticate the Lord Jesus as Messiah and King. The first three are miracles of healing (8:1–17). Healing **a leper** was a dramatic place to begin for there was no record of an Israelite leper being healed in the entire history of the nation except for Miriam (Num. 12:10–15).

8:2, 3 Before this miracle, the only record of an Israelite being healed of leprosy was the case of Miriam in Num. 12:10–15. The phrase **if You are willing** is important because it indicates genuine faith. It does not necessarily mean that if one simply believes, God *will* do something. But that He *can* do it (Dan. 3:17, 18). Normally, touching a leper would result in ceremonial defilement (Lev. 14:45, 46; Num. 5:2, 3; Deut. 24:8). In this case Jesus touched the leper and the leper became clean.

8:4 See that you tell no one: Perhaps Jesus gave this command so that the healed person would first obey the law before he became preoccupied with telling others about his healing. Jesus' command **show yourself to the priest** involved no small undertaking for the cleansed leper. He would need to make the journey from near the Sea of Galilee to Jerusalem and there offer the sacrifice required by Moses (Lev. 14:4–32). The purpose of Christ's command was not only to obey the Law of Moses, but also to be a testimony to the religious authorities in Jerusalem that the Messiah had arrived. Jesus also commanded the man to keep quiet because He did not want the Jewish people to act hastily on preconceived, erroneous ideas of the Messiah and His kingdom (John 6:14, 15).

8:5–9 In the NT, centurions (officers in charge of one hundred soldiers) are consistently looked upon in a favorable light. These soldiers were the equivalent of present-day sergeants. The centurion's response to Jesus indicated his clear understanding of **authority.**

8:10 He marveled: Only one other time

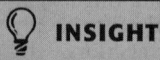 INSIGHT **Peter's Household**

Households in Jesus' day tended to be much larger than those of today, with more children and more relatives from the extended family.

But Peter's home (Matt. 8:14) was somewhat unusual in that his mother-in-law lived with the family. Peter was not required by law or custom to provide her with a home. A widow usually moved back to her father's home, if he were still alive, or else joined a son's household.

It was fortunate for Peter's mother-in-law that Peter befriended Jesus. The Lord's compassion extended to her. He healed her from her fever, and she began to serve Him, a response that indicated a changed life and a deeply grateful attitude.

does Scripture say Jesus marveled: when His own townspeople rejected Him (Mark 6:6). **I have not found . . . not even in Israel:** This commendation of the faith of the Gentile centurion was a strong rebuke of the Jewish people. The Israelites thought that they would have priority in the coming kingdom (Is. 45:14; Zech. 8:23; Rom. 9:3–5; Eph. 2:11, 12). Jesus made it clear that being just a physical descendant of Abraham did not guarantee entrance into His kingdom.

8:11 Sit down literally means "recline," as at a banquet table. The coming kingdom is commonly portrayed in terms of a feast, particularly a wedding feast (Matt. 22:1–14; Is. 25:6; Rev. 19:7–10).

8:12, 13 Sons of the kingdom refers to the Jews who had the covenants and the promises, and who should have been heirs of the kingdom. The idea that Gentiles would take their place in the coming kingdom was unthinkable to the Jews. **Outer darkness,** meaning "the darkness outside," speaks of the experience of those who do not endure and so will not reign in the kingdom (Matt. 22:13; Rom. 8:17; 2 Tim. 2:12, 13; 2 John 8; Rev. 3:11). Living with Christ in heaven is a gift (John 3:16; Rom. 4:1–8; 6:23) to be received without cost. But the reign with Christ is a prize to be won with great effort (compare 1 Cor. 9:24–27; Rev. 22:12).

8:14–17 This flurry of healing activity anticipated the future healings based on Christ's cross ministry that would take place in the kingdom age. The verse is a quotation of Is. 53:4. The death of Christ on the cross makes possible the healing that will belong to God's children in the coming messianic reign and in eternity. It is possible the sequence of miracles in Matt. 8:1–17 has significance. First, the Lord Jesus was manifested to Israel in His earthly ministry. Because He was rejected by them, He ministered to Gentiles in this present age (8:5–13). Then He will come to Israel and restore them as their promised Messiah and Redeemer (8:14–17).

8:17 took our infirmities . . . bore our sicknesses: In what way did Jesus take infirmity and sickness from us? Certainly, when He healed someone, He did not receive their disease and become sick Himself. The text of Isaiah regarding Messiah may mean at least two things. Christ bore our sickness in that He empathizes with our weaknesses. Repeatedly Jesus is said to have healed because He had compassion on the people (Matt. 9:36; 14:14; 20:34; Mark 1:41; 5:19; compare 6:34; Luke 7:13). He also bore our sicknesses by His vicarious suffering for sin on the cross. Our physical sickness is ultimately because of the Fall, the fact that we are sinners with its impact on our lives through the curse. Note Is. 53:4, 5 connects these two dimensions.

Photo by Howard Vos

Remains of a church at ancient Gergesa which memorializes Jesus' healing of the demoniac (Matt. 8:28–34). This region east of the Sea of Galilee was also known as Gadara and Gerasa.

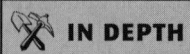

IN DEPTH   Supernatural Realities

Jesus often encountered demons like those that possessed the men at Gadara (Matt. 8:28–34). The mention of demons affirms the reality of powerful spiritual forces in the universe. Scripture has much to say about angels and demons.

Angels are members of an order of heavenly beings who are superior to humans in power and intelligence (Heb. 2:7; 2 Pet. 2:11; Zech. 3:1). However, unlike God, they are not all-powerful or all-knowing (Ps. 103:20; 2 Thess. 1:7). God often sends them to announce good news, such as the birth of Jesus (Luke 1:30, 31), or to warn of coming dangers, such as the destruction of Sodom (Gen. 18:16–19:29).

Angels played a particularly active role in the events surrounding Jesus' birth, resurrection, and ascension. They:

- counseled Joseph to wed Mary (Matt. 1:20);
- warned Joseph to flee to Egypt with Mary and the Christ child (2:13);
- instructed Joseph to return the family to Palestine (2:19);
- foretold to Zacharias the birth of John the Baptist (Luke 1:11–38);
- announced to shepherds the birth of Christ (2:8–15);
- appeared to Jesus in the Garden of Gethsemane to strengthen Him (22:43);
- rolled back the stone from Jesus' empty tomb (Matt. 28:2);
- appeared to women at the empty tomb to announce Jesus' resurrection (Luke 24:4–7, 23; John 20:12);
- promised Jesus' return after His ascension (Acts 1:9–11).

Since Pentecost, the frequency of angelic activity in human affairs appears to have diminished, perhaps because of the larger role played by the Holy Spirit in the lives of believers.

Demons are fallen angels that have been cast out of heaven. They seek to undermine the cause of righteousness in the world (1 Pet. 3:19, 20; 2 Pet. 2:4; Jude 6). Scripture describes them with various names: "unclean spirits" (Mark 6:7), "wicked or evil spirits" (Luke 7:21; Acts 19:12, 13), "spirit of divination" (Acts 16:16), "deceiving spirits" (1 Tim. 4:1), and "spirit of error" (1 John 4:6).

8:18–20 The term **Son of Man** is very important. In the Gospel records the expression is never found on anyone's lips but the Lord Jesus, and it was His favorite self designator (83 times). It looks back to Dan. 7:13, 14 and anticipates the messianic reign of Christ. In Matt. 8:20 it describes the Messiah in His humiliation in His first coming. He didn't come first to reign but to suffer. Next He will come to reign. The cross was before the crown but it was the crown that motivated Him (Heb. 12:2, 3). **foxes and birds:** Jesus indicates, in the midst of His teaching on discipleship, that sacrifice must be undertaken, even similar to the Lord Himself, who, as a man, had no dwelling place to call His own (compare Luke 9:57–62).

8:21, 22 This passage most likely describes a follower whose father was still alive, because by Levitical law the man would not be out in public if his father had just died. His father was aged, so the man wanted to go to his home, wait for his father to die, and then follow Christ. Jesus' answer means that we must never make excuses for refusing to follow Him. There is no better time than the present.

8:23–27 Jesus rebuked their **little faith** in light of the fact that He had commanded the trip across the Sea of Galilee.

8:28 The country of the Gergesenes may refer to (1) the village of Khersa, near the eastern shore of the Sea of Galilee; (2) Gerasa, about thirty miles southeast of the Sea of Galilee; or (3) Gadara, about six miles away. This was Gentile territory.

8:29–34 We learn several things about demons in this passage: (1) they recognize the deity of Christ; (2) they are limited in their knowledge; (3) they know they will ultimately be judged by Christ (Matt. 25:41; James 2:19; 2 Pet. 2:4; Jude 6; Rev. 12:7–12); and (4) they cannot act without the permission of a higher authority—Christ's.

9:1, 2 Their faith refers to the faith of the paralytic as well as that of the men who were carrying him.

9:3–8 Jesus' tactic caught the leaders off

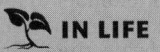 **IN LIFE** | **The Power of Forgiveness**

The crowd that watched Jesus heal the paralytic responded enthusiastically to His dramatic display of power (Matt. 9:8). But they overlooked His more significant ability to forgive sins—a power that deeply troubled the scribes (9:2, 3).

The power of forgiveness is immeasurable. Jesus challenged us as His followers to forgive others who have wronged or hurt us (6:14, 15; 18:21–35). That may seem like a simple act, but anyone who has struggled with pain and anger knows that it takes enormous power to authentically forgive—to lay aside one's hurt and reach out to an offender with the embrace of a pardon. On the other side, forgiveness can release the wrongdoer from paralyzing guilt and even turn around the course of that person's life (James 5:19, 20).

Forgiveness is as powerful and liberating as the healing of a paralytic. And it's a power that Jesus has delegated to His followers (John 20:23). We are called to forgive others as Christ has forgiven us (Col. 3:13).

guard. Though these leaders might deny His ability, or right, to forgive sins, the outward physical healing could not be denied. It was far easier to say **Your sins are forgiven you** because there would be no visible proof that the sins were forgiven. The healing of the paralytic, however, was proof that forgiveness of sins had occurred as well. Neither physical nor spiritual healing pose any difficulty for God's Son.

9:9–11 Matthew is called Levi in Mark 2:14; Luke 5:27. **The tax office** was a toll booth set up alongside a highway to levy taxes on merchandise transported on that road. Matthew probably worked for Herod Antipas, tetrarch of Galilee. Tax collectors were considered traitors by the Jews. They were despised because they generally collected more than necessary and pocketed the difference, vastly enriching themselves.

9:12, 13 Jesus quoted Hos. 6:6 (and again in Matt. 12:7) to make the point that God is more interested in a person's loyal love than in the observance of external rituals. Jesus refers iron-

ically to the Pharisees as **the righteous.** They were not righteous; that was only how they perceived themselves because of their pious and scrupulous law-keeping (Phil. 3:6). But Jesus explained, quoting from the familiar words of an OT prophet, that God had already judged sacrifices without mercy as worthless.

9:14, 15 Jesus used the picture of marriage to illustrate God's relationship with Israel (Is. 54:1–8; Jer. 3:1–20; Hos. 2:1–3:5). In referring to Himself as a **bridegroom,** Jesus was describing Himself as the Messiah. **Will be taken away from them** anticipates the Lord's violent death.

9:16, 17 The principle expressed here is that Jesus Christ has come to bring in a new dispensation altogether, which cannot be fitted into the forms of the old Jewish economy. The principle taught here by illustration is that the rule of the law must be replaced by that of grace, which will now have free reign in the hearts of all believers. **Unshrunk cloth** means unbleached cloth. The KJV reads "new." **Wineskins**

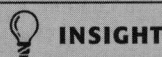 **INSIGHT** | **The Mourners**

In the ancient world, paid professional mourners (Matt. 9:23), most often women, aided families in their public expression of grief upon the death of a loved one. They composed poems or dirges praising the deceased, which they chanted to the accompaniment of a flute or other musical instrument to stir the audience emotionally. They usually wore sackcloth and scattered dust in the air and on their heads. Weeping, wailing, and beating their breasts, they created an unmistakable tone of grief. Here was no denial of death or a distancing themselves from loss.

Perhaps Jesus was making use of the image of the professional mourner when He spoke of those who mourn in the Sermon on the Mount (Matt. 5:2).

were frequently used in the ancient East as containers for liquids. The strength of fermentation of the new wine would be too much for the partly worn, old, or inelastic skins and would cause them to break.

9:18–26 a ruler: This was a magistrate. The other Gospels indicate that his name was Jairus (Mark 5:22–43; Luke 8:41–56). **Worshiped** suggests that he recognized Jesus' deity and authority. In the parallel passages we are told that she was dying when the father first came and that she died while he was en route. Matthew combines these two phrases into one, saying, **has just died.**

9:27–31 See that no one knows it: Jesus wanted to discourage the masses from coming to Him for physical healing alone, because His primary purpose was spiritual healing. Physical healing simply served to authenticate His claim to be the promised Messiah.

9:32–34 The Pharisees could not deny the reality of the miracles, so they attributed them to **the ruler of the demons.** The same rationalization is found in 12:24.

9:35 This verse is very similar to 4:23. Just as Matthew 4:23 brings one section to a conclusion and prepares the reader for a discourse, so does 9:35 here. The miracles of Matthew 8 and 9 prove Jesus as the Messiah is capable of bringing about kingdom conditions. The next chapter sees the Twelve sent out to proclaim the presence of the King and the nearness of the kingdom.

9:36 This verse is a terrible indictment of the religious authorities of Israel, who though

very religious, provided no spiritual guidance to their people. Here is a solemn reminder to those today who market and make merchandise of ministry. **compassion:** To bring them God's truth, Jesus' heart was moved toward those who were the victims of charlatans.

9:37, 38 The harvest will mark the beginning of the kingdom age. For the lost, it will mean doom; for the saved, it will mean blessing.

10:1, 2 The **twelve** are called "disciples" in 10:1; in v. 2 they are called **apostles.** The word *apostle* emphasizes delegated authority (1 Thess. 2:6); the term *disciple* emphasizes learning and following. Because the disciples had been given authority, they were now called apostles.

10:2–4 The disciples are named in pairs and probably were sent out that way (Mark 6:7).

10:5, 6 These commands stand in stark contrast to Matt. 28:19. The reason for commands in Matt. 10:5, 6 is the contingency of the coming of the kingdom. Its arrival was dependent on Israel's response to Jesus as the Messiah (compare Acts 3:19, 20). Between Matt. 10 and Matt. 28, the Jewish leaders and, consequently, the nation rejects the Messiah in spite of His obvious credentials. During the interim the gospel is to go to all the nations of the world. When Israel repents, the kingdom will come (compare Zech. 12:10).

10:7–42 The instructions given to the Twelve were specifically for their particular preaching mission to announce the nearness of the kingdom. If all of the commands in this address were meant to be followed explicitly

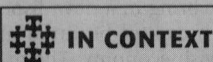 **IN CONTEXT** **Jesus—A City Preacher**

Popular opinion frequently regards the Bible in general and the ministry of Jesus in particular in rural terms. But that is somewhat misleading.

Palestine in Jesus' day was undergoing rapid urban development. Its population of around 2.5 million to 3 million people lived in numerous preindustrial cities and towns that revolved around Jerusalem, the hub of the region, which had a population conservatively estimated by modern scholars at between 55,000 and 90,000. (Josephus, a first-century Jewish historian, placed the number at 3 million; the Talmud puts it at an incredible 12 million.)

As Jesus carried out His ministry, He focused on the urban centers of Palestine (Matt. 9:35; 11:1; Luke 4:43; 13:22) and visited Jerusalem at least three times. This brought Him into contact with a greater number and wider variety of people—women, soldiers, religious leaders, the rich, merchants, tax collectors, Gentiles, prostitutes, beggars, the poor—than He would have encountered in a purely rural campaign. These He attracted in large crowds as He visited each city.

Jesus' urban strategy established a model for His disciples and the early church. When He sent the disciples on preaching tours, He directed them toward cities (Matt. 10:5, 11–14; Luke 10:1, 8–16). Later, the movement spread throughout the Roman Empire by using an urban strategy that planted communities of believers in no less than forty cities by the end of the first century.

In light of the vital role that cities played in the ministry of Jesus, our Lord's example in urban Palestine has much to teach us in our modern world.

today, the church could not have a worldwide mission (compare 10:5).

10:7, 8 The message is the same as that proclaimed by John (3:2) and the Lord Jesus (4:17). The king was present but the kingdom was not; it had drawn near and was ready to come.

10:9, 10 The disciples' mission was short-term. In essence, they were to do a national religious survey to determine the people's response to Jesus as Messiah. For the Twelve to cover an area that is at most 75 miles by 125 miles would not take very long. Thus they did not need extensive provisions.

10:11 Because the testimony of the apostles was at stake, they were to seek out homes with good reputations. Further, they were not to be constantly trying to find a more desirable residence.

10:12–14 To **greet** a household was to pronounce a blessing on it, "**Peace** to you." These messengers were to assume the best of their hosts when they arrived; however, if the home proved to be unworthy (the occupants rejected the message of the apostles), the apostles were to remove the pronouncement of blessing.

10:15 This verse, together with 11:22, 24, implies that there will be degrees of judgment and torment for the lost.

10:16 Snakes are commonly thought of as **wise,** perhaps because they are silent and dangerous, or because of the way they move (Gen. 3:1). **In the midst of wolves** meant that the apostles would be exposed to hatred and violence from men. **Harmless** literally means "unmixed," which may also indicate purity and innocence.

10:17 Beware of men helps to explain the **wolves** of v. 16. The whole emphasis on persecution seems to anticipate the period of tribulation prophesied in the OT (Dan. 9:26, 27; Jer. 30:4–6). It was anticipated that the Messiah would die and be resurrected (Dan. 9:26; Pss. 16: 10; 22; Is. 53:1–11). The time of Jacob's trouble would follow the death and resurrection of the Messiah (Dan. 9:26, 27; Jer. 30:7). Then the Messiah would return to end the tribulation and judge the world (Dan. 7:9–13, 16–27; 9:27; 12:1; Zech. 14:1–5). Then the Christ would establish His kingdom on this earth (Dan. 7:11–27; 12:1, 2; Is. 53:11, 12; Zech. 14:6–11, 20, 21). It appears this is the program the Lord Jesus is anticipating in this discourse. At this

 **IN COMPARISON**   **The Twelve**

Apostle	Description
Simon (Peter)	Fisherman from Galilee, Andrew's brother
Andrew	Fisherman from Galilee, Peter's brother
James	Son of Zebedee, brother to John; from Capernaum
John	Son of Zebedee, brother to James, from Capernaum
Philip	From Bethsaida
Bartholomew (Nathanael)	From Cana in Galilee
Thomas (Didymus)	Possibly also a fisherman
Matthew (Levi)	Tax collector in Capernaum; son of Alphaeus, possibly James's brother
James	Son of Alphaeus, possibly Matthew's brother
Lebbaeus Thaddaeus (Judas)	May have taken the name Thaddaeus ("warm-hearted") because of the infamy that came to be attached to the name Judas
Simon (the Cananite)	From Cana; one of the Zealots, Jewish revolutionaries who opposed Rome
Judas Iscariot	From Kerioth, and possibly the only Judean among the Twelve

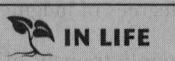 **IN LIFE**   **Affirm Other Leaders**

J esus invested Himself in the development of other people, particularly the Twelve. He gave them responsibility and authority, resisting the temptation to get the job done "right" by doing it Himself. With this approach, He accepted the risk that they might fail. Of course, He gave them adequate preparation before sending them out, and on their return He affirmed them on their successful completion of the mission and corrected their mistakes. If we want to be like Him, we will share the joys and risks of working together with our brothers and sisters.

point the temporary "setting aside" of Israel and the church age had not yet been revealed. They were yet mysteries (Matt. 16; Eph. 3). **scourge:** This reference to scourging in the synagogues shows (1) there will be opposition to the message of the apostles and (2) this resistance will be primarily on the part of Jewish leaders. Even during the tribulation Israel will be in unbelief until near the end of that seven-year period (compare Zech. 12:10 in the context of the entire chapter).

10:18–22 God would use Jewish rejection and persecution of the messengers to bring the gospel message to Gentiles. This occurred with Paul in Acts 21:26–36; 24:1–21; 25:13—26:32.

10:23 This verse has caused no little discussion. Some have even said the Lord Jesus made a mistake here! The only consistent interpretation is to say, as the comments on 10:17 indicate, that the church age had not yet been

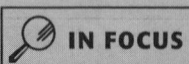 **IN FOCUS**   **"Beelzebub"**

(Gk. *Beelzeboul*) (Matt. 10:25; 12:24–27; Mark 3:22; Luke 11:15–19) Strong's #954: Most of the Greek manuscripts read *Beelzeboul,* which is probably the right form of this word. The other reading probably came from the OT word Baal-Zebub—an idol, the god of Ekron (2 Kin. 1:2). All idolatry was regarded as devil worship (Lev. 17:7; Deut. 32:17; Ps. 106:37; 1 Cor. 10:20), so there seems to have been something peculiarly satanic about the worship of this hateful god, which caused his name to become a synonym for "Satan." Though we nowhere read that Jesus was actually called Beelzebub, He was charged with being in league with Satan under that hateful name (Matt. 12:24, 26), and more than once He was charged with being possessed by "a devil" or "demon" (Mark 3:30; John 7:20; 8:48).

revealed and the great tribulation (Dan. 9:27; Matt. 24:15–31) appeared to be in the near future. The way that Christ presents imminent events, which might be much longer in time is consistent with the OT prophets. It is like looking at two mountain ranges, not viewing the large valley between them (compare Is. 61:1, 2 with Luke 4:16–21). The church age is a valley between the first and second comings of Christ. It was a mystery hidden in God and not revealed in the OT (Eph. 3:1–12).

10:24–26 do not fear: Do not be intimidated by opposition.

10:27, 28 Fear Him refers not to Satan but to God. **Destroy** does not indicate annihilation but ruination. The same verb is used in 9:17 of wineskins being ruined.

10:29–31 These verses show that an infinite God is concerned about and watches over an infinite number of details.

10:32, 33 Every act of our lives will be evaluated at the judgment seat of Christ (2 Cor. 5:10). To refuse to speak up for Christ because of intimidation or persecution will result in the believer's loss of reward and consequent loss of glory in the kingdom (Rom. 8:17; 2 Tim. 2:12).

10:34–36 To the disappointment of many Christians throughout the ages, it has often been those closest to them who have rejected them and their message, even to the point of betrayal. The Lord Himself experienced these feelings with the betrayal of Judas and the denial of Peter.

10:37 not worthy of Me: Those who will be glorified with Christ in His kingdom reign are those who have suffered for Him (Rom. 8:17; 2 Tim. 2:12). Those who refuse that kind of discipleship will experience great loss (1 Cor. 3:15; 2 Cor. 5:10; Rev. 3:11, 12).

10:38 Taking up a **cross** stands for commitment to the extent one is willing to die for a cause. This verse is not saying the only saved people are those who continually are totally committed. If this were true, who would be justified? Rather, when a person who is saved lapses, as Peter did and as a carnal Christian does (1 Cor. 3:1–4), that person certainly is not worthy of Christ and that act brings loss of reward. Of course, the same is always true of a lost individual. Even his finest work is ultimately worthless to him because it is done apart from acknowledgment and dependency on Christ (Rom. 3:12).

10:39 Finding **life** looks not at living life only for what one can obtain from physical life and the material world but how he or she can invest it today in the future reign with Christ (Matt. 6:19–21). We can't have it both here and there. As stewards of this life and all its resources, we shall be evaluated as to how well we invested (Luke 19:11–26). You can't take it with you, but you can send it ahead in the form of present wise investment.

10:40–42 these little ones is a figure of speech to describe the disciples. This is known by the identification of the prophet and the righteous person of v. 41. **Reward** is the last word of the chapter, and it summarizes the motivation Christ has been setting before the disciples. He doesn't want them to lose out on the future reign because of a wrong attitude toward the present. Furthermore, He wants them to understand that nothing shall miss His notice at the *bema* (2 Cor. 5:10), not even a **cup of cold water.**

11:1, 2 Verse 2 actually looks back to 4:12 and anticipates John's death recorded in 14:1–12. Probably John had expected the Messiah to come and immediately to judge Israel and to establish His earthly kingdom (compare 3:2–12). Christ's failure to act in a way even expected by the forerunner himself begins to cause doubt in John's mind. John expected immediate judgment on faithless Israel and pos-

sibly the overthrow of Israel's enemies since they all truly deserved it. Christ was longsuffering and came in mercy. We must be careful not to second-guess the Lord ourselves. This may cause doubt to arise in our own heart when we set forth a path for Christ's work in our lives that He has not Himself purposed.

11:3–6 The Coming One is a title for the Messiah (Ps. 118:26; Mark 11:9; Luke 13:35; 19:38; Heb. 10:37).

11:7–15 In the light of John the Baptist's question, some may have questioned his commitment to the Messiah. This may have prompted Jesus' supportive statements about John.

11:9, 10 John was **more than a prophet** in that he alone was the forerunner who announced the coming and presence of the Messiah. In doing so, he fulfilled Mal. 3:1.

11:11 Born of women means that John the Baptist had a human mother. A similar expression is used of the Lord Jesus in Gal. 4:4. The **least in the kingdom** refers to those who will be living in the coming kingdom. As great as John was during Jesus' day, his position as forerunner was inferior to that of the least person in the kingdom of heaven, because that person will have seen and understood the finished work of Christ on the Cross and through His resurrection—events that John would not live to see. Little wonder that Jesus gave such strong exhortations in Matt. 10:32–42 not to miss out on His future reign.

11:12 The violent take it by force in this context probably means that violent people forcibly oppose the kingdom with their hostility (23:13). As Christ's kingdom advances, so do the attacks against it.

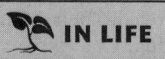 **IN LIFE**   ## What It Means to Be Like Jesus

Jesus' statement in Matt. 10:25 implies that His disciples will be like Him. To His first-century followers, that included the prospect of persecution and martyrdom. Eight portraits in Matthew's eyewitness account give us some clues about what else it means to be like Jesus:

#1: To be like Jesus means to accept our roots (1:1–17).

#2: To be like Jesus means to engage the world's pain and struggle (1:18—2:23).

#3: To be like Jesus means to commit ourselves to other believers, no matter how "weird" they appear to be (3:1–17).

#4: To be like Jesus means to admit our vulnerability to temptation (4:1–11).

#5: To be like Jesus means to openly proclaim the message of Christ (4:12–25).

#6: To be like Jesus means to commit ourselves to changed thinking and behavior (5:1–7:27).

#7: To be like Jesus means to serve others, especially those who are oppressed or without Christ (8:1–9:38).

#8: To be like Jesus means to affirm others in leadership (10:1–42).

 **IN FOCUS**   "Christ"

(Gk. *Christos*) (Matt. 11:2; 16:16; John 1:41; Acts 2:36; 2 Cor. 1:21) Strong's #*5547*: Many speak of Jesus Christ but do not realize that the title "Christ" is in essence a confession of faith. The word literally means "the Anointed One." In the OT, forms of its Hebrew equivalent *messiah* were applied to prophets (1 Kin. 19:16), priests (Lev. 4:5, 16), and kings (1 Sam. 24:6, 10), in the sense that all of them were anointed with oil, the symbol that God had set them aside for their respective offices. But the preeminent Anointed One would be the promised Messiah, for He would be anointed by God's Spirit to be the ultimate Prophet, Priest, and King (Is. 61:1; John 3:34). With his dramatic confession, "You are the Christ, the Son of the living God" (Matt. 16:16), Peter plainly identified Jesus as the promised Messiah.

11:13 The prophets and the law refers to the OT, which anticipated the coming of the Messiah. Because John the Baptist was the forerunner of Christ, the OT anticipated John's ministry as well.

11:14, 15 Malachi 4:5, 6 predicted the coming of Elijah before the judgment preceding the presence of the kingdom. If Israel had repented, the Baptist would have come in the spirit and power of Elijah. However, because Israel failed to respond as they should have, the prophecy of Malachi 4:5, 6 is yet to be fulfilled (Matt. 17:11; Mal. 3:1).

11:16–19 Because of their hardness of heart, Israel failed to accept either the ministry of John the Baptist or that of the Lord Jesus Christ.

11:20–22 Woe: Jesus pronounced a direct judgment on Israel. **Chorazin** was a village about two and a half miles north of Capernaum; **Bethsaida** was about three miles east. Both of these cities were in Galilee and both had witnessed Jesus' ministry firsthand. They would be judged for seeing the Messiah and then rejecting Him.

11:23, 24 Capernaum, on the north shore of the Sea of Galilee, was the base of operations for Christ's ministry. In Matt. 9:1 Capernaum is called "His own city."

11:25–28 You who labor and are heavy laden describes the Jews as suffering under a load of religious responsibilities laid on them by priests, rabbis, scribes, and Pharisees (Matt. 23:4; Acts 15:10). **Rest** is relief from this burden.

11:29, 30 You will find rest for your souls. These words are taken from Jer. 6:16. The LXX has "ye shall find purification unto your souls" and is corrected by Matthew to the original meaning in the Hebrew. **Easy** means good or kind. Verses 28–30 are peculiar to Matthew's gospel.

12:1, 2 The way Jesus observed the Sabbath was a primary point of contention between Himself and the religious authorities. The Pharisees and scribes recognized that the Sabbath was the sign of the Mosaic covenant. Therefore, to desecrate the Sabbath was to flaunt disobedience to the entire Law of Moses (Num. 15:30–36). While reaping was forbidden on the Sabbath (Ex. 34:21), the disciples were picking grain to eat, not for profit. They were not breaking God's law. The Pharisees had established thirty-nine categories of actions to be forbidden on the Sabbath, and according to them, the disciples were "harvesting" and therefore breaking the Sabbath. The Pharisees were trying to make Jesus into a lawbreaker and accuse Him of wrongdoing.

12:3–5 profane the Sabbath: On the Sabbath the priests carried out their work of ministry, showing that their official service had priority over the normal Sabbath observance.

12:7, 8 For a similar use of Hos. 6:6 see Matt. 9:13.

12:14 Because of Jesus' view of the Sabbath, the Pharisees concluded that He was trying to overthrow the entire Mosaic system and therefore had to be destroyed. Their antagonism toward Jesus was growing.

12:15, 16 withdrew: From this point on, the Lord's ministry was characterized by opposition, withdrawal from that opposition, and continued ministry to His followers.

12:17–21 This quotation of Is. 42:1–4 shows that the Messiah's quiet withdrawal was in keeping with the prophet's portrayal of Him. The most significant aspect of this prophecy is that Jesus' reserve in the face of Jewish opposition would lead to blessings on the Gentiles.

12:22–24 Could this be the Son of David may also be translated "This one can't be the Son of David, can he?" The question expected a negative answer.

12:25–28 Jesus' defense was in three parts. First, a kingdom, city, or even a family cannot continue to exist if it is divided against itself.

💡 **INSIGHT** **The Son of Man**

"Son of Man" (Matt. 12:8) is a designation that Jesus used freely for Himself throughout the Gospels. No one else except Stephen (Acts 7:56) referred to Him this way. The phrase seems to have originated with Ezekiel (Ezek. 2:1), where it stressed the prophet's full involvement with the people to whom he spoke. In Dan. 7:13, "One like the Son of Man" may refer to a divine or angelic being. As Jesus used the phrase, it seems to combine His humanity and divine authority.

Jesus may have used the phrase because His contemporaries had preconceived ideas that might make them misunderstand other titles. "Christ," for example, could refer to one who would establish an earthly kingdom.

"Son of Man" was a more flexible term. As the Son of Man, Jesus exercised authority over the Sabbath (Matt. 12:8) and forgave sins (9:6). The Son of Man must suffer and die to ransom sinners (Mark 8:31), yet He would come again in divine glory (Matt. 26:64) to gather His followers (Mark 13:26, 27) and to judge the world (Matt. 13:41–43).

Second, when the followers of the Pharisees exorcized demons, the Pharisees claimed it was accomplished by the power of God. Third, the casting out of demons by the Messiah indicated the nearness of the kingdom.

12:27 your sons: Probably Jews who cast out demons in God's name (Acts 19:13–18). **they shall be your judges:** Their own people recognized that only God could conquer demons.

12:29, 30 This verse shows how Jesus the King was confronting the kingdom of Satan. In His exorcisms, Jesus was binding Satan bit by bit. When He comes suddenly to establish His kingdom, He will bind Satan quickly and completely (Rev. 20:1–10).

12:31, 32 This passage discusses the infa-

mous "unpardonable sin." The first question to be answered is, "Why is blasphemy of the Son of Man pardonable, but not blasphemy against the Holy Spirit?" The key seems to be in the title "Son of Man." It describes Jesus or Messiah in human terms; He was a man. Someone could consider who Jesus was and conclude He was no more than a human being. However, if the Holy Spirit convicted a person of the fact that Jesus was more than a mere mortal, and this person refused to accept the ministry of the Holy Spirit, there would be no possible forgiveness. That the sin against the Holy Spirit is called "blasphemy" implies a final and unalterable decision has been made. The sin that is unforgivable is the stubborn refusal when the Holy Spirit convicts to accept the forgiveness Christ

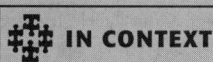 **IN CONTEXT** **Brood of Vipers**

Jesus' contemporaries considered the Pharisees to be model religious people. Yet in Matt. 12:34, Jesus called the Pharisees a brood, or offspring, of vipers. Calling a person a snake was an insult, but to call someone a child of a snake was worse.

An idea that the Greek historian Herodotus (484–425 B.C.) had about Arabian vipers was still circulating in Jesus' day. Although most reptiles lay eggs, people believed that viper eggs hatched inside their mother's stomach. The baby vipers would then eat their way out to be born, killing their mother in the process. Also, according to some ancient writers, including Herodotus, mother vipers ate the father vipers while the mothers were pregnant, so the baby vipers avenged their father by killing the mother.

Murdering one's mother or father was the crime ancient people thought most horrible. Even if one killed one parent to avenge it's murder of the other parent, the Greeks thought that the child who committed this kind of murder would be hounded by avenging spirits called "Furies." Jewish people also considered the murder of parents or other blood relatives to be terribly wicked.

By calling the Pharisees an "offspring of vipers," Jesus may have been comparing them with parent murderers, thus implying that they were quite vile and evil.

offers. Particularly in reference to the leaders of Israel, Jesus had offered them all the proof that could be expected—the ministry of John, the testimony of the Father, the prophecies of the OT, His own testimony, and the substantiation by the Holy Spirit. They rejected all proofs regarding Jesus as Messiah. Nothing else was to be given.

12:33–37 By your words does not refer to justification or condemnation on the basis of what one says, but to the outward evidence of the inward attitude of the heart. While the Pharisees asked for evidence of Christ's claim, they overlooked the clear evidence that was to be seen in His miracles.

12:38, 39 The demand for signs is evidence of unbelief rather than faith. **The sign of the prophet Jonah** is explained in v. 40 as the Resurrection.

12:40 Three days and three nights does not necessarily indicate three full days. In ancient Israel, a part of a day was considered a whole day (Esth. 4:16; 5:1); so a period of twenty-six hours could be called "three days."

12:41, 42 The men of Nineveh represent Gentiles who came to faith because of the words of God's prophets and kings, lesser people than Jesus Christ, God's only Son.

12:43–50 This difficult analogy most likely

leaders in ch. 12 is seen by Jesus as official rejection of His messiahship after which He deliberately turned from them. In the aftermath Jesus encountered the great pedagogical challenge of first teaching His close disciples about this change and then the multitudes that followed Him. His followers faced the problem of how He could be the Messiah if He had been rejected by the leaders, and how that would affect His kingdom program. To explain these monumental problems Jesus turned to the parabolic method. The parable is distinguished from an allegory in that it teaches basically one central truth which may be bolstered by several points in the story.

13:1–3 He spoke many things to them in parables: This teaching method, often used by the rabbis, utilized common scenes from everyday life to teach new truths about the kingdom.

13:4 Seed . . . by the wayside speaks of soil hardened by much human and animal traffic; thus it failed to allow penetration of the seed, leaving it fair game for the birds.

13:5, 6 Stony places refers to shallow soil resting on a shelf of rock. The thin layer of dust or dirt accelerated the seed's growth under the hot sun, but the plant could only live a short time because of the shallow soil.

 **INSIGHT** | **Family Loyalty**

Ancient society placed great emphasis on faithfulness to blood relatives (Num. 27:4). So Jesus' words in Matt. 12:48–50 must have sounded quite foreign to the crowd. He seemed to be breaking with tradition and disowning His family.

But notice: Jesus didn't deny that the woman and the men at the door were His family. He merely pushed beyond the normal understanding of family to a larger reality—the claims of spiritual kinship. This new "family" included anyone who did the will of His Father in heaven.

Far from denying the value or benefits of solid family relationships, Jesus, by calling attention to His Father, was underlining the significance of family.

---

describes the moral reformation that took place in Israel as a result of the ministries of John the Baptist and Jesus. The reformation, however, was not genuine (Matt. 3:7–10); therefore, Israel's unbelief and hardness of heart were worse than before.

13:1–58 Chapters 12 and 13 are critical to the understanding of Matthew's Gospel because they bring us to the watershed point in Jesus' ministry. In ch. 12 the unbelief of Israel is climaxed in the unpardonable sin of rejecting their Messiah. Chapter 13 continues Christ's response to this unbelief. This blasphemy by the religious

13:7 Among thorns suggests good soil occupied with wild growth.

13:8 Good ground refers to prepared or tilled soil that allows prosperous growth.

13:9 The statement **He who has ears to hear** goes beyond physical hearing and implies an inner spiritual reception of truth. This prompted the disciples' question as to why He had spoken to them in parables. Whereas He had used parables to illustrate His messages, now they formed the basis of the message.

13:10–15 it has been given to you: The purpose of this parable was both to reveal (v.

11) and to conceal the truth (v. 13). This hiding of the truth was a judgment for unbelief, as happened during Isaiah's ministry (Is. 6:9, 10).

13:11 the mysteries of the kingdom of heaven: The word *mystery* describes a truth that had not been previously revealed (Rom. 16:25, 26). The fact of the coming kingdom was introduced by 3:1 with no further explanation. There was no need, for it was thoroughly and repeatedly explained in the OT, and also by His previous presentation of the kingdom prophesied in the OT. But this expression **the mysteries of the kingdom of heaven** refers to new truths about the promised kingdom. It had drawn near; the Messiah was in the process of being rejected; now it was time to tell the disciples by means of parables some truths about God's kingdom program that had not been revealed up to this point. In light of Israel's rejection of the King, God's kingdom program would take a new track for an indefinite period of time. This is called the "interadvent kingdom" period.

13:12–17 whoever has, to him more will be given: Just as the failure to respond to truth brings blindness, so a positive response is rewarded with further understanding (Luke 8:16–18). This principle is applied to the leaders of Israel in fulfillment of many OT prophecies, especially Is. 6:9, 10. The leaders' rejection of Jesus' message further blinded them to the spiritual nature of His kingdom. Parables then became Jesus' effective tools both for revealing truth to the faithful and concealing it from those who would reject it. As emphasized by Mark 4:11, 12, Jesus' parables revealed the truths of His kingdom as well as the unbelief of many.

13:18–23 The parable of the soils (vv. 3–23 is a unit) contains no new truth; what is said here has always been true. The responses to truth are always like those of the soils. What then is the purpose of this parable? It serves as an introduction to the whole series of parables. Productivity is always dependent upon believing and receiving. We can never receive more than we believe, and we can't believe what we don't understand (Acts 8:30, 31). The differences, then, are not to be found in the Word but in the preparation of the soil to receive the Word (James 1:19–21).

13:24 The kingdom of heaven is like: This phrase introduces new truth regarding God's coming kingdom. The introductory formula does not mean that the kingdom is to be exactly identified with **a man,** or a mustard seed (v. 31), or leaven (v. 33). It simply means that some truth regarding the kingdom is found in the story. A parable was primarily intended to teach one point, not to be picked apart to find meaning in all of its details.

13:25–30 his enemy came and sowed

tares: Tares closely resemble wheat but are poisonous to humans. They are indistinguishable from wheat until the final fruit appears. Farmers would weed out tares just before the wheat harvest. Until Christ returns, both genuine believers and counterfeits will be allowed to remain together.

13:31, 32 The kingdom of heaven is like a mustard seed: The parable of the wheat and tares (vv. 24–30) reveals that the kingdom of heaven will be preceded by an age in which

INSIGHT | **Rainfall and Crops**

Jesus' parables taught spiritual truths through practical illustrations, such as the sowing of the seed. Plowing in ancient Israel was not deep, and it could be done either before or after the sower scattered the seed. Rainfall was irregular and often inadequate. The success of a growing season in a particular plot could not be predicted, and for that reason a good harvest was all the more appreciated (Matt. 13:8).

good and evil coexist. The parable of the mustard seed affirms that during that time period, the number of people who will inherit the kingdom will be very small at first. But though it begins like the smallest of seeds, the nucleus will enjoy growth completely out of proportion to its initial size. **The birds of the air** do not represent evil as they do in the parable of the soils (vv. 4, 19). In the OT a tree large enough to support nesting birds was considered prosperous and healthy (Ps. 104:12; Ezek. 17:23; 31:6; Dan. 4:12, 21). The kingdom, though having only a small number of people at the beginning of the age, will ultimately be large and prosperous.

13:33 The kingdom of heaven is like leaven: This second parable on growth is even shorter than the former and builds upon it. This very brief parable has occasioned a great deal of discussion. Does the leaven illustrate sin or is it parallel with the parable of the mustard seed to portray large results from small beginnings? It is generally believed that leaven in the Bible portrays evil. Its use in this verse has also often been taken to represent evil which will gradually interpenetrate Christendom (the kingdom of heaven). But it is doubtful that leaven refers to evil in this parable, especially since this parable is also given in Luke 13:20, where it describes the "kingdom of God," which can hardly be conceived as penetrated by evil. In the domestic context of Palestine, we should recall that leaven was properly used all but one week in the year. The parables were given to be understood by the common people, not the leaders who were concerned about deciphering theological symbols. If it is a picture of the dynamic character of yeast that once it starts it is impossible to stop, this could be a picture of the numerical growth of the kingdom. As the parable in vv. 31 and 32 dealt with the extent of the kingdom's growth, this one concerns the power and process of its growth. Its lesson is

13:44 the kingdom of heaven is like treasure hidden in a field: The parables of vv. 44–52 concern kingdom values and responsibilities. They are especially directed at believers. The first two are recorded by Matthew alone and appear to belong together. Stripped of their grand dreams of an immediate, powerful kingdom of David and facing the prospect of much opposition on all sides, the disciples were forced to count the cost. In the first story a man stumbles on a treasure trove, which he makes every effort to obtain. The central truth being

---

 INSIGHT | ## Fifty Pounds of Flour

When Jesus told the parable of the leaven (Matt. 13:33), laughter may have rippled through the crowd from the women who were listening. "Doesn't He know anything about baking?" they might have chuckled, or maybe Jesus was humoring them with an inside joke.

Jewish women did not use fresh yeast each day to leaven their barley or wheat bread; they used a small piece of fermented dough from the previous day's batch. However, three measures was an enormous amount of flour, close to fifty pounds. How could that much flour be leavened by the usual amount of previously leavened dough?

Jesus' parable, and its point, must have come to mind every day afterwards as the women kneaded their dough. Fifty pounds of flour leavened by such a small amount of dough . . . , the kingdom of God brought about by such a small number of faithful people.

---

related to the former in portraying how that great growth will take place. Rather than powered by outward armies or organizations, this kingdom will grow by an internal dynamic, later revealed as the Holy Spirit. As such it will not be hindered by opposition, but will rather thrive on it, as kneading enables leaven to penetrate and produce growth in dough. Consider this. It took from Pentecost to 1900 for Christians to number 2.5 percent of the world's population. From 1900 to 1970 it doubled to 5 percent. In the next twenty-two years it doubled again to 10 percent. There is a demographic explosion of Christendom taking place today, especially in Third World countries.

13:34, 35 The quotation of Asaph in Ps. 78:2 serves as a prophecy of Jesus' use of parables.

13:36 Jesus sent the multitude away: The parables of vv. 1–35 were addressed to the multitude. The phrase **went into the house** indicates that the parables of vv. 44–52 were for the disciples only. During this "private instruction," Jesus explained His previous stories and added four more.

13:37, 38 Sons of the kingdom refers to heirs of the kingdom.

13:39–43 The end of the age speaks of the time when the Son of Man will come to set up His righteous kingdom.

taught is that of the immense value of the kingdom, which far outweighs any sacrifice or inconvenience that one might encounter on earth to possess it.

13:45, 46 the kingdom of heaven is like a merchant seeking beautiful pearls: This second parable on kingdom values was evidently given to further underscore Jesus' optimism for the despondent disciples. His double encouragement indicates their great need at that time. This parable has a slightly different emphasis from the one in v. 44. Though the individual in v. 44 found his treasure by accident, the person here found it by diligent search. No matter how a person is led to Christ's kingdom, its values and delights will be beyond estimation. Christ laid down this basic investment principle for disciples (Matt. 6:19–21; 16:24–27). Two erroneous tendencies to allegorize these parables should be noted. One is the tendency urged by Origen to allegorize Christ as the hidden treasure or priceless pearl whom a sinner should seek to purchase. The other reverses the roles, making Christ to be the finder and purchaser of the church in a lavish allegory. Both, however, are bad theology (Christ is not for sale, nor did He sell Israel to buy the church), and both deal with problems foreign to the context. It is better simply to recognize the disciples' dilemma at that time and Christ's concern to imbue them with a high sense of calling to His new kingdom program.

13:47–50 the kingdom of heaven is like a dragnet: The last two parables speak of kingdom responsibilities for disciples. First, Jesus describes a large seine (net), which would encircle a large area and drag the bottom of a lake. This net gathers fish **of every kind,** without discrimination. Similarly, the responsibility of disciples would be to catch as many "fish" of every kind as possible. The work of judging or ferreting out the false catch, however, is not a job that the disciples are called or equipped to do. That work is assigned to **angels** at Christ's return.

13:51, 52 Things new and old refers to truths about the kingdom that were found in the OT and those that were freshly revealed in these parables. What were some of the new things? (1) Rather than the immediate coming of the kingdom, an age would intervene (compare Acts 1:6, 7) when good and evil would coexist, even among the ranks of those who professed to be heirs of the kingdom (13:37–43). (2) The number of the heirs of the kingdom would be very small at the inception of this new age. However, they would grow into a large group (13:31, 32). (3) Evil would invade this group and ultimately make it apostate (13:33). (4) The treasure of the kingdom though seen as near in the ministry of Christ would be hidden. He purchased it; it will yet be revealed. (5) The body of the redeemed is not just Jewish; it will be like a pearl and be comprised of many peoples in one group. (6) The anticipated judgment will occur at the conclusion of the present age. Just as the parable of the sower was used as an introduction to the six "kingdom parables," so this parable is a conclusion. It calls for action in view of what they have learned. They are to be responsible stewards and dispensers of these kingdom treasures (*thēsaurou*). That work, however, was made contingent on their understanding the previous lessons. Knowledge of the *things new and old* brings responsibility. Responsible stewards will distinguish between the covenant program for Israel (now temporarily on the sidetrack) and the new interadvent kingdom program which Jesus has introduced. He concludes by warning them that the two programs are not to be confused.

13:53–56 carpenter's son: "Carpenter" basically means skilled worker. Joseph may have been a stonemason or some other type of craftsman.

13:57, 58 A prophet is not without honor except in his own country: In this second mission of Jesus to Nazareth, His home-

town, He found that the people's unbelief had not abated (Luke 4:16–30). Because of their familiarity with Jesus, the people failed to recognize Him for who He is. Their eyes were blinded by unbelief. Matthew notes that it had in fact spread even to "his own household" (John 7:5). Though they based their unbelief on His being the "carpenter's son," Jesus did not refute that misinformation at this time. He saw it as mere intellectual facade to cover up their aversion to spiritual repentance (John 6:42). His change of ministry, if anything, appeared to enflame the unbelief of those closest to Him.

14:1, 2 John the Baptist had already been beheaded (how that happened is recorded in the following verses). According to Herod, the miracles of Christ were so wonderful that they could only be explained as the work of a resurrected prophet, perhaps John the Baptist.

14:3–12 Herod had gone to Rome, where he met Herodias, the wife of his half-brother Philip (not Philip the tetrarch). After seducing Herodius, Herod divorced his own wife and married Herodias. What is significant is the principle that laws of marriage and divorce pertain to both saved and lost people as a creation, not a redemptive, ordinance. Also interesting is that John believed it was a duty to rebuke the political authority for moral transgression, not only to preach the gospel.

14:13–21 Jesus' miraculous feeding of the crowd indicates several things: (1) He fulfills the expectations of those looking forward to a new Moses, based on Deut. 18:15 (John 1:21; Acts 3:22; 7:37); (2) He can supply the daily bread requested in 6:11; and (3) He is the Messiah who will provide the messianic banquet (Matt. 22:1–14; 26:29; Ps. 132:15; Is. 25:6). This miracle is so significant that it is the only precrucifixion sign recorded in all four Gospels.

14:22–26 The fourth watch would be between 3 A.M. and 6 A.M.

14:27 It is I may also be translated "I am." Some interpret this as a claim to deity (Ex. 3:14).

14:28 Peter answered Him in his characteristic impulsive manner.

14:28–36 Only the Gospel of Matthew records the miracle of Peter walking on the water. This was a valuable lesson for the disciples to learn. They could do the humanly impossible with the power of Christ.

15:1 The fact that **the scribes and Pharisees** had traveled **from Jerusalem** to Galilee to see Jesus indicates that Jesus' reputation was becoming widespread.

15:2 The tradition of the elders was not the Law of Moses, it was the oral tradition based on interpretations of the Law. They washed their hands ceremonially to remove defilement, not for hygienic purposes (Mark 7:2–4).

15:3 In typical rabbinical style, Jesus answered the accusations of the scribes and Pharisees with a question. Whereas they challenged Jesus for His disciples' violation of the teachings of former rabbis, Jesus challenged them for violating **the commandment of God.** The scribes and Pharisees were placing their own views above the revelation of God, and yet claimed to be following Him.

15:4–9 Jesus was referring to a practice whereby people would dedicate their possessions to God so that they could use their finances for themselves and not for others. For example, if parents needed money, the children could excuse themselves from helping because their resources were already "dedicated" to God. This ruse kept people from honoring their parents by taking care of them in their old age.

15:10–14 In vv. 3–9, Jesus rebuked the scribes and Pharisees for being so obsessed with traditions that they failed to observe basic commandments. Here He chided them for being so

concerned with external ceremonial washings and dietary regulations that they failed to deal with character. Both of these charges were an outgrowth of the accusations of the scribes and Pharisees recorded in v. 2.

15:15–20 As a person thinks in his **heart,** so is he. How do thoughts get into the heart, the seat of reflection? Through the eyes, ears, and other senses. The raw material of our actions is what we take into our mind and allow to settle in our heart. David put it this way: "Your word I have hidden in my heart, that I might not sin against You" (Ps. 119:11). The other side is seen in Ps. 101:3: "I will set nothing wicked before my eyes." Paul pictured the believer as "bringing every thought into captivity to the obedience of Christ" (2 Cor. 10:5).

15:21–23 The woman was a Gentile who would have had no natural claims on a Jewish Messiah.

15:24 This verse demonstrates Christ's commitment to **Israel,** whom He called **lost sheep.** Jesus would always give the Jews the first opportunity to accept Him as their Messiah.

15:25–28 The "children" that Jesus referred

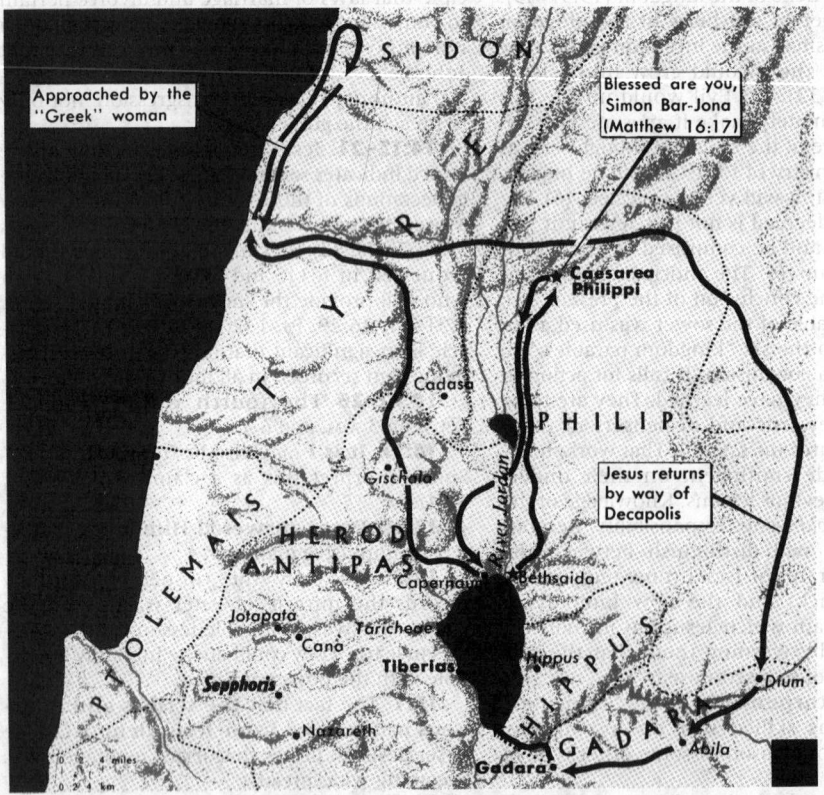

Jesus' Visit to Tyre, Sidon, and Caesarea Philippi

to were the people of Israel. **The little dogs** refer to Gentiles.

15:29–31 The scene changes from the region of Tyre and Sidon to a mountain near **the Sea of Galilee** but still in Gentile territory. Mark 7:31 identifies this region as the Decapolis. **they glorified the God of Israel:** The Gentiles believed and glorified Israel's God, while many in Israel remained blind to their Messiah.

15:32–39 This is not the same miracle recorded in 14:14–21. Jesus Himself identified two distinct feedings of multitudes (16:9, 10). This was a supernatural supply of food for Gentiles. The **seven** baskets of leftovers here contrasts with the twelve baskets that were gathered in ch. 14, and the word for **large baskets** in v. 37 is different from the word for "baskets" in 14:20.

16:1–4 sign from heaven: Perhaps the scribes and Pharisees were thinking of signs such as the fire from heaven that answered Elijah's prayer (1 Kin. 18:36–38), the plagues on Egypt (Ex. 7–12), or the sun standing still (Josh. 10:12–14).

16:4 And He left them: Previously Jesus had withdrawn in the face of opposition (12:15; 14:13; 15:21); here He "left" the Pharisees and Sadducees, meaning that He abandoned or forsook them. Jesus deserted these religious leaders as reprobates.

16:5 The other side refers to the other side of the Sea of Galilee, where the Gentiles lived.

16:6–12 In Scripture, **leaven** is often used as a symbol of evil. The doctrine of the Pharisees and Sadducees was hypocrisy, legalism, political opportunism, and spiritual hardness. Jesus' warning here was a result of the Pharisees' request for a sign in vv. 1–4.

16:13, 14 Caesarea Philippi was located north of the Sea of Galilee, at the base of the southwest slope of Mount Hermon. The place had long been associated with idol worship. The site for pagan worship centered on a massive stone facade, which Jesus referred to in His play on words concerning "rock" in v. 18. **Who do men say that I . . . am:** In the face of the surrounding idols, Christ led His disciples into a proclamation of His deity by first soliciting from them what other people said. In the end, however, what mattered was the apostles' own beliefs concerning Jesus.

16:15, 16 The Spirit of grace revealed to Peter the true identity of the Lord Jesus. **Son of the living God** refers to Jesus' deity. Several factors point to this conclusion: (1) He was born of a virgin (1:18–20); (2) He was called Immanuel, meaning "God with us" (1:23); (3) the title in Greek is emphatic: "the Son of the God, the living One"; and (4) later passages describe Christ as God (John 20:27–29).

16:17 has not revealed: People do not come to faith in Jesus Christ by scrutiny or searching but by the Father's revelation of the Son to them (John 6:65).

16:18 Peter in the Greek text is *Petros* and **rock** is *petra*. *Petros* is a moveable stone, large or small and *petra* is a ledge or shelf of rock. This statement by Christ may have been made with a gesture at the rocky structure nearby (see comment on 16:13). Some argue this distinction cannot be drawn because the Lord spoke Aramaic, a language in which such variations of meaning do not exist; however, the Holy Spirit in inspiration of the NT *did* use different vocabulary. Moreover, this perhaps was one of the times that Jesus spoke Greek, for He was trilingual, speaking Greek, Aramaic, and Hebrew. Otherwise the pun—*Petros, petra*—doesn't make sense, and why mention the Aramaic translation at other times in the book unless such usage was uncharacteristic and the Greek was more normal. The rock on which Christ would build His church is probably the confession of Peter. **I will build my church** shows that the church had not yet been started. Of the four Gospels, only in Matthew is the word "church" found, the other being in the context of church discipline (18:17). Obviously the disciples did not understand at this point the doctrine of the NT church with its equality of the Jew and Gentile (Eph. 2:11—3:7). They simply understood it to be the Lord's congregation or people. Even so, they knew this was a future group. Some believe **the gates of Hades** to be only a Jewish way of referring to death, so that Christ is simply saying death will not vanquish the church. One day by the power of Christ's resurrection the church and all the redeemed will be resurrected. Death will not hold the church captive. Others believe that the phrase refers to the fact that the forces of evil will not be able to conquer the people of God.

16:19 The keys of the kingdom may have a couple of meanings. It may refer to Peter's giving access to the kingdom to various groups of people (Jews in Acts 2, 3; Samaritans in Acts 8:14–17; Gentiles in Acts 10). The keys would open doors to lost people. However, this term may have a second significance. The keys seem to be explained by the binding and loosing discussed here. In rabbinic literature the terms "binding" and "loosing" referred to what was prohibited and what was permitted. In the context of Matt. 16:19 they are judicial (18:18). This explains the neuter **whatever**; it does not say "whomever." In other words this is referring to judgments Peter will make as to actions that are permitted and those forbidden. This also suits the idea of **keys,** which simply refers to authority. The tenses of **will be bound** and **will be loosed** are significant. It is written in such a way as to mean "will have been bound"

✠ IN CONTEXT | Party Politics in Jesus' Day

What were the politics of Jesus? We may speculate on what His preferences might be today, but what political ideals, if any, did He favor during His earthly life? What leaders did He endorse, if any? What causes did He support? For that matter, was political choice even an issue for Him? Did politics even matter?

It would be difficult if not impossible to determine any satisfactory answers. Yet Jesus seemed acutely aware of the power brokers in His society, and He showed remarkable skill with them when necessary, but He never addressed or practiced politics in any formal sense. And, of course, He lived in a system completely different from our own.

Even if we cannot know precisely what Jesus' affiliations were, we can at least understand some of the political dynamics at work in Palestine in the first half of the first century. For example, we know that there were at least five major political parties among the Hebrews of that day.

The Herodians—Loyal Defenders of the Status Quo

- Took their name from Herod the Great (37–4 B.C.) and his supporters.

- Supported the adoption of Graeco-Roman culture and policies in Palestine.

- Like the Pharisees, favored local political autonomy. Fearing military intervention by Rome, they stridently resisted challengers to the status quo, such as the Zealots, John the Baptist, Jesus, and the apostles.

- Joined forces with other parties in the plot to eliminate Jesus (Matt. 22:16; Mark 3:6; 12:13).

The Pharisees—Religious Legalists

- Probably derived from a group of the faithful called the Hasidim.
- Name means "to separate."
- Shared similar views with the Essenes but chose to stay within the larger society. Nevertheless, many chose to study the law on their own, having lost respect for the priesthood as a result of its corruption.
- Many served on the council (Acts 6:12).
- Considered the doctors of the law; scribes were considered laymen.
- Collected and preserved the Talmud and the Mishnah, voluminous products of oral tradition and OT commentary.
- By reputation, legalistic and fanatically devoted to rabbinic tradition. Some refused to eat with non-Pharisees for fear of being contaminated by food not rendered ritually clean.
- Like the Herodians, favored local political autonomy.
- Differed with the Sadducees over the doctrine of the resurrection.
- Understood the coming kingdom as a literal fulfillment of the promise to David for a King to reign over Israel forever.
- Maintained an elaborate theology of angels, believing them to intervene in human affairs.

The Sadducees—The Urban Elite

- May have derived from Zadok, high priest under King David.
- Tended to represent the aristocrats, priests, merchants, and urban elite in Jerusalem and other cities in Judea.

Party Politics *cont.*

- Hostile to Jesus and His followers.
- Many served on the council. Most of the high priests in the days of Jesus and the apostles were Sadducees.
- Denied the resurrection or life after death, along with the doctrines of everlasting punishment and a literal kingdom.
- Denied that God controls history, insisting on free will and the responsibility of humans to make wise choices according to the law.
- Held only to the Law of Moses (the first five books of the OT) as supremely authoritative.
- Denied the existence of angels.

The Zealots—Firebrands of Revolution

- Ardent nationalists who awaited an opportunity to revolt against Rome.
- Resisted paying taxes to Rome or to the temple.
- One particular tax revolt against Rome, led by Judas the Galilean (6 B.C.), secured Galilee's reputation as a seedbed of revolutionaries.
- Blamed by some for the collapse of Judea to Rome in the war of A.D. 66–70. Josephus, a Jewish historian, claimed that they degenerated into mere assassins or *sicarii* (dagger-men).
- Sided with the Pharisees in supporting Jewish law.
- Opposed the Herodians and Sadducees, who tried to maintain the political status quo.
- Intolerant of the Essenes and later of the Christians for their tendencies toward nonviolence.
- Two recruited by Jesus were Judas Iscariot and Simon the Cananite.

The Essenes—Detached Purists

- A sect of ascetics that thrived between the middle of the second century B.C. until the Jewish-Roman war in A.D. 66–70.
- Once members of the Hasidim but, unlike the Pharisees, separated from society, withdrawing into monastic communities like Qumran, where the Dead Sea scrolls were found.
- Known today mostly through secondary sources.
- Lived in societies that held property in common.
- Believed in the immortality of the soul, angels, and an elaborate scheme of end-times prophecies. Some were looking for as many as three different Messiahs.
- Known for celibacy, pacifism, opposition to slavery, caring for their own sick and elderly, trading only within their own sect, simplicity in meals and dress, and the rejection of all ostentatious display.
- Paid more attention to ceremonial purity than did even the Pharisees, and carefully guarded the Sabbath.
- Practiced ritual baptism and a communal dinner called the messianic banquet.
- May have influenced some early Christian practices and rituals.

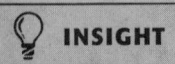

An Ancient Key

An ancient key was a piece of wood or metal that could be passed through a hole in a door and used to move the latch or crossbar inside. Protection was provided by making the shape of the key complex. The Egyptians put wooden pins in the crossbar that kept it from moving until the right key was used to push the pins just the right amount. The instruction of "keys" in Matt. 16:19 and Luke 11:52 signified access to spiritual teaching.

and "will have been loosed." In other words there is the promise of divine guidance in determining Peter's judgments. When will this be fulfilled? The term **kingdom of heaven** consistently refers to the future kingdom. To Peter is given the promise of authority in the future kingdom; this blessing will be extended to all twelve of the apostles in Matt. 19:28.

16:20 Because the public did not understand the concept of the suffering Messiah, they were not to be told **that He was Jesus the Christ.** Furthermore, the nation had already turned away from Christ. They had crossed the point of no return (12:31, 32).

16:21 The phrase **from that time** marks a new direction in Jesus' ministry. The expression occurs twice in the Book of Matthew, here and in 4:17, where it introduces the beginning of Jesus' ministry in announcing the nearness of the kingdom. Here in 16:21 it introduces the Cross and the ultimate rejection of the Messiah. **Elders and chief priests and scribes** refer to the makeup of the Jewish council, also called the Sanhedrin. Together with the mention of **Jerusalem,** this indicates that Jesus' rejection would be an official one. **Be killed** is the first of three predictions in Matthew concerning Christ's death (17:22, 23; 20:18, 19).

16:22 Evidently Peter heard nothing about the Lord's resurrection. Like so many Christians, he only perceived the negative. **rebuke him:** The same tongue that attributed deity to Him earlier (v. 1b) is now correcting deity!

16:23 To call Peter **Satan** was a very serious thing. But when Peter stood in the way of the plan of God, he was speaking for Satan! The mouth that was used as the vehicle of God's oracle is now the channel of Satan's lie. How fickle people are. And how patient God is!

16:24 If Christ died for the redeemed, the saved should commit themselves to Him to the point they are willing to die for Him.

16:25–27 **Soul** may simply refer to life, as is true of the same Greek word translated "life" in

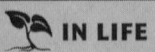

Living Within One's Limits

People are at times quick to step forward with a plan of action. As the exchange between Peter and the Lord in Matt. 16:22, 23 shows, there were times when Peter liked to take charge quickly and set the agenda for himself and others. But just as often, he found himself in over his head:

- When Jesus came walking on water to the storm-tossed boat that held His terrified disciples, Peter demanded that Jesus prove that it was He by bidding Peter also to walk on water. After a few steps on the water, Peter noticed the wind and the waves and promptly sank, requiring Jesus to rescue him again (Matt. 14:22–32).
- Peter overstated his commitment to Christ, claiming that "even if I have to die with You, I will not deny You!" (Matt. 26:35). Yet only a few hours later he denied having any association with the Lord (26:69–75).
- He took charge of defending Jesus against Roman soldiers when they came to arrest Him, even though he had failed to "watch and pray" with Christ, as He had requested (Matt. 26:36–46; John 18:1–11).
- He refused to allow Jesus to wash his feet at the Last Supper, but then he called on Him to wash his hands and his head as well (Matt. 13:5–11).

Eventually Peter's leadership skills were captured in a more controlled spirit and he became a significant figure in the early church. Like many of us, despite many false starts as a result of Peter's impetuous nature, Jesus enlisted this impulsive but loyal follower to feed His sheep (Matt. 21:17).

v. 25. It seems best to say it looks at the basic self. Here Christ is asking for commitment in order to receive rewards. That this is His point is seen in the following verse. The way we invest our life determines our reward at Christ's coming (Rev. 22:12).

16:28 coming in His kingdom: This verse anticipates the Transfiguration in ch. 17. Several reasons point to this conclusion: (1) It is Peter's interpretation in 2 Pet. 1:16–18; (2) the three synoptic Gospels (John omits the account of the Transfiguration) all place the Transfiguration immediately after this prediction; and (3) not all of the apostles saw the Transfiguration (19:27–30). In the Transfiguration, Peter, James, and John saw a preview of the kingdom.

17:1 The **high mountain** was probably a spur of Mount Hermon, which rises to about 9,400 feet.

17:2–4 Moses and Elijah: Their presence indicated that the OT Scriptures had been looking forward to the Messiah and His kingdom.

17:5–8 This is My beloved Son, in whom I am well pleased were the identical words spoken at Jesus' baptism in Matt. 3:17 (Ps. 2:7; Is. 42:1). **Hear Him** seems to refer to Deut. 18:15.

17:9 Tell the vision to no one: The command for silence was due to the fact that the masses of Israel had an incorrect concept of the Messiah (Matt. 8:4; 12:16). They expected a conquering king not a Suffering Servant.

17:10 The three disciples evidently did not comprehend the reference to Christ's death in v. 9. The problem they raised concerned the Transfiguration. They had just seen Elijah on the mountain. If the scribes were correct that Elijah must come before the kingdom would arrive, why should the disciples not inform everyone that Elijah had appeared on the mountain?

17:11 The Lord told His three apostles that the scribes were right in their interpretation of Mal. 3:1; 4:5, 6. The fact that Christ used the phrase **will restore all things** indicates that the prophecy still has a future fulfillment.

17:12, 13 Jesus indicates that the prophecies concerning **Elijah** had their fulfillment in **John the Baptist.** Yet because the restoration is not complete, some conclude that the role of Elijah will be taken up by one of the two witnesses of Rev. 11:3–6.

17:14–18 In this case, the epilepsy was caused by a demon (v. 18).

17:19–21 The disciples could not exorcize the demon because they failed in faith. The power was there, but they had failed to appropriate it.

17:22, 23 Jesus and the disciples began what would be Jesus' final journey to Jerusalem. Once again Jesus predicted His death and

resurrection (Matt. 16:21; 20:18, 19). Once again the disciples failed to understand the Resurrection; they seemed to have heard only His words about His coming death, because they became **exceedingly sorrowful.**

17:24 The temple tax was given annually by every adult Jewish male over twenty years of age for maintaining the temple. This tax was based on Ex. 30:13 and amounted to two day's wages for a common laborer. Evidently Jesus had not yet paid the tax, and the temple tax collector was following up on it.

17:25 Peter, desiring to maintain the best reputation and also assuming the best of his Master, replied to the tax collector (v. 24) that Jesus had paid the temple tax. **Anticipated** implies that Peter was about to speak, evidently about the matter of Christ paying the temple tax, when Jesus spoke first. **Their sons** may refer to citizens of a country as opposed to conquered peoples or **strangers.** However, citizens often pay customs and taxes. More likely the contrast is between the imperial family and the common people.

17:26 Jesus demonstrates that, as God's Son, He was free from the obligation to pay the temple tax. In fact, the temple belonged to Him (Mal. 3:1). The fact that He used the plural **sons** implies that Peter and the other disciples were also free from that obligation.

17:27 The half-shekel coin used to pay the tax was no longer in circulation, and it was therefore common for two men to pay the tax together with a *stater*, which was worth a full shekel.

18:1–35 (Mark 9:33–37; Luke 9:46–48) This chapter forms Jesus' longest recorded statement regarding the principle of forgiveness. Forgiving others is one of the most responsible and spiritual activities in our lives and must be repeated continually throughout one's life. This is the last great discourse before Jesus' journey to Jerusalem, and it is given in response to the disciples' jealousy of one another and to prepare them for the crucifixion, an act they will have to learn to forgive. Mark 9:33 indicates the message was given "in a house," probably Peter's.

18:1 Matthew 18 contains the fourth of five discourses in Matthew's Gospel (5:1—7:27; 10:1–42; 13:1–53; 24:1—25:46). The theme of this discourse is humility. Jesus outlines five reasons that humility is essential: (1) for entrance into the kingdom (vv. 2, 3); (2) for greatness in the kingdom (v. 4); (3) to prevent offenses (vv. 5–11); (4) to carry on proper discipline in the church (vv. 5–20); and (5) for forgiving one another (vv. 21–35). **Greatest in the kingdom** implies rank, a concept implied by Jesus Himself in Matt. 5:19.

18:2–5 Converted means to turn around (Luke 22:32).

18:6, 7 Causes . . . to sin literally means to put a snare, trap, or stumbling block in someone's way. A **millstone** was a heavy grinding stone so large that it had to be turned by a donkey.

18:8, 9 This same basic statement is found in reverse order in Matt. 5:29, 30. One of the keys to understanding this assertion is to recognize the present tense of **causes you to sin.** Although the warning was addressed to the disciples, it describes a person who has a lifestyle of sinning and needs drastic measures in order to change it (1 John 3:7–10).

18:10,11 One of these little ones describes either a little child or a believer. Verses 12–14 seem to indicate a believer. Here Jesus implies that **angels** watch over and serve His followers on earth (Heb. 1:14).

18:12–14 These little ones probably refers back to those who believe (v. 6). The Father watches over each of His little ones.

18:15–17 Jesus teaches His disciples about the process of restoring an erring believer. First, there should be a loving personal confrontation. The second step outlined in v. 16 is not as clear. The principle of witnesses is taken from Deut. 19:15, but what is it the witnesses attest? Evidently they witness that the offended brother is acting in good faith and in the right spirit in attempting to work out a reconciliation. They also would be witnesses to any agreement. If this does not bring peace, the offended brother

is to report it to the assembly. The church then is to do everything possible to convince the believer who has sinned to be reconciled or to right the wrong. If the erring one will not respond, that person is to be disciplined by being cut off from the fellowship. Such a loss would be extremely painful to the offender (1 Cor. 5:11; 2 Thess. 3:6, 14, 15).

18:18 bind: Binding refers to things that are not permitted; loosing refers to things that are permitted (16:19). As in 16:19, the tenses imply that what is loosed or bound on earth will have been determined already in heaven. In other words, this is a promise of divine direction for each local church.

18:19, 20 This passage is commonly used as a general prayer promise, which it is not. Quite obviously, one child of God has full access to the throne of grace. It doesn't take two or three for God to be present. Specifically it refers to church discipline. It is a promise for guidance for the two or three who confront, and it is a promise for the church to claim wisdom and restoration for the erring brother.

18:20 This is not a definition of a local church, but the promise of Christ to be in their midst in the carrying through of the process of discipline as delineated in the preceding paragraph.

18:21 Peter's question was a logical outgrowth of the teachings of vv. 15–20. Actually Peter was being very generous in his willingness

---

☙ IN LIFE **Commitment**

Some even call it the "C" word today, as if to shame commitment. The demands and costs of commitment seem too great to many people, and convenience often wins out over the sacrifice involved in being committed to someone or something.

It was the same in Jesus' day. As He began to unveil a new way of life, critics challenged Him on the difficulties of keeping the marriage commitment (Matt. 19:3, 7). Later, even His own disciples wanted to send away some "bothersome children" in order to deal with more "important" things (19:13). But Jesus remained committed to the children.

The discussion of divorce followed appropriately on the heels of Jesus' remarks about the merits of boundless forgiveness (18:21–35). What better way to lead into the topic of commitment? Jesus didn't ignore the problems and failures of human relationships. Those very shortcomings are what make forgiveness, which is a special kind of commitment to others, crucial.

The vital necessity of commitment is also reinforced in Jesus' next encounter, with a rich man who wanted to ensure his possession of eternal life (19:16–30). The man proposed rule-keeping as the standard by which he should be judged, but Jesus countered with an appeal for service (19:21). True wealth involved a higher commitment: serving the Lord and others rather than the idol of material gain (19:23, 29).

Followers of Christ are known for their commitments, to marriage, to family, to community, to work, and above all to Jesus Christ. Such loyalty today is much needed, when people often make vows of convenience rather than of commitment.

to forgive **up to seven times.** The traditional limit was three times, possibly because of the refrain in Amos 1:3, 6, 9, 11, 13; 2:1, 4, 6.

18:22 Seventy times seven may also mean "seventy-seven times." The point is not to keep count at all, but to always be willing to forgive.

18:23–31 Ten thousand talents was an enormous sum. A denarius was one day's wage for a laborer (20:2). A talent was worth about six thousand denarii. Ten thousand talents would be sixty million day's wages, a sum that would be impossible to repay. Thus Jesus graphically portrayed this man's hopeless predicament.

18:32–34 This parable reiterates the principle that we should forgive others (Matt. 6:12) because God forgives us.

18:35 This verse is a warning of discipline for not forgiving others (1 Cor. 11:30–32; Heb. 12:5–11). All of a Christian's sins are forgiven and forgotten forever (Ps. 103:12; Jer. 31:34; Heb. 8:12). But this parable illustrates the Christian duty to forgive others (Matt. 6:12, 14, 15; 2 Cor. 2:10; Eph. 4:32). If our forgiveness should be in direct proportion to the incredible amount that we have been forgiven (18:22), then we must always be willing to forgive.

19:1–3 This question could be dangerous. John the Baptist's answer had resulted in his imprisonment and ultimately his death (Matt. 14:3–11). That the problem is posed with malicious intent is seen in the participle **testing.** It means to tempt. The basis for the question was Deut. 24:1. The rabbis had been arguing about what was meant by the expression "uncleanness" (literally, "the nakedness of a thing"), which referred to some indecency in the opinions of most. One school of thought, the school of Shammai, was more strict and said the only grounds for divorce was immorality. The other viewpoint, the school of Hillel, was much more lenient and believed that anything that displeased the husband was sufficient to obtain a divorce. The question is framed as though the questioner may have been disposed to the view of Hillel, at least it appears they tilted the question in that direction.

19:4–6 Jesus avoids the Hillel-Shammai controversy and goes right to the Scripture. He gives three reasons for the permanence of marriage: (1) He made one male and one female. If God had intended more than one wife for Adam, He could and would have created more. The same would be true of husbands for Eve. The title **He who made them** is literally "the One who created" or "the Creator." The implication is that the Creator is Lord and is the One who determines what is the ideal in marriage. (2) God ordained marriage as the strongest bond in all human relationships (v. 5). A man leaves his parents and is **joined to his wife.** The language is very strong here. **Leave** is the verb "abandon" and **joined to** means "to be glued to." The most permanent relationship in the fabric of society is not between parent and child, which is broken to establish marriage (Gen 2:24), but is the marriage of a man and a woman. (3) **the two become one flesh** (Gen. 2:24): The basic element in marriage is a contract or covenant (Mal. 2:14); the result of that covenant is sexual intercourse. The physical union of a man and woman represents the union of their lives and their commitment to each other. That is why it is so wrong outside of marriage (1 Cor. 6:16). The physical union in marriage is a symbol of their unity in many areas. To break this physical union is to destroy a fundamental unity of life. Even if lost people are married and have conjugal relations, God has made them one, since marriage is a creation ordinance, not a redemptive one. By divorce, humans separate what **God has joined together.**

19:7 The opponents immediately catch the tenor of the Lord's answer and challenge His conclusions.

19:8 The Lord Jesus' reply is that Moses never commanded divorce; he only **permitted** it. And this permission was only because of the obstinate heart of humans. God's ideal was not to divorce.

19:9 Many problems come to the surface in this verse. For instance, what is meant by the word **wife?** Some have taken the divorce decree to be valid only during the engagement period, as in the case of Joseph and Mary (Matt. 1). Then "wife" means the woman to whom a man is engaged, a legitimate meaning. However, Deut. 24:1 is not talking about an engagement period, clearly the historical context to the discussion in Matt. 19. It specifically says the husband is to send her out of his house. They are already living together! Another question is the meaning of **immorality.** The word here (as is the term in Deut. 24:1) is a very general one and may refer to any kind of sexual immorality: premarital, extramarital, harlotry, homosexuality, and even bestiality. Of great importance is the problem of whether the exception clause only grants the right to divorce the wife or does it also give permission to remarry? Probably the latter is correct. In other words, immorality not only is grounds for divorce but also for remarriage. The last part of v. 9 probably means that a man who marries a woman who has been divorced because of her immorality commits adultery in marrying her. It should be noted that the bill of divorce protected the wife. A husband could not flippantly rid himself of his wife by a simple oral statement. He must have grounds and the decree was to be written. Even if there are sufficient grounds for divorce, it would be better for no divorce to take place. Lifetime marriages are God's ideal (v. 8). It is no accident that the passage on divorce in ch. 19 immediately follows the discussion on forgiveness in ch. 18.

19:10 Here the disciples enter into the discussion. They evidently were surprised at the Lord's stringent view. If the only basis for divorce is immorality, it would be **better not to marry.** But this was not the intent of Jesus because marriage was given to men and women for their good (Gen. 2:17).

19:11 Jesus indicates that remaining unmarried is only for a few people.

19:12 Some people do not marry because they were born with no sex drive. Others do not marry because they are castrated. Still others forgo marriage for the sake of serving God. Some have been given the spiritual gift of celibacy in order to do this (1 Cor. 7:7).

19:13–17 **Why do you call Me good** may be rephrased as, "Why are you asking me con-

cerning what is good?" The only One who can ultimately answer the question about goodness is God. The fact that Jesus went on to answer the question is a quiet claim to deity.

19:18 **Which ones** is really "What sort of?"

19:18, 19 The Lord responded by quoting from the last half of the decalogue climaxing with the fifth commandment and Lev. 19:18.

19:20–22 These verses do not teach salvation by works (Rom. 3:23, 24; Eph. 2:8, 9). Rather, Jesus was proving the error of the man's claim to have fulfilled God's law (v. 20). If the young man loved his neighbor to the extent required by the Law of Moses (v. 19; Lev. 19:18), he would have had no difficulty in giving away his wealth to needy people.

19:23–26 The comment that **it is hard for a rich man to enter the kingdom of heaven** shocked the disciples **(Who then can be saved?)**, who accepted the common notion of the day that the rich were blessed of God and therefore certainly saved. To correct that misunderstanding, Jesus explained the human difficulty for the rich to be converted. **Hard** (Gk. *duskolos*) implies with extreme difficulty,

---

✠ IN CONTEXT | ## The Children's Significance

When Jesus welcomed the little children (Matt. 19:14), He was making a major statement about their value and significance. Perhaps the disciples, who rebuked the mothers who brought their babies to Jesus (19:13), had adopted the prevailing Graeco-Roman view of childhood as an insignificant phase of life. To be sure, children were necessary for a family's survival, but they were not valued for their own sake.

Unwanted infants in pagan cultures were routinely abandoned on roadsides and at garbage dumps. Tragically, gender and economics often determined such a fate, and more girls than boys were "exposed" since girls represented a future financial burden while boys could eventually contribute to the family's income. Most exposed infants died, but some might be "rescued" and raised to become slaves, gladiators, or prostitutes. Children were held in such low esteem in Jesus' time that some professional beggars collected exposed children, mutilated them, and then used their misery to gain sympathy and thus increase profits from their begging.

Among the Jews, however, children were traditionally considered a blessing from God and childlessness a curse. Children were so desired by the Jews that barrenness became grounds for divorce.

Jewish fathers had ultimate authority over all aspects of their children's lives, but both fathers and mothers were instructed by the Law of Moses to nurture and care for their children. Fathers were particularly obligated to teach their children God's commands and to raise them as members of God's chosen people (Deut. 6:6–8). In return, children were obliged to honor both mother and father (Deut. 5:16). Jewish mothers usually took care of the infants, who typically nursed until the age of two or three.

In some wealthy Greek and Roman homes, mothers employed wet nurses and, as the children grew, slaves were assigned to their total care. Poor mothers often worked while their babies hung from slings on their backs, and as soon as the children were old enough, they were taught to help.

First-century parents, of course, did not have to confront the childcare dilemma faced by many parents today. Work and home were more tightly linked in those days, and so they did not have to surmount the peculiar challenges of specialization and separation of today's world.

though not hopeless. The illustration of **a camel** going through **the eye of a needle** has been interpreted differently, such as threading a camel hair rope through a needle's eye, or as an actual camel squeezing through a small gate, "the eye of a needle," next to the main gate at Jerusalem. It has also been interpreted as the absolute impossibility of a literal camel (Palestine's largest animal) trying to get through a tiny needle's eye. The latter is most likely, following a similar Talmudic proverb about an elephant. Note that they were not in Jerusalem at this time. The point is that the salvation of the rich is humanly **impossible**. In fact, all human nature is incapable of saving itself and must rely on God's efficacious grace for that which is humanly impossible to become **all things . . . possible** with God. The salvation of a rich sinner is just as miraculous as the salvation of a poor sinner. Both are only possible with God.

19:23, 24 Jesus' comment about a rich man's salvation would have been difficult for some Jewish people in this period to accept because they held to a form of "prosperity theology." If people prospered, it was evidence of God's blessing on them. Whereas v. 23 says **it is hard** for a rich man to become saved, v. 24 implies that it is as impossible as passing a camel **through the eye of a needle** (Mark 10:25; Luke 18:25).

19:25, 26 Christ's response affirmed no human could save himself; salvation is of God (John 2:9).

19:27 we have left all: The instruction Jesus gave to the rich man was precisely what Peter and the other disciples had done (4:18–22). The natural question then was **what shall we have?** Rather than upbraid Peter for what may seem like a selfish request, Jesus assured him that the life investment he and the other disciples had made (16:24–28) would have dividends "a hundredfold" (v. 29).

19:28 The apostles never forgot Jesus' promise about their place in His kingdom; it was still in their minds in Acts 1:15–26. **In the regeneration** looks ahead to the coming kingdom promised in Dan. 7:13, 14. **throne of His glory:** Christ is today seated at the right hand of the eternal throne of the Father. In the future kingdom, He will occupy the Davidic throne (Rev. 3:21). In that kingdom, the twelve apostles will **sit on twelve thrones, judging the twelve tribes of Israel.**

19:29 The expression **hundredfold** may be "manifold," but it makes no difference either in interpretation or application. The family of God is such that if one loses a family member, that member is replaced manifold, or hundredfold, by the followers of Christ, whose view is the extended family as contrasted to the nuclear family.

19:30 The chapter division here is unfortunate. This saying, or proverb, obviously parallels 20:16 and brackets the parable. The proverb serves as an *inclusio* and is a major theme of the parable. The proverb is even reversed in 20:16.

20:1–3 The third hour was about 9 A.M.

20:4 These workers, unlike those in v. 2, had no contract; they only trusted the landowner.

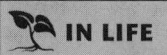 **IN LIFE** | **Unjust Pay?**

Anyone who feels that they are not paid what they are worth can appreciate the reaction of the workers in the parable about the wages that Jesus told in Matt. 20:1–16. He spoke of an employer who hired workers for a full day, others for two-thirds of a day, others for half a day, and others for even less. Yet he paid them all the same wages (20:9–11). Naturally those who had worked longer demanded, "What's going on here?" (20:11, 12).

Notice that none of the workers was employed before the landowner hired them (20:3, 6, 7), and thus they got their jobs due to the employer's goodwill and not to anything they brought to the situation. Furthermore, the landowner promised the first group fair wages of a day's pay, and he promised the others an undetermined amount ("whatever is right"). As it turned out, he paid them all an entire day's wage.

Jesus was trying to help people grasp something important about grace in the kingdom of God. His followers had been asking earlier about the kingdom's makeup and benefits (Matt. 19:16, 25, 27), and in this parable He was not encouraging unjust pay scales and discrimination. He was illustrating the nature of God's grace in terms that His followers could understand.

In the kingdom of God, grace is given because of the nature of the Giver, not the worthiness of the recipient. Receiving God's grace is a privilege for sinners who, after all, really deserve nothing but condemnation.

20:5 The sixth hour was about noon. **The ninth hour** was 3 P.M.

20:6, 7 The eleventh hour was about 5 P.M. There would have been only one hour left in the working day.

20:8–15 The first workers complained that their wages were the same as those who had been hired late in the day. However, the owner had not cheated them; everyone received the agreed-upon sum for his work. The early workers grumbled because they were evil in their outlook; their master, however, was sovereignly generous.

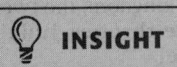

INSIGHT   The Denarius

The denarius (Matt. 20:9) was a common unit of currency in the Roman Empire for over four centuries. First minted in 211 B.C., this silver coin weighed about an eighth of an ounce, a weight between that of a penny and a nickel. Julius Caesar paid soldiers 225 denarii per year. Augustus paid the same but supplemented it with awards and gifts.

20:16 In the context of Matthew, the workers with the contract represent Israel; they had the promises and the covenants (Rom. 3:1, 2; 9:4; Eph. 2:11, 12). Those without an agreement represent the Gentiles, who would be made equal with the Jewish people when salvation became available to all through faith in Jesus Christ (Rom. 11:16, 17; Eph. 2:13–15; 3:6).

20:17–19 Once again the Lord Jesus anticipated His death and resurrection (Matt. 16:21; 17:9, 22, 23). For the first time He referred to the way He would die: crucifixion.

20:20, 21 What a contrast with vv. 17–19! Quite possibly, James and John had put their mother up to this. Further, a comparison of Matt. 27:56, Mark 15:40, and John 19:25 makes possible the idea that Mary, the mother of Jesus, and the mother of James and John were sisters. If so, the brothers were trading on their kinship with Jesus.

20:22, 23 and be baptized . . . baptized with is not in the earlier manuscripts. It was probably added from Mark 10:38.

20:24 The indignation of **the** other **ten** apostles was probably due to their own desire for these lofty positions. Jesus' response was addressed to all of them (vv. 25–28).

20:25–28 The measure of greatness is not position, power, or prestige; it is service.

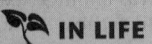

IN LIFE   How Jesus Handled Fame

It is easy to feel intimidated in the presence of a famous person. People of status and image can easily make us feel inferior, as if we have nothing to offer by comparison. Jesus, however, who became famous among His own people, stood fame on its head by modeling the traits of compassion and humility.

As He entered Jerusalem, the capital of Palestine, He gave us a new way for handling acclaim from crowds. The city was wild with excitement during its peak season of tourists and celebration. What a moment for Jesus to bring His campaign to a climax! He even had the prophecies of Zechariah (9:9) and Isaiah (62:11) to bolster His confidence. But instead of a parade of chariots and trumpets and a well-orchestrated ceremony, Jesus chose to ride into town on a donkey, a common beast of burden; no prancing war-horse for Him! Instead of walking arm-in-arm with powerful city officials and other celebrities, He was accompanied by a small band of common fishermen, rural Galileans, and even a former tax collector. For once, the common folks had a parade (Matt. 21:8, 10).

At the end of the parade route, Jesus did not go to the halls of the powerful. He marched into the place of worship, a national center for the Jews, and overthrew the tables of unjust businesses that manipulated the poor and made the temple a place of moneymaking (21:12, 13). He focused on the blind, the lame, and children (21:14–16). And when He had completed the day's tasks, He spent the night not in the fashionable home of a city leader but in a humble house in a nearby suburb, Bethany (21:17).

Even in His fame, Jesus' final activities before His death focused on those most ready to hear of His love, forgiveness, and hope—the little people in (or even outside) the system of privilege and power (Luke 4:18). Here is a new style of fame, which can help us when dealing with the temptations that can come when we seek to rub shoulders with the powerful and the elite.

20:29–33 Only Matthew mentions **two blind men;** Mark and Luke refer to one, probably the one who spoke. The fact that Matthew records two men especially suits his Gospel, which was written primarily for Jews who would have desired two witnesses (Deut. 17:6). **Son of David,** a messianic title (2 Sam. 7:12–16), identifies Jesus as the heir to David's throne. This cry, repeated in v. 31, shows the spiritual insight of these blind men.

21:1 The Mount of Olives was directly east of Jerusalem, across the deep ravine of the Kidron valley. **Bethphage** was on the eastern slope of the Mount of Olives.

21:2, 3 The Lord is Jesus. The owner of the animals was likely a follower, or at least an admirer, of Jesus.

21:4, 5 These actions fulfill Is. 62:11 and Zech. 9:9. The emphasis in these prophecies and Jesus' actions is on Jesus' humility.

21:6, 7 The disciples **laid their clothes** on both animals so that Christ could ride either one. Perhaps the mother donkey walked in front, followed by the colt on which Jesus was seated.

21:8 The great multitude were not the inhabitants of Jerusalem (compare v. 10) but the large crowd who had gone with Christ from Jericho (Matt. 20:29) to Jerusalem. The scene is a royal one (2 Kin. 9:13). Amazingly prior to this time the Lord Jesus had steadfastly avoided such a display (Matt. 8:4; 9:30; 12:16; 17:9). In the face of opposition, He had withdrawn (Matt. 12:15; 14:13; 15:21). Now He openly rides into Jerusalem as king! The point is obvious: the Lord Christ is presenting Himself to Israel as its Messiah and king. And isn't it interesting to contemplate that this may be the exact day Daniel had prophesied: 173,880 days from the day the decree of Artaxerxes went forth (Dan. 9:25). Note that Luke 19:42 mentions "your day."

21:9 Hosanna literally means "save now," as in Ps.118:25, but it had come to take on the idea of an ascription of joyous praise. **Blessed is He who comes in the name of the Lord** is a quotation of Ps.118:26. This Psalm anticipates the coming millennial age when in that day of kingdom Sabbath rest (Heb. 4:9) all will say "This is the day the Lord has made!" (Ps. 118:24). The whole scene anticipates the coming reign of Christ.

21:10 The city was moved is literally "the city was shaken." The same verb is used in Matt. 2:3 of Herod's reaction to the wise men who were asking about the birth of Israel's King.

21:10, 11 Here there is a contrast between the people of **the city,** who were ignorant of our Lord's identity, and **the multitudes,** who were able to answer the people's question. There were probably many Galileans in the latter group who had come up for the feast and who already knew our Lord through His preaching and healing ministry in the north. In Jewish history and tradition, the quoted Psalm was considered a messianic royal psalm, and the riding of an ass's colt (not a horse) marked the official entry of the king.

21:12 Two cleansings of the temple are recorded in the Gospels—one in John 2:14–17 at the beginning of Jesus' ministry and one in the synoptic Gospels at the end of His ministry

✠ IN CONTEXT — The Temple Courts

The temple in Jerusalem had always been divided into courts. Even in Solomon's temple there was a court in which some were forbidden. Everyone had access to the outer court, called the "great court" (1 Kin. 17:12). But the inner court was reserved for the priests only and was called the "court of the priests" (2 Chr. 4:9).

Herod's temple, though still under construction in Jesus' time (Matt. 21:12), was enormously impressive, consisting of four courts. The large outer Court of the Gentiles was an open-air quadrangle measuring some 500 yards long by 325 yards wide, enclosed by rows of tall columns. This was the only part of the temple open to Gentiles (non-Jews).

Each of the remaining three courts was restricted to other kinds of people. All three of these courts—the Court of Women, the Court of Israel, the Court of Priests—were located in the temple proper, which was a sublime edifice measuring some 150 yards by 100 yards. This complex stood in the middle of the Court of the Gentiles. Only Jews were allowed to enter its first court, the Court of Women, and only Jewish men were admitted to the Court of Israel.

When Jesus observed the tables of the money changers who "sold in the temple" (Matt. 21:12), He was standing in the Court of the Gentiles. Only here were merchants allowed to sell and to exchange currency. This was the site of the dramatic cleansing.

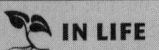 **IN LIFE** | # A Challenge to Authority

ooner or later, almost all leaders have their authority questioned. Sometimes they are challenged
directly, but more often indirectly by rumor and innuendo.
    Jesus faced a direct challenge to His authority from the chief priests and elders, the top leader-
ship in Israel (Matt. 21:23–27). In this instance He didn't argue with them but simply tossed the ball
back into their court. He showed that one effective way of responding to threatening questions is to
ask questions in return.
    Observe two aspects of the interaction between Jesus and the Jewish leaders:

- (1) The motives of the challengers. The scribes and Pharisees had no interest in an honest
  understanding of the nature or source of Jesus' authority. They were only concerned with protecting their own interests and power. Their behavior is indicative of times when we question or
  resist people in authority because we are afraid or jealous of them.

- (2) The security of Jesus. Jesus was neither upset nor caught off guard by His attackers. For one
  thing, He had endured their criticism before, and no doubt expected it to increase. But He also
  knew with absolute certainty about the very thing that His challengers were attacking: He knew
  who He was and whose authority He wielded (Matt. 28:18). His response is a reminder that
  intimidation is something we allow to occur. People may threaten and confront us, but only we
  allow ourselves to feel fear. The real question is: are we certain who we are as followers of the
  King?

(Mark 11:15–17; Luke 19:45, 46). **bought and
sold:** Financial corruption ran rampant in the
outer courts of the temple. Some of the gains
that were realized from this profiteering probably went to the family of the high priest. Some
churches today do not allow anything to be sold
in church, based on this episode. At least two
things are wrong with this reasoning. First,
Jesus was not condemning the selling of animals
for sacrifices or the exchanging of money. What
He was condemning was cheating, and extortion, and corrupt commercialism. Second, the
church building is not the **temple of God**
today; believers are. We would do well to stop
referring to a building as the temple or sanctuary. God dwells in people, not buildings. **The
money changers** exchanged coins with pagan
symbols on them for acceptable coins to be used
in the temple. They charged a premium for this
"service." **Those who sold doves** sold them at
top prices.
    21:13 **My house shall be called a house
of prayer** is quoted from Is. 56:7. **den of
thieves:** The temple had become a garrison for
bandits. Jer. 7:9, 10 says that the Jewish people,
after committing all sorts of sins, would plead
deliverance from the consequences of those sins
based simply on the fact that they came to the
temple. Thus in Jeremiah's day, it became a den
for robbers, just as it was in Jesus' day.
    21:14–16 In Ps. 8:2, which is quoted here, the
infants expressed praise in the face of enemies.

    21:17 The idea here is that Jesus abandoned
the chief priests and scribes, the temple, and the
city of Jerusalem. Instead of welcoming their
Messiah, the religious authorities had rejected
and opposed Him.
    21:18, 19 **He was hungry:** Jesus desired to
eat fruit from the fig tree one more time before
He died, but He could not. Fig trees do not bear
their fruit in the spring, during Passover, but in
the fall. However, fig trees do have a small, edible
fruit that appears in the spring before the
sprouting of the leaves. This tree was full of
leaves but had no fruit. It looked full of promise,
but it was empty, just like the city of Jerusalem
and its beautiful temple. **Immediately** does not
necessarily mean instantly; it may have the idea
of "very soon," as in Luke 19:11 (Mark 11:12–14,
20–24). This miracle—the only recorded miracle
of Jesus that involved judgment—illustrates
God's judgment on the Israelites, who professed
adherence to God but produced no fruit or spiritual reality.
    21:20–22 The withering of the fig tree illus-
trates God's judgment on unbelieving Israel, but
it also became a means for Jesus to teach His disciples that faith works miracles and is the basis
for answered prayer. A person does not increase
belief by trying harder to believe but by
increasing the object and content of belief. This
is why we need to know the will of God in order
to believe effectively (Jer. 9:23, 24).
    21:23 **These things** refers to the Triumphal

> ⚒ IN DEPTH | **Parables: More Than Stories**

Although Jesus lived among a story-telling people, His approach to instruction was still unusual. His stories were memorable, but they were not transparent. People heard them but did not necessarily understand them. They are clearer to us because of the apostle Paul's writings, but few of those who first heard the parables understood them. At one point the disciples asked in frustration, "Why do you speak to (the people) in parables?" (Matt. 13:10). The disciples did not grasp the stories any better than the the the crowd did.

Jesus' answer to the disciples reveals much about the purpose of His teaching. He quoted Is. 6:9, 10 to demonstrate that those with physical sight and hearing may still not be able to perceive the truths presented to them. For Isaiah, the "dullness" or hardness (Matt. 13:15) of the human heart directly affects spiritual insight and understanding. People need to soften their hearts, humble themselves before God, and honestly seek the truth in order to find it.

Jesus' stories are like wrapped gifts. The packaging of the story can either distract or captivate. But unless the package is opened, the gift itself remains unseen. Likewise unless one seeks the core of the parable—its truth and application—the lessons will remain hidden. Yet when discovered, these lessons prove to be extremely valuable. The testimony of millions of changed lives over two thousand years attests to this.

When unwrapped, Jesus' stories include powerful multiple applications. The same parable can strike people in different ways. For example, the parable of the Soils (Matt. 13:1–23) may be "heard" by at least four distinct people depending on their identification with one of the soils. The parable of the Lost Son (Luke 15:11–32) will affect a father quite differently than it would a rebellious son or a jealous brother.

When Jesus taught in Jerusalem during His last week, His parables focused on one's acceptance or rejection of Him. This time even the priests and the Pharisees "perceived He was speaking of them" (Matt. 21:45). They were stung by Jesus' parables, and they despised Him and His message. But they were unwilling to give up their pride, learn at Jesus' feet, and seek the forgiveness they so desperately needed. They sensed they would not appreciate what they found if they unwrapped the parables, so they refused to seek the truth any further. In doing this, they perfectly conformed to Isaiah's description of a people with dull hearts, hardness of hearing, and closed eyes. The religious leaders who should have been leading the people into the truth were the most blind to it.

Entry, the cleansing of the temple, and the accepting of the praise of children. That **the chief priests and the elders** opposed the Lord Jesus illustrates the unified antagonism of the Sanhedrin. Priests, elders, and scribes were the three representative groups in that body.

21:24, 25 It was a common rabbinic method to answer a question with a question.

21:26, 27 We do not know: The religious leaders' response not only released the Lord from having to answer their question, but also disqualified them as spiritual leaders.

21:28–32 Tax collectors and harlots is a proverbial phrase for moral reprobates. Jesus' phrase **enter . . . before you** not only established that these repentant sinners would enter the future kingdom, it also left the door open for the religious leaders to repent. But even though the self-righteous leaders saw the example of repentant tax collectors and prostitutes, they refused to believe. This parable condemned the leaders' conduct. Clearly God delights in the brokenness of sinners and in the humble faith of the morally upright.

21:33–41 The beginning of the parable of the wicked vinedressers is presented in the language of Is. 5:1, 2. However, there is a difference. In Is. 5, the vineyard and its provisions represented Israel; here the **vineyard** illustrates God's kingdom (compare 12:43 with Is. 5:7). The detailed description of the vineyard indicates that the **landowner** provided for its well-being with the utmost care. The owner of that vineyard was God; the **vinedressers** were the nation of Israel. As God's people, Israel was to bring forth fruits in anticipation of God's coming kingdom. The **servants** represent God's messengers, the prophets, who were so shamefully treated by the Jewish leaders (1 Kin. 18:4; 19:10; 22:24; 2 Chr. 24:20, 21; Neh. 9:26; Jer. 2:30; 20:1, 2; 26:20–23; 37:15; 38:6). The **son** is Jesus, the Messiah.

21:42 This verse explains that the rejection of the son (vv. 38, 39) was predicted in Ps.

118:22, 23. The rejected **stone** is the Messiah, who became **the chief cornerstone** (Mark 12:10, 11; Luke 20:17; Acts 4:11; Eph. 2:20; 1 Pet. 2:7).

21:43 In our time, **nation** refers to the church (Rom. 10:19; 1 Pet. 2:9). This does not mean, however, that the kingdom has been forever removed from Israel (Rom. 11:26, 27). This is impossible because of the promises given to Abraham, David, and the prophets. That Israel as a people and nation will yet be restored to the place of blessing is asserted by Paul in Rom. 11:26, 27. The church is now the custodian of the vineyard and is expected to bring forth fruits worthy of repentance. One day the kingdom will be restored to Israel (Matt. 19:28).

21:44–46 This paradoxical saying indicates that people can give two responses to Christ, the **stone.** A person may be broken with repentance as a result of falling on Christ. But if a person refuses to repent, judgment results. The reference to **powder** seems to look back to Dan. 2:35, 44, 45.

22:1 The plural **parables** refers to the parable of the two sons (21:28–32), the wicked vinedressers (21:33–44), and the wedding feast (21:1–14). This story is not the same one in Luke 14:15–24. The occasion is different in Luke and some details vary.

22:2 The kingdom of heaven is like indicates that the story contains principles or truths that relate to the kingdom of God. **Marriage** refers to a wedding feast (Rev. 19:6–10). Jewish weddings in biblical times involved a number of steps. First, the couple made a marriage contract, which was the basis of the marriage (Mal. 2:14). About a year later, the groom went to the bride's house, where the bride was presented to him. This was followed by a nighttime wedding procession to the groom's home (Matt. 25:1–13), where a festive wedding banquet was held (John 2:1–11). The banquet could last up to a week, depending on the resources of the groom's family. A feast, especially a wedding feast, is often used in Scripture to portray God's kingdom on earth (Matt. 8:11; 25:10; Is. 25:6; Luke 14:15–24; John 2:1–11; Rev. 19:7–9). In this parable, the **king** is God the Father and the **son** is Jesus.

22:3 Two invitations were sent out. The first was sent long before the celebration so that people would have plenty of time to prepare themselves for the banquet. **Those who were invited** had received this original announcement. A second invitation was sent to them to announce that the banquet was ready and so they should come right away.

22:4 The plea of this verse undoubtedly portrays the ministry of John the Baptist (Matt. 3:1–12), Jesus (4:17), and the disciples (10:5–42).

22:5 They made light of it means "they did not care about it." They were so preoccupied with the here and now that they had no concern for God's kingdom.

22:6 The indifferent response in v. 5 describes Israel at the time of Jesus' earthly ministry; the actions in this verse may be attributed to the religious authorities. These leaders approved John the Baptist's death at the hands of Herod Antipas (Matt. 21:25); they instigated Jesus' crucifixion (26:3–5, 14–16; 27:1, 2); and they initiated the persecution of the early church (Acts 4:1–22; 5:17–40; 6:12–15).

22:7 The burning of the **city** refers to the destruction of Jerusalem in A.D. 70 under Titus. A parallel prediction of the same event is found in Matt. 21:41.

22:8, 9 These verses describe the present age. The **wedding** or kingdom is still future, and the world, described by Christ as **as many as you find,** is being invited to participate in that future earthly kingdom, which had been promised to Israel.

22:10 Both bad and good probably refers to Jews and Gentiles. Both groups include some who are morally evil and others who are morally good. Whatever their condition, people need to respond to the gospel. The important point to recognize is that this group responded to the invitation, while those who had received special invitations had spurned the king's bidding.

22:11 did not have on a wedding garment: Like the others, this visitor had been invited to the wedding, but he failed to prepare himself for it (Rev. 3:18). In Revelation the garment of fine linen worn by the Lamb's bride is said to be the righteous deeds of the saints (Rev. 19:8). The **man** had ignored a basic obligation placed on him when he accepted the king's gracious invitation to the feast; he was supposed to wear clean clothes. To come to a wedding banquet unprepared, or in soiled clothing, would have been insulting. In this parable the garment may refer to the righteousness of Christ graciously provided for us through His death. To refuse to put it on would mean a refusal of Christ's sacrifice or arrogance in believing that the "garment" was somehow not needed. If we want to enter Christ's banquet, we must "put on" the righteousness He gives us (Eph. 4:24; Col. 3:10). Because this man was unprepared, the king declared him unworthy. His refusal resulted in the man being sent out of the banquet hall.

22:12 The normal word for **friend** in the NT is *philos;* the word used here is *hetaire,* a noun that occurs only in Matthew and always on the lips of the Lord Jesus and invariably to those who are able to be corrected (20:13; 26:50). The man had failed a basic obligation placed on him in accepting the king's gracious offer to the feast. We should not understand this man to be unsaved and the remaining guests as saved; all the guests accepted the invitation. Also he was not treated with enmity by the king. Because he failed to properly prepare himself for the joyous occasion, he was not permitted to enjoy the feast with the others and was placed outside the hall into the darkness.

22:13 Bind him hand and foot is a vivid picture of the man's inability to participate in Christ's kingdom. The clause **cast . . . into outer darkness** (Gk. *to skotos to exoteron,* literally, "the darkness outside") occurs in Matt. 8:12; 22:13 and 25:30 (the Greek expression occurs nowhere else in the NT) and is always used of the judgment that precedes the kingdom age. The phrase **weeping and gnashing of teeth** is found in 8:12; 13:42, 50; 22:13; 24:51 and 25:30 and always refers to the same judgment. Many persons have placed these two figures together and believed them to be a reference to eternal punishment. There really is no reason to do so. In this parable a person who had actually accepted the invitation from the king is in view. Though he was at the wedding, due to his lack of preparedness in having a wedding garment, he was not allowed to participate in the festivities of the wedding; the darkness outside is contrasted with the lights of the feast. Two other passages in Matthew use the figures of outer darkness and weeping and gnashing. In Matt. 8:12, the sons of the kingdom (a term used of believers in the parable of the tares, compare 13:38) are being discussed, not unbelievers. In Matt. 25:30 the one cast outside was a servant along with those rewarded; he simply did not receive the joyous award from the master. In all these references the failure is to prepare properly for the kingdom, not the rejection of God's salvation. The mention of weeping and gnashing has caused many to think of the torment of hell (likely there will be great anger in hell, not remorse). This is missing a very important cultural practice of the Jewish people. The figure refers to considerable remorse felt by persons at the loss of something or someone highly valued. When unprepared people are not permitted to enjoy all that will be shared by the prepared—in this parable the feast—there will be a great sense of loss for what might have been (1 Cor. 3:15; 2 Cor. 5:10; 2 Tim. 2:12; 1 John 2:28; 2 John 7, 8; Rev. 3:11). From a perspective of future events, the parable teaches that persons who fail in their discipleship will enter the millennial kingdom of Christ but will not be able to participate in all the joyous advantages of that reign.

22:14 many are called, but few are chosen: The word "called" in this instance refers to being "invited," not to the call of God as Paul used the word (Rom. 8:28, 29). All Israel had been invited, but only a few would accept and follow Jesus. Not all those invited will be among the chosen of God, for not all will believe. Note the weak response of Israel in Heb. 3 and God's warning to us to not neglect our salvation.

22:15 Entangle means "to snare," like a trapper catching his prey.

22:16 Nothing is known of **the Herodians** outside of the Gospels. Judging from their name, they were supporters of the Herodian dynasty in its collaboration with the Roman government. This would put them at the opposite end of the political spectrum from the Pharisees. Yet their common hatred of Christ was great enough that the Pharisees and Herodians joined forces against Him. **we know that You . . . teach the way of God in truth:** In a way, the Herodians and Pharisees were saying, "You truly teach God's word, no matter what people think of you."

22:17 The dilemma is obvious: side with the Pharisees and risk being accused of insurrection

C oins in circulation in Palestine included both Roman and local issues. The typical Roman coin had on one side a portrait of the emperor or another important person (Matt. 22:20). On the other side was a symbolic design, such as a temple. The lettering around the imperial portraits had recently begun to include the letters "DIV," signifying "divine." Julius Caesar was the first living person to appear on official Roman coins.

against the Roman government, or side with the Herodians and lose the favor of the masses. **Taxes** included an annual tax paid by every Jewish adult to the Roman government. The Jews despised paying this tax to their hated oppressors.

22:18 Test here means "to solicit to evil." The Lord called the Herodians and Pharisees **hypocrites** because they falsely pretended to have good intentions.

22:19, 20 The **tax money** was a **denarius,** a silver coin with an image of the emperor and the inscription calling him "divine." The **image and inscription** were repugnant to the Jews because they hated their Roman overlords and worshiped only the God of Israel.

22:21, 22 In responding to His opponents, the Lord changed the verb they used from "pay" (v. 17) to **render,** which literally means "to pay back." Christ's followers have an obligation to earthly governments and to God. Believers today are citizens of a heavenly kingdom and strangers and sojourners on the earth (1 Pet. 1:1; 2:11). It is the believers' responsibility to obey the law of the land until it becomes sinful to do so (Rom. 13:1–7; 1 Pet. 2:13–17). When the two realms are in conflict, Christians are to follow God (Acts 4:18–20; 5:29).

22:23 Some of the beliefs of **the Sadducees** are explained in Acts 23:8. These men looked on the first five books of Moses as their authoritative Scripture. To them, any religious argument had to come from the Pentateuch.

22:24 The law that is the basis of the Sadducees' question is found in Deut. 25:5, 6. It is known as the law of the levirate marriage (Gen. 38:1–26).

22:25–28 This theological riddle had probably been used by the Sadducees to confound the Pharisees on more than one occasion.

22:29, 30 The verb **mistaken** means to err, to drift off course. Essentially, Christ says, "You are wrong," a stinging rebuke to these Sadducees who were noted for their love of debate. These Sadducees, though among the leadership of Israel, had not understood or accepted the texts of Scripture which taught the doctrine of the resurrection and they underestimated the power of God to do the miraculous. He who created man and possessed life and death in His hands would have no problem raising the dead.

22:31, 32 Jesus quoted from the Pentateuch, Ex. 3:6, 15, to prove the doctrine of the resurrec-

They must be resurrected in order to receive God's promises in full. That God is called **the God . . . of the living** indicates that there is a present spirit world over which God presides and that will one day be revealed.

22:33 Jesus taught something that no one had seen clearly before: that the patriarchs are still living. The crowds were **astonished,** and they may also have been surprised that Jesus did not teach like the scribes and Pharisees, who appealed to rabbinic authority or prefaced their teachings with, "Thus says the Lord." Jesus appealed to His own authority when He taught them.

22:34 Undoubtedly the Pharisees were delighted to see their theological rivals muzzled; yet they were still intent on snaring Christ in some way (v. 15).

22:35, 36 The **lawyer** was a student of the Law of Moses. He put the Lord to a test with a question designed to reveal how much Christ knew about the law.

22:37 To answer the lawyer's question, Jesus quoted from the great Jewish confession of faith called *The Shema.* The confession is called this because it begins with the Hebrew word *shema,* meaning "hear:" "Hear, O Israel: The LORD our God, the LORD is one!" (Deut. 6:4, 5; 11:13–21). The **heart, soul,** and **mind** represent the whole person.

22:38 Some Greek texts place **great** before **first.** Nevertheless, love for God takes priority over every other command.

22:39 This command from Lev. 19:18 is not an imperative to love one's self. People naturally love themselves and are at least somewhat self-centered. Because we love ourselves, we want the best for ourselves; likewise, we should be concerned for the welfare of others.

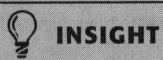 **INSIGHT** | **Roman Traditional Law**

The traditional law of Israel was part of Jewish education (Matt. 22:40). The Romans also had a traditional law called the Twelve Tables, which their children memorized. This law had civil, criminal, and religious provisions. Unlike the Law of Moses, the text of the Twelve Tables has been preserved only in fragments.

tion. That the Lord is **the God of Abraham, the God of Isaac, and the God of Jacob** is a title that recalls that God is the One who gave the promises to the patriarchs. In particular, God promised Abraham, Isaac, and Jacob the land of Canaan (Gen. 13:14–17; 15:7–21; 17:8; 26:2–5; 28:13–15; Deut. 30:1–5). Of course, the patriarchs did not receive the land in their lifetimes.

22:40 The Ten Commandments can be divided into two categories: those dealing with love for God (the first four) and those dealing with responsibilities toward other people (the last six). The same may be said for **all the Law and the Prophets.**

22:41–45 After answering three questions posed by Israel's religious leaders (vv. 15–22,

23–33, 34–40), Jesus turned to the Pharisees with a question of His own. The question had two parts, a first about the identity of the Messiah and a second about the interpretation of Ps. 110.

22:42 The answer to Jesus' question about the identity of the Messiah is in a number of OT passages (2 Sam. 7:12–16; Ps. 89:3, 4, 34–36; Is. 9:7; 16:5; 55:3, 4). The Messiah would come from David's royal line.

22:43 This verse affirms that **David** wrote Ps. 110. Furthermore, it declares that David wrote the psalm under the inspiration of **the Spirit.**

22:44–46 Verse 44, which quotes Ps. 110:1, describes Christ's presence in heaven until He comes to reign on earth (Heb. 10:11–13; Rev. 3:21). Other messianic psalms are built on the experiences of the psalmist (Ps. 2; 16; 22; 45), but Ps. 110 seems to be completely prophetic and messianic. Psalm 110:1 uses two different Hebrew words for God. The first, translated **Lord**, is the name Yahweh, the proper name of Israel's God. The second **Lord** means "Master." David, the great king of Israel, calls one of his offspring "Lord" or "Master," a title for deity. The implication is that Jesus, the Son of David, is God. He is a descendant of David and therefore human, but He is also divine.

23:1, 2 The synagogues had an official chair called **Moses' seat** (Luke 4:20). **The scribes** were official copiers of the OT Scriptures and were also teachers of the law (Matt. 7:29; 8:19).

23:3 The Pharisees and scribes took the Scriptures at face value, so their instructions were to be followed. However, Jesus warned the people of the Pharisees' legalism, which valued their own rules and regulations above the Scriptures. They followed their external laws meticulously and appeared to be righteous. Yet the people were not to imitate their actions, for although they appeared righteous, their hearts were filled with all kinds of envy, hatred, and malice.

23:4 Contrast the Pharisees' actions with Jesus' call to the people in Matt. 11:28–30.

23:5 One key aspect of hypocrisy is doing good deeds to attract applause from those who see them (Matt. 6:1–18). **Phylacteries** were small boxes containing Bible passages that were worn on the forehead or arm. This custom was based on Ex. 13:9, 16 and Deut. 6:8; 11:18. But from such passages as Prov. 3:3; 6:21; 7:3, the scribes should have known that Lord intended more than merely outward adornment. **Borders,** translated "hem" in Matt. 9:20, refers to the tassels that were worn on the corners of garments in order to remind the Israelites of God's laws (Num. 15:38; Deut. 22:12). In order to be

seen as especially righteous, some hypocrites would make their phylacteries conspicuously large and their tassels unusually long.

23:6 The best places were the positions of honor at banquets. The **best seats,** or "first seats," were a row of seats in the front of the synagogue facing the congregation.

23:7 Greetings in this context meant more than a passing "hello"; it was a respectful salutation given to a superior. **Rabbi** means "teacher."

23:8–10 This principle is not to be applied universally because these titles are used elsewhere in Scripture with no qualification or admonishment (Matt. 15:4–6; 19:5, 29; 2 Kin. 2:12; 1 Cor. 4:15; Gal. 4:2; Heb. 12:9). The hypocrites sought these titles for the prestige and power that went with them, not for the purpose of using the positions to serve others. **Teachers** may also mean "leaders."

23:11 Hierarchies of authority are not to be done away with in this world (1 Thess. 5:12, 13; 1 Tim. 5:17; Heb. 13:17); however, all leadership is to be carried out humbly in a spirit of servanthood.

23:12 Exaltation will be carried out in the future reign of Christ (Rom. 8:17; 2 Tim. 2:12).

23:13, 14 Jesus proclaimed **woe** on the scribes and Pharisees because of their outright opposition to the truth.

23:15 you travel land and sea: The Pharisees and scribes could never fairly be accused of being lazy, but they were clearly misdirected and dangerous to the cause of God.

23:16–22 The religious authorities taught that oaths based on **the temple, the altar,** and **heaven** were not binding; however, oaths sworn by **the gold of the temple, the gift** on the altar, or **God** were binding. Jesus pointed out the absurdity of such teaching and called the leaders **blind guides.**

23:23 Mint and anise were spices. **Cummin** was a tiny fruit. The **scribes and Pharisees** were meticulous about tithing tiny seeds, but they failed to be obedient in more significant matters, such as ensuring that all their actions were governed by **justice and mercy and faith** (Mic. 6:8). Jesus was not saying that tithing is unimportant; He was pointing out that the scribes and Pharisees were emphasizing one area at the expense of another. Similarly, we can become so preoccupied with external rules and regulations in the church that we forget the principles behind them.

23:24 Leviticus 11:41–43 contains a prohibition against eating anything that swarms, crawls on its belly, walks on all fours, or has many feet. The Pharisees would meticulously **strain out** the smallest unclean insect, the **gnat,** with a cloth filter before drinking liquids, especially wine. However, Jesus said they would

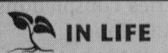 **IN LIFE**   **Tithing**

Jesus' words to the Pharisees in Matt. 23:23 raise the issue of tithing. Should Christians today pay tithes, or are we free from that practice? For that matter, what is a tithe? The word means "a tenth part." In the OT, God commanded the Israelites to give tithes—one-tenth of their produce or income—for one of three reasons:

(1) To support the Levites, who were responsible for the tabernacle and worship (Num. 18:20–24).
(2) To support various feasts and sacrifices (Deut. 14:22–26), some of which lasted more than one day and were times of joyous celebration and thanksgiving.
(3) To establish a pool of resources to help the poor, the orphans and widows, and the strangers in the land (Deut 14:28–29).

In the NT neither Christ nor the apostles gave any explicit instructions about tithing. However, Jesus clearly endorsed it, as He did all the Law (Matt. 5:17–20; 23:23). He denounced the hypocritical way that the Pharisees ignored the "weightier matters" of the Law: justice, mercy, and faith. But those "heavy duty" issues by no means negated such "lightweight matters" as tithing.

So what is the place of tithing for believers today? Several principles might be considered:

(1) As Christians, our allegiance is not to the OT Law, which was primarily given to Israel, but to Christ.
(2) Our giving needs to spring from a love of Christ, not a slavish obedience to a percentage standard. When Abraham gave the first tithe recorded in the Bible (Gen. 14:17–20), he did it as an expression of gratitude for God's deliverance of him in battle. Throughout Scripture, loving God and worshiping Him are at the heart of tithing.
(3) All of what we have ultimately comes from and belongs to God, not just what we give away, but also what we keep. So He has total claim on 100 percent of our income, not just 10 percent.
(4) Ten percent makes a great starting point for giving. However, studies indicate that, as a group, Christians in the United States give nowhere near that much of their income away to ministries or charities of any kind. In fact, while per capita income has increased, church members have actually decreased their contributions to churches.
(5) The NT is clear that vocational Christian workers have a right to financial support from those to whom they minister (1 Cor. 9:13, 14; Gal. 6:6). Likewise, many churches and other ministries assist the poor, the orphans and widows, and the strangers. So it seems legitimate to expect believers to donate money to those causes.
(6) No matter how much we give or to whom, Matt. 23:23 indicates that our first priority should be to ensure that justice is carried out around us, that we show mercy to our "neighbors," and that we practice our faith and not just talk about it. In the end, it is through our obedience that Jesus increases our faith.

easily **swallow** a large unclean animal, a **camel.** Jesus was exaggerating a point to illustrate how much the Pharisees had neglected justice, mercy, and faith (v. 23). He used a similar exaggeration in Matt. 19:24 to portray the difficulty a rich man has in obtaining salvation.

23:25, 26 The **inside** of the cup represents a person's character. Sometimes those who most loudly protest the sins of others are secretly guilty of those sins, or worse sins, themselves.

23:27–33 The generation of scribes, Pharisees, and hypocrites living at the time of Jesus had inherited all the guilt of their forefathers.

23:34 The present tense **I send** refers to the

prophets, **wise men,** and **scribes** sent by God to the apostolic church. The Book of Acts testifies to the accuracy of this prediction: the Israelites persecuted the early preachers and teachers of the Good News (Acts 7:51–60).

23:35 **Abel** was the first person murdered in the OT (Gen. 4:8); **Zechariah** was the last. Zechariah's death is recorded in 2 Chr. 24:20–22, the last book in the Hebrew canon. Jesus was saying that from the beginning of the Bible until the end, true followers of God had often been treated in this manner. **son of Berechiah:** In 2 Chr. 24:20, Zechariah is called the son of Jehoiada. Zechariah the prophet is called the son

💡 INSIGHT

Whitewashed Tombs

Jesus drew upon a grim, arresting image in His denunciation of the self-righteous Pharisees (Matt. 23:27, 28). At the end of a Jewish funeral procession, which everyone was obliged to join, the body was placed on a rock shelf in a tomb. Once the flesh had decomposed, the bones would be collected and removed, allowing the shelf to be reused. Since Jews were made ritually unclean by touching graves (Num. 19:16), rocks used to seal such tombs were whitewashed as a warning to stay away. The glaze gave the tombs a clean image on the outside, even though corpses were decomposing inside.

of Berechiah in Zech. 1:1. It is possible that Jehoiada was the grandfather of the murdered Zechariah and Berechiah was his father. It is less probable, although possible, that Zechariah's father had two names: Jehoiada and Berechiah.

23:36 This verse looks back to v. 32 and anticipates the destruction of Jerusalem in A.D. 70 (see commentary on 24:34).

23:37 Calling a name twice, as in **Jerusalem, Jerusalem,** indicates strong emotion (Matt. 27:46; 2 Sam. 18:33; Acts 9:4). The phrases **I wanted** and **you were not willing** illustrate the opposition of Israel to Christ's will (for another image of a mother hen, see Ps. 91:4).

23:38 **House** may refer to the temple, but it more likely refers to the Davidic dynasty (2 Sam. 7:16). Israel was never without a designated king to rule on David's throne, but often that king was not on the throne because of the disobedience of the nation. When the nation comes back to God, its captivity will end and Jesus will reign (Deut. 30:1–6). Just as the temple would be destroyed, so Israel would be under the judgment of God.

23:39 All of Israel's hopes rest in the adverb **till.** One day the nation will repent (Zech. 12:10–14) and Israel will be restored to its place

of blessing and prominence (Rom. 11:26). The quotation is from Ps. 118:26, a messianic Psalm anticipating the day when the rejected stone becomes the chief cornerstone (Ps. 118:22). "This is the day the LORD has made"; it will be a time of rejoicing (Ps. 118:24).

24:1 The discourse of 23:1–39 had evidently been given in the **temple** precincts. The NKJV gives the impression in 24:1 that the Lord Jesus had already left the temple area when the **disciples came up to show Him the buildings of the temple.** The Greek text clarifies that this happened as they were in the process of departing from the temple complex. The first temple built by Solomon was destroyed by the Babylonians in 586 B.C. The second temple built on the encouragement of Haggai and Zechariah and the leadership of Zerubbabel and Joshua (Hag. 1:1) was completed after considerable delay in 516 B.C. This second temple was totally renovated by Herod the Great, a master builder. He began the work some ten years before he died, and it was not completed during the lifetime of Christ (John 2:20). The actual work was not finished until A.D. 64. It stood completed only six years. The construction was massive and lavish. **The disciples** were justifiably proud of the temple area with its buildings.

24:2 The devastation of the temple by the

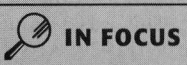 **IN FOCUS**

"hen"

(Gk. *ornis*) (Matt. 23:37; Luke 13:34) Strong's #3733: The Greek term simply means "bird." The English word *ornithology* (the study of birds) is a derivative of it. Throughout the OT there are references to God exercising His care for His people in the same way that a mother bird cares for her young (Deut. 32:10–12; Ruth 2:12; Ps. 17:8; 36:7; 61:4; 63:7; 91:4; Is. 31:5; Mal. 4:2). Many of these references speak of God's protective wings, under whose shelter the frightened could find refuge. The later rabbis had a beautiful expression for proselytes from the Gentiles: they had "come under the wings of the Shekinah" (Ruth 2:12). Jesus came to His people to give them that kind of motherly care, but they rejected that care and tender affection again and again.

Romans in A.D. 70 was so thorough that the precise location of the sanctuary is still unknown today.

24:3 Undoubtedly the disciples were immediately confounded by the Lord's prophecy; however, they held their tongues until they had left the temple mount, crossed the Kidron Valley, and had come to the **Mount of Olives.**

the rapture of the church, a truth not yet revealed (1 Thess. 4:14–17: 1 Cor. 15:51, 52). Instead they generally address matters which will occur during the Seventieth Week of Daniel, especially the Great Tribulation. The modern, western reader expects Jesus to be presenting a strictly sequential development, but in the manner of the east (see Book of Job intro-

Photo by Andy Schupack

A model of Jerusalem as it might have appeared in Jesus' time. Jesus was distraught about the city because of its unbelief (Matt. 23:37).

There Jesus **sat** in the manner of teachers (Matt. 5:1) and the **disciples** finally questioned Him about the destruction of the temple. Some say that the verse contains two questions: "When will the temple be destroyed?" and **what will be the sign of Your coming, and of the end of the age?** Others feel one basic question is in the disciples' minds. According to Zech. 14:1–9, the destruction of Jerusalem, the deliverance by the Messiah, and the end of the age will occur in order and very quickly. To the disciples, the devastation of the city and the coming of the Messiah were parts of one large event. The questions therefore should be taken as one, though the fulfillment comes in stages. An important matter that must be clarified, however, and which is often misunderstood by Bible teachers and lay persons alike, is that the teachings and signs of Matthew 24 do not concern

duction), the presentation is more cyclical with a broad panorama that fills in specific details.

24:4, 5 This warning was especially appropriate for the disciples. The destruction of Jerusalem did not necessarily mean the nearness of the end of the age. This was a point of confusion for them (Luke 19:11–27; Acts 1:6, 7).

24:6 Three markers of time are found in vv. 4–14. The first is found in v. 6, **the end is not yet. All these are the beginning of sorrows** is the second marker, in v. 8. The final indication of time is given in v. 14, **and then the end will come.** Verses 4–6 may describe the first part of Daniel's Seventieth Week (Dan. 9:25–27), but more likely they are a general picture of the present age. False messiahs, **wars and rumors of wars** are characteristic of fallen humans. When the Lord said **all these things must come to**

✠ IN CONTEXT | Herod, the Great Builder

More architectural remains in Israel date from the reign of Herod the Great (37–4 B.C.) than from any other historical personality. He initiated numerous diverse projects, including temples, gymnasiums, harbors, and other buildings.

In Jerusalem he had a number of important building projects. The Antonia Fortress, a combined palace and fortress that dominated the temple mount, was named after Mark Anthony. There was also a central palace, the largest of Herod's palaces, and a theater and amphitheater, and the most famous of all his projects: the temple mount. Because of the Roman destruction of Jerusalem in A.D. 70, nearly all of the material remains of Herod's period have disappeared.

In his eighteenth year (20–19 B.C.) Herod began rebuilding the Jerusalem temple and enlarging the sacred precincts around it, probably following the plan of the original temple but on a more elaborate scale. Modern excavations have exposed large sections of the western and southern temple mount walls, as well as a monumental stairway, a plaza, and evidence of adjoining roads. The "buildings of the temple" (Matt. 21:1) were therefore certainly an impressive sight in Jesus' day, even though construction was still in progress.

pass, He used a word for "must" that looks at divine or logical necessity. Such activities are necessary because of the sin of man. False messiahs existed before (Acts 5:36, 37; 21:38), and false preachers would come in the future (Acts 20:29, 30; 2 Cor. 11:13–15).

24:7, 8 This paragraph describes things that are characteristic of the end times generally. Verse 7, with its **nation . . . against nation, and kingdom against kingdom,** seems to be an advance over v. 6; they seem to be wars on a broader or worldwide scale. **The famines, pestilences, and earthquakes** are more fully described in Rev. 6:1; 8:5–13; 9:13–21; 16:2–21. The noun **sorrows** of v. 8 is literally "birth pangs." The earth continually has birth-pangs today (Rom. 8:22); during the coming seven year tribulation, these "sorrows" will increase in intensity and frequency until the kingdom age or time of regeneration is born (Matt. 19:28; Acts 3:21).

24:9–14 These verses seem to look at the last half of the Seventieth Week, for **the end will come** with the conclusion of these things.

24:9–11 The hatred of servants of Christ will be by **all nations** because the man of sin will rule the world. He will oppose any who do not worship him (Rev. 13:7, 8, 17).

24:12 Love needs the soil of righteousness in order to flourish. **Lawlessness** and **love** do not mix; in fact, the former stifles the latter.

24:13 The **end** here has mistakenly been taken to mean the end of one's life, but a careful look at the context (vv. 3, 6) makes it evident that it means the "end of the age." **Endures** cannot refer to personal self-effort at endurance resulting in eternal salvation, as some cults teach. Rather, it likely refers to physical deliverance from the devastating destruction of the Great Tribulation into the millennial reign with Christ on earth. They will enter the kingdom with physical bodies.

24:14 this gospel of the kingdom: The final evidence of the end times is the universal proclamation of the gospel. The antecedent of "this" must be v. 13. The "gospel" (literally, "good news") is that the final holocaust of the Great Tribulation known as Armageddon will not result in a genocide and the destruction of all people, for the Lord Jesus Christ will intervene bringing an end to the destruction and preserve a people for His kingdom on earth. It seems this will be accomplished by the 144,000 from Israel who are sealed and are described in Rev. 7:4–8. The innumerable polyglot multitude referred to in Rev. 7:9, 10 seems to be the result of the ministry of the 144,000. This in no way contradicts Paul's statement about "another gospel," for there he discusses no other means of redemption (Gal. 1:6–10).

24:15 This is the first specific time reference that Christ gives. From 24:4–14 the Lord Jesus spoke in general terms. In v. 15 He picks up on the emphasis on the temple. Even more awful than the destruction of the present temple is the desecration of the temple to come. This He does under the imagery of the **abomination of desolation,** the next prophetic sign that people can know. This term means the "abomination that makes desolate." As the Lord stated, it comes from Daniel, specifically 9:27; 11:31, and 12:11. In Dan. 9:27 and 12:11 it is totally prophetic; however, Dan. 11:31 looks to Antiochus IV, who desecrated the temple and set up an idol to Zeus in it. His actions were a prelude to what the ultimate man of sin will do. Significantly, Paul used the same event to indicate when the actual tribulation would be present (2 Thess. 2:3, 4, Rev. 13:14, 15).

24:15 The holy place is the temple.

24:16 In the period of the destruction of the temple in A.D. 70, many of the Hebrew Christians did flee, remembering the words of Jesus, and hid in the clefts of Petra. This deepened the schism between Jews who believed in Jesus and those who did not. The true setting of the verse, however, is in the future desecration of the temple, as it refers to the breaking of the covenant (Dan. 9:27), and the subsequent setting up of an image of the man of sin in the Holy of Holies of the temple. When that occurs, all **in Judea** are to **flee to the mountains.**

24:17–20 These warnings describe the severity of the situation.

24:21 great tribulation: Some may say the world always has had troubles; however, this period of testing will be greater than anything before or after it. It is unique (Dan. 12:1; Rev. 3:10).

24:22 Those days will be shortened (cut short) refers to the seven year period, especially the last three and a half years of the Tribulation. If the Tribulation had not been limited to seven years, all humanity would be destroyed. Note the "good news" of the kingdom in vv. 13, 14 (Zech. 14:2–4). Christ will intervene and stop a genocide.

24:23–25 Miracles by themselves do not prove something is of God (Matt. 7:21–23, 2 Thess. 2:9; Rev. 13:13–15). Miracles must be tested by correct doctrine (Deut. 13:1–5; 1 John 4:1–3) and the witness of God the Spirit (John 10:3–5, 27).

24:26, 27 It is impossible for Christ after His death and resurrection to be in some **desert** or **inner rooms** because when He comes again His coming will be so spectacular it will be impossible to miss. It will be self-attesting (v. 30).

24:28 In the parallel passage of Matt. 24:37–44 found in Luke 17:26–37, this statement of Matt 24:28 comes after the question in Luke 17:37 in answer to the question as to where those judged will be taken. This seems then to be a sweeping statement that conveys the image of the horrible carnage that will take place in the judgment at the coming of the Son of Man. This summary verse, therefore, anticipates the very descriptive parabolic expression that will be given in the rest of chs. 24 and 25.

24:29 immediately after: This is the second time reference (v. 15 is the first). Verse 29 moves chronologically to the close of that seven year period. It will be marked by monumental cosmic disturbances (Is. 13:10; 34:4; Ezek. 32:7, 8; Joel 2:30, 31; 4:15; Hag. 2:6; Zech. 14:6; Rev. 6:12–14).

24:30 The sign of the Son of Man has been taken to be a sign of the cross in the skies; more probably it is Christ Himself or the Shekinah glory (Matt. 16:1; Acts 1:11). Because the context of this discourse is Jewish, **the tribes of the earth** probably refers to Israel. This will be the national repentance of Israel predicted in Zech. 12:10, 12. **The Son of Man coming on the clouds** is in fulfillment of Dan. 7:13, 14.

24:31 Gather refers to the regathering of Israel predicted so often in the OT (Deut. 30:1–6; Is. 11:11, 12; 43:5, 6; 49:12; Jer. 16:14, 15; Ezek. 34:13; 36:24; 37:21–23). Many will have been scattered throughout the earth because of persecution (24:16) and the witness of the 144,000 will bring innumerable multitudes to Christ (Rev. 7:1–10). **Elect** speaks here specifically of Israel as God's chosen people.

24:32 The Lord has instructed His disciples about the Tribulation; now by means of a series of parables (24:32—25:30) He makes some application to life. **The fig tree** does not necessarily portray Israel here (Matt. 21:18–22; Luke 21:29 says, "Look at the fig tree and all the trees"). The lesson to be learned is the proximity of summer, when the branches of trees become **tender** and put forth **leaves.**

24:33 All these things must come to pass before one can say the end is near (i.e., initiation of the Great Tribulation by setting up the abomination of desolation). **it is near:** This is different from the imminency of Christ's coming for the church, which does not rely on a sequence of signs for its happening.

24:34 Generation (Gk. *genea*), as used in different contexts, may mean "race" or "generation." Some, therefore, take it to mean race here, so that Israel as a people will not cease existing until God fulfills His promises to them. Other peoples, like the Hittites and Amorites, have come and gone, but the Jew is still here. Another possibility is to say that *genea* describes a particular era in which people will see those end times. The events that happen will occur so rapidly that all will happen in one generation. Perhaps both are true. **All** includes the Antichrist, the Great Tribulation, and most importantly the stellar appearance of the Christ of glory.

24:35 The words of Christ are more sure than the very existence of the universe.

24:36 no one knows: In spite of such clear statements (vv. 42, 44; 25:13; Acts 1:6, 7), there are still multitudes that follow those who, in disobedience to Christ's word, still set dates for the coming of the Lord. The fact is that there are no prophesied events that have yet to take place before our Lord's rapture of the church. It is imminent; that is, it can happen at any time. Thus, we ought not to be looking for signs of a sign-less event. There are no signs of the time because we are not in the time of the prophesied signs (1 Thess. 1:10; 4:13–18; 1 Cor. 15:51, 52). The earliest Greek manuscripts add "nor the Son" after **the angels of heaven.** How can Jesus as God say, "I do not know" (Mark 13:32)? When the Lord Jesus was incarnate He volun-

24:42–44 This is the application of vv. 36–41. As Noah was vigilant in preparing for the flood so should people living in the tribulation be alert in preparation for Christ's return.

24:45–51 These two servants who belong to their master (Luke 19:11–26) illustrate two attitudes people will have to Christ's coming.

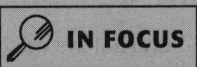 **IN FOCUS** | **The Kingdom of Heaven**

(Gk. *he basileia ton ouranon*) (Matt. 3:2; 4:17; 5:3, 10; 10:7; 25:1) Strong's #*932; 3772:* This phrase, used almost exclusively in Matthew's Gospel (33 times), is a Jewish way of saying "the kingdom of God." The Jews avoided saying the name of God out of respect for Him. Therefore they often used the word *heaven* as an alternative way to refer to God. The word *heaven* also points to the heavenly nature of Jesus' kingdom. His kingdom did not involve a political restoration of the nation of Israel, as many Jews had hoped. Instead He brought a heavenly kingdom with a spiritual domain, the hearts of His people. Such a kingdom demanded internal repentance, not just external submission. It provided deliverance from sin rather than political deliverance.

---

tarily limited His *use* of His divine attributes to His Father's will (Phil. 2:5–8; John 17:4, 5). Therefore He hungered and became thirsty and weary. Luke records that Jesus grew in knowledge and wisdom (Luke 2:52). This statement in v. 36, then, was made while He had surrendered the independent use of His divine omniscience.

24:37–39 the coming of the Son of Man will be **as the days of Noah:** The similarity that Christ is pointing out is not the wickedness of those days (Gen. 6:5) but the indifference of the people in Noah's day. There is nothing sinful about **eating and drinking, and marrying and giving in marriage.** The sin that Christ is referring to is living as though no judgment was coming. So it will be when Christ comes again. The fatal wickedness is seen in the words that they **did not know until the floods came.** One wonders if the comfort zone of evangelical Christians in the United States will grow until there is "no time for end times."

24:40, 41 Taken (Gk. *paralambanō*) is a word of judgment (Luke 17:36). This is not the Rapture; the Rapture is not found in Matt. 24—25. The "taking" of the people is removal in judgment and parallels the "taking away" in judgment in the flood as described in v. 39. It is true that different Greek verbs are used for **took** in v. 39 and **taken** in vv. 40, 41; however, the parallel with v. 39 is too obvious to miss. That being the case, those who are **left** behind go on into the kingdom of the millennium (Matt. 13:30, 40–43) just as Noah and his family were left to repopulate the planet.

The faithful and wise will be given larger responsibilities in the Lord's kingdom. The wicked will be **cut . . . in two,** a form of judgment used in the ancient world. **There will be weeping and gnashing of teeth** is a clause used throughout Matthew, always of remorse experienced when one has suffered great loss. Those who fail to be diligent servants of God will not share in all of God's blessings when they enter the millennial kingdom (Matt. 8:12; 13:42, 50; 22:13; 25:30).

25:1 The **ten virgins** in this parable were waiting for the wedding procession that went from the bride's home to the home of her husband. This nighttime procession would use lamps to light the way because ancient cities did not have streetlights.

25:2 The good servant of 24:45 is described as "faithful and wise." The parable of the ten virgins explains the need for wisdom (vv. 1–13). The following parable of the talents (vv. 14–29) shows the need for faithfulness. The word translated **wise** here and in 24:45 means "prudent."

25:3–9 Possessing **oil** illustrates the concept of being prepared. Lack of oil represents being unprepared for Christ's return.

25:10 The door was shut speaks of being shut out of the kingdom. The unwise virgins were not ready when Christ returned. Compare the wedding feast of Matt. 22:1–14 and Rev. 19:7, 8.

25:11 Lord, Lord is reminiscent of a similar cry in Matt. 7:21–23, where the same scene is portrayed. The repetition of *Lord* indicates strong emotion.

25:12, 13 Just as Jesus said, "I never knew you," in Matt. 7:23, so here He says, "I don't know you" (compare Matt. 10:32, 33; 2 Tim. 2:11–13).

25:14 The parable of the talents illustrates the faithfulness required of God's servants. The fact that the master traveled to a **far country** indicates that there would be ample time to test the faithfulness of the servants.

25:15–17 A talent was a large sum of money, about six thousand denarii. A denarius represented the day's wage for a typical working man (Matt. 20:2).

25:18, 19 It was believed that money hidden in the ground was as secure as it could be.

25:20, 21 ruler: This describes millennial rewards (compare Matt. 24:45).

25:22, 23 The first two servants received the same reward even though they had received different amounts of money. The reward was based on faithfulness, not on the size of their responsibilities. The smallest task in God's work may receive a great reward if we are faithful in performing it (Matt. 10:42).

25:24–28 The wicked servant was lazy and unfaithful, because if he really had feared his master, he would at least have deposited the **money with the bankers.** Then the master would have **received back** the investment plus **interest.**

25:29 This proverb illustrates that a person must use what God has given or else lose it (Heb. 5:11, 12). This includes abilities and spiritual gifts, as well as material possessions (1 Pet. 4:10).

25:30 The unprofitable servant is one who fails to be faithful to the tasks given by the master. This servant will not share in the rewards (Matt. 8:12; 13:42, 50; 22:13).

25:31 The final section of this discourse involves judgment. Matthew has been called "the Gospel of judgment" because the subject occurs so often (3:12; 6:2, 5, 16; 7:24–27; 13:30, 48, 49; 18:23–34; 20:1–16; 21:33–41; 22:1–14; 24:45–51; 25:1–12, 14–46). This is to be expected, since Matthew emphasizes the coming of the kingdom and thus the judgment that accompanies it. In the previous two parables, Jesus had been speaking of the judgment on those Israelites who were unprepared for the coming of the Messiah. In the last parable of this discourse, Jesus focuses His attention on all the nations of the earth. **When the Son of Man comes in His glory** recalls the words of Dan. 7:13, 14, 27 and anticipates the future reign of Christ (Rev. 5:9, 10; 19:11–18; 20:4–6).

25:32, 33 Nations here means Gentiles. **Sheep** and **goats** were clean animals according to the Levitical law; however, their natures are

very different. Shepherds regularly herded their sheep and goats together, but there came a point when the two had to be separated.

25:34–39 The kingdom prepared for you from the foundation of the world indicates that this kingdom has always been God's goal for humans.

25:40–45 Three groups are referred to in vv. 31–46: sheep, goats, and **My brethren.** At the very least, these "brethren" are believers in Jesus Christ.

25:46 Everlasting and **eternal** are used to describe both torment and **life,** indicating that one will last as long as the other. In fact, "everlasting" is used of God in Rom. 16:26.

26:1, 2 As is his style, Matthew brings the discourse of the Lord to a conclusion with the words, **Now it came to pass, when Jesus had finished** (Matt. 7:28; 11:1; 13:53; 19:1).

26:3 The wicked **Caiaphas** was **high priest** from A.D. 18 to 37. However, Luke 3:2 says that both Annas (father-in-law of Caiaphas) and Caiaphas were high priests; Acts 4:6 calls Annas the high priest. Although Caiaphas was officially the high priest, Annas still had influence over that office. Annas was so despicable that the Roman government deposed him from office. However, he continued to work behind the scenes through his wicked son-in-law.

26:4 The religious leaders knew they could not take Christ by argument or logic (22:46), and they did not dare take Him by force (21:46). Their only recourse was **trickery.**

26:5 This verse is to be compared with v. 2, which speaks of Christ's full knowledge of what was coming and His acceptance that it was part of God's plan (John 10:18). Despite what people plot, God still sovereignly controls all events.

26:6 Apparently Jesus spent His nights in the village of **Bethany,** just a few miles outside Jerusalem on the Mount of Olives. **Simon** was a **leper** who evidently had been cleansed by Jesus. He may have been the father of Lazarus, Mary, and Martha (John 12:1, 2).

26:7 The **costly fragrant oil** (Mark 14:3) was a perfume extracted from pure nard. The woman poured the costly perfume on both the head and feet of Jesus (John 12:3). She could have opened the flask in such a way that it would have trickled out; instead, she broke the flask and poured out the oil to cover Jesus' body (Mark 14:3).

26:8, 9 Just as 26:2 is to be contrasted with 26:5, so the women's attitude is in sharp distinction to that of the disciples.

26:10–13 Jesus saw the pouring of the **fragrant oil** on His body as an anticipation of His death (Mark 14:8). The perfumed ointment was placed on Jesus *before* His death; normally it would have been used after His death. The

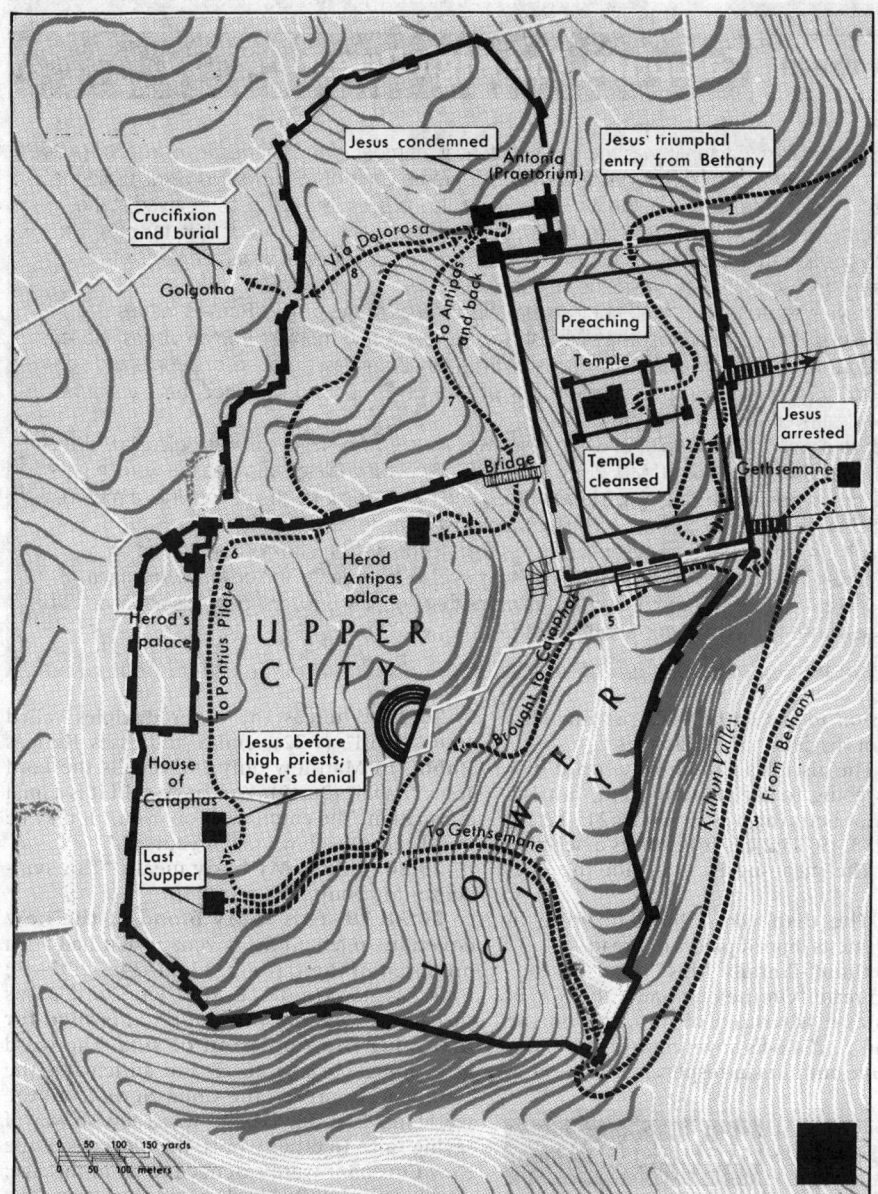

Jesus' Trial, Judgment, and Crucifixion

expensive oil points to (1) the value of Jesus' death and (2) the high cost of devotion to Him.

26:14 The enormity of Judas's sin is seen in the words **one of the twelve.** Jesus was betrayed by one of His inner circle. **Judas** must once have been considered a person of integrity or he would not have been trusted as treasurer.

26:15, 16 Thirty pieces of silver was the price of a slave (Ex. 21:32). Zechariah had fore-

shadowed this sum in his prophetic actions (Zech. 11:12, 13). Note the contrast between the costly devotion of the woman (vv. 7–13) and the small price of Judas's betrayal.

26:17–19 The first day of the Feast of the Unleavened Bread is also the day of the Passover (v. 18). **The disciples** were Peter and John (Luke 22:8).

26:20, 21 One of you will betray Me indicates the Lord's omniscience. Repeatedly—

 **IN DEPTH** **Caiaphas, the High Priest**

As the high priest, Caiaphas was the most influential member of the Sanhedrin, or council (Acts 6:12), which was the highest ruling body and supreme court of the Jews. However, while the position afforded him vast authority, it provided little job security. High priests served at the whim of Rome, and between A.D. 37 and A.D. 67, the empire appointed no fewer than twenty-eight men to the position. The fact that Caiaphas held on to the job for eighteen years is a tribute to his political savvy and, some felt, was evidence that he was in league with Rome.

There may be some truth to that, but if so, his concern was not to protect Rome's interests as much as Israel's. He was afraid that the slightest civil disorder would mobilize Roman troops and lead to Israel's downfall. So when Jesus came, drawing the attention of vast numbers of people and performing astounding miracles, especially the raising of Lazarus, Caiaphas determined that He would have to be destroyed (John 11:45–50).

This led to a well conceived plot in which Jesus was arrested. An illegal trial was held, and false evidence was brought against Him (Matt. 26:3, 4, 57–68). By playing Pilate, who was the Roman governor, and Herod the Jewish king against each other, and by whipping up the people into a mob (Luke 22:66—23:25), Caiaphas orchestrated Jesus' conviction leading to execution.

To Caiaphas's amazement, however, the sparks that he thought he had doused flamed up with renewed power. The apostles began preaching the gospel in Jerusalem (and beyond) with great effect. And, like Jesus, they began performing miracles that not only drew the people's attention but also their response to the message about Christ (Acts 3:1—4:13).

in submission to the Father—Christ unveiled evidences of His deity to His disciples.

26:22 The disciples had already heard that Jesus was going to die in Jerusalem, but His revelation of betrayal was new (16:21; 17:12, 22, 23; 20:18, 19; 25:2). **Is it I** expects a negative response. The meaning is: "I'm not the one, am I?"

26:23 The dish was a bowl of broth in which the guests dipped pieces of bread.

26:24 Quite literally this verse is constructed to read: "On the one hand, the Son of Man goes as it is written of him, but on the other hand . . ." God's sovereignty, therefore, does not rule out human responsibility.

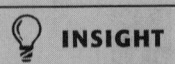 **INSIGHT** **Alabaster**

Alabaster is a soft, translucent stone that can be easily carved and polished. It was often used as a substitute for glass. Alabaster perfume bottles were sealed, disposable containers, opened by breaking and then discarded when empty (Matt. 26:7). The value of spices, ointments, and perfumes then was much higher relative to other goods than it is today.

26:25 Whereas the other disciples called Jesus "Lord" (v.22), Judas addresses Him as **Rabbi**. In Matthew only Judas calls the Lord Jesus "Rabbi" (26:49). **You have said it** is a mild affirmation. The emphasis is on "you." It may be translated, "You have said it yourself."

26:26 This is My body means "This symbolizes My body" (1 Cor. 10:4).

26:27, 28 This is My blood of the new covenant refers to the covenant that had been promised in the OT (Jer. 31:31–34; 32:37–44; Ezek. 34:25–31; 37:26–28). The Lord Jesus specifically said that His **blood . . . is shed for many for the remission of sins.** The word *many* looks back to 20:28 and anticipates the command to preach the Good News to all the world in 28:19, 20. "Many" was a Jewish way of saying "all." In other words, the blessings of the New Covenant were extended to all in this age; it will yet be fulfilled for Israel in the future. The expression **blood of the covenant** also seems to look back to the institution of the Mosaic covenant in Ex. 24:8.

26:29, 30 This verse anticipates God's kingdom when Christ will reign on the throne of David. Today He is seated with the Father on His throne and intercedes for us.

26:31 All of you will . . . stumble: All the disciples, not just Peter, would fall away. **I will strike the Shepherd . . . the flock will be scattered:** This OT prophecy is found in Zech. 13:7 (Ps. 118).

⚒ **IN DEPTH**   **Judas Iscariot, the Betrayer**

W hen the NT mentions Judas Iscariot it reminds the reader that he was the man who betrayed Jesus (Matt. 10:4; Mark 3:19; John 12:4). Consequently, to this day the name Judas is a symbol of betrayal.

Why did he do it? His portrayal in the Gospels suggests that he had a keen interest in money. But the amount that the priests paid him—thirty pieces of silver—was relatively small. Besides, he had access to the disciples' money box and apparently was known for helping himself to its contents (John 12:6).

Some have suggested that Judas thought that his betrayal of Jesus would force Jesus into asserting His true power and overthrowing the Romans. Others have suggested that Judas became convinced that Jesus was a false Messiah and that the true Messiah was yet to come. Or perhaps he was upset over Jesus' seemingly casual attitude toward the Law in regard to associating with sinners and violating the Sabbath.

No one knows what Judas's exact motives were for turning against Jesus. He remains a shadowy figure in the Gospel accounts, unknown by his companions, unfaithful to his Lord, and unmourned in his death. (The NT mentions more than one Judas, such as a brother of Jesus, who was probably author of the Book of Jude; Matt. 15:35.)

26:32 Several reasons may be offered as to why Christ went to Galilee to meet His disciples: (1) they were all from Galilee; (2) He wanted to be away from Jerusalem, the center of opposition; (3) He wanted to take up the work of shepherding His flock where He had ministered to them before; or (4) the most effective setting for the Great Commission given in 28:19, 20 would be Galilee (4:12–16).

26:33–35 The **rooster** crow is usually thought to refer to the third Roman watch, from midnight to 3 A.M.

26:36 Judas had already gone (John 13:21–30), so the Lord left eight of His disciples at this spot. **Gethsemane** (which means "oil press") was east of Jerusalem on the Mount of Olives. In the place where olives were crushed and ground, the One anointed with oil was crushed and rent.

26:37 This was the third time that Jesus singled out Peter, James, and John to accompany Him for a specific purpose (see the Transfiguration in 17:1–13 and the raising of Jairus's daughter in Luke 8:49–56).

26:38 My soul is exceedingly sorrowful, even to death seems to look back to Pss. 42:5, 6, 11; 43:5. **Watch** literally means "stay awake."

26:39 let this cup pass from Me: It was not the impending physical suffering, as terrible as it would be, that caused Jesus to pray this way. It was the reality of the sinless Son of God bearing the sins of the world and facing separation from His Father (2 Cor. 5:21; Gal. 3:13; Heb. 12:2; 1 Pet. 2:24). *Cup* is a figure of speech for wrath in the OT (Ps. 75:8; Is. 51:17). Jesus became a curse for us and took the brunt of God's righteous wrath against sin (Gal. 3:13).

26:40 Could you not watch with Me one hour: Although addressed to Peter, the question was meant for all three disciples. Earlier Peter had claimed that he would never forsake Jesus and that he would even die for Him (v. 35); yet Peter could not stay awake to pray with Jesus at the time of His greatest need.

26:41 The disciples needed to stay awake **and pray** because they were about to be tested themselves. Here the word **flesh** emphasizes human weakness. The contrast between the weakness of the disciples and the strength of the Lord is startling. Because the flesh is **weak,** every child of God needs supernatural empowerment (Rom. 8:3, 4).

26:42–44 The fact that Jesus **prayed the same words** indicates that there is nothing wrong with repetition from a devout heart. In the first prayer, Jesus made a positive request: "Let this cup pass from Me." In the second and third prayers, His request was negative. In obedience to His Father, Jesus committed Himself to **drink** the **cup,** whatever the cost.

26:45 Are you still sleeping: The disciples were resting while Jesus was sweating in prayer to the point of exhaustion (Luke 22:43, 44).

26:46 This verse shows Jesus' active submission to the Father's will, as He stated in v. 42. Jesus did not go reluctantly but with determination to do the Father's will.

26:47, 48 The fact that the multitude was armed **with swords and clubs** indicates that **Judas** did not really know the heart of Jesus. Christ went out to meet the multitude not to do battle, but to surrender.

26:49 The only person to address the Lord as **Rabbi** in the Book of Matthew was Judas (v.

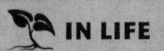 **IN LIFE** **"Choice" Leaders**

Shortly after Jesus' death, those whom He had trained would assume the reins of His new movement, and the transition would prove to be quite awkward. It didn't help that it was forced on the group by hostile outsiders, but an even more troubling aspect was that the group began to fall apart during Jesus' last days and hours. For instance:

- Bravado caused them to overstate their commitment (Matt. 26:35). When the moment of truth came, they deserted the Lord (26:56).
- Even though the Lord asked them to keep watch with Him during His final hours of freedom, they fell asleep twice (26:40, 43).
- At the very moment when Jesus was standing trial and enduring mockery and beatings, Peter, who had led the others in declaring their loyalty (26:35), denied any association with Him (26:6 9–75).

In short, the disciples hardly seem to have had the "right stuff" for leadership, for continuing the important work that Jesus began. Yet Jesus returned to that very group after His resurrection and declared that they were still His chosen representatives, the ones appointed to continue His work. And He affirmed His commitment to stick with them to the end (28:19, 20).

Jesus' treatment of these disciples shows that failure is not unforgivable. Rather, it seems to be the crucible out of which character is formed. It is certainly not a sifting-out process to eliminate weak or useless people. Christ does not look for perfect people but for faithful people who can experience His forgiveness and grow.

25). **Kissed** means to kiss as a display of affection. The same verb form is used in the parable of the Lost Son in Luke 15:20.

26:50 Friend: Even though He knew Judas's wicked heart and actions, Jesus offered him friendship and an opportunity to change his mind. The words translated **Why have you come** may also mean "Do what you have come to do."

26:51 John 18:10 explains that the impetuous swordsman was Peter. This action was performed with one of the two swords that the disciples had (Luke 22:38).

26:52, 53 A legion in the Roman army was about six thousand men. When one considers the power of one angel, as seen in the OT (Ex. 12:23; 2 Sam. 24:15–17; 2 Kin. 19:35), the power of more than 72,000 angels is beyond comprehension. Jesus had all of heaven's power at His disposal, yet He refused to use it. His Father's will was for Him to go to the Cross.

26:54 If Jesus had called for angelic aid, the prophetic Scriptures foretelling His betrayal, His death, and His resurrection would not have been fulfilled. This point is so important that it is stated twice (v. 56).

26:55, 56 all the disciples forsook Him and fled: Compare Peter's claim in v. 35 with Jesus' words in v. 41, "The spirit indeed is willing, but the flesh is weak."

26:57 The Lord Jesus was subjected to six trials—three Jewish and three Gentile. The first

Jewish trial was before Annas, who was not the actual high priest, but was a powerful influence on the high priest's office. This trial is mentioned only by John (John 18:12–23). The second trial was before **Caiaphas** and the Jewish council. Clearly the council had been hastily called together in anticipation of passing judgment on Jesus. Matthew does not mention Jesus' trial before Herod Antipas (Luke 23:6–12); he also combines the two trials before Pilate into one (27:2, 11–26). Jesus' opponents were trying desperately to find some legal basis for condemning Him to death.

26:58 John 18:15, 16 explains that Peter and John were both granted an entrance into the **courtyard** because John was known to the high priest. **The servants** were probably house-servants, not members of the mob who arrested the Lord. Apparently, Peter had forgotten the words of Jesus concerning His resurrection. For Peter, this was **the end.**

26:59–61 This was a misquotation and misapplication of Christ's words (John 2:19–21). At any rate, to say that Jesus had spoken against the temple was an action for which they could condemn Him (Acts 6:13, 14).

26:62 The high priest must have recognized that the accusers had no case against Jesus. His outburst was the result of frustration and desperation. In maintaining His silence, Jesus fulfilled the prophecy of Is. 53:7.

26:63 I put You under oath by the living

God: The high priest thought he needed to put Christ under oath in order to get a truthful confession. Christ needed no such oath; He had indicated His divine nature and unity with the Father on several occasions (John 8:58; 10:30–33).

26:64 Jesus answered the high priest's request (v. 63) in the affirmative and then fortified His answer by applying two clearly messianic passages to Himself (Ps. 110:1; Dan. 7:13).

26:65, 66 Jesus' claim of sitting at the right hand of God (v. 64) was an assertion of deity and was, to this unbelieving high priest, a clear case of **blasphemy.**

26:67, 68 Prophesy . . . who struck you: This is a sarcastic demand to be told by supernatural knowledge the names and identities of those who were strangers to Him.

26:69–74 The cursing by Peter means that he called curses upon himself if he knew the Lord. **Swear** shows he swore under oath that he did not know Christ Jesus. **immediately a rooster crowed:** Some have argued a contradiction between this passage, where the rooster is said to crow (presumably once) after Peter denies Jesus three times, and the statement in Mark's gospel that the rooster would crow twice. This then would mean that there are more than three crowings; there is a total of six (Mark 14:72). Others believe that to see a contradiction is simply forced reading of the text. Matthew, Luke, and John give the simple statement that a rooster would crow (Matt. 26:75; Luke 22:61; John 18:27), whereas Mark, which is Peter's gospel, emphasizes the exact number of times the rooster would crow. Obviously the number of times would be much more on Peter's mind than the other gospel writer's, who were concerned only with the general sign of the denials. These believe that there is no reason to posit two separate rooster crowings and six denials of Peter.

26:75 He went out and wept bitterly indicates Peter's genuine repentance. In His grace, the Lord later forgave Peter.

27:1 This was the third Jewish trial. The first two were illegal because they were held at night. This third meeting was held **when morning came** and was simply a "rubber stamp" of the one described in 26:57–68.

27:2 Pontius Pilate was **governor** of Judea, Samaria, and Idumea from A.D. 26–36. Because the Jews did not have authority to execute Jesus (John 18:31), they brought Him to Pilate.

27:3, 4 Judas felt remorse because he had not planned for this to happen. He may have betrayed Jesus in order to force Him to take action against His enemies and inaugurate His kingdom. But that was not God's timing and plan.

27:5 Acts 1:18 says that the death of Judas was due to a headlong fall. The likely explanation is that Judas **hanged himself** on a tree, only to have the rope or branch break. If the tree was over a rocky precipice, the account in Acts can be correlated with this account.

27:6 The religious leaders, who had no problem condemning an innocent person to death, suddenly became very scrupulous about the law. Because of Deut. 23:18, it was felt that blood money should not be used for religious purposes.

27:7, 8 Originally this plot of ground was known as **the potter's field,** a place where potters dug for clay. Consequently, it was full of holes, which would have made it easy to bury people who had no family tombs. It was purchased as a cemetery for strangers who died in Jerusalem. It is likely that Gentiles were also buried there.

27:9, 10 This prophecy is found in Zech. 11:12, 13; however, Matthew states that the prophecy was made by Jeremiah. The best solution to the problem seems to be that the prophecy **was spoken by Jeremiah** and recorded by Zechariah. A second option is that the name Jeremiah stands for the collection of prophetic writings in which Zechariah is found. It may also be that in the days of Christ, the Book of Jeremiah headed the books of the prophets. The quotation is then identified with the name of the first book in the section and not the name of the specific book within the group.

27:11–14 The title **King of the Jews** has not been used in Matthew's Gospel since 2:2. Clearly Pilate's charge against the Lord Jesus was prompted by Jewish religious leaders.

27:15–18 Barabbas was **notorious** because he was an insurrectionist and a murderer (Mark 15:7; Luke 23:19, 25). Evidently Pilate assumed the Jews would choose Jesus to be released over a murderer like Barabbas. Jesus had only gone about doing good.

27:19 Only Matthew records this incident concerning Pilate's wife. It highlights Pilate's sense of responsibility; he did not want to condemn an innocent man.

27:20–24 The religious authorities, who wanted to avoid a riot earlier, here used a **tumult** (the same Greek noun as in 26:5) to accomplish their goal. The tenure of Pilate had been rocked by conflicts with the Jews from the very beginning. He could scarcely have afforded another one on his record. Once again, Pilate pronounced Jesus to be innocent. The washing of **his hands** is recorded only by Matthew. The governor vainly attempted to rid himself of the guilt of condemning an innocent man to death (Deut. 21:1–9; Ps. 73:13).

27:25 His blood be on us and on our

IN DEPTH · The Meaning of Messiah

Matthew wrote his Gospel to demonstrate to his Jewish audience that Jesus is indeed the long-awaited Messiah. Who is the Messiah and why were the Jews waiting for such a person?

The Term
In Hebrew or Aramaic, the word *Messiah* means "anointed." The Greek equivalent of the word is the title "Christ."

Old Testament Background
In the OT, prophets, priests, and kings were literally anointed with oil to consecrate them for special service or to signify the endowment of the Spirit of God (Lev. 4:3; 8:12; 1 Sam. 10:1, 6; Ps. 105:15; Is. 61:1). These practices pointed to the promised arrival of God's Anointed One, who would fulfill all three offices as the Prophet, the Priest, and the King.

Titles for the Messiah
Seed of Abraham (Ps. 105:6); Son of David (Matt. 1:1); Son of Man (Dan. 7:13); My Son (Ps. 2:7); My Servant (Matt. 12:18); My Elect One (Is. 42:1); The Branch (Zech. 3:8; 6:12); Wonderful, Counselor, Mighty God, Prince of Peace (Is. 9:6)

Major Old Testament Prophecies of the Messiah
Gen. 3:15; 9:27; 12:3; 22:18; 49:8, 10; Deut. 18:18; 2 Sam. 7:11–16; 23:5; Pss. 2; 16; 22; 40; 110; Is. 2; 7; 9; 11; 40; 42; 49; 52; 53; Jer. 23:5, 6; Dan. 7:27; Hag. 2:9; Zech. 12:10–14; Mal. 3:1; 4:5, 6

Jewish Expectations for the Messiah
In the first century the Jews looked for a Messiah who would deliver the nation from Roman domination and become their King and rebuild the nation of Israel to its former glory. By looking for a military deliverer and a political Messiah, the Jews minimized the messianic roles of prophet and priest. Thus many Jews rejected Jesus as the Messiah because He came as a humble spiritual Savior and not a conquering political ruler.

The Messiah's Rule
Jesus indicated that He was the King for whom the Jews were looking. However, His kingdom was not an earthly kingdom but a heavenly kingdom. In Matthew there are thirty-two references to the "kingdom of heaven." This phrase, found in the NT only in Matthew's Gospel, is probably derived from the description of the kingdom of the Son of Man in Dan. 7:13–18. The phrase indicates the rule of heaven over all of the earth (Matt. 6:10).

Jesus' Claim
When asked specifically if He was the Christ, Jesus answered in the affirmative, incurring the wrath of the Jews (Matt. 26:63–65). In addition, Jesus praised Peter for recognizing Him as the Anointed One of God (Matt. 16:15–20).

Significance
The title Messiah implies the idea of deity. The great prophet Moses, the priest Melchizedek, and even the glorious King David pale in comparison to the messianic Prophet-Priest-King. In the words of Heb. 1:3, Jesus Christ is the "brightness of [God's] glory and the express image of His person." In short, He is God (Heb. 1:8).

children: The destruction of Jerusalem was one of the results of this sin (Matt. 23:32–39).

27:26 when he had scourged Jesus: Scourging was a life-threatening punishment. Evidently this was an attempt by Pilate to punish Jesus so severely that the people would have pity and say, "It is enough; release Him" (John 19:4,

[The disciple whom Jesus loved] It is the Lord (John 21:7)

And when they saw him they worshiped him (Matthew 28:17)

[Two disciples] Jesus himself stood among them (Luke 24:36)

[Mary Magdalene] I have seen the Lord (John 20:18)

[The disciples] We have seen the Lord (John 20:25)

Ascension

Then he led them as far as Bethany (Luke 24:50)

Resurrection

Jesus' Resurrection and Ascension

5). However, the mob cried out for Jesus to be crucified (John 19:6).

27:27 The Praetorium was the official residence of the governor when he was in Jerusalem. It was originally built as a palace for Herod the Great.

27:28–30 The soldiers mocked Jesus for claiming to be a king. Note the references to the

robe, the **crown,** the scepter (**reed**), and the praise.

27:31 crucified: Crucifixion, a practice probably adopted from Persia, was considered by the Romans to be the cruelest form of execution. This punishment was reserved for the worst criminals; Roman citizens were not crucified. The victim usually died after two or three days of agonizing suffering, enduring thirst, exhaustion, and exposure. The victim's arms were nailed to a beam, which was hoisted up and fixed to a post, to which the feet of the victim would be nailed. The body weight was supported by a peg on which the victim sat.

27:32 Compelled, the same verb used in 5:41, refers to the Roman government's right of impressment, the right of the Roman army to demand labor from a person. The scourging undoubtedly left Jesus weak and unable to carry His cross, so a Roman guard ordered Simon to carry it. **Simon** must have been (or later became) a Christian; it is unlikely that he would be referred to by name if he were a stranger to the Christian community. This Simon was the father of Alexander and Rufus (Mark 15:21). **Cyrene,** located in North Africa, was home to a large number of Jews (Acts 6:9).

27:33 The reason the site was called **Place of a Skull** is not known for certain; possibly the hill or mound looked something like a skull.

27:34 Sour wine mingled with gall would have dulled Jesus' pain and consciousness. Jesus refused it; He wanted to drink His cup of suffering fully aware of all that was happening (Ps. 69:21).

27:35 The executioners had the privilege of taking the victim's clothes. In **casting lots** for Jesus' **garments,** the soldiers fulfilled Ps. 22:18.

27:36 Perhaps the soldiers **kept watch** to prevent anyone from trying to rescue Jesus from the Cross.

27:37 Putting the Gospel accounts together, the **accusation** probably read "This is Jesus of Nazareth, the King of the Jews" (Mark 15:26; Luke 23:38; John 19:19).

27:38 two robbers were crucified with Him: This is in fulfillment of Is. 53:12, "He was numbered with the transgressors." Luke recorded that one of these robbers believed and was promised that he would join Jesus in paradise that very day (Luke 23:39–43).

INSIGHT | **Sunday Morning at the Tomb**

The Gospels agree that Jesus was raised bodily from the dead on Sunday. They also agree that Mary Magdalene was the first witness of the empty tomb, and most probably of the resurrected Lord. This is an important piece of historical evidence, since the testimony of a woman had no legal value in ancient Jewish society. If some early church writers had invented a story of the resurrection, they would not have emphasized Mary's witness in the narrative.

Like the crucifixion accounts, the resurrection accounts in the Gospels diverge in a number of particulars. Only Matthew reports an earthquake and the stone being rolled away (Matt. 28:2). Since Matthew also reported an earthquake at the crucifixion (27:51), the second earthquake may show the equal significance of the Resurrection. Matthew and Mark speak of one angel at the tomb (Matt. 28:5; Mark 16:5). Luke and John speak of two (Luke 24:4; John 20:12). Matthew and Mark report only the women at the tomb. Luke and John tell of a visit by Peter. John also relates a footrace between Peter and the beloved disciple to the tomb (John 20:3–8).

27:39 Psalm 22:7 predicted the insults that would be directed at the Messiah.

27:40 For a similar falsehood at Jesus' trial, see 26:61. Jesus' actual words were: "Destroy this temple, and in three days I will raise it up" (John 2:19). In three days Jesus rose from the dead, thereby fulfilling this prophecy.

27:41–44 Jesus would not come down from the Cross *because* He was the Son of God and the King of Israel (John 10:18). He was obediently following God's plan for Him; His obedience would lead to His exaltation as King over all (Phil. 2:8–11). Compare the religious leaders' taunts with Ps. 22:8.

27:45 The sixth hour was noon. The **darkness** was not due to an eclipse of the sun, since the Passover occurred at full moon. This was a supernatural occurrence.

27:46 The physical darkness was a demonstration of the agony of the Lord's human soul. **My God, My God, why have You forsaken Me:** The duplication of "My God, My God" indicates Jesus' deep sorrow. The fact that Jesus spoke in Aramaic, the tongue of His birth, may be another sign of the extreme stress He was encountering. No human can understand the theological significance of this cry. It graphically parallels 2 Cor. 5:21. This was not a cry of defeat, however. Christ was quoting from Ps. 22 and may have been alluding to the great victory that the psalm describes.

27:47–49 Sour wine was the cheap wine used by soldiers and the lower class. Christ may have accepted this in order to give Himself enough moisture and strength to cry out again with a loud voice (v. 50).

27:50 The **loud voice** (v. 46) indicates that Jesus was still fairly strong when He **yielded up His spirit.** The cry referred to by Matthew, "It is finished" (John 19:30), was not a cry of exhaus-

tion but of victory. The purpose for which Jesus came was fulfilled. Redemption for the sins of the world had been accomplished. Satan's judgment was a fact. The verb translated *yielded* means "dismissed." Even in dying the Lord demonstrated His royal authority.

27:51 the veil of the temple was torn in two from top to bottom: The temple had two veils or curtains, one in front of the holy place and the other separating the holy place from the Most Holy Place. It was the second of these that was torn, demonstrating that God had opened up access to Himself through His Son (Heb. 6:19; 10:19–22). Only God could have torn the veil from the top.

27:52, 53 many bodies of the saints . . . were raised: Because the Lord Jesus is the firstborn from the dead (Col. 1:18; Rev. 1:5) and the firstfruits of those who are asleep (1 Cor. 15:20, 23), these people could not have received their resurrection bodies. They probably were raised, as Lazarus was, to ordinary physical life. The fact that the people who were raised **appeared to many** in **the holy city** implies that they had been contemporaries of the people who saw them.

27:54 The centurion and those with him may have heard the exchanges between Pilate and Jesus (v. 11); they certainly witnessed the taunts recorded in vv. 40, 43. The supernatural signs convinced them that Jesus was indeed **the Son of God.** Significantly, this confession of faith came from a Gentile.

27:55, 56 Three women who where faithful to the Lord Jesus to the end are named: **Mary Magdalene; Mary the mother of James and Joses,** the wife of Clopas (John 19:25); and **the mother** of James and John, wife of Zebedee, named Salome (Mark 15:40).

27:57–60 Arimathea was about twenty

IN COMPARISON　The Appearances of the Risen Christ

Central to Christian faith is the bodily resurrection of Jesus. By recording the resurrection appearances, the New Testament leaves no doubt about this event.

- In or around Jerusalem:
  - To Mary Magdalene (Mark 16:9; John 20:11–18)
  - To other women (28:8–10)
  - To Peter (Luke 24:34)
  - To ten disciples (Luke 24:36–43; John 20:19–25)
  - To the Eleven, including Thomas (Mark 16:14; John 20:26–29)
  - At the Ascension (Mark 16:19, 20; Luke 24:50–53; Acts 1:4–12)
- To the disciples on the Emmaus road (Mark 16:12, 13; Luke 24:13–35)
- In Galilee (28:16–20; John 21:1–24)
- To five hundred people (1 Cor. 15:6)
- To James and the apostles (1 Cor. 15:7)
- To Paul on the road to Damascus (Acts 9:1–6; 22:1–10; 26:12–18; 1 Cor. 15:8)

miles northwest of Jerusalem. Mark 15:43 describes **Joseph** as "a prominent council member, who was himself waiting for the kingdom of God." Luke 23:50 describes him as "a good and just man." But Matthew describes him as **rich**, a fulfillment of Is. 53:9.

27:61 These two Marys, also mentioned in v. 56, were witnesses to the burial of Jesus.

27:62 The next day was the Sabbath. **The chief priests** were Sadducees. The **Pharisees'** and the Sadducees' common animosity toward Jesus united them.

27:63 The Sadducees and Pharisees described the Lord Jesus as **that deceiver** when, in reality, *they* were the deceivers (26:4) and hypocrites (23:13, 15, 23, 25, 27, 29).

27:64 For emphasis, the verb **secure** is used three times in vv. 64–66.

27:65 The noun translated **guard** is a Latin word, since the soldiers were Romans and not part of the temple guard.

27:66 To emphasize the impossibility of anyone stealing the body of Jesus, Matthew stressed that the tomb was sealed (Dan. 6:17).

28:1–20 Although Matthew is brief in his discussion of the resurrection of Christ, he defends it carefully. The Resurrection was attested by several witnesses, including an angel, various soldiers, and the women at the tomb (vv. 1–8). The tomb with Jesus' body in it was sealed (27:66), but later the body was not found there (vv. 6, 8). The excuse of the soldiers was illogical (vv. 11–15). No Roman soldier would admit to sleeping on the job, for the punishment for this was death. Finally, Jesus Himself appeared to many of His disciples, providing even more witnesses to His resurrection (vv.

16–20). Matthew presents the evidence for Jesus' resurrection with precision because the doctrine is essential to the Christian faith. The Resurrection is a sign that Jesus is the Messiah, the Son of God (Matt. 12:38, 39), and the Resurrection validates the Lord's own prophecies of it (Matt. 16:21; 17:22, 23; 20:17–19). In 1 Cor. 15:12–19, Paul emphasizes the importance of the Resurrection by listing a series of consequences if the doctrine is denied.

28:1 after the Sabbath: The Sabbath ended at sundown on Saturday. The events of this verse took place at dawn on Sunday morning. The two Marys are identified in 27:56, 61.

28:2 An **earthquake** marked the death of the Lord Jesus (27:51); here it evidenced His resurrection. The tomb was not opened to permit Christ to come out but to allow others in, so they could see that it was empty.

28:3, 4 Brilliance is a characteristic of heavenly beings (Matt. 17:2; Dan. 7:9; 10:5, 6; Acts 1:10; Rev. 3:4, 5; 4:4; 6:11; 7:9, 13; 19:14).

28:5, 6 He is risen, as He said: For Jesus' predictions of His resurrection, see Matt. 12:40; 16:21; 17:9, 23; 26:32.

28:7, 8 The Lord Jesus made post-resurrection appearances first in Jerusalem and Judea, then in Galilee, and then again in Jerusalem. Both Matt. 28 and John 21 emphasize the appearances in Galilee. Christ's command to "come, see" (v. 6) is followed here by **go . . . tell.** This is always the divine order: to tell others the Good News about our Lord.

28:9, 10 Galilee was the appointed location for Jesus' rendezvous with His disciples (v. 7; 26:32) and also the setting of the Great Commission (vv. 18–20). Note that the Lord referred

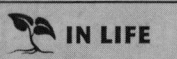 **IN LIFE** | **To All the Nations**

Jesus sent His followers to make disciples of all the nations (*ethne*, "peoples"; Matt. 28:19). That mandate may seem obvious to us today. After all, we live at the end of 2,000 years of Christian outreach. Christianity now is an overwhelmingly Gentile religion subscribed to by roughly one-third of the world's population. And with modern technology, it appears to be a relatively simple task to expand that outreach even further.

Yet in many ways we are just like Jesus' original disciples. They wanted a local hero, a Messiah just for Israel, one who would follow their customs and confirm their prejudices. So they were no doubt stunned by the scope and far-reaching implications of the global, cross-cultural vision that Jesus now presented. He was turning out to be more than the King of the Jews; He was the international Christ, the Savior of the entire world.

Actually, Jesus had been showing them this since the beginning of His ministry. Matthew recorded His work among the Gentiles (8:10; 15:24), and he cited Is. 42:1–4, that Jesus would "declare justice to the Gentiles [nations] . . . and [that] in His name Gentiles will trust" (Matt. 12:14–21). Yet the disciples had a hard time believing it. Could their Lord really be interested in "all the nations"? They did not seem to be. It is easy to pay lip service to the idea that Jesus cares for the whole world. But isn't it easier to follow a Christ that fits comfortably only into our own culture?

Culture, after all, is the key. Jesus told His Galilean followers to "make disciples," and they did— Jewish disciples. But they experienced profound culture shock when the Holy Spirit brought new groups into the fellowship, including Hellenist disciples, Samaritan disciples, and eventually Gentile disciples of all kinds (Acts 6:1–7; 8:4–25; 10:1–11:18; 15:1–21).

Today the bulk of new disciples are non-white and non-Western. Not surprisingly, they bring different cultural perspectives into the church. So one of the greatest challenges believers will face in the coming years is the same one that the original disciples faced at the inauguration of the movement: not only to believe but also to accept that Jesus really is for all the nations. For God's plan to make disciples of people throughout the world is part of His overall, long-term objective of making His name great among the nations (Mal. 1:11).

---

to His disciples as His **brethren** (Matt. 12:48–50; Ps. 22:22; Heb. 2:11, 12).

28:11 The Roman guards **reported to the chief priests** because they had been assigned for duty to the religious authorities (27:65).

28:12–14 His disciples . . . stole Him away while we slept: Besides being a lie, this was a very weak explanation. If a guard was found sleeping at his post or if a prisoner escaped, the guard would be put to death (Acts 12:19; 16:27, 28; 27:42). It may have been possible for one soldier to sleep, but it is highly improbable that all of them slept at the same time. Also, sleeping people do not make good witnesses. If they were asleep, how did they know what happened?

28:15 Until this day refers specifically to the time of the writing of Matthew's Gospel; however, this explanation is current even today.

28:16, 17 When **the eleven disciples went away into Galilee** they were probably accompanied by many more people. This may be the appearance to more than five hundred people mentioned by Paul in 1 Cor. 15:6. This may explain why **some doubted;** after all, the eleven were confirmed believers in the resurrected Christ by this time (John 20:19–28).

28:18 All authority has been given to Jesus, although He is not yet exercising all of it (Phil. 2:9–11; Heb. 2:5–9; 10:12, 13; Rev. 3:21). He will manifest this power when He returns in all His glory (Matt. 19:28; 1 Cor. 15:27, 28; Eph. 1:10). The word *authority* normally refers to delegated authority (as in 8:9; 9:6, 8; 10:1; 21:23, 24, 27). The Father would give this authority to the Son (Phil. 2:9–11). Here the Lord Jesus may have been recalling the prophecy of Dan. 7:13, 14.

28:19, 20 Often this verse is viewed as having three commands; namely, to go, to baptize, and to make disciples or teach. In reality the Great Commission revolves around one main imperative: **make disciples.** Making disciples involves three steps: going, **baptizing,** and **teaching,** especially the last two. Baptism looks at the decision to trust in Christ. It was assumed that when a person trusted in the Lord Jesus he would be baptized; the NT knows of no unbaptized believers. The word **name** is singular, indicating God is one in three Persons.

The Gospel According to

Mark

■

*M*ARK'S GOSPEL IS UNIQUE. IT IS NOT A biography of Jesus, like Matthew or Luke, for it does not dwell on Jesus' family history or career. Instead, this Gospel is a record of Jesus' actions and achievements. It presents Jesus as a Savior-King, who conquers demons, disease, and death. The emphasis on Jesus' mighty and miraculous works makes this Gospel action-packed, fresh, and vivid.

Mark constantly uses the present tense to create the impression of an eyewitness account—the kind presented by an on-the-spot reporter. And just like a reporter, he speaks directly to the reader. He uses rhetorical questions that readers would likely ask themselves, such as, "Who can this be, that even the wind and the sea obey Him!" (4:41). Sometimes he even addresses his audience with Jesus' words, "And what I say to you, I say to all: Watch!" (13:37). Mark wants to transform believers with his report, not merely inform them.

Moreover, his eyewitness accounts provide considerable detail—the emotional responses of Jesus and others, the sizes and reactions of crowds, and the appearance of men and women. The account of the Gadarene demoniac is an example of Mark's attention to detail. He uses twenty verses to tell that story, while Luke uses fourteen and Matthew writes a mere seven. Yet Mark's Gospel is the most concise of all of the Gospels, because he omits Jesus' longer discourses. In general, Mark presents the miracle-working Jesus, not the teaching Jesus.

Mark wrote for Gentile Christians, especially Romans. This conclusion is based on several facts: (1) Mark assumes some prior knowledge of the Christian faith on the part of his readers. John (the Baptist), baptism, and the Holy Spirit (1:4, 5, 8) are all mentioned without comment. (2) He does not assume a familiarity with Jewish Scripture. He directly quotes only one Old Testament passage (1:2, 3). (3) Furthermore, he regularly explains Jewish customs and geography (7:2–4; 13:3; 14:12). (4) Finally, Mark purposely omits Jesus' prohibition of preaching to the Samaritans and Gentiles (6:7–11; compare Matt. 10:5, 6).

Mark's Gentile readers faced persecution and martyrdom. He wrote his Gospel to strengthen and guide Roman believers through Nero's terrible persecutions. First of all, his readers needed to know that Jesus had also suffered. But, they also needed to know that Jesus, after his suffering, had triumphed over both suffering and death. The suffering Jesus was also the Son of God (1:1, 11; 14:61; 15:39), the Son of Man (2:10; 8:31; 13:26), the Christ (Messiah) (8:29), and the Lord (1:3; 7:28). After the death of Peter and other eyewitnesses to Jesus' life, this gospel message needed to be written down. Mark wrote the story down in order to verify these truths and to provide a way to pass them on to new generations of believers.

Mark introduces the main character of his action-packed narrative, Jesus, in thirteen quick verses. He weaves in this introduction both expectation ("Prepare the way of the LORD," 1:3) and conflict (Satan tempts Christ in v. 13). The large section that follows (1:14—8:30) heightens the conflict, as in a Greek tragedy. There are successes for Jesus, but there is also growing hostility. Triumph and conflict appear side by side. This long section culminates in Peter and the other disciples recognizing Jesus as the promised Messiah (8:29).

In the next section (8:31—15:47), Mark describes the final outcome for the Messiah— Jesus' passion and death. First, Jesus announces His coming death to His disciples (8:31; 9:31; 10:33) and prepares them for it. Then, He journeys to Jerusalem and is tried and put to death. But in the epilogue (16:1–20), the purpose of His death becomes clear. The drama comes to a rousing conclusion as Christ rises from the dead and encourages His followers. This is the Gospel of Mark—the Good News of Jesus Christ.

Peter was Mark's primary informant. In fact, the outline of events in Mark's Gospel follows precisely the outline of Peter's sermon to Cornelius at Caesarea (Acts 10:34–43; compare Acts 13:23–33). Oral preaching at that time, such as Peter's sermon, used established styles and rhetorical techniques to aid both instruction and recall; Mark's Gospel reflects these oral styles. Furthermore, Justin Martyr, writing at about A.D. 150 in Rome, confirmed that Mark wrote down Peter's recollection of events. He quoted

Mark 3:17 as being in "the Memoirs of Peter." In addition to recording Peter's memories, Mark may have added his own memories and consulted other documents.

Most agree that Mark wrote his Gospel in Rome under Peter's supervision. A second-century document, called the Prologue to Mark, states that the Gospel was composed in Italy. Furthermore, Irenaeus, writing about A.D. 180, specifically stated Rome. Since Mark was with Paul in Rome around A.D. 60–62 and may have returned around A.D. 65 at Paul's request (2 Tim. 4:11), there is little reason to doubt this evidence.

Several important early sources, including the AntiMarcionite Prologue and Irenaeus, stated that Mark composed his Gospel after Peter's death. In fact, Irenaeus dated its composition after both Peter and Paul's death around A.D. 67.

However, Clement of Alexandria and Origen, writing a few years after Irenaeus, insisted that Peter was still alive during Mark's writing of the book. Moreover, a later tradition, recorded by Eusebius about A.D. 340, stated that it was written earlier, during the reign of Claudius (A.D. 41–54). Finally, an inscription on later manuscripts dated Mark's composition at an even earlier date around A.D. 39–42. These early dates, however, seem doubtful because (1) Mark probably would not have written the Gospel before his first failed missionary journey, (2) Peter most likely was not in Rome until after A.D. 60, and (3) Paul's epistle to the Romans (about A.D. 56–57) greets many believers, but mentions neither Mark nor Peter.

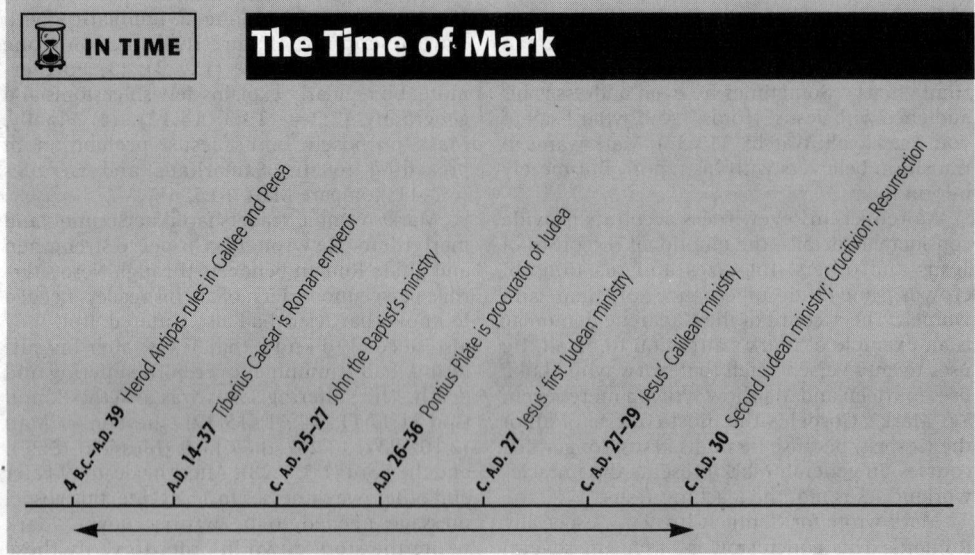

IN TIME

The Time of Mark

4 B.C.–A.D. 39 Herod Antipas rules in Galilee and Perea

A.D. 14–37 Tiberius Caesar is Roman emperor

C. A.D. 25–27 John the Baptist's ministry

A.D. 26–36 Pontius Pilate is procurator of Judea

C. A.D. 27 Jesus' first Judean ministry

C. A.D. 27–29 Jesus' Galilean ministry

C. A.D. 30 Second Judean ministry; Crucifixion; Resurrection

The most thoughtful estimate would place Mark's work sometime after Peter's death in A.D. 64 or 65, yet prior to A.D. 70, when Jerusalem was destroyed. In any event, the Gospel of Mark was penned within only three or four decades after the events it records.

The Gospel of Mark does not identify its author. However, numerous documents from the early church unanimously point to Mark as the author. Papias, bishop of Hierapolis (A.D. 140), claimed that Mark, as Peter's interpreter, wrote an accurate Gospel. The Roman Prologue to Mark, dating from A.D. 160–180, also named Mark as the author, and Irenaeus, in France around A.D. 180, claimed that Mark wrote down Peter's preaching. This is repeated by Tertullian and Clement of Alexandria, both in North Africa around A.D. 200.

Mark is mentioned ten times in the New Testament. His Jewish name was John (Acts 13:5, 13), but his Roman name was Mark (Acts 12:12, 25; 15:37). He lived in Jerusalem and was a cousin of Barnabas (Col. 4:10). He might have been the youth wearing a linen cloth at Jesus' arrest (14:51, 52), because only his Gospel mentions this incident, which occurred after all the disciples had already fled. The fact that Peter announced his miraculous jail escape at the home of Mary, Mark's widowed mother (Acts 12:12), indicates Mark had significant contact with Peter and the other leaders of the Jerusalem church.

In A.D. 46, Mark spent time with Barnabas and Saul in the Antioch church before he accompanied them as a helper on the first missionary journey. His unexpected departure from that expedition, however, caused Paul to lose confidence in him (Acts 15:37–39). Yet Mark later continued his missionary activity with Barnabas on Cyprus.

By A.D. 60–62, Paul again had placed his confidence in Mark and had complimented him as a fellow worker (Col. 4:10, 11; Philem. 24). In addition to helping Paul and Barnabas, Mark assisted Peter in "Babylon" (1 Pet. 5:13). Finally, Paul asked Mark to come to Rome to assist him while he was confined (2 Tim. 4:11). These short, positive references to Mark in the New Testament indicate that he faithfully and successfully served God as a missionary and apostolic helper throughout the period.

Mark Outline

I. Prologue: Identity of the Servant Son of God (1:1–13)

II. The Servant Son's initial message and ministry (1:14–8:30)

A. Fame and popularity (1:14–45)

  1. Preaching and discipling (1:14–20)

  2. Exercising power and authority (1:21–45)

B. Opposition and conflict (2:1–3:35)

C. Explanation of opposition (4:1–41)

  1. Jesus' parables (4:1–34)

  2. Jesus' power over the elements (4:35–41)

D. Belief and unbelief (5:1–8:30)

  1. Triumphs over demons, disease, and death (5:1–43)

  2. Unbelief around Nazareth (6:1–6)

  3. Greater ministry with the twelve (6:7–56)

  4. The Pharisees' defense of tradition (7:1–23)

  5. Jesus' withdrawal and teaching (7:24–8:26)

  6. Peter's confession (8:27–30)

III. The Servant Son's approach to the Cross (8:31–10:52)

A. Jesus' announcement of His coming death and resurrection (8:31–10:34)

B. Jesus' teaching and practice of servanthood (10:35–52)

IV. The Servant Son's ministry and death in Jerusalem (11:1–15:47)

A. Jesus' initial ministry in Jerusalem (11:1–33)

B. Rising opposition to Jesus (12:1–44)

C. The Olivet Discourse (13:1–37)

D. Jesus' preparation for His death (14:1–42)

E. Jesus' rejection by disciples, people, and His Father (14:43–15:47)

V. Epilogue: The living and victorious Servant Son (16:1–20)

Commentary

1:1 Writing three decades after the Resurrection of Christ, Mark starts his narrative with a simple declaration of the Good News about God's Son, the Lord Jesus Christ. As Luke notes in Acts 1:1, the Gospel stories describe what "Jesus began both to do and teach." The **gospel** refers to the basic story of the Good News to be found in Christ's life, ministry, death, and resurrection. **Jesus,** meaning "Yahweh saves," is the earthly name Jesus received at birth, whereas **Christ** is an OT title that designates Him as God's chosen servant. **Son of God** makes clear Jesus' deity and demonstrates His unique relationship to God.

1:2, 3 Other than by quoting Jesus, Mark makes only one reference to the OT. In this quotation from **the Prophets,** the gospel writer retells the work of Christ's forerunner, John the Baptist. **Messenger** and **make His paths straight** call forth the image of a king visiting his realm. In ancient times, a messenger was sent ahead to announce the coming of the king. Local communities would often repair rough roads to ensure the comfort of the king as he traveled. The quartet of Isaiah, Malachi, John the Baptist, and the writer Mark proclaims the coming of the King of all kings, Jesus Christ.

1:4 The mention of **John** without any introduction presupposes some knowledge of the Christian faith on the part of Mark's readers. John's **baptism of repentance** should not be confused with Christian baptism. The latter always follows conversion and symbolizes the spiritual death, burial, and resurrection with Christ that is accomplished in a believer's salvation experience (Acts 19:1–5; Rom. 6:3–6). It is performed in the name of the Father, the Son, and the Holy Spirit. John's baptism, on the other hand, prepared his followers to receive the new message about Christ and His kingdom. **For the remission of sins** does not mean that one is baptized in order to receive forgiveness of sins. The Greek preposition translated *of* in English probably means "with a view to," signifying that baptism looks to the forgiveness that God gives through the gift of repentance.

1:5 John's baptizing was a recurring popular event that attracted large crowds. Mark vividly portrays the continuous stream of followers who flocked to John. One may visualize throngs making the trek to the wilderness, with people waiting in line to be baptized. As each person was baptized by John, he or she would admit to individual sin and the need for the Messiah. The Sea of Galilee and the Jordan River are still the only fresh water sources in the land of Israel.

1:6 The angel Gabriel (the name means "mighty one of God") announced to Zacharias that his son, John, would "go before Him (Christ) in the spirit and power of Elijah" (Mal. 4:5; Matt. 17:10–13; Luke 1:13–17). John not only had the force of Elijah's personality, but apparently dressed like him as well (2 Kin. 1:8).

1:7 The tense of the verb **preached** indicates continuous action in past time. John's characteristic message was to promote expectancy and acceptance of the Lord Jesus Christ. He said he was **not worthy** to loosen the Messiah's **sandal strap.** Students often performed menial tasks for their rabbis, but even they were not expected to remove someone's sandals. That task was left to slaves. John humbly understood and accepted his own role in the coming kingdom.

1:8 John emphasizes the different tasks he and Christ would perform. The prediction that Christ **will baptize you with the Holy Spirit** appears in each Gospel (Matt. 3:11; Luke 3:16; John 1:33), and was repeated by Christ in Acts 1:5 as being "not many days from now." Though the NKJV uses **with water** and **with the Holy Spirit,** it is more Christian to translate the Greek preposition by *in.* The water is a physical representation of the future life in the Spirit that the Messiah's people would have. Presumably the Day of Pentecost marked the fulfillment of this promise.

1:9 Because He had no sins of which to repent, Jesus' baptism was unique. It showed His identity with John's work and with the sinner for whom He would die. It also foreshadowed His own death, burial, and resurrection for sinners.

1:10 **Immediately** occurs forty-one times in Mark's Gospel to indicate the swift action required of a servant (vv. 10, 12, 18, 20, 21). God places Christ in a confrontation with Satan early in His ministry. The Holy **Spirit** comes to empower and fill Christ for His future ministry. This passage (1:10, 11) also demonstrates the Trinity—one God who exists simultaneously as three distinct personalities—Father, Son, and Holy Spirit. The baptismal formula of Matt. 28:19 and many other texts teach this doctrine (2 Cor. 13:14; 1 Pet. 1:2).

1:11 Three times during Christ's earthly ministry **a voice came from heaven.** It was the Father's testimony to Christ's unique and divine Sonship. The other two confirming incidents were at the Transfiguration (9:7) and on the day of Christ's triumphal entry into Jerusalem (John 12:28).

1:12 Mark declares that **the Spirit drove** Christ into the wilderness. The verb used for **drove** was frequently used to describe Christ's expulsion of demons and appears two other times in this chapter (vv. 34, 39).

1:13 Mark introduces an event of conflict to seize his readers' attention. Being **tempted by Satan** is something that all believers face, but Jesus triumphed completely over his adversary. Mark alone mentions the **angels** who were ministering to Christ through the forty days. The mention of being with **wild beasts** might especially speak to Roman Christians who had seen those terrors in the arena.

1:14 Mark begins his account of Christ's ministry with events **after John was put in prison,** as do the other synoptic Gospel writers. John is the only writer who informs us of a number of events that took place *before* John the Baptist's imprisonment (John 3:24). Andrew, Peter, John, Philip, and Nathaniel were following Jesus in an itinerant yet intermittent manner. They were at the wedding in Cana (John 2:2), and even accompanied Jesus to Capernaum (John 2:12), to Jerusalem (John

✓ IN COMPARISON	**Baptism in the Bible**

Mark begins his account of Jesus' ministry by describing devout Israelites streaming out to the Jordan River to be baptized by John. Here is a summary of the subject of baptism in the Scriptures:

Etymology	The word baptism comes from the Greek verb *baptizō* meaning "to dip, immerse, submerge."
Definition	Baptism is a sacred rite that signifies purification, initiation, or identification of an individual with a leader, group, or teaching.
The Different Types of Baptism in the Scriptures	• Jewish baptism: a ceremonial cleansing prescribed for both people and articles (7:3; Ex. 19:10–14; Lev. 8:6; Heb. 9:10). • John's baptism: a preparatory act in which Jews expressed their belief in the imminent coming of the Messiah and their desire to turn away from sin and live righteous lives (1:4–8). • Jesus' baptism: an act of ceremonial righteousness. By being baptized, Christ was not admitting His sinfulness, as those who submitted to John's baptism were. Instead through baptism, Christ was consecrating Himself to His ministry (1:9–11). • Spirit baptism: the supernatural work of the Holy Spirit by which believers are joined to the body of Christ (Rom. 6:3, 4; 1 Cor. 12:13; Gal. 3:26, 27; Eph. 4:5; Col. 2:9–12). • Christian baptism: a ceremonial act instituted by Christ (Matt. 28:19) and practiced by the apostles (Acts 2:38) that depicts a believer's union and identification with Christ in His death, burial, and resurrection. • Baptism by fire: a possible reference either to the judgment at the Second Coming or to the coming of the Spirit at Pentecost (Matt. 3:9–12; Luke 3:16, 17).
Old Testament Types	The NT writers point to several events in the OT that foreshadow baptism as commanded by Christ. • Noah coming through the waters of the Flood (1 Pet. 3:17–22). • The Israelites' crossing of the Red Sea (1 Cor. 10:1, 2).

2:13-22), and through Judea where they baptized people (John 3:22, 23).

1:15 Jesus proclaimed **the kingdom of God.** It was the subject of much OT prophecy, and the theme was familiar to Jesus' listeners. **Repent, and believe** are both acts of faith. When a person accepts the only true and worthy object of faith, that person readily turns from inferior substitutes. Nothing and no one can fill that God-shaped vacuum but Christ. **The gospel:** the Good News about Jesus Christ—in this case as King.

1:16 Simon and Andrew had been disciples of John the Baptist. They had known Jesus (John 1:35–42), but were now being called to a lifetime of service.

1:17 Jesus called fishermen, hardworking and industrious people, to perform the most important task on earth: being **fishers of men.** Jesus characteristically used figures of speech that His listeners would readily understand.

1:18–20 left their nets . . . their father: Let neither occupation nor family keep you from following Christ. **immediately:** One of Mark's

favorite words (vv. 12, 18, 20, 28).This is the only reasonable response to the Lord of glory.

1:19 James . . . John: The scenes of vv. 16–20 are very colorful. Simon and Andrew are fishing when we encounter them; James and John are mending their nets. Such details indicate the testimony of an eyewitness, probably Peter.

1:21 Capernaum sits beside the northern edge of the Sea of Galilee, a pear-shaped freshwater lake eight miles wide and twelve miles long. It was a cross section of trade routes between Egypt and Syria (Cairo and Damascus), located on the Sea of Galilee on the primary trade route between Egypt and Damascus and points to the east. The town's name means "Village of Nahum." Capernaum was Christ's ministry "headquarters" and is mentioned twenty-two times in the Gospels. By contrast, only one recorded event during Christ's ministry occurred at Nazareth (Luke 4:16). The ruins of a **synagogue** at Capernaum, just a few hundred feet from the water's edge, date from the second to fourth century A.D.

 **IN CONTEXT** | **The Synagogue**

In Jesus' day, synagogues (Mark 1:21) were common throughout Palestine. Synagogues (from the Greek *sunagoge,* meaning "a leading or bringing together") were local congregations of Jews that met for the reading and explanation of Scripture and for prayer. The original emphasis was not on preaching but instruction in the Law of Moses.

Synagogues began during the Babylonian captivity experience. Lacking a temple but longing for communion with God, Jewish captives in Babylon met in local groups for worship and Torah reading. Some of the captives eventually returned to their land, where Zerubbabel rebuilt the temple and Ezra the scribe promoted the reading of the Law and prayer (Neh. 8). But many Jews remained in Persia and spread elsewhere, notably to Alexandria, Egypt. Both in and outside of Palestine, Jews continued to meet in synagogues, which became centers of community life.

Some synagogues functioned as local courts of justice which could sentence offenders as well as inflict the punishment of scourging (Matt. 10:17; 23:34). They also became grammar schools teaching children to read. And much of Jewish social life revolved around synagogue activities.

By Jesus' time, synagogues were well established and had customary officials, including:

Elders, a board made up of devout and respected men who regulated the policies of the synagogue. Custom seated the elders in the chief seats at the front of the synagogue (Matt. 23:6).

A ruler of the synagogue, appointed by the elders, whose duty was to attend to matters concerning the building and the planning of the services. There could be more than one ruler. On one occasion, a ruler named Jairus approached Jesus about healing his daughter (Mark 5:21–43).

The minister (chazzan), who had charge of the sacred scrolls kept in the ark, attended to the lamps, and kept the building clean. If an offender was found guilty by the council of elders, this official was the one who administered the number of lashes prescribed for the scourging. During the week he taught children how to read.

The delegate of the congregation. This was not a permanent office. Before each service the ruler chose a capable person to read the Scripture lesson, lead in prayer, and preach or comment on the Scripture. Jesus was selected for this office in the synagogue in Nazareth (Luke 4:16–20).

The interpreter. The Scriptures were written in Hebrew, but by Jesus' day most Jews in Palestine spoke Aramaic, a language related to Hebrew but different enough to call for an interpreter.

Almoners, two or three persons who received money or other necessities for the poor.

A synagogue could not be formed unless there were at least ten Jewish men in the community—apparently a condition met in a great many towns throughout the Roman world, as Paul found synagogues at Damascus (Acts 9:2), Salamis (13:5), Antioch in Pisidia (13:14), Iconium (14:1), Thessalonica (17:1), Berea (17:10), Athens (17:16, 17), and Ephesus (19:1, 8). Indeed, whenever Paul entered a city to preach the gospel, he invariably spoke first in the synagogue before reaching out to the larger community.

Not surprisingly, synagogue worship had a profound influence on Christian worship. The Jewish service began with a recitation of the shema by the people. *Shema* ("Hear") is the first Hebrew word in the passage, "Hear, O Israel: The LORD our God, the LORD is one!" (Deut. 6:4–9). The speaker for the day then led the congregation in prayer as they stood facing Jerusalem with hands extended. At the close of the prayer the people said "Amen."

The chosen speaker stood and read the Law while the interpreter translated it into Aramaic. Then a passage from the Prophets was read and translated. For the commentary or sermon, the speaker usually sat down. After the sermon, a priest, if one was present, pronounced a benediction and the people said "Amen." Since the earliest Christians were Jews, they tended to follow this synagogue pattern in their own assemblies.

1:22 Forty-two percent of Mark's verses contain some mention of teaching. Mark, however, omits most of Jesus' main discourses to emphasize His mighty works as the Servant Son of God. **astonished at His teaching:** Christ's teaching differed from that of scribes and Phar-isees because He did not lean on the wisdom of other teachers and rabbis. His authority came from Himself.

1:23 The term **unclean** (Gk. *akathartos*) bore special connotations to the Jewish mind. The OT frequently distinguished between what was lawful and unlawful, accepted and rejected, and therefore may mean ungodly. "Demon" is a designation used interchangeably with **unclean spirit.**

1:24, 25 The demon cried out **"Let us alone,"** not because it was speaking for other demons in the man (as was the case in 5:1–20), but because Jesus was a threat to *all* demons. Jesus constantly confronted demons and about 20 percent of the approximately thirty-five miracles recorded about Jesus involved helping those troubled by demons. The demon acknowledged Jesus as **the Holy One of God,** but Jesus refused the testimony from such a disreputable source.

1:26, 27 unclean spirit: This is another term for demon. The unholy anger of these demons seeks to cause as much damage as possible when forced to leave the man; they may resist but they know their doom is sure (v. 24).

1:28, 29 Mark notes the extent of recognition this great miracle brought Jesus by saying **His fame spread throughout all the region.** Mark creates suspense by contrasting the people who received Christ with the Pharisees and rulers who worked to bring about His death. The sad truth remains that often the religious of the world do more to keep people from Jesus Christ than most worldly atheists. But the gospel is not religion. It is Good News that can free even the most horrible sinner.

1:30 Simon's wife's mother: Paul notes the married state of Simon (Cephas) and others of the disciples (1 Cor. 9:5).

1:31 Jesus completely healed Simon Peter's mother-in-law. Not only did the **fever** leave, but her strength was renewed so that she **served** Jesus and His followers.

1:32 So as not to violate the Sabbath restriction on bearing burdens (v. 21; Neh. 13:19), the people waited until **evening.**

1:32–34 demon-possessed (Gk. *daimonizomai*): The healing and casting out of demons must have continued into the night. Jesus was constantly about His Father's business, realizing that He had only about three and one-half years to accomplish His mission.

1:35, 36 The tense of the verb **prayed** indicates a continued action, not just a brief moment. Jesus' prayer life was successful because it was planned, private, and prolonged. He got up early enough, got far enough away, and stayed at it long enough.

1:37, 38 Jesus' fame spread quickly, and the disciples' concern is evident in the statement **"Everyone is looking for you."** Refusing a comfortable existence, Jesus took seriously his mission to reach **the next towns.** He came to **preach** and to proclaim God's message. **for this purpose:** Christ modeled singleness of purpose.

He would not let anything distract Him—not the temptations of Satan (1:12, 13), not the well-intentioned advice of Peter (Matt. 16:22). Note his model in Heb. 12:1-3.

1:39, 40 A leper was an outcast from society. **You can make me clean:** Evidence of the man's faith in Jesus.

1:41–43 Jesus was **moved with compassion.** He not only healed but touched the leper. How often do we see the need but remain unmoved and uninvolved? Scripture has over four hundred passages admonishing us to care for the poor (8:2; Deut. 15:7–11).

1:44 After healing the leper, Jesus commanded him to **say nothing to anyone.** His demand for silence has several plausible explanations. (1) The report of Jesus' healing the man may have prejudiced the priest who needed to pronounce him clean. (2) Jesus did not want to be known primarily as a miracle worker, so He often commanded those who received His healing to remain quiet. (3) The man's testimony would possibly have hastened the confrontation between Jesus and the religious leaders.

1:45 The cleansed leper did not obey Jesus' simple injunction to keep quiet. As a result, Jesus had to remain in **deserted places** because the crowds swarmed to Him. Christ was working on a time line, and His time had not yet come.

2:1–28 Mark's first chapter establishes Jesus as a popular figure who experiences great success. Chapters 2 and 3 demonstrate rising opposition to His mission and teaching and suggest more drama and suspense to come.

2:2 Mark is largely a record of Christ's actions, but what Jesus said is not neglected. Here he describes how Jesus **preached the word,** the message of the coming kingdom.

2:3 The paralytic was borne by four men, apparently on some sort of stretcher that held his bed (v. 11).

2:4 Many in the crowd may have come expecting to see healings and miracles. The throng blocked entrance into the already packed room. The determination of the men is seen in the fact that **they uncovered the roof** over the room where Jesus was preaching. The roof was probably flat and constructed of tiles laid one on another.

2:5 their faith: Not only did the four men have faith, but the paralytic himself had it too. When Jesus announced to him, **your sins are forgiven,** He was implicitly acknowledging the paralytic's trust that He was the Messiah.

2:6, 7 Mark notes the opposition of **the scribes,** who under their breath accused Jesus of blasphemy. In Christ's day the scribes were commonly called "lawyers," because they studied the Law of Moses.

2:8–11 Jesus asked the **which is easier** question to demonstrate the truth of His claim to forgive the man's sins—something only God can accomplish. Anyone could assert the ability to forgive sins, since there was no earthly way of confirming the statement. But to say **arise, take up your bed and walk** to a paralytic could be tested immediately by whether he walked or not. By healing the paralytic, Jesus made His pronouncement of forgiveness far more credible. **Son of Man** is a term regularly used for the Messiah (8:31; Dan. 7:13; Mark 8:31).

2:12 all were amazed and glorified God: The crowd's reaction showed that they understood the significance of Jesus' miracle. It is possible that some scribes and Pharisees joined in the acclamation. But permanent, life-changing faith is what Christ sought, not temporary adoration from the crowd.

2:13 Jesus regularly taught the multitudes in retreat settings. This is indicated by the continuous tense of the verbs used here: They kept on coming, and Jesus kept on teaching.

2:14 Levi, also called Matthew (Matt. 9:9; 10:3), was Jewish, but he collected taxes for Rome. The Jews hated tax collectors. They had a reputation for taking more than they needed in order to add to their own wealth. Jesus' **"Follow me"** must have shook Matthew's very being, because he quit his profession and followed Jesus.

2:15, 16 Because **tax collectors** worked for the Romans or their representation, such as Herod Antipas, the Jews hated them and considered them great sinners. By eating with these people, Jesus showed that God's forgiveness is extended even to the worst. Believers must go to the lost since it is plain that the lost rarely come on their own seeking Jesus.

2:17 In this instance Jesus was speaking tongue-in-cheek when He used the word **righteous.** None are righteous, though some, such as the Pharisees, fancied themselves as such. Instead, Christ came to call **sinners, to repentance.** Jesus did not condone the activities of sinners, but required repentance—a change of mind that recognizes the need of a Savior and recognizes Jesus Christ as the only Savior.

2:18 fast: Jesus was not against fasting, if properly observed. He gave guidelines for fasting in the Sermon on the Mount (Matt. 6:16–18). Here, the Pharisees' fasting, perhaps twice each week (Luke 18:12), is contrasted with Jesus' feasting, probably at Levi's house. Some believe that the OT enjoins fasting on only one day each year—the Day of Atonement (Lev. 16:29), the "affliction of the soul" referring to fasting. This day is the only annual fast referred to in the NT (Acts 27:9).

2:19 Jesus' presence, as with a wedding celebration, called for rejoicing, not mourning.

2:20 Taken away from them may be a hint of Jesus' coming departure (John 14:19, 20; 16:5). After His crucifixion, Jesus' disciples **will fast,** perhaps figuratively in the sense of sorrowing over His loss.

2:21, 22 Mark records only four of Jesus' parables—two of which he includes here. The comparison implies that the newness of His message, and of the New Covenant to follow, cannot fit into the old molds of Judaism. The OT was preparation for the NT (Gal. 3:19–25).

2:23 Ripe grain can be eaten whole and is both tasty and nutritious. Plucking bits of grain from another's field for sustenance was permitted under Mosaic Law (Deut. 23:25). Wholesale reaping with a sickle, however, was prohibited.

2:24 The point to the Pharisees' accusation against Jesus and His disciples was that they had performed work **on the Sabbath,** but their charge was dubious. The act of plucking grain should not be confused with Sabbath work condemned in the law (Ex. 31:15). This incident is further proof of rising opposition to Jesus' ministry.

2:25, 26 Part of Jesus' defense was to recall the story of David's eating the **showbread** from the tabernacle. Since that bread was intended for the priests, it was **not lawful** for others to eat.

2:27, 28 Jesus does not declare directly the innocence of either David or His disciples, but instead reminds His critics of the meaning of the Sabbath for humans and His own Lordship over it. Human needs may at times overrule a ceremonial observance of the Sabbath.

3:1, 2 The **Sabbath** controversy continued as Jesus visited the synagogue. The Pharisees (3:6) **watched Him closely,** not to hear the words of life but to **accuse Him.** In similar fashion, coming to church with a hostile, fault-finding motive will rob one of spiritual benefit and bring bitterness into the soul.

3:3, 4 Christ put the meaning of the Sabbath to the test. Certainly it was more consistent with the intention of the law to restore this man's afflicted hand, even on the Sabbath, than to destroy his hopes for the sake of keeping human tradition. The Pharisees did not respond, for they knew that they would condemn themselves.

3:5 It is possible, as Paul exhorts, to be angry and not sin (Eph. 4:26). Jesus demonstrated this righteous **anger.** He was grieved with sin but did not sin Himself by retaliating or losing control of His emotions.

3:6 The Pharisees were religious experts who should have led the people in righteousness.

Instead, they **plotted** Jesus' death **with the Herodians,** their bitter enemies. They were willing to set aside differences to destroy a common foe. The Herodians were Jews who supported Rome and the Herods in particular. Herod Antipas, a son of Herod the Great, ruled Galilee during the same time that Pilate served as Roman governor over Judea and Samaria.

3:7 Because of this plot against His life, Jesus withdrew with the disciples from the area.

the Son of God not because the demons incorrectly identified Jesus, but because their testimony was untrustworthy. Christ doesn't need the affirmation of His enemies. Mark records even their testimony to Christ's deity.

3:13 Jesus had a large group of followers. John 6:66 indicates that even after the Twelve were appointed, He still had a large and continual following. Luke 10:1 notes that later Jesus sent out an additional seventy disciples.

 **INSIGHT**   ## The Twelve Apostles

These twelve men were called "apostles" (Gk. *apostolos,* "messenger") for they had been sent out to deliver Christ's message to others. Mark 6:30 actually uses the word *apostles* to describe the twelve who had been sent out (6:7) to preach, cast out demons, and heal sickness. This same word is found in the parallel passages in Matt. 10:2 and Luke 6:13, and Luke's Gospel uses the word five other times (Luke 9:10; 11:49; 17:5; 22:14; 24:10).

Many of Jesus' followers could rightly be called disciples, or learners, because they listened to and accepted Jesus' teachings. Yet Christ chose only a select group to entrust with the task of carrying the gospel throughout the world. These twelve formed the closest circle around Christ. (The language of Matt. 19:28 suggests that the twelve may have represented the twelve tribes of Israel. Given the largely Jewish audience for whom Matthew wrote, the symbolism would be powerful.) These twelve lived with Jesus, ate with Him, and most importantly listened to Him. They witnessed His ministry and were challenged by His rebuke. They joined together with Jesus to proclaim the Good News and serve others. Of these twelve, Peter, James, and John were perhaps Jesus' most trusted followers, for they alone witnessed the raising of Jairus' daughter, the Transfiguration, and Jesus' prayer in Gethsemane. Tragically, even in the intimate circle of these twelve men, Satan found opportunity to sow discontent, eventually resulting in Judas' betrayal of Christ. In three short years, Jesus molded these men into leaders of faith. Then after His resurrection, He empowered them with the Holy Spirit and sent them out to be His witnesses to the ends of the earth (16:15, 16; Acts 1:4, 5; 2:1–21).

Still crowds flocked to Him from north (Galilee), south (Judea), and beyond.

3:8 Idumea (the Edom of the OT), the birthplace of Herod the Great, was south of Judea. **Beyond the Jordan** refers to the Transjordan, the cities on the east side of the Jordan (10:1). **Tyre and Sidon** (Phoenicia in the OT), both on the Lebanese coast, were also cities Jesus visited during His earthly ministry (7:24) and mentioned in His teachings (Matt. 11:21, 22).

3:9 small boat: Christ knew the impact of His ministry on the multitudes and made preparation for being alone, which He highly prized.

3:10–12 Some unfortunate persons who met Christ were possessed by **unclean spirits,** or demons. These spirit beings have no bodily existence but frequently seek to inhabit humans or even animals. Mark says they **fell down before Him,** most likely by forcing to the ground the person they possessed. Jesus rebuked the demons who proclaimed **You are**

3:14 These **twelve** were Jesus' apostles—a chosen group sent out to fulfill a particular mission. Many could be disciples, or learners, but only a select group of men were chosen for certain leadership tasks. These twelve formed the closest circle to Christ, and of them Peter, James, and John were even more intimate on certain occasions, such as at the raising of Jairus's daughter, the Transfiguration, and in Gethsemane. **That they might be with Him** highlights the principle of association. Jesus worked with the group principle—not so much the one-on-one. We grow in relation, not in isolation. In our case this is even more important because on the one hand, we don't have all the gifts, and, on the other hand, we are sinful and give a distorted portrait of the Christ we seek to reflect. But a more balanced image will be given in the group.

3:15 Christ gave **power** or authority to the twelve apostles (Matt. 10:1–4). The apostle Paul called this authority "the signs of an apostle" (2

Cor. 12:12). Christ and the apostles authenticated their ministry through signs, miracles, and wonders (Heb. 2:3, 4).

3:16–19 Jesus **gave** Peter a new **name** because it was the Jewish custom to rename someone who had experienced a life-changing event. This renaming of the disciples has similarities to the renaming of Abram (Gen. 17:3–5) and of Saul (Acts 9). Jesus no doubt sent out His apostles in pairs as He did the seventy disciples (6:7–13; Matt. 10:5–15; Luke 9:1–6). This explains the listing of the apostles' names in groups of two. The coupling is especially evident in Matt. 10:1–4: Peter and Andrew, James and John, Philip and Bartholomew (Nathaniel), Matthew and Thomas, James (son of Alphaeus) and Thaddaeus, and Simon the Cananite and Judas. Even though Judas Iscariot had a close partner in the work for three years, no one yet suspected he would be the one **who also betrayed Him**. Close association with other believers, or even with Christ Himself, is no guarantee of salvation. Furthermore, fine external behavior doesn't prove the reality of my regeneration. Judas must have had a good reputation to be trusted to carry the money for the group.

3:20, 21 Opposition to Jesus came not only from His enemies. Jesus' **own people,** no doubt close friends and perhaps even relatives (vv. 31–35), heard of his teaching and assumed that He was **out of His mind.** This may have been due to the strenuous schedule Jesus kept.

He had only three and one-half years to minister, and He needed to make the most of this time. Even then, He had to withdraw at times to keep a balance physically, mentally, and spiritually.

3:22 The **scribes,** or teachers of the Jewish law, were more harsh and direct in their assessment of Jesus. They accused Him of being possessed by **Beelzebub** (literally, "Lord of the Flies"; 2 Kin. 1:3), another name for Satan. This false charge demonstrates a hardness of heart and is akin to blaspheming against the Holy Spirit (vv. 28–30).

3:23–26 Jesus' reply **in parables** was actually a threefold message that contrasted unity and disunity. Nothing—including Satan's kingdom—can stand if it is divided.

3:27 Whoever defeats Satan must be stronger than he. Jesus implies that He Himself has come to enter the house of the **strong man,** Satan, to seize his goods (1 John 3:8).

3:28–30 Assuredly (*Amēn, Amēn* in Gk.) indicates the solemnity of Jesus' declaration which follows. While the prophets said "thus saith the Lord," what Christ says is true on its own merit. While Jesus does not say that anyone in the crowd He addresses actually has committed the sin He describes, He nonetheless stresses the hopelessness of such a condition. Anyone who **blasphemes against the Holy Spirit** places himself totally outside the redeeming grace of God. It is apparently not a single act of defiant behavior, but a continued

☑ IN COMPARISON **Pagan Gods in the New Testament**

Name	Description	Reference
BEELZEBUB	A heathen god considered by the Jews to be the supreme evil spirit.	Mark 3:22
DIANA	In Roman mythology, the goddess of the moon, hunting, wild animals, and virginity.	Acts 19:24, 27, 28
HERMES	The Greek god of commerce, science, invention, cunning, eloquence, and theft.	Acts 14:12
MAMMON	The Aramaic word for riches, personified by Jesus as a false god.	Luke 16:9, 11
MOLOCH	National god of the Ammonites whose worship involved child sacrifice.	Acts 7:43
REMPHAN	An idol worshiped by Israel in the wilderness.	Acts 7:43
TWIN BROTHERS	In Greek mythology, the twin sons of Zeus.	Acts 28:11
ZEUS	The supreme god of the ancient Greeks.	Acts 14:12, 13

state of opposition entered into willfully, but irrevocably. The tense of **they said** indicates a continued action, not a one-time event. The words and works of Christ were spoken and performed by the power of the Holy Spirit. To attribute them to Satan is to attribute the credentials of heaven to hell. If one persists in that state there is no remedy. How someone can enter into this state of affairs today is a difficult question, but those who persist in denigrating Christ by insisting His person and works were motivated and empowered by Satan rather than by the Holy Spirit no doubt place themselves dangerously near non-regenerative hope (Matt. 12:31, 32).

3:31, 32 Opposition arose from Jesus' own immediate family, **His brothers and His mother.** We are not told precisely what they wanted to say, but it likely involved a concern for Jesus' safety or reputation, since He was becoming widely known as a preaching prophet (1:14, 15) and a worker of miracles (1:31; 2:12).

3:34, 35 Whoever does the will of God expresses a spiritual allegiance that goes beyond loyalty to one's biological family. Spiritual kinship is determined not by blood or race but by obedience to God. Thus, if our nuclear families are to prosper, we need to keep our focus on the extended family, the church family of God. These are those with whom we have eternal filial relationships.

4:1–34 Mark now shifts the emphasis of his

that hid large rocks just beneath the surface, fields overgrown with weeds, and excellent, rich soil here and there. The point of the parable is that the condition of the soil determines the potential for growth. The principle is true for Christians and non-Christians alike. Those who have become complacent and lackadaisical are not likely to receive the Word with benefit (James 1:22–25).

4:10 Apparently Jesus' extensive teaching of the multitude ended and the crowd was gone. Jesus may have taught for hours using many such parables (v. 2) during that time. But now He was alone except for His closest followers who **asked Him about the parable** (of the sower).

4:11 A **mystery** in Scripture is a truth God has revealed or will reveal at the proper time (Rom. 16:25, 26). Jesus apparently used parables for several reasons. First, they are interesting and grab the listener's attention. Second, such stories are easily remembered. Third, they reveal truth to those who are ready spiritually to receive it. Fourth, they conceal truth from those who oppose Christ's message. Frequently, Jesus' opponents failed to understand the lessons because of their own spiritual blindness (Matt. 21:45, 46).

4:12 Not all will understand the teaching of the kingdom. Compare this statement of Jesus with Is. 6:9, 10; 43:8.

4:13–14 In response to the disciples' request, Jesus explains the parable of the sower

---

 INSIGHT | **Old Testament Signs**

Mark told the story of Jesus much like the disciples must have told it after the Resurrection. He builds on the foundation of OT promises about the Messiah, beginning exactly where Malachi—the last book of the OT—ends. He starts by introducing John the Baptist as the promised forerunner to the Messiah.

When the disciples ask Jesus why He speaks in perplexing parables, Jesus shows that He is fulfilling the prophecy of Is. 6:9, 10 (Mark 4:10–13). And when Jesus warns the disciples that they will scatter when He is arrested, He confirms this by citing the prophet Zechariah (13:7; Mark 14:27).

Gospel from Jesus' works to His words. Both are important.

4:2 Parables go beyond mere entertainment or moralizing; they teach vital spiritual truths about the kingdom of God.

4:3–9 The story Jesus told was easy enough to comprehend. During the planting season, it was common to see men scattering seed by hand over their small fields. They cast the seeds over the kinds of soil Jesus describes—smooth pathways running through fields, rough terrain

and the four soils (or hearts, see v. 15). The number four is not important. Jesus could have used three or five or six types of soil to illustrate the fact that people will receive quite differently the truth of the **word** (v. 14), Jesus' message about His coming kingdom.

4:15 The pathway soil is trampled, hard, and unresponsive. The birds (v. 4) represent Satan, who quickly **takes away the word that was sown in their hearts.** Elsewhere we are told that Satan can blind the minds of those who do not believe (2 Cor. 4:4). The fuller rendering of Jesus' explanation in Matthew's parallel account (Matt. 13:19) says that this person "does not understand" and then the "wicked one comes and snatches away what was sown in his heart."

4:16, 17 The shallow soil overlaying the **stony ground** represents those who seem eager to receive Christ's message but whose commitment is superficial.

4:18, 19 The thorn-infested soil represents those **who hear the word** but lack single-mindedness and become completely unproductive. Worry (the normal **cares of this world**) and pleasure-seeking (**deceitfulness of riches** and the pursuit of **other things**) are both capable of producing a deadly spiritual apathy.

4:20 Only one soil produces fruit. Christ emphasizes the necessity to **hear the word, accept it, and bear fruit.** Their belief has encompassed reality, been activated and life-transforming. The word *accept* is the same word as *believe*. A person can receive only as much as he or she can believe. And one's belief will only be as valuable as the object of his or her belief. People believe many things, but only truth is worthy of ultimate belief (compare John 8:31, 32).

4:21–23 Jesus' lesson of the **lamp,** a small clay vessel that burned a wick set in olive oil, is that light reveals what it glows on. Like the lamp, Jesus' teachings reveal the motives of the human heart. Time would prove the reality of His teaching and bring the secret hidden things of men to light.

4:23 hear (Gk. *akouō*): Used four times in two verses. To hear the right things and respond properly is absolutely basic to spiritual prosperity. How important it is that we be selective in our listening and our looking. We are programming our actions all the time by what we look at and listen to (James 1:19).

4:24 To those **who hear**—who receive God's Good News—**more** spiritual truth **will be given.** A growing believer must be receptive and teachable.

4:25 Whoever has, meaning those who possess spiritual life, will continue to learn and grow. **Whoever does not have** spiritual life will lose even what little desire for God he or she seems to have.

4:26–29 Plants develop in a complex, intricate process that humans still do not fully understand even two thousand years after Jesus spoke these words. Yet plants grow and bear fruit and seeds just the same. God's kingdom likewise is growing, although we do not understand all that is happening. This parable, which appears only in Mark's Gospel, presents God's kingdom in brief, from first sowing to final

reaping. Truly, we are fellow workers with God. But we are also totally dependent on Him for growth.

4:30–32 A mustard seed is much smaller than a kernel of corn or a grain of wheat, yet its growth is more spectacular, reaching a height of ten to twelve feet. The point is the comparatively large result from such a humble and insignificant beginning. The kingdom that Jesus came to announce drew little support during His life but will find complete fulfillment when He returns. The mention of **birds** making their **nest under its shade** (v. 32) should not be confused with the birds in the parable of the sower (4:4). Most likely, these birds illustrate how large the mustard plant has become.

4:33, 34 Parables were Jesus' primary teaching tool.

4:35 To **cross over** the Sea of Galilee, a lake only eight miles wide, would not seem difficult at first glance. Yet its unique geography produces a greatly varying climate. The lake is situated seven hundred feet below sea level and is surrounded by mountains that rise three to four thousand feet above sea level on the west, north, and east. Tropical conditions prevail around the lake's surface, where even bananas are grown today. Yet the higher elevations can produce chilling night air.

4:36, 37 It is not unusual even today for a sudden **great windstorm** to appear on the Sea of Galilee during the evening hours. The warm tropical air from the lake's surface rises and meets the colder air from the nearby hills. The resulting turbulence stirs up great **waves** which make boating extremely treacherous.

4:38 The mention of Jesus being **asleep on a pillow** shows His true humanity. He was fully human and needed food and rest just as all people do.

4:39 Jesus' command over the wind and the sea demonstrates His full and complete deity. Only God the Creator can calm wind and sea.

4:40, 41 Mark uses the disciples' question **"Who can this be?"** to evoke a similar response in the minds of his readers. Mark relates the works and words of the One he calls "Jesus Christ, the Son of God" (1:1).

5:1–8:30 In the major section which begins here, Mark relates incidents of belief and unbelief, climaxing with Peter's confession of Jesus' deity.

5:1–20 Mark records the fullest account of Jesus' dealing with the demoniac of Gadara. Matthew uses only seven verses, while Luke covers the story in eleven. Mark is given to detail.

5:1 The country of the Gadarenes is on the eastern shore of the Sea of Galilee. Gergesenes is used in Matt. 8:28-34 and Gadarenes in

Luke 8:26, 27 and here; Gergesenes is merely a variant term but refers to the same place. No towns or villages exist along the lake's narrow eastern shore because cliffs several thousand feet high rise up from near the water's edge. The steep cliffs are less pronounced the farther south one proceeds toward Gadara, situated on the heights several thousand feet above the Jordan Valley

5:2 Apparently, right after leaving the boat and perhaps before ascending the nearby hills, Jesus was encountered by **a man with an unclean spirit** (1:23). The man was demon possessed, as v. 15 clearly states.

5:3, 4 the tombs: Caves in the rocks, often used for burial places. The man's natural strength was no doubt enhanced by the demon within.

5:6–8 Jesus distinguished between the man and the demon who possessed him. Although the man's physical body prostrated itself before Christ, it was the demon within who spoke to Jesus, and was likewise addressed by Jesus in return.

5:9 My name is Legion: By giving his name, the demon responded to Jesus' authority. A legion of the Roman army consisted of 4,000 to 6,000 soldiers. The **many** demons reflect the chaotic state of the man's mind.

5:10 out of the country: They considered this wild Gentile place their own country.

5:11 The presence of **swine** shows these people were Gentiles.

5:12, 13 It is not certain that the demons needed **permission** to leave the man and enter the swine, but they may have been trying to forestall permanent bondage by Christ. (The bottomless pit of Rev. 9:1 may be such a place of imprisonment.) Jesus bears no responsibility for the action the demons took; He did not direct them to run the swine into the sea. Even today, two thousand hogs is a very large herd. Their monetary value could easily have been worth a quarter of a million dollars in today's economy—a sizable loss for the owners.

5:14 The OT forbade Jews to have any contact with swine (Lev. 11:7, 8). However, the owners of these swine might not have been Jewish, since this area was inhabited largely by Gentiles (5:20).

5:17–20 Jesus was not well received in this region. His presence had caused financial loss for some, although it meant liberation to the demoniac. Jesus could have healed and saved in that region, but He was turned away by its fearful citizens. Yet He left a solid witness behind. All the people **marveled** when they heard what **Jesus had done for him.** Jesus later made an excursion through the Decapolis region (7:31). **Decapolis** literally means "ten

cities." The largest city was Scythopolis (ancient Bethshan) and included Damascus in the far north and Philadelphia (modern Amman, Jordan) on the southern extreme. The other seven cities were Pella, Abila, Gerasa (Jerash), Hippos, Dion, Raphana, and Gadara. This largely Gentile, Greek-speaking area was an important strategic link in Rome's military defense.

5:21 Jesus' crossing **by boat to the other side** brought Him to Capernaum, although Mark does not mention that here. Matthew 9:1 says He came to "His own city," a common designation of Capernaum, Jesus' headquarters for ministry activity.

5:22 Jairus, **one of the rulers of the synagogue,** was a lay leader charged with supervising services at the synagogue.

5:23 Aware of Jesus' miraculous powers, Jairus approached Jesus with perhaps the greatest need he had ever faced. He knew that Jesus could meet his need. However, he believed—falsely, it turned out—that Jesus had to actually touch his desperately ill daughter before she could be healed. Yet his faith was unshakable.

5:24 The multitude which was eagerly awaiting Jesus' arrival now **thronged Him.** People were being pressed against Jesus from all sides.

5:24–34 Intertwined with the incident of Jairus's daughter is the story of the woman with a persistent blood flow, perhaps a severe menstrual disorder. As a result, she was considered unclean, and anyone she touched would

IN FOCUS **"synagogue"**

(Gk. sunagōge) (1:21; 5:22; 6:2; 13:9): This word literally means "a place where people gather together." After Babylon destroyed the temple (587 B.C.), synagogues gradually emerged in many Jewish towns as places of worship and as schools for teaching the Mosaic Law. Jews met in synagogues on the Sabbath, recited prayers, and read from the Scriptures.

become unclean ceremonially for one day (Lev. 15:25–27). Still, she entered the crowd to touch Jesus.

5:26 Mark is not complimentary toward the **physicians** who had treated the woman, noting that **she had spent all that she had.** Luke, a physician himself, omits Mark's added detail that her condition actually **grew worse.**

5:27 The woman **touched His garment.**

 **IN COMPARISON** **Miracles in Mark**

Mark dedicates more of his account to Jesus' miracles than any of the other Gospel writers. For Mark, these miracles were demonstrations of Jesus' power—His power over disease, the forces of evil, even over nature. Many flocked to Him to be healed and fed. Some wondered who Jesus was. But others followed Him.

Miracle	Reference	What the Miracle Demonstrated	Response
Casting out an unclean spirit	1:23–28	Jesus' power over the forces of evil	The people of Capernaum were amazed and asked, "What new doctrine is this?"
Healing Peter's mother-in-law	1:29–34	Jesus' power over sickness	The people brought the sick and demon-possessed to be healed.
Cleansing a leper	1:40–45	Jesus' compassion and His power over sickness	The leper told everyone about Jesus and the people came from every direction to see Him.
Healing a paralyzed man	2:1–12	Jesus' power over sickness and His authority to forgive	The Pharisees questioned Jesus' authority to forgive, but the people glorified God.
Healing a man with a withered hand	3:1–6	Jesus' power over sickness and His authority to do good on the Sabbath	The Pharisees wanted to accuse Jesus of breaking the Sabbath and began to plot against Him.
Calming a storm	4:35–41	Jesus' power over nature	The disciples were afraid and asked, "Who can this be?"
Casting out demons	5:1–20	Jesus' compassion and His power over the forces of evil	The demon-possessed man told everyone what Jesus had done for him. Yet the people of Gadara pleaded with Jesus to leave the region.
Raising Jairus's daughter	5:21–24, 35–43	Jesus' power over death	The family of Jairus is overcome with amazement.
Healing a woman with a hemorrhage	6:25–34	Jesus' power over sickness	
Feeding the five thousand	6:30–44	Jesus' power to provide food	The disciples' hearts were hardened, and they did not understand what the miracle meant (v. 52).
Walking on the sea	6:45–52	Jesus' power over nature	The disciples were greatly amazed.
Casting out the demon from the Greek woman's daughter	7:24–30	Jesus' power over evil forces not in His immediate proximity.	
Healing a deaf-mute	7:31–37	Jesus' power over the ability to hear and speak	The people spread the news of Jesus and were astonished.
Feeding the four thousand	8:1–10	Jesus' power to provide food	
Healing a blind man	8:22–26	Jesus' power over sight	
Casting out a deaf and dumb spirit	9:14–29	Jesus' power over the forces of evil, and the source of His power: prayer	The disciples asked Jesus what was the source of His power.
Healing blind Bartimaeus	10:46–52	Jesus' power over sight	Bartimaeus followed Jesus.
Withering a fig tree	11:12–14, 20–24	Jesus' power over nature, and the source of His power: prayer	Peter was amazed.

Perhaps she had heard of another who was healed in a similar way. She must have feared having her embarrassing condition revealed to the crowd.

5:28 Her faith motivated her to act.

5:29, 30 The word **immediately** is used twice in this context. Both the woman and Jesus simultaneously knew what had happened. The woman had no idea that Jesus had consciously healed her. While she sought to disappear into the crowd, Jesus turned and asked, **"Who touched My clothes?"** He wanted to correct any mistaken notion she may have had about her healing. It was not any magical quality of His clothing, but His divine will that had made her well.

5:31 No one else was aware that the healing had happened. The disciples became dismayed, perhaps because they were anxious to reach Jairus's home.

5:32 **He looked around,** or literally, kept on looking around, gazing on the people crowded near Him.

5:33 Jesus' kind manner and tender words must have eased the fear this woman had of being revealed. She stepped forward **and told Him the whole truth.** Naturally, the time that Jesus took to care for the woman must have worried the already tense disciples.

5:34 Jesus used a tender word, **daughter,** to address this woman, and He noted that her **faith** made the difference, for it was correctly

Him—**Peter, James, and John.** Note that these same three were the ones permitted to see the Transfiguration (9:2) and accompanied Jesus for prayer in Gethsemane (14:32, 33).

5:38–40 Public mourning was loud and boisterous.

5:41 **Talitha, cumi** is Aramaic.

5:42 That **the girl arose** indicates that her life had been restored, just as in the case of the dead son of the widow of Nain (Luke 7:15) and of Lazarus, who had been dead for four days (John 11:44). All three would die again. Jesus' resurrection, however, was unique. Not only was He restored to life, but His body was transformed so that He would never again have to face death.

5:43 The command to keep the miracle a secret was a temporary measure, for certainly the girl's reappearance could not be hidden very long. Such orders would, however, allow Jesus to exit quietly. Jesus did not want to be known primarily as a miracle worker lest people seek Him for the wrong reasons.

6:1 Jesus now went to minister in **His own country,** the area where He grew up, around Nazareth.

6:2 The people readily acknowledged both Jesus' **wisdom** and His **mighty works,** but with insensitive hearts and spiritual callousness they rejected Jesus' message. He taught that He was the fulfillment of the messianic prophecies of the OT (Luke 4:16-21).

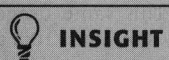 **INSIGHT** | ## Working-Class Savior

Like his earthly father before Him, Jesus worked as a carpenter (Mark 6:3). Possibly He continued to practice His trade while traveling about to teach and heal.

He certainly derived no income from His ministry. Only officials of the temple and religious courts drew salaries. The rest of the religious teachers and leaders were either independently wealthy or supported themselves through a trade or profession.

Jesus did receive support from several wealthy women. And He was welcomed as a guest into many homes. But of all the complaints that His enemies lodged against Him—that He failed to keep the Sabbath, that He ate and drank with sinners, that He made Himself out to be God—they never accused Him of being lazy. Indeed, Jesus' own townsfolk were amazed at His teaching because he was "just a carpenter."

---

placed in Him. Faith itself does not heal; rather, it is the proper object of that faith, Jesus, who heals.

5:35, 36 The implication of the girl's reported death is that her condition is now irreversible and without remedy. Jesus immediately corrects this thought by insisting that Jairus stop being **afraid** and continue to **believe.**

5:37 He permits only three disciples to join

6:3 The fact that Joseph is not mentioned here may indicate that he had died. Mark mentions Jesus' four **brothers** by name as well as His **sisters.** One brother, **James,** did not trust Christ prior to His crucifixion (John 7:5), but seems to have come to faith after Jesus' resurrection (Acts 1:14; 1 Cor. 15:7). He later became the leader of the church in Jerusalem (Acts 15:13; Gal. 1:19) and wrote the Epistle of

James. **Judas** later authored the Book of Jude (Jude 1).

6:4–6 A prophet is not without honor except in his own country is a maxim still repeated and still true today. Perhaps others were jealous of Jesus' popularity and huge following. Their envy even took the form of violence against Christ (Luke 4:29).

6:7 Going out **two by two** provides fellowship, support, encouragement, accountability, and adequate witness. This principle is still a good one to follow today in church visitation and calling.

6:8–11 These instructions accompanied the twelve on their assigned journey, the results of which are reported in Mark 6:30. These rules made for easier travel and encouraged the disciples to trust God for their food and shelter, which faithful Jewish hearers who heeded their teaching would provide.

6:12 That people should repent was part of the apostles' primary message. Repentance was necessary to cultivate the new life Christ offered.

6:13 Casting out demons and healing the sick would add authority to the apostles' message (2 Cor. 12:12; Heb. 2:3, 4).

6:14–29 These verses break from the narrative to describe the death of John the Baptist. So alarming was Jesus' sudden fame that Herod feared that John had risen from the dead. The disciples Jesus had sent out (6:7–13) undoubtedly added to Herod's worry. It appears that one of Mark's purposes in describing John's death was to foreshadow the violent death of Christ Himself and even of some who would follow Him.

6:14 King Herod is Herod Antipas, one of the sons of Herod the Great, the king who tried to kill the baby Jesus (Matt. 2:1–18). After Herod the Great's death in 4 B.C., his kingdom was divided between Archelaus, who received Judea and Samaria; Philip, who ruled Iturea and Trachonitis, north and east of Galilee; and Antipas, who controlled Galilee and Perea from 4 B.C. to A.D. 39. Jesus ministered largely in the territory ruled by Antipas.

6:15 This verse demonstrates the contrast in expectations that Israel had for its coming Messiah. It is clear that many did not recognize the divine mission that Jesus was fulfilling.

6:16, 17 The **prison** where John was kept was at Machaerus, in the hills which overlook the Dead Sea. A complete palace and fortress occupied that site. **Herodias** was a granddaughter of Herod the Great and the sister of Herod Agrippa I (Acts 12:1–23). She was married to **Philip,** a half brother of Herod Antipas, but not the Philip of Luke 3:1. Herodias's first husband was never a ruler. She divorced this

Philip in order to marry Herod Antipas. Herod likewise divorced his first wife, the daughter of Aretas IV, king of Arabia (2 Cor. 11:32).

6:18–21 John's message to Herod was that his divorce was **not lawful** as grounds for remarriage. John's declaration could be based on Jesus' stern words about divorce (10:11, 12) or on Lev. 20:21, which prohibits a man from taking his brother's wife.

6:22 Herodias's daughter, named Salome, was still unmarried at this point and danced seductively to please Herod Antipas. She later married Philip the Tetrarch, who ruled Iturea and Trachonitis and is mentioned in Luke 3:1.

6:23–25 Because she pleased him, Herod Antipas **swore to** Salome a solemn oath to give her **up to half** of his **kingdom** (an expression meaning a large amount but with limits), words that remind us of Xerxes' promise to Esther (Esth. 5:3, 6). This gesture was no doubt exaggerated, yet Salome seized the opportunity for her mother, Herodias, who hated John the Baptist.

6:26 exceedingly sorry: John's death by a ruler who thought him innocent is similar to Jesus' death at the hands of Pilate (15:14, 15).

6:27–29 To keep his oath, Herod dispatched **an executioner.** Here Mark uses a Latin word, *spekoulatora,* easily understood by his Roman readers.

6:30 The word **apostles** (Gk. *apostellō,* I send) in this context refers to the twelve men Jesus sent out in v. 7. The word has long been used as a technical term to designate the original twelve men Jesus chose. This same usage is found in the parallel passages in Matt. 10:2 and Luke 6:13, and although infrequent in Mark, is used regularly in this manner in Luke (17:5; 22:14; 24:10).

6:31, 32 The disciples had returned from their tours of ministry in Galilee begun at v. 7. Jesus sought the privacy of a **deserted place** belonging to the city of Bethsaida (Luke 9:10), but yet a distance from the city.

6:33–35 The Gospels record several times that when Jesus saw a need, He **was moved with compassion** (1:41; Ex. 34:6). That compassion led to action, despite an obvious lack of food in this instance.

6:36–38 The disciples sought to avoid responsibility for the hungry multitude, saying **send them away.** No doubt they thought they were showing compassion. But Jesus' reply, **"You give them something to eat,"** must have startled them. The Latin word **denarii** is the plural of *denarius,* a commonly used silver coin. It was the sum typically paid to a laborer for a day's work. Thomas calculated it would take the wages of two hundred days' labor to provide for that multitude.

6:39, 40 Details such as sitting **on the green grass,** which is possible only in late winter and early spring, and the fact that the groups were counted in **hundreds and in fifties** are indications that an eyewitness, probably Peter, recounted this story to Mark. John 6:4 informs us that this event occurred prior to the approaching Passover, always celebrated in March or April.

6:41 The tense of the verb **gave,** used by Mark and Luke (9:16), suggests that the multiplication of the loaves took place in Jesus' hands as He *continued* or *kept on giving* the bread and fish to the disciples.

6:42, 43 The **twelve baskets full of fragments** were small baskets commonly carried by

titude away because they were determined to make Him their king by force (John 6:15).

6:46 Jesus spent several nights in prayer during His ministry. Prayer was a vital part of Christ's communion with the Father and always preceded and accompanied especially difficult situations. This particular night followed a busy day when solitude was sought but not found. Jesus was also facing Satan's temptation to step out of the path that led to the Cross in order to become king prematurely.

6:47 In the middle of the sea does not mean the very center of the lake but simply out in the water. They were probably closest to the northern shore.

6:48 The fourth watch lasted from 3 A.M.

Photo by Willem A. VanGemeren

The Sea, or Lake, of Galilee on which Jesus walked during a storm to reassure His disciples and to show His mastery over the natural order (Mark 6:48–51).

travelers (contrast the baskets described in 8:8, which are larger). It is possible to conclude that the leftovers gave each disciple enough food for his own use. When we put the will of God first, He will care for our needs (Matt. 6:33) and provide our daily bread. God desires daily dependence on Him.

6:44 In addition to the estimated **five thousand men** were women and children as stated in Matt. 14:21, and as indicated by the presence of the lad who donated his lunch to Jesus (John 6:9).

6:45 Jesus had difficulty in sending the mul-

until 6 A.M. That Jesus **would have passed them by** does not indicate that He was on His way to somewhere else. He intended to reveal Himself to His disciples in a miraculous manner. He could easily have calmed the waves from shore, but He wanted His disciples to understand His deity and mastery over all nature.

6:49 When the disciples saw Jesus, they thought they saw a **ghost** (an apparition), a sign often interpreted as a foreshadowing of evil, even death.

6:50 Mark omits the added detail of Peter walking on the water to meet Jesus (Matt.

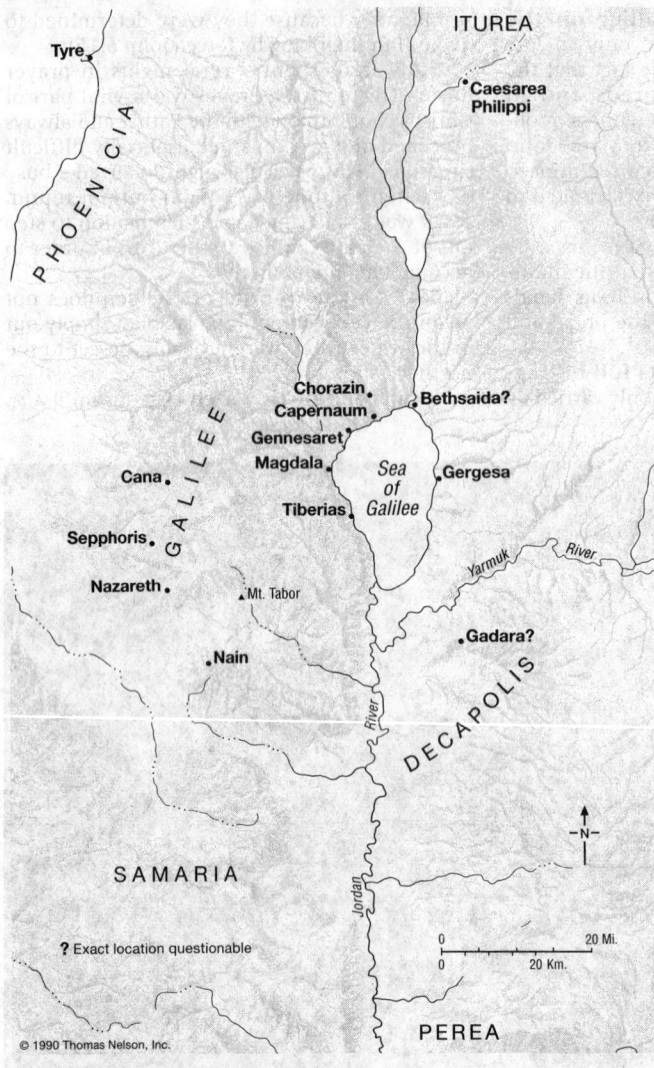

Cities of Jesus' Galilean Ministry

Jesus began His public ministry at Cana, where He graced a wedding party with His presence and turned water into wine (John 2:1–11). In the synagogue of Nazareth, Jesus announced that He was the fulfillment of prophecy from the Book of Isaiah (Luke 4:16–22). But his hometown rejected Him, so He went to Capernaum, a prosperous fishing town situated along an international trade route. There He established a base of ministry.

In Capernaum He called Matthew to be His disciple (Mark 2:14) and healed the paralyzed servant of a centurion (Matt. 8:5–13), as well as Peter's mother-in-law (Matt. 8:14, 15). The Sea of Galilee, with its fishing industry, was the setting for many miracles. At Nain, Jesus mercifully raised to life the only son of a widow (Luke 7:11–17). Chorazin and Bethsaida were cities Jesus chastised for their unbelief (Matt. 11:21). The area of Gergesa was possibly where Jesus healed the demoniacs (Matt. 8:28–34).

14:28–31). Mark almost certainly knew of the incident but does not want to exalt Peter.

6:51, 52 Three miracles are contained in this brief account (vv. 47–51). (1) In the darkness Jesus saw the disciples out in the storm miles away. (2) Jesus walked on the water. (3) Jesus showed complete control over His creation when **the wind ceased.**

6:53 They had set out for Bethsaida (v. 45) on the northeastern shore, but the storm apparently changed their course. The **land of Gennesaret** was on the northwest shore of the Sea of Galilee, just west of Capernaum. It was and still is a fertile agricultural area.

6:54–56 Mark summarizes Jesus' healing ministry, noting how widespread it was. The hem of a garment was significant, for it was often woven with tassels that reminded the wearer of God's commandments (5:27; Num. 15:37–41).

7:1–23 In this chapter, the scribes and Pharisees become more vocal in their opposition to Jesus. The breach between true spirituality and man-made tradition widens considerably.

7:1 Jerusalem was the central city of the Jewish faith. The Pharisees (Matt. 5:20) and scribes (teachers of the law) were no doubt sent by the Jewish religious authorities to ascertain Jesus' position on the issues they counted important. The Gospels present both good and bad scribes (Matt. 7:29; 8:19).

7:2 they found fault: It is so much easier to criticize than to encourage. Counselors say that people, especially children, need encouragement over criticism on an eight-to-one ratio. We make encouragement and uplifting easier when we make it a habit.

7:3, 4 These two verses explain the tradition of hand washing and various kinds of ceremonial uncleanness. Mark's intended readers in Rome likely needed more background on the Jewish faith to understand this controversy.

7:5 The tradition of the elders (Matt. 15:2) was a series of rules meant to bolster the ceremonial law of the Jews. Its authority was not supported by Scripture. The question indirectly challenged Jesus, for as the disciples' teacher He was judged responsible for their actions.

7:6, 7 Jesus did not directly answer the question but instead addressed two more significant issues: (1) the superiority of God's law over man-made tradition (vv. 6–13) and (2) the difference between ceremonial and true moral defilement (vv. 14–23). Jesus enters into the argument by calling His adversaries **hypocrites.** The term originally referred to actors who wore masks on stage as they played different characters. Thus the Pharisees were not genuinely religious; they were merely playing a part for all to see.

7:8, 9 In earlier times the Hebrews held the written Law of God, the Torah, in such esteem that they would not write down their reflections on it, lest they should tempt later generations to consider their words as important as God's law. But as time went on, written commentaries on the law, collected in the Talmud, assumed greater authority than the Torah itself.

7:10–13 But you say shows the absolute contrast between God's will and man's empty tradition. The **corban** was evidently a pious-sounding evasion of the requirement of honoring one's parents by supporting them financially.

7:14 A private question at mealtime bloomed into a controversy that now met the ears of **all the multitude** whom Jesus summoned. Jesus made a bold public statement that must have liberated His listeners and infuriated the Pharisees.

7:15, 16 No food we eat defiles us, but unbridled speech and conduct can. Here is a basic principle of conduct. Our actions are determined by the programming of our minds. Our actions are the blossom of our deepest thoughts. Notice also that the words of a **man** defile him even before others.

7:17–23 Jesus had to spell out exactly what He meant to His dull and seemingly imperceptive disciples. How often we try to blame our environment rather than observing this principle.

7:20 This may be the statement of Christ that indicates a transition from the dietary laws of Lev. 11 with the full change occuring in the teaching of the church in Acts 10—11.

7:24–8:26 After a forceful public confrontation with the Jewish authorities, Jesus withdrew to rest and to instruct His own disciples.

7:24 Jesus' travels **to the region of Tyre and Sidon** are the farthest beyond Israel He is reported to have gone during His public ministry. Of course, during His infancy, He traveled about three hundred miles from his birthplace into Egypt. Sidon is about fifty miles northeast of Capernaum.

7:25 Even in a house in faraway Sidon, Jesus could not find privacy.

7:26 The woman who approached Jesus was a Gentile, as the word **Greek** signifies here. She was a native of that area. **Syro-Phoenician** (see 1 Kin. 17:8–24 for the story of the widow at Zarephath) reflects the political situation of the Middle East at that time. Phoenicia (modern Lebanon) was part of the Roman province of Syria, which also included all of Palestine— Galilee, Samaria, Perea, Judea, Idumea, and other regions.

7:27 Jesus was in the midst of teaching or feeding His disciples, called figuratively His **children.** During a meal one does not stop to feed the house pets, **the little dogs.** Jesus is not attempting to insult the woman by using this metaphor. In fact, He is testing her faith. Matthew records Jesus' reaction to her reply, "O woman, great is your faith" (Matt. 15:28).

7:28 The woman understood Jesus' test and persistently replied that even during the meal **the little dogs** consume **the children's crumbs** that fall from the table.

7:29 Rewarding her persistence, Jesus granted her request. He cast the demons out, although the girl was not in His presence.

7:30 The verb **lying** indicates the position into which the girl was cast by the demon when it left her.

7:31 Jesus' route to Israel bypassed Galilee itself. Instead Jesus went east into the **Decapolis** region and then turned south past Mount Hermon until He reached **the Sea of Galilee.**

7:32–35 The healing of this **deaf** man (who also had a speech impediment) is one of the two miracles recorded by Mark only. (The other is the healing of the blind man recorded in 8:22–26.) Those who have never heard also frequently have problems pronouncing words.

7:34 Ephphatha is an Aramaic word. Mark provides an interpretation for his largely non-Jewish audience.

7:36 Jesus' command to **tell no one,** though unheeded, was meant to allow Him to move freely in the area. He knew that curiosity seekers could hamper His ministry.

7:37 the deaf . . . hear and the mute . . . speak: Signs that God's kingdom had come (Is. 35:5, 6).

8:1–30 Having concluded one narrative section with the approval voiced by the crowd,

Mark will reach a climax when he ends this section with Peter's confession.

8:1–5 Jesus desired to feed the multitude, but His disciples questioned **how.** They had witnessed the feeding of the five thousand a few days earlier but could not imagine Jesus duplicating this miracle. They were slow to comprehend who Jesus really was.

8:6, 7 The verb tenses for the words translated **took, gave thanks,** and **broke** specify action at a fixed moment in the past. Yet the verb translated **gave** is in the imperfect tense, which shows a continuing action. Thus, we may conclude that the miracle of multiplication was a continuing process that took place, at least initially, in Jesus' hands.

8:8 The **seven large baskets** contained leftovers—one basket from each original loaf. This was both a memorable witness to the miracle as well as a hint not to waste food. These baskets were much larger than the twelve small personal baskets mentioned in 6:43. It was this kind of larger basket that was used to lower Paul over the wall of Damascus (Acts 9:25).

8:9 The number **four thousand** does not specify men as with the five thousand, so the size of the gathering could have been significantly smaller. Since there are those who attempt to merge the two accounts into one event, the significant differences should be noted: the number of people fed, the place, the time, the numbers of fish, loaves, and baskets.

8:10 Apparently **Dalmanutha** and Magdala (Matt. 15:39) are different names for the same region. Both are mentioned only once in the NT. Dalmanutha was probably on the western side of the Sea of Galilee, about three miles north of modern Tiberias and about five miles southwest of Capernaum.

8:11, 12 The Pharisees' testing of Jesus was crafty and devious. Obviously these men did not heed the many signs and wonders that Jesus had already performed. John 20:30, 31 indicates that the signs were meant to produce faith. It is doubtful that the Pharisees would have changed their minds even if they had seen another miracle.

8:13, 14 Having fed the four thousand on the western side of the lake, Jesus led His disciples by boat **to the other side,** near Bethsaida (v. 22).

8:15 Jesus repeatedly commanded His disciples to **beware of the leaven,** the growing corruption of the Pharisees and of Herod Antipas which was spreading throughout Israel.

8:16–21 The disciples continued to show a lack of spiritual discernment despite the miracles they had witnessed. Jesus' rebuke was intended to make them recall what God had done for them. Like the apostles, we have short memories of God's provisions; we need to trust Him for our "daily bread."

8:22–26 Jesus' healing of the blind man in stages paralleled the disciples' imperfect perception of Jesus. Like the man, they were no longer blind, but they could not see clearly either. Only the Holy Spirit could clear their vision.

8:27 Caesarea Philippi is about twenty-five miles north of Bethsaida and the Sea of Galilee. It stands on the southern edge of Mount Hermon and is today called Banias. One of the sources of the Jordan River springs forth from under a large rocky cliff that rises a hundred or more feet above the village. Many idols were carved into the rock facade. The contrast between Jesus Christ and these local gods was striking—a perfect place for Christ to ask the question of v. 29. The name *Philippi* distinguishes this town from Caesarea by the sea.

8:28 The disciples' answers to Jesus' question about His identity restate popular misconceptions. They recall the statements made by Herod and others in 6:14, 15.

8:29 Jesus then emphatically asks His disciples for their understanding. The word **you** is prominent in Jesus' question. Peter answers for the group when he says, **"You are the Christ."** Jesus wants His disciples to grasp firmly His true identity before He reveals to them the necessity of His coming death and resurrection. In Mark's Gospel, only the disciples come to understand who Jesus is. The opposition of the religious leaders and the disciples' dullness is suddenly overshadowed by Peter's wonderful confession.

8:30 Jesus' warning to **tell no one about Him** may seem strange. Its explanation lies in the fact that the Jews expected the Messiah to be a political liberator. Jesus' first coming was meant to accomplish another kind of liberation—release from sin. Hence Jesus was careful not to use the name *Messiah* publicly, for it was misunderstood by the Jewish people, their leaders, and the Roman authorities.

8:31 This is the first of several clear predictions Jesus makes about His coming death and resurrection (9:31; 10:33, 34). **He began to teach them** signals this new disclosure of His death, burial, and resurrection to His apostles. The **Son of Man** is a title that only Jesus used of Himself. With it He defined His ministry in terms of initial suffering, followed by later glory, and avoided the use of titles such as Messiah which held other meanings for the Jewish mind. The **elders and chief priests,** former high priests, **and scribes** made up the Jewish ruling council, the Sanhedrin. These men would condemn Jesus to death (for the fulfillment of Jesus' prediction, see 14:53, 64).

8:32 Jesus **spoke . . . openly,** that is

plainly, not in parables. **Peter** understood clearly Jesus' prediction of death and could not accept or understand it, and so he **began to rebuke Him.**

8:33 Peter's thoughts, born of fear and concern, were probably well-intended, but they did not take in God's eternal purposes and plan. Peter was not indwelt by **Satan,** but Satan had certainly suggested his thoughts. If Peter had his way, Jesus' mission would not have been accomplished.

8:34 Deny himself does not mean to hate himself or to go without one or more things, but to give full control of his life to Christ. **take up his cross:** The person who carried a cross was on the way to execution. Thus, it is a graphic picture of one who is dead to his own will. He is ready to accept whatever costs are involved in a life of complete Christian commitment. Jesus' call for discipleship is addressed to **whoever desires to come after me.** It is restricted only by one's unwillingness to come. In Jesus' day, when one would **take up his cross** it would be primarily a public act, not a private decision.

8:35, 36 To preserve one's life eternally, one must surrender earthly possessions and relationships held so dearly (Matt. 16:24–27). Apparent earthly loss means eternal gain, whereas apparent earthly gain may be translated into eternal loss (Matt. 19:21). We are investing resources all the time. The dividends will be determined by the wisdom of the investment.

8:37 The worth of a single life (Gk. *psyche*) is of great consequence in the kingdom reign of Christ (Matt. 16:27). It is interesting that the same Greek word is used in vv. 35–38 but is usually translated "life" in v. 35 but "soul" in vv. 36, 37. The idea is not a spiritual side of a person lost for eternity but failing to live one's life faithfully for the King of the kingdom.

8:38 When He comes in the glory is the key of this address to the disciples (vv. 34–38). It is the first glimpse of the fulfillment of all history (1 Cor. 15:24–28). Those who will reign with Christ invest their lives in that which will last (v. 35). Those who are willing to confess Him today will be rewarded before the Father in heaven (Matt. 5:10–12; 2 Tim. 2:11–13; Rev. 2:26–28).

9:1 After Jesus predicted His own death, Peter and the other disciples needed reassurance that Jesus would ultimately triumph. His prediction that some of them would see **the kingdom of God present with power** must have alleviated their fears.

9:2, 3 After **six days** links Jesus' prediction of v. 1 with the events of vv. 2–8. The **high**

Our basic need is not trying harder but believing more.

mountain was most likely one of the foothills surrounding Mount Hermon. They probably did not stand on Mount Hermon itself, a snowy peak which rises to 9,232 feet. It is the highest point in all of Palestine. These mountains overlook Caesarea Philippi, where Peter's confession was made (8:27–29). Jesus' transfiguration deeply affected John and Peter, who mention it in their writings (John 1:14; 2 Pet. 1:16–18).

9:4 Elijah is mentioned in Mal. 4:5, 6 in connection with the future coming of Christ. This is why people asked John the Baptist if he were Elijah (John 1:21). **Moses** was the lawgiver and liberator, while Elijah was the first of the great prophets. Their presence confirmed the reality that Jesus is the Messiah of Peter's confession.

9:5, 6 The synoptic Gospels use three different words for Peter's addressing of Jesus. **Rabbi** (in Mark), Master (Luke 9:33), and Lord (Matt. 17:4) are separate Greek translations of whatever Hebrew or Aramaic word Peter used to address Jesus on the mount. Mark's emphasis is on Jesus' respected position among the disciples as their leader. Nathanael (John 1:19), Nicodemus (John 3:2), and even Judas (14:45) also used this title of Jesus. Although Peter knew that it was **good** to be there, he did not understand what was happening. **Three tabernacles** suggests that he wanted to stay on the mountain. But this experience was to prepare him to carry his cross in the day-to-day world. His answer tended to put Jesus, **Moses,** and **Elijah** on the same level.

9:7–10 The voice of God the Father was heard audibly three times during the life of Christ. The other two occasions were at Jesus' baptism (1:11) and during His triumphal entry into Jerusalem (John 12:28).

9:11, 12 This question is based on the words of Mal. 4:5, 6.

9:13 Jesus' comment that **Elijah has also come** is a reference to John the Baptist. John was not a reincarnation of Elijah, but one who ministered "in the Spirit and power of Elijah" (Luke 1:17) in preparing the way for Christ. **They did to him whatever they wished** refers to the ruthless way John the Baptist was imprisoned and murdered.

9:14–20 The boy had several problems. The **mute spirit** was a demon that kept the boy from speaking, but the demon also produced seizures. Verse 20 says **the spirit convulsed him.**

9:21, 22 if You can: Faith mixed with doubt.

9:23 Believe is a marvelous word—not work, pay, cry, or penance, but believe.

9:24–27 I believe; help my unbelief expresses the fact that even a grain of faith is sufficient, but also that a person's faith needs to grow and mature. One can only receive as much as he or she can believe. Our basic need is not trying harder but believing more.

9:28, 29 Jesus said that **prayer and fasting** were required to prevail in some difficult instances. Fasting may help focus one's energies on the resources available in our great God.

9:30 He did not want **anyone to know** of their return because He needed this time alone with His disciples.

9:31, 32 For the second time (8:31), Jesus tells plainly of His coming death and resurrection.

9:33–35 The disciples **kept silent,** refusing to tell Jesus about their discussion. But Jesus once again challenged their assumptions. He presented them with another paradox—that to be great in God's kingdom, one must be a servant. The example was modeled by Christ Himself.

9:36, 37 Children were given little status in the ancient world. The child here represents all needy people, but especially needy believers. Christ's disciples take a lowly place by ministering to the needs of the lowly. **receives Me:** This service is accepted as if done to Jesus who made Himself lowest of all.

9:39–40 Jesus is not endorsing all who claim to follow Him. Rather, this statement was meant to remind the disciples that God's work

feet across and about a foot thick, used to grind grain into meal.

9:43 Cut it off should be taken figuratively; it means to take whatever drastic action is necessary to avoid sin. The imagery of **hell** (frequently called *gehenna*) refers to a garbage dump outside the walls of Jerusalem. Jesus' hearers were familiar with the smoldering fires that always burned there. Obedience and self-control (v. 41, 47) are necessary to overcome sin. The longing of the disciples for greatness (vv. 33–37) needed to be reshaped according to God's purposes.

9:44–48 Many modern versions omit vv. 44 and 46, believing the phrase which appears in v. 48 was wrongly inserted in those two places. It could be that they are repeated. It seems that Jesus is emphasizing His point by a threefold repetition, a characteristic typical of Hebrew poetic style. This is similar to the sevenfold repetition of "he who has an ear, let him hear what the Spirit says to the churches" (Rev. 2—3).

9:49 The word **for** shows that Mark intended his readers to apply the preceding verses to their own lives. **Everyone will be seasoned with fire** may refer to the trials and judgments that all will face—believers with trials that purify faith, unbelievers with the eternal fire of God's judgment.

9:50 Have peace with one another aptly ends Jesus' explanation of servanthood begun in v. 35.

10:1 Jesus, now on His final journey to Jerusalem, comes to Capernaum (9:33). From

---

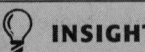 **INSIGHT** | **Divorce in New Testament Times**

In the first century, Jewish men were allowed to divorce their wives for many different reasons (Mark 10:2). Depending on which interpretation of the Torah one followed, a man could even send his wife away if she burned a meal.

By contrast, women were far more restricted in their grounds for divorce. One of the few had to do with her husband's occupation. If he were a copper smelter, tanner, or dung collector, she could get a divorce, even if she knew before she married what his trade was, on the grounds that she couldn't have known how awful the smell would be.

---

was not necessarily restricted to their small group.

9:41 a cup of water: The most trivial service given to encourage a Christian receives God's blessing. It is not the size of the task, but loving faithfulness that counts with God.

9:42 Jesus uses hyperbole, exaggeration for an effect, to state the seriousness of causing spiritual injury to others. **A millstone** is an extremely heavy circular stone, three to four

His Galilean ministry He will head south to Judea and even into Perea on the eastern side of the Jordan River.

10:2 The Pharisees' question about divorce was a trap. Perhaps they hoped He would contradict Moses (Deut. 24:1–4) or offend Herod Antipas as John the Baptist had (6:18). The only possibility for divorce under Jewish law was **for a man to divorce his wife.**

10:3, 4 A certificate of divorce was a document signed before witnesses. Its intent was to limit frivolous divorces. In Jesus' day, the interpretation of this custom varied widely. The disciples of Hillel allowed divorce for almost any reason, but the followers of Shammai permitted divorce only for sexual impurity.

10:5, 6 Jesus declares that divorce was a concession to **the hardness of your heart** and then turns the argument to God's original intentions for marriage as seen in Gen. 2:21–25. God's design of **male and female** shows that He held each to be equal in value and worth, but that they fulfilled a different function and role in His design.

10:7, 8 A man is to **leave** his parents, cleave to his wife, then weave a life of beauty with her. Jesus quotes almost verbatim from the Septuagint text of Gen. 2:24. The **one flesh** is a bond created sexually which encompasses the totality of man and woman, and this bond is comparable to that of a blood relationship.

10:9 Jesus indicates that God's original purpose in marriage is not to be broken by human beings. No exceptions are given. The exception in Matt. 19:9 may be accounted for by the Jewishness of that Gospel (compare Rev. 18).

10:10, 1 **Whoever divorces his wife:** Mark includes no exception to Christ's prohibition of divorce, nor is any exception listed in Luke 16:18; Rom. 7:1, 2; 1 Cor. 7:10, 11. Compare Matt. 5:32; 19:9, for the Jewish exception to this rule.

10:12 In Jewish society, it was not possible for **a woman** to divorce **her husband,** but Mark is presenting Jesus' words in a way his Roman audience would understand.

10:13, 14 **He was greatly displeased** expresses the emotion of a single verb (Gk. *aganakteō*) used in the NT only in the synoptic Gospels. Jesus felt emotional pain like all human beings do, but even then He expressed Himself in a controlled fashion. The term **little children** (Gk. *paidia*) includes infants to those at least age twelve. Jairus' daughter, who was twelve years old, is referred to by this same word (5:39).

10:15 **Receive the kingdom** indicates the continuing thrust of Jesus' message as He prepares His disciples for reigning in the coming kingdom. Children exhibit sincerity, eagerness, a trusting attitude, and total dependence on their parents. Thus, childlikeness is a fitting comparison for the qualities a disciple should have. Adults can become worldly wise, self-sufficient, and skeptical of religion and various plans for salvation. Heart attitude is basic to leadership in the kingdom.

10:16 Only Mark notes that Jesus **blessed** the children. Mark uses a compound verb (Gk. *kateulogei*) that appears only here in the NT. It

signifies Jesus' continuously tender but fervent blessing. Jesus' concern is not limited to adults only, but extends to little boys and girls as well.

10:17 In addressing Jesus as **Good Teacher,** the rich young ruler (Matt. 19:22; Luke 18:18)

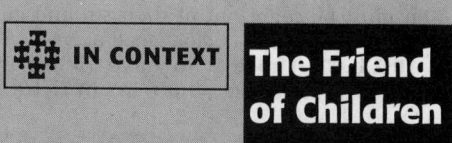

IN CONTEXT — The Friend of Children

In Jesus' day it was common for mothers to ask famous rabbis to bless their children. With Jesus, however, they sought more than a blessing; they wanted the touch of this rabbi (Mark 10:13). No doubt the power of His touch had become well known. Mark did not explain why the disciples tried to keep the children away. Perhaps they viewed the little ones as ritually unclean, or, like most of society, unworthy of an important man's attention. But Jesus rebuked the disciples and invited the children into His arms (10:16). The way He spoke to them and embraced them must have shocked those who stood by. Such tenderness and respect were rarely given children in that society.

meant no more than to issue a respectful formal greeting to a religious teacher.

10:18 The reply that **no one is good but One, that is, God,** can be construed as a claim to deity, which Jesus asks the young ruler to recognize.

10:19 Jesus recounts the seventh, sixth, eighth, ninth, and fifth commandments with the phrase **do not defraud** inserted just before the fifth commandment. All of these commands concern the fair and ethical treatment of other people (Ex. 20:12–17).

10:20 By his answer the man admits that something more than keeping the letter of the law is necessary for eternal life. Matthew remembered the young man asking Jesus, "What do I still lack?" (Matt. 19:20).

10:21 Jesus is not teaching salvation by works, i.e., by giving money to the poor. He is pointing out the need to admit and deal with self-righteousness and self-dependence so that trust may be transferred entirely to Christ. By driving the man to the ultimate conclusion of his premise—what shall I do (v. 17)—Jesus is showing him its impossibility and his need for utter dependence on Christ.

10:22 This was too much; he **went away**

sorrowful. Does this story teach that salvation is merited by good works? One must remember that prior to the acceptance of the gospel a man needs to recognize his need. Jesus was aware of the man's self-righteous attitude, trusting in his observance of rules. Therefore, his need was for Christ to point out **one thing you lack** (v. 21). Men must be cognizant of their sin and guilt before they can be ready for "good news."

10:23, 24 Those who have riches frequently also are **those who trust in riches,** a

own brothers (1 Cor. 9:5). Many times, however, they made heavy sacrifices for the **sake** of Christ **and the gospel.** In so doing, they were being true followers of the One who left His heavenly glory and took upon Himself servant-hood, suffering, and death (Phil. 2:6-11).

10:30 Spiritual rewards await those who follow Christ **in this time,** meaning during this age between Christ's first and second comings. Mark alone mentions that **persecutions** will follow as well—a point his Roman readers may

---

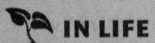 **IN LIFE** **"One Thing You Lack"**

He was young, well mannered, well educated, and well-off. He was sincere, honest, and above reproach. Maybe he also had an engaging personality and a winsome smile. Certainly Jesus found him likable; He even tried to recruit him (Mark 10:21). He was the man who had every-thing—except eternal life. And he could have had that, too. All he had to do was get rid of his money and follow Jesus.

But it wasn't to be. Elsewhere Jesus had said that no one can serve both God and money (Matt. 6:24). Here was living proof of that principle. In coming to Jesus, the rich young ruler came to a fork in the road. He had to choose which one he would serve—money or Jesus. Apparently he chose money.

Jesus never condemned people for being rich. Nor does Scripture condemn the possession or the accumulation of money. But Jesus warned people about what He called "the deceitfulness of riches" (Mark 4:19). He understood the powerful but ultimately fatal attraction of money as a substitute for God.

Jesus perceived that tendency in the rich young ruler. The man was placing far too much value on his wealth. So Jesus told him to give it away, to free himself from its entanglements. It's worth noting that Jesus did not give that same advice to every other rich person He encountered. But it was a requirement for this young ruler.

There are many rich young rulers today—people who have or are well on their way to having rela-tively sizable assets. Some are Christians and some are not. But sooner or later they all must answer the question that this man asked Jesus: "What shall I do that I may inherit eternal life?" (10:17).

---

dangerous condition for one seeking spiritual life.

10:25-27 This comparison of a **camel** going through a **needle** is a literal one (Matt. 19:24). In human terms, it is not just difficult, but totally impossible, for a rich man to be saved. But it is also impossible for anyone at all to be saved apart from God's grace and power. God provides the means of salvation, enlightens the sinner's understanding, and regenerates the believing soul.

10:28 Peter expressed what must have been in the mind of each disciple. They had given up a lot to follow Jesus even if the rich young, ruler did not. "What will we get in return?" they asked.

10:29 The **one who has left** all these things has not necessarily renounced them but has certainly reordered his priorities (Matt. 19:29). Peter still had his wife some twenty-five years later, as did the other apostles and Jesus'

have already known. After Christ's return, **in the age to come,** the incomparable reward will be **eternal life,** which is not simply extent of life but quality of life.

10:31 Human standards for reward will be overturned. Humility and servanthood lead to greatness in God's kingdom, not such worldly priorities as wealth, social standing, nobility, birth, or personal favoritism. Matthew follows this saying with an illustrative parable (Matt. 20:1-16).

10:32-34 Jesus revealed for the third time His imminent death and resurrection as the dis-ciples walked the road toward Jerusalem for Passover (see 8:31; 9:31 for His previous teaching on this subject). Since Jerusalem is in the hill country, one always goes **up to Jerusalem** as he approaches it (Acts 11:2; 21:4; 25:1), and down as he leaves it (3:22).

10:35 Matthew 20:20 says it was the mother of **James and John** who sought Jesus,

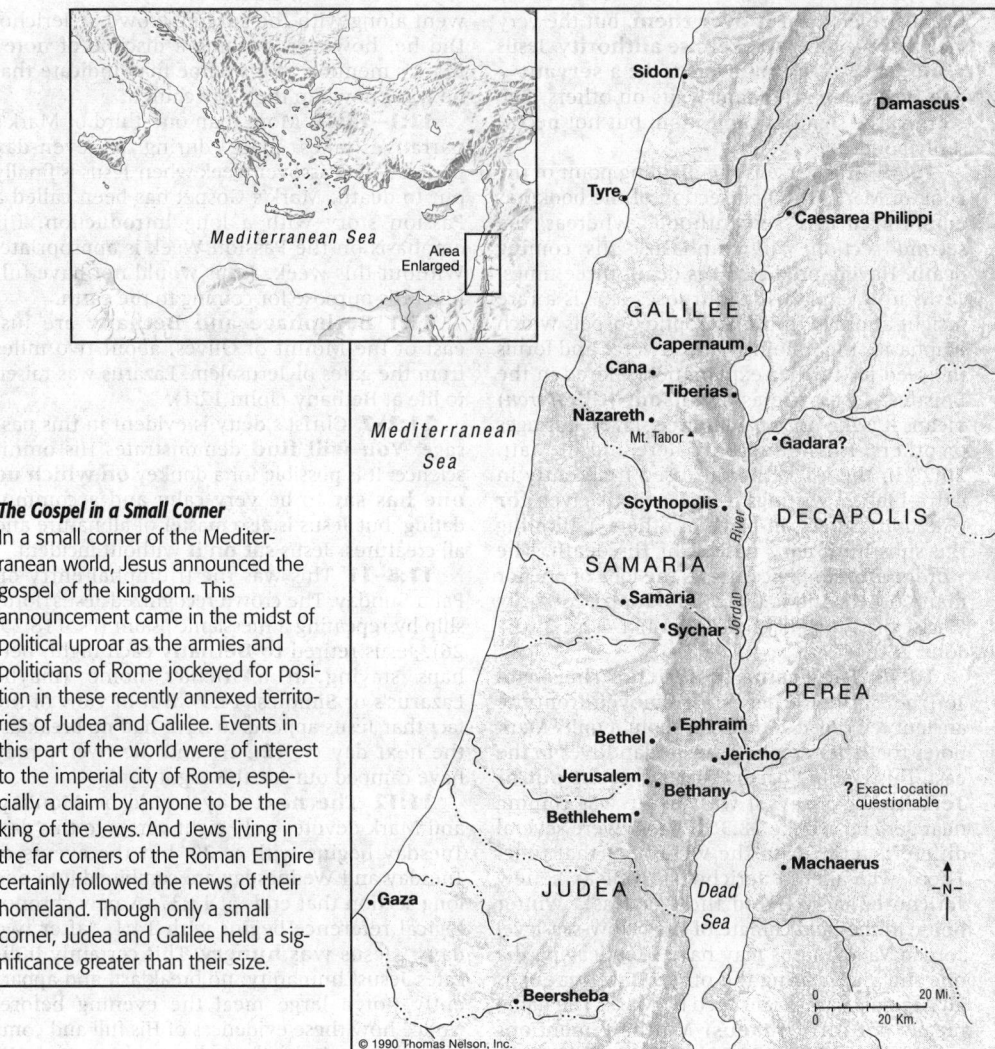

The Gospel in a Small Corner

In a small corner of the Mediterranean world, Jesus announced the gospel of the kingdom. This announcement came in the midst of political uproar as the armies and politicians of Rome jockeyed for position in these recently annexed territories of Judea and Galilee. Events in this part of the world were of interest to the imperial city of Rome, especially a claim by anyone to be the king of the Jews. And Jews living in the far corners of the Roman Empire certainly followed the news of their homeland. Though only a small corner, Judea and Galilee held a significance greater than their size.

© 1990 Thomas Nelson, Inc.

but it is likely that the sons themselves encouraged her to do it.

10:36, 37 To be seated at a king's **right hand** was to take the position of most prominence; the person seated at the **left** hand ranked just below that (Luke 22:24–30). Jesus was emphasizing servanthood while the apostles were practicing public and private one-upmanship. Jesus had to remind the disciples again about the price of greatness in God's kingdom. As they journeyed toward Jerusalem, "they thought the kingdom of God would appear immediately" (Luke 19:11), so they may have wanted to secure their power and authority as soon as possible.

10:38 **To drink the cup** and **be baptized** are references to the suffering and death that awaited Jesus (14:36). Jesus wanted His disci-

ples to understand the mocking, scourging, beating, and torture He would have to endure.

10:39, 40 Jesus agreed with their response, though they had not yet understood the cost of their commitment. Although not suffering the same level of spiritual agony that Jesus did, James would soon be executed by Herod Agrippa I in A.D. 44 (Acts 12:1, 2). John was the last apostle to die, being exiled for a while on the island of Patmos (Rev. 1:9). He was persecuted greatly and had to witness the deaths of more Christians than probably any of the other apostles.

10:41 The ten disciples who had not been part of the private discussion seeking special favors were **greatly displeased** because they had similar ambitions.

10:42–44 The point here is not the fact that

Gentile rulers **lord it over them,** but the very idea that they seek to **exercise authority.** Jesus wants each of His followers to be a **servant**— one who as an attendant waits on others. The word **slave** signifies subjection, but not necessarily bondage.

10:45 This verse is the dividing point of the book of Mark. The first section of the book has emphasized His servanthood, whereas the second section will emphasize His coming death. Having predicted His death three times, Jesus now explains its purpose. This is a rare insight afforded in the Synoptic Gospels which emphasize the training of the Twelve and forms the seed for further explanation offered in the Epistles. Jesus' life as a **ransom** (Gk. *lutron*) means it is the price paid to free slaves, hostages or others. It is found only here and in Matt. 20:28 in the NT, although used frequently in extra-biblical writings. Christ's life is given **for** (Gk. *anti*) others, in place of others, indicating the substitutionary nature of His death. The word **many** simply contrasts the idea of one for many others and is not a limitation. Certainly Christ died for all (2 Cor. 5:14; 1 Tim. 2:6; 1 John 2:2).

10:46 They came to Jericho: The site of Jericho in the NT period is removed from the ancient tell called Jericho by about a mile. Mark notes that after crossing the Jordan River to the east, this healing occurs as Jesus **went out of Jericho.** Luke says it was "as He was coming near Jericho" (Luke 18:35). There were several different Jerichos in the vicinity at that time. There was an old Jericho as well as a new Jericho built by Herod the Great as a winter home in the mild climate of the below-sea-level Jordan Valley. Jesus may have been leaving the one site and nearing the other. **Bartimaeus** is an Aramaic name translated by Mark. The name means **son of Timaeus.** Matthew mentions two beggars (Matt. 20:30), but Mark concentrates on only one.

10:47, 48 Son of David is a messianic title. Mark shows us the irony of a blind man who had spiritual insight, while many who could see—including the religious leaders—were spiritually blind.

10:49, 50 Mark's account has all the graphic details of an eyewitness account—Jesus **stood still;** then Bartimaeus was suddenly **throwing aside his garment** to rise and meet Jesus. Mark also notes the changed attitude of the crowd—they began by deriding Bartimaeus but later encouraged him.

10:51 Rabboni is a very tender Aramaic form of address meaning "master" or "teacher" (John 20:16).

10:52 We know that Bartimaeus **followed Jesus** for at least a short time **on the road.** He went along with the surging crowd at Jericho. Did he, however, become a disciple of note? Mark's mention of his name may indicate that he was known in the early church.

11:1–15:47 More than one-third of Mark's narrative takes place during a seven-day period—the Passover week when Jesus is finally put to death. Mark's Gospel has been called a Passion story with a long introduction. His emphasis on the Passion Week is appropriate. Without this week, Jesus would not have fulfilled His purpose for coming to the earth.

11:1 Bethphage and Bethany are just east of the Mount of Olives, about two miles from the gates of Jerusalem. Lazarus was raised to life at Bethany (John 12:1).

11:2–7 Christ's deity is evident in this passage. **You will find** demonstrates His omniscience. It is possible for a donkey **on which no one has sat** to be very calm and accommodating, but Jesus is also master of all nature and all creatures. Jesus **sat on it** without incident.

11:8–11 This was the triumphal entry on Palm Sunday. The crowd recognized Jesus' lordship by repeating a messianic psalm (Ps. 118:25, 26). Jesus retired **to Bethany** each night, perhaps staying in a friend's home (maybe Lazarus's or Simon's, 14:3). But in view of the fact that Jesus appears to have had no breakfast the next day (v. 12), He and the twelve may have camped outside this night.

11:12 The next day would be Monday, and Mark devotes only eight verses to this day. Tuesday begins with v. 20, but the events of Tuesday and Wednesday are combined into one long section that ends at 13:37. A new chronological reference begins with 14:1, "after two days." Jesus **was hungry.** This certainly indicates Jesus' humanity: no breakfast, and apparently not a large meal the evening before. Notice how these evidences of His full and complete humanity follow the evidences of His undiminished deity (vv. 2-10).

11:13, 14 Mark informs his readers that **it was not the season for figs.** Passover always comes in March or April, and fig season is not until May or June. However, fig trees generally produce a number of buds in March, leaves in April, and ripe fruit later on. Jesus was looking for the edible buds, the lack of which indicated that the tree would be fruitless that year.

11:15–18 By cleansing the temple, Jesus clearly claimed authority equal to God who first filled it with His glory (2 Chr. 5:13, 14).

11:15, 16 bought . . . sold: Animals considered clean for sacrifice. **money changers:** The temple had its own currency. Worshipers were required to exchange other currency for these coins when making temple gifts. This was Jesus' second time to set things straight in the temple.

Previously, near the beginning of His ministry, He performed the same duty (John 2:13-21). Being a carpenter (compare 6:3) built Jesus' strength and He had the boldness to oppose physically those who so desecrated God's house. Jesus must have been a fine picture of mature manhood.

11:17 Jesus quoted from the prophets Isaiah and Jeremiah (Is. 56:7; Jer. 7:11) to make His point about the despicable conduct of those who bought and sold in the temple. A **den of thieves** refers to the practice of cheating people, both Israelites and those of other nations, either through a crooked exchange of money or by selling inferior products.

11:18 The suspense of Mark's drama increases with the contrasting reactions to Christ. The religious leaders **sought** to **destroy Him** by plotting His death, while **the people** had just welcomed Him with a triumphal procession and **were astonished at His teaching.**

11:19, 20 Mark clearly indicates the transition from **evening** (Monday) to **the morning** (Tuesday).

11:21 Why was the **fig tree** both **cursed** and **withered?** The passage emphasizes the

---

 **Events of Holy Week**

The Gospel writers devoted much of their material to the events leading up to the crucifixion of Jesus. The final week of His earthly ministry began with the triumphal entry into Jerusalem and the "Hosannas" from the crowd that changed to cries of "Crucify Him" before the week was over. Jesus apparently spent most of the week teaching in the temple area during the day. His evenings were spent in the home of Mary, Martha, and Lazarus in Bethany. Significant events during this week included the plot of the Sanhedrin, Jesus' betrayal and arrest, the trials of Jesus, His journey to Golgotha down the Jerusalem street known today as the Via Dolorosa ("Way of Suffering"), and the Resurrection. After His resurrection, Jesus ministered another forty days before His ascension.

Day	Event	Biblical Reference
Sunday	The triumphal entry into Jerusalem	Mark 11:1–11
Monday	Cleanses the temple in Jerusalem	Mark 11:15–19
Tuesday	The Sanhedrin challenges Jesus' authority Jesus foretells the destruction of Jerusalem and His return Mary anoints Jesus at Bethany Judas bargains with the Jewish rulers to betray Jesus	Luke 20:1–8 Matt. 24; 25 John 12:2–8 Luke 22:3–6
Thursday	Jesus eats the Passover meal with His disciples and institutes the Memorial Supper Jesus prays in Gethsemane for His disciples	John 13:1–30; Mark 14:22–26 John 17
Friday	Jesus' betrayal and arrest in the Garden of Gethsemane Jesus questioned by Annas, the former high priest Jesus is condemned by Caiaphas and the Sanhedrin Peter denies Jesus three times Jesus is formally condemned by the Sanhedrin Judas commits suicide The trial of Jesus before Pilate Jesus' appearance before Herod Antipas Jesus is formally sentenced to death by Pilate Jesus is mocked and crucified between two thieves The veil of the temple is torn as Jesus dies Jesus' burial in the tomb of Joseph of Arimathea	Mark 14:43–50 John 18:12–24 Mark 14:53–65 John 18:15–27 Luke 22:66–71 Matt. 27:3–10 Luke 23:1–5 Luke 23:6–12 Luke 23:13–25 Mark 15:16–27 Matt. 27:51–56 John 19:31–42
Sunday	Jesus is raised from the dead	Luke 24:1–9

power of true faith. Some have suggested that the fig tree represented Israel, which bore no fruit and would soon face the judgment of God.

11:22, 23 The illustration of casting an enormous mountain into the sea is an extreme example of the absolutely impossible. That is the point. Having **faith in God** can accomplish the impossible. Mark had previously emphasized Jesus' insistence on simply believing (9:23, 24).

11:24 The key to prayer is to **believe.** However, other conditions are to ask for things that are "according to His will" (1 John 5:14), and to ask on the merits of Christ's name (John 15:16). That which makes believing powerful is the object of the belief—truth.

11:25, 26 To **forgive** is to release it to God, for all sin is ultimately against God and He alone has the right of vengeance (Rom. 12:19). The believer's experience of the Father's forgiveness is dependent on his or her willingness to forgive.

11:27, 28 The religious leaders (v. 27), who were now plotting Jesus' death (v. 18), asked Jesus about the (1) nature and (2) source of His authority, perhaps because He had not openly declared that He was the Messiah. **These things** refer to the authority Jesus used in cleaning out the temple (vv. 15–17).

11:29, 30 The intent of Jesus' question was to expose once again the insincerity of His detractors. The **baptism of John** refers to the authority of John's baptism. Was it **from heaven**—that is, ordained by God and worthy of obedience? Or was it merely **from men**—that is, of human contrivance and void of any spiritual authority and reality?

11:31, 32 They reasoned and debated the question and quickly discovered the answer. John's baptism was from heaven. Jesus' authority came from there as well.

11:33 We do not know was a dishonest reply, but perhaps the only one possible for men who wished only to save their reputations.

12:1 He began to speak to them in parables. Mark records only one parable here, but Matthew presents an additional one (Matt. 22:1–14). This parable represents God as carefully preparing the nation of Israel (**a vineyard**) and leaving it in the care of others (the **vinedressers;** Is. 5:1–7). Great care was taken to fence the vineyard, to prepare a **wine vat** for crushing the grapes, and to build a **tower** in order to keep watch and protect the property from thieves.

12:2–5 The **servants,** including the **many others** who were sent, represent the prophets who had gone before Jesus, perhaps culminating with John the Baptist, whose baptism Jesus had just mentioned (11:30).

12:6 Parables usually get across a significant truth, but the details are not meant to correspond exactly with particular spiritual realities. In this parable, the owner of the vineyard represents God, but God Himself was never so mistaken as to assume they would respect His Son. God is omniscient, whereas the vineyard owner in the parable is not. In addition, few owners would send a continuous stream of servants to their deaths when greater forces were available. This story illustrates the immense patience God had with Israel.

12:7–9 Jesus answered His own rhetorical question. The destruction of **the vinedressers,** the Israelites who rejected the Son of God, took place in A.D. 70 when the Romans smashed a revolt in Jerusalem and destroyed the temple. Giving **the vineyards to others** refers to the importance the Gentiles would assume in the growth of Christianity.

12:10, 11 Jesus became **the chief cornerstone** when God raised Him from the dead. His life, death, and resurrection are key to God's plan of salvation.

12:12 The chief priests, scribes, and elders **sought to lay hands on Him,** to arrest Jesus, and to carry out their plot to destroy Him (11:18). Only as the final points of the parable were made did these evil men realize that Jesus **had spoken the parable against them.** Parables gain a hearing and disguise the truth. Jesus' foes were the brunt of the story before they realized it.

12:13 The Herodians are mentioned in the NT three times, all in conjunction with the Pharisees. The Herodians wanted to kill Jesus because He threatened their authority (3:16; Matt. 22:16). Their attempt **to catch Him in His words** was their hope that Jesus would say something that could be grounds for His arrest.

12:14 You . . . care about no one was intended as a compliment. The teachers recognized that Jesus was partial to no one. The question, however, was a lose-lose proposition: a *yes* answer would alienate Jews who opposed Rome, while a *no* answer could be taken as treason against the state. The ruling emperor from A.D. 14 to 37 was Caesar Tiberius (Luke 3:1), the adopted son of Caesar Augustus (Luke 2:1). Here Mark uses a Latin word for **taxes** in order to communicate clearly to his Roman readers.

12:15 A **denarius** was worth an entire day's wages.

12:16 The **image and inscription** on the coin was **Caesar's.** His head faces to the right with the words TI CAESAR DIVI on the right and the words AUG AUGUSTUS continuing on the left side. These words mean "Tiberius Caesar, Son of the Divine Augustus." On the reverse side appear the words PONTIFEX MAXIMUS, meaning "High Priest."

12:17 The coin they showed Jesus contained the answer to their question. We pay taxes in support of the peace, protection, and services the government renders, but this does not mean we support every action taken by government. God's sovereignty overrules the emperor's authority.

12:18 The **Sadducees** were an elite group of religious leaders who denied the existence of angels, the immortality of the soul, and the Resurrection. They rejected the oral traditions and accepted only the validity of the Pentateuch, the first five books of the OT. But since resurrection is clearly taught in Job 19:26, Ps. 16:10, and Dan. 12:2, they must have spiritualized this teaching. They also seemed to place more authority in the Law of Moses than in other OT writings.

12:19–22 The custom of marrying the widow of one's brother was supported by Deut. 25:5, 6, but it was not absolutely binding (Deut. 25:7–10).

12:23 The purpose of this story was to discredit the doctrine of resurrection.

12:24 Two categories support the resurrection—**the Scriptures** and God's **power.** The Sadducees undoubtedly did know the Scriptures, but lacked spiritual insight to understand God's purposes.

12:25 **Angels** neither marry nor procreate. Luke 20:36 applies these restrictions to all angels without distinction.

12:26, 27 Jesus quotes from the Law—the Book of Exodus—to make His point. God said **I am** the God of the three patriarchs mentioned,

for several days to see if He had any imperfections (Ex. 12:5, 6).

12:29 The **Hear, O Israel** verse of Deut. 6:4 is commonly called the Shema (from a Hebrew word meaning "to hear") and is repeated by Jews the world over as expressing the essence of their faith in God.

12:30, 31 **The first commandment** summarizes the first four of the Ten Commandments. The **second** is the essence of commandments five through ten, which relate to the treatment of other people. Some interpreters have tried to find a third commandment—"love yourself." But that is not a command; rather, it is a given. We do love ourselves. That's why we run for the first-aid kit when we cut ourselves.

12:32, 33 People who professed to worship God brought **offerings and sacrifices.** But it is not professing to worship God that is important, but rather a love for God which leads to obedience and love for others. Such love makes our worship acceptable to Him.

12:34 Because of this scribe's humility and understanding of God's true purpose, he was **not far** from accepting Jesus as the Christ.

12:35 **In the temple** does not refer to the sanctuary (Gk. *naos*) itself, where only the priests were allowed to minister. The temple environs (Gk. *hieron*) included a number of porticos and courts. One was designated especially for women (and included the treasury, 12:41), another for men. Gentiles could view the temple from an outer area. Actually, even Jesus could not enter the *naos* because He was not an Aaronic priest. He only entered the

---

| IN LIFE | **Quality, Not Quantity** |

What did Jesus mean when He said that the widow had put more money into the treasury than anyone else (Mark 12:43)? Clearly, He was indicating that economic value is relative. The widow's contribution would have been nothing but spare change to the rich who preceded her. But to her, two mites represented enormous value. It was *all* that she had, her *whole* livelihood" (12:44, emphasis added). Replacing it would be difficult, if not impossible; as a poor widow, she was probably unemployable. Giving it to God meant that she could not use it to buy her next crust of bread.

But Jesus indicated that God placed moral rather than economic value on her tiny offering. Her gift showed that she was giving herself entirely to God and trusting in Him to meet her needs. Her use of money disclosed the moral and spiritual condition of her heart.

---

not "I was their God, but now they are dead." He still is their God because they are still alive. Their souls not only live after death, but their bodies will be raised anew as well.

12:28–34 The next test came almost immediately. Like the Passover lamb, Jesus was tested

hieron. Yet, when Scripture refers to us as the temple of God, it uses *naos* (1 Cor. 3:16; 6:19; Eph. 2:21).

12:36, 37 **David himself said by the Holy Spirit** is Jesus' clear affirmation of the doctrine of inspiration (2 Tim. 3:16; 2 Pet. 1:21).

Jesus' argument about the Messiah being Lord as well as Son showed that the Messiah, even though a descendant of David, would be superior to him. In fact, He would be His Lord. He was both man and God at the same time.

12:38–40 The **scribes** of Jesus' day were teachers of the law, often dependent on people's gifts for their support. Some, however, overstepped the bounds of humility, piety, and dignity by flaunting their position of respect and trust. They sought the glory that belonged to God and even took advantage of widows who helped feed and support them.

12:42 By contrast, the widow worshiped God out of deep humility and genuine devotion. Mark notes for his Roman readers that her **two mites** make a **quadrans,** a Roman monetary unit mentioned by Mark and Matthew (Matt. 5:26) only once. It was worth just a few cents.

12:43, 44 Jesus' comparison of the percentages contributed by the rich and the poor reminds us that God measures not how much we give, but how much we retain. Those with greater income have an obligation to return a larger percentage of it to God's work.

13:1–37 Jesus continued His last week of ministry in Jerusalem by teaching His apostles about future events. This speech is known as the Olivet Discourse, so named because Jesus sat on the Mount of Olives while speaking (v. 3).

13:1, 2 The disciples' excitement over the temple's tremendous **manner of stones and what buildings** are a natural reaction to splendid and majestic architecture; these stones weighed several tons each. Descriptions by Josephus (*Antiq.* 15.11.3–7) show its magnificence. There was nothing like it in all the world. Beautiful white marble stones with gold ornamentation comprised a one-hundred-foot-high structure begun by Herod the Great in 20 B.C. It was later completed by Herod's descendants before A.D. 66. This was surrounded by covered colonnaded walkways, courtyards, and stairways that filled twenty acres of the most prominent landscape in all Jerusalem. It all stood on a hill accentuated by the Tyropean and Kidron valleys. For Jesus to remark seriously that **not one stone shall be left upon another** was a startling attention getter. This prophecy was fulfilled in A.D. 70 when the Roman general Titus sacked the city. Titus's arch in Rome still stands over the Appian Way entrance to the Forum, where its murals depict Titus's conquest of Jerusalem.

> *Those with greater income have an obligation to return a larger percentage of it to God's work.*

13:3–4 Only Mark, given to detail, mentions the names of the four disciples who questioned Jesus. They want to know about (1) chronology—the time of the fulfillment and (2) circumstances—the sign of the fulfillment. A third question about Jesus' coming is recorded in Matt. 24:3. It is answered in Mark 13:24–37. Their question assumes that the temple's destruction will signal the end of the present age and the inauguration of the Messiah's reign. They wonder how near that event may be.

13:5–12 In general, the circumstances to be encountered will involve religious deception, belligerent nations, earthquakes and famines, religious betrayal, and the spread of the gospel.

13:5–7 The end is the end of the age (Matt. 24:3, 6, 13, 14).

13:8 The beginnings of sorrows is a phrase partaking of the imagery of birth pangs. Like a woman's contractions, these events will hasten the birth of the Messiah's kingdom.

13:9, 10 Four times in this discourse (vv. 5, 9, 23, 33), Jesus warns His disciples to take heed or **watch out** (Gk. *blepete*). Jesus' words have a practical application.

13:11–12 The promise that the **Holy Spirit** will guide one's speech in the hour of trial applies first to the twelve, and only secondarily to others who will experience persecution. But this promise does not assure immunity from trial or even freedom from being **put to death.**

13:13 He who endures to the end shall be saved is not referring to regeneration or justification but to physical deliverance from the tribulation (vv. 19, 20). The ones who physically endure will be delivered into Christ's (messianic) kingdom reign.

13:14–23 These verses answer the second question voiced by the disciples in v. 4 about "what will be the sign when all these things will be fulfilled?"

13:14 The chief sign for the Jewish remnant at the end of the age will be that of the **"abomination of desolation."** Daniel warned of this in Dan. 11:31 and 12:11 (compare Dan. 9:27). **Standing where it ought not** is a reference to the Antichrist's presence in the rebuilt Jewish temple of the tribulation period. There, midway through the tribulation period, he will declare himself to be God and demand the worship of all mankind (2 Thess. 2:3, 4). **Let the reader understand** points Mark's audience back to the Hebrew origins of this teaching that Jesus gave, namely the Book of Daniel. The command to **flee to the mountains** is because the supposed protector of the Jews, the Roman prince of Dan. 9:26, 27, now shows his true colors and begins to persecute the Jews of Israel.

13:15–18 To escape death, one must disregard everything but his life. No material object can safely be retrieved or carried away, and even recent motherhood and winter weather may imperil one's life.

13:19 In those days there will be tribulation. The events of Mark 13:14 will signal an unparalleled time of suffering. Matt. 24:31 calls it great (Gk. *megale*) tribulation, and Jer. 30:7 titles it the time of Jacob's trouble, emphasizing the Jewish nature of that period. This time of trouble cannot be a lengthy general period of history but must coincide with all or part of Daniel's seventieth week (Dan. 9:26, 27; 7:25; 12:7; Rev. 11:2, 3; 12:6, 14; 13:5).

13:20 He shortened the days refers to God's limiting or terminating the duration of this period of great tribulation.

13:21–23 To deceive, if possible, shows that the deception will not accomplish its purpose on **the elect.** One quality of being saved by God is that of being kept by God (compare 1 Pet. 1:3–5).

13:24, 25 But (Gk. *alla*) points to a marked distinction between the false prophets of v. 22 and the true coming of Christ in v. 26. **After that tribulation** tells when Jesus will return to set up His millennial kingdom. Great astrological disturbances will accompany Christ's glorious return. One of the four purposes for the sun, moon, and stars mentioned at the time of their creation is for signs (Gen. 1:14). These signs will be fulfilled at that time. Just imagine the universal fireworks that God will use to set the stage for the coming of His majestic Son to reign.

13:26 Jesus refers to Himself as **the Son of Man coming in the clouds.** This terminology is taken directly from Dan. 7:13, 14. In that passage, the Son of Man, who is obviously deity, receives the kingdom from God the Father. Daniel 7:27 shows the Son of Man sharing His rule with the saints (compare Rev. 2:26, 27). The tribulation martyrs are pictured as those who "lived and reigned with Christ for a thousand years" (Rev. 20:4).

13:27 It appears that the purpose for which Jesus will **send His angels** is to **gather together His elect.** This is not the Rapture. The Rapture will involve a sudden and instantaneous transformation of believers into the immediate presence and likeness of Christ (compare 1 Thess. 4:15–17; 1 Cor. 15:51, 52). The need for angel transportation for the elect at the conclusion of the tribulation period is because these believers will still occupy their natural bodies. They will continue to live in the natural state throughout the one thousand-year reign of Christ. Angels will transport them to Christ's inauguration.

13:28–29 Jesus likens the signs of the coming astrological events to the new sprouts of growth and leaves on a fig tree. Both signify something ahead, whether the return of summer or the glorious return of Christ.

13:30 Some scholars have argued that **this generation** (Gk. *genea*) refers to Jesus' contemporaries, or to a race or people, such as the Jews who are related racially. See discussion on this at Luke 21:32. A multiple fulfillment may be intended here to incorporate those who see an initial destruction of Jerusalem as well as those Jews living at the time Jesus returns who will see the final fulfillment of **all these things. Will by no means** is a double negative expressing strong certainty.

13:31 What Jesus foretells here about **heaven and earth** passing away is also in Is. 65:17, 2 Pet. 3:10, and Rev. 21:1. The new earth will have about seven times as much usable land because the oceans will be gone. Jesus' words, however, unlike this perishing planet, will never (Gk. *ou mē*, a strong double negative) **pass away.** What a comfort to have **words** we can count on.

13:32, 33 As One who was fully God and at the same time fully man, Jesus possessed all the attributes of deity, including omnipotence and omniscience. He knew what was in men's hearts (2:8) and He could still the waves (4:39). When Jesus became a man, however, He voluntarily relinquished the independent use of His attributes (compare Phil. 12:5–8). Like a father who tosses the ball ever so easily to his small boy, though he has the ability to reassert his full power, if necessary, to save the boy from running in front of a car. Of course today, glorified in heaven, Jesus now knows the **day and hour** of His return.

13:34–36 Jesus' parable of the absent master of the house is unique to Mark. The point is that He could return at any time, so all servants must be vigilant and watchful (compare Luke 19:11–27). The Romans divided the night into four watches as expressed in v. 35— the evening (6 P.M. to 9 P.M.), midnight (9 P.M. to midnight), rooster crowing (midnight to 3 A.M.), and dawn (3 A.M. to 6 A.M.).

14:1–42 In this section Mark portrays the preparations for Jesus' death. The loving anointing at Bethany (vv. 3–9) is placed between the accounts of the treachery of Judas and the chief priests and scribes (vv. 1, 2, 10, 11).

14:1, 2 After two days is the next time designation given since the mention of the events of Tuesday and Wednesday (11:12, 20). If the Crucifixion occurred on Friday, then the events of this chapter took place on Wednesday evening and Thursday. The **Passover** was celebrated on the fourteenth day of Nisan (March–April), while **the Feast of Unleavened Bread** followed on the fifteenth through the twenty-first days of Nisan. The Jewish feast of Passover commemorates the time in Egypt when the death angel passed over those homes which had applied the blood over the lintel and on the doorposts (Ex. 12:6–14). The feast of unleavened bread spoke of Israel's haste to leave Egypt so that they had no time to allow bread to rise with leaven (Ex. 12:15–20). The chief priests planned to **take** Jesus. In the Greek, this verb suggests physically grasping and laying hold of an object. They wanted to arrest Jesus, take Him away, and kill Him. They preferred to do it secretly, away from the crowd. **During the feast,** the population of Jerusalem would expand greatly as zealous Jews converged on the city in accord with the Law of Moses (Deut. 16:16). Many of Christ's admirers were present too, so the religious leaders wanted to defer the arrest and avoid conflict. Some obviously feared a Roman reprisal if a public arrest of Jesus resulted in a civic disturbance.

14:3 Simon the leper had been healed at some point in Jesus' ministry. Mark records a leper's healing in 1:40–42. **Alabaster** is a translucent stone still used to make ornamented

notes that she anointed Jesus' feet and used her hair as a towel (John 12:3).

14:4, 5 The **some who were indignant** were Jesus' disciples (Matt. 26:8), but Judas Iscariot, a thief who despised real givers, was their mouthpiece on this occasion (John 12:4–6). A single denarius represented a day's wages for a common laborer, so **three hundred denarii** was a considerable gift.

14:6, 7 Jesus' statement does not show callousness to **the poor** (Deut. 15:7–11). His compassion for those overwhelmed by sickness and poverty appears frequently in the Gospels, and He encouraged others to meet their needs (10:21). But He also wanted people to give freely and of their own volition. No one can coerce a gift from another; no one should criticize another's gift; and no one can read the heart of a giver. A giver's motive is known only to God.

14:8 Mary had tremendous spiritual insight when she anointed Jesus. She anointed His **body for burial.** She, unlike the disciples, understood that Jesus was soon to die.

14:9 The fact that this story is recorded in Matthew, Mark, and John is ample testimony to the fulfillment of this prediction of Jesus.

14:10, 11 Judas Iscariot decided to profit even further from his association with Jesus by betraying Him. The **chief priests** changed their plans when Judas came knocking at their door.

🌱 IN LIFE   **Worship, Not Waste**

What the disciples saw as waste (Mark 14:4–9) the Lord saw as worship. The woman's gift of costly oil was worth about one year's average wages, yet she poured it out, apparently sensing that her days with Jesus were drawing to a close.

This incident raises the issue of how one's material wealth enters into worship. While Jesus was still physically present and available to her, the woman did "what she could" (14:8). She took one of her most valuable possessions and gave it to Jesus in an unusual act of devotion. A waste? Not to the One she honored by it.

Today Jesus is not physically among us. Yet while we are alive, we control a certain measure of the world's resources. So we might ask: What act of worship might we give while we have opportunity? How might we honor the Lord materially?

There are no easy answers. But Jesus offered a clue when He told His disciples that just as the woman had done Him "a good work," so they could do good to the poor at any time (14:6).

---

jewelry boxes and other items of value. **Spikenard,** a precious perfume imported from India, was made from plants that grow in the high elevations of the Himalayas. This perfume is mentioned in the Song of Solomon (1:12; 4:13, 14). Mark relates that the woman **poured it on His head,** while John identifies the woman as Mary, the sister of Martha and Lazarus, and

14:12 The first day of Unleavened Bread was the fifteenth day of Nisan (Lev. 23:6). However, because the feasts of Passover and Unleavened Bread were so closely associated in the minds of many Jews, Mark clarified the precise time for his readers by adding **when they killed the Passover lamb.** The lamb was killed on the evening of the fourteenth of Nisan

(March–April). Here, Mark is speaking of the events of Thursday. The word **Passover** (Gk. *pascha*) can signify three different things. (1) In Mark 14:12, to kill the Passover means the Passover lamb, while (2) in the same text to eat the Passover (and in 14:16 to prepare the Passover) refers to the Passover meal. (3) The term may refer to the entire celebration as in Luke 2:41, the Feast of the Passover. Since the Passover meal was to be eaten in Jerusalem (Deut. 16:16, "in the place which He chooses"), the disciples asked Jesus **where** He wanted that to be.

14:13 Jesus had apparently already made arrangements for a place to eat. To divulge this location in an inconspicuous manner, Jesus **sent out two of His disciples,** Peter and John (Luke 22:8). It was unusual for **a man** to be **carrying a pitcher of water,** since this was normally a woman's task. This man may have been a servant.

14:14, 15 Although the identity of **the master of the house** is not positively known, there is reason to suspect it may have been Mark's father. The **guest room** is familiarly described as **a large upper room, furnished and prepared.** Mark himself may have been the young man of vv. 51, 52. Acts 12:12 indicates that this house was later used as a gathering place for many believers who prayed together. Tradition has it that this was also "the upper room" of Acts 1:13 where over one hundred believers met on Pentecost.

14:16 Although no mention is made of the fact here, Jesus' omniscience must have amazed Peter and John.

14:17, 18 Two memorial meals were observed **as they sat** (literally, reclined) **and ate.** First, they ate the regular Passover commemoration meal, during which time Jesus predicted His betrayal by one of the disciples. Second, after Judas had left (John 13:30), Jesus observed the Last Supper, which anticipated the imminent breaking of His body and shedding of His blood. The phrase **one of you who eats with Me will betray Me** recalls the messianic prophecy of Ps. 41:9.

14:19 In Greek **Is it I?** is actually a negative question that implies a negative answer. The phrase means "It is not I, is it?"

14:20, 21 Matthew and John both identify the culprit as Judas, even though Mark does not (Matt. 26:25; John 13:26). **Woe** shows great pain, distress, or calamity that will befall someone. Mark uses the term only here and of women who may be with child when the antichrist is revealed (13:17), which would impede a quick escape to safety. The statement that **it would have been good** for Judas **if he had never been born** points to the awful judg-

ment that awaited him. Judas was personally and morally responsible for his actions even though he acted in accordance with what had long been **written of** Christ.

14:22 Judas left the room after receiving the dipped portion of bread, prior to Jesus' act of breaking additional bread and explaining its significance (John 13:30). The Lord's Supper is a memorial for believers only and should be observed solely by those who are in right relationship with Christ—saved, baptized, and church members in good standing. The phrase **this is My body** is obviously a metaphor, meaning this bread represents the body of Jesus. It was not His actual body, for He sat whole before them. But it stood for the manner in which His body would be broken for them.

14:23 A single **cup** was passed around and **they all drank from it.** The old phrase "drink ye all of it" is not an exhortation to total consumption, but simply a command for all of the disciples to partake "of it," or from it.

14:24 Some interpret **this is My blood** metaphorically, meaning that the contents of this cup represented Jesus' blood that would be shed for our sins. Others give the statement a more literal interpretation. The sprinkling of blood was required to institute the Mosaic covenant in Ex. 29:12, 16, 20 (Heb. 9:18–22). In the same way, Jesus' blood shed on the cross initiated **the new covenant:** His blood was **shed for many.** He died on the cross in the place of many sinners from every nation. He paid the price for all of their sins. All those who believe in Him will receive eternal life.

14:25 Jesus foresees an earthly **kingdom of God.** He came announcing it (1:14, 15), promised the disciples rulership in it (Matt. 19:28), and will one day receive and administer it with the saints (Dan. 7:13, 14, 27; 2 Tim. 2:11, 12; Rev. 20:4). Jesus even said He would sit down in that kingdom to fellowship with Abraham, Isaac, and Jacob (Matt. 8:11).

14:26 The **hymn** they sang was no doubt from the Psalms. Frequently Pss. 113—118 were used in connection with the Passover, including "I shall not die, but live, / And declare the works of the LORD" and "The stone which the builders rejected / Has become the chief cornerstone" (Ps. 118:17, 22). Leaving the Upper Room, they crossed the Kidron Valley to the base of **the Mount of Olives.** Gethsemane (v. 32) is directly across from the Eastern Gate (sometimes called the Golden Gate) of Jerusalem.

14:27 Jesus knew more than just the future which He predicted in this verse in accord with Zech. 13:7. "The heart is deceitful above all things, and desperately wicked; Who can know it?" Jesus knows our hearts precisely and fully. The disciples would lose heart, run and hide, and in Peter's case even deny Jesus. The prediction was fulfilled, and the sheep were scattered.

14:28 This saying was repeated by one of the angels at the tomb shortly after Jesus' resurrection (16:7). Nevertheless, the disciples remained in Jerusalem for more than a week before eventually following their risen Shepherd into Galilee (John 20:26; 21:1). Matthew mentions the disciples meeting Jesus at a mountain in Galilee (Matt. 28:16) prior to His ascension at Bethany (Luke 24:50, 51).

14:29 Overconfidence is deadly. Peter did not heed the words of Prov. 16:18, "Pride goes before destruction / And a haughty spirit before a fall." Pride was Satan's downfall, and it can frequently be ours as well. Peter, so emphatic in his denial, soon realized the emptiness of his hasty declaration.

14:30 Only Mark mentions Christ's prediction of Peter's denial occurring **before the rooster crows twice.** The incident would have remained vivid in Peter's mind when he related the story to Mark. And only Mark records the two crowings of the rooster (14:68, 72).

14:31 Peter's intentions were good, but he could not keep them. **And they all said likewise** shows how easy it is to go along with the crowd, even in making good decisions, but so hard to keep those commitments. How patient our God is with us! And how careful we need to be in judging people by their fruit.

14:32–42 Sit here while I pray: Prayer consumed much time and energy in Jesus' earthly work. It crowned both the beginning (Luke 3:21) and ending (Luke 24:50, 51) of His public ministry. When necessary, He would take extraordinary measures to ensure privacy in order to pray (6:46; Matt. 14:22, 23; John 6:14, 15). Though the Lord Jesus did praise God (Luke 10:21) and thank the Father (8:6, 7) in His praying, most of His recorded prayers were petitions and intercessions.

14:32 Gethsemane, though famous today, is mentioned by name only twice in the Bible (here and in Matthew). John, however, informs us that Jesus and the disciples "often met there" and that it was a garden (John 18:1, 2). The admonition to **sit here** was directed to all but Peter, James, and John (14:33).

14:33 Jesus wanted His closest disciples **with Him,** to support Him with their presence and their prayers. All of us need such an inner circle. We are meant to live in relation to others, not in isolation.

14:34 Exceedingly sorrowful: The crushing realization of having to bear the sin of the world and to lose, even temporarily, the fellowship of God the Father was nearly more than Jesus' soul could bear. His extreme spiritual anguish must have affected His mental, emotional, and physical condition as well.

14:35 Jesus must have prayed for some time. Verse 37 mentions one hour. That was time enough for each of His accompanying disciples to be asleep when He returned. Mark records Jesus' petition that **the hour might pass from Him,** a reference to the time Jesus would bear the punishment for the sin of the world in His own body, becoming, as it were, sin for all. John uses the expression "the hour" or "His hour" frequently in his Gospel (John 2:4; 7:30; 8:20; 12:23, 27; 13:1; 17:1). Mark uses it only here and in v. 41.

14:36 Abba was what a little child would call his father. Jesus' relationship to His Father was close and tender. In addition to the term **hour** (v. 35), **this cup** foreshadows Christ's impending death (10:38). The cup figuratively holds the judgment of God for the sin of the world. The wicked will someday drink of "the cup of His indignation" (Rev. 14:10) and of "the winepress of the fierceness and wrath of the Almighty God" (Rev. 19:15). Jesus had a distinct human will, but he yielded His own will to that of His Father (Phil. 1:2–6).

14:37 Simon: The sleeping disciple is called by the name he had before he became a disciple (1:16). Peter was not exhibiting the characteristics of a rock at this time in his life (3:16).

14:38 Avoiding temptation demands constant vigilance, so much so that Christ included this admonition in the prayer He taught the disciples (Matt. 6:13; Luke 11:4). The dichotomy between Spirit and flesh is real. Our fallen human nature, even after conversion, wars against the work of God.

14:39–42 The three apostles were exhorted to watch and pray several times, and no doubt truly desired to uphold their Lord in His deepest hour of need. Yet physical fatigue overcame spiritual alertness. Their days were packed with activities and duties as ours are. Proper rest, sleep, and nutrition can go a long way toward spiritual living.

14:43–15:47 Mark now describes Jesus' complete rejection by His disciples, the religious leaders, and the people, and His time of separation from the Father.

14:43 Judas came with **a great multitude,** identified by John as a detachment of troops (John 18:3). It was one-tenth of a Roman legion, or roughly six hundred men. Although the size of such a detachment could vary somewhat, Mark's mention of a multitude points to a sizable crowd.

14:44 A **kiss,** usually a sign of affection, was now the signal for betrayal. **Lead Him away safely** is not an expression of concern for Jesus' safety, but rather an indication of how difficult it may have been to seize Jesus. A wonder worker like Jesus might escape unless extra precautions were taken. The fact is they never could have seized Him except that He stated, "The hour has come." We, too, serve the same sovereign God and no one can touch us until God allows it.

14:45 Mark's characteristic word, **immediately** (Gk. *euthus*), is used to describe Judas's haste to entrap Jesus.

14:46, 47 Only two of Jesus' disciples had swords that evening (Luke 22:38) and John tells us that Peter carried one of them (John 18:10, 26). Mark graciously avoids identifying Peter as being guilty of this well-meaning but pointless act. John, the eyewitness, identifies the servant as one named Malchus and says it was his right ear that was severed (John 18:10). Peter may have swung wildly, intending to cut off Malchus's head but succeeding only in wounding him. Luke the physician mentions that Jesus restored Malchus's ear.

14:48, 49 Jesus did not resist arrest but did shame His captors. The swarms of soldiers, the secluded location, the cover of night, and the **swords** and **clubs** all suggested that Jesus was some violent **robber** or revolutionary. Ironically, this same word is used to describe Barabbas (John 18:40) and the two who were crucified with Jesus (15:27). The cowardice of Jesus' captors was evident—why else would they arrest a peaceful teacher with such brute force? In the midst of such turmoil, Jesus' statement that **the Scriptures must be fulfilled** indicates great confidence and comfort because all was proceeding under God's sovereign plan. Jesus may have had in mind Zech. 13:7 ("Strike the Shepherd / And the sheep will be scattered") in view of His earlier prediction in v. 27 and the context of v. 50. Or perhaps His being "numbered with the transgressors" (Is. 53:12) was in mind, considering His response to His captors in v. 48.

14:50–52 Jesus was abandoned. The eleven disciples were gone, but **a certain young man followed Him.** Only Mark tells of this incident, and many believe that this young man was Mark himself. How else would he have known this story, and why else should he have included it? If it was Mark, and if the Last Supper was at his home that evening, he could easily have risen from bed, pulled on **a linen cloth,** and followed Jesus and the disciples. It is also likely that Judas and the mob may have first come to arrest Jesus at the house Judas left earlier in haste (John 13:30). Mark admits that rather than be captured with Jesus, he also **fled.**

14:53 The high priest at that time was Caiaphas (A.D. 18–37; John 18:13). The **chief priests** included others who had formerly been high priests, and **the elders** consisted of the heads of leading families in the community. The **scribes** were the Jewish experts and teachers of the commandments of God as well as the traditions of men (7:8, 9, 13). Together this group made up the Sanhedrin, always referred to in the Gospels and Acts as the Council (14:55; 15:1; Acts 5:27; 23:1).

14:54 Although we often criticize Peter, at least he was brave enough to come back to see what would happen to Jesus. John also returned and was admitted "with Jesus into the courtyard of the high priest" (John 18:15). Mark's note that Peter followed **at a distance** must have come from Peter himself.

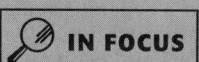

IN FOCUS   "rabbi"

(Gk. *rabbi*) (9:5: 10:51; 11:21; 14:45) Strong's #4461: In New Testament times, rabbi was not a formal office, but rather a respectful title for a teacher well versed in the Mosaic Law. The title, which derives from a Hebrew word meaning "great," is often translated "my master." *Rabboni,* an Aramaic form of this word, expresses affectionate respect. Both the disciples and teachers of the law honored Jesus with this title.

14:55, 56 The Sanhedrin was supposed to administer justice, but this council **sought testimony against Jesus to put Him to death.** The Jewish authorities had lost to Rome the right to pronounce a death sentence. Thus, they eventually had to appeal to Pilate (15:1). Because no real witnesses could testify to any grounds for Jesus' death, **false witness** was heard, but it was contradictory.

14:57–59 Finally, some tried to accuse Jesus of plotting to destroy the **temple** (John 2:19–21), but even that testimony was too inconsistent.

14:60–62 **He kept silent** in fulfillment of Is. 53:7. He remained silent before Pilate (15:3–5) and before Herod Antipas as well (Luke 23:9). Finally, when they could find nothing substantial with which to charge Him, Jesus affirmed that He was **the Christ, the Son of the Blessed.** What they specifically condemned Him to death for, however, was His declaration of being the majestic divine personage known as **the Son of Man,** described in Dan. 7:13, 14 as the One to whom the Father gives eternal dominion, glory, a kingdom, and Who receives divine worship. This was the term Jesus constantly used of Himself, rather than Messiah; but its full significance was not grasped by the Jewish leaders until Jesus explained it so graphically in the context of this verse.

14:63, 64 The trial was over, and Jesus stood falsely condemned for **blasphemy,** which in this context means laying claim to deity. Naturally, this is the boast of a liar or a lunatic—unless He is the Almighty God in human flesh, as Jesus was (John 1:1–3, 14; Phil. 2:5–8).

14:65 Those who **beat** and **struck** Jesus here were not applying the dreaded scourging, which could disembowel an individual. Compare 15:15 where the scourging itself is mentioned.

14:66–72 Some believe that Peter may have denied the Lord four distinct times. Three were around the fire, or inside the courtyard area, but John may record a separate denial that Peter made when confronted initially at the gate (John 18:16, 17). In Jesus' earlier prediction, only Mark specifically records Jesus' words that the three denials would precede a rooster's second crowing (14:30). Mark, who gives extra attention to detail, distinguishes an initial crowing in this verse with the words **and a rooster crowed.** It would seem strange, so it

only three denials, rather than six, do so because the other Gospel authors may be speaking in general terms about the rooster crowing while Mark, which reflects Peter's recollections, is more detailed in mentioning two crowings of the rooster. **Then he began to curse and swear.** Peter may have told Mark to include this report. None of Peter's actions were commendable, and his swearing illustrates the truth of Jer. 17:9, "The heart is deceitful above all things, / And desperately wicked; / Who can know it?" We are not told that Peter thought at all about Jesus' words when the **rooster crowed** the first time. If he did, maybe he tried to conceal his identity more carefully, but to no avail. Each of the other Gospel writers tells us that the rooster crowed immediately upon Peter's final denial (Matt. 26:74; Luke 22:60; John 18:27). This time **he thought about it,** and **he wept.**

15:1–47 Rejected by His disciples, condemned by the council, and denied by Peter, Jesus now faces the merciless Roman authorities and the hostile crowd.

15:1–3 Rather than murdering Jesus pri-

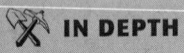 **IN DEPTH** | **"Give Us Barabbas!"**

But for a remarkable set of circumstances, Barabbas probably would have remained unknown to history. He was just another one of the *sicarii* ("dagger-men") who assassinated Roman officials in the vain hope of driving them out of Palestine. Occasionally, when political conditions were right, such men managed to gain a small following and create serious trouble. For example, in A.D. 6 Judas the Galilean led a tax revolt. But the Romans quickly executed him and scattered his followers.

In a similar way, the authorities had arrested Barabbas and others on charges of insurrection and murder (Mark 15:7; Luke 23:19). The prisoners knew well what fate awaited them—crucifixion, a grisly form of execution that the Romans reserved for political criminals. The public spectacle of nailing rebels to an upraised cross was a potent deterrent to political opposition.

But Barabbas was not to die in that manner. The arrest of Jesus, the political maneuverings of Caiaphas the high priest and of Herod and Pilate (Luke 23:6–12), and the custom of releasing a prisoner during the feast of the Passover (Mark 15:6) combined to open a way for Barabbas to go free.

What finally secured his liberty were the cries of the mob to have him released (John 18:40). Pilate found it hard to believe that they actually preferred Barabbas, and when they kept demanding that Jesus be crucified, Pilate asked, "Shall I crucify your king?" (19:15). At that point the chief priests claimed, "We have no king but Caesar!" and the governor released Barabbas. What a peculiar irony that a revolutionary against Rome should be released by the cry, "We have no king but Caesar!"

---

goes, for Mark to indicate that the rooster crowed **a second time** (v. 72), while omitting any reference to his first crowing. Others believe that there are three denials of Peter after a first crowing and three after a second rooster crowing. This is due to the difference in the accounts between Mark and the other Gospels. Those who believe that there were

vately, the Jewish politicians decided to seek Pilate's approval so they could execute the "blasphemer" legally. Their charges included **many things** but apparently centered on treason. Jesus claimed to be a king, thus defying Caesar (Luke 23:2). This crime was punishable in the Roman Empire by death.

15:4, 5 answered nothing: Throughout

His trial and crucifixion Jesus was the only one who did not act from fear, jealousy, or self-interest.

15:6–8 Pilate must have concluded that the charges against Jesus were groundless, for Mark

to the governor's official residence. *Praetorium* is a Latin word found eight times in the NT. The word is always transliterated in the NKJV, except in Phil. 1:13, where it is translated *palace guard*. The KJV sometimes translates Praetorium as

Photo by Gustav Jeeninga

This inscription from a theater in Caesarea mentions Pontius Pilate, prefect of Judea, who pronounced the death sentence against Jesus (Mark 15:15).

tells us he desired to release Jesus (v. 9). So his readers could understand the complexity of the situation, Mark parenthetically explains the local custom of releasing a prisoner during the feast as well as the facts about Barabbas. Although Matthew calls Barabbas a "notorious" prisoner, only Mark classifies him with **rebels** who **had committed murder.**

15:9–14 Pilate attempted to release Jesus, for he **knew** the charges against Jesus were insubstantial. Pilate adeptly judged the Jewish leaders' **envy** of Jesus. He mocked them subtly by referring to Jesus as **the King of the Jews.**

15:15 Pilate had Jesus **scourged:** This word, used only twice in the NT (Matt. 27:26 and here), describes a punishment more severe than flogging or beating. The prisoner was beaten with a whip fashioned of numerous strips of leather attached to a handle. To the leather strips were tied sharp pieces of bone and metal, which could rip and tear one's skin to shreds. Pilate may have hoped that the Jews would give up demands for Jesus' crucifixion after this brutal beating, but he was in no position to offend the Jews. Jesus was greatly weakened by this scourging.

15:16 The hall called Praetorium refers

judgment hall. The **whole garrison,** a Roman cohort, consisted of up to six hundred men. Those who gathered on this occasion were probably only those nearby, though still a considerable number.

15:17 The **purple** robe mocked Jesus' claim to be a king. The **crown of thorns** was no doubt a twisted, dried vine with sharp thorns more than an inch in length. Any thorn prick is extremely painful.

15:18–21 Jesus' reaction to all this misguided treatment was a calm, quiet assurance that He was in the center of His Father's will. They **led Him out to crucify Him** indicates that the place of crucifixion was outside the city itself (Heb. 13:12). All three synoptic Gospels identify Jesus' cross bearer as Simon of Cyrene, but only Mark adds that he was **the father of Alexander and Rufus.** These men may have been known to Mark's Roman audience, and it is interesting that Paul greets a Rufus in Rom. 16:13.

15:22 Golgotha is an Aramaic word meaning **Place of a Skull.** The hill may have resembled the bony features of a skull or was called this because it was a place of death. The name Calvary comes from the Latin word for skull. This place was very near the city wall (John 19:20).

15:23 This potion of **wine** (or vinegar) **mingled with myrrh** was intended to numb the pain. Jesus refused it, choosing to suffer the complete pain.

15:24 Casting lots for and dividing **His garments** fulfilled the prophecy of Ps. 22:18. In fact, Psalm 22 is the Good Shepherd psalm, picturing the One who gave His life for the sheep (John 10:11).

15:25 The third hour was 9 A.M., using a common Jewish system of marking the day. Jesus suffered on the Cross until at least 3 P.M., the ninth hour of v. 34. **And they crucified Him** was a terse summary for Mark's Roman readers, for they knew quite well the horrors of crucifixion.

15:26 The inscription placed over Jesus'

head appeared in three languages (John 19:20): Hebrew (Aramaic); Latin, the official language of government; and Greek, the common language spoken by many. If we piece together details from all four Gospels, the complete sign must have read, "This is Jesus the Nazarene, the King of the Jews." He claimed to be Messiah-King and was officially crucified on this charge.

15:27–31 Jesus was mocked and forsaken by nearly everyone—Pilate, Herod, soldiers, Jewish leaders, the crowd, even the robbers on either side (v. 32).

15:32 Jesus was called mockingly **the Christ,** or Messiah, by the chief priests and scribes. Their offer to **believe** in Christ if He would **descend . . . from the cross** was empty mockery. Jesus performed many miracles before their eyes, but they still refused to believe. True evidence alone does not turn a soul toward God.

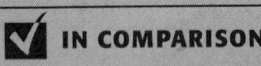 **IN COMPARISON** | **Mary Who?**

I n reading the NT, one discovers that Mary was a popular name in first-century Palestine. For example, we find:

- Mary of Nazareth, the mother of Jesus (Luke 1:26–2:52).
- Mary of Bethany, the sister of Martha and Lazarus (10:38–42; John 11). She anointed Jesus with perfume before His death (12:3).
- Mary of Magdala, a financial supporter of Jesus (Luke 8:2, 3). The Lord had cast seven demons out of her. She watched Jesus' crucifixion and was the first witness of His resurrection (Mark 15:40; 16:9).
- Mary the mother of James and Joses. She was present at Jesus' crucifixion and was probably the same woman described as the "other" Mary (Matt. 27:61; 28:1) and Mary the wife of Clopas (John 19:25).
- Mary the mother of Mark, making her a relative of Barnabas (Acts 12:12; Col. 4:10).
- Mary of Rome, known simply as a woman who worked hard for Paul and his companions (Rom. 16:6).

Why were so many Jewish women named Mary? The name is the Greek form of the Hebrew *Miriam*, which was the name of one of Israel's most famous women:

- Miriam was the sister of Moses (Num. 26:59) and one of the nation's first prophets (Ex. 15:20).
- She, her brother, and Aaron were the leadership team that God appointed to lead Israel out of Egypt and through the wilderness toward the Promised Land (Mic. 6:4).
- Miriam displayed courage early in life when she saved her baby brother from death (Ex. 2:4–7).
- Later, after Israel escaped across the Red Sea from the Egyptian army, she helped lead the people in songs of celebration and praise (15:20–21).
- However, on one occasion she spoke against Moses. As a consequence she experienced God's judgment by contracting leprosy. For seven days she was shut out of the camp, the time required before a person healed of leprosy could rejoin the community (Num. 12:1–15).
- While she was on "forced sick leave," the people remained in one place until she returned to her work of leading the people (12:15).

A sinful heart must be convicted of the need of God's salvation.

15:33 This **darkness** was a supernatural darkening of the skies.

15:34 Of the seven cries from the cross, this fourth one was the most passionate. Quoting Ps. 22:1, Jesus expressed the agony of being abandoned by His Father as He alone bore the sin of the world. Jesus' spiritual agony was intense, yet He still addressed His Father personally as **My God.**

15:35, 36 Those who mistook Jesus' words as a call for the prophet **Elijah** may have been unable to understand Him. The dehydration caused by crucifixion often made speech difficult. A sip from the **sponge full of sour wine** was supplied because Jesus said "I thirst" (John 19:28). This allowed Jesus to utter His final two sayings, "It is finished" (John 19:30) and "Father, into Your hands I commit My spirit" (Luke 23:46).

15:37 Jesus **breathed His last** after a **loud** conscious statement. Frequently, crucifixion produced a coma or unconsciousness prior to death, but Jesus was in control of all His faculties until the moment when He voluntarily gave up His life (John 10:17, 18). He willingly laid down His life for us.

15:38 The significance of the supernatural tearing of **the veil of the temple** is that access to God is now open to all. No longer through priests and the blood of bulls and goats do we approach God, but through the torn veil, which also symbolizes Jesus' broken and torn body (Heb. 10:20). **Top to bottom** reminds us that God Himself removed the barrier.

15:39 Only Mark uses (here and in vv. 44, 45) the Latin term **centurion,** a Roman captain in charge of one hundred men. The centurion's statement that Jesus **was the Son of God** can be construed as a confession of belief in Jesus' deity. But **the Son** could also be translated *a son.*

15:40, 41 These women were true disciples of Christ. They had ministered to Jesus' needs and would be the first witnesses of His resurrection. Mark does not name Jesus' mother here but includes other prominent women. Three Marys were present along with **many other women,** and **Salome,** whom only Mark mentions by name (16:1). Salome was the wife of Zebedee and the mother of the disciples James and John (Matt. 27:56). She may have been the unnamed sister of Jesus' mother (John 19:25). If so, James and John were Jesus' first cousins.

15:42 Mark explains for his Roman audience, unacquainted with Jewish customs, that the crucifixion took place on **the Preparation Day,** that is, Friday.

15:43 **Joseph of Arimathea** (a town twenty miles northwest of Jerusalem) is identified as **a prominent council** (Sanhedrin) **member.** He, according to Luke 23:51, "had not consented to their decision and deed." To ask Pilate **for the body of Jesus** was not just a gesture of kindness. It was an act of bravery, which placed

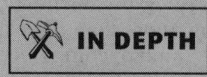

IN DEPTH

A Loving Tribute

How much should you spend on a funeral? A fortune, or only enough to pay for the barest essentials?

The four Gospel writers recorded that Jesus' body was treated as a rich man's corpse might be—which is not surprising since rich people buried Him:

- *Joseph of Arimathea* bought fine linen to wrap the body in before laying it in his own very expensive tomb (Mark 15:43–46; Matt. 27:60).
- *Nicodemus* helped with the arrangements and brought one hundred pounds of myrrh and aloes, costly substances used to perfume and wrap the body (John 19:39).
- *Women who had supported Jesus* in His ministry, including Mary Magdalene, Mary the mother of James, and Salome, prepared spices and fragrant oils to place on the body as soon as the Sabbath was over (Mark 16:1; Luke 23:56).

Those who took charge of Jesus' burial did so out of love, not guilt. And under the circumstances, they obviously were not trying to make a prideful show of their wealth. Rather they honestly expressed their grief, devotion, respect, adoration, and desire to protect the Lord's body from His enemies. They did what they could according to their desires and financial resources, and in keeping with the laws, customs, and traditions of their day.

Joseph in opposition to the Sanhedrin and identified him as a follower of Jesus.

15:44, 45 It was unusual for one to die so soon from crucifixion. Frequently bodies remained on crosses for several days. Joseph's haste to remove the body could have been based on Deut. 21:23, which instructs that persons put to death on a tree should have their corpses removed and buried the same day.

15:46 Joseph, assisted by another formerly silent disciple, Nicodemus (John 19:39), wrapped Jesus' body in **fine linen,** apparently encased with a large amount (about one hundred pounds) of a gummy, sticky resinous mixture of myrrh and aloes to retard decay and to mask the stench of a decaying body. John notes that this was the Jewish custom of burial (John 19:40). The **stone** used to cover the opening of the tomb may not have been more than three or four feet in diameter, since tomb openings were not usually as tall as doorways. In fact, John 20:5 plainly says that one had to stoop down to peer in. But since it fit into a sunken groove, it would be difficult to remove.

16:1–20 Mark's readers, who acknowledged Jesus as the Son of God, have seen Him cruelly rejected and killed. Now His resurrection fills those readers with hope and joy.

16:1, 2 The Sabbath is Saturday. The next day is **the first day of the week,** Sunday. The **spices** would conceal the stench of decay and were a symbol of the care and concern these women had for their beloved Master.

16:3, 4 The women thought about how **large** the stone was and how difficult it would be to dislodge it from the entrance. They expressed no concern over the seal on the tomb

16:7 Chosen by God as the first human witnesses to Christ's resurrection, these women were commanded to **go** and **tell.** The special mention of **Peter** signifies that Christ still accepted him, even though he had denied the Lord three times.

16:8 Initially, the women's fear caused them to say **nothing to anyone.** They recovered shortly, however, and brought word to the eleven disciples, including Peter (16:10; Matt. 28:8, 9; John 20:2).

16:9–20 This large section of twelve verses has been disputed as to authenticity. In light of this dispute it is best not to base doctrine on these verses. Those who doubt Mark's authorship of these verses point to two early manuscripts (fourth century) which do not contain these verses. Those favoring their inclusion point out that even these two manuscripts leave space for all or some of these verses, indicating that their copyists knew of their existence. The difficulty is knowing whether the space is for this longer version of Mark's ending or one of the alternate endings found in the manuscripts. Practically all other manuscripts contain vv. 9–20 and this passage is supported by such early church fathers as Justin Martyr (A.D. 155), Tatian (A.D. 170) and Irenaeus (A.D. 180). The

---

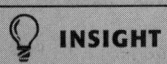 **INSIGHT**   **Different Details in the Gospels**

When you read the Gospels side by side, you'll notice some apparent discrepancies. For example, Mark reports that there were three women at the tomb of Jesus on resurrection Sunday, while Matthew speaks of only two. And Mark quotes Peter as declaring that Jesus is the Messiah, while Matthew quotes the apostle declaring Jesus is the Messiah and the Son of God.

If four members of a band wrote stories about life on the road with a famous musician, we would expect a lot of overlap, but also some variation. People see the same things differently.

The core issue is whether or not the Gospels witness truthfully in answering the question: Who is this Jesus? The Gospels are early written witnesses to Jesus: They express the testimony of those who had been with Jesus during His ministry, after His resurrection, and (after His ascension to heaven) through the outpoured Holy Spirit. Through all their differences, the Gospels agree that Jesus rose from the dead and is now "both Lord and Christ" (Acts 2:36). And they agree that how people respond to this Jesus determines whether they live or die, eternally.

---

or the presence of a Roman guard, apparently unaware of the precautions the Jews and Romans had taken (Matt. 27:62–66).

16:5, 6 Mark does not identify the **young man** who appeared **in a long white robe** as an angel, but clearly he is there to explain the mystery that confronts the women. The Greek voice of **He is risen,** which is passive, indicates that an act of God accomplished the raising up of Jesus. But the unexpected and strange scene **alarmed** the women.

internal evidence is more difficult to evaluate than the external. There is an abrupt change in subject between vv. 8, 9, and some words appear in vv. 9–20 that are not present in the rest of Mark; but the latter could be said of any section of twelve verses of Mark. It might also seem unusual for Mark's story to end with v. 8 on a note of fear.

16:9 Although the women had been commissioned to tell of Jesus' resurrection, none had actually seen Jesus until **He appeared first to**

Mary Magdalene. Only Mark and Luke (8:2) mention Jesus' exorcism of **seven demons** from Mary, which would explain her strong devotion to Him.

16:10 Only Mark mentions the disciples' mourning and weeping. They experienced personal and psychological loss with the execution of their Lord.

16:11 Jesus' resurrection was evidently not expected by anyone in spite of His repeated predictions. It had to have been the Resurrection event itself which resulted in faith, rather than an expectation of His resurrection which gave rise to stories concerning it.

16:12, 13 Jesus' appearance **in another form** (Gk. *hetera morphē*) may indicate that He is different from how He appeared to Mary (v. 9), or that He appeared differently to the two on the road than He had appeared to them before. The identity of the **two** who **walked** is not entirely stated, either here or in the longer account in Luke 24:13–35. However, one is identified as Cleopas (Luke 24:18), and it is quite possible that he was accompanied by his wife. There is no indication that the two had to be men.

16:14 After Judas's demise (Matt. 27:3–5; Acts 1:16–18), the disciples were known for a while as **the eleven.** Jesus upbraided these disciples for not believing the account of eye witnesses, but He pronounces a blessing on "those who have not seen and yet have believed" (John 20:29). Jesus' words would apply equally to Mark's original readers and present-day believers as well.

16:15 The great commission is contained here and in each of the other three Gospels

(Matt. 28:19, 20; Luke 24:47; John 20:21).

16:16 He who does not believe will be condemned. This negative statement shows that baptism is not a requirement for salvation. Otherwise the statement would read that he who does not believe and is not baptized will be condemned. However, the NT firmly teaches that baptism is to follow belief in Christ. In fact, one cannot find Christians in the NT who do not follow Christ in baptism.

16:17–18 Five **signs** (Gk. *sēmeia*) would authenticate the message Christians proclaimed. Three of these signs were displayed in the early church: (1) casting **out demons,** displaying victory over Satan (Acts 16:18); (2) speaking with **new tongues,** that is, in known languages as in Acts 2:4–11; and (3) healing **the sick,** as in Acts 28:8. But the two signs of (1) taking **up serpents** and (2) drinking **anything deadly** seem to express conditions that may be forced upon the follower of Christ, not some voluntary action he takes. There is no biblical warrant for snake handling and poison drinking today.

16:19 The final sign that Jesus was the Son of God is that **He was received up into heaven** to be seated **at the right hand** (the position of authority and power) **of God**. Mark's readers can rest assured in the complete deity of Christ and in His ability to save all who will trust in Him.

16:20 The obedience of Christ's disciples who **went out and preached everywhere** challenges us to engage in that same endeavor. We can be confident that as the **Lord** was **working with them,** He will also work with us.

The Gospel According to

Luke

SOMETIMES WE NEED TO TAKE A STEP BACK to gain perspective. It is one thing for three of Jesus' twelve disciples to write about the life of Christ; it is quite another for someone who did not know Him to write about Him. Luke never met Jesus, yet chose to follow Him. An obviously educated man who, as Col. 4:14 tells us, was a physician, Luke learned all that he could about Jesus and shared his findings with

us. Thus his Gospel provides a "step back," a unique perspective on Jesus' birth, ministry, death, and resurrection.

The Gospel of Luke is unique in several ways. It is the only Gospel that has a sequel, Acts. Both Luke and Acts include an account of the Ascension, an event that only Luke describes in detail. Second, Luke is the longest of the four Gospels. Third, Luke records a wide variety of miracles, teaching, and parables, making it the fullest portrait of Jesus' ministry. Much of the material in chs. 9–19 appears only in Luke; in all, about one-third of the Gospel of Luke is unique. Fourth, Luke is the only Gospel addressed to an individual. Luke writes for Theophilus, who was probably a Gentile believer.

For Luke, Jesus is the promised Messiah (1:31–35), the Son of God (9:35), the Servant through whom God works (4:16–18), and the Lord who is called to sit at God's right hand exerting His authority and giving the Spirit to those who believe (compare 22:69 with Acts 2:30–36). Though aspects of God's plan are fulfilled in Jesus' first coming, other parts of the plan remain to be fulfilled when Jesus returns (21:5–36; Acts 3:14–26).

Luke wrote his Gospel to reassure Theophilus that God was still at work in the Christian community founded by Jesus. Luke presents God's grace as revealed in Jesus' ministry on earth. He emphasizes that this grace is available to Gentiles, even though the promises relating to Jesus' ministry stretch back into Israel's history (1:1–4). For this reason Luke also concentrates on Jesus' relationship to the nation and leaders of Israel. The rejection of Israel does not mean the failure of God's plan. On the contrary, although they did not know it, their rejection was part of God's plan from the beginning (Acts 2:22–39). In fact, persecution of the Christian community would be the means by which the church would spread the Good News throughout the world. Jesus Himself had predicted that this would happen (24:45–48).

The first two chapters of Luke emphasize the Old Testament and its promises of a Messiah, while 3:1—4:13 demonstrate that Jesus is the Messiah who can resist the Evil One. Then, 4:14—9:50 introduce Jesus' power and teaching. In these chapters, Luke records Jesus' claims to authority and the numerous miracles that supported them. Even with these miracles as evidence, the people rejected Jesus while the disciples' faith in Him steadily grew. The growing rift between Jesus and the Jewish leadership is seen in 9:51—19:44. This breach is emphasized most in chs. 9–13, but in chs. 14–19 attention turns to Jesus' instruction of His disciples. The last section (19:45—24:53) portrays the final controversies, the trial, the death of Jesus, and the Resurrection and Ascension. The book ends with Jesus telling the disciples to wait for the coming of the Spirit. By now, they should have realized that everything that had taken place in Jesus' life was promised in the Law, the Prophets, and the Psalms (24:43–49). Jesus is the promised Messiah. Forgiveness of sin can be obtained only through Him. The disciples were witnesses to this fact; their mission was to share this Good News with all nations, not merely the Jews. Jesus gave them this task, but He also provided them with the power to carry it out (24:47). Thus it is clear that Luke's Gospel centers on God's plan to provide salvation to the world. It closes anticipating the spread of the gospel that is recorded in its sequel, the Book of Acts.

Neither Luke nor Acts has a byline, so we are left to deduce the author's identity. The author writes that he was not an eyewitness to the events surrounding Jesus but had gathered the reports of others. On the other hand, the author was present with Paul at some of the events described in Acts, events that belong to the "we sections" of Acts (Acts 16:10–17; 20:5–15; 21:1–18; 27:1—28:16). So the author must have been a lately converted Christian who knew Paul and sometimes traveled with him.

Early Christian writings, from the works of Justin Martyr to Tertullian, identify the author as Luke, an identification that was firmly in place by the third century A.D. Luke was an educated man by ancient standards. He was capable of writing in high Greek style, and Col. 4:10–14 seems to indicate that Luke was not "of the circumcision," that is, not Jewish. If so, Luke would be the only Gentile author of a New Testament book. Tradition says that after accompanying Paul on some of his missionary journeys, Luke settled in Philippi, investing his life in the ministry of the Philippian church.

Neither Luke nor Acts indicates when they were written, so this too must be deduced. The last event recorded in the Book of Acts is the first Roman imprisonment of Paul; therefore, the earliest Acts could have been written is A.D. 62. Most scholars choose between two times for the Gospel: early to late sixties, or mid-seventies to late eighties. Two factors determine the choice: the date of the other Gospels and the portrayal of the fall of Jerusalem in Luke.

Almost everyone considers Luke the second or third Gospel to be written, though they debate whether Mark or Matthew was the first. The first Gospel, whether Matthew or Mark, is usually dated in the sixties. Those who place Matthew and Mark in the sixties often date Luke after A.D. 70, to allow time for the circulation of Matthew and Mark. Another reason given for dating Luke after A.D. 70 is the claim that Luke presents Jesus' predictions of the fall of Jerusalem (19:41–44; 21:20–24) in such a way as to indicate that the city had already fallen.

Neither of these arguments is decisive. Given that the major figures of the early church had

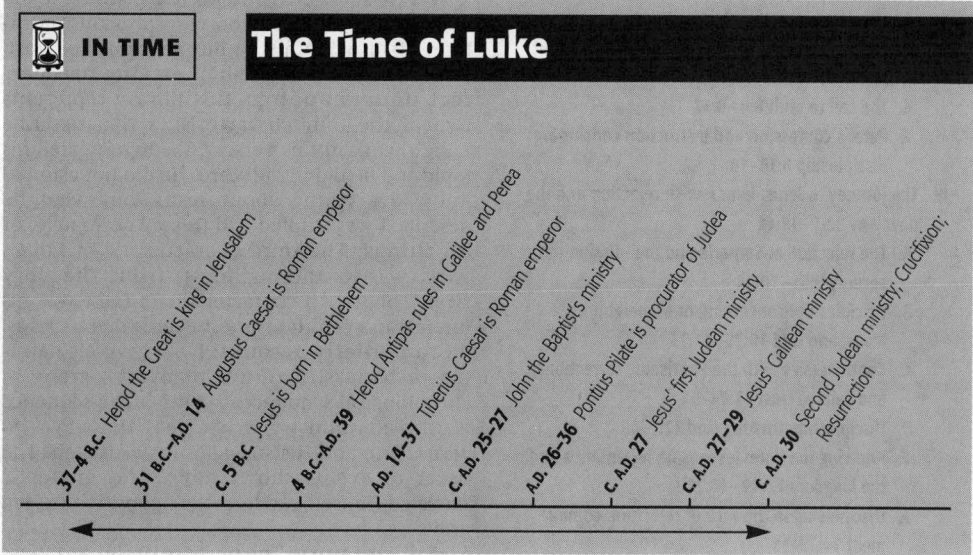

IN TIME   **The Time of Luke**

37–4 B.C. Herod the Great is king in Jerusalem

31 B.C.–A.D. 14 Augustus Caesar is Roman emperor

c. 5 B.C. Jesus is born in Bethlehem

4 B.C.–A.D. 39 Herod Antipas rules in Galilee and Perea

A.D. 14–37 Tiberius Caesar is Roman emperor

c. A.D. 25–27 John the Baptist's ministry

A.D. 26–36 Pontius Pilate is procurator of Judea

c. A.D. 27 Jesus' first Judean ministry

c. A.D. 27–29 Jesus' Galilean ministry

c. A.D. 30 Second Judean ministry; Crucifixion; Resurrection

contact with one another, there is no reason to assume that it took a decade for a major Gospel to get into circulation. The prediction of the fall of Jerusalem in Luke is unique among the Gospel accounts in focusing on the fall of the city and not merely the destruction of the temple. Thus, what Jesus describes is a judgment that is the result of covenant unfaithfulness, similar to the destruction of Jerusalem in 586 B.C. The fact that Luke includes Jesus' prediction of a second fall of the city does not mean the city had already been destroyed when the book was written. Since the sequel to Luke, the Book of Acts, does not record either Peter's death, Paul's death, or even the fall of Jerusalem (in the face of Jesus' clear prediction of it), it is most likely that Luke was written in the early to mid-sixties. A date in the later sixties is also possible.

Outline

I. Introduction to John the Baptist and Jesus 1:1–2:52
 A. Preface 1:1–4
 B. Birth and childhood of John the Baptist and Jesus 1:5–2:40
 C. Jesus' childhood wisdom 2:41–52
II. Preparation for the ministry 3:1–4:13
 A. John the Baptist, the one who goes before 3:1–20
 B. Jesus, the One who comes 3:21–4:13
III. Galilean ministry: the revelation of Jesus 4:14–9:50
 A. Overview of Jesus' ministry 4:14–44
 B. The gathering of disciples 5:1–6:16
 C. The sermon on the plain 6:17–49
 D. First movements to faith and questions about Jesus 7:1–8:3
 E. The call to faith 8:4–9:17
 F. Peter's confession and instruction concerning discipleship 9:18–50
IV. The journey to Jerusalem: Jewish rejection and the new Way 9:51–19:44
 A. The rejection at Samaria and the mission of the seventy 9:51–10:24
 B. Discipleship: concerning one's neighbors, Jesus, and God 10:25–11:13
 C. Controversies with the Pharisees, corrections, and calls to trust 11:14–54
 D. Discipleship: trusting God 12:1–48
 E. Knowing the time: lessons on repentance and the kingdom 12:49–14:24
 F. Discipleship in the face of rejection: commitment 14:25–35

 G. God's pursuit of sinners 15:1–32
 H. Generosity with money and possessions 16:1–31
 I. Lessons on false teaching, forgiveness, faith, and service 17:1–10
 J. Faith in the King and the kingdom's consummation 17:1–18:8
 K. Humility and trusting all to the Father 18:9–30
 L. Jesus' approach to Jerusalem 18:31–19:44
V. Jerusalem: the Innocent slain and raised 19:45–24:53
 A. Controversy in Jerusalem 19:45–21:4
 B. Jesus' prediction of Jerusalem's destruction 21:5–38
 C. The Last Supper and the last discourse 22:1–38
 D. Jesus' betrayal, trial, and death 22:39–23:56
 E. The Resurrection and the Ascension 24:1–53

Commentary

1:1, 2 many have taken in hand: Luke makes it clear that he was not the first to write a **narrative** of the ministry of Jesus. The theme of God's plan is introduced with the note that the subject of such narratives was the **things which have been fulfilled.** The sources for these narratives were **eyewitnesses** who **delivered** their testimony to the church. *Deliver* refers to the transmission of an authoritative account. These verses suggest that Luke was not an eyewitness to the events of Jesus' ministry, but that he had access to statements of those who were.

1:3 it seemed good to me also: Luke did not express dissatisfaction with previous narratives of Jesus' ministry, but he identified with those who went before him. **having had perfect understanding:** This phrase represents two of the four characteristics that describe Luke's work in this verse. Luke investigated his topic and he did it with care. He did not claim to know everything about Jesus, but what he described was studied and treated accurately. **of all things:** The third characteristic of Luke's work was its thoroughness. **from the very first:** The fourth characteristic of Luke was his interest in even the earliest events tied to Jesus' life. **an orderly account:** Luke gave his narrative a basic structure. Not every part is in chronological sequence, but the broad sequence is Christ's ministry in Galilee, His travel to Jerusalem, and His struggles in Jerusalem. The order of events shows how Jesus gradually revealed Himself and how the opposition to Him grew.

1:4 certainty: The purpose of this term was

to give assurance to Theophilus, possibly a young believer and someone very interested in the Christian message. It is likely that Theophilus was a Gentile, since so much of Luke and Acts is concerned with Jewish-Gentile relationships (Acts 10; 11; 15). He not only needed to know the truth and accuracy of what the church taught, but also needed to be reassured. He might well have been wondering what he as a Gentile was doing in a movement that was originally Jewish, especially when so many Israelites were rejecting the message. Can a dead Messiah really be the center of God's promise? Is the persecution of the church a sign of God's judgment on a movement that has made God's grace too generous by including Gentiles so directly without making them become Jews first? Luke wished to reassure Theophilus (and other readers of his work) that Jesus did bring the promise of God, that His ministry and especially His resurrection show that God is behind Him, and that any Gentile belongs in the movement. In addition, as Acts shows, the persecution of the church is like that which Jesus faced and has provided the opportunity for the Word of God to spread over the entire region, even as far as Rome.

1:5 In the days of Herod, the king: Luke is very exact in giving precise historical and chronological information. This is seen in these words, as well as other references to major historical persons, events and dates as in 2:1–3; 3:1, 2, 19, and 23. This Herod, known as Herod the

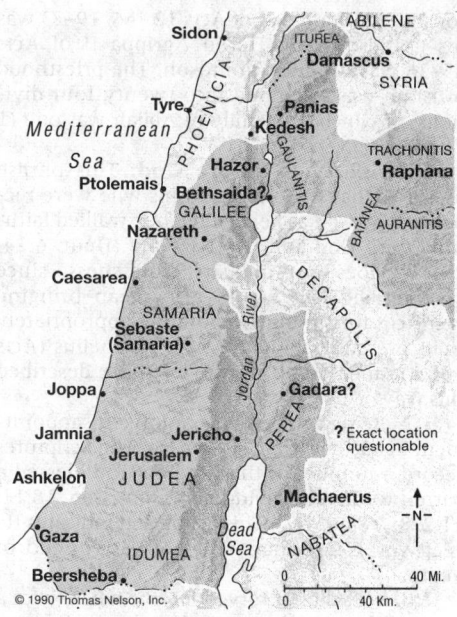

Herod's Kingdom at Jesus' Birth

Great, was a descendant of Esau (compare Gen 27:39–40). Born in 73 B.C., he was appointed King of the Jews by the Roman Senate in 40 B.C. He ruled until his death in March or April, 4 B.C. Archelaus (Matt. 2:22), Philip (Luke 3:1), and Herod Antipas (Luke 23:7–12, 15) were his

⚒ IN DEPTH Good News for Gentiles

Luke's Gospel (as well as Acts) is addressed to someone named Theophilus. Little is known about this person, though speculation abounds. Was this an individual or a group of believers? Was Theophilus, which means "lover of God," his given name or a name taken after conversion (a common practice)? The title "most excellent" (Luke 1:3) indicates prominence and a high rank in Roman society. However, the title is dropped in Acts 1:1. Did Theophilus lose his position in the intervening years?

One thing seems apparent: Luke was writing to and for a Gentile reader. In fact, a major emphasis of the account is that the gospel is not just for a select nation. Jesus offers forgiveness and salvation freely to all humanity, regardless of race, gender, or social merit. Luke shows that the Good News is for:

- Samaritans (Luke 9:52–56; 10:30–37; 17:11–19);
- Gentiles (2:32; 3:6, 8; 4:25–27; 7:9; 10:1; 24:47);
- Jews (1:32, 33, 54);
- women (1:26–56; 7:36–50; 8:1–3; 10:38–42);
- outcasts such as tax collectors, widows, lepers, and the disabled (3:12; 4:27; 5:27–32; 7:11–15, 22, 23, 37–50; 14:1–6; 15:1; 17:12; 19:2–10);
- the poor (1:53; 2:7; 6:20; 7:22); and
- the rich (19:2; 23:50).

sons. Herod Agrippa I of Acts 12:1–6, 19–23 was his grandson, and Herod Agrippa II of Acts 25–26 was his great-grandson. The priesthood of Israel was separated into twenty-four divisions, of which the family of Abijah was one (1 Chr. 24:10; Neh. 12:17).

1:6 righteous before God: This phrase indicates that the priest and his wife were recognized by God as believers. They walked faithfully with God and kept His law (Deut. 6:24, 25). It does not indicate sinlessness, since keeping the law would also mean bringing sacrifices for sin and responding appropriately to its presence. Simeon (2:25), Cornelius (Acts 10:22), and Joseph (Matt. 1:19) are described this way.

1:7 Being **barren** was a grave disappointment in ancient Israel (1 Sam. 1). The Scriptures record a number of times when God blessed a barren woman by giving her a son (Gen. 18:11; 21:2, 3; 1 Sam. 1:2). This act of God indicates He is at work, since they were both **advanced in years.**

1:8, 9 Zacharias served for one week twice a year at the temple, one of perhaps eighteen thousand priests who served in a year. Offering the incense was something a **priest** could do only once in a career. It was a great moment for Zacharias, all the more so because of the sovereign plan God had for him and his family.

1:10, 11 The hour of incense came twice a day, at 9 A.M. and 3:30 P.M. Probably the afternoon offering is in view here.

1:12 fear fell upon him: To be afraid at the presence of God or His messenger (v. 11) is common in Scripture (1:29, 65; 2:9; 5:8–10, 26; 7:16; 8:37; 9:34; Ex. 15:16; Dan. 8:16, 17; Acts 5:5, 11; 19:17).

1:13 Do not be afraid: Angels often calmed the fears of those to whom they appeared (v. 30; 2:10; Gen. 15:1; Dan. 10:12; Matt. 1:20; Acts 18:9; 27:24; Rev. 1:17). **your prayer is heard:** The angel was probably referring to the prayer for the redemption of Israel that Zacharias had recited in the holy place, or to his earlier prayers for a child. In fact, God's action starts a process that answers both requests at once. The meaning cannot be that he was praying for the child in the holy place, since v. 18 indicates he presently had no hope of having a child. **you shall call his name John:** When God names a child, greatness usually follows (Gen. 16:11; 1 Kin. 13:2; Is. 7:14).

1:14 Joy is a major theme throughout the writings of Luke (vv. 44, 47, 58; 2:10; 10:20; 13:17; 15:5–7; 19:6; 24:52; Acts 5:41).

1:15 great in the sight of the Lord: John had a great place in the plan of God, but it was inferior to Jesus' own unique role. John was a prophet, and as such he was **filled with the Holy Spirit** from before birth (Is. 49:1; Jer. 1:5). Being filled with the Spirit means being directed by Him and obedient to Him (Eph. 5:18). **wine nor strong drink:** As with Samuel and Samson, a vow was imposed on the child that indicated his special consecration to the Lord. Unlike Samson and Samuel, this vow was imposed by God, not by his mother. It is not clear whether this was a Nazirite vow, since nothing is said about refraining from cutting his hair (Num. 6:1–4; Judg. 13:5, 7).

1:16 The prophet John promised reconciliation to God for those who responded to his call to repent (3:1–14). **Turn** is a biblical term for conversion, indicating a change of orientation, a turning away from sin and towards God (1 Thess. 1:9, 10). John's mission was to prepare Israel for its Messiah.

1:17 in the spirit and power of Elijah: John was the forerunner of the Messiah. This description recalls Mal. 3:1; 4:5. John's ministry paralleled Elijah's, for both prophets called Israel to repentance (1 Kin. 17; 18). The reconciliation John brings involves both one's relationship to God (as people return to **the wisdom of the just**) and the relationship of people to one another (as fathers turn **to the children**). That John is "Elijah" does not mean that the Elijah hope is exhausted with John the Baptist. Both John and Jesus suggest the return of an Elijah-like figure at the end (Matt. 17:11, 12; John 1:21). John is like Elijah. As with many elements in God's plan, there is an initial fulfillment and a later fulfillment yet to come, which are distinct but related. Both John and Jesus may suggest the return of an Elijah-like figure in the end times (Matt. 17:11–13; John 1:21). **a people prepared:** The prepared people are those whom God has drawn to Himself for His special purposes. The closest OT parallel is 2 Sam. 7:24 (LXX), where the prepared people rejoice in the hope of Davidic promise, so the prepared people are those special people God has drawn to Himself for His special purposes. Davidic hope connections will reappear in Luke 1:31, 32.

1:18 How shall I know: Zacharias expressed his doubt and asked for a sign, a lack of faith that is addressed in vv. 64, 65. Zacharias completely ignored the divine source of the promise and the angelic messenger who delivered it. In order for the angel's words to come true, it would be necessary for God to reverse the natural processes of aging for Zacharias and to correct the malfunction of Elizabeth's womb. Did not this religious leader of Israel remember that a similar thing happened to Abraham, the father of the Jewish people? As David Gooding in his book *According to Luke* has poignantly said, "A miracle indeed; but if such a miracle is impossible, as Zechariah at first thought, all talk of redemption is idle talk, or at best a misnomer. A new body that had nothing at all to do with the old body, a new world that had nothing to do with the old world, this would certainly be a wonderful thing—but it would not be redemption. Redemption must mean turning back the decay of nature, renewing dying bodies, resurrecting dead ones, restoring fallen spirits."

1:19 One of two angels named in the Bible, **Gabriel** was often a messenger who communicated God's plan (Dan. 8:16; 9:21). Michael is the other angel whose name is given (Dan. 10:13, 21; Jude 9; Rev. 12:7).

1:20 mute: The sign is also an opportunity to reflect on lack of faith. It seems that Zacharias was not only unable to speak, but unable to hear as well (vv. 62, 63). The arrival of the child would break Zacharias's silence. The priest would be filled with joy, praising God for His faithfulness (see Zacharias's song in vv. 68–79).

1:21, 22 The **people** at the **temple** awaited the Aaronic blessing of the high priest (Num. 6:24–26). The conclusion of the offering occurred only after the priests emerged from the holy place.

blessing her even as He moved His plan for all of human history forward.

1:26–38 The announcement to Mary presents the declaration of a virginal conception of Jesus (vv. 27, 34, 35), but ties it to the OT less directly than Matt. 1:23, which actually cites Is. 7:14. Luke's account tells the story from Mary's perspective, while Matt. 1:18–25 focuses on Joseph. It parallels similar announcements in the OT (Isaac: Gen. 16:7–14; 17:15–22; 18:9–15; Gideon: Judg. 6:11–17; Samson: Judg. 13:3–23; Samuel: 1 Sam. 1:9–20). The announcement emphasizes Jesus' regal position as well as His unique origins. Luke makes it clear that Mary did not put together the theological significance of this birth, as her response in Luke 2:48 shows. Luke prefers to show how Jesus gradually revealed who He was and how people wrestled with who He was.

1:26, 27 In the sixth month means six months after John the Baptist was conceived. **Nazareth** was a little village in Galilee, a region north of Jerusalem.

1:28–31 blessed are you among women: Mary, like all other mortals, was a blessed recipient of God's grace, not a bestower of it. She had a special role, just as John the Baptist had a spe-

---

✠ IN CONTEXT   Betrothal

Betrothal (Luke 1:27) was a mutual promise or contract for a future marriage (Deut. 20:7; Jer. 2:2). Not to be entirely equated with the modern concept of engagement, betrothal followed the selection of the bride by the prospective husband. The contract was negotiated by a friend or agent representing the bridegroom and by the parents representing the bride. It was confirmed by oaths and was accompanied with presents to the bride and often to the bride's parents.

Betrothal was celebrated by a feast. In some instances, it was customary for the bridegroom to place a ring on the bride's finger as a token of love and fidelity. In Hebrew custom betrothal was actually part of the marriage process. A change of intention by one of the partners after he or she was betrothed was a serious matter, subject in some instances to a fine.

Betrothal was much more closely linked with marriage than our modern engagement. But the actual marriage took place only when the bridegroom took the bride to his home and the marriage was consummated in the sexual union.

1:23 Zacharias's **house** was located in the hill country south of Jerusalem (v. 39).

1:24 Why Elizabeth **hid herself** is not clear. The most likely suggestion is that she withdrew to give praise to God, as v. 25 suggests, and to prepare privately for the coming of her special child.

1:25 my reproach: In ancient Israel barrenness was seen as a cause for shame. The "opening of the womb" indicated God's grace (Gen. 21:6; 30:23; 1 Sam. 1; 2; Ps. 128:3). In this verse Elizabeth praises the Lord for mercifully

cial call. She was simply a **highly favored one** (v. 30).

1:32, 33 great . . . Son of the Highest: In contrast to Luke 1:15, Jesus is simply called **great** (perhaps Mic. 5:3 is alluded to here). The reference to "the Highest" is another way to refer to the majesty of God to which Jesus has a unique relationship as *Son*. His greatness and His sonship are defined by what follows. He fulfills promises made to David of an unending rule (i.e., He is Messiah). The OT introduces and develops this promise in great detail (2

Sam. 7:8–17, especially vv. 13, 16; 1 Kin. 2:24, 25; Pss. 2:1–12; 89:14, 19–29, 35–37; 110:1–7; 132:11, 12; Is. 9:6, 7; 11:1–5, 10; Jer. 23:5, 6). In Judaism this hope was very political and earthly in focus and also was expressed as the hope of unending rule or an unending line of rule (Psalms of Solomon 17 and 18, especially 17:4; 1 Enoch 49:1; 62:14; 2 Baruch 73:1). The NT does not lack this picture of an earthly focus to this rule, but portrays its most visible manifestations to the period of Jesus' return (Rev. 19 and 20). Luke does portray aspects of this rule and authority as already in evidence in Jesus' initial coming, though its most evident elements will be displayed in the future (18:39; 19:38; 22:69; Acts 2:30–36). The Davidic con-

birth is another reason the child can be called **Son of God.**

1:37 nothing will be impossible: God keeps His promises regardless of how difficult the circumstances may seem. Gabriel's statement about God should be our statement of faith: Nothing is impossible with God. The ultimate proof of the power of God is that the infinite Creator took upon Himself finiteness as a creature.

1:38 Maidservant suggests humility before the Lord and a readiness for faithful and obedient service, which should characterize every believer. Paul uses the masculine form of this word to describe himself (Rom. 1:1).

1:39–41 the babe leaped in her womb:

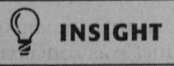

INSIGHT | A Rugged Journey

Mary's journey into the Judean hill country (1:39) was no leisurely stroll along a country road. Given the difficulties and dangers that the landscape posed, her support network—Elizabeth and family—must have been especially valuable to her.

The mountainous terrain that she traversed did have a certain rugged beauty: desert yellows, a glimpse of the Dead Sea, violet-red mountains, and perhaps a few groves of fruit trees grown on terraced slopes. One main north-south road linked the region's principal cities—Jerusalem to the north, Bethlehem, Beth-zur, and Hebron to the south.

Beyond that, the hill country was rather bleak. The eastern slopes were mostly impassable desert, stretching ten to fifteen miles from their highest point, 3,000 feet near Hebron, down to the Dead Sea, the lowest point on earth at 1,300 feet below sea level (Josh. 15:2). The vast wasteland was broken only by imposing cliffs and canyons and a few forts and oases, such as En Gedi (1 Sam. 23:29). It was an area fit for fugitives, rebels, and hermits—but certainly not for a pregnant woman.

nection is one Luke emphasizes in these early scenes (1:27, 32, 69; 2:4, 11). The hope is expressed in vv. 32, 33 in very national terms, as are most of the remarks in Luke 1 and 2. This is because the promise, as Paul puts it, was to the Jew first and then to the Greek (Rom. 1:17; 9:1–5).

1:34 How can this be: Mary did not ask for a sign, so this remark does not reflect unbelief. She accepts her role without question in v. 38, and thus is a model of faith even though she does not fully understand everything. The work of God in Mary introduces something unknown before or after: the birth into the human race of One who is both God and man.

1:35, 36 The Holy Spirit will come upon you: This is a direct declaration of Jesus' divine conception. The association of the Spirit with **power** is frequent for Luke (v. 17; 4:14; Acts 1:8; 6:8–10; 10:38). The child's conception means He is uniquely set apart, the **Holy One,** a phrase which is here not so much a title as a description of Jesus' sinless nature. The unique

Mary's coming brought a reaction from John in Elizabeth's womb. The Messiah's forerunner gave testimony to the Messiah even before he was born. The angel had predicted to Zacharias that his baby would be filled with the Holy Spirit even from the womb (v. 15).

1:42–44 why is this granted to me: Elizabeth marveled at the grace that allowed her a role in God's great plan. She knew God owed her nothing; but she also knew that God had mercifully given her much.

1:45 Mary's faith contrasts with the doubt of Zacharias. **Blessed is she who believed:** Mary's response of faith was exemplary. She was simply waiting on God to bring His promises to **fulfillment.**

1:46 Magnifies: This term provides the source for the name of this hymn, the "Magnificat," which comes from the Latin Vulgate translation. This hymn is personal in focus in vv. 46–49, while vv. 50–55 turn to the principles by which God acts. It is a declarative praise psalm, since Mary praises God with a recital of what He has done. The hymn is one of four hymns in Luke 1 and 2. Luke 1:67–79; 2:14; 2:29–32 are the others.

1:47 God my Savior: God's activity as Savior is highlighted in the hymn. Mary regards it as an honor to share in God's work. God the Father is the focus of this hymn as He is the source and executor of the plan. God's attributes are not discussed as abstractions but are related to His activities. The deliverance of the Savior is expressed in very earthly terms, so Mary has more in view here than just spiritual salvation. The variation in verb tense between this verse and the last **(magnifies/has rejoiced)** suggests the continual presence of praise.

1:48 henceforth: This phrase can also be translated "from now on." Things would never be the same again (5:10; 12:52; 22:69; Acts 18:6). **all generations will call me blessed:** Mary went from being a poor unknown Hebrew girl to the most honored woman in the history of the world.

1:49 He who is mighty: God is One who protects and fights for His children (Pss. 45:3; 89:8; Zeph. 3:17). **holy is His name:** God is unique and set apart from all other beings (Lev. 11:44, 45; Ps. 99:3; Is. 57:15).

1:50 The term **mercy** expresses the OT concept of God's loyal, gracious, faithful love (Ps. 103). **those who fear Him:** This is a key phrase in the hymn for it shows that God is not dealing with social classes and the humble without regard for their spiritual orientation. The hymn reflects covenant commitments (vv. 54, 55) as well as assuming response to God. God's mercy comes to those who look respectfully to Him. Therefore, use of the hymn to argue for political-social ends alone is not appropriate.

1:51–53 These verses portray a "reversal" in the end times, when those who have abused power will be judged and those who have suffered persecution will be exalted. The tenses, though past, look to the future since they portray the principles by which God acts and are expressed within the certainty of a past event. Mary was looking forward to the day when God's people are no longer oppressed, but are instead blessed by the Lord. God's **strength with His arm** figuratively describes His activity and power as Savior of His people (v. 47; Deut. 4:34; Pss. 89:13; 118:15).

1:54–56 His servant Israel: The idea of Israel as God's servant is found frequently in the Book of Isaiah (Is. 41:8, 9; 44:1, 2, 21; 48:20; 49:3). Israel has a special role in serving God and revealing Him. Mary sees a day when Israel will be delivered, and she can accomplish her commission. **He spoke to our fathers:** God's actions in the life of Mary were based on commitments He made centuries before (Gen.

12:1–3; 22:16–18). He will keep His promise, which is why Mary can be so confident.

1:57–59 they would have called him: It was an ancient custom to give the name of a family member to a newborn.

1:60, 61 John: The fact that Elizabeth does not follow custom shows their obedience to the Lord, who had given the name to Zacharias (v. 13).

1:62, 63 The fact that the people **made signs** to Zacharias indicates that he was deaf as well as mute (v. 20). **A writing tablet** was a wood tablet covered with wax.

1:64 Immediately: Zacharias has learned his lesson of faith as v. 63 indicates, so his sign-punishment comes to a swift end.

1:65, 66 fear: This is the normal response to the presence of God. This event brought two reactions: fear and reflective discussion.

1:67 filled with the Holy Spirit: Here the presence of the Spirit enabled Zacharias to announce God's promise. Zacharias's hymn is called the "Benedictus" from its first word in the Latin Vulgate translation. **prophesied:** Though Zacharias was a priest, the Spirit enabled him to prophesy. There are three types of prophecy in the Bible: foretelling future events, forthtelling the Word of God, and praising God. Zacharias's prophecy includes all three.

1:68 He has visited and redeemed: As also in Mary's hymn, God the Savior is the object of Zacharias's praise. The salvation referred to by Zacharias is both national (vv. 71, 74) and spiritual (vv. 75, 77, 79).

1:69, 70 The **horn** of an ox is a symbol of power (Deut. 33:17) and a picture of a warrior (1 Sam. 2:10; 2 Sam. 22:3; Pss. 75:4, 5, 10; 132:17; Ezek. 29:21). **David:** Jesus' royal ancestry is highlighted by Zacharias and tied to God's promise (v. 70).

1:71 God had promised to deliver the Israelites from their **enemies.** In Luke these enemies include both human and spiritual forces (4:16–30; 11:14–26).

1:72, 73 To perform the mercy . . . remember His holy covenant: God's actions represented His commitment to love the Israelites faithfully (v. 50) and to fulfill His promises to their ancestors (vv. 54, 73; Lev. 26:42).

1:74, 75 might serve Him: Zacharias longs to serve God in holiness and righteousness. Luke shows the priest has learned much through the events of this birth. Christ came to give us the freedom to **serve** God **without fear** of persecution by our **enemies,** and to live in **holiness** of heart before God and in **righteousness** of conduct toward others.

1:76 you will go before the face of the Lord: Though debated whether it is God the

Father or Jesus who is alluded to here, the subject of the praise and the activity is God the Father. This comment by Zacharias repeats the remarks of Luke 1:16, 17, where it is clear that God the Father is meant. Luke consistently portrays salvation and benefits as God's act mediated through Jesus (Acts 2:30–36). On the other hand, John is to prepare the way for Yahweh, a reference to being the forerunner for the Messiah.

1:77 To give knowledge of salvation: This is also John's task as prophet: to prepare the people by informing them of their need to repent (3:1–14) and of the hope that comes in the One who comes after him (3:15–18). This remark is also not about Jesus since the subject of the phrase found in v. 76 is John the Baptist. John's work was preparatory and opened the door for Jesus. Salvation came through the remission of sin, since one cannot happen without the other. John's baptism pictured this possibility, while the "greater baptism" which Jesus brought with the indwelling Spirit (3:15–18) reflects its presence.

1:78, 79 Dayspring is a reference to the coming of Messiah (Num. 24:17; Mal. 4:2). This Greek word was also used to translate the Hebrew word for "branch" or "sprout," a concept with messianic overtones (Is. 11:1–10; Jer. 23:5; 33:15; Zech. 3:8; 6:12). **To give light . . . To guide our feet:** As the Dayspring or the "Rising Sun," the Messiah will provide the light of truth and forgiveness to those blinded by the darkness of their sins. **Peace** describes a harmonious relationship with God.

1:80 the child grew: This refrain ends the story of the birth of John the Baptist. Two similar refrains greet the account of Jesus (2:39; 52). The doubling is another stylistic touch that highlights Jesus' superiority to John, as does the difference in wording between the refrains. John had to wait for thirty years for the Messiah to manifest Himself to Israel. John had not only great humility but tremendous patience.

2:1, 2 Caesar Augustus . . . Quirinius: Augustus was the emperor of Rome (31 B.C.–A.D. 14), and **Quirinius** was the administrator of a major census organized to facilitate the payment of taxes. The only known census tied to Quirinius in extra-biblical records dates to A.D. 6, but this is too late to be the one referred to here. As a result, many have regarded this note by Luke as erroneous; but it is possible that Quirinius served as governor twice in his career, since there is a gap in the governorship records between 4 B.C. and A.D. 1 in the period between Varus and Gaius Caesar. The problem is that the gap follows Herod's death, rather than preceding it, as the timing of Jesus'

birth requires (Matt. 2). It may well be that the census spanned the period from Varus to Quirinius and became associated with the name of the one who completed it sometime in the period immediately following Herod's death. In that case, Luke has historically compressed the data, as is common, and is not in error. Another possible explanation is that the term translated *first* can sometimes be translated "before" (John 15:18), in which case all Luke says is that this census preceded the governorship of Quirinius. Again, no error is present.

2:3, 4 The registration, following Jewish custom, took place at a person's ancestral home (2 Sam. 24). The journey from **Nazareth** to **Bethlehem** was about ninety miles, at least a three-day trip.

2:5 his betrothed wife: The fact that Mary made the journey with Joseph suggests that they were already married. However, the marriage had not yet been consummated (Matt. 1:24, 25).

2:6 the days were completed: There is a good historical basis as to why the traditional date of December 25, accepted by the ancient Greek and Latin churches, may be a good approximate date. The date of the birth can be fixed with some precision, since Matt. 2:19 makes it clear that Jesus was born near the time of Herod the Great. Josephus mentions that Herod's death occurred between an eclipse and Passover (*Antiq.* 18.167). The only eclipse recorded in this period was in March 4 B.C., while Passover would have been mid-April. So Jesus was born at least a few months before spring 4 B.C., either the winter of 5 B.C. or the following spring, which is why dates of Jesus' birth read 5 to 4 B.C. The fixing of the date of Christmas as December 25 dates at least from the time of Constantine (A.D. 306–337). The celebration became the church's way to celebrate Jesus' birth and have an alternative celebration to a popular pagan feast.

2:7 Swaddling cloths were strips of cloth wrapped around a baby to keep its arms and legs straight. **Firstborn Son** implies that Mary had other children (Matt. 1:25; 13:55; Mark 3:31–35). The **manger** was probably a feeding trough for animals. Jesus was probably born in a stable or in a cave that served as one. **The inn** was most likely a reception room in a private home or a space at a public shelter, not a large building with several individual rooms.

2:8 The night **watch** was kept to protect sheep from robbers and wild animals.

2:9 Glory refers to evidence of God's majestic presence, later associated with Jesus (Acts 7:55). In this scene the glory is the appearance of light in the midst of darkness.

2:10 good tidings . . . joy: The association

of these two ideas occurs only here and in Luke 1:14, but they sum up what the response to Jesus' presence should be.

2:11, 12 The city of David here refers to Bethlehem. In other passages, the phrase means Jerusalem (2 Sam. 5:7). **Savior . . . Christ . . . Lord:** These three titles together summarize the saving work of Jesus and His sovereign position. What God was called in 1:47, Savior, Jesus is called here. The word Christ means "Anointed," referring to Jesus' royal, messianic position. The word Lord was the title of a ruler. The meaning of the word is defined by Peter in Acts 2:30–36. Jesus is destined to sit and distribute salvation's benefits from God's side, ruling with the Father.

2:13 Heavenly host refers to an entourage of angels.

2:14 Glory here refers to praise given to God. **goodwill toward men:** The phrase means that people are the objects of God's goodwill. In ancient Judaism, this phrase described a limited group of people who were the objects of God's special grace. The promise of peace (1:79) and goodwill would come to those who welcome God's only Son.

2:15–20 marveled: Similar to John's birth (1:65, 66), Jesus' birth produced marvel and discussion.

2:21 eight days: According to the law, a Jewish boy was to be circumcised on the eighth day (Gen. 17:12; Lev. 12:3).

2:22–24 Her purification refers to a ceremony in which a new mother of a son was declared ceremonially clean again (Lev. 12:6).

did not have and could not afford to buy an animal. The journey **to Jerusalem** from Bethlehem was only five miles. **Present Him to the Lord** refers to the normal presentation of a firstborn son to God (Ex. 13:2, 12; Num. 18:6; 1 Sam. 1 and 2). Luke shows that Jesus' parents were faithful Jews who kept the requirements of the law.

2:25, 26 Simeon was waiting for **the Consolation of Israel,** the Comforter of Israel, a hope that parallels the hope of national deliverance expressed in the two hymns of ch. 1. This deliverance would involve the work of Messiah, as v. 26 suggests. **Holy Spirit:** Luke highlights the presence of the Spirit at the beginning of God's work in Jesus.

2:27, 28 into the temple: The location within the temple is not given, but Mary's presence suggests either the court of Gentiles or the court of women.

2:29 According to Your word: Simeon thanks God (blessed God) and first recalls the fulfillment of the promise of God (v. 26). This promise is the one that suggests Simeon is old, although his age is never given. Simeon, a picture of faith, can rest knowing God's plan will be completed, even though he will not see it come to full fruition in his lifetime.

2:30 Simeon identified God's **salvation** as being personified in Jesus. For Jesus to come was for God's salvation to come.

2:31 You have prepared: This suggests God's design and the fulfillment of a plan.

2:32 A light to bring revelation to the

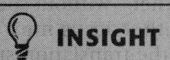 **INSIGHT**   **A Patient Believer**

There was nothing special about Simeon that qualified him to take up the Christ child in his arms and bless Him (Luke 2:28). To our knowledge he was not an ordained religious leader, and he had no credentials or special authority. He was simply a "just and devout" man who had a close walk with the Holy Spirit (2:25–27).

Thus, Simeon, whose name means "God hears," is an example of how God honors those who engage in lifetimes of quiet prayer and constant watchfulness. Simeon was a man of patient faith, yet his wait for the Messiah must have seemed interminable. He likely had many opportunities for doubt, as numerous would-be Messiahs sounded false alarms in the land.

Yet somehow he knew that the Redeemer would first come not as a great, heavenly champion wrapped in banners of nationalism, nor with a political agenda of violence, but as a Baby carried in the arms of His parents. His kingdom would prove to be a stumbling block to some and the Rock of salvation to others, both Jew and Gentile. Simeon also knew that the young couple standing before him would be hurt by the controversy that would eventually surround their Son (2:34, 35).

The ceremony took place forty days after the birth. At this ceremony, the mother could offer a lamb or two pigeons (Lev. 12:8). Jesus' family chose the pigeons (v. 24), suggesting that they

Gentiles . . . the glory of Your people Israel: This is the first explicit statement in Luke that includes both Jew and Gentile. Salvation is portrayed as light (1:79). It would be a revelation to

Gentiles because they would be able to participate in God's blessing with a fullness that had
not been revealed in the OT (Eph. 2:11–22;
3:1–7). Jesus is the glory of Israel because
through Him the nation would see the fulfillment of God's promises; the nation's special role
in God's plan would be vindicated (Is. 46:13;
60:1–3; Rom. 9:1–5; 11:11–29).

2:33–34 the fall and rising of many: This
is the first hint that Jesus' career is not all roses.
The plan is emphasized by the phrase **is destined.** The picture of the rise and fall is conceptually parallel to Is. 8:14, 15 and Is. 28:13–16,
which are used frequently in the NT to describe
the division Jesus brought in the nation (Rom.
9:33; 1 Pet. 2:6–8; Luke 20:17, 18). There is
some discussion whether one group in Israel
that rises and then falls is discussed here or
whether the reference is to a division of a nation
into two groups. The latter is more likely, given
Lucan appeal to the idea of division caused by
Jesus (6:20–26; 13:28, 29, 33–35; 16:25;
18:9–14; 19:44, 47, 48; 20:14–17, especially
12:51). The reference that Jesus will be a **sign . . .
spoken against** also adds to the note of division. In Acts, Luke shows many in the nation
responding, but most do not.

2:35 a sword: The image is of a large, broad
sword striking Mary. She will suffer much pain
in watching Jesus' rejection and in watching
Him form a new group with priorities that lead
to such rejection. The remark, as the text notes,
is a parenthesis. **thoughts . . . revealed:** This is
the recognition that Jesus is a litmus test for
where people stand before God. He is a judge
who will expose the thoughts of people (Acts
10:42, 43; 17:30–31).

2:36, 37 It is not clear whether **eighty-four
years** was Anna's age, or how long she had
been a widow. The testimony of this pious
woman complements Simeon's testimony. Both
men and women observed God's work early in
Jesus' life. Anna's work as a prophetess in the
temple court suggests that she addressed all who
would listen to her, as did Miriam (Ex. 15:20),
Deborah (Judg. 4:4), and Huldah (2 Kin. 22:14).
Philip's daughters are another example of
prophetesses in the NT (Acts 21:9).

2:38 Redemption in Jerusalem is another
way of speaking of the Consolation of Israel
(v. 25).

2:39 Galilee: The family finally returns to
what will be their home in Nazareth. Luke does
not note any of the visits or travels that Matt. 2
relates.

2:40 the Child grew: With this note, the
story of Jesus' infancy ends. The narrative picks
up in v. 41 some twelve years later. These two
verses reveal the growth of Jesus' human
nature, whereas in the divine nature He was

unchanging and infinite. Christians must balance both these natures when speaking of the
Lord Jesus. Failure to do this has resulted in
many unbiblical traditions about the boyhood of
Jesus.

2:41 The annual pilgrimage to **Jerusalem**
was customary for many who lived outside the
city. The law commanded three pilgrimages for
the men each **year:** for Passover, Pentecost, and
the Feast of Tabernacles (Ex. 23:14–17; Deut.
16:16). By the first century, most Jewish men
made annual pilgrimages to Jerusalem because
of the distance many had to travel due to the
dispersion of the Israelites across Asia Minor.

2:42 twelve years old: Jesus is now at the
age when intensive instruction for Him begins
in preparation for His reaching the age of
responsibility at thirteen, when a boy was
accepted into the religious community as a man
responsible to keep the law.

2:43–45 Entire families, including extended
families, frequently traveled together. This
would account for the parents of Jesus not
noting His absence until the evening encampment.

2:46–48 The teachers were Jewish rabbis.
Note that Jesus was not lecturing, but engaging
the rabbis in theological discussion (v. 47).

2:49 I must: Even at twelve, Jesus knew
that God had commissioned Him to accomplish
certain tasks on this earth (4:43; 9:22; 13:33;
17:25; 19:5; 22:37; 24:7, 44). **about My
Father's business:** This is the first indication in
Luke's Gospel that Jesus knew He had a unique
mission and a unique relationship to the Father.
The Greek text is elliptical here and reads, "I
must be in the . . . of my Father," without specifying a place or activity. Either Jesus must be
about the work of God, as the translation suggests; or he must be in the house of God, discussing God's truth. In the end the two
possibilities are not very different.

2:50–52 did not understand: Despite all
of the revelation to which Jesus' parents were
subject, they still were trying to understand
aspects of Jesus' mission. The disciples will have
similar troubles (9:45; 10:21–24; 18:34). The
realization of who Jesus is sometimes takes
time, since His person and mission are unique
and break new ground (Matt. 16:21–23; John
18:10, 11).

3:1 Tiberius Caesar began to rule after his
stepfather Augustus died in A.D. 14. **Judea** was
a senatorial province, ruled by a **governor** or
procurator. **Pontius Pilate** held this position
and was responsible for administering the
region and collecting taxes for Rome. **Herod** is
Herod Antipas, who ruled Galilee and Perea
from 4 B.C. to A.D. 39. Herod's brother Archelaus
had control of Judea and Samaria until A.D. 6,

when he was banished. Herod's other brother **Philip** ruled the northern area east of the Jordan River.

3:2 Annas the high priest (A.D. 7–14) was succeeded in office by **Caiaphas,** his son-in-law, around A.D. 18. Caiaphas served with brief breaks from then until A.D. 37. In addition to Caiaphas, all of Annas's five sons served as high priest at one point or another. It is clear that Annas retained the influence as well as the title of his former office. The various rulers that Luke lists show the complexity of the historical and political situation in Israel during Jesus' day. A first-century Israelite had to deal with the edicts of the Roman emperor, the regulations of the governor over Israel, and the judgments of the religious leaders of Israel. The date of these events about John the Baptist, given the date of A.D. 33 for the crucifixion and a date based on the arrival of Tiberius to total power, is A.D. 29 (23:12). **John:** The Baptist is also attested to in extrabiblical material (Josephus, *Antiq.* 18.116–119).

3:3 Baptism figuratively means "to be identified with," as an unbleached cloth is identified with the color in a vat of dye when it is dipped. As John the Baptist preached and the people identified with his message, they were baptized as an outward sign of their inward **repentance** or "change of mind."

3:4–6 Prepare the way: This citation from Is. 40:3–5 declares the coming of God's deliverance. Luke cites the text more fully than Matthew or Mark. He carries the passage through to its mention of **salvation** being seen by **all flesh** (v. 6), thus highlighting that the gospel is for all people. The preparation for the arrival of a king typically meant that a road was prepared for his journey. This is what Isaiah compares to the arrival of God's salvation, both after the Babylonian captivity and in God's final work of salvation. Isaiah 40 introduces the entirety of Is. 40—66, which discusses both these events (Is. 49:8–11; 52:11, 12; 62:6–10, especially 57:14–17). One event pictures, to a lesser degree, the other greater event, since God works in patterns. The Gospel writers compare John to the one who announces that the time is right to get ready for such an arrival. The preparation alluded to here is spiritual, the readiness of the heart, as his preaching shows.

3:7 As the **multitudes** flocked to hear John the Baptist, many people went through the outward motions of baptism, but their actions did not truly represent their inward attitude. These people were not genuinely interested in the kind of King and kingdom that John was presenting.

3:8, 9 John the Baptist warned that the fruits of repentance are necessary, not the claim of an ancestral connection to **Abraham.** External genealogical connections would not change one's attitude to God.

3:10–14 What shall we do: A genuine change of mind resulted in a change of action for the **people,** the **tax collectors,** and the **soldiers.** The repentant were instructed to give to those in need, to work at their jobs with

Photo by Howard Vos

Bust of Tiberius, emperor of the Roman Empire at the time when Jesus began His public ministry in Palestine (Luke 3:1)

integrity, to refrain from abusing their power, and to be content with earning a basic wage.

3:11 two tunics: One was an undergarment, and the other was an outer garment. A person did not need two when another person had none.

3:12–14 Tax collectors were Jewish agents employed by those who had purchased the right to collect taxes for the Roman state. Tax collectors often added interest to cover their own expenses and to pad their income. They were disliked both for their business practices and for their support of the occupying state.

3:15–17 One mightier than I: This is the first direct mention of Jesus by John. John's baptism was minor compared to what was coming from Jesus, who would bring **the Holy**

Spirit and fire (Matt. 3:11). These two facets of Christ's work relate to His first and second comings. Baptism in the Holy Spirit is referred to seven times in the NT—four times in the Gospels (Matt. 3:11; Mark 1:8; John 1:33), twice in Acts (Acts 1:5; 11:16), and once in the Epistles (1 Cor. 12:13). As a result of Christ's work at His first coming, believers are placed into one family (1 Cor. 12:13) and commended to the care of the Holy Spirit. When Christ comes a second time, He will come with the fire of judgment. Notice that in the Gospels, the two of the four parallel passages that refer to the hypocrisy also mention the fire of judgment. Chaff refers to useless shells of grain that were separated from the useful wheat by the winnowing fan, a wooden forklike shovel that lifted the grain in the air so that the wind could separate it. The chaff was burned, picturing those who will undergo judgment. The unquenchable fire indicates the thorough nature of the judgment.

3:18–20 he shut John up in prison: This event is related earlier in Luke than in Matthew (14:3–5) and Mark (6:17–20) and is clearly moved up in chronology, since John cannot baptize Jesus in vv. 21, 22 if John is in jail! Herod had first married the daughter of Aretas IV of Arabia but then divorced her to marry his own niece Herodias, who already had been his brother Philip's wife. Not only was the divorce problematic, but marrying such a close relative was a problem (Lev. 18:16; 20:21). Only Luke notes that this was but one issue John raised. John lost his head for this. His ministry was not very successful with the powerful, but it was faithful to God. Josephus also notes this event (Antiq. 18.116–119).

3:21, 22 a voice came from heaven: This is one of two heavenly endorsements of Jesus' ministry. The other is found in 9:35. You are My beloved Son; in You I am well pleased:

This statement combines two ideas. The idea of God's Son comes from Ps. 2:7, a psalm about God's chosen King. The idea of God's pleasure comes from the image of the Servant in Is. 42:1. This image depicts Jesus' election by God, and the special favor He enjoyed. The fact that Jesus is both King and Servant is fundamental to Jesus' identity.

3:23–38 as was supposed: People naturally assumed that Jesus was the physical son of both Joseph and Mary. Luke corrected this misunderstanding by emphasizing that Jesus was only apparently Joseph's physical son. Luke's genealogy is unlike Matthew's, although both go back to David and Abraham. Luke traces Jesus' line all the way back to Adam, showing Jesus' significance for all people. Matthew provides the legal lineage from David through Joseph to Jesus, while Luke provides the physical lineage from David through Mary to Jesus.

4:1, 2 The order of the temptations differs between Matthew and Luke. Luke has the temptation about Jerusalem last, probably because Jerusalem is the place Jesus is headed for His decisive confrontation with Satan (13:32–35). In His temptation Jesus demonstrated not only His ability to resist the devil, but also His allegiance to God. What Adam could not do, Jesus did. Where Israel had failed in the wilderness, Jesus succeeded.

4:3 If You are the Son of God: This is a conditional statement. In other words, Satan was saying: "Let's assume for the sake of argument that You are the Son of God." In fact, Satan was challenging Jesus' identity and authority.

4:4 It is written: Jesus responded to Satan's temptation by quoting Deut. 8:3. Jesus refused to operate independently of God. The Spirit had led Him into the wilderness to prepare Him for His ministry, so eating at Satan's

IN COMPARISON | From Defeat to Victory:
Adam and Jesus Confront Temptation

1 John 2:16	First Adam Genesis 3:6	Second Adam—Christ Luke 4:1–13
"the lust of the flesh"	"the tree was good for food"	"command this stone to become bread"
"the lust of the eyes"	"it was pleasant to the eyes"	"the devil . . . showed Him all the kingdoms"
"the pride of life"	"a tree desirable to make one wise"	"throw Yourself down from here"

instruction would have shown a lack of dependence on the Father.

4:5 all the kingdoms of the world: This temptation was an attempt to offer Jesus power by the wrong means. Satan's method involved a detour around the Cross, an inducement to "take the easy way" to power.

4:6, 7 this has been delivered to me: Satan's claim here is exaggerated. He has great authority over the earth (John 12:31; 14:30; 16:11; 2 Cor. 4:4; Eph. 2:2), but not the authority to deliver kingdoms.

4:8 Get behind Me, Satan: Later, Jesus makes the same statement to Peter when he becomes a channel for Satan's message (Matt. 16:23). In response to Satan's second temptation, Jesus cited Deut. 6:13. Jesus knew that only God is worthy of **worship,** that only God is to be served.

4:9 The pinnacle of the temple may refer either to the high temple gate or to the southeast corner of the temple that loomed over a cliff some 450 feet high, which Josephus described as making one dizzy (*Antiq.* 15.411–412).

4:10, 11 He shall give His angels charge over you: Satan cited Ps. 91:11, 12, reminding Jesus of God's promise of protection. However, the mere use of biblical words does not always reveal God's will, particularly if they are placed in the wrong context.

4:12 You shall not tempt the Lord: In response to Satan's third temptation, Jesus cited Deut. 6:16. God is to be trusted, not tested. The Deuteronomy passage refers to Israel's attempt to test God at Meribah (Ex. 17:1–7). Jesus would not repeat the nation's error of unfaithfulness to God.

4:13 until an opportune time: This was but the first of several encounters Jesus had with Satan and his forces (11:14–23).

4:14–17 Most **synagogue** services had a reading from the Law and one from the Prophets, with an exposition that tied the texts together. Jesus expounded from Is. 61. The scroll was kept in the synagogue and handed to Jesus by an attendant.

4:18, 19 By citing Is. 61, Jesus was claiming to be a royal figure and to have a prophetic mission (v. 24). Jesus healed **the brokenhearted,** referring to those who were discouraged because of their plight in life. Jesus proclaimed **liberty to the captives.** In the OT captivity refers to Israel's exile (1:68–74); here captivity refers to sin (1:77; 7:47; 24:47; Acts 2:38; 5:31; 10:43; 13:38; 26:18). Jesus gave **sight to the blind,** a reference to His miraculous works (7:22), though not without spiritual overtones (1:78, 79; 10:23, 24; 18:41–43). Jesus **set at liberty** the **oppressed.** This was originally the call of Israel, but the nation had failed in its assign-

ment (Is. 58:6). What Israel had failed to do, Jesus does. The image here addresses both physical and spiritual realities. Jesus proclaimed **the acceptable year of the Lord,** an allusion to Jubilee. This was every fiftieth year, in which all debt was forgiven, slaves were given their freedom, and ancestral lands were given back to its original family. The Year of Jubilee allowed for a new start (Lev. 25:10). Jesus offers a total cancellation of spiritual debt and a new beginning to those who respond to His message.

4:20 Jesus **closed the book** in the middle of the sentence (Is. 61:2). He did not continue because the next phrase—"the day of vengeance of our God"—was not being fulfilled then. This is a classic example of telescoping events that have significant time periods between them.

4:21 Jesus proclaimed the fulfillment of God's plan and promise in Himself, since He is the figure described in the passage. Luke often notes the presence of fulfillment by including a reference to **today** (2:11; 5:26; 12:28; 13:32, 33; 19:5, 9; 22:34, 61; 23:43).

4:22 marveled: They are amazed at the power of Jesus' words and the nature of His message. **Is this not?** Doubt remains, since a humble carpenter's son surely cannot be such a central figure in God's plan.

4:23 Physician, heal yourself: The request for more signs was for Jesus to prove His claim by repeating the type of miraculous work He had done in Capernaum (Mark 1:21–27). Such requests for signs often contained a mocking tone (11:16; 22:64; 23:8, 35–37).

4:24 Jesus made it clear that He is God's messenger who declares God's ways. However, Jesus also knew that a **prophet** is often rejected. This is a lesson of the OT to which Jesus and other NT authors allude (11:47–51; Acts 7:51–53).

4:25–27 Jesus speaks of a period of widespread unfaithfulness to God (1 Kin. 17; 18; 2 Kin. 5:1–14). During this period, judgment came on the nation in the form of **famine.** The only people to receive healing were Gentiles. With such an allusion, Jesus warned His listeners not to be unfaithful like their ancestors by rejecting His message.

4:28–30 filled with wrath: The crowd, which knew its OT history, got the point of Jesus' accusation. They wanted **to throw him down.** This is the first hint of rejection in Luke, but it is not time for the full rejection of Jesus. Thus, He is supernaturally delivered by **passing through** the violent crowd that had taken Him to the cliff.

4:31, 32 Luke emphasizes Jesus' **teaching** (v. 15). The perception of Jesus' **authority** probably arose as a result of His discussing issues directly, rather than merely noting tradition.

4:33, 34 Let us alone: The demon knew that Jesus possessed divine authority, and he wanted nothing to do with Him. **the Holy One of God:** Even a demon witnessed to Jesus' divinity. In the OT the title Holy One referred to a person with a special call from God (see "holy man" in 2 Kin. 4:9 and "saint" in Ps. 106:16). Luke records the demon's use of this title as proof that Jesus is the promised Messiah (v. 41; 1:31–35).

4:35–37 rebuked: This term in Aramaic was a technical term for calling evil into submission. Jesus' authority over evil forces is clear. He possessed the **authority and power** to grant salvation, as well as to confront all opponents to it. **Be quiet:** Jesus, not Satan and his demons, controlled who would testify to His messianic identity. Why Jesus silenced such a confession is not clear. Possibilities include the following: (1) A messianic confession might label Him as a political revolutionary, something He was not. (2) Jesus might have preferred that His works testify to His messianic identity (7:18–23). (3) The Israelites might have thought it was not appropriate for a messiah to be announced until messianic works were achieved. Others regarded as messiahs by the Jews in this period, such as the Teacher of Righteousness at Qumran and Simeon ben Kosebah, were also hesitant to make direct messianic claims. (4) Jesus might not have welcomed a testimony from a demon. (5) It might

not have been God's time for Jesus to reveal His messianic identity.

4:38, 39 The fact that Simon's mother-in-law served her guests **immediately** indicates that her recovery from **fever** was instantaneous. Miraculous healing in the Bible was always immediate (5:13).

4:40, 41 You are the Christ, the Son of God: This confession, unique to the Gospel of Luke, shows the close connection Luke makes between Jesus' sonship and messiahship.

4:42, 43 The **kingdom** is referred to thirty times in Luke and six times in Acts. Jesus announced the rule of God through His person, in dealing with sin (24:47), in distributing the Spirit as He mediates blessing from God's side (24:49), and in reigning with His followers according to the OT promise (Ps. 2:7–12; Acts 3:18–22).

4:44 Galilee: This probably refers to the whole of Palestine in this context (23:5; Acts 10:37; 11:1, 29; 26:20).

5:1 The Lake of Gennesaret is also known as the Sea of Galilee and the Sea of Tiberias.

5:2, 3 washing their nets: They were cleaning their nets from the evening's labor (v. 5).

5:4 let down your nets: This was a "parabolic action." Jesus commanded Simon to place his nets in the water in order to depict a spiritual reality. Jesus, in v. 10, explained the spiritual

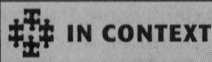 **IN CONTEXT** # Life on the Water

Fishing on the Sea of Galilee was big business. This now-famous body of water, eight miles wide and thirteen miles long, lay beside a fertile plain renowned for its agriculture. In Jesus' day, nine cities crowded its shorelines, each with no less than 15,000 citizens, possibly making the region's total population greater than Jerusalem's.

The names of the Galilean towns reflect the importance of fishing to the life and economy of the area. For example, at Tarichaea, "the place of salt fish," workers packed fish for shipment to Jerusalem and export to Rome. Bethsaida—from which at least four fishermen left their nets to follow Jesus (Matt. 4:18–22; John 1:44)—means "fish town"; most of the town was employed in the fishing industry.

Shoals just offshore were a fisherman's paradise. In Jesus' day, hundreds of fishing boats trawled the lake. Galileans ate little meat besides fish. It came highly salted, as there was no other way of preserving the "catch of the day."

Two kinds of nets were used—the sagene and the amphiblestron. The sagene (Matt. 13:47) was larger. Fitted with both weighted and buoyant material, it was used for trawling. In water, it stood almost upright and bagged fish as it was dragged behind a boat. The smaller amphiblestron was shaped like an umbrella and was used for casting off the side of a boat (Mark 1:16).

The fisherman's day did not end with a return to shore. Mending and washing nets, preserving fish, maintaining boats and supplies, training and supervising crews, and negotiating with merchants and others in the shipping industry made for long, tiring hours.

truth: Simon's new occupation would be fishing for people who would do the will of Jesus.

5:5, 6 at Your word I will let down the net: This is Peter's statement of faith. The fisherman noted that he and his companions had just failed to make a catch at the best time for fishing, the evening. The circumstances were not good for a catch at the time of Jesus' command, but Peter chose to obey His word and let down his nets anyway.

5:7 they began to sink: The success was overwhelming—two boats so full they were sinking.

5:8, 9 Peter's confession indicates that he recognized God's work through Jesus. Peter, as a **sinful man,** was not worthy to be in Jesus' presence, because Jesus was holy.

5:10 Do not be afraid: Jesus does not drive away the sinner who recognizes his or her wretched condition. He accepts the confessing sinner and offers that person the opportunity of reconciliation with God. Then He sends the forgiven sinner out to do the work of God. **catch men:** Peter's commission was to rescue men from the danger of sin.

5:11 forsook all and followed Him: Following Jesus became the main priority in the disciples' lives. Such priority is the essence of discipleship.

5:12 The term **leprosy** was used broadly in the ancient world. It included psoriasis, lupus, and ringworm. Lepers were isolated from the rest of society (Lev. 13:45, 46), but could be restored to the community when they recovered (Lev. 14). Leprosy is no longer a threat today but a similar equivalent in our culture to such ostracism may be AIDS.

5:13 The disease responded **immediately** to the Creator's touch (4:39). Jesus honored the leper's humble request for health because he recognized Jesus' power and authority.

5:14 show yourself to the priest: Jesus commanded that the regulation of Lev. 14 be followed. In silencing the healed leper, Jesus sought to avoid drawing excessive attention to His healing ministry. He wanted people to seek Him for spiritual healing, not merely physical healing. The leper's **testimony** was to God's faithfulness and His exercise of power through Jesus (7:22).

5:15, 16 to hear, and to be healed: Now it is teaching and healing that draw the crowds (Contrast 4:14, 15, but see 4:40).

5:17–19 The religious leadership of Israel began to watch Jesus closely. The **Pharisees** were a group of about six thousand pious, influential teachers in the synagogues. They were a group who meticulously followed the law, adhering to the traditional rules that kept a person from inadvertently breaking it. The

teachers of the law were officials trained in the Law of Moses. Also known as scribes, these men were in effect the religious lawyers of the

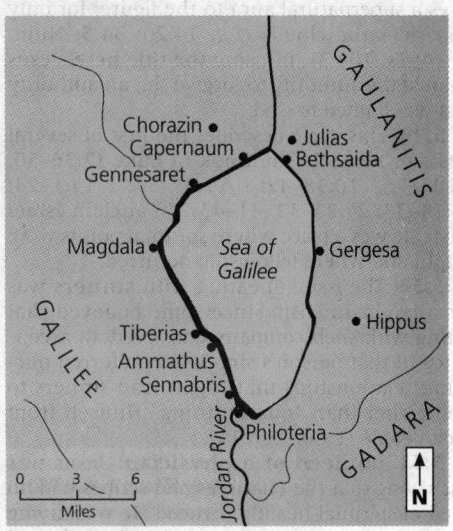

The Sea of Galilee

Pharisees. In the Judaism in the first century there was a wide range of factions, including the Sadducees and the Essenes. The Pharisees, despite their relatively low numbers, were very influential.

5:20 Luke directly links **faith** and forgiveness here. According to the OT, only God was able to forgive sin (Ps. 103:12). Rather than announcing that God would forgive the man's sin, Jesus proclaimed that the man's sins were **forgiven.** This act was blasphemous to the ears of Jesus' theologically sensitive audience.

5:21 blasphemies: The charge of **the scribes and the Pharisees** was that Jesus' claim dishonored God. This was a serious charge; the conviction of blasphemy would eventually lead to Jesus' death (22:70, 71).

5:22 perceived their thoughts: The reference here is to prophetic insight, since the leaders' thoughts had not been spoken. Jesus "knew what was in man" (John 2:25).

5:23 Jesus posed a riddle to His audience. From an external point of view, it would seem **easier** to declare sins forgiven than to actually heal a person. In reality, however, one has to possess more authority to forgive sin. Jesus linked the healing to what it represented, the forgiveness of sin. Jesus forgave the man's sins and healed him at the same time.

5:24–28 Son of Man is an Aramaic idiom that refers to a human being, meaning "someone" or "I." Jesus used this idiom as a title, taken from Dan. 7:13, 14 (21:27; 22:69; Mark 14:62). In the Book of Daniel, the phrase Son of Man describes a figure who shares authority with the Ancient of Days. Association with the clouds gives a supernatural aura to the figure, for only God rides the clouds (Ex. 14:20; 34:5; Num. 10:34; Ps. 104:3). In using the title here, Jesus claimed the authority to forgive sin, an authority that was limited to God.

5:29 This verse describes the first of several feasts or meals in the Book of Luke (7:36–50; 9:10–17; 10:38–42; 11:37–54; 14:1–24; 22:14–38; 24:28–32, 41–43). In ancient Israel the table was a place where spiritual points were taught and where fellowship occurred.

5:30 The issue of eating with **sinners** was sensitive in Judaism since some believed that eating with such company conveyed an acceptance of that person's sin. Jesus preferred pursuing relationships that might lead sinners to God rather than "quarantining" Himself from such people (1 Cor. 5:9–13).

5:31 no need of a physician: Jesus was not saying that the Pharisees and scribes had no need of spiritual healing. Instead He was saying that only those who know their spiritual need can be treated. As self-righteous people, the Pharisees would not come for aid, and in their own eyes, did not need a doctor.

5:32 Jesus' mission was to call sinners to **repentance.** Upon His ascension, Jesus commissioned His disciples to the same task (24:47; see also 3:3, 8; 13:1–5; 15:7–10; 16:30; 17:3, 4; Acts 26:20). In this passage repentance is pictured as a patient who recognizes that illness is present and that only Jesus, the Great Physician, can treat it. A humble approach to God for spiritual healing is the essence of repentance.

5:33 fast: The Pharisees fasted twice a week, on Mondays and Thursdays (18:12), as well as on the Day of Atonement (Lev. 16:29). They also fasted as an act of penitence (Is. 58:1–9) and to recall four times a year the destruction of Jerusalem (Zech. 7:3, 5; 8:19). The goal of fasting was to dedicate oneself to prayer and to focus on God. John led an ascetic life, which his followers also imitated (7:24–28; Matt. 11:1–19).

5:34 bridegroom: Jesus compared His presence to the joyous time of a wedding. In the OT this image was used for God's relationship to His people or to describe the messianic period (Is. 54:5, 6; 62:4, 5; Jer. 2:2; Ezek. 16; Hos. 2:14–23). Jesus explained that while He was on earth, the time was not right for fasts.

5:35 The image of the removal of the bridegroom is the first hint in Jesus' ministry of His approaching death (see 2:35 for the first allusion). The church will (and did) **fast** (Acts 13:1, 2; 14:23). Though such fasting returned, it was not required or regulated to the same degree as in Judaism.

5:36–38 the new makes a tear: Jesus pointed out that one cannot mix old things (Judaism) with new things (the new way He brings). The attempt to mix the two is compared to repairing clothes. The original cloth has already shrunk and when the new cloth shrinks a rip occurs. In addition, the two pieces do not match. Jesus' teaching here indicates the discontinuity between the old way and the new.

5:39 Jesus pointed out that someone who likes **old wine** will not even try **new wine,** since such a person is satisfied with the old. This analogy explained why some people in Israel had trouble turning to Jesus.

6:1 plucked . . . ate . . . rubbing: According to Jewish tradition, the disciples were reaping, threshing, and preparing food, and so were violating the commandment not to work on the Sabbath. It is clear that at this point the Pharisees were watching Jesus carefully (v. 7).

6:2 what is not lawful: The Pharisees wanted to know why the disciples had violated the traditions surrounding the Law of Moses (14:3; Matt. 12:12; 19:3; 22:17; 27:6; Mark 3:4; 12:14).

6:3, 4 In responding to the Pharisees' charges against His disciples, Jesus appealed to 1 Sam. 21:1–7; 22:9, 10. **David** and his men ate the **showbread** that only the priests could eat. This was **not lawful,** but God did not punish David for it. Such bread was taken from the twelve loaves placed on a table in the holy place and changed once a week (Ex. 25:30; 39:36; 40:22, 23; Lev. 24:5–9). Jesus pointed out that if David and his men could violate the law to satisfy their hunger, His disciples could do the same. Jesus may have been attempting to show that the law was never intended to be applied so absolutely that it would take precedence over the necessities of daily life (Mark 2:27).

6:5 Regardless of the laws and customs that the Pharisees cited (v. 2), Jesus has authority over the **Sabbath.** Jesus' claim of divine authority here is similar to His claim of authority to forgive sins in 5:21, 24.

6:6–8 knew their thoughts: Jesus functions like a prophet and whenever this phrase appears, one can expect Jesus either to act or correct improper thinking (5:22; 9:47; 11:17; 19:15; 24:38; John 2:25). The command to **stand** makes the healing a very public affair.

6:9 Is it lawful: The issue was the correct way of conducting oneself on the Sabbath (v. 2). Jesus chose to do good. The plots of the Pharisees represented doing evil and destroying. That was truly breaking the Sabbath (v. 7). **To save** here means simply to heal, as Jesus was about to do.

6:10–11 **Rage** here is irrational or mindless anger. The parallels in Matt. 12:14; Mark 3:6 make it clear that the Pharisees started to plot against Jesus in earnest after this confrontation.

6:12 **in prayer:** Here we find an example of Jesus spending time with God before an important event in His life (3:21; 22:41–44).

6:13 **chose twelve:** Jesus selected the main body of disciples, those who would become responsible for leading the early church (Matt. 10:2–4; Mark 3:16–19; Acts 1:13). The raw material was common humanity, but Christ shaped them to be the foundation stones of the church which was born at Pentecost (compare Eph. 2:20).

6:14 **Bartholomew** is probably Nathanael of John 1:45.

6:15 **Matthew** is Levi of 5:27–32 (Mark 2:14–17).

6:16 **Judas the son of James** is probably Thaddaeus (Matt. 10:3; Mark 3:18). This is not the Lord's half brother.

6:17, 18 **A level place** probably refers to a plateau on a mountain. The setting and the contents of the sermon that follows suggest that Luke is providing a shorter version of the Sermon on the Mount, omitting those portions that have to do with the law. Points of similarities between Luke's account here and Matthew's account in Matt. 5—7 are as follows: (1) Both begin with a series of beatitudes. (2) Both contain Jesus' teaching on loving one's enemies. (3) Both end with the parable of the two builders. The theme of the sermon is the disciple's walk. The audience for the sermon consisted of both **disciples** and the **great multitude.** Jesus did not restrict His remarks simply to those who believed. **Tyre and Sidon:**

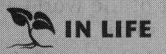 **IN LIFE**   **The Poverty of the Kingdom**

"**B**lessed are you poor, for yours is the kingdom of God." A consummate communicator, Jesus began His sermon with a sentence that certainly must have riveted His audience. Probably most of them were poor. Their lives were far from easy; their rough, worn hands attested to that fact. The difficulties and hardships of their lives drove them to travel the hot and dusty roads of Judea to listen to this prophet Jesus. Perhaps He would tell them more about the kingdom of God. Most of them had placed their hopes on the coming of this glorious kingdom. They longed for the day when the righteous Messiah, not the cruel Roman governor, would rule their lives.

Jesus began His sermon with an attention-grabbing, irony-filled series of blessings that have intrigued and puzzled Bible scholars and laymen for centuries. Often referred to as the Beatitudes, these statements contrast worldly goods and values with a heavenly estimation of people's affairs. The Beatitudes provide us with a heavenly perspective, evaluating the present in the light of eternity. They remind us that things are not always what they seem, and certainly not what they will one day be.

At face value, it appears that Jesus was making a blanket promise of salvation and blessing to anyone and everyone below the poverty line (6:20). Some have adopted just such an interpretation and have felt a special call to aim their ministries at the downtrodden. In this view, the poor are seen as God's chosen people. Though they suffer in this world, and perhaps because they suffer now, they can expect glorious blessing in the world to come. And the adherents of this view believe that while in this world the people of God should do everything possible to alleviate the suffering of the poor. In this way the kingdom of God is extended.

Many interpret the word *poor* as referring to the "poverty of spirit" that Jesus talks about in a very similar sermon, the Sermon on the Mount (Matt. 5:3). In other words, Jesus was offering hope and joy to those who freely recognize their spiritual poverty before God. These individuals are blessed because they come to God with nothing to offer Him except their great need. Thus Christ's offer of the kingdom of God is not a promise to every poor person. Rather it is a statement about the future condition of those who humbly choose to follow Him. When a person rejects worldly values and embraces the godly teachings of Jesus, then that individual begins to experience the reign of Christ in his or her life. This is how we enjoy the kingdom of God now in this fallen world. One day we will experience the joys of this kingdom in a fuller, more glorious way.

To summarize, anyone, rich or poor (and in a spiritual sense we are all poor), can taste the deep joy of God's rule and the blessing of His kingdom. But doing so requires that we renounce the ways of the world and humbly submit our ways to God (Is. 66:2). This kind of poverty, an emptying of ourselves of our self-centered desires, is what God expects from everyone.

Jesus' fame extended even into Gentile regions. The people were drawn by His teaching and healing ministry.

6:19 power went out from him: It is clear that Jesus' healing draws upon resources related to the special work of the Spirit through Him (Acts 10:38).

6:20 Though Jesus was speaking to the entire crowd, the beatitudes of vv. 20–23 were directed to the **disciples. Blessed** means "happy," referring to the special joy and favor that comes upon those who experience God's grace. **poor . . . kingdom of God:** In general, the disciples of Jesus were not wealthy (1 Cor. 1:26–29; James 2:5). They were poor men who had come humbly to trust in God. All of the promises of God's rule both now and in the future belong to such disciples.

6:21 The reason for the **hunger** and poverty is found in v. 22: persecution. Jesus promised that God would provide the disciples with all the sustenance they needed. **weep . . . laugh:** Any present suffering will be turned into joy.

6:22, 23 hate . . . exclude . . . revile you: Here is the cause of the disciples' precarious condition: persecution for **the Son of Man's sake.** Identification with Jesus usually leads to rejection and hardship, but the disciple who has left all to follow Jesus understands what placing Jesus first means. He or she also recognizes that God is aware of all suffering.

6:24 The woes of vv. 24–26 contrast with the beatitudes of vv. 20–23. A **woe** is a cry of pain that results from misfortune. Just as God presented blessings for obedience and curses for disobedience in Deut. 28, Jesus presented blessings and woes to His disciples who were anticipating the kingdom. The same blessings and woes apply to believers today when their works are evaluated (1 Cor. 3:12–15; 2 Cor. 5:10; 1 John 2:28; Rev. 22:12). **you who are rich . . . have received your consolation:** The background for this remark is found in Mary's song of praise in 1:51–53. All that the rich receive is what they acquire on earth (Matt. 6:19–21). Luke records many of Jesus' critical remarks about the wealthy. Their wealth typically blinds them to their spiritual poverty and their need for salvation (1:53; 12:16–21; 14:12; 16:1–14, 19–26; 18:18–25; 19:1–10; 21:1–4).

6:25, 26 full . . . hunger: This is called "eschatological reversal." Suffering will be their fate. **laugh . . . mourn and weep:** Again, comfort and ease is replaced with pain (1 John 2:28; Rev. 3:17, 18).

6:27, 28 The threat of religious persecution was very real when Jesus presented His command for extraordinary **love.** The reference to a cursing enemy suggests a context of religious persecution. **do good:** This makes love practical through visible expression.

6:29 offer the other: This is a description of being repeatedly vulnerable in the face of injustice. The one who seeks to love will always remain exposed and at risk. A **tunic** was an undergarment; a **cloak** was an outer garment.

6:30 do not ask them back: Jesus' instruction here is to forgive and forget. The commands of vv. 29, 30 are expressed in such absolute terms that they force the listener to reflect on them by contrasting them with the normal responses people would have to such injustices.

6:31 as you want men to do to you: This is the "golden rule." Note that Jesus' command is stated in the positive (contrast Lev. 19:18). Such love as Jesus describes recognizes the preferences of others and is sensitive to them.

6:32–34 what credit is that? Repeating the examples, Jesus' point is that a disciple's love is to be more than that of the world and that such love will require sacrifice.

6:35 The practice of loving one's enemies is modeled by God Himself, who is **kind to the unthankful and evil.** Jesus also notes that the **reward will be great** for the losses suffered while practicing this type of love. The divine compensation package is one hundredfold—that is, 10,000 percent (Matt. 19:28, 29).

6:36 be merciful: This is another way to define the essence of love. It is forgiving. The disciples are asked to apply a standard that matches what God does (**just as** God **is merciful**).

6:37 Judge not . . . Condemn not . . . Forgive: The idea here is not that one should ignore sin or refuse to discuss its consequences (11:39–52; Gal. 6:1, 2); rather, one should be gracious and quick to forgive.

6:38 good measure: This illustration comes from the marketplace where grain was poured out, shaken down, and then filled to overflowing so the buyer received the full amount purchased. Such is the full measure that will be returned to one who has been generous.

6:39 The blind here refers to teachers who cannot see where they are going and are unable to lead others. Jesus was warning against self-righteousness and arrogance. It is debated whether Jesus was describing the Pharisees here or simply warning His disciples about dangerous attitudes. The focus on the disciples' attitudes suggests the latter, though the remark would also have applied to the teachers with whom Jesus was in conflict.

6:40 will be like his teacher: Jesus remarks that usually the disciple will be like the teacher. The implication is, be careful who your teacher is.

6:41 A **speck** represents a small fault in another person in contrast to a **plank,** which represents a large fault in the one making the criticism.

6:42-45 First remove, and then: This makes it clear that confrontation about sin is to continue. Jesus says the confronter should look to see that sin is dealt with in one's own life, then he or she is in a position to help another person in that area.

6:46 Lord, Lord: Jesus pointed out that those who called Him by this title of respect acknowledged submission to Him. However, when these same people ignored His teaching, they were guilty of hypocrisy.

6:47–49 hears . . . and does: One who listens to and acts on Jesus' teaching can face any difficult circumstance. **heard and did nothing:** Not acting on Jesus' teaching will cause a person to be overwhelmed by circumstances, eventually resulting in total loss (1 Cor. 3:12–15; 2 John 8).

7:1 Capernaum was on the northwest shore of the Sea of Galilee. It was an important town in northern Galilee with an economy centered on fishing and agriculture. Heavily Jewish, it was the center for Jesus' Galilean ministry (4:31–44).

7:2–4 sent elders: The parallel in Matthew 8:5–13 does not mention emissaries at all. It is likely that Matthew has compressed his account as he often does (Matt. 9:2, 18, 19; 11:2, 3), since an emissary in ancient culture is regarded as speaking for the one who sends him (2 Kin. 19:20–34), just as today a White House press secretary speaks for the President. This verse also depicts exemplary cooperation between Jews and Gentiles in a culture where race was divisive. The elders were the Jewish leaders in the community.

7:5 built us a synagogue: The Roman government regarded synagogues as valuable because their moral emphasis helped maintain order.

7:6, 7 I am not worthy: The centurion, through messengers, communicates his exemplary humble attitude and faith, which Jesus commends in v. 9.

7:8 The centurion compared his authority as a commander of **soldiers** to Jesus' **authority** over life and health. The centurion knew that Jesus' word alone was sufficient to heal his servant.

7:9 not even in Israel: The centurion's

> *Jesus says the confronter should look to see that sin is dealt with in one's own life, then he or she is in a position to help another person in that area.*

example of faith came from outside the nation of Israel. This is one of only two cases where Jesus was said to "marvel" (Mark 6:6).

7:10 found the servant well: The healing occurred without Jesus being physically present, just as the centurion had believed.

7:11–13 a dead man was being carried out: This was a funeral procession. The cemetery was located outside the city gates. Funerals were normally held the day of death because keeping a body overnight rendered a house unclean. Before the funeral the body was anointed. In a town the size of Nain (v. 11) many would have stopped to share in the mourning.

7:14, 15 The fact that Jesus **touched** the coffin indicated that He preferred helping the dead man to remaining ceremonially clean (Num. 19:11, 16).

7:15 he who was dead sat up: An amazing contrast of description, which indicates the miracle was restoration to life. Other restorations are Jairus's daughter (8:40–56) and Lazarus (John 11:38–44). Again note the immediacy of response (4:39; 5:13, 25).

7:16, 17 The crowd recognized the parallel between Jesus' raising of the widow's son and the work of the **great** prophets Elijah (1 Kin. 17:17–24) and Elisha (2 Kin. 4:8–37).

7:18-21 Are You the Coming One: John's uncertainty may have been due to the fact that Jesus did not show signs of being the political and conquering messiah that most Jews were anticipating in that period.

7:22, 23 go and tell: Jesus prefers for His work to speak for His identity rather than make messianic claims. He appeals to His healing of the blind, the lame, the lepers, the deaf, and the dead, as well as emphasizing that He preaches the gospel. The allusions recall Luke 4:18, 19 and look back to OT texts, which describe what will happen when God brings salvation (Is. 35:5–7; 26:19; 29:18, 19; 61:1). The connections to Luke 3 and 4 show that Jesus claims to bring the end and, thus, is the figure whom John announced.

7:24–26 The questions that Jesus asked were designed to emphasize that John the Baptist played a special role in God's plan. The crowds did not go out to the wilderness to see scenery or a man dressed in special clothes, but to see a **prophet.**

7:27 My messenger: The citation here is from Mal. 3:1 (Matt. 11:10; Mark 1:2). John the

Baptist was the promised Elijah figure who would point the way to the arrival of God's salvation (1:16, 17; 3:4–6). The reference to Your way before You is a reference to the preparation of the people (1:17). This reference to "You" is unique to the NT citation and may contain an allusion to Ex. 23:20 where the cloud went before the people to guide and protect them. That Luke refers to the people here and not to Jesus is indicated by the fact that response is the issue in vv. 29, 30, and the passage alludes back to Luke 1:16, 17, which speaks of a prepared people.

7:28 he who is least in the kingdom of God: Jesus emphasizes the contrast between the old and new eras. John was the greatest prophet ever born. But the lowest person in the new era of God's kingdom is higher than the greatest prophet of the old era.

7:29, 30 Luke, in an aside, contrasts the responses to John's message. **The tax collectors justified God,** which means that they responded to John's message by submitting to John's baptism. The Pharisees, however, **rejected the will of God,** which means that

ating with sinners. No matter what the style of God's messenger was, the religious leaders complained and rejected him.

7:35 God's **wisdom** is vindicated by those who respond to it and receive blessing.

7:36 one of the Pharisees asked Him to eat with him: This event is not the same as the one in Matt. 26:6–13; Mark 14:3–9; John 12:1–8. The event described in those passages occurred in the house of a leper, a place where no Pharisee would ever have gone. **sat down to eat:** A meal with a religious figure in the ancient world was arranged so that the invited guest was at the main table while others were along the outside wall of the room listening to the conversation.

7:37, 38 The woman's sin is not specified. This woman is not Mary Magdalene of 8:2, since in that passage she is introduced as a new figure. The woman's anointing of Jesus was in response to Jesus' message of compassion for sinners (vv. 41–43, 50). **An alabaster flask** was made of soft stone to preserve the quality of the precious and expensive perfume. There is humility and devotion in the woman's act of service, as well

---

✠ IN CONTEXT | **A Pharisee Outdone**

The incident in Luke 7:36–50 contrasts a respectable Pharisee, Simon, against a disreputable, unnamed woman. Luke describes her as a "sinner" (7:37), a general term describing both those who failed to keep the ritual laws as well as those who flaunted the moral laws. How she gained entrance to Simon's feast is unclear.

The religious leader was probably restricted from even talking to the woman. Extensive Jewish religious laws had developed in the first century to ensure moral purity. Many men suspected women of being sexually aggressive and eager to trap unsuspecting men. So Jewish men in general and teachers of the Law in particular—such as Simon and Jesus—were to have as little to do with women as possible.

Jesus knew what kind of life the woman lived. Yet He accepted her anyway, violating taboos against speaking with her or allowing her to touch Him. In return, she gave to Jesus what Simon, the host, should have given—a kiss of welcome, a washing of the feet, and oil for the skin. These comforts were not merely symbolic but practical expressions of hospitality.

---

they refused to listen to John and were not baptized (Matt. 3:7–12).

7:31–34 Jesus made a comparison between **children** playing a game in the marketplace and the present **generation** of Israel, referring especially to the Jewish religious leaders. The leaders were like the children in that they complained no matter what tune was played. John the Baptist refused to eat bread or drink wine, and the religious leaders dismissed him as demon-possessed. In contrast, Jesus, **the Son of Man,** was accused of living loosely and associ-

as a great deal of courage, as she performed the deed in front of a crowd that knew her as a sinner. Although the woman does not say a word in the entire account, her actions speak volumes about her contrite heart.

7:39 if He were a prophet: The Pharisee doubted Jesus' credentials because He associated so openly with sinners. Jesus' association with sinners is a prominent theme in Luke (v. 34; 5:8, 30, 32; 13:2; 15:1, 2, 7, 10; 18:13; 19:7; 24:7). A Pharisee would reject such associations.

7:40 I have something to say: Jesus' reply

indicates that He knew the reputation of the woman, but was more interested in what the woman could become through the grace of God.

7:41 Jesus often compared sin to a monetary debt. A denarius was a day's wage for a basic laborer, so **five hundred denarii** was approximately the wages of one and a half years.

7:42, 43 which of them will love him more: Jesus' point is that the amount of love showered on the Savior will be in direct proportion with one's sense of the gravity of the sins that the Savior has forgiven. The woman knew she had been forgiven much, and as a result she would love much.

7:44–46 Jesus contrasted the actions of the woman with the actions of the Pharisee **Simon,** implying that the woman knew more about forgiveness than Simon (v. 47).

7:47, 48 her sins . . . are forgiven: Jesus confirmed that the love of the woman, which was visible in her actions toward Jesus, had come from being forgiven.

7:49 Who is this: The grumbling over Jesus' declaration concerning forgiveness indicates that at least some people in the audience rejected His authority.

7:50 Faith is the human channel for receiving God's gift (Eph. 2:8, 9).

8:1–3 The fact that **Mary called Magdalene** is introduced here as though for the first time makes it unlikely that she was the sinful woman of 7:36–50. Mary Magdalene is also distinct from Mary of Bethany in John 12:3. **Joanna the wife of Chuza, Herod's steward:** News of Jesus had reached Herod's palace. **provided for Him from their substance:** This is an example of how some women of means used their wealth to benefit the work of God.

8:4–8 In the ancient world, fields were sown sometimes before and sometimes after planting. Paths often cut through fields. Sometimes **seed** would take root on these paths, where it could not mature. In addition, some soil was rocky and also could not support a successful crop.

8:9, 10 Jesus' parables both concealed and revealed truths. His parables contained fresh teaching—**mysteries**—concerning **the kingdom of God.** The disciples were privileged to learn the truths of the parables. For other listeners, the parables served as judgments that concealed truth, as the reference to Is. 6:9 indicates. On occasion, a parable was understood by an outsider but was not accepted, thus still functioning as a message of judgment (20:9–19).

8:11 word of God: The parallel in Matt. 13:19 speaks of the seed as the "word of the kingdom," a point that Luke makes in v. 10. The soils do not represent individual moments of decision as much as a "career" of response to God's Word. The explanations make clear that

they cover a breadth of time.

8:12 Because **those by the wayside** never really gain an understanding (Matt. 13:19) of the word of God before Satan snatches it **away,** there is really no productivity at all.

8:13 believe for a while . . . fall away: Brief and superficial encounters with the word of God will not stand times of testing. A person needs to meditate on the truths in Scripture and establish them as principles for living in order to withstand the trials and temptations that will inevitably come.

8:14 According to this parable, **cares, riches, and pleasures of life** are three great obstacles to spiritual fruitfulness. The concerns of life can squelch spiritual growth. This type of "soil" is viewed as tragically unsuccessful (2 Tim. 2:4; 4:10).

8:15 keep it and bear fruit: This is the one praiseworthy group in the parable. The key here is a **noble and good heart.** This "soil" allows the word of God to settle in and become productive (John 15:2, 3; Col. 3:16, 17; James 1:21).

8:16 sets it on a lampstand: Continuing with the theme of the word of God introduced in vv. 4–15, Jesus compares His teaching to **light.** It

INSIGHT — Why Use Parables?

Jesus used parables often, the NT recording about forty separate stories. Jesus used parables for several reasons. (1) To attract attention. They have tremendous interest value, and everyone likes a story. (2) To prevent hearers from being repelled too quickly by normal direct statements. (3) To stimulate inquiry and to teach. These stories could easily be remembered, and were thus good vehicles for preserving the truth. (4) To reveal the truth, as some could understand a story taught in parabolic form more easily than regular teaching. (5) To conceal the truth. Often a story would protect the truth from the mockery of a scoffer who could not understand the meaning. One's spiritual condition frequently determined how much he would understand of what Jesus said.

should not be hidden, but displayed, so that people can benefit from the illumination it gives.

8:17 come to light: Eventually everything will be revealed by the light of the word of God (Heb. 4:12, 13).

8:18 take heed how you hear: Jesus explicitly warned His audience to listen to and follow the word of God (James 1:22–25). **what he seems to have will be taken:** This phrase introduces the principle of judgment. The one who responds to the word of God receives more. The one who does not respond to the word of God loses what he thought he had.

8:19, 20 Jesus' family was concerned about the direction of His ministry (Mark 3:31–35). Though some have suggested that the **brothers** here were sons of Joseph by a previous marriage or cousins of Jesus, most likely they were the sons of Joseph and Mary. Joseph's absence here may mean that he had died by this time.

8:21 My mother and My brothers: In a clear contrast to v. 19, Jesus declared that His true family consists of those who hear and do the **word of God.**

8:22, 23 windstorm: The calming of the wind is the first of four miracles in vv. 22–56 that demonstrate Jesus' authority over a variety of phenomena— nature, demons, disease, and death. Each enemy strikes nearer to the person and is overcome by Jesus, showing the comprehensiveness of His authority. This

first miracle took place on the Sea of Galilee. Cool air rushing down the ravines and hills of the area collides with warm air, causing sudden and strong storms. Even the experienced fishermen in the boat feared this kind of storm.

8:24 they ceased: At Jesus' word, all the chaos of the storm stopped. Such control over nature is attributed to God in the OT (Pss. 104:3; 135:7; Nah. 1:4).

WHY IT STORMS OVER GALILEE

Storms rapidly form over the Sea of Galilee when air masses from the surrounding higher plains and mountains are funneled through deep river ravines to meet the warm shore air rising off the lake.

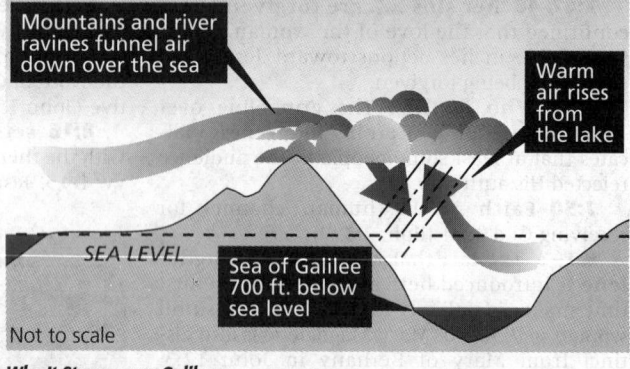

Mountains and river ravines funnel air down over the sea

Warm air rises from the lake

SEA LEVEL

Sea of Galilee 700 ft. below sea level

Not to scale

Why It Storms over Galilee

IN CONTEXT   What Kind of Storm Was This?

The Sea of Galilee was no place to be caught in a storm. The kind of weather that caught Jesus and His disciples occurs there to this day. As one traveler described it:

"The sun had scarcely set when the wind began to rush down towards the lake, and it continued all night long, with increasing violence, so that when we reached the shore the next morning the face of the lake was like a huge, boiling caldron. . . .

"We had to double-pin all the tent-ropes, and frequently were obliged to hang on with our whole weight upon them to keep the quivering tabernacle from being carried up bodily into the air."

The reason for such gale-force winds is the surrounding landscape. The lake is seven hundred feet below sea level, and is fed by rivers that have cut deep ravines surrounded by flat plains that are in turn hedged in by mountains. The ravines act like wind siphons or tunnels, gathering cooler air from the mountains as it crosses the plains. When the air mass runs into the hot lake shore, violent storms are whipped up with no warning.

Several of the disciples were experienced fishermen, well acquainted with such storms. However, they had never seen winds like those that attacked their boat (Luke 8:23), for they turned to the Lord in utter terror, certain that all was lost. Yet their fear of the wind and the waves gave way to wonder and awe when Jesus turned and calmed the sea.

8:25 Where is your faith: Jesus' question was a rebuke of His disciples. Because God was aware of their situation, they could trust in His protection, for He was powerful enough to control the mighty winds and waves. **Who can this be:** This is the real question of Jesus' entire Galilean ministry, the beginning of which is recorded in 4:14. All of the displays of Jesus' authority during this ministry were designed to raise this question of His identity. **they obey Him:** This reflection hints at the reply, since Jesus controls nature. The closest precedent to such power is Elijah (1 Kin. 17), but the miracles come with such frequency and variety that this category is too limiting. The disciples already sense that someone more than a prophet is present. Luke is honest about how the disciples grew in their understanding about Jesus. They learned about Him gradually. Their view of Jesus grew "from the earth up to heaven." The greater our knowledge of God, the greater will be our faith. Every sin we ever commit is the result of inadequate and erroneous thinking about God.

8:26 The city of the **Gadarenes** (Matt. 8:28) was probably a town about five miles southeast of the Sea of Galilee. Whatever its exact location, it was situated in a predominantly Gentile region.

8:27 no clothes . . . in the tombs: The demons destroy the self-esteem of the possessed. He is closer to death than life. The man is a pawn in a cosmic battle that pits the authority of the two sides against each other. Only Matt. 8:28 mentions a second man.

8:28 The demon's confession of Jesus as **Son of the Most High God** recalls the angel's announcement to Mary in 1:31, 32 and the demonic confessions of 4:34, 41.

8:29 broke the bonds: The power of the demons is made clear.

8:30 Legion: This name reflects the fact that the man was possessed by multiple demons. A *legion* was a Roman military unit of about six thousand soldiers; thus the name suggests a spiritual battle.

8:31 The abyss is an allusion to the underworld and the destruction of judgment (Rom 10:7).

8:32 Swine were unclean animals for Jews (Lev. 11:7; Deut. 14:8). Even though this incident took place in a Gentile area, it is still interesting to note that the unclean spirits sought out unclean animals.

8:33 drowned: The visible display of demonic destruction of the pigs graphically shows that the man was freed of his tormentors.

8:34–36 sitting at the feet of Jesus, clothed and in his right mind: This is a contrast to the same man who was roaming the tombs previously (vv. 27, 29). The man's position at Jesus' feet paints a picture of true discipleship (10:38–42).

8:37 There is some speculation that the reason the people asked Jesus to **depart** was to prevent further economic damage to their herds. According to Luke, the people were afraid of the authoritative presence of Jesus. Often economy is the bottom line.

8:38, 39 The man who was formerly demon-possessed wanted to go with Jesus and His disciples, but Jesus commissioned the man to be a witness in his own community. As an aside, it is helpful to notice how Jesus prioritizes His time and energy. There must have been many, like this man, who wanted to be His disciple but He limited them to twelve. The Synoptics are very instructive to us as we watch Jesus and the training of the Twelve. **Jesus had done:** Though Jesus wanted the Father to receive the credit for the man's healing, the man could not separate what God did from the role Jesus had played.

8:40 returned: Jesus apparently is back in Jewish territory.

8:41, 42 ruler: Jairus was the main elder of the synagogue. As such, he conducted the service and kept order.

8:43 Now a woman: The interruption of Jairus's request when his daughter was in such dire straits must have been heartrending.

8:44 her flow of blood stopped: This condition not only would have been embarrassing, it would have made the woman unclean (Lev. 15:25–31). It took great courage for her to seek out Jesus. Note that her action was not criticized, but commended (v. 48). The healing comes instantly; twelve years of suffering is halted in a moment (4:39; 5:13, 25; 7:15).

8:45, 46 Who touched Me? Jesus makes the woman's contact with Him known, especially since he felt **power going out** (v. 46) from Him.

8:47 she declared . . . the reason: The woman knew that she was **not hidden,** so she explained all. The knowledge that God's power is present and that He knows all should make one aware that hiding from Him is impossible.

8:48 your faith has made you well: Here Jesus commends the timid woman who has become bold in the knowledge that Jesus was aware of her desire to seek God's help.

8:49 Your daughter is dead: The delay caused by the woman with the blood disorder appeared to have been fatal for Jairus's daughter.

8:50 only believe: This miracle highlights not only the authority of Jesus, but also the response of faith that God honors.

8:51 He permitted no one to go in

except Peter, James, and John: The reason Jesus singled out these three disciples is not given. Luke records a similar action in 9:28. Matthew and Mark record a similar singling out at Gethsemane (Matt. 26:37; Mark 14:33). We do well to watch carefully the prioritizing exercised by Christ in the training of the Twelve.

8:52 Sleeping, a common metaphor for death, indicates in this passage that the girl's death was not permanent.

8:53 they ridiculed Him: The term used here suggests that the derision included laughter.

8:54, 55 immediately: Again, the healing is instantaneous (4:39; 5:13, 25; 7:15; 8:44).

8:56 The reason for Jesus' command for silence in this verse is not entirely clear, given that anyone could have deduced **what had happened.** The situation seems odd in light of Jesus' instruction to the demon-possessed man to proclaim what had occurred to him in 8:39, 45–47 and the public raising of the dead in 7:11–17. Jesus may have wanted to curtail such healings so that they would not become the center of His ministry.

9:1 gave them power and authority: Now Jesus shows that His authority can be extended through the Twelve. The nation to which He came as King (Matt. 10:5, 6) needed to witness His power and authority. The Twelve were delegated to accomplish this task.

9:2 to preach . . . to heal: The entire nation of Israel needed to see the evidence of the kingdom of God and make a decision concerning the King and His kingdom. Jesus commissioned His disciples to spread the word about God's kingdom through preaching and healing.

9:3–6 Take nothing: To cover a country 75 miles by 125 miles would not take a long time. The assignment had definite closure.

9:7–9 At Herod's palace, opinions varied as to whether Jesus was **John** the Baptist, **Elijah** (Mal. 3:1), or one of the **prophets.** Though this passage suggests that Herod was uncertain about Jesus' identity, Matt. 14:2 and Mark 6:16 indicate that Herod viewed Jesus as John the Baptist raised from the dead.

9:10–12 spoke . . . healed: Jesus had the same two-pronged ministry that the twelve disciples had: preaching and healing (v. 2). The topic of Jesus' preaching was always **the kingdom of God.**

9:13–17 This is the only miracle of Jesus' ministry that appears in all four Gospels (Matt. 14:13–21; Mark 6:30–44; John 6:5–14). The feeding of the five thousand demonstrated Jesus' ability to provide. **blessed and broke:** Some see an allusion here to the Lord's Table. Though this is not made clear in Luke's presentation, the description is similar to the table fellowship of the Last Supper (22:19) and Jesus' meal with some of the disciples after His resurrection (24:30).

9:17 twelve baskets: This is merely a striking sum noting the excess and probably should not be interpreted to mean anything more. The lesson for the disciples is that He is the source of their sustenance.

9:18, 19 praying: Another major event that Luke notes was accompanied by prayer. **say that I am:** This is the major issue for Luke. Who is Jesus? Luke's description of what Jesus does is important only because it raises the issue of who Jesus is.

9:20 The Christ of God: The emphasis here is on the messianic role of Jesus. He is the promised One who was ushering in a new era. However, Jesus would soon reveal to the disciples that His messiahship would have elements of suffering that the disciples did not expect (vv. 22, 23).

9:21 tell this to no one: Jesus knew that the messianic role that the people and the disciples expected was much different from His actual role as the Messiah. The element of suffering that the Messiah would endure was not a part of popular expectation. Thus Jesus' messiahship could not be openly proclaimed before the true nature of the Messiah was revealed.

9:22 must suffer . . . be rejected . . . be killed . . . be raised: This is the first of several predictions in Luke of Jesus' suffering and vindication (v. 44; 12:50; 13:31–33; 17:25; 18:31–33). The disciples struggled to understand what Jesus was saying (v. 45; 18:34). They could not comprehend how Jesus' predictions fit into God's plan. Only after Jesus' resurrection and His explanation of the Scriptures to them did they begin to understand (24:25–27, 44–49).

9:23 deny himself . . . take up his cross daily . . . follow Me: Here we see the real difference between sonship and discipleship. We receive the position and privilege of sonship as a gift (John 1:12) whereas we receive the prize or reward of sharing in Christ's glory in His coming kingdom reign (Matt. 5:10–12; Rom. 8:17; 1 Thess. 2:12; 2 Thess. 1:15; 2 Tim. 2:12) by the suffering we endure for Him with the life we received as a gift (Eph. 2:8, 9).

9:24, 25 It makes no sense to attempt to save our lives on earth only to lose everything when our lives quickly and inevitably pass away. The wise course is to invest our earthly resources—our time, talents, and wealth—in what is eternal. Even if we lose our lives for Jesus' sake, that investment will produce returns for all eternity (19:11–27; Matt. 6:19–21; 19:27–30).

9:26 Recognition of Jesus will be rewarded in the coming judgment. Failure to recognize

Him will lead to significant loss (1 Cor. 3:12–15; 2 Cor. 5:10; 2 Tim. 2:12; 1 John 2:28; 2 John 7, 8; Rev. 3:11; 22:12).

9:27 till they see the kingdom of God: Since these disciples died before Jesus' return, the reference here is no doubt to the Transfiguration (vv. 28–36). With this there is probably also a prediction of the descent of the Spirit at Pentecost (10:9; 11:20; 17:21).

9:28–29 At the Transfiguration Jesus was **altered** into a radiant figure, even down to His **white and glistening** clothes. The description here is similar to the description of the glory of Moses after seeing God (Ex. 34:29–35).

9:30, 31 Decease is literally **exodus.** This important allusion to the central OT event of salvation is unique to Luke's account of the Transfiguration. The comparison is made between Jesus' death and the journey to salvation that the nation of Israel experienced under Moses. Jesus' journey would take Him to the side of God, from which He will return to exercise authority (Acts 2:30–36; 10:42; 17:31).

9:32, 33 let us make three tabernacles: Peter desired structures for the two OT visitors and Jesus, perhaps as a means of prolonging their visit. **not knowing what he said:** This rebuke of Peter is probably for suggesting an equality between Moses, Elijah, and Jesus. In addition, he may have been rebuked here for wanting to celebrate the arrival of the *eschaton* before major events necessary for it have occurred. This is the first of several remarks in Luke 9 which suggest that the disciples have much to learn. We need to keep reminding ourselves that in the Gospels we are seeing Christ training the Twelve who are going to be put in place as the foundation stones (Eph. 2:20) of the church that was going to be inaugurated in Acts 2 at Pentecost. The ministry of Christ was not basically spent in reaching the masses but in training the Twelve. Christ operated on the principle that quality begets quantity, not vice versa. Church growth leaders today need to recapture this principle.

9:34, 35 This is My beloved Son: This is the second heavenly endorsement of Jesus (3:22). The reference to the *beloved Son* recalls the words of Ps. 2:7; Is. 42:1. The command to **hear Him** alludes to Deut. 18:15–18 and identifies Jesus as the Prophet promised in that passage. Jesus, as the new Prophet, would lead a new group of people into salvation (Matt. 21:43; Rom. 11:1–36; 1 Pet. 2:9, 10), just as Moses led

How much more we could accomplish for Christ and His kingdom if we did not care who got the credit.

the nation of Israel. As a Revealer of God's will, Jesus had much to teach the disciples about God's plan. The disciples needed to listen because they had much to learn.

9:36 told no one: In this passage, we are not told why the disciples remained silent about the Transfiguration. Matthew 17:8, 9; Mark 9:9, 10 note that Jesus commanded such silence and Mark makes it clear that the disciples did not yet understand the event (see 2 Pet. 1:16–21 for Peter's reflection on this experience).

9:37, 38 when they had come down: As three disciples had a great experience with Jesus, the others were struggling to perform a healing. The contrast and the failure is significant. Again, the disciples had much to learn.

9:39, 40 a spirit seizes him: The detailed description of symptoms shows the severity of the possession. The fact that the relative is an only child (v. 38) adds to the mood of the event.

9:41 O faithless and perverse generation: This rebuke suggests that the disciples lacked the faith to cast out the spirit described in vv. 38–40. There is also a hint of a competitive spirit among the disciples (v. 46). The same is true today. How much more we could accomplish for Christ and His kingdom if we did not care who got the credit.

9:42 rebuked the unclean spirit: Jesus' authority is again the issue.

9:43 all amazed: The **majesty of God** is what Jesus' authority reveals. There is a great popular reaction to Jesus, but He knows it will be short-lived (v. 44).

9:44 Note that Jesus predicted that He, the **Son of Man,** would be betrayed, even when many were still marveling at His ministry (v. 43).

9:45 they were afraid to ask: The indication here is that the disciples still had much to learn. Their fear shows that they understood something about what Jesus said, but they did not understand how and why Jesus could say such things about Himself, since He was the Messiah. The suffering of the Messiah was something the disciples did not yet understand. They would continue to be confused in their understanding of how such suffering fit into God's plan until Jesus' death and resurrection (24:25, 26, 43–49).

9:46 which of them would be greatest: Here is great irony. Jesus predicts His suffering, and the disciples are jockeying with each other about the kingdom (22:24; Mark 10:35–45). The disciples still have much to learn. We too have much to learn when we are seeking to build our own kingdom instead of building Christ's kingdom. There was nothing wrong with the desire to have positions of glory and honor in Christ's kingdom, but they were missing some basic principles that Christ gave them in the Upper Room (22:14–25; John 13:12–17; 33–35). It is as we seek to serve one another in love that we gain true greatness. All of these principles will be part of Christ's final evaluation of our stewardship of this life (9:23–24; 1 Cor. 4:5; 2 Cor. 5:10).

9:47, 48 he who is least . . . will be great: Jesus' point was that prominence is not measured by human standards of achievement, but by one's relationship to God. Anyone related to God is great, even "the least" of His disciples.

9:49 casting out demons in Your name: The issue here was that the disciples saw others who shared their gifts, and they thought it was wrong. They still were learning. Pastors of people today need to realize as well that their ministry is being fulfilled not when they do everything while the people look on but when they are training and enabling the people to use the gifts God has given them. It is not the role of leaders to be substitutes for the people but to be equippers of the people to do the work of the ministry.

9:50 Do not forbid him: Jesus notes that anyone exercising God's gifts, who is not opposed to Jesus and the disciples' ministry, is on their side and should be allowed to minister. Ministering for Jesus is not the privilege of a select few. All of God's children are gifted (Rom. 12:3–8; 1 Cor. 12:3–27; Eph. 4:1–16; 1 Pet. 4:10, 11). Again, we are not to be concerned with building our own little domains but rejoicing in the building of the kingdom of God regardless of who is doing it.

9:51 set His face to go to Jerusalem: This is the first indication that Jesus' attention was turning toward His final suffering in Jerusalem (v. 53; 13:22, 33–35; 17:11; 18:31; 19:11, 28, 41). The journey to Jerusalem was not direct, however. In 10:38–42, we find Jesus at Martha and Mary's house in Bethany. In 17:11 we find Him in Samaria and Galilee. The journey to Jerusalem proceeded only according to God's design and in His timing. Jesus was nearing the destiny of His mission—that is, His death. Luke's Gospel uniquely emphasizes this journey to Jerusalem. Luke records much of Jesus' teaching and parables on this journey as Jesus

> *Anyone related to God is great, even "the least" of His disciples.*

contrasted His way of suffering with the way of the Jewish religious leaders.

9:52 Samaritans were the descendants of Jews who had married Gentiles after the fall of the northern kingdom, Israel. The Samaritans eventually developed their own religious rites, which they practiced on Mount Gerizim instead of at the temple in Jerusalem. Though there was deep hostility between Jews and Samaritans, Jesus ministered to both groups.

9:53, 54 command fire to come down: James and John, the "sons of thunder," wanted Jesus to bring judgment upon the Samaritan villages that refused to respond to His message, just as Elijah had done in 2 Kin. 1:9–16. Their demand for judgment was antithetical to Jesus' loving response (v. 56).

9:55, 56 He turned: Jesus' action shows that He refuses the request. The disciples do not understand that they are to bring grace. The right of judgment lies in other hands for other times.

9:57–62 Here we gain insight into a class session with Jesus and a sampling of his disciples. Each of them is a distinct personality and each has a problem in advancing to the next level of discipleship. But all of their individual problems find their source in one main problem. See if you can discern it.

9:57 I will follow You: The first man volunteered without reservation. He was warm, ardent, and enthusiastic. His problem is that he has not realistically counted the cost. His enthusiasm is based on the feelings of the moment, which will not be strong enough to sustain him in the thick of battle.

9:58 Son of Man has nowhere to lay his head: Jesus warns the disciple that Jesus (Son of Man) does not have even the ordinary comforts of home, unlike the creatures of creation. And to follow Jesus today may require going without our beauty-rest mattress and goose-down pillow. This eliminates many candidates.

9:59 let me first go and bury my father: This aspiring disciple placed family responsibilities ahead of following Jesus. The concerns of home were this man's stumbling block. Unlike the previous volunteer (v. 57), this man was slow, meditative, and contemplative. He was counting the cost of discipleship. Cultic purity was viewed as very important in Jewish circles, so a quick burial of the dead was required (7:11–17).

9:60 Let the dead bury their own dead: Jesus makes it clear that a disciple is to have clear, biblically based priorities. The remark is rhetorical, because in fact the dead cannot bury their colleagues in death. It is an emphatic way to say the call of God receives priority. In periods of urgency such as the current time, burial is not necessary (Jer. 16:5–7). Social obligation is not to cancel the immediacy of ministry. It may well be the rhetorical remark about the "dead" refers to the spiritually dead; so the point is that the world can take care of the mundane matters of life and death, but the disciple is to prioritize ministry. His problem is that he did not have proper priorities and thus did not sense the urgency of taking action when Jesus called. Such improper priorities cause us to miss grand opportunities of investment (Phil. 4:15).

9:61 bid them farewell: This request is like the one Elisha made of Elijah (1 Kin. 19:19, 20), which was granted. The time of Jesus is more urgent so that now the request is denied.

9:62 looking back: Here is the vacillating disciple—hot and cold. Jesus makes it clear that entry into discipleship with Him in faith is something from which one does not turn back without great peril. The allusion to looking back recalls Lot's wife (Gen. 19:26). The remark about being **fit** (or usable) for the kingdom of God shows how seriously Jesus takes commitment to Him. The remark is a warning that the one who comes to Jesus should be prepared to stay with Him (1 Cor. 15:2; Col. 1:21–23; Matt. 7:21–23; 22:11–13; Luke 13:25–27). To put a **hand to the plough** is to engage in a task. Here, it is the task of serving the kingdom. **Looking back** militates against plowing straight furrows. The first disciple was too ready because he hadn't counted the cost. The second disciple was not ready at all because he hadn't sensed the urgency of moving when Jesus said move. And the third disciple was only half ready—hot to go when he looked forward but cold to go when he looked back. What lessons these are for those of us who aspire to discipleship and reign with Christ in His kingdom.

10:1 The account of Jesus calling **seventy** disciples is unique to the Gospel of Luke. The instructions that Jesus gave to these disciples are similar to the instructions He gave to the Twelve in 9:1–6.

10:2 The picture of a plentiful harvest suggests that a positive response awaited the laborers, even in the face of much rejection.

10:3–7 The image of **lambs among wolves** was popular in Judaism. It derived from Is. 40:11. Jesus uses a similar image in John 10:1–18. Actually, no one has even seen lambs *among* wolves. Lambs *in* wolves, yes! Lambs *among* wolves, no! This is naturally impossible. But it is made possible by the presence of the Shepherd. The key is the focus on the Shepherd.

10:8–12 kingdom . . . near to you: Like v. 11, 11:20, and 17:21, this text shows how aspects of kingdom authority accompanied Jesus' earthly ministry. The healing Jesus brought pictured what the kingdom offered (11:20). Jesus' ministry was the arrival of the initial stages of God's rule, which Jesus will consummate at His return (17:20–37). God's kingdom comes in stages. When Jesus came the first time, He was rejected. In His second coming, He will establish His complete rule over all.

10:13, 14 The **mighty works** of Jesus were so great that if they had been performed before the worst pagans of the old era, those people would have repented. Jesus' remark was meant to wake the people up to what their rejection of Him signified.

10:15 will be brought down: As with Luke 10:13, the cities are in view, not individuals. These judgments relate to the danger of the nation in rejecting Jesus, though they carry implications that apply to individuals who reject the offer.

10:16 He who hears you hears Me: Hearing the messenger is the same as hearing the One who sent him. Authority resides not in the messenger, but in the person the messenger represents, the source of the message.

10:17 even the demons are subject to us in Your name: The disciples rejoice at the authority that they exercise. The key, as they note, is the authority they have "in Jesus' name."

10:18 This verse provides a commentary on what the disciples' healing ministry meant. The reversal of the effects of sin and death, which **Satan** introduced through his deception in Gen. 3, are portrayed graphically as Satan falling from heaven. Jesus' ministry and what grows out of it represents the defeat of Satan, sin, and death.

10:19, 20 This verse records the transmission of Jesus' **authority** to His immediate circle of disciples. It should be noted that similar authority was not given beyond that circle of disciples. Note the authority that is given to the Eleven in Matt. 28:16–20; Acts 1:8. As Jesus makes clear in v. 20, authority was not the most important thing the disciples received. **your names are written in heaven:** More important than the disciples' authority over **spirits** was their position as God's children. Their names were known to God and were written in God's book. This was the disciples' greatest blessing.

10:21 Father: Here Jesus prays to His Father and reveals His joy that God has revealed His sovereign plan for the world to **babes.** Jesus' point is that it is not the great, in terms of human achievement and status, who receive these tremendous truths, but the simple who come to Him as dependent beings.

10:22 All things have been delivered to Me: This is Jesus' declaration of total authority as the Son of God (John 10:18; 17:2). He makes a similar statement in Matt. 28:18. **except the Father . . . except the Son:** Jesus declares His unique relationship with God the Father. The Lord reveals Himself only through Jesus. To know God, one must know His Son, Jesus.

10:23 Blessed are the eyes: Jesus notes the honor that comes from sharing in what He offers and teaches.

10:24 have not seen . . . heard it: Jesus contrasted the OT era of expectation, in which people desired to see the Messiah but did not, with the era in which the disciples were living. If they had the spiritual insight they could witness the fulfillment in Jesus of many of God's promises.

10:25, 26 The question posed by the lawyer is really a challenge, since the verse speaks of the testing of Jesus. This is a similar, though probably distinct, event from Matt. 22:34–40; Mark 12:28–34. To **inherit** something is to receive it. In other words, the man was asking, "What must I do to share in the reward at the resurrection of the righteous at the end?" (Phil. 3:11–14). The OT basis of this question is the

---

✔ IN COMPARISON | **Appearing Only in Luke . . .**

In Jesus' day the Samaritans were despised by orthodox Jews because most of the Jews from that region had intermarried with foreigners. The irony of the parable of the Good Samaritan is that a scorned Samaritan knows how to show love to his neighbor, whereas a priest and Levite, who had intimate knowledge of God's Law, do not. The Book of Luke highlights Jesus' love for a variety of groups who were not esteemed in His day.

Women	
Elizabeth	1:5–25, 39–45, 57–66
Mary	1:26–56; 2:1–20, 41–52
Anna	2:36–38
The widow of Nain	7:11–15
The sinner who anoints Jesus' feet	7:36–50
Women disciples	8:1–3
The woman searching for her lost coin	15:8–10
The persistent widow petitioning the unjust judge	18:1–8
The sorrowful women along the way to the Cross	23:27
The women who discover the empty tomb	24:1–10
Social Outcasts	
Gentiles	2:32; 24:47
Shepherds	2:8–20
The poor	6:20–23
The Samaritans	10:30–36; 17:16
Tax collectors and "sinners"	15:1
Lepers	17:11–17

hope of resurrection in Dan. 12:2. Jesus countered the lawyer's test by having him answer his own question.

10:27 you shall love the LORD . . . and your neighbor: The lawyer responded to Jesus' questions by quoting Deut. 6:5, a text that was recited twice a day by every faithful Jew. This text summarized the central ethical standard of the law. The lawyer also alluded to Lev. 19:18. The basis of the man's response is an expression of allegiance and devotion that also can be seen as the natural expression of faith, since the total person, **heart, soul, strength,** and **mind,** is involved. The theme of love for God is picked up in vv. 38–42 with its emphasis on devotion to Jesus, and in 11:1–13, where the disciples are taught to be devoted to God in prayer. In vv. 30–37 Jesus develops the theme of love for one's neighbor.

10:28 do this and you will live: Jesus was not saying that righteousness is the result of works. Rather He was saying that love for and obedience to God will be a natural result of placing one's faith in the Lord. Those who

that some people are neighbors while others are not. The lawyer was looking for minimal obedience while Jesus was looking for absolute obedience.

10:30 Jerusalem to Jericho: This was a seventeen-mile journey on a road known to harbor many robbers. They would hide in caves along the way and attack their victims.

10:31, 32 by chance: This is a nice literary touch. The man was in danger and now help seemed to come fortuitously his way. **passed by:** Both a priest and Levite consciously avoid giving aid. How easy it is for those who handle the rituals of religion to become calloused and treat the opportunities to minister as trivial and commonplace.

10:33 Part of the beauty of the story of the Good Samaritan is the reversal of stereotypes. The priest and Levite traditionally would have been the "good guys." The **Samaritan** would have been a "bad guy," a person who compromised in religious matters. However, the Samaritan knew how to treat his neighbor. The neighbor here was not someone the Samaritan

---

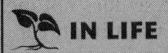 **IN LIFE** | ## Martha: Too Much Service?

Jesus' visit to Martha's home (Luke 10:38–42) has given rise to a caricature of Martha as obsessively "practical," as opposed to Mary, her "spiritual" sister. In fact, some would use this incident to reinforce a hierarchy of "spiritual" concerns over "secular" ones: it is more important to "sit at Jesus' feet"—that is, to engage in religious pursuits such as prayer or attending church—than to be "distracted" with everyday tasks such as work or household chores.

But it would be unfair to read Jesus' words to Martha as a rebuke for her preparations. After all, He had come as a guest to her home with His disciples. Someone was obligated to prepare a meal—a large meal. Assuming Jesus and the Twelve, plus Mary, Martha, and Lazarus, there were at least sixteen hungry people. No wonder Martha was "distracted [literally, drawn away] with much serving" (10:40). She could not sit and chat with her guests if she was to prepare the food.

So what was Jesus getting at in vv. 41 and 42? Only this: that in addition to her marvelous preparations, Martha needed to add spiritual sensitivity. He was in no way setting up a dichotomy between the sacred and the secular, but merely emphasizing that in the midst of her busyness, Martha should not lose sight of who He was and why He had come. Without question, Mary had that insight, and Jesus was keen to preserve it.

Apparently Martha profited from Jesus' exhortation, for when her brother Lazarus died, she recognized His ability as the Christ to raise him from the dead (John 11:27).

Like Martha, we today are called on to strike a balance between faithful, diligent service in our day-to-day responsibilities and a constant attitude of dependence on the Lord.

---

believe in Jesus and follow Him will receive eternal rewards. Jesus states this principle to Peter in Matt. 19:27–30.

10:29 Luke makes it clear that the lawyer was trying to place himself in the position of satisfying the highest demands of the law. **who is my neighbor:** This question was an attempt to limit the demands of the law by suggesting

knew or even someone of the same race, just someone in need.

10:34 Oil was used to soothe wounds. **Wine** was used as a disinfectant.

10:35 two denarii . . . I will repay: The Samaritan, if he paid a typical rate of one-twelfth of a denarius a day, paid for twenty-four days at the inn. Given the man had been robbed, such support was necessary. Compassion expressed itself concretely in both time and money. The Samaritan also was prepared to do more, if it was necessary. How different from the statement, "Be warmed and filled" (James 2:16).

10:36 which . . . was neighbor: The central issue is not determining who one's neighbor is, but being a good neighbor to all.

10:37 He who showed mercy: The lawyer apparently could not bring himself to say "Samaritan" and lend credence to the surprising reversal of stereotypes in the story.

10:38 a certain village: If this is the **Martha** and **Mary** of John 11:1—12:8, then the location is Bethany, just outside Jerusalem (John 11:1, 19; 12:1). This text suggests that the "Jerusalem journey" of 9:51—19:44 was not a direct trip to Jerusalem, but a journey of drawing near to the time for Jesus' death.

10:39 sat at Jesus' feet: A picture of discipleship, as Mary listens to Jesus teach.

10:40 Martha **was distracted** by the amount of **serving** she had to do. Her complaint to Jesus indicates that she was irritated that her sister was not helping her.

10:41 Jesus' tender reply is evident in the double address of **Martha, Martha** (6:46; 8:24; 13:34; 22:31). He notes that Martha was anxiety-ridden over ordinary matters.

10:42 that good part: Mary was a silent example. She said nothing, but did what was right by devoting herself to Jesus' teaching.

11:1 The Lord's Prayer illustrates the variety of requests that one can and should make to God, as well as displaying the humble attitude that should accompany prayer. The use of the plural pronoun **us** throughout the prayer shows that it is not just the prayer of one person for his or her own personal needs, but a community prayer.

11:2 Father: God is approached confidently as a caring figure. **Hallowed:** In the context of intimacy with God, there also is respect and recognition of His uniqueness. *Hallowed* means that God is holy, set apart, unique in His character and attributes. **Your kingdom come:** The reference here is to God's program and promise. This is more affirmation than request, highlighting the petitioner's submission to God's will and the desire to see God's work come to pass.

11:3 our daily bread: This request recognizes that one is dependent on God for daily needs.

11:4 forgive us our sins: This request recognizes that sin is a debt to God that needs to be acknowledged on the basis of His mercy. **we also forgive:** The petitioner recognizes that if mercy is to be sought from God, then mercy must be shown to others. We need to adopt the same standard that we expect others to follow. **do not lead us into temptation:** This remark is often misunderstood as suggesting that perhaps God can lead us into sin. The point is that if one is to avoid sin, one must follow where God leads. In short, the petitioner asks God for the spiritual protection necessary to avoid falling into sin.

11:5, 6 I have nothing to set before him: In ancient culture, to be a generous host was assumed. For his late night visitor the host had a choice—be rude or get food somewhere else. He chose to be a good host and seek some bread in the middle of the night.

11:7 Do not trouble me: The man responding does not wish to be disturbed. In an ancient house, all members of the family would have slept in one room. To pull the rod on the door would have awakened the children.

11:8 Persistence here refers to shameless boldness more than to tenacity. Jesus' point is that in prayer the disciple is to be bold. The example in the parable (vv. 5–7) is a man who goes boldly to his neighbor to seek what he requires. Likewise, the disciple is to go boldly to God for that which is needed.

11:9, 10 receives: This verse does not mean that we receive whatever we want in prayer. As v. 13 demonstrates, with its reference to receiving God's Spirit, the suggestion is that we receive what is spiritually beneficial.

11:11, 12 stone . . . serpent . . . scorpion: Here is another parable. What father gives a son worthless or destructive things when basic needs are requested?

11:13 how much more will your heavenly Father give: If people, who are evil, can give **good** gifts, imagine the value of God's gift of **the Holy Spirit.** If anyone does not have the Holy Spirit, that person does not belong to Christ (Rom. 8:9). In the triune Godhead, the Holy Spirit is the divine distributor (1 Cor. 12:11) of the good things purchased by the Son (Eph. 4:7, 8) and ordained by the Father (Eph. 3:1).

11:14, 15 If Jesus was not to be believed, His miracles had to be demonic in origin. This was the ultimate blasphemy—attributing the credentials of heaven to hell. The Latin name **Beelzebub** was originally a reference to the Philistine god Baal-Zebub worshiped at the city of Ekron (2 Kin. 1:2, 3, 6, 16). The name means "Lord of the Flies."

11:16 sought from Him a sign: Others wanted more evidence. There is irony here as well as stubbornness, as if the miracles were not enough (7:22).

11:17, 18 The attribution of Jesus' miracles to Satan was not only blasphemous, it was illogical. If Satan had cast out the demon (v. 14), he

 **IN DEPTH** | **Demons**

Scripture presents demons not as mythological creatures, but as real beings involved in historical events. Jesus, for example, frequently encountered demons during His ministry, as in the case of the demon-possessed mute (Luke 11:14).

Demons are fallen angels who joined with Satan in rebellion against God. The Bible does not explicitly discuss their origin, but the NT does speak of the fall and later imprisonment of a group of angels (2 Pet. 2:4; Jude 6). Their rebellion apparently occurred before God's creation of the world. Afterward, Satan and his followers roamed the new creation, eventually contaminating the human race with wickedness (Gen. 3; Matt. 25:41; Rev. 12:9). To this day they continue to oppose God's purposes and undermine the cause of righteousness.

Demon Possession

One of Jesus' primary purposes was to overcome the power of Satan, which is why He regularly challenged the demonic realm (Matt. 12:25–29; Luke 11:17–22; John 12:31; 1 John 3:8). One of His most compassionate activities was to release persons possessed by demons.

Our culture tends to dismiss demon possession as a quaint, archaic way of trying to explain physical and psychological conditions. But the Bible never suggests that all ailments are the result of demonic activity, only that demons can afflict people with physical symptoms such as muteness (Matt. 12:22; 9:17, 25), deafness (9:25), blindness (Matt. 12:22), and bodily deformity (Luke 13:10–17). The Gospels actually distinguish between sickness and demon possession (Matt. 4:24; Mark 1:32; Luke 6:17, 18).

Demons can also cause mental and emotional problems (Matt. 8:28; Acts 19:13–16). The demon-possessed might rant and rave (Mark 1:23–24; John 10:20), have uncontrolled fits (Luke 9:37–42; Mark 1:26), and behave in an antisocial manner (Luke 8:27, 35).

In casting out demons, Jesus and His disciples used methods that differed radically from the mystical rites so often employed in that time. Through His simple command Jesus expelled them (Mark 1:25; 5:8; 9:25). His disciples did the same, adding only the authority of Jesus' name to their command (Luke 10:17; Acts 16:18). Even some who were not His followers invoked the Lord's power (Luke 9:49; Acts 19:13).

Despite these straightforward means, Jesus' enemies accused Him of being in alliance with Satan's kingdom (Mark 3:22; Luke 11:15; John 8:48). The same accusation was made against Jesus' forerunner, John the Baptist (Matt. 11:18; Luke 7:33). But Jesus' works of goodness and righteousness showed that these claims could not be true (Matt. 12:25–29; Luke 11:17–22).

The Final Victory

Following the resurrection of Jesus and His return to heaven, demons have continued their warfare against Him and His followers (Rom. 8:38, 39; Eph. 6:12). Yet Satan and his allies will ultimately be overthrown by God. After Christ returns, the devil and his angels will be defeated and thrown into the lake of fire and brimstone (Matt. 25:41; Rev. 20:10)—a doom with which the demons are quite familiar (Matt. 8:29). God will achieve the final victory in a conflict that has been going on since the beginning of time.

---

would have been destroying the result of his own work.

11:19 by whom do your sons cast them out: Jesus' question and the implied reply to it can be taken in one of two ways: (1) How did Jewish exorcists expel demons? If the answer is by God's power, then why not give Jesus the same credit? (2) How did Jesus' disciples, who were the "sons" of Israel, drive out demons? The dissenters not only had to explain Jesus' miracles, but those of His followers. Most scholars prefer the former interpretation.

11:20 The finger of God is an allusion to God's power, like that demonstrated in the Exodus (Ex. 8:19; Deut. 9:10; Ps. 8:3). **the kingdom of God has come upon you:** Jesus' miracles represented the arrival of God's power and promise—in short, His rule. That rule comes in and through Jesus. The miracles of Jesus demonstrated God's victory over the forces of evil. The kingdom program, depicted as drawing near, will be consummated at the return of Jesus when this rule is manifested over every creature.

11:21, 22 Jesus portrays Himself as someone **stronger** than Satan who overruns Satan's house and gives the spoils of victory to those who are His (Eph. 4:8, 9 for a similar concept).

11:23 He who is not with Me . . . does not gather: Jesus' ministry forces everyone to make a choice. Neutrality is not an option. Either Jesus comes from God or He does not. Not to align with Jesus is to be against Him.

11:24 seeking rest: The picture is of an exorcised spirit seeking a home after God has acted on someone's behalf. **I will return:** The spirit decides to go back where he was.

11:25 swept: The exorcised person becomes like a clean house, although empty if God is not present, and still exposed to spiritual danger.

11:26 the last state . . . is worse: Jesus' point is that experiencing God's blessing and then ignoring it leaves one callous towards the work of God and exposed to the control of demonic forces.

11:27, 28 Blessed is the womb: The woman offered praise for Jesus' mother. Though Jesus always honored Mary, He commented carefully on the woman's blessing to keep the focus on the **word of God.** It is easy to allow traditional practices to take the place of the authority of the Scriptures. Jesus offers His blessing to those who respond concretely to God's will as expressed in the Bible.

11:29 The sign of Jonah here refers to his prophetic call to repentance rather than to the Resurrection foreshadowed by Jonah's return from the belly of the great fish.

11:30–32 Jesus warned that refusal to hear Him would result in condemnation from those in the OT who had responded to God's teaching. The examples Jesus offered included Gentiles such as the **queen of the South** (the queen of Sheba in 1 Kin. 10:1–10) and **the Ninevites** (Jon. 3). Because Jesus is **greater than** those who proclaimed God's word in those days—**Solomon** and **Jonah,** His word should have been heeded by the first-century Israelites.

11:33 may see the light: Light is to be a source of guidance. Luke 11:27–36 is about responding to the light of God's word as presented in Jesus' teaching. God has made it clear for all to see.

11:34, 35 It has been said that "you are what you eat." But even more accurately, you are what you see. This is why David said, "I will set nothing wicked before my eyes" (Ps. 101:3). A person who concentrates on what is **good** (God's teaching) is healthy. But a person who focuses on what is **bad** (the false teaching of the world) is **full of darkness.**

11:36 your whole body is full of light: A person can become like light, a living picture of what God's Word teaches, by concentrating on the light of the truth.

11:37, 38 He had not first washed before dinner: Such ceremonial washing is described in the OT (Gen. 18:4; Judg. 19:21), but not commanded.

11:39 make the outside . . . clean: These condemnations by Jesus are similar to those in Matt. 23. The Pharisees washed the outside of cups, making sure that the cups had not become unclean through contact with a dead insect (Lev. 11:31–38). Jesus pointed out that the Pharisees concerned themselves with outward appearances and ritual cleanness, while what was inside, what really counts, was full of selfishness and evil.

11:40 did not He who made: Jesus points out that the outside and inside were made by the same God and they demand equal care.

11:41 give alms: The giving of alms was the donation of support to the poor. As such, it pictures the labor of self-sacrifice and compassion. Jesus says that is the picture of the type of devotion one should give to the care of one's inner spiritual condition. Such care for the requirements of a needy soul lead to true cleanliness before God.

11:42 pass by: The Pharisees worried about tithing ten percent, even down to the smallest herbs, which were tithed according to the dictates of tradition, not the Law of Moses (Num. 18:21–32; Deut. 14:22–29; see also Lev. 27:30 for the practice of tithing herbs). The law spoke of tithing all produce, but what constituted food was debated. Some Pharisees took the strictest interpretation and counted almost anything, including spices. However, they neglected two basic things that the prophets also had spoken about: love and justice (Mic. 6:8; Zech. 7:8–10).

11:43 love the best seats . . . greetings: This condemns the pride of the Pharisees, but it also speaks volumes to every believer.

11:44 The Pharisees were like hidden **graves.** To have contact with a grave or with the dead was to become ceremonially unclean (Num. 19:11–19). Anyone or anything in the same room as the dead was considered in Jewish tradition to be impure. This is Jesus' stronger condemnation. The Pharisees, the paragons of purity, were in fact the height of uncleanness.

11:45 You reproach us also: One lawyer attempts to defend the Pharisees by noting their close relationship to the scribes. If one group is rebuked, so is the other.

11:46 Jesus applied His woes to **lawyers** as well as to the Pharisees. In everyday Greek, the term translated **burdens** refers to a ship's cargo. The idea is that a heavy strain was being imposed on the people and yet, in the end, this burden did not bring them closer to God. Here Jesus rebuked the tradition that had grown up around the Law of Moses. **you yourselves do not touch the burdens:** The meaning of this phrase is debated. Was Jesus accusing the scribes of hypocrisy in not practicing what they taught and in making distinctions that freed them from obligations, as they did with oaths (Matt. 5:33–37)? Or was Jesus simply accusing the scribes of not offering aid and compassion to those who tried to follow their rules? The second interpretation is more likely, since the Pharisees were known for adhering to the law.

11:47, 48 you build the tombs of the prophets: Jesus made a biting, ironic comparison between the current generation of Israel and the generations of the past. Jesus was saying that the current generation finished the job of slaying the prophets that the previous generation had started. The building and care of tombs was supposed to be an act of honoring the prophets, but Jesus pointed out that something else was really going on.

11:49 The wisdom of God refers to God's knowledge of the people. The **prophets and apostles** who would be persecuted and killed were the disciples and the prophets of the early church. This is the basis of Jesus' previous rebuke (vv. 47, 48). Those who would come in the current generation with the message of God would suffer the same fate as the prophets of old.

11:50 Generation seems to refer to the people or nation of Israel. They had received and would receive judgment for the way they treated God's prophets. The judgment here refers specifically to the fall of Jerusalem in A.D. 70, and ultimately to the final judgment of God in the Tribulation.

11:50, 51 Abel is pictured as the first prophet to be killed, going back to **the foundation of the world** (Gen. 4:10). **Zechariah** is probably the man described in 2 Chr. 24:20–25. He would be the last prophet slain in the OT if one considers the Hebrew order of the books of the OT.

11:52 Jesus charged the **lawyers** with doing the opposite of what they claimed their calling to be. Rather than bringing people nearer to God, they had removed the possibility of their entering into that **knowledge,** and had prevented others from understanding as well.

11:53, 54 seeking to catch Him: The

scribes and Pharisees began challenging Jesus in the hope that He might make a blunder that would allow them to destroy His ministry. They were **lying in wait** for Him (6:11; 19:47, 48; 20:19, 20; 22:2).

12:1, 2 Leaven here represents the presence of corruption. Unleavened bread is what the Jews ate at Passover (Ex. 12:14–20). The corruption in view here is **hypocrisy.** Practicing hypocrisy is senseless because eventually all deeds—both good and evil—will be exposed.

12:3 will be proclaimed on the housetops: All secrets will be revealed by God (Rom. 2:15, 16; 1 Cor. 4:5). The inner room was a storeroom that was surrounded by other rooms; it was the most private part of a house.

12:4 do not be afraid of those who kill the body: This verse anticipates the presence of severe religious persecution in response to Jesus' remarks in 11:39–54.

12:5 Even in the context of physical persecution, the only One believers should **fear** is God, who sees how we live and judges us. Jesus was not guaranteeing physical preservation in this life, but was opening the prospect of deliverance in the next life.

12:6 This verse emphasizes that God knows the most minute detail of what happens on earth. The **copper** coins mentioned were the smallest coin in circulation, worth about one-sixteenth of a basic day's wage.

12:7 Do not fear: Jesus emphasizes that God knows the person, even down to the number of hairs on one's head. One is not to fear, in the sense that placing one's life in God's care means He knows what we need. If God knows what happens to sparrows, He knows what happens to His children.

12:8 The issue here is faithfulness in testimony to Jesus, especially in the context of religious rejection. Acknowledging Jesus before men means being acknowledged by the **Son of Man** before God.

12:9 denies . . . will be denied: Every act of denial of Christ on earth will meet with commensurate denial of reward at the judgment seat (1 John 2:28). This is not speaking of the gift of salvation, but of the prize or reward (1 Cor. 9:24–27).

12:10 A word against the Son of Man is forgivable because His deity was veiled, but blasphemy against the Holy Spirit is flagrant rejection of the works and words of Christ (Matt. 12:31, 32, note).

> *If God knows what happens to sparrows, He knows what happens to His children.*

12:11 when they bring you to the syna-gogues: This is another indication that religious persecution is in view in these verses. **Magis-trates and authorities** governed civil proceed-ings, while synagogues conducted religious tribunals. In such situations, the disciple should not worry about what to say.

12:12 the Holy Spirit will teach you: The promise of God is that the faithful will receive ability to speak up for Jesus. Examples of the fulfillment of this passage include Acts 3—5 (especially 4:8); 7:51, 56 and the defense speeches of Paul in Acts 21—28.

12:13 tell my brother: Jesus is asked to intervene in a family dispute, as an ancient rabbi would be.

12:14 who made Me a Judge: Jesus refuses to enter into a dispute over money, which is clearly dividing a family. Such disputes over money destroy relationships, so Jesus tells a parable that explains the danger of focusing on wealth.

12:15 beware of covetousness: Jesus' warning is made explicitly. **life does not con-sist in the abundance of the things:** Jesus disagrees with the philosophy, "The one with the most toys wins." Such a focus is to make life consist of the things of creation and of man's creation, rather than to focus on God and the people He has created. Creation is not an object to be served or possessed by man. Life is found in the relationships one has, while the creation is designed to enhance those relationships. Things do not make life, God and people do. Only people will last. Thus, invest in what will last (2 Pet. 3:10–12)

12:16 parable: Jesus illustrates His point with the story of a man who "by chance" came into wealth and did not respond to its presence properly.

12:17 What shall I do? The man faces his dilemma as anyone might, by determining how to preserve his abundant resources.

12:18, 19 Including v. 17, the word **I** appears six times, showing the selfish focus this man has as a result of his fortune. His plan is to store his abundant resources for himself, as though the assets were his alone and should be hoarded. This focus on the self is what Jesus is condemning.

12:20 God's judgment on selfishness is clear. What did the rich **fool** have for the next life? He could not take his grain with him. What he owned was no longer of any value after death. In a single day, the rich man became poor. All

> *To be rich toward self without the greater priority of richness toward God is to be a double loser.*

earthly wealth is temporary and ultimately worthless (Matt. 6:19–21; 1 Tim. 6:6–10, 17–19; James 5:1–6).

12:21 so is he who lays up treasure for himself: Jesus highlights the negative example. Of course, the opposite is exhorted here by implication. To be rich toward self without the greater priority of richness toward God is to be a double loser.

12:22 do not worry: This is a call to faith to trust God to provide. One of the reasons a person desires possessions is to secure control of his or her life and have comfort and provi-sion. Jesus says that God will provide such needs.

12:23 Life is more than: Jesus mentions the basics of care here; food and clothing. He says that life is more than these basic things.

12:24 Jesus describes God's care of **ravens,** unclean crea-tures according to Jewish law and among the least respected of birds (Lev. 11:15; Deut. 14:14). Yet God even cares for them. **How much more value are you,** says Jesus, pointing out that God will surely care for the disciple as well.

12:25 It is uncertain whether Jesus is saying through His rhetorical question that worry cannot add to one's physical height or that worry cannot add to one's life span. In fact, worry can sometimes shorten life. What is clear is that worry is utterly useless and shows a lack of faith in God's plan for our lives.

12:26 If you then are not able to do the least: Jesus again highlights the pointlessness of worry. If worry does not help the basic things of life, why worry so much?

12:27–29 Even the wealthy King **Solomon** did not clothe himself as God has clothed the **lilies.** The illustration of **grass** indicates that God cares enough to provide beauty for the parts of His creation that have a short life. Why should we worry if God takes such care of even the smallest blade of grass? The Lord knows our problems and will provide us with what we need. **do not seek . . . nor have an anxious mind:** Since God will provide, there is no need for us to concentrate on mundane things such as food. This should not be our chief concern, but instead our first priority should be doing the will of God (v. 31).

12:30 The world pursues expensive food and luxurious clothing as ends in themselves. It has its heart set on things, without thinking of God and thanking Him for such pleasures. The materialistic world is like a group of passengers frantically scurrying to get the best deck chair on a sinking ship. When we are consumed with possessions, there can be little left in our heart for God. **your Father knows:** We can trust God to provide for us because God knows precisely what we need. It is not wrong to have possessions. The issue here is one of priorities.

12:31, 32 Jesus contrasts what the world pursues (v. 30) with what the disciple is to pursue (v. 31). Those who get their priorities right and overcome the world will receive power to reign with Christ in His kingdom (Rev. 2:25–29). Jesus desires to share His coming glory.

12:33 Sell what you have: In contrast to the world's hoarding of possessions, the disciple must be generous with what God gives. **money bags which do not grow old:** By serving God and others, you can invest in your eternal future. You cannot take possessions with you in the next life, but you can store up an eternal treasure by giving to others (see Paul's statement in Phil. 4:17).

12:34 What people consider valuable is **where** their energy will be spent. Knowing God and investing in His purposes should be the **treasure** we seek.

12:35 waist be girded . . . lamps burning: These are two pictures of readiness. A lamp was used at night, while girding the waist involved pulling up the hem of a robe so that one could run. Jesus was calling the disciples to be ready for service.

12:36 Jesus compared the disciples to servants who are ready to serve their master **immediately.** Paul also used this image in describing his relationship to God (Rom. 1:1).

12:37 Blessed: Here the blessing is on those who watch attentively for their master's return. Jesus was speaking of faithful and obedient service. One day Jesus will return to make an accounting of how people served Him (Rom. 14:10; 2 Cor. 5:10). In a reversal of the servant image, Jesus pointed out that the faithful servant will be served by Jesus on His return. Faithfulness will be rewarded.

12:38 This verse speaks of a return at an unusually late hour. The exact time referred to depends on which system of time was used. In the Roman system the **second** and **third** watch would be 9 P.M. to 3 A.M. By the Jewish method it would be 10 P.M. to 6 A.M. Luke usually uses the Roman pattern (Acts 12:4); but since Jesus is speaking, the Jewish system is also possible. The point is that constant attentiveness is necessary.

12:39, 40 he would have watched: Jesus changed the illustration slightly, comparing the watch to protecting against a robbery. Knowledge of the time would lead to vigilance. But since the time is not known, constant readiness is essential.

12:41 to us, or to all people: Peter asked if Jesus' teaching was for the disciples only or for all people. Jesus did not answer the question directly. Instead He described a variety of categories of servants. Servants are those who belong to the Master and have their stewardship evaluated (19:11–27). Several responses, from faithfulness to blatant disobedience, are described in vv. 42–48. The issue is who lives life in a way that looks for, and takes seriously, the return of Jesus (1 John 2:28).

12:42 Who then is that faithful and wise steward? This is the basic question. The faithful steward is the one who looks for the Lord's return and serves faithfully in His absence, knowing that such faithfulness is what the master desires (vv. 37, 40, 43, 44).

12:43 blessed: The waiting and faithful servant is the one whom Jesus calls blessed.

12:44 he will make him ruler: Such rule will be a part of the administration of Jesus' kingdom when He returns (19:11–27; 1 Cor. 6:2, 3; Rev. 20—22).

12:45 is delaying . . . begins to beat: This servant is depicted as consciously doing the opposite of caring for others and of treating the Master's return as irrelevant.

12:46 The image of being slain—**cut him in two**—indicates the severity of this judgment, especially in contrast to the whippings of vv. 47, 48. **Unbelievers** are those who did not take seriously the consequences of judgment (2 Cor. 5:10; Rev. 3:11).

12:47 knew . . . did not prepare himself or do: This is a category of disobedience, not as blatant as doing the opposite, but unfaithfulness nonetheless. This servant is disciplined **with many stripes,** though he is not rejected. Such evaluation of church leaders is described in 1 Cor. 3:10–15 and is broadened to apply to all believers in 2 Cor. 5:10.

12:48 Discipline for the ignorant is less severe—**beaten with few.** The parable suggests degrees of God's punishment: The faithful are rewarded, the ignorant are disciplined a little, the disobedient are disciplined moderately, and the blatantly disobedient are executed. In each case, the stewardship of the servant is evaluated.

12:49 I came to send fire: Fire is an image associated with God's judgment (Jer. 5:14; 23:29). Jesus' coming brings judgment on those who refuse to accept Him and divides the believers from the faithless. Though Jesus was ready for the judgment of humankind, other things had to happen first (v. 50).

12:50 As a figure for Jesus' death (Mark 10:38, 39), **baptism** in this verse refers to the coming of overflowing waters of divine judgment (Pss. 18:4, 16; 42:7; 69:1, 2; Is. 8:7, 8; 30:27, 28). Note Jesus' human response to what He recognized as His necessary death.

12:51 Part of Jesus' mission was to create a **division** within humankind. Other texts of Luke speak of Jesus bringing peace (2:14; 7:50; 8:48; 10:5, 6; Acts 10:36; Eph. 2:13–17). He offers peace to those who respond to Him.

12:52, 53 Jesus describes the division that enters into families.

12:54, 55 a cloud rising out of the west: In Israel a western breeze meant moisture coming from the Mediterranean Sea. **the south wind blow:** A **south wind** meant hot air coming from the desert.

12:56 Hypocrites: Jesus rebuked His audience for being able to discern the weather but not what God was doing through Him.

12:57 do you not judge what is right? A rhetorical question of reflection. They are to consider the wise course of action.

12:58, 59 make every effort . . . to settle with him: The picture here is of a magistrate who functions like a bailiff bringing a debtor into prison. Since the context of this passage is Jesus' mission, the **judge** likely represents God. The message of this parable is to become reconciled to God before judgment comes.

13:1 The details of the incident referred to here, in which Jewish blood was shed at or near the temple during a time of **sacrifices,** are not known. **Pilate** was known for his insensitivity to the Jewish people early in his rule. The event probably occurred during the Feast of the Passover or Tabernacles, when **Galileans** most likely would have been at the temple.

13:2 Do you suppose: Jesus' question reflected the opinion of His audience. The idea that judgment and death are the results of sin led to the belief that tragic death was the result of extreme sin. While such a view was common in Judaism, it was not always a correct conclusion (Ex. 20:5; Job 4:7; 8:4, 20; 22:5; Prov. 10:24, 25; John 9:1–3).

13:3 unless you repent: Jesus' point here is that everyone stands at the edge of death until repentance occurs. The death in view here is spiritual, not physical.

13:4 The event referred to here was a natural tragedy as opposed to the violent human act alluded to in vv. 1 and 2. However, the same question was raised. Were the people who suffered being judged for their sins? **Siloam** was

> *In order to have a relationship with God, one must embrace Jesus and come to know Him.*

located in the southeast section of Jerusalem.

13:5 The manner in which a person dies is not a measure of righteousness; what is important is not to die outside of God's grace and care. The way to avoid such a fate is to **repent,** to come to God through the care of the physician Jesus (5:32).

13:6 A fig tree often represents God's blessing or a people who have a special relationship with God (Mic. 7:1, 2). The man in this parable represents God; the fig tree represents Israel.

13:7 for three years: A fig tree was often given some time to bear good fruit since its root structure was complex and took time to develop. Three years would have been enough for the tree to yield some fruit.

13:8 this year also: The keeper asks that the tree have a little more time. It is an appeal for compassion. The keeper will try to care for the tree so it will produce a fruit.

13:9 But if not: If the tree, symbolizing Israel, would yield some fruit it could escape judgment; a failure to be fruitful would result in judgment. In v. 35, Jesus declares that the nation's house is desolate, so judgment comes. That judgment is described in 19:41–44. The fall of Jerusalem, which took place in A.D. 70, is in view. This theme is also addressed in 20:9–19.

13:10–12 loosed from your infirmity: This is a declaration that she is freed from Satan's power (v. 16).

13:13 immediately: The healing, as is common, occurs immediately and is followed by the praise of thanksgiving to God (4:39; 5:13; 25; 7:15; 8:44).

13:14 with indignation: The synagogue ruler is not pleased and tells the crowd, while rebuking Jesus, that such healings can wait until after the Sabbath, since God's Sabbath should be honored.

13:15 Hypocrite: When the ruler of the synagogue became indignant regarding Jesus' healing on the Sabbath (vv. 10–14), Jesus pointed out that if basic compassion was shown to animals on the Sabbath, how much more compassion should be shown to a suffering woman (v. 16). In fact, Jewish practice varied in such cases. Some Mishnaic texts show that some activity with cattle was allowed on the Sabbath, such as untying them, feeding them, and leading them to water, providing it was not too far; while at Qumran, an activity like the one Jesus describes is forbidden on the Sabbath, if one must go more than 2,000 cubits (about

1,000 yards) to get to the water. At Qumran, a man could only go 1,000 cubits out of town on the Sabbath for a journey (Num. 25:4); while in some instances, the Pharisees allowed up to 2,000 cubits.

13:16 daughter of Abraham: This description of the woman indicates how special she was. Jesus pointed out that there was no better day on which to overcome Satan than the Sabbath.

13:17 adversaries . . . multitudes: The contrasting responses show the division that Jesus brings (12:51).

13:18, 19 Jesus compared the growth of God's kingdom to a little **seed** that becomes a big tree where many birds can find shelter. A tree of the **mustard** family would grow to about twelve feet. The image of birds nesting in the trees is found frequently in the OT (Ps. 104:12; Ezek. 17:22–24; Dan. 4:10–12).

13:20, 21 In this illustration the **leaven** is hidden in **meal** or flour equaling about fifty pounds. Leaven permeates bread and makes it rise. Usually this image is negative, as in 1 Cor. 5:6; but in this parable, it is positive. The kingdom will start small, but will grow and eventually fill the earth. The emphasis is not so much on a process of growth as in the difference between the kingdom's beginning and its end.

13:22–24 the narrow gate: The suggestion here is that one must enter salvation on God's terms. Those who seek to enter but are unable are those who seek entrance on their own terms. Many will miss the blessings of God because they think they can achieve salvation on their own merit or on the basis of their own piety, rather than because they came to know God through Jesus (v. 25).

13:25 Once a person's life has ended, **the door** of opportunity to respond to Jesus is closed and access into God's presence cannot be gained. **I do not know you:** The issue here is being properly and personally related to God through Jesus. Verse 26 makes it clear that the **Lord** at the door is Jesus, since reference is made to His ministry. Those who seek entry after the door is closed will be rejected, since they did not come to God on His terms through Jesus.

13:26 We ate and drank . . . You taught: The appeal here is by people who experienced Jesus' presence. The passage primarily involves those Jews who witnessed Jesus' ministry. They were trying to gain entry into God's presence based simply on the fact that they had observed Jesus. Jesus refused them, pointing out that it was not enough for them to have been close to Him. In order to have a relationship with God, one must embrace Jesus and come to know Him.

13:27 I do not know you . . . Depart from Me: In this verse, Jesus turns a question about salvation (v. 23) into a question about personally knowing Him. Failure to seek salvation in Jesus means that sin remains in a person's life.

13:28 weeping and gnashing of teeth: This is a figure describing the reaction of someone to traumatic news. It is a figure of remorse, pain, and frustration. It is clear here (though not in every place of its occurrence) that the figure describes reaction to being excluded from salvation, as the reference to being **thrust out** also makes clear. Jesus says the great patriarchs and prophets will be inside, but the one who does not enter by the narrow way will be excluded.

13:29 east . . . west . . . north . . . south: The scene changes in v. 29 to those who will come from all corners of the earth for entrance into God's kingdom. This passage alludes to the inclusion of Gentiles.

13:30 There will be many surprises in God's kingdom. Those who are despised on earth—some Gentiles, for example—will be greatly honored in the kingdom. Conversely, those who are considered influential and powerful on earth may find themselves ashamed (compare John 2:28).

13:31–33 Herod wants to kill You: This warning from the Pharisees was apparently an effort to get Jesus out of the region and out of their hair. It is hard to know whether the warning was true. **fox:** The reference here is to Herod's viciousness. Jesus' reply seems to take the Pharisees' warning at face value. **I shall be perfected:** Jesus predicted His resurrection in Jerusalem. Because it was His call from God, Jesus could not avoid ministering in the region. The verb translated *perfected* means to complete something, which is why it alludes to Jesus' resurrection, the decisive moment of His ministry. The reference to **today, tomorrow, and the day following** is figurative, since Jesus was speaking of more than three remaining days in His ministry.

13:32 perfected: Jesus predicts His resurrection in Jerusalem. He cannot avoid ministering in the region. It is His call. The reference to **today, tomorrow** and the **third day** are figurative, since Jesus is speaking of more than three remaining days of total ministry. The verb translated *perfected* means "to complete something," which is why it alludes to Jesus' resurrection—the decisive moment of His ministry.

13:33 it cannot be: Jesus followed a long line of prophets that were executed in the nation's capital (1 Kin. 18:4, 13; 19:10, 14; 2 Chr. 24:21; Jer. 2:30; 26:20–23; 38:4–6; Amos 7:10–17).

13:34 Jerusalem, Jerusalem: The double address indicates Jesus' deep sorrow (2 Sam. 18:33; Jer. 22:29). The city had executed many of God's messengers. Stephen makes a similar point about the nation of Israel in Acts 7:51–53. **I wanted to gather:** As a prophet, Jesus spoke for God in the first person. He compared God's desire to gather the nation to a hen sheltering and protecting her young. Sadly, the nation was not willing to be gathered.

13:35 Your house is left . . . desolate: Jesus declared that the nation stood under a judgment similar to the exile to Babylon (Jer. 12:7; 22:5). God would abandon the nation

temple. Jesus used the language of this psalm to illustrate God's greeting to Him.

14:1 Sabbath: Luke covers yet another Sabbath event (4:16–30; 4:31–38; 6:1–11; 13:10–17). Luke notes that Jesus is being **watched closely.** The term used means "lurk about and watch closely."

14:2 Dropsy is a condition in which water is retained in the body, leading to swollen limbs (Num. 5:11–27). Dropsy is a symptom and not a specific disease.

14:3 Is it lawful: Note that Jesus raised the question of Sabbath law here, preempting the questioning he had faced in 6:2 (6:9).

 **IN CONTEXT** | **Keeping the Sabbath**

A man's withered hand is restored; a man with dropsy is healed. Most would rejoice in the restoration of health and marvel at Jesus' power over illness. But the Pharisees were filled with rage (6:11) or remained disapprovingly silent (14:4). Why?

To the Jewish leaders of Jesus' day, healing on the Sabbath was sacrilegious. They considered His healings to be work, and the Ten Commandments clearly prohibited work on the Sabbath (Ex. 20:8–11; Deut. 5:12–15). The Sabbath was holy, a day set apart for God. Just as the Israelites were commanded to tithe part of their earnings to God, they were to give Him their time as well. Breaking the Sabbath was a very grave matter, for God's law demanded death for those who ignored it (Ex. 31:14, 15; 35:2).

During the period of the second temple (515 B.C.–A.D. 70), scribes and rabbis pored over the words of Scripture, interpreting every detail. What constituted "work" on the Sabbath? What could be allowed "within the law?" According to the Law, burdens were not to be carried on the Sabbath. This meant that what exactly constituted a "burden" had to be clarified and defined. On the surface, the scribes had a good reason for interpreting the Law: they did not want anyone to break it inadvertently. But their interpretations increasingly emphasized external adherence to the Law instead of the cultivation of an attitude of submission before the Lord. Perfect obedience to the Law and its interpretation became a source of pride instead of a tangible expression of love for God. By Jesus' day, the rabbis and scribes had become so strict that they accused Jesus' disciples of breaking the Sabbath because they had simply plucked some heads of grain, rubbed them in their hands, and eaten them as they walked through a grainfield (6:1, 2).

Jesus' healings on the Sabbath enraged the religious teachers. It was obvious to them that healing was classified as work and prohibited by the fourth commandment (Deut. 5:14). But to Jesus it was common sense and a good deed. Jesus revealed the rabbis' hypocrisy with the example of an ox falling down a pit. The Pharisees would allow an ox to be rescued on the Sabbath, but they wanted to prohibit Jesus from rescuing a human being. Their outrage at Jesus' healing came from their own interpretation of the Law and not from the Law itself. The scribes and rabbis had thought through, categorized, and defined all the minutiae of the Law, but they had missed its central point. The Lord had given the Law to encourage the Israelites to love Him and to love others (Mark 12:30, 31). He had never prohibited doing good on the Sabbath.

---

until they responded to the Messiah. **Blessed is He:** This is a citation of Ps. 118:26. The people of Israel would not see the Messiah again until they were ready to receive Him and recognize that He was sent from God. Psalm 118 reflects the greeting of a priest to a group entering the

14:4 silent: The absence of reply shows a hesitation to enter into dialogue; then Jesus heals the man in their presence.

14:5 Which of you: Now Jesus explains that many Jews would rescue an animal on the Sabbath. As noted in Luke 13:15, various and somewhat different rules existed within the differing groups of Judaism for this kind of Sabbath activity.

14:6–11 they could not answer: Jesus has silenced his opponents.

14:12, 13 True hospitality and service is what is given to those who cannot repay. Disciples must have a special concern for the **poor, maimed, lame,** and **blind,** as Jesus does (4:16–19).

14:14 you shall be repaid: Even though there may be no reward in this life, God will not overlook what His servants have done to carry out His love and mercy (2 Cor. 5:10; Heb. 6:20).

14:15 Blessed is he: One of the guests at the meal reflected on the glory of sitting at the banquet table of God, an image of being saved and living in God's presence. The man probably assumed that many of the people attending the meal with Jesus would be present at God's banquet table. Jesus responded to the man's assumption with a warning.

14:16, 17 those who were invited: In the ancient world, invitations to a feast were sent out well in advance of the meal. Then on the day of the feast, servants would announce the start of the meal. This parable is similar to the one in Matt. 22:1–14, but was probably spoken on a different occasion.

14:18 I must go: Something gets in the way of the celebration. In the ancient world, closing the purchase could require a post-purchase inspection. Other things are more important.

14:19 going to test them: To own five oxen suggests wealth, since most landowners had only one or two. Again, something is more pressing.

14:20 I have married a wife: While the OT exempted a man from military duty because of marriage (Deut. 20:7; 24:5), marriage was not an excuse for avoiding social duties. The general point here is that the man regarded his own affairs as more important than the feast.

14:21 poor . . . maimed . . . lame . . . blind: This list matches that of v. 13. The maimed were excluded from full participation in Jewish worship (Lev. 21:17–23). The master's second invitation extended the scope of the offer to those who were rejected by society.

14:22 still there is room: The response has not filled the hall.

14:23 The master's second invitation extended beyond the city limits, encouraging even more people to come to the feast. This may picture the inclusion of Gentiles in God's salvation (Is. 49:6). The instruction to **compel them to come in** does not mean to force people in, but to urge them. As outsiders, the people might not feel comfortable coming.

14:24 none of those . . . invited: This speaks of most of the Jewish nation to whom Christ was originally offered. Because they rejected Him, they will not share in the meal.

14:25 great multitudes: Jesus did not hesitate to discuss the demands of discipleship with those who were interested in His claims.

14:26 does not hate: The essence of discipleship is giving Christ first place. To "hate" one's family and even one's life is rhetorical. It refers to desiring something less than something else. This instruction was especially appropriate in Jesus' day, since a decision for Jesus could mean rejection by family and persecution even to the point of death. Those who feared family disapproval or persecution would not come to Jesus.

14:27 Jesus' call here is to follow Him in the way of rejection and suffering. A **disciple** will be rejected by those in the world who do not honor Christ. Therefore, a disciple must be ready to face and accept such rejection.

14:28 count the cost: The picture of the tower is a call to consider what it will take to follow Jesus. Christ does not give some emotional appeal to follow Him. He asks for careful consideration of the action the disciple may choose to take and whether he or she will be faithful to the task (9:57, 58).

14:29, 30 was not able to finish: Their mocking centers on the dishonor that results from an inability to complete the task. Following Christ is not something to be taken up on a trial basis. It calls for ultimate commitment (9:62).

14:31, 32 The picture here is of a **king** assessing his ability to do battle with another more powerful king. The king **sends a delegation** only after appreciating the weight and consequences of his decision. Jesus urged the people to think about what it would mean to follow Him, and not to take it lightly.

14:33 forsake all: The essence of discipleship is to place all things in God's hands. Jesus wants the crowds to understand this. Following Jesus is not a trivial matter. It is not how little you can give to God, but how much God deserves. **cannot be My disciple:** One is not really being a disciple if one is not fully devoted to God.

14:34 In the ancient world, **salt** was often used as a catalyst for burning fuel such as cattle dung. The salt of the time was impure and could lose its strength over time, becoming useless. Jesus' point is that the same is true of a "saltless" disciple.

14:35 throw it out: Jesus warned that an ineffective commitment leads to being cast aside. This apparently is a reference to those who are judged as unfaithful believers (1 Cor. 11:30). Remaining useful to God means remaining faithful to Him (9:61, 62).

15:1 the tax collectors and the sinners: The three parables of ch. 15 explain why Jesus associated with despised groups while the Pharisees and scribes did not. The parables in this chapter are found only in Luke.

15:2 eats with them: In the ancient world, table fellowship indicated acceptance of the other guests. This is why the Jewish religious leaders complained about Jesus' companions at His meals (5:30–32; 19:10; Mark 2:15).

15:3, 4 A hundred sheep was a medium-sized flock. The average herd ran from twenty to two hundred head, while a flock of three hundred or more was considered large.

15:5, 6 The call to **rejoice** at finding the lost sheep would have been natural enough, since sheep were valuable property in the ancient world.

15:7 likewise: Jesus compared the joy of

In this second parable of ch. 15, more detail is given regarding the search effort than in the first parable of vv. 4–7.

15:9 I have found: The response parallels Luke 15:6.

15:10 likewise: The comparison to sinners is again made as in v. 7; but here the response of the angels as heaven's representatives is in view.

15:11 A certain man: This parable, Luke 15:11–32, is really about the father, who pictures God's compassion, and his reaction to his sons.

15:12 the portion of goods that falls to me: In the ancient world, this son most likely would have been in his teens and single. As the younger son he would have received half of what the elder son received (Deut. 21:17), or a third of his father's estate. The early Jews warned fathers against breaking up an estate too

The pods of the carob tree—probably the coarse food in Jesus' parable that the lost son was tempted to eat (Luke 15:16).

finding a lost sheep to the joy of heaven over a sinner's repentance. The unstated conclusion is that the hope of such a conversion was the reason Jesus associated with the undesirable of society. **Persons who need no repentance** is a rhetorical way of describing the scribes and Pharisees. A similar description is found in 5:31, where it is said that some do not need a physician. The scribes and Pharisees believed that they did not need to repent because they were not lost.

15:8 ten silver coins: A drachma was a silver coin equal to a day's wage for a basic laborer. The woman needed a **lamp** because she lived in a windowless house. Her broom for sweeping would have been made of palm twigs.

early. Here the father granted the request, illustrating how God permits each person to go his or her own way.

15:13 wasted his possessions: The verb here means "to scatter or disperse something." The term translated **prodigal** describes a debased, extravagant life (Prov. 28:7).

15:14 famine . . . began to be in want: Some of the son's hardship was made worse by circumstances which were beyond his control.

15:15 Feeding **swine** was an insulting job for a Jewish person, since pigs were unclean according to the Law of Moses.

15:16 pods that the swine ate: The unclean pigs eat better than the son does. This shows how low he fell. This type of "pod" or sweet bean was eaten only by the poorest people.

15:17 he came to himself: This means "he came to his senses." He knows his father's slaves are doing better than he is.

15:18, 19 I have sinned: The son's words represent the confession of a sinner. The son expected nothing and relied completely on the mercy of his father. So it is with the sinner who repents.

15:20 The description of the father's **compassion** in running to his son and kissing him illustrates the immediate acceptance of a sinner who turns to God.

15:21 no longer worthy to be called your son: Despite his awareness of being accepted by his father, the son continued his confession of his sin. He then asked to become one of his father's servants. Similarly, a sinner realizes that he or she brings nothing to and deserves nothing from God, but must rely completely on God's mercy.

15:22 The father accepted his son's confession but refused his request to make him a servant. Instead the returning son was made a full member of the family again. The **robe** probably represented the best clothes the father had to offer. The **ring** may have borne the family seal, signifying the son's acceptance back into the family. The son's confession of sin brought full restoration.

15:23 fatted calf: The father will celebrate with a great banquet. The fatted calf was usually kept for sacrifices on feast days and was specially fed for the occasion. Such a meal of meat was rare in ancient Palestine. The celebration parallels Luke 15:6, 9.

15:24 dead . . . alive . . . lost . . . found: The total transformation of the prodigal son is summarized in these two contrasts. Such a transformation is a reason to celebrate. It is also the reason Jesus chose to associate with the lost.

15:25–27 heard music and dancing: The party developed quickly, so that the other son, coming in at the end of the day, encounters the noise of the celebration as he approaches.

15:28 The older brother's unhappiness over a fatted calf (v. 27) being killed to celebrate the return of his undisciplined brother illustrates the response of the Pharisees and scribes at the prospect of sinners becoming acceptable to God.

15:29 I never transgressed . . . you never gave me: Note the contrast between the older son's attitude here and the younger son's attitude in vv. 19, 21. The older son proclaimed his righteousness and argued that justice had not been done.

15:30 harlots: We are never told whether in fact the charge of the older son is true. The complaint is a strong one, "Father, you honor immorality over faithfulness."

15:31 all that I have is yours: The father responded to his disgruntled older son by explaining that just because someone receives a blessing, that does not mean there is no blessing for others. The father also implied that the older son always had the opportunity to celebrate with a fattened calf, since the animals were his.

15:32 It was right: The father claims justice is being done and rejoicing should occur using the same dead/alive, lost/found contrast which appeared in v. 24. We are not told how the elder responds. The parable is left hanging for reflection. One is left to decide whether they rejoice at the return of the sinner like the father or complain like the elder son. If one is willing to rejoice at the presence of transformation in the sinner, one should also seek out the sinner who can benefit from it.

16:1 A steward was a servant who supervised and administered an estate. The charge brought against this steward is incompetence.

16:2 Give an account . . . you can no longer be steward: The rich man responded to the charge that his steward was incompetent by firing the steward and asking for his records to be brought up to date.

16:3 I cannot dig; I am ashamed to beg: The steward does not wish to engage in common labor or admit he is poor.

16:4 I have resolved: He says, "I have got it!" He produces a scheme that will encourage others to help him.

16:5, 6 A hundred measures of oil . . . fifty: Three explanations are commonly given concerning the steward's right to alter the amount his master was owed: (1) The steward simply lowered the price on his own authority; (2) the steward removed the interest charge from the debt, according to the law (Lev. 25:36, 37; Deut. 15:7, 8; 23:20, 21); or (3) the steward removed his own commission, sacrificing only his own money and not that of his master. The different rates of reduction reflect the different rates for different commodities.

16:7 hundred measures of wheat: This is the Hebrew measure of the "kor," which was ten ephahs or thirty seahs, though various standards are cited for the kor (also spelled "cor"), making an exact figure uncertain. By the highest standard used, this is around 1,100 bushels or 3,930 liters of grain, a yield of a 100-acre tract of land. It would be worth 2,500–3,000 denarii. On the smaller standard, it is only 5 percent of this total. More important than the exact size is the reduction of the bill.

16:8 The master recognized the foresight in the steward's generosity. It is debatable whether the steward was dishonest and robbed the master by such reductions or was **shrewd** in using his authority to discount the goods (vv. 6, 7). The fact that the master commended the steward may suggest that the master was not robbed, and that the steward's reduction was the result of either an adherence to the law or a lowering of the steward's own commission.

16:9 Mammon, or money, should be used generously to build works that last. Money is called **unrighteous** because it often manifests unrighteousness and selfishness in people (Tim. 6:6–10, 17–19; James 1:9–11; 5:1–6).

16:10 faithful . . . unjust . . . least . . . much: Small examples of selfishness now result in greater selfishness later. Likewise, small examples of generosity now result in greater generosity later.

16:11 mammon . . . true riches: This is the development of v. 10. A person who cannot handle money certainly cannot handle spiritual matters that are of much more value.

16:12, 13 another man's: Yet another application of v. 10. If one cannot handle something for someone else, why should he be entrusted to risk himself on his own possessions, where accountability is gone?

16:14–16 Jesus indicates a basic division in God's plan here. The time of promise extended from the Law and Prophets **until John** the Baptist. Now the promise of God's kingdom is preached. The new era approaches. **Everyone is pressing into it** can also be translated "all are urged insistently to come in," emphasizing the urgency of the message.

16:17 one tittle of the law to fail: Here the law is seen in terms of promise as v. 16 suggests. Jesus' point is not that all 613 commandments of the Torah remain in effect forever, but that the goal of the law, the promise of God's rule, is realized. The New Covenant fulfills and replaces the old (Acts 2:14–40; 3:14–26). This verse also is an important one for the doctrine of the inerrancy of Scripture. Christ says that the awesome act of the universe being destroyed is more likely than for something God has given in His Word to be inaccurate.

16:18 commits adultery: Jesus illustrates the moral demands of the law by citing the inviolate nature of marriage, so much so that a remarriage is seen as adulterous. In other texts (Matt. 5:32; 19:9), Jesus notes the exception of sexual immorality, which can be a ground for a permissible divorce, though divorce is never set forth as a preferred option. What the sexual immorality refers to and whether a "permissible divorce" exists and whether one can remarry after such a divorce are all heavily debated issues in the church. Jesus' point in Luke was not a detailed exposition of this question since the Matthean texts are more complete, but

simply serves as an illustration of the moral authority of His teaching. He is the ethicist of the kingdom. Other relevant texts to the issue of divorce are: Deut. 24:1–4; Mark 10:1–12; 1 Cor. 7:7–16. In Judaism there also was debate. The rabbinic school of Shammai only allowed divorce for immorality, while the school of Hillel allowed it for a wide variety of reasons (Mishnah, Gittim, 9:10).

16:19 clothed in purple: Purple clothes were extremely expensive because they were made with a special dye extracted from a kind of snail.

16:20, 21 To have his sores **licked** by **dogs** threatened Lazarus with infection as well as ritual uncleanness, since dogs fed on garbage, including dead animals.

16:22 Abraham's bosom was the blessed place of the dead. Angelic escorts for the dead were also known in Judaism. This verse indicates that the dead know their fate immediately.

16:23 Note the reversal of fortune from vv. 19–21. Here the rich man was suffering and Lazarus was at peace. **Hades** in the OT was the place where the dead are gathered. It is also called *Sheol* in Pss. 16:10; 86:13. In the NT, Hades is often mentioned in a negative context (10:15; Matt. 11:23; 16:18). Hades is where the unrighteous dead dwell.

16:24 I am tormented: The rich man desired relief from his suffering. The image of thirst for the experience of judgment is common (Is. 5:13; 65:13; Hos. 2:3).

16:25 The standard by which the rich man treated others was applied to him. In his **lifetime** he lacked compassion, so now there was no compassion for him.

16:26 a great gulf fixed: This detail illustrates the fact that the unrighteous, once they have died, cannot enter into the sphere of the righteous.

16:27, 28 The rich man asked for a heavenly envoy to be sent so that his **brothers** would not repeat his irreversible error. It is difficult to know if his concern for his brothers was sincere, or just a backhanded way of saying that in his own life he had not received adequate warning about the judgment.

16:29 They have Moses and the prophets: Abraham made it clear that the rich man's brothers should have known what to do, since they had the message of God in the ancient writings. The point here is that generosity with money and care for the poor were taught in the OT (Deut. 14:28, 29; Is. 3:14, 15; Mic. 6:10, 11).

16:30 from the dead: The rich man's premise is that a resurrection will bring repentance.

16:31 If they do not hear: A person who

rejects God's message will not be persuaded by resurrection. Though the rich man's request for a heavenly messenger is denied within the parable, it is honored in the telling of the account, because the parable is part of a gospel that announces Christ's resurrection.

17:1, 2 woe to him: Jesus warned that judgment awaits those who cause others to stumble. The severe form of the warning suggests that false teaching, or leading someone into apostasy, is in view here. **A millstone** was a heavy stone used in a grinding mill.

17:3 Take heed: This command probably closes the warning of Luke 17:1, 2. **sins . . . rebuke . . . repents . . . forgive:** Here Jesus makes disciples accountable to one another, but in a context that emphasizes being forgiving as v. 4 makes clear.

17:4 you shall forgive him: The repeated

race (9:52). A hated **foreigner** was the only former leper who gave **glory to God** for his cleansing.

17:19 Jesus commended the **faith** that heals, as He did in 7:50; 8:50. The Samaritan apparently received more than physical healing.

17:20 In ancient Israel there was an expectation that the **kingdom of God** would come with cosmic signs. Such expectation was rooted in texts that linked God's coming with great signs (Joel 2:28–32). Jesus' concept of the kingdom of God, however, was broader than the time of the final consummation, when such signs will be seen (Matt. 24:29).

17:21 within you: The marginal translation "in your midst" is clearer. Jesus would not tell Pharisees that the kingdom is in them. His point is that the kingdom comes with Him. They do not need to hunt in order to find it. This is

---

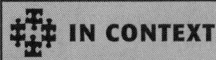 **IN CONTEXT** | **Only One Returned**

Once again Jesus chose a route that made it likely that He would encounter Samaritans (Luke 17:11). And once again Luke's account has to do with the tension between Jews and Samaritans.

It's easy to see why Jesus would ask, "Where are the nine?" (17:17). He was amazed at their lack of gratitude. But why did He call the one man who did return a "foreigner"? Luke singles out the fact that he was a Samaritan. That meant that he and Jesus were divided by a cultural wall that was virtually impenetrable. In fact, it was said to be unlawful for a Jew even to associate with a "foreigner" (compare Acts 10:28). Yet Jesus openly violated that taboo as He marveled at the Samaritan's thankful heart.

What of the other nine? Were they not Samaritans as well? Possibly, since this incident was taking place in or near Samaria. But is it not equally possible, given Luke's comment and Jesus' remark, that the other nine were not Samaritans, but Jews who had been driven away from the Jewish community to the Samaritans because of their leprous condition?

If so, their ingratitude was inexcusable. There was no racial wall separating them from Jesus. The only barrier had been their leprosy—and Jesus had removed that. They had every reason to turn in faith toward the Lord, but instead they turned away.

By contrast, a man who had every reason to stay away from Jesus returned and gave glory to God. As a result, he received what the other nine—and most of the rest of Israel—did not: spiritual healing, and not just physical.

---

request for forgiveness is to be honored. The disciple is to be generous with compassion.

17:5 Increase our faith: The disciples desire to grow in their faith.

17:6–10 Even faith the size of a tiny **mustard seed** can do wonderful things. The black **mulberry** tree has a vast root system that allows it to live up to six hundred years.

17:11–14 Samaria and Galilee: Though Jesus was traveling to **Jerusalem,** His journey did not follow a direct route.

17:15–18 The Samaritans were a despised

one of the most important texts on the kingdom, for it indicates that an aspect of kingdom promise came with Jesus in His first coming. The kingdom is the rule of God manifested over a realm (eventually the earth, but it is specially manifested in this present period among believers in the church). The kingdom of God is among the kingdoms of men today; but one day, the kingdom of God will swallow up the kingdoms of men (Rev. 11:15). Jesus makes clear by vv. 22–37 that the kingdom has two phases—one now and one to come. In the beginning of His kingdom on earth, God first prepares a King to rule; then He gathers a people for Him to rule over; and then He gives the Ruler a realm (the earth) in which to reign. King David provides a picture of this in the OT. He was declared to be king. Then he gathered a people. Then he took the realm. As such, the kingdom is not the same as the church, though the church is a part of the kingdom. The kingdom now is the presence of God alongside the kingdoms of men. The power of God is shown now in the distribution and work of the Spirit (Rom. 14:17; 1 Cor. 4:20). One day, however, Jesus will rule over a kingdom that will swallow up the kingdoms of men and will share that rule with the saints that are overcomers (Rev. 2:26, 27; 5:9, 10; 20:4–6).

17:22–24 Lightning is sudden and visible to all. Likewise, the sudden **day** of the **Son of Man** will be visible to all. When the Lord returns, He will come quickly and obviously. There will be no doubt as to what has occurred.

17:25 first He must suffer: Jesus makes clear that His death comes first.

17:26 In the days of Noah people paid little attention to God and faced judgment as a result (Gen. 6:5–13). The same will be the case at Jesus' return.

17:27 until the day: Jesus details how life went on normally until the Flood came.

17:28 likewise as it was also in the days of Lot: A second example from the godless time of Lot in Sodom and Gomorrah (Gen. 18:16—19:28).

17:29 destroyed them all: The day of the Son of Man will be a time of total judgment, as were the days of Noah (v. 27) and **Lot.**

17:30 Even so it will be: As God acted in the past, so He will act **when the Son of Man is revealed** (i.e., when Jesus returns).

17:31 let him not come down . . . let him not turn back: When the time comes, one is not to pause but to move quickly, not longing for the old life. One is to flee quickly to escape the coming wrath.

17:32 Lot's wife represents those who are attached to earthly things, those whose hearts are still in this world. Like Lot's wife, such people will perish (Gen. 19:26).

17:33 whoever loses his life will preserve it: Those who invest their lives in advancing Christ's kingdom, even to the point of suffering and death, will receive great privilege and glory in the climactic reign of Christ (Matt. 5:10–12; 19:27–30; 2 Tim. 2:12; Rev. 20:4–6).

17:34 one will be taken . . . the other will be left: Some have seen this as a picture of the separation at the rapture; however, "taken" is better understood as judgment (such as the

soldiers took Jesus to crucify Him). Furthermore, v. 37 makes it clear that those taken are taken to final judgment.

17:35-36 one taken . . . the other left: A second and third picture follow. The day of the Son of Man divides mankind into two groups— those taken to judgment and those left to live and reign with Christ.

17:37 Where, Lord? The disciples ask where the judgment will occur. **the eagles will be gathered:** Jesus does not answer the question directly. The term for eagles refers to vultures who gather over dead corpses. In effect, Jesus says that when the judgment comes, it will be final and tragic with the stench of death and the presence of vultures everywhere. Again, one will not need to look for it; the birds will reveal its presence. This language is heavily pictorial to evoke the foreboding mood of the climactic events described. Jesus brings salvation but also judgment, which is why a decision about Him is so important. He brings the kingdom (v. 20), and one either is with Him or suffers the fate of judgment.

18:1 always ought to pray . . . not lose heart: Luke makes clear why Jesus tells this parable.

18:2 The Romans allowed the Jews to manage most of their own affairs. This **judge** did not fear God, and was therefore probably a secular judge, not a religious one. The dishonest judge represents corrupted power.

18:3 The woman in this parable is a **widow,** dependent on society for her support. Luke often takes special note of the plight of widows (2:37; 4:25, 26; 7:12; 20:47; 21:2, 3; Acts 6:1–7; 9:39, 41). **Get justice:** Perhaps the woman was asking for help concerning a financial problem.

18:4, 5 The persistence of the widow is the lesson of the parable. God is a counterexample to the judge. God does not begrudge answering prayer. Jesus' point is that if an insensitive judge will respond to the **continual** requests of a widow, God will certainly respond to the continual prayers of believers.

18:6, 7 shall God not avenge His own elect: God will respond to injustice and religious persecution meted out to His people. In the end, He will avenge.

18:8 will He really find faith: Jesus' question here is whether upon His return believers will still be looking for Him. Persecution can cause the faithful to lose their enthusiasm. In asking this question, Jesus is exhorting believers not to lose heart (v. 1).

18:9 to some who trusted in themselves: Jesus always challenges religious pride and self-righteousness while commending humility (5:29–32; 7:36–50; 14:1–14).

18:10–12 God, I thank You: The tone of

the prayer reveals the Pharisee's problem. He uses the pronoun *I* five times in two verses. The Pharisee's attitude seems to be that God should be grateful to him for his commitment. The man obviously looked down on other people and was proud of his fasting and tithing.

18:13 This is an example of the humble spirit of repentance that Jesus commends. The **tax collector** knew that he could not say or bring anything to enhance his standing with God. He knew that only God's mercy and grace, and not his own works, could deliver him.

18:14 Jesus identified the contrast between the Pharisee and the tax collector as one between pride and humility, between those who exalt and those who humble themselves. God will bring down the proud and will exalt the humble (1:52; 14:11).

> *God will bring down the proud and will exalt the humble.*

18:15 they rebuked them: The disciples assumed that Jesus was too important and too busy for children. The parents' desire for Jesus to **touch** the children was probably a request to bless them.

18:16, 17 Jesus used the thoughtlessness of His disciples to make two points: (1) All people, even little children, are important to God. (2) The **kingdom of God** consists of those who respond to Him with the trust that a little child gives to a parent.

18:18–21 All these things I have kept: Like the Pharisee in vv. 11, 12, the ruler was certain of his own ability to live righteously.

18:22 Sell all that you have and distribute to the poor: This was a radical test of the ruler's concern for others (12:33, 34). Jesus was determining whether the ruler's treasure (Matt. 6:19–21) lay with God or money (16:13). Jesus was not establishing a new requirement for being saved. He was examining the ruler's orientation to God by directly confronting him with the very thing that was hindering him— namely, his wealth. By contrast, Zacchaeus was a wealthy man who responded to Jesus (19:8–10).

18:23 very sorrowful . . . very rich: Here is the sad commentary of his response. His wealth meant that he would not even consider Jesus' admonition.

18:24 How hard it is for those who have riches: Jesus knows that wealth can turn into a matter of pride and a sense of ownership. A wealthy person can easily think he has no need of God and that he is in control of life or is controlling it through things. This means becoming subservient to the creation and not the Creator.

So Jesus says that it is difficult for the wealthy to set proper priorities for God and His kingdom as contrasted with material things. This is even more tragic when one considers that the former lasts forever whereas the latter passes away quickly (2 Pet. 3:10–12).

18:25 easier for a camel: This is hyperbole. It is impossible for a camel to go through the eye of a sewing needle, but even that is easier than a rich person entering into God's blessing. This would shock any Jewish hearer who might assume that wealth meant the presence of God's blessing.

18:26, 27 Who then can be saved: Jesus answered this question by explaining that the change of heart one must experience in order to know God is **possible** only through Him. Any person who enters the kingdom does so only by the marvelous grace of God (John 3:3).

18:28 we have left all and followed You: Peter wanted reassurance about the disciples' sacrifice as compared to the ruler.

18:29 for the sake of the kingdom of God: Jesus assured the disciples that the sacrifices they made in leaving everything to follow Him would be rewarded without measure in His kingdom. The disciples' wise stewardship of their lives exemplifies the principle of 9:24; 17:33.

18:30 shall not receive many times more . . . eternal life: Here we see the clear division of time into the **present age** and **the age to come.** Blessings abound in both periods for disciples. In the future comes the very eternal life about which the ruler asked in v. 18. The quality of that life will be as abundant (John 10:10) as the sacrificial investment of the present (9:24). In fact, Jesus cites the divine compensation as one hundredfold (Matt. 19:29). The remuneration is always much greater with God than the renunciation we endure.

18:31 Though Jesus referred to the suffering He was going to face in **Jerusalem,** a suffering that was predicted **by the prophets,** His disciples did not understand the implication of His words until after His resurrection. The theme of Jesus' suffering is repeated in 24:25, 26, 44–47.

18:32, 33 The entire sequence of events of Jesus' trial, crucifixion, and resurrection is predicted here in detail.

18:34 understood none of these things: The disciples may have understood something of what Jesus said, but they could not understand why God's Chosen One would have to face such suffering. For those who were expecting the Promised One to be an exalted figure who would deliver God's people, it would be very difficult to reconcile such an expectation with such terrible suffering. **was hidden:** The disciples did not understand the implications of Jesus' suffering and death until it was explained to them in detail after Jesus was raised from the dead (24:25, 26, 44–47).

18:35–37 Jesus was nearing Jerusalem: **Jericho** was about seventeen miles from the city.

18:38 Note the irony in this verse. The blind man recognized who **Jesus** was, the **Son of David,** more clearly than many people who were blessed with physical sight. The blind man's cry for **mercy** demonstrated his belief that Jesus had the power to heal him.

18:39–41 he cried out all the more: The crowd's rebuke does not stop the vibrancy of the blind man's faith.

Jesus' Last Journey to Jerusalem.
During Jesus' last trip to Jerusalem (9:51–56), He was turned away by an unfriendly Samaritan village. Thus, instead of passing through Samaria, He apparently took a longer route from Scythopolis, crossing to the east bank of the Jordan River to travel south. Recrossing the Jordan near Jericho, He ascended the mountain to Bethany and finally arrived at Jerusalem.

18:42 your faith has made you well: Jesus again highlights the value of faith (7:50; 8:50; 17:19).

18:43 The gracious work of God led to **praise,** not only from the one who was blessed but also from those who saw the blessing.

19:1, 2 Zacchaeus, as **chief tax collector,** most likely bid for the right to collect taxes and then hired another tax collector to actually gather the money.

19:3, 4 A sycamore tree is similar to an oak tree, with a short trunk and wide lateral branches.

19:5 today I must stay at your house: Jesus takes the initiative with the tax collector. Jesus uses a key term for Luke, "today" (2:11; 4:21; 13:32, 33; 23:43). Jesus also says that He "must" stay there, using another key expression in Luke (2:49; 4:43; 9:22; 13:33; 17:25; 22:37; 24:7, 44). Together they suggest immediacy and the working out of Jesus' commission to fellowship with those who were rejected by society.

19:6 made haste: Zacchaeus does exactly as Jesus commanded in v. 5.

19:7 The crowd was not happy with Jesus' choice of whom to honor with His fellowship. In the crowd's opinion, Zacchaeus was a sinner. The term translated **complained** recalls the grumbling of 5:30 and 15:2, where the same issue was in view. Since tax collectors often took for themselves a high percentage of what they demanded, they were hated and despised in ancient Israel.

19:8 give half . . . restore fourfold: Zacchaeus determined to deal generously with others. In later Judaism, it was considered generous to give away up to 20 percent of one's belongings; giving away more than this was considered dangerous. Legal restitution for extortion was also 20 percent (Lev. 5:16; Num. 5:7).

19:9, 10 for the Son of Man: Jesus gives another mission statement. He declares that **the Son of Man has come to seek and save that which was lost.** Zacchaeus is an example of such success. The entire episode recalls the teaching of Luke 15, while the roots of the imagery go back to Ezek. 34:2, 4, 16, 22, 23 (John 10).

19:11 kingdom of God would appear immediately: Jesus corrects the disciples' thinking that when Jesus comes to Jerusalem, the consummation of the kingdom (judgment and rule) will come. They are still asking the same question in Acts 1:6. Jesus' answer is very appropriate for the many today who continue to set dates for the coming of Christ.

19:12 This parable is similar to Matt. 25:14–30, but the occasion is probably different. The story parallels in part what happened to Archelaus, a son of Herod the Great, who came to power in 4 B.C. The people disliked Archelaus, and they appealed to Augustus Caesar not to give him authority. Jesus is not retelling the story of Archelaus, but the historical events meant that the parable had a well-known plot. A significant detail is that the kingdom is received during the journey away from the land to be ruled. This corresponds to Jesus' leaving this earth to **receive** the **kingdom** following His resurrection.

19:13 Do business till I come: This detail shows that Jesus' return would not be immediate (v. 11). The **servants** represent Jesus' followers. They are to serve faithfully until Jesus returns. **ten minas:** Each servant received one mina, or about four months' wages for the average worker. The master, symbolizing Jesus Himself, wants to see fruit, or dividends from his investment. Did his servants put the money they received to good use?

19:14 his citizens hated him: This is a separate group from the servants and refers to those who reject Jesus outright.

19:15 how much every man had gained: Having returned with authority to rule, the nobleman asks the servants to give an account of their labor in his absence.

19:16 The first servant earned **ten** times the amount he was given originally.

19:17 you were faithful . . . have authority over ten cities: Faithfulness is commended and rewarded with greater opportunity. The authority given to the servant represents a role in administering Jesus' kingdom (1 Cor. 6:2, 3; Rev. 2:26–28; 5:9, 10; 20:1–6).

19:18 five minas: The second servant adds five times to the original investment.

19:19 five cities: This servant is also given further responsibility as a reward.

19:20–23 I feared you: The unfaithful servant's excuse for failure reflects a negative view of the nobleman. If the servant had really feared the master, he would have done something with the money. Even putting the **money in the bank** would have yielded **interest.** As it was, the servant failed to respond to the nobleman at all or even to understand him.

19:24 take . . . give: The third servant ends up with nothing while the faithful servant receives even more (1 Cor. 3:15).

19:25 he has ten minas: The crowd offers a mild protest to the additional reward.

19:26, 27 what he has will be taken away: Unfaithfulness brings loss of reward (Rev. 3:11). It is possible that the loss for some will be so great that they will be excluded from the millennial reign with Christ on earth (Matt. 22:13). This latter servant may be an example of such millennial disinheritance.

19:28 going up to Jerusalem: Jesus now approaches the city where He must die (Luke 13:33).

19:29, 30 Jesus was in control of the events of the last week of His life, even though those events led to His death. Here He prepared to enter the city riding a **colt. Bethphage** and **Bethany** were located just east of Jerusalem, within two miles of the city. The Mount of Olives was in a range of hills just outside of Jerusalem, directly across from the temple.

19:31 the Lord has need of it: Such borrowing of an animal was not as strange as it may appear. There was an ancient custom by which a political or religious leader could commandeer property for short-term use. Jesus was entering Jerusalem to celebrate the Passover and the Feast of Unleavened Bread, festivals that commemorated the great act of God's deliverance of the nation. Such feasts were often celebrated at this time with the hope that God's decisive deliverance would come.

19:32, 33 found it just as He had said: Jesus is in control of events and is aware of what is taking place. The events in Jerusalem did not catch Him by surprise.

19:34 The Lord has need of him: This occurs just as Jesus predicted. To control the major events of history (John 10:18), one must control all the events. Only God can do that.

19:35 The **clothes** were probably their outer garments. The scene recalls the declaration of Jehu as king in 2 Kin. 9:13. The ride on the **colt** or mule resembles the events of 1 Kin. 1:33, in which David made the new king, Solomon, ride to Gihon on a mule. Zechariah had prophesied that the coming King would ride into Jerusalem humbly on a donkey (Zech. 9:9). However, Luke does not emphasize these connections with OT prophecy as Matthew and John do (Matt. 21:5; John 12:15).

19:36 spread their clothes on the road: The actions here indicate that a dignitary was being greeted (2 Kin. 9:13). This is like "rolling out the red carpet" today.

19:37 disciples began to rejoice: Luke is more detailed than Matt. 21:8 and Mark 11:8 who attribute these actions to the crowd. Luke appears to be suggesting that what the disciples started, the crowd joined. The disciples **rejoice and praise God** for **the mighty works** they had seen. Here is the declaration of a regal figure (v. 38) who does the work of the *eschaton* (7:22). The last miracle that Luke described was a healing by Jesus as the Son of David (18:38–43).

19:38 This verse is a citation of Ps. 118:26, with the title of **King** added to it. The disciples recognized that Jesus was the promised King sent from God. He is the One who brings **peace** to the relationship between people and God (1:78, 79).

19:39 rebuke Your disciples: Some Pharisees were not pleased that Jesus allowed Himself to receive such honor; they wanted it stopped.

19:40 the stones would immediately cry out: Jesus replied ironically that if the disciples did not offer such praise, creation would. Creation is more sensitive than those who are making the complaint!

19:41 wept over it: Jesus knew that so many of the people of Israel had rejected Him that the nation would suffer judgment, in the form of the terrible destruction that came on Jerusalem in A.D. 70.

19:42 if you had known: They could have known if they had been in God's word (Deut. 9:24). In fact, **this your day** was a very specific day of prophecy. It was the 173,880th day from the going forth of the decree of Artaxerxes until Messiah the Prince (sixty-nine weeks of years is 483 x 360 days or 173,880. God picked out a specific day for the presentation of His Son as King to the nation, but they did not know "the time of their visitation" (v. 44).

19:43 build an embankment: This is a prediction of Rome's successful siege of Jerusalem under Titus. The details reflect a divine judgment for covenant unfaithfulness, similar to the Babylonian destruction of Jerusalem in 586 B.C. (Is. 29:1–4; Jer. 6:6–21; 8:13–22; Ezek. 4:1–3).

19:44 level you, and your children: The totality of the destruction is made clear in this further description of the siege of Jerusalem. Even children would die, and buildings would be destroyed. **your visitation:** Jesus gave the reason for the judgment. They did not recognize the time of God's coming in Messiah.

19:45 Jesus' entrance into Jerusalem begins the final section of Luke's Gospel. Jesus cleansed the **temple** in anger after seeing that the place of prayer had become an excuse for corrupt commerce. Merchants were selling sacrificial animals in the outer court of the temple (the court of the Gentiles) at exorbitant prices. Money changers were making an excessive profit exchanging currencies for the temple shekel. John records a temple cleansing in John 2:13–22, but it is not clear whether that event is the same as this one in Luke. Since John places the event early in Jesus' ministry, Jesus might have cleansed the temple twice. The synoptic Gospels place the cleansing of the temple in the last week of Jesus' ministry (Matt. 21:12–17; Mark 11:15–19). Some have suggested that John purposely placed the cleansing of the temple out of chronological order as a foretaste of Jesus' judgment on contemporary religious practices.

19:46 The holy place of worship had become a site for taking economic advantage of people. Jesus' remark about **a house of prayer**

alludes to Is. 56:7. His comment regarding the **den of thieves** comes from Jer. 7:11.

19:47 Jesus' actions at the temple, the most sacred location for Jews, caused the Jewish religious leaders to strengthen their resolve **to destroy Him.**

19:48 unable to do anything: The leadership is portrayed as paralyzed in the face of the people's interest in Jesus.

20:1–4 Here as throughout the Gospel of Luke, the ministries of **John** the Baptist and Jesus are linked (1:5–80; 3:10–18; 7:18–35). Jesus' question presented the Pharisees with a dilemma. If they recognized John's ministry as coming **from heaven,** they would be recognizing the same divine origin of Jesus' similar "independent," Spirit-directed ministry. But if the Pharisees denied that John was sent by God, they risked angering the majority of the people, who believed that John's ministry was divinely directed (vv. 5, 6).

20:5–8 they did not know: The religious experts, for expediency, claim ignorance on this key question.

20:9 In a variation of Is. 5:1–7, the **vineyard** here represents the promise made to Israel, while the **vinedressers** represent the nation of Israel. The **man** who **planted** the **vineyard** represents God. The imagery of the vineyard recalls the subject of Jesus' parable in 13:6–9. This parable is also found in Matt. 21:33–44 and Mark 12:1–12, with some slight variations of detail in each account.

20:10 beat him . . . sent him away empty-handed: The treatment of the servant in this parable represents the treatment of the OT prophets by the people of Israel. During the time of the prophets, the nation of Israel produced no fruit; disobedience abounded (11:49–51; 13:34; Acts 7:51–53).

20:11 beat . . . treated him shamefully . . . sent away empty-handed: Yet again, a servant is rejected. This shows such rejection was repeated.

20:12 wounded him . . . cast him out: A third servant is treated more harshly.

20:13 I will send my beloved son: This refers to Jesus (3:21, 22; 9:35).

20:14 This is the heir . . . let us kill him: The vinedressers hoped that with the son gone, the inheritance would fall to those who worked the property, a transfer that was possible in the ancient world. It should be noted that the details of this parable do not represent the thinking of those who crucified Jesus. The leaders of Israel thought they were stopping someone who was dangerous to Judaism, not that they were going to inherit Jesus' kingdom.

20:15 cast him out . . . killed him: The parallel here of course is Jesus' death. **what**

will the owner of the vineyard do to them: the parallel question is "What will God the Father do to those who reject and murder His Son?"

20:16 come and destroy those vinedressers: God will exercise judgment on those who killed His Son. He will **give the vineyard to others.** Jesus is alluding to the inclusion of Gentiles in the promise of God's kingdom.

20:17 The stone which the builders rejected: This passage, taken from Ps. 118:22, pictures the exaltation of the Righteous One, Jesus, after His rejection. Opposition will not stop God from making the One who is rejected the center of His work of salvation.

20:18 Jesus is the stone. Anyone who goes against the stone will be destroyed. Jesus' statement is similar to a late Jewish proverb: "If the stone falls on the pot, alas for the pot; if the pot falls on the stone, alas for the pot." The imagery of Jesus as a stone is also found in 1 Pet. 2:4–8, where Peter compares the believers to living stones built into a spiritual temple for the Lord. **chief cornerstone:** This could be the large stone that joins the foundation of two walls of a building, or else the capstone at the top of a doorway.

20:19 The Jewish religious leaders wanted Jesus removed because of His direct challenges to them. But because they **feared** the reaction of the crowd, they waited for a more favorable time to do away with Jesus.

20:20 The religious leaders **watched** Jesus very closely. They **pretended to be righteous,** which in this context means that they tried to look sincere. They wanted to trap Jesus into saying something that would make Him look like a political revolutionary, then they planned to hand Him over to the Roman **governor** Pilate.

20:21 teach the way of God: This flattery comes across as very dishonorable when placed next to v. 20.

20:22 Is it lawful for us to pay taxes to Caesar or not: This question concerned the poll tax to Rome, which was different from the taxes collected by the tax collectors. The poll tax was a citizenship tax paid directly to Rome, as an indication that Israel was subject to that Gentile nation. The Pharisees' query was a trick question. If Jesus answered yes, the people would be angry because He respected a foreign power. If He answered no, He could be charged with sedition.

Identifying with Jesus often means risking the rejection and denunciation of family, and in some cases martyrdom.

20:23 perceived their craftiness: Jesus, in control, knows their motives.

20:24 Whose image . . . does it have: Jesus' reply was clever. He had the Pharisees pull out a coin, indicating that they already recognized Roman sovereignty by using Roman coins themselves. A denarius was a silver coin that usually had a picture of the emperor Tiberius on it. On some of them the reverse bore an image of Tiberius's mother Livia portrayed as a goddess of peace, with the inscription "High Priest."

20:25 The Pharisees could not twist Jesus' wise reply into a charge of sedition (23:2). According to Jesus, **Caesar,** as the ruler of the empire, had the right to collect taxes. Yet at the same time, **God** should be honored above any ruler. Honoring God does not make a person exempt from supporting the basic functions of the state (Rom. 13:1–7), for all figures of authority have been ordained by God.

20:26 they marveled: Jesus escapes the trap, and the listeners are amazed.

20:27 The Sadducees, the Pharisees, and the Essenes were three major divisions in first-century Judaism. The Sadducees rejected the oral traditions that the Pharisees so stringently obeyed. Instead they based their teaching only on the first five books of the OT, the books of Moses. They denied that there could be a **resurrection,** and they contrived a ludicrous example to suggest that the doctrine was impossible.

20:28 In Judaism a childless widow would marry the **brother** of her late husband, according to the custom known as levirate marriage (Deut. 25:5; Ruth 4:1–12). The law was designed to perpetuate the name of a man who died childless.

20:29–32 seven brothers: The example goes through seven childless marriages and the woman's death.

20:33 whose wife does she become? This question was intended to show that resurrection leads to absurd results.

20:34, 35 Jesus contrasted life in the current age with life in the age to come. Because marriage will not be a part of the age to come, the Sadducees' absurd example (vv. 28–33) does not apply. Jesus upheld the doctrine of resurrection in His reply, speaking of both the **age** to come and the **resurrection,** so that the two concepts were clearly associated. Jesus also noted that only those **counted worthy** would receive the benefits of the age to come.

20:36 equal to the angels . . . sons of God: The everlasting life of a resurrected person makes that person something like an angel. Paul explains further that in the resurrection we will be given resurrection bodies similar to Christ's (1 Cor. 15:25–58). This will be a new experience that will not necessarily parallel experiences on this earth, such as marriage.

20:37 the God of Abraham . . . Isaac . . . Jacob: Jesus' reply here is more subtle. He says if God is the God of the patriarchs, then they must be raised and alive.

20:38 the God of the . . . living: Jesus points out that if God is the God of the patriarchs, then they must be raised and alive. God has a relationship only with those who are alive. Jesus' citation of the law (Ex. 3:1–6, 15) probably made an impact on the Sadducees, who revered the teachings of the books of Moses.

20:39, 40 scribes: The scribes, accepting the Pharisees' view of resurrection as derived from the Scripture, are pleased with the answer and commend Jesus.

20:41–43 Here Jesus takes His turn at raising a theological issue. The dilemma He poses is how the Messiah (the Hebrew word for **Christ**) could be called the **Son of David**, when David himself gave Him the title *Lord*. **my Lord:** This is a citation from Ps. 110:1 (22:69;

not answer His question. It is to be reflected upon. For Jesus, the key title is **Lord.** As the subsequent discussions of the passage show, Messiah is Son of David; but that is less important than being David's Lord.

20:45–47 devour widows' houses: Jesus noted the scribes' hypocrisy and their taking advantage of others. Such activity will be judged.

21:1 There were various places around the temple where people could leave contributions. Thirteen such locations were in the forecourt. The receptacles were made in the shape of trumpets. Each represented a different kind of offering. There was also a **treasury** room near the court of women.

21:2 The **poor widow** contributed **two mites,** small copper coins that were the smallest currency available.

21:3 has put in more than all: Jesus contrasted the giving of the rich (v. 1) with the sacrifice of the poor widow.

21:4 put in all the livelihood that she had: The widow did not refuse to give even when she needed more to live on. Her devotion to God through her contributions was her first priority (2 Cor. 8:1–5; 9:6–9).

21:5 how it was adorned: The temple was refurbished under Herod the Great with

---

💡 **INSIGHT**   **Poorer Than Poor**

Jesus called the widow in Luke 21:1–4 "poor." The word He used referred to a person so destitute that she was literally in danger of death.

It is hard to reckon what the two mites that she threw into the treasury would be worth in today's currency. But even in her day they were not much. Each mite was worth about one-thirty-second of a denarius, the daily wage of a soldier, which would be less than fifty cents today.

The important thing to note is that the two coins were "all the livelihood that she had" (21:4). She was truly destitute—the sort of widow who would later be eligible for support from the church (1 Tim. 5:5). Nevertheless, she gave generously to the temple. Jesus praised her for her faithfulness, even though it meant sacrifice.

In doing so, the Lord showed that God's accounting differs from ours. He pays attention to our attitudes in giving more than the absolute dollar amount of our gifts.

Acts 2:30–36). The Messiah was David's descendant and yet David gave Him the respect due to a superior, the reverse of what normally occurred in ancient times. Jesus was not denying the title *Son of David* to the Messiah, He was simply noting that the title *Lord*, meaning "Master," is more central. Even David one day will bow at the Messiah's feet and confess that He is Lord (Phil. 2:10).

20:44 how is He then his Son? Jesus does

new foundation walls and enlarged areas outside the temple. Great stones of twelve to sixty feet in length were used. The entire effort took from 20 B.C. to around A.D. 64. Thus the refurbishing was in progress during Jesus' visit, around A.D. 30. The **donations** were gift offerings for the decoration of the temple and included gold and silver plated gates, grape vine clusters, and Babylonian linen tapestries, which hung from the temple veil. Even Tacitus, the

Roman historian, called it an "immensely opulent temple."

21:6 not one stone: Jesus noted that the beautiful place of worship was temporary and would be destroyed. He was referring to the fall of Jerusalem in A.D. 70, which itself was a picture of the destruction of the last days.

21:7 when . . . what sign: The disciples want to know what will lead to such a tragedy and when it will occur.

21:8 Take heed: The first century and early second century were times of great messianic fervor in Judaism, as the Israelites sought freedom from Roman rule. Many people claimed to be the Messiah. Jesus warned His disciples not to be fooled by such claims.

21:9, 10 wars: These and other commotions will also come, but these events are not the coming of the **end.**

21:11 A wide variety of cosmic and natural events will occur before the end times. Verses 8–11 give signs before the end, while vv. 12–19 speak of events that will happen before the signs of vv. 8–11.

21:12 persecute you . . . for My name's sake: Jesus predicted the arrests and suffering that the disciples would face as a result of identifying with Him. Some of these events are detailed in Acts 3–5; 7; 21–28. The reference to **synagogues, kings,** and **rulers** indicates that all nations would share responsibility for the massacre of the disciples.

21:13 an occasion for testimony: Suffering can be an opportunity to advance the kingdom of God. This is why those who endure suffering and persecution are called blessed (Matt. 5:10–12).

21:14 settle it in your hearts: Jesus speaks here of resolve ahead of time to stand up for the faith in the midst of rejection.

21:15 I will give you a mouth and wisdom: Jesus promises the disciples that the Holy Spirit will assist them in giving testimony (12:11, 12). The initial fulfillment of this promise is found in Acts 4:8–14; 7:54; 26:24–32.

21:16 You will be betrayed: The persecution of the disciples would be painful and severe. Identifying with Jesus often means risking the rejection and denunciation of family, and in some cases martyrdom.

21:17 you will be hated . . . for My name's sake: Jesus forces a choice and some, not liking the option, react against those who have joined Him.

21:18 not a hair of your head shall be lost: Since Jesus has noted that some will die in v. 16, this must be read as referring to everlasting life. They may kill the body but not the life (12:4, 5). This is a note of assurance. The investment you make in this life for the next

will not be affected by "moth or rust" (Matt. 6:19–21).

21:19 possess your souls: Patient allegiance to Jesus leads to eternal life (9:24).

21:20 A siege would be the sign that the end was near for **Jerusalem** and the temple. The other synoptic Gospels (Matt. 24:15; Mark 13:14) allude to the abomination of **desolation** in Dan. 9:25–27; 11:31. This passage compares the desecration of the temple to what occurred in 167 B.C., when Antiochus Epiphanes erected an altar to Zeus in the temple. A similar desecration of the temple site occurred during the destruction of Jerusalem in A.D. 70.

21:21 let those in Judea flee: The siege will be a terrible time, so it is best not to be in Jerusalem.

21:22 days of vengeance: Jerusalem had become an object of divine judgment because of its unfaithfulness. Jesus warned of this consequence throughout His ministry (13:9, 34, 35; 19:41–44). The premise for such judgment goes back to the curses of the Mosaic covenant and the OT prophets' warnings of coming judgment (Deut. 28:49–57; 32:35; Jer. 6:1–8; 26:1–9; Hos. 9:7).

21:23 woe: Jesus says it will be a hard time for those who are pregnant and have young children. Judgment and war are never pleasant; divine judgment is no exception. **Great distress** is the fate of the nation.

21:24 fall . . . be led away captive: This verse elaborates on Jerusalem's fall. There would be death and captivity, just as the nation experienced under the Assyrians and Babylonians. **times of the Gentiles:** There would be a period in God's salvation plan when Gentiles would be dominant, of which the fall of Jerusalem would be a clear sign. The fact that the time of the Gentiles will run its course also suggests that Israel will once again play a significant role in God's plan (Rom. 9—11).

21:25, 26 signs: Jesus shifts His focus to the end times with His second mention of cosmic turmoil (v. 11; Is. 24:18–20; 34:4; Ezek. 32:7, 8; Joel 2:30, 31). **men's hearts failing them:** The terror of cosmic chaos will cause apprehension about what is coming.

21:27 the Son of Man coming in a cloud: The reference here is to the authoritative return of Jesus. The allusion to the cloud and the figure comes from Dan. 7:13, 14, with its picture of One who receives authority from the Ancient of Days. Jesus viewed this text in terms of an apocalyptic deliverance. The image of the cloud is important, since God is identified as riding the clouds in the OT (Ex. 34:5; Ps. 104:3). **with power and great glory:** The Son of Man has divine authority to judge the world.

21:28 lift up your heads . . . redemption

⚒ IN DEPTH | Jerusalem Trampled by Gentiles

Those living in Jerusalem at the time of Christ had reason to believe His prediction that the city would eventually fall to an invading army (Luke 21:20; see also 19:41–44). Political tensions were at a breaking point.

The Jews bitterly resented Rome's occupation of their homeland, which brought the corrupting influence of Greek culture, crushing taxes, and cruel government. Some, like the Zealots, fanned the flames of revolution by leading tax revolts and launching terrorist strikes against Roman troops and officials.

The final chapter of the drama began in A.D. 66 when a skirmish broke out between Jews and Gentiles over the desecration of the synagogue at Caesarea. Unable to prevail politically, the Jews retaliated religiously by banning all sacrifices on behalf of foreigners, even for the emperor himself. Furthermore, access to the temple grounds at Jerusalem would be strictly limited to Jewish countrymen.

Meanwhile, the Roman procurator ordered an enormous payment from the temple treasury. The Jews balked and assumed that the ruler would back down. Instead, he unleashed troops on the city who raped and pillaged at will, even resorting to flogging and crucifixion. The slaughter claimed about 3,600 Jewish lives, including children.

The city went into riot. Arsonists torched official buildings along with the home of the high priest, long suspected of collusion with the empire. Elsewhere, Jews overran Roman fortresses and ambushed a legion of reinforcements, capturing arms for the revolt at Jerusalem. In the end, the Romans retreated, temporarily leaving the Holy City in the hands of the rebels.

Yet no matter how brave or committed the Jewish revolutionaries may have been, they were no match for the professional armies of Rome. Emperor Nero dispatched Vespasian, his top general, to the region. Beginning in Galilee and working his way south, he systematically cut off Jerusalem's lines of supply—and escape—from Babylonia, the Mediterranean, and Egypt. By A.D. 70, he was poised to launch the final assault on Jerusalem.

However, Vespasian returned to Rome to succeed Nero as emperor, leaving his son Titus to complete the campaign. Advancing on the city from the north, the east, and the west, his legions erected siege walls and finally took the city, fulfilling Jesus' prophecy. Herod's temple was destroyed only six years after its completion (compare Luke 21:5, 6), the priesthood and the council were abolished, and all Jews were expelled from the remains of the city.

Jesus wept to think of such carnage (Matt. 23:37–39). Yet it was one of the prices His generation paid for rejecting Him as its Messiah.

---

draws near: This is the sign of the deliverance of Jesus' followers. The Son of Man acts on behalf of those who have suffered in His name.

21:29, 30 The tender buds that appear every spring on trees show that summer is approaching; the appearance of the signs Jesus describes will warn of the coming of the end times.

21:31 when you see . . . know: The cosmic signs and earthly chaos are indications that the decisive and consummate rule of God is approaching.

21:32 The most likely meaning of this verse is that when the end comes, it will come quickly. The events of the end times will fall within one **generation** from start to finish (17:22–24). The word *generation* can also refer to a race. Thus, it may mean that the Jews will continue to exist as a people until the end.

21:33 by no means pass away: The disci-

ples had the assurance that Jesus' promises concerning the end times were more certain than creation itself. God made an unconditional and unilateral covenant, and He will keep it (Gen. 12:1–3; 15:18–21; Ps. 89).

21:34 Though the events of the end times may not come to pass for a long time, believers should continue to look for their arrival. The **Day** of Jesus' return should not take us by surprise. We should live as if it is imminent.

21:35 a snare: The end is something all must deal with; it is like a trap for all on the earth. Judgment follows and one should be ready for it and live in light of its approach.

21:36–38 Watch . . . pray: Jesus encouraged His disciples to be persistent in prayer and faith, looking for the day when the **Son of Man** exonerates the faithful in the judgment, so that they are able **to stand** before Him (1 John 2:28).

✠ IN CONTEXT **Passover**

The Passover and Feast of Unleavened Bread (Luke 22:7) was the first of three great festivals of the Hebrews.

The name Passover recalls the deliverance of Israel from slavery in Egypt (Ex. 12:1–13:16). God sent His angel to kill all the firstborn sons of the Egyptians in order to persuade Pharaoh to let His people go. Hebrew families were instructed to sacrifice a lamb and smear its blood on the doorpost of their house as a signal to God that His angel should "pass over" them during the judgment.

Passover was observed on the fourteenth day of the first month, Abib (March–April), with the service beginning in the evening (Lev. 23:6). It was on the evening of this day that Israel left Egypt in haste. Unleavened bread was used in the celebration as a reminder that the people had no time to leaven their bread before they ate their final meal as slaves in Egypt.

In NT times, Passover became a pilgrim festival. Large numbers gathered in Jerusalem to observe the annual celebration. Thus an unusually large crowd was on hand to take part in the events surrounding Jesus' entry into the city (Luke 19:37–39) and His arrest, trial, and crucifixion (23:18, 27, 35, 48). Apparently many stayed on until the Feast of Pentecost, when they heard Peter's persuasive sermon (Acts 2:1–41).

Like the blood of the lambs that saved the Hebrews from destruction in Egypt, the blood of Jesus, the ultimate Passover Lamb, saves us from the power of sin and death.

22:1 This verse begins the "passion narrative," the account of Jesus' death and resurrection. **The Feast of Unleavened Bread** took place immediately following **Passover** (Ex. 12:1–20; Deut. 16:1–8). The two feasts were often considered as one. Passover commemorated the night of the tenth plague in Egypt, when the firstborn of Israel were "passed over" and spared by the angel of death. The Feast of Unleavened Bread celebrated the Exodus (Ex. 12; Lev. 23:5, 6). Many Jewish pilgrims traveled to Jerusalem to celebrate these feasts.

22:2 how they might kill Him: The leaders still want to remove Jesus, but fear of His popularity with the people stop them (19:47, 48; 20:19).

22:3 The journey to the Cross was not just a matter of human effort or Judas's plots. Cosmic forces were at work in the opposition to Jesus. **Satan** is mentioned in the temptations of Jesus, and in 10:18 and 13:16. The name derives from the Hebrew term for "adversary" (Job 1:9–11).

22:4 Judas's involvement in the plot to betray Jesus was fortunate from the point of view of the Jewish religious leaders. They could arrest Jesus secretly and later claim that the driving force to stop Him came from within His own group of disciples. The **captains,** Levites who were members of the temple guard, were the ones who could make the arrest.

22:5 glad . . . agreed to give him money: This detail is why Judas has been called greedy. Matt. 26:15 notes that Judas raised the issue of money. Judas's offer simplified matters enor-

mously, so the leadership was pleased and ready to pay.

22:6 in the absence of the multitude: The leadership did not want to get Jesus in public, lest a commotion break out.

22:7, 8 The synoptic Gospels are very clear that Jesus was betrayed on the day of **Passover** (Matt. 26:17–19; Mark 14:12–16).

22:9, 10 follow him: Jesus is again in control of events and tells the disciples where they will hold the meal.

22:11, 12 guest room: Such rooms were often made available to the thousands of pilgrims who came to Jerusalem for the celebration of Passover and the Feast of Unleavened Bread. Such a room would contain couches for guests at the feasts to recline for the meal. Access to the room was probably gained by stairs on the outside of the house.

22:13 as He had said: Jesus' remarks are correct, even in non-spiritual matters.

22:14–30 A comparison of this account with John 13:1–30 suggests that Luke has rearranged the order of events in a topical manner. Luke has the meal first and all the discourse afterward. In John's account, Judas was gone by the time the meal was shared. Luke's account does not mention Judas's departure. In addition, Luke mentions two cups, while the other three Gospels mention only one. A Passover meal had four courses and four cups. Thus, it is obvious that all the Gospel writers summarize the events of the meal. The words over the bread and cup recorded by Luke are very similar to those of 1 Cor. 11:23–26.

22:15 to eat this Passover: Jesus is able to enjoy the fellowship of His disciples one last time before suffering and is also able to give some basic teaching before He departs.

22:16 I will no longer eat of it until it is fulfilled: In the kingdom to come, when final victory is celebrated, Jesus again will eat (Rev. 19:9).

22:17, 18 I will not drink of the fruit: As is made clear in v. 16, Jesus will abstain from celebrating a meal until His return.

22:19 My body . . . do this in remembrance: Jesus instituted a new meal, which is not only a memorial of His death but also a fellowship meal of unity. It is a proclamation and a symbol of the believers' anticipation of Jesus' return, when all God's promises will be fulfilled (1 Cor. 10:16, 17; 11:23–26). The **bread** of the Lord's Supper represents the body of Jesus, offered on behalf of His disciples.

22:20 This cup is the new covenant: The wine of the Lord's Supper depicts the giving of life, a sacrifice of blood, which inaugurates the New Covenant for those who respond to Jesus' offer of salvation (Heb. 8:8, 13; 9:11–28). This is the strongest substitutionary image in the Gospel of Luke: Jesus died on the cross in our place and for our sins (Acts 20:28).

22:21, 22 Jesus would suffer as God's plan unfolded, and the one who betrayed Him would face **woe.**

22:23 which of them it was: The news creates discussion at the table as to which of these close associates would act against Jesus.

22:24 the greatest: Note the sad irony in this verse. While Jesus faced the reality of being betrayed and killed, His disciples argued about which of them was greatest.

22:25 benefactors: This title suggests that the people should be grateful for the generous leaders of their nation and that they should recognize their power and authority.

22:26 as the younger . . . as he who serves: Leadership in the church does not exalt; it serves. It shows respect to others, as a young person would show respect to an elder. True leaders labor for others, as a servant would. In short, the Lord's view of greatness is the exact opposite of the world's view.

22:27 as the One who serves: Jesus appeals to His own service as the example. It is intriguing to consider if Jesus is alluding to the foot washing, which only John 13 portrays, or is referring to the general tone of His ministry.

22:28 in My trials: Jesus recognized that the disciples had been present and had suffered with Him during His ministry.

22:29 Jesus passed on His **kingdom** authority to the apostles who would continue planting the church, a part of the kingdom. The authority that Jesus bestowed on them was like the authority that the **Father** had **bestowed** on Him.

22:30 eat and drink . . . sit on thrones judging: This is a promise of future blessing and authority. The disciples were promised a seat at the banquet of victory and the right to help Jesus rule over Israel on His return (Matt. 19:28; 2 Tim. 2:12).

22:31 Satan has asked for you: The Greek word for *you* here is plural, indicating that Satan had asked permission to trouble all of the disciples.

22:32 I have prayed for you . . . when you have returned: The Greek word for *you* here is singular, referring specifically to Peter. In effect, Jesus restored Peter even before his fall (vv. 54–62), and He instructed the disciple to shepherd the saints by strengthening them.

22:33 to death: Peter overestimates his loyalty and does not sense the danger in Jesus' remarks. Paul also said **"I am ready"** but his confidence was in the dynamic of the gospel (Rom. 1:15–17) rather than the vacillating enthusiasm of the flesh.

22:34 three times: Jesus predicts that a triple denial will come before the cock finishes his morning crow.

22:35, 36 When I sent you: The allusion here is to the disciples' mission recorded in 9:1–6; 10:1–24. When the disciples had depended on God to provide for their needs, those needs were met through generous people. However, the situation had changed. Jesus here instructed His disciples to take **a money bag, a knapsack,** and a **sword** on their journeys in order to be prepared for the rejection that was to come.

22:37 this which is written: Jesus cited Is. 53:12, which describes a righteous one who suffers as a criminal. Jesus noted that His death would fulfill Isaiah's prediction.

22:38 Misunderstanding Jesus' instructions in v. 36, the disciples indicated that they had weapons with which to fight (vv. 50, 51).

22:39 Mount of Olives: Matthew 26:36 gives the name Gethsemane, while John 18:1 speaks more generally of a garden.

22:40 Pray: Jesus advises the disciples to pray for God's protection in this hour.

22:41 prayed: Jesus does what He has told His disciples to do. **A stone's throw** would be several yards.

22:42 Jesus agonized over His approaching death and the effect of God's wrath. The **cup** is a figure of speech for wrath (Pss. 11:6; 75:7, 8; Jer. 25:15, 16; Ezek. 23:31–34).

22:43 strengthening Him: God's answer

to Jesus' prayer did not allow His Son to avoid suffering. However, God did provide angelic help for Jesus to face what was coming. Sometimes God answers prayer by eliminating trials; sometimes He answers by strengthening us in the midst of them.

22:44 His sweat became like great drops of blood: Jesus' earnest prayer and emotion (vv. 42–44) led to a physical reaction. Though Jesus probably did not bleed here, His sweat became like blood.

22:45 sleeping from sorrow: The disciples are weary and so sleep from the emotion that has overcome them, but it cost them time needed for prayer.

22:46 pray: Jesus repeats His call to prayer. They need it more than ever in these key stress-filled moments, when temptation is so likely.

22:47 to kiss Him: The betrayal takes place with an action that is a great lie.

Jesus mercifully healed the ear of one who was taking Him to His death. Jesus illustrated here the love for His enemies that He had commanded in 6:27–36.

22:52 as against a robber: The Greek term for *robber* was used of both highway bandits and revolutionaries. Jesus rebuked His captors for treating Him as though He were a dangerous lawbreaker.

22:53 you did not try to seize Me: Jesus notes their cowardice in that they did not seize Him publicly while He taught in the temple. **your hour . . . darkness:** Jesus notes that forces of evil are at work (John 8:44; 13:30; 14:30).

22:54 This is Jesus' first appearance before Annas (John 18:13).

22:55 Peter sat among them: The fire indicates that it is a cool evening. Peter has followed along just to see what happens.

 INSIGHT | **A Fortunate Miss**

Total confusion reigned in the Garden of Gethsemane as Judas led a band to arrest Jesus. The chaos boiled over when Peter drew a sword and swept the air with a stroke that lopped off the ear of Malchus, one of the arresting party (Luke 22:50; John 18:10).

Peter's impulsive act could have spelled disaster. Jesus and the Twelve were completely outnumbered and ill equipped to defend themselves against a mob that included soldiers from the Roman cohort. The arresting party might even have been looking for a pretext to use violence against this supposedly dangerous rabbi. Fortunately, Jesus acted swiftly to regain control of the situation by healing Malchus's ear and addressing the crowd (Luke 22:51–53).

Another stroke of fortune was probably Peter's bad aim. It's interesting that the account details an injury to Malchus's right ear. Modern readers might assume that Peter would have swung his sword laterally, with the blade parallel to the ground. But a first-century swordsman was more likely to sweep out his sword and come down on the head of an opponent with a vertical, chopping stroke. In battle, the idea was to place a well-aimed blow on the seam of an enemy's helmet, splitting it open and wounding the head.

Perhaps this was Peter's intention, but he aimed wide to the left. Perhaps, too, Malchus saw the blow coming and ducked to his left, exposing his right ear.

In any event, Peter caused no mortal injury. But he certainly drew attention to himself. Malchus happened to be a servant of Caiaphas, the high priest (Matt. 26:3). Later, one of Malchus's relatives recognized Peter warming himself by a fire outside Pilate's court. "Did I not see you in the garden?" he asked suspiciously, a claim that Peter denied (John 18:26).

22:48 Not only did Jesus remind Judas of what he had done, He also noted the irony of being betrayed **with a kiss.**

22:49 shall we strike? The disciples ask if they should fight.

22:50 one of them struck the servant: John 18:10 indicates that this impetuous disciple was Peter (Matt. 26:51; Mark 14:47). His violent act risked giving the impression that the disciples were seditious.

22:51 touched his ear and healed him:

22:56 was also with Him: The servant girl identifies Peter as a disciple.

22:57 denied: This is the first denial.

22:58 you also are of them . . . I am not: Denial number two followed after some time **(after a little while).**

22:59 for he is a Galilean: According to Mark 14:70, Peter's accent gave him away as being from the same region as Jesus.

22:60 I do not know what you are saying: The third denial brings Jesus' word to pass. **rooster crowed:** The sign of Jesus' prediction follows.

22:61, 62 looked at Peter: Apparently a window opened into the courtyard, and Peter knew that the Lord was aware of his denials. **wept bitterly:** The Lord knew Peter better than Peter knew himself (v. 34). Peter was greatly grieved that he had failed Jesus.

22:63 mocked Him and beat Him: Matthew 26:67; Mark 14:65 further describe the abuse of Jesus at the hands of the soldiers as involving speaking, spitting, and slapping.

22:64 Prophesy: The soldiers played a game to mock Jesus. They covered His head and asked Him to identify who was striking Him.

22:65 blasphemously: They dishonor or slander Him. Again, irony is present; for blasphemy is what Jesus will be charged with at the trial (Mark 14:64).

22:66–68 The description here is of a major morning trial that involved all the Jewish religious leaders, the entire **council** or Sanhedrin. This trial violated various Jewish legal rules given in later sources: meeting on the morning of a feast; meeting at Caiaphas's home; trying a defendant without defense; and reaching the verdict in one day instead of the two days that were required for capital cases.

22:69 Hereafter means "from now on." Jesus' point was that authority would reside with Him from this point on. Though He was on trial, in reality He is the ultimate Judge. **on the right hand of the power of God:** Jesus' reply here alludes to the regal enthronement image of Ps. 110:1. This reply is what convicted Him. Apparently what offended Jesus' audience was His claim to sit in God's presence and to exercise divine authority. In effect, His answer to their question about being the Christ was more than they expected. It was not blasphemous to claim to be Messiah. What was blasphemous was the claim to be the Judge of the Jewish people, with God's authority. Jesus' remark also implies the hope of vindication. Though the people would kill Him, Jesus would end up at God's side. The title of the Son of Man is an allusion to Dan. 7 (Matt. 26:64; Mark 14:62).

22:70 Son of God: The Jewish leaders sensed that Jesus was claiming great authority here. They sensed that Jesus was asserting a unique and highly exalted relationship with God, making Himself the equal of God. In their view, this was not possible. **You rightly say that I am:** Jesus notes that they have made the implication, and He does not reject it.

22:71 from His own mouth: The Jewish leadership concluded that Jesus had made a confession of guilt. Jesus was "convicted" by His claim to a relationship to God in which He exercises an authority like God's.

23:1 The Roman ruler **Pilate** was responsible for collecting taxes and keeping the peace. It may be that he was in Jerusalem for judicial hearings, a procedure called an "assize." The fact that others were crucified with Jesus makes this likely.

23:2 began to accuse: Three charges were lodged against Jesus: (1) **perverting the nation,** (2) **forbidding** payment of taxes to Rome, (3) claiming to be the **Christ.** The first charge, which was a general complaint, involved disturbing the peace. The other two charges could have been construed as challenges to Rome. The second charge was a blatant lie (20:20–26). The third charge was true, but not in the threatening sense that the prosecutors suggested. A three-part Roman procedure was followed at the trial: charges, examination, and verdict.

23:3 It is as you say: Jesus gave Pilate the same qualified reply He gave the Sanhedrin in 22:67, 68, 70. Jesus is a king, but He was not a threat to Rome (John 18:36).

23:4 I find no fault: Pilate's verdict was that Jesus was innocent. This is the first of several such declarations in this chapter (vv. 14, 15, 22, 41). Jesus' suffering and death were those of an innocent, righteous One (v. 47).

23:5 By mentioning the charge that Jesus stirred up the **people,** the leaders suggested that Pilate risked being found derelict in his duty if he let Jesus go.

23:6, 7 Herod's jurisdiction: Herod was responsible for Galilee, so Pilate "passed the buck" for the ruling and showed political courtesy at the same time.

23:8 he was exceedingly glad: Herod's curiosity about Jesus is noted in 9:7–9.

23:9 answered him nothing: Jesus may have remained silent because He had already been declared innocent and yet was still subjected to trial (Acts 8:32, 33).

23:10 vehemently accused Him: The pressure to convict Jesus continues.

23:11, 12 After deciding that he had nothing to fear from Jesus, Herod and his men entertained themselves at Jesus' expense. Dressing him in a **gorgeous robe** was probably a sarcastic reference to Jesus' claim to be king.

23:13, 14 I have found no fault: This is Pilate's second declaration of innocence.

23:15 neither did Herod: The report of Herod's verdict is **nothing deserving of death.**

23:16 chastise Him and release Him: Pilate hoped that a public whipping might satisfy the crowd and tame Jesus, avoiding the need to resort to the death penalty.

23:17 it was necessary . . . to release one to them: Pilate wanted to take advantage of this custom and let Jesus go (Matt. 27:15; Mark 15:6).

23:18, 19 Away with this Man: The entire crowd is portrayed as wanting Jesus to die. Luke makes it clear that Jesus' death was not only instigated by Jewish officials but approved by the Jewish people. **Barabbas:** The people preferred that a seditious murderer be freed instead of Jesus. The idea of Jesus' substitution for this noted murderer foreshadows the substitutionary death of Jesus for sinful people.

23:20–23 Luke mentions the **chief priests** separately from the crowd since they were the instigators of the plot against Jesus. Because Pilate feared the will of the people, he entered into the conspiracy and shared its guilt, agreeing to put to death someone he knew to be innocent (Acts 4:25–27).

23:24, 25 delivered Jesus to their will: Jesus is going to His death.

23:26 Jesus was apparently unable to carry His own cross. **Simon a Cyrenian,** a man from a leading city of Libya, was chosen to carry the cross for Him (Acts 6:9; 11:20; 13:1). Mark 15:20, 21 mentions that Simon's sons were Rufus and Alexander, believers known to Mark's audience.

23:27 The events of vv. 27–31 are unique to Luke's account. While such mourning for the dead was required by custom in the ancient world, Jesus' reply seems to take the people's mourning as sincere.

23:28 do not weep for Me: Though He was dying, Jesus pointed out that their weeping should be for Jerusalem and its inhabitants, since judgment was going to fall on the city (19:41–44). Jerusalem here represents the entire nation of Israel.

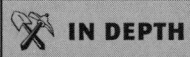 **IN DEPTH**   ## Crucifixion

The Romans used one of the most painful methods of torture ever devised to put Jesus to death (Luke 23:33). Crucifixion was used by many nations of the ancient world, including Assyria, Media, and Persia. The idea may have originated from the practice of hanging up the bodies of executed persons on stakes for public display. This discouraged civil disobedience and mocked defeated military foes (Gen. 40:19; 1 Sam. 31:8–13).

Crucifixion on a stake or cross was practiced by the Greeks, notably Alexander the Great, who hung 2,000 people on crosses when the city of Tyre was destroyed. During the period between Greek and Roman control of Palestine, the Jewish ruler Alexander Jannaeus crucified eight hundred Pharisees who opposed him. But such executions were condemned as detestable and abnormal even in that day as well as by the later Jewish historian Josephus.

From the early days of the Roman Republic, death on the cross was used for rebellious slaves and bandits. The practice continued well beyond the NT period as one of the supreme punishments for military and political crimes such as desertion, spying, revealing secrets, rebellion, and sedition. However, following the conversion of Constantine, the cross became a sacred symbol and its use as a means of execution was abolished.

Crucifixion involved attaching the victim with nails through the wrists or with leather thongs to a crossbeam attached to a vertical stake. Sometimes blocks or pins were put on the stake to give the victim support as he hung suspended from the crossbeam. At times the feet were also nailed to the vertical stake. As the victim hung dangling by the arms, blood could no longer circulate to his vital organs. Only by supporting himself on the seat or pin could he gain some relief.

But gradually exhaustion set in, and death followed, although usually not for several days. If the victim had been severely beaten, he would not live that long. To hasten death, the executioners sometimes broke the victim's legs with a club. Then he could no longer support his body to keep blood circulating, and death by suffocation quickly followed. Usually bodies were left to rot or to be eaten by scavengers.

To the Jewish people, crucifixion represented the most disgusting form of death: "He who is hanged is accursed of God" (Deut. 21:23). Yet the Jewish council sought and obtained Roman authorization to have Jesus crucified (Mark 15:13–15).

The apostle Paul summed up the crucial importance of His manner of death when he wrote, "We preach Christ crucified, to the Jews a stumbling block and to the Greeks foolishness, but to those who are called, both Jews and Greeks, Christ the power of God and the wisdom of God" (1 Cor. 1:23, 24). Out of the ugliness and agony of crucifixion, God accomplished the greatest good of all—the redemption of sinners.

23:29, 30 barren: In the days of judgment, the children, who were usually thought of as cursed, would be better off than those with family because the terror of that time would be so great. **Fall on us:** Fear of the judgment would be so great that people would prefer to die rather than suffer what was coming. There is an allusion here to Hos. 10:8 (Rev. 6:16). People who face God's judgment desire the relief of death rather than to endure His wrath.

23:31 what will be done in the dry: The idea here seems to be "If this is what is done to a live tree, what will happen to the dead one?" In other words, "If Jesus, the living tree, has not been spared, how much more will dead wood not be spared." This is Jesus' final lament over the nation of Israel.

23:32 Jesus' prediction of dying with the transgressors (22:37; see also Isaiah's prediction in Is. 53:12) was fulfilled when two **criminals** accompanied Him to death.

23:33 The name of the place in Aramaic is Golgotha, which means "Skull." **Calvary** is the Latin name for Golgotha. Possibly the name referred to a geographical feature of the locale, something that resembled a skull.

23:34 forgive them: Those who put Jesus to death acted in ignorance, not really understanding who it was they were killing. Jesus' example of interceding for His executioners was followed by Stephen in Acts 7:60. **divided His garments and cast lots:** The language here alludes to the suffering Righteous One of Ps. 22:18.

23:35 sneered: Jesus is mocked and called upon to save Himself if He is the Christ (John 10:18). There is irony as they mock Him, thinking they have stopped Him and that He cannot save Himself. God is preparing a vindication whereby He will be saved and will save others.

23:36 The drink referred to here was probably **wine** vinegar, which was inexpensive and quenched thirst better than water. It was a drink of the poor.

23:37 save Yourself: The sarcastic call to save continues, as does the irony.

23:38 KING OF THE JEWS: This inscription, which gave the charge against Christ, was written in three languages. Jesus was killed for who He is.

23:39 save Yourself: The mocking had come from the rulers (v. 35) and the soldiers (v. 37), and now what Luke calls blasphemy comes from one of the criminals.

23:40 Not everyone rejected Jesus at His crucifixion. The second criminal rebuked his companion in death, warning that he should fear God. The sarcastic thief, who would suffer judgment, was in no position to insult Jesus.

23:41 we indeed justly: One criminal knew the difference between those who had sinned and deserved to die and the One who did not.

23:42 remember me: This remark is amazing for its insight. While others mocked Jesus' seeming inability to save Himself, this thief recognized that Jesus would live and rule. He wanted to be saved and take part in Christ's kingdom.

23:43 you will be with Me: Jesus promised eternal life to the thief, doing what the mockers had asked Him to do in v. 39.

23:44 sixth hour . . . ninth hour: The first hour was sunrise, so the time was 12 P.M. to 3 P.M. During these three hours, signs of creation revealed that the hour was not one of light but of darkness (22:53).

23:45 the sun was darkened: This testimony of creation was designed to signal the importance of Jesus' death. Passover falls on the full moon, so this cannot have been an eclipse of the sun. The imagery is similar to that associated with the day of the Lord (Joel 2:10, 30, 31; Amos 8; 9; Zeph. 1:15). It is not clear whether the curtain that was torn was the one at the entrance to the tabernacle, or the inner curtain that separated the holy place from the Most Holy Place. The tearing of the veil symbolizes a renewed access to God through the death of Christ (v. 43; Heb 9; 10).

23:46 into Your hands: Jesus' final words are from Ps. 31:5, where this is the prayer of trust from a righteous sufferer. Jesus exercised that faith here.

23:47 In Matt. 27:54; Mark 15:39, the centurion's remark is noted as a confession of the Son of God. If Jesus was **righteous** and innocent, then He is who He claimed to be. Thus a second figure besides the thief on the cross had insight into Jesus' death.

23:48 beat their breasts: The customary mourning at death follows.

23:49 The Galileans **stood at a distance** to watch Jesus' crucifixion. Their sadness is further explained in 24:16–20.

23:50 Joseph, a council member: Not every Jewish religious leader opposed Jesus.

23:51 He had not consented: Joseph did not agree with the sentence of Jesus. Mark 14:64 suggests that "all" present were in favor of Jesus' execution, so Joseph may not have attended the trial. **waiting for the kingdom of God:** The description of Joseph in vv. 50, 51 recalls Zacharias and Elizabeth (1:5, 6) and Simeon and Anna (2:25, 38). The description suggests that Joseph was a follower of Christ.

23:52 the body of Jesus: There is no doubt that Jesus died. Efforts to explain the Resurrection as something like a return from a coma are more impossible than the idea of the Resurrection itself.

23:53 Jesus was given an honorable burial (Deut. 21:22, 23). The **linen** was probably fine cloth. The **tomb** had a stone to cover it in order to make it secure (Matt. 27:66). Guards were posted to stop anyone trying to steal the body (Matt. 27:65, 66).

23:54 Jesus was buried late on Friday on the day called **Preparation,** when everything was made ready for the Sabbath, the day when no labor could take place.

23:55 the women . . . observed the tomb: There is no doubt where Jesus was buried.

23:56 prepared spices and fragrant oils: On Friday the women prepared for the anointing of Jesus' body on the day after the Sabbath, since they could not make preparations on the Sabbath. The spices were used to delay decay and lessen the odor of the body. Mark 16:1 notes that spices were also purchased after the Sabbath. Apparently the women did not anticipate a resurrection.

24:1 very early: The women come early in the morning to anoint Jesus' body. John 20:1 notes that it was still dark, while Matt. 28:1 speaks of the dawn. Mark 16:2 says it was very early. Some manuscripts mention only the women of Luke 23:55 going.

24:2 Matthew 28:2 mentions that an earthquake moved the **stone,** which would have fit in a channel in front of the entrance to the tomb. Moving the stone would have been possible, though difficult, for a group of people. The earthquake settles the question of how the stone was moved.

24:3 did not find the body: The first citing of the empty tomb indicates that resurrection has occurred.

24:4, 5 It may be assumed that the **two men** who appeared were angels, based on the way their clothes are described as **shining garments** (v. 23). **Why do you seek the living:** Angels announced that Jesus was alive. Anointing Him would not be necessary.

24:6 is risen . . . Remember: The women were reminded that Jesus had predicted His resurrection as far back as **Galilee** (9:22).

24:7 delivered . . . crucified . . . rise: The contents of the predictions are reviewed and summarized (9:22, 18:32, 33).

24:8 remembered: The reminder triggers their memory.

24:9 told all these things: The first witnesses to the empty tomb give their report, which is summarized in Luke 24:23.

24:10 Three women are named: **Mary Magdalene** (8:2; Matt. 28:1; Mark 16:1; John 20:1), **Joanna** (8:3), and **Mary the mother of James** (Mark 15:40; 16:1). Other women also joined in the report of Jesus' resurrection. Mary, the last one at the Cross and the first one at the tomb, was given the privilege of relaying the first resurrection message.

24:11 Skepticism reigned among the disciples. It is clear that they did not expect a resurrection. **they did not believe:** The disciples thought the women's story was nonsense.

24:12 Peter arose and ran: Having already experienced a fulfilled prediction of the Lord (22:54–62), Peter hurried to the tomb to check out the women's story. It is hard to say whether Peter believed in the Resurrection when he left the tomb. Does his **marveling** indicate amazement or faith?

24:13–35 The Emmaus incident is recorded only in Luke.

24:13–16 eyes were restrained: The disciples could not recognize that Jesus was with them (v. 15). This indicates that Jesus was in the same, though glorified, body in which He died. Otherwise there would have been no need to keep them from recognizing Him.

24:17 What kind of conversation? Jesus asks about the topic that makes them so **sad.**

24:18 have you not known? Cleopas can't believe that their companion has not heard about what happened in Jerusalem.

24:19–21 Jesus of Nazareth . . . a Prophet: These disciples on the road to Emmaus regarded Jesus as the Revealer of God's way and the Doer of His work. **He who was going to redeem Israel:** The disciples had hoped that God would once again save Israel through Jesus.

24:22, 23 a vision of angels . . . said He was alive: The women reported that there was no body found in Jesus' tomb, and that angels had announced to them that Jesus lives. The fact that the men were still sad indicates that they did not believe the report. They were among the skeptics of v. 11.

24:24 As far as the disciples were concerned, there was still no decisive proof of Jesus' resurrection. They wanted to **see** the resurrected Jesus. Thomas was not alone in his doubts (John 20:25).

24:25 slow of heart to believe: Jesus, who at this time was still not known to the travelers, rebuked His companions and reminded them of the things that the prophets taught.

24:26 The prophets taught the suffering of **the Christ** and His entrance into **glory.** The passages referred to here would include Pss. 16; 100; Is. 53. See the Book of Acts for the apostle's use of these passages to prove that Jesus is the promised Messiah (Acts 2:14–36; 8:32, 33). Note how Jesus used the title of Christ (Messiah) to refer to Himself, while the disciples called Him merely a prophet (v. 19).

24:27 Going from the books of **Moses** to the **Prophets,** Jesus provided an overview of God's plan in the Scriptures. This plan is present throughout the entire OT (Acts 3:22–26; 10:43).

24:28, 29 Abide with us: This is an everyday use of a key verb in the first Epistle of John and in John's Gospel (John 15:1–8; 1 John

not a disembodied spirit. The presence of **flesh and bones** indicates that Jesus had been raised bodily, and that He was not a hallucination. He was raised in the same physical body in which He had been put to death. Otherwise it would have been a reincarnation, not a resurrection. The difference was that His resurrected body is not corruptible and not subject to death. Some have mistakenly taught that the character of the

Photo by Howard Vos

Modern Emmaus, named after the village toward which Cleopas and another disciple were traveling when Jesus appeared to them after His resurrection (Luke 24:13–27).

2:6). It means "to remain or to stay somewhere." They wish to have a meal with their interesting companion.

24:30–32 Did not our heart burn? They had sensed during the exposition that they were sharing in something special.

24:33, 34 Before the two travelers could report their experience, the other disciples reported that **Simon** had seen Jesus as well.

24:35 how He was known to them: The Emmaus experience is told to those who knew of Peter's sighting.

24:36 Jesus Himself stood in the midst: Though Jesus is "absent," He is present and appears to them again.

24:37 a spirit: The disciples had a difficult time adjusting to the fact that the physically raised Jesus was in their midst. They believed they were seeing a heavenly apparition (v. 39).

24:38 why do doubts arise: Jesus' appearances were designed to reassure the disciples about the reality of His vindication.

24:39 Jesus pointed out that a raised body is

resurrection body is to walk through walls or dematerialize at will. There is no proof that these capacities are inherent in a resurrected body; remember that Jesus walked on water, a violation of physical law, before the Resurrection. Paul discusses the resurrection body in 1 Cor. 15:35–58.

24:40, 41 joy . . . marveled: They are convinced as Jesus asks to share a meal with them.

24:42, 43 The physical nature of Jesus' resurrected body was confirmed by the fact that he **ate** something.

24:44, 45 The plan of God as outlined **in the Law of Moses and the Prophets and the Psalms** was being fulfilled in Jesus. This threefold categorization of the ancient Scriptures summarizes the contents of the OT. **opened their understanding:** The disciples' comprehension involved seeing how God's plan, as outlined in the Scriptures, fits together.

24:46 Christ to suffer and to rise: Two parts of God's plan had been fulfilled. Jesus had been crucified and raised from the dead. OT

☑ IN COMPARISON **Jesus in Isaiah**

Would you be able to explain to someone where the Scriptures speak about Jesus, "beginning at Moses and all the Prophets" (Luke 24:27)? That's what the Lord did with two of His disciples on the road to Emmaus. He explained how the OT—the only inspired Scriptures in existence at that time—foretold His coming as the Messiah.

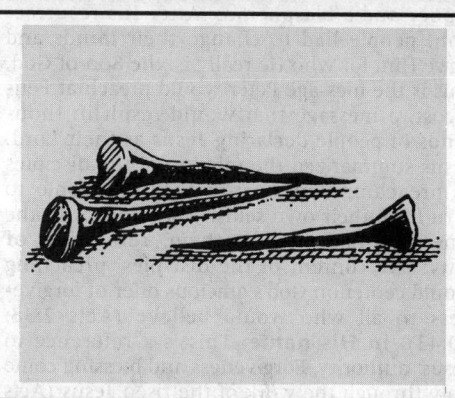

An entire list of the OT texts to which Jesus probably referred would be too lengthy to publish here. But one book that He undoubtedly spent a lot of time on was Isaiah. No other OT prophet made as many references to the coming Messiah as did Isaiah. Notice his emphasis on the Messiah as a suffering servant, a role that Jesus fulfilled:

Isaiah's Prophecy Fulfilled in Christ	
The Suffering Servant	**Jesus**
Would be widely rejected (Is. 53:1, 3)	Jesus "came to His own, and His own did not receive Him" (John 1:11; compare 12:37, 38).
Would be disfigured by suffering (Is. 52:14; 53:2).	Pilate had Jesus scourged (beaten); Roman soldiers placed a crown of thorns on His head, struck Him on the head with a stick, and spat on Him (Mark 15:15, 17, 19).
Would voluntarily accept the pain, suffering, and death that sinners deserve (Is. 53:7, 8)	As the Good Shepherd, Jesus laid down His life for His "sheep" (John 10:11; compare 19:30).
Would make atonement for sin through His blood (Is. 52:15)	Believers are redeemed and saved through the blood of Christ (1 Pet. 1:18, 19).
Would take upon Himself the grief of human sin and sorrow (Is. 53:4, 5)	Jesus was "delivered up because of our offenses" (Rom. 4:25); He "bore our sins in His own body on the tree," and by His stripes we were healed (1 Pet. 2:24, 25).
Would die on behalf of "the iniquity [sin] of us all" (Is. 53:6, 8)	God made Jesus "who knew no sin to be sin for us" (2 Cor. 5:21).
Would die in order to make "intercession for the transgressors" (Is. 53:12)	Jesus was crucified between two robbers, one on His right and the other on His left (Mark 15:27, 28; compare Luke 22:37). More generally, He is the one "Mediator between God and men" (1 Tim. 2:5).
Would be buried in a rich man's tomb (Is. 53:9)	Joseph of Arimathea placed the body of Jesus in his own new tomb (John 19:38–42).
Would bring salvation to those who believed in Him (Is. 53:10, 11)	Jesus promised that whoever believes in Him would not perish but have everlasting life (John 3:16). The early church proclaimed that same message (Acts 16:31).
Would be "exalted and extolled and be very high" (Is. 52:13)	God has "highly exalted [Jesus] and given Him the name" of Lord, to whom "every knee should bow" (Phil. 2:9–11)

texts that predict these events are Ps. 118:22 (Acts 4:11) and Ps. 22.

24:47 Jesus had been considered a pretender and a blasphemer. After His resurrection, people had to change their minds and serve Him for who He really is, the Son of God. This is the message Peter would preach at Pentecost, a message that would result in thousands of people declaring Jesus as their Lord. Jesus summarized the mission of the disciples as preaching **repentance,** calling people to turn from their own selfish ways to Christ, the One who had died for them. **remission of sins:** The content of the disciples' preaching would center on God's gracious offer of forgiveness to all who would believe (Acts 2:38; 10:43). **in His name:** This is a reference to Jesus' authority. Forgiveness and blessing come only through the work of the risen Jesus (Acts 2:30–39). The message of Jesus' salvation can go **to all nations,** to Jews and Gentiles alike. The offer is made to anyone who will receive it (Acts 10—15). The disciples' mission would begin in **Jerusalem** where Jesus died; from there, it would spread out into the entire world (Acts 1:8).

24:48 witnesses: Jesus pointed out that the disciples were called to testify to His work (Acts 1:8, 22; 3:15; 5:32; 10:39, 41; 13:31; 22:15; 26:16).

24:49 Promise of My Father: This is a reference to the baptism of the Holy Spirit at Pentecost (Acts 2). It was promised in Joel 2:28 (Acts 2:14–18), and in Jer. 31:31–33. Peter called this coming of the Spirit "the beginning" (Acts 11:15) because the real fulfillment of God's promise of salvation would start in those people united by the Spirit to establish the church. **tarry in the city of Jerusalem until you are endued with power from on high:** The disciples were to remain in Jerusalem until the Spirit empowered them on the day of Pentecost.

24:50 Bethany was just outside Jerusalem (19:29).

24:51 carried up into heaven: This is the first of two descriptions of the Ascension in Luke and Acts (Acts 1:9–11). Luke may be summarizing here what happened forty days later to create a link to the Book of Acts.

24:52 worshiped . . . joy: This is a proper response to the reality of the Resurrection and Ascension of Jesus.

24:53 continually in the temple praising and blessing God: The disciples' sorrow over Jesus' death had been totally reversed (v. 17). Now the disciples awaited the promise of God with joy. Luke's account continues in the Book of Acts. There he records the disciple's initial response to Jesus' commission to preach to all the nations (v. 47).

The Gospel According to

John

■

THE WORDS "READ THIS FIRST" HAVE TAKEN AN important role in the packaging of modern consumer products. Most consumers think life is too short for instruction manuals, so the packagers state it plainly: If you cannot read the manual, at least read this very important part. "Read This First"—it is for your own good. The Gospel of John makes a similar claim. It is the only book in the Bible that states

its purpose clearly and succinctly: It was written to tell individuals how to find eternal life (20:31). This clearly identified purpose sets the Gospel of John apart from the other Gospels. It is not so much a life of Jesus as it is a powerful presentation of His deity. Every chapter presents evidence—both signs and statements—for His divine authority. According to John, believing that Jesus is the Son of God, the Savior of the world, is the beginning of eternal life (3:14–17). What could be more important? John's statement about his Gospel is as good as a "Read This First" sticker for a person's entire life.

The Gospel of John is a persuasive argument for the deity of Jesus. It concentrates on presenting Jesus as the Word, that is, God (1:1) who became a man (1:14). Thus, John meticulously records the statements and describes the miracles of Jesus that can only be attributed to God Himself.

Jesus called Himself the bread of life (6:35, 41, 48, 51), the light of the world (8:12; 9:5), the door for the sheep (10:7, 9), the good shepherd (10:11, 14), the resurrection and the life (11:25), the way, the truth, the life (14:6), and the true vine (15:1, 5). Each of these statements

begins with the words, "I am," recalling God's revelation of His name, "I AM," to Moses (Ex. 3:14). Jesus did not say He gave bread; He said He *is* the Bread which gives life. He did not say He would teach the way, the truth, and the life; instead He said He *is* the Way, because He *is* the Truth and the Life. These are Jesus' clear claims to deity: He was not a mere man.

Then there are the signs of Jesus' deity. Miracles in the Gospel of John are called "signs" because they point to Jesus' divine nature. John records seven such signs: changing water into wine (2:1–11), healing a man's son (4:46–54), healing a lame man (5:1–9), multiplying bread and fish (6:1–14), walking on water (6:15–21), healing a blind man (9:1–7), and raising Lazarus (11:38–44). These miracles show that Jesus is God; He possesses power over nature. Other indications of Jesus' deity include the testimonies of John the Baptist (1:32–34), Nathanael (1:49), the blind man (9:35–38), Martha (11:27), and Thomas (20:28)—not to mention Jesus' own words (5:19–26).

Jesus was also fully man. His body grew weary (4:6), His soul was troubled (12:27; 13:21), and He groaned in His spirit (11:33). At the same time, this God-man was Israel's Messiah. Andrew told his brother, "We have found the Messiah" (1:41). Nathanael concluded, "You are the Son of God! You are the King of Israel!" (1:49). Even the Samaritan woman testified to Jesus' identity (4:25, 26, 29). Jesus the Messiah was and is the Savior of the world (4:42; 11:27; 12:13).

John urges us to trust in Jesus for eternal life. Our trust is built on our belief that (1) the Father is in Christ, and Christ is in the Father (10:38; 14:10, 11); (2) Christ came from God (16:17, 30), and God sent Him (11:42; 17:8, 21; see 6:29); and (3) He is the Son of God (6:69; 11:27; 20:31). John reveals the Bible's most important message: Believe and follow Jesus, because He is the way to eternal life.

The author of the Gospel of John does not identify himself by name, but his identity can be learned from the dialogue recorded in 21:19–24. The author calls himself "the disciple whom Jesus loved" (21:20), a designation that occurs four other times in the book (13:23; 19:26; 20:2; 21:7). This was the same "disciple who . . . wrote these things" (21:24). The author had to be one of the twelve apostles, because he is described as leaning on Jesus' bosom at the Last Supper, an event to which only the apostles were invited (13:23; Mark 14:17). These details imply that he was one of the three disciples closest to Jesus: Peter, James, or John (Matt. 17:1). He could not be Peter, because 21:20 states that Peter looked back and saw this one Jesus loved, and in another place asked a question of him (13:23, 24). On the other hand, James was martyred

too early to be the author of this Gospel (Acts 12:1, 2). Thus it is reasonable to conclude that this book was written by the apostle John. This conclusion is supported by early Christians such as Polycarp (A.D. 60–155), who was a follower of John.

In the nineteenth century, many critics claimed that the Gospel of John was written around A.D. 170. Then in 1935 C. H. Roberts discovered a scrap of papyrus in Egypt containing portions of 18:31–33, 37, 38 that disproved their theory. This fragment, the Rylands papyrus, was written around A.D. 125. The Gospel itself must have been written before A.D. 125, or even A.D. 110, allowing time for it to be copied and then carried to Egypt.

Conservative scholars typically date the book between A.D. 85 and A.D. 95. The book makes no reference to the destruction of Jerusalem in A.D. 70, implying that such a significant event must have occurred many years earlier. Moreover, the statement about Peter in 21:18, 23 seems to indicate that the Gospel was written when John was an old man. Only then would John have had to explain the death of Peter, or contend with a long-standing rumor of the early church. Others have suggested a date before A.D. 70 on the basis of 5:2, which indicates that Jerusalem was still standing. But there is a question about the interpretation of the tense of the verb *to be*. It is likely that the reason John used the present tense in this verse was to describe Jerusalem vividly, not to describe its present condition. Without more evidence than the tense of the verb in 5:2, the date of around A.D. 90 still seems most reasonable.

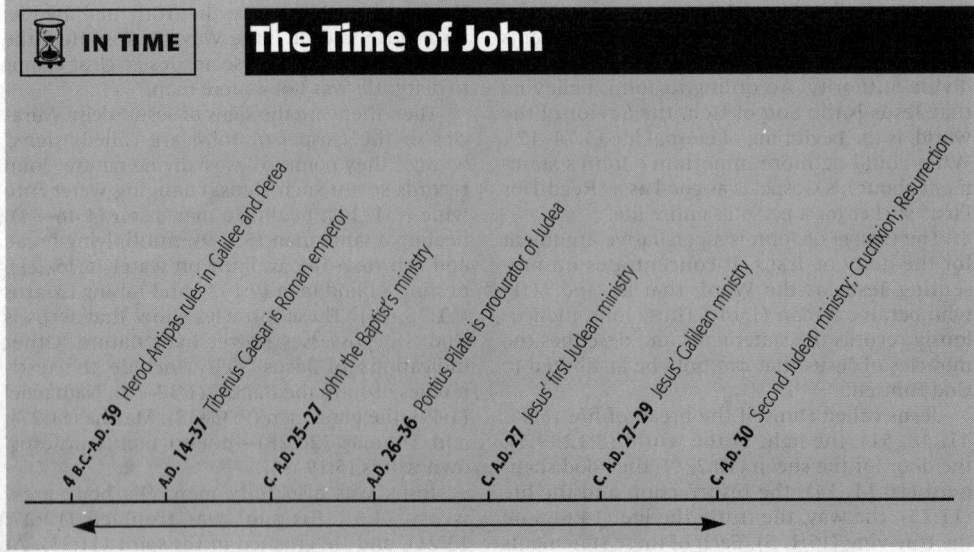

IN TIME **The Time of John**

4 B.C.–A.D. 39 Herod Antipas rules in Galilee and Perea

A.D. 14–37 Tiberius Caesar is Roman emperor

C. A.D. 25–27 John the Baptist's ministry

A.D. 26–36 Pontius Pilate is procurator of Judea

C. A.D. 27 Jesus' first Judean ministry

C. A.D. 27–29 Jesus' Galilean ministry

C. A.D. 30 Second Judean ministry, Crucifixion, Resurrection

Outline

Commentary

1:1–18 These first verses of the gospel according to the apostle John are among the most
elegant and profound that may be found in the
Word of God. They take us before the beginning
of creation and move us into the time and space
of human history. They reveal, like no other
portion of Scripture, that the Jesus who came
into human history (1:14) was the Creator God
of Gen. 1:1. These verses identify the eternal
relation of the Father and the Son and reveal
that we may have light and life through our
reception of Him—the One who is ultimate revelation of the Father.

1:1 In the beginning: Genesis 1:1 starts
with the moment of creation and moves

through time to the creation of humanity. John
1:1 commences with the beginning of creation
and contemplates eternity past. Before the creation of a material universe there was **the
Word** (Gk. *logos*). The Word was preexistent
(note the contrast with v. 14, where the eternal
Word "became" flesh). The term *Word* means
"that which is spoken, a statement, a speech." In
the Jewish translation of the OT into Aramaic,
this term was used for God. It was also used in
Greek intellectual circles to denote the controlling reason of the universe, the all-pervasive
mind which ruled and gave meaning to all
things. John has the OT concept in mind. *The
Word* here is the expression or the manifestation
of God (1:14, 18). John is obviously referring to
Jesus Christ (John 1:14, Rev. 19:13). Thus, this
Gospel begins with the thought that Jesus, the
Word, the unique manifestation of God, was
already continuously in existence when the
material universe was created. The fact that **the
Word was with God** suggests a face-to-face
relationship. In the ancient world, it was important that persons of equal station be on the same
level, or face-to-face, when sitting across from
one another. Thus the word *with* indicates a personal relationship, but also implies equal status.
The Word, Jesus Christ Himself, is an active
Person in communication with the Father (1
John 1:2). Moreover, **the Word was God.** The
Greek construction emphasizes that the Word
was of the very quality of God while still
retaining His personal distinction from the
Father. If John had used the definite article
before God, He would have taught a unitari-
anism of the Father rather than plurality in the
Godhead. Thus, the Gospel of John opens with a
simple, single sentence affirming the preexistence (eternality), personality and deity of the
Logos, Jesus Christ. He is distinct from God and
yet is God.

1:2 Neither the Person of Christ, nor His
Sonship, came into being at a point in time.
Rather, the Father and the Son have always
been in loving fellowship with one another.

1:3 All things were made (Gk. *ginomai*)
through Him: Before creation the Word was
(1:1). The tense speaks of continuous existence.
Creation itself, however, was made (1:3); matter
is not eternal. God the Father created the world
(Gen. 1:1) through God the Son (Col. 1:16, Heb.
1:2). Christ was not part of the creation. All that
is creation was made through Him; He is the
Creator God. The biblical teaching on creation,
confirmed in this verse, is that it is completed.
Some who hold to evolutionary views and to
reincarnation advocate an ongoing work of creation. Creation, however, ceased at the original
creation by God recorded in Gen. 1; He is now
sustaining His creative work (5:17).

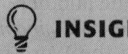

IN COMPARISON | The Seven Signs and Their Meanings

Turns water into wine (2:1–12)	Jesus is the source of life.
Heals a nobleman's son (4:46–54)	Jesus is master over distance.
Heals a lame man at the pool of Bethesda (5:1–17)	Jesus is master over time.
Feeds 5, 000 (6:1–14)	Jesus is the bread of life.
Walks on water, stills a storm (6:15–21)	Jesus is master over nature.
Heals a man blind from birth (9:1–41)	Jesus is the light of the world.
Raises Lazarus from the dead (11:17–45)	Jesus has power over death.

1:4 Note that **life** is not said to have been created; life existed in Christ (5:26; 6:57; 10:10; 11:25; 14:6; 17:3; 20:31). Humans are dependent on God for life. Our existence, spiritually and physically, depends on God's sustaining power. In contrast, the Son has life in Himself from all eternity. The life, Jesus Christ, is also **the light of men.** This image conveys the concept of revelation. As the light, Jesus Christ reveals both sin and God to humans (Ps. 36:9). Later in this Gospel, Christ declares Himself to be both the life (11:25) and the light (8:12). Death and darkness flee when the life and light enter. The dead are raised and the blind receive their sight, both physically and spiritually.

1:5 light shines in the darkness: Christ entered this dark world to give it spiritual light (Is. 9:2). The word translated **comprehend** can mean (1) to take hold of; (2) to overpower; or (3) to understand. Therefore, this verse may mean that darkness did not positively take hold of or understand the light, or that darkness did not negatively overcome the light. Both statements are true. Humans did not appropriate or understand the light, nor did they overtake or overpower it. Although Satan and his forces resist the light, they cannot thwart its power. In short, Jesus is life and light; those who accept Him are "sons of light" (12:35, 36). As the creation of light was the beginning of the original creation (Gen. 1:3), so when believers receive the light, they become part of the new creation (2 Cor. 4:3–6).

1:6 John the Baptist is here contrasted with Jesus Christ. Jesus is God (v. 1); John **was a man sent from God.** Jesus was the Light (v. 4); John was the lamp that bore witness to the Light (vv. 7, 8). Our task, like John's, is not to attract others to ourselves but to Christ. How great was the darkness so that God had to send a messenger to point out the light. Moral decay was not only in the world but in Israel and in the religious leadership of Israel. In the Gospel of John the name John never refers to John the apostle but always to John the Baptist. The

INSIGHT | John and the Other Gospels

Though all four Gospels trace the ministry of Jesus Christ, the fourth Gospel is different from the other three, containing 98 percent unique material. Unlike the synoptic Gospels which are in many ways alike, John does not include Jesus' genealogy, birth, baptism, temptation, casting out of demons, parables, transfiguration, the instituting of the Lord's Supper, Gethsemane, or His ascension. John also includes items the others do not such as the conversations with Nicodemus, the woman at the well, Jesus' "I am" statements, the Upper Room Discourse, and His high priestly prayer (John 17). The synoptics emphasize Jesus' Galilean ministry; John stresses Jesus' Jerusalem ministry. These differences are not contradictions, they are complementary. Each Gospel writer chooses material that supports his theme. In the case of John, his subject is Jesus, the Son of God and Messiah. The material he incorporates into his Gospel best develops that theme.

writer of this gospel had previously been a disciple of "the Baptist."

1:7, 8 To bear witness means "to testify" or "to declare." John uses the word translated *witness* thirty-three times as a verb and fourteen times as a noun in his Gospel. The term is particularly important to his purpose, which is to record adequate witnesses to Jesus as the Messiah so that individuals might believe in Him (20:30, 31). **Believe** means "to trust." John uses this verb almost one hundred times in his Gospel to express what must take place for a person to receive the gift of eternal life. The noun *faith* does not occur in the book nor does the word *repent*.

1:9 In order to give due notice to the incarnation of Jesus, this verse may be rephrased: "That was the true Light coming into the world, which enlightens every man." Jesus became man in order to reveal the truth to all people. Jesus Christ gives light to every human being by being the Creator. Creation gives light to every one on the earth that there is a Creator in heaven (Rom. 1:20). The inclusion of all people is in contrast to the exclusivism of the ancient world. The Jewish prophets taught and many Jewish people believed that in the last days Zech. 14 would be fulfilled and that Gentiles would be converted. This is in contrast to the Greek and Roman world. The Greek world never dreamed that knowledge was for every person. The Romans looked down on barbarians as the lesser breed without the law. Jesus Christ came to be the light to everyone, though not all would receive His light; this does not mean that all people would believe. John's part was to bear witness to that light. And we, today, should use every opportunity to reflect the light. Depending on the context, **world** can refer to (1) the universe; (2) the earth; (3)

humanity; or (4) the human system opposed to God.

1:10, 11 Receive here means "to receive with favor" and implies "welcome." Instead of a welcome mat, Jesus had a door slammed in His face. The themes of rejection and reception (v. 12) introduced in the prologue (1:1–18) appear again and again throughout the Gospel of John.

1:12 The phrase **believe in His name** occurs three times in the Gospel of John (1:12; 2:23; 3:18). *Name* does not refer to the term by which He is called, but to what His name stands for—*the Lord is salvation* (Ex. 3:14, 15). In this context, the phrase means to believe that Jesus is the Word, the life, and the Light—that is, He is the Christ, the Son of God (20:31). **To them He gave the right** refers to the legitimate entitlement to the position of **children of God.** None of us was naturally a child of God. We were by nature children of wrath and condemned apart from Christ. Imagine being a pauper and then being given the right to inherit the riches of a king and the position of royalty. By believing, undeserving sinners can become full members of God's family.

1:13 born . . . of God: This new spiritual birth is **not of blood,** that is, by physical generation or by parents. Nor is the new birth **of the will of the flesh,** that is, by personal effort. Neither is the birth **of the will of man,** that is, something accomplished by human effort. The new birth is the work of God alone. It is a gift to be received (4:10, 14), not a reward achieved by individual effort. The new birth is based on *relationship* with Christ, not personal *position*. The relationship, however, proceeds from the position of Christ as the mediator. Christ is life (1:4; 14:6). Those who trust Him are born of God, meaning they are given spiritual life.

 **IN FOCUS** | # God in Flesh

John 1:1 is probably the strongest passage in the NT for declaring the deity of Jesus Christ. Because of this many who deny this biblical doctrine, especially cultists, have attempted to undercut it by arguing that this passage only teaches that Jesus is "a god" and so not fully Deity. This confused position falls on at least two grounds. Such a view is polytheistic, the belief in more than one god. Second, it betrays a misunderstanding of Greek grammar. Verse 1 of the first chapter of John reads, "In the beginning was the Word, and the Word was with God, and the Word was God." The last portion of 1:1 is the major point of contention. It reads in the Greek *theos en ho logos,* or literally, "the Word was God." God, or *theos,* occurs in this verse without the Greek article *ho,* so that some have contended that the lack of the article in the Greek text should cause the statement to be translated "the Word was a god." The best understanding for the translation, however, as recognized by Greek scholars, is that since *theos* is a predicate and precedes the noun *logos* and a verb, it is natural for it to occur here without the article. Greek scholars are agreed that the verse should be translated as it regularly is in modern and ancient translations, clearly affirming that Jesus is indeed God.

1:14 The **Word** (Gk. *logos*) who was (continuous existence) God (1:1) **became** (point action; Gk. *ginomai*) **flesh** (Gk. *sarx*) (1:14). Verse 1 speaks of Christ's nature and works being outside of space and time, before creation. Verse 14 presents the irruption of Jesus Christ into time and space, even the history of humankind. The Son of God who was from all eternity, at a point in time, took humanity to deity (Phil. 2:5–9). God became human with limitations in time and space. Jesus Christ uniquely and thoroughly identified with us as both God and man. He was fully God and yet He became fully human (He did not have sin but then sin is not part of the nature of humanity, but is an intruder). Since nothing of the essential nature of deity was lost in this event, we might better understand "became" to mean "took to Himself" flesh. John uses the word *flesh* for the physical nature of persons, not for the sinful disposition (unlike the apostle Paul; Rom. 8:1–11). God the Son will forever exist as a man with a resurrected body (Acts 1:11; compare 1 John 4:2, 3). God **dwelt among us,** that is, among the apostles. *Dwelt* comes from the Greek word for tent. It was used in the Greek OT for the tabernacle where the presence of God dwelt. He was not an armchair dictator issuing orders from a parapet of heaven. Rather, He was a man among humanity. In the OT, **glory** refers to the divine presence (Ex. 33:18). As God manifested His glory in the tabernacle, so Jesus displayed His divine presence before the apostles (18:6; 20:26, 27). **Only begotten** (3:16, 18) means unique, one of a kind. The same term is used of Isaac (Heb 11:17), who was not the only physical son of Abraham, but was the unique son of promise. All who trust Christ are born of God. In the Gospel of John, these "born ones" are called children of God (vv. 12, 13), but Jesus Christ is the unique Son of God. He is the only Son who is fully God. He is also **full of grace and truth.** When God revealed Himself to Moses, He proclaimed Himself to be "abounding in goodness and truth" (Ex. 34:6). As applied to Jesus Christ, this phrase marks Him as the author of perfect redemption and perfect revelation.

1:15 He was before me: Jesus was born after John the Baptist (Luke 1:36) and began His ministry later than John the Baptist. Yet John the Baptist said Jesus was *before* him, meaning that Jesus' existence is from eternity past (v. 30). John is an excellent example of the single-mindedness that is needed to fulfill a person's ministry before God. He knew the specific message God gave him to preach and he did not deviate from that message.

1:16 Most people take the words of v. 15 to be John the Baptist's. Probably the words of vv. 16–18 are those of John the writer of this Gospel, although they too may be John the Baptist's. **Grace for grace** means grace piled upon grace. The background of this doubled term, as well as the use of the term in v. 17, is found in Ex. 32—34. Moses and the people had received grace, but they were in tremendous need of more grace (Ex. 33:13).

1:17 Throughout the NT, **grace** is God's favor expressed to sinful humankind apart from any human works or worth. **law was given through Moses:** John is not denigrating the law or Moses in this verse. Law and grace in the OT were not antithetical. Persons in the OT who were under the law were also saved by grace. The reference for the teaching here is probably Ex. 34:6, 7. In Ex. 34:6, 7a, Yahweh is seen as merciful and forgiving sin, while Ex. 34:7b says He will not clear the guilty. This conflict is reconciled in Jesus, who brings grace (forgiveness) and truth (judgment of law on sin) together in His person. He receives the judgment for sin in His body and consequently forgives the transgressors. John is not saying that Moses began the law but Jesus brought grace. He is only saying that in Christ grace and truth became full. Though there was abundant grace and truth expressed by God through the Law He gave Moses, it is in the person of Jesus Christ that grace and truth are realized to the fullest.

1:18 No one has seen God: God is Spirit (4:24) and is invisible (Col. 1:15, 1 Tim. 1:17) unless God chooses to reveal Himself. Humans cannot look at God and live (Ex. 33:20). Abraham, the friend of God, did not see God. Even Moses, the lawgiver, could not look at God's face (Ex. 33:22, 23). However, the Son is in intimate relationship with the Father, face-to-face with God (1:1; 6:46; 1 John. 1:2). God became visible to human eyes in the man Jesus. It is through seeing the Son that we see God. We cannot see Him today, but we know Him through His word. **The bosom,** or chest, is used here to designate a close and intimate relationship (13:23; Luke 16:23). The One who is the Father's **only begotten Son** and who knows God intimately came to earth and **declared Him.** *Begotten* speaks of His unique relationship to the Father. *Declared* can also mean "explained." Thus, Jesus Christ, who is of the essence of God (1:1), became a man (1:14) to explain God to us (1:18), especially the resolution of God's mercy and judgment (grace and truth). One of the many blessings of grace (1:17) is knowledge of God (1:18). As we continuously behold His glory as revealed in Scripture, we are transformed into His image (2 Cor. 3:18). Imagine it! We who were created in the image of God but were defiled through sin now are restored by beholding Christ, the very essence of God. What better investment of time could there be than beholding Christ? It is the key to victory in the race (Heb. 12:2, 3).

1:19—2:11 This passage records the events of a week at the beginning of the ministry of the Lord. On the first day John the Baptist testified to the Jewish leaders (1:19–28). On **the next day** (1:29) John bore witness again (1:29–34). **Again the next day** (1:35) John testified to two of his disciples who became followers of Christ (1:35–42). **The following day** (1:43) Jesus added two more disciples (1:43–51). **On the third day** (2:1), that is, the third day from the last day mentioned, Jesus took His new-found disciples to Canaan. Travel from Bethabara (Bethany) near Jericho of Judea (1:28) would probably take three days of walking. Thus, 1:19—2:11 carefully marks out the first week of witnesses.

1:19, 20 the Jews: That is, the Jewish leaders, the Sanhedrin. It is tragic that Christians and non-Christians have been guilty of anti-Semitism, ostensibly under the guise of all Jewish people being guilty of the death of Christ in some special way that is not true for all mankind for which He died. We must remember that Jesus and His disciples, and the many that He loved, were Jews. It is true that many among His people rejected Him, and especially many within the leadership of Israel, but no more blame should be placed on them than upon the Romans, and in fact each of us, for we have all rejected Him at some time in our lives. John primarily uses the phrase "the Jews" for the leadership of Israel and those who opposed the Lord Jesus. The Sanhedrin was responsible to examine anyone who was accused by someone of being a false prophet. The members of the Sanhedrin were divided into Sadducees and Pharisees. The delegation which came to investigate John the Baptist, was of the Pharisaic faction (1:24). **Who are you:** In the first century many people were waiting for the coming of the Messiah promised by the OT prophets. John did not claim to be the Messiah, but the rulers were concerned about maintaining peace under the eye of Rome, and they kept a close watch on all prospective messiahs. John was quick to acknowledge that he was **not the Christ.**

1:21, 22 Are you Elijah: The OT promised that Elijah would come before the great day of the Lord (Mal. 4:5). **Are you the Prophet:** Moses had predicted that a prophet like himself would come (Deut. 18:15). John denied being either; he didn't have a "Messiah complex." We, like John, must not think of ourselves more highly than we ought (Rom. 12:3).

1:23 The voice: Christ is the Word; John the Baptist was the voice. When pressed to identify himself, John the Baptist claimed that he was the fulfillment of Is. 40:3. In Isaiah's day there were few roads. When a king traveled, roads were built so that the royal chariot would not have to travel over rough terrain or be stuck in the mud. Isaiah was saying that before God appeared to manifest His glory, a voice would be heard, inviting Israel to make straight the way by which God Himself would come. John was identifying himself as that voice calling people to **make straight the way of the LORD.**

1:24 The Pharisees were an influential sect that numbered about six thousand. As strict interpreters of the Law in Israel, they were extremely zealous for ritual and tradition. Not all Pharisees were like the ones depicted by the

---

💡 **INSIGHT** **One God in Three**

The Gospel asserts that the Word, Jesus, "was God" (1:1). Jesus also said He was the Son of God, and "in the Father" (14:10). Yet when asked what the most important law was, He cited the creed of the Jewish people, first expressed in Deut. 6:4: "Hear, O Israel: the LORD our God, the LORD is one. And you shall love the LORD your God with all your heart (Mark 12:29, 30).

The Lord is one. Not two. Not three.

So how can the Lord be one, as Jesus admitted, and yet seem to be more than one, with the Son on earth praying to the Father in heaven?

The Gospel of John doesn't explain how, but the Prologue clearly asserts that the Word-Son-Jesus is God, yet distinct from God the Father (1:1–18). And the end of the book includes another testimony to Jesus' unique identity. After he touches the wounds of the risen Jesus, Thomas exclaims, "My Lord and my God!" (20:28). In telling us who Jesus is, John stresses both identity (Jesus is the Lord God) and distinction (the Son is closely related to but not identical with the Father or the Holy Spirit). The earliest Christians lived with this complex relationship but left it to theologians in later centuries to explain the complex oneness of God in the doctrine of the Trinity, when the divine nature of Jesus was challenged in the late third and early fourth centuries of the Christian era.

apostle (Matt. 5:20), but as a general rule these religious leaders failed to accept the Messiah.

1:25 Why . . . do you baptize: Performing the rite of baptism was regarded as making a claim to authority. The Pharisees were asking, "By what authority do you perform this religious rite?" The Jewish authorities believed that they had the right to accredit religious speakers. John, however, had his accreditation from God. John clearly saw his mission (1:26) and performed it in the spirit and power of Elijah (Luke 1:17).

1:26, 27 Undoing the sandal strap was the job of a slave. The Jewish Talmud says, "Everything that a servant will do for his master a scholar shall perform for his teacher, except the menial task of loosing his sandal thong." Thus John was saying that "Jesus Christ is the living

? Exact location questionable

Mediterranean Sea

0 ——— 40 Mi.
0 ——— 40 Km.

GALILEE
Nazareth
Scythopolis
Aenon?
Salim?
SAMARIA
DECAPOLIS
Jordan R.
PEREA
Jericho
Jerusalem
Wilderness of Judea
Bethabara
JUDEA
Dead Sea
Machaerus
—N—

© 1996 Thomas Nelson, Inc.

Jesus' Baptism and Temptation

Jesus came from Nazareth in Galilee to be baptized by John the Baptist. Though John had been baptizing in the Jordan River near Aenon and Salim (3:23), the exact location of Jesus' baptism is uncertain. Immediately after, Jesus was led by the Holy Spirit into the wilderness of Judea below Jericho. Following His temptation there Jesus returned to Galilee.

Lord and I am the voice, His servant and slave. Actually, I'm not even worthy to be His slave."

1:28 The location of **Bethabara** is unknown. Some think that Bethany is meant, but not the same Bethany as the familiar one near Jerusalem. **Beyond the Jordan** means east of

the Jordan River. Evidently, this was John's normal place for baptizing.

1:29 The Lamb of God: In the OT, the Israelites sacrificed lambs at the Passover feast (Ex. 12:21) and as offerings (Lev. 14:10–25). Jesus Christ is the Lamb that God would give as a sacrifice for the sins not only of Israel, but of the whole world (Is. 52:13—53:12). In one masterful sentence of introduction, John summarizes the whole redemptive program revealed throughout the OT.

1:30 preferred before me: Superior in rank or honor. **was before me:** Prior in existence.

1:31 I did not know Him: At first John did not know that Jesus was the Messiah. Apparently even though Mary and Elizabeth were relatives (Luke 1:36), there is no evidence of contact between them in the childhood years of John and Jesus. All John knew was that he was to baptize with water and that the Messiah would be manifested to Israel through him by that means. God had given John a sign by which he would know the Messiah—the descending of the Holy Spirit as a dove. When Christ came to be baptized, the Holy Spirit descended upon Him (v. 32), revealing to John Jesus' identity (v. 33). Matthew's account adds that a voice came from heaven saying, "This is my beloved Son in whom I am well pleased" (Matt. 3:17).

1:32–34 He who baptizes with (Gk. *en*) **the Holy Spirit:** Seven times the NT mentions this ministry of Jesus. Five are prophetic (Matt. 3:11; Mark 1:8; Luke 3:16; John 1:33; Acts 1:5), one is historical (Acts 11:16–18), and one is doctrinal (1 Cor. 12:13). Although the English translations vascillate between "with" and "in," the Greek consistently uses *en* which speaks of the sphere into which Christ baptizes. This action of the Messiah did not occur while He was on the earth. The baptism in the Holy Spirit first occurred at Pentecost (Acts 1:5; 11:15, 16) and became the common reality of all Christians at the time of the new birth (1 Cor. 12:13).

1:35 One of the **two** disciples of John the Baptist was Andrew (v. 40). The other is not named but was probably John, the author of this Gospel.

1:36, 37 John was willing to lose his disciples if they followed Jesus. After John introduces Jesus, he fades out of the picture in the Gospel of John except for one mention at the end of ch. 3 (vv. 22–36). **followed Jesus:** The disciples at this point not only physically followed Jesus at that time, but with John's blessing they changed their allegiance to the Lord.

1:38 What do you seek? This question is one of the most important questions that a follower of Christ must answer. The question of

Christ to these disciples is more profound than the response He received from them ("where are You staying?"). Christ was seeking to have them define their goals as new disciples. Were they looking for a revolutionary? Were they looking for an easy life? Christ, then, was not the choice. Jesus began to set forth the kind of commitment to Him that discipleship demands.

1:39 the tenth hour: There are six references to a time during the day in the Gospel of John (1:39; 4:6, 52; 18:28; 19:14; 20:19). The question is which system of telling time does John use? The Jews began their day either at approximately 6:00 in the morning (sunrise) or 6:00 in the evening (sunset). The Romans started the day at midnight as we do today. John, who probably wrote at Ephesus, apparently uses the Roman system. If John is not using the Roman system, then John 19:14 is in conflict with Mark 15:25. By the Jewish system of reckoning time, the tenth hour in this verse was 4:00 in the afternoon. According to the Roman system, the tenth hour was 10 A.M. Since John is evidently using the Roman system, the tenth hour here was 10:00 in the morning. Christ invited these disciples to spend virtually a whole day privately with Him during which they came to believe.

1:40–42 An early example of personal evangelism: **Andrew** brought his brother **Simon** the Good News, describing Jesus as **the Messiah.** Andrew appears two more times in the Gospel of John (6:4–9; 12:20–22); both times he is bringing someone to Jesus. Notice how Jesus uniquely meets the needs of each one. To Andrew He showed His humility. To Peter He showed His ability to change character. To Philip He showed His authority. To Nathanael He will show His omniscience. The testimony of each climaxes with the Son of God. **Cephas** is the Aramaic word for "rock" (Matt. 16:18). Jesus saw in Simon a rocklike character that would eventually enable him to become a leader and faithful witness.

1:43, 44 From this verse, it might appear that **Philip** followed Jesus without being evangelized by another disciple, but there are several indications that Philip was approached by Andrew and Peter before he actually met the Lord. Verse 44 says that Andrew and Peter were from the same city as Philip, suggesting that they had talked to him. Furthermore, when Philip told Nathanael what had happened, he said "we" have found the Messiah (v. 45).

1:45 Nathanael is not mentioned in the synoptic Gospels. But in every list of the apostles in Matthew, Mark, and Luke, the name Bartholomew is listed with Philip, as Nathanael is linked with Philip here. It is likely that Nathanael and Bartholomew were the same

person. **son of Joseph:** Philip did not have knowledge of the virgin birth at this time. However, soon all of the disciples would recognize Christ as the Son of God (v. 49).

1:46 Nazareth: Nathanael knew that the OT prophets had predicted that the Messiah would be born in Bethlehem. Furthermore, Nazareth was an obscure village. Nathanael simply could not fathom that such a significant person as the Messiah could come from such an insignificant place as Nazareth. **Come and see:** Notice that Philip did not arrive with Nathanael. Truth is not best imparted by argument but by gentle invitation to "come and see."

1:47 an Israelite indeed: In his younger life Jacob, the first Israelite, was a cunning, scheming fellow full of **deceit.** Nathanael was an Israelite, a descendant of Jacob, but he was genuine and sincere. Jesus read Nathanael's character like an open book (2:24).

1:48, 49 under the fig tree: In the OT, this expression often suggests being safe and at leisure (1 Kin. 4:25; Mic. 4:4; Zech. 3:10). Nathanael may have been meditating under the tree about the dream of Jacob referred to in vv. 50, 51. **I saw you:** Jesus manifested His supernatural knowledge. Apparently, this incident convinced Nathanael that since Jesus had such knowledge of him, He had to be the **Son of God,** the **King of Israel** (20:31). These titles referred to the Messiah.

1:50 greater things: Jesus assured Nathanael that he would see even greater supernatural manifestations in the future. Jesus' statement may have referred to the miracles performed in chs. 2—11; it may also refer to the future glory of Christ as the coming Son of Man (1:51; Dan. 7:13).

1:51 Jacob had a vision of angels ascending and descending a ladder from heaven (Gen. 28:12). The thought here is similar, namely that there will be communication between heaven and earth. **Son of Man,** an expression used in Dan. 7:13 of a heavenly being, was Jesus' favorite designation of Himself (Matt. 8:20; Mark 2:10).

2:1, 2 The third day refers to the third day from the last day mentioned (1:43). To walk from where John was baptizing to Cana would probably have taken three days. **Cana** was about four and a half miles northwest of Nazareth. The wording of the text, **the mother of Jesus was there . . . Jesus and His disciples were invited,** suggests that Jesus and His disciples were invited because of Mary. Her prominence in asking Jesus to help when the wine ran out (v. 3) may indicate that she was in some way related to the family holding the wedding.

2:3 Hospitality in the east was a sacred duty.

A wedding feast often lasted for a week. To run out of **wine** at such an important event would have been humiliating for the bride and groom. The family of Jesus was not wealthy, and it is likely their relatives and acquaintances were not either. This may have been a "low-budget" wedding feast. Although Christ had not publicly declared Himself to be the Son of God, the Messiah, Mary knew His divine position since surely she had not forgotten His miraculous birth. She remembered the words of the angel Gabriel (Luke 1:32, 33). But friends probably did not believe her. Perhaps she was anxious for the day

request. "Whatever He says to you, do it." That is great advice. It reminds us of passages such as Prov. 3:5, 6, Ps. 37:4, and Matt. 6:33. Full obedience brings joy, satisfaction, and transformation.

2:6 six waterpots: Each waterpot held **twenty or thirty gallons,** for a total of 120 to 180 gallons of the finest wine (v. 10). **purification of the Jews:** Jewish tradition required several kinds of ceremonial washings. Strict Jews washed their hands before a meal, between courses, and after the meal. This "purifying" extended not only to washing hands, but also to washing cups and vessels (Mark 7:3, 4).

Cana of Galilee in the area where Jesus grew up and the village where He performed His first miracle at the beginning of His public ministry (John 2:1–12).

she could be vindicated. But even though these ideas may have been swarming around in her head, technically she did not ask Him to do anything. She only told Him about the situation; she left all to His wisdom and will. Perhaps we could learn from Mary.

2:4 Woman was a term of respectful address (19:26). **My hour has not yet come** seems to mean that the time for Jesus to publicly work miracles, declaring Himself the Messiah, had not yet come. For the use of similar expressions, see 7:6, 8, 30; 8:20; 12:23; 13:1; 16:32; 17:1.

2:5 Jesus' response to Mary seems to have been a refusal to do anything about the situation. Yet she seemed to expect Him to do something. Perhaps something in the tone of Jesus' voice let Mary know that He would grant her

Because the roads were not paved and people wore sandals, water was needed for foot washing. At a large Jewish wedding, a large amount of water would have been required.

2:7–10 master of the feast: At a Jewish wedding, one of the guests served as a governor of the feast, similar to a master of ceremonies at a banquet. Our modern equivalent is probably a head waiter. This person was responsible for seating the guests and the correct running of the feast. **the good wine:** Usually the better wine was served first. Then, after the guests' palates were dulled, the everyday wine was served. But this wine was so good that the master of the feast was surprised to see it being served late in the celebration. Some have argued that the wine here is merely grape juice, but the Greek word for unfermented grape juice is never used in the NT. The context here also militates against such a view. The biblical view regarding wine is always against excess.

2:11 Signs (Gk. *semeion*): In the Gospel of John the miracles of Jesus are called *signs* to indicate that these miracles point to His Messiahship. There are seven signs in John, which are an organizing principle of this Gospel (4:46–54; 5:1–9; 6:1–14; 6:15–21; 9:1–7; and 11:38–44). Here the text specifically mentions that the sign signified Christ's glory, that is, His deity. When He transformed water into wine He demonstrated His creative power. He did in a moment what is ordinarily done in weeks or in months. Milton said, "The conscious water blushed when it saw its Maker." This is the first time the text says that His disciples **believed** in Him. Following sometimes precedes believing and believing sometimes precedes following.

2:12 down: Cana was in the highlands and Capernaum was on the northwestern shore of the Sea of Galilee, which was below sea level. To go from Cana to Capernaum they had to go

---

✠ IN CONTEXT | Water into Wine

Jesus' miracle of turning water into wine (John 2:1–12) was loaded with symbolism. Its placement at the beginning of John's Gospel is significant.

For Jews, wine represented life and abundance. No proper wedding would be without it. Wine symbolized the life of the party and the expectation of a good life to come for the newlyweds. But at Cana, just as the young couple prepared to launch a new life, the unthinkable happened—they ran out of wine. That may have been a common problem in that day, given that wedding festivities often lasted as long as a week. Nevertheless, it was discouraging and probably quite an embarrassment to the host. The party immediately began to wind down.

But Jesus used the moment to reveal to His followers something of who He was. By producing wine from water, He astounded His disciples and encouraged their faith (2:11).

However, the product was not merely wine, but the best wine (2:10). In the same way, Jesus was the new wine bringing abundant life to Judaism, which, like the wedding, had run out of life and become spiritually empty.

"down." Jerusalem, on the other hand, was situated on the top of a hill and one had to go "up" to get there (2:13).

2:13 the Passover of the Jews: Every male Jew was required to go to Jerusalem three times a year—for the Feast of Passover, the Feast of Pentecost, and the Feast of Tabernacles (Ex. 23:14–19; Lev. 23). **Jerusalem:** The synoptic Gospels—Matthew, Mark, and Luke—concentrate on Jesus' Galilean ministry. John focuses on Jesus' ministry in Jerusalem. The different accounts do not contradict each other; instead, they complement each other.

2:14 The synoptic Gospels place the cleansing of the temple at the conclusion of Jesus' ministry (Matt. 21:12, 13), whereas John puts it at the beginning (vv. 14–17). Apparently Jesus cleansed the temple two different times. The language of the synoptic Gospels and that of John differ considerably, indicating two separate events. The Law of Moses required that any animal offered in sacrifice be unblemished, and that every Jewish male over nineteen years of age pay a temple tax (Lev. 1:3; Deut. 17:1). As a result, tax collectors and inspectors of sacrificial animals were present at the temple. However, these officials would not accept secular coins because they had an image of the Roman emperor, whom the pagans worshiped as a god. To put such coins into the temple treasury was thought to be an offense. So in order to accommodate visitors in need of animals and the right kinds of coins, animal merchants and money changers set up shop in the outer court of the temple. These inspectors, collectors, and exchangers, however, charged high prices.

2:15 Jesus' **whip** was probably more a symbol than a weapon; nevertheless, it was effective in scattering the money changers and the animals they were selling. Jesus' actions were a sign of authority and judgment.

2:16, 17 The cleansing of the temple was the first public presentation of Jesus to Israel; He presented Himself as Messiah. The Messiah's ministry began in the temple; He came to purify (Mal. 3:1–3). The expression **My Father's house** was a distinct claim to messiahship. At the wedding in Cana, Jesus demonstrated His deity and power; here He showed His authority. Recalling the words of Ps. 69:9, the disciples understood that Jesus was claiming to be the Messiah.

2:18 The Jews apparently refers to the religious authorities of Israel (1:19), who also understood that Jesus was representing Himself as the Messiah; therefore, they asked for a **sign** (1 Cor. 1:22).

2:19 Destroy this temple: Jesus was not talking about the physical building; He was referring to His body, as John emphasizes in v.

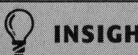

INSIGHT | Herod's Temple

During Jesus' time, the temple at Jerusalem was undergoing extensive reconstruction and renovation. Desiring favor among the Jews, King Herod pledged to build a magnificent temple that would perhaps recall some of the glory of Solomon's temple (1 Kin. 6:1).

At first the priests opposed Herod, suspicious that his real intent was to either do away with the temple altogether or erect something profane in its place. But Herod proved he was serious, hiring ten thousand laborers and ordering one thousand wagons for hauling cream-colored stone. When finished, the structure shone so brightly in the Mediterranean sun that it was difficult to look at directly.

21. Jesus was speaking of His death. **I will raise it up:** Note that Jesus did not say, "I will build it again." He was referring to His resurrection, three days after His death. The sign Jesus gave the Jews was the sign of His death and resurrection (Matt. 12:39; 16:4).

2:20 forty-six years: Herod began restoring the temple about A.D. 19. The work was not finished at the time of this conversation. In fact, it was not completed until around A.D. 64, under Herod Agrippa.

2:21, 22 The disciples understood that Jesus was the Messiah (v. 17; 1:41, 45, 49), but they did not understand that He was speaking of the resurrection of His body until it actually happened.

2:23 many believed in His name: John's purpose in recording Jesus' miracles was for people to believe and have eternal life (20:30, 31). Many have concluded that though the text says these people believed, they did not have true faith. Inasmuch as their faith was only based on Christ's miracles, they say it was not saving faith. Furthermore, they note that Christ did not commit Himself to them (v. 24); however, John says he recorded the miracles of Christ so that people would believe and have eternal life (20:30, 31). Also the text says they "believed in," a construction that everywhere else in the NT indicates saving faith. Moreover, they believed in His name, a phrase only used two other times in the Gospel of John and in both places it is of saving faith (John 1:12; 3:18).

2:24 Commit is the same Greek word translated "believe" in v. 23. There is a play on words here. These individuals trusted Jesus, but Jesus did not entrust Himself to them. Nicodemus is an illustration. John obviously ties these comments and the story of Nicodemus together. He says Christ "knew what was in man" (Gk. *anthrōpos*, 2:25) and then adds, "There was a man (Gk. *anthrōpos*) of the Pharisees named Nicodemus" (3:1). He, like Joseph of Arimathea, was a secret disciple (19:38, 39). Thus, the Lord did not commit Himself to him like He committed Himself to others, for

example, the apostles (15:15). We need to ask ourselves how trustworthy we are (Luke 16:1–13). Christ may be using the principle of readiness for receiving truth (notice, for example, 16:4 as well as 15:5).

2:25 In the Greek text **He** is emphatic. Without being told by others, Jesus knew the hearts of people. He reads people like people read billboards, another indication of His deity. In the OT God alone was said to know the hearts of all people (1 Kin. 8:39).

3:1 The phrase **ruler of the Jews** indicates that **Nicodemus** was a member of the Jewish council, the group that had sent a committee to investigate John the Baptist (1:24). Nicodemus no doubt knew that John the Baptist had denied being the Messiah (1:20), but had said that the Messiah was present (1:26, 27).

3:2 The fact that Nicodemus came to Jesus **by night** may reveal the timidity of his faith (12:42); however, his faith was developing (7:50, 51; 19:39).

3:3 born again: The Greek word translated "again" can mean either "from above" or "anew." The new birth, or regeneration (Titus 3:5), is the act by which God imparts spiritual life to one who trusts Christ. Without this spiritual birth, a person cannot perceive spiritual things (1 Cor. 2:10, 13–16), nor can he or she enter **the kingdom of God** (v. 5).

3:4 How? The construction of the questions assumed a negative response. Nicodemus misunderstood Jesus' statement as referring to a second physical birth. **old:** An adult.

3:5 born of water (Gk. *hudōr*) **and the spirit** (Gk. *pneuma*): *Of water* has been interpreted as: (1) water baptism. But the NT teaches that one is born again at the point of faith, not baptism (Acts 10:43–47); (2) a synonym for the Holy Spirit. The phrase could be translated "born of water, even the spirit"; (3) a symbol of the Word of God (Eph. 5:26; 1 Pet. 1:23); (4) physical birth; (5) John's baptism; or (6) a symbol, along with wind, in OT imagery for the work of God from above. The first three views are questionable since they must rely on future teaching in the Scripture which would not have been accessible to Jesus' listeners For interpretation 4, the idea is that Nicodemus brought up physical birth (3:4) and Jesus went on to say, "That which is born of the flesh is flesh" (3:6). If one could enter a second time into his mother's womb and be born, he would still be flesh. This position is not likely since Jesus' words would be trivial and do not advance the argument. Options 5 and 6 are the better choices for the meaning of the statement. Option 5 is a viable one since Nicodemus would probably be familiar with John's baptism. Jesus would be saying that one must identify with and accept John's message (baptism) and then one would receive Messiah's baptism in the Spirit as John promised (1:31–33). This view has both historical and theological support. Christ emphasizes by v. 6 that there are two realms, that of the flesh and the Spirit. Humans cannot save themselves but must rely on God's Spirit to regenerate them. Option 6 relies on the translation of *pneuma*, wind or spirit. Under this view the Greek term should be understood as *wind* rather than *spirit* and thus serve alongside of *water* as symbols for spiritual truths similar to how these terms are used in the OT (for example, Is. 44:3–5 and Ezek. 37:9, 10). Jesus, then, is contrasting the things from below (earthly womb) from the elements of water and wind from above (the divine work of the Spirit of God). A teacher of Israel should understand such OT imagery. Nicodemus may have been challenged by Christ, since he was a teacher of Israel, to understand the questions of Prov. 30:3–5: (1) Who has ascended into heaven, or descended? (2) Who has gathered the wind in His fist? (3) Who has bound the waters in a garment? (4) Who has established all the ends of the earth? (5) What is His name, and what is His Son's name? "Every word of God is pure; He is a shield to those who put their trust in Him" (compare John 3:15, 16).

3:6 flesh: (Gk. *sarx*). Flesh cannot be made into spirit. One must experience a spiritual birth (v. 7).

3:7 In the Greek text, **you** is plural. In v. 2, Nicodemus used the word *we*, probably referring to the Jewish ruling council, the Sanhedrin. Here Jesus spoke not only to Nicodemus, but to all whom he represented.

3:8 This conversation took place at night (v. 2). Conversations at night usually occurred on the flat roof of the house. Perhaps as they talked the wind was blowing. Jesus used **the wind** as an illustration of the work of the Holy Spirit. The Greek word translated "Spirit" also means "wind." As the wind seemingly blows where it wills, so the Holy Spirit sovereignly works. Likewise, no one knows the origin or destination of the wind, but everyone knows it is there. The same is true of the Holy Spirit.

3:9 Nicodemus wanted to know **how** he could experience the spiritual birth spoken of by Jesus.

3:10 Jesus answered Nicodemus's question (vv. 13–15), but first He rebuked Nicodemus for being a **teacher** of the Hebrew Scriptures and not knowing about spiritual birth (Prov. 30:4; Is. 44:3; Ezek. 36:26, 27).

3:11 you do not receive: Again *you* is plural (v. 7). Jesus had others in mind beyond Nicodemus. Here Jesus rebuked not only Nicodemus, but the other Pharisees as well.

3:12 Earthly things refers to things that occur on earth, like the new birth (vv. 3, 5–7), the wind (v. 8), and perhaps miracles. **Heavenly things** refers to events like Christ's ascension (6:61, 62) and the coming of the Holy Spirit (16:7). Nicodemus may have believed in Jesus' miracles (v. 2); the majority of the Jewish council did not (v. 11).

3:13 In v. 9, Nicodemus, referring to the new birth, asks, "How can these things be?" Here Jesus answers the question. New birth is by **the Son,** by the Cross (v. 14), and by faith (v. 15).

3:14 Every time the words **lifted up** occur in the Gospel of John there is a reference to Jesus' death (8:28; 12:32, 34). When **Moses lifted up the serpent in the wilderness** (Num. 21:9), those who looked at it lived. So it is with the Son of Man (1:51). Look and live! Look to the Lamb of God!

3:15 This is the first time **eternal life** is mentioned in John's Gospel (4:36; 5:39; 6:54, 68; 10:28; 12:25; 17:2, 3). When a person trusts Christ, he or she is born again and receives eternal and spiritual life, God's kind of life. The focus is not on our faith but on Christ, the object of our faith. Faith doesn't save. It is the channel to the One who saves—Christ.

3:16 God so loved the world: God's love is not restricted to any one nation or to any spiritual elite. *World* here may also include all of creation (Rom. 8:19–22; Col. 1:20). The Greek word for *only begotten* suggests a one and only son; it does not necessarily convey the idea of a birth. For example, Isaac is called Abraham's *only begotten* in Heb. 11:17 and in the Septuagint, the Greek OT (Gen. 22:2, 12, 16), when actually Abraham had two sons: Ishmael and Isaac. The Son of God is the Father's one and only, His unique Son.

3:17 At His first coming, Jesus came so that **the world through Him might be saved.** When Jesus comes again, He will come in judgment upon those who refused His offer of salvation.

3:18 To believe is to receive life (vv. 15, 16)

and avoid judgment. A person **who does not believe** not only misses life, but is **condemned already.** The idea of believing in Jesus' name is also found in 1:12.

3:19 Condemnation refers to the reason for judgment. The **light** referred to here is Jesus, the light of the world (1:7–9; 8:12; 9:5).

3:20 People offer many excuses for not accepting Christ. Some cite the presence of hypocrites in the church. Others claim inability to believe some of the truths about Christ or the gospel. These are merely attempts to conceal a heart in rebellion against God. The ultimate reason people do not come to Christ is that they do not want to.

3:21 The one **who does the truth** (1 John 1:5) is obviously already a believer because his or her **deeds** are **done in God.** Therefore, "coming to the light" is more than exercising faith. A person who **comes to the light** not only believes, but also openly identifies with the light so that his or her works can be seen as things done in union with God. One who believes on the Son and practices the truth can be trusted by God to be given revelation and responsibilities for service.

3:22 baptized: The impression here is that Jesus baptized. John corrects this idea in 4:2. Jesus provided the authority, but the disciples performed the baptisms.

3:23 Aenon was probably west of the Jordan River. **much water:** There were a number of springs at Aenon. **they came:** The people of the area.

3:24 The synoptic Gospels, particularly Matthew and Mark, give the impression that the imprisonment of John the Baptist came right after the baptism of Jesus. This verse indicates that there was an interval between Jesus' baptism and John's imprisonment during which both ministered.

3:25 The Greek word translated **then** often means "therefore." The disciples of Jesus and the disciples of John were both baptizing people; as a result, a question arose. The question came from John's disciples when they entered into a discussion with the Jews. **Purification** here refers to baptism.

3:26 John the Baptist's disciples were loyal to him. They were deeply concerned that one of his "disciples," Jesus, was competing with and surpassing him. In their astonishment, they exaggerated the predicament, saying, **all are coming to Him.** They were concerned that John was losing his audience to another preacher.

3:27, 28 John the Baptist clarified the relationship between himself and Jesus. First, he talked about himself (vv. 27–29); then he talked about Jesus (vv. 30–36). John explained that he

---

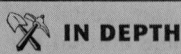 **IN DEPTH** | **God Takes All Kinds**

Jesus' nighttime meeting with Nicodemus (John 3:1–21) and His midday encounter with the Samaritan woman (4:5–42) show two of the many different ways in which He dealt with people. Whether it had to do with a respected urban leader like Nicodemus or a hardened, street-wise loner like the woman of Samaria, Jesus approached people on their own terms, as individuals with unique concerns. He modeled for us what it means to live, work, and communicate the gospel message in a pluralistic society.

Nicodemus was an upper-class Jew, a Pharisee from one of the prominent families of Jerusalem. He approached Jesus, alone, at night. The Lord confronted him with his need to be "born again," then let him go away to think things over. The next time we see him, he is defending Jesus on a procedural matter (7:45–52). But Nicodemus apparently didn't openly identify with Jesus until after the crucifixion, when he helped prepare His body for burial (19:39).

The Samaritan woman, on the other hand, had lived a scandalous lifestyle with a succession of husbands and then with a live-in companion. As a result, her community despised her. She also probably came from mixed ancestry, for which the Jews despised her. She was spoken to by Jesus in broad daylight, in public, first by herself but later in the company of others. He told her of "living water" and the need to worship in spirit and truth. She responded much more quickly than Nicodemus. Furthermore, hers may have been not so much an individual choice as a clan decision (4:39–41).

John went on to record many other ways Jesus dealt with people, and many ways they responded to Him. Some became believers after they were fed (6:4–14), others after they were healed (9:1–38), and others after they had seen the resurrected Christ (20:24–29). Some responded to the Lord's miracles, others to His teaching. There was no one kind of response to Jesus.

could not accept the position of supremacy that his disciples wanted to thrust upon him because he had not received it **from heaven.** To attempt to do any work, even God's work, must be done with divine approval. Too many of our tasks, even in the church, are patterned after the ways of the world. We need to be sensitive to follow God's commands, even if they fly in the face of what the world thinks is "smart." We don't have to be poured into the mold of this world's system. We can be transformed from the inside out by applying God's Word (Rom. 12:2).

3:29 In explaining why people were flocking to Jesus (v. 26), John the Baptist pointed out that **the bridegroom** receives **the bride.** John compared himself to **the friend of the bridegroom,** who was appointed to arrange the preliminaries of the wedding, to manage the wedding, and to preside at the wedding feast. When the friend of the bridegroom finished his job, he had to get out of the way. His **joy** came from the success of the bridegroom. John was satisfied with his position in life. He was content to be a "voice" (1:23) and a friend.

3:30 John the Baptist insisted that Jesus Christ had to **increase** in popularity and that he, John, had to **decrease.** John explained that Jesus had to increase because of (1) His divine origin (v. 31), (2) His divine teaching (vv. 32–34), and (3) His divine authority (vv. 35, 36). Even though John encouraged his disciples to also follow Jesus, there were still some found many years later in Ephesus (Acts 19).

3:31 **He who comes from above** refers to Jesus Christ. **He who is of the earth** refers to John the Baptist. John emphasized his earthly origin and its limitations. John proclaimed divine truth on earth; Jesus, on the other hand, is from heaven and **above all.**

3:32 **no one receives His testimony:** No one, apart from God's work in him or her (6:44), can accept Jesus Christ.

3:33 **Certified** means "to seal." In a society where many could not read, seals were used to convey a clear message, even to the illiterate. A seal indicated ownership to all and expressed a person's personal guarantee. To receive Jesus' testimony is to certify that **God is true** regarding what He has sealed.

3:34 Unlike human teachers, Jesus was not given **the Spirit by measure**—that is, in a limited way (Is. 11:1, 2). The Holy Spirit was given to Jesus completely. All three Persons of the Trinity are referred to in this verse: God the Father sent Christ the Son, and gave Him the Holy Spirit without measure.

3:35 God the Father not only gave Jesus, in His humanity, the Holy Spirit (v. 34), He also gave Him **all things,** including the authority to give life (5:21) and judge (5:22). The phrase **into His hand** signifies the Son's authority over the use of "all things."

3:36 The verb translated **has** is in the present tense. The one who **believes** has eternal life as a present possession. Likewise, the one who refuses to believe on Christ has the **wrath of God** abiding on him or her as a present reality.

4:1, 2 **Therefore** refers the reader back to 3:22–36. Christ's success in winning disciples had created jealousy among John's followers and provoked questions among the Pharisees. Since Jesus did not want to be drawn into a controversy over baptism at this stage of His ministry, He left Judea for Galilee (v. 3).

4:3 **again:** Jesus had been to Galilee before (1:43—2:12). He had left Capernaum to go to Jerusalem for the Passover.

4:4 The shortest route from Judea in the south to Galilee in the north went through Samaria. The journey took three days. Christ **needed to go through Samaria** if He wanted to travel the direct route. The Jews often avoided Samaria by going around it along the Jordan River.

4:5 Jacob had purchased a parcel of ground (Gen. 33:18, 19), which he bequeathed on his deathbed to Joseph (Gen. 48:21, 22).

4:6 the sixth hour: According to the Jewish system of reckoning time, the sixth hour was noon. By the Roman system it was 6 P.M. John seems to be using the Roman system (1:39, note).

4:7–9 Samaritans: When Assyria conquered the northern kingdom in 722 B.C., it exported half of the population to another country and imported Gentiles. The Jews who remained in the Northern Kingdom intermarried with the incoming foreigners; thus, they lost their racial purity. These racially mixed Jews were the Samaritans. When Babylon conquered and carried off the Judeans of the Southern Kingdom, they remained unalterably Jewish. After returning to the Holy Land, the pure Jews would have nothing to do with the Samaritans. To make matters worse, the Samaritans built a rival temple on Mount Gerizim. As a result of all this, the Judeans and the Samaritans hated each other.

4:10 Living water (7:37–39; Is. 12:1–6) springs from an unfailing source and is everflowing. Jesus, of course, was talking about eternal life (4:14; Rom. 6:23).

4:11–15 The Samaritan woman did not comprehend Jesus' spiritual message. She was thinking only of physical water and could not understand how Jesus could provide water without a means of drawing it, especially since the **well** was **deep.**

4:16 Jesus mentioned the woman's **husband** in order to expose her sin (v. 18).

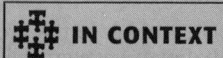 **IN CONTEXT**

"Jews Have No Dealings with Samaritans"

Hatred between Jews and Samaritans was fierce and long-standing. It dated to the fall of the northern kingdom of Israel in A.D. 722 The victorious Assyrians deported twenty thousand Israelites, mostly from the upper classes, and replaced them with settlers from Babylon, Syria, and several other nations. These foreigners introduced pagan idols and intermarried with the Hebrews, creating an ethnically mixed population.

When the Jews of Judah returned from the Babylonian captivity, they met resistance from the Samaritans as they tried to rebuild the temple, Jerusalem, and the rest of their society. They looked down on their northern cousins because of their mixed marriages and idolatrous practices. Soon, permanent walls of bitterness had been erected by both sides. By Jesus' day, the hostilities were so severe that the woman at the well was astonished that Jesus would even speak with her. As John explained, "Jews have no dealings with Samaritans" (John 4:9).

4:17, 18 The woman is definitely immoral, living in adultery with a man who is not her husband.

4:19 Because of what Jesus told her about herself, the woman concluded that Jesus Christ was a prophet, a person divinely inspired with supernatural knowledge (1 Sam. 9:9).

4:20 By mentioning the two different worship sites, the woman was perhaps trying to shift the conversation away from the subject of her own sins to theological questions. Or perhaps she realized that she was a sinner (v. 18), and knew that she was required to offer a sacrifice. The woman probably assumed that because Jesus was a Jew, He would insist that the sacrifice be offered in the temple at Jerusalem. The Jews insisted that the exclusive place of worship was Jerusalem. But the Samaritans had set up a rival worship site on Mount Gerizim, which according to their tradition was where Abraham went to sacrifice Isaac, and where later on he met Melchizedek. When the blessings and curses were read to the wilderness generation of Israel, the blessings were read from Mount Gerizim (Deut. 11:29; 27:12). Deuteronomy 27:4 instructed that an altar be erected on Mount Ebal, opposite Mount Gerizim. But the Samaritan scripture changed the verse to read "Mount Gerizim." The Samaritans altered history and tampered with the text of Scripture to glorify Mount Gerizim. This woman had

been reared to regard Mount Gerizim as the most sacred spot in the world and to despise Jerusalem. No wonder she brings up the issue of the place of worship. She thinks Mount Gerizim is the place of worship and sacrifice, and here is a Jew she is convinced is from God. She is sure He would tell her to go to Jerusalem.

4:21–23 The hour is coming: Christ reveals to the woman that where a person worships is unimportant. It is not limited to Mount

"Our fathers worshiped on this mountain" (John 4:20), the woman at the well told Jesus, referring to Mount Gerizim, still considered a sacred worship site by the Samaritans.

Gerizim or Jerusalem. The Samaritans worshiped what they did not know; they had created their own religion. The Jews had divine guidelines for worship. **Salvation is of the Jews** means that the Messiah would come from the Jewish people.

4:24 God is Spirit . . . worship Him . . . in spirit and truth: God is not limited by time and space. When people are born of the Spirit, they can commune with God anywhere. *Spirit* is the opposite of what is material and earthly, for example, Mount Gerizim. Christ makes worship a matter of the heart. *Truth* is what is in harmony with the nature and will of God. It is the opposite of all that is false. Here the truth is specifically the worship of God through Jesus Christ. The issue is not *where* a person worships, but *how* and *whom*.

4:25 The Samaritans believed that the prophet of Deut. 18:15 would teach **all things** when he came.

4:26 I . . . am He: Using the same words that God used when He revealed Himself to Moses (Ex. 3:14), Jesus clearly stated that He is the Messiah.

4:27 The disciples **marveled** that their rabbi was speaking to a woman (John 4:27). In their day it was considered disreputable and beneath his dignity for a rabbi to speak to a woman in public. But Jesus chose a more inclusive posture than His religious peers.

4:28, 29 all things that I ever did: In her excitement, the woman exaggerated. She did not report what Jesus actually told her, but what He *could have* told her. Note the woman's spiritual journey. She first viewed Christ as a Jew (v. 9), then as a prophet (v. 19), and finally as the Messiah.

4:30–33 As the Samaritan woman did not understand the switch from physical water to spiritual eternal life (4:15), neither did the disciples understand the switch from physical food to spiritual food. This is another instance of spiritual dullness. In 2:20 it was the Jews. In 3:4 it was Nicodemus; in 4:11 the Samaritan woman, and now the disciples (11:12; 14:5).

4:34 My food is to do the will of Him who sent Me: In v. 32 Jesus referred to the food He had and in this verse He tells what it is, namely, *doing* the will of His Father. Again, Jesus is modeling for His disciples."Food" is not simply knowing the will of God but doing it. Notice the difference between milk and solid food in Heb. 5:12. Milk is information or input but food is practice or output. Too often we stop with input rather than going on to output or productivity.

4:35 In vv. 35 to 38 Jesus puts before the disciples an opportunity for "doing" that will be "food" for them if they take advantage of it. The first part of v. 35 has been taken as a proverb

and as an actual fact. No such proverb is known. If this is factual, then this conversation took place in December/January because the harvest began in the middle of April. Actually, Christ is speaking about the approaching Samaritans. In them He sees a spiritual harvest opportunity for which they will not have to wait long.

4:36 The reaper of a spiritual harvest **receives wages**—that is, fruit which brings joy. In this case, Jesus sowed by giving the message to the woman. He was about to reap because He would see the whole city saved. Also the disciples were going to reap the harvest that Christ had sown. Note the "hundredfold" wages Jesus promises in Matt. 19:27–29 (1 Cor. 3:6–8; 2 Cor. 5:10).

4:37 One sows . . . another reaps: A vital lesson in discipleship. There are various tasks and laborers in the work of the Lord, but all receive honor alike (1 Cor. 3:6, 7).

4:38 Jesus applied what He had just said to His disciples. The **others** may have been John the Baptist and his disciples. They had labored in Judea (3:22–36). Thus, Jesus' disciples were reaping what others had sowed (vv. 1, 2).

4:39–41 The Samaritans readily **believed in** (Gk. *pisteuō eis*) **Him.** The Judeans rejected the testimony of their own Scriptures, John the Baptist, and Christ's miracles and teachings. The Samaritans accepted the testimony of an outcast woman. Sometimes God uses the most unlikely source to accomplish His work, while those who should have been at the forefront of the work of God fail to follow Him.

4:42 The title **Savior of the world** is used only here and in 1 John 4:14. The Judeans of Jesus' day taught that to approach God one first had to be a Jew. By including this incident in the Gospel, John demonstrates that Jesus is for all people of the world.

4:43, 44 His own country has been taken to mean: (1) Judea, (2) Nazareth, or (3) Galilee. Having no honor or reception in Nazareth, Jesus went elsewhere in Galilee.

4:45 The feast refers to the Passover (2:13–25). The Galileans who had gone to the feast received Jesus when He came to Galilee. The specially designed supernatural signs were doing their work as God intended (20:30, 31). This is pre-evangelism.

4:46 Nobleman is literally royal officer, one in service of the king. Herod Antipas was technically the "tetrarch" of Galilee, but he was referred to as a king.

4:47–49 The royal officer was under two false impressions about the power of Christ. He thought Christ would have to travel to Capernaum to heal, and that Christ did not have power over death **(before my child dies).** Christ was concerned that the man's faith was based only on **signs and wonders.**

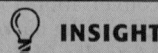

INSIGHT The Nobleman's Son

The key to understanding the significance of Jesus' second sign miracle (John 4:46–54) is geography. The nobleman and his dying son lived in Capernaum, the main city of the Galilee region (Luke 4:31). But Jesus was twenty miles away at Cana (where, significantly, His first sign miracle had taken place, John 2:1–12). That means that the nobleman walked a forty-mile round trip—a two-day trek by foot—to implore Jesus to heal his son. But Jesus merely spoke a word (4:50), producing results twenty miles away, in a world that knew nothing of phones, faxes, or modems. No wonder the incident produced faith (4:53). Jesus was the master of distance.

4:50–54 The nobleman is said to have **believed** twice, once in v. 50 and again in v. 53. In v. 50, he believed Jesus' promise that his son would not die. But believing that Jesus can and will heal is not enough to save. What was it that the nobleman believed in v. 53? The explanation is found in v. 54. The miracle that Jesus performed was His **second sign** (2:11). These signs were performed so that people might believe that Jesus is the Christ, the Son of God, and that by believing they might have life (20:31). When the Jewish nobleman realized that his son had been healed, he knew that Jesus was more than a mere mortal. The nobleman and his household placed faith in Jesus and were born from above (3:3). Often in the NT entire households would express faith in Christ (compare Acts 10:44–48; 16:31–34).

5:1 The **feast of the Jews** is probably not the Passover, which John usually refers to by name (2:13; 6:4; 11:55). It may have been Purim, which is not a divine institution but a Jewish-instigated feast to celebrate the deliverance of the Jews and Queen Esther. It is literally a feast of the Jews.

5:2 The **Sheep Gate** was a gate in the wall of Jerusalem near the temple, through which sheep were brought for sacrifice. The pool of **Bethesda** was a double pool surrounded by Herodian colonnades on four sides, with a fifth colonnade standing on the dividing wall that separated the northern and southern pools. The **five porches** were in the colonnades on the two sides, with two on each end and one in the middle.

5:3–4 By this pool there lay a group of sick people **waiting for the moving of the water.** All the oldest manuscripts were copied without the latter part of v. 3 and all of v. 4.

5:5 The exact nature of the **infirmity** is not stated. Apparently it affected his ability to walk (v. 7).

5:6, 7 Why ask a sick man if he wants to be healed? Some accuse the sick man of losing hope, but he is at the pool and is trying to be the first to get into the moving water ("while I am coming" in v. 7). Christ asks to verify that the man does indeed want to be healed and to focus his mind on the One able to heal.

5:8 The **bed** was a pallet, which was standard furniture for the people of Judea.

5:9 John records this miracle because it was a witness to Jesus' deity. Jesus Himself told John the Baptist that the proof of His messiahship was that the lame would walk (Matt. 11:1–5), for the prophet Isaiah had predicted this long before: "The lame shall leap like a deer" (Is. 35:1–6). Carrying a **bed** on **the Sabbath** was considered a violation of the Law of Moses (v. 10).

5:10 The Jews probably refers to Jewish leaders who were members of the council (1:19, note). The Law of Moses taught that the Sabbath must be different from other days. On it, neither people nor animals could work. The prophet Jeremiah had prohibited carrying bur-

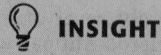

INSIGHT The Man at Bethesda

Jesus' third sign miracle revolves around the issue of time. The man at the pool of Bethesda had lain there for thirty-eight years—an entire lifetime as a helpless cripple. Indeed, he had probably started lying there before Jesus was even born. Imagine the disappointment he must have experienced time after time when the angel stirred up the pool, but always he had arrived too late to experience healing. Yet Jesus healed him and immediately he was able to walk. Jesus showed Himself to be the master of time. However, was Israel ready for Him (John 5:16)?

dens or working on the Sabbath (Jer. 17:21, 22). Nehemiah made it clear that trading on the Sabbath as if it were an ordinary day was forbidden (Neh. 13:15–19). Over the years, the Jewish leaders had amassed thousands of rules and regulations concerning the Sabbath. By Jesus' day, they had thirty-nine different classifications of work. One of these categories of work consisted of carrying a burden, including carrying a needle in one's robe. They even argued over whether a person could wear artificial teeth or a wooden leg. According to them, carrying furniture and even providing medical treatment on the Sabbath were forbidden. Jesus did not break the Law; He violated the *traditions* of the Pharisees which had grown up around the Law.

5:11–13 This man was healed without exercising faith. He did not know who Jesus was when he was healed (compare Acts 3:1–10) nor does he later express any thankfulness (v. 14). Perhaps we have here an illustration of the legitimacy of meeting a social need simply because there is a need, without any other purpose in view. This is pre-evangelism. **Jesus had withdrawn:** John records Jesus quietly withdrawing from a crowd on four occasions (8:59; 10:39; 12:36). However, Jesus caught up with the man later (v. 14).

5:14, 15 Sin (Gk. *hamartano*) **no more** (literally, "stop sinning") implies that this man's sickness was the result of sin, but this is not always so (9:1–3). The **worst thing** probably does not refer to hell. In this life, there are worse things than this man's sickness.

5:16 This is the first recorded declaration of open hostility toward Jesus in the Gospel of John.

5:17, 18 My Father: Jesus is "the only begotten Son" (1:14, 18; 3:16, 18)—that is, the unique Son of God. Here He claims not only a unique relationship with God the Father, but also equality with God in nature. Since God continually does good works without allowing

Himself to stop on the Sabbath, the Son does likewise, since He is equal with God. Certainly the Jewish leaders understood the implications of Jesus' claims (v. 18).

5:19–47 As a result of the miracle (5:1–9) and the dispute that followed (5:10–18), Jesus gives a lengthy discourse (5:19–47). In it He makes claims (5:19–30), offers proof of His claims (5:31–39), and challenges His opponents (5:40–47).

5:19 His first claim is a special relationship with the Father—equality. He explains this further with four statements, each beginning with "for" (5:19b–22). His second claim concerns His relationship to people, that He has the ability to give life and to judge (5:24–30). **The Son can do nothing of Himself** means that action by the Son apart from the Father is impossible because of the unity of the Father and the Son (v. 17). **Whatever He does, the Son also does** is a claim of deity and unity with the Father.

5:20 The Son does what the Father does (v. 19) because **the Father loves the Son.** Moreover, because the Father loves the Son, He reveals all to Him. The Father would show the Son **greater works** than the healing of the sick man. Jesus would raise the dead (v. 21) and eventually judge humanity (v. 22).

5:21 the Son gives life: As God raises people from the dead and gives them life, so Christ gives people spiritual life (v. 24). Jesus claimed the same power as God, thus claiming that He is equal with God.

5:22 all judgment to the Son: The Jews recognized that God alone had the right to judge humanity. In claiming that the Father committed all judgment to Him, Jesus again claimed equality with God.

5:23 honor the Son just as they honor the Father: To claim the same honor as the Father is to claim equality with the Father. Here Jesus claimed equal authority with God.

✠ **IN CONTEXT** | **Does God Work on Sundays?**

Jesus offered an odd retort to His critics in the controversy over observance of the Sabbath (John 5:16–17). God "rested" from His work on the seventh day of creation and "sanctified" it (Gen. 2:2, 3), or set it apart as something special. Later, one of the Ten Commandments made the seventh day a holy day, a Sabbath or day of rest in Israel (Ex. 20:8–11). This should not be confused with Sunday, which celebrates the resurrection of Christ from the dead.

According to rabbinical legal tradition, the healed man was violating the Sabbath rest by carrying his bed (John 5:10), as was Jesus by healing him on that day (5:16). But Jesus said that even God "breaks" His own Sabbath by continuing to work (5:17). Even though He has completed the Creation, He continues to maintain it and provide for His creatures—even on Sundays.

The point was that it's never the wrong day to do good.

5:24 The phrase **believes in Him who sent Me** is unusual. Christ, not the Father, is usually the object of this verb in John. The issue in this passage is the unity of the Father and the Son (vv. 17–23). All who believe in the One who sent Christ will believe in Christ. **shall not come into judgment:** A judgment to decide a person's eternal destiny is no longer possible for the one who has already been given eternal life. However, all believers will stand before the judgment seat of Christ (Rom. 14:10; 2 Cor. 5:10), not for punishment of sin, but to determine inheritance in Messiah's kingdom.

5:25 and now is: In the present, Christ gives spiritual life to the spiritually dead.

5:26, 27 For indicates that this verse explains the previous verse. Christ can give life because He Himself possesses life. He not only has a part in giving it, He is the source of it. This is another testimony to Jesus' deity, because only God has life in Himself.

5:28 the hour is coming: Christ not only gives spiritual life now (v. 25), He will give physical life later.

5:29 Two separate resurrections (Rev. 20:4, 5), the **resurrection of life** and the **resurrection of condemnation** are presented here in the fashion of the OT prophets, who often grouped together events of the future without distinction of time (Is. 61:2). Jesus was teaching the universality of resurrection, not the timing of it. **those who have done good:** The only "good" anyone can do is to believe on Christ, the One God sent (6:28, 29). All other good actions flow from that. Anything good that is done without that belief means nothing to God and will result in the resurrection of condemnation.

5:30 Christ's **judgment is righteous** because it is in accordance with God's divine will. In v. 19 Jesus said, "The Son can do nothing of Himself"; here He says He can **do nothing** independent of the Father. This verse is the climax and conclusion of vv. 19–29.

5:31–47 The term **witness** (testimony, v. 34) is a prominent concept in John. Though Jesus' testimony about Himself was true, under Jewish law one's self-testimony was not admissible in legal proceedings. **another** (v. 32): The Father Himself is Jesus' primary and ultimate witness (v. 37). Jesus also points His hearers to three other witnesses: **John** the Baptist (vv. 33–35), Jesus' own **works** (v. 36), and the **Scriptures** (v. 39), especially the writings of **Moses** (vv. 45–47).

5:31, 32 The other witness was John the Baptist (v. 33).

5:33, 34 You have sent to John: The religious leaders sent a delegation to interrogate John (1:19). **he has borne witness:** The testimony of John was that Jesus was the living Lord (1:27, 34; 3:31) and the dying Lamb (1:29). Jesus declares that witness to be true.

5:35 Jesus is the Light (1:4, 5). John was a **lamp. He was:** Jesus used the past tense because by this time John's work had been ended either by imprisonment or by death.

5:36 the works: John did not perform any signs (10:41). Those were specific works that the Son was to perform, as predicted in the OT (Is. 35:5, 6) to attest to the fact that He was sent by the Father (vv. 1–15; 2:1–11; 4:43–54).

5:37, 38 the Father Himself . . . has testified: This is not a reference to the voice from heaven at the baptism of Christ, but to Scripture (v. 39).

5:39 The Jewish religious leaders of Jesus' day diligently searched the OT **Scriptures,** but did not see Jesus as the Messiah and did not believe in Him (v. 38). There are also those today who master the Scriptures but do not allow the Scriptures to master them. God doesn't promise to bless Bible reading but, rather, Bible heeding (Rev. 1:3; James 1:22–25).

5:40 Their problem was not a lack of evidence; it was a lack of willingness to consider any evidence that would bring them to Christ.

5:41 Christ said He did not receive testimony from men (v. 34) nor honor from men (v. 41), meaning He did not seek either.

5:42 The love of God here is not love *from* God but love *for* God. Love from God is evidenced in Christ (3:16; Rom. 5:8). Since God loves us, we should love Him (Deut. 6:5; 1 John 4:19).

5:43 Jesus came in the **Father's name,** revealing God to the people, but they rejected Him. Ironically, if someone had come **in his own name,** giving his own ideas in harmony with the people's ideas, the people would have received him. How evident depravity is when people reject the truth and receive a lie, reject Christianity and receive the cults.

5:44 The people did not believe in Jesus because they did not seek **honor that comes from the only God.** This honor may be similar to Paul's view of the glory that will be revealed in us in the presence of God (Rom. 8:18). How transient and futile is the praise of man. Movie stars honor each other for performances, most of which will be forgotten in a decade. Sports heroes revel in victories that are short-lived. Plaques and trophies they win will one day be consumed by fire (2 Pet. 3:10–13). Jim Elliot once said, "He is no fool who gives what he cannot keep, to gain what he can never lose."

5:45 Trust means "hope." Christ will not have to accuse the people on Judgment Day because the one in whom they placed their hope, **Moses,** will. The people will be condemned by the very Law they professed to keep.

5:46 he wrote about Me: Moses wrote about Christ in the promises to the patriarchs, in the history of the deliverance from Egypt, in the symbolic institutions of the Law, and in the prediction of a Prophet like himself (Luke 24:25, 26). If the people had believed Moses, they would have received Jesus gladly. Over three hundred OT prophecies were specifically fulfilled in the First Coming of Christ.

5:47 you do not believe his writings: The ultimate problem was that the people did not believe the Word of God written through Moses.

6:1 After these things: About six months elapsed between 5:47 and this verse. Herod Antipas had killed John the Baptist and was seeking Jesus. The disciples had preached throughout Galilee, and many people were curious about Jesus (v. 5). John further identifies **the Sea of Galilee** as **the Sea of Tiberias,** an indication that his Gospel was written for those outside of Palestine. The Jewish people called this body of water the Lake of Gennesaret. The Romans called it Tiberias, after the city built on its western shore by Herod Antipas and named for the Emperor Tiberius.

6:2, 3 This was a world-renowned center of healing because of its hot mineral springs. Jesus apparently never went to Tiberias to do healing. If He wanted to gain worldwide reputation as a healer, that would have been the place to go. He had a different mission.

6:4 This is the second direct mention of **Passover** in John (2:23). At the time when His Jewish hearers were thinking of unleavened bread and manna, Jesus declared Himself to be the "bread of life" (v. 35).

6:5, 6 to test him: This was part of God's educational program (James 1:3, 13–15;1 Pet. 1:7). It is for refining Philip's faith, not tempting him to do evil.

6:7 One denarius was a day's wage for a laborer or field hand (Matt. 20:2). **Two hundred denarii** would have been almost two-thirds of a year's wages.

6:8, 9 Barley loaves were an inexpensive food of the common people and the poor.

6:10 men . . . about five thousand: Women and children were not included in this number (Matt. 14:21). The crowd possibly exceeded ten thousand. They sat in groups of fifty and one hundred (Mark 6:40) and thus were easy to count.

6:11 The miraculous multiplication of the food demonstrated Jesus' deity, because only God can create. This is the only miracle of Jesus that is recounted in all four Gospels.

6:12, 13 There were **twelve baskets** (Mark 6:43) of leftovers, perhaps one for each disciple.

The surplus emphasizes the sufficiency of the food created by Christ.

6:14 The Prophet is a reference to Deut. 18:15. The men's statement does not necessarily indicate that they believed Jesus was the Messiah. Some made a distinction between the Prophet and the Messiah (compare 1:20, 21). The bread (v. 11) may have reminded them of Moses and manna. Thus they concluded that Jesus was the Prophet that Moses had foretold.

6:15 make Him king: Moses had not only miraculously provided food for the Israelites, he had also led them out of bondage in Egypt. Perhaps these men felt that Jesus could lead them

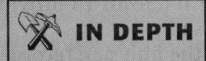

IN DEPTH — Feeding the Five Thousand

John writes that the crowd that followed Jesus did so in response to His miracles (John 6:2), a link to the healing of the lame man in 5:1–17. This leads to a fourth sign miracle, the feeding of the 5,000.

What Jesus did was remarkable in every way. Consider, for example, that even today very few facilities in the United States can accommodate 5,000 people for a sit-down meal. Yet Jesus miraculously provided for at least that many—with leftovers! John mentions that they filled twelve baskets—perhaps one for each disciple, or perhaps one for each of the twelve tribes of Israel. The overall result was faith: Jesus must be the Prophet promised by Moses (Deut. 18:15), the crowd concluded (John 6:14).

Yet doubt and rejection were soon to follow. Detractors pointed out that Jesus' lunch may have been impressive, but it was only one meal. By contrast, Moses had fed Israel in the wilderness for forty years (6:30, 31). Incredibly, they had missed the point of the sign: Jesus was not merely a deliveryman; He was the Bread of Life itself (6:32–58).

out of bondage to the Romans. Christ was at the zenith of His popularity, and the temptation to take the kingdom without the Cross must have been great (Matt. 4:8–10). The parallel passages say that He went to the mountain by Himself to pray (Matt. 14:23; Mark 6:46). Here is our greatest resource in times of testing.

6:16–18 His disciples went down to the

INSIGHT | Miracles at Sea

The fifth sign miracle that John included in his Gospel was a private affair for the disciples alone (John 6:15–21). What happened on the troubled Sea of Galilee revealed Jesus as master of the elements. John makes no explanatory comment on this incident, but its impact on the disciples is evident in Peter's words: "We have come to *believe and know* that You are the Christ, the Son of the living God" (6:69, emphasis added).

sea: In Mark 6:45 we discover that the disciples went to the sea because Jesus compelled them to do so. **It was already dark** by the time the disciples got out on the lake. The **wind** began to pick up, setting the stage for Jesus to provide another revelation of Himself.

6:19–21 This miracle, the fifth sign recorded by John, pointed to Jesus' deity. Only God could walk on water, calm the sea, and supernaturally transport the disciples to their destination.

6:22–71 After the two miracles, Jesus spoke to the multitude in general (6:22–40), then to the Jews who questioned Him (6:41–59), to the disciples (6:60–66), and finally to the Twelve (6:67–71).

6:22–25 The multitude had seen that there was only one boat **and that Jesus had not entered the boat with His disciples.** They assumed that Jesus was still there and were looking for Him.

6:26 Jesus rebuked their motives. He stated that although the people had seen the signs, they had not accepted them for what they were (proof of His true messiahship), and they were only interested in the physical.

6:27 Do not labor for the food: The impression that one must work for eternal life is quickly corrected when Jesus adds **which the Son of Man will give you.** The Son provides *life* as a gift (4:10). We are reminded of the servant who said, "Lord, I believe. Help my unbelief." We are surrounded by a world of religions that require works to be saved; thus, it seems so difficult to only believe. **Set His seal on Him** means that the Father has authorized and authenticated the Son as the Giver of life.

6:28, 29 This is the work (Gk. *ergon*) of God, rather than man's work for God, which the people were wanting to do (v. 28). Salvation is totally by God's undeserved favor.

6:30 When Jesus said "believe in Him whom He sent," (v. 29), the people must have understood that He was claiming to be the Messiah. Therefore, they asked for a **sign**—despite the fact that they had just witnessed the miracle of the feeding of the multitudes.

6:31 There was a tradition that said the Messiah would cause manna to fall from heaven

as Moses did (Ex. 16:4, 15). The people probably also saw this "miracle worker" as the perpetual provider of physical needs rather than spiritual ones.

6:32 The crowd misrepresented the truth, so Jesus corrected them. The manna had not come from Moses; it had been provided by God. Moreover, God still gives **true bread**—that is, eternal life (v. 33).

6:33 The bread is now called **the bread of God,** meaning it is bread from God—or Christ.

6:34 Lord can mean "sir," which is no doubt the meaning here (4:11, 15).

6:35 Bread of life means "bread which supplies life." Manna satisfied physical needs for a while; Christ satisfies spiritual need forever (4:13, 14).

6:36 seen . . . not believe: Seeing does not necessarily mean believing (v. 30; 11:46–57), although sometimes it does (11:45; 20:29). On the other hand, Christ blesses those who believe without having seen (20:29).

6:37 The Father gives implies divine election. **the one who comes** implies human agency. Election precedes human response (Acts 13:48).

6:38 For indicates an explanation of the previous statement. Christ will not cast out any who come to Him because He came to do the Father's **will.**

6:39, 40 The will of the Father is twofold: (1) that all who come to the Son will be received and not lost; (2) that all who see and believe on the Son will have **everlasting life.**

6:41 The Jews referred to representatives of the council. They **complained** that Jesus said He was **the bread which came down from heaven.** Although this exact phrase is not found in Jesus' statements, it is a fair summary of what He said (vv. 33, 35, 38). Jesus did claim that He was from heaven.

6:42 the son of Joseph: The religious leaders' proof that Jesus was not from heaven was that they knew His parents. To them, there was nothing supernatural about Jesus' origin.

6:43–44 Jesus returns to His message of life. In order for a person to come to the Bread of Life, the Father must **draw him.** This verb (Gk.

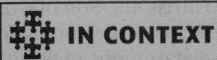

The Bread of Life

When Jesus called Himself the "bread of life" (John 6:35; also 6:32, 33, 41, 48), He was using as an image more than a staple of the diet, He was drawing on a rich symbol of Jewish life.

Bread played an important role in Israel's worship. During the celebration of Pentecost, two loaves of leavened bread were offered as sacrifices (Lev. 23:17). In the tabernacle, and later in the temple, the Levites placed twelve loaves of unleavened bread, or bread without yeast, before the Lord each week to symbolize God's presence with the twelve tribes (Ex. 25:30).

Throughout the Exodus, God miraculously sustained His people by sending manna from heaven each morning (Ex. 16). The bread-like manna was a "small round substance as fine as frost" (16:14). It looked "like white coriander seed" and tasted like "wafers made with honey" (16:31) or "pastry prepared with oil" (Num. 11:8).

It was this manna that Jesus was recalling when He called Himself "the true bread from heaven" (John 6:32), "the bread which came down from heaven" (6:41), and the "bread of life" (6:48–51, 58). Symbolically, Jesus is the heavenly manna, the spiritual or supernatural food given by the Father to those who ask, seek, and knock (6:45; Matt. 7:7, 8).

However, it's also interesting that Jesus' "bread of life discourse" (as John 6:26–58 is called) was given during Passover, also known as the Feast of Unleavened Bread (6:4, 22; see "Passover" at Luke 22:7). Passover celebrated the deliverance of Israel from slavery in Egypt. On the night before leaving Egypt, the Israelites made unleavened bread, as they had no time to let their bread rise before taking flight (Ex. 12:8; 13:6, 7).

In this context, Jesus had just fed at least 5,000 people (John 6:1–14), an event that led directly to the bread of life discourse (6:22–27). Clearly, He was indicating that He was God's provision for the people's deepest spiritual needs. Just as God had provided for His people as they came out of Egypt, so Jesus had provided physical food for the 5,000 and was ready to provide spiritual nourishment and life to all of them as well.

Tragically, the people balked at His teaching (6:30, 31, 41, 42, 52, 60). Their hearts were hardened in unbelief. Soon, many began to turn away (6:66). But to those who believed, like Peter who declared, "You are the Christ, the Son of the living God" (6:69), Jesus gave abundant and eternal life.

helkuō) is also translated "draw" in the sense of dragged (Acts 16:19; 21:30). People cannot be saved at all unless God through the Holy Spirit draws them.

6:45 God draws people by teaching them. Everyone, then, who hears and learns from the Father will come to Christ.

6:46, 47 Hearing and learning (v. 45) fall short of seeing the Father. John declares, "No one has seen God at any time" (1:18; 5:37). Here Jesus adds that only the Son **has seen the Father.** Though a person has not seen the Father, he or she can believe in Christ and have **everlasting life.**

6:48, 49 Christ is **the bread of life.** Those who believe in Him have life (v. 47). **The manna in the wilderness** did not ultimately sustain life. Those who ate it eventually died because it could not provide everlasting life.

6:50, 51 Eats of this bread is a synonym for faith (vv. 35, 48–50).

6:52 flesh to eat: They took in a nonfigurative way what was figurative.

6:53–54 Christ complicates the situation

further by adding **unless you . . . drink His blood.** The Jews were forbidden to drink blood (Lev 7:26, 27) and this additional statement must have added insult to injury. However, the Jews misunderstood. Lev. 17:11 clearly states that life is in the blood. Accepting the sacrifice of the body and blood of Christ is the basis for eternal life.

6:53–58 Eats my flesh and drinks my blood is not a reference to the Lord's table, which He would institute a year later. For one thing, Christ has made abundantly clear in this context that eternal life is gained by believing (vv. 29, 35, 40, 47). These verses are teaching that the benefits of Christ's death must be appropriated by each person. Christ has made explicitly clear that such appropriation is by faith.

6:59 the synagogue . . . in Capernaum: In the ruins of a synagogue at Capernaum, a large stone with a pot of manna engraved on it has been found. Some have suggested that perhaps the synagogue in this passage had such a symbol.

6:60 Disciple means "learner" and is used in a variety of ways in the NT. It can include unbelievers (v. 64), believers who go beyond initial faith to baptism and obedience (8:31), or it can mean the apostles in particular (2:11). The context determines what meaning is intended. Here it simply means learner. Some of the crowd were students; they came to learn. Not all of these had believed in Christ. It was **hard** for the Jewish learners to accept the idea of eating flesh and drinking blood. Jews were forbidden to even taste blood.

6:61, 62 Jesus was asking, "If the thought of eating flesh and drinking blood offends you, would you be further offended at the idea of My ascension?"

6:63, 64 Jesus was trying to get the religious leaders to see beyond the physical aspects of His teaching to the real issue—namely, that if they believed on Him they would have everlasting life. Because they did **not believe,** many of these disciples did not follow Jesus any longer (v. 66).

6:65 The people did not believe (v. 64) because it was not **granted** to them by the Father. There is a balance in this chapter between God's initiative and human response. The multitude is told about the election of the Father (v. 37), and yet all are invited to believe (v. 40). The same is true of the Jewish leaders (vv. 44, 47) and those called disciples (v. 63).

6:66 From that time could mean "for this reason." Because of Jesus' teaching, they ceased to travel with Him.

6:67 This is the first time in John's Gospel that the apostles are referred to as **the twelve** (though there is perhaps an indirect reference to the Twelve in 6:13).

6:68, 69 John wrote so that people might believe "that Jesus is the Christ, the Son of God" (20:31). The similarity between the confession of Peter and the purpose statement of John is inescapable.

6:70, 71 Judas Iscariot never made Peter's confession of faith in Christ. Though he was a disciple and even one of **the twelve,** it is never said that he believed.

7:1 The Jews here means the religious authorities, not the people in general (5:18). Many common people had responded to Jesus with joy (Mark 12:37).

7:2 The **Feast of Tabernacles** was one of the three great Jewish religious festivals (Passover and Pentecost were the other two). It was called the Feast of Tabernacles because for seven days the people lived in makeshift shelters made of branches and leaves. The feast commemorated the days when the Israelites wandered in the wilderness and lived in tents (Lev. 23:40–43). The festival was in September —October, about six months after the events of ch. 6.

7:3, 4 Jesus' brothers argued, "If You are really working miracles and thus claiming to be the Messiah, do not hide in obscure Galilee. If you are doing miracles at all, then do them in Jerusalem at the Feast to convince the whole nation." These words were sarcastic, as v. 5 explains.

7:5 brothers: Note that earthly kinship does not determine eternal life (1:13).

7:6 Earlier, Jesus had told His mother, "My hour has not yet come" (2:4; compare 12:23). Here He told His brothers also that the time for manifesting Himself to the world had not yet

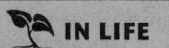 **IN LIFE**   **Not All Will Believe**

If you ever feel discouraged because family, friends, or coworkers refuse to accept the gospel, you may take some comfort from the fact that even Jesus' own brothers did not believe that He was the Christ (John 7:5). Even though they had seen His miracles and listened to His teaching, they still balked at the idea of placing faith in Jesus as the Son of God.

This is important to notice, because it shows that the person who hears the gospel bears responsibility for responding in faith, while the person who shares the gospel bears responsibility for communicating with faithfulness. If we as believers ever start holding ourselves responsible for whether unbelievers accept or reject the message of Christ, we are headed for trouble!

That's not to suggest that we can be careless in our witness or ignore our credibility. Notice that Jesus' brothers rejected Him *in spite of* His works and words. Is that true of us? Or do people dismiss our faith because our lives show little evidence that what we say we believe is true or that it makes any difference to us?

Eventually, at least some of Jesus' brothers did believe in Him. James, probably the oldest, became a leader in the church (Acts 15:13–21) and wrote the NT letter that bears his name. Likewise, the author of Jude may have been the half brother of Jesus.

come. Jesus mentioned on several occasions that the time for Him to be publicly manifested on the Cross was in the future (2:4; 7:6, 8, 30; 8:20).

7:7 The world cannot hate you: The world was not about to hate Jesus' brothers, because they were part of it.

7:8, 9 The Feast of Tabernacles was a festival for work accomplished. His work was not finished; His time had **not yet fully come.** Jesus on several occasions mentions that the time for Him to be publicly manifested (the cross) was yet in the future (2:4; 7:6, 8, 30; 8:20). Nothing could rush Him to this purpose. Only at the time of His intercessory prayer immediately before the arrest culminating in His death does He say His time had come (17:1).

7:10 When Christ did go to the Feast, He went **not openly** as His half brothers suggested (v. 4). He went "in secret"; He stayed concealed.

7:11–13 The Jews is a reference to the Jewish leaders, especially the members of the council (1:19).

7:14 The middle of the feast would have been the fourth day of the seven-day feast. During the first half of the festival Jesus remained in seclusion (v. 10). During the second half He began to teach publicly. This is the first mention in the Gospel of John of Jesus teaching in the temple.

7:15 Having never studied means never having attended a rabbinical school. Similar bewilderment was later expressed regarding Jesus' disciples (Acts 4:13).

7:16 not Mine, but His: Jesus' statement indicates that He did not receive His teaching from the rabbis, nor did He fabricate it. Instead His teaching came directly from God.

7:17 wills . . . shall know (Gk. *ginōskō*): Truth is imparted only to open hearts. God imparts the truth in accord with our ability to receive it (John 2:24, 25; 15:15–17; 16:4).

7:18, 19 is true: The test of a teacher is whether or not he delivers God's message. Jesus gave God's message; so did Moses. The religious leaders were breaking Moses' Law by seeking to kill Jesus.

7:20 The people from the provinces who had come for the feast knew nothing of the plan of the hierarchy to kill Christ. Thus, they perceived that He was demon-possessed. Those from Judea were better informed (v. 25). Perception often does not square with the facts (v. 24).

7:21 The **one work** was the healing of the impotent man in Jerusalem on the Sabbath a year before to this occasion (5:1–14; see especially v. 16).

7:22–24 Circumcision began with Abraham (Gen. 17:10). The Law of Moses required infants to be circumcised on the eighth day (Lev. 12:3). The Jews obeyed this law, even if the eighth day fell on **the Sabbath.** Jesus asked why the leaders were angry with Him for making a man **completely well** on the Sabbath.

7:25, 26 They are amazed that Christ spoke **boldly** (openly) and for a moment think that perhaps the rulers have been convinced that He is the Messiah.

7:27 The Jewish people seem to have expected the Messiah to appear suddenly from nowhere. They reasoned that since they knew where Jesus came from, He could not be the Messiah. They were ignorant of the Scriptures, for Micah had predicted the Messiah would come from Bethlehem (Mic. 5:2).

7:28, 29 Cried out signifies a loud cry of strong emotion. **You . . . know Me . . . where I am from:** Jesus reminded the leaders that they knew His origin. Their problem was that they did **not know** God, who sent Jesus. He explained to them that He knew God, was from God, and was sent by God.

7:30 take Him: Because of Jesus' public claims of divine origin (v. 29), the religious leaders sought to arrest Him. **because His hour had not yet come:** John passes over the immediate reason they were unable to arrest Him and gives the ultimate explanation (2:4). God is sovereign and He alone sets the time. As with Jesus, so with us; no one can touch us without the Father's consent (10:29).

7:31 In contrast to the leaders, many of the Jewish **people believed** because of the miracles Jesus performed (20:30, 31).

7:32 to take Him: The Jewish leaders decided earlier that they wanted to kill Christ (5:16), but this is the first real attempt on His life.

7:33 a little while longer: Jesus' time on earth was limited; soon He would be crucified and then ascend to the Father. His life was not determined by the Jewish religious leaders (v. 32), but by the Father.

7:34–36 you cannot come: Christ would be in heaven; the people would not be able to come to Him there. **Where does He intend to go:** The Jewish leaders did not comprehend what Jesus meant. They could only think of one of the various places where Jews had been scattered.

7:37–39 On each day of the feast, the people came with palm branches and marched around the great altar. A priest took a golden pitcher filled with water from the Pool of Siloam, carried it to the temple, and poured it on the altar as an offering to God. This dramatic ceremony was a memorial of the water that flowed from the rock when the Israelites

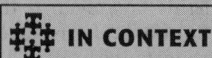 **IN CONTEXT** | **"We Interrupt This Program . . ."**

Jesus' cry in John 7:37 was far more dramatic than most modern readers realize. He chose a time when Jerusalem was packed with holiday visitors and a crucial moment in the festivities when He could attract the most attention. It would be as if someone broke into the broadcast of a presidential state-of-the-union address to announce, "We interrupt this program to bring you a special report."

The annual Feast of Tabernacles (or Booths, or Tents; John 7:2) swelled Jerusalem with an overflow of festive crowds. Every Jewish family within twenty miles of the city was required to move out of its home and live in a booth or tent in remembrance of Israel's wanderings in the wilderness. Many chose to move into the city for the week. Reunions and parties alternated with solemn processions from the temple down to the Pool of Siloam, a reservoir (9:7). Pushing its way through the crowded streets, the throng sang Pss. 113–118 in anticipation of God's righteous reign over Jerusalem.

Jesus chose to keep a low profile at this year's festival (7:2–10). He taught in the temple (7:14), but waited for the right moment to declare Himself publicly. It came on the last day of the feast (7:37), probably at the climax of the daily processional.

As on the previous six days, the high priest filled a goblet of water from Siloam and carried it back to the temple, where he poured it out for all the people to see. Each day at that point the crowds chanted, "Oh, give thanks to the LORD" (Ps. 118:1), and "Save now, I pray, O LORD; O LORD, I pray, send now prosperity" (118:25), and again, "Oh, give thanks to the LORD." Then they shook myrtle, willow, and palm branches toward the altar, as if to remind God of His promises. Then, after a pause, sacrifices were offered.

On the last day, however, just after the crowds had not only waved their branches but, as was the custom, literally shook them to pieces in a frenzy of enthusiasm, a voice suddenly cried out: "If anyone thirsts, let him come to *Me* and drink" (John 7:37, emphasis added). Jesus' timing couldn't have been more perfect or His claim more explicit: He was declaring Himself to be none other than the long-awaited Messiah who would pour out the Holy Spirit, as many in the crowd immediately recognized (7:39–43).

In many ways 7:37 acts as the pivot for John's account. From that point on, the hostility of Jesus' enemies mounted until they finally arrested Him (18:12) in vain hopes of shutting off the "living water."

traveled through the wilderness. On the last day of the feast, the people marched seven times around the altar in memory of the seven circuits around the walls of Jericho. Perhaps at the very moment that the priest was pouring water on the altar, Jesus' voice rang out: **If anyone thirsts, let him come to Me and drink.**

7:38 as the Scripture has said: The reference is not to a single passage, but to the general emphasis of such passages as Num. 24:7; Deut. 18:15; Is. 58:11; Zech. 14:8. In contrast to the small amount of water poured out each day during the feast, there will be a river of water coming out of those who believe in Christ. Not only will they be satisfied themselves, but they will also become a river so that others may drink and be satisfied (v. 39).

7:39 John explains that Jesus was speaking of **the Holy Spirit** who would satisfy personal thirst and produce a perennial fountain for the satisfaction of others. The Holy Spirit would come after Jesus' crucifixion and ascension. Jesus prepared His disciples for this in the Upper Room (14:16–20; 15:26, 27; 16:7–15).

7:40–44 Moses predicted that **the Prophet, the seed of David,** would come (Deut. 18:15, 18; 2 Sam. 7:14–16). These people knew that the Messiah was to come from **Bethlehem** (Mic. 5:2). However, they did not know that Jesus had been born there. They thought He was from **Galilee** (v. 41; Matt. 16:13, 14). They knew the Scripture, but they did not take the time to know the Messiah (5:39).

7:45, 46 The soldiers could have stated that they failed to arrest Christ because of the danger of the crowd but they did not. Instead, they reported that Jesus was not like anyone they had ever heard speak.

7:47, 48 After the soldiers reported that they did not take Jesus, the Pharisees gave a typical arrogant response, **Are you also deceived?** Surely, they reasoned, if the religious rulers did not believe in Jesus, He could not be the Messiah. In fact, though the poor heard Christ gladly, the religious rulers were among the least likely to believe in Christ. He threatened their positions. They had sold out to power and riches.

7:49 this crowd . . . is accursed: The Pharisees accused the people of being ignorant of the Law and thus under God's curse (Deut. 28:15). The irony of the situation was that it was the Pharisees, not the crowds, who were under God's wrath because they had rejected His Son (3:36).

7:50, 51 Nicodemus made a plea for justice (3:2; 12:42, 43), but his plea was rejected.

7:52 no prophet has arisen out of Galilee: Actually, the prophets Jonah, Hosea, Nahum, and perhaps Elijah, Elisha, and Amos were from Galilee or close to it.

8:1 The people went to their own houses (7:53). Jesus, who had no place to lay His head (Luke 9:58), spent the night on **the Mount of Olives.**

8:2 Early in the morning literally means "at dawn." **all the people came:** Because the Feast of Tabernacles had concluded the day before (7:2, 37), many visitors were still in Jerusalem. Attracted by the appearance of a noted rabbi, a crowd rapidly gathered. **He sat:** Teachers in ancient Israel sat when they taught. Jesus assumed the position of an authoritative teacher.

8:3 Abruptly bringing the adulterous woman into **the midst** of the proceedings was a rude disruption. The Pharisees were bent on confounding Jesus (7:45).

8:4, 5 such should be stoned: Stoning was specified in certain cases of adultery (Deut. 22:23, 24), though not all. The law required that both parties be stoned. Where was the male offender? They had already ignored the law by bringing the woman without the man. Why did the authorities intend to punish the woman but not the man? In the Greek text, the pronoun **You** is emphatic. The religious leaders were trying to trap Jesus into saying something that was contrary to the Law.

8:6 testing Him: If Jesus had said not to stone her, He would have contradicted Jewish law. If He had said to stone her, He would have run counter to Roman law, which did not permit Jews to carry out their own executions (18:31). What Jesus **wrote on the ground** is a matter of conjecture. Some suggest that He wrote the Ten Commandments recorded in Ex. 20. Had the content of His writing been critical, it would have been recorded. Perhaps the issue was not the content of what He wrote but the act of writing. In the OT, God wrote the law with His finger (Ex. 31:8). Maybe by writing the law Jesus is symbolically saying He is not the teacher of the law; He is the giver of the law. If He were merely a rabbi, He would only assert the Mosaic prescription of judgment. As the giver of the law, He could do for this woman what God had done for Israel at Sinai—He could forgive.

8:7 After pressing the issue, Jesus answered the accusers. In answering, He did not abolish Moses' law; rather, He applied that law to the lives of those who had accused the woman.

8:8 and again He . . . wrote: God wrote the Ten Commandments twice and here Jesus writes twice (8:6). Furthermore, in Ex. 31:18 and in John 8:6, the finger is only mentioned in the first instance.

8:9, 10 went out: Jesus had entered the temple at dawn (8:2). This scene could have happened in a few minutes. Thus, as this all happened, the sun was rising. As the scene was opened to the light of the sun, their guilty past was exposed by the light of the world (v. 12).

8:11 Sin no more implies that Jesus forgave her. He did not condemn her, but neither did He condone her sin. Some think the Lord will forgive them after they have done the best they can. Jesus forgave this woman after she did the worst she could. Jesus loves us just the way we are (Rom. 5:8), but He loves us too much to leave us that way.

8:12 I am the light of the world: As the sun is the physical light of the world, so Jesus is the spiritual light of the world. As the light of the world, Jesus exposes sin (vv. 1–11) and gives sight (9:1–7).

8:13–59 In vv. 1–11 the Jewish leaders attempted to discredit Christ. It did not work. Now they openly attack Him. In 8:13–59 they hurl a series of charges and questions at Him: (1) You have not proven Your case (vv. 12–18); (2) Where is Your Father? (vv. 19, 20); (3) Will He kill Himself? (vv. 21–24); (4) Who are You? (vv. 25–32); (5) How can You say, You will be made free? (vv. 33–38); (6) they claim Abraham and God as their father (vv. 39–47); (7) You have a demon (vv. 48–51); (8) Are You greater than Abraham? (vv. 52–56); (9) Have You seen Abraham? (vv. 57–59). Notice Christ's claims in this chapter: "I am the light of the world" (v. 12); "I know My origin and destiny" (v. 14);. "I judge no man" (v. 15); "I am from above" (v. 23); "I am not of this world" (v. 23); "I speak what I hear from My Father" (vv. 26, 29, 30); "I am of God" (v. 42); "I know God" (v. 55); "Before Abraham was I am" (v. 58).

8:13 Not true here does not mean "false"; it means "not sufficient." The Pharisees challenged Jesus on legal grounds, because no man on trial in a Jewish court was allowed to testify on his own behalf. Their point was that if Jesus was the only one testifying as to who He claimed to be, it would not be enough to prove His case.

8:14 My witness is true: In 5:31 Jesus argued on the basis of legality and offered other witnesses. Sometimes, however, an individual is the only one who knows the facts about himself. Thus, self-disclosure is the only way to truth (7:29; 13:3).

8:15 According to the flesh could mean either "according to appearance" or "by human standards." The religious leaders formed conclusions based on human standards and an imperfect, external, and superficial examination. Jesus did not judge according to human standards or outward appearances.

8:16–18 I am not alone: Jesus could claim that His pronouncements were true and accurate even though the Law of Moses required two witnesses for a testimony to be valid (Deut. 17:6; 19:15): Both He and the Father through the signs bore testimony to Jesus' words and works. The Pharisees charged Christ with not proving His case (v. 13). Christ's response is: your evaluation is superficial (vv. 14, 15). My proof, He says, is My Father and I (vv. 16–18).

8:19 Where is Your Father: Since the Father was part of Jesus' proof of Himself, the Pharisees wanted to know where this Father was. **You know neither:** Even if the Pharisees could see the Father, they would not receive what Jesus said. Jesus came to reveal the Father (1:18), and they had not received Him.

8:20 His hour: See 2:4.

8:21, 22 kill Himself: Later Jewish belief placed suicide on the same level with murder.

8:23 from beneath: Jesus was not referring to hell, but to **this world.**

8:24, 25 I am was God's designation of Himself (Ex. 3:14). Jesus was claiming to be God. This assertion was not understood by the religious leaders at this time. Later, Jesus' claim to be the "I AM" (v. 58) prompted the Jewish leaders to seek His life (v. 59).

8:26, 27 Jesus had **many things** to tell them which would add to their judgment. Those **things** were **true** because He received them from the Father. The Jews were blinded by prejudice and unbelief. Jesus had clearly explained on several occasions that the Father had sent Him (5:36, 37), and yet they did not accept it.

8:28 Lift up is a reference to the Crucifixion.

8:29 Imagine a mere mortal saying, **I always do those things which please Him.** This is a distinct claim to deity.

8:30 The Greek phrase translated **believed in** occurs almost exclusively in John's Gospel (1:12; 2:11; 3:15, 16, 18, 36; 6:29, 35, 40, 47; 7:38, 39; 9:35, 36; 10:42; 11:25, 26, 45; 12:44, 46). The phrase describes faith in Jesus' message (1 Cor. 1:21), which results in eternal life.

8:31 believed (Gk. *pisteuō*) **Him:** Some argue that these believers were not genuine believers. To support their claim, they point to the fact that "believe" in this verse is not fol-

---

✔ **IN COMPARISON** | **Jesus Takes on the Pharisees**

Jesus told the Pharisees . . .	The Pharisees responded . . .
I know where I came from and where I'm going (John 8:14–18)	You were born illegitimately (8:19).
You do not know God (8:19).	No response.
You will die in your sin (8:21, 24).	Who are You? (8:25).
[My] truth will make you free (8:31, 32).	We've never needed freedom (8:33).
You are the slaves of sin (8:34–38).	We are children of Abraham (8:39).
You are murderers and liars, doing the deeds of your father (8:39–41).	We are not illegitimate [like You]; besides, God is our Father (8:41).
Your father is the devil, a murderer and liar (8:42–47).	You're nothing but a Samaritan and have a demon! (8:48).
I have power even over death (8:49–51).	Who do You think You are? (8:52–54)
My Father honors Me [as His Son]; but you are liars (8:54–56).	You're just a young upstart, yet You claim to have seen Abraham! (8:57).
I AM (8:58; compare Gen. 17:1; Ex. 3:14).	They picked up stones to throw at Him (8:59).

lowed by "in." Jesus, however, is speaking to those who have genuinely trusted Him for eternal life. Thus, at least in this passage, there is no difference between "believe in Him" (v. 30) and "believe Him" (v. 31). **Abide** means to remain, to continue. A believer who continues to obey the Word is a disciple, a learner.

8:32 One who abides in the Word of God knows the **truth** (v. 31; 17:17). Notice that He does not say you shall know the *word* but that you shall know the *truth*. The antagonists searched the Scriptures, but they did not find Him who is the truth. Those who believed in Christ in v. 30 had to abide in words of Scripture to experience the truth. Such abiding leads to an experience of truth that sets us free. How a person abides is explained in ch. 15, especially v. 10. "If you keep my commandment you will abide in my love. The word **free** refers to freedom from the bondage of sin. Obedience to the Lord means fellowship with Him, protection from sin, and experiencing His love.

8:33 They answered Him: Throughout this chapter, Jesus was engaged in an exchange with His antagonists, the Pharisees (v. 13). They are also designated by the term *Jews* (vv. 22, 48, 52, 57) and the pronoun *they* (vv. 19, 25, 27, 33, 39, 41, 59). Verses 30–32 are a parenthesis to those in the crowd who believed in Him as they heard what He said to His opponents. In v. 33 the Jewish leaders once again speak. Thus, the objection in this verse is from Christ's antagonists, not the believers of vv. 30–32. **We . . . have never been in bondage:** The Pharisees' objection is startling. In their past the Israelites had been in bondage to the Egyptians, the Assyrians,

and the Babylonians. At the time they spoke, Israel was under the power of Rome.

8:34 slave of sin: Jesus was speaking of spiritual slavery. Such a slave cannot break away from his bondage. He must have someone else set him free (Rom. 8:34).

8:35, 36 A slave was not a permanent resident of a house. A son remained a family member with family privileges forever. This proverbial saying is applied in v. 36. The application proves that the "Son" here is Jesus Christ (see "the Son of Man" in v. 28). As a family member, the Son can bestow family privileges on others.

8:37 Abraham's descendants may have been physical heirs of Abraham, but they were not his spiritual descendants unless they had faith. But instead of trusting Christ to forgive their sins, the religious leaders wanted to kill Him. They heard the **word,** but did not believe it. Thus, they could not experience its truth (compare v. 31).

8:38 Note the contrast between **My Father** and **your father.** He would eventually tell them who their father was (8:44).

8:39 Abraham is our father: The Pharisees believed that being a descendant of Abraham guaranteed them a place in heaven. **The works of Abraham** included paying honor to those who spoke in the name of God (Gen. 14 and 18).

8:40 However, these people wanted to **kill** Jesus. Such works were not characteristic of Abraham; consequently, these people were not Abraham's children.

8:41 We were not born of fornication:

✠ IN CONTEXT — Jesus and "the Jews"

John is more hostile to "the Jews" than any of the other three Gospels. When the other Gospels talk about the opponents of Jesus, they specify Jewish leaders, such as priests or scholars. But John simply calls them "the Jews' (5:16). In the Gospel of John, "the Jews" is a technical term that means the opponents of Jesus, not all people who are racially Jews.

John reports Jesus going so far as to say the Jews didn't descend from Abraham: "Your father the devil" (8:44). Physically, they came from Abraham. But spiritually, there was no resemblance. Not all Jews, however, opposed Jesus. In fact, Jesus was a Jew. So were all of His twelve disciples. So were the vast majority of His many other followers.

John probably wrote his Gospel in the last quarter of the first century, shortly after Jewish leaders had grown so weary of Jewish Christians worshiping with them that they expelled them from the synagogues. If so, this book was written during the height of an us-them, Christian-Jew antagonism. Many of the Christians were Jews, racially. And many continued to honor Jewish traditions, such as the Sabbath and Jewish holidays. But more and more they were also beginning to think of themselves as distinct. Religiously speaking, they were followers of Jesus. The Jews still worshiping in the synagogue, however, were not.

From ancient times, this has been interpreted as a sneer, as if to say, "We are not illegitimate children, but You are." Apparently gossip had followed Jesus for many years, alleging that He had been conceived out of wedlock.

8:42, 43 not able: Sin had so blinded their eyes and hardened their ears that they could not receive the words of Jesus. They did not, and they could not.

8:44–47 your father: Jesus knew what was in the hearts of people (2:25), so He could trace their actions to their source. The devil is a **murderer;** his agents wanted to kill Christ.

8:48 The Jewish leaders charged Jesus with being **a Samaritan** and having **a demon.** In the process, they turned back to Jesus both charges that He had brought against them, namely, that they were not legitimate children of Abraham (vv. 39, 40) and that they were of the devil (v. 44). The conversation between Jesus and the Jewish rulers had become very heated. On the Pharisees' part, emotions were running high and reason was being set aside.

8:49 The Jewish leaders were dishonoring Jesus even though their eternal destiny depended on what they did with His message (v. 51).

8:50 One: God the Father will seek Christ's glory and judge those who dishonor Him.

8:51 Jesus graciously held out to the Jewish leaders the promise of forgiveness and eternal life. **My word** refers to the word concerning who He is. **Death** here refers not to physical death, but to spiritual death resulting in eternal separation from God.

8:52, 53 greater than . . . Abraham: Abraham and the prophets kept God's word and died. Jesus was claiming not that He would prevent physical death, but that He could give eternal life. To the Jewish leaders, this was proof that Jesus was demon-possessed.

8:54, 55 a liar like you: Notice the continuing candor of Christ as He charges the religious leaders. Religious hypocrisy brought His wrath! But He extended mercy to the woman taken in adultery.

8:56 My day: Abraham looked for the One who would fulfill all that was promised to him—promises that included blessings for all nations (Gal. 3:8, 9, 29).

8:57 They misunderstood what He said. He said Abraham saw His day (v. 56). They asked, **"have you seen Abraham?"**

8:58, 59 I AM: Jesus was not just claiming to have lived before Abraham; He was claiming eternal existence. He was claiming to be God Himself (Ex. 3:14). This time the Jewish leaders understood that Jesus was claiming to be God, so they **took up stones** to stone Him for blasphemy (Lev. 24:16).

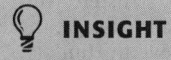

INSIGHT

Jesus Heals the Blind Man

The sixth sign miracle featured in John's Gospel reveals Jesus as the light of the world (John 9:5). He was also unique among the prophets in that none of them had cured blindness (9:30–33).

The healing of the blind man speaks to the problem of human suffering. Then as now, sickness was often assumed to be divine punishment for someone's sin. Like Job's counselors (Job 4:7–9; 8:2–8; 11:4–20), Jesus' disciples asked, "Whose sin caused this man's blindness?" (John 9:2). But Jesus replied with a radically new truth: God can use human suffering to reveal His glory (9:3). Jesus immediately showed what He was talking about by healing the man's blindness, thereby revealing Himself to be the Son of God.

9:1 The **man who was blind from birth** was a beggar (v. 8). Beggars waited by the gates of the temple for gifts from worshipers. Therefore, it is likely that this scene took place near the temple shortly after the confrontation recorded in ch. 8.

9:2 who sinned: It was commonly supposed that sickness was a result of sin. It would follow that sins committed by a baby still in the womb or sin committed by parents could result in a baby being born with a disease. Jesus rejected both suggestions (v. 3).

9:3 God allowed the man to be born blind so that Jesus could heal him and thus reveal **the works of God,** His healing power. Think of the years that this man carried the burden of blindness until the time it could be used for God's glory. May this comfort us in our pain and trial as we wait on the Lord.

9:4 work . . . while it is day; . . . night is coming: A reference to the earthly work of Jesus, which was soon to end.

9:5 For the second time Jesus claims **I am the light of the world** (compare note on 8:12).

9:6 Mixing **clay** with **saliva** was a common practice used for eye infections. Jesus may have used the clay to provide an opportunity for the man to exercise his faith in washing it off.

9:7 Siloam: Hezekiah had a tunnel cut through solid rock to transport water from Gihon (the "Virgin's Fountain") into the city of

In this detail from a Roman sarcophagus (about A.D. 330), Jesus touches the eyes of a blind man with a paste of spittle before sending him to the Pool of Siloam (John 9:1–7).

Jerusalem, to the Pool of Siloam (2 Kin. 20:20; 2 Chr. 32:30). John emphasizes that the name Siloam means "Sent," because Jesus had just announced that He had been sent by God (v. 4).

9:8–12 The **neighbors** were reluctant to acknowledge the miracle. See the cured man's understanding of Jesus grow: **A Man called Jesus** (v. 11), a prophet (v. 17), a Man from God (v. 33), the Son of God (vv. 35–38).

9:13, 14 Because the man had been healed on the Sabbath, the neighbors took him to the Pharisees. To make clay on the Sabbath was illegal.

9:15 His answer to the Pharisees is shorter than his explanation to his friends and neighbors (v. 11). Perhaps his impatience, which breaks out later (v. 27), is beginning to form at this point.

9:16 some of the Pharisees said . . . Others said: The Pharisees could not believe that Jesus was from God because He had healed on the Sabbath, thereby breaking the oral traditions that had grown up around the Law. But those who fairly evaluated Jesus' miraculous signs came to the conclusion that He was from God.

9:17–21 The blind man concluded that Jesus was **a prophet.** This does not mean he had decided that Jesus was the Messiah (1:20, 21; 6:14).

9:22, 23 To **be put out of the synagogue** was to be excommunicated. The Jews had three types of excommunication: one lasting thirty days, during which the person could not come within six feet of anybody else; one for an indefinite time, during which the person was excluded from all fellowship and worship; and one that meant absolute expulsion forever. These judgments were very serious because no one could conduct business with a person who was excommunicated.

9:24 The command to **Give God the glory** was a solemn charge to declare the whole truth (Josh. 7:19; 1 Sam. 6:5). Attempting to put words in the man's mouth, the Jewish leaders said they knew Jesus was **a sinner.** In their view, healing on the Sabbath was breaking the Law. So to them, Jesus was a sinner (5:16).

9:25 Not concerned about doctrinal disputes, the man gave his irrefutable testimony: **Though I was blind, now I see.**

9:26 How: Like a lawyer trying to disprove the testimony of a witness, they tried once more to shake the evidence.

9:27 Losing his patience with people who would not believe the facts before them, the man refused to relate the events again, saying sarcastically, **"Do you also want to become His disciple?"**

9:28, 29 You are His disciple: The healed man had not claimed to be Jesus' disciple. He only asked the Jewish leaders if they were interested in this case because they wished to become Jesus' disciples (v. 27).

9:30–33 unheard of: There is no healing of a blind man recorded anywhere in the OT.

9:34 Having no effective argument against the man's logic, the Pharisees resorted to abusing him. **born in sins:** Claiming that his blindness had been an evidence of sin, the very thing Jesus had denied (v. 3).

9:35, 36 Who is He: Faith must have a proper object. Jesus, not faith, saves. Faith is only a channel to the worthy object, the Lord Jesus Christ.

9:37, 38 Note the progression throughout this chapter of the healed man's understanding of the person of Christ. First, he called Jesus "a Man" (v. 11); then "a prophet" (v. 17); and finally he realized that Jesus is the Son of God (vv. 35–38). This is similar to the progression of understanding exhibited by the woman at the well in John 4.

9:39–41 For judgment I have come into

IN DEPTH Jesus and Physical Pain

- Most of the healings that Jesus performed were intended to reveal His divine power and authority (John 9:2, 3, 32, 33).
- He healed people from all walks of life, both the untouchables and the well-off and well-connected.
- He did not heal everyone (Matt. 13:58).
- He recognized and dealt with the emotional side of illness—feelings of sadness, anger, disorientation, anxiety, conflict, fear, and aggression.
- He exhibited patience, compassion, and courage when confronting the sick.
- He never used spells, charms, incantations, drugs, incense, or herbs to ward off evil spirits or to heal people of their diseases. His power came directly from His person.
- He drew a parallel between physical sickness and spiritual need (Mark 2:15–17).
- He often linked the healing of disease with faith and the forgiveness of sins.
- He refused to see all sickness as a sign of God's judgment.
- He refused to allow religious traditions and taboos to prevent Him from relieving pain and suffering.
- His power to heal threatened the established authorities.
- His immediate followers experienced the same power over physical maladies, a sign that their message was from God.
- Sometimes illness and death showed God's judgment (Acts 5:1–11; 12:19–23).
- His followers were not spared from physical afflictions. God used their sufferings to form character.
- We can look forward to a time when suffering, sorrow, pain, and disease will come to an end (Rom. 8:18; Rev. 21:4).

this world: Jesus did not come into the world to execute judgment (3:17). Nevertheless, the inevitable result of His coming is judgment, because some refuse to believe (3:18). As the light of the world, Jesus came that the blind might **see** and those who think they can see will be **made blind.**

10:1 In John 7, Jesus journeyed to Jerusalem for the Feast of Tabernacles (7:2, 10). All of the events between 7:10 and 10:39 take place on that visit to Jerusalem. Thus, chs. 9 and 10 are closely connected, suggesting that Jesus had the Pharisees of ch. 9 in mind when He spoke the opening words of ch. 10. A **sheepfold** was a walled enclosure or high fence made with stakes, and having one door or gate; often the enclosure was a cave. **some other way:** The Pharisees had secured their power by illegitimate means. A **thief** steals in secret; **a robber** plunders openly with violence.

10:2 In contrast to the thief, the true **shepherd** would come through **the door.**

10:3 **The doorkeeper** was the undershepherd. **Calls** expresses personal address rather than a general or authoritative invitation. **by name:** The naming of sheep was an ancient practice (Ps. 147:4; Is. 40:26). This was good practice for the undershepherd who has been given the charge of a portion of God's flock (1 Pet. 5:2).

10:4 **Brings out** is a translation of the same Greek word used in 9:34, 35 of the Pharisees casting out the man born blind. The false shepherds put out the sheep to rid themselves of trouble. The true shepherd puts out the sheep in order to feed them. The sheep know the voice of the true shepherd.

10:5 **A stranger** is anyone whom the sheep do not know, not necessarily a thief and a robber. Sheep would not follow a stranger's voice even if he used the shepherd's call and imitated his tone.

10:6 **They** are the Pharisees of 9:40.

10:7–18 All of God's undershepherds should read 1 Pet. 5:1–4 along with this passage.

10:7 In vv. 1–5, Jesus is the shepherd; here He is **the door.** Some shepherds lay down across the entry of the sheepfold at night to sleep. Wild beasts would be discouraged from entering, and sheep would not exit. Thus the shepherd was also the door.

10:8 The **thieves and robbers** were the Pharisees (v. 1).

10:9 Jesus, the shepherd, gives spiritual life and access to spiritual food.

10:10 **more abundantly:** The thieves take life; the shepherd gives it. Abundant life includes salvation, nourishment, healing (v. 9), and much more. **Life** here refers to eternal life,

 **IN COMPARISON** | **Jesus' Seven "I Am" Statements**

Jesus' "I am" statements would have particular significance to the first-century Jewish listener. God had revealed Himself to Moses with a resounding "I AM" (Ex. 3:14). Now Jesus was using the same words to describe Himself (4:26; 6:20; 13:19).

Title	Reference	Context	Significance
"I am the bread of life."	6:35, 41, 48, 51	After Jesus had fed the five thousand and the people wanted more free food.	As bread sustains physical life, so Christ offers and sustains spiritual life. The nourishment and satisfaction He offers are permanent.
"I am the light of the world."	8:12	During the Feast of Tabernacles. At this feast a huge candelabra was lit in the women's court of the temple. It reminded the Israelites of the pillar of fire, which guided their ancestors during the wilderness wanderings.	To a world stumbling about in the darkness of sin, Christ offers Himself as a constant guide. Light is also symbolic of holiness.
"I am the door of the sheep."	10:7, 9	During a discourse with Israel's religious leaders in which Jesus in essence declared them to be unfit shepherds of the nation.	Shepherds guided their flocks into stone enclosures each night to protect them. These structures had no doors. The shepherd would sit or lie in the opening to prevent predators from attacking. Thus Jesus was describing His care and constant devotion to those who are His.
"I am the good shepherd."	10:11, 14	Same as above.	Unlike hirelings who might run away and leave the flock unprotected, Jesus is committed to caring for and keeping watch over His people.
"I am the resurrection and the life."	11:25	After Lazarus had died.	Jesus is the Lord of all life and possesses the power to raise the dead. Death is not the final word, for all who are in Christ will live forever.
"I am the way, the truth, and the life."	14:6	When the disciples were confused about Jesus' statements about heaven.	Jesus is the one and only way to the Father. He is the source of all truth and the source for all knowledge about God. He offers to spiritually dead people the very life of God.
"I am the true vine."	15:1, 5	In the Upper Room Discourse on the night of His arrest.	The OT contains many references to Israel as God's vine (Ps. 80:8; Is. 5:1–7; Ezek. 15; Hos. 10:1). But because of the nation's unfruitfulness, Jesus came to fulfill God's plan. By attaching ourselves to Christ, we enable His life to flow in and through us. Then we cannot help but bear fruit that will honor the Father. In this metaphor, He is the Gardener.

God's life. It speaks not only of endlessness, but of *quality* of life. With Christ, life on earth can reach much higher quality, and then in heaven it will be complete and perfect.

10:11 Jesus is **the good shepherd** who **gives His life for the sheep** (3:16; 1 John 3:16), as opposed to the wicked thief who takes their lives. While *life* in v. 10 refers to eternal life, **life** here refers to physical life. Jesus laid down His physical life in order to give us eternal life.

10:12, 13 The **hireling** is a hired shepherd, a mercenary, who tends the flock for his own interest. When a hired shepherd sees a wolf coming he flees, not caring about the sheep.

10:14, 15 The **good shepherd** has an intimate knowledge of His sheep, and His **own** know Him. This interaction between Christ and His followers is something like the fellowship between the **Father** and His Son.

10:16 The **other sheep** were not Jews in heathen lands, but Gentiles. The Jewish people had asked if Jesus would go and teach the Gentiles (7:35). Jesus now declared that He had sheep among the despised heathen. **One flock** anticipates the salvation of the Gentiles and the formation of the church, in which converted Jews and Gentiles would form one spiritual body (1 Cor. 12:13; Gal. 3:28; Eph. 2:16).

10:17, 18 As the good shepherd, Jesus had the **power**—that is, the authority—not only to voluntarily **lay** down His life for the sheep (vv. 11, 15, 17), but also to **take it** up again. No one but God can do that.

10:19–21 After Jesus' analogy of the good shepherd, the editorial comment by John is fitting. In the analogy, Jesus was the good shepherd whose sheep hear His voice, implying that there are sheep who do not hear His voice. John's comment, true to the purpose of his Gospel, indicates that some believe and others do not. This is the same **division** that occurred in 9:16. People who look at the same evidence and hear the same testimony don't necessarily come to the same conclusions (12:9–11). See the apostle Paul's response to this in 2 Cor. 2:15–17.

10:22 The events of 7:1—10:21 occurred during the Feast of Tabernacles, which was about the middle of October. **The Feast of Dedication** was for eight days toward the end of December; thus, there was about two months between vv. 21, 22. This feast is also known as the Feast of Lights or Hanukkah. John notes that the events of 10:22 occurred in **winter,** not as a mark of time but as an explanation of why the Lord chose a sheltered spot to teach (v. 23).

10:23, 24 A pavilion surrounded the temple. **Solomon's porch** was a long, covered cloister or colonnade in the temple court, probably on the east side.

10:25 Jesus answered: Jesus reminded the Jewish leaders of His words and works. Jesus was the Messiah and said so. He told the woman at the well that He was the Messiah (4:25, 26), as well as the man born blind (9:35–37). His works include all the miracles He performed as signs pointing to His messiahship (20:31). Nevertheless, Christ usually did not claim publicly to be the Messiah. He had a reserve of dignity in not succumbing to their demands. Evidently, His method was to publicly tell everything about Himself that would lead to the conclusion He was the Messiah, but He stated His messiahship directly only to those who accepted it or were ready to accept it. Christ didn't develop robots as followers but people who could think. He followed a pattern of gradual self-disclosure to bring them to the day of discovery.

10:26 as I said to you: At the Feast of Tabernacles, Jesus had told the leaders that they were not among His sheep (vv. 14, 15; 8:42–44, 47).

10:27–29 Jesus described three characteristics of His sheep: (1) They **hear** His **voice** (v. 4). He knows them (Rom. 8:29). (2) **They follow** Him. The following of the sheep is a metaphor for faith. Other metaphors for faith in this Gospel include "drinking" water (4:14), eating bread (6:50, 51), eating flesh and drinking blood (6:54). (3) **they shall never perish:** In the Greek text there is a double negative with the word *perish,* "shall never, no never ever perish forever." Their eternal life can never be taken away. The **Father's hand** is more powerful than that of any enemy.

10:30 I and My Father are one: The Jewish opponents understood that Jesus was claiming to be God (vv. 31, 33).

10:31 again: This was not the first time that the Jewish leaders **took up stones** against Jesus (8:59). Those who cannot stand before the truth with arguments often find it necessary to silence the truth through forceful means.

10:32, 33 The Jewish antagonizers revealed the reason for their opposition to Jesus—He was claiming a unique unity with the Father, a unity that clearly indicated His own deity. The Jewish leaders considered this to be **blasphemy.**

10:34 In the OT, judges were called *gods.* They exercised godlike judicial sovereignty. This is also similar to Moses whom Yahweh said would be like a god to Aaron and Aaron would then be a voice or prophet for him. Psalm 82:6, the verse quoted here, refers to judges who violate the Law. Jesus' argument was that if the divine name had been applied by God to mere men, there could be neither blasphemy nor folly in its application to the incarnate Son of God Himself.

10:35, 36 Broken actually means "to loose, untie." This is a strong statement of the inerrancy of the Holy Scriptures. Notice how Jesus made the veracity of His argument rest on the absolute trustworthiness of Scripture.

10:37, 38 believe the works: Jesus asked the Jewish leaders to at least consider His miracles because these indicated and demonstrated His deity. Note that the heart of the issue is *belief.* John never deviates from this single means to being born again. The word translated *believe* is used ninety-nine times in this book.

10:39 escaped: No one could snatch His sheep out of His hand (v. 28), but He escaped out of theirs (see note on 5:13).

10:40–42 beyond the Jordan: This sojourn into Perea is also noted in Matt. 19:1; Mark 10:1.

11:1 Bethany, a small village on the southeast slope of the Mount of Olives, was located about two miles from Jerusalem (v. 18).

11:2 Mary who anointed: The anointing had not yet taken place (12:1–3). When John wrote, the anointing was well known, so he used the event to distinguish this Mary from other women with the same name.

11:3 The message simply states the facts. There is no request or plea, yet it implies a belief that Christ can and will heal him.

11:4 Not unto death means not having death as its final result. **may be glorified:** By raising Lazarus from the dead, Jesus would demonstrate His deity in an undeniable way.

11:5–8 stayed two more days: God's purpose was to glorify His Son (v. 4) and to cause the disciples to grow (v. 15). Had Jesus immediately rushed to Lazarus's bedside and healed him, Lazarus would not have died and Jesus would not have been able to manifest His glory by raising Lazarus. God's timing to accomplish His purpose is perfect. The disciples were skeptical. In their minds, for Jesus to go back to Judea would mean death.

11:9, 10 Twelve hours are the daylight hours during which work can be done. Jesus is saying that work must be done when there is opportunity. "I still have time, I will not die until my work is finished."

11:11–14 Lazarus sleeps: Death is often referred to as sleep (Gen. 47:30; Matt. 27:52; 1 Thess. 4:13). However, in no way do these passages teach a state of soul-sleep or unconsciousness. Death for the saint is restful sleep from the problems of this world, but a full consciousness of another world (Phil. 1:23).

> *Death for the saint is restful sleep from the problems of this world, but a full consciousness of another world.*

11:15 Jesus was not **glad** that Lazarus was dead. He was glad for the opportunity the disciples would soon have to see an amazing miracle. The disciples had already believed (2:11), but each new trial offered an opportunity for their faith to grow (compare 2 Pet. 1:5–8).

11:16 the Twin: In Thomas, the twins of belief and unbelief contended with each other for mastery. He seems to have combined devotion to Jesus with a tendency to see the dark side of things. Jesus said, "Let us go," that the disciples might believe (v. 15). Thomas said, **Let us also go, that we may die.** While the Lord saw their development in faith, Thomas saw their deaths. Yet in his loyalty, he followed anyway.

11:17–20 Note the contrast in personalities. Martha is a woman of action, whereas Mary is a woman of quiet reflection (Luke 10:38–42).

11:24 Pious Jewish belief included acceptance of the resurrection (compare Dan. 12:13), a belief rejected by the Sadducees (compare Matt. 22:23; Acts 23:8).

11:25–27 Christ is **the resurrection** for those who believe and are physically dead. He is **the life** for those who believe and have not yet died. When Jesus asked Martha if she believed, she responded with words similar to the ones John used to describe the purpose of his book (20:31). In order to have eternal life, a person must place his or her faith in Jesus, who is **the Christ, the Son of God,** who came into the world to bring eternal life to those who believe.

11:28–30 secretly: Martha told Mary privately that Jesus had come so Mary could meet the Lord alone.

11:31 followed her: The secrecy (v. 28) was spoiled. **To weep** means to lament and bewail. It refers to a loud expression of grief, wailing, and crying, not merely the shedding of tears.

11:32 if You had been here: Mary said the same thing to the Lord as Martha had (v. 21). No doubt they had expressed this thought to one another often in the previous few days.

11:33, 34 Groaned means to be deeply moved. **Troubled** means to be stirred up, disturbed. Jesus was moved by the mourning of Mary and indignant at the hypocritical lamentations of His enemies.

11:35, 36 Wept simply means "shed tears." Jesus did not weep aloud in hopeless grief like the others (v. 33). He knew what He was about to do, but His compassion for their pain moved Him to tears. It may also be that He truly felt empathy for the pain of death that Lazarus had endured.

11:37 Some people misinterpreted Jesus' tears as powerlessness. They complained that He had healed others, but now was impotent.

11:38, 39 a cave: Having a private burial place indicates that the family was wealthy.

11:40–42 Did I not say: Christ's statement here is apparently a reference to vv. 25, 26 and to the reply of the messengers in v. 4. Perhaps on both occasions more was said than is recorded. The key to receiving is believing.

11:43, 44 cried: This loud cry was either the result of strong emotion or in order that the multitude might hear. **Lazarus:** In a rhetorical flair, Augustine once said that if Jesus had not designated Lazarus by name, all the graves would have been emptied at His command (5:28). Raising Lazarus from the dead is the seventh sign of Jesus' messiahship, the greatest miracle of all, giving life back to the dead.

11:45–48 Place refers either to Jerusalem or to the temple. The real concern of the Jewish leaders is seen here. They were not as upset at Jesus' supposed blasphemy as they were about losing their positions of authority.

11:49–52 In the opinion of **Caiaphas,** Jesus should die rather than plunge the nation into destruction. John adds that by virtue of his office, Caiaphas pronounced a message of God unconsciously: **one man should die for the people.** Caiaphas was a prophet in spite of himself. John also saw in Caiaphas's words a prophecy that Jesus should die not only for Israel but for the Gentiles as well.

11:53 Humanly speaking, the resurrection of Lazarus was a major factor that led to the plot by the Jewish religious leaders to kill Christ. At this point the council decided informally, if not formally, to put Jesus to death. John marks the growth of the hostility step by step (5:16; 7:1, 32, 45; 8:59; 9:22; 10:39). It is ironic that these men believed they could put to death permanently One who could raise the dead.

11:54 no longer walked openly: Jesus withdrew from public life for a while. He met privately with His disciples. **Wilderness** usually refers to the desert of Judea, which extended to Jericho.

11:55–57 The Jews would **purify them-**

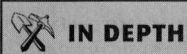 **IN DEPTH** | # Life to Lazarus, Death to Jesus

It was after the raising of Lazarus from the dead that the chief priests, Pharisees, and other religious leaders finally determined to put Jesus to death (John 11:53). Until now, the conflict between them and the upstart rabbi had been little more than a war of words. But the raising of Lazarus was an incredible miracle, witnessed by many. Jesus had raised at least two others, but those events had taken place in faraway Galilee (Mark 5:22–24, 35–43; Luke 7:11–17). By contrast, Lazarus's resurrection occurred in Bethany, a suburb of Jerusalem (John 11:18).

Not surprisingly, the miracle caused many to believe in Jesus (11:45). It provided undeniable proof that Jesus' bold claim must be true: "I am the resurrection and the life . . . and whoever lives and believes in Me shall never die" (11:25). Indeed, Lazarus became something of a curiosity, drawing numerous onlookers who wanted to see for themselves the man whom Jesus had brought back to life (12:9).

It was this kind of publicity that the leaders especially feared. Disputes over religious matters were one thing; a rapidly growing movement led by a popular Messiah-figure was something else. It was bound to have political repercussions, as the Romans were ever on the lookout for signs of rebellion (see "Jerusalem Trampled by Gentiles" at Luke 21:20).

It was Caiaphas the high priest (Matt. 26:3) who saw the usefulness of that fact. Why sacrifice the entire nation for the sake of Jesus, when Jesus could be sacrificed for the sake of the nation (John 11:49–52)? Thus the religious leaders began to scheme how they might bring Jesus before the Romans and, hopefully, have Him put away on a charge of rebellion. And even though Lazarus had just been brought back from the dead, they plotted to do away with him as well, as he was living evidence of Jesus' power (12:10, 11). The desire to kill a man raised from the dead, as well as the One who raised him, reveals the blindness of an unbelieving heart.

The plan succeeded brilliantly except for one detail that Caiaphas and his fellow leaders either overlooked or refused to believe: in arranging His death, they handed Him an opportunity to prove once and for all that He had spoken the truth when He said, "I am the resurrection and the life."

selves in preparation for **the Passover** by washing their bodies and their clothing so that they could enter the temple for worship. Some were looking for Jesus out of curiosity or loyalty (v. 56), but the **chief priests** (v. 57) sought to arrest Him.

12:1 six days before the Passover: If the crucifixion took place on a Friday, this dinner occurred during the evening of the previous Saturday. Verse 12 seems to support this conclusion, because the Jerusalem entry took place on Sunday.

12:2 They probably refers to the people of the village. The inhabitants of Bethany wished to express their thanks to Jesus, who by a glorious miracle had honored their obscure village. **Lazarus** was the guest of honor.

12:3–6 very costly oil: Judas Iscariot said that this oil cost three hundred denarii (v. 5). One denarius was a laborer's wage for one day (Matt. 20:2). Thus, the oil cost approximately a year's wages. **anointed the feet:** Mary also anointed Jesus' head (Matt. 26:7; Mark 14:3). The custom of that time was to anoint the heads of guests. Anointing Jesus' head was an act of honor; anointing His feet was a display of devotion.

12:7 My burial: Anointing was the first stage of embalming (19:39). Whether Mary knew it or not, she was anticipating Jesus' death, which would come within the week.

12:8 the poor you have with you always: We will never lack an opportunity to care for the poor (Deut. 15:11).

12:9–11 plotted to put Lazarus to death also: The chief priests were mostly Sadducees. They had an additional reason to kill Lazarus. He was a living refutation of their doctrine that there was no resurrection (11:57; Acts 23:8). Yet this was not a meeting of the Jewish council, nor was it a formal sentence of death. **on account of him:** The ultimate motivation for wanting to kill Lazarus was that because of him many were believing in Jesus. **Went away** implies that these individuals were withdrawing from the Jewish leaders.

12:12–15 took branches of palm trees: This was the Sunday before Christ arose, today called Palm Sunday. **cried out . . . King of Israel:** Until this point, Jesus had discouraged expressions of support from the people (6:15; 7:1–8). Here He allowed public enthusiasm. He entered Jerusalem on the back of a young donkey. This act fulfilled prophecy (Zech. 9:9) and as such was a symbolic proclamation that Jesus is the Messiah.

12:16 did not understand: The disciples did not catch the prophetic significance of Jesus' act. **when Jesus was glorified:** After Christ's death, resurrection, and ascension, the disciples finally understood that the OT prophecies concerning the Messiah had been fulfilled in Jesus.

12:17–19 These verses explain the series of events that led to the condemnation and crucifixion of Jesus.

12:20 The fact that these **Greeks** came to Jerusalem **to worship at the feast** indicates that they were Jewish proselytes. By recording this incident, perhaps John was hinting that the salvation rejected by many of the Jews was already passing to the Gentiles.

12:21, 22 Perhaps the Greeks came to **Philip** because he had a Greek name.

12:23 The hour has come: Prior to this, Jesus had stated that His hour had not yet come (2:4; 7:6, 30; 8:20). Now the time had come for Christ to die and be raised from the dead (13:1; 16:32; 17:1).

12:24 unless a grain . . . dies: When a seed dies, it produces fruit. Life comes by death. This principle is true not only in nature, but it is also true spiritually. Jesus was speaking first and foremost of Himself. He is the grain of wheat. His death would produce much fruit and would result in many living for God.

12:25, 26 The phrase **loves his life** describes those who serve only themselves. In a very short time, Jesus was going to give the disciples an opportunity to identify this problem in their lives (13:1–7). **Hates his life** involves serving Christ. Each believer must establish his or her priorities. We cannot give ourselves fully to this life and yet be committed to the life to come. **Follow Me** in this context means to follow Jesus' example of self-sacrifice (13:15). Jesus set the example of "hating" His life in this world so that He could accomplish eternal purposes (Phil. 2:5–8).

12:27 My soul is troubled: Jesus' agony over His impending death was not confined to Gethsemane, where He prayed, "O My Father, if it is possible, let this cup pass from Me" (Matt. 26:39). He felt the agony and expressed it almost a week before Gethsemane.

12:28, 29 Christ's ultimate desire is to glorify His Father's **name.** The Father answers from heaven that His Name has been glorified (through the obedient ministry of His Son), and it will be glorified again (through the death, burial, and resurrection of the Son).

12:30–33 The voice was also for the people so that they would recognize Christ as God. Christ is referring to His judgment of sin through His death, and His defeat of Satan (1 Cor. 15:54–57).

12:34 Christ remains forever: The people understood that **lifted up** meant removal from the earth by death. They argued that Scripture teaches that the Messiah would abide forever (Ps. 110:4; Is. 9:7; Ezek. 37:25). To them, the

Messiah would not have to die. They did not understand that He would be raised.

12:35, 36 Instead of answering the people's questions (v. 34), Jesus gave them a warning. **Walk while you have the light:** Jesus is the light (1:4; 8:12; 9:5). He wanted the people to believe and abide in Him (v. 46).

12:37 they did not believe: Their unbelief is startling. However Jesus' predicted suffering and death did not fit the people's idea of the Messiah.

12:38 the word of Isaiah . . . might be fulfilled: John quotes Is. 53:1 to prove that their unbelief is predictable.

12:39, 40 The consequence of repeated rejection is loss of the capacity to believe. Isaiah taught that some **could not believe** because God **hardened their hearts** (Is. 6:10) after they repeatedly rejected the truth.

12:41 John uses the words **His glory** to speak of the manifestation of God Himself. John quotes Is. 6:9 (v. 40) as a prophecy of the people's unbelief and their rejection of Christ. In that verse, Isaiah was talking about God Himself. Therefore in this passage John is teaching that Jesus is God.

12:42, 43 Rulers refers to members of the council. Because the rulers **did not confess Him,** some claim that their faith was not genuine. The text, however, says that they **believed in Him,** a construction in Greek that typically indicates saving faith (8:30). Moreover, the word **nevertheless** marks a stark contrast between these believers and the unbelief spoken of in vv. 37–41. These men were genuine believers. Their problem was that they feared the opinions of their fellow leaders. Such believers will be ashamed at Christ's return (1 John 2:28).

12:44, 45 not in Me but in Him: Jesus insisted that anyone who believed in Him was at the same time exercising belief in God the Father. Jesus explained that He was the personal manifestation of God (1:18; Col. 1:15; Heb. 1:3).

12:46, 47 I do not judge may be rephrased as "I do not execute judgment." Christ will judge, but at His first coming He did not come to judge but to save (3:17).

12:48–50 I . . . speak: Jesus spoke what the Father told Him. To reject His Word is to reject God's Word.

13:1–6 An important principle of knowing and doing is demonstrated here. Notice that vv. 1 and 3 relate what Jesus **knew** and vv. 4 and 5 tell what he did. Our actions are the blossom of our deepest thoughts. Jesus did what He did because He knew what He knew. As a person thinks in his heart, so is he (Prov. 23:7).

13:1 To the end means either "to the last" or "utterly and completely." What follows in vv. 1–11 demonstrates Jesus' complete love. Jesus loved His disciples, even though He knew that one would betray Him, another would deny Him, and all would desert Him for a time.

13:2 Being ended may also be translated "having begun." It was customary for slaves to wash guests' feet as the guests arrived, before they sat down to eat (vv. 4, 5). In any case, it appears that the supper had not ended, but was in progress. The statement of Jesus' complete love in v. 1 is contrasted with the fact that Judas would soon **betray Him.**

13:3 knowing (Gk. *oida*): Christ loved them (v. 1), knowing the worst about them (v. 2) and the best about Himself (v. 3).

13:4, 5 His garments: Jesus **laid aside** His outer garment, which would have impeded His movements. **towel:** By putting on an apron, Christ looked like the slave to whom the task of washing the feet of guests was assigned. Though the disciples realized what Jesus was doing, none of them offered himself for the task. Servanthood was not on their minds. Jesus loved them knowing all about them, including the worst one of them, Judas. All of the disciples knew what needed to be done. All of them could have done it but none of them did. Luke 22:24 gives us a clue to the reason. They were arguing about who was going to be greatest. That kind of thinking will not lead to servant actions (Phil. 2:3, 4). Our actions are the results of our deepest thoughts. Why would Jesus do what He did, that is, take the role of a servant? Because He knew what He knew and thought deeply (vv. 1, 3). It didn't intimidate Jesus to take the tempory role of a servant because He knew where He came from and He knew where He was going to and He knew what He was commissioned to do. Thus, Paul urges us, "Let this mind be in you which was also in Christ Jesus."

13:5 began: John does not say with whom the Lord started, but from early times some have conjectured that it was Judas. Still none, including John, jumped up to take the menial task from His hands. The subject of this story is love. The ultimate in love is service.

13:6, 7 Impulsive Peter strongly objected to this act of humility. Christ responded to Peter's question by implying that there is a deeper meaning in washing feet. One day Peter would understand that this was a graphic illustration of Christ's humility.

13:8 no part with Me: The washing was a symbol of spiritual cleansing (vv. 10, 11). If Peter did not participate in the cleansing, he would not enjoy fellowship with Christ (1 John 1:9).

13:9, 10 but also my hands and my

head: Given Jesus' dramatic statement, Peter had no choice but to submit. Only this time he went too far in the other direction. At first he wanted to tell the Lord what to do (v. 8). Now he wanted to dictate the manner in which Jesus did it. But Jesus told him he did not need a bath; he only needed Jesus **to wash his feet** that were dusty from the road. This is symbolic. A believer has already been "cleansed." He or she only needs the cleansing of daily sins that comes through confession (1 John 1:9). Thus Jesus' washing of the disciples' feet not only is a model of service, but it represents the ultimate in service—forgiveness of sins.

13:11 You are not all clean: This is the second indication of the presence of a traitor among the apostles (6:70). Apparently this comment did not attract much attention.

13:12, 13 Teacher and Lord were the ordinary titles of respect given to a rabbi.

13:14–17 you also ought to wash (Gk. *niptō*) **one another's feet:** Some have argued that the Lord instituted a foot-washing ordinance. Washing feet, however, was not a Jewish ordinance so they would not have understood that He was directing an ordinance, only an attitude. Christ did not tell them to do *what* He had done but **as,** or similar to, what He had done. What they needed was not an ordinance but simply one who was willing to do the thing that everyone knew needed to be done and everyone could have done but nobody did because they were too interested in being served rather than serving. Jesus is not instituting an ordinance but using His practical action to give **an example** of love to His disciples (13:1). Christ is not suggesting that a ritual of foot washing be established but that His humble example of love in self-sacrificing service and forgiveness be followed. The person who practices these things will be blessed.

13:18 Jesus quoted Ps. 41:9 to explain the action of Judas. Lifting up **his heel** was a gesture of insult, or a preparation to kick. The blow had not yet been given. This was the attitude of Judas at that moment. He was eating with the disciples, but he was ready to strike.

13:19, 20 I send: The betrayal of Judas should not hinder their faith (v. 19) or their service (v. 20). Not all had received Him, and not everyone would receive them (v. 16).

13:21 troubled: Faced with bereavement (11:33), His own death (12:27), and betrayal, Jesus was deeply stirred.

13:22 perplexed: They had no idea that

Judas was the one who would betray Christ. Matthew and Mark record that each of them began to ask "Is it I?" (Matt. 26:22; Mark 14:19).

13:23 leaning on Jesus' bosom: At this time people did not generally sit at a table to eat. They reclined on the left side of a low platform, resting on the left elbow and eating with the right hand, their feet extended outward. Reclining in such a way, a man's head was near the bosom of the person on his left. The disciple **whom Jesus loved** is never named in Scripture, but the tradition of the early church designates him as John, the author of this Gospel.

13:24, 25 Peter . . . motioned to him to ask: Evidently Peter was not sitting next to Jesus. He was nearer to John, so he beckoned John to ask Jesus who was going to betray Him.

13:26, 27 First, the devil put ideas in the head of Judas (v. 2); here **Satan entered** Judas. Note that Judas's actions were the result of the deepest thoughts of his heart.

13:28, 29 The whole company of disciples did not understand this. Christ had addressed His statement about the bread to John and consequently, he was the only one who understood its implications.

13:30 it was night: Not only did Judas go out into the darkness of the night, he had also entered into spiritual darkness, separated from Jesus, the Light of the World (8:12; 9:5).

13:31, 32 the Son of Man is glorified: Jesus would be revealed as the divine Son of God and Savior of the world by His death and resurrection, and the gift of the Holy Spirit. God would be **glorified in Him** in that God's love, truth, and righteousness would be revealed in what Jesus was doing.

13:33 The time had come for Jesus to announce His departure to His disciples. **Little children** is an expression of tender affection used nowhere else in the Gospels. John did not forget the expression; he used it repeatedly in 1 John.

13:34 The command to **love** was **new** because Jesus gave it a new standard. Moses said, "Love your neighbor as yourself" (Lev. 19:18). Jesus said the new standard was **as I have loved you.** Jesus gave His disciples the example of love that they were to follow (vv. 1–17).

13:35 By this: Unbelievers recognize Jesus' disciples not by their doctrinal distinctives, nor by dramatic miracles, nor even by their love for the lost. They recognize His disciples by their deeds of love for one another. (Compare a figu-

> The subject of this story is love. The ultimate in love is service.

rative literal correspondence to this plain literal meaning in 15:8). The early church caught hold of this fantastic principle of incendiary love (Acts 4:32–37, 1 Thess. 1:3). Francis Schaeffer called this "The Mark of a Christian." It is the greatest apologetic for Christ.

13:36 Lord, where are You going: This question, which Jesus had already addressed twice before, indicates that Peter completely missed the point of what Jesus said in vv. 34, 35. It leads to the next childish question of which we are all guilty too often—Why?

13:37 I will lay down my life: Peter was ready to die for Jesus. Unfortunately, he was not ready, at this point, to live for Him. He was ready to attack single-handed a cohort of soldiers with his sword (18:10), but he was not willing to wash the feet of his brothers as Jesus had just done (13:4). Actually, Peter had things backwards. Christ was about to lay down His life for Peter, instead of Peter laying down his life for Christ. In spite of all this, Christ did not give up on Peter (Luke 22:31, 32). Later Peter would die for Christ (21:18, 19). Church tradition states that Peter was crucified upside down, at his request, for he felt himself unworthy to be crucified like his Lord.

13:38 till you have denied Me three times: At these words of Jesus, Peter was stunned and said nothing. He is not mentioned again until 18:10. But Luke helps us to know that Christ had prepared him for this shocking news (Luke 22:31, 32). Surely Jesus was the master counselor, as Is. 42:3 and Matt. 12:20 prophesied of Him.

14:1 After announcing Judas's betrayal (13:21), His own imminent departure (13:33), and Peter's denial (13:38), Jesus told His disciples not to **be troubled,** but to trust Him. **believe . . . believe:** The simple but profound solution to all of our problems is believing. We do what we do because we believe what we believe. Our actions are nothing more than the product of our deepest convictions. The key is what we believe—the object of our faith. Right thinking is basic to right action and right thinking begins by thinking right about God. Thus, the entire fourteenth chapter is input from Christ, the master counselor, about what God is like. He does not say anything more about Peter's forthcoming denial. Rather, He gives him truth to believe about God the Father (twenty-three references in ch. 14), God the Son, and God the Holy Spirit. This lifting is what is going to keep Peter trusting as he goes through Satan's sifting process (Luke 22:31, 32).

14:2 Mansions refers to dwelling places. Everybody has a longing for a permanent, secure place. Such places have already been set aside for all of God's children. Jesus has gone

ahead to prepare our place. Peter never got over the wonder of his unfading, reserved, heavenly home (1 Pet. 1:3, 4). The Lord is telling them that though they are disturbed now, they will have rest and refreshment later.

14:3, 4 I will come again and receive you: Peter may have failed Jesus (13:38), but Christ will not fail to return for Peter and for everyone else who has believed in Him (1 Thess. 4:16, 17). Surely this is the essence of unconditional love. He loves us just the way we are, but He loves us too much to leave us the way we are. These are the kind of truths Christ was planting indelibly in their hearts. They will cause them to stand (Phil. 1:6).

14:5 where . . . how: Christ had just said He was going to His Father's house to prepare a place for them (v. 2) and they knew the way there (v. 4). Yet Thomas asks where He was going and how to get there! (see note on 14:8).

14:6 Through His death and resurrection, Jesus is **the way** to the Father. He is also **the truth** and **the life.** As truth, He is the revelation of God. As life, He is the communication of God to us.

14:7, 8 known My Father also: Jesus came to reveal the Father (1:18). To know Jesus is to know the Father (1 John 2:23). **show us the Father:** Jesus had just said that to see Him is to see the Father. Yet Philip asked to see the Father. Like Thomas, Philip seems to have been slow to comprehend (v. 5).

14:9 The Lord rebuked Philip because he should have known the answer to the question he asked. **He who has seen Me has seen the Father:** The Lord patiently explained again that He was revealing God the Father to them (v. 7). It is impossible to escape the claim Jesus was making. Clearly, He was claiming to be God.

14:10, 11 believe . . . believe: The Lord extends an appeal to believe because of His words (v. 10) and His works (v. 11). His words demonstrate who He is. He said I am "the water of life" (7:37), "the bread of life" (6:48), "the light of the world" (8:12; 9:5), and "the good shepherd who gives life" (10:11). He claimed to be equal with God (5:17, 18) and be sent from God (7:28, 29). He said He was the "I Am" (8:24, 28, 58) and that He and the Father were one (10:30). Furthermore, He stated the Father was in Him and He was in the Father (10:38). His works also demonstrate who He is. He changed water into wine (2:1–11). He healed people (4:43–54, 5:1–9), He miraculously produced bread and fishes (6:1–12), He calmed the sea (6:15–21), and He raised the dead (11:38–44). All along Christ has been informing and enriching their needs with truths to "believe" about God.

14:12 Jesus had accomplished the greatest

works possible, including raising the dead. How could He say that believers would do **greater works?** The answer is seen in the extent of what the apostles did. Jesus' work on earth was confined to Palestine; the apostles would preach everywhere and see the conversion of thousands. Peter's message at Pentecost brought more followers to Jesus than did Jesus' entire earthly ministry. The disciples were able to do this work because Christ would go to the Father and send the Holy Spirit to empower them.

💡 INSIGHT | A Helper

Jesus calls the Holy Spirit the Helper (John 14:16, 17). The Greek word, *paraklētos*, means "one called alongside to help." In giving us the Holy Spirit, Jesus shows that leadership is not so much the ability to walk ahead of someone as the willingness to walk beside someone. Followers need support as well as direction, a hand that helps as well as a finger that points.

14:13, 14 Note the relationship of works to prayer (Acts 1:14; 2:42; 3:1; 4:31). Effective prayer is **in My name.** This is prayer in agreement with the desires of Christ. The result of prayer is the glorification of the Father, not self-glorification.

14:15 Love is not sentimental emotionalism; it is obedience to the commandments of God.

14:16 All three members of the Trinity are mentioned here. Jesus prayed to the Father who would give the Holy Spirit.

14:16, 17 Verses 16 and 17 contain three different prepositions that describe the relationship of the Holy Spirit to the believer. He is said to be **with** (Gk. *meta*) them for fellowship (v. 16), to abide beside them (Gk. *para*), to defend them (v. 17), and to be **in** them (Gk. *en*) as a source of power (v. 17; Acts 2:1–4).

14:17 The Holy Spirit is called **the Spirit of truth** (15:26; 16:13; 1 John 4:6) because He is truth and guides us into all truth (1 Cor. 2:13; 2 Pet. 1:21). **Neither sees Him nor knows Him** does not mean merely that the world is not able to visually identify the Holy Spirit because He is spirit. Something more is meant: The Spirit of God is active in the world, but His acts go unnoticed by the world (1 Cor. 2:14).

14:18 orphans: Earlier, Jesus called the disciples "little children" (13:33). Here He told them He would not leave them fatherless; He would come to them. There are three suggested

interpretations as to when that statement would be fulfilled: (1) after the Resurrection, (2) at Pentecost, in the person of the Holy Spirit, and (3) at the Second Coming.

14:19 you will see Me: Jesus would come to the disciples (v. 18), but not with the same kind of presence they experienced at that moment. The world saw Jesus only in the flesh; the disciples would see Him in a spiritual sense.

14:20, 21 These two verses are the conclusion of Jesus' answer to Philip's request, "show us the Father" (v. 8). As the believer lovingly obeys Christ's commandments, he or she will experience a more intimate knowledge of Him.

14:22 The disciples had expected the Messiah to come publicly and deliver Israel from Rome and the corrupt priesthood of the temple. Jesus had said that the disciples would see Him, but the world would not (v. 19). Judas (not Iscariot) wanted to know how that could be.

14:23 loves Me . . . keep My word: In response to Judas's question (v. 22), Jesus explained that His manifestation to the disciples would be in response to their love and obedience. **make Our home with him:** If a believer loves and obeys the Lord, he or she will experience fellowship with God.

14:24 not love . . . not keep: If a person does not love Jesus, he or she will not obey Him. Disobedience is a serious matter, for Jesus' words are the words of God.

14:25, 26 Jesus told His disciples **these things** while He was with them, but when **the Holy Spirit** came, He would remind the disciples of **all things** that Jesus had said, and would **teach . . . all things** (1 Cor. 2:13). This promise was primarily fulfilled through the lives of the apostles in the writing of the NT. Matthew and John wrote down Jesus' words. Peter wrote about the gospel in his two letters and may have dictated some of his memories of Jesus to Mark.

14:27 Peace: The customary good-bye among the Jews was to say *shalom*, meaning "peace." The Lord was about to depart, so He added to this farewell by saying, **My peace.** The word *My* is emphatic. This is no conventional wish; this is Jesus' personal, special grant of peace. The peace that Christ gives banishes fear and dread from the heart, for Jesus is in control of all circumstances.

14:28 My Father is greater than I: This does not mean that Jesus is less than deity. *Greater* indicates a difference in rank. As the humble, submissive Son, Jesus submitted Himself to the authority of His Father (1 Cor. 11:3; 15:28).

14:29–31 He has nothing in Me indicates Jesus' sinlessness. Jesus' yielding to what was about to happen did not mean that Satan had any power over Him. Jesus would soon voluntarily yield to the death of the Cross, in loving obedience to the Father (v. 31).

15:1 vine: This word can describe a single grapevine or an entire vineyard. Either way, the image evokes the picture of corporate dependence. Israel was the vine of God's planting, but it failed to bear the proper fruit (Is. 5:1–7; Jer. 2:19–21). Jesus, with His believers incorporated in Him, is the true vine—the true fulfillment and actualization of the vine. As the entire race of Israel sprang from the patriarch Israel, the new generation of God's people is here viewed as originating from Christ, organically united to Him, as branches emanating from the vine. This is a fulfillment of Ps. 80, in which "the son of man" (Ps. 80:17) is said to be the vine planted by God.

15:2, 3 Every branch is said to be *in* Christ. Paul uses the phrase "in Christ" to speak of a Christian's legal and family position as a result of God's grace. The emphasis of **in Me** in this passage, however, is on deep, abiding fellowship. Jesus' purpose was to move His disciples from servants to friends (vv. 13–15). This would involve a process of discipline in regard to His commandments. **not bear fruit:** No plant produces fruit instantaneously; fruit is the result of a process. Such is also the case with believers. Those who are not bearing fruit the vinedresser **takes away** (Gk. *airō*) which has as its basic meaning "to lift up." When the winter weather was over and the time for productivity was approaching, the vinedresser would move through the vineyard lifting the branches from the ground, where they had been for the winter, and propping them up with stakes where they would receive the warmth of the sun. The heat promotes the ripening of the fruit. Furthermore, by getting the branches off the ground, it keeps them from sinking many little roots directly from the branch into the surface of the soil where the moisture is not sufficient to produce anything but hard, sour grapes. If the branch is lifted out of the dirt, however, it is forced to get its moisture from the deep roots of the vine and produces luscious fruit. **Prunes** (Gk. *kathairō*) means "cleanses." Once the fruit is on the vine, the vinedresser cleanses the fruit of bugs and diseases. The spiritual counterpart is cleansing which is done through the Word (v. 3). The primary reference here is the words that He has just been lifting them with in the Upper Room, especially ch. 14. It is that word which is going to transform the disciples from shrinking, cowardly disciples to stalwart soldiers for Christ. But it will be a process over time. The noun form of this word is rendered "clean" in v. 3. Thus, the vinedresser lifts up fruitless branches and cleanses fruitful ones so they can be more fruitful. The

point of the figure is not union but communion and consequent fruit.

15:4 For the branch to produce more fruit, it must **abide,** which means to dwell, to stay, to settle in, to sink deeper. The way to abide in Christ is to obey (15:10; 1 John 3:24). The believer who lovingly obeys the Word of God produces much fruit.

15:5 can do nothing: Apart from Christ, a believer cannot accomplish anything of permanent spiritual value.

15:6 Not abiding in Christ has serious consequences: (1) The person **is cast out as a branch,** indicating the loss of fellowship; (2) the person **is withered,** indicating a loss of vitality; (3) the person is **burned,** indicating a loss of reward. **The fire** here is figurative, symbolizing either fiery trials (1 Pet. 1:7; 4:12) or the fire at the judgment seat of Christ (1 Cor. 3:11–15). Failure to abide produces spiritual disaster. **they gather them:** Note the movement from "He" (the Father who is the vinedresser, v. 2) to "you" (the believer who does or does not abide, v. 4) to "they" (unbelievers looking for signs of life, 13:35).

15:7 abide in Me, and My words: There are five results of abiding in Christ: answered prayer (v. 7), fruit (v. 8), a fulfilled purpose, my Father is glorified (v. 8), experiencing love (vv. 9, 10), fullness of joy (v. 11) and effective evangelism (13:35; 15:8). Abiding in Christ involves personal communion with Him. Abiding in His Word includes obedience. Getting to know the Savior makes believing in Him an obvious response which leads to loving obedience. Notice how the apostle Paul presented this process (Phil. 3:10).

15:8 By this: Notice the striking parallel between this verse and 13:35. The love of 13:35 is pictured as **fruit** here. The text has come full circle in showing how strategic it is for disciples to love each other, as Christ's method of evangelizing the lost. "They shall know" becomes **so you will be** Christ's disciples. Where there is good fruit, there are also seeds for propagation.

15:9 As the Father loved Me, I also have loved you: The love of God the Father for God the Son is the measure of the love of the Son for believers.

15:10 abide in My love: Christ loves believers unconditionally (v. 9). But as believers obey Christ's Word and abide in His love, they come to experience and understand His love for them more and more (Eph. 3:14–19).

15:11 That your joy may be full is an expression peculiar to John (3:29; 16:24; 17:13; 1 John 1:4; 2 John 12). It describes a believer's experience of Christ's love: complete joy.

15:12 love one another: To abide, a

believer must obey (v. 10). To obey, a believer must love other believers (13:34, 35).

15:13 lay down one's life: In rashness and with confidence in the flesh, Peter had offered to lay down his life for Jesus. In actuality, he was not ready to die for Jesus; he was not even ready to live for Him (18:17, 18, 25–27). The supreme example of love is Jesus' humility in sacrificial service (13:15).

15:14 if you do: Jesus is our model for love (v. 13). Intimacy with Him is the motive for loving as He loves. If believers obey His command to love, they enjoy the intimacy of His friendship. Note that friendship, unlike sonship, is not a once-for-all gift, but develops as the result of obeying Jesus' command to love.

15:15 No longer . . . servants: Until this point, Jesus had called His disciples servants (12:26; 13:13–16). A servant does what he is told and sees what his master does, but does not necessarily know the meaning or purpose of it. **friends:** A friend knows what is happening because friends develop deep fellowship by communicating with one another.

15:16 I chose you: Jesus had initiated the relationship with His disciples (1 John 4:10). It started with selection, moved to servanthood, and grew to friendship. **that you should go and bear fruit:** Having chosen the disciples, Jesus commissioned them to bring forth permanent fruit through prayer.

15:17 Again Christ returns to the theme of love. Loving one another is a command, not an option.

15:18–21 hated Me: As Jesus spoke these words, the Pharisees were planning to kill Him (11:45–57). The world hated Him, so it should not be surprising that the world hates His followers.

15:22–25 no sin . . . no excuse: The world's hatred of Jesus was a sin against God, for He revealed the Father Himself to them. **My Father also:** Since Christ and the Father are one, those who hate Christ hate the Father. The testimony of Jesus' words (v. 22) and His **works** (v. 24) made those who rejected Him accountable for their **sin.** In v. 25 Jesus quotes Ps. 69:4 to show how evil and irrational it is to reject the love and goodness of Christ.

15:26, 27 The third time in Jesus' last hours with the disciples that He spoke of the coming of the Holy Spirit (14:16, 26). **Helper** is sometimes translated "Advocate" or "Counselor." The **Father** and Son are equally involved in the

> *The world hated Him, so it should not be surprising that the world hates His followers.*

coming of the **Spirit.** Both the Spirit and Spirit-empowered disciples will **testify** about Jesus.

16:1 made to stumble: Rejection by the world should confirm, not weaken, our faith. Both predictions of v. 2 were fulfilled in the lives of the apostles. **He will testify . . . you also will bear witness:** As the disciples spoke, the Holy Spirit would bring inner conviction to unbelievers concerning Christ. This in turn would make the disciples witnesses for Jesus.

16:2 They will put you out of the synagogues . . . kills you: The persecution that the disciples would face included excommunication and even execution. Excommunication had economic as well as religious implications, because much of the life of an ancient Jew revolved around the synagogue. **Offers** expresses the idea of offering a sacrifice. The murderers of believers would imagine that they were offering a sacrifice to God.

16:3 have not known (Gk. *ginōskō*) **the Father or Me:** The ultimate issue is the fact that the persecutors do not know Christ or the Father (1 Cor. 2:8).

16:4 at the beginning: Jesus had been preparing His disciples to assimilate the truth (Prov. 22:6). In His wisdom, the Lord never gives us more than we can handle. The process of learning is as important as the product.

16:5 one of you asks Me, "Where are You going?": Peter had asked this very question (13:36) and Thomas had suggested it (14:5). However, things were different now. The disciples had learned about denials, suffering, and death. To go with Jesus involved the most serious consequences.

16:6 sorrow (Gk. *lupē*) **has filled your hearts:** The prospects of separation and suffering shut out all thoughts of consolation and strength.

16:7 The disciples must have thought, "How can it be to our **advantage** to be alone? The Romans hate us because they see us as disturbers of the peace. The Jewish leaders hate us because they see us as blasphemers. You alone love us, and You are leaving us." So Jesus explained the benefits of His departure. When Jesus left, the believers would have (1) the provision of the Holy Spirit (vv. 7–15); (2) the potential of full joy (vv. 16–24); (3) the possibility of fuller knowledge (vv. 25–28); (4) the privilege of peace (vv. 29–33). **I will send Him:** Jesus explained that the Holy Spirit will convict the world (vv. 7–11) and communicate truth to the apostles (vv. 12–15). **to you:** The Holy Spirit would not be given to the world, but to believers. The coming of the Spirit would be more profitable to believers than even the physical presence of Christ, since the Spirit could dwell in all believers at the same time.

16:8 Convict means "convince" or "reprove." The Holy Spirit would demonstrate the truth of Christ beyond the fear of contradiction. The Holy Spirit convicts unbelievers through believers who witness about Christ (15:26, 27). Believers are the mouthpiece for God's voice. The content of the witness that the Spirit reinforces includes truth about **sin, righteousness,** and **judgment.**

16:9 of sin: Note the singular *sin,* not *sins.* Our witness should not focus on *sins* (adultery, gluttony, pride, and other sins), but on the full payment that Christ has made for *all sin.* Reception of the full pardon is the only cure for the disease of sin.

16:10 of righteousness: After Christ's departure the Holy Spirit would convict the world of the nature of righteousness and the need for righteousness. Jesus' work on the Cross was completely righteous. This is demonstrated by the Father's emptying of the tomb, signifying His satisfaction with the righteous payment and His acceptance of Christ into His presence.

16:11 of judgment: Satan, the ruler of this world, rules in the hearts of unregenerate people and blinds their minds (1 Cor. 2:6–8). Satan was judged at the Cross, and the Holy Spirit would convince people of the judgment to come. Satan has been judged, so all who side with him will be judged with him. There is no room for neutrality. A person is either a child of God or a child of the devil.

16:12 You refers to the apostles. Technically, what the Lord says about the ministry of the Holy Spirit in vv. 12–15 applies primarily to the apostles. The Holy Spirit's ministry to them was threefold: (1) He would guide them into all truth (v. 13); (2) He would tell them of the future (v. 13); (3) He would help them glorify Christ (vv. 14, 15). Jesus' words were fulfilled in the apostles' preaching and writings. The Holy Spirit guided the apostles by revealing to them not only the truths embodied in Jesus' life and death, but also the glorious future of all believers. The apostles, in turn, wrote it down in the NT, which glorifies—that is, reveals—Jesus Christ. The word **bear** means "to carry a burden" and is used later of Christ carrying the Cross (19:17). In other words, there were truths that they could not understand (v. 13) or handle until the Holy Spirit came at Pentecost.

16:13 Spirit of truth: The phrase means that the Holy Spirit is the source of truth (14:17; 15:26). **guide:** The Holy Spirit would not compel or carry the disciples into truth. He would lead; their job was to follow. **All truth** refers to the truth necessary to be mature saints and thoroughly equipped servants (2 Tim. 3:16, 17). **Things to come** includes truths about the church (Eph. 3:1–7), as well as future events.

16:14 For indicates that the last part of the verse explains **glorify Me.** The Holy Spirit glorifies Christ by declaring Him or making Him known. It is the work of the Holy Spirit to throw light on Jesus Christ, who is the image of the invisible God. Christ is to be on center stage; that is the desire of both the Father and the Spirit. The apostles received truth from the Holy Spirit, truth about things to come, and truth about Christ. Then under the guidance of the Holy Spirit they wrote those truths in documents known today as the NT (14:25, 26; 1 Cor. 2:13).

16:15 To say that the Holy Spirit will take what belongs to Christ (v. 14) does not mean He will concentrate on Christ to the exclusion of **the Father.** There is no division within the Godhead. What the Father has, the Son has

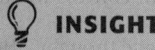
An alternative translation to *sorrow* (John 16:21) is "pain." There were few options available to first-century women for pain relief during labor. Since births took place at home, all of the disciples had probably heard a woman scream out in pain while giving birth.

As in most undeveloped countries today, childbearing in biblical times was often fatal for the child, the mother, or both. Many pagan women sought help from their gods, along with special charms, to protect them during pregnancy and delivery.

So Jesus was using a graphic metaphor by comparing the coming "sorrow" of His followers with that of a woman in labor. He was indicating that their pain could not be avoided. But He did give them a hope: He promised that they would see Him again, and when they did their joy would be as great as a woman whose baby has finally been delivered safely.

(17:10). What the Son has, the Spirit will declare (1 Cor. 2:13). However, the focus will be on Christ because He is the "image of the invisible God" (Col. 1:15). His steps are the only ones we can follow because He is the only one we have "seen."

16:16 You will see Me has been interpreted to mean: (1) the disciples would literally see Jesus after the Resurrection; (2) the disciples would spiritually see Jesus after the Ascension because of the work of the Holy Spirit. Verse 22 seems to support the literal sight after the Resurrection.

16:17 some . . . said: They were puzzled about the apparent contradiction of not beholding and yet seeing. The statement puzzled them also because He said He would depart. They were expecting a Messiah who would rule and reign, not die and depart (Luke 19:11; Acts 1:6).

16:18 A little while: The biggest question weighing on the disciples' minds was the time factor. They simply did not understand the strange intervals marked by their separation from Jesus.

16:19–21 weep and lament: When Jesus died, the disciples would openly express their intense sorrow. **The world** would **rejoice,** assuming that it was rid of Jesus. But the **sorrow** of the disciples would be **turned into joy.** This is not merely a case of sorrow being followed by joy, but of sorrow *becoming* joy. The sorrow itself would be transformed. The death of Jesus would be first a sorrow and then a joy. To explain His words (in v. 20), Jesus used the example of a pregnant woman. **A woman . . . in labor** has **sorrow,** but the very sorrow is transformed into **joy** in the birth of the child.

16:22 I will see you again refers to Jesus' postresurrection appearances. **your joy no one will take:** The disciples' sorrow would depart; their joy would remain. Jesus' death and resurrection brings the joy of forgiven sins (1 Pet. 1:8) that the world cannot take away.

16:23 In that day, that is, after the Resurrection and Ascension. **you will ask Me nothing:** Apparently Jesus means that they will not personally ask Him anything because He will not be physically present after the Ascension. Certainly they will ask Him through the work of the Holy Spirit.

16:24 in My name: After the Ascension they will pray as His representative and will receive answers to prayer that their **joy may be full.**

16:25 An example of **figurative language** is the allegory of the grapevine in 15:1–8, which presents the work of the Father in producing the fruit of love in believers. A figure of speech can be more vivid and graphic than ordinary prose.

16:26, 27 In My name means by Christ's authority. **I do not say . . . I shall pray the Father for you:** Because Jesus provides forgiveness of sins through His death and now intercedes for all believers at the right hand of the Father (Heb. 7:25), we have direct access to the Father. We do not need the intercession of a priest, because Jesus acts as our High Priest before God. **For** indicates that v. 27 explains the previous verse. After Jesus' departure, the disciples would be able to pray directly to God the Father, who loves them because they believed in and loved His Son, Jesus.

16:28 This verse is a summary of the whole visit of the Son to the world. It includes His mission, nativity, passion, and ascension.

16:29, 30 we believe: Jesus had read the disciples' hearts (v. 19) and answered their questions. Like the Samaritan woman, they concluded that He knew all things (4:39). To the disciples, Jesus' supernatural knowledge proved His divine mission.

16:31 now believe: We continue in the Christian life the same way we begin, by believing in Jesus. The more we learn of Christ, the more we have to believe. The more we place our trust in Jesus, the more we receive. The more we receive, the more we can accomplish for His glory.

16:32 you will be scattered: The disciples would desert Jesus. Knowing this, Jesus still loved them, an amazing example of unconditional love.

16:33 Tribulation is literally "pressure," and figuratively means "affliction" or "distress." **Be of good cheer** means "be confident and courageous." When we place our trust in God, He can give us peace in the midst of pressure. Read Phil. 1:27–30 for Paul's explanation of the principle of joy in suffering.

17:1, 2 the hour has come: Throughout the Gospel of John, Jesus referred to the Cross as His "hour" (2:4; 7:30; 8:20; 12:23; 13:1). The time for Him to die had arrived. **Glorify Your Son:** Jesus was asking that His mission to the world would be made known through the Cross. The reasons for this request are twofold: (1) **that Your Son also may glorify You.** In the Cross, Jesus reveals the Father to the world, that is, His love and justice; and (2) that through Jesus' death on the Cross, God would provide forgiveness of sins and **give eternal life** to all those who believe in His Son.

17:3 that they may know You: Eternal life consists of a growing knowledge of **the only true God,** as opposed to false gods.

17:4, 5 I have glorified You: Jesus made known the Father by completing the work God gave Him to do. **glorify Me:** Jesus looked to the Father to restore Him to the glory He had in heaven before He left (Phil. 2:6). This is another indication of Christ's preexistence and deity (1:1–14).

17:6–8 The men, i.e., the apostles, the ones Christ trained to be the foundation stones of the church which had its beginning at Pentecost. He prays for these that He will leave behind to accomplish His mission.

17:9, 10 I do not pray for the world indicates that Jesus was praying only for present and future believers (17:20; Luke 23:34). **I pray . . . for those whom You have given Me:** The apostle Paul observes the same priority (Col. 1:4, 9). Too often Christians pray for the unregenerate until they accept Christ and then drop them from their prayer list. The point at which Christ and the apostles intensively began prayer, we tend to stop.

17:11 This verse reveals Jesus' keen sensitivity to the plight of His disciples brought on by His departure. He was going to the Father, but they would be left behind. Jesus asked the Father to **keep** the disciples **through** His **name,** that is, to keep them true to the revelation of God that Jesus had given to them while He was with them. The disciples would have a new union with the Father and Son through the future indwelling of the Holy Spirit.

17:12 none of them is lost: Jesus protected the disciples during His earthly ministry (18:9). Judas, **the son of perdition,** is distinguished from the rest of the apostles. He was never really one of those given to Christ (18:8, 9). He had never really been a believer (6:64–71); he had not been cleansed (13:11).

17:13 I speak in the world: Jesus prayed aloud (v. 1) so that His words would comfort the apostles when they remembered that Jesus gave them into His Father's keeping.

17:14, 15 not of the world: This is undoubtedly the biggest challenge of spiritual warfare that the Christian faces. The Lord doesn't want us "out of the world" (v. 15) but neither does He want us "of the world" (v. 16). We are to be in it (v. 18) but not of it. The tendency is one of two extremes: to be in the world and so saturated with it that there is no difference between the Christian and the world system or to get out of the world system and to be so isolated from it that our commendable lifestyle is not seen by this world. Both saturation by the world system and isolation from the world system fall short of the penetration of the world system that Christ calls for. Christ said, "I send you forth as sheep in the midst of wolves" (Rom. 12:1, 2; Phil. 2:14–16). **take . . . out of:** Although the Father lifts (Gk. *airō*) branches off the ground (15:2), Christ doesn't want them lifted out of (Gk. *epairō*) the world. This further supports the meaning of "lift" in 15:2 rather

than "take out" or "cut off." **evil one:** This word can either be neuter (evil) or masculine (evil one, that is, Satan).

17:16–18 Sanctify means "to set apart." There are two ways to understand this statement: (1) as separate for holiness, or (2) as set apart for service. According to the first view, Jesus was praying not only that the disciples should be kept from evil, but that they should advance in holiness. However in v. 18, sanctification seems to refer to the disciples' mission, indicating that *sanctify* may also mean that Jesus was setting apart His disciples for this. **Your word is truth** is a strong statement of Jesus' confidence in the veracity of Scripture. People's opinions may vary, and experiences are notoriously untrustworthy, but God's Word always remains true.

17:19 I sanctify myself: Christ does not state that He is in the process of becoming holy; He is referring to His self-sacrifice and total commitment. It is His example that should stir His followers to that same type of surrender.

17:20 those who will believe: Jesus not only prayed for those the Father had given Him (v. 9) but for all future believers—for their unity (vv. 20–23) and their future glory (vv. 24–26). If you are a believer, these words are Jesus' prayer for you.

17:21 all may be one: The present tense of the verb "to be" indicates that Jesus was praying for the unity that takes place through the sanctification of believers. This is what Jesus was commanding in 13:34, 35: His followers had to love each other so that the world may believe in the reality of Jesus' love. The loving relationship of believers to each other is the greatest witness to Jesus Christ.

17:22 The glory, the revelation of Jesus Christ through His disciples, is the means to unity. Such unity begins with belief and correct thinking about Jesus and God the Father, that is, with doctrine. But correct belief must bear fruit—a life that demonstrates God's love and produces the unity between all the believers.

17:23 I in them, and You in Me: The mutual indwelling of the Father in the Son and the Son in the church is also the means to unity, the ultimate expression of God's love (3:35; Rom. 8:17).

17:24 May be with Me is a prayer for the future glorification of believers. **may behold My glory:** The apostles saw Christ's glory in His words and works (v. 22). Christ prayed for all believers to behold His glory, unveiled in the full revelation of His deity.

17:25, 26 Jesus concludes His prayer, summarizing several of the main themes: (1) knowing the **righteous** (holy) God; (2) Jesus' divine origin; (3) the revealing of the Father's

✓ IN COMPARISON | Jesus in Court

Before Jewish Religious Authorities	
• preliminary hearing before Annas (18:12–24).	Although the Romans had deposed Annas, in the eyes of the Jews he still functioned as the high priest because the office was for life. Annas questioned Jesus, but Jesus demanded a legal hearing.
• hearing before Caiaphas (Matt. 26:57–67; Mark 14:53–65)	Caiaphas was the high priest appointed by the Romans. Two false witnesses testified against Jesus and Caiaphas asked Jesus if He was the Messiah. Jesus answered yes, and Caiaphas concluded that Jesus was guilty of blasphemy.
• trial before the Sanhedrin (Matt. 27:1, 2; Mark 15:1; Luke 22:66–71)	The council of Jewish religious leaders confirmed Caiaphas's conclusion. In this trial, Jesus admitted He was the Son of God and declared that He would sit on the right hand of God the Father.
Before the Roman Authorities	
• first hearing before Pilate (18:28–37; Matt. 27:11–14; Mark 15:2–5; Luke 23:1–5)	The Jewish religious leaders brought Jesus to Pilate in order to get permission to execute Him. They accused Him of treason. Pilate saw Jesus' innocence, but briefly questioned Him. In this interview, Jesus revealed to Pilate that His kingdom was not of this earth.
• hearing before Herod (Luke 23:6–12)	Pilate sent Jesus to Herod because Jesus was from Galilee, the region ruled by Herod. Jesus remained silent before Herod.
• final hearing before Pilate (18:38—19:16; Matt. 27:15–26; Mark 15:6–15; Luke 23:13–25)	Pilate did not want to condemn an innocent man, but he was afraid of another Jewish uprising. Therefore, he finally gave in to the cries of the crowd: "Crucify Him."

name; and (4) the unity of mutual love between the **Father,** Son, and believers.

18:1, 2 The Brook Kidron was a ravine between Jerusalem and the Mount of Olives.

18:3 A detachment was a cohort of about six hundred men, or one-tenth of a legion. However, sometimes this Greek word was used for one-third of a cohort, or two hundred men. These soldiers were probably the experienced Roman troops stationed at the Antonia, a fortress near the temple. The **officers** who came with the detachment were members of the temple police under the command of the Jewish council, the Sanhedrin.

18:4, 5 knowing all things: Knowing He was about to be arrested, Jesus could have escaped, but He did not. He submitted Himself voluntarily to the ordeal that was ordained by God.

18:6 fell to the ground: For a moment, Christ unveiled His majesty. His statement of deity, **I am,** manifested such glory that it literally threw the soldiers to the **ground.**

18:7–9 For the third time in this passage, Jesus claimed to be **I am** (vv. 5, 6), echoing God's self-revelation in Ex. 3:14. **let these go:** As He was being arrested, Jesus demonstrated His love for the apostles.

18:10, 11 Note the contrast between Peter and Jesus. By fighting the guard, **Simon Peter** vehemently exercised his own self-will; Jesus in contrast voluntarily submitted to the will of God. One swung the sword of self-will; the other drank from the cup of God's will. See Matt. 16:22, 23 for another attempt by Peter to control God's plan for Jesus. **cut off his right ear:** Jesus mercifully restored the ear (Luke 22:51) that Peter cut off. He often does the same in our lives when we act rashly. His purposes are fulfilled in spite of us.

18:12 A captain was the chief officer of a Roman cohort (v. 3).

18:13 Annas was high priest from A.D. 7 to 14. He was deposed by the Romans. Then Caiaphas, Annas's son-inlaw, was appointed to the position and served from A.D. 18 to 37. However, according to Jewish law the high priest was a lifetime position, so the Jews still considered Annas to be high priest. So they took Jesus to Annas first. Caiaphas would soon be involved, however, since he had the authority to carry out the plan (v. 14).

18:14 In passing, John reminds the reader of the earlier prediction of **Caiaphas** (11:50–52): Jesus would die for the entire nation.

18:15 another disciple: Although this other disciple is never identified, the consensus is that he was John, the author of this Gospel.

18:16–18 I am not: This was the first of Peter's three denials prophesied by Jesus (13:38). An apparent contradiction exists between "the rooster crows" of Matthew, Luke, and John and "the rooster crows" twice of Mark 1:72. A possible solution has been given by Johnston M. Cheney and Stanley Ellisen in *The Greatest Story*.

18:19 The high priest: This refers to Annas (compare 18:13). This was not a true trial since the Sanhedrin had not been assembled. The purpose of this inquisition was probably to gather evidence. Annas was interested in Christ's **disciples** and His **doctrine.** He was interested in the number of followers that Christ had gained.

18:20 I spoke openly . . . in secret I have said nothing: Christ taught in public places. His purpose had not been concealed. He had not founded a secret society.

18:21 Ask those who have heard Me: According to the law, the witnesses for the defense had to be called first. Jesus should not have been questioned until witnesses had testified.

18:22 the officers . . . struck Jesus: This was illegal according to Jewish law. There was to be no punishment before conviction.

18:23, 24 bear witness: Jesus invited His accusers to present evidence that He had done something wrong.

18:25 I am not: This was the second of Peter's three denials prophesied by Jesus (13:38).

18:26, 27 Peter then denied again: For the third time, Peter denied the Lord, as Jesus had said he would (13:38). In the Upper Room, Peter had boasted that he would remain true to the Lord to the end (13:37; Matt. 26:33, 35). In the garden he surrendered to the desires of his body, by sleeping three times when the Lord had commanded the disciples to stay up in prayer (Mark 14:32–42). Now he submitted to the pressure of the world and denied the Lord three times.

18:28 The Praetorium was the Roman governor's official residence, probably the

Fortress Antonia near the temple. Early morning refers to the fourth watch of the night, from 3 to 6 A.M. A Roman court could have been held immediately after sunrise, and this scene could have taken place around 6 A.M. **defiled:** During Passover, if a Jew entered a house that contained leaven, he or she would be ceremonially defiled and unable to celebrate the feast. Thus Jews would not enter the residence of any Gentile for fear of being ceremonially defiled. **Passover:** The main meal of the Passover had taken place. The synoptic Gospels report that Jesus celebrated that meal the night before (Matt. 26:17–29; Mark 14:12–25; Luke 22:7–22). However, there were other ceremonial meals during the Passover, which lasted the entire week.

18:29, 30 What accusation: Pilate was not ignorant of the accusation. He was merely requesting that it be formally stated. **If He were not an evildoer:** Jesus' accusers had no charge that would stand up in a Roman court. Therefore they sullenly replied, "If He were not a criminal we would not have brought Him to you."

18:31 You take Him and judge Him: The accusations did not warrant a trial before Pilate. **It is not lawful:** The Romans did not allow the Jews to impose capital punishment. These Jewish leaders had no interest in a just trial; they simply wanted permission from Rome to have Jesus executed.

18:32 signifying by what death He would die: Jesus had said, "If I am lifted up from the earth," indicating the method of His death, crucifixion (12:32, 33). The Jewish method of execution was stoning. However, Jesus had already indicated that He would be crucified. John is pointing out that the Jewish leaders' inability to impose capital punishment themselves fulfilled Jesus' prediction describing His death.

18:33 Are You the King of the Jews: The Jews charged that Jesus claimed to be their king. From their standpoint, this was the most damaging accusation possible because it would be regarded by the Romans as treason and would be punishable by death. In the Greek text, *you* is emphatic, perhaps indicating that Pilate did not think the forlorn figure before him looked like the defiant rebels he was used to dealing with as claimants to the Jewish throne.

18:34 Are you speaking for yourself: In reply to Pilate, Jesus gave no violent protest of innocence, nor was He sullenly defiant. Jesus politely but directly asked whether Pilate was asking on his own initiative or whether the charge was secondhand. If Pilate's question originated with him, he was using *king* in the Roman sense of a political ruler. If not, then *king* was being used in the Jewish sense of the messianic King.

18:35 Am I a Jew: Pilate was asking, "Is it likely that I, a Roman governor, would have any interest in a Jewish question?"

18:36 My kingdom is not of this world: Jesus pointed out that though He was a king, he was no threat to Rome because His kingdom would not come by a worldly revolution.

18:37 bear witness to the truth: The truth was the seal of God. **hears My voice:** If Pilate wanted to know the truth, he would understand what Jesus was saying.

18:38 What is truth: This question has been interpreted as (1) a cynical denial of the possibility of knowing truth; (2) a contemptuous jest at anything so impractical as abstract truth; and (3) a desire to know what no one had been able to tell him. **No fault** is a legal term meaning that there were no grounds for a criminal charge. Teaching the truth was not against the law. Pilate pronounced Jesus not guilty.

18:39 you have a custom: It appears that some in the crowd suggested that a prisoner should be released in honor of the Passover (Mark 15:8, 11). Pilate jumped at the possible compromise. By promising to release Jesus on account of the custom rather than by proclaiming Him innocent, Pilate would avoid insulting the Jewish leaders, who had already pronounced Him guilty.

18:40 The people demanded that Pilate release **Barabbas,** who was not only **a robber,** but a rebel (Mark 15:7) and a murderer (Luke 23:19).

19:1 Pilate orders Jesus to be **scourged,** hoping that the Jews would accept this rather than execution. The scourge was made of thongs to which were attached sharp pieces of metal and pieces of bone. The prisoners were beaten across the back, having the flesh and sometimes the organs torn. Many prisoners died from this cruel punishment.

19:2 The **crown of thorns** was in mockery of a kingly crown. Placing a **purple robe** on Jesus made Him a caricature of a royal conqueror.

19:3 Hail, King of the Jews was probably a sarcastic echo of what the soldiers had heard at Jesus' triumphal entry or at His trial.

19:4 I am bringing Him out to you: Perhaps Pilate was appealing to the people's compassion so that he could release Jesus.

> *Jesus pointed out that though He was a king, he was no threat to Rome because His kingdom would not come by a worldly revolution.*

19:5, 6 Crucify Him: The Jewish leaders anticipated an outburst of pity. Therefore they began demanding Jesus' death. **You . . . crucify Him:** Pilate was enraged. **I find no fault in Him:** This was the third time Pilate declared that he could find no legal grounds for capital punishment (18:38; 19:4).

19:7 We have a law: The Jewish leaders were telling Pilate, "If you are appealing to us, we say that according to our law, He must die." As governor, Pilate was bound by Roman custom to respect Jewish law. **He made Himself the Son of God:** The Jewish leaders were accusing Jesus of violating the laws against blasphemy (Lev. 24:16).

19:8 he was the more afraid: Though not mentioned earlier, Pilate had no doubt become fearful. The claim of Jesus' deity further excited his fears.

19:9 Jesus gave . . . no answer: Three times Pilate had publicly pronounced Jesus innocent (18:38; 19:4, 6). If he had really wanted to know the truth, he would have believed what Jesus had already told him (18:37).

19:10 I have power: Pilate was irritated by Jesus' refusal to speak.

19:11 given you from above: Jesus acknowledged that Pilate had the power to take His life, but only because God allowed him that power. **The one who delivered Me to you** is a reference to Caiaphas (18:24, 28), who had **the greater sin** because as a religious leader he had that much greater a responsibility to recognize the Messiah.

19:12 not Caesar's friend: The Jews shifted their focus from the religious charge (v. 7) to the political charge (18:33), which they backed up with an appeal to Caesar's own political interest. This new plea forced Pilate to choose between yielding to an indefinite sense of right or escaping the danger of an accusation at Rome.

19:13 The Pavement no doubt referred to a large paved area in the Fortress Antonia.

19:14 The Preparation Day of the Passover refers to the Friday of Passover week (v. 31), the preparation for the Sabbath of the Passover. Some have suggested that this may be the Thursday before the Passover, the same time that the Passover lamb was offered as a sacrifice. However this interpretation appears to conflict with the narrative of the three synoptic Gospels, where it seems that Jesus is described as being crucified on Friday (Matt. 27:62). **The sixth hour** was 6 A.M. according to the Roman system of time.

19:15, 16 The Jewish leaders preferred proclaiming a heathen emperor as their **king** to acknowledging Jesus as their Messiah. Trapped by his own fear, Pilate handed over the innocent Jesus to endure a punishment Pilate knew He did not deserve.

19:17 The Place of a Skull probably got its name from the shape of the hill.

official languages of the day. Everyone could read the message in his or her own language.

19:21 The addition of the phrase **of the Jews** to the title **chief priests** (probably referring to Caiaphas and Annas) occurs nowhere else in the NT. The addition probably corresponds to the title given Jesus. The chief priest of the Jews objected to Jesus being called **King of the Jews.** They did not want a messianic designation connected with Him.

19:22 Pilate refused to change the title. As

An excavated area in ancient Jerusalem known as The Pavement (John 19:13), identified by some scholars as the place in the Fortress of Antonia where Pilate pronounced the death sentence against Jesus (John 19:13–16).

19:18 they crucified Him: Of all the apostles, John alone witnessed the crucifixion. However, he spares his readers the revolting details. The **two others** were thieves (Matt. 27:38; Mark 15:27).

19:19 wrote a title: It was a Roman custom to write the name of the condemned person and his crime on a plaque to be placed above his head at the execution. Mark calls this title "the inscription of His accusation" (Mark 15:26).

19:20 written in Hebrew, Greek, and Latin: Multilingual inscriptions were common. The title was written in the local, common, and

did Caiaphas, Pilate affirmed more than he ever intended. The title proclaimed to all that Jesus is indeed the promised Messiah.

19:23 the soldiers: According to Roman law, the **garments** of a condemned criminal belonged to the executioners. Jesus had two items of clothing. The cloak was a large, loose garment. The **tunic** was a close-fitting garment that went from the neck to the knees.

19:24 The outer garment could be conveniently divided, but the inner garment could not. Thus the soldiers divided the outer one and **cast lots** for the inner one. Unknowingly, the soldiers fulfilled David's prophecy in Ps. 22:18.

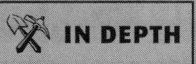 **IN DEPTH** | **The Women Around Jesus**

Jesus went to His death attended by a loyal following of women who had stood by Him throughout His ministry (John 19:25). Women played a major part in Jesus' life and work. It was a woman or women who . . .

- nurtured Him as He grew up (Luke 2:51);
- traveled with Him and helped finance His ministry (8:1–3);
- listened to Him teach (10:39);
- were featured in His parables (Matt. 13:33; 24:41);
- shared the good news that He was the Messiah (John 4:28–30);
- offered hospitality to Him and His companions (Mark 1:29–31);
- were treated by Him with respect and compassion (John 4:5–27; 11:32, 33);
- were healed by Him (Matt. 9:20–22; Luke 13:10–17);
- were praised by Him for their faith (Mark 7:24–30);
- were commended by Him for their generosity (12:41–44);
- worshiped Him and prepared His body for burial before His crucifixion (Matt. 26:6–13);
- stood by Him at the Cross (27:55; John 19:25);
- assisted in His burial (Mark 16:1; Luke 23:55—24:1);
- first saw Him resurrected (John 20:16); and
- went to tell the rest of His followers that He was risen from the dead (20:18).

This passage had long been considered a messianic prophecy.

19:25, 26 The disciple whom He loved refers to John, the author of this Gospel.

19:27 Behold your mother: Jesus placed Mary in the care of John.

19:28 that the Scripture might be fulfilled: Everything foretold concerning the earthly life of Jesus had been accomplished.

19:29 Sour wine was not the same as the drugged wine that had been offered to Jesus earlier ("wine mingled with myrrh"; Mark 15:23). Jesus did not take that wine because He wanted to die fully conscious. He did take a sip of this wine; one of the agonies of crucifixion was incredible thirst, added to the terrible pain.

19:30 It is finished . . . He gave up His spirit: Having fulfilled every command of the Father and every prophecy of Scripture, Jesus voluntarily died. This was not a cry of exhaustion, but of completion. Jesus had done what He had agreed to do.

19:31–33 The Preparation Day was Friday, the day before the Sabbath (v. 14). **bodies should not remain on the cross:** It is ironic that in the midst of a deliberate judicial murder the Jews were scrupulous about keeping the ceremonial law. According to Jewish law (Deut. 21:23), it was necessary to remove the bodies of executed criminals before sunset. To avoid breaking the Law, the Jews requested that the legs of the condemned be broken so that the men would die quickly and could be removed from their crosses. Breaking the legs was not always part of crucifixion. But with his legs broken, a victim could no longer lift his body in order to breathe and would soon suffocate. **High day** is literally "great day." The coming Sabbath was especially important because it was the Sabbath of the Passover Week.

19:34 To make certain that Jesus was dead, **one of the soldiers pierced His side with a spear.** After the soldier did this, **blood and water came out,** indicating that Jesus was already dead. Only blood would have flowed from a living body.

19:35 he who has seen: John's words can be trusted because he is giving an eyewitness account, so that his readers will believe that Jesus is the Savior.

19:36, 37 One should trust Christ not only because John gives an accurate account of His death (v. 35), but also because He fulfilled Scripture (v. 37), proving that He is the Messiah. Both the lack of broken bones and the piercing of His side fulfilled prophecies recorded in the OT (Ex. 12:46; Zech. 12:10).

19:38 Joseph, a rich member of the Jewish council (Matt. 27:57; Mark 15:43), had not agreed with their decision (Luke 23:50).

19:39 Nicodemus, like Joseph (v. 38), was a member of the council (3:1). At last, Nicodemus identified himself with the One who had come from above (12:42). **A hundred pounds** was a large amount. Nicodemus

✓ IN COMPARISON   Understanding Jesus' Death

The Jews viewed Jesus' death as a scandal. The church understood His death as fulfillment of OT prophecy.

Aspect of Jesus' Death	Old Testament Reference
In obedience to His Father (18:11)	Psalm 40:8
Announced by Himself (18:32; see 3:14)	Numbers 21:8, 9
In the place of His people (18:14)	Isaiah 53:4–6
With evildoers (19:18)	Isaiah 53:12
In innocence (19:6)	Isaiah 53:9
Crucified (19:18)	Isaiah 22:16
Buried in a rich man's tomb (19:38–42)	Isaiah 53:9

intended to cover Jesus' entire body with spices—a common burial custom.

19:40 The custom of the Jews, in contrast to the Egyptians, who removed the soft organs and dried the muscular tissue with preservatives.

19:41, 42 a new tomb: Matthew specifies that the tomb belonged to Joseph (Matt. 27:60). This too was a fulfillment of a prophecy: The Messiah would be buried in a rich man's grave (Is. 53:9).

20:1 while it was still dark: Apparently **Mary Magdalene** arrived ahead of the other women (Matt. 28:1; Mark 16:1; Luke 24:10). Mary Magdalene, out of whom Jesus had cast seven demons, was the last one at the Cross and the first one at the grave.

20:2 The other disciple, whom Jesus loved, was John, the author of this Gospel. **They have taken away the Lord:** Mary Magdalene jumped to the wrong conclusion. **we:** Other women were with Mary Magdalene (Matt. 28:1; Mark 16:1; Luke 24:10).

20:3, 4 John probably **outran** Peter because he was younger.

20:5 the linen cloths lying there: No one who came to steal the body would have taken the time to unwrap it and leave the cloths behind.

20:6 saw: The Greek term implies an intense stare, in contrast to the more casual look described in v. 5. Peter **went into the tomb** to get a good look. He carefully examined the place where Jesus' body had been.

20:7 folded together: The **handkerchief** around Christ's head had not been thrown aside, as might have been done by a thief. It had

been folded and laid aside. Perhaps the implication is that Christ did not rush out of the tomb, but left His grave clothes neatly folded.

20:8 The other disciple, commonly believed to be the apostle John, **saw** the tomb and the grave clothes and **believed** that Christ had been raised from the dead.

20:9, 10 they did not know the Scripture: The disciples believed because of what they saw in the tomb (v. 8), not because of what they knew from OT passages describing the Savior's resurrection (Luke 24:25–27). Jesus had prophesied His death and resurrection in the disciples' presence, but the disciples had not understood what He was talking about. Later Jesus would instruct them about how His life and death fulfilled the Scriptures (Luke 24:13–27, 44–47).

20:11–13 Mary must have returned with Peter and John (vv. 3, 4), lingering **outside . . . the tomb** after the men left. **Angels** (v. 12) are primarily God's messengers. Their message to Mary and the others is given in fuller form in Luke 24:4–7.

20:14–16 did not know: Overcome by grief, and with tear-dimmed eyes, **Mary** did not immediately recognize **Jesus.** When Christ uttered her name, **Mary** recognized His voice. Mary addressed Christ as **Rabboni,** an Aramaic term which John translates for his Greek readers. The Aramaic **Rabboni** means "my lord," but had become commonly used for **Teacher,** as had its Hebrew equivalent "Rabbi."

20:17, 18 Cling means "to fasten oneself to" or "to hold." Mary had grabbed Christ and was holding on to Him as if she would never turn

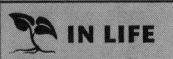 **IN LIFE** | **Lord over Doubt**

Have you ever struggled with doubts or troubling questions about Christ, the Christian faith, or the church? Do you sometimes feel that tough questions are not welcome or acceptable among believers?

Thomas (John 20:24) was a classic skeptic. Even though he had traveled with Jesus and learned from His teaching for at least three years, he needed time, evidence, and personal convincing before he would accept the Resurrection (20:25, 26). But Jesus responded to his doubt by inviting him to check it all out. He presented Himself for Thomas's inspection (15:26, 27) and did not chide him for wanting to be certain.

Jesus seeks to honor the mind and heart of every seeker or doubter. He knows that easily developed loyalties often lack staying power. By contrast, many tenacious people who probe the corners of their doubts and fears finally reach the truth—and faith in the truth is what Christ desires. He even promised that the Spirit would aid those who seek it (16:12–16).

The encounter with Thomas welcomes every skeptic to bring his or her doubts to God. He delights in hearing our arguments and questions.

Him loose. Christ explained to her that He could not stay because He had to ascend to His Father. **My brethren** referred to the disciples (v. 18). Jesus sent Mary to them with the first postresurrection testimony. Though it may be that Mary was formerly a woman of ill-repute, this did not keep Jesus from commissioning her to bring the gospel message to the apostles (Mark 16:11). **My Father and your Father:** God is the Father of Christ and of believers (1:14, 18; 3:16, 18).

20:19, 20 Jesus came and stood in the midst: Christ's appearance was miraculous, because **the doors were shut.** Jesus, as God, could perform a variety of miracles without requiring a change in His humanity. Here Christ's body was a physical body, the same body in which He died and was buried. The difference is that His flesh had been changed to take on immortality and incorruptibility (1 Cor. 15:53).

20:21 As indicates that the disciples were commissioned to carry on Christ's work, not to begin a new one.

20:22 Receive the Holy Spirit: The ministry to which Jesus called the disciples (v. 21; see also Matt. 28:16–20; Luke 24:47–49) required spiritual power. The reference here is to a special preparation of the apostles who were to become the foundation of the church at Pentecost. Here Jesus breathed the Spirit into the disciples. At Pentecost the Spirit unified the believers into one body and empowered them to testify of Jesus (1 Cor. 12:13). The reception of the Spirit here is reminiscent of the creative breath of God into Adam in Gen. 2:7. Yet the gift here was not a human spirit, but the Spirit of the living God.

20:23 If you forgive: The apostles did not

take Jesus' words to mean that they had the power to forgive sins (Acts 8:22). They knew that only God could forgive sins (Mark 2:7). Neither the apostles nor the church had the power to forgive specific sins or to prevent forgiveness for any individual. Fundamentally, Jesus was speaking of the responsibility of the church to declare the gospel to all the world, so that those who believe in Jesus can find the precious gift of forgiveness (Matt. 16:19).

20:24, 25 Thomas was not present when Jesus appeared to the disciples in the closed room (vv. 19–23). **Unless I see in His hands:** When Jesus appeared to the other disciples, He showed them His hands and His side (v. 20). No doubt they told Thomas about it; hence his request.

20:26, 27 In spite of his misgivings (v. 25), **Thomas** was **with them.** He had not left the group, nor had they excluded him (Rom 14:1).

20:28 My Lord and my God: In awestruck wonder, Thomas not only believed that Christ was risen from the dead, but he also saw that the Resurrection proved His deity.

20:29 Those who have not seen includes all who have believed in Christ since His ascension to the Father (1 Pet. 1:8, 9).

20:30, 31 John states the purpose of his book. His purpose was to convince his readers that Jesus is the Christ, the Messiah who fulfilled God's promises to Israel. Jesus is the Son of God, God in the flesh. By believing these things, a person obtains eternal life (1:12).

21:1 Sea of Tiberias: The Sea of Galilee was renamed for the Roman emperor Tiberias Caesar.

21:2 John, the author of this Gospel, was one of **the sons of Zebedee.** The omission of

IN DEPTH | Peter Forgiven

John is the only Gospel writer who records the account of Jesus restoring Peter to His ministry after Peter's three denials (18:17, 25–27; 21:15–19). Only a short time before this dramatic encounter with the risen Lord, Peter had boldly announced that he would give his life for Jesus. Jesus responded by informing Peter that he would actually *deny* Him three times that same night (13:37, 38).

Later that evening, Jesus was arrested. While He stood trial before the chief priest, Peter hid outside in the courtyard. Three times Peter was recognized as one of Jesus' followers; three times he denied knowing Jesus, thus fulfilling Jesus' words. Luke 22:62 tells us that when Peter realized what he had done, he "wept bitterly."

Imagine, then, Peter's emotions during his encounter with the resurrected Savior by the Sea of Tiberias. On the one hand, he was no doubt overjoyed to see the risen Lord. On the other hand, he may still have been ashamed and embarrassed about his desertion of Jesus in the hour of His greatest need.

Three times the Lord asked Peter if Peter loved Him. The first two times, Christ used the word *agapaō*, signifying a love of commitment, a love of the will. Peter responded with the word *phileō*, indicating his strong emotion for the Lord. The word suggests warmth, fondness, and friendship.

When Peter acknowledged that he loved Christ, the Lord gave him the task of feeding His lambs and taking care of His sheep. Expressing love for Christ implies accepting a duty to do the work of God and to be faithful. Peter had some difficulty with such faithfulness during Christ's earthly ministry. As Christ was getting ready to depart, He wanted to elicit a commitment from Peter.

The third time Jesus asked Peter if he loved Him He used the word *phileō*, indicating strong friendship. Christ had taught that a friend who loves will lay down his life for a friend. Peter, instead, had denied Christ three times. With Peter's final response, "You know that I love You," Christ had drawn a commitment from Peter and assured the other disciples of the bond between Himself and Peter. In the process, He demonstrated His complete forgiveness of Peter. With this exchange, the Lord restored Peter to a position of leadership in the ongoing ministry of the gospel.

---

his name here is consistent with his reserve about everything connected with himself in his book.

21:3 Peter said . . . "I am going fishing." Peter has been severely criticized for returning to his previous occupation, but there is nothing in the text to suggest that Peter did anything wrong. The Lord does not rebuke him for what he did.

21:4 the disciples did not know: Perhaps the apostles did not recognize Jesus because they were preoccupied with their work as Mary Magdalene had been with her sorrow (20:14). In addition, there was not much light at this time of day. **When the morning had now come** refers to daybreak.

21:5 have you any food: The question from the shore was probably regarded as a request to buy fish. The disciples answered that they had nothing to sell.

21:6 "Cast the net on the right side of the boat." Perhaps they thought the stranger had seen fish. Fish were sometimes detected in schools in the lake.

21:7 That disciple whom Jesus loved is commonly considered to be John, the author of this Gospel. **Peter . . . plunged into the sea:** John was the first to recognize the Lord; Peter was the first to act. Though Peter often made bad decisions, he had zeal that would eventually be channeled to good use (Acts 2:14–41).

21:8–10 Two hundred cubits is about a hundred yards.

21:11–14 The phrase **the third time** applies to the disciples as a group. John himself has related three appearances before this one, the first being to Mary Magdalene (20:19–23, 26–29).

21:15 More than these means more than the other disciples (Matt. 26:22). On two different occasions Peter had claimed extraordinary love for Christ, even comparing himself to other men (13:37; Matt. 26:33).

21:16 Tend means to shepherd. Lambs need to be fed (v. 15); **sheep** need to be guided. Peter would need to care for diverse people in different ways, as Christ had done with His disciples.

21:17 Peter denied the Lord at least three times. Here he affirmed his love for the Lord for **the third time.**

21:18, 19 Peter must have been bewildered by Christ's words to him. Jesus had just spoken of the future ministry of Peter; now He spoke of Peter's death. When Peter was younger, he **walked where** he **wished,** moving about without restriction. When Peter became older, he would **stretch out** his **hands,** looking for help. **Another will gird you** means that Peter would be bound as a condemned criminal. The day would come when Peter would be totally under the control of Roman executioners, who would **carry** him where he would **not wish** to go, to death (v. 19). His death is hinted at in 2 Pet. 1:13, 14. Jesus' words here confirm the early church tradition that Peter was crucified upside down.

21:20, 21 The disciple whom Jesus loved is commonly considered to be John, the author of this Gospel. **What about this man:** Peter wanted to know if John too would suffer a violent death.

21:22, 23 You follow Me: The Lord told Peter that he should be concerned with following God's will himself and not worrying about God's will for others. **this disciple would not die:** The rumor was that Jesus would return before John died.

21:24 This is the disciple: The disciple was the one whom Jesus loved (v. 20). This is basically John's signature to his Gospel.

21:25 there are also many other things that Jesus did: The Gospel of John is truthful (v. 24), but it is not exhaustive.

Acts
of the Apostles

◆

THE INFECTIOUS NEWS FIRST APPEARED IN Jerusalem, then spread quickly from person to person and from city to city. It faced opposition everywhere it went. But the world was ill-equipped to fight it. Empowered by the Holy Spirit, the followers of Christ relayed the Good News about Jesus everywhere. In less than thirty-five years, the gospel had reached cities from Jerusalem to Rome.

Luke wrote the Book of Acts to show the fulfillment of Jesus' words, "I will build My church, and the gates of Hades shall not prevail against it" (Matt. 16:18). Before Jesus ascended to heaven, He commanded His followers to make disciples of all nations (Luke 24:46–49). Luke begins Acts with a reiteration of that commission and a description of how it would be carried out (1:8). This commission not only ties the Book of Acts to the Gospel of Luke, but it also provides an outline for the book: the witness in Jerusalem and Judea (1:1—6:7); the witness in Judea and Samaria (6:8—9:31); and the witness to the ends of the earth (9:32—28:31).

The Book of Acts begins in Jerusalem with the disciples huddled in a room on the Day of Pentecost. Then the Holy Spirit came upon them and authorized them to be His witnesses. The rest of Acts describes the ripple effect of that great event. Jesus' followers first witnessed to the Jews in Jerusalem, with Peter at the center of the movement. Then persecution broke out (7:60), scattering believers into Samaria and the rest of the known world. Saul of Tarsus, once a leader of the persecution, became a leader of the persecuted. In ch. 11, the focus of the Book of

Acts moves from Peter's ministry to the Jews to Saul's ministry to the Gentiles. Under his more familiar name Paul, this converted persecutor established churches in Asia Minor and Europe. The Book of Acts records three of Paul's missionary journeys, as well as his voyage to Rome to face his trial. The book ends abruptly with Paul under house arrest in Rome. The ending is fitting, because the entire Book of Acts is itself just a prologue. Jesus has not finished His work on earth. The narrative begun by Luke in this book will not end until Jesus Christ returns in glory (1:11; 1 Cor. 15:28).

The Book of Acts provides a condensed history of the early church, an eyewitness account of the miraculous spread of the gospel from Jerusalem to Rome. The book details how the Holy Spirit authorized our spiritual forebears to carry out Jesus' mandate to be His witnesses throughout the world. The accounts in Acts include stirring examples for us to follow, but the recurring theme of the Book of Acts is that our spiritual ancestors were empowered by the Holy Spirit. That same power is available to us. God has not left us at the mercy of our own weaknesses; He has sent the Holy Spirit to help us follow their example (Eph. 5:17, 18), and to be Jesus' witnesses in all of the earth.

The Book of Acts is a historical narrative, but at the same time it has profound theological significance. A believer's faith rests upon the facts of history: the life, death, and resurrection of Jesus. These historical events were recorded by Luke in his Gospel in order to evoke belief. If the historical fact of Christ's resurrection is not true, then a believer's faith has no foundation. As Paul states, "If Christ is not risen, your faith is futile; you are still in your sins" (1 Cor. 15:17). The Book of Acts reassures believers that their faith in Christ rests on fact. The extraordinary growth of the early church was based directly on the resurrected Christ. His command and empowerment of the disciples through the Holy Spirit is the only reasonable explanation for the incredible and rapid spread of the gospel in the first century. The early Christians were not testifying about a dead Christ, but a living Christ whom they had seen with their own eyes (1:1–5; Luke 24:36–53; 2 Pet. 1:16). The same is true for us today. Jesus lives and continues to work through the church.

The Book of Acts begins with a reference to the author's "former account" written to a man named Theophilus (1:1), a clear reference to the Gospel of Luke (Luke 1:3). Even though the author does not mention himself by name in either the Gospel or Acts, early tradition identifies Luke as the author of both volumes. As early as the second century, ancient authors, such as Irenaeus (c. A.D. 180), indicate this.

Called "the beloved physician" by Paul (Col. 4:14), Luke was a doctor whom Paul met in Troas (16:8–11). He cared for Paul during the ill-

nesses he suffered on his missionary endeavors. Paul's references to Luke in 2 Timothy 4:11 and Philemon 24 portray Luke as Paul's faithful traveling companion. After the two met in Troas, Luke included himself with the missionary team recorded in Acts (16:10, the beginning of the so-called "we" sections in the book). Luke's faithful friendship to Paul continued until Paul's death in Rome, for Luke was one of the few people who did not desert him (2 Tim. 4:11).

The Book of Acts does not record Paul's death. Instead it ends abruptly during Paul's residence in Rome (28:30). Paul's house arrest in Rome occurred around A.D. 61, marking the earliest possible date for the book's completion. Acts makes no reference to the fall of Jerusalem in A.D. 70 or to Nero's persecution of Christians following the fire of Rome in A.D. 64. Surely Luke would have mentioned these significant events if they had occurred when he wrote. Moreover, the many references to Paul's vindication before Roman officials would not make sense if Nero had already started his vehement persecution of Christians. Therefore, it is reasonable to assume that Acts was written between A.D. 60 and 64.

Outline

I. The apostles' witness in Jerusalem 1:1–6:7
  A. The acts of the Holy Spirit 1:1–26
  B. The birth of the church 2:1–47
  C. The healing of a lame man 3:1–26
  D. Salvation in no one else 4:1–37

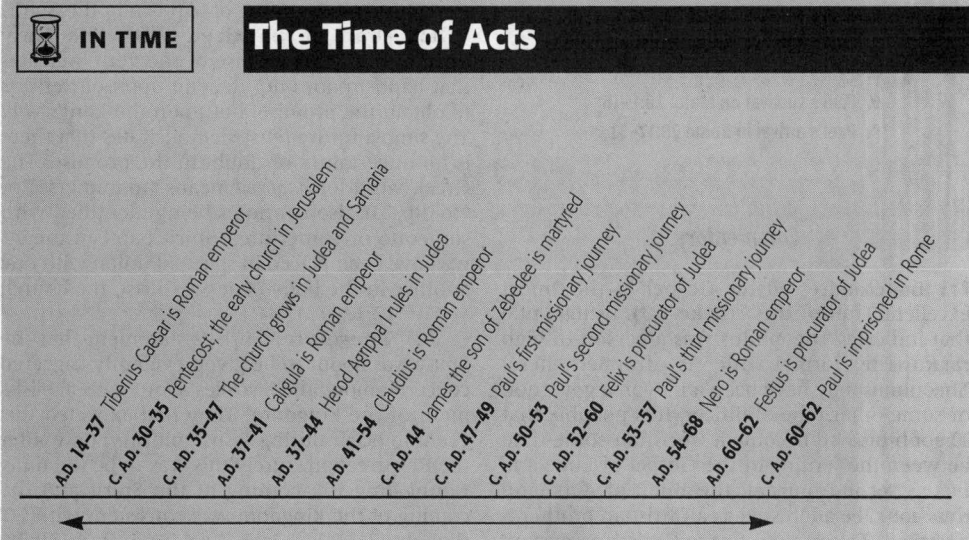

IN TIME — **The Time of Acts**

A.D. 14–37 Tiberius Caesar is Roman emperor
c. A.D. 30–35 Pentecost, the early church in Jerusalem
c. A.D. 35–47 The church grows in Judea and Samaria
A.D. 37–41 Caligula is Roman emperor
A.D. 37–44 Herod Agrippa I rules in Judea
A.D. 41–54 Claudius is Roman emperor
c. A.D. 44 James the son of Zebedee is martyred
c. A.D. 47–49 Paul's first missionary journey
c. A.D. 50–53 Paul's second missionary journey
A.D. 52–60 Felix is procurator of Judea
c. A.D. 53–57 Paul's third missionary journey
A.D. 54–68 Nero is Roman emperor
A.D. 60–62 Festus is procurator of Judea
c. A.D. 60–62 Paul is imprisoned in Rome

Commentary

1:1 Luke addressed his Gospel to the "most excellent **Theophilus**" (Luke 1:3), using a title that indicates Theophilus was a person of high rank. The formal title is dropped here. Theophilus may have been a mayor, a governor, or some other type of officer. It is possible that Theophilus had become a Christian some time between the writing of the Gospel of Luke and Luke's second journal, the Book of Acts, and thus could be addressed as a Christian brother.

1:2, 3 Taken up refers to Christ's ascension,

the end of His earthly ministry. These verses look back to Luke 24:51 and ahead to vv. 9, 22. **the apostles . . . to whom He also presented Himself alive:** The resurrected Jesus presented Himself "not to all the people, but to witnesses chosen before by God" (10:41). In the **forty days** between Jesus' resurrection and ascension, there are recorded some ten or eleven appearances of Jesus to believers confirming His resurrection from the dead. On the last of these appearances, Jesus gathered His apostles together and commanded them not to leave Jerusalem (v. 4). **Many infallible proofs** serve as the basis for the believer's confidence in the resurrection of our Lord. The Greek word translated *infallible proofs* speaks of "convincing, decisive proof." Christian belief is not built on speculation or myth but on the sovereign acts and words of God incarnate in the time-space universe. The birth, ministry, death, resurrection, and ascension of the Lord Jesus Christ are solidly rooted in history. **The kingdom of God** was the central topic of discussion between Christ and His apostles during the forty days between Jesus' resurrection and ascension. The goal of history is not the Cross, but the crown—the time when King Jesus reveals Himself in all His majesty and reigns in glory (Is. 11; Dan. 7:13, 14; 1 Cor. 15:24–28; Rev. 20:4–6).

1:4 As predicted by John the Baptist (Matt. 3:11; Mark 1:8; Luke 3:16; John 1:33) and reiterated by Jesus Himself, **the Promise of the Father** was the promise of baptism in the Holy Spirit. There are seven references in Scripture to baptism in the Spirit. Five are prophetic (v. 5; Matt. 3:11; Mark 1:8; Luke 3:16; John 1:33); one is historical (11:15, 16), referring to the Day of Pentecost; and one is doctrinal (1 Cor. 12:13), explaining the meaning of baptism in the Spirit.

1:5 shall be baptized with the Holy Spirit: The passive tense of the verb indicates that baptism does not depend upon our efforts to obtain the promise, but upon the Lord's will. The simple future tense demonstrates that there is no uncertainty or doubt in the promise. The Greek word for *baptized* means "to immerse" or "to dip." It also connotes being identified with someone or something. Spirit baptism means we have been placed in spiritual union with one another in the body of Jesus Christ, the church (1 Cor. 12:12, 13).

1:6 Therefore: Christ's statement that the Spirit was about to be given evidently triggered concern among the disciples about the establishment of the kingdom. They had expected this event to occur during Jesus' ministry; now, after the Resurrection, surely this was to be the time. Connecting the coming of the Spirit and the coming of the kingdom was consistent with OT thought (3:21; Is. 32:15–20; 44:3–5; Ezek. 39:28,

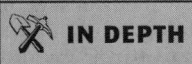 **IN DEPTH** | **A Worldwide Gospel**

Grand Strategy

Speaking on the Mount of Olives at Bethany (Acts 1:4, 12), Jesus outlined a vision that would affect the whole world (1:8). He began by pointing to the starting point of gospel penetration—Jerusalem, two miles to the west. From there the message would spread to the surrounding region, Judea, and its estranged cousin to the north, Samaria. Eventually it would reach the entire world (though the crowd in Acts 1 probably understood "the end of the earth" as meaning the extent of the Roman Empire).

While Jesus' mandate sounds admirable today, it probably met with less than enthusiasm then. All of the places mentioned represented trouble and danger, both real and imagined. Jews—which almost all of Jesus' listeners were—were a small minority in the Roman Empire.

In fact, most of the apostles came from the Galilee region, north of Samaria. Galileans endured the scorn of their Jewish brothers from Judea, especially those from Jerusalem, who considered themselves more pure and orthodox, less contaminated by foreign influences. The lake region was derided as "Galilee of the Gentiles." Even the Galilean accent was chided.

Jerusalem

Jerusalem was not the apostles' home, but it was Judea's key city, center of its religious, political, economic, and cultural life. Jesus' crucifixion had recently taken place there. Leaders still plotted to stamp out what was left of His movement.

Yet Christ told His followers to start their witness there, in the place of greatest hostility and intimidation. They must have wondered: Could He protect them from the inevitable opposition they would encounter? Would they suffer the same terrible end that He had?

Judea and Samaria

The relationship of Jerusalem to Judea was that of urban center to province, or of city to state. By penetrating the city, the gospel would also permeate the city's surroundings.

However, Jesus was careful to link Judea to Samaria, its cousin to the north. The two regions endured a bitter rivalry dating to the early eighth century B.C., when the Assyrians colonized Samaria with non-Jews who intermarried with Israelites and thereby "corrupted" the race. Judea, which means "Jewish," considered itself the home of pure Judaism and viewed Samaria with contempt. As John points out in his account of the woman at the well at Sychar, "Jews have no dealings with Samaritans" (John 4:9).

In reaching Judea with the gospel, the Galilean apostles would have to surmount barriers of regional pride and cultural arrogance. But in moving into Samaria, they would have to overcome long-held ethnic prejudices.

The End of the Earth

Talk of the gospel spreading to "the end of the earth" signaled the eventual inclusion of Gentiles—the ultimate shock to the apostles. In their mind, the world was divided into Jews and non-Jews (Gentiles or "foreigners"). Extremely orthodox Jews would have nothing to do with Gentiles. Even Jews like the apostles, who had grown up alongside of Gentiles, avoided contact as much as possible.

For the gospel to spread to the Gentiles, then, Jesus' followers would have to overcome centuries of racial, religious, and cultural prejudice and break down well-established walls of separation. Eventually they did—but not without great conflict and tension.

29; Joel 2:28—3:1; Zech. 12:8–10). **At this time** expresses the anxiety of the apostles as they anticipated the kingdom rule that Christ had spoken of in the preceding days and weeks (v. 3). The popular expectation and hope was that Christ would establish His kingdom immediately.

1:7 It is not for you to know: Jesus did not correct His disciples' views concerning the restoration of the kingdom to Israel (v. 6). Instead He corrected their views concerning the timing of the event. This was the same erroneous thinking that He had sought to correct with His parable in Luke 19:11–27, the parable of the minas. **times or seasons:** These words speak to the issue of timing differently. *Times* refers to chronology or the duration of time—

"how long." *Seasons* refers to the epochs or "events" that occur within time. The disciples were not to know how long it would be before Christ set up His kingdom, nor were they to know what events would transpire before the establishment of it. Peter points out that even the OT prophets did not know the timing between the sufferings of Christ and the glories that would follow (1 Pet. 1:11). All things will happen in God's time and in God's way. This verse alone should keep anyone from attempting to set dates for the return of Christ.

1:8 Instead of being concerned about the date of Christ's return, the disciples' job was to carry His message throughout the world. **you shall receive power:** This does not refer to personal power for godly living, as demonstrated in the lives of OT saints (see Abraham in Gen. 22; Joseph in Gen. 39; Moses in Ex. 14; Daniel in Dan. 6). This was power for a new task—namely, to take the gospel to the ends of the earth. **Be witnesses** is Christ's command to His disciples to tell others about Him regardless of the consequences. Church tradition tells us that all but one of the eleven apostles who heard this promise became martyrs (John died in exile). God empowered His disciples to be faithful witnesses even when they faced the most vehement opposition. That same power for witnessing is available to us today. Our task is not to convince people, but to testify of the truth of the gospel.

1:9–11 Jesus promised that He would not leave or forsake us, but would be with us always, even to the end of the age (Matt. 28:20; John 14:18). He fulfilled this promise in the form of the Holy Spirit, who dwells within believers (John 16:4–7). **taken up . . . cloud received Him . . . He went up:** These three statements portray the gradual, majestic departure of Jesus from the earth. The Ascension has very little place in the Gospel records. Rather, it is fitting that it should come at the beginning of Acts as the preparation for the Day of Pentecost, the birthday of the church, which is founded upon the death, resurrection, and ascension of its exalted head to the right hand of the Father. Christ had earlier said that the Holy Spirit would not come until He had departed (John 16:7), so Acts gives the leaving of Christ in ch. 1 and the coming of the Spirit in ch. 2 in juxtaposition to one another. **will so come:** The Second Coming of Christ and the establishment of His kingdom (vv. 6, 7) will occur the same way Jesus ascended: physically, visibly, and in the clouds.

1:12 A **Sabbath day's journey** was the distance permitted by Jewish custom for travel on a Sabbath day (Ex. 16:29; Num. 35:5; Josh. 3:4), about a half mile. Anyone who traveled farther than this would be regarded as breaking the fourth commandment.

1:13 **The upper room** could have been the room where Jesus spent the last Passover with His disciples, or the room in which He appeared to them after His resurrection (Luke 24). It is possible that the same room was the site of both events. This room may have belonged to Mary, the mother of John Mark. Her house is mentioned in 12:12 as a meeting place of the disciples. Jesus' followers **were**

✠ IN CONTEXT | Power with a Purpose

At the beginning of Acts, Jesus' followers appear confused and fearful. But by the end of the book they are well on their way to transforming the Roman world with the gospel. What accounts for this dramatic change? Acts 1:8 provides the answer: "You shall receive power." But notice:

(1) *The power promised was not force or political authority.* Israel had enjoyed superiority under David and Solomon, but those days were a distant memory. Jesus was not indicating a revival of Jewish dominance. Instead, the word "power" means ability or capacity. Jesus promised that once the Holy Spirit came upon them, His followers would have a new ability.

(2) *The ability had more to do with being than doing.* The believers would "be witnesses," not just "do witnessing." Evangelism is a process, not just an event. It involves a total lifestyle, not just occasional efforts.

(3) *The power came from without, not from within.* The believers were not to manufacture their own ways of proclaiming the gospel, but to look for supernatural ability from the Spirit to make them effective in gospel presentation. The power came when the Holy Spirit arrived, not before.

(4) *The believers were to be witnesses to Christ, not to themselves.* They were to make disciples not to themselves but to the risen Lord (Matt. 28:18–20).

staying in this upper room, waiting in Jerusalem as the Lord had directed, until they received the power Jesus had promised (v. 5). Except for Peter, James and John, this will be the last mention of the apostles by name. The unmentioned, along with Peter, James, and John, go on to significant ministries for our Lord, giving their lives to accomplish the goal of the Great Commission. Peter was crucified upside down. Thomas was speared to death for his faith. Matthew was murdered by being thrust through with a spear. Matthias was beheaded. James was put to death with a fuller's club. Jude, Philip, and Bartholomew were crucified. The story of the Resurrection is powerfully authenticated by the willingness of the apostles to die rather than repudiate the truth of their testimony. People may lie when it suits their convenience, but will they cheerfully sacrifice their lives in order to perpetrate what they know to be a hoax? Not one of the apostles denied that he had been an eyewitness to the death, burial and resurrection of Jesus. Not one of these men backed off their testimony and their personal witness to the resurrection of Jesus Christ; they sealed their witness with their own blood.

1:14 with one accord: This phrase, which is found eleven times in the Book of Acts, is made up of two words that mean "same" and "mind." The phrase speaks of people sharing the same mind or thinking like-mindedly. It does not refer to people who all think and feel the same way about everything, but to people who set aside personal feelings and commit themselves to one task—in this case witnessing to others about the Lord Jesus Christ (Rom. 15:5, 6). Jesus said the world would know that He was sent from the heavenly Father when people saw the love between believers (John 17:21): the unity among the believers described in Acts was a demonstration of this love. **Mary the mother of Jesus** receives special recognition in the group. While on the Cross, Jesus had requested that John care for His mother (John 19:25–27).

1:15–17 From the earliest days of the apostles' calling, **Peter** assumed a position of leadership. Though he often made mistakes, he was never bashful about dealing with problems. It was inevitable that the matter of Judas Iscariot be dealt with. In the upper room **a hundred and twenty** people gathered. No doubt the majority of them were among those who saw the risen Christ (1 Cor. 15:6). Though Christ spent most of His time with the Twelve, there were many other disciples who traveled with Jesus (John 6:66). **Holy Spirit spoke . . . mouth of David:** Peter equated the speech of David with the voice of the Holy Spirit. This is

an example of the biblical doctrine of inspiration, which asserts that the words of Scripture are equally the words of God and the words of men, with no error (2 Tim. 3:16; 1 Pet. 1:11; 2 Pet. 1:20, 21).

1:18, 19 purchased a field: The field that was obtained with the money Judas received for betraying Jesus was actually purchased by the priests after Judas hanged himself (Matt. 27:6–8). Since the money legally belonged to Judas, the priests purchased the field in his name. **burst open . . . entrails gushed out:** Apparently the noose Judas used to hang himself broke and his body fell, rupturing in the middle. This is why the place was called the **Field of Blood.**

1:20–23 Peter applied Pss. 69 and 109 to the apostles' situation. Psalm 69:25 speaks of the removal of the psalmist's enemy. Psalm 109:8 mentions the replacement of an enemy by someone else. Peter, enlightened by the teaching of Jesus (1:3; Luke 24:44–46), regarded these scriptural references as ultimately speaking of Judas the traitor. It was the defection of Judas, not his death, that caused Peter to ask the disciples to choose another to replace him. When James was later killed (12:2), no replacement was chosen for him. Peter specified two qualifications for the appointed apostle. First, he had to have accompanied the disciples from the beginning of Jesus' ministry, His **baptism.** The replacement had to be someone who had seen what the apostles had seen and heard what they had heard, an eyewitness to the miracles and teachings of Jesus. Second, he had to be an eyewitness of Jesus' **resurrection.**

1:24–26 cast their lots: It was customary for the Jews to determine the will of God on certain questions by this method. The names of Matthias and Justus, probably written on stones, were put in a jar that was shaken until one of the names fell out. The name that fell out of the vessel would be the one that God had chosen to take the place of Judas. The fall of the lot was determined not by chance but by God's sovereignty.

2:1 Pentecost was one of the three major Jewish festivals; the other two are the Passover and the Feast of Tabernacles. From the Greek word for "fifty," Pentecost was so named because it fell on the fiftieth day after the Sabbath of the Passover. Pentecost was also known as "the Feast of Weeks," "the Firstfruits of the Wheat Harvest," and "the Day of Firstfruits." During this harvest celebration, the Jews brought to God the firstfruits of their harvest in thanksgiving, expecting that God would give the rest of the harvest as His blessing. This particular Day of Pentecost was the day of firstfruits of Christ's church, the beginning of the great harvest of souls who would come to know Christ and be joined together through the work of the Holy Spirit. There are also some scholars who believe that Pentecost was an observance of the giving of the Law at Mount Sinai. This day in the Book of Acts is significant because it marks when God would begin writing that Law within our hearts. **they were all:** Many assume that the entire 120 persons mentioned in 1:15 were present when the Holy Spirit came on Pentecost. This is probably not the case. Several

imagine how the large crowd mentioned in v. 5 could have observed the activities in the upper room or congregated in the narrow streets outside the upper room of a house where the disciples were meeting.

2:2 A sound like a **rushing mighty wind** was needed to attract the multitudes to the small gathering of apostles who were **sitting,** the normal position for listening to someone speak, rather than standing for prayer.

2:3 there appeared to them divided tongues, as **of fire:** After the great crowd-gathering sound of v. 2 came the visual manifestation of God. Fire often indicated the presence of God. God initially appeared to Moses in a burning bush that was not consumed (Ex. 3). God guided the children of Israel with a pillar of fire by night (Ex. 13:21, 22), and He descended before them in fire on Mount Sinai (Ex. 19:18). God sent fire to consume Elijah's offering on Mount Carmel (1 Kin. 18:38, 39), and He used a vision of fire to warn Ezekiel of His coming judgment (Ezek. 1:26, 27). This fire, in the form of tongues which divided itself upon each

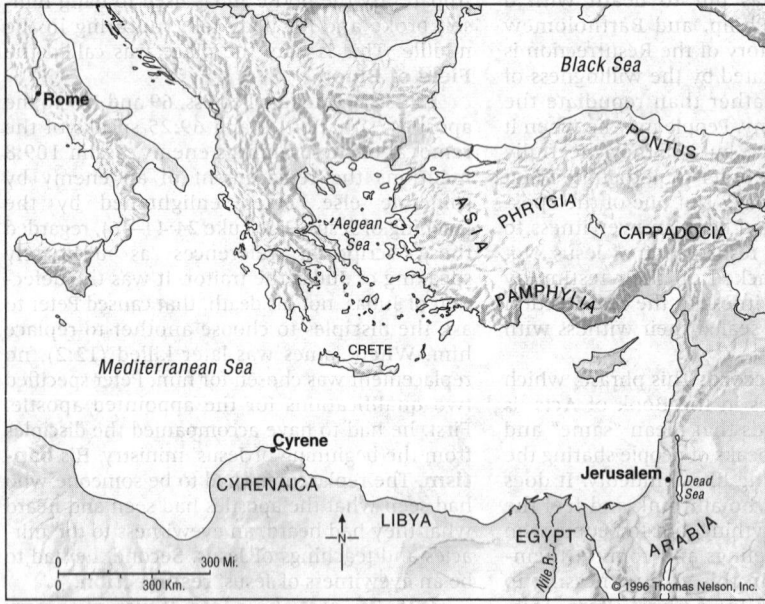

The Nations of Pentecost

In the first Christian century, Jewish communities were located primarily in the eastern Roman Empire, where Greek was the common language. There were Jewish communities as far west as Italy and as far east as Babylonia. In addition to people from the nations shown here, those present on the Day of Pentecost (2:9–11) included visitors from Mesopotamia and even farther east, from Parthia, Media, and Elam (present-day Iran).

days may have passed from the occurrence of Peter speaking of Judas until the happenings at Pentecost. Luke does not say *the next day,* following 1:26 but *when the day of Pentecost had come.* Second, the **they were all** most naturally refers to the last mentioned group, namely, the apostles in 1:26. Third, the ones who spoke in tongues of 2:1–4 are described as Galileans, reminiscent of 1:11 which referred only to the apostles (compare 1:2, 3). Last, when Peter stands to speak in 1:14, he is spoken as being with the eleven other apostles, not a larger group of disciples. **in one place:** The place may have been part of the temple. It is difficult to

one of them, would immediately bring back thoughts of all of these OT examples of fire.

2:4 The word translated **tongues** here is the normal Greek word for known languages. Speaking in "tongues" or diverse languages underscored the universal outreach of the church. These witnesses were speaking foreign dialects to the people who had gathered for Pentecost from other nations. The Day of Pentecost, as one of the three major Jewish celebrations, was a pilgrimage event. People who lived outside Israel traveled to Jerusalem to celebrate the festival. They came from Arabia, Crete, Asia, and even as far away as Rome. Many of these people stayed in Jerusalem for the entire fifty-day celebration. **Spirit gave them utterance:** Note that the text does not say that the Spirit spoke through the apostles, but that the Spirit gave them the ability to speak in languages that they had not previously known.

2:5–11 men . . . from every nation under heaven: People from all over the known world were in Jerusalem. Most of them probably knew Greek, but they also spoke the various languages of the Mediterranean world. **everyone heard them speak in his own language:** The visitors to Jerusalem probably expected the apostles to use Aramaic or Greek, but instead they heard their own dialect. The visitors were astonished because they knew this was most unlikely unless the speakers had come from their land. This was a sign from heaven, a supernatural event. **the wonderful works of God:** It appears that the "speaking in tongues" did not consist of proclaiming the gospel. Rather, the apostles were praising God's mighty works (10:46; 1 Cor. 14:16).

2:12, 13 A contrast is made between two groups of people, the Hellenists and the Hebraists (6:1). Both groups heard the apostles speaking in tongues. Verse 12 speaks of the reaction of the Hellenists, who were from various parts of the world: they understood the dialects in which the apostles spoke and consequently viewed the event as miraculous. On the other hand, those mentioned in v. 13 were Judeans and did not understand the foreign languages the apostles were speaking. They concluded the apostles were drunk and speaking gibberish.

2:14 Peter, the first disciple to recognize the truth about Jesus (Matt. 16:13–19), was also the first to bear witness of Him. Peter preached his sermon to **men of Judea** who had judged the whole episode as being the effect of too much wine (vv. 13, 15).

2:15 these are not drunk: It was only 9:00 in the morning. Jews abstained from eating and drinking on a holy day until later in the day.

2:16–21 Peter began his sermon by quoting Joel 2:28–32 from the Greek translation of the OT. In that passage, God had promised that there would be a time when all those who followed Him would receive His **Spirit,** and not just prophets, kings, and priests. Peter pointed out that that time had **come to pass.** God would speak to and through all those who would come to Him, whether in **visions, dreams,** or prophecy. This was the beginning of the last days. God's final act of salvation began with the pouring out of His Spirit. This final act

---

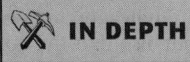 **IN DEPTH** ## The Spirit of Prophecy

Old Testament passages associate the Spirit with creation, with new life, and with empowerment for various divine missions, most often for the mission of a prophet. By Jesus' day, Jewish interpreters most frequently emphasized prophetic empowerment: the Spirit empowered God's servants to hear Him and to speak His message the way He desired.

Many Jewish people believed that God had withdrawn the Spirit after the death of the prophets Haggai, Zechariah, and Malachi. The general assumption was that prophecy continued occasionally on a lower level, but the full restoration of the Spirit was yet to come. Prophets like Isaiah and Ezekiel had promised the final restoration of the Spirit (Is. 44:3; Ezek. 39:29). Nevertheless, the Spirit was not expected until the end time, in the period in which the Messiah would come, and most Jewish people did not believe that the Messiah had come yet.

Peter, recognizing that the Messiah had come in Jesus and that the Spirit who empowered the prophets was now fully active among God's people, chose an OT text about the outpouring of the Spirit of prophecy (Joel 2:28–32). To make it clear that Joel's prophecy refers to the end time, Peter added explanatory words to his quote of Joel: "in the last days" (Acts 2:17).

Further, Peter was teaching that the end time had already begun because the Messiah had already come and taken His heavenly throne (2:34–36). Thus, *some* "signs in the earth" (2:19) had been fulfilled by Jesus (2:22). This in turn meant that the time of salvation of which Joel spoke had also arrived. Thus, Peter viewed the Spirit of prophecy as an end-time gift. God's servants should consider themselves to be empowered by the same Spirit who empowered Isaiah, Jeremiah, Huldah, Samuel, Deborah, and others.

So thoroughly did Peter wish to emphasize this point that he took a liberty used sometimes by Jewish interpreters in his day. He added some more explanatory words to the text he was quoting: "And they shall prophesy" (2:18).

of deliverance will continue to the end of this age.

2:22-24 being delivered by the determined purpose: Jesus Christ was God's provision for the judgment of sin; yet it was our sinfulness that made His death necessary. In other words, it was both the sinfulness of humanity and God's plan to save humanity that put Jesus to death on the Cross (Is. 53:10). God exercises sovereign control over all events—even the death of His Son. Yet at the same time, people are still responsible for their own sinful actions.

2:25-36 Joel prophesied that the Spirit would come; Jesus fulfilled that promise when He sent the Spirit (John 14:16). If Jesus was dead, He could not have sent the Spirit. Therefore, He must be alive. Furthermore, Jesus could not have sent the Spirit unless He had ascended as Lord to heaven. Therefore, Jesus is both our Master and our Savior. **let me speak freely:** Peter knew (v. 29) that no one could dispute the point he was about to make from Ps. 16:8-11, in which the Messiah is described as not decaying. Because David had been buried and had not come back to life, the psalm had to be speaking about someone else, David's heir. Peter pointed out that this heir is Jesus, who was put to death and resurrected. Not only had Jesus been raised from the dead, He is now at the right hand of God. As further proof of this Peter quoted David again. According to Ps. 110:1, the Messiah would sit at the right hand of God. David had not ascended to the heavens. But the apostles declared themselves to be witnesses of the very ascension spoken of in this psalm, the ascension of Jesus. Based on these points, Peter's conclusion is clear: Jesus, the One who had been crucified, is **both Lord and Christ.**

2:37 Peter's argument was irrefutable. **Cut to the heart,** the Judeans asked what they should do. This was the point of new birth. The Spirit of God brought conviction to their hearts, the springboard of action.

2:38 Repent: Repentance for the Judeans involved rejecting their former attitudes and opinions concerning who Jesus was. In faith they had to accept Him for who He declared Himself to be while on earth, a declaration that was confirmed by His resurrection and ascension. **be baptized:** When a person recognizes who Jesus Christ really is, the result is the desire to do what He commands. The first action that Jesus requires of a new believer is baptism (Matt. 28:19, 20), the outward expression of inward faith. The idea of an unbaptized Christian is foreign to the NT (v. 41; 8:12, 36; 9:18; 10:48; 16:15, 33; 18:8). Faith and baptism are integrally connected. Baptism comes after faith in Christ but it is the first Christian sign of faith in Christ. *Faith is to baptism what words are to ideas.* It is pos-

sible to have ideas without words but for the ideas to be understood by others words are needed. The same is true with baptism and trust in Christ. If a person says that he has placed his faith in Jesus Christ as his Savior, then he or she should want to obey Him as Lord and do what is pleasing in God's sight. **for the remission of sins:** Is Peter saying that we must be baptized to receive forgiveness of our sins? Scripture clearly teaches that we are justified by faith alone, not by works (Rom. 4:1-8; Eph. 2:8, 9). The critical word in this phrase is the word *for,* which may also be translated "with a view to." A comparison of Peter's message in 10:34-43 makes it clear that "remission of sins" comes to "whoever believes." Believers are baptized in view of God's work of forgiveness, not in order to receive that forgiveness. God's forgiveness in Christ gives baptism its significance. Baptism is a public declaration that a person's sins have been forgiven because of Christ's work on the Cross. Another grammatical option may be to understand it as "(you) repent for the remission of your sins, and let each of you be baptized in the name of Jesus Christ." Others have interpreted baptism as a sign and seal of God's grace, similar to circumcision, which was a sign of the Abrahamic covenant. **The gift of the Holy Spirit** was the promise of Jesus in John 14:16, 17. The Holy Spirit puts us in communion with the Father and the Son. This indwelling of the Spirit is a beautiful promise of the New Covenant (Jer. 31:33, 34), an indication not only that our sins are forgiven, but also that the Lord has placed His law within us.

2:39 Peter exhorted his listeners to repent. In other words, each person had to make the decision to turn away from his or her sinful habits and turn to God in faith (16:31, 33, 34). Then God would forgive that person's sins and declare them righteous because of Jesus' work on the Cross. **to you and to your children:** In first-century Israel, a father held tremendous influence in his home. When a father chose to receive Christ and be baptized, his children would follow his lead.

2:40-43 three thousand souls: The response to Peter's sermon was tremendous. Such impressive growth in the number of believers created additional needs and responsibilities. The apostles had the duty of training this large group and bringing them into fellowship with the other believers. This was a four-step process: (1) The new believers were to be trained in **the apostles' doctrine.** Uniformity of belief concerning the person of Jesus Christ—based on the eyewitness testimony of His followers—was essential. (2) The new believers were to be trained in the **fellowship** of the church. The Greek word translated *fellowship* means sharing in the lives of other believers. (3)

The new believers were to be trained in the **breaking of bread,** probably a reference to the Lord's Supper (1 Cor. 11:23, 24). Some believe this is a broader reference to the "love feast," a meal of fellowship in the early church. (4) The new believers were to be trained in the discipline of prayer. Corporate **prayers** were viewed as an essential part of the spiritual growth of the church. **Wonders and signs** apparently were given by the Lord to the apostles to validate their divinely ordained position and to verify the truthfulness of their witness in the establishment of the early church (Heb. 2:3, 4).

2:44, 45 The disposal and distribution of possessions in the early church was directed **among all, as anyone had need.** When a physical or spiritual need became known in the church, action was taken to address it (1 John 3:17). The NT believers demonstrated their love for one another by giving self-sacrificially. Was this a form of early communism? Most definitely not. Communism teaches that possessions should be distributed to everybody equally, so that nobody will have more than anyone else. Here, the disposal and distribution of the possessions of the early church was based on need. In communism the state uses the police power to accomplish the desired result. Here, the pooling of resources was not obligatory but a free expression of love to those who were poor and hurting. Communism desires a permanent restructuring of society, while the distribution in this case was limited and temporary until the severe crisis was dealt with because of the great influx of Christian converts.

2:46, 47 They continued with **one accord,** not in isolation, but **in the temple.**

3:1 went up . . . to the temple: The disciples of Jesus continued to follow Jewish tradition. A prayer service accompanied each of the two daily sacrifices, one in the morning and the other in the afternoon. **The ninth hour** would have been 3 P.M.

3:2, 3 The **lame** man was **laid** near the gate called **Beautiful.** This gate opened into the Court of the Women from the outer Court of the Gentiles. It served, in a sense, as the front door to the temple proper. The Beautiful Gate would have been an ideal place for the man to position himself for begging. Those who ignored the man's pleas may have found it difficult to worship due to the guilt they felt for refusing to help such a powerless person. Moreover, as people left the temple they would be more apt to give to someone who was waiting there for help.

3:4, 5 Look at us: It was important to get the man's undivided **attention,** even more important than an outstretched hand (Mark 10:51).

3:6 The apostles indicated immediately that they did not represent themselves in what they were about to do. They represented Jesus

---

✓ IN COMPARISON | The Powerful Name of Jesus

Using none of the sophisticated marketing strategies of today's corporate giants, a small-town carpenter's name managed to become a byword in the first-century world. Why? Because there was power in His name.

Jesus means "Jehovah {God} is salvation" or "Jehovah delivers." Early Christians discovered just how true to His name Jesus was. In Acts 3 and 4, Luke records a sequence of events resembling a five-act drama, in which the name of Jesus features prominently.

The Five-Act Drama of Acts 3 and 4		
Act One, 3:1–10	The lame man healed at the gate.	The name of Jesus healed him (3:6).
Act Two, 3:11–26	Peter's sermon identifies Jesus with the "I Am" of Israel's history. Jesus is Lord!	Faith in the name of Jesus brings salvation (3:16, 26).
Act Three, 4:1–12	Peter and John imprisoned and tried.	No other name but Jesus can be called on to bring salvation to all the earth (4:12).
Act Four, 4:13–22	Peter and John warned and released.	Though opposed, the name of Jesus rings true—"God delivers" (4:18, 21).
Act Five, 4:23–37	The church responds by worshiping Jesus, caring for each other, and witnessing about Christ.	Signs and wonders continue to be done through the name of Jesus (4:30).

Christ. Because of His **name**—who He is—the beggar would receive the miracle of God. The phrase "in the name of Jesus" is not a magical formula used to give some affirmation or guarantee to a prayer. A person's name represented that person's authority and influence. The power in the name of Jesus comes from what the Holy Spirit will do because of that name. Note that Peter and John did not lay their hands on the beggar and pray for God to heal him. Rather, as apostles with the power of God to perform signs and wonders, they simply told him to **rise up and walk.**

3:7, 8 his feet and ankle bones received strength: Luke, a physician by profession, described what took place. Instantly strength was given to the portions of the body that needed it. Blood supply was increased to the muscle. The brain sent signals to the nerve endings of the ankles and feet. The hardened fluid between the joints was softened, and the atrophied muscles and ligaments regained flexibility. The feet suddenly could bear the man's weight.

3:9 the people saw him: Public opinion was an important factor in the decision of the leaders, both in their condemnation of Jesus (Matt. 27:24) and in their treatment of the apostles (Acts 4:16, 17).

3:10 The people had seen the beggar day after day, maybe year after year. His healing was not a staged event. When the beggar stood and walked, the only reasonable explanation was that God had healed him.

3:11, 12 the people ran together to them: People were following after them, but the apostles immediately gave all the glory to Jesus.

3:13–16 glorified His Servant Jesus: Peter's reference to "His Servant" comes from Is. 52:13, a messianic psalm. Jesus can be considered the Servant of God because He gave His life as a guilt offering for the sins of all humanity. The Father raised Jesus from the dead as confirmation that His sacrifice was accepted. Peter pointed to the healing of the beggar as a sign of the glorification of Christ. The people had handed Jesus over to Pilate to be crucified. Yet God had raised the crucified Jesus from the dead. It was in the name of this very same Jesus that the crippled man was healed.

3:17, 18 you did . . . God foretold: Throughout Peter's sermon in ch. 2, he balances the human responsibility of the Jews and Romans with the eternal plan of God.

3:19, 20 The word translated **refreshing** refers to restoration of strength and nourishment. Strength is restored when hope is restored. Peter challenged the people to **repent** and **be converted,** to change their thinking about Jesus as their Messiah and to serve Him.

3:21 The **restoration** may allude to the expected rule of the Messiah after His return (1:11; 17:31).

3:22, 23 The Jewish leaders expected a fulfillment of the prediction in Deut. 18:15 (John 1:21, 22). Peter announced its fulfillment and identified the **Prophet** as Jesus.

3:24–26 sons of the prophets, and of the covenant: These Jewish people were the **first** recipients of the blessings promised to **Abraham,** prophesied by the prophets, and provided by Jesus. **all the families of the earth:** We too are included in the blessing of being turned away from our **iniquities** —God's purpose in sending Christ.

4:1–4 The **Sadducees** were **greatly disturbed** for two reasons. First, the Sadducees were skeptics who rejected all the OT except the books of Moses, and who denied the resurrection from the dead. Peter's teaching about the Resurrection challenged their beliefs and teaching. Second, the Sadducees were leaders of the Jews at that time. They came from wealthy families and consorted with the Roman government in order to maintain their position, influence, and wealth. The last thing the Sadducees

IN FOCUS **"filled with the Holy Spirit"**

(Gk. *plēthō pneumatos hagiou*) (2:4; 4:8, 31; 9:17; 13:9; Luke 1:15, 41, 67) Strong's *#4130; 4151; 40:* The Greek word *plēthō* is used for describing the filling of anything from a sponge to a boat (Matt. 27:48; Luke 5:7). Luke uses this common term to describe how the Holy Spirit influences a person. He uses the expression *filled with the Holy Spirit* eight times in his writings. In every case, the filling of the Holy Spirit enables the person so endowed to speak or preach for God. Thus, the filling of the Spirit is directly related to the prophetic ministry, the revelation or explanation of God's Word.

wanted was for a couple of Jewish men to declare the resurrection of a king. **laid hands on them . . . believed:** The attempt to silence God's truth by arresting His messengers did not hinder His work. Though God's servants are chained, His word is never chained (2 Tim. 2:9). The result of the Sadducees' taking two men into custody was that **five thousand** people believed the gospel message.

4:5, 6 were gathered together: The Sanhedrin, which consisted of 70 men plus the high
priest, was the highest Jewish court. The group
consisted of the wealthiest, most educated, and
most powerful Jewish men in Israel. **Annas the
high priest:** Annas had been removed as high
priest in A.D. 14 by the Romans. At the time of
Christ, the high priests were appointed by the
Roman governors. Apparently Annas had
become a political threat to Rome. The Jewish
people refused to acknowledge Roman
authority over such matters; so even though
Annas was officially removed from his office,
the Jewish people still considered him high
priest. **Caiaphas,** the son-in-law of Annas, was
the actual high priest. **John** was most likely the
son of Annas who succeeded Caiaphas in A.D.
37.

4:7 Because the healing of the lame man
was indisputable (3:1–10), the question was
how the man was healed and by whose
authority or **name** the healing had been performed.

4:8–10 Peter, filled with the Holy Spirit:
This is the second description in the Book of
Acts of someone being filled with the Holy Spirit
(v. 31; 2:4; 9:17; 13:9). The initial filling accompanied the baptism in the Spirit. This filling
brought boldness for God's work. Jesus had
promised His disciples that they would stand
before kings and rulers and that the Spirit of
God within them would implant in their minds
exactly what to say to these leaders (Matt.
10:16–20). It is interesting to compare the
actions of this Spirit-controlled Peter with the
Christ-denying Peter when he stood in the

courtyard intimidated about his faith before a
servant maid in Matt. 26:69–75. On that occasion, Peter denied Christ three times. Now, Peter
stood unafraid and unashamed before the Sanhedrin, the highest Jewish court in the land.

4:11 the chief cornerstone: The OT refers
to the cornerstone as the foundation of the
earth (Job 38:6), the foundation (Is. 28:16), the
stone for the corner (Jer. 51:26), the head cornerstone (Ps. 118:22), or the headstone (Zech.
4:7). Thus the image of a cornerstone is used as
both the chief stone and the stone at the corner
of a foundation. In the first century A.D., the
expression *chief cornerstone* was also used to refer
to the stone placed on the summit of the
Jerusalem temple. The cornerstone was the
uniting stone at the corner of two walls that
joined them together. It was the stone built into
one corner of the foundation of an edifice and
was the actual starting point of the entire
building. Thus, Peter used the phrase to point
out that when the people rejected Jesus Christ,
they rejected the One who completed the plan
of God for humankind. The phrase and its significance here would have been well understood in the first century, especially among the
Jewish rabbis and people who knew the Scriptures.

4:12 no other name: Only by placing faith
in the historical Jesus—the One who came,
died, and was raised again—can a person be
saved.

4:13 Even though **Peter and John** were
uneducated Galilean fishermen, they spoke
with confidence and freedom. Their presentation of the gospel was powerful because they

---

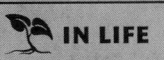 **IN LIFE**   **Sharing Things in Common**

The first Christians were extraordinarily generous. In fact, "they had all things in common" (Acts
4:32–35), an ideal that pure communism advocated but never achieved. So were these first
believers in some sense communists?

No. In the first place, they were not setting up an economic system here, but simply responding to
each other with gracious, Christlike compassion. Such behavior was one powerful result of the outpouring of the Spirit (2:1–4). Unfortunately, not all NT believers demonstrated that kind of concern
(5:1–11; 1 Cor. 6:8; James 4:1, 2).

Furthermore, Scripture never mandates an equal distribution of goods, nor does it call for the elimi-
nation of property or ownership. This passage (along with Acts 2:44, 45) is a historical account, not a
doctrinal treatise. It documents the work of God in building the early church.

In that day, as in ours, there were both rich and poor Christians (2 Cor. 8:2; 1 Tim. 6:17–19). And
when the NT does address issues such as wealth, care for the poor, work, equality, widows, slaves,
and public justice, it inevitably calls believers to compassion and generosity; but not to asceticism, the
idea that one can become more godly through self-denial and renouncing worldly wealth. In fact, Paul
warns against that (Col. 2:18–23). The Bible condemns the love of wealth, not its possession, as a
root of all kinds of evil (1 Tim. 6:9, 10).

were personal witnesses of everything they spoke about (1:22).

4:14–18 they could say nothing: The Sanhedrin knew that the miracle was real. The apostles offered their explanation: the miracles were the work of the resurrected Christ. But instead of believing, the members of the Sanhedrin concerned themselves with "damage control." They tried to intimidate the apostles by warning them not to **speak** or **teach in the name of Jesus.**

4:19–22 listen to you more than to God: There is no authority apart from God. When human authority rejects God's authority, it becomes twisted and loses its right to demand compliance (5:29). From the beginning, God's people have resisted any command that was against God's will (for example, the Jewish midwives of Ex. 1; Moses' parents in Heb. 11:23; Shadrach, Meshach, and Abed-Nego in Dan. 3).

4:23–31 The response of Peter and John's **companions** after the apostles' release was a spontaneous outburst of praise, song, and prayer.

4:32–37 Luke notes that for the early Christians, being filled with the Holy Spirit meant not only proclaiming the Word of God, but also sharing their possessions with those in **need.**

5:1, 2 Ananias and **Sapphira** wanted to have a reputation like that of Barnabas (4:36, 37), but they did not have the same character he had. At a time when others were seeking to serve their fellow believers, Ananias and Sapphira were seeking to serve themselves.

5:3 why has Satan filled your heart: Ananias and Sapphira believed in the Lord Jesus Christ; however, they had succumbed to the temptations of greed and pride. Note that the same word *filled* is used here in connection with Satan as is used in 4:8 of the Holy Spirit. The term means to take possession of or control. God's children, who have been freed from the tyranny of Satan, have the ability to choose whom they will allow to control them. When we choose to sin, we open the door to Satan. The Evil One tempted Ananias and Sapphira with wicked desires and thoughts, and they yielded their will to these temptations. **lie to the Holy Spirit:** The author of all lies is Satan (John 8:44). When Ananias and Sapphira deliberately lied, they took upon themselves the moral character of the one who is behind all lies, the devil himself.

5:4 You have not lied to men but to God: The Holy Spirit is the third person of the triune Godhead. To lie to Him (v. 3) is to lie to God. **in your own control:** Ananias and Sapphira could have kept a part of their proceeds or they could have kept it all; their stewardship was between them and the Lord. But the problem was that they wanted others to believe they had sacrificed everything when in fact they had given only a portion to the Lord.

5:5–7 fell down and breathed his last: The severity of the punishment may seem extreme to some people, much like the story of Achan in Josh. 7:16–26. However, Prov. 6:16–19 tells us how God feels about deception and division. The early church was vulnerable to great spiritual danger. Yet Jesus had promised (Matt. 16:18) that the power of hell would not destroy this fledging church in its infant stage. God

---

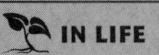 **IN LIFE**   **The Danger of Lying to God**

The dramatic account of Ananias and Sapphira (Acts 5:1–11) immediately after the mention of Barnabas (4:36, 37) draws a stark contrast between two kinds of people. On the one hand, Barnabas serves as a positive model of sincere faith, as evidenced by his open-handed generosity. On the other hand, Ananias and Sapphira serve as negative models.

Externally, they appeared the same. Like Barnabas, they sold land and brought money to the church, where they "laid it at the apostles' feet" (4:37; 5:2). But internally, they had a radically different commitment.

The sins that Peter named—lying to the Holy Spirit (5:3) and testing the Spirit (5:9)—indicate that they were playing games with God. Peter noted that the source of their deception was Satan. As the ultimate liar (John 8:44), Satan had filled their hearts with lies, in contrast to the Holy Spirit, who fills the heart with truth (14:16, 17; Eph. 5:6–21). And like Israel, they were testing the Spirit (1 Cor. 10:1–13), testing the limits of what He would permit, trying to see how much they could get away with.

God dealt severely with this couple by making an example of them. As a result, fear came upon the church (Acts 5:5, 11)—not a cringing fear of dread, but a heightened respect for God's holiness, His moral purity. The incident still stands as a bold warning to believers today about relating to God.

would move with great discipline to ensure its purity and survival.

5:8 Peter gave Ananias's wife an opportunity to **tell** the truth. Sapphira would not be disciplined for the sin of her husband. Even though Ananias and Sapphira were married, they were also brother and sister in Jesus Christ. Sapphira was responsible for her own personal relationship with God. When Sapphira committed the same sin of rebellion and deception that her husband had committed, she received her own punishment.

5:9 to test the Spirit: A challenge to God to expose their duplicity.

5:10, 11 the great fear: Evidences the great respect Ananias and Sapphira had among the believers. If God was so severe with these believers, they knew they had better watch their step.

5:12 Signs refers to supernatural occurrences that point to a warning, instruction, or encouragement from God. A sign gave credibility to the fact that what was being said was from God. **Wonders** points to the response to a sign. By its very nature a wonder caused awe in those who saw or heard it. Signs and wonders were given by God to confirm His word (Matt. 12:38, 39).

5:13 none . . . dared join them because of the recent discipline (5:1–11).

5:14 Not only did fear come upon the church because of the discipline, but **believers** were **increasingly** added to the Lord.

5:15 In the ancient world many people believed that a person's **shadow** could possess magical healing powers. The people referred to in this verse were not necessarily Christians, but those who believed that Peter, as an advocate of a new religion, had magical powers. The people imposed their superstitions upon this new faith.

5:16 they were all healed: God, working miracles through the apostles, never failed to bring complete physical restoration.

5:17 Sadducees . . . filled with indignation were threatened by the teaching of the apostles. The people were sympathetic to this movement that challenged the Sadducees' denial of the Resurrection and charged them with the murder of the Messiah.

5:18 The imprisonment of the **apostles** apparently was a common event in the early church.

5:19 an angel of the Lord: The word for *angel* basically means "messenger." The phrase "angel of the Lord" is commonly used in the OT to refer to a spiritual messenger of God, and probably refers to the preincarnate Christ in most instances. Considering the events of this particular passage, it is clear that a supernatural visitor is in view.

5:20 Note that the angel's orders were not to escape from the city, but to return to the **temple** courts, where the disciples had been first arrested, and speak to the people. The fact that the disciples would return to the place of their arrest was an open testimony to the Jewish leaders and the general public that these men were willing to die for the truth they were proclaiming.

5:21–25 While **the council** was meeting to deal with the problem, their prisoners were back at the temple **teaching the people** (v. 25).

5:26 How powerless the **captain** and the **officers** were before God's witnesses.

5:27, 28 bring this Man's blood on us: A response to the apostles' accusation that the Jewish leaders had personally crucified Jesus (v. 30 and note; 4:10). They were not rid of Jesus yet and felt increasingly on the defensive. They refused to accept Jesus as Messiah because they did not want to lose their authority.

5:29 We ought to obey God: As to the accusation of disobedience to authority, Peter put the charge in context. Jesus had said, "You shall be My witnesses" (1:8). The council said, "You shall not be His witnesses" (v. 28). All authority comes from God. When any authority commands what God has forbidden, or forbids what God has commanded, a Christian must obey the Author of all authority, God Himself. We submit to governmental authority because the One who instituted the authority is God Himself. When we submit to government, we are submitting to God.

5:30 Tree here refers to the Cross (Deut. 21:22, 23; 1 Pet. 2:24).

5:31, 32 The declaration that **God has exalted** Him **to His right hand** would have been understood by the Sanhedrin as a reference to the Resurrection. The apostles' claim regarded the resurrected Jesus as equal with God (John 5:18; 10:33).

5:33 The council **plotted to kill them,** as they had disposed of Jesus and later would also of Stephen, all in the name of religion.

5:34 Gamaliel was a highly respected Pharisee, the grandson of the famous Rabbi Hillel, a brilliant spiritual leader. Gamaliel was the teacher of Saul, who would later become the apostle Paul (22:3). Gamaliel was given the honored title of "Rabban," meaning "Our Teacher." It is said in the Mishna—the commentary on the Torah, the first five books of the OT—that when Gamaliel died, "the glory of the Torah ceased, and purity and sanctity died out also." This is an impressive eulogy for a Jewish teacher.

5:35–37 A certain **Theudas** is mentioned by the Jewish historian Josephus, who places

---

⚒ IN DEPTH | Transformed Disciples

Once you've read the early chapters of Acts, and compared them to the closing chapters of any of the Gospels, you can't help but notice the radical change in the disciples. On Passover weekend, in early spring, they run for their lives when Jesus is arrested. They are afraid to stand with Him when He faces death. Peter, the lead disciple, won't even admit to household servants that he is a disciple.

Fifty days later, each disciple is willing to face death alone on behalf of Jesus. In the temple court-yard, within the viewing of Jewish leaders who plotted the execution of Jesus, they speak the same words that got Jesus killed: they proclaim Him Messiah and Son of God.

Something happened during those 50 days to change the disciples—something that wiped away their fear of death.

They had seen the afterlife. They talked with the resurrected Jesus and ate fish with Him along the seashore. Months before they had heard His words, "Do not fear those who kill the body but cannot kill the soul" (Matt. 10:28). But now they believed Him. And then the Holy Spirit fell upon them, making them bold to witness to the risen Jesus, who is Lord over all.

Fearless of death, they witness to Jesus by continuing His teachings and actions. Eventually, early Christian writers report, this costs them their life. But, Jesus would quickly add, not their soul.

Theudas's revolt against Rome around A.D. 44. According to Gamaliel, the revolution by Theudas took place before **Judas of Galilee,** who began the Zealot movement around A.D. 6. The Romans quickly punished Theudas and his followers, forcing the movement underground. Some scholars believe Luke erred in placing Theudas before Judas of Galilee. However, it is more likely that Gamaliel and Josephus spoke of two different men. Theudas was a very common name. There were a number of insurrections and revolution attempts recorded: Josephus himself refers to ten thousand of them. Most likely, the revolution of Theudas that Gamaliel referred to took place before A.D. 6 and was led by a different Theudas than the person Josephus mentions in his history.

5:38, 39 This influential Pharisee argued boldly that the teaching of the apostles might be of God. If so, he knew that teaching would refute the position of the Sadducees that there was no resurrection.

5:40 they agreed with him: God first delivered the disciples from jail by supernatural means, sending an angel from heaven (vv. 19, 20). Then God delivered them through natural means, causing an enemy of Christianity to argue for their release. This passage is proof of the work of God's sovereign hand in history. He can even use the thoughts of those who oppose the gospel to preserve and protect His servants.

5:41 This verse provides the first instance of physical persecution against the followers of Jesus Christ—in this case against the leaders of the Christian movement. The apostles' response would set a precedent for other Christians who

would be persecuted. Instead of complaining or feeling sorry for themselves, they rejoiced that they were **counted worthy** by God to endure the abuse. The apostles knew that more important things than preserving their health and life were at stake. God was using the suffering of the disciples to bring people into His kingdom (Matt. 5:10–12; Phil. 1:29; 2 Tim. 2:12).

5:42 In defiance of the ban they continued **daily,** in public and in private, **teaching** the Good News that the Messiah had come.

6:1 The Hellenists were those of Jewish descent who grew up outside the land of Israel. They spoke Greek, were raised in Hellenistic culture, and used the Greek translation of the Hebrew OT, the Septuagint (2:5). **The Hebrews** were Palestinian Jews who spoke Aramaic and used the Hebrew OT. There may have been an animosity between the groups, even among the new believers, which gave rise to distrust and tension over the care of the **widows** who were **neglected.** In Jewish law, a woman did not receive an inheritance. She was dependent on her husband or another relative.

6:2 should leave the word of God: The issue here was not blame, but rather what could be done to remedy the apparent injustice. The apostles knew that the problem of supporting the needy required attention. Though the apostles were sensitive enough to recognize the problem, they were also careful to recognize the priorities that are placed on church leaders by God. They could not leave what God had called them to do—declaring and teaching the word of God and establishing the church in prayer. **serve tables:** In NT times, business was trans-

The Hebrews and the Hellenists

Tensions developed in the Jerusalem church over alleged discrimination on the basis of language and culture. Scholars differ in their descriptions of the two opposing groups: the "Hebrews" and the "Hellenists." The Hebrews are often described as Aramaic-speaking Jews native to Palestine. The Hellenists were possibly Greek-speaking Jews from outside of Palestine. Most Jews in Jerusalem, however, would have spoken Greek as at least one language, so more likely the Hellenists were Diaspora (foreign) Jews, or their children, who had settled in Jerusalem. Some of these foreign Jews probably had come from places such as Cyrene, Alexandria, Cilicia, or Asia (Acts 6:9).

Widows were a disadvantaged segment of ancient society, invariably poor and easily oppressed. Jewish people traditionally cared for the widows and other poor through the charity collections of local synagogues. The Hellenist synagogues, however, probably had more widows to care for than other synagogues, hence were stretched to the limit in their capacity to help. Since it was considered pious to spend one's last days in Jerusalem, many foreign Jewish men moved to Jerusalem when they retired, eventually leaving an inordinate number of foreign Jewish widows needing support.

This broader societal problem spilled over into the church: how would they care for the foreign Jewish widows among them? And how could they be sure to keep this minority group within the church from feeling second-class? Most people in antiquity simply told offended minorities to be quiet, but the apostles had a different solution: they selected members of the Hellenist minority to run the food distribution program. All seven of those selected have Greek names (6:5), suggesting that all or most were foreign Jews. These seven Hellenists were commissioned for the office of charity distributor, a highly respected position in Jerusalem (6:6).

acted over tables. The work of administrating and distributing care to those in need would have been carried on over tables and thus was a ministry of service rather than a ministry of speaking. The words *serve* here and *ministry* in v. 4 translate Greek words that are related to the English word *deacon*.

6:3 seek out: The leaders of the church included the congregation in the search process. The local council in Jewish communities usually consisted of **seven men** known as the "seven of the town." The men who would be chosen would be known among the people for their **good reputation** because they were **full of the Holy Spirit and wisdom.** The men's lives were consistent with their confession of faith. They knew the will of God and understood how to carry it out in their lives (Eph. 5:15–18). They could be trusted with responsibility and authority.

6:4 prayer and . . . word: Note the order here. Prayer was primary for the apostles (2:42).

6:5 they chose Stephen . . . Nicolas: All these names are Greek. The selection of Hellenists no doubt was a wise and gracious gesture to the people who had initially raised the complaint concerning the widows (v. 1).

6:6 The laying on of **hands** was not for these men to receive the Holy Spirit, because the seven men were already "full of the Holy Spirit" (vv. 3, 5). Instead the apostles were conferring on these men the responsibility of car-rying out the ministry. The laying on of hands was a meaningful tradition that dated back to the days of Moses (Num. 27:15–23), and it identified people with the ministries to be performed.

6:7 the word of God spread: What Jesus Christ had done in the lives of these people was spreading throughout the region. Men and women became **disciples** who lived in submission to Christ's lordship. They were not ashamed of their faith, but with great boldness they went out to bear witness to the truth of the gospel that had changed their lives. This is what Jesus promised would happen. Through people sharing with those who had yet to hear the Good News, the church experienced dramatic growth. Those who came to know Christ did not keep that knowledge to themselves, but went out and told others. **a great many of the priests:** It is estimated that in Jerusalem there were some eight thousand priests. Luke is not referring here to those who attacked the faith (4:1, 2; 5:17, 18). Most priests were not from the high priestly families. They had ordinary vocations that permitted them to serve their turn in the temple periodically—much like Zacharias, the father of John the Baptist. These were humble, devoted men of God who became **obedient to the faith,** recognizing Jesus as the Christ. Their service in the temple was enhanced because they understood the truth behind the rituals they performed.

6:8 Stephen was full of wisdom (v. 3), full of the Holy Spirit (v. 5), and **full of faith and power.** He had the gifts, the boldness, and the brilliance to be a powerful witness; yet even his witness would be rejected by the religious leaders. Hearts are opened only by God, not by our gifts, boldness, or brilliance.

6:9–11 the Synagogue of the Freedmen: A synagogue was a local place of worship, a community center for worship and studying the Scriptures. In contrast, the temple was the one worship center for all Judaism, the focus of Jewish rituals such as sacrifice. There were many synagogues both in Judea and throughout the Roman world. The one referred to in this verse was for Hellenistic Jews from outside Jerusalem.

6:12, 13 Resistance to the gospel had gone from discussion to debate, from debate to slander, and from slander to violence. The antagonist **stirred up the people** by convincing them that the essence of the Jewish faith—the things held as most sacred: the temple, the Law, Moses, and even God—was under attack by Stephen. The issue was not the work of Christ on the Cross but the core of traditional Jewish religion.

6:14 this place: The importance of the temple would be ended by the gospel that Stephen preached (7:48). That gospel would fulfill the revelation of God to **Moses,** but also **change the** Mosaic **customs** as understood by the Jewish leaders. The rest of Acts describes these conflicts (15:22–29; 21:27–29; 24:5–21).

6:15 Stephen was so full of the Spirit that his **face** was radiant (2 Cor. 3:18).

7:1 The high priest presumably was Caiaphas, the man who had presided over the Sanhedrin's trial of Jesus.

7:2, 3 The God of glory appeared: God intervened in history again and again to speak to His people. When God first spoke to **Abraham,** it was not in the temple of Jerusalem; it was not even in Palestine.

7:4 The text does not explain why Abraham settled **in Haran** when the Promised Land was Canaan. All we know is that Abraham chose to wait for his father to die before he journeyed to the Promised Land (Gen. 12:1).

7:5 gave him no inheritance in it: God moved Abraham along his spiritual pilgrimage from blessing to blessing. Possession was not the goal, apparently, since God would not let

---

✠ IN CONTEXT | The Synagogue

In nearly every city in which we find Jesus or Paul in the NT, we also find a synagogue for the Jewish population—even in Jerusalem, the home of the temple, the center of worship. No one knows when synagogues came into being. Some scholars believe that synagogues are hinted at in Ps. 74:8. Certainly instruction and debate must have occurred in some organized manner and in some building within the villages and cities away from Jerusalem during OT times.

Yet most scholars agree that the NT form of the synagogue probably began taking shape after the temple in Jerusalem had been destroyed and during the Exile. With their people scattered around the known world, displaced Jews needed meeting places within their new communities where they could learn about the faith of their fathers and worship God.

By the time of Jesus and Paul, synagogues served as local centers of worship, education, and government in the Jewish community. Although subject to the law of the land, each synagogue had its own government, led by elders who were empowered to exercise discipline and punish members. The rebuilt temple in Jerusalem remained the center for sacrificial worship and the site at which to celebrate appointed feasts. But the synagogue played an ever-increasing role in the religious instruction of the Jews. In fact, one tradition claims that there were anywhere from 394 to 480 synagogues within Jerusalem itself around A.D. 70.

According to tradition, a synagogue was established wherever there were as many as ten Jewish men. The principal meeting was on the Sabbath, and a typical service consisted of the recitation of the Shema, a confession of faith in the one God (Deut. 6:4–9), prayers, scripture readings from the Law and the Prophets, a sermon, and a benediction.

It was in first-century synagogues that the Christian faith began taking hold. Paul and other missionaries never rejected their Jewish faith, but rather saw Christ as the fulfillment of all that they had been taught in the synagogues. Their fellow worshipers also believed in the one true God, studied the Scriptures, and looked for the coming Messiah. For the early Christian missionaries, the local synagogues were the logical places to start their ministries.

Abraham settle down—to stagnate in God's past blessing.

7:6, 7 Before Abraham's **descendants** would be allowed to enjoy the land as their home, they would be tested in a furnace of affliction **in a foreign land.**

7:8 The covenant of circumcision was the symbol given to Abraham that he might never forget that God had promised to bless him. The sign of this promise was transmitted from generation to generation, from Gen. 17 to the time of Stephen's confrontation with the Sanhedrin. Abraham was saved by faith (Gen. 15:6), and the symbol of circumcision was an outward sign demonstrating the genuineness of

his faith. Similarly, God would bless Stephen's audience not because of their circumcision, but because of their faith.

7:9, 10 The patriarchs refers to Jacob, the grandson of Abraham, and his twelve sons. Jacob's name, meaning "Usurper," was changed by God to Israel, meaning something like "God's Defender." His twelve sons were the founders of the twelve tribes of Israel.

7:11–13 The **famine** proved to be the providential means of bringing Joseph's brethren to Egypt in search of grain—and more importantly, of reconciling them with Joseph.

7:14, 15 Stephen stated that **seventy-five** people in all went to Egypt. Genesis 46:26 indi-

---

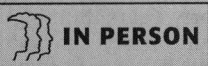 **IN PERSON** | # Stephen, the First Christian Martyr

Ethnic tension played a decisive role in the trial and death of Stephen, the church's first martyr. Other members of the early church faced the council (Acts 6:12; 4:1–23), but it was Stephen, probably a Hellenist, who first died for his faith.

Hellenists, Jews born outside of Palestine, were among those first attracted by the gospel. Treated as second-class citizens by native-born Jews, many found acceptance in the early church. But it could be that as the new faith threatened to further alienate Hellenistic Jews from the full-blooded majority, some Hellenists (6:9) had a motive to try to discredit the Christian movement.

Their opposition focused on Stephen, a dynamic, emerging leader who enjoyed in the church a prominence that would have been denied him in the Hebrew community. His trial and murder (ch. 7) show that the Hellenists were willing to sacrifice one of their own as a demonstration of loyalty to the ruling system.

The strategy worked. Stephen's death precipitated a great persecution of believers, sanctioned by the council and led by a new young leader, Saul of Tarsus (8:1–3; 9:1, 2).

The Council

The council, or Sanhedrin, was the highest ruling body and supreme court of the Jews.

- Led by the high priest, the most powerful Jewish official in the city.
- 71 members, including priests, leading men (elders), and experts in Mosaic law (scribes).
- In the first century, dominated by two major parties, Pharisees and Sadducees (see "Party Politics of Jesus' Day" at Matt. 16:1).
- Allowed by Rome to oversee religious, civil, and criminal issues in the province of Judea.
- Politically: could appoint kings and high priests, make war, gerrymander the city, and expand the temple.
- Judicially: could judge traitorous priests, false prophets, rebel leaders, and rebellious tribes.
- Religiously: could ordain certain services, such as the Day of Atonement.
- Had its own police force.
- Prevented by Rome from exercising capital punishment.
- Prominent members mentioned in the Bible:
    Joseph of Arimathea (Mark 15:43)
    Annas and Caiaphas, high priests (Luke 3:2)
    Nicodemus (John 3:1; 7:50)
    Gamaliel (Acts 5:34)
    Ananias (23:2)
    Possibly Tertullus, an orator (24:1, 2)
    Possibly Saul, a student of Gamaliel (22:3)

cates that sixty-six people accompanied Jacob to Egypt, not including Jacob, Joseph, and the two sons of Joseph. Stephen derived the number seventy-five from the Septuagint translation of the OT. The translators apparently added nine wives (Gen. 46:26 says the number sixty-six did not include the wives). It was only nine and not twelve because the wives of Judah and Simeon had died and Joseph's wife was already in Egypt.

7:16 Why did Stephen make the point that the patriarchs were buried in **Shechem?** At the time of Stephen's defense, Shechem was the center of Samaritan life. Nearby was Mount Gerizim, the site of another temple (John 4:20). Stephen was charged with speaking against the temple in Jerusalem as if this were tantamount to speaking against God Himself. Stephen's point was that God had been speaking and moving in the lives of His people in and out of Jerusalem, with and without a temple. The most important address God made to His people was at Mount Sinai, which was nowhere near Jerusalem.

7:17–19 Abraham's descendants enjoyed prosperity and great growth that proved threatening to the Egyptians and to Pharaoh, **who did not know Joseph.**

7:20, 21 One might say, "what an unfavorable time for Moses to be born." In reality, it proved to be very timely.

7:22 No person has been given the attention in Jewish tradition that **Moses** has. It is said that Pharaoh initially had no son; therefore, Moses was being prepared by Pharaoh's daughter to succeed to the throne. For this reason, Moses was educated **in all the wisdom of the Egyptians.** Later, Pharaoh had a son of his own to succeed him instead of Moses. Jewish tradition also states that Moses became a great captain among the Egyptians, leading them to victory against the Ethiopians. Thus he was **mighty in words and deeds.**

7:23–29 In the opinion of some Jewish rabbis, **forty** was the age at which a man had grown to maturity. Moses' life is divided into three parts: the first forty years in the palace of Pharaoh, the second forty years in the desert, and the third forty years carrying out God's will to deliver His people. Moses began his period of wilderness training after he had tried to free the Israelites in a way that God had not chosen. We must be careful to do God's work in God's way, in God's time, and for God's reasons. It has been said that Moses spent forty years thinking he was somebody, then spent forty years finding out he was nobody. Finally, he spent forty years finding out what God could do with somebody who was nobody.

7:30–34 In relating the burning bush incident, Stephen once again underscored the fact that God is free to reveal Himself wherever He pleases. Wherever God does so, that ground becomes **holy ground.**

7:35–41 Stephen pointed out that **Moses,** the very one the Jewish leaders accused him of speaking against (6:11), was rejected by the leaders' forefathers as God's appointed leader and redeemer—just as the leaders were rejecting Jesus. It was this same Moses who spoke of the coming of Jesus in Deut. 18. Stephen challenged the religious leaders of his day either to believe

---

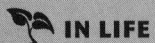 **IN LIFE**   **The Education of Moses**

"It doesn't matter whether you have an education," some people say, "God can use you anyway." True, God can use anyone, with or without formal education. But Moses' learning "in all the wisdom of the Egyptians" (Acts 7:22) proved to be a valuable asset when the Lord called him to lead Israel out of captivity.

Moses spent the first third of his life—40 years—in Egypt. Raised among royalty, he was exposed to the impressive culture of the pharaohs. The curriculum likely included political science, public administration, religion, history, literature, geometry, and perhaps even engineering and hydraulics.

But that was not the end of Moses' education. He spent another 40 years in "graduate school" in the desert, studying animal husbandry while interning as a shepherd. He also learned about public health and primitive communities. Altogether, the first two-thirds of Moses' life prepared him for his most challenging job—leading Israel through the wilderness.

Intelligence and education alone don't make someone fit to serve God. Indeed, an educated person can hide behind his or her learning in order to avoid dealing with God. Young Saul fell into that trap (Acts 22:3–5), as did his fellow Pharisees. So did the philosophers at Athens (17:16–34). But as Stephen pointed out, the problem is not with the intellect but with the will; the danger comes not from embracing knowledge but from resisting God (7:51).

all of what Moses taught or none of it. **our fathers would not obey:** The Talmud, the Jewish commentary on the OT, calls the rebellion involving the golden calf "that unspeakable deed." The rabbis did not want to talk about it, forbidding a translation of the account in the vernacular for the synagogue services. The Jewish religious leaders wanted to bury the incident, but Stephen wanted to dig it back up.

7:42, 43 God . . . gave them up: Stephen warns his accusers that God may abandon Israel if the light of the gospel is rejected, just as He once sent idolatrous Israel **beyond Babylon.**

7:44, 45 The ancient **tabernacle** had been the focus of the Israelites' national worship. Even after the miraculous deliverance from Egypt there was a tendency among the people to forget God's presence with them. The tabernacle was a constant testimony of God's presence no matter where the people went. Paul tells us that *we* are the tabernacle, the temple of God (1 Cor. 3:16). We can never move out of the presence of God, for we carry His presence with us (Ps. 139).

7:46–50 It was David's desire to give God a permanent **dwelling place.** The danger of David's request was that some might identify the presence of God with one place, as if God were confined to that location. God honored David's desire by permitting his son Solomon to build such a house and by filling it with the Shekinah glory, a demonstration of His presence. But God did not live in the temple. The Creator cannot be confined by anything He has made. His presence fills all that He has made. Solomon understood this when he dedicated the temple (1 Kin. 8:27–30). In his speech, Stephen emphasized that God could not be confined to **temples made with hands.**

7:51 You always resist the Holy Spirit: Here Stephen turned from history to direct accusation.

7:52 Which of the prophets: Stephen put the council on the spot. The members of the council wanted to appear open to God's truth, but they and their ancestors rarely wanted to hear God's truth through His messengers. Jesus made essentially the same charges in Matt. 23:34–36. Stephen did not shrink from accusing the Sanhedrin of handing Jesus over to death, thus becoming His **murderers.** He used even stronger language than Peter had (3:13–15).

7:53 Their guilt was deepened because they had received the **law** but refused to obey it. **Angels** were present at Sinai (Gal. 3:19; Heb. 2:2).

7:54 cut to the heart: An expression frequently used to express conviction of sin or anger (2:37). The Holy Spirit still works this way today.

7:55 Stephen at that moment was **full of the Holy Spirit,** which was evidenced by the fact that all he wanted to do was please God. He was consumed only with doing God's will by responding to this terrifying moment in the way that would glorify Him. Stephen completely trusted the Holy Spirit to empower him to respond in the proper way.

7:56 I see . . . the Son of Man: Gazing at death may be terrifying, but gazing past death to the presence of Jesus waiting for the believer is the hope that dissolves the fear. We have the opportunity to glorify God in the face of death, boldly declaring our confidence in the fact that we will spend eternity in the presence of God. Stephen's use of the title *Son of Man* is similar to the Lord's appellation of Himself in Matt. 16:13 and the apocalyptic statements about the Messiah in Dan. 7:13. The term usually carried the idea of the One who is God's coming ruler. Unusual here is that Jesus was standing rather than seated. His being seated indicates His rule, while the standing may indicate His coming, especially here in a pre-second coming to receive Stephen.

7:57 stopped their ears . . . with one accord: The truth was too painful to bear; anger unified them in a mob spirit.

7:58 They . . . stoned Stephen in violation of the law. The Romans did not permit the Jews to inflict capital punishment; Pilate had to authorize the death of Jesus. This is the first mention of **Saul** of Tarsus.

7:59, 60 Because Jewish law did not allow an execution within the walls of the Holy City, the religious leaders took Stephen outside the city walls. Jewish custom was that the first witness would push the condemned person face forward into a pit some twelve feet deep. If the man survived the fall, the body would be turned over and large boulders would be thrown down on his chest to crush his ribs. If he remained alive, stones would be thrown by the whole congregation. The situation may have been a little different with Stephen, perhaps due to the executioners' haste; the text indicates that Stephen knelt (v. 60). **Lord Jesus, receive my spirit:** Stephen's work was done. He was immediately ushered into the presence of Jesus (Luke 23:43; 2 Cor. 5:8; Phil. 1:21–23). **Lord, do not charge them:** As Jesus had done, Stephen requested mercy for his killers.

8:1, 2 The church father Augustine wrote that the church owes Paul to the prayer of Stephen. **Saul,** who later became the apostle Paul, never forgot the way Stephen died—he also did not conceal that he was in full agreement with the killing (22:20). God promises in Rom. 8:28 that all things work together for good. Even though Paul was struggling against the work of the early church and the **church** was experiencing its worst **persecution** up to that time, it was this struggle that would eventually lead Paul, the man who wrote at least half of the NT, to eternal life. **they were all scattered:** This phrase speaks of scattering seeds on the ground so that something will grow. The members of the church in Jerusalem may not have understood what was happening to them, but Jesus would not let His church become limited racially, culturally, or geographically. These early believers became missionaries as much as refugees. Previously the efforts to suppress the followers of Jesus were confined to beating and imprisoning the apostles. At this point the entire church began to pay the price of discipleship. Even today God is building His church and through His sovereignty will direct our ways. **except the apostles:** The initial target of the great persecution was the Hellenistic or Greek-speaking Jewish believers, in the person of Stephen.

8:3 Stephen's death supplied the spark for the persecution, and Saul supplied the leadership (v. 1). **He made havoc** describes a wild boar ravaging something in an attempt to destroy it (22:4, 19; 26:9–11). Saul had all the legal papers he needed to direct this persecution, and he had the authority to put people to death. Saul was arresting the Christians, **men and women,** and taking **them to prison.** After Saul was converted to Christ, the Lord appeared to Ananias, instructing him to go minister to Saul. However, because Ananias had heard about the tremendous pain and suffering Saul had afflicted upon the Jewish believers, he was afraid to go (ch. 9).

8:4 everywhere preaching the word: The church would no doubt increase greatly if more believers did this today.

8:5–12 Philip went to preach the gospel to Samaria as Jesus had commissioned (1:8). In the first century, the Jews and the Samaritans hated each other. The Jews considered the Samaritans half-breeds and religious deviants. Following the fall of the northern kingdom of Israel in 722 B.C., Samaria had been resettled by colonists brought to the land by the Assyrians. These colonists intermarried with the remaining Jews, and the Samaritans were descendants of these mixed marriages. The Samaritans rejected the OT Scriptures beyond the five books of Moses. Furthermore, they built a rival temple on Mount Gerizim. To express their disdain for the Samaritans, Jews traveling to Galilee would generally avoid Samaria by crossing over the Jordan River into Perea. But the gospel message transcended the first-century barrier between the Jews and Samaritans. The Spirit of God created a loving fellowship of believers out of the hate that existed. The formation of the Samaritan church indicates that there is no room for racism in the church (1 Cor. 12; Gal. 3:26–28), for Jesus died for the sins of the whole world.

8:13 Simon himself also believed: Though this man was baptized, he had a long way to go in Christian doctrine and personal growth. Some people believe Peter's words in v. 21 indicate that Simon's confession and baptism were not genuine. Church history later associates Simon with heresy and identifies him as an enemy of the Christian faith. His actions have given to the vocabulary of the church the word "simony," which means buying and selling of church offices.

8:14 the apostles . . . sent Peter and John: Jesus had given "the keys of the kingdom" (Matt. 16:19) to Peter. He was the one God would use to open the doors to the Jews (ch. 2), the Samaritans (ch. 8), and the Gentiles (ch. 10).

8:15, 16 that they might receive the Holy Spirit: Peter and John were the official messengers from Jerusalem to tell the Samaritans what had occurred at Pentecost. The Samaritans had to know that salvation came from the Jews; the Jews, in turn, had to understand that the same salvation had come to the Samaritans. Jesus said in John 17 that the world would know that Jesus came from the Father when the world saw the unity of the body of Christ. With the tremendous hatred that existed between the Jews and Samaritans, God demonstrated to both sides that they would be united together as a church. The dependence of the Samaritans upon the Jews to receive the gift of the Holy Spirit was the healing sign that the two sides were to become one. When Peter later preached to the Gentiles, they immediately believed and received the gift of the Holy Spirit without the laying on of hands (ch. 10). This served as a sign to the Jews that the same gift was being given to the Gentiles as well. The Holy Spirit was the unifying factor that would bring Jews, Samaritans, and Gentiles into one body.

8:17 laid hands on: A common practice in the early church (13:1–3; 1 Tim. 4:14). In this case it was evidently done in connection with the prayer for the Samaritan believers to receive the **Holy Spirit.**

8:18–25 Simon saw . . . the Holy Spirit was given: The text does not indicate what exactly Simon saw. The gift of tongues was a sign to the nation of Israel (1 Cor. 14:20–22), so it is likely that the same sign was present at each step of the opening of the gospel—at Jerusalem, at Samaria, and at the home of Cornelius (ch. 10). Alternatively, the word *saw* may simply mean that Simon perceived what was hap-

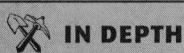 **IN DEPTH** | **Witness in Samaria**

Jesus said that His disciples were to be His witnesses not only in Jerusalem, but also to Judea, Samaria, and the ends of the earth (Acts 1:8). As ch. 8 opens, several years had probably gone by, but the church had not yet left Jerusalem. In fact, it took persecution to move the Lord's people to obedience.

Why was that? Jerusalem was not the apostles' home. The church had no buildings there. The authorities certainly had not welcomed it. Why, then, the reluctance to leave?

One probable factor was that the apostles had grown up in a culture deeply divided along ethnic lines. For them to preach the gospel to Jews at Jerusalem was a challenge, but a manageable one. But to preach to Samaritans was hard. Perhaps that's why the apostles chose to stay in Jerusalem despite Saul's persecution (Acts 8:1).

But a man who was probably a Hellenistic (Greek-speaking) Jew, Philip, crossed the Jewish-Samaritan barrier. A veteran of cross-cultural work (Acts 6:1–7), Philip knew by personal experience what it meant to be a second-class citizen. When he preached Jesus in the city of Samaria, multitudes responded. The gospel breached the wall of separation.

News of the revival reached the apostles in Jerusalem, and they dispatched Peter and John to investigate. The two Galileans must have been stunned and no doubt humbled by what they found. John, who once had asked to call down fire from heaven on unbelieving Samaritans (Luke 9:52–54), now joined Peter in praying for the Holy Spirit to come upon the new believers.

Ironically, Peter condemned Simon the magician for trying to purchase the Spirit's power with money. "I see that you are poisoned by bitterness and bound by iniquity," he told him (Acts 8:23). But the poison of bitterness and the bondage of iniquity also were behind those who allowed ethnic differences to prevent Samaritans and others from entering the kingdom.

As they returned to Jerusalem, Peter and John were changed men. Notice that they finally began to preach in the Samaritan villages (8:25). The wall of ethnic hatred was breaking down. Samaritans were now embracing the gospel—and at least two of the apostles were beginning to embrace Samaritans.

pening. **Give me this power:** Verse 13 indicates that Simon was a believer. However, he confused the work of God with his previous magical practices. Because others had paid him for the secrets of his magic, he may have simply thought that this was the best way to approach Peter. He soon learned the error of his ways.

8:26 go toward the south along the road: This road descended from Jerusalem **to Gaza,** southwest of Jerusalem, near the Mediterranean coast of Palestine. Gaza was the last settlement before the **desert** wasteland stretching to Egypt. This was the road most travelers took to Africa. God had a divine appointment for Philip to meet the Ethiopian eunuch. The gospel would take a leap from the Samaritans to the "end of the earth" (1:8)—in this case, Africa.

8:27 he arose and went: Compare Philip's response with the unquestioning obedience of Abraham (Gen. 22:3). Faith in God means being ready to move without explanation. **a eunuch of great authority:** Technically a *eunuch* is a man who has been emasculated. However, by the first century the term had become a government title used for important military or political officials. The ancient kingdom of Ethiopia was

ruled by a queen mother or **Candace,** who ruled on behalf of her son the king. Because the king was considered the child of the sun, he was too holy to become involved in secular affairs. Therefore, his mother took over the responsibility. The eunuch in this passage was the minister of finance, a prominent position in the Ethiopian regime. He was responsible for distributing the funds of the treasury based on the desires of the queen mother. **had come to Jerusalem to worship:** Many Gentiles in the first century had grown weary of the multiple gods and loose morals of their nations. They were searching in Judaism for the truth. If they accepted Judaism as their faith, they would obey all the rules and regulations of the Law of Moses. This would include being circumcised and baptized. This type of convert was called a *proselyte.* Gentiles who did not become proselytes but did attend the Jewish synagogues to listen to the Scriptures were called *God-fearers.* We cannot be sure which the Ethiopian eunuch was.

8:28, 29 The **chariot** referred to in this passage was probably an ox-drawn wagon. Most likely the eunuch was part of a caravan journeying in the same direction, moving slowly down the road. As was the practice of the day,

IN PERSON | Philip and the Ethiopian Treasurer

The Ethiopian treasurer was probably a convert to Judaism. He had a great yearning to know the God of Israel, as demonstrated by his reading of Is. 53 (Acts 8:28–33) and by the fact that he had to travel at least 750 miles one way to worship in Jerusalem. The trip would have taken him and his servants at least 30 days by chariot. How long would he have stayed? A month? Then he faced a return trip. So he spent at least a quarter of a year to travel to Jerusalem to worship God.

What he heard in the city about the followers of Jesus and their persecution is not recorded. But he responded warmly to Philip and the message about Christ, and became the first known witness—black or white—to Africa. For the second time in Acts 8, the gospel moved outside of the narrow confines of Jerusalem and Judea.

Once again God used Philip, the Greek-speaking Hellenist table-server, to accomplish the task rather than Peter, John, or the other apostles, who were just beginning to realize that the gospel reaches out to all peoples—Hellenists, Samaritans, even Gentiles of all colors and races.

the man was reading aloud. Philip, prompted by the Spirit, spoke to the man about the prophecy of Isaiah, explaining the prophetic words about Christ.

8:30–34 Do you understand what you are reading: This question indicates the dili-

gence that is required in the study of Scripture (2 Tim. 2:15). The Spirit of God does not eliminate the need for human teachers or diligent study. The Spirit is not given to make study needless but to make study effective.

8:35 preached Jesus to him: First-century Jews did not speak much about a suffering Messiah. The Jewish people, facing the yoke of Roman rule, believed that the Messiah would come as the Lion of Judah, a delivering King, not a weak lamb. They believed and taught that the suffering One spoken of by Isaiah was the suffering nation of Israel. Most likely this eunuch had heard the "official" teaching of this passage in Jerusalem but still had some questions. Philip showed him that suffering One was Jesus. He had to suffer on the Cross for the sins of all of humanity.

8:36–38 What hinders me from being baptized: Having heard the message of Christ's sacrifice for sin, the eunuch responded to the conviction of the Holy Spirit. Irenaeus, an early church father who lived between A.D. 130–202, wrote that the eunuch returned to Ethiopia and became a missionary to his own people.

8:39, 40 caught Philip away . . . Philip was found: The Greek word translated *caught* here is also used in 1 Thess. 4:17 for the catching away of the church into the air. Though this passage may say only that Philip went from the desert to **Azotus,** most likely the terminology indicates a miraculous transportation.

9:1 Saul was **still** restless in his zeal to defend his Jewish faith from the new, supposedly dangerous Jewish messianic sect (8:3). **the disciples:** Christians were orig-

DAMASCUS
Paul was converted on his way to this city.

The City of Damascus

Damascus was a transportation and commercial hub for Palestine and Egypt to the south, the Tigris and Euphrates River valleys to the east, and Antioch and Asia Minor to the north. It sat at the intersection of the two main international highways of the ancient Near East, the Way of the Sea and the King's Highway.

inally referred to as "disciples" and "belonging to the Way." Jesus Himself had used both of these titles (Matt. 28:19; John 14:6). *Disciple* means a follower, an imitator, one who has a master.

9:2 The **letters** were documents authorizing Saul to arrest Christians in Damascus, 140 miles northeast of Jerusalem. Rome permitted the Jewish Sanhedrin to control Jewish affairs. At this time the new church was a Jewish affair. **synagogues:** The early Jewish believers in Jesus were still attending the synagogues. The synagogues in Damascus had to cooperate with anyone who had the authorization that Saul possessed. Saul planned to take the followers of Jesus who had escaped to Damascus back to Jerusalem to stand trial before the Sanhedrin (26:9–11), and probably to face a death sentence. **The Way** was a title for the followers of Jesus (19:9, 23; 22:4; 24:14, 22; John 14:6).

9:3–9 A light shone that was brighter than the sun and continued to shine around Saul (26:13). The light was so intense and penetrating that Saul **fell to the ground,** as did everyone who was with him (26:14). **persecuting Me:** In persecuting the church, Saul was persecuting the body of Christ whose individual members are in Christ (1 Cor. 12:27). The arguments of Stephen in his final speech, the spread of the gospel, and the extraordinary response of believers to the gospel were like **goads** to Saul, but Saul in his fury continued to resist such promptings from the Holy Spirit. **hearing a voice but seeing no one:** The men with Saul stood speechless, hearing the voice but not seeing the individual speaking. In ch. 22, Paul indicates that those with him saw the light but did not understand the voice, even though they heard the sound of it. **when his eyes were opened he saw no one:** Ironically while Saul was blind, he would see his own spiritual blindness.

9:10 Not an apostle but a layman, **a certain disciple . . . named Ananias** was ready and available to be used by God. He did not know that God would send him to Saul, the man who had been vigorously persecuting the Christians.

9:11 In ancient Damascus, **the street called Straight** went from one end of the city to the other.

9:12 Saul had received God's revelation by a light, a man, and now, **in a vision.**

9:13 So far in Acts, Christians have been

called "disciples," "believers," and "those belonging to the Way" (5:14; 6:1; 9:2). Here the word **saints** is used. It means those set apart by God for use in His service. It has more to do with why we are here than with how good we are. God is not so much here for us; we are here for Him and His good pleasure.

9:14 authority . . . to bind: The hesitation of Ananias is not surprising. Those **who call on Your** (Jesus') **name** was one of several designations for early believers (v. 21; 11:26; 22:4; 24:5).

9:15, 16 he must suffer: The persecutor became the persecuted. Suffering was promi-

Entrance to the "street called Straight" in Damascus, Syria, where Ananias was sent by the Lord to restore the sight of the apostle Paul (Acts 9:10–19).

nent in Paul's life and his theology; it lent authenticity to his claim to apostleship (2 Cor. 11:23–31; Phil. 3:10).

9:17 Jesus, who appeared to you: Saul was not dreaming on the road to Damascus but instead had seen the resurrected **Lord.**

9:18–21 The people in Damascus **were amazed** that Saul was preaching, because Saul had come to kill Christians, not defend their faith. Saul's fame as a persecutor of Christians was well-known to the Jews in Damascus. The leaders of the synagogues were probably notified of his coming and instructed by the high priest to welcome this zealous defender of Judaism. They seem to have been unnerved at first, not only by the fact that Saul had become a Christian, but by the strength of his faith and of his argument from Scripture that Jesus was indeed the promised Savior of Israel, the Messiah.

9:22, 23 So powerful was Saul's argument from Scripture that Jesus is the Christ that the Jews **plotted to kill him.** They even enlisted the cooperation of the governor of Damascus

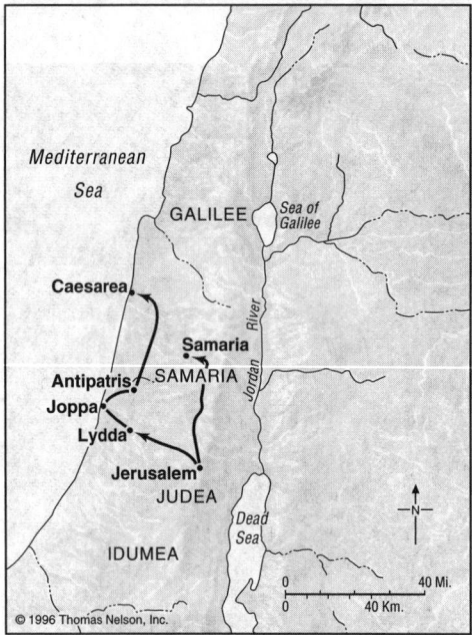

Peter's Missionary Journeys

Peter and John traveled to Samaria to join Philip in the revival there (8:14–25). Peter's missionary efforts described in 9:32–10:48 show the power of God at work. He traveled to Lydda where Aeneas was healed, and in Joppa he restored Dorcas to life and stayed many days with Simon the tanner. The vision of the unclean animals and birds prepared Peter to accept Cornelius's invitation to come to Caesarea, where the gospel was powerfully effective among the Gentiles.

under King Aretas IV of Arabia, who reigned from 9 B.C. to A.D. 40.

9:24, 25 let him down through the wall in a large basket: If the Jewish leaders had caught the Damascus disciples helping Saul pursue his service to the Lord, the result probably would have been widespread persecution. In ancient times city walls contained all kinds of openings—windows without glass. Saul's escape

here recalls the spies' escape from Jericho in Josh. 2:15 and David's escape from King Saul in 1 Sam. 19:12. *Basket* here refers to a wide, flexible container used to carry large quantities of things. This was the first of many attempts on Paul's life. Even with this kind of pressure upon Saul, he still did not hesitate to travel and preach, entrusting his protection and care to the sovereign hand of God.

9:26, 27 It is no wonder that the **disciples** in **Jerusalem** were cautious about Saul, wondering whether his "conversion" was actually an attempt to infiltrate their ranks and catch them all. **Barnabas,** who had the gift of encouragement, saw Paul's true heart and defended him to the other **apostles.**

9:28, 29 Stephen had also debated the Hellenistic Jews (6:9). In a sense, Saul picked up where Stephen left off. The sting of rage against Stephen is now felt by Saul.

9:30 Tarsus, the birthplace of Saul, was about three hundred miles north of Jerusalem and about ten miles inland from the Mediterranean Sea. Tarsus was a well-known university city, surpassed in educational opportunities only by Athens and Alexandria.

9:31–33 Then the churches . . . had peace: This peace was not due solely to Saul's conversion. Tiberius, the emperor of Rome, died around this time. He was replaced by Caligula, who wanted to erect a statue of himself in the temple at Jerusalem. Thus Jewish energy was directed away from persecuting Christians and toward Caligula. Here we see God's sovereign hand at work, giving the early church a short season of respite.

9:34, 35 Jesus the Christ heals you: Everyone who witnessed the healing believed. The outcome of the one physical healing was many spiritual healings. Many **turned to the Lord** because they saw more than a crippled man walking around; they saw proof that Jesus was alive from the dead and had authority over disease.

9:36–38 At Joppa there was a certain disciple named Tabitha. Today known as Jaffa, Joppa was a Mediterranean coastal city about ten miles northwest of Lydda. There also was a Christian community in which a certain disciple was named Tabitha or **Dorcas** (Gk. *dorkas,* meaning gazelle), who had endeared herself to that Christian community because she **was full of good works and charitable deeds.** However, Dorcas had fallen ill and died. She was prepared for burial and placed in the upper chamber. Apparently having heard of the healing of Aeneas by Peter, some disciples from Joppa sent to Lydda to fetch Peter, hoping that he could come and perform an even greater miracle on the behalf of their beloved Tabitha.

IN PERSON   **Peter's Missionary Work**

The Book of Acts records two missionary journeys made by Peter. On his first trip he confirmed the evangelistic work of Philip in Samaria (Acts 8:14). Peter subsequently made a trip along the Mediterranean coast from Joppa to Caesarea, where a Roman garrison was commanded by the officer Cornelius. Peter's ministry to the Gentile household of Cornelius was accepted by the Jerusalem church only when Peter convinced them that the Gentiles had become believers in the same sense as had Jesus' followers, who were filled with the Holy Spirit on the Day of Pentecost (11:1–18).

The church continued to grow as a result of persecution, for the scattered Christians shared their faith in their new home cities (11:19). Meanwhile, in Jerusalem, opposition to the church continued to mount: Herod Agrippa I, whom the emperor Caligula had given the title "king," had James executed and arrested Peter. Agrippa died in A.D. 44 of abdominal pains, according to Josephus (12:23).

The first church to include Gentile Christians was the church at Antioch. More innovative than the Jerusalem church, Antioch became the center of missionary outreach to Gentiles, yet still maintained close ties with Jerusalem. Josephus and other historians record the famine that occurred in A.D. 46 or 47, during the reign of Claudius Caesar (A.D. 41–54). Christians at Antioch sent to Judea by way of Barnabas and Saul their collection for famine relief (11:27–30).

9:39, 40 Tabitha, arise: Peter follows the example of the Master because he was with Jesus one day when the Lord addressed another little girl who had died (Mark 5:38–42). In Aramaic Jesus would have said, "Talitha cumi" ("little girl, arise"). In Aramaic Peter would have said, "Tabitha cumi"—the difference of only one letter. Immediately her life was restored. The power and authority of the risen Jesus was over life and death.

9:41–43 To be **a tanner** was not desirable or socially acceptable in Israel. A tanner had to deal with dead animals, contrary to Jewish ceremonial practices, not to mention the unpleasantness of the work itself and its attendant odor.

10:1, 2 The following two chapters mark an important turning point in the Book of Acts. Those who were scattered by persecution from Jerusalem had been preaching the gospel only to Jews (11:19). At this point, they began to overcome their prejudices and carry the message of Christ to the Gentiles. As a **centurion,** Cornelius would have been part of a cohort, a **regiment** of the Roman military. A legion numbered about six thousand men. Each legion had ten cohorts of about six hundred men each. The cohorts were divided into centuries of a hundred men, and each century was commanded by a centurion, something like a modern sergeant. **Cornelius** was a Gentile of Italian descent. He and his family were "God-fearers," similar to the Ethiopian eunuch (8:27). **Caesarea,** which was about thirty miles north of Joppa on the coast, was the capital of Judea under the Roman procurators.

10:3 The **ninth hour** (3 P.M.) was the hour of prayer in Jerusalem (3:1).

10:4 a memorial before God: Arising like incense in the temple. Prayers of all sincere seekers are effective, as Peter learned to his surprise.

10:5, 6 lodging with Simon, a tanner: God cut away Peter's prejudices by having him stay for many days not only with a Gentile, but with one whose trade Peter likely considered repulsive.

10:7 when the angel . . . departed, Cornelius called: Cornelius's desire was to be pleasing to God. The fact that he readily obeyed the angel is a sign of how much he desired the truth. With this kind of attitude, there is no question that Cornelius was open to receiving the truth of the gospel the moment he heard it.

10:8 Joppa: About 30 miles (48 km) south of Caesarea (v. 1).

10:9–16 While his host was preparing the noon meal, Peter fell into a trance during which he was commanded to kill and eat all kinds of animals, reptiles, and birds. The problem was that the animals were mixed: clean and unclean beasts were gathered together (Lev. 11). Jewish people were taught from childhood never to touch or eat any animal that was unclean. However, here Peter was being commanded by God to do just that. Three times God corrected Peter's resistance with the words, **what God has cleansed you must not call common.** Food may have been his first consideration, but Peter would soon understand the greater message. The vision was a sign from heaven that Jews were no longer to call Gentiles unclean. From that point on, these two groups would be on equal footing before the Father. God was breaking down Peter's prejudices.

10:17–23 Peter went away with them: Though Peter chose to travel in public with three Gentiles, who came from Cornelius, he was careful to take six believing Jewish brethren with him (11:12) as witnesses. Thus,

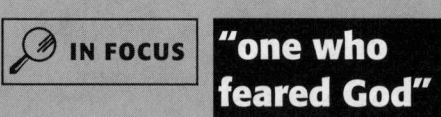

IN FOCUS "one who feared God"

(Gk. *phoboumenos ton theon*) (10:2, 22; 13:16, 26) Strong's #5399; 2316: Simply stated, this expression means "God-fearer." Luke identifies such a category of people throughout the Book of Acts (10:2, 22, 35; 13:16, 26 for the expression "fearing God," and 13:43, 50; 16:14; 17:4, 17; 18:7 for the expression "worshiping God"). The God-fearers were Gentiles who were interested in Judaism but were not necessarily converts or proselytes. They worshiped the same God and observed the same laws as the Jews did, but they did not become circumcised. Many of these God-fearers were the first Gentiles to become Christians. Cornelius was the prototype of such a God-fearer.

he would have double the number of witnesses required by law (Deut. 19:15) in case he was called into question for entering a Gentile house (11:2, 3).

10:24–26 Cornelius . . . worshiped him: The Greek term indicates veneration of God or of an important person. But Peter was quick to disclaim deity (14:15).

10:27, 28 many . . . had come together: The great faith of Cornelius is demonstrated by the fact that he had a house full of people when Peter arrived. They were eager to hear his message (v. 33).

10:29, 30 Fasting was practiced by devout Jews and those who commissioned Paul and Barnabas. As one who feared God, **Cornelius** followed this Jewish custom.

10:31–42 God shows no partiality: The Good News of the gospel is not for a certain population. **In every nation** every kind of person is welcome into the kingdom of God. This is precisely what Christ had told the apostles (Matt. 28:19).

10:43 In order to **receive remission of sins,** one has to believe—nothing more, nothing less.

10:44–46 the Holy Spirit fell upon all those who heard: The Jewish believers present were amazed because they saw that the Gentiles had received the same gift of speaking in **tongues** that they had received (ch. 2). Both here and in Acts 2:4, the Spirit came upon those listening to the word of God, not those praying for the Spirit (compare 11:17). The Jewish believers were amazed because they saw that these Gentiles had received the same gift, speaking in tongues as in Acts 2 and exalting God for His grace to them. This would complete the circle. The Good News had reached the Jews, the Samaritans, and now the Gentiles. All were united by the same faith in the same Lord with the same gift of the Holy Spirit.

10:47, 48 Willingness to **be baptized** is the consistent response in the Book of Acts of all who placed their faith in Christ. It is the appropriate response (Matt. 28:19, 20) of a regenerated heart (2:36–38).

11:1 The Jews were not fond of the **Gentiles.** In some rabbinical writings, the Gentiles were considered to have been created by God to kindle the fires of hell. They were called dogs (Matt. 15:26) and unclean (10:14). Later we will see Judaizers—Christian Jews—who are so legalistic that they tell the Gentiles they must become Jewish and follow all the rites of Moses, including circumcision, before they can come into the church. This was another sign of the prejudice Jews had toward the Gentiles.

11:2 Those of the circumcision refers to Jewish Christians who believed that Gentiles had to become Jews when they became Christians. The Jewish Christians had been circumcised as a seal of the Mosaic covenant and had kept the Jewish laws. They were not pleased that the Gentiles were considered equal to them in the eyes of God, based on nothing more than their faith in Christ. They wanted the Gentiles to be circumcised and to keep the Law of Moses in order to become Christians. **contended with him:** This was not a polite discussion, but an intense quarrel. The Jewish Christians were upset because Peter had broken Jewish law by going into the home of a Gentile and eating with him. The Jewish Christians justified their prejudice by claiming that it was God who had forbidden eating with Gentiles. However, the Levitical laws were not intended to teach ostracism.

11:3 You . . . ate with . . . uncircumcised men: Peter had violated one of the three tests of Jewish fidelity to the law. In their eyes this failure invalidated his Judaism.

11:4–10 in a trance I saw a vision: Because of the importance of the issue of personal

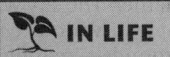 **IN LIFE** | **Overcoming Barriers**

A major breakthrough in race relations is described in Acts 10. For years a virtual wall between Jews and Gentiles had hampered the apostles in sharing Jesus with the Gentile world. But when Peter met Cornelius—an officer of Rome's occupation troops in Palestine—two conversions took place: Cornelius, his family, and his friends came to faith; and Peter came to realize that God wants Gentiles in the church.

God easily could have used Philip the evangelist (Acts 8:5) to bring the gospel to Cornelius. After all, he lived in Caesarea and had already shown his willingness to share the gospel across ethnic lines. But no, God called Peter to bring His message to the Roman centurion. Apparently He wanted to break down barriers against Gentiles in Peter's heart.

How Peter Saw Cornelius

- *Living in Caesarea,* Roman military capital of Palestine (Acts 10:1).
- *A centurion,* commander of 100 occupying Roman troops (10:1).
- *Of the Italian Regiment,* all men from Italy (10:1).
- *Gentile* (10:1).
- *Unclean,* like the unclean animals of the OT dietary laws (10:11–16).
- *Unlawful for a Jew to visit,* as he was from another nation (10:28).
- *Uncircumcised,* therefore not right to eat with (11:3).

In Peter's mind, these factors disqualified Cornelius from serving him dinner, let alone coming to faith. But Peter was following a "Jewish gospel."

God's intention had been that Hebrews would treat their Gentile neighbors cordially (Num. 35:15; Deut. 10:19; Ezek. 47:2). Of course, He also charged His people to exclude heathen practices, particularly idolatry (Lev. 18:24—19:4; Deut. 12:29–31). Inter-marriage was condemned, though sometimes allowed (compare Ex. 34:16; Deut. 7:3; Ezra 9:12; 10:2–44; Neh. 10:30). But the main concern was moral purity.

Through rabbinic tradition strict separation became the rule. By Peter's day, four hundred years of Greek and Roman oppression had only hardened Jewish resolve to avoid as much contact as possible with foreigners.

Peter and the other Jewish believers brought these attitudes with them into the church, which made it almost impossible for them to reach out to Gentiles.

How God Saw Cornelius

- *Devout* (Acts 10:2).
- *A God-fearer,* along with his household (10:2).
- *Generous to the poor* (10:2).
- *A man of prayer* whose prayers and alms were received by God (10:2, 4).
- *Obedient to God's angel* (10:7, 8).
- *Cleansed by God,* so not unclean (10:15).
- *Crucial for Peter to visit* (10:5, 19, 20).

God's view of Cornelius was a contrast to Peter's. Because of Christ, God was ready to throw the doors of faith wide open to Gentiles: "What God has cleansed you must not call common," He sternly declared to Peter (10:9–16). Because of Christ, the centurion could be "cleansed" from sin and be acceptable to God.

But Peter was confused. Should he break with his culture and visit this Gentile, violating traditional codes handed down as if carrying the force of God's law? He had at least two days to sort out his thoughts as he walked to Caesarea to meet Cornelius. His emotional struggle can be seen in his first words to the assembled group: "You know how unlawful it is for a Jewish man to keep company with or go to one of another nation" (10:28).

But God broke down the wall in Peter's heart by pouring out the Holy Spirit on these Gentile believers (10:44, 45).

prejudice, Luke repeats the account of the vision of the sheet and the unclean animals that God used to free Peter from his racial bigotry (10:9–16).

11:11 At that very moment (10:17) the timing of God is a beautiful thing to observe.

11:12–14 Peter had wisely taken **six brethren** with him when he visited Cornelius's home (10:23). He anticipated the argument from "those of the circumcision" (v. 2).

11:15 began to speak: Apparently Peter considered the words he spoke in Caesarea (10:34–43) to be just the introduction to the sermon he had intended to preach. **as upon us:** The manifestation of the Holy Spirit was the same to the Gentiles at Caesarea as it was to the Jews at Jerusalem (10:44). **At the beginning** is a reference to the Day of Pentecost (2:4), approximately ten years earlier.

11:16 baptized with the Holy Spirit: This statement is found seven times in the NT (1:5; Matt. 3:11; Mark 1:8; Luke 3:16; John 1:33; 1 Cor. 12:13). The reference is to a once-for-all act whereby Christ places believers in the care and safekeeping of the Holy Spirit until the day He returns.

11:17 the same gift: The Holy Spirit given to Jewish believers at Pentecost (2:4; 15:8). It is clear from vv. 15–17 that Peter considered Cornelius and his household to have become believers in the same sense as had Jesus' followers, who were filled with the Holy Spirit on the Day of Pentecost.

11:18 granted to the Gentiles repentance to life: This section begins a bold new step in the mission of the church. The Samaritans were part Jewish; the Ethiopian eunuch and Cornelius were Jewish proselytes. Finally the Jewish Christians that made up the early church understood Jesus' commission to them: they were to bring the gospel message to the Gentiles too (1:8).

11:19–21 This **persecution** began when Stephen was murdered for his faith (ch. 7). God often uses tough times to accomplish His will. Jesus said, "You shall be witnesses to Me in Jerusalem, and in all Judea and Samaria, and to the end of the earth" (1:8). God allowed persecution to be the impetus for spreading Christ's witness throughout the land. Those who face such persecution will receive "great reward" in heaven (Matt. 5:10–12). **the Jews only:** At this time it was primarily the Jewish believers who were being persecuted. Consequently, the Jewish Christians were the ones who were moving out and sharing the gospel of Jesus Christ in various regions. They shared the gospel with the Jews because they still met in the local synagogues and held on to many of the Jewish customs.

11:22–24 Seleucus I founded the city of **Antioch,** naming it after his father. The city was cosmopolitan, attracting people of various cultures and ethnic backgrounds—including people from Persia, India, and even China. The gospel proclaimed in Antioch would have had tremendous potential for reaching other areas of the world. Moreover, because the city was culturally diverse, it was not controlled by one religious group, making the people there more open to hearing the truth of the gospel message. **Barnabas,** nicknamed "Son of Encouragement" by the apostles (4:36), was sent to discern what God was doing in the lives of the new converts. When Barnabas saw the grace of God in these converts, he was true to his name and **encouraged** them in their new faith. **Purpose of heart** describes a resolve of the will to make up one's mind about one thing. The resolve here was to remain with the Lord. Barnabas was a man who understood commitment. We would do well to receive the encouragement of Barnabas in our lives. We waste so much of our lives being double-minded (James 1:6–8), not making up our minds about what we believe and what we are going to do.

11:25 Barnabas departed . . . to seek Saul: Because Barnabas was sensitive to the leading of the Holy Spirit (v. 24), God was able to bring Saul of Tarsus to his mind again. The disciples in Jerusalem were afraid of Saul and refused to believe that he was a disciple (9:26). Barnabas, however, had defended Saul before the apostles (9:27).

11:26 The believers were **called Christians** because they worshiped Christ, the Messiah. The historian Josephus called them "that tribe of Christians." Tacitus, the Roman historian, referred to them as "Christians, a name derived from Christ." Originally, the church called themselves "The Way." But later they began to refer to themselves as Christians, despite the fact that the name most likely was originally used to ridicule the believers.

11:27–30 And in these days prophets came from Jerusalem to Antioch. In the first-century church, a prophet belonged to a recognized order in the church (compare 2:17, 18; 13:1; 20:23; 21:9, 10; 1 Cor. 12:28, 29; Eph. 4:11). One of these prophets was a man named Agabus who indicated, prophesying under the influence of the Spirit of God, **that there was going to be a great famine throughout all the world.** Luke is interested in pinpointing the exact time of this famine. Thus he goes one step further in identifying it by saying that the famine occurred in the days of Claudius Caesar (A.D. 41–54). Many extrabiblical sources make note of a succession of bad harvests and extreme famine throughout the entire Roman Empire, especially Palestine, during the reign of Claudius. In response to this prophetic announcement, the believers at the church of Antioch **determined to send relief to the brethren** who lived in Jerusalem and its environs. Thus, they set aside a certain percentage of their income to collect a contribution to be sent to the believers of Judea. This relief fund was to be sent to the elders **by the hands of Barnabas and Saul.** This social and communal interest the church at Antioch had for the church at Jerusalem is not only a pleasing expression of the love of the Lord Jesus for the brethren (10:35), but it marks the beginning of the Pauline practice of accepting the responsibility for caring not only for the souls of those to whom he ministered but for the bodies as well. The church at the end of the twentieth century could well take a lesson from the church at the end of the first century.

12:1–3 Herod the king is Herod Agrippa I, the nephew of Herod Antipas who murdered John the Baptist, and the grandson of Herod the Great who had the children of Bethlehem put to death in his search for Jesus. Herod was not a Jew but an Edomite. The Jews resented this fact, and Herod knew it. **James** was the first of the twelve apostles to die for the sake of the gospel, and the only one whose death is recorded in the NT. Being put to death **with the sword** meant being beheaded. Jesus had told both James and

his brother John that they would drink the same cup of suffering He did (Matt. 20:20–23). For James, this suffering was execution. For John, it was exile. The killing of James by Herod was an attempt to win the favor of the Jewish leaders.

12:4 Four squads of soldiers were to see that Peter did not escape a second time (5:19).

12:5–10 Peter was arrested and slated to be executed like James (v. 2). However, Peter's execution was delayed because it was against Jewish law to have a trial or sentencing during the Feast of Unleavened Bread, better known as Passover. This was Peter's third arrest (4:3; 5:18). During a previous incarceration, Peter had miraculously escaped with the help of an angel of the Lord who opened the gates of the prison (5:19, 20). This time Peter was placed under maximum security in the care of four squads of soldiers of four men each. The soldiers worked three-hour shifts. Both of Peter's wrists were chained, and he had a soldier on each side. Outside Peter's cell, two more soldiers stood guard.

12:11 delivered me from the hand of Herod: Why was Peter's life spared while James's life was taken? The answer is the sovereign will of God. If we believe that God is good and wise, we can trust that what He allowed to happen was part of His wise plan for the good of all of His people. When we place our complete

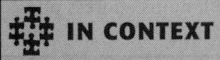 **IN CONTEXT** | ## A Gospel for the Cities

Christianity eventually prevailed as the dominant worldview and social force in the Roman world. One reason: it planted churches in dozens of the empire's major cities by the end of the first century. Christians spread the gospel "to the end of the earth" (Acts 1:8) by establishing strategic, visible communities in urban areas such as Antioch (11:22, 26; 13:1). These groups of believers stood apart from the culture in their beliefs and values, yet engaged the culture in their daily lives and work.

The NT word for "church," *ekklesia,* means assembly or congregation. In the Greek world, the *ekklesia* was a public assembly called together by a herald to discuss legal issues and make community decisions. For example, Paul faced such a gathering at Ephesus, a town meeting that turned into a riot (19:32–41). But *ekklesia* always referred to people—originally to the citizens of a city, and later to a gathering of believers. There is no evidence that it meant a church building until the fourth century A.D.

Interestingly, eight times out of ten the NT uses the word *ekklesia* to refer to all of the believers in a specific city, such as "the church that was at Antioch" (13:1) or "the church of God which is at Corinth" (1 Cor. 1:2). Elsewhere it implies all Christian believers, regardless of geographic location or time in history—what is often called the universal (or catholic) church (Eph. 1:22; 3:10, 21; 5:23–32).

In forming churches, the early Christians did not drop out of society, nor did they form congregations that competed with each other for members (though sometimes members competed with each other, 1 Cor. 1:10–12). Instead, they lived and worked as members of the larger community. Meanwhile, they related to the other believers in their cities as members of a common family in Christ.

trust in the goodness of God, we can find true peace. God is in control despite any appearance to the contrary.

12:12–15 You are beside yourself: It is interesting to note that those who were praying

so fervently for Peter's deliverance (v. 12) should regard as insane the person who informed them that their prayers had been answered. **It is his angel:** This statement may imply a belief in individual guardian angels

 **IN COMPARISON**

The Ministries of Peter and Paul Compared and Contrasted

	Peter	Paul
Formerly known as:	Simon	Saul
First encounter with Christ	Introduced by Andrew at Bethany (John 1:41)	A supernatural vision on the road to Damascus (9:1–6)
Occupation	Fisherman (Luke 5:1–11)	Tentmaker (18:3)
Formal religious training	A disciple of Christ (4:13; Mark 1:16, 17)	A disciple of Gamaliel (22:3); a Pharisee (23:5, 6; Phil. 3:5)
Role	Missionary to the Jews	Missionary to the Gentiles
Strength	Bold preacher and spokesman; leader of the early church	Intelligent defender of the faith and tireless church planter
Ministry experiences	Usually paired with John	Paired with Barnabas (13:1—15:39), then Silas (15:40—17:14), then a number of others
	Preached the great sermon at Pentecost when three thousand believed	Preached everywhere he went, including the famous address on Mars' Hill (17:16–33)
	Healed others (3:1–10; 5:15)	Healed others (14:8–10; 19:12)
	Raised Dorcas from the dead (9:36–42)	Raised Eutychus from the dead (20:7–12)
	Jailed frequently (4:3; 5:18; 12:3)	Jailed frequently (16:23, 24; 21:27–36)
	Gave impassioned sermons to religious authorities (4:5–12; 5:29–32)	Spoke boldly to religious rulers and leaders (22:30—23:6; 26:1–29)
	Experienced a vision in which he was commanded to take the gospel to Cornelius (10)	Experienced a vision in which he was commanded to take the gospel to Europe (16:6–10)
Writings	1 and 2 Peter	Romans; 1 and 2 Corinthians; Galatians; Ephesians; Philippians; Colossians; 1 and 2 Thessalonians; 1 and 2 Timothy; Titus; Philemon
Death	Church tradition says he was crucified upside down.	Church tradition says he was beheaded.

being assigned to believers (Dan. 10:21; Matt. 18:10).

12:16 Peter continued knocking because those praying inside could not believe their prayers had been answered.

12:17 James: The brother of Jesus (15:13; 21:18; Mark 6:3). **the brethren:** Other leaders of the church.

12:18, 19 Then as soon as it was day, there was no small stir among the soldiers. One can imagine the consternation that would have occurred in the minds of the two soldiers on either side of Peter, chained now to no one, the soldiers who stood guard outside the cell, now with no one to guard, and those who guarded the first two wards leading to the outside of the prison. No one had an explanation as to what happened to their prisoner. When Herod looked for him and the report came that he was not to be found, **he examined the guards and commanded that they should be put to death.** The penalty for losing a prisoner was severe in the Roman Empire, and these men took very seriously their responsibility in keeping prisoners secure. But now nothing could be done; the prisoner was gone. Because of this, Herod Agrippa I departed from Jerusalem and went to reside at Caesarea, his other capital.

Although these verses do not advance the narrative, they do provide great insight into the death of Herod Agrippa I. Luke is always interested in keeping a historical perspective in the Book of Acts. Thus, he includes these verses.

12:20 It is unclear why **Herod** was so **angry with the people of Tyre and Sidon.** Both cities were seaports, like Caesarea, the provincial capital of Judea. The dispute may have been an issue of seaport business, since competition was great. The important point was that the cities did not want the angry king to set an economic embargo against them. Through the royal official **Blastus,** the people of Tyre and Sidon received an appointment to present their case to the king.

12:21–24 The voice of a god: The Jewish historian Josephus also provides an account of this display, informing us that in an attempted appeasement of the king the people confessed that he was "more than a mortal." Herod, instead of rebuking the address of deity, enjoyed the adulation—until he discovered the consequence of such blasphemy. The essence of arrogance is the desire for personal divinity, the expectation of being treated as a god. The essence of humility is remembering that God is God and we are not.

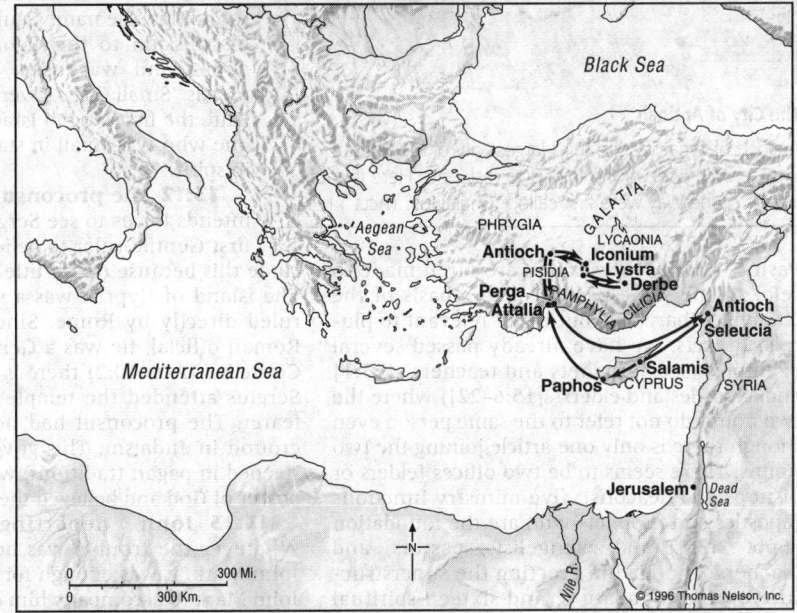

Paul's First Missionary Journey

Sent out from the church at Antioch (13:1–3), Paul and Barnabas went to Cyprus, then to the cities of Galatia in Asia Minor. The Jewish synagogues in these cities provided Paul a platform for preaching the gospel. However, at times he encountered opposition from the synagogues.

12:25 They had fulfilled their ministry, bringing famine relief from Antioch to Judea (11:29, 30).

13:1 Prophets functioned in the early church as proclaimers of God's revelation. **Teachers** explained the meaning of the revelation and helped the people apply it to their lives. In the early church the prophets were the preachers—the ones who communicated revelation directly from the Spirit of God. Evangelists, pastors, and teachers (Eph. 4:11) took what was taught or declared and made it applicable for the daily nurture of people's lives.

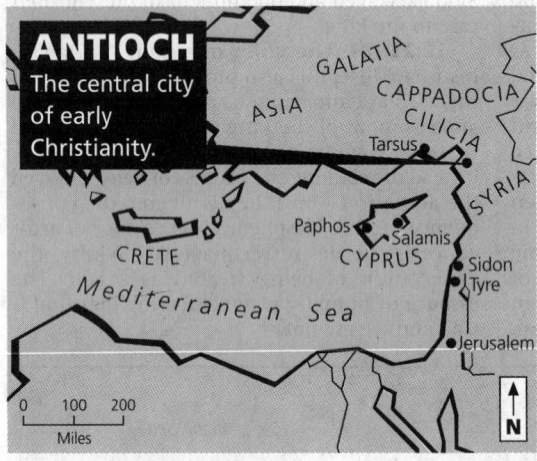

The City of Antioch

Antioch of Syria was the third largest city of the Roman Empire, with 500,000 to 800,000 residents. Here the followers of the Way were first called "Christians" (Acts 11:26).

Pastors and teachers today are often made to refer to the same person on the basis of the Granville-Sharp rule but is not relevant to plurals. In Acts, we have already passed several examples (see "prophets and teachers" [13:1] and "apostles and elders" [15:6–22]) where the two nouns do not refer to the same person even though there is only one article joining the two nouns. There seems to be two offices (elders or bishops and deacons); five ministry functions (apostles and prophets who are the foundation [Eph. 2:20]) and evangelists, pastors, and teachers who lead in erecting the superstructure on the foundation; and sixteen spiritual gifts (four sign gifts, five speaking gifts and seven serving gifts). **Antioch** was the base of operation for Saul.

13:2 ministered to the Lord: As the people carried out what God had given them to do as prophets or teachers, their ministry to the church became their ministry to the Lord.

Whenever we serve each other, God accepts that service as directly unto Him (Matt. 25:31–46). **fasted:** Fasting was practiced by the early church, a practice associated with Judaism. The abstention from food and other distractions was for the sake of praying. It was to help believers focus on what they were taking to God in petition. The idea of fasting was to be able to devote oneself with less distraction to the contemplation of divine things.

13:3 The laying on of **hands** was the church's way of identifying with and affirming the mission to which God had called a particular person.

13:4, 5 John was John Mark, the nephew of Barnabas (12:25).

13:6–12 Luke presents **Sergius Paulus** as the first Gentile ruler to believe the gospel. The island of Cyprus was a senatorial island, which means it was Roman-controlled. As a Roman official, Sergius was a Gentile. Unlike Cornelius (10:2), there is no evidence that Sergius attended the temple or was a God-fearer. This pagan government official was amazed at the power of God and believed the truth.

13:9–11 Saul, who also is called Paul: It was not unusual for a person to have two names. In Paul's Jewish surroundings, the name Saul was used. But in his mission to the Gentiles, his Roman name Paul was used. The name Paul means "Small One." Over against the name Saul, the first king of Israel, was now Paul, one who was small in stature and humble in spirit.

13:12 the proconsul believed: Luke intends for us to see Sergius Paulus as the first Gentile ruler to believe. We can conclude this because of the title given to Sergius. The island of Cyprus was a senatorial island, ruled directly by Rome. Since Sergius was a Roman official, he was a Gentile—and unlike Cornelius (Acts 10:2) there is no evidence that Sergius attended the temple and was a God-fearer. The proconsul had no religious background in Judaism. This government official, steeped in pagan traditions, was amazed at the power of God and believed the truth.

13:13 John, departing from them: Whatever the trouble was between Paul and John Mark, it was enough for Paul not to want John Mark to accompany him on a later journey (15:36–39). John Mark would prove faithful later in Paul's ministry (2 Tim. 4:11).

13:14 Why did Paul and his party pass through **Perga** without any reported sharing of the gospel there? Paul might have had some physical affliction that forced him from the lowlands of Perga to the cooler, higher altitudes of

IN PERSON | Paul, the Apostle to the Gentiles

Ironically, Paul's background not only prepared him to be the early church's chief opponent, but also to become its leading spokesperson. Devout, energetic, outspoken, stubborn, and exacting, Paul became far more troublesome to the Jews than he had ever been to the Christians, not in terms of violence, but ideology. Indeed, he lived with a price on his head as his former colleagues among the Jews sought to destroy him (Acts 9:23–25, 29; 23:12–15; 2 Cor. 11:26, 32, 33).

Perhaps the chief irony of Paul's life was his calling to be the "apostle to the Gentiles" (Acts 9:15; Gal. 1:16; 2:7–9). Paul had been a Pharisee, the very title meaning "to separate." Some Pharisees even refused to eat with non-Pharisees for fear of being contaminated by food not rendered ritually clean. They also separated from women, from lepers, from Samaritans, and especially from Gentiles (or "foreigners").

So for Paul to take the gospel to the Gentiles was a reversal of his life and a thorough repudiation of his background as a Pharisee. Perhaps three people proved invaluable in helping him make this dramatic change: Barnabas, who like Paul was a Hellenistic Jew and came from a Levite background—he embraced Paul and mentored him in the faith when no one else would come near him (Acts 4:36, 37); and Priscilla and Aquila, fellow tentmakers—they joined Paul in business in Corinth and probably discussed the faith and its implications with Paul much as they did with Apollos (18:1–3, 24–28; Rom. 16:3–5).

Paul eventually became Christianity's leading evangelist and theologian. But even as his status in the church rose, his perspective on himself changed. At first he saw himself as an important Christian leader, but then as "the least of the apostles" (1 Cor. 15:9). Later he realized that he was capable of "nothing good" (Rom. 7:18) and was "less than the the the least of all the saints" (Eph. 3:8). Finally he described himself as the "chief" of sinners (1 Tim. 1:15)—and threw himself on God's mercy and grace.

The fearsome Pharisee of Pharisees became the fearless apostle to the Gentiles whose credo was, "To live is Christ, and to die is gain" (Phil. 1:21).

Antioch in Pisidia, some 3,600 feet above sea level. Later, when Paul wrote to the Galatian churches, he spoke about an illness (Gal. 4:13). Paul's affliction may have affected his eyes in some way. Some think Paul had malaria, which left him with disabling headaches, described by the ancients as like a red-hot bar thrust through the forehead. Possibly this was what Paul meant when he referred to his "thorn in the flesh" (2 Cor. 12:7). Antioch in Pisidia was a different city from the Antioch located just north of Palestine in Syria (11:22).

13:15 It was customary for the **rulers of the synagogue** to invite guests to speak to the congregation.

13:16–19 Paul stood up: The rabbis usually remained seated to teach; Paul stood perhaps to be heard better (Luke 4:20, 21).

13:20, 21 Some early manuscripts apply the **four hundred and fifty years** to the period before the **judges** referred to in vv. 17–19. In either case the intended extent of the time reference is vague.

13:22–35 David . . . a man after My own heart: What God saw in David was a deep desire to do His will. Throughout David's entire

life that drive never changed. Unlike King Saul, who was a self-willed man, David confessed his sins and quickly repented of them (Ps. 51).

13:36, 37 He whom God raised up saw no corruption: Paul argued that David could not have been speaking of himself in Ps. 16:10 (v. 35). When David died, his body returned to dust just like everyone else's (see Peter's comments in 2:29–31). David was speaking of the Messiah, who would be raised from the dead as the final proof of His divine Sonship (Rom. 1:4).

13:38–44 everyone who believes is justified: Justification is a legal term meaning "declared innocent." It is a legal declaration that a person is acquitted and absolved. It is by justification that a person is righteous and acceptable to God. The death of Christ was the payment of our sin debt, so that we might be forgiven.

13:45 When Luke refers to **the Jews,** he is not speaking of all Jews. The Jews mentioned in v. 43, those who were urging Paul and Barnabas "to continue in the grace of God," honestly wanted to know the truth. The Jews in this verse were the Jewish leaders, those in the positions of religious authority. When the Jewish leaders saw the crowds following Paul, they changed their minds about Paul and became filled with jealousy, especially since many of the people who had gathered were Jews.

13:46–50 judge yourselves unworthy of everlasting life: A person who convinces himself that he does not need forgiveness from the Holy One has already condemned himself.

13:51, 52 Jews **shook off the dust** when they left a Gentile town. These Jews who rejected the gospel were no better off than unbelieving Gentiles.

14:1–5 Following their previously established pattern, Paul and Barnabas went first to the **synagogue of the Jews** which was located in **Iconium,** in the eastern district of **Phrygia.** The text indicates that **a great multitude** (v. 1) of both Jews and Greeks believed. However, the **unbelieving Jews** began to stir up opposition again to the message of the apostles. Since it took a while for the opposition to become effective, Paul and his team were able to remain there preaching for a **long time.** In Luke's typi-

cally historical fashion, he does not indicate how long a period of time this actually was, making an exact chronology of Paul's travels almost impossible. Finally, the hostile Jews succeeded in inciting a riot which caused Paul and Barnabas to have to leave Iconium. Verse 3 indicates that the message of the gospel was the **word of His grace** and that their ministry was also accompanied by **signs and wonders,** or miracles.

14:1–7 Paul and Barnabas **spoke** with authority because they spoke the truth. The power of God is not in the person who witnesses, but in what is witnessed to.

14:8–13 the gods have come down: The Roman poet Ovid told of an ancient legend in which **Zeus** and **Hermes** came to the Phrygian hill country disguised as mortals seeking lodging. After being turned away from a thousand homes, they found refuge in the humble cottage of an elderly couple. In appreciation for the couple's hospitality, the gods transformed

---

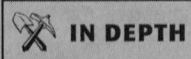 **IN DEPTH** | **Why Did John Mark Go Home?**

Luke does not tell us why John Mark returned to Jerusalem (Acts 13:13), giving rise to all kinds of speculation. A few possibilities:

He was young and felt homesick. Possibly, but we don't know exactly how old Mark was. He had been to Antioch (12:25), but otherwise might never have been outside Palestine.

He reacted negatively to the interaction with Gentiles. On the first leg of the trip (Cyprus), cultural and ethnic overload may have set in. We know how controversial the inclusion of Gentiles in the church proved to be for believers at Jerusalem (15:1–29). If Mark departed because of prejudice, it might explain Paul's refusal to take him on a later journey (15:37, 38). On the other hand, he had worked with the multiethnic church at Antioch with no apparent problems (12:25).

He didn't want to work with Paul. We know that Paul was a hard charger and that his standards were quite high. Perhaps Mark didn't measure up, or perhaps the relational chemistry didn't work, and so Mark decided to go home rather than endure a lengthy trip with a demanding person. But later Paul was eager to have him on board (2 Tim. 4:11) and included him among his fellow laborers (Philem. 24).

He got seasick. No evidence for that except that Mark left as soon as the party hit the mainland at Perga in Pamphylia. But why return home over seasickness?

He was afraid. In Antioch, Mark met a diverse community of believers who showed extraordinary concern and compassion for each other. But on Cyprus he encountered characters like Elymas the sorcerer (13:6–12) and discovered that in gospel outreach, opponents use live ammunition. So he might have left out of fear.

The pace was too hard. Luke calls Mark an "assistant" (13:5), which probably involved making arrangements for travel, food, and lodging, and possibly some teaching. Again, Paul's pace may have outstripped the young man's capacities, and once they arrived at Perga he decided to throw in the towel. But this is pure speculation.

Scripture doesn't tell us why John Mark made the decision to go home. But the encouraging thing is that his return didn't disqualify him from the faith or diminish his spirituality, no matter how strongly Paul felt about it later (15:38, 39). With time and the encouragement of Barnabas, Mark developed into one of the key leaders of the early church who had a lasting impact on the faith.

the cottage into a temple with a golden roof and marble columns. All the houses of the inhospitable people were then destroyed. This ancient legend may be the reason that the people treated Paul and Barnabas as gods. After witnessing the healing of the cripple, they did not want to make the same mistake as their ancestors.

14:14 tore their clothes: The tearing of robes was a Jewish expression of distress and grief. This custom went all the way back to Joshua and Caleb, who tore their clothes after hearing the people of Israel wanted to go back to Egypt instead of entering the Promised Land (Num. 14:6). Later, when the high priest accused Jesus of blasphemy, the high priest also tore his own clothes (Matt. 26:65). The tearing of clothes was from the neck down and usually extended about the length of one's hand. The Jews would also do this during times of distress (Josh. 7:6) and especially during seasons of sorrow (2 Sam. 1:11).

14:15–18 The sermon by Paul in these three verses is a condensed version of his sermon on the Areopagus in 17:22–31. These Gentiles did not know or believe in the Scriptures, so Paul preached truths that were self-evident to all and led his listeners to biblical truth.

14:19–22 supposing him to be dead: The physician Luke may be saying that Paul did not die here. However, some believe that the text speaks of Paul's resurrection. We're not sure whether Paul experienced a miracle of healing or a miracle of resurrection.

14:23, 24 appointed elders: It is difficult to know whether these elders were appointed by Paul and Barnabas or by a vote of the people. However, the process outlined in 6:1–7 for selecting the seven men may provide a clue to the process used for selecting elders here. Both the assembly and the apostles were involved in the selection process. **in every church:** Here is a clear passage presenting a plurality of elders for leadership in each church. This would parallel what we find in Acts 20:17 concerning the plurality of elders in the church at Ephesus.

14:25, 26 the word: The Good News that the Messiah has come to save from sin.

14:27, 28 all that God had done: God's action in saving **Gentiles** demanded a change in theology and church strategy.

15:1, 2 The Council of Jerusalem is one of the great turning points of the Book of Acts, as are the conversions of Paul and Cornelius. The relation between the Jewish and Gentile believers in terms of admission to membership in the church was the issue of this discussion. In the beginning, the church consisted almost entirely of converted Jews who had automatically been circumcised as OT believers. Even

Peter, earlier, had great difficulty making the transition to full fellowship with the Gentiles. The establishment of a predominantly Gentile church in Antioch and now the success of the Gentile mission in Galatia refocused attention upon fellowship with these growing churches. Church growth certainly underlies the basic themes represented by Luke in the Book of Acts. The power of the message of the gospel is demonstrated by the fact that it gains reception and response almost everywhere. When the Jewish converts from Judea arrived in Antioch, they insisted that believers must be **circumcised** in order to **be saved** (v. 1). The text later (v. 5) indicates that these converts were from among the Pharisees, the strictest of the sects of the Jews. The disputations would also seem to indicate that some of the early believers still looked upon Christianity as a movement within Judaism at this point.

15:1–4 Later those who taught the need for circumcision among new believers were known as Judaizers. They wanted the Christian faith to become a sect of Judaism. In other words, they wanted Gentile believers to become Jewish proselytes. As proselytes, the Gentile believers would need to be circumcised as a sign of coming into the covenant of God along with the Jews.

15:3–6 The Jerusalem church welcomed the delegation from Antioch and listen eagerly to the story of their successful evangelization of the Gentiles in Galatia, which caused **great joy to all the brethren.** Objections by the **Pharisees who believed** (or Christian converts from among the Pharisees) led to a formal conference of the **apostles and elders** with the delegation from Antioch. While the leaders were involved in the discussion, vv. 12, 22 show that the whole church participated in the ultimate decision. The wrong decision at this point would have thrown the church back under Jewish bondage to the law and would have stalled the expansion of the church as designed by her Lord.

15:5, 6 some of the sect of the Pharisees: These people believed in Jesus Christ but were still identified as Pharisees. Jews who became followers of Christ could still be Pharisees. The same could not be said for the Sadducees, for they denied that there was a resurrection, and thus could not believe that Jesus had been raised from the dead. **It is necessary to circumcise them:** This statement summarizes the problem. Is salvation granted through faith alone? Or does a person have to have faith plus the works of the law in order to be forgiven by God?

15:7–9 It was from the **mouth** of Peter that Cornelius and his Gentile friends heard the **gospel** of Jesus Christ (10:11–43).

15:10 Yoke here refers to the law (Gal. 5:1).

15:11 we shall be saved in the same manner as they: These are the last words of Peter in the Book of Acts. He leaves us with the eternal truth that we are saved through faith by grace alone. The emphasis in the Book of Acts now moves from Peter to Paul, from the presentation of the gospel message among the Jews to its presentation to the Gentiles.

15:12 Barnabas and Paul reported what God was doing in changing the lives of Gentiles with the gospel of Jesus Christ. Their testimony at this council was critical.

15:13, 14 The council listened to **James** because he was the first of the three pillars of

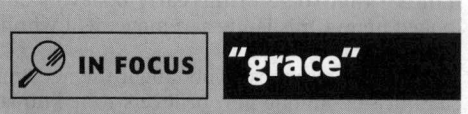

IN FOCUS **"grace"**

(Gk. *charis*) (15:11; Rom. 3:24; 5:15; Eph. 2:5; Titus 2:11) Strong's #*5485*: The Greek word for *grace* is probably equivalent to the Hebrew word *chesed* meaning "lovingkindness," a word frequently used by the psalmists to describe God's character. In the NT, the word *charis* usually means divine favor or goodwill, but it also means "that which gives joy" and "that which is a free gift." This is a noteworthy occurrence of the word *grace*, because while it was one of Paul's favorite words for God's free gift of salvation, here we see Peter using it in the same way.

the church (Gal. 2:9). He was the leader of the church in Jerusalem until he was stoned to death at the insistence of the high priest in A.D. 62. James was the Lord's half brother, the one who did not believe until the Lord appeared to him privately after the Resurrection (1 Cor. 15:7). He is probably the author of the Book of James, which explains to Jewish believers the true essence of genuine faith.

15:15–18 While the testimony of Peter, Barnabas, and Paul was important for the council in making their decision, something more than the experience of the Gentiles had to be taken into consideration. The council needed to know what the Word of God said. James pointed out that what was happening among the Gentiles was in full agreement with the OT (Amos 9:11, 12).

15:19, 20 The testimony of Paul and Barnabas—those who worked **among the Gentiles**—and most importantly the teaching

of Scripture, indicated to James that God was truly at work (v. 18). In view of this, he suggested that a letter be drafted that alleviated Jewish requirements for Gentiles who placed their trust in Jesus. Though James did not want to trouble Gentiles with Jewish ceremonial regulations, he believed certain practices should be followed. He mentioned four issues: eating food offered to **idols, sexual immorality,** eating food from animals that had been **strangled,** and eating food with **blood.** If Gentiles continued such practices, there would continually be tension between the Gentile and Jewish Christian communities. There is a debate as to whether these requirements were ceremonial or moral in nature. If they were ceremonial, "things polluted by idols" would refer to food offered in pagan temples (1 Cor. 8—10). "Sexual immorality" would refer to the marriage laws of Lev. 18:6–20. The prohibition against eating blood would be from Lev. 17:10–14. On the other hand, if these prohibitions were moral in nature, the food polluted by idols would relate to the problem of Rev. 2:14, 20. Evidently some Gentile Christians were attending the celebrations and banquets held in pagan temples that frequently involved sexual immorality. The prohibition against eating blood preceded the Law of Moses and extended back to the contract God made with Noah (Gen. 9:3, 4).

15:21 For Moses has had . . . those who preach him: James may have been saying that since there were Jewish communities in every city, it would be wise to remain sensitive to Jewish convictions. He may also have been saying that since the Gentile believers would learn more and more about the Scriptures, the Spirit of God would cultivate godly convictions in their hearts.

15:22–27 it pleased the apostles and elders: It is interesting to note the process the council followed in resolving this conflict. First, the problem was clearly stated: Each side was presented in a debate. Second, the facts were presented by those who were acquainted with them. Third, the counsel was given by a person who was trusted for his objectivity and wisdom. Fourth, unanimity was sought in the decision. Fifth, the attitude of preserving the unity of the Spirit remained utmost on the council's mind. This same formula would be helpful in resolving conflicts found within the church today. **chosen men of their own company:** The **apostles and elders** sent a representative from both sides of the dispute—a Judean (**Judas**) and a Hellenist (**Silas**)—along with Paul and Barnabas to bolster and confirm the ruling of the council.

15:28, 29 the Holy Spirit, and . . . us: The Jewish Christians showed a constant dependence on the guidance of the Spirit. The Spirit should have an equally large role in our spiritual decisions.

15:30–33 they rejoiced: Freed from unnecessary restrictions, salvation by grace through faith brings joy.

15:34, 35 Teaching and preaching are equally important.

15:36–38 Paul was adamant that John Mark not accompany him on his impending journey. Earlier John Mark had deserted Paul and Barnabas **in Pamphylia** (13:13). It is unclear why he did so. Some have speculated that John Mark returned to Jerusalem because he did not like the idea of Gentiles coming into the church by faith alone. Whatever the reason for the desertion, it is interesting to note that John Mark was reconciled to Paul and again helped him in his ministry. In 2 Tim. 4:11, Paul, who was in prison, writes, "Get Mark and bring him with you, for he is useful to me for ministry."

15:39–41 the contention became so sharp that they parted: There was a heated argument between Paul and Barnabas over John Mark's usefulness to them. Note that Luke does not assign blame for the disagreement. There are times when Christians will not agree on certain aspects of ministry. Perhaps the best course of action in some of those situations is to work separately. Barnabas left with John Mark, refusing to make the disagreement an issue before the church at Antioch. Barnabas had led the church in its early days (11:22–25). He was the church's main representative at the Jerusalem council, but he did not use his prominence to seek a reprimand of Paul. Instead he accepted the situation and proceeded to faithfully serve the Lord.

16:1 Timothy was the **son** of Eunice, a **Jewish woman** of great faith (2 Tim. 1:5). Eunice had taught the Holy Scriptures to Timothy from infancy (2 Tim. 3:15). The NT's silence about the faith of Timothy's father suggests he was not a believer.

16:2 Well spoken of may be rephrased as "well witnessed." In other words, people did not have to be told that Timothy was a Christian.

16:3 took him and circumcised him: In Jewish law, Timothy should have been circumcised and raised a Jew, even with a Gentile father. But in Greek law, the father dominated the home. The fact that Timothy was an uncircumcised Jew would have limited his effectiveness in ministering to the Jewish Christians. Salvation was not the issue here. Instead Timothy became circumcised so that God could use him to reach all people—even the Jews—with the message of the gospel.

16:4, 5 The council's decision (15:24–29) brought great joy and comfort to the Gentiles. Apparently the **decrees** from the Jerusalem council were considered reasonable and not burdensome.

16:6–10 sought to go to Macedonia: With both the southwesterly route and the northern path closed by the Holy Spirit (vv. 6, 7), Paul headed in the only direction left open to him—northwest—until he came to the Aegean port of Troas, where he could go no further. Paul was at the right place at the right time to receive the call to go to Macedonia. **We:** This is the first of four "we" sections in the Book of Acts (16:10–17; 20:5–15; 21:1–18; 27:1—28:16). This indicates that Luke, the author of Acts, accompanied Paul at least these four times.

16:11 Troas: A seaport of Asia Minor near the site of ancient Troy. **Samothrace:** A large island between Asia and Europe. The name **Neapolis** means "New City." It was the port for Philippi.

16:12 Named after the father of Alexander the Great, **Philippi** was a Roman **colony** loyal to the empire. The city itself was organized by the state of Rome and functioned as a military

---

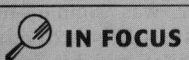 **IN FOCUS**   **"the Spirit"**

(Gk. *to pneuma*) (16:7; Rom. 8:9; Phil. 1:19; 1 Pet. 1:11) Strong's *#4151*: The Greek word for *Spirit* is derived from the verb *pneo,* meaning "to breathe" or "to blow." It is sometimes used to refer to the wind and sometimes to life itself (John 3:8; Rev. 13:15). It can refer to the life of angels (Heb. 1:14), demons (Luke 4:33), and human beings (7:59). Yet this word is also used for the Spirit of God (1 Cor. 2:11)—that is, the Holy Spirit (Matt. 28:19), the third Person of the Trinity, the One who lives inside believers (James 4:5; 1 John 4:13). This same Spirit is called "the Spirit of Jesus Christ" (Phil. 1:19), and as the marginal note indicates, many older manuscripts have the title *the Spirit of Jesus* in 16:7. This title emphasizes the unity of action between Jesus and the Spirit that permeates this book and its companion volume, the Gospel of Luke. During the days of Jesus' earthly ministry, the disciples were directed by Jesus; now, after His resurrection and ascension, by the Spirit of Jesus.

outpost. The people who settled the city were probably army veterans, who were given the rights of Roman citizens. Typically such a colony would possess an autonomous government and be immune from tribute and taxation. Because of its proximity to the sea as well as to one of the major roads to Europe, Philippi was a commercial center in Macedonia. Its influence throughout the region made it a good place to begin preaching the gospel of Jesus Christ.

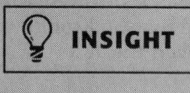

A New Direction for the Gospel

Paul's vision and subsequent trip from Troas to Neapolis (Acts 16:9–11) proved to be a major fork in the road for Western civilization. One small step for Paul became one giant leap for Christianity as it spread west, gaining a foothold at Philippi in Macedonia, moving on into Europe, and eventually pervading the entire western hemisphere.

16:13 where prayer was customarily made: According to Jewish custom, a congregation consisted of ten households. If ten male household heads could be found in a city, a synagogue was formed. If not, a place of prayer was established, usually near a river under the open sky. Paul's habit was to go first to the synagogue of a new city. However in Philippi, he searched for a Jewish prayer meeting.

16:14, 15 Thyatira was well known for **purple** dyes and cloth dyeing. Purple dye had to be gathered drop by drop from a certain shellfish. Because it was so expensive, purple dye was used on garments worn by royalty. As an artisan in purple dyes, **Lydia** was a wealthy woman who had come to Philippi to practice her trade. Paul preached the gospel, but **the Lord opened** Lydia's **heart** to it.

16:16 Luke's description of the **slave girl** in Greek indicates that she had a "spirit of Python." The python was a mythical serpent killed by Apollo, who took both the serpent's gift of predictions and sometimes its form. Apollo became known as Pythian Apollo. When it was said that one had a "spirit of Python," it meant that the person was controlled by an evil force. Apparently those who knew the girl did not regard her as insane or fraudulent. Rather they viewed her ability to foretell events as genuine. People paid the girl for her **divination** services, earning her

masters a lot of money. This particular cult was popular in Greece, especially in Corinth. The chief shrine to Apollo was at Delphi across the isthmus from Corinth.

16:17–19 greatly annoyed: Paul was upset not because what the girl said was untrue, but because the girl was being viewed as the source of truth.

16:20, 21 These claims were as false as those leveled first against Jesus and then Stephen. Those who desire to stop the truth of God are often unscrupulous about the truthfulness of their statements. Nothing Paul and Silas had preached remotely related to Roman **customs** or laws.

16:22–24 Before prisoners were **beaten with rods,** their garments were literally torn off so that their flesh would be exposed for the flogging. Paul experienced this particular Roman ordeal on three separate occasions. Later Paul would refer to this beating with wooden rods (2 Cor. 11:23, 25).

16:25 praying and singing . . . prisoners were listening: The word translated *listening* here means "to listen with pleasure," as if listening to beautiful music. It is in times of darkness that the light of a Christian witness shines brightest (Phil. 2:14–16).

16:26 immediately all the doors were opened: In ancient prisons each door was secured by a bar. The earthquake, as it passed along the ground, probably forced the doorposts apart so that the bars fell to the ground.

16:27–29 Under Roman law, a guard who allowed the escape of a prisoner was generally put to death. Believing that all the prisoners had escaped, **the keeper of the prison** assumed that death was certain for him.

16:30–36 what must I do to be saved: The events surrounding the arrest of Paul and Silas, the way they responded to suffering, and the mighty acts of God brought the jailer to his knees. He finally knew he needed God's salvation. But how could he be reconciled to God? Paul and Silas's answer was simple—just **believe on the Lord Jesus Christ.** No other work was needed. The jailer and his family placed their trust in God and immediately expressed that faith by being baptized.

16:37–40 Once the **magistrates** learned that Paul and Silas were Roman citizens, they realized that they were in danger of the wrath of Rome. It was unlawful to whip a Roman citizen or deny that person the right to due process. Paul refused to leave when he had the opportunity because he was protecting the infant church in Philippi. Because Paul and Silas were beaten in public, people probably believed that they had done something wrong. If Paul left quietly, then the perception would be that those associated with him, in particular the members of the Philippian church, had also done something wrong.

17:1-4 reasoned with them from the Scriptures: There was a great deal of evidence in Scripture that Paul could use in his argument. For example, Ps. 22, written over one thousand years earlier by David, describes the crucifixion of the Messiah. Paul could quote Is. 53 and Zech. 12 to demonstrate that the suffering, death, and resurrection of the coming Messiah was predicted by the prophets. The OT abounds with evidence of the Messiah's character and life that clearly matches that of Jesus (Luke 24:25–27).

17:5, 6 The Jews here refers to the Jewish leaders of the synagogue who felt threatened by the gospel because it contradicted their own teachings.

17:7, 8 acting contrary to the decrees of Caesar: In A.D. 49 the Roman emperor Claudius expelled all Jews from Rome due to riots that were ignited by a group of zealous Jews. These insurrectionists were advocating revolution against Rome and were opposing the installation of a new king. Paul's accusers were trying to paint him as a revolutionary who was bringing sedition to Thessalonica.

17:9, 10 had taken security from Jason: Taking security was similar to posting bond today. It was meant as an assurance that there would be no repetition of the trouble caused by the apostle Paul, and that he would not return to Thessalonica. Instead, Paul and Silas traveled 50 miles southwest to the city of **Berea.**

17:11-14 These Jews **searched the Scriptures** to discover the truth. It is God's plan for Christians also; that is why He gave us the Word.

17:15 Arriving in **Athens,** Paul apparently saw that he would need the help of **Silas** and **Timothy.** He sent word for them to join him there.

17:16 Paul was greatly distressed at the sight of numerous pagan temples and altars in **Athens.** In his letter to the Corinthians Paul explained why he was indignant (1 Cor. 10:20). The people's offerings were being sacrificed to demons. By doing this, the Gentiles were having fellowship with the powers of darkness. For these people to be so deceived by the devil was deeply troubling to Paul.

17:17 Paul was not a tourist. He was **in the marketplace** witnessing to those who passed by.

17:18 this babbler: Some of the philosophers in Athens mocked Paul, calling him a "seed picker" or gutter sparrow, a small bird that snatches up scraps of food. Paul was being accused of grabbing at bits of knowledge

without fully digesting or thinking through what he taught. Because Paul did not speak eloquently (1 Cor. 2:1), some philosophers in Athens arrogantly ridiculed him, arguing that he was not sophisticated enough to be taken

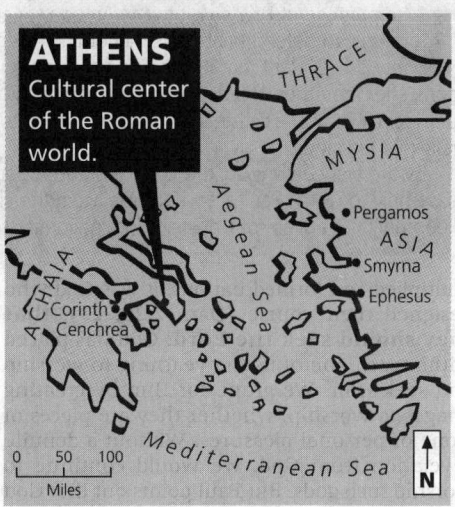

The City of Athens

Athens was the principal city of ancient Greece and capital of the district of Attica. Although Paul won several converts to the gospel in Athens, it may have been years later before a church began.

seriously. Others thought that Paul was advocating foreign gods named Jesus and Resurrection, incorrectly understood to be a male and female deity.

17:19-21 the Areopagus: Just southwest of the Acropolis in Athens was a hill called the Hill of Ares (Mars in Latin), the god of war. This was where court was held concerning questions of religion and morals. In Athens, the gospel message was examined by the supposed experts of philosophy and religion.

17:22-31 Because the men of Athens had scant knowledge of the Hebrew Scriptures, Paul started with the general revelation visible in creation itself. In the sixth century B.C. it was said that a poet from Crete named Epimenides turned aside a horrible plague from the people of Athens by appealing to a god of whom the people had never heard. An altar was built to honor this god, whom the Athenians now called the UNKNOWN GOD. Paul obviously knew of Epimenides; he quoted the poet in Titus 1:12. Thus Paul began his presentation of the gospel by appealing to natural revelation and to certain true statements of the Athenian poets. **He has made from one blood:** God sovereignly created one man, Adam. As Adam's descendants

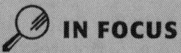 IN CONTEXT   Paul's Speech to the Areopagus

The purpose of Paul's visit to the Areopagus and its council is not certain, but he may have been on trial to defend his beliefs. Although ancient references to the council of the Areopagus are few, it is evident that it was an aristocratic body that advised the king. It then assumed royal functions after the Athenians deposed their monarchy (sometime before 800 B.C.). With the rise of democracy in 500 B.C. the council lost some of its power and became largely an esteemed group with religious functions.

By the first century A.D. the council of the Areopagus had regained much of its former authority. The assembly to which Paul preached was again the chief governing body in Athens, a position it would keep until the advent of Christian domination in the fourth century A.D.

---

multiplied and formed nations, it was God who designed their course (Dan. 2:20, 21). **that they should seek the Lord:** God has placed within each one of us the yearning to worship and seek Him. We grope for Him by creating images to worship, whether they are pieces of stone or personal pleasures. Without a definite revelation from God, we would continue to worship such gods. But Paul points out that God is not far away; we can have fellowship with Him. In fact, every day we depend upon Him for our life and breath. Our loving Creator has sent His Son, Jesus Christ, to demonstrate His love for us. It is our responsibility to respond to His Son and to follow Him.

17:32, 33 Paul's reference to **the resurrection of the dead** ignited a reaction among the Athenians. The Greeks repudiated the idea of a bodily resurrection. Though they embraced the concept of the soul living forever, they were repulsed by the idea of a bodily resurrection because they considered the body to be evil, something to be discarded. This idea, known as dualism, was derived from the teachings of the

Greek philosophers Socrates and Plato. It held that everything physical is evil and everything spiritual is good, and that it makes no difference what one does with one's body so long as the spirit is good. Tragically, the Athenians' adherence to this philosophy blinded them to the truth of the gospel.

17:34 some . . . believed: The sermon was not a failure, although with a different type of audience Paul decided to preach differently in Corinth (1 Cor. 2:1, 2). Believers in Athens included some influential people, even a judge—**Dionysius.**

18:1 Corinth was the political capital of Achaia. It was also a center for the worship of Aphrodite, the goddess of fertility, and it housed the major temple of Apollo. Because of the sensuous nature of the religious cult of Aphrodite, Corinth had a reputation for being a city of immorality. Beginning in the fifth century B.C., the Greeks used a word meaning "to act like a Corinthian" as a synonym for sexual immorality.

18:2, 3 All young rabbinical students had to learn a trade. **Tentmakers** were leather

---

🔍 IN FOCUS   "Epicurean and Stoic philosophers"

(Gk. *Epikoureioi kai Stoikoi philosophoi*) (17:18) Strong's #*1946; 2532; 4770; 5386*: The Epicureans were those who followed the teachings of Epicurus (341–270 B.C.), who said the chief end of humankind was pleasure and happiness. This pleasure, they believed, was attained by avoiding excess and the fear of death, by seeking tranquillity and freedom from pain, and by loving other people. They believed that if gods existed they were not involved in events on this earth. The Stoics were followers of Zeno (c. 334–262 B.C.). They got their name from the Greek word *stoa* (meaning "porch"), for Zeno taught at a place in Athens called the Stoa. The Stoics were pantheists who thought the universe was ruled by an absolute Purpose or Will, to which a person had to conform his or her will, unmoved by all external circumstances and changes. The person who did this would reach the perfection of virtue. The byproducts of such a philosophy were pride and self-sufficiency, as can be seen in their arrogant response to the gospel (17:18, 32).

workers. The province of Cilicia, from which Paul came, was noted for its cloth made from goats' hair. It is likely that Paul's skill involved making such cloth.

18:4–6 Paul's custom was to go to the Jews first whenever he entered a new city. Thus, in Corinth he began his proclamation of Jesus in the synagogues. After several attempts to reach the Jews of Corinth (v. 4), attempts that had few results, Paul turned his attention almost exclusively to the **Gentiles.**

18:7 Justus: Most Romans had three names. This man's name was Titius Justus. Based on Paul's letter to the Corinthians, it is likely that Justus was the man called Gaius in 1 Cor. 1:14.

18:8–11 In view of the severe treatment he had received elsewhere, Paul must have been very comforted by Christ's statement that he would not be **hurt** or beaten in Corinth (16:22–24).

18:12, 13 In the spring of A.D. 51 or 52, a **proconsul** named **Gallio** was appointed by the Roman senate to govern the province of **Achaia** (Greece). Gallio was a brother of the famous stoic philosopher Seneca, who possessed great influence in Rome. The Jewish leaders thought they would take advantage of the new governor and rid themselves of Paul and the gospel of Jesus Christ. Bringing Paul before the judgment seat of the governor was a momentous event. If the Roman governor ruled Christianity illegal, it would set a precedent and encourage immediate persecution of all Christians.

18:14–17 Paul did not even have to open his **mouth** to defend the faith. God had already provided for Paul's defense; he had prepared Gallio to make the correct decision. No crime had been committed against Rome. Gallio considered Christianity to be a Jewish sect. Because Judaism was an established religion in the Roman Empire, this "sect" was not in violation of Roman law. Gallio had his bailiffs drive the accusers out of his presence. Once again the sovereign hand of God preserved the life of His faithful servant.

18:18 Paul **had his hair cut** as part of a Nazirite vow he had made (Num. 6). Such a vow had to be fulfilled in Jerusalem, where the hair would be presented to God. Vows were made either in gratitude for God's blessing (like Paul's safekeeping in Corinth) or as part of a petition for future blessing. The vow involved abstinence from drinking wine and a commitment not to cut one's hair for a period of time. At the end of this set period, the hair was cut and then burned along with other sacrifices as a symbol of offering oneself to God (21:23–26). Paul redirected his entire travel schedule because he wanted to get to Jerusalem in time to make this vow.

18:19–21 Paul had tried to go to **Ephesus** before but was forbidden by the Holy Spirit (16:6). We are not told how or why, but during his second missionary trip, the Holy Spirit kept Paul from traveling the southwestern route, which would have taken him to Ephesus. Instead, Paul went northwest to the Aegean

---

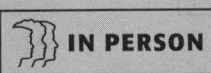 **IN PERSON** | **Dionysius and Damaris**

Apparently none of the Epicurean or Stoic philosophers of Athens responded to Paul's message about Christ, but Luke does name a council member and a woman as the nucleus of a group that believed (Acts 17:34). Dionysius was a member of the court and likely a person of some standing. Later writers name him as the first bishop of the church in Athens.

As for Damaris, it is remarkable that a woman should be among the first believers. Greek women of the day rarely took part in philosophical discourses. They generally stayed at home in seclusion while their husbands, freed by slaves from the menial tasks of life, pursued leisurely activities such as gymnastics, politics, and philosophy.

There are several possibilities to explain how Damaris managed to hear Paul and decide to follow Christ. One is that she was among a class of women known as *hetairai*, specially trained companions to wealthy men who were educated in subjects usually reserved for men, such as rhetoric and philosophy. Their purpose was to entertain their partners. The role of *hetairai* was not as respected as that of wives, but they enjoyed far more freedom and opportunity—including the opportunity to attend the philosophical discussions held daily in the marketplace and the Areopagus (17:17, 19).

Of course, there is no way to know for certain whether Damaris was a *hetaira*. But no matter what her role in the society was, she courageously went against the prevailing culture by siding with Paul, Dionysius, and the message about the resurrected Jesus.

port of Troas, where he received the Macedonian call to take the gospel to Europe. If we will entrust our way to God's timing as Paul did, we will end up at the right place at the right time.

18:22 Paul completed his vow (vv. 18–21) when he went to Jerusalem and **greeted the church** there. Paul then returned to his sending church in **Antioch,** completing his second missionary journey, one that covered over three hundred miles. **he went down:** Antioch was north of Jerusalem but lower in elevation.

city about 150 years before the birth of Jesus. The city was famous for its great library and was considered the cultural and educational center of the world.

18:25–27 John's **baptism** was a baptism of repentance in preparation for the coming of the Messiah. John's followers had scattered throughout Asia Minor and into Egypt. Apollos was a disciple of John the Baptist. Apparently he did not know about the finished work of Jesus Christ on the Cross, the Resurrection, the Ascension, and the sending of the Holy Spirit.

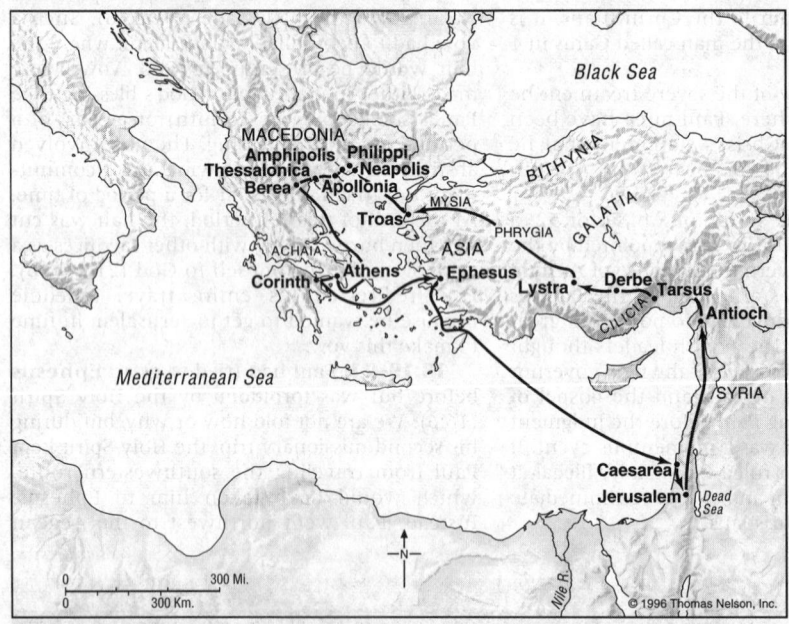

Paul's Second Missionary Journey

Starting from Jerusalem, Paul took Silas to visit the churches of Galatia. Timothy joined them in Lystra, and together they went to Macedonia and Achaia (present-day Greece). On this journey, the Philippian jailer was saved, the Bereans "searched the Scriptures daily" (17:11), and Paul preached at the Areopagus in Athens.

18:23 he departed and went over the region: On his third missionary journey Paul traveled back through Asia Minor to visit the churches that had been established on his previous trips. The cities included Derbe, Lystra, Iconium, Antioch, and Ephesus.

18:24 Apollos, born at Alexandria: This Jew with a Greek name was from the second largest city in the Roman Empire. Alexandria was a seaport on the northern coast of Egypt. Founded by Alexander the Great, the city was very cosmopolitan. Egyptians, Romans, and Greeks all lived there; over a quarter of the population was Jewish. The Greek translation of the Hebrew Scriptures had been produced in that

18:28 he vigorously refuted the Jews: Many of the believers in Corinth were Gentiles and were easy targets for opponents who knew the Hebrew Scriptures. However, the arguments of these Jews did not stand up against the brilliance of Apollos, the new Jewish Christian apologist (v. 26).

19:1, 2 These twelve men (v. 7) had been baptized into the baptism of John the Baptist, but they had never heard about the **Holy Spirit.** All they knew was that One mightier than John was to come. They did not know that Jesus the Messiah, the One mightier than John had already come. He had died for their sins, had been raised from the dead, had ascended to the Father, and had already sent the Holy Spirit. They needed to hear the rest of the gospel. As soon as this happened, these men could place their faith in Jesus and receive the Holy Spirit.

19:3, 4 Baptism was a ritual used by the Jews as a picture of cleansing and purification. Gentiles who converted to Judaism would go through the rite of purification as their first act of worship. They would dip themselves in water as a sign of being cleansed from their old way of life. Before entering into the temple to worship, Jews would dip themselves in ritual bathing pools to show their desire for purification. But the dipping performed by John the Baptist was a call for repentance rather than mere ritual cleansing. His baptism was a call to people to turn to God and to identify with the coming Messiah who would forgive their sins (Matt. 3:1–12).

19:5 in the name of the Lord Jesus: This phrase was a declaration of ownership, an identification with Jesus as Lord and Savior of one's life.

19:6, 7 laid hands on them: The Holy Spirit was received without the laying on of hands in 10:44–48. By laying on his hands here, Paul was demonstrating his apostolic authority. He was also affirming the unity of the new church in Ephesus with the church in Jerusalem, whose members also were empowered by the Holy Spirit to speak in foreign languages (2:4, 11). This speaking in tongues was a sign to others that they were part of the body of Christ (1 Cor. 14:22).

19:8–10 From Ephesus, other churches were born in **Asia** Minor—in Colosse, Smyrna, Pergamos, Thyatira, Sardis, Philadelphia, and Laodicea. Note the sequence of events. Paul tried **explaining the things of the kingdom of God** to the Jews in the **synagogue** for three months. After he was finally rejected, he took those who had believed and started a new "school" for the study of the Scriptures in the facilities of a philosopher named **Tyrannus.** During the two years that Paul conducted these classes, **all who dwelt in Asia** heard the gospel. This indicates that Paul and the students of the school did more than study; they must have witnessed to others as well.

19:11 God confirmed Paul's apostolic authority by performing **miracles** through him. The writer of the Book of Hebrews helps us understand why miracles were accomplished through the apostles (Heb. 2:3, 4). The miracles verified that the apostles represented God and that the gospel they preached was from heaven.

19:12 handkerchiefs or aprons: A handkerchief was a cloth used to wipe away perspiration and was usually worn tied around the head. The apron was tied around the waist. These were sweat rags used by Paul in his tent-making trade as he worked with leather. Why would God perform healings in this way? Ephesus was a focal point for magicians and wandering priests. The city was filled with wizards attempting to exercise power over the dark forces. God may have used such unusual means in order to show that His miraculous power was greater than the powers of darkness.

19:13–16 to call the name of the Lord Jesus: The use of magical names in incantations was common in the ancient world. Jewish practitioners of magic enjoyed great prestige because they claimed to know the true pronunciation of the sacred name of God, and thus were able to release God's full power. These practitioners had latched onto the name of Jesus to use as an incantation. **overpowered them:** The seven so-called exorcists found out that it was not enough to know the name of Jesus; they needed to know Jesus personally.

19:17–19 These **books** were filled with formulas, spells, and astrological forecasts. The volumes were expensive; **fifty thousand pieces of silver** would have taken ten laborers twenty years to earn. Burning the books indicated real repentance on the part of **those who had practiced magic.**

19:20 The word of the Lord . . . prevailed over pagan religion in this political and religious capital of the province of Asia (now western Turkey).

19:21, 22 Paul made plans, under the guidance of **the Spirit,** for his continuing ministry.

19:23–27 Silver shrines of Diana refers to small shrines containing a miniature image of the fertility goddess of Ephesus. Sales of these idols were falling off as people were introduced to the truth of Jesus Christ.

19:28, 29 into the theater: This amphitheater seated 25,000 people.

19:30, 31 The **officials of Asia** were prominent citizens, friendly to Rome. They had been given the title of honor, "Asiarch," and were also friends of Paul.

19:32–34 The Jews wanted to distance themselves from Paul, so they put **Alexander** forward to explain that the Jews had nothing to do with Paul. However, Alexander never got the chance to speak once the crowd discovered he was a Jew.

19:35–41 image which fell down from Zeus: Some feel that the first image of Artemis was possibly carved out of a meteorite. **we are in danger:** The riot at Ephesus could have brought the discipline of Rome down upon the city. The *Pax Romana,* the peace that the Roman Empire brought to the Mediterranean world,

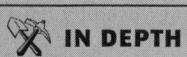 **IN DEPTH** | # The Gospel in Ephesus: A Case Study

Evangelism in Ephesus was explosive and unpredictable. People from vastly different backgrounds formed a diverse coalition of believers who had a far-reaching impact on the city's culture and economy (Acts 19:10).

Laypeople Laid a Foundation

Start-up began with Priscilla and Aquila, the entrepreneurial couple that Paul met in Corinth (Acts 18:1–3). Joining Paul's team, they sailed with him to Ephesus, a major city of 350,000. While he traveled to Palestine and Galatia, they remained and set up key contacts, working in the tent manufacturing industry (18:18–23).

One beneficiary of their efforts was Apollos, a powerful orator from Alexandria who stirred things up in Paul's absence. Eloquent in delivery but incomplete in his theology, he learned from them about Jesus. After mentoring him in the faith, they sent him to Greece where he strengthened the believers, including their old friends at Corinth (18:24–28; 1 Cor. 3:6).

The Message Took Hold

Returning to Ephesus, Paul encountered a new breed of religious zealots. Like Apollos, they were unaware of Jesus, knowing only of John the Baptist. But they became ecstatic as Paul related the fulfillment of John's ministry in Christ. Twelve of their number received the Holy Spirit, arousing the religious establishment (Acts 19:1–7).

Paul exploited the interest by initiating a three-month campaign in the local synagogue. However, his arguments met with opposition from obstinate synagogue Jews who maligned the movement publicly. In response, Paul relocated to the school of Tyrannus where for two years he engaged the Ephesians in a dialogue on Christianity during their midday, off-work hours (19:8–10).

Rapid Growth

Concentrated focus brought extraordinary results. The Christian message proved contagious among both open-minded Jews and intellectually curious Gentiles, impacting the city's educational system. Residents and merchants of Ephesus and from throughout Asia Minor were exposed. As word spread among workers in regional commerce, the arts, and the transportation system, "all . . . in Asia heard the word of the Lord" (Acts 19:10). Philemon's house church in Laodicea and probably other Asian churches were started by those attending Paul's "university lectureship."

Meanwhile, God validated Paul's message with dramatic miracles among the sick and diseased. This drew the notice of health professionals, including esoteric healing artists who become jealous. One group, the seven sons of Sceva, attempted to imitate the apostle through an occult ritual but were routed by the very powers over which they claimed to have mastery. The incident produced even more converts to Christianity, driving occult practitioners and publishers out of business (though not all; 2 Tim. 3:8). The growing community of believers lit a bonfire that consumed magic books valued at no less than 400,000 hours of wages (Acts 19:11–20).

Economic Impact

At this point the civic leaders started receiving complaints from artisans and craftsmen, particularly metalworkers, about the economic impact of the message. Paul's meddlesome habit of attacking idolatry threatened the city's thriving tourist trade, centered around the internationally acclaimed temple to Diana, one of the "Seven Wonders of the Ancient World." The metalworkers, led by Demetrius, mobilized the entire city to save a key industry. Recruiting their associates in other trade guilds, they fomented a riot and rushed to the amphitheater.

This brought city hall into the act. At great pains to keep law and order—as well as his job—a Rome-appointed civil servant finally silenced the crowd and urged them to use the court system for redress of their grievances. His tactic forestalled violence, bought time, and saved the economy. It also spared Paul and his companions (Acts 19:23–41).

The Gospel in Ephesus *continued*

An Established Community

The riot brought Paul's lecture series to an end, but not the impact of the gospel. Departing the city, he left behind a growing, dynamic church, pastored by his young protégé, Timothy (Acts 16:1–3; 1 Tim. 1:3). Not only did these believers continue to penetrate their own community with the message of Christ; they also reached out to the many travelers to and from their strategically placed import export city—tourists and religious pilgrims, shipping merchants, sailors and other transportation workers, military personnel, political refugees. Dozens of churches sprang up throughout Asia Minor, thanks to the Holy Spirit's coordinated use of three tentmakers (Priscilla, Aquila, and Paul), a fiery evangelist (Apollos), and countless unnamed laity.

was important to Rome. Therefore, the empire severely disciplined unruly cities. The Romans would not tolerate any kind of uprising or rebellion. Ephesus risked losing its freedom and being ruled directly by the Roman army.

20:1, 2 The word translated **encouraged** has a full range of meanings, from rebuking to comforting. Encouragement included instruction, appeal, affirmation, warning, and correction. People need to know that God has something to say to them and has said it in many ways. Paul didn't just bring sweetness and light. He told them everything they needed to hear—both the tough words and the kind words.

20:3–6 he decided to return through Macedonia: Often Jewish pilgrim ships left for Syria taking Jews to the Passover. Paul had intended to sail on such a ship, but after the plot against his life was discovered he decided he would celebrate the Passover with his friends in Philippi. It would have been easy for his enemies to arrange for Paul to "disappear" over the side of the boat and never be heard from again.

Paul was very sensitive to the leading of the Holy Spirit in his life and ministry. Sometimes the Spirit of God led him into difficult circumstances; other times the Spirit protected him from such circumstances.

20:7 The first day of the week was Sunday. The people gathered to worship on this day for the same reason we do today, to celebrate the day of the resurrection of Jesus Christ. The Jewish believers continued to worship on the Sabbath, which is Saturday. The Book of Hebrews tells us that Christ and His finished work is our Sabbath, our rest (Heb. 4:8–10). **to break bread:** The primary purpose of the gathering was the Lord's Supper.

20:8–12 Because the rooms had **many lamps,** it was probably stuffy and hot. No wonder **Eutychus** had difficulty staying awake.

20:13–16 to go on foot: Luke and the others left Troas for Assos, some 30 miles south by sea. Paul wanted to walk to Assos alone. Paul may have felt the need to spend some time alone with God, to pray and reflect on what God wanted him to do. When Paul met

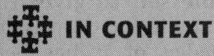 **IN CONTEXT** ## The Riot in Ephesus

Paul's work in Ephesus during his third missionary journey (c. A.D. 54) began to turn the allegiance of some from paganism to Christ. When the success of the gospel threatened the trade of silversmiths in Ephesus, money motivated an attack against Paul. A civil disturbance was instigated by Demetrius, a silversmith who manufactured devotional shrines for the worship of Diane (the Greek goddess Artemis).

"Diana of the Ephesians" (Acts 19:34) was the mother goddess of Asia. Her temple in Ephesus was one of the Seven Wonders of the ancient world, and people came from all parts of the Roman world to worship her. A legend told of an "image which fell down from Zeus" that was kept in Diana's temple (19:35). The "image" may have been a meteorite similar to others that were venerated at various places in the ancient world, most notably the "image of the Great Mother" brought to Rome from Pessinus.

up with the others in Assos, it is clear that he had received guidance. He was now in a hurry to get to Jerusalem to deliver the offering taken by the Gentile churches for the suffering church there.

20:17–21 The Greek term for **elders** is *presbuteros,* a term borrowed from the Jewish synagogue. It referred to those who were held in respect as the leaders of a particular fellowship.

kingdom and the honor of Christ, no matter what the earthly cost was.

20:25–28 with His own blood: It was the blood of the Son of God that was shed for the sins of the church.

20:29, 30 wolves . . . men: There are always two threats to the church, one from the outside and one from the inside. Unbelievers are a dangerous threat from the outside; the arro-

Photo by Howard Vos

The great outdoor theater at Ephesus, where Paul was almost mobbed by the worshipers of the pagan goddess Diana (Acts 19:21–41).

In v. 28 the elders are called "overseers" (Gk. *episkopos,* translated *bishop* in Titus 1:7). The terms appear to be interchangeable in the NT (Titus 1:5–7).

20:22, 23 I go bound in the spirit: Some say that Paul was out of the will of God in going to Jerusalem after the warnings of bonds and afflictions. But there is no evidence that Paul was rebelling against God. On the contrary, Jesus Himself confirmed that the trip was part of His good and perfect will (23:11). While Paul was in a Jerusalem prison, Jesus appeared to him to tell him to take courage. The Lord explained to Paul that just as he had solemnly witnessed for the cause of Christ at Jerusalem, he would do the same in Rome. There was no condemnation, but rather affirmation, of the fact that Paul bore witness to Jesus Christ in Jerusalem.

20:24 nor do I count my life dear to myself: Paul no longer desired to hold on to his life. He sought only the furtherance of God's

gant and self-serving are a threat from within.

20:31–34 Watch is reminiscent of Peter's warning about the devil in 1 Pet. 5:8. Elders protect the flock by their care and teaching.

20:35 It is more blessed to give: This saying of Jesus is not found in the Gospels, but through Paul's knowledge of it has been recorded here.

20:36–38 The touching farewell gives us a keen insight into the warm fellowship of the early church. **Paul knelt down and prayed with** his converts and they all **wept . . . and kissed him** (following the common early Christian greeting of the "kiss of peace"). It is also interesting to note that they sorrowed most because they would not have the opportunity to hear him speak again, more so than sorrowing over missing his presence. The implication here is clearly that their loyalty to Paul was based on his message of truth rather than on his personality.

21:1 When we had departed from them
may be rephrased as "after tearing ourselves
away from them." The apostle Paul's affection
for his fellow believers ran deep (20:37). It must
have been a difficult life for Paul, constantly

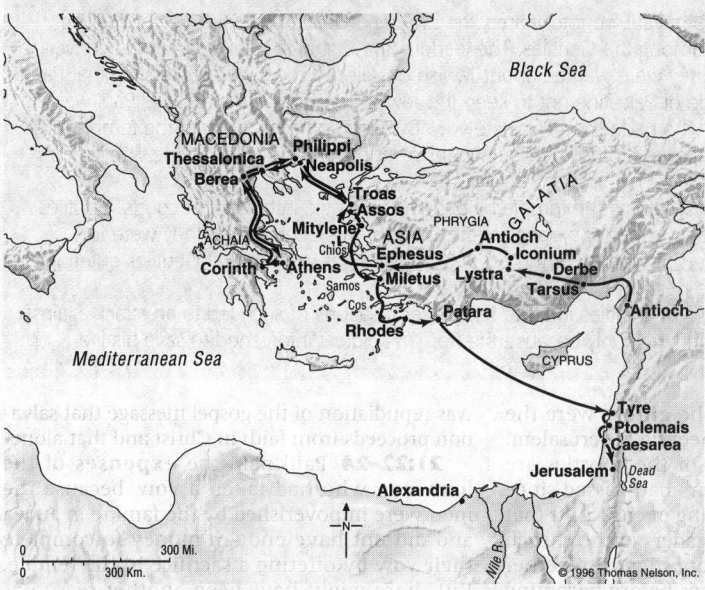

Paul's Third Missionary Journey

Paul visited the churches of Galatia for a third time, and then settled in Ephesus
for more than two years. Upon leaving Ephesus, Paul traveled again to Macedonia and Achaia (Greece) for a three-month stay. He returned to Asia by way of
Macedonia.

On this third journey Paul wrote 1 Corinthians from Ephesus, 2 Corinthians
from Macedonia, and the letter to the Romans from Corinth.

leaving friends and family as he traveled about
proclaiming the gospel. In **Patara,** a seaport,
Paul and his companions could find a larger ship
that would sail the four hundred miles directly
to Phoenicia, with its ports at Tyre and Sidon. In
the summer months, the wind of the Aegean
Sea blows from the north, beginning very early
in the morning. In the late afternoon the wind
dies away. Sunset brings a dead calm, and later a
gentle south breeze blows. If a ship was heading
down the coast, it would typically anchor at
evening and wait for the winds of the morning.
21:2, 3 finding a ship: Paul wasted no time
because he wanted to get to Jerusalem by Pentecost, which occurs just 50 days after Passover.
Paul had celebrated Passover with his friends in
Philippi more than three weeks earlier, so he
had less than 30 days to reach Jerusalem in time
for the festival.
21:4 In this verse, a warning was being
given by the Holy **Spirit** of the danger that was

waiting for Paul in Jerusalem. It is doubtful that
the warning meant that Paul was actually not
supposed to go. The warning did cause the disciples, who loved Paul and did not want to see
him hurt, to discourage Paul from continuing
his journey. But Paul
had already demon-
strated sensitivity to the
leading of the Holy Spirit
(16:6). He had already
said that he was "bound
in the spirit" to go to
Jerusalem (20:22). Later
Jesus Himself encour-
aged Paul concerning his
decision to go (23:11).
**21:5, 6 we knelt
down . . . and prayed:**
Kneeling must have
been their usual posture
when in prayer (Eph.
3:14).
21:7 Ptolemais:
The ancient seaport of
Acco (modern Acre) was
renamed by Ptolemy of
Egypt to perpetuate his
memory. **one day:** Haste
limited their visit with
the **brethren** there.
21:8 Some believe
that Philip's **house** was
the place where the
believers of **Caesarea**
assembled to worship
God.
**21:9 four virgin
daughters:** Here we see
a fulfillment of what
Peter said in ch. 2 about how young men and
women both would be gifted by the Spirit of
God to prophesy and proclaim the truth of God.
21:10–14 Agabus had predicted in
11:27–30 the famine that would fall upon
Judea. In response to his prediction, the Gentile
believers had collected money for the suffering
believers in Jerusalem. Here Agabus predicted
Paul's imprisonment and suffering. The Holy
Spirit did not forbid Paul to go to Jerusalem, but
warned him of what it would cost him.
**21:15, 16 we packed and went up to
Jerusalem:** Although they had been told
repeatedly that Paul would be beaten and
arrested in Jerusalem, Paul's traveling companions continued to travel with him. They would
not leave Paul in his moment of crisis. During
times of suffering, true friends stick close to provide comfort and assistance (Prov. 17:17).
Mnason of Cyprus possibly was one of the
original 120 mentioned in 1:15.

After arriving in Jerusalem, Paul went to James, the brother of Jesus, and to the elders, telling them about his work among the Gentiles. The leaders of the church rejoiced over the conversion of Gentiles, but they were worried about Jewish hostility. Rumors were circulating that Paul had taught Jews living outside of Palestine not to keep the Jewish law. To avoid a dispute, Paul was urged to join with four men who had taken a Nazirite vow. By accompanying them to the temple and paying the expenses of the sacrificial offerings, Paul would demonstrate that as a Jew he was keeping the law, despite his witnessing to Gentiles.

Paul was also accused of profaning the temple by bringing a Gentile into its inner courts. Gentiles were allowed in the outer court, called appropriately the Court of the Gentiles, but they were forbidden to come into the Court of Women or the Court of Israel. Signs warned that Gentiles entering these courts would be put to death.

Though Paul had not brought Gentiles into the temple, accusations of such led to an attack against him. The mob stopped beating Paul only because the Roman soldiers intervened to save his life.

21:17, 18 James and the **elders** were the leaders of house churches meeting in Jerusalem. It is interesting that none of the apostles are mentioned here. Seven years had passed since the Jerusalem council meeting of ch. 15. At that time, the apostles and the leaders of the church had gathered to settle the question of whether Gentiles had to become Jews before becoming Christians. That question was settled in the negative; the Scriptures and the Holy Spirit both taught that the gospel was for all people. Apparently the apostles left Jerusalem after that conference to carry out Jesus' commission to be witnesses to the "end of the earth" (1:8).

21:19 things which God had done: The evidence of how God changed the lives of Gentiles was presented to the Christians in Jerusalem. The strongest evidence was the Gentile believers themselves who had accompanied Paul to Jerusalem. At this time, Paul may have also given the money he had been collecting from the Gentile Christians (11:27–30; 1 Cor. 16:1). The love the Gentiles expressed to their suffering Jewish brethren was a mark of their genuine conversion.

21:20, 21 informed about you: Reports were circulating that Paul had been urging Jews to abandon Mosaic traditions. However, Paul never derided his Jewish heritage nor demanded that Jewish Christians renounce the Law of Moses. He only made it clear to everyone that the law could not function as a means of salvation. There is evidence that Paul was continuing to keep the Law when he stood before Felix in 24:11, 12. The fact that he was coming to Jerusalem to worship was evidence of this. What Paul *did* resist was any attempt to force Gentiles to become Jews. Salvation was through faith alone. Relying on adherence to the Jewish law

was repudiation of the gospel message that salvation proceeds from faith in Christ and that alone.

21:22–24 Paul paid the **expenses** of the four men who had taken a vow, because the men were impoverished by the famine in Judea and did not have enough money to complete their vow by offering a sacrifice in the temple. But there might have been another reason as well. The Jewish historian Josephus tells us that when Herod Agrippa I began his reign over Judea in A.D. 41, he paid for a considerable number of Nazirite vows to show his respect for the Mosaic Law. For the sake of showing his Jewish brethren that he had not forsaken the laws of Moses, Paul did what they asked. Reputation was an issue for the apostle, as it is for all believers (1 Tim. 3:7).

21:25 they should keep themselves: The Christian leaders were not asking Gentiles to live like Jews; neither did they want to compel Jews to live like Gentiles. The spiritual unity of the body of believers is realized in its diversity, not in its conformity. From our diverse backgrounds and cultures we honor the same Lord.

21:26–29 defiled this holy place: The temple in NT times was surrounded by three courts. The innermost court was the Court of Israel where Jewish men could offer their sacrifices. Only consecrated priests actually entered the temple building itself, and only the high priest could enter the inner sanctuary of the Most Holy Place—once a year on the Day of Atonement (Heb. 9:7). The second court was the Court of the Women where Jewish families could gather for prayer and worship. The outer court was the Court of the Gentiles, open to all who would worship God. If any Gentile went beyond the barrier into the second court, he or she would be liable to the death penalty. The Roman authorities, out of respect for the Jewish religion, authorized the death sentence for this trespass even for their own Roman citizens.

21:30, 31 garrison: Between six hundred and a thousand men were stationed in the Fortress Antonia on the northwest side of the temple. From a tower overlooking the temple courts they could watch for any trouble. When the riot broke out against Paul, at least two hundred soldiers were dispatched from the fortress into the Court of the Gentiles.

21:32–36 They stopped beating Paul only because the Roman soldiers intervened to save his life. **ran down to them:** Herod had built the Fortress of Antonia adjacent to the temple area. A tunnel permitted soldiers of the garrison to appear suddenly in the temple grounds to maintain order.

21:37–40 When Paul spoke Greek, the commander realized that he was **not the Egyptian** assassin who had come to Jerusalem in A.D. 54 claiming to be a prophet. This Egyptian had led four thousand fanatical Jews up to the Mount of Olives, promising that at his word the walls of Jerusalem would fall and the Roman Empire would be destroyed. Felix, the governor of Jerusalem at the time, ordered his men up the Mount of Olives, where they killed some four hundred Jews and captured another two hundred. However, the Egyptian and some of his followers slipped away into the desert. These followers were called *sicarii*, meaning "dagger men." They would mingle with the crowds in Jerusalem during festivals and murder pro-Roman Jews.

22:1 hear my defense: This was the first of five defenses Paul would make.

22:2 After speaking Greek to the commander (21:37), Paul addressed the people in the **Hebrew** dialect, most likely Aramaic. When the people heard him speaking to them in their own language they were reminded that Paul was not a Gentile but a Jew like themselves. Therefore, they listened to what he had to say.

22:3–5 as you all are today: Paul explained to the crowd that he understood why they were beating him and wanted him dead. They were zealous for God. Paul was not blaming them for what they had done to him. He pointed out that in his former zeal he would have done the same thing. Paul showed compassion even to his attackers; we should model that same type of compassion for all people who have not yet placed their faith in Jesus.

22:6–8 Now it happened: Paul shared his personal testimony. God has given to each of us a testimony of how He has changed our lives. We must share that testimony to everyone who will listen (1:8). Peter exhorts us in 1 Pet. 3:15

always to be ready to give an answer for the hope that lies within us.

22:9, 10 did not hear the voice: The men who had accompanied Paul heard the sound but could not understand the words that were being spoken to Paul. We are not told why they could not understand the sound they heard.

22:11 I could not see for the glory: Jesus told Paul to get up and go into Damascus. A divine appointment was waiting for him there. Paul arose but could not see. In the silence of his blindness there was deep repentance as he looked into the darkness of his own heart. In quiet times of honest reflection honest repentance may be experienced.

22:12–16 Calling on the name of the Lord saves us. Baptism is the declaration of that calling (Rom. 10:9–13).

22:17 returned to Jerusalem: Three years later (Gal. 1:17–19).

22:18–21 to the Gentiles: The Jews refused to hear him further because they believed that to share their privileges with non-Jews would jeopardize their nation's unique relation to God.

22:22, 23 they listened to him: The Jews did not hate all Gentiles. In fact, they permitted God-fearing Gentiles to worship in the Court of the Gentiles. A Gentile could even become a proselyte, recognized as a Jew, by being circumcised and obeying the laws of Moses. Thus the Jews in this passage were not upset about allowing Gentiles to worship God, but at the idea that Gentiles could be on an equal footing with them before God without being proselytes. The fact that the Gentiles could come to God directly by faith in Jesus Christ was offensive to them.

22:24 The scourge was a leather whip, studded with pieces of metal or bone, fastened to a wooden handle. Paul had been beaten before with whips and rods (2 Cor. 11:24, 25). But **scourging** was worse. The punishment was used to cripple for life or to kill. The victim endured this torture either stretched out on the floor, tied to a pillar, or tied to a hook suspended from the ceiling.

22:25 Is it lawful: The Roman law was that no Roman citizen could be chained, scourged, or killed without a proper trial. Failure to obey this law resulted in severe punishment for the one who commanded the illegal punishment. Paul had been chained and was about to be scourged without any formal charges having been made.

22:26–30 Originally the privileges of Roman citizenship were limited to free people living in the city of Rome. Later, citizenship was granted to others living in the Roman Empire. Sometimes the emperor would offer citizenship

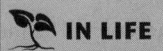 **IN LIFE** | **Faith and Rights**

Human rights" is not a new concept. Nearly every social structure has at least some rules to protect its members.

As a Roman commander arrested Paul and ordered that he be beaten, Paul used his Roman citizenship to protect his rights (Acts 22:25–29). He had done the same thing at Philippi after being illegally jailed (16:36–40). In Jerusalem, he insisted on due process rather than endure unjust mob retaliation. He set the record straight so that the authorities could intervene appropriately.

Rumor, anger, or distortion regarding the faith need to be met forthrightly, as Paul's example shows. There's no need to allow discrimination to hinder one's practice of Christianity in society, particularly in one's workplace. As believers, we need a clear understanding of the laws and rules and their application, and we need to ensure that they are applied fairly on behalf of everyone—including ourselves.

to those who had rendered outstanding service. Possibly Paul's father or grandfather had became a citizen this way with the result that Paul was **born** a Roman. Ultimately God used Paul's Roman citizenship to spread the gospel to Rome.

23:1–3 whitewashed wall: Whitewash is a thin paint used to make something dirty look clean. The fact that Ananias had someone else "do his dirty work" did not absolve him from the ordering of the act. Ananias deserved this rebuke because his having Paul slapped in the face was unlawful. No Israelite was to be struck in the face by another Israelite (Lev. 19:15).

23:4, 5 Note that Paul did not defend his behavior (v. 3), but rather repented of it. **I did not know:** There are several possible reasons why Paul did not know Ananias was the high priest. It could be that Paul's eyesight was poor, and he could not see Ananias clearly. Or perhaps this was not a normal assembly of the Sanhedrin, and the high priest was not wearing his normal robes or sitting in his usual place. It had been 20 years since Paul had associated with this group. Possibly he did not know who was the current High Priest.

23:6–8 The **Sadducees** did not believe in the resurrection of the dead, miracles, life after death, or the existence of angels. On the other hand, the **Pharisees** believed in the supernatural and affirmed the very things the Sadducees denied.

23:9, 10 let us not fight against God: Perhaps they remembered the warning of their famous teacher Gamaliel (5:39).

23:11 bear witness at Rome: Warned by friends not to go to Jerusalem, Paul may have begun to doubt his decision. The Lord encouraged Paul not to be afraid because he was under the sovereign care of God. As Paul had borne witness to Jesus as a prisoner in Jerusalem, so he would do as a prisoner in Rome. Paul's

chains would glorify God in ways that would have been impossible without them.

23:12–15 The willingness of the Jewish **council** to cooperate with the assassination plot against Paul shows how conscious they were of their weak case against him.

23:16–24 Paul was to be escorted out of the city under cover of darkness surrounded by hundreds of soldiers. Apparently the commander thought the threat of assassination was serious enough to commit almost half of the entire garrison at the Fortress of Antonia to escorting Paul at least part of the way to Rome.

23:25–30 He wrote a letter: Roman law required a subordinate officer to send a written statement of the case with a prisoner when he referred the case to his superior.

23:31, 32 Slipping out of Jerusalem when the city was quiet, the foot soldiers and cavalry probably attracted little attention. Ahead lay **Antipatris,** 40 miles away, by way of a winding downhill road where an ambush would have been disastrous. Antipatris was used by the Romans as a relay station for their troops. The rest of the journey was over open plain where there was no need for a large number of soldiers. The foot soldiers returned to Jerusalem, leaving the seventy horsemen to escort Paul the remaining distance to Caesarea, the capital of Judea. The hand of God over Paul's life can be seen in the provision of such extraordinary protection.

23:33, 34 the governor: Antonius Felix governed Judea from A.D. 52 to 60. Felix had been a slave, but had gained the status of freedman under the Emperor Claudius. Because Felix's brother was a friend of the emperor, Felix's political career blossomed, even though he was not popular among his peers. Felix was known for indulging in every kind of lust, and the writer Tacitus described him as "exercising the powers of a king with the character of a slave." **he was from Cilicia:** After reading the letter from Jerusalem, Felix wanted to know Paul's home province. When he learned it was Cilicia he decided to hear the case, because the political status of Cilicia did not require its natives to be sent back there for trial.

23:35 As the official residence built by Herod the Great, **Herod's Praetorium** included cells for prisoners (John 18:28; Phil. 1:13).

24:1–5 we have found this man: There were three basic charges against Paul: political treason, religious heresy, and temple desecration. His opponents argued that Paul had been causing riots throughout the empire, that he spoke against the Law of Moses, and that he had brought a Gentile into the Jewish temple courts.

24:6–12 Paul first addressed the charge of sedition, knowing that if he was found guilty it would mean his life. He demonstrated how

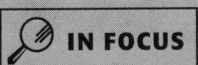

IN FOCUS "Nazarenes"

(Gk. *Nazōraios*) (24:5; Matt. 2:23) Strong's #3480: The name means "those who belong to the Nazarene." Jesus was called "the Nazarene" (Matt. 2:23). It was not a flattering designation, but an insulting one. The Jewish leaders never thought the Messiah could come from Nazareth, a small town in Galilee, a region that was populated by many Gentiles and therefore was held in contempt by orthodox Jews. The early church was stigmatized with the same name; they were known as "the sect of the Nazarenes" (Acts 24:5). This meant they were considered an aberrant Jewish group (or sect) that believed that Jesus of Nazareth was the Messiah.

ridiculous the charge was in that it had only been **twelve days** since he had come to Jerusalem. This was hardly enough time to incite riots or start revolutions in Judea.

24:13, 14 Paul openly admitted that he was a follower of **the Way,** but he contended that he still believed **the Law** and **the Prophets.** That is, he was a follower of Judaism, a religion protected by Rome.

24:15–17 offerings to my nation: Paul had brought a gift from the Gentile churches to the Christians at Jerusalem as an expression of thanks for the gospel (1 Cor. 16:1–4; 2 Cor. 8; 9; Rom. 15:25–33).

24:18, 19 The reference to **Jews from Asia**

indicated to Felix that Paul's real accusers were not present, creating some suspicion about the charges against the apostle.

24:20–22 having more accurate knowledge of the Way: How did Felix know about the Christian faith? His wife Drusilla was Jewish. She was the great-granddaughter of Herod the Great, who had tried to kill the baby Jesus. She was the great-niece of the Herod who killed John the Baptist. Her father was the man who had the apostle James put to death (12:1, 2). Also, Felix was well acquainted with Christianity from having governed Judea and Samaria for six years.

24:23–25 Felix had taken Drusilla from her former husband, the king of Emesa in Syria. She was Felix's third wife. His first wife was the granddaughter of Mark Antony and Cleopatra. His second wife was a princess whom he also divorced. When Paul talked about **righteousness, self-control,** and the coming **judgment,** Felix must have been reminded of his immoral life. He refused to talk any more about the Way because of the guilt he felt.

24:26 Felix may have hoped that Paul had **money** from the Gentile churches or that perhaps Paul's friends would pay a ransom for him. Felix wanted to talk about a payoff; Paul wanted to talk about righteousness (v. 25).

24:27 after two years: It may be that this was the time Luke wrote most of the Book of Acts, considering that he had access to people in Jerusalem and Caesarea for information about the early church. After two years, another riot broke out in Caesarea. Felix crushed it with such force that he was removed as governor around A.D. 60.

25:1–4 The Jews hated Felix, and they wrote letters to Rome detailing their outrage over his brutality against them. As a result, Felix was replaced as governor by Porcius **Festus.** Festus learned from the mistakes of Felix. Three days after arriving in Caesarea, Festus headed to Jerusalem to meet with the Jewish leaders to establish some sort of working arrangement with the high priest and the Sanhedrin. **they petitioned him:** The Jewish leaders pressured Festus not for a concession or a favor. They wanted Festus to send Paul back to Jerusalem for trial. Their plan was to assassinate Paul on the way (23:15).

25:5 see if there is any fault in him: Festus reopened Paul's case in an attempt to appease the Jewish leaders.

25:6–12 Paul knew that as a citizen of Rome he could insist on a trial before the Roman judgment seat, and not the Jewish Sanhedrin, where he would find little justice. The **appeal to Caesar** was the right of any Roman citizen. If a citizen thought he was not getting

✚ IN CONTEXT   Paul's Roman Citizenship

When it suited his needs, Paul used his status as a Roman citizen to frustrate his adversaries. His citizenship made kings and governors, soldiers and priests, and Romans and Jews all think twice about their intended actions toward him. But what did it mean to be a citizen of Rome?

The Roman Empire was the reigning power of its day. Being a citizen of the empire carried certain rights, responsibilities, and status. A citizen was liable for Roman property taxes and municipal taxes, but also had the right to vote in Rome (although during Paul's time different social classes had different rights). A Roman citizen was guaranteed a fair trial and was protected against certain forms of harsh punishment. A Roman citizen could not be executed without a trial and could not be crucified except by order of the emperor. A citizen could even appeal to Caesar in order to be tried in Rome.

Paul was born a Roman citizen, but how his family gained that citizenship is unknown. There were several ways to become a Roman citizen. Being born to a Roman parent was one way. Retiring from the Roman army was another. Citizenship could be granted by an emperor or a Roman general to an individual or to an entire group. Finally a person could purchase citizenship.

The empire of Rome was so powerful that few wished to incur its wrath by breaking its laws. Paul was intelligent enough to know all of his rights and savvy enough to know how to use them to his and especially God's advantage. Not only did his rights as a Roman citizen often save his life in dangerous situations (22:25), they also allowed him to carry the gospel message to jailers, shipmates, kings, and to the emperor in Rome (25:11).

justice in a provincial court, he could appeal to the emperor himself. If the appeal was declared valid, all other proceedings in the lower courts ceased and the prisoner was sent to Rome for disposition of his case.

25:13 Festus decided to present the problem to King Agrippa II (A.D. 53 to about 100). He and **Bernice** were children of Herod Agrippa I who died at Caesarea (12:23). Although Agrippa was king of only a small area in northern Palestine, he had the right of appointing the Jewish high priest and was considered an expert on Jewish affairs (26:3).

25:14–22 Festus laid Paul's case before the king: Festus had a problem. In the case of an appeal, a letter had to be written providing the details of the case. Festus did not understand what was going on with Paul or why the Jewish leaders hated him. When King Agrippa arrived to bring his official greetings, it gave Festus an opportunity to get an opinion from one who might have understood such things.

25:23–26 my lord: The Roman emperor, Nero (A.D. 54–68).

25:27 unreasonable . . . not to specify the charges: Hence the opportunity for Agrippa to hear Paul, which the king welcomed. Paul was equally pleased to bear witness before such a distinguished audience and a relatively friendly king.

26:1 Stretched out his hand: In salutation to the king.

26:2–5 I lived a Pharisee: The Jewish his-

torian Josephus described the Pharisees as "a body of Jews with the reputation of excelling the rest of the nation in the observances of religion, and as exact exponents of the laws." Paul pointed out that he was not some stranger or foreigner trying to start a new religion. He was a Jew, a Pharisee, who lived out his Jewish faith better than most.

26:6–9 for the hope of the promise: Paul was not being judged because he had done something wrong. He had not turned against his own Jewish heritage. Instead he fervently believed in the promises God had made to the nation of Israel: the promise of a coming Messiah and the reestablishment of the kingdom of God. Paul did not reject the hope of salvation for Israel. Instead he saw that hope fulfilled in the life, death, and resurrection of Jesus. The fact that Jesus had been raised from the dead confirmed to Paul that all believers would be raised from the dead to enjoy the blessings of the promised kingdom of God.

26:10 I cast my vote against them: Some have concluded that Paul must have been a member of the Sanhedrin at some time, since he mentions casting a vote. However, Paul was probably too young to belong to such a body of aged men or elders. Paul may have been the Sanhedrin's chief prosecutor, urging a verdict of guilty against those Christians he had hunted down in the course of his campaign of persecution.

26:11 The imperfect tense of the verb **com-**

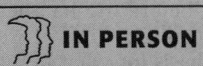

IN PERSON | Agrippa, Paul's Judge

Marcus Julius Agrippa was the Roman name of Agrippa II, the last of the Herodian dynasty of five Roman-appointed kings in Palestine. He and his father, Agrippa I, were descended from the Jewish-born Herod the Great, ruler of Judea at the time of Christ's birth (Matt. 2:1).

The writings of the Jewish historian Josephus (A.D. 37–100) provide the most information about Agrippa. Since he was too young to receive the throne of Judea in A.D. 44 when his father died, the Romans appointed a governor. Agrippa himself was given other territories to rule, notably in Galilee.

At the beginning of the Jewish revolt in A.D. 66 Agrippa came to Jerusalem to quell the disorder. Unsuccessful in this venture, he became an ardent Roman sympathizer. Josephus (*The Wars of the Jews* 2:345) attributes a speech to Agrippa in which he warned that the Romans were much too strong for the Jews to resist, and thus they should side with them. After the revolt in A.D. 70 the Romans gave Agrippa additional territory in reward for his loyalty.

In A.D. 59 the apostle Paul stood trial before Agrippa, who was considered an expert on Jewish affairs, and was interested in Paul's case (Acts 25:13—26:32). The king was accompanied at the trial by his sister Bernice (25:13, 23). Rumors about Agrippa, who apparently never married, having an incestuous relationship with Bernice were denied by Josephus while supported by the Roman writer Juvenal. Paul's judge was a Jewish king, a Roman sympathizer, and a man of questionable moral reputation. As Paul defended his Christian faith, he appealed to Agrippa's Jewish background, challenging even him to become a believing Jew (26:2, 3, 26, 27).

pelled does not tell us whether or not Paul had actually been successful in causing believers to **blaspheme** their faith, only that he had tried to compel them to do so.

26:12, 13 a light from heaven: Nothing less than an act of God could have changed the zealot Saul into the apostle Paul.

26:14 kick against the goads: A young ox, when it was first yoked, usually resented the burden and tried kicking its way out. If the ox was yoked to a single-handed plow, the plowman would hold a long staff with a sharpened end close to the heels of the ox. Every time the ox kicked, it struck the spike. If the ox was yoked to a wagon, a studded bar with wooden spikes served the same purpose. The point was that the ox had to learn submission to the yoke the hard way. Before his encounter with Jesus on the Damascus road, Paul was resisting God in a similar manner (1 Tim. 1:13).

26:15 I am Jesus, whom you are persecuting: You are sinning against Me, but I am forgiving you.

26:16, 17 Gentiles, to whom I now send you: Paul's primary calling was Gentile evangelism (Eph. 3:6, 7). The fact that Paul was born in the Gentile city of Tarsus uniquely qualified him for this ministry.

26:18 from darkness to light: God's enlightenment promised by the prophets had come (Is. 42:6, 7, 16; Col. 1:12). To follow Christ meant leaving the reign of **Satan** and submitting to the control of **God**. Both **forgiveness**

and sanctification come by **faith** in Christ. Those who are forgiven may **receive an inheritance among those who are sanctified.**

26:19 I was not disobedient: We must never forget that grace and faith must be followed by obedience.

26:20–22 Repentance indicates a complete change in thinking. In Rom. 12:2, Paul speaks of the "renewing of your mind." We do what we think is best, what makes sense to us. Paul was killing Christians because he thought it was the correct course of action. Christ's revelation changed his thoughts, but his preaching of the Good News was visible proof that he had repented of his former ways. Genuine repentance is evidenced by changed behavior.

26:23 Christ would suffer . . . rise . . . proclaim light: The gospel in a capsule.

26:24–32 Agrippa realized that Paul was doing more than just defending his faith; he was actually trying to persuade Agrippa to become a follower of Jesus Christ. If Agrippa had told those gathered that he did not believe the prophets, he would have angered the Jews. If he had acknowledged that he did believe the prophets, he would have had to give weight to Paul's words. Agrippa avoided being maneuvered into an embarrassing corner by sidestepping the issue. The interview was becoming too personal for Agrippa's comfort, so he ended the dialogue.

27:1 we: Luke accompanied Paul on this journey (for other "we" passages, see 16:10–17;

20:5–15; 21:1–18). **other prisoners:** Some of the other prisoners may have also appealed to Caesar, or they may have been under sentence of death and were on their way to Rome to appear as combatants in the arena.

27:2 The pronouns **we** and **us** indicate that Luke was also a member of the party.

IN FOCUS **"Christian"**

(Gk. *Christianos*) (11:26; 26:28; 1 Pet. 4:16) Strong's #5546: This word means "one who belongs to Christ." It was first used as a term of contempt against the believers at Antioch (11:26). In the NT, the word is found in only three places (26:28; 1 Pet. 4:16). In the early days of the church, the believers did not have a distinctive name. They called each other "brothers" (6:3), "disciples" (6:1), "believers" (1Tim. 4:12), followers of "the Way" (9:2), or "saints" (1 Cor. 1:2). Jews who denied that Jesus was the Messiah would never call believers Christians, but called them the Nazarenes (24:5). In Antioch, where many Gentiles were converted and where missionary work beyond the Jewish community began in earnest, the believers were no longer considered a Jewish sect, so their pagan neighbors began calling them by a new name, Christian.

27:3 Julius treated Paul kindly: Roman officials treated this prisoner with great respect (16:35–39; 18:12–16; 23:12–24).

27:4–6 the winds were contrary: This was not a good time for sailing. It was just before the winter months when sailing became difficult because of storms. Because of headwinds, the ship had to sail north of the island of Cyprus, using it and the mainland to break the force of the gale. Eventually the travelers reached the port of Myra where a larger ship was found to sail to Italy.

27:7–9 Paul and his shipmates neared **Cnidus** on the southwest tip of Asia Minor, some 130 miles from Myra, which would have been their last port of call before sailing across the Aegean Sea to the coast of Greece. However, the wind was so strong that the ship was forced southward. The ship sailed along the southern coast of the island of **Crete,** again using the island to break the force of the wind. Finally the ship docked at a small port called **Fair Havens.** The season for sailing was over, and continuing the journey would have been dangerous.

27:9–12 Paul advised them: Paul had been at sea many times before. He had been shipwrecked at least two other times (2 Cor. 11:25), so he had some basis for what he was saying. However, his counsel was rejected. Because Fair Havens was a little town, the sailors decided to try to reach Phoenix, the major port on the west side of Crete, some 60 miles away. It could be that the owner of the ship wanted to get his grain to a larger port so that he could sell it. Furthermore Julius, the centurion in charge, probably wanted a better place to winter his men. In other words, greed and the desire for comfort may have gotten in the way of good sense.

27:13–16 In the morning there was a calm over the sea and a breeze blowing from the south, so the travelers quickly set sail, hugging the shoreline for protection. Suddenly a violent northeasterly storm called **Euroclydon** (a name given to all northeasterly storms) hit the ship, preventing the crew from sailing into the wind. The word translated **tempestuous** is the root of our word *typhoon*. The storm drove the ship south of a small island named **Clauda,** which broke the force of the gale long enough for the crew to take some measures to save the ship.

27:17, 18 cables to undergird the ship: Because the ship's timbers could come apart, the sailors passed strong ropes under the ship, pulling up tight to hold the ship together. **run aground on the Syrtis Sands:** The sailors were fearful of the sandbars of Syrtis, just off the northern coast of Africa. The crew of Paul's ship let down a sea anchor, attempting to slow themselves down.

27:19 the ship's tackle: Everything that added weight to the hull.

27:20–27 no loss of life: Paul had been given absolute assurance by the all-powerful and all-knowing God that no one would be lost on the ship. Yet in v. 31 Paul warned that if the sailors were successful in escaping from the ship, the Roman soldiers would lose their lives. Because of Paul's comments, the soldiers stopped the sailors from leaving the ship and everyone made it ashore alive (v. 44). God fulfilled His purpose and promise through the warnings of Paul and the choices of the soldiers.

27:28 A fathom equals six feet (2 m).

27:29–41 place where two seas met: A shoal on the north side of Malta bears the name "Bay of St. Paul." Since Paul's visit in A.D. 60, without interruption, the inhabitants of the island have been Christian.

27:42, 43 The soldiers planned **to kill the prisoners** because they knew Roman military law. If a prisoner escaped, the soldier on guard would be liable for the punishment of the one who escaped.

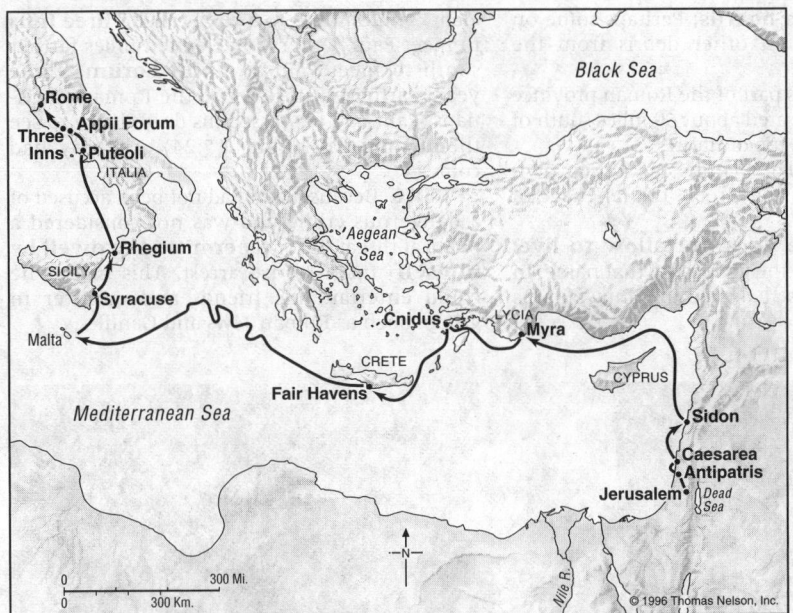

Paul's Journey to Rome

In Jerusalem after his third missionary journey, Paul struggled with Jews who accused him of profaning the temple (21:26–34). He was placed in Roman custody in Caesarea for two years, but after appealing to Caesar was sent by ship to Rome. After departing the island of Crete, Paul's party was shipwrecked on Malta by a storm. Three months later he finally arrived at the imperial city.

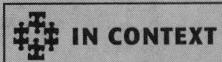 **IN CONTEXT** **From Malta to Rome**

Springtime on the Mediterranean meant the return of cargo-laden ships from Alexandria, Egypt. They used westerly winds to deliver their goods to the empire's key ports.

Paul was transported from Malta to Rome on one such vessel, a voyage that covered 180 nautical miles in less than two days at sea (Acts 28:11). On the journey he was able to visit three important cities and continue his movement-building work: Syracuse, the dominant city of Sicily; Rhegium, a key harbor town on the Italian side of the Strait of Messina; and Puteoli, gateway to southern Italy, just 33 miles from Rome.

Throughout Christian history, the gospel has invariably traveled the routes of commerce. For example, many have been introduced to the Good News through the witness of:

- merchants doing business in foreign countries;
- employees of multinational corporations stationed overseas;
- consultants advising governments and businesses worldwide;
- medical personnel serving in developing nations;
- faculty and students studying and teaching around the world; and
- soldiers in foreign lands during war or occupation.

27:44 some on boards: Perhaps some on planks and some on other debris from the broken ship.

28:1 Malta was part of the Roman province of Sicily and was located about 60 miles south of that island near the toe of Italy.

28:2 natives: The people spoke their own dialect instead of using Greek, the language of cultured people.

28:3, 4 justice does not allow to live: Justice may refer to the goddess of that name. In any case the Maltese believed the universe was under moral law.

eled 33 miles south to a place called **Three Inns** to meet Paul. Others traveled ten miles farther south to meet Paul at **Appii Forum.** Three years earlier in his letter to the Roman Christians, Paul had expressed his deep desire to see them some day (Rom. 15:24). The day had come.

28:16 Because Paul had not been accused of a dangerous crime and was not considered a political threat, he was **permitted to dwell by himself** under house arrest. This meant he could entertain his friends and minister to groups such as Roman Jews and Gentiles.

Photo by Howard Vos

Paul met a group of Christians from Rome at the town of Appii Forum, probably situated on this ancient Roman road known as the Appian Way (Acts 28:15).

28:5–8 lay sick of a fever: This fever was possibly Malta fever, which was common in Malta, Gibraltar, and other Mediterranean islands. The microorganism has since been traced to the milk of the Maltese goats. The fever usually lasted four months, but sometimes could last as long as two or three years.

28:9–11 This **Alexandrian ship** bore a figurehead of the sons of Zeus called the **Twin Brothers,** Castor and Pollux, the mythological figures revered by sailors as protectors on the sea.

28:12–15 Some Christians from Rome trav-

28:17 leaders of the Jews: By this time, the decree of the emperor Claudius (18:2) had been allowed to lapse, and Jews had returned to Rome.

28:18–22 The Jewish leaders had not **received** any news about Paul from **Judea.** It may be that after Paul's appeal to Caesar, Paul was on the first ship that made it to Italy. Or the Jewish antagonists may have given up their attacks on Paul, having already failed with Felix, Festus, and Agrippa. A third reason may be that the Jews, only recently back in Rome after the expulsion of Claudius, wanted to avoid trouble.

INSIGHT | Looking Beyond Rome

aul felt driven to get to Rome (Acts 19:21; Rom. 1:15), no doubt because it was the capital city. But he also intended to stop there on his way to Spain (15:28).

Why was Spain significant? It's impossible to say exactly what Paul had in mind. But the OT prophet Isaiah predicted that in the end times Gentiles would join Jews at Jerusalem to worship God, inaugurating a marvelous new era (Is. 66:19–24). Isaiah's text refers to "Tarshish," thought to mean Spain. Is it possible that Paul believed that getting the gospel to Rome meant being one step closer to the fulfillment of Isaiah's glorious vision (Acts 26:23; 28:28)? We don't know whether Paul ever made it to Spain.

28:23–25 some were persuaded . . . some disbelieved: These contrasting reactions were experienced by Jesus and by every evangelist thereafter.

28:26, 27 you will see, and not perceive: This quotation (Is. 6:9, 10) is cited five times in the NT to explain rejections of gospel truth.

28:28–30 two whole years: During this time Paul was permitted to minister to anyone who came to his rented house. Paul also wrote four of the NT letters (Ephesians, Philippians, Colossians, and Philemon) during this period.

28:31 Luke does not reveal what happened to Paul's case. Apparently it had not yet been decided when Luke finished Acts. There are good reasons for believing that Paul was released, since he had been found innocent by all Roman officials up to this point. Ancient tradition tells us that Paul actually went to Spain as he desired (Rom. 15:24). In his captivity letters, Paul expressed his hope of being released (Philem. 22) and his confidence that he would be released (Phil. 1:25). Paul's Pastoral Epistles contain items that cannot be fitted into the Book of Acts, suggesting that they were written later. For instance, Titus 1:5 implies that Paul ministered on the island of Crete, something that is not reported in the Book of Acts. Paul most likely resumed his missionary travels for two more years before being rearrested, retried, condemned, and executed as a martyr some time between A.D. 64–67.

The Epistle to the

Romans

■

ROMANS SERVES AS THE FLAGSHIP OF THE FLEET of Pauline letters within the New Testament. This letter has also loomed large in the history of Christianity. Countless men and women of faith have singled out Romans as the weapon God graciously used to bring about their surrender to Christ. Augustine, Martin Luther, John Wesley, and others received unexpected spiritual volleys from Romans that

pierced their defenses and ended their rebellion against God.

Romans combines breadth, logic, and a mature understanding of the Old Testament Scriptures into a powerful arsenal. By the time it was written, the Holy Spirit had shaped the apostle Paul into a skillful communicator of the faith. The result is his letter to the Romans, a theological treatise that perfectly fits Paul's description of all Scripture as "profitable for doctrine, for reproof, for correction, for instruction in righteousness" (2 Tim. 3:16). The letter represents a full expression of apostolic theology. Paul's arguments challenge the secular, pagan mind, yet they also pierce the shallow spiritual confidence of many nonpagans. Romans is a mighty leveler, for it declares that "all have sinned and fall short of the glory of God" (3:23). Since all are sinners, it comes as a delightful shock that "God demonstrates His own love towards us, in that while we were still sinners, Christ died for us" (5:8). This is the Good News, which Paul so eloquently and systematically defends in this theological treatise addressed to the Romans.

All of Paul's other letters arise from a partic-

ular occasion and have a definite purpose. Romans is different; from the content it seems to have a much more general didactic aim. Having said this, it is possible to see at least three purposes Paul had in writing the book.

His first purpose was to prepare the Romans for his planned journey to Rome and later to Spain. His immediate itinerary involved a trip to Jerusalem, but his vision was toward the west. He clearly suggests that he expects assistance from them in his endeavor to carry the gospel to Spain (15:24). But if that had been his only purpose, a brief note would have been enough. Obviously Paul had more in mind.

A second purpose involved Paul's understanding that the believers needed to "be established" (1:11). Paul wanted to give them a well-instructed faith. His letter is a kind of syllabus of Paul's apostolic teaching. Romans is a masterful presentation of God's plan of salvation for Jews and Gentiles.

The third purpose for the letter was pastoral. Paul wanted to exhort Jewish and Gentile believers to live in harmony. As in most of the early churches, the gospel brought different groups of people together who otherwise would have stayed apart, whether for reasons of nationality, status, or culture. Once they came together under one roof, the challenge was to preserve their oneness in Christ. Thus, throughout the letter, Paul deals with problems arising from Jewish and Gentile differences. He emphasizes what everyone shared. Since there is only one God, He is the God of both Jew and Gentile. Both groups are under sin (3:9), and both are saved through faith (3:30). This theme of Jew and Gentile living together surfaces most clearly in chs. 14 and 15, where Paul deals with the practical aspects of being together in one body. Paul hammers home his central theme: the righteous God justifies and ultimately glorifies both Jew and Gentile by grace through faith.

Romans includes the most systematic presentation of theology found anywhere in Scripture. It explains the meaning of the Cross for the believer's life. While expounding why Jesus died for all of humanity, Paul clarifies the core concepts of the Christian faith: sin and righteousness, faith and works, justification and election. The letter contains (1) a detailed description of the sinfulness of man (1:18—3:20); (2) an extensive discussion of justification by faith (3:21—5:11), including a clear interpretation of the death of Christ (3:24–26); (3) an elaborate explanation of sanctification (5:12—8:39); (4) a strong section on the doctrine of election (9:1–29); (5) a developed exposition of what happened to the nation of Israel and the destiny of God's people (9:1—11:36); (6) an extended section addressing spiritual gifts (12:1–8); and (7) instructions on the believers' relationship to government (13:1–14). Certainly Romans is the most doctrinal book in the Bible.

Because it provides a systematic outline of the essentials of the Christian faith, it is as useful to the mature believer as it is to someone who wants a short introduction to the Christian faith.

The author introduces himself in the first verses of Romans by name (Paul), by identity (bondservant), by vocation (apostle), and by purpose (separated to the gospel of God). Romans has been recognized as an epistle of Paul throughout church history. The character and message of Paul, which we read so much about in Acts, appear in Romans as his signature to the letter.

This letter was written to a vibrant church in the city of Rome. Although the origins of the church are unknown, it could have been established by new believers returning from Jerusalem following the Resurrection and the outpouring of the Holy Spirit at Pentecost. When Paul wrote this letter he had not personally visited Rome, although he had desired to do so for some time.

Few clues are included in the Epistle to the Romans about the Roman believers. Paul admired their faith and prayed regularly for them. It is evident that the church included both Jews and Gentiles. On the surface it does not appear that any problem in the church at Rome was the occasion for the epistle. However, there is some indication that the believers at Rome needed to be exhorted to live in harmony (14:1—15:13). Evidence in the Corinthian letters, in Romans, and in Acts indicates that Paul wrote to the Roman church from Corinth on his third missionary journey. When Paul composed the Corinthian epistles, he referred to a collection for the poor Christian believers in Jerusalem that

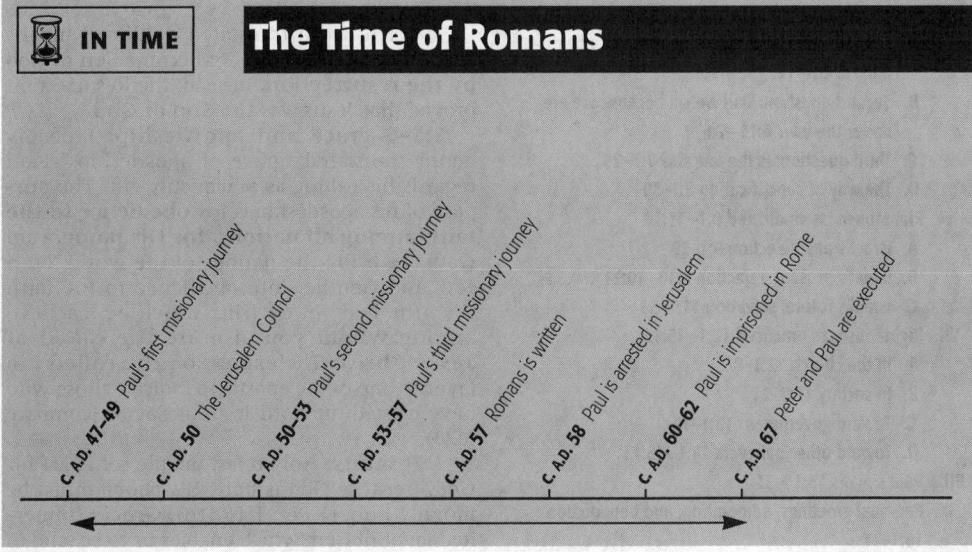

IN TIME

The Time of Romans

c. A.D. 47-49 Paul's first missionary journey
c. A.D. 50 The Jerusalem Council
c. A.D. 50-53 Paul's second missionary journey
c. A.D. 53-57 Paul's third missionary journey
c. A.D. 57 Romans is written
c. A.D. 58 Paul is arrested in Jerusalem
c. A.D. 60-62 Paul is imprisoned in Rome
c. A.D. 67 Peter and Paul are executed

was being gathered from the various Mediterranean churches (1 Cor. 16:1–3; 2 Cor. 8:1—9:1). By the time Romans was written that task had been completed and Paul was about to depart to Jerusalem to deliver the funds (15:22–29).

The implication is that Paul planned to sail for Judea directly from Corinth. Phoebe also, a fellow believer, was about to leave Corinth for Rome. She was presumably the bearer of the letter from Paul to the Romans. Since practically all navigation on the Mediterranean Sea ceased after November 11 and was not resumed again until March 10, Romans was likely written in the fall of A.D. 57.

A plot by the Jews, however, changed Paul's travel plans. Instead of taking a ship from Corinth, he went through Macedonia by foot (Acts 20:3) and eventually left for Jerusalem from Philippi the next spring (Acts 20:6). Little did Paul know that his eventual arrival in Rome would be in captivity (Acts 28:17–31).

Outline

Commentary

1:1–7 In NT times the opening section of a letter named the sender and the recipient. **Paul** (v. 1) wrote this letter to **all who are in Rome** (v. 7). In addition to his greetings, Paul includes a brief summary of the **gospel of God** to be treated in this epistle. That gospel was **promised** in the OT (v. 2), was about **Jesus Christ** (vv. 3, 4), and was the basis of Paul's **apostleship** and mission (vv. 5, 6).

1:1 Bondservant means "slave." Paul is talking about a slavery undertaken voluntarily out of love (Ex. 21:1–6), unlike the forced slavery well known to many in the Roman Empire. Paul emphasizes his personal subjection to Jesus Christ. By calling himself an **apostle,** Paul places himself on the level of the twelve apostles and claims authority from God for His work. **separated to the gospel of God:** Paul was set apart for the ministry of the gospel long before the Damascus road experience (Gal. 1:15). With the pedigree of Paul (Phil. 3:5, 6), he would have made an excellent minister to his people, the Jews. But in the providence of God, Paul was separated unto the gospel of God as an apostle to the Gentiles (Acts 9:15). Thus, a disastrous schism between the Jewish and Gentile factions of the early church was avoided through the unique ministry of Paul.

1:2, 3 Humanly speaking, Jesus was a descendent of **David** (Matt. 1:1). He was truly and completely human; but at the same time, He was God's Son. The fact that Jesus was a descendent of David also links Him to the Davidic covenant. When Christ returns to reign over all, He will fulfill God's promise to David to give him a dynasty that will last forever (2 Sam. 7:8–17).

1:4 The word translated **declared** means "designated." Jesus did not become Son of God **by the resurrection.** Instead, the Resurrection proved that Jesus was **the Son of God.**

1:5–6 grace and apostleship: Probably better translated "grace of apostleship," Paul regards his calling as a heavenly gift. The purpose of his apostleship is **for obedience to the faith among all nations, for His name.** Paul wants to bring the nations of the world, both Jew and Gentile, into obedience to the faith (i.e., the body of doctrine which he teaches). **among whom you also are the called of Jesus Christ:** The expression **the called** is a favorite one of the apostle to indicate those who have trusted the Lord Jesus as Savior (compare 8:28).

1:7 saints: Holy ones, people set apart for God. Because God is holy, His people must be morally holy (1 Pet. 1:15, 16). **Grace:** Unmerited favor of God, which enables us to be, and to do, what God wants. **peace:** Perfect harmony with God, others, and oneself—Christian wholeness. Only after we have experienced God's grace can we experience His peace.

1:8 your faith is spoken of throughout the whole world: So strong was the faith of these Roman believers that, as the church of the Thessalonians (1 Thess. 1:8), Paul speaks of it in worldwide terms. The expression **throughout the whole world** is the common one for "everywhere."

1:9, 10 always in my prayers: Paul prayed for them every time he prayed. In other words, they were on his prayer list. The greatest of saints, and even our Lord Jesus, knew they could not do their work for God or live their lives without praying.

1:11, 12 To impart . . . **some spiritual gift** does not mean that Paul would bestow spiritual gifts like teaching, healing, or prophecy. It means that he would exercise his spiritual gift and in so doing would bless them.

1:13 His ministry elsewhere **hindered** (Gk. *koluo*) Paul from coming to Rome sooner (15:22).

1:14 Paul felt he had a duty to preach to the cultured and uncultured, to the educated and uneducated. Although not many wise people are called, some are (1 Cor. 1:26–29); all need to hear.

1:15–17 Ready to preach the gospel states Paul's commitment. Verses 16 and 17 give his reason for that commitment and summarize the message of the entire epistle.

1:15 I am ready to preach: This expression appears to be the middle statement of a trilogy of three first-person statements concerning Paul's preaching of the gospel of Christ. The first segment is **I am a debtor.** The third statement is **I am not ashamed.** All of us are debtors to Christ. All of us should be unashamed of the gospel of Christ. But not all are ready to preach that gospel. Paul was not only able and willing, but he was ready to preach as well. He was a clean vessel, not just a chosen vessel. He was ready to be used of God.

1:16 The NT speaks of **salvation** in the past tense (Eph. 2:8), the present tense (2 Cor. 2:15), and the future tense (13:11). In the past, the believer has been saved from the penalty of sin. In the present, the believer is being saved from the power of sin. In the future, the believer will be saved from the very presence of sin (Matt. 5:10–12; 8:17; 2 Cor. 5:10; 2 Tim. 2:11–13; Rev. 22:12). **not ashamed:** Paul was ready to preach the **gospel of Christ.** When we really believe in it, we too are eager to make it known. **the power of God:** He was not ashamed because it works. **Salvation** delivers us from the judgment of God and the power of sin. It makes us

God's children, giving us peace with Him and a share in future glory. Christ's atonement makes salvation available to **everyone** who will accept His offer. **believes:** Accepts the truth about Jesus revealed by God and acts accordingly. **the Jew first:** The Jews were first in that God worked with them throughout the OT to prepare salvation for the entire human race. For Paul the term **Greek** includes all people who are not Jews.

1:17 From faith to faith means faith is at the beginning of the salvation process, and it is the goal as well. When a person first exercises faith in Christ, that person is saved from the penalty of sin and declared righteous. As the believer lives by faith, God continues to save him or her from the power of sin to live righteously (v. 16). **the righteousness of God:** A key concept in Romans. God is righteous because He always acts in accord with His holy character and His promises to people. Because He is righteous, He condemns sin and judges sinners (1:18—3:20). Because of that same righteousness, He has provided through Christ forgiveness for all who believe (justification; 3:21—5:21) and power for living a holy life in right relationship to Himself (sanctification; 6:1—8:39). God's righteousness shows itself in His faithful keeping of His promise to the Jews (9:1—11:36), and in His careful instructions for the Christian's daily walk of holiness (12:1—15:13).

1:18–32 God's judgment is a fact (v. 18). Rejection of the knowledge of God is the cause of His judgment (vv. 19–23); increased wickedness is the tragic result (vv. 24–32). There is repetition of the phrase **God gave them up** (vv. 24, 26) or **over** (v. 28), indicating a progression. Each time the phrase is used it indicates that they have become more degenerate.

1:18 As the next verse indicates, **the truth** is truth about God. Having departed from godliness and righteousness, people **suppress** the truth about God: that God is their loving Creator and deserves their worship and praise. Sinful people can mentally perceive the revealed truth of God (vv. 19, 20), but they have chosen to suppress it. They are without excuse. God's anger **is** being **revealed** (the present tense) **against** sin and the suppression of the truth.

1:19, 20 what may be known of God: Not only are divine attributes clearly seen in humanity, but they can be seen in the material universe as well (v. 20; 10:18; Ps. 19:1–4). Nature itself speaks eloquently of its Creator. From the intricate design of the human cell to the majestic strength of the Rocky Mountains, all of God's works testify to His wisdom and power. God's **invisible attributes,** such as His **eternal power** and **Godhead,** meaning His

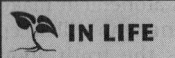 **IN LIFE**   ## Salvation

In the letter to the Romans we find the apostle Paul's clearest and most detailed explanation of the gospel message. After his customary salutation, Paul explains his unabashed passion for taking the Good News of Christ to the ends of the earth: "it is the power of God to salvation for everyone who believes" (1:16). The Greek word for *salvation* used by Paul literally means "deliverance" or "preservation." In a spiritual context, the idea is rescue from the power and dominion of sin. Paul's fervor for preaching the gospel was rooted in its power "to free" or "to rescue" people from the tragic consequences of their own sin.

Paul and the other NT writers portray Jesus Christ, on the basis of His sacrificial death on the Cross in the place of sinners, as the Author and Provider of salvation (3:24, 25; 5:21; Acts 4:12; Heb. 12:2). This spiritual deliverance is graciously and lovingly offered by God to all people, but only those who repent and trust in Jesus will experience its blessings (John 3:16; Eph. 2:8, 9; Heb. 2:3).

What exactly are those blessings? Some Bible teachers summarize them as salvation from the *penalty* of sin, salvation from the *power* of sin, and salvation from the *presence* of sin. Theologians use the terms justification, sanctification, and glorification. *Justification* is the divine act of declaring sinners to be righteous on account of their faith in Jesus. He paid for their sins completely and finally on the Cross, and through faith in Him their sins can be forgiven (3:21; 4:5; 5:1). Closely related to justification is regeneration, in which the Spirit of God indwells a repentant sinner and imparts eternal life to his or her spiritually dead soul (Eph. 2:1–5). *Sanctification* is the process in which God develops the new life of the believer and gradually brings it to perfection (6:11; Phil. 1:6). *Glorification* is the ultimate salvation of the whole person. This occurs when we are face to face with our Savior in His coming kingdom. At that time, God will completely mold us into the image of Christ (8:29, 30; Phil. 3:21). Then we will be able to enjoy complete fellowship with God, singing His praises forever.

Other benefits of salvation include reconciliation and adoption. When our sins are forgiven, we move from a position of being God's enemies to being His beloved children (John 1:12; Gal. 4:4, 5; Eph. 1:5).

Is it any wonder that the apostle Paul was so excited about the gospel and its power to save? The more we consider the marvelous truth of salvation, the more enthusiastic we will be, thankful to God and eager to share with others the hope that is in us (1 Pet. 3:15).

divine nature, can be **clearly seen** by contemplating His awesome works in all of creation.

1:21, 22 They knew, that is "perceived," truth about God through creation (v. 18). Nature reveals God as great and good. Its gentle rain and rich soils provide humans with all varieties of delicious food. God is good. Even with all this evidence in creation, people refuse to recognize their Creator, worship Him, or **glorify Him as God.**

1:23 The ultimate human folly (v. 22) is idolatry.

1:24 In God's present wrath (v. 18; there is also a wrath to come when Christ returns, see 1 Thess. 1:10), **He gave them up,** that is "over," to their sin (vv. 26, 28). God did not give up on humanity, but He did allow them to go deeper and deeper into sin. He gives us an opportunity to see how evil sin really is and how desperately wicked people can become.

1:25 The lie refers to idols. They are satanic counterfeits of God, void of truth and power.

1:26 The next verse makes clear that this

verse refers to unnatural sexual relations between women. Lesbianism is **against nature**; it is contrary to the intention of the Creator.

1:27 Homosexual acts are sin (Lev. 18:22). In this passage, the point is not that homosexuality is a sin that should be punished. Rather homosexuality itself is the punishment. Having rejected God and become idolaters, some men have been given over to their **shameful** passions (v. 26). Thus, they receive **in themselves the penalty of their error.**

1:28 a debased mind: A mind totally devoid of moral sensitivity.

1:29–32 These verses contain one of the most extensive lists of sins in all Scripture. The list shows the exhaustive sweep of human moral depravity (compare **all** in v. 29). Note that while society tends to rationalize certain sins, God judges all sin. These sins particularly reveal our rebellious hearts. All, without exception, deserve God's punishment.

2:1–16 How does God judge? He judges justly (v. 2), according to a person's **deeds** (vv.

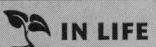

IN LIFE   Facing the Facts About Sin

The Bible is straightforward about the ultimate cause behind suffering and evil. It gives a sobering account of how we human beings, who were created as pure and noble creatures, have become wicked and hurtful toward each other. The Book of Romans speaks candidly about our condition, which it calls sin (Rom. 3:23). This separation from God has resulted in our thoughts becoming futile and our foolish hearts being darkened (1:21). God has given us up to the full outworking of our rebellion against Him (1:24). This has produced:

- *Sexual immorality,* wherein we dishonor the bodies that God gave us (1:24).
- *Idolatry,* wherein we turn away from our Creator and exalt the works of our own hands (1:25).
- *Vile passions,* wherein we become irrational pleasure seekers, often dominated by a perverted sensuality, rather than thoughtful servants of each other and responsible stewards of God's good gifts (1:26, 27).
- *A debased mind,* wherein we come under terrible spiritual bondage that makes us incapable of doing good; we become slaves to sin (1:28).

Paul concludes this severe but enlightening assessment with a list of ugly consequences, including approval of each other's sins (1:29–32). The candor of this list is painful, but honest. Any resistance to sin seems to be overridden by a compulsive search for freedom from all restraints to fulfill unbridled pleasure. Rules, laws, values, traditions, or any other restraints are steadily removed.

Thus, like the people of Sodom and Gomorrah, we are traveling the road to disaster. God declares that because of our sin, we are deserving of death (1:32), inexcusable (2:1), and treasuring up wrath and judgment for ourselves (2:5). This is true of every human being (3:10–12; compare Ps. 51:4).

The Book of Romans carefully spells out the eternal implications of this sinful rebellion. It warns us that sin is real. It is not just bad feelings or an overly sensitive conscience. We have alienated ourselves from a righteous and holy God, and there is a penalty to pay—the penalty of eternal death, of everlasting separation from Him.

However, Romans does not stop there. It tells of God's wonderful provision for us in Jesus Christ, who brought the opportunity for peace with God, access by faith to His grace, and hope of returning to His glory (Rom. 5:1–5). To demonstrate His love, Jesus paid the penalty for our sins on the Cross (5:8). Thus with Paul we can say, "Thanks be to God for His indescribable gift!" (2 Cor. 9:15).

6–10) and in the light of what one knows (vv. 11–16).

2:1 In 1:18–32, Paul declares that all unrighteous people are without excuse. Now he demonstrates that the self-righteous (those who **judge** others) are **inexcusable,** by revealing the standards by which everyone will be judged. Judgment will be (1) according to truth (vv. 1–5), (2) according to works (vv. 6–11), and (3) according to the light one has of the law (vv. 12–16).

2:2 Truth as used in this verse is different from the truth in 1:18, 25. There it referred to the evidence of God in creation; here it refers to the true condition of humanity.

2:3 The **man** who knows what is wrong, condemns it in others, but thinks his own sins will be overlooked by God.

2:4 Repentance literally means "to change one's mind." In this context, it means to reject one's sinful habits and turn to God. This is the only occurrence of this word in Romans.

2:5 Wrath as used here is different from the "wrath of God" in 1:18. There God's wrath was His present anger; here the word refers to God's future wrath. Most take this future wrath to refer to the day of judgment. Thus, people who continue in their rebellion against God are accumulating wrath for themselves.

2:6 who will render to each one according to his deeds: When unsaved men appear before the final judgment bar of God, the Great White Throne Judgment, salvation will not be the issue there. This is a judgment to determine the degree of punishment. Thus, God will mete out punishment in relation to the evil deeds of the individual. By the same token, at the judgment seat of Christ, where only believers appear, God will reward us according to our deeds.

2:7 According to this verse, it seems that **eternal life** can be gained by **doing good.** But Romans clearly teaches justification by faith (3:22). But Paul does not contradict himself.

The subject of this verse is judgment, not justification. Believers who continue in good works will receive rewards in the life to come. Whenever the NT speaks of eternal life as a present possession, it is a gift received by faith (John 3:16); but whenever it refers to eternal life as something to be received in the future by those who are already believers, it refers to eternal rewards (5:21; Gal. 6:8; 1 Tim. 6:17–19; Titus 1:2; 1 Pet. 1:7). Rewards will be based on works accomplished here on earth.

2:8, 9 The **self-seeking** and disobedient will experience God's punishment. **Tribulation** and **anguish** are the fate of every person who **does evil. Truth** refers to the gospel message (Gal. 2:5).

2:10 All believers doing **good** works will be rewarded.

2:11 For there is no partiality with God: An eternal truth is that as God deals in condemnation without favoritism, likewise He deals in salvation without favoritism. God is impartial because He does not change His pattern "to the Jew first," whether righteousness or unrighteousness is involved.

2:12 Those **without law** are the Gentiles (v. 14). Those **in the law** are the Jews.

2:13 hearers . . . doers: It is not enough to know God's will; only those who do His will are pleasing to God (Luke 6:46). **justified:** By having their sins forgiven and being accepted into right relationship with God.

2:14 by nature do the things in the law: Gentiles who do not have the Law still do such things as honor their parents, which indicates that they believe in a basic moral law (v. 15). They know within their hearts that there is a difference between right and wrong. This "law of conscience" serves as a judge to them in place of Moses' law.

2:15 The Law is not inscribed in our hearts, but the **work of the law** is **written** on our

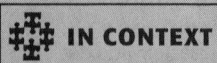 **IN CONTEXT** **The Law**

Paul's reference to "law" (Rom. 2:12) has to do not with laws in general, but with the specific code of rules and regulations that God gave to Moses on Mount Sinai. The Law was part of the covenant that set Israel apart as God's people. It governed their worship, their relationship to God, and their social relationships with one another. The Ten Commandments form a summary of that Law.

Israel was not the only nation to have a law code. Indeed, such collections were common in the ancient world. Most of them began by explaining that the gods gave the king power to reign, along with a pronouncement about how good and capable he was. Then came the king's laws grouped by subject. Finally, most of the codes closed with a series of curses and blessings.

What set the Mosaic Law apart from these other codes was, first of all, its origin. The Law was given by God Himself. It issued from His very nature; like Him it was holy, righteous, and good. Thus, all crimes in Israel were crimes against God (1 Sam. 12:9, 10). He expected all of the people to love and serve Him (Amos 5:21–24). As their final judge, He disciplined those who violated the Law (Ex. 22:21–24; Deut. 10:18; 19:17), though He also held the nation responsible for insuring that justice was carried out (13:6–10; 17:7; Num. 15:32–36).

Furthermore, God ruled over Israel, in effect, as the nation's King. Ancient kings often enacted laws to try to outdo their predecessors in image, economic power, and political influence. God, however, gave His law as an expression of love for His people, to advance their best interests (Ex. 19:5, 6).

The Law can be divided into three categories—moral laws, ceremonial laws, and civil laws. The latter regulated in great detail matters having to do with leaders, the army, criminal cases, crimes against property, humane treatment, personal and family rights, property rights, and other social behavior.

The ceremonial laws contained specifications regarding public worship and ritual, giving high priority to the concept of holiness. Because God is holy (Lev. 21:8), Israel was to be holy in all its religious practices.

The Law was given specifically to Israel, but it rests on eternal moral principles that are consistent with God's character. Thus, it is a summary of fundamental and universal moral standards. It expresses the essence of what God requires of people. That's why when God judges, He can be impartial. Gentiles will not be judged by the Law (Rom. 2:12), since it was not given to them, but they will still be judged by the same righteous standard that underlies the Law.

hearts. The Law of Moses was engraved in stone, and there is a similar moral law within every person.

2:16 According to the **gospel** Paul preached, God will **judge** not only people's actions, but their motives, or **secrets,** as well (1 Cor. 4:5).

2:17–29 Paul applies God's standards of judgment directly to His chosen people. They claim to be instructed in God's will and thus able to distinguish right from wrong. They aspire to teach others (vv. 17–20), yet their inconsistent conduct contradicts their knowledge (vv. 21–24). Their covenant of circumcision has been made useless by their faithless conduct (v. 25). The uncircumcised Gentile is made acceptable to God by his righteous conduct (vv. 26, 27). God looks at the attitude of a person's heart (vv. 28, 29).

2:17 Indeed you are called a Jew, and rest on the law: Israelites who remained in Israel, or who returned to it after the Babylonian captivity, were designated as "Jews," even though tribes other than Judah were included. Paul calls himself a "Jew" in Acts 21:39 but "an Israelite" in Rom. 11:1 and "a Hebrew" in Phil. 3:5. All three names refer to the same people; but in a technical sense "Hebrew" is the racial name, "Israel" is the national name, and "Jew" is the religious name of the sons of Jacob. The Jews rested on the law because it was described as "wisdom and . . . understanding in the sight of the peoples" (Deut 4:6). The Jew did not have to travel around the world to study in a distant university. He did not have to rely on the philosophy of the Gentiles. The Jew trusted his law to be all that he needed and the best education he could get. Thus, he boasted in the God who gave that law.

2:18 things that are excellent: What is morally important.

2:19, 20 The Jewish people Paul addressed were not only **confident** before God (vv. 17, 18), but they felt superior to others and considered themselves to be guides, lights, instructors, and teachers.

2:21–23 There is a touch of sarcasm in Paul's question, **You, therefore who teach another, do you not teach yourself?** The Jews were prepared to teach the heathen Gentiles the commandments of the law, but were themselves breaking these commandments. **Do you steal?** (the eighth commandment), **do you commit adultery?** (the seventh commandment), **do you rob temples?** (the second commandment). The Jews were ready to preach morality but their lives did not back up their message. They were stealing from one another, perhaps by collecting an extreme interest; they were committing adultery; they were profaning

the house of God by commercialism; and thus Paul asked the biting question, **You who make your boast in the law, do you dishonor God through breaking the law?** Transgression of the law brings dishonor to God. The Jews claim to have known the law but were silent in claims to have kept it.

2:21 Special privileges like having the law do not guarantee having righteousness.

2:22 Apparently it was not unusual for their enemies to accuse the Jews of robbing **temples.** Paul may be using the phrase in a figurative way as an equivalent of "to be sacrilegious or impious."

2:23, 24 Paul argues that these particular Jews who thought they were guides to the blind (v. 19) were actually breaking their own laws and dishonoring God (Matt. 15:3–9). Paul applies Is. 52:5 as proof of his point. As a result of their hypocrisy, the Gentiles themselves **blasphemed** God.

2:25, 26 Circumcision becomes a useless ritual unless the person develops an obedient heart that is completely submitted to God (1 Sam. 15:22; Is. 1:11–20). On the other hand, if a Gentile was keeping the law, circumcision would not matter. God judges a person according to the state of his or her heart, not according to external appearances.

2:27 judge you: These self-righteous Jews believed they would escape judgment. According to them, God's judgment was reserved for the Gentiles. However, Paul confronted their hypocrisy. A Gentile who kept the law would be able to judge a Jew who broke it.

2:28, 29 Paul pronounces **circumcision** as being of no value (vv. 25–27). Circumcision that is only outward is of no avail before God because God wants the outward demonstration to be the sign of an inward reality. Paul's teaching is consistent with the Law and the OT prophets, for both proclaimed the need for internal circumcision (Deut. 10:16; Jer. 4:4). **in the Spirit, not in the letter:** The change of heart that Paul describes with the image of internal circumcision is the work of the Holy Spirit, not the result of external obedience to the Law. In fact, God condemns external observance if it is not the product of a righteous heart (Is. 1:10–18).

3:1 What advantage then has the Jew? If the Jews are condemned along with the heathen, what advantage is there in being the chosen nation of God? **Or what is the profit of circumcision?** Since circumcision is the sign of Israel's covenant relationship with God, what advantage is that relationship if being Jewish will not save?

3:2 Much in every way: This verse indicates that the Jewish people have numerous advantages (9:4). The **oracles of God** refers to the entire OT, the laws and the covenants that had been given by God Himself to the nation of Israel. This phrase reaffirms the belief of the apostles of the inspiration of the OT. The Bible is God's Word for us.

3:3, 4 Even if some Jews do **not believe** the Word of God, God will be faithful to what He has promised (Ps. 89:30–37).

3:5 Speaking from a foolish human point of view, Paul asks: If humanity's **unrighteousness** reveals God's **righteousness,** why then should God punish unrighteousness? Paul explains that this is an absurd question that is nonetheless asked by many, when he adds parenthetically, **I speak as a man.** The suggestion that God is unjust is simply ridiculous.

3:6 Paul answers his own question (v. 5) with another question. If God does not punish unrighteousness, then He is not just and there will be no Day of Judgment. The flaw in logic is evident: God's justice demands that He **judge** unrighteousness. To claim that God is unjust *because* He judges is a ludicrous argument.

3:7 The question in this verse is the same basic objection as in v. 5, except this time the sinner objects to being called **a sinner** if his or her sin enhances God's truth.

3:8 Paul takes the erroneous argument a step further. If God can bring good out of evil, then we should not be judged for doing evil, because **good may come** of it. God will be proved righteous and in that way glorified by our sin. Obviously such a position is preposterous. Paul does not even try to argue against such a senseless view; he simply assigns those who hold it to God's judgment.

3:9–20 The Jews are not **better** than the Gentiles; both are guilty of **sin** (v. 9). Quotations from the Jewish OT (vv. 10–18) prove their guilt (v. 19). No man can earn a right relationship with God by doing the requirements of the Mosaic law (v. 20).

3:9 better than they: This question means "Do we Jews have an advantage over the Gentiles?" (v. 1). In other words, "Is there anything we can cling to for protection?" The answer is no, since **all** are **under sin.**

3:10–18 To prove that all are under sin Paul quotes without formal introduction a number of different verses from the OT. The collection of citations can be divided into two parts. The first half is made up of negative statements emphasizing humanity's deficiencies (vv. 10–12); the second half mainly exposes human depravity (vv. 13–18).

3:10 This is a quotation from Ps. 14:3 that says, "There is none who does good." Paul uses the word for **righteous** because he is discussing the unrighteous condition of all people (1:18). No one can be justified on the grounds of his or her own righteousness before God.

3:11 People do not understand spiritual truth (1 Cor. 2:14) nor do they diligently seek after God. At best, people are satisfied with externals, with being "religious."

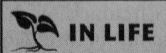 **IN LIFE**   **Good News for Sinners**

It's common today for people to excuse their faults with the attitude, "Hey, nobody's perfect!" True enough. People can only be expected to be human—and that means fallible.

Unfortunately, though, few people take that reality seriously enough. Indeed, when it comes to their standing before God, all too many take a different stance: they may not be perfect, but they're "good enough."

The question is, Are they good enough for God? Romans says they are not. That's what Paul means when he writes, "all are under sin" (Rom. 3:9) and then cites a number of OT passages to back up his claim (3:10–18).

It's not that people are evil through and through, or that they never do any moral good. Quite the contrary. People are capable of impressive acts of courage, compassion, and justice. But in light of God's holy (morally perfect) character, which is the ultimate standard against which people's goodness is measured, people are indeed far from perfect. Their good behavior turns out to be the exception rather than the rule.

The Good News that Paul writes about in Romans, however, is that God has reached out to humanity despite its imperfect ways. His attitude has not been one of rejection, as if to say, "They're not good enough for Me," but one of grace and compassion that says, in effect, "I will make them into good people—people as good as I AM—by means of Christ My Son."

3:12 turned aside: This means turning away from God's way. **unprofitable:** That is, useless to God or His good purposes. **Good:** Apart from God, people lack true goodness and kindness. While some unbelievers are gracious and kind, these acts ultimately have no value because they do not come from believing hearts that seek to glorify God (1:21). Even a "good person" can be rebelling against God and seeking his or her own welfare through goodness.

3:13 In showing humanity's total depravity, Paul quotes passages in the Psalms that describe the evil that can come from the throat, tongue, lips, mouth, feet, and eyes. The heart is compared to a **tomb,** for buried in it is the seed of death. The **throat** reveals the corruption inside, the spiritual decay. The **lips** are like the fangs of an asp; they contain deadly poison.

3:14 Humans apart from God are not blessing others; they are often **cursing** them. They are not loving; they are bitter.

3:15–17 swift to shed blood: People apart from God are prone to violence. They murder and kill because they have no respect for the life of another.

3:18 Fear of God is an OT expression for respect and reverence for God, and is said to be the very beginning of knowledge (Job 28:28; Prov. 1:7). Because people without God are spiritually dead, they produce only deceit, damage, and destruction.

3:19 Whatever the law says refers to vv. 10–18. **All the world,** whether Jewish or Gentile, stands in **guilty** silence **before God.**

3:20 A legal term used of the defendant in a trial, **justified** means "declared righteous." No one will be declared righteous by doing what God requires in the Law. This is confirmed by the fact that the Law was not given to justify sinners but to expose sin (v. 19).

3:21 In this context the **righteousness of God** is not an attribute of God, but an act of God whereby He declares a sinner righteous. This is righteousness *from* God. This righteousness is **apart from the law.** This expression is a strong expression categorically stating that righteousness is given totally apart from any law. See the same use of this word in Hebrews 4:15 where the Lord Jesus was tempted in all points as we are "yet without sin." Just as sin and Jesus Christ have nothing in common, so too the righteousness was not manifested in keeping the law but it was manifested at the Cross when "He (God the Father) made Him (God the Son) who knew no sin to be sin for us, that we might become the righteousness of God in Him" (2 Cor. 5:21).

3:22, 23 God revealed to people how they should live, but no one can live up to God's perfect way. **all have sinned:** No one can live up to what God created us to be; we all **fall short** of His glory. We cannot save ourselves because as sinners we can never meet God's requirements. Our only hope is **faith in Jesus Christ.**

3:24 Those who believe (v. 22) are **justified,** that is, "declared righteous," **freely,** without cost, by God's **grace,** or "favor." **Christ Jesus** died to provide **redemption,** which means He died to pay the price required to ransom sinners. By paying the penalty of their sin through His death, Jesus can free people from their sin and transfer His righteousness to those who believe in Him. On the basis of

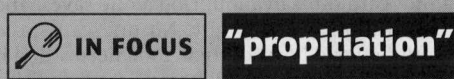

IN FOCUS **"propitiation"**

(Gk. *hilastērion*) (3:25; Heb. 9:5) Strong's #2435: This term is derived from the Greek verb *hilaskomai,* a word which has three meanings: (1) "to placate" or "to appease"; (2) "to be propitious and merciful"; or (3) "to make propitiation for someone." The NT never describes people appeasing God. Instead, as Luke 18:13 and 1 John 2:2 make clear, the NT describes God as being merciful to, or making propitiation, for us. God provides a merciful expiation, or atonement, of the sins of believers through the death of Christ. But since Paul also speaks of God's wrath, it must also speak of the conciliation of God's anger by means of a sacrifice—namely, the sacrifice of His Son. John states that God demonstrated His love to us by sending His Son to become "the propitiation for our sins" (1 John 4:10). Just as in the OT God met His people when the blood of the sin offering was sprinkled on the altar, so Christ's death brings us into fellowship with God.

Christ's righteousness alone, believers can approach God's throne with praise. Through God's initiative, they have been restored to a proper relationship with Him.

3:25, 26 By His death, Christ satisfied the justice of God. He paid the penalty of sin in full. Paul cites two reasons why the righteousness of God comes through Christ's death. The first is to **demonstrate** that God Himself is righteous, and did not judge the sins committed prior to the Cross. The second reason for the Cross is that God wanted to show that He is both righteous and at the same time the One who can declare sinners righteous. Because of Christ's death, God does not compromise His holiness when He forgives a sinner.

3:27 law of faith: Paul uses a wordplay here. The "law," or the standard of God, is commonly associated with "works." But here Paul says that a person can only boast in the standard of God that excludes human "works." This "law" is faith (John 6:28, 29). Thus, the Jews who were boasting in their knowledge of the law and their adherence to it were silenced by Paul (2:17, 23). The law could only condemn them, but God was the One who saved them. Therefore, their boast should only be in Him.

3:28 Man is justified, that is, "declared righteous" (v. 20), **apart** from doing what the law requires. Thus, salvation is through **faith** alone (4:23–25). No matter what we do, we cannot earn our salvation. God alone saves, and His salvation is a free gift. No one can stand before God and boast of their good deeds. God is the only One who is righteous, and for this reason He should be praised.

3:29 If God gave salvation through the Law of Moses, He would be the God of the **Jews only,** because only the Jews had that law.

3:30 one God: He is the God of both Jews and Gentiles. He will justify them both through **faith.**

3:30 Although a distinction may be made between "by" and "through" in the text, Paul is probably using variety to express the same idea that both the circumcised and uncircumcised are saved by the same method—faith.

3:31 Law can have three different meanings in this passage, and the gospel fulfills all of those meanings. If *law* here refers to the Law of Moses, the Pentateuch, then the passage is referring to the way Jesus completely fulfilled the requirements of the law. If *law* is the entire OT, then the gospel fulfills the promises of the coming of Christ and of the forgiveness of sins. If *law* is the moral law, then the gospel fulfills it because it is through Christ that people are empowered by the Holy Spirit to live in a way that pleases God.

4:1–25 This chapter is pivotal in establishing that justification is by God's grace through faith alone. Verses 1–8 demonstrate that justification is a gift and cannot be earned by works. Verses 9–12 argue that since Abraham was justified before he was circumcised, circumcision is not a basis of justification. Verses 13–17 prove that since Abraham was justified hundreds of years before the Mosaic Law, then justification cannot be based on the Law. Verses 18–25 summarize Paul's argument by concluding that Abraham was justified by his faith and not by his works.

4:1 According to the flesh means "according to his own labor." As the next verse indicates, Paul is asking, "Was Abraham justified before God by his works?"

4:2, 3 Paul quotes Gen. 15:6 to prove that **Abraham** was not justified by works. God made a promise to Abraham, and Abraham trusted God to fulfill it. Because of Abraham's faith, God credited Abraham with **righteousness.** In gaining this righteousness from God, Abraham did not obey some law or perform some ritual like circumcision; he simply **believed** God.

4:4 The fact that Abraham was **counted**

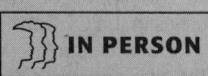 **IN PERSON** | **Abraham, Man of Faith**

A s father of the Hebrews, Abraham (Gen. 12:1; Rom. 4:1) features prominently in the NT. Here in Rom. 4 he is recalled as an individual. Elsewhere he represents the entire people of Israel, and especially those who have placed faith in God (Rom. 9:7; 11:1; Gal. 3:6–9).

Indeed, Abraham's faith is what makes him so important to the NT writers. God made important promises to him and his descendants, Isaac, Jacob, and Jacob's twelve sons—promises that God repeated throughout Israel's history. Abraham is remembered as the man who believed that God would do what He said He would do (Rom. 4:3)—a remarkable thing when we consider that at the time of the promises, Abraham had very little evidence that God would follow through, certainly far less than the NT writers or we who live today.

One of the most important promises was that God would send a Messiah, an "Anointed One." Jesus claimed to be that Messiah. So the central question of the NT becomes, Do we believe that? Do we take Jesus at His word? Do we accept His claim and its implications? Abraham believed God; do we?

Another important question raised by the coming of Jesus was, What happens to Israel? Even though many Jews believed Jesus' claims and followed Him, by and large the nation rejected Him. What did that mean for the promises of God? Paul deals with those issues in Rom. 9–11.

righteous when he believed is an indication that he did not work to earn it.

4:5 God gives **righteousness** to those who believe (v. 3). The person who **does not work,** who comes to God by faith alone without having performed rituals or followed Jewish laws—that person will be counted righteous. Paul continues to build his case that righteousness is apart from works of the law.

4:6–8 According to Jewish law, a question was settled by two or three witnesses. Paul calls two witnesses from the OT to testify to justification through faith: one from the Law (4:1–5) and one from the Prophets (4:6–8; see also 3:21; Acts 2:29, 30 where David is called a prophet).

4:9, 10 Given the understanding that people can become righteous by faith alone, apart from obeying the Jewish law, the obvious question from Paul's readers is: "Is this righteousness actually available to **the uncircumcised?**" Many of the Jews of Paul's day assumed that blessing from God and forgiveness applied only to those who had been circumcised, the Jews. **Abraham,** however, received righteousness from God before he was circumcised. This fact opens the door to a new understanding of God's grace. It is available to all people, both Jews and Gentiles.

4:11, 12 Abraham is a **father** both of the **uncircumcised** who believe as well as of the circumcised who believe. Circumcision was a **sign** and **seal.** As a *sign,* it pointed to the fact that Abraham possessed righteousness, and as a *seal* it verified that Abraham was righteous. Technically, circumcision was a sign and a seal of the covenant that God gave Abraham for the land. But God would not make a covenant with one who was not righteous. Note that the conditional promise of Gen. 12:1–3 becomes an unconditional covenant in Gen. 15:18. God declared His unconditional covenant with Abraham after declaring him righteous because of his belief (15:6).

4:13 The **promise** to Abraham was not through circumcision (vv. 9–12) nor **through the law** (vv. 13–16), but **through the righteousness of faith. Heir of the world** means that Abraham and his **seed,** in particular Christ, will inherit the earth, a promise that will be fulfilled in the kingdom to be established when Christ returns.

4:14 Those who are of the law is not a reference to the Jewish people but to any who depend on the law for their righteousness.

4:15 Transgression means "stepping over." The law draws the line that should not be crossed.

4:16 Therefore it is of faith: Paul concludes that God's promises to Abraham were founded on his faith so that it would be

acknowledged that salvation was only through **grace,** that is, God's favor. Since the promise was not based on adherence to any law or the performance of any ritual, such as circumcision, Abraham is the forefather of all who believe.

4:17 Gives life to the dead is a reference to the birth of Isaac from Abraham's "dead" body and Sarah's "dead" womb; both were far beyond the age of childbearing (v. 19).

4:18 When Abraham was physically beyond any **hope** of having a child, he based his hope on God's promises instead. He believed that his offspring would be as numerous as the stars of the heavens, because the all-powerful God had promised it.

4:19 deadness of . . . womb: Sarah had no children previously in her life, and by the time God gave this promise she was well past childbearing age.

4:20 glory: Glorifying God means declaring who God is. Abraham, by his faith, acknowledged that God was faithful and powerful enough to keep His promise.

4:21 Abraham was not just wistfully hoping that God would make him the father of many nations, but was **fully convinced that what He had promised He was also able to perform.** History teaches us that what God promises, He also performs.

4:22 Abraham's faith was credited to him as **righteousness** (v. 3, note).

4:23, 24 God had Abraham's faith recorded in Scripture not to immortalize Abraham but to be a model for others. **who raised up:** Abraham's faith was a model because he believed in a God who can raise the dead. We follow Abraham's example when we have faith, when we believe that God raised Jesus from the dead and will grant us eternal life also. Belief in Jesus' resurrection and ours is central to the gospel (1 Cor. 15:4).

4:25 Jesus was **delivered up** to death, taking the penalty of our sin on Himself. Just as God brought life from Abraham and Sarah, who thought they were unable to have children, so God **raised** Jesus back to life. Jesus' resurrection brought us justification before God because the Resurrection proves that God accepted Jesus' sacrifice for us.

5:1–11 Justification brings **peace with God** (v. 1), **grace** for present living (v. 2), **hope** for the future (v. 2), victory in **tribulations** (vv. 3, 4), and assurance brought by God's love put in our hearts by the **Holy Spirit** (v. 5). Because of God's great justifying love (vv. 6–8), we can rejoice that our **hope** of eternal reward will be fulfilled (vv. 9–11).

5:1 Peace here is not a subjective feeling of peace. Rather, this peace is the state of being at peace instead of at war. The hostility between

God and the believer has ceased. The believer has been reconciled to God.

5:2 To **have access** means "to approach," as if by introduction into a king's throne room. Believers have been granted admission to stand before God. Even though they were once rebels, they do not have to face His judgment. Instead they approach His throne in the realm of **grace**, or in the King's favor. **Rejoice** means "to boast" and **hope** means "expectation." Believers boast in the sure expectation of the **glory of God.**

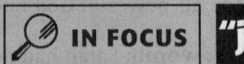 **IN FOCUS** **"justification"**

(Gk. *dikaiōsis*) (4:25; 5:18) Strong's #*1347:* The Greek noun for *justification* is derived from the Greek verb *dikaioō,* meaning "to acquit" or "to declare righteous" (used by Paul in 4:2, 5; 5:1). It is a legal term used of a favorable verdict in a trial. The word depicts a courtroom setting, with God presiding as the Judge, determining the faithfulness of each person to the Law. In the first section of Romans, Paul makes it clear that no one can withstand God's judgment (3:9–20). The Law was not given to justify sinners but to expose their sin. To remedy this deplorable situation, God sent His Son to die for our sins, in our place. When we believe in Jesus, God imputes His righteousness to us, and we are declared righteous before God. In this way, God demonstrates that He is both a righteous Judge and the One who declares us righteous, our Justifier (3:26).

They are confident, for God Himself has placed the Holy Spirit in their hearts (v. 5).

5:3 Glory is the same Greek word that is translated "rejoice" in v. 2. Believers can rejoice, glory, and boast not only in their future hope (v. 2) but also in their present troubles. **Tribulations** refers to physical hardship, suffering, and distress. **Perseverance** means "endurance." Trials and tribulation produce endurance when we exercise faith during those difficult times (James 1:2, 3). Such faith produces its own reward (Matt. 5:10–12; 2 Tim. 2:12).

5:4 Perseverance produces **character,** the quality of being approved. As believers endure tribulation, God works in them to develop certain qualities and virtues that will strengthen them and draw them closer to Him. The result is fortified **hope** in God and His promises.

5:5 The **hope** that believers have of their future glory with God will not **disappoint** them by being unfulfilled. They will not be put to shame or humiliated because of their hope. The reason the believer can be so confident is that **the love of God has been poured out.** The moment a person trusts in Christ, that person receives the Holy Spirit (8:9), who constantly encourages them in their hope in God.

5:6 Paul now explains the nature of God's love. God loved us when **we were still without strength** and **ungodly.** God loved us so much that He sent His Son to die for us (v. 8). God loves us just the way we are, but He loves us too much to leave us the way we are (John 15:16; Phil. 1:6).

5:7, 8 God's love is truly remarkable. It is unlikely that anyone would die for a **righteous** man (Gk. *dikaiōs*); the just man; the upright, respected citizen; or a **good** man (Gk. *agathos*); the helpful, benevolent man. **while we were still sinners, Christ died for us** (Gk. *hamartolos*): This is a clear demonstration of God's love. He receives us just as we are and then begins to make something beautiful.

5:9, 10 If God loved us when we were helpless, ungodly **enemies,** how much more will He love us now that we are His children? **By His blood . . . through the death of His Son** we have been **justified,** that is "declared righteous," and **reconciled,** meaning our state of alienation from God has been changed. Believers are no longer enemies of God; they are at peace with God (v. 1). **we shall be saved:** Many take these verses to refer to final salvation from the presence of sin. But in this context, Paul goes on to discuss being saved from the power of sin (ch. 6). Thus, *wrath* here is God's present wrath (1:18), and *His life* is the life of Christ in believers (v. 18). The point is that since God's love and the death of Christ have brought us justification, then as a result of that love, we can also expect salvation from God's wrath. To experience this truth, the believer must fully cooperate with the process that is explained in 6:1–14 (John 8:32). The believer must die to sin and present himself or herself to God as an "instrument of righteousness" (6:14).

5:11 Not only shall the justified person escape the wrath of God by the death of Christ, but also he or she shall obtain joy in God because of Christ's life. The word translated **rejoice** is the same as is translated **glory** in v. 3. The blessings which justification brings to its recipients terminate in joy **through our Lord Jesus Christ.** This last expression is identical to that found in v. 1 of this chapter. All that we have we owe to Him, the Lord Jesus Christ.

5:12–21 This paragraph contains a comparison between Adam and Christ which is interrupted with a parenthetical thought (vv. 13–17).

🔍 IN FOCUS **"reconciliation"**

(Gk. *katallagē*) (5:11; 11:15; 2 Cor. 5:18, 19) Strong's #*2643*: The Greek word basically means "change" or "exchange." In the context of relationships between people, the term implies a change in attitude on the part of both individuals, a change from enmity to friendship. When used to describe the relationship existing between God and a person, the term implies the change of attitude on the part of both a person and God. The need to change the sinful ways of a human being is obvious; but some argue that no change is needed on the part of God. But inherent in the doctrine of justification is the changed attitude of God toward the sinner. God declares a person who was formerly His enemy to be righteous before Him.

The comparison begins in v. 12, is formally stated in v. 18 and then explained in v. 19.

5:12 The **one man** is Adam. Through him **sin entered the world. Sin** brought **death.** The result is that death is now a universal experience. The phrase **because all sinned** does not mean just that "all have sinned" at some time in their lives, thus referring to individual sins. Paul takes his readers back to the beginning of human history, to the one sin that brought death upon us all. The unity of the human race is demonstrated here. In Adam, we all sinned (1 Cor. 15:22). The result is physical and spiritual death for everyone. From Adam we inherited a sin nature. Furthermore, as a result of our sin in Adam, we face a common judgment—death.

5:13, 14 Until the law, that is until the Law of Moses was given, sin was not **imputed.** *Imputed* means "to charge to one's account," as by an entry made in a ledger. In other words, sin was present in the world from Adam to Moses, but God did not keep an account of sins before the giving of the Law because there was no Law to obey or disobey. **not sinned:** Those after Adam and before Moses did not sin like Adam because there were no prohibitions similar to the Law of Moses. But they did sin, and the way we know this is that **death reigned.** They all died.

5:15 Through one man, Adam, death came. Yet through **one Man,** Jesus Christ, grace and **the gift** of God, eternal life, was given. **much more:** The works of the two men, Adam and Jesus, are not merely antithetical. Christ's work is greater, for it brings God's grace to those stuck in the sinfulness which originated in Adam.

5:16 Through Adam came **condemnation,** a word used only three times in the NT, and all three times in Romans (v. 18; 8:1). The word refers to "the punishment following a judicial sentence." In the face of this, through Christ came **the free gift** that **resulted in justification.** That is to say, the aim or goal of the gift is *justification,* or "righteousness." In v. 18, the

same word is translated "righteous act." In other words, the goal of the gift of eternal life is righteous living. This does not refer to justification by faith but to the practical outworking of faith through righteous acts (6:16). Thus, this verse contrasts the penal servitude of a sinner with the righteous life of a believer.

5:17 When **death** reigns, people are destroyed. When Christ reigns, we are given eternal **life** and share in His glory.

5:18 Here Paul completes the comparison begun in v. 12 between the sinful work of Adam and the righteous work of Jesus. Through Adam came **condemnation.** Through Christ came **justification of life,** a justification that produces life.

5:19 Made means "to make," "constitute." As the result of Adam's sin, people became sinners. By Christ's death **many will be made righteous** (in contrast to declared righteousness, see 4:3). That is, believers are actually being constituted or made righteous. Through the sanctifying work of the Holy Spirit, the believer who has been declared righteous by God is continually becoming more righteous.

5:20 the offense might abound: Law magnified sin. What was inherently wrong became formally and explicitly wrong once the Law was revealed. **grace abounded much more:** The Greek term Paul uses means "superabounded." Not only can sin never exceed the grace provided by God, sin loses its threat when compared to the superabounding grace of God.

5:21 This verse contains the double contrast between sin and righteousness and between death and life. From the very moment sin entered the universe it has reigned, bringing about physical and spiritual death. Its principle of rulership has been to separate mankind from his Creator and to cause his end to be a mortal one. But through the blood of Jesus Christ, sin has been dethroned and righteousness now rules in its stead. Whereas death was the order of the day in Adam's society, now life eternal is the order of the day for those who have believed in Jesus Christ. The contrast is a great one. It is a contrast between man's sin and Christ's obedience, between the wages of sin and the gift of God. Some have thought that universal salvation is taught in this passage, thinking that just because all were condemned, now all will be saved. Such is not the case. New birth is mandatory for eternal life and the qualifying expression, **those who receive** in v. 17, teaches that faith in Jesus Christ is absolutely essential for salvation.

6:1–14 As Christians we died to sin when we identified with Christ in faith (vv. 1–4); thus, we have been freed from the dominion of sin to live a life of obedience to God (vv. 5–11). This new beginning should become a continuing reality in our lives (vv. 12–14).

6:1 Since sin in a way makes grace more abundant (5:20, 21) why not **continue in sin?** This is certainly a possible conclusion, though a wrong one, from the teaching about grace in ch. 5. Apparently Paul had been accused of teaching this false doctrine, called antinomianism. To

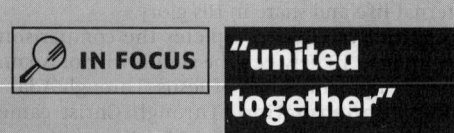

IN FOCUS   **"united together"**

(Gk. *sumphutos*) (6:5) Strong's #4854: The expression, which occurs only here in the NT, means "to grow in union" or "to plant in union." The word describes two plants that have been planted together and are growing together, closely entwined or even united. The context speaks of union, our union with Christ in His death (6:4) and resurrection (6:5). Our union with Christ in death is like being planted with Him. Like a seed, our sinful natures must die with Christ so that we might grow in Christ and bear spiritual fruit (John 12:24). Our union with Christ is now a loving union, in which we are growing with Him "in the likeness of His resurrection."

silence his accusers, Paul shows in this chapter that a believer who continues in sin would be denying his or her own identity in Christ.

6:2 Certainly not: The Greek expresses a response of shock, that has even been translated "God forbid." The thought of a believer living in sin in order to take advantage of grace was abhorrent to Paul. The reason believers should not live in sin is that they have **died to sin,** as is explained in vv. 3, 4.

6:3 baptized: Paul uses the common experience of believers being baptized as a picture of being identified with Jesus Christ. Baptism expresses faith the way a word expresses an idea. There can be an idea without words, but normally they are expressed in words. Water baptism is a symbol of the spiritual union of Christ and the believer. When a person trusts Christ, he or she is incorporated into, united to, Jesus Christ, which includes being united to **His death.** Jesus' death becomes our death. Christian baptism makes these spiritual realities vivid.

6:4, 5 newness of life: If the believer's identification with Christ means being identified with His death, then it logically follows that the believer also identifies with Jesus' resurrection. Having died and having been raised with Christ, the believer should live a new kind of life.

6:5–11 Verse 5 states that participation in Christ's death assures us that we shall share in His resurrection. Verses 6, 7 show that by this crucifixion we are freed (i.e., "justified")from sin. Verses 8–10 assure us that having been made free from sin, we are prepared to live with Christ. Verse 11 is a plea that this experience of having died to sin shall become a reality in our lives.

6:6 Some say **old man** refers to part of us, namely our old nature, our sinful disposition. However, the word *man* does not refer to part of a person; instead, the word describes the entire inner person before conversion, the person connected to the sin nature of Adam. The *old man* was **crucified with** Christ (Gal. 2:20). Simply put, a believer is not the same person he or she was before conversion; a believer is a new creation in Christ (2 Cor. 5:17). There are two reasons (see the two clauses that begin with **that**) for crucifying the *old man*. First is **that the body of sin might be done away.** The *body of sin* is either a reference to the physical body, that is, the body that is enslaved to sin, or the phrase is a figurative expression for the sin in a believer's life. Colossians 2:11, a parallel passage, indicates that sin in a believer's life is meant. The sinful nature of a believer is abolished when the old self is crucified with Christ. The second purpose is **that we should no longer be slaves of sin.** Believers are new people who are no longer enslaved to the old sinful nature.

6:7 Freed here translates the Greek word for "justification," which is a legal term. The idea is that the believer no longer has any obligation to sin.

6:8 Dying and living with Christ summarizes vv. 3–7. **Believe** introduces a new idea. Christians must not only know that they have died to sin (vv. 6–8) and have been made alive with Christ, they must also *believe* it.

6:9, 10 Christ died for sin once for all. He is

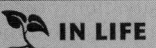 **IN LIFE** | **The Perilous Nature of Sin**

Some people scoff at the concept of sin by defining it as a prohibition against fun made by the few who hate it against the many who enjoy it. In a way, this was the original lie that the serpent told Eve. He suggested that God was withholding things from her that she truly needed and would benefit from (Gen. 3:4, 5).

But Scripture presents sin as anything but fun or beneficial. Sin has devastating consequences of which we need to be aware. As the Book of Romans points out, sin enslaves people and demands that they obey its lusts (Rom. 6:6, 12, 20).

Several phrases in the NT help to define the perilous nature of sin:

- To sin is to "fall short of the glory of God" (Rom. 3:23). People trapped in sin's tight snare cannot live up to the holy lifestyle that God intended when He created them.
- "Sin is lawlessness" (1 John 3:4). It involves living for "me first" rather than for God, being "a law unto oneself."
- "All unrighteousness is sin" (1 John 5:17). When we sin, we offend the God who loves justice and righteousness (Rom. 1:18).
- If we know what is good and yet do not do it, we sin (James 4:17). Thus sin involves conscious disobedience against what is right, even to the point of approving the sin of others (Rom. 1:32).

This is a sobering picture, but even more startling is that every human being is a part of this picture. "There is none righteous, no, not one" (Rom. 3:10; compare 2 Chr. 6:36; Rom. 5:12). "All have sinned and fall short of the glory of God" (Rom. 3:23).

Nor is sin limited to a few matters of religion or personal habits. Because God is the sovereign owner of the whole world—its lands, nations, people, and all resources—misuse of any part of the creation means sinning against Him. We are accountable for every dimension of life. Nothing is really "secular" in the sense of being outside His concern.

now alive at the right hand of God. Since believers have been joined to Christ and to His **death** and resurrection, they can now believe that they too are alive to God.

6:11 Reckon is an accounting term that means "to take into account," "calculate," or "decide." Verses 3–10 reveal the truth that believers have already died to sin because they have participated in Jesus' death. Since believers have died with Christ and have also been raised with Him, Paul now urges Christians to consider themselves **dead . . . to sin.** Although before conversion they were still enslaved to the power of sin, now they are free to resist it.

6:12 Though believers in Christ have died to sin, sin is still a problem. The sin principle is still present and can express itself through the **mortal body,** the body that is subject to death. The difference is that sin has no right to **reign.** Thus, Paul admonishes the believer not to **obey** it.

6:13 Verse 12 has the whole body in view; v. 13 focuses on the individual parts of the body such as the hands or mouth. Believers are not to **present** the parts of their bodies as a means of sinning. Simply put: Do not use your hands to

steal or your tongue to lie. Rather, believers should **present** themselves to God and the parts of their bodies as **instruments of righteousness.**

6:14 Not under law means not under the Law of Moses. Yet the believer with God's help, the believer **under grace,** fulfills the law (3:31; 13:8–10). The Mosaic system consisted of external laws which revealed the sin prevalent in human hearts. In contrast, God's grace places the believer in Christ, and the Holy Spirit in the believer. Therefore, a Christian does not have to sin; he or she can resist temptation and do what is right (2 Cor. 3:15–18).

6:15 Since believers are **not under law but under grace** (v. 14) and grace cancels sin (Col. 2:14), why not sin? This is similar to the question in 6:1. There the issue was whether believers should sin so grace could be displayed. Here it is whether believers should sin because they are not under the Mosaic law system.

6:16 slaves to obey: Paul highlights the principle that everyone is a slave to someone or something—whether it is a person, possession, or activity. But a Christian should be a slave to God's righteousness.

6:17 you: Paul moves from the principle (v. 16) to the experience of the Roman believers. **Form of doctrine** is a unique expression. *Form* means "pattern," "type," or "example." The gospel message is the pattern. It is the message that Christ died for our sins and rose from the dead (1 Cor. 15:3, 4). This message demands a response from the hearer and with it must be the command to believe (Acts 16:31). **Obeyed from the heart:** The Roman believers voluntarily obeyed the message. There was no external law imposed on them.

6:18 slaves of righteousness: Being a slave in the ancient world meant being owned by a master. Whether slaves obeyed did not change their status as slaves, although it would affect the relationship between slave and master (Luke 19:20–26). The question is one of obligation. A person who has been freed from sin can act as though still a slave to sin (v. 16), or that person can live as a "slave" to righteousness, as a servant to a kind master who gives great rewards.

6:19 In human terms refers to Paul's illustration of slavery. The analogy of slavery to the Christian life is imperfect, because Christians are God's children (8:15, 16). Having been set free from sin and having become a slave of righteousness (v. 18), the believer should serve righteousness **just as** he or she served sin before trusting Christ. The result will be **holiness.**

6:20, 21 The result of sin is **death.** The child of God who lives in sin lives in the sphere of death (1 John 3:14, 15). The ultimate result is physical death (James 1:13–15).

6:22 free from sin: (v. 7). The new relationship with God results in a new person, which makes a new kind of **fruit** possible: right-

eousness. This verse and the next present the beginning and end of the salvation process. Christians have been freed from sin so that they can be given eternal life. Eternal life is a gift (John 3:16) from God to each believer.

6:23 Paul explains that **sin** results in **death,** but God gives the **gift** of **eternal life.** Most often this verse has been used as a promise of regeneration. The phrase *eternal life* is used 42 times in the NT, and it usually refers to something we receive as a gift at the moment of belief in the gospel (John 3:16; 5:24; 6:40). But 11 of these 42 times, *eternal life* is presented as something to be attained (v. 22; 2:7; Matt. 19:16, 29; Mark 10:17, 30; Luke 10:25; 18:18–30; John 12:25, 26; Gal. 6:8). Thus, we learn from the Bible that eternal life is not simply a static entity. It is a dynamic and growing relationship with Jesus Christ Himself (John 10:10; 17:3). Through living in faith and obedience, Christians can fully enjoy God's free gift of eternal life.

7:1–3 Paul returns to the question of 6:15: Shall we continue to sin while under grace? Paul's answer is no, and now he illustrates his negative answer by a comparison with marriage. Marriage is lifelong. But if one partner dies, the other is no longer bound by the law and is free to marry someone else.

7:4 An exact application of the illustration would be that the law died, and now the believer is free to "marry" grace. Paul's words are that believers died **to the law.** Having died to the law, the believer is now free to marry God and **bear fruit** for Him. Out of the marriage relationship comes children. So out of intimacy with Christ comes the fruit of practical righteousness (6:22).

IN LIFE　　A Slave to Sin

The apostle Paul was willing to take a long, hard look at his deepest, darkest inner life. What he saw there was troubling, but true: he was a slave to sin (Rom. 7:15). In fact, he realized that nothing good lived in his flesh (7:18)—a fact that caused him to cry out in wretchedness (7:24). Paul was not just having a bad day when he wrote Rom. 7. He was not merely suffering from a sense of inadequacy and low self-esteem. Paul's realistic appraisal of his spiritual life came from measuring himself against the high and holy expectations that God has for all of us, what the Book of Romans calls the law (7:7). The more Paul became aware of what God wanted, the more aware he became of his inability, in his own strength, to live as God wanted.

The only answer to Paul's wretched condition—and to our own—is Jesus Christ (7:25). Only Jesus makes it possible to fulfill the righteous requirements of a holy God (8:3, 4). Thus, Paul's honesty led to hope.

The same is true for us. In confession we can find God's forgiveness. In admitting our weakness we can find His strength. If we deny our true condition, we deceive ourselves, and doom ourselves to lives enslaved to sin (1 John 1:8–10).

7:5 In the flesh refers to the period before the believer's conversion. In this context, those *in the flesh* are unregenerate, or not born again, and those *in* the Spirit are regenerate. On the other hand, both believers and unbelievers may walk *according to* the flesh, but only believers can walk *according to* the Spirit. The law **aroused** sinful desires that were expressed through the **members** of the body and resulted in death.

7:6 At conversion, believers **died** to the law (v. 4), with the result that they are now able to serve in newness of life (6:4). They have a new life in the Holy Spirit, not in the old way of **the letter,** the old way of trying to gain life by means of the law.

7:7–12 Sin and the law both held people in bondage. Is the law, then, something evil like sin? Not at all. The specific commandments of the law made the knowledge of sin clearer. Sin takes advantage of that clearer knowledge to stir us to rebel and thus leads us into greater sin. The good purpose of the law was to show us how to please God in order that we could have **life.** Sin twisted God's purpose for the law so that it actually brought spiritual **death** (v. 10).

7:7 The next logical question (6:1, 15) is: **Is the law sin? Certainly not!** (6:2, 15). Paul emphatically denies that the law is sinful. **I:** Beginning here and in the rest of the chapter, Paul uses his personal experience as an illustration. **The law** reveals sin.

7:8 The law also stirs up sin (v. 7). **sin was dead:** Sin can exist without the law (5:13), although without law it may be dormant. Without standards of right and wrong, there can be no judgment of what is sin and what is not. The law, however, with its commands against certain behaviors, can arouse the desire to perform those evil behaviors (v. 5).

7:9 I was alive: There was a time when Paul was alive to God (6:8, 11, 13) and without the law (vv. 4, 6; 6:14). Then some time after his conversion, when he was enjoying fellowship with God, he was confronted by the law, and he **died.** This is a figurative way of saying that his sin nature broke his fellowship with God.

7:10, 11 bring life: Since the law points out the path of righteousness, it points to life. But since sin reigns in our natures, the law means judgment and death for us. When we focus on the law we are **deceived** into sinning, which thus "kills" our spiritual lives.

7:12 The conclusion is that **the law** as a whole and the individual commandments are **holy.** Our problem with sin is not the fault of the holy law of God, only of how our sinful nature (vv. 8, 11, 13) responds to the law.

7:13–25 Verse 13 picks up the theme of v. 5: life in the flesh under the control of sin,

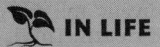 **IN LIFE** **Two Kinds of Sin**

Sin is what made necessary God's plan of salvation through Christ. In a technical sense any lack of conformity to God's will or standards is a sin—it is not in accord with His plan for us. Thus, in the OT there were sacrifices commanded for sins committed in ignorance. It is this broader conception of sin that leads some to believe that all Christians "sin in word, thought, and deed every day." The Scriptures, however, indicate that God holds us primarily accountable for *known* acts of transgression, rebellion, or omission (John 9:41; Rom. 1:20, 21; James 4:17).

The second form of sin described in the Bible is the quality of the fallen human nature that inclines people to commit individual acts of sin. Every person comes into the world with this inclination to evil, inherited from Adam (Rom. 5:12–14, 18, 19). This universal tendency to oppose God's will has been called "original sin," "the carnal mind," "inherited sin," "the old man," "inbred sin," "moral depravity," and "sinful nature." It is an inherent sinful disposition that inclines persons to sinful acts.

It is important to understand how Scripture distinguishes between acts of sin and a sinful nature. Acts of sin are commonly, though not always, referred to in the plural: "How many are my iniquities and sins?" (Job 13:23) and "forgive us our sins" (Luke 11:4). In contrast, the sinful nature is usually referred to as a single quality or disposition of the human spirit (Rom. 7:14, 17, 20, 25; 8:2).

When the difference between sin as nature and sin as an act is not indicated by the singular and plural terms for sin, the context must determine the writer's thought. Sin as nature is evident when the context emphasizes an inherent inclination to evil, as in Paul's criticism of the Corinthians in 1 Cor. 3:3, "Where there are envy, strife, and divisions among you, are you not carnal?" David's cry, "Create in me a clean heart, O God, and renew a steadfast spirit within me" (Ps. 51:10), reflects a sinful reality deeper than actions, a sinfulness that requires cleansing.

aggravated by the demands of the law. Verses 14–25 paint a picture of the experience of such an individual. Here is the moral person who attempts to deal with the demands of the law and the power of sin. But he is using only his own resources without the power of Christ and the enabling of the Holy Spirit. He wants to do what God requires, but he is not able. Non-Christians who have been convicted by the Holy Spirit live with this struggle. Also Christians who are not living a victorious life in the

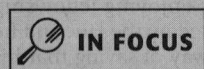

(Gk. *nomos*) (6:14; 7:21–23, 25; 8:2–4; Gal. 2:16; 5:3; Heb. 8:4) Strong's #*3551*: The Greek term for *law* here means an inward principle of action—either good or evil—operating with the regularity of a law. The term also designates a standard for a person's life. The apostle Paul described three such laws. The first is called "the law of sin" which was operating through his flesh, causing him to sin. Paul, like all other believers, needed another law to overcome "the law of sin": this is "the law of the Spirit of life in Christ Jesus," which makes us "free from the law of sin and death" (8:2). By following this law, believers can actually fulfill the righteous requirements of God's law (8:4)—which is the third law in this section; it is the standard for human action that corresponds to the righteous nature of God.

Spirit experience similar struggles, even though God has given them a measure of victory over sin (8:9; 1 Cor. 3:1–4).

7:13 Paul asks another rhetorical question (v. 7; 6:1, 15). **Has then what is good** (that is, the law, v. 12) **become death to me? Certainly not** is again Paul's emphatic denial (v. 7; 6:2, 15). The problem is not the law; the problem is **sin.** Sin used the good law to produce evil, that is, death. But through the law, sin is shown for what it is, and its evil and tragic consequences are clearly revealed.

7:14 spiritual: The law comes from God. In contrast, Paul said his problem (and that of all believers; see 1 Cor. 3:1–3) is that he was **carnal,** meaning he was like a slave **sold** over to **sin.** Even though Paul was a Christian dedicated to serving God (v. 25), he continued to fall short of God's moral standards.

7:15–17 Being fleshly, sold over to sin, involves a conflict that mystifies Paul and other

believers. Paul feels he does not understand himself. He finds himself defeated, not doing what he wants to do, and doing what he hates to do. The conflict indicates that there is battle between two identities in the believer. First, there is something that acknowledges that the **law . . . is good.** Second, there is something within, called **sin,** which produces evil.

7:18 The problem is the **flesh,** the part of the believer in which there is **nothing good.** The **will** is the desire to do good (v.12). Yet the ability to **perform** is lacking.

7:19 Basically a repetition of v. 15.

7:20 The same exact conclusion mentioned in v. 17.

7:21 Paul confesses that he is carnal, sold unto sin (v. 14), that more specifically the problem is in his flesh in which nothing good dwells (v. 18) and now that **evil** (Gk. *kakon*) **is present.**

7:22 The **inward man** is virtually synonymous with the mind (v. 23; 2 Cor. 4:16; Eph. 3:16), and it finds **delight in the law of God.** This delight causes believers in Christ to want to align themselves with the new nature that God has imparted to them.

7:23 The law of sin is a reference to the sinful nature's rejection of the law of the mind that seeks after God. The sinful nature seeks to draw us away from following God's work in us.

7:24 The **wretched,** or "distressed, miserable," **man** is the believer whenever he or she is defeated by sin (vv. 14, 23). This defeat occurs whenever the believer fails to live in the power supplied by the Spirit. **body of death:** This is a figurative expression for the sin nature. Paul wants to be freed from sin, which leads to death.

7:25 thank God: Paul breaks forth in jubilant praise to God that there is victory through **Jesus Christ,** who delivers believers from the body of death, the flesh. **So then:** Paul concludes that the problem is not the law; the problem is the flesh. From this argument, Paul moves into the solution—salvation found in Jesus Christ.

8:1–30 Paul described life "in the flesh" (7:5). Now he describes the opposite—life "in the newness of the Spirit" (7:6). The person controlled by the Spirit is not condemned by the law because his past is forgiven, and through the Spirit he is enabled to do what the law requires as he waits for his final resurrection into glory (vv. 1–11). The Spirit makes us God's children (vv. 12–17) and assures us of a wonderful future hope (vv. 18–30).

8:1 therefore: This Greek word does not draw a formal conclusion, but an informal inference, from 7:25. In contrast with the preceding vivid description of sinfulness, Paul depicts the freedom of living in the Spirit. **no condemna-**

tion: In Christ, we are no longer under the sentence of the law, but empowered by the Spirit to live for Christ.

8:2 the law of the Spirit: The *Spirit* refers to the Holy Spirit who energizes our renewed spirit. It is also possible that the word refers to the spirit in us that has now been brought to life.

8:3 The law could pronounce judgment on sin, but **the law could not** do anything about sin itself. It had no power to put sin to death in a person's life. **God** accomplished what the law could not do **by sending His own Son.** Jesus came in **the likeness of sinful flesh:** Jesus, as God, took on our human nature, a nature that was susceptible to temptation. Although He was tempted, He never gave in. He never sinned.

8:4 The purpose of the coming of Christ was that **the law might be fulfilled.** The believer gains the righteous standard of the law—love (13:8–10)—not by means of the law but by being in Christ and walking **according to the Spirit.**

8:5 The Greek word rendered **set their minds** includes a person's will, thoughts, and emotions. It also includes assumptions, values, desires, and purposes. Setting the mind **on the things of the flesh** or on the things of **the Spirit** means being oriented to or governed by those things on which we focus.

8:6 Peace is the resolution of the intense warfare described in ch. 7, as well as the inward harmony and tranquility that results from yielding to God.

8:7–11 A believer can live according to the flesh with the result of death (James 1:13–15), or else by the renewed spirit, so as to experience life. In vv. 7–11, Paul elaborates on these two possibilities, showing the possibility and the benefit of living according to the spirit.

8:7 The reason that being carnally minded results in death (v. 6) is that **the carnal mind** is an enemy of God. The mind of the flesh is hostile to God and can never submit itself **to the law of God.**

8:8 Being **in the flesh** is different from "walking according to the flesh." Being *in the flesh* means being unregenerate or sinful. People in that state **cannot please God.**

8:9 Christians no longer live according to the **flesh,** under control of their sinful human nature. Instead, with **the Spirit** living in them and empowering them, they can live in a way pleasing to God.

8:10 Dead because of sin refers not to physical death but to the "body of death" of 7:24 (v. 6). The problem that Paul is dealing with in this passage is how the "dead" body, in which sin dwells, can be made the vehicle for expressing the life of God.

8:11 The solution to the problem of the flesh is the Holy Spirit. He gives **life to your mortal bodies.** Being spiritually minded means overcoming the deadness of the body and experiencing life and peace. This is the resurrection life (Phil. 3:10).

8:12, 13 you will die: Death here does not refer to physical death, because those who live according to the Spirit also die physically. It refers to the experience of those who live their

---

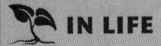 **IN LIFE**   **Transformed by the Spirit**

Paul's words about the Law being unable to produce righteousness because of the weakness of the flesh (Rom. 8:3) should not be interpreted as if he thought little of the Law. On the contrary, he took seriously the high calling and expectations that God revealed through Moses. In fact, walking "according to the Spirit" (8:4) involves the fulfillment of these expectations. That's why Paul urged believers to:

- Turn from evil to good (Rom. 12:2, 9).
- Seek love (1 Cor. 13).
- Not misuse liberty (Gal. 5:13–16).
- Choose to do good toward all people (Gal. 6:10).
- Live with a new, godly lifestyle (Eph. 2:1–3; 4:1–3).
- Learn how to serve others in humility, with love (Phil. 2:1–7).
- Undo patterns of sin within ourselves (Col. 3:5–11).
- Develop godly contentment with what we have (1 Tim. 6:6–11).

This is life in the Spirit—a lifelong adventure of reclaiming what God intended for us from the beginning (Eph. 5:8–10).

lives apart from God. **by the Spirit:** By walking according to the Spirit (v. 4), by being spiritually minded (v. 6), the believer can **put to death** sinful deeds and **live** for God.

8:14 Being **led by the Spirit** is virtually synonymous with walking according to the Spirit. "Walking" highlights the active participation and effort of the believer. "Being led" underscores the passive side, the submissive dependence of the believer on the Spirit. **these are sons of God:** Those led by the Spirit are God's children, and the sovereign Lord, in turn, is their Father (2 Cor. 6:18).

8:15 Believers are sons of God because they received **the Spirit of adoption.** In ancient Rome, an adopted son would possess all the rights of a son born into the family. Christians have been adopted into God's family, receiving an eternal inheritance. **Abba:** Jesus Himself prayed to God using this Aramaic word for Father (Mark 14:36).

8:16 A further indication of believers' sonship is that the Holy Spirit **bears witness with** their spirits. When believers cry out to the

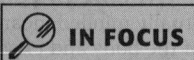

IN FOCUS   "adoption"

(Gk. *huiothesia*) (8:15; Gal. 4:5; Eph. 1:5) Strong's #5206: The Greek word for *adoption* is derived from the word *huios,* meaning "son," and the word *thesis,* meaning "placement." It is a legal term that in this context indicates that believers have been given the full privileges of sonship in God's family. Concurrent with this placement into sonship, God places the Spirit of His Son into our hearts so that we become, in effect, His natural-born children. As such, we are not just "adopted" (in the sense the word now conveys) but genuinely "begotten" by God. God makes children of men into children of God, just the reverse of what happened to Christ when the Son of God became the Son of Man.

Father in prayer (v. 15), the Holy Spirit intercedes for them (v. 26).

8:17 heirs: All of God's children have an inheritance based on their relationship to God, which is incorruptible, undefiled, and is reserved in heaven (1 Pet. 1:4). Their inheritance includes an expectation of eternal life (Titus 3:4–7). As **joint heirs** with Christ, they share His suffering now (Phil. 3:10) and will share His glory later (Phil. 3:11–14).

8:18 The **sufferings** of the present are slight when compared with the **glory** later. Paul calls the sufferings "light affliction" compared to the "eternal weight of glory" (2 Cor. 4:17). The divine compensation package is "a hundredfold" (Matt. 19:29).

8:19–27 The creation (vv. 19–22), believers (vv. 23, 24) and even the Holy Spirit Himself (vv. 25–27) groans now for the glory later.

8:19 Earnest expectation literally means "to watch with outstretched neck." **Creation** is impatient to see the revelation of the **sons of God.**

8:20 Futility, which means "vanity, emptiness," refers to the curse on creation (Gen. 3:17–19).

8:21 Creation awaits the coming glory because it also will be **delivered. The bondage of corruption** further describes the futility of v. 20. Nature is a slave to decay and death because of sin.

8:22, 23 The firstfruits of the Spirit may refer to the first workings of the Holy Spirit (8:9–11), which is a pledge of more work to come, like **the redemption of our body.** Otherwise, the expression *firstfruits* may be in apposition to the word *Spirit;* thus, *firstfruits* is the Spirit. The firstfruits of a harvest was a foretaste of the harvest to come. So the Spirit, or His work, is God's assurance of the greater blessings to come. Elsewhere the Spirit is called a "guarantee of our inheritance" (Eph. 1:14).

8:24 Hope is a constant expectation of an unseen reality. We are saved by faith, but our hope is in the return of Christ in all His glory and our complete deliverance from our sinful natures.

8:25 If we are expecting something unseen, we **wait** with **perseverance;** that is, we are willing to endure the present.

8:26 Though more may be involved in the concept of **weaknesses,** the primary reference here is to mental ignorance. The contrast offered by Paul in this verse is between our inability to know how to pray and the effective prayers of the Spirit Himself. The emphasis indicates that the Spirit Himself prays for us when we are incapable of praying. He intercedes on our behalf before the throne of God (1 John 2:1). But His intercession **cannot be uttered,** which means it is "unexpressed, unspoken." No language is in view here, only the inner groanings of the Spirit.

8:27, 28 As children of God, we do not always know what to pray for or how best to pray (v. 26), but we can know the purpose of God which the Holy Spirit desires to accomplish. **work together for good:** The primary reference of *all things* is the "sufferings of this present time" (v. 18). All circumstances will work together in cooperation for the believer's good—that is, the believer will be conformed to Jesus Christ now and reign with Him later. **Those who love God** are in fact **those who are the called** by God. Our love is our response to the work of the Holy Spirit in us. We are called **according to His purpose.** God does everything, including redemption, in order to accomplish His overarching plan.

8:29 God **foreknew**, which means simply "to know beforehand," but carries more than mere knowledge of people or events. It expresses knowing people, not merely knowing about them. This has been interpreted by some as God's free and merciful choice of certain people who receive His gift of salvation apart from any works they do. His knowledge of future events and people, however, do not determine His choice (1 Pet. 1:2). Instead, He chose those who would be saved out of His own free will and for His own purpose. *Only* God saves; people never earn salvation through any work.

8:30 God not only foreknew and predestined (v. 29), He also **called** believers through the preaching of the gospel message (2 Thess. 2:14). This, however, is not the general call of the gospel to all people. If it were, we would be forced to *universalism*, the view that everyone will be saved. Instead, those who are called by God have been foreknown, predestined, and **justified.** This *call* refers to the internal work of the Spirit in the hearts of God's elect to bring them to belief in Christ (Acts 16:14). Being justified means being "declared righteous." Finally, God **glorified.** Though glorification is in the future, it is stated here in the past tense. Everyone then, who was foreknown by God in eternity past, has such a certain future that the apostle speaks of their glorification as already accomplished.

8:31 Paul now asks a series of four rhetorical questions in relation to the eternal purpose of God. **What then shall we say to these things?** In essence, this verse is the conclusion Paul draws to the first eight chapters of Romans. What will our response be to what has been said? **If God is for us, who can be against us?** This is not one of the four rhetorical questions but rather the answer to the first question. Paul's only response is he has complete assurance that the eternal purpose of God will come to fruition because God is God. **Who can be against us?** does not mean that we have no adversaries. Verses 35 and 36 list a great number of adversaries. By this Paul means that there is no adversary too great to thwart the eternal purpose of God.

8:32 Paul answers the rhetorical question of v. 31 with a question. Since God has done the greatest thing, giving **His own Son,** will He not also **freely give us all things?**

8:33 This is a rhetorical question equivalent to an emphatic denial. **Elect** recalls God's eternal program (vv. 28–30). If God, the Supreme Judge, **justifies,** then who is going to successfully bring a charge against us?

8:34 Christ . . . died . . . makes intercession: Since Christ had fully justified us and is presently interceding for us, then no one can possibly condemn us. The death of the Lord Jesus on our behalf would avail little apart from His resurrection. It is the living Lord that insures the security of God's eternal purpose. Consequently, He is now sitting at the right hand of God where He is highly exalted in glory and sovereignty. By the authority which is innate to His deity, the Lord Jesus makes intercession for us to God the Father. By His victorious death, His victorious resurrection, His victorious ascension into heaven, and His victorious intercession for us, the Lord Jesus has sealed the eternal purpose of God. In the whole universe there is nothing which can provide greater assurance than the finished work of Christ.

8:35 If no one can successfully oppose us (v. 31), charge us (v. 33), or condemn us (v. 34)

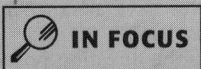 **IN FOCUS**   **"predestined"**

(Gk. *proorizō*) (8:29, 30; Acts 4:28; 1 Cor. 2:7; Eph. 1:5, 11) Strong's #4309: To *predestine* means "to mark out beforehand," "to establish one's boundary, or one's limits, beforehand." Our English word *horizon* is a derivative of this Greek word. The Christian's ultimate destiny or horizon has been fixed by God from all eternity: to be made like His Son. Note how the words *predestined, called, justified,* and especially *glorified* in Rom. 8:29, 30 are in the past tense. That is because God, from His eternal perspective, sees this process as having been completed already. From God's perspective, we have been glorified already because He sees us righteous because of the work of Jesus on the Cross. But still, in the march of time, we must undergo the process of being conformed to the image of God's Son.

with regard to our personal relationship with God, then it follows that no one can **separate** us from Christ's love for us. The list in this verse covers the full range of experiences that could seem to pose a challenge to the reality of Christ's love.

8:36 sheep for the slaughter: Those who love God (Ps. 44:17–22) have always had to face death daily (2 Cor. 4:11).

8:37 The trials and difficulties listed in v. 35 not only do not separate us from Christ's love; they make us **more than conquerors** by forcing us to depend even more on God.

8:38, 39 Absolutely nothing can **separate** believers from God's love. The apostle struggles for words to describe the absolute certainty of God's love for believers. Nothing hard or dangerous, neither death nor life, can separate us. If God, the uncreated One, is for us, and no created thing can separate us, then our security in Him is absolute.

9:1–3 At the end of ch. 8 Paul established that: (1) God has a purpose for believers, (2) nothing can prevent that purpose from being fulfilled, and (3) no one can separate God's people from His love. But what about the Jewish people? God had a purpose for Israel and God had said He loved Israel. Yet Israel appears to be excluded from God's program. Paul addresses this problem in chs. 9—11. **accursed from Christ:** Paul's pain was so great that he was willing, if possible, to be separated from Christ if it meant Israel could be united to Him (Ex. 32:32).

9:2, 3 great sorrow (Gk. *lupe*) **and continual grief** (Gk. *odune*): Paul begins with an expression of his sadness for Israel's unbelief.

9:4, 5 Paul lists some of the great privileges of Israel. For example, they were called **Israelites.** Israel was the name given to their ancestor Jacob as an expression of God's favor (Gen. 32:28). **Christ:** Their supreme privilege was that the Messiah came through them. **eternally blessed God:** Jesus Christ is God in the flesh.

9:6 The word of God in this context is a reference to God's promises to Israel. Paul is declaring that God's purposes and promises have not failed. **not all Israel:** Not all the physical descendants of Jacob (Israel) inherited the promises of God.

9:7 Abraham is another illustration of Paul's point that physical descent is no guarantee of a place in God's family. Abraham had two sons, Ishmael and Isaac; but Isaac inherited the promises, not Ishmael.

9:8 of the flesh: Just being a physical descendant of Abraham does not mean inheriting God's **promise** to Abraham and his offspring.

9:9 For this is the word of promise: At this time I will come and Sarah shall have a son: This quotation from Gen. 18:10 is in accordance with the promise that Isaac would be born, a promise which seemed so unlikely that it provoked Sarah to laughter (Gen. 18:12). Nevertheless, Isaac was born and, although not the firstborn of Abraham, he was God's choice as the son through whom the promises of God would be manifested. God chose Isaac. It was His purpose that, in "Isaac your seed shall be called" (Rom. 9:7). Paul advances Isaac as an illustration that God deals on the principle of His sovereignty, not human initiation.

9:10 The children of **Isaac** are still another illustration of Paul's point. God's promise to Isaac was never intended to be fulfilled through Esau.

9:11 not yet . . . born: God chose Jacob over Esau before they were born. Neither had **done any good or evil** at the time the choice was made. It was not based in any way on their **works.** It was solely based on **Him who calls.** God did not elect Jacob because of anything Jacob did; his election was based on grace.

9:12 older: The descendants of Esau. **younger:** The descendants of Jacob (Gen. 25:23 and note).

9:13 hated: Actually God made provision for Esau (Gen. 27:39; 36; Deut. 23:7). *Hated* is an idiom where the opposite is used to express a lesser degree. For example, Gen. 29:30 says Jacob loved Rachel more than Leah, but the next verse (literally translated) says that Leah was hated. What Paul is saying is that Esau was not the object of God's electing purpose.

9:14 If God chose some of Abraham's descendants (v. 6), like Isaac over Ishmael (vv. 7–9), or Jacob over Esau (vv. 10–13), then **is there unrighteousness with God?** The complaint is that if God chose Isaac or Jacob without regard to their works, then this would have been unrighteous or unjust. If God's election and rejection was based on the evil deeds of one or the good deeds of the other, the question of God's "fairness" would never have arisen. This question is the theme of chs. 9—11.

9:15 Paul's response to the question posed in v. 14 is not to justify God's actions or choices but to state the unequivocal sovereignty of God in doing as He wills. **I will have mercy:** In this passage from Exodus, God states His absolute right not to be questioned by His creatures about His decisions (Ex. 33:19). With these words about *mercy* and *compassion* God revealed His character to Moses when he asked to behold the glory of God. Those who question God in these matters have not seen the glory of God that Moses was allowed to see.

9:16 but of God: The basis of God's sovereign choice is not a person's conduct, but God's compassion. God is free to show mercy to whom He chooses.

9:17, 18 Pharaoh refused to obey the Lord (Ex. 5:2) and hardened his heart (Ex. 7:13, 14, 22; 8:15, 32; 9:7). God used Pharaoh's sin to demonstrate His **power** and magnify His **name. hardens:** God only gave Pharaoh over to what Pharaoh had already chosen to do. Nevertheless, the fact remains that God sovereignly chooses to have mercy on some and to withhold it from others.

9:19, 20 Find fault means "to blame." Paul again poses human questions that he will answer in vv. 20, 21. If God hardens whom He wills (v. 18), why blame the one who was hardened? **His will:** If God hardens, how can it be said that person is resisting God? Isn't the hardened one only doing what God has willed him to do? **Reply** means "to make a rejoinder," implying an argumentative attitude. Paul rebukes anyone who would raise such objections, which in the end are only protests against God's ways, and not a sincere request for an explanation.

9:21 The word translated **power** can mean "right" or "authority." Paul insists on God's right to do as He pleases.

9:22, 23 What if: Some insist that Paul is raising only the possibility of a vessel designed for destruction. Others take the passage literally, that God prepares some for eternal doom. **prepared for destruction . . . prepared beforehand for glory:** The grammatical structure of

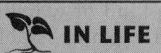 **IN LIFE** | **Righteousness**

What is righteousness? Most of us immediately think of a person trying to keep a list of rules, like a little boy or girl who never steps over the line. When Paul speaks of righteousness in Romans, he means far more than this commonsense understanding of the word. He draws on the OT concept of righteousness, which speaks of a proper relationship between God and a person, or between God and His people.

In the OT, righteousness is fundamentally an attribute of God (Pss. 71:15; 119:42). He alone is truly righteous. He is the One who remains faithful, to His promises, His covenant with Israel, and the Law. In turn, the Israelites as God's people had the responsibility to exemplify God's righteousness on this earth. Ultimately, this meant they had to love and worship the living God alone. The Law of Moses could be summed up in that command and its corollary, "You shall love your neighbor as yourself" (Lev. 19:18; Mark 12:31). Tragically, the Israelites did not comply. They proved unfaithful to the covenant, although God proved Himself as faithful. By sending prophets to His people, the Lord warned them again and again of their sinfulness. Finally He had to discipline them, with famine, military defeat, and even exile in Babylon. But God remained faithful, and He restored His people to the land and to Himself when they repented and turned to Him.

After their return from Babylon, the Israelites confused righteousness with a strict adherence to the Law as recorded in the Pentateuch. Indeed, the Jewish religious leaders added numerous amendments to the Law to ensure that no one would inadvertently break it. Zealous obedience to the Law was equated with righteousness. Yet mere external compliance to a set of rules did not please the Lord. What God wanted was repentant, humbled hearts that truly worshiped Him. He wanted to be the God of their hearts and minds, and the center of their devotion.

In his letter to the Romans, Paul clearly states that no one has achieved this standard; no one has completely loved and worshiped the Lord as they should (3:23). All have sinned. No good work or outward appearance of piety can restore a proper relationship with the Holy One (Is. 64:6). On the one hand, the Gentiles did not pursue a right relationship with their Creator, so they had been given over to all kinds of evil (1:18–31). On the other hand, the Jews through external obedience to the Law and their traditions were attempting to justify themselves before God (9:31, 32). Both failed. Jesus is the only One who can stand before the glorious God; He is the only One who is truly righteous. Remarkably, He has offered us a way out of our slavery to sin. By placing our faith and trust in Him, we can be declared righteous. We can have a righteousness that has nothing to do with our own works but instead relies on Jesus' sinless life and His sacrificial death for our sins. The Lord forgives us and declares us righteous because of our identification by faith with the righteousness of His Son (4:5). Through Jesus, we can finally be released from the guilt of our sins. Not only can we approach the Holy One in praise and thankfulness, but we can do God's will.

the first *prepared*, referring to the vessels of wrath, is different from the second *prepared*, referring to the vessels of mercy. The first may literally mean "prepared themselves," while the second is "which He prepared." If we are doomed, it is because of our rejection of God; if we are redeemed, it is because of the grace of God. The question is not: Why are some saved and some condemned? Everyone deserves condemnation. It is only by God's grace that anyone is saved.

9:24–29 God calls both **Jews** and **Gentiles.** Paul quotes several OT passages to support this point.

9:29 Unless God had been merciful, Israel would have been utterly destroyed.

9:30–32 The question is: Since **Israel** had the law and pursued **righteousness,** why have they not **attained** it? Was it because they were not elected? The answer is that they did not obtain righteousness because they did not believe. They tried obtaining righteousness **by the works of the law.** Being committed to a righteousness by works, they **stumbled** over the righteousness of faith offered in Christ.

9:32, 33 The great tragedy of the Jewish nation was that the Messiah they so long awaited became to them a stumbling stone rather than a shelter in which to hide. The quotation here is from Is. 28:16, which is set in the context of Israel trusting Egypt for deliverance from the Assyrians instead of trusting in the power of God. Those who trust in God need never fear that their trust has been ill-placed or is ill-founded. **Whoever believes on Him will not be put to shame:** Had Israel trusted in her God rather than her law and her neighbors, she would not have been confounded and dispersed throughout the world. But the partial blindness of Israel, in the eternal purpose of God, has resulted in good for the Gentiles and the world in general. God is now calling out a people unto His name from both Jews and the Gentiles.

10:1–21 The groundwork for ch. 10 has already been laid in 9:30–33. The emphasis here is on righteousness and why Israel lacks it. Paul will lay the responsibility for the lack of righteousness squarely on the shoulders of the individual. He knows that when sinners are brought into the presence of divine sovereignty, their frequent response is to justify themselves by placing the responsibility for their sin on God. Paul does not apologize in any way for what he has said about God's sovereignty in ch. 9. He does not retreat at all from his strong belief that God has always worked by the principle of election. However he does demonstrate that God is not responsible for the unbeliever's lost condition. Man alone is responsible and it is futile to try to hide behind divine sovereignty and the doctrine of election as an excuse for personal sin.

10:1 saved: This word is used in the NT in several different ways (1:16). In Romans, Paul seems to make a distinction between justification and salvation (5:9, 10); the reader must pay attention to the context. Justification is what takes place at the moment of faith in Christ. Salvation, at least in Romans, refers to the work of God in the believer that continues after justification. It is deliverance from God's wrath (1:18; 5:9, 10). The logical conclusion from ch. 9 is that Israel is under divine wrath (9:22). Paul's deep **desire** and **prayer** is that Israel may be justified and **saved** from His wrath.

10:2 Israel had a **zeal for God;** outwardly, they were very religious. But their effort was **not according to knowledge.** They lacked a correct understanding of the kind of worship God wanted from them. Paul explains Israel's ignorance in vv. 3–13.

10:3 God's righteousness is the righteousness that belongs to God, and more specifically in this context, the righteousness God gives when a person trusts Christ. **not submitted:** This means "to obey." Israel did not obey God's command to believe (1:5; 6:17; Acts 16:31).

10:4 End can mean "fulfillment"; that is, Christ fulfilled all the requirements of the law. It can also mean "goal," to say that Christ was the object to which the law led. The point is that Israel was ignorant of God's righteousness because they failed to comprehend what the law was intended to do. The law revealed sin and showed that people could not hope to keep the law. Christ came and fulfilled it, then offered us His righteousness through faith in Him.

10:5–8 There are two kinds of righteousness, by works or by faith. One is inaccessible, the other is very accessible. Paul uses the words of Deut. 30:11–14 to demonstrate that righteousness by faith is not far off and inaccessible, but is as **near** as a person's **mouth** and **heart.** All one has to do is repent, believe in Jesus, and confess that belief.

10:9 Confess comes before **believe** in this verse because "mouth" precedes "heart" in Deuteronomy (v. 8). The order is reversed in the next verse. One has to confess with the **mouth** to be **saved.**

10:10 For indicates that this verse explains v. 9. The condition for **righteousness,** that is for being justified, is internal faith. The condition of **salvation,** meaning deliverance from wrath and from the power of sin, is external confession (v. 1; 5:9, 10), which is calling on the Lord for help (vv. 12, 13).

10:11–13 Paul emphasizes the universal offer of salvation. **Whoever** in vv. 11, 13 means

✠ IN CONTEXT   Unity in the Body of Christ

By the time Paul wrote his letter to the Christians at Rome, Gentiles were probably becoming a majority of believers throughout the church. Jews had less and less influence theologically, culturally, or politically. Gradually—and tragically—the attitudes of pride and prejudice with which Jews had looked down on Gentiles were coming back to haunt them, as Gentile believers began to turn away from their Jewish brothers.

In Rom. 9—11, Paul pleaded with his Gentile readers to remember that God has not forgotten Israel. God made promises to the nation that He cannot forsake (11:29). Furthermore, Gentiles have no room for arrogance: they were not originally included among God's people, but were allowed in, like branches grafted onto a tree (11:17, 18).

Paul saw the possibility of a church divided, with Jewish and Gentile believers going their separate ways. If that happened, Gentiles would ignore the Jewish community altogether rather than show compassion and communicate the gospel so that Jews could be saved. That's why here, as elsewhere, Paul challenged believers to pursue unity in the body of Christ and charity among the peoples of the world.

"all." Verse 12 explains that this includes **Jew and Greek** (Gentile).

10:14, 15 If salvation is to be made possible for everyone, God must send preachers so people can **hear, believe** and **call.**

10:16 they: Israel. Not **all** Jews have **obeyed** the command to believe in Christ.

10:17 One must hear the **word of God** and then **believe.**

10:18–21 Israel **heard** but was **disobedient;** only a remnant believed the gospel.

11:1–36 Even though Israel heard and rejected the gospel (10:16–21), God has not entirely rejected them. Even now some Israelites have accepted God's grace (vv. 1–10). Moreover, the rejection of the nation as a whole is not final (vv. 11–24), for God wills to save both Gentiles and Jews by grace (vv. 25–32). Praise His name (vv. 33–36)!

11:1 One of the proofs that God has not **cast away** the Jewish people is Paul himself. He was an **Israelite,** a descendant of **Abraham**, a member of the **tribe of Benjamin.** He was a Jew, and he was chosen by God to be a believer and an apostle.

11:2 In this verse, **His people** refers to the nation of Israel and not just the elect within the nation. In vv. 4–7 Paul differentiates between the nation and the remnant, but his point there is that God's saving of the remnant proves that He has not abandoned His plan for the nation (v. 26). **whom He foreknew:** See 8:29.

11:3–5 Paul cites Elijah as an illustration. Elijah thought that the whole nation of Israel had fallen away, but he was wrong. The **remnant** in Elijah's day was proof that God had not cast off His people, and the remnant in Paul's day was continuing proof of His faithfulness.

11:6 if by grace, then it is no longer of works: *Grace* and *works* are mutually exclusive. God's election was established solely on the basis of grace (v. 5).

11:7 What Israel **seeks** is righteousness (9:31—10:3). The **elect** have **obtained** righteousness by faith. The others were **blinded** because they did not believe.

11:8–10 Paul quotes Isaiah and **David** to show that Israel's spiritual indifference was a continual pattern. Their rejection of Christ would bring untold misery on the nation.

11:11 fall: Does Israel's rejection mean the end of God's program for the nation? **Certainly not!** Israel's unbelief brought **salvation . . . to the Gentiles,** and it will ultimately lead to Israel's salvation (v. 26).

11:12, 13 fullness: The nation of Israel, chosen by God to receive salvation, will be saved along with believing Gentiles, resulting in great blessing for everyone (v. 26).

11:14 save some: Paul is revealing his great desire to see the salvation of all of Israel (vv. 12, 26).

11:15 life from the dead: The failure of Israel in rejecting Christ will make their eventual acceptance as vivid and wonderful as the resurrection that all believers will experience; it will be as if they had come back from the dead.

11:16 Firstfruit and **root** are references to the conversion of some Jews (v. 14) and the Gentiles (v. 15).

11:17 The **wild olive tree** is the Gentile Christians. The **olive tree** refers to Israel, those who inherited the promises of the Abrahamic covenant (Gen. 12:1, 2; 17:7, 8; Hos. 14:6). **grafted in:** Paul intentionally stretches the analogy of grafting in order to communicate his point that Gentiles have been supernaturally connected to the family of God.

11:18–24 If it had not been for the grace of God, Gentiles would never have been grafted into the life of God which the Jews enjoyed. The

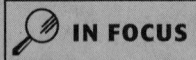

IN FOCUS "mystery"

(Gk. *mustērion*) (11:25; 16:25; 1 Cor. 2:7; Eph. 1:9; 3:3, 4, 9) Strong's #3466: The word *mystery*, so often used by Paul, does not mean something incomprehensible, but something that had been kept secret and now has been disclosed. In Paul's cultural and religious milieu, the term was often used with reference to the mystery religions. Adherents to the mystery religions used the term to speak of the secret knowledge of the religion revealed only to the initiated ones. In contrast, Paul uses the word to speak of a secret that has been openly revealed to all.

new life which enables them to produce fruit grows from the same root that the old stock of Israel grows. NT believers must not assume that they are better than the Jews because they were cut off for their unbelief. The Gentile church must never forget its reliance upon the divine grace of God, else her end will be the same as that of the old branches. The process of being grafted into the life of God finds its basis in the

grace of God. We must never lord the grace of God over those who have been cut from the tree, for it is much easier to put the natural branches back than to graft different branches in their place. We therefore must rest totally on the grace of God for our salvation, as the remnant does.

11:18 Gentiles, who have been grafted into the Abrahamic covenant and therefore become recipients of God's blessing, should not **boast**. Gentile believers should not despise the Jews, **the branches** of God's vine.

11:19 The reason Israel was **broken off** (v. 17), "cast away" (v. 15), and "has fallen" (v. 12) is so that Gentiles could be grafted into the tree.

11:20 Well said: Paul agrees with the objector (v. 19) that Israel was **broken off** because of **unbelief** and that Gentiles **stand by faith.** But he goes on to warn that Gentiles should not **be haughty, but fear.** Standing before God is based on faith. Feelings of superiority are out of place.

11:21 Paul was warning the Gentiles not to be arrogant (v. 20), but to remember that they depended on God and were accountable to Him no less than the Jews were.

11:22, 23 If Gentiles **continue** in God's **goodness,** they will not be **cut off,** and if Jews turn to God in faith, they can be grafted in again. This is not a reference to individual salvation but to God's program for Jews and Gentiles.

11:24 It is far more natural to expect Israel, the **natural branches**, to be **grafted in,** than to expect Gentiles, the **wild** branches, to be included.

11:25 If believers do not understand this **mystery,** chances were they will be **wise in**

IN COMPARISON **The Christian Life**

Description of the Christian:	Result:
Presents himself to God (12:1)	Becomes a sacrifice that is living, holy and pleasing to God (12:1)
Receives transformation by a renewed mind (12:2)	Discovers and displays the will of God (12:2)
Has spiritual gifts according to grace from God (12:6–8)	Uses spiritual gifts as part of Christ's body (12:6)
Honors civil law (13:1)	Honors God (13:1)
Loves others (13:8)	Fulfills God's law (13:8)
Pursues peace (14:19)	Serves to edify all (14:19)
Becomes like-minded toward others (15:5)	Glorifies God with others (15:6)

their **own opinion,** meaning they will be haughty (v. 20) and boast (v. 18). The mystery is that Israel has been temporarily and partially hardened, but God has not rejected them.

11:26 All Israel does not mean that every individual in the nation will turn to the Lord. It means that the nation as a whole will be saved, just as the nation as a whole (but not every individual in it) was now rejecting the Lord.

11:27 For this is My covenant with them, When I take away their sins: Paul continues the quotation of Is. 59:21, but then passes into the promise of Jer. 31:33 to indicate that God will not fail to keep His covenant with Israel.

11:28, 29 The Jews are **enemies** in that they reject the **gospel.** For the **sake of the fathers** refers to the promises God made to the patriarchs. **Irrevocable** means "not to repent." God does not change His mind. He made promises to the patriarchs (v. 28) and He will fulfill them.

11:30–32 Israel's **disobedience** (Gk. *apeitheō*) doesn't change the fact that God can still have mercy as He did on disobedient Gentiles.

11:33 God's method of dealing with Jews and Gentiles is a display of deep divine **wisdom.**

11:34, 35 The OT indicated in several places that God's wisdom is unobtainable by man in his own strength.

11:36 God is the source, means, and end of all things. He is the Creator, Sustainer, and the goal of everything. Therefore, He should be praised and glorified **forever.**

12:1–15:13 The transformation made by God in the spirit of the believer must be shown in the daily life. The practical instructions in 12:1—15:13 are based on Paul's doctrinal teaching in 1:18—11:36. Christian doctrine must lead to Christian ethics. In 12:1 and 2 is the basic commitment required of the Christian in light of all that God has done. The rest of this section describes how this commitment is carried out in the changing situations of daily life.

12:1 Based on God's mercy (9:11, 15, 16, 18, 23; 11:30–32), Paul entreats believers to **present** their **bodies** as **a living sacrifice,** meaning they should use their bodies to serve and obey God (6:13). Such giving of the body to God is more than a contrast with a dead animal sacrifice, it is "newness of life" (6:4). **Holy** means set apart for the Lord's use; **acceptable** means pleasing to Him; and **reasonable** indicates that such a gift is the only rational reaction to all the good gifts God has showered on us.

12:2 Conformed means "to form" or "mold." **World** is the normal word for "age" or "era." Instead of being molded by the values of this world, the believer should be **trans-**

formed, that is, changed **by the renewing of** the **mind.** Spiritual transformation starts in the mind and heart. A mind dedicated to the world and its concerns will produce a life tossed back and forth by the currents of culture. But a mind dedicated to God's truth will produce a life that can stand the test of time. We can resist the temptations of our culture by meditating on God's truth and letting the Holy Spirit guide and shape our thoughts and behaviors.

12:3–13 Instructions on how a person is to live within the Christian community. We Chris-

IN FOCUS **"transform"**

(Gk. *metamorphoō*) (12:2; Matt. 17:2; 2 Cor. 3:18) Strong's #*3339*: The Greek word means "to change form," as does the English derivative *metamorphosis.* In the NT, this word is used to describe an inward renewal of our mind through which our inner spirit is changed into the likeness of Christ. Paul told the Roman believers: "Be transformed by the renewing of your minds" (12:2). As our Christian life progresses, we should gradually notice that our thought life is being changed from Christlessness to Christlikeness. Transformation does not happen overnight. Our regeneration is instantaneous, but our transformation is continuous. We are conformed to Christ's image gradually as we spend time in intimate fellowship with Him (2 Cor. 3:18).

tians are closely united because we are all members of the **body of Christ** (vv. 3–8). In humility we are to use our God-given spiritual gifts to strengthen one another. Our conduct toward each other is best expressed as **love** (vv. 9–13).

12:3 think of himself: A renewed mind (v. 2) begins with thinking **soberly** about oneself. The first step in changing behavior is self-observation (1 Cor. 11:28–32). **to each one:** God has given everyone one or more gifts that can be used in His service. **dealt . . . a measure of faith:** The *measure* refers to God's sovereignly given gifts mentioned in vv. 6–8. These gifts are not the result of intense prayer or spirituality. Instead, God simply gives everyone certain gifts so each person can strengthen the church (1 Cor. 12:11, 18, 28).

12:4, 5 As the human body is a unity with **many members,** each having its own **function,** so is the body of Christ. The church is a unified body under the headship of Christ, but

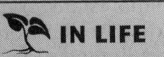 **IN LIFE**   **Antidote for Comparisonitis**

One of the most debilitating diseases of the modern world is "comparisonitis"—the tendency to measure one's worth by comparing oneself to other people. You won't find this illness listed in any of the standard medical textbooks, nor will your company's disability or health insurance or worker's compensation program reimburse you for it. But make no mistake: comparisonitis is a scourge as widespread and destructive as any physical or emotional malady known today.

Comparisonitis happens when people find ways to look down on others and think highly of themselves because they enjoy greater abilities, intelligence, status, or wealth than they. Comparisonitis is an ancient disease. Certainly Paul was aware of how deadly it could be. That's why he offered an antidote for it—to see ourselves not as we stack up against others, nor as others evaluate us, *but as God sees us* (Rom. 12:3). Ultimately, His estimation of our worth is what matters. And to Him we matter a *lot!*

God does not define us according to culturally defined externals. Even our gender, ethnicity, family heritage, or body type are not of primary importance to Him. No, He uses an altogether different set of criteria as the basis for how He deals with us, as several people in Scripture indicate:

- *Paul* found that God's grace made him who he was (1 Cor. 15:10). He also discovered that despite his past, God had made him into a new person (2 Cor. 5:17).
- *Peter* learned that God's power gave him everything he needed to live his life and pursue godliness (2 Pet. 1:3).
- *Job* realized that all he had—family, friends, possessions, health—was ultimately from God (Job 1:21).
- *One of the psalmists* understood that God Himself had created him, "fearfully and wonderfully." Imagine what that did for his self-image! (Ps. 139:14).

the members have different functions (1 Cor. 12:12–31).

12:6 gifts: The Greek word (*charismata*) refers to God-given abilities that should be used to build up other members in the church. Although they are "irrevocable" and, thus do not change (11:29), they are to be pursued and developed (1 Pet. 4:10). **prophecy:** This word is used here in a general sense for all types of gifts that involve speaking God's word. For example, in 1 Cor. 14:3 "exhortation" appears as a prophesying gift. In its narrower sense, *prophecy* means the revealing of God's will in a particular situation (Acts 13:1–3).

12:7, 8 Ministry means "service" and is in contrast to the speaking gifts (1 Pet. 4:11). The Scriptures list five speaking gifts: prophecy, teaching, encouragement, the word of wisdom, and the word of knowledge. In addition, seven serving gifts are named: helps, mercy, faith, discernment of spirits, leadership, managing, and giving.

12:9 Christian **love** is not mere emotion, but action. **Abhor . . . evil:** The Christian avoids "every form of evil" (1 Thess. 5:22).

12:10 There are at least four Greek words for love, not all of which are used in the NT. (1) The highest form of love is *agape*. This is a self-sacrificial love. It involves an act of the will

whereby one seeks the best for another. *Agapē* is used in v. 9. (2) The Greek word *philos* means "affectionate regard," and the derived form *philadelphia* is translated **brotherly love** in this verse. (3) *Philostorgos* means "family affection" and is translated **kindly affectionate** in this verse. (4) *Eros* means physical love and does not occur in the NT. **preference to one another:** The greatest proof of the truth of the gospel message and of the reality of Jesus' love is the love believers show to each other. Christ is the model for such self-sacrificial love (Phil. 2:3–8).

12:11 in diligence: Christians should not offer their service half-heartedly or in a lazy manner. Instead, Paul encourages the Romans to serve eagerly and in earnest.

12:12 The believer who is constantly praying will be **rejoicing in hope** and **patient** (Gk. *hupomenō*), or, enduring, **in tribulation.**

12:13 Hospitality means "love of strangers." The primary reference is to housing travelers, though all forms of hospitality are included. The progression in this verse is significant. As we dedicate ourselves to meeting the needs of our fellow believers, we will have opportunities to serve strangers and thus witness to them about the love of Christ.

12:14–21 As we relate to non-Christians, we are to respond in love to our persecutors (v.

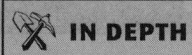 **IN DEPTH** | **Submitting to Authority**

cripture challenges us as believers to subject ourselves to whatever governments we live under (Rom. 13:1–7). Submission to authority is never easy. Human nature tends toward resistance and even rebellion, especially if government is imposed, incompetent, and/or corrupt. But as we struggle with how to respond to the systems in which we live, this passage offers some helpful perspectives:

(1) *God is the ultimate authority* (13:1). Government as an institution has been established by God to serve His purposes. God raises up and does away with leaders.

(2) *Both followers and leaders are ultimately accountable to God* (13:2). Submission to human authorities reflects our submission to God's authority.

(3) *God uses governments to carry out His good purposes on earth* (13:3). Without question, some governments sometimes persecute those who do good. Paul had firsthand experience with that. But mainly, it's the lawbreaker, not the law-abiding citizen, who has something to fear from government.

(4) *Obedience is a matter of inner conviction as well as external law* (13:5). Our motivation to obey must go beyond fear of punishment. As believers, we serve the highest of all authorities, God Himself.

Only when a government commands us to do what God prohibits (worship, taking of innocent life, etc.) or prohibits us from doing what God commands are we to be in disobedience.

---

14), to live at peace with unbelievers (v. 18), and to do good even to those who treat us badly (v. 20).

12:14 Bless means "to speak well of" or "praise."

12:15 rejoice . . . weep: Because believers are a body, when one part hurts, everyone feels the pain; when one is joyful, everyone can rejoice. Christians cannot be indifferent to the suffering or joy of their fellow believers (1 Cor. 12:25, 26).

12:16 Be of the same mind: Keep harmony among yourselves. Do not be haughty, conceited, or maneuver to associate with the great.

12:17 The word **good** in this verse means "morally good," "noble," or "praiseworthy." This is the positive side of the negative command not to return **evil for evil** (1 Pet. 3:9). A Christian should not concentrate on the evil in others, but instead should focus on what is good. By doing so, we encourage others around us to aspire to the good.

12:18 The believer's aim should be to **live peaceably.** But sometimes peace is not within our control; this is why Paul limits the command.

12:19 Believers are not to seek personal revenge, but rather to let God punish.

12:20, 21 Freed from vengeance, believers can give themselves to mercy, even toward their enemies. By acts of kindness, the believers will **heap coals of fire** on the head of their enemies, perhaps bringing shame and repentance to

them. It is possible for an enemy to become a friend. This is the phenomenal power of God's love that believers are connected to through Christ.

13:1 God, the supreme Sovereign, has ordained (v. 2) that there should be **governing authorities. Every** believer is to **be subject** to these various authorities, even if these authorities are evil as Nero (A.D. 54–68), the emperor of Rome who cruelly persecuted Christians. When Paul wrote this letter, Nero was in power. Yet Paul exhorted the Roman believers to submit to Nero's authority, because that authority was ordained by God Himself, although God may not approve of all acts that a government or leader may do.

13:2 Judgment does not necessarily include eternal punishment. God may judge people through the human authorities He appoints.

13:3 Government is to be obeyed because it is ordained to punish **evil** (Gk. *kakon*) and promote **good** (Gk. *agathos*).

13:4 The **sword** is an instrument of death. Government has the right in the proper circumstances to impose capital punishment as well as to wage war. In Paul's day, the common method of capital punishment was decapitation with a sword.

13:5 for conscience' sake: Believers must obey government not only because it is their civic duty, but because it is their spiritual duty before God.

13:6 Paying **taxes** is the most obvious and

 **IN COMPARISON** | **The Key Terms of Salvation**

Paul, in the Epistle to the Romans, attempts to portray God's plan of salvation in a concise and clear manner. In doing so, he uses Greek words whose meanings are not widely known today. Here is a brief glossary of the key terms of salvation in this book:

English Term	Greek Term	References	Meaning
Faith	*pistis*	(1:17; 4:9; 12:6)	"Belief, trust"; faith is the means by which sinful people can experience and enjoy all the blessings of salvation. It is a complete trust in Jesus for salvation from sin and the coming judgment.
Gospel	*euangelion*	(1:16, 11:28)	"Good News"; Paul uses this word to refer to the wonderful message of forgiveness and eternal life in Christ.
Grace	*charis*	(1:5; 5:2; 12:3)	"The unmerited favor of God"; this term refers to God's inexplicable giving of good things (especially salvation) to undeserving people who could never earn it. Salvation is a free gift made possible by Christ's death on our behalf.
Justification	*dikaiosis*	(4:25; 5:18)	"The act of being declared righteous"; a legal term used by Paul to describe the spiritual transaction whereby God (the Judge) declares those who trust in Christ and what He has done for them on the Cross, to be acceptable before Him. Such a verdict is possible only because Christ has settled all the claims of the Law against sinners.
Law	*nomos*	(2:12; 4:13; 7:12; 10:4; 13:8)	"The commandments given by God"; Paul emphasizes both the holy character of the Law and the inability of sinful people to live according to it. The Law becomes a burden and a curse, until we allow it to point us to Christ, who perfectly fulfills all its requirements.
Propitiation	*hilasterion*	(3:25)	"The satisfaction of God's holy wrath against sin"; rebellion against God results in the wrath of God and must be met with judgment. By dying in our place and taking our sins upon Himself, Jesus satisfies God's righteous anger against all who believe.
Redemption	*apolutrosis*	(3:24; 8:23)	"The act of freeing someone by paying a purchase price"; this economic term is used by Paul in a theological sense to describe how Christ paid the penalty required by God for our sins (that is, death) by giving His own life on the Cross. When we believe, Jesus frees us from sin.
Righteousness	*dikaiosune*	(3:5; 5:17; 9:30)	"God's standard of purity" or "God's own truthfulness and faithfulness"; God is holy, therefore He cannot tolerate sin. It is through Jesus Christ that we can find righteousness that is acceptable to God. Christ not only takes away our sin, but He grants us His perfect purity.
Salvation	*soteria*	(1:16; 10:10)	"Deliverance"; this word is often used in the Bible to describe someone being rescued from physical harm. The word is used by Paul chiefly to denote deliverance from sin and its deadly consequences.
Sin	*hamartia; hamartema*	(3:9; 5:12; 7:11; 8:2; 14:23)	"Missing the mark" or "disobedience to God's law"; several different Greek words are used by Paul to describe the tendency of humans to rebel against God. Sin can be broadly defined as any attitude or action that opposes the character and will of God. Sin is what brings death—that is, separation from God.

universal expression of support for civil government.

13:7 Civic loyalty and obedience to God normally run parallel (Mark 12:17). We are to **fear** and **honor** God above all others, but **taxes** and **customs** are likewise Christian obligations. In a democratic society the Christian has a share in civil authority and therefore must do what he can to see that its actions conform to God's moral law.

13:8 In the present context, **owe no one anything** primarily means respect and honor (v. 7). No doubt money is also included, but this passage does not prohibit borrowing (Ps. 37:21; Matt. 5:42). **except to love:** Love is a debt that is never paid in full.

13:9 as yourself: This verse is not a command to love ourselves. It is a recognition that we do love ourselves, and commands us to love others just as genuinely and sincerely as we love ourselves.

13:10 Love excludes murder, adultery, stealing, and lying (v. 9). Therefore when we love, we automatically fulfill the prohibitions of **the law.** If we attempt to live by the law, we quickly discover that we are breaking the law (7:5). But when we act in accordance with God's love, without being under the law, we fulfill it.

13:11 sleep: Believers are pictured as being asleep or inactive. **Salvation** here refers to the future, when believers will be saved from the presence of sin. Thus, *salvation* here speaks of the imminent return of Christ.

13:12, 13 Night is the present age during which we live in Satan's domain. **Day** is the beginning of a new life with Christ in His glorious reign. **At hand** means "is imminent"; the Lord could return at any moment (Phil. 4:5; James 5:8; 1 Pet. 4:7). Note that Paul puts **strife** and **envy** on the same level as **drunkenness** and **lust.**

13:14 put on the Lord Jesus Christ: Believers should clothe themselves with Christlike characteristics such as truth (John 14:6), righteousness (1 Cor. 1:30), and peace (Gal. 5:22, 23; Eph. 2:14; 6:10–17).

14:1—15:13 gives instructions to those strong in the faith (15:1) on their relationship to those weak in the faith (14:1).

14:1–13 Paul refers to **disputes** between those who are strong in faith and those who are weak (15:1). The strong were Christians who disregarded as nonessential certain prohibitions that were not specifically declared in Scripture. Their faith was strong enough to participate in such conduct without a guilty conscience (v. 22). The **weak in faith** were Christians whose consciences were troubled by these same prohibitions. Some Christians thought they could eat

anything served as food; others did not (v. 2). Some held that Jewish festival days should be kept as holy days; others did not (v. 5). Paul was concerned that, on these nonessential issues, the strong should not **despise** the weak as ignorant and the weak should not **judge** the strong as profane or worldly (v. 3). He reminds us that both the strong and the weak are accountable to God (v. 12; 1 Cor. 8:4–13).

14:1, 2 Those who were **weak in the faith** did have faith: they had trusted in Christ. Some of the Roman believers might not have accepted the apostle's teaching concerning certain practices, such as accepting that all food was clean if received with thanksgiving (1 Tim. 4:4, 5). Instead, they ate **only vegetables.** The strong in the faith are told to **receive** the weak and not to dispute over **doubtful things,** which literally means "reasonings" or "opinions." The mature believers were not to pass judgment or to enter into dispute with those who were less mature.

14:3 The strong are not to **despise** the weak, that is, to treat them with contempt. The weak are not to **judge** the strong by attempting to place excessive prohibitions on them.

14:4 another's servant: Christ's follower. In a particular issue, whether a person **stands** approved by God or **falls** into sin is God's decision, not ours. Paul prohibits a censorious interference with another's freedom.

14:5 one day above another: This verse probably relates to the many holy days of the OT ceremonial law. **fully convinced:** The exhortation does not mean it is wrong to have strong convictions, but that all people have a right to their own convictions. This principle is basic in dealing with disputes.

14:6 Days and diets are not the issue, but whether what is being done is committed **to the Lord.**

14:7–9 None of us refers to believers, not people in general. Believers belong to the Lord. They live and die in relation to Him. Therefore, Christians should aim to please Him.

14:10 Again (v. 3) Paul addresses the weak and the strong. The weak are not to **judge,** and the strong are not to **show contempt,** the same word that is rendered "despise" in v. 3. **All** believers are accountable to their Master, Jesus Christ, for they will appear before Him. At the **judgment seat of Christ,** every believer's life will be evaluated to determine his or her reward (1 Cor. 3:11–15; 2 Cor. 5:9, 10).

14:11 every knee: One day everyone will submit to God's authority. He will judge all people before His great throne (Rev. 20:11–15).

14:12, 13 Let us not judge sums up Paul's instruction in vv. 1–12 on how weak and strong Christians should behave toward each other.

✚ IN CONTEXT — Are Sundays Special?

In the OT, God commanded the Hebrews to set aside one day a week as a "Sabbath," a holy day of rest (Ex. 20:8–11; Is. 58:13, 14; Jer. 17:19–27). Yet here in Romans, Paul seems to take a nondirective posture toward the Sabbath (Rom. 14:5). Does that mean that there is no such thing as a "Lord's day," that God's people are no longer required to observe a Sabbath, whether it be Saturday or Sunday?

Not exactly. For Paul, *every day* should be lived for the Lord because we are the Lord's possession (14:8). If we act as if Sunday is the Lord's day but the other six days belong to us, then we've got a major misunderstanding. All seven days of the week belong to the Lord. The early church worshiped on the first day because it was the day of the Resurrection.

So the real question is, Should one of those days be observed in a special way, in light of God's instructions regarding a Sabbath? Paul says that neither pressure from other people nor tradition should bind our consciences. Instead, we are to seek guidance from the Spirit of God as to what we should do. Having inspired the Scriptures, God will help us determine what we should do as we study them.

but rather resolve: Addressed chiefly to the strong Christians whose position Paul deals with in vv. 14–23. **stumbling block:** Any action that causes others to fall into sin.

14:14 Unclean means "common" and refers to things prohibited by the Jewish ceremonial law. **to him:** If anyone considers some activity to be unlawful, then it is wrong for that person to engage in that activity (14:23).

14:15 Do not destroy: Paul here builds on the principle of *conviction* with the principle of *consideration* for the brother who is weak. This is a step in maturity. If eating meat (v. 2; 1 Cor. 8:7–11; 10:25–28) destroys a weak believer, then the strong believer should not eat it.

14:16 Your good is what you, the believer, consider to be *good*. **Be spoken of as evil** means "reviled" or "slandered." Do not cause your freedom, a good thing, to be reviled because of the way in which you use it.

14:17 The kingdom of God does not consist of external things like food, but in spiritual realities like **righteousness** in action and thought, **peace** that seeks harmony, and **joy** that comes from **the Holy Spirit.** Those who understand the spiritual realities of the kingdom will not choose the brief joy of satisfying selfish desires over the spiritual joy of putting aside those desires for the sake of others.

14:18 acceptable to God: Because our service to Christ is rooted in "righteousness and peace and joy" (v. 17). **approved by men:** Opposite to "spoken of as evil" (v. 16).

14:19, 20 The believer should **edify,** that is, "build up." **Do not destroy:** That is, do not "throw down" or "demolish." Paul has already exhorted mature believers to have consideration for the weak believers (v. 15). Here Paul exhorts the mature believer to identify ways to build up those weaker in the faith.

14:21 There is little distinction between **stumbles, offended,** and **made weak.** Paul uses all three words to reiterate that a mature believer should not cause the downfall of another believer (vv. 12, 13, 20).

14:22 Paul does not require the strong to abandon their convictions about things not condemned by the law. Instead he encourages them to **have faith** about such issues. Although mature believers may refrain from eating meat in front of weaker believers, they can still believe that Christ gives them the freedom to eat all types of food (v. 2) privately **before** Him (v. 5).

14:23 whatever is not from faith: Any action that violates my Christian conscience is a **sin.**

15:1, 2 scruples: Because there are no clear guidelines in Scripture for some issues, the **weak** are overcautious. We are not to **please ourselves** at the expense of others. Rather, we are to help our **neighbor** by doing what will strengthen him spiritually.

15:3 Christ is the ultimate model for the strong believer. He renounced self-gratification so that He could clearly represent God and His cause (Phil. 2:5–8).

15:4 Through **patience** (endurance) and the **comfort** (or encouragement) of Scripture, believers learn that they have **hope.** In this case, if strong believers are patient with the scruples of the weak, they have hope of being rewarded (14:10; 1 Cor. 9:17, 24–27).

15:5 the God of patience: Attributing to God the same virtues just ascribed to the Scriptures (v. 4), Paul prays for the unity of all believers.

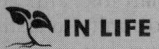 **IN LIFE**   **God's Rainbow**

S ocieties and their systems tend to encourage people to divide along racial, ethnic, and cultural lines, or else to abandon their distinctives by assimilating into the dominant power group. Paul called for a different approach. He didn't ask Jews to give up their Jewish heritage and become Gentiles, nor did he ask Gentiles to become Jews. Instead, he affirmed the rich ethnic backgrounds of both groups while challenging them to live together in unity (Rom. 15:7).

That kind of unity is costly, and the attempt to practice it is always under attack. Yet that is the church that God calls us to—a diverse body of people who are unified around Christ. Our backgrounds—whether Japanese, Anglo-Saxon, African, Middle Eastern, Puerto Rican, Chinese, Italian, or whatever—are God's gifts to each of us and to the church. He has placed us in our families as He has seen fit. We can rejoice in the background He has given us and be enriched by the background He has given others.

15:6 If believers are divided over some amoral issue, God will not be glorified by the unified whole (Phil. 1:27—2:2).

15:7 Therefore introduces the conclusion of the discussion begun in 14:1, where Paul began with the command to **receive** the weak believer. Thus, the command to **receive one another** is addressed not just to the strong believers, but to all believers.

15:8–13 Jesus Christ became a **servant** to the Jews for two purposes: (1) **to confirm** God's **promises** to Abraham, Isaac, and Jacob; and (2) to demonstrate God's mercy to the Gentiles so that they might **glorify** Him. Paul cites four passages from the OT to prove that God intended the Gentiles as well as the Jews to glorify Him. **as it is written:** Paul quotes from all three divisions of the OT (the Law, the Prophets, and the Psalms or Writings), and from three great Jewish leaders (Moses, David, and Isaiah), to demonstrate that God's purpose was always to bless the Gentiles through Israel. Although the nation of Israel has been set aside for the present (11:1–31), both Jews and Gentiles are being brought together in the church (3:1–12; Eph. 2:14–22). **root of Jesse:** This is a title for the Messiah. Jesse was the father of David, and the Son of David was the promised Messiah.

15:12 root of Jesse: Jesus was descended from David, whose father was Jesse.

15:13 A prayer that concludes Paul's exhortations. We are able to fulfill God's will only through the **power** that the **Holy Spirit** gives.

15:14 This is probably primarily a reference to the exhortations concerning doubtful things. They were **able . . . to admonish** (Gk. *noutheteo*) **one another** so they would not ignore the spiritual life of the weak.

15:15 as reminding (Gk. *epanamimnesko*): Paul did not write to teach them something they did not know but to remind them of what they

already knew (2 Pet. 3:1). Believers need to be reminded regularly of truths like these.

15:16 Ministering means rendering priestly service. Paul pictures himself as a priest offering a sacrifice to God. The sacrifice is Gentile believers who have been made **acceptable** to God because they have been **sanctified,** that is, set apart **by the Holy Spirit** for God's service.

 **IN FOCUS**   **"hope"**

(Gk. *elpis*) (15:13; 1 Cor. 9:10) Strong's #1680: The Greek term denotes "confident expectation" or "anticipation," not "wishful thinking" as in common parlance. The use of the word *hope* in this context is unusual and ironic, for it suggests that the Gentiles, who knew nothing or little about the Messiah, were anticipating His coming. However, we need only think of Cornelius (Acts 10) to realize that some Gentiles had anticipated the coming of the Jewish Messiah. For Jesus was sent, not only for the salvation of the Jews, but also for the Gentiles. Since God is the Author of our salvation, we can call Him the God of hope for He has given us hope (15:13).

15:17 Since his ministry was all by God's grace (v. 15), Paul could **glory** (Gk. *kauchesis*) in it (v. 18).

15:18 to make the Gentiles obedient (Gk. *hupakoe*), that is, to the command to believe on Christ.

15:19 By performing **mighty signs and wonders,** Paul demonstrated that God had granted him apostolic power (2 Cor. 12:12).

Illyricum is roughly modern-day Albania and north, between Greece and Italy.

15:20, 21 Paul's **aim to preach** where the gospel had not yet been heard is aptly expressed in v. 21 by the quotation from Isaiah.

15:22 For this reason: Paul's ambition to preach Christ where He was not yet known (vv. 20, 21) had **hindered** him from going to Rome.

15:23 a place (Gk. *topos*), that is, where Christ has not been preached (v. 20). **no longer having a place :** Having finished his work there.

15:24 Paul desired to **enjoy** (Gk. *empimplemi*) their fellowship, minister to them (1:10, 11) and be **helped** (Gk. *propempō*) by them. He did not specify the kind of help he had in mind. Paul had his eyes on **Spain,** the frontier of the Roman Empire in the West. He hoped the Romans would support him in his mission farther west.

15:25, 26 Paul planned **to minister** to the believers in Jerusalem by taking the **contribution** from Macedonia and Achaia (1 Cor. 16:1–4; 2 Cor. 8 and 9). This money was not only aid from Gentile believers to Jewish believers, but an expression of love that would unify the church even more.

15:27 Because the Jewish Christians had shared the gospel with the Gentiles, it was only right that the Gentile churches minister to the material needs of their Jewish brothers and sisters.

15:28 this fruit: The collection referred to in v. 26. **Spain:** No one knows for sure whether Paul ever got to Spain, but he had it on his travel itinerary.

15:29 when I come: Paul did get to Rome but not in the time frame or way he had thought. God had a special plan for Paul. The Lord would give him the opportunity to testify of his faith in the emperor's court, but he would do so as a prisoner (Acts 27 and 28).

15:30–32 strive together . . . in prayers: Intercession for his plan for Jerusalem was Paul's earnest request. He expressed three concerns: (1) deliverance from unbelievers in **Judea,** (2) the success of his mission to **Jerusalem,** and (3) a satisfying visit to the church in Rome.

15:31 Delivered means rescued from serious danger. He had been warned about the danger of a trip to Jerusalem (Acts 20:22, 23).

15:32 Be refreshed pictures rest and relaxation. Paul anticipated conflict in Jerusalem. He looked forward to a time of refreshment from the believers in Rome.

15:33 A blessed benediction.

16:1, 2 Servant is the word used for the office of deacon (Phil. 1:1; 1 Tim. 3:8, 10, 12). The fact that it is used here with the phrase **of the church** seems to suggest an official position. **Helper** means "patron" or "benefactor." It implies that Phoebe was a person of wealth and position.

16:3–16 This list of greetings is the longest in any of Paul's letters. Twenty-six people are mentioned, about one-third of them women.

16:3, 4 Priscilla and Aquila worked in the same trade as Paul, tentmaking (Acts 18:1–3), and labored with him in Corinth and Ephesus (Acts 18:1–3, 18, 26). This married couple is never mentioned separately, perhaps because they ministered so effectively together. The NT does not record how or where Priscilla and

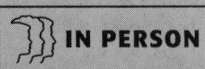 **IN PERSON**   **Phoebe, Paul's Helper**

Paul called Phoebe (Rom. 16:1) a *diakonos* (translated here as "servant," elsewhere as "deacon" or "minister") of the church at Cenchrea, the eastern port of Corinth. Does that mean she held a formal position of responsibility? Possibly. Paul frequently referred to himself as a *diakonos* and used the same term in writing about male coworkers such as Apollos, Tychicus, Epaphras, and Timothy (1 Cor. 3:5; Eph. 6:21; Col. 1:7; 4:7; 1 Thess. 3:2).

Our understanding of exactly what it meant to be a *diakonos* in the early church is incomplete. Where the word appears in secular literature of the first century, it refers to a helper of any sort who was not a slave. Whatever the role entailed, Paul commended Phoebe to the believers in Rome as a valued sister and one to be esteemed as one of his coworkers.

One important way that Phoebe may have assisted Paul was by taking his letter to Rome. The terms used to describe her suggest that she was a wealthy businesswoman of some influence. Perhaps she agreed to carry the document with her on business to the capital. Since couriers in the ancient world served as representatives of those who sent them, it is possible that Phoebe not only delivered the letter but also read it at different gatherings of Christians and discussed its contents with them.

Aquila **risked their own necks** for Paul, though it probably happened at Ephesus.

16:5 the church . . . in their house: In NT times churches met in private houses for worship.

16:6 Greet Mary, who labored much for us: The labor which this woman bestowed probably refers to her association with Priscilla and Aquila from the inception of the Roman church. We know nothing of her but that she bore the name Mary, one of the six persons so named in the NT.

16:7 Of note among the apostles as a phrase can mean either that they were well known to the apostles, or that they were distinguished as apostles. It is probable that they were known to the apostles because there is no mention of them in the Gospels or Acts.

16:8–10 Amplias . . . Urbanus . . . Stachys . . . Apelles were common slave names. The same names have been found in lists of slaves who served in the imperial household. **Aristobulus** was a familiar Greek name. In fact, the family of Herod the Great used the name often. Some have suggested that this Aristobulus was the grandson of Herod the Great and the brother of Agrippa I.

16:11 my countryman: Herodion must have been a Jew, like Paul. Some have suggested that this **Narcissus** was a famous freedman of that name who was put to death by Agrippa shortly after Nero came to power.

16:12 Greet Tryphena and Tryphosa, who have labored in the Lord: Tryphena and Tryphosa were probably sisters and possibly even twins. It was a common practice to name twins of the same root word. The name means those who live voluptuously. Although these names stem from a pagan, Anatolian root, Paul nevertheless associates them with labor in the Lord. **Greet the beloved Persis, who labored much in the Lord:** Persis (the name means Persian woman) is said to be **beloved** but with a woman Paul delicately avoids using the phrase "my beloved." Her name appears on Greek and Latin inscriptions as that of a slave or freedwoman.

16:13 Though a common name, this **Rufus** is often identified with the one in Mark 15:21. Since **chosen in the Lord** is true of all believers, many interpret this phrase to mean "outstanding" or "eminent." But it is possible that just as some believers demonstrate God's love and others reflect God's justice, so Rufus was an exceptional example of God's election.

16:14 Greet Asyncritus, Phlegon, Hermas, Patrobas, Hermes: Little is known of these believers other than that they were apparently of one community and were all men. Hermas is an abbreviation of some names such

as Hermogenes or Hermodorus and very common (compare *The Shepherd of Hermas* in apocryphal literature). Patrobas was abbreviated from Patrobius. Hermes was the name of the god of good luck and became a common slave name.

16:15 Greet Philologus, and Julia, Nereus, and his sister, and Olympas: Philologus and Julia were perhaps husband and wife. Both names occur several times in connection with the imperial household of Rome. Nereus, according to a tradition which goes back to the fourth century, is associated with Flavia Domitilla, a Christian woman who was banished to the Island of Pandateria by her uncle Emperor Domitian in A.D. 95. She was released after his death the following year. Olympas is an abbreviated form of Olympiodorus. These all appear to have been a community of faith.

16:16 holy kiss: This kiss on the cheek was practiced by the early church as a symbol of the love and unity among the early Christians (1 Cor. 16:20; 2 Cor. 13:12; 1 Thess. 5:26; 1 Pet. 5:14).

16:17 Cause divisions means "to stand apart" or "to cause dissension." In the NT it occurs only here and in Gal. 5:20. Strife and rivalry cause dissension, which eventually leads to divisions in a church (13:13; Gal. 5:20). Such dissension causes **offenses**—that is, it becomes a snare or stumbling block to others (this word occurs at 14:13). Contentious, divisive people can cause others to stumble, so they should be avoided. Paul teaches this type of church discipline in his other letters (1 Cor. 5:9–13; 2 Thess. 3:6; 2 Tim. 3:5; Titus 3:10).

16:18 Their motive was wrong. They were not serving **our Lord Jesus Christ.** They were serving **their own belly,** meaning they were selfish if not sensual. They were walking according to the flesh (8:4, 5). Furthermore, their methods were deceptive. **Smooth words** (Gk. *chrēstologia*) mean "good, kind, gracious." **Flattering speech** (Gk. *eulogia*) means smooth, praising speech. Thus, with gracious praise they **deceive** (Gk. *exapataō*) **. . . the simple** (Gk. *akakos*), the gullible.

16:19 Paul quickly explained that he didn't mean to imply that the Romans were simpletons. **Your obedience** (Gk. *hupakoē*) indicates there was no dissension in the Roman church for which Paul was **glad** (Gk. *agalliaomai*). But Paul wanted them to be **wise** (Gk. *sophos*) as well as obedient and **simple concerning evil.**

16:20 Divisive people destroy the peace and unity of the church, but **God,** who is the source of **peace,** will **crush** this work of **Satan** through the wisdom and obedience of believers. Ultimately, God will totally defeat Satan and bring peace to the whole church. Paul closes with his customary prayer that the **grace of** the **Lord Jesus Christ** would be with them.

16:21 Timothy worked with Paul and later received two letters from him. Some think **Lucius** here is Luke, the author of the third Gospel and Acts. But Paul includes this Luke among his **countrymen,** meaning he was a Jew. Luke the author was a Gentile. **Jason** is mentioned in Acts as Paul's host on his first

16:24, 25 The word **establish** is used only twice in Romans. At the beginning of the book, Paul expresses a desire to visit the Romans that he might impart some spiritual gift to them so that they would be "established" (1:11). Now he praises God who is able to do it. God used the **gospel,** which is **the preaching of Jesus Christ,** to establish the Roman believers. Paul speaks of his message as a **mystery** (11:25)

Photo by Gustav Jeeninga

A theater inscription at Corinth, mentioning the name Erastus. This may have been the same Erastus, "the treasurer of the city," who sent greetings to the Christians in Rome (Rom. 16:23).

journey to Thessalonica (Acts 17:5, 7, 9). **Sosipater** is likely the same person referred to in Acts 20:4.

16:22 Paul, the author of Romans, dictated the letter to a secretary named **Tertius,** who actually **wrote** the words. Tertius here sends his greetings to the Romans.

16:23 Gaius of Corinth (1 Cor. 1:14) not only gave Paul lodging, but also offered his house as a meeting place for the church. In Acts 19:22 a man named **Erastus** was sent by Paul to Macedonia. This may have been the same man.

because God's complete plan of salvation was at first hidden but now was being revealed. The revealed *mystery* is that the church will consist of both Jews and Gentiles united in the one body of Christ (Eph. 3:1–13).

16:26 by the . . . Scriptures . . . all nations, according to the commandment . . . for obedience: God has commanded that His Scriptures be preached in all nations so all people can obey His command to believe.

16:27 God in His wisdom saves people who, upon hearing the Scripture and especially the gospel, trust **Jesus Christ forever.**

The First Epistle to the

Corinthians

■

THE CHURCH AT CORINTH WAS A SERIOUSLY troubled church. Infected with sexual immorality, split by factions that dragged each other into court, and crippled by abuse of the spiritual gifts, this church was in need of radical spiritual surgery. Though true believers, the Corinthians had a lot of growing up to do. They had to stop following the immoral, selfish, and contentious ways of their pagan neighbors in

Corinth, the notoriously immoral city of that day. One can sense the disappointment of a hurt father in Paul's stern words for the Corinthians. Yet Paul, like a surgeon, diagnosed the problem and aimed his efforts straight at the source: pride and a lack of true love in the church.

First Corinthians is a reply to two letters. Paul had left the Corinthian church under the leadership of Aquila and Priscilla in the spring of A.D. 53 to continue his second missionary journey. On his third journey, during his stay at Ephesus, he received two letters from the Corinthian believers. One was a disturbing report from the household of Chloe (1:11). The report detailed the divisions and immorality in the church. These problems arose because the young Corinthian church had failed to protect itself from the decadent culture of the city. The immaturity of the Corinthians had given way to sectarian divisions. The believers were identifying themselves as followers of specific Christian leaders rather than as followers of Christ (3:1–9). They were also dragging each other into court (6:1). Their desire to sue each other rather than settle their disputes within the church betrayed their immaturity and mis-

placed trust in human wisdom. Sexual immorality had become a problem in the church in spite of a previous letter (that has not been preserved) in which Paul warned against it (5:9–11).

The second letter Paul received was a set of questions that Stephanas, Fortunatus, and Achaicus had brought from Corinth (16:15–18). The detailed questions were about marriage and singleness (7:1–40) and Christian liberty (8:1—11:1).

Paul wrote First Corinthians to answer both letters and to give some additional instructions. He taught about decorum in worship services (11:2–16), the solemnity of the Lord's Supper (11:17–34), and the place of spiritual gifts. Though the Corinthians were very gifted, in their immaturity and pride they had abused their gifts. Paul reminded the Corinthians that gifts come from God (12:11) and are to unify and edify the church (12:24, 25; 14:1–4). In conclusion, Paul corrected a doctrinal matter by writing the New Testament's most detailed explanation of the resurrection of Christ and Christians (15:1–58). Even though the church was riddled with problems, Paul ended his confrontational letter with a note of hope. The Corinthians could have victory over sin and death because Jesus in His death and resurrection had already decisively obtained it (15:57).

Corinth was an important city in ancient Greece. Geographically, it was an ideal hub for commerce between Italy and Asia. Along with the flow of merchandise, Corinth received travelers from both east and west, creating ethnic diversity among the city's inhabitants. Although Corinth was ransacked by the Romans in 146 B.C., it was rebuilt by Julius Caesar in 46 B.C. Roman control of Corinth allowed them to dominate east-west commerce as well as the Isthmian Games (9:24–27), which were surpassed in importance only by the celebrated Olympic Games.

Corinth's commercial success was rivaled only by its decadence. The immorality of Corinth was so well known that Aristophanes coined the Greek verb *korinthiazomai* (meaning "to act like a Corinthian") as a synonym for sexual immorality. Greek plays of the day often depicted Corinthians as drunkards and reprobates. The Corinthians drew attention to their lewdness through their worship of Aphrodite, the goddess of love and beauty. Yet Corinth was also a strategic location for the propagation of the gospel. The city's corrupt nature made for a unique opportunity to display to the Roman world the transforming power of Jesus Christ.

Acts 18:1–18 records the founding of the Corinthian church. Paul visited Corinth on his second missionary journey, after leaving Athens. This initial visit probably occurred in the fall of A.D. 52. Paul, Silas, Timothy, and Luke had left Troas for Macedonia about eight months earlier and had started churches in Philippi, Thessalonica, and Berea. Luke remained at Philippi and Silas and Timothy at Thessalonica, while Paul journeyed on to Athens. Paul's ministry at Athens proved disappointing, perhaps leaving him discouraged as he entered Corinth, where he made tents during the week and preached in the synagogue on the Sabbath. After the Jews of Corinth rejected Paul's message, he began to reach out to the Gentiles. He ministered in Corinth for eighteen months, eventually establishing a church. This church, like the city, had a mixture of nationalities. Though some Jews had been converted, most of the believers were Gentiles (12:2).

While the Corinthian church reflected the city's multinational character, it also mirrored some of Corinth's immorality. The sharp tone of First Corinthians results from Paul's urgent desire to get the church back on course.

First Corinthians twice names the apostle Paul as its writer (1:1, 2; 16:21). Paul's authorship of First Corinthians is almost unanimously accepted throughout biblical scholarship. One of the earliest witnesses to Paul's authorship of the book was Clement of Rome (c. A.D. 95).

Most likely Paul wrote the letter while he was ministering at Ephesus during his third missionary journey. In 16:8, Paul said that he would remain in Ephesus until Pentecost. This, coupled with Acts 20:31, indicates that he wrote it in the last year of his three-year stay in Ephesus, some time in the spring of A.D. 56. The Corinthian church would have been about four years old at that time.

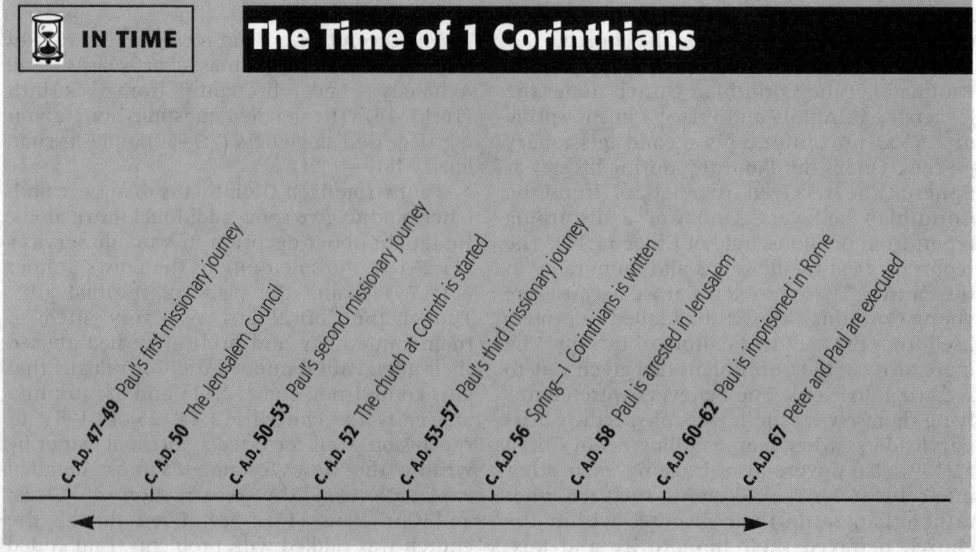

IN TIME   **The Time of 1 Corinthians**

c. A.D. 47-49 Paul's first missionary journey
c. A.D. 50 The Jerusalem Council
c. A.D. 50-53 Paul's second missionary journey
c. A.D. 52 The church at Corinth is started
c. A.D. 53-57 Paul's third missionary journey
c. A.D. 56 Spring–1 Corinthians is written
c. A.D. 58 Paul is arrested in Jerusalem
c. A.D. 60-62 Paul is imprisoned in Rome
c. A.D. 67 Peter and Paul are executed

Outline

Commentary

1:1–3 Paul's words of introduction are more than simple words of greeting. The first few verses introduce the themes of his letter. Thus in his greeting, Paul introduces his apostolic authority (9:1–27), the sanctification of his readers (5:1), and the unity of all believers (1:10–17), all major themes of the letter and concerns for the Corinthian believers.

1:1 through the will of God: The Corinthian church greatly valued human wisdom. This misplaced emphasis had caused some in the church to challenge Paul's authority (v. 12; 9:1, 2). They forgot that Jesus Christ Himself had called him to his ministry as an apostle of Jesus Christ (Paul uses the same title in 2 Cor. 1:1).

1:2, 3 A local **church of God** is a group of people who identify themselves with God and gather together to worship and serve Him. **sanctified in Christ Jesus:** The Corinthians' holiness came from their position in Christ, not from their own goodness. The tense of the verb *sanctified* indicates that God had sanctified the Corinthians at a specific time in the past, producing a condition that they still enjoyed in the present. **called to be saints:** The work of Jesus Christ makes a believer holy forever in God's eyes. But in everyday living, sanctification involves small, daily changes (Heb. 10:14). This is why Paul could call the Corinthian believers to become saints, even though the problems in their church testified that they were far from the goal of holiness. **In every place** is most likely a reference to local churches throughout the Roman Empire (1 Tim. 2:8).

1:4–9 The thanksgiving Paul offers to God for the Corinthians seems odd, considering the many problems the church was experiencing. However, Paul focuses his praise not on the troubled Corinthians but on the eternally faithful God. Paul does not praise the Corinthians for their good works as he does some other churches (Eph. 1:15); instead, he praises God who works in them. When we focus on people's faults, hope soon wanes and discouragement follows. But when we concentrate on the Lord, even the darkest hours can be filled with praise.

1:5, 6 Enriched means that the Corinthians had been spiritually destitute but had become abundantly prosperous through God's grace.

1:7 Gift here is probably a reference to the spiritual gifts described in chs. 12–14. Despite the Corinthians' boasting, their many gifts had come from God (12:11, 18, 28). The Corinthians were richly blessed with spiritual gifts because God was giving them everything they needed to do His will (12:14–27).

1:8, 9 Because God is faithful to His word, Paul was confident that even the sin-plagued Corinthians would stand **blameless** before Him. This blamelessness does not refer to the Corinthians' works, but to their standing in Christ, their justification (3:14, 15).

1:10–17 Paul began his response to the disturbing report concerning the Corinthian church by attacking the worldly wisdom which had divided the church.

1:10 Paul pleaded for an outward expression that comes from an inward spirit. Not only did Paul encourage the Corinthians to **speak the same thing** and have external unity; he also urged them to be **joined together in** a unity of hearts and minds that expresses the unity of the one body of Christ.

1:11 Paul avoided dealing in rumors or secrecy; he openly named his sources: **Chloe's household.** We know little of this woman and her household except what this verse implies. Chloe lived in Corinth or Ephesus, and the Corinthians respected her word.

1:12, 13 The Corinthian church was divided into at least four factions, following four prominent leaders.

1:14–16 Paul said **I thank God that I baptized none of you,** because the Corinthians had taken to identifying with their spiritual

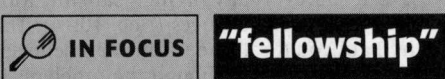

(Gk. *koinonia*) (1:9; Acts 2:42; Phil. 2:1; 1 John 1:3, 6, 7) Strong's *#2842*: The Greek term means "that which is shared in common." In the NT the word was used to denote the believers' common participation in the triune God—the Father, the Son, and the Holy Spirit. The Father and Son have enjoyed communion with each other before the creation of the world. When the Son entered into time, His fellowship with the Father also entered into time. During the days of His ministry, Jesus was introducing the Father to the disciples and initiating them into this fellowship. Then once the disciples were regenerated unto eternal life, they actually entered into fellowship with the Father and the Son. Thus, the unique fellowship between the Father and the Son begun in eternity was manifested in time through the incarnation of the Son, was introduced to the apostles, and then through the apostles was extended to each and every believer through the indwelling of the Holy Spirit (2 Cor. 13:14; Phil. 2:1).

mentors rather than Christ. **Crispus** was the ruler of the synagogue in Corinth when Paul began to preach there (Acts 18:8). He was instrumental in the conversion of many other Corinthians. **Gaius** may be the same person who hosted Paul and the entire church (Rom. 16:23). **Stephanas** was one of Paul's first converts in Achaia, the region of which Corinth was capital. Paul praised him and his household for their devotion to the ministry and for their assistance (16:15). Stephanas was one of the couriers who took correspondence to and from Corinth.

1:17 Paul's primary ministry was **to preach the gospel.** Baptism naturally followed conversion but was secondary in importance. With the

phrase **not with wisdom of words,** Paul addressed the Corinthians' tendency to place undue emphasis on human wisdom. The immature Corinthians were so impressed by clever oratory and learned debate that many of them ignored the relatively "simple" message of **the cross.**

1:18–25 In this section, Paul emphasizes that salvation is in the message of Christ, not in human philosophies. The powerful simplicity of Christ over human wisdom negates any cause for people to boast. Many people stumble over this simplicity because the religions of the world make the source of salvation something we do rather than a **message** we believe.

1:18 **The message of the cross** is the gospel, the Good News about Christ's death and resurrection for our sins. The gospel penetrates to the core of self-centeredness. For those who exalt self, the message sounds absurd. But for those who bow humbly in faith, it becomes the **power** that is able to snatch them from death and impart eternal life. No wonder Paul put such confidence in this message (Rom. 1:16).

1:19 In Is. 29:14, the Lord rebuked OT Israel for their hypocritical worship and their human rules for salvation (Is. 29:13). He declared He would confound their carnal wisdom. Paul used this quote to illustrate his point that God has voided any human attempts to find favor with God.

1:20, 21 **The wise** is probably a reference to Greek philosophers. **The scribe** is a technical term for a Jewish scholar trained to handle details of the Law. **The disputer** refers to a Greek person, especially one trained in rhetoric. These professionals tried to solve every problem with logic and debate. The point of this passage is that all human efforts to find favor with God fall woefully short (Rom. 3:9–28). Only through faith in Christ can we be saved from our sins.

1:22, 23 The **Jews** sought miraculous signs from the Messiah to signal the beginning of the deliverance God had promised (Mark 8:11; John 6:30). The **Greeks,** especially the philosophers, sought to use wisdom to answer their questions about God and life. To the Jews, who expected a political savior, Jesus was **a stumbling block.** To the Greeks, whose self-centered wisdom could not make sense of the cross, to believe in Jesus was **foolishness.**

1:24, 25 Paul uses a paradox to say that the most insignificant thought or work of God is greater than the most extraordinary achievement of humans.

1:26 **Wise** refers to the Greek philosophers. **Mighty** refers to influential, politically powerful people. **Noble** includes all the aristocratic upper classes. Most of the Corinthians came from the lower classes.

1:26–31 Although the Corinthians thought highly of themselves, Paul challenged them to survey their own congregation and realize that most of them came not from the upper classes, but from the lowly of the world. Paul attacked the pride that had caused schisms by comparing humans to God (1:20–25), then by comparing the church to the world around them (1:26–31). Both arguments display the greatness of God's wisdom in saving the insignificant of the world so that none have a basis for boasting.

1:27 God's plan of salvation does not conform to the world's priorities. In fact, it seems **foolish.** Yet in reality, eternal salvation is more valuable than all the fame, wealth, and success pursued by the world.

1:28 base . . . despised: Paul's use of these two terms for the slave class would capture the attention of his readers in Corinth, where many slaves lived. **the things which are not:** No doubt many of the Corinthian believers were people who did not count in the eyes of the world but had found grace in God's eyes.

1:29–31 God uses what is considered foolish and despised in this world to reveal His truth, so that He alone will receive the glory. Otherwise, the powerful would boast that they had found the truth. Instead, God sent His Son to become a humble carpenter and to die in the most despicable way, on a cross. Jesus' life and death reveals God and His **wisdom.** Since Christ not only imparts wisdom but also righteousness, the Christian cannot boast, except in **the Lord.**

2:1–5 Paul continued his illustration of the futility of human wisdom by using his own ministry in Corinth as an example. Paul's preaching, by human standards, was unimpressive (2:1), but it was the vehicle of God's Spirit to save the Corinthians. Paul's obvious weakness had moved his readers to trust not in Paul, but in God.

2:1, 2 excellence of speech or of wisdom: Paul did not rely on his eloquence or

---

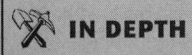 **IN DEPTH**   **The Message, Not the Messenger**

One of the main problems facing the first-century Corinthian church was division. When Paul wrote to Corinth, the church was divided into at least four factions, each of them aligned with one of four prominent Christian leaders. One group identified itself with the apostle Paul. The members of this faction may have been attracted by Paul's emphasis on his ministry to the Gentiles. A second group identified itself with Apollos, one of Paul's fellow missionaries. He may have attracted a following because of his eloquent speaking abilities (Acts 18:24–28). A third group identified itself with Cephas, another name for the apostle Peter. This group may have been mostly of Jewish background. A fourth group identified itself specifically with Christ. While on the surface it might seem that this group was the "godly" contingent of the Corinthian church, this may not have been the case. Paul does not commend any of the groups, not even the "I am of Christ" faction, suggesting that all of their professed allegiances were causing division and dissension in that church.

Paul uses three rhetorical questions, each expecting a negative response, to show the absurdity of the Corinthian divisions. "Is Christ divided? Was Paul crucified for you? Or were you baptized in the name of Paul?" Paul pointed out that in the act of baptism, a person identifies himself or herself with Christ, period. Baptism does not align the believer with any human leader or with any faction of Christianity, but with the Lord Himself. The Corinthians, who prided themselves on their wisdom and understanding, had misconstrued this truth. They had begun to identify themselves with the men who had performed the baptisms rather than with Jesus Himself.

We might be tempted to write off this problem, attributing it to "those silly, immature Corinthians," if it were not for the fact that the tendency to exalt dynamic leaders is still prevalent today. Witty, engaging Christian speakers and vibrant, charismatic spiritual leaders still have the power to mesmerize and motivate believers today. And there is nothing inherently wrong with such power. The danger comes when the speaker or leader, and not the message, becomes the focus of attention.

Christian speakers and leaders are merely vessels through whom God's Word is communicated. Exalting them for the message they proclaim is a misunderstanding of their purpose. Put simply, it's the message, not the messenger.

As believers today, we must guard ourselves against identifying too closely with human leaders or placing too much emphasis on them. Our loyalty and identification belong only to Jesus Christ and His message.

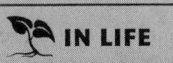 **IN LIFE** | **Is Christianity a Crutch for the Weak?**

Is Christianity just another crutch for people who can't make it on their own? In one sense, yes. "Those who are well have no need of a physician," Jesus said, "but those who are sick. I have not come to call the righteous, but the sinners, to repentance" (Luke 5:31, 32). Jesus bypasses those who pretend to be invincible, those who think they have it all together. Instead He reaches out to those who know that something is wrong, that their lives are "sick" with "illnesses" such as greed, lust, cruelty, and selfishness.

Jesus knows that no one is spiritually healthy. No one is righteous enough to stand before a holy God. That's why He came into this world, to restore people to God. The good news is that Christ gives us the power to overcome sin and the ways it pulls us down time after time.

What happens to the "weak" who avail themselves of this "crutch"? Consider Mother Teresa, who emerged from an insignificant nunnery to love the helpless and homeless of Calcutta and became a worldwide symbol of compassion. Or consider Alexander Solzhenitsyn, a forgotten political prisoner rotting away in the gulag system of Stalinist Russia. Surrendering himself to Jesus, he gained renewed strength to challenge a totalitarian regime on behalf of human dignity and freedom.

These are but two examples from the millions who have thrown away the self-styled crutches on which they used to limp along the road of life, opting instead for the seasoned wood of the cross of Christ which has transformed their weakness into strength.

In one sense, Christianity is a crutch for the weak. But those who dismiss it for that reaon usually do so to deny their own inadequacies. They use that excuse as a way to evade the claims God has on their lives. They cannot accept that He takes wounded, fractured people and makes them whole.

on Greek wisdom to convince his listeners. Instead, he gave **the testimony of God** which had not been explained before, but which was being revealed by the Holy Spirit (vv. 10–14). The focal point of Paul's preaching was **Jesus Christ.**

2:3–5 Whereas the Corinthians gloried in their strength, their wealth, and their gifts, Christ was glorified in His humility and death. Paul wanted to model Christ's humility by presenting his "weaknesses." Then the "strength" of the gospel message could be clearly seen. **My speech** probably refers to the way Paul spoke; **my preaching** probably refers to the content of his message. **not with persuasive words . . . but in demonstration of the Spirit:** Even though Paul had many strengths of his own (Phil. 3:4–9), he wanted to be counted among those who relied on God's strength. Rather than using the rhetoric of the day to win converts, he gave a straightforward message. **power of God:** Miraculous signs had sometimes accompanied Paul's preaching (2 Cor. 12:12; 1 Thess. 1:5; Heb. 2:3, 4). Such signs were intended to magnify God, not the human speaker.

2:6 among those who are mature: After having heard eloquent addresses by men like Apollos, the Corinthians may have viewed Paul's message as elementary or unpolished. Paul assured the Corinthians that he was imparting **wisdom**—instruction that mature Christians would appreciate. **rulers of this age:**

In some passages Paul used the word *rulers* to refer to spiritual beings (Eph. 6:12; Col. 2:15); here he referred to earthly rulers, the Roman and Jewish leaders who presided over Jesus' crucifixion. If these rulers had been among the wise, they would have worshiped the Lord instead of crucifying Him. **coming to nothing:** People look at beauty, wealth, and power as greatly desirable. But all earthly splendor will be rendered meaningless and worthless by death and the coming of God's judgment (Luke 16:19–29; 2 Pet. 3:10–13).

2:7 The **mystery** that Paul referred to here is defined in Rom. 16:25, 26 as "revelation . . . kept secret since the world began, but that now has been made manifest." The message was **hidden,** known only to God, until He chose to reveal it (Eph. 3:1–11). This is in contrast to the teachings of the Gnostics, a group of false religious teachers who would infiltrate the early church (1 John 2:18–27). They claimed that there existed a body of secret knowledge that was only available to those initiated into an inner circle of spiritual teachers.

2:8 Lord of glory: Though Jesus emptied Himself of His majesty when He became human, He remained fully equal with the Father.

2:9–12 through His Spirit: Only the Holy Spirit could reveal the truths of God (2 Pet. 1:19–21). **knows . . . know:** The first verb refers to innate knowledge; the second refers to experiential knowledge. We could never have

✠ IN CONTEXT   Judging All Things

Paul's claim about judging all things (1 Cor. 2:15) sounds rather presumptuous. Is he urging believers to become moral policemen, passing judgment on everyone and everything around us?

Yes and no. Paul was challenging the spiritually immature believers at Corinth to grow up by applying spiritual discernment to the world around them. In this passage he mentions three categories of people:

- *natural* (2:14), those without Christ, still living in the lost condition in which they were born;
- *spiritual* (2:15), believers in Christ who have been born of the Spirit and in whom the Spirit of God lives and is producing growth; and
- *carnal* (3:1), believers who remain immature in the faith because they don't allow the Spirit to work in their lives.

Spiritual people "judge" all things that come their way (2:15) in the sense of scrutinizing, examining, and investigating spiritual value and implications. This is not something that we should do merely as individuals, but also corporately with other believers. For example, in the workplace Christians in various occupations need to band together to explore how the faith applies to particular vocations. By analyzing work situations in light of Scripture, we can discern what the issues are and how we might respond with Christlikeness.

"Judging all things" has nothing to do with damning others, but with recognizing and doing what God would want. Instead of pride, it calls for humility, since God will be the final Judge of everything we do (2 Cor. 5:10).

discovered the mysteries of God or the benefits of Christ's death by ourselves. But we can know them by experience because they have been **freely given** to us by God.

2:13 the Holy Spirit teaches: Paul emphasized that the intellectuals of this world could not teach the knowledge he was giving to the Corinthian believers. Note that the Spirit did not simply dictate words to Paul and the other apostles; He taught them. The apostles related with their own vocabulary and style what they had learned from the Spirit. **comparing spiritual things with spiritual:** These words are difficult to translate and interpret. The Greek term translated *comparing* may also mean "to combine" or "to interpret." The two references to *spiritual* may mean interpreting spiritual truths to spiritual persons, or else combining spiritual truths with spiritual words. The latter seems better. In other words, the phrase teaches that the spiritual truths of God are combined with the spiritual vocabulary of the apostles (2 Pet. 1:20, 21; 2 Tim. 3:16).

2:14–16 natural man: The natural person does not have the Spirit of God, in contrast to the Christian who does have the Spirit (15:44–46). **Receive** here means "to welcome." This verb does not pertain to discovering the meaning of a passage, but *applying* the meaning to life.

3:1 Paul says he cannot speak to them as **spiritual** but **as to carnal.** How can a person be spiritual and yet carnal? Observe that the specific terms *carnal* and *natural* do not speak to the same truth. The natural person (2:14) is devoid of the Spirit of God. The carnal person is not equated with the natural person but with a babe *in Christ.* The person has not attained spiritual maturity but is considered in union with Christ. The carnal person is spiritual in the sense of having the Spirit of God but is not living consistently or maturely. This is often the experience with Christians today, but it was equally the problem of many Christians in the first century (Heb. 5:11–14).

3:2 fed . . . milk: Paul did not expect the Corinthians to be mature in Christ at the time of their conversion. By placing their faith in Christ, they had been justified. They had been united with Him and his death on the Cross (Rom. 6:3–5), and the Spirit of God had come to live in them (2:12; Rom. 8:9). They were considered righteous before God because of Jesus' righteousness. Thus, when Paul first established the church at Corinth he taught them as new converts, as those justified. Yet he expected them to grow in their faith—that is, become sanctified. The behavior of the Christians in Corinth should have begun to line up with their righteous position in Christ.

3:3, 4 for you are still carnal: An immature Christian naturally lacks many Christian
traits, but no one should expect this condition to
last. Paul was surprised that the Corinthians had
not yet grown into spiritual maturity or become

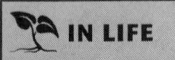

Who Gets the Credit?

Paul pointed out that the work of planting
the church at Corinth was a joint venture
between himself, Apollos, and the Lord
(1 Cor. 3:5–8). Actually, many others were
involved as well. But the point was that cooperation, not competition, is what God desires.

Paul was speaking about the start-up of a
church, but the principles apply in the workplace as well. An attitude of competition worries
about who gets the credit for success, which is
really a selfish concern. By contrast, cooperative
efforts over time generally result in achievements far greater than what any individual
could do in isolation. That's because the skill,
insight, and energy in an organization's work
force have enormous potential. But that potential will never be realized if everyone's chief
objective is to take credit for results.

able to distinguish between good and evil (Heb.
5:14).
3:5–10 Paul had **planted,** or started, the
church in Corinth; Apollos had **watered** it—
had a significant ministry there after Paul left.
But both men were only servants through
whom God worked. The ones who plant and
water have nothing to boast about because God
gives **the increase:** Only God draws unbelievers to Himself. It is our responsibility to do

our job no matter what the results, for God will
reward us for our efforts and the quality of our
work (9:24–27). We are like tools in the hands
of the craftsman. As long as we are usable, God
will use us. When we cease this function, we
could be put on the shelf or disqualified (1 Cor.
9:27). Paul develops four conclusions from his
observation in v. 6: (1) We are God's servants,
helpers of Christ who do our assigned tasks.
Without Him we can do nothing (John 15:5).
Even the faith of those who believe through us
is a gift from God. (2) The servants in their
diverse tasks are really one. They are not competing with one another. They are all doing the
work of God who gives the increase. (3) Even
though the servants are one, each person's
reward will be based on the quality of work
done. The kind of material used will determine
the kind of reward one gets. (4) Paul concludes
that the church is **God's building** to be worked
on by God's **fellow workers** (that is, Paul,
Apollos, and other ministers, v. 9).
3:11–15 Paul had established the church at
Corinth on the **foundation** of Christ. **gold,
silver, precious stones**, **wood, hay, straw:**
These building materials refer to the quality of
work done by the Corinthians, and possibly also
to their motivations or the kinds of doctrines
they taught. **The Day** speaks of the time when
Christ will judge the merits of His servants'
work (2 Cor. 5:10), not whether they receive
forgiveness of sin. Likewise, **fire** does not refer
to the "eternal fire" of damnation (Rev. 20:10)
but to the evaluation of believers' works (Rev.
2:18, 19; 3:18; 22:12). Fire proves the quality of
gold, but it consumes wood, hay, and stubble.
Some "good work" is actually self-centered
aggrandizement. The true value of such "service" will become obvious to all in the day of
God's judgment (Rev. 3:17, 18).
3:16, 17 Do you not know: This phrase,
found in nine other places in 1 Cor. (5:6; 6:2, 3,
9, 15, 16, 19; 9:13, 24), always introduces an
indisputable statement. **temple:** There are two

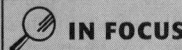

"futile"

(Gk. *mataios*) (3:20; 15:17; Titus 3:9; James 1:26) Strong's #*3152*: This word means "pointless" and
"purposeless." The NT writers, especially Paul, used it to depict the meaninglessness that pervades the
thought life of fallen human beings. Paul characterizes the "thoughts of the wise" as being futile
(3:20), and he describes the Gentiles as living "in the futility of their minds, having their understanding
darkened" because they are "alienated from the life of God" (Eph. 4:17, 18). The ideas of the unregenerate are futile and aimless because they lack divine insight; they produce a life of purposelessness
and ineffectiveness. Salvation from such futility comes from the indwelling Spirit of Christ in believers
(Rom. 8:10, 11, 26, 27).

words translated *temple* in the NT. One refers to the temple building and all its courts; the other refers strictly to the Most Holy Place where no one but the high priest could go. Paul uses the latter term to describe the local church, in whom **God dwells.** Unlike 6:19, where the word *temple* refers to the individual believer, and Eph. 2:21, where the word speaks of the church universal, these verses speak of the local church as God's temple. God takes very seriously our actions in the church. **destroy:** Any person who disrupts and destroys the church by divisions, malice, and other harmful acts invites God's discipline (11:30–32).

3:18–23 The wisdom of this world does not coincide with God's wisdom, the foolishness of Christ crucified (1:18–25). Paul quotes from Job 5:13 and Ps. 94:11 to urge the members of the Corinthian church to humble themselves. **all things are yours:** The Stoic literature of the time, which the Corinthians would have known, often spoke of the wise man as possessing everything. Everything God has done in the church, and in the entire universe, benefits all believers. There is no place for foolish boasting or competition among Christians.

3:21–23 let no one boast in men: This is the conclusion of ch. 3. The Corinthians had seriously limited themselves by boasting in different teachers, when Christ is the source of **all things.** Earthly teachers are simply God's servants for the benefit of His people (v. 5). **Life** and **death** belong to the Christian who lives and dies victoriously by the power of Christ (15:55–57). In Him we have nothing to fear from **things present** or **things to come.**

4:1–21 These verses escalate the discussion of workers as servants of Christ. First Corinthians 4:1–5 states that those called servants of Christ are also accounted as stewards or managers who have been committed a trust. Thus, we should not compare ourselves with other servants. Our accountability is to Christ.

4:1 Servants had no unique position, but **stewards** did. A steward was a slave who administered all the affairs of his master's household, though he himself owned nothing (compare the testimony of the early church in Acts 4:32). Joseph held such a position in the house of Potiphar (Gen. 39:2–19). As stewards, believers manage the message and ministry God has entrusted to them.

4:2–5 each one's praise will come from God: A steward was not to worry about the evaluations of those around him or even his own self-assessment; he needed only to please his master. Similarly, while believers can benefit from the constructive evaluations of fellow believers, their ultimate Judge is the Lord Himself. Since God is the Judge, we should be careful not to make any premature evaluations of others.

4:6–13 Paul upbraided the Corinthians for their immense pride (6). He reminded them that they boasted of gifts which God had graciously distributed (vv. 7, 8). Then, almost in a sarcastic manner, he contrasted their "greatness" with the servant attitude of Apollos and himself (vv. 9–13). The very men they exalted to the point of causing schisms in the church (1:11–17) viewed themselves as destitute servants of God (vv. 10–13).

4:6, 7 The Greek term translated **learn** is related to the word translated *disciple* in Matt. 28:19. It implies the use of a skill and not just knowledge. The Corinthians knew about humility, so Paul called on them to become humble. Greeks considered humility to be a fault, a characteristic of slaves. To the Christian, however, it exemplifies the attitude of Christ (Phil. 2:5–8). **in us:** Paul presented himself and Apollos as models to follow (v. 16; 11:1). **what is written:** This word is often used to introduce a quotation of the OT (Rom. 14:11). Paul was exhorting the Corinthians not to go beyond the teachings of Scripture. Then they would avoid the pride and divisions that were fracturing their church. A true minister of God's Word will use Scripture to unify and strengthen the church. Only those who want to exalt themselves will misuse Scripture and thus weaken and divide the church.

4:8 The Corinthians thought that Christians were to be **full, rich,** and to **reign** in the present. But Paul knew that we must go through trials now if we are to reign when Christ returns. **I could wish:** That you were indeed involved in the **reign** of Christ and that we might be united in His true kingdom.

4:9, 10 Spectacle alludes to the public executions carried out by the Romans. In these executions condemned men were brought into the coliseum, where they were tormented and killed by wild animals as cheering crowds looked on. Paul pointed out that the whole world and the angels were witnesses to the humiliation of God's servants. With biting sarcasm Paul contrasted the Corinthians' lofty evaluation of themselves with the world's evaluation of him. Paul knew that true strength is found in understanding our weakness and Christ's sufficiency (2 Cor. 12:7–10; Phil. 4:11–13).

4:11–13 Paul lists the hardships he had suffered in Christ's ministry, both physical challenges and verbal abuse (2 Cor. 11:22–30).

4:14 Although the Corinthians should have been ashamed of their conduct, Paul's aim in writing was to warn them of the serious consequences of their actions. **As my beloved**

children emphasizes the responsibility of parents to practice tough love in appropriate discipline.

4:15 instructors . . . fathers: Paul used these two terms to differentiate between his role and the role of the Corinthian teachers, slaves who took care of their masters' children. Paul was the Corinthians' spiritual father. He had final responsibility for them and the right to command them to follow his example.

4:16 Paul urged his readers to **imitate** him as he followed Christ (11:1). The word refers to the way a student would follow a teacher or the way an actor would play a role (11:1).

4:17 For some reason Paul could not come immediately to Corinth, but he had confidence in Timothy to teach the Corinthians properly. Timothy was already doing what Paul hoped his readers would begin to practice: following Paul's good example.

4:18–20 Some people in Corinth, probably the instructors who had caused divisions (v. 15), acted as though Paul would never return to hold them accountable for their actions. **puffed up:** These people were conceited and prone to boasting. **The kingdom of God** here does not refer to the future reign of Christ, but to Christ's present rule in the hearts of His people. This reality guaranteed that Paul would have the power to expose and discipline those who afflicted the Corinthian church.

4:21 Paul uses the same Greek word for **rod** here that Luke uses to describe the instrument that was used to beat Paul and Silas (Acts 16:22–24). The term also is used figuratively of Christ's authority to judge (Rev. 19:15). God had given Paul authority to punish the agitators in Corinth, though he preferred not to use that power.

5:1–13 Paul has just concluded a lengthy segment dealing with the divisions within the Corinthian church (1:10—4:21). Now he moves into the problem of incest in the church and the failure of the Corinthians to deal with it.

5:1 The **sexual immorality** of incest was forbidden by OT law (Lev. 18:8; Deut. 22:30) and by Roman law. Paul used the phrase **his father's wife** instead of "his mother" probably to indicate that the woman was the offender's stepmother. The omission of discipline for the woman implies that she was not a believer. The church is responsible for disciplining only its members, not unbelievers.

5:2 puffed up: The Corinthians had a twisted view of grace that caused them to be proud of their tolerance of the sexual offender. They believed that because God's grace is limitless, the freedom that every Christian enjoys is also limitless.

5:3–5 Paul displays the apostolic power he spoke of earlier (4:20, 21). He had already judged the sin and gave the church his authoritative command to remove the man from the congregation. When a person is living in sin, he or she is open game for Satan.

5:5 Destruction of the flesh may refer to God's turning the sexual offender over to **Satan** for physical affliction or even physical death. After being separated from the spiritual protection of the church, ideally the offender would recognize his sin, repent, and return to the church. All church discipline has restoration as its ultimate goal.

5:6–8 The backdrop for this passage is the Passover (Ex. 12), when the Israelites removed yeast from their homes in preparation for the feast. The removal of leaven was a reminder of the Israelites' quick departure from Egypt. They did not have time to wait for leavened bread to rise. The point here is that a little leaven has

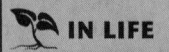 **IN LIFE** | **Danger from Within**

Evil can never be remedied by ignoring or hiding it. In fact, covering it up is the worst that can happen, for like yeast, evil does its terrible work from within (1 Cor. 5:6–8).

The same is true of believers who live in consistent disobedience to God's expressed will. Their behavior will badly infect the larger groups of which they are a part. It can even lead to a distorted perception of sin in which the group tolerates or even approves of disobedience among its own members yet condemns outsiders for the very same activity (Rom. 1:32; 1 Cor. 5:9, 10).

Paul challenged the Corinthians to confront the subtle deterioration they had allowed within their congregation (5:5). However, once the perpetrator had repented, they were then to seek his restoration. Even though corrective activity among believers may be severe, confrontation should always be to promote healing rather than to expel wrongdoers (compare Matt. 18:15–22; 2 Cor. 10:8). There are no throwaway people in the kingdom of God.

tremendous impact or influence on whatever it is in. The Corinthian church was tolerating sexual sin. This leaven of sin, though small in size, was dangerous, because it could spread through the church. Like cancer, sin demands drastic surgery.

5:6 Like a tiny pinch of **leaven** spreading through a loaf of bread, unchallenged sin can soon contaminate the whole church. The sexual offender was guilty of sin, but the whole congregation was also guilty of ignoring the man's disobedience and failing to hold him accountable. Left unchecked, this sin could have caused many new believers to commit sexual immorality.

5:7 Jewish people were required to sweep all **leaven** out of their houses in preparation for the Passover (Ex. 12:15). The *leaven* here symbolizes the powerful influence of sin.

5:8 The feast is a figure of speech for Christ. As Israel was to remove all leaven from the celebration of the Passover, so the Corinthians were not to contaminate their relationship with Christ with any **malice** or **wickedness.**

5:9–13 Paul here corrects a misunderstanding arising out of his previous letter (v. 9). He had commanded the Corinthians to withdraw themselves from sexually immoral people. In this letter, Paul explains that he was not speaking of the pagan culture around them. If they withdrew totally they would be unable to function in the world. Instead, he was talking about the immorality in their midst. They should judge the sin among themselves, while still reaching out to the lost in Corinth.

5:9 My epistle refers to an earlier letter from Paul to the Corinthians that no longer survives.

5:10 out of the world: Christians are called to influence the world, not run away from it (Matt. 5:13–16). They are agents of God to carry the light of Jesus Christ into a dark world (Phil. 2:14–16; 1 Pet. 2:11, 12).

5:11 not even to eat with such a person: Eating together is a key part of fellowship and closeness with others. The Corinthians were not to have fellowship with those who claimed to be Christians but whose lives were dominated by sin.

5:12, 13 do you not judge . . . God judges: The church's responsibility is to discipline its members while trusting the Lord to judge the world (Matt. 13:30).

6:1–11 In these verses, Paul instructs the Corinthians to stop taking their personal disputes into the pagan courts. The Corinthians had been carrying their conflicts to the Roman courts and thus were making a mockery of Christianity by feuding in public. Their inability

to settle personal disputes illustrated the sharp divisions in the church (1:10–17). Paul wanted to bring home several important ideas to these Corinthians: Public litigation is a disgrace to a Christian congregation (v. 1). Personal disputes should be settled within the church (vv. 2–6). The presence of contentions indicates spiritual defeat (vv. 7, 8). All unrighteousness, such as the disputes, should have been vanquished when the Corinthians became believers (vv. 9–11).

6:2 do you not know: Paul uses this phrase six times in this chapter (vv. 3, 9, 15, 16, 19) to introduce truths that the Corinthians should have known. This phrase must have deflated the pride of a church infatuated by its own knowledge and wisdom.

6:3 Believers will participate in judging fallen **angels** (Rev. 19:19, 20; 20:10). Paul suggested that if the Corinthians were going to be judging with Christ in His future kingdom (Matt. 19:28), then surely they had the means to settle their own personal differences.

6:4–6 Those who are least esteemed refers to judges in civil courts. The Corinthians, though they had the ability to judge the issues themselves, took their disputes to pagan court for the judges there to decide.

6:7, 8 cheated . . . cheat: In all of their bickering, the Corinthians made frivolous and even dishonest charges against one another. Paul suggested that it was better to be *cheated* by one of these dishonest people than to dishonor one's Christian witness before pagans.

6:9, 10 The kingdom of God here seems to refer to a future time when God will rule the earth in righteousness (Matt. 6:10; Luke 11:2). **do not be deceived:** Tragically, Christians sometimes deceive themselves into thinking that God does not require them to live righteously. Paul emphasizes that the kinds of people listed in these verses will not **inherit** or possess the kingdom of God.

6:11 In this verse, Paul uses three terms to describe the conversion of the Corinthians. The tense of all three verbs indicates an action in the past that is complete. **Washed** means spiritually cleansed by God. **Sanctified** means set apart as God's people. **Justified** means declared righteous by God because of Christ's work on the Cross.

6:12–20 Paul moves from his discussion of the relationship of the Corinthians to the law courts to personal integrity in body and spirit. Paul tackled the issue of Christian liberty by addressing three Corinthian slogans that reflected their attitudes toward sexual sins (vv. 12, 13, 18). In the process he presented a greatly elevated concept of the human body as created by God the Father, redeemed at great price and

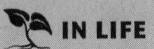 **IN LIFE** **Freedom from the Tyranny of Things**

As Christians we live under grace, not law. We enjoy a certain freedom of choice and commitment. But Paul reminds us that our choices and commitments, while freely made, do not always bring freedom (1 Cor. 6:12). Often they overpower us: we no longer possess our possessions—they possess us! We can be consumed by our jobs, our wealth, our houses, our hobbies, even our churches.

Are there any ways to manage this problem? Here are a few suggestions:

(1) Determine your limits. What can you actually handle? What is realistic?

(2) Let time go by before making decisions and commitments. Sooner or later you need to decide, but very few choices are better made sooner than later.

(3) Pay attention to agreement or disagreement with your spouse and/or a close friend or associate. There is wisdom in mutual decision making.

(4) To manage the commitment you are taking on, what are we willing to give up? Taking on new responsibilities means trading one set of problems for another. Are we prepared for that?

(5) Commit to giving away as well as taking on. That declares your freedom from the tyranny of things and responsibilities.

service to Christ the Son, and made the temple of God by the indwelling Spirit. Thus, the triune God is involved in what we do with our bodies. We call the room where the church meets the "sanctuary." Actually, *we* are God's sanctuary—His temple. What a difference it would make if we lived with that realization. Our bodies are not garbage dumps. They are temples!

6:12 All things are lawful for me was a slogan the Corinthians had coined to justify their immoral behavior. Paul reminded the Corinthians that freedom from the ceremonial laws of Moses did not give them license to sin or indulge their own selfishness. This would only enslave them in the sin from which Jesus had freed them. **under the power of any:** The only power that should control us is the Holy Spirit. Sin should never dominate our lives because the Spirit empowers us to fight temptation.

6:13, 14 Foods for the stomach and the stomach for foods was another phrase the Corinthians used to justify their sinful lifestyles (v. 12). Food was gratifying and essential for life. When the Corinthians became hungry, they ate. Following the same logic, whenever the Corinthians craved sex, they indulged themselves. In their opinion any physical activity should not affect one's spiritual life, just as digesting food did not affect one's spirituality. The Corinthians' reasoning had two faults: (1) The stomach and the digestive process are in a sense no more than earthly and without function in eternity. But the body, through the resurrection power of Christ, is eternal. It has been sanctified by God to bring Him glory (v. 20). (2) While the stomach's purpose is to digest food, it

is not the purpose of the body to commit immorality. Furthermore, by design God put restrictions on both eating and sexual activity. Eating to the point of gluttony and having wanton sex outside of marriage violate God's intent and are therefore sinful.

6:15–17 Believers' lives are greatly altered when they are joined to Christ. The union affects

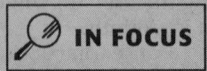 **IN FOCUS** **"temple"**

(Gk. *naos*) (3:16; 6:19; 2 Cor. 6:16; Eph. 2:21; Rev. 21:22) Strong's #*3485*: This Greek word for *temple* refers more to the building itself than *hieron*, which was used to indicate the entire temple complex. Paul told the believers that each one of their bodies was a *naos*, a sanctuary for God (6:19). Paul also said that the church, as Christ's body, is a spiritual *temple* for God (3:16, 17; 2 Cor. 6:16; Eph. 2:21). What a special privilege it is to be God's spiritual dwelling place, both individually and corporately. The glory of God filled the tabernacle (Ex. 40:34) and the temple (1 Kin. 8:10, 11). Now the glory of God in the person of the Holy Spirit dwells within every believer (John 14:16, 17) and thus inhabits the entire church. In the New Jerusalem, there will be no need for a physical temple because God and the Lamb will be the eternal temple (Rev. 21:22).

both the believer and Christ. When a believer commits immorality, he or she is dragging the union with Christ into the illicit relationship. By quoting Gen. 2:24, that **the two . . . shall become one flesh,** Paul illustrates the seriousness of sexual sin.

6:18 **Every sin that a man does is outside the body** was another slogan used by the Corinthians to justify their immorality (vv. 12, 13). Paul pointed out that the opposite is true: sexual sin is done **against** the body, not outside of it. Paul exhorted the Corinthians to **flee** any temptation to indulge in sexual sin (Gen. 39:1–12).

6:19 The **temple** (3:16, 17) was the congregation of believers. The temple was recognized as the sacred dwelling place of God. The Shekinah glory of Yahweh filled the tabernacle (Ex. 40:34) and the temple (1 Kin. 8:10, 11). Now, the glory of God in the person of the Holy Spirit dwells within every believer (John 14:16, 17) and thus inhabits the entire church. The OT priests took great pains to maintain a pure sanctuary for God's presence. Every Christian ought also to care diligently for his body, the temple of the Holy Spirit, in order to honor God and the church.

6:20 **Bought at a price** alludes to someone purchasing a slave at a slave auction. With His death Jesus Christ paid the cost to redeem us from our slavery to sin (Eph. 1:7; 1 Pet. 1:18, 19). While it is true that this is applicable to all people, even those who deny the Lord (2 Pet. 2:1), it has a very unique and special significance for the believer (compare 1 Pet. 2:9; 1 Tim. 4:10). Paul concludes with the imperative **therefore, glorify God in your body.** In other words, use your bodies in order that other people may see that you belong to God.

7:1 **things of which you wrote to me:** After addressing the problems reported by the people of Chloe's household (1:11), Paul began to answer questions that had been sent to him (7:1—14:40). **It is good for a man not to touch a woman:** There were two extreme positions in the Corinthian church. Both groups falsely separated the physical and the spiritual, believing that neither affected the other. One group was hedonistic. This group claimed that sin only had to do with the physical body, and that believers could sin in their body without any consequence to their spiritual lives. Paul corrects this misunderstanding in ch. 6. The other group believed that all things spiritual are good, and all things physical are bad, and that in order to be truly spiritual a person has to suppress every physical desire. Proponents of this view claimed that celibacy is the only proper lifestyle. Paul corrects their misunderstanding here and explains that while sexual relationships in marriage are good, he chose celibacy in his own personal situation.

7:2 Because of the rampant **immorality** in Corinth, Paul encouraged those who might be tempted to commit sexual sin to marry. It is better to develop a permanent relationship with a wife or husband than to lapse into sexual sin.

7:3–5 **affection:** Husbands and wives have a duty to maintain sexual relations with each other so that neither will be tempted by **Satan** to have sex outside of marriage.

7:6–9 I say this as a concession, not as a commandment: This brief clause reveals for us an important understanding of Paul's method of argument and also what we believers must consider as mandate over against option. If Paul had indicated this teaching was a commandment, we would have been under an obligation. The apostle Paul at times gave direct commands or spoke so directly to an issue that it is the teaching of the Lord. For example, 1 Cor. 11:28–34 provides commands of how things should be conducted at the Lord's Table. His teachings on gifts in 1 Cor. 12—14 are not mere opinion but apostolic truth. In v. 7 he stated his preference that the unmarried **remain even as** he is but recognized that God has different purposes and capabilities for His people. **good:** To ones who were married but now are widows, it is a *good* thing to be like Paul for this gives greater opportunity to work for Christ. On the other hand, he recognizes that few have the gift of **self-control** to refrain from sexual relationships. The *good* of v. 8 must be balanced with the teaching of Gen. 2:18 where God said it was "not good" for man to be alone. **it is better to marry than to burn:** Those who burn with passion should go ahead and marry rather than struggle with sexual passion.

7:10–16 Paul turns from the concerns of celibate persons to those who are married. He speaks of the commands that Christ gave on the subject while on earth, along with insight that he has as an apostle of the Lord.

7:10, 11 not I but the Lord: When Christ was on earth, He told us not to *divorce* a spouse; instead of *divorce,* Paul uses the word translated **depart,** which refers to wives leaving their husbands. The idea is the same: a believing husband and wife should not leave each other. The further statement that if the couple divorced they were to remain **unmarried** is consistent with Jesus' teaching (Mark 10:9–12).

7:12, 13 I, not the Lord, say: Paul now presents a problem that was not addressed by Jesus. Sometimes a husband or wife would become a Christian, but the spouse would not. Paul exhorts the believer to remain married if the unbelieving spouse does not want to divorce.

7:14 Sanctified primarily means "set

apart." Here the term refers to the special situation an unbelieving husband or wife enjoys when his or her spouse is a believer, being exposed to God's teachings. **Unclean** here probably means the opposite of *sanctified*. Children with one believing parent may learn about God and come to Christ.

7:15: If an unbeliever seeks to divorce a believing spouse, the Christian is **not under bondage** or obligation to continue the marriage. There is no conflict here between Paul's advice and that of our Lord in Matt. 5:32. The point is that the divine standard cannot be imposed upon the unregenerate. There is nothing the believer can do but submit to the divorce. The overriding principle is that **God has called us to peace.**

7:16 how do you know: The Greek grammar suggests that Paul asked the question expecting a negative answer. The promise given in 1 Pet. 3:1–6, however, reminds us that consistent obedience to God can make a skeptical spouse into a believing one.

7:17–24 so let him walk: This section develops the theme of faithfulness to the Christian calling rather than to social status. Whether you are **slave** or **free**—upper class or lower, powerful or powerless, married or single—is irrelevant; what matters is your calling from God (Col. 3:11).

7:25–40 I have no commandment from the Lord: Paul clearly distinguishes his words as an apostle from the words of Christ. **virgins:** This classification of the unmarried in the church is probably smaller than the one mentioned in v. 8, which included widows and those who had been married before. Though Paul is concerned with both celibate men and women, the attention here is on the women. Although the Greek term used in v. 25 could refer to either men or women, the other instances in this passage refer to women (vv. 28, 34, 36, 37). By the second century, the church had developed important offices for virgins, widows, and deaconesses. Since they were unencumbered with the duties of a wife, they could assist the pastors and deacons in baptizing, ministering to the sick, and other works of mercy.

7:26, 27 present distress: Paul saw turbulent days ahead for married Christians because in times of persecution, consideration for family can make it difficult to live out Christian convictions to the fullest extent. A virgin would have lesser family responsibilities and would not be deterred by the possibility of repercussions affecting her husband or children.

7:28–35 Paul does not want to be understood as prohibiting the marriage of virgins. Again, this is his preference, not an apostolic command. If the virgin or unmarried person should marry, they have not sinned. Even if they should marry, however, they should consider

---

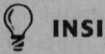 **INSIGHT** | **Divorce and Remarriage**

Jewish law permitted only the husband to initiate a divorce. Only under extreme circumstances could the wife request a court to compel a husband to divorce her. By contrast, Roman law viewed marriage as a matter of mutual consent, and so dissolved a marriage if either party requested it. Under Roman divorce, the children went to the father. Rapid remarriage was customary and society encouraged it (especially for young women), so the church congregation in Corinth probably included some new converts who had been remarried one or more times before their conversion.

Paul addressed the Christians who wanted to divorce spiritually incompatible spouses. Offering his own judgment, he contended that spiritual incompatibility did not provide adequate grounds for a divorce (1 Cor. 7:12–14). In addition, by giving the command of "the Lord" (1 Cor. 7:10, 11), he seemed to cite Jesus' general prohibition of divorce (Mark 10:11, 12).

Ancient interpreters commonly qualified general principles, modifying or interpreting them to account for specific situations. In this manner Paul interprets Jesus' general principle as needing to be qualified for those who are divorced against their will. In cases in which an unbelieving mate deserted the marriage, Paul declared, the believer was "not under bondage" (7:15).

In using the phrase "not under bondage," Paul was echoing the exact language of ancient divorce contracts, which spoke of marriage as "binding" a woman to her husband and divorce as "loosing" or "freeing" a woman for remarriage. Such divorce terminology appears in Jewish texts, such as the Mishnah, and in actual first-century Jewish divorce contracts that have been recovered. Ancient readers would have understood "not under bondage" as Paul's permission for an abandoned person to remarry.

themselves similar to those who are unmarried as far as their dedication to God's work. He admonishes them not to get caught up in the world around them because it is only temporary.

7:36–38 One interpretation of this passage is that **any man** refers to the father of an unmarried **virgin. She is past the flower of youth** indicates that the virgin is approaching an age at which marriage would be unlikely. Under these circumstances, it would be perfectly acceptable for the father to give **her in marriage.** A second interpretation suggests that the *any man* of v. 36 refers to a fiance who is maintaining a celibate state with a *virgin* but is having difficulty doing so. In this view, the Greek term otherwise translated "she is past the flower of youth" is translated "he has strong passions." If the man has difficulty in controlling his sex drive, he should **marry** (v. 9). On the other hand, if he can control himself (**has power over his own will**), he should maintain his celibacy (v. 8). **having no necessity:** If the man can control himself and keep himself from immoral action, he should stay single. On the other hand, if the man's will is weak, he should go ahead and marry.

7:39, 40 bound by law: This passage is similar to Rom. 7:2, where Paul used marriage to illustrate obligation to the law. Here he emphasizes that marriage should be lifelong. In a case where a marriage partner has died, the only restriction concerning remarriage is for the person to marry a fellow Christian. Even though remarriage is permitted, Paul still believes that it is wiser to remain unmarried (v. 8). **I also have the Spirit of God:** The Holy Spirit enabled Paul not only to speak with apostolic authority, but also with spiritual wisdom.

8:1–13 Chapter 8 answers their question on Christian liberties that goes through 11:1, with the first subject being meat sacrificed to idols. In ancient Corinth, when a person went to the marketplace to buy food, among the meat for sale was some which had been offered to a pagan god. Supposedly, a portion of a sacrifice would be taken by the god with the remainder to be eaten by the priests. What they did not eat would be taken to the marketplace. A Christian buying meat might inadvertently be eating meat offered to a false god. Two schools of thought developed at Corinth on this question. The first perspective was that such meat was tainted by

---

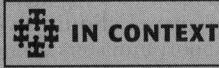 **IN CONTEXT** ## Women and Work in the Ancient World

Paul's observation that a married woman must care about "the things of the world" (1 Cor. 7:34) hints at the busy lives that first-century women lived, especially in the large cities of the Roman Empire.

The NT shows that women carried out a wide range of tasks: for example, drawing water, grinding grain, manufacturing tents, hosting guests, governing and influencing civic affairs, making clothes, teaching, prophesying and filling other spiritual functions, burying the dead, and doing the work of slaves, to name but a few. Additional evidence from the period reveals that women also served as wool workers, midwives, hairdressers, nurses, vendors, entertainers, political leaders, and even construction workers, among many other occupations.

If a woman was among the upper classes, she enjoyed relative economic security and social privileges. According to the Roman ideal, her role in society was to marry a citizen, produce legitimate heirs for him, and manage the household according to his orders. However, by the first century few families attained that ideal.

Wealthy women used slaves to perform such household tasks as cooking, making clothes, washing laundry, and caring for children. Slaves also functioned as nurses, midwives, hairdressers, stenographers, and secretaries, and it was common for a high-ranking slave to be designated the household manager.

Female slaves were not only considered to be household property, but sexual property as well. The master of the house could legally force a slave to have sex with him, or with anyone he chose. Any children that she bore became his property. In this way a citizen could increase his number of slaves.

Women who were former slaves, or freeborn, lacked the economic security of either the citizen or the slave. Nevertheless, many women sought to buy their way out of slavery. Some of these working-class women earned their living as vendors, selling fish, grain, vegetables, clothing, or perfume. Others became wet nurses, and some chose to become entertainers or prostitutes—occupations that were considered beneath the dignity of respectable women.

the pagan worship, while the other view held that this meat could be eaten by believers.

8:1 We know that we all have knowledge appears to have been a slogan used by certain Corinthian believers as an arrogant statement against weaker Christians. The weaker Christians believed that eating food offered to idols was a sin. Other Corinthian believers thought that such concerns were

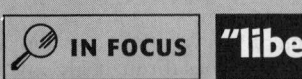

(Gk. *exousia*) (7:37; 8:9; 9:18; Matt. 7:29; Rom. 9:21) Strong's #*1849*: The Greek term usually denotes "right," "authority," or even "privilege." In certain contexts, as this one, it connotes the freedom to exercise one's right. Specifically, Paul was addressing the Corinthians' right to eat meat that may have come from pagan temples. To be clear, the eating of sacrificial food—the cultic meals in pagan temples—was censured by Paul because it was understood that the participants in those meals were uniting themselves to demons (10:19–21). However, Paul had no problem with those who purchased food that had been left over from these events and that was later sold in the marketplace. In his judgment if they ate it at home they were not participating in idolatry. They had the liberty—or right—to eat this food in good conscience. The exception was if they would be destroying a weaker believer by doing so. For the sake of such believers, one should abstain.

ridiculous. They argued that if the idols were worthless, then the meat offered to them was fine to eat. Paul agreed that food offered to idols was not contaminated, but he wanted the knowledgeable Christians not to flaunt their enlightened point of view. **Knowledge puffs up, but love edifies:** This is one of Paul's five attacks on the arrogance of some of the church members at Corinth (4:6, 18, 19; 5:2). These people belittled their weaker brothers and sisters with their knowledge. They had missed the point. They should have been using their knowledge to help other believers in the church.

8:2 We know nothing about God as we ought unless our knowledge leads us to love others.

8:3–6 The Corinthian believers who claimed to have knowledge readily admitted

that **an idol is nothing** (Is. 37:19; Jer. 16:20; Gal. 4:8) and that there is only one God (Deut. 6:4). But Paul did not dismiss the idea of idols altogether because though these gods are not real, they exist in the minds of those who worship them (10:20).

8:7–13 The knowledgeable believers were correct in their view of **idols,** but it did not matter. If the weaker brothers and sisters saw other believers eating **food** offered to idols, they might also eat, in violation of their own conscience. To go against the conscience was in fact sinning. By their knowledge the stronger believers were causing the weaker believers to stumble. Paul exhorted the strong believers to show love to the weaker ones by refraining from offending them.

9:1, 2 Am I not an apostle: Paul substantiated his apostleship with two arguments: (1) he had **seen** the resurrected **Lord** (Acts 1:21, 22), and (2) the church at Corinth was his work in the Lord, a **seal** of his **apostleship.**

9:3–18 Paul had the **right to eat and drink** whatever he wanted, to have a **wife,** and to receive wages for his ministry. But he did not exercise these rights. **Is it oxen God is concerned about:** God requires that ministers should be paid for their work just as He requires beasts of burden to be compensated for theirs. **those who preach the gospel should live from the gospel:** To support ministers of the gospel is commanded by God. Even as the priests in Israel were supported for their work, NT ministers were to be provided for as well (1 Tim. 5:17, 18).

9:19–23 I have made myself a servant to all, that I might win the more: Paul put his ministry of the gospel above his personal desires. He was willing to conform to the customs of other people, whether Jew or Gentile, in order to bring them to Christ. For example, in order to relate to the Jews in Jerusalem he made a Nazirite vow in the temple (Acts 21:23, 24). Around those who were under the Law—the Jews—Paul obeyed the Law. Around those who were outside the Law—the Gentiles—Paul did not observe Jewish custom. Paul clarified this, however, lest anyone misunderstand his actions. He obeyed God's law through obedience **toward Christ** (v. 21). This was a broader law than the Mosaic legislation; this was the fulfillment of Christ's will (11:1; Rom. 13:8; Gal. 6:2).

9:24–26 Paul had a passion to fulfill his ministry at all costs. This was similar to the kind of commitment that goes into preparing for athletic competition. **I run thus: not with uncertainty:** Paul had a clearly defined goal and knew that perseverance was needed to achieve it. In order to prepare properly for the race or boxing match, he knew he had to force himself

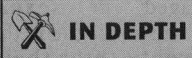 **IN DEPTH** | **The Race for the Crown**

What does it take to be a champion in a given sport? For one, it is necessary to have a dedication to succeed no matter what the cost. A passion for the game is certainly essential, as is a single-minded determination to accomplish the task at hand. A willingness to train incessantly is also required. And a burning desire for the trophy or prize awarded to the one who wins is an absolute must.

In his letter to the Corinthians, the apostle Paul drew a direct comparison between the Christian life and an athletic competition. This comparison would have had immediate resonance with Paul's Corinthian readers. Corinth was the site of the Isthmian games, a great athletic festival that was very similar to the Olympic games. Contestants in the Isthmian games endured ten months of mandatory training. Anyone who failed to complete this training was barred from competing in the games. The highlight of the Isthmian games was a great endurance race. It was this race that Paul used as an illustration to depict the faithful Christian life.

In the Isthmian games, several athletes competed for one prize; there could be only one winner. In contrast, the Christian life offers the opportunity for many people to be winners. The winner of the Isthmian games received a pine wreath crown. Those who faithfully complete the Christian life, on the other hand, will receive an imperishable crown.

Paul illustrates the "champion" mindset required to faithfully complete the Christian life with his statements, "I run thus: not with uncertainty" and "Thus I fight: not as one who beats the air" (9:26). Paul was not an aimless competitor. He had a clearly defined goal. Like an athlete preparing for a race or a boxing match, Paul knew that he had to discipline his body; he had to force himself to maintain the strenuous, consistent practice needed for success.

The race that Paul prepared himself for, the race that all Christians need to prepare themselves for, was the calling of God. Paul taught that Christians are rewarded for the calling that God gives them. Paul had an apostolic ministry for which he sacrificed all things. He knew that if he was faithful to his calling he would receive a reward from the Lord for his service (4:2). Paul also knew that if he ignored or treated lightly his mission he would not receive from God the victor's crown for service. Having seen some of his close friends forsake their calling (2 Tim. 4:10), Paul recognized that the loss of the victor's crown was a very real possibility for any believer, regardless of his or her standing in the Christian community. The apostle's overwhelming passion was to fulfill his ministry at all costs, to stay faithful to the "fight" (9:26) to the very end. In Paul's last letter, written shortly before his death, we discover that he accomplished his goal (2 Tim. 4:6–8).

Paul's spiritual training was the very best available. Yet he did not assume that he would automatically persevere to the end of the race. He continued to discipline himself, to fight, and to follow his calling from God. In doing so, Paul provided an ideal model for all Christians striving to become champions.

---

to maintain the strenuous, consistent practice needed for success.

9:27 I myself should become disqualified: The Greek word for *disqualified* means "disapproved after testing." Although some have cited this verse as evidence that Christians can lose their salvation, this clause most likely does not refer to salvation. A careful distinction should be made between the *prize* and the *gift*. The free gift of justification cannot be the result of good works (Rom. 4:1–8). However, the prize or crown is the reward for endurance and suffering for the cause of Christ (Phil. 1:29; 2 Tim. 2:12).

10:1–5 Paul places the story of Israel's unfaithfulness to God after his exhortation to the Corinthians to persevere in God's work. He emphasizes the blessings the Israelites enjoyed in the desert. They all had the protection and guidance of God. They all experienced God's miraculous deliverance. They all identified with their spiritual head, Moses. They all enjoyed the bread from heaven. Finally they all drank the water God provided. Paul's key point is that although all of the Israelites received these wonderful blessings from God, most failed to please Him.

10:1 For the ancient Israelites **under the cloud** in the wilderness, the *cloud* served two functions: (1) It provided protection (Ex. 14:19, 20), fire by night in the cold desert and shade by day from the blistering sun. (2) It guided the people through the desert (Ex. 13:21). **all passed through the sea:** Every Israelite who left Egypt in the Exodus experienced the deliverance of God at the Red Sea.

10:2 all were baptized into Moses: The acts of God **in the cloud and in the sea** joined the people with their spiritual head, Moses.

10:3–5 the same spiritual food . . . the same spiritual drink: They all followed the same God and the same laws (John 4:13, 14; 6:32–35).

10:6–10 our examples: The discipline of God exercised against the disobedient Israelites should serve notice to Christians that God will punish His people's sin.

10:6 The first failure of the ancient Israelites was that they **lusted,** or "craved." They were not satisfied with God's provision but looked back to the provision that they had in Egypt (Num. 11:4–34).

10:7, 8 The ancient Israelites were notorious **idolaters.** Even though the true God had brought them out of Egypt, they insisted on worshiping lifeless idols. Furthermore, the ancient Israelites engaged in **sexual immorality,** a sin that also plagued the Corinthians (5:1; 6:18). **twenty-three thousand:** The account in Numbers gives the figure twenty-four thousand (Num. 25:6–9). There are several possible reasons for the difference. Some have suggested that Paul's number reflects the number that died **in one day,** while the Numbers account may be a record of all who died in the plague. Another explanation may be that the Numbers account includes the death of the leaders (Num. 25:4) while Paul's figures do not.

10:9 tempt Christ: Apparently this phrase relates to the Israelites' questioning of the plan and purpose of God while on their way to Canaan (Num. 21:4–6).

10:10 The ancient Israelites **complained** against their God-given leaders so much that many **were destroyed,** or put to death (Num. 16:41–49).

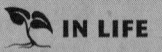 **IN LIFE** | ## Watch Out for Temptation

Opportunities for temptation are almost endless. And since human nature is not getting any better, nor is any of us immune to the corrupted appetites of the flesh, we need to take Paul's warning seriously and watch out for temptation, or we will surely fall. Yet Scripture offers several alternatives for dealing with temptation as we find it:

(1) We should *avoid* temptation whenever possible. Prov. 4:14, 15 urges us, "Do not enter the path of the wicked, and do not walk in the way of evil. Avoid it, do not travel on it." Often we know beforehand whether a certain set of circumstances is likely to lead to sin. Therefore, the obvious way to avoid sin is to avoid those circumstances. Paul described a "way of escape" from temptation (1 Cor. 10:13). Often the escape is to stay away from the place or the people where temptation lurks.

As believers, we can help others in this regard. We can avoid setting up situations that encourage people to do wrong. Teachers, for example, can help students avoid cheating by making assignments, giving tests, and communicating expectations in ways that reduce the need or incentive to cheat. Likewise, business owners and managers can devise procedures that don't needlessly place employees in a position where they might be tempted to steal cash, inventory, or equipment. It's not that a teacher or employer can't trust students or employees, but that no one can trust human nature to be immune from temptation.

(2) We should *flee* from powerful temptations. Earlier in this letter, Paul warned the Corinthians to flee sexual immorality (6:18). Here he warned them to flee idolatry (10:14). Elsewhere he warned Timothy to flee the lust for material possessions and wealth (1 Tim. 6:9–11), as well as youthful lusts (2 Tim. 2:22). The message is clear: don't toy with temptation. Flee from it!

(3) Chronic temptation is something we need to *confess* and offer to Christ, and ask for His cleansing work. Some temptations are powerful inner struggles, with thoughts and attitudes that graphically remind us of how fallen we really are. What should we do with that kind of temptation? Rather than deny it or try to repress it, we should bring it to Christ. He alone is capable of cleaning up the insides of our minds.

(4) Finally, we must *resist* temptation until it leaves us. When Christ was tempted by the devil, He resisted until the devil went away (Matt. 4:1–11). James encouraged us to do the same (James 4:7). Resistance begins by bathing our minds with the Word of God and standing our ground. We have the promise, after all, that the temptations we experience will never go beyond the common experiences of others, or beyond our ability to deal with them (1 Cor. 10:13). That is great news!

10:11 as examples: Paul emphasizes again that the things that happened to Israel are not merely historical events to be read but warnings to heed. This is especially true, in Paul's view, since the **ends of the ages have come.** God's plans were reaching culmination. The God bringing about the end of all things is the same God who brought judgment on the Israelites by killing them; he might do so again (compare 11:30; Rom. 11:22).

10:12 lest he fall: The Corinthians may have had the attitude that since they were justified by God, nothing could happen to them. The discipline of God, however, is not to be taken lightly. No one can sin with impunity (Gal. 6:7, 8).

10:13 Paul provides the Corinthians with a word of comfort. The various temptations they were experiencing were normal; all believers throughout the ages have had to resist temptation. God is so good that He will not let believers experience anything for which He has not prepared them. He will give every believer the grace and power to endure. Furthermore, endurance will bring its own reward (9:24–27).

10:14–11:1 In this section the apostle Paul addresses the problem of idolatry in the Corinthian church. Worship of various gods was totally ingrained in Greek culture. In the ancient Greek world there were idols on street corners and in houses. Various civic societies paid homage to their favorite gods. Cities adopted certain gods as their special protectors. The pagan temples were frequented often, especially in Corinth with its temple prostitution. Most of the food in the marketplace had been offered in worship to different gods. Paul first addresses the demonic nature of idol worship and then expounds on the nature of Christian liberty, especially concerning food offered to idols.

10:14–22 flee from idolatry: Pagan worship is a violation of the believer's union with Christ (v. 21). The idols themselves are not a threat (v. 19); the danger lies in the **demons** (v. 20) who, unknown to the worshipers, are the real objects of idol worship.

10:21 You cannot drink: Paul reminded the Corinthians of the fellowship and unity they had in their participation in the Lord's Supper. Participation in idol worship is a violation of that unity.

10:22–24 All things are lawful for me: Though we have freedom, we also have a responsibility to help others in their Christian growth. Our first duty is to others, not ourselves.

10:25, 26 Eat whatever is sold: Paul himself did not ask whether meat was sacrificed in the temple, because pagan worship could not contaminate what God had made clean (Ps. 24:1; Acts 10:15).

10:27–30 These verses present a scenario of a knowledgeable Christian being invited to a private home for dinner. If no one makes an issue of meat offered at the temple, the believer should not make a point of it; this strong believer accepts the truths enunciated in v. 26.

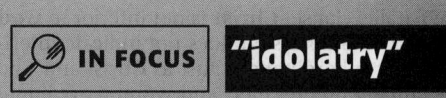

IN FOCUS **"idolatry"**

(Gk. *eidololatreia*) (10:14; Gal. 3:20; Col. 3:5) Strong's *#1495*: This word refers to the practice of worshiping idols. Related Greek words are translated "idolater" in 5:10, 11; 6:9; 10:7; "idol" in 8:4, 7; 10:19; 12:2; and "things offered to idols" in 8:1, 4, 7; 10:19, 28. The fullest discussion in the NT concerning idolatry is found in First Corinthians. Paul had told the Corinthians not to associate with those who called themselves believers but were still idolaters (5:9–11). The Corinthians must have asked Paul for clarification on this matter, for in First Corinthians Paul warns the believers to refrain from all forms of idol worship.

On the other hand, if a weak or unknowledgeable believer is present and brings to the strong Christian's attention that the meat is from idol worship, the knowledgeable Christian should refrain from eating out of consideration for the weaker Christian.

10:31–11:1 Doing **all to the glory of God** involves encouraging fellow Christians and spreading the good news about Christ. Paul accomplished this by refusing to offend **Jews, Greeks,** or **the church of God,** even if it meant restricting his freedom. Like **Christ,** Paul did not seek his own way or do things for his own pleasure; instead, he desired to help others (v. 24). This should be our desire as well.

11:2–34 These verses follow a lengthy section about the improper way the Corinthians had taken advantage of their freedom in Christ. After a series of gentle rebukes (1:10, 11; 3:1; 4:7–13, 18; 5:1–3; 6:1–6; 7:1–5; 8:9–12; 10:1–14) the apostle begins this section with praise because they were following certain traditions he had taught them.

11:2 Now I praise you reflects genuine appreciation on Paul's part. The Corinthians had made many mistakes, but they were not totally corrupt. The Corinthians had followed the apostle's instructions in certain areas.

11:3 But introduces an exception to the praise Paul had given the Corinthians in v. 2. He wanted to instruct the Corinthians on another point of confusion. **Head** primarily means "authority" when used in the context of human relationships. Some have said that *head* can also mean "source" or "origin," a claim now rejected by Greek lexical authorities. **the head of woman is man:** The relationship between men and women does not involve inferiority, for, in the parallel clause, **Christ** is not inferior to **God** the Father. Submission does not indicate inferiority, but subordination. Just as Christ and God are equally divine, men and women are equal beings. But just as Jesus and God the Father have different roles in God's plan of salvation, so men and women are given different roles.

11:4 Praying or prophesying may refer specifically to intercessory prayer similar to that of OT prophets (Gen. 20:7; 1 Sam. 12:23; Jer. 27:18), or Anna (Luke 2:36–38), or to the combination of tongues and prayer (14:13–16; Acts 2:4; 10:46). **Having his head covered** probably refers to the wearing up of hair on a man's head. **dishonors his head:** It is impossible to decide whether *head* here refers to the man's physical head or to Christ, the man's authoritative head (v. 3). Either interpretation is possible; Paul may even have meant the word to have a double meaning.

11:5, 6 every woman who prays or prophesies: Women were obviously allowed to pray and prophesy in the Christian assembly because it would have been meaningless for Paul to give instructions for something they were not permitted to do. **Dishonors her head** refers either to the woman's own physical head or to her husband as her head, or possibly both (v. 4). For a woman not to cover her head with her own hair was as shameful as having a **shaved** head, a sign of public disgrace.

11:7–9 man is not from woman, but woman from man: The woman was taken from the side of the man (Gen. 2:21). **Woman for the man** is Paul's way of stating the concept of the "helper" in Gen. 2:20. This does not mean the woman is inferior to the man; it refers only to the purposes of God for man and woman in the creative order.

11:10 Women were to wear a covering on their head **because of the angels.** Evidently God's angels are present at the meeting of the church and actually learn of God's work of grace through the lives and worship of God's people (Eph. 3:10). **symbol of authority:** This might be a symbol of the woman's authority to prophesy in the new church age, which was inaugurated with the giving of the Holy Spirit at Pentecost (v. 5). It also might refer to a symbol of the man's authority over the woman (v. 3).

11:11, 12 neither . . . independent: Men and women need each other, and as creatures of God, both depend on Him. Neither man nor woman can have any claim to special status other than what God has purposed for them as their Creator.

11:13–15 Nature seems to refer, in Paul's usage, to how things naturally ought to be (compare Rom. 1:26; 2:14, 27; also read 11:21, 24; Gal. 2:15; 4:8). To Paul, it is natural for men and women to be different. Women are able to manifest this by wearing their hair longer than men.

11:16 no such custom: Paul's question presupposes his pointed question in v. 13 and his view of what is natural in v. 14. To the question, "Is it proper for a woman to pray to God with her head uncovered?" one must answer a resounding, "Certainly not!"—that is, if one is to make any sense of Paul's discussion to this point. The Christians at Corinth should observe this universal custom. No other church allowed a woman to prophesy without covering her head, and the Corinthian church should not let this occur in their assembly.

11:17–34 This passage concerns the improper activities that were occurring when the church met to participate in the celebration of the Eucharist or Lord's Supper.

11:17 I do not praise you: In contrast to Paul's praise in v. 2, that the Corinthians had followed many of his teachings, here he expressed concern for their sinful practices at worship. **Come together** is a technical term for the meeting of the church and is used three times in this passage (vv. 18, 20).

11:18 divisions: It is tempting to equate the divisions here with the problems occurring in ch. 1, but the divisions in this verse seem to relate to events happening when the church met for the Lord's Supper. Possibly the difficulties were over class distinctions of rich and poor, or Jew and Gentile. When the church meets, all the parties should come together as equals, but such was apparently not the case at Corinth. Instead of the unity urged by Paul in 11:17 and emphasized again in chs. 12—14, there was fractionalism among the believers.

11:19 those who are approved: One of the positive results of division or **factions** in the church is that it becomes obvious who the genuine Christians are in the congregation.

11:20–22 The Lord's Supper was the centerpiece of early Christian worship. Gathered around one table, fellow believers met with the Lord and with each other in unity. Christ had expressed this type of humility and unity when He instituted the Supper (Matt. 26:26–30; Mark 14:22–26; Luke 22:14–23). Corinthian believers were taking their **own supper ahead of others,** violating the spirit and purpose of the meal. In acting this way, they showed contempt for **the church of God** and shamed those who had **nothing.**

11:21 For in eating ... one is hungry, and another is drunk: In the early church, the Lord's Supper was commonly preceded by a fellowship meal, later known as the Agape Feast. Eventually, so many problems accompanied these feasts that at the Council of Carthage (A.D. 397), they were strictly forbidden. And such was the case at Corinth. In their coming together, they were not eating together; hence it could not be called communion; and their behavior was so dishonoring to the Lord, it could hardly be called the Lord's Supper. Some were actually getting drunk.

11:22–25 I received speaks of Paul's revelation from Christ, which he had **delivered** to the people. Paul explained it again.

11:24, 25 Take, eat . . . broken, are all omitted in the best manuscripts. **this is My body:** Certainly not literally, but figuratively. He was there in the midst participating with the disciples in the element of the bread which signifies His incarnation. **which is . . . for you:** This signifies the sacrificial and vicarious character of

the death of Christ. Christ is memorialized at this table, not as a great example, or teacher, or even prophet, but as the Lamb of God that takes away the sin of the world. **do this in remembrance of me:** In contrast to the often thoughtless and reckless gathering of Corinthian believers at their so-called love feast, Jesus asked of His disciples, "Remember me."

11:26 you proclaim the Lord's death till He comes: The Lord's Supper looks back to Christ's death and forward to His second coming (Matt. 26:29; Mark 14:25; Luke 22:18).

11:27–29 In an unworthy manner refers to the way in which a person eats the Lord's Supper. The Corinthians had been making the meal a time of overeating and getting drunk rather than a time of reflecting on the death and resurrection of the Lord Jesus Christ.

11:30 Sleep here refers to the death of Christians (15:18; 1 Thess. 4:15, 16). In this passage, it refers to untimely death, a punishment suffered by some Christians who failed to **examine** themselves at the Lord's Supper (v. 28).

11:31, 32 If we would judge ourselves,

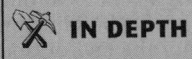 **IN DEPTH**   **The New Covenant**

The NT describes the new covenant (1 Cor. 11:25), or agreement, that God has made with humanity, based on the death and resurrection of Jesus Christ.

In the Bible, a covenant involves much more than a contract or simple agreement. A contract has an end date, but a covenant is a permanent arrangement. Furthermore, a contract generally involves only one aspect of a person, such as a skill, while a covenant covers a person's total being.

God entered into numerous covenants with people in the OT. For example: with Adam and Eve (Gen. 3:15); with Noah (8:21, 22; 2 Pet. 3:7, 15); with Abraham (Gen. 12:1–3); with Israel (Deut. 29:1–30:20); and with David (2 Sam. 7:12–16; 22:51).

The agreement with Israel was especially significant, because it established a special relationship between God and the Hebrews. They were made His "chosen people" through whom He would bring blessing and hope to the rest of the world. However, because the recipients of God's law could not keep it perfectly, further provision was necessary for them as well as for the rest of humanity.

That's why God promised a new covenant through the prophet Jeremiah. Under the new covenant, God would write His law on human hearts. This suggested a new level of obedience and a new knowledge of the Lord.

The work of Jesus Christ brought the promised new covenant into being. When Jesus ate His final Passover meal with the Twelve, He spoke of the cup as "the new covenant in My blood" (Luke 22:20), the words that Paul quoted to the Corinthians to remind them of the need for purity and propriety in their worship (1 Cor. 11:25–34).

The new covenant in Jesus' blood rests directly on the sacrificial work of Christ on the Cross (which was prefigured by Israel's system of sacrifices) and accomplishes the removal of sin and the cleansing of the conscience by faith in Him (Heb. 10:2, 22). So every time Christians celebrate the Lord's Supper, they remind themselves that God has fulfilled His promise: "I will be their God, and they shall be My people . . . I will be merciful to their unrighteousness, and their sins and their lawless deeds I will remember no more" (Heb. 8:10, 12; compare Jer. 31:33, 34).

God would not need to correct us. But when Christians are unwilling to do this self-examination, God Himself will chasten them.

11:33, 34 wait for one another: Paul concludes his discussion of the Lord's Supper with a practical exhortation that the Corinthian believers show proper concern for one another. He implies his disapprobation of the common love feast in the words **eat at home.** And he demonstrates again pastoral concern when he expresses the thought **lest you come together for judgment:** Paul takes no delight in the chastening hand of the Lord. **I will set in order** (Gk. *diatasso*) refers to outward practical arrangement (compare Matt. 11:1; 1 Cor. 9:14; 16:1; Gal. 3:19). Any other details pertaining to the Lord's Supper, Paul will clarify upon his visit to the city.

12:1–14:40 Paul continues his discussion of proper order in the church with the subject of the exercise of spiritual gifts in the church. He presents the proper interrelationship between unity of the body, yet diversity of gifts, the proper function of gifts, and the primacy of love in the operation of spiritual gifts.

12:1 Now concerning: The apostle is responding to another question in the letter from the Corinthians (7:1, 25; 8:1). **spiritual gifts:** The Greek text does not contain the word *gifts* but merely reads "spirituals" (*pneumatikon*), which may refer to spiritual things or to spiritual persons. Many have assumed it refers to the **gifts** (*charismata*) of 12:4–11 (Matt. 7:7–11; Luke 11:9–13), but this is probably not the case, in view of how the term is used in chs. 12—14, specifically 12:1–3; 14:1–3; and 14:37.

12:2 Gentiles were looked upon as barbarian or unlearned which Paul uses to emphasize their state of ignorance. Unfortunately, people who are ignorant don't like to admit it, so Paul has to drive it home. Because of their ignorance, they have been **carried away** or swept off their feet. Paul considers demonic forces behind idol worship (10:20) so this personal action of being captivated forcefully may be behind his expression. The term reflects the eroticism of much pagan religion in which the participant was taken by ecstasy and did not use self-control characteristic of the work of the Spirit as taught by the apostle in ch. 14. **Dumb idols** is an expression that would be immediately recognized by the Corinthians familiar with the OT idolatry (compare 1 Kin. 18:26–29; Ps. 65:4–8; Is. 46:7). Bruce suggests that Paul is contrasting the silence of the idols with the noisy (demon-inspired) outcry of their worshipers.

12:3 calls Jesus accursed . . . say that Jesus is Lord: A person truly speaking by means of the Holy Spirit will never curse (i.e.,

demean or defame) Jesus, and all who genuinely proclaim the lordship of Christ do so by the Spirit's enabling.

12:4–6 gifts: The first use of the word for gifts stands in contrast to *pneumatikon* of 12:1. *Charismata* refers to "grace-gifts" of God on the individual Christian through which He may strengthen His people. **diversities . . . differences . . . diversities** (same Greek word): Note the diversity in the work of the Trinity. In v. 4 the Spirit distributes each one to the believer (12:11). In v. 5 the Son of God assigns the believer the particular way the gift is manifested in the body (12:12–27). In v. 6, the Father provides the energy to the believer in exercising the gift (12:28). God works His will through His people in many ways. Not everyone is intended to be the same or perform the same function in the body. **same Spirit . . . same Lord . . . same God:** Though people are gifted differently by God, God and His work is unified. Regardless of which gifts various persons have or do not have, the one **God . . . works all in all.**

12:7–11 To each one for the profit of all expresses Paul's main teaching on the work of the Spirit. God works in believers to benefit the entire body, not simply the individual Christian (vv. 25, 26). The Christian is a vehicle through which God works toward the upbuilding and unity of the entire body, not the end of God's work. **For to one . . . to another:** The two Greek words (*allos . . . heteros*) point up the diversity and begin a list of *charismata* that are distributed by God throughout His body. No one is given every gift nor are all given one gift, like tongues. Rather, the various *charismata*, or grace gifts, are distributed so as to bring diversity among the unified body. The various gifts of **wisdom . . . knowledge . . . faith . . . gifts of healings . . . working of miracles . . . prophecy . . . discerning of spirits . . . kinds of tongues . . . interpretation of tongues** were probably very understandable to the Corinthians, but their exact nature is difficult for us to know two thousand years later. *Word of knowledge* appears to be the ability to discourse on doctrine; not the knowledge itself but the skill of discourse. *Word of wisdom* is quite the opposite of word of knowledge and refers to practical or ethical outworkings of the knowledge, similar to what one observes in the Proverbs. This gift helps solve the problem of the distribution of food in Acts 6. *Faith* appears to be the capacity to believe God for extraordinary deeds. *Miracles* would probably be the ability to do deeds similar to Moses, the prophets, or maybe some nature miracles one observes in the Gospels. Notice that God particularly used these gifts to confirm truth spoken through the early apostles (Heb. 2:3, 4). *Prophecy* is the forthtelling or foretelling of the revelation of God, either "new" revelation or divine elucidation of what is already known. More than merely teaching or preaching, this action results from the empowering but not inspiration of the Spirit. Peter demonstrated this gift at Pentecost. *Discerning of spirits* may refer to the ability to distinguish the works of God from demonic activity in the church. *Kinds of tongues* probably refers to the ability to speak various languages that one has not studied. *Interpretation of tongues* is the ability to explain or translate the tongues spoken in the congregation so that the entire group of believers might benefit from the prayer spoken (14:16) by the tongues-speaker (14:13, 28). **As He wills**, not as *we* will. Whether or not Christians are to seek for any of the gifts of the Spirit is discussed at 12:31.

12:12–31 Paul attempts to help the carnal Corinthian Christians to turn from selfish desires and to seek for the unity of the body and to serve with the gifts God has given (vv. 7, 25, 26).

12:12–14 For . . . For . . . For: Note the development of thought as the Spirit of God continues to give Christ the glory (John 16:12–14; 1 Cor. 12:3).

12:12, 13 so also is Christ: The analogy of the human body illustrates the need for unity in diversity in the body of Christ.

12:13 one . . . one . . . one: The apostle continues to emphasize unity: one **Spirit**, one **body,** one **Spirit;** Paul denies that the Spirit is partitioned into the groups mentioned in chs. 3 and 4. All believers (v. 3) are infused by the same God. **by one Spirit we were all baptized:** The verse might be better translated "in one Spirit we were all baptized into one body." Christ, the exalted and ascended Head of the body, is the active agent who places the new member of the body in the sphere of the Holy Spirit for His care and safekeeping. All believers are baptized into the body in the sphere of the Holy Spirit and thereby made part of the body of Christ, whether **Jews or Greeks, slaves or free.** No one has it over another in Christ's church; everyone enters the same way: by faith into the promise of Abraham (Gal. 3:26–29). Each of us has equal share in the same Spirit of God: we **have all been made to drink into one Spirit.** Some of the Corinthians—probably the *pneumatikon* (v. 1)—believed that only certain gifted individuals were especially in tune with the Spirit, but Paul puts every believer on an equal footing in the Spirit. It is unlikely that "drinking" refers to common participation in the cup of the Lord's Supper. The Spirit not only surrounds us in baptism; but since we have drunk of the Spirit He also dwells within us.

 **IN COMPARISON**

Spiritual Gifts vs. Spiritual Responsibilities

Spiritual gifts—or grace gifts, more accurately—are extraordinary abilities that the Spirit gives to a believer to build up the church. Even though such attributes as faith, teaching, and giving are considered gifts, all Christians are exhorted to develop these traits.

Some Christians are given . . .	But all believers are called . . .
Divine wisdom (12:8)	To live wisely (Rom. 16:19; Eph. 5:15; Col. 4:5)
Extraordinary faith (12:9)	To walk by faith (2 Cor. 5:7) and abound in faith (2 Cor. 8:7); to take up the shield of faith (Eph. 6:16) and pursue faith (1 Tim. 6:12; 2 Tim. 2:22)
Special teaching gifts (12:28; Rom. 12:7)	To teach others the truths of God (Matt. 28:20; 2 Tim. 2:2, 24)
Supernatural ability to help (12:28)	To serve one another in love (Gal. 5:13) and to minister to others (Rom. 12:7)
The gift of exhortation (Rom. 12:8)	To exhort one another daily (Heb. 3:13)
The ability to give with liberality (Rom. 12:8)	To give "not grudgingly or of necessity" but cheerfully (2 Cor. 9:7)
Divine power to show mercy (Rom. 12:8)	To be merciful (Luke 6:36; James 2:13)

12:14-27 These verses emphasize one major idea: the body is a magnificent picture of both unity and diversity at one and the same time (vv. 14-19, unity in diversity; vv. 20-27, diversity in unity). None should exalt themselves because of the gift given to them, nor should any think themselves less because they receive a gift some view as less significant.

12:25-27 That introduces the main purpose, namely, **no schism in the body. should have the same care for one another:** This emphasizes the purpose of the gifts as stated in v. 7—"for the profit of all." Rather than bickering with other Christians and being jealous about other people's positions or gifts, our task is to give of ourselves to others so that if any part of the body is having difficulty or is hurting we seek to minister and heal that part.

12:28-30 God has appointed continues to emphasize sovereign appointment of gifts by the Spirit (v. 11), Son (v. 18), and Father (v. 28). The gifts are not by our choice. The persons of **apostles, prophets,** and **teachers** are listed first and with ordinal numbers, probably

because they are foundational for the body of Christ, although the Corinthians had valued them less than the spectacular gifts, such as tongues. Sometimes "apostles," used in a general sense, approximates "missionary" (compare 15:7; 2 Cor. 11:5; 12:11; Gal. 1:17, 19; Rom. 16:7); used more specifically, it refers to a small group who witnessed the resurrected Christ and were specially appointed by Him as His representatives (the Twelve and Paul; 15:5 and 9:1; 15:8). The apostle speaks of OT prophets elsewhere (Rom. 1:2; 3:21; 9:3; 1 Thess. 2:15), but in 1 Corinthians and Eph. 2:20 he may use the term for only NT prophets, whose activity is referred to in ch. 14. As in OT prophecy, the chief job of prophets was not foretelling but forthtelling. NT prophets guided the church in its infancy, along with the apostles. Teachers expound the truth of the written revelation of God, as indicated in Gal. 6:6 and 2 Tim. 2:2. After these three major positions, the apostle Paul mentions a variety of other helpful gifts, listing tongues, their favorite, last. The concluding questions—Should we expect all to be

---

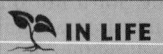 **IN LIFE** | ## Are Some Jobs More Important?

Does a hierarchy of gifts (1 Cor. 12:28-31) mean God values some jobs more than others? Judging by popular opinion, one might conclude that He does. In fact, for centuries Christians have subscribed to a subtle yet powerful hierarchy of vocations.

In our culture, that hierarchy tends to position *clergy* (missionaries and evangelists, pastors and priests) at the top, members of the *helping professions* (doctors and nurses, teachers and educators, social workers) next, and *secular* workers (business executives, salespeople, factory laborers, and farmers) at the bottom.

So what determines the spiritual value of a job? How does God assign significance? The hierarchy assumes sacred and secular distinctions, and assigns priority to the sacred. But does God view vocations that way? No.

All legitimate work matters to God. God Himself is a worker. In fact, human occupations find their origin in His work to create the world (Ps. 8:6-8). Work is a gift from Him to meet the needs of people and the creation.

God creates people to carry out specific kinds of work. God uniquely designs each of us, fitting us for certain kinds of tasks. He distributes skills, abilities, interests, and personalities among us so that we can carry out His work in the world. That work includes "spiritual" tasks, but also extends to health, education, agriculture, business, law, communication, the arts, and so on.

God cares more about character and conduct than occupational status. Paul's teaching in this passage is about gifts, not vocations. At the time Paul wrote it, there were few if any "professional" clergy in the church. Paul himself was a tentmaker by occupation, along with his friends, Aquila and Priscilla (Rom. 16:3-5; 1 Cor. 16:19). Other church leaders practiced a wide variety of professions and trades. God may assign rank among the spiritual gifts, but there's no indication that He looks at vocations that way.

Furthermore, Scripture says there is something "more excellent" than exercising certain gifts (1 Cor. 12:31). Chapter 13 reveals that to be the way of Christlike love and character. Implication: If we want status in God's economy, we should excel at love, no matter what we do for work. Love has the greatest value to God (13:13; Matt. 22:35-40).

apostles, or prophets, or teachers, or workers of miracles? Do all have the various gifts like healings, or tongues, or interpretation?—expect the answer no! What kind of body would it be that was one big hand, or toe, or tongue? This body would not be functional. It would be grotesque!

12:31 The translation of **earnestly desire** presents a problem: Should it be translated as the NKJV does, as an imperative, or as an indicative, a statement of fact: "You are desiring the sensational gifts"? The Greek word *zeloo*, normally a negative term, allows either. The imperative is chosen by most interpreters, but the indicative is possible and would fit with the correction at which chs. 12—14 aim. In contrast to such unprofitable desire, Paul directs them to **a more excellent way** in ch. 13, the way of exercising any and all gifts only in love.

13:1–13 The love chapter is divided into three sections: (1) the futility of gifts without the fruit of the Spirit, love; (2) the nature of love; and (3) the permanence of love in contrast to the temporality of the gifts.

13:1 tongues of men and of angels: The miraculous gift of "speaking in tongues" (*glosso-lalia*) involved human languages, self-evident by the wording here (tongues of men) and also in other passages (Acts 2:4, 6, 8, 11; 10:46). But were the tongues in the Corinthian church angelic languages or humanly unintelligible languages from God? The tongues-speakers may have thought so, but Paul may be using hyperbole: "even if I were to speak in some heavenly language." Either way, without love such a gift would be worthless. **Sounding brass or a clanging cymbal** were standard instruments used in pagan worship. The exercise of the grace gifts apart from Christian love would differ little from the activities of various pagan and mystery religions.

13:2 gift of prophecy . . . all mysteries and all knowledge . . . all faith: All three are listed in ch. 12. All these gifts, employed without love, amount to nothing.

13:3 Bestow all my goods: People can do works of charity without the proper motivation (4:5). **Body to be burned:** With this ultimate gift, Paul has extended each gift to the nth degree in hyperbole to show their worthlessness apart from love. They are "wood, hay, and stubble" (3:12–15) at the judgment seat of Christ.

13:4–7 Paul now advances from the superiority of the fruit of the Spirit, **love,** to the important traits of love. Love **suffers long,** or puts up with people that it is easy to give up on. Love is **kind,** namely, treats well people who have treated us poorly. Love doesn't **envy** (Gk. *zeloo*) nor **parade itself** and is **not puffed up.** Self-promotion plagued Corinth and challenges

us today. **Behave rudely** means to act in an unfair or unseemly manner, as Paul discussed in 7:36. **seek** (Gk. *zeteo*) **its own:** A person who loves is willing to set aside his or her own plans or entitlements for another's good. **Not provoked** speaks of not being irritated or over-sensitive to others, easily angered. **thinks no evil:** When we love someone we do not immediately assume evil on their part. Furthermore, if we understand "think" (*logizomai*), or "consider," as an accounting term, the text would mean that we do not keep a record or account of evils done to us. **does not rejoice in iniquity . . . rejoices in the truth:** Love does not delight in evil in any form, including the fall of a brother or sister. Instead, love delights in all that expresses the gospel, both in word and deed. **bears . . . believes . . . hopes . . . endures all things:** The word for *bears* literally means to "support." Love is the foundation for all acts that please God. Love believes all things in that love never gives up and never loses hope. Love endures any hardship or rejection, revealing its superior strength. In the face of confrontation, love simply continues. To love is the great commandment (compare John 13:34, 35) and no other force promotes righteousness more.

13:8–10 This third section of ch. 13 moves from the nature of love to its permanence. **Love never fails:** This uncompromising affirmation contrasts with grace-gifts, which are transitory at best. One day *all* the gifts will be needed no longer, but love will continue forever. **prophecies . . . tongues . . . knowledge:** Paul focuses on three of the sixteen gifts to demonstrate the temporariness of them all. **prophecies . . . will fail:** The word translated "fail" (*katageo*) is in the passive voice. Literally the translation is "prophecies will be stopped." **tongues . . . will cease . . . knowledge . . . will vanish away [be stopped]:** Prophecy and knowledge (which are among the twelve body gifts for edification) are **in part** (Gk. *ek merous*). They, with all the gifts of ch. 12, serve the body of Christ, but only for now. **we know** in part, **we prophesy** in part. These "in part" (*ek merous*) gifts will continue until **that which is perfect** (Gk. *teleios*, complete) **has come** (v. 10). The perfection in view here has been interpreted quite differently: (1) the end of the apostolic era, by which time the core doctrines of the church had been revealed and taught; (2) the completion of the canon of Scripture, which secured the inspired and authoritative source of all true Christian doctrine; and (3) the second coming of Christ, at which point the role and relationship of all believers and the church will be transformed, and the "partial" will no longer by needed. This time of completion (whichever view is embraced) supercedes and replaces all the "only for now," "in part" gifts. Unlike these, love endures forever.

13:11, 12 Child is used five times in v. 11. Paul uses the growth from childhood to adulthood as an illustration to explain his comments in vv. 8–10 about movement to completion. It is normal and expected for a child to act and think like a child. But when a person becomes an adult, the acts and toys of childhood need to stop. **now** (used twice) **we see in a mirror dimly:** The mirror is likely the revelation of God, which, while incomplete, is accompanied by these three gifts. **But then** (used twice in balance with "now") refers to the "perfect" when we shall **know . . . as . . . known.** Thus there will be no further need for the body gifts.

13:13 greatest is love: **Faith, hope**, and love are permanent Christian virtues, yet love clearly stands over the other two. Faith is the foundation (Heb. 11:6) and love is the capstone. Doctrine is the foundation (3:10; Jude 3) and experience is the practical expression which attracts (John 13:35).

14:1 Like 12:31, this verse is a hinge which connects the preceding to the following.

14:1, 2 Pursue love: The Greek word for pursue (*dioko*) carries such meanings as "hasten," "run," "run after," "aspire to." We can take or leave many things in life, but not love. We should pursue or strive for love as a priceless treasure. The fruit of the Spirit prepares believers for the exercise of the grace-gifts of the Spirit. **desire spiritual gifts** (*pneumatikon*; compare 12:1) Most interpreters take this to mean that believers are to seek certain gifts—prophecy, especially—in order to serve Christ's body. Two matters may speak against such a view. First, the Greek word for desire (*zeloo*) is the same as in 12:31 and may indicate a negative desire, not positive. 14:1 would then read, "Pursue love, but you are desiring spirituals, when you should rather prophesy." Secondly, *gifts* is not in the Greek text and, as in 12:1, should be omitted. The context seems to indicate that spirituals (*pneumatika*) is an adjective describing specific utterances, perhaps ecstatic tongues. Therefore, in contrast to the "spirituals" (ecstatic tongues?) they desire improperly, they should desire prophesying. Why? Because the main purpose of gifts is to edify one another, but the person who **speaks in a tongue** is understood only by God. Thus **no one understands. . . in the spirit**.

14:3–5 He who prophesies here may incorporate all of the speaking gifts (Rom. 12:6; 1 Pet. 4:11) that edify others, as is demonstrated by the results in vv. 3 and 4. **edification . . . exhortation . . . comfort:** Paul prefers for the Corinthians to exercise this gift in their midst instead of "speaking in a tongue," by which one

merely **edifies himself**. **I wish you all spoke in tongues:** Perhaps the apostle is contrasting the Spirit-given gift of tongues (note the plural) with speaking in a tongue (the singular), which may be a reference to ecstatic speech. Or perhaps Paul recognizes value in private, personal prayer uttered in a tongue, even as he aims to correct the abuse of tongues in public worship. Another possibility is that we should not read too much into this comment. Elsewhere the apostle wished that all were celibate like him (7:7) but certainly he did not expect such to be the case. Paul saw benefit in the true gift of tongues but a limited one. **prophesies is greater . . . unless indeed he interprets:** When interpreted, the gift of speaking in tongues will benefit the church.

14:6 what shall I profit you: If Paul had first come to the Corinthians speaking in tongues that they did not know, what benefit

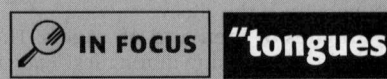

IN FOCUS "tongues"

(Gk. *glossa*) (12:10; 14:2, 4–6, 9, 13, 14, 18, 27; Acts 2:4; 10:46; 19:6) Strong's #*1100*: The Greek term *glossa* means "tongue" or "language." When the early believers were empowered by the Holy Spirit on the Day of Pentecost, they were given the ability to speak in many different languages, so that those visiting from all around the Roman world could hear the glories of God being uttered in their native tongue (Acts 2:4–11). The household of Cornelius also spoke in different languages when they were baptized in the Holy Spirit (Acts 10:46). And the same happened with the new disciples from Ephesus (Acts 19:6). Other than these instances, priority mention of tongue speaking is at Corinth, where they spoke in different languages as a way of praying to God. When these languages were spoken outside the corporate worship setting, interpretation was not needed; when they were spoken in the meetings, Paul required interpretation so that the others could understand and be edified (14:2–27).

would it have been to them? Their response would probably have been one of disinterest (v. 11) or derision (v. 23). Rather than this fruitless approach he came with a **revelation** (compare 2:10), **prophecy** (12:29), **knowledge** (compare 2:12) and **teaching** (12:29; compare 14:26).

14:7–9 Like musical instruments that must

be used at the proper time and in the proper way for them to serve their proper function, so tongues being exercised outside these guidelines are like **speaking into the air.** Even if the languages sound beautiful, are spoken fluently, or contain great ideas or even praise of God, they are irrelevant if no one can understand what is being said.

14:10, 11 Paul again forms an analogy to further drive home his point. **many kinds of languages:** No one can master all the languages in the world, but they have one point in common: they all convey meaning (**significance**). **Meaning** is essential to communication in language and it is no different with the languages from the Spirit. Without meaning they make the speaker a **foreigner** (literally, barbarian, making meaningless sounds like "barbar") to listeners.

14:12 spiritual gifts: The word for spiritual here is different from Paul's usage to this point (gifts is not in the Greek text). Rather than *pneumatikon* or *pneumatika,* he uses the common word *pneuma,* meaning "spirits." They are desirous for spirits (v. 2). Paul may be speaking with tongue in cheek, describing their fall back to former practices in Greek pagan worship. Or he may use "spirits" to refer to their speaking in tongues. Paul seeks to redirect their zeal toward legitimate manifestations of the Holy Spirit that will benefit fellow worshipers.

14:13 pray that he may interpret: If one "speaks in a tongue" (possibly with ecstacy), no one around can understand (14:2). Consequently, the speaker should beseech God for the ability to interpret so that the entire church may benefit.

14:14 pray in a tongue: But if one prays in a tongue (i.e., without interpreting) and there is no interpretation (which seemed to be the Corinthian practice), then there is no understanding and consequently no benefit to the person or the church.

14:15 Pray with the spirit refers contextually to the spirit of the person, not the Spirit of God (v. 2). Paul desires to pray to God both with his spirit and with **understanding.** Paul is unwilling to become schizoid in his spiritual life, turning off his mind while giving free sway to his spirit.

14:16, 17 Otherwise: From v. 12 on, Paul shows the absurdity of their promoting their favorite "gift" in an unedifying way rather than building the body into unity as taught in ch. 2. Here, then, he forces them through his logic to channel their zeal (12:31; 13:5; 14:1; 14:12). **place of the uninformed:** Possibly a new convert is in view. However, anyone who does not have the gift of interpretation could fill this place. **Amen at your giving of thanks:** It was

common in Jewish, and apparently early church, worship for the congregation to indicate its agreement with the prayer by responding with "amen" (Deut. 27:14–26; Rev. 5:14). Such a response would be impossible when no one understands.

14:18, 19 more than you all: Apparently Paul quantitatively spoke numerous languages. Or he spoke in tongues more often than even the zealously tongues-speaking Corinthians. Either way, **in the church** the speaking of five words that were understandable (presumably prophesying) had more benefit than a countless number of words **in a tongue.** All speaking in tongues in Acts occurred in public. Paul's teaching here focuses on such public utterance, although v. 18 may have in view Paul's tongues-speech in private, personal prayer. Possibly, in view of vv. 20–22, the apostle prayed publicly in various languages when he visited the different synagogues as he traveled from town to town through the Roman Empire.

14:20–22 Brethren: In this new paragraph (possibly picking up now from 13:11) Paul challenges the Corinthians to reorient their thinking. They are to be **mature,** while in **malice** they are to be **babes.** The Corinthians still had much to learn. At the time of Paul's writing they had poor ethical judgment though they had a high opinion of themselves. **In the law:** Paul evaluates the purpose of tongues and the mature use of them by the Scriptures rather than by personal experience. The quotation from Is. 28:11 indicates that "law" here refers to the OT rather than simply the Pentateuch.

14:23–25 At this point Paul advances from the theological debate to the application to the congregation. Having demonstrated that their tongue-speaking had limited value for the church and was even harmful to it, Paul displays vividly what their disorderly tongues-speaking was doing to unbelievers. Whenever the church met and the **uninformed or unbelievers** entered the assembly and the Corinthians were speaking in tongues (presumably without interpretation), these Christians appeared mad. However, when these non-Christians heard the congregation **prophesy,** the message **convicted** them, so that they fell **down on** their faces and worshiped God.

14:26 Paul now sets forth to the Corinthians a sample of the way that a local church meeting should be conducted. If **each of you** brings to the meeting the special ability that God has given and everything is done for **edification,** the church as a whole will be benefited. **Psalm** probably refers to the singing of an OT psalm (compare Col 3:16; Eph. 5:19). **Teaching** would most likely consist of the presentation of some

OT truth or teaching of the apostles. Though the apostle has sought to curtail the excess, he still recognizes that there was a proper place for the gift of tongues (**has a tongue**) with **an interpretation.** The one who receives a **revelation** may be the prophet who speaks the word of God (vv. 29–32).

14:27 The apostle puts forth some guidelines designed to keep the gift of tongues under control and yet allow the Spirit of God to use the gift through the church. He limits the number of manifestations of this gift in one church meeting to **three,** and in order (**in turn**), and each one of these manifestations is to be interpreted. Before speaking in tongues, they need to be sure that someone is present to **interpret** or the tongues-speakers themselves should interpret (compare vv. 5, 13).

14:28 if . . . no interpreter . . . keep silent: If no one interprets what is said, then the tongues-speaker is not to speak. The Greek word for "silent" (*sigao*) means "to say nothing," "stop speaking," "hold one's tongue."

14:29 two or three prophets speak: As beneficial as prophesying is, even here Paul seeks to order the activity. There is only so much time in a meeting of the church and there is much to be done. **Let the others judge** indicates that no one, not even a person exercising a grace-gift, is exempt from the judgment of the church (6:5; 11:29, 31). This judgment might be by the other prophets present.

14:30 Revealed surely indicates that the prophesying is more than what we view as preaching or speaking from the texts of Scripture. This is akin to OT prophecy in which God gives revelation to a servant for him to give that revelation to God's people. **Let the first keep silent** is similar to the admonition in v. 28 concerning tongues-speakers. The speakers are not to be interrupting each other. All things are to be done orderly (v. 41).

14:31, 32 One by one is similar to "in turn" of v. 27 regarding the tongues-speakers. Since the purpose of prophesying is that the congregation may **learn** and **be encouraged,** only this orderly procedure will assure the result. **Subject to the prophets** is added lest someone should claim, "I simply can't help myself when God brings a revelation to me from the Spirit." Paul teaches that the Holy Spirit does not overpower the individual he empowers. The will of the Christian is not broken but must cooperate with the work of God.

14:33 God is not the author of confusion: Confusion is exactly what the Corinthians had been experiencing. This comes not from God but from the sinful flesh. **As in all the churches of the saints** may go with the first part of v. 33 or as the beginning of v. 34. The clause seems to fit better with v. 34 regarding behavior in the church meetings.

14:34 Paul commands that **women** are to be **silent** in the church meetings. This is a stronger and more inclusive statement than is given in 1 Tim. 2:12. In 1 Timothy the reference is to teaching men; here all talking appears prohibited. This seems to disagree, however, with the previous allowance of women prophesying in ch. 11. Some have argued that the speaking refers to speaking in tongues, while others believe disruptive talk is prohibited. Still others believe Paul is attempting to inhibit a feminist group at Corinth. The solution is likely otherwise. The immediate context concerns self-control and judging the prophets. The prohibition relates to women not being involved in judging the prophets. Such judging would be an expression of authority over men, which was forbidden.

14:35 Ask their own husbands at home seems to indicate the **women** are older women who are already married. The idea of younger unmarried women seeking to address the church probably never entered the apostle's mind. **Shameful** indicates the strong feeling of the apostle and the early church in general of having women instruct men in the church or exercise authority over them. However, when women were covered and prophesied, this was acceptable and not viewed as exercising authority over the men (compare 11:3–10).

14:36 Come originally from you is another argument for the Corinthians to accept Paul's teaching. The Corinthians did not invent the truth Paul teaches. It began at Jerusalem and has now traveled throughout most of the Roman world.

14:37 To further establish his arguments and the authority of his teaching, Paul now asserts that as an apostle what he teaches are the **commandments of the Lord.** They are not opinions and are not optional. **Thinks himself to be a prophet or spiritual** further demonstrates that two primary classes of gifted persons are in view in ch. 14, namely, the prophet and the tongues-speaker.

14:38–40 To the person who refuses to heed the apostle's admonition, Paul simply says if that person wants to be **ignorant, let him be ignorant.**

15:1, 2 Paul's **gospel** to the Corinthians centered on the physical death and resurrection of Jesus Christ, the eternal Son of God who became human yet never sinned (Gal. 1:6–10). Paul had started the Corinthian church; the gospel that the Corinthians had originally **received** came from him (2:2).

15:3 Paul did not originate the proclamation of Jesus that he **delivered** to the Corinthians;

he simply gave the Corinthians what he himself had **received.** He viewed himself as a link in a long chain of witnesses to the truth of the death and resurrection of Christ. **Christ died for our sins:** Christ's death dealt decisively with our sins. He suffered in our place to endure the just wrath of God against us. **according to the Scriptures:** Christ lived and died in accordance with the prophecies about Him in the OT (Ps. 16:10; Is. 53:8–10).

15:4 The Resurrection verifies the fact that Christ's death paid the full price for sin. The Greek term translated **rose** here is in the perfect tense, emphasizing the ongoing effects of this historical event. Christ is a risen Savior today.

15:5–8 At the time of Paul's writing, a person could have verified the truthfulness of the apostle's statements. The majority of the **five hundred** people who saw the risen Christ, as well as **all the apostles** and **James** (the half brother of Jesus), were still living. **Born out of due time** is probably Paul's comment on the unique way he became an apostle. Unlike the other apostles, who had the benefit of an initial training period with Christ, Paul became an apostle abruptly, with no opportunity for earthly contact with Christ or His teaching.

15:9 Paul considered himself **the least of the apostles** because at one time he had persecuted the church (Acts 22:4; Eph. 3:8; 1 Tim. 1:15, 16).

15:10 I labored more abundantly: Even

 **IN COMPARISON** | **Facts About the Resurrection**

The resurrection of Christ was proclaimed eagerly by the early church. This miracle was considered an essential part of the gospel message. Surely Christ had died, but more importantly, He had been raised. More than just a suffering Savior, Jesus is our living Lord.

Christ's resurrection was prophesied in the OT Scriptures (Ps. 16:10).	15:4
The risen Christ appeared to more than five hundred witnesses, including Paul.	15:5–8
If Jesus did not rise from the dead, the gospel message is pointless, empty, and dishonest. Jesus Christ would not be alive, interceding for us, and we would not be able to place our hope in a glorious future with Him. The Resurrection is central to the gospel.	15:14, 15
According to Paul, "if Christ is not risen, your faith is futile; you are still in your sins" (15:17; Rom. 4:25). Christ's resurrection, not merely His death on the Cross, secured our justification. His resurrection was a sign of God's approval of Christ's sacrifice for our sins. In short, no Resurrection equals no forgiveness of sin.	15:17–19
The resurrection of Christ was designed to reveal what lies ahead for those who put their trust in Jesus (15:20–57). Paul called Christ "the firstfruits of those who have fallen asleep" (15:20). This OT image (Ex. 23:16–19) means that Christ serves as both an example and a guarantee of what we can expect. Because He has conquered death (15:26, 27, 54–57), we need not fear death. Because He now enjoys a glorified body, we also can expect to inherit a "spiritual body" (15:44–46) after this mortal one wears out.	15:20–26
Our dead, physical body will one day be resurrected.	15:42
We will once again be both material and immaterial beings, our soul being reunited with our resurrected body.	15:43, 44
The power behind this marvelous, yet mysterious, event is Jesus, the self-declared "resurrection and the life" (John 11:25).	15:45
Our physical body will be altered and changed to prepare us for the life to come. If Jesus is the prototype, we will still be recognizable, but our new body will be capable of supernatural activities (Luke 24:31, 36, 51).	15:51–54
Our resurrection will take place when Jesus returns (1 Thess. 4:13–18).	15:53

though Paul got a late start and did not have the discipleship training that the other apostles did, he traveled further, established more churches, and wrote more Scripture than all of them (2 Cor. 11:23–27). But Paul attributed his success to **the grace of God.**

15:11 whether . . . I or they: Paul did not care who got credit for the Corinthians' faith. He cared only that the Corinthians believed.

15:12, 13 Some of the Corinthians were teaching **that there is no resurrection.** These opponents of Paul may have been denying the reality of Christ's resurrection. They may also

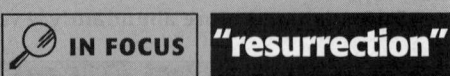

IN FOCUS "resurrection"

(Gk. *anastasis*) (15:12, 13, 21, 42; Acts 17:32; Rom. 1:4; 1 Pet. 1:3) Strong's #386: The Scriptures often speak of Christ's resurrection with the phrase that is literally "resurrection out from among dead ones." This is the wording in the first half of 15:12 and in other verses (Acts 17:31; 1 Pet. 1:3). When Scripture speaks of the resurrection in general, commonly the phrase is "a resurrection of dead ones." This is the wording in the second half of 15:12 (15:13, 42). In Rom. 1:4, Christ's resurrection is spoken of as "a resurrection of dead ones." The same terminology is used in 15:21, where the Greek text literally reads: "For since through a man death came, so also through a Man came a resurrection of dead persons." This shows that Christ's resurrection included the resurrection of believers to eternal life. When He arose, many arose with Him, for they were united with Him in His resurrection (Rom. 6:4, 5; Eph. 2:6; Col. 3:1).

have been teaching that resurrection is only spiritual rather than physical. Or they may have been teaching that the Resurrection had already happened (2 Tim. 2:18). Whatever the case, they contradicted the essential teaching that Christ had been physically raised from the dead and that believers in Him will some day also be resurrected.

15:14 preaching is empty . . . faith is also empty: It is not enough that a person believes something. It is absolutely essential that *what* one believes is true. The object of our faith is important. A dead Savior cannot take away sins, rescue us from God's wrath, or develop a relationship with us.

15:15 false witnesses: In vv. 5–8, Paul

listed several people, including himself, who had witnessed the resurrected Christ. To deny the Resurrection was to deny the truth of their testimony.

15:16, 17 you are still in your sins: Christ's death without His resurrection would not succeed in saving us from our sins.

15:18 Without the resurrection of Christ, those who are **asleep in Christ**—the dead—have **perished** or been destroyed. The Greek word translated *futile* in this passage speaks of something that has no results. Without the resurrection of Christ, the Christian faith brings no forgiveness and no future life in God's presence.

15:19 we are of all men the most pitiable: If Christians have no hope for the future, the pagans could justifiably consider Christians fools since believers would have suffered for nothing.

15:20–28 Paul changes mood and tone in these verses. He declares the truthfulness of Christ's and the believer's resurrection.

15:20 Jesus is the **firstfruits** of all others who believe in Him. This is an OT image of the first installment of a crop which anticipates and guarantees the ultimate offering of the whole crop (16:15; Rom. 8:23). Because Christ rose from the dead, those who are **asleep** in Christ (v. 18; 1 Thess. 4:15, 16) have a guarantee of their own resurrection.

15:21, 22 by man came death: The first man, Adam, transgressed God's law and brought sin and death into the world (Gen. 2:17; 3:19; Rom. 5:12–21); the second Man, Jesus Christ, was the perfect sacrifice to take away sin and to bring life and resurrection to those who believe in Him (Rom. 5:15–21). **in Christ all shall be made alive:** The principle here is similar to that in Rom. 5:18, 19, where Paul explains that by one man's (Adam's) sin many were made unrighteous, whereas by one Man's (Christ's) obedience many will be made righteous.

15:23 Each one in his own order indicates that God has a certain design for the resurrection. The word *order* is a Greek military term that might also be translated "rank." The Commander is raised first; His troops afterward. In 1 Thess. 4:13–18, **His coming** is described as Christ's coming with those who have "fallen asleep" (the dead), who are then united with their physical bodies. Following this is the removal of all living Christians from the earth.

15:24 The end here refers to all remaining prophetic events that will occur after the rapture of the church and during the climax of history, when Christ **puts an end to all rule** (vv. 25–28). **delivers the kingdom to God the Father:** When Christ and the church are joined at His coming, God will establish His *kingdom* on this earth, culminating in a new heavens and a

Using Authority Wisely

Some day all authority, rule, and power will end—a sobering thought (1 Cor. 15:24). Peter mentioned a similar idea when he asked, In light of the end of the present time, what sort of people should we be (1 Pet. 3:10–13)? How should we live? No matter how hard we've worked to acquire and accrue power and position, it will eventually come to an end. That thought should challenge us to hold on lightly to the trappings of authority, and use it wisely and responsibly for God's purposes.

new earth. **puts an end to all rule and all authority:** Until the time of *the end,* the Father subjugates everything to the Son (Ps. 110:1; Dan. 2:44; 7:14, 27). Christ is Lord over the universe (Col. 1:15–17).

15:25, 26 all enemies: God has allowed His enemy Satan to rule as the "prince of the power of the air" (Eph. 2:2) and the "god of this age" (2 Cor. 4:4), but his final judgment before God is certain. **The last enemy . . . death:** The conquering of *death* is final proof of God's victory and the inauguration of the new day of the Lord (Rev. 20:14).

15:27, 28 it is evident: Paul clarified the verses that he had been quoting from the OT. The texts say that everything is put under the Son, but God the Father **is excepted,** or excluded from this subjugation, because the **Son** must be **subject to** the Father. **God may be all in all** indicates that there will be no challenge to the sovereign rule of God over all the universe. There will be universal peace and prosperity.

15:29 There are scores of interpretations as to what is meant in this verse by **baptized for the dead.** The most natural interpretation is that some of the Corinthians, in conformity to their prior pagan practices which allowed such rites, were baptized for some in the Corinthian church who had died without baptism. Certainly whether they were baptized or not relates in no way to whether they were justified or not but may have served some ritualistic function within the church. The apostle does not approve or disapprove of the unusual practice in so many words though it is informative that he says *they* rather than *we* when speaking of the ceremony. No other evidence is found among the church in the first century of such a practice except for a heretical sect (i.e., the Marconites). He desires, rather, to get to the heart of the problem: **If the dead do not rise . . . Why then:** To deny the Resurrection and yet be involved in such activities surely makes that look foolish.

15:30–32 why do we stand in jeopardy:

Paul risked his life **daily.** To do so would have been of no **advantage** without the hope of a resurrection. Why else should Paul have endured difficulties like fighting **beasts at Ephesus?** It would have been better for him to take the position of the Epicureans, who sought pleasure and avoided pain. The reference to *beasts* might be a figurative reference to Paul's human

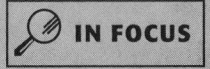 **IN FOCUS** **"life-giving spirit"**

(Gk. *pneuma zoopoioun*) (15:45; 2 Cor. 3:6; 1 Pet. 3:18) Strong's #4151; 2227: The Greek expression denotes "the spirit that gives life" or "the spirit that makes alive." The Lord Jesus entered into a new kind of existence when He was raised from the dead because He was glorified and simultaneously became life-giving spirit. The verse does not say Jesus became "the Spirit," since the Second Person of the Trinity did not become the Third Person. Rather, Jesus became spirit in the sense that His mortal existence and form were changed into that which is spiritual. As One now united with the Spirit in a glorified body, Jesus is no longer bound by His mortal body. He is alive in the Spirit (1 Pet. 3:18), to give life to all who believe. This is why Paul speaks of the Spirit of life in Christ Jesus (Rom. 8:2).

enemies at Ephesus. Acts 19 does not record any confrontation with animals.

15:33, 34 Paul had already warned the Corinthians to avoid fellow believers who lived immoral lives (5:9–13). Quoting a proverb from the poet Menander, **evil company corrupts good habits,** Paul warned the Corinthians to stay away from those who teach false doctrine (2 Cor. 6:14—7:1).

15:35–37 Some people objected to the Resurrection on the grounds that it was too hard to understand. Paul called these people **foolish.** Difficulty understanding the nature of the Resurrection should not cause a person to doubt its reality, any more than not understanding how a seed becomes a plant should cause disbelief in the coming harvest.

15:38–41 The variety found in nature among living beings such as **men, animals, fish,** and **birds,** and among objects such as

term translated *spiritual* here refers to a body directed by the Spirit, as opposed to one dominated by the flesh (2:15; 10:4). **First man . . . second Man** contrasts the sinful nature that every person inherits with the new righteous nature that comes through Christ.

15:50 Mere **flesh and blood** cannot enter into the glorious existence of an immortal body (vv. 35–49). Something must happen to this *flesh* so that it becomes incorruptible (v. 42).

Photo by Ben Chapman

Just as God raised Jesus from the dead, Paul declared, believers will also be victorious over death through the grace and power of Jesus Christ (1 Cor. 15:50–57).

celestial bodies and terrestrial bodies reflects the Creator's power and will. The varying brightness of the **sun, moon,** and **stars** serves as a good illustration of the differences between the earthly human body and the heavenly human body. All these different celestial and terrestrial objects are evidence that God the Creator can certainly create new resurrected human bodies out of our old bodies.

15:42–44 The earthly body has various weaknesses, while the heavenly body is devoid of these weaknesses. The body from the earth is corruptible, has **dishonor,** is weak, and is governed by natural instincts. The body from heaven is incorruptible, glorious, powerful, and is governed by the spirit energized by God.

15:44–49 natural . . . spiritual: The contrast is not between a material body and an immaterial body, but between a body subject to death and a body that is immortal. The Greek

15:51, 52 we shall all be changed: The teaching here is similar to the teaching given to the Thessalonians (1 Thess. 4:13–18). Whereas the dead in Christ will be raised first, the living believers will be instantly transformed into their immortal bodies when Jesus returns.

15:53–57 The living will receive a body that is not subject to death (v. 50). Satan's apparent victories in the Garden of Eden (Gen. 3:13) and at the Cross (Mark 15:22–24) were reversed by Jesus' death (Col. 2:15) and resurrection. From the vantage point of Jesus' victorious return, **Death** and **Hades** (the grave) have no power over Christians, because Jesus has already conquered both. We participate in His **victory.**

15:58 The Corinthians were to continue **steadfast** in the **work** of Christ, specifically because of the Resurrection. **your labor is not in vain:** All the work that we do for Christ will be rewarded (2 Cor. 5:10; Rev. 22:12).

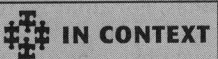 **IN CONTEXT** | **Help for Needy Believers**

Money is powerful. It can bring out the best or the worst in a person. In our drive to gain lots of it or use it for personal comfort and convenience, we can become very cold and manipulative (1 Tim. 6:10). But that ought not to be the way for God's followers.

In 1 Cor. 16, we see that Paul was coordinating a fund-raising drive to help some needy believers. He could have focused on the plight of the recipients. They were Christians in Jerusalem, perhaps suffering from persecution or famine. But instead he concentrated on how the Corinthians should initiate a regular pattern of giving to meet the need (1 Cor. 16:2). Their participation would be an act of loving worship as they met together on the first day of the week.

Paul also pointed out that the transfer of the funds would be carried out by responsible people chosen by the Corinthians themselves (16:3). That guaranteed accountability and integrity. Apparently Paul was quite realistic about the human tendency toward manipulation and greed.

16:1–4 Now concerning: Paul once again addressed a question asked by the Corinthians (7:1, 25; 8:1; 12:1) about giving (Acts 11:29, 30; 24:17; Rom. 15:25–28; 2 Cor. 8; 9). **The first day of the week** was the regular weekly meeting day of the early church. **Lay something aside** expresses the concept of Christian giving in the NT. The OT tithe (altogether coming to about 23 percent) was not adopted by the NT church, though certainly Christ practiced it. NT believers were encouraged to give liber-ally, but never a specified amount or percentage (Rom. 12:8). Paul wanted to make sure that the Corinthians' offering would be collected before he arrived so that he would not need to pressure the people when he saw them (2 Cor. 9:5). **Whomever you approve** refers to the person who would accompany Paul (v. 4) to **Jerusalem** to deliver the gift on behalf of the Corinthian church.

16:5–7 Now I will come to you: Paul had hoped to leave Ephesus soon to visit Corinth,

 **IN PERSON** | **Friends in the Faith**

Paul had once been a dangerous enemy to the followers of Christ. But his dramatic encounter with the Savior and subsequent change of heart brought him into the family of God (Acts 9:1–30). Courageous Christians such as Ananias (Acts 9:10) and Barnabas (Acts 4:36, 37) began to nurture and aid the new believer. He had become a brother.

In the same way, Christ makes believers today into a new family. Having experienced the same gift from God—forgiveness and hope—we are now brothers and sisters in Christ.

Paul acknowledged several of his family of faith as he closed 1 Corinthians:

- *Young Timothy* (1 Cor. 16:10, 11), who needed acceptance and affirmation.
- *Gifted Apollos* (16:12), one of the Corinthians' former leaders (1:12), who was unable to go to them at that time (Acts 18:24–28).
- *Stephanas* (16:15, 16), baptized by Paul in the early days of the Corinthian church; the Corinthians needed to respect him.
- *Fortunatus and Achaicus* (16:17, 18), encouragers of Paul who may have delivered to him the letter from the Corinthians that he was answering with 1 Cor.; like Stephanas, they too needed recognition.
- *Priscilla and Aquila* (16:19), cofounders of the Corinthian work and business partners with Paul (Acts 18:1–4); they now were leading a similar work at Ephesus and sent warm greetings to their brothers and sisters across the Aegean Sea.

Once an enemy, Paul became a true friend, partner, and advocate of other believers. Just as others had once cared for him and his needs, he wrote to the Corinthians of the needs and concerns of his brothers and sisters in Christ.

perhaps even spending **the winter** with the Corinthians. Travel by sea during the winter was hazardous (Acts 27:9–44). Paul eventually did make it to Corinth, but not according to the schedule he planned here. This failure to come caused him trouble later with the Corinthians (2 Cor. 1:15—2:1).

16:8, 9 The opportunities for Paul's ministry **in Ephesus,** a major city of Asia Minor, were great, as was the persecution he endured there.

16:10–12 Though Paul could not leave immediately for Corinth, he wanted to be represented among the Corinthians by his fellow workers. He planned to send **Timothy,** a young man at this time. Paul encouraged the Corinthians to go easy on Timothy, for although he was trustworthy, he was more timid than Paul.

16:13, 14 Watch is often used in the NT to indicate anticipation of some future event (Mark 13:37; Rev. 3:3). Paul's exhortation to **stand fast in the faith** is especially important in view of the susceptibility of the Corinthians to false teaching (2 Cor. 11:3). **Be brave** may also be translated "play the man," emphasizing not only bravery but maturity. Paul's command to do everything **with love** serves as a balance to these strong exhortations.

16:15–18 The household of Stephanas was among the first in **Achaia** to respond to Paul's preaching. **Stephanas, Fortunatus, and Achaicus** probably were the ones who confirmed the bad news brought by Chloe's household in 1:11. They were also probably the bearers of the letter that the Corinthians sent to Paul (7:1).

16:19, 20 The churches of Asia may be those mentioned in Rev. 2 and 3. **Aquila and Priscilla** were tentmakers who had met Paul in Corinth. They followed him to Ephesus and made their house available for the meetings of the church (Rom. 16:3–5). They would have been known to many in the Corinthian church. **a holy kiss:** This custom, adopted by the early Christians, symbolized love, forgiveness, and unity.

16:21–24 my own hand: From this point on, Paul stopped dictating (Rom. 16:22; Gal. 6:11) and completed the letter in his own handwriting. **let him be accursed:** It may seem harsh that Paul would wish God's damnation on those who do not love Jesus. But the acceptance or rejection of Christ is serious business. Those who reject the Lord Jesus are enemies of God (Gal. 1:8, 9). In the next breath Paul desires the coming of our Lord with an Aramaic expression, *marana tha,* meaning "Lord, come."

The Second Epistle to the

Corinthians

SECOND CORINTHIANS IS THE MOST AUTOBIOGRAPHICAL of Paul's letters and probably the most difficult letter that Paul had to write. In previous letters, Paul had exhorted the Corinthian church to correct some abuses that were occurring in the congregation. However, some false teachers in the congregation were antagonized by Paul's rebuke and rejected his warnings. As a result, in this letter Paul was forced to defend his

character, and more importantly his apostolic authority, in the face of slanderous accusations. His defense reveals the trials and tribulations, the problems and the pressures of his itinerant ministry more than any other book in the Bible. Yet like the rest of Paul's letters, Second Corinthians points past Paul's sweat and tears to the power that lay behind his actions and words: the Lord Jesus Christ.

In First Corinthians, Paul had instructed the believers in Corinth to discipline an incestuous member (1 Cor. 5), and to take a collection for the poor saints in Jerusalem (1 Cor. 16:1–4). Titus gave Paul a report that was on the whole encouraging (2:14; 7:5–7). The Corinthians had responded properly to First Corinthians. They had faithfully carried out the discipline necessary (2:5–11). But Titus also informed Paul about the presence of "false apostles" (11:13) who accused Paul of walking according to the flesh (1:12, 17; 10:2), being deceitful (2:17; 4:2; 12:16), intimidating the church with his letters (10:9, 10), unjustly mistreating someone to the point of ruining that person (7:2), and defrauding people (7:2). These false teachers probably pointed out that Paul had not returned

as he promised, and used this as evidence for his duplicity (1:15–17, 23, 24). They even attempted to discredit Paul by charging that he was raising money to enrich himself (7:2; 8:16–23). Inevitably these accusations raised doubts in the minds of the Corinthians about the integrity of the apostle Paul.

Paul wrote Second Corinthians out of his concern for the Corinthian church (7:12). He wanted to offer the church some further instructions concerning the repentant offender (2:5–11) as well as about the collection for the poor saints in Jerusalem (9:1–5). However, Paul's main purpose for writing Second Corinthians was to defend his ministry. Paul's opponents in Corinth had severely attacked him. He wrote this letter to prove that his ministry was sincere and genuine, and to reassert his authority as an apostle of Christ.

Second Corinthians is primarily a personal letter, defending Paul's ministry among the Corinthians and appealing to the factions in the church to reconcile themselves to each other. Yet Paul still uses doctrine to address this church's problems. He speaks of the foundational doctrines of the Christian faith: the Trinity

(1:21, 22; 13:14), as well as the deity (1:12, 19; 4:5), humanity (8:9), death (5:19, 21), and resurrection of Christ (5:15). Paul reaffirms that all believers have been sealed by the Holy Spirit (1:22) and have been given the Spirit as a deposit (1:22; 5:5). The believing Corinthians are in Christ (5:7) and Christ is in them (13:3, 4). They will be resurrected (4:14; 5:1–8) and evaluated at the judgment seat of Christ (5:10), where they will either be ashamed (5:3) or rewarded (5:9, 10). Paul points out that part of the reason for the Corinthians' difficulties and divisions was Satan's opposition to the church. He blinds unbelievers to truth (4:4) and uses every opportunity to divide the believers (2:11). That is why Paul exhorts the Corinthians to lead holy lives, to repent of the sins of the past, and to be reconciled to each other. Thus, in this personal letter defending his ministry and authority, Paul still weaves doctrine into the fabric of his discussion. For Paul, the essence of Christian faith touched on every facet of life, not only divisions and controversies like those that disturbed the Corinthian church.

Second Corinthians begins by identifying the author as Paul (1:1; 2:1). The style of the letter confirms Paul's authorship, as does the testimony of the early church. Some critics theorize that chs. 10—13 were not part of the original letter because the tone is different from chs. 1—9. The spirit of the first nine chapters is joyful and jubilant, while the spirit of the last four is one of sorrow and severity. Many of these critics claim that chs. 10—13 are part of a lost letter referred to in 2:4. However, the final chapters of Second Corinthians are firm, not "sorrowful."

Moreover, no early manuscript or author can be cited to support such a theory. The difference in tone can be accounted for by the change of subject in those chapters.

Paul wrote First Corinthians during the last year of his ministry at Ephesus, on his third missionary journey, probably in the early spring of A.D. 56. Second Corinthians was written shortly after First Corinthians. Thus, the date of Second Corinthians is probably the fall of A.D. 56.

In order to understand the purpose of Second Corinthians, one must know about the background to the letter, that is, what had occurred between the writing of First Corinthians and this letter. Reconstructing that background, however, is complicated.

The issues are: (1) How many visits did Paul make to Corinth before he wrote Second Corinthians (2:1; 12:14)? (2) How many letters had he written (2:3, 4, 9; 7:18)? (3) Who was "the offender" (2:5; 7:12)? There are two basic ways of reconstructing the life and letters of Paul to explain these references. The traditional view takes the references in Second Corinthians to a previous letter to refer to First Corinthians. In this case, the "offender" is the incestuous person of 1 Cor. 5. A more recent interpretation contends that the data in Second Corinthians does not fit First Corinthians; therefore, there must have been another letter written by Paul to Corinth between First and Second Corinthians. Either that letter was lost, or else it is chs. 10—13 of Second Corinthians. Those holding this theory usually maintain that Paul must have visited Corinth briefly between the writing of First and Second Corinthians, based on the word "again"

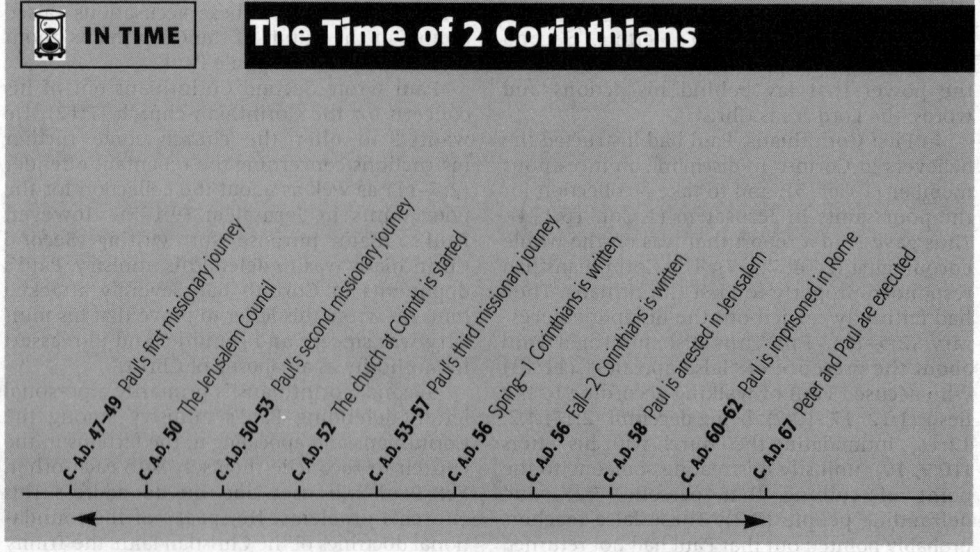

IN TIME **The Time of 2 Corinthians**

c. A.D. 47–49 Paul's first missionary journey

c. A.D. 50 The Jerusalem Council

c. A.D. 50–53 Paul's second missionary journey

c. A.D. 52 The church at Corinth is started

c. A.D. 53–57 Paul's third missionary journey

c. A.D. 56 Spring—1 Corinthians is written

c. A.D. 56 Fall—2 Corinthians is written

c. A.D. 58 Paul is arrested in Jerusalem

c. A.D. 60–62 Paul is imprisoned in Rome

c. A.D. 67 Peter and Paul are executed

in 2:1. This is sometimes called the "painful visit." According to this view, the "offender" was not the incestuous person of 1 Cor. 5, but the leader of a party opposed to Paul.

The traditional view contends that the data of Second Corinthians does fit the facts of First Corinthians. Therefore the "previous letter" is First Corinthians and "the offender" is the incestuous member. According to this view, there was "no painful visit," for the word "again" in 2:1 does not necessarily mean that Paul made a visit between writing First and Second Corinthians. It simply means he did not want to return "in sorrow." The reference in 12:14 and 13:1, 2 to a "third time" does not mean Paul was coming for his third time; it simply means that he was "ready" to come for a third time. He had planned to come (1 Cor. 16:5–9), evidently was ready to come (12:14), and then did not actually make the trip (1:15–17, 23).

Thus, the background of Second Corinthians may be pieced together as follows: Paul founded the Corinthian church (Acts 18:1–17; 1 Cor. 3:6, 10). After eighteen months he departed from Corinth and wrote a letter which is now lost (1 Cor. 5:9). Paul then talked to some members of Chloe's household about quarrels in the Corinthian church (1 Cor. 1:11). Perhaps at this point, Paul sent Timothy on a trip that included Corinth (1 Cor. 4:17; 16:10). Then a committee arrived from Corinth with questions for Paul (1 Cor. 7:1; 16:7). Then Paul wrote the book now called First Corinthians to correct disorders and answer questions from the Corinthian church. Paul probably sent Titus to Corinth with First Corinthians. After sending him, Paul became deeply concerned about how the Corinthians would respond to what he had written. He had called them carnal (1 Cor. 3:1) and proud (1 Cor. 4:18). In the meantime, serious difficulties arose at Ephesus, so he left ahead of schedule (Acts 20:1). He stopped at Troas to preach the gospel (2:12). But because he did not find Titus there and was still eager to hear about the Corinthians, he hastened to Macedonia (2:13). There Paul found Titus. According to an early tradition, Paul wrote Second Corinthians from Philippi.

Outline

Commentary

1:1, 2 Second Corinthians opens the way most ancient letters did: salutation, author, recipients, and greeting. The author was **Paul, an apostle.** His identification with **Jesus Christ** is especially important in this letter because false apostles (11:12–15; 1 Cor. 4:14–16) had opposed him in Corinth and caused confusion in the church. **Timothy** is listed as coauthor. This companion of Paul is not mentioned in the introduction to 1 Cor., presumably because Timothy had already been sent to Corinth (1 Cor. 4:17; 16:10). That he appears here indicates that he has since rejoined the apostle, given his report concerning the affairs at Corinth, and traveled with him to Macedonia. Paul and Timothy wrote this letter to the church **at Corinth** and all believers in **Achaia,** what is today southern Greece. **Grace to you and peace** was Paul's standard greeting. With it, Paul was expressing his prayer that the Corinthians would experience God's favor and the joy that results from being in a proper relationship with the Lord.

1:3 A word of thanks often followed a letter's salutation (vv. 1, 2). **Blessed** expresses adoration and praise. Paul called God the **God**

CORINTH
Greece's center of commerce, transportation, and paganism.

MACEDONIA
Philippi
Thessalonica
Berea
Aegean Sea
Athens
Cenchrea
ACHAIA
CRETE
Area of detail
0   50   100
Miles
N

The City of Corinth

Corinth was a major city of Greece situated on the Isthmus of Corinth between the Ionian Sea and the Aegean Sea. A transportation hub for both land and sea travel, it was also a major center for pagan religions. More than twelve temples have been excavated at Corinth, including the magnificent temple of Apollo, with its 38 Doric columns 24 feet high. The temple of Aphrodite, goddess of love, employed at least 1,000 temple prostitutes. The city had a widespread reputation for gross immorality.

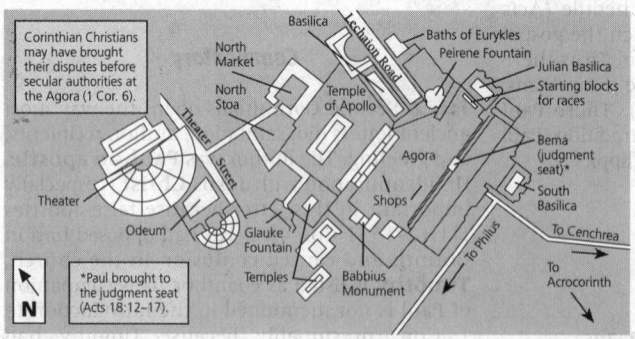

Corinthian Christians may have brought their disputes before secular authorities at the Agora (1 Cor. 6).

Basilica
North Market
North Stoa
Temple of Apollo
Theater Street
Theater
Odeum
Glauke Fountain
Temples
Babbius Monument
Lechaion Road
Baths of Eurykles
Peirene Fountain
Julian Basilica
Starting blocks for races
Agora
Bema (judgment seat)*
Shops
South Basilica
To Cenchrea
To Philus
To Acrocorinth

*Paul brought to the judgment seat (Acts 18:12–17).
N

and Father of Christ. Even though Jesus is God, as the incarnate Son He was dependent on God the Father. Thus, God the Father was His God. **Comfort** here means "exhortation," "encouragement," "cheer." Paul used this word, sometimes translated "consolation," ten times in

the following five verses (vv. 3–7). This is the purpose of our gathering in the church (Heb. 10:24, 25), and it is Paul's subject in ch. 7 (7:12, 13). When they meet, believers should encourage each other in the faith.

1:4 Tribulation means distress or of affliction. God comforts us not only to make us comfortable but also to make us comforters. The comfort that God gives to us becomes a gift we can give to others (7:6; Acts 9:10–19). Our willingness to share it reflects the sincerity of our faith (John 13:35).

1:5 Tribulation (v. 4) is called **the sufferings of Christ.** Christ suffered as a bearer of our sins (1 Pet. 3:18) and as a servant to His disciples (John 13:1–17). Those who follow Christ also will experience the same suffering while they serve (John 15:20), for which they will receive a reward, "a far more exceeding and eternal weight of glory" (4:17).

1:6 Paul's example when **afflicted** encouraged the Corinthians to endure.

1:7 our hope for you: All who take part in **sufferings** for Christ are certain to be rewarded. **Consolation** here means the grace, strength, and deliverance that Christ gives to His servants (Luke 9:23, 24).

1:8 Paul's commitment to Christ and His service did not by any means exempt him from trouble. By **Asia** Paul meant the Roman province in western Asia Minor, present-day Turkey. It is not known exactly where Paul was experiencing this **trouble,** but it was probably at Ephesus. Most likely it was the uproar stirred up against Paul by Demetrius the silversmith (Acts 19:23–41; 1 Cor. 15:31, 32).

1:9, 10 the sentence of death: Paul returns to the theme of death and resurrection several times in this letter (2:16; 4:7–14; 5:1–10; 13:4). Here Paul is probably referring to the life-threatening persecution he faced when he preached the gospel (Acts 14:19, 20).

1:11 As Paul trusted the Lord and as the Corinthians prayed, God delivered him (v. 10).

We should pray for one another so **that thanks may be given.** If many people intercede, many will thank God when He answers. Whenever we face difficulties, we should let others know so they can pray and God can be praised. Answers to **prayer** should always receive public praise, for our Deliverer deserves our adoration.

1:12 Paul's critics accused him of living for his own selfish interest (10:2). They used his failure to return to Corinth as evidence of his lack of sincerity. Paul began the body of this letter by defending his integrity (1:12—2:4). **Fleshly wisdom** refers to selfish interest (contrast with Paul's admonition and Christ's example of humility in Phil. 2:3–8). Paul's **godly sincerity** was **more abundantly** clear to the Corinthians than to others; he spent 18 months with them (Acts 18:11).

1:13, 14 Paul's critics had accused him of being insincere in his letters, of **writing** one thing and doing the opposite (10:10). Paul denied these charges. He meant what he wrote; there were no hidden agendas in his letters.

1:15, 16 Paul had intended to visit the Corinthians (1 Cor. 16:5–7), but he had failed to come. This prompted some of the members of the Corinthian church to accuse him of living according to "fleshly wisdom" (vv. 12, 17). The **second benefit** was the benefit of two visits, one on his way to Macedonia and the other after leaving (v. 16).

1:17 when I was planning this: Paul rhetorically asked: When he made plans to visit the Corinthians, was he joking, guided by self-interest, or inconsistent? The Greek text indicates that these questions expected a negative answer. Paul explained later why he changed his plans (1:22—2:4).

1:18 Before finishing the defense of his personal integrity (1:23—2:4), Paul defended his preaching: it was both true and trustworthy (vv. 18–22). **Our word** is a reference to teaching of Paul (v. 19).

1:19 Paul's preaching was not **Yes and No** at the same time—not inconsistent or contradictory. Instead, his preaching reflected the truthfulness and faithfulness of God, because his teaching was based on the Scriptures and the teachings of Christ.

1:20 All of God's **promises** concerning Christ are true and trustworthy: a **Yes.**

1:21, 22 In the Greek text, **anointed** is connected to **establishes.** God confirmed Paul and his fellow workers by anointing them. This anointing probably refers to special empowerment by the Holy Spirit, similar to the anointing John described in 1 John 2:20, 27. **sealed:** Sealing indicates ownership and security. The *sealing* and the *giving* of the Holy Spirit are also

linked. The Holy Spirit is a **guarantee,** the down payment that there is more spiritual blessing to come and that the believer will receive eternal life.

1:23 Paul had promised to come and use his authority, if necessary, to straighten out the

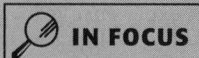

IN FOCUS | **"sealed"**

(Gk. *sphragizo*) (1:22; Eph. 1:13; 4:30) Strong's #4972; guarantee (Gk. *arrabon*) (1:22; 5:5; Eph. 1:14) Strong's #728: The Greek word translated *sealed* here was a technical term denoting a seller's guarantee of the validity of a purchase. As such, God's gift of the Holy Spirit is our guarantee. In the ancient world people commonly branded or marked personal possessions as they sealed letters, with a seal identifying the owner or sender. In this passage, Paul was describing believers as being marked as God's possession with the seal of the Holy Spirit. This seal will remain until we, as God's possession, are completely redeemed (Eph. 1:13, 14; 4:30). Paul often used another term with *sealed,* namely *arrabon,* translated *guarantee.* This Greek term was commonly used for the promissory first installment that guaranteed a full, final payment. The word was also used by the ancients to refer to an engagement ring. As Christians, we have received the Spirit as a first installment, guarantee, and foretaste of the full inheritance yet to be given (Eph. 1:13, 14).

problems at Corinth (1 Cor. 4:21). To **spare** them the pain of correction and give them an opportunity to correct themselves, he did not come. God is patient with us too. But Paul had warned them previously that their weakness, sickness, and even death was due to their failure to correct themselves (1 Cor. 11:30).

1:24 As an apostle, Paul had authority to discipline (10:2), but it was not his place to order the Corinthians around.

2:1 Paul changed his travel plans partly because he did not want to come to Corinth **again in sorrow.** Some have interpreted this verse to mean that Paul had made a painful visit to Corinth and wanted to avoid another one. Although the narrative in Acts does not indicate such a visit, some have proposed that Paul visited Corinth between the writing of the two letters, 1 and 2 Corinthians. However, the text

does not necessarily say that he had made a previous painful visit, only that he did not want his
next visit to Corinth to be in sorrow.

2:2 If there are those in the assembly who
think Paul derived any degree of satisfaction
from his previous visit, Paul assures them that it
inflicted no small amount of hurt to his own
heart. **if I make you sorrowful, then who is
he who makes me glad?** The greatest joy the
minister of the gospel can experience is to see
that his spiritual children are walking in the
truth (compare 2 John 4). Conversely, nothing
is more painful than to have to employ the rod
of correction. Paul derived no joy from that last
encounter and the anxiety is still with him, as
reflected in these verses.

2:3, 4 I wrote: Traditionally commentators
have identified the previous letter to which Paul
refers in these verses as 1 Corinthians. Many

recent commentators believe that Paul is
speaking about a letter written between 1 and 2
Corinthians that has been lost. Some have identified chs. 10—13 as this "lost letter" because the
tone of those chapters seems to match the
description of these verses, a letter of **much
affliction and anguish of heart.**

2:5–11 Paul wrote of someone who had
caused grief. The traditional interpretation has
been that this offender was the incestuous man
of 1 Cor. 5. Lately some commentators have
suggested that the offender may be another
person who had wronged Paul during the
"painful visit" that he made between the writing
of 1 and 2 Corinthians (vv. 3, 4).

2:6 Punishment means "warning," "censure," or "rebuke." This is a reference to the
church discipline Paul had instructed the
Corinthians to use on the person mentioned in

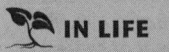 **IN LIFE**   ## Accountability in the Body of Christ

The discipline of a Corinthian believer (2 Cor. 2:6) points to one of the important functions of the
body of Christ—to hold its members accountable for how they conduct their lives. In the case
mentioned here, the censure of the church caused the offender to repent and change his ways,
restoring his spiritual life and bringing joy to the church.

Accountability is easy to talk about but difficult to practice. No one likes to be judged by others. In
modern society it's especially easy to feel that one's personal life is no one else's business. But a study
of Scripture reveals a number of important principles about accountability:

(1) *As believers, we are accountable not only for our actions, but also for our attitudes.* In the per-
formance-oriented work world, evaluations tend to measure results alone—higher sales, greater cost
control, more clients served. Everything is quantitative. But God is interested in our innermost heart.
He looks at the quality of our character. As God told Samuel, "The Lord does not see as man sees; for
man looks at the outward appearance, but the Lord looks at the heart" (1 Sam. 16:7).

(2) *Accountability depends on trust.* To hold ourselves accountable to others is to trust their judgment and to believe that they are committed to the same truths and values that we are. It also helps if
we can sense that they have our best interests at heart. That's why Paul pleaded with the Corinthians
to forsake their divisions and "be perfectly joined together in the same mind and in the same judgment" (1 Cor. 1:10). Without that unity, they would never submit to each other.

(3) *Accountability is directly related to the principle of submission.* Every person must struggle with
the natural tendency toward rebellion against God. Accountability involves allowing others to enter into
that struggle with us. But that means that sometimes we must defer to the judgment or counsel of
another, especially when they challenge us with clear-cut Scriptural truth or the wisdom of personal
experience. Paul told the Ephesians that part of living in the will of the Lord involves "submitting to one
another in the fear of God" (Eph. 5:21).

It's not surprising that participation in the body of Christ would involve accountability, because all of
us experience accountability in many other areas of life. For example, the government holds us
accountable for obeying the law and paying taxes. Likewise, government officials are accountable to
the public for their decisions. Employees are accountable to the boss for their work. Likewise, corporate officers are accountable to stockholders for quarterly financial results. In short, accountability
touches us at home, at work, at church, and even at play.

But our attitudes toward accountability in general ultimately reflect our attitude toward accountability to God. If we are rebellious toward the One who created us and loves us most, how will we be
able to submit to others?

v. 5. It was tough love, but it worked. The man repented.

2:7, 8 forgive and comfort him: The purpose of church discipline is repentance and restoration. Forgiveness should always follow the correction, just as Christ instructed (Matt. 18:15–35). There is no place for vindictiveness; instead the love of Christ is to be expressed through us. Serious consequences are promised to those who fail to forgive. Continuing failure to forgive will bring loss at the judgment seat of Christ.

2:9, 10 in all things: Following Paul's instructions to discipline the offender had proved their obedience. For Paul, obedience was always to Christ and only to Paul as he followed Christ (10:5; 1 Cor. 11:1).

2:11 One of Satan's **devices,** or designs, is to cheat the believer out of true forgiveness. The devil will try to divide the church any way he can.

2:12, 13 Troas was a city on the Aegean coast, where Paul had received his call to preach the gospel in Macedonia (Acts 16:8). Paul **had no rest** because he was deeply concerned about the Corinthians and was looking for Titus, who was on his way back from Corinth. Paul then crossed the Aegean Sea and arrived in **Macedonia,** probably at the city of Philippi.

2:14 When Titus gave Paul good news about the Corinthians (7:5–7), Paul burst forth with a hymn of praise. This interruption became an extended digression. Paul did not resume the story of his trip to Macedonia and his meeting with Titus until 7:5 (verses 2:14—7:4 give a long account of his ministry). **God . . . leads us in triumph:** Paul used the metaphor of the Roman triumphal procession to praise God. When a Roman general was victorious in a war, he led his army and the captives in a parade down the main street. God is the general who has conquered. Paul is one of His officers following in His train. In the Roman procession, priests carrying censers filled with incense followed the conqueror. Paul the priest set forth the fragrance of Christ by preaching the gospel.

2:15 In v. 14 the **fragrance** was the knowledge of Christ; here it was Paul, who was a sweet smell to God for his faithfulness in preaching the gospel. Fragrance is sweet on the basis of faithfulness to the preaching of the gospel, not on success in response. Too often a person's ministry is judged by whether he or she draws large crowds or has spectacular buildings or church productions. God's standards are different. He asks for faithfulness to the truth and to our calling. God alone gives the increase according to His sovereign purpose.

2:16 The leader in a Roman procession was followed by priests (dispensing incense), officers, soldiers, and captives. The **aroma** of the event represented victorious life to the soldiers and slavery or **death** to the captives. In the same way, the gospel message gives life to those who accept it, but it represents death and judgment to those who reject it. The answer to Paul's question **who is sufficient for these things** is given in 3:5. It is God who makes us sufficient.

2:17 Peddling means "to make merchandise of," "to sell." Some people use religion for personal gain. To them the gospel is merchandise to be peddled for profit. Thus, they corrupt or compromise it. This is the first reference in this epistle to false teachers. It may be a subtle reference to Paul's opponents. Paul, unlike some others, was sufficient for the gospel ministry because he was sincere; his motives were pure.

3:1–18 Paul contrasts the life-changing work of the Spirit in the lives of his readers with the letters of **commendation** carried by other religious teachers (vv. 1–6) and with the Law of Moses **engraved on stones** (vv. 7–18).

3:1 Having again declared his sincerity (2:17), Paul asked if he needed a letter of **commendation** to back him up, **as some others** did. The language implies that the false apostles mentioned later in this letter (11:13) had tried to gain acceptance by using such references.

3:2 You are . . . written in our hearts: The Corinthians were Paul's letter of recommendation. These verses do not mean that letters of recommendation should not be used. Paul himself used such letters before his conversion (Acts 9:1, 2) and after (8:22; Rom. 16:1; 1 Cor. 16:10; Col. 4:10). In this case Paul did not need one because he already had one: the believing Corinthians and his ministry among them. Paul's love for the Corinthians was known to all who were acquainted with his ministry. One of the qualifications for ministry is love for people, both God's people and the lost.

3:3 an epistle of Christ: Paul appealed to the Corinthians themselves for proof of his ministry's authenticity. God had changed them—an obvious matter of public record.

3:4 trust: The Greek word means "confidence" (2:14–3:3; Phil. 4:19). Paul was convinced that Christ would make his ministry effective.

3:5, 6 Sufficient means "adequate," or "competent." Paul placed his confidence not in himself or his own abilities but in the Lord. This is the answer to the question asked in 2:16, Who is sufficient? **The letter** is a reference to the old covenant—that is, the Ten Commandments written on stone. The letter **kills** because all break the law, and the penalty is death.

3:7–11 Paul now lists three contrasts between the OT ministry and the NT ministry. Each contrast begins with "if" (vv. 7, 9, 11). In

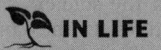 **IN LIFE**   ## The Importance of Image

A s Paul traveled through the cities of the Roman Empire, he always gave thought to how he
would be perceived, but his biggest concern was whether observers would see Jesus in him.
To illustrate this principle, Paul recalled a phenomenon that occurred during the period in
which Moses received the law (2 Cor. 3:7, 13). As Israel wandered through the wilderness, God
revealed Himself to the people through what looked like a consuming fire (Ex. 24:17). But to Moses
He spoke face to face (33:11). This encounter with the living God had such an effect on Moses that
his face would shine with an afterglow whenever he returned to the people. To dispel their fear, he put
a veil over his face to hide the glory that resulted from his proximity to God.

Paul argues that we as believers have an even closer proximity to God than Moses did, for God
Himself lives inside us (2 Cor. 3:8). Thus, when we meet others, they ought to see the glory of God
shining out of us (3:9–11, 18). In other words, they ought to see Jesus.

each case, the NT ministry is said to be more glorious than the OT ministry (vv. 8, 9, 11).

3:7, 8 Paul lists the first of three contrasts
between the OT ministry and the NT ministry
(vv. 7, 9, 11). First, the OT ministry **engraved
on stones** (a reference to the Ten Commandments) was glorious, but the ministry of the
Spirit is **more glorious,** because the glory of the
ministry of the law given through Moses **was
passing away.** Besides, though the law itself is
holy (Rom. 7:12), the ministry of the law is the
ministry of death, whereas the ministry of the
Spirit is the ministry of life (v. 6). The Holy Spirit
produces eternal life.

3:9, 10 The second contrast (vv. 7, 11) is
that the OT ministry was a **ministry of condemnation,** but the NT ministry is more glorious because it is a **ministry of
righteousness.** God declares righteous those
who believe in His Son, and then the Holy Spirit
empowers the believer to live righteously. This
first work of God is called justification, and the
second is called sanctification.

3:11 The third contrast (vv. 7, 9) is that one
ministry is **passing** while the other ministry
remains. The new covenant would supersede
the old covenant established at Mount Sinai
between God and the nation of Israel.

3:12 Paul used **boldness of speech**, a
phrase that means "freedom of speech" or
"frankness." Instead of being fearful or reluctant, Paul was frank and courageous.

3:13 unlike Moses: What follows is an allegorization of the account given in Ex. 34:29–35.
put a veil over his face: The veil was not to
hide the glory but to obscure it. The people saw
his brightness but not directly. Not only did this
veil actually conceal the brightness of the glory
but it also concealed the **end of what was
passing away.** The transience of the glory
which accompanied the old covenant was not

manifestly evident to the children of Israel. And
for Paul this has typical significance.

3:14, 15 The **veil** on the face of Moses
reminded Paul of another veil. As Moses' veil
concealed the fading glory of his ministry, so
there is a veil on the hearts of people concealing
the fading away of the old covenant.

3:16 taken away: Whenever Moses turned
to the Lord, he took off the veil (Ex. 34:34).
Likewise, we find freedom in Christ by looking
to Him.

3:17 the Lord is Spirit: The Holy Spirit is
God Himself, like the Father and like the Son.
liberty: The Spirit gives us freedom from sin,
death, and the condemnation of the law (vv.
7–12).

3:18 All believers behold the **glory of the
Lord** in the Scripture and are **transformed** into
the image of God. Christ is the image of God
(4:4). **glory to glory:** An ever-growing glory. As
believers behold the glory of God in the Word of
God, the Spirit of God transforms them into the
likeness of Jesus Christ. This is a description of
the gradual process of sanctification. If we want
to become like Christ, we must spend quality
time focusing on Him in the Word of God. This
reflection then becomes the raw material that
the Spirit of God uses to form Christ in us.

4:1–3 Paul now draws a conclusion from
what he said about his ministry in 3:4–18. **This
ministry** is the NT ministry (3:6), a ministry of
the Spirit (3:6), of life (3:7), and of righteousness (3:9). It is a glorious ministry (3:7–12) of
liberty (3:17). Paul did not achieve this ministry
by his own human ability but by God's **mercy**
(3:5, 6). **Lose heart** means "to become weary,"
"to become tired," or "to despair." No matter
how difficult the task or how great the opposition, Paul did not retreat in silence but spoke
boldly because he was motivated by the grace of
God (3:12; 1 Thess. 2:1–12). **Hidden** means

"secret." Paul rejected **craftiness**—that is, being unscrupulous or **handling the Word of God deceitfully** (2:17). Apparently, Paul had been accused of being crafty (12:16) and of being deceitful in the way he preached. Paul defended his ministry because it was based on the truthfulness of the Word of God.

4:4, 5 Unbelievers have a barrier to overcome: **the god of this age has blinded** their minds. Because of Satan's deception, sometimes what the world thinks is obviously true is painfully wrong (Prov. 14:12). **image of God:** Jesus Christ is God's Son, and He perfectly reveals God the Father to us. Although human beings have been created in the image of God, through sin they have fallen from a perfect relationship with God. Jesus Christ is restoring believers to what they were originally created to be (3:18; Gen. 1:26). **Christ Jesus the Lord:** Paul's message is that Jesus is divine. **bondservants:** Paul describes himself and those who minister with him as slaves to people. They served the Corinthians **for Jesus' sake.**

4:6 As God **commanded** the **light** to shine in the darkness at creation (Gen. 1:3), so he "turns on" the light in peoples' **hearts** so they can see who Jesus Christ is. People who do not

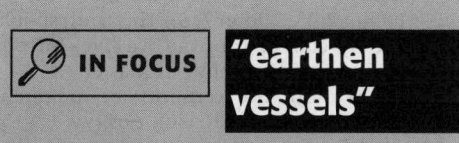

IN FOCUS   **"earthen vessels"**

(Gk. *ostrakinos skeuos*) (4:7; 2 Tim. 2:20) Strong's *#3749; 4632*: This Greek phrase means "clay pots." In ancient times it was a common practice to bury treasures inside clay jars. Two recent discoveries of biblical manuscripts—the Chester Beatty Papyrus and some of the Dead Sea Scrolls—reveal that these manuscripts were hidden away in jars for nearly two thousand years. As these treasures were enclosed in earthen vessels, so the indwelling Christ lives within our earthly bodies.

believe are blinded by Satan (v. 4). But believers see the light.

4:7 The **treasure,** or the divine revelation of Jesus Christ, is in a common clay pot! The reason why God places such a valuable treasure in a lowly vessel is that it might be apparent that the power of the gospel is of God and not the vessel.

4:8 Hard pressed is translated *afflicted* in 1:6. In the Greek text, an identical expression

occurs in 7:5, where it is rendered "troubled on every side." But in 7:5 Paul adds, "Outside were afflictions, inside were fears." Thus, **every side** means "inside and outside." Yet Paul was not **crushed,** a compound Greek word from the words for *narrow* and *space*. **Perplexed** is derived from two Greek words: the word for *no* plus the word for *way*. Thus, *perplexed* means "to be at a loss." One is perplexed when one sees no way out. Yet Paul was not **in despair,** which means "utterly at a loss." As believers, we will face trials. But we must remember that God controls trials and uses them to strengthen His people. God's glory is manifested through broken vessels, through people who endure troubles by relying on His power.

4:9 The picture behind the word **persecuted** is pursuit by someone determined to harm someone else. Paul was not **forsaken** by the Lord, but he was **struck down.** This literally happened (Acts 14:19). In Lystra a crowd stoned Paul, leaving him for dead. But he was **not destroyed,** that is, killed (11:23–33). The Lord spared his life so he could continue to preach the Good News and testify to God's deliverance.

4:10, 11 The expression **carrying about in the body the dying of the Lord Jesus** is explained as being **delivered to death for Jesus' sake.** In his service for Christ, Paul constantly faced death so that **the life of Jesus may also be manifested.** God's deliverance of Paul was evidence that Jesus is alive (1:8–10). For Paul, the death and resurrection of Jesus was a model for his ministry. In his suffering, he participated in Jesus' suffering and death. But Paul's endurance of all types of hardships produced eternal life in those to whom he preached the gospel. In the same way, Jesus' death was merely a precursor to His resurrection to eternal life.

4:12 life in you: Had Paul not been willing to risk death to bring the gospel to Corinth, the Corinthians would not have received eternal life.

4:13 therefore I spoke: Quoting Ps. 116:10, Paul explained why he was willing to risk his life for the gospel. His belief in the gospel compelled him to tell others.

4:14 He who raised up: Paul's belief was focused upon the God of resurrection power, which motivated him to face difficulties, danger, and death for Christ's sake. **knowing:** Paul rested in what he knew about God, not how he felt.

4:15 your sakes: All the suffering that Paul endured (vv. 8–11) brought good to others and glory to God.

4:16 Paul concluded that the Corinthians should **not lose heart,** because God would raise them up with Jesus (v. 14). Here is a great principle. A proper focus on our glorious future with Christ will empower us to endure any kind of trouble. The **outward man** is the physical body, called in this section "the earthen vessel" (v. 7), "the body" (v. 10), "mortal flesh" (v. 11), "earthly house" (5:1), and "tent" (5:1). The afflictions (4:17) Paul encountered (4:8–10) contributed to the perishing process. Those pressures afflicted his physical frame. The inward man is "renewed" on a daily basis. Although the external is degenerating and dying, the internal does not lose heart but is renewed, reenergized, and revitalized.

4:17 Working means "producing," or "accomplishing." Afflictions produce glory. But the glory is out of proportion to the affliction: trials are light and temporary compared to the eternal glory we will receive (Mark 10:30). Paul's focus on the future enabled him to assess problems properly and see how small they were compared to their **eternal** results.

4:18 Look means "to keep one's eye on," "to consider," or "to contemplate." The noun form of this verb means "goal" (Phil. 3:14). In order not to lose heart, the believer needs to shift his or her focus from that which is seen to that which is **not seen,** from temporary problems to the glorious eternal rewards he or she will receive (v. 17).

5:1 Paul explains in more detail what he has just said (4:16–18). The human body, like a demolished house or a dismantled tent, will be destroyed unless death is preceded by the Rapture. The believer's future house, his resurrected body, is a God-made building, which is eternal.

5:2 Suffering makes believers **groan** with longing for their glorious future in heaven (Rom. 8:22, 23).

5:3 not be found naked: Paul looks forward not only to his resurrected body but also to the reward he would receive in the future. What the believer does with the salvation he has been given will determine what will be worn in the kingdom reign with Christ.

5:4 The believer's future experience is called **life,** meaning the full experience of eternal life in Christ. The life experience of the future is being determined by how we invest this life today (4:17).

5:5 guarantee: The Holy Spirit's work in believers' lives can be compared to a deposit or down payment (1:22). The presence of the Holy Spirit assures believers that God has purchased them. They are no longer slaves to sin, but His children. They will receive all the rights and privileges of children of God when their Savior returns.

5:6 Because the believer has God's guarantee (v. 5), he or she can be **confident,** a word that means "to be of good cheer" or "to be of courage."

5:7 Sight means "appearance." Christ is not

physically present, so believers live by faith (John 20:29).

5:8 After the parenthetical thought of v. 7, Paul resumes where he left off in v. 6. He was not only confident (v. 6) that he was going to be with the Lord; he was **pleased** that he would be **with the Lord** after his death. This is one of the passages in the NT that indicates where believers will go immediately after their death; they will be with Jesus in heaven (Phil. 1:23). Jesus' promise to the repentant criminal on the cross next to Him indicates this: "Today you will be with Me in Paradise" (Luke 23:43).

5:9, 10 Wanting to be with Christ (v. 8) produces the ambition to please Him (Luke 19:17). We strive to please the Lord not only because we know we will be with Him (v. 8) but also because He will evaluate our work—**whether good or bad**—and reward us accordingly. The person unconcerned about doing good deeds shows a grave lack of vision. **Appear** means "to make visible" or "to make known." Here it may refer to nothing more than an appearance, such as appearing in court before a judge. Or it may mean believers will stand before the Lord with their true character revealed. **Receive** means "to receive back," "to get an equivalent," or "to get one's due." The believer will be either approved or ashamed (5:3; Luke 19:11–26; 1 Cor. 3:14, 15; 9:27; 1 John 2:28; 2 John 7, 8). This truth should dramatically change the way we live, for our actions will be evaluated by our Master.

5:11–21 Both the certainty of judgment (v. 11) and the **love of Christ** for us (vv. 12–15) motivated Paul to proclaim the transforming (vv. 16, 17, 21) and reconciling (vv. 18–20) work of Christ.

5:11 Therefore indicates that this verse is a conclusion drawn from the previous one. The **terror of the Lord** is the fear of standing before the Lord and having one's life exposed and evaluated. The reality of giving an account to the Lord motivated Paul to **persuade** people, in this context meaning to convince the Corinthians of his sincerity and integrity.

5:12 Paul was defending the integrity of his ministry, not to win the approval of the Corinthians again (3:1), but so the Corinthians could answer those who bragged about their outward appearance, such as the false apostles present among them (11:18). **Opportunity** literally means "a base of operation." This letter would be a foundation or base for those who wanted to defend Paul's authority and ministry in the Corinthian church.

5:13 If Paul was beside himself in exposing himself to danger, it was **for God.** If he was of a **sound mind,** it was for the sake of the Corinthians. The point is that Paul's motive for ministry was for the glory of God and the

☑ IN COMPARISON	The Judgment Seat of Christ
What does it involve?	Only believers will appear before the judgment seat of Christ. The "great white throne" judgment described in Rev. 20:11–15 is for unbelievers.
What is it?	At his judgment seat, Jesus will determine a believer's faithfulness to Him and reward each person appropriately (1 Cor. 3:11–15). This will not be a determination of one's eternal destiny; that issue is decided the moment a person believes in Christ.
Who will preside?	The risen Christ.
Where will it occur?	Heaven (5:8).
When will it occur?	The Scriptures do not specify when this will occur. It is obviously at a time when all Christians are gathered in heaven.
What is the nature of these eternal rewards?	Some commentators consider the various "crowns" mentioned in the NT as the rewards (1 Cor. 9:25; 2 Tim. 4:8; James 1:12; 1 Pet. 5:4; Rev. 2:10). These will eventually be placed before the throne of God (Rev. 4:10). Others point to the parable of the minas in Luke 19:11–27 and see the prospects of serving and ruling in eternity as being directly tied to our faithfulness on earth. We do not know the exact nature of the "new heavens and new earth" or "the kingdom of God." But the Scriptures do seem to imply that eternity will involve serving and reigning (Matt. 25:21, 23; Rev. 22:3, 5).
Why is this doctrine significant?	Knowing that in the future we will stand before Jesus Christ and face a review of our lives should motivate us to live righteously and faithfully in the present.
How can we prepare for our eternal "audit"?	Walk by faith, not by sight (5:7). Develop a longing for heaven (5:8). Make it our chief aim in life to please the Lord (5:9). Keep the judgment seat of Christ in view (5:10).

good of others, not his own glory. Thus, the Corinthians could justly defend him.

5:14 The phrase **the love of Christ** can mean either (1) Christ's love for us or (2) our love for Christ. The last part of the verse indicates that Paul had in mind Christ's love for us. **Died for all** refers to Christ's death for all believers. **all died:** In Christ believers die to sin (Rom. 6:1–14).

5:15 **That** in the phrase "that those" indicates the purpose of Christ's death for believers was that they should no longer live for themselves, but for Him.

5:16 Believers should not evaluate Christ or anyone else **according to the flesh,** that is, the way people typically evaluate each other (v. 12).

5:17 **in Christ:** Paul is presenting the results of Christ's death for the believer and the believer's death with Him (v. 14). Because believers are united with Jesus both in His death and resurrection, they participate in the new creation. That is, they receive the benefits of being

restored by Christ to what God had originally created them to be (Gen. 1:26; 1 Cor. 15:45–49). **All things have become new:** A believer's life should change, because he or she is being transformed into the likeness of Christ (3:18). Instead of living for oneself, a believer lives for Christ (v. 15). Instead of evaluating others with the values of the world, a believer looks at this world through the eyes of faith (v. 16).

5:18 **reconciled us to Himself:** Because of Christ's propitiation, His satisfaction of God's righteous demands, God is now able to turn toward us. God has made us new creatures in Christ and has given us the ministry of **reconciliation,** a word meaning "a change of relation from enmity to peace." We who have been reconciled to God have the privilege of telling others that they can be reconciled to Him as well.

5:19 God could change His relationship toward us because our sins have been imputed (reckoned) to Christ, instead of to us. In other words, God placed our sins on Christ, who knew no sin. His death was in our place and for our sins. If we believe in Jesus, God counts Jesus' righteousness as our righteousness (v. 21). The **word of reconciliation** that has been entrusted to us is to tell all people that God wants to restore them to a relationship with Himself (Rom. 5:8). This is the Good News that everyone needs to hear.

5:20 Ambassadors are more than messengers. They are representatives of the sovereign who sent them. In the Roman Empire, there were two kinds of provinces, the senatorial and the imperial. The senatorial provinces were generally peaceful and friendly to Rome. They had submitted to Roman rule and were under the control of the Senate. The imperial provinces, however, had been acquired later, and were not as peaceful. These provinces were under the authority of the emperor himself. Syria, including Judea, was such an imperial province. To these provinces, the emperor sent ambassadors to govern and maintain peace. Christians have been called by their King to serve as ambassadors in a world that is in rebellion against Him. However, God has given His representatives a message of peace and reconciliation. In this way, believers are God's ambassadors, whose mission is to implore people to be reconciled to God, to listen to the forgiving voice of their Creator.

5:21 no sin: Jesus never did anything wrong. Yet He died for our sins, so that we could be declared righteous, that is to say, justified (v. 19).

6:1 plead: In 5:20, Paul describes God as pleading for people to be reconciled to Him. Here Paul pleads (the same Greek word occurs in 5:20) with the Corinthians also. **in vain:** If believers live for themselves (5:15), they will have received the grace of God, but they will miss out on a heavenly reward for their service to Him (5:10; 1 Cor. 3:15). In Phil. 2:12 Paul encourages those who have been saved to work out or develop their salvation. The Corinthians were failing at this very point. They were saved and stuck, so to speak. They were not continually working out their salvation. Paul was encouraging them to consider their lives and realign them more closely to Christ.

6:2 Paul quoted Is. 49:8 to remind the Corinthians that God was ready to listen to them and to help them. Salvation (Gk. *soterias*) begins with justification, continues through sanctification, and ends with glorification. He would deliver them, if only they turned to Him in faith.

6:3 Offense means "an occasion of stumbling." Paul did not do anything that would cause others to stumble in their faith. **be blamed:** The word means "to find fault with" and implies ridicule. In other words, no one could find fault with Paul's work among the Corinthians.

6:4–10 In many different types of situations (11:23–28), Paul and his coworkers conducted themselves as righteous ministers of God. These verses list the different types of experiences in which Paul and his fellow workers found themselves: (1) vv. 4, 5 describe the suffering they endured; (2) vv. 6, 7 describe how they conducted themselves; and (3) vv. 8–10 describe their paradoxical experiences.

6:4–10 In much patience is followed by three triplets that indicate specific situations in which their endurance was demonstrated. **Sleeplessness** is not insomnia but going without sleep voluntarily in order to spend more time in ministry (11:27).

6:11–7:4 This section is the high point of emotion for the whole epistle. It begins and ends with Paul asking the Corinthians to open their hearts to God, Paul's intense desire to be reconciled with the **Corinthians.** The accusations against him and their own sinful entanglements resulted in the Corinthians withdrawing from him, at least emotionally. He had been

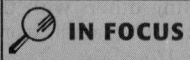 **IN FOCUS** "righteousness of God"

(Gk. *dikaiosune theou*) (5:21; Rom. 1:17; 3:21, 22; 10:3) Strong's #*1343; 2316*: The *righteousness of God* is a righteousness that comes from God; it is God's way of making a sinner right, or just, before Him. Luther defined the *righteousness of God* as a "righteousness valid before God, which a man may possess through faith." Luther said that this righteousness is the first and last need of any sinful individual. The word *righteousness* in Paul's letter to the Romans carries a double sense, and may be labeled both legal and moral. In other words, the word refers to the legal action God takes in declaring believers righteous, but it also refers to perfect righteousness, a characteristic that can only be attributed to God Himself in Scripture and is the lofty standard for human behavior. This lofty standard cannot be achieved by anyone's effort, so God has to act to bring His people into a right relationship with Himself.

totally open to them, but they had not responded to him in the same spirit.

6:11 O Corinthians: Paul addressed his readers by name on only two other occasions (Gal. 3:1; Phil. 4:15). When he did this he was expressing strong emotion.

6:12, 13 The suspicions planted by Paul's enemies had **restricted** their **affections** for Paul (2 Tim. 4:10). Paul had been **open** with the Corinthians (v. 11) and asked that they be open with him.

6:14 unequally yoked: Paul's use of "yoke" comes from Deut. 22:10, where the Israelites were directed not to yoke an ox and donkey together. The ox was a clean animal but the donkey was not (Deut. 14:1–8). Moreover, from a practical standpoint, the two animals had different work styles and different natures. As this relates to Corinth, history reveals that the Corinthians were notorious for their association-alism. They had guilds, societies, or associations for practically everything. Every society had its own idol or protective deity. To fail to do obeisance to this idol would be to anger the god and bring its wrath down on the guild. Thus, the Corinthians tried to go along with this idol even though they did not believe in it. Evidently, the Corinthians were shutting Paul out of their hearts (vv. 11–13) and developing a dangerous affection for the false apostles (11:4, 13; Prov. 4:23).

6:15 The term **Belial** for Satan occurs only here in the NT. It refers to one who is vile and wicked and causes destruction.

6:16 you are the temple: A reference to Lev. 26:11, 12 as well as perhaps other passages such as Jer. 32:38 and Ezek. 37:27, to remind the Corinthians of their relationship with God. Since the Holy Spirit was living in them, they were God's new dwelling place (1 Cor. 6:19).

6:17, 18 Verse 17 is derived from Is. 52:11 with words from Ezek. 20:34 added. Verse 18 is taken from 2 Sam. 7:14 with words added from Is. 43:6. **come out . . . be separate:** Paul was not encouraging isolation from unbelievers (1 Cor. 9:5–13) but discouraging compromise with their sinful values and practices. He was urging them (and us) to maintain integrity in the world just as Christ did (John 15:14–16; Phil. 2:14–16).

6:18 father: This passage is not teaching that God will be a Father and an individual will be His child if that person withdraws from unbelievers. It is saying that since you are a believer and therefore God dwells in you, act like His child and you will enter fully into the experience of God being your Father. He will take care of you.

7:1 Based on the promises that God would receive them with favor (6:17) and provide for and protect them as a father does his children

(6:18), Paul exhorted the Corinthians to cleanse themselves **from all filthiness.** In other words, they were to wash away all dirt from both **flesh and spirit,** meaning those actions and attitudes that came from having the false teachers in their midst (6:14). The point of cleansing is **perfecting holiness.** This means dedicating ourselves to Christ and living righteously (Heb. 6:1).

7:2 With the admonition **open your hearts** Paul resumed the discussion of 6:11–13. **cheated:** Perhaps the false teachers were charging that Paul had collected money for the poor saints at Jerusalem (1 Cor. 16:1–4) but had spent it on himself.

7:3 I do not say this to condemn: Paul was not blaming anyone; he was defending himself.

7:4 Paul was **filled with comfort** and joy because of the report he received from Titus about the Corinthians (v. 7).

7:5 Paul cared very much for the Corinthians. **our bodies had no rest:** Earlier he wrote, "I had no rest in my spirit" in Troas (2:12, 13). **troubled on every side:** The same expression, though translated differently, is used in 4:8 to express Paul's suffering in his ministry.

7:6 The Lord **comforted,** that is, encouraged Paul by allowing him to see Titus again.

7:7 but also by: Paul was encouraged to learn how Titus had been received by the Corinthians and had seen that they were accepting Paul's exhortations.

7:8, 9 Paul regretted that he had to write a "severe letter" to the Corinthians. But since it did cause the Corinthians to repent and turn to God, his sorrow was transformed into joy. Traditionally this **letter** has been identified as 1 Corinthians, but some recent commentators have suggested that it was another letter that Paul wrote after 1 Corinthians, but that has not been preserved (2:3, 4).

7:10 Godly sorrow produces repentance: True sorrow for sins leads to a change of mind and a turning to God. Since repentance means turning to God, who is the Savior, repentance results in spiritual deliverance, or **salvation** (6:2). But the kind of sorrow the world experiences **produces death.**

7:11 sorrowed in a godly manner: Although Paul had been harsh in his previous letter (v. 8), he generously praised the Corinthians for how they responded to his admonition.

7:12 care: Paul wrote the "severe letter" (v. 8) not only to correct the one who had sinned but also to tell the Corinthians that he cared for them (1 Cor. 4:14).

7:13 Therefore we have been comforted in your comfort: The comfort Paul could not find (v. 5), is supplied by the report of the spiritual progress at Corinth.

7:14 I have boasted: Paul bragged to Titus

that they would be obedient to his instructions in 1 Cor. 5. His prophecy came true.

7:15, 16 fear and trembling: We should always receive God's messengers and God's word with reverence and respect. Such attitudes bring blessings from God (Luke 18:13, 14) and increase the **confidence** of Christian leaders in their converts.

8:1—9:15 On his third missionary journey

Paul raised an offering to relieve the poverty of the Christians in Jerusalem and to demonstrate the unity of the Jewish and Gentile churches (1 Cor. 16:1–4; Rom. 15:25–28 and notes. He here encourages the Corinthians to participate in this offering and explains how it will be administered.

8:1 Macedonia corresponds to the northern part of present-day Greece. Paul had estab-

---

 **A Faithful Minister**

In his most autobiographical epistle, Paul defends his ministry, giving us clear insights into the numerous difficulties he faced as a servant of Christ.

Reference	Difficulties Paul Faced	Paul's Response
1:3–7	Tribulation, sufferings	Turned to God for comfort
1:8–11	Life-threatening trouble	Trusted in God
1:12–24	Charges by his opponents that he was unreliable and untrustworthy	Explained his pure motives for changing his itinerary and postponing his trip to Corinth
2:1–4	Emotional anguish over an unpleasant visit with the Corinthian church	Expressed his great love
2:5–12	An unpleasant church discipline situation	Urged forgiveness and comfort for the repentant sinner
2:17; 4:2, 5	Motives suspected	Clarified his sincere motives
4:7—5:11	Trials, persecution, and pressure	Persevered, clinging to the truth that Jesus was being manifested and God was being glorified
6:3–10	Apostolic credentials questioned	Recited his record of faithfulness in a wide variety of difficult circumstances
7:2	Allegations of misconduct	Maintained innocence; stated his affection; pleaded for a more loving response
7:5–7	Conflict, fear, and discouragement	Found comfort in the arrival of Titus and in the news that the Corinthians cared about his situation
8:1–9:15	Having to write about the uncomfortable subject of giving	Cited the sterling example of the Macedonian Christians; courageously challenged the Corinthians to give
10:9–11	Criticism from the false apostles	Refused to compare; sought the Lord's commendation
11:5–33	Comparisons to the false apostles	Set forth his long history of sacrificial service
12:1–10	A "thorn in the flesh"	Prayed for the removal of this ongoing, unpleasant affliction; then realized it was God's grace to him, forcing him to rely on God's strength and not his own

lished churches in the Macedonian cities of Philippi, Thessalonica, and Berea.

8:2–5 The Macedonians were a great example of giving because they gave (1) during **affliction,** (2) in spite of great **poverty,** (3) with great **joy,** (4) beyond their means, and (5) **freely.** In fact, (6) they pleaded for the privilege of sharing their wealth with other believers, and (7) they **gave themselves to the Lord** and to others.

8:6 Titus had begun the collection when he was in Corinth (2:13; 7:6, 7, 13–15). Paul wanted him to complete it.

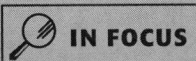

IN FOCUS **"liberality"**

(Gk. *haplotes*) (8:2; 9:11, 13; 11:3; Rom. 12:8) Strong's #572: The Greek term *haplotes* is derived from *haplous,* meaning "single" or "simple." Thus, *haplotes* expresses "simplicity" and "generosity." Combining these two notions together, the word connotes "glad and gracious giving." Paul is the only NT author to use this word. Normally he uses it to describe the way certain believers happily gave generous contributions to other believers who were suffering hardship.

8:7 The Corinthians had an abundance of spiritual gifts and graces (1 Cor. 1:4–7). They had the gift of **faith** (1 Cor. 12:9; 13:2), gifts of **speech,** such as prophecy (1 Cor. 1:5; 12:10), and the gift of **knowledge** (1 Cor. 1:5; 12:8). They were also blessed with **diligence** (7:11) and **love** for Paul (7:7).

8:8–15 Some of the guidelines for grace giving are (1) giving should be motivated by love (8:8, 9), (2) giving should be regulated by willingness and ability to give (8:10–12), and (3) giving should be generated by equality (8:13–16).

8:8 testing: Generosity is the natural result of sincere love.

8:9 The Corinthians did not need a command (v. 8), because the example of Christ taught them about sacrificial giving. **He was rich:** See John 17:5; Col. 1:16. **He became poor:** See Phil. 2:7, 8 for an eloquent description of all that Jesus gave up to come to this earth. **You . . . might become rich** refers to the spiritual riches that Jesus gives to all who place their trust in Him: He offers forgiveness, justification, regeneration, eternal life, and glorification. Jesus purchases us from slavery to sin and makes us children of God. He gives us the right

and privilege to approach God with requests and praise.

8:10-15 Advantage means "profit." Giving now would profit the Corinthians at the judgment seat of Christ (Phil. 4:17). Such giving is an investment (Matt. 6:19–21; Rev. 22:12).

8:16–23 is a letter of recommendation for three men who were coming to Corinth to handle the collection. The first was Titus, who cared about the Corinthians (8:16, 17). The second was a brother with an excellent reputation, who was chosen by the church to accompany Titus (8:18–21). The third was another brother who, like the others, could be trusted (8:22, 23).

8:16, 17 thanks be to God: Paul asked Titus to go, but Titus went **of his own accord,** probably at his own cost. Paul attributed this desire in **the heart of Titus** to God (Phil. 2:12, 13).

8:18 The brother has been variously identified as Luke, Barnabas, Silas, Timothy, John Mark, and others. The churches of the first century knew who he was, but no one today knows.

8:19 Like Titus, he was **chosen by the churches to travel with us with this gift:** He was selected by the churches to assist the apostles in overseeing the collection for Jerusalem. Most likely, he was one of the men cited in Acts 20:4.

8:20-24 These honest men were sent to handle the collection in order to do what was **honorable** before **the Lord** and **men,** and to prevent anyone from blaming Paul for mishandling the funds. Verse 21 is a quotation from Prov. 3:4.

9:1 In this verse, the collection for the Jerusalem believers is called **the ministering to the saints.**

9:2 Their willingness stirred up the majority of the Macedonians to give.

9:3, 4 Paul was in Macedonia when he wrote this letter (2:13; 7:5). When he left Macedonia to come to Corinth, some of the Macedonians would no doubt come with him. He did not want them to find that the Corinthians had not completed the collection (8:11) and thus **be ashamed.**

9:5 The brethren mentioned here are the delegation of 8:16–20.

9:6 reap sparingly: The law of the harvest is referred to repeatedly in Scripture (Prov. 11:24, 25; 19:17; Luke 6:38; Gal. 6:7). Paul applied it to giving. Giving is like sowing seed. The amount of the harvest is determined by the amount of the seed sown.

9:7 Knowing the law of the harvest (v. 6), each believer should give **as he purposes in his heart.** The believer is to give freely and cheerfully, not out of compulsion, and without regret.

9:8 If we give, **God is able** to give us more so that we can perform other good works. In

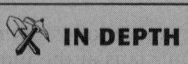 **IN DEPTH** | **New Testament Giving**

The most detailed passage on giving in the NT is found in Second Corinthians (chs. 8; 9). The primary reason that Paul addressed this topic here was that false teachers in Corinth were questioning Paul's motives for ministry. Evidently they were suggesting that Paul was pocketing contributions earmarked for the poor believers in Jerusalem. Consequently the Corinthians, despite their announced willingness to help, had not donated to the cause.

Taking pen in hand, Paul defended his integrity (1:12). Using the churches in Macedonia as his example, Paul gave the Corinthians a wonderful summary of why and how believers ought to give. Here are the highlights of Paul's sermon:

First, who should give? All believers can and should contribute to the cause of Christ. The church at Macedonia was notoriously poor, yet they asked for the privilege of being allowed to give (8:4) out of "their deep poverty"(8:2).

In what spirit should we give? We ought to give willingly (8:12; 9:2) and cheerfully, "not grudgingly or of necessity" (9:7). It is a privilege to share in the work of God. Moreover, it is the appropriate response to God's "indescribable gift," His own Son (9:15).

How much should we give? Nowhere does the NT give us a specified percentage or amount. In this passage, Paul simply exhorts each of the members of the Corinthian church to give "as he purposes in his heart" (9:7). Ideally, our gifts would be "generous" (9:5) and given with "liberality" (9:11). The overall tenor of this passage suggests sacrificial giving. Again, by way of example, the Macedonians, like the poor widow praised by Christ in Luke 21:1–4, gave not merely their "leftovers," but more than they could afford (8:3).

How should monetary gifts be handled? Paul took special care to explain that the Corinthians' contributions would be handled with integrity by Titus (8:16–20, 23) and another unnamed brother (8:22). These were men of the highest character. They were trustworthy and above reproach in the handling of money. We should entrust our church finances to men of this caliber.

Why is giving so important? In Paul's words, it tests the sincerity of our love for God and others (8:7, 8). To paraphrase the words of Christ (Matt. 6:19–21), how we handle material wealth is a barometer of our spiritual health.

What will be the results of our giving? We should not give primarily to get, but Paul makes it clear that giving does lead to abundance. Cheerful givers experience God's love in a special way (9:7). They enjoy the spiritual blessing of participating in a rich harvest of righteousness (9:10).

---

other words, God sees to it that the generous giver will not suffer want. Instead, God generously provides for those who give so that they can continue to do so.

9:9 His righteousness: The good person's acts of generosity. **endures forever:** These acts will bring eternal blessing to those who receive and to those who give (Matt. 25:31–40).

9:10 This verse is Paul's prayer for God's blessing to be poured out on the Corinthians. The words **supply seed to the sower and bread for food** are adapted from Is. 55:10. The latter part of the verse is a reflection of Hos. 10:12.

9:11 enriched in everything: The Christian who is generous in God's work will be blessed for it. God knows our needs and supplies them. **causes thanksgiving:** Those who experience the generous spirit of God's people often, as a result, offer thanks to God Himself (vv. 12–14).

9:12, 13 Giving consummates in a twofold grace. It **supplies the needs of the saints,** and

it is **abounding** ("overflowing") by means of **many thanksgivings to God.** The final result is that God is glorified. It will be noted that this process is cyclical. Out of the riches of God's grace He supplies the needs of the believer. The believer, in an expression of gratitude and liberality, shares of his abundance with others. They, in turn, direct their expressions of thanksgiving ("grace") to God from whom the supply originated. Thus, the cycle is complete. And so Paul says, **they glorify God for the obedience of your confession to the gospel of Christ, and for your liberal sharing with them.** The act of giving is evidence of obedience to the gospel.

9:14 their prayer for you: Paul anticipated that God's grace would lead the Jerusalem Christians to pray for the Corinthian believers and to be deeply concerned about them.

9:15 God's **indescribable gift** is His Son, Jesus Christ. Our gifts can never compare to God's sacrifice for us.

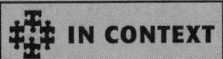 **IN CONTEXT** | **Paul's Collection for Jerusalem**

Paul's collection for the Jerusalem church seems to have originated at the so-called "Jerusalem Council" (Acts 15; Gal. 2:1–10). While the apostles and elders of the council agreed that Paul could pursue his mission to the Gentiles, they asked that he "remember the poor" (Gal. 2:10), indirectly referring to an offering for the Jerusalem church. The collection, therefore, stood at the very foundation of Paul's missionary work.

The offering remained a cornerstone in Paul's ministry. He mentioned the collection in writing to churches at Corinth (1 Cor. 16:1–4) and at Rome (Rom. 15:25–27). He praised churches in Macedonia and Achaia for their generosity in giving (Rom. 15:26; 2 Cor. 8:1–4).

Why would Jerusalem ask for such an offering, and why would Paul keep the offering central to his mission among the Gentiles, the non-Jews? Possibly because he saw his ministry as fulfilling the promises of the Jewish Scriptures, the OT. In the resurrection of Jesus Christ, as Paul believed, the end time had already begun, and through Jesus, God had begun to fulfill the end time promises found in the Scriptures. Among these eschatological promises, especially those in the Book of Isaiah, Jerusalem bore special prominence. Isaiah looks toward a new age centered in Jerusalem, where God unites both Jew and Gentile in worship to Him (Is. 66:16–21).

No wonder the collection was central to Paul's mission. The offering brought the wealth of the Gentiles to Jerusalem, signaling the fulfillment of God's plan for Israel through Jesus. Paul finally returned to Jerusalem with the offering and delivered it to the church there around A.D. 57 (Acts 21:15–17; 24:17).

10:1 I, Paul . . . myself: Timothy and Paul together wrote the first nine chapters of this letter (1:1). In this section, Paul alone addresses the Corinthians. **in presence . . . lowly . . . absent . . . bold:** This is a quotation from Paul's critics in the Corinthian church. They accused him of being weak when present, and bold only in his letters (vv. 9, 10).

10:2 By saying **I beg,** Paul was gently asking the Corinthians to deal with his critics before he came so that he would not have to be stern with them. Paul's critics said that he **walked according to the flesh** and that he was thinking only of himself when he did not come as promised (1:17).

10:3 Walk: Paul concedes that he lived in the flesh (Gk. *sarx*) but insists that he did not war according to the flesh (Gk. *sarx*). He meant

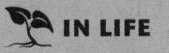 **IN LIFE** | **Aid for the Poor**

By comparison to the many modern Christians who live in affluence, the Corinthian believers would appear poor. Yet Paul described the Christians of Macedonia as living in "deep poverty" (2 Cor. 8:2), so they were much poorer even than the Corinthians. What does Scripture mean, then, when it says that God "has given to *the poor*" (9:9, emphasis added)? And what does that mean for believers today who are relatively affluent?

The word for *poor* (8:9) described someone who toiled for a living, what we would call a day laborer. Such persons were distinct from the truly destitute. The former may have had a difficult life, but at least they were in no danger of losing it. By contrast, the truly poor were in immediate danger of perishing if they didn't receive charitable aid.

Paul described God as dispersing to the poor, the day laborers, not food for survival but seed that they could sow to raise a crop (8:9, 10). He indicated that God would aid the Corinthians so that they, in turn, could aid the completely destitute believers in Jerusalem.

So what does that mean for us as Christians today if we work at relatively stable, well-paid jobs, own our own homes, and manage to salt away at least some money for retirement? Paul would doubtless identify us as rich. We may work hard, but we have disposable income that most first-century Christians could have only imagined.

he did not conduct his ministry in a self-serving way that was opposite of what God is like.

10:4, 5 strongholds . . . high thing: Overlooking ancient Corinth was a hill 1,857 feet high. On top of it was a fortress. Paul used that imagery as an illustration of the spiritual warfare he waged. He destroyed strongholds, cast down towers, and took captives. The fortress,

---

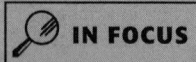 **IN FOCUS** **"service"**

(Gk. *leitourgia*) (9:12; Phil. 2:17, 30; Heb. 8:6) Strong's #*3009*: This term indicates "public ministry" or "official duty." The related word *leitourgos* is used frequently in Greek literature to designate a man who performed some public service (Rom. 13:6). In general, it means a public servant or administrator. Paul used *leitourgia* in connection with the service of those who labored to benefit the church.

---

towers, and captives represent the **arguments,** thoughts, and plans that Paul was opposing. Paul cast down all rationalizations. He took captive **to the obedience of Christ** every perception and intention of the heart that was against God. Our actions reveal our thoughts. We should not cling to thoughts that do not conform to the life and teachings of Christ. Paul did not walk according to the flesh or his worldly desires; instead he conquered the flesh. He explains his strategy in 1 Cor. 9:24–27: "I discipline my body and bring it into subjection."

10:6 After Paul destroyed strongholds, cast down towers, and took prisoners, he was ready to punish or "do justice" to the **disobedience** of the "some" (10:2).

10:7 In this context, being **Christ's** means more than merely belonging to Him. It means being His servant or His disciple (v. 8).

10:8, 9 Paul had **authority** as an apostle **for edification,** a word that means "building up." His exhortation in his letter was aimed at correcting abuses, not the **destruction** of the church. The word **destruction** means "tearing down." Paul repeated his authorization at the end of his letter (13:10).

10:10 they say: Paul spoke simply so that the power of God would remain evident. He did not use complicated rhetorical techniques to sway his audience. His critics at the Corinthian church had turned his simple, unpretentious style against him (11:6; 1 Cor. 1:17; 2:1–5).

10:11 On the contrary, he intends to demon-

strate that his actions will correspond to his words. **Such we will also be in deed when we are present.** He does not give empty threats.

10:12 They, Paul's critics, commended themselves (3:1), measured themselves by their own personal opinions, and compared themselves with others. Contrast Paul's advice to esteem others above oneself (Phil. 2:3, 4).

10:13–15 Paul boasted only within the **sphere** of ministry God had given him, but that sphere included the Corinthians. By implication, Paul's critics were boasting of what they had not worked at or cultivated, perhaps the results of Paul's ministry in Corinth.

10:16 regions beyond you: In the Book of Romans, which Paul wrote around this time, he said his ambition was to preach the gospel in Spain (Rom. 15:24).

10:17 The Christian leader does not **glory** in his own achievements, but **in the Lord** and what He has done.

10:18 Paul began this section by saying he was not going to place himself among the group that commended themselves (v. 12). The reason he would not was that **the Lord** would commend Him as a faithful worker (1 Cor. 4:5). Throughout this passage, Paul has been very careful to boast only in the Lord and His work in order to establish his credentials as an apostle to the Corinthians.

11:1–15 Paul boasts about his financial policy. He gives three reasons for this boast: (1) He is deeply concerned about them (11:2, 3). (2) They seem willing to endure those who preached another gospel (11:4). (3) He is not inferior to the most eminent apostles (11:5, 6).

11:1 Paul must cite some of his own virtues in order to counter the criticisms against him. To him this boasting of self was **folly,** even though in this case a necessary self-defense.

11:2 Paul loved the Corinthians and was legitimately **jealous** because, as their spiritual father (1 Cor. 4:15), he had **betrothed** them to Christ and wanted to present them to Him as a **chaste virgin.** He did not want them corrupted by false teachers (vv. 3, 4).

11:3 Paul was afraid that Satan would deceive them, causing their minds to be corrupted or turned away from the simplicity that is in Christ. The Greek word translated **simplicity** is used in 2 Corinthians of sincerity (1:12) and generosity (8:2, 9). The Corinthians had a sincere singleness of heart toward Christ, which expressed itself in generosity. If Satan could get them to believe something not true, he would destroy their genuine attitude toward the Lord. One practical effect would be to kill their commitment to completing the collection. We should never underestimate the strategies of the great deceiver. The best antidote to his influ-

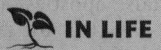 **IN LIFE** | **Paul's Defense**

I speak as a fool" (11:23). These words jump out of the pages of 2 Corinthians; they seem out of place in the Bible. Why would an apostle speak foolishly? A closer look reveals the reason behind Paul's words. The church at Corinth had been infiltrated by insidious false teachers. Although no one knows what philosophical or theological group these false teachers belonged to, we can ascertain some of their beliefs from Paul's two letters to the Corinthians. Evidently they were a group who prided themselves on their Jewish heritage (11:22). This group may also have held to what some have called an "incipient Gnosticism." They placed value on spiritual knowledge and experiences (1 Cor. 8:1) that were only accessible to gifted teachers, perhaps those who were especially skilled in Greek rhetoric (11:6). These "false teachers" were not only slandering Paul; they were denying his authority (12:11) and the truthfulness of what he preached. Some have postulated that there were several different groups that opposed Paul. That may have been the case, for Paul speaks of several different factions in the church (1 Cor. 1:12, 13).

To counter the accusations of his opponents, Paul took great pains to present his apostolic credentials. He opened his life and ministry for all to review. But he was doing more than defending himself; the great apostle wrote with an additional goal in mind. This was to warn the Corinthians of the dangers the false teachings posed. Thus, Paul reluctantly painted a stark contrast between his own ministry and that of his rivals. According to Paul, these false teachers preached "another Jesus" and a "different gospel" (11:4). He regarded them as "deceitful workers" (11:13). Unlike Paul, these impostors collected fees for their services (11:7–9). And unlike Paul, they enjoyed comfortable, easygoing ministries. To defend himself, Paul was forced to "boast" in his ministry. But his boast was unusual, for it was in his weaknesses and suffering. He did not boast of his own accomplishments, but in the troubles and difficulties that clearly showed the power of Christ in his life (12:9).

Many centuries later, the cast of characters has changed, but the story remains the same. The church continues to be infiltrated by those who advocate unbiblical ideas. Many of these present-day "false teachers" appear to be very sincere. They speak with great passion and eloquence. Their ideas seem to make perfect sense. But we must exercise extreme caution. The lucrative potential of modern mass communications has attracted hucksters who tickle the "itching ears" (2 Tim. 4:3) of their audiences in an attempt to profit personally. Every message must be weighed against the Word of God.

And what is a church body to do if it detects false teachers in its midst? On this issue, the NT is clear: Those who foster division within the church by persistently advocating unbiblical beliefs are to be removed from fellowship (6:14; Rom. 16:17, 18; 1 Tim. 6:3–5; Titus 3:9–11; 2 John 9–11). There is to be no toleration. When unaddressed, false doctrine is like a cancer that permeates a body, weakening it, and ultimately bringing about its demise.

ence is to focus on Christ, the light that exposes the darkness.

11:4 Another Jesus would be one who was a man but not God, or crucified but not risen. **A different spirit** would be one of fear, not faith (4:13)—of bondage, not freedom (3:17; Gal. 5:1). **A different gospel** would be one of law and not grace, one of works and not faith.

11:5 Some take the **eminent apostles** as a sarcastic reference to the false apostles in Corinth (v. 13). Others believe that Paul was comparing himself here to the genuine apostles of Christ, as he did later in the book (12:11, 12).

11:6 By **untrained in speech,** Paul meant he was not schooled in professional rhetoric. This does not mean that he was a poor speaker, only that he was not trained in Greek oratory.

He did not lack **knowledge.** He had received direct revelation from the Lord (Gal. 1:11, 12).

11:7, 8 free of charge: In Paul's day, professional philosophers and teachers in Greek society charged for teaching. Paul did not. He labored (1 Thess. 2:9) and received support from other churches. Those who preach the gospel should make a living from the gospel (1 Cor. 9:14). Although Paul had the right to take money from the Corinthians, he chose not to do so in order to demonstrate his integrity (1 Cor. 9:12).

11:9 The brethren who came from Macedonia were probably from Philippi (Phil. 4:14–18).

11:10 Paul's **boasting** was that he preached without charge (vv. 7, 8).

11:11 Paul poses the question as to why he did not take money from them. He rejects the suggestion that it was because he did not love them.

11:12 Paul did not accept money from the Corinthians because he did not want to give his critics **the opportunity** to put themselves on the same level as himself.

11:13 Paul's critics apparently called themselves **apostles of Christ,** but Paul said they were **transforming themselves.** The word means "to change in appearance," "to disguise," or "to masquerade." They were false teachers.

11:14, 15 And no wonder: If Satan, the prince of darkness, can disguise himself as an angel of light, then his servants, the ministers of evil, can disguise themselves as **ministers of righteousness.** Satan's main tool is deception.

11:16 Also indicates that his opponents were boasting.

11:17 Not according to the Lord means "not according to the Lord's standard." This kind of boasting was not characteristic of the Lord. Jesus Christ was an example of humility, not boasting (Phil. 2:5–11).

11:18, 19 The false apostles were boasting **according to the flesh,** that is, they measured themselves by their own standards rather than by God's. Unfortunately, the Corinthians were listening to them (vv. 19, 20).

11:20 The Corinthians were doing more than just listening. They were willing to put up with being enslaved, being consumed, being taken advantage of, being lorded over, and being insulted.

11:21 Paul's critics had accused him of being weak (10:10). He sarcastically said that he was **too weak** to rule the Corinthians harshly as the false apostles had done.

11:22–12:10 This section is sometimes known as the "Fool's Speech" (11:23; 12:6, 11). Paul boasts of his heritage (11:22), of his suffering as a minister of Christ (11:23–33), and of his spiritual experiences (12:1–10). Yet all of these things point out how God's strength was manifested through Paul's weakness (12:10).

11:22 So am I: Paul's adversaries were Jewish and apparently felt that this made them superior not only to Gentiles but also to Greek-speaking Jews. Paul boasted that he was just as Jewish as they were.

11:23–33 Paul's long list of problems includes physical suffering, long and difficult travel, toil, and weaknesses. He suffered profoundly for following Christ. Anyone who ever imagined that the Christian faith always leads to health, wealth, and comfortable circumstances has forgotten Paul. This apostle was under no such delusions. He knew very well that faithfulness to God brings difficulty, not ease (12:9, 10). Yet temporal difficulties for the cause of the gospel bring their own eternal reward.

11:23-26 Paul's opponents were not **ministers of Christ.** They were "false apostles" (v. 13), "ministers of Satan" (v. 15). But for the sake of argument, he responded to their claim as if it were true. **I speak as a fool:** Paul was hesitant to brag about his spiritual "accomplishments," because he knew that only God had made his preaching and service effective. He was merely God's instrument, and God was the One who deserved the glory. Paul's boast was in the Lord (10:17).

11:27 Hunger and thirst means involuntarily going without food and drink; **fastings** means voluntarily going without food for the sake of the ministry (6:5).

11:28, 29 Paul's pastoral anxiety for **all the churches,** especially for the weak, climaxes his list of trials. He cared for the **weak** so deeply that he identified with their weakness. He was indignant with those who caused others to **stumble** into sin.

11:30, 31 Infirmity means "weakness." Paul explains his weakness further in 12:7–10.

11:32 Aretas the king: Aretas IV (9 B.C.–A.D. 40), the father-in-law of Herod Antipas, was king of Nabatea, a kingdom whose capital was Petra. Nabatea included the city of Damascus before the city was incorporated into the Roman province of Syria. Aretas was able to appoint a governor over Damascus because the Emperor Caligula (A.D. 37–41) gave Aretas control over the city.

11:33 Escaping from Damascus **in a basket** was Paul's example of boasting in his weakness (v. 30).

12:1 Paul prepared to boast about **visions and revelations** he received from God, possibly to counter similar claims by the false teachers; but he set them in contrast to the trials he had suffered in his ministry (vv. 7–10).

12:2 It becomes apparent later in the passage (vv. 5–7) that Paul was writing here about himself, but he modestly presented this experience about **a man in Christ** as if it had happened to someone else. Paul wrote 2 Corinthians in A.D. 56; **fourteen years** before would have been A.D. 42, probably when he was in Antioch (Acts 11:26). **the third heaven:** It was common to speak of three "heavens": The first is the atmosphere where the birds fly; the second is the place of the sun, moon, and stars; the third is where God dwells.

12:3, 4 Heaven (v. 2) is here called **Paradise.** This experience should be compared to others in the Bible. God came down and met Moses on Sinai. Moses and Elijah came down from heaven to meet Christ. Peter, James, and John saw Christ glorified on the Mount of Transfiguration. John saw visions of the heavenly throne. And Paul is said to have been transported to heaven and returned. The experience probably helped Paul to endure suffering for the cause of Christ. Yet Paul never placed the focus of his message on this experience; instead he always preached Christ crucified (4:1–5).

12:5 Of such a one (Gk. *hyper tou toioutou*, "regarding such a one"). Again, the direction of Paul's boast is not toward himself but in regard to the experience the Lord afforded him. **I will boast:** Such a divine favor and privilege justifies his response. **Yet of myself I will not boast, except in my infirmities:** Paul is careful to keep the attention of his readers upon the true object of his boast.

12:6 sees me to be: It is easy to claim a spiritual experience but others can verify our faith only by observing our lives. Paul wanted to be evaluated by his words and deeds.

12:7 Thorn means "splinter," "stake," or "something pointed." **Flesh** can refer to the body or to the sinful nature. Three basic suggested interpretations of the thorn are as follows: (1) If flesh is a reference to the body, then it is a physical ailment like an earache, headache, eye trouble, epilepsy, or recurrent fever. (2) If flesh is a reference to the fallen nature, then the thorn could be a temptation. (3) If the expression is figurative, it could refer to persecution or opposition. Most commentators interpret it as a physical ailment. Many suggest that it was eye trouble, on the basis of Gal. 4:15. **messenger of Satan:** God permitted Satan to afflict Paul as He did Job (Job 1; 2). **Buffet** means "to strike with the fist" (Matt. 26:67). Paul's thorn was a painful, humiliating experience given to prevent pride.

12:8 pleaded: I argued my case, entreated the Lord.

12:9 infirmities . . . power: When believers are without strength and look to the Lord (v. 8), He provides power by His grace.

12:10 Paul not only boasted about his weaknesses (v. 9), he said **I take pleasure,** a word meaning "to think good," "to be well-pleased" in them. In Paul's weaknesses, Christ's power was made more apparent to others. It would bring praise to the only One who deserved it.

12:11 The Corinthians **compelled** Paul to boast because they listened to the false apostles (11:4) and were taken in by them (11:12).

12:12 When Paul established the church in Corinth, he performed **the signs of an apostle,** miracles, or supernatural evidences that proved his authority as an apostle (Acts 14:3).

12:13 For what is it in which you were inferior to other churches: In what respect do you find your church handicapped, for not having been founded by one of the other apostles (1 Cor. 1:6, 7)? **Except that I myself was not burdensome to you:** The only fault of his ministry was that he showed them preferential treatment. Against such ingratitude Paul's irony deals a mortal blow. Then, as though the blade did not penetrate enough, he gives it an additional twist with the words, **Forgive me this wrong.**

12:14 for the third time I am ready to come: Paul's first visit to Corinth was on his second missionary journey (Acts 18:1–18). Because of Paul's mention of a "painful visit" in 2:1, some consider Paul's second visit as occurring some time when he was staying in Ephesus and before he wrote this letter (Acts 19:1–14). Others discount a second visit before this time. They insist that *ready* in this verse indicates that Paul had prepared to come to Corinth, but did not make the trip (1:15, 16, 23; 2:1–4). He promised not to be **burdensome,** that is, to take financial support from them.

12:15 for your souls: For your total well-being. It sometimes seems that the more we pour out ourselves in Christian **love** for some people, the less we are **loved** by them. But Paul did not stop loving the Corinthians even though some did not return his love.

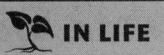 **IN LIFE** | ## Strength Through Weakness

Our world prizes strength—the physical strength of athletes, the financial strength of companies, the political strength of office-holders, and the military strength of armies. But Paul put a new twist on the notion of strength: weakness can make a person strong (2 Cor. 12:7–10).

Most of us would have no problem with God using our natural areas of strength, such as speaking, organizing, managing, or selling. But suppose He chose instead to use us in areas where we are weak? Moses claimed to be a poor speaker (Ex. 4:10), yet God used him as His spokesman on Israel's behalf. Peter tended to be impulsive and even hot-headed, yet God used him as one of the chief architects of the early church.

Weakness has a way of making us rely on God far more than our strengths do.

12:16, 17 Earlier Paul said he was "not walking in craftiness" (4:2). He also pointed out that Satan was deceitful (11:3) and that the false apostles were like Satan (11:13, 14). Now he sarcastically echoes his critics' charge that he was **being crafty.** But how did he trick them?

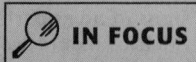 **IN FOCUS** **"apostle"**

(Gk. *apostolos*) (1:1; 12:12; Matt. 10:2; Acts 2:37; Rom. 1:1; Heb. 3:1) Strong's #652: The Greek word simply means "sent ones." Out of Jesus' many disciples, He selected twelve to be His apostles. These were the men who were sent by Jesus to take His message to the world and then raise up churches. Paul also became an apostle by the appointment of the risen Christ, who encountered Paul on the road to Damascus (Acts 9). Paul's apostleship was accompanied by a great deal of suffering; and then to add to it, some false teachers in the Corinthian church doubted his authority. Thus, in 2 Corinthians, Paul repeatedly defended the genuineness of His apostleship.

He tricked them into not supporting him. Through sarcasm, Paul was vindicating himself against the charge of both trickery and fraud.

12:18 Apparently **Titus** was being implicated through the false apostles' accusations because Paul had recommended Titus for the collection task (8:16, 17). However they did not have any evidence against Titus. He was above reproach.

12:19 excuse ourselves to you: Paul was not trying to justify himself before the Corinthians; **God** was his Judge. He only

wanted to do everything for their spiritual upbuilding.

12:20–13:10 Paul explains in detail exactly why he wrote. What he has to say can be outlined by the verbs that he uses of himself: (1) He feared (12:20), (2) he mourned (12:21), (3) he would not spare (13:2), (4) he prayed (13:7), and (5) he wrote (13:10).

12:20 as I wish . . . as you do not wish: If Paul did not find the Corinthians living Christlike lives, he would have to discipline them; then they would not be happy with him. **Contentions** and other unchristian actions listed arise from self-seeking and pride. **backbitings:** Criticizing people behind their backs; slandering their characters.

12:21 humble me: Paul would be humbled if his converts were not living as they should. Their conduct will cause him to **mourn** for them, not boast about them. Instead of coming in joy (3:2) he would be coming in sorrow (2:1–3). **Uncleanness** describes the types of sexual immorality in which the Corinthians had indulged before their conversion. Paul perhaps feared that some had again become involved in these sins and had not repented of them.

13:1 The third time has been interpreted two different ways. Those who hold that Paul had visited Corinth twice before writing this letter take this statement at face value, that Paul had been there twice and was now ready to come a third time. Those who say that Paul had been to Corinth only once point to 12:14 and say that he was prepared to come again but did not actually do so.

13:2 told you before: In 1 Corinthians, Paul warned against sexual immorality (1 Cor. 6:12–20). By writing this letter, he was warning them a second time (12:21). **Not spare** means he would confront them if necessary.

13:3 Paul would confront those who were sinning (v. 2) since the Corinthians were

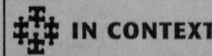 **IN CONTEXT** **How to Use Authority**

I f you exercise leadership among other believers, you'll want to study carefully Paul's comment about his authority (2 Cor. 13:10). Like many of us, Paul liked to be in charge, and he felt frustrated when people failed to follow his lead, as the Corinthians had. As an apostle, he had spiritual authority over them, which at times led him to deal severely with them (1 Cor. 4:21; 5:5; compare Titus 1:13).

But it's important to notice how Paul exercised his authority, especially as he grew older in the faith. He didn't lord it over others or try to use his authority to personal advantage. Nor did he abuse his power by using it to work out his own anger. Instead, he recognized that spiritual authority is given "for edification and not for destruction" (2 Cor. 10:8; 13:10), for building others up, not for tearing them down.

seeking **a proof of Christ speaking** in him. Apparently Paul's critics claimed that an apostle should be a strong individual. Paul was saying that when he came again he would be strong.

13:4 For indicates that Paul was going to explain how Christ, who is strong, could be speaking through Paul, who was weak. As Christ appeared to be weak when he was crucified, but was raised by **the power of God,** so Paul was weak, but by the power of God he would live with Christ in strength toward them. Paul was not speaking of the future resurrection but of his next visit.

13:5 The Corinthians had been seeking proof of Christ's speaking in Paul; he told them to examine themselves to see if they were **in the faith** (1 Cor. 16:13; Titus 1:13). Paul did not doubt that they were true believers (1:1, 24; 7:1; 8:1; 12:14). He wanted them to ask themselves whether they were walking according to the gospel that they professed. He wanted them to apply the same standard to themselves that they were applying to him.

13:6 But I trust that you will know that we are not disqualified: Regardless of how the Corinthians came out in the test, they are to be assured that the apostle was genuine.

13:7–9 Paul prayed they would **do no evil,** which is probably a reference to the sins listed in 12:20, 21, and that they would be made **complete.** The Greek word for *complete* was used to describe the setting of bones and the reconciling of alienated friends. Paul was praying that there would be reconciliation of the divisions (12:20), and restoration. If his prayer was answered, he would **seem disqualified,** for he would not have to exercise his apostolic authority to discipline them.

13:10 I write: Paul confronted the Corinthians on paper so that he would not have to do it in person (v. 2; 10:11; 12:20).

13:11 Here, as in other passages, **farewell** no doubt means "rejoice" (Phil. 3:1; 1 Thess. 5:16).

13:12 fellowship: This is what Paul desired for everyone in the church. They should love and enjoy one another, not fight and do battle with one another (12:20). They needed grace, not self-seeking; love, not anger; communion, not contention.

13:13 All the saints: The other Christians in the place from which Paul was writing.

13:14 Paul's concluding benediction invokes the blessing of the triune God: **grace** from **the Lord Jesus Christ** (8:9), the **love of God** (v. 11), and the **communion of the Holy Spirit.** At the end of his letter, Paul identifies the solution to many of the Corinthians' problems. The Holy Spirit, who dwelled in each of them, could empower them to live righteously. Furthermore, the Spirit could reconcile them to each other. They could love and encourage each other instead of fighting each other (12:20). They needed God's grace, not selfishness; God's love, not anger; and communion, not conflict.

The Epistle to the

Galatians

---

*I*N THE WHOLE BIBLE, THERE IS NO MORE passionate, comprehensive, yet concise statement of the truth of the gospel than Galatians. Salvation is through faith in Jesus Christ alone (2:16; 3:11, 12). No work can earn salvation. Paul's succinct refutation of the Judaizers in this letter has transformed the lives of many—from Martin Luther to John Wesley. In general, people want to earn their salvation by

works that can easily be identified. In this letter, Paul reveals the arrogance of such thinking. It amounts to a desertion of the truth of the gospel and a turning away from God (1:6). We can stand justified before God only through faith in Jesus Christ; nothing else will save us.

Apparently Paul became aware of a perversion of the gospel of grace that was actively infecting the Galatian churches. The false teachers who had come to Galatia since Paul's ministry there were advocating salvation by "the works of the law"—that is, by keeping the law. Specific emphasis was placed on the Jewish rite of circumcision.

Paul's letter to the Galatians was a swift and decisive attempt to counter this message, which was a different gospel. Paul had to convince his "little children" in the faith, whom he had evangelized personally, that the new teaching was in fact a distortion of the gospel of Christ. In his argument Paul reasserted his authority as an apostle, which apparently had been minimized by the Judaizing teachers. Paul wrote not out of anger, but out of love. He saw the Galatians leaving the correct path by their additions to the gospel message, and he

loved his fellow believers too much to allow them to go astray.

Galatians contains the three standard elements of a typical first-century letter: introduction (1:1–5), body (1:6—6:10), and conclusion (6:11–18). However, Galatians differs from many of Paul's other letters. For example, most of Paul's other letters contain an introductory thanksgiving section that serves as a prologue (Phil. 1:3–11). The startling absence of such a thanksgiving at the beginning of Galatians probably indicates the severity of the situation in Paul's eyes. There is virtually nothing for which Paul can be thankful, since some of the Galatians were abandoning the gospel they had once embraced. Likewise, the letter contains no concluding greetings, whether long, like Rom. 16:3–23, or short, like 2 Cor. 13:12, 13. There is only a terse benediction and concluding salutation (6:16, 18).

If there is one repeated phrase that summarizes the subject of Galatians, it is "the truth of the gospel." Unlike Romans, which presents the gospel as the answer to universal human sinfulness (Rom. 3:23; 6:23), Galatians clarifies the gospel message against the subtle but deadly danger of works salvation. No sinful person has ever been granted eternal life based on works. What is more, everyone who lives by such a confidence in works is "cursed," because no one can perfectly obey the law (3:10). Thus, to add works, rituals, or the law to the message of what it takes to become a Christian is to overturn the Good News. The proper place of the law is to convict us of our sin, demonstrating the urgent need for the redemption provided by Jesus Christ.

What then is the basic gospel that Paul goes to such lengths to clarify and safeguard? The only way a person can be justified before God is by faith in Jesus Christ (2:16). Paul emphasizes this point over and over. Faith in Christ, nothing more and nothing less, is the proper response to the gospel. This emphasis on faith is not about the historical dimension of the gospel that is open to reasonable inquiry: Jesus perfectly kept the Law of Moses (4:4), died on the Cross (2:20), and rose from the dead (1:1). Rather, Paul underscores faith in Christ because the controversies in Galatia raged around the reception of the gospel in the lives of new believers.

Paul also addresses themes dealing with the Christian life, or living out the new freedom the believer possesses in Christ. Between the extremes of legalistic sanctification and hedonistic license, Paul charts a middle course of "faith working through love" and the power of the Holy Spirit (5:5, 6). Thus, not only is justification by faith alone, but so is sanctification.

Paul variously describes this life of faith as walking in the Spirit (5:16, 25), being "led by the Spirit" (5:18), producing "the fruit of the Spirit"

(5:22, 23), and sowing "to the Spirit" (6:8). Concretely, "faith working through love" (5:6) expresses itself in love for neighbors, especially other believers, and in bearing one another's burdens (5:14; 6:2, 6). The ever-present danger is that rather than relying upon the power of the Spirit, the believer will start displaying the corrupt "works of the flesh." Works can be truly good only when they are accomplished in the power of the Holy Spirit given to those who place their faith in Christ (6:7–10).

The writer of Galatians identifies himself as Paul (1:1). He claims to be an apostle, and then goes on to argue at length for the apostolic authority behind his gospel message. Much of the personal information he gives in the course of his defense corresponds to the narratives about Paul in the Book of Acts, as well as to the autobiographical material in Phil. 3:4–6. The use of the Old Testament in chs. 3 and 4 fits Paul's rigorous training in Judaism. Finally, the theology presented in this letter corresponds perfectly with the theology Paul expresses in his other writings, notably the Epistle to the Romans.

Paul addresses his letter "to the churches of Galatia" (1:2) and to readers he expressly calls "Galatians" (3:1), but it is not easy to determine what this means precisely. At the time Paul was writing, the word *Galatians* could be used with an ethnic or with a political meaning.

To a great extent, assigning a date for Galatians depends on making a decision about the destination of the letter If the churches of Galatia were founded on Paul's second missionary journey in the northern part of Galatia (Acts 16:6), the earliest the epistle could have

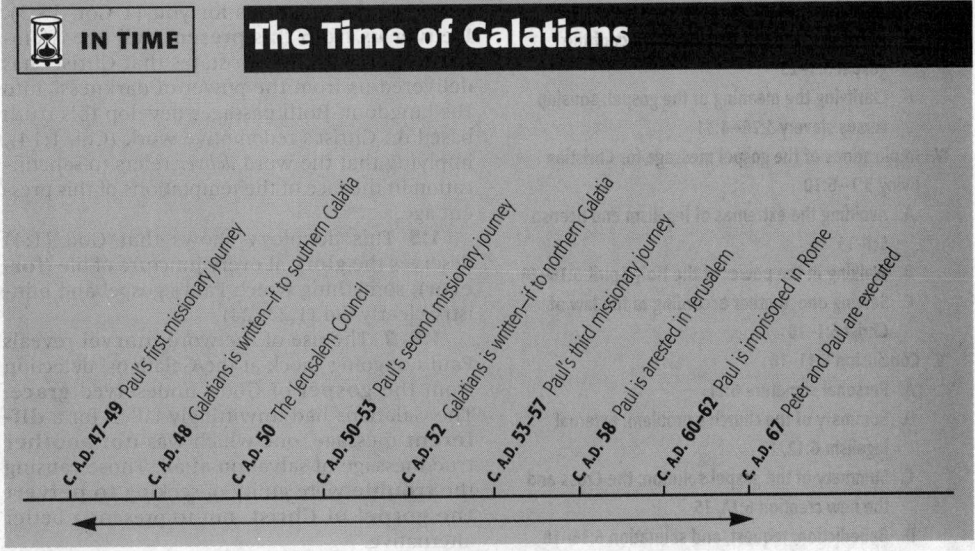

IN TIME

The Time of Galatians

c. A.D. 47–49 Paul's first missionary journey
c. A.D. 48 Galatians is written–if to southern Galatia
c. A.D. 50 The Jerusalem Council
c. A.D. 50–53 Paul's second missionary journey
c. A.D. 52 Galatians is written–if to northern Galatia
c. A.D. 53–57 Paul's third missionary journey
c. A.D. 58 Paul is arrested in Jerusalem
c. A.D. 60–62 Paul is imprisoned in Rome
c. A.D. 67 Peter and Paul are executed

been written was around A.D. 52. The similarity in content between Galatians and Romans, among other things, has led some to date the letter in the mid-50s. On the other hand, if Galatia is understood to be southern Galatia, including Lystra, Iconium, and Pisidian Antioch (Acts 14:21), congregations planted on Paul's first missionary journey, the letter could have been written as early as A.D. 48.

To determine the date, the possible role of the Jerusalem Council (Acts 15) in the controversies addressed in Galatians must also be considered. If Galatians was written after the Jerusalem Council had made its authoritative decisions, Paul most likely would have centered his argument on those decisions, or at least made an unmistakable reference to them. Since he did not, Galatians probably dates from A.D. 48. This means it is one of the earliest New Testament books.

Outline

I. **Introduction 1:1–9**
  A. Salutation and preview of the letter's themes 1:1–5
  B. Occasion of the letter: condemnation of error 1:6–9
II. **Defense of the apostolic authority of the gospel message 1:10–2:21**
  A. Apostolic call: the divine source of Paul's gospel 1:10–16
  B. Apostolic confirmation: human agreement with Paul's gospel 1:17–2:21
III. **Scriptural basis of the gospel message 3:1–4:31**
  A. Identifying the Old Testament roots of the gospel 3:1–25
  B. Clarifying the meaning of the gospel: sonship versus slavery 3:26–4:31
IV. **Implications of the gospel message for Christian living 5:1–6:10**
  A. Avoiding the extremes of legalism and license 5:1–15
  B. Walking in the power of the Holy Spirit 5:16–26
  C. Serving one another according to the law of Christ 6:1–10
V. **Conclusion 6:11–18**
  A. Personal signature 6:11
  B. Summary of the church's problem: external legalism 6:12, 13
  C. Summary of the gospel solution: the Cross and the new creation 6:14, 15
  D. Benediction, request, and salutation 6:16–18

Commentary

1:1–5 The introduction of the letter includes the three standard elements found in epistolary salutation sections: (1) the writer **Paul** (1:1); (2) the addressees—**to the churches of Galatia** (1:2); and (3) the greeting—**grace to you and peace** (1:3).

1:1 Paul calls himself **an apostle** to assert his divinely given authority to speak to the problem confronting the Galatian churches. **Through Jesus Christ and God the Father** refers to Paul's unique call to be an apostle (vv. 15, 16), which came to him at the same time as his salvation on the road to Damascus (Acts 26:12–18). **Raised Him from the dead** is a reference to the resurrection of Jesus Christ, a central belief of the Christian faith (1 Cor. 15).

1:2 and all the brethren who are with me: Paul implies that there were with him a goodly number of Christian believers, members of the household of faith. Paul associates these unnamed fellow workers with him in sending greetings. **churches of Galatia:** Galatians is a circular letter, intended for several churches.

1:3 Grace is a variation from the standard greeting of ancient letters in Paul's time. **Peace** is the Greek translation of the traditional Hebrew greeting. Paul commonly combines the two ideas of grace and peace in the introductions of his letters (1 Cor. 1:3; 2 Cor. 1:2). The true message of salvation is based solely on God's grace (1:6; 2:21) received by faith (Eph. 2:8), and it provides peace with God (Rom. 5:1).

1:4 gave Himself for our sins: This phrase looks ahead to Paul's discussion of redemption in 3:13, 14. It is a quick summary of the Good News: Christ's death is for you (1 Cor. 15:3). **Deliver us from this present evil age** is similar to Col. 1:13, which states that Christ "has delivered us from the power of darkness" into His kingdom. Both passages develop this truth based on Christ's redemptive work (Col. 1:14), implying that the word *deliver* refers to sanctification in the face of the temptations of this present age.

1:5 This doxology shows that God (1:4) deserves the **glory** at every juncture of life (**forever**), something which Paul's gospel and ministry clearly did (1:23, 24).

1:6, 7 The use of the word **marvel** reveals Paul's ongoing shock at the Galatians' defection from the **gospel** of God's undeserved **grace**. The Galatians had unwittingly fallen for a **different** message, one which was **not another** true message of salvation at all. Those causing the **trouble** were guilty of seeking **to pervert the gospel of Christ,** not to present a better alternative.

1:8, 9 Paul moves from the hypothetical (vv. 6, 7) to the actual in denouncing the Galatians' perversion of the **gospel.** If even the apostles or an **angel from heaven** were to **preach** a false gospel, they would be **accursed.** That being the case, **anyone** who proclaimed a perversion of the message that the Galatians had **received** from Paul fully deserved eternal destruction. Paul's concern for the purity of the gospel mes-

the longest autobiographical sections in Paul's epistles (2 Cor. 11:22—12:10).

1:11, 12 There was no human creativity flavoring the **gospel** Paul **preached.** Paul knew it only because he **received** it by special **revelation** from **Jesus Christ** at his conversion (Acts 26:12–18).

1:13, 14 Judaism means the Jewish way of life, which was based partly on the OT and

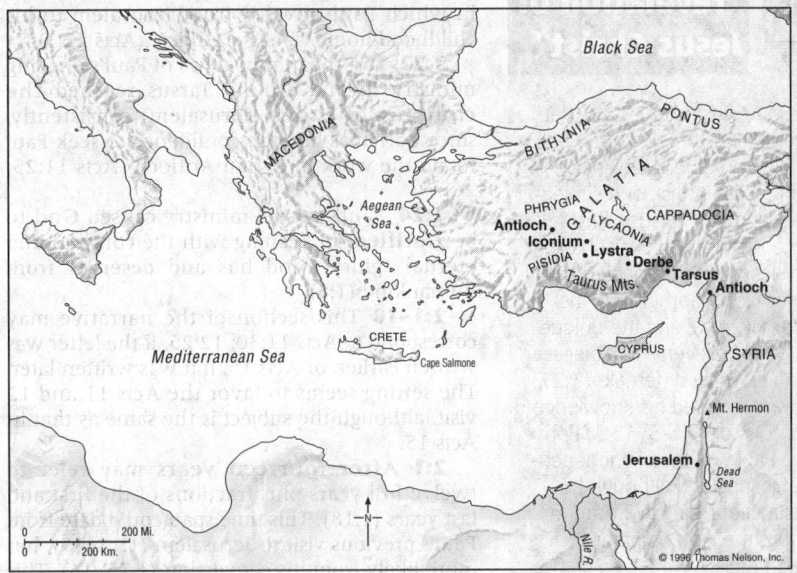

Galatia

sage is revealed by his assertion that he would condemn to destruction anyone who taught a false gospel.

1:10 To **please men** was neither Paul's motivation nor the source of his authority (v. 1). Paul continually sought the approval of God. He did not base his decisions on the opinions of other people. Instead he single-mindedly aimed at pleasing God (Phil. 3:14). As an apostle Paul was a leader, but he was always **a bondservant of Christ.**

1:11–2:14 This extended passage is one of

partly on additional **traditions** of the **fathers,** or leaders of the people (Matt. 15:2). Paul's **conduct** before his conversion had greatly distinguished him in Judaism in two ways: (1) He painstakingly kept the law and traditions, certainly more so than the Judaizers in Galatia (6:13). (2) He **persecuted the church of God** in order to **destroy it** (Phil. 3:6), doing so under the authority of Jewish religious leaders (Acts 8:3; 9:1, 2).

1:15–17 In words echoing the calling of the messianic Servant (Is. 49:1) and Jeremiah the

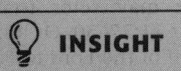 **INSIGHT**   ## The Churches of Galatia

Two possible locations are suggested for the "churches of Galatia." The "North Galatia" theory points to the region in the heart of Asia Minor whose boundaries included Bithynia and Pontus on the north, Phrygia on the southwest, and Cappadocia on the east. The "South Galatia" theory understands Galatia to refer to the Roman province of that name, which included Pisidia, Lycaonia, and parts of Phrygia and Cappadocia.

prophet (Jer. 1:5), Paul relates that God had chosen him to be an apostle (v. 1) before his birth. Paul, like the Judaizers in Galatia, had previously tried to earn his salvation by works (v. 14). However, his apostolic call and conversion both came through God's **grace,** His unde-

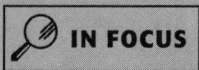

IN FOCUS **"revelation of Jesus Christ"**

(Gk. *apokalupsis Iesou Christou*) (1:12; 1 Pet. 1:13; Rev. 1:1) Strong's #602; 2424; 5547: In the Greek this could be an objective genitive—a revelation concerning Jesus Christ, or a subjective genitive—a revelation from Jesus Christ. Both thoughts are consistent with the context. Paul's "revelation of Jesus Christ" enabled him to see that Christ was God's Son (1:16), the sole object of our faith (2:16), and the unique source of oneness of all believers—whether Jew or Gentile, bond or free, male or female (3:27, 28; Eph. 3:1–11). Paul received his knowledge by special revelation (1 Cor. 11:23; 15:3; Eph. 3:3; 1 Thess. 4:15). Paul was thus an independent witness to the gospel; and although he had received no instructions directly from the apostles but only from the Holy Spirit, his teachings agreed with theirs.

served favor. If Paul's gospel message was made by men, he would have had to **confer** with other people to receive or validate it. To do this, Paul would have had to travel **to Jerusalem,** where the other **apostles** were, for such a conference. Instead, when he left **Damascus,** where he had stayed immediately after his conversion to Christianity (Acts 9:1–22), he went **to Arabia** (2 Cor. 11:32, 33). This was the kingdom of the Nabatean Arabs, extending from Damascus to the Red Sea, including parts of modern Syria, Jordan, Israel, and Saudi Arabia.

1:18 after three years: This could be thirty-six months, or else a shorter period measured from the end of one year, through a complete year, and ending early in the third year. The three years could begin at the time of Paul's conversion (vv. 15, 16) or of his departure to Arabia (v. 17). Undoubtedly Paul and **Peter** talked at length about Christ and the gospel during the **fifteen days** Paul was in **Jerusalem.**

1:19, 20 The apparent reference to **James, the Lord's brother,** as being one of **the other apostles** indicates that the word *apostles* was

not always restricted to "the Twelve" (Matt. 10:1–4; 1 Cor. 15:5). The sequence of 1 Cor. 15:7–9, where **James,** Paul, and "all the apostles" are listed as having seen the resurrected Christ, implies that Paul may have accepted **James** as possessing at least partly parallel apostolic qualifications to his own (Acts 1:21–26).

1:21 Following his brief trip to Jerusalem (vv. 18, 19), Paul **went** to **Syria and Cilicia,** likely the same journey mentioned in Acts 9:30, in which Paul traveled from Jerusalem to his childhood home, Tarsus in Cilicia (Acts 22:3).

1:22, 23 Apparently, news of Paul's ongoing ministry in and around Tarsus reached **the churches of Judea** (Jerusalem) consistently, since Barnabas had the confidence to seek Paul to aid the work in Syrian Antioch (Acts 11:25, 26).

1:24 Paul's gospel ministry caused **God** to be **glorified,** in keeping with the constant and eternal "glory" God has and deserves from humankind (1:5).

2:1–10 This section of the narrative may correspond to Acts 11:30; 12:25, if the letter was written earlier, or Acts 15, if it was written later. The setting seems to favor the Acts 11 and 12 visit, although the subject is the same as that in Acts 15.

2:1 After fourteen years may refer to twelve full years plus fractions of the first and last years (1:18). This time span could date from Paul's previous visit to Jerusalem (1:18, 19), but more likely from his conversion (1:15, 16). This was the point at which Paul received the gospel message, the focus of discussion throughout this extended section (1:11—2:14). **I went up again to Jerusalem:** If Galatians was written before the Jerusalem Council, this journey is the one recorded in Acts 11:30. Otherwise, it is a reference to the Jerusalem Council (Acts 15). **Barnabas** is a Hebrew nickname meaning "Son of Encouragement" (Acts 4:36). Barnabas met Paul briefly in **Jerusalem** during Paul's first postconversion visit (Acts 9:26, 27). Later they served together in the events narrated in Acts 11:25–30; 12:25—15:39. **Titus** is not mentioned in Acts, but he was a convert of Paul's (Titus 1:4) and an effective ministry associate over a number of years (2 Cor. 2:13).

2:2 Revelation here may refer to the prophecy of Agabus in Acts 11:27–30. Or it may refer to a private revelation of the Lord to Paul, perhaps similar to the one he received in Jerusalem earlier (Acts 22:17–21). Later Jesus appeared to Paul in another vision (Acts 23:11). **Them** may refer to the Jerusalem church at large, or it may be only **those who were of reputation,** presumably the inner core made up of James, Cephas (Peter), and John (v. 9). For Paul to have **communicated** with these leaders **privately** does not mean he considered altering his gospel, as the following section clearly shows (vv. 3–10). **In vain** does not reflect on the effectiveness of Paul's **gospel,** but rather on his efforts to maintain a unity in the church without sacrificing "the truth of the gospel" (v. 5).

2:3 Titus (v. 1) was a "test-case" Gentile. The term **circumcised** introduces a central topic of the Jewish false teachers, one which Paul addresses repeatedly in Galatians (5:2, 3, 6). Unlike Timothy, whom Paul had circumcised because Timothy's mother was Jewish, Titus was not circumcised. Circumcising him would have been a sign to all other Gentiles that following Jewish law was required for a person to become a Christian. As Paul explains in this letter, that would be a rejection of the Good News that salvation is God's gift to those who believe in His Son.

2:4 false brethren: This phrase apparently indicates that although these people passed themselves off convincingly as Christians, there was reason to view their profession as a sham. These pseudo-Christians did not announce their purpose, which was to curtail Christian **liberty** (5:1, 13) and to bring Paul and his converts into the **bondage** of Jewish legalism (6:12–15). These false brethren maintained that one had to keep the Jewish law in order to be saved. They refused to confess that salvation was God's gift through faith alone. For this reason, Paul would not recognize them as genuine Christians.

2:5 Paul's message about **the truth of the gospel** had never given way to the message of the false teachers, whether in Jerusalem (vv. 1–10), Syrian Antioch (vv. 11–14), or Galatia. **you:** The Galatian Christians could trust Paul's consistent advocacy of his gospel, which was revealed by God (1:11, 12).

2:6 While Paul recognized the leadership roles of James, Cephas (Peter), and John (v. 9)

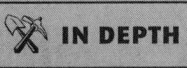 **IN DEPTH** — ## Who Were the Galatians?

It is difficult to decide who Paul was writing to in the Book of Galatians. In Paul's time the word *Galatians* had both an ethnic and a political meaning.

The ethnic Galatians were Celts who migrated from central Europe to Asia Minor in the third century B.C. They settled in the area around Ankara, the capital of present-day Turkey. In Paul's day the native Galatian dialect was still spoken there, although Greek had been accepted as the language of business and diplomacy.

By NT times there was a Roman province called Galatia that was larger than the original ethnic area. Territory to the south which was not ethnically Galatian was included in the province. Pisidia as well as sections of Phrygia and Lycaonia were formally part of political Galatia.

Whether Galatia refers to the people or to the province would indicate who the original readers of the letter to Galatians were. The usual view until the last two centuries was that Paul addressed "North Galatia," or congregations of ethnic Galatians located in the northern part of the province. Personal contact of the apostle with these churches may be alluded to in Acts 16:6 and 18:23. However, a "South Galatian" theory is more widely held today. According to this view Paul wrote to churches in the southern part of the province, that is, to the churches he founded on his first missionary journey (Acts 13:14—14:24) and later revisited (Acts 16:1–5).

An obvious strength of the North Galatian view is that the northern part of the province was Galatia in both senses: ethnic and political. Also, it has been asserted that Paul's description of the fickleness of his readers was a well-known characteristic of the ethnic Galatians in the north.

On the other hand, a strong case can be made for the South Galatian view. Paul normally used Roman provincial names, as did Luke in the Book of Acts. Also, the most natural understanding of Acts 16:6 and 18:23 is that Paul retraced his steps from the first missionary journey (Acts 13; 14) at the beginning of his second and third journeys.

With the biblical and historical evidence divided as it is, there have been notable scholars on both sides of the Galatian question. Neither theory is clearly superior, though it seems that the South Galatian view fits better with Acts. The question is important for assigning a date to the letter.

In either case, it is obvious that the book was addressed to a church which was struggling with the Judaizers, a group that insisted that the Gentile converts keep the requirements of the law. Paul's letter was a stern rebuke of this faction in the church. By adding the law to the gospel message, this group was in effect rejecting Jesus' free offer of salvation.

as "pillars" of the Jerusalem church, he pointed out that they were in no way superior to him in their understanding of the gospel. **added nothing to me:** The other apostles were satisfied with Paul's understanding of the gospel.

2:7–10 There were not two different gospels, one for **the uncircumcised** Gentiles and another for **the circumcised** Jews. Rather, the primary scope of Paul's apostolic ministry was to the Gentiles (Rom. 11:13), while Peter's **apostleship** was, first and foremost, targeted toward the Jews. The fact that God **worked effectively** through **Peter** in reaching Jews and just as effectively through Paul in reaching **the Gentiles** was strong evidence to the leaders in Jerusalem of Paul's apostolic commission (Rom. 1:5). **The right hand of fellowship** was a common sign of acceptance and friendship. It indicated full recognition of Paul by the representatives of the Jerusalem church. The request to **remember the poor,** almost certainly the poor among the church in Judea

(Acts 11:29, 30), reflects an ongoing concern of Paul's (Rom. 15:26).

2:11, 12 Antioch was the largest city of the Roman province of Syria. It became a center for missionary outreach to other Gentile cities in Asia Minor and Macedonia (Acts 13:1–3). After the earlier meeting in Jerusalem (vv. 1–10), the behavior of **Peter** in Antioch was contradictory and hypocritical (vv. 12, 13). Given Peter's immense influence, Paul had little choice but to point out the hypocrisy directly (vv. 11, 14). Paul confronted Peter because refusing to **eat with the Gentiles** contradicted what Peter had long since recognized, that the gospel was for the Gentiles too. **Certain men came from James** indicates that they came with the authority of James, one of the leaders of the Jerusalem church (v. 9). However, it is unlikely that they accurately represented the views of James (vv. 7–10). Whatever they said to Peter caused a strong reaction in which he **withdrew and separated himself** from table fellowship

---

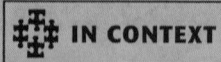 **IN CONTEXT** | **The Circumcision**

The fact that a certain group in the early church was referred to as "the circumcision" (Gal. 2:12) reflects how deeply controversial the ancient practice of circumcision had become by the first century A.D. Originally mandated by God as a sign of His covenant relationship with Israel (Gen. 17:9–14), circumcision became a mark of exclusivity, not only among the Jews, but among the early Jewish Christians.

Circumcision involved the surgical removal of a male child's foreskin. The Hebrew people came to take great pride in this rite. In fact, it became a badge of their spiritual and national superiority. This attitude eventually fostered a spirit of exclusivism instead of compassion to reach out to other nations as God intended. They came to regard Gentiles as the "uncircumcision," a term of disrespect implying that non-Jewish peoples were outside the circle of God's love. Thus, the terms "circumcised" and "uncircumcised" became charged with emotion, as is plain from the discord the issue brought about in the early church.

A crisis erupted at Antioch when believers from Judea, known as Judaizers, taught the believers, "Unless you are circumcised according to the custom of Moses, you cannot be saved" (Acts 15:1). In effect, the Judaizers insisted that a person from a non-Jewish background must first become a Jew ceremonially by being circumcised before he could be admitted to the Christian faith.

A council of apostles and elders was convened at Jerusalem to resolve the issue (Acts 15:6–29). Among those attending were Paul, Barnabas, Simon Peter, and James, leader of the Jerusalem church. To insist on circumcision for the Gentiles, Peter argued, would amount to a burdensome yoke (15:10). This was the decision handed down by the council.

Years later, reinforcing that decision, the apostle Paul wrote the believers at Rome that Abraham, the "father of circumcision" (Rom. 4:12), was saved by faith rather than by circumcision (4:9–12). He declared circumcision to be of no value unless accompainied by an obedient spirit (2:25–26).

Paul also spoke of the "circumcision of Christ" (Col. 2:11), a reference to His atoning death which "condemned sin in the flesh" (Rom. 8:3) and nailed "the handwriting of requirements" to the cross (Col. 2:14). In essence, Paul declared that the new covenant of Christ's shed blood has made forgiveness available to both Jew and Gentile and has made circumcision unnecessary. All that ultimately matters for both Jew and Gentile is a changed nature—a new creation that makes them one in Jesus Christ (Eph. 2:14–18).

with Gentiles. Apparently Peter was **fearing** damage to his reputation as apostle to **the circumcision** (2:7, 8).

2:13 Peter's example was so decisive that **the rest of the Jews** in the church at Syrian Antioch, including **Barnabas,** followed suit. However, Peter's actions did not represent conviction, but **hypocrisy.**

2:14 Peter's hypocritical example implied that Gentiles had to behave like Jews in order to receive God's grace. Thus, Peter was **not** being **straightforward about the truth of the gospel** of God's grace. It had already been decided (vv. 1–5) that it was not proper to **compel Gentiles to live as Jews** because salvation was through faith alone.

2:15–21 This section may represent the continuation of Paul's confrontation with Peter, or it may represent a statement of the central point of his letter: that Christians are justified by faith in Jesus Christ alone.

2:15–17 Paul is not denying that those who are **Jews** by birth are **sinners,** as are all **Gentiles** (Rom. 3:23). Rather, he is implying that Jews enjoy spiritual privileges (Rom. 9:4, 5) that should make them more knowledgeable about how to be justified before God (3:6; Gen. 15:6). The Jews should have been aware that no person can be declared righteous or justified by obedience to the Law of Moses (3:10–21).

2:16 By the grace of God (v. 21), the only way to be **justified** (declared righteous or pardoned) is through **faith in Jesus Christ.** Any other way allows **works,** whether keeping **the law** of Moses or performing good deeds in general, to play a role in justification. This is the main point of Paul's letter to the Galatians: salvation or righteousness cannot be obtained by obeying the law. Salvation is only through faith in Jesus Christ (Rom. 3:20).

2:17–19 Paul strongly rejects the erroneous conclusion that being **justified by** faith in **Christ** actually made Jews **sinners,** thus painting Christ as a promoter of **sin.** Those who attempt to be justified through "the works of the law" are "cursed" (3:10). If anyone attempts to reassert the "works of the law" as having any part in justification before God, **the law** itself convicts that person of being **a transgressor** (3:19–25). The law itself is not sinful; its purpose is to convince individuals of their personal spiritual deadness in sin outside of faith in Christ (Rom. 7:7–13).

2:20 Paul and every believer were **crucified with Christ** in order to die to sin, the law, and "this present evil age" (1:4). While believers live on physically, **Christ** also **lives** within them spiritually. Christ's resurrection power through the Spirit is worked out through the Christian (Rom. 6:4–11) who chooses to **live by faith in the Son of God.**

2:21 If **righteousness** is attainable **through** keeping **the law** of Moses, then God's gracious act of sending **Christ** to die on the Cross to pay for sin was unnecessary and useless (Rom. 3:4–26).

3:1 **Foolish** does not indicate lack of intelligence but lack of wisdom. Paul wonders whether something like an evil spell had prevented the Galatians from recalling the gospel of the **crucified** Christ, which had been **clearly portrayed** or preached to them. He uses a play on words—**before whose eyes**—to highlight their duplicity as contrasted with the truth he had carefully explained to them.

3:2 In this verse, Paul contrasts obedience to the law with faith. **The hearing of faith** is probably what Paul had in mind in Rom. 10:17 when he said, "So then faith comes by hearing, and hearing by the word of God." It may also be closely related to Paul's concept of obedience to the faith, since the Greek word for "hear" can also be translated "listen" or "obey" (Rom. 1:5; 16:26).

3:3 Paul reminds the Galatians that their Christian life was **begun in the Spirit** by faith alone (v. 2; 2:16). **Being made perfect by the flesh** indicates that the Galatians were mistakenly trying to achieve perfection through their own efforts, especially through circumcision.

3:4 This statement implies that the Galatian Christians had previously **suffered** for their faith, before they were tricked by the false gospel.

3:5 What Paul meant here by the working of **miracles** is uncertain. Perhaps his resuscitation from near death after being stoned (Acts 14:19, 20) is part of what he had in mind.

3:6 There are several reasons for Paul's reference to Abraham's faith as an example. (1) Abraham was the father of the Jewish nation (Gen. 12:1–3). (2) Abraham is the clearest example of justification in the OT. (3) The Judaizers almost certainly were pointing back to Abraham, probably in connection with circumcision (2:3; 5:2, 3). The example of Abraham's faith is also developed in Rom. 4; Heb. 11; James 2. Paul quotes Gen. 15:6 from the Greek translation of the OT to show that **Abraham** was justified by faith alone. This verse communicates precisely what Paul called "the truth of the gospel" (2:5, 14).

3:7 **Those who are of faith** are spiritual **sons of Abraham,** even if they are not Jews. They are part of God's people.

3:8, 9 **Scripture** is personified as a preacher who foretells that **Abraham** and his example of faith (Gen. 15:6) would become a life-changing blessing to all **nations** (Gen. 12:3; Matt. 28:19) as the **gospel** spread. All who have **faith,** as Abraham did, join in his **blessed** status.

Believing (Gk. *pistos*) could also be translated "faithful," but the context favors *believing* or "believer." This is the only use of the word in Galatians.

3:10 Being **under the curse** through trying to be justified by **the works of the law** is contrasted with being blessed as a believer (v. 9). The quotation from Deut. 27:26 says that those who do not keep the whole law are **cursed,** proving that all are *cursed* who follow the law, because all fall short of the law's standards (Rom. 1:17; 3:10–18, 23).

3:11, 12 Paul quotes Hab. 2:4 to demonstrate that a person can only be **justified** through **faith.** He cites Lev. 18:5 to prove that keeping **the law** to gain salvation is utterly incompatible with faith.

3:13, 14 Paul knew that many of his readers would perceive that they were actually under **the curse of the law** (v. 10; Deut. 27:26). For them as for us, it is incredibly comforting to know that **Christ** became that curse **for us** on the Cross (Deut. 21:23). The picture is that of the wrath of God hanging over us—as Damocles' sword—but Christ took that wrath. Thus, the *curse* is lifted **through faith** in Christ's redemption and **the blessing of Abraham** and **the promise of the Spirit** to all believers. It is likely that the Jewish false teachers were stating that *blessing* came through keeping the Mosaic law, and that people were **cursed** if they did not.

3:15 Covenant here probably means a "last will and testament," which is unchangeable after it is **confirmed.** Most of the uses of the word in the NT refer to a solemn agreement or contract God made with His people.

3:16 Jesus **Christ** is the fulfillment of the covenant (v. 15) God made with **Abraham.** Although in one sense all Jews are the physical seed of Abraham, Christ is the final focus of God's **promises,** the ultimate **Seed.** Christians are the spiritual seed of Abraham (v. 29).

3:17 Four hundred and thirty years was the period of time Israel was in Egypt before the Exodus (Ex. 12:40, 41). **The law,** which was put into force at the end of those centuries, could not override or **annul** the standing **covenant** with Abraham (Gen. 15:18).

3:18 The law of Moses and the **promise** God made to **Abraham** were at odds with each other. Paul demonstrated that the false teachers' view that the law was the fulfillment of the Abrahamic covenant had no scriptural basis.

3:19, 20 The **purpose** of **the law** of Moses was not to justify humankind in God's eyes (2:16). Rather, the law was **added** after God's promise to Abraham (vv. 16, 17) to clarify the issue of sin until Christ **the Seed** (v. 16) came. According to Stephen's sermon in Acts 7, the

law was given **through angels** to Moses as the human **mediator** (Acts 7:38). This view was in line with Jewish teaching of the NT era. No mediator, or go-between, was needed with the Abrahamic covenant since it was a one-party, or unilateral, **promise.** God put Abraham into a "deep sleep" and consummated the ceremonial enactment of the covenant alone (Gen. 15:12–17).

3:21, 22 The relationship of **the law** and **the promises of God** is not competition, but need and fulfillment. The law was not designed by God to give eternal **life** and **righteousness.** Rather, the law showed humanity's need for the **promise** of **life** through **faith in Jesus Christ** (v. 9; 2:16), having **confined all** people **under** their **sin** (Rom. 3:23; 6:23).

3:23–25 Paul gives two different illustrations concerning the function of **the law** until **Christ** came (4:4, 5). The law acted as a jail **guard** to hold humankind in custody until faith in Christ was **revealed.** But the law also served as a **tutor.** A tutor in ancient Greek culture would accompany the children in his care, instructing and disciplining them when necessary. The law was like a tutor because it both corrected and instructed the Israelites in God's ways until Christ was revealed, and such a tutor was no longer needed (4:1, 2).

3:26, 27 Through faith in Christ Jesus believers are not only blessed as sons of

IN FOCUS   "tutor"

(Gk. *paidagogos*) (3:24, 25; 1 Cor. 4:15) Strong's #3807: The Greek term means "custodian" or a person who attends a child. In Greek households a faithful servant was given the responsibility of taking care of a boy from childhood to puberty. The servant kept him from both physical and moral evil, and went with him to his amusements and to school. Paul used the word to say that the law functioned as a child-custodian. The law acted as an outward check on desires, thus making the consciousness of sin more acute. And since none of us is able to deal with sin by ourselves, the law guides us to Christ, our only Rescuer and Savior.

Abraham (vv. 7, 9) but also as **sons of God** (John 1:12) and God's heirs (4:7). Believers have been adopted by God Himself. Although we were His enemies, we have been made His sons. Although we deserve judgment, we will receive an eternal inheritance from our Father.

3:28 The context of this verse is justification by faith **in Christ Jesus,** the fact that Jesus has redeemed all those who believe on Him, whether Jew or Gentile (3:26—4:27). Racial, social, and gender distinctions that so easily divide in no way hinder a person from coming to Christ in order to receive His mercy. All people equally can become God's heirs and recipients of His eternal promises (4:5–7).

3:29 To be **Christ's** through faith (3:26, 27) also means to be **Abraham's** sons **(seed)** (3:7) and blessed **(heirs)** with him (3:9), **according to** God's **promise** (Gen. 12:3).

4:1, 2 Drawing upon the illustration of the "tutor" and "heirs" in 3:24–29, Paul develops the idea of what it means to be an adopted son of God. In ancient society **a child** had to wait until the proper time before he could inherit what was his. Paul uses this to explain why God delayed Jesus Christ's coming, leaving people with His law as a guide (3:23–25).

4:3 We were children in bondage parallels "child" and "slave" in v. 1. Some believe that the **elements** Paul refers to in this verse are "elemental spiritual forces." As in astrology today, the ancients associated spiritual forces with "the elements," such as earth, air, fire, and water. But the context, and Paul's use of the word elsewhere (Col. 2:8, 20), favors an understanding of *elements* as "elementary principles or regulations," perhaps the Jewish law or aspects of it (compare Heb. 5:12—6:3). This is con-

firmed in the context, for *elements of the world* parallels "guardians and stewards" in v. 2, as well as the role of the law in 3:23–25. These elements are described as "weak and beggarly" in v. 9 and are linked to what appears to be Jewish calendar observances in v. 10.

4:4, 5 The fullness of the time is "the perfect time" in history, the "time appointed" by **God** the Father (v. 2) for **His Son** to be born, and later to die for the sins of the world. **Born of a woman** speaks of Christ's humanity and perhaps alludes to His role as the ultimate "Seed" of the woman (3:16; Gen. 3:15). **Born under the law** means Christ was subject to the Jewish law (Matt. 5:17–19), further establishing His identification with all people who are subject to the law. **Redeem,** meaning "to buy from the slave market," is a term used only by Paul in the NT (3:13; Eph. 5:16; Col. 4:5). The verb describes Christ's supreme and final payment for the sins of humanity (Rom. 3:23–25). This payment, His death on the Cross, frees those who believe on Him from the curse of the law and slavery to sin. This decisive payment and resulting freedom clears the way for Christians to become God's **sons.** Although there is only one natural Son in God's family, Jesus Christ (vv. 4, 6), God has graciously adopted all believers as His sons. We are no longer slaves to sin, nor children under the guardianship of the law.

4:6 Just as "God sent forth His Son" in "the fullness of the time" in world history (v. 4), so

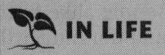 **IN LIFE**　　**Rights**

We live in a time when it seems that everyone is concerned about exercising their "rights." Indeed, society has become somewhat polarized as various groups form around their perceptions of rights that they feel they are being denied. The more intense the struggle to achieve those rights, the more social conflict seems to escalate.

Paul indicated to the Galatians that before God, no one has any rights; whatever rights humanity once had have been forfeited as a result of sin. To bring this situation home to his readers, Paul used the metaphor of a slave (Gal. 4:1–3), an image that the Galatians probably knew well, as the Roman Empire depended heavily on slave labor (Rom. 6:16).

The Galatians had become children of God, but before that they were in bondage to sin, to the "elements of the world" (Gal. 4:3; compare Col. 2:8, 20). As slaves to sin, they had no rights before God. He owed them nothing. They belonged to sin, which they were forced to serve. Emancipation from that position had to come from a source other than their own power, ingenuity, or morality.

Such is the plight of all sinners before God—helpless and hopeless (Rom. 3:23, John 3:19, 20). But just as God gave life, resources, and responsibility to humanity in the beginning (Gen. 1:26—2:4), so now He has given Christ His Son to rescue or "redeem" people from sin and grant them all the privileges of adoption into the family of God (Gal. 4:4–7). No one deserves that, which is why receiving Christ's new life and the rights therein is truly a gift.

If as believers we have received these treasures from God, then we ought to let others know that the same opportunity is available to them.

🔍 IN FOCUS　"elements"

(Gk. *stoicheion*) (4:3, 9; Col. 2:8, 20; Heb. 5:12; 2 Pet. 3:10) Strong's #4747: This Greek word can mean (1) "elementary or rudimentary principles" or (2) "elemental spirits." The word itself means things placed in line or in a row, like an alphabet. It was used to speak of rudimentary principles (Heb. 5:12) or basic elements of the universe, whether physical (2 Pet. 3:10) or spiritual. If Paul was thinking of elementary principles, he meant that people are in bondage to the basic elements of religion (Col. 2:20); if he meant spirits, he was saying that people are in bondage to the "elemental spirits," meaning certain gods or demons. *Principles* suits the overall context of Galatians, whereas *spirits* accords with 4:8–10. In either case, Paul was saying that people were in bondage until Christ came.

God has sent forth the Spirit of Christ at just the right time for every person who believes in Christ. **into your hearts:** Christians can know intimacy with the Father because of the indwelling Spirit (Rom. 8:1–17).

4:7 Paul summarizes the illustrations and teaching of the preceding section (vv. 1–6) by speaking of the transformation of the believer from being a spiritual **slave** to being a **son** with full rights. To be an **heir of God** is true of all "sons" unconditionally. This should be distinguished, however, from being an heir of the kingdom. The Scripture speaks of two inheritances (Rom. 8:17). All children of God by faith (John 1:12) have an inheritance in heaven which can never fade (1 Pet. 1:3–5), but the inheritance in the earthly reign of Christ is earned as a result of our sufferings for Him (2 Tim. 2:12).

4:8, 9 The words **in bondage** and **elements** refer back to v. 3. Paul was in effect asking the Galatians, "Is it spiritual progress **again** to be enslaved to **weak and beggarly** rituals and observances (v. 10)? How could you **have known God** and turned away to 'childish' (v. 3) things?" The Galatians had come to **know God** through faith in Jesus Christ (John 17:2, 3). He had adopted them as His own sons, but they were turning back to the law that had once enslaved them. They were in the process of leaving the light and liberty of Christianity for the shadow and slavery of legalism. Ritualistic observances are heathenish in principle. They are a system of bondage opposed to God's grace. How can anyone want to exchange the robe of Christ's righteousness for the filthy rags of heathenism, Judaism, or any other "ism"?

4:10 The word **days** likely refers to Sabbaths or special feasts. **Months and seasons** pertain to longer observances, such as the celebrations between the Passover and the Day of Pentecost. **Years** probably indicates the Year of Jubilee, the fiftieth year in which slaves were to be freed, family lands returned to their original owners, and the land left fallow (Lev. 23—25). The Jews commemorated all these feasts in order to please God.

4:11 In this section (4:8–20) Paul uses two variations on the idea of labor: (1) He initially speaks of having **labored for you** in "preaching the gospel to you" (4:13); (2) Then he uses the analogy of labor pains related to a baby's birth to describe the difficulty of furthering the Christian growth of the Galatians "until Christ is formed in you" (Eph. 4:13).

4:12 **I urge you:** To get beyond the present dilemma, Paul appeals to the Galatians to follow his example (1 Cor. 11:1). He had abandoned the ceremonial rules and regulations connected with Judaism so that he could freely preach the gospel of Christ to Jew and Gentile alike in the cities of Galatia. They too should not hinder the gospel of Christ with laws and regulations.

4:13–15 Paul describes the closeness and understanding that had existed between him and the Galatians when he had **preached the gospel** to them initially. He recalls how the Galatians had cared for him in his illness, treating him as they would **an angel,** or even **Christ** Himself. Paul's **physical infirmity** could have been an illness contracted en route to Galatia, a consequence of having been blinded on the road to Damascus (Acts 9:3, 8) or a consequence of being stoned (Acts 14:19). Some have suggested that Paul was practically blind. This would explain the reference to **your own eyes,** as well as the size of Paul's handwriting, referred to in 6:11. This might have been the infirmity about which Paul wrote in his letter to the Corinthians. Paul had repeatedly asked God for healing, but God refused to heal him because his weakness demonstrated God's strength (2 Cor. 12:7–10).

4:16 A person with pure motives and real friendship does not always say things that are pleasant to hear. Paul was telling the Galatians the **truth,** and as a result was being labeled as their **enemy.** Sometimes the truth hurts; but a faithful friend would courageously confront another.

4:17, 18 Paul's own career of persecuting Christians proved that **zealous** behavior can be tragically misguided (1:13, 14). Paul was strongly implying that the false teachers in Galatia were making the same mistake he had made prior to his conversion. Their zeal for the law was blinding them to the freedom and truth to be found in Jesus Christ.

4:19 In a most tender way, Paul calls the Galatian Christians his **little children** because of their lack of spiritual growth and depth. The apostle also portrays himself as the Galatians' "spiritual mother." He was feeling the **labor** pains of their **birth** all over **again** because they had fallen into serious error.

4:20 Paul concludes his highly personal appeal to the Galatians (4:8–20) by stating his desire to **be present with** them, and for things to be different. But in light of the erroneous teaching in their midst, he has good reason to **have doubts about** their spiritual status.

4:21–31 In this section Paul develops an allegory to complement his argument that justification has always been by faith and that was not changed by the emergence of the law (3:6–25). Although there are other biblical examples of allegory, the giving of figurative meaning to the details of a story (Is. 5:1–7), Paul is not recommending, or even condoning, the use of allegorical interpretation. An allegory is a legitimate figure of speech for conveying a literal truth, whereas allegorization is an illegitimate distortion of historical facts in order to create a deeper, hidden spiritual meaning. Paul is drawing upon a common Jewish approach of the day, likely used by the false teachers in Galatia to attempt to support their views. Paul may be "turning the tables" by using their method to discredit their position.

4:21, 22 Once again Paul speaks of **the law** and the experience of **Abraham,** addressing the false teachers' foundational respect for Abraham (3:6–9) and the Galatians' infatuation with living **under** the law. To clinch his lengthy argument about the bondage of the law and the freedom found in Christ, Paul uses as examples the **two sons** of Abraham. These are Ishmael, who was born of the **bondwoman** Hagar (v. 24); and Isaac, who was born of Sarah, the rightful wife of Abraham and a **freewoman.** Appropriately, Paul counters the Jewish false teachers' zeal for the law with an argument based on the Law, the Pentateuch (Gen. 16:15; 21:2). He uses allegory to prove his point because it was a rhetorical technique the false

teachers used. In other words, Paul was demonstrating that he could argue from the Law just as well as they could, but to prove that the Law of Moses pointed to the Messiah, Jesus Christ.

4:23 In Gen. 16, Abraham and Sarah attempted to fulfill God's **promise** through their own strength, using Hagar, **a bondwoman.** In spite of the complications caused by that "fleshly" alternative, Sarah, **a freewoman,** eventually saw the miraculous outworking of God's promise in the birth of Isaac (Gen. 12:2; 15:4).

4:24 symbolic: Paul was using the common Jewish allegorical method of the day to make his point. He used this approach to draw a stark contrast between **two** biblical **covenants** at odds with each other in the churches in Galatia: the Abrahamic promise (Gen. 12:1–3) and the Law of Moses that God gave Israel at **Mount Sinai.**

4:25 Paul compared **Jerusalem,** the center of Jewish life, to **Mount Sinai,** the birthplace of the Law of Moses.

4:26 The Jerusalem above represents the Jewish hope of heaven finally coming to earth (Rev. 21; 22). Since **us all** obviously refers to those who are **free** through faith in Christ (v. 7), Paul was strongly implying that the question at hand was not allegiance to Jerusalem, but allegiance to *which* Jerusalem—the new or the old? Would the Galatians follow the shortsighted present Jerusalem and its legalism or the liberty of the heavenly Jerusalem?

4:27 Paul quotes Is. 54:1, using the prophesied restoration of Israel from judgment and exile to illustrate how the later-born **children** of promise would eventually far outnumber the earlier offspring.

4:28–30 This portion of Paul's allegory is based on Gen. 21:9, 10. **Isaac** was continually **persecuted** by his older half brother Ishmael. Eventually, Ishmael and his mother Hagar were expelled because Ishmael had no standing in God's eyes as **heir** of Abraham. In creating a parallel between the story from Genesis and the Galatians' situation, Paul points out that (1) the persecution by the Jewish legalists of his day was not unexpected, and (2) it would not go on indefinitely because the legalists would soon be cast out.

4:31–5:1 So then represents the conclusion of the previous section, while **therefore** signals that Paul is going to apply this spiritual truth to the lives of the Galatian believers. To be **children of the bondwoman** is to be enslaved to the covenant from Mount Sinai (4:24, 25), the Law of Moses. To be **of the free** is to follow Abraham's example of faith (3:6–9), to be "born according to the Spirit" (3:2; 4:29), and to be destined for the "Jerusalem above" (4:26).

Understanding such realities, the believer in **Christ** must continually **stand fast** in the **liberty** of not having to keep the Law of Moses in order to be saved. The Galatians were on the verge of becoming enslaved to the law again.

5:2–4 The legalistic Jewish teachers in Galatia were urging believers to be **circumcised** (6:12, 13). Paul points out that being circumcised changes the entire orientation of salvation away from God's grace to one's own actions. One who is circumcised in an attempt to gain God's acceptance is obligated **to keep the whole law,** which history has abundantly demonstrated no one can do (Rom. 3:10–18). It is a double loss: No one can be **justified by** *law* (2:16), and the person who attempts to do so is completely **estranged from Christ,** deriving no **profit** from Christ's redemptive death on the cross. What the Jewish legalistic teachers did with respect to circumcision is not different in principle from legalistic teachers in every age.

5:4 Fallen from grace is understood by some to refer to the loss of salvation. However, *fallen from* may refer to their attitude and to the message that it communicates, rather than to their eternal salvation.

5:5 Faith in Christ brings about not only justification before God, but also growth in the Christian life until we are completely glorified by God and freed from the presence of sin. This is **the hope of righteousness.** We can be assured that we will be declared righteous before the Lord on that last day, because we have a foretaste of that righteousness from the Spirit who lives within us (2 Cor. 5:5).

5:6 By **faith** it is possible to fulfill Christ's command to **love** one's neighbor (vv. 13, 14; John 13:34, 35).

5:7, 8 You ran well: The Galatians' splendid start in the race of the Christian life had not continued. Their detour into legalism was certainly not God's will.

5:9, 10 Leaven symbolizes the intruders, with their false doctrine and sinister influence. They were taking the gospel of free forgiveness away from the Galatians. The one who causes

---

 **IN COMPARISON**   **Grace vs. the Law**

The Galatian believers, under pressure from Jewish legalists, were considering rejecting the gospel of grace and reverting back to dependence on the Mosaic law for salvation. Paul wrote this letter to outline the dramatic differences between the two approaches to God.

Grace . . .	Law . . .
• is based on faith (2:16).	• is based on works (2:16).
• justifies sinful men (2:16, 17).	• is incapable of resulting in justification (2:16; 3:11).
• begins and ends with Christ (2:20).	• makes Christ nothing (5:3).
• is the way of the Spirit (3:2, 3, 14).	• is the way of the flesh (3:3).
• is a "blessing" (3:14).	• is a "curse" (3:13).
• is God's desired end for His people (3:23–25).	• was intended to be only a means to an end (3:23–25).
• results in intimacy with Christ (3:27).	• results in estrangement from Christ (5:4).
• makes one a son of God and an heir of Christ (4:6, 7).	• keeps one a slave (4:7).
• brings liberty (5:1).	• results in bondage (5:1).
• depends on the power of the Holy Spirit (5:16–18, 22, 23).	• depends on human effort (5:19–21).
• is motivated by love (5:13, 14).	• is motivated by pride (6:3, 13, 14).
• centers on the cross of Christ (6:12–14).	• centers on circumcision (5:11; 6:12–15).

such harm will experience God's **judgment** (2 Cor. 5:10).

5:11 And I, brethren: Paul contrasts himself with the legalists. The legalists charged Paul with inconsistency and duplicity. They had misconstrued Paul's act of having Timothy circumcised (Acts 16:3). Paul could not be preaching both circumcision and the Cross, for they are contradictory. **The cross** gives **offense** because it proclaims God's unmerited grace (2:21), leaving no place for people's good works.

5:12 cut themselves off: The spiritual damage caused by legalistic teaching regarding circumcision and the law was so serious that Paul used strong, sarcastic words to emphasize his point. The false teachers should go beyond mere circumcision and castrate themselves. This exaggerated statement reveals Paul's frustration with those who muddied the clear gospel message of God's grace.

5:13, 14 Liberty presents an opposite temptation from legalism. A person can be tempted to view freedom in Christ as a selfish **opportunity for the flesh,** in other words, an opportunity to do whatever one wants to do. But Paul points out that true Christian **liberty** is the freedom to **serve one another** in **love** (vv. 5, 6).

5:15 When Christians follow their sinful desires (v. 13), they begin to criticize and contend with **one another.** Such self-centered behavior is self-defeating. Those who criticize and attack usually end up being **consumed** in worthless struggles.

5:16–18 These verses introduce the contrast between the work of the **Spirit** and the work of the flesh in the believer's life. Should "Spirit" be understood as a reference to the Holy *Spirit* or the human *spirit?* The flesh is the sinful propensity that dwells in us as a result of the fall. Satan works through the flesh to move us toward sin, whereas God works through our human *spirit* by His Holy *Spirit* to produce Christian virtues that please Him. However we understand *Spirit* or *spirit,* this does not change the truth of these verses.

5:16 The only consistent way to overcome the sinful desires of our human nature (the **flesh**) is to live step-by-step in the power of the Holy **Spirit** as He works through our spirit (v. 25). **Shall not** is a striking promise. Walking each moment by faith in God's word under the Spirit's control assures absolute victory over the desires of our sinful nature.

5:17 The potential of **the flesh** energized by Satan in the life of the Christian should not be underestimated. Given free rein, the flesh will direct our choices, making us do what we know we should not do. This inner conflict between the flesh and the **Spirit** is very real, but there is

considerable disagreement as to its precise meaning. Some believe that *flesh* here refers to a "sinful nature" continuing after salvation, while others view it as simply the physical flesh and its natural tendencies. Still others focus on the "fleshly" or "worldly" habits and patterns that continue after justification. Although the precise meaning of *flesh* in unclear, Paul's intent is plain. The desires of our flesh are at odds with what the Holy Spirit desires for us: to be free from sin.

5:18 Those who **are led by the** Holy **Spirit** exhibit a quality of behavior (5:22, 23) which is above and beyond the requirements of the Mosaic code.

5:19–21 The works of the flesh include, but go well beyond, the destructive **contentions** and **jealousies** portrayed in v. 15. Where there is such behavior, it is positive proof that the person is not living in the power of the Holy Spirit (vv. 16, 18, 22, 23) but is being energized by Satan and his hosts (Matt. 16:23; Acts 5:3). **The flesh** expresses itself in sexual

IN FOCUS   **"flesh"**

(Gk. *sarx*) (5:19, 24; 6:8, 12, 13; Rom. 7:18; 8:3, 13) Strong's #4561: In Greek literature, the word *sarx* usually meant nothing more than the human body. It was also used this way in the NT (John 1:14; Rev. 17:16; 19:18, 21). However, Paul often used the word to denote the entire fallen human being—not just the sinful body but the entire being, including the soul and mind, as affected by sin. Thus, Paul often pitted the "flesh" against the "Spirit" as being two diametrically opposed forces. The unbeliever can live only in the flesh, but the believers can live in the flesh or in the Spirit. Paul repeatedly encourages the believers to overcome the deeds of the flesh by living in the Spirit.

immorality and indecency **(adultery . . . lewdness),** idolatrous and occult worship **(sorcery),** and other acts like **murders, drunkenness,** and wild carousing **(revelries).** But it also manifests itself in such socially acceptable sins as **hatred, wrath** (anger), **selfish ambitions, dissensions, heresies** (Gk. *haireseis,* "false beliefs" or "factions"), even **envy. And the like** shows that this is a representative rather than a complete list of such sins (read 1 Cor. 6:9, 10 for a different listing).

5:22, 23 Spirit: There is a question here whether Paul means specifically the works done by a person's regenerated human spirit, or works done by the Holy Spirit Himself in the believer's life. The **fruit** analogy is reminiscent of Jesus' teaching on the vine, branches, and fruitful harvest (John 15:1–5). It is well for the Christian to remember that, without Christ and His Spirit (Gal. 4:6), "you can do nothing" (John 15:5). Since **fruit** is singular, it apparently sees the following characteristics **(love . . . self-control)** as a harmonious unity. It is a multifaceted prism that displays its beauty in diverse but integrated ways. Thus, to the same extent that there is love, there will be self-control. Because *love* has been spoken of in 5:6, 13, 14 in a way that summarizes the positive quality of Christian living, it is likely that *love* is listed first as either the most basic or comprehensive of the items in the list. Certainly this composite description of character resembles that of Jesus Christ, which is fitting for the believer who is "in Christ Jesus" by faith (5:5, 6), and who has His Spirit dwelling within (4:6) and guiding his steps (5:18).

5:24 Christians are spiritually "crucified with Christ" (2:20). They no longer have to follow the values or desires of the world (6:14). However, it remains difficult for Christians to apply this spiritual reality to the **passions** (affections) **and desires** (lusts) of **the flesh** (v. 16). Those who have mastered these sinful desires are those who have kept their focus on God (Jer. 9:23, 24; Dan. 11:32; John 17:3; Heb. 12:1–3).

5:25, 26 In these verses, Paul exhorts the Galatians to walk in the Spirit because they are already living in the Spirit. Such an action should be natural, but unfortunately we are at war with the flesh. **Walk in the Spirit** means to obey the prompting of the Holy Spirit. A believer following the Spirit's lead (v. 16) will not **become conceited,** provoke others, or envy others.

6:1–5 Paul turns from dealing with the believer's responsibility for sin to address the spiritual restoration of sinners (6:1) and over-burdened **brethren** (6:2) before further consideration of personal responsibility (6:3–5).

6:1 Any trespass probably recalls the sinful "works of the flesh" in 5:19–21. **Overtaken** means to be caught off guard, perhaps at a vulnerable point. A believer devastated by sin needs to be approached with **gentleness** (5:23) by fellow believers. Those not controlled by the Holy Spirit would tend to boast by comparing themselves to the fallen believer (vv. 3, 4). Even as a doctor can catch a disease from treating a patient, so one restoring a fallen sinner can **be tempted** to fall into sin. That danger is well worth **considering.**

6:2 The law of Christ referred to here is probably the summation of the law: "Love your neighbor" (5:14; Matt. 22:39; John 13:34, 35). The term **fulfill** suggests that choosing to **bear** another Christian's **burdens** (or restore another Christian from burdensome sin, v. 1) is precisely what **Christ** expects of all believers. The Greek word for *burdens* refers to something beyond the normal capacity to carry, as opposed to a "load" (v. 5), which is what a person could be expected to carry.

6:3, 4 Anyone who concludes that he is **something** special, through shortsighted self-comparison with those who seem to have fallen, truly **deceives himself.** Instead of examining and judging others, a Christian should always examine **his own work** to see if he is closely following Christ's example (1 Cor. 11:31; 2 Cor. 13:5).

6:5 Each Christian must **bear** (6:2) **his own load** so as not to overload, or unduly "burden" (6:2), other believers. While it is a priority to "do good," particularly to other Christians (6:10), there are limits of time and other resources that must be considered.

The Epistle to the

Ephesians

∎

N ROME, PAUL WAS IN OFFICIAL CUSTODY. Although his movements were restricted, he continued to guide the early church and preach the gospel. The Romans could imprison Paul, but they could not imprison the spread of the Good News. Numerous local assemblies had sprouted up along the routes of Paul's three missionary journeys. The members of these churches were still proclaiming the gospel,

not only by what they said, but also with their lives. Paul wrote the letter to the Ephesians to strengthen these congregations. He wanted them to understand the spiritual reality behind the numerous groups that gathered in houses all over the Mediterranean world, and he wanted them to encourage each other in the faith. They were the body of Christ.

Ephesians, like so much of Paul's writing, underscores the truth that salvation is by faith alone and not through works or human striving. The first half of the epistle (chs. 1—3) addresses the central doctrines of the Christian faith, while the second half of the letter (chs. 4—6) describes how those spiritual truths should be reflected in a Christian's behavior. Some would divide the second half of the letter into two sections—first the Christian's conduct and then spiritual conflict with the forces of evil. Such a division highlights the familiar passage describing the spiritual armor of a Christian.

The whole letter emphasizes the truth that all believers are united in Christ because the church is the one body of Christ. In the early chapters, Paul describes how God formed this new body from Jews and Gentiles with His Son

as the Head. Through Jesus' death, God reconciled sinful people to Himself. This reconciliation with God has its effects on earth. People who were normally divided, like the Jews and the Gentiles in the first century, were reconciled to each other through Christ. In Ephesians, Paul exhorted his readers to live out the spiritual truth of being joined together with Christ. Whether Jew or Gentile, they had to work together to make the unity of the church a reality. In the rest of his letter, Paul gives a number of practical ways for church members to unite against the forces of evil. Each individual has to do his or her part in order for the whole body to function properly. Each person has to display Christ's love, patience, humility, and gentleness as they use their gifts to build up the church. From parent to child, employer to employee, each person has a unique task in the body of Christ (5:22–33).

Paul identifies himself as the author of Ephesians at the beginning and in the middle of the letter (1:1; 3:1). Internal evidence supports Pauline authorship. The fact that the author describes himself as being imprisoned points to Paul, for Luke describes Paul as being under house arrest in Rome in Acts 28. The letter is similar in content to Colossians, suggesting that both letters were written during the same imprisonment in Rome, around A.D. 60. The vocabulary and thought of the letter are typical of Paul, with his characteristic emphasis on justification by faith (2:8). New uses of old words are merely examples of the apostle's genius and versatility. Finally, the early church fathers were unanimous in ascribing the letter of Ephesians to Paul.

Modern scholars have recognized the clear Pauline themes in the letter, but some have used this characteristic of the letter to prove an alternative theory about the authorship of Ephesians. These scholars contend that when the body of Pauline epistles was collected, someone else constructed Ephesians as an introduction to Paul's writings. However, this elaborate theory still has to surmount the convincing evidence for Paul's authorship of the letter.

Ephesus was the capital of the Roman province of Asia (today part of Turkey). Located at the intersection of several major trade routes, Ephesus was a vital commercial center of the Roman Empire. It was the site of a famous temple for the fertility goddess Diana that was one of the seven wonders of the ancient world. Most importantly, however, Ephesus figured prominently and dramatically in early church history, for Paul used the city as a center for his missionary work in that region.

Paul visited Ephesus briefly at the end of his second missionary journey. When he departed, he left behind Priscilla and Aquila to continue the ministry in that city (Acts 18:18–21). On Paul's third missionary journey, he spent about three years in Ephesus. When the apostle's gospel message was rebuffed by the Jews in the Ephesian synagogue, Paul taught Scripture to both Jews and Greeks in the school of Tyrannus. Paul's ministry at Ephesus was marked by several Spirit-empowered miracles. As a result, the city became a center for evangelistic outreach to the rest of the province of Asia (Acts 19:18–20). In fact, so many people in Ephesus turned to Christ and renounced their pagan ways that some craftsmen in the city started a riot because the gospel threatened their trade of making and selling idols.

In Acts 20:17–38 Paul warned the elders of the Ephesian church about "savage wolves" who would not spare the congregation. About four decades later, the Lord Jesus Himself dictated to the apostle John a letter to the same congregation (Rev. 2:1–7). He commended the Ephesians for hearing Paul and not tolerating false teachers, but He exhorted them to recapture their first love for God.

There is much evidence that the Epistle to the Ephesians was originally a circular letter sent to several congregations in the province of Asia, where Ephesus was the capital. Some manuscripts lack "in Ephesus" in 1:1. Another clue that Ephesians is a circular letter is its lack of personal references. The phrases in 1:15 and 3:2 imply that Paul had only heard of the recipients of the letter but had never met them. This is especially noteworthy since Paul had spent three years ministering at Ephesus. It seems likely that the apostle would have mentioned at least some of the Ephesians by name in his

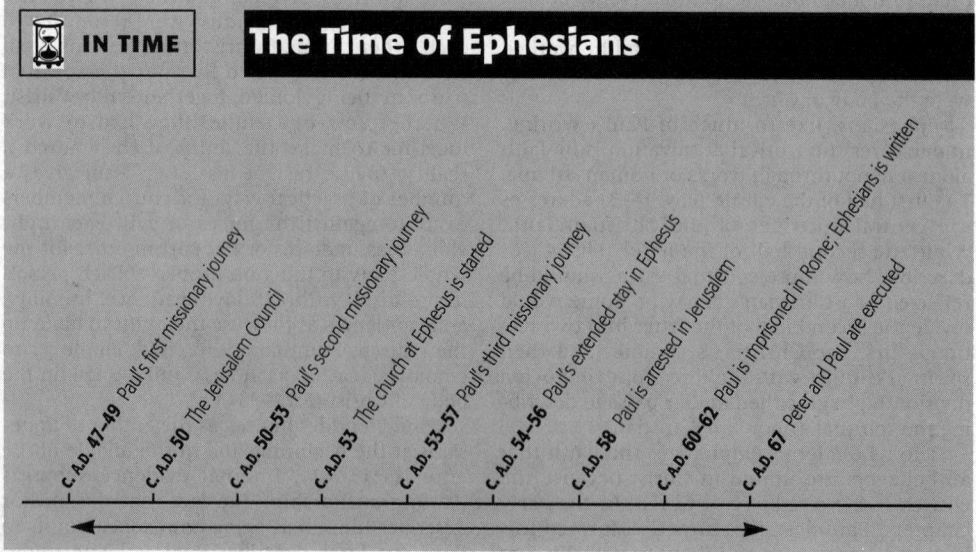

IN TIME

The Time of Ephesians

c. A.D. 47–49 Paul's first missionary journey

c. A.D. 50 The Jerusalem Council

c. A.D. 50–53 Paul's second missionary journey

c. A.D. 53 The church at Ephesus is started

c. A.D. 53–57 Paul's third missionary journey

c. A.D. 54–56 Paul's extended stay in Ephesus

c. A.D. 58 Paul is arrested in Jerusalem

c. A.D. 60–62 Paul is imprisoned in Rome; Ephesians is written

c. A.D. 67 Peter and Paul are executed

letter. In addition to the lack of personal references, the content and teaching of the letter is itself very general. Paul refers to the church as the body of Christ as a whole, and not to a specific local church. If the letters to the Corinthians bristle with local congregational problems, Ephesians lacks such allusions entirely.

The idea that Ephesians is a circular letter is not unparalleled. In a way, all the New Testament epistles are circular in the sense that they eventually were circulated among many churches. While the question of destination is interesting, it does not strongly affect the meaning or the relevance of the letter. To a greater or lesser extent, all the letters in the New Testament are for the general edification of the church.

Ephesians Outline

I. **Doctrines for members of Christ's body 1:1–3:21**
   A. Paul's greeting of grace 1:1, 2
   B. God's election 1:3–12
   C. The Spirit's sealing 1:13–23
   D. Salvation by grace through faith 2:1–10
   E. The unity of Christ's body 2:11–22
   F. The mystery of Christ's body 3:1–21

II. **Duties of the members of Christ's body 4:1–6:24**
   A. To walk worthy 4:1–6
   B. To build up the body through one's gift 4:7–16
   C. To put on the new person 4:17–32
   D. To be imitators of God 5:1–21
      1. By walking in love 5:1–7
      2. By walking in light 5:8–14
      3. By walking in wisdom 5:15–17
      4. By walking in the Spirit 5:18–21
   E. To promote domestic harmony 5:22–6:9
      1. Between wives and husbands 5:22–33
      2. Between children and parents 6:1–4
      3. Between slaves and masters 6:5–9
   F. To put on God's full armor 6:10–20
   G. Paul's salutation of grace 6:21–24

Commentary

1:1–3:21 The first half of Ephesians, like that of a number of Paul's epistles, stresses the doctrines or beliefs upon which the duties and behavior of the second half are built.

1:1, 2 The salutations in NT epistles follow the form of the typical first-century letter: the writer is mentioned first and the recipient next,

followed by a blessing or best wishes for good health. The difference lies in the content of the blessing: pagan letters mentioned non-existent gods and goddesses such as Diana or Apollo; the apostles call upon the one true God and His Son Jesus Christ to bless their readers. In Ephesians, Paul refers to himself as an **apostle** because he was personally commissioned by Jesus Christ with special authority to preach the gospel. **Saints** in the NT refers to all believers set apart by God in Christ. **Ephesus:** This letter may have been a circular letter for the churches around Ephesus.

1:2 The free gift of salvation which is God's **grace** leads to **peace** and the wholeness of life. The deity of the **Lord Jesus Christ** is made clear by associating Him parallel with the **Father.**

1:3–12 Right at the beginning of the letter, Paul bursts out in praise for the God who chose Him before the foundation of the world. It was in Christ that He elected them to be both blessed and a blessing to others. The emphasis is not merely on escaping punishment, but on acting like real saints and bringing praise to God's glory.

1:3 The blessings of Christianity are largely **spiritual.** God does not guarantee health, wealth, and prosperity to the NT believer. The phrase **in the heavenly places** suggests that a Christian living anywhere in the world is even now in a spiritual sense seated with Christ on high.

1:4, 5 **Love** here is *agape* in Greek, the love that is by choice or one's will, not just a sentimental feeling. **having predestined us:** Predestination is not a cold-hearted determinism or set fate, but rather a loving choice on God's part. **According to** (Gk. *kata*) is a significant term in Ephesians, but not apt to be noticed since it is a common preposition. Paul uses it eleven times in this epistle. In ch. 1 we read "according to the good pleasure of His will" (v. 5), "according to the riches of His grace" (v. 7), "according to His good pleasure" (v. 9), and "according to the purpose of Him who works all things according to the counsel of His will" (v. 11). In ch. 3 we read "according to the riches of His glory" (v. 16) and "according to the power that works in us" (v. 20). The point of all this is that God does not merely lavish His grace on us "out of" (*ek*) abundance, but in accordance with (*kata*) His abundance. This has been well illustrated by the millionaire giving out dimes on the street. If he gave like God gives, "according to his riches," he would be giving out one hundred dollar bills.

1:6 **The Beloved** may also be translated "the One He Loves," namely, Jesus Christ. In Col. 1:13 Paul uses the similar title "the Son of His love." *The Beloved* is a messianic title, referring to God's Son. Jesus is not simply one among others who are loved by God. He is *the* Beloved Son.

1:7, 8 redemption: The word means "buy back" or "ransom." In ancient times, one could buy back a person who was sold into slavery. In the same way, Christ through His death bought us from our slavery to sin. **His blood:** The blood of Christ is the means by which our redemption comes. The OT and the NT both clearly teach that there is no forgiveness without the shedding of blood. Blood here is a vivid symbolic equivalent of death. It recalls the sacrificial system of the old covenant, which looked forward to the self-sacrifice of Jesus Christ that took away the sin of the world..

1:9 The mystery is not a puzzle to solve, or knowledge only for the few and the initiated, as in the mystery religions of Paul's day. In Paul's usage, the word *mystery* refers to an aspect of God's will that was once hidden or obscure, but now was being revealed by God (Rom. 11:25).

1:10 The word translated **dispensation** means "house rule." The English word *economy* is derived from this Greek word. The word refers to God's administration or arrangement of all history to fulfill His plan of salvation. While God never changes, His plan for the salvation of humanity has distinct phases. In this context, *dispensation* probably refers to the time when God will establish His eternal kingdom.

1:11, 12 We Jews **have obtained an inheritance** in Christ, far better than the inheritance promised under the old covenant. This was not something new, but was **predestined** (planned) **according to the purpose** of God from the beginning.

1:13–23 In this paragraph Paul switches from those who, like him, were born into Jewish homes ("we") to those with Gentile ethnic roots ("you"). The emphasis is on the work of the Holy Spirit. He seals every believer, thus making him or her God's special possession through faith. The Holy Spirit Himself is the seal and guarantee of our acceptance by God through faith in Christ. The goal of the Holy Spirit is to produce a fully perfect "Christ," namely, Jesus Christ the head and Christians the body! What an amazing thought, that we who were once alienated from God now help fill out what Paul calls the "Christ."

1:14 The guarantee of our inheritance is the Holy Spirit Himself. Interestingly, the Greek word for *guarantee* can also be used to indicate an engagement ring. As Christ is the Bridegroom and the church is the bride, so the Holy Spirit is the down payment, the earnest money, in the long-awaited marriage of the two (Rev. 19:7, 8). **purchased possession:** The OT described the nation of Israel as God's special treasure, one He had purchased by His mighty acts of deliverance during the Exodus (Ex. 19:5; Deut. 7:6). Here Paul describes Christians as the Lord's own possession, one bought with the blood of His own Son.

1:15–23 Here is Paul's earnest prayer of intercession for these Christians. After giving thanks for them (vv. 15, 16), he prays that they will have spiritual insight (v. 17) into **the hope of His calling** (v. 18), into the **glory of His inheritance** (v. 18), and into the **exceeding greatness of His power** (vv. 19–23).

1:15 after I heard (Col. 1:5, 9): Paul doesn't mention praying for them before he heard of their faith. How different from most of our prayers. We tend to plead for the salvation

---

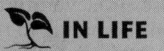 **IN LIFE**   ## What's In It for Me?

Peter and the other disciples wondered what they were going to get out of following Christ. "We have left all and followed You," Peter told Jesus. "Therefore what shall we have?" (Matt. 19:27). In other words, "What's the payoff? What's in this for me?"

Paul describes some of the "payoff" for believers here in Eph. 1:3–14. Because so much of it lies in the future, in another mode of existence, the language is strange and hard to understand. But in 1:11 he mentions an inheritance that is coming to us. What is it that we are going to receive "in Christ"?

Simply this: all that God has prepared for Christ in "the fullness of the times" is going to be ours as well (Rom. 8:15–17). This includes salvation from sin (Heb. 1:14), everlasting life (Matt. 19:29), and the kingdom of God (25:34). In fact, we will inherit God Himself.

Is this just wishful thinking? No, God is already giving us glimpses of that inconceivable future. The Holy Spirit lives inside us as a guarantee of things to come (Eph. 1:14). He "seals" us, assuring that we remain in God's family and do not lose our inheritance. And while we move toward that day, He works within our lives to make us like Christ. Paul describes what that looks like inchs. 4–6.

of lost persons and then drop them once they come to faith in Christ. Paul did just the opposite. Perhaps he learned from the Lord's pattern of prayer (John 1:7, 9, 20).

1:16, 17 my prayers: It is instructive to study Paul's prayers and learn about the nature of intercession. Much of our praying falls short of effective intercession.

1:18, 19 The eyes of your understanding refers to spiritual understanding. To describe this, Paul uses words that picture the heart looking out with eyes that have been brightened with divine illumination. **what is the hope:** A Christian may hope many things, but there is one hope that all Christians have in common (4:4), the Lord Jesus Christ (Col. 1:5, 27). In Him we find true hope and true riches.

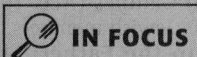

IN FOCUS "purpose"

(Gk. *prothesis*) (1:9, 11; 3:11; Rom. 8:28) Strong's #4286; counsel (Gk. *boule*) (1:11; 1 Cor. 4:5; Heb. 6:17) Strong's #1012; will (Gk. *thelema*) (1:1, 9, 11; 2:3; 5:17; Rom. 1:10; 1 Cor. 1:1) Strong's #2307: Three key words, all related conceptually, appear in this verse. One of these words (*thelema*) has been used by Paul twice before in this chapter (1:1, 9). The word conveys the idea of desire, even a heart's desire, for the word primarily expresses emotion instead of volition. Thus, God's will is not so much God's intention, as it is His heart's desire. The word *prothesis* denotes an intention or a plan; it literally means "a laying out beforehand" like a blueprint. This plan was created in God's counsel, a translation of the Greek word *boule*, which means the result of deliberate determination. But behind the plan and the counsel was not just a mastermind but a heart of love.

1:20 worked in Christ: The resurrection of Christ from the dead was the expression of God's power. The Resurrection is also proof of what God can do in us and for us. **seated Him:** Christ Jesus was not only raised from the dead; He was given a position at the **right hand** of God. Jesus received this position as the Son of David in fulfillment of the messianic prophecies of Pss. 2; 110. Jesus Christ will remain at the Father's right hand until the enemies of God have been subjugated and it is time for Christ to return.

1:21 The Jews of Christ's time understood

the end times to be divided into two time periods, the age in which they were living and the coming age. The Messiah, called "the Coming One," would rule in the age **which is to come.**

1:22, 23 In Ephesians Paul emphasizes Christ as **head,** just as his letter to the Colossians, written during the same imprisonment, emphasizes the body of Christ. **The church** here does not refer to any one local assembly but to all believers.

2:1–10 This is probably the clearest exposition of the gospel in all of Paul's epistles: We are saved by grace through faith totally apart from human merit or works. It is not that Christians do not do good works (we were created for this purpose), but that they are not a requirement or proof of acceptance with God. Luther summarized it succinctly: "It is not against *works* that we contend, but against *trust* in works."

2:1 Dead in trespasses and sins means spiritually dead and lost.

2:2 you once walked: Walking is a biblical expression that pictures a believer's steady, normal progress with God (Ps. 1:1). Paul here refers to a believer's old walk. Whether it was a path of moral carelessness or the dark alley of evil, believers should no longer walk according to their past evil ways (4:17). Believers are saved so that they can have a lifestyle characterized by good works (v. 10). They are to walk worthy of their calling (4:1), which means to walk in love (5:2), in light (5:8), and in wisdom (5:15). Paul points out to the Ephesians that they formerly walked according to the world's ways and after **the prince of the power of the air**—namely, the adversarial **spirit** Satan. **Sons of** is a Hebrew way of saying "those characterized by." Thus, the **sons of disobedience** are people who disobey, whether Christians or non-Christians (Matt. 16:23; Luke 22:31, 32; Acts 5:3).

2:3 Lusts means "strong desires." Even with the modifier **of our flesh,** this word pertains to more than merely sensual cravings. The natural human desires for fame, power, and riches are meant as well (Gal. 5:19–21).

2:4–7 we were dead: Because of Adam's sin, the entire human race is spiritually dead. Only God can grant new life and save us from this predicament. Out of His mercy, God gave His Son for us while we were yet His enemies. He loved us long before we loved Him (1 John 4:9, 10). In addition to making us spiritually **alive,** He determined that we would sit in **heavenly places** with our Savior, Jesus Christ. **in the ages to come:** God desires to demonstrate **His kindness** throughout eternity through **Christ Jesus** His Son. This has nothing to do with our own merit. It is only

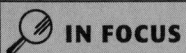

IN FOCUS   "workmanship"

(Gk. *poiema*) (2:10; Rom. 1:20) Strong's #4161: The word literally means "a thing made"; it comes into English as *poem*. The word indicates a handiwork, a masterpiece. God's church is His "poem," His masterpiece, His workmanship, just as all creation is (Ps. 19:1; Rom. 1:20). As He is the Author of His handiwork, He should get all the credit (Ps. 19:1–6).

because He is merciful and kind that He reaches out to save us.

2:8–10 Christians **have been saved** by **grace.** The grace of God is the source of salvation; **faith** is the channel, not the cause. God alone saves. Salvation never originates in the efforts of people; it always arises out of the lovingkindness of God. Truly, "salvation is of the LORD" (Jon. 2:9). The past tense of the verb *saved* in this passage indicates that the believer's salvation has already occurred in the past, at the Cross. **the gift of God:** We cannot do anything to earn our salvation. Some suggest that *the gift of God* modifies the word *faith* in this verse. Thus, Paul is saying that even our belief in God does not originate in ourselves. This too is a gift, so no one can take pride in his or her position as a Christian. Everything is received from our merciful and gracious Father.

2:11–22 In vv. 1–10, Paul taught the salvation of individual Jews and Gentiles by grace through faith. In the second half of ch. 2, he teaches the formation of one new and holy temple of God composed of former Jews and Gentiles now united upon the foundation of apostles and prophets, Jesus Christ Himself being the cornerstone.

2:11 Because the sign of the Abrahamic covenant was circumcision, the Jews proudly referred to themselves as **the Circumcision.** Somewhat less kindly, they called Gentiles the **Uncircumcision.**

2:12, 13 Paul painted vividly the bleak condition of pagans. They had no hope, for God had not reached out to them to establish a covenant relationship. However, the shed **blood of Christ** could bring the Gentiles back to their Creator.

2:14 The **middle wall of separation** between Jews and Gentiles was vividly portrayed by an actual partition in the temple area, with a sign warning that any Gentile going beyond the Court of the Gentiles would receive swift and sudden death.

2:15, 16 having abolished . . . the law: Paul was not saying that God had rejected the righteous standards of the law. Rather, in Christ the righteous standards that people could never

reach have been accomplished. He is our righteousness; in Him, believers fulfill the law (Matt. 5:17, 20; Rom. 3:21, 22, 31). The Christian church, composed of both Jews and Gentiles, is described as **one new man.** In the earliest days of Christianity, the church was largely made up of Jews. But under the direction of God's Spirit, the believers witnessed to Gentiles (Acts 10), who then outnumbered the Jewish members.

2:17, 18 access . . . to the Father: The blessed privilege of every Christian. All members of the Trinity—Christ, the **Spirit,** and the **Father**—are involved in our salvation.

2:19 When Gentiles become one with the people of God, they are not simply patched on. They, along with Jewish believers, are made **fellow citizens** of the kingdom of God and equal **members** of God's family.

2:20 The **apostles and prophets** were the foundation of the church because they pointed to and witnessed to Jesus. The early church was established on their teaching and preaching (Acts 2). Yet Christ Himself is the rock foundation on which the whole church rests (1 Cor. 3:11). The **cornerstone** was the first large stone placed at the corner of a building. The builders would line up the rest of the structure to the chief cornerstone (1 Pet. 2:1–9).

2:21, 22 Being fitted together pictures the process in Roman construction whereby laborers (usually slaves) would turn huge rocks around until they fit each other perfectly. For example, columns appeared to be one piece, but were actually separate cylinders of stone resting on each other. In similar fashion, God fits believers together into the **holy temple** He is building for Himself.

3:1–21 If we compare 3:1 with 3:14, we see that everything between the two times Paul uses the expression "for this reason" is a digression. This is a common feature of the apostle's writing style. These are real letters, not books of systematic theology (although next to Romans, Ephesians probably constitutes the most closely reasoned theology in the NT). The parenthetical material details God's revelation to Paul of the "mystery," that is, the sacred secret that in the dispensation (or stewardship) of God's grace,

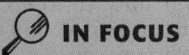

"stewardship"

(Gk. *oikonomia*) (1:10; 3:2; 1 Cor. 9:17; 1 Tim. 1:4) Strong's #3622: The word means "household management." In ancient times, the word was often used to describe the work of a person who took care of all the financial affairs of a large household or business (Luke 16:1, 2). Paul was entrusted with the stewardship of God's economy, to dispense the riches of Christ to God's household and to preach the Good News (3:2–11). Paul uses this same word to describe God's own administration or government of time (1:10).

Jews and Gentiles would be on an equal level and in one body.

3:1–4 The **dispensation** (stewardship) that God gave Paul for the benefit of the Ephesians had previously been a mystery. Now God was revealing this mystery more fully in Paul's ministry to the Gentiles. The mystery was that Jews and Gentiles were to have an equal status in the church, the body of Christ.

3:5, 6 People who lived in the **other ages,** before Pentecost, had a great deal of knowledge about God and His grace, as the OT demonstrates. However, that knowledge was not as all-embracing as the revelation that we receive in Christ Jesus. The OT predicted that God's grace would come to the Gentiles (Gen. 12:3), but equality with the Jews in one body was a secret never before **revealed.**

3:7 The word translated **minister** here means "servant." **the gift of . . . grace:** It took divine grace to transform Paul from a blasphemer into a saint, from a Pharisee into an apostle, and from a persecutor of Christians into a preacher of Christ. Then it took divine power

and authority to enable Paul to function as a minister of God.

3:8 Paul was not expressing false humility when he called himself **less than the least of all the saints.** He was truly humble because he previously had persecuted Christ's church. In another place Paul refers to himself as the chief of sinners (1 Tim. 1:15). He is ever conscious of his demerit and never thinks of himself more highly than he ought to think (Rom. 12:3). **the unsearchable riches of Christ:** The contents of the message, the wealth beyond description which God provides for all men in the person and work of Christ. It is a vast and measureless resource, this love and grace of God. If Christ were not too big for our mental comprehension, He would be too little for our spiritual need.

3:9 Paul's mission as an apostle was to enlighten all people about the **mystery** of God's grace in Christ, which was not understood in previous times but which had become clear with the coming of Jesus Christ.

3:10–13 God's **manifold wisdom** is to be displayed to the angelic beings by the members

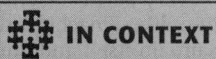

The Power of Prayer

Our troubles can easily cause us to lose the larger picture about life. Daily routines and pressures can create doubts about our significance. And because we are bound in a world of time, it's easy to assume that difficulties such as sickness, conflict, loneliness, insecurity, or fear will become a permanent state of affairs.

The Ephesian believers lived with a lot of pressure. Their faith was born in a crucible of riots, courtroom conflict, and economic change (Acts 19:23–40). Later, when Paul wrote this letter to the Ephesians, he encouraged them to develop and maintain God's perspective on their lives and faith:

- *Looking back,* he rehearsed what God had done for them before they were even born (Eph. 1:3–8).
- *Looking forward,* he listed the future benefits that their faith would bring (1:9–14).
- *In the meantime,* he prayed that they would be aware of and comprehend these realities, and experience God's power (1:15–23). He also prayed that their identity would be rooted in eternal truths and in God's present power in them (3:14–21).

of the church. God's ways are not only "mysterious," but also varied. Angels are also learning about God's wisdom as they watch His grace working in us (1 Cor. 11:10).

3:14–21 These verses express the essence of Paul's prayer for these Ephesian believers. He recognizes the fatherhood of God as well as His position as the great Creator and sustainer. He asks not for material possessions for these Christians but strengthening in the inner person. He desires that they come to understand the love of Christ. The apostle closes with a beautiful statement of his grand vision of God's work in believers. This is an excellent model prayer that all believers might use in their praying for others.

3:14, 15 Father and **family** are related words in the original text. All families of people and angels derive from God the Father, their Creator.

3:16, 17 Paul seems to be speaking of that second experience of the Christian in which the Holy Spirit cleanses and empowers the heart. To be thus **strengthened** by the **Spirit,** to have the indwelling **Christ,** and to be established in **love** are basic to Christian growth. **Dwell** is from the Greek word used for permanent residence. We are to be **rooted** like a tree and **grounded** in the love that God has for us and gives to us.

3:18, 19 The **love of Christ** is so great that it is beyond our understanding. The **fullness of God** is the abundance of gifts that flows from God.

3:20, 21 These two verses form a doxology, or praise, to God in which Paul points out that God can **do exceedingly abundantly above** anything we may **ask.** Neither God's love nor His power is limited by human imagination.

4:1 The second half of Ephesians, like that of a number of Paul's epistles, emphasizes the behavior that should result from the doctrines or beliefs taught in the first half. Note that the Christian life is not compared here to running or standing still, but to a walk. **walk worthy:** A believer's life should match the excellency of Christ's calling.

4:2 lowliness and gentleness, with long-suffering: These are the attitudes that Jesus demonstrated when He was on earth (Phil. 2:5–8). These attitudes do not come naturally, but must be cultivated by the determination to place others above ourselves. Only the Spirit can empower us to treat people this way consistently. **Bearing** is close to our expression "putting up with"; however, Paul's use of the term has positive connotations. It describes being patient with the shortcomings of others. Often we ask God to be patient with our own failings, and yet do not exercise the same type of patience ourselves.

4:3 unity of the Spirit: All Christians are one in the Spirit. It is our duty to **keep** or observe that unity, recognize it as real, and act upon it without a sectarian spirit (John 17:20–26) **Endeavoring** means to make every effort, to work hard at maintaining the unity of the Spirit.

4:4 There is one body: The church is a living organism composed only of living members (i.e., blood-bought, born-again, Bible-believing saints). This one body has one Head and many members (1 Cor. 12:12, 13). **one Spirit:** The Holy Spirit who is the life and breath of that body, who was instrumental in the regeneration of each member, and who now maintains a vital connection of each member with the other members and with the head. **one hope of your calling:** The same ultimate, glorious reality for both Jews and Gentiles.

4:5 One baptism may refer to the baptism in the Spirit that places all believers into the body of Christ, the church (1 Cor. 12:13). It may also refer to water baptism, the sign or seal that a person is a member of the body of Christ. At the time of the early church, public baptism clearly identified a person as a Christian.

4:6 one God and Father of all: For all; not a separate God for each nation. **who is above all:** This speaks of His transcendence and His unshared sovereign power. **and through all:** This speaks of His immanence, His pervading action. **and in you all:** This speaks of His indwelling presence of believers, His personal relationship. The one God rules over all, works through all, and dwells in all.

4:7 Like Peter (1 Pet. 4:10), Paul taught that all Christians have a spiritual **gift** or gifts. The gifts are given sovereignly by the ascended Christ in order to build up the church (1 Cor. 12:11). Thus, the body of Christ is to function like a machine in which every part is essential for getting a job done. But unlike a machine, the body of Christ should maintain itself and build every one of its members up so that they can do good works (1 Cor. 12:7).

4:8 Paul quotes Ps. 68:18 to picture the **ascended** Messiah, triumphant over Satan and his hosts, distributing spiritual **gifts** to His people. The faithful stewardship of our gifts on earth will determine our position of service in Christ's messianic reign.

4:9 Many people take this descent to refer to Christ's entering Hades (specifically the saved portion of that unseen world) after His crucifixion to take saints to heaven when He rose from the dead. On the other hand, **lower parts of the earth** may also be translated "lower parts, the earth," so as to refer to Christ's coming to our humble planet as a man. This is the more likely meaning here (Phil. 2:5–8).

4:10 The One who humbled Himself as a lowly Servant is the same One **who ascended far above all the heavens** in universal supremacy (Phil. 2:9–11; Col. 1:18).

4:11 Apostles, meaning "envoys," or "ambassadors," in its strict sense refers to those who saw Christ in resurrected form, performed miracles, and were specially chosen by Christ to tell others about Him from their eyewitness accounts. As such, there are no apostles today. **Prophets** delivered direct revelations from God before the NT was written (1 Cor. 14). They foretold God's actions in the future, and they proclaimed what God had already said in the Scriptures. **Evangelists** are gospel preachers who help bring people into the body of Christ. They do so by presenting Christ's offer of free salvation by grace through faith (2:8, 9). Since each of these categories is responsible for equipping believers, evangelists may also train other believers to share their faith effectively. **Pastors** do all for the church that a literal shepherd does for sheep: feeds, nurtures, cares for, and protects them from enemies. A shepherd's task is not to acquire sheep. However, if a shepherd does what he is supposed to do, he will have healthy sheep and his flock will grow. **teachers:** While the Greek ties the two titles *teachers* and *pastors* closely together here, elsewhere they are listed separately (Rom. 12:7; 1 Pet. 5:2).

4:12, 13 Three stages of growth are presented here: Gifted leaders are responsible for **the equipping of the saints;** the well-equipped saints do **the work of ministry;** and the result is that **the body of Christ** is built up. The final goal is maturity, truth, and love.

4:14 Children are gullible, vulnerable, and easily victimized. The church needs to work diligently at moving babes in Christ on to maturity (1 Pet. 2:2).

4:15 Speaking the truth in love suggests that all that believers say or do should be honest and true, and said or done in a loving manner.

4:16 Note the use of the body metaphor here to present the same truth as the building metaphor in 2:21. **Every joint . . . every part** is essential to full growth. There are no insignificant parts in the body (1 Cor. 12:14–27). Anything that builds up believers and the church can be said to be **edifying.**

4:17–19 Those who are so insensitive to moral darkness as to be **past feeling** have been hardened by years of sin and debauchery.

4:20, 21 The **if indeed** is assumed to be true. Paul is not casting doubt on their Christian experience.

4:22–24 Paul compared the Christian life to stripping **off** the dirty clothes of a sinful past and putting on the snowy white robes of Christ's righteousness.

4:25 Quoting Zech. 8:16, Paul calls for believers to speak the **truth** to each other, because all believers are united in Christ. The Proverbs identify a lying tongue as one of the six things God abhors (Prov. 6:17).

4:26 Paul uses Ps. 4:4 to illustrate that not all **wrath** is sinful. However, anger should not be allowed to fester or continue for long (Mark

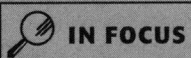

IN FOCUS | "new man"

(Gk. *kainos anthropos*) (4:24; Col. 3:10) Strong's #2537; 444: This Greek word for *new* does not mean something more recent in time, but something having a different quality or nature. Thus, the *new man* is the new humanity created in Christ, of which all believers partake, both individually and corporately. Since Paul has already spoken of the new man created in Christ in terms of a new unified corporate humanity (2:14, 15), the new man in this verse must also be thought of corporately (Col. 3:9–11). In the immediate context, Paul is exhorting each believer to put on his or her new human nature.

11:25). Christians may respond in controlled anger to injustice and sin, but they should never be consumed by this anger. Instead they should seek opportunities to express Christ's love to everyone.

4:27 nor give place to the devil: Satan waits for opportunity to get his foot in the door. The Greek present imperative means: Do not have the habit of giving place to Satan. Uncontrolled anger is an open door and an invitation for Satan to enter in to disrupt and corrupt the body. He can only hurt and harm as he finds a place in some life to do his evil work.

4:28 something to give him who has need: Instead of taking what belongs to someone else, a Christian should earn enough to share some of his or her own earnings with the needy. This is not merely a call to stop stealing or being greedy. Rather, this is a call to be generous, to have a true change of attitude.

4:29 Standards of speech for Christians are extremely high: **no corrupt word** is permitted.

4:30 The Holy Spirit of God should never be pushed away, ignored, or rejected. If we would remember that the One who lives in us is God's own Spirit, we would be much more selective about what we think, read, watch, say, and do. Note that Paul acknowledges that evil thoughts and actions are temp-

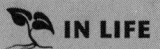 **IN LIFE**   **From Deadbeat to Donor**

D oes Christ affect people's work life? Yes, and Paul gives a concrete illustration of what "putting on the new man" means (Eph. 4:24, 28). After Christ comes into his life, a person who has been a no-account thief stops stealing and takes an honest job. He becomes a contributing, productive member of society, doing good work. As a result, he is able to provide for his own needs and those of his family.

But the transformation doesn't stop there. As God prospers him through his labor, he is able to give money away to help meet the needs of others. Christ changes a deadbeat into a donor!

tations even for those who are **sealed** by the Holy Spirit.

4:31, 32 The old life comes from a hostile heart of **bitterness,** seeks its own way, speaks **evil** and wishes evil on others. How do we put away **all** bitterness? By letting God fill our hearts with His perfect love. The new life is **tenderhearted,** shows itself in acts of kindness, and is ready to forgive wrongs suffered from others.

5:1, 2 Believers are to follow the example of God's actions. He loved us when we were still His enemies. As **imitators,** believers should demonstrate that type of self-sacrificial love.

5:3 Ephesus, with its pagan temple dedicated to the Roman goddess Diana (Acts 19:23–31), was similar to our society in that sexual immorality and greed ran rampant. Paul warned the believers in Ephesus to avoid these pitfalls.

5:4 The Christian's life must not be degraded by **filthiness, foolish talking, coarse jesting.** These do not honor God nor give Him **thanks** for redeeming us.

5:5 The modern laxity of morals in many religious circles is contrary to God's word. **Unclean** and greedy people will have no **inheritance in the kingdom.**

5:6 See note at 2:2 for the phrase **sons of disobedience.** God's **wrath** is aimed at those who practice the vices mentioned in v. 5.

5:7–10 The believer's position has changed from **darkness** (sin) to **light (righteousness).** Believers are to change their **walk** to correspond to their position in Christ (Rom 12:2).

5:11, 12 Have no fellowship with evil persons in their evil deeds, nor participate in their wickedness. We **expose** (reprove) evil deeds when we avoid them and let others know how God feels about them.

5:12, 13 in secret: This verse effectively bans Christians from indulging in the modern preoccupation with examining the lurid details of evils such as the occult and other perverted practices.

5:14 Awake, you who sleep: This may be

a fragment of a first-century Christian hymn, or an original thought by Paul alluding to Is. 26:19, a promise of God's coming salvation.

5:15 To **walk circumspectly** is to step gingerly. We should watch our path to avoid contact with undesirable influences.

5:16 Redeeming the time means taking advantage of opportunities for service. We each have a limited amount of time on this earth. Paul exhorts us to use as much of that time as possible for advancing Christ's purposes in this world.

5:17 do not be unwise, but understand: Discerning the will of the Lord is not a matter of feeling or emotion, but of mental understanding, applying our minds to Scripture.

5:18 Just as a person who is **drunk with wine** is under the control of alcohol, so a Spirit-filled believer is controlled by the Spirit. **filled:** Filling is a step beyond the sealing of the Holy Spirit (1:13). Sealing is an action God took at the point of our new birth. The tense of the Greek word translated *filled* indicates that filling is a moment-by-moment, repeatable action. It is something Paul commands the believers at Ephesus to do. In other words, not all Christians are Spirit-filled, but all have been sealed (4:30).

5:19 One of the natural outcomes of being filled with the Spirit is **singing and making melody** to God. Some take the three types of music that Paul mentions in this verse to refer to different parts of the Book of Psalms. Most believe that these words refer to three larger categories: (1) the 150 **psalms** in the Psalter, plus other psalmlike poems throughout the Scripture; (2) **hymns,** compositions addressed directly to God, like the modern song "How Great Thou Art"; (3) **spiritual songs,** hymns about the Christian experience, like "Amazing Grace."

5:20 giving thanks . . . all things: When we truly believe 1:11, we will have much less trouble with 5:20.

5:21, 22 Verse 21 completes the thought of the previous verses (vv. 18–20), which address how being filled with the Spirit manifests itself

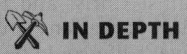

The Concept of Submission

What kind of submission is Paul advocating in Ephesians? Some hold that Paul is speaking of mutual submission in this passage (5:21–6:4). They point to the phrase "submitting to one another in the fear of God" (5:21), as the overall theme of the verses following it (5:21–6:4). According to this view, husbands and wives, parents and children, masters and slaves all submit to each other in different ways.

This passage certainly teaches a proper Christian response to each other at different levels, as the mutual submission view holds. It is clear that Paul develops two ideas side by side—submission and the appropriate response of the one to whom submission is given. But the mutual submission view does not adequately reflect the meaning of *submission* in Greek. The Greek term for *submission* has military origins, emphasizing being under the authority of another. The word does not connote a forced submission; instead it is a voluntary submission to a proper authority. Thus, Paul seems to be saying that wives should voluntarily place themselves under the authority of their husbands. The same word is used to describe Christians voluntarily submitting to governmental authorities (1 Pet. 2:13) and younger people submitting to the wisdom of their elders (1 Pet. 5:5). In this passage, Paul gives the illustration of the church's submission to Christ. After encouraging wives to submit to their husbands, Paul goes on to describe how children should obey their parents, and slaves their masters. Their subordination is described in terms of obedience, instead of in terms of voluntary submission.

But Paul's major emphasis in this passage is not on the submission of wives, but on the duty of those who are in authority. Husbands should imitate the love of Christ. Parents should not provoke children. Masters are not to threaten their slaves. The apostle argues that serving is more important than being in authority over others; Christ should be our model. Although He, as God's Son, could demand obedience from all, He did not shrink from performing duties that were customarily the task of a servant. Jesus washed the feet of His disciples (John 13:12–16). A husband is to be a godly leader; he is to be a servant-leader. His role is to lead his wife, but to do so by taking everything about her into consideration and by using his position to give her the greatest opportunity to succeed.

in the believer's life. It also introduces the next section (5:22—6:4), about how members of a Christian family should relate to each other. **submitting:** The Greek word for *submitting* does not refer to being under the absolute control of another but, in this context, to voluntarily placing oneself under the authority of another.

5:22–24 Just as Christ is not inferior to the Father, but is the second person in the Trinity, so **wives** are equal to their **own husbands.** Yet in a marriage relationship, a husband and wife have different roles. **to the Lord:** A wife's voluntary submission arises out of her own submission to Christ.

5:25 Husbands, love: Paul does not emphasize the husband's authority; instead, he calls on husbands to love self-sacrificially. Husbands are to emulate Christ's love, the kind of love that is willing to lay down one's life for another person and serve that person even if it means suffering.

5:26, 27 In these verses, Paul briefly outlines what Jesus has done for the church. First of all, He loved the church so much that He was willing to suffer and die for it. His actions not only saved the church; they also sanctified it. In other words, Jesus wanted to develop the

church into what it should be, the holy temple of God.

5:28 as their own bodies: As they love themselves. This depth of love for the wife was never expected in the pagan world of Rome and Greece.

5:29 A husband who realizes that his wife is truly **his own flesh** will treat her with love and care.

5:30 We Christians are **members** of Christ's **body.**

5:31 the two shall become one flesh: Paul quotes Gen. 2:24, which teaches that the special union between husband and wife supersedes the original family ties.

5:32 The mystery, a sacred secret revealed, is that Christian marriage parallels the union that exists spiritually between **Christ** and His bride, **the church.**

5:33 Men need respect; women who put down their husbands, especially in public, are destroying their marriage. It works both ways. Men who treat their wives in an unloving or ungracious way are also endangering their marital happiness.

6:1–4 This paragraph has the beautiful balance we expect to find in God's Word: children are to obey their parents, and parents are to treat their children in such a way that the children will want to obey. **Children** must obey their **parents** for Christ's sake, even if their parents are not believers. This is supported by the only one of the Ten Commandments followed by a **promise** (Deut. 5:16). Of course, Christian children should not do anything sinful even if their parents should command them to. In such a case, children must obey God rather than men (Acts 5:29). **do not provoke:** Parents should not be unreasonably severe with children or ridicule them.

6:5 A very large percentage of the population of the Roman Empire was made up of **bondservants** or slaves. These people were considered mere property and could be abused and even killed by their masters with no resulting investigation by the state. In the church, wealthy slave owners and their slaves broke bread together at the Lord's Table as equals. No doubt some slaves were gifted spiritual leaders and ministered the word to people far above them on the social ladder.

6:6 not with eyeservice: Servants and employees should serve faithfully even when no one is looking. After all, God sees all that we do.

6:7 If every job were done as **to the Lord,** what a difference it would make in the quality of our work!

6:8 Receive the same refers to future rewards (Col. 3:23–25).

6:9 Christian **masters** should not use **threatening** language to their servants but should remember that they too are servants of a much higher **Master . . . in heaven,** who is completely fair.

6:10–20 This practical passage is one of the most famous and richly rewarding in all of the NT. Paul probably had plenty of time to contemplate the parts of a Roman soldier's armor. After all, he was constantly guarded during his house arrest in Rome.

6:10 Be strong may also be translated "be made strong." The passive voice would suggest that we cannot do it ourselves.

6:11 The whole armor of God is the believer's protection against evil and the Evil One. Paul presented the extended metaphor of the battle dress roughly according to the order in which the various pieces were put on. **Wiles of the devil** are Satan's subtle tricks to defeat Christians in spiritual warfare (2 Cor. 11:3).

6:12 Our real battle is not with human cultists, false religionists, atheists, agnostics, and pseudo-Christians, but with the demonic beings working through them, of which even the **flesh and blood** opponents themselves are sometimes unaware.

6:13 The evil day is taken by some to refer to the end times when the Evil One will launch a ferocious campaign against Christ and His army. A more common view is that any great spiritual contest in a believer's life could be in view here.

6:14 Verses 14–17 present the six pieces of spiritual armor. Four are mentioned specifically and the belt and shoes are implied. Soldiers **girded** themselves with a belt, from which hung strips of leather to protect the lower body. **Truth** is considered crucial by Paul (4:15, 25), because a dishonest Christian cannot hope to withstand the father of lies himself. The truth referred to here is integrity, a life of practical truthfulness and honesty. The **breastplate** of Roman times went completely around the body, so that the back of a warrior was also protected. The breastplate was made of hard leather or metal. The **righteousness** that the breastplate represents is not the righteousness of Christ, which all believers possess, but the practical, righteous character and deeds of believers.

6:15 A Roman soldier's **feet** were **shod** with hard, studded shoes. Paul used this image to represent **the preparation of the gospel of peace.** This may mean either that the gospel is

Photo by Howard Vos

A Roman soldier in combat gear, demonstrating some of the pieces of "spiritual armor" needed in the believer's battle against Satan (Eph. 6:10–18).

the firm foundation on which Christians are to stand or that the Christian soldier should be ready to go out to defend and spread the gospel.

6:16 Above all may mean that the **shield**

is to be used against everything. It may also mean that the shield is to cover the whole armor. A Roman soldier's shield typically measured two and a half feet by four feet. The Christian's shield offers protection against **all the fiery darts of the wicked one.** Flaming arrows could not penetrate the fireproof shield of the ancient Roman soldier, nor can the assaults of Satan penetrate to the believer who places his or her faith in God.

6:17 the helmet of salvation: The intricately designed Roman helmet protected the soldier's head and also made him look taller and more impressive. **The sword of the Spirit** is the only offensive weapon in the believer's armor. This weapon is not necessarily the Bible as a whole, but the specific word that needs to be spoken in a specific situation. To have the precise word ready, a person must know the Bible intimately.

6:18–23 Paul, the man of prayer (1:15–23; 3:14–21), ends this great section of his letter to the believers at Ephesus with an exhortation to prayer.

6:18 Without **prayer,** all the armor in the world would be of no use. **praying always:** General prayers and specific petitions in the Spirit are to be made **for all** believers and at all occasions. Perseverance and patience in prayer are essential.

6:19 The apostle Paul was not ashamed to ask other believers to pray that he would have the courage to proclaim the gospel. Even as a prisoner, Paul still wanted to be a faithful witness for the Lord.

6:20 Paul was **an ambassador in chains** in Rome for the gospel of Christ. His prayer was that he might **speak boldly,** as an ambassador for the King of kings **ought to speak.**

6:21–24 The last verses of Ephesians reveal Paul's appreciation of the ministry of others, especially the ministry of Tychicus (Col. 4:7). The fact that this letter does not conclude with personal greetings as Paul's other letters do (Rom. 16) may indicate that this was a circular letter, one intended for a number of churches around Ephesus. **Sincerity** may also be translated "without corruption."

The Epistle to the

Philippians

ROM BEATINGS TO IMPRISONMENT, PAUL
had endured much suffering for the cause of Christ.
These trials had taught Paul to be content in all circumstances, an ability that Paul encouraged the Philippians to cultivate (4:11). In fact, his letter to the Philippians is a testimony to
this attitude. Even though he was in prison, facing an uncertain
future, Paul wrote this thank you letter to the Philippians, a letter

that expresses Paul's abundant joy in what God
was accomplishing through them.

The most prominent theme of the Epistle to
the Philippians is joy, specifically the joy of
serving Jesus. The general tone of the letter
reflects Paul's gratitude toward the Philippians
and his joy in God. This may seem strange
because Paul wrote this letter while he was in
prison. Paul, however, had the ability to recognize opportunities for sharing the gospel even in
apparent setbacks. This was the origin of Paul's
joy: he saw God working through the difficult
situations he faced.

Another theme of Paul's letter is "partnership in the gospel." Paul uses the Greek word
koinonia in this letter in various ways: "fellowship" (1:5; 2:1; 3:10), "partakers" (1:7), and
"shared" (4:15). All of these passages highlight
the Philippians' active involvement in Paul's
own ministry. By supporting Paul, the Philippians had become partners with him to further
the Good News of Jesus Christ. Paul illustrates
this concept of "partnering" or "fellowship" with
the lives of Jesus Christ (2:5–11), Timothy
(2:19–23), Epaphroditus (2:25–30), and Euodia
and Syntyche (4:2, 3).

Since the Philippian Christians already possessed great joy and had demonstrated their
partnership in sharing the gospel, Paul took the
opportunity to identify a few weak areas that
could be improved (4:2). For example, fellowship has two components: love and discernment. The Philippians had expressed the former
but were lacking the latter (1:9; 4:10–16). Thus,
Paul exhorted the Philippians to grow in knowledge and discernment, words that in the Greek
refer to a relational understanding (1:9). In
other words, the Greek word for knowledge
focuses on a person-to-God relationship,
whereas the Greek word for discernment points
to a person-to-person relationship. Paul wanted
the Philippians not only to abound in love but
also to experience more of God so that they
could grow into a mature understanding of His
ways.

All this shows that Paul had more than one
purpose for his letter to the Philippians. Today's
readers will continue to find wonderful passages
of encouragement in this short, joyful letter. Situations such as bickering among church members, living in this evil world, giving to
missionaries, and finding contentment are still

current issues for today's Christians. In this letter, Paul provides God's wisdom and encouragement. But most importantly, he holds up Jesus' life as the model for believers.

Church tradition unanimously agrees with the statement in Philippians (1:1) that Paul wrote this letter. The events described in this letter parallel the life of Paul.

To determine when Paul wrote his letter to the Philippians requires identifying the location from which he wrote. He says that he was in prison (1:13). But to which imprisonment was Paul referring? The answer must be guided by three factors: evidence of Paul's imprisonment in a given city, whether the Praetorian Guard was in that city, and the distance of that city from Philippi, which has to allow for several trips between the two cities.

Some speculate that Paul was writing from Corinth, and therefore date the letter around A.D. 50. Proponents of this view typically refer to Acts 18:10, a passage in which the Lord indicates to Paul that He would protect him from harm in Corinth. However, that passage does not explicitly speak about imprisonment.

Others point to the city of Ephesus (and hence a date of A.D. 53–55) on the basis of its proximity to Philippi and the definite possibility that the Praetorian Guard was stationed there. Once again, although several passages reveal that Paul experienced difficulties in Ephesus (Rom. 16:4, 7; 1 Cor. 15:32; 2 Cor. 1:8–23), there is no clear record that he was ever imprisoned there.

Still others advocate Caesarea as the location from which Paul wrote the letter (about A.D. 58–59). The Praetorian Guard may have been garrisoned at Caesarea, and the guard was at times considered to be part of Caesar's household (4:22). However, Paul's expectation that he would soon be set free (1:19, 26; 2:24) does not fit the circumstances of this imprisonment. In Caesarea, release from prison was only a remote possibility. In fact, Paul had to appeal to Caesar in order to escape Jewish influence over the judicial process (Acts 25:6–11). Furthermore, Caesarea was far from Philippi. It is an improbable origin for Paul's short letter to the Philippians.

Most students have favored Rome (about A.D. 60–62) as the city from which Paul wrote this epistle. Although the distance between Rome and Philippi is great, Paul was in Rome long enough for messages to travel back and forth to that city. Furthermore, Paul's imprisonment in Rome is well established in Scripture (Acts 28:16–31). Because his situation allowed him freedom to preach the gospel (1:12, 13; Acts 28:23–31), he undoubtedly felt confident that his release from prison was imminent.

While on his second missionary journey, and in response to a vision from God, Paul left Troas in the province of Asia (part of present-day Turkey) and traveled to Macedonia (in present-day Greece) to establish the first church in Europe, the church in the city of Philippi (Acts 16:6–12).

Named for Philip II of Macedon, the father of Alexander the Great, Philippi was strategically located on a major road, the Egnatian Way, that connected the eastern provinces of the Roman Empire to Rome. Thus, Philippi became the leading city of Macedonia. In 42 B.C. the Romans granted Philippi the highest status possible for a

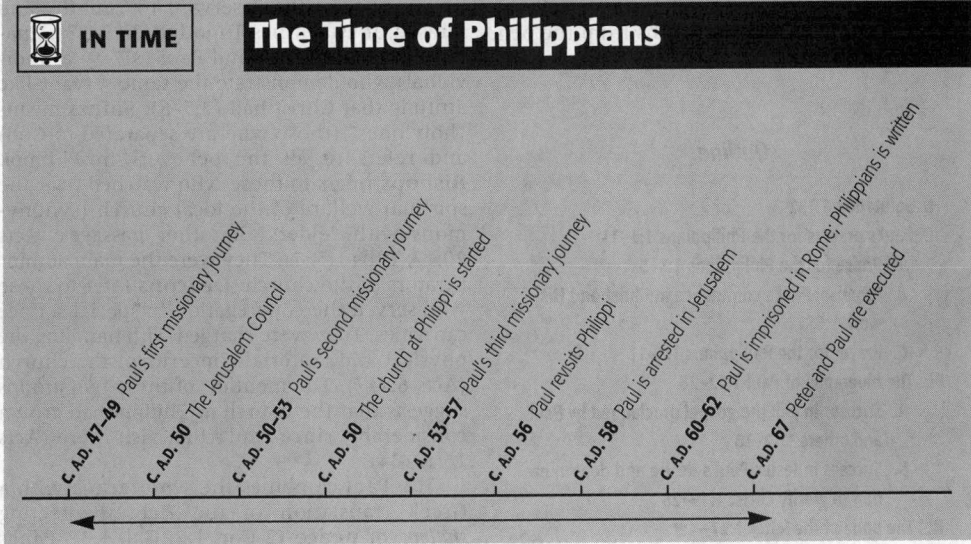

IN TIME

The Time of Philippians

C. A.D. 47–49 Paul's first missionary journey

C. A.D. 50 The Jerusalem Council

C. A.D. 50–53 Paul's second missionary journey

C. A.D. 50 The church at Philippi is started

C. A.D. 53–57 Paul's third missionary journey

C. A.D. 56 Paul revisits Philippi

C. A.D. 58 Paul is arrested in Jerusalem

C. A.D. 60–62 Paul is imprisoned in Rome; Philippians is written

C. A.D. 67 Peter and Paul are executed

provincial city, the status of a Roman colony. This meant that the citizens of Philippi could purchase, own, or transfer property. They also had the privilege of filing civil lawsuits in Roman courts and were exempted from paying both poll and land taxes. Their elevated status and wealth gave them not only confidence but a pride that bordered on arrogance.

Philippians closely follows the normal form of Paul's letters: (1) an identification of author and readers; (2) a pronouncement of God's grace and peace; (3) thanks offered to God because of the readers; (4) the body of the letter; (5) a personal desire to see the readers or to send someone to them; (6) greetings to the readers from those with Paul; and (7) a statement of blessing which serves as the conclusion of the letter. The only variation from this basic pattern is that Paul places the desire-to-send section (2:19–30) in the body of the letter. Paul does this in order to illustrate his point concerning humble service with the lives of Timothy and Epaphroditus.

Although the letter follows Paul's normal pattern, some have suggested that the letter is actually three letters combined into one. They do so on the basis of Paul's use of the Greek words for *finally* in 3:1 and 4:8. They argue that those words signal actual conclusions at those two points, thus indicating that Philippians is actually three different letters.

Yet the Greek words for *finally* can function as a transitional phrase (1 Thess. 4:1), in essence meaning "besides" or "furthermore." The strongest evidence for the unity of Philippians is a Greek manuscript from around A.D. 200 that includes all three sections of the letter (1:1—2:30; 3:1—4:7; 4:8–23). But whether Philippians is a unity or a compilation of several letters, it contains timeless truths from the pen of the apostle Paul.

Outline

Commentary

1:1–11 In the first few verses, Paul reveals his great love for the Philippians. He thinks of them often (vv. 3–6), he is concerned about them (vv. 7, 8), and he regularly prays for them (vv. 9–11). These verses not only reveal Paul's relation to the Philippians but also his view of God. The Lord does not merely start a wonderful work in us; He finishes what He starts. This is a comfort for those Christians who are in times of distress or suffering. God will continue His work in us.

1:1 bondservants: In his other prison epistles (Ephesians, Colossians, and Philemon), Paul calls himself an apostle. In this letter he begins by giving the title of servant to Timothy and himself. It establishes Timothy (2:19–23), Epaphroditus (2:25–30), and Paul (3:7–9) as individuals who demonstrate the same servant-like attitude that Christ had (2:5–8). **Saints** means "holy ones" (those who are separated to God) and refers to all the believers in Philippi. **Bishops** refers to those who watched over the spiritual welfare of the local church (synonymous with "elders" in other passages; Acts 20:17; Titus 1:5, 7). They were the main administrators of the church. **Deacons** refer to those who served the congregation in special service capacities. They were charged with handling the physical and material concerns of the church (Acts 6:1–7). The mention of these two groups suggests that the church at Philippi had grown considerably since Paul's first visit there (Acts 16:12–34).

1:2 Paul combines the word **grace** with a Greek translation of the Hebrew greeting *shalom,* or **peace** (2 Cor. 1:2; Gal. 1:3). Paul's association of the **Lord Jesus Christ** with **God our Father** underscores the equality and unity of these two persons of the Godhead.

1:3 I thank: The tense of the Greek verb indicates that Paul was continually thankful to God for the Philippian Christians. **upon every remembrance of you:** Every time God brought them to his mind, Paul gave thanks.

1:4 Joy, a prominent theme in Philippians, filled Paul's prayers for the Philippians even when he interceded for their needs. This is the first of five uses of the Greek word for *joy* in the letter (v. 25; 2:2, 29; 4:1). Paul also uses the Greek word for *rejoice* nine times in this letter (v. 18; 2:17 {twice}, 18 {twice}, 28; 3:1; 4:4 {twice}).

1:5 Fellowship is a commercial term for a joint-partnership in a business venture in which all parties actively participate to ensure the success of the business. In the Christian community, the word expresses intimacy with Christ (1 Cor. 1:9) and other believers (2 Cor. 8:4, 1 John 1:7). In this case, Paul may be using the word *fellowship* to refer to the financial contributions the Philippians had given Paul **from the first day until now** (4:14, 15). Immediately upon becoming Christians and continually thereafter, the Philippians had dedicated themselves to living and proclaiming the truth about Jesus Christ, and specifically to helping Paul in his ministry.

1:6 being confident: Paul had become convinced some time in the past that God would complete His good work among the Philippians, and his confidence remained unshaken. **in you:** Since *you* is a plural pronoun, the good work that God was doing was taking place "among" the believers rather than "in" any isolated believer. **Until** can also be translated "as far as." It expresses progress toward a goal and indicates that a time is coming when God will completely finish His work among the Philippian Christians. **the day of Jesus Christ:** The ministry in which the Philippians participated continues (like a relay race) up to the present, and it will continue until Christ returns. Paul calls Christ's return "the day of Christ" (2:16). On that day, Christ will judge nonbelievers and evaluate the lives of believers (2 Tim. 2:11–13).

1:7 The word **right** conveys a sense of moral uprightness (in keeping with God's law) and is often translated throughout the NT as "righteous." In this context, the word indicates that Paul's thoughts regarding the Philippians were in perfect accord with God's will. **because I have you in my heart:** *Heart* refers to the innermost part of a person, the place where one thinks and reflects. Since **defense** implies speech, we can be certain that Paul was not silent while in prison, but boldly spoke about Jesus Christ. Paul may have also been indicating that he would testify about Christ at his judicial proceedings. **confirmation:** Used only here and

---

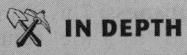 **IN DEPTH** **The Believers at Philippi**

Racial, ethnic, and social segregation are as old as society itself. Wherever people live, they form groups along these lines, then put up walls around them to keep others out.

In Philippi, as elsewhere, Paul offered the gospel first to the Jews. There must have been very few Jews in Philippi because the city did not have a synagogue, and in first-century Judaism it took only ten Jewish men to justify building a synagogue for worship. The Jews who did live in Philippi went outside the city gate to the banks of the Gangites River for worship and prayer. Yet the Christian church to which Paul wrote must have flourished, because in his letter he referred to levels of leadership in the church, such as overseers and deacons.

Philippi was a culturally diverse Roman city on the main highway (the Egnatian Way) from the eastern provinces to Rome, and the church at Philippi had a diverse group of believers. The NT specifically mentions an Asian, a Greek, and a Roman. On the surface, these people had little in common. One was a businesswoman who sold purple cloth to the rich; one was a slave girl who had been possessed with a spirit of divination; the third was a jailer. Three different races, three different social ranks, and probably three different religious loyalties before encountering Christ. But Paul taught them that all were equal in the body of Christ; all were sinners saved by God's grace. They were to humble themselves as Jesus had done, and be unified in the love of Christ. In a world segregated along class and ethnic lines, the church at Philippi broke the rules: "There is neither Jew nor Greek, there is neither slave nor free, . . . for you are all one in Christ Jesus" (Gal. 3:28). This church was one of the most integrated places in the Mediterranean world.

in Heb. 6:16 in the NT, this word is a legal and commercial term meaning "a validating guarantee." *Defense* and *confirmation* are the negative and positive aspects of Paul's ministry. He defended the gospel against its opponents' attacks, and he confirmed the gospel through powerful signs. Since these are both legal terms, Paul's usage may indicate that he was looking ahead to his forthcoming trial.

1:8 God is my witness: Much as if he had taken an oath in a court of law, Paul conveyed the seriousness and the truth of what he was about to say. **I long for you:** Paul had a strong

IN LIFE   **Paul's Broad Perspective**

Paul was deeply committed to the truth and integrity of the gospel. But in Phil. 1:12–18 he generously credits others who were doing ministry, even though they had impure motives.

This sets an important example for Christians today who feel strong loyalty to their particular tradition or institution. Like Paul, we need to accept and celebrate the fact that other believers with different perspectives and approaches may be helping people and accomplishing tasks that we never could.

desire that is directed toward the Philippians; he is anxious for their spiritual well-being. **all:** Paul emphasizes that every one of the Christians at Philippi (not merely the leadership) is the focus of his attention. **affection of Jesus Christ:** The word translated *affection* literally means the internal organs, regarded by the first-century reader as the center of the deepest feelings. Whereas the heart is the seat of reflection, Paul now speaks of his affection, his deep feelings for the believers. In modern terminology, Paul revealed that he had the "heart" of Jesus Christ. His feelings for the Philippians were like those of Jesus Christ, who loved them and died for them.

1:9 I pray: Verses 9–11 give the content of his prayer for them. He is desirous that this fervent love will continue to burn hotly but within the splendor of full knowledge and spiritual discernment. Love without knowledge is like water without a channel. Water uncontrolled is disastrous but is productive when controlled. The **love** that Paul sought for the believers is the highest form of Christian love, based on a lasting, unconditional commitment, not on an

unstable emotion. **knowledge:** The first of two terms on which a directed love is built, *knowledge* suggests an intimate understanding based on a relationship with the person. Here the focus of this knowledge is God. **discernment:** Found only here in the NT, the Greek word means moral or ethical understanding based on both the intellect and the senses. The word implies perception or insight into social situations.

1:10 that you may approve: This verb is used in ancient literature for the testing of gold to determine its purity, and for trying oxen to assess their usefulness for the task at hand. The purpose of increasing in love, controlled by knowledge, is to be able to evaluate people and situations correctly. **sincere:** This term, literally meaning "judged by sunlight," does not mean "honestly trying hard," but rather pure, unmixed, and free from falsehood. Any spot in a garment or imperfection in merchandise could be seen by holding the object up to the sunlight. Christ died to free the church from every blemish (Eph. 5:27). **without offense:** Using still another graphic term to describe the Christian, Paul conveys the sense of not striking out at someone. Here the phrase means not leading others into sin by one's own behavior. **day of Christ:** The goal ahead for the believer is the *day of Christ* in which the believer will stand for evaluation before the Savior, who is the faithful and true witness (v. 6; 1 Cor. 1:8; 5:5). This joyous yet sobering prospect should motivate us to purify our own lives (1 John 2:28; 3:2, 3).

1:11 fruits of righteousness: This phrase is best understood either as "fruit that results from being justified" or "fruit characterized by morally correct conduct." *Righteousness* describes the source or the nature of the fruit, the behavior. **glory and praise of God:** The final result of growing in love and of living a wise and pure life that overflows with righteousness is that God will be honored and pleased. Each day we are expanding our capacity to enjoy Him and bring glory to Him forever.

1:12–26 Paul reveals the external and internal pressures that he is facing. He rejoices because, despite physical persecution and social ostracism, the Word of God is being proclaimed with much success. Furthermore, although he desires to be in heaven with Jesus, he realizes that God is keeping him on earth in order to help the Philippians to continue their successful proclamation of that same Word.

1:12 I want you to know: Paul uses this or similar statements to introduce an important declaration regarding a misunderstood matter. Because of this love for Paul and their confidence in his ministry, they had given repeatedly and generously, even out of their poverty for the support of this missionary outreach. They saw this as a great investment in the kingdom. **actually turned out:** Paul wanted the Philippians to know that his imprisonment was advancing, not hindering, the gospel. Such words would comfort the Philippians, who were concerned about Paul's welfare and who needed assurance that their prayers for Paul and their gifts to him had not been in vain. **furtherance:** This word could suggest a pioneer beating or cutting a path through a densely forested area. Paul's imprisonment was a strategic advance in the kingdom of God because it was clearing the way for the gospel to penetrate the ranks of the Roman military (v. 13) and even the royal house (4:22). These were two areas that under normal circumstances would have been closed to the gospel.

1:13 Paul's imprisonment furthered the gospel in two ways. First, the palace guard heard it as Paul preached in prison. Second, **all the rest**—Paul's visitors—heard the gospel. Some of his visitors were leaders of the Jews in Rome (Acts 28:17). The **palace guard** (Praetorian Guard) consisted of several thousand highly trained, elite soldiers of the Roman Empire who were headquartered at Rome. For the one to two years that Paul had been under house arrest in Rome, different soldiers had taken turns guarding him. Because they were chained to Paul, they had no other choice but to listen to him proclaim the gospel; they could not beat him into silence because he was a Roman citizen (Acts 16:37, 38). Although Paul could not go to the world to preach, in this way God brought the world to Paul. In an ironic twist, they were the captives and Paul was free to preach. **in Christ:** Paul considered his imprisonment to be the result of God's sovereign will.

1:14 most . . . bold: Many Christians who saw Paul in chains in Rome became encouraged to preach the gospel with boldness, emphasizing the outward aggressive demonstration of an inward character and feeling of courage. **without fear:** Although they too could be imprisoned as Paul was, the Roman Christians were emboldened by Paul's courage and were able to proclaim the message about Jesus Christ fearlessly.

1:15 Those preaching **from envy and strife** were not heretics, since they were preaching Christ. But apparently they were jealous of the attention Paul received, and they determined to sow seeds of dissension in order to cause him trouble. **some . . . from goodwill:** Other Christians preached Christ with good motives. They thought well of Paul and of the gospel message and were dedicated to serving God faithfully.

1:16, 17 Some manuscripts reverse the order of vv. 16 and 17. **selfish ambition:** The motives of these believers were anything but good. The term for *selfish ambition* implies that they did not preach to honor God or to help Paul but rather to gain applause and followers for themselves (2:3). **not sincerely:** Paul reemphasized the fact that these Christians were not acting with pure motives. **to add:** The word Paul uses here literally means "to raise up" or "to cause." In other words, Paul believes that these preachers actually desired to cause him additional problems while he was in prison.

1:18 What then: In essence Paul is saying, "Their motives are between them and God." **in**

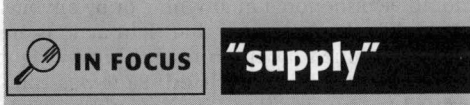

(Gk. *epichoregia*) (1:19; Eph. 4:16) Strong's #2024: The Philippians' prayer would generate the Spirit's *supply*. The Greek word was used to describe what a choir manager would provide for all the members of a Greek choir who performed in Greek drama. In short, he took care of all their living expenses. The word came to mean a full supply of any kind. Paul was looking forward to getting a full supply of Jesus Christ's Spirit as a result of the Philippians' prayers.

pretense or in truth: Whether the preaching was done for false motives or pure, whether for appearance's sake or for the sake of what was right, Paul was pleased that the gospel was being spread. Notice that Paul is not condoning error. He called a curse down on those who corrupt the gospel (Gal. 1:6–9). The issue was motive and attitude, not doctrine. **I rejoice:** This means simply "to be glad." What a contrast is his noble and magnanimous spirit. How did he rejoice rather than grow angry and vengeful? It came from focusing on Jesus Christ (Heb. 12:2, 3).

1:19–26 Paul's own life provides a model of bringing glory to Christ whether **by life** or **by death** (v. 20).

1:19 will turn out: Paul expresses his positive attitude and confidence about how the sovereign God would work out this difficult situation. **deliverance:** The Greek word translated *deliverance* is usually translated "salvation." In the NT this word is used for physical healing, rescue from danger or death, justification, sanctification, and glorification. Here Paul refers to his daily empowering to endure the troubling situation before him. He may also be indicating his confidence that he would be delivered from prison (v. 25). **your prayer:** Here is the channel for his deliverance. The prayer of believers on behalf of other believers is vitally important because by it, and together with the work of the Holy Spirit, God produces positive results. **supply:** Originally this word was used to refer to a wealthy benefactor defraying the expenses of a chorus or dance troupe. Later and more generally, it meant to supply the abundant resources that would meet someone's need.

1:20 earnest expectation: This phrase translates a Greek word which pictures the outstretched hand of someone straining to focus attention on an object. **hope:** This is not just wishful thinking but confident expectation. **in nothing . . . ashamed:** Paul was determined not to be dishonored in anything or by anyone. He vividly demonstrated that right actions are not determined by environment but by right thinking. **will be magnified:** Paul was committed to ensuring that Christ would be made even more conspicuous in his own life than ever. He was not relying on himself to exalt Christ but looked to the Holy Spirit (v. 19) to magnify Christ in him (John 16:14; 2 Cor. 3:18). **by life or by death:** There was no difference between life and death as far as Paul was concerned, as long as that life or death magnified, glorified, and exalted Christ before others.

1:21 For to me is similar to the common expression: "As far as I'm concerned." **Christ . . . gain:** Paul would experience *gain* in his own death because he would be with Christ (v. 23). In fact, Paul may have been expressing his confidence that since his imprisonment had furthered the gospel, God would also use his death to further His kingdom.

1:22 fruit from my labor: If Paul continued to live, he would have the opportunity to preach the gospel to others and see spiritual victory in the lives of the Philippians. **what I shall choose:** Paul was in a dilemma because he clearly saw the advantages of both life and death for the Christian. Life meant an opportunity to minister to people like the Philippians (v. 24), while death meant being with Christ his Savior.

1:23 Paul felt **pressed** in on every side, much like a besieged city with no hope of relief

from its affliction. He was torn between the prospect of seeing the Lord and his passion for ministering to the Philippians. A **desire** here means more than a wish; it indicates an intense longing. **to depart:** In relation to Paul's profession as a tentmaker, the term *depart* means to strike, or take down, the tent to be ready to travel elsewhere. Paul saw death not as the end of life but as a time of moving from one home to another. **far better:** In Paul's mind, there was no real comparison between life and death because death was **far better** (literally, "much more better"). Jesus said He was going to prepare a place for us (John 14). The place is already there in the Father's house.

1:24 remain: The idea contained in **remain** is to "abide fully" or "persevere." It is an intensive form of the Greek word for "remain" in v. 25. **more needful:** The Greek word used here counterbalances the **far better** of v. 23. The fact that God wanted him to continue living was, according to Paul, totally necessary for the spiritual growth of the Philippians (v. 25).

1:25 your progress: Paul was not satisfied that the Philippian Christians should simply be saved, but that they should advance to maturity in Christ. He felt a responsibility to continue to teach them.

1:26 rejoicing for me: Paul knew that, because the Philippians loved him greatly, they would be overjoyed that God had preserved his life in prison and that Paul was confident that their joint ministry would continue. "Rejoicing" literally means "boasting" or "glorying." **more abundant:** Their rejoicing was to grow dramatically because of the work of the Lord.

1:27—4:9 Paul devotes the main section of his letter to instructing the Philippians on the importance of conducting their lives as servants who have dedicated themselves to their Lord. He illustrates this teaching by referring to the manner in which Jesus Christ, Timothy, Epaphroditus, and he himself lived.

1:27 let your conduct: The word used could refer to discharging the obligations of a citizen. Because Philippi held the privileged status of a Roman colony, its citizens understood

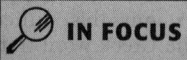 **IN FOCUS** **"striving together"**

(Gk. *sunathleo*) (1:27; 4:3) Strong's #4866: The image in Greek is drawn from athletic contests. Usually, athletes competed one against another; in 1:27 Paul asks the church at Philippi to compete together as a team of athletes to help advance the faith that comes through the preaching of the gospel. In the same epistle, he also mentions Euodia and Syntyche as those who were contending for the gospel side by side with himself (4:2, 3).

the responsibilities associated with citizenship. Paul here commanded them (the first command in the letter) to shift their perspective from the earthly realm to the heavenly one. They should live in this world as citizens of another world, the heavenly kingdom. Their conduct should reveal their heavenly citizenship. **stand fast:** They were not to stand alone in isolation but together in oneness of spirit and mind, united for a common goal. **striving together:** Teamwork is the key concept expressed by this Greek word, which literally means "to engage together in an athletic contest." **for the faith:** God never intended believers to be alone. His plan is that we should gather together in a church in order to strengthen and encourage each other (2:2). Paul was urging them to strive together, not just for the sake of their individual faith, but also on behalf of the truth of Christianity, their common faith.

1:28 The word translated **terrified** is a strong term that is used of the terror of a panicked horse. The Philippians are not to be terror-stricken in the face of their enemies. Their courage would be proof of their salvation and of the ultimate failure of their foes. **proof of perdition:** By striving together in love and confidence, the Philippians would be living *proof* (a legal term denoting proof obtained by an analysis of the facts) to their opponents that the message of Jesus Christ is true. This would confirm the lost state of their adversaries. Because Paul contrasted **salvation** to **perdition,** his focus here undoubtedly was on eternal matters. Contrast this with Paul's focus on his own present salvation, or "deliverance," in v. 19.

1:29 to suffer: Suffering is actually a gift from God, for in the midst of suffering He comforts us (2 Cor. 1:5) and enables us to rejoice (1 Pet. 4:12, 13). Suffering is a blessing because it brings eternal reward (Matt. 5:1–12; 2 Cor. 4:17; 2 Tim. 2:12; Rev. 22:12). God sees suffering as a tool to accomplish His purposes both in His Son (Heb. 2:10) and in His children (1 Pet. 1:6, 7). Suffering, moreover, matures us as Christians in the present (James 1:2–4) and enables us to be glorified with Christ in the future (Rom. 8:17).

1:30 the same conflict: The same struggles Paul was experiencing, the Philippians would also experience. They needed to learn how to be victorious in the midst of their trials by following Paul's example in the face of his persecution.

2:1 The Philippians' biggest battle was not with their external circumstances but with those internal attitudes that destroy unity. Paul had demonstrated his own refusal to let external circumstances control his attitudes (1:12–18). The **therefore** ties together his conflict and their conflict. **if . . . if . . . if . . . if:** The condi-

tional clauses in this verse indicate certainties, not "maybes." Each *if* here expresses the idea of "since," and each following clause may be considered to be true. **fellowship:** Scripture teaches that our fellowship is not only with God the Holy Spirit as seen here, but also with God the Father (1 John 1:3) and God the Son (1 Cor. 1: 9; 1 John 1:3), as well as with other Christians (1 John 1:7). **affection:** See 1:8. **mercy:** The Greek term means compassionate desires that develop in response to a situation and that stimulate a person to meet recognized needs in that situation.

2:2 In this verse the apostle sets forth a fourfold appeal, an appeal that expresses one major idea—namely the unity of the church. **like-minded:** This expresses Paul's concern for humility (4:2). Paul illustrates this attitude in 2:3, 4 and then describes the greatest example of humility, Jesus Christ Himself, in 2:5–8. **same love:** See 1:9. **one accord:** Paul here is stressing a unity of spirit between Christians (Ps. 133), literally "a togetherness of soul." **one mind:** The words Paul uses to indicate *one mind* are virtually identical to the words translated *like-minded* earlier in this verse. Paul was strongly emphasizing the unity that should exist between believers and how they must single-mindedly strive together to advance the gospel of Jesus Christ.

2:3 Here Paul attempts to correct any misunderstanding that may arise from what he said earlier in the letter about some preaching out of selfish motives (1:15, 16). He was concerned that someone might think he was condoning **selfish ambition,** so long as the gospel was being preached. **conceit:** Paul uses a Greek term meaning "empty pride," or "groundless self-esteem." Pride should not be a Christian's motivation; instead, everything should be done in the power of the Holy Spirit. **lowliness of mind:** The Greek word suggests a deep sense of humility. Although the pagan writers used the word negatively, in effect to mean abjectness or groveling, Paul did not. What Paul was calling for was an honest evaluation of one's own nature. Such an evaluation should always lead to a glorification of Christ. For without Him, we can do nothing (John 15:5). **let each esteem:** This verb indicates a thorough analysis of the facts in order to reach a correct conclusion about the matter. In other words, each Philippian Christian was to properly assess himself or herself. Such an assessment would lead to valuing others. **others better than himself:** The honest self-examination that Paul was calling for leads to true humility. This enables a person to hold others above himself or herself, to value people over material possessions or personal plans.

2:4 look out: This verb means to direct one's attention at something. Since the word implies the exertion of much mental concentration, Paul wanted his readers to do everything in their power to be involved in meeting the needs of others, as well as their own.

2:5 These verses (vv. 5–8) present one of the most significant statements in all of Scripture on the nature of the Incarnation, the fact that God

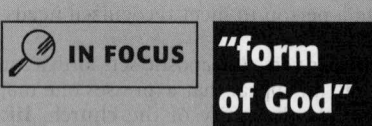

IN FOCUS — "form of God"

(Gk. *morphe theou*) (2:6) Strong's *#3444; 2316*: The Greek word for *form* was generally used to express the way in which a thing exists and appears according to what it is in itself. Thus, the expression *form of God* may be correctly understood as the essential nature and character of God. To say, therefore, that Christ existed in *the form of God* is to say that apart from His human nature Christ possesses all the characteristics and qualities belonging to God because He is, in fact, God.

became man. Also, through this wonderful description of Christ, Paul vividly illustrates the principle of humility (vv. 3, 4). **Let this mind be:** All godly action begins with the "renewing of the mind." Right thinking produces right actions. Our actions are the fruit of our deepest thoughts. **in you:** Thinking and being like Christ are requirements not only for an individual but also for the corporate body of believers. Together we need to think and act like one being, like the person of Jesus Christ.

2:6 form: Paul carefully uses the Greek word *morphe* with the present participle to indicate that the nature that Christ continually possesses is "the specific character or essential substance" of God. This word always expresses the nature of the being with which it is associ-

ated. That which God was, Jesus is. That status which God possesses, Jesus possessed. Hence, because Jesus' nature is God's nature, Jesus is God. **robbery:** Because Christ was God, He did not look on sharing God's nature as *robbery,* that is, as "a thing to be seized," as though He did not already possess it, or as "a thing to be retained," as though He might lose it. **equal:** As used in this verse, this word speaks of equality of existence. Christ was fully God, but He limited Himself in such a way that He could also be completely human. In Christ, God became man.

2:7 made Himself of no reputation: This phrase can be translated "He emptied Himself." Christ did this by taking on the form of a servant, a mere man. In doing this, He did not empty Himself of any part of His essence as God. Instead, He took upon Himself existence as a man. While remaining completely God, He became completely human. **form:** Jesus added to His divine essence (v. 6) a servant's essence, that is, the essential characteristics of a human being seeking to fulfill the will of another. Paul does not say that Christ exchanged the form of God for the form of a servant, involving a loss of deity or the attributes of deity. Rather, in the Incarnation, Christ continued in the very nature of God but added to Himself the nature of a servant. **bondservant:** In this context, the term refers to the lowest status on the social ladder (Heb. 10:5), the exact opposite of the term *Lord,* a title by which all will one day recognize the risen and exalted Christ (v. 11). It is truly amazing, therefore, that the God who created the universe (John 1:3; Col. 1:16) and who rules over all creation (Col. 1:17) would choose to add to His person the nature of a servant. **likeness:** This word does not mean that Christ only appeared to be a man. Rather, the term emphasizes identity. In reality He was a man, possessing all the essential aspects of a human being, although unlike all others He was sinless.

2:8 appearance: This is the third word Paul uses to show the Philippians that Jesus Christ who is fully God from all eternity is also fully man. In the previous verses, Paul describes Jesus as possessing the nature of God and taking on the nature of a servant. Jesus came to the

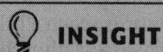

INSIGHT — Downward Mobility

In contrast to the many people today who seek upward mobility, Jesus was, in a sense, downwardly mobile (Phil. 2:5–8), moving from a position of ultimate power to utter powerlessness. In making this transition, He set the best possible example of servant-leadership (Matt. 20:25–28; John 13:2–17). However, Paul paints a different portrait of the Lord in Colossians.

earth with the identity of a man. Here the word *appearance* points to the external characteristics of Jesus: He had the bearing, actions, and manners of a man. **He humbled Himself:** Jesus willingly took the role of a servant; no one forced Him to do it. **obedient:** Although He never sinned and did not deserve to die, He chose to die so that the sins of the world could be charged to His account. Subsequently He could credit His righteousness to the account of all who believe in Him (2 Cor. 5:21; Gal. 1:4). **even the death of the cross:** Paul describes the depths of Christ's humiliation by reminding his readers that Christ died by the cruelest form of capital punishment, crucifixion. The Romans reserved the agonizing death of crucifixion for slaves and foreigners, and the Jews viewed death on a cross as a curse from God (Deut. 21:23; Gal. 3:13).

2:9 Note the contrast between Jesus' placing Himself in a debased status (v. 8) with God the Father's elevation of Jesus to a **highly exalted** status. On earth Christ was God, but appeared as man; back in heaven. He retained His humanity, but He manifests His prerogatives of deity. God graciously granted to Him the name. On earth Christ was crowned with thorns (Matt. 27:29); back in heaven He is crowned with glory and honor (Rev. 5:12–14). **and given Him the name which is above every name:** Paul is referring to the OT passage speaking of the divine name Yahweh (Lord).

2:10 every knee: Although all will one day worship Christ, only those who put their faith in Him in this life will have an everlasting relationship with Him after death (Rev. 20:13–15). **those under the earth:** Paul refers here to those who will already have died at the time of Christ's return, in contrast to the angels in heaven and those who will still be living on earth.

2:11 confess: The term Paul uses is a strong, intensive verb, which means "agree with" or "say the same thing." Essentially Paul is saying that everyone will unanimously affirm what God the Father has already stated (Is. 45:23): that Jesus Christ is Lord.

2:12 Therefore: Paul desires the Philippians to respond positively to his admonition to have the mind of Christ (vv. 5–8). The command is to the entire group since the word **you** is plural. The subject is their mutual, corporate salvation (1:19, 28; Luke 22:24–30). **work out:** The Greek term speaks of the present deliverance of the Philippians. The word translated *work out* is used by the first century author Strabo to speak of digging silver out of silver mines. Thus, salvation can be compared to a huge gift that needs to be unwrapped for one's thorough enjoyment. Note that Paul is encour-

aging the Philippians to develop and *work out* their salvation, but not to work *for* their salvation. **with fear and trembling:** Demonstrating God's grace and power to the world by our unity and love (compare John 13:34, 35) is a very serious responsibility. This is not fear that is cowardice but respect for great value. They were to take great pains and care to discharge their duties correctly. They were not to fear the responsibility but to handle it as a commission of the highest order. The results would determine their position of privilege and glory in Christ's kingdom.

2:13 God Himself is at work in our lives and all that He does in our lives is done for His **good pleasure** (Rom. 8:28). It pleases God to do good for us. But He can only bless obedience to His will (John 15:10). Our ultimate goal should be to please Him in all we do. God supplies both the desire and the enablement to accomplish His will. We only need to appropriate what He supplies.

2:14–16 These verses give specific instructions on how the Philippians were to work out all things. The apostle had shown them in 1:27—2:13 the kind of attitude and actions they were to follow. They were to demonstrate in their corporate and individual life the kind of conduct that would prove worthy of the great calling that God has given them. He uses **all things** to emphasize the inclusiveness of this command.

2:14 The Philippians have been secretly discontented and have been **complaining** (2:1–4). But the word used suggests that loud dissension had not yet broken out.

2:15 This verse focuses on the testimony of the church. The purpose of the command in v. 14 is that the Philippians might be **blameless** light bearers in their world. They should deserve no censure because they are free from fault or defect in relation to the outside world (3:6). If the Philippian believers were going to have a testimony in their community, they had to be blameless in their actions and attitudes, both inside and outside the church (1 Tim. 3:2). **without fault:** This term is a technical word used to denote anything that is fit to be offered as a sacrifice to God, without spot or blemish, untainted by sin. **crooked and perverse generation:** Paul describes the world as being the opposite of Christian. On the one hand the world is turned away from the truth, while on the other hand it exerts a corrupting influence that is opposed to the truth. **shine as lights:** Paul depicts believers as stars whose light penetrates the spiritual darkness of a perverted world. Jesus said, "I am the light of the world." He also said, "You are the light of the world" (Matt. 5:14). Christ is inherently light. We are the light of the world as long as we reflect Christ.

2:16 The Greek verb translated **holding fast** contains two thoughts: holding fast and holding forth. The former concept suggests a steadfastness in which our lights (v. 15) blaze continually for God. The latter concept implies projecting our lights into the darkness of this world. **Run** suggests energetic activity, while **labored** indicates the toil of Paul's ministry.

2:17 being poured out: Both Jews and Greeks sometimes poured wine out on an altar in connection with religious sacrifices (Num. 15:1–10). Some have interpreted this figure of speech as depicting Paul's own martyrdom for the cause of Christ. However the content of the letter reveals by contrast that Paul assumes he will live (1:25) and expects to be released from prison shortly (v. 24). Thus, Paul probably was saying that he was presently being poured out as a living **offering** on behalf of the faith of the Philippians. **sacrifice:** This means primarily the act of offering something to God. **service:** Paul chooses a Greek term that depicts a person who fulfills the duties of a public office at his or her own expense. In the Christian context, this word speaks of worship humbly offered to God.

2:18 for the same reason: Because Paul is joyful in the midst of his sufferings on behalf of the Philippians (v. 17), he expects the Philippians to look on his suffering not as a matter of sadness but as a source of joy. He had caught the spirit of true blessing from Jesus (Matt. 5:10–12).

2:19–30 Paul sent two of his ministry companions, Timothy and Epaphroditus, to minister to the Philippians. Both of them exemplified the humility, unity, and sacrificial service which Paul had been teaching (2:1–18). These men could serve as object lessons of Paul's teaching, living epistles to be read by the Philippians. Our lives can speak much more forcefully than the greatest preacher.

2:19 Paul balanced the previous somber passage (vv. 12–18) with the optimistic hope of sending his coworker **Timothy,** whose name means "One Who Honors God" and was from a believing family. Both his mother Eunice and his grandmother Lois had become Christians (2 Tim. 1:5). He had accompanied Paul on the second missionary journey, during which time they had established the church at Philippi. Timothy apparently was well-loved by the Philippians, and he in turn exhibited a great concern for them (vv. 20–22).

2:20 like-minded: Timothy and Paul had the same quality of concern for the Philippians (read Paul's command in v. 2 for the Philippians to be like-minded).

2:21 all: An overstatement for emphasis.

Most people tend to be selfish, but Paul knows that Timothy is different. He exhorts the Philippians (v. 3) that they too can break free from this way of life if they have the mind of Christ (2:5–8). That is still Christ's way for us.

2:22 Timothy had shown his faithful **character** both to the Philippians, who knew of his ten years of ministry with the apostle Paul. **as a son:** In NT times, a son who **served** his father did so to learn the family trade. Serving in this way meant learning all about the business and being willing to obey the teacher in order to become as skillful as possible in the work.

2:23 I see: Before sending Timothy to the Philippians, Paul needed to assess carefully his own situation. He explained this need through the use of a Greek term which means "to turn one's eyes from all else and to concentrate them on one thing."

2:24 Paul waited to send Timothy until Paul saw the outcome of his case. Apparently, Paul expected a legal ruling soon on his present imprisonment. **in the Lord:** All the thoughts, attitudes and actions of Christians should spring from the fact that they are "in the Lord" (2:19). **shortly:** Paul anticipates being released from prison in the near future.

2:25 Epaphroditus was a Philippian Christian sent by the church in Philippi to take a gift to Paul (4:18) and to assist Paul in his ministry. He is described with a series of complimentary terms: a "brother," a "fellow worker," a "fellow soldier," a "messenger" to the Philippians, and a "minister" to Paul. He is mentioned in the Bible only in this letter. **fellow worker:** Paul considers Epaphroditus to be an equal in the work of the gospel. The title of **fellow soldier** was given only to those who had fought honorably alongside another. Paul thus offered high praise to Epaphroditus for his faithful service in the cause of Christ. **your messenger:** Here Paul uses the Greek term usually translated "apostle" in its nontechnical sense. Both Paul and Epaphroditus are messengers, but Paul's authority is greater than Epaphroditus's. Paul had a direct commission from Jesus Christ, while Epaphroditus was sent by the Philippians.

2:26 longing: Paul declares that Epaphroditus demonstrates the same concern for the Philippians as he himself does (1:8). Thus, they are one in their work for the Lord (v. 25), and they are one in their love for the Lord's people.

2:27 sick almost unto death: Paul was making certain that the Philippians understood the effort that Epaphroditus had made for the cause of Jesus Christ. Epaphroditus's condition had been far worse than perhaps they had imagined. Paul viewed Epaphroditus's healing as God's direct intervention. Though Paul exercised apostolic powers (2 Cor. 12:12), those powers were useless outside of the will and timing of God.

2:28 more eagerly: Paul returns Epaphroditus to the Philippians sooner than they expected him to do so. He does so for two reasons: (1) to encourage the Philippians to rejoice by letting them know that Epaphroditus is physically well and has fulfilled their spiritual service to him, and (2) to lessen a burden that he, Paul, is bearing (i.e., **to be less sorrowful**) because of his concern that the Philippians might be thinking less highly of Epaphroditus than they should.

2:29 Receive him: This term contains the idea of a favorable reception, an embrace of the one who comes. **esteem:** The Philippians are to hold Epaphroditus in high honor; they are to consider him a "precious," "prized," or "highly valued" servant.

2:30 not regarding his life: Paul informs the Philippians of the commitment that Epaphroditus had for the work that they had given him to do. **to supply what was lacking:** Paul acknowledges the work that the Philippians had already done for him. Epaphroditus was able to do what the Philippians could not do: be physically present to minister to him.

3:1 To sum up all that he has said about living worthy of Christ, Paul adds, **rejoice in the Lord.** This rejoicing is in the Lord, not in circumstances. God is always in charge, so even in prison Paul can rejoice. Consequently, it is not **tedious** (troublesome) for Paul to encourage the Philippians to rejoice. It will be a safeguard for their conduct because they will have the right attitude. **safe:** Paul is concerned that the Philippians do not fall into the trap set forth by those within the church who support heresy.

3:2 In NT times, **dogs** were hated scavengers. The term came to be used for all who had morally impure minds. **evil workers:** Since the term *workers* was occasionally used to identify those who propagated a religion, the words *evil workers* probably refers to teachers who are spreading destructive doctrines. **mutilation:** Paul here points sarcastically and specifically to those who desire to reinstate Jewish religious practices as necessary for salvation. He chooses a term that literally means "to cut." By doing so, he suggests that these people do not even understand the truth about the OT practice of circumcision but understand it merely as a cutting of the flesh.

3:3 Paul defines true **circumcision** as a matter of the heart and not of the flesh. He reveals three aspects of true circumcision: (1) worshiping **God in the Spirit;** (2) rejoicing in **Christ;** and (3) placing no **confidence** in any human honor or accomplishment as a means to reach God. The OT also taught that circumcision was more than a ritual of the flesh (Lev. 26:41; Deut. 10:16, 30:6; Jer. 4:4; Ezek. 44:7).

3:4–9 Paul speaks as though he had **confidence in the flesh** to show that the reason he did not rely on Jewish credentials was not that he did not possess them, but that they could not achieve the righteousness only God could provide.

3:5 eighth day: Paul's parents obeyed God's law and had Paul circumcised on the appropriate day after his birth (Lev. 12:2, 3). The people of Israel are called the people of God. That Paul states he is of the **stock of Israel** implies that he is able to trace his origins to the true line of Israel, to Jacob and not Esau. **tribe of Benjamin:** The *tribe of Benjamin* was highly regarded by Israelites because that line had produced the first king of Israel and had remained loyal to David. Furthermore, that tribe had joined Judah after the Exile to form the foundation for the restored nation (1 Sam. 9:15–21; 1 Kin. 12:21–24). **Hebrew of the Hebrews:** This description of Paul may indicate that (1) both his parents were Jews, (2) he was a model Jew,

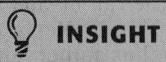 **INSIGHT**   **Paul's Drivenness**

As we read Paul's description of his younger days (Phil. 3:4–6), we discover a profound drivenness, as if he were out to prove something. Several clues suggest that he probably was. He was born outside of Palestine, in Tarsus, rather than in Judea. He devoted his life to intensive study of the Law. He attacked Christians with unusual vengeance. Perhaps it all added up to an intense desire to be accepted by the Jewish society in Jerusalem.

There are two major ways that minorities and other outsiders cope with rejection or discrimination by the larger society. One is to turn inward and refuse to participate in the dominant culture. The other is to remove or diminish differences and blend in with the majority. Perhaps one might be accepted, even if never treated as an equal. Paul seems possibly to have chosen the latter course.

or (3) he was educated completely as a Jew. **Pharisee:** Pharisees were highly educated Jewish leaders who spearheaded the opposition against Jesus while He was on earth, and later against the Christian church. They rigorously followed and defended the letter of the Jewish law. Paul himself came from a line of Pharisees (Acts 23:6) and had studied under Gamaliel, a highly respected Pharisee of that day (Acts 22:3).

3:6 persecuting the church: Prior to becoming a Christian, Paul vigorously attacked those who believed in Christ, even to the point of having them put to death (Acts 7:58—8:3; 9:1, 2).

3:7 gain: See 1:21. **loss:** This word indicates that which is damaged or of no further use (v. 8; Acts 27:10, 21). Those things that Paul thought to be important became unimportant after confronting the resurrected Messiah.

3:8 excellence: The value of knowing Christ surpasses all else (2:3; 4:7). **rubbish:** This word means anything that is detestable or worthless. All the things of this world are rubbish compared to Christ. Even "our righteousnesses are like filthy rags" (Is. 64:6). **I may gain:** The former *gain* (v. 7) is here substituted for the latter *gain:* Christ Jesus (1:21).

3:9 from the law: In vv. 6 and 7, Paul reveals the uselessness of righteousness that is in the law. Here he divulges that his own righteousness that had been in that law was also in vain. **through faith in Christ:** Paul recognizes that true righteousness is a matter of faith, not of works. It is God's righteousness that comes through Christ, not our own righteousness.

3:10 Paul indicates that he rejected his own righteousness in order to secure not merely an intellectual knowledge of Christ but also a relational knowledge, in fact, an intimate knowledge of **Him. power of His resurrection:** Paul does not say the power "in" His resurrection, which would specify the power of the one-time event of His resurrection. Rather, Paul seeks the ongoing power that is the day-to-day experience of being in Christ. Paul may also be alluding to his desire to be clothed with his own resurrection body. **fellowship of His sufferings:** Paul sees the value of participating in the persecutions or struggles that naturally accompany one who is in partnership (that is, fellowship, 1:5) with Christ and His sufferings (James 1:2–4; 1 Pet. 2:21–24). **being conformed to His death:** Paul desires to imitate Christ—even in His death. In other words, Paul wants to be completely obedient to God the Father, just as Jesus was obedient to His Father's will (Luke 22:42).

3:11 Attain to means "to arrive at" as well as to "become a partaker of." Paul was not doubting his participation in the resurrection but was instead viewing it in expectation (1 Cor. 15:1–34). Paul desired to be with those Christians who, through their victory in Christ, would receive special reward in the **resurrection** (Heb. 11:35).

3:12 not . . . attained: Paul chooses a different Greek word from that translated in v. 11 as *attain.* Here he indicates he has not yet "gained possession of" or "laid hold of" all that he seeks to be. **perfected:** The Greek term means mature or complete, finished. It does not specifically mean a moral or sinless perfection. Paul is not speaking of moral perfection or righteousness but of reaching the state of completion as a Christian. **press on:** Paul "pursues with all deliberate speed" the goal that is before him. The verb form indicates that he is doing this continually. **lay hold of:** This phrase adds the idea of overtaking by surprise to the sense of seizing some object. Paul urgently wants to "grab hold of" God as God had **laid hold of** him (Acts 9:1–22). Christ had dramatically and suddenly seized Paul on the road to Damascus, and his life was never the same after that.

3:13 Paul could not obliterate the past from his memory, but he refused to let his past obstruct his progress toward his goal. He wanted to forget his self-righteous past (vv. 4–7). By using the present tense for **forgetting,** Paul was indicating that it is an ongoing process. He might even be implying that he wanted to forget everything so that he would not rest on his past successes in Christ, but continue to labor for the Lord. **reaching forward:** This verb means "fully extended." It is used of a horse stretching and straining to gain the victory in a race.

3:14 goal: This word specifically refers to the marker at the end of a race on which runners intently fix their eyes. The **prize** is the reward for victory. Paul evidently takes to heart what he teaches in 1 Cor. 9:24. **upward call:** In the NT this speaks of the divine call to complete salvation. It may refer to the judgment seat of Christ, the place of reward. Paul does not say that he is pressing on for the call of God but rather for the prize of that call. He is not working for his salvation but rather for a reward.

3:15 mature: Paul uses the adjectival form (Gk. *teleios*) of the verb form (Gk. *teleioo*) he records in 3:12 ("perfected"). One way to understand how these words are related is to recognize that in verse 15 Paul is speaking about one's standing or position in Christ whereas in v. 12 he is discussing the level of one's spiritual growth in Christ. Another way to connect these two words is to assume that Paul is using a touch of sarcasm or irony in v. 15. Thus, when he speaks of those who are "mature," he may be mocking the heresy spreaders among the Philippians who believed that they had already attained perfection.

3:16 let us walk: Paul commands the Philippians to conduct themselves as soldiers who "march in line" together, organized, each in his proper position.

3:17 The word **pattern** indicates an exact representation of the original. The example of Paul's life is so evident that one can readily see it and use it as a pattern for living.

3:18–21 Unlike Paul, Timothy, and Epaphroditus (2:17—3:17), **many** people have **set their mind on earthly things** (v. 19). As believers we are to concentrate our attention and efforts on reaching heaven because that is where we hold our **citizenship** (v. 20).

3:18 The term **weeping** reveals Paul's compassion and concern for those who most tragically are **the enemies of the cross.** In v. 2, he offers a stern warning against them, but here he weeps for them.

3:19 In this verse **destruction** indicates the opposite of eternal salvation (1:19, 28). **belly:** The physical appetites of the "many" (v. 18) control and consume them. **glory is in their shame:** The things in which they take pride actually are the things that will bring "disgrace" or "humiliation" to them, things of which they should have been ashamed.

3:20 Christians need to remember that

though we are in this world we are not of this world; our ultimate **citizenship is in heaven. eagerly wait:** Here Paul presents a direct contrast to the earthly focus of the enemies of the Cross in v. 19. The eager desire of Christians is not earthly things, but a heavenly Person, the Savior, **the Lord Jesus Christ** (Rom. 8:19–25).

3:21 Paul guarantees that Christ **will transform,** or "change in appearance," the believer. **lowly body:** What God will transform is the physical body. **conformed to His glorious body:** In v. 10, Christians are conformed to Christ's death; here they are conformed to His life. Our body now is weak and susceptible to sin, disease, and death. But God will change our bodies to resemble Christ's glorious resurrection body.

4:1 Paul's transition ("therefore") closes the previous section (3:17–21) and introduces the following exhortations. **joy and crown:** Paul considers the lives of these beloved Philippians to be the crowning reward for the work he has done. **stand fast:** With this command that requires continuous action on the part of the Philippians, Paul begins a series of ten commands that extends through v. 9.

4:2, 3 I urge: This word implies a certain level of familiarity; it introduces a request, not a demand. **true companion:** The identity of this person is unknown. It may be a specific person named Syzygos (the Greek word for *companion*),

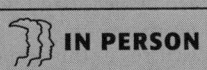 **IN PERSON** | **Euodia and Syntyche**

Paul's letters provide insight into the social makeup of the small early Christian communities in the Greco-Roman world. In his letter to the Philippian church, the first two persons he mentions by name are women: Euodia and Syntyche (Phil. 4:2). When Paul describes them as "these women who labored with me in the gospel" and includes them in the category of "fellow workers" (4:3), he indicates that they joined with him as equal partners in his missionary and teaching activity.

The exact nature of their leadership roles in the church at Philippi is not certain. The authority of both women in the church was sufficient, however, for Paul to encourage them to seek harmony with one another (4:2). He even called on someone addressed as "true companion" to "help these women" (4:3). Perhaps he was concerned that competition between them for the Philippians' loyalty and affection might fracture the young Philippian church. Perhaps the church met in the houses of these two women; competition between them, then, would have been a temptation.

Paul was concerned that Euodia and Syntyche "be of the same mind in the Lord" (4:2). His concern could not have run too deep, though. Along with Clement, he believed that both Euodia's and Syntyche's names were "in the Book of Life" (4:3). Nevertheless, both women needed to seek the mind of Christ, not their own.

Women played important leadership roles in Paul's churches, two examples being Phoebe in the church at Cenchrea (Rom. 16:1) and Priscilla in Ephesus (1 Cor. 16:19). Particularly in Macedonia, where women often assumed prominent roles in religious cults, it would be natural to find female leaders in a church. Paul supported women's roles in the Christian communities and instructed believers: "There is neither male nor female; for you are all one in Christ Jesus" (Gal. 3:28).

someone else particularly close to Paul, or any of the faithful Christians in the church who could help resolve the dispute. **help:** This verb means literally "to assist by holding together" and suggests that the women's dispute is not minor but potentially divisive. The **Book of Life** refers to a book in heaven where the names of believers are recorded (Dan. 12:1; Rev. 21:27).

4:4–8 Paul exhorts the Philippians to strive after four basic Christian virtues: (1) "rejoice in the Lord always" (v. 4), (2) be gentle to all people (v. 5), (3) be prayerful, not anxious (v. 6), and (4) meditate on excellent things (v. 8).

4:4 In the midst of difficulties, in the midst of all situations, Christians are to **rejoice.** The joy of Christians is not based on agreeable circumstances, instead it is based on their relationship to God. Christians will face trouble in this world, but they should rejoice in the trials they face because they know God is using those situations to improve their character (James 1:2–4).

4:5 gentleness: This noun identifies a person who manifests a calmness and fairness of spirit. A person who is gentle is willing to sacrifice his or her own personal rights to show consideration to others. **at hand:** The Lord's return could occur at any moment. Paul uses that fact to motivate the Philippians to honor God with their lives.

4:6 Paul exhorts the Philippians to pray about their circumstances instead of worrying over them. **be anxious for nothing:** Although the same word in 2:20 describes Timothy's concern for the Philippians, here Paul uses the word to refer to worry. He prohibits the Philippians from worrying about their own problems. Instead they are to commit their problems to God in prayer, trusting that He will provide deliverance.

4:7 will guard: Paul's choice of a military term implies that the mind is in a battle zone and needs to be "protected by a military guard." Since the purpose of such a guard in a wartime situation is either to prevent a hostile invasion or to keep the inhabitants of a besieged city from escaping, the **peace of God** operates in the same way: to protect the mind from external corrupting influences and to keep the mind focused on God's truth.

4:8 noble: This term describes that which is of honorable character. **pure:** This word is closely associated with the Greek word for *holy* and thus means "sacred" or "immaculate." **meditate on:** Paul commands the Philippians "to deliberate," "to evaluate," "to compute over and over" what is good and pure. In this way, Christians can renew their minds so that they will not conform to the evil habits of this world (Rom. 12:2).

4:9 learned: This verb conveys not only the concept of "increasing in intellectual knowledge" but also the idea of "learning by habitual practice." In some areas of their Christian development the Philippians had been excellent disciples of Paul, practicing what he had taught. **received:** This verb (Gk. *paralambano*) literally means "to take alongside oneself." It indicates a reception without rejection or disobedience. **do:** The Philippians are to "put into practice" or "undertake to do" all they had gained from Paul.

God of peace: As the Philippians do all that Paul commands, they will realize the presence of God, who is characterized by peace and who is the only source of true peace.

4:10–20 What Paul discusses in this section may be the reason why he wrote this letter. The Philippians had given him a gift and he desired to thank them for it. In this section, Paul indicates that the Philippians would be rewarded for their gift and that God would meet all their needs.

4:10 flourished again: Paul uses an agricultural word found only here in the NT to picture a plant that "shoots up" or "sprouts again," describing a condition of prosperity or abundance. **lacked opportunity:** Paul politely lets the Philippians know that he is aware of their continual concern for him.

4:11 content: The word literally means "self-sufficient." In Stoic philosophy this Greek word described a person who dispassionately accepted whatever circumstances brought. For the Greeks, this contentment came from personal sufficiency. But for Paul true sufficiency is found in the strength of Christ (v. 13).

4:12 to be abased: This term in its passive form means "to be demoted to a lower rank" or "to be humiliated by frugal circumstances." **to abound:** Paul also knows how to "live in affluence" and to "be richly supplied to the point of abundance." According to this verse, Paul knows what Job had learned centuries before: "The LORD gave, and the LORD has taken away; blessed be the name of the LORD" (Job 1:21). **I have learned:** This Greek verb indicates that Paul "was initiated into the secrets" of dealing with a satisfied or hungry stomach. He was, as this verb suggests, "intimately acquainted with" both conditions since he had become "accustomed" to both. **to suffer need:** Paul indicates

accrues interest. But Paul was not as concerned with their *gift* as with the development in the Philippians of the spiritual ability to give.

4:18 sweet-smelling aroma: Paul cherishes the gift that the Philippians sent him because he sees it as more of an offering to God than as a gift to him. **an acceptable sacrifice:** By giving to Paul, the Philippians had offered themselves as a gift to God (Rom. 12:1, 2).

4:19 In v. 18 Paul says that he is full because they gave. In this verse he writes that

 **IN COMPARISON** **The Christian Quest**

SEEK	Christ above all (1:21; 3:7, 8) and FIND righteousness in Christ and the power of His resurrection (3:9–11).
	Christlike humility (2:5–7) and FIND God's will in the believer (2:12, 13).
	A divinely appointed goal (3:14) and FIND the prize of eternal salvation (3:14).
	All things that are true, noble, just, pure, lovely, virtuous, and praiseworthy (4:8) and FIND the presence of the God of peace (4:9).

that there are times when he is "devoid," "falling short of," or "suffering the lack" of what others would call essentials.

4:13 I can do: The basic meaning of this verb is "to have power," especially to possess the physical strength that allows one to accomplish difficult tasks.

4:14 you shared: Though Paul relied on Christ to sustain him, he wanted the Philippians to know that their gift was appreciated.

4:15 giving and receiving: Paul considers the relationship between himself and the Philippians to be a two-way street, with both parties actively involved in the sharing of both material and spiritual gifts.

4:16 my necessities: Even the apostle had needs, and God used others to meet them.

4:17 Paul has in mind in this verse the material **gift** that the Philippians sent to him. **account:** Paul uses business terminology. The Philippians' gift was producing spiritual profit just as money deposited in a bank account

God will **supply all** their needs. The Philippians, in turn, will be full because of the gifts God will give them. **according to His riches:** Out of His abundant wealth, God will more than amply take care of the Philippians.

4:20 The Jewish practice of closing prayers with the word **amen** carried over to the Christian church as well. When found at the end of a sentence as it is here, the word can be translated "so be it," or "may it be fulfilled." At the beginning of a sentence, it means "surely," "truly," or "most assuredly."

4:21 brethren: Paul reminds them that they are part of the family of the Lord Jesus Christ.

4:22 those . . . of Caesar's household: These believers may have been officials in the Roman government (such as members of the Praetorian Guard; 1:13) or servants who lived and served in the emperor's palace.

4:23 As the letter opened with a blessing of grace, so also it closes. It is a fitting picture of the Christian life.

The Epistle to the
Colossians

∎

*J*UST AS A CHILD NEEDS PROPER INSTRUCTION early in life, so the early believers needed to be set on the proper path with correct teaching. Paul wrote this letter to deal with a doctrinal heresy that was creeping into the Colossian church. Although we are not told specifically what this heresy was, we can pick up clues from Paul's response. The error was probably a mixture of Judaism and an early form of

Gnosticism. The Colossian church was experiencing the same problems other early churches had encountered. Certain members were teaching that the observance of Jewish rules about food, the Sabbath, and special festivals would help believers to earn their salvation (Gal. 3:23–25; 4:10, 11). At Colosse, however, some of the Gentile members were apparently also promoting a form of mysticism that claimed that Jesus was a higher being, but not God. Paul refutes these false doctrines by pointing to Christ. Jesus had been the focus of Paul's preaching from the beginning. In Colossians, Paul reiterates the supremacy of Christ. It was because Jesus is divine that His death reconciles believers to their Creator.

As in all of his epistles, Paul seems to write as though he had our own society in mind. Even today, new cults claim to be Christian yet deny the deity of Christ and the basic beliefs of Christianity. Many today view Jesus as no more than "a great teacher." Paul's patient correction of the Colossian believers should remind us that we need to keep the worship of Jesus Christ central in our churches.

The city of Colosse was about a hundred miles east of Ephesus, in the valley of the Lycus River. During the Persian wars of the fifth century B.C., Colosse was a large and strategic city. By the time of the apostle Paul, however, it had declined into the shadows of its two sister cities, Laodicea and Hierapolis, and had become a small merchant town on the trade route from Rome to the east.

Evangelization of Colosse probably took place during Paul's three-year stay in Ephesus. Luke records in Acts 19:10 that people throughout the Asian region heard the gospel. Apparently Epaphras was converted in Ephesus, and after being instructed by Paul returned home to Colosse to proclaim the gospel. Evidently the church that emerged was largely composed of Gentiles, for Paul refers to their "uncircumcision," a word employed by Paul to designate Gentiles (2:13; Rom. 2:24–27; Eph. 2:11).

Pauline authorship of this letter has been universally recognized throughout church history. Paul identifies himself as the author of the letter three different times, describing himself as "an apostle of Jesus Christ" and as a servant of the gospel. Furthermore Paul closes the epistle with a handwritten greeting, a characteristic of several of his letters (1 Cor. 16:21; 2 Thess. 3:17). The Muratorian fragment (a document written around A.D. 180 that lists books considered by the early church to be divinely inspired) includes Colossians as a Pauline epistle. Many church fathers also upheld Paul as the author of Colossians. These include Justin Martyr, Irenaeus, Clement of Alexandria, Tertullian, and Origen.

Paul probably wrote Colossians while imprisoned in Rome around A.D. 60. Some have argued for other places of origin, such as Ephesus and Caesarea, but there is not enough evidence to displace the traditional theory that Paul wrote from his prison in Rome. Colossians is one of the four prison epistles of Paul, along with Ephesians, Philippians, and Philemon. Because Colossians, Ephesians, and Philemon have several similarities, many believe that the three were written at about the same time.

The many parallels between Colossians and Ephesians indicate that the two letters were written about the same time. Both letters reveal the centrality of Christ and His relationship to the church. Ephesians shows Christ as head of the church, while Colossians extends that imagery of His authority over all creation (1:16–18; 2:10). In Ephesians, Paul highlights how Christians are the members of the body of Christ, who is the head. In Colossians, he places emphasis on Christ the head, of whose body Christians are members.

The differences in the epistles are significant as well. Colossians stresses the completeness of the believer in Christ; Ephesians points to Christian unity that is found in Christ. The mystery in Colossians is that Christ is in believers (1:26, 27), while the mystery in Ephesians is the unity of Jew and Gentile in Christ. Colossians speaks of Jesus as Lord over all creation, while Ephesians concerns itself with Christ's authority over the church. Finally, Colossians has a stronger tone because it confronts a specific false teaching in Colosse. Ephesians has a softer tone; it does not address a specific heresy.

But with all their similarities and differences, Ephesians and Colossians together present a mature understanding of who Christ is and what His life and death mean for the believer. From prison, Paul was teaching the churches in Asia Minor how central the person of Jesus Christ is to the Christian faith. He is the image of God, the source of all wisdom, and the head of the church. He is the One who reconciles us to God and to our fellow believers. As our Savior and Deliverer, He deserves our sincere adoration and praise.

Outline

I. Introduction 1:1, 2
II. The preeminence of Christ in the life of the Colossians 1:3–14
    A. Paul's thanks for the Colossians' faith in Christ 1:3–8
    B. Paul's prayer for the Colossians' understanding and fruitfulness 1:9–14
III. The preeminence of Christ in His nature and work 1:15–29
    A. The divine nature of Christ 1:15–20

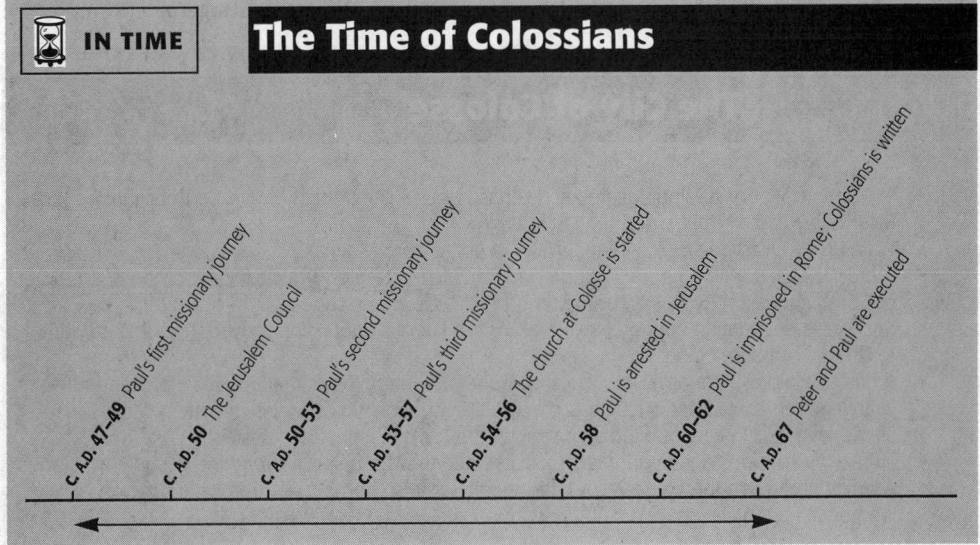

IN TIME · **The Time of Colossians**

C. A.D. 47-49 Paul's first missionary journey

C. A.D. 50 The Jerusalem Council

C. A.D. 50-53 Paul's second missionary journey

C. A.D. 53-57 Paul's third missionary journey

C. A.D. 54-56 The church at Colosse is started

C. A.D. 58 Paul is arrested in Jerusalem

C. A.D. 60-62 Paul is imprisoned in Rome; Colossians is written

C. A.D. 67 Peter and Paul are executed

B. The glorious work of Christ 1:21–23

IV. Paul's ministry in general and for the Colossians
1:24—2:7

V. The preeminence of Christ over false religion
2:8–23

  A. The superiority of Christ over false philosophy
2:8–15

  B. The reality of Christ instead of false worship
2:16–19

  C. The power of Christ versus false asceticism
2:20–23

VI. The preeminence of Christ in Christian
living 3:1—4:6

  A. Christ, the foundation of the believer's life
3:1–4

  B. The virtues of the believer's life in Christ
3:5–17

  C. Christ in relationships 3:18—4:6

    1. Family relationships 3:18–21

    2. Business relationships 3:22—4:1

    3. Personal relationships 4:2–6

VII. Conclusion 4:7–18

Commentary

1:1 Paul calls himself **an apostle,** a word whose root means "to send." This Greek word was first used of a cargo ship or fleet, but later denoted a commander of a fleet. The NT employs the word to signify an approved spokesman sent as a personal representative. Although not every Christian is called by God to minister like Paul or the twelve apostles, every Christian is sent by God to represent Him before the people with whom he or she comes in contact. **by the will of God:** This speaks of Paul's divine appointment. His appointment was not by the Twelve, by religious leaders, by his family, nor by himself. This is an assertion of his divine authority, a declaration of his independence of all human authority, and he disclaims any individual merit or personal power. **and Timothy our brother:** Timothy was not an apostle; he was a brother. This trusted companion was with Paul in Rome. As an act of courtesy, Paul includes Timothy in the salutation. Timothy was Paul's spiritual son (1 Tim. 1:2, 18; 2 Tim. 1:2; 1 Cor. 4:17).

1:2 The Greek term translated **saints** means "holy people." The essence of "holiness" is being set apart to God. All believers are saints, not because they are perfect, but because they belong to God. **in Christ:** This is a favorite expression of the apostle Paul, used some 80 times in his letters. Paul saw all of Christian experience growing out of the believer's position in Christ. **Grace . . . peace:** Paul combines the Greek word for grace with the standard Hebrew greeting, *peace.* He broadens and deepens his meaning by reminding his readers that the ultimate source of "favor" and "wholeness" is in **God our Father and the Lord Jesus Christ** (Rom. 1:7).

1:3 The apostle indicates the tender concern that he has for these Christians; he is **praying always** for them. This common phrase of Paul's (Eph. 1:16; Phil. 1:4; 1 Thess. 1:2), which combines intercessory prayer and thanksgiving, means that each time Paul prayed, he interceded for the Colossians and offered praise for God's work among them.

1:4–8 faith . . . love . . . hope: Paul often uses these three terms together (Rom. 5:2–5;

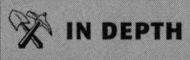 **IN DEPTH** | **The City of Colosse**

- A Roman city of Asia Minor located at the base of 8,000-foot-high Mount Cadmus in the Lycus River valley east of Ephesus.
- Watered by a cascade descending through a gorge from Mount Cadmus.
- A prosperous industrial center especially famous for its textiles, but clearly in decline at the time of Christ, squeezed by its increasingly competitive neighbor, Laodicea.
- Survived a devastating earthquake in A.D. 61, but later its population moved three miles south to Chonai (modern Honaz).
- Judaism, Platonism, and mystery cults from the surrounding mountain peoples blended into strange, often contradictory religious practices. Cultic worship of angels persisted, with Michael as the favorite. He was credited with sparing the town in a time of disaster.
- Home of Archippus and Epaphras, associates of Paul who helped spread the gospel throughout Asia, up and down the Lycus Valley. The region was also home to Onesimus, a runaway slave who became a believer.

1 Cor. 13:13; 1 Thess. 1:3; 5:8). *Faith* is in Christ. This is the thrust of the passage. The Colossians' faith was grounded in the nature and work of Jesus Christ. *Love* flows from faith and proves the genuineness of one's faith (James 2:14–26). The Colossians' sacrificial love **for all the saints** proved their true belief in Christ. *Hope* refers to the result of faith, the treasure **laid up . . . in**

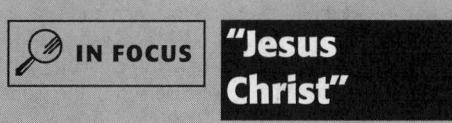

IN FOCUS   **"Jesus Christ"**

(Gk. *Iesous Christos*) (1:1; Matt. 1:1, 18; Mark 1:1; John 1:17; 17:3; 1 Cor. 1:2–10) Strong's #2424; 5547: "Jesus Christ" is not the first and last names of Jesus, as people are commonly named today. *Jesus* is His human name, whose meaning relates to His mission to "save" us (Matt. 1:18). *Christ* is a description of His office: He is "the Anointed One," anointed by God to be our King, Prophet, and High Priest. The combination of name and title is rare in the Gospels (occurring only five times) because Jesus was still in the process of revealing Himself as the Christ. Once this was recognized by His followers, the combination was used prolifically throughout the Book of Acts and the Epistles to express the belief that Jesus is the Christ, the promised Messiah. Paul uses the combined form at the start of Colossians to indicate the theme of his letter, the supremacy of Jesus Christ.

heaven where our faith will find its fulfillment in the presence of Christ. **Epaphras** is also mentioned in 4:12, 13 and Philem. 23. Epaphras probably was Paul's convert and fellow prisoner. He most likely started the church in his hometown of Colosse.

1:9–12 Paul's prayer for the Colossian Christians is a model for us. As soon as he heard of the new faith of the Colossians, he began interceding with God for them, asking Him to give them knowledge, wisdom, strength, and joy. He prayed that the new believers at Colosse would grow into Christian maturity so that they might walk before God, pleasing Him and producing good works.

1:9 Paul's chief concern is that the Colossians might have full **knowledge** of God's **will**. The desire to serve God will be in vain without a proper understanding of the One we want to serve. Thus, Paul prays that the Colossians might be filled with full knowledge that encompasses **all wisdom and spiritual understanding.** *Wisdom* is the practical outworking of knowledge (James 3:17), and that knowledge cannot be separated from the *spiritual understanding* that comes through the discernment given by the Holy Spirit.

1:10 In addition to the full knowledge of the Lord's will mentioned in v. 9, Paul desires that the Colossians **may walk worthy of the Lord.** Paul wanted the Colossians to live in a manner that adequately reflected what God had done for them and was doing in them. Being "worthy of God" is a phrase that occurs in ancient pagan inscriptions throughout Asia. It pictures someone's life being weighed on scales to determine its worth. If these devotees to false gods knew they had to walk in a worthy manner, certainly Christians should dedicate their lives to the living God in order to please Him.

1:11 according to His glorious power: This phrase means that believers are empowered not in proportion to their need but according to God's strength. So then, Paul desires to see nothing less than the very power of God Himself at work in the Colossian believers. Like Samson's (Judg. 14:19), a believer's strength comes from God alone. **patience:** Literally, "remaining under." This is the opposite of cowardice and despondency. It is forbearance, steadfast endurance, fortitude, and the capacity to see things through. It means remaining under difficulties without succumbing to them. **longsuffering:** This is the opposite of wrath and revenge. It is self-restraint, even-temperedness, holding out long. Longsuffering does not retaliate in spite of injury or insult (compare James 5:7–11). **with joy:** Not with a long face, not with a sickly smile, but with psalms in the night. "The joy of the Lord is your strength" (Neh. 8:10).

1:12 qualified: The word means to be able or authorized for a task. Believers can never be qualified on their own; instead God must make them sufficient through Jesus Christ. The tense of the verb points to "qualifying" as an act in the past rather than a process. Ordinarily to qualify for an event or a position, we have to prove ourselves. However the **inheritance** (v. 5) that believers receive is not one that they have earned but is based on being *qualified* by God. The Father "qualifies" us for eternal life with Him, whereas the Son will reward us at the end of the race (Rev. 22:12). The term **saints** probably does not refer to the angels of God as in 1 Thess. 3:13. Instead Paul uses the word for the believers at Colosse.

1:13 Delivered . . . conveyed: God has liberated believers from the dominion of darkness. The apostle uses the common symbolism of light and darkness for good and evil, for God's

---

🔍 IN FOCUS — **"firstborn"**

(Gk. *prototokos*) (1:15; Rom. 8:29; Heb. 1:6) Strong's #4416: The first part of this word (*proto*) can indicate "first in time" (temporal priority) or "first in place" (preeminence). In this context, preeminence is in the forefront. Moreover, the phrase carries either an active or passive sense, bearer of one born, here the former. Thus, the Son of Man is the "chiefbearer" of all God's creatures. In Ex. 4:22; Deut. 21:16, 17; Ps. 89:23, the Greek OT *prototokos* is used to express the idea of preeminence and first cause. This designation in no way indicates that Christ Himself was created by God; the verse moreover asserts that all things were created in, through, and for Christ. As a participant in the creation of all things, Christ cannot be a created being. Instead, He is the Son of God, the second person of the Godhead, who has existed from eternity.

---

kingdom and Satan's kingdom, that is found throughout the NT. The kingdom from which believers have been rescued is the kingdom of darkness (see this imagery in John 1:4–9; Eph. 5:8; 1 Thess. 5:5; 1 Pet. 2:9; 1 John 1:5). This realm of darkness had a brief apparent triumph against our Lord (Luke 22:53), but His ultimate victory on the Cross brings victory over the kingdom of darkness to His saints. That deliverance transferred them into a new kingdom. **Conveyed** was used of resettling colonists as citizens of a new country. The final consummation is not yet; but in some sense, believers are already ushered into Christ's kingdom. There is a tension in Paul's theology here that he delicately balances. The future earthly manifestation of the kingdom is coming, but there is already a foretaste of the gloriousness of that future time.

1:14 The Greek word **redemption** points naturally to the payment of a price or ransom for the release of a slave. The slavery from which believers are released is not physical but spiritual. They are freed from bondage to sin by **forgiveness of sins** through the blood of Jesus Christ (Eph. 1:7). People today tend to avoid speaking of sin. Often when a person has committed wrongs or even crimes, these are dismissed as disease or dysfunction. The Bible speaks forthrightly of sins for which persons must be forgiven. The wages of sin is death. The only release comes from the forgiveness of God based on the death of His Son (Rom. 3:24, 25).

1:15–20 Paul interrupts his description of his prayers for the Colossians with a song of praise. These verses are generally recognized as an early Christian hymn celebrating the supremacy of Jesus Christ.

1:15 firstborn over all creation: *Firstborn* could devote a priority in time or in rank. The word does not describe Christ as the first being created in time because the hymn proclaims that all things were "created by Him" and that

"He is before all things." Jesus is the eternal One who was before all creation. The idea of *firstborn* in the Hebrew culture did not require that one be the first son born. This was not the case with either Isaac or Jacob. But they were the *firstborn* in the sense that they were rightful heirs to the line of their fathers. Being *firstborn* referred more to rank and privilege than to order of birth. Since Christ is God, He is supreme in rank over all creation. Yet He is not only the transcendent deity who created us; He is the One who died on our behalf (Phil. 2:6–18) and was subsequently raised from dead. Thus, He is also the *firstborn* from the dead (v. 18), the first One who experienced the true resurrection (1 Cor. 15:20).

1:16 This early Christian hymn emphasizes the superiority of Christ over all creation. Christ is the One who created all things, whether they be material or immaterial, seen or unseen. This idea is in direct contradiction to the false teaching, later known as Gnosticism, that was developing in the Colossian church. In general, Gnostics believed that various angelic beings were the creators of the earth and that Christ was one among many of these angels. **all things were created through Him and for Him:** Not only did Jesus create all things; everything was created for His purposes (Heb. 1:2, where Christ is said to be the "heir of all things"). But the glory of the earth, the heavens, or the sun, moon, and stars cannot be compared with the glory of His new creation (2 Cor. 5:17).

1:17 before all things: Both in time and in supremacy. Because of Christ's supreme authority and oversight, all things **consist** (hold together).

1:18 Following the celebration of Christ's authority over all creation, this early Christian hymn proceeds to proclaim His authority over the church. He is the **head** of His own **body,** which is the church. No one should underestimate the significance of the church, for it is in

✠ IN CONTEXT Christ, the Lord of the World

In Col. 1:15–18, Paul presents Jesus as the cosmic Christ, Creator of the universe, Sustainer of earth and all of its ecological systems, and Ruler over the competing power networks of the world. This is quite a contrast from Jesus the Servant, as presented in Phil. 2:5–8. There He is Lord of the personal and the private, the One who speaks to someone's heart. Here in Colossians, Paul offers the Lord of the public who transcends individual needs to deal with global concerns.

These are not two different Christs, but the same Christ, Lord of all. And His rule over both domains—the public and the private—suggests the kinds of activities in which His followers need to engage. On the one hand, Christ lives in us to transform us personally. He wants to affect our individual jobs, our families, our local communities, and our personal relationships. On the other hand, Christ is at work globally, using people to transform societies and their systems, confront principalities and powers, and work for public justice and human rights.

fact Christ's body. The sovereign Creator of the universe, as head of the church, provides leadership and oversight over it. No wonder He is so jealous for it (1 Cor. 3:16, 17). **firstborn from the dead:** Christ was the first to be raised from the dead. His own resurrection guarantees that the church will one day be resurrected (1 Cor. 15:12–28).

1:19 fullness: The opponents of Paul, and later the Greek Gnostics, seem to have used this word as a technical term for the sphere between heaven and earth where a hierarchy of angels lived. The Gnostics viewed Christ as one of many spirits existing in this hierarchy between God and all people. However, Paul used the term *fullness* to refer to the complete embodiment of God. Christ is the only Intercessor for human beings and fully embodies all of God's nature (1 Tim. 2:5). No other intermediary, whether person or group, is able to stand in our place before the Father. Only Jesus can do this.

1:20, 21 reconcile all things . . . now He has reconciled: This phrase shows the significance of Christ's work on the Cross. It does not mean that all people will be saved, since many passages clearly say that unbelievers will suffer eternal separation from God (Matt. 25:46). The work of Christ will overthrow the damage effected by the Fall and change all of creation from a position of enmity to a relationship of peace and friendship (Rom. 8:20–23; 2 Cor. 5:18–20).

1:22 body of His flesh: The false teachers at Colosse were telling the believers that redemption could only be accomplished through a spiritual being. They rejected Christ's incarnation. According to them, Jesus could not have had a physical body. Thus, Paul uses two terms, *body* and *flesh*, to clearly state that Christ became man and experienced a physical death. **holy . . . blameless . . . above reproach in His**

sight: We who were once enemies of God and alienated by our own wicked works will one day be presented as above reproach on account of Christ's death for us.

1:23 if indeed you continue in the faith: The perseverance of the Colossians was proof of the reconciling work of Christ on their behalf (vv. 21, 22). **every creature under heaven:** Paul uses this exaggeration to illustrate the rapid spread of the gospel. Compare Acts 17:6, where the apostles are said to have turned the world upside down, even though their ministry up to that point had been limited to a small portion of the eastern Mediterranean region.

1:24–29 Paul received a **stewardship from God** (v. 25) to preach this divine Christ (vv. 9–18) who had reconciled the world (vv. 19–23). It was Paul's ministry, but we, too, are responsible to God to preach Christ.

1:24 In this verse, Paul is not saying that Christ's death was insufficient (2:11–15) or that somehow he was a coredeemer with Christ. Paul is making the point that a Christian will endure the **sufferings** that Christ would be enduring if He were still in the world (2 Cor. 1:5; 4:11). Christ had told His disciples that if the world hated Him it would hate His followers. If people persecuted Him they would persecute His followers (John 15:19, 20). Paul believed he was suffering the afflictions God wanted him to endure. Instead of facing his difficulties with dread, Paul saw his troubles as a time of joy (Rom. 8:17; Phil. 1:29; 1 Thess 1:6; 2:2; 3:3–5; 2 Tim. 3:12), because they were producing an eternal reward (2 Cor. 4:17).

1:25 I became a minister: Become a servant. Paul's appointment made him a minister of the gospel (Eph. 3:7; Col. 1:23) a minister of God (2 Cor. 6:4); a minister of Christ (1 Cor. 4:1); and a minister of the New Covenant (2 Cor. 3:6). **stewardship:** Divine ordering (Gk.

oikonomia), administration, trusteeship. This was Paul's high privilege and sacred trust. Paul was a steward in God's economy; a trustee in God's household; and an administrator of God's business. Paul was on business for the King. **given:** Not usurped. **for you:** For your benefit and for your blessing. **to fulfill the word of God:** God's purpose was Paul's purpose, and God's Word was Paul's message. Therefore, Paul's message was pure and uncorrupted by false teaching (Rom. 15:19; 2 Tim. 4:2–5).

1:26, 27 The **mystery** referred to in these verses is similar to the mystery spoken of in Eph. 3:8–10. In Greek pagan religions, a mystery was a secret teaching reserved for a few spiritual teachers who had been initiated into an inner circle. Paul uses the word to refer to knowledge that had been "hidden from the ages and generations" (2:2, 4:3; 1 Cor. 2:7; 4:1; Eph. 3:4, 9; 5:32; 6:19; 1 Tim. 3:9, 16), but was now being revealed by God. The Lord had revealed this mystery to Paul and called him to be a steward of it (Eph. 3:5). The mystery is that Christ now lives within Gentile believers: **Christ in you, the hope of glory.** This is in harmony with Ephesians. In that letter, Paul states that the mystery is the union of Jews and Gentiles in one body, Christ's church (Eph. 3:6).

1:28 Here is a great discipling verse. Paul was not content to see people born again. He took the responsibility of leading them on to maturity. He moved them from infancy to infantry. Spiritual babies have great potential, but they became a serious drain on the church and a source of untold problems if they remain in the nursery forever. **perfect:** The concept of perfection in the NT means completeness or maturity. Here the reference is probably to the coming of Christ, when every believer will experience the completion of Christ's work in him or her (1 Cor. 13:10).

1:29 Paul toiled and agonized for the perfection of his fellow believers (v. 28), not in his own strength but by the power of God working in him.

2:1–5 Paul's ministry included Christians like the Colossians whom he had never **seen.** He had **a great conflict** for them in care, desire, and prayer (vv. 1–3). He was concerned lest someone **deceive** them (v. 4), and he was **rejoicing** at their **steadfastness** (v. 5). Paul is a model of pastoral concern.

2:1 Laodicea was a sister city of Colosse about eleven miles away. The two churches were to share their letters from Paul (4:16).

2:2, 3 Though the false teachers at Colosse spoke of initiating people into a superior knowledge, Paul tells his readers that they can understand the **mystery** (1:26, 27) of God without this false philosophy. The Gnostics sought

knowledge as an end in itself, but Paul reminds the Colossians that true knowledge will demonstrate itself by bringing people together in Christian love in the church. Note how Paul joins the **Father** and **Christ** together, emphasizing their common deity and unity. The Gnostics would view Jesus only as an emanation from the Father, sharing a portion of the attributes of deity. Paul not only emphasizes Jesus' deity, but also explains that He possesses all wisdom and knowledge. The Gnostics thought only certain "knowledgeable" people could join their elite group; Paul teaches that every believer has access to complete wisdom found in Christ.

2:4 Do not let the **persuasive** but deceptive **words** of false teachers lead you from the true "wisdom" (v. 3) in Christ.

2:5 absent . . . with you: Although Paul did not know the Colossians and Laodiceans personally (2:1), his strong feelings for them

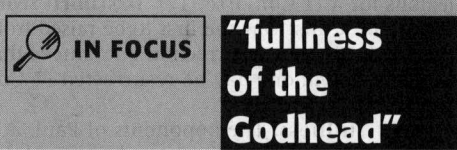

IN FOCUS

"fullness of the Godhead"

(Gk. *pleroma tes theotetos*) (2:9) Strong's #4138; 2320: The Greek word *pleroma* indicates "plenitude" and "totality." The Gnostics used the word to describe the totality of all deities. Both Paul and John used the word to describe Christ, who is the fullness, the plenitude of God, for all the fullness of the Godhead dwells in Him bodily (1:19; 2:9). Since all of God's fullness resides in Christ, every spiritual reality is found in Christ. In Him, we lack nothing. The Greek word *theotetos* for Godhead is used only here in the NT and designates the totality of God's nature and person. All the fullness of the Godhead "dwells" or "permanently resides" in the body of Jesus, the God-man.

and the vivid report from Epaphras (1:7) made him feel present with them in spirit (1 Cor. 5:3–5).

2:6, 7 Just as the Colossian believers had begun with Christ, so Paul encourages them to continue in their **walk** with Him. Paul uses four words to describe the Colossians' walk with Christ. The tense of the word translated **rooted** denotes a complete action; the believers *have been* rooted in Christ. The next three words, **built up, established,** and **abounding,** are in the present tense, showing the continual growth that should characterize every Christian's walk with Christ.

2:8 This verse has been used at times to teach that Christians should not study or read **philosophy.** This is not Paul's meaning. Paul himself was adept at philosophy, evidenced by his interaction with the Stoic and Epicurean philosophers in Athens (Acts 17:1–34). Paul was warning the believers not to be taken in by any philosophy that does not conform to a proper knowledge of Christ. The false teachers at Colosse had combined worldly philosophies with the gospel. These philosophies are spoken of by Paul as the **basic principles** of the world, which some have interpreted as "spirits" or "angels" who supposedly control a person's life (Gal. 4:3, 9). It seems more likely that the term *principles* refers to the elementary rules and regulations that certain teachers were seeking to impose on believers according to the dictates of human philosophies. Paul's strongest indictment against the heretics was that their teaching was **not according to Christ,** and thus they were not walking with Christ (vv. 6, 7).

2:9 In this verse Paul clearly proclaims the Incarnation, the fact that God became a man **bodily.** This contradicts the Gnostic idea of the inherent evil of physical bodies and the claim that Jesus is merely a spirit. The Gnostics thought **the fullness** of God had been divided among a number of angelic beings, the last creating the material world. In contrast, Paul says that the fullness of God exists in Christ.

2:10 Paul illustrates the adequacy of Christ by demonstrating how the Colossian believers are **complete.** In Christ, the Colossians have put off the power of sin and the flesh (v. 11), have received new life (vv. 12, 13), have been forgiven, have been delivered from requirements laid down by human traditions (v. 14), and have been freed from the powers of spirit beings (v. 15). There is nothing that the Christian needs to add to what was received in Christ at the time of conversion. Paul emphasizes the sufficiency of Christ in order to refute the Gnostics and the Judaizers who respectively believed that special knowledge or works were necessary to make a Christian complete.

2:11 Whereas all Jewish males were required to receive physical **circumcision,** the circumcision that is from Christ is **without hands** (Deut. 10:16). Rather than the mere removal of flesh, Christian circumcision is the spiritual removal of sin from the heart, taking part in the New Covenant of Jesus Christ.

2:12, 13 buried . . . in baptism: Baptism is the symbol of the believer's association with Christ's death on the Cross. Water baptism itself does not bring forgiveness of sins, but Paul uses

the rite to help explain the work of the Spirit. The early church would never have understood the idea of an unbaptized Christian. Baptism and faith were considered to be the outward and inward realities of being a Christian (Acts 2:38; 10:47, 48; 16:33; Rom. 6:3–5). Some have highlighted Paul's close association of baptism and circumcision in this passage as an indication that water baptism is a sign of the New Covenant, just as circumcision was a sign of the Abrahamic covenant.

2:14 nailed . . . to the cross: Not only were our personal sins forgiven at the Cross, but those rules that condemned us have also been removed by the death of Christ.

2:15 Principalities and powers allude to Satan and the fallen angels. Paul is describing Christ's victory on the Cross over the powers that opposed Him and that were against God's faithful people. To describe this victory, Paul uses the spectacle of the military triumph, when prisoners of war were stripped and paraded before the populace behind the conquering general. Satan and his forces thought the Cross would be their victory and Christ's defeat. In reality, at the Cross the Lord vanquished His foes, took away their weapons, and **made a public spectacle of them.** This is a dramatic contrast to the victory that Satan had over our first parents in the garden. Satan was the victor in that instance, but at the Cross he was the clear loser. In view of this victory by Christ, we should be wary of those who emphasize demonism or play up the power of demons over Christians. By giving Satan recognition, we give him power. This is not to deny demonic forces, only to keep in proper perspective their limited power over Christ's kingdom now and their final destiny at the end of the world.

2:16–19 In view of Christ's victory over His enemies, we should not be controlled by those powers and practices over which Christ has already triumphed. The false teachers in Colosse were tempting the Colossians to bind themselves with the outward observances of Judaism, such as the Jewish dietary restrictions. These were merely a **shadow** of Christ. Judaism and its rites pointed to Christ. Paul warns the believers in Colosse not to let others bind them to regulations from which Christ has already freed them. **false humility:** People who do not champion salvation in Christ alone often appear to be humble. But their search for a new spiritual experience or advocacy of some work as necessary for salvation is actually human pride. They do not want to submit to God's plan of salvation revealed in the Bible.

2:20–23 regulations: Since believers have been released from ritualistic observances, why should they let others bind them down again

(Rom. 6:3–14)? No human work can be added to the merit of Christ's death. His work on the Cross is the only acceptable work in God's eyes. The legalistic commands of others are a **self-imposed religion** and **are of no value** for salvation.

3:1–4 Paul's exhortations in ch. 3 are practical applications of the doctrine he has presented in ch. 2. **if . . . you were raised with Christ:** Paul ties his ethical teaching (v. 5) to the doctrine of the Resurrection (2:12, 13). **set your mind on things above:** The false teachers were instructing the Colossians to concentrate on temporal observances; in contrast, Paul instructs them to concentrate on the eternal realities of heaven. The Greek verb for *set* emphasizes an ongoing decision. Christians must continually discipline themselves to focus on eternal realities, instead of the temporal realities of this earth. A Christian's life is no longer dictated by this world but is **hidden with Christ.** The Greek word for *hidden* indicates that God has accomplished this in the past so that it is a present reality.

3:5–8 While obedience to rules cannot bring salvation, those who are saved ought to live worthy of that salvation. Thus, Paul gives the Colossians instructions concerning proper conduct. He states in negative and positive terms the kind of life that God wants Christians to live. Although the believers at Colosse were once captivated by the evil practices listed in vv. 5, 8, 9, they were to abandon such practices.

3:9 The analogies between the **old man** and our old sinful ways and the **new man** and our new lives in Jesus Christ parallel Paul's discussion in Rom. 6 about dying to sin and living for Christ. The two words *old man* and *new man*

do not refer to the Christian's fleshly and spiritual natures. Instead, Paul describes our former unredeemed life as the *old man,* and our life as God's child as the *new man.* The new man has the image of the new creation in Christ, just as the old man bears the image of our fallen nature. The old man is under an old master, Satan, while the new man has a new master, the Spirit of God living within.

3:10 and have put on the new man: Have clothed yourselves with the new man. The new man is the person you are after having been saved. The new man is received from Christ at the time of the second birth, and is the regenerated man, the new nature. **renewed:** This present passive participle (Gr *anakaineo*) indicates constantly being renewed. This is a continuous process; the new man has not yet matured and is ever in the state of development.

3:11 barbarian: In the Roman Empire a person who did not speak Greek was despised. **Scythian:** An uncultured person who came from the area around the Black Sea. **Greek . . . Jew . . . slave . . . free:** This list is similar to the list in Gal. 3:28. In both places the point is not the functions of the persons in the body of Christ, but equal acceptance of all the groups into God's family.

3:12 elect of God: God calls all people to salvation; those who accept are the elect from the foundation of the world (compare Eph. 1:3–14). They become God's own special people. As God is **holy,** we who are **beloved** by God must be holy and **put on** His characteristics. Exploitation of others was the old way of life; the new must be characterized by concern.

3:13 A **forgiving** spirit is an essential char-

 **IN COMPARISON** ## The Preeminence of Christ

CHRIST				
In universal government	In reconciliation	In wisdom and knowledge	In religious observance	In Christian living
• The visible image of God (Col. 1:15)	• Pleases the Father (1:19, 20)	• The source of all treasures (2:2, 3)	• We are alive in Him (2:11–13)	• He is our life (3:3)
• The agent of creation (1:16)	• Reconciles us through His death (1:21, 22)	• Worldly philosophy does not conform to Him (2:8)	• No need for legalism and ritualism (2:16–23)	• We can avoid immorality and can bless others (3:5–14)
• The Sustainer (1:17)	• Lives in us as our hope of glory (1:27)			
• The Head of the church (1:18)				

acteristic for one who has been forgiven by Christ.

3:14 But above all these things: On top of all these things, like an outer garment. **put on love:** Love is the basis and cloak of all the graces (1 Cor. 13:13). **bond:** The bond that binds the others together. **perfection:** This means completeness, full grown, mature.

3:15 The **peace of God** rules in our **hearts** when we are completely surrendered to God's will, and thus our whole being is unified in obedience to Him. Christ's reconciling work makes this surrender possible.

3:16 Let the word of Christ dwell in you richly is apparently a parallel thought to Paul's statement in Eph. 5:18 where he says to be "filled with the Spirit." Both here and in Ephesians, the result of being "filled" with the Spirit or the word of Christ is singing (Eph. 5:19–21). The **psalms** are the *psalms* found in the OT, the "songbook" of the early church as well as of

Israel. The **hymns** would be the songs of the church that reflected the new truth in Christ. Examples of such hymns are found in 1:15–20; Phil. 2:5–11; l Tim. 3:16. **Spiritual songs** may have been other kinds of songs praising God.

3:17 In this verse, Paul sums up how Christians should live. We should commit everything we do or say to **Jesus** and continually thank God for all His good gifts (Eccl. 12:13, 14).

3:18–4:1 These verses show Christians how to do everything in the home "in the name of the Lord Jesus" (v. 17). All members of the household are responsible to Christ. There are three balanced pairs of exhortations: to wives and husbands (3:18, 19); to children and fathers (3:20, 21); and to servants and masters (3:22—4:1).

3:18, 19 Based on the kind of Christian life to which believers are called, Paul gives some practical guidance. General applications like "be good" or "love everybody" are very difficult to

 **IN DEPTH** ## False Teaching at Colosse

Good truths are often corrupted. The apostle Paul spent much of his time battling false teachers who came behind him and added their own "spin" to the gospel. He wrote to the Christians at Colosse partly to correct a heresy about God and spirituality that had begun to take root there.

Even at this early stage in the church's life, before any heresies had developed far enough to be labeled with names, Jewish mysticism, Jewish legalism, and Greek philosophy had mixed in with true Christian doctrine. The kind of doctrine that was infecting Colosse would eventually be called Gnosticism. This was a prominent Christian heresy in the second and third centuries. Gnosticism taught that special knowledge was needed for a soul to break from the physical realm into the spiritual realm. As this false doctrine developed, it claimed that salvation could only be obtained through such special knowledge. In this way the Gnostics replaced faith with intellect.

Gnosticism followed the Greek philosophy that matter was inherently evil. Only nonphysical, "spiritual" realities were good. Hence, Gnostics did not believe that God created the world or that Christ came in a physical body. According to the Gnostics, an angel or secondary god created the material universe. Paul corrected this error in Colosse by stating clearly that Christ is the Creator and Sustainer of all, the supreme Head over the church and over all other authorities.

Gnosticism affected a person's morality in one of two ways. One tendency was indulgence. This sort of Gnostic reasoned that since the body was evil and the spirit was good, nothing done by the body could harm the spirit. These Gnostics tended to give in to every sensual desire, denying themselves nothing. They believed that because they had God's grace and because the physical body was of no account, they could do whatever they wanted with their bodies. The apostle John dealt with this type of Gnosticism in 1 John, as did Paul in 1 Corinthians.

The second moral outcome of Gnosticism was asceticism. Ascetics reasoned that because the body is bad, it should be denied every pleasure. They hoped that denial of the body would elevate the spirit. Paul's opponents at Colosse were ascetics. They found legalism alluring, and the strict Jewish laws (2:16) meshed easily with their harsh, self-denying rituals. Paul warned his readers that such rituals are useless and have no spiritual value (2:20–23).

The main problem with the heresy at Colosse was its denial of who Christ is. These false teachers denied that Jesus is the Creator who came in the flesh, that He is God who became man. Their rejection of the deity of Christ led them to seek salvation through their intellect or through the abuse of one's body. Such efforts served only to hide the truth, that salvation is found only in Christ.

follow, so Paul seeks to apply moral truths to the daily lives of the Colossians (Eph. 5:21—6:9). The Colossian home would usually consist of father, mother, children, and servants. Paul gives instructions to each group. The first is for **wives** to **submit.** The word *submit* is a military

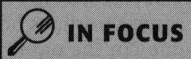

IN FOCUS **"peace"**

(Gk. *eirene*) (1:2; 3:15; Eph. 2:17; Phil. 1:2; 4:7) Strong's #*1515*; rule (Gk. *brabeuo*) (3:15) Strong's #*1018*: The Greek term *eirene* has a variety of meanings, including "unity," "tranquility," and "concord," and corresponds to the Hebrew word *shalom,* which primarily means "wholeness." In the NT, the Greek word is used for a harmonious relationship between people (Rom. 14:19), the order produced by a ruling government (Acts 24:2), and the reconciliation between God and a person through the saving work of Christ (Eph. 2:17). In 3:15, Paul encourages the believers to let "the peace of God rule" in their hearts. The Greek word for *rule* means "to act as umpire" or "to arbitrate." The peace of God should act as our umpire when anger, envy, and other such passions arise in our hearts.

term meaning to "arrange oneself under another" and indicates a voluntary submission, not an unthinking obedience. It is clear that submission does not denigrate the one who submits. The husband is commanded to **love** his wife (Eph. 5:25 says as Christ loved the church). In his headship, he is to seek her highest good, not his own welfare. He is to honor her and be considerate of her, and not to be bitter or harsh.

3:20, 21 Children and **fathers** also have admonitions from the apostle. Children are to obey. Yet the **all things** should not be taken as an absolute. When God's truth and anyone's demands come into conflict, a child should obey God. Furthermore, a father should be careful not to frustrate his children or discourage them. Regulations should be reasonable, not arbitrary. The father should train his children the same way God disciplines and teaches him.

3:22–25 Bondservants, obey . . . your masters: The question of slaves and masters may appear to be out-of-date and inapplicable to modern society, but on second glance there are important principles in this passage. Even though slavery might not be officially condoned or practiced today, the admonition to work hard

as though one was working for God, and not people, applies to employees. **the reward of the inheritance:** The strong motivation to serve someone well is found in the future reward that Christ gives to those who are faithful in this service. We normally think we receive eternal rewards for spiritual practices like reading the Bible, prayer, or evangelism. Here Paul asserts that all work done to the honor of Christ will bring an eternal reward (1:22, 23; 2:18).

4:1 Masters: Paul does not concern himself only with servants or employees. Employers also have a duty not to take advantage of employees. Instead they should offer a just wage, proper benefits, and adequate rest. In contemporary societies, many of these benefits are required by government regulations. But how much better when Christian employers treat their employees well for the Lord's sake, knowing that they too have **a Master in heaven.**

4:2 Paul encourages the Colossians to be diligent in thanksgiving and prayer, especially praying for himself and his coworkers as they worked at spreading the gospel. Even the apostle Paul requested and needed the prayers of others to support him.

4:3 Even while in prison, Paul felt his need of prayer for God to **open . . . a door**—an opportunity to spread the gospel. **the mystery of Christ:** The Good News of salvation for all which can be known and experienced only through Christ.

4:4 that I may make it manifest: Paul's chief concern is to make the message clear and plain. **as I ought to speak:** As it is my duty; as it is necessary for me to speak (1 Cor. 2:4; 2 Cor. 2:14, 17).

4:5 Walk in wisdom toward those who are outside: Early Christians were often viewed with suspicion, distrust, and disdain. They were considered atheists because they would not worship the gods of Rome and Greece. Many labeled them as unpatriotic because they would not burn incense before the image of the emperor. Some accused the early Christians of participating in orgies because of their talk of "love feasts" (Jude 12). Others harbored suspicions that Christians were really cannibals, who ate and drank the blood and the body of the Lord. With such misrepresentations of Christian belief and practice running rampant, it was very important for misunderstandings to be dispelled by the virtuous and impeccable lives of Christian believers.

4:6 Let your speech always be with grace: Christ was full of grace and truth (John 1:14). Christians are to be gracious, pleasant, attractive, winsome, and courteous. **seasoned**

with salt: Not insipid, not flat, not dull, not tasteless. Christians are to have an edge of liveliness, and to be marked by purity, wholesomeness, and hallowed pungency. **that you may know . . . answer each one:** In order that we can adapt the message to the situation and speak appropriately to each and every person.

Gospel of Mark. At the beginning of his second missionary journey, Paul had refused to take Mark with him (Acts 15:37–40). Evidently the two had been reconciled, for Paul commends him here and in 2 Tim. 4:11. **Luke** is the author of the Gospel of Luke and the Book of Acts. He

---

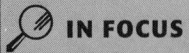 **IN FOCUS** | **"perfect"**

(Gk. *teleios*) (1:28; 4:12; Rom. 12:2; Phil. 3:15; James 1:4) Strong's #*5046*: This Greek word is an adjective derived from the word *telos,* meaning "end," "limit," or "fulfillment." Paul uses *telos* to speak of Jesus Christ as the complete fulfillment of God's law (Rom. 10:4). In his letter to the Colossians, Paul uses *teleios* to speak of the completion or perfection of Christians (1:28; 4:12). The "perfect Christian" is a mature Christian, who has endured trials (James 1:4) and has learned to express God's love to others (3:14). By loving others, we not only are made complete in and through Christ but we also see God's love "perfected" in us (1 John 4:12). Just as Paul pressed on toward the goal of perfection (Phil. 3:12–14) to which Christ had called him, so we too should make perfection in Christ our goal, a goal that will be completely achieved when "that which is perfect" comes (1 Cor. 13:10).

4:7, 8 Tychicus was an intimate friend of Paul's who came from the province of Asia. He had accompanied Paul on part of the third missionary journey. He probably delivered this letter and answered questions about Paul's condition in prison.

4:9 The slave **Onesimus** probably accompanied Tychicus to Colosse. Paul's letter to Philemon would have been carried along with the letter to the Colossians. It dealt with a personal situation between Philemon and his slave Onesimus, so Paul wrote a separate letter to him.

4:10–15 Paul greets a number of friends and introduces and commends several who work with him. The apostle's great warmth and true appreciation for his beloved coworkers comes through in these few verses. This should remind us that no one is an island. We all need the support of each other in the work of God. **Aristarchus,** a Jew from Thessalonica, had been traveling with Paul since the riot that occurred in Ephesus on his third missionary journey (Acts 19:29; 20:4). Evidently he remained with Paul even when he was imprisoned in Rome (27:2). **Mark** is the author of the

accompanied Paul on many of his missionary journeys. **Demas** would later abandon Paul (2 Tim. 4:10).

4:16 There are numerous theories as to the identity of the Laodicean letter mentioned in this verse. Whether it is one of the other NT letters, like 1 or 2 Thessalonians or Ephesians, or whether it is a lost **epistle** probably cannot be determined.

4:17 And say to Archippus: He is mentioned in Philem. 2 in such a way as to suggest that he was a member of Philemon's household, probably his son. **Take heed:** Keep an eye on. **you have received in the Lord:** Archippus was called of the Lord, and most probably had some ministerial responsibility in the church at Colosse. **that you may fulfill it:** That you keep on filling to the full, discharge fully. This is a lifetime job. God does not discharge His servants.

4:18 This salutation by my own hand: The apostle dictated his letters to a secretary, but it was his custom to give a greeting in his own handwriting at the end (2 Thess. 2:1, 2; 3:17). This served to personalize and authenticate the letter.

The First Epistle to the

Thessalonians

●

*N*EARLY ALL NEW BELIEVERS HAVE QUESTIONS about their faith. As a seasoned missionary, Paul knew this. For this reason, he sent Timothy back to Thessalonica shortly after establishing the church there. Timothy's job was to find out how the young church was doing. When he returned, he was loaded down with their questions. First Thessalonians is Paul's patient reply. He reinforces the basic

gospel message, instructs them further in the faith, and provides practical applications for spiritual truths.

First Thessalonians gives us an intimate introduction to how Paul mentored young believers. As this epistle demonstrates, his teaching for young converts was rich in doctrine and application, accurately describing salvation in its full dimensions.

In 1 Thessalonians, Paul reviewed some of the basics of the faith and applied these truths to the believers' lives. He challenged them to persevere in godly living despite persecution. He extended the comfort of the Resurrection to those who were in mourning, and he spoke about details of the Second Coming. In addition, Paul responded to the angry attacks of his Jewish opponents, who were jealous because Christians were drawing God-fearing Gentiles away from the local synagogue. Paul's opponents may have charged that his failure to return to Thessalonica proved that he was insincere. Paul devoted the first three chapters of his letter to correcting this false impression.

In a brief space Paul covered a wide spectrum of the essential doctrines of Christianity. These

include such beliefs as the Trinity (1:5, 6), the deity of Christ (3:11, 12), the power of the Holy Spirit (1:5, 6), the nature of Scripture (2:13), the timing and the events of the Second Coming (1:10; 2:19; 3:13; 4:13–17; 5:23), the day of the Lord (5:1–3), assurance of salvation (1:5), conversion (1:9), sanctification (4:3; 5:23), the Resurrection (4:14–18), the relation of faith to works (1:3), the relation of love to service (1:3), and the relation of patience to hope (1:3).

Because 1 Thessalonians is one of Paul's earliest letters, it reveals much of what Paul preached during his second missionary journey. Evidently the return of Christ was central to his message, for Paul answers many questions about the Second Coming. In fact, perhaps the most significant doctrinal contribution of this small letter is its detailed explanation of Christ's return.

Paul's authorship of 1 Thessalonians has not been seriously questioned except by a few modern liberal scholars. Paul refers to himself as the author in the letter (1:1; 2:18), and the early church recognized him as such. The canon of Marcion lists 1 Thessalonians as being a work of Paul. Early church fathers such as Irenaeus,

Tertullian, and Clement of Alexandria also acknowledged it as being by Paul.

The letter was probably written from Corinth around A.D. 51 and is considered to be one of Paul's earliest epistles. In fact, Galatians may be the only one written before it.

Thessalonica was one of the first cities to be evangelized by Paul and Silas when they landed on the continent of Europe. A divine vision of a man from Macedonia inviting Paul to preach the gospel had drawn the two missionaries to that region (Acts 16:9, 10). After preaching in Philippi, Paul traveled another one hundred miles to Thessalonica. This was a port city and commercial center located in the northwest corner of the Aegean Sea. The Egnatian Way linking Rome to Byzantium passed through it. This important highway and the thriving port made Thessalonica one of the wealthiest trade centers of the Roman Empire. It was the capital and the largest city of the province of Macedonia, with a population of about two hundred thousand.

Because of its strategic location, Thessalonica became a base for the spread of the gospel in Macedonia and Greece. This was Paul's plan. A church planted in a geographic center would become the evangelistic hub for the surrounding region. Evidently this was especially true of Thessalonica, for Paul commends them for their evangelistic work (1:8).

Paul started the Thessalonian church by preaching for three Sabbath days in the Jewish synagogue. He had great success, not only among the Jews but also among God-fearing Greeks. But some Jews who rejected Paul's message and were envious of his success hired thugs to attack him. When Paul could not be found, the Jews brought the owner of the house where Paul was staying, Jason, before the magistrates. They charged him with treason because he was harboring someone who was teaching that there was another king, Jesus. The magistrates took a bond from Jason and let him go. Consequently, Paul and Silas considered it best to leave immediately, and went to the next important town, Berea. Here they also had a good reception. But when the Jews in Thessalonica heard of it, they went there to stir up more opposition to Paul and Silas. Paul moved on to Athens. After a brief stay there, he went to Corinth, where he was joined by Silas and Timothy (Acts 18:5). Concerned about the welfare of the Thessalonian converts, Paul sent Timothy back to Thessalonica to see how the believers were doing.

After a brief, encouraging ministry in Thessalonica, Timothy rejoined Paul in Corinth and brought a good report of the faithfulness of the Thessalonians even under persecution. They did have some questions about the faith, and Paul undertook to answer these.

Outline

I. Thanksgiving for the Thessalonians' salvation
1:1–10

II. Paul's defense of his ministry in Thessalonica
2:1–12

  A. His integrity in his ministry 2:1–4

  B. His selfless and loving ministry 2:5–9

  C. His blameless behavior 2:10–12

III. Paul's prayer for their spiritual growth 2:13–3:13

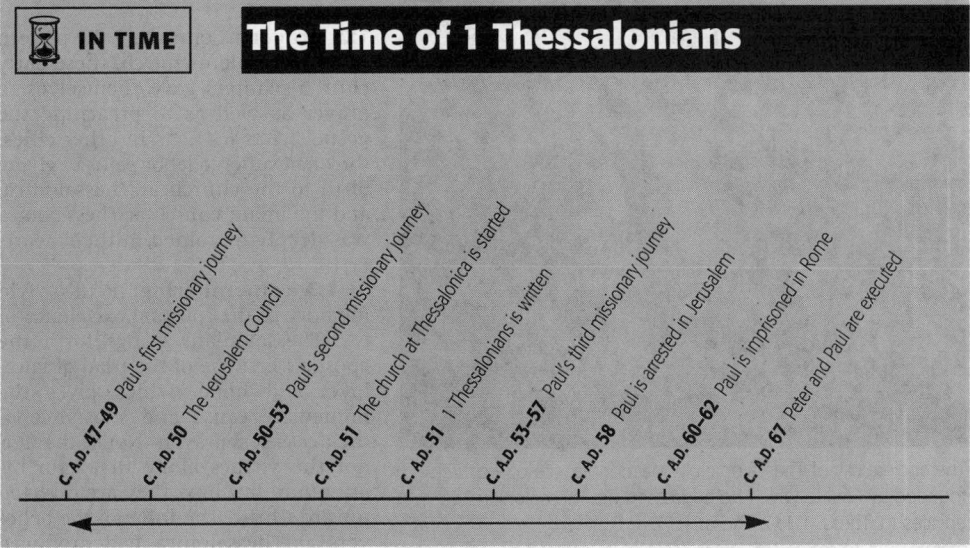

IN TIME   **The Time of 1 Thessalonians**

C. A.D. 47–49 Paul's first missionary journey

C. A.D. 50 The Jerusalem Council

C. A.D. 50–53 Paul's second missionary journey

C. A.D. 51 The church at Thessalonica is started

C. A.D. 51 1 Thessalonians is written

C. A.D. 53–57 Paul's third missionary journey

C. A.D. 58 Paul is arrested in Jerusalem

C. A.D. 60–62 Paul is imprisoned in Rome

C. A.D. 67 Peter and Paul are executed

   A. His concern for their suffering 2:13–16
   B. His earnest desire to see them 2:17–20
   C. His expression of love through Timothy 3:1–8
   D. His prayer 3:9–13
IV. Paul's exhortation for their sanctification 4:1–12
   A. His command that they abstain from sexual immorality 4:1–8
   B. His exhortation to brotherly love rather than sexual impurity 4:9, 10
   C. His exhortation to proper Christian life 4:11, 12
   D. The return of Christ 4:13–18
VI. The day of the Lord 5:1–11
VII. Paul's concluding exhortations 5:12–28

Commentary

1:1 Paul follows the customary form of ancient letters, giving the writer first, the destination second, and a brief greeting third. Paul mentions **Silvanus,** Silas's Roman name, and Timothy, but he is the writer of the epistle (4:9). When Paul uses the pronoun *we* (v. 2), he may

The ancient city of Thessalonica in Macedonia, site of a church founded by Paul to which he addressed his Thessalonian epistles (1 Thess. 1:1; 2 Thess. 1:1).

be referring to Silas and Timothy as editors with him of the letter. After Paul separated from Barnabas (Acts 15:36–40), Silas became Paul's traveling companion on the second missionary journey, and he may have served as Paul's secretary. He was a leader of the Jerusalem church (Acts 15:22, 23), and he accompanied Paul and Barnabas to Antioch to deliver the decree of the Jerusalem Council (Acts 15: 22, 23). He and Paul suffered a beating at Philippi (Acts 16:22–24), and he had helped found the church at Thessalonica (Acts 17:1–4). **Timothy** was also with Paul on the second missionary journey. Paul considered him like a son and loved him dearly (Acts 16:3; 1 Tim. 1:2). This letter is a response to Timothy's report from the church in Thessalonica. **To the church:** The Greek word *ekklesia* was a familiar term meaning any gathering or assembly. In its NT usage this common Greek word calls to mind the relationship of believers to one another and to Christ. Note that Paul addresses the believers at Thessalonica as a body, and not as individual believers. In the early church, belief in Christ always led to joining a fellowship of believers, the body of Christ (Acts 2:42–47; 1 Cor. 12:27). The expression **grace to you and peace,** though similar to common salutations, eloquently expresses the main concepts of the Christian faith. The word *grace* means "unmerited favor and blessing," and the word *peace* describes the relation Christians have with God and should cultivate with other people. The order of the two terms in the greeting is always maintained in the NT, since God's grace is the only basis for His people's peace.

1:2 prayers: Continuing the pattern of the Jerusalem church, these early church planters gave themselves to prayer as well as to preaching the gospel (Acts 6:4). As in other cities, they had suffered labor pains in giving birth to the church at Thessalonica, and the infant church at Thessalonica was deeply ingrained in their hearts (2:13, 17; 3:5, 6).

1:3 remembering: Paul's vivid memory of the spiritual excellence of the Thessalonians brings forth the apostle's first use of the triad of faith, love, and hope, which gives the immediate cause and substance of their ceaseless prayers. Notice that it is not the virtues alone that gain his attention, but how they are directed toward Christ. The **faith** of the believers at Thessalonica had produced true repentance. When they turned to God, they turned away from idols (v. 9). Note that Paul views the Thessalonians' repentance as a result of their faith, not vice versa. **labor of love:** The Thessalonians' love for Christ resulted in serving (v. 9) in the midst of persecution (v. 6). Note the contrast between *work* and *labor*. Whereas work may be pleasant and stimulating, labor often involves strenuous effort to the point of fatigue and even exhaustion. **patience of hope:** The believers at Thessalonica fixed their hope solidly on the return of Jesus Christ (v. 10). Notice that each of the virtues has Christ as its object. Jesus is constantly the focus. This is a good standard for evaluating any Christian service: Does it glorify Christ?

1:4 knowing . . . your election: The missionaries gave thanks not only for the good works arising from the Thessalonians' faith (v. 3), but more importantly for what God had done for them. God had chosen them to be His holy people. In vv. 5–10, Paul lists the indisputable proof of their election by God: their joyful response to the gospel, their strong faith, and their progress in holiness. God had graciously chosen them, a clear reason to rejoice (v. 2; Eph. 1:3–14).

1:5 Paul does not define his **gospel** at this point, but he had preached it clearly when he was with them: for three weeks he had "reasoned with them from the Scriptures, explaining and demonstrating that the Christ had to suffer and rise again from the dead" (Acts 17:2, 3). This message of a crucified Christ was far different from the messianic expectations that Paul knew from his own training as a Pharisee. The Jews of that day were not looking for a suffering savior but a conquering champion. Thus, Paul had to demonstrate from the OT Scripture that the prophets had foretold the suffering, death, and resurrection of the Messiah. **not . . . in word only, but also in power:** Paul did not neglect a careful, precise, and persuasive use of the Scriptures in his preaching. But he realized that apart from the convicting work of the Holy Spirit, no one could or would turn to Christ (John 16:8). But with God's blessing, Paul's preaching persuaded some of the Jews in the synagogue, together with "a great multitude of the devout Greeks, and not a few of the leading women" (Acts 17:4).

1:6 followers of us and the Lord: Everyone needs teachers, especially new converts. At times, Paul encouraged new believers to imitate him (1 Cor. 11:1) as he was imitating Christ. All the writers of the NT lead their readers back to the footprints of Christ as shown in the Gospels (Phil. 2:5; Heb. 12:2; 1 Pet. 2:21; 1 John 2:6). This should be our goal also, to lead others to Christ by our own virtuous example.

As we focus on Jesus, we will reflect His image to others (2 Cor. 3:18). **Having received** is not the usual word for reception, but a word expressing a warm welcome. The Thessalonians seized the gospel with joy, even if it meant facing persecution.

1:7 The effect of the gospel was so powerful that the Thessalonians became examples to the whole province of Macedonia, of which their town was the capital. The word **examples** (Gk. *tupos*) is singular in the original and refers not to a number of individual examples of Christian living, but rather to the single pattern of response to the Word. It was this willingness to obey the Good News and believe in Christ as the Messiah promised in the OT that Paul praised.

1:8 Your faith . . . has gone out: Testimony of the Thessalonians' remarkable faith rang out throughout Greece and Macedonia. Since Thessalonica was a port city and was on the much-traveled Egnatian Way, those who saw the virtuous life and persistent faith of the Thessalonian Christians would spread the word throughout the entire region. The same had occurred at the Jerusalem church (Acts 6:7); that is, vital Christian living was making an

 **INSIGHT** **Work, Labor, and Patience**

It's easy to see Paul's emphasis on faith, hope, and love, the trinity of Christian virtues (1 Thess. 1:3). But notice the words that precede these qualities: work of faith, labor of love, and patience of hope. These are marketplace terms. Christians in the workplace understand that useful results come only from hard work, diligent labor, and patience. The same is true in spiritual growth. (Heb. 6:9–12 mentions these same values.)

impact on the people who lived in and traveled through the city.

1:9 they themselves declare concerning us: These reports were not from missionaries but from ordinary travelers who were giving their impressions of the Thessalonian believers. **turned to God from idols:** The truth of the gospel exposed the falsehood of idolatry. Since Jews avoided idolatry, Paul was primarily speaking to a Greek audience (Acts 17:4).

1:10 to wait for His Son: Paul hoped for the Lord's return to occur at any moment. The phrase *to wait for* pictures an eager and expectant looking forward to the return of our Lord

Jesus who **delivers us from the wrath to come.** This is a future deliverance, but this verse does not make clear whether Paul is referring to a specific time or to the outpouring of God's wrath on unbelievers in a more general sense. The general teaching of 1 Thessalonians

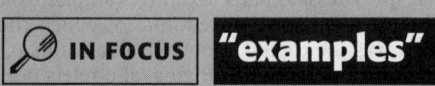

(Gk. *tupos*) (1:7; 1 Cor. 10:6; 2 Thess. 3:9; 1 Pet. 5:3) Strong's #*5179*: The Greek word *tupos* is derived from a root meaning "strike" or "hit." It means an impression left by a blow, and by extension a "type," "example" or "model." The members of the church at Thessalonica made it a model for the other churches in the region. Thessalonica was not only the largest city in Macedonia and the capital of the province but also the center of evangelistic activity in the region. The extraordinary perseverance of the members of that church was held up as exemplary or typical of what a church should be.

would favor the former. Because Christ endured God's wrath at Calvary, all who are in Christ will escape all aspects of God's wrath (5:9). Thus, they have nothing to fear.

2:1–12 A person's ministry will not be **in vain** (v. 1) if he has pure motives (v. 3), if he seeks God's approval (vv. 4–6), and if he loves his people with a mother's self-giving love (vv. 7–9) and a father's encouraging and correcting love (vv. 10–12).

2:1, 2 Paul's motives for coming to Thessalonica had apparently been attacked after he left by pagan Gentiles and by Jews clinging to their traditional faith. Paul pointed out what the Thessalonians knew, that he had not preached to them **in vain** (1:9) but had declared his message in the face of opposition, including the painful experience of being beaten and put in the stocks in **Philippi** (Acts 16:22–24). Only the unbelievers questioned Paul's motives in an attempt to undermine the faith of the Thessalonian Christians. Paul's response is to let the record speak for itself. Paul's response is so different than ours. Even a simple criticism or a disgusting look can pour cold water on our witnessing. May God help us to tell the good news of God in Christ in spite of the persecution we encounter.

2:3, 4 Answering criticism of his motives for preaching, Paul asserted that he used the truth, not **error;** his motives were pure, not from

uncleanness; his presentation was in sincerity, not in **deceit** (a word used also of a fishing lure to catch fish, suggesting trickery). In contrast to these criticisms, Paul asserted that he and his coworkers were **approved** messengers, missionaries shown by testing to be genuine. Their ministry was not their personal choice, but God's appointment.

2:5–8 Paul denied that in his visit to the Thessalonians he had used flattery. Instead, he preached boldly that everyone was a sinner who needed to be saved by the grace of God. His preaching did not serve as a **cloak for covetousness,** that is, as a mask to hide greed. Here he appeals to God as his **witness** because no person could examine his motives. Moreover, he and his companions were not seeking praise or desiring positions of authority. Paul did not even exercise his right for financial support (1 Cor. 9:3–14; 2 Cor. 11:7–11). Instead, here as in Corinth he paid his own way. In contrast to the enemies' accusations, Paul and his companions had demonstrated their loving care for the Thessalonians. While a professional nurse would know how to provide for the physical needs of an infant, a mother **cherishes her own children** with maternal love. Paul emphasizes the extent of his love: he would have sacrificed his own life for them if necessary.

2:9 Paul's affection for the Thessalonians was demonstrated by his **labor.** As in 1:3, this word indicates strenuous work that produces weariness and fatigue. Paul made tents to provide for his financial needs, working early and late, in order that he might not be a burden to his converts. Paul's actions showed that his ministry was motivated by an unselfish desire to promote the well-being of others rather than to advance his own needs.

2:10–12 In addition to their avoiding any need for financial support (v. 9), the morality and devotion to God demonstrated by Paul and his companions backed up their message. They both comforted and challenged the Thessalonians like a loving **father** (v. 7). Paul's ultimate goal for them was that they would **walk worthy of God,** or live in a way measuring up to the God they served. It seems an impossible standard. But Paul reminds the Thessalonians that God had called them for this purpose, and He would surely empower them, for "He who has begun a good work in you will complete it" (Phil. 1:6). Christians should have the same goals Paul had, of divine approval and the reward at the judgment seat of Christ (2 Cor. 5:9, 10).

2:13 Paul and his companions were thankful for the way the Thessalonians had welcomed the Word of God. **effectively works:** Gentile Christians in Thessalonica could contrast the pure Word of God, with its transforming effect, to the immoral pagan religions, which only perverted people even more. Likewise, Jewish believers could contrast the love and grace of God in the gospel to the legalism and pride often produced by the Jewish religion. What was true of the spoken Word of God in Thessalonica is also true of the written Word of God, which is "living and powerful, and sharper than any two-edged sword" (Heb. 4:12). **Believe** is present tense; they continued to believe. Those who keep on believing keep on receiving—a strong reminder of Jesus' word to Peter in John 14:1.

2:14 As the church in Judea had been persecuted by unbelieving Jews, so the Thessalonians were being persecuted by both Jews and Gentiles, and they became **imitators** of those in Judea (1:6). Sometimes suffering comes because of our own failures (1 Pet. 4:15), but these believers were suffering because they stood for God's truth (1 Pet. 4:16).

2:15 and have persecuted us: Paul tells the Thessalonians that they should not be surprised at suffering for Christ's sake, since fellow believers in Judea, including himself, had already suffered for the cause of the gospel. Such hostility toward the church actually represents hostility toward Christ (read Christ's words to Paul in Acts 9:4, 5).

2:16 to fill up . . . their sins: The implication is that God will allow a nation, group, or individual to accumulate only a certain amount of sin before His judgment falls on them (Gen. 15:16). In this case, Paul says that the judgment is near. Just as walking in Christ will lead to complete salvation and a reward, the sins of the wicked will lead to ultimate punishment.

2:17, 18 Contrary to what Paul's accusers were asserting, Paul eagerly desired to return. But he may have been **hindered** (Dan. 10:13), among other things, by the bond that Jason had deposited for him (Acts 17:9). If Paul returned and a riot ensued, Jason's bond would have been forfeited (Acts 17:1–9). **Having been taken away** literally means "orphaned," as a parent is separated from a child 2:7, 2:11. Paul was heartbroken about being taken from them, especially in their infancy in Christ. The many expressions of endearment in this letter indicate the genuine concern Paul had for these new converts.

2:19, 20 In spite of persecution and satanic opposition, Paul looked beyond the present trials (2 Cor. 4:16–18) to the joy of being **in the presence of our Lord Jesus Christ** and being with the Thessalonian Christians who had found the Lord through him. The Thessalonians would be Paul's **crown** (the wreath presented to the winner of Greek athletic contests) because they would prove the genuineness of his work for Christ.

3:1 When forced to leave Thessalonica, Paul and Silas went to Berea, the next city west of

---

✠ IN CONTEXT | ## Painful Expectations

Thessalonica proved to be a hostile environment for the gospel. Not only did Paul and Silas have to leave the city prematurely, but their opponents followed them to Berea and created problems for them there (Acts 16:35—17:15).

Paul reminded his Thessalonian friends that they had become believers "under fire" (2:14). He had tried to strengthen their young faith with warnings about the suffering they would experience (3:4). But he was concerned about the survival of the church because he had had so little time to lay a solid foundation there.

Paul decided to take action. He traveled alone to Athens while Timothy traveled to Thessalonica to "establish" and "encourage" (3:2) the Christians there, and then undoubtedly to bring fresh news to Paul from that church. Paul based his first letter to the Thessalonians on the encouraging report he received from Timothy.

The Thessalonian experience illustrates a key aspect of the spread of the gospel. The truth takes root in resistant soil. When the "tempter" (3:5) cannot prevent the Good News from bringing life to someone, his tactic changes in order to make the young Christian ineffective. Pressure and persecution are inevitable. They may come camouflaged as vague cultural disapproval, or they may be open hostility, but in one way or another spiritual growth will always meet resistance.

Persecution is demoralizing, but it can also be a cause for taking heart. Without resistance, how can growth be recognized? Trials and tribulations test character (James 1:2–4). Absence of pressure may indicate a lack of growth. Paul's encouraging words still ring true today. The fellowship that comes from suffering together promotes Christian maturity (2:14–16; 3:3, 7).

Thessalonica. The Jews in Thessalonica who opposed Paul, upon learning that he was at Berea, went there also and stirred up opposition. Paul's friends then escorted him south to **Athens** (Acts 17:13–15). There Paul left word for Silas and Timothy to join him. But before they arrived, Paul left for Corinth, a short distance west of Athens.

3:2 Because Paul himself could not go to Thessalonica, he sent Timothy in his place. Apparently Silas went back to Philippi, their first stop in Macedonia. Paul sent Timothy to strengthen the church at Thessalonica and to **encourage** them **concerning** their **faith.** The Thessalonians, now that they were saved, needed to be built up in the faith and fortified against the ever-present opposition. Because Timothy was young and lacked the maturity of Paul, a special word of commendation was expressed for him as a **brother** in Christ, and more importantly as a **minister of God,** and a **fellow laborer in the gospel.** Paul showed his strong confidence in Timothy by sending him, not only to the Thessalonians, but later to the Corinthians (1 Cor. 16:10, 11) and to the Philippians (Phil. 2:19–23).

3:3, 4 Difficulties are to be expected in the Christian life, and Paul had warned the congregation of their coming **afflictions.** The Scripture teaches that those who live godly lives should expect persecution (2 Tim. 3:12). In fact, Christ warned His disciples that they would experience the same type of rejection He had experienced (John 15:18–21). Suffering from persecution should not cause Christians to be downcast. Instead they should rejoice that they have been considered worthy of sharing in Christ's sufferings (Matt. 5:10–12).

3:5–8 our labor might be in vain: Paul was concerned that the Thessalonians might succumb to the temptations of Satan and forsake their Christian faith. **if you stand fast:** Paul's joy was based on the Thessalonians' faithfulness to Christ.

3:6 But now that Timothy has come to us from you: The sense of the original here is that Timothy has just now arrived with the news when Paul sat down to write. This clearly shows the occasion and purpose of the letter. When Timothy arrived, his news was good; so good in fact, that **brought us good news** is the same word often translated "preach the gospel." Paul was glad to hear of their faith and love, and the fact that they had wanted to see him just as much as he had wanted to see them.

3:7, 8 therefore, brethren . . . we were comforted (Gk. *parakaleō*). This is again the word that means "help" or "encourage." Another translation has, "we have been encouraged about you." The encouragement was badly needed.

Paul was himself in **affliction and distress.** Both of these words are strong. The first (Gk. *anankē*) is related to the word from which we get "anxiety," while the second (Gk. *thlipsis*) means "rubbing" or "pressure," and is the word often translated in the NT as "tribulation." The thing that gave Paul the needed encouragement was the faith of these converts.

3:9 Paul made prayer a priority. In his prayers, he did not forget to thank God for what He was doing. Christians should follow Paul's example by offering praise and thanksgiving along with their petitions.

3:10 Paul's desire to see the Thessalonians was not primarily to satisfy his own love and emotion but to **perfect,** or complete, their own **faith.** There is always room for improvement. The Thessalonians' endurance under persecution demonstrated the growth of their faith, but Paul wanted them to mature in it.

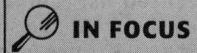 **IN FOCUS   "coming"**

(Gk. *parousia*) (3:13; 4:15; 5:23; 2 Thess. 2:1, 8; 2 Pet. 1:16) Strong's #3952: The Greek word *parousia* literally means "presence." The word was commonly used in NT times to describe the visitation of royalty or of some other important person. Thus, the word signals no ordinary "coming." The NT writers also use the word to describe Christ's second coming, when He will return to earth in His ultimate, glorious visitation as the King over all.

3:11–13 Christ had told His disciples that His followers would be identified by their love for one another (John 13:35). Here Paul prays that the Thessalonians would love each other more and more. Finally, Paul expresses his desire that their **hearts** would be **blameless in holiness,** not simply before people but before **God.** The word **saints** can refer both to saved people and to holy angels. Angels will participate in the Second Coming (4:16; Jude 14; Rev. 19:14).

4:1, 2 Finally does not mean that Paul was coming to a conclusion but serves as a transition to the main section of the letter, addressing doctrine and its application to life. In the first three chapters Paul dealt with the readers as a "nursing mother" gently cares for her children (2:7). Now in these last two chapters he urges and charges them with the authority of a father (4:1, 2). Paul commonly uses the word **walk** as a description of a Christian life (Rom. 6:4; 2 Cor.

🔍 **IN FOCUS** | **"sanctification"**

(Gk. *hagiasmos*) (4:3, 4, 7; Rom. 6:19, 22; 1 Cor. 1:30; 2 Thess. 2:13; Heb. 12:14) Strong's #38: The Greek term for *sanctify* means to "set apart" for God's special use, to make distinct from what is common—hence, to be made like God who is distinct from all else and therefore holy. The Greek word for *sanctify* refers to a process that is perfect in principle though not yet attained. Though we are not yet completely holy, we stand in relation to God as though we were. This is indicated in Heb. 10:10, where the verb *sanctified* is in a tense that indicates the present result of a past action. Thus, Christ sanctified by His one sacrifice, and that sanctification has the lasting result that it continues to work in us, making us holy. Sanctification has been done once for all, but its effect still continues as stated in Heb. 10:14, in "those who are being sanctified."

5:7; Gal. 5:16; Col. 1:10; 2:6; 4:5). The Christian life not only begins with faith, but it continues as a daily walk of faith. Just as people are dependent on their limbs to support them in every step, so Christians walk in dependence on God. As walking has a direction, so does the Christian life. Christians are not to walk like unsaved Gentiles (Eph. 4:17); instead, they are to walk worthy of their calling from God (Eph. 4:1). John exhorts Christians to walk in the light, that is, in the revealed will of God (1 John 1:7).

4:3–8 A major problem for the early church was maintaining sexual purity (1 Cor. 5:1, 9–11). Pagan religions often condoned **sexual immorality** as part of their rites, and ancient Roman culture had few sexual boundaries. In contrast, Paul strongly urged the Thessalonians not to participate in any sexual activity outside of marriage. He reminded them that the human body is God's temple and should be kept holy (1 Cor. 6:18–20). The body should be honored as created by God and should be sanctified in keeping with its holy purpose. Believers should have a personal passion for sexual purity that surpasses the passion that the world has for sexual experiences. Sexual involvement outside of marriage dishonors God, one's marriage partner or future spouse, and even one's own body. There is always a price to pay, for God often allows Christians to reap what they sow.

4:6–8 that no one should take advantage of and defraud his brother in this matter: Several words need explanation here. First, **take advantage of** means quite literally "to overstep" or "break laws." In this context it obviously means to break this moral law. Secondly, if he does break this moral law, a man will, by that very fact, **defraud** (Gk. *pleonekteō*) his brother. This word denotes "robbing," or "cheating someone" through greed. A comment is also needed on the phrase **in this matter.** The construction in the original language of the NT (an article of previous reference) allows only

one meaning here. It is not just any **matter** that is in view, but specifically this matter which has just been mentioned—unethical sexual activity. The sense of the passage is that when a man does not live with his own wife as he should, but instead commits adultery with someone else's, he must know that he has violated, or "robbed" his brother by so doing, and that he deserves the vengeance of God. To show the seriousness of his sin, Paul alludes to Ps. 94:1 where God is called the God of vengeance. Note that according to v. 7, this kind of conduct is the opposite of **holiness** and is called **uncleanness.** To be sanctified according to God's will must mean to be pure or clean in this matter. Rejecting **holiness** is rejecting God and the ministry of the Holy Spirit within us.

4:9, 10 The Thessalonian believers already had a good record of loving one another, but Paul desired that love to **increase more and more.** This was the commandment of Jesus (John 13:34, 35; 15:12, 17) and is an important basis of evangelism. In a world that is filled with self-serving individuals, the genuine love of Christians should attract others to the faith.

4:11, 12 Summarizing his preceding instructions, Paul exhorted the Thessalonians believers to lead **a quiet life,** not referring to a lack of activity but rather to an inner quietness and peace befitting the Christian faith (2 Thess. 3:12; 1 Tim. 2:11). They should not be busybodies but should **mind** their **own business.** Usually people who are busy running other people's affairs do not run their own affairs well. A Christian's house should be in order as a testimony to others. Paul also exhorted the Thessalonians **to work with** their **own hands** as he had done among them (2:9). Possibly because of their enthusiasm for the coming of the Lord, some Thessalonians had become idle. They might also have been influenced by the general Greek abhorrence for physical labor. But Paul admonished the Christians to be dedicated and productive workers so that they might bring honor to Christ's name. Christians are to be dedicated, productive workers. Failure to work hard is a negative witness to the world. It also produces an unhealthy dependence on other believers. Paul had set a good example as a worker in his making of tents.

4:13 fallen asleep: This is a metaphor for dying. Though Paul had taught the Thessalonians about Christ's return when he was there, apparently Timothy had encountered further questions on the subject, possibly arising from the death of some of the new converts. In answer to these questions, Paul stated that he wanted them to be informed, and also to be comforted by the hope of seeing their loved ones again. This was a hope their pagan neighbors did not have.

4:14 This hope (v. 13) for the dead Christians was as certain as the fact of the death and resurrection of Christ. Paul says that **God will**

bring with Him those who sleep in Jesus. Some have inferred from this statement that departed Christians are unconscious until the Second Coming. But the Bible indicates that to be absent from our present body is to be present with the Lord Jesus (5:10; 2 Cor. 5:8; Phil. 1:23). Accordingly, when a Christian dies, it is the body that sleeps; the soul goes to heaven. Thus when Christ returns, He will need to bring with Him from heaven to earth the souls of Christians who have died, confirming their previous residence in the presence of God. This return of Christ is also a physical and bodily return, though Christ is everywhere present in His deity (Matt. 28:20) and resides in the believer (John 14:23). This will be a crowning event as Christ comes physically from heaven to earth to receive the believers.

4:15 Paul believed that Christ could come in his lifetime, and so did the Thessalonians (1:10). **precede those who are asleep:** Evidently the

---

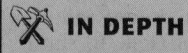 **IN DEPTH** | **Sexual Immorality**

Even though the Thessalonians were living in a sexually charged culture, the apostle Paul urged them to "abstain from sexual immorality" (4:3). According to the Bible, what exactly is sexual immorality? The following is a quick summary.

What is sexual immorality?

The Greek word used by Paul is the term from which we get the English word *pornography* (4:3). It is a broad term, encompassing any illicit sexual activity.

What specific sexual activities does Scripture prohibit?

- Lust may be a strong desire for anything. But in sexual contexts, lust is defined as "the sinful desire for illicit sex." Lust is forbidden by Scripture because it gives birth to sin, which leads to death (4:5; Matt. 5:28; Rom. 13:13; James 1:14, 15; 1 Pet. 4:3).
- Adultery is extramarital sex. It is strictly condemned in the Scriptures. The seriousness of this sin is demonstrated by its inclusion in the Ten Commandments (Ex. 20:14) and by its warranting the death penalty under OT law (Lev. 20:10). Proverbs states that it "destroys" the guilty party's soul (Prov. 6:32).
- Incest, sex with a close relative other than one's spouse, is prohibited and said to be worthy of the sentence of death (Lev. 18:6–18; 20:11, 12, 17; Deut. 27:20, 22, 23).
- Homosexuality, sex with a person of one's own gender, is condemned in no uncertain terms in several OT and NT passages (Lev. 18:22; 20:13; Rom. 1:26, 27; 1 Cor. 6:9; 1 Tim. 1:10).
- Bestiality is sex with an animal. This sexually deviant behavior is outlawed in the Bible. It was punished with death in ancient Israel (Ex. 22:19; Lev. 18:23; 20:15, 16; Deut. 27:21).

Does the Bible take a prudish view of sex?

No. Sex within marriage is viewed as a good gift from God to be enjoyed and celebrated by both husband and wife (Prov. 5:15–20; Heb. 13:4).

How can believers stay pure in an impure world?

- By living carefully according to God's Word (Ps. 119:9), and hiding it in our hearts (Ps. 119:11).
- By making the conscious choice not to lust (Job 31:1).
- By walking under the control of the Holy Spirit (Gal. 5:16–25).
- By fleeing sexual temptations and pursuing righteousness (2 Tim. 2:22).

Thessalonians were concerned that believers who had died would miss the glory associated with the return of Christ for the church. Paul answers their question by affirming that actually those who were dead would go before (v. 16) those living on earth.

4:16 Accompanying the descent of Christ from heaven will be the voice of an archangel, perhaps Michael, who is portrayed as the leader of the army of God (Dan. 10:13, 21; Jude 9; Rev. 12:7–9). The only other angel named in Scripture is Gabriel, who is given a prominent role as a messenger of God (Dan. 8:16; 9:21; Luke 1:19, 26). The archangel's voice will be one of triumph because of the great victory at the coming of Christ, culminating thousands of years of spiritual conflict with Satan. The final signal will be the trumpet of God. The three elements consisting of the **shout** of the Lord Himself, the **voice** of an archangel, and the **trumpet** of God will perhaps be separate events occurring in rapid succession. The doctrine of the Resurrection is a central doctrine of the Christian faith, including as it does the resurrection of Christ and, ultimately, the resurrection of all people. The answer to the question as to how the dead can be raised when the remains of their bodies are in some cases totally scattered is not a problem for a supernatural God who created the world. Clearly the Resurrection will be a physical resurrection in which bodily existence will be restored, as con-

firmed in 1 Cor. 15:51–53. The resurrected bodies of Christians will be like that of Christ (1 John 3:2), incorruptible and immortal, and yet they will be bodies of flesh and bone (Luke 24:39, 40; John 20:20, 25, 27). They all will be recognizable, as was the resurrected body of Christ.

4:17 Living Christians will be **caught up** together with the other believers in the clouds to meet the Lord in the air. (The English word *rapture* comes from the Latin verb meaning "caught up.") **In the clouds** probably refers to atmospheric clouds that also will attend the Second Coming (Rev. 1:7), or it may be the resurrected multitudes who are referred to as a cloud (Heb. 12:1). In the Bible the Lord is often accompanied by clouds, signifying His glory (Pss. 68:4; 97:2). The important result is that **we shall always be with the Lord.**

4:18 The wonderful truth described (vv. 13–17) is to be a **comfort** to the Thessalonians and to all Christians. They had mistakenly thought that only those who were alive at the time of the coming of Christ would witness and share in the glory of it. The fact is that Christians who have died will be raised first and so go before the living to the gathering in the sky. Observe that Paul expects a practical, immediate response to this great doctrinal teaching of the Second Coming. The Thessalonians should remind one another of this truth as a source of comfort in the face of death. The sentence is in

---

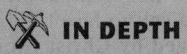 **IN DEPTH**   ## Pictures of the End Time

The "voice of an archangel" and the "trumpet of God" (1 Thess. 4:16) emphasize the divine authority behind Paul's description of Jesus' return. The images and pictures Paul uses for the end time overlap with those of other Jews of his time, though he omits most elements found in contemporary Jewish descriptions. What Paul does describe especially matches Jesus' picture of the end time (trumpet, clouds, angels, times and seasons, sudden destruction).

Jewish readers familiar with the OT recognized the importance of trumpets for gathering the assembly, sometimes to battle. Gentile readers probably knew the Roman use of trumpets to gather troops or to send signals in battle. Most relevant, Jewish tradition, as emphasized in a daily synagogue prayer, portrayed the gathering of Israel in the end time as accompanied by the sounding of a trumpet.

The highest archangel, according to Jewish tradition, was Michael (Dan. 10:13), who was also the special patron for Israel. Each nation had a guardian angel, but Michael was especially powerful, as the guardian of God's chosen people. Jewish traditions sometimes gave Michael special prominence in the final battle, though, for Paul, Jesus fulfilled this function Himself (1 Thess. 4:16).

The "shout," conjoined with the trumpet, may picture the battle cry offered by a commander. The OT sometimes portrays God as a divine warrior, occasionally mentioning His battle cry (Is. 42:13).

Jesus' teaching about the end time (Matt. 24) is probably the background for Paul's own teaching, which he claimed was by "the word of the Lord" (1 Thess. 4:15). As Jesus described the coming Son of Man, He applied to Himself a variety of end-time descriptions that the OT and Judaism normally reserved only for God (Matt. 24:30, 31). Similarly, Paul applies these same descriptions to the coming Christ.

the present tense, indicating that it should be a constant comfort to us to think each day that the Lord may come.

5:1 But concerning: This expression characteristically introduces a different topic. From the discussion of the Rapture the apostle turns to the day of the Lord. **the times and the seasons:** This reminds us of the same expression used by our Lord in Acts 1:7. *Times* probably emphasizes quantity, duration, or measurement, whereas *seasons* draws attention to the quality, character, or critical nature of the times. **no need that I should write:** In the previous verses (4:13–18) Paul addressed a matter of ignorance; now he addresses a matter of knowledge. He is not informing as much as he is exhorting them to live in the light of what they already know.

5:2–11 In these verses Paul develops the topic of the day of the Lord. This expression was familiar to those who knew the Hebrew Scriptures. The day of the Lord in the OT was characterized by two phases: God's judgment against sinful people and God's eternal reign over His people. God's judgment will be a time of darkness and an expression of God's wrath (Joel 2:1, 2; Amos 5:18–20; Zeph. 1:14, 15). His reign will be a time of God's blessing (Is. 2:1–3; 11:1–9; 30:23–26; Zech. 14:1, 7–11, 20, 21; Matt. 19:28; Acts 3:19–21).

5:2 In contrast to the certainty in the previous paragraph of Christ's coming, Paul now deals with the uncertainty of the timing of the coming **day of the Lord.** This period is the subject of considerable prophecy in the OT (Is. 13:9–11; Joel 2:28–32; Zeph. 1:14–18; 3:14, 15). The Book of Joel as a whole is an exposition of the day of the Lord, describing it as a terrible time of judgment. In the OT, the phrase *the day of the Lord* is used for any period where God intervenes in judgment on the earth. There were "days of the Lord" predicted in the OT that have already been fulfilled (Amos 5:18). Here Paul uses the expression to refer to Christ's return and the coming judgment. **thief in the night:** The day of the Lord will come when no one expects it. The day of the Lord as a time period begins before the events of the day of the Lord come, as illustrated in an ordinary day beginning at midnight with few events signaling the beginning of the new day. But when daylight come and events begin to happen, it is clear that the day of the Lord comes. So it will be at the end time. When the Rapture occurs, there probably will not be immediate earthshaking events, but in due time major events will take place which make clear that the day of the Lord has begun. These are mentioned in 2 Thess. 2 as the emergence of the man of sin (v. 3) and the removal of the restrainer of sin (v.

7). These two major events will make evident that the day of the Lord is underway, even though all the events will not happen at the same time.

5:3 when they say: Paul does not include himself and his readers among the *they.* Evidently he is speaking about unbelievers. The world will be absorbed in the cares of this life and will be lulled into a false sense of safety and security. **Peace** gives the idea of no feeling of alarm, and **safety** conveys an idea of security from external threats from God or people. The world will have turned a deaf ear to the repeated warnings of coming judgment. Paul uses the image of **labor pains** to stress the suddenness of the day of the Lord. A woman's first contraction comes suddenly and unexpectedly.

5:4, 5 But you, brethren: Though the day of the Lord will overtake the unsaved world unexpectedly, it will not overtake Christians, because they will be looking forward to and expecting it. In his characteristic style, Paul first addresses the readers' beliefs (vv. 1–5) and then their behavior (vv. 6–11). The fact that Christ could come at any moment should motivate unbelievers to accept His forgiveness and believers to live daily for Him.

5:6, 7 Because Christians are informed concerning future events, they should not be spiritually asleep but should **watch and be sober.** While every Christian is prepared to go to heaven in the sense of having been saved, not every Christian is prepared at every moment to present the quality of his or her spiritual life to God. Accordingly, this is a call to face the fact that our lives will be judged by Christ (Rom. 14:10, 11; 1 Cor. 3:11–15; 9:24–27; 2 Cor. 5:10).

5:8 In contrast to what unbelievers do, the Christian should be **sober,** living a disciplined life, not only free from drunkenness but alert to spiritual realities. The believer should put on the **breastplate of faith.** Here again is the familiar triad of faith, hope, and love, the basic essentials of a Christian life. In contrast to the unbelief of the world, with its love of self and of material wealth (1:3), Christians should place their faith in God and give their love to God and to other people. In addition to demonstrating faith and love, Christians should adopt **the hope of salvation** and live in the light of the Lord's return.

5:9, 10 Paul states that **God did not appoint us** (believers) **to wrath** (1:10). There will be wrath at the day of the Lord, but it will be God's wrath on the unbelieving world that has spurned and mocked Christ (Rev. 6:12–17). When we think about divine judgment, we should offer thanks to Christ for saving us from that horrible fate by dying **for us.** Whether we are still living at the coming of Christ, or whether we have died and our bodies are in the

✠ IN CONTEXT | Helping the Needy

Paul begins the concluding words of his letter with four sharp exhortations (1 Thess. 5:14). The "unruly"—the lazy, the undisciplined, those looking for a free ride—need a bit of a jolt. (Paul later gave them one in 2 Thess. 3:6–12.) Those who are losing heart need encouragement. And everyone needs patience.

But Paul's third directive, "uphold the weak," has to do with one's responsibilities toward the poor. Wherever Scripture raises this issue, it challenges us to share at least some of our material wealth with people in desperate need. It is the only Christlike response there is.

Indeed, Christ serves as the ultimate model of compassion. He even staked His credibility on His work among the downtrodden and destitute when John the Baptist inquired as to whether He was the Christ.

Paul hardly needed to challenge the Thessalonian believers to be generous. He knew by experience that even though they lived in deep poverty, they were willing to give "beyond their ability" (2 Cor. 8:3) to help others in need.

tomb, it is assured that we will **live together with Him** forever.

5:11 While the Rapture is an encouraging hope (4:18), so is the prospect of the Lord's return. Freedom from the judgments of the day of the Lord should be a constant encouragement. It is also a doctrine that will **edify,** or build one another up. Teaching on future events is designed by God to produce present results in the form of godly living (2 Pet. 3:11). Doctrinal truth is not intended just to satisfy our curiousity, but to change our lives.

5:12–19 Paul moves from his presentation of prophetic teaching to practical admonition. It is important that he has two different audiences in mind in giving his instruction. The "brethren" of v. 12 are the entire community of Christians at Thessalonica. They are to honor their leaders and to live with one another peacefully. The second "brethren" are the leaders of the congregation. They have several duties to the people to ensure the spiritual growth of the believers and to maintain order in the church. The leadership of the church can either cause God's people to glorify Christ and to grow spiritually or it can destroy the effectiveness of God's people. Not all division and difficulties facing the church today are caused by false teachers entering the church or contentious church members. Sometimes the leadership is not following the Spirit or heeding the admonition of the apostles concerning the manner for leading God's people (1 Pet. 5:2, 3).

5:12, 13 Significantly, Paul combines prophecy with practical teachings for the Christian life. God never intended prophecy as a field for academic debate but as a truth that would provide believers hope and direction in their lives. In vv. 12–22, Paul describes the characteristics of

a person who is living in the light of Christ's imminent return. **recognize those:** Because everyone in the Thessalonian church was a recent convert, it may have been difficult for some to recognize the leadership of others. Paul teaches the Thessalonians submission rather than individualism and rejection of authority (Eph. 5:21). He emphasizes that the leaders' authority was from the **Lord.** Paul admonishes the believers to appreciate and submit to those congregational leaders. They should be held in high esteem because of the important work they were doing. At the same time, the believers were to work together in maintaining the peace among themselves. Notice the plural pronouns; the Thessalonians followed the pattern of the Jerusalem church and all NT churches by having more than one person in leadership (Acts 6:1–7).

5:14 The Thessalonians had to face the fact that some of them were not living as Christians should, but were **unruly.** They needed to be warned about their behavior. Some were **fainthearted** and needed **comfort.** The congregation should also **uphold the weak** and be **patient** toward all, recognizing that all Christians have faults. To be most effective in promoting positive change in people's lives, believers should respond to individuals according to each one's particular needs.

5:15 renders evil for evil: For a Christian to try to get revenge is a denial of basic Christian love (Rom. 12:17; 1 Pet. 3:9), and it goes against Jesus' teaching (Matt. 5:38–42; 18:21–35).

5:16 Regardless of difficult circumstances (3:2, 3), a Christian **always** has grounds for rejoicing. The Lord is a sovereign ruler and will accomplish His purpose. Christian joy is not based on circumstances but on a growing

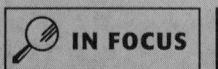

IN FOCUS "spirit"

(Gk. *pneuma*) (5:23; Luke 8:55; 1 Cor. 5:5) Strong's #*4151*; soul (Gk. *psuchē*) (5:23; Eph. 6:6; Phil. 1:27) Strong's #*5590*; body (Gk. *sōma*) (5:23; Matt. 6:22; Heb. 4:12) Strong's #*4983*: This is the only place in the NT where the tripartite being of a person is implied. Yet in this passage, all three constitute a person in his or her entirety. The *spirit* enables a person to contact the divine Spirit and is that part of a person that the Spirit quickens at the time of regeneration (John 3:6; Rom. 8:16). The Greek word *psuche* translated *soul*, means "life." The NT writers use this word to speak of a person's personality or inward, animating essence. Finally, the NT writers identify the *body*, a person's physical being, as separate from one's soul or spirit. As this verse indicates, God works from the inside out, sanctifying our entire being so that we can live with Him forever.

awareness of God and the certain future of eternal life with Christ (Rev. 21:1–7).

5:17 Paul exhorts the Thessalonians to maintain a faithful prayer life like his own (1:2, 3; 2:13; Rom. 1:9, 10; Eph. 6:18; Col. 1:3; 2 Tim. 1:3). Praying **without ceasing** does not mean praying constantly, but being persistent and consistent in prayer.

5:18 Thankfulness should characterize the Christian life in every circumstance, not thanks *for* everything but thanks **in everything.** Paul emphatically states **this is the will of God.** An OT example of this was when Job lost his money, his children, and his health. He blessed the name of God in spite of his personal tragedies, not because of them. Nothing speaks more powerfully of a walk with God than continuous thankfulness.

5:19, 20 To **quench the Spirit** means to resist His influence, like trying to smother a fire. One of the fundamental rules of walking with God is that we should not say no to the Spirit of God.

5:21, 22 It is difficult to determine the eternal value of much in our modern world. Christians are told to **test all things.** This takes time and a system of values. That which survives the test should be held fast. Verses 12–22 provide numerous characteristics of a person who is living in the light of Christ's imminent return.

5:23 Paul's prayer for the Thessalonians is that they may be sanctified in all aspects of their life, **spirit, soul, and body.** Every part of a Christian's life should bear evidence that he or she is set apart as holy to God. This will result in being **blameless at the coming of our Lord Jesus Christ.** Christians are already saints in the sense that they have been set apart to God. Paul exhorts the Thessalonians to express holiness in this life so that the Lord would approve of their conduct upon His return. *Blameless* does not mean sinless, but free from causes for reproach and regret.

5:24 As a believer pursues the Christian life, he can be assured that God is **faithful** and that he cannot do it himself but that God **will do it.**

5:25 pray for us: Paul was faithful in prayer for the Thessalonians, but he also recognized the need and importance of their prayers for him.

5:26 Greeting one another **with a holy kiss** on the cheek was customary, something like our modern handshake. It could have had more significance than just a handshake, signifying spiritual reconciliation.

5:27 This epistle was not a private letter. It was meant for all the Christians at Thessalonica—and for us.

5:28 The greatest benediction Paul could express is that the **grace** of Jesus Christ would be with them. Christians are saved by grace and live by grace, enjoying undeserved blessing from their loving God.

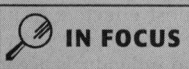

IN FOCUS "epistle"

(Gk. *epistolē*) (5:27; 2 Cor. 3:1–3; 2 Thess. 2:2, 15; 2 Pet. 3:1, 16) Strong's #*1992*: This Greek word has come into English as *epistle*. It signifies a written letter, whether personal correspondence (such as 2 and 3 John; 2 John 12; 3 John 13), or official correspondence (such as Acts 15:23–29; 23:26–30), or a formal treatise (such as Romans; Rom. 16:22). Sometimes letters of recommendation were sent along with emissaries in order to establish their credentials among those they were visiting. In 2 Cor., Paul called the believers in Corinth his epistles, or his living letters of recommendation from God (2 Cor. 3:1–3). Here Paul exhorts the Thessalonians to read his letter to the entire church so that everyone could profit from its teaching.

The Second Epistle to the

Thessalonians

A SIMPLE PHONE CALL COULD HAVE CLEARED UP some of the problems encountered by believers in the early church. But of course there were no telephones in the ancient world. Paul had to be personally tracked down wherever he was and given a letter with questions. The apostle then had to dictate his response and have someone hand-deliver a letter in return. Because of the distances and slow modes of

transportation, this process took weeks or even months. The intervening time span often allowed false beliefs to spread or become ingrained in new churches. Second Thessalonians is an example of just such a situation. Paul had to write this letter to correct false ideas about the Second Coming that had arisen in that church.

Paul had encountered stiff opposition when he first preached the gospel in Thessalonica (Acts 17:1–9), forcing him to flee at night to Berea. His travels soon brought him to Corinth. From that city, he sent Timothy back to Thessalonica to ascertain the condition of the church there. Timothy returned with an encouraging report: the Thessalonian Christians were enduring despite persecution. Not only that, but the testimony of the Thessalonians' steadfast faith was spreading throughout Macedonia (1 Thess. 1:8). Paul wrote a letter to encourage the young church and to answer a few questions that they had sent with Timothy. He wrote 2 Thessalonians soon after to correct some misunderstandings about the end times and to counter false teachings that had crept into the church.

Since the writing of 1 Thessalonians, reports

had come to Paul of continued progress in the Thessalonian church, indicating their faithfulness to the gospel. However, doctrinal problems had also arisen. False teachers had begun to tell the believers in Thessalonica that the day of the Lord was already at hand. These teachers were misapplying and possibly even twisting Paul's teaching that the day of the Lord would come suddenly (1 Thess. 5:2). Most likely because of this, some of the believers had stopped working and were simply waiting for the Lord. Mounting persecution may have also fueled these extreme beliefs about the Second Coming.

In 2 Thessalonians, Paul stated emphatically that he had never taught that the day of the Lord had already come. To counter false doctrine, Paul gave the Thessalonians a good dose of the truth, explaining to them the emergence of the man of lawlessness and the prevalence of sin during the end times. Furthermore, he reminded them they had been called by God and saved through Christ's work. In view of this fact, he exhorted them to stand firm in Christ (2:13) and to work hard (3:12), always patiently waiting for Jesus' return.

Paul identifies himself as the author of

2 Thessalonians, and even calls attention to his own handwriting at the end of the letter (1:1; 3:17). Although many of the early church fathers, including Irenaeus, Tertullian, and Clement of Alexandria, confirm that this letter came from Paul, some modern scholars have questioned the letter's authenticity. Some have asserted that 1 and 2 Thessalonians teach contradictory doctrines about the Second Coming. The first letter is said to teach an imminent return of Christ, but the second to include an intervening period of "lawlessness" before Christ's return. A closer examination of the question reveals that the instructions of the two letters concerning the end times are complementary, not contradictory. First Thessalonians emphasizes the suddenness of the Lord's coming to those who are unprepared, while 2 Thessalonians highlights some of the events that will occur before Jesus returns. Since Paul wrote 2 Thessalonians to correct a misunderstanding that had arisen from his first letter, the difference between the two letters is understandable.

Second Thessalonians was written from Corinth shortly after 1 Thessalonians, or around A.D. 51 or 52.

Outline

I. Encouragement to faithfulness in spite of persecution 1:1–12
  A. Salutation 1:1, 2
  B. Thankfulness for their faithfulness 1:3–5
  C. Assurance of judgment on their persecutors 1:6–10
  D. Prayer for their glorification 1:11, 12
II. Explanations concerning the day of the Lord 2:1–17
  A. Correction of the false teaching that the day of the Lord had begun 2:1, 2
  B. Evidence that the day of the Lord had not begun 2:3–12
  C. God's work in believers and the believers' response 2:13–17
III. Exhortation to continued faithfulness to God 3:1–15
  A. Desire for prayer and continued service for God 3:1–5
  B. Idleness condemned 3:6–15
IV. Benediction of grace and peace 3:16–18

Commentary

1:1 Paul, Silvanus, and Timothy were also the authors and editors of 1 Thessalonians. **Silvanus** (Latin for Silas) had been Paul's traveling companion ever since the start of the second missionary journey. He had participated in the founding of the church at Thessalonica (Acts 17:1–4). **Timothy** also was accompanying Paul on his second missionary journey. His report from the Thessalonian church had been the occasion for the writing of 1 Thessalonians (1 Thess. 3:6–8). **To the church:** The Greek word *ekklesia* means "gathering" or "assembly." Even though the Thessalonians were experiencing persecution and were being infiltrated by false teachers, Paul still addresses them as an

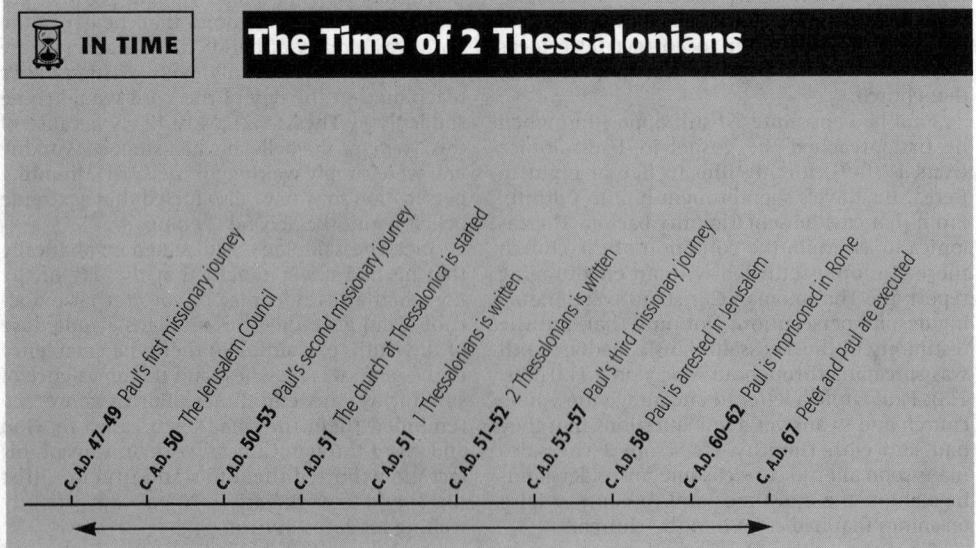

IN TIME

The Time of 2 Thessalonians

c. A.D. 47-49 Paul's first missionary journey
c. A.D. 50 The Jerusalem Council
c. A.D. 50-53 Paul's second missionary journey
c. A.D. 51 The church at Thessalonica is started
c. A.D. 51 1 Thessalonians is written
c. A.D. 51-52 2 Thessalonians is written
c. A.D. 53-57 Paul's third missionary journey
c. A.D. 58 Paul is arrested in Jerusalem
c. A.D. 60-62 Paul is imprisoned in Rome
c. A.D. 67 Peter and Paul are executed

assembly in **God the Father and the Lord Jesus Christ.** Their troubled circumstances did not change their position before God.

1:2 Paul's salutation is similar to those in other ancient letters (Gal. 1:3; Col. 1:2; 1 Thess. 1:2), but his expression is filled with spiritual meaning. **Grace** is the unmerited favor God gives to believers through Jesus Christ. **Peace** refers to the end of enmity between God and people. The Thessalonians could experience peace with God even during severe persecution.

1:3–12 Paul thanks God for the progress of the Thessalonian Christians, especially for their endurance of persecution (vv. 3, 4). He encourages them by imparting how those who are persecuted now will be glorified at Christ's return (vv. 5–10). He prays that they will continue in holiness and thereby be ready when the Lord comes (vv. 11, 12).

1:3 The faithfulness of the Thessalonian church in persecution gave Paul reason to praise God. Satan persecutes Christians in order to discourage and defeat them. These Christians had experienced persecution but continued to grow in Christ, in agreement with the apostle's earlier prayer in his first letter to them (1 Thess. 3:10; 4:9, 10). Here the apostle praises God because the Thessalonians' faith is growing **exceedingly.** They were growing beyond all natural expectation. **Abounds** pictures an expansive growth similar to the sudden surge of flood waters. The Thessalonians' steadfast faith not only strengthened them to withstand difficult circumstances; it also motivated them to express genuine love for others. A Christian's faith in Christ should always culminate in true love for others (read Christ's command in John 13:34, 35).

1:4 Persecution not only tests faith but reveals it and causes it to grow. Continued faith and endurance through **persecutions** provide a testimony for Christ, of which Paul was boasting to the other churches.

1:5–10 Paul encourages them to endurance in view of the coming judgment at Christ's return. The definite article together with the use of the singular leaves no doubt that he is referring to an event in the future when the righteous Judge shall set right the tremendous disparities that now exist.

1:5, 6 Although the Thessalonians were enduring persecution (Acts 17:5–9; 1 Thess. 2:14), Paul explains that their persecutors would be repaid by God. The **judgment of God** requires that the unrighteous be punished for their persecution of the righteous (Pss. 9; 10; 17; 137; Rev. 6:9, 10). Also if the believers handle their persecutions properly, they will be counted worthy of great reward in the coming kingdom of God (Matt. 5:12; 1 Pet. 2:19, 20). Christians are called to endure suffering in this world, for they will receive a far greater reward in the next (2 Tim. 2:12).

1:7–9 Rest is the relief from affliction that will come at Christ's return (Rev. 6:11). The Christian's race or warfare on this earth necessarily includes tension. At the coming of Christ we will experience release from that tension forever, even as we remain active in His service. This promise of future eternal rest helps the suffering Christian to endure present trials (v. 4). **when the Lord Jesus is revealed:** Presently the Lord Jesus is enthroned in glory at the right hand of the Father (John 17:5). Stephen saw this glory before he was martyred (Acts 7:55, 56), but one day, and it may be soon, "every eye will see Him" (Rev. 1:7). Notice the threefold description of His appearance: **from heaven, with His mighty angels, in flaming fire.** Although other passages picture His coming in the clouds, this one describes Him as encircled with leaping flames of fire, taking vengeance on those who have rejected Him. John the Baptist prophesied of this baptism by fire (Matt. 3:11, 12; Luke 3:16, 17). Right now, Christ baptizes those who come to Him with the Holy Spirit;

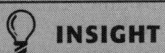 **INSIGHT** | **Finishing Well**

When Paul wrote to the believers in Thessalonica, they were in the midst of intense suffering (2 Thess. 1:4, 5). But Paul encouraged them to look beyond their immediate troubles to the return of Christ and the affirmation they would receive from Him at that time (1:6, 7). Their enemies, who were really enemies of the Lord, would be judged and dealt with (1:8, 9). By contrast, they would join with their Savior in joy and praise (1:10). Paul went on in the next chapter to expand on this theme and its impact on the Thessalonians' current difficulties (2:1–12).

God calls us as His people to finish our lives well by holding on to the truths that last (2:15). He challenges us to maintain lifelong faithfulness and not to be entirely caught up in the here and now, whether good or bad.

but when He comes in judgment He will baptize with fire. Today is the day of salvation, but that day will be the day of vengeance on **those who do not know God** (unbelieving Gentiles; Eph. 2:11, 12) and **those who do not obey the gospel** (unbelieving Jews who knew about God but who rejected His Son; Rom. 10:1, 16). There were both Jewish and Gentile converts in the Thessalonian church (Acts 17:1–5). Therefore, the persecuted Thessalonian believers could be

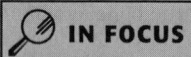

(Gk. *olethros*) (1:9; 1 Cor. 5:5; 1 Thess. 5:3; 1 Tim. 6:9) Strong's *#3639*: The Greek word for *destruction* does not mean annihilation, which as nonexistence could not be eternal, but rather the loss of everything worthwhile. In 1 Corinthians, Paul uses the word to speak of the devastating temporal consequences of sin (1 Cor. 5:5). Here and in 1 Tim. 6:9, Paul uses the same word to refer to the eternal consequences of sin. The penalty for sin is not annihilation, but eternal ruin, eternal separation from the love of Christ. Just as endless life belongs to Christians, endless ruin belongs to those who are opposed to Christ.

encouraged by the fact that when Jesus is revealed from heaven with His angels, He will bring flaming fire and **everlasting destruction** on the enemies of God, the ones who were persecuting them (Rev. 19:12, 17–19; 20:10–15). The word *destruction* does not mean annihilation; it refers to the awful fate of those who reject Jesus, eternal separation from God (Matt. 25:42–46).

1:10–12 In contrast to the destruction of the wicked, Christ will be **glorified in His saints.** Christ will be glorified not only among but also in the saints, for believers reflect His glory. Paul continued to pray that the Thessalonian believers would live in a manner **worthy** of God, in a way that would glorify Christ (1 Thess. 2:12). Believers are determining today, by what they do with the grace that has been given to them, the extent to which they will be worthy to glorify Christ in the reign to come (2 Tim. 2:12).

2:1–12 This paragraph is the heart of the letter. Not only is it very strategic prophetically, but no other portion of the prophetic Scriptures covers the specific points of revelation found here.

2:1, 2 After writing 1 Thessalonians, Paul had received word that the believers in Thessalonica were being misled by false teachers, who were confusing the believers with erroneous ideas about the Second Coming. Paul's second letter was his attempt to correct these misunderstandings. The Greek word translated **gathering together** is found in the NT only here and in Heb. 10:25. There it refers to the local congregation, while here it is the congregation of the whole church. This will be the first time the whole church, including every believer, will be gathered before the Lord to worship Him. The phrase seems to refer to the event described in 1 Thess. 4:17, where Paul speaks of meeting the Lord in the air. The false teaching was that the day of the Lord (called the **day of** here, but compare 1 Thess. 5:2–4) had already come, bringing with it the tribulations they were experiencing. Thus, some Thessalonian believers thought Christ's coming had passed them by. Paul states that they were not to believe such teaching, whether **by spirit or by word or by letter,** as though it had come from him. Paul had taught them that the day of the Lord begins after the Rapture (1 Thess. 5:1–11). But if the day of the Lord had already come, either they had missed the Rapture or the Rapture had not been properly taught by Paul earlier. Paul sensed the need to give further instruction to calm their hearts.

2:3 When Paul wrote 1 Thessalonians, the believers were in danger of losing hope in the Second Coming. In this letter Paul was correcting the opposite extreme—that Jesus had already come. Paul restores balance to the church by describing some of the major events that would precede the day of the Lord (1 Thess. 5:1–11), in particular the **falling away,** and the revealing of the **man of sin.** The falling away, Paul declared, must come first. The Greek term translated *falling away* commonly means a military rebellion. But in the Scriptures, the word is used of rebellion against God. Thus, some have interpreted this verse to refer to a general defection from the truth during this time. This rebellious apostasy would prepare the way for the Antichrist. Others translate the term as *departure* and understand it to be a reference to the Rapture. That is to say, the man of sin cannot be revealed until Christ comes to take His church to be with Him. As far as the word itself is concerned, it could refer to a spiritual departure (falling away), or it could refer to a physical departure (the Rapture). Whichever way one understands it, it is an event that occurs before the man of sin is revealed. Paul does not use the title Antichrist for this man, but his description of him parallels John's description of the Antichrist (1 John 2:18; Rev. 13). The man of

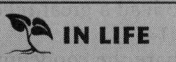 **IN LIFE**   **Thinking About the Future**

Like many people today, the believers in Thessalonica were vulnerable to urgent warnings and announcements related to the future (2 Thess. 2:1, 2). In fact, certain false teachers of the day pandered to people's interest in such things, playing to their greatest hopes and worst fears about the return of Christ (2:3; 1 Thess. 5:2–5). In response, Paul appealed for reason and critical thinking based on the clear instructions he had given (2 Thess. 2:3–12, 15).

As we read 2 Thessalonians today, we, like the letter's original readers, need to "stand fast and hold the traditions which {we} were taught," the truths of God's Word. We should avoid fanciful, fearful guesswork about events related to the Lord's return and instead be busy about our responsibilities at hand (3:6–13).

sin will lead the world into rebellion against God (v. 10), perform wonders through Satan's power (v. 9), and finally will present himself as a god to be worshiped (v. 4).

2:4 The man of sin will proclaim himself to be divine and will sit **in the temple of God,** acting as if he is a god. Many leaders in history have called themselves gods, and the Antichrist is the final declaration of that blasphemy. He will tolerate no one else being worshiped but himself (Rev. 13:6–8). Note the contrasts between the true God and the Antichrist. Though many people have wanted to be gods, the true God became a man, humbled Himself, and redeemed us through the shedding of His own blood (Acts 20:28; Phil. 2:6–8). The One who deserves all worship and praise does not command worship but instead came to this world as a servant. In contrast, the one who deserves only contempt presents himself as a god. The man of sin will probably stand in a physical temple in Jerusalem to declare himself to be god, the ultimate fulfillment of the "abomination of desolation" spoken of by Daniel (Dan. 7:23; 9:26, 27; 11:31, 36, 37; 12:11) and Jesus (Matt. 24:15; Mark 13:14). These prophecies may have been partially fulfilled when Antiochus Epiphanes erected a pagan altar to Zeus in the temple in Jerusalem in 167 B.C. (175–164 B.C.), or when Titus destroyed the temple in A.D. 70. Others have interpreted Paul's reference to the temple of God as a reference to the church. In other words, the man of sin will attempt to divert the church's true worship of God to himself.

2:5 Do you not remember: Paul reminds the Thessalonians of his previous teaching about the Second Coming, confirmed in his first letter to them (1 Thess. 4:13—5:11). He had taught them that they would not experience the night of judgment overtaking the world in the day of the Lord or be the recipients of the wrath of God (1 Thess. 5:9).

2:6 This **restraining** power is not identified. Perhaps it is the civil order established by God to curb the power of evil (Rom. 13:1–7). Since in v. 7 the restraining power is spoken of as a person, perhaps it is the Roman emperor, the embodiment of Roman law. Others believe that Paul has in view the sum total of moral power that resides in the church through the person of the Holy Spirit. Whatever the case, God is in charge. The man of sin cannot appear until God permits it.

2:7 already at work: The evil and deception that the man of sin embodies already exist in this world. John states that there are many antichrists presently at work (1 John 2:18). Anyone who opposes Christ and His church and seeks to deceive others into worshiping false gods is against Christ, and in that case is an antichrist. **He who now restrains:** There was a good reason why the man of sin had not been revealed. The present restrainer, probably the Spirit of God, had to be taken out of the world. God has restrained sin in the world through the power of the Holy Spirit. The Spirit works directly through the Bible, godly people, and His holy angels to advance God's kingdom and restrain evil. Some have interpreted **taken out of the way** in this verse as a reference to the Rapture, for the church cannot exist without the Spirit's presence. Thus, the removal of the church through the Rapture will be in effect the removal of all restraint on the power of sin in this world. There are a variety of other interpretations for this verse and the identity of the restrainer. The Roman state, the emperor of Rome, Paul's missionary work, the Jewish state, or the principle of law and government embodied in the state have all been proposed as the restrainer of lawlessness.

2:8, 9 Although the man of sin will be revealed as extremely powerful (Rev. 13:7), he will be destroyed by Christ and cast into the lake of fire when the Lord comes (Rev. 19:19, 20).

The **power, signs,** and **lying wonders** of the **lawless one** will be overshadowed by the glory and brightness of Christ in His second coming. It is significant that Satan, in order to promote his lie at the end of the age and pass himself off as a god, will use the same kind of power, signs, and wonders that the Spirit of Christ used at the beginning of the age to authenticate the truth about Himself as God (2 Cor. 12:12; Heb. 2:4).

2:10, 11 The condemnation of the man of sin extends to those who follow him who did not receive the love of the truth, in order that they might be saved. Although many will come to Christ after the Rapture, those who reject Christ before the Rapture will not receive Him

---

🔍 IN FOCUS   **"the lawless one"**

(Gk. *ho anomos*) (2:8; 1 Tim. 1:9; 2 Pet. 2:8) Strong's #459: The Greek word *anomos* literally means "without law." Thus, this word is depicting the "man of rebellion." Just as Christ embodies righteousness, so the "man of lawlessness" will embody rebellion against God's righteous law. This figure is probably the same person described by John as "the Antichrist" (1 John 4:2, 3) and "the beast" (Rev. 13:1). With his open defiance of the sovereign Ruler of the universe, this man is the embodiment of evil and the great opponent of Christ and His kingdom.

---

after the Rapture. No doubt many who have superficially heard the gospel and turned away can still be saved after the Rapture, but those who were under conviction of the Spirit and deliberately turned away will not.

2:11, 12 God will send them strong delusion: God is not the author of deception, but He allows those who reject the truth to be misled by falsehood. Following such falsehood, they are eternally **condemned.** We are lost when we choose **unrighteousness** and it becomes our source of **pleasure.** Paul's teaching on the Second Coming as found in both Thessalonian letters may be integrated. Christians who have died will certainly share in the return of Christ (1 Thess. 4:13–18). Christians who are alive should be prepared so that His return will not take them by surprise, as it will unbelievers (1 Thess. 5:1–11). On the other hand, Christians must not think that the Second Coming has occurred and they have been left

out. Although Christ may come very soon, first a "lawless one" will arise to lead a great rebellion against God (2 Thess. 2:1–12).

2:12 Unbelievers will share the condemnation of those who rejected the truth and took **pleasure** in their own **unrighteousness.** Rejection of the truth of the gospel always results in condemnation. Even those who never hear the gospel can reject the revelation of God in nature (Rom. 1:18–21).

2:13 Paul in these verses emphasizes the importance of believing the truth. Again he begins with thanksgiving (1:3; 1 Thess. 1:2; 2:13; 3:9). Paul was continually giving **thanks** to the Lord for the believers. He was thankful for their **salvation,** which was based on God's choice of them, His work in them through the Spirit and the Word, and their ultimate glorification. **chose:** The Greek tense of this word indicates that in the past God had chosen the Thessalonians to be His people, set apart as holy to Him. Their salvation was accomplished by the Spirit when they placed their faith in Christ. Yet note the balance of the Spirit and the **truth** (the Word). The Spirit without the Word is mute; He has nothing to say. The Word without the Spirit is lifeless; it has no power to act. The work of the Spirit is always united with the work of the Word to convict the believer of the truth.

2:14 our gospel: In 1 Thess. 1:5, Paul uses this expression to speak of the Good News that Jesus died for us. In other passages he calls it the gospel of Christ (1 Thess. 3:2) and the gospel of God the Father (1 Thess. 2:8). This is the message that Paul had confidently proclaimed among the Thessalonians with the power of the Holy Spirit (1 Thess. 1:5). **obtaining of the glory:** Paul makes it clear that the Thessalonians have already been saved (v. 13) and **called** by God alone. But now he indicates the Thessalonians' responsibility to respond to God's work in them. Through the power of the Spirit (v. 13), the Thessalonians were to prepare on this earth for a glorious future with Christ by living in a holy manner (1:10; 1 Thess. 4:1, 2).

2:15 Traditions refers to instructions passed on from one person to another. Sometimes the word refers to human traditions, people's opinions, and speculations. But in this case Paul is referring to the revealed truth of God that contains no error. This is what Paul had passed on to them. He had communicated some of God's truth when he was preaching among them, further truth by his first **epistle,** and now he was communicating more truth through a second letter. The NT had not yet been written, and the essential beliefs of the Christian faith were being communicated through the apostles' preaching and letters. Having believed the truth, the Thessalonian believers were now to maintain it and stand fast in their faith. A sure way to retain truth is to use it. If you do not use it, you lose it. If the Thessalonians had been steadfast in the truth, it would have prevented the confusion over Christ's coming that Paul was now having to correct.

2:16, 17 In preparation for the instructions that follow in ch. 3, Paul prays that God would encourage the Thessalonians and establish them in the truth (a similar prayer is found in 1 Thess. 3:11–13). It was only because God had graciously chosen them as His own people, **loved** them, and **given** them everlasting salvation that they could have **hope.** Paul uses the singular verbs **comfort** and **establish** with the plural subject, **Jesus Christ** and the **Father,** to indicate the unity and equality of these two persons of the Godhead (1 Thess. 3:11).

3:1, 2 Paul not only prayed for the Thessalonians, but he also sensed his own need for their prayers. He asked them to pray for the advance of the gospel and for his own deliverance from human opposition. **Run swiftly** refers to the rapid spread of the gospel, while **glorified** expresses the idea of being triumphant. The verbs suggest not a single victory but a continuing series of victories marking the progression of the gospel throughout the world. **Unreasonable** means the men are capable of harmful deeds, while **wicked** indicates that they are evil in themselves and desire to corrupt others. These men may have been unbelieving Jews in Corinth who were persecuting Paul at the time he wrote this letter (Acts 18:12, 13). Justice in this world may never come for Christians, but they can certainly pray for deliverance from the wicked.

3:3 Although Paul was aware that the Thessalonians might be tempted and prove unfaithful, he was confident that God would **establish** or strengthen them (2:17; l Thess. 3:2, 13). He knew that God would **guard** or protect them (Phil. 1:6; 1 Thess. 5:24). In the previous verse, he had warned them concerning evil men (v. 2). Here Paul assures them that God will faithfully stand watch over them so that not even the **evil one,** Satan himself, could get hold of them. This passage must have been especially comforting to the Thessalonians, for they were still experiencing severe persecution on account of their faith (1:4).

3:4 Paul had **confidence** that the Thessalonians would obey his commands, but his confidence was in the Lord and based on what the Lord would do to help the Thessalonians stand true. Paul had a similar confidence regarding the church in Philippi (Phil. 1:6).

3:5 With the prayer **may the Lord direct your hearts,** Paul was indicating that the heart, the seat of a person's will, is the place were spiritual renewal begins. There God plants His love and patience, traits that will produce a harvest of good works. Paul uses the word *direct* to indicate that God will clear away the obstacles that may stand in the way of their progress toward **love** and **patience.** Paul prays that the Thessalonians, when faced with persecution, will be able to show the same type of patience Jesus expressed when people rejected Him.

3:6 Paul uses here the strong word **command** (v. 4; 1 Thess. 4:2, 11). This is not simply a suggestion but a binding order with the authority of the Lord Jesus Christ. The same

---

✠ IN CONTEXT | Busy Waiting

Every generation of Christians must face the dilemma of how to live in the tension between the possibility of Christ's immediate return and the impossibility of predicting the moment. Many Christians unfortunately settle the problem by living as if Christ will not return. Meanwhile, others dabble in various fruitless but persistent schemes to "figure out" the time of Christ's return.

The young Thessalonian church struggled with persecution from the outset. Facing such difficulties, many of them found hope in the promise of Christ's return. Others misapplied the lesson by becoming lazy. After all, they reasoned, if Christ is already on His way, why participate in the details and responsibilities of life? Why sow if we will not be here to reap?

For those who had chosen to "coast" until Christ's return, Paul had blunt words: "If anyone will not work, neither shall he eat" (3:10). Paul understood the strong temptation to hide irresponsibility under a cover of spirituality. The integrity of the gospel was at stake.

In his final words of encouragement in 2 Thessalonians, Paul touched on the daily challenge for every person seeking to live for Christ: "But as for you, brethren, do not grow weary in doing good" (3:13). Herein lies the secret of being ready for Christ's return. If the hope of His arrival stirs up a wholehearted commitment to do good for His sake, we will be ready for Him. We must be busy waiting.

word, found also in vv. 10, 12, is used of a military command that one must obey or else face the penalty of treason. Paul instructs the Thessalonians to **withdraw,** or withhold fellowship, from a disobedient person. Among other things this would include not allowing the person to participate in love feasts and the Lord's Supper (1 Cor. 5:9–13). Read Jesus' instructions in Matt. 18:15–17.

3:7, 8 Some Thessalonians, perhaps using the impending return of the Lord as an excuse, had refused to work and were expecting others in the church to feed them. In his previous letter Paul had already exhorted them to work (1 Thess. 4:11, 12). Evidently they had not heeded Paul's instruction, for in this letter Paul tells the church to discipline them (v. 6). As an example to all, Paul had **worked . . . night and day** when he preached among them. His goal was to avoid being a burden to anyone. Both the

Greeks and the Romans despised manual labor; typically they used slaves for all such tasks. By contrast, the Jews regarded work as an evidence of good character and trained their children to work in a trade. Paul made tents in order to provide for his needs whenever this became necessary on his missionary journeys (Acts 18:1–3).

3:9 Christian workers can expect financial support, and the church is obligated to pay those who serve them (Luke 10:7; 1 Cor. 9:6–14; Gal. 6:6; 1 Tim. 5:17, 18). Yet Paul did not want to use his **authority** to demand payment. Rather, he wanted to be an **example** for others to follow. The fact that he worked would also cut off any opportunity to accuse him of greed. He wanted nothing to hinder the spread of the gospel (1 Cor. 9:12).

3:10 Again using the expression **we commanded you this,** Paul laid down the rule that if anyone does not work, neither should he eat.

 **IN COMPARISON** | **Church Discipline**

In 2 Thess. 3:14, Paul instructs the Thessalonians to discipline one of their church members. What does church discipline involve? When should it be employed? What does the Scripture say about it? The following chart attempts to sort out a frequently misunderstood process.

The Definition	Church discipline is ultimately the denying of fellowship to a believer in Christ who is involved in open sin.
The Occasion	Church discipline involves Christians engaged in overt sin (Matt. 18:15–17; 1 Cor. 5:9–13), especially sexual immorality; those creating division within the body of Christ (Rom. 16:17; Titus 3:10); and those in open defiance of God's appointed leadership in the church (3:6, 7, 14; Heb. 13:17).
The Reason	A church must exercise discipline because the church must remain pure (1 Cor. 5:8).
The Goal	The goal of church discipline is to cause the sinning person to repent (James 5:19, 20); to "gain back" or restore an erring brother (Matt. 18:15; Gal. 6:1); to make the sinful person feel ashamed enough to change (3:14).
The Steps	There are several distinct steps to church discipline. First, meet one-on-one with the person. Second, if necessary meet with the person and another church member. Third, if there is no change in behavior, announce the matter to the congregation so that the whole church can corporately encourage the person to repent. Finally, if all else fails, put the sinning person out of the assembly (Matt. 18:15–17).
The Attitude	The tone of church discipline should be firm gentleness (Gal. 6:1). The people exercising church discipline should put away any spite, hatred, or malice so that they can facilitate true restoration.
The Commands	Matt. 18:15–17; Rom. 16:17; 1 Cor. 5:1–13; Gal. 6:1; 2 Thess. 3:6, 7, 14, 15; Titus 3:10, 11; Heb. 13:17; James 5:19, 20

This applies to those unwilling to work, not to those unable to work.

3:11 Idleness breeds sin. Those who are **disorderly,** not working at all, become **busybodies,** causing trouble and division in the church.

3:12 Again Paul says **we command and exhort** (vv. 6, 10). He urges the Thessalonians to **eat their own bread** and to do so in a quiet manner, not causing division and disruption. Paul's cure for gossip is hard work.

3:13 The Thessalonian believers were exhorted not to be discouraged in work by those who did not work, but rather to continue in doing good.

3:14 do not keep company with him: Again (v. 6) the believers were to withdraw fellowship and not associate with anyone who disregarded the words of this authoritative letter from the apostle Paul. Otherwise their pagan neighbors might think the Thessalonian Christians approved of that person's actions.

3:15 admonish him as a brother: The disobedient one is not an enemy, but one who needs correction. Even though rebellion was to

be dealt with, Paul demonstrates his tremendous compassion for fellow believers. He hated the sin but not the sinner.

3:16 In view of the possibility of disharmony in the church, Paul prayed that the **Lord of peace** would guide their actions, granting peace and unity to the church.

3:17 with my own hand: Paul dictated many of his epistles to a secretary. He adds a personal word in his own handwriting as evidence of the authenticity of this letter (Col. 4:18). This proof was necessary in this case because Paul suspected that the Thessalonians might have received a letter falsely attributed to him (2:2). To guard against this, Paul explicitly tells the Thessalonians that his handwriting at the end of a letter is the official **sign** that a letter was from him.

3:18 To all the difficulties that faced the Thessalonians and Paul as well, the solution was the **grace of our Lord Jesus Christ.** Not only was Jesus the Thessalonians' ultimate hope, but it was He who lovingly strengthened them to endure trials. It was Paul's prayer that this would be evident in their midst.

The First Epistle to
Timothy

SOMETIMES THE MOST DIFFICULT PART OF A TEACHER'S job is to let the students go, to let them graduate and make their way in the world. One can sense this kind of anxiety in Paul's first letter to Timothy. He affectionately calls Timothy "a true son" (1:2), charging him again and again to remain faithful to what he had taught him (1:18; 5:12–16, 21; 6:11–13). The letter concludes with Paul's heartfelt cry: "O Timothy! Guard

what was committed to your trust" (6:20). Timothy had accompanied Paul for years (Acts 16:1–3; 17:10; 20:4), assisting him and acting as his liaison to a number of churches. Paul had not only taught Timothy the essentials of the Christian faith; he had modeled Christian leadership to him. Now Paul was leaving Timothy in charge of the church at Ephesus. From Macedonia, Paul wrote to encourage his "son" in the faith. In effect, this letter is Timothy's commission, his orders from his concerned teacher, the apostle Paul.

The central purpose of 1 Timothy is found in 3:15: "I write so that you may know how you ought to conduct yourself in the house of God, which is the church of the living God, the pillar and ground of the truth." The church is God's primary vehicle for accomplishing His work on earth (Matt. 16:18–20). The Lord has ordained that men and women who have trusted Him as Savior should be involved in working out His will in local assemblies around the world (1 Thess. 1:1; Heb. 10:24, 25).

Paul wrote 1 Timothy in order to instruct his young protégé on how the church should function and on how mature men and women of

God should interact in it (6:11–16). Specifics are given on developing and recognizing godly leadership and avoiding false doctrine in the church (3:1–13; 4:1–6). Paul insists that Christian maturity should be expected in leadership, while it is developed in the lives of all believers (4:6–10). Paul offers Timothy a whole list of extremely practical advice for leading a church. As he faced the problems and hardships of ministry in a local church, Timothy must have repeatedly read Paul's letter for the valuable insights it offers (4:15).

Timothy was a native of Lystra in Phrygia (Acts 16:1–3). His father was Greek, and his mother, Eunice, and grandmother, Lois, were godly Jewish women (2 Tim. 1:5; 3:14, 15). It was through the influence of these women that Timothy learned the Hebrew Scriptures as a child. Paul calls Timothy a "true son in the faith" (1:2), suggesting that he was converted during Paul's first missionary visit to Lystra (Acts 14:6, 19).

At the beginning of Paul's second missionary journey, Timothy was chosen by Paul to accompany him and Silas (Acts 16:3). Since they would be preaching to Jews, Paul had Timothy circumcised (Acts 16:3), and evidently the leadership of the church laid hands on Timothy (4:14; 2 Tim. 1:6). He traveled with Paul and Silas helping them in their evangelization of Philippi and Thessalonica. Apparently he remained in Thessalonica (Acts 17:10) and then joined Paul and Silas in Berea. In Corinth, Paul employed Timothy as a liaison between himself and the church in Thessalonica. Later he used Timothy as a liaison again, this time to the church in Corinth, to teach the believers there (1 Cor. 4:17; 16:10). Acts does not record Timothy's travels during this period. He reappears in Ephesus (Acts 19:22), where Paul commissioned Timothy and Erastus to prepare the churches in Macedonia for his arrival. Timothy remained in Macedonia and accompanied Paul to Corinth, where presumably Paul wrote his letter to the Romans (Rom. 16:21).

Then Timothy, along with six others, spearheaded Paul's journey to Troas (Acts 20:4, 5). Later he comforted Paul in Rome during the apostle's first imprisonment (A.D. 60–62), sending greetings to the Colossians (Col. 1:1), Philemon (Philem. 1), and the Philippians (Phil. 1:1). During Paul's imprisonment, Timothy traveled to Philippi to encourage the believers there and then report back to Paul in Rome (Phil. 2:19). After Paul's release, Timothy traveled with him to Ephesus. Timothy stayed there to confront the false teachers who were infiltrating the church, and Paul went on to Macedonia, where he wrote his first letter to Timothy (1:3). He wrote his second letter to him from prison (2 Tim. 1:8), imploring Timothy to come quickly. This was probably Paul's last letter, for he was soon to die. If Timothy did

come quickly, he would have been with him as his "true son" in the final days before his execution (2 Tim. 4:11, 21).

The letter names Paul as its author, and the author's statements about his life in 1:12, 13 are consistent with what is known of him. The early church fathers Clement of Rome and Polycarp accepted the letter as one of Paul's, as did Irenaeus, Tertullian, and Clement of Alexandria.

Early in the nineteenth century, some scholars began to question Paul's authorship of the Pastoral Epistles (1 and 2 Timothy and Titus). Critics claimed that these letters were "pious forgeries" written in the second century. They leveled four different attacks on the integrity and authenticity of these letters. First is a historical problem. Since the chronological references in these letters do not correspond with the Book of Acts, critics assume that the letters were written at a much later time by an impostor. However, the letters could have been written soon after the events described in the Book of Acts. Many scholars hold that Paul was acquitted and released from the imprisonment described in Acts 28, and then traveled for several years in Asia Minor and Macedonia. During this time he wrote the disputed letters. Eventually he was imprisoned in Rome again, and then died in Nero's persecution.

Second, critics argue that the Pastoral Epistles do not fit Paul's writing style. These letters contain a number of words that occur only here in the New Testament but are common in the writings of the second century. This is taken as evidence that the letters are from the second century. The weakness of this argument is that

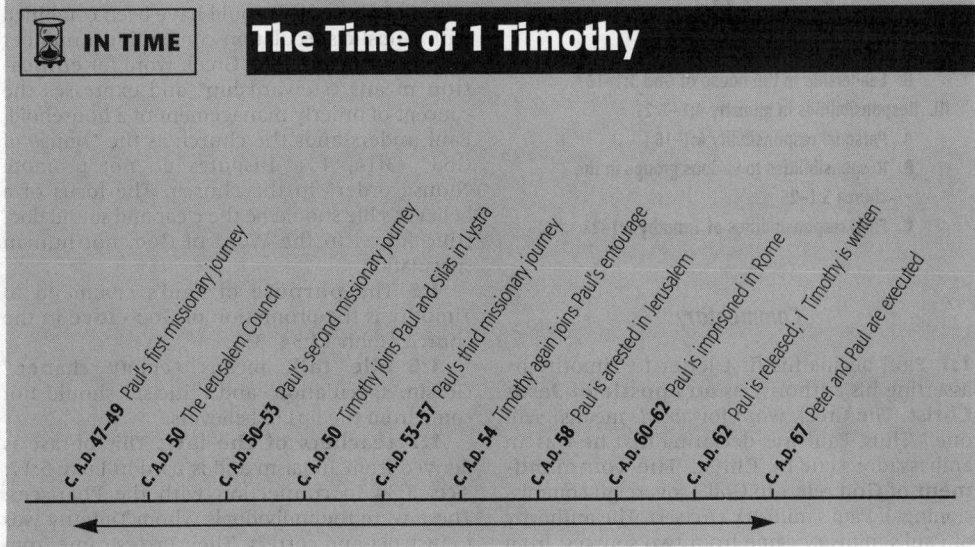

IN TIME | **The Time of 1 Timothy**

C. A.D. 47–49 Paul's first missionary journey
C. A.D. 50 The Jerusalem Council
C. A.D. 50–53 Paul's second missionary journey
C. A.D. 50 Timothy joins Paul and Silas in Lystra
C. A.D. 53–57 Paul's third missionary journey
C. A.D. 54 Timothy again joins Paul's entourage
C. A.D. 58 Paul is arrested in Jerusalem
C. A.D. 60–62 Paul is imprisoned in Rome
C. A.D. 62 Paul is released; 1 Timothy is written
C. A.D. 67 Peter and Paul are executed

there is a limited body of literature from the second century from which to draw such a dogmatic conclusion.

The third point relates to the form of church leadership described in the Pastoral Epistles. The structure of authority, including elders and deacons, seems to represent a more developed, second-century church. However, it is clear from Phil. 1:1 that the offices of elder and deacon were already functioning during Paul's ministry.

The fourth argument involves theology. Critics claim that the heresy combated in the Pastoral Epistles is the full-grown Gnosticism of the second century. While it is true that Gnosticism was not fully developed until the second century, it is also certain that the heresy began slowly and evolved before it became a complete theological system. Paul dealt with similar false teachings in Colosse (Col. 1:9–15). The heresy in 1 Timothy appears to be an early form of gnostic teaching that combined elements of Judaism (1:7), Persian thought, and Christianity.

There is no reason, therefore, to conclude that 1 and 2 Timothy are not authentic Pauline Epistles. First Timothy was probably composed shortly after Paul's release from his first Roman imprisonment. This means the book was composed in Macedonia around A.D. 62.

Outline

I. Reminders in ministry 1:1–20
   A. Warnings concerning false doctrine 1:1–17
   B. Warnings concerning good warfare 1:18–20
II. Regulations in ministry 2:1–3:16
   A. Women in worship 2:1–15
   B. Leadership in the house of God 3:1–16
III. Responsibilities in ministry 4:1–6:21
   A. Personal responsibility 4:1–16
   B. Responsibilities to various groups in the church 5:1–25
   C. Final responsibilities of Timothy 6:1–21

Commentary

1:1 Paul begins his first letter to Timothy by asserting his authority as **an apostle of Jesus Christ.** The Greek word for *apostle* means "sent one." Thus, Paul was declaring that he was an ambassador sent by Christ. **The commandment of God** refers to God's sovereign commissioning of Paul's ministry (Acts 9). The authority of Paul's ministry came from two sources: from

God our Savior and from **the Lord Jesus Christ.** The title *Savior* identifies God as the source of our salvation, both our justification and sanctification. Paul speaks of Christ as **our hope** because He is the reason we can expectantly look forward to eternal life in glory.

1:2 Timothy was a young believer from Lystra who traveled with Paul during his second and third missionary journeys (Acts 16:2, 3). **True son** refers to a legitimate child who possessed all the rights and privileges of membership in a family. Paul was indicating total acceptance of Timothy as a believer. The salutation is **Grace** (Gk. *charis*), the Greeks' "hello." It means to get what you don't deserve. Salvation is by grace (Eph. 2:8, 9). **Mercy** (Gk. *eleos*) means you don't get what you do deserve. It is only in the Pastoral Epistles that Paul breaks from his usual pattern of saying "grace and peace" and includes "mercy." Preachers need mercy. **Peace** (Gk. *eirēnē*) means "to bind together that which has been separated." Christ is our peace (Eph. 2:14) and binds us to God.

1:3–11 Paul exhorts Timothy to correct false teaching because it leads to a corrupt way of life.

1:3 It is not certain when Paul traveled to **Macedonia.** His request for Timothy to **remain in Ephesus,** ministering to believers there, demonstrates Paul's confidence in the young man.

1:4 The word **fables** is used in Titus 1:14 in connection with Jewish fables. **Genealogies** is used in Titus 3:9 within the context of the Law. The errors that Paul left Timothy to correct in Ephesus appear to have been primarily Jewish in nature, involving unrestrained speculation about genealogies and allegorical interpretations of the Law like those found in rabbinical literature. In Ephesus this could have been combined with Gnostic speculation concerning a number of spiritual beings. The Greek word for **edification** means "stewardship" and expresses the concept of orderly management of a household. Paul understands the church as the "house of God" (3:14, 15). Disputes do not promote "house order" in the church. The focus of a believer's life should be the clear and sound doctrine found in the Word of God, not human speculation.

1:5 The **purpose** of Paul's command to Timothy is the promotion of God's **love** in the church (John 13:34, 35).

1:6 Idle talk means "empty chatter." Gossip, speculation, and criticism should not come from the lips of believers.

1:7 teachers of the law: This phrase is derived from Judaism and is used in Luke 5:17; Acts 5:34 in connection with the Pharisees. These were the individuals whom Timothy was to instruct and correct. Their errors came from their relation to the law. These men were loveless, legalistic teachers with impure hearts and motives. Instruction without love promotes legalism.

1:8–11 Even something good like the **law** can be used improperly. Its purpose is to teach us about right and wrong and to curb **sinners.** It is not given to bring those who are **righteous** through Christ into legalistic bondage (Rom. 7:12, 13). The sins listed in vv. 9, 10 are flagrant violations of the Ten Commandments.

1:8 The proper function of the **law** is to make sinners aware of their sinfulness (Rom. 3:20).

1:9 Paul's list of those who have violated the law appears to parallel the order of the Ten Commandments (Ex. 20:3–17). The first three pairs of violations recall the first four commands, which address a person's relationship

with God: **the lawless and insubordinate, the ungodly and . . . sinners, and the unholy and profane.** Following these are eight violations that parallel five of the last six commands of the Ten Commandments. Covetousness is not mentioned.

1:10 Fornicators are persons involved in sexual immorality in general. **Sodomites** are specifically male homosexuals (1 Cor. 6:9). But heterosexual and homosexual immorality are violations of the seventh commandment. **kidnappers . . . liars . . . perjurers:** These are violations of commandments eight and nine. **Sound doctrine** may also be translated "healthy teaching." *Sound* is derived from the Greek for "in good health." Doctrine is a key theme in 1 Timothy (4:1, 6, 13, 16; 5:17; 6:1).

1:11 according to the glorious gospel: This phrase should be interpreted in its imme-

 **IN COMPARISON** | **Practical Advice for the Ministry**

Timothy was a young minister, appointed to lead the apparently contentious church at Ephesus. He had already learned the essentials of the gospel; now he had to learn how to lead. In this letter, Paul was passing on all the wisdom he had accumulated in his years of ministry. His insights are extremely practical, and valuable even today.

Exhortations: what to do	Warnings: what to avoid
• Command others to teach no other doctrine than the true doctrine of Christ (1:3).	• Do not listen to fables or endless genealogies, which cause disputes (1:4).
• Teach the Good News that Christ saves sinners (1:15–18).	• Reject fables (4:7).
• Pray and intercede for everyone (2:1).	• Do not neglect your gift (4:14).
• Choose church leaders who are worthy of the office (3:1–15).	• Do not rebuke older men, but exhort them (5:1).
• Instruct others in sound doctrine (4:6).	• Do not receive an accusation against an elder unless there are two witnesses (5:19).
• Train oneself in godliness (4:7, 8).	• Do not govern the church with prejudice; be impartial (5:21).
• Be an example to the believers in word, in conduct, in love, in spirit, in faith, and in purity (4:12).	• Do not hastily lay hands on anyone (5:22).
• Honor widows (5:3).	• Withdraw from those who reject Paul's teaching and are constantly arguing over words (6:4, 5).
• Stay pure (5:22).	• Flee from those who are greedy and want to become wealthy from the ministry (6:5–11).
• Pursue righteousness, faith, love, patience, and gentleness (6:11).	• Avoid profane and idle talk, which is falsely called knowledge (6:20).

diate context, a discussion about the purpose of the law. The proper use of the law is to demonstrate human sinfulness and our need for the Good News that Christ has saved us from bondage to the law and our own sins.

1:12 I thank Christ Jesus our Lord: There was no arrogance in Paul. The world is "unthankful." He did not take his privilege for granted. **enabled me** (literally, "put strength"): Paul knew well his "strength is made perfect in weakness" (2 Cor. 12:9). **faithful:** This is required of stewards with a trust (1 Cor. 4:1, 2). **ministry:** No man takes this honor to himself (Heb. 4:5) and Paul did not "handle the Word of God deceitfully" (2 Cor. 4:2), as did the legalizers.

1:13 Before Paul trusted in Christ as Savior, he was **a blasphemer,** speaking against God; **a persecutor,** pursuing Christians like a hunter pursuing his prey (Acts 8:3; 9:1–5); and **an insolent man,** a violent person acting out of personal pride. **but I obtained mercy:** If the apostle Paul could find mercy after the terrible things he did against Christ, then God surely offers salvation with "open arms" to all people (2:4).

1:14 Grace is God's undeserved, unearned, freely given favor. The grace given to Paul was **exceedingly abundant,** overflowing beyond all expectations.

1:15 Paul summarized the heart of the gospel (v.11): **Christ Jesus came into the world to save sinners.** *World* refers to all humanity. *Save* means to deliver or rescue. Christ came to die for the sins of humanity. **of whom I am chief:** Paul saw the degradation of sin and understood the sinfulness of human beings. Because of this, he placed himself first among sinners.

1:16 believe on Him: Over 185 times in the NT the sole condition given for salvation is belief, having faith or trust in Jesus Christ. The gospel is that Christ died for our sins, was buried, and rose on the third day. All those who place their trust in Jesus for salvation will be saved from the coming judgment. To add any other condition to faith for salvation is to make justification a matter of works (Rom. 11:6; Gal. 2:16).

1:17 In the middle of his explanation of the gospel Paul cannot contain himself. He must give praise to such a merciful God.

1:18 Apparently earlier in his ministry **prophecies** had been made about Timothy and his future role in the church. Paul urges Timothy to **wage the good warfare.** According to this powerful imagery, Christian ministry is spiritual warfare directed against God's enemies.

1:19 having the **faith:** The definite article is here speaking of "the faith" once delivered (Jude 3). "Stay true to the Word" is the meaning

today. **good conscience:** Six times in the Pastoral Epistles Paul speaks concerning the conscience. Some people need an amplifier for that still small voice. It can only be kept clear by judging oneself and confessing sin (1 Cor. 11:30–32; 1 John 1:9). Once the conscience is seared (4:2), even a preacher is capable of committing gross sin. David's conscience wasn't cleared; his sin was ever before him (Ps. 51:3), until he confessed it. **shipwreck:** Many a shipwreck began with unconfessed small sins.

1:20 Hymenaeus and Alexander: Paul offered examples of two men (2 Tim. 2:17, 18; 4:14) who were failing to fight the good fight (vv. 18, 19). The phrase **delivered to Satan** is similar to 1 Cor. 5:5. The authority to "deliver over" was apostolic in nature. Paul did not deliver the two men because they were unbelievers, but so that they would **learn not to blaspheme.** In the NT the word translated *learn* is used only of God's discipline of believers (1 Cor. 11:32; Heb. 12:6, 7, 10). Paul was indicating that these men should be excluded from the church so that they might abandon their evil ways (1 Cor. 5:1–5).

2:1, 2 Therefore: Here Paul elaborates on what will build up the church (1:4). In these verses, Paul uses four of the seven NT terms for prayer. **Supplications** emphasizes personal need. The verb from which the noun is derived has the idea of "petition." **Prayers** is the general word for prayer. The term is always directed toward God with reverence or worship. **Intercessions** means "approaching with confidence," suggesting free access to God. **Giving of thanks** is an attitude of gratitude, the act of praising God for what He has done for us. Each of these aspects of prayer should be included in the prayer life of a church. **For all men** is the first object of prayer. This generic expression for male and female alike cannot be restricted to believers; it also includes nonbelievers, such as **kings and all who are in authority. Peaceable** refers to internal composure or an amiable attitude. The idea of praying for kings has a twofold emphasis. First, it is a specific way to pray for all men, because the actions of a king affect society as a whole. Second, it reminds believers that God is the ultimate Sovereign. He is in control, and our prayers affect decisions at the highest level.

2:3 Good (Gk. *kalos*) means "useful," "excellent," or "suitable" (compare 1:8). The prayer is good because it is in accordance with the will of God. **In the sight of God our Savior** indicates the saving power of God (1:15).

2:4 Who desires all men to be saved does not mean that God has willed that everyone should come to salvation, for elsewhere Paul clearly teaches that only those who believe in Christ will receive salvation (Rom. 1:16, 17; 3:21–26; 5:17). This is also the clear teaching of Jesus (John 3:15–18). Thus, universal salvation is not the *determinative will* of God, by which He sovereignly rules the world. Instead what Paul might be saying here is that the Savior God extends the offer of salvation to all. Christ died for the sins of all, but only those who believe receive the benefits of that sacrifice (John 3:16; 2 Cor. 5:14, 15). **The knowledge of the truth** refers to Christian growth after being saved. God's desire is not only our salvation (justification) but also our growth in the truth (sanctification), so that we will not be led astray by false teachers (1:3, 4).

2:5 One God is a central truth of the Hebrew Scriptures. The only living God desires all to be saved. He is the only One to whom our prayers should be addressed. **Mediator** is a concept derived from the ceremonial worship prescribed in the OT. In the tabernacle and later in the temple, the priests mediated between God and the Israelites by offering animal sacrifices to atone for the sins of the people and by interceding to God for the nation. In their position as mediators, the priests were the only ones eligible to enter the Holy Place, the place where God had made His presence known. The **one** Mediator is **the Man Christ Jesus** (Heb. 9:11–15). There is one God from whom salvation is available. There is only one way to Him, through the Mediator, Christ Jesus, who has the full nature of God and the full nature of man. Christ has identified with us; He understands us perfectly and represents us at the right hand of God the Father (Rom. 8:34).

2:6 The work of the Mediator (v. 5) is described as giving **Himself a ransom for all.** The Greek word translated *ransom* is found only here in the NT. It specifically refers to a ransom paid for a slave. In Greek it is formed with a prefix that reinforces the idea of substitution (Matt. 20:28; Mark 10:45). In other words Christ substituted His life for ours. Our sins had separated us from God. Christ paid the penalty for our sins so that we could be reconciled to our Father.

2:7 Teacher of the Gentiles describes the ministry to which Paul had been commissioned (Acts 9:15; Rom. 11:13). **Faith** refers to one's initial salvation (justification); **truth** relates to the believer's growth in salvation (sanctification). Paul was called not only to preach the gospel to the Gentiles but also to guide their growth in the truth. This is why he left Timothy at Ephesus. Timothy was to charge the Ephesians not to teach other doctrines, fables, or endless genealogies (1:4).

2:8–10 These instructions concern how people should conduct themselves in public worship, but the principles taught have a wider application to the behavior of believers. Holiness of life (v. 8) and modesty of dress (vv. 9, 10) are especially appropriate for the Christian.

2:8 The men refers to those involved in leading public worship. Leadership in public worship is not restricted to elders or those with

IN FOCUS **"ransom"**

(Gk. *antilutron*) (2:6) Strong's #487: The word *ransom* in Greek is *antilutron,* made up of *anti* (signifying substitution) and *lutron* (the word used for the ransom of a slave or prisoner). The *antilutron* is a payment given instead of a slave or prisoner—that is, in substitution for him or her. The person holding the slave accepts the payment as a substitute. According to Gal. 3:13, Christ redeemed us from the curse of the law. The law held us captive in its condemnation, and no one but Christ could pay the price to release us from this bondage.

specific gifts. Prayer is one of the central features of Christian worship. The Greek word translated *men* in this verse refers to males distinguished from females. Some have insisted that this means that males are to be the only leaders in public worship. On the other hand, Paul describes women as praying in public in some of his other letters (v. 9; 1 Cor. 11:5). **Lifting up holy hands** is a Hebrew way of praying (1 Kin. 8:22; Ps. 141:2). *Holy* means "morally and spiritually clean." Biblical prayer must be done with a clean heart and life (Heb. 10:22). **without wrath and doubting:** *Wrath* is a slow, boiling type of anger. *Doubting* literally means "to think backward and forward." It carries the idea of disputing. Prayer is to be offered without resentment or disputing among those in the church. If believers do not have good relations with others in the church, they should not lead in public worship.

2:9 in like manner also: This expression probably continues the discussion of prayer begun in v. 8. In other words, when men pray they are to possess sincere and holy attitudes; when women pray, they should be modest. **modest apparel:** The emphasis is that women should dress appropriately when at worship, and not put on extravagant clothes that draw attention to themselves. **Propriety** means reverence and respect, shrinking away from what is inappropriate. **Moderation** may also be translated "sound judgment" or "self-control."

2:10 Paul exhorts the women at Ephesus to be concerned about clothing themselves with godly character instead of wearing inappropriate and lavish clothes. **with good works:** A Christian woman's beauty is found in her godly character and her love for the Lord as demonstrated in all types of good works.

2:11–15 These restrictions may have been based on the inappropriate behavior of some women recently converted from paganism. Paul himself did not disapprove of women praying and prophesying in public provided they were properly attired (1 Cor. 11:4, 5). Also Paul freely acknowledged his debt to a considerable group of women who helped in the NT church (Rom. 16:1–15).

2:11–12 Paul uses a literary device called an inclusio in these verses to frame his argument on women not teaching or exercising authority over men in the church. Moreover, he uses two pairs of words to convey his meaning. We may understand it as follows:

v. 11   women in silence (*hēsuchia*)
        let them learn (*manthaneto*)
            full submission (*en pase hupotagē*)
v. 12   teaching (*didaskein*)
        exercise authority (*authentein*)
           [women] be in silence (*hēsuchia*)

2:11 Let a woman learn is a command. Women are encouraged to learn in the local assembly but with a proper attitude. Here Paul rises above the Greek culture, since the first-century woman in Greece was not considered able to learn. Paul disavows that myth and exhorts Timothy to provide opportunity for women to learn. The apostle who made such full use of women in ministry (Rom. 16:3–15) set a great example for Timothy. **In silence** (Gk. *hēsuchia*) is to be her attitude or disposition ("peaceable" in 2:2 and "gentle and quiet" in 1 Pet. 3:4) while learning, as should be true of all believers. Paul is not saying that a woman may not speak in the local assembly (compare 1 Cor. 11:2–16). A different Greek term (*sigas*) means to say nothing or not to speak. Though Paul grants this new privilege and freedom, he cautions that women are to learn with an attitude of **all submission,** not in a debating, unruly manner. The new freedom for those who have been kept in ignorance and consequent immaturity may easily be abused as was the case in Ephesus (5:11–15).

2:12 I do not permit is a present tense and indicates an abiding attitude. The apostle expresses his abiding personal authority as an apostle in regard to the matter of women teaching men in the local church (compare Rom. 12:1). **to teach** (Gk. *didaskein*): The

---

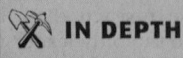 **IN DEPTH**   **A New Way to Worship**

What is the proper way to worship God? For those who had grown up in the religious climate of Ephesus before the gospel, Christian worship called for altogether different behavior than they were used to practicing. So Paul offered guidelines for worship to the men and women in the Ephesian church (1 Tim. 2:8–15).

Ephesus was world-renowned for its magnificent temple of Artemis. Pagan cults flourished there, along with occult practices. In fact, books with magic recipes came to be known as "Ephesian books."

Nevertheless, the gospel bore great fruit there and the community of believers grew rapidly. Yet some of the new converts brought their old way of life into the church and began teaching other doctrines (1 Tim. 1:3–7). When it came to worship, many were used to wild rites and festivals. Ephesian women were particularly unacquainted with public behavior, having been excluded for the most part from public gatherings, except pagan rituals.

So Paul described the correct way of worship. Men, who were apparently given to anger and doubts, needed to stop wrangling and start praying (1 Tim. 2:8). Likewise, women needed to focus on godliness and good works rather than clothing, jewelry, and hairstyles (2:9–10). And because some were apparently disruptive, they needed to practice restraint (2:11)—not necessarily complete silence, but "quiet" (as the word is translated in 2 Thess. 3:12), since they likely participated in the prayers and other expressive parts of the worship gatherings (compare 1 Cor. 11:5; Eph. 5:19).

Today the message of Christ continues to attract people from a variety of backgrounds. Some, like the Ephesians, need to learn for the first time about worshiping God. Others bring cultural norms and expectations that are worth using in the worship experience, so long as they preserve biblical guidelines such as those that Paul gave to the Ephesians.

apostle uses the Greek word to express the type of teaching found in the Jewish communities from which Paul had come. It was more than the impartation of information to students. It included the call by a rabbi, or teacher, to have his disciples to listen, believe, and practice the words of the teacher. Such teaching was built upon the revelation of God and assumed the functions exercised in the early church by the elders (doctrine, correction, discipline, and reproof; compare 2 Tim. 3:17; 1 Tim. 4:11; 4:16—5:2; 2 Tim. 4:1–4; Titus 2:15; 3:8–11). Generally, those who exercised this responsibility in the early church had the spiritual gift of teaching (compare Rom. 12:7; 1 Cor. 12:28) but not every exercise of this spiritual gift (by men or women) would be, necessarily, over the congregation. **Have authority** (Gk. *authentein*) is not the normal word for authority (which is *exousia*, "to have the right"). The word is found only this one time in the NT and because of this has been the subject of misunderstanding. The generally accepted understanding of *authenteō* in recognized scholarly dictionaries and recent scholarly studies shows with little question that the idea is that women are not to exercise authority over men. The connective **or** (Gk. *oude*) seems to indicate that *teach* is being defined by the term "have authority." Some have wrongly thought that the two terms should be joined and translated "to teach in a domineering manner." Thus, if women teach with a proper attitude, they may (it is said) teach men in the congregation. This introduces a grammatical idea simply not found in this text and one not characteristic of the apostle's writing style. Certainly Paul would not want anyone—men or women—to teach improperly. Moreover, the text nowhere indicates that the apostle is prohibiting the teaching of false doctrine (which would be prohibited for men and women alike). Rather the apostle is prohibiting any teaching of men by women (congregational teaching is obvious in the context, vv. 8–12) or of women being in congregational authority over men. When one examines the 144 NT examples of the same construction found here in v. 12, one discovers that *or* is used for reinforcement or intensification of a concept to which both elements relate (the first specific and the latter general: here teach and exercise authority) *not* to indicate a single idea (namely, teaching in a domineering way). Paul, then, does not disallow the teaching by women because of cultural reasons or the aptitude or education of women. The exhortation relates to theology alone, to the creation order and the fall, where one aspect of the judgment of the woman was for her exercising authority in an area apparently reserved for the husband—a reversal of the creation order (compare Gen. 3:16; 4:7). It seems best to understand this passage as teaching that women may exercise any of the spiritual gifts they have received and developed in a variety of ministries in a local assembly (2 Tim. 3:14, Titus 2:3, 4), other than teaching men, when done under appropriate male (elder) leadership. Women may serve the body of Christ in many types of ministries, but men function as God's official leadership in the local assembly.

2:13, 14 For: Paul offers reasons for the directives of vv. 9–12. **Adam was formed first** refers to Gen. 2:7–25. In God's order of creation (1 Cor. 11:9), Adam was made before Eve. This is an implied reference to the privileges that a firstborn received in ancient society. These privileges were not given on the basis of inherent

---

✠ IN CONTEXT Eve's Legacy

When Paul wrote that Eve "fell into transgression" (1 Tim. 2:14), he was pointing out how easily a person can be led into temptation and sin with disastrous results. In Eve's case, Paul explicitly stated that "Adam was not deceived," but Eve was (compare 2 Cor. 11:3). Was the apostle making a statement about women in general? Opinions differ, but either way it seems clear that he was using Eve to illustrate an important point related to the women in the congregation at Ephesus.

Most women in the first century were not formally educated. In Greece they led relatively isolated lives at home and did not often engage in public discourse. Most of what they knew they learned either from their husbands or from other women. But that made them susceptible to deception. It's no wonder, then, that Paul urged that the Ephesian women not be permitted to teach. In addition to recognizing Adam's priority in creation as a basis for women not teaching men, Paul also wanted them to avoid the error of Eve, who helped to bring sin into the world because she accepted the lies of the serpent.

superiority but instead on being born first, something controlled by God Himself. The second reason for the prohibitions in vv. 9–12 is related to the Fall. **Adam was not deceived** points to the fact that Adam sinned with his eyes open; he knew what he was doing (Rom. 5:12). **woman being deceived:** The verb indicates that Eve was "completely deceived." Paul's argument from creation and the Fall in these verses seem to indicate that the prohibitions in vv. 9–12 are permanent. (Some have argued that Paul was drawing an analogy between creation and the Fall and the present situation in the Ephesian church, where men were teaching and some women were being misled by false teachers, but no passage in 1 Timothy supports this view.)

2:15 saved in childbearing: Some believe this verse refers to the birth of Christ and that the woman is Mary. However, it may refer to the woman's special task of bearing children (Titus 2:3–5). The salvation referred to here is not justification, but daily sanctification. Most likely, Paul is referring to being delivered from the desire to dominate by recognizing one's appropriate place in God's creation order. **If they continue** suggests that this salvation (sanctification) is conditioned upon women's continued walk in the faith, in love, in holiness, and in self-control.

3:1–16 In discussing how to behave in the house of God, Paul now turns to the leader. There are two scriptural officers of the church: the bishop (Gk. *episkopos*), the pastor or overseer today, and the deacon (Gk. *diakonos*). The overseer, the pastor or preacher of the gospel, is to live by the gospel (1 Cor. 9:14). This is his calling. The deacon serves in the church but does not live by this service. He is nowhere told he is called to this as a living. There are no double standards of Christian living. What *ought* to be true of every believer *must* be true of leaders in the house of God. It is very proper to have standards of conduct for leaders in a local church. Here is a good list to go by.

3:1 bishop: This Greek word refers to a person who oversees a congregation. In many NT passages, the Greek words for *bishop* and *elder* are used interchangeably for the same office (Titus 1:5–7).

3:2 Blameless means "not laid hold of." The idea is not that a bishop is sinless but that he displays mature, consistent Christian conduct that gives no reason for anyone to accuse him of anything. **Husband of one wife** literally means "a one-woman kind of man." This expression has been interpreted as a general exclusion from office of all who are sexually immoral or of polygamists, or as referring specifically to those who have remarried after divorce. This is also a qualification of deacons (v. 12).

Temperate means "without wine," sober or clear-headed. **Sober-minded** means that an overseer must have control of his body and mind. It is a balanced state of mind arising out of self-restraint. **Of good behavior** means "orderly." **Hospitable** means "loving strangers." An overseer's home should be open for purposes of ministry. **Able to teach** could also be translated "qualified to teach," or "teachable." Since the passage is about character, it

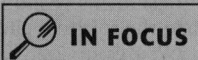

IN FOCUS "bishop"

(Gk. *episkopos*) (3:2; Acts 20:28; Phil. 1:1; Titus 1:7) Strong's #*1985*: The Greek term *episkopos* means "one who oversees." In the NT, elders are described as overseeing a congregation. In Acts 20:17; 20:28 the *elders* of the church at Ephesus are called *overseers*. Elders were responsible for the internal affairs of the church; and there seem to have been several elders in positions of responsibility in any given congregation (Acts 14:23; Titus 1:5–7). After NT times, it became the custom to appoint one elder as the presiding elder and to give him the title of *bishop*.

seems best to understand this qualification as being teachable, a necessity for a man of God (see 5:17; 2 Tim. 2:24; Titus 1:9 for the requirement that an elder should be able to teach).

3:3 Not given to wine means "not addicted to wine." **Not violent** means "not a striker." An elder should not be prone to violence or to striking others. **not greedy for money:** An overseer is not to have a materialistic attitude toward money or possessions. Part of this qualification is a warning to those in church leadership concerning proper management of God's finances. **Not quarrelsome** means "without fighting." This is the quality of being peaceable. A bishop or overseer should contend for the faith without being contentious. **Not covetous** means "not a lover of silver" (6:9). Note that this is a second warning about money. Certain Ephesian elders were receiving financial support from the ministry (5:17, 18). Paul exhorted them not to allow their desire for money to become a priority.

3:4 Rules means "stands before" or "manages." **his own house:** An elder must manage his own family well. His children must submit to his leadership with **reverence** or respect.

3:5 If a man is unable to lead in his family, he will not be able to **take care** of the church. A

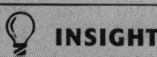

The Character Factor

In 1 Tim. 3:3, Paul outlines the criteria that qualify people for leadership in the church community. All of the items mentioned have to do with character. God seems far more concerned with the personal integrity of leaders than with their education, eloquence, or charisma.

Without question, the standards are high, but that doesn't imply a higher standard for church leaders than "ordinary" Christians. *All* believers are called to these same high standards of Christlikeness. Paul is not creating a class of the spiritually elite here. He is simply indicating that the church should select its leadership from among people who are generally living up to the ideals of the gospel.

shift from *rule* to *care* emphasizes the tenderness of the shepherding function of an elder in the church.

3:6 Novice means "newly planted." An elder is not to be a new believer. Being a new convert could put him in danger of **being puffed up with pride.** Such pride is described as the **condemnation** of **the devil** (Ezek. 28:11–19).

3:7 good testimony: An elder must have a good reputation in the community (Acts 6:3). A non-Christian should not be able to **reproach** or insult an elder. The elder's good testimony avoids the **snare of the devil,** the traps or pitfalls of Satan (2 Tim. 2:26).

3:8–13 Likewise: Similar qualifications apply to **deacons,** who were also ministers in the church. They had special responsibility for visiting and ministering to those in need. The seven chosen in Acts 8:3–6 to relieve the twelve apostles of distributing food to the poor may have been the first deacons (Acts 6:2–4).

3:8 Deacons fill a second leadership position in the local assembly. The Greek word for *deacon* means "servant." Although the word itself is not used in Acts 6, the seven godly men selected there to distribute food to widows appear to be the forerunners of this office and ministry. This verse and Phil. 1:1 indicate that the office of deacon was an established office in the early church. **not double-tongued:** This phrase speaks of the dangers of gossip, specifically saying one thing to one person and another to someone else.

3:9 The mystery of the faith is the doctrine clarified in v. 16 as the incarnation of God in the flesh. The Son of God becoming flesh to serve humanity (Mark 10:43–45) is the embodiment of service.

3:10 tested: Deacons are to be evaluated, observed, and approved before being appointed to office. Their character in this approval process is to be **blameless** or "without accusation."

3:11 Likewise, their wives: The similar phrasing of v. 8 seems to indicate that Paul was speaking of another office in the local body, the deaconess. These women, like deacons (vv. 8–10, 12, 13), served under the leadership of the elders. However some interpret this verse as referring to the wives of deacons and not to an office.

3:12, 13 A twofold encouragement is given to deacons who serve well. First, they will receive a good **standing,** or respect. This relates primarily to their standing in the congregation, but also to their greater rewards for service at the judgment seat of Christ (Rom. 14:10; 1 Cor. 3:10–15, 2 Cor. 5:10). Second, they develop **boldness in the faith.** Faithful servants develop confidence and assurance in their Christian walk.

3:14 Paul desires to join Timothy at Ephesus (1:3).

3:15 Paul's purpose in writing his first letter to Timothy was to give him instructions on how a local assembly and its leadership should function. **church of the living God:** The church universal is manifested in local assemblies around the world. **the pillar and ground of the truth:** Misconduct and disorder in the local church weaken the support of God's truth in the world. Godly men and women gathering together in local assemblies to worship the Lord produce an orderly church, a church that testifies to others of the truth of God.

3:16 This verse contains an early hymn of the church. The hymn is three couplets. **Manifested in the flesh** refers to Christ's incarnation, the fact that Jesus became man (John 1:14). **Justified in the Spirit** refers to the Holy Spirit's work in Jesus' ministry and resurrection (Matt. 3:15–17; John 16:7, 10; Rom. 1:4). **Seen by angels** refers to the angelic witness of Christ's ministry and resurrection. **Preached among the Gentiles** refers to the proclamation of Christ to the nations (Col. 1:23). **Believed on in the world** refers to the response of individuals to God's plan of salvation (1 Cor.

1:18–25). **Received up in glory** refers to the Ascension; Christ is seated in God's presence in heaven (Acts 1:9; Heb. 1:3, 4).

4:1 Paul begins a series of instructions specifically for Timothy. **the Spirit expressly says:** Paul may be referring to various prophecies inspired by the Holy Spirit concerning defection from God's truth (Dan. 7:25; 8:23; Matt. 24:4–12), or he might be speaking of a revelation the Spirit had given to him. **Depart** here means literally "to stand away from." There are various seasons in which **some** people will depart from their faith (1:19, 20). The reference here is not to a loss of salvation but to a failure to walk obediently (John 19:25–27; 1 Cor. 3:1–3; 11:29, 30). The impact of satanic attack and influence is described in vv. 1–3. **Doctrines of demons** refers to following occult practices.

4:2 conscience seared: How can they believe such things? As your finger is numb when it has been burned with a hot iron, so too their consciences are numbed by the searing of sin.

4:3, 4 The false teachers at Ephesus evidently disparaged the material world as evil, which became a central doctrine of the full-grown Gnosticism of the second century. In Gen. 1:31, God's creation is called "very good." Believers are to enjoy the **good** things God creates and gives them to manage.

4:5 Sanctified means "set apart." Marriage, eating, and possessions are, in reality, spiritual issues. They are to be enjoyed as the believer recognizes their proper purposes before God.

4:6–6:21 Paul has been instructing Timothy how he should conduct himself "in the house of God" (3:15). Here he deals with Timothy's personal life (4:12–16; 5:23–25; 6:11–16, 20, 21) and discusses how he should treat various people (5:1, 2), especially **widows** (5:3–16), **elders** (5:17–22), **bondservants** (6:1, 2), the contentious (6:3–5), and the **rich** (6:6–10, 17–19).

4:6 Continued growth in the church occurs through **words of faith** and instruction in **good doctrine.** Sound doctrine is the basis of a healthy ministry and correct practice.

4:7 Exercise is the normal term for the physical training of Greek athletes. True spirituality requires one to train at godliness in one's walk with the Lord.

4:8 Profits a little contrasts the short-term value of physical exercise with the long-term benefits of **godliness** for **all things.** Discipline in godliness affects both the present and future life of the believer. The present aspect includes obedience and a life of purpose (John 10:10). The future aspect involves greater rewards in the coming reign of Christ (1 Cor. 3:10–15; 2 Cor. 5:9, 10).

4:9 This is . . . worthy of all acceptance and that no one can deny. The wise become doers of the Word.

4:10, 11 Savior of all men describes God as the One who gives life, breath, and existence to all. **Especially of those who believe** draws a contrast between God's common grace to all and His special saving grace to those who trust Him as their Savior.

4:12 Youth was a term applied to men until they were forty. Timothy might have been between thirty-five and forty years old at this time. The antidote for his *youth* was his life. He was to set an example in six areas: (1) **in word,** meaning conversation; (2) **in conduct,** or

---

 **IN LIFE**   **Good Advice for a Novice**

Timothy was young in age and relatively untested as a trainee under Paul, his mentor. His pastorate in Ephesus was his first solo assignment. So Paul offered him some seasoned wisdom and perspective:

- Tough times are to be expected in a broken world (1 Tim. 4:1–3).
- We need to accept God's gifts with thanksgiving (4:4, 5).
- Affirm the truth with others who share your faith (4:6).
- Avoid getting caught up in the folklore that occurs in every environment (4:7). It's not that stories are bad, but always search out the truth and make it your trademark (4:8–11).
- Overcome the skepticism of others with the basics like love, edifying conversation, and purity (4:12).
- Work on your own skills and abilities with diligence (4:13, 14).

Over the long haul, perspectives like these will hold one in good stead.

behavior; (3) **in love,** which is the love of God; (4) **in spirit,** the attitude or power of the Holy Spirit; (5) **in faith,** meaning trust in God; and (6) **in purity,** both in sexual matters and in thoughts (5:2). These godly elements are not only for the young, but should be desired and practiced by all. These qualities should be developed early in a Christian's life.

4:13 Give attention (Gk. *proseche*) is a present command for personal preparation and diligence. Three specific areas of responsibility in the house of God are defined. **Reading** is a command for public reading of the Scriptures (Acts 13:15). **Exhortation** is an encouragement to obey the Scriptures. **Doctrine** is formal teaching and instruction in the Word of God (2:12).

4:14 Paul encourages Timothy to be diligent. The **gift** is the spiritual gift Timothy received from Christ (Eph. 4:7, 8). **by prophecy:** Timothy's gift was given through a prophetic message (1:18) and **with the laying on of . . . hands,** probably at Lystra (Acts 16:1). The laying on of hands signified the elders' commission and recognition of God's work in Timothy's life. Paul himself was part of the group that laid their hands on Timothy (2 Tim. 1:6).

4:15 Meditate (Gk. *meleta*) is a present command for Timothy continually to practice Paul's instruction. **Give yourself** (Gk. *isthi*) is another present command. Paul's care for Timothy, his "son in the faith" (1:2), is evident. He was instructing Timothy so that his **progress** would be **evident** to everyone in the church.

4:16 Take heed (Gk. *epeche*) is another present command alerting Timothy to himself, his character, and actions along with **the doctrine** (Gk. *tei didaskalia*), teaching. **Continue** (Gk. *epimene*) is a present command to stay or remain in the things Paul has written. **Save . . . yourself** is not a reference to justification by works but to sanctification, the Christian's daily walk of faith (Mark 8:34–38; John 12:25, 26). **Those who hear you** refers to the members in the church to whom Timothy was reading, exhorting, and teaching.

5:1–25 Paul encourages Timothy in various relationships in the church: older and younger men, older and younger women, widows, and elders.

5:1 Rebuke (Gk. *epiplēssō*) means to strike sharply. Younger men should avoid sharply reprimanding older men.

5:2 All purity is a word of caution to young men. They must respect the purity of the younger women as the purity of a sister.

5:3 Honor is a command to show respect, a respect demonstrated by one's attitude and through financial support (vv. 4, 8). **Widows** are those who have family to help support them (vv. 4, 16); the one who is **really a widow** is one without family support. If this type of personal concern toward family were exercised by

---

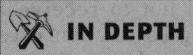 **IN DEPTH** | **Widows in the Household**

The fundamental social institution of the Greco-Roman world was the household. The ancient household included far more people than the modern nuclear family of a husband, wife, and two and one-third children. Everyone involved in the "family business" under the rule of a male administrator, called the "father," was part of the household. Thus, the Greco-Roman household consisted of relatives plus various dependents: the father's wife, his slaves, children, as well as clients—those who gave the father honor and influence in exchange for material favors.

Households, particularly the fathers, ranked themselves socially in terms of honor, prestige, and influence. The more honor a father received, the more prestige and influence he gathered. Wealth, therefore, was not important to accumulate in order to gain more wealth. Wealth was important so that a father might parade his honor. Wealth enabled a father to lavish gifts on his dependents, thereby making more people honor their father as their benefactor.

One household member who especially needed protection was the widow. In NT times, widows had virtually no means of supporting themselves. The early church felt responsible to care for Christian widows, but problems arose in ministering to their needs. As new structures and guidelines had to be developed, the church eventually distinguished between widows who really needed support and those who should be commended to the care of their household (1 Tim. 5:3–5, 8). A Christian father who did not provide for a widow of his household was deemed "worse than an unbeliever" (5:8). Even in non-Christian households of the Greco-Roman world, the head of the household supported poor widows.

Christians today, especially toward parents whom they are to honor, there would be little need for government welfare.

5:4 Family members are instructed to care for widows. **Piety** is respect, reverence, or obligation. **repay:** Honoring our **parents** includes caring for them physically and financially as they grow older. In effect, we are returning the time and energy they gave to us while we were young.

5:5 Trusts means to have hope or confidence in God.

5:6 This verse identifies widows living ungodly lives, who are not to be supported by the church. **Lives in pleasure** refers to a life of comfort focused on one's own desires. **Dead** means separated from fellowship (James 2:26). Widows in the church who choose to live for themselves are separating themselves from fellowship with God and the church.

5:7 blameless: Maintain a good reputation for themselves and for the church.

5:8 A believer is to **provide** for **his own** (his near relatives) and **his household** (his immediate family). Failure to provide for one's family is equal to denial of **the faith** (Ex. 20:12; Mark 7:9–12; Eph. 6:2). If a Christian cannot even care for his or her own family, how can that person sincerely love and care for others? **worse than an unbeliever:** Some unbelievers take better care of their families than believers do.

5:9 Taken into the number means to write down on a list. The list referred to here was most likely a list of widows whom the church was to assist. Widows who were enrolled on the list were to be at least **sixty years old** and **the wife of one man.** Some have maintained that this list was an official order of widows. These widows were to pray for the church (v. 5) and practice works of charity (v. 10).

5:10 Children refers either to the widow's own children or possibly to orphans. **Lodged strangers** indicates an attitude of hospitality. **Washed the saints' feet** demonstrates a servant's heart. **Relieved the afflicted** suggests giving aid to those facing adversity. **Followed every good work** indicates a commitment to serving.

5:11, 12 Refuse is a command to not put **younger widows,** those less than sixty years old, on the list of widows to be supported by the church. The reason for this refusal is that younger widows may **grow wanton,** which means to experience sexual desire, and thus **desire to marry,** presumably an unbeliever, since the marriage is said to be outside their **first faith.**

5:13, 14 It is best for those younger widows to remarry (1 Cor. 7:39, 40). Otherwise, they might become **idle,** without work. **gossips and busybodies:** Paul was concerned that younger widows would not have enough to do, and thus would bother everyone else with worthless talk or even harmful and divisive words.

5:15 Some of these younger widows had ignored the biblical pattern for remarriage and had **turned aside after Satan.**

5:16 Responsibility for support rests first upon the family (vv. 4, 8). When Christian families meet their own responsibilities, the church is able to care for those who have no family resources.

5:17–20 Paul now addresses the topic of elders.

5:17 The primary function of **elders** is to **rule well.** The word **honor** was used in ancient writings outside the Bible to refer to financial remuneration. **Double** refers to two types of honor: (1) respect for ruling well and (2) adequate pay for their diligent care of the church (1 Cor. 9:1–14). **Those who labor in the word and doctrine** are those elders who preach and teach the Scriptures.

5:18 For the Scripture says: With two quotations, one from Deut. 25:4 and the other from the words of Christ in Luke 10:7, Paul provides proof for the principle of providing adequate financial care for elders. The Luke passage is especially noteworthy because it shows that Paul considered that Gospel to be Scripture along with the Book of Deuteronomy.

5:19 An elder is protected against malicious attacks by the command not to **receive an accusation,** a charge or legal accusation, except when it comes from **two or three witnesses** (Deut. 19:15; Matt. 18:16). Charges against elders are to be factual, not based on a single opinion or rumor.

5:20 Those who are sinning refers to elders who fail in their leadership, whether in the local church, in their social life, or in their home life. **Rebuke** is a command to bring a sin to light, to expose it before **all,** including other elders and the church body. **the rest also may fear:** The public rebuke of a sinning elder is to serve as a warning to other believers. God's discipline is consistent from leadership to laity. Sin is a serious matter in the lives of believers, especially those in leadership (1 Pet. 4:17). When leaders sin with impunity, church members might erroneously start justifying their own sins.

5:21 I charge you: Discipline must be exercised in the church. But it should be done without **prejudice** (personal bias) or **partiality** (preferential treatment).

5:22 This verse warns against too **hastily** restoring a leader who has fallen. Correction in

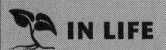 **IN LIFE** | **The Challenge of Contentment**

Paul's young disciple Timothy had his hands full in Ephesus. The apostle had left Timothy in that city to oversee the organization of the church. Timothy was to provide consistent teaching, help the church choose leaders, and model personal integrity as a leader.

Paul's first letter to Timothy contains both direction and encouragement for Timothy. Among his memorable objectives Paul included the following: "Now godliness with contentment is great gain" (6:6). Obviously, the absence of both godliness and contentment would indicate great loss, especially in the Christian life. Godliness without contentment would be a joyless and legalistic righteousness. Contentment without godliness describes a person sadly disconnected from God's truth.

What kind of life was Paul describing when he speaks of godly contentment? Paul describes such a person as having a firm understanding of the passing nature of life. The things of this world are here when we arrive and are left behind when we leave. Neither godliness nor contentment can be found in accumulating them. Things beyond God's provision of our basic needs ("food and clothing," 6:8) can be enjoyed without becoming a necessity. Paul understood that if godliness (our desire to see God's character reproduced in us) and contentment (our acceptance of God's will in our lives) depend on our environment or circumstances, both will always be unstable.

Elsewhere, Paul indicates that godly contentment must be a learned response (Phil. 4:11–13). Developing godly contentment lies well beyond our abilities. That is why along with Paul we must appeal to the right source for such a character trait: "I can do all things through Christ who strengthens me" (Phil. 4:13).

love and restoration to fellowship should occur as soon as possible, but restoration to leadership should not be made without time and biblical evaluation. Another interpretation of this verse suggests that it is a command to evaluate carefully anyone being considered for leadership, not just former leaders who want to be restored (3:1–14). **Keep yourself pure** is a caution for Timothy not to share responsibility for another person's sins by restoring or appointing someone who is not qualified.

5:23 Paul recalls Timothy's inclination toward a stomach disorder. This could certainly be the case if he were involved in the discipline of an elder, especially in light of his apparent timidity! The apostle encouraged Timothy to use **wine** as a medical help for his **stomach's sake** and **frequent infirmities.** Our physical condition often affects clear judgment. The wisdom of avoiding major decisions until feeling well is well-advised.

5:24, 25 cannot be hidden: Unnoticed good works will become evident, if not in this life then at the judgment seat of Christ (1 Cor. 3:10–15).

6:1 Bondservants . . . under the yoke refers to believers who are slaves. Believing slaves were to give their unbelieving masters **all honor** or respect. The life and actions of a Christian slave were to represent the Christian faith and Christ Himself. In same way we should watch how we act at work. It is extremely important, for our actions testify to the reality of Christ's power in our lives.

6:2 Teach: Paul moves to the conclusion with a final warning for Timothy to instruct his congregation in order to combat the false teachings that were infiltrating that church (vv. 4, 5). The Greek word for *teach* means the formal presentation of doctrine (2:12), while the Greek word for **exhort** implies less formal instruction, a "coming alongside" to guide. **These things** is probably best understood as the contents of this letter.

6:3, 4 If anyone teaches otherwise: Here Paul refers to false teachers. He contrasts their "sick" teaching with the **wholesome words** ("sound doctrine" in 1:10) of the **Lord Jesus Christ.** These false teachers were more interested in theory and debate than putting the truth into practice. They had a morbid desire to argue over words.

6:5 Destitute of the truth describes the uselessness of speculative religious arguments. These false teachers were using religion for their own financial **gain.** Probably they were hoping that their debates on religion would gain them a following and financial support. Sound doctrine and exhortation are the basis of a healthy church—not glitz, glamour, and greediness of false teachers.

6:6 True gain is in godliness with **contentment** (Gk. *autarkeia*), or "sufficiency of life needs."

6:7 This is the reason we should be content—we will all die eventually!

6:8 The two physical needs of believers are **food,** or nourishment, and **clothing** and shelter. These two areas with godliness provide the basis of being truly **content** (Phil. 4:12).

6:9 Two types of people are described in relation to wealth (v. 17). The first type are those who **desire to be rich.** An inner lack of godliness and contentment leaves a vacuum filled with greed. This greed drives people into **temptation,** snares, and **foolish and harmful lusts. Drown** literally means to drag to the bottom. Paul was painting a graphic word picture of a greedy person drowning under the tremendous weight of material desires. **Destruction and perdition** are synonymous with ruin and irretrievable loss. This loss may be experienced in this life, as through a wrong purpose for living, or it may be experienced in the afterlife if material desires lead a person away from Christ (1:16; 2:4; Luke 16:1–14).

6:10 Money in and of itself is not a problem, but the **love of money** is. Love of money is **a root,** though not *the* root, of **evil.** The love of money can drive a person into all types of evil. **Greediness** may cause a believer even to stray **from the faith.** Christians may be blinded by greed and materialism to such a degree that they break away from their faith. **many sorrows:** A life focused on material things produces only pain.

6:11 Paul issues a powerful warning against materialism. **Flee** is a strong command. **Pursue** is a command to hunt or chase after some object. **Righteousness, godliness,** and **faith** are character qualities. **Love, patience,** and **gentleness** are fruit of the Spirit-controlled life (Gal. 5:22). Men and women of God should pursue godliness, not materialism, with all of their being.

6:12 lay hold on eternal life: Eternal life is viewed as a free gift (John 3:16; Eph. 2:8–10), a present experience (John 10:10), and a reward (Mark 10:29, 30; Luke 18:29, 30). Here Paul is not speaking of Timothy's salvation, but instead of his fruitfulness in this life and his rewards in the next. **The good confession** is Timothy's call and ministry. Paul was urging Timothy to continue his ministry of preaching the Word of God.

6:13 urge: Charge, or command. Once again Paul presents the seriousness of what he had said. Timothy is to keep this charge, not for Paul's sake, but before God who **gives** or "preserves life" and Christ Jesus, who gave a good witness before **Pontius Pilate.** Pilate said, "I find no fault in Him at all" (John 18:38).

6:14 commandment: In the immediate context, Paul was exhorting Timothy to avoid empty religious argumentation (6:3–5) and the greed of materialism (6:6–10). Timothy was to remain faithful to Christ until He appeared again. Thus, Paul was encouraging Timothy to focus on the return of Christ, not on temporal gain. The imminent return of Christ should be a motive for godly living (2 Pet. 3:10–16; 1 John 2:28).

6:15, 16 God will **manifest** the return of Christ **in His own time.** This will happen at a specific point in time that Jesus declared was known only to the Father (Acts 1:6, 7). The last half of v. 15 and all of v. 16 form a doxology of praise to the Lord Jesus. **Immortality** may also

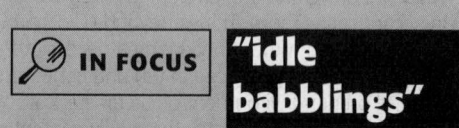

IN FOCUS **"idle babblings"**

(Gk. *kenophōnia*) (6:20; 2 Tim. 2:16) Strong's #2757: This Greek word literally means "empty words." In Paul's writings, the Greek word *kenos* expresses the ultimate emptiness of all that is not filled with spiritual meaning. In other words, human achievement amounts to nothing if it does not come from the will of God. Nothing comes from this nothingness; it is futility. Paul uses a derivative of this word to describe the hollow words (6:20; 2 Tim. 2:16) spoken by Judaizers trying to entice the believers with their foolish philosophies (Eph. 5:6; Col. 2:8). But the teaching committed to Paul and the apostles was not futile; it would last throughout eternity because it originated in God's unchanging will (Matt. 5:18; 1 Cor. 15:12–15).

be translated "without death." Jesus is God and therefore can never die.

6:17 those who are rich: Paul has already condemned those who are attempting to become rich through the ministry (vv. 6–10). The second group of people Paul addresses in regard to wealth (v. 9) are those who are already wealthy. Paul encourages Timothy to tell the rich not to be high-minded or proud and not to **trust in uncertain riches.** Only **the living God** can provide for all of our needs.

6:18 Those with wealth are commanded to recognize God as the true source of their wealth and to be generous with their riches. The material blessings of God are to be enjoyed and used for the advancement of His kingdom, not for self-centered living.

6:19 Storing up may also be translated "treasuring up," a phrase similar to Jesus' challenge in Matt. 6:19–21 to lay up treasure in heaven. A believer's daily obedience to God builds a **good foundation** for the **time to come.** The Scriptures teach that a believer's works will be evaluated to see what his or her life in Christ has produced (1 Cor. 3:10–15).

6:20 The Greek term for **committed** is found only here and in 2 Tim. 1:12, 14. The deposit that Timothy had to guard was the truth revealed in this letter. **Knowledge** is the Greek word *gnōsis,* from which the word Gnosticism is derived. Evidently an early form of Gnosticism had infiltrated the Ephesian church. This heresy taught that salvation came through the "knowledge" of spiritual mysteries. In unequivocal terms, Paul warns Timothy not to be caught up in this false teaching (1:3, 4; 6:3–5).

6:21 First Timothy closes as it begins (1:2), with an emphasis on God's **grace.** The Greek word for **you** is plural, perhaps indicating that this letter was to be read to the church in Ephesus.

The Second Epistle to

Timothy

■

⸻

HEN DEATH NEARS, PRIORITIES CHANGE. IN LIGHT of mortality, what used to seem significant may dim in comparison to one's ultimate fate. That is why we listen to a person's "last words." When all is said and done, everyone wants to know what gave that person hope in the face of death. Second Timothy is Paul's "last words." From a cold, lonely Roman prison, the aged apostle Paul wrote his final

instructions to his protégé Timothy. Paul knew that this letter might well be his final contact with Timothy; his execution was most likely imminent. He implored Timothy to come quickly to his side. But in case he did not make it, Paul imparted his last words of encouragement to his "son" in the faith.

Paul's primary purpose for writing this letter was to offer final instructions to Timothy regarding the Christian life. Second Timothy has an intensely personal nature and tone. One senses Paul's strong love and concern for Timothy. Paul encourages his close friend to use his spiritual gifts. He writes to strengthen Timothy's loyalty to Christ in the face of the suffering and persecution that would come. The apostle challenges Timothy to handle the Word of God accurately, faithfully instructing others in the truths of the faith. Warnings and instructions are given concerning how a believer should relate to the world in times of apostasy. In the closing chapter, Paul offers Timothy his final word of advice: "Preach the word! Be ready in season and out of season." This was Paul's own mission, to preach the gospel to the Gentiles; now he was passing it on to his beloved son in the faith, Timothy.

Paul's second purpose for writing this letter was to urge Timothy to join him in Rome. Paul knew that he was soon to die. He longed to see and have fellowship with his child in the faith one last time.

Paul was well aware that hardships and conflict are a part of Christian ministry. One of the essential characteristics of a faithful servant of Christ is endurance in the midst of difficulties. To encourage Timothy in this virtue, the apostle reminds him that Jesus Christ is "of the seed of David" and "was raised from the dead" (2:8). Mention of the seed of David links Christ with the Davidic covenant (2 Sam. 7:11–16), which states that a Son of David will rule on his throne forever. Furthermore, Christ has been resurrected; He is alive. The promise of ruling and reigning with Him (2:11–13) is set before Timothy as a motive for faithful endurance in ministry. A special crown will be given to those who faithfully serve the Lord and wait for His return (4:8).

Chapter 3 develops the theme of apostasy in the latter days. Paul warns Timothy that difficulties are coming for believers, and he instructs him about how Christians are to respond and behave. Jesus had predicted that such times would come (John 15:18–25; 16:33; 17:15–18), and Paul himself had referred previously to these times (1 Thess. 3:1–8). Although he would not live to see these dreadful days, Paul still cared enough to urge Timothy to be bold in the work of the Lord, even in the midst of troubling times.

The Book of Acts ends with Paul under house arrest in Rome (Acts 28). But many scholars believe that Paul was acquitted, as he had expected (Phil. 1:19). From sporadic evidence in the Pastoral Epistles, we can trace Paul's travels after his imprisonment. He probably visited Crete (Titus 1:5), Ephesus (1 Tim. 1:3), Macedonia, and perhaps Colosse (Philem. 22) and Spain (Rom. 15:24). Timothy traveled with Paul to Ephesus and was left there to confront the false teachers that were infiltrating the church in that city (1 Tim. 1:3).

Many believe that Paul was put in prison when Nero began his campaign of persecution, shortly after Rome burned in A.D. 64. Nero blamed the Christians for starting the fire, and executed many of them with extreme cruelty. Soon afterward, the apostle Peter died for his faith by being crucified upside down, according to the church father Origen. As Paul penned his second letter to Timothy, he was aware of his coming death (4:6–8). A number of believers had deserted him (4:16), and only Luke was with him at the writing of this letter (4:11). At the end of the letter, one can sense Paul's concern. He implores Timothy: "Be diligent to come to me quickly" (4:9). Paul did not want to leave this earth without seeing Timothy and Mark to give them some final words of wisdom (4:9–13).

Paul's concern for Timothy arose out of their long relationship with each other. Ever since the beginning of the second missionary journey, Timothy had been close to Paul, assisting him in his ministry, acting as his liaison, and learning from his godly example. Timothy's devout mother, Eunice, and grandmother, Lois, had provided him with a grounding in the Hebrew Scriptures on which Paul could build (2 Tim. 1:5; 3:14, 15). Although evidently Timothy was slightly timid because of his young age (1:7; 1 Tim. 4:12), Paul developed his son in the faith by placing more and more responsibility on his shoulders. Timothy had functioned as Paul's representative to Thessalonica (1 Thess. 3:2) and Corinth (1 Cor. 4:17). But leaving Timothy at Ephesus was a major step for Paul; as a concerned mentor, he wrote a letter to Timothy repeatedly charging him to remain faithful to the essentials of the Christian faith (1 Tim. 1:18; 5:12–16, 21; 6:11–13). Paul had served as Timothy's spiritual mentor throughout his life. Now as he neared his death Paul wanted to see him one last time. And if that could not be, he wanted at least to give Timothy some final words of encouragement.

The author of 2 Timothy identifies himself as Paul (1:1). Other remarks in the book are characteristic of Paul's ministry (3:10, 11; 4:10, 11, 19, 20). Many of the early church fathers such as Polycarp, Justin Martyr, and Irenaeus support Pauline authorship. For an explanation of the challenges to Pauline authorship of 2 Timothy, see the Introduction to 1 Timothy. Most of these challenges are based on the erroneous assumption that the theology and Greek style of this letter can only fit the context of the second century.

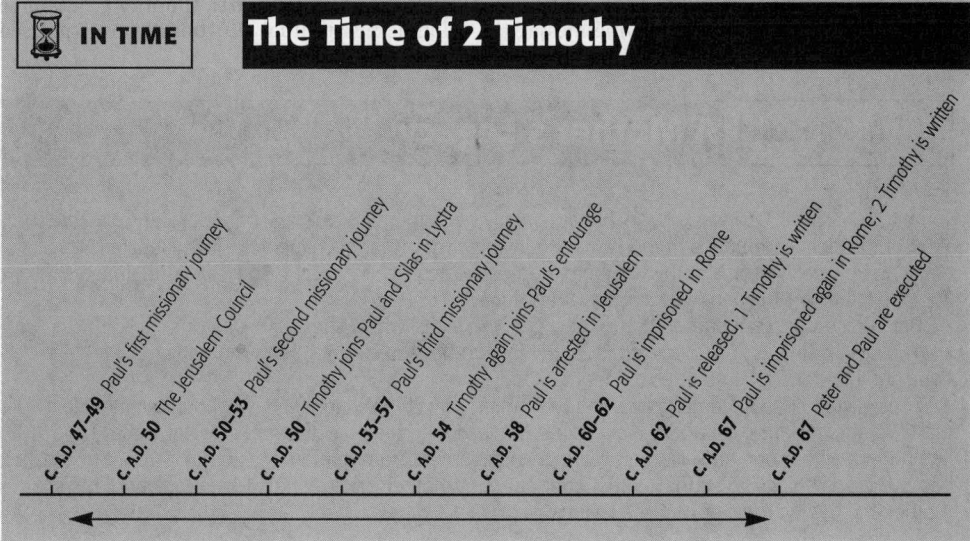

IN TIME

The Time of 2 Timothy

c. A.D. 47–49 Paul's first missionary journey

c. A.D. 50 The Jerusalem Council

c. A.D. 50–53 Paul's second missionary journey

c. A.D. 50 Timothy joins Paul and Silas in Lystra

c. A.D. 53–57 Paul's third missionary journey

c. A.D. 54 Timothy again joins Paul's entourage

c. A.D. 58 Paul is arrested in Jerusalem

c. A.D. 60–62 Paul is imprisoned in Rome

c. A.D. 62 Paul is released; 1 Timothy is written

c. A.D. 67 Paul is imprisoned again in Rome; 2 Timothy is written

c. A.D. 67 Peter and Paul are executed

Many scholars believe that 2 Timothy was written during a second imprisonment of Paul in Rome (1:8, 16, 17; 4:6–13). According to the fourth-century church historian Eusebius, Paul was martyred during Nero's regime, some time before A.D. 68. Since this letter was written immediately before Paul's death, it was probably written around A.D. 67.

Outline

I. Encouragement in ministry 1:1–18
  A. Using spiritual gifts 1:1–7
  B. Suffering for the gospel 1:8–18
II. Examples in ministry 2:1–26
  A. Comparisons to a soldier, an athlete, and a farmer 2:1–13
  B. Challenge to handle God's Word accurately 2:14–26
III. Exhortations in ministry 3:1–17
  A. Warnings of apostasy 3:1–9
  B. Ways to face apostasy 3:10–17
IV. Encouragements in ministry 4:1–22
  A. Preach the Word 4:1–5
  B. Final exhortations and encouragements 4:6–22

Commentary

1:1 Paul speaks of himself in 1 Timothy as **an apostle** "by the commandment of God" (1 Tim. 1:1). In 2 Timothy he calls himself an apostle **by the will of God** (2 Cor. 1:1; Eph. 1:1; Col. 1:1). **according to the promise of life:** Paul considers himself a bearer of a life-giving message.

This message of life stands in ironic contrast to the fact that Paul was writing from a Roman prison, facing his execution. The characteristic phrase **in Christ,** found in other Pauline letters, also appears in this letter, further indicating that it came from Paul.

1:2 beloved son: In his first letter to Timothy, Paul referred to him as a "true son in the faith" (1 Tim. 1:2). Paul's deep love and concern for this younger man of God is shown throughout this letter.

1:3 I serve is a priestly phrase often associated with worship. **Forefathers** were the patriarchs of the faith: Abraham, Isaac, and Jacob. Paul had a great love for Israel (Rom. 9:1–5). The reason he connects himself with Israel's forefathers may be to demonstrate that he is not advocating a new religion but one of which the godly of the past are also a part. **remember you in my prayers:** Although he was most likely held in a cold and damp prison (4:13), the aged apostle was still worshiping God and offering prayers on behalf of Timothy. Christian service and worship go hand in hand in ministry. No matter what their circumstances, believers should pray to their heavenly Father, committing everything to His loving hands.

1:4 desiring to see you: Paul longed to see Timothy, possibly because the apostle realized his life would end soon (4:6–17).

1:5 The word translated **genuine faith** means "unhypocritical." Paul rejoices when he recalls Timothy's faithful **grandmother Lois** and **mother Eunice,** whose name means "Good Victory." The prayers, witness, and faith of his godly mother and grandmother were central factors in the spiritual development of Timothy (1 Tim. 2:15).

1:6 stir up the gift: Timothy is urged to rekindle his spiritual gift (this idea is expressed

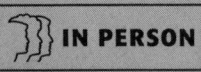 **IN PERSON** | **A Mother's Legacy**

Eunice (2 Tim. 1:5) was Jewish, but apparently her father was not very orthodox: he violated one of the clear commands of the Law in arranging a match for his daughter with a Gentile (Acts 16:1). Later, when Timothy was born, he wasn't circumcised (16:3). So it seems that neither Eunice's father nor husband were observant of Judaism.

But Eunice was. Paul praised her for her "genuine faith," which she shared in common with Lois, her mother (2 Tim. 1:5). Eunice imparted that faith to her son, Timothy, and more than anyone else equipped him for a lifetime of usefulness for God.

Eunice is an encouragement for every woman faced with the daunting task of nurturing the spiritual life of her children, especially if she can't count on the help of a strong male. Eunice may have had no formal religious education and little encouragement from her family, except for Lois. But she had two crucial things going for her that offer hope for mothers today—the inherent power of being a mother and the dynamic power of a loving God.

in the negative in 1 Tim. 4:14). The desire to discover, develop, and deploy our specific spiritual gifts should be like a fire blazing within us. The constant struggle of Christians is to be diligent about our work for God and not to slacken our pace in this spiritual race. We need to make a conscious effort to exercise our gift for the common good of the body of Christ.

1:7 The Holy Spirit is the One who gives us spiritual gifts and empowers us to use them. God's Spirit does not impart **fear** or cowardice,

INSIGHT

The Spirit of Power

Second Timothy 1:6, 7 offers both encouragement and exhortation. Paul links power—the ability to make things happen—with love and a sound mind. Conversely, power exercised without love and wisdom is inevitably destructive.

but **power, love,** and **a sound mind,** or "self-control." The Spirit imparts power for the various circumstances of ministry. The love the Spirit gives to us should be directed toward other individuals. Furthermore, as we use our spiritual gifts to build up the church, we should exercise self-control, using our abilities only at the appropriate times.

1:8 Timothy is encouraged not to be **ashamed** or shrink back from the **testimony of our Lord.** *Testimony* is the witness of the Lord; the Greek term is the source of the English word *martyr.* Church tradition says that most of the apostles died as martyrs. Paul is concerned that in the face of vehement opposition Timothy might be afraid to witness. **Share with me in the sufferings** indicates that at times a faithful witness for the Lord will involve adversity. Paul's call for boldness in vv. 7–9 may indicate that Timothy was timid. Every once in a while, he needed a gentle push to be bold.

1:9 God's saving and calling of believers is **not according to . . . works.** It is impossible for people to earn their way into heaven. Salvation is according to God's **own purpose** or sovereign plan (Rom. 8:28–30; Eph. 1:11). **Grace** is God's unearned favor. The Lord called us and saved us **in Christ Jesus before time began.**

1:10 The manifestation of God's plan and grace has been **revealed,** or brought to light, in the **appearing of our Savior Jesus Christ. abolished death:** Fear of dying might have caused believers to shrink from testifying about

their faith. The Greek term translated **life** is typically used of eternal life in the NT. God's life, unlike the life of humans, is immortal; He cannot die. Through their faith in Christ, believers have inherited eternal life. We have nothing to fear, not even death. Therefore, we can proclaim with boldness our trust in Christ.

1:11 Paul's mission for the gospel was three-fold: **preacher, apostle,** and **teacher** (1 Tim. 2:7).

1:12 Paul's confidence in the gospel and his Savior enabled him to suffer without any shame. The phrase **whom I have believed** expresses Paul's unshakable trust in his Savior. **What I have committed** does not refer to something Paul had done for Christ, but to something he had entrusted to Him, like a deposit in a bank. This speaks not of Paul's confidence in himself but of Christ's trustworthiness. Paul was certain that God would **keep** his deposit, his life and the eternal rewards of his ministry. The apostle was preparing for imminent death, but in spite of this he was hopeful. He had spent his time, resources, and even his life on proclaiming the gospel, and this investment in Christ's kingdom would bring him an abundant reward in eternity (Luke 19:15; 1 Cor. 3:10–15; Rev. 11:15, 18). God will protect us in life and in death. He will not forget a life of faithful service to Him when He returns. Sometimes people are unappreciative or forgetful of the good that we do for them; however, all that we do in faithful service for our Savior will be remembered and rewarded (Matt. 10:42).

1:13 Hold fast is a command to Timothy to persist in the **sound words** of healthy teaching (1 Tim. 1:3–10). Many who say they speak for Christ proclaim false doctrine. Like Timothy, we need to pursue sound teaching and avoid all teaching that does not conform to the Scriptures, no matter how good certain teachers might sound or how large their following might be.

1:14 That good thing may be rephrased as "the good deposit." Here the phrase refers to Paul's teachings to Timothy (1 Tim. 6:20). **Keep** means "to guard" or "to protect." **Who dwells in us** describes the indwelling of the **Holy Spirit** in believers.

1:15–17 These verses describe those who had abandoned Paul. Yet even here, Paul recalls **Onesiphorus** (a name meaning "Help Bringer"). This man from Ephesus had **refreshed** Paul as if by a cup of cold water. We too should be a refreshment to other believers.

1:18 how many ways he ministered to me: Without complaining Paul seems to cover a multitude of problems and the help Onesiphorus gave. Few people ever realize the enormous pressures and problems a pastor faces as included in the daily "care of all the churches" (2 Cor. 11:28). What reward there will be **in that Day** for those who minister to the ministers!

2:1–13 Paul continues to encourage Timothy to endure and to pass on the gospel faithfully (vv. 1, 2). He cites three examples from everyday life (vv. 3–7) and refers to his own sufferings and to Christ's victory (vv. 8–13).

2:1 In light of the defections of others (1:15), Paul exhorts Timothy to be faithful. But Paul's call is for Timothy to **be strong in the grace that is in Christ Jesus.** The emphasis is on the strength of Christ, not on Timothy's own power. If we trust in ourselves, we are doomed to fail.

2:2 Timothy is commanded to **commit** Paul's teaching to **faithful men.** Faithful believers then have the responsibility of teaching others. This would be the basis for an endless chain of Christian discipleship, the teaching of Christian teachers (Matt. 28:18–20). **among many witnesses:** Discipleship may

occur in large groups, small groups, or one-on-one encounters. Here Paul emphasizes a group setting.

2:3–6 Three illustrations are given for faithfulness. The first is a **soldier.** The Christian walk is often presented as spiritual warfare. Effective service calls for singleness of purpose. The second illustration comes from **athletics.** The Greek games were important and demanded strenuous training (1 Cor. 9:25). No competitor could be **crowned** unless he competed in accordance with **the rules.** Here the reference is to a victor's wreath given in an athletic contest. Faithful believers will receive a victor's crown, not the royal crown that belongs to Jesus. Paul is saying that spiritual activity must be conducted within the directives of biblical faith and doctrine. To defect from true doctrine is to lose our reward (2 John 7, 8). The third illustration is that of a **hardworking farmer.** Conscientious, hard labor is necessary before a farmer can enjoy a bountiful harvest. Laziness cannot be a character trait of faithful Christians.

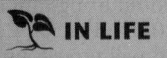 **IN LIFE** **The Handbook for a Life's Work**

In his final and intimate letter to his "son in the faith," Paul reminded Timothy of the essentials of the faith, the basis of Christian ministry. Paul did not want Timothy to drift away from the truth, as Phygellus and Hermogenes had done (1:15). Therefore, he passionately exhorted Timothy to hold on tightly to the faith and to the sound teaching that Paul had entrusted to him (1:13).

Paul knew that consistency and personal integrity (2:22–26) would be significant factors in the young pastor's effectiveness. So Paul warned Timothy about associations with others (3:1–5), encouraging him to reflect on their years together as an example of ethical consistency in the midst of difficulty (3:10–15). In fact, Paul wrote, "all who desire to live godly in Christ Jesus will suffer persecution" (3:12). Timothy certainly had vivid memories of trials in ministry to illustrate Paul's point (Acts 19:21–20:6).

But Paul also made sure that whatever other counsel he gave his pupil, Timothy would find beneath it all a rock-solid dependence on God's Word. Timothy's authority would not come from his own wisdom, Paul's endorsement, or the acceptance of others. His teaching would stand only to the degree that it was based on Scripture.

Paul's ringing tribute to the authority and practicality of God's Word (3:16, 17) completes a section that begins in 2:2 with his charge to Timothy to "commit" what he had learned to "faithful men who will be able to teach others also." In 3:17, Paul offered the central test for measuring whether the gospel torch had been successfully passed from one generation to the next. The application of God's Word in four distinct ways would ensure that the next generation would become "complete, thoroughly equipped for every good work" (3:17). Effective teaching would include (1) doctrine, the basic truths of the faith; (2) reproof, or challenging and confronting each other with the Word of God; (3) correction, by providing guidance from the truths in Scripture; and (4) instruction in righteousness, the personal and practical application of biblical truths.

Paul was encouraging Timothy not only to pass the truths of Scripture on to the next generation, but also to pass on the basis of those truths, the Word of God itself. As we follow in Paul's footsteps, we too must make it clear that the authority of our teaching comes from the Bible. If we teach the truth but do not teach the source of truth, we will not succeed in passing on our faith. Our affirmations and actions have to be founded on God's Word or they will be little more than wishful thinking.

☑ **IN COMPARISON** | **Descriptions of the Christian Life**

In describing how Christians should live, Paul often resorts to analogies or metaphors. This chart lists some of the metaphors of the Christian life found in the NT.

Christians are called to be like . . .	Text	Meaning
Soldiers	2 Tim. 2:3, 4	Like a single-minded soldier, we should respond to the orders of our commanding officer, the Lord Jesus, with unquestioning obedience.
Farmers	2 Tim. 2:6	Farmers labor strenuously and consistently in order to reap a fruitful harvest. We also must work hard in serving the Lord.
Athletes	2 Tim. 2:5	Athletes follow strict training rules so as to avoid being disqualified from their race; we must display a similar measure of self-control.
Workers	2 Tim. 2:15	Our work is to "rightly divide" or correctly handle God's Word so as to avoid shame.
Vessels	2 Tim. 2:20, 21	We must take care to keep ourselves pure, like a clean dish, so that we will be "useful for the Master."
Fishers of men	Matt. 4:19	As fishermen, we are called to "catch" men with the Good News of Christ.
Salt	Matt. 5:13	As salt, we act as a godly preservative in an evil society; moreover, we make people thirsty to know their Creator.
Light	Matt. 5:14–16	As light, we point the way to reconciliation with God, and we reflect God's character, for He is the Light (John 1:7)
Branches	John 15:5	As branches, we bear godly fruit as long as we are attached to the Vine, Christ.
Stewards	1 Cor. 4:1, 2	Like administrators, we have responsibilities to manage. God will evaluate how we handled the resources He has given us.
Ambassadors	2 Cor. 5:20	We are representatives of God's kingdom to the lost citizens of this world.
Living stones	1 Pet. 2:5	In former days, God dwelt in a physical temple; now He dwells in His people, the church.
Priests	1 Pet. 2:5, 9, 10	Like priests, we have the privilege of approaching near to God, and the responsibility of helping others in reconciling themselves to Him.
Sojourners	1 Pet. 2:11	As children of God, we do not belong to the world. This world is not our home; we are only "passing through."

2:7 Consider means to contemplate or reflect on Paul's teachings.

2:8 Timothy is commanded to **remember** Christ's resurrection. **The seed of David** emphasizes Jesus' humanity and the fact that He would fulfill all the promises God had given to David (2 Sam. 7:11–16). **Raised from the dead** emphasizes that our Savior lives today seated at the right hand of God the Father.

2:9 Human circumstances cannot confine the **word of God.** Whether through a tract, a book, a Bible, or a simple statement, God uses His word to accomplish His purposes. There are numerous examples of people who were antagonistic to God's truth but who surrendered their lives to God when He kept after them (see Paul's conversion in Acts 9:1–25). We must not hide the gospel, but instead let it go forth unchained in spite of our own limitations.

2:10 Paul is able to **endure** his present difficult circumstances—his own imprisonment—because he knows that God's work is still progressing among the **elect,** God's chosen ones. The final outcome of their salvation will be the **eternal glory** of God's coming kingdom.

2:11–13 This section is possibly a hymn or confession of the early church. The form resembles the parallelism of Hebrew poetry. The hymn reflects the themes of Christ's death and resurrection introduced by Paul in v. 8.

2:11 if we died . . . We shall also live: Believers are united with Christ in His death and resurrection (Rom. 6:8), which become our death and resurrection the moment we believe (Rom. 6:1–4).

2:12 If we endure: Persevering in the faith even in the face of hardship or persecution will result in a reward when Christ returns (Luke 19:11–27; Rom. 8:17; Rev. 3:21).

2:13 Faithless describes the life of an immature believer who lives for himself and not for the Savior (1 Cor. 3:1–3, 15). **He remains faithful:** Even when believers fail the Savior, He remains loyal. For Christ to abandon us would be contrary to His faithful nature (John 10:27–30; Heb. 10:23; 13:5). Christ's relationship with Peter is a great example of God's faithfulness (Luke 22:31–34).

2:14–26 The Christian leader's moral and spiritual life is important in dealing with false teachers and those deceived by them.

2:14 these things: The momentous facts of vv. 11–13 are of such importance that it is foolish to get involved and strive about insignificant words to no profit. A faithful pastor will keep off the side issues. Paul told Timothy to keep reminding those he teaches to do the same.

2:15 What is **approved** is what remains after testing, like metals that have been refined

by fire. **Rightly dividing** literally means "cutting straight." **word of truth:** Truth defines the nature of Scripture. It is a beacon of truth in the darkness of all kinds of falsehoods. Teachers of the Bible should make every effort to handle His truth accurately. Failure to do so will lead to divine judgment (James 3:1).

2:16–18 Paul warns Timothy about two men, **Hymenaeus and Philetus,** who taught that the resurrection of believers had already occurred (1 Tim. 1:20). This was probably an early form of Gnosticism that emphasized a spir-

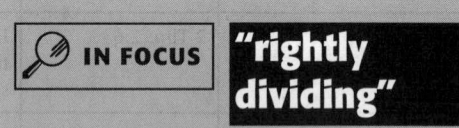

IN FOCUS **"rightly dividing"**

(Gk. *orthotomeō*) (2:15) Strong's #*3718*: This word, which occurs only here in the NT, means "to cut straight," as to cut a straight road or to keep a straight course. The idea could also be that of plowing a straight furrow or of squaring and cutting a stone to fit it in its proper place. In the Greek OT, the word is used in Prov. 3:6; 11:5 to depict God's provision of a straight path for the righteous. Paul encouraged Timothy to handle the word of truth in a straight way, like a road that goes straight to its goal, without being turned aside by useless debates.

itual resurrection over against the Christian belief in a future bodily resurrection.

2:19 In spite of the unfaithful actions of some, the **solid foundation of God stands.** The tense of the verb indicates that Paul saw God's truth as standing not only in the past but also in the present. Isaiah 40:8 reveals that God's Word will also stand firmly in the future, since it is eternal. **The Lord knows those who are His:** This is an intimate, experiential knowledge that can only be obtained in a relationship. **depart from iniquity:** Our sure relationship with our Father in heaven should motivate us to a life of purity.

2:20, 21 The imagery of the **house** is used to describe two categories of believers. **Gold and silver** represent believers who are faithful and useful in serving Christ. **Wood and clay** represent believers who fail to honor the Lord (1 Cor. 3:12–15). **Master** is a strong term for God's authority over the lives of believers regardless of their level of spiritual maturity. We choose to serve the Lord in the power of the Holy Spirit in order to be useful to our Master.

2:22, 23 Flee . . . pursue . . . avoid: In these verses Paul describes in practical terms how Timothy can be a useful vessel for God's work.

2:24 Quarrel translates a military term for hand-to-hand combat. The Lord's servant must not battle with words, but instead must be **gentle** and kind to all.

2:25, 26 Correcting means "training" or "bringing to maturity." **Those who are in opposition** are those who place themselves in conflict with the preaching of God's truth, such as Hymenaeus and Philetus (v. 17). The aim of correction is **repentance,** or a "change of thinking." Paul exhorts Timothy to persevere in correcting his opponents because it is imperative that they should **know the truth,** even though they might oppose the truth at present with their false teachings about the Resurrection (v. 18). It was Paul's hope that they would finally **come to their senses,** or become sober again. False teaching has an intoxicating effect that dulls the mind to God's truth. Timothy's persistence in correcting them might enable them to **escape the snare of the devil.** The devil takes **captive** believers who teach false doctrine, leading others astray. One of Satan's tactics is to cause divisions in the church.

3:1–9 The rise of false teachers and the increase in moral decay that comes with them is a fact of the Christian era. The Christian leader should expect these things and deal decisively with them.

3:1 The exhortations of ch. 2 to endure hardship, be diligent, rightly divide the Word, and be a vessel fit for the Master's use are given in the context of difficult, even **perilous** times. **Last days** includes the whole time from the writing of this letter until the return of Christ.

3:2–5 A long list of traits characteristic of those who do not serve Christ.

3:2 lovers of themselves . . . money: See 1 Tim. 6:10. Self-centeredness heads this list of evil attitudes. **blasphemers:** Abusive and irreverent, without respect for either God or people. **disobedient:** In violation of God's command. **unthankful, unholy:** God desires the exact opposites.

3:3 Unloving connotes a lack of natural affection, as for parents and children (Rom. 1:31). **unforgiving:** Unwilling to come to terms with other persons, implacable. **Without self-control** contrasts with "the fruit of the Spirit" (Gal. 5:22, 23).

3:4 haughty: Puffed up (1 Tim. 6:4). **lovers of pleasure:** The indulgent pursuit of self-satisfaction becomes their god.

3:5 This verse is the climax of three verses containing dark descriptions of fallen humanity. **A form of godliness** is an outward appearance of reverence for God. **Denying its power** describes religious activity that is not connected to a living relationship with Jesus Christ. As time progresses, people would begin to participate in religious activities that are empty. Their activities have nothing to do with a true relationship with God or with individual faith in Jesus Christ. This kind of religion provokes God's anger (Is. 1:10–18; Matt. 23:25–28). **Turn away** is a command for Timothy to avoid the evil persons described in vv.

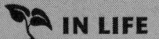 **IN LIFE**   ## Counterfeit Christianity

Wherever people accept the truth of God and begin practicing it, counterfeits soon surface. That's what Paul found at Ephesus, and what he warns Timothy about (2 Tim. 3:8, 9).

He mentions two characters, Jannes and Jambres, whose names mean "he who seduces" and "he who is rebellious." Neither name is in the OT, but Jewish legend held that these were the names of two Egyptian magicians who opposed Moses' demand of Pharaoh to free the Israelites. They tried to duplicate the miracles of Moses in an attempt to discredit him. But God showed that Moses' authority was more powerful (Ex. 7:11, 12, 22).

Paul faced a similar experience at Ephesus. For two years he taught the message of Christ there, in a culture heavily steeped in pagan idolatry and occultism. God confirmed his teaching through powerful miracles and the release of many from evil spirits. But local exorcists attempted to duplicate the miracles. Their scheme backfired, however, to the benefit of the gospel (Acts 19:8–20).

Counterfeits to the truth of Christ abound today, as Paul predicted they would. If we effectively communicate the gospel to friends and coworkers, we can virtually count on the fact that competing systems and worldviews will soon appear. That's why we must "continue in the things which you have learned and been assured of," basing our lives and our witness on the firm foundation of Scripture (2 Tim. 3:14–17).

2–5. We are not to link up in common cause with them (1 Cor. 15:33).

3:6 creep into households: The empty religious individuals of vv. 2–5 use deception to gain a hearing. **Make captives** is a military term for taking prisoners in war. The imagery of spiritual combat is clear in these verses. **Gullible women** are the target of attacks by false teachers. Evidently the false teachers at Ephesus had made significant inroads among a group of women in that church (1 Tim. 5:13–15). Here is the danger of ignorance. Hence, Paul instructs Timothy to "let a woman learn" (1 Tim. 2:11).

3:7 This verse describes the women who have a desire to learn yet fail to comprehend the real truth. **Knowledge** (Gk. *epignōsin*) includes both intellectual and experiential knowledge.

3:8 Paul gives a specific example of two men who resisted truth in Moses' time. **Jannes and Jambres** are not named in the OT, but according to Jewish tradition, they were two of the Egyptian magicians who opposed Moses (Ex. 7:11). People of **corrupt minds** resist the truth because it unveils their shameful thinking and behavior.

3:9 their folly will be manifest: The character and empty religion of false teachers will ultimately be exposed because our actions are the blossom of our deepest thoughts (Prov. 23:1–8).

3:10–17 Timothy's life must contrast with that of the false teachers. He has carefully followed Paul's example of enduring hardship for Christ (vv. 10–13). Now he must continue in the teachings that he has received. Their truth is assured by the character of those who taught them (v. 14) and, above all, by their scriptural basis (vv. 15–17).

3:10, 11 you have carefully followed: Paul draws a sharp contrast between a Christian testimony and the way of the false teachers (vv. 2–9). He notes ten different qualities of his own teaching and life that Timothy had had opportunity to observe.

3:12 Those who want to live godly lives must be prepared for **persecution,** literally "to be hunted." God does not promise us deliverance from persecution but deliverance through it. Persecution is one of the means God uses to develop our capacity to reign with Him in His kingdom (2:12; Matt. 5:10–12; Rev. 2:10).

3:13 The Greek word translated **impostors** can also mean sorcerers or swindlers. **deceiving and being deceived:** False teachers deceive themselves as well as others (Matt. 15:18–20). Deception and self-deception are intrinsic elements of sin.

3:14 Timothy is exhorted to **continue** or abide in things he has **learned** (2:2). Remaining in God's truth is essential for godly living.

3:15 from childhood: Paul emphasizes Timothy's godly heritage (1:5). His mother, Eunice, and his grandmother, Lois, had faithfully taught him the **Holy Scriptures.** The truths of God's Word directed Timothy to Christ. God's Word and the Spirit of God are both essential for our salvation. The Word of God without the Spirit of God is lifeless; it has no power to act. But the Word of God empowered by the Spirit of God becomes a living force in our lives.

3:16 Paul emphasizes the preeminence of **all Scripture. Given by inspiration** is literally "God-breathed." In this verse, Paul teaches that God was actively involved in the revelation of His truth to the apostles and prophets, who wrote it down. The Author of the Bible is God Himself. Thus, Scripture is true in all that it affirms and is completely authoritative (1 Pet. 1:20, 21). The study of the Bible is profitable in at least four different ways. **Doctrine** is teaching. Paul highlights correct teaching first; Luke also emphasizes the Jerusalem church's commitment to doctrine first (Acts 2:42).

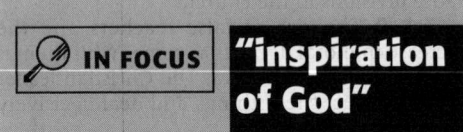

IN FOCUS "inspiration of God"

(Gk. *theopneustos*) (3:16) Strong's #*2315*: The Greek word means "God-breathed," from *theos* (God) and *pneo* (to breathe). Although it is difficult to fully recreate the thought of this Greek expression in English, we are fairly sure that Paul meant to say that all Scripture was breathed out from God. This is the primary meaning. God not only inspired the authors who wrote the words of the Bible, but He also illuminates those who read it with a heart of faith.

Reproof is conviction. This is not simply a rebuke; it is demonstrating some truth beyond dispute. **Correction** refers to setting something straight (2:15). **Instruction** refers to the process of training a child. In this list, only one of these terms is oriented to knowledge and information—that is, *doctrine* (1 Pet. 2:2). The other three in the list involve a change of life. Knowledge that does not change one's life is useless. On the other hand, living without any understanding of who God is and what He expects of us is dangerous.

3:17 The study of Scripture will make a believer **complete,** meaning "capable" or "pro-

(1:10; 4:1, 8; 2 Thess. 2:8; 1 Tim. 6:14; Titus 2:13)

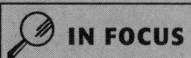

IN FOCUS | **"appearing"**

(Gk. *epiphaneia*) (1:10; 4:1, 8; 2 Thess. 2:8; 1 Tim. 6:14; Titus 2:13) Strong's #*2015*: This word literally means "a shining forth" and was used in Greek literature to denote a divine appearance. The English word *epiphany* is a close equivalent. The NT writers use the word to refer to Jesus' first coming, the time when He entered this world as a man (1:10). They also use the word to speak of Jesus' second coming, specifically to His appearance to all the world (Matt. 24:27).

ficient." **Thoroughly equipped** means "fully prepared." The person who masters the Word of God will never lose his or her way. **every good work:** Paul emphasizes the essential link between knowing God's Word and applying it to one's daily life. Right doctrine should produce right practice.

4:1–8 These verses are the climax of the letter. Paul gives Timothy a final charge to fulfill his ministry (vv. 1–5) and backs up this charge with his own testimony of faithfulness in face of imminent martyrdom (vv. 6–8).

4:1, 2 I charge: Paul underscores the importance of his command to Timothy by calling on God and Jesus to be witnesses to it. He reminds Timothy that Jesus will return in judgment. Paul's charge to Timothy is to **preach the word.** The foundation of any ministry is God's Word. Preaching God's truth is a sacred and demanding task, requiring perseverance and courage. **Be ready** means to take a stand. Timothy was to be alert at all times to his responsibilities, even when it was inconvenient. This type of ministry is not for a novice (James 3:1). **longsuffering . . . teaching.** Patience and instruction are two necessary components of an effective ministry. True spiritual growth occurs over a period of time, through consistent teaching and application of God's Word.

4:3 Timothy needs to be alert and ready to preach God's Word. **Sound** teaching is essential for spiritual maturity, but will not always be tolerated. There will come a time when people will seek out teachers to tell them

what they want to hear and what makes them feel good.

4:4 People **turn their ears** to avoid **truth.** This is the sixth time that Paul uses the word *truth* in this short letter (2:15, 18, 25; 3:7, 8). He had used the word five times in the first letter to Timothy (1 Tim. 2:4, 7; 3:15; 4:3; 6:5). As Paul faced execution, he was evidently concerned that his son in the faith would be tempted to depart from truth, lured by deceptive false teachers.

4:5 Watchful means "sober." **Endure afflictions** refers to the hard toil of ministry, which will have its own reward (2:12). **work of an evangelist:** *Evangelist* is one of five offices mentioned by Paul in Eph. 4:11. An evangelist equips and encourages believers to share the Good News.

4:6 Paul is aware that the time of his death is near. A **drink offering** was an offering performed by pouring wine out on the ground or altar (Num. 28:11–31). Paul's life was already being poured out in service to Jesus Christ, the

Photo by Howard Vos

Starting blocks for runners at a stadium in the Greek city of Delphi. Paul spoke of his service to Christ as a race in which he persevered until the very end (2 Tim. 4:7).

Lamb (Rev. 5:4–6). **my departure is at hand:** Paul was confident that no one could touch him until the heavenly Father ushered him into his eternal home with a victory celebration.

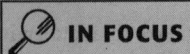 **IN FOCUS** | **"books"**

(Gk. *biblion*) (4:13; Luke 4:17; John 20:30; 21:25; Rev. 1:11) Strong's #975; parchments (Gk. *membrana*) (4:13) Strong's #3200: The word *biblion* is common in the NT but not the word *membrana*, which occurs only here. It is a word derived from Latin that means an animal skin used for writing. The two words in this passage have been interpreted in three different ways: (1) "The scrolls" were copies of OT books, and "the parchments" were copies of various NT books; (2) "the books" were copies of OT and NT books, and "the parchments" were blank writing material or notebooks containing rough drafts; or (3) the two words signified the same thing: "the books—that is, the parchment notebooks." If the third interpretation is correct, it suggests that Paul was anxious to recover some rough drafts he had left behind when he was arrested.

4:7 Paul had been vigilant in his service to God. Note that Paul did not make these comments until the end of his race, until he was about to die. He did not presume or rely on his past service. Instead he persevered, struggled, and served God until the end (1 Cor. 9:24–27).

4:8 Paul understood the eternal potential of a lifetime of faithful service to Christ. Jesus would return with rewards for those who stick it out over the long haul. **The crown of righteousness** is a special reward given to those who serve God faithfully on this earth (Matt. 5:10–12). There will be as many crowns as there are runners who finish the race well. **All who have loved His appearing** are those believers in Christ who have lived faithfully in the hope of His return (Titus 2:11–15; 1 John 2:28).

4:9 Paul is in prison and sends a heartfelt plea to Timothy, asking his young friend to **come . . . quickly.** Paul desired Christian fellowship and some words of encouragement from Timothy, the one he had trained in the faith.

4:10 Demas, Paul's trusted coworker (Col. 4:14, Philem. 24), had fled because he **loved this present world.** He could not endure the hardships of ministry and instead followed worldly pleasures and comfort.

4:11, 12 Only Luke is with me: The value of a trusted friend in the midst of hard times cannot be overstated. Paul's reference to **Mark** as **useful** is a note of tender restoration. Mark's desertion of Paul in Pamphylia on his first missionary journey had led to the separation of Paul and Barnabas at the beginning of Paul's second missionary journey (Acts 15:36–40). But later Paul and Mark were reconciled, and Mark served Paul in the ministry (Col. 4:10). Now at the end of his life, Paul expresses his appreciation of Mark's service. **to Ephesus:** Paul was sending a faithful coworker Tychicus

(Acts 20:4; Eph. 6:21; Col. 4:7) to replace Timothy at Ephesus.

4:13 the cloak: Paul was probably in an unheated prison. **Carpus** appears only here in Scripture. **books . . . parchments:** Perhaps (1) Paul's legal papers, (2) the OT Scriptures, (3) written accounts of Jesus' words and works, or (4) other NT materials, including copies of Paul's epistles.

4:14, 15 Timothy is warned about **Alexander.** This is possibly the person named in 1 Tim. 1:20 or Acts 19:33 who caused **harm** to Paul's ministry in Ephesus. Jesus warned the apostles that they could expect opposition (John 15:18–21). We don't need to look for opposition, but if we don't have any it is possible that we are not on the cutting edge of ministry.

4:16 Paul echoes the forgiving attitude of Christ. Although many had abandoned him, he asked God not to hold them accountable for their actions.

4:17 In spite of the failure of his friends, Paul was supported by the Lord, who always strengthens and empowers. Often people will fail us in troublesome times. The Lord, however, never fails His children, no matter how difficult the circumstances are (Luke 22:32; Heb. 7:25). God had consistently empowered Paul during his life so that he could continue to preach the truth to the Gentiles. **Lion** is probably a reference to execution by lions. It is also possible that Paul is using the word as a metaphor for the spiritual conflict from which he was delivered.

4:18 Paul's expression of confidence in God builds to a crescendo of praise, ending with **Amen.**

4:19–21 Paul closes the epistle with a number of instructions regarding various individuals in his ministry. **Greet Prisca and Aquila:** Prisca is another name for Priscilla.

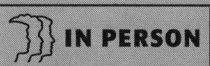

Alexander, the Enemy

Wherever the gospel enjoys unusual success, believers will soon find someone determined to oppose it. In fact, it seems that the greater the impact that the message of Christ has, the more strident and determined will be the opposition.

The man Alexander (1 Tim. 4:14) became a confirmed enemy of Paul and the church at Ephesus. Some identify him as a Jew who lived in the city during the riots instigated by Demetrius and the silversmiths to oppose Paul's preaching (Acts 19:21–41). The Jews tried to use Alexander to convince the Gentile Ephesians that they (the Jews) had nothing to do with Paul and the burgeoning Christian movement (19:33).

Others, however, believe that Alexander was one of two heretical teachers at Ephesus mentioned by Paul (1 Tim. 1:19, 20). With his associate Hymenaeus, Alexander was said to have "suffered shipwreck" concerning the faith, indicating that at one point he may have been counted among the believers. But Paul, apparently using his apostolic authority, "delivered {him} to Satan," which may have been some form of excommunication from the church.

Whoever Alexander was, Paul counted him as a confirmed enemy and warned Timothy to watch out for him (2 Tim. 4:15). However, rather than attack him, Paul left his fate in the Lord's hands, to repay him "according to his works."

Who are the confirmed enemies of the gospel where you live and work? Are you on guard against their attempts to discredit the cause of Christ?

Paul had met both Priscilla and Aquila in Corinth on his second missionary journey (Acts 18:1–3), and they had assisted in God's work in Ephesus (Acts 18:18, 19). **One-siphorus:** This greeting indicates that Timothy was probably still at Ephesus, for Onesiphorus was from there (1:16–18; 1 Tim. 1:3). **Trophimus,** a member of the church of Ephesus (Acts 21:29), had traveled with Paul to Jerusalem (Acts 20:4).

4:22 The final note of this book and of Paul's ministry is **grace,** a fitting conclusion for this man of God and his faithful service to the **Lord Jesus Christ.** The fact that the pronoun **you** is plural may indicate that Paul intended this letter to be read before the congregation.

The Epistle to
Titus

·

"POINT MAN," "PINCH HITTER," "CLUTCH PLAYER," "go-getter." These terms describe a person who can be counted on, someone who knows what to do and how to do it and who works tirelessly to get it done. Titus was that kind of person.

Titus had to be. Much of his work, like the apostle Paul's, was dangerous, unpopular, difficult, and tiring. It involved traveling,

introducing strangers to new ideas, constantly making new friends, consistently battling new enemies, and even deflecting threats on one's life. The number of people who could share such a load was small, but the early church desperately needed them. Not just anyone could start and maintain a new church in a hostile world. Yet Titus rose to the challenge.

The believers in Crete lacked leadership and were suffering as a result. False teachers were taking advantage of the absence of sound doctrine. Judging from Paul's exhortations, the harmony and morals of the young congregation were disrupted. Paul relied on Titus to help them establish their leadership and make up their other deficits. Their struggles are repeated in every age, and this letter is as relevant today as it was to Titus.

Although Titus contains only forty-six verses, it covers a wide range of topics. It is a key New Testament book for church organization, with its guidelines for elders, pastors, and other believers. Furthermore, it contains one of the clearest statements about God's grace in all of the New Testament (2:11–14; 3:3–7). It explicates the significance of Christ's first (2:11) and

second coming (2:13). The book contributes to our understanding of the work of the Holy Spirit in salvation and the Christian life (3:5). But it is known most for its practical instruction about the roles of men, women, and servants (2:2–10) and its instruction for dealing with false teaching (1:9–16; 2:1, 7, 8, 12, 15; 3:2, 8–11, 14). A church needs organization, sound doctrine, and good teaching to survive. In this letter, Paul gives Titus a succinct overview on how to lead a church.

Whereas the letters to Timothy emphasize sound doctrine, the letter to Titus emphasizes good works (1:16; 2:7, 14; 3:1, 5, 8, 14). There were influential people in the church who were motivated by personal interest and selfish gain (1:11). In his letter, Paul exposes the ways this was affecting the doctrine (1:11) and practice (1:16) of the church and urges Titus to champion purity, service, and kindness toward others (2:11–15; 3:3–7). Paul reminds Titus that salvation is not based on our own "works of righteousness" (3:5) but rather is the result of God's work of kindness and love toward us (3:4). We are unable to do good works in our disobedient and selfish state (3:3). Salvation in Christ frees us to do good works, and the "washing of regeneration and renewing of the Holy Spirit" (3:5) enables us.

God wants His people to devote themselves to doing good works (2:11, 12; 3:1, 8, 14). Older men (2:2), older women (2:3), young women (2:4, 5), young men (2:6–8), and servants (2:9, 10) should "adorn the doctrine of God our Savior in all things" (2:10). In his letter, Paul exhorts the believers at Crete to display the testimony of good works to outsiders (2:11, 12; 3:1, 8, 14). While good works are a Christian duty, they are also a gift from God. Through justification in Christ (3:7), God declares us righteous. We must have this legal standing in order to qualify before God to do good works. Redemption (2:14) removes us from the jurisdiction of Satan by paying the debt incurred by our sins. At the same time, it places us in the family of God so that we might be "His own special people, zealous for good works" (2:14).

This letter says it was written by the apostle Paul (1:1), and there is little reason to doubt that he wrote it. Although some scholars have raised objections in the last two hundred years, these objections rest mainly on the assumption that Paul died at the end of the imprisonment described in Acts 28 and did not make the journey implied in the letter to Timothy and Titus. The historical details within Titus itself give us no reason to abandon the traditional view that Paul wrote this letter. Because the arguments against Pauline authorship are the same ones suggested against the Pastoral Epistles in general, see the Introduction to 1 Timothy for more information.

It seems that Paul wrote Titus some time between his two Roman imprisonments, between A.D. 62 and 65. Tradition holds that Titus was written shortly after 1 Timothy, around A.D. 63.

Crete is a large island, approximately 160 miles long and 35 miles wide, in the Mediterranean Sea. The island is located one hundred miles southeast of Greece. The Cretans developed a relatively prosperous agriculture and trading economy, creating one of the best-known business centers of the ancient world. Such prosperity also fostered a great deal of excess. In 1:12, Paul quotes the Greek poet Epimenides, who wrote, "Cretans are always liars, evil beasts, lazy gluttons."

Paul may have planted a church on the island of Crete during a missionary trip after his first imprisonment in Rome, which ended about A.D. 62. When Paul departed from Crete, he left Titus behind to "set in order the things that {were} lacking" in the church (1:5).

Titus is mentioned numerous times in the New Testament as one of Paul's most trusted assistants. He was a Greek and was converted by Paul (Gal. 2:3). He assisted the apostle on some of his missionary journeys (2 Cor. 7:6, 7; 8:6, 16) and went with him to the Jerusalem council (Acts 15:2; Gal. 2:1–3). Paul mentioned Titus several times in Second Corinthians (2 Cor. 2:13; 7:6, 13, 14; 8:6, 16, 23; 12:18). Titus carried the letter to Corinth. While at Corinth, Titus was entrusted with collecting funds from the Corinthian church. Later Titus went to Dalmatia at Paul's request (2 Tim. 4:10). Early church tradition says that Titus returned to Crete and spent the remainder of his life there.

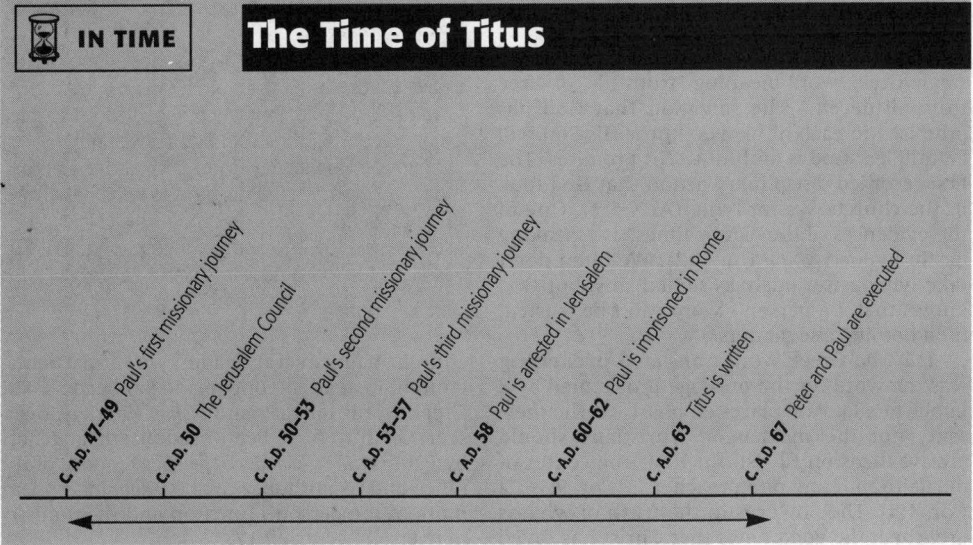

IN TIME — The Time of Titus

- C. A.D. 47-49 Paul's first missionary journey
- C. A.D. 50 The Jerusalem Council
- C. A.D. 50-53 Paul's second missionary journey
- C. A.D. 53-57 Paul's third missionary journey
- C. A.D. 58 Paul is arrested in Jerusalem
- C. A.D. 60-62 Paul is imprisoned in Rome
- C. A.D. 63 Titus is written
- C. A.D. 67 Peter and Paul are executed

Outline

Commentary

1:1–4 The standard opening format for Greek letters (1) identifies **Paul** as sender, (2) names **Titus** as recipient, and (3) extends a brief greeting. In identifying himself, Paul emphasizes the purpose of his apostleship in a way that makes this introduction more detailed and solemn than those in the epistles to Timothy.

1:1 Paul introduces the theme of the book, good works, in the first verse with the term **godliness.** *Good works* or *works* appears eight times in this epistle (twice in v. 16; 2:7, 14; 3:1, 5, 8, 14). At least two other phrases parallel the good works theme: "reverent in behavior" (2:3) and "adorn the doctrine of God" (2:10). Neither truth nor faith is in isolation from the practical outworking of the Christian life.

1:2 cannot lie: This phrase translates a single Greek word meaning "truthful," or "free from all deceit." The salvation that God has promised to each of us who know His Son will be fulfilled; God is faithful to His promises. The first recorded disciplinary action that God took in the church was for lying (Acts 5:3). One of the evidences of the "latter times" is "speaking lies in hypocrisy" (1 Tim. 4:2). We often don't take lying as seriously as sexual sins; but God knows that if a person's word can't be trusted, then nothing else matters.

1:3 The Greek word translated **preaching** was the word for the message proclaimed by a public herald. Paul places emphasis on the message, not the messenger. Christians should always focus on Christ, for He is the center of our faith, not any one preacher (1 Cor. 9:16; 2 Cor. 4:5). The power is in the truth of what is preached, the good news that Christ has saved

us from our sins (Rom. 1:15, 16; 1 Cor. 2:4). **committed to me:** A king's commission is a definite, official act, giving a person a task and authority to carry it out. Paul's commission was as God's "imperial secretary," carrying the royal message of salvation.

1:4 true son: Legitimately born. Titus was another of Paul's converts. What a blessed event. **common faith:** Faith held in common. **Grace, mercy, and peace:** Paul's usual greeting in the Pastoral Epistles.

1:5–9 Paul instructs Titus to appoint leaders for the churches in Crete. Those appointed must have their family life in order (v. 6), avoid the vices of v. 7, and cultivate the virtues of v. 8. Their ministry must be one of faithfully teaching the truth of the gospel (v. 9).

1:5 Lacking indicates an unfinished organization of the churches in Crete due to the brevity of Paul's visit. Paul identifies three specific areas of shortcoming: (1) a lack of organization in the churches (vv. 5–9); (2) unchallenged false teachers (vv. 10, 11; 3:10, 11); (3) a need for teaching in doctrine and practical living (2:1–10; 3:1, 2). Titus was left behind to **set in order** these deficiencies. Titus's first step toward completing his task was to **appoint elders in every city** (Acts 14:23). Apparently the early

IN FOCUS   **"slave"**

(Gk. *doulos*) (1:1; John 13:16; 1 Cor. 7:21; Philem. 16; Rev. 6:15; 13:16) Strong's *#1401*: This Greek word means "a bondslave," one who is subject to the will of his master. The Roman Empire depended on slavery, and many Christians were slaves. The NT does not endorse slavery, nor does it promote a political crusade against it. Instead, Paul encouraged slaves to get their freedom if they could do so within the confines of the law (1 Cor. 7:21), and it seems that Paul was asking Philemon to set Onesimus free (Philem. 15, 16). To express his complete submission to God's will, Paul described himself as slave to God (Rom. 1:1; Gal. 1:10).

church had several leaders in a particular church instead of one principal leader. The Greek words for *elder* and *bishop* (literally, overseer) seem to have been used interchangeably by Paul (v. 7). *Elder* perhaps speaks more of the office and its authority, while *bishop* may speak more of the person's function and the ministry of oversight (Acts 20:17).

1:6 Blameless means to have nothing in one's conduct on which someone could base an accusation (1 Tim. 3:2). Such is to be the overall characteristic of an elder. Yet Paul further defines this blamelessness with sixteen qualities. These qualities are in three areas: family life (v. 6), personal life (vv. 7, 8), and doctrinal beliefs (v. 9). The contrast between the blameless behavior of church elders and the base behavior of the false teachers should have been evident to all (vv. 10–16). **husband of one wife:** This phrase is found only in the Pastoral Epistles (1 Tim. 3:2, 12; 5:9). Its exact meaning is debated. The apostle might be barring a polygamist, a

should also have children who demonstrate faithfulness to God. If a man has children who reject the ways of God, this reflects on the father's ability to lead others outside his home. This rule would apply to children who are not yet fully grown, but possibly not to adult children.

1:7–9 Elders were not to be **self-willed,** but **self-controlled.** If they were self-seeking, like the false teachers on Crete (vv. 10–16), they would not possess the character required to promote good works and sound doctrine among the believers. **Convict** means to rebuke in such a way as to produce repentance and confession

Photo by Howard Vos

The central plain of the island of Crete in the Mediterranean Sea. Paul left Titus in charge of the church on this island (Titus 1:5).

divorced or remarried man, or a man known to be unfaithful to his wife. Whatever the exact meaning of this phrase, it is clear that Paul was emphasizing, as Jesus did (Matt. 19:5), the importance of marital faithfulness. Marriage is the uniting of a man and a woman into "one flesh." **faithful children:** Not only should the man have a good relationship with his wife; he

of sin (John 16:8). A rebuke can have the positive results of producing change in a person's life.

1:10–16 Leaders must be appointed (vv. 5–9) in order to stop false teachers from spreading a doctrine that leads to immoral living.

1:10, 11 many insubordinate: In these

verses, Paul describes the characteristics of the false teachers whose teaching was contrary to the truth and was undermining the authority of church leaders. **those of the circumcision:** Apparently there were Jewish Christians in the churches of Crete who were limiting the Christian freedom of Gentile Christians by requiring an adherence to Jewish laws (Gal. 3).

1:12 Cretans are always liars, evil beasts, lazy gluttons: Paul is quoting the Cretan poet Epimenides, who wrote these words around 600 B.C. The Cretans were so much regarded as liars in the Mediterranean world that the expression "to Cretanize" meant to lie. Paul was contrasting the Cretans' reputation with God's. The Lord was incapable of lying (v. 2).

1:13 This testimony is true: Paul confirms these as facts and says **rebuke them sharply.** There was no place for timidity here. **Sharply** (Gk. *apotomōs*) meant "to cut off abruptly." **That** meant the purpose of the rebuke was that they may be **sound** or "healthy" in the faith.

Rebuke was not vindictive but curative, as it should be always.

1:14 The word *fable* is always used in contrast to Christian doctrine (1 Tim. 4:6, 7). These **Jewish fables** were probably legends about OT figures, like some that survive to this day in nonbiblical writings. This speculation was not only opposed to the **truth,** but it also undermined the faith (v. 13). **commandments of men:** The rules that come from false doctrine are contrasted with the good works (v. 16) that should proceed from sound doctrine (see Mark 7:1–16 for examples of fables and commandments of men).

1:15 In this verse Paul highlights the mistaken asceticism of the Cretan false teachers. They had identified certain foods and practices as defiled when in reality it was their minds that were **defiled and unbelieving.** On the other hand, **to the pure all things are pure.** Because the Cretan believers had placed their trust in Christ focusing their minds on Him, they would be empowered by God's Spirit to lead

---

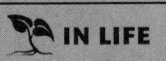 **IN LIFE**　　**Personal Training**

In a world where education seems to be offered everywhere, the biblical description of the church as God's training center for holy living is often overlooked (2:1–15). This error becomes obvious when a church lacks leaders. Effective leadership in a church is the result of proper training. When young believers have not been trained, the church begins to flounder.

Paul was one of the most effective leaders of the early church. He preached the gospel tirelessly, founded a succession of churches throughout Asia Minor and Greece, and grounded these churches in God's Word and the essentials of the Christian faith. But to be truly effective, Paul had to nurture others to follow in his footsteps and faithfully lead the church into the next century. Titus was one of the young men Paul was training for leadership. He had accompanied Paul early in his ministry (Gal. 2:1–3), had served as Paul's representative (2 Cor. 7:5–16), and was considered a "fellow worker" (2 Cor. 8:23). When Paul wrote this letter, he had begun to pass the reins of leadership to this capable young man who was overseeing the churches on the island of Crete.

In his instructions to Titus, Paul reminds him of the traits of a spiritual leader (1:5–16). Paul had chosen Titus as a helper because he had evidenced these qualities. Now he had to model such traits to others, searching for those who could become leaders in the newly planted churches.

Paul instructed Titus to place the responsibility of moral leadership on the elders. Older men and women (2:1–5) had to lead the way in personal holiness. If their lives demonstrated the transforming power of the gospel, they would leave a lasting impact on following generations. Young men who saw older men diligently maintaining their faith in Christ would do likewise (2:2). Young women who heard older women encourage them to "love their husbands, to love their children" (2:4) would be more likely to take the counsel to heart if they saw their mentors doing that themselves. Titus himself was to exhort "young men" (2:6), while making sure that he was consistently following the pattern of life he was teaching (2:7).

The degree to which sound training exists in a local church practically determines the health of that church. The pastor may be the designated teacher, but the Bible makes everyone both a trainer and a trainee. Church members should rely on each other for spiritual guidance. The older generation should pass on to the next generation their vital Christian faith by word and example. The character that results from this process of spiritual training truly is an eye-catching advertisement for the gospel.

pure lives. Jesus taught the same principle in Matt. 15:11. Physical objects or external practices do not defile a person, but a mind focused on evil thoroughly corrupts. Although present-day believers are typically not concerned with Jewish ritual observances, the principle is still applicable. We should be more concerned about renewing our mind and focusing it on Jesus than observing a list of rules that have no biblical support.

1:16 They profess . . . but: Profession and performance should not contradict. Faith and works go together. True faith produces true works. **Disqualified** has the idea of being tested but disapproved.

2:1–10 Paul gives Titus instructions for various members of the Christian household—older people, younger people, and bondservants.

2:1 Paul normally follows a rebuke of false doctrine with an admonition of how the believer should act (2 Tim. 3:10, 14). **Sound** means "healthy." Paul makes frequent use of the term in the Pastoral Epistles. He uses it five times in Titus (1:9, 13; 2:2, 8). Paul views sound doctrine as the root that produces the fruit of sound practice (good works), such as faith, love, and patience (v. 2), as well as sound speech (v. 8). Right thinking is the raw material for right actions (Ps. 119:11; Prov. 23:7; Rom. 12:2; James 1:13–15). Our actions will naturally reveal the direction of our thoughts.

2:2 Older men refers to men older than about fifty. The same is true of older women (v. 3). The character of those who are mature should serve as a spiritual example to all. Maturity is not determined simply by age or even by how much a person knows; it is determined by how skilled a person is in applying the truth to life and in distinguishing good from evil (Heb. 5:13, 14).

2:3 In keeping with the theme of good works (vv. 1, 2), **older women** are not to engage in evil practices like slander, gossip, or drunkenness; instead, they are to teach younger women (v. 4). Paul outlines a tremendous cur-

riculum here that can be implemented with great profit in any local church. If greater emphasis were given to women teaching women, especially when it comes to intimate and domestic relations, there would likely be much less temptation for men to abuse marital fidelity.

2:4 In this verse the word **admonish** means "to give encouragement through advice." Older women are to pass on their insights to their younger counterparts. **love their husbands:** Paul speaks here not of romantic love, but of the commitment of a woman to her husband's welfare. Husbands and wives must be challenged to learn and practice this love by an act of their will.

2:5 homemakers: The importance that Paul places on the role of women in the home may also be seen in 1 Tim. 5:2–16 and Prov. 31. **obedient to their own husbands:** Women are not under the authority of men in general, but rather the authority of their own husbands. The Greek word translated *obedient* is a military term that indicates voluntary submission to the one in authority (Eph. 5:21). **that the word of God may not be blasphemed:** Paul wanted the older women to teach the younger women so that their actions would glorify God, build His kingdom, and strengthen the family. Failure to follow Paul's instructions would result in the Word of God being maligned in the pagan community. When children of God do not follow the instructions of their Father in His Word, unbelievers are led to reject the sincerity of their religious profession and the truth of the Word of God.

2:6 Young men are to pursue the character qualities that older men should possess already.

2:7, 8 a pattern of good works: Paul concludes his instructions to various age groups by reminding Titus that his personal life is an essential aspect of his teaching. More people will learn from our daily actions than from what we say. Therefore, we must pay careful attention that our lives are in line with our beliefs.

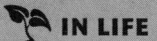 **IN LIFE** | **The Case for Women Teaching and Counseling Women**

Paul in Titus 2:3 makes a case for a special ministry in the church—older women teaching and counseling other women. Women know and understand other women better than men. Every woman needs another woman to confide in—and what better place for this to happen than in the church.

The phrase "older women" speaks of the maturity required for the woman who conducts such a ministry to others. She should be a maturing, praying, trusting, godly Christian.

2:9, 10 bondservants: About half of those who lived in the Roman Empire in the early church were slaves. Good works from a Christian slave would make **the doctrine of God** very attractive to a non-Christian master.

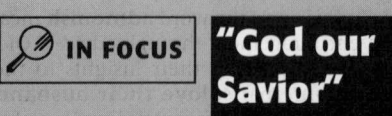

IN FOCUS "God our Savior"

(Gk. *soter hemon theos*) (1:3; 2:10; 3:4; 1 Tim. 1:1; 2:3) Strong's #4990; 2257; 2316: In the Pastoral Epistles, this expression or similar ones appear often. In each of these verses, the appellation seems to describe God the Father. The OT writers speak of God as Savior (Ps. 24:5; Is. 12:2; 45:15, 21) and so do a few other NT writers (Luke 1:47; Jude 25). The Son is called Savior in the Pastoral Epistles (1:4; 2:13; 3:6; 2 Tim. 1:10), and in 2:13 the Son is called "our God and Savior," thus clearly identifying Jesus as God.

Believing the teachings of Scripture is proper and good, but living those truths will influence the nonbelievers with whom we rub shoulders every day.

2:11 appeared: Twice in this context Paul speaks of Christ's appearance in history. The first time Christ came in **grace** to save people from their sins; the second time He will come in glory (v. 13) to reign.

2:12, 13 The appearance of the grace of God is to produce two results in the lives of believers: First, we are to resist the evil temptations of this world, living godly lives in this present age. Second, we are to look for Christ's return. Paul reminded Timothy that there is a special crown

awaiting "all who have loved his appearing." (2 Tim. 4:8). **great God and Savior Jesus Christ:** This is one of the strongest statements of the deity of Christ in the NT.

2:14 Redeem means "to purchase." With His death on the Cross, Christ paid the price to release us from the bondage of sin (Eph. 1:7) to which every unbeliever is a slave (Rom. 6:6, 7, 17, 20). God's purpose in redeeming us is not only to save us from hell; He also wants to free us from sin so that we can produce good works that glorify Him (Eph. 2:8–10).

2:15 rebuke: For the third time in this letter (1:11, 13), Paul strongly commands Titus to confront false teachers.

3:1–11 God's grace in us should be evident by the respect we give to **rulers** (v. 1) and by the way we treat others (v. 2). We once were just like our ungodly neighbors (v. 3), but God has totally changed us (vv. 4–7). Therefore, we should **maintain good works** (v. 8), **avoid foolish disputes** (v. 9), and admonish **divisive** people (vv. 10, 11).

3:1, 2 Remind: Paul had already instructed the Cretans regarding submission and obedience to the authorities in their communities. Titus was to remind them of their duty to be good citizens, a virtue that the Cretans notoriously lacked (1:12). **rulers and authorities:** This phrase often refers to the angelic realm, including both good (Eph. 3:10) and evil angels (Eph. 6:12). Here it refers to civil leaders and institutions. Disobedience permeated the Cretans' lifestyle, both in the church (v. 10) and in government. Titus must advise them to get along with civil authorities and to live peacefully with their neighbors. This type of life would reflect positively on the Christian faith and thus glorify God.

3:3 Paul provides another motive for good works by explaining the rationale for the Christian life. The believers were supposed to treat others the way God in His grace had treated

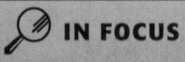

IN FOCUS "washing of regeneration"

(Gk. *loutron palingenesias*) (3:5) Strong's #3067; 3824: The Greek word for *washing* can signify the receptacle of washing (the basin) or the act of washing itself. In Eph. 5:26, the only other NT occurrence of this word, the natural meaning is "washing". Here also the action of washing is presented. Quite simply, the text says that regeneration is characterized by or accompanied by the action of washing. The regenerative activity of the Holy Spirit is characterized elsewhere in Scripture as cleansing and purifying (Ezek. 36:25–27; John 3:5). The Greek term for *regeneration* literally means "being born again"—indicating a new birth effected by the Holy Spirit (John 3:6; Rom. 8:16; Gal. 4:6). Thus, God saved us through one process with two aspects: the washing of regeneration and the renewing of the Holy Spirit.

them when they were involved in the ungodly activities noted in this verse (Rom. 5:8).

3:4 But when: Amazing grace! **God our Savior** describes the Father (1:3). God's **love** for us appeared in Jesus Christ, who is thus called our Savior (v. 6).

3:5 not by works of righteousness: Since Paul has been exhorting Titus to emphasize good works in his ministry with the Cretans, he wants to make it clear that such works have no value in saving a person. Rather, it is solely on the basis of God's **mercy** that we are delivered

This emphasizes the practical benefit of good works.

3:9–11 Paul was admonishing Titus to avoid anything that would promote wickedness among the believers. **Reject a divisive man:** Titus was to cut off the church's relationship with any person who would not submit to correction after two warnings (2 Thess. 3:14, 15). The Greek word for **warped** here suggests that Satan is perverting this person. **Sinning** indicates that the man will not change his ways and thus continues to rebel against God.

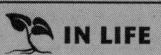 **IN LIFE**   ## United for the Work

Working without phones, faxes, cars, or planes, a dedicated, diverse team of first-century believers spread the good news about Jesus throughout the Roman world. Paul mentioned several of these coworkers to Titus—Artemas, Tychicus, Zenas the lawyer, and Apollos (Titus 3:12, 13)—but there were many others; for example, Barnabas (Acts 4:36, 37), Priscilla and Aquila (Rom. 16:3–5), Silas (Acts 15:34), and Junia (Rom. 16:7).

The task of proclaiming the gospel in the face of sometimes fierce opposition knit these early believers together. They planned their travel not only around the tasks of ministry, but also around their relationships with each other. For example, Paul encouraged Titus to come to him at Nicopolis during a seasonal break (Titus 3:12). They also took care to provide necessities for each other (3:13).

The principle emerges from this pattern that the cause of Christ goes forward even in the face of opposition when the workers are united for the work.

---

from the penalty of our sin. **washing of regeneration:** This phrase refers to the work of the Holy Spirit, who in a moment makes a person new by the cleansing of regeneration (the new birth). This new nature is the ground for living the Christian life and performing good deeds. **renewing of the Holy Spirit:** The continual process of Christian living is enabled by the Holy Spirit, resulting in growth in character and good works.

3:6 poured out . . . abundantly: Richly, lavishly (Acts 2:33). The Father sent the promised Holy Spirit through the work of Jesus (Luke 24:49; Acts 1:4, 5).

3:7 we should become heirs: God justifies believers so that they might become coheirs with Jesus Christ in His coming reign (Rom. 8:17; 2 Tim. 2:12).

3:8 This is a faithful saying: Paul is emphasizing that what he has written (vv. 4–8) is a trustworthy statement, one that is central to the Christian faith. There are four other places in the Pastoral Epistles where Paul labels his teaching as a faithful saying (1 Tim. 1:15; 3:1; 4:9; 2 Tim. 2:11–13). It is significant that the faithful saying in Titus includes an admonition to **maintain good works,** the theme of the letter. **These things are good and profitable:**

3:12, 13 Tychicus, one of Paul's assistants, is also mentioned in Acts 20:4; Eph. 6:21; Col. 4:7; 2 Tim. 4:12. The city of **Nicopolis** was on the Adriatic coast of Greece. **Apollos** was a fellow worker of Paul's (Acts 18:24; 19:1; 1 Cor. 1:12; 3:4–6, 22; 4:6; 16:12), an Alexandrian who had been taught by Priscilla and Aquila and had eloquently preached the gospel at Ephesus and Corinth (Acts 18:24—19:1).

3:14 Paul ends his letter to Titus with an emphasis on **good works,** the theme of this letter (1:1). **to meet urgent needs:** Paul gives the Cretans a practical way they can start demonstrating their faith in good works: they can begin meeting the needs of other people. **that they may not be unfruitful:** A recurring theme throughout the NT is that believers should live up to their holy calling. They should continue being sanctified (Heb. 10:14, 23–26). Justification is a gift solely from God, but we will be rewarded according to what we do on this earth (Rev. 22:12). What a tragedy it will be for some to stand ashamed at Christ's return (1 John 2:28). How much better it will be to abound in good works that the Holy Spirit empowered us to do (Phil. 4:17).

3:15 those who love us: Paul's Christian friends in Crete.

The Epistle to

Philemon

NDER ROMAN LAW, A SLAVE WHO RAN AWAY from his master could face the death penalty. In spite of this possibility, the apostle Paul sent Onesimus, a runaway slave and a recent convert to Christianity, back to his owner Philemon to make restitution. The Epistle to Philemon is Paul's plea that Onesimus no longer be viewed as a runaway slave, but rather as a "beloved brother" (vv. l6, 17; Col. 4:9). Obedience to

these requests would require forgiveness and restoration, actions that no other slave owner would have to contemplate in the ancient world. But Christians were called to a higher calling, one that contradicted the expectations of the culture at large. While the world pursued power and glory, Christians were to pursue the way of the Cross—the way of forgiveness, servanthood, suffering, and love.

The greeting and the content of the letter indicate that Philemon is the intended recipient. Philemon was a slave owner whose home served as the meeting place for a local church. Philemon probably lived in Colosse, a city in the Roman province of Asia Minor. He was a convert to Christianity as a result of Paul's ministry, possibly during the apostle's stay in Ephesus (Acts 19:26). Apphia was probably his wife, and Archippus may have been his son, possibly serving at this time as the pastor of the church that met in Philemon's house (Col. 4:17).

Philemon owned a slave named Onesimus, a common name for slaves in that period. Onesimus ran away and had apparently stolen something from his master. Having fled to Rome, the escaped slave providentially came into contact

with Paul, became a Christian, and remained with the apostle for some time, serving him in prison. However, restoration and restitution needed to be made. It was agreed that Onesimus would return to Philemon, even though this could result in the former's death. Paul wrote a letter to his friend Philemon, pleading the cause of Onesimus. At the same time he wrote a letter to the church at Colosse and sent it with Tychicus (Col. 4:7–9). The New Testament does not reveal what finally happened to Onesimus. Some have taken him to be the Onesimus who eventually became the bishop of Ephesus, mentioned by Ignatius in the early second century.

The Epistle to Philemon was not written to refute theological error or to teach doctrine. However, into this short letter Paul skillfully weaves the concepts of salvation (vv. 10, 16), substitution (v. 17), imputation (v. 18), and redemption (v. 19). Although here these ideas speak of Paul's relationship with Onesimus, they remind us of Christ's relationship with us (Gal. 4:1–7). We were once slaves to sin, but Christ redeemed us from our awful fate, death.

This letter is basically an earnest plea for a Christian love that would confront the cruelty and hatred embodied in the cultural institutions of that day. Paul commends Philemon for already expressing that type of love (vv. 5, 7). But to ensure that this love would be shown to Onesimus, Paul offers to pay Onesimus's debt (v. 19). Paul's love for Onesimus went beyond mere words; he was willing to give out of his own poverty to guarantee this slave's well-being.

Three times in this book (vv. 1, 9, 19) Paul identifies himself as its author. The vocabulary and style are clearly his, for many of the phrases in this letter are found in Paul's other letters (compare v. 4 with Phil. 1:3, 4). Also, many of those who sent their greetings with this letter are the same ones who did so in the letter to the Colossians. This fact indicates the close relationship between the two letters (Col. 4:12–15).

Paul was a prisoner when he wrote this epistle, but his location is uncertain. Three possibilities have been suggested: Ephesus, Caesarea (Acts 24—26), and Rome (Acts 28). But most hold that Paul wrote this letter during the first Roman imprisonment around A.D. 60, along with the other Prison Epistles—Ephesians, Philippians, and Colossians.

Outline

I. Introductory greetings 1–3
II. Paul's prayer for Philemon 4–7
III. Paul's plea to Philemon 8–22
   A. The authority behind the plea 8, 9
   B. The person involved in the plea 10, 11
   C. The explanation necessary for the plea 12–14
   D. The providence behind the plea 15, 16
   E. The content of the plea 17–21
   F. The proof of the reception of the plea 22
IV. Closing blessing 23–25

Commentary

1 Paul identifies himself not as an apostle, but as **a prisoner,** because of his surrender to the cause of Christ and the fact that he was writing from prison in Rome (vv. 9, 10, 13, 23). **Timothy** was with Paul in Rome (Col. 1:1) and in Ephesus. **To Philemon:** All we know about Philemon is contained in this short letter. Residing at Colosse, Philemon was apparently a model Christian. He was an active worker for Christ and also the owner of the slave Onesimus, who had run away. Philemon is called **beloved.** Paul's plea (vv. 9, 10) will be built on the concept of love. **Fellow laborer** indicates someone who is united with Paul in the work of Christ.

2 Apphia may have been the wife of Philemon. **Archippus** may have been the son of Philemon or perhaps an elder of the Colossian church (Col. 4:17). **fellow soldier:** This term implies more than *fellow laborer* (v. 1). It is used only one other time in the NT, when Paul speaks of Epaphroditus (Phil. 2:25). **in your house:** The church was meeting in Philemon's house. Philemon may have been an active leader in the church.

3 Grace to you, and peace: Grace (Gk. *charis*) was the common Greek greeting, just as **peace** (Heb. *shalom*) was the ordinary Hebrew

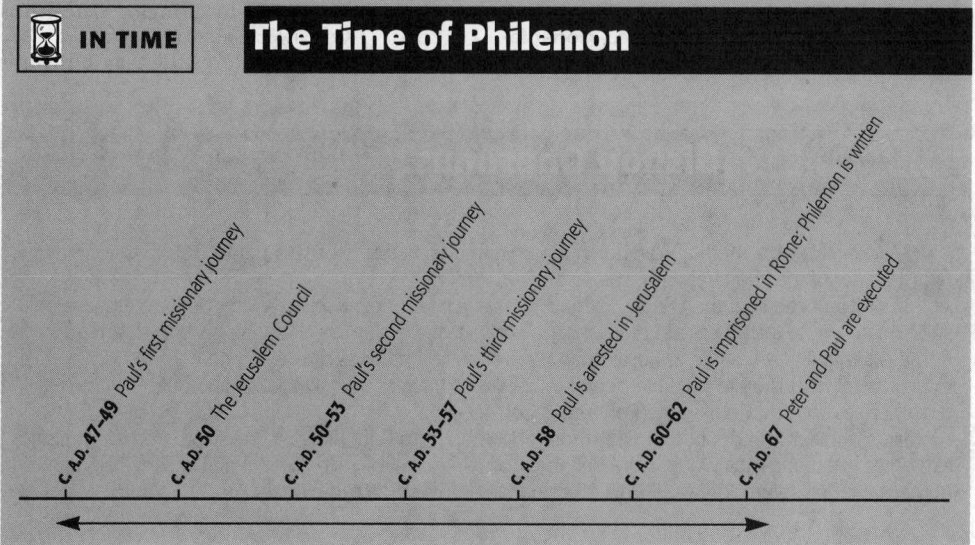

IN TIME

The Time of Philemon

c. A.D. 47-49   Paul's first missionary journey

c. A.D. 50   The Jerusalem Council

c. A.D. 50-53   Paul's second missionary journey

c. A.D. 53-57   Paul's third missionary journey

c. A.D. 58   Paul is arrested in Jerusalem

c. A.D. 60-62   Paul is imprisoned in Rome; Philemon is written

c. A.D. 67   Peter and Paul are executed

salutation. Paul combines both of these terms, heightened with the full Christian meaning of all the blessings of salvation that freely come to us through Christ, and the peace of God that we have because Christ has made peace with God on our behalf. The fact that God the Father and the Lord Jesus Christ together send this grace and peace illustrates their equality in the Godhead.

4–7 In vv. 4–7 Paul lays the basis for the plea in a commendation of Philemon.

4, 5 in my prayers: Philemon's Christian life was a continual cause for thanksgiving whenever Paul prayed. **hearing:** Paul continually heard of Philemon's love and faith from others around him. Philemon was a model believer, both before the Lord, and with regard to other believers. This naturally has a bearing on the request Paul makes of Philemon. **love and faith . . . toward the Lord Jesus and toward all the saints:** This may be an example of the literary device called a chiasmus, where parallel phrases are connected in reverse order. Thus, the word *faith* refers to Christ, and the word *love* refers to the saints. *Saints* speaks of all believers. True love is expressed in action and not just in words (1 Cor. 13:1–7).

6 Paul prays that Philemon's **faith** will be **effective**—a term that speaks of being in good working order (Heb. 4:12, where *powerful* translates the same word). Working faith is a sharing faith; it is the **acknowledgment** of what Christ has done in the believer's life (Eph. 3:17–19). That kind of faith will also result in the sharing of possessions with other believers (vv. 17, 18).

7 Rather than merely being happy because of Philemon's love, the apostle remarkably stated that he had **joy,** even when he was in chains (v. 1). A Christian's joy in trying circumstances is a testimony to God's peace. **Consolation** may also be translated "encouragement."

Philemon's **love** brought joy and encouragement to Paul. **Hearts** refers to the inner emotional nature of a person (vv. 12, 20). Paul had heard that the hearts of the saints were also being **refreshed** by Philemon's love (Matt. 11:28; 1 Cor. 16:18). Paul is not desiring to argue theologically to Philemon, but from the heart. If Philemon expresses this kind of love toward Onesimus, he will be restored and Paul will rejoice and be encouraged. Expressed Christianity is an encouragement to others. Accepting a slave back without any punishment whatsoever was striking at the very heart of the Roman social and economic order.

8 Therefore: In light of the foundation that has been laid (vv. 4–7), Paul is ready to make his plea. **very bold:** This phrase speaks of "free and open speaking" (2 Cor. 3:12; Eph. 6:19). Paul's apostolic authority and Philemon's spiritual condition made Paul confident that he could **command** Philemon to do what is proper (Col. 3:18).

9 Rather than commanding Philemon (v. 8), Paul preferred to **appeal** to Philemon on the basis of love. *Appeal* is the same word translated *consolation* in v. 7. **Paul, the aged:** The apostle is speaking either of the office of elder or of his old age.

10 appeal: Notice the carefulness of the apostle Paul in never asserting his authority in winning Philemon to his position. Each of us could learn a lesson in diplomacy from Paul's manner in this epistle. Force often begats force; love can break down the barriers that divide. **My son** is the Greek word for "child." The imagery of a father and child is used at other times by Paul when speaking of his converts (1 Tim. 1:2; Titus 1:4). **begotten:** The apostle was personally responsible for bringing **Onesimus** to Christ (1 Cor. 4:15; Gal. 4:19).

11 Paul uses an interesting play on words

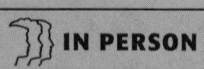 **IN PERSON** **Bishop Onesimus?**

About fifty years after Paul, a church leader named Ignatius wrote a letter to Bishop Onesimus, leader of the church in Ephesus.

It's uncertain if this bishop is the same slave who once lived in nearby Colosse. But it is possible. If Paul wrote the letters of Ephesians, Colossians, and Philemon all during his imprisonment in Rome—as many believe—the Ephesian people may have met Onesimus while he was on his way back to his master. This is quite possible because Onesimus traveled with Tychicus, who delivered the letters of Ephesians and Colossians (Eph. 6:21; Col. 4:7–9).

Many scholars who doubt that Paul wrote Philemon from Rome suspect he wrote from jail in Ephesus. If so, the Ephesians would have become acquainted with Onesimus during his conversion and perhaps after his return to Paul, if Philemon took the hints and freed him.

here. Having just mentioned Onesimus, whose name means "Useful" (v. 10), the apostle describes him as someone who was formerly **unprofitable** (not useful) but is now **profitable.** Paul is saying that Onesimus had become good and useful, even more so than Philemon could have imagined. That is what God's grace can do.

12 I am sending him back: Paul is referring the case back to Philemon for a decision. He encourages Philemon not to view Onesimus as a runaway slave. In fact, Onesimus had become a part of Paul's **own heart** (vv. 7, 20).

13 wished: Paul wanted to keep Onesimus in Rome, helping in the ministry, confident that Philemon would approve. Onesimus had been serving Paul in place of Philemon, giving Paul the aid Philemon could not.

14 Paul expressed his desire to have Philemon involved in the decision of whether Onesimus could remain with him. Therefore, he would act only with Philemon's **consent.** Philemon's **good deed** had to be **voluntary.** Service for Christ is never forced. Paul had given Philemon several good reasons to forgive Onesimus, but here he returns to the foundation of his argument: Philemon's actions had to proceed from his own love (v. 9).

15 perhaps: After appealing to the emotions of Philemon for Paul, the apostle turns to Philemon's mind and view of God. "Philemon, did you ever wonder why Onesimus left?" might be a good way to paraphrase Paul's meaning. **departed for a while:** It was God's plan that Onesimus would run away. **receive him forever:** Paul contrasts the temporary separation because of Onesimus's running away to the eternal benefit of his salvation, from a temporary slave to an eternal son, from a demeaning condition to an eternal relation with Christ and fellow believers. Thus is the transforming power of God's grace.

16 no longer as a slave but . . . a beloved brother: Paul contrasts the lowly position of a slave to the high privilege of a Christian brother. Though the pagan mysteries of the time recognized an initiated slave to be a free man to his former owner, the Christian perspective is higher. The slave becomes a brother, truly part of the family of the former Christian master. **in the flesh and in the Lord:** Not only will Onesimus be useful on the human level; he will be useful for the work of the Lord.

17, 18 partner . . . owes: Onesimus had probably stolen something from Philemon when he left. Furthermore, he owed Philemon for the time he was gone. Paul uses business imagery in offering to pay for any loss Philemon suffered because of Onesimus's actions. *Partner* is a form of the Greek word for *fellowship.* Philemon was to receive Onesimus as he would his partner in Christ, Paul. **put that on my account:** This accounting imagery reminds us of the theological truth that our sins were charged over to Christ even though He had not earned them. Forgiveness is costly (Is. 53:6).

19 my own hand: Paul wrote this note himself because it was a personal note, but also because the letter could be considered a legal document obligating him to pay the damages Onesimus had caused. **I will repay:** Paul

---

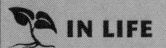 **IN LIFE** | **Big Lessons from a Little Letter**

The Onesimus-Philemon story holds a number of significant lessons:

- It shows that in Christ there is always room for reconciliation and a second chance for people.
- It illustrates how God works behind the scenes to bring people to faith and restore relationships.
- It shows the power of the gospel to work at a distance and effect change from city to city, coast to coast, and continent to continent.
- It shows the value of mentoring relationships, the way that older, seasoned believers can help younger followers of Christ work out problems and conflicts.
- It shows a measure of irony behind God's patience and providence: He had to send Onesimus thousands of miles away from his Christian master in order to bring him to faith!
- It shows that in Christ, people can change. Consider the many stages that Onesimus went through: from slave, to thief and runaway, to refugee, to convert, to penitent, to brother, and possibly to bishop.

promises to pay Onesimus's debt to assure the runaway slave's gracious reception by his owner. **you owe me:** The mention of Philemon's spiritual debt to Paul is not an attempt to cancel his own promise to pay; Paul chooses not to appeal to Philemon on the basis of this obligation.

20 The word translated **joy** in this verse is different from the one used in v. 7. The term here may also mean "benefit." Philemon's restoration of Onesimus would benefit Paul. **refresh:** What Philemon had done for other believers (v. 7), he could do for Paul by his kind treatment of Onesimus.

21 obedience: Paul is expecting Philemon to be compassionate to his former slave Onesimus (vv. 5, 7, 9). **more than I say:** Paul is intimating his expectation of the release of Onesimus. Obedience is costly. Love goes the second mile.

22 prepare a guest room: Hospitality is a Christian virtue (Rom. 12:13; 1 Tim. 3:2). Paul's mention of a possible visit adds weight to his request of Philemon. The term translated **granted** here is related to the Greek word for *grace*. Paul expects to be released from prison (Phil. 2:24).

23 Epaphras, my fellow prisoner: Epaphras was well known to the Colossians (Col. 1:7; 4:12, 13). To call him a fellow prisoner (as he did Aristarchus, Col. 4:10) must mean that these men were so constantly with Paul that it seemed they were prisoners too.

24 Marcus: John Mark had recovered from his failure on the first missionary journey (Acts 13:13; 15:36–41) and was now with Paul again (compare 2 Tim. 4:11). **Aristarchus** was one of Paul's converts from Thessalonica who accompanied Paul on much of the third missionary journey (Acts 20:4) and on the trip to Rome (Acts 27:2; Col. 4:10). **Demas,** sad to say, later turned back from following Christ (2 Tim. 4:10). **Luke,** the beloved physician, the author of Luke and Acts, was faithful to the very end (2 Tim. 4:11). These all sent their greetings to Philemon. Of the eleven persons mentioned in this short letter, Onesimus is precisely in the middle, and is the central character.

25 Paul ends this letter as he began it, with the **grace of our Lord Jesus Christ** directed toward Philemon's entire household. All grace resides in Him who freely gave all He had for us. "Thanks be to God for His indescribable gift" (2 Cor. 9:15). Philemon's response to grace would be to treat Onesimus as a brother.

The Epistle to the

Hebrews

A T FIRST CHRISTIANITY WAS JEWISH. JESUS WAS a Jew, His disciples were Jews, and the first converts were Jews. Their first meetings took place in synagogues, and their first controversies concerned adherence to Jewish laws. Christianity's first critics knew it as a Jewish sect. But for the first Jewish believers, believing in Christ raised many questions. What about the temple and animal sacrifices? What

about the Law of Moses? Did believing in Christ negate so much that they had grown up believing? Was it really enough to trust in Christ? The Old Testament did not answer these questions.

Answers were needed right away for those who lived in the time of this book's writing. Tolerance would soon give way to torture and executions. Nero would not leave this odd group alone forever. Believing in Christ would be a life-or-death proposition, and the temptation for Jewish believers to go back to their old ways would be irresistible—unless they could know for sure they had made the right choice.

The Book of Hebrews was written to address the doubts of those who were second-guessing their conversion to Christianity. "You began with God's plan of salvation," it says in effect. "You believed in His word and followed His plan of salvation through the temple sacrifices. And then when His once-for-all final sacrifice was made in Jesus Christ, you believed. That was as it should be. That was God's plan. Do not go back on the steps you have taken!"

The author of Hebrews set out to show that Christianity is the true successor to Judaism. He

centers his attention on three topics: (1) priesthood, or divine mediation (7:1–28; 10:19–22); (2) sacrifice, or divine redemption (9:11—10:18); and (3) covenant, or divine promises (8:8–13; 9:15–22). He uses three Old Testament passages to prove his point: (1) Ps. 110:4, which announces a new priesthood providing the necessary divine mediation; (2) Ps. 40:6–8, which speaks of the new and final sacrifice providing divine redemption; and (3) Jer. 31:31–34, which announces a New Covenant that provides full and final forgiveness.

According to the author of Hebrews, all of this points to the supremacy and sufficiency of Christ. True spirituality comes through access to God (7:19; 10:19–22); and this spirituality can be found only through the Son of God, Jesus Christ. The Book of Hebrews establishes the supremacy and sufficiency of Christ over all (1:1–4; 9:11–14). His sacrifice was enough to take away our sin; He is all we need to come to God today.

The original audience of Hebrews is not named. Some scholars have said that the book was written to Gentile Christians, arguing from the author's use of the Septuagint and from the absence of any mention of Gentile-Jewish controversy. Others have suggested that the letter was addressed to a mixed group of Jews and Gentiles.

But most scholars suppose that the addressees were Jewish Christians because of the book's heavy emphasis on Jewish topics and themes, especially the detailed discussion of the superiority of Jesus Christ over angels, Moses, Joshua, and Old Testament believers. Quotes of Old Testament passages appear throughout the book. Many of the author's themes assume an in-depth knowledge of Old Testament priesthood and sacrifice. Jews living outside of Jerusalem would almost certainly have been Greek-speaking, explaining the use of the Septuagint. The recipients are addressed as "brethren" throughout, and in the early church this would have included a large number of Jews. The title "To the Hebrews" is not from the author's hands, but it is dated as early as the second century.

Where did the readers live? The expression "they who are from Italy" (13:24) may refer to those in Italy or originally from Italy but presently away from there. It seems most reasonable to think of the readers as Jewish believers at Rome. The letter was first known at Rome, and the concluding salutation easily fits this view (13:24; Acts 18:2). The reference to false teaching about food in 13:9 matches a similar problem in the Roman church (Rom. 14:1—15:3).

The structure of Hebrews is unique among the epistles of the New Testament. Was it a letter or a sermon? It has the ending of a letter but not the salutation of one. It does not name its author or its intended audience, yet it contains personal greetings, assumes that the readers knew who was writing to them, and mentions some well-known mutual acquaintances, such as Timothy (13:23). This mix of elements has caused much debate over what the Book of Hebrews really is, with no solid conclusion. The author himself calls it "the word of exhortation" (13:22).

No one knows for sure who wrote Hebrews. No one in the early church could say with certainty that they knew, though the church at Alexandria (Egypt) strongly believed it to be the apostle Paul's work. Yet Hebrews has been accorded one of the most respected places in the Bible. This book won its place in the New Testament by its merit, not by the esteem of its author.

Did Paul write Hebrews? The letter's vocabulary, style, and theology differ greatly from Paul's letters. Unlike the author of Hebrews, Paul always identified himself in his writings; in fact, in one of them he offered his name as proof of the letter's authenticity (2 Thess. 3:17, 18). The language of Hebrews is polished, deliberate, and without the outbursts of emotion so characteristic of Paul. Typically Paul used Greek, Hebrew, and other sources in his Old Testament quotations, while the author of Hebrews used only the Greek Septuagint. Hebrews 2:3 seems to say that the author did not hear the word of salvation directly from the Lord, whereas Paul did. If Paul wrote Hebrews, he left none of the usual clues.

Tertullian suggested that Barnabas wrote it.

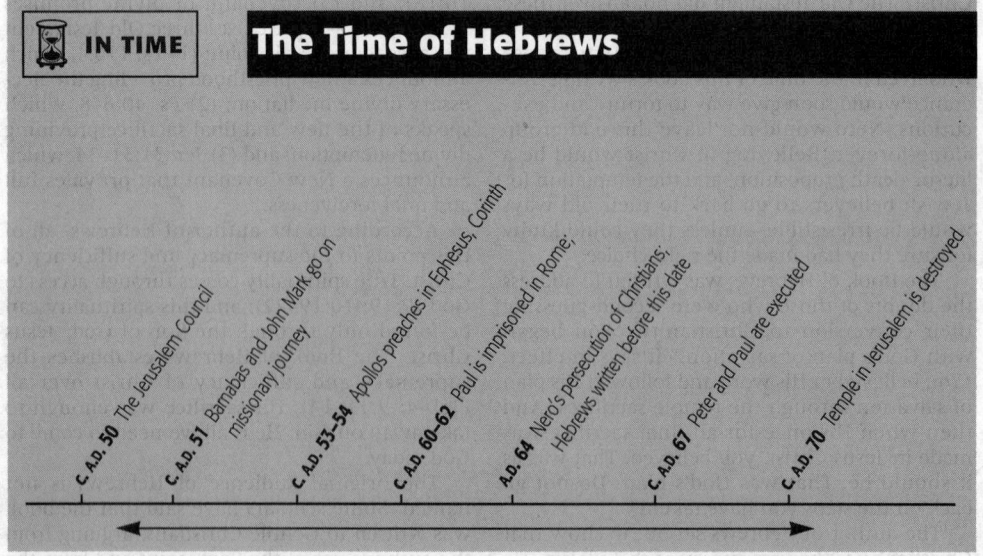

IN TIME | **The Time of Hebrews**

c. A.D. 50 The Jerusalem Council

c. A.D. 51 Barnabas and John Mark go on missionary journey

c. A.D. 53-54 Apollos preaches in Ephesus, Corinth

c. A.D. 60-62 Paul is imprisoned in Rome;

A.D. 64 Nero's persecution of Christians; Hebrews written before this date

c. A.D. 67 Peter and Paul are executed

c. A.D. 70 Temple in Jerusalem is destroyed

Barnabas was from Cyprus, where the Greek was of good quality, and Hebrews represents the Greek of the educated and cultural classes more than any other New Testament book. Barnabas was also a Levite (Acts 4:36), a person who would be very familiar with Judaism's sacrificial system, central to the book's theme. Barnabas's name is translated in Acts 4:36 as "Son of Consolation" or "Son of Exhortation," a parallel to the description in Heb. 13:22.

Martin Luther and many contemporary scholars have speculated that Apollos wrote Hebrews. Apollos was a Jew, an Alexandrian, and a knowledgeable, eloquent man (Acts 18:24). But none of the church fathers named him. And if Apollos did write Hebrews, the Alexandrian church would probably have known it because Apollos was an Alexandrian.

Could the author have been Priscilla, as the scholar Adolf Harnack suggested (Acts 18:26)? The masculine participle in 11:32 probably rules that out. The original recipients knew who wrote it (13:18, 22–24), but they left no clue for us.

No one knows exactly when Hebrews was written either, although guessing a date is easier than guessing the author. If it was written to the Jewish believers at Rome, as is commonly assumed, then the fact that the community had not yet been called upon to suffer death for their faith suggests that the epistle should be dated before Nero's persecution of Christians in A.D. 64.

Outline

I. Prologue: God has spoken through His Son 1:1–4

II. The superiority and sacrificial work of Christ 1:5–10:18

   A. Christ's superiority 1:5–7:28

     1. Christ's superiority to angels 1:5–14

     2. Exhortation to pay attention to the greater salvation 2:1–4

     3. Christ as the perfect Man 2:5–18

     4. Christ's superiority to Moses 3:1–6

     5. Christ's superiority to the rest of Israel 3:7–4:13

     6. Christ as High Priest in the order of Melchizedek 4:14–5:10

     7. A rebuke for lack of understanding and immaturity 5:11–6:20

     8. The priesthood of Melchizedek 7:1–28

   B. Christ, the minister and High Priest of the New Covenant 8:1–10:18

     1. The New Covenant in relation to the old 8:1–9

     2. The better covenant explained 8:10–13

     3. The new sanctuary and the perfect sacrifice 9:1–28

     4. The New Covenant at work 10:1–18

III. Elements of the faith 10:19–13:17

   A. Description of the faith 10:19–25

   B. Description of those who reject the faith 10:26–39

   C. Examples of the life of faith 11:1–40

   D. Christ, the supreme example of faith 12:1–4

   E. The Father's love made known through chastening 12:5–11

   F. Christian conduct under the New Covenant 12:12–29

   G. Christian life in daily practice 13:1–17

IV. Epilogue 13:18–25

Commentary

1:1 Various times refers to the periods of OT history. **Various ways** refers to the different methods God used to communicate, including visitations, dreams, signs, parables, and events (Is. 28:10).

1:2 By His Son may be rephrased as "in such a person as a Son." The emphasis rests on the character of the revelation. It is a revelation of the Son, a revelation not so much in what He has said as in who He is and what He has done. **heir of all things:** Jesus will inherit everything because He is the eternal Son of God Himself (Is. 9:6, 7; Mic. 5:2). His inheritance is universal dominion. He will rule over everyone and everything (Rom. 4:13; Rev. 11:15). **made the worlds:** The Greek word for *worlds* can also mean "ages." Thus, *worlds* indicates the entire created universe, all space throughout all time. The Son is the Lord of all history. He has managed the universe throughout its history as Mediator under the Father.

1:3 The Son is **the brightness of** God's **glory,** meaning the radiance that comes from God's essential glory (John 1:14; 2 Cor. 4:4, 6). The author of Hebrews is emphasizing that this is not a reflected brightness like the light of the moon. Instead this is an inherent brightness like a ray from the sun. Jesus' glorious brightness comes from being essentially divine. The phrase **express image** occurs only here in the NT and means "exact representation" or "exact character." In Greek literature the word was used of stamping a coin from the die. The Son is the exact representation of God's being because He is God Himself (Col. 1:15). In fact, the Greek word translated **person** here means "nature" or "being." As Jesus said, "He who has seen me has seen the Father" (John 14:9). **Upholding**

means "bearing" or "carrying," referring to movement and progress toward a final end. The Son not only created the universe by His powerful word but also maintains and directs its course. He is the Governor of the universe. The laws of nature are His laws, and they operate at His command. **Purged** means "cleansed" or

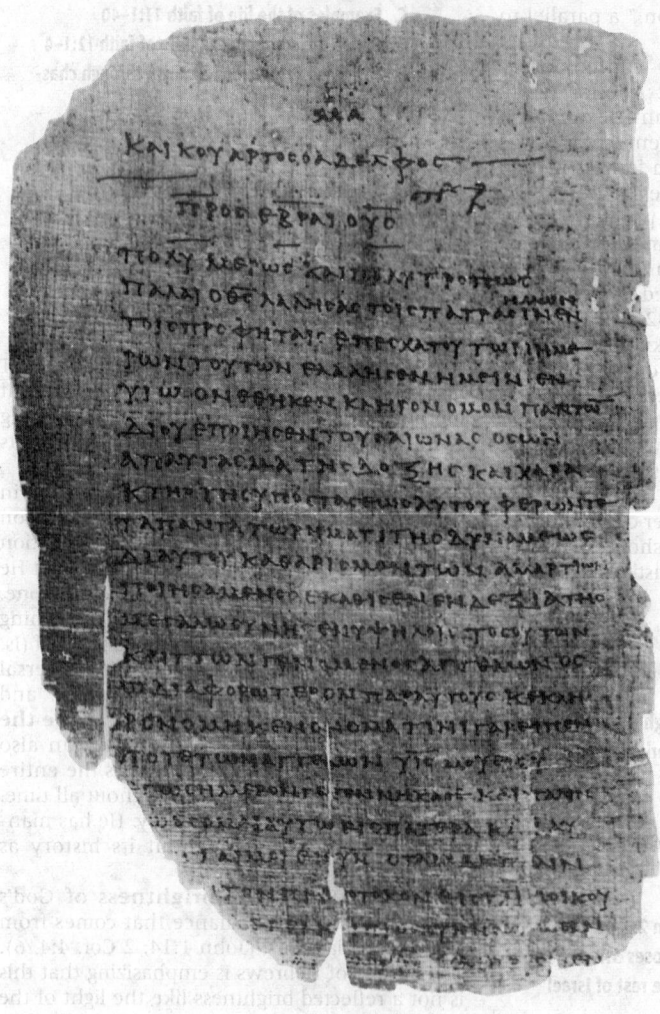

This ancient papyrus manuscript contains the end of the Epistle to the Romans and the beginning of the Epistle to the Hebrews, written in *koine* Greek—the language of the New Testament.

"purified." The glory of redemption is far greater than the glory of creation. The Son of God came down not to dazzle us with His splendor but to purge our sins. **Sat down** suggests the formal act of assuming the office of High Priest and implies a contrast to the Levitical priest, who never finished his work and sat down

(10:11–13). In the OT we meet a seatless sanctuary. In the NT we find a seated Savior.

1:4 The Son is **better than the angels,** or higher in rank, because He sits at the right hand of God (v. 3) and because of His eternal inheritance. The Son has obtained a greater name than the angels. This majestic picture builds up to the dramatic invitation in 4:16 for us to come boldly into the Son's presence.

1:5–14 The author of Hebrews uses seven OT citations to explain why the Son is superior to angels.

1:5 Angels are "sons" collectively, in that they were created by God (Job 1:6). In contrast, Christ is uniquely and eternally the **Son.** He is superior to the angels. **Today I have begotten You** probably refers to the day Christ sat down at the Father's right hand after He accomplished His work as the Messiah. On that day the eternal Son entered into the full experience of His Sonship. **I will be to Him a Father:** This passage quotes 2 Sam. 7:14 and is a prophecy of Christ as the eternal Person in whom the Davidic line and kingdom culminates.

1:6 When He again brings is a reference to the Second Coming. **Firstborn** here refers to rank, meaning one who ranks above all others (Ps. 89:27). The Son does not worship but is worshiped by angels. The quotation in this verse is either from the Septuagint version of Deut. 32:43 or from Ps. 97:7, where the Septuagint correctly renders the Hebrew text *angels.* The angels will **worship** the Son when He is enthroned as the King over the entire earth (2:5–9), after taking revenge on His enemies and restoring His people.

1:7 The Son is superior to angels because He is the Sovereign who is worshiped, while the angels are **ministers**, that is, servants of God. The author of Hebrews quotes Ps. 104 because that psalm places angels in a long list of created objects that God sovereignly controls.

1:8 O God: Jesus Christ is accorded the

🔍 IN FOCUS | "brightness"

(Gk. *apaugasma*) (1:3) Strong's #541; express image (Gk. *charakter*) (1:3) Strong's #5481: These two expressions occur only here in the NT. The Greek word for *brightness* expresses the brilliance emanating from a glorious source of light, such as the beams of the sun. Christ, as the effulgence of God's glory, is the radiance of God, revealing God's glory to humanity. The Greek word translated *express image* can mean the instrument used in engraving or stamping, but usually it means the image engraved or stamped. In this context, the word means that Christ is the exact representation of God's nature. Since God's essence, nature, and being are invisible, the Son reveals God to us, for He is an exact visible likeness of God.

rank of full deity. The Son has an eternal **throne,** which means He possesses an eternal kingdom.

1:9 Companions comes from a word that means "close associates" or "partners." The concept of believers being companions with Christ is key in Hebrews (3:1, 14; 6:4; 12:8). The term refers to those who will be participants with Christ in His reign. As the Son obtained the right to rule and joy through a righteous life, so will His partners—believers who live godly lives and who will rule with the Son in His kingdom.

1:10–12 The context of Ps. 102, from which these verses are taken, clearly indicates that the "LORD" is the One who would appear in the future to Israel and the nations (Ps. 102:12–16). Thus, the psalm can only refer to Jesus, the Second Person of the Trinity, the only One who would become incarnate. Jesus is God become man. The universe will **perish** (2 Pet. 3:10–13; Rev. 21:1), but the Son will **remain** forever. The universe will **be changed,** but the Son will remain **the same** (13:8).

1:13 Christ sits at the **right hand** of God until the final victory over all His **enemies** (1 Cor. 15:25–28).

1:14 Angels are mere servants (v. 7) who serve **those who will inherit salvation.** *Salvation* here is not justification because it is in the future, not in the past. The reference is to believers who inherit the Kingdom or rule in God's kingdom as a reward for their service to the Son (9:28; Col. 3:24). The author is speaking about "the world to come" (2:5). References to salvation in 2:3, 10; 5:9; 6:9 probably also concern the future.

2:1 The author issues the first of five exhortations (vv. 1–4; 3:1—4:16; 5:11—6:20; 10:19–39; 12:1–29). Believers **have heard** from the Lord God because we have heard the gospel message. His very majesty demands that we listen attentively to what He says. **drift away:** The author's audience was marked by immaturity and spiritual sluggishness (5:11, 12). The author warned

them not to be carried away by the popular opinions that surrounded them. Instead they were to hold fast to Christ's words because they were the words of God. How easy it is to drift with the currents. Think of how far "righteous Lot" drifted from Abraham when he turned his eyes toward Sodom. All of us are continually exposed to the currents of opinion that seem so reasonable and comfortable as contrasted to the task of fighting the rapids with our eyes focused upon our Captain (Rom. 12:2).

2:2 the word spoken through angels: The Law was delivered from God to Moses by angels (Deut. 33:2; Acts 7:38, 53; Gal. 3:19). Disobedience or obedience to the law was punished or rewarded. This discipline is discussed at length in 12:5–11 (Deut. 28—30). When a person broke the law, the punishment he received was not loss of justification or regeneration. Instead, he lost temporal blessing and was disciplined (compare Heb. 12:5–11).

2:3 how shall we escape: If the people who heard the message delivered through angels were justly punished when they disobeyed the Law, how can believers expect to escape punishment when they neglect the even greater message delivered through the greater Messenger, the Son? *We* is found five times in vv. 1, 3. The author warns these believers, including himself, about neglecting salvation and losing out on the opportunity to reign with Christ. The **great salvation** (Phil. 2:12, 13) cannot be a reference merely to justification because this salvation was **first . . . spoken by the Lord.** Justification was spoken of in the OT (Gen. 15:6); but it was the Lord who first spoke of His followers inheriting His kingdom and reigning with Him (v. 10; Luke 12:31, 32; 22:29, 30). **those who heard Him:** The author includes himself among those who had not heard the Lord Himself. The fact that the third generation had the message confirmed to them by the second generation who apparently worked the miracles implies that the confirming miracles had ceased by the third generation. The past tense of **confirmed** supports this conclusion. The original readers may have seen the miracles, but they did not perform them.

2:4 Signs and wonders refers to the miracles performed by the **Holy Spirit** through the Lord and His apostles in fulfillment of the ancient promises regarding the coming of the Messiah (Acts 2:22, 43; 4:30; 5:12; 6:8; 14:3; 15:12; 2 Cor. 12:12).

2:5 The author returns to the theme of ch. 1 that the Son is superior to the angels. **For** connects this passage with 1:4–14, as the mention of angels in this verse and the allusion to Ps. 110 (v. 8) indicate. **The world to come** is the future rule of the Son and His companions (1:9) on the earth.

2:6–8 Since the Son's humanity might appear to be an obstacle to the claim of His superiority, the author of Hebrews cites Ps. 8, a lyrical reflection on Gen. 1, to prove that God has placed humanity over all created things, which includes the angelic world.

2:8 But now: The rule of human beings over God's creation has been delayed because of sin (v. 15). Humanity's collusion with Satan has brought all people into collision with God. **Not yet** indicates that the delay is only temporary.

2:9 Human beings will rule over creation, but it will be through Jesus Christ. **But we see Jesus:** The author uses Christ's human name *Jesus* for the first time in this letter. Citing

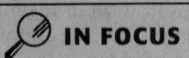

IN FOCUS **"captain"**

(Gk. *archēgos*) (2:10, 12:2; Acts 3:15; 5:31) Strong's #747: The Greek word for *captain* means "pioneer" or "leader." It literally means "the first one to lead the way" from *archē* ("the first") and *agō* ("to lead"). To express this idea of leadership, the word is translated in Acts 3:15; 5:31 as the "Prince" and in Heb. 12:2 as "the author." Thus, the writer of Hebrews is emphasizing that Jesus endured suffering and temptation on this earth in order to become a perfect leader. He is not only sinless but also can sympathize with our difficulties in following His perfect way, the Way that leads to glory.

phrases from Ps. 8, the author points out that Christ, by His humiliation and exaltation, has regained what Adam lost, the original calling for human beings to rule over God's creation (Phil. 2:6–11; Rev. 5:1–14).

2:10 Bringing many sons to glory is not a reference to taking believers to heaven. It is bringing fellow sufferers to future glory (2 Cor. 4:17). When believers suffer, they become sons in the sense that they are like their Father. Jesus used the word *sons* in this way (Matt. 5:44, 45). The Greek word for **captain** means "leader" or "originator." The word describes a pioneer or pathfinder. Jesus' endurance of **sufferings** on this earth makes Him our leader. He has already experienced the sufferings we must go through on this earth. He not only endured them but triumphed over sin, death, and Satan through them. His sinless life has blazed a path to God, a path we must follow. Jesus is our model, our leader, and our Captain. He understands our pain because He Himself went through suffering. **Salvation** refers to our future salvation, our glorification in Christ's coming kingdom (1:14).

2:11–13 By a statement followed by three supporting quotations from the OT, the writer demonstrates the unity between the Son and the many sons.

2:11 all of one: This phrase refers either to the common humanity that Jesus shares with all believers, or to the fact that Jesus and believers all belong to God. Because the children of God and the Son Himself are from the same Father (John 20:17), Jesus can call all believers His **brethren.**

2:12 Psalm 22, which is quoted here, describes the agony of a righteous sufferer. Ultimately the psalm is messianic. It depicts the sufferings of Christ. Jesus quoted Ps. 22:1 on the Cross (Matt. 27:46). In this psalm, the Messiah refers to **My brethren,** identifying Himself with all those who place their faith in God.

2:13 The citations are from Is. 8:17, 18 and refer to a prophet, who, like the Lord Jesus, was persecuted and rejected but became a rallying point for the faithful.

2:14–16 Having established the unity between the Son and believers, the author concludes that there are two purposes of this close identification. The Son became human so that He could destroy the devil (v. 14) and release those who were in bondage to sin (v. 15).

2:14 shared the same: Jesus Christ shared in our humanity by humbling himself to become a man (Phil. 2:5–11). **power of death:** The devil tempts people to sin and then accuses them of rebelling against God (Gen. 3; Job 1). By inducing them to sin, Satan delivers people over to death, the due penalty for their sin (Rom. 5:12). The devil is still active today (1 Pet. 5:8), but his power over death has been taken away from him. Christ's death fulfilled the penalty for sin. Thus, by placing our trust in Christ, we can be free from Satan's evil grasp (Luke 10:18; 2 Tim. 1:10; Rev. 1:18). The judgment of Satan was rendered by the Cross, but the execution lies in the future (1 Cor. 15:54–57; Rev. 20:10).

2:15 The devil uses the **fear of death** to enslave us. Through His death (v. 14), the Son eliminated such fear and broke the **bondage** of sin and death.

2:16 The seed of Abraham refers either to the physical descendants of Abraham or the spiritual children of Abraham—that is, the ones who, like Abraham, have placed their faith in God (Gal. 3:7, 29). The author may have used this expression because the recipients of this letter were primarily Jewish believers. The author is pointing out that Christ came to the aid of Abraham's sons, not of the angelic hosts.

2:17 In all things includes Jesus' humanity (v. 14) and His suffering (v. 18). Jesus participated in our nature and in our sufferings on earth so that He could be a sympathetic Mediator between God and humanity. He understands our weaknesses and intercedes for us in the presence of God the Father. He is a **merciful** (sympathetic) and **faithful** (trustworthy) **High Priest.** This is the first time the title High Priest occurs in Hebrews, and the first time the title is applied to Jesus Christ in the Bible. **Make propitiation** refers to the satisfaction of the claims of a holy and righteous God against sinners who have broken His law. Christ appeased God's righteous wrath by dying on the Cross in our place (Rom. 3:21–26). Although completely perfect and sinless, Christ voluntarily submitted to the penalty of sin, this agonizing death on the Cross. This voluntary sacrifice of Himself for our welfare satisfied the justice and holiness of God. The benefits of His sacrifice are applied to all who place their faith in Him.

2:18 being tempted: Christ's suffering included temptation. He experienced the lure of sin, but He never surrendered Himself to it. He knows what it is like to be tempted, so He knows how to assist those who are being tempted.

3:1–4:16 The second exhortation (2:1-4). **Holy brethren** links them with the concept of sanctification in 2:11.

3:1, 2 Partakers is the same Greek word that is translated *companions* in 1:9. The **heavenly calling** of these *companions* is to inherit salvation (1:14) and their future glory in Christ (2:10). The author of Hebrews invites Jewish believers to **consider** the faithfulness of Christ Jesus. **Apostle** means "one who is sent." This is the only passage in the NT that labels Jesus as the Apostle. The title indicates that Jesus was "sent" by God to reveal the Father (John 4:34; 6:38; 7:28, 29; 8:16). The phrase **in all His house** is taken from Num. 12:7. *House* refers to the tabernacle, the center of Israelite worship.

Moses had faithfully obeyed God's instructions concerning the tabernacle. In the same way, Jesus had been obedient to the mission the Father had given Him. Through His obedience, God established a new house of God, the church.

3:3, 4 He who built all things is God: The author of Hebrews equates Jesus with God. Thus, Jesus is certainly **worthy of more glory than Moses** (1:2, 8, 10). The implication is that the covenant established through Jesus' death is more glorious than the covenant established at Mount Sinai.

3:5 The author of Hebrews continues the comparison between Moses and Jesus. While Moses was faithful **as a servant,** Christ's faithfulness was greater because it was performed by **a Son. Things . . . spoken afterward** indicates that Moses' work pointed forward to Christ (9:10; 10:1–3). The regulations of the Law of Moses pointed out both the sin of humanity and the need for a perfect sacrifice to reconcile people to their holy Creator.

3:6 a Son over His own house: The Son is the One who will sit on the throne in the coming kingdom (1:8). He presently rules over the church and will rule over all creation when His opponents are completely defeated. His house consists of all those who believe in Him. **hold fast the confidence . . . to the end:** Those who endure to the end, steadfastly placing their hope in the Son, will live with Him in eternity.

3:7–11 The author of Hebrews quotes Ps. 95:7–11 to warn the Jewish Christians about hardening their hearts to God and the salvation He offers. Moses' generation had refused to trust in God to provide for their needs in the wilderness (Ex. 17:1–7), and the readers of this letter were in danger of not trusting in the salvation offered through God's Son. If they were to hold fast to the end (v. 6), they could not **harden** their hearts to God now (vv. 8, 13, 15). Instead they had to renew their belief in God's Word (vv. 12, 19), place their trust in Christ, and obey Him (v. 18). **Rest** is a key concept in Hebrews. In the OT, the conquest of the Promised Land and the cessation of fighting in the land was viewed as a form of rest (Deut. 3:20; 12:9; 25:19; Josh. 11:23; 21:44; 22:4; 23:1). In the NT, *rest* speaks of the believer's eternal home and the joy that he or she will experience in Jesus' presence (4:1).

3:12 The author is definitely speaking to genuine believers. He addresses them as **brethren** (Gk. *adelphoi;* compare "holy brethren" in v. 1) as is the uniform treatment throughout the book. Nowhere is there the slightest suggestion that they were mere professors as over against genuine Christians as is widely believed. **an evil heart of unbelief:** This refers to serious spiritual heart trouble. An unbelieving heart is evil because unbelief is evil. **departing** (Gk. *aphistēmi*): This word has the idea of "standing off." **from the living God:** Serious losses accrue to unbelieving believers, those who refuse to listen and turn a cold shoulder to God. Evidently this describes a relapse from Christianity into Judaism. Jesus is God. To depart from Him is to depart from the living God. This is contrasted with the "hold fast" of v. 6.

 **IN COMPARISON** **The Majesty of Christ**

Hebrews is perhaps the greatest Christological book in the Bible, giving us a detailed description of the attributes and accomplishments of Jesus Christ. The following chart is a summary.

Christ is . . .	This means . . .
heir of all things (1:2)	As God's "firstborn" Son, Christ will inherit infinite glory and honor.
the One through whom God made the worlds (1:2)	Christ was the Agent who created the universe.
the brightness of God's glory (1:3)	Christ reflects the majesty of God.
the express image of His person (1:3)	Christ is God made visible, in the flesh.
upholding all things by the word of His power (1:3)	Christ holds the universe together (Col. 1:17).
seated at the right hand of the Majesty on high (1:3)	Christ is reigning and ruling with God the Father as Lord over all.
better than the angels (1:4)	Christ is to be exalted more than the angels, no matter how glorious and awe-inspiring they are.
captain of our salvation (2:10)	Christ is the founder of the effort to "bring many sons to glory" (5:9).
the destroyer . . . of . . . the devil (2:14)	In dying for our sins, Christ overcame our greatest enemies—death and the devil.
a merciful and faithful High Priest (2:17)	Christ brought the ultimate sacrifice before God—His own blood—so that we might have fellowship with God.
worthy of more glory than Moses (3:3)	Unlike Moses, who was merely a servant in the house of God, Christ is the "Son over His own house" (3:6).
a High Priest who can sympathize with our weaknesses (4:15)	While on this earth, Jesus experienced the temptations and trials of living in a fallen world. He understands the struggles we face and has compassion for us.
always alive to make intercession (7:25)	Christ's priesthood is eternal. We will always have a perfect representative for us before the throne of God.
Mediator of a better covenant (8:6)	The old covenant with its earthly tabernacle and imperfect priests has been superseded by the sinless Christ. He is our High Priest who is interceding for us before God in heaven.
our model for enduring hostility from sinners (12:2, 3)	When we are discouraged, we can find strength and inspiration in Christ's willingness to persevere.
that great Shepherd of the sheep (13:20)	Christ will care for us and lead us to our eternal home.

3:13, 14 Exhorting each other to continue in the faith is important. Believers must hold their faith firmly to the end of their lives if they are to be **partakers of Christ** (vv. 15–19). *Partakers* is the same word translated *companions* in 1:9. Faithful believers will be partners with Christ in His future kingdom (Rev. 2:26, 27).

3:15–19 The author of Hebrews speaks of the Israelites' unbelief as sin (v. 17) and disobedience (v. 18). The Israelites did not **enter** God's **rest,** the Promised Land (v. 11), because they did not believe in God's promises to them (Num. 1:1–34). They failed to possess their inheritance because they did not trust in God (Deut. 12:9; Josh. 13:7). The Jewish Christians to whom this letter was addressed were in danger of following in their ancestors' footsteps. They were tempted to doubt the words of Jesus. With the rhetorical questions in these verses, the author of Hebrews was encouraging them to place their faith firmly in Christ (10:26; 12:1, 2).

4:1–11 In 3:12–19 Israel's failure to enter the rest God had provided is a warning to Christians. The author now explains what this **rest** is and shows why it is available for us today.

4:1 The tragic unbelief of the desert generation of Israelites (3:7–19) serves as a warning for believers today to enter into God's **rest,** which is still offered to the faithful (vv. 6–11).

4:2 The gospel was preached is the translation of a single Greek word meaning "the good news was announced." The good news of God's rest (v. 1) had been proclaimed to the Israelites. The generation led by Moses had failed to enter their rest, which was the Promised Land (Deut. 12:9), because of their lack of **faith.** In the same way, the gospel of Christ that had been proclaimed to the author's audience was calling them into God's rest, but their unbelief would hinder them from entering into it.

4:3 from the foundation of the world: The creation rest of God is the archetype and type of all later experiences of rest.

4:4 God rested: The theme of rest has its beginning in God's own rest after creation. The fact that Genesis makes no mention of the evening of the seventh day of creation provides a basis for some Jewish commentators to conclude that the rest of God lasts throughout all of history.

4:5, 6 They: There was a rest later for God's people, and the Exodus generation failed to enter into it.

4:7, 8 By merely entering the Promised Land, the Israelites had not entered God's rest, for David (years after Joshua had led the Israelites into the land) had warned his generation to not **harden** their hearts, so that they could enter God's rest (3:7–11). Like David, the author of Hebrews called the present generation

to respond to God **today** (3:13), which is the day of repentance.

4:9 The Greek word for **rest** in this verse is different from the word used in vv. 1, 3, 5, 10, 11; 3:11, 18. This word means "Sabbath rest" and is found only here in the NT. Jews commonly taught that the Sabbath foreshadowed the world to come, and they spoke of "a day which shall be all Sabbath."

4:10 rest from his own work: This may refer to the rest believers will enter in when they finish their work for God's kingdom on this earth (Rev. 14:13).

4:11 us: Including himself as well as his readers, the author exhorts believers to be **diligent,** a phrase meaning "make every effort." **to enter that rest:** The rest is not automatic. Determined diligence is required. The danger is that believers today, like the Israelites of the past, will not stand, but **fall** in **disobedience.**

4:12 The **word of God** is the measuring stick Christ will use at the judgment (2 Cor. 5:10). God's message is alive and active, penetrating the innermost parts of a person. It distinguishes what is natural and what is spiritual, as well as the **thoughts** (reflections) and **intents** (insights) of a person. The word of God exposes the natural and spiritual motivations of a believer's **heart** (v. 7; 3:8, 10, 12, 15; 8:10; 10:16, 22; 13:9).

4:13 Naked and open suggests complete exposure and defenselessness before God. All believers must **give account** to the all-seeing, all-knowing God (Rom. 14:10–12; 2 Cor. 5:10).

4:14–10:18 This section on the high priesthood of Christ is the heart of Hebrews. The subject was mentioned in 2:17. It is reintroduced here in 4:14–16, discussed briefly in 5:1–10, and considered at length in 7:1—10:18. Our High Priest is just the kind we need: He can cleanse the sinful human heart.

4:14 Then refers back to the subject of the high priesthood of Christ (2:17—3:6). **We have** indicates possession. In the OT the high priest of Israel passed through the courts and veils into the Most Holy Place. Our High Priest has **passed through the heavens** to the very presence of God, where He sits at God's right hand (1:3). The title **Jesus . . . the Son of God** underlines His two natures—His humanity and deity.

4:15 Sympathize means "to suffer with" and expresses the feeling of one who has entered into suffering. **In all points tempted** means Jesus experienced every degree of temptation (2:18). **without sin** (7:26; 2 Cor. 5:21): Only those who do not yield to sin can know the full intensity of temptation. Only Jesus did not yield to temptation.

4:16 Come is the same Greek word translated *draw near* in 10:22. What a contrast to the

---

🔍 **IN FOCUS**   **"mercy"**

(Gk. *eleos*) (4:16; Rom. 15:9; Eph. 2:4; Titus 3:5; Jude 21) Strong's #*1656*: The Greek word for *mercy* denotes an outward demonstration of pity, a sympathy that expresses itself in helping a person in need instead of remaining completely passive. The word *eleos* is often used in conjunction with the Greek word *charis,* translated *grace* (Eph. 2:4, 5; 1 Tim. 1:2; 1 Pet. 1:2, 3). A similar idea is expressed by the Hebrew word *chesed,* often translated *lovingkindness* or *goodness.* It is the "loyal love" that God freely showed the Israelites because of His covenant with them. The ultimate expression of God's mercy is His voluntary offering of His only Son for our sins, even when we were still His enemies (Eph. 2:4, 5). Since Jesus, our Intercessor at the right hand of God (7:25), has experienced every kind of temptation we endure (4:15), we can approach Him with boldness, knowing that we will find sympathy and mercy. We who have experienced God's mercy and forgiveness should, in turn, show mercy to others (James 2:13).

"stay away in order that you die not" of the OT which these people and all their forebears grew up under. How beautiful was the difference summed up by John the Baptist in his introduction of Jesus. "Behold, the Lamb of God who takes away the sin of the world." No longer would there be the death of animals as sacrifices. No longer would only the high priest have access to the holiest. **Boldly** is the same word that is rendered *confidence* in 3:6 (10:19) and means "plainness of speech," "fearlessness," or "courage." Believers should courageously approach God in prayer because His is a **throne of grace,** and our High Priest sits at His right hand interceding for us.

5:1–4 These verses explain what it means to be a **high priest.** A high priest must be a person (vv. 1–3) called by God (v. 4). A priest represents the people and thus must identify with their human nature. But he also represents God to the people and thus must be called by God to his office.

5:1 gifts and sacrifices: The primary reference here is to the work of the high priest on the Day of Atonement, the one day of the year when a priest entered into the Most Holy Place (9:7–10) to atone for the sins of the people and intercede for them.

5:2 Ignorant and going astray describes those who unintentionally sinned among the people (Num. 15:30–36).

5:3 The high priest was required to offer a sacrifice **for himself** on the Day of Atonement (9:7; Lev. 16:6).

5:4 called by God: Aaron was appointed to the position of priest by God Himself (Ex. 28:1), as were his successors (Num. 20:23–28; 25:10–13). Those who challenged Aaron's call or appointed themselves as priests were put to death by God (Num. 16).

5:5, 6 Christ did not call Himself to the office of **High Priest;** the Father called Him to the honor. Both Pss. 2:7 and 110:4 are cited to prove this fact. Psalm 2:7 is also quoted in 1:5 to prove Christ's superiority to the angels, and now the writer uses the quote to prove Jesus' special relationship with God the Father. The quote from Ps. 110:4 highlights the eternal nature of Jesus' priesthood. He will be Mediator between God and us forever.

5:7 Christ did not offer sacrifice for Himself. Rather, He **offered up** for us the **prayers, supplications, cries and tears** of an obedient life and death. He was **heard** and His sacrifice accepted because of His **godly fear** (reverent obedience). He was saved **from death** through the Resurrection.

5:8 He learned obedience: Jesus did not need to learn to obey as if disobedient previously, but He did have to go through the experience of obeying His Father's will. He learned the nature of obedience.

5:9 having been perfected: This phrase does not suggest that Jesus had not been perfect before. It means that He successfully carried out God's plan for Him. He endured suffering and temptation so that He could truly function as our High Priest, understanding our weaknesses and interceding before God for us. **Author** means "cause" or "source." Jesus' obedience to the Father led to Calvary, His own death on the Cross. The sacrifice of this sinless One in our place makes Him the source of our **salvation.**

5:10 Called here means "designated" and introduces Christ's formal title, **High Priest.**

5:11 Though the author of Hebrews has much more to say about Jesus' priesthood, it will be **hard to explain** to the readers of this letter because they are **dull of hearing.** *Dull* means "sluggish." When these people heard the word of God they were not quick to accept it (6:11, 12). They had grown even more lazy in the faith, so explaining the truth to them would be difficult.

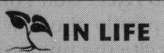 **IN LIFE**   # Lessons in Leadership

Leadership is often understood in terms of power, manipulation, assertiveness, and ambition. The literature of the work world is cluttered with "how to" books that profile the famous and successful who have fought and won by these cruel values. In the first century, the Roman Empire was dominated by very powerful and manipulative family dynasties riddled with competition, violence, greed, and dirty tricks.

But Jesus modeled a different way of leadership. Throughout the NT we are shown glimpses of His life and character. In them we discover a stark contrast to our world's soap opera of abuse and distortion.

Hebrews 5 is one such picture. It describes a true leader as a priest who is:
- focused on people and how they connect with God (Heb. 5:1).
- compassionate with the weak and ignorant (5:2).
- required to face sin head-on (5:3).
- not self-appointed, but rather called by God into his role (5:4).

Jesus was the perfect priest (5:5–10). The writer admits that this portrait is hard to grasp (5:11–14). However, those who seek to grow into Christlike maturity need to consider it carefully. Jesus provides for those who seek His help. All we need to do is ask (4:14–16).

5:12—6:20 The author prepares his readers to receive the teaching on the high priesthood of Christ. He first chides them for their spiritual immaturity (5:12—6:3) and the fact that they have fallen away from progress unto maturity (6:4–8; all five participles in vv. 4–6 are *past* action). He then recalls their spiritual achievements (6:9–12) and reminds them of God's promise (6:13–20).

5:12 By this time you ought to be teachers suggests all believers ought to be teachers not in the formal sense (compare 1 Cor. 12:29; James 3:1), but in the sense that those who have been taught ought to impart to others what they have learned through the gifts God has given them. **First principles** are basic truths (6:1, 2). The phrase refers to the letters of the alphabet in writing or to addition and subtraction tables in arithmetic. First principles are the elements out of which everything else develops. **have come to need:** They have retrogressed because of disuse. If you don't practice what you see and hear, you lose it and have to be told it again and again. To not use it is to lose it. **milk . . . solid food:** The author illustrates the ingredients of growth. Milk equals input. Solid food equals output. We start with the input of truth (1 Pet. 2:2), exercising the principle of readiness for learning. We gradually implement the principle of practice for retention of truth. Consistent and persistent practice of truth results in growth to maturity (this same formula is applied to the Corinthians by Paul in 1 Cor. 3:1–4).

5:13 unskilled in the word of righteous- **ness:** The readers of this letter did not necessarily lack information concerning righteousness; they lacked experience in practicing the information they had. Maturity comes from practice. As we practice righteousness, we will have less difficulty in determining good from evil. **Babe** is a description of the spiritually immature. Babies have little discernment or self-discipline. They must be constantly told "no." Mature believers are able to know right from wrong and to control their sinful appetites.

5:14 Full age describes the spiritually mature. **Reason of use** means "practice" or "habit." Those who make a habit of obeying the message of righteousness mature in the faith and are able to distinguish **good and evil.**

6:1, 2 The author urges the readers of his letter to leave the basics (5:12) and **go on to perfection,** meaning "maturity." He lists six items in three couplets that he calls **the elementary principles of Christ** ("the first principles" in 5:12). (1) **Repentance from dead works** refers to a change of mind about the demands of the Law of Moses (9:14). Even though the Law was good (1 Tim. 1:8), it was weak because of the weakness of our sinful nature (Rom. 8:3). (2) What is needed for salvation is not lifeless works that cannot save, but **faith** directed **toward God.** (3) **Baptisms** refers either to the various baptisms in the NT (the baptism of Christ, of John, of believers, and the spiritual baptism of believers), or to the various ritual washings practiced by the Jewish people. (4) In the Book of Acts, the **laying on of hands** was used to impart the Holy Spirit

(Acts 8:17, 18; 19:6). It was also used for ordination for ministry (Acts 6:6; 13:3). This practice is also found in the OT in commissioning someone to a public office (Num. 27:18, 23; Deut. 34:9) or in the context of presenting a sacrificial offering to the Lord (Lev. 1:4; 3:2; 4:4; 8:14; 16:21). (5) **Resurrection from the dead**

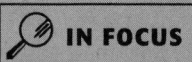 **IN FOCUS** **"oracles"**

(Gk. *logion*) (5:12; Acts 7:38; Rom. 3:2; 1 Pet. 4:11) Strong's *#3051*: The Greek term *logion* is a diminutive of the word *logos* (in 5:13). Here it is not "the Word of God," but "words from God" or "divine communications." Peter uses the word for the teaching of Christian preachers (1 Pet. 4:11), while Paul employs the word to refer to the writings of the OT prophets (Rom. 3:2). Stephen uses the word to speak of God's utterances on Mount Sinai and His promises concerning the coming of the Messiah. The author of Hebrews uses this word for the basics of Christian doctrine, perhaps consciously contrasting this word to the *logos,* "the word of righteousness," which is for the mature Christian (5:13).

---

refers to the resurrection of all people at the end time (Rev. 20:11–15). The resurrection is an OT teaching (Is. 26:19; Dan. 12:2) which was widely taught in first-century Judaism, especially by the Pharisees. To Christians, belief in the bodily resurrection of Jesus was essential, for without His resurrection there is no forgiveness of sin (1 Cor. 15:12–17). (6) **Eternal judgment** refers to the belief that everyone will be judged by the great Judge. The Scriptures indicate that there are two judgments: one for believers, in which Jesus determines every believer's reward (1 Cor. 3:12–15), and the other a judgment of condemnation on unbelievers (Rev. 20:11–15).

6:3 Using **we,** the author includes himself. **if God permits**—that is, Lord willing (James 4:15)—indicates the imperative of God's empowering if it is to happen.

6:4–6 This difficult passage concerning "falling away" has been interpreted in various ways. Some insist that the author of Hebrews is speaking of nominal Christians who heard the truth and appeared to believe in Christ, but eventually demonstrated their shallow adherence to Christ by publicly renouncing Him. Others view these verses as a hypothetical argument. In other words, the author of Hebrews is using this hypothetical case to warn the spiritually immature (vv. 1–3) not to reject God's offer of salvation (v. 6; 3:12). Typically those who postulate these two positions cite the numerous passages that speak of a true believer's eternal security (John 6:39, 40; 10:27–29; Rom. 8:28–30). Once God has saved us, nothing can separate us from His love (Rom. 8:35–39). Still others insist that the author is speaking of genuine Christians who renounce Christ and cease to be Christians. They claim that this is a clear reading of this text and cite the numerous warnings in the NT to resist the deceptions of false teachers as additional evidence for their interpretation (2 Cor. 11:1–4, 13–15; 2 Tim. 2: 17, 18; 1 John 2:21–25). Most likely, the passage concerns true believers in Jesus, who are Jewish, and under persecution are tempted to mesh in with the Jewish religion and its rituals from which they had been freed in Christ. Rather than speaking of a loss of justification, it refers to failure to grow further into maturity. The believer who is tempted in "falling to the side," as the Greek better translates, after making much progress in the Christian walk as evidenced by the characteristics of Christian growth found in verses 4 and 5 and have subsequently fallen (not from Christ but in the Christian race) place themselves in danger of being stagnated in Christian growth.

6:6 The phrase **if they fall away** may better be rendered "having fallen to the side" and depicts a runner who has fallen to the side of the track during a race. The Greek does not possess a conditional conjunction. Rather, one should understand this participle as the last of those describing a person for whom it is impossible to have a "change of mind" or repentance while being involved in those activities that mitigate against His profession of Christ. **To renew** (Gk. *anakainizō*) means to restore. It is impossible for continuous effort on the part of anyone in the Christian community to restore a person back to fellowship with God. This is the reason for the strong warning of Heb. 3:13 to exhort one another to avoid a hardened heart. Continuing immaturity is dangerous. Think of those you have known who were radiant witnesses for Christ who were sidetracked and are now cold as stone. The reason the author gives is that they **crucify again . . . put Him to an open shame.** By departing from Christian growth, apostates put themselves in the position of those who actually had Christ crucified and exposed to public shame. If the original readers were Christian Jews contemplating returning to Judaism, then they were joining the ranks of those who crucified Christ. It amounts, in essence, to a fresh public rejection, a crucifixion (symbolically) of Christ all over again.

6:7, 8 An illustration from nature is used to convey two truths: (1) A piece of land that receives rain (a "heavenly gift," v. 4) and is productive, that is, useful to others and blessed by God (v. 7). (2) The same piece of land (v. 8) receives rain (a "heavenly gift," v. 4) but is unproductive, that is, **rejected** (Gk. *adokimos*), a word which means "disqualified" and is used of believers being disqualified from receiving rewards (1 Cor. 9:27; 2 Cor. 13:5, 7). The ground is not cursed; it is **near to being cursed** (1 Cor. 11:29–31). The ultimate end is burning, which is not hell but the temporal judgment of God. In the OT God's judgment on His people is likened to the burning of a field (Is. 9:18, 19; 10:17) which was physical death, not eternal death. Perhaps there is also an allusion here to the fire of the judgment seat of Christ (1 Cor. 3:11–15). There was an ancient practice of burning the ground to destroy the weeds and make the field useful again. If such an allusion is intended, then this passage is teaching that while all human attempts to restore apostates are futile (v. 6), there is hope for production again. It is possible for a person to shipwreck his faith and learn from the experience (1 Tim. 1:18–20).

6:9 With the warmth and affection of the title **beloved,** the author assures the Hebrews that he is **confident of better things** for them. Their good works were signs to the author that they had genuinely received Christ (v. 10).

6:10 They will be rewarded or punished because **God is not unjust.** He will reward them for what they have done.

6:11 Christians are always in danger of not continuing to trust fully in the **hope** they have in Christ. We must keep this commitment firm to **the end.**

6:12 Sluggish is the same word that is translated *dull* in 5:11 and initiates this exhortation to the Hebrews to grow in their faith (5:11—6:12).

6:13–15 Abraham is an example of faith and patience in God's **promise** (v. 12). He waited twenty-five years from the time the promise was first made until Isaac, the promised son, was born (Gen. 12:4; 21:5).

6:16, 17 Confirmation means "guarantee." An **oath** is used to guarantee an agreement.

6:18 The Lord confirmed His oath to Abraham by swearing by Himself (v. 13) because He alone is beyond deceit. The **two immutable things** are God's Word and God's oath. Since God does not lie and since He is all-powerful, He will fulfill all His promises. This unchanging nature of God is the believer's **consolation** and encouragement.

6:19 The believer's **hope** in Christ is secure, like an **anchor.** Furthermore, this anchor is not

in sand, but in the very presence of the Almighty. **Behind the veil** refers to the Most Holy Place, the place where God dwells.

6:20 The Greek word for **forerunner** was used in the second century A.D. of the smaller boats sent into the harbor by larger ships unable to enter due to the buffeting of the weather. These smaller boats carried the anchor through the breakers inside the harbor and dropped it there, securing the larger ship. *Forerunner* presupposes that others will follow. Thus, Jesus is not only the believer's anchor but He is like a runner boat that has taken our anchor into port and secured it there. There is thus no doubt as to whether this vessel is going into port. The only question, is whether it will go in with the sleekness of a well-trimmed sailing vessel or like a water-laden barge. Believers who have such a hope in the presence of God should come boldly before the throne of grace (4:14–16). Moreover, since the hope of believers is sure and cannot be shaken loose, they should use it persistently.

7:1–25 Chapter 7 is the beginning of the advanced teaching for the mature (5:14). Verses 1–10 describe the superiority of Melchizedek's priesthood. According to Gen. 14:18–20, he was greater than Abraham and Levi. Verses 11–25 describe the superiority of Christ, the priest like Melchizedek. According to Ps. 110:4 He is "a priest forever." Therefore, He is greater than the Levitical priests who descended from Aaron (vv. 11–25).

7:1 The mention of **Melchizedek** recalls the author's reference to this ancient priest in 5:10, 11. Melchizedek was both a **king** and a **priest,** a common combination in ancient times. **Salem** was later renamed Jerusalem.

7:2 The name Melchizedek means **king of righteousness. Salem** means **peace.** The ideal king rules in righteousness, which assures peace (Is. 32:17).

7:3 without father . . . mother . . . genealogy: Genesis, a book with many genealogies, has none for Melchizedek. The author is not saying that Melchizedek was born without a father and mother, only that there is no record of his birth in the genealogies of Genesis. This description of Melchizedek prefigures the eternal priesthood of Jesus. Like Melchizedek, Jesus is both a Priest and a King, belonging to a righteous priesthood that is independent of Aaron's. Some commentators have cited this passage as evidence that Melchizedek is a preincarnate manifestation of Jesus. This is unlikely for the author states that Melchizedek is **like the Son of God,** not the same as Him.

7:4–7 Melchizedek was **great** because **Abraham** gave him a tithe. In the Greek text the word **patriarch** is emphatic. The greatness of Abraham, the one who possessed the promises of God (v. 6), underscores the even greater rank of Melchizedek, the priest of righteousness.

7:8–10 Melchizedek was not only superior to Abraham; he was superior to the Levitical priesthood in two ways. First, the Levitical priests were **mortal**—that is, they died; and thus different priests represented the people at different times. In contrast, Melchizedek **lives**, meaning the OT does not record his death (v. 3).

(Gk. *aphomoioō*) (7:3) Strong's #*871*: This Greek word literally means "to make a facsimile," or "to produce a model or copy." Thus, the author of Hebrews was highlighting the similarities between the Son of God and the way Scripture presents Melchizedek. In other words, the ancient priest-king of Salem was a copy of Jesus.

Second, in a sense, Levi paid tithes to Melchizedek through Abraham's gift. **So to speak** indicates that Levi, who was not yet born, did not literally pay tithes. However, because he descended from Abraham, he is counted as having paid tithes to Melchizedek too.

7:11–25 Why does Christ, the priest after Melchizedek's order, replace the **Levitical priesthood?** Interpreting Ps. 110:4 phrase by phrase, the author of Hebrews gives the answer: Christ's priesthood was prophesied (vv. 11–14); His priesthood was based on **the power of an endless life** (vv. 15–19); the **oath** of God established our Lord's priesthood (vv. 20–22); Christ has no successor but **continues forever** (vv. 23–25). Under this new plan, the **law** (v. 12) has been replaced by **a better hope** (v. 19) and **a better covenant** (v. 22).

7:11 If the **Levitical priesthood** had been able to bring people to **perfection**, then a superior priest from **the order of Melchizedek** would not have been needed (Ps. 110:4). If the priests under the Law of Moses could offer permanent reconciliation between God and His people, there would be no need for a coming Messiah, One who would restore the Israelites to their relationship with God.

7:12 Change means "removal" (12:27). If the Melchizedek priesthood removed the Levitical priesthood, then the Mosaic Law is also removed. In short, the believer is not under the Law but instead relies on the righteousness of

Christ (Rom. 6:14; Gal. 3:24, 25). Any system of religion that tries to be under the law cannot have Christ because Christ does not minister the law. It's either Christ or the law but not both.

7:13–19 The author gives two more arguments to demonstrate that the law has been superseded. The first is in vv. 13, 14 and the second is in vv. 15–19.

7:13, 14 He of whom these things are spoken is the Lord, who arose from **another tribe**, namely Judah. According to the Law, the tribe of Judah had nothing to do with the priesthood. The argument hinges on Ps. 110:4 (5:6). If the OT said that another priest was coming from another tribe, then clearly the Law was going to be superseded.

7:15–19 The law, which regulated the priesthood, was **fleshly** in the sense that it regulated a person's external actions. The Lord, however, is a Priest **according to the power of an endless life.** This is proved by Ps. 110:4, quoted in v. 17. Jesus is a different kind of Priest, another indication that the Law has been changed. There has been an **annulling**, a putting away, of the Law.

7:20–28 Having proven that the Law has been superseded, the author argues that it has been replaced by something better.

7:20–22 Christ's priesthood is superior to the Levitical priesthood because it was established by an **oath** ("the LORD has sworn" in Ps. 110:4).

7:23, 24 Because Christ lives **forever,** His priesthood is **unchangeable.** In the Levitical system, the high priest's office was always changing hands. When one high priest died, another assumed the office. Josephus estimated that there were eighty-three different high priests between Aaron and the fall of the temple in A.D. 70.

7:25 Christ **is . . . able to save** because He is fully God and fully human (2:18; 4:15). Since this verse speaks of Jesus' present intercession for us, the word *save* in this verse speaks of our sanctification, the continuing process by which we are freed from the power of sin. This continuing process of salvation will eventually be completed in our glorification, when we our saved from the presence of sin. The word **uttermost** may speak of this glorification, this "complete" or "whole" salvation. **come:** The Greek verb for *come* is in the present tense. Therefore, the word indicates that Jesus continues to save those who keep coming to Him. Our justification is a once-for-all event accomplished on the Cross, but our sanctification is a continuing process. Since Christ has a permanent priesthood, He can **save to the uttermost** (Gk. *panteles*), a word which means "completely," or "wholly." To be saved completely (1 Thess.

5:23), believers must come to God through Christ and Christ must intercede for them. This is the last and greatest of the three great "ables" in the book (2:18; 4:15).

7:26–28 The author concludes this chapter with a summary of why Jesus' priesthood is superior to any other. **Higher than the heavens** means Christ is exalted above all and sits in glory at the right hand of the Father (1:3; 2:9; 4:14). **daily, as those high priests:** The high priest offered an annual sacrifice on the Day of Atonement for the atonement of the people's sins (9:7; 10:1), but the priests also offered sacrifices every day before the Lord (Ex. 29:36). In contrast, Jesus offered Himself **once,** a perfect, sinless sacrifice for the sins of all. Since Jesus is perfect, He did not have to offer sacrifices for His own sins. The permanent, eternal nature of Jesus' priesthood established by an **oath** of God is in sharp contrast to the temporal, weak nature of the Levitical priesthood.

8:1–6 Christ's priestly ministry belongs to the heavenly realm. He ministers in heaven, not in the Mosaic **tabernacle** (vv. 1, 2, 5). His sacri- fice was appropriate for heaven; it was not **gifts according to the law** (vv. 3, 4). Therefore, He mediates a **better covenant** (v. 6). These themes are further developed in 8:7—10:18.

8:1 The main point of this section of Hebrews (vv. 1–6) is the High Priesthood of Christ, mentioned in 2:17—3:1 and developed in 4:14—7:28.

8:2, 3 The sanctuary refers to the heav- enly reality represented by the Most Holy Place (9:2, 8, 24; 10:19; 13:11). This reality is the pres- ence of God. Our High Priest serves there and desires to bring us there (10:19).

8:4 according to the law: Only men from the tribe of Levi could serve as priests. Christ was not from that tribe (7:13, 14).

8:5 The Levitical priesthood served as a **copy** of the **heavenly** Priest. The same goes for the tabernacle. Moses was shown a **pattern,** a type or model, of the true tabernacle (Ex. 25:40).

8:6 Christ not only serves in a better sanc- tuary (vv. 1–5); He has a **more excellent min- istry** and is **mediator of a better covenant** based on **better promises** (vv. 10–12).

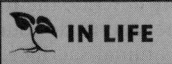 **IN LIFE**   # The Superiority of Jesus

When it comes to spiritual matters, people are peculiar. They become obsessed with angels, but somehow ignore or forget the God who created and directs these heavenly messengers. They devote themselves to seeking and understanding "truth," but they never encounter the Holy One who encompasses all truth. They engage in all sorts of rituals and practices to try to find and reach out to their Creator; but they somehow miss the fact that He has already reached down to them.

This is the case today, just as it was in the first century. In fact, this spiritual "peculiarity" is one of the reasons the Spirit of God inspired the letter to the Hebrews. To Jewish Christians who were dealing with persecution and hardship, who were doubting the truth of the gospel and the New Covenant, and who were considering the idea of turning away, the writer of Hebrews sent this clear message: Christ is the Ultimate.

More than a mere prophet, Christ is God in the flesh (1:2, 3, 8). He is Creator (1:10–12) and Sus- tainer of all (1:3). As the "holy, harmless, undefiled" High Priest who is "separate from sinners" and "who does not need to offer up sacrifices . . . for His own sins" (7:26, 27), Jesus Christ alone is capable of providing salvation and sanctification (2:10, 11).

Given these facts, it is easy to see why the author of Hebrews states that Christ is better than the angels (1:4). It is clear why even Moses pales in comparison. No wonder Hebrews states that Christ is the Author and Mediator of a better covenant (7:22; 8:6), that He offered a better sacrifice for sin (9:23), that He possesses a more excellent name (1:4), and that He carries out a more excellent min- istry (8:6).

We must resist the temptation to settle for a superficial spirituality. Angels, rituals, and human role models all have their place. But none of these things compares to Christ. And therein lies the stag- gering promise of the gospel: Jesus Christ comes to us and offers Himself. Because of His perfect pay- ment for sins, we can find the forgiveness we so desperately need. More than that, we can experience eternal life, which Jesus Himself described as an intimate, never-ending relationship with God the Father and God the Son. Given that mind-boggling opportunity, why would we look anywhere else or settle for anything less?

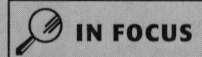

IN LIFE   A New Covenant

Thousands of years of Jewish history were built on God's covenant with Israel. But Christ came to rewrite the script of history. He offers a superior covenant rooted in better promises and without fault (Heb. 8:6, 7). As the prophet Jeremiah had foreseen, under the new arrangement wickedness will be forgiven, sins will be forgotten, and the old covenant will fade into the shadows before vanishing altogether (8:12, 13; Jer. 31:31–34).

What an amazing message! We can have a fresh start. Bondage to old, seemingly unbreakable patterns can be broken and replaced. But first we must confess our condition and accept God's provision, which includes His agenda for change (1 John 1:8–10). Therein lies a fresh start for our lives.

8:7 **That first covenant** is the Mosaic covenant (v. 9; Ex. 19:5).

8:8–12 A quotation from Jer. 31:31–34 demonstrates that even the OT recognized there was another or "second" (v. 7) covenant.

8:8, 9 The **new covenant** is the "better covenant" of v. 6. This covenant was made with **Israel** and **Judah,** yet the church enjoys the spiritual blessings of this covenant now. The Abrahamic covenant was made with Abraham and his physical descendants (Gen. 17:7), who would inherit the land (Gen. 12:7; 13:14, 15). Yet the Abrahamic covenant also contained spiritual promises (Gen. 12:3) in which the church participates (Rom. 11:11–27; Gal. 3:13, 14). The New Covenant in fact is a fulfillment of the spiritual redemption promised in the Abrahamic and Davidic covenants (Matt. 26:26–29; Luke 22:20).

8:10–12 There are four provisions of the New Covenant: (1) God's law will be written on believers' minds and **hearts.** This is in contrast to the Mosaic Law, which was written on tablets of stone. (2) Believers will have a relationship with God fulfilling the promise of Lev. 26:12 (2 Cor. 6:16). (3) **All** will **know** God. No longer will Pharisees and scribes have to teach the intricacies of the Law to the people. (4) God will forgive the sins of believers and remember them no more. The continual sacrifice of animals for the atonement of sin will cease.

8:13 The presence of a **new,** better covenant not only demonstrates that the **first** covenant is not sufficient (v. 7); it also shows that the first covenant is **obsolete** and **ready to vanish away.** At the time the author of Hebrews wrote these words, the ceremonies of the Mosaic covenant were still being conducted in the temple in Jerusalem. In A.D. 70 the Roman general Titus destroyed the temple, fulfilling these words.

9:1–10:10 Verses 1–10 of ch. 9 describe the Day of Atonement sacrifices in the earthly tabernacle (Lev. 16). These sacrifices could not cleanse the conscience. By contrast, Christ's offering of Himself gained Him entrance into the heavenly sanctuary (9:11–14), established a New Covenant (9:15–22), and thus provided for our salvation once and for all (9:23–28). His obedience made His sacrifice effective (10:1–10).

9:1 The **first** (Mosaic) **covenant** included an **earthly sanctuary,** the tabernacle (v. 2), in which **divine service** was offered.

9:2–5 These verses simply describe the furniture of the **tabernacle.** The tabernacle courtyard contained an altar for animal sacrifice, a

IN FOCUS   "know"

(Gk. *ginosko*) (8:11; John 21:17; Gal. 4:9) Strong's #*1097*; (Gk. *oida*) (8:11; John 21:15–17; 2 Cor. 5:16; Gal. 4:8, 9) Strong's #*1492*: In the statement "know the Lord, for all shall know me," there are two different Greek words for *know.* The first word (*ginosko*) means "to come to know" or "to know personally." It can designate ongoing, personal knowledge, which implies a relationship between the knower and the person who is known. The second word (*oida*) is derived from the Greek verb meaning "to see." Thus, *oida* means "to perceive" or "to know absolutely." It suggests complete knowledge, while *ginosko* means a growing knowledge.

laver for ceremonial washings, and the tent itself (the word *tabernacle* literally means "tent"). The tabernacle was divided into two rooms by a veil. The first part was the **sanctuary** or holy place, housing the lampstand, the table for the showbread, and the altar of incense. The second room was the Most Holy Place (v. 3) containing the

ark of the covenant, in which were stored symbols of the Mosaic covenant. The **pot of manna** reminded the people of God's miraculous provision for them in the wilderness. **Aaron's rod** was a sign of the authority of the priesthood. God had ordained Aaron and his sons to be representatives of the people before Him. The tablets were the Ten Commandments given to the nation at Mount Sinai. On top of the ark was the **mercy seat,** the place where God made His presence known. **golden censer:** In this passage, it sounds as if the censer was placed in the Most Holy Place, when in fact it was just outside the veil that separated the Most Holy Place from the holy place. Because of its function, the censer was commonly associated with the Most Holy Place (Ex. 30:6; 40:6).

9:6 Every morning and every evening **the priests** entered the holy place to burn incense on the golden altar and trim the lamps (Ex. 30:7, 8). Every week on the Sabbath, the showbread was changed (Lev. 24:5–8).

9:7 Only **the high priest** could enter the Most Holy Place. **Once a year,** on the Day of Atonement, the high priest offered a **blood** sacrifice **for himself** and for the sins of **ignorance** committed by everyone in the nation of Israel (Lev. 16). In the provisions of the Mosaic covenant, access to God was limited (compare the promises of the "new covenant" in Heb. 8:10, 11).

9:8 The fact that the high priest could enter the **Holiest of All** only once a year indicates the striking failure of the Mosaic covenant to bring believers into the presence of God.

9:9 The tabernacle was **symbolic,** an illustration of spiritual truths. **The present time** refers to the OT period. **cannot make . . . perfect:** The Mosaic covenant covered sins of ignorance (v. 7), but not premeditated sins or the sinful nature of all people (Ps. 51). In other words, the old system was lacking. It did not completely reconcile the people to God.

9:10 fleshly ordinances: This indicates they were external and temporary. **Reformation** (Gk. *diorthōsis*) means "new order." The temporary nature of the Mosaic law appears again.

9:11–14 The "first covenant" (v. 1) had a sanctuary (vv. 2–5) and a service of sacrificial worship (vv. 6–10). Christ, too, had a sanctuary (v. 11) and offered a sacrifice (vv. 12–14).

9:11 Christ's tabernacle is better than the OT tabernacle (vv. 1–5). **The good things to come** include access to God (8:10–12). The preposition **with** in this context means "in connection with." Therefore, **the greater and more perfect tabernacle** is not a reference to Christ's body but to the "true tabernacle" (8:2).

9:12 The service of the Levitical priest obtained a limited, recurring, symbolic type of redemption. Christ, **with His own blood,** obtained **eternal redemption.** His sacrifice never has to be repeated because it is perfect. Millions and millions of animal sacrifices were fulfilled in the one climactic sacrifice of Jesus our Savior. The "with" is more accurately rendered "through." It is not as though He took a bowl of blood. Rather, His shed blood was the channel of access.

9:13 According to Mosaic Law, **the blood of bulls and goats** from the sacrifices made on the Day of Atonement would atone for the people's sins (v. 12). **The ashes of a heifer** were mixed with water and were used to cleanse a person who had become ceremonially defiled by touching a corpse (Num. 19). The author of Hebrews points out that these ceremonies could purify only a person's exterior, not a person's heart.

9:14 The eternal Spirit is the Holy Spirit; all three persons of the Trinity are involved in cleansing. **cleanse your conscience:** The defilement is internal, not external (v. 13). Christ's death has the power to purify a person's mind and soul. **Dead works** are the rituals of the Mosaic Law that could not give life (6:1). Placing faith and confidence in what has already served its purpose and has now passed away is useless. It is disobedience. The author of Hebrews commands his audience to free their conscience from regulations of Mosaic Law and instead cling to Christ for cleansing. In doing so, they could truly **serve the living God** and not dead works.

9:15 The **New Covenant** provides two gifts to a believer: redemption and inheritance. Believers receive **redemption** from the sins committed under the Law. In other words, Christ paid the price to free us from our own sin. His death substitutes for our death, the penalty of our sins. Like the Israelites, believers receive an inheritance, but our inheritance is **eternal** (v. 14). By imitating the faith and patience of Abraham, believers are assured that they will inherit the marvelous promises God has made (6:12; 8:6–12).

9:16, 17 Testament is the same word translated *covenant* in v. 15. It means a legal will. Before the provisions of a will take effect, the one who made it must die.

9:18–21 The Mosaic covenant was ratified by **blood,** that is to say, death. It was not the death of the one making the covenant, but the death of the animals offered as a sacrifice to God (Ex. 24:1–8). To support the proposition that death is necessary for ratification of a covenant, the author illustrates the point by appealing to the ratification of the Mosaic covenant (Ex. 24:3–8).

9:22 Almost indicates that there were exceptions to blood purification (Lev. 5:11–13), but that they were few in comparison with the central importance of sacrifices made for the remission of sins (Lev. 17:11).

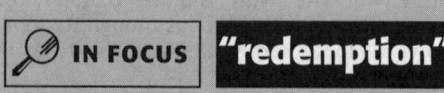

IN FOCUS "redemption"

(Gk. *apolutrōsis*) (9:15; Rom. 3:24; Eph. 1:14; Col. 1:14) Strong's #629: Two related words, *lutrōsis* and *apolutrōsis*, are both translated *redemption* and are frequently used by the NT writers. The first word indicates the act of freeing or releasing by paying a ransom price; the second, the act of buying back by paying a ransom price. Christ paid the ransom price with His own blood (1 Pet. 1:18, 19) and thus freed us from the demands of the law and its curse on sin to become children of God (Gal. 3:13; 4:5).

9:23 If the **copies** had to be cleansed by blood, then an even **better** sacrifice was necessary for the realm of the true sanctuary.

9:24 Christ's sacrifice was better than sacrifices made under the Mosaic covenant because Christ did not enter a man-made sanctuary, which was a copy; instead, He entered the true sanctuary, which is in heaven—the very **presence of God.**

9:25, 26 Christ's sacrifice was better than sacrifices made under the Mosaic covenant because He did not offer an annual sacrifice of animals, but offered **Himself** once. **at the end of the ages:** The coming of Christ is the climax of the OT period.

9:27, 28 As people **die once,** so **Christ** died once—not like the repeated sacrifices of the Levitical system. Unlike people, Christ did not die and face judgment. He died once to appear a

second time **for salvation** (1:14). Those who **eagerly wait for Him** are not necessarily all believers, but those who look for His return, those who are steadfast to the end.

10:1–4 Not the very image means "not the exact representation." **Perfect** refers to the removal of the consciousness of sins (v. 2; 8:12; 9:9). The sacrifices of the Mosaic covenant prefigured Christ's ultimate sacrifice of Himself. Therefore, these imperfect sacrifices of mere animals could not completely purify the person who offered them. If they had been able to, these sacrifices would have **ceased.** Instead of thoroughly atoning for the sins of the people, the annual sacrifice on the Day of the Atonement was a visible reminder of the people's sins.

10:5–7 Therefore: Based on the inadequacy of animal sacrifices, a conclusion is drawn. **it is written of Me:** The author presents Ps. 40 as a messianic psalm, for only Christ, and not David, could have fulfilled the prophecies of *the book*, the OT. **To do Your will:** The OT prophets had warned the Israelites that sacrifices alone would not please God. He desired obedience as well (Ps. 51:16, 17; Is. 1:13–17; Mark 12:33). This messianic psalm indicates that Jesus' obedience to God the Father was one of the reasons His sacrifice was better than the OT sacrifices.

10:8, 9 The author explains Ps. 40, concluding that God **takes away the first,** meaning the Levitical sacrificial system, to **establish the second,** namely, the Son's obedient sacrifice. The verb translated *takes away* means "abolishes." The imperfect sacrifices were abolished so that the perfect Sacrifice could impart true life.

10:10 Sanctified means "set apart." Believers have been separated from their sins and set apart to God by the once-for-all sacrifice of Christ.

10:11, 12 The author of Hebrews contrasts the Levitical priests with Jesus, our High Priest. The Levitical priests always stood before God. There were no seats in the sanctuary, for the

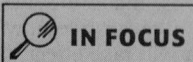

IN FOCUS "covenant"

(Gk. *diathēkē*) (9:15, 16, 17, 18, 20; 13:20; Matt. 26:28; Gal. 3:17) Strong's #1242: The word *diathēkē* can refer either to an agreement or a will (or testament). In 9:15–20, the author of Hebrews explains why the second covenant (8:7) has succeeded the first one made at Mount Sinai. The explanation employs an analogy to a "will." Thus, the author uses the word *diathēkē* throughout the section, employing the two different meanings of the word and tying them together. Just as the stipulations of a will go into effect when a person dies, so Christ died to initiate the New Covenant, the covenant that frees us from bondage to the first covenant.

priests' job was never done. There were always more sins for which to atone. In contrast, Christ **sat down** (1:3; 8:1) after offering Himself as a sacrifice. Sitting indicates that His work of atonement is finished. His final words on the Cross, "It is finished," declare this spiritual reality (John 19:30).

10:13 Christ's work of redemption is so finished that all He has to do is wait until **His enemies are made His footstool.**

10:14 The finished work of Christ in dying for sin once for all (v. 10) has **perfected** (v. 1) **forever those who are being sanctified,** that is, those who have been set apart to God (v. 10). Notice that the sanctification spoken of in v. 10 is positional; it refers to our justification, the fact

Restoring a right relationship with God then prompts believers to restore their relationships with others. Love for God demonstrates itself in love for others. The author exhorts his readers to faith, hope, and love through three commands: "let us draw near" (v. 22); "let us hold fast" (v. 23); and "let us consider" (v. 24).

10:19 Therefore recalls the *therefore* of 4:16. The author has spent five chapters explaining the superiority of Christ's priesthood to the Levitical priesthood and the superiority of the New Covenant to the Mosaic covenant. Unlike the Israelites, who approached God at Mount Sinai with fear and trembling (Ex. 20:18–21), believers can approach God with **boldness** (3:6; 4:16; 10:35) because we possess

Photo: Amsterdam Bible Museum

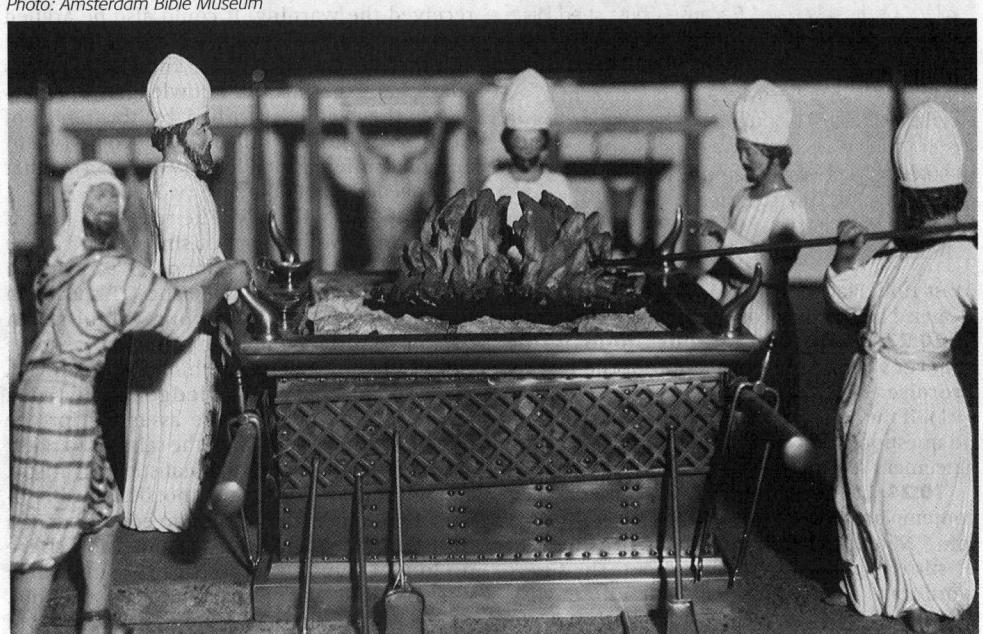

Christ's once-for-all sacrifice of Himself for human sin is superior to the animal sacrifices offered "daily" and "repeatedly" by the Levitical priesthood (Heb. 10:11, 12).

that we have been declared righteous. However, in this verse sanctification refers to the gradual process by which believers are being made more and more perfect.

10:15–18 If full and final forgiveness has been achieved so that God does not remember sin any longer (v. 17), then no further sacrifice for sin is necessary. To **remember** sins **no more** does not mean to forget, but not to hold sin against us any longer.

10:19–25 In these verses, the author of Hebrews demonstrates the relationship between faith, hope, and love. Faith in God leads believers to place their hope in His promises.

Christ's righteousness and not our own. The **Holiest** refers to the very presence of God. On this earth, most of us do not have immediate access to a president or monarch. But through Christ's **blood,** we have perpetual access to God Himself.

10:20 The OT high priest passed through a **veil** to get to the Most Holy Place. Now believers enter God's presence through Christ's **flesh,** meaning His sacrificial death.

10:21 Believers have **a High Priest** who, having been tempted Himself, can sympathize with their weaknesses and perfectly represent them before God (4:14, 15).

10:22 Draw near is the same word rendered *come* in 4:16. **Full assurance** means "certainty" (6:11). **our hearts sprinkled . . . our bodies washed:** Our consciences can be cleansed through the blood of Christ (9:14). Just as the high priest washed before entering the

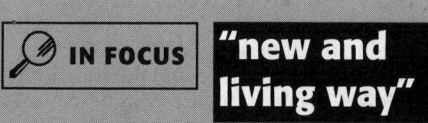

IN FOCUS "new and living way"

(Gk. *hodos prosphatos kai zōsa*) (10:20) Strong's #3598; 4372; 2532; 2198: The Greek word for new is *prosphatos*, meaning "recently killed" or "freshly slain." Because Christ shed His blood to prepare the way for us to enter the Most Holy Place, this way is "a freshly slain way," a way ever fresh because of the eternal efficacy of Jesus' blood. At the same time, this is the living way, for this way leads to our source of spiritual life, namely God Himself. Therefore, this way, prepared by Jesus' death, leads to eternal life.

Most Holy Place (Lev. 16:3, 4), so believers are cleansed before they come before the Holy One.

10:23 Confession of our hope is the believer's confident expectation of the future. **Promised** here may refer to the promise of rest (4:1). If the believer does his or her part, there is no question that God will fulfill His part of the agreement (2 Tim. 2:11, 12).

10:24, 25 Consider means "to observe," "to contemplate," or "to have an intelligent insight into." Note that **love and good works** need to be stirred up; they do not just occur. The Greek word translated **stir up** has come into English as *paroxysm*, which means a "convulsion." In this context the Greek word speaks forcefully of the tremendous impact believers can have on each other. That is why the author exhorts the Hebrews to gather together. Evidently some believers had stopped attending the worship services of the church, perhaps because they feared persecution. The author does not use the usual Greek word for *church*, perhaps because the term had come to mean the spiritual, invisible body of believers. Instead he uses a compound form of the word *synagogue*, which specifically means the local, physical gathering of believers (Ps. 40:9, 10; 42:4). **Exhorting** means coming alongside and inspiring another with the truth. The local assembly is where the gospel message is preached, but also where the Word of God is applied to the circumstances of our lives. **Approaching** may also be translated

"at hand" (Rom. 13:12; Phil. 4:5; James 5:8; 1 Pet. 4:7; Rev. 1: 3). Knowing that Christ's return is imminent, the believers were to encourage each other even more to remain faithful to Him (3:13).

10:26–39 The warnings found in these verses are similar to the warnings in Heb. 6. The additional element in Heb. 10 is the statement regarding intentional sin and the harsher language used of the judgment on the offender. Many have concluded that vv. 26–39 are directed toward the unregenerate, but these verses are clearly addressed to believers. The word **for** indicates that this passage explains the preceding paragraph, which is an exhortation to believers (vv. 19–25). **We** demonstrates the author included himself with those who received the warning. It could also be argued that they "received the knowledge of the truth" and that the Greek word for knowledge means "personal experimental knowledge." Furthermore, they were sanctified by the blood of Christ (v. 29), were called God's people (v. 30) and had suffered for Christ (vv. 32–34). What they needed was endurance (v. 36).

10:26 sin willfully: The reference here is not to an occasional act of sin (which can be confessed and forgiven, 1 John 1:8, 9), but to a conscious rejection of God. The OT speaks in Num. 15:30, 31 of committing willful sin. A person who sinned presumptuously was to be cut off from the people. In this verse, willful sin **after** receiving **the knowledge of the truth** about the centrality of the assembly for the upbuilding and maturing of the saints is to reject it and go one's own individualistic, privatistic, and selfish way. God's plan is not building in isolation but building in relation to each other. If a Christian rebels against God's provision **there no longer remains a sacrifice for sins.** There was no sacrifice for the presumptuous sin (Num. 15:29–31). Such action is to despise the word of the Lord.

10:27 With no hope of forgiveness (v. 26), all that one can expect is **judgment,** described here as a **fiery indignation.** Many have assumed this is a reference to hell. But fire is used in Scripture of other things. The fire here is either temporal judgment or the judgment seat of Christ, similar to the OT in which Yahweh's anger toward His people who sinned is described by the metaphor of fire (Is. 9:18, 19; 10:17). Those who choose to disobey God become His **adversaries** (James 4:4).

10:28, 29 The specific sin in the OT that required **two or three witnesses** was idolatry (Deut. 17:2–7). The judgment for idolatry was death by stoning. If idolatry was punished with physical death, **how much worse punishment** should someone receive who treats the word of Christ with disrespect or disdain? **Counted the blood . . . a common thing** means the blood of Christ is treated as no different from the blood of an ordinary man or the blood of an animal sacrifice. **Insulted the Spirit of grace** is a reference to the Holy Spirit, the agent of God's gracious gift of salvation. A believer who commits these offenses will be judged with a punishment worse than physical death. This is not a reference to spiritual death, or hell. There are forms of temporal judgment that are worse than physical death—some that make physical death a welcomed relief (Lam. 4:6, 9; compare 2 Chr. 26:21).

10:30, 31 The author quotes two passages from Deut. 32 to support his claim that judgment belongs to the Lord and that God's people are not excused from God's judgment. **It is a fearful thing to fall into the hands of the living God** because there is no other sacrifice for sin than Christ's sacrifice on the Cross (v. 26), only a fearful expectation of judgment (v. 27). All sin not covered by the blood of Christ will result in great loss at the judgment seat (1 Cor. 3:15; 2 Cor. 5:10).

10:32–12:17 Those who live the life of faith in God will suffer. These sufferers include the readers of Hebrews (10:32–39), the OT faithful (11:1–40), and, more than anyone else, Jesus Himself (12:1–4). God uses suffering to strengthen His true children (12:5–11). Therefore, be encouraged (12:12–17).

10:32, 33 To encourage his readers, the author urges them to **recall** their **former** endurance, which occurred right after they were **illuminated** or converted (6:9–12). They had endured even though they were ridiculed because of their faith.

10:34 The people to whom Hebrews was written had shown **compassion** on the author when he was in prison and had **joyfully accepted** economic hardship.

10:35, 36 To **cast away** one's **confidence** is to lose conviction about the value of one's Christian commitment. For the recipients of Hebrews to return to the safety of Judaism would mean a loss of eternal **reward** at the judgment seat of Christ.

10:37, 38 These verses focus the attention of a person facing trial on the imminent return

---

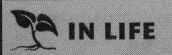 **IN LIFE** | **Growing Faith**

For some followers of Christ, faith is not merely a private matter but a timid one as well. It's as if faith is such a delicate thing that unless one carefully protects it, the world will surely destroy it. However, Hebrews challenges believers to a different way of living. Faith that is alive and growing need not be treated like a pet bunny rabbit that is periodically brought out of its cage to be adored and fed on special occasions, but then quickly returned to its haven of safety. To be sure, we live in a world of roaring lions (1 Pet. 5:8) and therefore must be on guard. Yet the safest way to live in a world of spiritual dangers is to build up our strength, not to hide our faith in secrecy. Hebrews offers some suggestions:

- We can *take confidence* by freely entering into God's presence through Christ (Heb. 10:19, 22).
- Our faith can *rest in full assurance* that because of Christ's work on our behalf, our sins have been forgiven (10:21, 22).
- We can *keep a firm grip* on the basics of our faith, which rest on the integrity of Christ (10:23).
- As believers we can *stir each other up* to loving, active faith (10:24).
- We can *meet with other believers* regularly for encouragement, accountability, worship, and prayer (10:25).
- We can *leave judgment and repayment up to God,* who is the ultimate Judge of people (10:29–31).
- We can *keep a loose grip* on privilege, comfort, and possessions and instead show compassion toward those in need, such as prisoners (10:32, 33).
- We can *condition ourselves for the long haul* so as to finish well (10:35–39).

Spiritual strength and health means integrating our faith with every area of life. Faith is not just one more thing on a list of a hundred things, but rather the foundation of who we are. If our walk with Christ is real, it should become evident to others (James 2:14, 26; 3:13). Faith that is alive and growing is faith unleashed!

of the Lord and the need to endure **by faith** (3:12, 13).

10:39 Those who draw back are in danger of destruction. The writer is confident that he and his readers **believe to the saving of the soul.** Those who live by faith (v. 38) invest their physical lives for eternal dividends.

11:1–39 Having concluded the fourth exhortation with the statement that believers should live by faith (10:38, 39), the author now discusses faith in detail, giving many OT examples of people who trusted God.

11:1 This verse is not a definition of **faith,** but a description of what faith does. **Substance** means "essence" or "reality." Faith treats **things hoped for** as reality. **Evidence** means "proof" or "conviction." Faith itself proves that what is unseen is real, such as the believer's rewards at the return of Christ (2 Cor. 4:18).

11:2 The elders are the believers of the OT. **Good testimony** refers to God's approval; He considered them righteous because of their faith (vv. 4, 5, 7).

11:3 worlds: Faith understands that the invisible God created the vast universe.

11:4 Abel's sacrifice was acceptable to God because of his **faith,** and was therefore declared **righteous.** Evidently Cain offered his sacrifices without faith (Gen. 4). Abel **still speaks** to us because his righteous deeds have been recorded in Scripture.

11:5, 6 The word **comes** is used repeatedly in Hebrews to refer to the privilege of drawing near to God (4:16; 7:25; 10:1, 22). Here the author of Hebrews explains that faith is mandatory for those who approach Him (10:22). **rewarder:** God rewards not only those who seek Him, but those who do good works in the Holy Spirit's power (Rev. 22:12).

11:7 Noah had never **seen** (v. 1) the flood God revealed to him. Yet he believed God in spite of this and heeded His warnings. His faith not only saved him from the deluge but also from God's judgment, for He became an **heir** of **righteousness.**

11:8, 9 Abraham did not know **where he was going,** yet he still placed His trust in God. Faith means obediently stepping into the unknown (v. 1). Abraham did this, and God

---

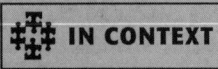 **IN CONTEXT** **Heros of Faith**

The Jewish Christians to whom the Epistle to the Hebrews is addressed were demoralized and discouraged. Christianity had proven difficult for them. It was radical. It set aside centuries of tradition. It emphasized a new but troubling kind of spiritual freedom. In short, it incurred the wrath of the Jewish religious establishment.

Many converts were ready to turn back and to leave the uneasy, uncharted waters of faith for the comfortable, familiar life of works and moral effort. This was the choice they faced: depending on the Law or following Jesus, trying to appease God or trusting in Him, a complicated religious system or a simple relationship with the living God through Christ.

After reminding these immature believers of the superiority of Jesus Christ, the writer of Hebrews, beginning in 10:19, demonstrates for them the superiority of faith. Faith means we cannot see the outcome, we are not sure what lies ahead (11:1). But we are convinced of the reality of God (11:6). In other words, "We're not sure what the future holds, but we know Who holds the future." Faith means clinging to the hope that God will eventually triumph; He will come back to earth in judgment, to reward those who have sought after Him (11:6). And so we obey. We do God's bidding, even when submission is hard.

It is the response of obedience that qualifies the characters in ch. 11 as people of great faith. Abraham and Sarah believed God; consequently, they obeyed Him, regardless of the consequences. It is this kind of willing trust that pleases God (11:6). Anything less will not do.

Those who do not have faith cannot see past the physical world around them. They are limited by their temporal circumstances and are blind to what God is doing. But those who open their spiritual eyes can see the spiritual realities that transcend this world. Their hope is in God's strength and in His faithfulness. In that hope they find the strength to endure. When it comes to faith, the world scoffs. Faith, at best, seems like a great waste; at worst, it seems almost suicidal. Do we really want to give up all the pleasures of this world for something elusive and ethereal?

Faith is never easy. But the more convinced we are of the reality of an all-good, all-powerful God, the more our trust will grow, and the less we will be overwhelmed by doubts and temptations.

considered him righteous because of it (Gen. 15:6; Rom. 4:1–12).

11:10 The city here is the New Jerusalem (Rev. 21:2, 10). Abraham lived in the land waiting for the future yet unseen New Jerusalem.

11:11, 12 Though the Book of Genesis does not explicitly say so, Sarah evidently believed that nothing was too hard for the Lord (Gen. 18:15). As a result, God blessed her with the **promised** son, though she was **past the age** of childbearing. **stars . . . sand:** This comparison used to be considered ridiculous. But now astrophysicists recognize the legitimacy of the comparison of the "stars of the sky" and the "sand of the seashore."

11:13, 14 These all refers to Abraham, Isaac, Jacob, and Sarah (vv. 8, 9, 11), who **died** before taking possession of the land or seeing any of the other provisions of God's covenant. Nevertheless, they endured in the faith, even to the end of their lives. **strangers and pilgrims on the earth:** These men and women of faith knew that this world was temporary, that their eternal home would be with God.

11:15, 16 The patriarchs and Sarah did not **return** to Ur, even though they could have if they had wanted to. The recipients of Hebrews were to follow the patriarchs' example and refuse to return to the religion of their ancestors, a religious system that no longer provided atonement for sin (8:7–13). Similarly, present-day believers should refuse to return to the attractions of this world (2 Tim. 2:3, 4; 4:10).

11:17–19 When **Abraham** was **tested,** he believed that God could **raise** Isaac **from the dead** (Gen. 22:5) if necessary. The incident is figurative of what God has done for us. Isaac was as good as dead, but God provided a ram to sacrifice in his place (Gen. 22:9–14). With God everything is possible. He is the Almighty, and His Son has triumphed over death (John 11:38–44; 1 Cor. 15:54–57; Rev. 1:18).

11:20–22 Isaac, Jacob, and **Joseph** all believed until the ends of their lives in the unseen future God had promised.

11:23 The **parents** of **Moses** had faith in God in the midst of opposition.

11:24–28 Moses believed God by refusing a high position in Pharaoh's court. Instead, he chose suffering, forsook Egypt, and instituted the Passover.

11:25 The **sin** for Moses would have been to abandon God's people (10:25).

11:26 The reproach of Christ refers to the earthly disgrace Christ received. Like Christ, Moses chose to suffer the indignities associated with God's people, instead of embracing the worldly pleasures of Pharaoh's court. The possibility of **reward** is the most frequently mentioned motivation for enduring in the faith (Matt. 5:10–12; 16:24–27; 1 Cor. 3:12–15; 2 Cor. 4:16–18; 2 Tim. 2:11–13; 1 John 2:28; Rev. 22:12).

11:27 forsook Egypt: Some commentators interpret this as a reference to Moses' flight to Midian. However, the mention of **not fearing the wrath of the king** in this verse fits the events of the Exodus better. At that time Moses showed true courage, a resolute faith in the Lord (Ex. 14:13, 14).

11:28 God told Moses to sprinkle **blood** on the doorposts. Moses believed God's word, heeded His warning, and as a result the firstborn of every Israelite family was saved (Ex. 12:1–13).

11:29 dry . . . drowned: Some have tried to explain away the miracle of the Red Sea crossing by saying it was a marshy place. If so, it would have been a major miracle that the Egyptian army drowned in a marsh!

11:30–34 It took **faith** for the warriors of Israel to destroy the walled city of **Jericho** by such unconventional means. Yet this act of faith brought the results they desired; God gave them victory over their enemies (Josh. 6). God's ways do not always appear the best or most logical to human understanding (Is. 55:8), but they always accomplish God's purposes.

11:35, 36 The reference to **women** who **received their dead** is probably a reference to the raising of the son of the widow of Zarephath (1 Kin. 17:17–24) and of the Shunammite woman (2 Kin. 4:32–37). But the author of Hebrews also points out that not all who had faith won victories, at least not in the same hour. **tortured:** This is usually understood to be an allusion to the heroic martyrs of Maccabean times, who were well known. **A better resurrection** is a reference to a richer resurrection, an abundant entrance into the Kingdom (2 Pet. 1:11), which is our eternal reward.

11:37, 38 Zechariah was **stoned** (2 Chr. 24:20, 21). According to Jewish tradition, the prophet Isaiah was **sawn in two.** Urijah was **slain with the sword** (Jer. 26:20–23). **Wandered about in sheepskins and goatskins** is probably a reference to Elijah (2 Kin. 1:8).

11:39, 40 Made perfect means "made complete." This completion, the realization of all of God's promises in Christ's coming kingdom, awaits all believers.

12:1 The **cloud of witnesses** refers to the people of faith mentioned in ch. 11. They are not actually spectators watching us; they are witnesses testifying to the truth of the faith (11:2, 4–6). **Weight** is anything that hinders a runner.

12:2 Looking here means "fixing one's eyes trustingly." We need to focus consistently

 **The Imperative of Faith**

What is faith?	• Faith is the substance of things hoped for, the evidence of things not seen (11:1).
Why is faith important?	• Without faith it is impossible to please God (11:6).
In what does faith believe?	• Faith believes that God is, and that He is a rewarder of those who diligently seek Him (11:6).
What does faith look like in a person's life?	• Abel offered a costly sacrifice (11:4). • Enoch lived in a way that pleased God (11:5). • Noah obeyed divine warnings and built a giant ark (11:7). • Abraham left Ur at God's calling and went out, not knowing where he was going (11:8). • Sarah bore Isaac in her old age (11:11). • Abraham was willing to offer up Isaac, his only son, trusting that God was able to raise him up (11:17–19). • Isaac blessed his sons and exhorted them to obey the covenant (11:20). • Jacob likewise reminded his sons of God's promises (11:21). • Joseph expressed his confidence that God would bring the Israelites out of Egypt (11:22). • Moses' parents refused to carry out the commands of Pharaoh to kill their child (11:23). • Moses turned his back on the passing pleasures of sin and sided with the downtrodden children of Israel, leading them out of Egypt and obediently carrying out the difficult commands of God (11:24–29). • The Israelites, led by Joshua, trusted God to give them victory over the city of Jericho (11:30). • Rahab believed in the power of God and helped the Israelite spies (11:31). • Many other OT people of faith trusted God for power and victory and refused to compromise their faith in God, even in the midst of life-threatening circumstances (11:32–38).
What happens to the faithful?	• Some died without having received the promises (11:13). • Some have to find consolation in the truth that they will not realize the full blessings of God until they enter heaven (11:14–16). • Some experience miraculous deliverance (11:33–35). • Others, despite their implicit trust in God, experience torture, mockings, scourgings, imprisonment, stonings, destitution, affliction, and torment (11:35–38).
What is God's verdict on those who faithfully endure?	• They are those of whom the world is not worthy (11:38).
How should the lives of faithful believers affect us?	• We should be motivated to lay aside every weight, and the sin which so easily ensnares us, and . . . run with endurance the race that is set before us (12:1).

on Christ instead of our own circumstances. **finisher:** Christ has done everything necessary for us to endure in our faith. He is our example and model, for He focused on the **joy that was set before Him.** His attention was not on the agonies of the Cross, but on the crown, not on the suffering, but the reward. **sat down:** Jesus is now at the right hand of the Father's throne, waiting for His enthronement on His throne (Rev. 3:21).

12:3 Consider here involves the idea of comparison, as an accountant would compare the various columns of a balance sheet. Believers should compare their sufferings to the torture Christ endured on their behalf (v. 4).

12:4 not yet resisted to bloodshed: Christ died (v. 3); but the community that received the letter to the Hebrews had not yet suffered deadly persecutions.

12:5–11 Christians are the adopted **sons** of God through the high priestly work of Christ, the eternal Son. Sinners who persecute us mean it for harm (v. 3). But God takes their persecution and changes it into **chastening**—His own fatherly discipline that trains us to become like Him.

12:5, 6 Proverbs 3:11, 12 teaches that divine discipline demonstrates divine love. **Scourges** means "whips," and is used figuratively of punishment. In the context of these verses, this discipline includes persecution (vv. 3, 4).

12:7 for what son: Sons are naturally disciplined out of love by their fathers. They should accept and learn from this discipline. In the same way, God disciplines us because He wants to make us better.

12:8 In Roman society an **illegitimate** son was one who had no inheritance rights. Without enduring discipline (literally, child training), believers are not sons in the sense that they are not like their Father (2:10). Neither do they receive an inheritance or reward (1:14) in the Kingdom.

12:9 Believers should not only endure God's discipline; they should **readily be in subjection** to their heavenly Father.

12:10, 11 our profit: Although fathers discipline for a while as they see fit, God disciplines us with our good welfare in mind. With every trial, God is fashioning us into a holy people, set apart for His good purposes (v. 14; 10:10). **The peaceable fruit of righteousness** suggests that the result of God's **chastening** is peace and righteousness.

12:12, 13 Borrowing the language of Is. 35:3, the author admonishes his readers to renew their strength so that they can endure the race of faith (v. 1).

12:14 See is sometimes taken to mean "to be in the presence of the Lord" and then the conclusion is drawn that **without holiness** no person can be in God's presence. But Satan comes before God (Job 1) and one day all will bow their knees before Him (Phil. 2:10, 11). The verse means: "Holiness, meaning practical righteousness, determines a person's perception." Such righteousness in this life allows us to see the Lord now (Gen. 32:30; Ex. 24:9–11).

12:15–17 Believers pursuing peace and practical righteousness (v. 14) should watch for three dangers: (1) falling **short of** God's **grace**—that is, refusing Christ's gracious offer of salvation and His provision for their needs (4:16); (2) allowing a **root of bitterness** to grow in their assembly—perhaps allowing idol worshipers to remain in the church (Deut. 29:18); and (3) becoming sexually immoral or irreligious. Esau illustrates those who are irreligious. Under the Law, the eldest son was to receive a double inheritance (Deut. 21:17). Esau lost his inheritance, which included God's gracious promises, by despising it and valuing the pleasure of food over it (Gen. 25:34).

12:18–24 In these verses, the author of Hebrews contrasts the Mosaic covenant

IN FOCUS   **"Mediator"**

(Gk. *mesitēs*) (8:6; 9:15; 12:24; Gal. 3:19, 20; 1 Tim. 2:5) Strong's #3316: This Greek word means "a go-between," an intermediary between two parties. Paul describes Moses as a mediator of the first covenant: he acted as a liaison between God and the Israelites, communicating the obligations of the covenant to Israel and pleading the Israelites' case before God (Gal. 3:19, 20). In a similar way, Jesus is the Mediator of the New Covenant. He established it through His own death, commissioning His disciples to preach the Good News. Now He sits at the right hand of God interceding for us (7:25).

with the New Covenant by contrasting two mountains: Mount Sinai and Mount Zion. At Mount Sinai, the Israelites received the Law from God with fear and trembling, for God displayed at that time His awesome power (Ex. 19:10—20:26). In contrast, Christian believers have come to a heavenly Jerusalem on Mount Zion through Jesus' blood. This mountain is a celebration of the Holy One, attended by angels, believers, and righteous people. The author makes the contrast between the two covenants vivid, and then once again exhorts

his readers not to reject Christ's offer of salvation (vv. 25–29).

12:23 In the OT the **firstborn** received a
double inheritance (Deut. 21:17). These then
are heirs who are in heaven awaiting the
Kingdom (1:14). **Just men made perfect**
refers to all believers who have died. They are
just because they have been justified, and perfect because they are now "complete" in
heaven.

12:24 The blood **of Abel** cried out for
revenge (Gen. 4:10); **the blood** of Christ speaks
of redemption.

12:25 Him who speaks from heaven is
Christ, who spoke on earth and is now in
heaven. **much more:** Greater revelation means
greater responsibility (2:1–4). If the Israelites
were judged for not believing in God's promises

(Num. 14:20–25), we too will be judged for disbelief.

12:26–28 The earth shook at Mount Sinai.
The earth and **heaven** will shake in the latter
days (Matt. 24:29). But the kingdom of God will
not be shaken, for it will endure throughout all
eternity (Luke 18:29).

12:29 our God is a consuming fire: The
author concludes His lengthy warning to those
who are tempted to abandon the faith (2:1—
12:29) with a vivid description of God's judgment (Deut. 4:24). The Lord will judge His
people (10:27, 30).

13:1–19 These concluding practical instructions show us how to "serve God acceptably"
(12:28).

13:1 continue: The recipients of this letter
had practiced **brotherly love** (6:10); but the

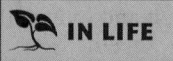 **IN LIFE** | **Time for a Checkup**

A timeworn adage that makes a lot of sense in the world of business and industry is, "If it ain't
broke, don't fix it!" However, that definitely does not apply when it comes to people's health.
In fact, health experts report that preventive care can not only lead to better health and
reduced risk from disease, but vastly reduce medical costs. People are unwise to neglect their physical condition.

This truth has its parallel in the spiritual realm, as the writer to the Hebrews shows. Twice the book
warns its readers to pay attention to their spiritual condition (Heb. 6:1–20; 12:14–29). Notice the
strong language used in Heb. 12 to describe what can happen to us if we neglect our walk with Christ:

- We can fall short of the grace of God (12:15).
- Bitterness can take root and sprout up, causing trouble (12:15).
- Many people can become defiled (12:15).
- We may make a foolish or even catastrophic mistake like Esau did (12:16, 17; Gen. 25:27–34;
  27:1–45).
- We may refuse to listen when God speaks to us (Heb. 12:25).
- God's judgment may consume us (12:29).

Those are dire consequences! Fortunately, the writer offers some ways to check our spirituality and
make corrections where we detect trouble:

- Are we pursuing peace with others (12:14)? For example: how do we respond to conflicts at
  home, work, or school?
- Are we pursuing holiness (12:14)? For example: is our thought life focused on that which puri-
  fies (Phil. 2:1–13; 4:8, 9; 1 Thess. 4:1–8)?
- Are we listening carefully to God (Heb. 12:25)? For example: do we regularly wrestle with Scrip-
  ture, allowing it to challenge us and keep us accountable?
- Do we live in grace, serving God in an acceptable way with reverence and respect (12:28)? For
  example: are we growing in our appreciation for God and His salvation, and for other believers?
  Do we express that clearly and regularly? Would others describe us as "thankful" (1 Tim. 4:4;
  Col. 3:17)?

How is our spiritual condition? Are there any symptoms to be concerned about? Any functions that
seem weak or absent? What changes do we need to make to build ourselves up into spiritual health
and strength?

author feared that the idea of returning to some form of Judaism might be hindering them from encouraging each other in the faith (10:24, 25).

13:2 Entertained angels is a reference to men in the OT who encountered heavenly beings. These men included Abraham (Gen. 18), Lot (Gen. 19), Gideon (Judg. 6), and Manoah (Judg. 13). The idea is that when you practice hospitality you may be helping a messenger of God without realizing it.

13:3 Remember the prisoners probably refers to believers who were being persecuted for the faith. The recipients of this letter had remembered those who were suffering (10:32–34). **In the body** is not a reference to the body of Christ, but to the physical body. The recipients of this letter were vulnerable to similar persecution as long as they were alive.

13:4 Marriage is honorable among all: The author now turns to some problems regarding physical love. To determine the full intent of this verse, one grammatical point must be resolved. In the Greek clause, the verb is omitted and must be supplied by the reader, as is common in both Hebrew and Greek. One may supply an indicative verb, **marriage is,** and make it a declarative sentence (KJV). Or one may supply a subjunctive verb, "let marriage be," and make it an exhortation (NASV). The latter seems preferable since the context is hortatorical and the author is bringing up a new subject for exhortation. Also, if the first half is exhortation, the second half of the verse fits better. Thus, this is a command to purity, rather than a declaration against the ascetic teaching that regarded the marriage relation itself as unwholesome. Ascetic teaching was a problem at this time (compare 1 Tim. 4:3). But this does not seem to be the intent of our author. Marriage is honorable and the marriage bed undefiled. It must be kept that way. **But** (Gk. *gar*) could better be translated "for." Keep marriage relationships, for God will judge those who do not. The **fornicators** are those who indulge in sexual relationships, heterosexual and homosexual, outside of marriage bonds. The **adulterers** are those who are unfaithful to their marriage vows.

13:5, 6 Covetousness is addressed in the last of the Ten Commandments (Ex. 19:17). This attitude destroys a person's inheritance in the Kingdom (1 Cor. 6:9, 10). **I will never leave you nor forsake you:** This quotation is one of the most emphatic statements in the NT. In Greek it contains two double negatives, similar to saying in English, " I will never, ever, ever forsake you." Jesus uses the same technique to express the certainty of eternal life for believers (John 10:28).

13:7 those who rule over you: Also translated "your rulers." The reference is probably to Christian leaders who have died. Perhaps they were those who had first **spoken the word of God** to the readers of Hebrews. The **outcome** of the lives of saints whom we have known inspires us to endurance. Verse 17 speaks of respect for present leaders.

13:8 the same: The unchanging nature of the Son was mentioned at the beginning of this book (1:12). **yesterday:** Christ gave His grace to the former leaders who trusted Him (v. 7). **today, and forever:** Christ's grace is presently and permanently available to all who believe in Him.

13:9 Strange doctrines implies ideas foreign to the gospel message. Many of the ideas that the author of Hebrews was confronting were Jewish in origin—pertaining to ritual observances, sacrificial feasts, and various laws identifying what was clean and unclean.

13:10, 11 The word **altar** is used figuratively of the sacrifice of Christ. On the Day of Atonement, the high priest did not have the **right to eat** the sacrificed animal because it had atoned for the people's sins. Instead, it was **burned outside the camp.** The believer has a sacrifice, Jesus Christ. He atoned for the sins of humanity with His death on the Cross. But unlike the high priests of the OT, believers receive their sustenance from Christ in a symbolic way, by believing in Him (John 6:41–58).

13:12, 13 To be **outside the gate** was considered a disgrace to Jews because it meant being separated from the community. The author exhorts his readers to take on Christ's **reproach** or disgrace (11:26). In essence, the author's command to **go forth to** Christ was a command to abandon Judaism. Anyone found with Christ—outside of the city gate—would be considered outside the Jewish community.

13:14 Believers do not have a permanent home on earth. They seek the eternal **city** that is in an eternal kingdom (11:10, 16; 12:22, 28).

13:15, 16 Although the OT sacrifices are now obsolete (8:13), believers are to offer spiritual sacrifices, which include their **praise,** their possessions, and even their lives (Rom. 12:1, 2).

13:17 The current leaders would give an account of their service at the judgment seat of Christ (Rom. 14:10–12).

13:18, 19 A good conscience is one that is not accusing. **that I may be restored to you:** Something hindered the author's coming, though it was probably not prison (v. 23).

13:20 The title **God of peace** is used five other times in the NT (Rom. 15:33; 1 Cor. 14:33; 2 Cor. 13:11; Phil. 4:9; 1 Thess. 5:23). Whenever the title was used, some sort of difficulty existed among the recipients of the letter. This is also the case here: the readers of Hebrews were wondering whether they should reject Christianity and return to Judaism in the face of increasing persecution. Jesus is the **great Shepherd of the sheep,** having laid down His life for them (John 10:15) and now continuing to make intercession for them (7:25). The New Covenant is an **everlasting covenant;** it will never become obsolete like the Mosaic covenant (8:13).

13:21 The purpose of this blessing is that God may **make you complete.** This is not the same perfection that the author earlier stated to be the result of Christ's once-for-all sacrifice (10:14; 11:40). That word (Gk. *teleioō*) involves the positional sanctification of the redeemed. Our word in 13:21 (Gk. *katartizō*) has more the idea of to mend or to equip for a task. The equipping needed here is to do **every good work.**

13:22 The word of exhortation refers to the whole Epistle to the Hebrews. It is an exhortation not to depart from the living God (3:12), but to go on to maturity (6:1) and endure in the faith to the end (3:6, 14). **In few words** is used as a comparison to what more could have been said (5:11; 9:5).

13:23 Timothy was a well-known associate of Paul. Two NT letters are addressed by name to him. **Set free** probably means released from prison.

13:24 Those from Italy may refer to people living in Italy, or else to people from there who were now living elsewhere. Because of its ambiguity, this phrase does not reveal the location of the author or of the recipients.

13:25 In light of what has been said about **grace** in the letter (v. 9; 2:9; 4:16; 10:29; 12:15), this closing is particularly appropriate.

The Epistle of

James

F ROM FIXING A CAR TO WALLPAPERING A bedroom, "how-to" books explain how things are done, with helpful pointers and colorful illustrations. The Epistle of James is the "how-to" book of the Christian life. It is one of the most practical books in the New Testament because it offers instruction and exhortation to Christians who are experiencing problems, as all of us do.

As if the trials themselves were not bad enough, James points out the dangers that come with them. Besides the obvious pitfall of failing to place our trust in the Lord and thus not enduring, James speaks of prejudice, improper speech, judging one another, leaving God out of our plans, and even bitterness. Like the author of a "how-to" book, James explains in a few words the responsibilities of a Christian, while supplying apt illustrations from real-life categories such as shipping and horseback riding.

The Epistle of James is more practical than doctrinal. Nevertheless, James contains theological statements. God is "the Father of lights, with whom there is no variation" (1:17), meaning that He is the Creator and is unchangeable. Jesus is "the Lord of glory" (2:1), a reference to Jesus' deity. James asserts that Jesus is coming again (5:7, 8), and when He does, He will judge all of humanity (5:9).

But the major theological issue in James is faith and works (2:14–26). Many contend that James is talking about true faith versus false faith. But it seems apparent that James is not questioning whether the recipients were genuine believers; he repeatedly calls them "brethren," "my brethren," or "my beloved brethren" (2:1, 14). These are clearly people who were exercising saving faith. Thus, what James is discussing is faith that is alone, meaning without works. He calls faith without works "dead," indicating that it was faith that was once alive (2:17, 26). For James, works is a natural result of faith. When a person truly believes in something, he or she will act on that belief. With this letter, James was sounding a wake-up call to all Christians: "Get your life in line with what you believe!"

The salutation identifies the readers of James as "the twelve tribes which are scattered abroad." Some believe this letter was directed to all Jews living outside of Palestine, including both Christian and non-Christian Jews. This seems unlikely, however, since James identifies himself as a follower of Christ and refers to his readers as a community of believers (1:18; 2:1, 7; 5:7). Others hold that the salutation is a figurative reference to all Christian churches, represented symbolically by ancient Israel. This too is improbable since the letter contains recognizable Jewish elements. There is also a third possibility, that the readers were Jewish Christians living outside of Palestine. Since this letter was a circular letter that was passed from church to church, no specific geographical destination is pinpointed.

Most of the recipients seem to have been poor and suffering from oppression imposed by their fellow Jews, among whom they were living. Evidently some of these Jewish Christians had been imprisoned and deprived of their possessions and livelihoods. Under such conditions, they fell into the clutches of worldliness, fought among themselves, favored the rich over the poor, and lost their original love for one another.

The author of this epistle identifies himself with the phrase "James, a bondservant of God and of the Lord Jesus Christ." James is a common name in the New Testament. The accompanying phrase could have described any Christian, suggesting that this particular James must have been a church leader who needed no further introduction.

Four men named "James" are mentioned in the New Testament: (1) James, the son of Zebedee and brother of John (Matt. 4:21), a disciple and apostle of Christ; (2) James, the son of Alphaeus (Matt. 10:3), called "the Less" or "the Younger," also one of the apostles; (3) James, the father of an apostle named Judas (Luke 6:16); and (4) James, the half brother of Jesus, traditionally called "the Just" (Matt. 13:55). He became the leader of the Jerusalem church (Acts 15:3; Gal. 2:9) and seems to be the most probable author of this epistle. If he was the author, it is noteworthy that he did not mention his relation to Jesus in this letter. Instead his sole

claim to authority was his spiritual servanthood to the Lord Jesus Christ (1:1).

Though not universally agreed upon, the evidence is strong that James is one of the oldest books in the New Testament. Since the letter contains no specific references to time or events that would indicate a particular date, one must consider the Jewish tone of the letter and the letter's accurate reflection of the general situation found in the early apostolic church. Many scholars assign a date somewhere between A.D. 44 and 62. The first date is the time when James became the leader of the Jerusalem church, taking Peter's place after he was released from prison in the year Herod Agrippa I died (Acts 12:5–23). The second date is the date given by Josephus, the first-century Jewish historian, for the martyrdom of James. In the end, an early date of around A.D. 46 seems reasonable for this letter.

Outline

I. Salutation 1:1

II. Prologue 1:2–18
  A. Responding to trials 1:2–11
  B. Responding to temptations 1:12–18

III. The themes: being swift to hear, slow to speak, slow to wrath 1:19, 20

IV. Being swift to hear 1:21–2:26
  A. Doing good works as a result of hearing the Word of God 1:21–27
  B. Excluding partiality 2:1–13

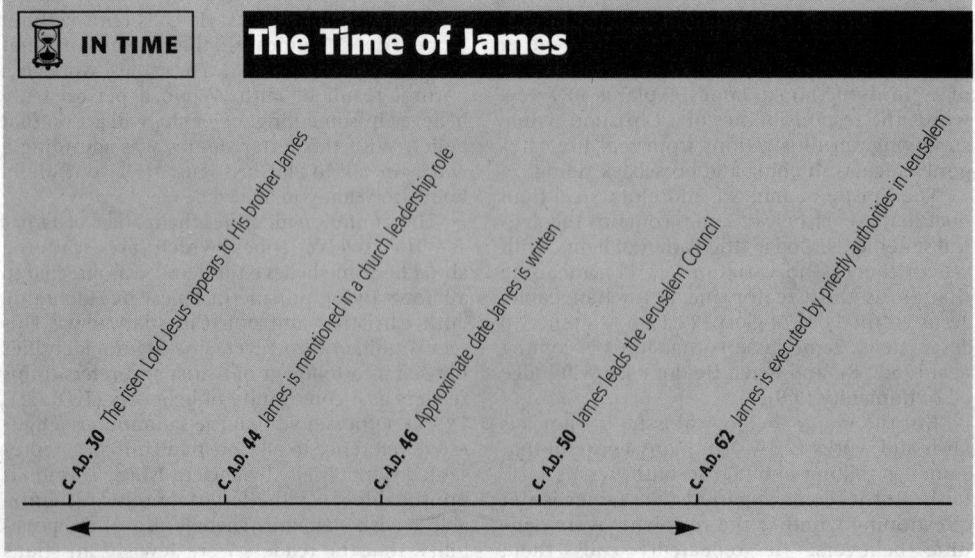

IN TIME — **The Time of James**

c. A.D. 30 The risen Lord Jesus appears to His brother James

c. A.D. 44 James is mentioned in a church leadership role

c. A.D. 46 Approximate date James is written

c. A.D. 50 James leads the Jerusalem Council

c. A.D. 62 James is executed by priestly authorities in Jerusalem

Commentary

1:1 Early church tradition identifies the author **James** as the half brother of Christ (1 Cor. 15:7). **To the twelve tribes:** This salutation probably means the letter is for Jewish Christians living outside of Palestine. The letter was not intended for one specific church but was to be passed around among various local assemblies.

1:2–27 James instructs us on how to face difficulties (vv. 2–4), the need for spiritual insight and faith (vv. 5–8), the proper attitude toward riches (vv. 9–11), and how to overcome temptation (vv. 12–18). He cautions us against a heart filled with anger (vv. 19, 20), and urges us to a life of doing God's word (vv. 21–27).

1:2 **Trials** are of outward circumstances—conflicts, sufferings, and troubles—encountered by all believers. Trials are not pleasant and may be extremely grievous, but believers are to consider them as opportunities for rejoicing. Troubles and difficulties are a tool that refines and purifies our faith, producing patience and endurance.

1:3 The word translated **testing of your faith** occurs only here and in 1 Pet. 1:7. The term, which means "tested" or "approved," was used for coins that were genuine and not debased. The aim of testing is not to destroy or afflict, but to purge and refine. It is essential to Christian maturity, for even Abraham's faith had to be tested (Gen. 22:1–8). The meaning of **patience** transcends the idea of bearing affliction; it includes the idea of standing fast under pressure, with a staying power that turns adversities into opportunities.

1:4 If a believer endures a trial, he or she will be **perfect**, meaning "having reached the end," and **complete**, meaning "whole."

1:5 The **wisdom** God gives is not necessarily information on how to get out of trouble but rather insight on how to learn from one's difficulties (Prov. 29:15). It is not more information about how to avoid times of testing but instead a new perspective on trials. The wisdom

of God begins with a genuine reverence for the Almighty ("the fear of the LORD" in Ps. 111:10; Prov. 9:10) and a steadfast confidence that God controls all circumstances, guiding them to His good purposes (Rom. 8:28).

1:6, 7 **Doubting** means "to be divided in one's mind" or "to debate." The term does not describe a momentary doubt but a divided allegiance, an uncertainty.

1:8 **Double-minded** is literally "two souls." If one part of a person is set on God and the other is set on this world (Matt. 6:24), there will be constant conflict within.

1:9–11 James offers two examples of trials (vv. 2–8): one is of a **lowly brother** and the other is about a **rich** man. Probably *lowly* means "poor," in contrast to the other man who is rich. The poor believer is to **glory** ("count it all joy" in v. 2) in the fact that God has exalted him by allowing him to experience difficult circumstances, for these will only perfect his character and faith (v. 4). The rich believer can also glory when a trial brings him low because it teaches

 **INSIGHT** **God's Three-Stage Plan**

God has a three-stage "human resource development" program for believers (James 1:2–5). Stage one involves trials—as many as we need, as hard as they need to be. That leads to stage two, patience—waiting for God with trust and perseverance. The final result is stage three, wisdom, which is God's goal of growth for personnel in His kingdom.

Do we want wisdom? We should be careful when we ask for it; we could get a healthy dose of trials that demand patience. Eventually the process leads to wisdom—if we let it work.

him that life is short, and that **his pursuits,** that is, his business, will **fade away.** The rich man should always trust the Lord, not himself or his money.

1:12 The believer who **endures** trials demonstrates that he or she loves Jesus and therefore **will receive the crown of life** (Rev. 2:10) at the judgment seat of Christ. The Bible describes the believer's reward (2 Cor. 5:10; Rev. 22:12) under various vivid images such as precious metals (1 Cor. 3:8–14), garments (Rev. 3:5, 18; 19:7, 8), and crowns (1 Cor. 9:25; Rev. 2:10; 3:11).

1:13 The focus of the chapter turns from trials (vv. 2–12) to temptation (vv. 13–18). **nor does He . . . tempt anyone:** Enticement to sin does not come from God. God will never deliberately lead a person to commit sin because that would not only go against His nature, but it would be opposed to His purpose of molding His creation into His holy image. Yet God does sometimes place His people in adverse circumstances for the purpose of building godly character (Gen. 22:1, 12). These rewards will be our respective capacities or positions of privilege and service to the glory of Christ in His coming reign (Rev. 4:10; 5:10).

1:14, 15 Turning a test into a temptation to do wrong is only possible when one allows strong desire to take control. **Drawn away** and **enticed** express the intensity with which desire lures an individual until he or she is tragically entrapped. Sin does not force itself on the unwilling, but is chosen because of its attractions. **Conceived** suggests the image of a person's will bending toward and finally seizing evil. This same idea is vividly illustrated by the tragic path of an addict: a habit once acquired by an individual in the end completely controls that person. **Full-grown** suggests bringing a goal to completion. The idea here is that sin has

 **IN COMPARISON** **Rich or Poor**

In ancient Israel, there were grasses that sprouted out of the ground in the morning and by the afternoon would wither away under the intense heat of the summer sun. James compares the instability of wealth to this type of grass; it is here today and gone tomorrow. The following chart delineates what Scripture says about riches.

The World's View of Riches	The Word's View of Riches
• Money brings freedom.	• The desire for money can be enslaving and lead to destruction; only Christ brings true freedom (1 Tim. 6:7–10).
• Money brings security.	• Worldly wealth is very insecure; it will quickly pass away (1:10). Real security is found in knowing and trusting God (Jer. 9:23, 24; 1 Tim. 6:17–19).
• Money is what matters.	• Christ and the kingdom of God are what matters (Matt. 6:33; Phil. 3:7–10).
• Money is power.	• Power comes from being filled with the Spirit (Acts 1:8; 3:1–10).
• Money establishes not only your net worth, but your worth as a person.	• Your worth is based on what God says, not what your bank statement says (John 3:16; Eph. 1:3–14).
• Money makes you successful.	• Success comes from knowing and doing what God says (Josh. 1:8).
• Money gives you options.	• God is the One who ultimately gives you options (Eph. 3:20).
• Money brings happiness.	• The happiness that money brings is short-lived. And in the long run, money can actually produce "many sorrows" (1 Tim. 6:10). Lasting joy comes from knowing God (5:1–6; John 15:11; 16:24).
• Money is your reward. Save it, and spend it on yourself.	• Give as much as you can (Matt. 6:19–24; Acts 20:35; 2 Cor. 9:6–11; 1 Tim. 6:18).
• Money is your possession. Spend it on whatever you want.	• All that you have is God's to do with as He pleases. You are merely a manager of His possessions (Ps. 24:1; Luke 19:11–27; 2 Cor. 5:10).

reached its maturity and has possessed the very character of the individual. **Death** here refers to physical death (Prov. 10:27; 11:19; Rom. 8:13).

1:16–18 James again illustrates (vv. 9–11). God does not tempt with evil (v. 13). He gives **good** and **perfect** gifts such as spiritual life (v. 18).

1:19 The conclusion of the introduction of James (vv. 2–18) is that enduring trials leads to a

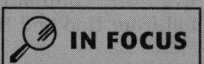

(Gk. *dosis agathē*) (1:17) Strong's #*1394; 18*; perfect gift (Gk. *dōrēma teleion*) (1:17) Strong's #*1434; 5046*: In the Greek text there are two separate words to describe God's giving. The first word (*dosis*) means "the act of giving" and is accompanied by the adjective for *good*, while the second (*dōrēma*) denotes the actual gifts received and is preceded by the adjective for *perfect*. The first expression emphasizes the goodness of receiving something from God, while the second, the perfect quality of whatever God gives. God's giving is continuously good; and His gifts are always perfect.

crown of life (v. 12) and yielding to temptation can lead to physical death (v. 15). Since that is the case, the believer in the midst of a trial needs to be **swift to hear, slow to speak,** and **slow to wrath.** These three exhortations reveal the outline of this letter (1:21—2:26 for "swift to hear"; 3:1–18 for "slow to speak"; 4:1—5:18 for "slow to wrath").

1:20 If a believer gets angry in difficult circumstances, the practical **righteousness of God** will not be evident in his or her life. When someone wrongs us, the natural reaction is to retaliate, at least verbally (v. 19). But this response does not glorify God. Holding one's tongue, trying to understand the other person's position, and leaving vindication to God demonstrates godly love in tense situations (Rom. 12:17–21).

1:21 The **word** of God that has been **implanted** in the believer's heart should be received with **meekness**—describing a teachable spirit—without resistance, disputing, or questioning. Receiving God's Word in this way will **save** the believer's *soul*, a word meaning "life." Sin leads to death (v. 15). Obedience prevents death; it protects a believer from sinful behavior that can lead directly or indirectly to physical death (v. 15; 1 Cor. 11:30).

1:22 be doers of the word, and not hearers only: Believers who hear the Word of God (v. 19) must receive it with a teachable spirit (v. 21), applying it to their daily lives. To hear and not obey is to be deceived.

1:23–24 He who follows this form of irrational thinking sees **his natural face in a glass** (mirror) and **goes away.** He observes, becomes entirely cognizant of the flaws, and promptly **forgets.**

1:25 The **perfect law of liberty** is the law of love. Loving God and loving one's neighbor sums up the Law (Matt. 26:36–40). But it is Christ's love (Eph. 3:17–19) that frees us from our sins to truly love others (John 8:36–38; Gal. 5:13).

1:26, 27 Pure (Gk. *katharos*) versus impure is the issue, not true versus false. Some people go through **religion** (Gk. *thrēskos*), or the external aspects of worship, with an unclean heart. James is confirming that the externals of religious activities are not acceptable to God unless accompanied by a holy life and loving service. Rites and rituals have never been an adequate substitute for service and sacrifice. Corporate worship within the church cannot take the place of individual works outside the church. Private profession must be coupled with the public expression of one's faith. **To visit** comes from the Greek word usually translated *bishop*, a person who oversees God's people (1 Tim. 3:1). **Orphans and widows** were among the most unprotected and needy classes in ancient societies (Ezek. 22:7). Pure religion does not merely give material goods for the relief of the distressed, it also oversees their care (Acts 6:1–7; 1 Tim. 5:3–16).

2:1–13 James gives an example of partiality to the rich (vv. 1–4), adding four reasons why we should not show such partiality: (1) God has accepted many poor people as His own (v. 5); (2) the rich often persecute Christians (vv. 6, 7); (3) being partial violates Christ's law of love (vv. 8–11); and (4) God will judge those who violate that law (vv. 12, 13).

2:1 The **faith of our Lord Jesus Christ** includes the fact that God loves the world and that Christ died for it. If God and Christ show grace and mercy without favoritism, so should believers (vv. 8, 13).

2:2–4 A clear illustration dismisses all excuses and exceptions. One might imagine two visitors arriving at a church on a Sunday morning. A chauffeured limousine exhibits a man arrayed in expensive clothing. Another man approaches in an old jalopy, and his cheap suit has almost worn through. When the ushers favor the wealthy man, they show **partiality** and become **judges with evil thoughts. Partiality** comes from the same verb as wandering

(1:6). By their partiality the offenders have "wavered" in their faith.

2:5 God has chosen to use **poor** people who are **rich in faith** to advance His kingdom. Those who **love Him** and obey Him (John 14:15; 15:9–17) and endure the testing of their faith (1:12) will inherit the **kingdom.** This inheritance means more than entering the Kingdom; it also involves ruling with Christ (1 Cor. 6:9; Gal. 5:21; 2 Tim. 2:12).

2:6 Dishonored involves not only attitudes but shameful treatment, as when Jesus was "dishonored" by the Jewish leaders (John 8:49). **Oppress** refers to the arrogant flaunting of governmental authority over Christians, as tyrants over helpless peasants. James has Jewish officials in mind when he says they **drag you into the courts.** Acts 9:2, where Saul traveled to Damascus with official letters to arrest Christians, testifies to the authority that Rome handed over to the Jews.

2:7 Not only do they despise the poor and oppress Christians, but the rich direct their assaults against the Lord Himself. **They . . . blaspheme** (Gk. *blasphēmeō*) or "speak evil against" **that noble name by which you are called,** i.e., Christians (Acts 11:26).

2:8, 9 The royal law is the law of love (1:25; Lev. 19:18; Matt. 22:39), a law superior to all other laws. **if you show partiality, you commit sin:** James alludes to Lev. 19:15, which prohibits favoritism to either the poor or the rich.

2:10 he is guilty of all: God does not allow selective obedience. We cannot choose to obey the parts of the Law that are to our own liking and disregard the rest. Some of the Pharisees were guilty of this. They carefully observed some of the requirements of the Law, such as keeping the Sabbath, and ignored others, such as honoring their parents (see Jesus' comments in Matt. 15:1–7). Sin is violation of the perfect righteousness of God, who is the Lawgiver. James is saying that the whole divine law has to be accepted as an expression of God's will for His people. The violation of even one commandment separates an individual from God and His purposes.

2:11 A basketball, whether it misses the hoop by an inch or a yard, still fails to score. Likewise, he who shows partiality becomes **a transgressor** just as readily as if he had murdered or committed adultery.

2:12, 13 Believers **will be judged by the law of liberty,** which is the law of love (1:25). Believers who do not practice partiality, but who practice love (vv. 5, 8) and **mercy,** will triumph at the judgment seat. Those who have not shown mercy will not receive mercy.

2:14–19 Faith is more than an intellectual belief in God. If that belief does not lead us to a holy life of righteousness and mercy, it is not a saving faith (Matt. 7:21–23). James gives three arguments in support of this truth: (1) Faith without **works** is no better than words without deeds (vv. 15–17). (2) Faith can be neither seen nor verified unless it shows itself in works (v. 18). (3) Even the **demons** have an intellectual

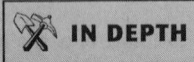 **IN DEPTH** ## Faith and Works

The great reformer Martin Luther, champion of the doctrine of salvation through faith alone, never felt good about the Epistle of James. He called it an "epistle full of straw" in the preface to his 1522 edition of the NT, and he put the book in the appendix. He preferred Paul's wording of the faith-works equation: "A man is justified by faith apart from the deeds of the law" (Rom. 3:28).

In a sense, Luther had little choice. He was surrounded by men who said that good works could save you. He knew that God alone could save through faith alone, and his mission was to tell them.

But Luther went too far, when he put James in the appendix to the NT. Neither faith nor works can be cut off and thrown away. James was taking aim at freeloaders, those who claimed to have no need for good deeds since they had faith. The reality is that if you have faith, works will naturally be a product. You cannot get rid of works just because they do not save you. You cannot sever the effect from the cause. Just as an apple tree will bear apples, so faith will produce good works (Luke 6:43, 44).

Paul had the opposite problem in view when he wrote Romans. His letter targeted those who placed their faith in the Law of Moses. Their trust was in their own good works, and not in God. That is why Paul wrote a defense of faith, and that is why Luther preferred it to James's defense of works.

Faith and works are not enemies. True faith and righteous works go hand in hand. They are two parts of God's work in us. Faith brings a person to salvation, and works bring that person to faithfulness. Faith is the cause, works are the effect. James believed it, and so did Paul.

belief in God, but it does not lead to their salvation (v. 19).

2:14 Some claim the faith mentioned in this passage is not genuine faith that produces eternal life. But James addresses this section to believers ("my brethren" in v. 14), that is, people who have exercised genuine faith. The issue in this paragraph is not true faith versus false faith; it is faith that is alone, meaning

The mound at the left in the background is believed to be the site of Haran, where Abraham stopped on his way to Canaan. The writer of James commended Abraham for his stalwart faith and obedience of God's command (James 2:21–23).

without works (v. 17) versus faith that is accompanied by works. **Saved** (Gk. *sōzō*) is used five times in James (1:21; 2:14; 4:12; 5:15; 5:20). Each time it refers to the saving of the temporal life, not saving from the penalty of sin (5:15). In this context James is referring to being "saved" from the judgment without mercy at the judgment seat of Christ (v. 13) and possibly the saving of one's life from physical death (1:21). **Works** are actions that follow the "royal law" of love (vv. 8, 15, 16). James is implying in this verse that faith in Christ will demonstrate itself

in love for others (see Jesus' command to His disciples in John 13:34, 35).

2:15–16 When Christians say empty platitudes without actually helping those in physical need, **what does it profit?** How many words fill a hungry stomach?

2:17 A faith . . . dead (Gk. *pistis*) that is now dead must have once been alive. Works keep faith thriving (1 Pet. 1:5–9). The absence of works brings death (James 1:14, 15) to faith (2:26).

2:18 The expression **But someone will say** introduces an objector (1 Cor. 15:35). Some manuscripts have the word **without,** while others have a Greek word which is translated "out of" (Gk. *ek*). If the latter is understood, then there is no apparent difference between the two statements of the objector—in English. In the Greek text, however, the objector changes the word order. In one he begins with faith and in the other he begins with works. He seems to be saying that it doesn't matter which one you start with—there is no relationship between faith and works. This explanation fits James's answer.

2:19 The objector continues by suggesting that **you,** that is James, believe **there is one God** and as a result you do **well** (Gk. *kalos*), which means you do something good (3 John 6). On the other hand, demons believe there is one God and they do not do good works. Their faith has the wrong object. They do not believe Jesus died for them. They only tremble. The objector is arguing that there is no relationship between faith and works.

2:20 James now answers the objector (vv. 22, 23): **Man** (Gk. *anthrōpos*) is in the singular and he calls this individual **foolish** (Gk. *kenōs*), meaning he is empty headed.

2:21 James clearly teaches justification by faith, for he quotes Gen. 15:6 in v. 23, which obviously connects the crediting of righteousness, that is, salvation, to Abraham's belief (see Paul's explanation of Gen. 15:6 in Rom. 4:1–12). The justification **by works** of which James is speaking is a different type of justification. This type of justification is before other people. In other words, James is using the word **justified** to mean "proved." We prove to others our genuine faith in Christ through our works. But the justification that comes through faith is before God, and we do not "prove" ourselves to Him; instead, God declares us righteous through our association with Christ, the One who died for our sins (Rom. 3:28).

2:22 The point James is making to the objector is that faith works together with works, that is, there is a relationship between the two and the relationship is works make faith **perfect** (Gk. *teleioō*), that is, mature.

2:23 By offering Isaac (Gen. 22:1–12), **Abraham** endured the test and demonstrated his complete trust in God. His obedience made him a friend of God (John 15:14).

2:24 **You** is in the plural, indicating that James now turns his attention to the reader. **You see** (not God) that a person is justified by works.

2:25 **Rahab's** works were done by faith (Heb. 11:31), but actions were necessary to affirm her inner change. Had she remained in sin while acclaiming faith, she would never have been declared righteous (justified).

2:26 The **body** (Gk. *sōma*) represents **faith** (Gk. *pistis*). Breathing (works) demonstrates the body is alive. Works demonstrate that faith is alive.

3:1–12 Christian **teachers** (v. 1) and preachers will be held more accountable (Luke 20:47) because their speaking has great influence over others. It is so easy to sin in our speech (v. 2), and a sinful word has such far-reaching consequences (vv. 3–6). By ourselves we cannot control our speaking (vv. 7, 8); it will continue to be a hypocritical mixture of good and evil (vv. 9–12). Only God's grace, the wisdom from above described in v. 17, can give us mastery over evil speaking.

3:1 we shall receive a stricter judgment: James does not give the warning of judgment to others without applying it to himself. **Teachers** will stand before the judgment seat of Christ and be judged more strictly than others. Their greater influence translates into greater responsibility. Judgment here most likely does not refer to eternal separation from God; rather, it suggests a thorough judgment of teachers before Christ (Matt. 5:19; Rom. 14:10–12). Leadership imposes responsibility. When the honor is great, the responsibility is greater; when the requirements are heavy, the penalty for failure is correspondingly more severe. All the heresies, most of the divisions, and many of the failures of the church throughout history have been due to teachers without godly wisdom and understanding.

3:2 The verb **stumble** means to trip, and thus, the clause may be rendered, "We all are stumbling in many areas." None of us has reached perfection. **Perfect** (Gk. *teleios*) describes the man who has reached his goal, the man who is self-controlled. That being the case in speech, he is **able also to bridle the whole body,** because the tongue resists control more than any other area of behavior. **Bridle** pictures restrained guidance.

3:3–4 Two illustrations emphasize that often what holds the greatest influence may appear insignificant, size having nothing to do with importance. In comparison to the total dimensions of a horse, a **bit** in the mouth appears trivial, yet the animal obeys it. **Ships,** enormous and **driven** by awesome winds, may be steered by a **very small rudder** or helm. **Wherever the pilot desires** in contemporary language may be translated, "Wherever the pilot wants it to go."

3:5 See how great a forest a little fire kindles: The tongue may be compared to a match in size, but its effect is like a raging forest fire.

3:6 An uncontrolled **tongue** can defile the **whole body,** or the whole person. **Course of nature** may also be translated "wheel of life," meaning the whole course of life. The tongue can damage all of a person and all of his life. Moreover, **by hell** indicates that Satan can put words in the believer's mouth by putting ideas in his mind (Mark 8:33; Acts 5:3).

3:7, 8 no man can tame the tongue: The instincts of animals can be subdued through conditioning and punishment, but the sinful nature that inspires evil words is beyond our control. Only the work of the Holy Spirit within us can bring this destructive force under control.

3:9 Bless our God may refer to the Jewish practice of saying "blessed be He" whenever God's name was mentioned. James is pointing out the inconsistency of blessing God while cursing people who are created in His image. **similitude of God:** God created human beings, both man and woman, in His own image (Gen. 1:26). Today, people still reflect God's image, though badly marred by sin (Gen. 9:6).

3:10–12 Pouring salt water into fresh produces salt water; and mixing bad fruit with good fruit produces a bushel of rotten fruit. Likewise, mixing the contradictory speech of **blessing** and **cursing** will only produce negative results.

3:13–18 A contrast between the wisdom that God gives (vv. 13, 17, 18) and the wisdom of fallen humanity (vv. 14–16).

3:13 The solution for the problem of controlling our tongues is to seek divine **wisdom** (1:5). The person who possesses godly wisdom (v. 17) will meekly show it with works, not just words. That is, believers should be slow to speak (1:19).

3:14 If you have worldly wisdom (vv. 15, 16), which is nothing more than self-interest, don't boast about it. Don't just be slow to speak; rather, don't speak lies at all.

3:15 If wisdom displays itself apart from good conduct and meekness, it is not from above. In fact, it is characterized as earthly, wise by the world's standards, sensual (Gk.

psuchikos), meaning natural as distinguished from spiritual, and **demonic.**

3:16 Evil produces confusion. On the other hand, God brings harmony and wisdom (1 Cor. 14:33). Anyone who is involved in **envy** and strife is confused. This confusion corrupts human relationships. It is likely that the Jewish Christians to whom James was writing were going through turmoil because of sinful acts like the ones mentioned here. James wanted his readers to set aside their petty attitudes and seek reconciliation.

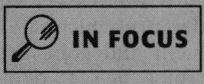

"similitude of God"

(Gk. *homoiōsis theou*) (3:9) Strong's *#3669; 2316*: The Greek expression means "God's likeness." Although human beings have lost much of Godlikeness, there is still enough in our make-up to hint at what we once were like and what we can become again through the work of Christ. It is interesting how the ancient Alexandrian Christians understood Gen. 1:26, where man and woman are created in the "image" and "likeness" of God. The "image" was that Godlike part of us that we never lost in the Fall, while the "likeness" was that Godlike part of human being that we have yet to acquire. By "image" they meant a person's physical and intellectual nature; by "likeness" they meant a person's moral being.

3:17 The main characteristic of godly wisdom is that it is **pure,** meaning "free from defilement." Bitterness, envy, and selfish behavior thoroughly corrupt a person (vv. 14, 16). Godly wisdom is also **peaceable,** describing a spirit of tranquillity and calmness. It does not suggest compromising truth just for the sake of peace, which would promote falsehood. In addition, godly wisdom is undivided, without favoritism, unwavering, and consistent. **without hypocrisy:** True wisdom is sincere and unpretentious.

3:18 This section, "slow to speak" (1:19), has focused around the uncontrolled tongue. Inner qualities are what season one's speech, and here **peace** is emphasized in two ways: (1) **righteousness is sown,** that is, it has its beginnings in peaceful conditions, not **envy and self-seeking** (v. 16); and (2) righteousness appears in those who practice peace. The glaring blemish of evangelical churches is inner turmoil

and bickering, yet Christian living depends upon **peace.**

4:1–10 Cleansing for carnal Christians (1 Cor. 3:1–4): (1) evidences of struggle with sin (vv. 1–4); (2) God's yearning to give **more grace** (vv. 5, 6); (3) the way of blessing (vv. 7–10).

4:1 The conflict *within* us is between our sinful **desires for pleasure** and the desire for God's will, an attitude the Holy Spirit has placed within us (v. 5).

4:2 The source of conflict *among* believers is often material things. James attributes fighting, murder, and war to materialism. John also warns believers of lusting after "the things in the world" (1 John 2:15, 16).

4:3 because you ask amiss: Some might have protested James's admonition (vv. 1, 2) by claiming that they had not received an answer to their prayers (Matt. 7:7). James responds by suggesting that they were praying for the wrong things. Instead of praying for their sinful desires, they should have been praying for God's good will for them. Often the reason God does not supply what a person desires is simply that He knows it would not benefit that person (Phil. 4:19). God is not obliged to answer our prayers in the affirmative. He will not act in ways that are contrary to His will, even if He is besieged by fervent prayers. Anytime we seek to further our personal **pleasures** through prayer, we are asking *amiss* (Matt. 6:33). In prayer, God does not bow to our will; instead we submit to His good will for our lives.

4:4 This verse does not speak of God's attitude toward the believer but of the believer's attitude toward God. The difference between the world and God is so vast that as we move toward **the world** we alienate ourselves from God. In the world, sin is considered acceptable and pleasurable. Ultimately believers lose their awareness of sin, and thus sin has become habitual. James's concern is not for occasional sins but for the attitude of heart that leads a person to turn his back on God and his face to the world. Rather than knowing sin by observation or personal experience, a Christian is supposed to use his God-given mind to discern good from evil without tasting of evil itself.

4:5 Scripture says: James probably does not have any specific OT reference in mind; instead he is speaking of a general concept in Scripture. The jealous yearning in this verse most likely refers to God's jealousy for His people, a concept prevalent in the OT (Ex. 20:5; 34:14; Pss. 78:58; 79:5) and an idea that fits the context. The friendship with the world mentioned in v. 4 would naturally provoke God's jealousy. However, the expression **Spirit who dwells in us** could also indicate our individual human spirit. Then the jealous yearning would be the covetous desire of people, recalling the theme of v. 2.

4:6 God resists the proud: James quotes from Prov. 3:34 to prove his point. Those who submit to divine wisdom will receive the necessary **grace** from God to put into practice the kind of life James describes (3:13–18). On the other hand, those who elevate themselves will face a formidable foe (v. 4). God Himself will fight against their plans because they are not on His side.

4:7 submit to God: We must follow in order the two commands in this verse. First we must submit to God by abandoning our selfish pride (vv. 1–6). Submitting to the Lord also involves putting on the whole armor of God, an image that includes everything from placing our faith in Him to immersing ourselves in the truth of God's Word (Eph. 6:11–18). Second, we must resist any temptation that the **devil** throws our way. Then the Evil One will have no choice but to **flee,** for we will belong to the army of the living God.

4:8 He will draw near: God is always ready to accept those who truly come to Him. **Cleanse your hands . . . purify your hearts:** The **double-minded** are those Christians divided in their heart's love between God and the world.

4:9 Lament and mourn and weep: When a believer who has fallen into sin responds to God's call for repentance, he or she should place laughter and joy aside to reflect on the sin with genuine sorrow (2 Cor. 7:9, 10). In this verse, **laughter** seems to refer to the loud revelry of pleasure-loving people. They immerse themselves in a celebration of their sins in an effort to forget God's judgment. A Christian should never laugh at sin. However, Christian sorrow leads to repentance; repentance leads to forgiveness; and forgiveness leads to true joy over one's reconciliation with God (Pss. 32:1; 126:2; Prov. 15:13).

4:10 Humble yourselves: The man who submits himself to the Lord will be exalted in ways that he himself could never accomplish. This primarily refers to one's spiritual relationship with God.

4:11, 12 There is one Lawgiver: The NT teaches us not to judge (Matt. 7:1) for God is the ultimate Judge and the One who will take vengeance on those who practice evil (Rom. 12:9; Heb. 10:30). Yet the Scriptures also exhort the church to exercise judgment over its members (1 Cor. 6:2–5). This type of judgment is corporate discipline exercised in accordance with biblical truths and the pattern in Matt. 18:15–20.

4:13–16 The sin of these people was not

that they made plans, but rather that they ignored the brevity of human **life** (v. 14) and did not consult **the Lord** in making their plans (v. 15). That kind of pride is **evil.**

4:13 we will go . . . make a profit: The problem here is not the plan or the concept of planning; it is leaving God out of the plan (v. 15).

4:14 you do not know: In spite of human frailty and ignorance of tomorrow, man arrogantly predicts his life's course. **For what is your life:** This question hopes to shake someone out of apathy and cause him to reassess his priorities. **Vapor** (Gk. *atmis*) is used of smoke (Acts 2:19), incense (Ezek. 8:11), and of steam. It makes no difference which one is chosen, for all are transient and gone in a moment. Compared to eternity, the span of our lives appears insignificant.

4:15 The command does not mean to keep adding the phrase, **If the Lord wills,** to everything a person says. To do such could become another form of pride. At the same time a person's behavior and plans should consistently demonstrate dependence upon the Lord. He may determine that at the present time patience through tribulation (Rom. 5:3) is a greater need than attaining our goals.

4:16 Boast could be translated "rejoice." The noun, **boastings** (Gk. *alazoneia*), connotes vain pretensions. A man who brags about future plans while ignoring God's sovereignty is foolish, but more than that his attitude is **evil.** The extent of this marks the depravity of contemporary society.

4:17 Therefore: The reference is not to people in general but to a particular merchant who made his plans without God. Apparently, he succeeded in making money, which he assumed came as a result of his own ingenuity and not as a gift from God. The idea is that the merchant determined to make money and then to spend it on himself. James summarizes what has already been said for every reader of his epistle: It is sin to doubt whether an action is right and yet go ahead and do it; it is also a sin to know what is right and yet not do it (Rom. 14:23). This is a stern warning against sins of omission (Luke 16:19–31 for an example of neglecting to do what is right).

5:1–6 In the spirit of the OT prophets, James pronounces judgment on employers who treat their employees unjustly (Is. 3:14, 15; 10:2). God will judge those who oppress the poor (Ezek. 18:12, 13).

5:1–3 In the ancient world food, costly **garments,** and precious metals were conspicuous signs of wealth. James pronounces judgment and destruction on all three.

5:4 Uncontrolled appetites for worldly accumulations have carried them to the worst extremes. Not only did they strive for the greatest profits, but they cheated employees in order to do so. **By fraud** they tricked the laborers out of their wages. The resulting desperate **cries** seemed to be in vain, but eternity reveals them to have **reached the ears of the Lord of Sabaoth.** That title, often translated "Lord of Hosts," emphasizes His omnipotence; in spite of how things may appear, He is sovereign!

5:5 In a day of slaughter may be taken in two ways. Some explain the slaughter as the excess killing of animals to prepare for a great feast. Thus, preparations for further indulgence seem to be in order. Others find eschatological significance to the phrase (Jer. 12:3), making it refer to their self-fattening process for their own slaughter. Perhaps the author had both ideas in mind. They anxiously make ready for another "day of slaughter" and feasting, while being ignorant of their ensuing judgment.

5:6 The just does not refer to Christ. It is a common OT expression that emphasizes a believer's faithful life. **Resist** has nothing to do with the good man's opposition to the oppressor's wickedness. It deals with the victim's mute response toward the tyrant's abuse.

5:7–11 Christ's imminent return encourages us to bear sufferings patiently (v. 8). Nor should we let hard times cause us to **grumble** or be bitter toward our Christian **brethren** (v. 9). The **farmer** (v. 7), the **prophets** (v. 10), and **Job** (v. 11) are models for us of this patient endurance.

5:7 be patient: James urges believers to maintain an attitude of patience while suffering injustices. Though every effort should be made to improve conditions and achieve justice, believers must keep a spirit of patient endurance, even in the midst of cruel treatment. The early church lived in the expectation of the imminent **coming of the Lord.** Their hope was that at that time justice would be handed both to the oppressor and the oppressed. At Christ's coming, wrongs will be righted and believers will be rewarded for their faithfulness to Christ (Prov. 14:14; Matt. 5:12).

5:8, 9 Expressions like **at hand** and **the Judge is standing at the door** indicate that the Lord could return at any moment.

5:10 A man undergoing trying circumstances may be comforted to learn that others

INSIGHT — Unjust Wealth

When James blasts the rich (James 5:1–6), is he condemning the possession of wealth? Is wealth inherently evil? No, but he is clearly warning those who get their wealth unjustly (5:4) and live lavishly while ignoring their neighbors (5:5, 6). Wealthy people of that kind are storing up judgment for themselves (5:1). God will call us to account for how we earn and spend our money.

have endured worse situations. The word **example** (Gk. *hupodeigma*) is positioned first in Greek to receive emphasis. A man's outspoken testimony for the Lord not only attributes a positive stand for the gospel; it frequently occasions harsh opposition from its enemies. **Of suffering and patience** both have definite articles in the original, which signifies "an example of the suffering affliction and the patience" that James has been discussing. **The prophets** stood loyal to their Lord, suffered for it, and now their experience encourages us.

5:11 We count them blessed holds somewhat of a paradox, although it may not have been intended. Objectively as we observe suffering in others, we urge them to endure, because victory will eventually arrive. Yet when we ourselves **fall into various trials** (1:2), our immediate human response often is negative. Job, who endured loss of property, family and

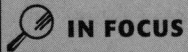 **IN FOCUS** — "Lord of Sabaoth"

(Gk. *kurios Sabaōth*) (5:4; Rom. 9:29) Strong's #2962; 4519: The name means "the Lord of hosts," "the Lord of armies," or "the Master of creation." It was suitable for James to use this familiar OT title (Ps. 24:10) in a letter to Jewish Christians, for they would have understood that the choice of this particular name of God was especially appropriate in this context. The rich oppress the poor because they think no one will stand up for them. But the Lord of all the hosts of heaven and earth is their Defender, and He is coming back to make all things right (5:7).

health, stands out as a specimen of enduring faith. His case not only asserts his patience but demonstrates the purpose and character of his Lord. **The end . . . of the Lord** (Gk. *telos*) may be better rendered "the Lord's goal." Our Lord permits suffering, because it leads to His excellent purposes (Rom. 8:28; Phil. 1:6). Moreover, while critics blaspheme God because of human suffering, Job's record shows the Lord to be **compassionate and merciful.** Suffering, then, must be attributed either to the means for God's ultimate purposes or (more often) man's own doing through corrupt leaders or personal sin.

5:12, 13 James is not forbidding a believer from taking an **oath** in court or invoking God as witness to some significant statement (1 Thess. 2:5). Instead he is prohibiting the ancient practice of appealing to a variety of different objects to confirm the veracity of one's statement. This practice was extremely close to idolatry, for it implied that such objects contained spirits. The warning in these verses can serve as a reminder to us to watch what we say. We should not use God's name in a reckless manner; and we should be careful to speak the truth.

5:14 Literally the Greek term translated **elders** meant those advanced in years (1 Tim. 5:1). However, the word also referred to those holding positions of authority in the community

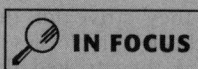

IN FOCUS "anointing"

(Gk. *aleiphō*) (5:14; Matt. 6:17; Mark 6:13; Luke 7:38; John 11:2; 12:3) Strong's #*218:* The Greek word *aleiphō* was commonly used in Greek literature to describe a medicinal anointing. Another Greek word, *chriō,* was used to describe a sacramental anointing. The distinction is still observed in modern Greek, with *aleiphō* meaning "to daub," or "to smear," and *chriō* meaning "to anoint." Furthermore, oil was one of the most common medicines of biblical times. Thus, James was prescribing both prayer and medicine in this verse.

or in a local congregation. As church officers, *elders* were responsible for pastoral supervision and spiritual leadership. The term is used interchangeably with *bishop* in the NT (1 Tim. 3:1; 5:17; Titus 1:5–9). **Anointing him with oil** may refer to medicinal treatment (Luke 10:34). Yet in this passage it most likely refers to the healing power of the Holy Spirit, for v. 15 speaks of prayer saving the person. In either case, there

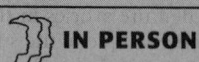

IN PERSON Elijah: A Prayer Model

What sort of person does it take to pray effectively? James offers Elijah as a model (James 5:17, 18).

In a way, Elijah seems an unlikely choice to be a model for ordinary people. After all, he was one of Israel's greatest prophets. He took on the evil Ahab and Jezebel, brought a punishment of drought on the land, called down fire from heaven, and was translated to heaven in a whirlwind accompanied by fiery chariots (1 Kin. 17—22, 2 Kin. 1 and 2). How much do we have in common with such a man? How could our prayers possibly emulate his?

Yet James insists that "Elijah was a man with a nature like ours." So apparently he did not pray because he was a great man; perhaps he became a great man because he prayed.

James shows some reasons why Elijah's prayer life was so effective:

- He prayed; one cannot be effective in prayer unless one prays in the first place.
- He prayed fervently; he was aware of what he was praying, and kept praying with diligence and discipline.
- He prayed an "effective" prayer (James 5:16); that is, he expected results.
- He was a righteous man (5:16); he did not allow sin to cloud his conversation with God.
- He prayed specifically, first for a drought, then for rain, in accordance with God's word (for example, Deut. 28:12, 24); he prayed according to Scripture.

Elijah was a great prophet granted extraordinary results by God. Nevertheless, there is no reason why any believer today cannot pray using the same principles as he did. Imagine what God might do in our world if Christians began praying like Elijah!

is no indication that calling the elders excludes the use of a physician or medicine. **Anointing him with oil** could be a medicinal act (Luke 10:34), but in this passage it is no doubt symbolic of the Holy Spirit because it is not the oil but prayer which heals (v. 15).

5:15 James certainly does not see the prayer and the oil, or the oil alone, as a sacrament, but he assigns the healing itself to the prayer of faith. The language seems to apply to any case of sickness, but the connection implies that the one mentioned, in addition to his bodily ailment, was also suffering spiritually. The Bible teaches that sickness can be a consequence of sin (Matt. 9:2). In such cases, confession of one's sin is a prerequisite to terminating a sickness as prescribed even here by James in v. 16. Praying for people to be made well ought not to be that they may be restored to their old manner of life but that their sins may be forgiven and their lives devoted to the service of God. **the prayer of faith:** Whether a believer is healed through medicine or through miraculous means, all healing is ultimately from the Lord. That is why prayers should be consistently offered for the sick (see 4:3 for an improper attitude towards prayer). **if he has committed sins:** The NT teaches that sickness may be the consequence of sin (Matt. 9:2), but not invariably (John 9:1–3). Yet when sin is involved, confession is a prerequisite to healing (v. 16).

5:16-18 Confess: This confession is not necessarily between the sick person and the elders, though this is not ruled out altogether. Instead, this exhortation is intended for the sick person and any person with whom the sick one needs to be reconciled. **Effective, fervent prayer . . . much:** This can mean either that (1) prayer is effective when it is used or (2) fervent prayer accomplishes great results. The illustration of **Elijah** may favor the latter meaning, for he prayed **earnestly.**

5:19, 20 The **death** (Gk. *thanatos*) spoken of here is physical death (1:14, 15; 1 Cor. 11:30; Acts 5:1–11). The covering of **sins** is an OT image for forgiveness (Ps. 32:1).

The First Epistle of

Peter

— • —

RETURNING GOOD FOR EVIL SOUNDS NOBLE, and Christians agree that it is the right thing to do; however, in the midst of trials and persecutions, showing kindness to our persecutors can be extremely difficult. The Christians of Asia Minor who received this letter from Peter had discovered this. They had found that a life lived for God is often a life of many difficulties. Some of their troubles came from

their neighbors, while some came from government authorities. Peter wrote to these Christians to encourage them, to explain to them why suffering occurs, and to remind them of their eternal reward at the end of this earthly life.

Peter blended five different themes in this letter. (1) He emphasized that Christians can expect suffering as a natural part of a life dedicated to Christ. Suffering was God's tool to shape godly character within them (1:6, 7; 3:14; 4:12–14). (2) He went on to exhort Christians to live righteous and holy lives in the face of the evils they were experiencing (1:13–16, 22; 2:1–5, 11, 12; 3:15; 4:1, 2, 7–11; 5:8–10). No matter how tempting it was, Christians were not to return evil for evil. That is a worldly and not a Christian response to persecution. (3) No matter how much suffering they experienced, Peter assured the Christians in Asia Minor they did not deserve it. Their suffering was a part of their service to God and His kingdom (2:20; 3:16, 17; 4:15–19). Although Christians would suffer injustice on this earth, there would come a time when God would right every wrong and reward those who have endured persecution for His name. (4) In light of this, Peter encouraged

Christians to submit themselves to others for the sake of the gospel and for the sake of harmonious interpersonal relationships (2:13–19; 3:1–9; 5:1–7). Christ would eventually judge their actions, and the difficulties they were experiencing would not be an excuse for rebellion and dissension. (5) Finally, Peter used this letter as an opportunity to drive home the central truth of the gospel, that Jesus endured the agony of the Cross to save us from our bondage to sin (1:2–5, 7–11, 17–21; 2:21–24; 3:18–22). Christ's example—His sinless life, His quiet endurance of suffering, and His commitment to the truth—should be our model in all the difficulties of this life.

To reach the centers of the provinces of ancient Asia Minor (present-day Turkey) to which Peter was writing, his letter had to travel many hundreds of miles over rugged terrain and treacherous seas. The bearer of the letter would have encountered Jews and Gentiles, Christians and pagans, free citizens and slaves. Some of the places in which the letter was read were cosmopolitan trade centers that were links between the Middle East and Europe. Other places were isolated villages. Yet throughout Asia Minor, small groups of Christians of a wide variety of social, ethnic, and cultural backgrounds would gather to hear God's word, to praise God, and to encourage one another in the faith.

Although cultural progress may not have touched many of the cities in which Christians lived, hostility to the gospel and to Christians themselves was there. Christians were targets of attack because they no longer participated in pagan religious practices. Since they were the ones who abandoned the so-called gods of the people, Christians were blamed for everything from natural disasters to economic downturns. They were even more vulnerable because they were often strangers in a city, having been driven out of other cities by persecution or having come from a Jewish background. These early Christians often had little security, low social status (many were slaves), and little recourse to government protection. Peter wrote to encourage them. They were pilgrims in this world heading to their glorious home in heaven.

Early church tradition affirms that the apostle Peter was the author of the letter known as 1 Peter. Those in the modern era who challenge his authorship argue that the vocabulary and literary style of the letter is more advanced than the vocabulary of an "uneducated and untrained" fisherman (Acts 4:13). Many of these critics also assert that the theology of the letter is too much like Paul's. It reflects Paul's thought rather than the experiences of the earthly life of Jesus Christ, as one might expect from Peter, one of Jesus' closest friends. Finally, these critics claim that the persecutions described in this letter could not have taken place during Peter's lifetime. But none of these

arguments is conclusive. Peter was from Galilee, a region that was bilingual. People who grew up there had to know two languages, Greek and Aramaic. As a fisherman, functioning in the business world of his day, Peter must have been reasonably fluent in Greek. Moreover, Peter, having "been with Jesus" (Acts 4:13), must have learned how to express himself from the Master Communicator Himself. As one of the first teachers and preachers of the gospel, Peter would have been able to express himself eloquently in Greek (Acts 2). If his own Greek style was not sufficiently polished, Peter could certainly have dictated this letter, perhaps to Silvanus (5:12), who would have polished his presentation (Acts 15:22–29).That Peter's letter reflects ideas similar to those found in the writings of the apostle Paul is understandable because the two men knew each other (Gal. 2:7–9). Peter had read Paul's letters (2 Pet. 3:15, 16), and both men were under the guidance of the Holy Spirit when they wrote. Thus, finding Pauline concepts in this letter is not a strong argument that Peter cannot be the author.

The issue about the author's seeming unfamiliarity with the earthly life of Jesus is best handled by looking at the letter itself, which reveals that the author is thoroughly acquainted with Christ's earthly sufferings and claims to be an eyewitness to them (2:21–23; 3:18; 4:1; 5:1). Moreover, the purpose of the letter was not to provide a record of the life of Christ. Instead, Peter was encouraging Christians with the comforting spiritual realities behind the persecution they faced.

Finally, the sporadic and local persecution before Nero's reign (before A.D. 68) is the perse-

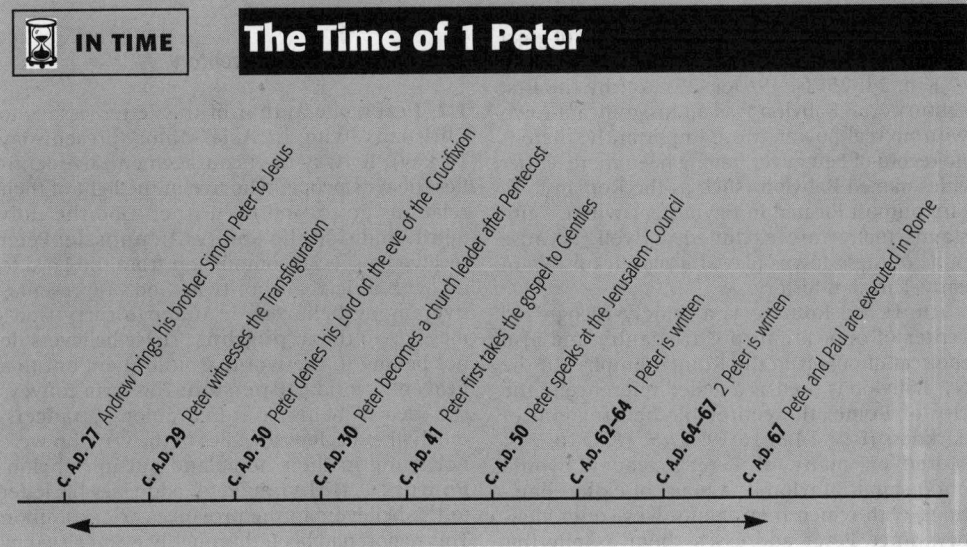

IN TIME

The Time of 1 Peter

C. A.D. 27 Andrew brings his brother Simon Peter to Jesus

C. A.D. 29 Peter witnesses the Transfiguration

C. A.D. 30 Peter denies his Lord on the eve of the Crucifixion

C. A.D. 30 Peter becomes a church leader after Pentecost

C. A.D. 41 Peter first takes the gospel to Gentiles

C. A.D. 50 Peter speaks at the Jerusalem Council

C. A.D. 62–64 1 Peter is written

C. A.D. 64–67 2 Peter is written

C. A.D. 67 Peter and Paul are executed in Rome

cution that Peter is probably addressing in this letter. Although severe official persecution did not begin until the reigns of Domitian (A.D. 95) or Trajan (A.D. 112), early Christians experienced oppressive local persecution from the beginning (Acts 14:19). In conclusion, there is no substantial evidence that contradicts the plain assertion of the letter that it is from the apostle Peter (1:1).

Church tradition tells us that Peter died in Rome during the anti-Christian persecution that took place during the reign of Nero (A.D. 54–68), so A.D. 67 is probably the latest this letter could have been written.

There are several indications that Peter wrote the letter around A.D. 62–64. First, Paul makes no reference to Peter being in Rome when Paul was writing his letters from there (Ephesians, Philippians, Colossians, and Philemon), some time between A.D. 60–62. Moreover, in his letter Peter makes no reference to Paul as being in Rome, identifying only Silvanus and Mark as his companions (5:12, 13). These facts suggest that Peter was writing after A.D. 62. But the fact that Peter admonishes his readers to submit to governmental authorities in 2:13–15 may indicate a date before the more severe persecution which occurred after the burning of Rome in A.D. 64.

Of course, this dating assumes that Peter wrote this letter from Rome and not from some other location. Peter concludes the letter by sending greetings from "she who is in Babylon" (5:13). Three locations are generally suggested for this reference: Babylon on the Euphrates River in Mesopotamia, a lesser-known city in the ancient world also called Babylon, and Rome.

The argument in favor of the Mesopotamian Babylon is its identity in the OT as a city of great power, a city feared and hated by the Israelites (2 Kin. 24; 25; Is. 39; Jer. 25). Yet by the first century A.D., Babylon was an insignificant town with no real power. More importantly, there is no record of Peter ever having been there. Other cities named Babylon (such as the Roman military outpost located in Egypt near where Cairo stands today) are excluded as well, because none of these towns played a significant role in early Christian history.

However, Rome was a widely-recognized center of opposition to Christianity and also the seat of power in the Roman Empire. In the NT, Babylon is used as a veiled reference to the city of Rome, the center of the kingdom of darkness (Rev. 14:8; 16:19; 17:5; 18:2, 10, 21). Moreover, many of Peter's readers would understand Babylon as a place of exile, something with which they themselves could identify, since Peter addresses them as pilgrims

scattered throughout Asia Minor. In this way Peter was concluding his letter where it began, with a sense that he and his fellow Christians had not yet arrived "home." Peter was using Babylon as a code word readily understood by early Christians to mean Rome, yet at the same time symbolizing more than just that earthly city.

Outline

I. Comfort and reassurance in suffering 1:1–25
   A. Salutation 1:1, 2
   B. Reassurance in God's grace and salvation 1:3–12
   C. Reassurance in holiness 1:13–25
II. Practical holiness 2:1–3:22
   A. The foundation of holiness 2:1–3
   B. Participation in a holy community 2:4–10
   C. Unimpeachable living, the answer to persecution 2:11–3:13
   D. Victory in unjust suffering 3:14–22
III. The spiritual significance of suffering 4:1–19
   A. Physical suffering: a type of death to the flesh 4:1–6
   B. Love for one another despite suffering 4:7–11
   C. The purifying fires of persecution 4:12–19
IV. Divine love as a guide in church life 5:1–11
   A. Elders to rule in love 5:1–7
   B. The devil to be resisted through divine grace 5:8–11
V. Closing salutation and benediction 5:12–14

Commentary

1:1 Peter, the author of this letter, writes to Christians living in **Asia** Minor (present-day Turkey). By way of encouragement, he identifies them as people who live in the light of their relationship to God the Father, God the Holy Spirit, and God the Son (v. 2). **apostle:** Peter received a special commission from the Lord to act with official authority as God's representative among believers, in order to carry God's message to them. **pilgrims:** These believers do not belong to the world around them but to a heavenly world. **Dispersion:** This term conveys the idea of being scattered among strangers, much like the Jewish exiles of the OT who were not living in their homeland but in Babylon. **Pontus . . . Bithynia:** Peter addresses his letter to the believers in the provinces of Asia Minor. This region had been thoroughly evangelized by

Paul during his missionary journeys (Acts 2:9–11; 16:6, 7; 18:23; 19:26).

1:2 Believers are chosen to be included in God's family, not on the basis of what they have done or who they are, but on the basis of God's eternal wisdom. **Sanctification** is the ongoing process whereby the Holy Spirit works in believers, making their lives holy, separated from their old ways and to God in order to be more like Him. **obedience:** One reason that God chooses us is so that we might serve Him. **sprinkling of the blood:** This concept, the second reason why God chooses us, draws our attention to three situations in the OT when the Israelites were sprinkled with the blood of animals: (1) Moses' sprinkling of blood on the Israelites at Mount Sinai, to symbolize their initiation into the covenant (Ex. 24:5–8); (2) the sprinkling of Aaron and his sons to be the priests of Israel (Ex. 29:19–21); and (3) the sprinkling of blood performed by priests over healed lepers to symbolize their cleansing (Lev. 14:1–9). Any of these three cases could be the one that Peter has in mind here.

1:3–11 God provides all our needs for this life and the future life. As a result, we are able to face our daily pressures with joy, knowing that God is in control of our present existence and our destiny. What He has given us is special—so special that the OT saints desired to understand it and the angels of heaven look in amazement at it.

1:3 according to His abundant mercy: Our salvation is grounded in God's mercy, His act of compassion toward us despite our condition of sinfulness. **has begotten us again:** God has given believers a new, spiritual life that enables us to live in an entirely different dimension than the one our physical birth allowed. **to a living hope:** *Hope* here does not imply a wishfulness but rather a dynamic confidence that does not end with this life but continues throughout eternity. "Hope is one of the Theological virtues," C. S. Lewis said. "This means that a continual looking forward to the eternal world is not (as some modern people think) a form of escapism or wishful thinking, but one of the things a Christian is meant to do. It does not mean that we are to leave the present world as it is. If you read history you will find that the Christians who did most for the present world were just those who thought most of the next. The Apostles themselves, who set on foot the conversion of the Roman Empire, the great men who built up the Middle Ages, the English Evangelicals who abolished the Slave Trade, all left their mark on Earth, precisely because their minds were occupied with Heaven. It is since Christians have largely ceased to think of the other world that they have become so ineffective in this. Aim at Heaven and you will get earth "thrown in": aim at earth and you will get neither." **through the resurrection:** Although this phrase may modify the phrase "to a living hope," the context suggests that it is to be understood as the means of our salvation rather than the means of our hope (1 Cor. 15:12–19).

1:4 The Greek word translated **inheritance** here suggests both a present and a future reality. God has already determined what we will one day experience in its totality. Note that Peter says that one of two reasons why God has given

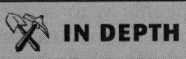 **IN DEPTH** | **Persecution in Bithynia**

Bithynia, combined with the nearby territory of Pontus, formed a Roman province in northwest Anatolia. It had been an important kingdom during the Hellenistic period, and a center of Greek language and culture. Although Paul did not evangelize in the region (Acts 16:7), the salutation in 1 Pet. 1:1, addressing Christians in Pontus and Bithynia, shows that Christianity had reached there by other means.

One of the earliest evidences of the Roman awareness of Christianity comes from Bithynia. The letters to the emperor Trajan from Pliny the Younger describe various reasons for the persecution of Christians (*Epistulae* 10.95–96). Pliny was the provincial governor of Bithynia and Pontus in A.D. 111–113. In his official correspondence he expresses to Trajan his alarm regarding the spread of Christianity.

The correspondence between this governor and his emperor offers one look at how the Romans dealt with the Christian religion in Bithynia and Pontus. According to Pliny, it appears that persecution had trimmed the ranks of Christians in the area. Trajan responds to Pliny that Christians should not actively be sought out. However, he allows that those who refused to perform certain Roman orders were to be punished. The letter of 1 Peter to Christians in Bithynia, Pontus, and other regions offers encouragement during similar persecutions (1 Pet. 1:6, 7).

us new life in Jesus Christ (v. 3) is to receive this never-to-end, never-to-be-spoiled, and never-to-lose-its-special-attraction inheritance. **reserved:** At this point, Peter must have thought back to our Lord's expression of unconditional commitment to Him as expressed in John 14:1–4 after revealing the prophecy of Peter's denials.

1:5 who are kept: God keeps His people safe from external attack and safe within the protective boundaries of His kingdom. Peter uses a twofold military concept to indicate that God keeps His people both safe from external attack and safely within the protective boundaries of His kingdom. **revealed:** We do not now see or understand fully the salvation that God has prepared for us, but one day we will (1 Cor. 4:5; 1 John 3:2)

1:6 grieved: While there is much rejoicing because of the salvation God has prepared for us, there will also be agony because of the pressures and difficulties of life. **by various trials:** In this context (v. 7), *trials* refers to ordeals that we encounter in life rather than those things that would induce us to sin. Note that no one particular problem is in view here, but rather all the testings of life.

1:7 genuineness: As the purity of gold is brought forth by intense heat, so the reality and purity of our faith are revealed as a result of the fiery trials we face. Ultimately the testing of our faith not only demonstrates our final salvation but also develops our capacity to bring glory to the Lord **Jesus Christ** when He comes into His kingdom and we reign with Him (Rom. 8:17; 2 Tim. 2:12; Rev. 5:9–12).

1:8 having not seen: Only a few believers had the privilege of walking and talking with Jesus when He was on earth (John 20:29). Most of us have shared the experience of Peter's addressees, who never had a personal physical relationship with Jesus but loved and believed in Christ anyway. **joy inexpressible:** This combination of words is used in the NT only here. It depicts an all-consuming joy that overwhelms us so that we are unable to express our feelings of gratitude to our glorious God.

1:9, 10 receiving the end: There is a final, positive outcome for trusting God through all the difficulties of life—our **salvation,** which here has an eschatological sense. **salvation of your souls:** This phrase refers to our glorification in heaven and perhaps the rewards we will receive for following Christ (Matt. 16:24–27; James 1:21). **the prophets:** Peter indicates that the OT prophets knew of the gracious salvation we would one day receive and, as a result, studied it carefully and intensively.

1:11 The focus of the OT prophets' study (v. 10) was not the **what** of our salvation but the **when.** They wanted to know when the Messiah

would suffer and when the glories of the end times would be revealed. Note that **the Spirit of Christ,** rather than the prophets themselves, was prophesying (2 Pet. 1:20, 21). The prophets were mouthpieces for God, not inventors of their own new ideas.

1:12 was revealed: God made known to the prophets that they would not experience all that we experience in Christ, that they were serving God for our benefit. **by the Holy Spirit:** Although humans may preach God's message of salvation, ultimately the Holy Spirit is the One who proclaims these great truths. Even the **angels** are amazed at what a wonderful salvation God has enacted on our behalf (Eph. 3:10).

1:13–25 Believers are challenged to live holy lives and to serve God faithfully because of the amazing work that He has done for us on the Cross and because our time on earth is so short.

1:13 gird up the loins of your mind: Just as people in biblical times would gather up their long robes and tie them around their waists so that they could move quickly and freely, we need to do whatever it takes to focus our thoughts on those things that allow us to serve God successfully, all the while eliminating any thoughts that would trip us up (Heb. 12:1). **be sober:** Peter's concern here is primarily using mentally or spiritually sound judgment. **rest your hope:** We need to exhibit confidence that God will accomplish all that He promised He would do (v. 3; Rom. 8:24, 25). **grace. . . at the revelation:** From beginning to the end, we are recipients of God's abounding grace (Rom. 8:28–30).

1:14 as obedient children: This idiom suggests that we should be people who actively obey because we, by our new nature, are children of obedience. **not conforming yourselves:** Believers should not pattern their lives after the desires that controlled them when they were not Christians, when they did not know God's ways (Rom. 12:2).

1:15–19 Three reasons why we should be holy: God is holy (vv. 15, 16); God who sees our inner attitudes judges justly (v. 17); and we are redeemed by the blood of Christ (vv. 18, 19).

1:15 but: Peter uses this term to indicate that the way we are to be (i.e., holy) is completely different than the way we used to be (1:14). **Holy** refers to being set apart or separate. We are to live so as to be dedicated totally to God and separated totally from the sin of this world.

1:16 because it is written: The coming of Christ did not lower or change God's expectations of His people. During OT times, they were to be holy; during NT times, they were to be holy; and today, we also are to be holy (Lev. 11:44).

1:17 who without partiality judges: Our heavenly Father is also our earthly Judge. Moreover, our relationship to Him as His children does not imply that we will escape judgment. God does not show favoritism in judgment but invokes His judgment on all people **according to** their works. **in fear:** For Christians, this phrase should be understood as something between terror and reverential awe. We need to remember that God is both our merciful Savior (vv. 3, 18–21) and our holy Judge (vv. 15–17). Thus, we should not see Him solely as an object of horror from whom we should run away nor should we think of Him merely as an object of respect.

1:18 Redeemed suggests the idea of offering something, usually money, in exchange for the freedom of a slave or a prisoner of war. God bought our freedom, paying for us with His Son's life (v. 19). **your aimless conduct:** Peter's focus is not on any specific action, but on the way of life that his readers inherited from their ancestors. Those old ways were futile, empty of power and incapable of securing salvation. Peter's readers needed to be snatched from their hopeless condition.

1:19 precious blood: God's way of salvation is contrasted to human attempts at gaining salvation through the use of earthly means (v. 18). **a lamb:** Peter describes Christ as the ultimate sacrificial Lamb, who is offered in our place to pay the price for our sins. The analogy here may be a reference either to the Passover lamb (Ex. 12:3–6) or to the many lambs without blemish that were offered as part of the OT sacrificial system (Lev. 23:12; Num. 6:14; 28:3). First-century believers recognized Jesus as the spotless Lamb of God who pays the price for the sin of the world (John 1:29).

1:20 foreordained: God has known (v. 2) the One who would bring salvation, even as He has known those to whom that salvation is offered and secured (Rom. 11:2). **but was manifest:** This phrase contrasts with the first half of the verse. What was known only to God before the creation of the world is now made known to us.

1:21 so that: Christ's coming results in our being able to place our trust and confidence in God.

1:22 Peter does not say that we purify our own **souls** but that we accomplish the purification of our souls by obedience to God's **truth.** It is unclear whether this obedience is a reference to the conversion process or to the sanctifying process after one's conversion. The former seems more likely in the context of vv. 20, 21; the latter seems more likely in light of Peter's

general theme of holiness in this letter. **sincere love:** An unfeigned love is one that is genuine, pure, and without hypocrisy. **love one another fervently:** We are to love our fellow Christians intensely, out of a true commitment of love.

1:23 born again: Though this phrase is commonly used by Christians today, it is rarely found in the NT (see John 3:3–8 for Jesus' use of the phrase). Christians are dead in sin before their life is renewed by the Spirit (Eph. 2:1). The same idea is expressed by "the washing of regeneration" (Titus 3:5) and the concept of "children of God" in John's first letter (1 John 3:1, 2).

1:24 withers . . . falls away: Peter reminds his readers of our transitory nature with an OT quote, comparing us to the temporary things of this world—a direct contrast to God's permanent work and His eternal word (vv. 23, 25; Is. 40:6–8).

1:25 the word which by the gospel was preached: A better understanding of this phrase is "the word, the gospel which was preached." Thus, the Good News of Jesus Christ, the gospel, is that which will last forever.

IN FOCUS "word"

(Gk. *logos*) (1:23; 2:8; 3:1, 15; 4:5; Rom. 9:6; Eph. 1:13) Strong's #3056; (Gk. *rhema*) (1:25; Rom. 10:17; Eph. 5:26) Strong's #4487: In 1:23 the Greek expression for *word* is *logos*, referring primarily to the idea. In 1:25 the Greek term is *rhema*, referring primarily to the spoken word. The spoken word is the gospel preached and proclaimed (the use of *rhema* in Rom. 10:17, 18). "The word of the Lord" is the gospel message about the Lord Jesus Christ. This word can regenerate men and women. Peter adapted the OT text (which says "the word of our God" in Is. 40:6–8) to its NT context.

2:1–10 God desires that Christians turn from the things of the world and seek His ways fully. By doing this, they acknowledge that they have accepted what the world has rejected and that they are rejecting what the world accepts. They recognize this reality in their lives because they have been chosen out of this world by God so they might act not as people of this world but as the people of God.

2:1 malice: This is a general term that conveys the idea of evil or wickedness, and encompasses both thoughts (i.e., desiring someone else's harm) and actions (i.e., the actual harming of another). **Deceit** is a general term for sin (2:22; 3:10) and suggests the deliberate use of guile or treachery in order to mislead someone. **hypocrisy:** Peter uses a plural noun to indicate that every act of hiding of one's evil intentions toward another behind a mask of piety is wrong and thus should be avoided. **envy:** Also a plural noun, this term presents those feelings of ill will or jealousy that an individual harbors against someone else because of a real or perceived advantage that that person has acquired. **evil speaking:** Words which are designed to ruin an individual's reputation or position (i.e., slander).

2:2 Desire does not mean merely to want something, but rather to long for something with all of one's being. **that you may grow:** The purpose of studying God's truth is not only to learn more, but to become mature in the faith.

2:3 if indeed you have tasted: The Greek grammatical construction here assumes this to be true: Peter's readers have experienced in personal terms the fact that Christ is gracious.

2:4 living stone: This phrase anticipates the OT quotations in vv. 6–8. Jesus, as a living stone, is superior to the OT temple. These words also may be a subtle attack on the dead stone idols that the Gentiles worshiped prior to becoming Christians. Thus, Jesus is greater than the traditions received from the fathers (1:18), He is greater than the temple in Jerusalem, and He is greater than the traditions of the Gentiles with their lifeless stone idols. The new building of God, of which Jesus is the Cornerstone, is living: it is the assembly of all believers, the church (v. 5). **rejected:** Not to receive Christ is to reject Him (John 3:18; Rom. 1:18–23).

2:5 Christians are part of God's great spiritual building project. **Stones** here refers to stones that are shaped and ready for use in construction, as opposed to natural rock. **a holy priesthood:** Unlike the OT priesthood, in which only those who were born into a certain tribe could be priests, all who are reborn into God's family, that is, all believers, are priests who have the privilege and responsibility of offering **spiritual sacrifices** to God (Rom. 12:1, 2; Heb. 13:15, 16).

2:6 chief cornerstone: Jesus is the foundation stone from which the placement of all other living stones in the spiritual house (v. 5) is

---

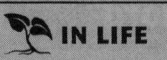 **IN LIFE**　　　**The Christian Calling: Holiness**

Writing to believers in Christ who were experiencing extreme persecution at the hands of a pagan culture, Peter advocated holy living. Seven times in Peter's first letter, we find the word *holy* (*hagios* in Greek) used in reference to conduct or behavior. And even when the word is not explicitly used, pure conduct is called for again and again.

Holy implies sacredness, being consecrated to God, or being worthy of God. In order to qualify for this label, a person or thing has to be free from impurity. There can be no hint of moral pollution or spiritual defilement. To be holy is to be free from anything that would offend a perfect God.

This state may seem impossible to achieve. After all, how can imperfect, fallen creatures like ourselves live up to the command to "be holy in all {our} conduct" (1:15)? The answer is found in the opening sentence of Peter's letter. *Sanctification,* the process by which we are made holy, is "of the Spirit" (1:2). The Holy Spirit of God, who indwells us at the moment of salvation, is able to transform us. By the power of the Spirit we find the ability to "abstain from fleshly lusts which war against the soul" (2:11). As we yield ourselves to God, and as we soberly and vigilantly resist the devil (5:9) and all his temptations, we will find that God is able to "perfect, establish, strengthen, and settle" us (5:10).

Holy living should be our goal not merely because God commands it, but also because it befits our true identity. In Christ we are no longer citizens of a sinful world, but the "people of God" (2:10). We are "sojourners and pilgrims" in this world, on our way to our true home, which is heaven (2:11).

Furthermore, holiness serves an evangelistic purpose. It is a "holy nation" and "special people" who are able to "proclaim the praises of Him who called you out of darkness into His marvelous light" (2:9). It is our "honorable" conduct and "good works" that cause evildoers to glorify God (2:12).

Finally, Peter speaks of the day when we will stand before God and give an account for the way we have lived. Those who have maintained a lifelong fear (reverence) of God resulting in holy living will be best prepared for that day of reckoning (1:17).

determined (Is. 28:16). In ancient buildings, the cornerstone was first situated on the foundation and then all of the other stones were aligned to it. Thus, as part of the house of God, we need to keep our focus on our Cornerstone (Heb. 12:2). **put to shame:** Those who trust in Jesus will never be embarrassed by making Him the focus of their lives.

2:7 to you who believe, He is precious: The Greek more precisely reads, "the honor is to you who believe." The honor or privilege that we experience is that we will never be ashamed of our relationship to Jesus Christ (v. 6) nor will we stumble because of Him (v. 8). **those who are disobedient:** This phrase (one word in Gk. *apistousin*) presents those who are the opposite of "you who believe," and is rendered literally, "those who are disbelieving." **Rejected** suggests that unbelievers, after examining Jesus to see if He meets their needs, declared Him to be useless or undesirable. Though He was not what they wanted, He is specifically the One whom God the Father has chosen to be the foundation of His eternal work.

2:8 stone of stumbling . . . rock of offense: Unbelievers, because they do not follow God's Word, find Jesus to be repugnant, an obstacle in their way and a cause for disapproval and anger. **they also were appointed:** The Greek does not clearly indicate whether those who are presently unbelieving (v. 7) are appointed to stumbling, to being disobedient, or to both. However, the context reveals that it is God who does the appointing.

2:9 But you: This verse provides a direct contrast to the previous verse, a contrast between those who believe in Jesus Christ and those who do not. **a chosen generation:** God has not left to chance those who will be part of a unique body of people, a group who will serve Him. He has reserved that decision for Himself. **a royal priesthood:** Believers are transformed not only internally (v. 5, which describes us as being made into "a holy priesthood") but also externally. We are a priesthood that functions in a ruling capacity, as kings. **a holy nation:** Believers are a unified group of people who are set apart for God's use. **His own special people:** God protects those whom He has adopted into His family. **proclaim the praises of Him:** The purpose for our having been transformed into these marvelous wonders is that we might declare to the world the works of our glorious God.

2:10 obtained mercy: Although we once deserved condemnation because of unbelief (John 3:18, 36; Eph. 2:1–3), we no longer are under the sentence of judgment (Eph. 2:4–7).

2:11–25 Remaining true to God implies exhibiting a life that constantly does what is right—a life that is submissive to others for the sake of God. Remaining true to God also may involve suffering for Him and demonstrating the same attitudes that Jesus maintained when He suffered in His earthly ministry (Rom. 8:17; Phil. 1:29).

2:11 sojourners and pilgrims: With these words, Peter reminds believers (1:1) that this earth is not our home. We are foreigners here, traveling to our eternal home, heaven. The word translated **abstain** literally means "to hold away from one's person." In other words, we must distance ourselves from our own self-indulgent urges. **war:** Life is not a game but a war to be waged, and that war is a matter of eternal life or death (Rom. 7:23; James 4:1). Yet the war is not necessarily fought on a physical, temporal plane, but on a spiritual one.

2:12 having your conduct honorable: Peter's emphasis here is the actual behavior of Christians. When internal struggles come (v. 11), responding with right actions is crucial because as we live in a world in which we are considered outsiders. **Gentiles** here refers to those who are not believers in Christ, not to those who are not Jews. **they speak against you as evildoers:** Despite our good works, those who are unbelievers will slander us. **they observe:** The Greek word for *observe*, used only here and in 3:2, implies a conscious, ongoing examination—in this case, of the actions of believers. **The day of visitation** probably refers to the final day of judgment when all people, believers and unbelievers alike, will fall on their knees and acknowledge who Jesus Christ is and what He has done through His people.

2:13 Peter forcefully commands Christians to **submit** voluntarily to governing authorities. He does not make submission a matter of personal conviction or choice. He decrees that it is an obligation for all Christians. **to every ordinance of man:** This phrase suggests that the submission of Christians is not to be exercised solely in relation to civil authorities (v. 14), but to all kinds of rules that Christians encounter (2:18; 3:1). **for the Lord's sake:** The command to submit is to be carried out not grudgingly or under compulsion but joyfully and willfully for the glory of God. Christians are not to have an attitude of rebellion.

2:14 governors: This term was used by the Greeks for all people, apart from the supreme ruler of a nation (v. 13), who exercise authority on behalf of the government of a country. **punishment of evildoers:** One role of government officials is the exercise of judgment against those who do wrong. **praise of those who do good:** Peter does not say, "for those who are Christians," but "for those who do good," whether they are Christian or non-Christian. One of the primary responsibilities of government is the rewarding of those who serve as good citizens.

2:15 the will of God: The authority backing Peter's command for civil obedience is the God of the universe, the Sovereign Ruler

IN LIFE **Enduring Hardship**

How should Christians react to injustices in the workplace? Healthy confrontation may be called for. There's a time to claim one's own rights or stand up for the rights of others. Scripture provides many examples and guidelines. For instance, Jesus gave instructions on how to deal with a believer in sin (Matt. 18:15–17), and Paul appealed to Caesar when he realized that justice was being withheld from him (Acts 25:8–12).

On the other hand, there is also a time to quietly suffer injustice as a matter of testimony, as Peter indicates (1 Pet. 2:18–21). Jesus told His followers the same thing (Matt. 5:38–42), and Paul discouraged lawsuits among believers for the sake of their testimony (1 Cor. 6:7).

Either way, Christians should never just ignore injustice. We may decide to quit if our employer is grossly unjust. But we should do so not out of cowardice or an unwillingness to endure hardship, but to honor Christ or else to find a constructive, godly alternative elsewhere.

over all citizens and governments and over all Christians and non-Christians. **put to silence:** Our actions should make our accusers speechless, like a muzzle placed over their mouths. **ignorance of foolish men:** The world is totally in the dark (v. 9) when it comes to recognizing the hand of God at work.

2:16 not using liberty: Freedom in Christ must be used wisely (1 Cor. 6:12, 13; 10:23–31). **A cloak for vice** may be understood either as an excuse made up before the fact (a reason for wrongdoing), or after the fact (a cover-up for wrongdoing). The context here seems to support the second. **as bondservants of God:** We should submit all our actions to God, for He is our Master.

2:17 Honor all people: We need to treat all people with great respect. **Love the brotherhood:** We are to have a special relationship with those who are our fellow Christians (Gal. 6:10). **Fear God:** Our reverence for God should be the

basis of our relationships with others. All people are created in His image, and He is the One who has placed some people in authority over us. Therefore, we should treat everyone with love and respect. **Honor the king:** We are to demonstrate great respect to those who are in positions of authority.

2:18–20 The Christian attitudes of these verses may be applied to employer/employee relationships today. **Servants:** Household slaves. **with all fear:** Out of reverence for God. **do good** (v. 20): In God's eyes. When we **patiently** bear undeserved persecution, God is pleased because His grace is at work in our lives.

2:18 Servants: Somewhere from one-third to half of the population of the Roman Empire were slaves. The percentage of Christians who were slaves may have been even higher. **be submissive . . . with all fear:** Workers are to take their responsibilities seriously. **but also to the harsh:** Christians are to serve even the worst of bosses with respect.

2:19 Those who suffer faithfully but unjustly as a result of their service to God please Him. Such suffering has a great reward (Matt. 5:10–12; Rom. 8:17, 18; Phil. 1:19; 2 Tim. 2:12). Peter himself had asked Jesus about this and received an exciting encouragement about the divine compensation package (Matt. 19:27–30). **endures:** Believers are not merely to survive the difficulties that come their way; rather, they are to bear patiently their heavy loads. **Grief** here is not the result of loss but of being afflicted. **wrongfully:** This verse is about injustice, about people being treated worse than they deserve.

2:20 Credit suggests benefit or personal gain. There is no advantage to believers for successfully enduring a deserved punishment for wrongdoing, yet there is great value when we honor God with our actions when we are unfairly condemned by others (3:17). **take it patiently:** Endurance and perseverance in the face of suffering please God.

2:21 For to this you were called: Part of being a Christian is the privilege of serving God faithfully when we encounter undeserved judgment (Phil. 1:29). **leaving us an example:** Observing how Christ handled unjust punishment gives us insight as to how we also may endure such trials.

2:22 Who committed no sin: Christ was perfect in everything He did, even when He was wrongly condemned to death by the world. **Nor was deceit found:** In His thoughts and attitudes, Jesus was perfect.

2:23 reviled: Although He was insulted and abused, Jesus remained in control of His words and did not utter slanderous remarks in return. **threaten:** Although He suffered physical pain,

Jesus did not cry out that He would get even or even that He desired to inflict pain on those who were causing Him agony. **committed Himself:** The Greek does not have *Himself*, and thus does not say whom or what Jesus kept giving over to God. Most likely, He constantly entrusted both Himself and His revilers to the power of God in order to let God deal with both as a righteous judge. When we pray, we are to forgive (i.e.

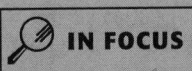 **IN FOCUS** **"example"**

(Gk. *hupogrammos*) (2:21) Strong's #*5261*: In common Greek usage, this word designated a tablet that contained the entire Greek alphabet. Students would use this to trace the alphabet, learning each letter from alpha to omega. The life of Jesus, a life of suffering, is just such a tracing tablet. We, the learners of Jesus, are to trace this life, beginning from alpha and going on to omega.

release to God) any offenses. It is not ours to "get even" (Mark 11:25, 26).

2:24 who Himself bore our sins: The Greek wording emphasizes Jesus' personal involvement in the act of paying the price for our sins. It also emphasizes that it is our sins that Jesus bore on the Cross. **The tree** is the Cross. **that we . . . might live for righteousness:** The purpose of Christ's bearing our sins is that we might live to please Him. **by whose stripes:** The Greek word for *stripes* is singular rather than plural. Thus, our spiritual healing comes neither from Jesus' day-to-day sufferings nor from His sufferings that led to the Cross, but from the one ultimate wound—His death.

2:25 Shepherd: This title portrays Christ as One who tenderly and wisely provides for all our needs. **Overseer:** Christ is also our Guardian, our Protector, the One who watches over us. This is the only place where the titles Shepherd (Pastor) and Overseer (Bishop or Elder) are used in the singular. No one else is qualified to be the one Shepherd and Overseer of our souls—only Christ is. For this reason the NT regularly describes the church and its congregations as having more than one leader (Titus 1:5).

3:1–7 Because of what Christ has done for us on the Cross, both wives and husbands are to make their marriages reflect Jesus Christ, even when difficulties arise (Eph. 5:32, 33).

3:1 In the same manner that citizens are to relate to their government leaders (2:13–17) and employees to their employers (2:18–25), so wives are to relate to their husbands. **be submissive:** Wives are commanded to place themselves willingly under the guidance and control of their husbands, living in such a way that their husbands will be challenged to live in obedience to God's truth. **do not obey the word:** Peter here is referring to non-Christian husbands (v. 20; 2:7, 8; 4:17). **without a word:** A godly wife does not preach to her husband with words but with the Christlike beauty of her daily life. **may be won:** The goal of her actions is to see the unbelieving husband become a Christian (1 Cor. 9:19–22).

3:2 chaste conduct: The Christian wife is to live without moral defect or blemish. **Fear** here refers to respect for God.

3:3 Do not let your adornment be merely outward: Christians are to spend more time developing their inner character than attempting to make themselves look beautiful on the outside (1 Sam. 16:7). Peter is not condemning women who wear jewelry. He is emphasizing the importance of a woman's character. We can spend most of our lives on things that are transitory rather than on things that are permanent—such as what clothes or jewelry we wear, or the car we drive. It is not wrong to be involved in temporal things, but we must put special effort into the development of inner character (compare 1 Tim. 2:9, 10).

3:4 the hidden person of the heart: The Christian wife is to be concerned with developing those intangible aspects of her life which are not flashy, but which are interwoven throughout all life. **Incorruptible beauty** involves inner qualities that do not decay or fade like makeup, jewelry, and clothes (v. 3). **gentle and quiet spirit:** Peter encourages Christian wives to exhibit attitudes that do not demand personal rights, attitudes that are not harsh and grating but are soothing and tranquil.

3:5 in this manner: These methods have been tested and proven to be God-honoring and effective by the spiritual women of previous generations.

3:6 calling him lord: Sarah was not worshiping Abraham; she was showing him respect. **not afraid:** Fear of her husband should not be the driving force that causes a Christian wife to practice the principles of godly marital relations.

3:7 Christian **husbands** are to demonstrate toward their wives the same unselfish spirit as Christian citizens (2:13–17), Christian subordinates (2:18–25), and Christian wives (vv. 1–6). **with understanding:** A Christian husband should be intimately aware of his wife's needs, her strengths and weaknesses, and her goals and desires. He should know as much about her

---

| **IN PERSON** | **Sarah's Example** |

Sarah (1 Pet. 3:6) was no doubt well known to the Jewish believers to whom Peter was writing. Just as Jewish men valued their connection with Abraham (compare Matt. 3:9; John 8:39; Acts 13:26), so women regarded themselves as daughters of Sarah. Peter affirmed that desire by describing what it would mean for Christian women facing severe persecution: doing good and not giving in to fear.

The Book of Genesis does not record Sarah calling her husband "lord," but the term was commonly used by members of a clan to show esteem to the head of the clan. By using such a title of respect, Sarah was honoring Abraham and demonstrating her submission to God by following her husband's leadership (3:1, 5).

Sarah exerted some leadership of her own by arranging for her servant Hagar to bear Abraham a son (Gen. 16:2–4), and later by urging him to send Hagar and her son Ishmael away (21:10–14). It's interesting that God instructed Abraham to listen to (obey) Sarah, even though Abraham was displeased with her plan.

In holding up Sarah as a model, Peter emphasized her good works and courageous faith (compare Heb. 11:11). She followed Abraham into some risky situations where courage and righteous living were required (Gen. 12:15; 20:2). In a similar way, Peter's readers were undergoing "fiery trials" as a result of their faith in Christ (1 Pet. 4:12). The key to their survival was not to capitulate to cultural standards of worth, but to develop a Christlike inner character, which is both beautiful and enduring (3:3, 4).

---

as possible in order to respond in the best way to her. **giving honor:** A Christian husband gives honor to his wife because she deserves honor (vv. 1–6). **weaker vessel:** The weakness in view here is primarily physical weakness, since the term *vessel* means the human body. **being heirs together:** The relationship described here is one between a Christian husband and his Christian wife, since all Christians and only Christians are heirs **of the grace of life** (Rom. 8:17). **that your prayers may not be hindered:** A Christian husband's spiritual relationship with God is directly affected by the way he treats his wife.

3:8 be of one mind: The idea is that of two people traveling the same mental path together. (Phil. 2:1–4). **having compassion for one another:** Used only here in the NT, the one Greek word (*sumpatheis*) for the five English words means having the same feelings as or suffering together with another person (Rom. 12:15). **be tenderhearted:** Christian affection should be demonstrated toward all people. **be courteous:** Literally, the Greek term (*tapeinophrones*) means to have a mind that does not rise far from the ground (i.e., to have an attitude of humility).

3:9–17 Only when we return good for **evil** do we receive the **blessing** that God wants to give us (v. 9). Verses 10–12 quote from Ps. 34:12–16 to support this truth. Verses 13–17 declare that it is better to do the right thing even if we suffer for it.

3:9 reviling for reviling: Peter encourages Christians to act like the Lord Jesus. He endured suffering and ridicule in silence, entrusting His just cause to the ultimate Judge (2:23). **but on the contrary blessing:** Peter emphasizes the contrast between our natural tendency as human beings, to get even when we are offended, with the way we should act as believers: returning good to those hurt us (Eph. 4:25, 29). **that you may inherit a blessing:** Christ will reward us for any suffering we endure in His name (Matt. 5:10–12; 19:27–30).

3:10 refrain: Christians are to cease and desist from speaking those things that might harm or deceive another. **speaking deceit:** Deceit means ensnaring someone through trickery, falsehood, or guile.

3:11 turn away from evil: Christians are to avoid what is sinful. **seek peace and pursue it:** Believers are not merely to desire peace; they are to run eagerly toward the goal of peace, yet always honoring God in their actions.

3:12 Peter uses the imagery of **eyes** and **ears** to remind his readers that God knows everything about believers, especially their suffering, and that He listens and responds to their cries for help (Heb. 4:12–16). **the face of the LORD is against:** In direct contrast to God's all-knowing and all-caring interest in His children who serve Him, He is diametrically opposed to those who do not follow His path of righteousness.

3:13 who will harm you: Under normal

circumstances, those who do what is right are less likely than those who do what is wrong to be hurt by others. **you become followers:** The idea conveyed is that of someone who is enthusiastic about doing good.

3:14 Since not everything in the world functions as it should, even those who do God's will may undergo suffering. **for righteousness' sake:** Believers should make certain that when they suffer it is only because they have served God faithfully and not because they have done anything wrong (4:14, 15). **you are blessed:** God especially honors those who suffer for doing what is right (Matt. 5:10–12).

3:15 sanctify the Lord God: Believers should acknowledge the eternal holiness of

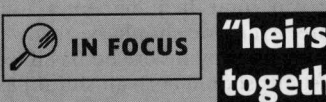

IN FOCUS   **"heirs together"**

(Gk. *sunkleronomos*) (3:7; Rom. 8:17; Eph. 3:6; Heb. 11:9) Strong's #4789: The Greek word means "joint-heirs" or "co-heirs." For Christian couples to be "joint-heirs" is for them to have an equal share and joint-participation in the Father's kingdom. The concept of inheritance is prominent both in the OT and NT (Num. 26:56; Ps. 25:13; Is. 60:21; Matt. 5:5; Gal. 3:29). For believers, Jesus promises an eternal inheritance in His kingdom. Paul uses the same Greek word to describe Christians' participation with Christ in glory (Eph. 3:6).

Christ by revering Him as the Lord of the universe who is in control of all things. **to give a defense:** Peter assumes that the Christian faith will be falsely accused. He therefore encourages Christians to have rational answers to respond to those false accusations. **Meekness** is the same term translated *gentle* in v. 4. Meekness is not weakness. Scripture indicates that both Moses and Christ were meek men; however, they were certainly not weak men. Fear implies a high degree of reverence or respect.

3:16 those who revile: Peter uses a different term here than in 2:23 and 3:9 for revile. In this verse, "revile" (Gk. *epreazo*) indicates false accusation or abusive treatment.

3:17 for it is better: Peter is not encouraging believers to seek out situations in which they will experience suffering. Instead, he is saying that believers should make certain that when they suffer it is the result of having been faithful to God rather than because they have

done evil (2:19, 20). **if it is the will of God:** Suffering may be part of God's perfect and wise plan for a believer (Matt. 5:10–12).

3:18 once for sins: Christ's death on the Cross was a once-for-all event. He died once for our sins; He does not have to be "recrucified" each time we sin. **that He might bring us to God:** Christ died so that we can be reconciled to God.

3:19, 20 There are various interpretations of the meaning of these verses, primarily because of the ambiguity of the phrase **spirits in prison.** The Greek term translated *spirits* can refer to human spirits, angels, or demons. There are three main interpretations: (1) Some interpret these verses as describing Jesus going to the place where fallen angels are incarcerated and declaring His final victory over evil in His work on the Cross. These commentators suggest that Peter is referring to **the days of Noah** because these fallen angels were typified by the gross immorality of those "spirits" who married human women at that time (Gen. 6:1–4; 2 Pet. 2:4; Jude 1:6). Depending on the commentator, this proclamation is assigned to the time between Christ's crucifixion and resurrection, or to a time after Christ's ascension to heaven. (2) Others hold that **spirits** refers to human spirits. Thus, Christ preached to human beings who had died in Noah's day and were in the realm of the dead (hell or Hades). Although some have insisted that Christ's preaching included an offer of salvation to these people, this is at best unlikely and at worst misleading, for Scripture never concedes a "second chance" for sinners after death. The content of Christ's preaching was most likely a proclamation of His victory over sin. (3) Finally, another major interpretation understands this passage as describing Christ preaching through Noah to the unbelievers of his day. Since they rejected Noah's message of salvation, they were presently **in prison**—that is, hell.

3:21 an antitype which now saves us: The symbolic act of **baptism** is the **answer of a good conscience** of one who has been saved from the penalty of sin (Rom. 4:1–6) by trusting in the death, burial, and **resurrection** of Christ (Rom. 6:4, 5). The floodwaters symbolize the baptismal waters, which in turn symbolize the salvation that can be obtained through Christ's death (Matt. 28:19, 20; Acts 2:38).

3:22 Being **at the right hand of God** means that Christ is in a position of power and authority. **subject to Him:** One day not only will authorities and powers—authorities and powers indicating different classes of angelic beings—recognize Christ's authority, but so will all people, believers and unbelievers alike (Phil. 2:9–11).

4:1–11 Suffering teaches Christians to live in such a way that they honor God. Christians are to be serious and joyful as they reveal through their lives the love and spiritual abilities that God has given to them.

4:1 in the flesh: Christ's suffering was real because He took on our human nature. **arm yourselves:** In order to fight the good fight successfully, believers must take on the **same mind** as Christ (Phil. 2:5). **He who has suffered** in this context refers to suffering Christians. **has ceased from sin:** Those who serve God faithfully in the midst of suffering take on a different attitude toward sin than what they previously held. Sin no longer holds the same grip on them. The phrase **has ceased** here does not suggest that those who have suffered become sinlessly perfect or that they will never sin again.

4:2 that: The focus of the lives of those who suffer for Christ is on doing God's will, rather than on living according to sinful passions.

4:3 Lewdness speaks of insolent, shameless behavior that goes unchecked in a person's life. **Revelries** refers to long, protracted feasts that involve much drinking and immorality. **abominable idolatries:** The idea here is that some forms of idolatry may have been detestable even to the civil authorities. Of course, all types of idolatry are hateful to God (Ex. 20:3–5; Deut. 7:25; 32:16, 17).

4:4 they think it strange: Unbelievers cannot understand the transformed lives of believers. **flood of dissipation:** In contrast to believers, who live in order to please God, unbelievers live without thought of the eternal consequences of their acts. They fill their lives with evil deeds that have no eternal value. **speaking evil of you:** Unbelievers typically ridicule those who refuse to follow them in their frivolous and wicked lifestyles.

4:5 They will give an account: Although unbelievers think they are free to do as they please, they are greatly mistaken. There are consequences to what they do. One day they will stand defenseless before God and give an account of all of their wickedness (Rev. 20:11–15).

4:6 There are four main interpretations of whom Peter refers to when he speaks of the **dead** in this verse. (1) Some see a connection between the gospel preached in this verse and the proclamation of Christ in 3:19, 20. Accordingly, they understand this verse to be about Christ offering salvation to those who lived in pre-Christian times (3:19, 20). This is most likely mistaken, because there is no indication in Scripture that anyone gets a "second chance" to be saved after death. (2) Another group of commentators also connects this preaching to

3:19, 20, but holds that this verse is speaking of Christ preaching the gospel only to the righteous people of OT times. The other two interpretations maintain that this verse is not connected to 3:19, 20: (3) One view has Peter speaking of the gospel which was preached to believers who are *now* dead. They had died just like other people, but they were now living with God. (4) The final and perhaps the most sound interpretation of this verse is that Peter is referring to the *spiritually* dead. The gospel was being preached to them so that they could come alive spiritually.

4:7–11 We will be ready for **the end** if we keep our relationship with God current through **serious** and **watchful** prayer, and if we maintain **fervent love** for one another (v. 8, explained in vv. 9–11).

4:7 Christ can come in judgment at any time. Therefore, everyone should be ready to give a reason for the way he or she has lived. **serious:** Christians should curb all sinful passions in light of the coming of the Lord. **watchful:** Peter urges his readers to be sober-minded and disciplined so that they can offer their **prayers** to God.

4:8 have fervent love among yourselves: Christian commitment for the good of one another is to be intense, stretched out to the maximum, holding nothing back. **love will cover a multitude of sins:** Peter is not suggesting that one Christian's love atones for

IN FOCUS "love"

(Gk. *agape*) (4:8; Rom. 5:5, 8; 1 John 3:1; 4:7, 8, 16; Jude 21) Strong's #26: This Greek word was rarely used in Greek literature prior to the NT. When it was used, it denoted showing kindness to strangers, giving hospitality, and being charitable. In the NT, the word *agape* took on a special meaning: It was used by the NT writers to designate a volitional love as opposed to the purely emotional kind. It is a self-sacrificial love, a kind naturally expressed by God but not so easily by men and women.

another Christian's sins. Rather, by introducing this proverb from the OT (Prov. 10:12), he is reminding us that love does not stir up sins. We can demonstrate our love for our fellow believers by truly forgiving them and not talking openly about their past sins.

4:9 Be hospitable: In NT times, hospitality

typically meant housing and feeding travelers for two to three days with no expectation of payment in return. **without grumbling:** Being truly hospitable required personal sacrifice. Therefore, many who performed such acts of kindness to strangers sometimes complained behind the backs of their guests about the hardships of caring for them. In this letter, Peter exhorts those Christians to serve others cheerfully.

4:10, 11 This is one of the most succinct but concentrated passages on the believer's spiritual gifts. Other key passages are Rom. 12:3–8; 1 Cor. 12—14; Eph. 4:1–16.

4:10 As each one has received a gift: Every believer is gifted to serve. **one another:** This is crucial for us to understand especially in a society that is fast becoming more and more addicted to privatism and individualism. It is God's plan to bring growth through relation, not through isolation. **Stewards** are managers or trustees who will be held accountable for using their gift in the best interest of the One who gave it to them.

4:11 as the oracles of God: Those who teach God's truth to others should teach it in a reverent manner so that their hearers will respect the Word of God. **with the ability which God supplies:** Not relying on their own strength, Christians should use the power God gives them to do His will on earth.

4:12–19 Peter instructs Christians regarding suffering. Some suffering, that which is experienced and for Christ, is natural and thus is to be expected. Some suffering, however, will come specifically from Christ and will have serious, eternal consequences. This suffering will be directed toward both Christians and non-Christians but the outcome for these groups will be significantly different.

4:12 do not think it strange: Apparently Peter's readers were astonished that they had to suffer as Christians, especially to the extent that they were suffering. The Greek word translated **fiery trial** here was also used to speak of the intense fire that burned away impurities in metals (1:6, 7). **to try you:** For Christians the purpose of suffering is to prove their true character, to clear away the dross of sin and to allow the pure nature of Christ to show itself. **some strange thing:** Christians should expect and prepare for suffering.

4:13 rejoice: That these early Christians were rejoicing in the midst of their suffering is evident. Peter, by using the Greek present tense of the command *rejoice*, urged them to keep on rejoicing. **when His glory is revealed:** Suffering will be part of the Christian experience until Christ returns (Rom. 8:18–22).

4:14 reproached: Christians may be unjustly blamed because of their association with **Christ.** Peter calls this situation **blessed**

These underground catacombs were used by early Christians as a place of refuge from persecution by the Roman authorities. Peter encouraged believers experiencing such persecution to persevere and remain loyal to Christ (1 Pet. 4:12, 13).

because it brings great reward in the next life (Matt. 5:10–12). **rests upon you:** When Christians suffer unjustly on behalf of Christ, they will discover that the close relationship they have with God during that period will refresh their spirit.

4:15, 16 But let none of you suffer as a murderer, a thief, an evildoer, or as a busybody: Peter again returns to this truth mentioned before in 2:20 and 3:17, to show that it is not suffering in itself which is virtuous, but suffering for the name of the Lord, or as a Christian, which counts. None of his readers should suppose that just punishment for sin by the government would bring the praise of God. The name "Christian" was applied in NT times as a term of derision (Acts 11:26; 26:28). Just being a Christian was at times punishable by death, or lesser penalties. History indicates that many have been killed for admitting to being Christians in these times of persecution by the government. **Let him not be ashamed,** that is, of this name of being a "Christian." Let him rather be proud of it, and use this derogatory name as a means and instrument for bringing glory to God.

4:17 the time has come for judgment: Judgment does not always imply condemnation in Scripture. When used in relation to Christians, it consistently refers to the evaluation of a believer's works for the purpose of reward (1 Cor. 3:10–15). **the house of God:** The focus here is not on a building but on believers. **those who do not obey:** Throughout this letter, Peter speaks of those who are not part of God's eternal family as being disobedient (2:7, 8; 3:1, 20).

4:18 scarcely saved: No one deserves to be saved, and no one is able to be saved by his or her good works (Eph. 2:8, 9). Since everyone deserves condemnation, the fact that anyone is saved is solely the result of God's grace. **appear:** If God does not hold back judgment from His own people, imagine the end of the enemies of God who have no one to justify them before Him (Ps. 1:4–6; Rev. 20:11–15).

4:19 Christians are to entrust their very lives to God, especially in the midst of suffering, always recognizing that He is the **faithful Creator** who is in control of all things. God never gives us more than we can handle (1 Cor. 10:13); everything He does always has a good purpose (Rom. 8:28).

5:1–4 Christian leaders are to serve God faithfully, remembering that God's divine compensation package is incomparable. Christ had made that clear to Peter in Matt. 19:27–29.

5:1 Peter sees himself on the same level as the rest of **the elders. Partaker** is a key term in the Epistle to the Hebrews (Heb. 3:1, 14). It speaks of sharing in Christ's reign in the coming kingdom (Rom. 8:17; Rev. 2:26–28; 5:9, 10). Peter considers himself to be already participating partly in **the glory** that one day he will experience fully.

5:2 Shepherd the flock of God: An ancient Israelite shepherd would go before his sheep to lead them; he would not drive the sheep in front of him. Church leaders should lead the people of God in the same way: feeding, protecting, and guiding them (John 21:15–17). Christian leaders should also remember that they have been given responsibility for tending a flock that belongs to God, not to themselves. **serving as overseers:** Church leaders must do everything in their power to ensure that the

Christians under their care are living according to God's Word. **not by compulsion:** The work of the ministry is to be done joyfully, not merely as a duty. **not for dishonest gain:** Christian leaders need to make certain that their work is not motivated by money, but by a passion for the good of those believers put in their charge (1 Tim. 3:3, 8; Titus 1:11).

5:3 nor as being lords over: Echoing a command that Peter heard directly from Jesus during His earthly ministry, Peter reminds all Christian leaders that they need to perform the role of servants, not of masters, to those whom God has assigned to their care (Matt. 20:25–28; Mark 10:42–45). **being examples:** Christian leaders should be a godly model to other believers (Phil. 3:17; 2 Thess. 3:9; 1 Tim. 4:12). Christ Himself set the example for all of us (John 13:15).

5:4 Chief Shepherd: Elsewhere Jesus is called the Shepherd (2:25), the good Shepherd (John 10:11, 14), and the great Shepherd (Heb. 13:20). **crown of glory:** God guarantees that those ministers who serve Him faithfully, in accordance with the guidelines of vv. 2, 3, will receive an eternal reward in Christ's coming kingdom.

5:5–11 God's people are to humble themselves before God, being wary of our enemy the devil but at the same time mindful that God brings a victory that lasts for eternity.

5:5 submit: Young men specifically are reminded not to usurp the authority of church leaders but to place themselves as subordinates under those leaders. The "swift to hear, slow to speak" of James is very appropriate. **resists:** God acts in direct opposition to those who are arrogant, contemptuous, or haughty—traits which are particularly evident in those who do not display an attitude of submission.

5:6 humble yourselves: All people will one day humble themselves under God's power (3:21; Phil. 2:9–11). We as believers need to do it now.

5:7 casting all your care upon Him: We need to present all our worries, anxieties, and problems to God in order to let Him handle them.

5:8 Be sober means to be self-disciplined, to think rationally and not foolishly. **Be vigilant** means to be alert to the spiritual pitfalls of life and take appropriate steps to make certain that we do not stumble. **your adversary:** Satan is our avowed enemy. He never ceases from being hostile toward us; he is constantly accusing us before God (Job 1:9—2:7; Zech. 3:1; Luke 22:31; Rev. 12:10). **like a roaring lion:** Satan is both cunning and cruel. He attacks when least expected and desires to destroy completely those whom he attacks.

5:9 Resist him: We are not commanded to run, but to resist—to fight rather than flee. Victory comes when we remain committed to God, because He is greater than our enemy (1 John 4:4). **knowing:** Realizing that other Christians are undergoing the attacks of Satan and are being successful against him gives us the courage to press on and to secure the victory as well.

 **IN COMPARISON** **Church Leaders**

Peter concludes his first letter with an exhortation for overseers to "shepherd the flock of God" (5:2). The following is a summary of the responsibilities and qualification of overseers and of deacons, the other church official mentioned in the NT.

	Overseers/Bishops/Elders	Deacons
Meaning	The Greek word *presbuteros* literally means "aged," which explains the common translation elder.	The Greek word *diakonos* literally means "servant."
Responsibilities	• To pastor or "shepherd" God's church—to feed, lead, guide, and nurture (Acts 20:28; 1 Pet. 5:2) • To administrate or rule God's church (1 Tim. 5:17; Titus 1:5) • To teach and preach (Eph. 4:12, 13; 1 Tim. 3:2; 5:17) • To represent the church (Acts 20:17) • To pray for the sick (James 5:14)	• To tend to physical needs among the believers (Acts 6:1–6) • To free up the elders for their ministry in teaching and prayer (Acts 6:1–6)
Qualifications from 1 Timothy 3	• Blameless (v. 2; Titus 1:6) • Husband of one wife (v. 2; Titus 1:6) • Temperate (v. 2) • Sober-minded (v. 2; Titus 1:8) • Of good behavior (v. 2) • Hospitable (v. 2; Titus 1:8) • Able to teach (v. 2; Titus 1:9) • Not given to wine (v. 3; Titus 1:7) • Not violent, but gentle (v. 3; Titus 1:7) • Not greedy for money (v. 3; Titus 1:7) • Not quarrelsome (v. 3) • Not covetous (v. 3) • Rules own house well (v. 4) • Has submissive children (v. 4; Titus 1:6) • Not a novice (v. 6) • Has a good testimony (v. 7)	• Blameless (v. 10) • Husband of one wife (v. 12) • Not given to wine (v. 8) • Not greedy for money (v. 8) • Rules own house well (v. 12) • Reverent (v. 8) • Not double-tongued (v. 8) • Has a pure conscience (v. 9) • Tested (v. 10)
Qualifications from Titus 1	• Not self-willed (v. 7) • Not quick-tempered (v. 7) • A lover of what is good (v. 8) • Just (v. 8) • Holy (v. 8) • Self-controlled (v. 8)	

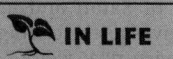 **IN LIFE** | ## The Business of the Church

There are many reasons why people seek positions of authority in a church. Some do it because they have authority at their normal job and therefore feel they should have authority at church. Some do it for just the opposite reason: authority is denied them at work, so they seek it in the church.

Peter reminds overseers (1 Pet. 5:2–4) that the presence or absence of authority or success on the job is more or less irrelevant to positions of authority at church. That may shock church members and leaders who have uncritically adopted models of church management from the business world. It's not that churches can't benefit from many of the practices found in business. Certainly in administration and finances, churches have much to learn from the efficient and effective policies of the marketplace. But the church is not a business, and philosophies and practices from that sphere need to be carefully evaluated and sifted in light of Scripture before they are put into effect.

5:10 perfect: Like a doctor setting a broken bone, God will mend our broken lives and make us whole. **establish:** God will make our way stable, despite the instability we feel living in a world that inflicts suffering upon us. **strengthen:** God will give us the ability to succeed in all that we do for Him. **settle:** As a consequence of our facing the attacks of our enemy, God will build in us a firm foundation that will make us steadfast and immovable.

5:11 the glory and the dominion: God is in control of all things both in this world and throughout eternity. **Amen:** Responding to the Word of God by saying "amen" echoes a Jewish practice of declaring that everything that had been said is true and that the hearers were committed to putting into practice that truth (Phil. 4:20).

5:12–14 By his concluding greetings, Peter reminds his readers that Christians are to build one another up through the exercise of God's grace and love.

5:12 Silvanus, whose Aramaic name was Silas, worked closely with both Peter and Paul (Acts 15:40; 16:19, 25, 29; 2 Cor. 1:19; 1 Thess. 1:1). **testifying:** Peter uses an intensive verb form here to show the intensity of his commit-

ment to witness unashamedly of God's truth. Contrast Peter's cowardly behavior prior to Jesus' crucifixion (Matt. 26:69–75; Mark 14:66–72; Luke 22:54–62; John 18:25–27).

5:13 She indicates the people who comprise the local church in the city from which Peter was writing (the Greek word for *church* is a feminine noun). Peter uses the term **Babylon** to refer to Rome. By the first century, the original Babylon was a small and insignificant town. **elect together with you:** All of the people of God are chosen by Him to be His people (1:2). **Mark my son:** John Mark (Acts 12:12, 25; 15:37, 39) was Peter's spiritual son, not his physical one. What is being conveyed here is that the relationship between Peter and Mark is like that of father and son.

5:14 a kiss of love: Early Christians and Jews greeted fellow believers with a kiss on the cheek. Here Peter is encouraging believers to treat fellow believers as part of one large spiritual family of God (Rom. 16:16; 1 Cor. 16:20; 2 Cor. 13:12; 1 Thess. 5:26). **peace:** Once again Peter desires that these Christians who are undergoing much suffering will experience God's perfect peace in their lives (1:2).

The Second Epistle of

Peter

EACHING AND LEARNING IS IMPORTANT BECAUSE it involves truth and error. What a student learns becomes ingrained in the heart and soul. The student develops an attachment to it. If this "learning" is false—if the student comes to believe that something untrue is actually true—so much the worse. It will be hard to convince the person otherwise. And if the truth or error involves our eternal destiny, the

stakes only go up. This is why Peter wrote his second epistle. The Christian faith that Peter had faithfully preached was not just a matter of philosophy. It was a matter of eternal life and death. Yet there were those who were peddling their own propaganda, falsehoods that contradicted the truth. Peter had to say something; he had to confront these falsehoods so they would not be mistaken for the truth.

With its emphasis on holy living and its efforts to refute false teachings, 2 Peter stresses sanctification. Ultimately Peter traces the motivation for leading a holy life back to the imminent return of Christ and the punishment and rewards Jesus would bring. The letter groups these teachings into five different themes. (1) Initially Peter asserts his own authority and the authority of the apostles' teaching. Their instruction would help the readers of 2 Peter to distinguish truth from error. (2) Evidently the recipients of this letter were having trouble establishing the connection between following Christ and leading a holy life. Peter reiterated to them that discipleship to Christ means putting away all kinds of immorality. (3) Furthermore, Peter warned them not to imitate the arrogance

of the false teachers, who were slandering spiritual beings. (4) To encourage them to persevere and to remain faithful to the truths of the faith, Peter depicted the day of the Lord, which would result in a new heaven and new earth. (5) Toward the end of his letter, Peter encouraged his readers to be patient. God had good reasons for delaying Christ's return and the fulfillment of His prophetic program. The day of the Lord had been delayed, but it was still imminent. For this reason, they should vigilantly watch their belief and practice so that they would not be deceived by falsehood.

The obvious similarities between 2 Peter and Jude call for an explanation (compare ch. 2 with Jude 4–18). Some have suggested that Peter borrowed from Jude, while others have maintained the opposite. In addition, some have suggested that both authors borrowed from another, anonymous source. This type of borrowing was fairly common in the first century. For example, it is evident that Luke used other sources when he wrote his Gospel (Luke 1:1–4). Most scholars agree that the more complete and precise statements in Jude point to Peter borrowing from Jude. The fact that the early church treated James, a half brother of Jesus, with utmost respect (Acts 12:17; 15:13; 21:18; Gal. 1:19) may help explain why Peter borrowed from the letter of another half brother of Jesus, Jude.

Second Peter is one of the NT books that struggled the longest to gain acceptance into the NT canon. Church authorities such as Origen (around A.D. 240) accepted it as canonical but admitted that is was a "disputed" book. Early critics believed it was written in the second century by a disciple of Peter who used Peter's name. They based their belief on differences of language and style between it and 1 Peter, as well as differences in subject matter and approach. Furthermore, they noted the similarities between 2 Peter and Jude, asserting that the unknown writer of 2 Peter borrowed from Jude, something the apostle Peter would have never done.

Nevertheless, by the fourth century A.D. the church councils had accepted 2 Peter as one of Peter's authentic letters. Modern studies have shown that the differences with 1 Peter are not nearly so great as earlier critics contended, and the stylistic differences can be accounted for by the use of different secretaries. First Peter may have been written with the help of Silvanus (1 Pet. 5:12). It is quite likely that Peter either wrote the second letter himself or employed another scribe to write it down—perhaps Mark. Although 2 Peter does not refer to as many events in the life of Jesus as 1 Peter does, it accurately describes the Transfiguration, the prophecy of Peter's own death, the day of the Lord's coming as a thief in the night, and the prediction of the appearance of false prophets. All of these are clear allusions to Jesus' life as recorded in the Gospels.

There is clear evidence from the early centuries of Christianity that the church did not tolerate those who wrote in an apostle's name. In one instance (specifically *The Acts of Paul* and *Thecla*), the author of such a work was disciplined for doing so. Paul also condemned such practices in his Thessalonian letters (2 Thess. 3:17). From the preceding evidence, it is reasonable to maintain that Simon Peter wrote this letter, just as the letter itself asserts (1:1).

Second Peter can be dated some time between A.D. 64 and 68. It was probably written from Rome, where early church tradition has the apostle spending the closing years of his life. Peter died a martyr in A.D. 68, and the epistle was written shortly before that (1:14, 15).

Peter addressed his letter "to those who have obtained a like precious faith with us" (1:1), a way of saying "to all believers everywhere." He had written 1 Peter to the widely scattered Christians in the Asia Minor provinces of Pontus, Galatia, Cappadocia, Asia, and Bithynia. By the time he wrote 2 Peter, they were no doubt even more widely scattered. Some have noted that 2 Peter seems to be addressed to a group whom Peter knows well and who were facing a specific false teaching. Even if this is the case, the readers seem to be largely Gentiles (because of the multiple references to licentious lifestyles, a characteristic of Gentiles) or a mixed group of Jews and Gentiles, probably living in one of the provinces mentioned above. Word of their difficulties with false teachers had reached

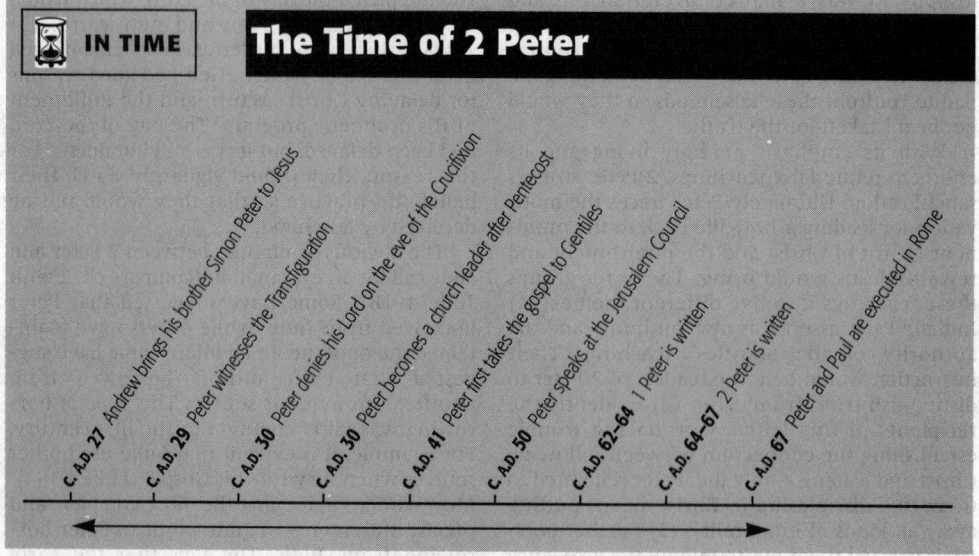

IN TIME

The Time of 2 Peter

c. A.D. 27 Andrew brings his brother Simon Peter to Jesus

c. A.D. 29 Peter witnesses the Transfiguration

c. A.D. 30 Peter denies his Lord on the eve of the Crucifixion

c. A.D. 30 Peter becomes a church leader after Pentecost

c. A.D. 41 Peter first takes the gospel to Gentiles

c. A.D. 50 Peter speaks at the Jerusalem Council

c. A.D. 62-64 1 Peter is written

c. A.D. 64-67 2 Peter is written

c. A.D. 67 Peter and Paul are executed in Rome

Peter in Rome, and he dispatched this letter to them to encourage them and warn them of the dangers they faced.

Outline

I. Salutation: the spiritual resources of a Christian 1:1–4

II. Essential Christian virtues 1:5–15
  A. Efforts for Christian faithfulness 1:5–9
  B. Confirmation of election 1:10, 11
  C. Need for reminders 1:12–15

III. Christ's divine authority 1:16–21
  A. Witnessed by the apostles 1:16–18
  B. Proven by divine prophecy 1:19–21

IV. False prophets and teachers 2:1–22
  A. Some warnings against false teachers 2:1–3
  B. The judgment of false teachers in the past 2:4–9
  C. The immorality of false teachers 2:10–16
  D. The uselessness of false teachings 2:17–22

V. Christ's return 3:1–18
  A. The certainty of the day of the Lord 3:1–10
  B. The ethical implications of the day of the Lord 3:11–16
  C. The need to guard against error 3:17, 18

Commentary

1:1 apostle: With this term Peter identifies himself as an authorized spokesman for the truth that Christ proclaimed. In vv. 1–4 Peter describes the resources his readers have that will make growth in grace and knowledge possible. His apostleship is the first of these resources. **like precious faith:** Anyone who has faith in Jesus has the same access to God as any other believer. This access is the second great resource that Peter's readers possess. It was obtained when they were given the gift of **righteousness** (justification). The righteousness believers are given is the righteousness of Christ Himself. **our God and Savior Jesus Christ:** This title of Jesus reflects Peter's great confession in John 6:69: "You are the Christ, the Son of the living God."

1:2 Grace and peace is a common Christian greeting in the epistles, combining Greek and Hebrew salutations. However, the phrase is more than a salutation to Peter. He sees grace and peace as blessings that spring from **the knowledge of God** and Jesus. The Greek word translated *knowledge* is a key word in this letter.

It describes a special kind of knowledge, a kind that is complete. Since our knowledge of Jesus grows as we mature in the faith, we will experience His grace and peace on many different occasions in our Christian walk.

1:3 The apostle Paul identifies the **divine power** referred to here as "the power of His resurrection" (Phil. 3:10; 4:13). This power is the third resource for godly living that Peter lists in this letter (v. 1). **by glory and virtue:** These words suggest the qualities of Jesus that attract believers to Him. The glory that John saw in Jesus (John 1:14) was His authority and power. The glory that Peter saw probably was manifested at the Transfiguration (vv. 16–18). Jesus' virtue is His moral excellence that continually awed His disciples.

1:4 Great and precious promises refers to the numerous offers of divine provision found in Scripture. These promises offer us the glory and virtue of Christ as the basis for our growing participation in the divine nature. We have Christ within us, as He promised (John 14:23), to enable us to become increasingly Christlike (2 Cor. 3:18). Because we have become new creatures in Christ, we have already **escaped the corruption** (the moral ruin) **that is in the world through lust** (perverted desire). We should make our escape from this world evident to all by our godly behavior and the renewing of our mind (Rom. 12:2). These promises are the fourth resource (vv. 1, 3) upon which believers may draw for sustaining help.

1:5 add: This is the same word rendered "supplied" in v. 11. As we add these qualities to

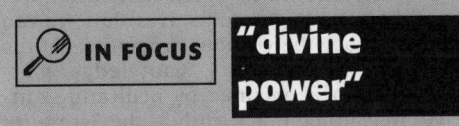

IN FOCUS **"divine power"**

(Gk. *theios dunamis*) (1:3) Strong's *#2304; 1411*; divine nature (Gk. *theios phusis*) (1:4) Strong's *#2304; 5449*: These are unique expressions in the NT. The divine power is the power God used in raising Christ from the dead and is that same power available to the church (Eph. 1:19, 20). This divine power has provided us with the spiritual ability to live a godly life. The divine nature is the nature that characterizes God, the nature that is expressed in holiness, virtue, righteousness, love, and grace (1:5–7). By being regenerated with the divine nature, believers can exhibit the same characteristics.

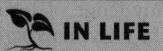 **IN LIFE** | **The Source of Power**

Do we think we have what it takes to "make it" in life? According to 2 Pet. 1:3, we do. Peter says that God's power gives us what we need to experience real life in a way that pleases Him. God wants to affect every area of our lives—work, marriage and family, relationships, church, and community.

How can we make God's power operational in our experience? Peter says that it comes "through the knowledge of Him who called us." In other words, we must grow closer to Christ. Real power comes from having an understanding of our place in God's purposes and relying on His provisions.

our faith, God will "add" to us an "abundant entrance" into the everlasting kingdom. The verb *epichorego* has a colorful and fascinating history. In Greek drama the plays were put on by the combined effort of a poet (who wrote the script); the state (which provided the theater); and a wealthy individual called a *choregos*, who paid the expenses. This called for a generous but sometimes costly effort on his part. In Peter's view, God has written in the blood of Jesus the captivating script for a Christian life; the world is the theater where it will be played out; but the believer must cooperate by expending his diligent efforts to make the script come alive in vivid display. This exhortation begins a section (vv. 5–11) in which Peter describes the responsibilities that result from possessing the godly resources described in vv. 1, 3, 4. **Faith** marks the beginning of the Christian life (Acts 3:16; Rom. 3:28; Heb. 11:6). Through genuine faith, God grants eternal life to a spiritually dead person (Eph. 2:1). **Virtue** is the same word used in v. 3 in reference to Christ's character. We cannot produce virtue ourselves; but we can choose to obey the virtuous promptings of the Holy Spirit who lives in us. **Knowledge** (practical wisdom) is obtained by dedicating ourselves to learning God's truth in the Scriptures and putting that truth into action.

1:6 Self-control means mastering one's emotions rather than being controlled by them. The false teachers whose views Peter was exposing believed that knowledge freed people from the need to control their passions. **perseverance:** A person who exercises self-control will not easily succumb to discouragement or the temptation to quit. Viewing all circumstances as coming from the hand of a loving Father who is in control of all things is the secret of perseverance.

1:7 The Greek word for **godliness** was used by ancient pagans to describe a religious individual who kept in close touch with the gods. Here Peter uses the word to speak of the need for Christians to be continually aware of God's

presence. Knowing that all of our life is in His hands should influence every aspect of our life. We should live for God and not for ourselves. **Brotherly kindness** is so closely linked with *godliness* that 1 John 4:20 says, "If someone says, 'I love God,' and hates his brother, he is a liar." As Jesus taught in John 15:12–17, love involves serving one another, sharing with one another, and praying for one another. **Love** here refers to God's kind of love, which originates not in the one loved but in the one who loves. God loves because He is love; we are to love because we are from God. Such love reaches beyond the Christian community to anyone, anywhere, seeking that person's highest good—even at a cost to ourselves.

1:8 neither barren nor unfruitful: The presence of the qualities listed in vv. 5–7 marks a healthy Christian and assures productivity in our lives. Thus, a person who asks how he or she can experience fruitfulness has the process laid out step by step

1:9 The lack of fruitfulness (v. 8) in a believer's life may be caused by two factors: **blindness** and forgetfulness. A **shortsighted** person is one who looks only at earthly and material values—what is close at hand—and does not see the eternal spiritual realities. Concerned only with this present life, such a person becomes blind to the things of God, forgetting the wonderful sense of cleansing that comes from turning oneself over to Christ.

1:10 In v. 10, Peter urges his readers to confirm **call and election,** not memory. It does not seem likely that a person could forget it if his sins had been washed away by the atoning death of Christ, but the whole matter could escape his notice if he were not urged to make sure about it. We cannot be sure of **call and election** if we have not been **purged** (v. 9) from our former sin. On the other hand, if these are confirmed by the fact that we have been cleansed from our old sins, it is certain that we **shall never stumble.**

1:11 entrance . . . abundantly: Peter distinguishes between a just-barely-made-it entrance into the eternal kingdom and a richly abundant one. The Scripture indicates that fruitful and faithful living here will be rewarded by greater privileges and rewards in glory (Rev. 22:12).

1:12 to remind you: Three times in vv. 12–15 Peter speaks of his desire to remind his readers of the truth he has already shared. To do otherwise would be negligence on his part, since even established Christians can lose sight of the importance of pressing on to the end. Perhaps Peter is thinking of his own wavering which led to a repeated denial of his Lord even when he was most confident that he would never fail Him.

1:13, 14 Peter is conscious of the short time he has to be in his body. Paul also viewed his body as a **tent** or tabernacle, a temporary residence (2 Cor. 5:1). Jesus had told Peter that when he was old he would be taken captive and put to death (John 21:18, 19). Now that he had little time left, Peter encouraged his readers to seize the opportunity to display Christ's love while they still could.

1:15 careful to ensure: Several early church fathers took these words to be Peter's promise to leave behind a testimony of the truth for his readers, which they considered to be the Gospel of Mark (a Gospel widely regarded as Peter's testimony of the life of Jesus). Peter describes his **decease** as an exodus or departure (Paul's use of the term in 2 Tim. 4:6).

1:16–21 Peter reminds his readers to be faithful because the Second Coming of Christ is no **fable.** That coming is assured by two things: (1) Peter himself witnessed the **majesty** of Christ at the Transfiguration (vv. 16–18), which was a preview of His second coming in glory. (2) The **prophetic word** of the OT also foretold Christ's coming (v. 19).

1:16 False teachers were claiming that Jesus' resurrection and return, as well as the Holy Spirit's indwelling of believers, were all **cunningly devised fables.** Peter countered their faith claims with an eyewitness account. Peter himself had actually seen the **power** and **coming** of the **Lord Jesus Christ.** These are the twin themes of this letter: the power of Jesus available for holy living and the coming of Jesus as the glorious hope of each believer.

1:17, 18 Along with James and John, Peter heard the **voice** of the **Father** during the Transfiguration (Matt. 17:1–13). That voice conferred **honor** upon Jesus by identifying Him as "My beloved Son, in whom I am well pleased" (Matt. 17:5). Jesus' **glory** was displayed in His shining garments (Mark 9:3). Thus, the apostolic witness of Jesus is established by three senses: they *saw* the transfigured Lord; they *heard* the voice of the Father (and the conversation with Moses and Elijah though Peter does not mention the

latter here); and they *remembered* the event as taking place on the holy mountain. This grounds the event in history and removes it from the realm of myth or fable.

1:19 We have the prophetic word confirmed may be rephrased as "we have the prophetic word as a surer confirmation." As strong as an eyewitness account (vv. 16–18) may be, there is an even stronger confirmation that Jesus is who He said He was. The written Scriptures are even more trustworthy than the

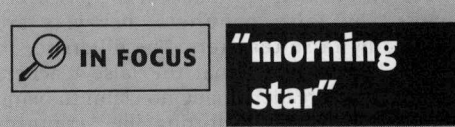

(Gk. *phosphoros*) (1:19) Strong's #5459: The Greek term means "light-bearer" or "light-bringer." Christ is the morning star, as elsewhere He is called the Bright and Morning Star (Rev. 22:16) and the Dayspring, that is, the rising sun (Luke 1:78). Presently, Christ shines in our hearts; when He returns, He will arise in our hearts and bring us into a perfect day. His outward coming will be matched by an inward rising, "an illuminating transformation" of our spirits.

personal experience of the apostle Peter. They cast **a light that shines** like a lamp **in a dark place** and will continue to do so until the **morning star rises** (Rom. 13:12–14). In other words, the truths in the Bible will continue to point to the source of all truth, Christ, until He returns in glory.

1:20 of any private interpretation: Although some have taken this phrase to mean that no individual Christian has the right to interpret prophecy for himself or herself, the context and the Greek word for *interpretation* indicates another meaning for the verse. The Greek word for *interpretation* can also mean "origin." In the context of v. 21, it is clear that Peter is speaking of Scripture's "origin" from God Himself and not the credentials of the one who interprets it. There is no private source for the Bible; the prophets did not supply their own solutions or explanations to the mysteries of life. Rather, God spoke through them; He alone is responsible for what is written in Scripture. This is why Christians should study the Bible diligently. It is God's Word.

1:21 prophecy never came by the will of man: No mere mortal chose to utter his own thoughts as though they were God's. On the contrary, God chose holy men to be His spokesmen, men who uttered thoughts given to them by the Holy Spirit. The metaphor "borne along" or "moved" is that of a ship raising its sails into the wind and going in the direction the wind blows. This may possibly reflect Peter's memory of Jesus' words to Nicodemus recorded in John 3:8.

2:1–22 Peter describes the **false teachers** who are leading Christians astray (vv. 1–3, 11–22) and assures his readers that these teachers will be judged (vv. 4–10).

2:1 Just as God's prophets of the past were opposed by **false prophets,** believers are opposed by **false teachers.** The difference in terminology suggests that the false teachers among Peter's readers made no claim to being prophets, but were distorting the Scriptures with heretical interpretations. Peter's certainty that there will be such false teachers probably rests on Jesus' predictions (Matt. 24:4, 5). False

teachers could be recognized by their secretive approaches, their doctrinal errors (such as a denial of Christ), and by their abrupt departure from the Christian community (1 John 2:19).

2:2 destructive ways: Peter is addressing here the ethical implications of false teaching. The Greek word translated *destructive* means "shameful" or "deliberately immoral." The false teachers gloried in the privileges of Christianity but treated its moral demands with indifference. **blasphemed:** The truth of Christian redemption is held in contempt by many because of the immoral behavior of professing Christians.

2:3 covetousness: The false teachers did not hesitate to take advantage of their followers in order to enrich themselves. **judgment . . . destruction:** Peter turns from the description of the false teachers to a description of their fate. Verses 4–8 provide three vivid examples of judgment on false teachers of the past.

 **IN COMPARISON** **Right Living in a Wretched World**

Writing to beleaguered Christians in an evil world where false teachers were aggressively spreading dangerous heresies, Peter urged, "Grow in the grace and knowledge of our Lord and Savior Jesus Christ" (3:18). The following is a summary of the components of spiritual growth Peter advocated.

Practice	Passage	Principles
Godly Living	1:1–15	• Through Christ we have been given everything we need to live godly lives. • We are partakers of the divine nature • We have been freed from the power of the old corrupt, sinful nature.
Reliance on the Scriptures	1:16–21; 3:1, 2	• Christian doctrine is not just another point of view; it is not a fable. • The Scriptures can be trusted because they were written by prophets and apostles inspired by the Holy Spirit. • The Scriptures function as a light in a dark age; they are an absolute in a relativistic world.
Opposition to False Teaching	2:1–22	• We are not to be swayed by the large numbers of people who are persuaded by unbiblical ideas. • Judgment is guaranteed for all who oppose the truths of God. • We should exercise discernment granted by the Holy Spirit to detect the deceptive teachings and alluring promises of the ungodly.
Watchfulness	3:3–18	• By looking for the return of Christ, we can avoid the sinful traps of the world. • We need to take care that we do not become lax in our thinking—God has set a day which will mark the end of this world as we know it. • God's promise of judgment should prompt us to encourage others to repent and believe in Christ.

2:4–9 Peter uses three illustrations of God's judgment against sin to prove that He will punish these false teachers: **angels who sinned** (v. 4), the **ancient world** of Noah's day (v. 5; Gen. 6:5—8:22), and **Sodom and Gomorrah** (v. 6; Gen. 19:1–26). He then gives two illustrations to show that God will deliver His own when they prove faithful in trials (v. 9): **Noah** (v. 5) and **righteous Lot.**

2:4 the angels who sinned: There are two main interpretations of this passage, depending on one's understanding of Gen. 6:1–6. Some think that Peter is referring to "sons of God" in Gen. 6:2. According to this interpretation, the "sons of God" were angels who rebelled against God and their role in creation. They began to engage in forbidden practices with the daughters of men. Their outrageous conduct was met with immediate judgment: the angels were **cast** into **hell,** or Tartarus, a place of final punishment. Tartarus involves severe limitation of action, symbolized by **chains,** and almost total lack of understanding, symbolized by **darkness.** A second group of commentators balk at the suggestion of sexual relations between angels and women. They consider this verse to be simply a reference to those angels who fell with Satan.

2:5 did not spare the ancient world: Peter's second example of God's judgment (v. 4) is **the flood** that came upon **the ungodly** in Noah's day (3:6; 1 Pet. 3:20). **Noah** is called a **preacher of righteousness** because his righteous life put to shame the immoral lives of his neighbors. Noah's building of the ark would certainly have given him the opportunity to explain the coming judgment and to invite people to repent and believe in God. But his entreaties fell on deaf ears, just as the truth of Christ's atonement fell on the deaf ears of the false teachers of Peter's day. Such indifference and unbelief brought the ungodly of Noah's world to certain destruction.

2:6 Sodom and Gomorrah is Peter's third example of God's judgment (vv. 4, 5). Genesis 19 makes it clear that sexual perversion was the primary cause of the **destruction** of Sodom and Gomorrah. This was intended to be a fearful example of the seriousness of not observing the sexual distinctions which God has determined. From time to time these distinctions have been cast aside, and widespread breakdowns in social structures have inevitably followed.

2:7, 8 Three times in these two verses **Lot** is described as a **righteous** man. The Genesis account seems to portray Lot as a man influenced by the values of the world. Here we are told of Lot's reaction to evil: he was depressed **by the filthy conduct of the wicked** and upset at their **lawless** actions. Lot was considered righteous by God because he refused to join in the immoral revelry of that city. For this reason he was delivered by divine intervention. This example emphasizes the importance of grieving over the conditions of the lost, and refusing to accommodate to their amoral standards.

2:9–11 the Lord knows how: God is in full control of all events. He delivers **the godly out of,** but not away from, their trials. He also sees that the **unjust** do not escape their day of **punishment.** Two particular groups are singled out for judgment: those who live in unclean **lust** and those who hold **authority** in contempt. **presumptuous, self-willed:** These words describe the character and methods of false teachers. Their actions are characterized by boldness; they recklessly defy both God and man. Behind their presumption is a commitment to their own desires. The **dignitaries** that the false teachers slander are probably angels, although the word can refer to people in authority. The reference here is almost certainly to Jude 9, where the archangel Michael, disputing with Satan over the body of Moses, does not revile the devil but simply says, "The Lord rebuke you."

2:12 like natural brute beasts: False teachers are compared to animals in their behavior because they act in ignorance of the realities of death and judgment. Like animals, they also react only to present circumstances, without giving thought to the consequences of their actions. They pour abuse on things which they do not understand, like an angered dog attacks someone whom it thinks is threatening him. Since they act like animals, they will end up like animals; their inner corruption will be the cause of their destruction, as a mad dog is sometimes shot to death to keep him from harming others. The phrase **perish in their own corruption** can actually mean "corrupted by their own corrupt living." That is the irony of sinful living: its very pleasures in the end become distasteful. Sensuality is self-destructive.

2:13 False teachers are perverse in their display of evil, like those who **carouse in the daytime.** Even pagan societies thought it strange and unnatural to hold drunken revels in broad daylight. However, the false teachers had no qualms about practicing their erroneous concept of Christian liberty in clear daylight. As a result, they would **receive the wages of unrighteousness,** that is, spiritual death (Rom. 6:23). The **feast** mentioned here may have been the *agape,* or love feast, built around the celebration of the Lord's Supper. On the other hand, the term may simply refer to social contact with the heretical teachers. The heretics were so self-deceived that they actually thought they were celebrating their freedom in Christ with their drunken revelry at the Lord's Table. In fact, they were **spots and blemishes,** disfiguring and degrading the purity of the Lord's feast.

2:14 The **eyes** of the false teachers were **full of adultery.** They looked lustfully at women. They could not **cease from sin** because their fantasizing had become habitual. As a consequence, they convinced certain **unstable souls** in the church that adultery was acceptable Christian behavior and lured them into sexual immorality. **Enticing** means "to catch with bait." These new, unstable converts, not yet fully grounded in Christ, were easily hooked into an immoral lifestyle. **trained in covetous practices:** The latter half of v. 14 belongs with vv. 15, 16, since Balaam is an example of the covetous ways of the heretics. Peter's charge is serious for he maintains the false teachers have deliberately trained their **hearts** in greedy practices. Covetousness (Gk. *pleonexia*) is used both to refer to greed for money and greed for bodies (i.e., illicit or unnatural sex). Here it is primarily greed for money or comforts. But, as Jesus plainly stated, "You cannot serve God and mammon (money)" (Matt. 6:24). To attempt it is to put oneself under the curse of God—to be doomed to perish with the world in its rejection of God's grace.

2:15, 16 The account of Balaam in Num. 22—24 is used here, as well as in Jude 11 and Rev. 2:14, to depict the danger of forsaking **the right way** and going **astray.** Balaam's primary downfall was that he **loved the wages of unrighteousness.** He sold his prophetic powers to the pagan king Balak and, for a promised monetary reward, sought to curse the children of God. On his way to do this he was rebuked by his donkey, who saw what Balaam could not see—a mighty angel with drawn sword standing in the path. By this story Peter is encouraging those unstable souls who were easily impressed by the teaching of the heretics Though Balaam's subsequent sin of introducing immorality into the camp of Israel is not mentioned here, it is significant that both avarice and lust were the major motivations of the false teachers described here. These two sins are seldom far apart!

2:17 wells . . . clouds: Peter accuses the heretical teachers of awakening false expectations, like springs that contain no water or storm clouds that darken but produce no rain.

2:18 Allure, like *enticing* in v. 14, means "to catch with bait." The bait is **great swelling words of emptiness,** high-sounding promises that prove to have no real content. The hook is

the **lusts of the flesh,** normal sexual desires that are practiced in wrong ways. The heretical teachers clearly were implying that once the soul is saved, what is done in the body is of no importance. **those who live in error:** The guarding of the flock from "wolves in sheep's clothing," as Jesus described false teachers, was one of the primary concerns of the apostles and is one of the chief tasks of pastors.

2:19 The irony of false teaching is that it promises great freedom while its advocates are already **slaves** to sin. The gospel offers release from the **corruption** of the world, but the false teachers were involved in moral ruin by their immoral practices (vv. 14–18) and greedy motivations (v. 3). These false teachers were probably twisting the Christian concept of freedom from the law into a license for sinning (Paul's condemnation of this type of thinking in Rom. 6).

2:20–22 The persons referred to in these verses have caused considerable difference of opinion among commentators. Generally, four views have been posited. First, some believe that the word *they* refers to the false teachers mentioned in the preceding verses rather than those persons deceived by them. A second view says that the apparent connection between the end of v. 18 ("the ones who have actually escaped from those who live in error") and the beginning of v. 20 ("if, after they have escaped the pollutions of the world") probably means that the "they" refers to unsaved people who were merely "listeners" of the gospel (v. 18). Third, some think that both the false teachers and their converts are in view and that they can lose their salvation. The fourth perspective proposes that the "they" refers to new converts who are warned against being entangled with a life of sensuousness only to find a less fulfilling life than before they were saved.

2:20 they have escaped: The subject of this phrase is the heretical teachers who are called "slaves of corruption" in v. 19. This verse seems to indicate that the teachers had formerly turned from the pollution of the world through a full and experiential knowledge of Christ. Now, however, they have fallen again into immorality, even becoming teachers of sinful lifestyles. As a result, **the latter end is worse for them than the beginning.** This phrase is almost certainly taken from Jesus' words in Matt. 12:45 and probably reflects Peter's memory of that occasion.

2:21 better . . . not to have known: Knowledge without obedience is dangerous. Jesus said of Judas that it would have been better for him not to have been born than to have turned from the truth he had known (Matt. 26:24). The phrases **way of righteous-**

ness and **holy commandment** emphasize the ethical content of the knowledge the false teachers had (v. 20). They knew what was right and holy, but they deliberately chose to do what was wrong and corrupt.

2:22 according to the true proverb: Jews considered dogs and pigs among the lowest of animals, so Peter chooses these animals to describe people who have known the truth but have turned away from it. The first proverb is found in Prov. 26:11; the second is from the Syrian story of Ahikar, known to Peter and his readers. Jesus used dogs and pigs as pictures of mankind far away from God (Matt. 7:6). A review of the whole chapter shows that yielding to the money-mad, sex-obsessed, materialistic and anti-authoritarian drives of modern society are indications that an individual's heart is not in touch with Christ's lordship, but has succumbed to the delusions of the devil. Pride in knowledge is the point of attack.

3:1–18 Peter reminds us about Christ's second coming (vv. 3–9) and how we should live in the light of that event (vv. 10–18).

3:1 Peter returns to his exhortation of the believers, addressing them as **beloved** (vv. 8, 14, 17). **this second epistle:** It is natural to assume that the first epistle Peter implies here is 1 Peter. However, 1 Peter is not really a letter of reminder, as Peter suggests here (1:12–15). In addition, 1 Peter was sent to a wide range of readers living in five different provinces (1 Pet. 1:1), while this letter seems to be addressed to a single church (or nearby churches) whose people and circumstances Peter knows well. For these reasons, many believe that the first letter referred to here was one written to the same readers as 2 Peter, but now lost to us (see Paul's reference to an earlier letter in 1 Cor. 5:9). In both letters to this congregation, Peter sought to awaken his readers' **pure minds** to the dangers of phony leaders who claimed to be Christians.

3:2 words which were spoken before: The only way Peter's readers could recognize the errors of the heretical teachers was to compare their teaching with the teaching of the **holy prophets** and **apostles.** As Peter had already reminded his readers in 1:21, "holy men" spoke words given to them by the Holy Spirit, which were therefore utterly reliable. These completely reliable words are in the Bible, God's Word. The **commandment** of the apostles probably refers to the new commandment Jesus gave, that believers should love one another (John 13:34, 35). As the apostles developed that in their writings, it is clear that such love was to be pure and clean, free from sexual wrongdoing (1 Tim. 1:5).

3:3 A primary motivation for righteous living was the expectation of Christ's return (1 John 3:2, 3). However, the unforeseen delay in that coming would soon produce **scoffers** who would mock the coming, because they desired to live in ways that fulfilled their self-indulgent desires. The suggestion is that the scoffers here and the heretical teachers of ch. 2 are one and the same. The apostles had predicted that such scoffing would occur (2 Tim. 3:1–5; James 5:3; Jude 18). **The last days** refers to the present age (Heb. 1:2). Throughout the centuries, scoffers have denied the Second Coming whenever hedonism and humanism have prevailed in the church.

3:4 all things continue: The basis for denying the supernatural reappearance of Jesus is that nothing of that nature has occurred in the past. Several Christian and even secular documents of the first two centuries report the dismay that spread among Christians when the

---

IN LIFE | **Looking Toward Eternity**

As Peter neared the end of his life, he wrote a letter in which he offers some insight into the nature of time and eternity. He beckons us to view time in both thousand-year units and as mere days (2 Pet. 3:8), recalling the beginnings of creation (3:4–6). He also projects into the future, when judgment will be rendered and new heavens and earth will be home to those who fear God (3:10–13). Peter reminds us that God values a day as much as a thousand years, affirming the importance of the here and now (3:8). But he also affirms God's activity long before we came on the scene (3:9).

Peter's perspective challenges us to live with a view toward eternity and values that last—purity, holiness, and righteousness (3:11, 14). We need to avoid getting caught up in the here and now and losing sight of our eternal destiny. Neither the joys of today nor the problems of this week can quite compare with what God has prepared for us in eternity. Peter urges us to stick with the basics of the faith and resist the fleeting enticements offered in this present moment (3:17, 18).

promise of Jesus about coming soon seemed unfulfilled. The **fathers** who **fell asleep** refers to the OT patriarchs.

3:5, 6 they willfully forget: The scoffing teachers would choose to overlook events such as creation and the Flood. The people of Noah's time did not believe in Noah's warning because they had never experienced a flood. They forgot, as the false teachers later would, that God created the entire universe by His **word,** something that they also had not experienced. Just as creation was by His **word,** the world is being sustained by His word. Likewise, the world's judgment and destruction would be by His word. God is in control, no matter what happens to this world.

3:7 by the same word: Peter expands his prophetic look from the world that then existed (v. 6) to **the heavens and the earth** that now exist. Water was the chief element in the world before the Flood; fire is the destructive force in the present universe. But as the water of the pre-flood world was under the control of God, so the fire of the present age is kept **preserved** (in restraint) by that same word. The fire is just as literal as the water was in v. 5. Since the explosion of the hydrogen bomb, people have little reason to doubt this prediction. We cannot take for granted that our environment will continue to support human life forever. Everywhere Scripture predicts a coming day of judgment when the ungodly will be made to submit forever to the horror they have chosen in existence without God.

3:8–10 Again Peter reminds his readers that there is something that they must keep in mind when thinking of the parousia of Christ. First, vv. 1–7 have assured his readers that the scoffing is unfounded, based on the desire of the scoffers not wanting to know the truth (v. 5) and one day their faith in the truths of God will be vindicated when God, under His own timetable, destroys this world with the ungodly. There is considerable difference between the question "where is the promise of His coming?" and "when is the Lord coming?" The former is of the unbeliever and the latter is of a perplexed believer. Peter provides a fourfold answer to his questioner regarding the delay of the Second Coming.

3:8 a thousand years: God will surely accomplish His purposes and promises, even though it may appear that He is slow in doing so. His timing is always perfect.

3:9 The delay of God's judgment is not due to **slackness,** but to the Lord's **longsuffering** attitude toward His people. **not willing that any should perish:** This text does not teach that God actually decrees that all will be saved

(universalism). The reference here is not to God's decree, but to His desire. Obviously everything that a sovereign God decrees will occur. Here Peter is describing the sovereign God's desire that all people would turn to Him and turn away from unprofitable lives (1 Tim. 2:4).

3:10 Day of the Lord here describes the end-time events, the Second Coming (descriptions of the end times are found in Dan. 9:24–27; 1 Thess. 5:2; 2 Thess. 2:1–12). At the end of this age in the day of the Lord's judgment, the **heavens will pass away with a great noise** and the **elements will melt,** presumably by fire (v. 12). The description that Peter gives of the judgment of God on the old heavens and old earth especially speak to our current age when we have seen the awesome destructive power of the atom. Some have thought that Peter is prophesying of the destruction of the earth by atomic warfare. Something much more destructive than what humans can do is in view here.

3:11 what manner of persons: The primary purpose of prophetic teaching is not to satisfy our curiosity but to motivate us to change our lives. Rather than working for things that will ultimately be destroyed, we should work for things that are eternal.

3:12–14 Verse 12 continues to mark the contrast in the way the Day is viewed by the ungodly and the godly; they tremble because it

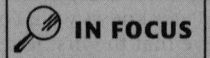 **IN FOCUS** "knowledge"

(Gk. *gnosis*) (1:5; 3:18; Eph. 3:19; Phil. 3:8; Col. 2:3) Strong's *#1108*: This Greek word for *knowledge* usually connotes progressive, experiential, and personal knowledge; it is knowledge that can grow. We need to grow in our actual, personal knowledge of Jesus Christ; such knowledge is the greatest protection against false teachings. One of the prominent themes in this epistle is Peter's exhortation to the believers to attain a fuller, more thorough knowledge of Jesus Christ (1:8; 2:20; 3:18).

means punishment and destruction, while the Christian is **looking for and hastening the coming of the day. Looking for** (Gk. *prosdokao*) is used in this context with the sense of "anticipation" with the word **hastening** (Gk. *pseudo*) which means "hurry," or "get busy," and is translated "be diligent" in v. 14. The hope or expectation of the Christian, **new heavens and a new earth in which righteousness dwells,** is the basis for the exhortation to blamelessness and purity of conduct. There will be no false teachers in heaven.

3:15, 16 Note that Peter equates the letters of **Paul** with **the rest of the Scriptures,** indicating that Peter considered the apostle Paul's writings to be the Word of God. Note that Peter considers Paul's writings on the end times to be **hard to understand.** This should be a comfort to each of us who attempts to interpret the writings of Paul on the coming of Christ. Even Peter found them difficult. Because of this, however, Peter says some **people** who are **untaught and unstable** destroy themselves. *Untaught* refers to one whose mind is untrained and undisciplined in habits of thought. *Unstable* refers to one whose conduct is not properly established on the truths of God's Word.

3:17, 18 Peter admonishes his readers that since they know truth, they should depart from **the error of the wicked** and **grow in the grace and knowledge** of the **Lord.**

The First Epistle of

John

———————————————— ■ ————————————————

*P*ART OF THE ARROGANCE OF HUMAN NATURE is to think that we know more than others do. In this letter, the apostle John addresses the problem of false teachers who were making lofty claims about their knowledge regarding the deity and nature of Christ. John counters their false claims by reminding his readers of the eyewitness accounts of the apostles, including himself. Jesus Christ came in human flesh,

lived a human life, died, and then was raised from the dead. He was fully human and fully God. Anything else being taught by others was false. In this letter, John sounded the alarm: False teaching could not be tolerated. Falsehoods would lead to immorality, and immorality would lead to eternal death. In contrast, the truth would demonstrate itself in love, and love would lead to eternal life. For John, what one believed truly mattered.

John most likely wrote this letter with two purposes in mind—one pastoral and one polemical. John's pastoral purpose was to promote fellowship (1:3). But for the believers to have true fellowship, they needed to understand the true nature of God (1:5; 2:29; 4:7, 8). Thus, the pastoral purpose naturally leads to the polemical purpose (2:26), which was to protect his readers against the deceptive ideas of false teachers. If the believers were deceived by false doctrine, they would eventually lose their unity, which is possible only in the love of Christ. Evidently some deceivers had arisen among the believers (2:18, 19, 26). If Christians could sort out truth from falsehood, they would be able to maintain their unity in the faith and have an opportunity

to show love to their fellow believers (3:11). For John, a person's behavior was naturally a result of that person's belief.

In accordance with John's purpose, fellowship dominates the first portion of this letter (1:5—2:27), while assurance of salvation dominates the remainder. Key concepts in the letter include eternal life, knowing God, and abiding in the faith. In addition, John develops theological ideas in this letter through explicit contrasts, such as walking in light or in darkness, children of God or of the devil, life or death, love or hate. With these contrasts John was attempting to draw a clear line between true and false teachers. John was writing to believers who were dealing with a particular type of false teaching, the contagious heresy of early Gnosticism. He wrote this letter to encourage them to abide in what they had heard from the beginning so that they could maintain their fellowship with God and their love for fellow believers. In short, he exhorted them to make their belief in Christ evident to all, so that correct doctrine could be identified by their righteous life and their wholehearted love for others.

Gnosticism was a problem that threatened

the church in Asia Minor during the second century A.D. Gnosticism was a teaching that blended Eastern mysticism with Greek dualism (which claimed that the spirit is completely good, but matter is completely evil). This teaching was present in the church in a seminal form during the latter years of the first century. By the middle of the second century it had become a fully developed theological system, which included Gnostic gospels and epistles. John recognized the danger of Gnosticism and wrote to counteract its influence before it could sweep through the churches of Asia Minor. Based on the concept that matter is evil and spirit is good, some Gnostics concluded that if God was truly good He could not have created the material universe. Therefore, some lesser god had to have created it. According to them, the God of the OT was this lesser god. The dualistic views of Gnosticism were also reflected in the prevalent belief that Jesus did not have a physical body. This teaching, called Docetism, claimed that Jesus only appeared to have a human body and never actually suffered pain and death on the Cross.

Another heresy that John addressed in this letter and personally confronted at Ephesus was Cerinthianism. This heresy taught that Jesus was just a man upon whom the "Christ" descended at His baptism, that the Christ then departed from Jesus just before His crucifixion, and that thus the spiritual Christ did not really suffer and die for humanity's sins on the Cross, but only appeared to do so.

There are several indications that John was addressing these heresies in this epistle. Note the use of expressions like "which we have looked upon, and our hands have handled" (1:1); "every spirit that confesses that Jesus Christ has come in the flesh is of God" (4:2); and "He who came by water and blood" (5:6). All of these phrases use explicit and vivid language to describe the Incarnation, the truth that Jesus is both completely God and completely human.

The author of this letter is understood to be John, the beloved apostle. Though he does not identify himself in this letter, the similarity of vocabulary and writing style between this book and the Gospel of John argues convincingly that both were written by the same person. The writings of the early church fathers, from Ignatius to Polycarp, also identify John as the author of this letter. Furthermore, in the epistle's first few verses (1:1–4), the author places himself among the eyewitnesses of the earthly life of Christ, as one who literally saw and touched "the Word of life." Obviously such a description fits an apostle but not a second-generation church leader. Finally, the author virtually calls himself an apostle (the "we" of 1:1–3; 4:14 seems to refer to the apostles).

Although some have argued that the epistle was written before the destruction of Jerusalem in A.D. 70, a later first-century date allows for the appearance of the ideas that later developed into Gnosticism, ideas that John was probably addressing in this letter. On the other hand, the letter could not have been written later than the end of the first century, when John died. Also, the evidence of early second-century writers who knew of the epistle and quoted from it demonstrates that it was written prior to then. Thus, 1 John probably was written just a few years before the Book of Revelation.

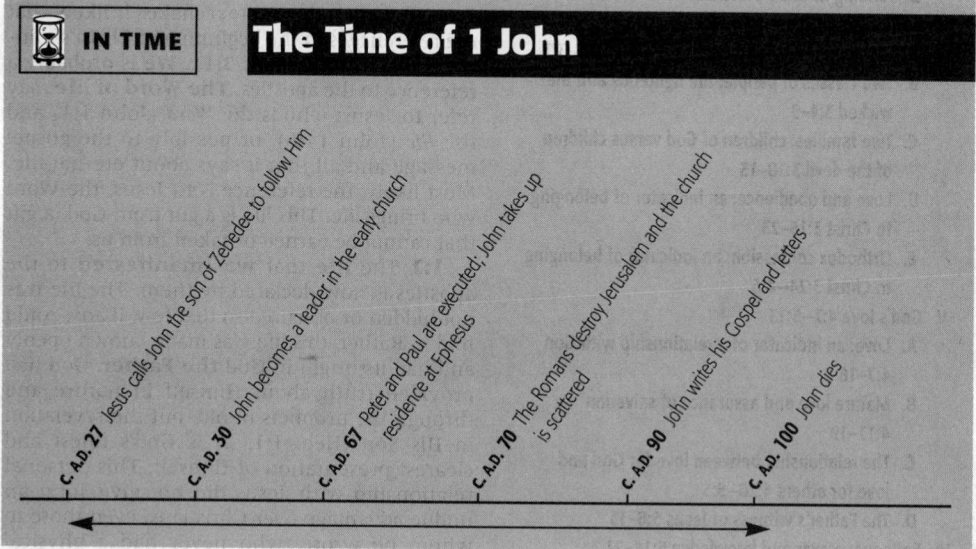

IN TIME

The Time of 1 John

C. A.D. 27 Jesus calls John the son of Zebedee to follow Him

C. A.D. 30 John becomes a leader in the early church

C. A.D. 67 Peter and Paul are executed; John takes up residence at Ephesus

C. A.D. 70 The Romans destroy Jerusalem and the church is scattered

C. A.D. 90 John writes his Gospel and letters

C. A.D. 100 John dies

In determining the date of the writing, several factors should be considered. First, the tone of the book and especially the attitude of the author toward the readers suggest an older person addressing a younger generation. Second, Irenaeus indicates that John lived in Ephesus and wrote to the churches of Asia. John's letters to the churches of Asia in Revelation (Rev. 2; 3) substantiate Irenaeus's comment. It is natural to conclude that 1 John is directed to these same believers. Third, Paul visited Ephesus several times between A.D. 53 and 56, using the city as the center of his evangelism efforts. Timothy was in Ephesus with Paul around A.D. 63 and was still there when Paul wrote him around A.D. 67. There is no indication that Timothy and John were at Ephesus at the same time, so John must have visited Ephesus after Timothy's departure. This would put the date of the writing of 1 John after A.D. 67 but before A.D. 98. A date around A.D. 90 seems reasonable.

Outline

Commentary

1:1–4 These verses show similarities to the prologue of the Gospel of John (John 1:1–18). However, while the Gospel of John emphasizes the metaphysical nature of Jesus, **the Word,** these verses emphasize the personal experience of the apostles with the incarnate Word. The memory of Jesus Christ burned in the mind of John as he reflected on the three and one-half years that he and the other disciples were with the Lord. Now he wanted to be sure that the churches under his care enjoyed **fellowship** with the resurrected Lord and with other disciples. Verses 1–4 also introduce the message of the book. The Prologue contains a purpose statement in v. 3 which some see as controlling the message of the epistle, making fellowship the central issue which John addresses. In contrast, most scholars see 5:13 as the epistle's purpose statement, emphasizing the need of belief in Christ for eternal life. Actually, both purposes are worked out in the epistle.

1:1 **That which** could refer to (1) the revelation about Christ, (2) the teachings of Christ, (3) the eternal life manifested by Christ, or (4) Christ Himself. The words **heard, seen, looked upon,** and **handled** indicate that Christ Himself is the likely subject. **The beginning** may refer to creation or to the beginning of Christ's ministry. If it is creation, it is like the statement about Christ and creation in the Gospel (John 1:1). However, the context makes it likely that the reference is to the beginning of Christ's ministry, similar to 2:7, 24; 3:11. **We** is probably a reference to the apostles. **The Word of life** may refer to Jesus, who is the *Word* (John 1:1) and the *life* (John 14:6), or possibly to the gospel message and all that it says about eternal life. Most likely, the reference is to Jesus, the Word who brings life. This life is a gift from God, a gift that cannot be earned or taken from us.

1:2 The **life** that **was manifested** to the apostles is now declared by them. The life was not hidden or obscured so that few, if any, could find it. Rather, this life was made known openly and had its origin in God **the Father.** God had provided truth about Himself in nature and through the prophets of old, but the revelation in His Son (Heb. 1:1, 2) is God's finest and clearest presentation of Himself. This personal relationship with Jesus did not give John an undue advantage over Christians, even those to whom he wrote, who never had a physical encounter with Christ. John's experience with Jesus was one of revelation and faith (Matt. 16:17; 1 Pet. 1:7–12). We must not think that to have known Jesus personally would bring greater faith in Him. Many of those who actually saw and heard Jesus rejected Him. Acceptance of Christ is an act of faith, a reception of revelation from God in Scripture. Even when the personal experience with Christ was years away, the apostles and those who knew Jesus held to Him by faith, not by sight (John 20:29). God insured that the revelation of Christ had guaranteed testimony through the written gospels.

1:3 The primary reason John writes is to provide his readers with an understanding of what they must do to **have fellowship** with the apostles and God. *Fellowship* carries both the idea of a positive relationship that people share and participation in a common interest or goal. The fellowship John promotes is not only vertical, between believer and God. He writes that they may have fellowship "with us." Since John considered his readers to be Christians (2:12–14), we should not interpret *fellowship* as equal to being a Christian.

1:4 A Christian can have no real **joy** except in a proper relationship with God and others (Pss. 16:11; 51:12; John 15:11). If the false teachers against whom John writes should have undue impact on his readers, they may fail to maintain their close bond and Christian joy. Thus, he writes to give them the truth they need

to sustain their relationship with the people of God and with the apostles.

1:5 God is light by nature, in His essential being, just as He is Spirit (John 4:24) and love (4:8). *Light* refers to God's moral character. **no darkness at all:** God is holy, untouched by any evil or sin. Because God is light, those who desire fellowship with Him must also be pure. **At all** stresses the absoluteness of John's emphasis. This is crucial to the thrust of this book.

1:6 Verses 6–10 contain three contrasts between words and works, or saying one thing and doing another. Following each contrast is the result of the action. **If we say:** The first false claim is to have **fellowship with** God while failing to reflect His moral character. **Walk** refers to a way of life or daily practice. To walk **in darkness** means to live contrary to the moral character of God, to live a sinful life. To claim fellowship with God without living a moral life or practicing **the truth** is to live a lie, since God cannot compromise His holiness to accommodate sin.

1:7 To **walk in the light** is to live in such a way that one is enlightened by the truth of who God is. John did not say "according" to the light, which would demand sinless perfection. **with one another:** When a Christian's conduct reflects God's moral character, then real fellowship is possible with other Christians. But it may be that *one another* refers to fellowship with God

---

🌱 IN LIFE Freedom from Guilt

No one likes to feel guilty. Like an unwelcome guest, guilt shows up at the worst possible time and does not go away no matter how much you wish it would.

Yet the truth is that we need guilt. It is the only proper response to any offense, whether a selfish thought or a premeditated murder. Even a nonbeliever wants a burglar to feel remorse for his theft. Why? Because he *should*. Guilt exposes the truth that we wish to avoid: we have all sinned. John puts it this way: "If we say that we have no sin, we deceive ourselves, and the truth is not in us" (1:8).

But John does not leave us with this dismal picture of ourselves. Instead, he goes on to paint a glorious portrait of a forgiving God. This is our only hope: "If we confess our sins, He is faithful and just to forgive us our sins and to cleanse us from all unrighteousness" (1:9). Guilt does more than just deliver the distressing news. It unlocks the door to forgiveness. Progress, change, reform, and most important of all, God's forgiveness all start with confession.

Confession works against the worst part of human nature, the part that imagines itself to be better than it really is. What person has not felt, "I'm not perfect, but I'm not as bad as my next-door neighbor"? This mindset always stops short of confessing; it would rather ignore or ease feelings of guilt than admit them. But only open confession of our sins will completely cleanse us. Only when we admit that we are sinners, unworthy of God's grace, can we make a fresh start.

C. S. Lewis said that "no man knows how bad he is till he has tried very hard to be good." Similarly, we can never know how much we need freedom until we try to unload our burden of sin. Yet God's forgiveness will liberate us to begin anew on the path of righteousness.

rather than fellowship with other believers. Our fellowship with God is dependent on walking in God's light, where sin is revealed. Such revelation enables us to stay clean before Him. Only **the blood of Jesus Christ** can cleanse us **from all sin,** making it possible for imperfect believers to have fellowship with a holy God.

1:8 The second false claim (v. 6) is **that we have no sin.** The idea would be that our sin nature is completely gone. To say this is to **deceive ourselves** (2 Chr. 6:36; John 9:41). The fact that we are not conscious of sin does not mean we are without it. It is so easy to cover over sin (Prov. 28:13). We will not deceive others; they usually see us clearly. Our problem is not seeing ourselves for who we really are. Every Christian can identify with David because he is a prime example of the believer who committed great sin but failed to see his sinfulness. He tried to carry on as the Lord's anointed one without the Lord's blessing. When Nathan the prophet confronted him, he was indignant at the man who took and killed the other man's sheep, yet could not see himself in Nathan's story (2 Sam. 11; 12). **The truth** is God's revelation, which says just the opposite. To have no sin is to have no need of a Savior, which would make the coming of Jesus unnecessary.

1:9 Though John uses **we** primarily to refer to himself and the other apostles as eyewitnesses of Christ (v. 1), here the term includes all believers who **confess** (acknowledge) sin. God says that we are sinners in need of forgiveness. To *confess* is to agree with Him, to admit that we are sinners in need of His mercy. If a believer confesses his or her specific sins to God, He will cleanse **all unrighteousness** from that person. The believer need not agonize over sin of which he is not aware. Forgiveness and cleansing are guaranteed because God is **faithful** to His promises. Those promises are legitimate because God is **just.** God can maintain His perfect character and yet forgive us because of the perfect and righteous sacrifice of Jesus, His own Son (2:2). Our salvation costs us nothing; it is a gift of God. But salvation is costly; it cost God the death of His Son. Since John is speaking to believers, the forgiveness here is not for their initial justification-salvation. His concern is sanctification-salvation. Christ accomplished the first portion of our salvation on the Cross while on earth (John 17:4). The second part of our salvation is before the throne of God, where Christ makes intercession for us (Heb. 4:15, 16; 7:23–28). **the sins:** The Greek text does not really say "our" sins, as is indicated by the italics in the English text. Literally the text reads, "If we confess our sins, He is faithful and just to forgive us *the* sins." It is probably that the sins of which John speaks are those we confess, not just any and every sin we commit. John proceeds on to say that Christ also, along with this forgiveness, cleanses us from all unrighteousness in our hearts. We should be careful to distinguish this family forgiveness of the Father for His children from the forgiveness we received at our redemption. This passage is written to those who are already saved from eternal judgment due to their sins but now are children of God in need of forgiveness for failures in their children walk.

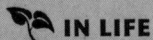 **IN LIFE**   **Communicating Christ to Others**

What exactly does it mean to "witness"? Many people associate the term with street evangelism. But street preachers can sometimes alienate people, although the boldness of their faith is acknowledged by all. What else, then, is needed for someone to be an effective representative for Christ?

John was one of Jesus' closest associates. In this first chapter of his first letter, John notes several basic elements of what it means to communicate Christ to others:

- Our message grows out of our knowledge and experience of Christ (1 John 1:1–4).
- We make clear to others what we have heard from Christ (1:5).
- We live out our faith on a continuous basis, thereby avoiding lives that contradict our message (1:6–7). "Walk" is a metaphor for living used often in the NT (John 8:12; Rom. 4:12; Col. 3:7).
- When we fall short (as we all will, 1 John 1:10), we own up to it, avoiding deception about our walk or Christ's work (1:8–10).

Truthfulness, clarity, consistency, and honesty should be basic qualities of Christ's followers. They are things that last in the eyes of God, and they matter most to those evaluating the faith. We should offer nothing less.

1:10 we have not sinned: We may admit to having a sin nature while still denying any personal sin and therefore any need for confession. The Greek verb translated *we have not sinned* indicates a denial in the past that continues to the present. Unlike v. 8, which speaks of the guilt of sin or a sinful nature, this verse is about the denial of any particular sins. To make this denial is to call God **a liar** because God's **word** emphasizes the penetrating nature of sin (Rom. 7:14–24). Denying that sin is in us indicates that God's **word is not in us.** In other words, a person who denies committing sinful acts does not have the Word of God changing his or her life.

2:1 With fatherly concern, the aged apostle John addresses his readers affectionately as **children.** He is the aged apostle with fatherly concern. He uses this Greek word seven times in this letter (vv. 1, 12, 28; 3:7, 18; 4:4; 5:21) and once in his Gospel (John 13:33). He also uses two similar words, *tekna* in John 1:12; 11:52; 1 John 3:2, 10 (twice); 5:2; 2 John 1, 4, 13 and *paidia* in 1 John 2:13, 18. **that you may not sin:** John's statements about sin (1:8, 10) were designed to make believers aware of sin's ever-present danger and to put them on guard against it. Lifeboats are on a ship not to make it sink but in case it does. According to Greek grammar, the **if** before **anyone sins** carries the added sense of "and it is assumed that we all do." This statement is not an encouragement to sin but a warning to all Christians to be on guard against sinful tendencies. **Advocate:** This Greek word is also used of the Holy Spirit in John 14:16, referring to a Helper for us in understanding the truth of God's Word. Here the word describes the intercessory work of the Son. When we sin, Jesus represents us as our *Advocate* **with the Father** to plead our cause in heaven's court. Satan, on the other hand, is the accuser of believers (Zech. 3; Rev. 12:10).

2:2 Propitiation brings about the merciful removal of guilt through divine forgiveness. In the Greek OT (the Septuagint), the Greek term for *propitiation* was used for the sacrificial mercy seat on which the high priest placed the blood of the Israelites' sacrifices (Ex. 25:17–22; 1 Chr. 28:2). On seeing these sacrifices the righteous anger of God was turned aside from Israel. Sometimes the term is understood by people to refer to the appeasement of a wrathful god who can be "bribed" with gifts by his devotees. This is foreign to the biblical perspective. But the word does indicate that God's anger against sin must be satisfied. In coming into the world as a man, God became the receiver of His own wrath and the means to providing escape from that wrath (the just and justifier, Rom. 3:26). Jesus Christ became this sacrifice in His death and satisfied

God's wrath on the Cross. The sacrifice of Jesus' sinless life is so effective that it can supply forgiveness **for the whole world** (2 Cor. 5:14, 15, 19; Heb. 2:9). Christ's death is *sufficient* for all, but efficient only for those who believe in Christ. Not everyone will be saved, but Jesus offers salvation to all (Rev. 22:17).

2:3–11 In this section, three false claims are exposed, each introduced by the phrase "he who says."

2:3 we know Him: The NT speaks of knowing God in two senses. A person who has trusted Christ knows Him (John 17:3), that is to

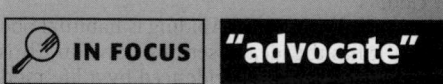

IN FOCUS   "advocate"

(Gk. *parakletos*) (2:1; John 14:16, 26; 15:26; 16:7) Strong's #3875: The Greek word literally means "one who is called to our side." This could be a comforter, a consoler, or a defense attorney. In John 14:26 and 15:26, the Holy Spirit is called our *parakletos*, our Comforter. Here Christ is called our *parakletos*, our Advocate. While the Holy Spirit works within us to comfort and help us, Christ represents us before the Father in heaven. The two paracletes work together in perfect harmony (Rom. 8:26, 27, 34).

say, has met Him. Someone who has previously met the Lord can also come to know Him intimately (Phil. 3:10). In this verse John is talking about knowing the Lord intimately. In all of 1 John, the apostle uses "know" in this second sense. For example, he says everyone who loves is born of God and knows God (4:7), yet he says not to love does not mean that a person is not born of God, only that he or she does not know God (4:8). Therefore, in 1 John, knowing God is knowing Him intimately. Assurance that a believer has really gotten to know the Lord intimately is his or her attitude of wanting to obey God's commands (John 14:15, 20, 23, 24; 15:10–17).

2:4 does not keep His commandments: Disobedience shows a lack of personal knowledge of Christ. To claim to know Christ while disobeying His Word is to lie. **truth is not in him:** Not only does the conflict of word and action make a person **a liar,** but it also shows that the truth is not a controlling influence in that person's life (1:6, 8, 10).

2:5 but: In contrast to being a liar, keeping His commandments demonstrates a valid relationship with Christ and shows that God's love is expressed fully in the Christian. **perfected:** This verb expresses the idea of maturity and completeness. **The love of God is** *perfected* may mean one of two things: (1) The believer's love for God grows as he or she keeps God's Word, or (2) as the believer pursues fellowship and obedience, God's love for him or her is more fully completed. The second is indicated here. The believer begins to **know** by experience **that he** or she is **in Him.** As John explains in the next verse, *in Him* means "abiding in Him." **Word** is a synonym for *commandment* in vv. 3, 4. *The love of God* here may refer to (1) God's love for men, (2) a godly kind of love, or (3) a person's love for God.

2:6 abides in Him: Abiding is habitual obedience. It has the idea of settling down in Christ or resting in Him. It is evidenced by a life modeled after Christ. A Christian may fail to abide in Christ as evidenced by His repeated commands to abide in John 15:4–10. **ought . . . to walk:** The admonition to live by the teaching of Jesus reveals that this conformity comes from us. Slaves *must* follow the commands of their masters or they will be punished. Employees *need* to do their work to keep their jobs. However, the Christian as a child of God *ought* to obey God because of a sincere desire to do so. It should be a joy to follow in the footsteps of the One who died for us.

2:7 old commandment: In vv. 3–6, John insists that the test of personal intimacy and knowledge of God is obedience to Christ's commandments. But which ones? John emphasizes that he has no new obligation in mind, but rather what the believers have known **from the beginning** (v. 24; 1:1; 3:11; 2 John 5). This may look back to Jesus' command to love one another in John 15, or it may refer to the Mosaic law (Lev. 19:18). They had heard this commandment from the beginning of their Christian lives.

2:8 The **new commandment** that John refers to is love (v.10). It may be that John is simply repeating the statement of Christ in John 13:34, where Christ calls this a "new" commandment He gave to the disciples. Moses said, "Love your neighbor as yourself" (Lev. 18:19). Jesus said, "Love one another as I have loved you (John 13:34). This is the basis on which the world will know that we belong to Christ. It is the Christian's greatest apologetic. It is the divine imperative for missions. It is absolutely basic to the advance of Christ's kingdom. **true in Him and in you:** The command to love reached its truest and fullest expression in the life of Christ. He demonstrated what true love is by coming into our world and giving His life for us. Christians should follow His supreme example. We know that the new command-

ment is in effect **because the darkness is passing away, and the true light is already shining.** This new commandment of love belongs to the new age begun by Christ.

2:9 Brother here refers to a fellow believer. Can a person be a believer in Jesus Christ and hate his brother at the same time? Apparently so, for John sees his readers as fellow Christians. Moreover, there is no possibility that unbelievers do not hate fellow spiritual brothers. Unfortunately, it is not only possible, but often practiced. Biblical history provides examples of believers in the true God who acted like unbelievers in their attitudes and actions. For example, King David was guilty of murder which is the final expression of hate (Matt. 5:21, 22). But we can no longer harbor hatred and say we walk with God. If the Christian has a proper relationship with the Christ of love, he will love his brother.

2:10 Him refers to the loving Christian. He does not cause his brother to commit sin. **Him** can also be translated **it,** meaning that the light provides an environment which helps the Christian avoid committing sin.

2:11 he who hates his brother: Hating one's brother opposes the teaching of Christ to love one another. The idea that one could hate a brother and yet claim fellowship with God shows the utter **darkness** that has **blinded** the Christian to the truth. The believer who hates is in darkness and not light, in sin and not in fellowship with God. **does not know where he is going:** A believer who hates his brother has lost his spiritual perspective and sense of direction (2 Pet. 1:9). The person who loves his brother walks in the light of God and does not have the inward "stumbling block" that causes him to fall into all sorts of sin.

2:12–14 These verses contain two sets of three items, describing John's readers as **little children, fathers,** and **young men.** These three classifications are not physical age groups or spiritual stages. Rather, it seems that each group is a reference to all of John's readers. For example, viewed as little children, they know their sins are forgiven. Viewed as fathers, they not only have a relationship with God, but they also have knowledge of God that comes from obedience to His commandments. Viewed as young men, they are strong. The repetition of the triplet is for emphasis. John articulates that the purpose for writing this epistle was their spiritual progress. The second reference to children (v. 13) should be translated as **have written** rather than in the present tense, leaving the three groups balanced.

2:15–17 Having strongly affirmed their spiritual attainments, John now warns them of the dangers that surround believers, no matter how advanced their Christian walk. Love of the world denies a love for our holy God and identifies us with a system doomed to destruction.

2:15 Do not love the world may be rephrased as "stop loving the world." John's readers were acting in a way that was inconsistent with the relationship with Christ. *World* here is the morally evil system opposed to all that God is and holds dear. In this sense, the *world* is the satanic system opposing Christ's kingdom on this earth (v. 16; 3:1; 4:4; 5:19; John 12:31; 15:18; Eph. 6:11, 12; James 4:4). **love of the Father:** This refers either to the love felt toward God in response to His love or to God's love felt toward us. More likely, the former is the meaning. It is not possible to love the world and love God at the same time (James 4:4).

2:16 the lust of the flesh, the lust of the eyes, and the pride of life: The world is characterized by these three lusts, which have been interpreted as corresponding to the three different ways Eve was tempted in the garden (Gen. 3:6), or the three different temptations Jesus experienced (Luke 4:1–12). However, the correspondences are not close enough to make it certain that John was alluding to either of these. Instead, John was probably making a short list of the different ways believers could be lured away from loving God. *The lust of the flesh* refers to desires for sinful sensual pleasure. *The lust of the eyes* refers to covetousness or materialism. *The pride of life* refers to being proud about one's position in this world.

2:17 passing away: John highlights the brevity of life. To be consumed with this life is to be unprepared for the next. What a tragedy to invest our resources in what will not last.

2:18–23 John now goes behind the world system to the devil, the god of this world, and his spokesmen, the **Antichrist.** The *antichrist* is revealed by his denial of Jesus as the Christ. These verses do not teach that anyone who leaves a given church is not a Christian. Rather, those who leave the apostolic teachings and deny the deity of Jesus are opposed to Christ, even if they claim the name *Christian.*

2:18 last hour: John views the rise of those who deny the truth of Christ from within the Christian community as an indication of the beginning of the end of all things. We should not understand *hour* as signifying a duration of time but a kind of time. God's countdown has begun, but He does not reckon time as we do (2 Pet. 3:8). Any attempt to date the ending of the world or Christ's coming is doomed to failure and often brings ridicule to the proclamation of Christ. **Antichrists** is a combination of two Greek words: *anti*, meaning "instead of" or "against," and *christos*, meaning "anointed one."

Antichrists most likely means those who seek to take the place of Christ. The **many antichrists** are the false teachers John opposed in this letter (v. 22; 4:3; 2 John 7). They are reminiscent of the *false christs* Jesus told the disciples about (Matt. 24:24). They are forerunners of the future **Antichrist,** also known as the *beast* in the Book of Revelation (Rev. 13:1–18), who will exalt himself above God (Dan. 9:27; 11:31; 12:11; Matt. 24:15). As we are waiting for the any-moment return of Jesus Christ, there will be a growing prevalence of the counterfeits (Matt. 24:4, 5, 23–26).

2:19 When the false teachers **went out from** among the believers, they revealed that they did not belong to the Christian community; they were never true believers. **they . . . us:** In the opening verses of this book, John made a distinction between *we* and *you* (1:1, 3). *We,* the apostles, were the eyewitnesses of Christ; *you* were the readers. That same distinction is probably maintained here (v. 20). Thus, when John says these false teachers were **not of us,** he means they did not agree with the teaching of the apostles. These antichrists had departed

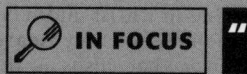

IN FOCUS   **"anointing"**

(Gk. *chrisma*) (2:20; 2 Cor. 1:21) Strong's #5545: The Greek term *chrisma* is related to the title Christ, which means "Anointed One," and is used in the Greek OT (the Septuagint) for the anointing of a high priest (Ex. 29:17). The *anointing* here depicts the impartation of the Holy Spirit to a person (Is. 61:1). As Christians, now indwelt by the Holy Spirit, we are joined to the Anointed One and share in His anointing (2 Cor. 1:21, 22). Therefore, we can know all things with respect to truth and falsehood. Because the Spirit lives within us, we know all that we need to know in order to resist the temptations of false teachers and to live godly lives in this world.

from the apostolic churches, and their attitudes and actions were not of the apostolic persuasion. If they had been in harmony with the apostles, they would have remained in fellowship with them (1:1–3).

2:20, 21 Anointing here refers either to the Holy Spirit or to Scripture. This anointing is the protection that believers have against the false teachers. John says that these believers are in contrast to the ones who went out (v. 19), who were representatives of the Antichrist. The true Anointed One, Jesus, also has representatives who are anointed. Since only God knows everything, the phrase **all things** must be limited in some way. In this context, *all things* is all the truth the believers needed to resist the antichrists (v. 21). One of the main heresies the first-century church faced was Gnosticism, whose followers claimed to have secret knowledge of the truth that led to salvation. Here John was opposing this teaching by asserting that all believers knew the truth. As an apostle, John was merely reminding them of what they already knew, not acting as an exclusive source of the truth.

2:22, 23 Denying the deity of Jesus is the same as denying the **Father and the Son.** In John's epistles, denying **that Jesus is the Christ** includes denying that He came in the flesh (1:1–3; 4:3; 2 John 7). A person cannot worship God while denying Jesus' full deity and full humanity.

2:24 let that abide in you: If John's readers would *abide* in the truths of the gospel, then they would *abide* in the Son and in the Father. Again, this is not a reference to eternal life, which is a gift, but to proper fellowship with the Son and the Father. By allowing Scripture to impact our lives, we abide in Christ and have fellowship with God. The message they **heard from the beginning** was that Jesus is the Christ (v. 22), the Son of God (v. 22) who had come in the flesh (1:1–3). If John's readers would resist the lies of the antichrists and hold on to the truth they had been taught from the beginning, they would continue abiding in fellowship with **the Son** and **the Father.**

2:25 Eternal life speaks of both the quality of life in the present, a life filled with the joy of God, and the promise of a future life in eternity.

2:26 Those who try to deceive you refers to false teachers, or antichrists. *You* indicates that it is possible for believers to be deceived by false teaching.

2:27 We are to base our walk with the Lord on the truth He has given us. Believers who know God's standards and desires for us but fail to put these truths into practice in their lives will also not mature in Christ (Heb. 5:11—6:12).

2:28–4:6 Because God is righteous, the divine sonship of Christians is revealed through righteous living, which includes love of fellow believers and orthodox belief in the deity of Jesus. This section moves from John's emphasis on fellowship to its basis, assurance of salvation.

2:28 John has been urging his readers to let what they have heard from the beginning abide in them (vv. 24–27). Here he advises them to **abide in** Christ Himself. If we abide in Christ we will avoid embarrassment when He returns. **ashamed:** The shame is the result of not having had a lifestyle of obedience when Christ returns.

2:29 Since God **is righteous,** those who practice **righteousness** will be recognized as being **born of** God. This verse does not say that everyone who is born of God practices righteousness. Believers can walk in darkness and sin (1:6, 8; 2:1). The point here is that when a child exhibits the nature of his or her father, he or she is perceived as the child of the father.

3:1 Behold what manner of love: John stands in amazement of God's love. But the greater amazement and appreciation is for the fact that God's love is expressed to human beings, that Christians are included in His family. God loves all believers, the weak as well as the strong. John describes Jesus on the night of His betrayal as "having loved His own who were in the world," and writes that "He loved them to the end" (John 13:1). God's love is in stark contrast to the love of the world. The world loves those who love them, while God loves even those who disobey Him.

3:2 When John admits ignorance of what we shall be when Jesus appears, his statement should cause us to be humble and cautious about detailed pronouncements of future events and the nature of our heavenly existence. God has chosen not to tell us many things either because we would not understand or because it might distract us from our responsibilities as

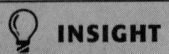

INSIGHT   The Promise of Eternal Life

From beauty creams to vitamins to aerobics, many people today are pursuing a "fountain of youth." They want to avoid growing old, perhaps because it leads to the final, ultimate reality, death. That reality is so painful to most people that they won't even consider it. They make little or no preparation for their death and its aftermath.

John offers the one way that a person can actually do something about his or her death. He speaks of a revolutionary promise that God has made—we can live happily forever (1 John 2:24, 25)! God makes that promise of eternal life for those who put their faith in Jesus Christ.

believers (Acts 1:6–8). **be like Him:** Though we do not know all the specifics of our future existence, we do know that we will have a body like Christ's (Phil. 3:21). Believers will put on immortality and become free from the sin nature that presently plagues us.

3:3 **Everyone who has** the **hope** of seeing Christ and being like Him (v. 2) realizes that Christ is morally pure. This realization helps a person pursue purity even more.

3:4–9 The two classes of people described are those whose lifestyles are characterized by righteousness and those who are characterized by sin. A vital relationship with God is revealed by a righteous lifestyle. The practice of sin denies a relationship with Jesus since He came to take away sin.

3:4 The **sin** described in this verse is not occasional sin but a consistent lifestyle of sin. **Lawlessness** is not the absence of law but active rebellion against the law.

3:5, 6 If Christ is sinless and the purpose of His coming was to remove sin, then **whoever abides in Him does not sin.** Habitually sinful conduct indicates an absence of fellowship with Christ. Thus, if we claim to be a Christian but sin is our way of life, our status as children of God can legitimately be questioned. Some understand sins to refer to even occasional sin rather

than the habitual practice of sin. For them the true Christian either does not sin at all, or attains to a sinless state at some point. The affirmation of 1:9—2:2 shows that Christians do indeed sin on occasion. John is not contradicting himself here since the present tense verb can have the sense of practicing sin rather than just committing a single sin. **neither seen Him nor known Him:** In the act of sin there is no vision of God. Sin is the result of blindness and ignorance toward God (2 Pet. 1:9). Every sin that a believer commits is the result of wrongly thinking about God. In fact, if a believer never thought wrong about God, he or she would never sin. Little wonder that the apostle Paul urges us to bring "every thought into captivity to the obedience of Christ" (2 Cor. 10:5). Any thought that we entertain that cannot pass that test may well be Satan's opportunity to take charge (Acts 5:2, 3).

3:7 **let no one deceive you:** Evidently the antichrists who were denying the doctrine of Christ (2:22) were also claiming to know God, yet were living in unrighteousness (1:6). John insists that to deny the doctrine of Christ is to not have Christ (2:23), and since God is righteous (2:29) and Christ is pure (v. 3) and has no sin (v.5) those who are born of God (2:29) have God's nature, and as they abide in Christ (v. 6)

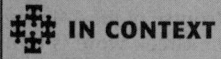 **IN CONTEXT**   **Sinless Perfection?**

Most followers of Christ would agree that they should pursue the highest moral integrity that they can. But John's statements in 1 John 3:6 appear to raise that standard to the point of sinless perfection. In fact, if the person who sins "has neither seen [Christ] nor known Him," then what hope is there for believers who fail?

Here is a case where the English language fails us. In English the word "sins" appears absolute and final: one sin and you're cut off from God. However, the form of the Greek verb here (*hamartanei*) conveys a sense of continuous action: "No one who abides in Christ makes a habit of continually sinning." The point is that true believers diminish their old patterns of sin as they grow in Christ, replacing them with new patterns of faith and love.

The situation is similar to losing weight by changing one's eating habits. No one obtains instant health, but over time and by sticking to a disciplined diet, one can make great strides in that direction.

Of course, the fact that we won't obtain sinless perfection in this life does not mean that we should deal lightly with sin. To do so would be an offense to God, as well as destructive to ourselves. Yes, God forgives individual sins, but if we persist in sinful patterns, we keep the power of Christ from operating in our lives. We also risk grave spiritual consequences, such as losing the ability to repent (Heb. 6:1–12).

Do we keep falling into a particular area of sin? John says that the way out of that frustrating predicament is to learn to continually "abide" in Christ. We need to confess our sins to Him and then concentrate not so much on avoiding sin as on maintaining our relationship with Him. After all, He has come to keep us from sin (1 John 2:1, 2). But if we turn away from Him and yield to sin's mastery, then, as John has written, we can neither see Him working in our lives nor know the joy of His presence.

they do not sin (v.6). True believers practice **righteousness** because the One in whom they dwell is **righteous.** God's righteousness is revealed in His children through their conduct. Righteous conduct does not *produce* righteous character, but reveals its presence in us.

3:8 Satan's sinful nature is shown through the lives of those who belong to him. Jesus' purpose in coming was to **destroy** the devil's **works.** A person **who sins,** even a believer, **is of the devil** in the sense that he is participating in the devil's activity (2:19). Thus, John is indicating that it is possible for believers to do that which is of the devil (Mark 8:31–33, James 3:6).

3:9 The **seed** that **remains** is probably the divine nature in which believers can participate (2 Pet. 1:4). But the *seed* has been variously interpreted as Jesus, the Holy Spirit, Scripture, or the gospel message. In other words, this verse is saying that habitual **sin** is not consistent with the Christian walk.

3:10 Christians **manifest** their nature by practicing **righteousness** (2:7). **Children of the devil** display their basic nature by sinning. Believers who sin are not expressing their nature as **children of God;** instead, they are following the devil's pattern.

3:11 John identifies loving **one another** as absolutely basic to living for Christ and advancing His kingdom.

3:12 Cain is identified as a spiritual child of the devil. His brother Abel is identified as a child of God. Cain's act of murder was the epitome of hatred, and thus came from **the wicked one** (v. 8).

3:13 This looks back to 3:1. **The world** is the evil world system whose people respond to righteous Christians the same as Cain did to Abel (v. 1; John 15:18–20).

3:14 Love for fellow believers is experiential evidence that one has **passed from** the realm of **death** to the sphere of **life.** The tense of the verb *have passed* indicates that something experienced in the past has continuing and abiding results in the present. Christians experience a permanent passage from death to life at the time of salvation. Salvation is evidenced by our love for Christians. It is not a result of our love. The person who hates his brother is abiding in death. Having said this, it is important to realize that the assurance of salvation would be impossible if based solely on a believer's love for others. Thus, John is saying that Christians who have experienced Christ's salvation in the past should demonstrate their salvation by loving their fellow believers in the present. We have already seen in the epistle (1:8, 10; 2:2) that no one lives a sinless life. Such a subjective judgment of loving one's brethren could never allow anyone any certainty about eternal life,

for how would one be sure at all times that one has fulfilled this command? John, then, in this passage is emphasizing that one cannot experience the life given by God in salvation if at the same time one is not loving one's brothers and sisters in the Lord; this does not speak of one's position in Christ.

3:15 eternal life abiding in him: Those who do not love their fellow Christians are not living in the light but instead are living in the darkness (2:11). They are not abiding in life but in death (v. 14). What they are doing is not of God but of the devil (v. 8). Eternal life is not *abiding* in these believers in the sense that it is not the controlling factor in their lives.

3:16–23 Love shown to the brethren and obedience to His commands reveals a healthy relationship with God. Murder and hate take life; **love** gives one's life. Jesus is the supreme example. Cain sacrificed his brother; Christ sacrificed Himself. Christ's example is not just to be admired; it is to be copied (2:6).

3:16 God's love is expressed through self-sacrifice, not simply words. Actions speak much louder than all the promises and pronouncements that we might make. John stated in vv. 14, 15 the need to love other believers like we love ourselves. Here, however, he goes a step further in urging us to love other believers more than we love ourselves, to be willing to give our lives for others, even as Christ gave His Life for us.

3:17 Goods means "course of life," "living," or "livelihood." This same Greek word is translated *life* in 2:16. It refers to the material objects that sustain life. Therefore, the **need** that is mentioned is for food, clothing, and shelter. A believer gives his life (v. 16) by giving that which cost part of his life and will sustain the life of another. John uses a rhetorical question, then, to communicate that self-sacrificial love means sharing material goods as much as it means dying for someone. If one claims love for the brother or sister in Christ, but his actions deny that love, does the love of God abide in that Christian? The answer to the question is no. Love is revealed by its fruit. **love of God:** This does not speak to the Christian being loved by God or our love for God. Probably it refers to God's love working through the actions of the believer. If a believer does not act in love, then God's love has not found a residence in him.

3:18 To **love in word** is to feel love and speak loving words but stop short of doing anything. To love **in tongue** is to profess what one does not have at all. The opposite of loving "in word" is to love **in deed** and the opposite of loving "in tongue" is to love **in truth.** Love from the heart and with actions.

3:19 We can be assured of the presence of

eternal life within us when we demonstrate self-sacrificial love to others. Believers who begin to truly love (v. 18) will know their behavior has its source in the truth and therefore will have confidence before God (v. 21). Thus, love benefits the giver and the receiver both. **Of the truth** means being identified with Him who is the Truth. **Before Him** recalls 2:28, 29 and refers to the Christian's appearance before the judgment seat of Christ.

3:20–22 Our heart condemns us in that we recognize that we do not measure up to the standard of love and feel insecure in approaching God. Our conscience may not acknowledge the loving deeds we have done in the power of the Holy Spirit, but **God** does, and He is superior to our heart. Unlike our conscience, God takes everything into account, including Christ's atoning work for us. God is more compassionate and understanding toward us than we sometimes are toward ourselves.

3:23 In this context, faith in **the name of . . . Christ** is in relationship to prayer (John 14:12–15; 16:24, 1 John 5:5, 13–15). Notice that although **believe** is sufficient for receiving eternal life (John 20:30, 31), believe and **love one another** is essential for experiencing the results of this life (vv. 19, 22).

3:24–4:6 Orthodox confession reveals a living relationship. Fellowship with God is evidenced by those who listen to the apostles rather than false teachers.

3:24 Abides in this verse describes the mutual indwelling of Jesus and the Christian. The believer abides in Christ by keeping **His commandments.** Christ abides in the obedient believer as One who is "at home" with that believer. Jesus spoke of this mutual abiding in

John 15:4, 5, 7. This is evidenced further by the reference to the **Spirit** being given to the Christian (4:1–3). *Proof* of one's salvation is obedience (the *basis* of one's salvation is the grace of God in Christ, and the *medium* of salvation is faith, Eph. 2:8, 9). This is not to say that one is not redeemed if we do not judge their actions to be in conformity to Christ—only that obedience indicates that a new life created by God and lack of obedience causes questions about whether this new life is present. This looks back at the Upper Room promises in John 14—16. This verse connects this paragraph with the previous section by the use of **Spirit,** a reference to the Holy Spirit in contrast to the spirits of the false teachers.

4:1 John speaks of the **spirits** of teachers in a way similar to what Paul says about the spirits of the prophets in 1 Cor. 14:32. John is not referring here to demon possession, but to teachers who promote error. Believers have the Holy Spirit (3:24); but **false prophets** obey evil spirits. A true prophet is one who receives direct revelation from God. A false prophet claims to have received direct revelation from God but in fact promotes erroneous ideas.

4:2 By this you know: One test of whether a person is led by the Holy Spirit is whether that person's beliefs agree with the truth of God's Word (2:22; 1 Cor. 12:3). **Jesus Christ has come in the flesh:** This test seems to be aimed at Docetists. They taught that Christ did not have a physical body. The test may also be aimed at the followers of Cerinthus who claimed that Jesus and "the Christ" were two separate beings, one physical and the other spiritual. In this letter, John is careful to use the name and title of **Jesus Christ** together to

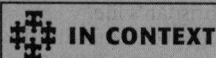 **IN CONTEXT** **Tough-Minded Faith**

hristianity rightly has been characterized as a religion of love, but it's important not to take that emphasis to an unhealthy extreme. If, in the name of love, we uncritically accept every idea or value of others, we open ourselves up to error. God never asks us to put our brains in neutral when it comes to matters of faith.

John repeatedly appeals for love (1 John 2:10; 3:3, 10–24; 4:7–12, 16–21), but he also places a premium on truth—not the wishy-washy opinions that pass for "truth" in our society, but the absolute, eternal truths of God's Word. For example, John challenges us to "test the spirits" (4:1) and learn to discern between truth and error (4:6). He calls for us to avoid sin, which requires that we discern what is sinful (2:1; 3:4–10). He tells us to distinguish between the things of the world and the will of God (2:15–17), and he appeals for us to identify deceivers and avoid them (2:18–29; 3:7).

Paul echoes this appeal to be tough-minded when it comes to our faith. To be spiritual, he writes, means to be able to "judge" (discern or test) all things (1 Cor. 2:15). Likewise, we are to have the mind of Christ: tough in discernment, loving toward all, and fearless in the face of judgment (Phil. 2:5–11, 17, 18).

clearly express the complete union of the two titles in one person.

4:3 Cerinthus, a false teacher of John's day, denied the Incarnation by teaching that the divine Christ descended on the human Jesus at His baptism and then departed before His crucifixion (2:22). John teaches that Jesus did not merely enter into an already existing human being, but He came as a human being. The Greek tense of the verb **has come** and the meaning of the noun **flesh** indicate that not only did Jesus come as a human being; He was still a human being even as John wrote. God the Son is forever fully God and fully man. He is immortal and has received a resurrected human body of flesh that does not age or die. A denial of Jesus' full and true humanity proves that a teacher is **not of God.**

4:4 Of God means more than "belonging to." It indicates that the source of the original reader's attitude and actions was God (2:19). We must identify with either God or the devil. We can **overcome** by recognizing false teachers and refusing to follow them. **He who is in you** is the Holy Spirit. **He who is in the world** is the devil (5:19).

4:5 They is a reference to the false prophets (v. 1) who have the spirit of the Antichrist (v. 3). The false teachers, being a part of the **world** system ruled by Satan, are accepted by the world. **The world** believes their false teachings and receives them into fellowship.

4:6 We refers to the apostles, who find acceptance only among those who know God. **He who knows God** (2:3) listens to what the apostles have to say. This passage, then, gives two tests of the spirit: (1) the confession of Jesus as the Christ, the Son of God come in the flesh (vv. 1–3); (2) the acceptance of the teaching of the apostles.

4:7 Love for **one another,** which here means fellow Christians, proves our spiritual birth and our relationship with God. **Born of God** recalls Jesus' conversation with Nicodemus in John 3:3–6. **Knows God** recalls Jesus' words in John 14:7.

4:8 Know God here refers to an intimate, experiential knowledge (v. 6; 2:3) of God, rather than just information about God. John never says that those who do not love are not born of God (v. 7). Yet it is impossible to know God intimately without loving others, for **God is love:** Anyone in whom God dwells reflects His character. To claim to know God while failing to love others is to make a false claim (1:6).

4:9 The love of God for His children was visibly demonstrated through Jesus' work on the Cross on our behalf. **Only begotten Son** expresses the sense of uniqueness, not a literal birth (Heb. 11:17). John is the only NT author who calls Jesus this (John 1:18; 3:16, 18). In other words, Jesus is the unique Son of God; no other person is God's Son in the way He is.

4:10 propitiation: See 2:2. God initiated the provision for our need.

4:11 An exhortation to remember when we are tempted to be unloving. Our love must not be a mere sentiment. God asks us to give ourselves for the good of others, just as He gives.

4:12–16 Love for one another and an orthodox confession are evidences of a vital relationship with God, He abiding in us and we in Him.

4:13 By this looks forward to the evidence of His Spirit rather than back to the evidence of love (vv. 7–11) for proof **that we abide in Him . . . and He in us** (3:24). Mutual abiding refers to the fellowship we have with God as a result of our salvation. The evidence that God abides in us and we in Him is the experience of the Holy **Spirit** dwelling in us. In the remainder of this passage (vv. 12–16), John explains how a believer can know that the Spirit is working in his or her life (vv. 15, 16).

4:14 We refers to John and the other eyewitnesses of Jesus (1:1; 4:6). Though Jesus came as **Savior of the world,** this does not mean that every person is automatically saved. This is made clear in v. 15.

4:15 A sincere confession of belief is an indication that the confessor is saved. **Abides** in this context refers to salvation rather than the fellowship that results from salvation. To be a Christian, a person must believe **that Jesus is the Son of God.**

4:16 And we have known is parallel to "and we have seen" in v. 14. **Abides in love** means the Christian lives within the sphere of God's love. That love is both experienced and expressed through the Christian's life.

4:17–19 When we express mature love toward one another and understand God's love for us, we will experience assurance of salvation.

4:17 The mature expression of **perfected** love (v. 12) produces confidence as a Christian anticipates Jesus' **judgment** of the **world.** A person who abides in love will not be ashamed when Jesus returns (2:28; John 15:9–17).

4:18, 19 A mature understanding of God's **love** removes any **fear** of God's judgment.

4:20–5:5 An absence of love toward Christians denies love toward God. Fellowship with God is revealed by our confession that Jesus is the Christ and by our obedience and love of the brethren.

4:20–21 If expresses a Greek idea indicating that there are some who say and think what follows. John uses **someone** rather than we, and so dissociates himself from this group. The backdrop behind this question is probably the fact that the antichrists were claiming to **love God** while obviously being unloving.

5:1 The condition for being **born of God,** for being a child of God, is believing or trusting in Jesus Christ. Only correct, sincere belief produces spiritual birth. This birth is reflected in love for others who also have been born into the family of God (2:3–11).

5:2 By this points to the remainder of the verse which develops the theme of love further. The false teachers are probably in view. It is likely that they were guilty of excluding other Christians from their fellowship. Loving God's children is linked directly to obedience.

5:3 The love of God demands obedience (John 14:15). However, rather than being **burdensome,** God's commands free believers to be the people they were originally created to be: holy beings who clearly reflect the image of God.

5:4 Whatever speaks of the new nature of the child of God. Regeneration (that is, our spiritual rebirth) provides **victory** over the **world** that is opposed to God. The **faith** that overcomes the world is faith in Jesus Christ as the Son of God (v. 5), who died for us (v. 6). The one who overcomes **the world** obeys God rather than following the expectations of the world. If we love God, we will find obeying Him a pleasure.

5:5 The faith which overcomes the evil **world** system involves the orthodox conviction that **Jesus is the Son of God.**

5:6–13 The Father bears witness that Jesus came in the flesh and is the source of eternal life in all who believe.

5:6 Water and blood have been interpreted in at least four ways: (1) as Jesus' baptism and death, (2) as His incarnation, (3) as the water and blood that flowed from His side on the Cross, and (4) as the baptism of the believer and the Lord's Supper. Most scholars favor the first interpretation. John is correcting the false teacher Cerinthus, who claimed that the Spirit came on Jesus at His baptism but left Him before His death (4:2, 3).

5:7, 8 The Holy Spirit testifies in accord with **the water** and **the blood** (v. 6) that Jesus is the Son of God.

5:9 We accept the **witness of men** so we should accept the **witness of God.**

5:10 The witness looks back to the anointing of the believer described in 2:27 and refers either to the Holy Spirit or to the testimony of the Scripture. The last part of the verse suggests that the Scripture is meant. John is

contrasting those who accept and those who reject what God says. A person who trusts in Jesus possesses the witness, namely, the truth of God (v. 9). The one who rejects God's **testimony** is claiming that God is **a liar.**

5:11 This is the testimony is the same phrase as what is translated "this is the witness" in v. 9. God's witness or testimony is that He **has given us eternal life . . . in His Son.** Eternal life is not a wage to be earned, but a gift to be received from God (Rom. 6:23).

5:12 John clearly states that our relationship with **the Son** determines whether we possess eternal **life.**

5:13 Some assume that the phrase **these things** refers to the whole book of 1 John and conclude that the way to know that one has eternal life is not only to believe in the Son but also to live a righteous life and love fellow believers. However, the phrase does not refer to the whole book; but to the immediately preceding verses and similar expressions throughout this letter (vv. 9–12; 2:1, 12–14, 21,

IN FOCUS | **"sin"**

(Gk. *hamartia*) (1:7, 9; 2:2; 3:4, 9; 4:10; 5:16; Gal. 1:4) Strong's #266: The word literally means "to miss the mark," to err. In this verse, there is one kind of sin one can recover from and another kind of sin from which one can't recover. The difference is one which John's readers were expected to recognize. We can only conjecture. The content of this letter suggests that those who had abandoned the Christian community (2:18, 19) in pursuit of heretical, "antichrist" teachings were irrecoverable. Their denial of Jesus' true person (4:1–3) leads to unrepentant sin, which finally produces spiritual death.

26; 4:1). In other words, the foundation of assurance of salvation is belief in God's Word and His Son, of whom the Spirit and Scripture testify (vv. 11, 12). Those who trust Christ can know they have eternal life because God says they have it.

5:14–17 Assurance of our relationship with God produces confidence in prayer and an active concern for brethren who have sinned.

5:14, 15 Now connects the Christian's **confidence** in prayer with assurance of a vital relationship with God which includes enjoyment of eternal life. Continuing to believe in the name of the Son of God includes continuing to practice believing prayer (3:22; John 14:12–14). The key to knowing that God **hears** our prayers is to pray **according to His will.**

Photo by Gustav Jeeninga

Idols or pagan gods, which John exhorted his readers to "keep yourselves from" (1 John 5:21) were numerous in the first-century world. One of the most popular false gods was Diana, a fertility goddess of the ancient Romans.

5:16, 17 A believer should intercede for a sinning fellow Christian provided that (1) the believer **sees** the **brother sinning** and (2) the sin **does not lead to death.** *Death* may refer either to spiritual or physical death, though physical death is probably the case here. **give him life:** The believer can pray with confidence, knowing that it is the will of God that sinning believers should stop sinning. **A sin leading to death** may refer to blaspheming the Holy Spirit, rejecting Christ as Savior, rejecting the humanity or deity of Jesus, a specific sin such as murder (3:12, 15), or a life of habitual sin. Whatever it is, the sin seems to be a flagrant violation of the sanctity of the Christian community (Acts 5:1–11; 1 Cor. 5:5; 11:30). In other words, John is encouraging us to help fellow believers who are straying; we can be the tools God uses to restore an erring brother or sister to true fellowship.

5:18–20 These verses contain three concluding absolute truths, each of which is introduced by the phrase **we know** (vv. 18–20). The general idea of this concluding section is that a proper relationship with God results in confidence of our position in Christ within a hostile world. **We** is possibly another reference to the apostles (1:1). **Does not sin** conveys the idea of not practicing sin as a habitual lifestyle. The phrase cannot mean that believers do not sin because John just spoke of seeing a believer sinning (v. 16).

5:19 The apostles are **of God,** meaning He is the source of their actions and attitudes (2:19). Satan does not touch the one born of God (v. 18), but he does have **the whole world** in his grip and under his dominion.

5:20 The **understanding** that Christ gives enables us to **know** God in a personal, intimate sense. **Jesus Christ** is **the true God;** to know Him is to have **eternal life.**

5:21 Idols here may refer to literal idols, foods sacrificed to idols, false ideas in contrast to God's truth, or the doctrines of false teachers. John has just reminded his readers of the true God (v. 20). It is appropriate that he closes by exhorting them to stay away from false gods.

The Second Epistle of

John

—■—

THE EARLY CHURCH HAD ITS HANDS FULL with false teachers. First there were the Judaizers, who held that Gentiles who did not observe Jewish rituals could not be Christians. Then there were false apostles, who specialized in attacking Paul's credibility. Later came Docetists, Gnostics, and many others who distorted the truth. Each brought their own version of the truth.

Second John is testimony to the fact that no question consumed more time than "Who is Jesus?" The false teachers who prompted John to write this letter were promoting a heresy about this question. This heresy, called Docetism, was the teaching that Christ did not actually come in the flesh. In other words, Christ did not have a body but only *seemed* to have a body and to suffer and die on the Cross (v. 7). Yet these teachers claimed to be Christians, teaching the truths of Jesus' life and death.

John would have none of it. He urged the believers to cling to the truth: Jesus Christ came in the flesh. The word *truth* appears five times in the first four verses. John wanted believers to guard against falsehood, and the best way to do that would be to arm themselves with the truth.

The early church made a practice of supporting traveling ministers and teachers with gifts and hospitality. Christians in each church would house these missionaries and provide for their needs (3 John 5, 6). Since false teachers also relied on this hospitality, John urged his readers to show discernment and not to support traveling teachers "who do not confess Jesus Christ as coming in the flesh" (v. 7).

John wrote this letter "to the elect lady and her children." This is either a figurative reference to a church community or a literal reference to a specific person. Several arguments favor the figurative meaning and several favor the literal. In defense of the figurative, the issues addressed seem to reflect the problems faced by a church more than an individual. The plural pronouns in vv. 6, 8, 10, 12 imply an audience of more than just one person. Neither the lady nor her children are named directly, although in 3 John three names appear. The fact that both Paul and John personified the church as a woman in other passages provides supporting evidence for the theory that this letter was addressed to the church as a whole (2 Cor. 11:2; Eph. 5:25–27, 31, 32; Rev. 21:2, 9; 22:17). And finally, the greeting of v. 13 makes better sense when it is understood as a greeting from one congregation to another rather than from a group of relatives to their aunt.

It is just as possible that John wrote this letter to a literal woman. The phrase "elect lady" makes sense as a title for a well-known and respected woman. The reference to her children walking in the truth also makes sense when taken literally. The greeting from her sister's children in v. 13 would fit this interpretation. The Greek word translated *elect* could be a woman's name, with *lady* added as a title of respect, as in "Lady Eklekta." As for the greeting, Paul forwarded greetings from others in his personal letter to Philemon (Philem. 23–25), so for John to do so in v. 13 of this letter would not be unprecedented. And finally, the plural references in vv. 6, 8, 10, and 12 could well refer to the woman and her children. The proof is not conclusive for either possibility, so the true identity of John's audience for this letter probably will always remain unknown. Yet the message of the letter remains clear: vigilantly guard against false teaching, and persevere in the truth.

The evidence is that the apostle John wrote this letter. Some have argued that there were two Johns, the apostle and a church leader known as John the Elder. But as with 1 John, evidence from the early church fathers identifies this letter with the apostle. Other evidences favoring John the apostle as the author of this letter are the similarity of the language and content of 1 and 2 John. John may have used the title Elder as an affectionate description of himself, since his authority as an apostle would not be in question at this late date.

This epistle was probably written soon after 1 John, for it assumes that the readers will understand what is meant by "antichrist" in v. 7. No firm date can be given because there is insufficient information in the letter itself and from church fathers. A date between A.D. 80 and 100 would fit. Early church writers stated that John was based in Ephesus following the fall of Jerusalem in A.D. 70, and it is likely that this letter was written there.

Outline

I. Opening greeting 1–3
II. Walking in the truth 4–11
   A. Walking in truth and love 4–6
   B. Responding to deceivers 7–11
III. Closing greeting 12, 13

Commentary

1–3 The opening of this epistle follows the classic Greek formula of identifying the author and recipient and extending a greeting. John's introduction is similar to the introductions of Paul's letters: he identifies himself and his readers, and assures them of God's **grace, mercy,** and **peace.** In v. 3 are two distinctive themes of this letter: (1) the **truth** about Jesus Christ and (2) the necessity of **love** for others.

1 **The Elder** is probably the apostle John. The title can refer either to an old man, an older person deserving respect, or a church leader. Here the word probably refers to the author's authority in the church. **The elect lady** may be a specific person, or the phrase may be a figurative description of the local church. **I love in truth:** John links truth and love. The second

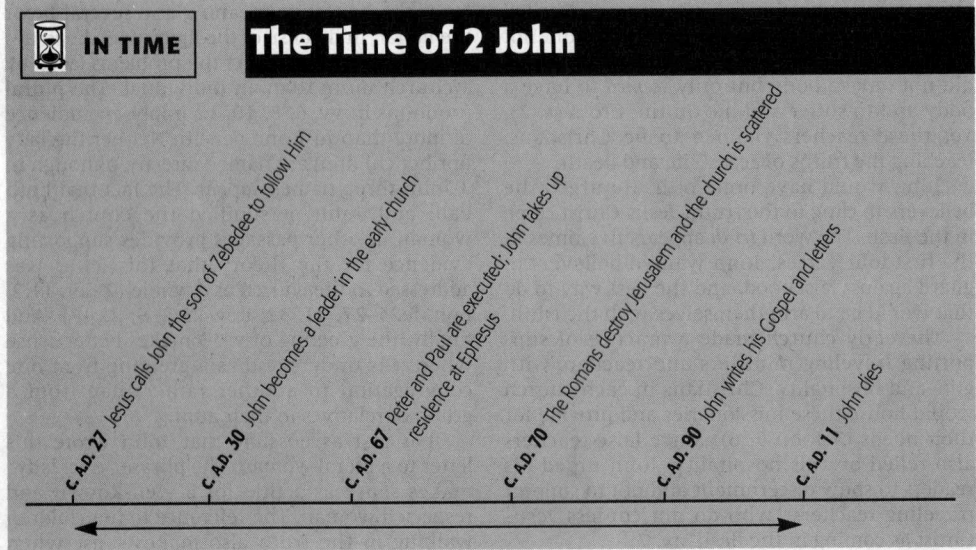

IN TIME — **The Time of 2 John**

c. A.D. 27 Jesus calls John the son of Zebedee to follow Him

c. A.D. 30 John becomes a leader in the early church

c. A.D. 67 Peter and Paul are executed; John takes up residence at Ephesus

c. A.D. 70 The Romans destroy Jerusalem and the church is scattered

c. A.D. 90 John writes his Gospel and letters

c. A.D. 11 John dies

use of **truth** refers to the body of doctrine that is true. This is God's revelation, the clear teachings and commands of Scripture.

2 truth: The reason that believers love each other is because of the indwelling **truth** (which is the Holy Spirit, the Spirit of Truth).

3 If we wish to experience God's **grace, mercy, and peace,** we must commit ourselves to His **truth** and communicate His **love.** Blessing comes from the **Father** and **Son** equally. John affirms the deity of Jesus by affirming the Son's equality with the Father.

4 Walking in truth means having an authentic relationship with God. Our walk with the Lord, if genuine, must be based upon His Word.

5 Specifically, our walk with God is based on His **commandment** to **love one another** (John 13:34, 35).

6 God's love is the basis of His desire for our obedience and, it is the reason He has revealed His will through **His commandments** in His Word. We prove our obedience to Him by demonstrating love toward one another. Love is an unlimited resource readily available to us, and it is tremendously effective in furthering the work of Christ.

7–11 Walking in truth means responding properly to deceivers by guarding against them and rejecting them. Having established that we are to obey God by demonstrating love toward one another, John must now address the problem of false teachers in the church. He shows that love for God means supporting the truth and rejecting those who stand against it.

7 One of the stumbling blocks to Christians is the **many deceivers** who subtly blur the truth about Jesus. Walking in truth means responding to deceivers by guarding against and rejecting them. **Coming in the flesh** refers to the Incarnation, the fact that Jesus is the God-man. The humanity of Jesus provides a test by which false teachers can be identified. The Gnostic heresy, against which John wrote in 1 and 2 John, included a denial of the physical body of Christ. People who deny the physical reality of Jesus are not Christians, but antichrists.

8 Being seduced by false teachers is one way that Christians can lose their reward at the judgment. With this in mind, John writes that the reason to guard against deceivers is our own desire not to **lose** our reward at the judgment seat of Christ. Jesus cautioned the church at Philadelphia to "hold fast what you have, that no one may take your crown" (Rev. 3:11). Every believer has the potential of a **full reward** or a complete loss of reward (1 Cor. 3:15). The determining factor is our faithfulness to Christ. Justification is not in view here because it is not something **we worked for,** but something we received as a gift from God (Rom. 4:1–6; Eph. 2:8).

9 Transgresses has the strong sense of running too far ahead, going too far. This is probably an allusion to the Gnostics, who considered themselves as having advanced beyond basic Christianity. Departure from Christ into doctrinal error indicates that a person does **not have God.** Love for God

---

✠ IN CONTEXT Needed: Christian Discernment

We live in a day in which any and everything is tolerated. No matter how outlandish or how strenuously we disagree with what others cherish or embrace, we accept their right to their opinion. There seems to be no basis for saying "no" any more. Ours is an age of "I'm okay, you're okay."

But that is just not true. It would be more honest to affirm, "I'm *not* okay and you're *not* okay. We both need help that we can count on."

The early church faced a similar predicament. After Jesus' death and resurrection, many claimed to know Him and His message, even though their versions of the story differed remarkably. For instance, Paul faced a conflicting gospel in Galatia and at Philippi and vehemently challenged his opponents' claims (Gal. 1:6–9; Phil. 3:1–4). Likewise, John warned against those who distort the truth (1 John 2:18–29; 4:1–6; 3 John 9–11).

The recipient of 2 John, possibly a woman (2 John 1), was given to hospitality (10)—a wonderfully Christlike virtue. But John was concerned to help her become more discerning and not lend the reputation of her household to those who would distort the truth about Christ (7, 11). He knew that not all who claim Christ are true followers. So believers must develop discernment if they are to remain loyal to truth.

means supporting the truth and rejecting those who stand against it.

10 This doctrine refers to the Christian belief that Jesus is God come "in the flesh" (v. 7), He is completely human and completely divine. A Christian should not only refuse to **receive** false teachers in the sense of supporting them while they visit the community; a Christian should also avoid appearing to endorse their teachings. The proper response to deceivers is to reject them as unbelievers. This shows how seriously we should take the Scriptures and how careful we should be in evaluating the teachings of everyone.

11 greets him shares: To greet someone

means to identify with that person publicly. This can refer to a personal greeting by an individual (v. 1) or to the church's public welcome of a false teacher (v. 10).

12, 13 Having many things to write to you: Second John is a mini-version of 1 John. The author is saying that although he could go on and write much more, he prefers to be with them and speak to them **face to face** (which in the first-century idiom is vividly "mouth to mouth") in order that he might, as it were, restore them to spiritual life in Christ. The greeting from the **elect sister** is, of course, another congregation, perhaps a larger one where John lived.

The Third Epistle of

John

S TRUGGLES WITH FORCES OUTSIDE THE CHURCH can be harmful enough, but struggles within a church can be devastating. Third John was written in response to one such struggle within a local church. One of the church leaders, Diotrephes, had asserted control over the congregation to such an extent that he was prohibiting representatives of other churches from ministering to his congregation. Worse yet, he

began driving away members of his own church who dared to help the representatives after he had refused to accept them. Diotrephes's actions violated Christ's command to love one another.

This was not a case of doctrinal deviation but of moral failure. However, it was as much a threat to the life of the church as the false teaching addressed in 1 and 2 John. Faithful members of the church community were being hurt by Diotrephes's arrogant attitude. The apostle John felt the need to deal with the problem and was planning a personal visit. In the meantime, the letter's recipient Gaius needed encouragement, and Demetrius needed support in his ministry.

The background of this epistle is similar to that of John's first two epistles, though the problem threatening the addressees of 3 John is made clearer from the content of the letter.

The early church had the practice of sending out itinerant ministers as messengers of the apostles or churches. These men would minister in a local church for a period of time, providing spiritual encouragement and doctrinal instruction. They were the equivalent of our modern evangelists, ministers, and missionaries who

travel from their home churches to provide teaching and encouragement to other believers. Itinerant ministers were expected to know and teach the doctrines of the apostles, and while they were with the church, the community of Christians benefiting from their ministry was expected to support them. Titus's ministry as Paul's representative to the church in Corinth (2 Cor. 2:12, 13; 7:6–15; 8:6) and to the churches of Crete (Titus 1:5) is an example of this. As the itinerant ministers traveled from one place of ministry to the next, they would seek assistance and comfort from the churches of the communities through which they passed. This practice is reflected in Paul's instructions to Titus to assist Zenas and Apollos as they traveled (Titus 3:13).

As is true today, some leaders, filled with personal ambition instead of the love of Christ, sought to control their local congregations with an iron hand. In this case, a man named Diotrephes was trying to assert his leadership even against the apostles. Diotrephes had asserted his influence and was driving out legitimate representatives of the apostles in order to maintain his personal control.

The recipient of the letter was a Christian

named Gaius, though no other record of him has been found to date. He was likely a member of one of the churches in Asia Minor to which John's influence had spread during his Ephesian ministry. He seems to have had the resources to show hospitality to itinerant preachers, and he was certainly a prominent and trustworthy person to whom John could give the task of standing firm against the authoritarianism of Diotrephes until the apostle could come to deal with the problem himself.

As with 1 and 2 John, the author of this epistle is generally accepted to be the apostle John. Similarities among the letters and early church tradition speak strongly of John's authorship. Although some have proposed that there were two Johns, the apostle and a church leader known as John the Elder, the consensus remains that the apostle wrote this letter.

No information is given within the epistle to indicate its date. The circumstance addressed in 3 John is markedly different from that of John's first two letters, and it is not possible to say whether it was written before or after 1 and 2 John. The letter was probably sent from Ephesus, where early church tradition says John located his ministry following the fall of Jerusalem in A.D. 70.

Outline

I. Opening greeting to Gaius 1–4
II. Gaius's responsibility 5–12
  A. Gaius's support of fellow believers 5–8

B. Diotrephes's opposition 9–11
C. Endorsement of Demetrius 12
III. Closing greetings 13, 14

Commentary

1–4 Introduction: John's response to Gaius's walk in truth was joy and prayer for his blessing.

1 The Elder is the apostle John. The word *Elder* can refer to an old man, an older person deserving respect, or a church leader. Here the word is an appeal to the writer's authority in the church. **Gaius** was a common Roman name. The Gaius to whom John wrote was a Christian in one of the churches of Asia Minor. It cannot be said with certainty that this Gaius identifies with Gaius of Derbe (the traditional view, compare Acts 20:4), Gaius of Macedonia (Acts 19:29), or Gaius of Corinth (1 Cor. 1:14; Rom. 16:23). The traditional view is quite possible; at least we know that this Gaius was a leader in the church, he was very hospitable, and that he was a dear friend, perhaps a convert of John's.

2 may prosper . . . be in health . . . soul prospers: John's greeting may imply that Gaius was physically weak, though spiritually strong. More probably John is simply following the pattern of greetings common to Greek letters.

3 The reason for John's prayer is the testimony of others that Gaius walks **in the truth.** *Truth* here refers to the body of truth given to the church through the apostles and prophets, that is, the Scripture. Gaius walks according to

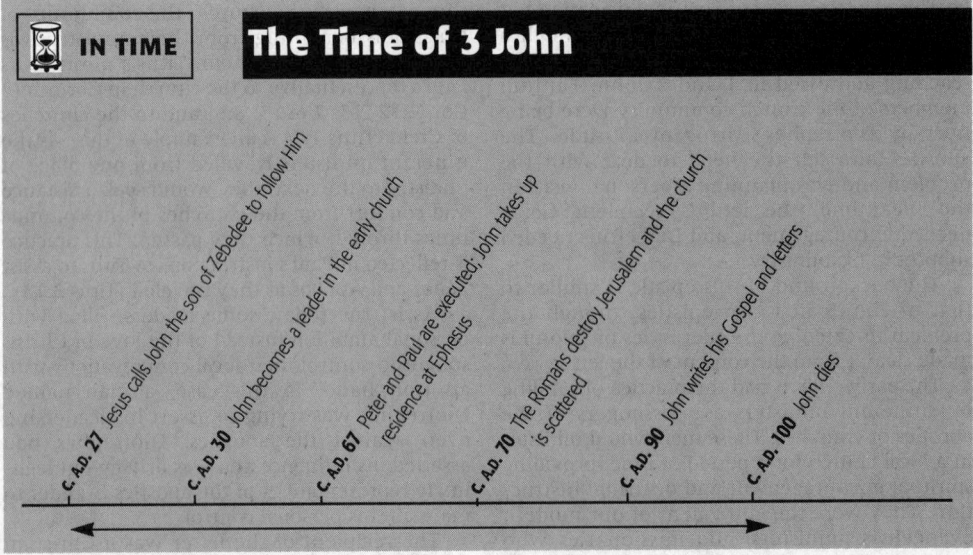

IN TIME — The Time of 3 John

C. A.D. 27 Jesus calls John the son of Zebedee to follow Him

C. A.D. 30 John becomes a leader in the early church

C. A.D. 67 Peter and Paul are executed; John takes up residence at Ephesus

C. A.D. 70 The Romans destroy Jerusalem and the church is scattered

C. A.D. 90 John writes his Gospel and letters

C. A.D. 100 John dies

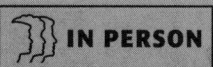 **IN PERSON** | **Gaius and Prosperity**

John's greeting (3 John 2) raises an important issue. It is clear that he expects God to give physical and material well-being to Gaius. Is that what believers today should be asking God for? Should we expect God to prosper us physically and financially? Is this verse an indication that He will? Notice some important things:

(1) John is praying for Gaius's prosperity, not Gaius praying for his own prosperity.

(2) This is part of a formal greeting or blessing. We say very similar things today like, "Good luck," or "Have a good day," or "Stay healthy, kid."

(3) The Greek word here for prosper means "to travel well on a journey." That fits with its use in a blessing. Furthermore, it is not something one should actively pursue, but rather a gift that one should look for, a sense of "wholeness" like the OT concept of *shalom* that people enjoy when they follow God's precepts and live in His power.

(4) We don't know what Gaius's circumstances may have been, only that his soul was prospering. John may be saying, "You are doing so well in the faith; I wish you were doing as well in your health and the rest of your life."

(5) John's main concern is that Gaius would walk in the truth (3, 4), not that he would have a big bank account or be in tip-top shape.

Overall, it would be foolish to construct a general principle of material blessing from this verse, especially when so many other passages warn against that very thing.

the Word of God rather than the ways of the world.

4 My children is a description Paul uses of those he has led to saving faith in Christ (1 Cor. 4:14–17) and may indicate that Gaius was one of John's converts. It may also be a term John uses to describe those under his pastoral care, as reflected in 1 John 2:1, 12, 18, 28; 3:7, 18; 4:4; 5:21. To **walk in truth** means to walk according to God's Word, the revelation of His truth.

5–12 In these verses John affirms Gaius's responsibility to assist Demetrius despite the opposition of Diotrephes and his expulsion of those who received traveling missionaries. In the first part of this section (vv. 5–8), John says that Gaius's support of itinerant preachers should be continued in order for him to be a fellow worker in the truth. In the last part of the section (vv. 9–11), John promises that Diotrephes's opposition will be addressed by him when he arrives. Meanwhile, John endorses Demetrius as a legitimate teacher who is deserving of shelter and support (v. 12).

5 you do faithfully: Gaius's support of **the brethren,** including those he does not know personally, reflects his faithfulness to the Lord. This emphasizes the importance of serving the Lord by being faithful in our responsibilities within our local churches.

6 worthy of God: These people had reported to others about Gaius's ministry in their lives.

7 Gentiles here refers to unbelievers, not to Gentile Christians. The majority of Christians in the churches of Asia Minor were Gentile converts rather than Jewish.

8 We **become fellow workers** in the Lord's service when we support the ministries of others, publicly as well as financially. To **receive** means to identify with people publicly, welcome them into our homes, and supply their needs.

9 I wrote: John had written an earlier letter that was either lost or possibly destroyed by **Diotrephes,** who was asserting his control over the church out of his own personal ambition (1 Pet. 5:1–5). John had probably written asking Diotrephes's church to extend hospitality to the traveling missionaries the apostle had sent out (v. 10), and Diotrephes had refused to heed John's request.

10 If I come reflects the idea of "when I come." John intends to come and take Diotrephes to task for his attitudes and actions, and to exercise his apostolic authority in punishing him. This is a warning similar to those of Paul in 2 Cor. 10:2; 13:1, 2. Diotrephes's sins include verbal attacks on John and his representatives, as well as active opposition to those who wanted to support legitimate ministers.

11 The proof of our commitment to God is that we personally reject evil and embrace a life patterned after that which **is good.** The idea of **has not seen God** is explained more fully in 1 John 3:4–9. The lifestyle that we exhibit is a

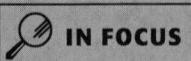 **IN FOCUS** | **"church"**

(Gk. *ekklesia*) (vv. 6, 9, 10; Matt. 16:18; Acts 8:1; Rom. 16:1; Rev. 1:4) Strong's #*1577*: The Greek term simply means "an assembly." It was used in secular Greek to speak of any gathering of people to a political or festive assembly. It was used by the NT writers to mean a local assembly of believers or the whole body of believers. In John's third epistle we see an example of both uses: "the church" in v. 6 connotes a large, unspecified group of believers, whereas "the church" in vv. 9, 10 has to be a specific local church. According to the overall pattern of the NT, it appears that the Christians of each city were unified under one group of elders (Acts 14:23; 15:2, 4; 20:17, 18; Titus 1:5). Within the local church in the city there were probably several "assemblies" or "meetings" of believers, held in various homes.

direct reflection of the extent to which we have seen God. If we were to see God perfectly, we would never sin. Our sin is a result of a faulty vision of God. Therefore, the Scriptures encourage us to look at Christ (2 Cor. 3:18; 4:16–18; Heb. 12:2, 3), for the day when we see Him perfectly will be the day that we will be like Him (1 John 3:2, 3).

12 Gaius can trust John's endorsement of **Demetrius,** who not only has a good reputation but also has a testimony **from the truth itself.** In other words, Demetrius's life measured up to the teaching of Scripture and Christ's commands. His conduct matched his theology.

13–15 The brevity of the letter reflects John's plan to speak to Gaius soon. The apostle closes with a greeting of **peace,** a common feature of Greek letters. **by name:** John probably knew the church members well and asks Gaius to give each one a personal greeting.

The Epistle of

Jude

F EW BOOKS IN THE NEW TESTAMENT HAVE more to say to our generation than the Epistle of Jude. Distorters of the faith will find the book distasteful because of its warnings and uncompromising stance against defectors from the truth of Jesus Christ. But to those who approach the book with receptive hearts, Jude's words speak as clearly and forcefully today as they did almost two thousand years ago.

This small epistle strikes the imagination with its vivid pictures of false teachers. The writer commands our attention with his appeals for defending the faith and growing in grace. The primary focus of the book is on the faith, the believers, and God—not on the errors and character of the heretics. It is notable that with all of the blunt descriptions of false teachers, Jude gives us neither a command to confront these troublemakers (only to avoid them) nor a plan of disciplinary action. He simply indicates they are under the condemnation of God.

The literary form of Jude is the common style of correspondence of that day. The letter opens with the author's name, a description of the recipients, and a conventional wish that they are well. Yet as with other NT epistles, the eloquence and depth of thought rises far above the usual business and personal correspondence. Jude comes quickly to his point. Not content merely to expose error, he forcefully exhorts his readers and concludes with a truly eloquent benediction.

From his opening sentence, the author assaults error, threatens judgment, and encourages holiness. The description of the errors of the false teachers is poetic in its imagery (vv. 12, 13). Jude likes to arrange his thoughts in groups of three. In v. 1 Christians are "called, sanctified . . . and preserved"; in v. 2 the author wishes for his readers "mercy, peace, and love"; in vv. 5–7 there are three illustrations of sin and judgment from the OT; in v. 8 the false teachers are described as defiling the flesh, rejecting authority, and speaking evil of dignitaries; in v. 11 three examples of rebellion—Cain, Balaam, and Korah—are given. All of this persuasive prose results in a strong encouragement to the faithful to "contend earnestly for the faith" (v. 3).

The obvious similarities between Jude and 2 Pet. 2 seem to show that one has borrowed from the other. The vocabulary of the two books is similar; both books use the OT for illustrations, and neither quotes it directly. The books deal with similar situations, though their approaches are different. Peter seems to be anticipating difficulty with false teachers (the future tense is used in 2 Pet. 2:1–3), while Jude uses the past tense to describe the situation (v. 4). On the other hand, because of the more precise language in Jude, many scholars believe that Jude was first and Peter borrowed from him, but this cannot be known for certain.

The author of this epistle calls himself Jude, and there is no reason to think that this is a pseudonym. There are six individuals named Jude in the NT, but only two are likely to have written this book: (1) the apostle Jude (Luke 6:16; Acts 1:13), who is probably Thaddaeus of Matt. 10:3; (2) Jude the brother of James and the half brother of the Lord Jesus. The brothers of the Lord are named in Matt. 13:55 as "James, Joses, Simon, and Judas."

Since the author does not claim apostolic authority, and since v. 17 indicates that the apostles are a group that does not include the writer, we are left with the second candidate—Jude, the brother of the Lord and of James. This identification is confirmed by the author's reference to his brother James (v. 1) and a reference in a letter of Clement of Alexandria (around A.D. 153–217).

We might wonder why Jude did not assert that he was the brother of the Lord Jesus, but his first readers would already have known this. Also, even in the years following the Resurrection, there were already some superstitions surrounding the "holy family" that Jude might have wished to avoid.

Although assigning an exact date for the writing of Jude is impossible, it is likely that the book was written between A.D. 60–64. It was almost certainly written before A.D. 70, since Jude does not make any reference to the fall of Jerusalem in A.D. 70. If he had been writing after this event, he would doubtless have mentioned it, since it would serve as an example of God's judgment.

Outline

Commentary

1 Instead of flaunting his honored relationship as a half brother to Jesus, **Jude** calls himself a **bondservant,** a servant of the Son of God. There were basically two types of slaves in the Roman world. One became a slave by force and the other by choice. The latter bonded himself to his master for life. This pictures the type of slave that Jude was. **called:** This is the primary description of Jude's readers: they had been chosen by God to represent Him in this world.

2 Mercy, peace, and love be multiplied: These words in Greek express a strong desire. Though *mercy* is mentioned in a greeting only four other times in the NT, those occurrences

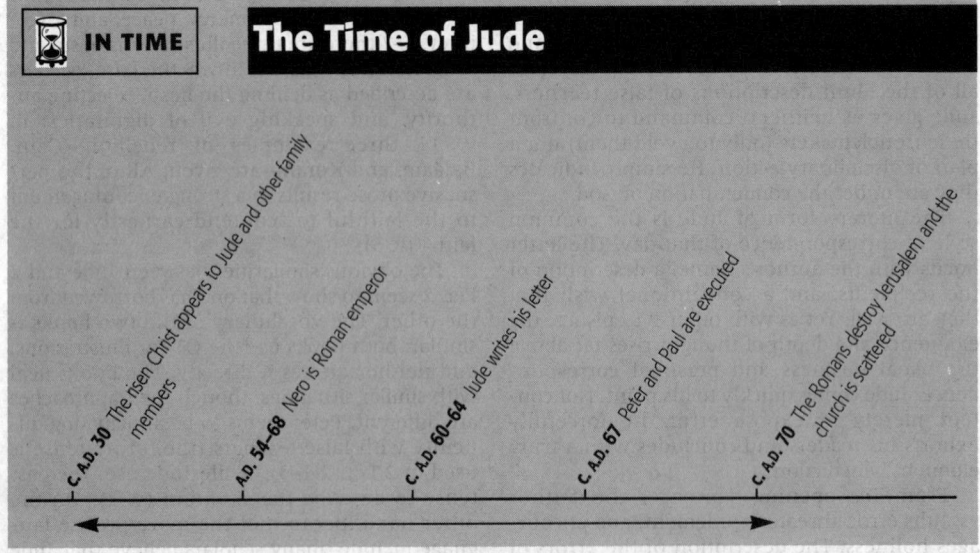

🕰 **IN TIME**   **The Time of Jude**

C. A.D. 30 The risen Christ appears to Jude and other family members

A.D. 54–68 Nero is Roman emperor

C. A.D. 60–64 Jude writes his letter

C. A.D. 67 Peter and Paul are executed

C. A.D. 70 The Romans destroy Jerusalem and the church is scattered are important because they also precede a warning against false teaching (1 Tim. 1:2; 2 Tim. 1:2; Titus 1:4; 2 John 3). Mercy is God's undeserving favor on us. Peace is the state of a person who rests in God completely for salvation and protection. The spiritual result of mercy and peace is love. Love is a response to God's work toward Him and others around us. Mercy might be seen looking up, peace looking inward, and love looking outward.

3–16 These verses serve as the center of Jude's argument and purpose for writing. Verse 3 reveals the deep concern and passionate personality of the writer. Though he desires to pursue a subject of theological importance to the readers, namely "our common salvation," an urgency to give them warning takes precedence. The book divides his readers from the false teachers that he warns against and describes. At several places in the letter he turns his attention to his readers with the pronoun "you" (vv. 3, 5, 12, 18 20–22, 24) in contrast to their ungodly distracters (vv. 4, 8, 10–12, 14–16, 19). Constant attention to exhort, inform, and comfort his readers reveals that Jude has the mind of a theologian but the heart of a shepherd.

3 Jude intended to write a more general doctrinal letter, but the present crisis demanded this short, pointed attack on doctrinal error. When Jude speaks of **common salvation,** he is referring to the unity all believers have in Christ. But due to the crisis of the infiltrating heretics, Jude does not dwell on the subject of the common salvation. **Contend earnestly** translates a Greek word that is the basis of the English word *agonize*. Christians are not called to passive service, but to vigilance in the cause of Christ (Phil. 1:27). **The faith** here does not have its usual sense of personal belief in Christ for salvation; here it means the body of teaching passed down in the church by the apostles (v. 17). This is similar to traditions about the Lord Jesus spoken of by the apostle Paul in 1 Cor. 11:1; 15:3–8. The revelation was not ongoing but **once for all delivered,** final and complete (Heb. 1:2). The world today is in flux. New fads and ideas come and go so fast that it is difficult to keep up with them. The truth of God, however, never changes. What God has said can always be trusted. This provides great comfort to the people of God.

4 The heretics were subtle. Their primary tactics were to pervert God's **grace** and to **deny** the authority of the Lord (Prov. 1:29). They were clever enough to have infiltrated the Christian community, even though they were **ungodly.** Jesus anticipated this kind of people when He spoke about wolves in sheep's clothing (Matt. 7:15). **turn the grace of our God into**

lewdness: The teaching of grace can be dangerous when perverted by false teachers or carnal people who believe that because they have been saved by grace they may live as they please (Rom. 6:1, 2). **the only Lord God and our Lord Jesus Christ:** These false teachers not only lived immorally; they rejected the authority of Christ. The first Greek word translated *Lord* here means "Master." It identifies one who possesses absolute power and thus commands obedience. In the original wording it is clear that the entire statement refers to Christ: Jesus is both our absolute Sovereign and our God. Titus 2:13 uses a similar Greek construction in another significant passage that teaches the deity of Jesus.

5–11 These verses expand the twofold statement of v. 4. There the ungodly men were fleshly in their spiritual life. In vv. 5–7 Jude illustrates such sinful activity by three examples from the OT: the children of Israel, the fallen angels, and the residents of Sodom and Gomorrah. Verses 8–11 develop the rejection of Christ's Lordship (v. 4). These people reject the leadership of Christ's church (v. 11), though even the angel Michael did not express such an attitude with Satan. Three examples of such rebellion are seen in the stories of Cain, Balaam, and Korah.

5 though you once knew this: These Christians were given fair warning concerning false teachers from the words of Christ and the apostles (vv. 17, 18) but they had become negligent and were no longer on guard. **destroyed those who did not believe:** The Israelites of the Exodus had a magnificent beginning in Egypt but a disastrous ending in the wilderness. That we have begun with the Lord does not mean that we will have the glorious conclusion we might have envisioned at the beginning of our salvation journey. The false believers who had infiltrated God's people would be judged, just like the false believers who rejected God in the wilderness (Num. 25:1–9).

6 The meaning of this verse is disputed, as is a similar reference in 2 Pet. 2:4. It is clear that **the angels** to which Jude refers are not holy angels of God. Instead these angels could be those who had previously fallen with Satan. Some think that these angels are "the sons of God" of Gen. 6:2, who took on human form and married women before the Flood. According to this interpretation, these perverted angels were condemned by God to **chains** and **darkness** and are presently awaiting the final judgment of Satan and all his angels (2 Pet. 2:4).

7 in a similar manner to these: As the angels had committed sexual immorality with humans, so the citizens of **Sodom and Gomorrah** had pursued all kinds of sexual perversion (here **strange flesh** refers to homosexual acts; Gen. 19:5). They were also judged by God with fire from heaven (Gen. 19:24).

8 The false teachers were arrogant and had their own agenda. They had not been commissioned by the church nor called by the Holy Spirit. Jude calls these ungodly persons **dreamers,** perhaps because they claimed divine revelation, but more likely because they denied the Lord and thus were living in an unreal world of deception. They were creating their own false world in which indulging in immorality went hand in hand with salvation. **reject authority, and speak evil of dignitaries:** The false teachers even rejected those who were placed in positions of authority in local congregations. They not only preferred error to truth but also demeaned and rejected those who taught the truth.

9 Jude's description here is probably taken from an apocryphal book called *The Assumption of Moses,* written in the first century A.D. There is no record in the Bible itself of the archangel's encounter with Satan, or a detailed account of Moses' body (there is a reference to it in Deut. 34:6). Although Jude uses an extrabiblical source to illustrate the arrogance of the false teachers, this does not invalidate the inspiration of this letter, and it does not mean the source from which Jude quotes was inspired (see Paul's use of pagan authors in Acts 17:28; Titus 1:12).

The name **Michael** means "Who Is Like God?" The desire to be like God was the initial sin of Satan (Is. 14:14). It was also the enticement that Satan offered Eve: "You will be like God" (Gen. 3:5). Michael, though opposing Satan, refused to bring **a reviling accusation** against him. Michael would not even accuse Satan, the chief of blasphemers, of being a blasphemer. Instead, he left judgment to God. This reverence for the prerogatives of God stands in great contrast to the heretics who were slandering anyone and everyone (vv. 8, 10).

10 The false teachers **do not know** the truth of the gospel. They speak on matters that they do not understand, as natural people and not as spiritual people (1 Cor. 2:14). They have understanding not of the Spirit of God, but only of what they share in common with the animal world, things far less than God's intent for His human creatures.

11 The heretics are compared to three OT failures. **Cain,** a tiller of the soil, did not place his faith in the Lord. The way of Cain is the way of pride and self-righteousness (Gen. 4:3–8; Heb. 11:4; 1 John 3:12). **Balaam** epitomized the sin of greed. He was a pagan prophet, an enemy of God, who believed he could profit from doing the work of God (Num. 31:16; 2 Pet. 2:15; Rev. 2:14). Similar to Balaam, the ungodly teachers in the church appeared to be religious. They sought to mix in with the people of God,

---

✚ IN CONTEXT The Use of Apocryphal Sources

The Jewish Apocrypha consists of books and writings that were never recognized as part of the canon of Scripture, but which served a devotional purpose for many believers of ancient times, including some of the authors of the NT. Jude cites two books of the Apocrypha in his letter. Jude 9 apparently comes from *The Assumption of Moses,* and v. 14 comes from *The Book of Enoch.* Today we do not have a complete text of *The Assumption of Moses,* but two early church fathers, Clement of Alexandria and Origen, testify that v. 9 is a reference to that book.

Jude is not the only NT author who quotes extrabiblical sources. In 1 Cor. 10:4, Paul apparently made use of a Hebrew commentary (the Midrash) to support his interpretation of Israel's wilderness wanderings. In Acts 17:28 and Titus 1:12, he quoted from pagan poets to support some of his assertions. Though we do not know where the names Jannes and Jambres come from (2 Tim. 3:8), Paul did not hesitate to use their story as an example of godlessness for Timothy.

Should the NT writers have quoted from apocryphal sources? Surely God had no trouble guiding the biblical writers in selecting material from these sources. Luke knew of "many" accounts of the life of Christ (Luke 1:1), which he set out to better with his own "orderly account" (1:3). Along the same lines, Paul had at least one letter from the Corinthian church to guide his responses in 1 and 2 Corinthians. Even the devil is quoted in Matt. 4:3, 6, 9. This does not mean that these sources are inspired, or even accurate, but it does mean that sometimes NT writers drew from the written sources God had given them to communicate effectively what He wanted them to say. The writers of Scripture wrote all that, and only that, which God had inspired them to say. We must affirm with Peter that the ultimate origin of Scripture is the mind of God (2 Pet. 1:19–21).

and they were even accepted by the believers. However, their true motive was greed. **Korah** was a Levite (Num. 16:1–3, 31–35) who resented the prominent positions of Moses and Aaron as God's representatives. The Lord brought judgment on him and his followers for rebelling against those He had placed in authority. Christians need to be careful not to speak against spiritual leaders in a careless way (Titus 3:1, 2).

12, 13 spots in your love feasts: The people of God had been deceived by people who appeared to be messengers of God but instead were ministers of Satan (2 Cor. 11:4, 13–15). The Greek word for *spots* may also be translated "hidden reefs"; it serves as a strong warning to be on guard against deceivers. **clouds without water . . . trees without fruit:** Clouds may look like they will bring rain until the wind blows them away (Prov. 25:14). Trees may look productive until autumn arrives, the time for fruit to be picked. The ministers of Satan promise spiritual growth but do not satisfy the hunger of God's people for the truth. Not only are they without fruit, but they are rootless and incapable of bearing, since they are unable to tap the true source of sustenance (Ps. 1:3). They talk about God but are truly godless. **raging waves . . . foaming . . . wandering stars:** These godless people put on a great show but lacked any substance. They boasted of liberty but placed the people of God in bondage to sin (2 Pet. 2:19). After they had done their evil deeds and made their profits, they, like wandering stars, moved on to other places to exploit God's people again. **darkness forever:** These deceivers might not be punished for their evil deeds in this world, and their true character and deeds might fail to be discovered by Christians, but their punishment is certain.

14 Enoch, the seventh from Adam: Jude quotes from the apocryphal *Book of Enoch* here. This was a book supposedly by Enoch, who was taken to heaven by the Lord before he died (Gen. 5:21–24). **Ten thousands** is a Hebrew expression meaning a limitless number.

15 ungodly: This word is repeated four times, making the verse one of the most striking in the letter. In view of the wicked nature of evil persons, how could the church allow them to stay in their midst? They are ungodly, yet they are with God's people, claiming to represent God. Just as Judas Iscariot appeared to be a follower of Christ right up to the end, so do these religious leaders (note the contrast with believers in v. 1; John 13:18–30).

16 grumblers, complainers: This verse describes various ways evil people misuse their tongues. Instead of praising God, they boast; instead of encouraging, they whine and complain. Their lives are characterized by intense selfishness and a slavery to personal desires. By using flattering words, they try to gain a following for themselves that opposes the proper authorities in local congregations.

17 The **words** of the **apostles** are important because they express the will of God. In discerning the spirit (v. 19) of anyone claiming to speak for God, the only sure standard for evaluation is the Bible. Those who attack the central truths of Scripture, the ones concerning God, Christ, and salvation by God's grace through faith, must be avoided.

18 Jude points out that nothing that has been observed about the false teachers should have taken the believers by surprise. The apostles had given warning (v. 17) that in the end times evil deceivers would come among them. The description of the heretics as **mockers** indicates that one of their main tactics to gain credibility was to tear down godly leaders.

19 When Jude declares that the false teachers are without the **Spirit,** he leaves no doubt as to their eternal destiny. They are merely worldly **persons** and do not belong to God.

20, 21 Jude tells us how to **keep** ourselves **in the love of God.** It is clear that Jude is

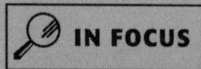

IN FOCUS   **"sensual"**

(Gk. *psuchikos*) (v. 19; 1 Cor. 2:14; 15:44; James 3:15) Strong's #5591: The Greek term literally means "of the soul" or "natural," as opposed to "spiritual," or "having the Spirit." It is translated "the natural man" in 1 Cor. 2:14. According to the Scripture, a person's being, both soul and body, should be ruled by "the spirit," that part of a person which is influenced by the Holy Spirit. But in the "natural" person, the spirit is subservient to the natural soul, which is worldly in its motives and aims.

encouraging us in this verse to cultivate our love for Christ, for we cannot be separated from His love for us (Rom. 8:35–39).

22, 23 We have certain obligations to other believers. First, we need to show mercy to those in any kind of spiritual or physical need. Second, we need to use discernment (**making a distinction**) in helping our brothers and sisters in the church. Some will require tender care and patience to help them grow in Christ. With others, we may need to use drastic action to rescue them from the temptations of sin. In rescuing our fellow believers, there is always the need to use wisdom and caution to prevent getting caught up in the sin that caused them to fall. **Hating even the garment defiled by the flesh** is a metaphor for staying wary of sin—as Paul says, "considering yourself lest you also be tempted" (Gal. 6:1).

24, 25 Jude concludes his letter with exuberant praise for the Lord, who alone could keep the readers from being deceived. **Stumbling** probably refers to the possibility of being tripped up by the false teachers' errors. Note

that Jude does not use the word *falling*, but *stumbling*. Only a person who is already walking or running (frequent biblical images of the Christian life) can stumble (Gal. 5:7; 1 Thess. 4:1; Heb. 12:1; 1 John 2:6). God is able to keep us from stumbling (Pss. 37:23, 24; 121:3; Prov. 4:11, 12). He guards us in this life, despite all the dangers and pitfalls that deceivers put in our way. **Faultless** is a Greek word used of sacrificial animals that had no blemish and thus were fit to be offered to God. Only God can save us, cleanse us from our sins, and present us to Himself as *faultless*, for God is the Author and Perfecter of our faith (Heb. 12:2).

The Revelation

of Jesus Christ

■

AS OUTSIDE PERSECUTION AGAINST CHRISTIANS increased, the first-century church also faced internal problems. They struggled with suffering, spiritual warfare, heretical doctrine and practice, and spiritual apathy. Christ had promised to return—but when? And how? And what would He do about the problems facing the church when He did come back? Confronted with these circumstances, the original readers of

Revelation needed to be both encouraged and exhorted. On the one hand, Revelation was intended to be a promise of divine protection from God's judgment on the world. On the other hand, those who read the book were to take it to heart and obey, worshipfully standing for the Word of God and the testimony of Jesus, as the apostle John had. In recording the Revelation of Jesus Christ, John wanted to reassure his readers that Jesus Christ controls the course and climax of history.

God's overriding purpose in all of history is the establishment of the promised messianic kingdom. Associated with this ultimate divine objective is the opportunity for believers to persevere by faith in a life of obedience. The prospect for these overcomers or victors is the destiny of reigning with Christ as co-heirs in His kingdom.

The book titles itself "The Revelation of Jesus Christ" (1:1). Christ is pictured as the glorified Son of Man (1:12–16), the Lion of Judah (5:5), the worthy Lamb (5:8–13), the Son who will rule all (12:5), the Bridegroom (19:7–9), the conquering King of kings and Lord of lords (19:16), and the rightful Ruler of His earthly

(20:4–6) and eternal (22:1, 3) kingdoms. It must never be forgotten that "the testimony of Jesus is the spirit of prophecy" (19:10). His person, victory, and rule result in worship and praise throughout the Book of Revelation.

The book details Christ's directions to the churches (chs. 2; 3) and describes "the wrath of the Lamb" (6:16), His judgments on the sinful world (chs. 6; 8; 9; 14; 16—18) prior to His second coming (19:11–21). This focus on the last times is completed by a brief description of the Lord's thousand-year reign (20:2–6), His judgment of the entire existing created order (20:4, 11–15), and His eternal rule (21:1—22:5).

The death, resurrection (1:5), and ascension (12:5) of Jesus Christ are the historical backdrop for His gracious offer of redemption from sin and eternal life (22:14, 17). Believers (2:5) and unbelievers (9:20, 21) both are urged to repent and to overcome by "the blood of the Lamb" (12:11). Those who obey are a royal priesthood for the Lord (1:6; 5:9, 10) and will reign with Him (20:4, 6). Their prayers are continually before God's heavenly throne (5:8; 8:3, 4).

In the power of the Holy Spirit, John received great visions (1:10; 4:2; 17:3; 21:10)

as well as crucial messages that the church needed to hear (2:7). In the spiritual realm, Revelation depicts a divine struggle against Satan and his demons (2:9, 10, 13, 24; 3:9). Yet this battle against the deceiver of the world and the "accuser of our brethren" has already been won by the blood of the Lamb (12:9–11). All that remains is for Satan and his followers to be sentenced to their just, eternal punishment by the Lord (19:20—20:3, 10). Their doom is sure.

From about A.D. 53 the apostle Paul used the great city of Ephesus as a center for evangelism and church planting throughout the Roman province of Asia (Acts 19:10). Probably the seven churches of Revelation were founded during this time or shortly thereafter.

While imprisoned in Rome (around A.D. 60–62), Paul wrote his letters to the Ephesians, the Colossians, the Philippians, and Philemon. Colossians was to be read "in the church of the Laodiceans" and "the epistle from Laodicea" was to be heard in the congregation in Colosse (Col. 4:16). Apparently the practice of writing epistles for wider circulation than a single individual or group was an accepted one, as seen in chs. 2 and 3 of Revelation.

Reliable historical sources dating from the second century A.D. place the apostle John in Ephesus and ministering throughout the province of Asia from about A.D. 70–100. It is likely that 1, 2, and 3 John were written by the apostle to Christians in that region around A.D. 80–100. During the latter part of this period, the emperor Domitian intensified his persecution of Christians. John was undoubtedly placed on the island of Patmos because of his Christian testimony. He was released after eighteen months by Emperor Nerva (A.D. 96–98), after which the apostle returned to Ephesus to resume his leadership role there.

The author of Revelation refers to himself as John. He is associated with the seven churches in the Roman province of Asia (present-day southwest Turkey) in their suffering, blessing, and perseverance. His stand "for the Word of God and for the testimony of Jesus Christ" (1:9) caused him to be exiled to Patmos, a small island located about sixty miles southwest of Ephesus in the Aegean Sea.

The author writes with prophetic authority. Allusions to Old Testament and extrabiblical Jewish literature saturate Revelation, suggesting that the writer is a Jew. Furthermore, striking parallels exist between the Gospel of John and Revelation. Thus, it is extremely likely that both books were written by the same author.

These lines of evidence do not prove that the apostle John wrote Revelation; however, John, who was one of the fiery "Sons of Thunder" (Mark 3:17) in his younger days, is the most likely candidate. The earliest witnesses in church history, such as Justin Martyr in the second century A.D., agreed that the apostle authored Revelation. However, a century later, Dionysius, bishop of Alexandria, determined that the book was written by another John, called "John the Elder." His view was based on differences between the language, style, and thought of Revelation and the more commonly acknowledged writings of John.

Through the ensuing centuries, Dionysius's

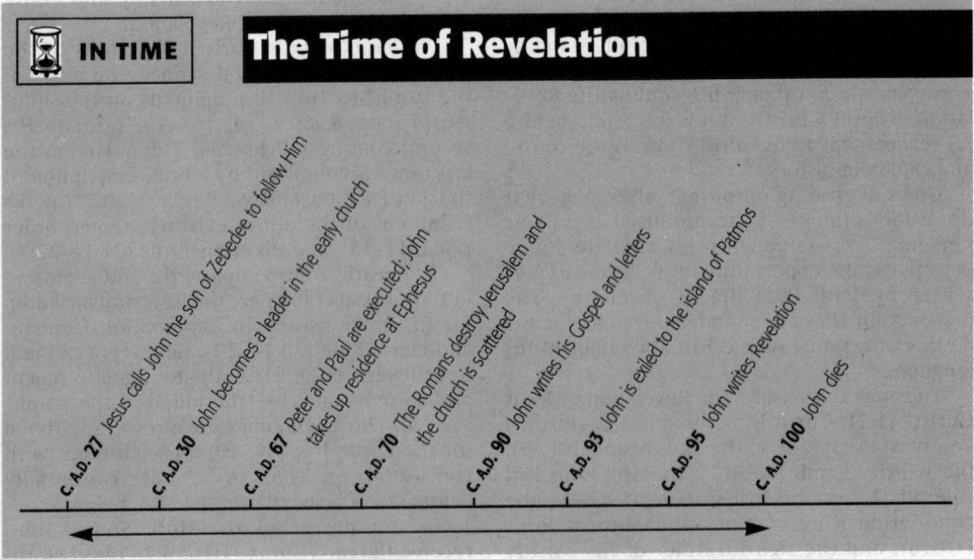

IN TIME **The Time of Revelation**

C. A.D. 27 Jesus calls John the son of Zebedee to follow Him

C. A.D. 30 John becomes a leader in the early church

C. A.D. 67 Peter and Paul are executed; John takes up residence at Ephesus

C. A.D. 70 The Romans destroy Jerusalem and the church is scattered

C. A.D. 90 John writes his Gospel and letters

C. A.D. 93 John is exiled to the island of Patmos

C. A.D. 95 John writes Revelation

C. A.D. 100 John dies

conclusion has attracted some followers, including Martin Luther during the Reformation. Yet the external evidence of history still strongly supports John the son of Zebedee as God's inspired writer of the Revelation of Jesus Christ.

As for the date of its writing, clearly Revelation emerged during a time when Christians were suffering persecution. The dates most widely suggested are an early one, before A.D. 70, and a later one, around A.D. 95.

The strength of the late sixties date rests on the popular myth of that period that the deranged emperor Nero would be revived. This myth parallels much of the imagery of ch. 13. Reference to "the temple of God" and "the altar" (11:1) in Jerusalem, which were both destroyed in A.D. 70, also supports the earlier dating. But the later date, near the end of Domitian's reign as emperor (A.D. 81–96), is more likely. The picture of suffering seen in Revelation seems closer to what is known of the persecution under Domitian. There is also the statement of Irenaeus, in about A.D. 185, that John wrote Revelation "at the close of Domitian's reign." This would be around A.D. 95.

Outline

I. **Introduction 1:1–20**
  A. Prologue 1:1–3
  B. Salutation and doxology 1:4–8
  C. The Son of Man and the churches 1:9–20

II. **Letters to the seven churches of Asia 2:1–3:22**
  A. To the church in Ephesus 2:1–7
  B. To the church in Smyrna 2:8–11
  C. To the church in Pergamos 2:12–17
  D. To the church in Thyatira 2:18–29
  E. To the church in Sardis 3:1–6
  F. To the church in Philadelphia 3:7–13
  G. To the church in Laodicea 3:14–22

III. **Visions of the end of this age and the new heaven and earth 4:1–22:5**
  A. The heavenly throne room, the sealed scroll, and the Lamb 4:1–5:14
    1. The scene around God's throne 4:1–11
    2. The seven-sealed scroll and the triumphant Lamb 5:1–14
  B. The opening of the seven seals of the scroll 6:1–8:1
    1. The first six seals: preparing for the day of God's wrath 6:1–17
    2. Interlude: sealing of the 144,000 7:1–17
    3. The seventh seal: silence in heaven 8:1

  C. The sounding of the seven trumpets announcing judgment 8:2–11:19
    1. The angels, the golden censer, and the prayers of the saints 8:2–5
    2. The first six trumpets: intensifying destruction and woe 8:6–9:21
    3. Interlude: the little scroll and the two witnesses 10:1–11:14
    4. The seventh trumpet: loud voices in heaven 11:15–19
  D. The seven signs and characters before the final judgment 12:1–14:20
    1. The mother of the future Ruler and the dragon 12:1–17
    2. The beasts from the sea and the earth 13:1–18
    3. The Lamb and the 144,000 14:1–5
    4. The climactic proclamation of the gospel 14:6–20
  E. The seven bowls of the wrath of God 15:1–19:5
    1. The seven angels with the bowls 15:1–8
    2. The first six bowls: God's righteous wrath 16:1–16
    3. The seventh bowl: climactic judgment on Babylon 16:17–21
    4. The mother of harlots and the beast 17:1–18
    5. The Fall of Babylon the Great 18:1–19:5
  F. The coming again and reign of the King of kings 19:6–20:15
    1. The announcing for the marriage of the Lamb 19:6–10
    2. The heavenly Ruler's victory over the beast 19:11–21
    3. The millennial reign of Christ 20:1–6
    4. The final rebellion and destiny of Satan 20:7–10
    5. The great white throne judgment 20:11–15
  G. The new heaven and earth and the New Jerusalem 21:1–22:5
    1. The proclaiming of the new eternal state 21:1–8
    2. The glory of New Jerusalem 21:9–27
    3. The river of life and the tree of life: an eternal Eden 22:1–5

IV. **Conclusion 22:6–21**
  A. The assurance of Christ's imminent return 22:6–15
  B. The final offer of the water of life 22:16–19
  C. Benediction 22:20, 21

Commentary

1:1 Revelation (a word meaning "unveiling" or "disclosure") indicates that this book is a type of literature known as *apocalyptic*. The Revelation of **Jesus Christ** can mean it comes from Christ, or is about Him—or in this case most likely both, since He is the subject of the entire book. Christ's **servants** are believers. The phrase **must shortly take place** is an allusion to Dan. 2:28, 29, 45, since *shortly* seems to indicate that the things that must come to pass in the last days will take place in quick succession. **John** (v. 4) is the human writer of Revelation, whereas Jesus is the divine Author.

1:2 The word of God and . . . the testimony of Jesus Christ are the reasons John was exiled to the island of Patmos (v. 9) and are often the reasons Christians are still persecuted today. **All things that he saw** are the visions of the Book of Revelation.

1:3 Blessed, meaning spiritually "happy" from God's perspective, signals the first of seven beatitudes in Revelation (14:13; 16:15; 19:9; 20:6; 22:7, 14). This is the first of many groups of seven throughout the book, a number signifying completeness.

1:4 John addressed Revelation to **seven churches** in the Roman province of **Asia,** which today is southwestern Turkey. The churches fit within a square fifty miles on each side, and their names are given in order going clockwise from the southwest. **Grace** is the Christian version of a common Greek greeting; **peace** is a common Hebrew greeting. **Him who is and who was and who is to come** describes God, who not only exists now, but always has and always will exist (Heb. 13:8). **The seven Spirits** may refer to the angels of the seven churches (chs. 2; 3), to seven other angels (8:2), or to the fullness of the Holy Spirit (Is. 11:2).

1:5 Jesus Christ . . . the firstborn from the dead guarantees the Christian's future resurrection through His own resurrection (1 Cor. 15:20, 23). Though He is the rightful **ruler,** Christ will not fully exert His authority (Matt. 28:18) **over the kings of the earth** until His second coming (19:17–21). At that time, He will establish His kingdom on earth (19:6) and will appoint prepared rulers who will share His sovereignty in submission to Him (2:26, 27; 3:21; 5:10; 20:4; 21:24).

1:6 Kings and priests echoes the description of Israel in Ex. 19:6, a description which is also applied to the church by the title "royal priesthood" in 1 Pet. 2:9. Christ's sacrifice of Himself (v. 5) has set apart believers as royal priests to offer spiritual sacrifices to God (Rom. 8:17; Heb. 3:1, 14; 13:15, 16).

1:7 Coming with clouds recalls Daniel's vision of the Son of Man (Dan. 7:13; Matt. 24:30). Jesus applies Daniel's vision to His glorious second coming (Matt. 24:30; Acts 1:11). **Every eye** indicates that Christ will be universally visible at His second coming, in contrast with His first coming in Bethlehem. The phrase **pierced Him** speaks of Christ's crucifixion (John 19:34) and Zechariah's prophecy that Israel will come to a point of mourning their rejected Messiah (Zech. 12:10; John 19:34, 37). In fact, **all the tribes of the earth will mourn** over Christ and regret their unbelief.

1:8 The Lord God's self-description as **the Alpha and the Omega,** the first and last letters of the Greek alphabet, means He is **Almighty** from **the Beginning** to **the End** of all creation. This knowledge can be a great comfort to a person who is suffering (v. 9). The Lord is sovereignly guiding history toward its consummation, the victory of Christ over all (1 Cor. 15:24–28).

1:9 John strongly identifies with his readers as a **brother and companion in the tribulation,** a tribulation which some were already suffering (2:9, 10). The apostle Paul said there would be many tribulations (Acts 14:22) for the believer before the coming of the **kingdom** (11:15). Such trials develop **patience** and maturity (James 1:2–4) in **Christ.** Enduring trials that come our way is a prerequisite for reigning with Christ (Rom. 8:17; 2 Tim. 2:12). The immediate suffering of John was related to his exile on the small **island** of **Patmos** in the Aegean Sea. Although John had been exiled in an effort to silence **the word of God** and **the testimony of Jesus Christ** (the Greek word translated *testimony* literally means "witness" and is the basis for the English word *martyr*), His witness continued in the writing of Revelation (vv. 1, 2).

1:10 In the Spirit describes John's state of spiritual exaltation as he received the visions of the Apocalypse (4:1, 2).

1:11 The seven churches in the province of Asia each received the whole Book of Revelation, and each received an individual letter from Christ (2:1—3:22).

1:12 The seven golden lampstands represent the seven churches named in v. 11 (v. 20).

1:13 One like the Son of Man is a reference to Dan. 7:13. Comparison of these two passages, along with Jesus' common use of the name Son of Man (Matt. 20:28) for Himself, indicate that Christ is the subject of vv. 12–18. **In the midst** speaks of love and familiarity. Christ was fully man and fully God. The long **garment** and **band** (sash) indicate that the glorified Christ is dressed like a high priest (Ex. 28:4).

1:14 The **white** appearance is parallel to the description of the "Ancient of Days" in Dan. 7:9 and of Christ on the Mount of Transfiguration (Matt. 17:2). The similar descriptions demonstrate the purity and eternality of both God the Father and God the Son. Additionally,

and over their present resting place, which will be emptied and destroyed at the time of the great white throne judgment (20:11–15).

1:19 The phrase **write the things which you have seen** expands and clarifies Christ's earlier command, "What you see, write" (v. 11).

Photo: Religious News Service

The rocky, barren island of Patmos in the Mediterranean Sea—the place where John received the messages from God which he recorded in the Book of Revelation.

overcoming believers will be "clothed in white garments" (3:5; 19:8) in Christ's presence, symbolizing purity. Christ's **eyes like . . . fire** indicate His righteousness, as well as His judgment of everything impure (Dan. 10:6; 1 Cor. 3:13).

1:15 **His feet** of **fine brass** may speak of respect or power, as well as His treading everything underfoot (1 Cor. 15:25).

1:16 The **seven stars** are "the angels of the seven churches," according to v. 20. These probably are literal angels, since it would be unlikely to interpret one symbol by using another. **A sharp two-edged sword** was a fierce long sword. This sword, coming **out** of Christ's **mouth**, is symbolic of the judging power of the Word of God (Is. 49:2; Heb. 4:12).

1:17, 18 When Christ speaks of Himself as **He who lives, and was dead, and** is **alive forevermore,** He is referring to His eternal existence, His becoming a man and dying on the Cross, and His glorified resurrection state. **The keys of Hades and of Death** describes Christ's authority over those who have died physically

"The things which you have seen" apparently refers to the vision of vv. 10–18. **The things which are, and the things which will take place after this** may refer to the present state of the churches in Asia (chs. 2; 3), followed by

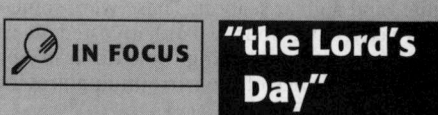

IN FOCUS   **"the Lord's Day"**

(Gk. *kuriakos hemera*) (1:10) Strong's #*2960*; *2250*: This is the only mention of the Lord's Day in the NT. This was most likely the first day of the week, a day on which Christians gathered to worship and celebrate the Lord's Supper (1 Cor. 11:20) because Jesus rose from the dead on that day. The early church father Ignatius seems to allude to "the Lord's Day," as does Irenaeus.

the visions of the future (chs. 4—22). The use of *after this* in combination with the vision of "One like the Son of Man" (v. 13) is an echo of Dan. 2:29, 45.

1:20 The angels of the seven churches have sometimes been understood to be human messengers or ministers. The normal NT meaning of the word *angel,* as in Revelation (v. 1; 5:2), is of spirit beings, who minister to believers (Heb. 1:14). It is not unreasonable to view angels as having authority over and responsibility for churches in the present age. This situation will be reversed in the kingdom of God: believers will judge angels (1 Cor. 6:2, 3). **The seven churches** have the glorified Son of Man in their midst (vv. 12, 13), recalling Christ's promise that "where two or three are gathered together in My name, I am there in the midst of them" (Matt. 18:20).

2:1–3:22 The seven letters are, with minor exceptions, organized in the following general pattern: (1) a description of Christ derived from the vision of ch. 1; (2) a commendation of the congregation; (3) a rebuke for spiritual deficiencies; (4) a correction for what is wrong; and (5) a promise to overcomers. The seven churches were congregations in Asia Minor in John's day. Sometimes they are interpreted as representing seven stages of church history. But this interpretation is unlikely, since there is disagreement among interpreters about what part of Revelation represents which period in history. More likely, these seven assemblies are examples of the kind of churches that exist throughout history (2:7). This means that all seven letters are warnings to every church in every age (2:7).

2:1 The angel of the church is either its guardian angel (Heb. 1:14) in spiritual warfare (Dan. 10:13) or some human leader. **Ephesus** was the most important city in Asia Minor when Revelation was written. It was the center of the worship of Artemis (or Diana; Acts 19:28), the goddess of fertility. It was a strategic commercial center and a great seaport. These were some of the reasons the apostle Paul invested nearly three years in establishing the church in Ephesus and the cities of the surrounding province (Acts 19:10; 20:31).

2:2 I know your works is a phrase that appears in each letter (vv. 9, 13, 19; 3:1, 8, 15), as a statement of recognition from the omniscient, omnipresent Judge.

2:3 persevered . . . patience . . . not become weary: These are qualities that produce character (Rom. 6:3, 4) and maturity (James 1:3, 4), as the believer faces trials and suffering.

2:4 The **first love** of the church may mean first in point of time, or first in importance. The greatest commandment is to "love the Lord your God" (Matt. 22:37, 38). Leaving the *first love* means a great diminishing of the church's initial love, or a turning away from the love of the Lord.

2:5 Remember . . . from where you have fallen speaks of a considerable drop-off of love (v. 4) in the Ephesian church. A generation earlier the same church was commended for love (Eph. 1:15, 16; 6:24), although it was also strongly commanded to grow in love (Eph. 4:2, 15, 16). **Repent** means to change one's thinking. It is clearly connected with changed behavior, as seen in the phrase **and do the first works.** The Ephesian Christians were to regain the lifestyle that they had before they departed from their first love (v. 4). To **remove your lampstand** would be to judge the church **quickly** or immediately.

2:6 Even if the Ephesian church did not love as it should have (v. 4), at least the Lord could positively say, **you hate the deeds of the Nicolaitans.** The Nicolaitans were a heretical group that troubled the churches at Ephesus and Pergamos (v. 15). Apparently their teaching and practice were immoral, perhaps even idolatrous (v. 14). Some church fathers connected this sect with Nicolas, one of the seven elected leaders in the Jerusalem church in Acts 6:5.

2:7 He who has an ear, let him hear is reminiscent of Jesus' warnings to His hearers after giving the parable of the sower (Matt. 13:9). When **the Spirit** of God speaks **to the churches,** it is to represent Christ (v. 2), for He is the Spirit of Christ (Gal. 4:6) who guides believers into all truth, and does not speak on His own authority (John 16:13). The one **who overcomes** is the believer who perseveres in obedience and is victorious in the face of trials. There are three main views about the nature of the *overcomer* in vv. 7, 11, 17, 26; 3:5, 12, 21. The first view is that the promise to the overcomer is experienced by all believers. In other words, all genuine believers are overcomers, and failure to overcome means that there was no true salvation in that person's case. The second view holds that the promises are experienced only by those believers who are faithful and obedient, and failure to overcome means there has been a loss of salvation. The third view is that the promises are experienced only by believers who are faithful and obedient, and failure to overcome means a loss of *rewards,* not salvation (1 Cor. 3:15). None of these is without difficulties, but the correct interpretation would be the one that most consistently handles the details of all seven "overcomer" passages. This means the last view is most likely. Some promises to the overcomer are clearly conditional (i.e., 2:26) and cannot be predicated of all believers. The promise appears to be a reward for doing something that not all believers do. The overcomer is the Christian who overcomes the specific threat to him and his church by his faithful conduct/obedience. If every believer is an "overcomer" the reader would expect the phrase "he who believes" rather than "he who overcomes," which suggests some distinction between believing and overcoming. The singular, "he who overcomes", implies that the victory is made on an individual basis, that not all Christians attain it. "A command that everyone keeps is superfluous and a reward that everyone receives for a virtue that everyone has is nonsense." (Fuller). There is no point in warning Christians about something they will all do. There is no motivation to obey the warnings if every believer receives the "reward." There would be no true reward. Some have argued that the term "he who overcomes" in Revelation 2 and 3 applies to all believers because of its use in 1 John 5:4, 5, where clearly all believers are in view. However, words take their meaning from the situation or context in which they are used. Other than the use of the same word, there is nothing about the context of 1 John 5 that reminds us of the context of Revelation 2 and 3. The context of 1 John 5 is a general promise to all believers without a condition. In Revelation 2 and 3, there are specific warnings and commands tied to the promises. In a general sense, by virtue of their faith, all Christians will overcome and live forever with God (1 John 5). However, not all Christians overcome to the same degree in this life and therefore will not be rewarded equally (Rev. 2 and 3). First John 5:4 and 5 is overcoming by faith in Christ and receiving a gift. Revelation 2 and 3 is overcoming by faithfulness to Christ and receiving a reward. There are two aspects of overcoming for the Christian. By their initial faith in Jesus Christ a believer overcomes by receiving eternal life (1 John 5:4, 5). By continued faith and faithfulness, a believer can overcome specific temptations and tests and receiver an eternal reward. This view seems to best fit the context as will be demonstrated in the notes on each "overcomer" passage. John is telling the Ephesian believers that they have spiritual obstacles to overcome. The problem in the church at Ephesus was a lack of fervent love for Christ. The church is commanded to "repent and do the first works" (v. 5), which suggests a lapse in Christian living. The reward for those who obey is the promise that they will eat of the **tree of life.** Eating of the tree of life is a promise of special intimacy with the Lord, a promise of renewing the fellowship lost before the Fall (22:14; Gen. 2:9; 3:22, 24; Prov. 11:30). The privileged access once denied Adam (Gen. 3:24) will be enjoyed by the overcomer. **Paradise** is the place Jesus told the believing thief he would

go to after his death on a cross (Luke 23:43). Paul uses the term interchangeably with "the third heaven" in 2 Cor. 12:2, 4.

2:8 Smyrna was an important seaport thiry-five miles north of Ephesus. The presence of a Roman imperial cult and a large Jewish population made life difficult for believers in Smyrna. However, the churches of Smyrna and Philadelphia are the only two of the seven not rebuked by Christ in some way.

2:9 Although there will yet be great tribulation (7:14) unparalleled in world history (Matt. 24:21), believers must expect to suffer much

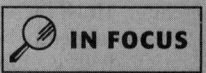

IN FOCUS — **"the tree of life"**

(Gk. *xulon tes zoes*) (2:7; 22:2, 14) Strong's #3586; 2222: The term in Greek denotes "a tree that gives life," that is, eternal life (John 20:31). This tree symbolizes the eternal life God has made available to humankind. The tree of life was present in the Garden of Eden, but its fruit was not eaten because Adam and Eve had fallen into sin (Gen. 2:9; 3:24). Jesus came to earth to restore humankind and to again offer them the tree of life (Rev. 2:7). Those who are in the new paradise, the New Jerusalem, will partake of the tree of life forever (Rev. 22:2).

tribulation even in the present age (Acts 14:22). Christians hindered by **poverty** in this life can take consolation in the fact that they possess great spiritual riches in Christ (Eph. 1:18). **Those who say they are Jews and are not** are either Jewish proselytes or Jews who refuse to believe the scriptural proof that Jesus is the promised Messiah (Rom. 2:28, 29). Calling these Jews **a synagogue of Satan** probably indicates that they were persecuting the believers.

2:10 You will have tribulation ten days has been understood as ten short outbreaks of persecution during the NT era, but more likely it means suffering for ten actual days, or one brief period. **The crown of life** may be the "victory wreath" of the martyr, following the normal Greek use of *crown* for the garland given to winners in athletic events. James 1:12 also promises the crown of life to believers who persevere under trial. Such perseverance will result in the ultimate enjoyment of life in God's kingdom.

2:11 He who overcomes by faith (1 John

...ed not fear the unending torment of ...believer in the lake of fire, **the second ...th** (20:14). Some understand this statement to imply that those believers who do not overcome will be harmed by the lake of fire in the sense that when their works are tried by fire (1 Cor. 3:11–15) they will suffer loss of reward. However, this promise is best understood as a figure of speech where the positive idea is stated by negating its opposite. The second death refers to the experience of eternal death in the lake of fire (20:14, 15). No believer will experience the second death; the overcomer will suffer no loss whatsoever. The believer who is faithful to death is promised the crown of life, a wonderful experience of life in the hereafter. Thus, there is not only deliverance from the second death, but an experience of life to a rich degree (John 10:10).

2:12 Pergamos, the ancient capital of the province of Asia, was said to be the place where parchment was first used. Pergamos means "Citadel" in Greek. It was located fifty miles north of Smyrna and was situated on a high hill dominating the valley below. **The sharp two-edged sword** is the powerful word of Christ's mouth (1:16; Heb. 4:12).

2:13 Satan's throne implies that Satan's authority and power were honored either openly or in effect. **Antipas** (not Herod Antipas) had already suffered martyrdom, thus receiving the promised "crown of life." **Hold fast to My name** may well refer to the Arian controversy, which lasted for over a century and was finally settled in A.D. 325 by the Council of Nicea (southeastern France on the Mediterranean Sea). They did not deny Christ's name, for the essential deity of the Lord Jesus Christ was maintained.

2:14 The doctrine of Balaam is explained from its background in the OT (Num. 22—25; 31). **Balak** hired Balaam to turn the hearts of **Israel** away from the Lord. Apparently, similar seduction was taking place in the church at Pergamos, especially in regard to **idols** and **sexual immorality** (Acts 15:20).

2:15 The doctrine of the Nicolaitans, already seen in the church at Ephesus (v. 6), was apparently similar to that of Balaam (v. 14).

2:16 Repent; or else I will come to you quickly: The church was called upon to exercise its discipline. The coming mentioned is a judicial visitation in speedy judgment according to the Word of God.

2:17 The person who **overcomes** by faith amidst terrible circumstances (vv. 13–15) will receive **hidden manna to eat.** The hidden manna, **white stone,** and **new name** are all prospective rewards for faithfulness to God. The hidden manna recalls the food from heaven that sustained Israel in the wilderness (Ex. 16:4, 14, 15, 31), a portion of which was placed inside the ark as a memorial (Ex. 16:32, 33; Heb. 9:4). Believers in Pergamos were involved in pagan feasts, where they ate food sacrificed to idols and committed sexual immorality (v. 14). The promise, then, is for those who refuse to compromise and partake of the feasts. For them there will be a better banquet in heaven. The hidden manna also suggests special intimacy with Christ (Luke 14:7–11; 22:28–30). Overcomers are promised supernatural sustenance in the resurrected state to enable them to function effectively as co-rulers in Christ's kingdom. In John's day the *white stone* could signify acquittal from legal charges, but it seems best to relate this either to a custom in the Greek athletic games of giving a white stone to the victor in a contest, or to gladiators at the Roman games who had won the admiration of the public and had been allowed to retire from further combat. This symbol of victory over the enemies of God cannot be separated from a *new name*, which identifies the obedient believer in terms of his or her distinctive character.

2:18 Thyatira was a city with a large military detachment about thirty miles southeast of Pergamos. Recognized for its wool and dye industries, the city was also noted for its trade guilds. The description of Christ as having **eyes like a flame** and **feet like fine brass** virtually repeats the wording of Dan. 10:6.

2:19 This church has much evil in it, but Christ looks first at what can be commended. These are the strongest words of commendation addressed to any of the churches. **faith . . . patience . . . works:** Devotion and zeal did exist in the Middle Ages in spite of the apostasy and corruption of the majority. **the last are more than the first:** The darker the night, the more ardent was the company of the godly minority.

2:20 Whether **Jezebel** is an actual name or a nickname, this woman's wicked actions parallel Queen Jezebel's in 1 Kin. 16 and 2 Kin. 9. **Sexual immorality** and **things sacrificed to idols** link the activities of Jezebel to the sins in Pergamos (v. 14). This description is strikingly similar to Babylon, "the great harlot" in Rev. 17:1–6. Behavior in the church can, on occasion, be tragically similar to the enemies of the Lord.

2:21 time to repent . . . she did not repent: In His grace and forbearance God gave this church time to repent. Godly men called upon the church to repent, but she refused to do so. Therefore, there is no call to repent in this letter. Only judgment remains. This church remains apart from the truth of God until she is joined with all the systems of religious evil of the world (compare chs. 18—19).

2:22 A sickbed is where a believer involved in prolonged, unconfessed sin may end up. The next step of God's discipline is death (1 Cor. 11:30). Sin can bring **great tribulation** into an individual believer's life, although this is not the great tribulation that will come upon the world prior to Christ's return (7:14).

2:23 Church members in Thyatira had apparently committed the sin unto **death** (James 5:20). **Death** is the eventual outcome for such sinful **works** (Rom. 6:23).

2:24 The depths of Satan may be the secrets known by those initiated into the things of the devil. There was considerable satanic influence in Asia Minor in John's day (vv. 9, 13; 3:9). Contrast *the depths of Satan* with "the deep things of God" (1 Cor. 2:10).

2:25 hold fast . . . till I come: Since there is no hope that the corrupt church will repent, the godly in her can only look for the coming of the Lord in faithful holding to the truth. The fact that the Thyatira saints are seen to go on to the time of Christ's coming reveals that the church as such goes on beyond its original period in the Middle Ages.

2:26, 27 Note that **he who overcomes** is further identified as the one who **keeps My works until the end.** To this faithful believer Christ promises the privilege of ruling and reigning with Him in His kingdom and sharing in His royal splendor (Luke 16:11; 19:17–19; Rom. 8:17; 2 Tim. 2:12). While all believers share the glory of Christ by being glorified with Him, it seems that not all believers will share His royal splendor with the accompanying privilege of reigning with Him. The words **power over the nations** and the quote from Ps. 2:9, which prophecies the Messiah's all-powerful role, link overcoming believers with the earthly rule of Christ in 20:4, 6. Only those believers who are overcomers and who persevere in obedience to the end of life have the promise of being co-heirs with Christ. He will share His sovereignty

with messianic partners who have proven their trustworthiness in this life by doing the will of God to the end. This is the exalted destiny to which all believers should aspire.

2:28, 29 The morning star is Christ Himself in 22:16. For the overcoming believer, Christ's presence is the light in the dark and difficult times before the dawn of the Son's coming. Moreover, *morning star* refers to the faithful believer's share in the glory or splendor of Christ. Christ gives every faithful believer the privilege of being like Him in royal splendor, to various degrees (Dan. 12:3).

3:1 Sardis, located thirty miles southeast of Thyatira, had been the capital of Lydia. The worship of the Roman Caesar and of Artemis, goddess of fertility, were active here. **The seven Spirits** may be the Holy Spirit, or perhaps seven angels (1:4). **The seven stars** are "the angels of the seven churches" (1:20).

3:2 No one's **works** are completely **perfect before God** (Rom. 3:23). Unbelievers, those whose names are not "written in the Book of Life" (20:15), will be judged solely according to their works (20:12, 13).

3:3 Christ's warning that He will **come** unexpectedly **as a thief** echoes His repeated emphasis in Matt. 24:36—25:13: Be alert and ready for My coming (16:15).

3:4 Those **who have not defiled their garments** are those who have remained faithful to Christ. Unlike some of the believers, they have had victory over sin and have demonstrated a practical righteousness. The Lord promises those who have not defiled their garments that they will **walk with** Him in **white, for they are worthy.** This image probably describes righteous acts, not the imputed righteousness of Christ (19:8).

3:5, 6 The **white garments** probably symbolize the Lord's recognition of godly character and faithful service in this life (v. 4; 6:11; 19:7, 8). White is the color of the garments the

---

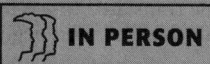 **IN PERSON** | **Jezebel**

The name Jezebel (Rev. 2:20; 1 Kin. 19:1) instantly signified evil for John's readers. King Ahab's wife, Jezebel, left a bad taste in Israel (1 Kin. 16:31; 21:25; 2 Kin. 9:7–10, 22). After her passing, Jews avoided naming their daughters Jezebel.

Here in Rev. 2, a Jezebel is teaching people to worship false gods and encouraging immorality. The pagan religions of the day, including the emperor-worship of the Romans, usually involved idol worship and sometimes included sexual activity.

This Jezebel was no follower of Christ, but a false prophet leading people astray. Yet the believers at Thyatira stood by, watching and tolerating her teaching and promotion of sexual promiscuity in the name of religion.

redeemed will wear in the Lord's presence (7:13, 14). **The Book of Life** is the list of the eternally redeemed (20:12, 15). To not **blot out** is a figure of speech, affirming a positive by negating its opposite. Thus, it means "I will include their names." *Blot out* likely alludes to Ex. 32:32, 33, where God says He will blot out sinners, but not faithful ones like Moses, from His Book. Christ will make sure the faithful believer's name and works are not erased, but remembered and honored. **confess his name before My Father and before His angels:** The text does not state that any believer will have his name blotted out of the Book of Life (Luke 10:20). Rather, the faithful believer will be resoundingly confessed before the saints, the angels, and the Father by the Son (Matt. 10:32, 33; 2 Tim. 2:12). To have the Lord publicly confess one's name is to have the Lord's approval of one's character and service (Matt. 10:32, 33; 1 Tim. 2:12, 13).

3:7 Philadelphia, which means "brotherly love" in Greek, was a small city located about forty miles southeast of Sardis. Its location, vineyards, and wine production made it wealthy and commercially important. **The key of David** represents authority as the One **who opens** and **shuts** the door in the Davidic kingdom (Is. 22:22), a prerogative that is Christ's as the rightful "Son of David" (Matt. 1:1).

3:8 The **door** that **no one can shut** seems, in this context, to be entrance into heaven and "the New Jerusalem" (v. 12, 21, 22). It is possible that the open door is also an opening for witness or service (Col. 4:3). Despite their having **little strength,** the believers at Philadelphia had obediently **kept** Christ's **word** (1:3; Matt. 28:20) and had **not denied** His **name.**

3:9 Those in Philadelphia who ultimately belonged to **Satan,** though they claimed to be **Jews** outwardly (Rom. 2:28, 29), would ultimately be forced to **worship** before the church and to acknowledge that Christ has **loved** His own (20:4, 6).

3:10 Christ's promise to **keep** the believers **from the hour of trial** is most likely a promise that He will remove them before the period of unparalleled tribulation. However, some take this promise to mean that believers will not be removed but rather protected, during the trial. The *hour of trial* is another way of referring to the unparalleled judgment of "the great tribulation" (7:14) predicted in Dan. 12:1; Matt. 24:21.

3:11 The Christian must always be ready for Jesus' **coming** (3:3). Christ's return with expected suddenness is an incentive to persevere in faithful service. Through misconduct one can lose a **crown** that had been previously attained (2 John 8). The crown signifies the royal authority given to the victorious co-heirs of Christ. The judgment seat of Christ will be an occasion of either reward or regret (2 Cor. 5:10).

3:12 Christ promises that the faithful believer will be a **pillar,** the most stable and permanent part of a building. To be a pillar **in the temple** implies a prominent place of service in Christ's kingdom (Is. 22:23; Luke 19:16–19). **He who overcomes:** The overcomer is identified with the names of **God** (signifying His ownership); **the city of God, the New Jerusalem** (citizenship in the heavenly city); and Christ's **new name** (the full revelation of His character). The latter also implies special intimacy (vv. 4, 21; 2:7, 17). The overcomer is associated with the ultimate rulers and the governing center of the universe throughout all eternity (21:9—22:21).

3:13 He who has an ear, let him hear: Openness to the truths of the Word of God is a necessity for understanding the special destiny of the overcoming Christian.

3:14 Laodicea was forty-five miles southeast of Philadelphia and ninety miles east of Ephesus. It was a wealthy city with thriving banks, a textile industry, and a medical school. The city was also known for its sparse water supply. All of these characteristics are played upon in Christ's message to the church (vv. 15–18). References to Christ as the **Amen** (meaning "The True One"), **the Faithful and True Witness,** and **the Beginning** (meaning "The First Place" or "The Ruler") of God's **creation** indicate that the lethargic Laodicean church (vv. 15–18) should pay close attention to His words. The phrase about creation has been interpreted by some to teach that Jesus is the first being that God created. This is certainly not required by Greek grammar, and is contrary to other biblical passages. Christ is described in other passages of the NT as eternal (John 1:1–3) and as being God Himself (John 8:58; Phil. 2:6; Titus 2:13). Revelation speaks of Him as the First and the Last, the Alpha and Omega, the Beginning and the End. In fact, the Greek phrase in this verse can be translated in a more active sense, so as to read "the One who begins the creation of God."

3:15, 16 Cold water is refreshing; **hot** water is useful for medical purposes. **Lukewarm** water is neither. By analogy, the **works** of the Laodicean church made Christ want to **vomit** the believers **out of His mouth.** In very vivid terms, the Lord rejects the halfhearted efforts of self-satisfied Christians.

3:17, 18 The Laodicean church was spiritually self-deluded. Because the church was **wealthy** it assumed that it had **need of nothing,** when in actuality it was spiritually impoverished. The church believed that because it had expensive **garments** it was well-clothed, when it was really spiritually **naked.** It believed that physical sight indicated the ability to **see** spiritually, when it was actually **blind** to spiritual realities. Fortunately, Christ provides spiritual **gold,** heavenly **white garments** (7:13, 14; 19:7, 8), and healing **eye salve** to all who repent (v. 19).

3:19 God's **love** for His children manifests itself in **rebuke** and chastening when they go astray (vv. 15–18). The intent of the Lord's discipline is for our "profit, that we may be partakers of His holiness" (Heb. 12:10). The proper response to God's loving discipline is to **repent** (to change our wrong outlook) and be **zealous** to move away from a dangerous, lukewarm spiritual state (vv. 15, 16). These believers needed to change their perspective and seek the spiritual riches of the ultimate Overcomer.

3:20 I stand at the door and knock pictures the Lord Jesus seeking entrance into His own church (v. 14) for the purpose of renewed fellowship. Though it is often understood as

Christ knocking at the door of an individual unbeliever's heart, the context makes that improbable.

3:21, 22 To him who overcomes: The promises to the faithful Christian reach a climax as the believer shares the actual **throne** with Christ. Those who share Christ's victorious experience on earth will have a victory similar to His. The victory of Christ led to His present position at the right hand of God in heaven, while the victory of believers leads to the privilege of sharing Christ's own earthly throne (2:26, 27; Luke 19:16–19; 2 Tim. 2:12). Jesus Christ **overcame** by humble obedience, even to the point of death (Phil. 2:6–8). As a result, the Lord Jesus **sat down . . . on His throne** and will be highly exalted (Phil. 2:9–11). Just as Christ overcame through faithful obedience, a believer today who overcomes by humble, obedient faith will sit with Christ on His throne (20:4, 6). God's purpose in the church is to raise up co-heirs who will share Christ's authority in His kingdom. These co-heirs must overcome

 **IN COMPARISON**

The Seven Churches of the Apocalypse

	Commendation	Criticism	Instruction	Promise
Ephesus (2:1–7)	Rejects evil, perseveres, has patience	Love for Christ no longer fervent	Do the works you did at first	The tree of life
Smyrna (2:8–11)	Gracefully bears suffering	None	Be faithful until death	The crown of life
Pergamos (2:12–17)	Keeps the faith of Christ	Tolerates immorality, idolatry, and heresies	Repent	Hidden manna and a stone with a new name
Thyatira (2:18–29)	Love, service, faith, patience are greater than at first	Tolerates cult of idolatry and immorality	Judgment coming; keep the faith	Rule over nations and receive morning star
Sardis (3:1–6)	Some have kept the faith	A dead church	Repent; strengthen what remains	Faithful honored and clothed in white
Philadelphia (3:7–13)	Perseveres in the faith, keeps the word of Christ, honors His name	None	Keep the faith	A place in God's presence, a new name, and the New Jerusalem
Laodicea (3:14–22)	None	Indifferent	Be zealous and repent	Share Christ's throne

as Christ did by persevering in the faith despite suffering (Rom. 8:17; 2 Tim. 2:12).

4:1—5:14 This scene in heaven introduces the remainder of the Book of Revelation. Its characteristic movement of focus back and forth between heaven and earth is initiated here with the proclamation that Christ, "the Lamb who was slain" (5:12), is worthy to open the scroll revealing God's plan (5:9), to reign, and to receive the praise of all creatures (5:10, 12, 13, 14).

4:1 This verse signals the beginning of a new section of the Book of Revelation, which reveals the terrifying events that will occur in the future. This is the main section of the Apocalypse, and it continues through 22:5. **Come up here** is also the command given to the two resurrected witnesses in 11:12. Some consider this command to refer to the rapture of the church before "the great tribulation" (7:14; Matt. 24:21). However, it may be simply a phrase in apocalyptic style that introduces John's revelatory vision (v. 2).

4:4 Twenty-four elders occupy other **thrones.** The identity of the elders is not certain. Some think that they represent the church or believers in heaven, but it seems preferable to view the elders as angels who comprise a heavenly ruling council (Jer. 23:18, 22). Authority is invested in those who by reason of age or experience are best qualified to rule. While it may refer to elders who represent the church, it must be noted that the seventieth week of Daniel is about to begin and God is once again dealing with Israel while the church in heaven is for a time out of view. It is also unlikely (logically and sequentially) that the church as the bride would be enthroned before their Lord and husband is recognized as being worthy to rule (5:8, 9). In fact, the church is to share His throne which has yet to be established (3:21). These elders function as ruling priests in the present age. Michael, an angel, is identified as one of these chief princes (Dan. 10:13; Col. 1:16). In contrast, the church is not prepared to rule until 19:7, 8. The

white robes and **crowns of gold** point to those who are confirmed in righteousness and who possess ruling authority. The wearing of the crowns indicates that the elders had already been judged and rewarded.

4:5 Lightnings and **thunderings** reflect the awesome majesty of God and recall the divine authority to judge (6:1; 8:5; 11:19; 14:2; 16:18; 19:6). **Seven Spirits of God** as represented by **seven lamps** presents the fullness of the sevenfold character of the Holy Spirit (Is. 11:2, 3). The seven lamps or torches signify the unique role of the Holy Spirit in executing judgment.

4:6 The **sea of glass, like crystal,** makes the appearance of the heavenly throne room even more awe-inspiring. It will be the "victory stand" for believing martyrs in 15:2. The **four living creatures** are strikingly similar to the cherubim (angels) Ezekiel saw close to God's throne (Ezek. 10:1–20). **Full of eyes** means that these creatures see everything.

4:7 The **lion, calf, man,** and **eagle** have been understood as referring to the four Gospels with their distinctive portrayals of Christ. However, the description recalls the four cherubim in Ezek. 1:4–10, and thus the four figures probably represent four different angels (Ezek. 10). These living creatures or angels seem to be associated with creation and its ultimate redemption.

4:8–11 Rest is a physical necessity of earthly life, but in heaven it is unnecessary. There is constant worship **day** and **night. Holy, holy, holy** recalls the similar heavenly scene in Is. 6:1–10. **Was and is and is to come** speaks of the eternal nature of God, past, present, and future. The elders **cast their crowns before the throne,** symbolizing the willing surrender of their authority in light of the worthiness of God as Creator. Because no one but God can create, He alone should be worshiped and recognized as sovereign.

5:1 A scroll . . . sealed with seven seals cannot be read until all the seals have been

---

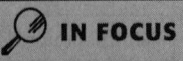 **IN FOCUS** "seven Spirits"

(Gk. *hepta pneumata*) (1:4; 3:1; 4:5; 5:6) Strong's #2033; 4151: This term connotes the "sevenfold Spirit." Since the number *seven* represents completeness, this description of the divine Spirit depicts the sevenfold energy of the Holy Spirit, His perfect, complete, and universal energy. The term *sevenfold* probably corresponds to the earlier reference to the seven churches. The Spirit of God is one in His essence but numerous in His gracious influences. The origin of this expression could have been a popular interpretation of Is. 11:1, 2 in the Greek OT, which was taken as a reference to the sevenfold spiritual blessings.

opened. The scroll apparently contains the judgments and redemption seen in later chapters. It may also be the scroll that was sealed in Dan. 12:4. There appears to be an allusion to the scroll the Lord handed Ezekiel in Ezek. 2:9, 10.

5:2–4 No creature in all of creation was **found worthy to open** the **seals** on the **scroll** in God's hand (v. 1).

5:5, 6 Here we see the consummation of God's twofold purpose in history: to reclaim His kingdom and to redeem His people. This twofold victory over Satan is first predicted in Gen. 3:15 and then covenanted to Abraham in the promise of a land and a Seed (Gen. 12:1–3, Deut. 30:1–5, 2 Sam. 7:12–16).

5:5 The Lion of the tribe of Judah (Gen. 49:8–10) and **the Root of David** (Is. 11:1, 10) are messianic titles for Jesus Christ. **Prevailed** refers to the death and resurrection of Christ on behalf of those who would be redeemed (v. 9).

5:6 The **Lamb** that **had been slain** is Christ, whom John the Baptist called "the Lamb of God who takes away the sin of the world" (John 1:29). How striking that Christ's worthiness is seen by John more in terms of a lowly lamb than a regal lion (5:5)! In the Bible, **horns** stand for power, strength, and the authority to rule (Dan. 7:8, 20, 24). **Sent out into all the earth** indicates that the **Lamb** knows exactly what is going on in the rest of the created realm while He is in the heavenly throne room.

5:7 The reception of the **scroll** from the Father demonstrates that judgment and authority over the earth is committed to the Son (Dan. 7:13, 14). The scroll is likely the same one sealed by Daniel (Dan. 12:9).

5:8 The prayers of the saints (believers) play an important role in the Lamb's opening of the **scroll** and the ensuing judgment (8:1–6). **Golden bowls** are also used to pour out God's wrath on the earth (15:7; 16:1–21).

5:9 The **new song** celebrates the redemptive work of the Son as the basis of His right to judge. Divine rule has its basis in creation (ch. 4) and redemption. Christ is **worthy** to open **the scroll** because He was slain on the Cross, purchasing with His blood believers out of every nation. True authority links both sovereignty and love, might and morality.

5:10 Many claim that the **reign** of the saints **on the earth** is a fancy. It is claimed that it is carnal and Jewish. The saints in heaven, who are made **kings and priests** (1:6), do not so regard it. That reign is not first spoken of in 20:4, because it has been stated in 3:21 in a promise and here in praise (compare Matt. 25:31).

5:11, 12 Innumerable **angels** join the **living creatures** and the **elders** in offering praise to Christ. They have a new appreciation for the loving heart of their Creator and sovereign Lord. They recognize His deserved right to rule and ascribe to Him all the necessary attributes for ruling. **thousands of thousands:** A host that could not be counted.

5:13, 14 Loud sevenfold praise for the Lamb spills over from the heavenly throne room and is joined by **every creature . . . on the earth . . . under the earth . . . in the sea,** as is seen in Pss. 148 and 150. **Blessing and honor and glory and power:** From the vantage point of heaven, these verses look forward to the climactic point when "every tongue should confess that Jesus Christ is Lord" (Phil. 2:11).

6:1–8:1 This section details the opening of the seven seals on the scroll by the Lamb who was found worthy. The scroll cannot be opened and read until all the seals have been broken. Therefore, the narrative of 6:1—8:1 apparently represents events prior to the outpouring of God's judgment contained in the scroll. The unsealing of the scroll follows the general pattern of the signs called "the beginning of sorrows" (Matt. 24:8) in the Olivet Discourse (Matt. 24:1–31). Some think that a number of these events have already taken place or will take place before the tribulation begins. Others think this section describes the beginning of the tribulation period.

6:1, 2 Because the first rider is on a **white horse** and is **conquering,** some take it to be Christ (19:11). If so, His full conquest is considerably delayed (19:11—20:6). Other widely held views are that this is the Antichrist, or a spirit of conquest and delusion (Matt. 24:3–6). The **bow** indicates that the rider is a warrior. The **crown** suggests that he is a ruler. The bow without the arrow could point to peaceful political conquest founded on military might. The emergence of this first rider most likely occurs at the beginning of the seventieth week of Daniel (Dan. 9:25–27).

6:3, 4 The **red** color of the second horse stands for bloodshed, and killing with the **sword,** for war instead of **peace** on **earth** (Matt. 24:6, 7). Man's efforts to effect a lasting peace will be frustrated. Mankind is now introduced to a version of history apart from the influence of the divine restrainer (2 Thess. 2:7, 8).

6:5, 6 The **black horse** apparently symbolizes famine, since the prices for the **wheat** and **barley** are extraordinarily high, as they would be in a time of extreme drought.

6:7, 8 Pale, which means literally "yellowish-green," is the color of a corpse. Thus, it is fitting that the pale **horse** is ridden by a figure named **Death. Hades** follows after Death to claim those who have died. This fourth judgment is the inevitable consequence of the first three. It is the greatest destruction of human life in recorded history. Up to this point, these three are characterized as the sword, famine, and pestilence. They are the same means that God used to bring the nation of Israel to repentance (1 Kin. 8:33–39; 1 Chr. 21:12), and in Revela-

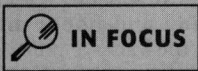

"Hades"

(Gk. *hades*) (6:8; 20:13, 14; Luke 16:23; Acts 2:27, 31) Strong's #86: The Greek term means "the place of the unseen." It designates the invisible world of the dead, as does the Hebrew word *sheol*. All people who die go to Hades because all pass from the visible world to the invisible. The association between death and Hades is therefore a natural one. Unfortunately, this word has often been associated with hell, a place of eternal punishment. But there is a different Greek word for *hell*; it is *gehenna* (Mark 9:43–45). We cannot avoid Hades, but we can avoid hell, by believing in Jesus and receiving eternal life.

tion a godly nucleus does arise as a result of these judgments (7:3–8).

6:9, 10 The fifth seal focuses on martyrs slain for standing for **the word of God** and Christ's **testimony,** the very reasons John was exiled to Patmos (1:9). These martyrs' souls are **under the altar** because sacrificial blood was poured beside the base of the altar in the temple (Ex. 29:12). The martyrs are impatient for the **Lord** to **avenge** their **blood** and to **judge** all **those** who are not among His redeemed (5:9).

This vengeance will not be carried out completely until 19:2.

6:11 Each martyr is **given** the **white robe** of the overcomer (3:5) and told to **rest . . . until** God's appointed time. "Vengeance is mine," says the Lord (Deut. 32:35; Rom. 12:19); it will come in His perfect timing.

6:12, 13 A great earthquake also occurs in 11:13; 16:18. The effects on the **sun, moon,** and **stars** are worded similarly to Matt. 24:29, placing these events in proximity to the coming of the Son of Man (Matt. 24:30). **Late figs** appeared in the winter, the off-season, and were easily blown off the tree.

6:14 The description of the **sky . . . rolled up** could be related to the effects on the sun, moon, and stars (vv. 12, 13). It may also be describing the scene of the Son of Man coming on the clouds of heaven (Matt. 24:30). The moving of **every mountain and island** would cause seismic damage in excess of any recorded earthquake.

6:15–17 Wrath means "anger." God's wrath is presently revealed against unbelievers by letting them go their way and face the consequences of their behavior (Rom. 1:18–32). However, **the great day** of His wrath (Rom. 2:5) is still to come. **Has come** may mean "has taken place" or "has begun." **Who is able to stand** is answered in the surrounding context. Unbelievers, no matter how strong, cannot stand. Those protected by the Lord are enabled to stand, whether on earth (7:1–8) or in God's presence in heaven (7:9–17).

7:1 There are two visions in this chapter: the 144,000 servants of God (vv. 1–8) and the innumerable multitude now in heaven (vv. 9–17). The **four angels** seem to be God's divine agents associated with the judgments. The **four winds** represent destructive forces from every direction.

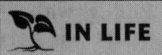

Worship or Wrath?

For some people, Christ makes very little difference in how one looks at life. Faith doesn't really matter. But in Rev. 4—10, John provides us with a peek into the future and the prospect of life or death forever. Clearly, the time we spend on earth is but a brief preamble to something much larger.

This section offers us a bird's-eye view of the coming apocalypse on earth and the promised joy of heaven (Rev. 4:1). The contrasts are severe. Those who embrace Christ and His provision for sin can anticipate a celebration that exceeds their greatest expectations. Those without Christ have cause to tremble for their refusal to accept His offer of deliverance from the wrath to come.

The message is plain: only in Christ is there hope of escaping wrath. That way of escape is offered right now. Waiting to accept Christ's offer only increases the risk of experiencing adverse judgment. It also deprives a person of new life today.

7:2, 3 Before the judgments are unleashed, God prepares to seal 144,000 of His servants **on their foreheads.** Seals are signs of ownership or authority that in ancient times were stamped onto a document by pressing a signet or cylinder into a lump of clay at the point where the document was opened and closed. God has the authority to open whatever seal He wishes (Matt. 27:66) or to place a seal on His child which no one else can break (Eph. 1:13; 4:30). Both perspectives lend confidence and security to a believer. In this case, the seal guarantees their preservation during the tribulation. Their identification as servants in an open fashion (**on their foreheads**) indicates that they are regenerated through faith in Christ and openly confess their faith.

7:4 One hundred and forty-four thousand may be taken either as an actual number or as a number symbolizing completeness (12 x 12 x 1000), referring to all who will be saved. The first option is more likely because of the details developed in vv. 5–8. **The children of Israel** is understood by some as the church, the new Israel (Gal. 6:16), and by others as the nation of Israel.

7:5–8 **Judah** is placed first in this list of the Israelite tribes because Christ, the Messiah, is the "Lion of the tribe of Judah" (5:5; Gen. 49:8–10). **Reuben** is next as Jacob's firstborn (Gen. 49:3, 4). Dan and Ephraim are omitted, perhaps because of their gross idolatry during the period of the judges, demonstrated by the incident in Dan (Judg. 18). **Joseph** and his son **Manasseh** are both included, as is Levi, bringing the number of tribes to twelve.

7:9, 10 The **great multitude,** in addition to praising **God** and **the Lamb** for providing **salvation,** will later glorify God for judging Babylon (19:1–3) and will proclaim "the marriage of the Lamb" (19:6, 7). This multitude of a multinational character might very well represent the evangelistic fruit of the labor of the 144,000 during the seven-year tribulation period. In His anger God will remember mercy. **White robes** may be the garments of overcoming believers (3:5, 18) or of martyrs (6:11). **Palm branches** were typically waved by crowds at victory celebrations (John 12:13).

7:11, 12 The intensifying scene of worship continues in the heavenly throne room (chs. 4; 5) with the added element of **thanksgiving** (7:12), apparently for the "salvation" of the "great multitude" (7:9). Salvation in Christ is something for which to be eternally grateful!

7:13 **One of the elders** (since he is part of the church in heaven, he knows the answer, compare 1 Cor. 13:12) asked John the identity of the great company, evidently to focus attention on their essential nature.

7:14 This vast multitude has **come out of the great tribulation,** referring to "the hour of trial which shall come upon the whole world" (3:10). In view of the great loss of life during this time period, martyrdom is most likely the means of their escape. Tribulation was already being experienced by the church in John's day (2:10; Acts 14:22). However, the great tribulation, predicted in Dan. 12:1, will be of an intensity "such as has not been since the beginning of the world until this time, no, nor ever shall be" (Matt. 24:21). **Washed their robes . . . in the blood of the Lamb** may imply martyrdom, but it more likely refers to forgiveness of sins through faith in Christ and His shed blood (1:5; 5:9).

7:15 The great multitude (v. 9) will **serve** the Lamb **day and night.** The 144,000 are later described as "the ones who follow the Lamb wherever He goes" (14:4). To *serve* indicates priestly service before the Lord (1:6; 5:10). The priesthood of Christians will enter a new phase in the presence of God in heaven. **Temple** actually refers to the inner sanctuary of the temple rather than the outer courts (11:19). The word translated **dwell** means "to live in a tent" or "to tabernacle." This verse echoes John 1:14. Believers who did not see Christ when He lived on this earth in His first coming will go to heaven, where He will dwell **among them.**

7:16, 17 **Shepherd them and lead them to living fountains of waters** recalls Ps. 23. The Lord who is the Shepherd in Ps. 23:1 is equated here with the **Lamb.** Both King David and the great multitude (v. 9) will "dwell in the house of the LORD forever" (Ps. 23:6), with Christ as their pastor. The "living" waters explain why there is no thirst (v. 16). The water of life is freely available to all who will come to Christ by faith (22:17). **God will wipe away every tear** means that there will be no crying, sorrow, or pain in the presence of the Lord.

8:1 **The seventh seal** on the scroll (5:1) is **opened,** finally allowing it to be unrolled. **Silence in heaven for about half an hour** seems to mark a brief but significant break between the unsealing of the scroll (6:1—8:1) and the trumpet judgments (8:6—11:19). This silence is broken only by a heavenly offering and "the prayers of all the saints" (vv. 3, 4). It is, however, the eerie silence before the storm as all of heaven awaits the coming judgment.

8:2 The judgments of the **seven trumpets** unfold in a pattern parallel to the unsealing of the seven-sealed scroll (6:1—8:1). This has led some to conclude that both describe the same time period from different angles, but greatly increased severity of the trumpet judgments makes this unlikely. The sounding of a trumpet had more than one significance in the OT. It was

 **IN DEPTH**   **Revelation as Apocalyptic Literature**

The word *revelation* (1:1) is a translation of the Greek word *apokalupsis,* from which we get the English words *apocalypse* and *apocalyptic.* An apocalypse is a special kind of prophecy. It features what most people associate with prophetic works of all kinds—dramatic, symbolic predictions of the future communicated to a prophet in a vision. The OT contains apocalyptic sections in Daniel, Ezekiel, and Zechariah, which were written around the sixth century B.C. Much of the Book of Revelation is apocalyptic.

Jewish apocalyptic literature outside the Bible flourished from the second century B.C. through at least the first century A.D. In most cases, these works were written to encourage and comfort the Jewish people, who were enduring the hardships of oppressive foreign rule. Some of these works are found in the Apocrypha and the Dead Sea Scrolls.

Because of its many symbols, apocalyptic prophecy is harder to interpret than any other kind of Scripture. Sometimes explicit interpretations (1:20) or an obvious reference to OT imagery or visions interpreted in previous passages (Dan. 7) give strong clues. In other cases, we must guess or infer the meaning. Revelation's four horsemen, the locusts, the dragon, and the beasts have all challenged commentators ever since John first wrote of them.

It helps to remember that like the nonbiblical apocalyptic literature of its day, Revelation's purpose is to comfort and challenge its readers. It affirms God's sovereign control over history and the certainty of His plan for the future. It reminds us that our present difficulties have a connection to the future, a future firmly in God's hands.

Though most of the Book of Revelation is apocalyptic, not all of it is. Revelation also contains straightforward prophecy (1:3) and seven letters of admonition (1:4). As prophecy, it focuses on our present duties and their relationship to the future. As a letter, it gives advice and encouragement to the believers at seven churches (1:4, 11; 2:1–3:22). In the final analysis, the Book of Revelation is a hybrid of apocalypse and prophecy written within the framework of an ancient Greek letter. The purpose of this letter is to inspire us to overcome all obstacles by steadfastly holding on to our faith (2:7, 17, 25, 26; 3:5, 11, 12, 21). The central message of the letter is clear: God is in control of all of history. He is coming back; and He will come in judgment, rewarding those who have remained faithful to Him (22:7, 12, 13, 20).

used to gather the Lord's people (Num. 10:7, 8), to assemble the Lord's army (Num. 10:9), to announce a new king (1 Kin. 1:34–39), and to proclaim the Year of Jubilee (Lev. 25:9). In this context, the sounding of trumpets indicates a declaration of war.

8:2–6 The seven angels who stand before God are likely "the angels of the seven churches" (1:20). The **prayers** of God's **saints** seem to have a part in the judgment of God. The **censer** is a firepan used for burning **incense. The golden altar** reflects the splendor of the heavenly throne room (4:2, 3). *Incense* here may speak of the fragrance of the infinite perfections of Christ that accompanies the prayers of all the saints or is mingled with their prayers. The addition of this incense is necessary to make our prayers acceptable before the throne. In breaking the silence in heaven (v. 1), the prayers of God's people for God to act in just judgment (6:10) are heard and responded to with **noises, thunderings, lightnings, and an earthquake.**

8:7–12 As in the sequence of the first four seals, the angels sound the first four trumpets in rapid succession. But the effects of the trumpet judgments on earth are far more devastating than the seal judgments. **A third** of all **trees** and **grass; a third** of **the sea, the living creatures in the sea,** and **the ships** on the sea; a **third** of all **rivers** and **springs of water;** and apparently **a third** of all daylight and moonlight are affected by the trumpet judgments. The first four judgments seem designed to reverse in part the original creation of God. The Lord initially assaults the environment. Food is destroyed; distribution of goods is crippled; water supply is severely limited; production is cut drastically.

8:7 When **the first angel** sounds the trumpet, a storm of **hail, fire,** and **blood** breaks forth. This incredible blend of destruction and horror sounds like a combination of the imagery of the first (Ex. 7:19, 20) and seventh (Ex. 9:22–25) plagues of God upon Egypt. **A third** here could be figurative for widespread, but not yet complete, destruction.

8:8, 9 A great mountain burning suggests a massive island volcano erupting explosively over a far-flung section of ocean waters. The description of the effects on the sea, however, indicates that this is much more than wind-blown pollution from volcanic ash. The sea becoming **blood** and the **creatures in the sea** dying are like an extension of the first plague on the Egyptians, the turning of the waters of the Nile River into blood (Ex. 7:17–21).

8:10 Star here translates the same term used for the angelic star in 9:1 and for Christ as "the Bright and Morning Star" in 22:16. But the precise meaning of each word must be carefully interpreted in its context. Here the star seems to be a huge asteroid that falls **from heaven** to earth, **burning like a torch** as it enters the atmosphere. The star could fall **on a third of the rivers and . . . springs** by disintegrating as it passes through the earth's atmosphere. It is also possible that the pollution of the headwaters of a number of the world's major rivers and underground water sources could rapidly spread to a third of the planet's waters.

8:11 Wormwood is a plant found in the Middle East, known for its bitter taste. Here and elsewhere (Lam. 3:19) the term is figurative for bitterness. Normally wormwood is not poisonous, but the plague of the third trumpet involves effects far more potent than the taste of this bitter plant: **many men** die **from the water.** Rapid pollution of **a third** of the world's drinking water would set off a chaotic crisis. The Lord will now expose the infidelity of the human heart in an unmistakable fashion (9:21).

8:12 Reference to darkening of the **sun, moon,** and **stars** is reminiscent of the ninth plague upon Egypt (Ex. 10:21, 22), and of the heavenly disturbances involved in Christ's description of His second coming (Matt. 24:29, 30). It is also similar to the phenomena of the sixth seal (6:12). **A third of the day did not shine** could mean that the sun, moon, and stars will not be seen for several hours of the normal cycle of day and night. But probably what is meant is that the intensity of light during the day and night is reduced by a third because of cosmic and atmospheric disturbances (vv. 7, 8, 10).

8:13 Woe, woe, woe refers to the impact of the three **remaining . . . trumpet** judgments on the unbelieving **inhabitants of the earth.** The first woe is the fifth trumpet (9:12); the second woe is the sixth trumpet (11:14). The third woe is said to be "coming quickly" and may be the same as the seventh trumpet (11:15–19), although that is not stated. If not, the final woe may be focused on Babylon, the great harlot, because of the climactic use of "woe" (translated *alas* in 18:10, 16, 19).

9:1 The **star fallen . . . to the earth** may be a demon (v. 11), Satan himself (12:9), or an angel serving God (20:1). It most likely is Satan or one of his subordinates who is given authority to release a vast demonic host which had been imprisoned in the pit. Satan will launch one final massive effort to prevent the establishment of God's kingdom on earth. **The bottomless pit** is the interim jail for some demons (Luke 8:31). It is also the place of origin of the beast (11:7; 17:8). Furthermore, it will be the place where Satan will be imprisoned during Christ's reign (20:2, 3).

9:2 Smoke is an accurate visual description of a huge locust swarm seen at some distance. Since the smoke **arose out of the pit,** the swarm is undoubtedly demonic (11:7).

9:3 Locusts, or grasshoppers, were greatly feared in ancient agricultural societies because they devoured crops. In Ex. 10:12–15, a plague of locusts wiped out what was left of Egypt's crops. Joel 1:2 tells of an invasion of locusts that the Lord used to judge unrepentant Judah, which was a foreshadowing of the day of the Lord. Perhaps that passage is a basis of the imagery in vv. 2–10. **Scorpions** sting with their tails, causing great pain and even death (v. 10). The only point of comparison between the locusts and the scorpions is the "stings in their tails" (v. 10).

9:4 God controls the locusts' actions, causing them to avoid those who **have the seal of God** (7:2–4). Since no **harm** is to be done to **the grass** or **any tree**—just unbelieving people who do not possess the seal of God—these insects are not ordinary locusts (vv. 7–10). A seal is placed on the 144,000 "of all the tribes of the children of Israel" (7:2–4) to protect them during "the great tribulation" (7:14). All those who have believed the gospel of salvation through Jesus Christ are "sealed with the Holy Spirit" (Eph. 1:13) until the final day of redemption and inheritance (Eph. 1:14).

9:5, 6 The **torment** apparently lasts **five months** because that is the life span of a locust. Many unbelieving **men will seek death,** but unsuccessfully. The passage does not say how their death wish is frustrated. However, this time period is an additional opportunity for these unbelievers to repent before the Lord (vv. 20, 21) and to be saved through Christ.

9:7 The phrase **like horses prepared for battle** may be further explained in v. 9 as "like breastplates of iron." If so, this means **the locusts** have some sort of armor. **Crowns . . . like gold** may imply that the locusts have high status among the demons but still rank below their king, Abaddon or Apollyon (v. 11). **faces of men:** The locusts have some humanlike characteristics.

9:8 Hair like women's may refer to the long antennae of insects. **Teeth . . . like lions'** suggests strength and cruelty, a description similar to that of the beast in 13:2.

9:9–11 The organization of the locusts out of the bottomless pit (9:2) under a **king** and wearing crowns themselves (9:7) implies that these may be in a hierarchy like "principalities . . . powers . . . rulers of the darkness of this age" (Eph. 6:12). **The angel of the bottomless pit** is demonic and controls the demonic locusts (vv. 3–10). If this angel serves God, this is another instance where the activity of Satan or his demons is under the Lord's sovereign control (2 Cor. 12:7, 9). The **name** of the angel in **Hebrew** as in **Greek** means "Destruction."

9:12 The first **woe** spoken of in 8:13 is the demonic locust plague that comprises the fifth trumpet (vv. 1–11). This implies that the **two** remaining **woes** are the sixth (vv. 13–21; 11:14) and seventh trumpets (11:15–19).

9:13 The fact that John heard **a voice** instead of a symphony of the voices of all the martyrs (6:9, 10), and a voice of authority instead of an angel's voice (8:3–5), indicates that the speaker is the Lamb who was slain and has redeemed His people (5:9).

9:14–16 The great river Euphrates is the eastern boundary of the land promised to Abraham and his descendants in Gen. 15:18, as well as the geographic area from which powerful enemies like Assyria and Babylon came to invade Israel (Is. 8:5–8). It may represent the seat of Satan's former victory (in the Garden of Eden). The **release** of **the four angels** at the exact **hour and day** is in keeping with apocalyptic literature's portrayal of God's sovereign control of the timing of His plan (Dan. 9:24–27). **The army of . . . two hundred million** will **kill a third of mankind,** under the command or influence of the four angels who were released. A third of humankind could number in the billions. Coupled with the former destruction of one-fourth of humanity, over one-half of the world's population will have been killed. Some hold that *a third* here is merely a stylistic feature of the trumpet judgments (8:7–12). Note also that widespread killing had already visited a fourth of the earth during the opening of the fourth seal (6:8), and many died during the catastrophes of the first three trumpets (8:7–11), further reducing the world population.

9:17–19 Although it is the horsemen for whom the number of two hundred million is given (v. 16), **the horses** they ride and their killing **power** are primarily described. There are similarities between the horses of the sixth trumpet judgment and the locusts shaped "like horses" (v. 7) of the fifth trumpet. The mention of **breastplates** (vv. 9), the comparison with

lions (vv. 8), and the **power** in their **tails** (vv. 5, 10) could suggest that these two passages offer different perspectives on the same demonically inspired force. This is unlikely, however, because the locusts are not given authority to kill (v. 5), but only to torment, while the horses kill **a third of mankind.**

9:20, 21 The rest of mankind who do **not repent** does not include those who "have the seal of God on their foreheads" (v. 4; 7:2–4). The unwillingness to repent despite the incredible devastation of the **plagues** is reminiscent of Pharaoh's attitude toward most of the plagues that came upon Egypt (Ex. 7:22; 9:7). *Repent* here means to change one's mind about ungodly **works,** to stop trusting **demons** and **idols** and to turn to the Lord Jesus Christ in faith (Luke 24:47; Acts 26:20).

10:1–11:14 This section serves as an interlude between the sixth and seventh (11:15–19) trumpet judgments much as Rev. 7 was a parenthesis between the sixth and seventh seals. Again there are two scenes: the little scroll (ch. 10) and the two witnesses (11:1–14), as there were in the first interlude (7:1–8; 7:9–17).

10:1 This **mighty angel** could be the "strong angel" of 5:2 or the angel "having great authority" of 18:1. It is unlikely that this is Michael, who is referred to by name elsewhere (12:7; Dan. 12:1), or Christ, since He is never called an angel in the NT. Furthermore, unlike Christ, this angel comes to earth before the time of tribulation is over.

10:2 The **little book** is not the same as the scroll that was unsealed in 6:1—8:1. It is more likely the scroll eaten by Ezekiel (Ezek. 2:9—3:3), although this scroll causes John's *stomach* to become bitter (vv. 9, 10), not just his spirit (Ezek. 3:14). The angel standing with one **foot on the sea** and the other **on the land** conveys the image of taking possession. A majestic representative of God's throne is intervening in the affairs of the earth.

10:3, 4 The devil and his hordes present themselves as fierce lions (9:8, 17; 1 Pet. 5:8). The victorious **lion** of Judah (5:5) also has an angelic servant who **roars** like a lion. It cannot be known what the **seven thunders uttered** because a heavenly **voice,** perhaps Christ's, commanded John to **seal up** what he had heard (Dan. 12:4, 9). Perhaps the seven thunders constitute absolute justice with no place for mercy and no remembrance of God's covenants with Israel. There will be no total obliteration of Israel, and He will not totally destroy the earth.

10:5, 6 swore by Him who lives forever: Only by the all-powerful authority of the eternal Creator can the mighty angel (v. 1) make the declaration about how and when "the mystery of God would be finished" (v. 7). After the sounding of the seventh trumpet (11:15–19), there will be **no** more **delay** in the unfolding of events leading toward Christ's return (19:11–21). All will happen in rapid-fire order. Delay (Gk. *chronos,* "time") means time prolonging the final outworking of the mystery of God, not delay caused by God arbitrarily putting off the final stanza of earthly history foretold by the prophets (v. 7).

10:7 The mystery of God, truth that has not been previously revealed (Eph. 3:9), will be revealed and **finished** as the events of the final half of the Apocalypse develop. Significant aspects of this mystery have already been revealed through the OT and NT **prophets,** but much remains that will be understood only when the events take place.

10:8–11 As words of judgment, the book would **make** John's **stomach bitter,** in the same way that Ezekiel's spirit had become bitter (Ezek. 3:14). The events of Ezek. 2 and 3 occurred soon before God's judgment on Judah and Jerusalem and were in effect the prophet's commission. John may have sensed a similar commission here to **prophesy** his message of judgment to the world. John's prophecy about **peoples, nations, tongues, and kings** may refer specifically to the remainder of the second woe (11:1–14), since there is a focus on the testimony of the two witnesses. However, the use of similar expressions in 13:7; 14:6; and 17:15 implies that John's commission to prophesy most or all of the Book of Revelation, a prophecy which speaks of all the events leading up to Christ's second coming (19:11–21).

11:1 John is given **a reed like a measuring rod,** much like that used by Ezekiel (Ezek. 40:3, 5) in his vision of the measuring of the temple (Ezek. 40—48). **measure the temple . . . altar:** This is the temple of the tribulation period that will eventually be desecrated (13:14, 15; Dan. 9:27; Luke 21:24; 2 Thess. 2:4). The measuring of **those who worship there** may mean that those who worship the Lord in the temple will be protected, while unbelieving Gentiles will not.

11:2 Luke 21:24 prophesies that **the Gentiles** will **tread the holy city underfoot** until "the times of the Gentiles are fulfilled." Apparently the period of **forty-two months** is the conclusion of "the times of the Gentiles." *Gentiles* here may also be translated "nations" (v. 9; 10:11).

11:3 Forty-two months (v. 2) is the same length of time as **one thousand two hundred**

> *Apparently the period of forty-two months is the conclusion of "the times of the Gentiles."*

. . . **sixty days** (12:6). Almost certainly "a time and times and half a time" (12:14) is also a period of three and a half years made up of forty-two thirty-day lunar months. These expressions draw from the prophecies in Daniel (Dan. 12:6, 7, 11, 12). The **two witnesses** will **prophesy** for 1260 days with astounding **power** (vv. 5, 6). Therefore, it seems that the beast's period of domination (v. 7; 13:5) follows the ministry of the witnesses, each occupying roughly half the tribulation period. The two unnamed witnesses are striking similar to Elijah (vv. 5, 6; 1 Kin. 17; Mal. 4:5) and Moses (v. 6; Ex. 7—11), who appeared together with Christ on the Mount of Transfiguration (Luke 9:29–32). It is also possible that these two witnesses symbolize all faithful believers testifying during the tribulation. **Clothed in sackcloth** means the witnesses are mourning for the unrepentant world to which they prophesy (Matt. 11:21).

11:4 The witnesses are described as **two olive tree** and **two lampstands,** linking them to the vision in Zech. 4 of "the two anointed ones, who stand beside the Lord of the whole earth" (Zech. 4:14). There the two anointed ones are Zerubbabel and Joshua the priest. But the overarching principle for these and all other witnesses for the Lord is that their testimony to the truth is "not by might nor by power, but by My Spirit" (Zech. 4:6).

11:5 Fire coming out of the **mouth** of the two witnesses so that **anyone** who opposes them is **killed** is close to the description of the plague of death brought about by the army of horsemen in 9:16–18. Apparently their ministry is unstoppable for three and one-half years (11:3) until "they finish their testimony" (11:7). The fire is also reminiscent of two of Elijah's miracles (1 Kin. 18; 2 Kin. 1).

11:6 The two witnesses have the authority to prevent **rain** during **the days of their prophecy,** identifying them with Elijah, whose prayer caused it not to rain for three and one-half years (James 5:17). Turning the **waters** into **blood** (Ex. 7:17–21) and striking **the earth** with **plagues** (Ex. 7—11) is reminiscent of Moses in Egypt.

11:7, 8 Finish translates the same word Jesus shouted climactically and triumphantly from the Cross: "It is finished" (John 19:30). **The beast** is allowed to **kill** the two witnesses in the same city where Jesus was put to death. The beast, who emerges as the satanically empowered world ruler in chs. 13; 17, emerges from **the bottomless pit,** as did the demonic locust plague of the fifth trumpet (9:1–10). **The great city** in Revelation is often Babylon (14:8), which possibly represents Rome (1 Pet. 5:13). But the further description **where also our Lord was crucified** seems to refer to Jerusalem. Some see the phrase as symbolic, meaning the sinful world in which Christ was crucified. **Sodom** was the prototype for the moral degeneration of this great city (Gen. 19); **Egypt** was the prototype for its rampant idolatry.

11:9, 10 The peoples, tribes, tongues, and nations are those to whom the gospel witness must continue until "the end of the age" (Matt. 28:19, 20). **Those who dwell on the earth** are those upon whom God's judgment falls (6:10, 8:13). Being **dead** for **three-and-a-half days** recalls the three and one-half year ministry of the witnesses (v. 3). The death of the **two prophets** (v. 7) will set off a global celebration among unbelievers who have hated their message of truth.

11:11 Breath . . . from God entered them recalls Ezekiel's prophecy of the resuscitation of the dry bones (Ezek. 37). Such a public resurrection could cause **great fear** worldwide if it were broadcast by means of modern satellite technology. The entire sequence of events would serve to remind Israel of the ministry of Jesus Christ—His death, resurrection, and ascension.

11:12 Come up here is the same command given to John in 4:1. **Ascended . . . in a cloud** recalls the description of Christ's ascension (Acts 1:9) and Paul's teaching about the Rapture in 1 Thess. 4:17. Some hold that the rapture of the church takes place at this point. But it is difficult to reconcile this description of death and resurrection (11:9–11) with the taking up of living believers (that is, the Rapture).

11:13 In the same hour: Soon after the two witnesses ascend to heaven, **a great earthquake** (6:12) will destroy **a tenth of the city,** resulting in **seven thousand** casualties. Those who survive will be terrified and will glorify God.

11:14 The second woe includes the sixth trumpet (9:12–21) and a second interlude (10:1—11:13). **The third woe** is apparently the seventh trumpet (vv. 15–19), since it is said to be **coming quickly,** and since 8:13 relates the woes to the last three blasts of the trumpet. The final woe may extend further since the word *woe* recurs in 12:12.

11:15 Our Lord . . . shall reign forever anticipates the return of Christ (6:12–17; 19:11–21).

11:16–18 The twenty-four elders were previously seen as continually worshiping God

(4:10, 11) and the Lord Jesus (5:8–10). Here their thanksgiving to the **Lord God Almighty** enters a new phase: they praise God's **power** and **wrath** and the corresponding distribution of **reward** and judgment. This stanza of heavenly thanks seems to reflect on the fulfillment of the great messianic prophecy in Ps. 2.

11:17 Reigned may refer to a present rule in heaven, or to the fact that Christ has already come to earth to subdue the nations (v. 18) by this point. It is also possible that this is a past tense of certainty, signifying a future event as good as done in God's plan for the world. For example, in Rom. 8:30, the believer is said to be *justified* and already *glorified* (past tense), although glorification in fact takes place later, when the Christian comes into Jesus' presence.

11:18 Here God's **wrath has come** (6:16, 17). The wrath of Satan will also be seen in 12:12, but the divine wrath cannot be rivaled (14:19). **The time of the dead** includes the bestowing of rewards upon God's people, His **servants, prophets,** and **saints** (2 Cor. 5:10), and the pronouncement of everlasting judgment on the unbelieving **nations** (Matt. 25:46). This is what the martyrs prayed for in 6:10; it is not completed until 20:12–15. **Those who fear God's name** are those who have responded by faith to "the everlasting gospel" (14:6, 7), possibly including those who feared and glorified God in v. 13.

11:19 The temple of God here is not the one in vv. 1, 2. That earthly temple had an outer court "given to the Gentiles" (v. 2); this temple is **in heaven.** An **ark** of the **covenant** is spoken of here, even though the ark of the covenant made by Moses was probably destroyed by the Babylonians when they looted and burned the temple in Jerusalem (2 Chr. 36:18, 19). The ark represented God's presence, leadership, and protection of Israel in the wilderness (Num. 10:33–36) and in the Promised Land (Josh. 3:3, 15–17). The ark here may represent similar blessings related to the New Covenant and Christ's return (Heb. 9:1, 4, 11, 23–28). It may also look ahead to God's protection of "the woman" who gave birth to the Messiah in "the wilderness" in 12:5, 6, 14. **Lightnings . . . thunderings** proceed from God's throne in heaven (4:5), and were poured out on earth at the beginning of the trumpet judgments (8:5), along with **an earthquake** (8:5), then **hail** (8:7).

12:1 In Revelation a **sign** is a person or event that looks beyond itself to some greater significance. In John's Gospel, each *sign* points to the divinity of Christ (John 2:11). In Revelation, besides the additional **great** signs in **heaven** (v. 3; 15:1), there are demonic signs on earth (13:13, 14; 16:14; 19:20). The **woman**

clothed with the sun is interpreted by some as the church, by others as believing Jews, and by still others as ethnic Israelites. The **garland of twelve stars** is a reference to the twelve tribes of Israel, or perhaps to the twelve apostles (21:12–14). The stars recall Joseph's vision (Gen. 37:9–11), which signified the preeminence of Joseph over his brothers.

12:2 The description of **labor** and **pain** before giving **birth** to the Child who becomes ruler of the nations (v. 5) may speak specifically of Mary, the mother of Jesus (Mic. 5:3; Luke 2:5–7). Later details (vv. 6, 13–17), however, suggest that the woman probably has a broader reference. Since similar imagery is used of Israel in Mic. 4:9, 10, it may picture the Jewish nation or the believing remnant within the nation. In addition, the first prophecy of the Bible, Gen. 3:15, serves as the ultimate backdrop to this struggle between a woman and Satan.

12:3 The **sign** of the **fiery red dragon** is interpreted in v. 9 as Satan, who first appears in Scripture as the serpent in the Garden of Eden (Gen. 3). The imagery is in keeping with OT and extrabiblical usage (Is. 27:1). The dragon with the seven heads and ten horns refers to Satan and the empire over which he rules during the course of time. **Seven heads, ten horns,** and **seven diadems** refer to Satan's (v. 9) brilliance, power, and glory as "god of this age" (2 Cor. 4:4). This description is almost identical to that of the beast from the sea in 13:1.

12:4 The reference to **a third of the stars** may link this event to the earlier trumpet judg-

ments in which *a third* is the characteristic proportion of destruction (8:7), including a "third of the stars" (8:12). However, many understand this reference to speak of the rebellion of a third of the angelic host following Satan. The attempt of **the dragon** to **devour** the newborn Christ **Child** reveals that the strategy of Herod to kill the baby Jesus (Matt. 2:3–16) was satanically inspired.

12:5 The **male Child** who will **rule . . . with a rod of iron** is the messianic figure of Ps. 2:8, 9; however, there is no earthly rule over **all nations** at this point. From the perspective of this heavenly scene, the Child-Ruler is soon **caught up** to the **throne** of God, apparently referring to the ascension of Christ (Acts 1:9).

12:6 The wilderness here is **a place** of protection **prepared by God** (Hos. 2:14) for the woman. The reference to God's feeding the woman in the wilderness recalls the Lord's miraculous provision for Israel in the Sinai wilderness (Ex. 16). **One thousand two hundred and sixty days** is the period of provision and protection for the woman in the wilderness. The detailed way in which this same length of time is expressed ("a time and times and half a time" in v. 14) suggests half of a literal seven-year tribulation period (Dan. 9:27).

12:7, 8 Michael is an archangel (Jude 9). According to Dan. 12:1, he is a special guardian angel for the nation of Israel. Apparently he commands an army of **angels.** Michael and the heavenly forces are victorious, making heaven off-limits to Satan and his demons.

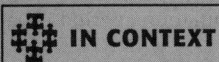 **IN CONTEXT** **Symbolic Pictures of Heavenly Conflict**

The Book of Revelation frequently uses visons, symbols, and images that the first readers would have understood. The vision of the woman clothed with the sun, moon, and stars (Rev. 12:1) portrays the salvation struggle between good and evil.

Throughout the Greco-Roman world people told stories of divine deliverers destined to defeat evil dragons. The dragon tried to slay the newborn deliverer, but the deliverer miraculously survived, grew up, and returned to slay the dragon. In one version of the story, the emperor seems to have claimed to be the dragon-slayer. In Revelation, the wicked emperor is himself a pawn of the dragon, and the true ruler, the Child Jesus, is the One who will triumph over all the world's kingdoms (Rev. 12:5).

The writer of Revelation has interwoven echoes from the OT. The woman with the sun, moon, and twelve stars can be interpreted as Israel (Gen. 37:9), as in some later Jewish traditions about twelve stars. The OT portrays the faithful remnant of Israel as God's virgin bride, in contrast to a portrayal of unfaithful Israel as a prostitute. The OT and the Dead Sea Scrolls portray the righteous remnant of Israel laboring and giving birth to a child, symbolizing the future restoration of God's people (Is. 66:7–10; Mic. 5:3).

In Revelation, the woman's first Child (Rev. 12:2–5) is often interpreted as Jesus and her other "offspring" as Christian believers (12:17). As John wrote to first-century churches in Asia (Rev. 1:4, 11), his imagery of a woman birthing her Child and of conflict with the dragon would have been familiar to his readers.

12:9 The devil's expulsion from heaven **to the earth** means that this world becomes his base of operations, and that his anger is vented toward the remaining inhabitants of the earth (v. 12). Thus, it is likely that the end times will be the greatest period of spiritual warfare (Eph. 6:10–18) in history.

12:10, 11 The heavenly defeat of Satan (vv. 7–9) is followed by reference to his earthly setbacks, including the crucifixion of Christ (**the blood of the Lamb**), the verbal witness of believers (**the word of their testimony**), and the martyrdom of some of the **brethren.** All these events precede the coming of **the kingdom of our God.**

12:12 Those in the **heavens** have good reason to **rejoice,** because of the permanent expulsion of **the devil.** On the other hand, the **earth and the sea** (natural creation) now has an additional **woe** (8:13; 9:12; 11:14) to contend with—the **great** anger of the devil, who **knows** his **time** is **short.** Soon Satan is to be bound in the bottomless pit for a thousand years (20:1–3).

12:13–16 Much of the imagery in these verses seems to be parallel to the Exodus period in which Israel was pursued by Pharaoh and his army (Ex. 14). The later reference to "the song of Moses" (Ex. 15) in Rev. 15:3 lends support to this understanding.

12:13 The defeated earth-bound **dragon** (Satan, 12:9) now angrily **persecuted** the people from whom the Messiah comes, represented by **the woman** who bore the **male** ruler (12:1, 2, 4, 5). This may be ethnic Jewish people, or, if this group is in view in 12:10, 11 (brethren, blood of the lamb, testimony), it must be Jewish believers.

12:14 The **woman** (vv. 1–6) is somehow brought to her place of protection from **the serpent, the wilderness,** as if carried on the **wings of a great eagle.** This is reminiscent of how Israel escaped the Egyptians and came to Mount Sinai (Ex. 19:4; Deut. 32:11, 12). **A time** probably equals one year, so the period of protection here is three and one-half years, which corresponds to the length of the two witnesses' testimony in 11:3. It is also equivalent to the period of the beast's authority ("forty-two months" in 13:5), which includes his ability "to make war with the saints and to overcome them" (13:7; Dan. 7:25; 12:7).

12:15, 16 The danger of the **flood** to the **woman** is averted when **the earth** opens up, perhaps as it did to claim the rebellious Korah and his followers in Num. 16:30–33. There is no way of determining whether this describes an actual flood or figuratively describes the onslaught of Satan against those protected by God.

12:17 **Enraged** by his inability to destroy the **woman,** Satan, **the dragon,** resorts to **war** against a related group. **The rest of her offspring** are believers in Christ, since they **keep the commandments of God** and the **testimony of Jesus Christ.** It is not clear whether they are Jewish believers (physical offspring of the woman) or Gentile believers (spiritual offspring; Gal. 3:29). In desperation, Satan opposes every trace of a biblically oriented faith in Christ.

13:1, 2 The description of the first **beast** (**seven heads . . . ten horns . . . ten crowns**) is very similar to that of the great **dragon** (that is, Satan) in 12:3. Whereas the crowns are on the heads of the dragon, they are on the *horns* of the sea beast. The seven-headed beast may refer to Gentile world power as it relates to Israel, especially in the end times. The heads are identified both as mountains and as rulers (17:9, 10). A mountain is typically a symbol for a kingdom (Dan. 2:34, 35, 44, 45). The seven heads could be Egypt, Assyria, Babylon, Greece, Persia, Rome, and a restored Roman Empire. The ten horns may signify the final form of Gentile world power. The beast receives his **power** and **authority** from the dragon. The parallel to the four beasts (especially the fourth) in Dan. 7 and the explanation of the beast given in 17:8–11 make it seem that the beast symbolizes both a revived Roman Empire, which exercises universal authority, and a specific ruler, whom John calls the "Antichrist" in 1 John 2:18. The **blasphemous name** may be the common claim of ancient Roman emperors to be divine, or blasphemy against the name of the true God (vv. 5, 6) as Daniel predicted of the "willful king" during the tribulation period (Dan. 11:36).

13:3, 4 **One of his heads** may stand for a specific ruler, but more likely it stands for an empire. The unbelieving **world** is enticed (12:9) by Satan to follow and worship the **beast.** Those who **worshiped** the beast also unwittingly worshiped the devil, **who gave authority to the beast.** Any false worship or idolatry is ultimately demonic and satanic (1 Cor. 10:20–22). The beast is worshiped because the world is convinced that no one is **like** him and that no one can successfully **make war** against him.

13:5–7 **Forty-two months** is the duration of the beast's worldwide supremacy, in keeping with the prophecy of Dan. 7:25. He likely gained his full measure of power after killing the two witnesses (11:7) at the end of their three and one-half year ministry (11:3). The two consecutive figures together add up to a total of seven years, the overall length of the tribulation period.

13:6, 7 This first use of the word **tabernacle** in Revelation (15:5; 21:3) may look back to the time when the power and presence of God were undoubted because the glory of God was seen clearly in the wilderness tabernacle. It may also look ahead to the time when God's tabernacle will be among His people in the new heaven and earth (21:3). In the meantime, there is no visible answer to the beast's **blasphemy.** He will appear to be victorious over God's people.

13:8 The Book of Life is the register of those who will receive eternal life, in contrast to those destined to the lake of fire (20:12, 15). Just as it was God's plan before **the world** began that Jesus Christ, the **Lamb** of God, would be **slain** for humanity's sin, so the **names** of believers have been included in the Book of Life from the beginning (17:8).

13:9 If anyone has an ear, let him hear seems to imply that either the following saying (v. 10) or the wider context has significant present application, not just future reference. Therefore, widespread spiritual delusion and blasphemy, as well as persecution and martyrdom, should not surprise believers at any point in history.

13:10 Even when believers face **captivity** or are being **killed,** they can have **patience** and **faith,** knowing that God will vindicate them (Rom. 12:19) on "the day of wrath and . . . righteous judgment" (Rom. 2:5).

13:11 Another means "another of the same kind," speaking of the close relationship between this **beast** from **the earth** and the previous beast that emerged from the sea (v. 1), even though their outward appearance is markedly different. This beast's actions described in vv. 12–17 make it virtually certain that he is the false prophet spoken of in 16:13; 19:20; 20:10. The two beasts may also symbolize the intermingling of secular, political power and religion during the Roman period and during the last days. This is the only place in Revelation where **lamb** does not refer to Christ. The lamb with **two horns** here is an emblem of Jewish worship and religious authority. **Spoke like a dragon** probably indicates that the second beast's message comes from the dragon (Satan), just as the first beast took his power and authority from the dragon (13:2).

13:12–15 Great signs, such as calling **fire** from **heaven** and giving **breath** and speech to the **image** of the first beast, are persuasive. These signs are very similar to those performed by the two witnesses (11:5, 6). The performance of great signs by the power of Satan is part of the mass deception prophesied by Paul in 2 Thess. 2:8, 9.

13:16, 17 The **mark** is equivalent to **the name of the beast** and **the number of his name.** Apparently the mark of the beast is some sort of identifiable proof of ownership and loyalty placed on the **right hand** or the forehead. Since there is no evidence of such a practice in first-century society, this mark is apparently an evil counterfeit of the seal on the foreheads of the servants of God in 7:3; 14:1.

13:18 After the preceding description of the tyranny of **the beast,** an explanatory comment designed to impart **wisdom** and **understanding** to the reader is given. The **number** (the "name" in v. 17) of the beast is **666;** it is also described as **the number of a man.** The beast is merely a man, not a god, as the signs might suggest. The number 6, just short of 7 (the number of completeness), is intensified as 666—the number of the most powerful man who is not God. This man's identity will some day be understood in relation to the number 666. It is a key for identifying the Antichrist.

14:1 Mount Zion is a synonym for the earthly Jerusalem, focusing on the hill where the temple was built. There is some difficulty in deciding whether this is a reference to the earthly or to the heavenly Mount Zion (Heb. 12:22). The **one hundred and forty-four thousand** have God's **name written on their foreheads,** instead of the name of the beast (13:17). In 7:2–4 the protection for this group is referred to as a seal on their foreheads. This is intended to be a contrast to the mark of the beast (13:16, 17), or it may be a sign visible only in heaven and in the new earth and heaven (3:12; 22:4).

14:2, 3 The **new song** is probably the one sung **before** God's **throne** in 5:9, 10. Since that song is about redemption and victory in Christ, apparently only those already in heaven and those **redeemed from the earth,** like the **hundred and forty-four thousand,** are allowed to **learn** it.

14:4 The **virgins** are symbolic of spiritual purity (2 Cor. 11:2). Redeemed believers will not compromise with evil. They will reject false doctrine and refuse to worship the beast. In the NT, the **firstfruits** are the first part of a crop to be gathered, implying a much larger harvest to come later (1 Cor. 16:15). At times, the term emphasizes only the sanctified nature of a sacrifice (James 1:18). Certainly the commitment of

> *The Book of Life is the register of those who will receive eternal life, in contrast to those destined for the lake of fire.*

the 144,000 to God emphasizes that they are holy ones, set apart to God. However, the continuing offer of the gospel (v. 6) and the harvest imagery (v. 15) also implies that many others will come to faith in Jesus Christ (vv. 12, 13).

14:5 The 144,000 were not sinless in their earthly lives (Rom. 3:23), but they were without **deceit** and **fault** with regard to their testimony for Christ. In particular, they did not participate in falsehood, because they rejected the lie of the Antichrist (2 Thess. 2). They were without fault or blemish because they refused the mark of the beast.

14:6, 7 The **angel** who preaches the **gospel** to **every nation, tribe, tongue, and people** helps to fulfill God's promise that the gospel "will be preached in all the world as a witness to all the nations" (Matt. 24:14) before Christ returns. The word *gospel*, which literally means "good news," is used here only in Revelation. Even at this late stage in God's judgment He continues to offer **everlasting** life to the world (John 3:16). The gospel message at this point beseeches unbelievers to **fear God and give glory to Him** and to escape **the hour of His judgment.** Earlier, some people had responded in this manner after the miracle of the two witnesses' resurrection (11:11–13). The activity of this angel may be behind the scenes, prompting a worldwide proclamation of the gospel by those who will declare the truth even at the cost of their lives.

14:8 **Another angel** proclaims part of the bad news of judgment to those among **all nations** (Matt. 28:19) who will not receive the

Good News of the gospel (v. 6). **Babylon** is first mentioned in Revelation here, and it becomes the focus of God's judgment in the following section (chs. 16—18). The **great city** here is Babylon; earlier the phrase was used to describe the city where "our Lord was crucified" (11:8), perhaps meaning Jerusalem in that reference.

14:9–11 **A third angel** announces with a **loud voice** the tragic eternal destiny of the one who rejects the offer of the gospel (vv. 6, 7) and **worships the beast** (ch. 13). In Romans, Paul speaks of the **wrath of God** as being revealed from heaven (Rom. 1:18) against unbelievers, as God allows them to receive the just consequences of their own ungodly behavior. In 6:17, "the great day of His wrath" was announced (11:18). Now it will be experienced in its **full strength** by those who follow the beast. In the just outworking of God's wrath, unbelievers who worship the beast will **be tormented . . . forever and ever,** with **no rest day or night.**

14:12 The **patience of the saints** echoes 13:10, as well as John's place as a partner with his readers in the "patience of Jesus Christ" (1:9). Those who patiently **keep the commandments of God and the faith of Jesus,** even in very difficult times (ch. 13), will receive a special divine blessing (v. 13).

14:13 **Blessed** signals the second of seven beatitudes in Revelation (1:3; 16:15; 19:9; 20:6; 22:7, 14). Six of the seven are clustered in the latter third of the Book of Revelation, perhaps as promises to encourage exemplary Christian response in the extremely difficult circum-

---

 INSIGHT | **Babylon: A Symbol of Evil**

In Revelation, Babylon (Rev. 14:8) probably represents, more than a city, an entire world system in rebellion against God. The OT prophets often prophesied the fall of Babylon, the capital of an empire that destroyed Jerusalem and carried away God's people into captivity. So here Babylon becomes a fitting image for a society that persecutes believers but which God will ultimately destroy.

In the first century, Babylon may have been a code word for Rome, built as it was on seven hills (17:9). Under the Roman emperor Domitian (A.D. 81–96), Christians were severely persecuted, especially for refusing to participate in the cult of emperor worship. Each mention of Babylon in Revelation shows that it is linked with evil and resistance to God.

Historically, Babylon oppressed and captured Judah. In the same way, John's figurative Babylon oppresses the people of God and holds them captive under its mighty grip. History is a war between two cities: "Babylon," the capital of idolatry and oppression, and "Jerusalem," the center of Christ's peace and justice.

John's buildup to the clash of these two titans is epic in scope and drama. The climax comes here in ch. 14, where judgment finally falls on Babylon, and the bowls, plagues, and intoxicating wine of God's wrath are poured out on her. A tremendous tidal wave of evil sloshes back and forth in the passage, like the last great battles of World War II. But the outcome is assured; Christ will prevail.

stances of the end times. **From now on** may mean from the point in the tribulation John is referring to, or from the time John was writing to his original readers. Spiritual **rest** is available to anyone who comes to Jesus Christ in faith (Matt. 11:28). The martyrs under the fifth seal had been told by the Lord to rest "a little while longer" (6:11), until God's plan was complete. Here the believers who have died are also told to rest **from their labors,** in the knowledge that their good **works** will be remembered and rewarded (1 Tim. 5:25).

14:14, 15 The reference to the **Son of Man** with a **golden crown** on His head indicates that the figure is Jesus Christ (1:13; Dan. 7). Some, however, hesitate to make this identification, largely because **another angel** gives the first figure the command to **reap,** which seems improper if "One like the Son of Man" is Christ. Yet there is no impropriety in having a representative of God the Father entrust judgment to the Son of Man (John 5:22). The Son will judge humankind as one who shares human nature. A **sharp** flint or iron **sickle** was the primary tool for an ancient grain **harvest.** Since the 144,000 have been received by God as the firstfruits (v. 4) of His harvest, the rest of the harvest **of the earth** is surely **ripe** for salvation (Matt. 13:37–43), as well as judgment.

14:16 The power of the Son of Man (Jesus Christ) is shown in that, with one **thrust** of **His sickle,** the harvest of **the earth** is **reaped.** This pictures the events of chs. 16—19 as parts of one rapid succession of judgment. Thus, this judgment is experienced by the inhabitants of the entire world.

14:17, 18 Another angel is placed in charge of the harvest of the **clusters** of **grapes** that are also **ripe,** meaning worthy of judgment. The other **angel,** referred to as having **power over fire,** may be the angel at **the altar** in 8:3–5. Perhaps the fire will burn the tares separated in the harvest (Matt. 13:38–43).

14:19, 20 A **winepress** was a trough in which workers **trampled** grapes with their bare feet, causing the juice to flow down into a vat. This common OT sign of God's **wrath** and judgment (Is. 63:3) apparently also explains how "the wine of the wrath of God" (v. 10) is produced. The image of the winepress is symbolic of an unbelievable quantity of shed **blood.** This description of the flow of blood indicates an unparalleled slaughter of life. **One thousand six hundred furlongs** is nearly two hundred miles. This great bloodshed is probably the result of Christ's defeat of the collected human armies (19:17–19) as He returns before "the supper of the great God" (19:17), which some hold to be the Battle of Armageddon (16:16).

15:1 **Another sign** looks back to 12:1, 3,

where the symbolism of the woman and the dragon also appeared **in heaven.** This sign is **great and marvelous,** apparently because it deals with **the seven last plagues** sent by the Lord. The plagues, "the bowls of the wrath of God" (16:1), are much stronger and more widespread than the trumpet judgments in 8:2—11:19. **The wrath of God is complete** with the seven last plagues (15:1—19:5). They are immediately followed by the Second Coming and the marriage supper of the Lamb (19:6–21).

15:2 A **sea of glass** is mentioned in 4:6 as a place of worship before the throne of God. Here it is seen **mingled with fire,** which is often a sign of God's judgment. The fire shows that the wrath of God acting in judgment has reached its zenith. The sea of glass also serves as the Lord's victory stand for all of His overcomers. **Those who have the victory over the beast** are believing martyrs who "did not love their lives to the death" (12:11).

15:3, 4 **The song of Moses** is a reference to Ex. 15:1–18, in which Israel celebrated its deliverance from Egyptian bondage, specifically from Pharaoh's army (Ex. 14). That song, remembering the great OT redemption, was sung by Jews in their Sabbath gatherings, as well as by early Christians at Easter. **The song of the Lamb** compares the completed redemptive work of Jesus Christ with God's deliverance in the Exodus. Perhaps the victorious overcomers in v. 2 are "safe on the other side," and the intensifying judgments of the preceding chapters are comparable to the climactic destruction of Pharaoh's army when the Red Sea closed in upon them. Considering God's **great . . . works** and character, every person should **fear** the Lord and **glorify** His **name** by trusting Jesus Christ. **All nations** is the same phrase found in Matt. 28:19 and Luke 24:47, expressing the scope of the Great Commission, Jesus' command to proclaim Good News to all nations. **Worship** means "to prostrate oneself," calling to mind Paul's description of the time when "every knee should bow" to Jesus Christ, the Lord (Phil. 2:10, 11).

15:5 **The temple of the tabernacle** links the powerful imagery of the heavenly temple in 11:19 with the strong parallels in ch. 15 to the Exodus period, when the majestic presence of God was clearly seen in the tabernacle. The tabernacle **of the testimony** calls attention to the Law or the tablets of testimony given to Moses (Ex. 31:18; 32:15). In the new heaven and new earth the tabernacle of God will be with believers because He will dwell eternally with them (21:3).

15:6 **Seven angels** come forward to administer the **seven plagues,** which are the last plagues (v. 1) God will send forth before Christ returns. **clothed in pure bright linen . . . golden bands:** Because their garments signify purity and righteousness, the angels are representatives of spotless justice.

15:7 The **golden bowls** of wrath recall the similar golden bowls that in 5:8 hold incense, representing the prayers of the saints.

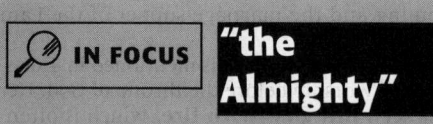

IN FOCUS   "the Almighty"

(Gk. *pantokrator*) (4:8; 11:17; 15:3; 16:7, 14; 19:6, 15; 21:22; 2 Cor. 6:18) Strong's #3841: The Greek word means "one who has power over everything"—in other words, the One in total control. God commands all the hosts of powers in heaven and earth, and He is able to overcome all His foes. The title Almighty occurs often in Revelation as this book unveils God's awesome control over all the universe and throughout all history.

15:8 The **smoke** that **filled** the **temple** had its source in the power and glory of God and prohibited access into the most holy place. The smoke signified God's resolve to act in judgment as an expression of His character and authority. Judgment was now irreversible, with no place for intercession (Lam. 3:44).

16:1 The **loud voice from the temple** is likely the voice of God, since no other heavenly being could enter the heavenly temple "till the seven plagues of the seven angels were completed" (15:8).

16:2 The effect of the **first . . . bowl** being **poured out** is a terrible **sore** upon all **who had the mark of the beast** (13:16, 17). The Egyptians faced a similar affliction during the sixth plague of the Exodus (Ex. 9:9–11). Just as God's great power could not be denied by the Egyptians and their magicians (Ex. 9:11), so unbelieving people will be unable to deny God's sovereign justice as the bowls of God's judgments rapidly progress (vv. 9, 11, 21).

16:3 The **second . . . bowl** turns the **sea** into **blood**, as did the second trumpet (8:8). However, only a third of the sea was affected by the trumpet (8:8, 9). This bowl brings about the death of **every living creature** in the sea. This verse is similar to Ex. 7:17–21, in which the Nile River is turned to blood; however, the judgment here is infinitely worse because of its global scope.

16:4 The **third . . . bowl,** like the third trumpet (8:10), targets **the rivers and springs of water.** This time, however, the impact is worldwide (compare 8:10, 11), and the water sources turn to **blood** instead of just becoming "bitter" (8:11).

16:5 The **angel of the waters** is probably the same angel who poured out the third bowl (v. 4), and not a separate figure. Because God is eternally **righteous,** His judgment of the inhabitants of the earth (v. 10) and their violent, unrighteous works is completely just.

16:6 God forces the unrepentant (v. 9) unbelievers who **have shed the blood** of God's people to **drink** blood in order to avenge the deaths of the martyrs, as some of them requested in 6:10. **Saints** refers to those who are set apart because of their relationship with Jesus Christ. In Revelation, saints may be Christians in general (5:8), or those believers facing persecution and martyrdom (13:7). **Prophets** may refer to all of God's spokesmen who have been killed as a result of persecution, or specifically to the two witnesses who prophesied for three and one-half years (11:3–13, 18).

16:7 In 6:9, 10 the martyred saints cried out for God to show His righteousness by judging the wicked. Because God is now doing that, they affirm that His judgment is **true** and **righteous.**

16:8 The **fourth . . . bowl** is reminiscent of the fourth trumpet in its effect on the **sun** (8:12). But in this plague, the sun's heat is intensified instead of diminished.

16:9 Those who followed the beast here blaspheme **the name of God,** just as the beast himself did (13:5, 6). They cannot argue against the existence or **power** of God, but even so they will **not repent and give** God **glory** (v. 11, 21). The Good News of Christ is still in effect even just before His return (19:11–21), though it is apparently rejected by all unbelievers who are still alive.

16:10, 11 The **fifth . . . bowl** is focused against the **throne of the beast,** apparently referring to his worldwide **kingdom** and authority (13:7). The phrase "Satan's throne" is used in 2:13 to speak of the satanic foothold in Pergamos as a result of the prevalence of emperor worship there. (All other uses of *throne* in Revelation refer to the Lord's throne.) The **darkness** in 6:12–17 caused even world leaders to fear "the wrath of the Lamb" (6:16). At this late date, the beast and his followers still blaspheme **the God of heaven** and refuse to **repent of their deeds. Pains** and **sores** may be roughly parallel to the torment suffered by those stung by the demonic locusts during the fifth trumpet judgment (9:5–10). However, it is more likely that *pains* refers to the scorching by

---

🔍 **IN FOCUS**   **"Armageddon"**

(Gk. *armageddon*) (16:16) Strong's #717: This Greek term, which appears only here in the NT, appears to be derived from the word *har,* which means a mountain, and the word *Megiddo,* a name of a city in Manasseh. In this area, God overthrew the Canaanite kings by miraculously aiding Deborah and Barak (Judg. 4). Josiah, the ally of Babylon, was also defeated and slain here. The name Megiddo comes from a Hebrew root meaning to "cut off" and thus means "slaughter" (Joel 3:2, 12, 14). Just the mention of the famous battleground of Armageddon to a Jew would suggest a horrific slaughter.

---

the sun in vv. 8, 9 and *sores* to the effects of the first bowl (v. 2).

16:12–14 The sixth bowl involves the Euphrates River, as does the sixth trumpet (9:14). Both judgments deal with demonically inspired military forces. The army of two hundred million (9:16) will kill a third of all humankind (9:18); the army in vv. 12–14 will do battle against God (19:19–21).

16:12 With the **water** of the **river Euphrates** completely **dried up,** invasion from the east would be much easier. **The kings from the east** have been understood as the Parthian armies that menaced the eastern half of the Roman Empire, though any powerful force from Asia would fit the wording of this verse.

16:13, 14 **Unclean spirits** spread forth the authoritative words of **the dragon** (Satan; 12:9), **the beast,** and **the false prophet**—an unholy trinity. There will be great deception involved in the **signs** (13:13, 14) that are used to persuade **the kings of . . . the whole world** to gather for battle against **God.** In 6:15, 16, the kings of the earth recoil in fear before the judgment of the Lamb. Here the kings are willing to wage war against God. The difference seems to be their confidence in the power of the beast, since they reason, "Who is able to make war with him?" (13:4). **The battle of that great day** takes place at Armageddon (v. 16; 19:17–21).

16:15 **Blessed** indicates that this is the third of seven beatitudes in Revelation (1:3; 14:13; 19:9; 20:6; 22:7, 14). **Coming as a thief** looks back to Jesus' warning to believers to be vigilant because of the unexpected timing of His return (Matt. 24:43, 44).

16:16 The **place** of the battle spoken of in v. 14 is **Armageddon,** a Hebrew word meaning "Mount of Megiddo." Some believe that this is not an actual place, but rather a symbol of the final battle between good and evil.

16:17 The **seventh . . . bowl** is the climax of all of Revelation's judgments. **It is done:** This is God's final act of judgment before Christ comes.

16:18 **A great earthquake as had not occurred** before goes well beyond the great seismological damage throughout history and the earlier earthquakes in Rev. 6:12; 8:5; 11:13; and 11:19.

16:19, 20 **The great city** of **Babylon** (11:8) seems to be the epicenter of the most destructive earthquake the world will ever see. The quake seems to be worldwide, wreaking havoc on **the cities of the nations.** Babylon had not been forgotten **before God.** Here He acts on His earlier promise that Babylon would fall (14:8) and that the **cup** of His **wrath** would be dispensed (14:10). Babylon here may refer to the rebuilt ancient city, or it may be a symbolic name for Rome (17:9). It may also be a way of referring to any proud human society that attempts to exist apart from God. Babylon's classic manifestations of rebellion against God are the Tower of Babel (Gen. 11:1–9) and the Babylonian Empire under Nebuchadnezzar (Dan. 4:30).

16:21 **Hail** falling **from heaven,** with each stone weighing about seventy-five pounds (a **talent**), would be phenomenally destructive. Still, unbelievers **blasphemed** against **God** instead of repenting (16:9, 11). Apparently by this point, their hearts are so hardened they will not respond properly to the Lord no matter what His display of power and judgment.

17:1, 2 The reference to **one of the seven angels who had the seven bowls** marks this passage as a continuation of 16:17–21. The coming reference to "BABYLON THE GREAT" (v. 5) has the same linking effect. **Many waters** are interpreted in v. 15 as "peoples, multitudes, nations, and tongues." Although Babylon is only called the **harlot** in vv. 1, 5, 16, and 19:2, her habitual **fornication** was introduced in 14:8, as was her imminent and well-deserved **judgment.** Both the **kings of the earth** and the **inhabitants of the earth** are seduced into committing spiritual adultery with Babylon. The indication is that she made them **drunk with** power, material possessions, false worship, and pride. The **wine** of Babylon's fornication (14:8) is judged forcefully and finally by God in "the wine of the fierceness of His wrath" (16:19).

17:3 In the Spirit describes John's spiritually exalted state as he receives the various visions of the Book of Revelation (1:10). **The wilderness** is where the **woman** identified as

may imply that Babylon is ultimately subordinate to the beast (13:16, 17). **MYSTERY** may be the first part of the title for **BABYLON THE GREAT.** But based on the use of the word *mystery* in v. 7, this verse should probably read, "on her forehead a mysterious name was

The ruins of the ancient city of Babylon are testimony to the destruction of this pagan city described in the Book of Revelation (Rev. 16:19).

"Babylon, the mother of harlots" (v. 5) is seen sitting on a **scarlet beast** (12:3; 13:1). Since this woman normally "sits on many waters" (v. 1) and since the woman who gave birth to the Child-Ruler fled into the wilderness as a place of protection (12:6, 14), perhaps Babylon here is seen as being in league with the dragon and the beast as they ferociously pursue God's people (12:13–16). The description of the scarlet beast clearly identifies him with the beast from the sea—the Antichrist—in 13:1, 5, 6. The *ten horns* are interpreted in v. 12 as ten kings; they may represent the ten toes of Nebuchadnezzar's vision (Dan. 2:41).

17:4 The **woman**, Babylon, is dressed like a queen (18:7), wearing **purple, scarlet, gold,** and **pearls.** Though the appearance of "the great harlot" (vv. 1, 5) is regal, her royal **golden cup** is **full of abominations and . . . filthiness,** speaking of idolatry and unclean acts that disgust God. This description is given first from the standpoint of people, who look at the outer appearance, and then from the perspective of God, who knows the heart (1 Sam. 16:7).

17:5 The **name** on Babylon's **forehead**

written." The title itself suggests that all spiritual harlotry and abominable acts in history are somehow the offspring of Babylon.

17:6 The woman Babylon is **drunk with the blood of the saints** and Christian **martyrs** (Matt. 24:21), as well as by "the wine of her fornication" (v. 2). Thus, her actions are doubly repugnant to the Lord, as are the acts of anyone who persecutes God's people. The woman's hatred of Christianity is clearly portrayed in this verse. Being drunk from saints' blood implies a time of extraordinary slaughter.

17:7 What the apostle John saw still needed to be explained to him in its details. Since the disclosure was granted him, not to perplex but to instruct him, the angel (compare v. 1) promises to clarify **the mystery of the woman and of the beast.**

17:8 The description of **the beast** as one who **was, and is not, and will ascend . . . and go to perdition** is a conscious contrast to the description of God in 1:4, 8. *Was* apparently indicates that the beast had been manifested in the past (Dan. 7). *Is not* suggests that the beast was not working his evil in John's day. *Will*

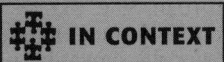 **IN CONTEXT** | **The Sinful City and the Antichrist**

The great harlot, identified with Babylon (Rev. 17:5), is a powerful and wealthy center of human civilization that leads the kings and all the earth in rebellion against God. As ancient Babylon led people away from God and into idolatry and wickedness, so the harlot sets the nations against Him. Rome in the first century may have been one manifestation of the harlot; the "seven mountains" (17:9) could recall the original city of Rome that was built on seven hills.

Other societies and governments in human history have also seemed to be in open rebellion against God. This great harlot is empowered by the beast, the Antichrist. The church, by contrast, is likened to a wife united with her Husband, Christ, at His return (19:7, 8). John's vision continues as the beast and his armies prepare for a battle that cannot be won. Christ has already secured the victory. The beast and his prophet are captured, and his armies are destroyed by the sword from Christ's mouth (19:15).

ascend . . . to perdition suggests eternal ruin or punishment. Those **whose names are not written in the Book of Life** (13:8; 20:12, 15) are deceived by the beast because they do not know its certain eternal destiny. All they **see** is one who once existed and has now made an incredible reemergence.

17:9, 10 The mind which has wisdom possesses divinely aided spiritual understanding, which is a mind receptive to God's truth (1:3). The clause may possibly be connected with v. 8 rather than v. 9, and may refer specifically to wisdom in understanding who the beast is. It may also refer to the following verses, the interpretation of the heads, the beast, the horns, and **the woman** (vv. 1–6). The **seven heads** of the beast (v. 3) symbolize both **seven mountains** and **seven kings.** Since the word *mountains* also means "hills" in Revelation (14:1), most interpreters understand this as referring to the seven hills along the Tiber River, a well-known designation of the city of Rome. However, *seven mountains* may also refer to successive world empires, since mountains are typically symbols of earthly kingdoms or empires (Ps. 30:7; Jer. 51:25; Dan. 2:44, 45). According to this view, **five** would be past kingdoms (perhaps Egypt, Assyria, Babylon, Medo-Persia, and Greece), with sixth being the Roman Empire and seventh another which **has not yet come.** Perhaps it is to be a revived Roman Empire. *Kings* may refer to Roman emperors, but this is unlikely since more than five had reigned before the writing of Revelation.

17:11, 12 The beast . . . is . . . the eighth, and is of the seven: The beast is related to the seventh king, but also has a separate identity. The obscure wording may express the worldwide amazement that the beast was healed from a deadly wound to rule the world again (13:3). It seems that the eighth world empire is some form of a revived Roman Empire over which the Antichrist establishes the imperial authority of a dictator. He will overcome three horns, or nations (Dan. 7:20), and will claim universal authority. **one hour:** A limited time is allotted to the **ten kings,** or **ten horns** (1:3; Dan. 2:34, 41, 42), who will **receive authority** to rule alongside **the beast** (18:10, 17, 19). The Lord's sovereignty is not threatened in these statements of sequence and duration because the beast cannot change the fact that he, because of God's just judgment, **is going to perdition.** The time frame for these events may coincide with 16:14, in which the preparations for the battle at Armageddon are described.

17:13 The ten kings who ultimately rule under the authority of the beast (v. 12) cooperate fully and **give** back **their power and authority to the beast.** Some understand these ten rulers to be provincial heads in the Roman Empire in John's day, while others take *ten* symbolically to mean a host of national powers aligned with the beast. Still others see a ten-nation confederacy, perhaps a revived latter-day Roman Empire (Dan. 7:7, 19, 20, 23, 24).

17:14 The ten kings in league with the beast will be so bold as to **make war** against **the Lamb** (Christ). He, the all-powerful **Lord of lords and King of kings** (19:16), will easily **overcome them** at His second coming (19:19–21). This wording is in direct contrast with 13:7, where the beast and his forces are allowed by God "to make war with the saints and to overcome them." Many of those whom the beast defeated and even killed are now numbered in the conquering army of the Lamb. The Lord's army is composed of the **called, chosen, and faithful**—probably the heavenly soldiers of 19:14.

17:15 The waters of 17:1 are interpreted as all the peoples and nations of the world.

17:16, 17 The ten horns (the kings of v. 12) will grow to hate Babylon, the harlot. As a result, they will expose and then utterly destroy her. Since this description is similar to God's judgment on Babylon in 18:8, it seems that the Lord sovereignly uses the forces of the beast as His instrument of judgment on the kingdom of Antichrist (ch. 18) before they themselves are destroyed (19:19–21). With the advent of the beast as a supreme ruler given to self-deification (Dan. 11:36; Matt. 24:15; 2 Thess. 2), Satan has originated an entirely new order. This order is so radically different from the great harlot, that the beast, or perhaps the political aspect of Babylon, turns upon and destroys the religious aspect of Babylon.

17:18 The woman in John's vision (vv. 1–6) is the great city Babylon (16:19), yet is also the ancient "mother of harlots" (v. 5). Thus, the satanic influence of this city over the world's leaders has continued from Babel through Babylon to Rome (v. 9, 10), its classic manifestation in the first century A.D.[NSB]

18:1 The angel which John now saw had great (divine) authority, not just short-term authority like the ten horns and the Beast (17:12, 13). In coming from the glorious abode of God, this angel still reflects the Lord's glory upon the earth (15:8), perhaps much as Moses' face shone with God's glory after being in His presence (2 Cor. 3:7–11).

18:2 Babylon . . . is fallen continues the thought introduced in 14:8 and 16:19, describing the city's destruction. The normal dwelling place of demons is the bottomless pit (9:1, 2). A prison is a place of banishment. Thus, Babylon, in the wake of her fall and judgment, will become a virtual hell on earth.

18:3 This unparalleled judgment from God has come because of Babylon's spiritual fornication (idolatry and abominations; 17:4) with the nations and their kings, largely through rich commerce, providing many merchants an abundance of wealth.

18:4, 5 Come out . . . my people is a command that echoes Is. 52:11 and especially Jer. 51:45, prophecies proclaimed at a time when the Babylonian Empire was ripe for judgment.

18:6–8 God will avenge Babylon's long history of iniquities and sinful works to the fullest extent and beyond (double; Is. 51:19). Instead of glorifying God, Babylon glorified herself (14:7; Rom. 1:21) with a royal lifestyle. She had thrived on pleasure and excess, but now judgment will leave her with only torment and sorrow. The climactic judgment of ancient Babylon also arrived in one day ("one hour" in

vv. 10, 17, 19), as Darius the Mede invaded the city and killed Belshazzar (Dan. 5:30, 31).

18:9–19 This section is framed like an ancient lament and is especially similar in content to Ezekiel's lament over the destruction of Tyre (Ezek. 27).

18:9, 10 The world's kings, the illicit partners of Babylon, will see her burning and weep out loud, probably as much for their loss as hers. They will, however, stay at a distance (v. 15) to escape her torment.

18:11–13 The merchandise includes purple, an expensive dye; citron wood, valuable material for cabinet making; and fragrant oil (literally "myrrh") and frankincense, both of which the wise men gave as gifts to the infant Jesus (Matt. 2:11). Bodies and souls refers to the slave trade.

18:14–16 clothed . . . adorned: The description of wealthy Babylon is almost identical to that of the harlot Babylon in 17:4.

18:17–19 Those who make their living from trade on the sea also lament the judgment and burning by which Babylon is made desolate. They throw dust on their heads in an expression of great sorrow, which is also seen in Ezek. 27:30 in the lament over Tyre.

18:20 This call to rejoice is a compressed introduction to the longer praise hymn in 19:1–5. Judgment for killing God's prophets is mentioned in 16:6, but this is the only place in Revelation other than 21:14 where Christ's apostles are mentioned. If specific apostles are in mind here, Peter and Paul's deaths at the hands of the state in Rome probably apply here. If Babylon is the symbol of all the enemies of God and His people, and not just the Babylonian or Roman manifestations, even the killing of James in Acts 12:1, 2 is being avenged here.

18:21, 22 The concluding lament over the fall of the great city Babylon comes from an angel powerful enough to hurl a huge millstone weighing thousands of pounds into the sea as an illustration of the swiftness and violence of Babylon's judgment.

18:23 From this point on in Revelation, the voice of bridegroom and bride is heard only in regard to "the marriage of the Lamb" (19:7–9) and the New Jerusalem, "a bride adorned for her husband" (21:2). Sorcery (literally "magic arts") is used in 9:21 to refer to the sins of humankind at large. Perhaps Babylon's influence is seen as corrupting all the nations.

18:24 The blood of the slain seem to refer to all the martyrs for the cause of Christ throughout history (6:10; 17:6). However, it may refer specifically to those who were slain during the tribulation, particularly during the beast's reign (13:7, 15).

19:1 The great multitude here is the

"great multitude which no one could number" in 7:9. The reference to **salvation** (7:10) and the later reference to the twenty-four elders and four living creatures (v. 4; 7:11, 13) seem to support this understanding. However, some contend that *multitude* here refers to angels. **Alleluia** represents the Hebrew word meaning "praise the LORD." The Hebrew word is well known in the OT from its frequent use in the Psalms ("praise the LORD" in Ps. 150:1, 6). The Greek transliteration of it appears in the NT only in Revelation (vv. 1, 3, 4, 6).

19:2 God has proven **true** to His Word (6:10) and **righteous** in His just **judgments** (16:5, 6) upon Babylon, **the great harlot** (17:1, 5, 6). All Christians are God's **servants** (1:1), but some of these **servants** have died as martyrs. All can look forward to serving God forever (22:3).

19:3 Alleluia: God is praised because evidence of Babylon's just judgment will continue eternally.

19:4 The twenty-four elders and the four living creatures constantly worship **God** (4:2–11; 5:8–14; 11:16; 14:3). The representatives of the angelic realm praise the Lord for the destruction of the system that originated in a fallen angel, Satan.

19:5 With so much praise and adoration filling the scene, one would not expect further summons to praise and extol God. But even after the third "Alleluia," it must be stressed that God is worthy of nothing less than eternal **praise.** All God's bondservants, of whatever rank or position, **both small and great,** are included in the invitation to praise Him; for the word of invitation comes from the seat of God's government.

19:6 sound of many waters: Now a heavenly multitude. The **Lord God Omnipotent** enters His reign after the destruction of sin and the Antichrist (vv. 11–21). **Reigns** is a Greek aorist tense, normally translated "reigned." But here it more likely means "is beginning to reign." An entirely new and different government is coming, not a democracy, but a theocracy—a government by God when the "Lord God Omnipotent" shall reign in righteousness (Is. 11).

19:7 Here the Lord is glorified specifically because **the marriage of the Lamb has come** at last. In both the OT (Hos. 2:19, 20) and the NT (Eph. 5:23, 32), God's people are viewed as the Lord's betrothed bride or **wife.** The bride of that time would make **herself ready** by bathing, rubbing on oil, and using perfume. Her hair would be specially fixed and she would wear her wedding gown.

19:8 fine linen: The bride of the Lamb wears a garment of precious **fine linen** that symbolizes the good works of believers. The fine linen, clean and white, refers not to the imputed righteousness of Christ, but to righteous acts of the **saints.** The garment signifies faithfulness in the habitual doing of good works. The garment is one that the believer must put on himself and consists of godly works produced in dependence upon the Holy Spirit. It is an outward reflection of character and conduct which is developed in this life (Matt. 22:11, 12). The reward for such godly character and conduct at the judgment seat of Christ consists of this garment and all the rights and privileges which are promised to the overcomer. Believers are not only heirs of God and thus have a home in heaven as a free gift (John 14:1, 2; 1 Pet. 1:3–5) but the overcomers (those who endure to the end of this life) and co-heirs with Christ and shall reign with Him (Rom. 8:17). John admonishes us to abide in Christ so that when we see Him, we will be confident and not be ashamed at His coming (1 John 2:28).

19:9 Blessed introduces the fourth of the seven beatitudes in Revelation (1:3; 14:13; 16:15; 20:6; 22:9, 14). **The marriage supper** of John's day would begin on the evening of the wedding, but the celebration might continue for days. The marriage supper here is a time of joyous feasting to be enjoyed by the church and especially by the overcomers who will reign with Christ. The key to being able to participate in the wedding banquet is faithfulness to God.

19:10 To **worship** any person or object other than **God** is a form of idolatry (Ex. 20:3–5). The angel rebukes John for his error (22:8, 9) and tells John that he is simply a **fellow servant** with him and his believing **brethren. The testimony of Jesus** here refers to the witness about Jesus (1:2, 9). Biblical **prophecy** looks to or is dependent upon the work of Christ and its proclamation (1 Pet. 1:12).

19:11 This verse answers the question asked about the beast in 13:4: "Who is able to make war with him?" Christ can defeat him.

19:12 Eyes . . . like a flame of fire parallels the description of the glorified Christ in 1:14. **Many crowns** show Christ to be more powerful than either Satan (12:3) or the beast (13:1). In ancient society, a **name** was more than a title. It revealed a person's character. **No one knew except Himself** apparently means

> *The key to being able to participate in the wedding banquet is faithfulness to God.*

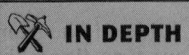 **IN DEPTH** | **Interpreting Revelation**

Interpreting Revelation has caused much debate, and at least four standard methods for interpreting the book have developed. *Preterists* view the book as referring almost exclusively to first-century events. *Historicists* view the book as referring to the unfolding of church history until Christ's second coming. *Idealists* see the book as symbolizing the eternal conflict between good and evil. *Futurists* see the book as mainly about the end times. Sometimes interpreters blend two or more of these approaches.

Furthermore, the "thousand years" of 20:2–6 has been the basis of three different views of the *millennium* (the Latin word for "thousand years"). The *amillennial* (no millennium) interpretation sees Christ as ruling spiritually in the church now; Satan has been bound or at least hindered during this present church era. According to this view, there will be no literal thousand-year reign; instead, Christ reigns through the church for an unknown number of years before He returns. The *postmillennial* (after the millennium) interpretation understands that by the spread of the gospel the world will become progressively more Christian. When the world becomes completely Christian there will be a millennium, then Jesus will return in glory. The *premillennial* (before the millennium) view holds that Jesus Christ will return to earth to set up His visible kingdom. At that time Satan will be bound for a thousand years.

Those who accept the premillennial position take specific views on when Christ will remove believers from the earth before He returns (19:11–21). A comparison of the common symbolism of Daniel and Revelation, as well as time references in Dan. 7:25; 9:27; 12:7 along with those in Rev. 11:2, 3; 12:6, 14; 13:5, seem to indicate that a seven-year period (Dan. 9:24–27), often called the Tribulation, will precede Christ's return. Five different views have tried to explain the timing between the rapture of the church and the Tribulation. (The word *rapture* comes from the Latin translation of "caught up" in 1 Thess. 4:17.) *Pretribulationists* expect the Rapture to take place before seven years of tribulation. *Midtribulationists* say the Rapture will occur midway through the seven-year period. The *posttribulation view* states that the church will go through the Tribulation, but will be removed at the time of Christ's second coming. The *prewrath view* places the Rapture between the mid- and post-tribulational points, before the climactic wrath of God.

Each of these positions depends on a different view of how the text of Revelation should be interpreted. It is a good idea to keep this in mind whenever you try to understand a position or talk about it with others. The central idea on which all these views agree is that Christ will return some time in the future, and that His return will be a welcome sight to His people. Our hope and prayer is the same as the apostle John's: "Come, Lord Jesus!" (22:20).

---

that there are parts of the character of the eternal and limitless God (1 Tim. 6:15, 16) that only God knows, though Christ may reveal such matters at His second coming.

19:13 **A robe dipped in blood** may speak of Christ's redemptive death on the Cross (7:9), or His trampling of the "winepress of the wrath of God" (v. 15; 14:19, 20), or both. **The Word of God** cannot be the name that no one knew except Christ (v. 12) because that name is revealed in John 1:1, 14.

19:14 **The armies in heaven** may be angelic hosts (5:11; Matt. 26:53), but 17:14 speaks of those with the Lord at His coming as being "called, chosen, and faithful," all terms for believers (Rom. 1:7; Eph. 1:1; 1 Pet. 2:9). The garments of **fine linen,** like that of the Lamb's bride in v. 8, supports this interpretation. **White horses,** a common symbol of victory, would be

appropriate for those who are already victorious over the beast (15:2).

19:15 The **sharp sword** that comes out of Christ's **mouth** is the two-edged sword spoken of in 1:16. **Strike the nations** may be a general statement of judgment or a specific reference to the armies of the earth being "killed with the sword" in v. 21. Christ **will rule . . . with a rod of iron** in fulfillment of the messianic prophecies in Ps. 2:8, 9; Is. 11:4. **Treads the winepress of** God's **wrath** recalls the command in 14:18–20 to gather the grapes of the earth for the "great winepress of the wrath of God."

19:16 **KING OF KINGS** means the One who is supreme over all earthly rulers. The phrase "Lord of lords and King of kings" is found in 17:14, anticipating the Second Coming.

19:17, 18 **The birds** are told to **gather** to

feast on the carcasses of the fallen armies gathered in opposition against Christ.

19:19–21 This picture of **the beast** and his extensive force has already been seen in 17:14 and is almost certainly the same as those gathered for "the battle of that great day of God Almighty" (16:14) at Armageddon (16:16). The beast (13:1–10) and **the false prophet** (13:11–17) are **captured** and **cast alive into the lake of fire,** the eternal destiny of all unbelievers (20:10, 14, 15). They are apparently the first to suffer the torment of the lake of **brimstone. The rest** of the beast's allies are **killed** by **the sword** from **the mouth** of the victorious Christ. Apparently all those who now suffer death go to Hades (Matt. 16:18), to which Jesus has the keys (1:18), until Death and Hades are emptied and cast into the lake of fire (20:13–15).

20:1–3 The **angel** here may be the same one who had the **key to the bottomless pit** in 9:1, 2. The bottomless pit is presently the place of imprisonment of some demons (Luke 8:31) and will be the place from which the beast ascends (17:8). Thus, it is fitting that **the Devil** will be held there for a **thousand years. The dragon** of 12:3, 9, known as **Satan,** was in control of the **serpent** in the Garden of Eden (Gen. 3). God has a sovereign plan for Satan. He will be **shut . . . up** in the abyss for a thousand years and then will be briefly released to **deceive the nations** one final time (vv. 7–9) before being cast into the lake of fire (v. 10). **Must be released** indicates that Satan will not escape from the pit but instead will be allowed to go forth from the pit to fulfill God's sovereign plan.

20:4–6 The interpretation of the thousand-year reign of Christ has been the subject of much controversy. Some understand **a thousand years** as a specific statement of time, while others take it figuratively as a round number for a long but undetermined period.

20:4 Thrones . . . reigned indicates that believers will participate significantly **with Christ** during His millennial rule (1:6; 2:26, 27; 5:10). This may be a partial fulfillment of Dan. 7:18, 27. The aspect of **judgment** in ruling is referred to in 1 Cor. 6:2–4. At the onset of the kingdom, authority is officially transferred from angels to men (Heb. 2:5, 8). A new world order is established with the overcoming saints of the church age ruling together with Christ in His kingdom (Rom. 8:17). **Those who had been beheaded** are believers martyred by **the beast** (13:7, 15) and may also be the victorious throng who sing praises to the Lamb in 15:2–4. John could identify with those who lost their lives because of **their witness to Jesus** and God's **word,** since John was exiled to the island of Patmos for the same reasons (1:9).

20:5 Did not live again indicates that the **resurrection** of the dead will not encompass all people at the same time, as passages like Dan. 12:2 and John 5:29 may also indicate. Like 1 Cor. 15:23, 52, this passage indicates that there will be a **first** resurrection of dead believers before **the thousand years** of Christ's reign and a final resurrection after the millennium is **finished,** before the great white throne judgment (vv. 11–13).

20:6 Blessed begins the fifth of seven beatitudes in Revelation. The other six (1:3; 14:13; 16:15; 19:9; 22:9, 14) all look forward to life with **Christ** beyond **the first resurrection** (v. 5). The first resurrection is assured for all believers. But the blessedness mentioned here belongs more precisely to those who have a **part** in the first resurrection. It is possible that this refers only to those believers who qualify to function as king-priests in Christ's kingdom. This might be what Paul was referring to when he spoke of his goal of obtaining the prize of Christ (1 Cor. 9:27; Phil. 3:10–14). **The second death** is the everlasting death of torment in the lake of fire for unbelievers who face the great white throne judgment (vv. 11–15). John has previously stated that the one who overcomes will not be hurt by the second death (2:11).

20:7–9 At the conclusion of Christ's thousand-year reign, **Satan will be released** by God to **deceive the nations . . . of the earth**

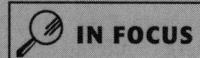

IN FOCUS   **"Devil"**

(Gk. *diabolos*) (2:10; 12:9, 12; 20:2, 10; Matt. 4:1; Acts 10:38) Strong's *#1228*; Satan (Gk. *Satanas*) (20:2, 7; Matt. 4:10; Rom. 16:20) Strong's *#4567*: The word *diabolos* signifies a slanderer, one who accuses another. Hence that other name given him: "the accuser of our brethren" (Rev. 12:10). The name Satan signifies an adversary, one who lies in wait for or sets himself in opposition to another. These and other names of the same fallen spirit point to different features of his evil character and deceitful operations.

(vv. 2, 3) again as he has throughout history (12:9). As a result of satanic deception, the world's armies will gather for battle against God again as they had done before Christ's second coming (16:13, 14; 19:19, 20). **Gog and Magog** was a common rabbinical title for the nations in rebellion against the Lord, and the names recall

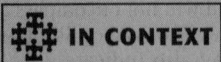 **IN CONTEXT** **The Millennium**

The term "millennium," coming from the Latin *mille*, "one thousand," is used to identify the 1,000-year rule of Christ with His saints (Rev. 20:4–7). This is the only place in the NT where such a period is described. Christians are divided over how to interpret the 1,000-year reign and the events surrounding it.

Some believe that the binding of Satan represents Christ's victory on the Cross. The 1,000 years is, then, symbolic of the church age during which the saints will rule spiritually with Christ. Satan's rebellion at the end of the 1,000 years is his final desperate attempt to challenge God before the return of Christ to judge the world. This view is called amillennialism because it does not believe in a millennial period separate from the church age.

Others believe that the victories of Christ (19:1–21) and the binding of Satan (20:1–3) represent the gradual triumph of the gospel throughout the church age. The millennium is, then, symbolic of an indeterminate time of earthly harmony after the progress of the gospel has resulted in the kingdom of God on earth. Only after this time will Christ return to finally defeat Satan (20:7–10) and judge the world (20:11–15). This view is known as postmillennialism because it teaches that Christ will not return until after the millennium.

Other Christians believe that 19:1–21 depicts Christ's second coming which will culminate in the binding of Satan (20:1–3), after which the saints will be raised and rule with Christ on earth for a period symbolized by 1,000 years (20:4–6). At the end of this period Satan will be released for one last rebellion and will be destroyed (20:7–10). Then the unrighteous will be raised and all will be judged (20:11–15). This position is called premillennialism since it teaches the return of Christ before the millennium.

the prophesied invasion of Israel in Ezek. 38; 39. Some hold that the battle of vv. 8, 9 is the one spoken of in Ezekiel, but there are major differences as well as similarities in the two passages. The use of **fire . . . out of heaven** to destroy gathered armies is also seen in Ezek. 38:22; 39:6. **Camp** is used elsewhere to refer to armies (Heb. 11:34) or the barracks of such forces (Acts 23:10). Some interpret the camp **of the saints** as being symbolic of the unity of the people of God. **The beloved city** may symbolically refer to the home of God's people. However, the New Jerusalem is commonly called "the city of My God" (3:12) and "the holy city" (21:2). The city here may be the renewed earthly Jerusalem, ready to give way to the everlasting sinless glory of the New Jerusalem (21:1—22:5).

20:10 When the final rebellion is put down by the Lord (vv. 8, 9), **the devil** will join **the beast and the false prophet** (19:20) in torment **forever** in **the lake of fire** (14:10, 11; Is. 66:22–24; Mark 9:48).

20:11 The **great white throne** is a picture of God's holy rule and judgment. The One occupying the throne may be God the Father (1 Cor. 15:24–28) or both the Father and the Lamb (Christ), as in the New Jerusalem (22:1, 3). **The earth and the heaven fled** is a poetic way of describing the burning up of this creation and its related works, as described in 2 Pet. 3:10–13. There is **no place** for this sin-polluted creation

in the new heaven and new earth (21:1—22:5).

20:12 The dead, called "the rest of the dead" in v. 5, are raised and made to stand before God's throne of judgment. To some, the first resurrection (v. 5) includes only martyrs (v. 4), so that both believers and unbelievers will stand before the great white throne. Others point to the broad promises to Christians in the Book of Revelation of ruling with Christ (1:6; 2:26, 27; 5:10) as evidence that all Christians will experience the first resurrection and thus will not have to endure the great white throne judgment. **Books** refers to the record of all **works** done in this life. Since all have sinned and fall short of God's standard (Rom. 3:23), the opening of these books would certainly lead to eternal sentences in the lake of fire. **The Book of Life,** God's register of those who are saved (17:8), is also opened. So although no one will be judged acceptable based on works (Eph. 2:9), many will be saved by God's grace received by faith in Jesus Christ (Eph. 2:8).

20:13, 14 The sea is the resting place of unburied bodies. **Death and Hades** refers not only to dying, but to existence beyond the grave (1:18; 6:8). The picture here is of all intermediate abodes of human bodies giving them up to God's judgment. While unbelieving humanity is judged **according to** its **works,** Death and Hades, the Lord's final enemy (1 Cor. 15:26), is also destroyed by being **cast into the lake of**

fire. The second death is spiritual and eternal, the just punishment of the wicked. The first death is physical dying. Both are included in the overall meaning of the death that came upon the human race because of Adam and Eve's sin (Gen. 2:16, 17; 3:1–19; Rom. 5:12).

20:15 Only God's elect, those whose names are **written in the Book of Life,** will escape **the lake of fire.** The rejection of the eternal gospel results in eternal condemnation (14:6, 7).

21:1, 2 New here suggests freshness, not just a second beginning. This is the fulfillment of the prophecies of Is. 65:17; 66:22; 2 Pet. 3:13. Significantly, this eternal renewal has already begun in the life of the believer because, using the same term, Paul says, "If anyone is in Christ, he is a *new* creation" (2 Cor. 5:17). The present **heaven and . . . earth,** including the **sea,** were burned up in the great white throne judgment (20:11, 13), and thus have **passed away** before the arrival of the new heaven and earth. The fact that there will be a continuation of some features of the present creation in the new heaven and new earth is implied by the description of the **New Jerusalem** as **the holy city,** a title that is applied to the present Jerusalem in 11:2. Yet the drastic difference in the new

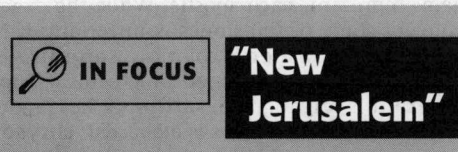

IN FOCUS   **"New Jerusalem"**

(Gk. *Ierousalem kaine*) (3:12; 21:2) Strong's #2419; 2537: The Greek term denotes "the brand-new Jerusalem." The New Jerusalem that comes out of heaven is plainly distinct from the earthly Jerusalem, the former capital of Israel. This is the city Abraham looked for, the city that has foundations, whose builder and maker is God (Heb. 11:10). This is the city that exists even now in heaven, for Paul calls it the Jerusalem that is above (Gal. 4:26).

eternal state is obvious from the fact that there will be **no more** sea, which was a major part of the original creation (Gen. 1:6–10). It is impossible to tell whether the New Jerusalem will sit on the new earth, since all three references to it describe the holy city as **coming down out of heaven** (v. 10; 3:12). **Prepared as a bride** is essentially the imagery of 19:7, 8, where God's people—or, more specifically, Christ's church—are prepared for "the marriage . . . of the Lamb" (19:9). **Her husband** refers again to Christ, the

Lamb (v. 9), but the bride is the New Jerusalem, according to vv. 9, 10. In other words, Christ's bride (v. 9) is the redeemed inhabitants of the holy city (vv. 3–7, 24–27).

21:3 In this verse, God is described as dwelling among His people. This recalls the Incarnation, the fact that Jesus "became flesh and dwelt among us" (John 1:14), and is a fulfillment of the promise in 7:15 that **God** will dwell among His redeemed people. A virtually identical promise was given to Israel in Ezek. 37:27, 28.

21:4, 5 Wipe away every tear fulfills the promises in 7:17 and Is. 25:8. **No more death . . . no more pain** goes far beyond the earlier promise of 7:16, which promises freedom from hunger, thirst, and scorching heat. **Former things have passed away** echoes both v. 1 and 2 Cor. 5:17. The believer's rebirth through faith in Christ brings newness to that person's life, but it is only in the eternal state that God will **make all things new.**

21:6 It is done echoes the voice from the throne in 16:17 that proclaims the completion of God's wrath being poured out on Babylon. Here the completion of the new creation by Him who is **the Alpha and the Omega** of all things is the focus. **Water of life** may be recalling Jesus' references to living water in John 4:14; 7:38, in connection with eternal life and life in the Holy Spirit. This water is further described in 22:1. A similar offer of God's grace **to him who** spiritually **thirsts** is repeated in 22:17.

21:7 He who overcomes will inherit not only the specific promises to the churches in 2:7, 11, 17, 26–28; 3:5, 12, 21, but **all things.** The most wonderful part of this inheritance is that the believer **will be** a **son** (a person who is a rightful heir) of **God** forever. Sonship as a concept embraces more than a relationship based upon a shared nature. It is a special honor associated with the Davidic covenant, including privileged intimacy and ruling authority (2 Sam. 7:14). While adoption as a son is all of grace (Gal. 4:5) and all Christians are adopted sons by virtue of spiritual birth, not all sons fulfill the requirements of such an exalted status (Matt 5:9, 43–45). A person can be a son and not necessarily behave as a son. A true son reflects a life of obedience (Jer. 7:23; 11:4). A willingness to yield to the leading of the holy spirit is characteristic of the sons of God (Rom. 8:14).

21:8 The characteristics of those who are not in Christ through faith—the **unbelieving**—are described. These unbelievers are destined for **the lake** of **fire,** eternal **death** after God's final judgment (20:12–14). All whose names are not written in the Book of Life (20:15) are judged according to their works (20:12), and are shown to be worthy of endless death (Rom. 6:23). In 1

Cor. 6:9–11, Paul makes essentially the same point.

21:9, 10 Since the beginning of this passage is similar to the beginning of ch. 17, it seems that **the Lamb's wife,** the New **Jerusalem,** is being contrasted with Babylon, "the great harlot" (17:1, 5). **In the spirit** is the exalted

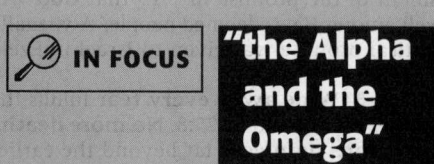

IN FOCUS   **"the Alpha and the Omega"**

(Gk. *to A kai to O*) (1:8; 21:6; 22:13) Strong's #*1; 2532; 5598*: Alpha and omega are the first and last letters of the Greek alphabet. In every context this phrase is used, it is difficult to tell whether the title applies to the Father or to Christ or to both. Most likely it can be attributed to both. God in Christ comprises everything, all that goes between the Alpha and the Omega, as well as being the First and the Last. This expresses God's fullness, comprehensiveness, and all-inclusiveness. He is the Source of all things and will bring all things to their appointed end.

state in which John received the apocalyptic visions of this book (1:10), the last of which **carried** him **away** (17:3) to a **high mountain** overlooking Jerusalem.

21:11 This description of the eternal city, New Jerusalem, emphasizes God's **glory,** which is a source of the **light** for the city (21:23). God's heavenly glory is like a **jasper stone** (4:3); the light in the New Jerusalem will be similar to the brilliant crystalline reflection of priceless jasper.

21:12, 13 The description of the **great and high wall** that contains **twelve gates** named after **the twelve tribes . . . of Israel** echoes Ezek. 48:30–35. Commentators variously interpret these twelve gates as representing all of God's people, including both Israel and the church, or as representing strictly the Israelites.

21:14 The **twelve foundations,** the huge stones upon which the wall of the New Jerusalem rests, contain the **names of the twelve apostles** of Christ (Luke 6:13–16), calling to mind Paul's imagery of the apostles as the foundation of the house of God in Eph. 2:20 (Jesus' promise to His apostles that they would occupy a prominent place in His kingdom in Matt. 19:28).

21:15–17 The reference to the **reed to measure the city** recalls Ezek. 40; 41, as does

the reference in 11:1, 2. The city seems to be **laid out** as a cube, since **its length, breadth, and height are equal.** The cube was an ancient symbol of perfection. The Most Holy Place in the OT tabernacle and in the temple were cubic in design. The symmetrical measurements of the city are so vast (**twelve thousand furlongs,** or about 1400 miles) and the wall is so thick (**one hundred and forty-four cubits,** or over 200 feet) that they almost surpass the imagination. The imagery indicates that the city is the dwelling place of God's presence, just as the tabernacle and temple had been. It is impossible to be certain whether ordinary measurements should be applied to the eternal state, though the reference to **the measure of a man** (human standards) may imply that they should.

21:18 As thick as the walls of New Jerusalem are (200 feet; v. 27), they are as transparent as crystalline **jasper.** The vast city itself (v. 16), especially the streets (v. 21), are also **like clear glass,** even though they are made of **pure gold.** The overall effect is that of an incredibly beautiful and transparent city, symbolizing never-ending glory and purity.

21:19, 20 The **stones** that serve as **foundations of the wall** for the New Jerusalem are named for the twelve apostles (v. 14), although there is no way to know which of the **precious** gems represents each apostle. While the exact color of some of the stones is uncertain, it is probable that **jasper** is colorless, **sapphire** is blue, **chalcedony** is green or greenish-blue, **emerald** is bright green, **sardonyx** has layers of red and white, **sardius** is blood-red, **chrysolite** is yellow, **beryl** is blue or blue-green, **topaz** is golden, **chrysoprase** is apple-green, **jacinth** is blue or blue-purple, and **amethyst** is purple or violet.

21:21 The **twelve gates** of the eternal city, representing the twelve tribes of Israel (v. 12), are **each** made from **one** huge **pearl.** What is immediately striking is that **the street** in the New Jerusalem is **gold** (v. 18), but it is also significant that only one street is mentioned (22:2).

21:22 There will be **no temple** building in the New Jerusalem because the Father and the Son (**the Lamb**) will be there. Recall that Christ referred to His body as a temple (John 2:19, 21) and that the church itself is called "a temple of God" (1 Cor. 3:16), "a holy temple," and the "dwelling place of God" (Eph. 2:21, 22).

21:23 Because of the **light** provided by God's **glory** and **the Lamb,** there is **no need of the sun or of the moon** in the eternal state (contrast Gen. 1:14–19). It is speculated that God's glory was the source of the light mentioned before the creation of the sun and moon in Genesis (Gen. 1:3–5, 16).

21:24 From all **the nations** (Matt. 28:19;

Luke 24:47), Christ redeemed His people (5:9), continually calling unbelievers to repent of their sins and believe in Him (14:6, 7). Great multitudes who may be among this group in the eternal Jerusalem have come into the Lord's presence in 7:9 and 15:1–4. Others hold that *the nations* here refers to believers from nations that existed during the millennium (20:1–10).

21:25 The **gates** to the eternal city will not need to **be shut** because everything that could threaten the city has been defeated (v. 27) and consigned to the lake of fire (20:15).

21:26 This verse builds on the truth of v. 24. But notice its **glory.** In the worship of Israel no Gentile could enter into the holy precincts without serious repercussions. Remember the persecution Paul suffered when some inferred that he had brought a Gentile into the temple (Acts 21:22–29). But no barriers will be found in the New Jerusalem.

21:27 Never again can the devil (12:9), the one behind every **abomination** and **lie** (John 8:44), emerge to instigate sin (Gen. 3). His eternal destiny in the lake of fire is certain (20:10). Only believers, whose names **are written in the Lamb's Book of Life,** are allowed by God to **enter** the New Jerusalem.

22:1 The **river** flowing with the **water of life** is reminiscent of the water coming from the temple in Ezek. 47, as well as of Jesus' expression "rivers of living water" (John 7:38), symbolizing the new covenant ministry of the Holy Spirit (7:39).

22:2 The **tree of life** in the original creation was in the middle of the Garden of Eden (Gen. 2:9), from which all of humanity was excluded after sin entered the world (Gen. 3:22–24). Ezekiel's apocalyptic vision included trees bearing fruit every month with medicinal leaves (Ezek. 47:12). Since only one tree of life is mentioned here—even though it is on both sides **of the river**—it is probably meant as a parallel to Gen. 2, implying that a new, better, and everlasting Eden has come.

22:3 No more curse means that the affliction of sin, especially on the human race and creation (Gen. 3:14–19), will be erased. As **God** had fellowship with Adam and Eve before their fall into sin (Gen. 3:8), so the Lord will again be with His **servants** eternally. In turn, His servants will worshipfully **serve Him** (Rom 12:1).

22:4 The believer's hope today is to **see** the Lord **face** to face (1 Cor. 13:12), something neither Moses nor any other human was previously allowed to do (Ex. 33:20). The **name . . . on their foreheads** is both in contrast to the mark of the beast (13:16, 17) and in fulfillment of the promise to the faithful believers at Philadelphia (3:12). It may also extend the imagery of the 144,000 in 14:1.

22:5 No night . . . no lamp fulfills Christ's proclamation of Himself as "the light of the world" (John 8:12; 9:5; 12:46). The eternal inhabitants of the New Jerusalem (20:15; 21:27) **shall reign forever** with the Lord, as implied in 1:6 and stated in Dan. 7:18, 27.

22:6, 7 The visions of Revelation are meant to inform the **servants** of **God,** true believers who will serve and reign with the Lord eternally (vv. 3, 5), as to what could **take place** very soon. **Blessed** begins the sixth of seven beatitudes in Revelation (v. 14; 1:3; 14:13; 16:15; 19:9; 20:6).

22:8, 9 John makes the mistake of worshiping an **angel** for a second time (19:10). Again the angel reminds John that he is merely a **fellow servant** of God and admonishes him to **worship** only **God.**

22:10 Earlier John was commanded to seal up (that is, not to write down) the utterances of the seven thunders in 10:4, as Daniel had been instructed to do (Dan. 12:4, 9). The reason John is now told not to **seal** the **book** is that **the time** of its fulfillment is potentially very near.

22:11 unjust . . . filthy . . . righteous . . . holy: This verse, on the surface, seems to be a prediction that believers and unbelievers will live out their lives true to their nature until the final judgment (20:12–15). However, it is almost certainly an implied, indirect evangelistic appeal based on the continuing offer of the gospel in v. 17 and 14:6, 7.

22:12, 13 The rewarding of each believer according to his or her works is taught in 2 Cor. 5:10. Christ's rewards are meant to provide a powerful incentive for an obedient life. Little wonder that the apostle Paul rigorously disciplined himself so that he would not be disqualified from the reward of reigning with Christ (1 Cor. 9:24–27). The judgment seat of Christ can be a time of great regret, or it can be an occasion of supreme joy (2 Cor. 5:9–11). After Christ comes again, He will give rewards to His own. This can be counted on because Christ is in control of all history and eternity.

22:14, 15 Blessed introduces the last of the seven beatitudes in Revelation (v. 7; 1:3; 14:13; 16:15; 19:9; 20:6). Since the **tree of life** is literal but is also viewed figuratively (Prov. 3:18; 11:30; 13:12; 15:4), it suggests a quality of life involving an intimate fellowship with Jesus Christ based upon a persevering obedience. This may be a fulfillment of Christ's provision of life, and more abundant life (John 10:10). Since no one can **enter . . . into the city** unless their name is written in the Lamb's Book of Life (21:27), this beatitude is speaking of those justified by faith who express that faith in obedience (Eph. 2:8–10). The obedient overcomer is promised the reward of entering through the gates of the city, possibly a privilege reserved for those who share in the Lord's victory procession.

22:15 Dogs was a common expression used by Jews to speak of Gentiles (Matt. 15:26); here, however, it more likely speaks of false teachers (Phil. 3:2). **Loves and practices a lie** indicates a life dominated by falsehood (21:8).

22:16 the Root and the Offspring of David: Jesus is both the Source and Son of David, echoing the wording of Is. 11:1, 10. Jesus is both greater than David and the rightful heir to the throne of David. **Bright and Morning Star** means that for the Christian, Jesus is the comforting light in a dark world until the dawn of His return (2:28).

22:17 This invitation by the Spirit remains open to anyone who will **come** by faith to Christ to accept the Lord's gracious offer of eternal life.

22:18, 19 The Book of Revelation was intended to be heard and obeyed (v. 7; 1:3), not tampered with. The person who either **adds to** or **takes away** from its contents will receive from **God** the strictest punishment, a punishment with eternal consequences. This terrifying warning is even stronger than that of Deut. 4:2 and Prov. 30:6.

22:20 The fact that Jesus is **coming quickly** within the scope of God's overall plan for this creation is a repeated theme in Revelation (3:11; 22:7, 12). John adds the hope of all believers to the declaration of Christ by praying, **come, Lord Jesus.**

22:21 The grace of our Lord Jesus Christ begins and concludes the Book of Revelation (1:4), implying that the message of grace and the free gift of eternal life in Christ (Eph. 2:8, 9)—not merely the message of judgment upon unbelievers—can be found in this book.

APPENDIXES

APPENDIXES

Important Archaeological Discoveries and the Bible*

Definition and Importance of Biblical Archaeology

HE LAST 150 YEARS HAVE WITNESSED THE BIRTH, growth, and phenomenal development of the science of biblical archaeology. This new science has performed many wonders in furnishing background material and in illustrating, illuminating, and in many cases authenticating the message and meaning of the Old and New Testament Scriptures. Biblical archaeology may be defined as a study based on the

excavation, decipherment, and critical evaluation of the records of the past as they affect the Bible. While the general field of archaeology is fascinating, much more so is the study of biblical archaeology, since it deals with the Holy Scriptures. This is the reason for the growing enthusiasm for biblical archaeology. The attraction lies in the supreme importance of the message and meaning of the Bible. The Scriptures, by virtue of their character as the inspired revelation of God to people, have naturally held a paramount place in the interest and affection of humankind. Biblical archaeology, illustrating the Bible in its historical background and contemporary life, attracts a measure of the interest that lies in the Bible itself. Accordingly, this science has a worthy ministry of expanding biblical horizons on the human plane. No field of research has offered greater challenge and promise than that of biblical archaeology.

Until the beginning of the 19th century very little was known of biblical times and biblical backgrounds, except what appeared on the pages of the Old Testament or what happened to be preserved in the writings of classical antiquity. This was considerable for the New Testament era but very little indeed for the Old Testament period. The reason for this is that Greek and Latin historians catalogued very little information before the fifth century B.C. As a result, the Old Testament period was very little known extrabiblically, and what was known was confined to what the Bible gave. This from the viewpoint of contemporary secular history was sparse. The result was that before the beginning of the science of modern archaeology there was practically nothing available to authenticate Old Testament history and literature. One can therefore imagine the fervor aroused among serious Bible students by illuminating discoveries in Bible lands, especially from about 1800 to the present. In fact, modern archaeology may be said to have had its beginning in 1798, when the rich antiquities of the Nile Valley were opened up to scientific study by Napoleon's Egyptian expedition.

*Revised and updated by Dr. Charles R Page, II, Academic Dean, Jerusalem Center for Biblical Studies. Many of the place names mentioned in this article can be located on one of the maps on pages 1780 and 1781.

Foundational Discoveries of the 19th Century

Although the most notable discoveries affecting the Bible and particularly the Old Testament were not made until the 20th century, foundational discoveries were made in the 19th century and prepared the way for the modern era.

The Rosetta Stone—Key to Egypt's Splendid Past

This very important monument was discovered in 1798 at Rosetta (Rashid), near the westernmost mouth of the Nile River, by an officer in Napoleon's expedition to Egypt. It was a slab of black basalt trilingually inscribed, which may be said to be the key that unlocked the door to knowledge of the language and literature of ancient Egypt and turned out to be the inscription that opened the modern era of scientific biblical archaeology.

The three languages in which this monument was found to be inscribed were the Greek of 200 B.C. and two forms of Egyptian writing—the older, more complicated hieroglyphic script and the later simplified and more popular demotic writing, which was the common language of the people. The Greek could at once be read and provided the clue to the decipherment of the other two ancient Egyptian scripts. Sylvester de Sacy of France and J. D. Akerblad of Sweden succeeded in unraveling the demotic Egyptian by identifying the Greek personal names it contained, namely Ptolemy, Arsinoe, and Berenike. Thomas Young of England then proceeded to identify the name of Ptolemy in the hieroglyphic portion, where groups of characters enclosed in oval frames, called cartouches, had already been surmised to be royal names. From this point on, the young Frenchman Jean François Champollion, 1790–1832, was able to decipher the hieroglyphics of the monument, show the true nature of this script, make a dictionary, formulate a grammar, and translate numerous Egyptian texts, from the year 1818 to 1832.

Champollion's achievement formally opened up the science of Egyptology. Scholars from henceforth were able to read Egyptian monumental inscriptions and reliefs. From that time forth the literary treasures of the Nile Valley have been opened to scholarly study. Today many universities maintain chairs in the language and culture of ancient Egypt. These studies have opened up vistas of history hitherto unknown so that, from the beginning of Egypt about 2800 B.C. to 63 B.C. when Rome took over, the entire history of the land of the Nile can fairly well be traced.

All of this has tremendous bearing on the background of the Bible. Egypt figures largely in the patriarchal narratives and the Book of Exodus and all through the Pentateuch. As a result, the background of the story of Joseph and of the sojourn of the children of Israel in Egypt, their deliverance under Moses, and much of their sojourn in the desert and later history in Canaan can now be set in the general framework of Egyptian history. It can be said that the whole context of the Old Testament history, in its broad span from Abraham to Christ, is made immeasurably clearer because of the vast strides in our knowledge of Egypt. That great nation of antiquity interacted with the mighty Assyro-Babylonian empires on the Tigris-Euphrates and with the Hittite power on the Halys across the tiny bridge that was ancient Palestine.

The Behistun Inscription—Gateway to Assyro-Babylonian Antiquity

This famous monument was the key to the languages of Assyria and Babylonia. It consists of a large relief panel containing numerous columns of inscription, which was boldly carved on the face of a mountain about five hundred feet above the surrounding plain of Karmanshah on the old caravan route from Babylon to Ecbatana. Unlike the Rosetta Stone written in ancient Egyptian hieroglyphics, and later in popular demotic and in the Greek of the third century B.C., the Behistun Inscription was written in the wedge-shaped characters of ancient Assyria Babylonia. It contained about twelve hundred lines of inscription. The three languages in which it was inscribed were all written in cuneiform characters, consisting of Old Persian, Elamite, and Akkadian. The third language, the Akkadian, was the wedge-shaped language of ancient Assyria and Babylonia, in which thousands upon thousands of clay tablets discovered in the Tigris-Euphrates region are inscribed.

Early excavations revealed a mass of material on which this curious wedge-shaped Babylonian-Akkadian writing appeared. But it was an unsolved riddle. Practically no progress was made until a young English officer in the Persian army, Henry C. Rawlinson, in 1835 and the following years made the dangerous climb to the Behistun Inscription and made copies and plaster of paris impressions of it. Rawlinson knew modern Persian and set to work to decipher the old Persian, the cuneiform part of the inscription. After a decade of labor, he finally succeeded in translating the five columns, nearly four hundred lines of the old Persian portion of the Behistun Inscription, and sent it to Europe in 1845. The text translation and commentary on it were published in 1847 in the Journal of the Royal Asiatic Society.

In conjunction with the literary part of the

monument was a life-sized figure with numerous individuals bowing before it. This person turned out to be Darius the Great (522–486 B.C.), the Achemenid prince who saved the Persian Empire from a rebellion. The scene depicts the king, as Rawlinson's translation of the Persian portion of the inscription shows, receiving the submission of the rebels. The emperor is portrayed at the top of the relief accompanied by two attendants. His foot is placed upon the prostrate form of a leading rebel. The king's left hand holds a bow, while his right hand is lifted toward the winged disc symbolizing Ahura-Mazda, the spirit of good, whom Darius, an ardent follower of Zoroaster, worshiped. Behind the rebel stands a procession of rebel leaders, roped together by their necks. Beside and beneath the sculptured panel the numerous columns of the inscription appear, relating in three languages how Darius defended the throne and crushed the revolt.

Working on the supposition that the other inscriptions told the same story, scholars were soon enabled to read the second language, which was the Elamite or Susian. Then last, but most important, they could decipher the Akkadian or Assyro-Babylonian. This was a great discovery, for this wedge-shaped character of writing is recorded on numerous literary remains from the Tigris-Euphrates Valley. It opened up a vast new field of biblical background, so that today, as in the case of the Rosetta Stone opening up the science of Egyptology, the *Behistun Inscription* has given birth to the science of Assyriology. Moreover, both Egyptology and Assyriology offer great help in understanding biblical backgrounds and biblical history. No Bible dictionary, Bible handbook, or commentary that is up-to-date can ignore the great findings of these sciences.

The task of deciphering cuneiform is increasing with every decade. Numerous cuneiform libraries have been discovered from antiquity. Two unearthed at Nineveh contained thousands of clay tablets. The library of Ashurbanipal (669–625 B.C.) contained some twenty-two thousand tablets. Among the tablets unearthed in this collection and sent to the British Museum were Assyrian copies of the Babylonian creation and flood stories. The identification and decipherment of these particular tablets by George Smith in 1872 produced great excitement in the archeological world.

Not only in Babylonia but in many other places large bodies of cuneiform literature have been uncovered. For example, the famous *Amarna Letters* from Egypt were discovered in 1886 at Tell el-Amarna about two hundred miles south of modern Cairo. These Amarna Tablets proved to be diplomatic correspondence of petty princes of Palestine in the 14th century B.C. with the Egyptian court at Amarna. The *Amarna Letters* give an inside glance into conditions in Palestine just before the conquest by Joshua and the Israelites. Many scholars actually think that they describe aspects of that invasion. One of the documents from the governor of Jerusalem (Urusalim) tells Amenophis IV that the "Habiru" (perhaps the Hebrews) were overrunning many Palestine cities and could not be held back.

Other important bodies of cuneiform literature bearing upon the Bible have been retrieved from Boghaz-Keui and Kanish in Asia Minor. Others come from Susa and Elam, others from the city of Mari on the middle Euphrates, others from Ras Shamra (ancient Ugarit), mentioned in the *Amarna Letters* and located in North Syria. Others stem from various sites within and without Babylonia.

The Moabite Stone—A Sensational Literary Find

This important inscription, found in 1868, offers another example of the discoveries of the 19th century that prepared the way for the great finds of the 20th century. The inscription dates from about 850 B.C. It was erected by Mesha, king of Moab, and is often styled the *Mesha Stone*. It tells of the wars of Mesha of Moab with Omri, king of Israel, and Omri's successors. It also tells of Mesha's wars with the Edomites. The material recorded on the *Moabite Stone* parallels biblical history recorded in 2 Kings, chapters 1 and 3. Numerous places mentioned in the Old Testament occur on the stele (inscribed monument). Among them are Arnon (Num. 21:13; Deut. 2:24), Ataroth (Num. 32:34), Baal Meon or Beth Baal Meon (Josh. 13:17), Beth Bamoth or Bamoth Baal (Josh. 13:17), Beth Diblathaim (Jer. 48:22), Bezer (Josh. 20:8), Dibon (Num. 32:34), Jahaza (Josh. 13:18), Medeba (Josh. 13:9), and Nebo (Num. 32:38).

This inscribed monument or stele measures 3 feet 8 1/2 inches in height, 2 feet 3 1/2 inches in width, and 1 foot 1 3/4 inches in thickness. Its thirty-four lines constitute the longest single literary inscription yet recovered extrabiblically dealing with Palestine in the period 900–600 B.C. It records that Moab had been conquered by Omri and his son Ahab but was set free from the Israelite yoke by Mesha's god Chemosh. This deity is represented as commanding King Mesha to go to war against Israel, who, according to 2 Kings 3:27, offered up his eldest son as a burnt offering upon the wall to propitiate the god Chemosh and to secure his favor.

The *Moabite Stone* is written in the language of Moab, which was very similar to the Hebrew of the time of Omri and Ahab. This inscription, therefore, has great value in tracing the development of early Hebrew through the centuries. When it was discovered, the *Mesha Stone* was not only the longest and oldest Phoenician-Hebrew inscription then in existence, it was the only one. Now the *Gezer Calendar* is known and dates from c. 925 B.C. It is a school boy's exercise written in perfect classical Hebrew. This small limestone tablet, found at ancient Gezer, gives an incidental sidelight on Palestinian agriculture as well as on ancient Hebrew writing. Such discoveries as the *Gezer Calendar* and the *Mesha Stone* not only give glimpses into the background of the Bible but form important links in the culture and history of the people outside the pale of Israel.

Great Discoveries of the 20th Century

Although such discoveries as the Rosetta Stone, the *Behistun Inscription*, and the Moabite Stone are important for their time and laid the foundations of scientific archaeology in the 19th century, it remained for the 20th century to produce the most thrilling and outstanding archaeological finds. During this period biblical archaeology came to be a refined and precise science, adding to the frontiers of biblical knowledge on the human plane and making tremendous contributions to the background, historical and cultural, of the written Word of God.

The Code of Hammurabi—Light on Mosaic Laws

Hammurabi (actually named Hammurapi), the sixth king of the first dynasty of Babylon who ruled in Babylon from 1728 to 1676 B.C., was not always the great world power as we think of him today. Instead, according to the *Mari Documents* (*see* Mari Texts under a separate heading in this article), he was somewhat of a minor power when compared to other kings of his day in the early years of his reign. Yet, he is memorialized for eternity with the discovery of the Code of Hammurabi, discovered in 1901. The code, a copy of which was discovered by Jacques de Morgan at Susa in Elam, where it had been carried off by the Elamites from Babylon, is inscribed on a stele of black diorite over seven feet tall and approximately six feet wide. On the stele the code contains some 250 laws or stipulations. At the top of the stele is a bas-relief showing the king receiving the law code from the god Shamash, the god of justice and law.

The code, which is not actually a code per se,

but more of a collection of laws, written near the end of Hammurabi's reign, is important in furnishing background material for comparison with other ancient bodies of law. It is natural that it should offer comparative data for the study of the law of the Torah or Pentateuch. This type of code contains a form of laws known as casuistic law or case law, based on specific cases of human conduct. The formula for this type of law is: "If someone does this to another human being (and the infraction is defined), then the penalty is (whatever is prescribed in the code)." James West, in his book *Introduction to the Old Testament* (Macmillan, 1981, page 180), states, "The social, civil, and criminal laws in the Pentateuch are cast in this form. The subjects covered include the various facets of a complex society, but, as compared with Hebrew laws, the extra-biblical codes exhibit a greater concern with property rights, a less rigorous attention to persons, and scarcely any regulation at all of religion and cult."

It is believed by some scholars that the Code of Hammurabi was not actually written to be used in the practice of law, but is more of an expression of philosophical, intellectual, or literary ideas and ideals to demonstrate the ethical and legal thinking of the day. Furthermore, the code was certainly not written by Hammurabi himself, but most likely by scribes in his employment who penned his name to the document.

For Jewish and Christian tradition the code has value because it enables us to better understand some of the legal writings found in the Pentateuch, such as the Covenant Code (from Exodus 21—23). But the law found in the Torah (Pentateuch) is also very different in places. For example, much of the law found in the Torah is known as apodictic law, which take the form of imperatives such as "You shall . . . , or You shall not . . . ." A good example of apodictic law is found in the Ten Commandments.

The Elephantine Papyri—Light on the Ezra-Nehemiah Era

Discovered in 1903 on the island of Elephantine at the First Cataract of the Nile in Egypt, these important documents give an interesting glimpse of one of the outlying regions of the Persian Empire in the latter part of the fifth century B.C. *The Elephantine Papyri* come from a Jewish military colony settled at that place. Inscribed in Aramaic, the language of diplomacy and trade throughout western Asia in the Persian period and that was gradually replacing Hebrew as the everyday tongue of the Jewish people, the contents are varied, ranging from the copy of the *Behistun Inscription* of Darius to such a document as a Jewish marriage contract. The letters tell us about the sacking of a Jewish temple at Elephantine in an anti-Jewish persecution about 411 B.C. The Jews at this far-off colony worshiped the Lord whom they referred to by the name of Yahu.

Other letters from Elephantine that have in recent years become known and have been published by the Brooklyn Museum demonstrate that the temple was rebuilt after its destruction. They contain mention of Yahu as "the god who dwells in Yeb, the fortress." Compare Psalm 31:3. These new papyri demonstrate that Egypt was still under the authority of Persia in the first years of Artaxerxes II (404–359 B.C.).

The Elephantine Papyri therefore illuminate the general background of the period of Ezra-Nehemiah and the earlier Persian period. They shed important light on the life of the Jewish dispersion in a remote frontier place such as Elephantine in Egypt. They also are invaluable in giving the scholar a knowledge of the Aramaic language of that period, and many of the customs and names that appear in the Bible are illustrated by these important literary finds.

The Hittite Monuments from Boghaz-Keui– Mementos of an Imperial People

In 1906 Professor Hugo Winkler of Berlin began excavations at Boghaz-Keui, a site that lies ninety miles east of Ankara in the great bend of the Halys River in Asia Minor. It was discovered that this was an ancient Hittite capital. Numerous clay tablets were dug up written in texts containing six different languages. A large number of these were inscribed in the cuneiform characters of the Hittite language. Eventually deciphered through the labors of three men and particularly of the Czech scholar Friedrich Hrozny, this language proved to be the key to a great deal of background of interest to the biblical student.

Before the Boghaz-Keui tablets revealed the Hittites to be an ancient people, the biblical references to them used to be regarded in critical circles as historically worthless. In the five books of Moses, references to the Hittites as inhabiting the land of Canaan and as among those whom the Israelites drove out occur in several places (Ex. 33:2; Deut. 7:1; 20:17; Josh. 3:10; 24:11). In the various lists the order varies, and there is not an inkling that one reference might be the name of a powerful imperial people and the other a small local tribe. Less than a century ago the "Hittites" meant little

more to the reader of the Bible than the "Hivite" or the "Perizite" still does.

It was commonly known from the biblical record that when Abraham settled in Hebron he had Hittites as neighbors. It was everyday knowledge that one of David's eminent soldiers was Uriah, a Hittite. But who would have expected that "Hittites" were more prominent than "Gadites" or "Beerothites"?

Now it is known that two great periods of Hittite power are to be noted. The first goes back to about 1800 B.C., and the second is dated from around 1400 to 1200 B.C. In this latter period of Hittite supremacy the powerful rulers reigned at Boghaz-Keui. One of these was named Suppiluliuma. This great conqueror extended his empire to the confines of Syria Palestine. The great Rameses II of Egypt, in the famous battle of Kadesh, collided with Hittite power. A Hittite treaty of peace with the pharaoh in the twenty-first year of the latter's reign was confirmed by a royal marriage.

About 1200 B.C. the great Hittite Empire collapsed, and the Hittite city of Boghaz-Keui fell. However, important centers of Hittite power remained at Carchemish, Sengirli, Hamath, and other places in north Syria. As a result of the excavation and decipherment of various Hittite monuments, the whole context of the ancient biblical world has been illuminated.

Because of this increased background knowledge, such allusions as those to the "kings of the Hittites" (1 Kin. 10:29; 2 Chr. 1:17) are much better understood. Also Ezekiel's reference to unfaithful Jerusalem as having an Amorite for a father and a Hittite for a mother (Ezek. 16:45) are now comprehensible. The manner in which archaeology has brought to light the ancient Hittites furnishes a good example of the way this important science is expanding biblical horizons.

The Religious Texts from Ras Shamra (Ugarit)– Canaanite Cults Exposed

One of the most important discoveries of the 20th century was the recovery of hundreds of clay tablets that had been housed in a library situated between two great temples, one dedicated to Baal and another dedicated to Dagon, in the city of *Ugarit*—modern *Ras Shamra* in north Syria. These clay tablets date from the 15th to early 14th centuries B.C. They are inscribed in the earliest-known alphabet written in wedge-shaped signs. Professor H. Bower of the University of Halle recognized this new writing as Semitic. Numbers of scholars such as E. Dhorme and Charles Virolleaud began working on the decipherment of this new Semitic language.

First intimations of the archaeological importance of the ancient city of Ugarit, which was unknown until 1928, came in the spring of that year when a Syrian peasant plowing in his field a little north of present-day Minet el-Beida suddenly came across some antiquities. On April 2, 1929, work began at Minet el-Beida under the direction of Claude F Schaffer. After a month's work he changed to the nearby tell of Ras Shamra. Only a few days' work demonstrated the importance of the new location. On May 20 the first tablets were uncovered. Schaffer continued excavations from 1929 to 1937. Between 1929 and 1933, the bulk of significant religious texts were recovered in the royal library in the area. Many of these were inscribed in an early Canaanite dialect of the late Bronze and early Iron periods.

The City of Ugarit

This flourishing second-millennium city, which had been known by scholars from Egyptian inscriptions from the *Tell el-Amarna Letters* and Hittite documents, was located on the north Syrian coast opposite the island of Cyprus, about eight miles north of Latakia and fifty miles southwest of Antioch. It was situated on a bay and had a port that could be used by seagoing trade ships. It was a harbor town known in Greek times as Leukos Limen, the white harbor. It is now called Ras Shamra, "hill of fennel," because fennel grows there.

The hill that comprises the ruin of the ancient city has the form of a trapezium with the long side about 670 yards north and south and the longer diagonal about 1,100 yards. The hill is about twenty-two yards high. The site was located on the important trade route along the coast from Egypt to Asia Minor, which was connected by a road with Aleppo, Mari on the Euphrates, and Babylon. The sea route from Ugarit to Alashiya—that is, Cyprus—was a short one.

Very early, Ugarit struck up a brisk trade with the Aegean Islands. It became an important harbor. One of the main exported articles was copper, which was used in the production of bronze. Copper was imported from Asia Minor and Cyprus. Bronze was produced in Ugarit. Being a Phoenician town, Ugarit, like its sister cities, delivered timber to Egypt. Not only cedars from the interior were exported but other kinds of wood as well. There were also blue dye factories. Great heaps of murex shells indicate this. These shells, abundantly found along the east Mediterranean coast, produced a famous dye of antiquity.

Literary Importance of the Texts

After preliminary work by many scholars, Cyrus Gordon worked out a *Ugaritic Grammar* and later put out an edition of the texts called *Ugaritic Literature*. The decipherment of the texts showed the important parallels between Ugaritic and Hebrew literary style and vocabulary. By 1936 H. L. Ginsberg had made some far-reaching observations with regard to common structural elements. Ginsberg's study showed that Canaanite poetry, like Hebrew, was basically accentual, that is, it consisted of numbers of feet, each of which was accented. Since the Ugaritic language is very closely connected with biblical Hebrew, much light has been shed upon Hebrew lexicography. Any recent lexicon of Hebrew must take into consideration the vocabulary used at Ugarit. Future Hebrew dictionaries will include many words hitherto misunderstood or only partially known.

For example, the word *beth-heber* (Prov. 21:9; 25:24) hitherto rendered "house" has been shown from Ugaritic and Assyrian to mean specifically "a storehouse." These verses could then be rendered "It is better to dwell in a corner of the housetop, than with a contentious woman and in a storehouse." It is of interest to note that the Egyptian proverbs of Amenemope, which have many parallels to the biblical Book of Proverbs, employs a word for "storehouse" in exactly the same sense.

Religious Significance of the Ugaritic Inscriptions

By far the most important contribution of the religious texts from Ras Shamra (Ugarit) is in giving the Bible student background material for the study of Old Testament religions. The epics set forth very clearly the Canaanite pantheon. We now know that this pantheon of the Canaanites was headed up by the god El, the supreme Canaanite deity. This is also a name by which God is known in the Old Testament (cf. Gen. 33:20). This name, El, often occurs in Old Testament poetry (Ps. 18:31, 32; Job 8:3). It occurs frequently also in prose in compound names, for example, *El Elyon*, the God Most High (Gen. 14:18); *El Shaddai*, Almighty God (Gen. 17:1); *El Hai*, the living God (Josh. 3:10). El is a common Semitic word for God.

Later Excavations at Ugarit

During World War II excavations at Ras Shamra were discontinued. They were resumed in 1948 and have been going on regularly. Work under the direction of C. F. Schaffer has been centered upon uncovering the great palace. The most important discoveries in connection with this structure were the royal archives. These archives, discovered in the palace, were of a historical nature in contrast to the mythological ritual texts of the early years, 1929–1937. The archives in the west wing of the building contained administrative documents to a large degree relating to the royal estates. Those in the east wing had documents relating to the capital city. Those in the central archive were mainly legal finds. Almost all documents were inscribed in the common language of these centuries, namely Akkadian. A few were written in Hurrian and Ugaritic. The names of twelve Ugaritic kings were found in the documents that date from the 18th to the 13th centuries B.C. The seals of the royal acts are remarkable as they all are identical in design at the top, without regard to the name of the reigning king. The motif is well known from Babylonian glyptic art and shows homage being paid to the deified king.

Numbers of fine objects have been recovered from the palace, especially pieces from the king's bedroom. Especially noteworthy was the large ivory foot panel of the royal bedstead, perhaps the largest single piece of ivory carving yet recovered in the Near East. Another remarkable piece found in the campaign of 1952–1953 is the ancient Ugaritic alphabet of thirty letters. This piece is now housed in the National Museum at Damascus.

The Nuzi Tablets and the Biblical Horites

From this city east of ancient Asshur and a short distance west of Arrapkha, which flourished in the middle centuries of the second millennium B.C., have come several thousand cuneiform texts. These texts have proved of immense value, illustrating the rise of the Hurrians and patriarchal customs. The present site of Nuzi is Yoghlan-Tepe. It is a mound 150 miles north of Baghdad near the foothills of southern Khurdistan. Nuzi was excavated in 1925–1931 by the American School of Oriental Research in Baghdad and Harvard University. The name "Nuzi" was used during its occupation by the Hurrians.

Before the time of the Hurrian settlement the site of Nuzi was occupied by a different ethnic group, called the Subarians. In this older period, the city bore the name of Gasur, and its earliest occupation goes back to prehistoric times. But the vital interest in the town stems from its occupation by the Hurrians and the cuneiform texts that have been excavated from it and from nearby Arrapkha, modern Kirkuk, some nine miles to the east.

The Nuzi Tablets and the Hurrians

Modern archaeology has not only resurrected the ancient Hittites, who were for centuries practically unknown except for sporadic references on the pages of the Bible, but also the enigmatic Horites. In the books of the Pentateuch there are numbers of references to a perplexing people called Horites. These people were defeated by Chedorlaomer and the invading Mesopotamian army (Gen. 14:6). They were governed by chiefs (Gen. 36:20–30). They are said to have been destroyed by Esau's descendants (Deut. 2:12, 22).

This unknown people used to be thought of as a very local, restricted group of cave dwellers. The name "Horite" was thought to be derived from the Hebrew *hor;* "hole" or "cave." Other than this etymological description the Horites remained completely obscure, not appearing outside the Pentateuch or in extrabiblical literature. Within the last thirty-five years, however, archaeology has performed a miracle in resurrecting the ancient Hurrians, the biblical Horites. They are known not to be a local, restricted group but to be a prominent people who took a preeminent place on the stage of ancient history. It is now known that they not only existed but played a far-reaching role in ancient Near Eastern cultural history. As a result of the discovery of the Hurrians, the popular etymology that connects them with "cave dwellers" has had to be abandoned.

The Hurrians or Horites were non-Semitic peoples who, before the beginning of the second millennium B.C., migrated into northeastern Mesopotamia. Their homeland was in the region south of the Caucasus. They appear first upon the horizon of history about 2400 B.C. in the Zagros Mountains east of the Tigris River. In the period around 2000 to 1400 B.C., the Hurrians were very common and widespread in Upper Mesopotamia.

The Nuzi Tablets and the Patriarchs

The main interest of the Nuzi tablets lies in the illumination of patriarchal times and customs. In the patriarchal narratives, many local practices have been quite obscure to the modern reader. Numerous clay tablets from Nuzi and nearby Arrapkha have in many cases illuminated these customs, so that now we see them as they existed in the general historical background of the time. Although the Nuzi tablets are to be dated in the 15th and 14th centuries B.C., sometime after the patriarchal period (c. 2000–1800 B.C.), nevertheless, they illustrate the times of the patriarchs. The reason is that when the patriarchs came out of Ur, they sojourned in Haran and mingled in west Hurrian society. But the same customs prevailed by extension among the west Hurrians as among the east Hurrians at Nuzi and Arrapkha. Hence, the results obtained at Nuzi are valid by extension for the west Hurrians, as well as for a period considerably later than the patriarchs.

In Genesis 15:2 Abraham laments his childless condition and the fact that his servant Eliezer was to be his heir. In the light of this situation, God assures the patriarch that he is to have a son of his own to inherit his property. The Nuzi tablets explain this difficult matter. They tell how a trusted servant, an apparent outsider, could be heir. At ancient Nuzi, it was customary in Hurrian society for a couple who did not have a child to adopt a son to take care of his foster parents as long as they lived, take over when they died, and then in return for his filial duty to become their heir. But it is important to note that if a natural son was born, this agreement was nullified, at least in part, and the natural son became heir. Eliezer was plainly Abraham's adopted son. But the miraculous birth of Isaac, as the promised posterity, altered Eliezer's status as heir.

At Nuzi a marriage contract occasionally included the statement that a given slave girl is presented outright to a new bride, exactly as in the marriage of Leah (Gen. 29:24) and Rachel (29:29). Other marriage provisions specify that a wife of the upper classes who was childless was to furnish her husband with a slave girl as a concubine. In such a case, however, the wife was entitled to treat the concubine's offspring as her own. This last provision illuminates the difficult statement in Genesis 16:2 with its punning: "I shall obtain children by her," which means "I may be built up through her." It is interesting to note that the related law of Hammurabi, paragraph 144, offers no complete parallel. There the wife is a priestess and is not entitled to claim the children of the concubine for herself.

It is thus seen that in Nuzian law and society in which the patriarchs moved for a time, marriage was regarded primarily for bearing children and not mainly for companionship. In one way or another, it was considered necessary for the family to procreate. After Isaac's birth, Abraham's reluctance to comply with Sarah's demand that Hagar's child be driven out is illustrated by local practice at Nuzi. In the event the slave wife should have a son, that son must not be expelled. In Abraham's case, only a divine dispensation overruled human law and made the patriarch willing to comply.

Cases involving rights of the firstborn occurring in Genesis are also illustrated. In the Bible Esau sells his birthright to Jacob. In the Nuzi tablets one brother sells a grove that he has inherited for three sheep. Evidently this is quite comparable in value to the savory food for which Esau sold his right.

In Hurrian society birthright was not so much the matter of being the firstborn as of paternal decree. Such decrees were binding above all others when handed down in the form of a deathbed declaration introduced by the following formula: "Behold now, I am old." This situation helps to illuminate Genesis 27, the chapter that tells of Jacob stealing the family blessing.

The obscure *teraphim* are also explained in Nuzian law. We now know that the teraphim were small household deities. Possession of them implied headship of family. In the case of a married daughter, they assured her husband the right to her father's property. Laban had sons of his own when Jacob left for Canaan. They alone had the right to their father's gods. The theft of these important household idols by Rachel was a notorious offense (Gen. 31:19, 30, 35). She aimed at nothing less than to preserve for her husband the chief title to Laban's estate.

The texts from Arrapkha and Nuzi have at last supplied details for explaining these difficult customs. In special circumstances the property could pass to a daughter's husband, but only if the father had handed over his household gods to his son-in-law as a formal token that the arrangement had proper sanction.

Another custom illuminated is that found in Genesis 12:10–20; 20:2–6; 26:1–11, where the wife of a patriarch is introduced as his sister with no apparent worthy reason. The texts from Nuzi, however, show that among the Hurrians marriage bonds were most solemn, and the wife had legally, although not necessarily through ties of blood, the simultaneous status of sister, so that the terms "sister" and "wife" could be interchangeable in an official use under certain circumstances. Thus, in resorting to the wife-sister relationship, both Abraham and Isaac were availing themselves of the strongest safeguards the law, as it existed then, could afford them.

Critical Value

Discoveries such as those at Nuzi and Arrapkha are forcing higher critics to abandon many radical and untenable theories. For example, not long ago it was customary for critics to view the patriarchal stories as retrojections from a much later period and not as authentic stories from the Mosaic age, namely, the 15th century B.C. But now the question rises, How could such authentic local color be retrojected from a later age? The Nuzi tablets have done a great service to students of early Bible history in not only attesting the influence of social customs in the patriarchal age and in the same portion of Mesopotamia from which the patriarchs come but also have demonstrated these narratives are authentic to their time. Such discoveries add greatly to our historical background and enable us in our modern day to reveal them in their genuine local color and historical setting.

The Mari Letters—Light on the World of the Patriarchs

One of the most historically and archaeologically rewarding sites that has been discovered in Mesopotamia and Bible lands is the city of *Mari*, modern Tell el-Hariri on the Middle Euphrates, about seven miles northwest of Abu-Kemal, a small town on the Syrian side of the Syro-Iraq frontier.

The ancient city owed its importance to being a focal point on caravan routes crossing the Syrian desert and linking the city with Syria and the Mediterranean coast and with the civilizations of Assyria and Babylonia. This site was further identified by William Foxwell Albright in 1932.

Mari began to be excavated in 1933 by Andre Parrot under the auspices of the Musée du Louvre. The results were the digging up of an ancient imperial city of great importance and splendor. World War II interrupted excavations in 1939, after six highly successful campaigns had taken place. In 1951 this work was resumed. After four further campaigns it was broken off in 1956, as a result of the trouble over the Suez Canal.

Among the most important discoveries at Mari was the great *temple of Ishtar*, for the Babylonian goddess of propagation, and a temple-tower or ziggurat. The temple itself had courts of the Sumerian type, columns, and a cella. The ziggurat or temple-tower was similar to that at Ur and other Mesopotamian sites. Statuettes were uncovered to illustrate the popularity of the Ishtar fertility cult. One of the palace murals depicts the fact that the ruling monarch at Mari was believed to have received his staff and ring, the emblems of his authority, from Ishtar.

Another important discovery at Mari was the *royal palace*. A sprawling structure contemporary with the first dynasty of Babylon, it was built in the center of the mound and contained almost three hundred rooms. The throne room furnished some rare specimens of well preserved wall paintings. This huge building with its beautifully colored mural paintings, its royal apartments, administrative offices, and scribal

school is considered one of the best preserved palaces of the Middle East. The structure was built by later Amorites, who worshiped the deities Adad and Dagon. In the postwar campaign the excavation centered mainly around the older strata going back to buildings of the pre-Sargonic period from the time of the dynasty of Akkad.

The Royal Archives

The most interesting finds, however, were the so-called *Mari Letters*, some twenty thousand clay tablets dug up, which have revolutionized knowledge of the ancient biblical world. These documents were written in the dialect of Old Babylonian. They date from the era of Hammurabi, about 1700 B.C., the same monarch whose code was discovered in 1901 at Susa. These records constitute memoranda of the king and governors of the city-state of Mari and belong to the time of the kings Yasmah-Adad, under whose reign the construction of the palace was begun, and Zimri-Lim, under whom it was completed. Some of the correspondence is that of King Yasmah-Adad with his father, the powerful empire builder King Shamshi-Adad I ofAssyria, as well as with the representatives of the provinces of his realm. King Zimri-Lim's correspondence also figures in exchanges of diplomatic correspondence with King Hammurabi of Babylon, as well as with the king of Aleppo and other vassals. Two letters dispatched from Aleppo to Zimri-Lim deal with prophetic utterances delivered in the name of the god Adad of Aleppo. The subject and tenor of these remind one of biblical prophecies.

Biblical Value of the Mari Texts

These records are of great value to biblical students because they stem from the region that was the home of the Hebrew patriarchs for a number of years before going on to Canaan. At the time of the third dynasty of Ur, Mari was ruled by the governors of the kings of Ur. Eventually, however, a prince of Mari, Ishbi-Irra, who had brought the city-state of Isin under his dominion about 2021 B.C., was instrumental in bringing about the downfall of the city of Ur.

Nahor, which figures prominently in the patriarchal narratives (Gen. 24:10), is mentioned quite often in the *Mari Letters*. One letter from Nahor is sent from a woman of that town to the king and runs as follows:

"To my lord say, Thus Inib-Sharrim, thy maid

✕	Important excavation	
(R)	One of the 6 cities of refuge	
(L)	One of the 48 Levitical cities	
?	Location uncertain	
- - -	Approximate tribal boundary	

Scale:
0   10   20   30   40 miles
0   20   40   60 kms

Tyre ✕
Kanah?
Hammon? ✕
Yiron?
Leshem (Laish)
Kedesh
Edrei?
Achzib • Abdon (L)
Achshaph? •
Beth-emek? •
Acco •
Rehob? (L) •
Aphek? •
Hazor ✕
NAPHTALI
Beth-anath? •
Neiel? • Rimmon •
ASHER
ZEBULUN
Kabul •
Neah? • Valley of Iphtah-el
Helkath? (L) •
Beten? •
CARMEL
Bethlehem? Shimron? •
Mareal? •
Jokneam (L) •
Dabbesheth? •
Dor •
Shihor-libnath? ✕
Megiddo ✕
Taanach (L) ✕
ISSACHAR
Hannathon? (L) •
Chaloth-tabor
Gath-hepher? •
Jabneel? •
Chesulloth
Sarid
Japhia •
Hukkok
Chinnereth
Rakkath •
Zer (Madon)? •
Adami-nekeb •
Hammath (L) •
Jabneel? •
Daberath (L) •
Beth-shemesh? •
En-dor •
Shunem •
Golan? (RL) •
Jezreel ✕
Beth-shan •
The Villages of MANASSEH Jair
En-gannim (L) •
Ibleam
Ramoth in Gilead (RL)
GREAT SEA
MANASSEH
Zaphon? •
Shechem (RL) ✕
Succoth? •
Michmethath ✕
Janoah •
Taanath-shiloh? •
Mahanaim? (L) •
Ramath-mizpeh? •
Torrent of Kanah
Tappuah? •
Ataroth •
GAD
Joppa •
Bene-berak •
Azor •
Jehud •
Shiloh •
Betonim •
Jazer? (L) •
Timnath-serah •
EPHRAIM
Zemaraim •
Beth-horon (L) •
Ophrah •
Beth-nimrah? •
Gibbethon (L)
Shaalabbin? •
Geba (L) •
Jericho ✕
Beth-arabah? •
Jabneel? •
Ekron? ✕
Gezer (L) ✕
Aijalon (L) •
BENJAMIN
Almon (L) •
Beth-hoglah •
Mephaath? (L) •
Eltekeh? (L) •
Eshtaol? •
Anathoth (L) •
Beth-peor? •
Beth-haram? •
Ashdod •
DAN
Zorah •
Jebus •
Beth-jeshimoth? •
Heshbon (L) •
Timnah ✕
Beth-shem •
Qumran •
Sibmah? •
Nebo •
Bezer? (RL) •
Azekah ✕
Bethel? •
Bamoth-baal? •
Medeba •
Ashkelon ✕
Beth-baal-meon •
Gedor? •
Tekoa •
Murabba'at ✕
REUBEN
Gath? ✕
Mareshah •
Zereth-shahar? •
Kedemoth? (L) •
Lachish ✕
Beth-zur ✕
Kiriathaim? •
Jahaz? (L) •
Gaza •
Beth-tappuah •
Hebron (RL) •
Engedi •
Dibon ✕
Aroer •
JUDAH
Ziph •
DEAD SEA
Torrent of the Arnon
Juttah (L) •
Eshtemoa (L) •
Ziklag? •
En-rimmon •
Bethuel? •
Sharuhen? ✕
Shema? •
SIMEON
Hazar-shual? •
Beer-sheba •
Hormah? •
Moladah? •
Eltolad? •
Ararah (Adadah)? •

PHILISTINES

© 1995 by Thomas Nelson

THE SETTLEMENT IN CANAAN

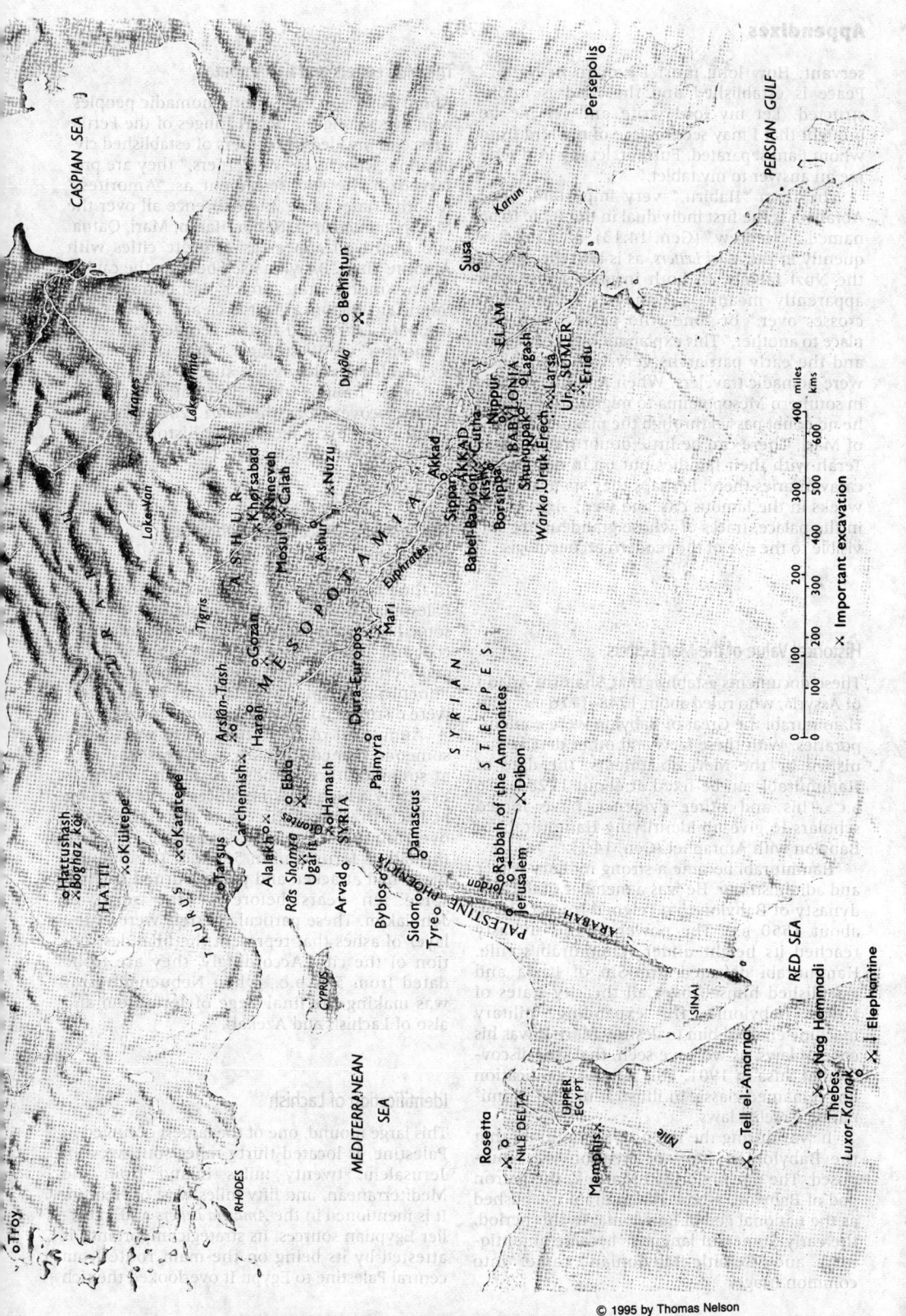

THE ANCIENT NEAR EAST

© 1995 by Thomas Nelson

servant. How long must I remain in Nahor? Peace is established and the road is unobstructed. Let my lord write and let me be brought that I may see the face of my lord from whom I am separated. Further, let my lord send me an answer to my tablet."

The term "Habiru," very important since Abraham is the first individual in the Bible to be named a "Hebrew" (Gen. 14:13), is found frequently in the *Mari Letters*, as is also the case in the Nuzi tablets. In both instances the term apparently means "a wanderer," "one who crosses over," or "one who passes from one place to another." This explanation fits Abraham and the early patriarchs very well since they were nomadic travelers. When Abraham left Ur in southern Mesopotamia to migrate to Canaan, he no doubt passed through the magnificent city of Mari. There can be little doubt that he and Terah with their families put up in one of the caravansaries there. Perhaps they spent days or weeks in the famous city and went sightseeing in the palace, traces of whose grandeur are still visible to the eye of the modern archaeologist.

Historical Value of the Mari Letters

These documents establish that Shamshi Adad I of Assyria, who ruled about 1748–1716 B.C., and Hammurabi the Great of Babylon were contemporaries. With these facts and other details furnished by the Mari documents, the date of Hammurabi can be fixed at about 1728–1676 B.C. This and other evidence have forced scholars to give up identifying Hammurabi of Babylon with Amraphel (Gen. 14:1).

Hammurabi became a strong military leader and administrator. He was a member of the first dynasty of Babylon that reigned from 1830 to about 1550 B.C. The power of this dynasty reached its height under Hammurabi's rule. Hammurabi defeated Rim-Sin of Larsa and established himself over all the city-states of Lower Babylonia. His expanding military machine enabled him to destroy Mari. It was his code of laws, as we have seen, that was discovered at Susa in 1901. This famous codification has remained classic in illustrating and illuminating Israelite laws.

It was during the reign of Hammurabi that the Babylonian story of creation was composed. The poem glorified Marduk, the patron god of Babylon, whom Hammurabi established as the national god of Babylonia. In this period, the early Sumerian language became an antiquity and Semitic-Babylonian came into common usage.

The Mari Letters and the Amorites

About 2000 B.C. the Semitic-nomadic peoples, who lived along the desert fringes of the Fertile Crescent, invaded the centers of established civilization. Known as "Westerners," they are preserved in the Old Testament as "Amorites." Amorite states came into existence all over the Mesopotamian area. Nahor, Haran, Mari, Qatna, and Ugarit all appear as Amorite cities with Amorite kings. Babylon itself became the capital of an Amorite state under Hammurabi. This important historical fact is clearly reflected in the *Mari Letters* and in the peoples known as "Amorites" or "Westerners." In such a manner archaeology is slowly but surely outlining the historical framework of the patriarchal age. Such discoveries as the *Mari Letters* prove of incalculable assistance to the historian of the ancient biblical world.

The Lachish Ostraca—Jeremiah's Age Lives Again

In the excavations of Lachish, a southwestern Palestinian city, the most astonishing finds were some letters embedded in a layer of burnt charcoal and ashes. They were eighteen in number and were in Hebrew writing done in the ancient Phoenician script. Three more of these letters were discovered in later campaigns in 1938.

Almost all of the letters were written by someone named Hoshiah, who was stationed at some military outpost, to Jaosh, who was evidently a high-ranking officer in the garrison at Lachish. It was the era of the Babylonian overrunning of Palestine several years before the fall of Jerusalem in 586 B.C. The Babylonians had attacked and partly burned Lachish some ten years before in the reign of Jehoiakim. These particular letters were in the layer of ashes that represent the final destruction of the city. Accordingly, they are to be dated from 587 B.C., when Nebuchadnezzar was making the final siege of Jerusalem and also of Lachish and Azekah.

Identification of Lachish

This large mound, one of the largest occupied in Palestine, is located thirty miles southwest of Jerusalem, twenty miles inland from the Mediterranean, and fifty miles west of Hebron. It is mentioned in the *Amarna Letters* and in earlier Egyptian sources. Its strategic importance is attested by its being on the main route from central Palestine to Egypt. It overlooked the rich

Shephelah (terrain that descended to the coastal lowland). The fortress city was an ideal barrier between the Philistine plains and the elevated Judean country. It was one of the principal fortified cities of Judah and one of the bastions taken by the Israelites in their conquest of Palestine (Josh. 10:31–35). The site of Umm-Lakis was first thought to be Lachish. Then the location was sought at Tell el-Hesy by Sir Flinders Petrie, a pioneer archaeologist. William Foxwell Albright finally identified it correctly with the large mound of Tell el-Duweir.

Nebuchadnezzar captured Lachish in 588–586 B.C. (Jer. 34:7). Marks of a huge conflagration on the road leading up to the gate and on the adjacent wall display that the attackers relied largely upon fire, for which felled olive trees not yet harvested supplied the fuel.

Excavations at Lachish

The Wellcome-Marston Archaeological Expedition in 1933 commenced work there, under the direction of J. L. Starkey. In 1938 Starkey was killed by Arab brigands, and the work was carried on by Lankester Harding and Charles H. Inge.

Besides evidences of earlier occupation, Lachish disclosed settlement by the Hyksos about 1720–1550 B.C. These people overran Egypt during this period. A typical Hyksos defense ditch or *fosse*, with a ramp of clay and lime that apparently provided an enclosure for their horses, was brought to light. In the fosse three Canaanite Egyptian temples built between 1450 and 1225 B.C. were excavated. A Persian temple of a much later period was also found. Cemeteries at Lachish yielded a great quantity of pottery, jewelry, scarabs, and skeletal evidence. A well, 200 feet deep, was located within the city, the remains of a tremendous engineering excavation for water storage, which was not completed. A shaft of about 85 feet terminates in a rectangle 80 x 70 feet cut to a depth of 80 feet. The aim was a water system that would have been much larger than that provided by Hezekiah for Jerusalem in the Siloam Tunnel and comparable to similar systems at Gezer and Megiddo.

A good quantity of inscribed material has been removed from the Lachish excavations. A bronze dagger from about 1700 B.C. contains four pictographic signs, samples of the early script. A bowl and a ewer contain specimens of the same early writing as that found at Serabit el-Khadem. The name "Gedaliah" was found on a jar handle and may be the official whom Nebuchadnezzar set over the land after the fall of Jerusalem (cf. Jer. 40—42).

Contents of the Lachish Letters

But of all the epigraphic discoveries at Lachish, the most important are the *Lachish Letters*. These letters may be briefly described as follows: Letter 1 lists names, the majority of which are found in the Old Testament. Letters 2 and 5 consist largely of greetings. Letter 3, the longest, contains the most information. This concerns movements of Jewish troops and also makes an interesting note to an unnamed prophet and his word of warning. Letter 4 states that Hoshiah, though observing the signals of Lachish, cannot see those of Azekah. Azekah may well have fallen earlier, for this letter states, "We are watching for the signal station at Lachish according to all the signals you are giving, because we cannot see the signals of Azekah." Letter 6 contains the biblical expression, "to weaken the hands of the people." This recalls Jeremiah, who uses a similar expression (Jer. 38:4).

Historical Importance of the Letters

The *Lachish Letters* give us an independent view of conditions in Judah in the last days before the fall of Jerusalem. As the Neo-Babylonian army advanced, the doom of Jerusalem was sealed, in contrast to its deliverance under the Assyrian, Sennacherib, as Isaiah had predicted (2 Kin. 19:20, 32–36). Relentlessly, Nebuchadnezzar advanced on the city after a terrible eighteen-month siege in 587–586 B.C. The walls of the city were broken down, the houses and the temple burned, and the people carried away to exile (2 Kin. 25:1–12).

Jeremiah conducted his difficult ministry in these agonizing times. His reference to Azekah and Lachish is most interesting. "When the king of Babylon's army fought against Jerusalem and all the cities of Judah that were left, against Lachish and Azekah; for only these fortified cities remained of the cities of Judah" (Jer. 34:7).

Tell Zakariya in the Shephelah region has been identified as Azekah. In 1898 it was excavated by Frederick K. Bliss of the Palestine Exploration Fund. It had a strong inner fortress buttressed with eight large towers.

The *Lachish Letters* concern the time just prior to the fall of the city and present the same conditions of turmoil and confusion that are revealed in the Book of Jeremiah. Numerous place names that occur in the Bible are found in the letters, as well as personal names. Hoshaiah appears in Jeremiah 42:1 and Nehemiah 12:32. God is referred to by the four-letters YHWH, which are the consonants of the name "Jehovah" or "Yahweh." It is also interesting to note that many of the men's names have

Yahweh endings. A prophet like Jeremiah is referred to in the letters. But this is most probably not Jeremiah himself.

So complete was the destruction by the Babylonians that it took many centuries for Judah to recover. The returned remnant was tiny and weak. The small Jewish state stamped its coins with the name "Yehud," that is, Judah, but not until after 300 B.C. do substantial archaeological remains appear, and then they are not abundant. Certainly the Babylonians did a thorough job of destroying Jewish power for many centuries.

The Paleographic Importance of the Letters

Being inscribed in biblical Hebrew, in which the Old Testament Scriptures were written, and with stylistic and vocabulary similarities to the Book of Jeremiah, these letters are of great paleographic importance. They help the scholar to trace the evolution of the Hebrew alphabet, noting the formation of the letters and their style. They also enable one to see how the Old Testament Scriptures, which were then written, appeared.

Surely research of this type, that makes it possible for the scholar to look back, to resurrect the past, and to see how the language of the Old Testament developed, is fascinating. Great strides are being made in this field of enquiry. It is one truly bright spot in original biblical studies. This type of study is of immense value in expanding historical backgrounds and illuminating Holy Scripture on the human plane.

The Dead Sea Scrolls

The middle of the 20th century saw the greatest manuscript discovery of modern times. In 1947 a young Bedouin shepherd stumbled upon a cave south of Jericho, containing many leather scrolls of Hebrew and Aramaic writing and about six hundred fragmentary inscriptions. Great excitement prevailed in the archaeological world. In 1952 new caves containing fragments of later scrolls in Hebrew, Greek, and Aramaic were found. These other startling manuscript discoveries have been followed by news of additional manuscripts found in other caves in the Dead Sea area.

The Date of the Scrolls

After intensive study of the manuscripts from the Dead Sea area, scholars define three periods: 1. The Archaic Period, about 200–150 B.C.; 2.

the Hasmonean Period, about 150–30 B.C.; and 3. the Herodian Period, about 30 B.C. to A.D. 70. The great majority originated in the second and third periods, especially the last half of the second period and last half of the third period.

Although attacks have been made against the antiquity and authenticity of these manuscripts, two lines of evidence substantiate their antiquity. The evidence of *radiocarbon count*, a scientific method of dating, places the linen in which the scrolls were wrapped in the general era of 175 B.C. to A.D. 225. Scholars relying on *paleographic evidence* date these documents by the form of the letters and the way they are written in comparison with other eras of writing. They are able to demonstrate that they come in the intermediate period between the script of the third century B.C. and of the middle of the first century A.D. W. F. Albright observes, "All competent students of writing conversant with the available material and with paleographic method date the scrolls in the 250 years before A.D. 70."

The Contents of the Scrolls

Literally hundreds of scrolls and scroll fragments were found through the excavation at Qumran. A summary of these findings are as follows:

In Cave One there were seven major scrolls found. Among these were two copies of Isaiah, one complete and one partially complete; The *Manual of Discipline; Pesher on Habakkuk* (a commentary); *Thanksgiving Hymns; The War Scroll;* and *Genesis Apocryphon.* There were also additional fragments from other scrolls found here. In Cave Two there were thirty-three fragments discovered. From Cave Three fourteen fragments were reclaimed. Cave Four produced the largest collection of materials. Literally thousands of scroll fragments were found here, both biblical and sectarian. In Cave Five twenty-five fragments were found. Cave Six contained some thirty fragments. Cave Seven contained nineteen fragments written in Greek. This was unique because most of the other scrolls and scroll fragments were written in Hebrew or Aramaic. In Cave Eight there were five fragments. Cave Nine produced only one fragment. From Cave Ten the archaeologists recovered an inscribed piece of pottery. Finally, in Cave Eleven approximately eighteen fragments were discovered.

Copies of every book of the Hebrew Scriptures were found here with the exception of the Book of Esther. Sectarian books found here include the *Manual of Discipline, The War Between the Children of Light and Darkness, The Book of Jubilees,* and *The Copper Scroll.* From these sectarian scrolls and scroll fragments we have been able to learn much about first-century Palestinian Judaism and also about the Essene sect, the scribes who copied the Dead Sea Scrolls. The biblical books found are the earliest extant copies to date. Before the discovery of the Dead Sea Scrolls, the earliest manuscript of the Hebrew Scriptures dated to the ninth century A.D.

Most of the scrolls are written in either Hebrew or Aramaic, but we have some scroll fragments written in Greek. The scrolls are usually written in one of four types of script: archaic, Hasmonean, Herodian, or ornamental.

Other Manuscript-Yielding Sites

In 1952 a cave was uncovered at Murabbaat in another part of the desert. This yielded manuscripts chiefly from the second century A.D. in Hebrew, Greek, and Aramaic, including a few texts of Genesis, Exodus, Deuteronomy, and Isaiah. Several Hebrew letters were discovered from the period of Simon ben Keseba, that is, Bar Kochba, who led the revolt in A.D. 132–135. A notable exception to the second century A.D. date of this material is an archaic Hebrew papyrus piece, a palimpsest, a list of names and numbers, dated in the sixth century B.C.

In the same general area, other caves have been found, one group in Khirbet Mird, northeast of the monastery of Mar Saba. These contain Arabic papyri, Greek and Christo-Palestinian-Syrian documents, with fragments of biblical codices, all late Byzantine and early Arabic. Another group of manuscripts date from the period of the bulk of the Murabbaat material. Among them is a version of the minor prophets in Greek and a corpus of Nabatean papyri, both of great biblical and historical importance.

Excavations at Khirbet Qumran

Khirbet Qumran was excavated between 1951 and 1954. This Essene community, with the nearby caves, proved to be the richest manuscript-yielding center. Members of this community copied these manuscripts and preserved them by hiding them in the caves. The Essenes at Khirbet Qumran, seven miles south of Jericho near the shores of the Dead Sea, were next to the Pharisees and Sadducees in importance in sectarian Judaism. This site has become one of the most publicized places in Palestine because of the phenomenal manuscript finds in the cave-dotted cliffs.

Excavations at Khirbet Qumran have fully authenticated this site as the center of Essenic Judaism. As the result of the recovery of coins, pottery, and architectural remains, the story of

Qumran's occupation can now be told. Four periods in the later history of the site are traced.

Period 1

The first period extends from its founding about 110 B.C. under John Hyrcanus. Numerous coins of this ruler were dug up, as well as of other Hasmonean rulers including Antigonus, 40–37 B.C., the last ruler of this line, to the seventh year of Herod, 31 B.C. At this time an earthquake apparently leveled the site.

Period 2

The second period at Qumran dates from the rebuilding and enlargement about A.D. 1 until the Roman destruction in June, A.D. 68. During this era in the lifetime of Jesus, John the Baptist, and the early Christian apostles, Qumran flourished, influencing Judaism and the early Christian church. Coins have been found dating from the reign of Archelaus, 4 B.C. to A.D. 6, and from the time of the Roman procurators down to the second year of the first Jewish revolt in A.D. 66–70. The Roman army, which took Jericho in June, A.D. 68, evidently likewise captured Qumran. One coin, marked with an X, belonged to the Tenth Legion. Iron arrowheads were found in a layer of burned ash in the excavation.

Qumran Fell to Roman Occupation

Some coins describe Judaea Capta. These date from the reign of Titus, A.D. 79–81, and mark Period 3 as the Roman occupation after Jerusalem's destruction in A.D. 70. Evidence that Qumran structures were converted into army barracks indicates that a Roman garrison was stationed there from about A.D. 68 to A.D. 100. At this time the site apparently was abandoned.

Period 4

Qumran is distinguished by reoccupation of the site during the second Jewish revolt, A.D. 132–135. Coins dating from this era indicate that here the Jews made their last stand to drive the Romans from their country. After that Qumran sank into obscurity.

Architectural Remains at Qumran

The main edifice at Qumran is 100 feet by 120 feet and formed the communal center and hub of the complex. At the northwest corner was a massive defense tower with thick walls enforced by stone embankments. Some coins from the time of the second Jewish revolt (A.D. 132–135) attest its use as a fortress against Roman power.

Alongside the general meeting room is the largest hall of the main building. Here was located the scriptorium. Several inkwells of the Roman period, and even some dried ink, indicate that the manuscripts had been copied by the community's scribes.

Also in the complex were two cisterns (artificial reservoirs) carefully plastered. There were installations for ablutions and baptisms. Of the possibly forty cisterns and reservoirs, the bulk of them must have been used for storage of water in the very hot, dry climate.

Of great interest is the cemetery, containing about one thousand burial places. De Vaux excavated many of these tombs. They are noted for their lack of jewelry and any evidences of luxury.

Khirbet Qumran and the Essenes

Not only do the excavations at Khirbet Qumran demonstrate that it was the headquarters of Essenic Judaism but three authorities who were contemporary witnesses attest the same fact, namely, Josephus, Philo, and Pliny. Pliny, for example, locates the Essenes at precisely the spot where Qumran is situated, namely, "on the west side of the Dead Sea." He also designates the town of En Gedi as situated "below the Essenes."

Josephus relates their unselfish character, industry, and communal life. He extols their love for common toil, says they dressed in white, and describes their three-year probationary period before admission to the sect, and other phases of discipline. He also mentions their various lustrations and says that they numbered about four thousand. He comments on their celibacy, piety, convictions concerning immortality, and their belief in rewards for righteousness.

Philo gives a similar description of this group in Judaism. The library at Qumran attests their delight in the Bible and literature. This is reflected in information given by Philo and Josephus. The Essenes carefully copied Holy Scripture and took pains to preserve it.

Recent Excavations in Jerusalem

The Ophel Garden

One of the most exciting excavations to take place in Jerusalem in the past three decades is also one of the most recent: the excavations to the south of the Temple Mount, known as the Ophel Garden. Here we find a collection of buildings and architectural styles representing various periods dating from the Turkish Period all the way back to the time of King Solomon. The stones found here were used in the construction of buildings from the Second Temple Period, from the temple of Herod the Great. These are the stones pushed from the temple walls by the Romans when they destroyed the temple in A.D. 70.

What makes this excavation so special? It reveals additional walls of the temple from the Second Temple Period (37 B.C. to A.D. 70). Up until the early 1980s, all we had of the Herodian temple was that small part of the outside wall known as the Western Wall or the "Wailing Wall." Now a new section of the wall to the west and the south has been opened for public viewing. This new section helps us to better see and understand just how magnificent the temple must have been. Some of the stones revealed here weigh an estimated eighty tons—some of the largest building stones ever found anywhere in the world! But there is also more.

The archaeologists who supervised most of the work are two very prominent Israeli scholars, Benjamin Mazar and Meir Ben-Dov. Much of their work has been published in an excellent work entitled *In the Shadow of the Temple* (Jerusalem: Keter Publishing, 1982). There is such a wealth of knowledge from their work that we cannot possibly do this excavation justice here. We can, however, lift up a few of their findings.

First, from their work we have learned of a long street that ran the entire length of the western wall of the temple, more than five hundred meters long. Along this wall, at its base, were shops, probably for the sale of religious articles used in the home (such as the menorah, mezzuzah, tefilin, or talit). In addition, deep in the ground beneath the southwestern corner a stone was found upon which was written the inscription "To the place of trumpeting." This must have fallen from the wall above during the Roman destruction. According to Jewish historical sources, the "place of trumpeting" was known as the "Pinnacle of the Temple," the place from which the shofar or ram's horn was blown to announce the beginning and ending of the Sabbath or Shabbat, daily temple worship, festivals, feast days, and holidays. It is this very place that is identified with one of the temptations of Jesus reported in the New Testament Gospels. Until this discovery it had been assumed that the pinnacle of the temple was located on the southeastern corner of the temple wall because it stood high overlooking the Kidron Valley. This, of course, would make no sense at all, since most of the people who needed to hear the trumpeting were living inside the wall in the lower city and near to the Temple Mount.

Second, Mazar and Ben-Dov found a collection of ancient, first-century miqvot or miqvah baths (Jewish ritual immersion baths) in the area of the southern steps that led into and out from the temple (these will be discussed in detail later). These miqvot would have been used by men entering the temple for worship and prayer, particularly priests, to satisfy ritual cleanliness for which religious Jewish men had a passion. Perhaps Jesus even used these baths when he entered the temple from the south.

Third, there are two sets of gates found here for entering and exiting the temple. Both sets are now sealed or closed. The eastern gate (known as the Eastern Huldah Gate, named for the prophetess Huldah) was for entrance into the Court of the Gentiles, the large court that surrounded the temple itself. The western gate (known as the Western Huldah Gate) was for exiting from the temple. However, there was a provision that stated that a person in mourning could enter through the exit and exit from the entrance. By this people would know that they were in mourning and could offer words of comfort.

Finally, here we find the remains of a massive staircase leading into the temple area. These steps were not only an entrance, but also a place where rabbis could teach privately, in a non-traditional way. When a rabbi would teach publicly he would teach inside the Court of the Gentiles, in a colonnade known as the "Royal Stoa." These teaching sessions were characterized with questions and answers, a common Jewish style of teaching, and open to anyone who wanted to listen or dialogue. This public teaching would take place on the Temple Mount. But if a rabbi wanted to teach more privately and in a manner not open to questions (in other words, if the teacher wanted to deliver a lecture), this would take place on the steps at the southern end of the Temple Mount. These steps were known colloquially as the "Teaching Steps." Perhaps it was here that Jesus spoke the words found recorded in Matthew 23.

All in all, this excavation has vastly increased our knowledge of these areas found outside of the Temple Mount to the south and southwest and has given us a clearer picture of the vastness of the temple.

The Essene Quarter

Where was the place of the Last Supper? This has been a hotly debated question for centuries. At last we think we have an answer! For centuries, when Christian pilgrims would visit Jerusalem, they would be taken to an "Upper Room" at present-day Mount Zion; and here they would read or tell the story of the Last Supper. In fact, this is a traditional site that cannot be dated back any farther than the Crusader Period, and this room was used as a place of prayer by the Muslims during the Turkish Period. This is certainly not the place where Jesus shared the Passover meal with His disciples the night of His arrest. That place has been long since destroyed.

If, then, this is not the place of the Last Supper, where should we look? Our answer lies in two unrelated sources: the New Testament and the writings of Josephus Flavius, a first-century Jewish historian. According to Luke 22:10–13, we find "'Behold, when you have entered the city, a man will meet you carrying a pitcher of water; follow him into the house which he enters. Then you shall say to the master of the house, "The Teacher says to you, 'Where is the guest room where I may eat the Passover with My disciples?'" Then he will show you a large, furnished upper room; there make ready.' So they went and found it just as He had said to them, and they prepared the Passover." For those who know a little of Jewish culture, there is something strange here. In the first century men did not usually carry water. This would have been considered as women's work. Why would a man be carrying water? Perhaps because he was an Essene monk.

Josephus tells us that there was a major earthquake in 31 B.C., and during this earthquake the Essene monastery of Qumran was destroyed. Herod the Great gave the Essenes a place in the Upper City of Jerusalem to establish a monastery there and they moved their headquarters to Jerusalem. This area was known as the Essene Quarter. Following the death of Herod the Great in 4 B.C., the Essenes moved back to the wilderness of Judea and rebuilt their monastery at Qumran. However, they left behind a small group of monks to maintain their monastery in Jerusalem. Perhaps it was here that Jesus shared the Last Supper, the Passover, with His disciples. There is no better explanation of why this man would be carrying water and why Jesus wanted His disciples to follow this man.

Where was this Essene monastery of Jerusalem located? Until the mid–1980s no one knew. At about that time, however, the remains of a gate was found not far from the traditional

Upper Room, behind the Dormition Abbey on Mount Zion, with the inscription "The Essene Gate." We now know where the monastery was located and a new excavation is under way to recover this place where Jesus had the Last Supper with His disciples.

Ebla

The modern Arabic name for this 140-acre mound in the Northwest corner of Syria is Tell Mardikh. Archaeologists of the University of Rome began digging this mound in 1964 and found an inscription in 1968 that identified this site as ancient Ebla. They uncovered portions of impressive buildings from the time of the biblical patriarchs (1900–1700 B.C.); and beneath these were palaces and temples of the Early Bronze Age (2400–2250 B.C.). This was the discovery of an early but advanced civilization that was previously unknown.

In 1974, 1975, and 1976, three rooms of one palace yielded almost seven thousand well-preserved clay tablets and about thirteen thousand fragments of other tablets with cuneiform writing on them. This archive of ancient Sumerian and Canaanite literature is very important. The tablets contain economic, political, and legal records of Ebla. (Understanding the cultures of Israel's neighbors aids biblical interpretation.) They show that Ebla was a merchant empire. Its rulers controlled trade routes that reached into the Mesopotamian Valley, into the mountains of modern-day Turkey, and to the edge of the Nile Valley.

But more importantly, some tablets are dictionaries—the earliest known—providing the meanings of words used in both the Sumerian and early Canaanite (Eblaite) languages. (Languages help archaeologists understand the cultures.) Many Canaanite words at Ugarit and Hebrew words in the Old Testament can be understood more accurately because they also occur on these early tablets.

Many place names occur in the Ebla records, including those familiar to readers of the Bible:

Haran, Damascus, Hazor, Beth Shan, Shechem, Joppa, Eshkelon, Jerusalem, Dor—and some scholars believe also Sodom and Gomorrah. Since the Bible itself presents these as real places, the Ebla tablets help support its historical reliability.

About ten thousand names of people are found on the tablets. Among them are biblical names such as Adam, Eve, Noah, Jubal, Abram, Ishmael, Hagar, Keturah, Bilhah, Israel, Micah, Michael, Saul, David, Jehorum, and Jonah. Although these names do not refer to the biblical personages, they establish that the names in Scripture are authentic.

Sometimes, however, the tablets contain mythic and legendary stories that conflict with the Scriptures (e.g., different creation accounts). Such cases illumine the biblical authors' polemics against pagan worldviews.

The excavation project continues until the present and may be expected to cast more light on the Bible's meaning and reliability.

The Thrilling Story of Biblical Archaeology Is Not Yet Completed

Other great discoveries as a result of continuous research in Bible lands promise even greater contributions to biblical studies in future years. For example, the recovery of thirteen Coptic codices from Nag Hammadi in Upper Egypt, since 1945, have almost rivaled the Dead Sea Scrolls in actual biblical importance. These even include the apocryphal "Gospel of Thomas" and are of inestimable value, especially from a critical standpoint in dating New Testament literature.

What new and exciting discovery affecting the Bible may we expect the archaeologist's spade to turn up next? The prospect should engender a love for the Scriptures and a desire to study them employing history, linguistics, and archaeology as the means under the Holy Spirit to a more accurate understanding of the Bible's message to humankind.

Backgrounds to Modern Church History

How the Three Main Branches of Christianity Came About

T HE ORGANIZED CHURCH OF MODERN TIMES IS composed of three large branches: Orthodox, Roman Catholic, and Protestant. These three segments of Christendom developed over a period of fifteen centuries. The Christian church of the first several centuries was unified structurally and had not yet taken on the threefold division that is so familiar to us today. Only in the developments of the next several centuries did these particular designations begin.

Originally the early church had major centers throughout the Roman Empire, over each of which arose a bishop who directed the affairs of the church in his particular region. The major centers of the second century were Jerusalem, Antioch, Alexandria, Ephesus, and Rome. Ephesus later lost influence, and the influence of Jerusalem was reduced following its destruction in A.D. 70 and the paganizing of Israel by the Romans after the Bar Kokhba revolt in A.D. 135. Prior to the sixth century there was no one bishop who was viewed as being over the entire church of Christ throughout the empire; instead there were five separate patriarchs who shared equal oversight.

Starting with the bishop of Rome called Gregory the Great, however, that bishop began to be recognized as chief among his peers. Based on this, one could place the formalization of the Roman Catholic Church at the end of the sixth century. Meanwhile, the eastern church retained considerable freedom from Rome and eventually became known as the Orthodox Church. Its leadership came from the bishop of Constantinople, the eastern capital of the Roman Empire.

The Protestant branch of Christendom separated from the Roman Catholic Church in the sixteenth century after the Reformation led by Martin Luther. The Reformation, which emphasized Scripture and deemphasized tradition as the standard of church doctrine, completed a split with Rome which had been initiated by Christian dissenters as early as the thirteenth century.

Historical Factors Prior to the Protestant Reformation

Heresies

Errors of doctrine began in the Christian church almost as soon as the church began. The apostles contended with false teachings about the requirements for justification before God (legalism), and about the nature of the physical body of Christ and of reality itself (early forms of gnosticism). Between the first century and the

(cont'd on p. 1792)

Protestant Church History at a Glance

Period	People
ANCIENT Early Church (30–100)	The apostles; also Clement of Rome (c. 30–c. 100); Papias (c. 60–c. 130); Polycarp (c. 69–c. 160); Ignatius of Antioch (d. c. 117); Hermas (d. c. 140)
Emerging Church (100–325)	Justin Martyr (c. 100–c. 165); Tatian (c. 110–c. 172); Irenaeus (c. 130–c. 200); Theophilus (d. 181); Clement of Alexandria (c. 150–c. 215); Tertullian (c. 150–c. 220); Hippolytus (c. 170–c. 246); Origen (c. 185–c. 254); Arius (c. 250–336); Eusebius of Caesarea (c. 263–339); Athanasius (c. 296–373); Apollinaris (c. 310–390); Alexander of Alexandria (d. 328)
Conquering Church (325–600)	Hilary of Poitiers (c. 315–c. 368); Cyril of Jerusalem (315–386); Constantine I (d. 337); Gregory of Nazianzus (330–389); Gregory of Nyssa (331–395); Basil the Great (c. 329–379); Ambrose of Milan (c. 340–397); Cyril of Alexandria (376–444); John Chrysostom (c. 345–407); Jerome (c. 345–420); Augustine of Hippo (354–430); Pelagius (c. 360–c. 420); John Cassian (c. 360–c. 435); Nestorius (d. c. 451); Patrick (c. 387–461); Leo I (d. 461); Gregory the Great (c. 540–604)
MEDIEVAL Roman Church Ascendancy (600–1300)	Maximus the Confessor (c. 580–662); Bede (c. 673–735); Boniface (c. 680–754); John of Damascus (c. 676–754); Charlemagne (747–814); Gottschalk (d. 868); Anselm (1033–1109); Peter Abelard (1079–1142); Bernard of Clairvaux (1090–1153); Francis of Assisi (1181–1226); Thomas Aquinas (1225–1274); John Duns Scotus (c. 1265–1308); William of Ockham (c. 1285–1349)
Reformation Church (1300–1550)	John Wycliffe (c. 1329–1384); John Hus (c. 1370–1415); Martin Luther (1483–1546); Huldreich Zwingli (1484–1531); Johann Mayer of Eck (1486–1543); William Tyndale (c. 1490–1536); Menno Simons (1496–1561); Philip Melanchthon (1497–1560); Felix Manz (c. 1498–1527); John Calvin (1509–1564); John Knox (c. 1513–1572); Jacobus Arminius (1560–1609)
MODERN Denominational Church (1550–1800)	John Cotton (1585–1652); Oliver Cromwell (1599–1658); John Milton (1608–1674); John Bunyan (1628–1688); George Fox (1624–1691); William Penn (1644–1718); Matthew Henry (1662–1714); Jonathan Edwards (1703–1758); John Wesley (1703–1791); George Whitefield (1714–1770); Frances Asbury (1745–1816); Timothy Dwight (1752–1817); William Wilberforce (1759–1833); William Carey (1761–1834); Alexander Campbell (1788–1866)
Global Church (1800–Present)	Charles G. Finney (1792–1875); John Darby (1800–1882); George Mueller (1805–1898); William Booth (1829–1912); J. Hudson Taylor (1832–1905); Charles H. Spurgeon (1834–1892); Dwight L. Moody (1837–1899); C. S. Lewis (1898–1963); Billy Graham (b. 1918); Martin Luther King, Jr. (1929–1968)

Events	Factors
Day of Pentecost (c. 30); conversion of Paul (c. 35); Council of Jerusalem (c. 49); martyrdom of Paul and Peter (c. 67); destruction of Jerusalem (70); first major persecution by emperor Domitian (c. 90–96); death of apostle John (c. 100)	The descent of the Holy Spirit; the New Testament books written; unity of Jews and Gentiles in one church; early gnosticism
First universal persecution under emperor Decius (c. 250); churches begin to own property for their assemblies; Constantine defeats Maxentius under sign of the cross (312); Edict of Milan legalizing Christianity (313); Christianity becomes official religion of empire (321); church council at Nicaea (325)	Clarification of doctrines of Trinity and deity of Jesus Christ
Building of Constantinople; Councils of Constantinople (381 and 553); Council of Ephesus (431); Council of Chalcedon (451)	Heresies of: Macedonianism, Nestorianism, Apollinarianism, Monothelitism, Monophysitism, Eutychianism, Pelagianism; Augustine's teaching on sin, predestination; identification of church with state
Iconoclastic controversy; development of monastic lifestyle; conversion of European peoples; Council of Nicaea (787); schism between western and eastern church; reformation of papacy (eleventh century); inquisition	Double predestination (Gottschalk); age of Scholasticism; use of icons; movement from Platonic to Aristotelian thought; natural theology of Aquinas
Rise of pre-Reformation groups such as the Waldenses and Lollards; reformation in Germany, Switzerland, and the Netherlands; counter-reformation; Council of Trent	Nationalism; priesthood of believers; justification by faith alone; authority of Scripture affirmed
Synod of Dort; English Civil War; Puritan migration; rise of Methodism; Great Awakening; beginning of modern missions movement	Calvinist/Arminian theological division; Socinianism; Enlightenment ideas; republican government in America; skepticism
Schism in American denominations due to Civil War; rise of Mormonism, Jehovah's Witnesses, Christian Science; ecumenical movement; World Council of Churches; National Association of Evangelicals; mass evangelistic crusades	Theological liberalism; Pentecostalism; Fundamentalism; neo-orthodoxy; rise of eastern and New Age religions; evangelical resurgence

modern era numerous heresies have arisen: Ebionites denied the true deity of Christ, as did later Dynamic Monarchianists and Arians; Modalists denied the Trinity; Eutychians and Nestorians struggled with the doctrine of the person of Christ in His human nature. These are only some of the more prominent errors, many of which are found in contemporary cults. Other heresies concerned the matter of human sin (Pelagianism) and the nature of the atonement. Heresy did have the positive result of forcing the church to more clearly define orthodox biblical doctrine, much of which has been expressed in the various creeds.

Persecutions

The early church went through ten separate persecutions. The harshest and most pervasive were the persecution of Domitian at the end of the first century (c. 90–96), the persecution of Decius (249–51) in the midst of the celebration of the 1,000th anniversary of the founding of Rome, in which there was a major push for return to the ancient religions; and, last and most severe, the persecution of Diocletian (303–311). The church braved these tribulations, however, and grew even stronger.

Constantine

Soon after the persecution of Diocletian, a subsequent emperor, Constantine, became a Christian. He began to use the machinery of the Roman government to strengthen his newfound faith, and he finally declared Christianity to be the official religion of the empire. Constantine's mother Helena, who was also a Christian, heard of the disrepair of many of the biblically significant sites in the Holy Land and traveled there to secure their protection through the building of shrines, some of which are now situated under ancient churches. Constantine was instrumental in bringing about an affirmation of Christ's deity at the Council of Nicaea, as expressed in the consequent Nicean Creed.

Mohammed

In the seventh century an Arabian named Mohammed claimed to have revelations from God, which ultimately gave rise to the Koran and the faith of Islam. Mohammed claimed that this faith was the final revelation of God, though he recognized the genuineness of earlier revelations given through Moses and Jesus, both of whom he considered great prophets. He enforced this new faith through the power of the sword, and eventually conquered many of the lands that had been largely Christian. These events eventually led to the Crusades of the eleventh through the thirteenth centuries.

Crusades

A call to deliver the Holy Land from the Muslim conquerors began in the late eleventh century. The first crusade was successful in capturing the major cities of Asia Minor and the city of Jerusalem. Following this came several other crusades which turned out not to be of lasting success. To attract soldiers for these crusades some prospective enlistees were offered immediate entrance to heaven if killed, or forgiveness of debts and freedom from taxes if they lived.

The Reformation

The Roman branch of the church held unfettered sway in the west from the sixth century until the Reformation of the sixteenth century, which sought to restore the ancient faith of the first several centuries. The centers of the Reformation were Germany with Martin Luther; Switzerland with John Calvin and Huldreich Zwingli; and Scotland with John Knox.

How Christianity Has Affected Secular History

What would life be like if Christ had not come and Christianity had not spread throughout the world? It would most likely be much different. Although Greece gave western civilization much art, philosophy and literature, and Rome provided law and government, it was the Christian worldview that provided the basis for modern science, efforts to alleviate poverty, universal education, and the ideals of equality and liberty enshrined in the documents of the many governments. The God of order and beauty provided for the view that nature was predictable and orderly. The Christian belief that all humanity is a creation of God gave a foundation to the self-evident truth of life, liberty and pursuit of happiness. Since people are made in the image of God they are valuable apart from their station in life, amount of wealth, or utility to society. People are helped, educated, and protected simply because they are made in God's image. Loss of these Christian ideals would undoubtedly be a tragic loss to the well-being of humanity.

General Bibliography

∎

Bible Atlases and Maps

Recommended: *Nelson's Complete Book of Bible Maps and Charts, Updated and Revised* (Nashville: Thomas Nelson, 1996). Reproducible.

Aharoni, Yohanan, Michael Avi-Yonah, and Anson F. Rainey. *The MacMillan Bible Atlas* (New York: MacMillan Publishing, 1993).

Brisco, Thomas V. *Holman Bible Atlas* (Nashville: Broadman and Holman, 1992).

Dowley, Tim, ed. *Atlas of the Bible and Christianity* (Grand Rapids: Baker, 1995).

Frank, Harry T. *Atlas of the Bible Lands* (Nashville: Broadman and Holman, 1994).

Jenkins, Simon. *Nelson's 3-D Bible Mapbook* (Nashville: Thomas Nelson, 1995).

Paterson, John H., Donald J. Wiseman, John J. Bimson, and John P. Kane. *New Bible Atlas* (Downers Grove: InterVarsity, 1992).

Pfeiffer, Charles F. *Baker's Bible Atlas* (Grand Rapids: Baker, 1990).

Pritchard, James B., ed. *The HarperCollins Concise Atlas of the Bible* (San Francisco: HarperCollins, 1994).

Rasmussen, Carl G. *Zondervan NIV Atlas of the Bible* (Grand Rapids: Zondervan, 1990).

Smith, Marsha E. *Holman Book of Biblical Charts, Maps, and Reconstructions* (Nashville: Broadman and Holman, 1994).

Wright, G. Ernest, and Floyd V. Filson. *Westminster Historical Maps of Bible Lands* (Louisville: Westminster-John Knox Press, 1995).

Bible Background, Customs, and Facts

Recommended: Vos, Howard F. *Nelson's New Illustrated Bible Manners & Customs* (Nashville: Thomas Nelson, 1999).

Anderson, Ken. *Where to Find It In the Bible* (Nashville: Thomas Nelson, 1993).

Archer, Gleason. *Encyclopedia of Bible Difficulties* (Grand Rapids: Zondervan, 1992).

Batchelor, M. K. *Nelson's Illustrated Bible Companion* (Nashville: Thomas Nelson, 1995.

Bell, Albert A. Jr. *Exploring the New Testament World* (Nashville: Thomas Nelson, 1998.

Bimson, John J., ed. *Baker Encyclopedia of Bible Places* (Grand Rapids: Baker, 1993).

Hepper, F. Nigel. *Baker Encyclopedia of Bible Plants: Flowers and Trees, Fruits and Vegetables, Ecology* (Grand Rapids: Baker, 1992).

Keener, Craig S. *The IVP Bible Background Commentary: New Testament* (Downers Grove: InterVarsity, 1997).

Millard, Alan. *Nelson's Illustrated Wonders and Discoveries of the Bible* (Nashville: Thomas Nelson, 1997).

Packer, J.I., and M.C. Tenny, eds. *Illustrated Manners and Customs of the Bible* (Nashville: Thomas Nelson, 1980).

Packer, J.I., M.C. Tenny, and William White Jr., eds. *Nelson's Illustrated Encyclopedia of Bible Facts* (Nashville: Thomas Nelson, 1995).

Smith, Jerome H. *The New Treasury of Scripture Knowledge* (Nashville: Thomas Nelson, 1992).

Walton, John H. *The IVP Bible Background Commentary: Genesis—Deuteronomy* (Downers Grove: InterVarsity, 1997).

Bible Concordances

Recommended: Strong, James, ed. *The New Strong's Exhaustive Concordance of the Bible* (Nashville: Thomas Nelson, 1994).

Goodrick, Edward W., and John R. Kohlenberger. *The NIV Exhaustive Concordance* (Grand Rapids: Zondervan, 1990).

Kohlenberger, John R., ed. *The NRSV Concordance, Unabridged* (Grand Rapids: Zondervan, 1991).

New King James Version Exhaustive Concordance (Nashville: Thomas Nelson, 1994).

Thomas, Robert L., ed. *New American Standard Exhaustive Concordance of the Bible* (Nashville: Holman Bible Publishers, 1992).

Young, Robert. *Young's Analytical Concordance to the Bible* (Nashville: Thomas Nelson, 1989).

Youngblood, Ronald F. *Nelson's New Comfort Print Bible Goncordance* (Nashville: Thomas Nelson, 1995).

Youngblood, Ronald F. *Nelson's Quick Reference Bible Concordance* (Nashville: Thomas Nelson, 1993).

Bible Dictionaries and Encyclopedias

Recommended: Youngblood, Ronald F., F.F. Bruce, and R.K. Harrison. *Nelson's New Illustrated Bible Dictionary* (Nashville: Thomas Nelson, 1995).

Bromiley, G.W., ed. *The International Standard Bible Encyclopedia*. 4 vols. (Grand Rapids: Eerdmans, 1988).

Couch, Mal, ed. *Dictionary of Premillennial Theology* (Grand Rapids: Kregel, 1996).

Douglas, J.D. *The NIV Compact Dictionary of the Bible* (Grand Rapids: Zondervan, 1989).

Drane, John, ed. *Nelson's Illustrated Encyclopedia of the Bible* (Nashville: Thomas Nelson, 1998).

Elwell, Walter A., ed. *Evangelical Dictionary of Biblical Theology* (Grand Rapids: Baker, 1996).

Elwell, Walter A., ed. *Evangelical Dictionary of Theology* (Grand Rapids: Baker, 1984).

Green, Joel B., Scot McKnight, and I. Howard Marshall, eds. *Dictionary of Jesus and the Gospels* (Downers Grove: InterVarsity, 1992).

Hawthrone, Gerald F., Ralph Martin, and Daniel G. Reid, eds. *Dictionary of Paul and His Letters* (Downers Grove: InterVarsity, 1993).

Holman Concise Bible Dictionary (Nashville: Broadman and Holman, 1994).

Marshall, I. Howard, A.R. Millard, J.I. Packer, and D.J. Wiseman. *New Bible Dictionary* (Downers Grove: InterVarsity, 1996).

Martin, Ralph P., and Peter H. Davids, eds. *Dictionary of the Later New Testament and Its Development* (Downers Grove: InterVarsity, 1997).

Nelson's Three-in-One Bible Reference Companion (Nashville: Thomas Nelson, 1993).

Richards, Lawrence O. *The Revell Bible Dictionary*, Deluxe Color Edition, 2nd ed. (New York: Wynwood Press, 1994).

Smith, William. *Smith's Bible Dictionary* (Nashville: Thomas Nelson, 1991).

Tenny, Merrill C. *The Zondervan Pictorial Bible Dictionary* (Grand Rapids: Zondervan, 1988).

Bible Handbooks

Recommended: Richards, Lawrence O. *Richards' Complete Bible Handbook* (Nashville: Thomas Nelson, 1987).

Beers, V. Gilbert. *The Victor Handbook of Bible Knowledge* (Colorado Springs: Cook Communications, 1995).

Boa, Kenneth and Bruce Wilkinson. *Talk Thru the Bible* (Nashville: Thomas Nelson, 1992).

Butler, Trent C., ed. *Holman Bible Handbook* (Nashville: Broadman and Holman, 1996).

Miller, Stephen M. *How to Get Into the Bible* (Nashville: Thomas Nelson, 1998).

Wiersbe, Warren. *With the Word: The Chapter-by-Chapter Bible Handbook* (Nashville: Thomas Nelson, 1994).

Bible Introductions and Basic Theologies

Recommended: Geisler, Norman L., and William E. Mix. *A General Introduction to the Bible* (Chicago: Moody Press, 1991).

Barclay, William. *A Beginner's Guide to the New Testament* (Louisville: Westminster-John Knox, 1995).

Gromacki, Robert G. *New Testament Survey* (Grand Rapids: Baker, 1989).

Guthrie, Donald. *New Testament Introduction*. Revised Edition (Downers Grove: InterVarsity, 1990).

Guthrie, Donald. *New Testament Theology* (Downers Grove: InterVarsity, 1981).

Kaiser, Walter C. *Toward an Old Testament Theology* (Grand Rapids: Zondervan, 1993).

Ryrie, Charles C. *Biblical Theology of the New Testament* (Chicago: Moody Press, 1987).

Smith, Ralph L. *Old Testament Theology: Its History, Method, and Message* (Nashville: Broadman and Holman, 1993).

Zuck, Roy B., ed. *A Biblical Theology of the New Testament* (Chicago: Moody Press, 1994).

Zuck, Roy B., ed. *A Biblical Theology of the Old Testament* (Chicago: Moody Press, 1991).

Biblical Word Studies

Recommended: Vine, W.E., Merrill F. Unger, and William White Jr. *Vine's Complete Expository Dictionary of Old and New Testament Words* (Nashville: Thomas Nelson, 1993).

Barclay, William. *New Testament Words* (Louisville: Westminster-John Knox, 1997).

Bromiley, Geoffrey W. *Theological Dictionary of the New Testament: Abridged in One Volume* (Grand Rapids: Eerdmans, 1985).

Harris, R. Laird, Gleason L. Archer, and Bruce K. Waltke, eds. *Theological Wordbook of the Old Testament*. 2 vols. (Chicago: Moody Press, 1988).

Richards, Lawrence O. *The Expository Dictionary of Bible Words* (Grand Rapids: Zondervan, 1991).

Strong, James. *The New Strong's Complete Dictionary of Bible Words* (Nashville: Thomas Nelson, 1993).

Wuest, Kenneth. *Word Studies in the Greek New Testament* (Grand Rapids: Eerdmans, 1980).

Electronic Bible Reference (CD-ROM)

Nelson's Electronic Bible Reference Library (Nashville: Thomas Nelson, 1997). Available in both a Deluxe Edition (39 Bibles and reference books unlocked) and a Professional Edition (76 Bibles and reference books unlocked). Windows compatible.

Commentaries on Genesis

Atkison, David. *The Message of Genesis 1—11*. The Bible Speaks Today Series. J.A. Motyer and John R.W. Stott, eds. (Downers Grove: InterVarsity, 1994).

Baldwin, Joyce G. *The Message of Genesis 12—50*. The Bible Speaks Today Series. J.A. Motyer and John R.W. Stott, eds. (Downers Grove: InterVarsity, 1994).

Briscoe, Stuart. *Genesis*. The Communicator's Commentary. Lloyd J. Ogilvie, ed. (Dallas: Word Publishing, 1991). Also available in

paperback in the Mastering the Old Testament series.

Davis, John J. *Paradise to Prison: Studies in Genesis* (Grand Rapids: Baker, 1994).

Kidner, Derek. *Genesis*. Tyndale Old Testament Commentary Series. D.J. Wiseman, ed. (Downers Grove: InterVarsity, 1993).

Ross, Allen P. *Creation and Blessing: A Guide to the Study and Exposition of Genesis* (Grand Rapids: Baker, 1988).

Stevens, Sherrill G. *Genesis*. Layman's Bible Book Commentary (Nashville: Broadman, 1995).

Vos, Howard F. *Genesis*. Everyman's Bible Commentary Series (Chicago: Moody Press, 1995).

Commentaries on Exodus

Cate, Robert L. *Exodus*. Layman's Bible Book Commentary (Nashville: Broadman, 1995).

Cole, R. Alan. *Exodus*. Tyndale Old Testament Commentary Series. D.J. Wiseman, ed. (Downers Grove: InterVarsity, 1993).

Dunnam, Maxie D. *Exodus*. The Communicator's Commentary. Lloyd J. Ogilvie, ed. (Dallas: Word Publishing, 1991). Also available in paperback in the Mastering the Old Testament series.

Youngblood, Roland F. *Exodus*. Everyman's Bible Commentary Series (Chicago: Moody Press, 1995).

Commentaries on Leviticus

Allen, Ronald B. *Numbers*. The Expositor's Bible Commentary, Vol. 2. Frank E. Gaebelein, ed. (Grand Rapids: Zondervan, 1990).

Demarest, Gary D. *Leviticus*. The Communicator's Commentary. Lloyd J. Ogilvie, ed. (Dallas: Word Publishing, 1991). Also available in paperback in the Mastering the Old Testament series.

Harrison, R.K. *Leviticus*. Tyndale Old Testament Commentary Series. D.J. Wiseman, ed. (Downers Grove: InterVarsity, 1993).

Honeycutt, Roy L. *Leviticus-Deuteronomy*. Layman's Bible Book Commentary (Nashville: Broadman, 1995).

Schultz, Samuel. *Leviticus*. Everyman's Bible Commentary Series (Chicago: Moody Press, 1995).

Commentaries on Numbers

Jensen, Irving L. *Numbers: Journey to God's Rest-Land.* Everyman's Bible Commentary Series (Chicago: Moody Press, 1995).

Philip, James. *Numbers.* The Communicator's Commentary. Lloyd J. Ogilvie, ed. (Dallas: Word Publishing, 1991). Also available in paperback in the Mastering the Old Testament series.

Wenham, Gordon J. *Numbers.* Tyndale Old Testament Commentary Series. D.J. Wiseman, ed. (Downers Grove: InterVarsity, 1993).

Commentaries on Deuteronomy

Brown, Raymond. *The Message of Deuteronomy.* The Bible Speaks Today Series. J.A. Motyer and John R.W. Stott, eds. (Downers Grove: InterVarsity, 1994).

Maxwell, John. *Deuteronomy.* The Communicator's Commentary. Lloyd J. Ogilvie, ed. (Dallas: Word Publishing, 1991). Also available in paperback in the Mastering the Old Testament series.

Schutz, Samuel. *Deuteronomy.* Everyman's Bible Commentary Series (Chicago: Moody Press, 1995).

Thompson, J.A. *Deuteronomy.* Tyndale Old Testament Commentary Series. D.J. Wiseman, ed. (Downers Grove: InterVarsity, 1993).

Commentaries on Joshua

Hess, Richard. *Joshua.* Tyndale Old Testament Commentary Series. D.J. Wiseman, ed. (Downers Grove: InterVarsity, 1993).

Huffman, John. *Joshua.* The Communicator's Commentary. Lloyd J. Ogilvie, ed. (Dallas: Word Publishing, 1991). Also available in paperback in the Mastering the Old Testament series.

Jensen, Irving L. *Joshua.* Everyman's Bible Commentary Series (Chicago: Moody Press, 1995).

Kent, Dan G. *Joshua-Ruth.* Layman's Bible Book Commentary (Nashville: Broadman, 1995).

Redpath, Alan. *Victorious Christian Living : Studies in the Book of Joshua* (Grand Rapids: Fleming H. Revell, 1993).

Commentaries on Judges and Ruth

Atkinson, David. *The Message of Ruth.* The Bible Speaks Today Series. J.A. Motyer and John R.W. Stott, eds. (Downers Grove: InterVarsity, 1994).

Cundall, Arthur E. , and Leon Morris. *Judges and Ruth.* Tyndale Old Testament Commentary Series. D.J. Wiseman, ed. (Downers Grove: InterVarsity, 1993).

De Hann, M.R. *The Romance of Redemption: Studies in the Book of Ruth* (Grand Rapids: Kregel, 1995).

Jackman, David. *Judges, Ruth.* The Communicator's Commentary. Lloyd J. Ogilvie, ed. (Dallas: Word Publishing, 1991). Also available in paperback in the Mastering the Old Testament series.

Lewis, Arthur. *Judges and Ruth.* Everyman's Bible Commentary Series (Chicago: Moody Press, 1995).

Wilcock, Michael. *The Message of Judges.* The Bible Speaks Today Series. J.A. Motyer and John R.W. Stott, eds. (Downers Grove: InterVarsity, 1994).

Wiseman, Luke H. *Practical Truths from Judges* (Grand Rapids: Kregel, 1995).

Wood, Leon. *Distressing Days of Judges* (Grand Rapids: Zondervan, 1975).

Commentaries on 1 and 2 Samuel

Baldwin, Joyce G. *1 and 2 Samuel.* Tyndale Old Testament Commentary Series. D.J. Wiseman, ed. (Downers Grove: InterVarsity, 1993).

Chafin, Kenneth L. *1, 2 Samuel.* The Communicator's Commentary. Lloyd J. Ogilvie, ed. (Dallas: Word Publishing, 1991). Also available in paperback in the Mastering the Old Testament series.

Lewis, Joe O. *1 and 2 Samuel, 1 Chronicles.* Layman's Bible Book Commentary (Nashville: Broadman, 1995).

Commentaries on 1 and 2 Kings

Dilday, Russell. *1, 2 Kings.* The Communicator's Commentary. Lloyd J. Ogilvie, ed. (Dallas: Word Publishing, 1991). Also available in paperback in the Mastering the Old Testament series.

Hubbard, Robert L. *1 and 2 Kings.* Everyman's Bible Commentary Series (Chicago: Moody Press, 1995).

Wiseman, Donald J. *1 and 2 Kings*. Tyndale Old Testament Commentary Series. D.J. Wiseman, ed. (Downers Grove: InterVarsity, 1993).

Commentaries on 1 and 2 Chronicles

Allen, Leslie. *1, 2 Chronicles*. The Communicator's Commentary. Lloyd J. Ogilvie, ed. (Dallas: Word Publishing, 1991). Also available in paperback in the Mastering the Old Testament series.

Cate, Robert L. *2 Chronicles*. Layman's Bible Book Commentary (Nashville: Broadman, 1995).

Sailhamer, John. *1 and 2 Chronicles*. Everyman's Bible Commentary Series (Chicago: Moody Press, 1995).

Selman, Martin J. *1 and 2 Chronicles*. Tyndale Old Testament Commentary Series. D.J. Wiseman, ed. (Downers Grove: InterVarsity, 1993).

Wilcock, Michael. *The Message of Chronicles*. The Bible Speaks Today Series. J.A. Motyer and John R.W. Stott, eds. (Downers Grove: InterVarsity, 1994).

Commentaries on Ezra, Nehemiah, and Esther

Andrews, Gini. *Esther: The Star and the Sceptre* (Grand Rapids: Zondervan, 1980).

Baldwin, Joyce G. *Esther*. Tyndale Old Testament Commentary Series. D.J. Wiseman, ed. (Downers Grove: InterVarsity, 1993).

Kidner, Derek. *Ezra and Nehemiah*. Tyndale Old Testament Commentary Series. D.J. Wiseman, ed. (Downers Grove: InterVarsity, 1993).

Laney, J. Carl. *Ezra and Nehemiah*. Everyman's Bible Commentary Series (Chicago: Moody Press, 1995).

Owens, Mary F. *Ezra-Job*. Layman's Bible Book Commentary (Nashville: Broadman, 1995).

Redpath, Alan. *Victorious Christian Service: Studies in the Book of Nehemiah* (Grand Rapids: Fleming H. Revell, 1993).

Roberts, Mark. *Ezra-Nehemiah*. The Communicator's Commentary. Lloyd J. Ogilvie, ed. (Dallas: Word Publishing, 1991). Also available in paperback in the Mastering the Old Testament series.

Whitcomb, John. *Esther: Triumph of God's Sovereignty*. Everyman's Bible Commentary Series (Chicago: Moody Press, 1995).

Commentaries on Job

Andersen, Francis I. *Job*. Tyndale Old Testament Commentary Series. D.J. Wiseman, ed. (Downers Grove: InterVarsity, 1993).

Atkinson, David. *The Message of Job*. The Bible Speaks Today Series. J.A. Motyer and John R.W. Stott, eds. (Downers Grove: InterVarsity, 1994).

McKenna, David. *Job*. The Communicator's Commentary. Lloyd J. Ogilvie, ed. (Dallas: Word Publishing, 1991). Also available in paperback in the Mastering the Old Testament series.

Zuck, Roy B. *Job*. Everyman's Bible Commentary Series (Chicago: Moody Press, 1995).

Commentaries on Psalms

Alden, Robert. *Psalms*. Everyman's Bible Commentary Series (Chicago: Moody Press, 1995).

Kidner, Derek. *Psalms 1—72*. Tyndale Old Testament Commentary Series. D.J. Wiseman, ed. (Downers Grove: InterVarsity, 1993).

Kidner, Derek. *Psalms 73—150*. Tyndale Old Testament Commentary Series. D.J. Wiseman, ed. (Downers Grove: InterVarsity, 1993).

McEachern Alton H. *Psalms*. Layman's Bible Book Commentary (Nashville: Broadman, 1995).

Scroggie, W. Graham. *A Guide to the Psalms* (Grand Rapids: Kregel, 1995).

Williams, Donald. *Psalms 1—72*. The Communicator's Commentary. Lloyd J. Ogilvie, ed. (Dallas: Word Publishing, 1991). Also available in paperback in the Mastering the Old Testament series.

Williams, Donald. *Psalms 73—150*. The Communicator's Commentary. Lloyd J. Ogilvie, ed. (Dallas: Word Publishing, 1991).

Commentaries on Proverbs

Alden, Robert L. *Proverbs: A Commentary on an Ancient Book of Timeless Advice* (Grand Rapids: Baker, 1983).

Arnot, William. *Studies in Proverbs* (Grand Rapids: Kregel, 1995).

Atkinson, David. *The Message of Proverbs*. The Bible Speaks Today Series. J.A. Motyer and John R.W. Stott, eds. (Downers Grove: InterVarsity, 1994).

Hubbard, David A. *Proverbs*. The Communicator's Commentary. Lloyd J. Ogilvie, ed. (Dallas: Word Publishing, 1991). Also available in paperback in the Mastering the Old Testament series.

Ironside, Henry A. *Proverbs* (Grand Rapids: Loizeaux Brothers, 1997).

Johnson, L.D. *Proverbs-Song of Solomon*. Layman's Bible Book Commentary (Nashville: Broadman, 1995).

Kidner, Derek. *Proverbs*. Tyndale Old Testament Commentary Series. D.J. Wiseman, ed. (Downers Grove: InterVarsity, 1993).

Commentaries on Ecclesiastes

Eaton, Michael. *Ecclesiastes*. Tyndale Old Testament Commentary Series. D.J. Wiseman, ed. (Downers Grove: InterVarsity, 1993).

Garrett, Duane A. *Proverbs, Ecclesiastes, and Song of Songs*. The New American Commentary (Nashville: Broadman and Holman, 1993).

Glenn, Donald R. *Ecclesiastes*. The Bible Knowledge Commentary: Old Testament (Colorado Springs: Cook Communications, 1994).

Hubbard, David A. *Ecclesiastes, Song of Solomon*. The Communicator's Commentary. Lloyd J. Ogilvie, ed. (Dallas: Word Publishing, 1991). Also available in paperback in the Mastering the Old Testament series.

Kaiser, Walter. *Ecclesiastes*. Everyman's Bible Commentary Series (Chicago: Moody Press, 1995).

Kidner, Derek. *The Message of Ecclesiastes*. The Bible Speaks Today Series. J.A. Motyer and John R.W. Stott, eds. (Downers Grove: InterVarsity, 1994).

Commentaries on Song of Songs

Carr, G. Lloyd. *The Song of Solomon*. Tyndale Old Testament Commentary Series. D.J. Wiseman, ed. (Downers Grove: InterVarsity, 1993).

Dillow, Joseph C. *Solomon on Sex* (Nashville: Thomas Nelson, 1982).

Gledhill, Tom. *The Message of the Song of Songs*. The Bible Speaks Today Series. J.A. Motyer and John R.W. Stott, eds. (Downers Grove: InterVarsity, 1994).

Glickman, S. Craig. *A Song of Lovers* (Downers Grove: InterVarsity, 1992).

Ironside, Henry A. *Song of Solomon* (Grand Rapids: Loizeaux Brothers, 1996).

Commentaries on Isaiah

Butler, Trent C. *Isaiah*. Layman's Bible Book Commentary (Nashville: Broadman, 1995).

Ironside, Henry A. *Isaiah* (Grand Rapids: Loizeaux Brothers, 1996).

Martin, Alfred. *Isaiah*. Everyman's Bible Commentary Series (Chicago: Moody Press, 1995).

McKenna, David. *Isaiah 1—39*. The Communicator's Commentary. Lloyd J. Ogilvie, ed. (Dallas: Word Publishing, 1991). Also available in paperback in the Mastering the Old Testament series.

McKenna, David. *Isaiah 40—66*. The Communicator's Commentary. Lloyd J. Ogilvie, ed. (Dallas: Word Publishing, 1991). Also available in paperback in the Mastering the Old Testament series.

Redpath, Alan. *Faith for the Times: Studies in the Book of Isaiah* (Grand Rapids: Fleming H. Revell, 1993).

Vine, W.E. *Vine's Expository Commentary on Isaiah* (Nashville: Thomas Nelson, 1992).

Webb, Barry. *The Message of Isaiah*. The Bible Speaks Today Series. J.A. Motyer and John R.W. Stott, eds. (Downers Grove: InterVarsity, 1994).

Commentaries on Jeremiah and Lamentations

Dalglish, Edward R. *Jeremiah and Lamentations*. Layman's Bible Book Commentary (Nashville: Broadman, 1995).

Goddard, Burton L. *Meet Jeremiah* (Grand Rapids: Kregel, 1990).

Guest, John. *Jeremiah, Lamentations*. The Communicator's Commentary. Lloyd J. Ogilvie, ed. (Dallas: Word Publishing, 1991). Also available in paperback in the Mastering the Old Testament series.

Harrison, R.K. *Jeremiah and Lamentations*. Tyndale Old Testament Commentary Series. D.J. Wiseman, ed. (Downers Grove: InterVarsity, 1993).

Huey, F.B. *Jeremiah, Lamentations*. The New American Commentary (Nashville: Broadman and Holman, 1993).

Jensen, Irving. *Jeremiah and Lamentations*. Everyman's Bible Commentary Series (Chicago: Moody Press, 1995).

Kidner, Derek. *The Message of Jeremiah*. The Bible Speaks Today Series. J.A. Motyer and John R.W. Stott, eds. (Downers Grove: InterVarsity, 1994).

Commentaries on Ezekiel

Alexander, Ralph. *Ezekiel*. Everyman's Bible Commentary Series (Chicago: Moody Press, 1995).

Cooper, Lamar E. *Ezekiel*. The New American Commentary (Nashville: Broadman and Holman, 1994).

Feinberg, Charles L. *The Prophecy of Ezekiel: The Glory of the Lord* (Chicago: Moody Press, 1969).

Huey, F.B. *Ezekiel-Daniel*. Layman's Bible Book Commentary (Nashville: Broadman, 1995).

Ironside, Henry A. *Ezekiel* (Grand Rapids: Loizeaux Brothers, 1997).

Stuart, Douglas. *Ezekiel*. The Communicator's Commentary. Lloyd J. Ogilvie, ed. (Dallas: Word Publishing, 1991). Also available in paperback in the Mastering the Old Testament series.

Taylor, John B. *Ezekiel*. Tyndale Old Testament Commentary Series. D.J. Wiseman, ed. (Downers Grove: InterVarsity, 1993).

Commentaries on Daniel

Anderson, Sir Robert. *Daniel in the Critics Den* (Grand Rapids: Kregel, 1988).

Baldwin, Joyce G. *Daniel*. Tyndale Old Testament Commentary Series. D.J. Wiseman, ed. (Downers Grove: InterVarsity, 1993).

De Hann, M.R. *Daniel the Prophet* (Grand Rapids: Kregel, 1995).

Ferguson, Sinclair. *Daniel*. The Communicator's Commentary. Lloyd J. Ogilvie, ed. (Dallas: Word Publishing, 1991). Also available in paperback in the Mastering the Old Testament series.

Ironside, Henry A. *Daniel* (Grand Rapids: Loizeaux Brothers, 1996).

McDowell, Josh. *Daniel in the Critics' Den: Historical Evidence for the Authenticity of the Book of Daniel* (San Bernardino: Here's Life Publishers, 1990).

Miller, Stephen R. *Daniel*. The New American Commentary (Nashville: Broadman and Holman, 1994).

Wallace, Ronald S. *The Message of Daniel*. The Bible Speaks Today Series. J.A. Motyer and John R.W. Stott, eds. (Downers Grove: InterVarsity, 1994).

Whitcomb, John. *Daniel*. Everyman's Bible Commentary Series (Chicago: Moody Press, 1995).

Wood, Leon. *A Commentary on Daniel* (Grand Rapids: Zondervan, 1973).

Commentaries on Hosea

Cohen, Gary C., and H. Ronald Vandermey. *Hosea, Amos*. Everyman's Bible Commentary Series (Chicago: Moody Press, 1995).

Feinberg, Charles L. *The Minor Prophets* (Chicago: Moody Press, 1990).

Hubbard, David A. *Hosea*. Tyndale Old Testament Commentary Series. D.J. Wiseman, ed. (Downers Grove: InterVarsity, 1993).

Kidner, Derek. *The Message of Hosea*. The Bible Speaks Today Series. J.A. Motyer and John R.W. Stott, eds. (Downers Grove: InterVarsity, 1994).

Ogilvie, Lloyd J. *Hosea, Joel, Amos, Obadiah, Jonah*. The Communicator's Commentary. Lloyd J. Ogilvie, ed. (Dallas: Word Publishing, 1991). Also available in paperback in the Mastering the Old Testament series.

Smith, Billy K. *Hosea-Jonah*. Layman's Bible Book Commentary (Nashville: Broadman, 1995).

Commentaries on Joel and Amos

Finley, Thomas J. *Joel, Obadiah, and Micah*. Everyman's Bible Commentary Series (Chicago: Moody Press, 1995).

Hubbard, David A. *Joel and Amos*. Tyndale Old Testament Commentary Series. D.J. Wiseman, ed. (Downers Grove: InterVarsity, 1993).

Motyer, J.A. *The Message of Amos*. The Bible Speaks Today Series. J.A. Motyer and John R.W. Stott, eds. (Downers Grove: InterVarsity, 1994).

Commentaries on Obadiah, Jonah, and Micah

Baker, David W., Desmond Alexander, and Bruce Waltke. *Obadiah, Jonah, and Micah*. Tyndale Old Testament Commentary Series. D.J. Wiseman, ed. (Downers Grove: InterVarsity, 1993).

Kaiser, Walter C. Jr. *Micah, Nahum, Habakkuk, Zephaniah, Haggai, Zechariah, Malachi*. The Communicator's Commentary. Lloyd J. Ogilvie, ed. (Dallas: Word Publishing, 1991). Also available in paperback in the Mastering the Old Testament series.

Kelly, Page H. *Micah-Malachi*. Layman's Bible Book Commentary (Nashville: Broadman, 1995).

Commentaries on Nahum, Habakkuk, and Zephaniah

Baker, David W. *Nahum, Habakkuk, and Zephaniah.* Tyndale Old Testament Commentary Series. D.J. Wiseman, ed. (Downers Grove: InterVarsity, 1993).

Coggins, Richard J., and S. Paul Reemi. *Nahum, Obadiah, and Esther: Israel Among the Nations* (Grand Rapids: Eerdmans, 1995).

Maier, Walter A. *The Book of Nahum* (Grand Rapids: Baker, 1992).

Robertson, O. Palmer. *The Books of Nahum, Habakkuk, and Zephaniah* (Grand Rapids: Eerdmans, 1994).

Commentaries on Haggai, Zechariah, and Malachi

Baldwin, Joyce G. *Haggai, Zechariah, and Malachi.* Tyndale Old Testament Commentary Series. D.J. Wiseman, ed. (Downers Grove: InterVarsity, 1993).

Kaiser, Walter C. *Malachi: God's Unchanging Love* (Grand Rapids: Baker, 1994).

Laney, J. Carl. *Zechariah.* Everyman's Bible Commentary Series (Chicago: Moody Press, 1995).

Unger, Merrill F. *Zechariah: Prophet of Messiah's Glory* (Grand Rapids: Zondervan, 1991).

Wolf, Herbert. *Haggai, Malachi: Rededication and Renewal* (Chicago: Moody Press, 1991).

Wright, Charles H. *Zechariah and His Prophecies* (Grand Rapids: Kregel, 1995).

Commentaries on Matthew

Augsberger, Myron S. *Matthew.* The Communicator's Commentary. Lloyd J. Ogilvie, ed. (Dallas: Word Publishing, 1991). Also available in paperback in the Mastering the New Testament series.

Crissey, Clair M. *Matthew.* Layman's Bible Book Commentary (Nashville: Broadman, 1995).

France, R.T. *Matthew.* Tyndale New Testament Commentaries. Leon Morris, ed. (Grand Rapids: Eerdmans, 1994).

Keener, Craig S. *Matthew.* IVP New Testament Commentary Series. D. Stuart Briscoe and Haddon Robinson, eds. (Downers Grove: InterVarsity, 1992).

Stott, John R.W. *The Message of the Sermon on the Mount.* The Bible Speaks Today Series. J.A. Motyer and John R.W. Stott, eds. (Downers Grove: InterVarsity, 1994).

Toussaint, Stanley D. *Behold the King: A Study of Matthew* (Portland: Multnomah Press, 1980).

Walvoord, John F. *Matthew: Thy Kingdom Come* (Chicago: Moody Press, 1974).

Commentaries on Mark

Cole, R. Alan. *Mark.* Tyndale New Testament Commentaries. Leon Morris, ed. (Grand Rapids: Eerdmans, 1994).

Earle, Ralph. *Mark: Gospel of Action.* Everyman's Bible Commentary Series (Chicago: Moody Press, 1995).

English, Donald. *The Message of Mark.* The Bible Speaks Today Series. J.A. Motyer and John R.W. Stott, eds. (Downers Grove: InterVarsity, 1994).

Garland, David E. *Mark.* The NIV Application Commentary (Grand Rapids: Zondervan, 1996).

Godwin, Johnnie C. *Mark.* Layman's Bible Book Commentary (Nashville: Broadman, 1995).

McKenna, David L. *Mark.* The Communicator's Commentary. Lloyd J. Ogilvie, ed. (Dallas: Word Publishing, 1991). Also available in paperback in the Mastering the New Testament series.

Commentaries on Luke

Benware, Paul. *Luke: Gospel of the Son of Man.* Everyman's Bible Commentary Series (Chicago: Moody Press, 1995).

Bock, Darrell L. *Luke.* IVP New Testament Commentary Series. D. Stuart Briscoe and Haddon Robinson, eds. (Downers Grove: InterVarsity, 1992).

Dean, Robert J. *Luke.* Layman's Bible Book Commentary (Nashville: Broadman, 1995).

Larson, Bruce. *Luke.* The Communicator's Commentary. Lloyd J. Ogilvie, ed. (Dallas: Word Publishing, 1991). Also available in paperback in the Mastering the New Testament series.

Morris, Leon. *Luke.* Tyndale New Testament Commentaries. Leon Morris, ed. (Grand Rapids: Eerdmans, 1994).

Wilcock, Michael. *The Message of Luke.* The Bible Speaks Today Series. J.A. Motyer and John R.W. Stott, eds. (Downers Grove: InterVarsity, 1994).

Commentaries on John

Carter, James E. *John*. Layman's Bible Book Commentary (Nashville: Broadman, 1995).

Frederickson, Roger L. *John*. The Communicator's Commentary. Lloyd J. Ogilvie, ed. (Dallas: Word Publishing, 1991). Also available in paperback in the Mastering the New Testament series.

Laney, J. Carl. *John*. Everyman's Bible Commentary Series (Chicago: Moody Press, 1995).

Milne, Bruce. *The Message of John*. The Bible Speaks Today Series. J.A. Motyer and John R.W. Stott, eds. (Downers Grove: InterVarsity, 1994).

Tasker, R.V.G. *John*. Tyndale New Testament Commentaries. Leon Morris, ed. (Grand Rapids: Eerdmans, 1994).

Vine, W.E. *Vine's Expository Commentary on John* (Nashville: Thomas Nelson, 1992).

Commentaries on Acts

De Hann, M.R. *Pentecost and After: Studies in the Book of Acts* (Grand Rapids: Kregel, 1995).

Fernando, Ajith. *Acts*. The NIV Application Commentary (Grand Rapids: Zondervan, 1996).

Larkin, William J. *Acts*. IVP New Testament Commentary Series. D. Stuart Briscoe and Haddon Robinson, eds. (Downers Grove: InterVarsity, 1992).

Marshall, I. Howard. *Acts*. Tyndale New Testament Commentaries. Leon Morris, ed. (Grand Rapids: Eerdmans, 1994).

Maddox, Robert L. *Acts*. Layman's Bible Book Commentary (Nashville: Broadman, 1995).

Ogilvie, Lloyd J. *Acts*. The Communicator's Commentary. Lloyd J. Ogilvie, ed. (Dallas: Word Publishing, 1991). Also available in paperback in the Mastering the New Testament series.

Ramsay, William M. *Historical Commentary on Acts* (Grand Rapids: Kregel, 1989).

Ryrie, Charles R. *Acts of the Apostles*. Everyman's Bible Commentary Series (Chicago: Moody Press, 1995).

Commentaries on Romans

Briscoe, D. Stuart. *Romans*. The Communicator's Commentary. Lloyd J. Ogilvie, ed. (Dallas: Word Publishing, 1991). Also available in paperback in the Mastering the New Testament series.

Bruce, F.F. *Romans*. Tyndale New Testament Commentaries. Leon Morris, ed. (Grand Rapids: Eerdmans, 1994).

Haldane, Robert. *Commentary on Romans* (Grand Rapids: Kregel, 1989).

Ironside, Henry A. *Romans* (Grand Rapids: Loizeaux Brothers, 1996).

Johnson, Alan. *Romans: The Freedom Letter*. Everyman's Bible Commentary Series (Chicago: Moody Press, 1995).

MacGorman, J.W. *Romans, 1 Corinthians*. Layman's Bible Book Commentary (Nashville: Broadman, 1995).

Pridham, Arthur. *Notes on Romans* (Grand Rapids: Kregel, 1984).

Commentaries on 1 Corinthians

Blomberg, Craig L. *1 Corinthians*. The NIV Application Commentary (Grand Rapids: Zondervan, 1996).

Chafin, Kenneth L. *1, 2 Corinthians*. The Communicator's Commentary. Lloyd J. Ogilvie, ed. (Dallas: Word Publishing, 1991). Also available in paperback in the Mastering the New Testament series.

De Hann, M.R. *Studies in First Corinthians* (Grand Rapids: Kregel, 1995).

Morris, Leon. *1 Corinthians*. Tyndale New Testament Commentaries. Leon Morris, ed. (Grand Rapids: Eerdmans, 1994).

Prior, David. *The Message of 1 Corinthians*. The Bible Speaks Today Series. J.A. Motyer and John R.W. Stott, eds. (Downers Grove: InterVarsity, 1994).

Redpath, Alan. *The Royal Route to Heaven: Studies in First Corinthians* (Grand Rapids: Fleming H. Revell, 1993).

Commentaries on 2 Corinthians

Barnett, Paul. *The Message of 2 Corinthians*. The Bible Speaks Today Series. J.A. Motyer and John R.W. Stott, eds. (Downers Grove: InterVarsity, 1994).

Belleville, Linda L. *2 Corinthians*. IVP New Testament Commentary Series. D. Stuart Briscoe and Haddon Robinson, eds. (Downers Grove: InterVarsity, 1992).

George, David C. *2 Corinthians-Ephesians*. Layman's Bible Book Commentary (Nashville: Broadman, 1995).

Hughes, Robert B. *2 Corinthians*. Everyman's Bible Commentary Series (Chicago: Moody Press, 1995).

Kruse, Colin. *2 Corinthians*. Tyndale New Testament Commentaries. Leon Morris, ed. (Grand Rapids: Eerdmans, 1994).

Redpath, Alan. *Blessings Out of Buffetings: Studies in Second Corinthians* (Grand Rapids: Fleming H. Revell, 1993).

Commentaries on Galatians

Cole, R. Alan. *Galatians*. Tyndale New Testament Commentaries. Leon Morris, ed. (Grand Rapids: Eerdmans, 1994).

De Hann, M.R. *Studies in Galatians* (Grand Rapids: Kregel, 1995).

Dunnam, Maxie D. *Galatians, Ephesians, Philippians, Colossians, and Philemon*. The Communicator's Commentary. Lloyd J. Ogilvie, ed. (Dallas: Word Publishing, 1991). Also available in paperback in the Mastering the New Testament series.

Hensen, G. Walter. *Galatians*. IVP New Testament Commentary Series. D. Stuart Briscoe and Haddon Robinson, eds. (Downers Grove: InterVarsity, 1992).

McKnight, Scot. *Galatians*. The NIV Application Commentary (Grand Rapids: Zondervan, 1996).

Stott, John R.W. *The Message of Galatians*. The Bible Speaks Today Series. J.A. Motyer and John R.W. Stott, eds. (Downers Grove: InterVarsity, 1994).

Vine, W.E. *Vine's Expository Commentary on Galatians* (Nashville: Thomas Nelson, 1992).

Commentaries on Ephesians

Foulkes, Francis. *Ephesians*. Tyndale New Testament Commentaries. Leon Morris, ed. (Grand Rapids: Eerdmans, 1994).

Liefield, Walter L. *Galatians*. IVP New Testament Commentary Series. D. Stuart Briscoe and Haddon Robinson, eds. (Downers Grove: InterVarsity, 1992).

Snodgrass, Klyne. *Ephesians*. The NIV Application Commentary (Grand Rapids: Zondervan, 1996).

Stott, John R.W. *The Message of Ephesians*. The Bible Speaks Today Series. J.A. Motyer and John R.W. Stott, eds. (Downers Grove: InterVarsity, 1994).

Commentaries on Philippians

Martin, Ralph P. *Philippians*. Tyndale New Testament Commentaries. Leon Morris, ed. (Grand Rapids: Eerdmans, 1994).

Motyer, J.A. *The Message of Philippians*. The Bible Speaks Today Series. J.A. Motyer and John R.W. Stott, eds. (Downers Grove: InterVarsity, 1994).

Thielman, Frank. *Philippians*. The NIV Application Commentary (Grand Rapids: Zondervan, 1996).

Tolbert, Malcolm O. *Philippians-Philemon*. Layman's Bible Book Commentary (Nashville: Broadman, 1995).

Walvoord, John F. *Philippians*. Everyman's Bible Commentary Series (Chicago: Moody Press, 1995).

Commentaries on Colossians and Philemon

Garland, David E. *Colossians, Philemon*. The NIV Application Commentary (Grand Rapids: Zondervan, 1996).

Harrison, Everett F. *Colossians*. Everyman's Bible Commentary Series (Chicago: Moody Press, 1995).

Lucas, R.C. *The Message of Colossians and Philemon*. The Bible Speaks Today Series. J.A. Motyer and John R.W. Stott, eds. (Downers Grove: InterVarsity, 1994).

Wall, Robert W. *Colossians and Philemon*. IVP New Testament Commentary Series. D. Stuart Briscoe and Haddon Robinson, eds. (Downers Grove: InterVarsity, 1992).

Wright, N.T. *Colossians and Philemon*. Tyndale New Testament Commentaries. Leon Morris, ed. (Grand Rapids: Eerdmans, 1994).

Commentaries on 1 and 2 Thessalonians

Demarest, Gary D. *1, 2 Thessalonians, 1, 2 Timothy, Titus*. The Communicator's Commentary. Lloyd J. Ogilvie, ed. (Dallas: Word Publishing, 1991). Also available in paperback in the Mastering the New Testament series.

Morris, Leon. *1 and 2 Thessalonians*. Tyndale New Testament Commentaries. Leon Morris, ed. (Grand Rapids: Eerdmans, 1994).

Ryrie, Charles R. *1 and 2 Thessalonians*. Everyman's Bible Commentary Series (Chicago: Moody Press, 1995).

Stott, John R.W. *The Message of 1 and 2 Thessalonians*. The Bible Speaks Today Series. J.A. Motyer and John R.W. Stott, eds. (Downers Grove: InterVarsity, 1994).

Vine, W.E. *Vine's Expository Commentary on 1 and 2 Thessalonians* (Nashville: Thomas Nelson, 1992).

Commentaries on 1 and 2 Timothy and Titus

Guthrie, Donald. *The Pastoral Epistles*. Tyndale New Testament Commentaries. Leon Morris, ed. (Grand Rapids: Eerdmans, 1994).

Hiebert, D. Edmond. *2 Timothy*. Everyman's Bible Commentary Series (Chicago: Moody Press, 1995).

Hiebert, D. Edmond. *Titus and Philemon*. Everyman's Bible Commentary Series (Chicago: Moody Press, 1995).

Stock, Eugene. *Practical Truths from the Pastoral Epistles* (Grand Rapids: Kregel, 1995).

Stott, John R.W. *The Message of 2 Timothy*. The Bible Speaks Today Series. J.A. Motyer and John R.W. Stott, eds. (Downers Grove: InterVarsity, 1994).

Towner, Philip H. *1-2 Timothy and Titus*. IVP New Testament Commentary Series. D. Stuart Briscoe and Haddon Robinson, eds. (Downers Grove: InterVarsity, 1992).

Commentaries on Hebrews

Brown, Raymond. *The Message of Hebrews*. The Bible Speaks Today Series. J.A. Motyer and John R.W. Stott, eds. (Downers Grove: InterVarsity, 1994).

De Hann, M.R. *Studies in Hebrews* (Grand Rapids: Kregel, 1995).

Evans, Louis H. Jr. *Hebrews*. The Communicator's Commentary. Lloyd J. Ogilvie, ed. (Dallas: Word Publishing, 1991). Also available in paperback in the Mastering the New Testament series.

Guthrie, Donald. *Hebrews*. Tyndale New Testament Commentaries. Leon Morris, ed. (Grand Rapids: Eerdmans, 1994).

Hodges, Zane C. *Hebrews*. The Bible Knowledge Commentary: New Testament (Colorado Springs: Cook Communications, 1994).

Pffeifer, Charles. *Hebrews*. Everyman's Bible Commentary Series (Chicago: Moody Press, 1995).

Stedman, Ray C. *Hebrews*. IVP New Testament Commentary Series. D. Stuart Briscoe and Haddon Robinson, eds. (Downers Grove: InterVarsity, 1992).

Valentine, Foy. *Hebrews-2 Peter*. Layman's Bible Book Commentary (Nashville: Broadman, 1995).

Commentaries on James

Cedar, Paul A. *James, 1, 2 Peter, Jude*. The Communicator's Commentary. Lloyd J. Ogilvie, ed. (Dallas: Word Publishing, 1991). Also available in paperback in the Mastering the New Testament series.

Doerksen, Vernon. *James*. Everyman's Bible Commentary Series (Chicago: Moody Press, 1995).

Hodges, Zane C. *The Epistle of James: Proven Character Through Testing*. The Grace New Testament Commentary Series (Dallas: Redencion Viva Publishers, 1987).

Moo, Douglas. *James*. Tyndale New Testament Commentaries. Leon Morris, ed. (Grand Rapids: Eerdmans, 1994).

Motyer, J.A. *The Message of James*. The Bible Speaks Today Series. J.A. Motyer and John R.W. Stott, eds. (Downers Grove: InterVarsity, 1994).

Nystrom, David P. *James*. The NIV Application Commentary (Grand Rapids: Zondervan, 1996).

Stulac, George M. *James*. IVP New Testament Commentary Series. D. Stuart Briscoe and Haddon Robinson, eds. (Downers Grove: InterVarsity, 1992).

Commentaries on 1 Peter

Barbieri, Louis. *1 and 2 Peter*. Everyman's Bible Commentary Series (Chicago: Moody Press, 1995).

Clowney, Edmund. *The Message of 1 Peter*. The Bible Speaks Today Series. J.A. Motyer and John R.W. Stott, eds. (Downers Grove: InterVarsity, 1994).

Grudem, Wayne. *1 Peter*. Tyndale New Testament Commentaries. Leon Morris, ed. (Grand Rapids: Eerdmans, 1994).

Marshall, I. Howard. *1 Peter*. IVP New Testament Commentary Series. D. Stuart Briscoe and Haddon Robinson, eds. (Downers Grove: InterVarsity, 1992).

McKnight, Scot. *1 Peter*. The NIV Application Commentary (Grand Rapids: Zondervan, 1996).

Commentaries on 2 Peter and Jude

Coder, S. Maxwell. *Jude: Acts of the Apostates.*
Everyman's Bible Commentary Series
(Chicago: Moody Press, 1995).

Green, Michael. *2 Peter and Jude.* Tyndale New
Testament Commentaries. Leon Morris, ed.
(Grand Rapids: Eerdmans, 1994).

Lucas, David, and Christopher Green. *The Message
of 2 Peter and Jude.* The Bible Speaks Today
Series. J.A. Motyer and John R.W. Stott, eds.
(Downers Grove: InterVarsity, 1994).

Moo, Douglas J. *2 Peter, Jude.* The NIV
Application Commentary (Grand Rapids:
Zondervan, 1996).

Commentaries on 1, 2, and 3 John

Burdick, Donald. *Epistles of John.* Everyman's
Bible Commentary Series (Chicago: Moody
Press, 1995).

Burge, Gary M. *The Letters of John.* The NIV
Application Commentary (Grand Rapids:
Zondervan, 1996).

Jackman, David. *The Message of John's Letters.*
The Bible Speaks Today Series. J.A. Motyer
and John R.W. Stott, eds. (Downers Grove:
InterVarsity, 1994).

Hodges, Zane C. *1, 2, and 3 John.* The Bible
Knowledge Commentary: New Testament
(Colorado Springs: Cook Communications,
1994).

Howard, Fred D. *1 John-Revelation.* Layman's
Bible Book Commentary (Nashville:
Broadman, 1995).

Palmer, Earl F. *1, 2, 3 John, Revelation.* The
Communicator's Commentary. Lloyd J.
Ogilvie, ed. (Dallas: Word Publishing, 1991).
Also available in paperback in the Mastering
the New Testament series.

Stott, John R.W. *The Letters of John.* Tyndale
New Testament Commentaries. Leon Morris,
ed. (Grand Rapids: Eerdmans, 1994).

Thompson, Marianne M. *1-3 John.* IVP New
Testament Commentary Series. D. Stuart
Briscoe and Haddon Robinson, eds.
(Downers Grove: InterVarsity, 1992).

Commentaries on Revelation

Gregg, Steven, ed. *Revelation: Four Views*
(Nashville: Thomas Nelson, 1994).

Ironside, Henry A. *Revelation* (Grand Rapids:
Loizeaux Brothers, 1997).

Michaels, J. Ramsey. *Revelation.* IVP New
Testament Commentary Series. D. Stuart
Briscoe and Haddon Robinson, eds.
(Downers Grove: InterVarsity, 1992).

Morris, Leon. *Revelation.* Tyndale New
Testament Commentaries. Leon Morris, ed.
(Grand Rapids: Eerdmans, 1994).

Ryrie, Charles R. *Revelation.* Everyman's Bible
Commentary Series (Chicago: Moody Press,
1995).

Seiss, Joseph A. *The Apocalypse: Exposition of the
Book of Revelation* (Grand Rapids: Kregel,
1995).

Wilcock, Michael. *The Message of Revelation.* The
Bible Speaks Today Series. J.A. Motyer and
John R.W. Stott, eds. (Downers Grove:
InterVarsity, 1994).